Merriam-Webster's
School
Dictionary

Merriam-Webster's School Dictionary

Merriam-Webster, Incorporated
Springfield, Massachusetts, U.S.A.

A GENUINE MERRIAM-WEBSTER

The name *Webster* alone is no guarantee of excellence. It is used by a number of publishers and may serve mainly to mislead an unwary buyer.

Merriam-Webster™ is the name you should look for when you consider the purchase of dictionaries or other fine reference books. It carries the reputation of a company that has been publishing since 1831 and is your assurance of quality and authority.

Library of Congress Cataloging-in-Publication Data

Merriam-Webster's school dictionary
p. cm.
ISBN 978-0-87779-680-0
1. English language—Dictionaries, Juvenile. [1. English language—Dictionaries.] I. Merriam-Webster, Inc.

PE1628.5.M47 2004
423—dc22

2004042674

Made in the United States of America

1st Printing Quad Graphics Versailles, KY February 2015

Contents

Preface

Merriam-Webster's School Dictionary is the most advanced of a series of dictionaries prepared especially for elementary and secondary students. It is preceded by *Merriam-Webster's Intermediate Dictionary* and prepares students to move on easily to *Merriam-Webster's Collegiate Dictionary*. *Merriam-Webster's School Dictionary* is intended for use primarily by students at the high school level. The range of vocabulary covered is suited to the needs of older high school students, but the definitions have been written in everyday language that will be clear to younger students.

The dictionary has been written and edited by Merriam-Webster's permanent staff of trained and experienced lexicographers. They have included words chiefly on the basis of their occurrence in textbooks and other materials in all subjects. The editors have also had access to the many millions of examples of English words used in context that form the extensive Merriam-Webster citation files and that underlie the entire family of Merriam-Webster dictionaries, including *Webster's Third New International Dictionary* and *Merriam-Webster's Collegiate Dictionary*.

By basing their work on this broad body of evidence, the editors have ensured that the current general vocabulary of English has received its proper share of attention, while also giving the language of special subjects—such as mathematics, science, history, and computers—the full coverage that today's students need.

Merriam-Webster's School Dictionary will give students all of the information they need about how words are spelled, how they are pronounced, and what they mean. In addition, it also includes many of the features found in more advanced dictionaries. There are etymologies that show the origin and development of words, explanatory paragraphs on synonyms to help students distinguish among closely related words and select the most appropriate for a particular context, and guidance on standard usage. In addition, there are separate sections in the back of the book for common abbreviations; signs and symbols; biographical, biblical, and mythological names; geographical names; and a handbook of style to describe standard usage of punctuation, italics, and capitalization.

More than 950 pictorial illustrations supplement and enrich the information given in definitions on such topics as Egyptian hieroglyphs, the parts of a cell, and the difference between an Asian and an African elephant. Special tables throughout the dictionary answer questions about such matters as the symbol for or atomic weight of a chemical element, the relation of a U.S. measure to its metric equivalent, or the diameter of a planet in our solar system.

Merriam-Webster's School Dictionary can be a very valuable book for students facing the special challenges of developing language skills and knowledge across a broad range of topics. The more a student uses the dictionary, the more useful it becomes. However, using a dictionary is not always an easy and obvious matter. To assist students in understanding the full range of information included in their dictionary, this dictionary includes an introductory section called "Using the Dictionary." Students should read this section carefully and become thoroughly familiar with it in order to get the most from their dictionary.

Using the Dictionary

Dictionary Entries

The entries in the dictionary are all the words printed in **boldface** type. The **main entries** are the entries that are listed in alphabetical order at the far left in a column.

Most main entries are single words, but a main entry can also be a single letter, like *a, b,* or *c,* or a combination of letters, like *ESP*. Many are combinations of words, like *hitchhike, nitty-gritty,* and *French horn.* There are also main entries that are only parts of words. These include prefixes like *anti-,* suffixes like *-ism,* and combining forms like *bio-* and *-ectomy* that are used only to form other words.

Run-on Entries

At the end of many entries are additional boldface words and sometimes boldface phrases. These are known as **run-on entries.** These words and compounds are derived from the main-entry word in different ways. They may come about through a shift in function (as the noun *implant* comes from the verb *implant*) or they may be formed by the addition of suffixes (as the adverb *closely* and the noun *closeness* come from the adjective *close*). These derived words are run on without definitions when their meaning is obvious. But if the meaning of a derivative word is not obvious from the meaning of the base word and the meaning of any added suffix, we always enter it as a main entry with a definition.

Boldface phrases that are common idioms whose meanings are more than the sum of the meanings of the individual words, are run on with definitions as the last element of many entries. These phrases are generally entered under the first major element (for example, a noun or verb or sometimes an adjective or adverb, rather than a preposition or article).

For example, the phrases *on board, in any case,* and *to date* will appear at the entries *board, case,* and *date* respectively. *Break camp, cast lots, pull one's leg,* and *now and then* appear respectively under *break, cast, pull,* and *now*.

All run-ons, whether derivative words or idiomatic phrases, are introduced with a dash. Run-on derivatives always have a part-of-speech label, usually have centered dots to indicate end-of-line division, and often have a pronunciation. Run-on phrases have none of these.

Order of Entries

Throughout the dictionary, words are alphabetized by first letter, then second letter, and so on, regardless of spaces or hyphens. For example, you will find the word *basenji* coming after *basement* and before *base on balls* and *houri* between *hourglass* and *hourly*.

Words spelled with a numeral will be found in the place they would occupy if spelled out. *A-1* follows *A-OK* and comes before *aorta* and *4-H* appears between *four-footed* and *four-hand*. Words that often begin with the abbreviation *St.* in common usage have the abbreviation spelled out: *Saint Bernard*.

When main entries are spelled exactly alike but have different functions in the sentence or have different origins, they are called **homographs.** Each homograph is entered at its own place and distinguished from other homographs by a small raised numeral at the very beginning.

^{1}**American** . . . *n*
^{2}**American** *adj*

Related homographs (all those having the same origin) are grouped together. Thus, ^{2}*bow* ("a bending of the head or body in respect, submission, agreement, or greeting"), which is related to ^{1}*bow* ("to bend the head, body, or knee in greeting, reverence, respect, or submission"), comes before ^{3}*bow* ("RAINBOW"). And ^{4}*bow* ("to bend into a curve") follows the related ^{3}*bow* and is ahead of ^{5}*bow* ("the forward part of a ship").

Full words are entered before parts of words made up of the same letters, and beginning word elements come ahead of final word elements.

ad . . . *n*
ad- . . . *prefix*
-ad . . . *adv suffix*

Entries printed in small letters come before capitalized ones.

^{1}**box·er** . . . *n*
^{2}**boxer** *n*
Box·er . . . *n*

Compounds that are written as one word are entered before hyphenated compounds, and hyphenated compounds are entered ahead of those made up of separate words.

lay·off . . . *n*

lay off . . . *vb*

lay–up . . . *n*

lay up . . . *vt*

low·down . . . *n*

low–down . . . *adj*

Guide Words

To aid you in finding the right word quickly, *Merriam-Webster's School Dictionary* has a pair of **guide words** at the top of every page. The entries that fall alphabetically between the guide words are found on that page. Any boldface term—a main entry, a variant spelling, an inflected form, a word run on undefined at the end of an entry, a phrase run on and defined at the end of an entry, or even a word in a list of undefined words—can be a guide word as long as it is alphabetically the first or last word on the page.

The first word of the pair of guide words is normally the first main entry on the page and the second is usually the last main entry. But it is important to remember that this is not always the case. On page 153, for example, the last main entry is *certification mark,* but the last guide word for that page is *certificatory,* which is alphabetically later and which is an undefined run-on at [2]*certificate.*

The guide words themselves are always in alphabetical order. When the alphabetically last word on one page would follow the first guide word on the next page, it is not picked as a guide word. Thus, on page 142 the alphabetically last boldface term is *carpentry* (an undefined run-on at *carpenter*). But since *carpentry* would come after the first guide word on page 143 (which is *carpenter ant*), it cannot be used as the guide word on page 142.

Variant Entries

A number of main entries have a second or sometimes a third spelling shown in boldface type. These alternate spellings are called **variants.**

Variants separated by the word *or* are equal variants. That means each is current in standard English usage and either spelling is correct for you to use. When equal variants are used with about the same frequency, we list them in alphabetical order.

bobby socks *or* **bobby sox**

But when the evidence indicates that one spelling is somewhat more common than another, the variants are listed in the order of relative frequency of use even if that means they are not listed in alphabetical order.

[1]**bo·gey** *or* **bo·gy** *or* **bo·gie**

pol·ly·wog *or* **pol·li·wog**

When the word *also* separates variants, it means that the following variant is considerably less common in standard English. Nevertheless, the *also* variant is a part of standard English usage and you may freely use it without being wrong, although many people prefer the more common spelling.

mor·tise *also* **mor·tice**

Occasionally we use both *or* and *also* in separating a number of variants at a single entry.

[1]**-an** *or* **-ian** *also* **-ean**

In this instance, the first two spellings are roughly equal in frequency and the last is of a secondary nature.

Whenever one variant form is more common with one meaning than with others, it is listed before the particular definition with some indication of how common or prominent it is.

[1]**nick·el** . . . **2 a** *also* **nick·le**

[1]**la·bor** . . . **5** *usually* **La·bour**

Centered Dots and Hyphenation

Merriam-Webster's School Dictionary shows you how to divide words for two distinct purposes: first, for end-of-line division by the use of **centered dots** in the entry words, and second, for syllabification by the use of **hyphens** in the pronunciations. It is important to understand that the centered dots in the entry words do *not* necessarily separate the syllables of a word.

Printers, typists, and writers often have to divide a word at the end of a line if it is too long to fit on one line. The centered dots in the boldface entry words show you acceptable places to put a hyphen when the word is broken at the end of a line. For example, *mor·al·is·tic* may be divided at any of three places.

mor-
alistic

or

moral-
istic

or

moralis-
tic

We use centered dots in all boldface entries except as follows.

Only the first of two or more homographs is divided if the pronunciation and division are the same for each.

[1]mas·ter . . . *n*

[2]master *vt*

[3]master *adj*

A word in a compound made up of two or more separate words is divided only if it is not entered as an individual entry. For example, we show no division for the entry *gamma radiation* because there are entries for *gam·ma* and *ra·di·a·tion.* The first word in the entry *Mo·lo·tov cocktail* is divided but the second is not, because there is no separate entry for *Mo·lo·tov* but there is for *cock·tail.* There are no entries for the individual elements of *pri·ma don·na,* thus both elements of the compound are divided.

It is customary to avoid breaking a word so as to leave a single letter at the end of one line or at the beginning of the next, so we do not show any division for single letters at the beginning or end of words, as in *idea* or *flighty.*

The syllables of a word are indicated by the use of hyphens in the pronunciation. You should rely on only these hyphens, and not the centered dots, for syllabification, since the placement and number of centered dots is not always the same as the placement and number of hyphens in the pronunciation.

eter·ni·ty \i-ˈtər-nət-ē\

When a boldface entry word is broken at the end of a line, a hyphen replaces the centered dots at that point. *Merriam-Webster's School Dictionary* also uses a special **double hyphen** at the end of a line any time the word that is divided is normally spelled with a hyphen. When you see the double hyphen, you will know to keep the hyphen even when you write the word all on one line.

all–pur·pose \ˈȯl-ˈpər-pəs\ *adj* : suitable for many uses ⟨*all=purpose* flour⟩

The double hyphen here indicates that when you write *all-purpose,* you should always spell it with a hyphen.

Pronunciation

There are two major ways in which we use the English language: writing and speaking. The spelling of written words is related to the sounds of spoken words. However, the relationship between spelling and sound in English is not always very close. It is often hard to tell from the spelling how to pronounce a word. On the one hand, different letters may be used to spell the same sound in different words. For example, the words *day, weigh, steak,* and *prey* all contain the same vowel sound. *Sight, site,* and *cite* are all pronounced alike. On the other hand, one letter or group of letters may be used to spell different sounds. For example, in *bat, late, any,* and *above* the letter *a* stands for a different sound in each word. In addition, there are many words that are pronounced in more than one way, although there may be only one accepted spelling.

In order to be able to indicate the sounds of words in a written form, we use a special alphabet of pronunciation symbols. Each pronunciation symbol stands for only one sound, and each sound is represented by only one symbol.

The pronunciation of most entry words is shown immediately following the boldface entry. To indicate that pronunciation symbols are being used and not regular letters, the symbols are always shown between slant lines \ \.

A complete list of pronunciation symbols used in this book appears on page 22a. A shorter list of symbols you may need to be reminded of is printed at the bottom of the right column on odd-numbered pages throughout the dictionary. After most of the symbols on the chart are words containing the sound of the symbol they follow. The boldface letters in these words are the letters which stand for the same sound as the symbol. If you say the sample words in your normal voice, you will be able to hear the sound meant by each symbol. In some cases the complete pronunciation of a sample word is given.

Hyphens are used with the pronunciation symbols to indicate the syllables of a word.

beast \ˈbēst\ (1 syllable)

be·cause \bi-ˈkȯz\ (2 syllables)

cast·away \ˈkas-tə-ˌwā\ (3 syllables)

des·po·tism \ˈdes-pə-ˌtiz-em\ (4 syllables)

Of course the syllables of words are not separated when we speak. One sound is connected to another without pause.

You will notice that in two of the above examples the number and position of the hyphens do not match the number and position of the centered dots in the headwords. The reason is that the centered dots do not separate syllables. Only the hyphens show syllables; the dots mark acceptable places to divide the word at the end of a line.

Some syllables of a word are spoken with greater force or emphasis than others. This relative emphasis is called **stress.** Three levels of stress are shown in *Merriam-Webster's School Dictionary.* **Primary** (or strong) **stress** is indicated by a high vertical mark \ˈ\ placed *before* the stressed syllable. **Secondary** (or medium) **stress** is indicated by a low vertical mark \ˌ\ placed *before* the stressed syllable. **Weak stress** is given to syllables which have no stress mark.

man•ner \ˈman-ər\ (primary \ˈman-\, weak \-ər\)

ob•vi•ate \ˈäb-vē-ˌāt\ (primary \ˈäb-\, weak \-vē-\, secondary \-ˌāt\)

Many words can be pronounced in more than one way. **Variant** pronunciations are separated by commas and sometimes groups of variants are separated by semicolons. The order of variants does not mean that the first variant is any better than the following ones. All the variants shown in this book are perfectly acceptable and are used by large numbers of educated English speakers. When learning a new word, you should choose the pronunciation variant which sounds most natural to you.

In many entries the variants are shown in full

of•ten \ˈȯ-fən, ˈȯf-tən\

but for words of two or more syllables, the variation may occur only in part of the word. For such words only the syllables that vary may be repeated.

hor•ri•ble \ˈhȯr-ə-bəl, ˈhär-\

pro•cess \ˈpräs-ˌes, ˈprōs-, -əs\

In some words there may be variation in the number of syllables pronounced. For instance, *celery* is pronounced both \ˈsel-rē\ and \ˈsel-ə-rē\, and *wiggler* is pronounced both \ˈwig-lər\ and \ˈwig-ə-lər\. To save space in the dictionary some of the syllables that do not change are not repeated.

cel•ery \ˈsel-rē, -ə-rē\

wig•gler \ˈwig-lər, -ə-lər\

A pronunciation variant following the word *also* is heard less frequently than the variants before it. A variant following *sometimes* is heard much less frequently than others. If a variant is used mostly in a particular region, the region may be identified.

help \ˈhelp, *South also* ˈhep\

kha•ki \ˈkak-ē, ˈkäk-, *Canadian often* ˈkärk-\

In general, no pronunciation is indicated for open compounds consisting of two or more English words that are entered at their own alphabetical place in the dictionary.

life jacket *n*

A pronunciation is shown, however, for any element of an open compound that does not have entry at its own alphabetical place.

letters of marque \-ˈmärk\

If an incomplete pronunciation is given for an entry word, the missing portions may be found at a preceding entry word.

cat•bird \ˈkat-ˌbərd\

cat•boat \-ˌbōt\

Thus, the full pronunciation of *catboat* is \ˈkat-ˌbōt\. If the pronunciation and end-of-line divisions of homographs are the same, the pronunciation is given only for the first.

¹cheer \ˈchiər\ *n*

²cheer *vb*

¹her•ald \ˈher-əld\ *n*

²herald *vt*

Some run-on entries have no pronunciation shown. In these cases the pronunciation of the run-on is the pronunciation of the main entry plus the pronunciation of the suffix, which may be found at its own place in the dictionary.

deft \ˈdeft\ *adj* . . . — **deft•ly** *adv* — **deft•ness** *n*

This tells you that *deftly* is pronounced \ˈdeft-lē\ and *deftness* is pronounced \ˈdeft-nəs\.

The Function of Words

Words are used in many different ways in a sentence. A word may serve as the name of something, or be used to indicate an action or to describe a thing or the way something happens. The several different functions of words are known as **parts of speech.** *Merriam-Webster's School Dictionary* identifies the function of most entry words with one of eight traditional part-of-speech labels, abbreviated and italicized and placed immediately after the boldface entry or after the pronunciation, when one is shown.

gui•tar \gə-ˈtär, gi-\ *n* (noun)

I \ī, ˈī, ə\ *pron* (pronoun)

³fit *vb* (verb)

snide \ˈsnīd\ *adj* (adjective)

hap·pi·ly \ˈhap-ə-lē\ *adv* (adverb)
for \fər, fȯr, ˈfȯr\ *prep* (preposition)
and . . . *conj* (conjunction)
ouch \ˈau̇ch\ *interj* (interjection)

When the main entry is a noun that is always used in the plural, the label *n pl* is used.

munch·ies . . . *n pl*

An entry word may be spelled as a plural and be considered a plural in some uses—such as being used with a plural verb—and yet be considered singular in other uses—such as being used with a singular verb. This variation in construction will be indicated as part of the functional label.

ac·ro·bat·ics . . . *n sing or pl*

The word *acrobatics* may be singular in such constructions as "acrobatics is a strenuous activity" or plural in "you make these acrobatics look easy."

Some entries that are singular in most uses may have one or more specific plural uses.

fix·ing . . . *n* . . . **2** *pl* : TRIMMINGS ⟨a turkey dinner with all the *fixings*⟩

Other entries will have one or more senses that are always spelled as plural but when used as the subject of a sentence will take a singular verb.

lanc·er . . . **2** *pl but sing in constr*

An example of this use might be "the lancers is an interesting dance."

A pronoun, too, is labeled if it takes a plural verb or if it may take either a singular or plural verb in construction.

²both *pron, pl in constr*
²any *pron, sing or pl in constr*

Both is plural in meaning and always takes a plural verb, as in "both are doing well." In the second example, *any* may be used with a singular verb, as in "I want some pie. Is there any left?" or with a plural verb, as in "are any of you tired?"

When variant plural forms are shown for an entry but only one is used with a particular meaning, that plural is shown at the definition *following* the abbreviation *pl.*

²die . . . *n, pl* **dice** . . . *or* **dies** . . . **1** *pl dice* : . . . **2** *pl dies* : . . .

The plural form for the first meaning of *die,* the little cube with dots on it, is *dice*: "roll the dice." The plural form for meaning 2, a tool to stamp an impression, is *dies*: "it takes two dies to stamp both sides of a coin."

When a particular meaning is only plural and only one variant plural form is used for that meaning, the form is shown *ahead* of the abbreviation *pl.*

¹folk . . . *n, pl* **folk** *or* **folks** . . . **4** *folks pl* : . . .

In this meaning, the word is always plural and only the form *folks* is used: "I'm going home to see my folks."

The label *vb* is used for verb entries that have both transitive uses (those that take a direct object) and intransitive uses. Verb entries that are used only as transitive verbs or only as intransitive verbs are given a specific *vt* (transitive verb) or *vi* (intransitive verb) label.

an·nul . . . *vt*
be·long . . . *vi*

In addition to the traditional part-of-speech labels, there are a number of other function labels that we use in this dictionary. *Prefix, suffix,* and *combining form* are relatively common and have already been introduced. The following identifying labels appear much less frequently.

may . . . *auxiliary verb*
me·thinks . . . *vb impersonal*
gid·dy·ap . . . *imperative vb*
an . . . *indefinite article*
the . . . *definite article*
Fris·bee . . . *trademark*
Au·to·mat . . . *service mark*
Realtor . . . *collective mark*
NC–17 *certification mark*
-nd *symbol*

Prefixes, suffixes, and combining forms are sometimes shown with a part-of-speech label when all compounds formed are of one part of speech.

-al·gia . . . *n combining form*
-ana . . . *n pl suffix*

In these examples, the compounds formed by either of these elements are always nouns, and in the second example the compounds are always plural nouns.

Sometimes an entry has more than one function label.

ago . . . *adj or adv*
betwixt . . . *adv or prep*

The *or* in these two examples indicates that the entry may at one time function as one part of speech and at another time as another part of speech without any significant difference in meaning.

We do not show part-of-speech labels or other function labels for idiomatic phrases defined at the end of a main entry or for main entry phrases that consist of two nouns joined by a preposition, like *act of God* and *man in the street*.

Capitalization

Most entries in *Merriam-Webster's School Dictionary* begin with a lowercase letter. A few of these have a label in italics *often cap*, which indicates that the word is as likely to be capitalized as not, that it is as acceptable with an uppercase initial as it is with one in lowercase. Some entries begin with an uppercase letter, which indicates that the word is usually capitalized. The absence of an initial capital or of an *often cap* label indicates that the word is ordinarily not capitalized.

fore•arm . . . *n*
gar•gan•tu•an . . . *adj, often cap*
Mo•hawk . . . *n*

The capitalization of entries that are open or hyphenated compounds is similarly indicated by the form of the entry or by an italicized label.

hot spring *n*
cesarian section . . . *n, often cap C*
neo–im•pres•sion•ism . . . *n, often cap N&I*
un–Amer•i•can . . . *adj*
Dutch oven *n*
Old Glory *n*

A word that is capitalized in some senses and lowercase in others shows variations from the form of the main entry by the use of italicized labels at the appropriate senses.

pat•er•nos•ter . . . *n* **1** *often cap*
Cae•sar . . . *n* . . . **2 a** *often not cap*
Cay•use . . . *n* . . . **2** . . . *not cap*

The Forms of Words

The plurals of nouns (and a few pronouns and adjectives), the past tense, past participle, and present participle forms of verbs, and the comparative and superlative forms of adjectives and adverbs are known as **inflected forms.** For most entries, these inflected forms are regular (that is, they are formed by the addition of *-s* or *-es* to nouns, *-ed* and *-ing* to verbs, and *-er* and *-est* to adjectives and adverbs), and these regular forms, since they normally present no problems in spelling, are not shown in *Merriam-Webster's School Dictionary.*

We do show irregular inflected forms, such as those that involve a change in the spelling of the base word or a doubling of a final letter, and any that we feel you might have reasonable doubts about.

NOUNS

Plurals are shown in this book when there is no change made in the base word,

deer . . . *n, pl* **deer**

when a final *-y* changes to *-i-* before the addition of *-es,*

ba•by . . . *n, pl* **babies**

when the plural involves a change in the spelling of the base word,

ax•is . . . *n, pl* **ax•es**
[1]that . . . *pron, pl* **those**

and when the word has kept a foreign plural.

se•ta . . . *n, pl* **se•tae**

Plurals are also shown for all nouns that end in *-o* or *-ey,*

ego . . . *n, pl* **egos**
don•key . . . *n, pl* **donkeys**

when a final consonant is doubled,

quiz . . . *n, pl* **quizzes**

for those that are pluralized in a way you may not expect,

[3]dry *n, pl* **drys**
goose•foot . . . *n, pl* **goosefoots**

and for any others we think you might have questions about.

[1]pi . . . *n, pl* **pis**
ninth . . . *n, pl* **ninths**

Most compounds pluralize the final element. These are considered regular plurals, and they are not shown when the final element is a recognizable word entered at its own place in the dictionary, such as *charwoman* or *thimbleberry.* We do show plurals for compounds that pluralize any element but the last,

moth•er–in–law . . . *n, pl* **moth•ers–in–law**
postmaster general *n, pl* **postmasters general**

and for all entries that have variant plural forms.

bis•cuit . . . *n, pl* **biscuits** *also* **biscuit**
[1]fish . . . *n, pl* **fish** *or* **fish•es**

Plurals are not shown for nouns that do not regularly have a plural use, like *paleontology*.

To save space, cutback inflected forms are used when the noun has three or more syllables. The form is usually cut back to the point that corresponds to the last indicated end-of-line division in the main entry.

anom·a·ly . . . *n, pl* **-lies**

VERBS

Principal parts are usually not shown for regular verbs—those that simply add *-ed* and *-ing,* either directly to the base word or after dropping a final *-e*—but they are shown for verbs that inflect in other ways. In such cases the past tense and present participle forms are always shown. The past participle is shown only when it differs from the past tense, and when it is shown it comes between the past tense and the present participle.

Inflections are shown when one or more principal parts change the spelling of the base word,

[1]**know** . . . *vb* **knew** . . . ; **known** . . . ; **know·ing**

when a final consonant is doubled before the addition of *-ed* or *-ing,*

[2]**crib** *vb* **cribbed; crib·bing**

and when a final *-y* becomes *-i-* before *-ed.*

[1]**hur·ry** . . . *vb* **hur·ried; hur·ry·ing**

Inflections are also shown for verbs when the final *-c* is changed to *-ck* before *-ed* and *-ing,*

[2]**picnic** *vi* **pic·nicked; pic·nick·ing**

when the base word ends in *-ee* or *-ey,*

agree . . . *vb* **agreed; agree·ing**
con·vey . . . *vt* **con·veyed; con·vey·ing**

when there are variant forms of the inflections,

[3]**bias** *vt* **bi·ased** *or* **bi·assed; bi·as·ing** *or* **bi·as·sing**

and when we feel you might have reasonable doubts about the forms.

[2]**visa** *vt* **vi·saed** . . . ; **vi·sa·ing**

Inflected forms of verbs with more than two syllables are cut back to the last indicated end-of-line division in the main entry.

mod·i·fy . . . *vb* **-fied; -fy·ing**

The cutback form is also used for verbs that end in *-l* when there are space-consuming variant forms,

[1]**can·cel** . . . *vb* **-celed** *or* **-celled; -cel·ing** *or* **-cel·ling**

and for verb compounds when the second element is a recognizable verb with irregular inflections.

fore·see . . . *vt* **-saw** . . . ; **-seen** . . . ; **-see·ing**

ADJECTIVES & ADVERBS

Most adjectives and adverbs form their comparatives and superlatives with *more* or *most* or with the addition of *-er* and *-est,* either directly to the base word or after dropping a final *-e.* These are considered regular formations and are not shown in *Merriam-Webster's School Dictionary.* We do show all irregularly formed inflections of adjectives and adverbs, and many of these are cut back in the superlative to just *-est.*

Comparative and superlative forms are shown for entries that change the base word,

[1]**good** . . . *adj* **bet·ter** . . . ; **best**
[3]**well** *adv* **bet·ter** . . . ; **best**

for those that double the final consonant before *-er* or *-est,*

[1]**flat** . . . *adj* **flat·ter; flat·test**

for those that change the final *-y* to an *-i* before the suffixes,

handy . . . *adj* **hand·i·er; -est**

for any adjectives or adverbs ending in *-ey,*

ca·gey . . . *adj* **ca·gi·er; -est**

and for those with variant forms.

dry . . . *adj* **dri·er** *also* **dry·er** . . . ; **dri·est** *also* **dry·est**
far . . . *adv* **far·ther** . . . *or* **fur·ther** . . . ; **far·thest** *or* **fur·thest**

The superlative forms of adjectives and adverbs of two or more syllables are usually cut back.

[3]**fancy** *adj* **fan·ci·er; -est**
[1]**ear·ly** . . . *adv* **ear·li·er; -est**

Whenever one inflected form but not another is in current use, we show only the current form in full with an appropriate label.

[2]**mere** *adj, superlative* **mer·est**

Sometimes we write out in full regular inflections or inflections that might normally be cut back in order to show the pronunciation of one or more forms.

daz·zle . . . *vt* **daz·zled; daz·zling** \ˈdaz-ling, -ə-ling\
[2]**model** *vb* **mod·eled** *or* **mod·elled; mod·el·ing** *or* **mod·el·ling** \ˈmäd-ling, -l-ing\

[1]**long** . . . *adj* **long·er** \ˈlȯng-gər\; **long·est** \ˈlȯng-gəst\

The comparative and superlative forms of adverbs are not shown when they are identical to the inflected forms of a preceding adjective homograph.

[1]**hot** . . . *adj* **hot·ter; hot·test**

[2]**hot** *adv*

The Meaning of Words

The **definition** is the core of the dictionary. It gives the meaning of the entry word. Every definition in *Merriam-Webster's School Dictionary* is introduced by a boldface colon whether or not there is a number before it.

blue jeans *n pl* : pants usually made of blue denim
blue law *n* **1** : one of many strict laws regulating morals and conduct in colonial New England

Often an entry or numbered meaning has more than one definition separated by a colon.

[1]**glad** . . . **1 a** : experiencing pleasure, joy, or delight : made happy

[2]**glint** *n* **1** : a small bright flash of light : SPARKLE

These different definitions, known as **substitutes,** are so close in meaning that either one can be substituted for the entry word in context without any change in meaning. Often the only difference between substitutes is in the point of view from which they are written.

When a main entry has a number of different **meanings** or **senses,** the senses are separated using boldface numerals and are arranged in historical order, with the oldest recorded meaning coming first, then the next oldest, and so on. The most recent meanings will normally be given last. With this method of ordering senses, you can follow the development of a word as the meanings have changed over the years.

The historical ordering of senses should not be taken to mean, however, that each sense necessarily developed directly from the earlier one. In many instances, each of the various successive senses may all have derived independently from the original meaning.

In addition to the division of definitions into numbered senses, some entries have the meanings further broken down into **subsenses.** These subsenses, marked by letters (**a, b, c,** etc.) are used when related meanings are grouped together. The order of subsenses is historical insofar as the dates can be established, but subsenses may not be in strict historical order with respect to the broader numbered senses.

[1]**bag** . . . *n* **1 a** : a flexible usually closed container for holding, storing, or carrying something **b** : PURSE; *esp* : HANDBAG **c** : SUITCASE **2** : something resembling a bag: as **a** (1) : a pouched or pendulous bodily part or organ; *esp* : UDDER (2) : a puffy sagging area of loose skin ⟨*bags* under the eyes⟩ **b** : a puffed-out sag or bulge in cloth **c** : a square white canvas container to mark a base in baseball **3** : the amount contained in a bag **4** : a quantity of game taken or permitted to be taken **5** : a slovenly unattractive woman

In this example, the numbered senses of *bag* are all in historical order and the subsenses within a numbered sense grouping are also offered by date of first occurrence. But sense 1c, meaning "a suitcase," properly belongs with the other senses that refer to a container—yet it actually came into use much later than sense number 4. And the baseball sense, 2c, also developed after sense 4, but it is grouped with the other senses at 2 because it is related in the idea of "something resembling a bag."

When further subdivision of a sense is needed, we indicate it by numerals in parentheses, as in senses 2a(1) and 2a(2) of *bag.*

Sometimes senses are divided by one of two italic labels. We use the sense divider *esp* (especially) to introduce the most common meaning covered by the more general definition immediately before it (as in senses 1b and 2a(1) of *bag*). We use *also* to introduce a closely related use obviously derived from the basic sense.

base·ball . . . *n* : a game played with a bat and ball between two teams of nine players each on a field with four bases that mark the course a runner must take to score; *also* : the ball used in this game

Cross-references

Words printed in small capitals are **cross-references.** A cross-reference in a definition is called a **synonymous cross-reference.** It is a *synonym* of the word, another word that means the same thing as the main entry word.

You may see a synonym appearing as a second substitute or standing in place of a definition.

Sometimes a synonymous cross-reference includes a sense number, meaning that only one sense of the synonym is the same as the entry word.

[3]**dab** *n* **1** : DAUB 1

[2]**daub** *n* **1** : something daubed on

When we use a cross-reference, it is always to a word that is of the same part of speech as the entry word. For example, a cross-reference at a noun entry word is always to another noun. When the synonym has two homographs that are the same part of speech, we use a homograph number with the cross-reference.

fly ball *n* : [2]FLY 5

[2]**fly** *n, pl* **flies** . . . **5** : a baseball hit high into the air

When a synonymous cross-reference is to a word with more than one sense and the cross-reference does not indicate a specific sense, you know that the words are synonymous in all senses.

cow·punch·er . . . *n* : COWBOY

cow·boy . . . *n* **1** : one who tends or drives cattle; *esp* : a usually mounted cattle ranch hand **2** : a participant in rodeos

Many entries or senses are defined only by two synonymous cross-references separated by a comma. You might think of these paired synonyms as two substitutes at a sense. When the first cross-reference is to an entry that has several senses, it usually includes a sense number,

¹charge . . . *n* . . . **3 a** : OBLIGATION 2, REQUIREMENT

unless both synonyms are common words that together help define the entry word and leave no doubt as to the intended meaning.

¹charge . . . *n* . . . **4** : INSTRUCTION, COMMAND

In addition to the synonymous cross-references in the definitions, there are three other types of cross-references used in *Merriam-Webster's School Dictionary*. Cross-references that follow a dash and the words *see* or *compare* (usually at the end of a definition) are called **directional cross-references.** They direct the reader to look at another entry for an explanation or related information.

digital computer *n* : a computer that operates with numbers in the form of digits — compare ANALOG COMPUTER

li·ter *or* **li·tre** \ˈlēt-ər\ *n* : a metric unit of capacity equal to one cubic decimeter — see METRIC SYSTEM table

The "see" directional cross-reference may also be used in place of a definition.

four . . . **1** — see NUMBER table

The **cognate cross-reference** is used when a variant form of a word is entered at its own alphabetical place in the dictionary and the reader is directed to see the entry at the more common variant.

lichee *variant of* LYCHEE

des·patch *chiefly British variant of* DISPATCH

sith . . . *archaic variant of* SINCE

The **inflectional cross-reference** is used when an inflected form of an entry is entered at its own alphabetical place. It tells you to go to the base word.

sought *past and past participle of* SEEK

was *past 1st & 3rd sing of* BE

Synonym Paragraphs

Merriam-Webster's School Dictionary also treats a number of synonyms in individual synonym articles set off as separate paragraphs at the end of entries. These synonym paragraphs help the reader discriminate among a number of similar words. Each paragraph begins with a list of the words to be discussed in it, followed by a statement of the element of meaning that the words have in common. At the entry for every word that is discussed in a synonym paragraph, there is a cross-reference, indicated by "***synonyms*** see . . . ," to the entry where the paragraph is located.

al·lo·cate . . . ***synonyms*** see ALLOT

ap·por·tion . . . ***synonyms*** see ALLOT

al·lot . . .

synonyms ALLOT, APPORTION, ALLOCATE mean to give as one's share. ALLOT may imply haphazard or arbitrary distribution ⟨*alloted* himself an hour daily for exercise⟩. APPORTION implies a dividing according to some regular principle ⟨*apportioned* a share to each person⟩. ALLOCATE implies a fixed appropriation for a particular use ⟨*allocated* tasks among the workers⟩.

The Usage of Words

New or unusual words, even when they have been defined, may sometimes seem like nothing more than abstractions to you until you understand how the words are actually used in writing or speaking. And there are times when an example of how a word is used can do more than a definition to convey meaning and proper usage. Sometimes too the meanings of individual senses are similar, but the way the senses are normally used in sentences is quite different. To help you better understand how the words are actually used, *Merriam-Webster's School Dictionary* gives brief examples of the words in everyday language as illustrations of idiomatic usage for many of the entries and senses. These **verbal illustrations** follow the definitions and are enclosed in angle brackets ⟨ ⟩, and the entry word, or an inflection of it, is printed in italics.

¹ar·rest \ə-ˈrest\ *vt* **1 a** : to stop the progress or movement of **b** : CHECK, SLOW ⟨*arrest* a disease⟩ **2** : to take or keep in custody by authority of law ⟨*arrested* on suspicion of robbery⟩ **3** : to attract and hold the attention of ⟨colors that *arrest* the eye⟩

Merriam-Webster's School Dictionary also gives information about word usage in two other ways. The first is by means of italic labels immediately following the part-of-speech or function label or, when the information applies only to one sense, just after the sense number or letter. These labels indicate limited areas of use in the English-speaking world or special subject matter with which a word or sense is used. They also indicate when a word's use is restricted with respect to a standard usage and when you should capitalize the word.

Many words or senses have use limited to a particular region of the United States.

pone . . . *n, Southern & Midland* : CORN PONE

And some words may be encountered only in dialect, but the use is over so wide an area that no specific regional label applies.

lar·rup . . . *vt* **1** *dialect* : WHIP 2a

A word or sense limited in use to one of the other countries of the English-speaking world has an appropriate regional label. The label *British* indicates that a word or sense is current in the United Kingdom or in one or more than one nation of the Commonwealth (as the United Kingdom, Australia, or Canada).

long–sight·ed . . . *adj, chiefly British* : FARSIGHTED

foot·ball . . . **1** . . . **a** *British* : SOCCER

laird . . . *n, chiefly Scottish* : a landed proprietor

Italic labels are also used to indicate that various entries or individual senses are not current in English usage. We enter a few words in this dictionary because of their historical importance in literature, but the words have not been an active part of the language for many years. The label *obsolete* tells you a word or sense has not been used in more than 200 years.

[2]all . . . **2** *obsolete* : ONLY 1b, SOLELY

Old words and meanings that are used only occasionally or not at all today or that may occur only in special uses (for example, in church liturgies) we label *archaic.*

[1]fain . . . **1** *archaic* : GLAD, HAPPY

Some of the entries in the dictionary, although commonly used, are still not a part of what is considered standard usage. To help the student recognize these words and meanings, most of which are not appropriate for formal writing, three additional labels are used: *substandard,* for words that have some currency in all areas of the United States but which are not normally used by educated writers and speakers; *nonstandard,* for words that are sometimes used by well-educated people but which nevertheless are not always considered appropriate for good usage; and *slang,* words and senses that convey a flavor of extreme informality, consist of colorful and sometimes unconventional coinages and figures of speech, and are used chiefly by a particular cultural group, such as students.

learn . . . **2** *substandard* : to cause to learn : TEACH

[1]lay . . . **12** *nonstandard* : [1]LIE

[2]grand . . . **2** . . . *slang* : a thousand dollars

The labels *disparaging* and *offensive* are used for those words or senses that in common use are intended to hurt or shock or that are likely to give offense even when they are used without such an intent.

USAGE NOTES

The italic labels that appear before the definitions are one way we give information on how words are used. Another way is through **usage notes** that follow the definitions. A usage note is set off from the definition by a dash. These notes are normally used to give information on usage that is not a proper part of the definitions and that cannot be given adequately by labels.

Usage notes usually show a limited range of application of the word

[2]bias . . . — used chiefly of fabrics and their cut

le·ga·to . . . *adv or adj* . . . — used as a direction in music

dick·ens . . . — used chiefly as a mild oath

or give information about context.

[1]dint . . . — used chiefly in the phrase *by dint of*

Sometimes when usage for a sense is mostly plural—but not enough to permit a *pl* label before the definition—we give you that information in a usage note.

[2]narrow . . . — usually used in plural

There are times when we use usage notes in place of definitions if the word has a special use that cannot be easily explained in the definition.

[2]please *adv* **1** — used as a function word to express politeness . . .

Ms. . . . *n* — used instead of *Miss* or *Mrs.* as a courtesy title (as when the marital status of a woman is unknown or irrelevant)

USAGE PARAGRAPHS

Brief paragraphs on usage have been placed at a number of entries for terms that are considered to present problems of confused or disputed usage. A usage paragraph may give some historical background of the usage issue and the opinions associated with it, often compares these opinions with the current evidence about how the word is used, and usually offers some advice to the dictionary user. Each paragraph is signaled by an indented boldface italic ***usage.*** At the entry for every word that is discussed in a usage paragraph, there is a cross-reference, indicated by "***usage*** see . . . ," to the entry where the paragraph is located.

[2]**affect** *vt* . . . ***usage*** see EFFECT

[3]**affect** *n* . . . ***usage*** see EFFECT

[2]**effect** . . .
usage *Effect* and *affect* are often confused because of their similar spelling and pronunciation. The verb [2]*affect* usually has to do with pretense ⟨she *affected* a cheery disposition despite feeling down⟩. The more common [3]*affect* denotes having an effect or influence ⟨the weather *affected* everyone's mood⟩. The verb *effect* goes beyond mere influence; it refers to actual achievement of a final result ⟨the new administration hopes to *effect* a peace settlement⟩. The uncommon noun *affect*, which has a meaning relating to psychology, is also sometimes mistakenly used for the very common *effect*. In ordinary use, the noun you will want is *effect* ⟨waiting for the new law to take *effect*⟩ ⟨the weather had an *effect* on everyone's mood⟩.

The History of Words

Merriam-Webster's School Dictionary shows when and how the various main-entry words originated and developed in the **etymology**, which is in square brackets following the definition.

The etymology traces the word as far back in English as possible, sometimes all the way to Old English, the earliest language of the English people —from about A.D. 600 to about 1100. In the etymology, the entry word's ancestors are given in italics and their meanings in quotation marks.

[3]**bit** *n* **1** : a small piece or amount . . . ⟨a little *bit* of luck⟩ . . . [Old English *bita* "piece bitten off"]

When the etymology gives a language from which the main-entry word derived but does not show the word form in that language, it means the form of the word in the earlier language was the same as that of the main entry. When there is no meaning given in the etymology, the meaning of the older word was the same as the *first* sense of the main entry.

[1]**arm** . . . **1 a** : a human upper limb; . . . [Old English *earm*]

[1]**blind** . . . **1 a** : SIGHTLESS . . . [Old English]

In the first example, the etymology shows that the modern English word *arm* can be traced back to the Old English word *earm* which had the same meaning as the first sense of *arm*. The second example tells us that the Old English word *blind*, meaning "without sight," was the ancestor of our modern English word *blind*.

When the etymology shows that an entry word has been traced back only into Middle English (from about 1100 to about 1500), it indicates that there is no evidence of it from Old English manuscripts and no indication that it was borrowed from another language.

[1]**bur·row** . . . [Middle English *borow*]

The etymologies in *Merriam-Webster's School Dictionary* trace the development of words in reverse order, giving the most recent ancestors first and moving backward to the oldest. Whenever a word form or a meaning is not shown at a particular stage in the etymology, it is the same as the form or meaning given before, or if none has been given before in the etymology, the same as that of the main entry.

pope . . . *n, often cap* : the head of the Roman Catholic Church [Old English *pāpa*, from Late Latin *papa*, from Greek *pappas, papas* title of bishops, literally, "papa"]

[1]**fi·nance** . . . **1** *pl* : liquid resources (as money) . . . [Middle English, "ending, payment," from Medieval French, from *finer* "to end, pay," from *fin* "end," from Latin *finis*]

In the first example the modern English word *pope* is derived from Old English *pāpa*, meaning "pope," which in turn came from the Late Latin word *papa*, also meaning "pope." The Latin word came from Greek *pappas*, which meant literally "papa" and had been used as a title of bishops. In the second example, the modern English word *finance* meaning "money resources" came from the Middle English word *finance*, which meant "payment" or "ending." This Middle English word was derived from a Medieval French word that had the same spelling and the same meaning as the Middle English word *finance*. This Medieval French word came from an earlier Medieval French word *finer*, which meant "to end" or "to pay," which was itself derived from the early Medieval French word *fin*, which meant "end." And the early Medieval French word *fin* was derived from the still earlier Latin word *finis*, which also meant "end."

Words borrowed directly into modern English show first the language from which the word was borrowed.

ro·deo . . . **1** : ROUNDUP 1 . . . [Spanish, from *rodear* "to surround," from *rueda* "wheel," from Latin *rota*]

te·pee . . . [Dakota (Siouan language of the Dakota Indians) *tʰípi*, from *tʰi-* "to dwell"]

caf·tan *also* **kaf·tan** . . . [Russian *kaftan*, from Turkish, from Persian *qaftān*]

gin·seng . . . [Chinese (Beijing dialect) *rénshēn*]

Words that are formed in modern English from other English words do not normally have etymologies, since the origin is usually obvious. Thus, the entry *likable* does not have an etymology because the word is derived from English *like* by addition of an ordinary English suffix *-able*. However, etymologies are given for words that are made up of parts of other words.

aero·sol . . . [*aer-* + [3]*sol*]

brunch . . . [*b*reakfast + l*unch*]

¹GI . . . [galvanized *i*ron; from abbreviation used in listing such articles as garbage cans, but taken as abbreviation for *government issue*]

ra·dar . . . [*ra*dio *d*etecting *a*nd *r*anging]

When a word comes from a person's name, we show that in the etymology,

der·by . . . **1** : any of several horse races . . . [Edward Stanley, died 1834, 12th earl of *Derby*]

but we do not show the name of a person who first used a word—unless the word was coined, that is, created as an original word that did not exist before in English or any other language.

blurb . . . [coined by Gelett Burgess, died 1951, American humorist]

For a number of entries whose origins are particularly interesting, we give additional information in a ***Word History*** **paragraph** beyond what is found in the etymology. In some cases the paragraph also contains information on how the meaning of the word has changed in English over the centuries.

¹dream \\'drēm\\ *n* **1** : a series of thoughts, images, or emotions occurring during sleep **2** . . . [Old English *drēam* "noise, joy"]

Word History Not until the 13th century was our word *dream* used in the sense of "a series of thoughts, images, or emotions occurring during sleep." But the word itself is considerably older. In Old English *dream* means "joy," "noise," or "music." Yet the shift in sense did not come simply from the development of a more specialized sense. Rather it appears that after many Scandinavian conflicts, conquests, and settlements in Britain the Old Norse *draumr*, meaning "a dream during sleep," influenced the meaning of the similar and probably related English word. By the end of the 14th century the earlier meanings had been entirely replaced.

Lists of Undefined Words

Lists of words without definitions appear at the following prefix entries in *Merriam-Webster's School Dictionary:*

anti-
co-
counter-
hyper-
inter-
mis-
multi-
non-
out-
over-
post-
pre-
re-
sub-
super-
ultra-
un-

The meanings of the compounds formed with these prefixes are readily understandable from the meaning of the prefix and the meaning of the base word, and these words are entered here to indicate to the reader that they are relatively common words and to show spelling. Compounds that are not readily understandable from the sum of the elements are given own-place entry with definitions.

Abbreviations Used in This Dictionary

A.D.	anno Domini
adj	adjective
adv	adverb
a.m.	ante meridiem
B.C.	before Christ
C	Celsius, centigrade
cap	capitalized
conj	conjunction
constr	construction
E	east, eastern
ENE	east-northeast
ESE	east-southeast
esp	especially
F	Fahrenheit
interj	interjection
n	noun
N	north, northern
NE	northeast, northeastern
NNE	north-northeast
NNW	north-northwest
n pl	noun plural
NW	northwest, northwestern
pl	plural
p.m.	post meridiem
prep	preposition
pron	pronoun
S	south, southern
SE	southeast, southeastern
sing	singular
SSE	south-southeast
SSW	south-southwest
SW	southwest, southwestern
U.S.	United States
U.S.S.R.	Union of Soviet Socialist Republics
usu	usually
vb	verb
vi	verb intrasitive
vt	verb transitive
W	west, western
WNW	west-northwest
WSW	west-southwest

Pronunciation Symbols

ə .... (called *schwa* \ˈshwä\) banana, collide, abut; in stressed syllables as in humdrum, mother, abut

ᵊ .... used when needed to indicate that the following symbol stands for a syllabic consonant, as in shrapnel \ˈshrap-nᵊl\

ər .... further, merger

a .... map, mat, mad, gag, snap, patch

ā .... day, fade, mate, drape, cape, aorta

ä .... bother, cot and, with most American speakers, father, cart

ȧ .... father as pronounced by those who do not rhyme it with *bother*; French patte

au̇ .... now, loud, out

b .... baby, rib

ch .... chin, match, nature \ˈnā-chər\; (actually, this sound is \t\ + \sh\)

d .... did, adder

e .... bed, pet

ē .... beat, easy, carefree; in unstressed syllables as in easy, daily, creation

f .... fifty, cuff

g .... go, big

h .... hat, ahead

hw .... whale as pronounced by those who do not pronounce *whale* and *wail* the same

i .... bid, tip, active, banish

ī .... site, side, buy; (actually, this sound is \ä\ + \i\, or \ȧ\ + \i\)

j .... job, gem, judge; (actually, this sound is \d\ + \zh\)

k .... kin, cook, ache

k̲ .... German ich, Buch; one pronunciation of loch

l .... lily, pool, build, cold, battle, handle

m .... murmur, dim, lamp, happen \ˈhap-ən, ˈhap-m\

n .... no, own, cotton, maiden

ⁿ .... indicates that a preceding vowel or diphthong is pronounced with the nasal passages open, as in garçon \gär-ˈsōⁿ\

ng .... sing \ˈsiŋ\, singer \ˈsiŋ-ər\, finger \ˈfiŋ-gər\, ink \ˈiŋk\, lock and key \ˈläk-ŋ-ˈkē\; (actually, this is a single sound, not two)

ō .... bone, know, soap

ȯ .... saw, all, taut

œ .... French boeuf, German Hölle

œ̄ .... French feu, German Höhle

ȯi .... coin, destroy

p .... pepper, lip

r .... red, rarity, rhyme, car

s .... source, less

sh .... shy, mission, machine, special; (actually, this is a single sound, not two)

t .... tie, attack, hot, water

th .... thin, ether; (actually, this is a single sound, not two)

th̲ .... this, either; (actually, this is a single sound, not two)

ü .... rule, youth, few \ˈfyü\, union \ˈyün-yən\

u̇ .... pull, wood, foot, curable \ˈkyu̇r-ə-bəl\

ue .... German füllen, hübsch

ue̅ .... French rue, German fühlen

v .... vivid, give

w .... we, away

y .... yard, young, cue \ˈkyü\, union \ˈyün-yən\

ʸ .... indicates that the sound represented by the preceding character is pronounced with the front of the tongue in the approximate position it has for the first sound of *yard*, as in French *digne* \dēnʸ\

yü .... youth, union, cue, few, music

yu̇ .... curable, fury

z .... zone, raise

zh .... vision, azure \ˈazh-ər\; (actually, this is a single sound, not two)

\ .... slant line used in pairs to mark the beginning and end of a transcription

, ; .... a comma separates variant pronunciations; a semicolon separates groups of variants

ˈ .... mark preceding a syllable with primary (strongest) stress: \ˈpen-mən-ˌship\

ˌ .... mark preceding a syllable with secondary (next-strongest) stress: \ˈpen-mən-ˌship\

- .... a hyphen separates syllables in a transcription

A

[1]**a** \ˈā\ *n, pl* **a's** *or* **as** \ˈāz\ *often cap* **1 :** the 1st letter of the English alphabet **2 :** the musical tone A **3 :** a grade rating a student's work as superior

[2]**a** \ə, ā, ˈā\ *indefinite article* **1 :** some one unspecified ⟨*a* person in the street⟩ ⟨*a* dozen⟩ **2 :** the same : ONE ⟨two of *a* kind⟩ ⟨birds of *a* feather⟩ **3 :** ANY ⟨*a* person who is sick can't work⟩ — used in all senses before words beginning with a consonant sound; compare [1]AN [Middle English *an, a,* from Old English *ān* "one"]

[3]**a** \ə\ *prep* **1** *chiefly dialect* **:** ON, IN, AT **2 :** in, to, or for each — used before words with an initial consonant sound ⟨twice *a* week⟩ ⟨dime *a* dozen⟩ [Old English *an, on, a-*]

[1]**a-** \ə\ *prefix* **1 :** on : in : at ⟨*a*bed⟩ **2 :** in a specified state or condition ⟨*a*fire⟩ ⟨*a*sleep⟩ **3 :** in (such) a manner ⟨*a*loud⟩ **4 :** in the act or process of ⟨gone *a*-hunting⟩ [Old English]

[2]**a-** \ā, ˈā *also* a, ˈa, ä, ˈä\ *or* **an-** \an, ˈan\ *prefix* **:** not : without ⟨*a*sexual⟩ — *a-* before consonants other than *h* and sometimes even before *h, an-* before vowels and usually before *h* ⟨*an*astigmatic⟩ ⟨*an*hydrous⟩ [Greek]

aah *also* **ah** \ˈä\ *vb* **:** to exclaim in amazement, joy, or surprise ⟨oohing and *aahing* at the fireworks⟩

aard·vark \ˈärd-ˌvärk\ *n* **:** a large burrowing nocturnal African mammal with a long sticky tongue which it uses to feed on insects and especially termites [Afrikaans, literally, "earth pig"]

aardvark

Aa·ron·ic \a-ˈrän-ik, e-\ *adj* **:** of or relating to the lower order of the Mormon priesthood [*Aaron,* brother of Moses]

ab- *prefix* **:** from : away : off ⟨*ab*normal⟩ [Latin *ab-, abs-, a-*]

ab·a·ca \ˌab-ə-ˈkä\ *n* **:** a strong fiber obtained from a banana plant native to the Philippines — called also *manila hemp* [Spanish *abacá,* from Tagalog *abaká*]

aback \ə-ˈbak\ *adv* **1** *archaic* **:** BACK, BACKWARD **2 :** by surprise : UNAWARES ⟨taken *aback* by the turn of events⟩

aba·cus \ˈab-ə-kəs, ə-ˈbak-əs\ *n, pl* **aba·ci** \ˈab-ə-ˌsī, -ˌkē; ə-ˈbak-ˌī\ *or* **aba·cus·es** **1 :** a slab that forms the uppermost part of the capital of a column **2 :** an instrument for making calculations by sliding counters along rods or in grooves [Latin, from Greek *abax* "board, slab"]

[1]**abaft** \ə-ˈbaft\ *adv* **:** toward or at the stern : AFT [Middle English, from [1]*a-* + *baft* "in the rear," from Old English *bæftan,* from *be* "by" + *æftan* "behind"]

[2]**abaft** *prep* **:** to the rear of; *esp* **:** toward the stern from

ab·a·lo·ne \ˌab-ə-ˈlō-nē, ˈab-ə-ˌ\ *n* **:** any of several mollusks with flattened slightly spiral shells perforated along the edge and lined with mother-of-pearl [American Spanish *abulón,* from Rumsen (American Indian language of Monterey Bay, Calif.)]

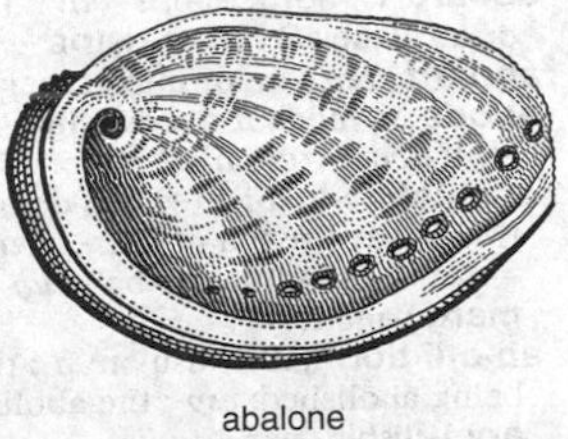

abalone

[1]**aban·don** \ə-ˈban-dən\ *vt* **1 :** to give up completely ⟨*abandon* a difficult task⟩ **2 :** to withdraw from often in the face of danger ⟨*abandon* ship⟩ **3 :** to withdraw protection, support, or help from ⟨*abandoned* the dog⟩ **4 :** to give (oneself) over to an emotion without restraint [Middle French *abanduner,* from *a bandun* "in one's power"] — **aban·don·er** *n* — **aban·don·ment** \-dən-mənt\ *n*

synonyms ABANDON, DESERT, FORSAKE mean to leave without intending to return. ABANDON may stress withdrawing protection or care from ⟨*abandon* a property⟩. DESERT implies leaving in violation of a duty or promise ⟨*desert* a military post⟩. FORSAKE implies breaking ties with something familiar or cherished ⟨could not *forsake* his family⟩.

[2]**abandon** *n* **:** a complete yielding to natural impulses; *esp* **:** carefree enthusiasm : EXUBERANCE ⟨laughing with *abandon*⟩

aban·doned \ə-ˈban-dənd\ *adj* **1 :** that has been deserted : FORSAKEN ⟨an *abandoned* house⟩ **2 :** completely free from restraint ⟨*abandoned* laughter⟩

abase \ə-ˈbās\ *vt* **:** to lower in rank or position : HUMBLE, DEGRADE [Medieval French *abesser*] — **abase·ment** \-mənt\ *n*

abash \ə-ˈbash\ *vt* **:** to destroy the self-possession or self-confidence of : DISCONCERT [Medieval French *esbaiss-,* stem of *esbair* "to be astonished," from *ex-* + *baer* "to open wide, gape"] ***synonyms*** see EMBARRASS — **abash·ment** \-mənt\ *n*

abate \ə-ˈbāt\ *vb* **:** to reduce or decrease in degree, amount, or intensity ⟨may *abate* their anger for the sake of peace⟩ ⟨*abate* a tax⟩ [Medieval French *abatre* "to beat down"] — **abat·er** *n*

abate·ment \ə-ˈbāt-mənt\ *n* **1 :** the act or process of abating : the state of being abated **2 :** an amount abated; *esp* **:** a deduction from the full amount of a tax

ab·at·toir \ˈab-ə-ˌtwär\ *n* **:** SLAUGHTERHOUSE [French, from *abattre* "to beat down"]

ab·ax·i·al \ab-ˈak-sē-əl\ *adj* **:** situated or facing away from the axis ⟨the *abaxial* or lower surface of the leaf⟩ [*ab-* + *axis*]

ab·ba·cy \ˈab-ə-sē\ *n, pl* **-cies :** the office, term of office, position, or jurisdiction of an abbot

ab·ba·tial \ə-ˈbā-shəl, a-\ *adj* **:** of or relating to an abbot, abbess, or abbey

ab·bé \a-ˈbā, ˈab-ˌā\ *n* **:** a French cleric not in a religious order — used as a title [French, from Late Latin *abbas* "abbot"]

ab·bess \ˈab-əs\ *n* **:** the superior of a convent of nuns

ab·bey \ˈab-ē\ *n, pl* **abbeys** **1 a :** a monastery governed by an abbot **b :** a convent governed by an abbess **2 :** a church that once belonged to an abbey ⟨Westminster *Abbey*⟩ [Medieval French *abbaie,* from Late Latin *abbatia,* from *abbas* "abbot"]

ab·bot \ˈab-ət\ *n* **:** the superior of a monastery for men [Old English *abbod,* from Late Latin *abbas,* from Late Greek, from Aramaic *abbā* "father"]

ab·bre·vi·ate \ə-ˈbrē-vē-ˌāt\ *vt* **:** to make briefer; *esp* **:** to reduce (as a word) to a shorter form intended to stand for the whole [Late Latin *abbreviare,* from Latin *ad-* + *brevis* "short, brief"] ***synonyms*** see SHORTEN — **ab·bre·vi·a·tor** \-ˌāt-ər\ *n*

ab·bre·vi·a·tion \ə-ˌbrē-vē-ˈā-shən\ *n* **1 :** the act or result of abbreviating : ABRIDGMENT **2 :** a shortened form of a written word or phrase used in place of the whole

ABC \ˌā-ˌbē-ˈsē\ *n, pl* **ABC's** *or* **ABCs** \-ˈsēz\ **1 :** ALPHABET — usually used in plural **2 a :** the rudiments of reading, writing, and spelling — usually used in plural **b :** the fundamentals of a subject — usually used in plural

Ab·di·as \ab-ˈdī-əs\ *n* **:** OBADIAH

ab·di·cate \ˈab-di-ˌkāt\ *vb* **:** to give up sovereign power, office, or responsibility usually formally : RENOUNCE [Latin *abdicare,* from *ab-* + *dicare* "to proclaim"] — **ab·di·ca·tion** \ˌab-di-ˈkā-shən\ *n* — **ab·di·ca·tor** \ˈab-di-ˌkāt-ər\ *n*

ab·do·men \ˈab-də-mən, ab-ˈdō-mən\ *n* **1 :** the part of the body between the chest and the pelvis; *also* **:** the body cavity containing the chief digestive organs **2 :** the hind portion of the body behind the thorax or cephalothorax in an arthropod [Latin] — **ab·dom·i·nal** \ab-ˈdäm-ən-l\ *adj* — **ab·dom·i·nal·ly** \-l-ē\ *adv*

A abdomen 2

ab·du·cens nerve \ab-ˈdü-ˌsenz, -ˈdyü-\ *n* **:** either of the 6th pair of cranial nerves supplying muscles of the eyes — called also *abducens* [Latin, "leading away"]

\ə\ **abut**	\au̇\ **out**	\i\ **tip**	\ȯ\ **saw**	\u̇\ **foot**
\ər\ **further**	\ch\ **chin**	\ī\ **life**	\ȯi\ **coin**	\y\ **yet**
\a\ **mat**	\e\ **pet**	\j\ **job**	\th\ **thin**	\yü\ **few**
\ā\ **take**	\ē\ **easy**	\ng\ **sing**	\t͟h\ **this**	\yu̇\ **cure**
\ä\ **cot, cart**	\g\ **go**	\ō\ **bone**	\ü\ **food**	\zh\ **vision**

ab·duct \ab-ˈdəkt\ *vt* **1 :** to carry (a person) off by force **2 :** to draw (a part of the body) away from the median axis of the body or bodily part; *also* **:** to move (similar parts) apart ⟨*abduct* adjoining fingers⟩ [Latin *abducere,* literally, "to lead away," from *ab-* + *ducere* "to lead"] — **ab·duc·tion** \-ˈdək-shən\ *n*

ab·duc·tor \-ˈdək-tər\ *n* **:** one that abducts; *esp* **:** a muscle that draws a body part (as an arm or finger) away from the median axis of the body or bodily part — compare ADDUCTOR

abeam \ə-ˈbēm\ *adv or adj* **:** on a line at right angles to a ship or plane's length

abed \ə-ˈbed\ *adv or adj* **:** in bed

Ab·er·deen An·gus \ˈab-ər-ˌdēn-ˈang-gəs\ *n* **:** ANGUS [*Aberdeen* and *Angus,* counties in Scotland]

ab·er·rant \a-ˈber-ənt\ *adj* **1 :** straying from the right or normal way **2 :** deviating from the usual or natural type **:** ATYPICAL [Latin *aberrare* "to go astray," from *ab-* + *errare* "to wander, err"] — **ab·er·rance** \-əns\ *n* — **ab·er·ran·cy** \-ən-sē\ *n* — **ab·er·rant·ly** *adv*

ab·er·ra·tion \ˌab-ə-ˈrā-shən\ *n* **1 :** the act of deviating especially from a moral standard or normal state **2 :** failure of a mirror or lens to produce exact correspondence between an object and its image **3 :** unsoundness or disorder of the mind **4 :** a small periodic change of apparent position in heavenly bodies due to the combined effect of the motion of light and the motion of the observer **5 :** an aberrant individual — **ab·er·ra·tion·al** \-shnəl, -shən-l\ *adj*

abet \ə-ˈbet\ *vb* **abet·ted; abet·ting :** to encourage or aid in achieving a purpose ⟨*abetted* the thieves in making their getaway⟩ [Medieval French *abeter,* from *a-* "ad-" + *beter* "to bait"] ***synonyms*** see INCITE — **abet·ment** \-mənt\ *n* — **abet·tor** *also* **abet·ter** \-ˈbet-ər\ *n*

abey·ance \ə-ˈbā-əns\ *n* **:** a temporary suspension of activity ⟨plans held in *abeyance*⟩ [Medieval French *abeance,* from *abaer* "to expect, await," from *a-* "ad-" + *baer* "to yawn, gape"] — **abey·ant** \-ənt\ *adj*

ab·hor \ab-ˈhȯr, əb-\ *vt* **ab·horred; ab·hor·ring :** to feel extreme disgust for **:** LOATHE [Latin *abhorrēre,* from *ab-* + *horrēre* "to shudder"] ***synonyms*** see HATE — **ab·hor·rence** \-ˈhȯr-əns, -ˈhär-\ *n* — **ab·hor·rer** \-ˈhȯr-ər\ *n*

ab·hor·rent \-ˈhȯr-ənt, -ˈhär-\ *adj* **1 :** feeling or showing disgust **2 :** not agreeable ⟨a notion *abhorrent* to their beliefs⟩ **3 :** DETESTABLE ***synonyms*** see REPUGNANT — **ab·hor·rent·ly** *adv*

abid·ance \ə-ˈbīd-ns\ *n* **1 :** the act or state of abiding **2 :** COMPLIANCE ⟨*abidance* by the rules⟩

abide \ə-ˈbīd\ *vb* **abode** \-ˈbōd\ *or* **abid·ed; abid·ing 1 :** to wait for **:** AWAIT **2 a :** to endure without yielding **:** WITHSTAND **b :** to bear patiently **:** TOLERATE **3 :** to accept without objection ⟨*abide* the court's decision⟩ **4 :** to remain stable or fixed in a state **5 :** to reside or continue in a place **:** DWELL [Old English *ābīdan,* from *ā-,* prefix denoting completion + *bīdan* "to bide"] ***synonyms*** see STAY — **abid·er** *n* — **abide by :** to accept the terms of **:** be obedient to ⟨*abide by* the rules⟩

abiding *adj* **:** LASTING, CONTINUING ⟨an *abiding* interest in nature⟩ — **abid·ing·ly** \-ing-lē\ *adv*

abil·i·ty \ə-ˈbil-ət-ē\ *n, pl* **-ties 1 a :** the quality or state of being able; *esp* **:** physical, mental, or legal power to do something **b :** competence in doing **:** SKILL **2 :** natural talent or acquired proficiency **:** APTITUDE

-abil·i·ty *also* **-ibil·i·ty** \ə-ˈbil-ət-ē\ *n suffix, pl* **-ties :** capacity, fitness, or tendency to act or be acted on in a (specified) way ⟨melt*ability*⟩ ⟨read*ability*⟩

abio·gen·e·sis \ˌā-ˌbī-ō-ˈjen-ə-səs\ *n, pl* **-e·ses** \-ˌsēz\ **:** SPONTANEOUS GENERATION

abi·ot·ic \ˌā-bī-ˈät-ik\ *adj* **:** not living or composed of living things ⟨soil acidity is an *abiotic* environmental factor⟩

ab·ject \ˈab-ˌjekt\ *adj* **1 :** sunk to a low condition **2 a :** having no pride or spirit ⟨made *abject* by suffering⟩ **b :** showing utter resignation **:** HOPELESS ⟨*abject* surrender⟩ **3 :** expressing or offered in a humble often ingratiating spirit ⟨an *abject* apology⟩ [Latin *abjectus,* from *abicere* "to cast off," from *ab-* + *jacere* "to throw"] — **ab·ject·ly** \ˈab-ˌjekt-lē, ab-ˈ\ *adv* — **ab·ject·ness** \-ˌjekt-nəs, -ˈjekt-\ *n*

ab·jure \ab-ˈju̇r\ *vt* **1 a :** to refuse to follow through one's oath ⟨*abjure* allegiance⟩ **b :** to reject solemnly **:** REPUDIATE ⟨*abjure* one's old beliefs⟩ **2 :** to abstain from **:** AVOID ⟨*abjure* extravagance⟩ [Latin *abjurare,* from *ab-* + *jurare* "to swear"] — **ab·ju·ra·tion** \ˌab-jə-ˈrā-shən\ *n* — **ab·jur·er** *n*

ab·late \a-ˈblāt\ *vb* **1 :** to remove or destroy by cutting, wearing away, evaporation, or vaporization **2 :** to undergo ablation

ab·la·tion \a-ˈblā-shən\ *n* **:** the process of ablating: as **a :** surgical removal **b :** removal of a part (as the outside of a nose cone) by melting or vaporization

ab·la·tive \ˈab-lət-iv\ *adj* **:** of, relating to, or constituting a grammatical case expressing typically the relations of separation and source and also frequently such relations as cause or instrument [Latin *ablat-,* alternate stem of *auferre* "to carry away, remove," from *au-* "ab-" + *ferre* "to carry"] — **ablative** *n*

ablative absolute *n* **:** a construction in Latin that consists of a noun or pronoun and its modifier both in the ablative case and together forming an adverbial phrase expressing generally the time, cause, or an attendant circumstance of an action

ablaze \ə-ˈblāz\ *adj* **1 :** being on fire **2 :** radiant with light, bright color, or emotion

able \ˈā-bəl\ *adj* **abler** \-bə-lər, -blər\; **ablest** \-bə-ləst, -bləst\ **1 a :** having enough power, skill, or resources to do something ⟨*able* to swim⟩ **b :** free from restrictions preventing an action ⟨*able* to vote⟩ **2 :** marked by intelligence, knowledge, skill, or competence ⟨an *able* news editor⟩ [Medieval French, from Latin *habilis* "handy, apt," from *habēre* "to have, hold"] — **ably** \ˈā-blē\ *adv*

synonyms ABLE, CAPABLE, COMPETENT mean having power to do or accomplish. ABLE may further imply skill that is above average and proved by performance ⟨an *able* trial lawyer⟩. CAPABLE stresses having necessary qualities or skill for a specified function or action ⟨a student *capable* of working independently⟩. COMPETENT suggests having necessary training, experience, or special knowledge ⟨a *competent* judge of figure skating⟩.

-able *also* **-ible** \ə-bəl\ *adj suffix* **1 :** capable of, fit for, or worthy of (being so acted upon or toward) — chiefly in adjectives derived from verbs ⟨eat*able*⟩ ⟨resist*ible*⟩ **2 :** tending, given, or likely to ⟨knowledge*able*⟩ ⟨perish*able*⟩ [Latin *-abilis, -ibilis*]

able–bod·ied \ˌā-bəl-ˈbäd-ēd\ *adj* **:** having a sound strong body **:** physically fit

able seaman *n* **:** an experienced deckhand qualified to perform routine duties at sea — called also *able-bodied seaman*

abloom \ə-ˈblüm\ *adj* **:** being in bloom

ab·lu·tion \a-ˈblü-shən, ə-ˈblü-\ *n* **:** the washing of oneself especially as a religious rite [Latin *abluere* "to wash away," from *ab-* + *lavere* "to wash"]

ABM \ˌā-ˌbē-ˈem\ *n, pl* **ABM's** *or* **ABMs :** ANTIBALLISTIC MISSILE

ab·ne·gate \ˈab-ni-ˌgāt\ *vt* **1 :** to give up or surrender (as a right or privilege) **:** RELINQUISH **2 :** to deny to or reject for oneself **:** RENOUNCE ⟨*abnegate* outworn beliefs⟩ — **ab·ne·ga·tion** \ˌab-ni-ˈgā-shən\ *n* — **ab·ne·ga·tor** \ˈab-ni-ˌgāt-ər\ *n*

ab·nor·mal \ab-ˈnȯr-məl, ˈab-ˈ\ *adj* **:** differing from the normal or average **:** UNUSUAL ⟨*abnormal* behavior⟩ — **ab·nor·mal·ly** \-mə-lē\ *adv*

ab·nor·mal·i·ty \ˌab-nər-ˈmal-ət-ē, -nȯr-\ *n, pl* **-ties 1 :** the quality or state of being abnormal **2 :** something abnormal

[1]**aboard** \ə-ˈbōrd, -ˈbȯrd\ *adv* **1 :** on, onto, or within a car, ship, or airplane **2 :** ALONGSIDE

[2]**aboard** *prep* **:** on or into especially for passage ⟨go *aboard* ship⟩

abode \ə-ˈbōd\ *n* **:** a dwelling place **:** RESIDENCE [Middle English *abod,* from *abiden* "to abide"]

abol·ish \ə-ˈbäl-ish\ *vt* **:** to do away with wholly **:** put an end to [Medieval French *aboliss-,* stem of *abolir,* from Latin *abolēre*] — **abol·ish·able** \-ə-bəl\ *adj* — **abol·ish·er** *n* — **abol·ish·ment** \-mənt\ *n*

ab·o·li·tion \ˌab-ə-ˈlish-ən\ *n* **:** the act of abolishing **:** the state of being abolished; *esp* **:** the abolishing of slavery — **ab·o·li·tion·ary** \-ˈlish-ə-ˌner-ē\ *adj*

ab·o·li·tion·ist \-ˈlish-nəst, -ə-nəst\ *n* **:** a person who is in favor of abolition especially of slavery — **ab·o·li·tion·ism** \-ˈlish-ə-ˌniz-əm\ *n*

ab·oma·sum \ˌab-ō-ˈmā-səm\ *n, pl* **-sa** \-sə\ **:** the fourth or true digestive stomach of a ruminant (as a cow) [Latin *ab-* + *omasum* "ox's tripe"] — **ab·oma·sal** \-səl\ *adj*

A–bomb \ˈā-ˌbäm\ *n* **:** ATOMIC BOMB

abom·i·na·ble \ə-ˈbäm-nə-bəl, -ə-nə-\ *adj* **1 :** deserving or causing loathing or hatred **:** DETESTABLE **2 :** quite disagreeable ⟨*abominable* weather⟩ — **abom·i·na·bly** \-blē\ *adv*

abominable snow·man \-ˈsnō-mən, -ˌman\ *n, often cap A&S* **:** a creature with human or apelike characteristics thought to exist in the Himalayas and usually held to be a bear

abom·i·nate \ə-ˈbäm-ə-ˌnāt\ *vt* **:** to hate or loathe intensely [Latin *abominari,* literally, "to deprecate as an ill omen," from *ab-* + *omen* "omen"] — **abom·i·na·tor** \-ˌnāt-ər\ *n*

abom·i·na·tion \ə-ˌbäm-ə-ˈnā-shən\ *n* **1 :** something detestable **2 :** extreme disgust and hatred **:** LOATHING

ab·o·rig·i·nal \ˌab-ə-ˈrij-nəl, -ən-l\ *adj* **1 :** being the first or earliest known of its kind in a region **:** INDIGENOUS **2 a :** of or relating to aborigines **b** *often cap* **:** of or relating to the indigenous peoples of Australia ***synonyms*** see NATIVE — **ab·o·rig·i·nal·ly** \-ē\ *adv*

ab·o·rig·i·ne \ˌab-ə-ˈrij-ə-ˌnē\ *n* **1 :** a native inhabitant especially as contrasted with an invading or colonizing people **2** *often cap* **:** a member of any of the native peoples of Australia [Latin *aborigines,* pl., from *ab origine* "from the beginning"]

aborn·ing \ə-ˈbȯr-niŋ\ *adv* **:** while being born or produced

abort \ə-ˈbȯrt\ *vb* **1 :** to bring forth or cause to bring forth stillborn, nonviable, or premature offspring **2 :** to become checked in development ⟨pollen grains that *aborted*⟩ **3 :** to put an end to prematurely ⟨*abort* a project⟩ [Latin *abortus,* past participle of *aboriri* "to miscarry," from *ab-* + *oriri* "to rise, be born"]

abor·tion \ə-ˈbȯr-shən\ *n* **1 :** a premature birth whether natural or induced artificially that is accompanied by, results in, or follows the death of the fetus **2 :** failure of a project or action to reach full development; *also* **:** a result of such failure

abor·tion·ist \-shə-nəst, -shnəst\ *n* **:** a person who induces abortions

abor·tive \ə-ˈbȯrt-iv\ *adj* **1 :** failing to achieve the desired end **:** UNSUCCESSFUL ⟨an *abortive* attempt⟩ **2 :** imperfectly formed or developed **:** RUDIMENTARY — **abor·tive·ly** *adv* — **abor·tive·ness** *n*

abound \ə-ˈbau̇nd\ *vi* **1 :** to be present in large numbers or in great quantity ⟨wildlife *abounds*⟩ **2 :** to be filled or abundantly supplied ⟨a stream *abounding* in fish⟩ [Medieval French *abunder,* from Latin *abundare,* from *ab-* + *unda* "a wave"]

[1]about \ə-ˈbau̇t\ *adv* **1 :** on all sides **:** AROUND ⟨had neighbors living all *about*⟩ **2 a :** with some approach to exactness in quantity, number, or time **:** APPROXIMATELY, NEARLY ⟨*about* three years⟩ **b :** ALMOST ⟨*about* ready to go⟩ **c :** on the verge of ⟨is *about* to graduate⟩ — used with a negative to express intention or determination ⟨not *about* to quit⟩ **3 :** HERE AND THERE ⟨pace *about*⟩ **4 :** in the vicinity **:** NEAR ⟨people standing *about*⟩ **5 :** in the opposite direction ⟨face *about*⟩ [Old English *abūtan,* from [1]*a-* + *būtan* "outside," from *be* "by" + *ūtan* "outside," from *ūt* "out"] ***usage*** see SOME

[2]about *prep* **1 :** on every side of **:** AROUND ⟨houses *about* the lake⟩ **2 a :** in the immediate neighborhood of **:** NEAR ⟨fish are abundant *about* the reef⟩ **b :** on or near the person of ⟨always carried money *about* her⟩ **c :** in the nature of ⟨something strange *about* them⟩ **d :** at the command of ⟨keep your wits *about* you⟩ **3 :** engaged in ⟨do it thoroughly while you're *about* it⟩ **4 :** with regard to **:** CONCERNING ⟨told me *about* it⟩ **5 :** over, through, or in different parts of ⟨traveled *about* the country⟩

about–face \ə-ˈbau̇t-ˈfās\ *n* **1 :** a reversal of direction **2 :** a reversal of attitude or point of view — **about–face** *vi*

[1]above \ə-ˈbəv\ *adv* **1 :** in or to a higher place **:** OVERHEAD **2 :** higher on the same page or on a preceding page **3 :** in or to a higher rank or number [Old English *abufan,* from [1]*a-* + *bufan* "above," from *be* "by" + *ufan* "above, over"]

[2]above *prep* **1 :** in or to a higher place than **:** OVER **2 a :** superior to (as in rank, quality, or degree) ⟨a captain is *above* a lieutenant⟩ **b :** out of reach of ⟨*above* criticism⟩ **c :** too proud or honorable to stoop to ⟨*above* such petty tricks⟩ **3 :** exceeding in number, quantity, or size **:** more than ⟨*above* the average⟩ **4 :** as distinct from and in addition to ⟨heard the whistle *above* the roar of the crowd⟩

[3]above *n* **:** something that is above ⟨none of the *above*⟩

[4]above *adj* **:** located or written higher on the same page or on a preceding page ⟨the *above* diagram⟩

above all *adv* **:** before every other consideration **:** ESPECIALLY

[1]above·board \ə-ˈbəv-ˌbōrd, -ˌbȯrd\ *adv* **:** in a straightforward manner **:** OPENLY

[2]aboveboard *adj* **:** free from concealment or deceit **:** STRAIGHTFORWARD

above·ground \ə-ˈbəv-ˌgrau̇nd\ *adj* **:** located or happening on or above the surface of the ground ⟨an *aboveground* pool⟩

ab·ra·ca·dab·ra \ˌab-rə-kə-ˈdab-rə\ *n* **1 :** a magical charm or spell **2 :** unintelligible language **:** JARGON [Late Latin]

abrade \ə-ˈbrād\ *vb* **1 :** to rub or wear away especially by friction **:** ERODE **2 :** to irritate or roughen by rubbing [Latin *abradere* "to scrape off," from *ab-* + *radere* "to scrape"] — **abrad·er** *n*

abra·sion \ə-ˈbrā-zhən\ *n* **1 :** a rubbing or wearing away by friction ⟨protect the surface from *abrasion*⟩ **2 :** a place where the surface has been rubbed or scraped off ⟨had an *abrasion* on my knee⟩ [Medieval Latin *abrasio,* from Latin *abradere* "to abrade"]

[1]abra·sive \ə-ˈbrā-siv, -ziv\ *adj* **1 :** having the effect of abrading **2 :** causing annoyance ⟨an *abrasive* manner⟩ — **abra·sive·ly** *adj* — **abra·sive·ness** *n*

[2]abrasive *n* **:** a substance (as emery, pumice, fine sand) used for grinding, smoothing, or polishing

abreast \ə-ˈbrest\ *adv or adj* **1 :** side by side with bodies in line ⟨soldiers standing five *abreast*⟩ **2 :** up to a standard or level especially of knowledge ⟨keep *abreast* of the times⟩

abridge \ə-ˈbrij\ *vt* **1 a** *archaic* **:** DEPRIVE **b :** to reduce in scope **:** DIMINISH ⟨forbidden to *abridge* the rights of citizens⟩ **2 :** to shorten in duration or extent ⟨modern transportation that *abridges* distance⟩ **3 :** to shorten by omitting words without sacrificing the sense **:** CONDENSE [Medieval French *abreger,* from Late Latin *abbreviare* "to abbreviate"] — **abridg·er** *n*

abridg·ment *or* **abridge·ment** \ə-ˈbrij-mənt\ *n* **1 :** the action of abridging **:** the state of being abridged **2 :** a shortened form of a work retaining the general sense of the original

abroad \ə-ˈbrȯd\ *adv or adj* **1 :** over a wide area **:** WIDELY **2 :** away from one's home **3 :** in or to foreign countries ⟨travel *abroad*⟩ **4 :** in wide circulation ⟨rumors were *abroad*⟩

ab·ro·gate \ˈab-rə-ˌgāt\ *vt* **1 :** to do away with or cancel by authoritative action ⟨*abrogate* a law⟩ **2 :** to treat as nonexistent ⟨*abrogating* their responsibilities⟩ [Latin *abrogare,* from *ab-* + *rogare* "to ask, propose"] — **ab·ro·ga·tion** \ˌab-rə-ˈgā-shən\ *n*

abrupt \ə-ˈbrəpt\ *adj* **1 a :** SUDDEN ⟨*abrupt* change in the weather⟩ **b :** impolitely curt or brief ⟨an *abrupt* manner⟩ **c :** marked by sudden changes in topic **:** DISCONNECTED ⟨an *abrupt* style of speaking⟩ **2 :** seemingly broken off; *esp* **:** rising or dropping steeply ⟨a high *abrupt* bank bounded the stream⟩ [Latin *abruptus,* from *abrumpere* "to break off," from *ab-* + *rumpere* "to break"] — **abrupt·ly** *adv* — **abrupt·ness** \ə-ˈbrəpt-nəs, -ˈbrəp-\ *n*

ab·scess \ˈab-ˌses\ *n* **:** a localized collection of pus surrounded by inflamed tissue [Latin *abscessus,* literally, "departure," from *abscedere* "to go away," from *ab-, abs-* + *cedere* "to go"] — **abscessed** \-ˌsest\ *adj*

ab·scis·sa \ab-ˈsis-ə\ *n, pl* **-scis·sas** *also* **-scis·sae** \-ˈsis-ē\ **:** the horizontal coordinate of a point in a plane Cartesian coordinate system obtained by measuring parallel to the x-axis — called also *x-coordinate*; compare ORDINATE [New Latin, from Latin *abscindere* "to cut off," from *ab-* + *scindere* "to cut"]

ab·scis·sion \ab-ˈsizh-ən\ *n* **1 :** the act or process of cutting off **2 :** the natural separation of flowers, fruit, or leaves from plants at a special separation layer

ab·scond \ab-ˈskänd\ *vi* **:** to depart secretly and hide oneself [Latin *abscondere* "to hide away," from *ab-, abs-* + *condere* "to store up, conceal," from *com-* + *-dere* "to put"] — **ab·scond·er** *n*

ab·sence \ˈab-səns\ *n* **1 :** the state of being absent ⟨was conspicuous by its *absence*⟩ **2 :** the time that one is absent ⟨a three-week *absence*⟩ **3 :** WANT, LACK ⟨an *absence* of detail⟩ **4 :** inattention to things present ⟨*absence* of mind⟩

[1]ab·sent \ˈab-sənt\ *adj* **1 :** not present or attending **:** MISSING **2 :** not existing **:** LACKING **3 :** lost in thought **:** PREOCCUPIED ⟨an *absent* mood⟩ [Latin *absens,* from *abesse* "to be away," from *ab-* + *esse* "to be"] — **ab·sent·ly** *adv*

[2]ab·sent \ab-ˈsent\ *vt* **:** to keep (oneself) away ⟨*absented* herself from the group⟩

ab·sen·tee \ˌab-sən-ˈtē\ *n* **1 :** one that is absent **2 :** a proprietor that lives elsewhere — **absentee** *adj*

absentee ballot *n* **:** a ballot submitted (as by mail) before an election by a voter who cannot be present at the polls

---

\ə\ **abut**	\au̇\ **out**	\i\ **tip**	\ȯ\ **saw**	\u̇\ **foot**
\ər\ **further**	\ch\ **chin**	\ī\ **life**	\ȯi\ **coin**	\y\ **yet**
\a\ **mat**	\e\ **pet**	\j\ **job**	\th\ **thin**	\yü\ **few**
\ā\ **take**	\ē\ **easy**	\ŋ\ **sing**	\t͟h\ **this**	\yu̇\ **cure**
\ä\ **cot, cart**	\g\ **go**	\ō\ **bone**	\ü\ **food**	\zh\ **vision**

ab·sen·tee·ism \ˌab-sən-ˈtē-ˌiz-əm\ *n* **1** : prolonged absence of an owner from his or her property **2** : chronic absence (as from school)

ab·sent·mind·ed \ˌab-sənt-ˈmīn-dəd\ *adj* : lost in thought and unaware of one's surroundings or actions — **ab·sent·mind·ed·ly** *adv* — **ab·sent·mind·ed·ness** *n*

ab·sinthe *or* **ab·sinth** \ˈab-ˌsinth\ *n* : a green liqueur flavored with aromatic herbs (as wormwood and anise) [French *absinthe,* from Latin *absinthium* "wormwood," from Greek *apsinthion*]

ab·so·lute \ˈab-sə-ˌlüt, ˌab-sə-ˈ\ *adj* **1 a** : free from imperfection : PERFECT **b** : free or relatively free from mixture : PURE ⟨*absolute* alcohol⟩ **c** : OUTRIGHT ⟨an *absolute* lie⟩ **2** : completely free from constitutional or other restraint or limitation ⟨an *absolute* monarch⟩ **3 a** : lacking grammatical connection with any other word in a sentence ⟨the *absolute* construction *this being the case* in "this being the case, let us go"⟩ **b** : standing alone without modifying a noun ⟨the *absolute* adjective *blind* in "help the blind"⟩ ⟨the *absolute* possessive pronoun *ours* in "your work and ours"⟩ **c** : having no object in a particular construction though normally taking an object ⟨*kill* in "if looks could kill" is an *absolute* verb⟩ **4** : having no restriction, exception, or qualification ⟨*absolute* freedom⟩ **5** : free from doubt : CERTAIN, UNQUESTIONABLE ⟨*absolute* proof⟩ **6 a** : independent of standards of measurement : ACTUAL ⟨*absolute* brightness of a star⟩ ⟨*absolute* motion⟩ **b** : relating to or derived from the fundamental units of length, mass, and time ⟨*absolute* electric units⟩ **c** : relating to the absolute-temperature scale ⟨10° *absolute*⟩ **7** : perfectly embodying the nature of a thing ⟨*absolute* justice⟩ [Latin *absolutus,* from *absolvere* "to set free, absolve"] — **absolute** *n* — **ab·so·lute·ness** \-ˌlüt-nəs, -ˈlüt-\ *n*

ab·so·lute·ly \ˈab-sə-lüt-lē, ˌab-sə-ˈlüt-\ *adv* : in an absolute way : completely or definitely ⟨*absolutely* straight⟩ ⟨you are *absolutely* right⟩

absolute pitch *n* : the ability to sing a note asked for or name a note heard without having heard any identified note beforehand — called also *perfect pitch*

absolute temperature *n* : temperature measured on a scale that has absolute zero as the zero point

absolute value *n* **1** : a nonnegative number equal to a given real number with any negative sign removed ⟨the *absolute value* of -3 is 3⟩ **2** : the positive square root of the sum of the squares of the real and imaginary parts of a complex number

absolute zero *n* : a hypothetical temperature characterized by complete absence of heat and motion and equivalent to approximately –273.15°C or –459.67°F

ab·so·lu·tion \ˌab-sə-ˈlü-shən\ *n* : the act of absolving; *esp* : a forgiving of sins pronounced by a Catholic priest

ab·so·lut·ism \ˈab-sə-ˌlüt-ˌiz-əm\ *n* **1 a** : a political theory that absolute power should be held by one or more rulers **b** : government by an absolute ruler or authority **2** : advocacy of absolute standards or principles — **ab·so·lut·ist** \-ˌlüt-əst\ *n or adj* — **ab·so·lu·tis·tic** \ˌab-sə-ˌlü-ˈtis-tik\ *adj*

ab·solve \əb-ˈzälv, -ˈsälv, -ˈzȯlv, -ˈsȯlv\ *vt* **1** : to set free from an obligation or from the consequences of guilt **2** : to forgive (a sin) by absolution [Latin *absolvere,* from *ab-* + *solvere* "to loosen"] — **ab·solv·er** *n*

ab·sorb \əb-ˈsȯrb, -ˈzȯrb\ *vt* **1** : to take in or swallow up : INCORPORATE ⟨the corporation *absorbed* three small companies⟩ **2** : to suck or take up or in ⟨a sponge *absorbs* water⟩ **3** : to engage or hold the interest of : ENGROSS ⟨*absorbed* in thought⟩ **4 a** : to receive without recoil or echo ⟨a sound-*absorbing* surface⟩ **b** : to transform (radiant energy) into a different form usually with a resulting rise in temperature ⟨the earth *absorbs* the sun's rays⟩ [Latin *absorbēre,* from *ab-* + *sorbēre* "to suck up"] — **ab·sorb·abil·i·ty** \əb-ˌsȯr-bə-ˈbil-ət-ē, -ˌzȯr-\ *n* — **ab·sorb·able** \əb-ˈsȯr-bə-bəl, -ˈzȯr-\ *adj* — **ab·sorb·er** *n*

synonyms ABSORB, ASSIMILATE mean to take in. ABSORB may imply that matter or energy enters a body and is retained without essential change to itself or to the receiving body ⟨plant roots *absorb* moisture⟩. ASSIMILATE may apply to an active process of incorporating substance into the substance of the receiving body ⟨the body *assimilates* nourishment from milk⟩.

ab·sor·ben·cy \əb-ˈsȯr-bən-sē, -ˈzȯr-\ *n, pl* **-cies** : the quality or state of being absorbent

ab·sor·bent \-bənt\ *adj* : able to absorb ⟨as *absorbent* as a sponge⟩ — **absorbent** *n*

ab·sorb·ing \-bing\ *adj* : fully taking one's attention : ENGROSSING — **ab·sorb·ing·ly** \-bing-lē\ *adv*

ab·sorp·tion \əb-ˈsȯrp-shən, -ˈzȯrp-\ *n* **1** : the process of absorbing or being absorbed: as **a** : the passing of digested food through the intestinal wall into the blood or lymph **b** : interception especially of light or sound waves **2** : complete occupation of the mind — **ab·sorp·tive** \-ˈsȯrp-tiv, -ˈzȯrp-\ *adj*

ab·stain \əb-ˈstān\ *vi* : to refrain voluntarily especially from an action ⟨*abstain* from voting⟩ [Medieval French *abstenir,* from Latin *abstinēre,* from *ab-, abs-* + *tenēre* "to hold"] ***synonyms*** see REFRAIN — **ab·stain·er** *n*

ab·ste·mi·ous \ab-ˈstē-mē-əs\ *adj* : sparing especially in eating and drinking [Latin *abstemius,* from *ab-, abs-* + *temetum* "intoxicating drink"] — **ab·ste·mi·ous·ly** *adv*

ab·sten·tion \əb-ˈsten-chən\ *n* : the act or practice of abstaining; *esp* : a usually formal refusal to vote ⟨3 ayes, 5 nays, and 2 *abstentions*⟩ [Late Latin *abstentio,* from Latin *abstinēre* "to abstain"] — **ab·sten·tious** \-chəs\ *adj*

ab·sti·nence \ˈab-stə-nəns\ *n* **1** : an abstaining especially from indulgence of appetite or from eating certain foods **2 a** : habitual abstaining from alcoholic liquors **b** : abstaining from sexual intercourse [Latin *abstinēre* "to abstain"] — **ab·sti·nent** \-nənt\ *adj* — **ab·sti·nent·ly** *adv*

[1]**ab·stract** \ab-ˈstrakt, ˈab-ˌ\ *adj* **1 a** : considered apart from a particular instance or object ⟨an *abstract* entity⟩ **b** : difficult to understand ⟨*abstract* problems⟩ **c** : insufficiently factual : purely formal ⟨possessed only an *abstract* right⟩ **2** : expressing a quality considered apart from an object ⟨the word *poem* is concrete; the word *poetry* is *abstract*⟩ **3 a** : dealing with a subject in purely hypothetical terms : THEORETICAL ⟨*abstract* algebra⟩ **b** : IMPERSONAL ⟨the *abstract* compassion of a surgeon⟩ **4** : having only generalized form with little or no attempt to create a realistic picture ⟨*abstract* painting⟩ [Medieval Latin *abstractus,* from Latin *abstrahere* "to draw away," from *ab-, abs-* + *trahere* "to draw"] — **ab·stract·ly** \ab-ˈstrak-tlē, -lē, ˈab-ˌ\ *adv* — **ab·stract·ness** \ab-ˈstrakt-nəs, -ˈstrak-, ˈab-ˌ\ *n*

[2]**abstract** \ˈab-ˌstrakt, *in sense 2 also* ab-ˈ\ *n* **1** : a brief statement of the main points or facts : SUMMARY ⟨an *abstract* of a book⟩ **2** : an abstract thing or state **3** : ABSTRACTION 4

[3]**ab·stract** \ab-ˈstrakt, ˈab-ˌ, *in sense 3 usually* ˈab-ˌ\ *vt* **1** : REMOVE, SEPARATE ⟨add or *abstract* baser metal during minting⟩ **2** : to consider apart from application to a particular instance ⟨*abstract* the idea of roundness from a ball⟩ **3** : to make an abstract of : SUMMARIZE **4** : to draw away the attention of **5** : to take away secretly or dishonestly : STEAL — **ab·strac·tor** *or* **ab·stract·er** *n*

ab·stract·ed \ab-ˈstrak-təd, ˈab-ˌ\ *adj* : PREOCCUPIED, ABSENTMINDED — **ab·stract·ed·ly** *adv* — **ab·stract·ed·ness** *n*

ab·strac·tion \ab-ˈstrak-shən\ *n* **1 a** : the act or process of abstracting : the state of being abstracted **b** : an abstract idea or term ⟨a mind full of *abstractions*⟩ **2** : inattention to one's surroundings : ABSENTMINDEDNESS **3** : abstract quality or character **4** : an artistic composition or creation characterized by designs that do not precisely represent actual objects or figures — **ab·strac·tive** \-ˈstrak-tiv\ *adj*

ab·strac·tion·ism \ab-ˈstrak-shə-ˌniz-əm\ *n* **1** : the creation of abstractions in art **2** : the principles or ideals of abstract art — **ab·strac·tion·ist** \-shə-nəst, -shnəst\ *adj or n*

ab·struse \ab-ˈstrüs, əb-\ *adj* : hard to understand [Latin *abstrusus,* from *abstrudere* "to conceal," from *ab-, abs-* + *trudere* "to push"] — **ab·struse·ly** *adv* — **ab·struse·ness** *n*

ab·surd \əb-ˈsərd, -ˈzərd\ *adj* : ridiculously unreasonable, unsound, or incongruous [Middle French *absurde,* from Latin *absurdus,* from *ab-* + *surdus* "deaf, stupid"] — **ab·surd·ly** *adv* — **ab·surd·ness** *n*

ab·sur·di·ty \əb-ˈsərd-ət-ē, -ˈzərd-\ *n, pl* **-ties** **1** : the state of being absurd **2** : something that is absurd

abun·dance \ə-ˈbən-dəns\ *n* **1** : an ample or overflowing quantity **2** : AFFLUENCE, WEALTH ⟨a life of *abundance*⟩ **3** : relative quantity or amount : degree of plentifulness ⟨the *abundance* of various species⟩

abun·dant \-dənt\ *adj* : existing in or having abundance : ABOUNDING [Latin *abundare* "to abound"] ***synonyms*** see PLENTIFUL — **abun·dant·ly** *adv*

[1]**abuse** \ə-ˈbyüz\ *vt* **1** : to attack in words : REVILE **2 a** : to put to a wrong or improper use : MISUSE ⟨*abuse* a privilege⟩ **b** : to use excessively ⟨*abuse* alcohol⟩ **3** : to use or treat so as to injure or damage : MISTREAT ⟨*abused* the car⟩ ⟨*abused* the dog⟩

[Medieval French *abuser,* from Latin *abuti* "to misuse," from *ab-* + *uti* "to use"] — **abus·er** *n*

[2]**abuse** \ə-ˈbyüs\ *n* **1 :** a corrupt practice or custom ⟨election *abuses*⟩ **2 :** improper or excessive use or treatment **:** MISUSE ⟨drug *abuse*⟩ **3 :** abusive language **4 :** physical maltreatment ⟨child *abuse*⟩

synonyms ABUSE, INVECTIVE, VITUPERATION mean vigorous condemnation. ABUSE stresses the offensive character of the language used ⟨scathing verbal *abuse*⟩. INVECTIVE may add additional suggestion of logical effectiveness and serious purpose in directing abuse ⟨blistering political *invective*⟩. VITUPERATION suggests fluent and sustained abuse ⟨a torrent of *vituperation*⟩.

abu·sive \ə-ˈbyü-siv, -ziv\ *adj* **1 :** using or characterized by improper use or action ⟨*abusive* financial practices⟩ **2 a :** containing or using harsh insulting language ⟨an *abusive* crowd⟩ **b :** causing physical harm — **abu·sive·ly** *adv* — **abu·sive·ness** *n*

abut \ə-ˈbət\ *vb* **abut·ted; abut·ting 1 :** to touch along a border or with a projecting part **:** BORDER ⟨the farm *abuts* on the road⟩ ⟨stores *abut* the sidewalk⟩ **2 a :** to end at a point of contact **b :** to lean for support [Medieval French *aboter* "to border on," from *a* "to" + *bout* "blow, end"] — **abut·ter** *n*

abut·ment \ə-ˈbət-mənt\ *n* **1 :** the place of abutting **2 :** something against which another thing rests its weight or pushes with force ⟨*abutments* that support a bridge⟩

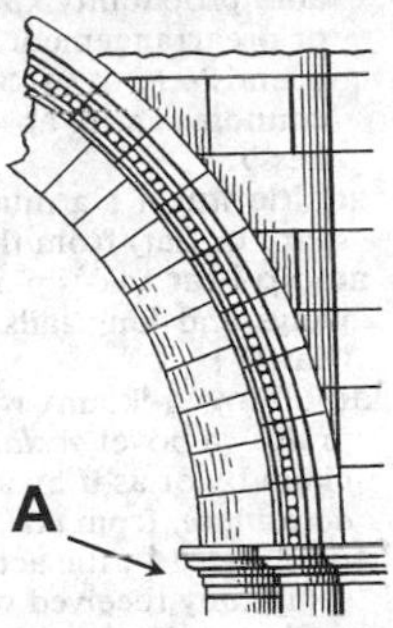

A abutment 2: abutment of an arch

abut·tals \ə-ˈbət-lz\ *n pl* **:** the boundaries of lands with respect to bordering lands

abysm \ə-ˈbiz-əm\ *n* **:** ABYSS [Medieval French *abisme,* from Late Latin *abyssus*]

abys·mal \ə-ˈbiz-məl\ *adj* **1 :** resembling an abyss **:** immeasurably deep or huge **2 :** ABYSSAL 2 — **abys·mal·ly** \-mə-lē\ *adv*

synonyms ABYSMAL, ABYSSAL mean unfathomable by ordinary means. ABYSMAL applies chiefly to figurative depths that seem to be without a lower limit ⟨*abysmal* ignorance⟩ ⟨*abysmal* poverty⟩. ABYSSAL refers to the ocean bottom at great depths ⟨fauna of the *abyssal* zone⟩ ⟨*abyssal* sediments⟩.

abyss \ə-ˈbis\ *n* **1 :** the bottomless gulf, pit, or chaos in old accounts of the origins of the universe **2 :** an immeasurably deep gulf or great space [Late Latin *abyssus,* from Greek *abyssos,* from *abyssos* "bottomless," from *a-* + *byssos* "depth"]

abys·sal \ə-ˈbis-əl\ *adj* **1 :** impossible to understand **:** UNFATHOMABLE **2 :** of or relating to the bottom waters of the ocean depths ***synonyms*** see ABYSMAL

Ab·ys·sin·i·an cat \ˌab-ə-ˈsin-ē-ən-, -ˈsin-yən-\ *n* **:** any of a breed of medium-sized slender domestic cats of African origin with short usually brownish hair ticked with darker color

Abyssinian cat

ac- — see AD-

-ac \ˌak, *in a few words* ik *or* ək\ *n suffix* **:** one affected with ⟨insomni*ac*⟩ [Greek *-akos,* variant of *-ikos* "of or relating to"]

aca·cia \ə-ˈkā-shə\ *n* **1 :** GUM ARABIC **2 :** any of numerous shrubs or trees of the legume family having ball-shaped white or yellow flower clusters and growing in warm regions [Latin]

ac·a·deme \ˈak-ə-ˌdēm\ *n* **1 a :** a place of instruction **:** SCHOOL **b :** the academic environment **2 :** PEDANT 2

ac·a·de·mia \ˌak-ə-ˈdē-mē-ə\ *n* **:** ACADEME 1b

ac·a·dem·ic \ˌak-ə-ˈdem-ik\ *adj* **1 :** of or relating to school or college ⟨*academic* excellence⟩ **2 :** literary or general rather than technical or vocational ⟨an *academic* course⟩ **3 :** conforming to the traditions or rules of a school (as of literature or art) or an official academy **:** CONVENTIONAL ⟨*academic* verse⟩ **4 :** having no practical significance **:** THEORETICAL ⟨an *academic* question⟩ — **ac·a·dem·i·cal·ly** \-ˈdem-i-kə-lē, -klē\ *adv*

academic freedom *n* **:** freedom to teach or to learn without interference (as by government officials)

ac·a·de·mi·cian \ˌak-əd-ə-ˈmish-ən, ə-ˌkad-ə-\ *n* **:** a member of an academy for promoting science, art, or literature

ac·a·dem·i·cism \ˌak-ə-ˈdem-ə-ˌsiz-əm\ *also* **acad·e·mism** \ə-ˈkad-ə-ˌmiz-əm\ *n* **:** a formal academic manner, style, or content

acad·e·my \ə-ˈkad-ə-mē\ *n, pl* **-mies 1** *cap* **:** the school of philosophy founded by Plato **2 a :** a school usually above the elementary level; *esp* **:** a private high school **b :** an institution for training in special subjects or skills **3 :** a society of learned persons united to advance art, science, or literature [Greek *Akadēmeia,* gymnasium in the suburbs of Athens where Plato established his school]

Aca·di·an \ə-ˈkād-ē-ən\ *n* **1 :** a native or inhabitant of Acadia **2 :** a Louisianian descended from French-speaking immigrants from Acadia

acan·thus \ə-ˈkan-thəs, -ˈkant-\ *n, pl* **acan·thus·es** *also* **acan·thi** \-ˈkan-ˌthī\ **1 :** any of a genus of prickly herbs of the Mediterranean region **2 :** a decoration representing the leaves of the acanthus [Greek *akanthos*]

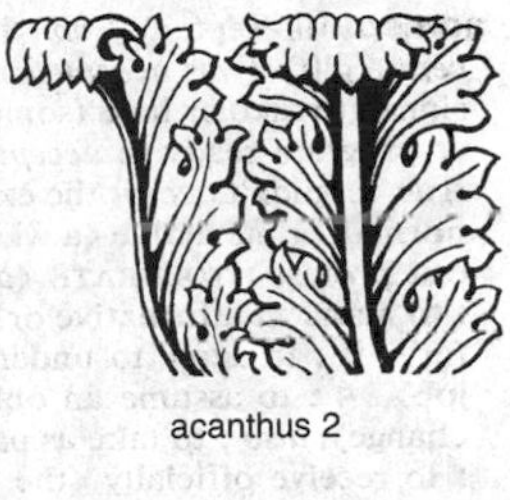
acanthus 2

a cap·pel·la *also* **a ca·pel·la** \ˌäk-ə-ˈpel-ə\ *adv or adj* **:** without instrumental accompaniment [Italian *a cappella* "in chapel style"]

ac·cede \ak-ˈsēd\ *vi* **1 a :** to become a party (as to an agreement) ⟨were invited to *accede* to the treaty⟩ **b :** to give consent **:** AGREE ⟨*accede* to a proposed plan⟩ **2 :** to enter upon an office or position ⟨*acceded* to the throne in 1838⟩ [Latin *accedere* "to go to," from *ad-* + *cedere* "to go"] ***synonyms*** see ASSENT

ac·ce·le·ran·do \ä-ˌchel-ə-ˈrän-dō\ *adv or adj* **:** gradually faster — used as a direction in music [Italian]

ac·cel·er·ate \ik-ˈsel-ə-ˌrāt, ak-\ *vb* **1 :** to bring about at an earlier time ⟨*accelerated* their departure⟩ **2 a :** to hasten the ordinary progress or development of **b :** to speed up (a course of study) **3 a :** to add to the speed of **b :** to cause to undergo acceleration; *esp* **:** to increase the velocity of **c :** to move or progress faster [Latin *accelerare,* from *ad-* + *celer* "swift"] — **ac·cel·er·a·tive** \-ˌrāt-iv\ *adj*

ac·cel·er·a·tion \ik-ˌsel-ə-ˈrā-shən, ak-\ *n* **1 :** the act or process of accelerating **:** the state of being accelerated **2 :** change of velocity or the rate of such change with respect to time

acceleration of gravity : the acceleration of a freely falling body under the influence of gravity expressed as the rate of increase of velocity per unit of time with the value being about 9.81 meters (32.2 feet) per second per second

ac·cel·er·a·tor \ik-ˈsel-ə-ˌrāt-ər, ak-\ *n* **:** one that accelerates: as **a :** a pedal in a motor vehicle used for varying the supply of fuel-air mixture to the combustion chamber and so controlling the speed of the motor **b :** an apparatus for imparting high velocities to charged particles (as electrons and protons)

ac·cel·er·om·e·ter \ik-ˌsel-ə-ˈräm-ət-ər, ak-\ *n* **:** an instrument for measuring acceleration or vibrations

[1]**ac·cent** \ˈak-ˌsent\ *n* **1 :** a peculiar or characteristic manner of speech shared by a group ⟨foreign *accent*⟩ **2 :** special prominence given to one syllable of a word ⟨*before* has the *accent* on the last syllable⟩ **3 :** rhythmically significant stress on the syllables of a verse usually at regular intervals **4** *archaic* **:** UTTERANCE **5 :** a mark (as ´, `, ˆ) used chiefly to indicate a specific sound value, stress, or pitch — compare ACUTE, CIRCUMFLEX, GRAVE **6 :** greater stress given to one musical tone than to its neighbors; *also* **:** a mark indicating this **7 a :** special concern or attention **:** EMPHASIS 2 ⟨an *accent* on youth⟩ **b :** a small detail in sharp contrast with its surroundings ⟨a color scheme of grays with red *accents*⟩ **8 :** a mark (as a prime or double prime) placed to the right of a letter or number and usually slightly above it [Middle French, "intonation," from Latin *accentus,* from *ad-* + *cantus* "song, chant"]

\ə\ **abut**	\au̇\ **out**	\i\ **tip**	\ȯ\ **saw**	\u̇\ **foot**
\ər\ **further**	\ch\ **chin**	\ī\ **life**	\ȯi\ **coin**	\y\ **yet**
\a\ **mat**	\e\ **pet**	\j\ **job**	\th\ **thin**	\yü\ **few**
\ā\ **take**	\ē\ **easy**	\ng\ **sing**	\t͟h\ **this**	\yu̇\ **cure**
\ä\ **cot, cart**	\g\ **go**	\ō\ **bone**	\ü\ **food**	\zh\ **vision**

[2]**accent** \ak-ˈsent, ˈak-ˌ\ *vt* **1 a :** to utter with accent : STRESS ⟨*accent* the first syllable of *after*⟩ **b :** to mark with a written or printed accent **2 :** to give prominence to or increase the prominence of

accent mark *n* **1 :** ACCENT 5 **2 :** one of several symbols used to indicate musical accent

accent mark 2

ac·cen·tu·al \ak-ˈsench-wəl, -ə-wəl\ *adj* **:** of, relating to, or characterized by accent — **ac·cen·tu·al·ly** \-ē\ *adv*

ac·cen·tu·ate \ak-ˈsen-chə-ˌwāt\ *vt* **1 :** to pronounce or mark with an accent **2 :** EMPHASIZE ⟨dark clouds *accentuated* an atmosphere of mystery⟩ — **ac·cen·tu·a·tion** \ˌak-ˌsen-chə-ˈwā-shən\ *n*

ac·cept \ik-ˈsept, ak-\ *vb* **1 a :** to receive or take willingly ⟨*accept* a gift⟩ ⟨was *accepted* as a member⟩ **b :** to be able or designed to take or hold (something applied or added) ⟨a computer program ready to *accept* commands⟩ **2 a :** to recognize as true ⟨couldn't *accept* the explanation⟩ **b :** to regard as proper, normal, or inevitable ⟨a widely *accepted* idea⟩ **c :** to take without protest : TOLERATE ⟨*accept* poor living conditions⟩ **3 a :** to make an affirmative or favorable response to ⟨*accept* an offer⟩ **b :** to agree to undertake the responsibility of ⟨*accept* a job⟩ **4 :** to assume an obligation to pay ⟨*accept* a bill of exchange⟩; *also* **:** to take as payment ⟨we don't *accept* checks⟩ **5 :** to receive officially ⟨the Senate *accepted* the report⟩ [Medieval French *accepter,* from Latin *acceptare,* from *accipere* "to receive," from *ad-* + *capere* "to take"] — **ac·cept·er** *or* **ac·cep·tor** \-ˈsep-tər\ *n*

ac·cept·able \ik-ˈsep-tə-bəl, ak-\ *adj* **1 :** capable or worthy of being accepted : SATISFACTORY ⟨an *acceptable* excuse⟩ **2 :** barely adequate ⟨plays an *acceptable* game⟩ — **ac·cept·abil·i·ty** \-ˌsep-tə-ˈbil-ət-ē\ *n* — **ac·cept·able·ness** \-ˈsep-tə-bəl-nəs\ *n* — **ac·cept·ably** \-blē\ *adv*

ac·cept·ance \ik-ˈsep-təns, ak-\ *n* **1 a :** the act of accepting **b :** favorable reception : APPROVAL **2 :** the quality or state of being accepted or acceptable

ac·cep·ta·tion \ˌak-ˌsep-ˈtā-shən\ *n* **1 :** ACCEPTANCE; *esp* **:** favorable reception **2 :** the generally accepted meaning of a word or expression

[1]**ac·cess** \ˈak-ˌses\ *n* **1 :** a sudden outburst of intense feeling **2 a :** permission, liberty, or ability to enter, approach, communicate with, pass to and from, or make use of ⟨*access* to the president⟩ ⟨blocked *access* to the Web site⟩ **b :** a way or means of approach ⟨a nation's *access* to the sea⟩ **c :** the act or an instance of accessing **3 :** an increase by addition ⟨a sudden *access* of wealth⟩ [Latin *accessus* "approach," from *accedere* "to go to," from *ad-* + *cedere* "to go"]

[2]**access** *vt* **:** to get at : gain access to

ac·ces·si·ble \ak-ˈses-ə-bəl, ik-\ *adj* **1 :** capable of being reached ⟨*accessible* by train or car⟩ **2 :** open to influence ⟨a mind *accessible* to reason⟩ **3 :** capable of being used, seen, or known : OBTAINABLE ⟨*accessible* information⟩ — **ac·ces·si·bil·i·ty** \ˌak-ˌses-ə-ˈbil-ət-ē, ik-\ *n* — **ac·ces·si·ble·ness** \ak-ˈses-ə-bəl-nəs, ik-\ *n* — **ac·ces·si·bly** \-blē\ *adv*

ac·ces·sion \ak-ˈsesh-ən, ik-\ *n* **1 :** something added : ACQUISITION ⟨new *accessions* to the museum⟩ **2 :** ADHERENCE ⟨*accession* to a treaty⟩ **3 a :** increase by something added **b :** acquisition of additional property (as by growth or increase) **4 :** the act of assenting or agreeing ⟨*accession* to a proposal⟩ **5 :** the act of coming to high office or a position of honor or power ⟨the *accession* of a king⟩ **6 :** a sudden fit or outburst — **ac·ces·sion·al** \-ˈsesh-nəl, -ən-l\ *adj*

ac·ces·so·rize \ak-ˈses-ə-ˌrīz, ik-\ *vb* **:** to wear or decorate with accessories

[1]**ac·ces·so·ry** \ak-ˈses-rē, ik-, -ə-rē\ *n, pl* **-ries 1 a :** a thing of secondary or lesser importance **b :** an object or device not essential in itself but adding to the beauty, convenience, or effectiveness of something else ⟨automobile *accessories*⟩ **2 :** a person who aids or encourages another in committing a crime or attempting to escape justice

[2]**accessory** *adj* **:** aiding or contributing in a secondary way

accessory fruit *n* **:** a fruit (as the apple or the strawberry) of which a conspicuous part consists of tissue other than that of the ripened ovary

access time *n* **:** the time lag between the time stored information (as in a computer) is requested and the time it is delivered

ac·ci·dence \ˈak-səd-əns, -sə-ˌdens\ *n* **:** the part of grammar that deals with inflections

ac·ci·dent \ˈak-səd-ənt, -sə-ˌdent\ *n* **1 a :** an event occurring by chance or from unknown causes **b :** lack of intention or necessity : CHANCE ⟨we met by *accident*⟩ **2 :** an unintended and usually sudden and unexpected happening and especially one resulting in loss or injury ⟨an automobile *accident*⟩ **3 —** used euphemistically to refer to an involuntary act of urination or defecation ⟨the baby had an *accident*⟩ **4 :** a nonessential quality : ATTRIBUTE ⟨the *accident* of nationality⟩ [Medieval French, from Latin *accidens* "nonessential quality, chance," from *accidere* "to happen, befall," from *ad-* + *cadere* "to fall"]

[1]**ac·ci·den·tal** \ˌak-sə-ˈdent-l\ *adj* **1 :** arising from secondary causes : NONESSENTIAL **2 a :** occurring unexpectedly or by chance ⟨an *accidental* discovery of oil⟩ **b :** happening without intent or from carelessness often with unfortunate results ⟨an *accidental* collision⟩ — **ac·ci·den·tal·ly** \-ˈdent-lē, -ˈdent-l-ē\ *adv* — **ac·ci·den·tal·ness** \-ˈdent-l-nəs\ *n*

synonyms ACCIDENTAL, CASUAL, FORTUITOUS mean happening by chance. ACCIDENTAL implies an absence of immediate intention ⟨an *accidental* discovery⟩ or reasonably foreseeable probability ⟨*accidental* death⟩. CASUAL stresses absence of prearrangement or premeditation ⟨*casual* encounters with friends⟩. FORTUITOUS stresses chance so strongly that it often connotes entire absence of cause ⟨*fortuitous* presence of a witness⟩.

[2]**accidental** *n* **:** a musical note whose pitch is altered (as by a sharp or flat) from that indicated by the key signature

ac·cip·i·ter \ak-ˈsip-ət-ər\ *n* **:** any of various hawks with short wings and long tails that dart in and out among trees [Latin, "hawk"]

[1]**ac·claim** \ə-ˈklām\ *vb* **1 :** to welcome with applause or great praise ⟨a novel *acclaimed* by the critics⟩ **2 :** to declare or proclaim by or as if by acclamation ⟨was *acclaimed* a hero⟩ [Latin *acclamare,* from *ad-* + *clamare* "to shout"] — **ac·claim·er** *n*

[2]**acclaim** *n* **1 :** the act of acclaiming **2 :** APPLAUSE, PRAISE ⟨the symphony received worldwide *acclaim*⟩

ac·cla·ma·tion \ˌak-lə-ˈmā-shən\ *n* **1 :** a loud eager expression of approval, praise, or assent **2 :** an overwhelming affirmative vote by voice rather than by ballot

ac·cli·mate \ə-ˈklī-mət, ˈak-lə-ˌmāt\ *vt* **:** to adapt to a new temperature, altitude, climate, environment, or situation — **ac·cli·ma·tion** \ˌak-ˌlī-ˈmā-shən, -lə-\ *n*

ac·cli·ma·tize \ə-ˈklī-mə-ˌtīz\ *vb* **:** ACCLIMATE — **ac·cli·ma·ti·za·tion** \ə-ˌklī-mət-ə-ˈzā-shən\ *n*

ac·cliv·i·ty \ə-ˈkliv-ət-ē, a-\ *n, pl* **-ties :** a rising slope [Latin *acclivitas,* derived from *ad-* + *clivus* "slope"]

ac·co·lade \ˈak-ə-ˌlād\ *n* **1 :** a ceremonial embrace **2 :** a formal salute (as a tap on the shoulder with the blade of a sword) that marks the granting of knighthood **3 a :** a mark of recognition of merit : COMMENDATION **b :** AWARD 1 [French, from *accoler* "to embrace," derived from Latin *ad-* + *collum* "neck"]

ac·com·mo·date \ə-ˈkäm-ə-ˌdāt\ *vb* **1 a :** to make fit or suitable : ADAPT **b :** to adapt oneself; *esp* **:** to undergo visual accommodation **2 :** to bring into agreement ⟨*accommodate* the differences⟩ **3 :** to do a favor for : OBLIGE ⟨*accommodated* me with a ride⟩ **4 :** to furnish with something desired: as **a :** to provide with lodgings **b :** to have or make room for [Latin *accommodare,* from *ad-* + *commodus* "convenient, suitable"]

synonyms see ADAPT, CONTAIN — **ac·com·mo·da·tive** \-ˌdāt-iv\ *adj* — **ac·com·mo·da·tive·ness** *n*

ac·com·mo·dat·ing \-ˌdāt-ing\ *adj* **:** inclined to be helpful or obliging — **ac·com·mo·dat·ing·ly** \-ˌdāt-ing-lē\ *adv*

ac·com·mo·da·tion \ə-ˌkäm-ə-ˈdā-shən\ *n* **1 a :** something supplied for convenience or to satisfy a need **b** *pl* **:** lodging and food or traveling space and related services ⟨overnight *accommodations*⟩ **2 :** the act of accommodating : the state of being accommodated: as **a :** the provision of what is needed or desired for convenience ⟨tables for the *accommodation* of picnickers⟩ **b :** an adjustment of differences : SETTLEMENT **c :** the automatic adjustment of the eye for seeing at different distances

ac·com·pa·ni·ment \ə-ˈkəmp-nē-mənt, -ə-nē-\ *n* **1 :** music to support or complement a principal voice or instrument **2 :** an accompanying object, situation, or event

ac·com·pa·nist \ə-ˈkəmp-nəst, -ə-nəst\ *n* **:** one (as a pianist) that plays an accompaniment

ac·com·pa·ny \ə-ˈkəmp-nē, -ə-nē\ *vb* **-nied; -ny·ing** **1 :** to go with or attend as an associate or companion **2 :** to perform an accompaniment to or for **3 :** to be or cause to be in association with ⟨a thunderstorm *accompanied* by high winds⟩ ⟨*accompanied* their advice with a warning⟩

ac·com·plice \ə-ˈkäm-pləs, -ˈkəm-\ *n* **:** one associated with another in wrongdoing [archaic *complice* (in the phrase *a complice*), from Late Latin *complic-, complex,* from Latin, "closely connected," from *complicare* "to fold together"]

ac·com·plish \ə-ˈkäm-plish, -ˈkəm-\ *vt* **:** to bring to a successful finish **:** PERFORM [Medieval French *accompliss-,* stem of *accomplir,* derived from Latin *ad-* + *complēre* "to fill up, complete"] — **ac·com·plish·able** \-ə-bəl\ *adj*

ac·com·plished \-plisht\ *adj* **1 :** established as true ⟨an *accomplished* fact⟩ **2 a :** skilled or polished through practice or training **:** EXPERT ⟨an *accomplished* pianist⟩ **b :** very successful ⟨the school's most *accomplished* graduate⟩

ac·com·plish·ment \ə-ˈkäm-plish-mənt, -ˈkəm-\ *n* **1 :** the act of accomplishing **:** COMPLETION **2 :** something accomplished **:** ACHIEVEMENT **3 :** an ability, a social quality, or a special skill acquired by training or practice

[1]**ac·cord** \ə-ˈkȯrd\ *vb* **1 :** to grant as suitable or proper ⟨*accords* the right of appeal⟩ **2 :** to agree or bring into agreement ⟨the decision *accords* with our sense of justice⟩ [Medieval French *acorder,* derived from Latin *ad-* + *cord-, cor* "heart"]

[2]**accord** *n* **1 a :** AGREEMENT, HARMONY ⟨were in *accord* with the company's policy⟩ **b :** an agreement between parties ⟨the disputants reached an *accord*⟩ **2 :** voluntary or spontaneous impulse to act ⟨went of their own *accord*⟩

ac·cor·dance \ə-ˈkȯrd-ns\ *n* **1 :** AGREEMENT, CONFORMITY ⟨in *accordance* with a rule⟩ **2 :** the act of granting

ac·cor·dant \-ˈkȯrd-nt\ *adj* **1 :** CONSONANT 1, AGREEING **2 :** HARMONIOUS ⟨*accordant* tones⟩ — **ac·cor·dant·ly** *adv*

ac·cord·ing as \-ˈkȯrd-ing-\ *conj* **1 :** in accord with the way in which **2 a :** depending on how **b :** depending on whether **:** IF

ac·cord·ing·ly \ə-ˈkȯrd-ing-lē\ *adv* **1 :** in accordance **:** CORRESPONDINGLY ⟨was grateful and acted *accordingly*⟩ **2 :** CONSEQUENTLY, SO ⟨felt ill and *accordingly* went home⟩

according to *prep* **1 :** in agreement or conformity with ⟨lined up *according to* height⟩ **2 :** as stated by ⟨*according to* our teacher⟩ **3 :** depending on ⟨will succeed or fail *according to* circumstances⟩

[1]**ac·cor·di·on** \ə-ˈkȯrd-ē-ən\ *n* **:** a portable keyboard wind instrument in which the wind is forced past metallic reeds by means of a hand-operated bellows [German *Akkordion*] — **ac·cor·di·on·ist** \-ē-ə-nəst\ *n*

[2]**accordion** *adj* **:** folding or creased or hinged to fold like an accordion ⟨*accordion* doors⟩

accordion

ac·cost \ə-ˈkȯst\ *vt* **:** to approach and speak to often in a challenging or aggressive way [Middle French *accoster,* derived from Latin *ad-* + *costa* "rib, side"]

[1]**ac·count** \ə-ˈkau̇nt\ *n* **1 a :** a record of money paid out and money received covering transactions involving a particular item, person, or concern **b :** a statement of transactions during a fiscal period and the resulting balance **2 :** an explanation of one's conduct **3 a :** a formal business arrangement providing for regular dealings or services and involving the establishment and maintenance of an account; *also* **:** CLIENT, CUSTOMER **b :** a sum of money deposited in a bank and subject to withdrawal by the depositor **c :** an arrangement in which a person uses the Internet or e-mail services of a particular company **4 a :** VALUE, IMPORTANCE ⟨a person of little *account*⟩ **b :** ESTEEM ⟨held in high *account*⟩ **5 :** PROFIT, ADVANTAGE ⟨used our knowledge to good *account*⟩ **6 a :** a statement of reasons, causes, or motives **b :** a reason for an action ⟨on that *account* we refused the offer⟩ **c :** careful thought **:** CONSIDERATION ⟨take *account* of the unexpected⟩ **7 :** a statement of facts or events ⟨newspaper *accounts* of the trial⟩ — **on account :** on credit — **on account of :** for the sake of **:** by reason of — **on no account :** under no circumstances — **on one's account :** for one's benefit or sake ⟨don't do it just *on my account*⟩

[2]**account** *vb* **1 :** to think of as ⟨*account* oneself lucky⟩ **2 :** to furnish a detailed analysis or a justifying explanation ⟨*account* for your expenditures⟩ **3 a :** to be the reason ⟨poor diet *accounts* for many illnesses⟩ **b :** to bring about the capture or destruction of something ⟨*accounted* for two rabbits⟩ [Medieval French *acunter,* from *a-* "ad-" + *cunter* "to count"]

ac·count·able \ə-ˈkau̇nt-ə-bəl\ *adj* **1 :** responsible for giving an account (as of one's acts) **:** ANSWERABLE ⟨*accountable* to one's superiors⟩ **2 :** capable of being accounted for **:** EXPLAINABLE — **ac·count·abil·i·ty** \-ˌkau̇nt-ə-ˈbil-ət-ē\ *n* — **ac·count·able·ness** \-ˈkau̇nt-ə-bəl-nəs\ *n* — **ac·count·ably** \-blē\ *adv*

ac·coun·tan·cy \ə-ˈkau̇nt-n-sē\ *n* **:** the profession or practice of accounting

ac·coun·tant \ə-ˈkau̇nt-nt\ *n* **:** a person professionally trained in the practice of accounting

ac·count·ing \ə-ˈkau̇nt-ing\ *n* **1 :** the system or practice of recording and analyzing money transactions of a person or business **2 :** the action of giving an account ⟨management is required to make an *accounting* to the stockholders⟩

ac·cou·tre *or* **ac·cou·ter** \ə-ˈküt-ər\ *vt* **-cou·tred** *or* **-cou·tered; -cou·tring** *or* **-cou·ter·ing** \-ˈküt-ə-ring, -ˈkü-tring\ **:** to provide with equipment or furnishings [French *accoutrer*]

ac·cou·tre·ment *or* **ac·cou·ter·ment** \ə-ˈkü-trə-mənt, -ˈküt-ər-mənt\ *n* **1 :** an accessory item of clothing or equipment — usually used in plural **2 :** an identifying often superficial characteristic — usually used in plural ⟨*accoutrements* of power⟩

ac·cred·it \ə-ˈkred-ət\ *vt* **1 a :** to send with credentials and authority to act as an official representative ⟨*accredit* an ambassador to France⟩ **b :** to vouch or recognize as conforming with a standard **c :** to recognize (an educational institution) as maintaining standards that qualify the graduates for admission to higher or more specialized institutions or for professional practice **2 :** to give credit to — **ac·cred·i·ta·tion** \ə-ˌkred-ə-ˈtā-shən\ *n*

ac·cre·tion \ə-ˈkrē-shən\ *n* **1 :** the process of growth or enlargement; *esp* **:** increase by external addition or accumulation **2 :** a product or result of accretion [Latin *accretio,* from *accrescere* "to increase," from *ad-* + *crescere* "to grow"] — **ac·cre·tion·ary** \-shə-ˌner-ē\ *adj*

ac·cru·al \ə-ˈkrü-əl\ *n* **1 :** the action or process of accruing **2 :** something that accrues or has accrued

ac·crue \ə-ˈkrü\ *vb* **1 :** to come about as a natural growth or addition ⟨benefits *accrue* to society from education⟩ **2 :** to accumulate over a period of time ⟨*accrued* interest⟩ [Medieval French *acreue* "increase," from *acreistre* "to increase," from Latin *accrescere*] — **ac·crue·ment** \-mənt\ *n*

ac·cul·tur·a·tion \ə-ˌkəl-chə-ˈrā-shən\ *n* **1 :** modification of the culture of an individual, group, or people by adapting to or borrowing traits from another culture; *also* **:** a merging of cultures through continuous and prolonged contact **2 :** the process by which a human being acquires the culture of a particular society from infancy — **ac·cul·tur·ate** \-ˈkəl-chə-ˌrāt\ *vt*

ac·cu·mu·late \ə-ˈkyü-myə-ˌlāt\ *vb* **1 :** to pile up or gather especially little by little **:** AMASS ⟨*accumulated* old newspapers⟩ **2 :** to increase gradually in quantity or number ⟨rubbish *accumulates* quickly⟩ [Latin *accumulare,* derived from *ad-* + *cumulus* "heap, pile"]

synonyms ACCUMULATE, AMASS mean to collect so as to form a large quantity. ACCUMULATE implies building up by successive small increases ⟨knickknacks *accumulate* dust⟩. AMASS suggests a more vigorous action during a limited time and applies especially to a putting together of something valuable ⟨*amass* a fortune⟩.

ac·cu·mu·la·tion \ə-ˌkyü-myə-ˈlā-shən\ *n* **1 :** a collecting together **:** AMASSING **2 :** increase or growth by addition especially when continuous or repeated ⟨*accumulation* of interest⟩ **3 :** something that has accumulated or has been accumulated

ac·cu·mu·la·tive \ə-ˈkyü-myə-ˌlāt-iv, -lət-\ *adj* **:** CUMULATIVE — **ac·cu·mu·la·tive·ly** *adv* — **ac·cu·mu·la·tive·ness** *n*

ac·cu·mu·la·tor \ə-ˈkyü-myə-ˌlāt-ər\ *n* : one that accumulates; *esp* : a part (as in a computer) where numbers are totaled or stored

ac·cu·ra·cy \ˈak-yə-rə-sē\ *n, pl* **-cies** **1** : freedom from mistake or error : CORRECTNESS **2 a** : conformity to a standard : EXACTNESS **b** : degree of conformity of a measure to a standard or a true value

ac·cu·rate \ˈak-yə-rət\ *adj* **1** : free from mistakes especially as the result of care **2** : conforming exactly to truth or to a standard : EXACT ⟨providing *accurate* color⟩ **3** : able to give an accurate result [Latin *accuratus,* from *accurare* "to take care of," from *ad-* + *cura* "care"] ***synonyms*** see CORRECT — **ac·cu·rate·ly** \-yə-rət-lē, -yərt-\ *adv* — **ac·cu·rate·ness** \-nəs\ *n*

ac·cursed \ə-ˈkərst, -ˈkər-səd\ *or* **ac·curst** \ə-ˈkərst\ *adj* **1** : being under or as if under a curse **2** : DETESTABLE, DAMNABLE — **ac·curs·ed·ly** \-ˈkər-səd-lē\ *adv* — **ac·curs·ed·ness** \-ˈkər-səd-nəs\ *n*

ac·cus·al \ə-ˈkyü-zəl\ *n* : ACCUSATION

ac·cu·sa·tion \ˌak-yə-ˈzā-shən\ *n* **1** : the act of accusing : the state or fact of being accused **2** : a charge of wrongdoing

ac·cu·sa·tive \ə-ˈkyü-zət-iv\ *adj* **1** : of, relating to, or being the grammatical case that marks the direct object of a verb or the object of any of several prepositions — compare OBJECTIVE **2** : ACCUSATORY ⟨an *accusative* tone⟩ — **accusative** *n*

ac·cu·sa·to·ry \ə-ˈkyü-zə-ˌtōr-ē, -ˌtȯr-\ *adj* : expressing accusation

ac·cuse \ə-ˈkyüz\ *vb* : to charge with a fault or especially with a criminal offense [Medieval French *acuser,* from Latin *accusare* "to call to account," from *ad-* + *causa* "lawsuit, cause"] — **ac·cus·er** *n* — **ac·cus·ing·ly** \-ˈkyü-zing-lē\ *adv*

ac·cused \ə-ˈkyüzd\ *n, pl* **accused** : one charged with an offense; *esp* : the defendant in a criminal case

ac·cus·tom \ə-ˈkəs-təm\ *vt* : to make familiar through use or experience : HABITUATE

ac·cus·tomed \-təmd\ *adj* **1** : often used or practiced : CUSTOMARY ⟨her *accustomed* lunch hour⟩ **2** : adapted to existing conditions ⟨eyes *accustomed* to the dark⟩ **3** : being in the habit or custom ⟨*accustomed* to making decisions⟩ ***synonyms*** see USUAL

[1]**ace** \ˈās\ *n* **1 a** : a die face or domino end marked with one spot **b** : a playing card bearing in its center one large figure **2** : a very small amount or degree ⟨came within an *ace* of winning⟩ **3** : a point scored on a stroke (as in tennis) that an opponent fails to touch **4** : a golf hole made in one stroke **5** : a combat pilot who has brought down at least five enemy airplanes **6** : one that excels at something ⟨a computer *ace*⟩ [Medieval French *as,* from Latin, "unit, a copper coin"]

[2]**ace** *vt* **1** : to score an ace against (as a tennis opponent) **2 a** : to earn a grade of A on (an examination) **b** : to perform very well in ⟨he *aced* every subject⟩

[3]**ace** *adj* : of first or high rank or quality ⟨an *ace* reporter⟩

acel·lu·lar \ˈā-ˈsel-yə-lər\ *adj* : not made up of cells

-a·ceous \ˈā-shəs\ *adj suffix* **1** : characterized by : consisting of : having the nature or form of ⟨carbon*aceous*⟩ ⟨sapon*aceous*⟩ **2** : of or relating to a group of animals characterized by (such) a form or (such) a feature ⟨cet*aceous*⟩ ⟨test*aceous*⟩ [Latin *-aceus*]

acerb \ə-ˈsərb, a-\ *adj* : ACERBIC [Latin *acerbus*]

acer·bic \ə-ˈsər-bik\ *adj* : sharp or biting in temper, mood, or tone — **acer·bi·cal·ly** \-bi-kə-lē, -klē\ *adv*

acer·bi·ty \ə-ˈsər-bət-ē\ *n, pl* **-ties** : sharpness of temper, manner, or tone

acet- *or* **aceto-** *combining form* : acetic acid : acetic ⟨*acet*yl⟩ [Latin *acetum* "vinegar"]

ac·e·tab·u·lum \ˌas-ə-ˈtab-yə-ləm\ *n, pl* **-lums** *or* **-la** \-lə\ : the cup-shaped socket in the hipbone [Latin, literally, "vinegar cup"]

ac·et·al·de·hyde \ˌas-ə-ˈtal-də-ˌhīd\ *n* : a colorless volatile water-soluble liquid compound C_2H_4O used chiefly in making organic chemicals

ac·et·amin·o·phen \ˌas-ət-ə-ˈmin-ə-fən\ *n* : a crystalline compound $C_8H_9NO_2$ used in chemical synthesis and in medicine to relieve pain and fever

ac·et·an·i·lide *or* **ac·et·an·i·lid** \ˌas-ə-ˈtan-l-ˌīd, -l-əd\ *n* : a white crystalline compound C_8H_9NO made from aniline and acetic acid and used especially to relieve pain or fever

ac·e·tate \ˈas-ə-ˌtāt\ *n* **1** : a salt or ester of acetic acid **2** : cellulose acetate or one of its products **3** : a phonograph record made of an acetate or coated with cellulose acetate

ace·tic \ə-ˈsēt-ik\ *adj* : of, relating to, or producing acetic acid or vinegar [Latin *acetum* "vinegar"]

acetic acid *n* : a colorless pungent liquid acid $C_2H_4O_2$ that is the chief acid of vinegar and that is used especially in synthesis (as of plastics)

ac·e·tone \ˈas-ə-ˌtōn\ *n* : a volatile fragrant colorless flammable liquid compound C_3H_6O used chiefly as a solvent and in organic synthesis

ace·tyl \ə-ˈsēt-l\ *n* : the radical CH_3CO of acetic acid

ace·tyl·cho·line \ə-ˌsēt-l-ˈkō-ˌlēn\ *n* : a compound $C_7H_{17}NO_3$ released at autonomic nerve endings that functions in the transmission of nerve impulses

ace·tyl·cho·lin·es·ter·ase \-ˌkō-lə-ˈnes-tə-ˌrās, -ˌrāz\ *n* : an enzyme that promotes the hydrolysis of acetylcholine

ace·tyl–CoA \ə-ˌsēt-l-ˌkō-ˈā\ *n* : a compound $C_{25}H_{38}N_7O_{17}P_3S$ formed as an intermediate in metabolism and active as a coenzyme in biological reactions involving addition of an acetyl radical

acetyl coenzyme A *n* : ACETYL–COA

acet·y·lene \ə-ˈset-l-ən, -l-ˌēn\ *n* : a colorless gaseous hydrocarbon C_2H_2 made especially by the action of water on calcium carbide and used chiefly as a fuel in welding and soldering and in organic synthesis

ace·tyl·sal·i·cyl·ic acid \ə-ˈsēt-l-ˌsal-ə-ˌsil-ik-\ *n* : ASPIRIN 1

[1]**Achae·an** \ə-ˈkē-ən, -ˈkā-\ *adj* **1** : of or relating to or characteristic of Achaea **2** : of or relating to Greece

[2]**Achaean** *n* **1** : a native or inhabitant of Achaea **2** : GREEK

[1]**ache** \ˈāk\ *vi* **1** : to suffer a usually dull persistent pain **2** : to long earnestly : YEARN [Old English *acan*]

[2]**ache** *n* : a usually dull persistent pain — **achy** \ˈā-kē\ *adj*

achene \ə-ˈkēn\ *n* : a small dry one-seeded fruit (as of the sunflower) that ripens without bursting its sheath [[2]*a-* + Greek *chainein* "to yawn, gape"]

achieve \ə-ˈchēv\ *vb* **1** : to carry out successfully : ACCOMPLISH ⟨*achieved* our purpose⟩ **2** : to get by effort ⟨*achieve* greatness⟩ [Medieval French *achever,* from *a-* "ad-" + *chef* "end, head"] — **achiev·able** \-ˈchē-və-bəl\ *adj* — **achiev·er** *n*

achieve·ment \-mənt\ *n* **1** : the act of achieving **2** : something achieved especially by great effort or persistence ⟨heroic *achievements* of the early settlers⟩ ***synonyms*** see FEAT

Achil·les' heel \ə-ˈkil-ēz-\ *n* : a vulnerable point [from the legend that Achilles was vulnerable only in the heel]

Achilles tendon *n* : the strong tendon joining the muscles in the calf of the leg to the bone of the heel

ach·ing·ly \ˈā-king-lē\ *adv* **1** : in a manner that causes aching ⟨an *achingly* sad song⟩ **2** : to an extreme degree ⟨*achingly* complicated⟩

achon·dro·pla·sia \ˌā-ˌkän-drə-ˈplā-zhē-ə, -zhə\ *n* : failure of normal development of cartilage resulting in dwarfism [[2]*a-* + Greek *chondros* "grain, cartilage"] — **achon·dro·plas·tic** \-ˈplas-tik\ *adj*

ach·ro·mat·ic \ˌak-rə-ˈmat-ik\ *adj* **1** : giving an image practically free from colors not in the object ⟨*achromatic* lens⟩ **2** : being black, gray, or white : COLORLESS

[1]**ac·id** \ˈas-əd\ *adj* **1** : sour, sharp, or biting to the taste : resembling vinegar in taste **2** : sour in temper : CROSS ⟨*acid* remarks⟩ **3** : of, relating to, or having the characteristics of an acid [Latin *acidus,* from *acēre* "to be sour"] ***synonyms*** see SOUR — **ac·id·ly** *adv* — **ac·id·ness** *n*

[2]**acid** *n* **1** : a sour substance **2** : any of various typically water-soluble and sour compounds that are capable of reacting with a base to form a salt, that redden litmus, that are hydrogen-containing molecules or ions able to give up a proton to a base, or that are substances able to accept an unshared pair of electrons from a base **3** : LSD

ac·id–fast \ˈas-əd-ˌfast\ *adj* : not easily decolorized by acids

acid·ic \ə-ˈsid-ik\ *adj* **1** : acid-forming **2** : ACID

acid·i·fy \ə-ˈsid-ə-ˌfī\ *vb* **-fied; -fy·ing** **1** : to make acid **2** : to change into an acid — **acid·i·fi·ca·tion** \ə-ˌsid-ə-fə-ˈkā-shən\ *n*

acid·i·ty \ə-ˈsid-ət-ē\ *n, pl* **-ties** **1** : the quality, state, or degree of being acid : TARTNESS **2** : the quality or state of being abnormally or excessively acid : HYPERACIDITY

ac·i·doph·i·lus \ˌas-ə-ˈdäf-ə-ləs\ *n* : a lactobacillus that is used especially in the production of yogurt and is normally found in parts of the body (as the intestines) [New Latin, literally, "acid-loving"]

ac·i·do·sis \ˌas-ə-ˈdō-səs\ *n* : an abnormal state characterized by reduced alkalinity of the blood and of the body tissues — **ac·i·dot·ic** \-ˈdät-ik\ *adj*

acid precipitation *n* : precipitation (as rain or snow) with increased acidity caused by environmental factors

acid rain *n* : rain with increased acidity that is caused by environmental factors (as atmospheric pollutants)

acid snow *n* : acid precipitation in the form of snow

acid test *n* : a severe or crucial test

acid·u·late \ə-ˈsij-ə-ˌlāt\ *vt* : to make acid or slightly acid — **acid·u·la·tion** \ə-ˌsij-ə-ˈlā-shən\ *n*

acid·u·lous \ə-ˈsij-ə-ləs\ *adj* : acid in taste or manner : HARSH ⟨an *acidulous* remark⟩

ack–ack \ˈak-ˌak\ *n* : an antiaircraft gun; *also* : antiaircraft fire [British signalmen's pronunciation of *AA*, abbreviation of *antiaircraft*]

ac·knowl·edge \ik-ˈnäl-ij, ak-\ *vt* **1** : to admit the truth or existence of ⟨*acknowledged* our mistake⟩ **2** : to recognize the rights, authority, or status of **3 a** : to express gratitude or obligation for ⟨*acknowledge* a gift⟩ **b** : to make known that something has been received or noticed ⟨*acknowledge* a letter⟩ [*ac-* (as in *accord*) + *knowledge*]

synonyms ACKNOWLEDGE, ADMIT, CONFESS mean to disclose against one's will or inclination. ACKNOWLEDGE implies disclosing what has been or might be denied or concealed ⟨*acknowledged* an earlier mistake⟩. ADMIT implies some degree of reluctance in disclosing or conceding ⟨*admitted* involvement in the scandal⟩. CONFESS implies admitting a weakness, failure, or guilt usually under compulsion ⟨*confessed* a weakness for sweets⟩.

ac·knowl·edged \-ijd\ *adj* : generally recognized or accepted ⟨the *acknowledged* leader of the group⟩ — **ac·knowl·edged·ly** \-ijd-lē, -ij-əd-\ *adv*

ac·knowl·edg·ment *or* **ac·knowl·edge·ment** \ik-ˈnäl-ij-mənt, ak-\ *n* **1 a** : the act of acknowledging **b** : recognition or favorable notice of an act or achievement **2** : a thing done or given in recognition of something received

ACL \ˌā-(ˌ)sē-ˈel\ *n* : ANTERIOR CRUCIATE LIGAMENT

ac·me \ˈak-mē\ *n* : the highest point : PEAK ⟨the *acme* of a scientist's ambition⟩ [Greek *akmē*]

ac·ne \ˈak-nē\ *n* : a skin disorder caused by inflammation of skin glands and hair follicles and characterized by pimples especially on the face [Greek *aknē* "eruption on the face," from *akmē*, literally, "point"]

ac·o·lyte \ˈak-ə-ˌlīt\ *n* **1** : a person who assists a member of the clergy in a service **2** : one that attends or assists : FOLLOWER [Medieval French *acolit*, Medieval Latin *acoluthus*, from Greek *akolouthos* "following," from *a-*, *ha-* "together" + *keleuthos* "path"]

ac·o·nite \ˈak-ə-ˌnīt\ *n* **1** : MONKSHOOD **2** : a drug obtained from the poisonous root of the common Old World monkshood [Greek *akoniton*]

acorn \ˈā-ˌkȯrn, -kərn\ *n* : the roundish one-seeded thin-shelled nut of an oak tree usually having a woody cap composed of hardened bracts [Old English *æcern*]

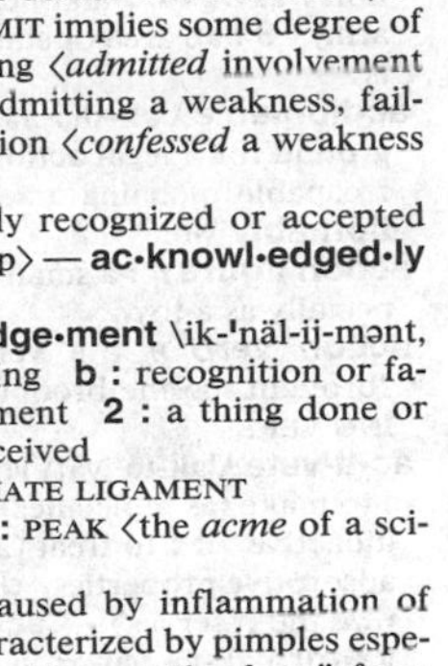

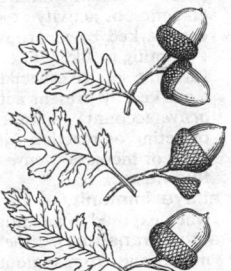

acorn: *top* white oak, *middle* black oak, *bottom* red oak

acorn squash *n* : an acorn-shaped dark green winter squash with a ridged surface and mildly sweet yellow to orange flesh

acorn worm *n* : any of a group of burrowing marine animals resembling worms that have an acorn-shaped proboscis and are usually classed with the hemichordates

acous·tic \ə-ˈkü-stik\ *or* **acous·ti·cal** \-sti-kel\ *adj* **1** : of or relating to the sense or organs of hearing, to sound, or to the science of sounds: as **a** : deadening or absorbing sound ⟨*acoustic* tile⟩ **b** : operated by or utilizing sound waves **2** : of, relating to, or being a musical instrument whose sound is not electronically modified ⟨an *acoustic* guitar⟩ [Greek *akoustikos* "of hearing," from *akouein* "to hear"] — **acous·ti·cal·ly** \-sti-kə-lē, -klē\ *adv*

ac·ous·ti·cian \ˌak-ü-ˈstish-ən, ə-ˌkü-\ *n* : a specialist in acoustics

acous·tics \ə-ˈkü-stiks\ *n sing or pl* **1** : the science dealing with sound **2** *also* **acous·tic** \-stik\ : the qualities in a room or hall that make it easy or hard for a person in it to hear distinctly

ac·quaint \ə-ˈkwānt\ *vt* **1** : to cause to know socially ⟨became *acquainted* through mutual friends⟩ **2** : to make familiar ⟨*acquainted* us with our duties⟩ [Medieval French *acuinter*, *aquaynter*, derived from Late Latin *accognoscere* "to recognize," from Latin *ad-* + *cognoscere* "to know"]

ac·quain·tance \ə-ˈkwānt-ns\ *n* **1** : knowledge gained by personal observation, contact, or experience ⟨had some *acquaintance* with the subject⟩ **2** : a person one knows but who is not a close friend — **ac·quain·tance·ship** \-ˌship\ *n*

acquired immune deficiency syndrome \ə-ˈkwīrd-\ *n* : AIDS

acquired immunity *n* : immunity that develops following exposure (as through infection or vaccination) to a disease-causing agent

acquired immunodeficiency syndrome *n* : AIDS

ac·qui·esce \ˌak-wē-ˈes\ *vi* : to accept, agree, or comply silently or passively [French *acquiescer*, from Latin *acquiescere*, from *ad-* + *quiescere* "to be quiet"] — **ac·qui·es·cence** \-ˈes-ns\ *n*

ac·qui·es·cent \-ˈes-nt\ *adj* : acquiescing or tending to acquiesce — **ac·qui·es·cent·ly** *adv*

ac·quire \ə-ˈkwīr\ *vt* **1** : to come into possession of especially by one's own efforts : GAIN ⟨*acquired* great wealth⟩ **2 a** : to come to have as a characteristic, trait, or ability often by sustained effort ⟨*acquired* good study skills⟩ **b** : to develop after birth usually as a result of environmental forces ⟨an *acquired* disease⟩ **3** : to locate and hold (a desired object) in a detector ⟨*acquire* a target by radar⟩ [Medieval French *aquerre*, from Latin *acquirere*, from *ad-* + *quaerere* "to seek"] — **ac·quir·able** \-ˈkwī-rə-bəl\ *adj*

ac·quire·ment \-ˈkwīr-mənt\ *n* **1** : the act of acquiring **2** : a physical or mental skill usually resulting from continued effort ⟨the *acquirements* expected of a high-school graduate⟩

ac·qui·si·tion \ˌak-wə-ˈzish-ən\ *n* **1** : the act of acquiring ⟨the *acquisition* of property⟩ **2** : something acquired or gained ⟨the book was a recent *acquisition*⟩ [Latin *acquisitio*, from *acquirere* "to acquire"]

ac·quis·i·tive \ə-ˈkwiz-ət-iv\ *adj* : strongly desirous of acquiring — **ac·quis·i·tive·ly** *adv* — **ac·quis·i·tive·ness** *n*

ac·quit \ə-ˈkwit\ *vt* **ac·quit·ted; ac·quit·ting** **1** : to set free or discharge completely (as from an obligation or accusation) ⟨the court *acquitted* the prisoner⟩ **2** : to conduct (oneself) usually satisfactorily ⟨*acquitted* themselves well⟩ [Medieval French *aquiter*, from *a-* "ad-" + *quite* "free of"] — **ac·quit·ter** *n*

ac·quit·tal \ə-ˈkwit-l\ *n* : the setting free of a person from the charge of an offense by verdict, sentence, or other legal process

ac·quit·tance \-ns\ *n* : a document (as a receipt) showing a release from an obligation

acr- *or* **acro-** *combining form* **1** : beginning : end ⟨*acronym*⟩ **2 a** : peak : height ⟨*acrophobia*⟩ **b** : extremity of the body ⟨*acromegaly*⟩ [Greek *akros* "topmost, extreme"]

acre \ˈā-kər\ *n* **1** *pl* : property consisting of land : ESTATE **2** : a unit of area equal to 43,560 square feet (about 4047 square meters) — see MEASURE table **3** : a broad expanse or great quantity ⟨*acres* of publicity⟩ [Old English *æcer*]

acre·age \ˈā-kə-rij, -krij\ *n* : area in acres : ACRES

acre–foot \ˈā-kər-ˈfu̇t\ *n* : the volume (as of irrigation water) that would cover one acre to a depth of one foot and that is equal to 43,560 cubic feet (about 1233 cubic meters)

ac·rid \ˈak-rəd\ *adj* **1** : biting or bitter in taste or odor **2** : bitterly irritating to the feelings ⟨an *acrid* remark⟩ [Latin *acr-*, *acer* "sharp"] — **acrid·i·ty** \a-ˈkrid-ət-ē, ə-\ *n* — **ac·rid·ly** \ˈak-rəd-lē\ *adv* — **ac·rid·ness** *n*

ac·ri·mo·ni·ous \ˌak-rə-ˈmō-nē-əs\ *adj* : marked by acrimony : BITTER, RANCOROUS ⟨an *acrimonious* dispute⟩ — **ac·ri·mo·ni·ous·ly** *adv* — **ac·ri·mo·ni·ous·ness** *n*

ac·ri·mo·ny \ˈak-rə-ˌmō-nē\ *n, pl* **-nies** : harsh or biting sharpness especially of words, manner, or disposition [Latin *acrimonia*, from *acr-*, *acer* "sharp"]

ac·ro·bat \ˈak-rə-ˌbat\ *n* **1** : one that performs feats requiring agility and balance **2** : one skilled at swiftly changing position or viewpoint [Greek *akrobatēs*, from *akros* "topmost" + *bainein* "to step, go"] — **ac·ro·bat·ic** \ˌak-rə-ˈbat-ik\ *adj* — **ac·ro·bat·i·cal·ly** \-ˈbat-i-kə-lē, -klē\ *adv*

\ə\ **abut**	\au̇\ **out**	\i\ **tip**	\ȯ\ **saw**	\u̇\ **foot**
\ər\ **further**	\ch\ **chin**	\ī\ **life**	\ȯi\ **coin**	\y\ **yet**
\a\ **mat**	\e\ **pet**	\j\ **job**	\th\ **thin**	\yü\ **few**
\ā\ **take**	\ē\ **easy**	\ng\ **sing**	\th\ **this**	\yu̇\ **cure**
\ä\ **cot, cart**	\g\ **go**	\ō\ **bone**	\ü\ **food**	\zh\ **vision**

ac·ro·bat·ics \ˌak-rə-ˈbat-iks\ *n sing or pl* **1** : the art or performance of an acrobat **2** : a striking performance involving great agility or complexity ⟨a singer's vocal *acrobatics*⟩

ac·ro·meg·a·ly \ˌak-rō-ˈmeg-ə-lē\ *n* : a disorder caused by excessive secretion of the pituitary gland and marked by progressive enlargement of hands, feet, and face [*acr-* + Greek *megal-, megas* "large"] — **ac·ro·me·gal·ic** \-mə-ˈgal-ik\ *adj*

ac·ro·nym \ˈak-rə-ˌnim\ *n* : a word (as *radar*) formed from the initial letter or letters of each of the successive parts or major parts of a compound term [*acr-* + *-onym* (as in *homonym*)]

ac·ro·pho·bia \ˌak-rə-ˈfō-bē-ə\ *n* : abnormal dread of being in a high place : fear of heights — **ac·ro·pho·bic** \-bik\ *adj*

acrop·o·lis \ə-ˈkräp-ə-ləs\ *n* : the upper fortified part of an ancient Greek city [Greek *akropolis,* from *akros* "topmost" + *polis* "city"]

[1]**across** \ə-ˈkrȯs\ *adv* **1** : in a position reaching from one side to the other ⟨boards sawed directly *across*⟩ **2** : to or on the opposite side ⟨got *across* in a boat⟩ **3** : so as to be understandable, acceptable, or successful ⟨put a point *across*⟩ [Medieval French *an crois-,* from *an* "in" + *crois* "cross," from Latin *crux*]

[2]**across** *prep* **1** : to or on the opposite side of ⟨*across* the street⟩ **2** : so as to intersect or pass at an angle ⟨lay one stick *across* another⟩ **3** : into an accidental meeting or contact with ⟨ran *across* an old friend⟩ **4** : THROUGHOUT ⟨sprung up *across* the nation⟩

across–the–board *adj* **1** : placed in combination to win, place, or show ⟨an *across-the-board* bet⟩ **2** : including or affecting all classes or categories ⟨an *across-the-board* change⟩

acros·tic \ə-ˈkrȯs-tik, -ˈkräs-\ *n* : a composition usually in verse in which sets of letters (as the initial or final letters of the lines) taken in order form a word or phrase or a regular sequence of letters of the alphabet [Greek *akrostichis,* from *acr-* + *stichos* "line"] — **acrostic** *adj* — **acros·ti·cal·ly** \-ti-kə-lē, -klē\ *adv*

[1]**acryl·ic** \ə-ˈkril-ik\ *adj* : of or relating to acrylic acid or its derivatives ⟨*acrylic* polymers⟩ [derived from Latin *acr-, acer* "sharp"]

[2]**acrylic** *n* **1 a** : ACRYLIC RESIN **b** : a paint in which the vehicle is acrylic resin **2** : ACRYLIC FIBER

acrylic acid *n* : an unsaturated liquid acid $C_3H_4O_2$ that polymerizes readily to form useful products (as a constituent of paint)

acrylic fiber *n* : a quick-drying synthetic textile fiber made by the polymerization of acrylonitrile

acrylic resin *n* : a glassy plastic made especially from acrylic acid and used for cast and molded parts or as coatings and adhesives

ac·ry·lo·ni·trile \ˌak-rə-lō-ˈnī-trəl, -ˌtrēl\ *n* : a colorless flammable liquid C_3H_3N used chiefly in polymerization

[1]**act** \ˈakt\ *n* **1** : something that is done voluntarily ⟨an *act* of kindness⟩ **2** : the doing of something ⟨caught in the *act*⟩ **3** : a law made by a governing body (as a legislature) ⟨an *act* of Congress⟩ **4** *often cap* : a formal record of something done or transacted **5 a** : one of the main divisions of a play or opera **b** : one of the successive parts of a variety show or circus **6** : a display of insincere behavior : PRETENSE [Latin *actus* "action" and *actum* "thing done," both from *agere* "to do"]

[2]**act** *vb* **1** : to represent or perform especially on the stage **2** : to play the part of ⟨*act* the villain⟩ **3 a** : to behave in a manner suitable to ⟨*act* your age⟩ **b** : to conduct oneself ⟨*act* like a fool⟩ **4** : PRETEND 2 **5** : to take action : MOVE ⟨think before you *act*⟩ **6 a** : to perform a specified function : SERVE ⟨trees *acting* as a windbreak⟩ **b** : to produce an effect : WORK ⟨wait for a medicine to *act*⟩ **7** : to make a decision ⟨*act* on a proposal⟩ — **act·abil·i·ty** \ˌak-tə-ˈbil-ət-ē\ *n* — **act·able** \ˈak-tə-bəl\ *adj*

ACT *trademark* — used for a standardized achievement test to evaluate suitability for college admission

ACTH \ˌā-ˌsē-ˌtē-ˈāch\ *n* : a protein hormone of the anterior lobe of the pituitary gland that stimulates the cortex of the adrenal gland [*a*dreno*c*ortico*t*rophic *h*ormone]

ac·tin \ˈak-tən\ *n* : a protein of muscle that with myosin is active in muscular contraction [Latin *actus* "action"]

[1]**act·ing** \ˈak-ting\ *adj* : serving temporarily or in place of another ⟨*acting* president⟩

[2]**acting** *n* : the art or practice of representing a character on a stage or before cameras

ac·tin·ic \ak-ˈtin-ik\ *adj* : relating to chemical changes produced by radiant energy

ac·ti·nide \ˈak-tə-ˌnīd\ *n* : any of the chemical elements in the series of increasing atomic numbers beginning with actinium or thorium and ending with lawrencium

ac·tin·i·um \ak-ˈtin-ē-əm\ *n* : a radioactive metallic element found especially in pitchblende — see ELEMENT table [Greek *aktin-, aktis* "ray"]

ac·ti·no·my·cete \ˌak-tə-nō-ˈmī-ˌsēt, -mī-ˈsēt\ *n* : any of an order (Actinomycetales) of filamentous or rod-shaped bacteria including soil saprophytes and disease producers [derived from Greek *aktis* "ray" + *mykēs* "fungus"]

ac·ti·no·my·co·sis \ˌak-tə-nō-mī-ˈkō-səs\ *n* : infection with or disease caused by actinomycetes — **ac·ti·no·my·cot·ic** \-ˈkät-ik\ *adj*

ac·tion \ˈak-shən\ *n* **1** : a proceeding in a court of justice by which one demands or enforces one's right **2** : the working of one thing on another so as to produce a change ⟨the *action* of acids on metals⟩ **3** : the doing of something usually in stages or with the possibility of continuation ⟨the *action* of singing⟩; *also* : such an action expressed by a verb **4 a** : a thing done : DEED **b** *pl* : BEHAVIOR, CONDUCT **c** : readiness to engage in daring activity : INITIATIVE ⟨a person of *action*⟩ **5** : combat in war **6** : the unfolding of the events of a drama or work of fiction : PLOT **7** : an operating mechanism ⟨the *action* of a firearm⟩ **8** : an area or state of vigorous activity ⟨where the *action* is⟩

ac·tion·able \ˈak-shə-nə-bəl, -shnə-\ *adj* **1** : subject to or giving ground for a legal action or lawsuit ⟨*actionable* negligence⟩ **2** : capable of being acted on ⟨*actionable* information⟩ — **ac·tion·ably** \-blē\ *adv*

action figure *n* : a small scale figure (as of a superhero) used especially as a toy

action verb *n* : a verb that expresses action ⟨*brought* in "brought me the broom" is an action verb⟩ — compare LINKING VERB

ac·ti·vate \ˈak-tə-ˌvāt\ *vt* : to make active or more active: as **a** : to make (as molecules) reactive **b** : to make (a substance) radioactive **c** : to treat (as carbon or alumina) so as to improve adsorptive properties **d** : to place on active military duty ⟨*activate* the reserves⟩ — **ac·ti·va·tion** \ˌak-tə-ˈvā-shən\ *n* — **ac·ti·va·tor** \ˈak-tə-ˌvāt-ər\ *n*

activation energy *n* : the minimum amount of energy required to convert a stable molecule into a reactive molecule

ac·tive \ˈak-tiv\ *adj* **1** : characterized by action rather than contemplation **2** : producing, requiring, or involving action or movement ⟨an *active* sport⟩ ⟨an *active* child⟩ **3** : of, relating to, or constituting a verb form or voice indicating that the person or thing represented by the grammatical subject performs the action represented by the verb ⟨*hit* in "they hit the ball" is *active*⟩ **4** : quick in physical movement : LIVELY **5 a** : disposed to action : ENERGETIC ⟨*active* interest⟩ **b** : engaged in an action or activity : PARTICIPATING ⟨an *active* club member⟩ **c** : marked by vigorous activity : BUSY ⟨an *active* mind⟩ **d** : erupting or likely to erupt ⟨an *active* volcano⟩ **6** : involving full-time service especially in the armed forces ⟨*active* duty⟩ **7** : marked by present action, operation, movement, or use ⟨an *active* account⟩ ⟨a student's *active* vocabulary⟩ **8 a** : capable of acting or reacting ⟨*active* ingredients⟩ **b** : tending to progress or increase ⟨*active* tuberculosis⟩ — **ac·tive·ly** *adv* — **ac·tive·ness** *n*

active immunity *n* : immunity produced by the individual when exposed to an antigen — compare PASSIVE IMMUNITY

active transport *n* : the movement of substances across a cell membrane from regions of lower concentration to those of higher concentration by the expenditure of energy

ac·tive·wear \ˈak-tiv-ˌwaər, -ˌweər\ *n* : SPORTSWEAR

ac·tiv·ism \ˈak-ti-ˌviz-əm\ *n* : a doctrine or practice that emphasizes vigorous action especially in support of or opposition to one side of a controversial issue — **ac·tiv·ist** \-vəst\ *n or adj*

ac·tiv·i·ty \ak-ˈtiv-ət-ē\ *n, pl* **-ties** **1** : the quality or state of being active **2** : vigorous or energetic action : LIVELINESS **3 a** : natural or normal function **b** (1) : a process that an organism carries on or participates in by virtue of being alive (2) : a similar process actually or potentially involving mental function; *esp* : an educational exercise designed to teach by firsthand experience **4** : an active force **5 a** : PURSUIT 2 **b** : a form of organized, supervised, often extracurricular recreation

act of God : an extraordinary interruption of the usual course of events by a natural cause (as a flood or earthquake) that could not reasonably have been foreseen or prevented

ac·to·my·o·sin \ˌak-tə-ˈmī-ə-sən\ *n* : a contractile complex of actin and myosin that functions together with ATP in muscular contraction

ac·tor \ˈak-tər\ *n* **1 a :** one that acts : DOER **b :** one that acts a part; *esp* : a theatrical performer **2 :** PARTICIPANT

act out *vb* **1 :** to represent in action ⟨*acted* out the story⟩ **2 :** to behave badly especially as a way of venting emotions

ac·tress \ˈak-trəs\ *n* : a woman who is an actor

Acts \ˈaks, ˈakts\ *or* **Acts of the Apostles** *n* : a book in the New Testament narrating the beginnings of the Christian church — see BIBLE table

ac·tu·al \ˈak-chə-wəl, -chəl; ˈaksh-wəl\ *adj* **1 a :** existing in fact or reality ⟨our *actual* intentions⟩ **b :** really acted on or carried out and not merely a possibility ⟨the *actual* conditions⟩ **2 :** not false : GENUINE **3 :** present or active at the time [Middle English *actuel,* from Late Latin *actualis,* from Latin *actus* "act"] ***synonyms*** see REAL

ac·tu·al·i·ty \ˌak-chə-ˈwal-ət-ē\ *n, pl* **-ties 1 :** the quality or state of being actual **2 :** something that is actual ⟨face the *actualities* of the situation⟩

ac·tu·al·ize \ˈak-chə-wə-ˌlīz, -chə-ˌlīz, ˈaksh-wə-\ *vb* : to make or become actual — **ac·tu·al·i·za·tion** \ˌak-chə-wə-lə-ˈzā-shən, -chə-lə-, ˌaksh-wə-\ *n*

ac·tu·al·ly \ˈak-chə-wə-lē, -chə-lē, ˈaksh-wə-, ˈaksh-lē\ *adv* : in fact : in truth : REALLY ⟨can *actually* read Latin⟩

ac·tu·ary \ˈak-chə-ˌwer-ē\ *n, pl* **-ar·ies :** a person who calculates insurance and annuity premiums, reserves, and dividends [Latin *actuarius* "shorthand writer, record keeper," from *actarius,* from *actum* "thing done, record"] — **ac·tu·ar·i·al** \ˌak-chə-ˈwer-ē-əl\ *adj* — **ac·tu·ar·i·al·ly** \-ē-ə-lē\ *adv*

ac·tu·ate \ˈak-chə-ˌwāt\ *vt* **1 :** to put into action ⟨the windmill *actuates* the pump⟩ **2 :** to move to action : arouse to activity ⟨were *actuated* by competition⟩ [Medieval Latin *actuare,* from Latin *actus* "act"] ***synonyms*** see MOVE — **ac·tu·a·tion** \ˌak-chə-ˈwā-shən\ *n*

act up *vi* : to act or function in an unruly, abnormal, or annoying way

acu·ity \ə-ˈkyü-ət-ē\ *n* : keenness of perception : SHARPNESS ⟨visual *acuity*⟩ [Medieval French *acuité,* derived from Latin *acutus* "sharp"]

acu·men \ə-ˈkyü-mən\ *n* : keenness of insight especially in practical matters : SHREWDNESS [Latin, literally, "point," from *acuere* "to make sharp"]

acu·pres·sure \ˈak-yə-ˌpresh-ər\ *n* : the application of pressure (as with the fingertips) to the same points on the body stimulated in acupuncture

acu·punc·ture \ˈak-yu̇-ˌpəng-chər, -ˌpəngk-\ *n* : an originally Chinese practice of inserting fine needles through the skin at specific points especially to cure disease or relieve pain [Latin *acus* "needle" + English *puncture*]

acute \ə-ˈkyüt\ *adj* **1 a :** being or forming an angle measuring less than 90 degrees ⟨an *acute* angle⟩ **b :** composed of acute angles ⟨an *acute* triangle⟩ **2 a :** marked by keen discernment or intellectual perception especially of subtle distinctions : PENETRATING **b :** responsive to slight impressions or influences ⟨*acute* hearing⟩ **3 :** marked by sharpness or severity ⟨an *acute* pain⟩ **4 :** felt, perceived or experienced intensely ⟨in *acute* distress⟩ **5 a :** having a sudden onset and short duration ⟨*acute* disease⟩ **b :** seriously demanding urgent attention : CRITICAL ⟨an *acute* emergency⟩ **6 :** of, marked by, or being an accent mark having the form ´ [Latin *acutus* "sharp," from *acuere* "to sharpen," from *acus* "needle"] ***synonyms*** see SHARP — **acute·ly** *adv* — **acute·ness** *n*

ad \ˈad\ *n* : ADVERTISEMENT 2

ad- *or* **ac-** *or* **af-** *or* **ag-** *or* **al-** *or* **ap-** *or* **as-** *or* **at-** *prefix* **1 :** to : toward — usually *ac-* before *c, k,* or *q* ⟨acculturation⟩ and *af-* before *f* and *ag-* before *g* and *al-* before *l* ⟨*al*literation⟩ and *ap-* before *p* and *as-* before *s* and *at-* before *t* ⟨*at*tune⟩ and *ad-* before other sounds but sometimes *ad-* even before one of the listed consonants ⟨*ad*sorb⟩ **2 :** near : adjacent to — in this sense always *ad-* ⟨*ad*renal⟩ [Latin, from *ad* "to"]

-ad \ˌad, əd\ *adv suffix* : in the direction of : toward ⟨caud*ad*⟩ [Latin *ad* "to"]

ad·age \ˈad-ij\ *n* : an old and well-known saying that expresses a general truth [Middle French, from Latin *adagium*]

[1]ada·gio \ə-ˈdäj-ō, -ˈdäj-ē-ˌō, -ˈdäzh-\ *adv or adj* : in an easy graceful manner : SLOWLY — used chiefly as a direction in music [Italian, from *ad* "to" + *agio* "ease"]

[2]adagio *n, pl* **-gi·os 1 :** a musical composition or movement in adagio tempo **2 :** a ballet duet by a man and woman or a trio of dancers displaying difficult feats of balance, lifting, or spinning

Adam *adj* : of or relating to an 18th century style of furniture characterized by straight lines, surface decoration, and conventional designs (as festooned garlands and medallions) [Robert *Adam,* died 1792, and James *Adam,* died 1794, Scottish designers]

[1]ad·a·mant \ˈad-ə-mənt *also* -ˌmant\ *n* **1 :** a stone (as a diamond) formerly believed to be of impenetrable hardness **2 :** an extremely hard substance [Medieval French, from Latin *adamas* "hardest metal, diamond," from Greek]

[2]adamant *adj* : unshakable or immovable especially in opposition : UNYIELDING — **ad·a·man·cy** \-mən-sē\ *n* — **ad·a·mant·ly** *adv*

ad·a·man·tine \ˌad-ə-ˈman-ˌtēn, -ˌtīn\ *adj* **1 :** made of or having the quality of adamant **2 :** rigidly firm : UNYIELDING **3 :** resembling the diamond in hardness or luster

Ad·am's apple \ˈad-əmz-\ *n* : the projection in the front of the neck formed by the largest cartilage of the larynx

adapt \ə-ˈdapt\ *vb* : to make or become suitable; *esp* : to change so as to fit a new or specific use or situation ⟨*adapt* to life in a new school⟩ ⟨*adapt* the novel for children⟩ [Latin *adaptare,* derived from *ad-* + *aptus* "apt, fit"] — **adapt·abil·i·ty** \-ˌdap-tə-ˈbil-ət-ē\ *n* — **adapt·able** \-ˈdap-tə-bəl\ *adj*

synonyms ADAPT, ADJUST, ACCOMMODATE, CONFORM mean to bring one into correspondence with another. ADAPT implies suiting or fitting by modification and may suggest pliability or readiness ⟨*adapted* themselves to the warmer climate⟩. ADJUST implies bringing into close or exact correspondence ⟨*adjusted* the schedule to allow for vacations⟩. ACCOMMODATE implies adapting or adjusting to by yielding or compromising ⟨*accommodated* his political beliefs in order to win⟩. CONFORM implies bringing or coming into accord with a pattern or principle ⟨refused to *conform* to society's values⟩.

ad·ap·ta·tion \ˌad-ˌap-ˈtā-shən, -əp-\ *n* **1 :** the act or process of adapting : the state of being adapted **2 :** adjustment to environmental conditions: as **a :** adjustment of a sense organ to the intensity or quality of stimulation **b :** inherited modification of an organism that increases its chances for survival in its environment; *also* : a change or structure resulting from such modification **3 :** something that is adapted; *esp* : a composition rewritten into a new form ⟨the movie is an *adaptation* of the book⟩ — **ad·ap·ta·tion·al** \-shnəl, -shən-l\ *adj* — **ad·ap·ta·tion·al·ly** \-ē\ *adv*

adapt·ed \ə-ˈdap-təd\ *adj* : SUITABLE 1

adapt·er *also* **adap·tor** \ə-ˈdap-tər\ *n* **1 :** one that adapts **2 a :** a device for connecting two parts (as of different diameters) of an apparatus **b :** an attachment for adapting apparatus for uses not originally intended

adap·tive \ə-ˈdap-tiv\ *adj* : showing or having a capacity for or tendency toward adaptation — **adap·tive·ly** *adv*

ad·ax·i·al \ˈa-ˈdak-sē-əl\ *adj* : situated on the same side as or facing the axis ⟨the *adaxial* or upper surface of the leaf⟩

add \ˈad\ *vb* **1 a :** to join or unite to a thing so as to enlarge or improve it ⟨*add* a wing to the house⟩ **b :** to unite or combine in a single whole **2 :** to say further ⟨let me *add* a word⟩ **3 :** to combine (numbers) into a single number that has the same total value [Latin *addere,* from *ad-* + *-dere* "to put"] — **add·able** *or* **add·ible** \ˈad-ə-bəl\ *adj*

ad·dax \ˈad-ˌaks\ *n, pl* **ad·dax·es :** a large light-colored antelope of the Sahara with long spiralling horns [Latin]

ad·dend \ˈad-ˌend, ə-ˈdend\ *n* : a number that is to be added to another number [short for *addendum*]

addax

\ə\ **abut**	\au̇\ **out**	\i\ **tip**	\ȯ\ **saw**	\u̇\ **foot**
\ər\ **further**	\ch\ **chin**	\ī\ **life**	\ȯi\ **coin**	\y\ **yet**
\a\ **mat**	\e\ **pet**	\j\ **job**	\th\ **thin**	\yü\ **few**
\ā\ **take**	\ē\ **easy**	\ng\ **sing**	\th\ **this**	\yu̇\ **cure**
\ä\ **cot, cart**	\g\ **go**	\ō\ **bone**	\ü\ **food**	\zh\ **vision**

ad·den·dum \ə-ˈden-dəm\ *n, pl* **-den·da** \-ˈden-də\ : a thing added (as to a book) : ADDITION [Latin, from *addere* "to add"]

[1]**ad·der** \ˈad-ər\ *n* **1** : a poisonous European viper; *also* : any of several related snakes **2** : any of several harmless North American snakes (as a hognose snake) [Middle English *nadder* (the phrase *a nadder* being understood as *an adder*), from Old English *nædre*]

[2]**add·er** \ˈad-ər\ *n* : one that adds

ad·der's–tongue \ˈad-ərz-ˌtəng\ *n* **1** : a fern whose spore-bearing stalk resembles a snake's tongue **2** : DOGTOOTH VIOLET

[1]**ad·dict** \ə-ˈdikt\ *vt* **1** : to devote or surrender (oneself) to something habitually or obsessively ⟨*addicted* to gambling⟩ **2** : to cause (a person) to become physically or mentally dependent upon a drug [Latin *addicere* "to favor," from *ad-* + *dicere* "to say"]

[2]**ad·dict** \ˈad-ikt, -ˌikt\ *n* **1** : one who is addicted (as to a drug) **2** : DEVOTEE ⟨a detective novel *addict*⟩

ad·dic·tion \ə-ˈdik-shən\ *n* **1** : the quality or state of being addicted ⟨*addiction* to reading⟩ **2** : compulsive physical or mental need for a habit-forming substance (as cocaine or nicotine)

ad·dic·tive \ə-ˈdik-tiv\ *adj* : causing or characterized by addiction ⟨an *addictive* drug⟩

Ad·di·son's disease \ˈad-ə-sənz-\ *n* : a disease marked by deficient secretion of hormones by the cortex of the adrenal gland [Thomas *Addison,* died 1860, English physician]

ad·di·tion \ə-ˈdish-ən\ *n* **1** : the result of adding : INCREASE **2** : the act or process of adding **3** : the operation of adding numbers to obtain their sum **4** : a part added (as to a building) **5** : direct chemical combination of substances into a single product — **in addition** : [2]BESIDES, ALSO — **in addition to** : over and above

ad·di·tion·al \-ˈdish-nəl, -ˈdish-ən-l\ *adj* : being an addition : ADDED ⟨an *additional* charge⟩ — **ad·di·tion·al·ly** \-ē\ *adv*

[1]**ad·di·tive** \ˈad-ət-iv\ *adj* : relating to, characterized by, or produced by addition — **ad·di·tive·ly** *adv*

[2]**additive** *n* : a substance added to another in relatively small amounts to add or improve desirable properties or suppress undesirable properties ⟨food *additives*⟩

additive identity *n* : an element (as zero in the set of real numbers) of a mathematical set that leaves every element of the set unchanged when added to it

additive inverse *n* : a number that when added to a given number sums to zero — compare OPPOSITE 2

ad·dle \ˈad-l\ *vb* **ad·dled; ad·dling** \ˈad-ling, -l-ing\ **1** : to make or become confused **2** : to become rotten : SPOIL ⟨*addled* eggs⟩ [from earlier *addle* "rotten, empty," from Old English *adela* "filth"]

[1]**ad·dress** \ə-ˈdres\ *vt* **1 a** : to direct the attention of (oneself) ⟨*addressed* myself to my work⟩ **b** : to deal with : TREAT ⟨failed to *address* the issues⟩ **2 a** : to communicate directly to a person or group ⟨*addressed* his thanks to his host⟩ **b** : to deliver a formal speech to ⟨*address* the convention⟩ **3** : to mark directions for delivery on ⟨*address* a letter⟩ **4** : to greet by a prescribed form **5** : to identify (as a computer peripheral or memory location) by an address or a name for information transfer [Medieval French *adrescer,* from *a-* "ad-" + *drescer* "to direct, put right, dress"] — **ad·dress·er** *n*

[2]**ad·dress** \ə-ˈdres, *for 4, 5, & 7 also* ˈad-ˌres\ *n* **1** : dutiful attention especially in courtship — usually used in plural **2** : readiness and capability for dealing (as with a person or problem) skillfully **3 a** : BEARING, MANNER ⟨a person of rude *address*⟩ **b** : the manner of speaking or singing : DELIVERY **4** : a formal communication; *esp* : a prepared speech **5 a** : a place where a person or organization may be communicated with **b** : directions for delivery on the outside of an object (as a letter or package) **c** : the designation of place of delivery above the salutation on a business letter **6 a** : a location (as in the memory of a computer) where particular information is stored **b** : a series of symbols (as numerals or letters) that identifies the location of information in a computer's memory or on the Internet or that specifies the source or destination of an e-mail message

ad·dress·able \ə-ˈdres-ə-bəl\ *adj* : accessible through an address ⟨*addressable* registers in a computer⟩

ad·dress·ee \ˌad-ˌres-ˈē, ə-ˌdres-ˈē\ *n* : one to whom something is addressed

ad·duce \ə-ˈdüs, -dyüs\ *vt* : to offer as example, reason, or proof in discussion or analysis [Latin *adducere,* literally, "to lead to," from *ad-* + *ducere* "to lead"] — **ad·duc·er** *n*

ad·duct \ə-ˈdəkt\ *vt* : to draw (a part of the body) toward or past the median axis of the body; *also* : to bring (similar parts) together [Latin *adductus,* past participle of *adducere* "to lead to, adduce"] — **ad·duc·tive** \-ˈdək-tiv\ *adj*

ad·duc·tion \ə-ˈdək-shən\ *n* **1** : the action of adducting : the state of being adducted **2** : the act or action of adducing or bringing forward

ad·duc·tor \ə-ˈdək-tər\ *n* **1** : a muscle that draws a body part toward the median axis of the body or bodily part — compare ABDUCTOR **2** : a muscle that closes the valves of a bivalve mollusk

add up *vi* **1 a** : to come to a total and especially the expected total **b** : to make sense ⟨her story just doesn't *add up*⟩ **2** : to amount to a lot ⟨just a little each time, but it all *adds up*⟩

-ade \ˈād\ *n suffix* **1** : act : action ⟨block*ade*⟩ **2** : sweet drink ⟨lime*ade*⟩ [derived from Latin *-ata,* feminine of *-atus* "-ate"]

ad·e·nine \ˈad-n-ˌēn\ *n* : a purine base $C_5H_5N_5$ that codes hereditary information in the polynucleotide chain of DNA and RNA — compare CYTOSINE, GUANINE, THYMINE, URACIL [Greek *adēn* "gland"; from its presence in glandular tissue]

[1]**ad·e·noid** \ˈad-n-ˌȯid, ˈad-ˌnȯid\ *n* : either of two masses of lymphoid tissue at the back of the pharynx that usually obstruct breathing when abnormally enlarged — usually used in plural [Greek *adenoeidēs* "glandular," from *adēn* "gland"]

[2]**adenoid** *adj* **1** : of or relating to the adenoids **2** : relating to or affected with abnormally enlarged adenoids

ad·e·noi·dal \ˌad-n-ˈoid-l\ *adj* : exhibiting the characteristics (as voice nasality) of one affected with abnormally enlarged adenoids : ADENOID ⟨an *adenoidal* tenor⟩ — not usually used technically

aden·o·sine \ə-ˈden-ə-ˌsēn\ *n* : a compound $C_{10}H_{13}N_5O_4$ that is a constituent of RNA and ATP and that is composed of adenine and ribose [blend of *adenine* and *ribose*]

adenosine di·phos·phate \-dī-ˈfäs-ˌfāt\ *n* : ADP

adenosine mo·no·phos·phate \-ˌmän-ə-ˈfäs-ˌfāt, -ˌmō-nə-\ *n* : AMP

adenosine tri·phos·phate \-trī-ˈfäs-ˌfāt\ *n* : ATP

[1]**ad·ept** \ˈad-ˌept\ *n* : a highly skilled or well-trained individual : EXPERT [New Latin *adeptus* "alchemist who has attained the knowledge of how to change base metals to gold," from Latin *adipisci* "to attain," from *ad-* + *apisci* "to reach"]

[2]**adept** \ə-ˈdept\ *adj* : thoroughly proficient : EXPERT ***synonyms*** see PROFICIENT — **adept·ly** *adv* — **adept·ness** \-ˈdep-nəs, -ˈdept-\ *n*

ad·e·quate \ˈad-i-kwət\ *adj* **1** : suitable or fully sufficient for a specific requirement **2** : barely sufficient or satisfactory ⟨their performance was *adequate* but not really good⟩ [Latin *adaequare* "to make equal," from *ad-* + *aequus* "equal"] ***synonyms*** see SUFFICIENT — **ad·e·qua·cy** \-kwə-sē\ *n* — **ad·e·quate·ly** \-kwət-lē\ *adv* — **ad·e·quate·ness** *n*

ad·here \ad-ˈhiər, əd-\ *vi* **1** : to give support or maintain loyalty (as to a cause) **2** : to hold fast or stick by or as if by gluing **3** : to agree to observe ⟨*adhere* to a treaty⟩ [Latin *adhaerēre* "to stick to," from *ad-* + *haerēre* "to stick"] ***synonyms*** see STICK

ad·her·ence \-ˈhir-əns\ *n* **1** : the action or quality of adhering **2** : steady or faithful attachment : FIDELITY ⟨*adherence* to a cause⟩

[1]**ad·her·ent** \-ˈhir-ənt\ *adj* **1** : able or tending to adhere **2** : connected or associated with something ⟨nations *adherent* to the world organization⟩ — **ad·her·ent·ly** *adv*

[2]**adherent** *n* : one that adheres: as **a** : a follower of a leader or party **b** : a believer in or advocate of something (as an idea or church)

ad·he·sion \ad-ˈhē-zhən, əd-\ *n* **1** : steady or firm attachment : ADHERENCE **2** : the action or state of adhering **3** : the abnormal union of tissues by fibrous tissue following inflammation (as after surgery) **4** : the molecular attraction exerted between the surfaces of bodies in contact [Latin *adhaesio,* from *adhaerēre* "to adhere"] — **ad·he·sion·al** \-ˈhēzh-nəl, -ˈhē-zhən-l\ *adj*

[1]**ad·he·sive** \ad-ˈhē-siv, əd-, -ziv\ *adj* **1** : tending to remain in association or memory **2** : tending to adhere **3** : prepared for adhering : STICKY — **ad·he·sive·ly** *adv* — **ad·he·sive·ness** *n*

[2]**adhesive** *n* : an adhesive substance (as glue or cement)

adhesive tape *n* : tape coated on one side with an adhesive and used especially for fixing bandages or supporting injuries

ad hoc \ad-ˈhäk, ˈad-, -ˈhōk\ *adv or adj* **:** for the particular purpose or case at hand ⟨a decision made *ad hoc*⟩ ⟨an *ad hoc* committee⟩ [Latin, "for this"]

ad ho·mi·nem \ad-ˈhäm-ə-ˌnem, ˈad-\ *adj* **:** appealing to feelings or prejudices rather than intellect especially through attack on an opponent's character rather than response to the opponent's arguments ⟨an *ad hominem* argument⟩ [New Latin, literally, "to the man"]

adi·a·bat·ic \ˌad-ē-ə-ˈbat-ik, ˌā-ˌdī-ə-\ *adj* **:** occurring without loss or gain of heat ⟨*adiabatic* expansion of a gas⟩ [Greek *adiabatos* "impassable," from *a-* + *dia-* + *bainein* "to go"] — **adi·a·bat·i·cal·ly** \-ˈbat-i-kə-lē, -klē\ *adv*

adieu \ə-ˈdü, -ˈdyü\ *n, pl* **adieus** *or* **adieux** \-ˈdüz, -ˈdyüz\ **:** FAREWELL 1 — often used interjectionally [French, from *a* "to" + *Dieu* "God"]

ad in·fi·ni·tum \ˌad-ˌin-fə-ˈnīt-əm\ *adv or adj* **:** without end or limit [Latin]

ad in·ter·im \ad-ˈin-tə-rəm, ˈad-, -ˌrim\ *adv or adj* **:** for the intervening time ⟨serving *ad interim*⟩ ⟨an *ad interim* appointment⟩ [Latin]

adi·os \ˌäd-ē-ˈōs, ˌad-\ *interj* — used to express farewell [Spanish *adiós,* from *a Dios,* literally, "to God"]

ad·i·pose \ˈad-ə-ˌpōs\ *adj* **:** of or relating to animal fat **:** FATTY [Latin *adip-, adeps* "fat"] — **ad·i·pos·i·ty** \ˌad-ə-ˈpäs-ət-ē\ *n*

adipose tissue *n* **:** tissue in which fat is stored and which has the cells swollen by droplets of fat

ad·ja·cent \ə-ˈjās-nt\ *adj* **1 a :** not distant ⟨the city and *adjacent* suburbs⟩ **b :** having a common border ⟨a field *adjacent* to the road⟩ **2 :** having a vertex or a vertex and side in common ⟨*adjacent* angles⟩ ⟨*adjacent* sides of a rectangle⟩ [Latin *adjacēre* "to lie near," from *ad-* + *jacēre* "to lie"] — **ad·ja·cen·cy** \-n-sē\ *n* — **ad·ja·cent·ly** *adv*

ad·jec·ti·val \ˌaj-ik-ˈtī-vəl\ *adj* **:** ADJECTIVE — **ad·jec·ti·val·ly** \-və-lē\ *adv*

[1]**ad·jec·tive** \ˈaj-ik-tiv\ *adj* **:** of, relating to, or functioning as an adjective ⟨*adjective* clause⟩ [Late Latin *adjectivus,* from Latin *adjicere* "to throw to, add to," from *ad-* + *jacere* "to throw"] — **ad·jec·tive·ly** *adv*

[2]**adjective** *n* **:** a word typically serving as a modifier of a noun to denote a quality of the thing named, to indicate its quantity or extent, or to specify a thing as distinct from something else

ad·join \ə-ˈjȯin\ *vt* **1 :** to add or attach by joining **2 :** to lie next to or in contact with

ad·join·ing *adj* **:** touching or bounding at a point or line ⟨*adjoining* lots⟩

ad·journ \ə-ˈjərn\ *vb* **1 :** to suspend further proceedings or business for an indefinite or stated period of time ⟨Congress *adjourned*⟩ ⟨*adjourn* a meeting⟩ **2 :** to move to another place ⟨*adjourn* to the study after dinner⟩ [Medieval French *ajorner* "to order to appear in court on a certain day," from *a-* "ad-" + *jour* "day"] — **ad·journ·ment** \-mənt\ *n*

ad·judge \ə-ˈjəj\ *vt* **1 :** to decide or rule upon as a judge **:** ADJUDICATE **2 :** to hold or pronounce to be **:** DEEM ⟨*adjudged* the book a success⟩

ad·ju·di·cate \ə-ˈjüd-i-ˌkāt\ *vt* **1 :** to settle judicially ⟨*adjudicate* a claim⟩ **2 :** to act as judge [Latin *adjudicare,* from *ad-* + *judicare* "to judge"] — **ad·ju·di·ca·tive** \-ˌkāt-iv\ *adj* — **ad·ju·di·ca·tor** \-ˌkāt-ər\ *n*

ad·ju·di·ca·tion \-ˌjüd-i-ˈkā-shən\ *n* **1 :** the act or process of adjudicating **2 :** a judicial decision — **ad·ju·di·ca·to·ry** \-ˈjüd-i-kə-ˌtōr-ē, -ˌtȯr-\ *adj*

[1]**ad·junct** \ˈaj-ˌəngt, -ˌəngkt\ *n* **1 :** something joined or added to another thing but not an essential part of it **2 :** a word or word group that modifies or completes the meaning of another word or other words and is not a major structural element in its sentence ⟨in the sentence "most children eat heartily," *most* is an *adjunct* to the subject *children* and *heartily* is an *adjunct* to the verb *eat*⟩ **3 :** a person associated with or assisting another [Latin *adjunctum,* from *adjungere* "to adjoin," from *ad-* + *jungere* "to join"] — **ad·junc·tive** \a-ˈjəng-tiv, -ˈjəngk-\ *adj*

[2]**adjunct** *adj* **1 :** added or joined as an accompanying object or circumstance **2 :** a lower ranked or temporary member of a staff ⟨an *adjunct* faculty member⟩

ad·jure \ə-ˈju̇r\ *vt* **1 :** to command solemnly under or as if under oath **2 :** to urge or advise sincerely [Latin *adjurare,* from *ad-* + *jurare* "to swear"] — **ad·ju·ra·tion** \ˌaj-ə-ˈrā-shən\ *n* — **ad·jur·a·to·ry** \ə-ˈju̇r-ə-ˌtōr-ē, -ˌtȯr-\ *adj*

ad·just \ə-ˈjəst\ *vb* **1 :** to bring to a more satisfactory state: **a :** SETTLE, RESOLVE ⟨*adjust* conflicts⟩ **b :** RECTIFY ⟨*adjust* an error⟩ **c :** to make suitable or conformable **:** ADAPT **2 :** to move the parts of an instrument or a piece of machinery until they fit together in the best working order ⟨*adjust* a watch⟩ ⟨*adjust* the brakes on a car⟩ **3 :** to determine the amount of an insurance claim **4 :** to adapt oneself to external conditions ⟨had to *adjust* to city living⟩ [Medieval French *ajuster* "to make conform," from *a-* "ad-" + *juste* "exact, just"] ***synonyms*** see ADAPT — **ad·just·able** \-ˈjəs-tə-bəl\ *adj* — **ad·just·er** *also* **ad·jus·tor** \-ˈjəs-tər\ *n*

ad·just·ment \ə-ˈjəst-mənt, -ˈjəs-\ *n* **1 :** the act or process of adjusting **2 :** a settlement of a claim or debt **3 :** the state of being adjusted **4 :** a means of adjusting one part (as in a machine) in relation to another ⟨an *adjustment* for focusing a microscope⟩ **5 :** a correction or modification to reflect actual conditions — **ad·just·ment·al** \ə-ˌjəst-ˈment-l, -ˌjəs-\ *adj*

ad·ju·tan·cy \ˈaj-ət-ən-sē\ *n* **:** the office or rank of an adjutant

ad·ju·tant \ˈaj-ət-ənt\ *n* **1 :** a staff officer (as in the army) assisting the commanding officer and responsible especially for correspondence **2 :** one who helps **:** ASSISTANT [Latin *adjutare* "to aid"]

adjutant general *n, pl* **adjutants general :** the chief administrative officer of an army or of one of its major units (as a division or corps)

ad·ju·vant \ˈaj-ə-vənt\ *n* **:** something (as a drug or procedure) that enhances the effectiveness of medical treatment [Latin *adjuvare* "to aid"]

[1]**ad–lib** \ad-ˈlib, ˈad-\ *adj* **:** spoken, composed, or performed without preparation

[2]**ad–lib** *vb* **ad–libbed; ad–lib·bing 1 :** to deliver spontaneously **2 :** to improvise lines or a speech

ad lib *adv* **:** without restraint or limit [New Latin *ad libitum* "in accordance with desire"]

ad li·bi·tum \ad-ˈlib-ət-əm, ˈad-\ *adj* **:** freely as a performer wishes — used as a direction in music [New Latin]

ad·man \ˈad-ˌman\ *n* **:** one who writes, solicits, or places advertisements

ad·min·is·ter \əd-ˈmin-ə-stər\ *vb* **ad·min·is·tered; ad·min·is·ter·ing** \-stə-ring, -string\ **1 :** to manage or supervise the execution, use, or conduct of ⟨*administer* a trust fund⟩ **2 a :** to give out as deserved **:** DISPENSE ⟨*administer* justice⟩ **b :** to give ritually ⟨*administer* last rites⟩ **c :** to give as a remedy ⟨*administer* a drug⟩ **3 :** to furnish aid or relief ⟨*administer* to an ailing friend⟩ — **ad·min·is·tra·ble** \-strə-bəl\ *adj* — **ad·min·is·trant** \-strənt\ *n*

ad·min·is·tra·tion \əd-ˌmin-ə-ˈstrā-shən, ˌad-\ *n* **1 :** the act or process of administering **2 :** performance of supervising duties **:** MANAGEMENT **3 :** the execution of public affairs as distinguished from policy-making **4 a :** a group of people who administer **b** *often cap* **:** the people who make up the executive branch of a government **c :** a governmental agency or board **5 :** the term of office of a managing officer or body

ad·min·is·tra·tive \əd-ˈmin-ə-ˌstrāt-iv, -strət-\ *adj* **:** of or relating to administration ⟨an *administrative* position⟩ — **ad·min·is·tra·tive·ly** *adv*

ad·min·is·tra·tor \əd-ˈmin-ə-ˌstrāt-ər\ *n* **1 :** one that is legally appointed to administer an estate **2 a :** one that administers especially business, school, or governmental affairs **b :** a priest appointed to administer temporarily a diocese or parish

ad·min·is·tra·trix \-ˌmin-ə-ˈstrā-triks\ *n, pl* **-is·tra·tri·ces** \-ˈstrā-trə-ˌsēz\ **:** a woman who administers an estate

ad·mi·ra·ble \ˈad-mə-rə-bəl, -mrə-bəl\ *adj* **:** deserving the highest esteem **:** EXCELLENT — **ad·mi·ra·ble·ness** *n* — **ad·mi·ra·bly** \-blē\ *adv*

ad·mi·ral \ˈad-mə-rəl, -mrəl\ *n* **1 a :** a naval officer of flag rank **b :** an officer rank in the Navy and Coast Guard above vice admiral **2 :** any of several brightly colored butterflies [Medieval Latin *admirallus,* from Arabic *amīr-al-bahr* "commander of the sea"]

Word History It is a curiosity of history that *admiral,* a word meaning "naval commander," ultimately has its source in Arabic, the language of a desert people who acquired their seafaring skills largely from the Mediterranean peoples they dominated after the great expansion of Islam in the 7th century A.D. As the name for a Muslim chieftain, the Arabic word *amīr* appears as a loanword in the 9th century in Medieval Latin documents, in spellings such as *amiratus, admirandus,* and *admirallus.* These words display a variety of suffixes and an extra *d,* through confusion with the Latin verb *admirari,* "to admire." The ending *-allus* is probably from the Arabic definite article *al,* which actually belongs to the following word in phrases such as *amīr al-ʿalī,* "supreme commander." The specific application of *admirallus* to a commander of a fleet originated in 12th century Sicily, when it was ruled by the Normans. The usage was acquired by the Genoese and then spread to the rest of western Europe, including France and England.

[1]**ad·mi·ral·ty** \ˈad-mə-rəl-tē, -mrəl-\ *n* **1** *cap* **:** a body of officials formerly having general authority over the British navy **2 :** a court having jurisdiction of maritime law; *also* **:** the system of law administered by admiralty courts

[2]**admiralty** *adj* **:** of, relating to, or having jurisdiction over maritime affairs ⟨*admiralty* law⟩

ad·mi·ra·tion \ˌad-mə-ˈrā-shən\ *n* **1 :** an object of admiring esteem **2 :** a feeling of delighted approval

ad·mire \əd-ˈmīr\ *vt* **1** *archaic* **:** to marvel at **2 :** to look at with a feeling of pleasure ⟨*admire* the view⟩ **3 :** to think highly of ⟨*admired* their capacity for work⟩ [Middle French *admirer,* from Latin *admirari,* from *ad-* + *mirari* "to wonder"] ***synonyms*** see REGARD — **ad·mir·er** \-ˈmīr-ər\ *n*

ad·mis·si·ble \əd-ˈmis-ə-bəl\ *adj* **:** that can be or is worthy to be admitted or allowed **:** ALLOWABLE ⟨*admissible* evidence⟩ — **ad·mis·si·bil·i·ty** \-ˌmis-ə-ˈbil-ət-ē\ *n*

ad·mis·sion \əd-ˈmish-ən\ *n* **1 a :** a granting of an argument or position that has not been fully proved ⟨an *admission* of guilt⟩ **b :** acknowledgment that a fact or statement is true **2 :** the act of admitting **3 :** the right or permission to enter ⟨standards of *admission* to a school⟩ **4 :** the price of entrance to a place [Latin *admissio,* from *admittere* "to admit"] ***synonyms*** see ADMITTANCE — **ad·mis·sive** \-ˈmis-iv\ *adj*

ad·mit \əd-ˈmit\ *vb* **ad·mit·ted; ad·mit·ting 1 :** to allow room for **:** PERMIT ⟨a question that *admits* of two answers⟩ **2 a :** to allow entry **:** let in ⟨*admit* a state to the Union⟩ **b :** to accept into a hospital as a patient ⟨was *admitted* for chest pains⟩ **3 :** to concede as true or valid ⟨reluctantly *admitted* failure⟩ [Latin *admittere* "to allow entry, permit," from *ad-* + *mittere* "to send, let go"] ***synonyms*** see ACKNOWLEDGE — **ad·mit·ted·ly** \-ˈmit-əd-lē\ *adv*

ad·mit·tance \əd-ˈmit-ns\ *n* **:** permission to enter a place **:** ENTRANCE

synonyms ADMITTANCE, ADMISSION mean permitted entrance. ADMITTANCE applies usually to mere physical entrance into a building or locality ⟨no *admittance* without proper dress⟩. ADMISSION implies formal acceptance that carries with it rights, privileges, or membership ⟨applied for *admission* to the club⟩.

admittedly *adv* **1 :** as has been or must be admitted ⟨an *admittedly* easy test⟩ **2 :** it must be admitted ⟨*admittedly,* we took a chance⟩

ad·mix \ad-ˈmiks\ *vt* **:** to mix in ⟨*admix* soil and gravel⟩ [back-formation from obsolete *admixt* "mingled (with)," from Latin *admixtus*]

ad·mix·ture \ad-ˈmiks-chər\ *n* **1 a :** the act of mixing ⟨made by *admixture* of chemicals⟩ **b :** the fact of being mixed **2 a :** something added by mixing **b :** a product of mixing **:** MIXTURE

ad·mon·ish \ad-ˈmän-ish\ *vt* **1 :** to scold gently but seriously **:** warn of a fault **2 :** to give friendly advice or encouragement to [Medieval French *amonester,* from Latin *admonēre* "to warn," from *ad-* + *monēre* "to warn, remind"] — **ad·mon·ish·er** *n* — **ad·mon·ish·ing·ly** \-ˈmän-i-shing-lē\ *adv* — **ad·mon·ish·ment** \-ˈmän-ish-mənt\ *n*

ad·mo·ni·tion \ˌad-mə-ˈnish-ən\ *n* **:** a gentle or friendly criticism or warning [Latin *admonitio,* from *admonēre* "to admonish"]

ad·mon·i·to·ry \ad-ˈmän-ə-ˌtōr-ē, -ˌtȯr-\ *adj* **:** expressing admonition **:** WARNING

ad nau·se·am \ad-ˈnȯ-zē-əm\ *adv* **:** to a sickening degree ⟨went on *ad nauseum* about her vacation⟩ [Latin]

ado \ə-ˈdü\ *n* **:** FUSS, TROUBLE ⟨much *ado* about nothing⟩

ado·be \ə-ˈdō-bē\ *n* **1 :** a brick made of sun-dried earth and straw **2 :** a building made of adobe bricks [Spanish, from Arabic *aṭ-ṭub* "the brick"]

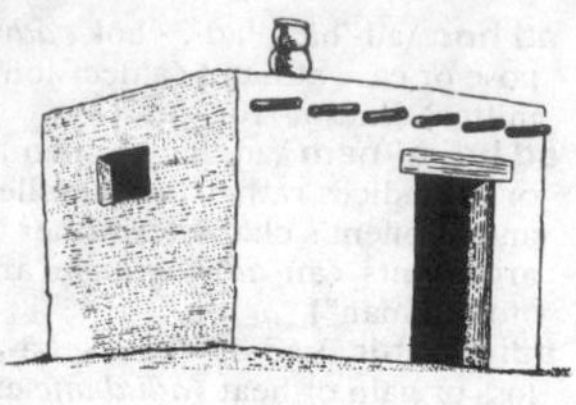

adobe 2

ad·o·les·cence \ˌad-l-ˈes-ns\ *n* **:** the state or process of growing up; *also* **:** the period of life from puberty to maturity

[1]**ad·o·les·cent** \-nt\ *n* **:** one that is in the state of adolescence **:** a person not fully mature [Latin *adolescere* "to grow up"]

[2]**adolescent** *adj* **:** of, relating to, or being in adolescence

adopt \ə-ˈdäpt\ *vt* **1 :** to take legally as one's own child **2 :** to take up and practice as one's own ⟨*adopt* a point of view⟩ **3 :** to accept formally and put into effect ⟨the assembly *adopted* a constitution⟩ **4 :** to choose (a textbook) for required study in a course [Latin *adoptare,* from *ad-* + *optare* "to choose"] — **adopt·abil·i·ty** \ə-ˌdäp-tə-ˈbil-ət-ē\ *n* — **adopt·able** \ə-ˈdäp-tə-bəl\ *adj* — **adopt·er** *n*

adop·tion \ə-ˈdäp-shən\ *n* **:** the act of adopting **:** the state of being adopted

adop·tive \ə-ˈdäp-tiv\ *adj* **:** made by or associated with adoption ⟨*adoptive* parents⟩ — **adop·tive·ly** *adv*

ador·able \ə-ˈdōr-ə-bəl, -ˈdȯr-\ *adj* **1 :** deserving to be adored **2 :** extremely charming ⟨an *adorable* child⟩ — **ador·abil·i·ty** \ə-ˌdōr-ə-ˈbil-ət-ē, -ˌdȯr-\ *n* — **ador·able·ness** *n* — **ador·ably** \ə-ˈdōr-ə-blē, -ˈdȯr-\ *adv*

adore \ə-ˈdōr, -ˈdȯr\ *vt* **1 :** WORSHIP ⟨*adore* God⟩ **2 :** to be extremely fond of [Medieval French *aurer, adourer,* from Latin *adorare,* from *ad-* + *orare* "to speak, pray"] — **ad·o·ra·tion** \ˌad-ə-ˈrā-shən\ *n* — **ador·er** \ə-ˈdōr-ər, -ˈdȯr-\ *n*

adorn \ə-ˈdȯrn\ *vt* **:** to decorate with ornaments **:** BEAUTIFY [Latin *adornare,* from *ad-* + *ornare* "to furnish, ornament"]

synonyms ADORN, DECORATE, EMBELLISH mean to improve the appearance by adding something that is not essential. ADORN implies enhancing appearance by adding something beautiful in itself ⟨*adorned* with jewels⟩. DECORATE suggests relieving plainness or monotony by adding color or design ⟨*decorate* a birthday cake with colored icing⟩. EMBELLISH often stresses the adding of superfluous ornament ⟨*embellish* a page with floral borders⟩.

adorn·ment \-mənt\ *n* **1 :** the action of adorning **:** the state of being adorned **2 :** something that adorns

ADP \ˌā-ˌdē-ˈpē\ *n* **:** a derivative of adenosine that is formed in living cells and is reversibly converted to ATP by the addition of a phosphate group [adenosine *di*phosphate]

[1]**ad·re·nal** \ə-ˈdrēn-l\ *adj* **:** of, relating to, or derived from adrenal glands or their secretions [*ad-* + *renal*]

[2]**adrenal** *n* **:** ADRENAL GLAND

adrenal cor·ti·co·tro·phic hormone \-ˌkȯrt-i-kō-ˈtrō-fik-\ *n* **:** ACTH

adrenal gland *n* **:** either of a pair of complex endocrine organs occurring one near each kidney and consisting of an outer cortex that produces steroid hormones and an inner medulla that produces epinephrine

Adren·a·lin \ə-ˈdren-l-ən\ *trademark* — used for a preparation of adrenaline

adren·a·line \-l-ən\ *n* **:** EPINEPHRINE

ad·ren·er·gic \ˌad-rə-ˈnər-jik\ *adj* **:** liberating or activated by adrenaline or a substance like adrenaline ⟨an *adrenergic* nerve⟩ [Greek *ergon* "work"]

ad·re·no·cor·ti·cal \ə-ˌdrē-nō-ˈkȯrt-i-kəl\ *adj* **:** of, relating to, or derived from the cortex of the adrenal glands

ad·re·no·cor·ti·co·tro·phic hormone \ə-ˌdrē-nō-ˌkȯrt-i-kō-ˈtrō-fik-\ *or* **ad·re·no·cor·ti·co·trop·ic hormone** \-ˈträp-ik-\ *n* **:** ACTH

adrift \ə-ˈdrift\ *adv or adj* **1 :** without motive power, anchor, or mooring ⟨a damaged ship *adrift* in the storm⟩ **2 :** without guidance or purpose

adroit \ə-ˈdrȯit\ *adj* **:** having or showing skill, cleverness, or resourcefulness in handling situations ⟨an *adroit* leader⟩ ⟨*adroit* tactics⟩. [French, from *à droit* "properly," from *à* "to, at" + *droit* "right"] ***synonyms*** see DEXTEROUS — **adroit·ly** *adv* — **adroit·ness** *n*

ad·sorb \ad-ˈsȯrb, -ˈzȯrb\ *vt* **:** to take up and hold by adsorption [*ad-* + *-sorb* (as in *absorb*)] — **ad·sor·bent** \-ˈsȯr-bənt, -ˈzȯr-\ *adj or n* — **ad·sorb·er** *n*

ad·sorp·tion \-ˈsȯrp-shən, -ˈzȯrp-\ *n* **:** the adhesion in an extremely thin layer of molecules (as of gases, solutes, or liquids) to the surfaces of solid bodies or liquids with which they are in contact — compare ABSORPTION — **ad·sorp·tive** \-ˈsȯrp-tiv, -ˈzȯrp-\ *adj*

ad·u·late \ˈaj-ə-ˌlāt\ *vt* **:** to flatter or admire excessively or slavishly [derived from Latin *adulari* "to fawn on (of dogs), flatter"] — **ad·u·la·tion** \ˌaj-ə-ˈlā-shən\ *n* — **ad·u·la·tor** \ˈaj-ə-ˌlāt-ər\ *n* — **ad·u·la·to·ry** \ˈaj-ə-lə-ˌtōr-ē, -ˌtȯr-\ *adj*

[1]**adult** \ə-ˈdəlt, ˈad-ˌəlt\ *adj* **1 :** fully developed and mature **:** GROWN-UP **2 :** of, relating to, intended for, or characteristic of adults [Latin *adultus,* past participle of *adolescere* "to grow up"] — **adult·hood** \ə-ˈdəlt-ˌhu̇d\ *n* — **adult·ness** \ə-ˈdəlt-nəs, ˈad-ˌəlt-\ *n*

[2]**adult** *n* **1 :** a fully grown person, animal, or plant **2 :** a person after an age (as 18) specified by law

adul·ter·ant \ə-ˈdəl-tə-rənt\ *n* **:** something used to adulterate another thing

adul·ter·ate \ə-ˈdəl-tə-ˌrāt\ *vt* **:** to weaken or make impure by adding a foreign or inferior substance; *esp* **:** to prepare for sale by replacing more valuable with less valuable ingredients [Latin *adulterare,* from *ad-* + *alter* "other"] — **adul·ter·a·tion** \ə-ˌdəl-tə-ˈrā-shən\ *n* — **adul·ter·a·tor** \ə-ˈdəl-tə-ˌrāt-ər\ *n*

adul·tery \ə-ˈdəl-tə-rē, -trē\ *n, pl* **-ter·ies :** voluntary sexual intercourse by a married person with anyone other than his or her spouse [Latin *adulterium,* from *adulter* "adulterer," back-formation from *adulterare* "to adulterate"] — **adul·ter·er** \-tər-ər\ *n* — **adul·ter·ess** \-tə-rəs, -trəs\ *n* — **adul·ter·ous** \-tə-rəs, -trəs\ *adj* — **adul·ter·ous·ly** *adv*

adult–onset diabetes *n* **:** TYPE 2 DIABETES

ad·um·brate \ˈad-əm-ˌbrāt, ə-ˈdəm-\ *vt* **1 :** to foreshadow vaguely **:** INTIMATE **2 :** to suggest or disclose partially [Latin *adumbrare,* from *ad-* + *umbra* "shadow"] — **ad·um·bra·tion** \ˌad-ˌəm-ˈbrā-shən\ *n* — **ad·um·bra·tive** \ə-ˈdəm-brət-iv\ *adj* — **ad·um·bra·tive·ly** *adv*

ad va·lo·rem \ˌad-və-ˈlōr-əm, -ˈlȯr-\ *adj* **:** based on a percentage of the monetary value of the goods ⟨an *ad valorem* tariff⟩ [Latin, "according to the value"]

[1]**ad·vance** \əd-ˈvans\ *vb* **1 :** to move forward ⟨*advance* a few yards⟩ **2 :** to further the progress of ⟨*advance* the cause of freedom⟩ **3 :** to raise or rise to a higher rank ⟨was *advanced* from clerk to assistant manager⟩ **4 :** to bring forward in time **:** to make earlier ⟨*advance* the date of the party⟩ **5 :** to supply in expectation of repayment ⟨*advance* a loan⟩ **6 :** to bring forward for consideration **:** PROPOSE ⟨*advance* a new plan⟩ **7 :** to raise or rise in rate or price ⟨gasoline *advanced* another two cents⟩ [Medieval French *avancer,* derived from Late Latin *abante* "before," from Latin *ab* "from" + *ante* "before"] — **ad·vanc·er** *n*

[2]**advance** *n* **1 :** a forward movement **2 :** progress in development **:** IMPROVEMENT ⟨*advances* in medicine⟩ **3 :** a rise in price, value, or amount **4 :** a first approach **5 a :** the giving of something in payment (as money) before goods or services are received ⟨needs an *advance* on his salary⟩ **b :** the money or goods supplied — **in advance :** BEFORE, BEFOREHAND ⟨knew of the change two weeks *in advance*⟩ — **in advance of :** AHEAD OF

[3]**advance** *adj* **1 :** made, sent, or furnished ahead of time ⟨*advance* payment⟩ **2 :** going or situated before ⟨an *advance* scout⟩

ad·vanced \əd-ˈvanst\ *adj* **1 :** far on in time or course ⟨a man *advanced* in years⟩ **2 a :** being beyond others in progress or ideas **b :** being beyond the elementary or introductory ⟨*advanced* mathematics⟩ **c :** being far along in progress or development ⟨an *advanced* civilization⟩ **d :** having changed from a more primitive ancestral state ⟨*advanced* insects as the wasps and bees⟩

advance directive *n* **:** a legal document (as a living will) signed by a competent person to provide guidance for medical decisions in the event the person becomes incompetent to make such decisions

Advanced level *n* **:** A LEVEL

ad·vance·ment \əd-ˈvans-mənt\ *n* **1 :** the action of advancing **:** the state of being advanced: **a :** promotion to a higher rank **b :** progression to a higher stage of development **2 :** an improved feature **:** IMPROVEMENT

ad·van·tage \əd-ˈvant-ij\ *n* **1 :** superiority of position or condition ⟨high ground gave the enemy the *advantage*⟩ **2 :** BENEFIT, GAIN; *esp* **:** benefit resulting from a course of action ⟨changing jobs will be of *advantage* to you⟩ **3 :** something that benefits its possessor ⟨speed is an *advantage* in sports⟩ **4 :** the first point won in tennis after deuce [Medieval French *avantage,* from *avant* "before," from Late Latin *abante*] — **to advantage :** so as to produce a favorable impression or effect

ad·van·taged \-ijd\ *adj* **:** having or providing an advantage and especially a financial or social advantage over others ⟨an *advantaged* position⟩

ad·van·ta·geous \ˌad-ˌvan-ˈtā-jəs, -vən-\ *adj* **:** giving an advantage **:** HELPFUL, FAVORABLE ***synonyms*** see BENEFICIAL — **ad·van·ta·geous·ly** *adv* — **ad·van·ta·geous·ness** *n*

ad·vec·tion \ad-ˈvek-shən\ *n* **:** the horizontal movement of a mass of air causing weather changes (as a drop in temperature) [Latin *advectio* "act of bringing," from *advehere* "to carry to," from *ad-* + *vehere* "to carry"] — **ad·vec·tive** \-ˈvek-tiv\ *adj*

Ad·vent \ˈad-ˌvent\ *n* **1 :** the period beginning four Sundays before Christmas and observed by some Christians as a season of prayer and fasting **2 :** the coming of Christ at the Incarnation or on Judgment Day **3** *not cap* **:** first or new appearance ⟨the *advent* of spring⟩ [Medieval Latin *adventus,* from Latin, "arrival," derived from *advenire* "to arrive, happen," from *ad-* + *venire* "to come"]

Ad·vent·ist \əd-ˈvent-əst, ad-ˈ, ˈad-ˌ\ *n* **1 :** one who believes Christ's second coming is near at hand **2 :** SEVENTH DAY ADVENTIST — **Ad·vent·ism** \ˈad-ˌvent-ˌiz-əm\ *n* — **Adventist** *adj*

ad·ven·ti·tious \ˌad-(ˌ)ven-ˈtish-əs, -vən-\ *adj* **1 :** coming from an outside source and not a fundamental part ⟨*adventitious* additions to a plan⟩ **2 :** appearing in other than the usual or normal place ⟨*adventitious* roots⟩ [Latin *adventicius* "coming from outside," from *advenire* "to arrive"] — **ad·ven·ti·tious·ly** *adv* — **ad·ven·ti·tious·ness** *n*

Advent Sunday *n* **:** the first Sunday in Advent

[1]**ad·ven·ture** \əd-ˈven-chər\ *n* **1 :** an undertaking involving unknown dangers and risks **2 :** the encountering of risks **3 :** an unusual or exciting experience [Medieval French *aventure* "chance, risk," derived from Latin *advenire* "to arrive, happen," from *ad-* + *venire* "to come"]

[2]**adventure** *vb* **-ven·tured; -ven·tur·ing** \-ˈvench-ring, -ə-ring\ **1 :** RISK 1, VENTURE ⟨*adventure* their capital in foreign trade⟩ **2 :** to venture upon **3 :** to proceed despite danger or risk

ad·ven·tur·er \-ˈvench-rər, -ə-rər\ *n* **1 :** one that adventures: as **a :** SOLDIER OF FORTUNE **b :** one that engages in risky commercial enterprises for profit **2 :** a person who seeks undeserved wealth or status

ad·ven·ture·some \-ˈven-chər-səm\ *adj* **:** inclined to take risks

ad·ven·tur·ess \-ˈvench-rəs, -ə-rəs\ *n* **:** a woman adventurer; *esp* **:** one who seeks status or money by questionable means

ad·ven·tur·ous \əd-ˈvench-rəs, -ə-rəs\ *adj* **1 :** ready to seek adventure or to cope with the new and unknown **2 :** characterized by unknown dangers and risks — **ad·ven·tur·ous·ly** *adv* — **ad·ven·tur·ous·ness** *n*

synonyms ADVENTUROUS, VENTURESOME, DARING mean exposing oneself to more danger than is required. ADVENTUROUS stresses a willingness to try the unknown regardless of possible or probable danger ⟨*adventurous* pioneers⟩. VENTURESOME may stress the tendency to take chances ⟨*venturesome* stunt pilots⟩. DARING heightens the implication of fearlessness in accepting risks that could be avoided ⟨*daring* mountain climbers⟩.

ad·verb \ˈad-ˌvərb\ *n* **:** a word used to modify a verb, an adjective, another adverb, a preposition, a phrase, a clause, or a sentence and often used to show degree, manner, place, or time [Medieval French *adverbe,* from Latin *adverbium,* from *ad-* + *verbum* "word, verb"] — **adverb** *adj*

ad·ver·bi·al \ad-ˈvər-bē-əl\ *adj* **:** of, relating to, or having the function of an adverb ⟨*adverbial* phrase⟩ — **adverbial** *n* — **ad·ver·bi·al·ly** \-bē-ə-lē\ *adv*

ad·ver·sar·i·al \ˌad-vər-ˈser-ē-əl\ *adj* **:** of, relating to, or characteristic of an adversary or adversary procedures **:** ADVERSARY

[1]**ad·ver·sary** \ˈad-vər-ˌser-ē, -və-\ *n, pl* **-sar·ies :** one that contends with, opposes, or resists ***synonyms*** see OPPONENT

[2]**adversary** *adj* **:** having or involving opposing parties or interests

\ə\ abut	\au̇\ **out**	\i\ **tip**	\ȯ\ **saw**	\u̇\ **foot**
\ər\ further	\ch\ **chin**	\ī\ life	\ȯi\ **coin**	\y\ **yet**
\a\ mat	\e\ pet	\j\ **job**	\th\ **thin**	\yü\ **few**
\ā\ take	\ē\ **easy**	\ng\ **sing**	\th\ **this**	\yu̇\ **cure**
\ä\ cot, cart	\g\ **go**	\ō\ bone	\ü\ **food**	\zh\ **vision**

ad·ver·sa·tive \ad-ˈvər-sət-iv\ *adj* : expressing opposition or adverse circumstance ⟨the *adversative* conjunction *but*⟩ — **ad·ver·sa·tive·ly** *adv*

ad·verse \ad-ˈvərs, ˈad-ˌ\ *adj* **1** : acting in a contrary direction ⟨*adverse* winds⟩ **2** : opposed to one's interests ⟨*adverse* testimony⟩; *esp* : UNFAVORABLE ⟨*adverse* criticism⟩ **3** : causing harm : HARMFUL ⟨*adverse* effects of a drug⟩ ⟨an *adverse* impact on the environment⟩ [Medieval French *advers,* from Latin *adversus,* from *advertere* "to turn toward," from *ad-* + *vertere* "to turn"] — **ad·verse·ly** *adv* — **ad·verse·ness** *n*

ad·ver·si·ty \ad-ˈvər-sət-ē\ *n, pl* **-ties** : a condition or experience of serious or continued misfortune

ad·vert \ad-ˈvərt\ *vb* : to direct attention : REFER ⟨*advert* to a previous remark⟩ [Medieval French *advertir*]

ad·ver·tise \ˈad-vər-ˌtīz\ *vb* **1** : to announce publicly especially by a printed notice or a broadcast ⟨*advertise* a sale⟩ **2** : to call public attention to especially by emphasizing desirable qualities so as to arouse a desire to buy or patronize ⟨*advertise* a new book⟩ **3** : to issue or sponsor advertising ⟨*advertise* for a secretary⟩ [Medieval French *advertiss-,* stem of *advertir* "to pay heed, observe, notify," from Latin *advertere* "to turn toward"] — **ad·ver·tis·er** *n*

ad·ver·tise·ment \ˌad-vər-ˈtīz-mənt, əd-ˈvərt-əz-\ *n* **1** : the act or process of advertising **2** : a public notice; *esp* : one published or broadcast

ad·ver·tis·ing \ˈad-vər-ˌtī-zing\ *n* **1** : the action of calling something to the attention of the public especially by paid announcements **2** : ADVERTISEMENTS **3** : the business of preparing advertisements for publication or broadcast

ad·vice \əd-ˈvīs\ *n* **1** : recommendation regarding a decision or course of conduct : COUNSEL **2** : information or notice given : NEWS — usually used in plural [Medieval French *avis* "opinion"]

ad·vis·able \əd-ˈvī-zə-bəl\ *adj* : reasonable or proper under the circumstances : WISE, PRUDENT ⟨it is *advisable* to bring a snack⟩ ***synonyms*** see EXPEDIENT — **ad·vis·abil·i·ty** \əd-ˌvī-zə-ˈbil-ət-ē\ *n* — **ad·vis·ably** \əd-ˈvī-zə-blē\ *adv*

ad·vise \əd-ˈvīz\ *vb* **1 a** : to give advice to : COUNSEL **b** : RECOMMEND ⟨they *advised* caution⟩ **2** : to give information or notice to : INFORM ⟨*advised* them of bad flying conditions⟩ **3** : to talk over a problem or decision : CONSULT ⟨they *advised* with friends⟩ — **ad·vis·er** *or* **ad·vi·sor** \-ˈvī-zər\ *n*

ad·vised \-ˈvīzd\ *adj* : THOUGHT-OUT, CONSIDERED — often used in combination ⟨an ill-*advised* plan⟩ — **ad·vis·ed·ly** \-ˈvī-zəd-lē\ *adv*

ad·vis·ee \əd-ˌvī-ˈzē\ *n* : a person who is advised

ad·vise·ment \əd-ˈvīz-mənt\ *n* : careful consideration ⟨take a matter under *advisement*⟩

^{1}**ad·vi·so·ry** \əd-ˈvīz-rē, -ə-rē\ *adj* **1** : having the power or right to advise ⟨an *advisory* committee⟩ **2** : giving or containing advice ⟨an *advisory* opinion⟩ — **advisory** *n*

^{2}**advisory** *n* : a report giving information and often recommending action to be taken ⟨a weather *advisory*⟩

ad·vo·ca·cy \ˈad-və-kə-sē\ *n* : the act of advocating or supporting a cause or proposal

^{1}**ad·vo·cate** \ˈad-və-kət, -ˌkāt\ *n* **1** : one that pleads the cause of another especially before a court **2** : one that argues for, recommends, or supports a cause or policy [Medieval French *advocat,* from Latin *advocatus,* from *advocare* "to summon," from *ad-* + *vocare* "to call"]

^{2}**ad·vo·cate** \-ˌkāt\ *vt* : to speak in favor of : SUPPORT 2 ⟨*advocate* a new plan⟩

adze *also* **adz** \ˈadz\ *n* : a cutting tool that has a thin arched blade set at right angles to the handle and is used for shaping wood [Old English *adesa*]

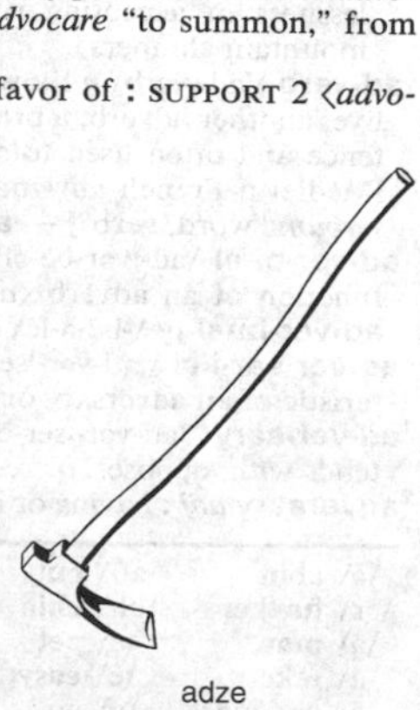
adze

ae \ˈā\ *adj, chiefly Scottish* : ONE [Middle English (Scots) *a*]

aë·des \ā-ˈēd-ēz\ *n, pl* **aëdes** : any of a genus of mosquitoes including carriers of disease (as yellow fever) [Greek *aēdēs* "unpleasant," from *a-* + *ēdos* "pleasure"]

ae·dile \ˈē-ˌdīl\ *n* : an official in ancient Rome in charge of public works and games, police, and the grain supply [Latin *aedilis,* from *aedes* "temple"]

ae·gis \ˈē-jəs\ *n* **1** : PROTECTION 1, DEFENSE ⟨under the *aegis* of the law⟩ **2** : PATRONAGE 1, SPONSORSHIP ⟨under the *aegis* of a museum⟩ [Greek *aigis* "shield made of goatskin"]

-ae·mia *chiefly British variant of* -EMIA

aeolian *variant of* EOLIAN

Aeolian *n* : one of a group of ancient Greeks colonizing Lesbos and the adjacent coast of Asia Minor

aeolian harp *n* : a box-shaped musical instrument that produces musical sounds when air currents pass over stretched strings

ae·on *or* **eon** \ˈē-ən, ˈē-ˌän\ *n* **1** : an immeasurably or indefinitely long period of time : AGE **2 a** *usually* **eon** : a very large division of geologic time usually longer than an era **b** : a unit of geologic time equal to one billion years [Latin, from Greek *aiōn*]

aer- *or* **aero-** *combining form* **1** : air : atmosphere ⟨*aer*ate⟩ **2** : gas ⟨*aero*sol⟩ **3** : aviation ⟨*aero*drome⟩ [Greek *aēr*]

aer·ate \ˈar-ˌāt, ˈer-\ *vt* **1** : to supply or impregnate with air **2** : to supply (blood) with oxygen by respiration **3** : to combine or charge with gas — **aer·a·tion** \ˌar-ˈā-shən, ˌer-\ *n* — **aer·a·tor** \ˈar-ˌāt-ər, ˈer-\ *n*

^{1}**ae·ri·al** \ˈar-ē-əl, ˈer-; ā-ˈir-ē-əl\ *adj* **1 a** : of, relating to, or occurring in the air or atmosphere **b** : living or growing in the air rather than on the ground or in water **c** : operating or operated overhead on elevated cables or rails **2 a** : lacking substance : THIN **b** : IMAGINARY, FANCIFUL **3 a** : of or relating to aircraft **b** : designed for use in, taken from, or operating from or against aircraft [Latin *aerius,* from Greek *aerios,* from *aēr*] — **ae·ri·al·ly** \-ē-ə-lē\ *adv*

^{2}**aer·i·al** \ˈar-ē-əl, ˈer-\ *n* **1** : ANTENNA 2 **2** : FORWARD PASS

ae·ri·al·ist \ˈar-ē-ə-ləst, ˈer-, ā-ˈir-\ *n* : a performer of feats above the ground especially on a flying trapeze

aerial root *n* : a root (as for clinging to a wall) that does not enter the soil

ae·rie \ˈaər-ē, ˈeər-, ˈiər-\ *n* **1** : the nest of a bird on a cliff or a mountaintop **2** : a dwelling or room placed high up [Medieval Latin *aerea,* from Medieval French *aire*]

aer·o·bat·ics \ˌar-ə-ˈbat-iks, ˌer-\ *n sing or pl* : spectacular flying feats and maneuvers [*aer-* + *-batics* (as in *acrobatics*)] — **aer·o·bat·ic** \-ik\ *adj*

aer·o·bic \ˌa-ˈrō-bik, ˌe-\ *adj* **1** : living, active, or occurring only in the presence of oxygen **2** : of, relating to, or caused by aerobic organisms (as bacteria) **3** : involving or increasing oxygen consumption ⟨*aerobic* exercise⟩; *also* : relating to or used in aerobics [French *aérobie* "aerobe," from *aéro-* "aer-" + *-bie* (from Greek *bios* "life")] — **aer·obe** \ˈar-ˌōb, ˈer-\ *n* — **aer·o·bi·cal·ly** \ˌa-ˈrō-bi-kə-lē, ˌe-, -klē\ *adv*

aer·o·bics \-biks\ *n sing or pl* : a system of physical conditioning that involves exercises (as running or swimming) intended to improve the body's ability to take in and use oxygen

aero·drome \ˈar-ə-ˌdrōm, ˈer-\ *n, British* : AIRFIELD, AIRPORT

aero·dy·nam·ics \ˌar-ō-dī-ˈnam-iks, ˌer-\ *n* : a branch of dynamics that deals with the motion of gaseous fluids (as air) and with the forces acting on bodies in motion relative to such fluids — **aero·dy·nam·ic** \-ik\ *adj* — **aero·dy·nam·i·cal·ly** \-i-kə-lē, -klē\ *adv*

aero·naut \ˈar-ə-ˌnȯt, ˈer-, -ˌnät\ *n* : one who operates or travels in an airship or balloon [French *aéronaute,* from *aér-* "aer-" + Greek *nautēs* "sailor"]

aero·nau·tics \ˌar-ə-ˈnȯt-iks, ˌer-\ *n* **1** : a science dealing with the construction and operation of aircraft **2** : the art or science of flight — **aero·nau·tic** \-ˈnȯt-ik\ *adj* — **aero·nau·ti·cal** \-ˈnȯt-i-kəl\ *adj* — **aero·nau·ti·cal·ly** \-i-kə-lē, -klē\ *adv*

aero·pause \ˈar-ō-ˌpȯz, ˈer-\ *n* : the level above the earth's surface where the atmosphere becomes ineffective for human and aircraft functions

aero·plane \ˈar-ə-ˌplān, ˈer-\ *chiefly British variant of* AIRPLANE

aero·sol \-ˌsäl, -ˌsȯl\ *n* **1** : a suspension of fine solid or liquid particles (as smoke or fog) in gas **2** : a substance (as an insecticide) dispensed from a pressurized container; *also* : the container itself [*aer-* + ^{3}*sol*]

^{1}**aero·space** \ˈar-ō-ˌspās, ˈer-\ *n* **1** : the earth's atmosphere and the space beyond **2** : a physical science dealing with aerospace

^{2}**aerospace** *adj* : of or relating to aerospace, to the manufacture or use of vehicles used in aerospace, or to travel in aerospace

aery \ˈaər-ē, ˈeər-\ *adj* **aer·i·er; -est** : having an aerial quality : ETHEREAL

Ae·so·pi·an \ē-ˈsō-pē-ən\ *adj* **1** : of, relating to, or characteristic of Aesop or his fables **2** : conveying an innocent meaning to an outsider but a concealed meaning to an informed member

of a conspiracy or underground movement ⟨*Aesopian* language⟩
aes•thete *also* **es•thete** \ˈes-ˌthēt\ *n* : one having or pretending sensitivity to the beautiful especially in art
aes•thet•ic *or* **es•thet•ic** \es-ˈthet-ik, is-\ *adj* **1** : having to do with beauty or with what is beautiful ⟨a work of *aesthetic* value⟩ **2** : appreciative of or responsive to what is beautiful ⟨an *aesthetic* person⟩ [derived from Greek *aisthanesthai* "to perceive"] ***synonyms*** see ARTISTIC — **aes•thet•i•cal•ly** \-ˈthet-i-kə-lē, -klē\ *adv*
aes•thet•i•cism *also* **es•thet•i•cism** \es-ˈthet-ə-ˌsiz-əm, is-\ *n* : devotion to or emphasis on beauty or the cultivation of the arts
aes•thet•ics *also* **es•thet•ics** \es-ˈthet-iks, is-\ *n sing or pl* **1** : a branch of philosophy that studies and explains the principles and forms of beauty especially in art and literature **2** : a pleasing appearance or effect : BEAUTY
aestivate *variant of* ESTIVATE
af- — see AD-
¹**afar** \ə-ˈfär\ *adv* : from, to, or at a great distance
²**afar** *n* : a great distance ⟨a voice from *afar*⟩
afeard *or* **afeared** \ə-ˈfiərd\ *adj, chiefly dialect* : AFRAID
af•fa•ble \ˈaf-ə-bəl\ *adj* **1** : being pleasant and at ease in talking to others ⟨an *affable* host⟩ **2** : characterized by ease and friendliness ⟨an *affable* manner⟩ [Latin *affabilis,* from *affari* "to speak to," from *ad-* + *fari* "to speak"] — **af•fa•bil•i•ty** \ˌaf-ə-ˈbil-ət-ē\ *n* — **af•fa•bly** \ˈaf-ə-blē\ *adv*
af•fair \ə-ˈfaər, -ˈfeər\ *n* **1 a** *pl* : personal, commercial, professional, or public business ⟨government *affairs*⟩ **b** : MATTER, CONCERN ⟨not your *affair* at all⟩ **2 a** : EVENT, ACTIVITY ⟨a social *affair*⟩ **b** : PRODUCT, THING ⟨the house was a 2-story *affair*⟩ **3** *also* **af•faire a** : a typically brief romantic or passionate relationship **b** : a matter causing public anxiety, controversy, or scandal [Medieval French *affaire,* from *a faire* "to do"]
¹**af•fect** \ə-ˈfekt, a-\ *vt* **1** : to be given to : FANCY ⟨*affect* flashy clothes⟩ **2** : to make a display of liking or using ⟨*affect* a worldly manner⟩ **3** : to put on a pretense of : PRETEND ⟨*affect* indifference⟩ [Latin *affectare* "to aim at," from *afficere* "to act on, influence"]
²**affect** *vt* : to produce an effect upon: as **a** : to produce a physical effect upon or change in ⟨lungs *affected* by cancer⟩ **b** : to act upon (as a person or a person's feelings) so as to bring about a response ⟨criticism *affected* their efforts⟩ ***synonyms*** see ASSUME, INFLUENCE ***usage*** see EFFECT
³**affect** *n* : an observable display of emotion ⟨a patient with a normal *affect*⟩ ***usage*** see EFFECT
af•fec•ta•tion \ˌaf-ˌek-ˈtā-shən\ *n* **1** : an assuming or displaying of an attitude or kind of behavior not natural or not genuine **2** : artificial speech or behavior

synonyms AFFECTATION, MANNERISM, POSE mean an adopted way of speaking or behaving. AFFECTATION applies to a specific trick of speech or behavior that impresses others as being deliberately assumed and insincere ⟨the accent is an *affectation*⟩. MANNERISM designates a peculiarity or eccentricity in behavior that is not deliberately assumed but results from unconscious, accidentally acquired habit ⟨talking with her hands is her most noticeable *mannerism*⟩. POSE implies an attitude deliberately assumed in order to impress others ⟨his shyness was just a *pose*⟩.

af•fect•ed \ə-ˈfek-təd, a-\ *adj* : not natural or genuine ⟨an *affected* interest in art⟩ — **af•fect•ed•ly** *adv* — **af•fect•ed•ness** *n*
af•fect•ing \-ting\ *adj* : arousing pity, sympathy, or sorrow ⟨an *affecting* story⟩ — **af•fect•ing•ly** *adv*
¹**af•fec•tion** \ə-ˈfek-shən\ *n* **1** : a tender feeling of attachment : FONDNESS **2** : INCLINATION 2, BENT
²**affection** *n* : DISEASE, DISORDER ⟨an *affection* of the brain⟩
af•fec•tion•ate \ə-ˈfek-shə-nət, -shnət\ *adj* : feeling or showing a great liking for a person or thing : TENDER — **af•fec•tion•ate•ly** *adv*
af•fec•tive \a-ˈfek-tiv\ *adj* : relating to, arising from, or influencing feelings or emotions : EMOTIONAL
af•fer•ent \ˈaf-ə-rənt, ˈaf-ˌer-ənt\ *adj* : bearing or conducting inward; *esp* : conveying impulses toward the central nervous system — compare EFFERENT [Latin *afferre* "to bring to," from *ad-* + *ferre* "to carry"]
af•fi•ance \ə-ˈfī-əns\ *vt* : to solemnly promise (oneself or another) in marriage : BETROTH ⟨the *affianced* couple⟩ [Medieval French, from *affier* "to pledge, trust," from Medieval Latin *affidare* "to pledge," derived from Latin *ad-* + *fides* "faith"]
af•fi•da•vit \ˌaf-ə-ˈdā-vət\ *n* : a sworn written statement; *esp* : one made under oath before an authorized official [Medieval Latin, "he has made an oath," from *affidare* "to pledge"]
¹**af•fil•i•ate** \ə-ˈfil-ē-ˌāt\ *vb* : to connect closely often as a member, branch, or associate ⟨*affiliated* themselves with a political party⟩ ⟨a school *affiliated* with the university⟩ [Medieval Latin *affiliare* "to adopt as a son," from Latin *ad-* + *filius* "son"] — **af•fil•i•a•tion** \ə-ˌfil-ē-ˈā-shən\ *n*
²**af•fil•i•ate** \ə-ˈfil-ē-ət\ *n* : an affiliated person or organization
af•fin•i•ty \ə-ˈfin-ət-ē\ *n, pl* **-ties** **1** : relationship by marriage **2 a** : sympathy marked by community of interest : KINSHIP ⟨felt a strange *affinity* for each other⟩ **b** : an attraction to or liking for ⟨an *affinity* for politics⟩ **c** : an attractive force between substances or particles that causes them to enter into and remain in chemical combination **3 a** : likeness based on relationship or causal connection **b** : a relation between biological groups indicating community of origin [Latin *affinitas,* from *affinis* "bordering on, related by marriage," from *ad-* + *finis* "end, border"]
af•firm \ə-ˈfərm\ *vb* **1 a** : CONFIRM, RATIFY ⟨*affirm* a contract⟩ **b** : to state positively or with confidence : declare to be true **2** : to make a solemn and formal declaration or assertion in place of an oath [Medieval French *afermer,* from Latin *affirmare,* from *ad-* + *firmus* "firm"]
af•fir•ma•tion \ˌaf-ər-ˈmā-shən\ *n* **1** : the act of affirming **2** : something affirmed
¹**af•firm•a•tive** \ə-ˈfər-mət-iv\ *adj* **1** : asserting that the fact is so ⟨an *affirmative* answer⟩ **2** : capable of being applied in a constructive way ⟨an *affirmative* approach to the problem⟩ **3** : favoring or supporting a proposition or motion — **af•firm•a•tive•ly** *adv*
²**affirmative** *n* **1** : an expression (as the word *yes*) of affirmation or agreement **2** : the affirmative side in a debate or vote
affirmative action *n* : an active effort to improve the educational and employment opportunities of members of minority groups, women, and other disadvantaged persons
¹**af•fix** \ə-ˈfiks\ *vt* **1** : to attach physically : FASTEN ⟨*affix* a stamp to a letter⟩ **2** : to attach in any way : ADD ⟨*affix* one's signature to a letter⟩ — **af•fix•a•tion** \ˌaf-ˌik-ˈsā-shən\ *n*
²**af•fix** \ˈaf-ˌiks\ *n* : one or more sounds or letters attached to the beginning or end of a word and serving to produce a derivative word or an inflectional form — **af•fix•al** \-ˌik-səl\ *or* **af•fix•i•al** \a-ˈfik-sē-əl\ *adj*
af•fla•tus \ə-ˈflāt-əs\ *n* : a divine imparting of knowledge or power : INSPIRATION [Latin, "act of blowing or breathing on," from *afflare* "to blow on"]
af•flict \ə-ˈflikt\ *vt* **1** : to distress so severely as to cause continued suffering ⟨people *afflicted* by famine⟩ **2** : to have a harmful effect on ⟨political theories *afflicted* with confused thinking⟩ [Latin *affligere* "to cast down," from *ad-* + *fligere* "to strike"]

synonyms AFFLICT, TORMENT, TORTURE, RACK mean to inflict on a person something that is hard to bear. AFFLICT is general and applies to the causing of pain, annoyance, or distress ⟨ills that *afflict* the elderly⟩. TORMENT suggests persecution or the repeated inflicting of suffering or annoyance ⟨a horse *tormented* by biting flies⟩. TORTURE adds the implication of causing unbearable pain or suffering ⟨*tortured* by guilt⟩. RACK stresses straining or wrenching ⟨a body *racked* by pain⟩.

af•flic•tion \ə-ˈflik-shən\ *n* **1** : the state of being afflicted **2** : a cause of continued pain or distress
af•flic•tive \ə-ˈflik-tiv\ *adj* : causing affliction : DISTRESSING — **af•flic•tive•ly** *adv*
af•flu•ence \ˈaf-ˌlü-əns *also* a-ˈflü- *or* ə-ˈflü-\ *n* **1** : an abundant flow or supply **2** : abundance of wealth or property
¹**af•flu•ent** \-ənt\ *adj* **1** : flowing in abundance : COPIOUS **2** : having an abundance of material possessions : WEALTHY, RICH [Latin *affluere* "to flow to," from *ad-* + *fluere* "to flow"] — **af•flu•ent•ly** *adv*
²**affluent** *n* : a tributary stream
af•ford \ə-ˈfōrd, -ˈfȯrd\ *vt* **1** : to manage to do, give, or bear without serious harm ⟨you can't *afford* to waste your strength⟩

\ə\ **abut**	\au̇\ **out**	\i\ **tip**	\ȯ\ **saw**	\u̇\ **foot**
\ər\ **further**	\ch\ **chin**	\ī\ **life**	\ȯi\ **coin**	\y\ **yet**
\a\ **mat**	\e\ **pet**	\j\ **job**	\th\ **thin**	\yü\ **few**
\ā\ **take**	\ē\ **easy**	\ng\ **sing**	\th\ **this**	\yu̇\ **cure**
\ä\ **cot, cart**	\g\ **go**	\ō\ **bone**	\ü\ **food**	\zh\ **vision**

2 : to manage to pay for ⟨unable to *afford* a new car⟩ 3 : to make available or provide one with : PROVIDE 4, FURNISH ⟨playing tennis *affords* healthful exercise⟩ [Old English *geforthian* "to carry out"] ***synonyms*** see PRESENT — **af·ford·able** \-ə-bəl\ *adj*

af·for·es·ta·tion \ˌa-ˌfȯr-ə-ˈstā-shən, -ˌfär-\ *n* : the act or process of establishing a forest especially on land not previously forested

af·fray \ə-ˈfrā\ *n* : a noisy quarrel or fight : BRAWL [Medieval French, from *affraier, effreer* "to attack, brawl, disturb, frighten"]

af·fri·cate \ˈaf-ri-kət\ *n* : a stop immediately followed by a related fricative (as the \d\ and \zh\ that make up the \j\ sounds of *judge*)

[1]**af·fright** \ə-ˈfrīt\ *vt, archaic* : FRIGHTEN 1, ALARM

[2]**affright** *n, archaic* : sudden and great fear : TERROR

[1]**af·front** \ə-ˈfrənt\ *vt* 1 : to insult especially to the face by language or behavior : OFFEND 2 : to face in defiance : CONFRONT [Medieval French *afrunter* "to defy," derived from Latin *ad-* + *frons* "forehead"] ***synonyms*** see OFFEND

[2]**affront** *n* : a deliberately offensive act or utterance
synonyms AFFRONT, INSULT, INDIGNITY mean words spoken or an action done for the purpose of hurting another's feelings. AFFRONT implies an open, deliberate act of disrespect ⟨his absence at the occasion was an *affront* to the family⟩. INSULT implies an attack intended to humiliate and degrade ⟨took the remark as a personal *insult*⟩. INDIGNITY suggests an outrageous offense to one's personal dignity ⟨balked at the *indignity* of wearing the costume⟩.

Af·ghan \ˈaf-ˌgan *also* -gən\ *n* 1 : a native or inhabitant of Afghanistan 2 : PASHTUN 3 *not cap* : a blanket or shawl of colored wool knitted or crocheted in strips or squares — **Afghan** *or* **Af·ghani** \af-ˈgan-ē, -gän-\ *adj*

Afghan hound *n* : any of a breed of tall slim swift hunting dogs originating in Afghanistan with a coat of silky thick hair and a long silky topknot

Afghan hound

afi·cio·na·do \ə-ˌfish-ē-ə-ˈnäd-ō, -ˌfis-ē-\ *n, pl* **-dos** : a person who likes, knows about, and appreciates an interest or activity : DEVOTEE, FAN [Spanish]

afield \ə-ˈfēld\ *adv* 1 : to, in, or on the field 2 : away from home 3 : out of a regular, planned, or proper course : ASTRAY ⟨remarks that went too far *afield*⟩

afire \ə-ˈfīr\ *adj or adv* : being on fire : BLAZING

aflame \ə-ˈflām\ *adj or adv* : AFIRE

af·la·tox·in \ˌaf-lə-ˈtäk-sən\ *n* : any of several toxic substances produced by fungi especially in stored agricultural crops (as corn) [*afla-* from initial letters of *Aspergillus flavus*, a species of mold]

afloat \ə-ˈflōt\ *adv or adj* 1 a : borne on or as if on the water ⟨fallen leaves *afloat* on the water⟩ b : at sea 2 : free of difficulties : SELF-SUFFICIENT ⟨enough money to keep the business *afloat*⟩ 3 : circulating about : RUMORED ⟨strange stories were *afloat* about them⟩

aflut·ter \ə-ˈflət-ər\ *adj* 1 : fluttering quickly 2 : nervously excited

afoot \ə-ˈfu̇t\ *adv or adj* 1 : on foot ⟨they traveled *afoot*⟩ 2 : in the process of development : under way ⟨a plan was *afoot* to seize power⟩

afore \ə-ˈfōr, -ˈfȯr\ *adv or conj or prep, chiefly dialect* : BEFORE

afore·men·tioned \-ˌmen-chənd\ *adj* : mentioned previously

afore·said \-ˌsed\ *adj* : said or named previously

afore·thought \-ˌthȯt\ *adj* : previously in mind : DELIBERATE ⟨with malice *aforethought*⟩

a for·ti·o·ri \ˌä-ˌfȯrt-ē-ˈōr-ē, ˌā-fȯrt-ē-ˈōr-ˌī, -ˈȯr-\ *adv* : with greater reason or more convincing force — used in drawing a conclusion that is inferred to be even more certain than another ⟨the man of prejudice is, *a fortiori*, a man of limited mental vision⟩ [New Latin, literally, "from the stronger (argument)"]

afoul of \ə-ˈfau̇l-əv\ *prep* 1 : in or into collision or entanglement with ⟨one ship ran *afoul of* the other⟩ 2 : in or into conflict with ⟨they fell *afoul of* the law⟩

afraid \ə-ˈfrād, *South also* -ˈfreəd *or* -ˈfred\ *adj* 1 : filled with fear or dread ⟨*afraid* of snakes⟩ 2 : filled with concern or regret over a possibly unfavorable occurrence ⟨*afraid* that they might be late⟩ 3 : having a dislike for something ⟨not *afraid* to work hard⟩ [Middle English *affraied*, from past participle of *affraien* "to frighten," from Medieval French *affraier*]

afresh \ə-ˈfresh\ *adv* : from a new start : AGAIN

Af·ri·can \ˈaf-ri-kən\ *n* 1 : a native or inhabitant of Africa 2 : a person and especially a black person of African ancestry — **African** *adj*

African–American *n* : an American of African and especially of black descent — **African–American** *adj*

African elephant *n* : ELEPHANT a

African sleeping sickness *n* : SLEEPING SICKNESS 1

African violet *n* : a tropical African plant related to the gloxinias and widely grown as a houseplant for its velvety fleshy leaves and showy purple, pink, or white flowers

Af·ri·kaans \ˌaf-ri-ˈkäns, -ˈkänz\ *n* : a language developed from 17th century Dutch that is one of the official languages of the Republic of South Africa [Afrikaans, from *afrikaans* "African"]

Af·ri·ka·ner \-ˈkän-ər\ *n* : a native South African of European descent whose native language is Afrikaans [Afrikaans]

Afro \ˈaf-ˌrō\ *n, pl* **Afros** : a hairstyle of tight curls in a full evenly rounded shape — **Af·roed** \ˈaf-ˌrōd\ *adj*

Afro

Af·ro–Amer·i·can \ˌaf-rō-ə-ˈmer-ə-kən\ *n* : AFRICAN-AMERICAN — **Afro–American** *adj*

Af·ro–Asi·at·ic languages \ˌaf-rō-ˌā-zhē-ˈat-ik-, -zē-\ *n pl* : a family of languages widely distributed over southwestern Asia and northern Africa including the Semitic, Egyptian, Berber, Cushitic, and Chadic subfamilies

aft \ˈaft\ *adv* : near, toward, or in the stern of a ship or the tail of an aircraft [Old English *æftan* "from behind, behind"]

[1]**af·ter** \ˈaf-tər\ *adv* : following in time or place : LATER, BEHIND ⟨returned 20 years *after*⟩ [Old English *æfter*]

[2]**after** *prep* 1 a : behind in place ⟨following *after* them⟩ b : following in time or order ⟨*after* dinner⟩ c : subsequent to and in view of ⟨*after* all our advice⟩ 2 — used as a function word to indicate an object or goal ⟨go *after* gold⟩ ⟨ask *after* a friend⟩ 3 a : in accordance with ⟨*after* an old custom⟩ b : with the name of or a name derived from that of ⟨named Pennsylvania *after* William Penn⟩ c : in imitation or resemblance of ⟨patterned *after* a Gothic cathedral⟩

[3]**after** *conj* : later than the time when ⟨opened the door *after* she knocked⟩

[4]**after** *adj* 1 : later in time : SUBSEQUENT ⟨in *after* years⟩ 2 : located toward the stern of a ship or tail of an aircraft

after all *adv* : in spite of expectations to the contrary : NEVERTHELESS ⟨decided to go *after all*⟩

af·ter·birth \ˈaf-tər-ˌbərth\ *n* : the placenta and fetal membranes that are expelled from the uterus after delivery

af·ter·burn·er \-ˌbər-nər\ *n* 1 : an auxiliary burner attached to the tail pipe of a turbojet engine for injecting fuel into the hot exhaust gases and burning it to provide extra thrust 2 : a device for removing unburned carbon compounds from exhaust gases (as of a car)

af·ter·care \-ˌkeər, -ˌkaər\ *n* : the care, treatment, help, or supervision given to a person released from an institution (as a hospital)

af·ter·deck \-ˌdek\ *n* : the rear half of the deck of a ship

af·ter·ef·fect \-ə-ˌfekt\ *n* : an effect that follows its cause after some time has passed or after a first effect has subsided ⟨the *aftereffects* of surgery⟩

af·ter·glow \-ˌglō\ *n* 1 : a glow remaining (as in the sky after sunset) where a light has disappeared 2 : a pleasant effect or feeling that occurs after something is done, experienced, or achieved ⟨basking in the *afterglow* of success⟩

af·ter·guard \ˈaf-tər-ˌgärd\ *n* : the sailors stationed on the poop or after part of a ship

af·ter·im·age \-ˌim-ij\ *n* : a usually visual sensation continuing after the stimulus causing it has ended

af·ter·life \-ˌlīf\ *n* 1 : an existence after death 2 : a later period in one's life

af·ter·math \ˈaf-tər-ˌmath\ *n* **1** : a second-growth crop especially of hay **2** : EFFECT 1, RESULT ⟨felt guilty as an *aftermath* of the accident⟩ **3** : the period immediately following a usually ruinous event ⟨in the *aftermath* of the war⟩ [Old English *mæth* "mowing," from *māwan* "to mow"]

af·ter·noon \ˌaf-tər-ˈnün\ *n* : the part of day between noon and sunset — **afternoon** *adj*

af·ter·noons \-ˈnünz\ *adv* : in the afternoon repeatedly ⟨*afternoons* we take a nap⟩

af·ter·shave \ˈaf-tər-ˌshāv\ *n* : a usually scented lotion for use on the face after shaving

af·ter·taste \ˈaf-tər-ˌtāst\ *n* : a sensation (as of flavor) continuing after the stimulus causing it has ended

af·ter·thought \-ˌthȯt\ *n* **1** : an idea occurring later **2** : something (as a part or feature) not thought of originally ⟨the porch was added as an *afterthought*⟩

af·ter·ward \ˈaf-tər-wərd, -tə-\ *or* **af·ter·wards** \-wərdz\ *adv* : at a later time

af·ter·world \ˈaf-tər-ˌwərld\ *n* : a future world : a world after death

ag- — see AD-

again \ə-ˈgen, -ˈgin, -ˈgān\ *adv* **1** : in return ⟨give them the message and bring us word *again*⟩ **2** : another time : ANEW ⟨come see us *again*⟩ **3** : in addition ⟨half as much *again*⟩ **4** : on the other hand ⟨we may, and *again* we may not⟩ **5** : FURTHER, MOREOVER ⟨*again*, there is another matter to consider⟩ [Middle English, "opposite, again," from Old English *ongēan* "opposite, back," from *on* + *gēan* "still, again"]

against \ə-ˈgenst, -ˈginst, -ˈgānst\ *prep* **1 a** : in opposition or hostility to ⟨campaign *against* the enemy⟩ **b** : contrary to ⟨*against* the law⟩ **c** : in competition with ⟨racing *against* each other⟩ **d** : as a basis for disapproval of ⟨I have nothing *against* them⟩ **2** : directly opposite : FACING ⟨over *against* the park⟩ **3 a** : in preparation for ⟨storing food *against* the winter⟩ **b** : as a protection from ⟨a shield *against* aggression⟩ **4 a** : in the direction of and into contact with ⟨ran *against* a tree⟩ **b** : in contact with ⟨leaning *against* the wall⟩ **5** : in a direction opposite to ⟨walk *against* the wind⟩ **6** : in exchange for ⟨lend money *against* a promissory note⟩ **7** : before the background of ⟨green trees *against* the blue sky⟩ [Middle English, from *again*]

[1]**aga·pe** \ä-ˈgä-ˌpā, ˈäg-ə-ˌpā\ *n* **1** : LOVE FEAST 1 **2** : LOVE 3a [Greek *agapē*, literally, "love"]

[2]**agape** \ə-ˈgāp *also* ə-ˈgap\ *adj or adv* **1** : wide open ⟨with mouth *agape*⟩ **2** : being in a state of wonder ⟨tourists *agape* at the scenery⟩

agar \äg-ər\ *also* **agar–agar** \ˌäg-ər-ˈäg-ər\ *n* **1** : a jellylike extract of a red alga used especially in culture media or to give firmness to foods **2** : a culture medium containing agar [Malay *agar-agar*]

aga·ric \ˈag-ə-rik, ə-ˈgar-ik\ *n* : any of a family including both poisonous and edible fungi with the spore-producing body usually resembling an umbrella with numerous gills on the underside of the cap — compare FLY AGARIC [Greek *agarikon*, a kind of fungus]

ag·ate \ˈag-ət\ *n* **1** : a fine-grained variegated quartz having its colors arranged in stripes, blended in clouds, or showing mosslike forms **2** : a child's playing marble of agate or of glass resembling agate **3** : a small size of type approximately 5½ point [Middle French, from Latin *achates*, from Greek *achatēs*]

agateware *n* : pottery veined and mottled to resemble agate

aga·ve \ə-ˈgäv-ē\ *n* : any of a genus of plants that have spiny-edged leaves and flowers in tall branched clusters and some of which are cultivated for fiber or for ornament [Greek *Agauē*, a daughter of Cadmus]

[1]**age** \ˈāj\ *n* **1 a** (1) : the time of life when a person attains some right or capacity ⟨voting *age*⟩ (2) : MAJORITY ⟨come of *age*⟩ **b** : the time from birth to a specified date ⟨a child six years of *age*⟩ **c** : normal lifetime **d** : the later part of life **2** : a period of time in history or in the development of human beings or in the history of the earth; *esp* : one characterized by some distinguishing feature ⟨machine *age*⟩ ⟨*Age* of Discovery⟩ ⟨*Age* of Reptiles⟩ **3** : a long period of time ⟨it happened *ages* ago⟩ [Medieval French *aage*, derived from Latin *aetas*] ***synonyms*** see PERIOD

[2]**age** *vb* **aged; ag·ing** *or* **age·ing** **1** : to become old : show the effects of increasing age **2** : to become or cause to become mellow or mature : RIPEN ⟨letting cheese *age*⟩ **3** : to cause to seem old especially prematurely (as by strain or suffering)

-age \ij\ *n suffix* **1** : aggregate : collection ⟨mile*age*⟩ **2 a** : action : process ⟨haul*age*⟩ **b** : cumulative result of ⟨break*age*⟩ **c** : rate of ⟨dos*age*⟩ **3** : house or place of ⟨orphan*age*⟩ **4** : state : rank ⟨vassal*age*⟩ **5** : fee : charge ⟨post*age*⟩ [Medieval French, from Latin *-aticum*]

aged \ˈā-jəd, *in senses 1b and 2b* ˈājd\ *adj* **1** : grown old: as **a** : of an advanced age ⟨an *aged* man⟩ **b** : having reached a specified age ⟨a person *aged* 40 years⟩ **2 a** : typical of old age **b** : having gained a desirable quality with age ⟨*aged* whiskey⟩ — **aged·ness** *n*

age·ism *also* **ag·ism** \ˈā-ˌjiz-əm\ *n* : prejudice or discrimination against people of a particular age and especially against the elderly — **age·ist** \-jist\ *adj*

age·less \ˈāj-ləs\ *adj* **1** : not growing old or showing the effects of age ⟨an *ageless* face⟩ **2** : TIMELESS, ETERNAL ⟨an *ageless* story⟩ — **age·less·ly** *adv* — **age·less·ness** *n*

age·long \ˈāj-ˌlȯŋ\ *adj* : lasting for a long time : EVERLASTING

agen·cy \ˈā-jən-sē\ *n, pl* **-cies** **1 a** : the office or function of an agent **b** : the relationship between a principal and that person's agent **2** : the capacity, condition, or state of acting or of exerting power : OPERATION **3** : a person or thing through which power is exerted or an end is achieved ⟨sued through the *agency* of my lawyer⟩ **4** : an establishment engaged in doing business for another ⟨advertising *agency*⟩ **5** : an administrative division (as of a government) ⟨Central Intelligence *Agency*⟩

agen·da \ə-ˈjen-də\ *n* **1** : a list of things to be considered (as at a meeting) or done **2** : an underlying often ideological plan or program ⟨a political *agenda*⟩ [Latin, "things to be done," from *agere* "to do"]

agent \ˈā-jənt\ *n* **1 a** : something that produces or is capable of producing an effect ⟨a cleansing *agent*⟩ **b** : a chemically, physically, or biologically active principle **2** : one that acts or exerts power **3** : one who acts for or in the place of another and by the other's authority ⟨government *agents*⟩ ⟨a real estate *agent*⟩ [Medieval Latin *agens*, derived from Latin *agere* "to drive, lead, act, do"]

agent pro·vo·ca·teur \ˌäzh-ˌä^{n}-prō-ˌväk ə-ˈtər, ˈā-jənt-\ *n, pl* **agents provocateurs** \ˌäzh-ˌä^{n}-prō-ˌväk-ə-ˈtər, ˈā jənts-prō-\ : a person paid to associate with members of a suspected group and to pretend sympathy with their aims so as to incite them to a legally punishable act [French, literally, "provoking agent"]

Age of Fishes : DEVONIAN 1

Age of Mammals : CENOZOIC 1

age of reason *n* : the 18th century in England and France characterized by a prevailing belief in the use of reason

Age of Reptiles : MESOZOIC 1

age–old \ˈāj-ˈōld\ *adj* : having existed for ages : ANCIENT ⟨*age-old* customs⟩

ag·er·a·tum \ˌaj-ə-ˈrāt-əm\ *n* : any of a genus of tropical American composite herbs often cultivated for their small showy heads of usually blue or white flowers [Greek *agēratos* "ageless," from *a-* + *gēras* "old age"]

age spots *n pl* : harmless flat spots of dark pigment on the skin (as from exposure to the sun) occurring especially among older people — called also *liver spots*

Ag·ge·us \a-ˈgē-əs\ *n* : HAGGAI

[1]**ag·glom·er·ate** \ə-ˈgläm-ə-ˌrāt\ *vb* : to gather into a ball, mass, or cluster [Latin *agglomerare* "to heap up," from *ad-* + *glomus* "ball"]

[2]**ag·glom·er·ate** \-rət\ *n* **1** : a jumbled mass or collection **2** : a rock composed of volcanic fragments of various sizes

ag·glom·er·a·tion \ə-ˌgläm-ə-ˈrā-shən\ *n* **1** : the action or process of collecting in a mass **2** : a heap or cluster of dissimilar elements — **ag·glom·er·a·tive** \ə-ˈgläm-ə-ˌrāt-iv\ *adj*

ag·glu·ti·nate \ə-ˈglüt-n-ˌāt\ *vb* **1** : to cause to adhere : FASTEN **2** : to cause to clump **3** : to unite into a group or gather into a mass **4** : to form words by agglutination [Latin *agglutinare*, from *ad-* + *gluten* "glue"]

ag·glu·ti·na·tion \ə-ˌglüt-n-ˈā-shən\ *n* **1** : the action or process of agglutinating **2** : a mass or group formed by the union of separate elements **3** : the formation of derivative or compound words by putting together constituents of which each expresses a single definite meaning **4** : a reaction in which parti-

\ə\ **abut**	\au̇\ **out**	\i\ **tip**	\ȯ\ **saw**	\u̇\ **foot**
\ər\ **further**	\ch\ **chin**	\ī\ **life**	\ȯi\ **coin**	\y\ **yet**
\a\ **mat**	\e\ **pet**	\j\ **job**	\th\ **thin**	\yü\ **few**
\ā\ **take**	\ē\ **easy**	\ng\ **sing**	\th\ **this**	\yu̇\ **cure**
\ä\ **cot, cart**	\g\ **go**	\ō\ **bone**	\ü\ **food**	\zh\ **vision**

cles (as red blood cells or bacteria) suspended in a liquid collect into clumps usually as a response to a specific antibody — **ag·glu·ti·na·tive** \ə-ˈglüt-n-ˌāt-iv\ *adj*

ag·glu·ti·nin \ə-ˈglüt-n-ən\ *n* : an antibody causing agglutination

ag·gran·dize \ə-ˈgran-ˌdīz, ˈag-rən-\ *vt* : to make great or greater (as in power or resources) [French *agrandiss-*, stem of *agrandir*, from *a-* "ad-" + *grandir* "to increase"] — **ag·gran·dize·ment** \ə-ˈgran-dəz-mənt, -ˌdīz-; ˌag-rən-ˈdīz-mənt\ *n* — **ag·gran·diz·er** *n*

ag·gra·vate \ˈag-rə-ˌvāt\ *vt* **1** : to make worse, more serious, or more severe ⟨problems *aggravated* by neglect⟩ **2** : to rouse to displeasure or anger by usually persistent often petty goading [Latin *aggravare* "to make heavier," from *ad-* + *gravis* "heavy, grave"] ***synonyms*** see INTENSIFY

ag·gra·va·tion \ˌag-rə-ˈvā-shən\ *n* **1** : the act of making something worse or more severe : an increase in severity ⟨the treatment caused an *aggravation* of the pain⟩ **2** : something that aggravates ⟨the cold winter was an *aggravation* of their misery⟩ **3** : the act of irritating or annoying

1ag·gre·gate \ˈag-ri-gət\ *adj* **1** : formed by the collection of units or particles into a whole ⟨*aggregate* expenses⟩ **2** : clustered in a dense mass or head ⟨an *aggregate* flower⟩ [Latin *aggregare* "to cause to join together," from *ad-* + *greg-*, *grex* "flock"] — **ag·gre·gate·ly** *adv* — **ag·gre·gate·ness** *n*

2ag·gre·gate \-ˌgāt\ *vt* **1** : to collect or gather into a mass or whole **2** : to amount to altogether : TOTAL 2

3ag·gre·gate \-gət\ *n* **1** : a collection or sum of units or parts somewhat loosely associated **2** : the whole sum or amount : SUM TOTAL **3 a** : any of several hard inert materials (as sand or gravel) used for mixing with a cementing material to form concrete, mortar, or plaster **b** : a clustered mass of individual soil particles considered the basic structural unit of soil ***synonyms*** see SUM

aggregate fruit *n* : a compound fruit (as a raspberry) made up of the several separate ripened ovaries of a single flower

ag·gre·ga·tion \ˌag-ri-ˈgā-shən\ *n* **1** : the collecting of units or parts into a mass or whole **2** : a group, body, or mass composed of many distinct parts : ASSEMBLAGE

ag·gres·sion \ə-ˈgresh-ən\ *n* **1** : a forceful action or procedure; *esp* : an unprovoked attack **2** : the practice of making attacks or encroachments **3** : hostile, injurious, or destructive behavior or outlook especially when caused by frustration [Latin *aggressio*, from *aggredi* "to attack," from *ad-* + *gradi* "to step, go"]

ag·gres·sive \ə-ˈgres-iv\ *adj* **1 a** : tending toward or practicing aggression ⟨an *aggressive* nation⟩ **b** : showing readiness to fight or attack ⟨an *aggressive* dog⟩ **2 a** : marked by initiative and vigor ⟨an *aggressive* sales campaign⟩ **b** : obtrusively self-assertive ⟨annoyed by an *aggressive* salesperson⟩ **3** : growing, developing, or spreading rapidly ⟨*aggressive* weeds⟩ — **ag·gres·sive·ly** *adv* — **ag·gres·sive·ness** *n*

ag·gres·sor \ə-ˈgres-ər\ *n* : one that commits or practices aggression

ag·grieved \ə-ˈgrēvd\ *adj* **1** : troubled or distressed in spirit **2** : having a grievance; *esp* : suffering from injury or loss ⟨*aggrieved* minority groups⟩

aghast \ə-ˈgast\ *adj* : struck with terror, amazement, or horror : SHOCKED [Middle English *agast*, from *agasten* "to frighten," from *gast*, *gost* "ghost"]

ag·ile \ˈaj-əl, -ˌīl\ *adj* **1** : able to move quickly and easily : NIMBLE **2** : mentally quick [Middle French, from Latin *agilis*, from *agere* "to act, do"] — **ag·ile·ly** \-əl-lē, -ə-lē\ *adv*

agil·i·ty \ə-ˈjil-ət-ē\ *n, pl* **-ties** : the quality or state of being agile ⟨the grace and *agility* of a gymnast⟩

aging *present participle of* AGE

agism, agist *variant of* AGEISM, AGEIST

ag·i·tate \ˈaj-ə-ˌtāt\ *vb* **1** : to shake jerkily : set in violent irregular motion ⟨water *agitated* by wind⟩ **2** : to stir up : EXCITE, DISTURB ⟨*agitated* by bad news⟩ **3** : to attempt to arouse or influence public interest in something especially by discussion or appeals ⟨*agitate* for better schools⟩ [Latin *agitare*, from *agere* "to drive, act, do"] ***synonyms*** see DISTURB, SHAKE — **ag·i·tat·ed·ly** \-ˌtāt-əd-lē\ *adv* — **ag·i·ta·tion** \ˌaj-ə-ˈtā-shən\ *n*

agi·ta·to \ˌaj-ə-ˈtät-ō\ *adv or adj* : in a restless and agitated manner — used as a direction in music [Italian]

ag·i·ta·tor \ˈaj-ə-ˌtāt-ər\ *n* : one that agitates: as **a** : one who stirs up public feeling on controversial issues **b** : a device for stirring or shaking

agleam \ə-ˈglēm\ *adj* : BRIGHT, SHINING ⟨eyes *agleam* with tears⟩

agley \ə-ˈglā, -ˈglē, -ˈglī\ *adv, chiefly Scottish* : AWRY 2, WRONG [Scots, from 1*a-* + *gley* "to squint"]

aglit·ter \ə-ˈglit-ər\ *adj* : GLITTERY, SPARKLING

aglow \ə-ˈglō\ *adj* : glowing (as heat, light, or emotion) strongly

ag·nos·tic \ag-ˈnäs-tik, əg-\ *n* : a person who holds that whether God exists is not known and probably cannot be known [Greek *agnōstos* "unknown, unknowable," from *a-* + *gnōstos* "known," from *gignōskein* "to know"] — **agnostic** *adj* — **ag·nos·ti·cism** \-ˈnäs-tə-ˌsiz-əm\ *n*

Ag·nus Dei \ˌäg-ˌnu̇s-ˈdā-ˌē, ˌän-ˌyüs-, -ˈdā; ˌag-nəs-ˈdē-ˌī\ *n* **1** : a liturgical prayer said or sung to Christ as Savior **2** : an image of a lamb often with a halo and a banner and cross as a symbol of Christ [Late Latin, "lamb of God"; from its opening words]

ago \ə-ˈgō\ *adj or adv* : earlier than the present time ⟨a week *ago*⟩ [Middle English *agon*, *ago*, from *agon* "to pass away," from Old English *āgān*, from *ā-*, prefix denoting completion + *gān* "to go"]

agog \ə-ˈgäg\ *adj* : full of intense interest or excitement : EAGER ⟨kids all *agog* over new toys⟩ [Middle French *en gogues* "in mirth"]

a–go–go \ä-ˈgō-ˌgō\ *n* : a nightclub for dancing to popular music [*Whisky à Gogo*, cafe and nightclub in Paris, France, from French *à gogo* "galore"]

ag·o·nal \ˈag-ən-l\ *adj* : of, relating to, or associated with agony and especially agony in death or dying

ag·o·nize \ˈag-ə-ˌnīz\ *vb* **1** : to suffer or cause to suffer extreme physical or mental pain or anguish **2** : to strive desperately : STRUGGLE — **ag·o·niz·ing·ly** \-ˌnī-zing-lē\ *adv*

ag·o·ny \ˈag-ə-nē\ *n, pl* **-nies** **1 a** : intense physical or mental pain : ANGUISH, TORTURE **b** : the throes of death **2** : a strong sudden display of emotion ⟨an *agony* of delight⟩ [Greek *agōnia* "struggle, anguish," from *agōn* "gathering, contest for a prize"] ***synonyms*** see DISTRESS

Word History In ancient Greece *agōn* was a public assembly or gathering, especially one for games and athletic contests. *Agōnia* was the struggle for the prize in such contests. From the meaning "a struggle for victory in the games," *agōnia* came to be used first for any physical struggle, then for any activity involving difficulty or pain, and finally for mental anguish as well. Our English word *agony* is a descendant of this Greek *agōnia*.

ag·o·ra \ˈag-ə-rə\ *n, pl* **-ras** *or* **-rae** \-ˌrē, -ˌrī\ : the marketplace or place of assembly in an ancient Greek city [Greek]

ag·o·ra·pho·bia \ˌag-ə-rə-ˈfō-bē-ə\ *n* : abnormal fear of being helpless in an embarrassing or inescapable situation that is characterized especially by the avoidance of open or public spaces — **ag·o·ra·pho·bic** \-ˈfō-bik, -ˈfäb-ik\ *adj*

agou·ti \ə-ˈgüt-ē\ *n* **1** : a tropical American rodent about the size of a rabbit **2** : a grizzled color of fur resulting from the barring of each hair in several alternate dark and light bands [French, from Spanish *agutí*, derived from Tupi *akutí*]

agouti 1

1agrar·i·an \ə-ˈgrer-ē-ən, -ˈgrar-\ *adj* **1** : of or relating to fields or lands or their ownership ⟨*agrarian* reforms⟩ **2** : of, relating to, or concerned with farmers or farming interests ⟨an *agrarian* political party⟩ **3** : AGRICULTURAL 2 ⟨an *agrarian* country⟩ [Latin *agrarius*, *agr-*, *ager* "field"]

2agrarian *n* : a member of an agrarian party or movement

agrar·i·an·ism \-ē-ə-ˌniz-əm\ *n* : a social or political movement designed chiefly to improve the economic status of the farmer

agree \ə-ˈgrē\ *vb* **agreed; agree·ing** **1** : to give one's approval : CONSENT ⟨*agree* to a plan⟩ **2** : ADMIT, CONCEDE ⟨*agreed* it was a good idea⟩ **3** : to be alike : CORRESPOND ⟨both copies *agree*⟩ **4** : to get on well together **5** : to come to terms ⟨*agree* on a price⟩ **6** : to be fitting or healthful : SUIT ⟨the climate *agrees* with them⟩ **7** : to correspond grammatically in gender, number, case, or person [Medieval French *agreer*, from *a gre* "at will," *a-* "ad-" + *gre* "will, pleasure," from Latin *gratus* "pleasant, agreeable"]

agree·able \ə-ˈgrē-ə-bəl\ *adj* **1 :** pleasing to the mind or senses ⟨an *agreeable* climate⟩ ⟨an *agreeable* fragrance⟩ **2 :** ready or willing to agree **3 :** being in harmony : CONSONANT — **agree·able·ness** *n* — **agree·ably** \-blē\ *adv*

agree·ment \ə-ˈgrē-mənt\ *n* **1 a :** the act of agreeing **b :** harmony of opinion, action, or character : CONCORD ⟨all are in *agreement*⟩ **2 :** a mutual arrangement or understanding as to a course of action; *also* **:** a written record of such an agreement **3 :** the fact of agreeing grammatically

ag·ri·cul·tur·al \ˌag-ri-ˈkəlch-rəl, -ə-rəl\ *adj* **1 :** of, relating to, or used in agriculture **2 :** engaged in or concerned with agriculture ⟨an *agricultural* society⟩ — **ag·ri·cul·tur·al·ly** \-ē\ *adv*

ag·ri·cul·ture \ˈag-ri-ˌkəl-chər\ *n* **:** the science, art, or occupation of cultivating the soil, producing crops, and raising livestock : FARMING [Middle French, from Latin *agricultura,* from *ager* "field" + *cultura* "cultivation"] — **ag·ri·cul·tur·ist** \ˌag-ri-ˈkəlch-rəst, -ə-rəst\ *or* **ag·ri·cul·tur·al·ist** \-ˈkəlch-rə-ləst, -ˈkəlch-ə-rə-ləst\ *n*

ag·ri·mo·ny \ˈag-rə-ˌmō-nē\ *n, pl* **-nies :** a common yellow-flowered herb of the rose family having toothed leaves and fruits like burs [Latin *agrimonia*]

agron·o·my \ə-ˈgrän-ə-mē\ *n* **:** a branch of agriculture that deals with the raising of crops and the care of the soil [Greek *agros* "field" + *nomos* "law"] — **ag·ro·nom·ic** \ˌag-rə-ˈnäm-ik\ *adj* — **ag·ro·nom·i·cal·ly** \-ˈnäm-i-kə-lē, -klē\ *adv* — **agron·o·mist** \ə-ˈgrän-ə-məst\ *n*

aground \ə-ˈgraund\ *adv or adj* **1 :** on or onto the shore or the bottom of a body of water ⟨a ship run *aground*⟩ **2 :** on the ground ⟨planes aloft and *aground*⟩

ague \ˈā-gyü\ *n* **1 :** a fever (as malaria) marked by outbreaks of chills, fever, and sweating that recur at regular intervals **2 :** a fit of shivering : CHILL [Medieval French *aguë,* from Medieval Latin *febris acuta,* literally, "sharp fever"] — **agu·ish** \ˈā-ˌgyü-ish\ *adj*

[1]**ah** \ˈä\ *interj* — used to express delight, relief, regret, or contempt [Middle English]

[2]**ah** *variant of* AAH

aha \ä-ˈhä\ *interj* — used to express surprise, triumph, or derision [Middle English]

ahead \ə-ˈhed\ *adv or adj* **1 a :** in a forward direction or position : FORWARD ⟨go *ahead*⟩ **b :** in front ⟨the car *ahead*⟩ **2 :** in, into, or for the future ⟨think *ahead*⟩ **3 :** in or toward a more advantageous position ⟨trying to get *ahead*⟩ **4 :** in advance ⟨make payments *ahead*⟩

ahead of *prep* **1 :** in front or advance of **2 :** in excess of : ABOVE

ahem *a throat-clearing sound; often read as* ə-ˈhem\ *interj* — used especially to attract attention or to express disapproval or embarrassment [imitative]

-ahol·ic *also* **-ohol·ic** \ə-ˈhȯl-ik, -ˈhäl-\ *n combining form* **1 :** one who feels compulsively the need to (do something) ⟨wor*kaholic*⟩ **2 :** one who likes (something) to excess ⟨choco*holic*⟩ [*alcoholic*]

A ho·ri·zon \ˈā-hə-ˌrīz-n\ *n* **:** the outermost dark-colored layer of a soil consisting of topsoil containing partly disintegrated organic debris

ahoy \ə-ˈhȯi\ *interj* — used in hailing ⟨ship *ahoy*⟩ [*a-* (as in *aha*) + Middle English *hoy,* interjection]

[1]**aid** \ˈād\ *vb* **1 :** to provide with what is useful or necessary in achieving an end **2 :** to give assistance [Medieval French *aider,* from Latin *adjutare,* from *adjuvare,* from *ad-* + *juvare* "to help"]

[2]**aid** *n* **1 a :** the act of helping **b :** help given : ASSISTANCE **2 a :** an assisting person or group **b :** something (as a device) by which assistance is given ⟨a visual *aid*⟩

aide \ˈād\ *n* **:** one that acts as an assistant; *esp* **:** a military officer acting as assistant to a superior [short for *aide-de-camp*]

aide–de–camp \ˌād-di-ˈkamp, -ˈkäⁿ\ *n, pl* **aides–de–camp** \ˌādz-di-\ **:** a military aide [French *aide de camp,* literally, "camp assistant"]

AIDS \ˈādz\ *n* **:** a disease of the human immune system that is characterized by greatly reduced numbers of helper T cells thereby making the subject highly vulnerable to life-threatening infections and that is caused by infection with HIV commonly transmitted in infected blood especially during illicit intravenous drug use and in bodily secretions (as semen) during sexual intercourse [*a*cquired *i*mmuno*d*eficiency *s*yndrome]

AIDS–related complex *n* **:** a group of symptoms (as fever, weight loss, and enlarged lymph nodes) that is associated with the presence of antibodies to HIV and that may be followed by the development of AIDS

AIDS virus *n* **:** HIV

ai·grette \ā-ˈgret, ˈā-ˌ\ *n* **:** a plume or decorative tuft for the head [French]

ai·ki·do \ˌī-ki-ˈdō\ *n* **:** a Japanese art of self-defense characterized by the use of techniques that cause the attacker's own momentum to work against him or her [Japanese *aikidō,* from *ai-* "match, coordinate" + *ki* "breath, spirit" + *dō* "art"]

ail \ˈāl\ *vb* **1 :** to be the matter with : TROUBLE ⟨what *ails* you?⟩ **2 :** to have something the matter; *esp* **:** to suffer ill health ⟨has been *ailing* for years⟩ [Old English *eglan*]

ai·lan·thus \ā-ˈlan-thəs, -ˈlant-\ *n* **:** TREE OF HEAVEN [Kamarian (an Austronesian language of the Moluccas) *ai lanito,* literally, "sky tree"]

ai·le·ron \ˈā-lə-ˌrän\ *n* **:** a movable portion of an airplane wing or a movable airfoil external to the wing for imparting a rolling motion [French, from *aile* "wing," from Medieval French *ele,* from Latin *ala*]

ail·ment \ˈāl-mənt\ *n* **:** a bodily disorder : SICKNESS

[1]**aim** \ˈām\ *vb* **1 a :** to direct a course ⟨a goal to *aim* for⟩ **b :** to point a weapon at an object **2 :** to direct one's efforts : ASPIRE **3 :** to have as a purpose : INTEND ⟨*aims* to win⟩ **4 :** POINT 5a ⟨telescopes *aimed* toward Mars⟩ [Medieval French *aesmer* "to aim, estimate," from Latin *aestimare* "to estimate"]

[2]**aim** *n* **1 a :** the pointing of a weapon or a missile at a mark **b :** the ability to hit a target ⟨your *aim* is deadly⟩ **2 :** GOAL 2, PURPOSE ***synonyms*** see INTENTION

aim·less \ˈām-ləs\ *adj* **:** lacking aim or purpose ⟨*aimless* wandering⟩ — **aim·less·ly** *adv* — **aim·less·ness** *n*

ain't \ˈānt\ **1 a :** are not **b :** is not **c :** am not **2 a :** have not **b :** has not [probably contraction of *are not*]

usage Although widely disapproved as nonstandard and more common in the habitual speech of less educated speakers and writers, *ain't* is flourishing in American English. It is used by educated speakers and writers to catch attention and to gain emphasis. It is used in journalistic prose as part of a consistently informal style. This informal *ain't* is commonly distinguished from the habitual *ain't* of less educated speakers and writers by its frequent occurrence in fixed constructions and phrases ⟨you *ain't* seen nothing yet⟩ ⟨two out of three *ain't* bad⟩. In fiction, *ain't* is used for the purpose of characterization.

Ai·nu \ˈī-nü\ *n* **1 :** a member of an indigenous people of Japan living chiefly in the northern islands **2 :** the language of the Ainu people [Ainu *aynu* "person"]

[1]**air** \ˈaər, ˈeər\ *n* **1 a :** the invisible mixture of odorless tasteless gases (as nitrogen and oxygen) that surrounds the earth **b :** a light breeze **2 a :** empty space **b :** NOTHINGNESS — usually used in the phrase *into thin air* ⟨vanished into thin *air*⟩ **3 :** TUNE 1, MELODY **4 a :** outward appearance : apparent nature ⟨an *air* of dignity⟩ **b** *pl* **:** an artificial or affected manner : HAUGHTINESS ⟨put on *airs*⟩ **c :** a surrounding or pervading influence : ATMOSPHERE ⟨an *air* of mystery⟩ **5 :** COMPRESSED AIR ⟨*air* sprayer⟩ **6 a :** AIRCRAFT ⟨*air* attack⟩ ⟨travel by *air*⟩ **b :** AVIATION ⟨*air* safety⟩ ⟨*air* rights⟩ **c :** AIR FORCE ⟨*air* headquarters⟩ **d** (1) **:** the medium of transmission of radio waves (2) **:** RADIO, TELEVISION ⟨went on the *air*⟩ **7 :** an air-conditioning system ⟨turn on the *air*⟩ **8 :** the height achieved in performing a maneuver in the air ⟨a skateboarder catching big *air*⟩ [Medieval French, from Latin *aer,* from Greek *aēr*]

[2]**air** *vt* **1 :** to place in the air for cooling, refreshing, or cleansing **2 :** to make known in public ⟨*air* one's complaints⟩

air bag *n* **:** an automobile safety device that is a bag designed to inflate automatically especially in front of an occupant in case of a collision

air base *n* **:** a base of operations for military aircraft

air bladder *n* **1 :** a sac in a fish containing gases (as

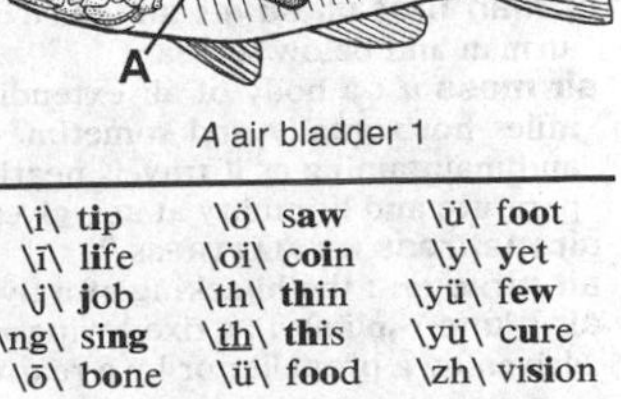

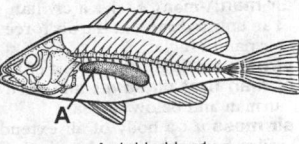

A air bladder 1

\ə\ **abut**	\au̇\ **out**	\i\ **tip**	\ȯ\ **saw**	\u̇\ **foot**
\ər\ **further**	\ch\ **chin**	\ī\ **life**	\ȯi\ **coin**	\y\ **yet**
\a\ **mat**	\e\ **pet**	\j\ **job**	\th\ **thin**	\yü\ **few**
\ā\ **take**	\ē\ **easy**	\ng\ **sing**	\t͟h\ **this**	\yu̇\ **cure**
\ä\ **cot, cart**	\g\ **go**	\ō\ **bone**	\ü\ **food**	\zh\ **vision**

oxygen and nitrogen) and serving as a float regulating buoyancy or assisting respiration — called also *swim bladder* **2 :** a gas-filled cavity of various algae that keeps the algae afloat

air·borne \-ˌbōrn, -ˌbȯrn\ *adj* **:** supported or transported by air

air brake *n* **1 :** a brake operated by a piston driven by compressed air **2 :** a surface that may be projected into the air for lowering the speed of an airplane

[1]**air·brush** \-ˌbrəsh\ *n* **:** an atomizer for applying by compressed air a fine spray (as of paint)

[2]**airbrush** *vt* **:** to paint, treat, or change (as to hide imperfections) with or as if with an airbrush ⟨*airbrush* a photograph⟩

air–con·di·tion \ˌaər-kən-ˈdish-ən, ˌeər-\ *vt* **:** to equip with an apparatus for cleaning air and controlling its humidity and temperature; *also* **:** to subject (air) to these processes — **air con·di·tion·er** \-ˈdish-nər, -ə-nər\ *n* — **air–con·di·tion·ing** \-ˈdish-ning, -ˈdish-ə-ning\ *n*

air–cool \ˈaər-ˈkül, ˈeər-\ *vt* **:** to cool the cylinders of (an internal combustion engine) solely by the use of air

air·craft \ˈaər-ˌkraft, ˈeər-\ *n, pl* **aircraft :** a machine (as an airplane, blimp, or helicopter) for navigation of the air that is supported either by its own buoyancy or by the action of the air against its surfaces

aircraft carrier *n* **:** a warship with a deck on which aircraft can be launched and landed

air·crew \ˈaər-ˌkrü, ˈeər-\ *n* **:** the crew manning an airplane

air dam *n* **:** a device attached to the underside of the front of an automobile to improve stability, aerodynamic performance, and engine cooling by redirecting the flow of air

air·drome \-ˌdrōm\ *n* **:** AIRPORT

air·drop \-ˌdräp\ *n* **:** delivery of cargo, emergency supplies, or personnel by parachute from an airplane in flight — **air–drop** \-ˌdräp\ *vt*

Aire·dale \ˈaər-ˌdāl, ˈeər-\ *n* **:** any of a breed of large terriers with a hard wiry coat that is dark on the back and sides and tan elsewhere [*Airedale,* valley of the Aire River, England]

air·field \ˈaər-ˌfēld, ˈeər-\ *n* **1 :** the landing field of an airport **2 :** AIRPORT

air·flow \-ˌflō\ *n* **:** a flow of air; *esp* **:** the motion of air relative to the surface of a body surrounded by the air

air·foil \-ˌfȯil\ *n* **:** an airplane surface (as a wing or rudder) designed to produce reaction (as lift or drag) from the air through which it moves

air force *n* **:** the military organization of a nation for air warfare

air·frame \-ˌfrām\ *n* **:** the structure of an airplane or rocket without the power plant

air gun *n* **:** any of various hand tools that work by compressed air; *esp* **:** AIRBRUSH

air hole *n* **1 :** a hole to admit or discharge air **2 :** AIR POCKET

air lane *n* **:** an airway that is customarily followed by airplanes

air letter *n* **1 :** a letter sent by airmail **2 :** a sheet of airmail stationery that can be folded and sealed with the message inside and the address outside

air·lift \ˈaər-ˌlift, ˈeər-\ *n* **:** a system of transporting cargo or passengers by aircraft to or from an area otherwise impossible to reach — **airlift** *vt*

air·line \-ˌlīn\ *n* **:** an air transportation system including equipment, routes, and personnel

air line *n* **:** a straight line through the air between two points

air·lin·er \-ˌlī-nər\ *n* **:** an airplane operated by an airline

air lock *n* **:** an air space with two airtight doors for permitting movement between two spaces with different pressures or different atmospheres

air·mail \ˈaər-ˌmāl, ˈeər-\ *n* **:** the system of transporting mail by airplanes; *also* **:** the mail transported — **airmail** *vt*

air·man \-mən\ *n* **1 :** a civilian or military pilot or aviator **2 :** an enlisted rank in the air force above airman basic and below airman first class

airman basic *n* **:** the lowest enlisted rank in the air force

airman first class *n* **:** an enlisted rank in the air force above airman and below sergeant

air mass *n* **:** a body of air extending hundreds or thousands of miles horizontally and sometimes as high as the stratosphere and maintaining as it travels nearly uniform conditions of temperature and humidity at any given level

air mattress *n* **:** MATTRESS 2

air piracy *n* **:** the hijacking of a flying airplane

air·plane \-ˌplān\ *n* **:** a fixed-wing aircraft heavier than air that is driven by a propeller or by a rearward jet and supported by the reaction of the air against its wings [alteration of *aeroplane,* from French *aéroplane,* from *aéro-* "aer-" + *-plane,* probably from *plan* "flat, level," from Latin *planus*]

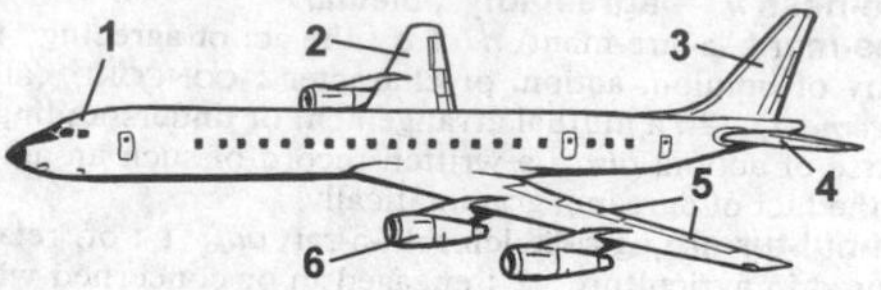

airplane: *1* cockpit, *2* wing, *3* vertical stabilizer, *4* horizontal stabilizer, *5* flaps, *6* jet engine

air plant *n* **1 :** EPIPHYTE **2 :** any of several kalanchoes

air pocket *n* **:** a condition of the atmosphere (as a downdraft) that causes an airplane to drop suddenly

air police *n* **:** the military police of an air force

air·port \ˈaər-ˌpōrt, ˈeər-, -ˌpȯrt\ *n* **:** a tract of land or water that is maintained for the landing and takeoff of airplanes and for receiving and discharging passengers and cargo and that usually has facilities for the shelter, supply, and repair of planes

air pump *n* **:** a pump for exhausting air from a closed space or for compressing air or forcing it through other apparatus

air raid *n* **:** an attack by armed aircraft on a surface target

air rifle *n* **:** a rifle that shoots BBs or pellets by compressed air

air sac *n* **1 :** one of the air-filled spaces connected with the lungs of a bird **2 :** one of the thin-walled microscopic pouches in which gases are exchanged in the lungs — called also *alveolus*

air·ship \ˈaər-ˌship, ˈeər-\ *n* **:** a lighter-than-air aircraft having propulsion and steering systems

air·sick \-ˌsik\ *adj* **:** affected with motion sickness associated with flying — **air·sick·ness** *n*

air·space \-ˌspās\ *n* **:** the space lying above a nation and coming under its jurisdiction

air·speed \-ˌspēd\ *n* **:** the speed of an airplane relative to the air as opposed to its speed relative to the earth

air·strip \-ˌstrip\ *n* **:** a runway without normal airport facilities

air·tight \-ˈtīt\ *adj* **1 :** so tightly sealed that no air can get in or out **2 :** leaving no opening for attack ⟨*airtight* defenses⟩

air·wave \-ˌwāv\ *n* **:** the medium of radio and television transmission — usually used in plural

air·way \-ˌwā\ *n* **1 :** a passage for a current of air; *esp* **:** one through which air passes to and from the lungs **2 :** a regular route for airplanes from airport to airport; *esp* **:** such a route equipped with navigational aids **3 :** AIRLINE

air·wor·thy \-ˌwər-thē\ *adj* **:** fit or safe for operation in the air ⟨a very *airworthy* plane⟩ — **air·wor·thi·ness** *n*

airy \ˈaər-ē, ˈeər-\ *adj* **air·i·er; -est 1 a :** of or relating to air **:** ATMOSPHERIC **b :** high in the air **:** LOFTY ⟨*airy* perches⟩ **2 :** consisting of air **3 :** performed in the air **:** AERIAL ⟨*airy* leaps⟩ **4 :** lacking a sound or solid basis ⟨*airy* romance⟩ **5 a :** being light and graceful in movement and manner **:** SPRIGHTLY ⟨an *airy* dancer⟩ **b :** extremely light, delicate, or refined ⟨an *airy* perfume⟩ **6 :** open to the air **:** BREEZY ⟨an *airy* room⟩ — **air·i·ly** \ˈar-ə-lē, ˈer-\ *adv* — **air·i·ness** \ˈar-ē-nəs, ˈer-\ *n*

aisle \ˈīl\ *n* **1 :** the side of a church separated by piers from the nave **2 a :** a passage (as in a theater) between sections of seats **b :** a passage (as in a store) for inside traffic [Medieval French *ele* "wing," from Latin *ala*]

ajar \ə-ˈjär\ *adj or adv* **:** slightly open ⟨a door *ajar*⟩ [earlier *on char,* from *on* + *char* "turn," from Old English *cierr*]

akim·bo \ə-ˈkim-bō\ *adj or adv* **1 :** having the hand on the hip and the elbow turned outward **2 :** set in a bent position ⟨legs *akimbo*⟩ [Middle English *in kenebowe*]

akin \ə-ˈkin\ *adj* **1 :** related by blood **:** descended from a common ancestor or prototype **2 :** essentially similar or related **:** ALIKE

Ak·ka·di·an \ə-ˈkād-ē-ən\ *n* **1 :** an extinct Semitic language of ancient Mesopotamia **2 :** one of a Semitic people inhabiting central Mesopotamia before 2000 B.C. — **Akkadian** *adj*

al- — see AD-

[1]**-al** \əl, ᵊl\ *adj suffix* **:** of, relating to, or characterized by ⟨direction*al*⟩ ⟨fiction*al*⟩ [Latin *-alis*]

[2]**-al** *n suffix* **:** action **:** process ⟨rehears*al*⟩ [Medieval French *-aille,* from Latin *-alia,* neuter plural of *-alis*]

ala \ˈā-lə\ *n, pl* **alae** \-ˌlē\ **:** a wing-shaped anatomical process or part **:** WING [Latin] — **alar** \ˈā-lər\ *adj* — **ala·ry** \-lə-rē\ *adj*

à la *also* **a la** \ˌä-ˌlä, ˌä-lə, ˌa-lə\ *prep* **:** in the manner of [French *à la*]

al·a·bas·ter \ˈal-ə-ˌbas-tər\ *n* **1 :** a compact fine-textured usually white and translucent gypsum that is carved into objects (as vases) **2 :** a hard compact calcite that is translucent and sometimes banded [Latin *alabaster* "vase of alabaster," from Greek *alabastros*]

à la carte *also* **a la carte** \ˌä-lə-ˈkärt, ˌa-\ *adj or adv* **:** according to a menu or list that prices each item separately ⟨an *à la carte* dinner⟩ [French *à la carte* "by the bill of fare"]

alack \ə-ˈlak\ *interj, archaic* — used to express sorrow, regret, or reproach [Middle English]

alac·ri·ty \ə-ˈlak-rət-ē\ *n* **:** promptness in response **:** a cheerful readiness to do something [Latin *alacritas,* from *alacer* "lively, eager"] ***synonyms*** see CELERITY — **alac·ri·tous** \-rət-əs\ *adj*

à la mode *also* **a la mode** \ˌä-lə-ˈmōd, ˌal-\ *adj* **1 :** FASHIONABLE, STYLISH **2 :** topped with ice cream ⟨pie *à la mode*⟩ [French *à la mode* "according to the fashion"]

al·a·nine \ˈal-ə-ˌnēn\ *n* **:** an amino acid $C_3H_7NO_2$ formed especially by the hydrolysis of proteins [German *Alanin,* derived from *Aldehyd* "aldehyde"]

¹alarm \ə-ˈlärm\ *also* **alar·um** \ə-ˈlär-əm, -ˈlar-\ *n* **1** *usually alarum, archaic* **:** a call to arms **2 a :** a signal (as a loud noise or flashing light) that warns or alerts **b :** a device that warns or signals **3 :** fear caused by a sudden sense of danger [Medieval French *alarme,* from Italian *all'arme* "to arms"]

²alarm *also* **alarum** *vt* **1 :** to notify of danger **:** put on the alert **2 :** to strike with fear **:** FRIGHTEN **3 :** to equip with an alarm ⟨*alarm* the car⟩ — **alarm·ing·ly** \-ˈlär-miŋ-lē\ *adv*

alarm clock *n* **:** a clock that can be set to sound an alarm at a desired time

alarm·ist \ə-ˈlär-məst\ *n* **:** one inclined to alarm others especially needlessly — **alarm·ism** \-ˌmiz-əm\ *n*

alas \ə-ˈlas\ *interj* — used to express unhappiness, pity, or concern [Medieval French, from *a* "ah" + *las* "weary," from Latin *lassus*]

Alas·kan malamute \ə-ˈlas-kən-\ *n* **:** any of a breed of powerful heavy-coated working dogs of Alaskan origin with erect ears, heavily cushioned feet, and bushy tail

Alas·ka time \ə-ˈlas-kə-\ *n* **:** the time of the 9th time zone west of Greenwich that includes most of Alaska

alate \ˈā-ˌlāt\ *adj* **:** having wings or a winglike part [Latin *alatus,* from *ala* "wing"]

alb \ˈalb\ *n* **:** a full-length white linen vestment with long sleeves worn by a priest at Mass [Medieval Latin *alba,* from Latin *albus* "white"]

al·ba·core \ˈal-bə-ˌkōr, -ˌkȯr\ *n, pl* **-core** *or* **-cores :** a large pelagic tuna with long pectoral fins that is the source of most canned tuna; *also* **:** any of several other tunas [Portuguese *albacor,* from Arabic *al-bakūra* "the albacore"]

Al·ba·nian \al-ˈbā-nē-ən, -nyən\ *n* **1 :** a native or inhabitant of Albania **2 :** the Indo-European language of the Albanian people — **Albanian** *adj*

al·ba·tross \ˈal-bə-ˌtrȯs, -ˌträs\ *n, pl* **-tross** *or* **-tross·es :** any of various large web-footed seabirds that are related to the petrels and include the birds of the sea with the greatest wingspread [probably alteration of *alcatras* "frigate bird," from Portuguese or Spanish *alcatraz* "pelican"]

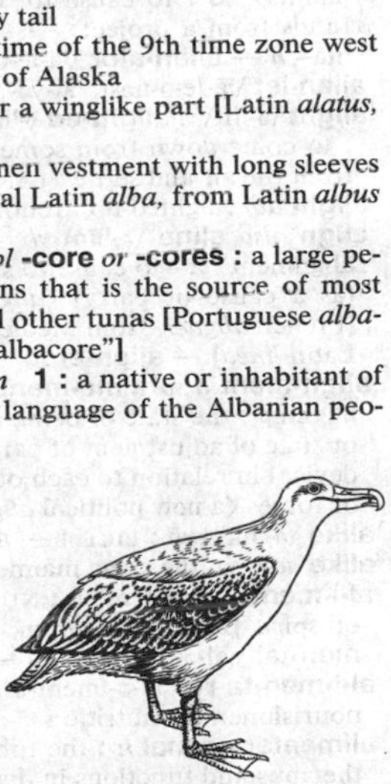

albatross

al·be·do \al-ˈbēd-ō\ *n* **:** the fraction of incident radiant energy reflected from a surface (as of the earth) [Late Latin, "whiteness," from Latin *albus* "white"]

al·be·it \ȯl-ˈbē-ət, al-\ *conj* **:** even though **:** ALTHOUGH [Middle English, literally, "all though it be"]

al·bi·no \al-ˈbī-nō\ *n, pl* **-nos :** an organism deficient in coloring matter; *esp* **:** a human being or animal that is congenitally deficient in pigment and usually has a milky or translucent skin, white or colorless hair, and eyes with pink or blue iris and deep red pupil [Portuguese, from Spanish, from *albo* "white," from Latin *albus*] — **al·bi·nism** \ˈal-bə-ˌniz-əm, al-ˈbī-\ *n* — **al·bi·nis·tic** \ˌal-bə-ˈnis-tik\ *adj* — **albino** *adj* — **al·bi·not·ic** \ˌal-bə-ˈnät-ik, -ˌbī-\ *adj*

al·bite \ˈal-ˌbīt\ *n* **:** a usually white feldspar containing sodium [Swedish *albit,* from Latin *albus* "white"]

al·bum \ˈal-bəm\ *n* **1 a :** a book with blank pages used for a collection (as of photographs) **b :** a container for a phonograph record **c :** one or more recordings (as on tape or disc) produced as a single unit **2 :** a collection usually in book form of literary selections, musical compositions, or pictures **:** ANTHOLOGY [Latin, "white tablet," from *albus* "white"]

al·bu·men \al-ˈbyü-mən\ *n* **1 :** the white of an egg **2 :** ALBUMIN [Latin, from *albus* "white"]

al·bu·min \al-ˈbyü-mən\ *n* **:** any of numerous heat-coagulable water-soluble proteins found especially in blood plasma, the whites of eggs, and various animal and plant tissues [Latin *albumen* "white of an egg"]

al·bu·min·ous \al-ˈbyü-mə-nəs\ *adj* **:** relating to, containing, or having the properties of albumen or albumin

al·ca·zar \al-ˈkäz-ər, -kaz-\ *n* **:** a Spanish fortress or palace [Spanish *alcázar,* from Arabic *al-qaṣr* "the castle"]

al·che·my \ˈal-kə-mē\ *n* **1 :** a medieval chemical science and philosophy aiming to achieve the conversion of base metals into gold, the discovery of a universal cure for disease, and the discovery of a means of indefinitely prolonging life **2 :** a power or process of transforming something common into something precious [Medieval Latin *alchymia,* from Arabic *al-kīmiyā'* "the alchemy," from Late Greek *chēmeia* "alchemy"] — **al·chem·i·cal** \al-ˈkem-i-kəl\ *adj* — **al·chem·i·cal·ly** \-kə-lē, -klē\ *adv* — **al·che·mist** \ˈal-kə-məst\ *n*

al·co·hol \ˈal-kə-ˌhȯl\ *n* **1 a :** ethanol especially when used as the substance in fermented or distilled liquors (as beer or whiskey) that can make one drunk **b :** any of various carbon compounds that are similar to ethanol in having one or more hydroxyl groups **2 :** drink (as beer, wine, or whiskey) containing ethanol [Medieval Latin, "powdered antimony," from Spanish, from Arabic *al-kuḥul* "the powdered antimony"]

¹al·co·hol·ic \ˌal-kə-ˈhȯl-ik, -ˈhäl-\ *adj* **1 :** of, relating to, caused by, or containing alcohol **2 :** affected with alcoholism — **al·co·hol·i·cal·ly** \-i-kə-lē, -klē\ *adv*

²alcoholic *n* **:** a person affected with alcoholism

al·co·hol·ism \ˈal-kə-ˌhȯ-ˌliz-əm\ *n* **:** continued excessive and usually uncontrollable use of alcoholic drinks; *also* **:** the abnormal state associated with such use

al·cove \ˈal-ˌkōv\ *n* **1 :** a small recessed section of a room **:** NOOK **2 :** an arched opening (as in a wall) [French *alcôve,* from Spanish *alcoba,* from Arabic *al-qubba* "the arch"]

Al·deb·a·ran \al-ˈdeb-ə-rən\ *n* **:** a red star that is seen in the eye of Taurus and is the brightest star in the Hyades [Arabic *al-dabaran,* literally, "the follower"]

al·de·hyde \ˈal-də-ˌhīd\ *n* **1 :** ACETALDEHYDE **2 :** any of various highly reactive organic compounds typified by acetaldehyde and characterized by the group –CHO [German *Aldehyd,* from New Latin *al. dehyd.,* abbreviation of *alcohol dehydrogenatum* "dehydrogenated alcohol"]

al·der \ˈȯl-dər\ *n* **:** any of a genus of toothed-leaved trees or shrubs that bear catkins, are related to the birches, and that grow especially in moist ground [Old English *alor*]

al·der·man \ˈȯl-dər-mən\ *n* **1 :** a high Anglo-Saxon government official **2 :** a member of a governing or legislative body of some counties, cities, towns, or boroughs [Old English *ealdorman,* from *ealdor* "elder, parent"] — **al·der·man·ic** \ˌȯl-dər-ˈman-ik\ *adj*

al·der·wom·an \-ˌwu̇m-ən\ *n* **:** a female member of a legislative body of some counties, cities, towns, or boroughs

al·dol·ase \ˈal-də-ˌlās, -ˌlāz\ *n* **:** an enzyme of living things that catalyzes reversibly the cleavage of a fructose ester into sugars with three carbon atoms [*aldehyde* + *-ol* + *-ase*]

al·do·ste·rone \al-ˈdäs-tə-ˌrōn, ˌal-dō-stə-ˈrōn\ *n* **:** a steroid hormone of the adrenal cortex that functions in the regulation of the salt and water balance of the body [derived from *aldehyde* + *sterol*]

al·drin \ˈȯl-drən, ˈal-\ *n* **:** a very poisonous formerly used insecticide $C_{12}H_8Cl_6$ [Kurt *Alder,* died 1958, German chemist]

ale \ˈāl\ *n* **1 :** an alcoholic beverage brewed from malt and hops that is usually heavier bodied and more bitter than beer **2 :** an

\ə\ abut	\au̇\ **out**	\i\ **tip**	\ȯ\ **saw**	\u̇\ **foot**
\ər\ **further**	\ch\ **chin**	\ī\ **life**	\ȯi\ **coin**	\y\ **yet**
\a\ **mat**	\e\ **pet**	\j\ **job**	\th\ **thin**	\yü\ **few**
\ā\ **take**	\ē\ **easy**	\ŋ\ **sing**	\t͟h\ **this**	\yu̇\ **cure**
\ä\ **cot, cart**	\g\ **go**	\ō\ **bone**	\ü\ **food**	\zh\ **vision**

English country festival at which ale is the chief beverage [Old English *ealu*]

alee \ə-ˈlē\ *adv* **:** on or toward the lee

ale·house \ˈāl-ˌhau̇s\ *n* **:** a place where ale is sold to be drunk on the premises

alem·bic \ə-ˈlem-bik\ *n* **:** an apparatus formerly used in distillation [Medieval Latin *alembicum,* from Arabic *al-anbīq* "the still," derived from Greek *ambix* "cap of a still"]

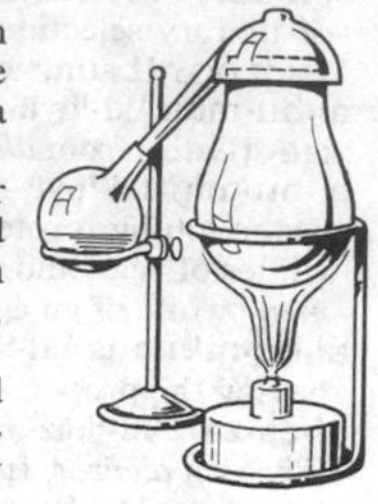
alembic

aleph–null \ˈäl-ˌef-ˈnəl, -əf-\ *n* **:** a number that is the smallest infinite number and that is equal to the number of elements in the set of all whole numbers [from *aleph,* the first letter of the Hebrew alphabet]

[1]**alert** \ə-ˈlərt\ *adj* **1 a :** watchful and prompt to meet danger **b :** quick to perceive and act **2 :** briskly active **:** LIVELY ⟨an *alert* movement⟩ [Italian *all'erta* "on the watch," literally, "on the height"] ***synonyms*** see CLEVER, WATCHFUL — **alert·ly** *adv* — **alert·ness** *n*

[2]**alert** *n* **1 :** a state of careful watching and readiness especially for danger or opportunity ⟨on 24-hour *alert*⟩ **2 :** a signal of danger **3 :** the period during which an alert is in effect

[3]**alert** *vt* **:** to call to a state of readiness **:** WARN

al·eu·rone \ˈal-yə-ˌrōn\ *n* **:** granular protein matter in the endosperm of a seed [Greek *aleuron* "flour"]

Aleut \ə-ˈlüt\ *n* **1 :** a member of a people of the Aleutian and Shumagin islands and the western part of the Alaska Peninsula **2 :** the language of the Aleuts [Russian]

A level *n* **:** the second of three standardized British examinations in a secondary school subject used as qualification for university entrance; *also* **:** successful completion of an A-level examination in a particular subject — called also *Advanced level;* compare O LEVEL, S LEVEL

ale·wife \ˈāl-ˌwīf\ *n* **:** a typically anadromous food fish of the Atlantic coast that is related to the herring

Al·ex·an·dri·an \ˌal-ig-ˈzan-drē-ən, ˌel-\ *adj* **:** HELLENISTIC [from the prominence of Alexandria, Egypt, in the intellectual and cultural life of the Hellenistic period]

al·ex·an·drine \-ˈzan-drən\ *n, often cap* **:** a line of poetry consisting of six iambic feet [Middle French *vers alexandrin,* literally, "verse of Alexander"; from its use in a poem on Alexander the Great]

al·fal·fa \al-ˈfal-fə\ *n* **:** a deep-rooted southwest Asian plant of the legume family with purple flowers and leaves like clover that is widely grown for hay and forage [Spanish, from Arabic dialect *al-faṣfaṣa* "the alfalfa"]

al·fres·co \al-ˈfres-kō\ *adv or adj* **:** in the open air ⟨an *alfresco* lunch⟩ [Italian]

al·ga \ˈal-gə\ *n, pl* **al·gae** \ˈal-jē\ **:** a plant or plantlike organism (as a seaweed) that includes forms mostly growing in water, lacking a vascular system, and having chlorophyll often masked by brown or red coloring matter [Latin, "seaweed"] — **al·gal** \ˈal-gəl\ *adj*

al·ge·bra \ˈal-jə-brə\ *n* **:** a branch of mathematics that is a generalization of arithmetic and in which numbers and letters representing numbers are combined according to the rules of arithmetic [Medieval Latin, from Arabic *al-jabr,* literally, "the reduction"] — **al·ge·bra·ist** \-ˌbrā-əst\ *n*

al·ge·bra·ic \ˌal-jə-ˈbrā-ik\ *adj* **1 :** of or relating to algebra ⟨*algebraic* expression⟩ **2 :** involving only a finite number of repetitions of addition, subtraction, multiplication, division, extraction of roots, and raising to powers — **al·ge·bra·i·cal·ly** \-ˈbrā-ə-kə-lē, -klē\ *adv*

-al·gia \ˈal-jē-ə, -jə\ *n combining form* **:** pain ⟨neur*algia*⟩ [Greek *algos*]

al·gin \ˈal-jən\ *n* **:** any of various colloidal substances from marine brown algae including some used especially as thickeners or emulsifiers

Al·gol \ˈal-ˌgäl, -ˌgȯl\ *n* **:** a binary star in the constellation Perseus whose larger component revolves about and eclipses the smaller brighter star causing periodic variation in brightness [Arabic *al-ghūl,* literally, "the ghoul"]

AL·GOL *or* **Al·gol** \ˈal-ˌgäl, -ˌgȯl\ *n* **:** a computer programming language used especially in mathematics and science [*algo*rithmic *l*anguage]

al·gol·o·gy \al-ˈgäl-ə-jē\ *n* **:** PHYCOLOGY

Al·gon·qui·an \al-ˈgän-kwē-ən, -ˈgäng-\ *n* **1 :** a family of American Indian languages spoken from Labrador to the Carolinas and westward to the Great Plains **2 :** a member of the peoples speaking Algonquian languages — **Algonquian** *adj*

al·go·rithm \ˈal-gə-ˌrit͟h-əm\ *n* **:** a step-by-step procedure for solving a problem (as finding the greatest common divisor) or accomplishing a goal that uses a limited number of steps and that often repeats sets of steps [Medieval Latin *algorismus,* from Arabic *al-khuwārizmi,* from *al-Khuwarizmi,* flourished 825 A.D., Islamic mathematician] — **al·go·rith·mic** \ˌal-gə-ˈrit͟h-mik\ *adj*

[1]**alias** \ˈā-lē-əs, ˈāl-yəs\ *adv* **:** otherwise called **:** otherwise known as ⟨John Doe *alias* Richard Roe⟩ [Latin, "otherwise," from *alius* "other"]

[2]**alias** *n* **:** an assumed name

[1]**al·i·bi** \ˈal-ə-ˌbī\ *n* **1 :** a plea made by a person accused of a crime of having been at another place when the crime occurred; *also* **:** the fact or state of having been elsewhere at the time **2 :** an excuse intended to avoid blame (as for failure) [Latin, "elsewhere," from *alius* "other"]

[2]**alibi** *vb* **-bied; -bi·ing 1 :** to offer an excuse **2 :** to make an excuse for ⟨tried to *alibi* for showing up late⟩

[1]**alien** \ˈā-lē-ən, ˈāl-yən\ *adj* **1 a :** belonging or relating to another person or place **:** STRANGE **b :** relating, belonging, or owing allegiance to another country **:** FOREIGN ⟨*alien* residents⟩ **c :** EXOTIC 1 **3 :** wholly different in nature or character ⟨an effect *alien* from the one intended⟩ **4 :** differing in nature or character typically to the point of incompatibility ⟨a detail *alien* to the argument⟩ [Latin *alienus,* from *alius* "other"]

[2]**alien** *n* **1 :** a person of another family, race, or nation **2 :** a foreign-born resident who has not been naturalized and is still a subject or citizen of a foreign country **3 :** an extraterrestrial being **4 :** EXOTIC

alien·able \ˈāl-yə-nə-bəl, ˈā-lē-ə-nə-\ *adj* **:** transferable to the ownership of another ⟨*alienable* property⟩ — **alien·abil·i·ty** \ˌāl-yə-nə-ˈbil-ət-ē, ˌā-lē-ə-nə-\ *n*

alien·ate \ˈā-lē-ə-ˌnāt, ˈāl-yə-ˌnāt\ *vt* **1 :** to transfer (as a title, property, or right) to another **2 :** to cause to lose feelings of love, loyalty, or attachment ⟨*alienated* by their constant complaints⟩ **3 :** to cause to be withdrawn or diverted ⟨*alienate* funds from a project⟩ — **alien·ation** \ˌā-lē-ə-ˈnā-shən, ˌāl-yə-ˈnā-\ *n* — **alien·ator** \ˈā-lē-ə-ˌnāt-ər, ˈāl-yə-ˌnāt-\ *n*

alien·ist \ˈā-lē-ə-nəst, ˈāl-yə-nəst\ *n* **:** PSYCHIATRIST

[1]**alight** \ə-ˈlīt\ *vi* **alight·ed** \-ˈlīt-əd\ *also* **alit** \ə-ˈlit\; **alight·ing 1 :** to come down from something **:** DISMOUNT **2 :** to descend from the air and settle **:** LAND

[2]**alight** *adj* **:** lighted up **:** ILLUMINATED

align *also* **aline** \ə-ˈlīn\ *vb* **1 :** to bring or come into line or alignment **2 :** to cause to support or to disapprove something (as a cause or party) ⟨*aligned* himself with the opposition⟩ [French *aligner,* from Medieval French, from *ligne* "line," from Latin *linea*] — **align·er** *n*

align·ment *also* **aline·ment** \ə-ˈlīn-mənt\ *n* **1 a :** the act of aligning **:** the state of being aligned **b :** the proper positioning or state of adjustment of parts (as of a mechanical or electronic device) in relation to each other **2 :** an arrangement of groups or forces ⟨a new political *alignment*⟩

[1]**alike** \ə-ˈlīk\ *adj* **:** LIKE 1 — **alike·ness** *n*

[2]**alike** *adv* **:** in the same manner, form, or degree

al·i·ment \ˈal-ə-mənt\ *n* **:** NUTRIMENT; *also* **:** food for the mind or spirit [Latin *alimentum,* from *alere* "to nourish"] — **al·i·men·tal** \ˌal-ə-ˈment-l\ *adj* — **al·i·men·tal·ly** \-l-ē\ *adv*

al·i·men·ta·ry \ˌal-ə-ˈment-ə-rē, -ˈmen-trē\ *adj* **:** of or relating to nourishment or nutrition

alimentary canal *n* **:** the tube that extends from the mouth to the anus and functions in digestion and absorption of food and in elimination of residual waste

al·i·mo·ny \ˈal-ə-ˌmō-nē\ *n, pl* **-nies :** an allowance of money made to one spouse by the other for support during or after legal separation or divorce [Latin *alimonia* "sustenance," from *alere* "to nourish"]

al·i·phat·ic \ˌal-ə-ˈfat-ik\ *adj* **:** belonging to a group of organic compounds whose structure is in the form of a chain whose ends are not joined [Greek *aleiphar* "oil"]

al·i·quot \ˈal-ə-ˌkwät, -kwət\ *adj* **:** contained an exact number of times in another ⟨5 is an *aliquot* part of 15⟩ [Medieval Latin *aliquotus,* from Latin *aliquot* "some, several"]

alive \ə-ˈlīv\ *adj* **1 :** having life **:** LIVING ⟨the proudest person *alive*⟩ **2 :** still in existence, force, or operation **:** ACTIVE ⟨keep hope *alive*⟩ **3 :** knowingly aware or conscious **:** SENSITIVE

⟨*alive* to the danger⟩ **4 :** filled with life, energy, or activity **:** SWARMING ⟨blossoms *alive* with bees⟩ — **alive·ness** *n*

aliz·a·rin \ə-ˈliz-ə-rən\ *n* **:** an orange or red crystalline compound $C_{14}H_8O_4$ made synthetically and used as a red dye and in making red pigments [probably from French *alizarine*]

al·ka·li \ˈal-kə-ˌlī\ *n, pl* **-lies** *or* **-lis** **1 :** a substance (as a hydroxide or carbonate of an alkali metal) having marked basic properties **2 :** ALKALI METAL **3 :** a soluble salt or a mixture of soluble salts present in some soils of arid regions [Medieval Latin, from Arabic *al-qili* "the soda ash"]

alkali metal *n* **:** any of the univalent mostly basic metals of the group lithium, sodium, potassium, rubidium, cesium, and francium

al·ka·line \ˈal-kə-ˌlīn, -lən\ *adj* **:** of, relating to, or having the properties of an alkali; *esp* **:** having a pH of more than 7 — **al·ka·lin·i·ty** \ˌal-kə-ˈlin-ət-ē\ *n*

alkaline battery *n* **:** a long-lasting battery containing alkaline chemicals

alkaline earth metal *n* **:** any of the strongly basic metals comprising beryllium, magnesium, calcium, strontium, barium, and radium — called also *alkaline earth*

al·ka·loid \ˈal-kə-ˌlȯid\ *n* **:** any of numerous usually colorless, complex, and bitter organic bases (as morphine or codeine) that contain nitrogen and usually oxygen and occur especially in seed plants — **al·ka·loi·dal** \ˌal-kə-ˈlȯid-l\ *adj*

al·kane \ˈal-ˌkān\ *n* **:** any of a series of compounds of carbon and hydrogen in which each carbon atom is attached to four other atoms [*alk*yl + *-ane*]

al·kyd \ˈal-kəd\ *n* **:** any of numerous synthetic resins that are used especially for protective coatings and in paint [blend of *alkyl* and *acid*]

al·kyl \ˈal-kəl\ *adj* **:** having or being an organic group derived especially from an alkane by removal of one hydrogen atom [probably from German, from *Alkohol* alcohol]

¹all \ˈȯl\ *adj* **1 a :** the whole of ⟨sat up *all* night⟩ **b :** the greatest possible ⟨told in *all* seriousness⟩ **2 :** every member or individual part of ⟨*all* students will go⟩ **3 :** the whole number or sum of ⟨*all* the angles of a triangle are equal to two right angles⟩ **4 :** EVERY ⟨*all* manner of hardship⟩ **5 :** any whatever ⟨beyond *all* doubt⟩ **6 a :** completely taken up with or absorbed by ⟨became *all* attention⟩ **b :** having or seeming to have a prominent physical feature ⟨*all* thumbs⟩ **c :** paying full attention with ⟨*all* ears⟩ **7 :** being more than one person or thing ⟨who *all* was there⟩ [Old English *eall*]

²all *adv* **1 a :** WHOLLY, ALTOGETHER ⟨sat *all* alone⟩ ⟨*all* across the country⟩ **b :** selected as the best (as at a sport) within an area or organization — used in combination ⟨*all*-league halfback⟩ **2** *obsolete* **:** ONLY 1b, SOLELY **3** *archaic* **:** quite as indicated **:** JUST **4 :** so much ⟨*all* the better for it⟩ **5 :** for each side **:** APIECE ⟨the score is two *all*⟩

³all *pron, sing or pl in construction* **1 a :** the whole number, quantity, or amount ⟨*all* that I have⟩ ⟨*all* of us⟩ **b** — used in such phrases as *for all I know, for all I care,* and *for all the good it does* to show a lack of knowledge, interest, or effectiveness **2 :** EVERYBODY, EVERYTHING ⟨sacrificed *all* for love⟩ ⟨known to *all*⟩ — **all in all :** on the whole ⟨*all in all,* it could be worse⟩ — **and all :** and everything else especially of a kind previously mentioned ⟨photographed, warts and *all*⟩

all- *or* **allo-** *combining form* **:** other **:** different **:** atypical ⟨*allo*tropy⟩ [Greek *allos* "other"]

¹al·la breve \ˌal-ə-ˈbrev, ˌäl-ə-ˈbrev-ˌā\ *adv or adj* **:** in duple or quadruple time with the beat represented by the half note [Italian, literally, "according to the breve"]

²alla breve *n* **:** the sign ¢ marking a piece or passage to be played alla breve; *also* **:** a passage so marked

Al·lah \ˈäl-ə, ˈal-ə, ˈäl-ˌä, ä-ˈlä\ *n* **:** GOD 1 — used in Islam [Arabic *Allāh*]

all along *adv* **:** all the time ⟨knew the truth *all along*⟩

all–Amer·i·can \ˌȯl-ə-ˈmer-ə-kən\ *adj* **1 :** representative of American ideals ⟨an *all-American* city⟩ **2 :** selected as the best in the U.S. ⟨the *all-American* team⟩ — **all–American** *n*

al·lan·to·is \ə-ˈlant-ə-wəs\ *n, pl* **al·lan·to·ides** \ˌal-ən-ˈtō-ə-ˌdēz\ **:** a fetal membrane of reptiles, birds, and mammals that is supplied with blood vessels and joins with the chorion in formation of the placenta in mammals [New Latin, derived from Greek *allas* "sausage"] — **al·lan·to·ic** \ˌal-ən-ˈtō-ik\ *adj*

al·lar·gan·do \ˌäl-ˌär-ˈgän-dō\ *adv or adj* **:** gradually slower with the same or greater volume — used as a direction in music [Italian, literally, "widening"]

all–around \ˌȯ-lə-ˈrau̇nd\ *also* **all–round** \ˈȯl-ˈrau̇nd\ *adj* **1 :** considered in or including all aspects ⟨the best *all-round* performance so far⟩ **2 :** competent in many fields ⟨an *all-around* performer⟩ **3 :** having general usefulness ⟨an *all-around* tool⟩ — **all around** *adv*

al·lay \ə-ˈlā\ *vt* **-layed; -lay·ing** **1 :** to make less severe **:** RELIEVE ⟨*allay* pain⟩ **2 :** CALM ⟨*allay* fears⟩ [Old English *ālecgan,* from *ā-,* prefix denoting completion + *lecgan* "to lay"]

all but *adv* **:** very nearly **:** ALMOST ⟨would be *all but* impossible⟩

all clear *n* **:** a signal that a danger has passed

al·le·ga·tion \ˌal-i-ˈgā-shən\ *n* **1 :** the act of alleging **2 :** something alleged; *esp* **:** an assertion unsupported by proof

al·lege \ə-ˈlej\ *vt* **1 :** to assert without offering proof ⟨*alleged* he was guilty⟩ **2 :** to offer as a reason or an excuse ⟨*allege* illness to avoid work⟩ [Medieval French *aleger* "to submit as evidence, adduce," probably from Medieval Latin *allegare,* from Latin, "to send as a representative, adduce in support of a plea," from *ad-* + *legare* "to depute"]

al·leged \ə-ˈlejd, -ˈlej-əd\ *adj* **:** said or thought to be so without proof ⟨the *alleged* criminal⟩ — **al·leg·ed·ly** \ə-ˈlej-əd-lē\ *adv*

al·le·giance \ə-ˈlē-jəns\ *n* **1 :** loyalty and obedience owed to one's country or government **2 :** devotion or loyalty to a person, group, or cause [Medieval French *allegeance,* from *ligeance,* from *lige* "liege"] ***synonyms*** see FIDELITY

al·le·go·rize \ˈal-ə-ˌgōr-ˌīz, -ˌgȯr-, -gər-\ *vt* **1 :** to make into allegory **2 :** to treat or explain as allegory — **al·le·go·ri·za·tion** \ˌal-ə-ˌgōr-ə-ˈzā-shən, -ˌgȯr-\ *n* — **al·le·go·riz·er** *n*

al·le·go·ry \ˈal-ə-ˌgōr-ē, -ˌgȯr-\ *n, pl* **-ries :** a story in which the characters and events are symbols expressing truths about human life [Latin *allegoria,* from Greek *allēgoria,* from *allēgorein* "to speak figuratively," from *allos* "other" + *-ēgorein* "to speak," from *agora* "public assembly"] — **al·le·gor·i·cal** \ˌal-ə-ˈgȯr-i-kəl, -ˈgär-\ *adj* — **al·le·gor·i·cal·ly** \-kə-lē, -klē\ *adv*

al·le·gret·to \ˌal-ə-ˈgret-ō, ˌäl-\ *adv or adj* **:** faster than andante but not so fast as allegro — used as a direction in music [Italian, from *allegro*]

¹al·le·gro \ə-ˈleg-rō, -ˈlā-grō\ *n, pl* **-gros :** a piece of music in allegro tempo

²allegro *adv or adj* **:** in a brisk lively manner — used as a direction in music [Italian, literally, "merry," derived from Latin *alacer* "lively"]

al·lele \ə-ˈlēl\ *n* **:** any of the several forms of a gene that may occupy identical places on homologous chromosomes and which determine alternate forms of one or more genetic traits [German *Allel,* short for *Allelomorph,* from Greek *allēlōn* "of one another" + *morphē* "form"] — **al·le·lic** \-ˈlē-lik, -ˈlel-ik\ *adj*

al·le·lop·a·thy \ə-ˈlē-lə-ˌpath-ē, -ˈlel-ə-\ *n* **:** the suppression of growth of one plant species by another due to the release of toxic substances [*allelo-* "reciprocal" (from Greek *allēlōn* "of another") + *-pathy*]

al·le·lu·ia \ˌal-ə-ˈlü-yə\ *interj* **:** HALLELUJAH

Al·len wrench \ˈa-lən-\ *n* **:** an L-shaped hexagonal metal bar used to turn a screw or bolt [*Allen* Manufacturing Co., Hartford, Conn.]

al·ler·gen \ˈal-ər-jən\ *n* **:** a substance (as pollen) that induces allergy — **al·ler·gen·ic** \ˌal-ər-ˈjen-ik\ *adj*

al·ler·gic \ə-ˈlər-jik\ *adj* **1 :** of, relating to, affected with, or caused by allergy ⟨an *allergic* reaction⟩ ⟨*allergic* to cat fur⟩ **2 :** having a dislike for ⟨*allergic* to hard work⟩

al·ler·gist \ˈal-ər-jəst\ *n* **:** a specialist in treating allergies

al·ler·gy \ˈal-ər-jē\ *n, pl* **-gies** **1 :** exaggerated or abnormal immunological reaction (as by sneezing, itching, or rashes) to substances, situations, or physical states that do not have such a strong effect on most people **2 :** a feeling of dislike [German *Allergie,* from Greek *allos* "other" + *ergon* "work"]

allergy shot *n* **:** an injection containing very small amounts of an allergen (such as mold or grass pollen) to which an individual is sensitive that is given at regular intervals usually over a period of several years to desensitize the immune system and reduce allergic symptoms

al·le·vi·ate \ə-ˈlē-vē-ˌāt\ *vt* **1 :** to make more bearable : RELIEVE ⟨*alleviate* pain⟩ **2 :** to remove or correct in part ⟨*alleviate* a labor shortage⟩ [Late Latin *alleviare,* from *ad-* + *levis* "light"] ***synonyms*** see RELIEVE — **al·le·vi·a·tion** \ə-ˌlē-vē-ˈā-shən\ *n* — **al·le·vi·a·tive** \ə-ˈlē-vē-ˌāt-iv\ *adj*

[1]**al·ley** \ˈal-ē\ *n, pl* **al·leys 1 :** a garden or park walk bordered by trees or bushes **2 :** a place for bowling or skittles; *esp* **:** a hardwood lane for bowling **3 :** a narrow street or passageway between buildings; *esp* **:** one giving access to the rear of buildings [Medieval French *alee,* from *aler* "to go"]

[2]**alley** *n, pl* **alleys :** a playing marble of superior quality [from *alabaster*]

alley cat *n* **:** a stray cat

al·ley·way \ˈal-ē-ˌwā\ *n* **1 :** a narrow passageway **2 :** ALLEY 3

All Fools' Day *n* **:** APRIL FOOLS' DAY

all fours *n pl* **:** all four legs of a four-legged animal or the two legs and two arms of a person ⟨down on *all fours*⟩

all get–out \ˌȯl-ˈget-ˌau̇t; -get-ˈau̇t, -git-\ *n* **:** the highest degree ⟨talented as *all get-out*⟩

all hail *interj* — used to express greeting or acclamation

All·hal·lows \ȯl-ˈhal-ōz, -əz\ *n* **:** ALL SAINTS' DAY

all hours *n pl* **:** a very late time ⟨stayed up until *all hours*⟩

al·li·ance \ə-ˈlī-əns\ *n* **1 a :** the state of being allied **b :** a bond or connection between families, parties, or individuals **2 a :** an association (as by treaty) of two or more nations to further their common interests **b :** a treaty of alliance

al·lied \ə-ˈlīd, ˈal-ˌīd\ *adj* **1 :** joined together ⟨two families *allied* by marriage⟩ **2 a :** joined in alliance especially by treaty ⟨*allied* nations⟩ **b** *cap* **:** of or relating to the nations united against Germany and its allies in World War I or World War II **3 :** related especially by common properties, characteristics, or ancestry ⟨chemistry and *allied* subjects⟩

al·li·ga·tor \ˈal-ə-ˌgāt-ər\ *n* **1 :** either of two large short-legged reptiles resembling crocodiles but having a shorter and broader snout **2 :** leather made from alligator's hide [Spanish *el lagarto* "the lizard"]

alligator 1

alligator clip *n* **:** a clip that has jaws resembling an alligator's and is used to make temporary electrical connections

alligator pear *n* **:** AVOCADO

all–im·por·tant \ˌȯ-lim-ˈpȯrt-nt, -ənt\ *adj* **:** of very great importance

al·lit·er·ate \ə-ˈlit-ə-ˌrāt\ *vb* **1 :** to form an alliteration **2 :** to arrange so as to make alliteration

al·lit·er·a·tion \ə-ˌlit-ə-ˈrā-shən\ *n* **:** the repetition of a sound at the beginning of two or more neighboring words (as in *wild and woolly* or *a babbling brook*) [*ad-* + Latin *littera* "letter"] — **al·lit·er·a·tive** \ə-ˈlit-ə-ˌrāt-iv, -rət-\ *adj* — **al·lit·er·a·tive·ly** *adv*

al·li·um \ˈa-lē-əm\ *n* **:** any of a genus of bulbous herbs related to the lilies and including the onion, garlic, chive, and leek [Latin, "garlic"]

allo- — see ALL-

al·lo·cate \ˈal-ə-ˌkāt\ *vt* **1 :** to divide and distribute for a specific purpose or among particular persons or things ⟨*allocate* funds among charities⟩ **2 :** to set aside for a particular purpose ⟨*allocate* materials for a project⟩ [Medieval Latin *allocare,* from *ad-* + *locare* "to place," from *locus* "place"] ***synonyms*** see ALLOT — **al·lo·ca·tion** \ˌal-ə-ˈkā-shən\ *n*

al·lo·path·ic \ˌal-ə-ˈpath-ik\ *adj* **:** relating to or being a system of medicine that aims to combat disease by using remedies (as drugs or surgery) which produce effects different from or incompatible with those of the disease being treated [German *Allopathie* "an allopathic system of medicine," from *allo-* "all-" + *-pathie* "-pathy"]

al·lo·pat·ric \ˌal-ə-ˈpat-rik\ *adj* **:** occurring in different geographical areas or in isolation ⟨*allopatric* speciation⟩ — compare SYMPATRIC [*all-* + Greek *patra* "fatherland," from *patēr* "father"]

al·lo·phone \ˈal-ə-ˌfōn\ *n* **:** one of two or more variants of the same phoneme ⟨the \t\ of *tip* and the \t\ of *pit* are *allophones* of the phoneme \t\⟩ — **al·lo·phon·ic** \ˌal-ə-ˈfän-ik\ *adj*

all–or–none \ˌȯ-lər-ˈnən\ *adj* **:** marked either by entire or complete operation or effect or by none at all

al·lo·sau·rus \ˌal-ə-ˈsȯr-əs\ *n* **:** any of a genus of very large carnivorous North American dinosaurs of the Jurassic period that had small forelegs, walked on the hind legs, and were related to the tyrannosaurus [Greek *allo-* "all-" + *sauros* "lizard"]

al·lot \ə-ˈlät\ *vt* **al·lot·ted; al·lot·ting :** to assign as a share or portion : ALLOCATE ⟨*allot* 10 minutes for each speech⟩ [Medieval French *aloter,* from *a-* "ad-" + *lot* "lot," of Germanic origin]

synonyms ALLOT, APPORTION, ALLOCATE mean to give as one's share. ALLOT may imply haphazard or arbitrary distribution ⟨*allotted* himself an hour daily for exercise⟩. APPORTION implies a dividing according to some regular principle ⟨*apportioned* a share to each person⟩. ALLOCATE implies a fixed appropriation for a particular use ⟨*allocated* tasks among the workers⟩.

al·lot·ment \ə-ˈlät-mənt\ *n* **1 :** the act of allotting **2 :** something that is allotted

al·lot·ro·py \ə-ˈlä-trə-pē\ *n* **:** the existence of a chemical element in two or more different forms in the same phase that show different chemical or physical properties ⟨diamond and graphite show the *allotropy* of carbon⟩ [Greek *tropos* "turn, manner"] — **al·lo·trope** \ˈal-ə-ˌtrōp\ *n* — **al·lo·trop·ic** \ˌal-ə-ˈträp-ik\ *adj*

all–out \ˈȯ-ˈlau̇t\ *adj* **:** made with maximum effort : EXTREME ⟨an *all-out* effort to win⟩

all out *adv* **:** with maximum effort ⟨go *all out*⟩

all·over \ˈȯ-ˌlō-vər\ *adj* **:** covering the whole extent or surface

[1]**all over** *adv* **1 :** over the whole extent **2 :** EVERYWHERE ⟨looked *all over* for my glasses⟩ **3 :** in every respect : THOROUGHLY ⟨she is her mother *all over*⟩

[2]**all over** *prep* **1 :** in eagerly affectionate, attentive, or aggressive pursuit of ⟨the band's fans were *all over* them⟩ **2 :** in or into a state marked by all-out criticism of ⟨reporters were *all over* the coach after the loss⟩

al·low \ə-ˈlau̇\ *vb* **1 a :** to assign as a share or suitable amount (as of time or money) **b :** to allot as a deduction or an addition ⟨*allow* a gallon for leakage⟩ **2 :** ADMIT 3, CONCEDE ⟨*allowed* that the situation was serious⟩ **3 a :** PERMIT ⟨gaps *allow* passage⟩ ⟨refused to *allow* smoking⟩ **b :** to fail to restrain or prevent : LET ⟨*allow* the roast to burn⟩ **4 :** to make allowance ⟨*allow* for growth⟩ [Medieval French *alouer* "to place, apportion, allow," from Medieval Latin *allocare*] ***synonyms*** see LET — **al·low·able** \-ə-bəl\ *adj* — **al·low·ably** \-blē\ *adv*

al·low·ance \ə-ˈlau̇-əns\ *n* **1 a :** a share or portion allotted or granted **b :** a sum granted ⟨a weekly *allowance*⟩ ⟨*allowance* for expenses⟩ **c :** a reduction from a list price or stated price ⟨a trade-in *allowance*⟩ **2 :** an allowed dimensional difference between mating parts of a machine **3 :** the act of allowing : PERMISSION **4 :** the taking into account of things that may partly excuse an offense or mistake ⟨make *allowances* for inexperience⟩

[1]**al·loy** \ˈal-ˌȯi, ə-ˈlȯi\ *n* **:** a substance composed of two or more metals or of a metal and a nonmetal united usually by being melted together [French *aloi,* from Medieval French, from *aloier, alier* "to ally, combine," from Latin *alligare* "to bind"]

[2]**al·loy** \ə-ˈlȯi, ˈal-ˌȯi\ *vt* **1 :** to reduce the purity of by mixing with a less valuable metal **2 :** to mix so as to form an alloy **3 :** to debase by admixture

all–pur·pose \ˈȯl-ˈpər-pəs\ *adj* **:** suitable for many uses ⟨*all-purpose* flour⟩

[1]**all right** *adj* **1 :** SATISFACTORY, CORRECT **2 :** SAFE, WELL

[2]**all right** *adv* **1** — used interjectionally especially to express agreement or acceptance or to indicate the resumption of a discussion ⟨*all right,* I'll be there⟩ **2 :** beyond doubt : CERTAINLY ⟨that's fast, *all right*⟩ **3 :** reasonably well ⟨does *all right* in school⟩

all–round *variant of* ALL-AROUND

All Saints' Day *n* **:** November 1 observed as a church festival in honor of the saints

All Souls' Day *n* **:** November 2 observed in some churches as a day of prayer for the souls of the faithful departed

all·spice \ˈȯl-ˌspīs\ *n* **:** the berry of a West Indian tree of the myrtle family; *also* **:** a mildly pungent and aromatic spice prepared from the dried berries

all–star \ˌȯl-ˌstär\ *adj* **:** made up chiefly or entirely of stars ⟨an *all-star* cast⟩ ⟨an *all-star* team⟩ — **all–star** \ˈȯl-ˌstär\ *n*

all–terrain vehicle *n* **:** a small motor vehicle with three or four wheels for use on various types of terrain

all told *adv* **:** with everything or everyone counted : in all

al·lude \ə-'lüd\ *vi* : to make indirect reference ⟨the sequel *alludes* to scenes in the earlier book⟩ [Latin *alludere,* literally, "to play with," from *ad-* + *ludere* "to play"] ***synonyms*** see REFER

[1]al·lure \ə-'lu̇r\ *vt* : to attract by something tempting or fascinating — **al·lure·ment** \-mənt\ *n*

[2]allure *n* : power of attraction : CHARM

al·lu·sion \ə-'lü-zhən\ *n* **1** : an implied or indirect reference **2** : the act of alluding to or hinting at something [Late Latin *alludere* "to play with"] — **al·lu·sive** \ə-'lü-siv, -ziv\ *adj* — **al·lu·sive·ly** *adv* — **al·lu·sive·ness** *n*

al·lu·vi·al \ə-'lü-vē-əl\ *adj* : relating to, composed of, or found in alluvium

al·lu·vi·um \-vē-əm\ *n, pl* **-vi·ums** *or* **-via** \-vē-ə\ : soil material (as clay, silt, sand, or gravel) deposited by running water [Late Latin, from Latin *alluere* "to wash against," from *ad-* + *lavere* "to wash"]

all–wheel \'ȯl-'hwēl, -'wēl\ *adj* : supplying power to turn each of the four wheels of an automotive vehicle ⟨*all-wheel* drive⟩

[1]al·ly \ə-'lī, 'al-ˌī\ *vb* **al·lied; al·ly·ing 1** : to form (as by marriage or treaty) a connection or relation between : join in an alliance : UNITE **2** : to form (as by likeness or compatibility) a relation between [Medieval French *alier,* from Latin *alligare* "to bind to," from *ad-* + *ligare* "to bind"]

[2]al·ly \'al-ˌī, ə-'lī\ *n, pl* **al·lies 1** : a plant or animal linked to another by genetic or evolutionary relationship ⟨ferns and their *allies*⟩ **2 a** : one associated or united with another for a common purpose **b** *pl, cap* : the Allied nations in World War I or World War II

-al·ly \ə-lē, lē\ *adv suffix* : [2]-LY ⟨terrific*ally*⟩ — in adverbs formed from adjectives in *-ic* with no alternative form in *-ical* [[1]*-al* + *-ly*]

al·ma ma·ter \ˌal-mə-'mät-ər\ *n* : a school, college, or university that one has attended [Latin, "fostering mother"]

al·ma·nac \'ȯl-mə-ˌnak, 'al-\ *n* **1** : a publication containing astronomical and meteorological data arranged according to the days, weeks, and months of the year and often including various other information **2** : an annual publication containing statistical and general information [Medieval Latin *almanach,* probably from Arabic *al-manākh* "the almanac"]

al·man·dine \'al-mən-ˌdēn\ *n* : ALMANDITE

al·man·dite \-ˌdīt\ *n* : a deep red garnet containing iron and aluminum [derived from Medieval Latin *alabandina,* from *Alabanda,* ancient city in Asia Minor]

al·mighty \ȯl-'mīt-ē\ *adj* **1** *often cap* : having absolute power over all ⟨*Almighty* God⟩ **2 a** : relatively unlimited in power ⟨an *almighty* board of directors⟩ **b** : having or regarded as having great power or importance ⟨the *almighty* dollar⟩ **3** : MIGHTY — used as an intensive ⟨an *almighty* shock⟩

Almighty *n* : GOD 1 — used with *the*

al·mond \'äm-ənd, 'am-; 'al-mənd, 'äl-\ *n* : a small tree related to the roses and having flowers similar to a peach tree; *also* : the edible kernel of its fruit used as a nut [Medieval French *alemande,* from Late Latin *amandula,* from Latin *amygdala,* from Greek *amygdalē*]

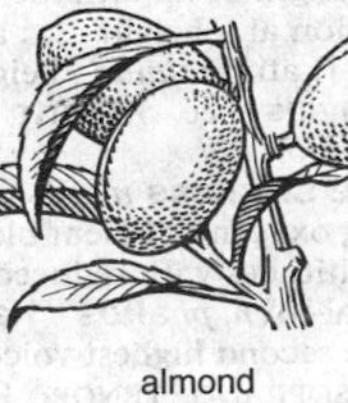

almond

almond eye *n* : a somewhat triangular obliquely set eye — **al·mond–eyed** \-'īd\ *adj*

al·mo·ner \'al-mə-nər, 'äm-ə-\ *n* : a person who distributes alms [Medieval French *almener,* from *aumone* "alms," from Late Latin *eleemosyna*]

al·most \'ȯl-ˌmōst, ȯl-'\ *adv* : only a little less than : NEARLY

alms \'ämz, 'älmz\ *n, pl* **alms** : something (as money) given to help the poor [Old English *ælmesse,* from Late Latin *eleemosyna,* from Greek *eleēmosynē* "pity, alms"] — **alms·giv·er** \-ˌgiv-ər\ *n* — **alms·giv·ing** \-ˌgiv-ing\ *n*

alms·house \-ˌhau̇s\ *n* : POORHOUSE

al·ni·co \'al-ni-ˌkō\ *n* : a powerful permanent-magnet alloy containing iron, nickel, aluminum, and one or more of the elements cobalt, copper, and titanium [*al*uminum + *ni*ckel + *co*balt]

al·oe \'al-ō\ *n* **1** : any of a large genus of succulent chiefly southern African plants related to the lilies with spikes of often showy flowers **2** *usually pl* : the dried bitter juice of the leaves of an aloe used especially formerly as a purgative and tonic **3** : ALOE VERA [Late Latin, from Latin, "dried juice of aloe leaves," from Greek *aloē*]

aloe vera \-'ver-ə, -'vir-ə\ *n* : an aloe plant with leaves containing a gelatinous substance soothing to the skin; *also* : such a substance or a preparation consisting mostly of such a substance [New Latin, literally, "true aloe"]

aloft \ə-'lȯft\ *adv or adj* **1** : at or to a great height **2** : in the air; *esp* : in flight **3** : at, on, or to the masthead or the higher rigging of a ship [Old Norse *ā lopt,* from *ā* "in" + *lopt* "air"]

alo·ha \ə-'lō-ə, ä-, -ˌhä\ *interj* — used to express greeting or farewell [Hawaiian *aloha* "love"]

[1]alone \ə-'lōn\ *adj* **1** : separated from others : ISOLATED ⟨*alone* in my room⟩ **2** : exclusive of anyone or anything else ⟨I *alone* know the secret⟩ [Middle English, from *al* "all" + *one* "one"]

synonyms ALONE, LONELY, LONESOME mean isolated from others. ALONE stresses the objective fact of being entirely by oneself ⟨everyone needs to be *alone* sometimes⟩. LONELY adds the suggestion of longing for companionship ⟨felt *lonely* with no other children around⟩. LONESOME may add an impression of being deserted or desolate ⟨an adopted dog no longer *lonesome* and forsaken⟩.

[2]alone *adv* **1** : without any other : SOLELY, EXCLUSIVELY ⟨the proof rests on that statement *alone*⟩ **2** : without company, aid, or support ⟨I'd rather do it *alone*⟩

[1]along \ə-'lȯng\ *prep* **1** : in a line matching the length or direction of ⟨walk *along* the beach⟩; *also* : at a point or points on ⟨a house *along* the river⟩ **2** : in accordance with ⟨a new agreement *along* the lines of the first⟩ [Old English *andlang,* from *and-* "against" + *lang* "long"]

[2]along *adv* **1** : progressively onward ⟨hurry *along* toward home⟩ **2** : as a companion or associate ⟨brought the child *along*⟩ ⟨work *along* with colleagues⟩ **3** : at or to an advanced point ⟨plans are far *along*⟩ **4** : in addition : ALSO ⟨the bill came *along* with the package⟩ **5** : at or on hand ⟨had their umbrellas *along*⟩

along·shore \-ˌshōr, -ˌshȯr\ *adv or adj* : along the shore or coast

[1]along·side \-ˌsīd\ *adv* : along or close at the side : in parallel position ⟨a guard with a prisoner *alongside*⟩

[2]alongside *prep* : side by side with; *esp* : parallel to

[1]aloof \ə-'lüf\ *adv* : at a distance : out of involvement ⟨stood *aloof* from their quarrels⟩ [obsolete *aloof* "to windward"]

[2]aloof *adj* : removed or distant in interest or feeling : RESERVED ⟨a shy, *aloof* manner⟩ — **aloof·ly** *adv* — **aloof·ness** *n*

al·o·pe·cia \ˌa-lə-'pē-shē-ə\ *n* : loss of hair, wool, or feathers : BALDNESS [Greek *alōpekia* "mange, baldness," from *alōpēx* "fox"]

aloud \ə-'lau̇d\ *adv* **1** *archaic* : LOUDLY **2** : so as to be clearly heard ⟨read *aloud*⟩

alp \'alp\ *n* **1** : a high rugged mountain **2** : a mountain pasture [from *Alps,* mountain system of Europe]

al·paca \al-'pak-ə\ *n* **1** : a mammal with fine long woolly hair domesticated in Peru and related to the llama **2** : wool of the alpaca or a thin cloth made of it; *also* : a rayon or cotton imitation of this cloth [Spanish, from Aymara (American Indian language of the Central Andes) *allpaqa*]

alpaca 1

[1]al·pha \'al-fə\ *n* **1** : the 1st letter of the Greek alphabet — Α or α **2** : something that is first : BEGINNING **3** : the chief or brightest star of a constellation

[2]alpha *adj* : socially dominant especially in a group of animals ⟨an *alpha* male wolf⟩

al·pha·bet \'al-fə-ˌbet, -bət\ *n* **1** : the characters (as letters) of a written language arranged in their customary order **2** : a system of signs or signals that serve as equivalents for letters [Greek *alphabētos,* from *alpha* + *bēta* "beta"]

\ə\ **abut**	\au̇\ **out**	\i\ **tip**	\ȯ\ **saw**	\u̇\ **foot**
\ər\ **further**	\ch\ **chin**	\ī\ **life**	\ȯi\ **coin**	\y\ **yet**
\a\ **mat**	\e\ **pet**	\j\ **job**	\th\ **thin**	\yü\ **few**
\ā\ **take**	\ē\ **easy**	\ng\ **sing**	\th\ **this**	\yu̇\ **cure**
\ä\ **cot, cart**	\g\ **go**	\ō\ **bone**	\ü\ **food**	\zh\ **vision**

al·pha·bet·ic \ˌal-fə-ˈbet-ik\ *or* **al·pha·bet·i·cal** \-ˈbet-i-kəl\ *adj* **1** *usually alphabetical* : arranged in the order of the letters of the alphabet **2** : of, relating to, or employing an alphabet — **al·pha·bet·i·cal·ly** \-i-k(ə-)lē\ *adv*

al·pha·bet·ize \ˈal-fə-bə-ˌtīz\ *vt* : to arrange in alphabetical order — **al·pha·bet·i·za·tion** \ˌal-fə-ˌbet-ə-ˈzā-shən\ *n* — **al·pha·bet·iz·er** \ˈal-fə-bə-ˌtī-zər\ *n*

alpha helix *n* : the coiled structural arrangement of many proteins consisting of a single amino-acid chain that is stabilized by hydrogen bonds

al·pha·nu·mer·ic \ˌal-fə-nü-ˈmer-ik, -nyü-\ *adj* : consisting of both letters and numbers

alpha particle *n* : a positively charged particle that is identical with the nucleus of a helium atom, consists of 2 protons and 2 neutrons, and is ejected at high speed in various radioactive transformations

alpha ray *n* **1** : an alpha particle moving at high speed **2** : a stream of alpha particles — called also *alpha radiation*

alpha wave *n* : a brain wave that is often associated with a state of wakeful relaxation — called also *alpha rhythm*

al·pine \ˈal-ˌpīn\ *n* : a plant native to alpine or boreal regions

Alpine *adj* **1** *often not cap* **a** : relating to or resembling the Alps or any mountains **b** : of, relating to, or growing on upland slopes above timberline **2** : of or relating to competitive ski events consisting of slalom and downhill racing

al·ready \öl-ˈred-ē\ *adv* **1** : before a stated or implied time : PREVIOUSLY ⟨we had *already* been there⟩ **2** : so soon ⟨surprised to find it done *already*⟩

al·right \öl-ˈrīt, ˈäl-; ˈöl-ˌ\ *adv or adj* : ALL RIGHT

Al·sa·tian \al-ˈsā-shən\ *n* : GERMAN SHEPHERD [*Alsace*]

al·sike clover \ˈal-ˌsak-, -ˌsīk-\ *n* : a European perennial clover widely grown as a forage plant [*Alsike,* Sweden]

al·so \ˈöl-sō\ *adv* **1** : LIKEWISE 1 **2** : in addition : TOO

al·so–ran \-ˌran\ *n* **1** : a horse or dog that finishes out of the money in a race **2** : a contestant that does not win

Al·ta·ic \al-ˈtā-ik\ *adj* : of, relating to, or constituting the Turkic, Tungusic, and Mongolian language families collectively [*Altai* Mountains, Asia] — **Altaic** *n*

Al·tair \al-ˈtīr, -ˈtaər, -ˈteər\ *n* : the first-magnitude star in Aquila [Arabic *al-ṭā'ir,* literally, "the flier"]

al·tar \ˈöl-tər\ *n* **1** : a usually raised structure or place on which sacrifices are offered or incense is burned in worship **2** : a table used in consecrating the eucharistic elements or as a center of worship or ritual [Old English, from Latin *altare*]

altar boy *n* : ACOLYTE 1

altar call *n* : an appeal by an evangelist to worshippers to come forward and commit their lives to Christ

al·tar·piece \ˈöl-tər-ˌpēs\ *n* : a work of art to decorate the space above and behind the altar

altar server *n* : ACOLYTE 1

al·ter \ˈöl-tər\ *vb* **1** : to change partly but usually not completely ⟨*alter* a dress⟩ ⟨my opinion has never *altered*⟩ **2** : CASTRATE, SPAY [Medieval Latin *alterare,* from Latin *alter* "other (of two)"] ***synonyms*** see CHANGE — **al·ter·abil·i·ty** \ˌöl-tə-rə-ˈbil-ət-ē, -trə-ˈ\ *n* — **al·ter·able** \ˈöl-tə-rə-bəl, -trə-bəl\ *adj* — **al·ter·ably** \-blē\ *adv* — **al·ter·er** *n*

al·ter·ation \ˌöl-tə-ˈrā-shən\ *n* **1** : the act or process of altering **2** : the result of altering : MODIFICATION

al·ter·ca·tion \ˌöl-tər-ˈkā-shən\ *n* : a noisy or angry dispute : WRANGLE [Latin *altercari* "to wrangle," from *alter* "other"]

al·ter ego \ˌöl-tər-ˈē-gō *also* -ˈeg-ō\ *n* **1** : a trusted friend or personal representative **2** : oneself in a changed form [Latin, literally, "second I"]

¹al·ter·nate \ˈöl-tər-nət *also* ˈal-\ *adj* **1** : occurring or succeeding by turns ⟨a day of *alternate* sunshine and rain⟩ **2 a** : occurring first on one side and then on the other at different levels along an axis ⟨*alternate* leaves⟩ — compare OPPOSITE **b** : arranged one above or alongside another ⟨*alternate* layers of cake and filling⟩ **3** : every other : every second ⟨works on *alternate* days⟩ **4** : being an alternative ⟨took the *alternate* route⟩ [Latin *alternare* "to alternate," from *alternus* "alternate," from *alter* "other"] — **al·ter·nate·ly** *adv*

²al·ter·nate \-ˌnāt\ *vb* **1** : to do, occur, or act by turns **2** : to cause to alternate

³al·ter·nate \-nət\ *n* **1** : ALTERNATIVE **2** : a person named to take the place of another whenever necessary

alternate angle *n* **1** : one of a pair of angles on opposite sides of a line intersecting two other lines and between the two intersected lines — called also *alternate interior angle* **2** : one of a pair of angles on opposite sides of a line intersecting two other lines and outside the two intersected lines — called also *alternate exterior angle*

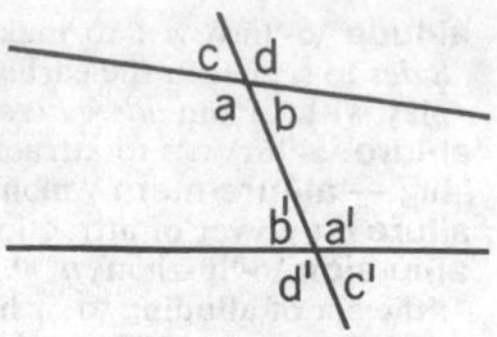

alternate angles: a, a'; b, b'; c, c'; d, d'

alternating current *n* : an electric current that reverses its direction at regular intervals — abbreviation *AC*

alternating series *n* : a mathematical series in which consecutive terms are alternatively positive and negative

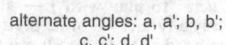

al·ter·na·tion \ˌöl-tər-ˈnā-shən *also* ˌal-\ *n* **1** : the act or process of alternating **2** : alternate position or occurrence : SUCCESSION

alternation of generations : the alternate occurrence of two or more different forms and especially of a sexual and an asexual generation in the life cycle of a plant or animal

¹al·ter·na·tive \öl-ˈtər-nət-iv *also* al-\ *adj* **1** : offering or expressing a choice ⟨*alternative* sources of energy⟩ **2** : different from the usual or conventional **3** : of, relating to, or being rock music that is regarded as an alternative to conventional rock — **al·ter·na·tive·ly** *adv* — **al·ter·na·tive·ness** *n*

²alternative *n* **1** : a chance to choose between two things ⟨the *alternative* of going by train or by air⟩ **2 a** : one of two or more things among which a choice is to be made **b** : something which can be chosen instead **3** : alternative rock music ***synonyms*** see CHOICE

alternative medicine *n* : any of various systems of healing or treating disease (as chiropractic or homeopathy) involving approaches not conventionally taught or practiced in the U.S.

al·ter·na·tor \ˈöl-tər-ˌnāt-ər *also* ˈal-\ *n* : an electric generator for producing alternating current

alt·horn \ˈalt-ˌhörn\ *n* : the alto member of the saxhorn family used chiefly in bands where it often replaces the French horn [German, from *alt* "alto" + *Horn* "horn"]

al·though *also* **al·tho** \öl-ˈt͟hō\ *conj* : in spite of the fact that : THOUGH

al·tim·e·ter \al-ˈtim-ət-ər, ˈal-tə-ˌmēt-ər\ *n* : an instrument for measuring altitude; *esp* : an aneroid barometer that registers changes in atmospheric pressure accompanying changes in altitude [Latin *altus* "high" + English *-meter*]

al·ti·tude \ˈal-tə-ˌtüd, -ˌtyüd\ *n* **1 a** : the angular height of a celestial object above the horizon **b** : the vertical distance of an object above sea level **c** : a perpendicular line segment from a vertex of a geometric figure (as a triangle or a pyramid) to the opposite side or the opposite side extended or from a side or face to a parallel side or face or the side or face extended **d** : the length of an altitude **2 a** : vertical distance or extent **b** : position at a height **c** : an elevated region — usually used in plural [Latin *altitudo* "height, depth," from *altus* "high, deep"] ***synonyms*** see HEIGHT — **al·ti·tu·di·nal** \ˌal-tə-ˈtüd-nəl, -ˈtyüd-n-əl\ *adj*

altitude sickness *n* : the effects (as nosebleed and nausea) of having oxygen-deficient blood and tissues as a result of being at high altitudes with reduced atmospheric pressure

al·to \ˈal-tō\ *n, pl* **altos** **1 a** : COUNTERTENOR **b** : CONTRALTO **c** : the second highest voice part in a 4-part chorus — compare BASS, SOPRANO, TENOR **2** : the second highest member of a family of musical instruments; *esp* : ALTHORN [Italian, literally, "high," from Latin *altus*]

al·to·cu·mu·lus \ˌal-tō-ˈkyü-myə-ləs\ *n* : a fleecy cloud formation consisting of large whitish globular masses with shaded portions

¹al·to·geth·er \ˌöl-tə-ˈge͟th-ər\ *adv* **1** : WHOLLY, THOROUGHLY ⟨*altogether* useless⟩ **2** : in all : ALL TOLD ⟨comes to $25 *altogether*⟩ **3** : on the whole ⟨*altogether* it compares favorably⟩

²altogether *n* : NUDE 2 ⟨posed in the *altogether*⟩

al·to·stra·tus \ˌal-tō-ˈstrāt-əs, -ˈstrat-\ *n* : a uniform layer of gray cloud similar to cirrostratus but darker and at a lower level

al·tri·cial \al-ˈtrish-əl\ *adj* : having the young hatched in a very immature and helpless condition so as to require care for some time — compare PRECOCIAL [Latin *altrix* "nurse," from *alere* "to nourish"]

al·tru·ism \ˈal-trü-ˌiz-əm\ *n* **1** : unselfish interest in or care for the welfare of others **2** : behavior by an animal that benefits others of its species but that is not beneficial to or may be harmful to itself [French *altruisme,* from *autrui* "other people," derived from Latin *alter* "other"] — **al·tru·ist** \ˈal-trü-əst\ *n* — **al·tru·is·tic** \ˌal-trü-ˈis-tik\ *adj* — **al·tru·is·ti·cal·ly** \-ˈis-ti-kə-lē, -klē\ *adv*

al·um \ˈal-əm\ *n* **1 :** either of two colorless crystalline sulfate compounds containing aluminum $KAl(SO_4)_2 \cdot 12H_2O$ or $NH_4Al(SO_4)_2 \cdot 12H_2O$ that have a sweetish-sourish taste and a puckering effect on the mouth and are used in medicine (as to check local sweating or to stop bleeding) **2 :** ALUMINUM SULFATE [Medieval French *alum, alun,* from Latin *alumen*]

alu·mi·na \ə-ˈlü-mə-nə\ *n* **:** the oxide of aluminum Al_2O_3 that occurs native as corundum and in bauxite and is used as a source of aluminum, as an abrasive, and as an absorbent

al·u·min·i·um \ˌal-yə-ˈmin-ē-əm\ *n, chiefly British* **:** ALUMINUM

alu·mi·nize \ə-ˈlü-mə-ˌnīz\ *vt* **:** to treat or coat with aluminum

alu·mi·num \ə-ˈlü-mə-nəm\ *n* **:** a silver-white malleable ductile light metallic element with good electrical and thermal conductivity and resistance to oxidation that is the most abundant metal in the earth's crust — see ELEMENT table [Latin *alumen* "alum"]

aluminum oxide *n* **:** ALUMINA

aluminum sulfate *n* **:** a white aluminum salt $Al_2(SO_4)_3$ made from bauxite and used in making paper, purifying water, and tanning

alum·na \ə-ˈləm-nə\ *n, pl* **-nae** \-ˌnē\ **:** a girl or woman who has attended or has graduated from a particular school, college, or university [Latin, feminine of *alumnus*]

alum·nus \ə-ˈləm-nəs\ *n, pl* **-ni** \-ˌnī\ **:** a person who has attended or graduated from a particular school, college, or university [Latin, "foster son, pupil," from *alere* "to nourish"]

al·ve·o·lar \al-ˈvē-ə-lər\ *adj* **1 :** of, relating to, resembling, or having alveoli **2 :** pronounced with the tip of the tongue touching or near the teethridge — **al·ve·o·lar·ly** *adv*

al·ve·o·lus \al-ˈvē-ə-ləs\ *n, pl* **-li** \-ˌlī, -ˌlē\ **1 :** a small cavity or pit: as **a :** a socket for a tooth **b :** AIR SAC 2 **2 :** TEETHRIDGE [Latin, from *alveus* "cavity, hollow," from *alvus* "belly"]

al·ways \ˈòl-wēz, -wəz, -ˌwāz\ *adv* **1 :** at all times ⟨I'm *always* right⟩ **2 :** through all time **:** FOREVER ⟨remember me *always*⟩

alys·sum \ə-ˈlis-əm\ *n* **1 :** any of a genus of herbs of Europe and Asia related to the mustards and having small usually yellow flowers **2 :** SWEET ALYSSUM [Greek *alysson,* a plant believed to cure rabies, from *a-* + *lyssa* "rabies"]

Alz·hei·mer's disease \ˈälts-ˌhī-mərz-, ˈalts-\ *n* **:** a brain disease typically occurring in late middle age or in old age and characterized by degeneration of brain neurons with progressive memory loss, impaired thinking, and disorientation — called also *Alzheimer's* [Alois *Alzheimer,* died 1915, German physician]

am *present 1st singular of* BE [Old English *eom*]

AM \ˈā-ˌem\ *n* **:** a system of broadcasting using amplitude modulation; *also* **:** a receiver of radio waves broadcast by such a system — **AM** *adj*

amah \ˈäm-ə, ˈäm-ˌä\ *n* **:** a female servant in eastern Asia; *esp* **:** a Chinese nurse [Portuguese *ama* "wet nurse," from Medieval Latin *amma*]

amain \ə-ˈmān\ *adv* **1 :** with all one's might **2 a :** at full speed **b :** in great haste

amal·gam \ə-ˈmal-gəm\ *n* **1 :** an alloy of mercury with some other metal or metals that is used for tooth filling **2 :** a combination or mixture of different ingredients [Medieval French *amalgame,* from Medieval Latin *amalgama*]

amal·gam·ate \ə-ˈmal-gə-ˌmāt\ *vb* **1 :** to unite in an amalgam **2 :** to merge into a single body — **amal·gam·ator** \-ˌmāt-ər\ *n*

amal·gam·ation \ə-ˌmal-gə-ˈmā-shən\ *n* **1 a :** the act or process of amalgamating ⟨the *amalgamation* of mercury with silver⟩ **b :** the state of being amalgamated **2 :** the result of amalgamating **3 :** a merger of business entities — **amal·gam·ative** \-ˈmal-gə-ˌmāt-iv\ *adj*

am·a·ni·ta \ˌam-ə-ˈnīt-ə, -ˈnēt-\ *n* **:** any of various mostly poisonous white-spored fungi with a bulbous sac about the base of the stem [Greek *amanitai,* a kind of fungus]

aman·u·en·sis \ə-ˌman-yə-ˈwen-səs\ *n, pl* **-en·ses** \-sēz\ **:** a person employed to write from dictation or to copy manuscript [Latin, from *servus a manu* "slave with secretarial duties"]

am·a·ranth \ˈam-ə-ˌranth\ *n* **1 :** an imaginary flower that never fades **2 :** any of a large genus of herbs including pigweeds and various forms cultivated for their colorful leaves or spikes of flowers [Latin *amarantus,* a kind of flower, from Greek *amaranton,* from *a-* + *marainein* "to wither, fade"]

am·a·ran·thine \ˌam-ə-ˈran-thən, -ˈran-ˌthīn\ *adj* **:** relating to or resembling an amaranth **:** UNFADING, UNDYING

am·a·ryl·lis \ˌam-ə-ˈril-əs\ *n* **:** any of various plants of a family related to the lily family; *esp* **:** a South African bulbous herb grown for its cluster of large showy flowers [probably from the name of a shepherdess in Virgil's *Eclogues*]

amass \ə-ˈmas\ *vt* **1 :** to collect for oneself **:** ACCUMULATE ⟨*amass* a fortune⟩ **2 :** to pile up into a mass **:** GATHER ⟨*amass* evidence⟩ ***synonyms*** see ACCUMULATE — **amass·er** *n*

am·a·teur \ˈam-ə-ˌtər, -ət-ər, -ə-ˌtür, -ə-ˌtyür, -ə-ˌchür\ *n* **1 :** a person who takes part in an activity (as a study or sport) for pleasure and not for pay **2 :** a person who is not skillful at an activity [French, literally, "lover," from Latin *amator,* from *amare* "to love"] — **amateur** *adj* — **am·a·teur·ish** \ˌam-ə-ˈtər-ish, -ˈtür-, -ˈtyür-, -ˈchür-\ *adj* — **am·a·teur·ish·ly** *adv* — **am·a·teur·ish·ness** *n* — **am·a·teur·ism** \ˈam-ə-ˌtər-ˌiz-əm, -ət-ər-, -ə-ˌtür-, -ə-ˌtyür-, -ə-ˌchür-\ *n*

am·a·to·ry \ˈam-ə-ˌtōr-ē, -ˌtòr-\ *adj* **:** of, relating to, or expressing sexual love

amaze \ə-ˈmāz\ *vt* **:** to surprise or astonish greatly **:** fill with wonder **:** ASTOUND [Old English *āmasian*]

amaze·ment \ə-ˈmāz-mənt\ *n* **:** great surprise or astonishment

amaz·ing \-ˈmā-zing\ *adj* **:** causing amazement or wonder — **amaz·ing·ly** \-ˈmā-zing-lē\ *adv*

am·a·zon \ˈam-ə-ˌzän, -ə-zən\ *n* **1** *cap* **:** a member of a race of female warriors of classical mythology **2** *often cap* **:** a tall very strong woman

Am·a·zo·nian \ˌam-ə-ˈzō-nē-ən, -ˈzō-nyən\ *adj* **1 :** of, relating to, or resembling an Amazon **2 :** of or relating to the Amazon River or its valley

am·bas·sa·dor \am-ˈbas-əd-ər, əm-, -ˈbas-ə-ˌdòr\ *n* **1 :** an official envoy; *esp* **:** a diplomatic agent of the highest rank who is the resident representative of his or her own government or appointed for a special temporary assignment **2 :** an authorized representative or messenger [Medieval French *ambassateur,* of Germanic origin] — **am·bas·sa·do·ri·al** \am-ˌbas-ə-ˈdōr-ē-əl, -ˈdòr-\ *adj* — **am·bas·sa·dor·ship** \am-ˈbas-əd-ər-ˌship\ *n*

am·ber \ˈam-bər\ *n* **1 :** a hard yellowish to brownish translucent fossil resin that takes a fine polish and is used mostly for jewelry **2 :** a dark orange yellow [Medieval French *ambre,* from Medieval Latin *ambra,* from Arabic *ʿanbar* "ambergris"] — **amber** *adj*

Amber Alert *n* **:** a widely publicized bulletin that alerts the public to a recently abducted or missing child [*Amber* Hagerman, died 1996, victim of an abduction, later read as acronym for *A*merica's *M*issing *B*roadcast *E*mergency *R*esponse]

am·ber·gris \ˈam-bər-ˌgris, -ˌgrēs\ *n* **:** a waxy substance from the sperm whale that is used in the manufacture of perfumes [Medieval French *ambre gris,* literally, "gray amber"]

ambi- *prefix* **:** both ⟨*ambi*valent⟩ [Latin, "both, around"]

am·bi·dex·trous \ˌam-bi-ˈdek-strəs\ *adj* **:** using both hands with equal ease [Latin *ambi-* + *dexter* "right hand"] — **am·bi·dex·trous·ly** *adv*

am·bi·ence *or* **am·bi·ance** \ˈam-bē-əns, äⁿ-byäⁿs\ *n* **:** a feeling or mood associated with a particular place, person, or thing **:** ATMOSPHERE [French *ambiance,* from *ambiant* "ambient"]

am·bi·ent \ˈam-bē-ənt\ *adj* **:** surrounding on all sides **:** ENCOMPASSING ⟨*ambient* sounds⟩ [Latin *ambiens,* present participle of *ambire* "to go around"]

am·bi·gu·i·ty \ˌam-bə-ˈgyü-ət-ē\ *n, pl* **-ties** **1 :** the quality or state of being ambiguous in meaning **2 :** an ambiguous word or passage

am·big·u·ous \am-ˈbig-yə-wəs\ *adj* **1 :** doubtful or uncertain especially from being obscure or indistinct ⟨an *ambiguous* color⟩ **2 :** capable of being understood in more than one way [Latin *ambiguus,* from *ambigere* "to wander about," from *ambi-* "around" + *agere* "to lead, drive"] — **am·big·u·ous·ly** *adj* — **am·big·u·ous·ness** *n*

am·bi·tion \am-ˈbish-ən\ *n* **1 a :** a strong desire for status, fame, or power **b :** desire to achieve a particular end **:** ASPIRATION **2 :** the object of ambition ⟨attain your life's *ambition*⟩ **3 :** desire to work or be active ⟨I have no *ambition* today⟩ [Latin *ambitio* "canvass for votes," literally, "going around," from *ambire* "to go around," from *ambi-* "around" + *ire* "to go"]

\ə\ **abut**	\au̇\ **out**	\i\ **tip**	\ȯ\ **saw**	\u̇\ **foot**
\ər\ **further**	\ch\ **chin**	\ī\ **life**	\ȯi\ **coin**	\y\ **yet**
\a\ **mat**	\e\ **pet**	\j\ **job**	\th\ **thin**	\yü\ **few**
\ā\ **take**	\ē\ **easy**	\ng\ **sing**	\t͟h\ **this**	\yu̇\ **cure**
\ä\ **cot, cart**	\g\ **go**	\ō\ **bone**	\ü\ **food**	\zh\ **vision**

Word History The literal meaning of Latin *ambitio,* a derivative of *ambire* "to go around," was "going around." The word also meant "soliciting of votes," because candidates for public office in ancient Rome were in the habit of going about the city for that purpose. From this political sense *ambitio* was extended a bit further, to mean "desire for honor or power." This is the meaning of English *ambition,* derived from Latin *ambitio.*

synonyms AMBITION, ASPIRATION mean strong desire for advancement. AMBITION implies a strong desire for personal advancement and may apply either to a praiseworthy or an inordinate desire ⟨driven by *ambition*⟩. ASPIRATION implies a striving after something higher than oneself which may be admirable and ennobling or merely presumptuous ⟨an *aspiration* to become president someday⟩.

am•bi•tious \am-ˈbish-əs\ *adj* **1 a :** having or driven by ambition ⟨an *ambitious* politician⟩ **b :** having a particular ambition ⟨*ambitious* to be captain of the team⟩ **2 :** showing ambition ⟨an *ambitious* plan⟩ — **am•bi•tious•ly** *adv*

am•biv•a•lence \am-ˈbiv-ə-ləns\ *n* **:** simultaneous attraction toward and repulsion from something or someone — **am•biv•a•lent** \-lənt\ *adj* — **am•biv•a•lent•ly** *adv*

am•bi•vert \ˈam-bi-ˌvərt\ *n* **:** a person having characteristics of both extrovert and introvert — **am•bi•ver•sion** \ˌam-bi-ˈvər-zhən\ *n*

[1]am•ble \ˈam-bəl\ *vi* **am•bled; am•bling** \-bə-ling, -bling\ **:** to go at an amble [Medieval French *ambler,* from Latin *ambulare* "to walk"] — **am•bler** \-bə-lər, -blər\ *n*

[2]amble *n* **1 :** an easy gait of a horse in which the legs on the same side of the body move together **2 :** a leisurely walk

am•bly•opia \ˌam-blē-ˈō-pē-ə\ *n* **:** reduced vision in one eye that results from the poor development of the visual pathway of the brain which serves the affected eye — called also *lazy eye* [Greek *amblyōpia,* from *amblys* "dull" + *-ōpia* "vision"]

am•bro•sia \am-ˈbrō-zhē-ə, -zhə\ *n* **1 :** the food of the Greek and Roman gods **2 :** something extremely pleasing to taste or smell [Latin, from Greek, literally, "immortality," from *ambrotos* "immortal"] — **am•bro•sial** \-zhē-əl, -zhəl\ *adj* — **am•bro•sial•ly** \-ē\ *adv*

am•bu•lance \ˈam-byə-ləns\ *n* **:** a vehicle equipped for transporting the injured or the sick [French, "field hospital," from *ambulant* "itinerant," from Latin *ambulare* "to walk"]

am•bu•lant \ˈam-byə-lənt\ *adj* **:** moving about; *esp* **:** AMBULATORY

am•bu•late \-ˌlāt\ *vi* **:** to move or walk from place to place

[1]am•bu•la•to•ry \ˈam-byə-lə-ˌtōr-ē, -ˌtȯr-\ *adj* **1 :** of, relating to, or adapted to walking **2 :** able to walk about ⟨*ambulatory* patients in a hospital⟩ [Latin *ambulare* "to walk"]

[2]ambulatory *n, pl* **-ries :** a sheltered place (as in a cloister or church) for walking

am•bus•cade \ˈam-bə-ˌskād\ *n* **:** AMBUSH [Middle French *embuscade*] — **ambuscade** *vb* — **am•bus•cad•er** *n*

[1]am•bush \ˈam-ˌbu̇sh\ *vt* **1 :** to station (as troops) in ambush **2 :** to attack from an ambush **:** WAYLAY [Medieval French *embuscher,* from *en* "in" + *busche* "firewood"]

[2]ambush *n* **:** a trap in which concealed persons lie in wait to attack by surprise; *also* **:** the persons so concealed or their position

ameba, ame•boid *variant of* AMOEBA, AMOEBOID

am•e•bi•a•sis \ˌam-i-ˈbī-ə-səs\ *n, pl* **-a•ses** \-ə-ˌsēz\ **:** infection with or disease caused by amoebas

amebic dysentery *n* **:** acute intestinal amebiasis of humans marked by dysentery, abdominal pain, and injury to the intestinal wall

ame•lio•rate \ə-ˈmēl-yə-ˌrāt\ *vb* **:** to make or grow better or more tolerable **:** IMPROVE [alteration of *meliorate*] — **ame•lio•ra•tion** \-ˌmēl-yə-ˈrā-shən\ *n* — **ame•lio•ra•tive** \-ˈmēl-yə-ˌrāt-iv\ *adj* — **ame•lio•ra•tor** \-ˌrāt-ər\ *n* — **ame•lio•ra•to•ry** \-rə-ˌtōr-ē, -ˌtȯr-\ *adj*

amen \ˈā-ˈmen, ˈä-; ˈä- *when sung*\ *interj* — used to express solemn agreement or hearty approval [Hebrew *āmēn*]

ame•na•ble \ə-ˈmē-nə-bəl, -ˈmen-ə-\ *adj* **1 :** liable to be called to account ⟨*amenable* to the law⟩ **2 :** easily influenced or managed **:** RESPONSIVE ⟨*amenable* to discipline⟩ **3 :** WILLING 1 ⟨I was *amenable* to spending time at home⟩ [Medieval French, from *amener* "to bring, compel," from *a-* "ad-" + *mener* "to lead," from Late Latin *minare* "to drive"] — **ame•na•bil•i•ty** \-ˌmē-nə-ˈbil-ət-ē, -ˌmen-ə-\ *n* — **ame•na•bly** \-ˈmē-nə-blē, -ˈmen-ə-\ *adv*

amend \ə-ˈmend\ *vb* **1 :** to change for the better **:** IMPROVE **2 :** ALTER 1; *esp* **:** to alter formally by modification, deletion, or addition ⟨*amend* the constitution⟩ [Medieval French *amender,* from Latin *emendare* "to emend"] ***synonyms*** see CORRECT — **amend•able** \-ˈmen-də-bəl\ *adj* — **amen•da•to•ry** \-ˈmen-də-ˌtōr-ē, -ˌtȯr-\ *adj* — **amend•er** *n*

amend•ment \ə-ˈmend-mənt, -ˈmen-\ *n* **1 :** the act or process of amending especially for the better **2 :** a modification, addition, or deletion (as to a law, bill, or motion) made or proposed

amends \ə-ˈmenz\ *n sing or pl* **:** something done or given to make up for a loss or injury one has caused ⟨make *amends*⟩

ame•ni•ty \ə-ˈmen-ət-ē, -ˈmē-nət-\ *n, pl* **-ties 1 :** the quality of being pleasant or agreeable **2 :** something that makes life easier or more pleasant — usually used in plural [Latin *amoenitas,* from *amoenus* "pleasant"]

ament \ˈam-ənt, ˈā-mənt\ *n* **:** CATKIN [Latin *amentum* "thong, strap"]

[1]Amer•i•can \ə-ˈmer-ə-kən\ *n* **1 :** a native or inhabitant of North America or South America; *esp* **:** a citizen of the U.S. **2 :** the English language used in the U.S.

[2]American *adj* **1 :** of or relating to America or its inhabitants ⟨the *American* coastline⟩ **2 :** of or relating to the U.S. or its inhabitants

Amer•i•ca•na \ə-ˌmer-ə-ˈkan-ə, -ˈkän-ə, -ˈkā-nə\ *n pl* **:** materials about America, its civilization, or its culture; *also* **:** a collection of such materials

American chameleon *n* **:** GREEN ANOLE

American cheese *n* **:** a mild process cheese made from American cheddar cheese

American dream *n, often cap D* **:** an American social ideal that stresses egalitarianism and especially material prosperity

American elm *n* **:** a large ornamental elm common in eastern North America

American Indian *n* **:** a member of any of the indigenous peoples of the western hemisphere except often the Eskimos; *esp* **:** an American Indian of North America and especially the U.S. — **American Indian** *adj*

Amer•i•can•ism \ə-ˈmer-ə-kə-ˌniz-əm\ *n* **1 :** a characteristic feature of American English as used in the U.S. **2 :** attachment or loyalty to the traditions, interests, or ideals of the U.S. **3 :** a custom or trait peculiar to the U.S. or to Americans

Amer•i•can•ize \-kə-ˌnīz\ *vb* **:** to make or become American — **Amer•i•can•i•za•tion** \ə-ˌmer-ə-kə-nə-ˈzā-shən\ *n*

American pit bull terrier *n* **:** any of a breed of medium-sized stocky dogs that have powerful jaws and great strength and that were originally bred for dogfighting

American plan *n* **:** a hotel plan whereby the daily rate covers the cost of both room and meals — compare EUROPEAN PLAN

American Sign Language *n* **:** a sign language for the deaf

American Staf•ford•shire terrier \-ˈstaf-ərd-ˌshir-, -shər-\ *n* **:** any of a breed of dogs similar to the American pit bull terrier

American Standard Version *n* **:** an American version of the Bible based on the Revised Version and published in 1901

am•er•i•ci•um \ˌam-ə-ˈrish-ē-əm, -ˈris-\ *n* **:** a radioactive metallic chemical element produced by bombardment of plutonium with high-energy neutrons — see ELEMENT table [New Latin, from *America*]

Am•er•in•di•an \ˌam-ə-ˈrin-dē-ən\ *also* **Am•er•ind** \ˌam-ə-ˈrind\ *n* **:** AMERICAN INDIAN — **Amerindian** *also* **Amerind** *adj*

am•e•thyst \ˈam-ə-thəst\ *n* **1 :** a clear purple or bluish violet variety of crystallized quartz used as a gem **2 :** a moderate purple [Greek *amethystos,* from *a-* + *methyein* "to be drunk"; from its supposed usefulness as a remedy for drunkenness]

Word History Gemstones were once believed to have magical and medicinal properties. An amethyst, for example, was supposed to have the power to prevent or cure drunkenness in its wearer. For this reason the Greeks gave it a name, *amethystos,* derived from the prefix *a-,* meaning "not," and *methyein* "to be drunk," from *methy* "wine."

ami•a•ble \ˈā-mē-ə-bəl\ *adj* **1 :** generally agreeable ⟨an *amiable* comedy⟩ **2 :** having a friendly and sociable disposition [Medieval French, from Late Latin *amicabilis* "friendly," from Latin *amicus* "friend"] — **ami•a•bil•i•ty** \ˌā-mē-ə-ˈbil-ət-ē\ *n* — **ami•a•ble•ness** \ˈā-mē-ə-bəl-nəs\ *n* — **ami•a•bly** \-blē\ *adv*

am•i•ca•ble \ˈam-i-kə-bəl\ *adj* **:** characterized by friendly goodwill **:** PEACEABLE ⟨an *amicable* settlement of differences⟩ — **am•i•ca•bil•i•ty** \ˌam-i-kə-ˈbil-ət-ē\ *n* — **am•i•ca•ble•ness** *n* — **am•i•ca•bly** \ˈam-i-kə-blē\ *adv*

am·ice \'am-əs\ *n* : a white linen cloth worn about the neck and shoulders under other vestments by a priest at Mass [derived from Latin *amictus* "cloak"]

amid \ə-'mid\ *or* **amidst** \-'midst, -'mitst\ *prep* : in or into the middle of : AMONG ⟨*amid* the crowd⟩

am·ide \'am-ˌīd, -əd\ *n* : a compound resulting from replacement of an atom of hydrogen in ammonia by a metal or radical or of one or more atoms of hydrogen in ammonia by univalent acid radicals [*ammonia* + *-ide*]

amid·ships \ə-'mid-ˌships\ *adv* : in or near the middle of a ship

amine \ə-'mēn, 'am-ˌēn\ *n* : any of various compounds derived from ammonia by replacement of hydrogen by one or more univalent hydrocarbon radicals [*ammonia* + [2]*-ine*]

ami·no \ə-'mē-nō\ *adj* : relating to or containing the group NH_2 united to a radical [*amine* + *-o-*]

amino acid *n* : any of numerous organic acids that contain the amino group NH_2 and include some which can combine in chains to form proteins and are synthesized by living cells or are obtained as essential components of the diet

amir *variant of* EMIR

Amish \'äm-ish, 'am-, 'ām-\ *adj* : of or relating to a strict Mennonite sect who were followers of Amman and settled in America [Jacob *Amman* or *Amen,* flourished 1693, Swiss Mennonite bishop] — **Amish** *n* — **Amish·man** \-ish-mən\ *n*

[1]**amiss** \ə-'mis\ *adv* **1** : in a mistaken way : WRONGLY ⟨if you think he is guilty, you judge *amiss*⟩ **2** : ASTRAY ⟨something had gone *amiss*⟩

[2]**amiss** *adj* : not satisfactory : WRONG, FAULTY ⟨something is *amiss* here⟩

ami·to·sis \ˌā-mī-'tō-səs\ *n, pl* **-to·ses** \-'tō-ˌsēz\ : cell division in which simple cleavage of the nucleus is followed by the division of the cytoplasm without the appearance of chromosomes or a spindle [[2]*a-* + *mitosis*] — **ami·tot·ic** \-'tät-ik\ *adj*

am·i·ty \'am-ət-ē\ *n, pl* **-ties** : friendly relations especially between nations [Medieval French *amité,* from Medieval Latin *amicitas,* from Latin *amicus* "friend"]

am·me·ter \'am-ˌēt-ər\ *n* : an instrument for measuring electric current in amperes [*ampere* + *-meter*]

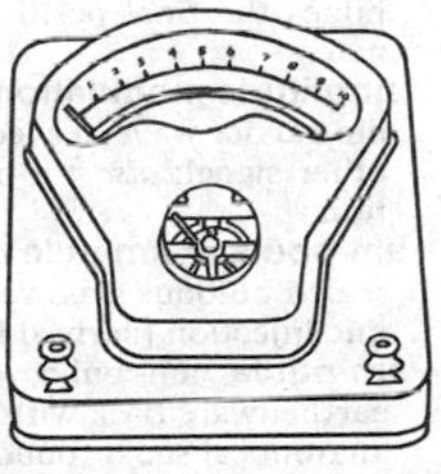
ammeter

am·mo \'am-ō\ *n, pl* **ammos** : AMMUNITION

am·mo·nia \ə-'mō-nyə\ *n* **1** : a colorless gas NH_3 that is a compound of nitrogen and hydrogen, has a sharp smell and taste, is very soluble in water, can be easily liquefied by cold and pressure, is used in the manufacture of fertilizers and explosives, and is the chief nitrogenous waste product of many aquatic organisms **2** : a solution of ammonia in water — called also *ammonia water* [Latin *sal ammoniacus* "sal ammoniac," literally, "salt of Ammon"; from its extraction near a temple of the Egyptian god Ammon (Amon)] — **am·mo·ni·a·cal** \ˌam-ə-'nī-ə-kəl\ *adj*

am·mo·ni·fi·ca·tion \ə-ˌmän-ə-fə-'kā-shən, -ˌmō-nə-\ *n* : decomposition with production of ammonia or ammonium compounds especially by the action of bacteria on nitrogenous organic matter — **am·mo·ni·fy** \-ˌfī\ *vb*

am·mo·nite \'am-ə-ˌnīt\ *n* : any of numerous flat spiral fossil shells of mollusks especially abundant in the Mesozoic age [Latin *cornu Ammonis,* literally, "horn of Ammon (Amon)"]

Am·mon·ite \'am-ə-ˌnīt\ *n* : a member of a Semitic people living in Old Testament times east of the Jordan River [*Ammon,* son of Lot] — **Ammonite** *adj*

am·mo·ni·um \ə-'mō-nē-əm\ *n* : an ion NH_4^+ derived from ammonia by combination with a hydrogen ion

ammonium chloride *n* : a white crystalline volatile salt NH_4Cl used in dry cells and as an expectorant — called also *sal ammoniac*

ammonium hydroxide *n* : a compound NH_4OH that is formed when ammonia dissolves in water and that exists only in solution

ammonium nitrate *n* : a colorless crystalline salt NH_4NO_3 used in explosives and fertilizers

ammonium phosphate *n* : a white crystalline compound $(NH_4)_2HPO_4$ used especially as a fertilizer and as a fireproofing substance

ammonium sulfate *n* : a colorless crystalline salt $(NH_4)_2SO_4$ used chiefly as a fertilizer

am·mu·ni·tion \ˌam-yə-'nish-ən\ *n* **1** : something (as a bullet, shell, grenade, or bomb) propelled by or containing explosives **2** : material for use in attacking or defending a position ⟨new evidence providing more *ammunition*⟩ [obsolete French *amunition,* alteration of *munition*]

am·ne·sia \am-'nē-zhə\ *n* : loss of memory due usually to brain injury, shock, fatigue, repression, or illness [Greek *amnēsia* "forgetfulness"] — **am·ne·si·ac** \-zhē-ˌak, -zē-\ *or* **am·ne·sic** \-zik, -sik\ *adj or n*

am·nes·ty \'am-nə-stē\ *n, pl* **-ties** : a general pardon granted by a ruler or government to a large group of persons [Greek *amnēstia* "forgetfulness," from *a-* + *mnasthai* "to remember"] — **amnesty** *vt*

am·nio·cen·te·sis \ˌam-nē-ō-ˌsen-'tē-səs\ *n, pl* **-te·ses** \-'tē-sēz\ : the surgical insertion of a hollow needle through the abdominal wall and uterus of a pregnant female into the amnion to obtain amniotic fluid for the determination of sex or especially of chromosomal abnormality in the fetus [*amnion* + Greek *kentesis* "puncture," from *kentein* "to prick"]

am·ni·on \'am-nē-ˌän, -ən\ *n, pl* **-nions** *or* **-nia** \-nē-ə\ : a thin membrane forming a closed sac about the embryo or fetus of a reptile, bird, or mammal and containing a watery fluid in which the embryo or fetus is immersed [Greek, "caul"]

am·ni·ot·ic \ˌam-nē-'ät-ik\ *adj* : of or relating to the amnion ⟨*amniotic* fluid⟩

amoe·ba *also* **ame·ba** \ə-'mē-bə\ *n, pl* **-bas** *or* **-bae** \-ˌbē\ : any of a large genus of naked rhizopod protozoans that have lobed and separate pseudopodia and no permanent cell organs or supporting structures and are widespread in fresh and salt water and in moist soils [Greek *amoibē* "change"] — **amoe·bic** \-bik\ *adj*

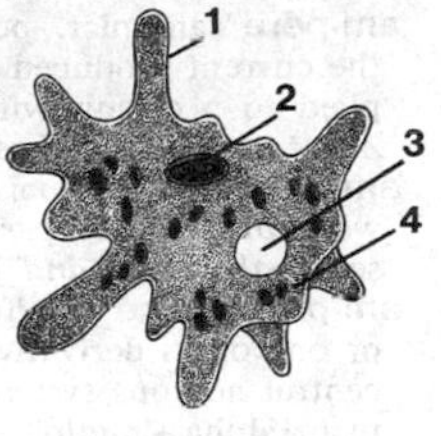

amoeba: *1* pseudopodium, *2* nucleus, *3* contractile vacuole, *4* food vacuole

amoe·boid *also* **ame·boid** \-ˌbȯid\ *adj* : resembling an amoeba especially in moving or changing in shape by means of protoplasmic flow

amok \ə-'mək, -'mäk\ *or* **amuck** \-'mək\ *adv* **1** : in a violently frenzied state ⟨run *amok*⟩ **2** : in an undisciplined, uncontrolled, or faulty manner ⟨machines run *amok*⟩ [Malay]

among \ə-'məng\ *also* **amongst** \-'məngst, -'məngkst\ *prep* **1** : in or through the midst of ⟨*among* the crowd⟩ **2** : in company with ⟨living *among* artists⟩ **3** : through all or most of ⟨discontent *among* the poor⟩ **4** : in the number or class of ⟨wittiest *among* poets⟩ **5** : in shares to each of ⟨divided *among* the heirs⟩ **6** : through the joint action of ⟨made a fortune *among* themselves⟩ [Old English *on gemonge* "in the crowd"] ***usage*** see BETWEEN

amon·til·la·do \ə-ˌmän-tə-'läd-ō\ *n, pl* **-dos** : a pale dry sherry [Spanish, literally, "done in the manner of Montilla (town in Andalusia)"]

amor·al \ā-'mȯr-əl, a-, 'ā-, 'a-, -'mär-\ *adj* : neither moral nor immoral; *esp* : outside the sphere to which moral judgments apply — **amor·al·ly** \-ə-lē\ *adv*

Am·o·rite \'am-ə-ˌrīt\ *n* : a member of one of various Semitic peoples living in Mesopotamia, Syria, and Palestine during the 3rd and 2nd millenniums B.C.; *esp* : one of the group founding the first Babylonian empire [Hebrew *Ĕmōrī*] — **Amorite** *adj*

am·o·rous \'am-rəs, -ə-rəs\ *adj* **1** : inclined to love : easily falling in love ⟨an *amorous* nature⟩ **2** : of, relating to, or caused by love ⟨an *amorous* glance⟩ [Medieval French, from Medieval Latin *amorosus,* from Latin *amor* "love," from *amare* "to love"] — **am·o·rous·ly** *adv* — **am·o·rous·ness** *n*

amor·phous \ə-'mȯr-fəs\ *adj* **1** : having no definite form : SHAPELESS **2** : having no crystalline form [Greek *amorphos,* from *a-* + *morphē* "form"] — **amor·phous·ly** *adv* — **amor·phous·ness** *n*

\ə\ **abut**	\aù\ **out**	\i\ **tip**	\ȯ\ **saw**	\ù\ **foot**
\ər\ **further**	\ch\ **chin**	\ī\ **life**	\ȯi\ **coin**	\y\ **yet**
\a\ **mat**	\e\ **pet**	\j\ **job**	\th\ **thin**	\yü\ **few**
\ā\ **take**	\ē\ **easy**	\ng\ **sing**	\t͟h\ **this**	\yù\ **cure**
\ä\ **cot, cart**	\g\ **go**	\ō\ **bone**	\ü\ **food**	\zh\ **vision**

am·or·tize \ˈam-ər-ˌtīz *also* ə-ˈmȯr-ˌtīz\ *vt* **:** to pay off (as a mortgage) gradually usually by periodic payments of principal and interest or by payments to a sinking fund [Medieval French *amortir* "to kill," from Latin *ad-* + *mors* "death"] — **am·or·ti·za·tion** \ˌam-ərt-ə-ˈzā-shən *also* ə-ˌmȯrt-ə-\ *n*

Amos \ˈā-məs\ *n* **:** a prophetic book of canonical Jewish and Christian Scriptures — see BIBLE table

[1]**amount** \ə-ˈmau̇nt\ *vi* **1 :** to add up ⟨the bill *amounted* to 10 dollars⟩ **2 :** to be equivalent ⟨acts that *amount* to treason⟩ [Medieval French *amounter,* from *amount* "upward," from *a-* "ad-" + *mont* "mountain"]

[2]**amount** *n* **1 :** the total number or quantity **:** AGGREGATE **2 :** the whole effect, significance, or import **3 :** a principal sum and the interest on it ***synonyms*** see SUM

amour \ə-ˈmu̇r, a-, ä-\ *n* **:** a love affair; *esp* **:** a secret love affair [Medieval French, "love," derived from Latin *amor*]

amour pro·pre \ˌam-ˌu̇r-ˈprōpr, ˌäm-\ *n* **:** SELF-ESTEEM [French *amour-propre,* literally, "love of oneself"]

amox·i·cil·lin \ə-ˌmäk-sə-ˈsil-ən\ *n* **:** a semisynthetic antibiotic derived from ampicillin [*am*ino + *ox-* + pen*icillin*]

[1]**amp** \ˈamp\ *n* **1 :** AMPERE **2 :** AMPLIFIER

[2]**amp** *vt* **:** EXCITE ⟨trying to *amp* up the crowd⟩; *also* **:** HEIGHTEN ⟨*amp* up the drama⟩

AMP \ˌā-ˌem-ˈpē\ *n* **:** a compound composed of adenosine and one phosphate group that is reversibly convertible to ADP and ATP in metabolic reactions [*a*denosine *m*ono*p*hosphate]

am·per·age \ˈam-pə-rij, -prij, -ˌpiər-ij\ *n* **:** the strength of a current of electricity expressed in amperes

am·pere \ˈam-ˌpiər, -peər\ *n* **:** a unit of electric current equal to the current produced by a potential difference of one volt applied to a circuit with a resistance of one ohm [André M. *Ampère,* died 1836, French physicist]

am·per·sand \ˈam-pər-ˌsand\ *n* **:** a character & standing for the word *and* [*and* (&) *per se and,* literally, "(the character) & by itself (is the word) *and*"]

am·phet·amine \am-ˈfet-ə-ˌmēn, -mən\ *n* **:** a compound $C_9H_{13}N$ or one of its derivatives used medically as a stimulant of the central nervous system but often abused for its stimulant effects [*a*lpha + *m*ethyl + *phe*n- + *et*hyl + *amine*]

amphi- *or* **amph-** *prefix* **:** on both sides **:** of both kinds **:** both ⟨*amphi*oxus⟩ [Greek *amphi* "around, on both sides"]

am·phib·ia \am-ˈfib-ē-ə\ *n pl* **:** AMPHIBIANS

am·phib·i·an \-ē-ən\ *n* **1 :** an amphibious organism; *esp* **:** any of a class (Amphibia) of cold-blooded vertebrate animals (as frogs and salamanders) that are intermediate in many respects between fishes and reptiles and have gilled aquatic larvae and air-breathing adults **2 :** an airplane designed to take off from and land on either land or water **3 :** a flat-bottomed vehicle that moves on tracks having finlike extensions by means of which it is propelled on land or water — **amphibian** *adj*

am·phib·i·ous \-ē-əs\ *adj* **1 :** able to live both on land and in water ⟨*amphibious* plants⟩ **2 a :** relating to or adapted for both land and water ⟨*amphibious* vehicles⟩ **b :** trained or organized for invasion from the sea; *also* **:** executed by amphibious forces [Greek *amphi-* + *bios* "life, mode of life"] — **am·phib·i·ous·ly** *adv* — **am·phib·i·ous·ness** *n*

am·phi·bole \ˈam-fə-ˌbōl, ˈamp-\ *n* **:** any of a group of white, gray, green, or black rock-forming minerals that are complex hydrous silicates and contain calcium, magnesium, iron, aluminum, and sodium [French, from Late Latin *amphibolus,* from Greek *amphibolos* "ambiguous"]

am·phi·ox·us \ˌam-fē-ˈäk-səs, ˌamp-\ *n, pl* **-oxi** \-ˈäk-ˌsī\ *or* **-oxus·es :** LANCELET [New Latin, from *amphi-* + Greek *oxys* "sharp"]

am·phi·pod \ˈam-fi-ˌpäd, ˈamp-\ *n* **:** any of a large group (Amphipoda) of small crustaceans (as the sand flea) with a laterally compressed body — **amphipod** *adj*

am·phi·the·ater \ˈam-fə-ˌthē-ət-ər, ˈamp-\ *n* **1 :** a round or oval building with seats rising in curved rows around an open space on which games and plays take place **2 :** something resembling an amphitheater (as a piece of level ground surrounded by hills) [derived from Greek *amphitheatron,* from *amphi* "around" + *theatron* "theater"]

am·pho·ra \ˈam-fə-rə, ˈamp-\ *n, pl* **-pho·rae** \-ˌrē, -ˌrī\ *or* **-pho·ras :** an ancient Greek jar or vase with two handles that rise almost to the level of the mouth; *also* **:** such a jar or vase used elsewhere in the ancient world [Latin, from Greek *amphoreus,* from *amphi* + *pherein* "to carry"]

am·pho·ter·ic \ˌam-fə-ˈter-ik, ˌamp-\ *adj* **:** capable of reacting chemically either as an acid or as a base [Greek *amphoteros* "each of two," from *amphō* "both"]

am·pi·cil·lin \ˌam-pə-ˈsil-ən\ *n* **:** an antibiotic of the penicillin group that is effective against many bacteria [*am*ine + *p*en*icillin*]

am·ple \ˈam-pəl\ *adj* **am·pler** \-pə-lər, -plər\; **am·plest** \-pə-ləst, -pləst\ **1 :** generous in size, scope, or capacity **:** COPIOUS ⟨*ample* room for a garden⟩ **2 :** enough to satisfy **:** ABUNDANT ⟨*ample* money for the trip⟩ [Medieval French, from Latin *amplus*] ***synonyms*** see PLENTIFUL — **am·ple·ness** *n* — **am·ply** \-plē\ *adv*

amphora

am·pli·fi·ca·tion \ˌam-plə-fə-ˈkā-shən\ *n* **1 :** an act, example, or product of amplifying **2 a :** matter by which a statement is expanded **b :** an expanded statement

am·pli·fi·er \ˈam-plə-ˌfīr\ *n* **:** one that amplifies; *esp* **:** an electronic device used to obtain amplification of voltage, current, or power

am·pli·fy \ˈam-plə-ˌfī\ *vt* **-fied; -fy·ing 1 :** to make larger; *esp* **:** to expand with clarifying details or illustration ⟨*amplify* a statement⟩ **2 :** to increase (voltage, current, or power) in magnitude or strength **3 :** to make louder ⟨*amplify* the voice by using a megaphone⟩

am·pli·tude \ˈam-plə-ˌtüd, -ˌtyüd\ *n* **1 :** the quality or state of being ample **:** FULLNESS, ABUNDANCE **2 :** the extent or range of something: as **a :** the extent of a vibratory movement (as of a pendulum) measured from the mean position to an extreme **b :** the height or depth of a periodic wave (as an alternating current) compared to its average value **3 :** the angle that determines the final position of the radius vector in polar coordinates

amplitude modulation *n* **:** modulation of the amplitude of a radio carrier wave in accordance with the strength of the audio or other signal; *also* **:** a broadcasting system using such modulation

am·poule *or* **am·pule** *also* **am·pul** \ˈam-ˌpyül, -ˌpül\ *n* **:** a small sealed bulbous glass vessel used to hold a solution for hypodermic injection [derived from Latin *ampulla* "flask"]

am·pul·la \am-ˈpu̇l-ə, -ˈpəl-\ *n, pl* **-lae** \-ˌē, -ˌī\ **1 :** a glass or earthenware flask with a globular body and two handles **2 :** an anatomical sac or pouch [Latin] — **am·pul·lar** \-ər\ *adj*

am·pu·tate \ˈam-pyə-ˌtāt\ *vt* **:** to remove by or as if by cutting; *esp* **:** to cut (as a limb) from the body [Latin *amputare,* from *am-, amb-* "around" + *putare* "to cut, prune"] — **am·pu·ta·tion** \ˌam-pyə-ˈtā-shən\ *n* — **am·pu·ta·tor** \ˈam-pyə-ˌtāt-ər\ *n*

am·pu·tee \ˌam-pyə-ˈtē\ *n* **:** one that has had a limb amputated

amuck *variant of* AMOK

am·u·let \ˈam-yə-lət\ *n* **:** a small object worn as a charm against evil [Latin *amuletum*]

amuse \ə-ˈmyüz\ *vt* **1 :** to entertain or occupy with something pleasant ⟨*amuse* a child with a toy⟩ **2 :** to appeal to the sense of humor of ⟨the story *amused* everyone⟩ [Medieval French *amuser,* from *a-* "ad-" + *muser* "to muse"] — **amus·ing·ly** \-ˈmyü-zing-lē\ *adv*

synonyms AMUSE, ENTERTAIN, DIVERT mean to pass or cause to pass the time pleasantly. AMUSE implies engaging the attention so as to keep one interested usually lightly or frivolously ⟨*amuse* yourselves while I prepare dinner⟩. ENTERTAIN suggests supplying amusement by specially prepared activity or performance ⟨a magician *entertained* the children at the party⟩. DIVERT stresses distracting the attention from worry or routine concern especially with something causing laughter or gaiety ⟨a light comedy *diverted* the tired worker⟩.

amuse·ment \ə-ˈmyüz-mənt\ *n* **1 :** the condition of being amused **2 :** pleasant diversion **3 :** something that amuses

amusement park *n* **:** a commercially operated park with various devices (as a merry-go-round or roller coaster) for entertainment

am·yl \ˈam-əl\ *n* **:** a univalent hydrocarbon radical C_5H_{11} occurring in various isomeric forms [derived from Greek *amylon* "starch"]

amyl acetate *n* : BANANA OIL
amyl alcohol *n* : any of eight isomeric alcohols $C_5H_{12}O$ used especially as solvents
am·y·lase \ˈam-ə-ˌlās, -ˌlāz\ *n* : an enzyme that accelerates the hydrolysis of starch or glycogen
am·y·lop·sin \ˌam-ə-ˈläp-sən\ *n* : the amylase of the pancreatic juice [*amyl* + *-o-* + *-psin* (as in *trypsin*)]
amyo·tro·phic lateral sclerosis \ˌā-ˌmī-ə-ˈtrō-fik-\ *n* : a rare fatal disease usually beginning in middle age and characterized especially by increasing and spreading muscular weakness and wasting — called also *Lou Gehrig's disease* [[2]*a-* + *my-* + *trophic*]
[1]**an** \ən, an, ˈan\ *indefinite article* : [2]A [Old English *ān* "one"]
usage *An* is usually found in speech and writing before words beginning with a vowel sound ⟨*an* oak⟩ ⟨*an* hour⟩ ⟨*an* X-ray⟩. It is also found usually in speech and less often in writing before *h*-initial words with an unstressed first syllable in which \h\ is often lost after *an* ⟨*an* historian⟩. *An* is sometimes used, though less frequently than in the past, before words whose initial letter is a vowel and whose initial sound is a consonant ⟨*an* unique occurrence⟩ ⟨such *an* one⟩.
[2]**an** \ən, an\ *prep* : [3]A 2 — used before words with an initial vowel sound ⟨once *an* afternoon⟩ ⟨fifty cents *an* hour⟩ [Old English *an, on, a-* "on, in"]
[3]**an** *or* **an'** *conj* **1** *see* AND\ : AND **2** \ˈan\ *archaic* : IF 1
an- — see A-
[1]**-an** *or* **-ian** *also* **-ean** *n suffix* **1** : one that belongs to ⟨Ameri*can*⟩ ⟨Boston*ian*⟩ ⟨crustac*ean*⟩ **2** : one skilled in or specializing in ⟨magic*ian*⟩ [Latin *-anus, -ianus,* adjective and noun suffix]
[2]**-an** *or* **-ian** *also* **-ean** *adj suffix* **1** : of or belonging to ⟨Ameri*can*⟩ ⟨Florid*ian*⟩ **2** : characteristic of : resembling ⟨Mozart*ean*⟩
[3]**-an** *n suffix* **1** : unsaturated carbon compound **2** : anhydride of a carbohydrate [alteration of *-ane*]
ana- *or* **an-** *prefix* : up : upward ⟨*ana*bolism⟩ [Greek, "up, back, again"]
-ana \ˈan-ə, ˈän-ə, ˈā-nə\ *or* **-i·ana** \ē-ˈ\ *n pl suffix* : collected items of information especially anecdotal or bibliographic concerning ⟨Americ*ana*⟩ ⟨Johnson*iana*⟩ [Latin, neuter plural of *-anus, -ianus* "-an"]
Ana·bap·tist \ˌan-ə-ˈbap-təst\ *n* : a Protestant of one of several 16th century sects rejecting infant baptism [Late Greek *anabaptizein* "to rebaptize"] — **Anabaptist** *adj*
anabolic steroid *n* : any of several synthetic hormones that are used medically to promote tissue growth, are sometimes abused by athletes to increase muscle size and strength, and may have harmful effects (as stunted growth in teenagers)
anab·o·lism \ə-ˈnab-ə-ˌliz-əm\ *n* : the part of metabolism concerned with building up the substance of plants and animals — compare CATABOLISM [*ana-* + *-bolism* (as in *metabolism*)] — **an·a·bol·ic** \ˌan-ə-ˈbäl-ik\ *adj*
anach·ro·nism \ə-ˈnak-rə-ˌniz-əm\ *n* **1** : the placing of persons, events, objects, or customs in times to which they do not belong **2** : a person or thing especially from a former age that is out of place in the present **3** : the state or condition of being out of place in time [Late Greek *anachronizein* "to be late," from Greek *ana-* + *chronos* "time"] — **anach·ro·nis·tic** \ə-ˌnak-rə-ˈnis-tik\ *adj* — **anach·ro·nis·ti·cal·ly** \-ti-kə-lē, -klē\ *adv*
an·a·co·lu·thon \ˌan-ə-kə-ˈlü-ˌthän\ *n, pl* **-tha** \-thə\ *also* **-thons** : lack of connection between the parts of one continuous stretch of speech or writing especially as the result of a shift from one construction to another in the middle of a sentence (as in "you really ought — well, do it your own way") [Greek *a-* + *akolouthos* "following"]
an·a·con·da \ˌan-ə-ˈkän-də\ *n* : a large semiaquatic South American snake that kills its prey by squeezing in its coils [probably from Sinhalese *henakandayā,* a kind of snake]
an·a·dem \ˈan-ə-ˌdem\ *n, archaic* : a wreath for the head [Latin *anadema,* from Greek *anadēma,* from *anadein* "to wreathe"]
anad·ro·mous \ə-ˈnad-rə-məs\ *adj* : ascending rivers from the sea for breeding ⟨shad and some salmon are *anadromous*⟩ — compare CATADROMOUS [Greek *anadromos* "running upward"]
anae·mia *chiefly British variant of* ANEMIA
an·aer·obe \ˈan-ə-ˌrōb; an-ˈar-ˌōb, -ˈer-\ *n* : an anaerobic organism
an·aer·o·bic \ˌan-ə-ˈrō-bik; ˌan-ˌa-ˈrō-, -ˌe-ˈrō-\ *adj* : living, active, or occurring in the absence of free oxygen ⟨*anaerobic* bacteria⟩ — **an·aer·o·bi·cal·ly** *adv*
anaerobic respiration *n* : FERMENTATION 1
an·aes·the·sia, an·aes·thet·ic, anaes·the·tist, anaes·the·tize *chiefly British variant of* ANESTHESIA, ANESTHETIC, ANESTHETIST, ANESTHETIZE
ana·gram \ˈan-ə-ˌgram\ *n* : a word or phrase made out of another by changing the order of the letters ⟨*rebate* is an *anagram* of *beater*⟩ [derived from Greek *anagrammatizein* "to transpose letters," from *ana-* + *gramma* "letter"]
anal \ˈān-l\ *adj* : of, relating to, situated near, or involving the anus — **anal·ly** \-l-ē\ *adv*
anal fin *n* : an unpaired median fin behind the vent of a fish
an·al·ge·sia \ˌan-l-ˈjē-zhə, -zhē-ə, -zē-ə\ *n* : loss of ability to feel pain without loss of consciousness [Greek *analgēsia,* derived from *a-* + *algos* "pain"] — **an·al·ge·sic** \-ˈjē-zik, -sik\ *adj or n* — **an·al·get·ic** \-ˈjet-ik\ *adj or n*
analog computer *n* : a computer that operates with numbers represented by directly measurable physical quantities — compare DIGITAL COMPUTER
an·a·log·i·cal \ˌan-l-ˈäj-i-kəl\ *adj* **1** : of, relating to, or based on analogy **2** : expressing or implying analogy — **an·a·log·i·cal·ly** \-kə-lē, -klē\ *adv*
anal·o·gous \ə-ˈnal-ə-gəs\ *adj* **1** : showing an analogy or a likeness permitting one to draw an analogy **2** : similar in biological function but different in structure and origin ⟨the wing of a bird is *analogous* to the wing of a butterfly⟩ [Latin *analogus,* from Greek *analogos,* literally, "proportionate," from *ana* "up, in accordance with" + *logos* "reason, ratio"] ***synonyms*** see SIMILAR — **anal·o·gous·ly** *adv* — **anal·o·gous·ness** *n*
an·a·logue *or* **an·a·log** \ˈan-l-ˌȯg, -ˌäg\ *n* : something that is analogous or similar to something else
anal·o·gy \ə-ˈnal-ə-jē\ *n, pl* **-gies** **1** : an inference that if two or more things agree with one another in some respects they will probably agree in others **2 a** : resemblance in some particulars between things otherwise unlike : SIMILARITY **b** : comparison based on such resemblance **3** : correspondence in function between anatomical parts of different structure and origin — compare HOMOLOGY
anal–re·ten·tive \ˈān-l-ri-ˈtent-iv\ *adj* : exhibiting or typifying personality traits (as frugality and obstinacy) held to be psychological consequences of toilet training
an·a·lyse *chiefly British variant of* ANALYZE
anal·y·sis \ə-ˈnal-ə-səs\ *n, pl* **anal·y·ses** \-ˈnal-ə-ˌsēz\ **1** : separation of a whole into its parts **2 a** : an examination of a whole to discover its elements and their relations **b** : a statement of such an analysis **c** : an examination and interpretation of the nature and significance of something (as a news event) **3** : the identification or separation of ingredients of a substance **4** : proof of a proposition by assuming the result and deducing a valid statement by a series of reversible steps **5** : PSYCHOANALYSIS [Greek, from *analyein* "to break up," from *ana-* + *lyein* "to loosen"]
an·a·lyst \ˈan-l-əst\ *n* **1** : a person who analyzes or who is skilled in analysis ⟨a news *analyst*⟩ **2** : a specialist in psychoanalysis : PSYCHOANALYST
an·a·lyte \ˈan-ə-ˌlīt\ *n* : a chemical substance that is the subject of analysis
an·a·lyt·ic \ˌan-l-ˈit-ik\ *adj* **1 a** : of or relating to analysis; *esp* : separating something into its parts or elements **b** : skilled in or using analysis ⟨a keenly *analytic* person⟩ **2** : involving or applying the methods of algebra and calculus rather than geometry ⟨*analytic* trigonometry⟩ — **an·a·lyti·cal** \-i-kəl\ *adj* — **an·a·lyt·i·cal·ly** \-kə-lē, -klē\ *adv*
analytic geometry *n* : a branch of mathematics that studies geometric properties by using algebra to represent geometric figures in a coordinate system — called also *coordinate geometry*
an·a·lyze \ˈan-l-ˌīz\ *vt* : to make an analysis of; *esp* : to study or determine the nature and relationship of the parts of by analysis — **an·a·lyz·a·ble** \-ˌī-zə-bəl\ *adj* — **an·a·lyz·er** \-ˌī-zər\ *n*
an·a·pest \ˈan-ə-ˌpest\ *n* : a metrical foot consisting of two unaccented syllables followed by one accented syllable (as in *the accused*) [Latin *anapaestus* "foot of two short syllables followed by one long," from Greek *anapaistos,* literally, "struck back,"

from *ana-* + *paiein* "to strike"; from its being a dactyl reversed] — **an·a·pes·tic** \ˌan-ə-ˈpes-tik\ *adj*

ana·phase \ˈan-ə-ˌfāz\ *n* **:** the stage of mitosis and meiosis in which the chromosomes move toward the opposite poles of the spindle

ana·phy·lax·is \ˌan-ə-fə-ˈlak-səs\ *n* **:** hypersensitivity (as to a drug) resulting from sensitization during an earlier exposure to the causative agent [*ana-* + *-phylaxis* (as in *prophylaxis*)] — **ana·phy·lac·tic** \-ˈlak-tik\ *adj*

an·ar·chic \a-ˈnär-kik, ə-\ *adj* **:** of, relating to, or tending toward anarchy **:** LAWLESS — **an·ar·chi·cal** \-ki-kəl\ *adj* — **an·ar·chi·cal·ly** \-ki-kə-lē, -klē\ *adv*

an·ar·chism \ˈan-ər-ˌkiz-əm, -ˌär-\ *n* **1 :** a political theory that holds all governmental authority to be unnecessary and undesirable and advocates a society based on the voluntary cooperation of individuals and groups **2 :** the support or practice of anarchistic principles

an·ar·chist \ˈan-ər-kəst, -ˌär-\ *n* **1 :** a person who rebels against any authority, established order, or ruling power **2 :** a person who believes in, supports, or promotes anarchism; *esp* **:** one who uses violent means to overthrow the established order — **anarchist** *or* **an·ar·chis·tic** \ˌan-ər-ˈkis-tik, -ˌär-\ *adj*

an·ar·chy \ˈan-ər-kē, -ˌär-\ *n* **1 :** the condition of a society without a government **2 :** a state of lawlessness, confusion, or disorder **3 :** an ideal society made up of individuals who have no government and enjoy complete freedom [Greek *anarchia,* from *a-* + *archein* "to rule"]

synonyms ANARCHY, CHAOS mean absence, suspension, or breakdown of government, law, and order. ANARCHY stresses the absence of government ⟨a war-torn country in *anarchy*⟩. CHAOS implies the utter absence of order ⟨was *chaos* on the field after the series-winning game⟩.

an·as·tig·mat \a-ˈnas-tig-ˌmat, ˌan-ə-ˈstig-\ *n* **:** an anastigmatic lens

an·astig·mat·ic \ˌan-ə-stig-ˈmat-ik, ˌan-ˌas-tig-\ *adj* **:** not astigmatic — used especially of lenses that are able to form approximately point images of object points

anas·to·mose \ə-ˈnas-tə-ˌmōz, -ˌmōs\ *vb* **:** to connect or communicate by anastomosis

anas·to·mo·sis \ə-ˌnas-tə-ˈmō-səs\ *n, pl* **-mo·ses** \-ˌsēz\ **1 :** the union of parts or branches (as of streams or blood vessels) so as to intercommunicate or interconnect **2 :** NETWORK, MESH [Greek *anastomōsis,* derived from *ana-* + *stoma* "mouth, opening"]

anath·e·ma \ə-ˈnath-ə-mə\ *n* **1 a :** a ban or curse solemnly pronounced by church authority and accompanied by excommunication **b :** a vigorous denunciation **:** CURSE **2 :** one that is cursed or intensely disliked [Greek]

anath·e·ma·tize \-ˌtīz\ *vt* **:** to pronounce an anathema upon **:** DAMN

anat·o·mist \ə-ˈnat-ə-məst\ *n* **:** a specialist in anatomy

anat·o·mize \-ˌmīz\ *vt* **1 :** to dissect so as to show or to examine the structure and use of the parts **2 :** ANALYZE

anat·o·my \ə-ˈnat-ə-mē\ *n, pl* **-mies 1 :** a branch of knowledge that deals with the structure of organisms; *also* **:** a writing on bodily structure **2 :** structural makeup especially of an organism or any of its parts **3 :** separation into parts for examination **:** ANALYSIS [derived from Greek *anatemnein* "to dissect," from *ana-* + *temnein* "to cut"] — **an·a·tom·i·cal** \-ˈtäm-i-kəl\ *or* **an·a·tom·ic** \ˌan-ə-ˈtäm-ik\ *adj* — **an·a·tom·i·cal·ly** \-kə-lē, -klē\ *adv*

-ance \əns, ᵊns\ *n suffix* **1 :** action or process ⟨further*ance*⟩**:** instance of an action or process ⟨perform*ance*⟩ **2 :** quality or state **:** instance of a quality or state ⟨protuber*ance*⟩ **3 :** amount or degree ⟨conduct*ance*⟩ [Latin *-antia,* from *-ans* "-ant"]

an·ces·tor \ˈan-ˌses-tər\ *n* **1 :** one from whom an individual, group, or species is descended **2 :** FORERUNNER 2, PROTOTYPE [Medieval French *ancestre,* from Latin *antecessor* "predecessor," from *antecedere* "to go before"]

an·ces·tral \an-ˈses-trəl\ *adj* **:** of, relating to, or derived from an ancestor — **an·ces·tral·ly** \-trə-lē\ *adv*

an·ces·tress \ˈan-ˌses-trəs\ *n* **:** a female ancestor

an·ces·try \ˈan-ˌses-trē\ *n* **1 :** line of descent **:** LINEAGE **2 :** individuals making up a line of descent **:** ANCESTORS

[1]an·chor \ˈang-kər\ *n* **1 :** a heavy iron or steel device attached to a boat or ship by a cable and so made that when thrown overboard it digs into the bottom and holds the boat or ship in place **2 :** something that secures or steadies or that gives a feeling of stability **3 a :** ANCHORMAN 1 **b :** ANCHORPERSON [Old English *ancor,* from Latin *anchora,* from Greek *ankyra*]

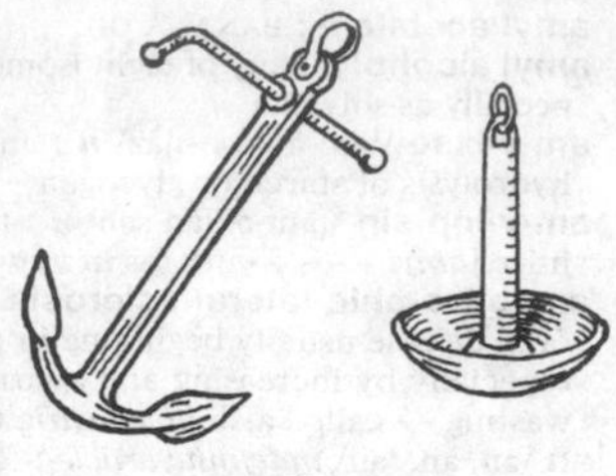

anchor 1

[2]anchor *vb* **an·chored; an·chor·ing** \-kə-ring, -kring\ **1 :** to hold in place by means of an anchor ⟨*anchor* a ship⟩ **2 :** to secure firmly ⟨*anchor* the cables of a bridge⟩ **3 :** to drop anchor **:** become anchored ⟨the boat *anchored* in the harbor⟩ **4 :** to act as an anchorperson

an·chor·age \ˈang-kə-rij, -krij\ *n* **1 :** a place where boats may be anchored **2 :** a secure hold to resist a strong pull **3 :** a means of security **:** REFUGE

an·cho·rite \ˈang-kə-ˌrīt\ *n* **:** a person who gives up worldly things and lives in solitude usually for religious reasons [Medieval Latin *anchorita,* derived from Late Greek *anachōrētēs,* from Greek *anachorein* "to withdraw"]

an·chor·man \ˈang-kər-ˌman\ *n* **1 :** one who competes or is placed last ⟨the *anchorman* on a relay team⟩ **2 :** ANCHORPERSON

an·chor·per·son \-ˌpərs-n\ *n* **:** a broadcaster who reads the news and introduces reports of other broadcasters

an·chor·wom·an \-ˌwu̇m-ən\ *n* **:** a woman who anchors a broadcast

an·cho·vy \ˈan-ˌchō-vē, an-ˈ\ *n, pl* **-vies** *or* **-vy :** any of numerous small fishes resembling herrings that include several that are important food fishes used especially for sauces and relishes [Spanish *anchova*]

an·cien ré·gime \ä^{n}s-ˈya^{n}-rā-ˈzhēm\ *n* **1 :** the political and social system of France before the Revolution of 1789 against the monarchy and aristocracy **2 :** a system or mode no longer prevailing [French, literally, "old regime"]

[1]an·cient \ˈān-shənt, -chənt; ˈāng-shənt, ˈāngk-\ *adj* **1 :** having existed for many years **:** very old ⟨*ancient* customs⟩ **2 :** of or relating to a period of time long past or to those living in such a period; *esp* **:** of or relating to the historical period from the earliest civilizations to the fall of the western Roman Empire in A.D. 476 **3 :** having the qualities of age or long existence **:** as **a :** VENERABLE **b :** OLD-FASHIONED, ANTIQUE [Medieval French *ancien,* derived from Latin *ante* "before"] ***synonyms*** see OLD — **an·cient·ness** *n*

[2]ancient *n* **1 :** an aged person **2** *pl* **:** the civilized peoples of ancient times and especially of Greece and Rome

an·cient·ly \-lē\ *adv* **:** in ancient times ⟨a tool used *anciently*⟩

an·cil·lary \ˈan-sə-ˌler-ē, an-ˈsil-ə-rē\ *adj* **1 :** SUBSIDIARY 1b ⟨the main factory and its *ancillary* plants⟩ **2 :** serving to aid or assist **:** SUPPLEMENTARY ⟨the need for *ancillary* evidence⟩ [Latin *ancilla* "female servant"]

-an·cy \ən-sē, ᵊn-sē\ *n suffix, pl* **-ancies :** quality or state ⟨piqu*ancy*⟩ [Latin *-antia* "-ance"]

and \ənd, ən, and, an, ˈand, *usually* ᵊnd *or* ᵊn *after* t, d, s, z, *often* ᵊm *after* p *or* b, *sometimes* ᵊng *after* k *or* g\ *conj* **1 :** added to ⟨2 *and* 2 make 4⟩ **2 :** AS WELL AS ⟨you *and* I⟩ — used as a function word to join words or word groups of the same grammatical rank or function (as two nouns that are subjects of the same verb) [Old English] — **and so forth 1 :** and others or more of the same or similar kind **2 :** more in the same or similar manner — **and so on :** and so forth

[1]an·dan·te \än-ˈdän-ˌtā, an-ˈdant-ē\ *adv or adj* **:** moderately slow — used as a direction in music [Italian, literally, "going"]

[2]andante *n* **:** a musical piece or movement in andante tempo

an·dan·ti·no \ˌän-ˌdän-ˈtē-nō\ *adv or adj* **:** somewhat quicker in tempo than andante — used as a direction in music [Italian, from *andante*]

an·des·ite \ˈan-di-ˌzīt\ *n* **:** an extrusive usually dark grayish rock consisting essentially of feldspar [*Andes* Mountains] — **an·des·it·ic** \ˌan-di-ˈzit-ik\ *adj*

and·iron \ˈan-ˌdīrn, -ˌdī-ərn\ *n* **:** either of a pair of metal supports for firewood in a fireplace [Medieval French *aundyre, andier*]

and/or \ˈand-ˈȯr\ *conj* — used as a function word to indicate that either *and* or *or* may apply ⟨cats *and/or* dogs means cats *and* dogs or cats *or* dogs⟩

an·dra·dite \an-ˈdräd-ˌīt, ˈan-drə-ˌdīt\ *n* : a garnet ranging from yellow and green to brown and black and containing calcium and iron [José B. de *Andrada* e Silva, died 1838, Brazilian geologist]

an·dro \ˈan-drō\ *n* : androstenedione

an·dro·gen \ˈan-drə-jən\ *n* : a male sex hormone [Greek *andr-*, *anēr* "male"] — **an·dro·gen·ic** \ˌan-drə-ˈjen-ik\ *adj*

an·drog·y·nous \an-ˈdräj-ə-nəs\ *adj* : having both male and female characteristics [Greek *andr-*, *anēr* "man, male" + *gynē* "woman"] — **an·drog·y·nous·ly** *adv* — **an·drog·y·ny** \an-ˈdräj-ə-nē\ *n*

An·drom·e·da \an-ˈdräm-əd-ə\ *n* : a northern constellation directly south of Cassiopeia between Pegasus and Perseus

an·dro·stene·di·one \ˌan-drə-ˌstēn-ˈdī-ōn\ *n* : a steroid sex hormone $C_{19}H_{26}O_2$ that is an intermediate product in the synthesis of testosterone and estrogen by the body [*androst*erone, a hormone + *-ene* + *di-* + *-one* (as in *ketone*)]

-ane \ˌān\ *n suffix* : saturated or completely hydrogenated carbon compound (as a hydrocarbon) ⟨meth*ane*⟩ [alteration of *-ene*, *-ine*]

an·ec·dote \ˈan-ik-ˌdōt\ *n* : a short narrative of an interesting, amusing, or biographical incident [French, derived from Greek *anekdotos* "unpublished," from *a-* + *ekdidonai* "to publish," from *ex-* "out" + *didonai* "to give"] — **an·ec·dot·al** \ˌan-ik-ˈdōt-l\ *adj* — **an·ec·dot·al·ly** \-l-ē\ *adv*

ane·mia \ə-ˈnē-mē-ə\ *n* **1** : a condition in which the blood is deficient in red blood cells, in hemoglobin, or in total volume and which is commonly marked by fatigue, weakness, pale skin, shortness of breath, and irregular heartbeat **2** : lack of vitality [Greek *anaimia* "bloodlessness," derived from *a-* + *haima* "blood"] — **ane·mic** \-mik\ *adj* — **ane·mi·cal·ly** \-mi-kə-lē, -klē\ *adv*

an·e·mom·e·ter \ˌan-ə-ˈmäm-ət-ər\ *n* : an instrument for measuring the force or speed of the wind [Greek *anemos* "wind"]

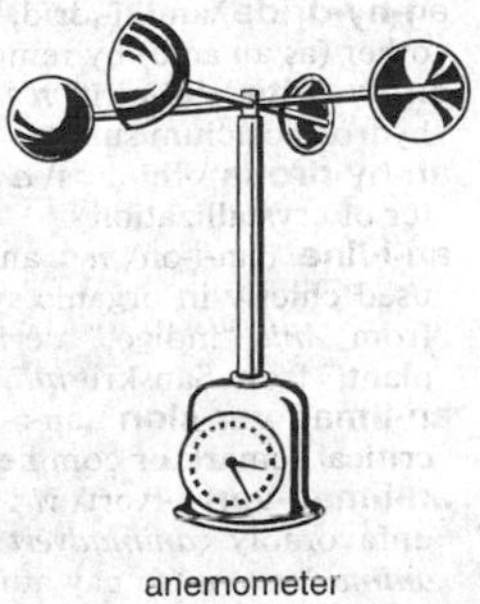
anemometer

anem·o·ne \ə-ˈnem-ə-nē\ *n* **1** : any of a large genus of herbs related to the buttercups that have showy flowers without petals but with conspicuous often colored sepals — called also *windflower* **2** : SEA ANEMONE [Latin, from Greek *anemōnē*]

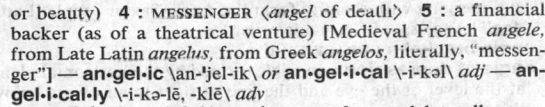

anent \ə-ˈnent\ *prep* : ABOUT 4, CONCERNING [Old English *on efen* "together, alongside," from *on* + *efen* "even"]

an·er·oid barometer \ˈan-ə-ˌrȯid-\ *n* : a barometer in which a change in atmospheric pressure is made to move a pointer [French *anéroïde* "without liquid," from *a-* + Late Greek *nēron* "water"]

an·es·the·sia \ˌan-əs-ˈthē-zhə\ *n* : loss of bodily sensation with or without loss of consciousness [Greek *anaisthēsia* "insensibility," derived from *a-* + *aisthanesthai* "to perceive"]

an·es·the·si·ol·o·gist \-ˌthē-zē-ˈäl-ə-jəst\ *n* : ANESTHETIST; *esp* : a physician specializing in anesthesia and the administration of anesthetics — **an·es·the·si·ol·o·gy** \-jē\ *n*

[1]**an·es·thet·ic** \ˌan-əs-ˈthet-ik\ *adj* : of, relating to, or capable of producing anesthesia — **an·es·thet·i·cal·ly** \-ˈthet-i-kə-lē, -klē\ *adv*

[2]**anesthetic** *n* : a substance that produces anesthesia in all or part of the body

anes·the·tist \ə-ˈnes-thət-əst\ *n* : a person who administers anesthetics

anes·the·tize \ə-ˈnes-thə-ˌtīz\ *vt* : to make insensible to pain especially by the use of an anesthetic

an·eu·rysm *also* **an·eu·rism** \ˈan-yə-ˌriz-əm\ *n* : an abnormal blood-filled bulge of a blood vessel and especially an artery resulting from weakening (as from disease) of the vessel wall [Greek *aneurysma*, from *aneurynein* "to dilate," from *ana-* + *eurynein* "to stretch," from *eurys* "wide"]

anew \ə-ˈnü, -ˈnyü\ *adv* **1** : over again : another time ⟨begin *anew*⟩ **2** : in a new or different form ⟨a story told *anew* as a movie⟩

an·gel \ˈān-jəl\ *n* **1 a** : a spiritual being serving God especially as a messenger or as a guardian of people **b** : a usually robed winged figure of human form in fine art **2** : an attendant spirit or guardian **3** : a person felt to resemble an angel (as in virtue or beauty) **4** : MESSENGER ⟨*angel* of death⟩ **5** : a financial backer (as of a theatrical venture) [Medieval French *angele*, from Late Latin *angelus*, from Greek *angelos*, literally, "messenger"] — **an·gel·ic** \an-ˈjel-ik\ *or* **an·gel·i·cal** \-i-kəl\ *adj* — **an·gel·i·cal·ly** \-i-kə-lē, -klē\ *adv*

an·gel·fish \ˈān-jəl-ˌfish\ *n* **1** : any of several laterally compressed brightly colored bony fishes of warm seas **2** : a black and silver laterally compressed South American fish of the cichlid family popular as an aquarium fish

angel food cake *n* : a usually white sponge cake made of flour, sugar, and whites of eggs

an·gel·i·ca \an-ˈjel-i-kə\ *n* : a biennial or perennial herb of the carrot family whose seeds and fruits furnish a flavoring oil

An·ge·lus \ˈan-jə-ləs\ *n* **1** : a Roman Catholic devotion that commemorates the Incarnation and is said morning, noon, and evening **2** : a bell announcing the time for the Angelus [Medieval Latin, "angel"; from the first word of the opening versicle]

[1]**an·ger** \ˈang-gər\ *n* : a strong feeling of displeasure and usually of antagonism ⟨easily aroused to *anger*⟩ [Middle English, "affliction, anger," from Old Norse *angr* "grief"]

synonyms ANGER, RAGE, WRATH, FURY mean an intense emotional state caused by displeasure. ANGER is the general term for an emotional reaction of displeasure in any degree of intensity that may or may not be shown ⟨tried to hide her *anger*⟩. RAGE implies loss of self-control from violence of emotion ⟨screaming with *rage*⟩. WRATH implies usually righteous rage with a desire to avenge or punish ⟨in his *wrath* the king ordered the rebels to be executed⟩. FURY suggests a violence of emotion amounting to temporary madness ⟨in her *fury* she accused everyone around her of betrayal⟩.

[2]**anger** *vt* **an·gered; an·ger·ing** \-gə-ring, -gring\ : to make angry

An·ge·vin \ˈan-jə-vən\ *adj* : of, relating to, or characteristic of Anjou or the Plantagenets [French, derived from Medieval Latin *Andegavia* "Anjou"] — **Angevin** *n*

an·gi·na \an-ˈjī-nə, ˈan-jə-\ *n* : a disorder marked by spasmodic attacks of intense pain: as **a** : a severe inflammatory condition of the mouth or throat **b** : ANGINA PECTORIS [Latin, "throat inflammation," from Greek *anchonē* "strangling"] — **an·gi·nal** \an-ˈjīn-l, ˈan-jən-\ *adj*

angina pec·to·ris \-ˈpek-tə-rəs, -trəs\ *n* : a heart disorder marked by brief recurrent attacks of intense chest pain caused by insufficient supply of oxygen to the heart muscles by the blood [New Latin, literally, "angina of the chest"]

an·gio·plas·ty \ˈan-jē-ə-ˌplas-tē\ *n* : surgical repair of a blood vessel; *esp* : surgery that opens a blocked artery by compressing the fatty blockage with the inflatable tip of a catheter [Greek *angeion* "vessel" + English *-plasty*]

an·gio·sperm \ˈan-jē-ə-ˌspərm\ *n* : FLOWERING PLANT [Greek *angeion* "vessel" + *sperma* "seed"] — **an·gio·sper·mous** \ˌan-jē-ə-ˈspər-məs\ *adj*

[1]**an·gle** \ˈang-gəl\ *n* **1** : a sharp projecting corner **2** : the figure formed by two lines extending from the same point or by two planes extending from the same line **3** : a measure of the amount that one line or plane of an angle would have to be turned to be in exactly the same place as the other line or plane ⟨a 90 degree *angle*⟩ **4 a** : POINT OF VIEW, ASPECT ⟨consider the problem from a new *angle*⟩ **b** : a special approach or technique for accomplishing an objective ⟨try a new *angle*⟩ **c** : an often improper method of obtaining an advantage ⟨a scam artist looking for an *angle*⟩ **5** : an abruptly diverging course or direction ⟨the road went off at an *angle*⟩ [Medieval French, from Latin *angulus* "corner, angle"] — **an·gled** \-gəld\ *adj*

[2]**angle** *vb* **an·gled; an·gling** \-gə-ling, -gling\ **1** : to turn, move, or direct at an angle **2** : to present (as a news story) from a particular often biased point of view : SLANT

[3]**angle** *vi* **an·gled; an·gling** \-gə-ling, -gling\ **1** : to fish with hook and line **2** : to use sly means to get what one wants [Middle English *angelen*, from *angel* "fishhook," from Old English, from *anga* "hook"]

An·gle \ˈang-gəl\ *n* : a member of a Germanic people conquering England with the Saxons and Jutes in the 5th century A.D.

and merging with them to form the Anglo-Saxon people [Latin *Angli* "Angles," of Germanic origin]

angle bracket *n* : BRACKET 3b

angle of depression : an angle formed by the horizontal plane at the level of the eye and the line of sight to an object below this plane

angle of elevation : an angle formed by the horizontal plane at the level of the eye and the line of sight to an object above this plane

angle of incidence : the angle that a line (as a ray of light) falling on a surface makes with a perpendicular to the surface at the point of incidence

angle of reflection : the angle between a reflected ray and the perpendicular to a reflecting surface drawn at the point of incidence

an·gler \ˈang-glər\ *n* **1** : FISHERMAN; *esp* : a person who fishes for sport **2** : ANGLERFISH

an·gler·fish \-ˌfish\ *n* : any of various bottom-dwelling marine fishes having a large flat head with projections that attract other fish within reach of its broad mouth

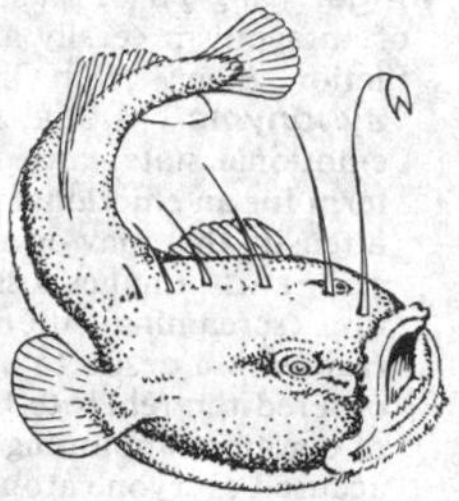

anglerfish

an·gle·worm \ˈang-gəl-ˌwərm\ *n* : EARTHWORM [[3]*angle*]

An·gli·can \ˈang-gli-kən\ *n* : a member of the established Church of England or of one of the related churches in communion with it [Medieval Latin *anglicus* "English," from Latin *Angli* "Angles"] — **Anglican** *adj* — **An·gli·can·ism** \-kə-ˌniz-əm\ *n*

an·gli·cism \ˈang-glə-ˌsiz-əm\ *n, often cap* **1** : a characteristic feature of English occurring in another language **2** : adherence or attachment to English customs or ideas

an·gli·cize \ˈang-glə-ˌsīz\ *vt, often cap* **1** : to make English (as in habits, speech, character, or outlook) **2 a** : to borrow (a foreign word, name, or phrase) into English without changing form or spelling and sometimes without changing pronunciation **b** : to change (a name) to its English equivalent ⟨*anglicize* "Juan" as "John"⟩ — **an·gli·ci·za·tion** \ˌang-glə-sə-ˈzā-shən\ *n, often cap*

an·gling \ˈang-gling\ *n* : the act or sport of fishing with hook and line

An·glo- *combining form* **1** \ˈang-ˌglō, -glə\ : English ⟨*Anglo*-Norman⟩ **2** \-ˌglō\ : English and ⟨*Anglo*-Japanese⟩ [Late Latin *Angli* "English people," from Latin, "Angles"]

An·glo–Amer·i·can \ˌang-glō-ə-ˈmer-ə-kən\ *n* **1** : an inhabitant of the U.S. of English origin or descent **2** : a North American whose native language is English and especially whose culture or ethnic background is of European origin — **Anglo–American** *adj*

An·glo–French \ˌang-glō-ˈfrench\ *n* : the French language used in medieval England

An·glo–Nor·man \-ˈnȯr-mən\ *n* **1** : one of the Normans living in England after the Norman conquest **2** : the form of Anglo-French used by Anglo-Normans

An·glo·phile \ˈang-glə-ˌfīl\ *n* : a person who greatly admires or favors England and English things

An·glo·phobe \-ˌfōb\ *n* : a person who strongly dislikes England and English things

An·glo–Sax·on \ˌang-glō-ˈsak-sən\ *n* **1** : a member of the Germanic people conquering England in the 5th century A.D. and forming the ruling class until the Norman conquest — compare ANGLE, JUTE, SAXON **2** : a native or inhabitant of England **3** : a person of English ancestry **4 a** : OLD ENGLISH 1 **b** : direct plain English — **Anglo–Saxon** *adj*

an·go·ra \ang-ˈgōr-ə, an-, -ˈgȯr-\ *n* **1** : yarn or cloth made from the hair of the Angora goat or the Angora rabbit **2** *cap* **a** : ANGORA CAT **b** : ANGORA GOAT **c** : ANGORA RABBIT

Angora cat *n* : any of a breed of cats having a long graceful body and silky medium-length hair; *also* : a long-haired domestic cat [*Angora* (Ankara), Turkey]

Angora goat *n* : any of a breed of domestic goats raised for their long silky hair which is the true mohair

Angora rabbit *n* : any of a breed of usually white rabbits raised for their long fine soft hair

an·gry \ˈang-grē\ *adj* **an·gri·er; -est** **1 a** : stirred by anger : ENRAGED ⟨became *angry* at the insult⟩ **b** : showing or arising from anger ⟨*angry* words⟩ **c** : threatening as if in anger ⟨an *angry* sky⟩ **2** : painfully inflamed ⟨an *angry* rash⟩ — **an·gri·ly** \-grə-lē\ *adv* — **an·gri·ness** \-grē-nəs\ *n*

angst \ˈängst, ˈangst\ *n* : a feeling of anxiety : DREAD [German]

ang·strom \ˈang-strəm\ *n* : a unit of length used especially of wavelengths (as of light) and equal to one ten-billionth of a meter — abbreviation *Å* [Anders J. *Ångström,* died 1874, Swedish physicist]

an·guish \ˈang-gwish\ *n* : extreme pain or distress of body or mind [Medieval French *anguisse,* from Latin *angustiae* "straits, distress," from *angustus* "narrow"] ***synonyms*** see SORROW

an·guished \ˈang-gwisht\ *adj* : full of anguish : TORMENTED ⟨an *anguished* call for help⟩

an·gu·lar \ˈang-gyə-lər\ *adj* **1 a** : forming an angle : sharp-cornered ⟨an *angular* mountain peak⟩ **b** : having one or more angles **2** : measured by an angle ⟨the *angular* distance between two stars as observed from earth⟩ **3 a** : stiff in character or manner : lacking smoothness or grace **b** : being lean and bony ⟨an *angular* figure⟩ — **an·gu·lar·i·ty** \ˌang-gyə-ˈlar-ət-ē\ *n* — **an·gu·lar·ly** *adv*

angular acceleration *n* : the rate of change per unit of time of angular velocity

angular velocity *n* : the rate of rotation around an axis per unit of time

An·gus \ˈang-gəs\ *n* : any of a breed of usually black hornless beef cattle originating in Scotland

an·hin·ga \an-ˈhing-gə\ *n* : a fish-eating bird having a long neck and sharply pointed bill and occurring from the southern U.S. to Argentina [New Latin, probably derived from an unattested Tupi word]

an·hy·dride \an-ˈhī-ˌdrīd, ˈan-\ *n* : a compound derived from another (as an acid) by removing a molecule of water

an·hy·drite \-ˈhī-ˌdrīt\ *n* : a mineral $CaSO_4$ consisting of an anhydrous calcium sulfate

an·hy·drous \-ˈhī-drəs\ *adj* : free from water and especially water of crystallization

an·i·line \ˈan-l-ən\ *n* : an oily liquid poisonous amine C_6H_7N used chiefly in organic synthesis (as of dyes) [German *Anilin,* from *Anil* "indigo," derived from Arabic *al-nīl* "the indigo plant," from Sanskrit *nīlī,* from *nīla* "dark blue"]

an·i·mad·ver·sion \ˌan-ə-ˌmad-ˈvər-zhən, -məd-, -shən\ *n* **1** : a critical remark or comment **2** : unfriendly criticism

an·i·mad·vert \-ˈvərt\ *vi* : to make a critical remark : comment unfavorably ⟨*animadvert* on a display of bad manners⟩ [Latin *animadvertere* "to pay attention to, censure," from *animum advertere* "to turn the mind to"]

[1]**an·i·mal** \ˈan-ə-məl\ *n* **1** : any of a kingdom (Animalia) of multicellular living organisms typically differing from plants in capacity for active movement, in rapid response to stimulation, and in lack of photosynthetic activity and cellulose cell walls **2 a** : one of the lower animals as distinguished from humans **b** : MAMMAL [Latin, from *animalis* "animate," from *anima* "breath, soul"]

[2]**animal** *adj* **1** : of, relating to, or derived from animals **2** : of or relating to the physical nature of a person as contrasted with the intellectual; *esp* : SENSUOUS

an·i·mal·cule \ˌan-ə-ˈmal-kyül\ *n* : a very small organism that is invisible or nearly invisible to the naked eye [New Latin *animalculum,* from Latin *animal*]

animal heat *n* : heat produced in the body of a living animal by its chemical and physical activity

animal husbandry *n* : a branch of agriculture concerned with the production and care of domestic animals

an·i·mal·ism \ˈan-ə-mə-ˌliz-əm\ *n* : ANIMALITY — **an·i·mal·is·tic** \ˌan-ə-mə-ˈlis-tik\ *adj*

an·i·mal·i·ty \ˌan-ə-ˈmal-ət-ē\ *n, pl* **-ties** **1** : a quality typical of animals: **a** : VITALITY **b** : a natural unrestrained unreasoned response to physical drives or stimuli **2** : the animal nature of human beings

animal kingdom *n* : a basic group of natural objects that includes all living and extinct animals — compare MINERAL KINGDOM, PLANT KINGDOM

animal starch *n* : GLYCOGEN

[1]**an·i·mate** \ˈan-ə-mət\ *adj* **1** : having life : ALIVE **2** : ANIMATED 1b, c, LIVELY [Latin *animare* "to give life to," from *anima* "breath, soul"] — **an·i·mate·ly** *adv* — **an·i·mate·ness** *n*

2an·i·mate \ˈan-ə-ˌmāt\ *vt* **1 :** to give life to : make alive ⟨belief that the soul *animates* the body⟩ **2 :** to give spirit and vigor to : ENLIVEN **3 a :** to make in such a way as to create lifelike movement ⟨*animate* a cartoon⟩ **b :** to make as an animated cartoon ⟨*animate* a story⟩

an·i·mat·ed \-ˌmāt-əd\ *adj* **1 a :** ALIVE 1, LIVING **b :** full of movement and activity **c :** full of vigor and spirit : LIVELY ⟨an *animated* discussion⟩ **2 :** having the appearance or movement of something alive ⟨an unusually *animated* sculpture⟩ **3 :** made in the form of an animated cartoon ⟨an *animated* movie⟩ ***synonyms*** see LIVELY — **an·i·mat·ed·ly** *adv*

animated cartoon *n* **:** a motion picture that is made from a series of drawings, computer graphics, or photographs of inanimate objects (as puppets) and that simulates motion by means of slight progressive changes in each frame

an·i·ma·tion \ˌan-ə-ˈmā-shən\ *n* **1 :** SPIRIT 4, LIVELINESS ⟨discussed their plans with *animation*⟩ **2 a :** ANIMATED CARTOON **b :** the preparation of animated cartoons

an·i·ma·to \ˌan-ə-ˈmät-ō\ *adv or adj* **:** with animation — used as a direction in music [Italian]

an·i·ma·tor \ˈan-ə-ˌmāt-ər\ *n* **:** one that contributes to the making of an animated cartoon

an·i·me \ˈan-ə-ˌmā, ˈä-nē-\ *n* **:** a style of animation originating in Japan that is characterized by stark colorful graphics depicting vibrant characters in action-filled plots often with fantastic or futuristic themes [Japanese]

an·i·mism \ˈan-ə-ˌmiz-əm\ *n* **:** attribution of conscious life to nature as a whole or to inanimate objects — **an·i·mist** \-məst\ *n* — **an·i·mis·tic** \ˌan-ə-ˈmis-tik\ *adj*

an·i·mos·i·ty \ˌan-ə-ˈmäs-ət-ē\ *n, pl* **-ties :** ill will tending toward active hostility [Late Latin *animositas,* derived from Latin *animus* "spirit, mind, courage, anger"] ***synonyms*** see ENMITY

an·i·mus \ˈan-ə-məs\ *n* **1 :** basic attitude : INTENTION **2 :** deep-seated hostility : ANTAGONISM [Latin, "mind, spirit, anger"]

an·ion \ˈan-ˌī-ən\ *n* **:** a negatively charged ion [Greek, from *anienai* "to go up," from *ana-* + *ienai* "to go"] — **an·ion·ic** \ˌan-ī-ˈän-ik\ *adj*

an·ise \ˈan-əs\ *n* **:** an herb related to the carrot with aromatic seeds; *also* : ANISEED [derived from Greek *anison*]

ani·seed \ˈan-ə-ˌsēd, -əs-\ *n* **:** the seed of anise often used as a flavoring in liqueurs and in cooking

an·iso·trop·ic \ˌan-ˌī-sə-ˈträp-ik\ *adj* **:** having properties that differ when measured from different directions ⟨an *anisotropic* crystal⟩

ankh \ˈängk\ *n* **:** a cross having a loop for its upper vertical arm and serving especially in ancient Egypt as an emblem of life [Egyptian *ʿnḫ* "live"]

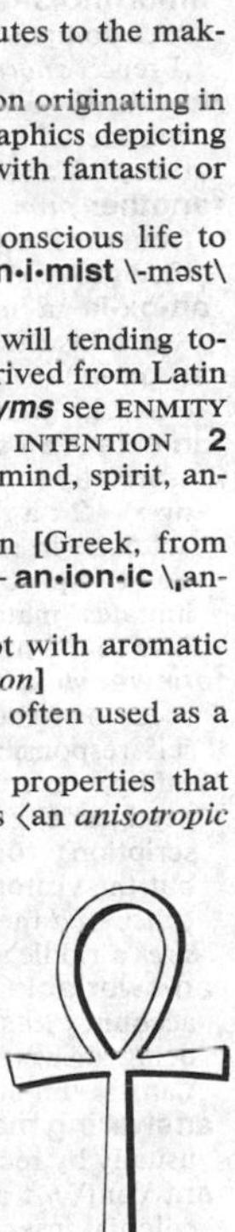

ankh

an·kle \ˈang-kəl\ *n* **:** the joint between the foot and the leg; *also* : the region of this joint [Old English *ancleōw*]

an·kle·bone \-ˈbōn, -ˌbōn\ *n* **:** TALUS 1

an·klet \ˈang-klət\ *n* **1 :** something (as an ornament) worn around the ankle **2 :** a short sock reaching slightly above the ankle

an·ky·lo·saur \ˈang-kə-lō-ˌsȯr\ *n* **:** any of several plant-eating dinosaurs of the Cretaceous period having a thickset body with bony plates covering the back [Greek *ankylos* "crooked" + *sauros* "lizard"]

an·ky·lo·sis \ˌang-ki-ˈlō-səs\ *n, pl* **-lo·ses** \-ˌsēz\ **1 :** stiffness or immobility of a joint by disease or surgery **2 :** a growing together of parts (as bones) into a rigid whole [derived from Greek *ankylos* "crooked"] — **an·ky·lose** \ˈang-ki-ˌlōs, -ˌlōz\ *vb*

an·nal·ist \ˈan-l-əst\ *n* **:** a writer of annals : HISTORIAN — **an·nal·is·tic** \ˌan-l-ˈis-tik\ *adj*

an·nals \ˈan-lz\ *n pl* **1 :** a record of events arranged in yearly sequence **2 :** historical records : CHRONICLES **3 :** records of the activities of an organization [Latin *annales,* from *annalis* "yearly," from *annus* "year"]

An·nam·ese \ˌan-ə-ˈmēz, -ˈmēs\ *n, pl* **Annamese 1** *or* **An·nam·ite** \ˈan-ə-ˌmīt\ **:** a native or inhabitant of Annam **2 :** VIETNAMESE 2 [*Annam,* region of Vietnam] — **Annamese** *adj*

an·nat·to \ə-ˈnä-ˌtō\ *n, pl* **-tos :** a yellowish red substance used for dyeing that is made from the pulp around the seeds of a tropical tree; *also* : the tree from which annatto is derived [Carib *annoto* "tree producing annatto"]

an·neal \ə-ˈnēl\ *vt* **1 :** to heat and then cool (as steel or glass) for softening and making less brittle **2 :** STRENGTHEN, TOUGHEN ⟨*annealed* by hardship⟩ [Old English *onǣlan* "to set on fire," from *on* + *ǣlan* "to burn"]

an·ne·lid \ˈan-l-əd\ *n* **:** any of a phylum (Annelida) of long segmented invertebrate animals (as an earthworm or a leech) having a body cavity [derived from Latin *annellus* "little ring," from *annulus* "ring"] — **annelid** *adj*

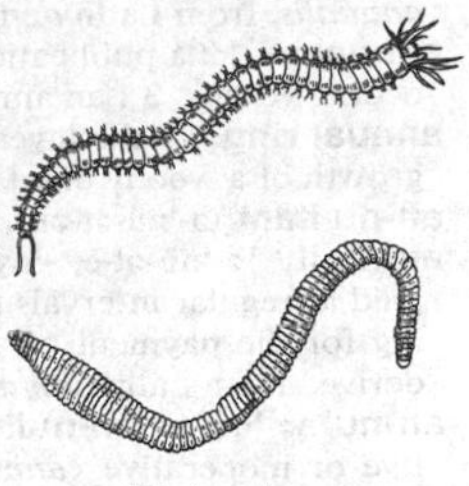

annelid: *top* clam worm, *bottom* earthworm

1an·nex \ə-ˈneks, ˈan-ˌeks\ *vt* **1 :** to add as an additional part : APPEND ⟨a protocol *annexed* to the treaty⟩ **2 :** to incorporate (a territory) within one's own domain ⟨the United States *annexed* Texas in 1845⟩ [derived from Latin *annexus* "attached," from *annectere* "to bind to," from *ad-* + *nectere* "to bind"] — **an·nex·a·tion** \ˌan-ˌek-ˈsā-shən\ *n* — **an·nex·a·tion·al** \-shnəl, -shən-l\ *adj* — **an·nex·a·tion·ist** \-shə-nəst, -shnəst\ *n*

2an·nex \ˈan-ˌeks, -iks\ *n* **:** something annexed or appended; *esp* : a part (as a wing) added to a building

an·ni·hi·late \ə-ˈnī-ə-ˌlāt\ *vt* **:** to destroy completely ⟨*annihilate* an entire army⟩ [Latin *annihilare* "to reduce to nothing," from *ad-* + *nihil* "nothing"] ***synonyms*** see DESTROY — **an·ni·hi·la·tion** \-ˌnī-ə-ˈlā-shən\ *n* — **an·ni·hi·la·tor** \-ˈnī-ə-ˌlāt-ər\ *n*

an·ni·ver·sa·ry \ˌan-ə-ˈvərs-rē, -ə-rē\ *n, pl* **-ries 1 a :** the annual recurrence of a date marking a notable event **b :** a date that follows such an event by a specified period of time measured in units other than years ⟨the 6-month *anniversary* of the accident⟩ **2 :** the celebration of an anniversary [Latin *anniversarius* "returning annually," from *annus* "year" + *vertere* "to turn"]

an·no Do·mi·ni \ˌan-ō-ˈdäm-ə-nē, -ˈdō-mə-, -ˌnī\ *adv, often cap A* — used to indicate that a time division falls within the Christian era; abbreviation *A.D.* [Medieval Latin, "in the year of the Lord"]

an·no·tate \ˈan-ə-ˌtāt\ *vb* **:** to make or furnish critical or explanatory notes or comment — **an·no·ta·tor** \-ˌtāt-ər\ *n*

an·no·ta·tion \ˌan-ə-ˈtā-shən\ *n* **1 :** the act of annotating **2 :** a note of comment or explanation

an·nounce \ə-ˈnau̇ns\ *vb* **1 :** to make known publicly : PROCLAIM **2 a :** to give notice of the arrival, presence, or readiness of ⟨*announce* dinner⟩ **b :** to indicate beforehand : FORETELL **3 :** to serve as an announcer [Medieval French *annuncier,* from Latin *annuntiare,* from *ad-* + *nuntiare* "to report," from *nuntius* "messenger"] ***synonyms*** see DECLARE

an·nounce·ment \ə-ˈnau̇ns-mənt\ *n* **1 :** the act of announcing **2 :** a public notice announcing something

an·nounc·er \ə-ˈnau̇n-sər\ *n* **:** one who announces: as **a :** a person who introduces television or radio programs, makes commercial announcements, or gives station identification **b :** a person who describes and comments on the action in a broadcast sports event

an·noy \ə-ˈnȯi\ *vb* **:** to disturb or irritate especially by repeated acts : VEX [Medieval French *anuier, ennoier,* from Late Latin *inodiare* "to make hateful," from Latin *in* "in" + *odium* "hatred"] — **an·noy·er** *n* — **an·noy·ing·ly** \-ing-lē\ *adv*

synonyms ANNOY, VEX, IRK, BOTHER mean to upset a person's composure. ANNOY implies a wearing on the nerves by persistent petty unpleasantness ⟨their constant complaining *annoys* us⟩. VEX implies greater provocation and stronger disturbance and usually connotes anger but sometimes perplexity or anxiety ⟨*vexed* by her son's failure to clean his room⟩. IRK stresses difficulty in enduring and the resulting weariness or impatience of spirit ⟨careless waste *irks* the boss⟩. BOTHER suggests interference with comfort or peace of mind ⟨don't *bother* me while I'm reading⟩.

an·noy·ance \ə-ˈnȯi-əns\ *n* **1 a :** the act of annoying or of being annoyed **b :** the state or feeling of being annoyed : VEXATION **2 :** a source of irritation : NUISANCE

\ə\ **abut**	\au̇\ **out**	\i\ **tip**	\ȯ\ **saw**	\u̇\ **foot**
\ər\ **further**	\ch\ **chin**	\ī\ **life**	\ȯi\ **coin**	\y\ **yet**
\a\ **mat**	\e\ **pet**	\j\ **job**	\th\ **thin**	\yü\ **few**
\ā\ **take**	\ē\ **easy**	\ng\ **sing**	\t͟h\ **this**	\yu̇\ **cure**
\ä\ **cot, cart**	\g\ **go**	\ō\ **bone**	\ü\ **food**	\zh\ **vision**

1**an·nu·al** \ˈan-yə-wəl, ˈan-yəl\ *adj* **1 :** covering the period of a year ⟨*annual* rainfall⟩ **2 :** occurring or performed once a year : YEARLY ⟨an *annual* reunion⟩ **3 :** completing the life cycle in one growing season or single year ⟨*annual* plants⟩ [Late Latin *annualis,* from Latin *annus* "year"] — **an·nu·al·ly** \-ē\ *adv*

2**annual** *n* **1 :** a publication appearing yearly **2 :** an event that occurs yearly **3 :** an annual plant

annual ring *n* **:** the layer of wood produced by a single year's growth of a woody plant

an·nu·itant \ə-ˈnü-ət-ənt, -ˈnyü-\ *n* **:** a beneficiary of an annuity

an·nu·ity \ə-ˈnü-ət-ē, -ˈnyü-\ *n, pl* **-ties 1 :** a sum of money paid at regular intervals (as every year) **2 :** a contract providing for the payment of an annuity [Medieval French *annuité,* derived from Latin *annuus* "yearly," from *annus* "year"]

an·nul \ə-ˈnəl\ *vt* **an·nulled; an·nul·ling 1 :** to make ineffective or inoperative ⟨*annul* a drug's effect⟩ **2 :** to declare or make legally void ⟨*annul* a marriage⟩ [Late Latin *annullare,* from Latin *ad-* + *nullus* "not any"] ***synonyms*** see NULLIFY

an·nu·lar \ˈan-yə-lər\ *adj* **:** of, relating to, or forming a ring [Latin *annulus* "ring"]

annular eclipse *n* **:** an eclipse in which a thin outer ring of the sun's disk is not covered by the smaller dark disk of the moon

an·nu·late \ˈan-yə-lət, -ˌlāt\ *adj* **:** furnished with or composed of rings : RINGED

an·nul·ment \ə-ˈnəl-mənt\ *n* **:** the act of annulling or state of being annulled; *esp* **:** a legal declaration that a marriage is invalid

an·nu·lus \ˈan-yə-ləs\ *n, pl* **-li** \-ˌlī, -ˌlē\ *also* **-lus·es :** RING; *esp* **:** a part, structure, or marking resembling a ring ⟨*annuli* of the earthworm⟩ [Latin]

an·nun·ci·ate \ə-ˈnən-sē-ˌāt\ *vt* **:** ANNOUNCE — **an·nun·ci·a·tor** \-ˌāt-ər\ *n* — **an·nun·ci·a·to·ry** \-sē-ə-ˌtōr-ē, -ˌtȯr-\ *adj*

an·nun·ci·a·tion \ə-ˌnən-sē-ˈā-shən\ *n* **:** the act of announcing

Annunciation *n* **:** March 25 observed as a church festival in commemoration of the announcement of the Incarnation to the Virgin Mary

an·ode \ˈan-ˌōd\ *n* **1 :** the positive electrode of an electrolytic cell to which the negative ions are attracted — compare CATHODE **2 :** the negative terminal of a primary cell or of a storage battery that is delivering current **3 :** the electron-collecting electrode of an electron tube [Greek *anodos* "way up," from *ana-* + *hodos* "way"] — **an·od·ic** \a-ˈnäd-ik\ *adj*

an·od·ize \ˈan-ə-ˌdīz\ *vt* **:** to subject (a metal) to electrolytic action as the anode of a cell in order to coat with a protective or decorative film

1**an·o·dyne** \ˈan-ə-ˌdīn\ *adj* **:** serving to relieve pain : SOOTHING [Greek *anōdynos,* from *a-* + *odynē* "pain"]

2**anodyne** *n* **:** an anodyne drug or agent

anoint \ə-ˈnȯint\ *vt* **1 :** to rub over with oil or an oily substance **2 a :** to apply oil to as a sacred rite **b :** to choose by or as if by divine election; *also* **:** to name as if by a ritual anointment ⟨critics *anointed* the author as the bright new talent⟩ [Medieval French *enoindre,* from Latin *inunguere,* from *in-* + *unguere* "to smear"] — **anoint·er** *n* — **anoint·ment** \-mənt\ *n*

anointing of the sick : a sacrament that consists of anointing a usually critically ill person and praying for his or her recovery and salvation

ano·le \ə-ˈnō-lē\ *n* **:** any of various chiefly tropical arboreal lizards that are able to change color and in the males have a usually brightly colored dewlap [of American Indian origin]

anom·a·lous \ə-ˈnäm-ə-ləs\ *adj* **1 :** deviating from a general rule or method or from accepted notions of order **2 :** being not what would naturally be expected : IRREGULAR, UNUSUAL [Late Latin *anomalus,* from Greek *anōmalos,* literally, "uneven," from *a-* + *homalos* "even," from *homos* "same"] — **anom·a·lous·ly** *adv* — **anom·a·lous·ness** *n*

anom·a·ly \ə-ˈnäm-ə-lē\ *n, pl* **-lies 1 :** deviation from what is usual or expected **2 :** something anomalous : something different, abnormal, peculiar, or not easily classified

anon \ə-ˈnän\ *adv* **1** *archaic* **:** at once : IMMEDIATELY **2 :** SHORTLY 2a, SOON **3 :** after a while : LATER ⟨more of that *anon*⟩ [Old English *on ān,* from *on* "in" + *ān* "one"]

an·o·nym·i·ty \ˌan-ə-ˈnim-ət-ē\ *n, pl* **-ties 1 :** the quality or state of being anonymous **2 :** one that is anonymous

anon·y·mous \ə-ˈnän-ə-məs\ *adj* **1 :** having or giving no name ⟨an *anonymous* author⟩ **2 :** of unknown or unnamed source or origin ⟨*anonymous* gifts⟩ ⟨an *anonymous* letter⟩ **3 :** lacking individuality or personality ⟨the *anonymous* faces in the crowd⟩ [Late Latin *anonymus,* from Greek *anōnymos,* from *a-* + *onyma* "name"] — **anon·y·mous·ly** *adv* — **anon·y·mous·ness** *n*

anoph·e·les \ə-ˈnäf-ə-ˌlēz\ *n* **:** any of a genus of mosquitoes that includes all mosquitoes which transmit malaria to humans [Greek *anōphelēs* "useless"] — **anoph·e·line** \-ˌlīn\ *adj or n*

an·o·rak \ˈan-ə-ˌrak\ *n* **:** PARKA [Inuit (Greenland) *annoraaq*]

an·orex·ia \ˌa-nə-ˈrek-sē-ə, -ˈrek-shə\ *n* **:** ANOREXIA NERVOSA [Greek, "loss of appetite," from *a-* + *orexis* "appetite"]

anorexia ner·vo·sa \-nər-ˈvō-sə, -zə\ *n* **:** a serious eating disorder primarily of young women in their teens that is characterized especially by an abnormal fear of weight gain leading to faulty eating patterns and usually excessive weight loss [New Latin, literally, "nervous loss of appetite"]

1**an·orex·ic** \ˌan-ə-ˈrek-sik\ *adj* **:** affected with anorexia nervosa; *also* **:** seemingly affected with anorexia nervosa as by being excessively skinny

2**anorexic** *n* **:** a person affected with anorexia nervosa

an·or·thite \ə-ˈnȯr-ˌthīt\ *n* **:** a white, grayish, or reddish feldspar [French, from Greek *a-* + *orthos* "straight"]

an·or·tho·site \ə-ˈnȯr-thə-ˌsīt\ *n* **:** a granular plutonic igneous rock composed chiefly of a plagioclase feldspar (as labradorite) [French *anorthose,* from Greek *a-* + *orthos* "straight"]

1**an·oth·er** \ə-ˈnəth-ər\ *adj* **1 :** different or distinct from the one considered ⟨from *another* angle⟩ **2 :** some other ⟨at *another* time⟩ **3 :** being one more in addition ⟨bring *another* cup⟩

2**another** *pron* **1 :** an additional one **2 :** one that is different from the first or present one **3 :** one of an indefinite or unspecified group ⟨for one reason or *another*⟩

an·ox·ia \a-ˈnäk-sē-ə\ *n* **:** a condition (as at high altitudes) in which insufficient oxygen reaches the tissues

an·ox·ic \an-ˈäk-sik\ *adj* **1 :** of, relating to, or affected with anoxia **2 :** greatly deficient in oxygen ⟨*anoxic* water⟩

1**an·swer** \ˈan-sər\ *n* **1 a :** something spoken or written in reply especially to a question **b :** a correct response ⟨knows the *answer*⟩ **2 :** a reply to a charge or accusation : DEFENSE **3 :** an act done in response ⟨his *answer* was to walk out⟩ **4 :** a solution to a problem ⟨more money is not the *answer*⟩ **5 :** one that imitates, matches, or corresponds to another ⟨television's *answer* to the news magazines⟩ [Old English *andswaru*]

2**answer** *vb* **an·swered; an·swer·ing** \ˈans-ring, -ə-ring\ **1 :** to speak or write in reply or in reply to **2 a :** to be or make oneself responsible or accountable ⟨*answered* for the children's safety⟩ **b :** to make amends : ATONE ⟨must *answer* for their negligence⟩ **3 :** CONFORM, CORRESPOND ⟨*answered* to the description⟩ **4 :** to act in response ⟨the home team scored first but the visitors *answered* quickly⟩ **5 :** to be adequate : SERVE ⟨*answered* the purpose⟩ **6 :** to offer or find a solution for ⟨*answer* a riddle⟩ — **an·swer·er** \ˈan-sər-ər\ *n*

an·swer·able \ˈans-rə-bəl, -ə-rə-\ *adj* **1 :** subject to be called to account : RESPONSIBLE ⟨*answerable* for a debt⟩ **2 :** capable of being answered ⟨an *answerable* question⟩ — **an·swer·abil·i·ty** \ˌans-rə-ˈbil-ət-ē, ˌan-sə-\ *n*

answering machine *n* **:** a machine that receives telephone calls usually by recording messages from callers

ant \ˈant\ *n* **:** any of a family of colonial insects that are related to the wasps and bees and have a complex social organization with various castes performing special duties [Middle English *ante, emete,* from Old English *æmette*] — **ants in one's pants :** impatience for action or activity : RESTLESSNESS

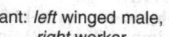

ant: *left* winged male, *right* worker

ant- — see ANTI-

1**-ant** \ənt, ᵊnt\ *n suffix* **1 a :** one that performs (a specified action) ⟨cool*ant*⟩ **b :** one that promotes (a specified action or process) ⟨expector*ant*⟩ **2 :** one that is acted upon (in a specified manner) ⟨inhal*ant*⟩ [Latin *-ant-, -ans,* present participle suffix of some verbs]

2**-ant** *adj suffix* **1 :** performing (a specified action) or being (in a specified condition) ⟨somnambul*ant*⟩ **2 :** promoting (a specified action or process) ⟨expector*ant*⟩

ant·ac·id \ant-ˈas-əd, ˈant-\ *n* **:** an agent that prevents or neutralizes acidity — **antacid** *adj*

an·tag·o·nism \an-ˈtag-ə-ˌniz-əm\ *n* **1 a :** active opposition or hostility **b :** opposition between two conflicting forces, tendencies, or principles **2 :** opposition in physiological action (as of two drugs or muscles) ***synonyms*** see ENMITY

an·tag·o·nist \-nəst\ *n* **1** : one that opposes another especially in combat : ADVERSARY **2** : an agent of physiological antagonism; *esp* : a drug that opposes the action of another ***synonyms*** see OPPONENT

an·tag·o·nis·tic \an-ˌtag-ə-ˈnis-tik\ *adj* : characterized by or resulting from antagonism — **an·tag·o·nis·ti·cal·ly** \-ti-kə-lē, -klē\ *adv*

an·tag·o·nize \an-ˈtag-ə-ˌnīz\ *vt* **1** : to act in opposition to : COUNTERACT **2** : to incur or provoke the hostility of ⟨his constant criticism *antagonized* his coworkers⟩ [Greek *antagōnizesthai,* from *anti-* + *agōnizesthai* "to struggle," from *agōn* "contest"]

ant·arc·tic \ant-ˈärk-tik, ˈant-, -ˈärt-ik\ *adj, often cap* : of or relating to the South Pole or to the region near it [Latin *antarcticus,* from Greek *antarktikos,* from *anti-* + *arktikos* "arctic"]

antarctic circle *n, often cap A&C* : the parallel of latitude that is approximately 66½ degrees south of the equator

An·tar·es \an-ˈtaər-ˌēz, -ˈteər-\ *n* : a giant red star of very low density that is the brightest star in Scorpio [Greek *Antarēs*]

ant bear *n* : AARDVARK

ant cow *n* : an aphid from which ants obtain honeydew

[1]**an·te** \ˈant-ē\ *n* : a poker stake usually put up before the deal to build the pot [*ante-*]

[2]**ante** *vt* **an·ted; an·te·ing** : to put up (an ante); *also* : PAY 1 — often used with *up*

ante- *prefix* **1 a** : prior : earlier ⟨*ante*date⟩ **b** : anterior : forward ⟨*ante*room⟩ **2** : prior to : earlier than ⟨*ante*diluvian⟩ [Latin *ante* "before, in front of"]

ant·eat·er \ˈant-ˌēt-ər\ *n* : any of several mammals (as an echidna or aardvark) that feed largely or entirely on ants; *esp* : an edentate with a long narrow snout and very long extensible tongue

an·te·bel·lum \ˌant-i-ˈbel-əm\ *adj* : existing before a war; *esp* : existing before the American Civil War [Latin *ante bellum* "before the war"]

[1]**an·te·ce·dent** \ˌant-ə-ˈsēd-nt\ *n* **1** : a noun, pronoun, phrase, or clause referred to by a personal or relative pronoun ⟨in "the house that Jack built," *house* is the *antecedent* of *that*⟩ **2** : the first term of a mathematical ratio **3** : a preceding event, condition, or cause **4 a** : a predecessor in a series; *esp* : a model or stimulus for later developments **b** *pl* : ANCESTORS, PARENTS [Latin *antecedens* "what precedes," from *antecedere* "to go before," from *ante-* + *cedere* "to go"]

[2]**antecedent** *adj* : coming earlier in time or order ***synonyms*** see PRECEDING — **an·te·ce·dent·ly** *adv*

an·te·cham·ber \ˈant-i-ˌchām-bər\ *n* : ANTEROOM

an·te·date \ˈant-i-ˌdāt\ *vt* **1** : to date (as a check) with a date prior to that of actual writing **2** : to precede in time ⟨automobiles *antedate* airplanes⟩

an·te·di·lu·vi·an \ˌant-i-də-ˈlü-vē-ən, -dī-\ *adj* **1** : of or relating to the period before the Flood described in the Bible **2** : very old or old-fashioned : ANTIQUATED [*ante-* + Latin *diluvium* "flood"] — **antediluvian** *n*

an·te·lope \ˈant-l-ˌōp\ *n, pl* **-lope** *or* **-lopes** **1 a** : any of various ruminant mammals chiefly of Africa and southwest Asia that are related to the goats and oxen and have a slender lean build and usually horns directed upward and backward **b** : PRONGHORN **2** : leather from antelope hide [Middle English, a fabulous heraldic beast, probably from Middle French *antelop,* a savage animal with sawlike horns, derived from Late Greek *antholops*]

an·te me·ri·di·em \ˌant-i-mə-ˈrid-ē-əm, -ē-ˌem\ *adj* : being before noon — abbreviation *a.m.* [Latin]

an·ten·na \an-ˈten-ə\ *n, pl* **-ten·nae** \-ˈten-ˌē\ *or* **-tennas** **1** *pl usually antennae* : one of a pair of slender movable segmented sensory organs on the head of an arthropod (as an insect or a crab) **2** *pl usually antennas* : a usually metallic device (as a rod or wire) for sending or receiving radio waves [Latin, "sail yard"]

Word History Latin *antenna* meant "sail yard" — a sail yard is a long spar that supports and spreads the sail on a sailing vessel. The Greek word for a sail yard was *keraia,* but "sail yard" was only the secondary meaning of this word. The primary meaning was "horn." The philosopher Aristotle used *keraiai* for the feelers of insects, probably because of their resemblance to the horns of some larger animals. In a Latin translation of Aristotle's work made during the Renaissance, the word *antennae* was used for Greek *keraiai.* In English we still use *antennae* for insects' feelers. And now we also use *antenna* with a regular English plural ending *-s* for the metal rods which pick up radio waves and seem to feel the air like the antennae of an insect.

an·ten·nule \an-ˈten-yül\ *n* : a small antenna (as of a crayfish)

an·te·nup·tial \ˌanti-ˈnəp-shəl, -chəl\ *adj* : PRENUPTIAL

an·te·pen·di·um \ˌant-i-ˈpen-dē-əm\ *n, pl* **-di·ums** *or* **-dia** \-dē-ə\ : a hanging for the front of an altar, pulpit, or lectern [Medieval Latin, from Latin *ante-* + *pendēre* "to hang"]

an·te·pe·nult \ˌant-i-ˈpē-ˌnəlt\ *n* : the 3rd syllable of a word counting from the end ⟨"-cu" is the *antepenult* in "accumulate"⟩ — **an·te·pen·ul·ti·mate** \-pi-ˈnəl-tə-mət\ *adj or n*

an·te·ri·or \an-ˈtir-ē-ər\ *adj* **1 a** : situated before or toward the front **b** : situated near or toward the head or the part most nearly corresponding to a head **2** : coming before in time : ANTECEDENT [Latin, comparative of *ante* "before"] — **an·te·ri·or·ly** *adv*

anterior cru·ci·ate ligament \-ˈkrü-shē-ˌāt\ *n* : a cross-shaped stabilizing ligament of the knee that attaches the front of the tibia with the back of the femur and that is subject to injury especially by tearing — called also *ACL* [New Latin *cruciatus* "cross-shaped," from Latin *cruc-, crux* "cross"]

an·te·room \ˈant-i-ˌrüm, -ˌrum\ *n* : a room used as an entrance to another room or as a waiting room

anth- — see ANTI-

an·them \ˈan-thəm, ˈant-\ *n* **1** : a sacred vocal composition with words usually from the Scriptures **2** : a song or hymn of praise or gladness **3** : a usually rousing popular song that is representative of a particular subculture, movement, or point of view ⟨*anthems* of teenage rebellion⟩ [Old English *antefn* "antiphon," from Late Latin *antiphona*] — **anthemic** *adj*

an·ther \ˈan-thər, ˈant-\ *n* : the part of a stamen that produces and contains pollen and is usually borne on a stalk [Latin *anthera* "medicine made of flowers," from Greek *anthēra,* from *anthos* "flower"] — **an·ther·al** \-thə-rəl\ *adj*

an·ther·id·i·um \ˌan-thə-ˈrid-ē-əm, ˌant-\ *n, pl* **-ia** \-ē-ə\ : the male reproductive organ of a spore-producing plant (as a moss or fern) — **an·ther·id·i·al** \-ē-əl\ *adj*

ant·hill \ˈant-ˌhil\ *n* : a mound thrown up by ants or termites in digging their nest

an·tho·cy·a·nin \ˌan-thə-ˈsī-ə-nən, ˌant-\ *n* : any of various soluble pigments producing blue to red coloring in flowers and plants [Greek *anthos* "flower" + *kyanos* "dark blue"]

an·thol·o·gist \an-ˈthäl-ə-ˌjist\ *n* : a compiler of an anthology

an·thol·o·gize \an-ˈthäl-ə-ˌjīz\ *vt* : to compile or publish in an anthology ⟨the story has often been *anthologized*⟩ — **an·thol·o·gist** \-jəst\ *n*

an·thol·o·gy \an-ˈthäl-ə-jē\ *n, pl* **-gies** **1** : a collection of selected literary pieces or passages **2** : a collection of selected pieces in any art form (as songs, recordings, or paintings) [Greek *anthologia* "gathering of flowers," from *anthos* "flower" + *legein* "to gather"]

an·tho·zo·an \ˌan-thə-ˈzō-ən, ˌant-\ *n* : any of a class (Anthozoa) of marine coelenterates (as the corals and sea anemones) having polyps with radial partitions [Greek *anthos* "flower" + *zōion* "animal"] — **anthozoan** *adj*

an·thra·cene \ˈan-thrə-ˌsēn, ˈant-\ *n* : a crystalline hydrocarbon $C_{14}H_{10}$ obtained from coal-tar distillation

an·thra·cite \ˈan-thrə-ˌsīt, ˈant-\ *n* : a hard glossy coal that burns without much smoke or flame [Greek *anthrakitis,* from *anthrax* "coal, carbuncle"] — **an·thra·cit·ic** \ˌan-thrə-ˈsit-ik, ˌant-\ *adj*

an·thrax \ˈan-ˌthraks\ *n* : an infectious disease of warm-blooded animals (as cattle and sheep) that is caused by a spore-forming bacterium, is transmissible to humans, and is characterized by ulcerating skin nodules or by often fatal lesions in the lungs; *also* : the bacterium causing anthrax [Latin *anthrax* "carbuncle," from Greek, "coal, carbuncle"]

anthrop- *or* **anthropo-** *combining form* : human being ⟨*anthropo*centric⟩ [Greek *anthrōpos*]

an·throp·ic \an-ˈthräp-ik\ *or* **an·throp·i·cal** \-i-kəl\ *adj* : of or relating to human beings or the period of their existence on earth

\ə\ **abut**	\au̇\ **out**	\i\ **tip**	\ȯ\ **saw**	\u̇\ **foot**
\ər\ **further**	\ch\ **chin**	\ī\ **life**	\ȯi\ **coin**	\y\ **yet**
\a\ **mat**	\e\ **pet**	\j\ **job**	\th\ **thin**	\yü\ **few**
\ā\ **take**	\ē\ **easy**	\ng\ **sing**	\t͟h\ **this**	\yu̇\ **cure**
\ä\ **cot, cart**	\g\ **go**	\ō\ **bone**	\ü\ **food**	\zh\ **vision**

an·thro·po·cen·tric \ˌan-thrə-pə-ˈsen-trik, ˌant-\ *adj* : interpreting or regarding the world in terms of human values and experiences

an·thro·po·gen·ic \ˌan-thrə-pə-ˈjen-ik, ˌant-\ *adj* : of or relating to the influence of human beings on nature ⟨*anthropogenic* pollutants⟩

[1]**an·thro·poid** \ˈan-thrə-ˌpȯid, ˈant-\ *adj* : of, relating to, or being an anthropoid ⟨*anthropoid* apes⟩

[2]**anthropoid** *n* **1** : APE 1b **2** : a person resembling an ape (as in behavior)

an·thro·pol·o·gy \ˌan-thrə-ˈpäl-ə-jē, ˌant-\ *n* : a science that deals with human beings and especially with their physical characteristics, origin, environmental and social relations, and culture — **an·thro·po·log·i·cal** \-pə-ˈläj-i-kəl\ *adj* — **an·thro·po·log·i·cal·ly** \-ˈläj-i-kə-lē, -klē\ *adv* — **an·thro·pol·o·gist** \-ˈpäl-ə-jəst\ *n*

an·thro·pom·e·try \ˌan-thrə-ˈpäm-ə-trē, ˌant-\ *n* : the study of human body measurements — **an·thro·po·met·ric** \-pə-ˈme-trik\ *adj*

an·thro·po·mor·phic \ˌan-thrə-pə-ˈmȯr-fik, ˌant-\ *adj* **1** : described or thought of as having a human form or human attributes ⟨*anthropomorphic* deities⟩ **2** : ascribing human characteristics to nonhuman things ⟨*anthropomorphic* interpretations of animal behavior⟩ — **an·thro·po·mor·phi·cal·ly** \-fi-kə-lē, -klē\ *adv* — **an·thro·po·mor·phism** \-ˌfiz-əm\ *n*

an·thro·po·mor·phize \-ˈmȯr-ˌfīz\ *vt* : to attribute human form or personality to

an·thro·poph·a·gous \ˌan-thrə-ˈpäf-ə-gəs, ˌant-\ *adj* : feeding on human flesh — **an·thro·poph·a·gy** \-ˈpäf-ə-jē\ *n*

[1]**an·ti** \ˈan-ˌtī, ˈant-ē\ *n* : one that is opposed [*anti-*]

[2]**anti** *prep* : opposed to : AGAINST

anti- *or* **ant-** *or* **anth-** *prefix* **1** : opposite in kind, position, or action ⟨*anti*climax⟩ ⟨*anti*clockwise⟩ ⟨*anti*matter⟩ **2 a** : hostile toward ⟨*anti*clerical⟩ ⟨*anti*-Semite⟩ **b** : opposing in effect or activity : counteracting ⟨*ant*acid⟩ ⟨*anti*coagulant⟩ **3** : serving to prevent or cure ⟨*anti*malarial⟩ **4** : combating or defending against ⟨*anti*aircraft⟩ ⟨*anti*ballistic missile⟩ [Greek *anti* "against"]

antiacademic
antiadministration
antiaggression
antiaging
antialcohol
antialcoholism
antialien
antiapartheid
anti–Arab
antiaristocratic
antiarmor
antiarthritic
antiarthritis
anti–Asian
antiasthma
antiauthoritarian
antiauthoritarianism
antibias
antibillboard
anti–Bolshevik
antibourgeois
antiboycott
anti–British
antibureaucratic
antiburglar
antiburglary
anticapitalism
anticapitalist
anticarcinogen
anticarcinogenic
anticaries
anti–Catholic
anti–Catholicism
anticensorship
anticholesterol
anti–Christian
anti–Christianity
antichurch
anticigarette
anticlassical
anticlotting
anticollision
anticolonial
anticolonialism
anticolonialist
anticommercial
anticommercialism
anticommunism
anticommunist
anticonservation
anticonservationist
anticonsumer
anticonventional
anticorrosion
anticorrosive
anticorruption
anticrime
anticruelty
anticultural
antidandruff
anti–Darwinian
anti–Darwinism
antidepression
antidiabetic
antidiarrheal
antidiscrimination
antidogmatic
antieconomic
antiemetic
anti–English
antienvironmental
antiepilepsy
antiepileptic
antiestablishment
antievolution
antievolutionary
antievolutionism
antievolutionist
anti–fascism
anti–fascist
antifatigue
antifemale
antifeminine
antifeminism
antifeminist
antiflu
antiforeign
antiforeigner
antifraud
anti–French
antifriction
antigambling
anti–German
antiglare
antiglobalization
antigovernment
antigrowth
antiguerrilla
antigun
antihijacking
antihomosexual
antihuman
antihumanism
antihumanist
antihumanistic
antihumanitarian
antihunter
antihunting
antihysteric
anti–icing
anti–immigrant
anti–immigration
anti–imperialism
anti–imperialist
anti–infective
anti–inflation
anti–inflationary
anti–institutional
anti–integration
anti–Irish
anti–Italian
antijam
antijamming
anti–Japanese
anti–Jewish
anti–Judaism
antilabor
antiliberal
antiliberalism
antilibertarian
antilitter
antilittering
antilynching
antimalaria
antimale
antiman
antimanagement
antimaterialism
antimaterialist
antimerger
antimilitarism
antimilitarist
antimilitaristic
antimilitary
antimiscegenation
antimonarchist
antimonopolist
antimonopoly
antimosquito
antinausea
anti–Nazi
antinepotism
antinoise
antiobesity
antiobscenity
antiorganization
antipapal
antiparasitic
antipesticide
antiplaque
antipleasure
antipoaching
antipolice
antipornographic
antipornography
antipoverty
antiprofiteering
antiprogressive
antiprostitution
antirabies
antiracism
antiracist
antiracketeering
antiradical
antirape
antirealism
antirealist
antirecession
antireflection
antireflective
antireform
antirejection
antireligion
antireligious
antirepublican
antirevolutionary
antirheumatic
antiriot
antiromantic
antiromanticism
anti–Russian
antirust
antiscience
antiscientific
antisecrecy
antisegregation
antisentimental
antisex
antisexist
antisexual
antisexuality
antishock
antishoplifting
antislavery
antisleep
antislip
antismoke
antismoker
antismoking
antismuggling
antismut
anti–Soviet
antispam
antispending
antistrike
antisubmarine
antisubversion
antisubversive
antisuicide
antisyphilitic
antitank
anti–tarnish
antitax
antitechnological
antitechnology
antiterrorism
antiterrorist
antitheft
antitheoretical
antitobacco
antitotalitarian
antitraditional
antitubercular
antituberculosis
antituberculous
antitumor
antityphoid
antiulcer
antiunemployment
antiunion
antiuniversity
antiurban
antiviolence
antiviral
antivivisection
antivivisectionist
antiwar
antiwear
anti–West
anti–Western
antiwoman
antiwrinkle
anti–Zionism
anti–Zionist

an·ti·abor·tion \ˌant-ē-ə-ˈbȯr-shən, ˌan-ˌtī-\ *adj* : opposed to abortion and especially to the legalization of abortion — **an·ti·abor·tion·ist** \-shə-nist\ *n*

an·ti·air·craft \ˌant-ē-ˈaər-ˌkraft, -ˈeər-\ *adj* : designed or used for defense against aircraft — **antiaircraft** *n*

an·ti–Amer·i·can \-ə-ˈmer-ə-kən\ *adj* : opposed or hostile to the people or the government policies of the U.S. — **an·ti–Amer·i·can·ism** \-kə-ˌniz-əm\ *n*

an·ti·art \-ˈärt\ *n* : art based on premises antithetical to traditional or popular art forms

an·ti·bac·te·ri·al \ˌant-i-bak-ˈtir-ē-əl, ˌan-ˌtī-\ *adj* : directed or effective against bacteria

an·ti·bal·lis·tic missile \ˌant-i-bə-ˌlis-tik-, ˌan-ˌtī-\ *n* : a missile for intercepting and destroying ballistic missiles

an·ti·bi·o·sis \-bī-ˈō-səs, -bē-\ *n* : antagonistic association between organisms to the detriment of one of them or between one organism and a metabolic product of another

an·ti·bi·ot·ic \-bī-ät-ik, -bē-\ *n* : a substance produced by or derived from a microorganism (as a fungus or bacterium) that in dilute solution inhibits or kills another microorganism — **antibiotic** *adj* — **an·ti·bi·ot·i·cal·ly** \-ˈät-i-kə-lē, -klē\ *adv*

an·ti·black \ˌant-ē-ˈblak, ˌan-ˌtī-\ *adj* : opposed or hostile to black people

an·ti·body \ˈant-i-ˌbäd-ē\ *n* : any of various proteins in the blood that are produced by specialized cells in the body and that react with specific antigens to counteract their effects or those of the pathogens on which the antigens may occur

an·ti·busi·ness \ˌant-ē-ˈbiz-nəs, ˌan-ˌtī-\ *adj* : antagonistic toward business and especially big business

an·ti·bus·ing \ˌant-i-ˈbəs-ing, ˌan-ˌtī-\ *adj* : opposed to the busing of schoolchildren

¹an·tic \ˈant-ik\ *n* **1 :** a silly, playful, or ludicrous act or action **:** CAPER ⟨carnival *antics*⟩ **2** *archaic* **:** CLOWN, BUFFOON [Italian *antico,* adj., "ancient," from Latin *antiquus*]

Word History In the ruins of ancient Roman buildings Renaissance Italians found fantastic mural paintings. In Renaissance England any similarly fantastic painting of more modern date that showed strange combinations of human, animal, and floral forms was called *antike* or *anticke,* from the Italian word for "ancient," *antico.* And any odd gesture or strange behavior reminiscent of the ancient Roman paintings became in English an *antic.*

²antic *adj* **1** *archaic* **:** GROTESQUE, BIZARRE **2 :** whimsically grotesque or extravagant ⟨an *antic* comedy⟩

an·ti·can·cer \ˌant-i-ˈkan-sər, ˌan-ˌtī-\ *adj* **:** used or effective against cancer ⟨*anticancer* drugs⟩

An·ti·christ \ˈant-i-ˌkrīst\ *n* **1 :** one who denies or opposes Christ; *esp* **:** a great antagonist expected to fill the world with wickedness but to be conquered forever by Christ at the second coming **2 :** a false Christ

an·tic·i·pate \an-ˈtis-ə-ˌpāt\ *vb* **1 a :** to take into consideration in advance ⟨*anticipate* the result of an action⟩ ⟨*anticipate* a plan⟩ **b :** to deal with before the expected or proper time ⟨*anticipate* a bill⟩ **2 a :** to deal with before another can act or interfere ⟨an idea *anticipated* by an earlier inventor⟩ **b :** to act before (another) often so as to check or counter **3 :** to use in advance of actual possession ⟨*anticipate* one's income⟩ **4 :** to look forward to **:** EXPECT ⟨*anticipate* a holiday⟩ ⟨*anticipate* your visit⟩ [Latin *anticipare,* from *ante-* + *capere* "to take"] ***synonyms*** see FORESEE — **an·tic·i·pa·tor** \-ˌpāt-ər\ *n*

an·tic·i·pa·tion \ˌan-ˌtis-ə-ˈpā-shən\ *n* **1 a :** a prior action that takes into account or forestalls a later action **b :** the act of looking forward; *esp* **:** pleasurable expectation **2 :** a picturing beforehand of a future event or state — **an·tic·i·pa·to·ry** \an-ˈtis-ə-pə-ˌtōr-ē, -ˌtȯr-\ *adj*

an·ti·cler·i·cal \ˌant-i-ˈkler-i-kəl, ˌan-ˌtī-\ *adj* **:** opposed to the influence of the clergy in secular affairs — **anticlerical** *n* — **an·ti·cler·i·cal·ism** \-ˈkler-i-kə-ˌliz-əm\ *n*

an·ti·cli·max \ˌant-i-ˈklī-ˌmaks\ *n* **1 :** the usually sudden change in writing or speaking from a significant idea to a trivial or ludicrous idea; *also* **:** an instance of such change **2 :** an event, period, or outcome that is strikingly less important than expected — **an·ti·cli·mac·tic** \-klī-ˈmak-tik\ *adj* — **an·ti·cli·mac·ti·cal·ly** \-ti-kə-lē, -klē\ *adv*

an·ti·cline \ˈant-i-ˌklīn\ *n* **:** an arch of stratified rock in which the layers bend downward in opposite directions from the crest — compare SYNCLINE [Greek *klinein* "to lean"]

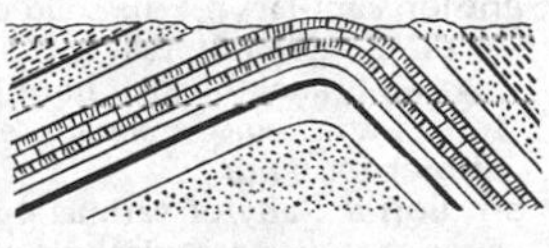

anticline

an·ti·clock·wise \ˌant-i-ˈkläk-ˌwīz, ˌan-ˌtī-\ *adj or adv* **:** COUNTERCLOCKWISE

an·ti·co·ag·u·lant \-kō-ˈag-yə-lənt\ *n* **:** a substance that hinders clotting of blood — **anticoagulant** *adj*

an·ti·co·don \-ˈkō-ˌdän\ *n* **:** a group of three nucleotide bases in transfer RNA that binds to a complementary codon in messenger RNA during protein synthesis at a ribosome

an·ti·com·pet·i·tive \-kəm-ˈpet-ət-iv\ *adj* **:** tending to restrict free competition

an·ti·cy·clone \ˌant-i-ˈsī-ˌklōn\ *n* **:** a system of winds that rotates about a center of high atmospheric pressure clockwise in the northern hemisphere and counterclockwise in the southern, that usually advances at 20 to 30 miles (about 30 to 50 kilometers) per hour, and that usually has a diameter of 1500 to 2500 miles (about 2400 to 4000 kilometers) — **an·ti·cy·clon·ic** \-sī-ˈklän-ik\ *adj*

an·ti·dem·o·crat·ic \ˌant-ē-ˌdem-ə-ˈkrat-ik, ˌan-ˌtī-\ *adj* **:** opposed or hostile to the theories or policies of democracy

an·ti·de·pres·sant \ˌant-i-di-ˈpres-nt, ˌan-ˌtī-\ *also* **an·ti·de·pres·sive** \-di-ˈpres-iv\ *adj* **:** used or tending to relieve mental depression — **antidepressant** *n*

an·ti·dote \ˈant-i-ˌdōt\ *n* **1 :** a remedy to counteract the effects of poison **2 :** something that relieves, prevents, or counteracts ⟨an *antidote* to unemployment⟩ [Latin *antidotum,* from Greek *antidotos,* derived from *anti-* + *didonai* "to give"]

an·ti·drug \ˈan-ˌtī-ˌdrəg, ˌan-tī-ˈ\ *adj* **:** acting against or opposing illegal drugs ⟨an *antidrug* program⟩

an·ti·dump·ing \ˌant-ē-ˈdəm-ping\ *adj* **:** designed to discourage the importation and sale of foreign goods at prices well below domestic prices ⟨*antidumping* tariffs⟩

an·ti·elec·tron \ˌant-ē-ə-ˈlek-ˌträn, ˌan-ˌtī-\ *n* **:** POSITRON

an·ti–fed·er·al·ist \ˌant-i-ˈfed-rə-ləst, ˌan-ˌtī-, -ə-rə-\ *n, often cap A&F* **:** a member of the group that opposed in 1787–88 the adoption of the U.S. Constitution

an·ti·fer·til·i·ty \-fər-ˈtil-ət-ē\ *adj* **:** intended to control excess or unwanted fertility **:** CONTRACEPTIVE

an·ti·freeze \ˈant-i-ˌfrēz\ *n* **1 :** a substance (as ethylene glycol) added to a liquid (as the water in an automobile radiator) to prevent its freezing **2 :** any of various substances found in some living organisms (as certain fish) that serve to lower the freezing point of body fluids

an·ti·fun·gal \ˌant-i-ˈfəng-gəl, ˌan-ˌtī-\ *adj* **:** destroying fungi or inhibiting their growth — **antifungal** *n*

an·ti·gen \ˈant-i-jən\ *n* **:** a substance (as a toxin or enzyme) that when introduced into the body stimulates the production of an antibody — **an·ti·gen·ic** \ˌant-i-ˈjen-ik\ *adj* — **an·ti·gen·i·cal·ly** \-ˈjen-i-kə-lē, -klē\ *adv* — **an·ti·ge·nic·i·ty** \-jə-ˈnis-ət-ē\ *n*

antigen–presenting cell *n* **:** any of various cells (as a macrophage) that take up and process an antigen into a form that when displayed on the cell surface serves to activate a specific helper T cell

an·ti·he·mo·phil·ic factor \ˌant-i-ˌhē-mə-ˈfil-ik-, ˌan-ˌtī-\ *n* **:** FACTOR VIII

an·ti·hero \ˈant-i-ˌhē-ˌrō, ˈan-ˌtī-, -ˌhiər-ˌō\ *n* **:** a principal character (as in a story or play) completely lacking in heroic qualities — **an·ti·he·ro·ic** \ˌant-i-hi-ˈrō-ik, ˌan-ˌtī-\ *adj*

an·ti·his·ta·mine \ˌant-i-ˈhis-tə-ˌmēn, ˌan-ˌtī-, -mən\ *n* **:** any of various drugs that counteract histamine in the body and are used for treating allergic reactions and cold symptoms

an·ti–in·flam·ma·to·ry \ˌant-ē-in-ˈflam-ə-ˌtōr-ē, ˌan-ˌtī-\ *adj* **:** counteracting inflammation ⟨*anti-inflammatory* medications⟩ — **anti–inflammatory** *n*

an·ti–in·tel·lec·tu·al \ˌant-ē-ˌint-l-ˈek-chə-wəl, ˌan-ˌtī-\ *adj* **:** opposing or hostile to intellectuals or to an intellectual view or approach — **anti–intellectual** *n* — **an·ti–in·tel·lec·tu·al·ism** \-ˈek-chə-wə-ˌliz-əm\ *n*

an·ti·knock \ˌant-i-ˈnäk\ *n* **:** a substance that when added to the fuel of an internal combustion engine helps to prevent knocking

an·ti·lock \ˈan-ˌtī-läk, ˈant-i-\ *adj* **:** being a braking system for a motor vehicle designed to keep the wheels from locking and skidding

an·ti·log \-ˌlȯg, -ˌläg\ *n* **:** ANTILOGARITHM

an·ti·log·a·rithm \ˌant-i-ˈlȯg-ə-ˌrith-əm, ˌan-ˌtī-, -ˈläg-\ *n* **:** the number corresponding to a given logarithm ⟨if the logarithm in base *x* of *a* equals *b* then the *antilogarithm* in base *x* of *b* equals *a*⟩

an·ti·ma·cas·sar \ˌant-i-mə-ˈkas-ər\ *n* **:** a covering to protect the back or arms of furniture [*anti-* + *Macassar* oil, a hair dressing]

an·ti·ma·lar·i·al \ˌant-i-mə-ˈler-ē-əl, ˌan-ˌtī-\ *adj* **:** serving to prevent, control, or cure malaria — **antimalarial** *n*

an·ti·mat·ter \ˈant-i-ˌmat-ər\ *n* **:** matter composed of antiparticles

an·ti·mi·cro·bi·al \ˌant-i-mī-ˈkrō-bē-əl\ *adj* **:** destroying or inhibiting the growth of microorganisms and especially pathogenic microorganisms — **antimicrobial** *n*

an·ti·mo·ny \ˈant-ə-ˌmō-nē\ *n* **:** a metallic silvery white crystalline element that is used especially as a constituent of alloys and in medicine — see ELEMENT table [Medieval Latin *antimonium*] — **an·ti·mo·ni·al** \ˌant-ə-ˈmō-nē-əl\ *adj*

an·ti·neu·tri·no \ˌant-i-nü-ˈtrē-ˌnō, ˌan-ˌtī-, -nyü-\ *n* **:** the antiparticle of the neutrino

an·ti·neu·tron \-ˈnü-ˌträn, -ˈnyü-\ *n* **:** the antiparticle of the neutron

an·ti·node \ˈant-i-ˌnōd, ˈan-ˌtī-\ *n* **:** a region of maximum amplitude occurring between two adjacent nodes in a vibrating body ⟨identify the nodes and *antinodes* of the standing wave⟩

an·ti·nu·cle·ar \ˌant-ē-ˈnü-klē-ər, -ˈnyü-, ˌan-ˌtī-\ *adj* **:** opposing the use or production of nuclear power

\ə\ **abut**	\au̇\ **out**	\i\ **tip**	\ȯ\ **saw**	\u̇\ **foot**
\ər\ **further**	\ch\ **chin**	\ī\ **life**	\ȯi\ **coin**	\y\ **yet**
\a\ **mat**	\e\ **pet**	\j\ **job**	\th\ **thin**	\yü\ **few**
\ā\ **take**	\ē\ **easy**	\ng\ **sing**	\th\ **this**	\yu̇\ **cure**
\ä\ **cot, cart**	\g\ **go**	\ō\ **bone**	\ü\ **food**	\zh\ **vision**

an·ti·nuke \-ˈnük, -ˈnyük\ *adj* : ANTINUCLEAR

an·ti·ox·i·dant \ˌant-ē-ˈäk-səd-ənt, ˌan-ˌtī-\ *n* : a substance that inhibits oxidation or reactions promoted by oxygen, peroxides, or free radicals — **antioxidant** *adj*

an·ti·par·ti·cle \ˈant-i-ˌpärt-i-kəl, ˈan-ˌtī-\ *n* : an elementary particle identical to another in mass but opposite to it in electric or magnetic properties that when brought together with its counterpart produces mutual annihilation

an·ti·pas·to \ˌant-i-ˈpas-tō, ˌänt-i-ˈpäs-\ *n, pl* **-pas·ti** \-tē\ : any of various typically Italian hors d'oeuvres; *also* : a number of these served especially as the first course of a meal [Italian, from *anti-* "before" (from Latin *ante-*) + *pasto* "food," from Latin *pastus*]

an·tip·a·thy \an-ˈtip-ə-thē\ *n, pl* **-thies** **1** : strong feeling against someone or something : AVERSION **2** : a person or thing that arouses strong dislike — **an·ti·pa·thet·ic** \ˌant-i-pə-ˈthet-ik\ *adj* — **an·ti·pa·thet·i·cal·ly** \-i-kə-lē, -klē\ *adv*

an·ti·per·son·nel \ˌant-i-ˌpərs-n-ˈel, ˌan-ˌtī-\ *adj* : designed for use against military personnel

an·ti·per·spi·rant \-ˈpər-spə-rənt, -sprənt\ *n* : a preparation used to reduce excessive perspiration

an·ti·phon \ˈant-ə-fən, -ˌfän\ *n* **1** : a psalm, anthem, or verse sung alternately by divisions of a choir or congregation **2** : a verse usually from Scripture said or sung before and after a canticle, psalm, or psalm verse [Late Latin *antiphona,* from Late Greek *antiphōna,* from Greek *antiphōnos* "responsive," from *anti-* + *phōnē* "sound"]

an·tiph·o·nal \an-ˈtif-ən-l\ *adj* : performed by two alternating groups ⟨*antiphonal* singing⟩ — **an·tiph·o·nal·ly** \-l-ē\ *adv*

an·tip·o·dal \an-ˈtip-əd-l\ *adj* **1** : of or relating to the antipodes; *esp* : situated at the opposite side of the earth **2** : diametrically opposite **3** : differing greatly

an·ti·pode \ˈant-ə-ˌpōd\ *n, pl* **an·tip·o·des** \an-ˈtip-ə-ˌdēz\ **1** : the parts of the earth diametrically opposite — usually used in plural **2** : the exact opposite or contrary [Latin *antipodes* "persons living at opposite points on the globe," from Greek, from *antipous* "with feet opposite," from *anti-* + *pous* "foot"] — **an·tip·o·de·an** \ˌan-ˌtip-ə-ˈdē-ən\ *adj*

an·ti·pol·lu·tion \ˌant-i-pə-ˈlü-shən, ˌan-ˌtī-\ *adj* : intended to prevent, reduce, or eliminate pollution ⟨*antipollution* laws⟩

an·ti·pope \ˈant-i-ˌpōp\ *n* : one elected or claiming to be pope in opposition to the pope canonically chosen

an·ti·pro·ton \ˌant-i-ˈprō-ˌtän, ˌan-ˌtī-\ *n* : the antiparticle of the proton

an·ti·psy·chot·ic \ˌant-i-sī-ˈkät-ik\ *n* : any of various powerful tranquilizers used especially to treat psychosis — **antipsychotic** *n*

an·ti·py·ret·ic \-pī-ˈret-ik\ *n* : an agent that reduces fever [Greek *pyretos* "fever," from *pyr* "fire"] — **antipyretic** *adj*

[1]**an·ti·quar·i·an** \ˌant-ə-ˈkwer-ē-ən\ *n* : ANTIQUARY

[2]**antiquarian** *adj* : of or relating to antiquaries or antiquities

an·ti·quary \ˈant-ə-ˌkwer-ē\ *n, pl* **-quar·ies** : a person who collects or studies antiquities

an·ti·quate \ˈant-ə-ˌkwāt\ *vt* : to make old or obsolete

an·ti·quat·ed *adj* **1** : OBSOLETE 1 **2** : OLD-FASHIONED, OUTMODED **3** : advanced in age

[1]**an·tique** \an-ˈtēk\ *n* : an object of an earlier period; *esp* : a work of art, piece of furniture, or decorative object made at an earlier period

[2]**antique** *adj* **1** : belonging to antiquity **2** : belonging to an earlier period ⟨*antique* furniture⟩ **3** : belonging to or resembling a former style or fashion : OLD-FASHIONED ⟨silver of an *antique* design⟩ [Middle French, from Latin *antiquus,* from *ante* "before"] ***synonyms*** see OLD — **an·tique·ly** *adv* — **antique·ness** *n*

an·tiq·ui·ty \an-ˈtik-wət-ē\ *n, pl* **-ties** **1** : ancient times; *esp* : those before the Middle Ages **2** : the quality of being ancient **3** *pl* **a** : relics or monuments of ancient times **b** : matters relating to the life or culture of ancient times

an·ti·re·tro·vi·ral \ˌant-i-ˈret-rō-ˌvī-rəl, ˌan-ˌtī-\ *adj* : acting, used, or effective against retroviruses ⟨*antiretroviral* drugs⟩ — **antiretroviral** *n*

an·ti·scor·bu·tic \ˌant-i-skȯr-ˈbyüt-ik, ˌan-ˌtī-\ *adj* : tending to prevent or relieve scurvy

an·ti–Sem·ite \-ˈsem-ˌīt\ *n* : a person who is hostile to or discriminates against Jews — **anti–Se·mit·ic** \-sə-ˈmit-ik\ *adj* — **an·ti–Sem·i·tism** \-ˈsem-ə-ˌtiz-əm\ *n*

an·ti·sep·sis \ˌant-ə-ˈsep-səs\ *n* : the inhibiting of the growth and multiplication of microorganisms by antiseptic means

[1]**an·ti·sep·tic** \ˌant-ə-ˈsep-tik\ *adj* **1** : preventing or stopping the growth of germs that cause disease or decay ⟨*antiseptic* agents⟩ **2** : relating to or characterized by the use of antiseptic substances ⟨*antiseptic* treatments⟩ **3 a** : free from living microorganisms : ASEPTIC ⟨*antiseptic* wounds⟩ **b** : protecting or protected from what is undesirable ⟨lives in *antiseptic* seclusion⟩ **c** : extremely neat or orderly; *esp* : neat to the point of being bare or uninteresting **d** : coldly impersonal ⟨an *antiseptic* greeting⟩ [*anti-* + Greek *sēptikos* "putrefying, septic"] — **an·ti·sep·ti·cal·ly** \-ti-kə-lē, -klē\ *adv*

[2]**antiseptic** *n* : a substance that inhibits the growth or action of microorganisms especially in or on living tissue

an·ti·se·rum \ˈant-i-ˌsir-əm, ˈan-ˌtī-, -ˌser-\ *n* : a serum that contains specific antibodies and is used to prevent or cure disease

an·ti·so·cial \ˌant-i-ˈsō-shəl, ˌan-ˌtī-\ *adj* **1** : contrary or hostile to the well-being of society; *esp* : being or marked by behavior deviating sharply from the social norm **2** : disliking or avoiding the company of others : UNSOCIABLE

an·ti·stat·ic \-ˈstat-ik\ *adj* : reducing, removing, or preventing the buildup of static electricity

an·tith·e·sis \an-ˈtith-ə-səs\ *n, pl* **-e·ses** \-ə-ˌsēz\ **1** : the rhetorical contrast of ideas by means of parallel arrangements of words, clauses, or sentences **2 a** : a direct or striking contrast **b** : the second of two contrasted things **3** : the direct opposite ⟨dictatorship is the *antithesis* of democracy⟩ [Late Latin, from Greek, literally, "opposition," from *antitithenai* "to place opposite, oppose," from *anti-* + *tithenai* "to put"] — **an·ti·thet·ic** \ˌant-ə-ˈthet-ik\ *adj* — **an·ti·thet·i·cal** \-ˈthet-i-kəl\ *adj* — **an·ti·thet·i·cal·ly** \-i-kə-lē, -klē\ *adv*

an·ti·tox·in \ˌant-i-ˈtäk-sən\ *n* : an antibody that is capable of neutralizing a particular toxin, is formed in response to the introduction of toxin into the body, and is produced commercially in animals for use in treating human diseases (as tetanus) in which such a toxin is present; *also* : a serum containing antitoxins — **an·ti·tox·ic** \-sik\ *adj*

an·ti·trust \ˌant-i-ˈtrəst, ˌan-ˌtī-\ *adj* : opposing or designed to restrict the power of trusts and similar business combinations ⟨*antitrust* laws⟩

an·ti·ven·in \ˌant-i-ˈven-ən, ˌan-ˌtī-\ *n* : a serum containing an antitoxin to a venom (as of a snake)

an·ti·ven·om \-ˈven-əm\ *n* : ANTIVENIN

an·ti·white \ˌan-tē-ˈhwīt, ˌan-ˌtī-, -ˈwīt\ *adj* : opposed or hostile to white people

ant·ler \ˈant-lər\ *n* : the solid often branched horn of an animal of the deer family that is cast off and grown anew each year; *also* : a branch of such horn [Medieval French *antiler,* derived from Latin *ante-* + *oculus* "eye"] — **ant·lered** \-lərd\ *adj* — **ant·ler·less** *adj*

ant lion *n* : any of various 4-winged insects with a long-jawed larva that digs a conical pit in which it lies in wait to catch insects (as ants) on which it feeds

an·to·nym \ˈant-ə-ˌnim\ *n* : a word of opposite meaning ⟨*hot* and *cold* are *antonyms*⟩ [*anti-* + Greek *onyma, onoma* "name"] — **an·ton·y·mous** \an-ˈtän-ə-məs\ *adj*

ant·sy \ˈant-sē\ *adj* : RESTLESS, IMPATIENT

an·uran \ə-ˈnu̇r-ən, a-, -ˈnyu̇r-\ *n* : any of an order (Anura) of amphibians (as the frogs and toads) which lack a tail in the adult stage and have long hind limbs often suited to leaping and swimming [derived from [2]*a-* + Greek *oura* "tail"] — **anuran** *adj*

anus \ˈā-nəs\ *n* : the posterior opening of the alimentary canal [Latin]

an·vil \ˈan-vəl\ *n* **1** : a heavy usually steel-faced iron block on which metal is shaped **2** : INCUS [Old English *anfilt*]

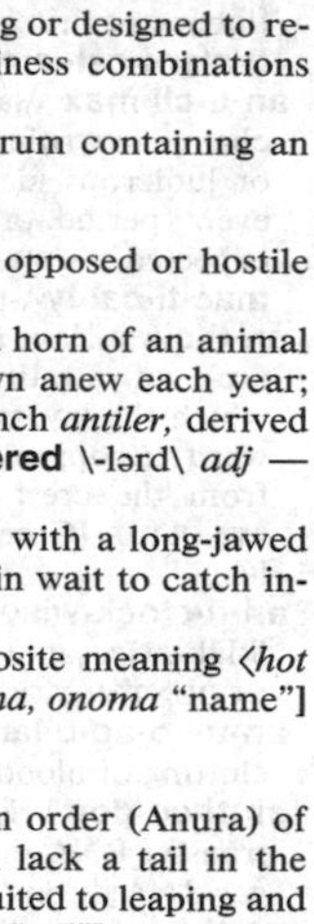

anvil 1

anx·i·ety \aŋ-ˈzī-ət-ē\ *n, pl* **-eties** **1 a** : painful or fearful uneasiness of mind usually over an impending or anticipated event **b** : a cause of such uneasiness **2** : a strong concern or desire mixed with doubt and fear ⟨*anxiety* to succeed⟩ [Latin *anxietas,* from *anxius* "anxious"]

anx·ious \ˈaŋ-shəs, ˈaŋk-\ *adj* **1** : fearful of what may happen : WORRIED ⟨*anxious* about their son's health⟩ **2** : desiring earnestly ⟨*anxious* to make good⟩ [Latin *anxius*] ***synonyms*** see EAGER — **anx·ious·ly** *adv* — **anx·ious·ness** *n*

[1]any \ˈen-ē\ *adj* **1 a :** one taken at random ⟨*any* person you meet⟩ **b :** EVERY — used to indicate one selected without restriction ⟨*any* child would know that⟩ **2 :** one, some, or all indiscriminately of whatever amount, number, or extent ⟨have you *any* money⟩ ⟨need *any* help they can get⟩ **3 :** unmeasured or unlimited in amount, number, or extent ⟨*any* quantity you desire⟩ [Old English *ǣnig*]

[2]any *pron, sing or pl in construction* **1 :** any person or persons **:** ANYONE ⟨wasn't believed by *any*⟩ **2 a :** any thing or things ⟨do *any* work?⟩ **b :** any part, quantity, or number ⟨no, I don't want *any*⟩

[3]any *adv* **:** to any extent or degree **:** AT ALL ⟨can't go *any* farther⟩ ⟨you're not helping *any*⟩

any·body \ˈen-ē-ˌbäd-ē, -bəd-\ *pron* **:** ANYONE

any·how \-ˌhau̇\ *adv* **1 :** in any way, manner, or order **2 :** at any rate **:** in any case

any·more \ˌen-ē-ˈmōr, -ˈmȯr\ *adv* **:** at the present time **:** NOWADAYS ⟨we never see them *anymore*⟩

any·one \ˈen-ē-wən, -wən\ *pron* **:** any person at all

any·place \-ˌplās\ *adv* **:** in any place **:** ANYWHERE

any·thing \-ˌthiŋ\ *pron* **:** any thing at all

any·way \ˈen-ē-ˌwā\ *adv* **:** ANYHOW

any·ways \-ˌwāz\ *adv, chiefly dialect* **:** in any case

any·where \-ˌhweər, -ˌhwaər, -ˌweər, -ˌwaər\ *adv* **:** in, at, or to any place

any·wise \-ˌwīz\ *adv* **:** in any way whatever **:** AT ALL

A–OK \ˌā-ˌō-ˈkā\ *adv or adj* **:** very definitely well or fine

A1 \ˈā-ˈwən\ *adj* **:** of the finest quality **:** FIRST-RATE

aor·ta \ā-ˈȯrt-ə\ *n, pl* **aortas** *or* **aor·tae** \-ˈȯrt-ē\ **:** the main artery of the circulatory system that carries blood from the heart to be distributed by branch arteries through the body [Greek *aortē,* from *aeirein* "to lift"] — **aor·tic** \-ˈȯrt-ik\ *adj*

aou·dad \ˈau̇-ˌdad, ˈä-u̇-\ *n* **:** a wild sheep of North Africa [French, from Berber *audad*]

[1]ap- — see AD-

[2]ap- *or* **apo-** *prefix* **:** away from **:** off ⟨*aphelion*⟩ [Greek *apo* "away, off"]

apace \ə-ˈpās\ *adv* **:** at a quick pace **:** SWIFTLY

Apache \ə-ˈpach-ē, in sense 2 ə-ˈpash\ *n, pl* **Apache** *or* **Apach·es** \-ˈpach-ēz, -ˈpash-əz\ **1 :** a member of a group of American Indian peoples of the southwestern U.S. **2** *not cap* **a :** a member of a gang of criminals especially in Paris **b :** RUFFIAN [sense 1 from Spanish; sense 2 from French, from *Apache* "Apache Indian"]

[1]apart \ə-ˈpärt\ *adv* **1 :** at a distance in space or time ⟨two towns five miles *apart*⟩ **2 :** as a separate unit **:** INDEPENDENTLY ⟨considered *apart* from other points⟩ **3 :** ASIDE ⟨joking *apart,* that's probably true⟩ **4 :** into pieces ⟨tear a book *apart*⟩ [Medieval French *a part,* literally, "to one side"]

[2]apart *adj* **1 :** different or separated from others ⟨a breed *apart*⟩ **2 :** holding different opinions **:** DIVIDED — **apartness** *n*

apart from *prep* **:** other than **:** BESIDES, EXCEPT FOR

apart·heid \ə-ˈpär-ˌtāt, -ˌtīt\ *n* **:** a policy of racial segregation formerly practiced in the Republic of South Africa [Afrikaans, literally, "separateness"]

apart·ment \ə-ˈpärt-mənt\ *n* **1 :** a room or set of rooms used as a dwelling **2 :** ROOM 2a **3 :** APARTMENT BUILDING

apartment building *n* **:** a building divided into individual dwelling units — called also *apartment house*

ap·a·thet·ic \ˌap-ə-ˈthet-ik\ *adj* **1 :** having or showing little or no feeling or emotion **:** SPIRITLESS **2 :** having little or no interest or concern **:** INDIFFERENT ***synonyms*** see IMPASSIVE — **ap·a·thet·i·cal·ly** \-ˈthet-i-kə-lē, -klē\ *adv*

ap·a·thy \ˈap-ə-thē\ *n* **1 :** lack of feeling or emotion **2 :** lack of interest or concern **:** INDIFFERENCE

ap·a·tite \ˈap-ə-ˌtīt\ *n* **:** any of a group of minerals of variable color that are phosphates of calcium usually with some fluorine and that are used as a source of phosphorus and its compounds [German *Apatit,* from Greek *apatē* "deceit"]

apat·o·sau·rus \ə-ˌpat-ə-ˈsȯr-əs\ *n* **:** BRONTOSAURUS [Greek *apatē* "deceit" + *sauros* "lizard"]

[1]ape \ˈāp\ *n* **1 a :** MONKEY; *esp* **:** one of the larger tailless or short-tailed forms **b :** any of two families of large tailless primates (as the chimpanzee, gorilla, orangutan, and gibbon) with incompletely upright bodily posture **2 a :** MIMIC **b :** a large uncouth person [Old English *apa*] — **ape·like** \ˈā-ˌplīk\ *adj*

[2]ape *vt* **:** to copy closely but often awkwardly ***synonyms*** see IMITATE — **ap·er** *n*

ape–man \ˈāp-ˈman, -ˌman\ *n* **:** a primate (as an australopithecine) intermediate in character between true humans and the higher apes

ape·ri·ent \ə-ˈpir-ē-ənt\ *n* **:** LAXATIVE [Latin *aperire* "to open"] — **aperient** *adj*

aper·i·tif \ˌäp-ˌer-ə-ˈtēf, ə-ˈper-ə-\ *n* **:** an alcoholic drink taken (as a cocktail) before a meal as an appetizer [French *apéritif,* derived from Latin *aperire* "to open"]

ap·er·ture \ˈap-ər-ˌchu̇r, ˈap-ə-, -chər\ *n* **1 :** an opening or open space **2 :** the opening in a lens that admits light; *also* **:** the diameter of this opening [Latin *apertura,* from *aperire* "to open"]

apex \ˈā-ˌpeks\ *n, pl* **apex·es** *or* **api·ces** \ˈā-pə-ˌsēz, ˈap-ə-\ **1 a :** the uppermost point **:** TOP ⟨the *apex* of a mountain⟩ **b :** the narrowed or pointed end **:** TIP ⟨*apex* of a leaf⟩ **2 :** the highest or culminating point ⟨*apex* of a career⟩ [Latin] ***synonyms*** see SUMMIT

apha·sia \ə-ˈfā-zhē-ə, -zhə\ *n* **:** loss or impairment of the power to use and understand words [Greek, from *a-* + *phasia* "speech," from *phanai* "to say"] — **apha·sic** \-zik\ *n or adj*

aph·elion \a-ˈfēl-yən\ *n, pl* **-elia** \-yə\ **:** the point of a planet's or comet's orbit most distant from the sun — compare PERIHELION [*apo-* + Greek *hēlios* "sun"]

aphe·re·sis \ˌaf-ə-ˈrē-səs\ *n, pl* **-re·ses** \-ˌsēz\ **:** withdrawal of blood from a donor, removal of one or more blood components (as plasma or platelets), and return of the remaining blood back into the donor [derived from Greek *aphairesis* "taking off," from *aphairein* "to take away," from [2]*ap-* + *hairein* "to take"]

aphid \ˈā-fəd, ˈaf-əd\ *n* **:** any of numerous soft-bodied insects that suck the juices of plants

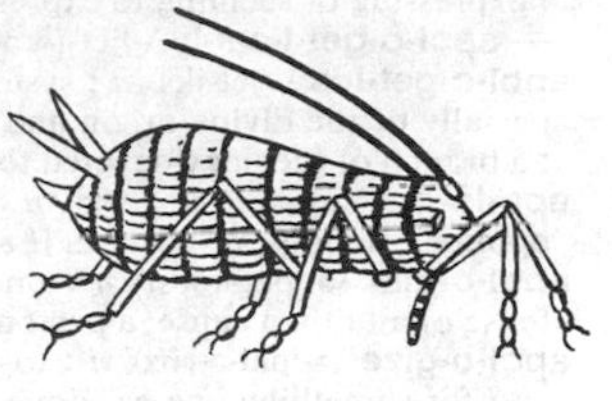
aphid

aphis \ˈā-fəs, ˈaf-əs\ *n, pl* **aphi·des** \ˈā-fə-ˌdēz, ˈaf-ə-\ **:** APHID [New Latin *Aphid-, Aphis,* genus name]

aph·o·rism \ˈaf-ə-ˌriz-əm\ *n* **:** a short sentence stating a general truth or practical observation [derived from Greek *aphorismos* "definition, aphorism," from *aphorizein* "to define," from *apo-* + *horizein* "to bound"] — **aph·o·rist** \-rəst\ *n* — **aph·o·ris·tic** \ˌaf-ə-ˈris-tik\ *adj* — **aph·o·ris·ti·cal·ly** \-ti-kə-lē, -klē\ *adv*

apho·tic \ā-ˈfōt-ik\ *adj* **:** being the deep zone of an ocean or lake receiving too little light to permit photosynthesis [[2]*a-* + *photic*]

aph·ro·dis·i·ac \ˌaf-rə-ˈdē-zē-ˌak, -ˈdiz-ē-\ *n* **:** something (as a food) that arouses or is held to arouse sexual desire [Greek *aphrodisiakos* "sexual," derived from *Aphroditē* "Aphrodite"] — **aphrodisiac** *also* **aph·ro·di·si·a·cal** \ˌaf-rəd-ə-ˈzī-ə-kəl, -ˈsī-\ *adj*

api·ary \ˈā-pē-ˌer-ē\ *n, pl* **-ar·ies :** a place where bees are kept; *esp* **:** a collection of hives of bees kept for their honey [Latin *apiarium,* from *apis* "bee"]

ap·i·cal \ˈā-pi-kəl *also* ˈap-i-\ *adj* **:** of, relating to, or situated at an apex [Latin *apic-, apex* "apex"] — **ap·i·cal·ly** \-kə-lē, -klē\ *adv*

apiece \ə-ˈpēs\ *adv* **:** for each one ⟨ten cents *apiece*⟩

ap·ish \ˈā-pish\ *adj* **1 :** extremely silly or affected ⟨*apish* antics⟩ **2 :** given to slavish imitation — **ap·ish·ly** *adv*

aplomb \ə-ˈpläm, -ˈpləm\ *n* **:** complete composure or self-assurance **:** POISE [French, literally, "perpendicularity," from *à plomb* "according to the plumb line"]

apo- — see [2]AP-

apoc·a·lypse \ə-ˈpäk-ə-ˌlips\ *n* **1 a :** one of the Jewish and Christian writings of 200 B.C. to A.D. 150 marked by the use of pseudonyms, symbolic imagery, and the expectation of an imminent cosmic cataclysm in which God destroys the ruling powers of evil and raises the righteous to life in a messianic kingdom **b** *cap* **:** the biblical book of Revelation **2 a :** something viewed as a prophetic revelation **b :** ARMAGEDDON **3 :** a great disaster ⟨an environmental *apocalypse*⟩ [Late Latin *apocalypsis,* from Greek *apokalypsis,* literally, "uncovering," from *apo-* + *kalyptein* "to cover"] — **apoc·a·lyp·tic** \ə-ˌpäk-ə-ˈlip-tik\ *adj* — **apoc·a·lyp·ti·cal·ly** \-ˈlip-ti-kə-lē, -klē\ *adv*

\ə\ **abut**	\au̇\ **out**	\i\ **tip**	\ȯ\ **saw**	\u̇\ **foot**
\ər\ **further**	\ch\ **chin**	\ī\ **life**	\ȯi\ **coin**	\y\ **yet**
\a\ **mat**	\e\ **pet**	\j\ **job**	\th\ **thin**	\yü\ **few**
\ā\ **take**	\ē\ **easy**	\ŋ\ **sing**	\t͟h\ **this**	\yu̇\ **cure**
\ä\ **cot, cart**	\g\ **go**	\ō\ **bone**	\ü\ **food**	\zh\ **vision**

apoc·o·pe \ə-ˈpäk-ə-ˌpē\ *n* **:** the loss of one or more sounds or letters at the end of a word (as in *sing* from Old English *singan*) [Late Latin, from Greek *apokopē,* literally, "cutting off"]

apoc·ry·pha \ə-ˈpäk-rə-fə\ *n sing or pl* **1 :** writings or statements of dubious authenticity **2** *cap* **a :** books included in the Septuagint and Vulgate but excluded from the Jewish and Protestant canons of the Old Testament — see BIBLE table **b :** early Christian writings not included in the New Testament [Medieval Latin, from Late Latin *apocryphus* "not canonical," from Greek *apokryphos* "obscure," from *apokryptein* "to hide away," from *apo-* + *kryptein* "to hide"]

apoc·ry·phal \-fəl\ *adj* **1** *often cap* **:** of or resembling the Apocrypha **2 :** of doubtful authenticity **:** SPURIOUS — **apoc·ry·phal·ly** \-fə-lē\ *adv* — **apoc·ry·phal·ness** *n*

apo·gee \ˈap-ə-ˌjē\ *n* **1 :** the point farthest from the center of a celestial body (as the earth or moon) reached by an object (as a satellite) orbiting it — compare PERIGEE **2 :** the farthest or highest point **:** CULMINATION [French *apogée,* derived from Greek *apo-* + *gē* "earth"]

apogee 1

apol·o·get·ic \ə-ˌpäl-ə-ˈjet-ik\ *adj* **1 :** offered in defense or by way of excuse or apology **2 :** expressing or seeming to express apology ⟨an *apologetic* face⟩ — **apol·o·get·i·cal·ly** \-ˈjet-i-kə-lē, -klē\ *adv*

apol·o·get·ics \-ˈjet-iks\ *n* **:** systematic argument in defense especially of the divine origin and authority of Christianity; *also* **:** a branch of theology devoted to the defense of a religious faith

apo·lo·gia \ˌap-ə-ˈlō-jē-ə, -jə\ *n* **:** a defense especially of one's opinions, actions, or position [Late Latin]

apol·o·gist \ə-ˈpäl-ə-jəst\ *n* **:** one who speaks or writes in defense of a faith, a cause, a person, or an institution

apol·o·gize \ə-ˈpäl-ə-ˌjīz\ *vi* **:** to make an apology **:** express regret for something one has done — **apol·o·giz·er** *n*

apol·o·gy \-jē\ *n, pl* **-gies** **1 :** a formal justification or defense **2 :** an admission of error or discourtesy accompanied by an expression of regret **3 :** a poor substitute [Late Latin *apologia,* from Greek, from *apo-* + *logos* "speech"]

synonyms APOLOGY, EXCUSE mean matter offered in explanation or defense. APOLOGY implies that one has been actually or apparently in the wrong; it may offer an explanation or it may simply acknowledge error and express regret ⟨*apologized* for her lateness⟩. EXCUSE implies an intent to remove blame or censure for a wrong, mistake, or failure ⟨too easily *excused* the child's misbehavior⟩.

apo·mix·is \ˌap-ə-ˈmik-səs\ *n, pl* **-mix·es** \-ˌsēz\ **:** reproduction (as parthenogenesis) involving specialized generative tissues but not dependent on fertilization [*apo-* + Greek *mixis* "act of mixing"]

apoph·a·sis \ə-ˈpäf-ə-səs\ *n* **:** the bringing up of an issue by claiming not to mention it (as in "we won't discuss his past crimes") [Greek, "denial, negation," from *apophanai* "to deny," from *apo-* + *phanai* "to say"]

ap·o·plec·tic \ˌap-ə-ˈplek-tik\ *adj* **1 :** of, relating to, or caused by stroke ⟨*apoplectic* symptoms⟩ **2 :** affected with or inclined to stroke ⟨*apoplectic* patients⟩ **3 :** highly excited or angry ⟨was *apoplectic* over the news⟩ — **ap·o·plec·ti·cal·ly** \-ti-kə-lē, -klē\ *adv*

ap·o·plexy \ˈap-ə-ˌplek-sē\ *n, pl* **-plex·ies** **:** STROKE 5 [Late Latin *apoplexia,* from Greek *apoplēxia,* from *apoplēssein* "to cripple by a stroke," from *apo-* + *plēssein* "to strike"]

ap·o·pto·sis \ˌap-ə-ˈtō-səs\ *n, pl* **-pto·ses** \-ˌsēz\ **:** a genetically directed process of cell self-destruction that is a normal physiological process for eliminating DNA-damaged, extra, or unneeded cells [Greek *apoptōsis* "a falling off," from *apopiptein* "to fall off," from *apo-* + *piptein* "to fall"]

apos·ta·sy \ə-ˈpäs-tə-sē\ *n, pl* **-sies** **1 :** renunciation of a religious faith **2 :** abandonment of a previous loyalty **:** DEFECTION [Late Latin *apostasia,* from Greek, literally, "revolt," from *aphistasthai* "to revolt," from *apo-* + *histasthai* "to stand"]

apos·tate \ə-ˈpäs-ˌtāt, -tət\ *n* **:** one who commits apostasy — **apostate** *adj*

apos·ta·tize \ə-ˈpäs-tə-ˌtīz\ *vi* **:** to commit apostasy

a pos·te·ri·o·ri \ˌä-pä-ˌstir-ē-ˈōr-ē, -pō-, -ˌster-, -ˈȯr-\ *adj* **:** relating to or derived by reasoning from known or observed facts [Latin, literally, "from the latter"] — **a posteriori** *adv*

apos·tle \ə-ˈpäs-əl\ *n* **1 :** one sent on a religious mission: as **a** *often cap* **:** one of an authoritative New Testament group made up especially of Christ's twelve original disciples and Paul **b :** the first Christian missionary to a region **2 a :** one that first advocates a cause or movement **b :** an ardent advocate or supporter [Late Latin *apostolus,* from Greek *apostolos,* literally, "one sent forth," from *apo-* + *stellein* "to send"] — **apos·tle·ship** \-əl-ˌship\ *n*

Apostles' Creed *n* **:** a Christian creed ascribed to the Twelve Apostles that begins "I believe in God the Father Almighty"

apos·to·late \ə-ˈpäs-tə-ˌlāt, -lət\ *n* **1 :** the office or mission of an apostle **2 :** a group dedicated to the spreading of a religion or a doctrine

ap·os·tol·ic \ˌap-ə-ˈstäl-ik\ *adj* **1 a :** of or relating to an apostle **b :** of or relating to the New Testament apostles or their times or teachings **2 a :** of or forming a succession of spiritual authority from the apostles held in Catholic tradition to be perpetuated by successive ordinations of bishops and to be necessary for the validity of sacraments and orders **b :** PAPAL — **apos·to·lic·i·ty** \ə-ˌpäs-tə-ˈlis-ət-ē\ *n*

apostolic delegate *n* **:** a representative of the Holy See in a country with which it has no formal diplomatic relations

[1]**apos·tro·phe** \ə-ˈpäs-trə-fē\ *n* **:** the rhetorical addressing of an absent person as if present or of an abstract idea or inanimate object as if capable of understanding (as in "O grave, where is thy victory?") [Latin, from Greek *apostrophē,* literally, "act of turning away," from *apo-* + *strephein* "to turn"]

[2]**apostrophe** *n* **:** a mark ' or ʼ used to show the omission of letters or figures (as in *can't* for *cannot* or *'76* for *1776*), the possessive case (as in *Chicago's*), or the plural of letters or figures (as in *cross your t's, six 7's*)

apos·tro·phize \ə-ˈpäs-trə-ˌfīz\ *vb* **1 :** to address by or in apostrophe **2 :** to make use of apostrophe

apothecaries' measure *n* **:** a system of liquid units of measure used chiefly by pharmacists

apothecaries' weight *n* **:** a system of weights used chiefly by pharmacists — see MEASURE table

apoth·e·cary \ə-ˈpäth-ə-ˌker-ē\ *n, pl* **-car·ies** **1 :** DRUGGIST, PHARMACIST **2 :** PHARMACY 2 [Late Latin *apothecarius* "shopkeeper," from Latin *apotheca* "storehouse," from Greek *apothēkē,* from *apotithenai* "to put away"]

apo·thegm \ˈap-ə-ˌthem\ *n* **:** a concise instructive saying or formulation **:** APHORISM [Greek *apophthegma,* from *apo-* + *phthengesthai* "to utter"]

apo·them \ˈap-ə-ˌthem\ *n* **:** the perpendicular from the center of a regular polygon to one of the sides [*apo-* + Greek *thema* "something laid down, theme"]

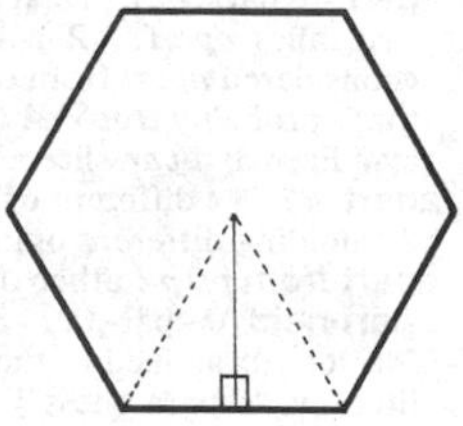
apothem

apo·the·o·sis \ə-ˌpäth-ē-ˈō-səs, ˌap-ə-ˈthē-ə-səs\ *n, pl* **-o·ses** \-ˈō-ˌsēz, -ə-ˌsēz\ **1 :** elevation to divine status **:** DEIFICATION **2 :** a perfect example [Late Latin, from Greek *apotheōsis,* from *apotheoun* "to deify," from *apo-* + *theos* "god"] — **ap·o·the·o·size** \ˌap-ə-ˈthē-ə-ˌsīz, ə-ˈpäth-ē-ə-\ *vt*

app \ˈap\ *n* **:** APPLICATION 6

ap·pall \ə-ˈpȯl\ *vt* **:** to overcome with fear or dread **:** HORRIFY, SHOCK ⟨we were *appalled* by his rude behavior⟩ [Middle French *apalir* "to make pale," from *a-* "ad-" + *palir* "to grow pale"]

ap·pall·ing \ə-ˈpȯl-ing\ *adj* **:** inspiring horror or dismay **:** SHOCKING ⟨living under *appalling* conditions⟩ — **ap·pall·ing·ly** \-ˈpȯ-ling-lē\ *adv*

Ap·pa·loo·sa \ˌap-ə-ˈlü-sə\ *n* **:** any of a breed of rugged saddle horses developed in western North America that have a white or solid-colored coat with small spots [origin unknown]

Appaloosa

ap·pa·nage \ˈap-ə-nij\ *n* **1 :** a grant (as of land or revenue) made by a sovereign or a legislative body to a member of the royal family or a person of noble rank

2 : a customary or rightful possession or privilege [French *apanage,* from Medieval French, from *apaner* "to provide for a younger offspring," from Medieval Latin *appanare,* from Latin *ad-* + *panis* "bread"]

ap·pa·rat \ˈap-ə-ˌrat, ˌäp-ə-ˈrät\ *n* : APPARATUS 2 [Russian]

ap·pa·ra·tchik \ˌäp-ə-ˈräch-ik\ *n, pl* **-ratchiks** *also* **-ra·tchi·ki** \-ˈräch-ə-ˌkē\ : a member of a Communist apparatus [Russian, from *apparat*]

ap·pa·ra·tus \ˌap-ə-ˈrat-əs, -ˈrāt-\ *n, pl* **-tus·es** *or* **-tus** **1 a** : the equipment used to do a particular kind of work **b** : an instrument or appliance for a specific operation **2** : the system of persons and agencies through which an organization functions; *esp* : the administrative machinery of a Communist party [Latin, from *apparare* "to prepare," from *ad-* + *parare* "to prepare"]

[1]**ap·par·el** \ə-ˈpar-əl\ *vt* **-eled** *or* **-elled; -el·ing** *or* **-el·ling** **1** : CLOTHE, DRESS **2** : ADORN, EMBELLISH [Medieval French *appareiller* "to prepare," derived from Latin *apparare*]

[2]**apparel** *n* : personal attire : CLOTHING

ap·par·ent \ə-ˈpar-ənt, -ˈper-\ *adj* **1** : open to view : VISIBLE ⟨the flaw in the material was *apparent*⟩ **2** : clear to the understanding ⟨it was *apparent* that the road was little used⟩ **3** : seemingly real or true ⟨an *apparent* contradiction⟩ [Latin *apparent-, apparens,* from *apparēre* "to appear"] — **ap·par·ent·ly** *adv* — **ap·par·ent·ness** *n*

synonyms APPARENT, EVIDENT mean readily perceived or grasped. APPARENT implies having outward signs that may prove on deeper analysis to be misleading ⟨the *apparent* cause of the accident⟩. EVIDENT suggests an appearance unmistakably corresponding with reality ⟨our *evident* delight at your gift⟩.

ap·pa·ri·tion \ˌap-ə-ˈrish-ən\ *n* **1** : an unusual or unexpected sight : PHENOMENON **2** : GHOST 2 [Late Latin *apparitio* "appearance," from Latin *apparēre* "to appear"] — **ap·pa·ri·tion·al** \-ˈrish-nəl, -ən-l\ *adj*

[1]**ap·peal** \ə-ˈpēl\ *n* **1 a** : a legal proceeding by which a case is brought before a higher court for review of the decision of a lower court **b** : a request for such a proceeding **2 a** : a request made to an authority for a confirmation or decision ⟨an *appeal* to the referee⟩ **b** : an earnest request : PLEA ⟨an *appeal* for financial support⟩ **3** : the power of arousing a sympathetic response : ATTRACTION ⟨movies had a great *appeal* for him⟩

[2]**appeal** *vb* **1** : to take action to have a case or decision reviewed by a higher court or authority ⟨*appeal* to the supreme court⟩ **2** : to call upon another for corroboration or vindication **3** : to make an earnest request ⟨*appealed* to them for help⟩ **4** : to arouse a sympathetic response ⟨that idea *appeals* to her⟩ [Medieval French *apeler,* literally, "to call, summon," from Latin *appellare*] — **ap·peal·abil·i·ty** \-ˌpē-lə-ˈbil-ət-ē\ *n* — **ap·peal·able** \ə-ˈpē-lə-bəl\ *adj*

ap·peal·ing \ə-ˈpē-ling\ *adj* : having appeal : ATTRACTIVE ⟨an *appealing* design⟩ — **ap·peal·ing·ly** \-ˈpē-ling-lē\ *adv*

ap·pear \ə-ˈpiər\ *vi* **1** : to come into sight : become evident : SHOW ⟨stars *appeared* in the sky⟩ **2** : to come formally before an authoritative body ⟨*appear* in court⟩ **3** : to have an outward aspect : SEEM ⟨things are not always as they *appear*⟩ ⟨*appear* to be tired⟩ **4** : to come out into public view ⟨the book *appears* next month⟩ ⟨she *appeared* on television last year⟩ [Medieval French *aparer, aparoir,* from Latin *apparēre,* from *ad-* + *parēre* "to show oneself"]

ap·pear·ance \ə-ˈpir-əns\ *n* **1 a** : external show : SEMBLANCE ⟨attempted to maintain an *appearance* of neutrality⟩ **b** : outward aspect : LOOK ⟨had a fierce *appearance*⟩ **c** *pl* : outward indication or show ⟨keep up *appearances*⟩ **2** : the act, action, or process of appearing **3 a** : something that appears : PHENOMENON **b** : an instance of appearing : OCCURRENCE

ap·pease \ə-ˈpēz\ *vt* **1** : to make calm or quiet **2** : to make less severe : ALLAY ⟨*appeased* my hunger⟩ **3** : to make concessions to (a potential aggressor) usually at the sacrifice of principles : CONCILIATE [Medieval French *apeser, apaiser* from *a-* "ad-" + *pais* "peace"] ***synonyms*** see PACIFY — **ap·pease·ment** \-mənt\ *n* — **ap·peas·er** *n*

ap·pel·lant \ə-ˈpel-ənt\ *n* : one that appeals; *esp* : one that appeals from a judicial decision or decree

ap·pel·late \ə-ˈpel-ət\ *adj* : of, relating to, or recognizing appeals ⟨*appellate* jurisdiction⟩; *esp* : having the power to review the decisions of a lower court ⟨an *appellate* court⟩

ap·pel·la·tion \ˌap-ə-ˈlā-shən\ *n* : an identifying or descriptive name or title : DESIGNATION

ap·pel·lee \ˌap-ə-ˈlē\ *n* : one against whom an appeal is taken

ap·pend \ə-ˈpend\ *vt* : to add as a supplement ⟨*append* a postscript to a letter⟩ [Latin *appendere* "to hang, weigh out," from *ad-* + *pendere* "to weigh"]

ap·pend·age \ə-ˈpen-dij\ *n* **1** : something attached to a larger or more important thing **2** : a usually projecting part of an animal or plant body; *esp* : a limb or an analogous part

ap·pen·dec·to·my \ˌap-ən-ˈdek-tə-mē\ *n, pl* **-mies** : surgical removal of the human appendix

ap·pen·di·ci·tis \ə-ˌpen-də-ˈsīt-əs\ *n* : inflammation of the appendix

ap·pen·dic·u·lar \ˌap-ən-ˈdik-yə-lər\ *adj* : of or relating to an appendage and especially a limb ⟨the *appendicular* skeleton⟩

ap·pen·dix \ə-ˈpen-diks\ *n, pl* **-dix·es** *or* **-di·ces** \-də-ˌsēz\ **1** : supplementary material usually attached at the end of a piece of writing **2 a** : a small tubular outgrowth from the cecum of the intestine — called also *vermiform appendix* **b** : a bodily outgrowth or process other than the appendix of the intestine [Latin, "appendage," from *appendere* "to append"]

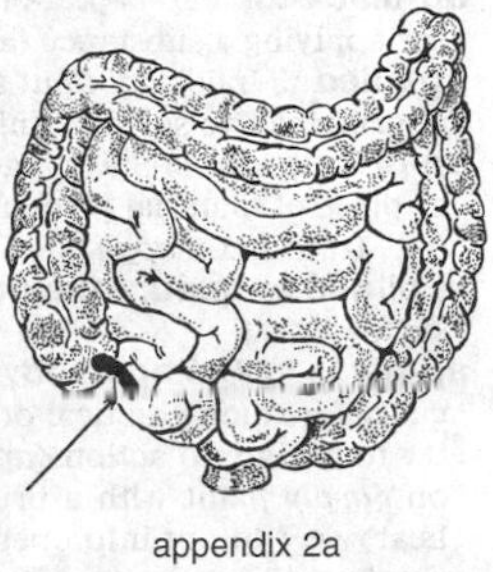

appendix 2a

ap·per·ceive \ˌap-ər-ˈsēv\ *vt* : to understand (something perceived) in terms of previous experience

ap·per·cep·tion \ˌap-ər-ˈsep-shən\ *n* : the process of apperceiving — **ap·per·cep·tive** \-ˈsep-tiv\ *adj*

ap·per·tain \ˌap-ər-ˈtān\ *vi* : to belong or be connected as a possession, part, or right : PERTAIN ⟨duties that *appertain* to the office of governor⟩ [Medieval French *apurtenir,* derived from Latin *ad-* + *pertinēre* "to belong"]

ap·pe·tite \ˈap-ə-ˌtīt\ *n* **1** : one of the instinctive desires necessary to keep up organic life; *esp* : the desire to eat **2 a** : an inherent craving ⟨an *appetite* for adventure⟩ **b** : TASTE 5, PREFERENCE [Medieval French *apetit,* from Latin *appetitus,* from *appetere* "to strive after," from *ad-* + *petere* "to go to"]

ap·pe·tiz·er \-ˌtī-zər\ *n* **1** : a food or drink that stimulates the appetite and is usually served before a meal **2** : something that creates a desire for more

ap·pe·tiz·ing \-ˌtī-zing\ *adj* : appealing to the appetite — **ap·pe·tiz·ing·ly** \-zing-lē\ *adv*

ap·plaud \ə-ˈplȯd\ *vb* **1** : PRAISE, APPROVE ⟨*applaud* her efforts⟩ **2** : to show approval especially by clapping the hands [Latin *applaudere,* from *ad-* + *plaudere* "to clap"] — **ap·plaud·able** \-ə-bəl\ *adj* — **ap·plaud·ably** \-blē\ *adv* — **ap·plaud·er** *n*

ap·plause \ə-ˈplȯz\ *n* : approval publicly expressed (as by clapping the hands) : ACCLAIM [Medieval Latin *applausus,* from Latin *applaudere* "to applaud"]

ap·ple \ˈap-əl\ *n* : a rounded fruit with a red, yellow, or green skin, firm white flesh, a seedy core, and a tart or mildly sweet taste; *also* : the tree of the rose family that bears this fruit [Old English *æppel*]

ap·ple·cart \-ˌkärt\ *n* : PLAN, SCHEME ⟨upset the *applecart*⟩

ap·ple·jack \-ˌjak\ *n* : brandy distilled from cider

apple–pie \ˈap-əl-ˌpī\ *adj* **1** : EXCELLENT, PERFECT ⟨in *apple-pie* order⟩ **2** : of or relating to traditional American values ⟨*apple-pie* wholesomeness⟩

ap·ple·sauce \-ˌsȯs\ *n* : a sauce or dessert made of sweetened stewed apples

ap·plet \ˈap-lət\ *n* : a small computer application [*appl*ication + *-et*]

ap·pli·ance \ə-ˈplī-əns\ *n* **1** : a piece of equipment for adapting a tool or machine to a special purpose : ATTACHMENT **2** : an instrument or device designed for a particular use; *esp* : a piece of household equipment that is operated by gas or electricity

ap·pli·ca·ble \ˈap-li-kə-bəl, ə-ˈplik-ə-\ *adj* : capable of being or suitable to be applied : APPROPRIATE — **ap·pli·ca·bil·i·ty** \ˌap-li-kə-ˈbil-ət-ē, ə-ˌplik-ə-\ *n*

\ə\ **abut**	\au̇\ **out**	\i\ **tip**	\ȯ\ **saw**	\u̇\ **foot**
\ər\ **further**	\ch\ **chin**	\ī\ **life**	\ȯi\ **coin**	\y\ **yet**
\a\ **mat**	\e\ **pet**	\j\ **job**	\th\ **thin**	\yü\ **few**
\ā\ **take**	\ē\ **easy**	\ng\ **sing**	\t͟h\ **this**	\yu̇\ **cure**
\ä\ **cot, cart**	\g\ **go**	\ō\ **bone**	\ü\ **food**	\zh\ **vision**

ap·pli·cant \ˈap-li-kənt\ *n* : a person who applies for something ⟨an *applicant* for work⟩ ⟨*applicants* for admission⟩

ap·pli·ca·tion \ˌap-lə-ˈkā-shən\ *n* **1** : the act or an instance of putting to use ⟨*application* of a new technology⟩ **2** : the act of laying or spreading on ⟨the proper *application* of paint⟩ **3** : close attention ⟨succeeds by *application* to her studies⟩ **4 a** : REQUEST, PETITION ⟨an *application* for a job⟩ **b** : a form used in making a request ⟨fill out an *application*⟩ **5** : capacity for being put to use ⟨the theory has practical *applications*⟩ **6** : a computer program that performs one of the major tasks (as word processing) for which a computer is used [Latin *applicatio,* from *applicare*]

ap·pli·ca·tor \ˈap-lə-ˌkāt-ər\ *n* : one that applies; *esp* : a device for applying a substance (as medicine or polish)

ap·plied \ə-ˈplīd\ *adj* : put to practical use; *esp* : applying general principles to solve definite problems ⟨*applied* sciences⟩

[1]**ap·pli·qué** \ˌap-lə-ˈkā\ *n* : a cutout decoration fastened to a larger piece of material [French, past participle of *appliquer* "to put on," from Latin *applicare*]

[2]**appliqué** *vt* **-quéd; -qué·ing** : to apply (an appliqué) to a larger surface

ap·ply \ə-ˈplī\ *vb* **ap·plied; ap·ply·ing** **1 a** : to put to use especially for some practical or specific purpose ⟨*apply* knowledge⟩ **b** : to bring into action ⟨*apply* the brakes⟩ **c** : to lay or spread on ⟨*apply* paint with a brush⟩ **d** : to place in contact ⟨*apply* heat⟩ **e** : to put into operation or effect ⟨*apply* a law⟩ **2** : to employ diligently or with close attention ⟨*apply* yourself to your work⟩ **3** : to have relevance or a connection ⟨this law *applies* to everyone⟩ **4** : to make an appeal or request especially in the form of a written application ⟨*apply* for a job⟩ [Medieval French *aplier,* from Latin *applicare,* from *ad-* + *plicare* "to fold"] — **ap·pli·er** \-ˈplī-ər\ *n*

ap·pog·gia·tu·ra \ə-ˌpäj-ə-ˈtu̇r-ə\ *n* : an embellishing note or tone preceding an essential melodic note or tone and usually written as a note of smaller size [Italian, literally, "support"]

ap·point \ə-ˈpȯint\ *vt* **1** : to fix or set officially ⟨*appoint* a day for a meeting⟩ **2** : to name officially especially to an office or position ⟨the president *appoints* the members of the cabinet⟩ [Medieval French *appointer,* from *a-* "ad-" + *point* "point"]

ap·point·ed \ə-ˈpȯint-əd\ *adj* : FURNISHED, EQUIPPED ⟨a well-*appointed* house⟩

ap·poin·tee \ə-ˌpȯin-ˈtē, ˌa-ˌpȯin-\ *n* : a person appointed to a position or an office

ap·point·ive \ə-ˈpȯint-iv\ *adj* : of, relating to, or filled by appointment ⟨an *appointive* office⟩

ap·point·ment \ə-ˈpȯint-mənt\ *n* **1** : the act or an instance of appointing : DESIGNATION ⟨holds office by *appointment*⟩ **2** : a position or office to which a person is named but not elected ⟨received an *appointment* from the president⟩ **3** : an agreement to meet at a fixed time ⟨an *appointment* with the dentist⟩ **4** : EQUIPMENT, FURNISHINGS — usually used in plural ⟨a house with modern *appointments*⟩

ap·por·tion \ə-ˈpōr-shən, -ˈpȯr-\ *vt* **-tioned; -tion·ing** \-shə-ning, -shning\ : to divide and distribute proportionately ⟨time carefully *apportioned* among various projects⟩ ***synonyms*** see ALLOT

ap·por·tion·ment \-shən-mənt\ *n* : the act or result of apportioning; *esp* : the apportioning of representatives or taxes among states or districts according to population

ap·pose \a-ˈpōz\ *vt* : to place near or in close relationship [Medieval French *aposer,* from *a-* "ad-" + *poser* "to place, pose"]

ap·po·site \ˈap-ə-zət\ *adj* : highly pertinent or appropriate : APT ⟨*apposite* remarks⟩ [Latin *appositus,* from *apponere* "to place near," from *ad-* + *ponere* "to put"] — **ap·po·site·ly** *adv* — **ap·po·site·ness** *n*

ap·po·si·tion \ˌap-ə-ˈzish-ən\ *n* **1 a** : a grammatical construction in which a noun or noun equivalent is followed by another that explains it (as *the poet* and *Burns* in "a biography of the poet Burns") **b** : the relation of one of such a pair of nouns or noun equivalents to the other **2 a** : the deposition of new layers (as in cell walls) upon those already present **b** : the state of being in close relationship — **ap·po·si·tion·al** \-ˈzish-nəl, -ən-l\ *adj*

[1]**ap·pos·i·tive** \ə-ˈpäz-ət-iv\ *adj* : of, relating to, or standing in grammatical apposition — **ap·pos·i·tive·ly** *adv*

[2]**appositive** *n* : the second of a pair of nouns or noun equivalents in apposition

ap·prais·al \ə-ˈprā-zəl\ *n* **1** : an act or instance of appraising **2** : a determination of the value of property by an appraiser; *also* : the value so determined

ap·praise \ə-ˈprāz\ *vt* **1** : to set a value on; *esp* : to give an expert judgment of the money value of ⟨a house *appraised* at $139,000⟩ **2** : to estimate the significance or status of ⟨*appraise* the situation⟩ [derived from Medieval French *a-* "ad-" + *preiser* "to prize, praise"] ***synonyms*** see ESTIMATE — **ap·praise·ment** \-mənt\ *n*

ap·prais·er \ə-ˈprā-zər\ *n* : one that appraises; *esp* : an official who appraises real estate and personal property for purposes of taxation

ap·pre·cia·ble \ə-ˈprē-shə-bəl *also* -ˈprish-ə-\ *adj* : large enough to be recognized and measured or to be felt ⟨an *appreciable* difference in temperature⟩ — **ap·pre·cia·bly** \-blē\ *adv*

ap·pre·ci·ate \ə-ˈprē-shē-ˌāt *also* -ˈprish-ē-ˌāt\ *vb* **1 a** : to grasp with full knowledge and understanding ⟨*appreciate* the difference between right and wrong⟩ **b** : to value or admire greatly ⟨*appreciates* the artist's work⟩ **c** : to be fully aware of ⟨had to see it to *appreciate* it⟩ **d** : to recognize with gratitude ⟨I *appreciate* your help⟩ **2** : to increase in number or value ⟨savings *appreciate* over time⟩ [Late Latin *appretiare,* from Latin *ad-* + *pretium* "price"] — **ap·pre·ci·a·tor** \-ˌāt-ər\ *n*

ap·pre·ci·a·tion \ə-ˌprē-shē-ˈā-shən *also* -ˌprē-sē- *or* -ˌprish-ē-\ *n* **1** : the action or an instance of appreciating **2 a** : awareness or grasp of worth or value **b** : expression of appreciation ⟨this commendation in *appreciation* of your work⟩ **3** : a gain in value

ap·pre·cia·tive \ə-ˈprē-shət-iv, -shē-ˌāt-iv *also* -ˈprish-ət-, -ˈprish-ē-\ *adj* : having or showing appreciation ⟨an *appreciative* audience⟩ — **ap·pre·cia·tive·ly** *adv* — **ap·pre·cia·tive·ness** *n*

ap·pre·hend \ˌap-ri-ˈhend\ *vb* **1** : ARREST, SEIZE ⟨*apprehend* a thief⟩ **2 a** : to become aware of : PERCEIVE **b** : to anticipate especially with anxiety, dread, or fear **3** : to grasp with the understanding : UNDERSTAND [Latin *apprehendere,* literally, "to seize," from *ad-* + *prehendere* "to seize, grasp"] — **ap·pre·hen·si·ble** \-ˈhen-sə-bəl\ *adj* — **ap·pre·hen·si·bly** \-blē\ *adv*

ap·pre·hen·sion \ˌap-ri-ˈhen-chən\ *n* **1** : COMPREHENSION 2, UNDERSTANDING ⟨a person of keen *apprehension*⟩ **2** : CAPTURE, ARREST ⟨*apprehension* of a burglar⟩ **3** : fear of what may be coming : dread of the future [Late Latin *apprehensio,* from Latin *apprehendere* "to seize"]

ap·pre·hen·sive \ˌap-ri-ˈhen-siv\ *adj* **1** : feeling or having apprehension **2** : fearful of what may be coming — **ap·pre·hen·sive·ly** *adv* — **ap·pre·hen·sive·ness** *n*

[1]**ap·pren·tice** \ə-ˈprent-əs\ *n* **1** : a person legally bound to serve a master for a specified period to receive instruction in an art or trade **2** : one who is learning a trade, art, or calling by practical experience under skilled workers [Medieval French *aprentiz,* from *aprendre* "to learn," from Latin *apprehendere* "to apprehend"] — **ap·pren·tice·ship** \-ə-ˌship, -əsh-ˌship, -əs-ˌship\ *n*

[2]**apprentice** *vt* : to bind or set at work as an apprentice

ap·prise \ə-ˈprīz\ *vt* : to give notice to : INFORM [French *appris,* past participle of *apprendre* "to learn, teach," from Latin *apprehendere* "to apprehend"]

[1]**ap·proach** \ə-ˈprōch\ *vb* **1 a** : to draw close : come near or nearer **b** : to be almost the same as ⟨her talent *approaches* that of her father⟩ **2 a** : to make offers to ⟨the actor was *approached* by many producers⟩ **b** : to take preliminary steps toward ⟨*approach* the subject with an open mind⟩ [Medieval French *aprocher,* from Late Latin *appropiare,* from Latin *ad-* + *prope* "near"]

[2]**approach** *n* **1 a** : an act or instance of approaching ⟨the *approach* of winter⟩ **b** : APPROXIMATION ⟨in this book he makes his closest *approach* to greatness⟩ **2 a** : a preliminary step toward an end **b** : way of dealing with something ⟨try a new *approach*⟩ **3 a** : a means of access : AVENUE **b** : the descent of an aircraft as it prepares to land

ap·proach·able \ə-ˈprō-chə-bəl\ *adj* **1** : capable of being approached : ACCESSIBLE **2** : easy to meet or deal with ⟨a friendly and *approachable* person⟩ — **ap·proach·abil·i·ty** \-ˌprō-chə-ˈbil-ət-ē\ *n*

ap·pro·ba·tion \ˌap-rə-ˈbā-shən\ *n* **1** : the act of approving formally or officially **2** : COMMENDATION, PRAISE [Latin *approbare* "to approve"]

[1]**ap·pro·pri·ate** \ə-ˈprō-prē-ˌāt\ *vt* **1** : to take exclusive possession of **2** : to set apart for a particular purpose or use ⟨Congress *appropriated* funds for the research⟩ **3** : to take without

permission : STEAL [Late Latin *appropriare,* from Latin *ad-* + *proprius* "one's own"] — **ap·pro·pri·a·tor** \-ˌāt-ər\ *n*

[2]**ap·pro·pri·ate** \-prē-ət\ *adj* : especially suitable or fitting : PROPER ⟨an *appropriate* response⟩ ***synonyms*** see FIT — **ap·pro·pri·ate·ly** *adv* — **ap·pro·pri·ate·ness** *n*

ap·pro·pri·a·tion \ə-ˌprō-prē-ˈā-shən\ *n* **1** : an act or instance of appropriating **2** : something that has been appropriated; *esp* : a sum of money formally set aside for a specific use

ap·prov·al \ə-ˈprü-vəl\ *n* : an act or instance of approving : APPROBATION — **on approval** : subject to a prospective buyer's acceptance or refusal ⟨goods sent *on approval*⟩

ap·prove \ə-ˈprüv\ *vb* **1** : to have or express a favorable judgment : take a favorable view **2 a** : to accept as satisfactory ⟨*approved* the date of the meeting⟩ **b** : to give formal or official sanction to ⟨the senate *approved* the bill⟩ [Medieval French *apruer, approver,* from Latin *approbare,* from *ad-* + *probare* "to prove"] — **ap·prov·ing·ly** \-ˈprü-ving-lē\ *adv*

synonyms APPROVE, ENDORSE, SANCTION mean to have or express a favorable opinion of. APPROVE may imply no more than this or it may suggest some degree of admiration ⟨the parents *approve* of the marriage⟩. ENDORSE adds the implication of support with an explicit statement ⟨publicly *endorsed* her for Senator⟩. SANCTION implies both approval and authorization ⟨the President *sanctioned* the military strike⟩.

[1]**ap·prox·i·mate** \ə-ˈpräk-sə-mət\ *adj* : nearly correct or exact ⟨the *approximate* cost⟩ [Late Latin *approximare* "to come near," from Latin *ad-* + *proximus* "nearest, next"]

[2]**ap·prox·i·mate** \-ˌmāt\ *vb* **1** : to bring or come close together ⟨*approximate* two boards⟩ **2** : to find the approximate value of ⟨*approximate* a cost⟩

ap·prox·i·mate·ly \-mət-lē\ *adv* : reasonably close to ⟨*approximately* five miles⟩ ***usage*** see SOME

ap·prox·i·ma·tion \ə-ˌpräk-sə-ˈmā-shən\ *n* **1** : the act or process of approximating **2** : the quality or state of being close especially in value **3** : something that is approximate; *esp* : a nearly exact estimate of a value or cost

ap·pur·te·nance \ə-ˈpərt-nəns, -n-əns\ *n* **1** : a secondary right (as a right-of-way) attached to a principal property right **2** : a subordinate part **3** *pl* : accessory objects ⟨sold the house, its furniture, and all other *appurtenances*⟩ [Medieval *apurtenance,* from *apurtenir* "to appertain"] — **ap·pur·te·nant** \-ˈpərt-nənt, -n-ənt\ *adj*

ap·ri·cot \ˈap-rə-ˌkät, ˈā-prə-\ *n* : an oval orange-colored fruit resembling the related peach and plum in flavor; *also* : a tree that bears apricots [derived from Arabic *al-birqūq* "the apricot"]

April \ˈā-prəl\ *n* : the 4th month of the year according to the Gregorian calendar [Latin *Aprilis*]

April fool *n* : a person who is tricked on April Fools' Day

April Fools' Day *also* **April Fool's Day** *n* : April 1 characteristically marked by the playing of practical jokes

a pri·o·ri \ˌä-prē-ˈōr-ē, -ˈȯr-\ *adj* **1** : of or relating to reasoning from self-evident propositions **2** : estimated from available facts without close examination : PRESUMPTIVE [Latin, "from the former"] — **a priori** *adv*

apron \ˈā-prən, -pərn\ *n* **1** : a garment worn on the front of the body to protect the clothing **2** : something that suggests or resembles an apron in shape, position, or use : as **a** : the part of the stage in front of the proscenium arch **b** : a shield (as of concrete, planking, or brushwood) along the bank of a river to prevent erosion **c** : the extensive paved part of an airport immediately adjacent to the terminal area or hangars [Middle English *napron* (the phrase *a napron* being understood as *an apron*), from Medieval French *naperon,* from *nape* "cloth," from Latin *mappa* "napkin"]

[1]**ap·ro·pos** \ˌap-rə-ˈpō, ˈap-rə-ˌ\ *adv* **1** : at the right time : SEASONABLY **2** : by the way : INCIDENTALLY [French *à propos,* literally, "to the purpose"]

[2]**apropos** *adj* : being to the point : PERTINENT ⟨*apropos* comments⟩

apropos of *prep* : with regard to : CONCERNING

apse \ˈaps\ *n* : a usually semicircular projection on the end of a building (as a church) [Medieval Latin *apsis,* from Latin, "arch, orbit," from Greek *hapsis,* from *haptein* "to fasten"] — **ap·si·dal** \ˈap-səd-l\ *adj*

apt \ˈapt\ *adj* **1** : FITTING, SUITABLE ⟨an *apt* quotation⟩ **2 a** : having a tendency : LIKELY ⟨plants *apt* to suffer from drought⟩ **b** : ordinarily disposed ⟨*apt* to worry⟩ **3** : keenly alert : quick to learn ⟨an *apt* pupil⟩ [Latin *aptus,* literally, "fastened," from *apere* "to fasten, fit"] — **apt·ly** *adv* — **apt·ness** \ˈap-nəs, ˈapt-\ *n*

usage Both *liable* and *apt* when followed by an infinitive are used nearly interchangeably with *likely. Apt* and *likely,* however, are common in situations having a positive or neutral outcome ⟨he's *apt* to be praised⟩ ⟨is *likely* to come⟩ or a negative outcome ⟨is *apt* to falter⟩ ⟨was *likely* to get caught⟩. *Liable,* on the other hand, is generally limited to situations having a negative outcome ⟨is *liable* to get lost⟩.

ap·ti·tude \ˈap-tə-ˌtüd, -ˌtyüd\ *n* **1** : capacity for learning **2** : a natural inclination or ability : TALENT ⟨an *aptitude* for math⟩

aqua \ˈäk-wə\ *n* : a light greenish blue color [Latin, "water"]

aqua·cade \ˈak-wə-ˌkād, ˈäk-\ *n* : an elaborate water spectacle consisting of exhibitions of swimming, diving, and acrobatics accompanied by music [*Aquacade,* a water spectacle originally at Cleveland, Ohio (1937), from Latin *aqua* "water" + English *-cade* (as in *cavalcade*)]

aqua·cul·ture *also* **aqui·cul·ture** \ˈak-wə-ˌkəl-chər, ˈäk-\ *n* : the cultivation of aquatic organisms (as fish or shellfish) especially for food [Latin *aqua* "water" + English *-culture* (as in *agriculture*)] — **aqua·cul·tur·al** \-ˌkəlch-rəl, -ə-rəl\ *adj*

aqua·for·tis \ˌak-wə-ˈfȯrt-əs, ˌäk-\ *n* : NITRIC ACID [New Latin *aqua fortis,* literally, "strong water"]

aqua·ma·rine \ˌak-wə-mə-ˈrēn, ˌäk-\ *n* **1** : a transparent semiprecious bluish or greenish stone that is a variety of beryl **2** : a pale blue to light greenish blue [Latin *aqua marina* "sea water"]

aqua·naut \ˈak-wə-ˌnȯt, ˈäk-, -ˌnät\ *n* : one that lives for an extended period in an underwater shelter which serves as a base for research [Latin *aqua* + English *-naut* (as in *aeronaut*)]

aqua·plane \ˈak-wə-ˌplān, ˈäk-\ *n* : a board towed behind a speeding motorboat and ridden by a person standing on it — **aquaplane** *vi* — **aqua·plan·er** *n*

aqua re·gia \ˌak-wə-ˈrē-jē-ə, ˌäk-, -jə\ *n* : a mixture of nitric and hydrochloric acids that dissolves gold or platinum [New Latin, literally, "royal water"]

aquar·ist \ə-ˈkwar-əst, -ˈkwer-\ *n* : one who keeps an aquarium

aquar·i·um \ə-ˈkwar-ē-əm, -ˈkwer-\ *n, pl* **-i·ums** *or* **-ia** \-ē-ə\ : a container (as a glass tank) in which living aquatic animals or plants are kept; *also* : an establishment where aquatic collections of living organisms are kept and shown [probably from *aquatic vivarium*]

Aquar·i·us \ə-ˈkwar-ē-əs, -ˈkwer-\ *n* **1** : the 11th sign of the zodiac; *also* : one born under this sign **2** : a zodiacal constellation south of Pegasus [Latin, literally, "water carrier"]

[1]**aquat·ic** \ə-ˈkwät-ik, -ˈkwat-\ *adj* **1** : growing or living in or frequenting water ⟨*aquatic* animals⟩ **2** : performed in or on water ⟨*aquatic* sports⟩ [Latin *aquaticus,* from *aqua* "water"] — **aquat·i·cal·ly** \-i-kə-lē, -klē\ *adv*

[2]**aquatic** *n* **1** : an aquatic animal or plant **2** *pl* : water sports

aq·ua·tint \ˈak-wə-ˌtint, ˈäk-\ *n* : an etching in which the printing plate is treated to produce an effect resembling a drawing in watercolors or india ink [Italian *acqua tinta* "dyed water"] — **aquatint** *vt*

aq·ue·duct \ˈak-wə-ˌdəkt\ *n* **1** : an artificial channel for carrying flowing water **2** : a structure that carries the water of a canal over a river or hollow [Latin *aquaeductus,* from *aqua* "water" + *ductus* "act of leading"]

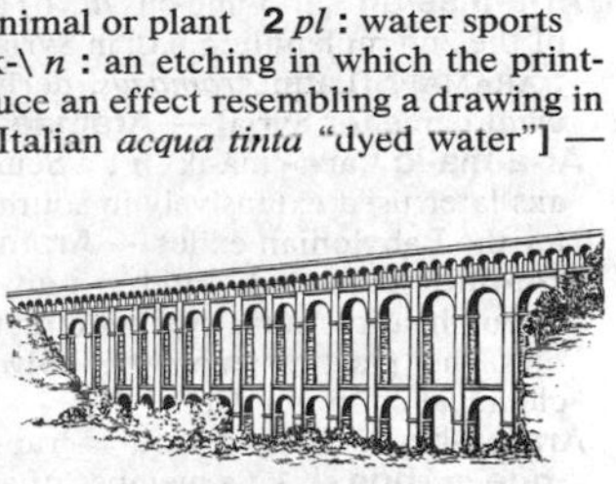

aqueduct 2

aque·ous \ˈā-kwē-əs, ˈak-wē-\ *adj* **1** : of, relating to, or resembling water **2** : made of, by, or with water ⟨an *aqueous* solution⟩

aqueous humor *n* : a clear fluid between the lens and the cornea of the eye

aq·ui·fer \ˈak-wə-fər, ˈäk-\ *n* : a water-bearing stratum of permeable rock, sand, or gravel — **aquif·er·ous** \a-ˈkwif-ə-rəs, ä-\ *adj*

Aq·ui·la \ˈak-wə-lə\ *n* : a northern constellation in the Milky Way south of Lyra and Cygnus [Latin, literally, "eagle"]

\ə\ **abut**	\au̇\ **out**	\i\ **tip**	\ȯ\ **saw**	\u̇\ **foot**
\ər\ **further**	\ch\ **chin**	\ī\ **life**	\ȯi\ **coin**	\y\ **yet**
\a\ **mat**	\e\ **pet**	\j\ **job**	\th\ **thin**	\yü\ **few**
\ā\ **take**	\ē\ **easy**	\ng\ **sing**	\th\ **this**	\yu̇\ **cure**
\ä\ **cot, cart**	\g\ **go**	\ō\ **bone**	\ü\ **food**	\zh\ **vision**

aq·ui·le·gia \ˌak-wə-ˈlē-jē-ə, -jə\ *n* : COLUMBINE [New Latin, genus name]

aq·ui·line \ˈak-wə-ˌlīn, -lən\ *adj* **1** : of, relating to, or resembling an eagle **2** : curving like an eagle's beak ⟨an *aquiline* nose⟩ [Latin *aquilinus,* from *aquila* "eagle"]

-ar \ər *also* ˌär\ *adj suffix* : of or relating to ⟨molecul*ar*⟩ : being ⟨spectacul*ar*⟩ : resembling ⟨oracul*ar*⟩ [Latin *-aris,* alteration of *-alis* "-al"]

Ar·ab \ˈar-əb\ *n* **1 a** : a member of the Semitic people of the Arabian Peninsula **b** : a member of an Arabic-speaking people **2** : ARABIAN HORSE — **Arab** *adj*

ar·a·besque \ˌar-ə-ˈbesk\ *n* : an ornament or a style of decoration consisting of interlacing lines and outlines usually of flowers, foliage, or fruit and sometimes animal and human figures [French, from Italian *arabesco* "Arabian in style"] — **arabesque** *adj*

[1]**Ara·bi·an** \ə-ˈrā-bē-ən\ *adj* : of or relating to Arabia or the Arabs

[2]**Arabian** *n* : a native or inhabitant of Arabia : ARAB

Arabian camel *n* : DROMEDARY 2

Arabian horse *n* : any of an ancient breed of horses originating in Arabia and adjacent regions and noted for their graceful build, speed, intelligence, and spirit

[1]**Ar·a·bic** \ˈar-ə-bik\ *adj* **1** : ARABIAN, ARAB **2** : expressed in or utilizing Arabic numerals ⟨21 is an *Arabic* number⟩ ⟨*Arabic* notation⟩

[2]**Arabic** *n* : a Semitic language of Arabia spoken in a wide region of southwestern Asia and northern Africa

Arabic numeral *n* : one of the number symbols 1, 2, 3, 4, 5, 6, 7, 8, 9, and 0 — see NUMBER table

ar·a·ble \ˈar-ə-bəl\ *adj* : fit for or cultivated by plowing or tillage : suitable for producing crops [Latin *arabilis,* from *arare* "to plow"] — **ar·a·bil·i·ty** \ˌar-ə-ˈbil-ət-ē\ *n* — **arable** *n*

arach·nid \ə-ˈrak-nəd, -ˌnid\ *n* : any of a class (Arachnida) of arthropods including the spiders, scorpions, mites, and ticks and having a segmented body divided into two regions of which the front part bears four pairs of legs but no antennae [derived from Greek *arachnē* "spider"] — **arachnid** *adj*

arach·noid \-ˌnȯid\ *n* : a thin membrane of the brain and spinal cord that lies between the dura mater and the pia mater [derived from Greek *arachnē* "spider, spider web"] — **arachnoid** *adj*

arach·no·pho·bia \ə-ˌrak-nə-ˈfō-bē-ə\ *n* : fear or loathing of spiders

ara·go·nite \ə-ˈrag-ə-ˌnīt, ˈar-ə-gə-\ *n* : a mineral that is chemically the same as calcite but is denser and has different crystalline form [German *Aragonit,* from *Aragon,* Spain]

Ar·a·mae·an \ˌar-ə-ˈmē-ən\ *n* **1** : a member of a Semitic people of the 2nd millennium B.C. in Syria and Upper Mesopotamia **2** : ARAMAIC [Latin *Aramaeus,* derived from Hebrew *ʼĂrām,* ancient name for Syria] — **Aramaean** *adj*

Ar·a·ma·ic \ˌar-ə-ˈmā-ik\ *n* : a Semitic language of the Aramaeans later used extensively in southwest Asia (as by the Jews after the Babylonian exile) — **Aramaic** *adj*

ar·a·mid \ˈar-ə-məd, -ˌmid\ *n* : any of a group of light but very strong heat-resistant synthetic materials used especially in textiles and plastics [*ar*omatic poly*amid*e, name of a group of chemical compounds]

Arap·a·ho *or* **Arap·a·hoe** \ə-ˈrap-ə-ˌhō\ *n, pl* **-ho** *or* **-hos** *or* **-hoe** *or* **-hoes** **1** : a member of an American Indian people of the central western plains **2** : the Algonquian language of the Arapaho

Arau·ca·ni·an \ə-ˌrau̇-ˈkän-ē-ən\ *n* : a member of a group of Indian peoples of Chile and Argentina [Spanish *araucano,* from *Arauco,* province in Chile] — **Araucanian** *adj*

Ar·a·wak \ˈar-ə-ˌwäk\ *n, pl* **-wak** *or* **-waks** : a member of an Indian people chiefly of Guyana

ar·bi·ter \ˈär-bət-ər\ *n* **1** : ARBITRATOR, UMPIRE **2** : a person having absolute authority to judge and decide what is right or proper ⟨an *arbiter* of taste⟩ [Latin "observer, judge"]

ar·bit·ra·ment \är-ˈbi-trə-mənt\ *n* **1** : ARBITRATION **2** : a decision or award made by an arbiter

ar·bi·trary \ˈär-bə-ˌtrer-ē\ *adj* **1** : depending on choice or discretion rather than defined by law ⟨an *arbitrary* settlement of a dispute⟩ **2** : not controlled or restrained by law : DESPOTIC ⟨*arbitrary* use of power⟩ **3 a** : based on opinion, preference, or whim ⟨made an *arbitrary* choice⟩ **b** : existing or coming about seemingly at random or by chance ⟨an *arbitrary* sampling⟩ — **ar·bi·trar·i·ly** \ˌär-bə-ˈtrer-ə-lē\ *adv* — **ar·bi·trar·i·ness** \ˈär-bə-ˌtrer-ē-nəs\ *n*

ar·bi·trate \ˈär-bə-ˌtrāt\ *vb* **1** : to settle a dispute after hearing and considering the arguments of both sides : hear and decide as an arbiter ⟨a committee appointed to *arbitrate* between the company and the union⟩ **2** : to submit to arbitration ⟨agreed to *arbitrate* their differences⟩ [Latin *arbitrari* "to observe, judge," from *arbiter* "judge"] — **ar·bi·tra·ble** \-bə-trə-bəl\ *adj* — **ar·bi·tra·tive** \-ˌtrāt-iv\ *adj*

ar·bi·tra·tion \ˌär-bə-ˈtrā-shən\ *n* : the act of arbitrating; *esp* : the settling of a dispute in which both parties agree beforehand to abide by the decision of an arbitrator or body of arbitrators — **ar·bi·tra·tion·al** \-shnəl, -shən-l\ *adj*

ar·bi·tra·tor \ˈär-bə-ˌtrāt-ər\ *n* : a person chosen to settle differences between two parties in a disagreement

[1]**ar·bor** \ˈär-bər\ *n* : a shelter of vines or branches or of latticework covered with climbing shrubs or vines [Medieval French *erber, herber* "garden," from *herbe* "herb, grass"]

[2]**arbor** *n* : a shaft on which a revolving cutting tool is mounted or on which work is mounted for turning [Latin, "tree, shaft"]

Arbor Day *n* : a day in April set aside for planting trees

ar·bo·re·al \är-ˈbōr-ē-əl, -ˈbȯr-\ *adj* **1** : of, relating to, or resembling a tree **2** : living in or frequenting trees [Latin *arboreus,* from *arbor* "tree"] — **ar·bo·re·al·ly** \-ē-ə-lē\ *adv*

ar·bo·res·cent \ˌär-bə-ˈres-nt\ *adj* : resembling a tree in growth, structure, or appearance; *esp* : branching repeatedly like a tree — **ar·bo·res·cence** \-ns\ *n* — **ar·bo·res·cent·ly** *adv*

ar·bo·re·tum \ˌär-bə-ˈrēt-əm\ *n, pl* **-re·tums** *or* **-re·ta** \-ˈrēt-ə\ : a place where trees, shrubs, and herbaceous plants are grown for scientific and educational purposes [Latin, "plantation of trees," from *arbor* "tree"]

ar·bor·ist \ˈär-bə-rəst\ *n* : a specialist in the care and maintenance of trees

ar·bor·vi·tae \ˌär-bər-ˈvīt-ē\ *n* : any of various evergreen trees and shrubs related to the cypresses that have leaves closely overlapping like scales and are often grown for ornament and in hedges [New Latin *arbor vitae,* literally, "tree of life"]

ar·bu·tus \är-ˈbyüt-əs\ *n* **1** : any of a genus of shrubs and trees of the heath family with white or pink flowers and red berries **2** : a trailing plant of the heath family that has fragrant pinkish flowers borne in early spring and is found in eastern North America [Latin, a kind of tree of the heath family]

[1]**arc** \ˈärk\ *n* **1 a** : something arched or curved **b** : a curved path **2** : a sustained luminous discharge of electricity across a gap in a circuit or between electrodes **3** : a continuous portion (as part of the circumference of a circle) of a curved line [Medieval French, "bow," from Latin *arcus* "bow, arch, arc"]

[2]**arc** *vi* **arced** \ˈärkt\; **arc·ing** **1** : to form an electric arc **2** : to follow an arc-shaped course

ar·cade \är-ˈkād\ *n* **1** : a row of arches with the columns that support them **2** : an arched or covered passageway; *esp* : one lined with shops [French, from Italian *arcata,* from *arco* "arch"] — **ar·cad·ed** \-ˈkād-əd\ *adj*

arcade game *n* : VIDEO GAME

ar·ca·dia \är-ˈkād-ē-ə\ *n, often cap* : a region or scene of simple pleasure and quiet [*Arcadia,* region of ancient Greece often chosen as a setting for pastoral poetry] — **ar·ca·di·an** \-ē-ən\ *adj or n, often cap*

ar·cane \är-ˈkān\ *adj* : SECRET 1a, MYSTERIOUS [Latin *arcanus,* from *arca* "chest for valuables"]

ar·ca·num \är-ˈkā-nəm\ *n, pl* **-na** \-nə\ : mysterious or specialized knowledge known only to the initiate [Latin, from *arcanus* "secret"]

[1]**arch** \ˈärch\ *n* **1** : a usually curved structural member spanning an opening and serving as a support (as for the wall above the opening) **2** : something resembling an arch in form or function; *esp* : either of two portions of the bony structure of the foot that impart elasticity to it and cushion it against shock (as in running and walking) **3** : ARCHWAY [Medieval French *arche,* derived from Latin *arcus* "bow, arch"]

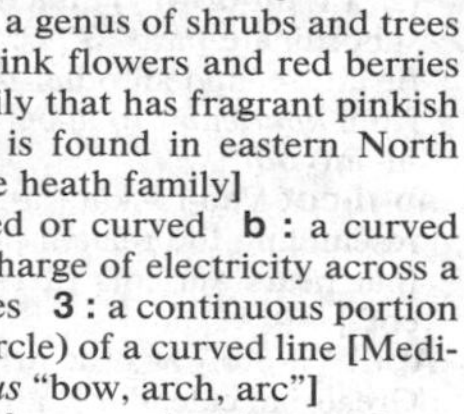

arch 1: *1* round, *2* lancet, *3* trefoil, *4* ogee

[2]**arch** *vb* **1** : to cover or provide with an arch **2** : to form or bend

into an arch **3** : to move in an arch : ARC

³arch *adj* **1** : PRINCIPAL, CHIEF ⟨their *arch* opponent⟩ **2** : playfully saucy : ROGUISH, MISCHIEVOUS ⟨an *arch* smile⟩ [*arch-*] — **arch·ness** *n*

arch- *prefix* **1** : chief : principal ⟨*arch*enemy⟩ **2** : extreme [derived from Greek *arch-, archi-,* from *archein* "to begin, rule"]

archae- *or* **archaeo-** *also* **archeo-** *combining form* : ancient : primitive ⟨*Archeo*zoic⟩ [Greek *archaios* "ancient," from *archē* "beginning"]

ar·chaea \är-ˈkē-ə\ *n pl* : single-celled organisms that are prokaryotes often of harsh environments (as hot springs) and include forms that produce methane [Greek *archaios* "ancient"]

ar·chae·bac·te·ri·um \ˌär-kē-ˌbak-ˈtir-ē-əm\ *n* : any of a group of primitive single-celled microogranisms that resemble bacteria and include methane-producing forms and others that inhabit very salty or very hot and acidic environments

ar·chae·ol·o·gy *or* **ar·che·ol·o·gy** \ˌär-kē-ˈäl-ə-jē\ *n* : the scientific study of material remains (as fossil relics, artifacts, and monuments) of past human life and activities — **ar·chae·o·log·i·cal** \-kē-ə-ˈläj-i-kəl\ *adj* — **archaeologically** *adv* — **ar·chae·ol·o·gist** \-kē-ˈäl-ə-jəst\ *n*

ar·chae·op·ter·yx \ˌär-kē-ˈäp-tə-riks\ *n* : a primitive extinct European bird of the Jurassic period of geological history with reptilian characteristics (as teeth) as well as wings and feathers [Greek *pteryx* "wing"]

ar·cha·ic \är-ˈkā-ik\ *adj* **1** : of, relating to, or characteristic of an earlier or more primitive time : ANTIQUATED **2** : having the characteristics of the language of the past and surviving chiefly in specialized uses ⟨the *archaic* words "methinks" and "saith"⟩ **3** : surviving from an earlier period ⟨an *archaic* plant⟩ [Greek *archaïkos,* from *archaios* "ancient," from *archē* "beginning"] ***synonyms*** see OLD

ar·cha·ism \ˈär-kē-ˌiz-əm, -kā-\ *n* **1** : the use of archaic words **2** : an archaic word or expression

arch·an·gel \ˈärk-ˌān-jəl\ *n* : an angel of high rank

arch·bish·op \ˈärch-ˈbish-əp\ *n* : the bishop of highest rank in a group of dioceses

arch·bish·op·ric \-ˈbish-ə-prik\ *n* **1** : the see or province over which an archbishop exercises authority **2** : the jursidiction or office of an archbishop

arch·dea·con \ˈärch-ˈdē-kən\ *n* : a clergyman having the duty of assisting a bishop

arch·dea·con·ry \-ˈdē-kən-rē\ *n, pl* **-ries** : the district or residence of an archdeacon

arch·di·o·cese \ˈärch-ˈdī-ə-səs, -ˌsēz, -ˌsēs\ *n* : the diocese of an archbishop — **arch·di·oc·e·san** \ˌärch-dī-ˈäs-ə-sən\ *adj*

arch·du·cal \ˈärch-ˈdü-kəl, -ˈdyü-\ *adj* : of or relating to an archduke or archduchy

arch·duch·ess \ˈärch-ˈdəch-əs\ *n* **1** : the wife or widow of an archduke **2** : a woman having in her own right the rank of archduke

arch·duchy \-ˈdəch-ē\ *n* : the territory of an archduke or archduchess

arch·duke \-ˈdük, -ˈdyük\ *n* : a sovereign prince; *esp* : a prince of the imperial family of Austria — **arch·duke·dom** \-dəm\ *n*

Ar·che·an *or* **Ar·chae·an** \är-ˈkē-ən\ *adj* **1** : of, relating to, or being the earliest eon of geological history or the corresponding system of rocks — see GEOLOGIC TIME table **2** : PRECAMBRIAN [Greek *archaios* "ancient"] — **Archean** *n*

ar·che·go·ni·um \ˌär-ki-ˈgō-nē-əm\ *n, pl* **-nia** \-nē-ə\ : a flask-shaped female sex organ found especially in mosses and ferns [Greek *archegonos* "originator," from *archein* "to begin" + *gonos* "procreation"] — **ar·che·go·ni·al** \-nē-əl\ *adj*

arch·en·e·my \ˈärch-ˈen-ə-mē\ *n* : a principal enemy

arch·en·ter·on \är-ˈkent-ə-ˌrän, -rən\ *n* : the cavity of the gastrula of an embryo

Ar·cheo·zo·ic \ˌär-kē-ə-ˈzō-ik\ *n* : ARCHEAN 1 — **Archeozoic** *adj*

ar·cher \ˈär-chər\ *n* : a person who uses a bow and arrow [Medieval French, derived from Latin *arcus* "bow"]

ar·chery \ˈärch-rē, -ə-rē\ *n* **1** : the art, practice, or skill of shooting with bow and arrow **2** : a body of archers

ar·che·type \ˈär-ki-ˌtīp\ *n* : the original pattern or model of a work or the model from which others are copied : PROTOTYPE [Latin *archetypum,* from Greek *archetypon,* from *archein* "to begin" + *typos* "type"] — **ar·che·typ·al** \ˌär-ki-ˈtī-pəl\ *also* **ar·che·typ·i·cal** \-ˈtip-i-kəl\ *adj* — **ar·che·typ·al·ly** \-ˈtī-pə-lē\ *also* **ar·che·typ·i·cal·ly** \-ˈtip-i-kə-lē, -klē\ *adv*

arch·fiend \ˈärch-ˈfēnd\ *n* : a principal fiend; *esp* : DEVIL 1

arch·foe \-ˈfō\ *n* : a principal foe : ARCHENEMY

ar·chi·epis·co·pal \ˌär-kē-ə-ˈpis-kə-pəl\ *adj* : of or relating to an archbishop [Late Latin *archiepiscopus* "archbishop," from Late Greek *archiepiskopos,* from *archi-* "arch-" + *episkopos* "bishop"]

Ar·chi·me·des' principle \ˌär-kə-ˈmē-dēz-\ *n* : a law of fluid mechanics: a body in a fluid is lifted up with a force equal to the weight of the fluid displaced by the body [*Archimedes*]

Archimedes' screw *n* : a device made especially of a helical tube and used to raise water

ar·chi·pel·a·go \ˌär-kə-ˈpel-ə-ˌgō, ˌär-chə-\ *n, pl* **-goes** *or* **-gos** **1** : an expanse of water with many scattered islands **2** : a group of islands [*Archipelago* "Aegean sea," from Italian *Arcipelago,* literally, "chief sea," from *arci-* "arch-" + Greek *pelagos* "sea"] — **ar·chi·pe·lag·ic** \-pə-ˈlaj-ik-\ *adj*

ar·chi·tect \ˈär-kə-ˌtekt\ *n* **1** : a person who designs buildings and oversees their construction **2** : a person who designs and guides a plan or undertaking ⟨the *architect* of U.S. foreign policy⟩ [derived from Greek *architektōn* "master builder," from *archi-* "arch-" + *tektōn* "builder, carpenter"]

ar·chi·tec·ton·ic \ˌär-kə-ˌtek-ˈtän-ik\ *adj* : of, relating to, or according with the principles of architecture : ARCHITECTURAL

ar·chi·tec·ton·ics \-ˈtän-iks\ *n sing or pl* : structural design : STRUCTURE, ORDER, PLAN

ar·chi·tec·tur·al \ˌär-kə-ˈtek-chə-rəl, -ˈtek-shrəl\ *adj* : of, relating to, or conforming to the rules of architecture — **ar·chi·tec·tur·al·ly** \-ē\ *adv*

ar·chi·tec·ture \ˈär-kə-ˌtek-chər\ *n* **1** : the art or science of designing and building habitable structures **2** : architectural work or product : BUILDINGS **3** : a method or style of building ⟨a church of modern *architecture*⟩ **4** : a unifying or organizing form or structure ⟨the *architecture* of a good novel⟩

ar·chi·trave \ˈär-kə-ˌtrāv\ *n* : the lowest division of an entablature resting immediately on the capital of the column in an ancient Greek or Roman building [Middle French, from Italian, from *archi-* "arch-" + *trave* "beam," from Latin *trabs*]

¹ar·chive \ˈär-ˌkīv\ *n* **1** : a place in which public records or historical documents are preserved; *also* : the material preserved — usually used in plural **2** : a collection especially of information [Latin *archivum,* from Greek *archeia* "government documents," from *archē* "beginning, rule, government"] — **ar·chi·val** \är-ˈkī-vəl\ *adj*

²archive *vt* : to file or collect in or as if in an archive ⟨was *archiving* documents⟩

ar·chi·vist \ˈär-kə-vəst, -ˌkī-\ *n* : a person in charge of archives

arch·ly \ˈärch-lē\ *adv* **1** : in an arch manner **2** : to an extreme degree ⟨*archly* conservative⟩

ar·chon \ˈär-ˌkän, -kən\ *n* : one of the chief magistrates in ancient Athens [Latin, from Greek *archōn,* from *archein* "to rule"]

ar·cho·saur \ˈär-kə-ˌsòr\ *n* : any of a subclass of reptiles comprising the dinosaurs, pterosaurs, and crocodilians [Greek *archos* "chief" + *sauros* "lizard"]

arch·ri·val \ˈärch-ˈrī-vəl\ *n* : a principal rival

arch·way \ˈärch-ˌwā\ *n* : a way or passage under an arch; *also* : an arch over a passage

-ar·chy \ˌär-kē, *in a few words also* ər-kē\ *n combining form, pl* **-ar·chies** : rule : government ⟨squire*archy*⟩ [Greek *-archia,* from *archein* "to rule"]

arc lamp *n* : a lamp whose light is produced when an electric current passes between two hot electrodes surrounded by gas — called also *arc light*

arc minute *n* : MINUTE 1b

arc second *n* : ³SECOND 1a

¹arc·tic \ˈärk-tik, ˈärt-ik\ *adj* **1** *often cap* : of, relating to, or suitable for use at the north pole or the region around it ⟨*arctic* waters⟩ ⟨*arctic* animals⟩ **2** : very cold [Latin *arcticus,* from Greek *arktikos,* from *arktos* "bear, Ursa Major, north"]

²arc·tic \ˈärt-ik, ˈärk-tik\ *n* : a rubber overshoe reaching to the ankle or above

arctic circle *n, often cap A&C* : the parallel of latitude that is approximately 66½ degrees north of the equator

\ə\ **abut**	\au̇\ **out**	\i\ **tip**	\ȯ\ **saw**	\u̇\ **foot**
\ər\ **further**	\ch\ **chin**	\ī\ **life**	\ȯi\ **coin**	\y\ **yet**
\a\ **mat**	\e\ **pet**	\j\ **job**	\th\ **thin**	\yü\ **few**
\ā\ **take**	\ē\ **easy**	\ng\ **sing**	\t͟h\ **this**	\yu̇\ **cure**
\ä\ **cot, cart**	\g\ **go**	\ō\ **bone**	\ü\ **food**	\zh\ **vision**

arctic fox *n* : a small fox of arctic regions that is blue-gray or brownish in summer and white in winter

arctic fox

Arc·tu·rus \ärk-ˈtu̇r-əs, -ˈtyu̇r-\ *n* : a large bright fixed star in Boötes [Latin, from Greek *Arktouros,* literally, "bear watcher"]

-ard \-ərd\ *also* **-art** \ərt\ *n suffix* : one that is characterized by performing some action, possessing some quality, or being associated with some thing especially conspicuously or excessively ⟨bragg*art*⟩ ⟨dull*ard*⟩ [Medieval French, of Germanic origin]

ar·dent \ˈärd-nt\ *adj* **1 a** : characterized by warmth of feeling : PASSIONATE ⟨an *ardent* admirer⟩ **b** : ZEALOUS, DEVOTED ⟨an *ardent* champion of justice⟩ **2** : extremely hot : FIERY ⟨the *ardent* sun⟩ [Medieval French, from Latin *ardent-, ardens, ardēre* "to burn"] ***synonyms*** see IMPASSIONED — **ar·den·cy** \-n-sē\ *n* — **ar·dent·ly** *adv*

ar·dor \ˈärd-ər\ *n* **1** : a warmth of feeling or sentiment **2** : ZEAL, EAGERNESS [Latin] ***synonyms*** see PASSION

ar·du·ous \ˈärj-wəs, -ə-wəs\ *adj* : extremely difficult : LABORIOUS, STRENUOUS ⟨an *arduous* climb⟩ [Latin *arduus* "steep, high, difficult"] — **ar·du·ous·ly** *adv* — **ar·du·ous·ness** *n*

[1]**are** *present 2nd singular or present plural of* BE [Old English *earun,* present plural]

[2]**are** \ˈaər, ˈeər, ˈär\ *n* — see METRIC SYSTEM table [French, from Latin *area* "open space"]

ar·ea \ˈar-ē-ə, ˈer-\ *n* **1** : a particular piece of ground or extent of space often set aside for special use ⟨a picnic *area*⟩ ⟨a waiting *area*⟩ **2** : the suface inside a figure or shape; *esp* : the number of unit squares equal to the amount of space the surface covers ⟨a circle with an *area* of 500 square meters⟩ **3 a** : REGION ⟨a farming *area*⟩ **b** : a field of activity ⟨*area* of knowledge⟩ **4** : a part of the cerebral cortex having a particular function [Latin, "open space, threshing floor"] — **ar·e·al** \-ē-əl\ *adj* — **ar·e·al·ly** \-ē-ə-lē\ *adv*

area code *n* : a usually 3-digit number that identifies a particular telephone service area (as in the U.S. or Canada)

area·way \-ē-ə-ˌwā\ *n* : a sunken space affording access, air, and light to a basement

are·na \ə-ˈrē-nə\ *n* **1** : an area in a Roman amphitheater for gladiatorial combats **2 a** : an enclosed area used for public entertainment **b** : a building containing an arena **3** : a sphere of interest or activity [Latin, "sand, sandy place"]

arena theater *n* : a theater having the stage in the center of the auditorium with the audience seated on all sides

aren't \ärnt, ˈärnt, ˈär-ənt\ : are not

are·o·la \ə-ˈrē-ə-lə\ *n, pl* **-lae** \-ˌlē\ *or* **-las** : a colored ring (as about the nipple) [Latin, "small open space," from *area*] — **are·o·lar** \-lər\ *adj*

arête \ə-ˈrāt\ *n* : a sharp-crested ridge in rugged mountains [French, literally, "fish bone," from Latin *arista* "beard of grain"]

[1]**ar·gent** \ˈär-jənt\ *n* : the heraldic color silver or white [Latin *argentum* "silver"]

[2]**argent** *adj* : resembling silver : SILVERY, SHINING

ar·gen·tite \ˈär-jən-ˌtīt\ *n* : a dark gray mineral Ag_2S that is a sulfide of silver and a valuable ore of silver

ar·gil·la·ceous \ˌär-jə-ˈlā-shəs\ *adj* : of, relating to, or containing clay or the minerals of clay [Latin *argilla* "clay"]

ar·gi·nine \ˈär-jə-ˌnēn\ *n* : an amino acid $C_6H_{14}O_2N_4$ found in various proteins [German *Arginin*]

Ar·give \ˈär-ˌjīv, -ˌgīv\ *adj* : of or relating to the Greeks or Greece and especially to the Achaean city of Argos or the surrounding territory of Argolis — **Argive** *n*

ar·gon \ˈär-ˌgän\ *n* : a colorless odorless inert gaseous chemical element found in the air and in volcanic gases and used especially as a filler for electric bulbs — see ELEMENT table [Greek, neuter of *argos* "idle, lazy," from *a-* + *ergon* "work"; from its relative inertness]

ar·go·naut \ˈär-gə-ˌnȯt, -ˌnät\ *n* **1** *cap* : one of a band of heroes sailing with Jason in quest of the Golden Fleece **2** : PAPER NAUTILUS [Greek *Argonautēs,* from *Argō,* name of Jason's ship + *nautēs* "sailor"]

ar·go·sy \ˈär-gə-sē\ *n, pl* **-sies** : a large ship; *esp* : a large merchant ship [Italian *ragusea* "vessel of Ragusa," from *Ragusa,* Dalmatia (now Dubrovnik, Croatia)]

ar·got \ˈär-gət, -gō\ *n* : a more or less secret vocabulary used by a particular class or group — compare DIALECT [French]

ar·gu·able \ˈär-gyə-wə-bəl\ *adj* : open to argument, dispute, or question — **ar·gu·ably** \-blē\ *adv*

ar·gue \ˈär-ˌgyü\ *vb* **1** : to give reasons for or against ⟨*argue* in favor of lowering taxes⟩ **2** : to debate or discuss some matter : DISPUTE ⟨*argue* about politics⟩ **3** : to persuade by giving reasons ⟨tried to *argue* their parents into getting a new car⟩ **4** : INDICATE ⟨your manner *argues* your guilt⟩ [Latin *arguere* "to demonstrate, prove" and Medieval French *arguer* "to reprove, argue"] ***synonyms*** see DISCUSS — **ar·gu·er** *n*

ar·gu·ment \ˈär-gyə-mənt\ *n* **1 a** : a reason for or against something **b** : a discussion in which arguments are presented : DISPUTE, DEBATE **2** : a heated dispute : QUARREL

ar·gu·men·ta·tion \ˌär-gyə-mən-ˈta-shən, -ˌmen-\ *n* **1** : the act or process of forming reasons and of drawing conclusions and applying them to a case under discussion **2** : DEBATE, DISCUSSION

ar·gu·men·ta·tive \ˌär-gyə-ˈment-ət-iv\ *adj* : marked by or given to argument : DISPUTATIOUS — **ar·gu·men·ta·tive·ly** *adv*

Ar·gus–eyed \ˌär-gə-ˈsīd\ *adj* : vigilantly observant

ar·gyle \ˈär-ˌgīl, är-ˈ\ *n* : a geometric knitting pattern of variously colored diamonds on a single background color; *also* : a sock knit in this pattern [*Argyle,* branch of the Scottish clan of Campbell, from whose tartan the design was adapted]

aria \ˈär-ē-ə\ *n* : MELODY, TUNE; *esp* : an accompanied elaborate melody sung (as in an opera) by a single voice [Italian, literally, "atmospheric air," from Latin *aer,* from Greek *aēr*]

-ar·i·an \ˈer-ē-ən, ˈar-\ *n suffix* **1** : believer ⟨Unit*arian*⟩: advocate ⟨latitudin*arian*⟩ **2** : producer ⟨disciplin*arian*⟩ [Latin *-arius* "-ary" + English *-an*]

ar·id \ˈar-əd\ *adj* **1** : very dry; *esp* : having too little rainfall to support agriculture **2** : lacking in interest : DULL [Latin *aridus*] — **arid·i·ty** \ə-ˈrid-ət-ē, a-\ *n* — **ar·id·ness** *n*

Ar·ies \ˈer-ˌēz, ˈer-ē-ˌēz, ˈar-\ *n* **1** : the 1st sign of the zodiac; *also* : one born under this sign **2** : a zodiacal constellation between Pisces and Taurus [Latin, literally, "ram"]

aright \ə-ˈrīt\ *adv* : RIGHTLY, CORRECTLY ⟨if I remember *aright*⟩

ar·il \ˈar-əl\ *n* : an outer covering or appendage of some seeds that develops after fertilization [probably from Medieval Latin *arillus* "raisin, grape seed"]

arise \ə-ˈrīz\ *vi* **arose** \-ˈrōz\; **aris·en** \-ˈriz-n\; **aris·ing** \-ˈrī-ziŋ\ **1** : to move upward : ASCEND **2** : to get up from sleep or after lying down **3** : to come into existence : spring up ⟨a dispute *arose* between the leaders⟩ [Old English *ārisan,* from *ā-,* prefix denoting completion + *rīsan* "to rise"]

ar·is·toc·ra·cy \ˌar-ə-ˈstäk-rə-sē\ *n, pl* **-cies** **1** : government by the best individuals or by a small privileged class **2 a** : a government in which power is exercised by a minority especially of those felt to be best qualified **b** : a state with such a government **3 a** : a governing body or upper class usually made up of a hereditary nobility **b** : a group felt to be superior in birth, wealth, culture, or intelligence [derived from Greek *aristokratia,* from *aristos* "best" + *-kratia* "-cracy"]

aris·to·crat \ə-ˈris-tə-ˌkrat, a-; ˈar-ə-stə-\ *n* **1** : a member of an aristocracy; *esp* : NOBLE **2** : one with habits and viewpoints typical of the aristocracy — **aris·to·crat·ic** \ə-ˌris-tə-ˈkrat-ik, a-ˌris-tə-, ˌar-ə-stə-\ *adj* — **aris·to·crat·i·cal·ly** \-i-kə-lē, -i-klē\ *adv*

Ar·is·to·te·lian *also* **Ar·is·to·te·lean** \ˌar-ə-stə-ˈtēl-yən\ *adj* : of, relating to, or characteristic of Aristotle or his philosophy — **Aristotelian** *n* — **Ar·is·to·te·lian·ism** \-yə-ˌniz-əm\ *n*

arith·me·tic \ə-ˈrith-mə-ˌtik\ *n* **1** : a branch of mathematics that deals with real numbers and their addition, subtraction, multiplication, and division **2** : an act or method of computing : CALCULATION ⟨a mistake in *arithmetic*⟩ [Medieval French *arismatike,* from Latin *arithmetica,* from Greek *arithmētikē,* from *arithmein* "to count," from *arithmos* "number"] — **ar·ith·met·ic** \ˌar-ith-ˈmet-ik\ *or* **ar·ith·met·i·cal** \-ˈmet-i-kəl\ *adj* — **ar·ith·met·i·cal·ly** \-kə-lē, -klē\ *adv*

arith·me·ti·cian \ə-ˌrith-mə-ˈtish-ən\ *n* : a person skilled in arithmetic

arithmetic mean \ˌar-ith-ˈmet-ik-\ *n* : a number equal to the sum of a set of numbers divided by how many numbers are in the set ⟨the *arithmetic mean* of 3, 4, 6, and 7 is 5⟩

arithmetic progression \ˌar-ith-ˈmet-ik-\ *n* **:** a sequence of numbers (as 3, 5, 7, 9, . . .) in which the difference between any term and the term before it is the same

arithmetic scale *n* **:** a scale on which the value of a point corresponds to the number of graduations the point is from the scale's zero — compare LOGARITHMIC SCALE

-ar·i·um \ˈar-ē-əm, ˈer-\ *n suffix, pl* **-ar·i·ums** *or* **-ar·ia** \-ē-ə\ **:** thing or place relating to or connected with ⟨planet*arium*⟩ [Latin, from neuter of *-arius* "-ary"]

ark \ˈärk\ *n* **1 a :** a boat or ship held to resemble that in which Noah and his family were preserved from the Flood **b :** something that affords protection and safety **2 a :** a sacred chest in which the ancient Hebrews kept the two tablets of the Law **b :** a place of deposit in or against the wall of a synagogue for the scrolls of the Torah [Old English *arc,* from Latin *arca* "chest"]

[1]**arm** \ˈärm\ *n* **1 a :** a human upper limb; *esp* **:** the part between the shoulder and wrist **b :** a corresponding limb of a lower vertebrate **2 :** something resembling an arm: as **a :** a lateral branch of a tree **b :** an inlet of water (as from the sea) **c :** a slender usually functional projecting part (as of a machine) **3 :** POWER, MIGHT ⟨the *arm* of the law⟩ **4 :** a support (as on a chair) for the elbow and forearm **5 :** SLEEVE 1 **6 :** a division of an organization [Old English *earm*] — **armed** \ˈärmd\ *adj* — **arm·less** \ˈärm-ləs\ *adj* — **arm·like** \-ˌlīk\ *adj* — **arm in arm** **:** with arms linked together ⟨walked down the street *arm in arm*⟩

[2]**arm** *vb* **1 :** to provide with weapons ⟨*arm* a regiment⟩ **2 :** to provide with a means of defense ⟨*arm* oneself with facts⟩ **3 :** to provide oneself with arms and armament ⟨the country *armed* for war⟩ **4 :** to equip or ready for action or operation ⟨*arm* a bomb⟩ [Medieval French *armer,* from Latin *armare,* from *arma* "weapons, tools"]

[3]**arm** *n* **1 a :** a means of offense or defense **:** WEAPON; *esp* **:** FIREARM **b :** a combat branch of an army (as the infantry or artillery) **c :** a branch of the military forces (as the navy) **2** *pl* **:** the designs on a shield or flag of a family or a government **3** *pl* **a :** active hostilities **:** WARFARE ⟨a call to *arms*⟩ **b :** military service

ar·ma·da \är-ˈmäd-ə, -ˈmad-, -ˈmād-\ *n* **1 :** a large fleet of warships **2** *cap* **:** the fleet sent by Spain against England in 1588 **3 :** a large number of usually moving things (as vehicles) [Spanish, from Medieval Latin *armata* "army, fleet," from Latin *armare* "to arm"]

ar·ma·dil·lo \ˌär-mə-ˈdil-ō\ *n, pl* **-los :** any of several small burrowing chiefly nocturnal mammals of warm parts of the Americas having body and head encased in small bony plates [Spanish, from *armado* "armed one," from Latin *armare* "to arm"]

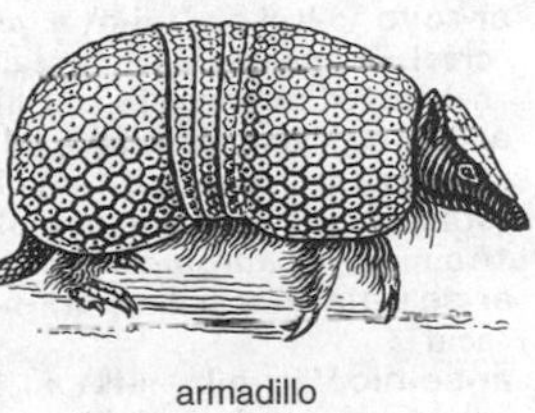

armadillo

Ar·ma·ged·don \ˌär-mə-ˈged-n\ *n* **1 a :** a final and conclusive battle between the forces of good and evil **b :** the site or time of Armageddon **2 :** a vast decisive conflict [Greek *Armageddōn,* scene of the battle foretold in Revelation 16:14–16]

ar·ma·ment \ˈär-mə-mənt\ *n* **1 :** the whole military strength and equipment of a nation **2 :** means of protection or defense **:** WEAPONS **3 :** the process of preparing for war

ar·ma·ture \ˈär-mə-chər, -ˌchu̇r\ *n* **1 :** a protective or defensive mechanism or covering (as the spines of a cactus) **2 :** the part of an electric generator that consists of coils of wire around an iron core and that induces an electric current when it is rotated in a magnetic field **3 :** the part of an electric motor that consists of coils of wire around an iron core and that is caused to rotate in a magnetic field when an electric current is passed through the coils **4 :** the movable part of an electromagnetic device (as an electric bell) **5 :** a framework used by a sculptor to support a figure being modeled (as in clay) [Latin *armatura* "armor, equipment," from *armare* "to arm"]

[1]**arm·chair** \ˈärm-ˌcheər, -ˌchaər\ *n* **:** a chair with armrests

[2]**armchair** *adj* **1 :** remote from direct dealing with problems ⟨an *armchair* strategist⟩ **2 :** sharing enjoyment or knowledge from another's experiences without experiencing them oneself ⟨an *armchair* traveler⟩

armed *adj* **1 :** furnished with weapons ⟨an *armed* guard⟩ **2 :** furnished with something that provides security or strength ⟨*armed* with knowledge⟩

armed forces *n pl* **:** the combined military, naval, and air forces of a nation

Ar·me·ni·an \är-ˈmē-nē-ən, -nyən\ *n* **1 :** a member of a people native to Armenia **2 :** the Indo-European language of the Armenians — **Armenian** *adj*

arm·ful \ˈärm-ˌfu̇l\ *n, pl* **arm·fuls** \-ˌfu̇lz\ *or* **arms·ful** \ˈärmz-ˌfu̇l\ **:** as much as a person's arm can hold ⟨an *armful* of books⟩

arm·hole \ˈärm-ˌhōl\ *n* **:** an opening for the arm in a garment

ar·mi·stice \ˈär-mə-stəs\ *n* **:** a pause in fighting brought about by agreement between the two sides **:** TRUCE [New Latin *armistitium,* from Latin *arma* "arms" + *-stitium* (as in *solstitium* "solstice")]

Armistice Day *n* **:** VETERANS DAY [from the *armistice* which ended World War I on November 11, 1918]

arm·let \ˈärm-lət\ *n* **:** a bracelet or band for the upper arm

ar·mor \ˈär-mər\ *n* **1 :** defensive covering for the body; *esp* **:** covering (as of metal) used in combat **2 :** something that provides or allows for protection ⟨safe in the *armor* of wealth⟩ **3 :** a protective covering (as the steel plates of a battleship or a sheathing for wire) **4 :** armored forces and vehicles (as tanks) [Medieval French *armure,* from Latin *armatura,* from *armare* "to arm"]

ar·mored \-mərd\ *adj* **1 :** protected by armor ⟨an *armored* car⟩ ⟨*armored* reptiles⟩ **2 :** supplied with armored equipment ⟨an *armored* force⟩

ar·mor·er \ˈär-mər-ər\ *n* **1 :** one that makes armor or arms **2 :** one that repairs, assembles, and tests firearms

ar·mo·ri·al \är-ˈmōr-ē-əl, -ˈmȯr-\ *adj* **:** of, relating to, or bearing heraldic arms

ar·mo·ry \ˈärm-rē, -ə-rē\ *n, pl* **-ries 1 :** a supply of arms **2 :** a place where arms are stored; *esp* **:** one used for training military reserve personnel **3 :** a place where arms are manufactured

armor 1

ar·mour \ˈär-mər\ *chiefly British variant of* ARMOR

arm·pit \ˈärm-ˌpit\ *n* **:** the hollow beneath the junction of the arm and shoulder

arm·rest \-ˌrest\ *n* **:** a support for the arm

arm wrestling *n* **:** a contest of strength in which two opponents face each other and place usually their right elbows on a surface, grasp hands, and seek to force the other person's arm down

ar·my \ˈär-mē\ *n, pl* **ar·mies 1 a :** a large body of persons organized and armed for land warfare **b :** a military unit capable of independent action and consisting usually of a headquarters, two or more corps, and auxiliary troops **c** *often cap* **:** the complete military organization of a nation for land warfare **2 :** a great number of persons or things ⟨an *army* of insects⟩ **3 :** a body of persons organized to advance a cause [Medieval French *armee,* from Medieval Latin *armata* "army, fleet," from Latin *armare* "to arm"]

army ant *n* **:** any of various nomadic tropical ants that live in colonies and prey especially on insects and spiders

ar·my·worm \-ˌwərm\ *n* **:** any of numerous moth larvae that are often abundant on and destructive to crops (as grasses or grain); *also* **:** any other stage of this insect

ar·ni·ca \ˈär-ni-kə\ *n* **1 :** any of a genus of yellow-flowered herbs related to the daisies **2 :** dried flower heads of a European arnica that are used especially in the form of a tincture as a liniment; *also* **:** this tincture [New Latin, genus name]

aro·ma \ə-ˈrō-mə\ *n* **1 :** a distinctive and usually pleasing smell ⟨the *aroma* of fresh coffee⟩ — compare FRAGRANCE **2 :** a distinctive quality or atmosphere ⟨the *aroma* of suspense⟩ [Medi-

\ə\ **abut**	\au̇\ **out**	\i\ **tip**	\ȯ\ **saw**	\u̇\ **foot**
\ər\ **further**	\ch\ **chin**	\ī\ **life**	\ȯi\ **coin**	\y\ **yet**
\a\ **mat**	\e\ **pet**	\j\ **job**	\th\ **thin**	\yü\ **few**
\ā\ **take**	\ē\ **easy**	\ng\ **sing**	\t͟h\ **this**	\yu̇\ **cure**
\ä\ **cot, cart**	\g\ **go**	\ō\ **bone**	\ü\ **food**	\zh\ **vision**

eval French *aromat* "spice," from Latin *aroma,* from Greek *arōma*] ***synonyms*** see SMELL

aro•ma•ther•a•py \ə-ˌrō-mə-ˈther-ə-pē\ *n* : the use of aromas (as of fragrant oils extracted from fruits or flowers) to enhance a feeling of well-being

ar•o•mat•ic \ˌar-ə-ˈmat-ik\ *adj* **1** : of, relating to, or having aroma **2** : of, relating to, or characterized by the presence of at least one benzene ring — used of hydrocarbons and their derivatives — **aromatic** *n*

arose *past of* ARISE

[1]**around** \ə-ˈraůnd\ *adv* **1 a** : in circumference ⟨a tree five feet *around*⟩ **b** : in, along, or through a curving or circular course ⟨the road goes *around* by the lake⟩ **2 a** : on all or various sides ⟨papers lying *around*⟩ **b** : NEARBY ⟨stick *around*⟩ **3 a** : here and there in various places ⟨traveled *around* from state to state⟩ **b** : to a particular place ⟨come *around* for dinner⟩ **4 a** : in rotation or succession ⟨pass the candy *around*⟩ **b** : from beginning to end ⟨mild the year *around*⟩ **c** : to a customary or improved condition ⟨the medicine brought the patient *around*⟩ **5** : in or to an opposite direction or position ⟨turned *around* and waved goodbye⟩ **6** : APPROXIMATELY ⟨a price of *around* $20⟩

[2]**around** *prep* **1 a** : on all or various sides of ⟨yard with a fence *around* it⟩ ⟨fields *around* the village⟩ **b** : so as to encircle or enclose ⟨seated *around* the table⟩ **c** : on or to another side of ⟨voyage *around* Cape Horn⟩ **d** : in the neighborhood of : NEAR ⟨somewhere *around* here⟩ **2** : here and there in or throughout ⟨traveling *around* the country⟩

[3]**around** *adj* **1** : moving from place to place ⟨will be up and *around* in no time⟩ **2** : being in existence, evidence, or circulation ⟨one of the best drummers *around*⟩

arous•al \ə-ˈraů-zəl\ *n* : the act of arousing or the state of being aroused

arouse \ə-ˈraůz\ *vb* **1** : to awaken from sleep **2** : to rouse to action : EXCITE [*a-* (as in *arise*) + *rouse*]

ar•peg•gio \är-ˈpej-ō, -ˈpej-ē-ˌō\ *n, pl* **-gi•os** : production of the tones of a chord in succession and not simultaneously; *also* : a chord so played [Italian, from *arpeggiare* "to play on the harp," from *arpa* "harp," of Germanic origin]

arquebus *variant of* HARQUEBUS

ar•raign \ə-ˈrān\ *vt* **1** : to call before a court to answer to an indictment : CHARGE **2** : to accuse of wrong, inadequacy, or imperfection [Medieval French *areisner, arener,* from *a-* "ad-" + *raisner* "to address," derived from Latin *ratio* "reason"] — **arraign•ment** \-mənt\ *n*

ar•range \ə-ˈrānj\ *vb* **1** : to put in order; *esp* : to put in a particular order ⟨*arrange* books on shelves⟩ **2** : to make plans for ⟨*arrange* a meeting⟩ **3** : to come to an agreement about : SETTLE ⟨*arranged* the release of prisoners⟩ **4** : to make a musical arrangement of [Medieval French *arenger,* from *a-* "ad-" + *renc* "row, rank"] — **ar•rang•er** *n*

ar•range•ment \ə-ˈrānj-mənt\ *n* **1** : a putting in order : the order in which things are put ⟨the *arrangement* of furniture in a room⟩ **2** : preparation or planning done in advance ⟨made travel *arrangements*⟩ **3** : something made by arranging ⟨a flower *arrangement*⟩ **4** : an adaptation of a musical composition to voices or instruments other than those originally intended

ar•rant \ˈar-ənt\ *adj* : being utterly or notoriously such : EXTREME ⟨*arrant* fools⟩ [alteration of *errant*] — **ar•rant•ly** *adv*

[1]**ar•ray** \ə-ˈrā\ *vt* **1** : to set in order : draw up : MARSHAL **2** : to dress or decorate especially splendidly or impressively [Medieval French *arraier,* of Germanic origin] — **ar•ray•er** *n*

[2]**array** *n* **1** : regular order or arrangement; *also* : military order ⟨troops in *array*⟩ **2** : rich or beautiful apparel : FINERY **3** : an imposing group : large number ⟨an *array* of problems⟩ **4** : a group of mathematical elements (as numbers or letters) arranged in rows and columns

ar•rears \ə-ˈriərz\ *n pl* **1** : the state of being behind in paying debts owed ⟨two months in *arrears* on their rent⟩ **2** : an unpaid and overdue debt [Medieval French *arrere* "behind, backward," from Latin *ad* "to" + *retro* "backward"]

[1]**ar•rest** \ə-ˈrest\ *vt* **1 a** : to stop the progress or movement of **b** : CHECK, SLOW ⟨*arrest* a disease⟩ **2** : to take or keep in custody by authority of law ⟨*arrested* on suspicion of robbery⟩ **3** : to attract and hold the attention of ⟨colors that *arrest* the eye⟩ [Medieval French *arester* "to stop, arrest," from Latin *ad-* + *restare* "to remain"]

[2]**arrest** *n* **1 a** : the act of stopping **b** : the state of being stopped **2** : the act of taking or holding in custody by authority of law

ar•rest•ing *adj* : catching the attention : STRIKING

ar•rhyth•mia \ā-ˈrith-mē-ə\ *n* : an irregularity in the rhythm of the heartbeat

ar•riv•al \ə-ˈrī-vəl\ *n* **1** : the act of arriving ⟨await the *arrival* of guests⟩ **2** : a person or thing that has arrived ⟨late *arrivals*⟩

ar•rive \ə-ˈrīv\ *vi* **1** : to reach a destination ⟨*arrive* home at six o'clock⟩ **2** : COME 4a ⟨the moment has *arrived*⟩ **3** : to be successful [Medieval French *ariver,* from Latin *ad* "to" + *ripa* "shore"] — **arrive at** : to reach by effort or thought ⟨*arrive at* a decision⟩

ar•ro•gance \ˈar-ə-gəns\ *n* : a sense of one's own superiority that shows itself in an offensively proud manner : HAUGHTINESS

ar•ro•gant \-gənt\ *adj* **1** : exaggerating one's own worth or importance in an overbearing manner **2** : marked by arrogance ⟨*arrogant* remarks⟩ [Latin *arrogare* "to claim," from *ad-* + *rogare* "to ask"] ***synonyms*** see PROUD — **ar•ro•gant•ly** *adv*

ar•ro•gate \ˈar-ə-ˌgāt\ *vt* **1** : to take or claim for one's own without justification ⟨the dictator *arrogated* the powers of parliament⟩ **2** : to attribute to another especially without good reason — **ar•ro•ga•tion** \ˌar-ə-ˈgā-shən\ *n*

ar•ron•disse•ment \ə-ˈrän-dəs-mənt, ˈar-ˌō^{n}-dē-ˈsmä^{n}\ *n* **1** : the largest division of a French governmental department **2** : an administrative district of some large French cities [French]

ar•row \ˈar-ō\ *n* **1** : a missile that is intended to be shot from a bow and that usually has a slender shaft, a pointed head, and feathers at the butt **2** : a mark (as on a map or signboard) to indicate direction [Old English *arwe*]

ar•row•head \-ˌhed\ *n* **1** : the usually wedge-shaped piercing tip fixed to the front of an arrow **2** : something (as a wedge-shaped mark) resembling an arrowhead **3** : any of a genus of aquatic plants with leaves shaped like arrowheads

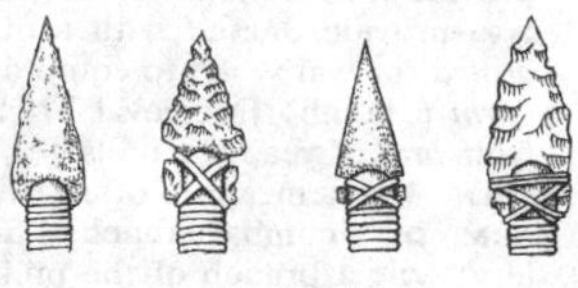

arrowhead 1

ar•row•root \-ˌrüt, -ˌrůt\ *n* : any of several tropical American plants with starchy tuberous roots; *also* : an edible starch from these roots

ar•row•worm \-ˌwərm\ *n* : any of a phylum (Chaetognatha) of small wormlike marine organisms with bristles on either side of the mouth

ar•royo \ə-ˈrȯi-ə, -ˈrȯi-ō\ *n, pl* **-roy•os** **1** : a watercourse (as a creek or stream) in a dry region **2** : an often dry gully or channel carved by water [Spanish]

ar•se•nal \ˈärs-nəl, -n-əl\ *n* **1 a** : a place where arms are manufactured or stored **b** : a collection of weapons **2** : STORE 2, SUPPLY ⟨the team's *arsenal* of players⟩ [Italian *arsenale,* derived from Arabic *dār ṣināʿa* "house of manufacture"]

ar•sen•ate \ˈärs-nət, -n-ət, -n-ˌāt\ *n* : a salt or ester of arsenic acid

ar•se•nic \ˈärs-nik, -n-ik\ *n* **1** : a solid poisonous chemical element commonly metallic steel-gray, crystalline, and brittle — see ELEMENT table **2** : a white poisonous trioxide As_2O_3 or As_4O_6 of arsenic used especially as an insecticide or weed killer — called also *arsenic trioxide* [Latin *arsenicum,* from Greek *arsenikon* "yellow orpiment"]

ar•sen•ic acid \är-ˈsen-ik-\ *n* : a white crystalline poisonous compound $H_3AsO_4 \cdot \frac{1}{2}H_2O$

ar•sen•i•cal \är-ˈsen-i-kəl\ *adj* : of, relating to, or containing arsenic ⟨an *arsenical* drug⟩ — **arsenical** *n*

ar•se•no•py•rite \ˌärs-n-ō-ˈpī-ˌrīt\ *n* : a silver-white mineral consisting of iron, arsenic, and sulfur

ar•sine \är-ˈsēn, ˈär-ˌ\ *n* : a colorless flammable extremely poisonous gas AsH_3 with an odor like garlic

ar•son \ˈärs-n\ *n* : the willful or malicious burning of property (as a building) especially with criminal intent [Medieval French *arsoun,* derived from Latin *ardēre* "to burn"] — **ar•son•ist** \ˈärs-nəst, -n-əst\ *n*

ars•phen•a•mine \ärs-ˈfen-ə-ˌmēn, -mən\ *n* : an arsenic-containing substance formerly used in the treatment of diseases caused by spirochetes [*arsenic* + *phen-* + *amine*]

[1]**art** \ärt, ˈärt, ərt\ *archaic present 2nd singular of* BE [Old English *eart*]

[2]**art** \ˈärt\ *n* **1** : skill in performance acquired by experience, study, or observation : KNACK ⟨the *art* of making friends⟩ **2** : an occupation that requires knowledge or skill ⟨the *art* of

cooking⟩ **3 :** a branch of learning; *esp* **:** one of the nonscientific branches of learning (as history or literature) — usually used in plural ⟨College of *Arts* and Sciences⟩ **4 :** the use of skill and creativity especially in the making of things that are beautiful to look at, listen to, or read **5 :** the works (as pictures, poems, or songs) produced by artists [Medieval French, from Latin *art-, ars*]

synonyms ART, SKILL, CRAFT mean the ability to carry out what one has planned. ART may be distinct from the other two in implying personal, unanalyzable creative or imaginative power and resource ⟨the *art* of choosing the right word⟩. SKILL stresses technical knowledge and proficiency gained through practice and experience ⟨the *skill* of a surgeon⟩. CRAFT implies expertness in workmanship ⟨the *craft* of a master goldsmith⟩.

-art — see -ARD

art de·co \ˌär-dā-ˈkō, ˌärt-; ˌärt-ˈdek-ˌō\ *n, often cap A&D* **:** a decorative style of the 1920s and 1930s characterized by bold outlines, geometric shapes, and the use of new materials (as plastic) [French *Art Déco,* from *Exposition Internationale des Arts Décoratifs,* an exposition of decorative arts held in Paris, France in 1925]

artefact *chiefly British variant of* ARTIFACT

arteri- *or* **arterio-** *combining form* **:** artery **:** arterial and ⟨*arteriovenous*⟩

[1]**ar·te·ri·al** \är-ˈtir-ē-əl\ *adj* **1 a :** of or relating to an artery **b :** being the bright red oxygen-rich blood present in most arteries **2 :** of, relating to, or being routes for through traffic ⟨*arterial* roads⟩ — **ar·te·ri·al·ly** \-ē-ə-lē\ *adv*

[2]**arterial** *n* **:** a through street or highway

ar·te·ri·ole \är-ˈtir-ē-ˌōl\ *n* **:** a very small artery connecting a larger artery with capillaries — **ar·te·ri·o·lar** \-ˌtir-ē-ˈō-ˌlär, -lər\ *adj*

ar·te·rio·scle·ro·sis \är-ˌtir-ē-ō-sklə-ˈrō-səs\ *n* **:** a chronic disease in which the arterial walls are abnormally thickened and hardened — **ar·te·rio·scle·rot·ic** \-ˈrät-ik\ *adj or n*

ar·te·rio·ve·nous \är-ˌtir-ē-ō-ˈvē-nəs\ *adj* **:** of, relating to, or connecting the arteries and veins

ar·tery \ˈärt-ə-rē\ *n, pl* **-ter·ies** **1 :** one of the tubular branching muscular-walled and elastic-walled vessels that carry blood from the heart through the body **2 :** a channel (as a river or highway) of transportation or communication; *esp* **:** the main channel in a branching system [Latin *arteria,* from Greek *artēria*]

ar·te·sian well \är-ˈtē-zhən-\ *n* **1 :** a drilled well from which water flows up like a fountain **2 :** a deep well [French *artésien,* literally, "of Artois," from *Artois,* region of France where such wells were common]

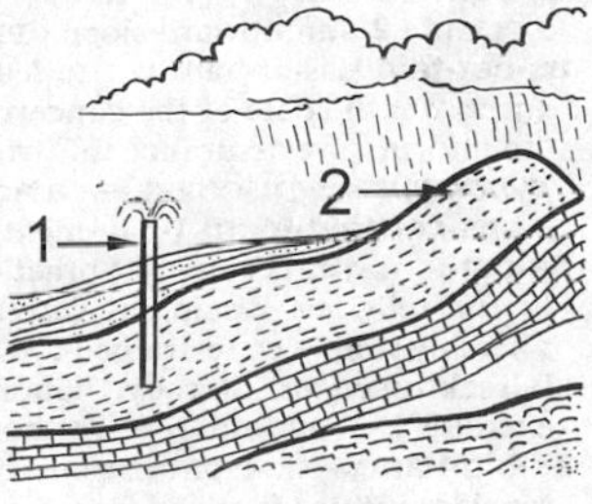

artesian well 1: *1* well, *2* catchment area

art·ful \ˈärt-fəl\ *adj* **1 :** performed with or showing art or skill ⟨an *artful* violin performance⟩ **2 :** produced by art **:** ARTIFICIAL **3 a :** using or characterized by art and skill **:** DEXTEROUS ⟨an *artful* writing style⟩ **b :** skillful or ingenious in gaining an end **:** WILY ⟨an *artful* cross-examiner⟩ ***synonyms*** see SLY — **art·ful·ly** \-fə-lē\ *adv* — **art·ful·ness** *n*

ar·thri·tis \är-ˈthrīt-əs\ *n* **:** inflammation of the joints [Latin, from Greek, from *arthron* "joint"] — **ar·thrit·ic** \-ˈthrit-ik\ *adj or n* — **ar·thrit·i·cal·ly** \-ˈthrit-i-kə-lē, -klē\ *adv*

ar·thro·pod \ˈär-thrə-ˌpäd\ *n* **:** any of a phylum (Arthropoda) of invertebrate animals (as insects, arachnids, and crustaceans) with a segmented body, jointed limbs, and an exoskeleton usually of chitin [derived from Greek *arthron* "joint" + *pod-, pous* "foot"] — **arthropod** *adj* — **ar·throp·o·dan** \är-ˈthräp-əd-ən\ *adj*

ar·thro·scope \ˈär-thrə-ˌskōp\ *n* **:** a fiber-optic surgical instrument inserted through an incision near a joint (as the knee) and used to visually examine the joint interior [Greek *arthron* "joint" + English *-scope*] — **ar·thro·scop·ic** \ˌär-thrə-ˈskä-pik\ *adj*

ar·ti·choke \ˈärt-ə-ˌchōk\ *n* **1 :** a tall herb resembling the thistle; *also* **:** its edible immature flower head which is cooked as a vegetable **2 :** JERUSALEM ARTICHOKE [Italian dialect *articiocco,* derived from Arabic *al-khurshūf* "the artichoke"]

[1]**ar·ti·cle** \ˈärt-i-kəl\ *n* **1 :** a distinct often numbered part of a document (as a contract or treaty) dealing with a single subject **2 :** a nonfictional prose composition forming an independent part of a publication and usually dealing with a single topic ⟨an *article* on winter sports⟩ **3 :** a word (as *a, an,* or *the*) used with a noun to limit it or make it clearer **4 :** a member of a class of things; *esp* **:** COMMODITY b ⟨*articles* of value⟩ [Medieval French, from Latin *articulus* "joint, division," from *artus* "joint"]

[2]**article** *vt* **-cled; -cling** \-kə-ling, -kling\ **:** to bind by the articles of a contract ⟨an *articled* apprentice⟩

ar·tic·u·lar \är-ˈtik-yə-lər\ *adj* **:** of or relating to a joint

[1]**ar·tic·u·late** \är-ˈtik-yə-lət\ *adj* **1 a :** divided clearly into words and syllables **:** INTELLIGIBLE **b :** able to speak; *esp* **:** able to express oneself clearly or effectively **2 :** consisting of segments united by joints **:** JOINTED ⟨*articulate* animals⟩ [Latin *articulus* "joint"] — **ar·tic·u·late·ly** *adv* — **ar·tic·u·late·ness** *n*

[2]**ar·tic·u·late** \-ˌlāt\ *vb* **1 a :** to speak in distinct syllables or words **b :** to express clearly and distinctly ⟨*articulate* every shade of meaning⟩ **2 :** to unite or become united or connected by or as if by a joint

ar·tic·u·la·tion \är-ˌtik-yə-ˈlā-shən\ *n* **1 :** the action or manner of articulating **:** the state of being articulated **2 :** the making of articulate sounds (as in pronunciation) **3 :** a joint between rigid parts of an animal; *esp* **:** one between bones or cartilages — **ar·tic·u·la·to·ry** \är-ˈtik-yə-lə-ˌtōr-ē, -ˌtȯr-\ *adj*

ar·tic·u·la·tor \är-ˈtik-yə-ˌlāt-ər\ *n* **:** a movable vocal organ (as a lip or the tongue)

ar·ti·fact \ˈärt-ə-ˌfakt\ *n* **:** a usually simple object (as a tool or ornament) showing human work or alteration and remaining from a particular period [Latin *arte factum* "made by skill"] — **ar·ti·fac·tu·al** \ˌärt-ə-ˈfak-chə-wəl, -chəl\ *adj*

ar·ti·fice \ˈärt-ə-fəs\ *n* **1 a :** a wily or artful device **:** TRICK **b :** false or insincere behavior ⟨social *artifices*⟩ **2 :** clever or artful skill **:** INGENUITY [Middle French, from Latin *artificium,* from *artifex* "artificer," from *art-, ars* "skill" + *facere* "to make"]

ar·tif·i·cer \är-ˈtif-ə-sər, ˈärt-ə-fə-sər\ *n* **:** a skilled or artistic worker

ar·ti·fi·cial \ˌärt-ə-ˈfish-əl\ *adj* **1 :** built, performed, or produced by humans often following a natural model or process ⟨an *artificial* lake⟩ **2 :** lacking in natural quality **:** FORCED ⟨an *artificial* smile⟩ **3 :** made to resemble something natural **:** IMITATION ⟨*artificial* flavors⟩ — **ar·ti·fi·ci·al·i·ty** \-ˌfish-ē-ˈal-ət-ē\ *n* — **ar·ti·fi·cial·ly** \-ˈfish-lē, -ə-lē\ *adv* — **ar·ti·fi·cial·ness** \-ˈfish-əl-nəs\ *n*

synonyms ARTIFICIAL, SYNTHETIC, ERSATZ mean made by people and not found in nature. ARTIFICIAL may apply to anything that is not the result of natural process or conditions ⟨the state is an *artificial* society⟩ but especially to something that has a natural counterpart ⟨*artificial* teeth⟩. SYNTHETIC applies especially to a manufactured substance or to a natural substance that is treated to resemble and substitute for another ⟨*synthetic* silk⟩. ERSATZ often implies the use of an inferior substitute for a natural product ⟨a football field of *ersatz* turf⟩.

artificial insemination *n* **:** introduction of semen into the uterus or oviduct by artificial means

artificial intelligence *n* **:** the power of a machine to imitate intelligent human behavior

artificial respiration *n* **:** the rhythmic forcing of air into and out of the lungs of a person whose breathing has stopped

artificial selection *n* **:** the process of modifying organisms by selection in breeding controlled by the breeder

ar·til·lery \är-ˈtil-rē, -ə-rē\ *n* **1 :** large-caliber crew-operated mounted firearms (as guns, howitzers, or rockets) **2 :** a branch of an army armed with artillery [Medieval French *artillerie* "weapons (as bows and slings) for discharging missiles," from *artiller* "to equip, arm"] — **ar·til·lery·man** \-mən\ *n*

\ə\ **abut**	\au̇\ **out**	\i\ **tip**	\ȯ\ **saw**	\u̇\ **foot**
\ər\ **further**	\ch\ **chin**	\ī\ **life**	\ȯi\ **coin**	\y\ **yet**
\a\ **mat**	\e\ **pet**	\j\ **job**	\th\ **thin**	\yü\ **few**
\ā\ **take**	\ē\ **easy**	\ng\ **sing**	\th\ **this**	\yu̇\ **cure**
\ä\ **cot, cart**	\g\ **go**	\ō\ **bone**	\ü\ **food**	\zh\ **vision**

ar·tio·dac·tyl \ˌärt-ē-ō-ˈdak-tl\ *n* : any of an order (Artiodactyla) of hoofed mammals (as the camel or ox) with an even number of functional toes on each foot [Greek *artios* "fitting, even-numbered" + *daktylos* "finger, toe"]

ar·ti·san \ˈärt-ə-zən\ *n* : a person (as a carpenter) who works at a trade requiring skill with the hands [Middle French, from northern Italian dialect form of *artigiano,* from *arte* "skill," from Latin *ars*]

art·ist \ˈärt-əst\ *n* **1** : a person skilled in one of the arts (as painting, sculpture, music, or writing); *esp* : PAINTER **2** : a person showing unusual ability in an occupation requiring skill ⟨a makeup *artist*⟩

ar·tiste \är-ˈtēst\ *n* **1** : a skilled adept performer; *esp* : a musical or theatrical entertainer **2** : an artistic or creative person [French]

ar·tis·tic \är-ˈtis-tik\ *adj* **1** : relating to or characteristic of art or artists **2** : showing imaginative skill in arrangement or performance — **ar·tis·ti·cal·ly** \-ˈtis-ti-kə-lē, -klē\ *adv*

synonyms ARTISTIC, AESTHETIC mean having to do with art. ARTISTIC implies the point of view of one who produces art and thinks in terms of creating beautiful forms ⟨an *artistic* rendering of the historic event⟩. AESTHETIC stresses the point of view of one who analyzes and reflects upon the effect a work of art has ⟨the *aesthetic* aspects of the building's design⟩. Either term may suggest a contrast with the practical, the functional, or the moral aspects of anything.

art·ist·ry \ˈärt-ə-strē\ *n* **1** : artistic quality of effect or workmanship **2** : artistic ability

art·less \ˈärt-ləs\ *adj* **1** : lacking art, knowledge, or skill : UNCULTURED **2 a** : made without skill : CRUDE ⟨an artless *attempt* to win⟩ **b** : being simple and natural ⟨*artless* grace⟩ **3** : free from guile or deceit — **art·less·ly** *adv* — **art·less·ness** *n*

art nou·veau \ˌär-nü-ˈvō, ˌärt-\ *n, often cap A&N* : a decorative style of late 19th century origin characterized by curving lines and leaflike forms [French, literally, "new art"]

art·sy \ˈärt-sē\ *adj* : ARTY

arty \ˈärt-ē\ *adj* **art·i·er; -est** : showily or pretentiously artistic — **art·i·ly** \ˈärt-l-ē\ *adv* — **art·i·ness** \ˈärt-ē-nəs\ *n*

ar·um \ˈar-əm, ˈer-\ *n* : any of a family of plants (as the jack-in-the-pulpit or the skunk cabbage) having heart-shaped or arrow-shaped leaves and flowers in a fleshy spike enclosed in a leafy sheath [Latin, from Greek *aron*]

[1]**-ary** *usually* ˌer-ē *after an unstressed syllable,* ə-rē *or* rē *after a stressed syllable, in Britain usually* ə-rē *or* rē *in all cases*\ *n suffix, pl* **-aries** : thing or person belonging to or connected with ⟨syllab*ary*⟩ ⟨function*ary*⟩ [Latin *-arius, -aria, -arium,* from *-arius,* adjective suffix]

[2]**-ary** *adj suffix* : of, relating to, or connected with ⟨budget*ary*⟩ [Latin *-arius*]

[1]**Ary·an** \ˈar-ē-ən, ˈer-, ˈär-yən\ *adj* **1** : INDO-EUROPEAN **2** : of or relating to the Aryans **3** : of or relating to a hypothetical ethnic type represented by early speakers of Indo-European languages

[2]**Aryan** *n* **1** : a member of the subgroup of Indo-European speakers ancestral to speakers of Indo-Aryan and Iranian languages **2 a** : NORDIC 2 **b** : GENTILE 1 [Sanskrit *ārya* "noble, Aryan"]

[1]**as** \əz, az, ˌaz\ *adv* **1** : to the same degree or extent ⟨*as* light as a feather⟩ **2** : for instance ⟨various trees, *as* oak or pine⟩ [Old English *eallswā* "likewise, just as," from *eall* "all" + *swā* "so"]

[2]**as** *conj* **1** : AS IF ⟨felt *as* I were weightless⟩ **2** : in or to the same degree that ⟨bright *as* day⟩ **3** : in the way or manner that ⟨do *as* I do⟩ **4** : WHILE, WHEN ⟨spilled the milk *as* I got up⟩ **5** : regardless of the degree to which : THOUGH ⟨strange *as* it seems, it's true⟩ **6** : for the reason that : BECAUSE ⟨stayed home *as* they had no car⟩ **7** : that the result is — used after *so* or *such* ⟨so clearly guilty *as* to leave no doubt⟩ — **as is** : in its present condition

[3]**as** *pron* **1** : THAT, WHO, WHICH — used after *same* or *such* ⟨attends the same school *as* my sister⟩ **2** : a fact that ⟨is a tourist, *as* is evident from the camera⟩

[4]**as** *prep* **1** : LIKE 2 ⟨all rose *as* one person⟩ **2** : in the character or position of ⟨working *as* an editor⟩

[5]**as** \ˈas\ *n, pl* **as·ses** \ˈas-ˌēz, ˈas-əz\ **1** : an ancient Roman unit of value **2** : a bronze coin representing one ancient Roman as [Latin]

as- — see AD-

as·a·fet·i·da *or* **as·a·foe·ti·da** \ˌas-ə-ˈfet-əd-ə\ *n* : an ill-smelling gum resin of the root of several Asian plants related to the carrot used as a flavoring especially in Indian cooking and formerly used in medicine [Medieval Latin *asafoetida,* from Persian *azā* "mastic" + Latin *foetidus* "fetid"]

as 2

as·bes·tos \as-ˈbes-təs, az-\ *n* : a mineral (as chrysotile) that readily separates into long flexible fibers suitable for use as a fireproof, nonconducting, and chemically resistant material [Latin, from Greek *asbestos* "quicklime," from *asbestos* "inextinguishable"]

as·ca·rid \ˈas-kə-rəd\ *n* : any of a family of roundworms that includes the common large roundworm parasitic in the human intestine [derived from Greek *askaris* "intestinal worm"]

as·ca·ris \ˈas-kə-rəs\ *n, pl* **as·car·i·des** \a-ˈskar-ə-ˌdēz\ : ASCARID

as·cend \ə-ˈsend\ *vb* **1** : to go up or upward : CLIMB, RISE ⟨*ascend* a hill⟩ ⟨smoke *ascends*⟩ **2** : to succeed to : OCCUPY ⟨*ascended* the throne⟩ [Latin *ascendere,* from *ad-* + *scandere* "to climb"] — **as·cend·able** *or* **as·cend·ible** \-ˈsen-də-bəl\ *adj*

synonyms ASCEND, MOUNT, CLIMB, SCALE mean to move upward or toward the top. ASCEND simply implies upward movement ⟨the balloon *ascended*⟩. MOUNT implies reaching the top ⟨*mount* the top stair⟩. CLIMB suggests effort and often the use of hands and feet ⟨*climbed* the ladder⟩. SCALE implies the use of a ladder or rope in climbing vertically ⟨*scaled* the cliff wall⟩.

as·cen·dan·cy \ə-ˈsen-dən-sē\ *or* **as·cen·dance** \-dəns\ *n* : governing or controlling influence : DOMINATION
synonyms see SUPREMACY

[1]**as·cen·dant** \ə-ˈsen-dənt\ *n* **1** : the sign of the zodiac that rises above the eastern horizon at a given moment **2** : a state or position of dominant power or importance

[2]**ascendant** *adj* **1** : moving or directed upward : RISING **2 a** : in a superior position **b** : inclined to control

as·cen·sion \ə-ˈsen-chən\ *n* : the act or process of ascending

Ascension Day *n* : the Thursday 40 days after Easter observed by Christians in commemoration of Christ's ascension into heaven

as·cent \ə-ˈsent\ *n* **1** : the act of rising or moving upward : CLIMB **2** : an upward slope : RISE

as·cer·tain \ˌas-ər-ˈtān\ *vt* : to learn with certainty : FIND OUT ⟨*ascertain* the date of the concert⟩ [Medieval French *acerteiner* "to inform, give assurance to," from *a-* "ad-" + *certein* "certain"]
synonyms see DISCOVER — **as·cer·tain·able** \-ˈtā-nə-bəl\ *adj* — **as·cer·tain·ment** \-ˈtān-mənt\ *n*

as·cet·ic \ə-ˈset-ik\ *adj* **1** : practicing strict self-denial especially for religious discipline ⟨*ascetic* in their way of life⟩ **2** : harshly simple or restrained : AUSTERE ⟨*ascetic* surroundings⟩ [Greek *askētikos,* literally, "laborious," from *askein* "to work, exercise"] — **ascetic** *n* — **as·cet·i·cism** \ə-ˈset-ə-ˌsiz-əm\ *n*

as·cid·i·an \ə-ˈsid-ē-ən\ *n* : any of various solitary or colonial sessile tunicates [derived from Greek *askidion* "little wineskin," from *askos* "wineskin, bladder"]

ASCII \ˈas-kē, -ˌkē\ *n* : a computer code for expressing numerals, letters, and other symbols [*A*merican *S*tandard *C*ode for *I*nformation *I*nterchange]

as·co·carp \ˈas-kə-ˌkärp\ *n* : the fruiting body of an ascomycetous fungus

as·co·my·cete \ˌas-kō-ˈmī-ˌsēt, -mī-ˈsēt\ *n* : any of a class (Ascomycetes) of higher fungi (as yeasts or molds) with septate hyphae and spores formed in asci — called also *sac fungus* [Greek *askos* "wineskin, bladder" + *mykēs* "fungus"] — **as·co·my·ce·tous** \-mī-ˈsēt-əs\ *adj*

ascor·bic acid \ə-ˈskȯr-bik-\ *n* : VITAMIN C [[2]*a-* + New Latin *scorbutus* "scurvy"]

as·co·spore \ˈas-kə-ˌspōr, -ˌspȯr\ *n* : a spore produced in an ascus

as·cot \ˈas-kət, -ˌkät\ *n* : a broad neck scarf that is looped under the chin [*Ascot* Heath, English racetrack]

as·cribe \ə-ˈskrīb\ *vt* : to refer to a supposed cause, source, or author : ATTRIBUTE [Latin *ascribere,* from *ad-* + *scribere* "to write"] — **as·crib·able** \-ˈskrī-bə-bəl\ *adj*

synonyms ASCRIBE, ATTRIBUTE, IMPUTE, CREDIT mean to lay something to the account of a person or thing. ASCRIBE suggests inferring or conjecturing the cause, source, or author of something ⟨forged paintings formerly *ascribed* to famous artists⟩. ATTRIBUTE implies more definiteness or stronger evidence for ascribing ⟨a quotation *attributed* to Plato⟩. IMPUTE suggests ascribing something that brings discredit by way of accusation or blame ⟨tried to *impute* bad motives to my actions⟩. CREDIT implies ascribing a thing to a person or other thing as its agent, source, or explanation ⟨*credited* his teammates for his success⟩.

as·crip·tion \ə-ˈskrip-shən\ *n* **:** the act of ascribing

as·cus \ˈas-kəs\ *n, pl* **as·ci** \ˈas-ˌī, -ˌkī, -ˌkē\ **:** a membranous oval or tubular spore sac of an ascomycete usually bearing eight spores [Greek *askos* "wineskin, bladder"]

-ase \ˌās, ˌāz\ *n suffix* **:** enzyme ⟨malt*ase*⟩ [French, from *diastase* "diastase, enzyme"]

asep·sis \ā-ˈsep-səs, ə-\ *n* **:** the condition of being aseptic; *also* **:** the methods of making or keeping aseptic [[2]*a-* + *sepsis*]

asep·tic \-ˈsep-tik\ *adj* **1 :** preventing infection ⟨*aseptic* surgical procedures⟩; *also* **:** free or freed from disease-causing microorganisms **2 a :** lacking life, emotion, or warmth ⟨*aseptic* essays⟩ **b :** being emotionally detached **:** OBJECTIVE ⟨an *aseptic* view of life⟩ — **asep·ti·cal·ly** \-ti-kə-lē, -klē\ *adv*

asex·u·al \ā-ˈsek-shə-wəl, ˈā-, -shəl\ *adj* **1 :** lacking sex or functional sex ograns ⟨*asexual* organisms⟩ **2 :** occurring or formed without the production and union of two kinds of gametes ⟨*asexual* reproduction⟩ — **asex·u·al·ly** \-ē\ *adv*

as for *prep* **:** with regard to **:** CONCERNING ⟨*as for* me⟩

As·gard \ˈas-ˌgärd, ˈaz-\ *n* **:** the home of the Norse gods [Old Norse *āsgarthr*]

[1]**ash** \ˈash\ *n* **1 :** any of a genus of trees related to the olive with thin furrowed bark and winged seeds **2 :** the hard strong wood of an ash [Old English *æsc*]

[2]**ash** *n* **1 a :** the solid residue left when material is thoroughly burned or is oxidized by chemical means **b :** fine particles of mineral matter from a volcanic vent **2** *pl* **a :** the last traces of something **:** RUINS **b :** the remains of a dead human body especially after cremation **3 :** something that symbolizes grief, repentance, or humiliation **4** *pl* **:** extreme paleness [Old English *asce*]

ashamed \ə-ˈshāmd\ *adj* **1 :** feeling shame, guilt, or disgrace ⟨*ashamed* of your behavior⟩ **2 :** kept back by pride ⟨*ashamed* to beg⟩ — **asham·ed·ly** \-ˈshā-məd-lē\ *adv*

Ashan·ti \ə-ˈshant-ē, -ˈshänt-\ *n, pl* **Ashanti** *or* **Ashantis :** a member of a people of southern Ghana

[1]**ash·en** \ˈash-ən\ *adj* **:** of, relating to, or made from the wood of the ash tree

[2]**ashen** *adj* **1 :** of the color of ashes **2 :** deadly pale **:** BLANCHED ⟨*ashen* with fear⟩

Ash·ke·nazi \ˌash-kə-ˈnaz-ē\ *n, pl* **-naz·im** \-ˈnaz-əm\ **:** a member of one of the two great divisions of Jews comprising the eastern European Yiddish-speaking Jews — compare SEPHARDI [Hebrew *Ashkĕnāzī*] — **Ash·ke·naz·ic** \-ˈnaz-ik\ *adj*

ash·lar \ˈash-lər\ *n* **1 :** dressed or squared stone; *also* **:** masonry of such stone **2 :** a thin squared and dressed stone used for facing [Medieval French *aiseler* "traverse beam," derived from Latin *assis* "board"]

ashore \ə-ˈshōr, -ˈshȯr\ *adv* **:** on or to the shore

ash·tray \ˈash-ˌtrā\ *n* **:** a container for tobacco ashes and cigarette and cigar butts

Ash Wednesday *n* **:** the first day of Lent

ashy \ˈash-ē\ *adj* **ash·i·er; -est 1 :** of, relating to, or resembling ashes **2 :** [2]ASHEN 2

Asian \ˈā-zhən, ˈā-shən\ *n* **1 :** a native or inhabitant of Asia **2 :** a person of Asian descent — **Asian** *adj*

Asian–Amer·i·can \-ə-mer-ə-kən\ *n* **:** an American of Asian descent — **Asian–American** *adj*

Asian elephant *n* **:** ELEPHANT b

Asian influenza *or* **Asian flu** *n* **:** influenza caused by a mutant strain of the influenza virus discovered in China in 1957

Asi·at·ic \ˌā-zhē-ˌat-ik, -zē-\ *adj, sometimes offensive* **:** ASIAN — **Asiatic** *n, sometimes offensive*

Asiatic cholera *n* **:** cholera of Asian origin marked by violent vomiting and purging

[1]**aside** \ə-ˈsīd\ *adv* **1 :** to or toward the side ⟨stepped *aside*⟩ **2 :** out of the way **:** AWAY ⟨put money *aside* for school⟩ **3 :** out of one's thought or consideration ⟨*all* kidding aside⟩

[2]**aside** *n* **1 :** words meant to be inaudible to someone; *esp* **:** an actor's words supposedly not heard by others on the stage **2 :** a straying from the theme **:** DIGRESSION

aside from *prep* **1 :** in addition to **:** BESIDES **2 :** except for

as if *conj* **1 :** as it would be if ⟨it was *as if* you had never left⟩ **2 :** as one would do if ⟨spoke *as if* he had done it⟩ **3 :** THAT ⟨it seemed *as if* the day would never end⟩

as·i·nine \ˈas-n-ˌīn\ *adj* **:** extremely foolish ⟨an *asinine* statement⟩ [Latin *asininus,* from *asinus* "ass"] — **as·i·nine·ly** *adv* — **as·i·nin·i·ty** \ˌas-n-ˈin-ət-ē\ *n*

ask \ˈask\ *vb* **1 :** to seek information **:** INQUIRE **2 a :** to make a request ⟨*ask* for help⟩ **b :** to make a request of ⟨*asked* his father for permission⟩ **3 :** to set as a price ⟨*ask* $20 for a bicycle⟩ **4 :** INVITE ⟨*ask* friends to a party⟩ **5 :** to seek or look for punishment or retaliation ⟨*asking* for trouble⟩ [Old English *āscian*] — **ask·er** *n*

synonyms ASK, REQUEST mean to try to obtain by making known one's wants. ASK implies simply the statement of the desire ⟨*ask* a favor of a friend⟩. REQUEST suggests some formality or courtesy in asking and implies an expectation of an affirmative response ⟨*requests* the pleasure of your company⟩.

askance \ə-ˈskans\ *adv* **1 :** with a side glance **2 :** with disapproval or distrust ⟨they eyed the stranger *askance*⟩ [origin unknown]

askew \ə-ˈskyü\ *adv or adj* **:** out of line **:** AWRY ⟨the picture hung *askew*⟩ ***synonyms*** see CROOKED

[1]**aslant** \ə-ˈslant\ *adv or adj* **:** in a slanting direction

[2]**aslant** *prep* **:** over or across in a slanting direction

[1]**asleep** \ə-ˈslēp\ *adj* **1 :** being in a state of sleep **2 :** lacking sensation **:** NUMB ⟨my *arm* is asleep⟩ **3 :** not alert **:** SLUGGISH

[2]**asleep** *adv* **:** into a state of sleep

as long as *conj* **1 :** provided that ⟨the team can fool around *as long as* they win⟩ **2 :** INASMUCH AS 2, SINCE ⟨*as long as* you're going, I'll go too⟩

aso·cial \ā-ˈsō-shəl\ *adj* **:** rejecting or lacking the ability for social interaction; *also* **:** ANTISOCIAL

as of *prep* **:** ON, AT, FROM ⟨takes effect *as of* July 1⟩

asp \ˈasp\ *n* **:** a small venomous snake of Egypt [Latin *aspis,* from Greek]

as·par·a·gine \ə-ˈspar-ə-ˌjēn\ *n* **:** an amino acid $C_4H_8N_2O_3$ that is derived from aspartic acid [French, from Latin *asparagus*]

as·par·a·gus \ə-ˈspar-ə-gəs\ *n* **:** a tall branching perennial herb related to the lilies and widely grown for its thick edible young shoots [Latin, from Greek *asparagos*]

as·par·tame \ˈas-pər-ˌtām, ə-ˈspär-ˌtām\ *n* **:** a crystalline compound $C_{14}H_{18}N_2O_5$ used as a low-calorie sweetener [*aspart*ic acid + *a*lanine + *me*thyl + est*er*]

as·par·tic acid \ə-ˈspärt-ik-\ *n* **:** a crystalline amino acid $C_4H_7NO_4$ found especially in plants [derived from Latin *asparagus*]

as·pect \ˈas-ˌpekt\ *n* **1 a :** the position of planets or stars with respect to one another held by astrologers to influence human affairs **b :** a position facing a particular direction **:** EXPOSURE ⟨the house has a southern *aspect*⟩ **2 :** a particular way in which something appears or may be regarded ⟨studied every *aspect* of the question⟩ **3 :** the appearance to the eye or the mind [Latin *aspectus,* from *aspicere* "to look at," from *ad-* + *specere* "to look"] — **as·pec·tu·al** \a-ˈspek-chə-wəl, -chəl\ *adj*

aspect ratio *n* **:** the ratio of one dimension (as width) to another (as height)

as·pen \ˈas-pən\ *n* **:** any of several poplars with leaves that flutter in the lightest breeze [Old English *æspe*]

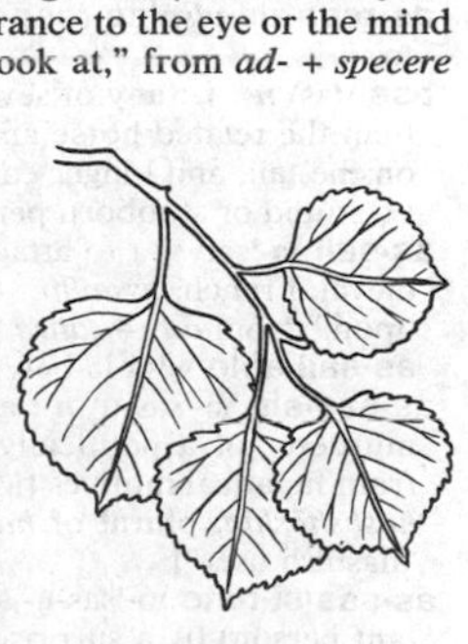
aspen

as·per·i·ty \a-ˈsper-ət-ē, ə-ˈsper-\ *n, pl* **-ties 1 :** RIGOR 3, SEVERITY ⟨the *asperities* of winter weather⟩ **2 :** roughness of surface (as of a leaf) **:** UNEVENNESS **3 :** harshness of temper, manner, or tone ⟨*argued* with asperity⟩ [Medieval

French *aspreté,* from *aspre* "rough," from Latin *asper*]

as·perse \ə-ˈspərs, a-\ *vt* : to attack with evil reports or false charges : SLANDER ⟨*asperse* someone's character⟩ [Latin *aspergere,* literally, "to sprinkle," from *ad-* + *spargere* "to scatter"]

as·per·sion \ə-ˈspər-zhən\ *n* : an injurious or offensive charge or implication ⟨cast *aspersions* on a person⟩

[1]**as·phalt** \ˈas-ˌfȯlt\ *or* **as·phal·tum** \as-ˈfȯl-təm\ *n* **1** : a brown to black substance that is found in natural beds or obtained as a residue in petroleum refining and that consists chiefly of hydrocarbons **2** : any of various compositions of asphalt having diverse uses (as for pavement or for waterproof cement or paint) [Late Latin *aspaltus,* from Greek *asphaltos*] — **as·phal·tic** \as-ˈfȯl-tik\ *adj*

[2]**asphalt** *vt* : to cover with asphalt

as·pho·del \ˈas-fə-ˌdel\ *n* : any of several herbs related to the lilies with white or yellow flowers in long erect spikes [Latin *asphodelus,* from Greek *asphodelos*]

as·phyx·ia \as-ˈfik-sē-ə\ *n* : a lack of oxygen or excess of carbon dioxide in the body that is usually caused by interruption of breathing or inadequate oxygen supply and resulting in unconsciousness and often death [Greek, "stopping of the pulse," from *a-* + *sphyzein* "to throb"]

as·phyx·i·ate \as-ˈfik-sē-ˌāt\ *vt* : to cause asphyxia in — **as·phyx·i·a·tion** \ˌas-ˌfik-sē-ˈā-shən\ *n* — **as·phyx·i·a·tor** \as-ˈfik-sē-ˌāt-ər\ *n*

as·pic \ˈas-pik\ *n* : a jelly (as of fish or meat stock) used cold especially to mold meat, fish, or vegetables [French, literally, "asp"]

as·pi·dis·tra \ˌas-pə-ˈdis-trə\ *n* : an Asian plant related to the lilies with large basal leaves that is often grown as a houseplant [derived from Greek *aspid-, aspis* "shield"]

as·pi·rant \ˈas-pə-rənt, -prənt, ə-ˈspī-rənt\ *n* : one that aspires

[1]**as·pi·rate** \ˈas-pə-ˌrāt\ *vt* **1** : to pronounce with an initial \h\ sound ⟨we do not *aspirate* the word "hour"⟩ **2 a** : to remove (as blood) by suction **b** : to take into the lungs by aspiration [Latin *aspirare* "to breathe on, aspire"]

[2]**as·pi·rate** \ˈas-pə-rət, -prət\ *n* **1** : an independent sound \h\ or a character (as the letter *h*) representing it **2** : a consonant having as its final element an \h\-like sound in the same syllable ⟨\t\ in English *toe* is an *aspirate*⟩

as·pi·ra·tion \ˌas-pə-ˈrā-shən\ *n* **1 a** : audible breath that accompanies a speech sound **b** : the pronunciation or addition of an aspiration; *also* : the symbol of an aspiration **2** : a drawing of something in, out, up, or through by or as if by suction **3 a** : a strong desire to achieve something high or great **b** : an object of such desire ***synonyms*** see AMBITION

as·pi·ra·tor \ˈas-pə-ˌrāt-ər\ *n* : an apparatus for producing suction or moving or collecting materials by suction

as·pire \ə-ˈspīr\ *vb* : to seek to attain something high or great ⟨*aspired* to the presidency⟩ [Latin *aspirare* "to breathe on, favor, aspire," from *ad-* + *spirare* "to breathe"] — **as·pir·er** *n*

as·pi·rin \ˈas-pə-rən, -prən\ *n* **1** : a white crystalline drug $C_9H_8O_4$ used as a remedy for pain and fever **2** : a tablet of aspirin [*a*cetyl + *spir*aeic acid (former name of salicylic acid), from New Latin *Spiraea,* genus of shrubs]

as regards *also* **as respects** *prep* : in regard to : with respect to

ass \ˈas\ *n* **1** : any of several mammals resembling but smaller than the related horse and having a shorter mane, shorter hair on the tail, and longer ears; *esp* : DONKEY **2** *sometimes vulgar* : a stupid or stubborn person [Old English *assa*]

as·sail \ə-ˈsāl\ *vt* : to attack violently with blows or words [Medieval French *assaillir,* derived from Latin *assilire* "to leap upon," from *ad-* + *salire* "to leap"] ***synonyms*** see ATTACK — **as·sail·able** \-ˈsā-lə-bəl\ *adj* — **as·sail·ant** \-ˈsā-lənt\ *n*

as·sas·sin \ə-ˈsas-n\ *n* : a person who commits murder; *esp* : a murderer of a politically important person either for hire or from fanatical motives [Medieval Latin *assassinus,* from Arabic *ḥashshāshīn,* plural of *ḥashshāsh* "worthless person," literally, "hashish user"]

as·sas·si·nate \ə-ˈsas-n-ˌāt\ *vt* **1** : to murder (a usually important person) by a surprise attack often for political reasons **2** : to injure or destroy unexpectedly and treacherously ⟨*assassinate* a person's character⟩ ***synonyms*** see KILL — **as·sas·si·na·tion** \ə-ˌsas-n-ˈā-shən\ *n*

[1]**as·sault** \ə-ˈsȯlt\ *n* **1** : a violent physical or verbal attack : ONSLAUGHT **2** : an apparent attempt or a threat to do harm to another — compare BATTERY 1b [Medieval French *assaut,* derived from Latin *assilire* "to assail"]

[2]**assault** *vt* : to make an assault upon ***synonyms*** see ATTACK

assault rifle *n* : any of various automatic or semiautomatic rifles designed for military use — called also *assault weapon*

[1]**as·say** \ˈas-ˌā, a-ˈsā\ *n* **1** *archaic* : TRIAL, ATTEMPT **2** : analysis (as of an ore, a metal, or a drug) to determine the presence, absence, or quantity of one or more substances [Medieval French *essai, assai* "test, essay, effort"]

[2]**as·say** \a-ˈsā, ˈas-ˌā\ *vb* **1** : TRY, ATTEMPT **2 a** : to analyze (as an ore) for one or more valuable substances **b** : to judge the worth of : ESTIMATE — **as·say·er** *n*

as·se·gai *or* **as·sa·gai** \ˈas-i-ˌgī\ *n* : a slender hardwood usually iron-tipped spear used in southern Africa [derived from Arabic *az-zaghāya* "the assegai"]

as·sem·blage \ə-ˈsem-blij\ *n* **1** : a collection of persons or things : GATHERING **2** : the act of assembling : the state of being assembled **3** : an artistic composition made by putting together scraps or junk

as·sem·ble \ə-ˈsem-bəl\ *vb* **-bled; -bling** \-bə-ling, -bling\ **1** : to collect into one place or group ⟨*assembled* the crew⟩ **2** : to fit together the parts of ⟨*assemble* a bicycle⟩ **3** : to meet together ⟨the right to *assemble* peacefully⟩ [Medieval French *assembler,* derived from Latin *ad-* + *simul* "together"] ***synonyms*** see GATHER

as·sem·bler \ə-ˈsem-blər, -bə-lər\ *n* **1** : one that assembles **2 a** : a computer program that automatically converts instructions written in an assembly language into the equivalent machine language **b** : ASSEMBLY LANGUAGE

as·sem·bly \ə-ˈsem-blē\ *n, pl* **-blies** **1** : a body of persons gathered together (as for discussing and making laws, worship, or entertainment) **2** *cap* : a legislative body; *esp* : the lower house of a legislature **3** : the act or state of coming together : ASSEMBLAGE **4** : a signal for troops to assemble **5** : a collection of parts that go to make up a complete machine, structure, or unit **6** : the translation of assembly language to machine language by an assembler **7** : a meeting of a student body and usually faculty for educational or recreational purposes

assembly language *n* : a code for programming a computer that is a close approximation of machine language but is more easily understood by humans

assembly line *n* : an arrangement of machines, equipment, and workers in which work passes from operation to operation in direct line until the product is assembled

as·sem·bly·man \ə-ˈsem-blē-mən\ *n* : a member of a legislative assembly

as·sem·bly·wom·an \-ˌwu̇m-ən\ *n* : a woman who is a member of a legislative assembly

[1]**as·sent** \ə-ˈsent\ *vi* : to agree to something especially after thoughtful consideration : CONCUR [Medieval French *assenter,* derived from Latin *assentire,* from *ad-* + *sentire* "to feel"]

synonyms ASSENT, CONSENT, ACCEDE mean to agree with what has been proposed. ASSENT implies the action of the understanding or judgment toward propositions or opinions ⟨voters *assented* to the proposal⟩. CONSENT involves the will or the feelings and indicates acceptance or approval of or compliance with what is desired or requested ⟨*consented* to their daughter's wishes⟩. ACCEDE suggests a yielding, often under pressure, of assent or consent ⟨*acceded* to the workers' demands⟩.

[2]**assent** *n* : an act of assenting : AGREEMENT

as·sert \ə-ˈsərt\ *vt* **1** : to state clearly and strongly : declare positively ⟨*assert* an opinion⟩ **2** : to defend forcefully ⟨*assert* your rights⟩ [Latin *asserere,* from *ad-* + *serere* "to join"] — **assert oneself** : to act or speak up in a manner that makes others recognize one's rights

synonyms ASSERT, DECLARE, AFFIRM, AVOW mean to state positively usually in anticipation of denial or objection. ASSERT implies stating confidently without need for proof or evidence ⟨*asserted* that modern music is just noise⟩. DECLARE often adds to ASSERT an implication of open or public statement ⟨*declared* her support for the candidate⟩. AFFIRM implies conviction of truth and willingness to stand by one's statement ⟨*affirmed* the existence of life on other planets⟩. AVOW implies open and emphatic declaration and personal responsibility for a statement ⟨*avowed* that all customers would be given a full refund⟩. ***synonyms*** see in addition MAINTAIN

as·ser·tion \ə-ˈsər-shən\ *n* : the act of asserting; *also* : something asserted : DECLARATION

as·sert·ive \ə-ˈsərt-iv\ *adj* : characterized by self-confidence

and boldness in expressing opinions — **as•sert•ive•ly** *adv* — **as•sert•ive•ness** *n*
asses *plural of* ASS *or of* ASS
as•sess \ə-ˈses\ *vt* **1 :** to fix the rate or amount of ‹*assessed* damages of $5000› **2 :** to set a value on (as property) for tax purposes ‹a house *assessed* at $140,000› **3 :** to lay a tax or charge on ‹the city *assessed* all car owners $51.00› **4 :** to determine the importance, size, or value of ‹*assess* your chances of winning› [probably from Medieval Latin *assessus,* past participle of *assidēre* "to assess," from Latin, "to sit beside, assist in giving judgment," from *ad-* + *sedēre* "to sit"] ***synonyms*** see ESTIMATE — **as•sess•able** \ə-ˈses-ə-bəl\ *adj*
as•sess•ment \ə-ˈses-mənt\ *n* **1 :** the act of assessing : APPRAISAL **2 :** the amount or value assessed
as•ses•sor \ə-ˈses-ər\ *n* **:** an official who assesses property for taxation
as•set \ˈas-ˌet\ *n* **1** *pl* **:** all the property (as cash, securities, real estate, or goods) of a person, corporation, or estate that may be used in payment of debts **2 :** ADVANTAGE, RESOURCE ‹a real *asset* to the team› [back-formation from obsolete *assets,* singular, "sufficient property to pay debts and legacies," from Medieval French *asez* "enough," from Latin *ad* "to" + *satis* "enough"]
as•sev•er•ate \ə-ˈsev-ə-ˌrāt\ *vt* **:** to state firmly or earnestly [Latin *asseverare,* from *ad-* + *severus* "severe"] — **as•sev•er•a•tion** \ə-ˌsev-ə-ˈrā-shən\ *n*
as•si•du•i•ty \ˌas-ə-ˈdü-ət-ē, -ˈdyü-\ *n* **:** the quality or state of being assiduous : DILIGENCE
as•sid•u•ous \ə-ˈsij-wəs, -ə-wəs\ *adj* **:** steadily attentive : DILIGENT [Latin *assiduus,* from *assidēre* "to sit beside," from *ad-* + *sedēre* "to sit"] — **as•sid•u•ous•ly** *adv* — **as•sid•u•ous•ness** *n*
as•sign \ə-ˈsīn\ *vt* **1 :** to transfer (property) to another ‹*assign* a patent to the heirs› **2 a :** to appoint to a post or duty **b :** to give out as a duty or task ‹*assign* homework› **3 :** to fix or set authoritatively ‹*assign* a limit› **4 :** to attribute as a motive or reason [Medieval French *assigner,* from Latin *assignare,* from *ad-* + *signare* "to mark," from *signum* "mark, sign"] — **as•sign•able** \ə-ˈsī-nə-bəl\ *adj* — **as•sign•er** \ə-ˈsī-nər\ *or* **as•sign•or** \ˌa-sə-ˈnȯr, ˌa-sī-, ə-ˌsī-\ *n*
as•sig•na•tion \ˌas-ig-ˈnā-shən\ *n* **1 :** ASSIGNMENT **2 :** TRYST 1
as•sign•ee \ə-ˌsī-ˈnē, ˌas-ˌī-; ˌas-ə-ˈnē\ *n* **:** a person to whom something is assigned
as•sign•ment \ə-ˈsīn-mənt\ *n* **1 :** the act of assigning ‹*assignment* of seats› **2 :** something assigned : an assigned task ‹an *assignment* in arithmetic› ***synonyms*** see TASK
as•sim•i•late \ə-ˈsim-ə-ˌlāt\ *vb* **1 a :** to take something in and make it part of and like the thing it has joined ‹*assimilate* nutrients into the body› ‹the nation *assimilated* millions of immigrants› **b :** to comprehend thoroughly : ABSORB **2 a :** to make similar **b :** to alter by assimilation [Medieval Latin *assimilare,* from Latin *assimulare* "to make similar," from *ad-* + *simulare* "to make similar, simulate"] ***synonyms*** see ABSORB — **as•sim•i•la•bil•i•ty** \-ˌsim-ə-lə-ˈbil-ət-ē\ *n* — **as•sim•i•la•ble** \-ˈsim-ə-lə-bəl\ *adj* — **as•sim•i•la•tor** \-ˈsim-ə-ˌlāt-ər\ *n*
as•sim•i•la•tion \ə-ˌsim-ə-ˈlā-shən\ *n* **1 :** the act or process of assimilating; *esp* **:** the bodily process of converting nutrients (as of digested food) into components of cells and tissues **2 :** change of a sound in speech so that it becomes identical with or similar to a neighboring sound ‹in the word "cupboard" the \p\ sound of the word "cup" has undergone complete *assimilation*› — **as•sim•i•la•tive** \-ˈsim-ə-ˌlāt-iv, -lət-\ *adj*
[1]**as•sist** \ə-ˈsist\ *vb* **:** to give support or aid : HELP [Latin *assistere* "to help, stand by," from *ad-* + *sistere* "to stand"]
[2]**assist** *n* **1 :** an act of assistance : AID **2 :** the action of a player who by passing a ball or puck enables a teammate to make a putout or score a goal
as•sis•tance \ə-ˈsis-təns\ *n* **:** the act of assisting or the aid supplied : SUPPORT
as•sis•tant \ə-ˈsis-tənt\ *n* **:** one that assists — **assistant** *adj*
assisted suicide *n* **:** suicide especially by a person with a fatal disease that is facilitated by the aid of another person and usually a physician
as•sis•tive \ə-ˈsis-tiv\ *adj* **:** providing aid or assistance especially to disabled persons ‹walked with an *assistive* device›
as•size \ə-ˈsīz\ *n* **:** a session of an English superior court formerly held periodically for the trial of civil and criminal cases in most counties by judges traveling on circuit — usually used in plural [Medieval French *assise* "session, legal action," from *asseer* "to seat," derived from Latin *assidēre* "to sit beside"]
[1]**as•so•ci•ate** \ə-ˈsō-shē-ˌāt, -sē-ˌāt\ *vb* **1 :** to join or come together as partners, friends, or companions **2 :** to connect or bring (as ideas) together or into a relationship ‹*associate* hot chocolate with winter› **3 :** to combine or join with other parts : UNITE [Latin *associare* "to unite," from *ad-* + *sociare* "to join," from *socius* "companion"]
[2]**as•so•ci•ate** \ə-ˈsō-shət; ə-ˈsō-shē-ət, -ˈsō-sē-, -ˌāt\ *n* **1 :** a fellow worker : COLLEAGUE **2 :** COMPANION 1, COMRADE **3** *often cap* **:** a degree conferred especially by a junior college ‹*associate* in arts› — **associate** *adj*
as•so•ci•a•tion \ə-ˌsō-sē-ˈā-shən, -ˌsō-shē-\ *n* **1 :** the act of associating : the state of being associated **2 :** an organization of persons having a common interest : SOCIETY **3 :** a feeling, memory, or thought connected with a person, place, or thing ‹pleasant *associations* with the beach› **4 :** the formation of polymers by linkage through hydrogen bonds **5 :** an ecological unit marked by uniformity and usually two or more dominant plant species — **as•so•ci•a•tion•al** \-shnəl, -shən-l\ *adj*
association football *n* **:** SOCCER
as•so•ci•a•tive \ə-ˈsō-shē-ˌāt-iv, -ˈsō-sē-, -ˈsō-shət-iv\ *adj* **1 :** of, relating to, or involved in association and especially mental association ‹*associative* powers of the mind› **2 :** dependent on or acquired by association or learning **3 :** of, having, or being the property of producing the same mathematical value no matter how an expression's elements are grouped so long as the order of those elements is the same ‹addition is *associative* since (a + b) + c = a + (b + c)› — **as•so•ci•a•tive•ly** *adv* — **as•so•cia•tiv•i•ty** \ə-ˌsō-shē-ə-ˈtiv-ət-ē, -ˌsō-sē-ə-, -ˌsō-shə-ˈtiv-\ *n*
associative neuron *n* **:** INTERNEURON
as•so•nance \ˈas-ə-nəns\ *n* **1 :** resemblance of sound in words or syllables **2 :** repetition of vowels without repetition of consonants (as in *story* and *holy* or *red hen*) used in poetry [French, from Latin *assonare* "to answer with the same sound," from *ad-* + *sonare* "to sound"] — **as•so•nant** \-nənt\ *adj or n*
as soon as *conj* **:** immediately at or just after the time that ‹left *as soon as* the meeting was over›
as•sort \ə-ˈsȯrt\ *vb* **1 :** to distribute into groups of a like kind : CLASSIFY **2 :** to agree in kind : HARMONIZE [Medieval French *assortir,* from *a-* "ad-" + *sorte* "sort"] — **as•sort•a•tive** \ə-ˈsȯrt-ət-iv\ *adj* — **as•sort•er** *n*
as•sort•ed \ə-ˈsȯrt-əd\ *adj* **1 :** consisting of various kinds **2 :** suited by nature, character, or design ‹an ill-*assorted* pair›
as•sort•ment \ə-ˈsȯrt-mənt\ *n* **1 a :** arrangement in classes **b :** the state or quality of being made up of various kinds **2 :** a collection of assorted things or persons
as•suage \ə-ˈswāj\ *vt* **1 :** to lessen the intensity of (as pain) : EASE **2 :** to put an end to by satisfying : QUENCH ‹*assuage* thirst› [Medieval French *asuager,* derived from Latin *ad-* + *suavis* "sweet, pleasant"] — **as•suage•ment** \-mənt\ *n*
as•sume \ə-ˈsüm\ *vb* **1 :** to take up or in or on : RECEIVE ‹what values may x *assume*› **2 a :** to take to or upon oneself ‹*assume* a responsibility› **b :** PUT ON 1b **3 :** to take as one's right or possession : SEIZE ‹*assume* control› **4 :** to put on in appearance only : FEIGN ‹*assumed* an air of cheerfulness› **5 :** to take for granted : SUPPOSE ‹*assumed* you already knew› [Latin *assumere,* from *ad-* + *sumere* "to take up, take," from *sub-* "up" + *emere* "to take, buy"]
synonyms ASSUME, AFFECT, PRETEND, SIMULATE, FEIGN, COUNTERFEIT, SHAM mean to put on a false or deceptive appearance. ASSUME often implies a justifiable motive rather than an intent to deceive ‹*assumed* an air of cheerfulness around the patients›. AFFECT implies making a false show of possessing, using, or feeling ‹*affected* an interest in art›. PRETEND implies an overt and sustained false appearance ‹*pretended* that nothing had happened›. SIMULATE suggests a close imitation of the appearance of something ‹cosmetics that *simulate* a suntan›. FEIGN implies more artful invention than PRETEND, less specific mimicry than SIMULATE ‹*feigned* sickness›. COUNTERFEIT implies achieving the highest degree of verisimilitude of any of these words ‹an actor *counterfeiting* drunkenness›. SHAM implies an obvious falseness that fools only the gullible ‹*shammed* a most unconvincing limp›.

as·sumed \ə-ˈsümd\ *adj* **1 a :** PRETENDED ⟨an *assumed* role⟩ **b :** FALSE ⟨an *assumed* name⟩ **2 :** taken for granted ⟨the *assumed* reason for absence⟩

as·sum·ing *adj* **:** ARROGANT 1, PRESUMPTUOUS

as·sump·tion \ə-ˈsəm-shən, -ˈsəmp-\ *n* **1** *cap* **:** August 15 observed as a church festival in commemoration of the taking up of the Virgin Mary into heaven **2 :** a taking to or upon oneself **3 :** the act of laying claim to or taking possession of something **4 a :** an assuming that something is true **b :** a fact or statement taken for granted [Late Latin *assumptio* "taking up," from Latin *assumere* "to take up, assume"]

as·sur·ance \ə-ˈshu̇r-əns\ *n* **1 :** the act of assuring **:** PLEDGE **2 :** the state of being sure or certain **3 :** SAFETY 1 **4** *chiefly British* **:** INSURANCE 1 **5 :** freedom from self-doubt or uncertainty; *esp* **:** extreme self-confidence **:** PRESUMPTION

as·sure \ə-ˈshu̇r\ *vt* **1 :** to make safe (as from risks) **:** INSURE **2 :** to give comfort or confidence to **:** REASSURE 2 ⟨tried to *assure* the worried neighbors⟩ **3 :** to make sure or certain **:** CONVINCE **4 :** to inform positively ⟨can *assure* you of their dependability⟩ [Medieval French *assurer,* from Medieval Latin *assecurare,* from Latin *ad-* + *securus* "secure"]

[1]**as·sured** \ə-ˈshu̇rd\ *adj* **1 :** characterized by certainty or security **:** GUARANTEED ⟨an *assured* market⟩ **2 a :** SELF-CONFIDENT ⟨an *assured* dancer⟩ **b :** marked by excessive confidence **:** SELF-SATISFIED **3 :** satisfied as to the certainty or truth of a matter **:** CONVINCED ⟨rest *assured* we will be there⟩ — **as·sur·ed·ly** \-ˈshu̇r-əd-lē\ *adv* — **as·sur·ed·ness** \-əd-nəs\ *n*

[2]**assured** *n* **:** a person whose life or property is insured

As·syr·i·an \ə-ˈsir-ē-ən\ *n* **1 :** a native or inhabitant of ancient Assyria **2 :** the dialect of Akkadian spoken by the Assyrians — **Assyrian** *adj*

as·ta·tine \ˈas-tə-ˌtēn\ *n* **:** a radioactive chemical element discovered by bombarding bismuth with helium nuclei — see ELEMENT table [Greek *astatos* "unsteady," from *a-* + *statos* "standing," from *histanai* "to cause to stand"]

as·ter \ˈas-tər\ *n* **1 :** any of various mostly fall-blooming leafy-stemmed composite herbs usually with showy white, pink, purple, or yellow flower heads **2 :** a system of radiating fibers about a centriole of a cell occurring especially during mitosis and meiosis [Latin, from Greek *astēr,* literally, "star"]

as·ter·isk \ˈas-tə-ˌrisk\ *n* **:** a character * used to refer a reader to a note or to show the omission of letters or words [Late Latin *asteriscus,* from Greek *asteriskos,* literally, "little star," from *astēr* "star"] — **asterisk** *vt*

as·ter·ism \ˈas-tə-ˌriz-əm\ *n* **:** a star-shaped figure of light exhibited by some crystals and caused by reflection from internal imperfections

astern \ə-ˈstərn\ *adv* **1 :** behind a ship or airplane **:** in the rear **2 :** at or toward the stern of a ship or aircraft **3 :** BACKWARD

as·ter·oid \ˈas-tə-ˌrȯid\ *n* **:** one of thousands of small rocky bodies chiefly between Mars and Jupiter with diameters from a fraction of a kilometer to nearly 800 kilometers [Greek *asteroeidēs* "starlike," from *astēr* "star"]

asteroid belt *n* **:** the region of interplanetary space between the orbits of Mars and Jupiter in which asteroids are formed

as·the·nia \as-ˈthē-nē-ə\ *n* **:** lack or loss of strength **:** DEBILITY [Greek *astheneia,* from *asthenēs* "weak," from *a-* + *sthenos* "strength"]

as·then·ic \-ˈthen-ik\ *adj* **1 :** of, relating to, or exhibiting asthenia **:** WEAK **2 :** characterized by slender build and slight muscular development **:** ECTOMORPHIC

as·theno·sphere \as-ˈthen-ə-ˌsfiər\ *n* **:** a zone of the earth which lies beneath the lithosphere and within which material yields readily to persistent stresses [Greek *asthenēs* "weak" + English *sphere*]

asth·ma \ˈaz-mə\ *n* **:** a lung disorder that is marked by recurrent episodes of labored breathing with wheezing, a feeling of tightness in the chest, and coughing [Medieval Latin *asma,* from Greek *asthma*] — **asth·mat·ic** \az-ˈmat-ik\ *adj or n* — **asth·mat·i·cal·ly** \-ˈmat-i-kə-lē, -klē\ *adv*

as though *conj* **:** AS IF

astig·ma·tism \ə-ˈstig-mə-ˌtiz-əm\ *n* **:** a defect of an optical system (as of the eye) that prevents light from focusing accurately and results in a blurred image or unclear vision [[2]*a-* + Greek *stigma* "mark"] — **as·tig·mat·ic** \ˌas-tig-ˈmat-ik\ *adj* — **as·tig·mat·i·cal·ly** \-ˈmat-i-kə-lē, -klē\ *adj*

astir \ə-ˈstər\ *adj* **1 :** being in a state of activity **2 :** being out of bed **:** UP

as to *prep* **1 :** with regard or reference to **:** AS FOR, ABOUT ⟨at a loss *as to* how to explain the mistake⟩ **2 :** ACCORDING TO, BY ⟨graded *as to* size and color⟩

as·ton·ish \ə-ˈstän-ish\ *vt* **:** to strike with sudden wonder **:** surprise greatly **:** AMAZE [probably from earlier *astony,* from Medieval French *estoner* "to stun," from Latin *ex-* + *tonare* "to thunder"] ***synonyms*** see SURPRISE

as·ton·ish·ing *adj* **:** causing astonishment **:** AMAZING — **as·ton·ish·ing·ly** \-ˈstän-i-shing-lē\ *adv*

as·ton·ish·ment \ə-ˈstän-ish-mənt\ *n* **1 :** the state of being astonished **2 :** a cause of amazement or wonder

as·tound \ə-ˈstau̇nd\ *vb* **:** to fill with bewilderment and wonder [Middle English *astoned,* past participle of *astonen* "to astonish," from Medieval French *estoner*] ***synonyms*** see SURPRISE

astrad·dle \ə-ˈstrad-l\ *adv or prep* **:** ASTRIDE

as·trag·a·lus \ə-ˈstrag-ə-ləs\ *n, pl* **-li** \-ˌlī, -ˌlē\ **:** [2]TALUS 1 [New Latin, from Greek *astragalos*]

as·tra·khan \ˈas-trə-kən, -ˌkan\ *n, often cap* **1 :** karakul of Russian origin **2 :** a cloth with a usually wool, curled, and looped pile resembling karakul [*Astrakhan,* Russia]

as·tral \ˈas-trəl\ *adj* **1 :** of or relating to the stars **:** STARRY **2 :** of or relating to a cell aster **3 a :** VISIONARY **b :** elevated in station or position [Latin *astrum* "star," from Greek *astron*] — **as·tral·ly** *adv*

astray \ə-ˈstrā\ *adv or adj* **1 :** off the right path or route **:** STRAYING **2 :** into error **:** MISTAKEN

[1]**astride** \ə-ˈstrīd\ *adv* **:** with one leg on each side

[2]**astride** *prep* **:** on or above and with one leg on each side of

as·trin·gen·cy \ə-ˈstrin-jən-sē\ *n* **:** the quality or state of being astringent

[1]**as·trin·gent** \ə-ˈstrin-jənt\ *adj* **1 :** able or tending to shrink body tissues ⟨*astringent* lotions⟩ ⟨an *astringent* fruit⟩ **2 :** rigidly severe **:** AUSTERE 1a ⟨an *astringent* manner⟩ [Latin *astringere* "to bind fast, contract," from *ad-* + *stringere* "to bind tight"] — **as·trin·gent·ly** *adv*

[2]**astringent** *n* **:** an astringent agent or substance

astro- *combining form* **:** star **:** heavens **:** astronomical ⟨*astrophysics*⟩ [Greek *astron* "star"]

as·tro·labe \ˈas-trə-ˌlāb\ *n* **:** a compact instrument used to observe the positions of celestial bodies before the invention of the sextant [Medieval Latin *astrolabium,* derived from Greek *astrolabos,* from *astron* "star" + *lambanein* "to take"]

astrolabe

as·trol·o·ger \ə-ˈsträl-ə-jər\ *n* **:** one who practices astrology

as·trol·o·gy \-jē\ *n* **:** the study of the supposed influences of the stars and planets on human affairs by their positions in relation to each other — **as·tro·log·i·cal** \ˌas-trə-ˈläj-i-kəl\ *adj* — **as·tro·log·i·cal·ly** \-ˈläj-i-kə-lē, -klē\ *adv*

as·tro·naut \ˈas-trə-ˌnȯt, -ˌnät\ *n* **:** a traveler in a spacecraft; *also* **:** a trainee for spaceflight [*astro-* + *-naut* (as in *aeronaut*)] — **as·tro·nau·ti·cal** \ˌas-trə-ˈnȯt-i-kəl\ *adj* — **as·tro·nau·ti·cal·ly** \-i-kə-lē, -klē\ *adv*

as·tro·nau·tics \-ˈnȯt-iks\ *n* **:** the science of the construction and operation of spacecraft

as·tron·o·mer \ə-ˈsträn-ə-mər\ *n* **:** one who is skilled in astronomy or who observes celestial phenomena

as·tro·nom·i·cal \ˌas-trə-ˈnäm-i-kəl\ *or* **as·tro·nom·ic** \-ˈnäm-ik\ *adj* **1 :** of or relating to astronomy **2 :** extremely or unimaginably large ⟨an *astronomical* amount of money⟩ — **as·tro·nom·i·cal·ly** \-ˈnäm-i-kə-lē, -klē\ *adv*

astronomical unit *n* **:** a unit of length used in astronomy equal to the mean distance of the earth from the sun or about 93 million miles (150 million kilometers)

as·tron·o·my \ə-ˈsträn-ə-mē\ *n* **:** the science of the celestial bodies and of their physical characteristics, relative motions, composition, and history [Medieval French *astronomie,* from Latin *astronomia,* from Greek, from *astron* "star" + *nomos* "law"]

as·tro·phys·ics \ˌas-trə-ˈfiz-iks\ *n* **:** a branch of astronomy dealing with the physical and chemical makeup of the celestial bodies — **as·tro·phys·i·cal** \-ˈfiz-i-kəl\ *adj* — **as·tro·phys·i·cist** \-ˈfiz-ə-səst\ *n*

as·tute \ə-ˈstüt, a-, -ˈstyüt\ *adj* **:** CLEVER ⟨an *astute* business person⟩; *also* **:** SLY 1 [Latin *astutus,* from *astus* "craft"] ***synonyms*** see SHREWD — **as·tute·ly** *adv* — **as·tute·ness** *n*

asun·der \ə-ˈsən-dər\ *adv or adj* **1 :** into parts ⟨torn *asunder*⟩ **2 :** apart from each other in position

¹as well as *conj* **:** and in addition ⟨brave *as well as* loyal⟩ ⟨fish for food *as well as* for sport⟩

²as well as *prep* **:** in addition to **:** BESIDES ⟨*as well as* being a poet, she is an exciting story teller⟩

asy·lum \ə-ˈsī-ləm\ *n* **1 :** a place of refuge and protection giving shelter to criminals and debtors **2 :** a place of retreat and security **:** SHELTER **3 :** protection afforded by or as if by an asylum **:** REFUGE ⟨a political refugee given *asylum* in the embassy⟩ **4 :** an institution for the relief or care of the sick and especially the insane [Latin, from Greek *asylon,* from *asylos* "inviolable," from *a-* + *sylon* "right of seizure"]

asym·met·ri·cal \ˌā-sə-ˈme-tri-kəl\ *or* **asym·met·ric** \ˌā-sə-ˈme-trik\ *adj* **:** not symmetrical — **asym·met·ri·cal·ly** \-tri-kə-lē, -klē\ *adv* — **asym·me·try** \ˈā-ˈsim-ə-trē\ *n*

asymp·tom·at·ic \ˌā-ˌsimp-tə-ˈmat-ik\ *adj* **:** presenting no symptoms of disease

as·ymp·tote \ˈas-əm-ˌtōt, -əmp-\ *n* **:** a straight line that is approached more and more closely by a curve that never actually meets it no matter how far the curve is extended [Greek *asymptōtos* "not meeting," from *a-* + *sympiptein* "to meet," from *syn-* + *piptein* "to fall"] — **as·ymp·tot·ic** \ˌas-əm-ˈtät-ik, -əmp-\ *adj*

asyn·de·ton \ə-ˈsin-də-ˌtän\ *n, pl* **-de·tons** *or* **-de·ta** \-dət-ə\ **:** omission of the conjunctions ordinarily expected (as in "I came, I saw, I conquered") [Late Latin, from Greek, from *asyndetos* "unconnected," from *a-* + *syndein* "to bind together," from *syn-* + *dein* "to bind"] — **as·yn·det·ic** \ˌas-n-ˈdet-ik\ *adj* — **as·yn·det·i·cal·ly** \-ˈdet-i-kə-lē, -klē\ *adv*

at \ət, at, ˈat\ *prep* **1** — used to indicate location in space or time ⟨staying *at* a hotel⟩ ⟨be here *at* six⟩ ⟨sick *at* heart⟩ **2** — used to indicate a goal that an action is aimed towards ⟨aim *at* the target⟩ ⟨laugh *at* him⟩ **3** — used to indicate a condition one is in ⟨*at* work⟩ ⟨*at* liberty⟩ ⟨*at* rest⟩ **4** — used to indicate how or why ⟨sold *at* auction⟩ ⟨angry *at* their answer⟩ **5** — used to indicate the rate, degree, age, or position in a scale or series ⟨the temperature *at* 90⟩ ⟨retire *at* 65⟩ [Old English *æt*]

at- — see AD-

at all \ət-ˈȯl, ə-ˈtȯl, at-ˈȯl\ *adv* **:** in any way or respect **:** to the least extent or degree **:** under any circumstances ⟨not *at all* likely⟩ ⟨doesn't mind *at all*⟩

at·a·vism \ˈat-ə-ˌviz-əm\ *n* **1 :** recurrence in an organism of a character typical of a more primitive ancestral form and usually due to genetic recombination **2 :** an individual or character manifesting atavism [French *atavisme,* from Latin *atavus* "ancestor"] — **at·a·vis·tic** \ˌat-ə-ˈvis-tik\ *adj*

atax·ia \ə-ˈtak-sē-ə, ā-\ *n* **:** inability to coordinate voluntary muscular movements [Greek, "confusion," from *a-* + *tassein* "to put in order"] — **atax·ic** \-sik\ *adj*

ate *past of* EAT

¹-ate \ət, ˌāt\ *n suffix* **1 :** one acted upon (in a specified way) ⟨distill*ate*⟩ **2 :** chemical compound derived from a (specified) compound or element; *esp* **:** salt or ester of an acid with a name ending in *-ic* ⟨bor*ate*⟩ [Latin *-atus, -atum,* masculine and neuter of *-atus,* past participle ending]

²-ate *n suffix* **1 :** office **:** function **:** rank **:** group of persons holding a (specified) position, office, or rank ⟨elector*ate*⟩ **2 :** state **:** dominion **:** jurisdiction ⟨emir*ate*⟩ ⟨khan*ate*⟩ [Latin *-atus*]

³-ate *adj suffix* **:** marked by having ⟨chord*ate*⟩ [Latin *-atus,* past participle ending]

⁴-ate \ˌāt\ *vb suffix* **1 :** cause to be modified or affected by ⟨camphor*ate*⟩ **2 :** cause to become ⟨activ*ate*⟩ **3 :** furnish with ⟨aer*ate*⟩ [Middle English *-aten,* from Latin *-atus,* past participle ending]

ate·lier \ˌat-l-ˈyā\ *n* **1 :** an artist's or designer's studio **2 :** WORKSHOP [French]

a tem·po \ä-ˈtem-pō\ *adv or adj* **:** in time — used as a direction in music to return to the original rate of speed [Italian]

Ath·a·na·sian Creed \ˌath-ə-ˈnā-zhən-, -ˌnā-shən-\ *n* **:** a Christian creed originating in Europe about A.D. 400 and relating especially to the Trinity and Incarnation [*Athanasius,* died 373, bishop of Alexandria]

athe·ism \ˈā-thē-ˌiz-əm\ *n* **:** the belief that there is no God **:** denial of the existence of a supreme being [Middle French *athéisme,* from Greek *atheos* "godless," from *a-* + *theos* "god"]

athe·ist \-thē-əst\ *n* **:** a person who believes there is no God — **athe·is·tic** \ˌā-thē-ˈis-tik\ *or* **athe·is·tic·al** \-ˈis-ti-kəl\ *adj* — **athe·is·ti·cal·ly** \-ˈis-ti-kə-lē, -klē\ *adv*

ath·e·ling \ˈath-ə-ling, ˈat͟h-\ *n* **:** an Anglo-Saxon prince or nobleman [Old English *ætheling,* from *æthelu* "nobility"]

ath·e·nae·um *or* **ath·e·ne·um** \ˌath-ə-ˈnē-əm\ *n* **1 :** a literary or scientific association **2 :** LIBRARY 1 [Latin *Athenaeum,* a school in ancient Rome for the study of arts, from Greek *Athēnaion,* a temple of Athena, from *Athēnē* "Athena"]

ath·ero·scle·ro·sis \ˌath-ə-rō-sklə-ˈrō-səs\ *n* **:** an arteriosclerosis in which fatty substances are deposited in the inner layer of the arteries [Latin *atheroma* "tumor containing matter resembling gruel," from Greek *athērōma,* from *athēra* "gruel"] — **ath·ero·scle·rot·ic** \-sklə-ˈrät-ik\ *adj*

athirst \ə-ˈthərst\ *adj* **1** *archaic* **:** THIRSTY **2 :** having a strong desire **:** EAGER ⟨*athirst* for knowledge⟩ [Old English *ofthyrst,* past participle of *ofthyrstan* "to suffer from thirst," from *of* "off, from" + *thyrstan* "to thirst"]

ath·lete \ˈath-ˌlēt\ *n* **:** a person who is trained in or good at games and exercises that require physical skill, endurance, and strength [Latin *athleta,* from Greek *athlētēs,* from *athlein* "to contend for a prize," from *athlon* "prize, contest"]

athlete's foot *n* **:** ringworm of the feet

ath·let·ic \ath-ˈlet-ik\ *adj* **1 :** of, relating to, or characteristic of athletes or athletics **2 :** VIGOROUS 1, ACTIVE **3 :** characterized by strength and muscular development **4 :** used by athletes — **ath·let·i·cal·ly** \-ˈlet-i-kə-lē, -klē\ *adv*

ath·let·ics \ath-ˈlet-iks\ *n sing or pl* **:** games, sports, and exercises requiring strength and skill

athletic supporter *n* **:** an elastic pouch for the genitals worn by men participating in sports or other strenuous activities

-athon \ə-ˌthän\ *n combining form* **:** event or activity lasting a long time or involving a great deal of something [*marathon*]

¹athwart \ə-ˈthwȯrt, *nautical often* -ˈthȯrt\ *adv* **:** ACROSS 1

²athwart *prep* **1 :** ACROSS **2 :** in opposition to

atilt \ə-ˈtilt\ *adj or adv* **:** in a tilted position

-a·tion \ˈā-shən\ *n suffix* **:** action or process **:** something connected with an action or process ⟨discolor*ation*⟩ ⟨flirt*ation*⟩ [Latin *-ation-, -atio*]

-a·tive \ˌāt-iv, ət-\ *adj suffix* **1 :** of, relating to, or connected with ⟨authorit*ative*⟩ **2 :** tending to ⟨talk*ative*⟩ [Latin *-ativus,* from *-atus* "-ate" + *-ivus* "-ive"]

At·lan·tic salmon \ət-ˈlant-ik-\ *n* **:** SALMON 1a

Atlantic time *n* **:** the time of the 4th time zone west of Greenwich that includes the Canadian Maritime provinces, Puerto Rico, and the Virgin Islands

at·las \ˈat-ləs\ *n* **1 a :** a book of maps often including descriptive text **b :** a book of tables, charts, or illustrations ⟨an *atlas* of anatomy⟩ **2 :** the first vertebra of the neck [*Atlas,* a Titan of Greek mythology]

Word History Atlas was one of the Titans or giants of Greek mythology, whose rule of the world in an early age was overthrown by Zeus in a mighty battle. Atlas was believed to be responsible for holding up the sky, a task which he tried unsuccessfully to have Hercules assume. In his published collection of maps, the 16th century Flemish cartographer Gerhardus Mercator included on the title page a picture of Atlas supporting the heavens, and he gave the book the title *Atlas.* Other early collections of maps subsequently included similar pictures of Atlas, and such books came to be called *atlases.*

ATM \ˌā-ˌtē-ˈem\ *n* **:** a computerized machine that performs basic banking functions (as issuing cash withdrawals)

at·mo·sphere \ˈat-mə-ˌsfiər\ *n* **1 a :** the whole mass of air surrounding the earth **b :** a gaseous mass surrounding a celestial body (as a planet) **2 :** the air in a particular place ⟨the stuffy *atmosphere* of this room⟩ **3 :** a surrounding influence or environment ⟨a friendly *atmosphere*⟩ **4 :** a unit of pressure equal to the pressure of the air at sea level or about 14.7 pounds per square inch (about 10 newtons per square centimeter) **5 a :** the overall mood or feeling of a work of art **b :** a unique or appealing effect or mood ⟨a restaurant with *atmosphere*⟩ [Greek *atmos* "vapor" + Latin *sphaera* "sphere"] — **at·mo-**

\ə\ **abut**	\au̇\ **out**	\i\ **tip**	\ȯ\ **saw**	\u̇\ **foot**
\ər\ **further**	\ch\ **chin**	\ī\ **life**	\ȯi\ **coin**	\y\ **yet**
\a\ **mat**	\e\ **pet**	\j\ **job**	\th\ **thin**	\yü\ **few**
\ā\ **take**	\ē\ **easy**	\ng\ **sing**	\t͟h\ **this**	\yu̇\ **cure**
\ä\ **cot, cart**	\g\ **go**	\ō\ **bone**	\ü\ **food**	\zh\ **vision**

spher·ic \ˌat-mə-ˈsfiər-ik, -ˈsfer-\ *adj* — **at·mo·spher·i·cal·ly** \-i-kə-lē, -klē\ *adv*

at·mo·spher·ics \ˌat-mə-ˈsfiər-iks, -ˈsfer-\ *n pl* **:** static produced by atmospheric electrical phenomena (as lightning); *also* **:** the electrical phenomena causing such disturbances

atoll \ˈa-ˌtȯl, -ˌtäl, -ˌtōl, ˈā-\ *n* **:** a ring-shaped coral island or string of islands consisting of a coral reef surrounding a lagoon [*atolu,* from a language of the Maldive Islands]

atoll

at·om \ˈat-əm\ *n* **1 :** a tiny particle **:** BIT **2 a :** the smallest particle of an element that can exist either alone or in combination ⟨an *atom* of hydrogen⟩ **b :** ATOMIC ENERGY [Latin *atomus* "indivisible particle," from Greek *atomos,* from *atomos* "indivisible," from *a-* + *temnein* "to cut"]

Word History Some ancient philosophers believed that matter is infinitely divisible, that any particle, no matter how small, can always be divided into smaller particles. Others believed that there must be a limit, that everything in the universe must be made up of tiny indivisible particles. Such a hypothetical particle was called in Greek *atomos,* which means "indivisible." According to modern atomic theory, all matter is made up of tiny particles called *atoms* after the ancient Greek *atomos,* and the atoms of any one chemical element are identical. Although the atom is the smallest particle of an element that has the characteristics of that element, it has turned out that atoms are not indivisible after all. Indeed, the splitting of atoms has been used, as in the explosion of atom bombs, to produce vast amounts of energy.

atom·ic \ə-ˈtäm-ik\ *adj* **1 :** of, relating to, or concerned with atoms, atomic bombs, or nuclear energy ⟨*atomic* physics⟩ ⟨the *atomic* age⟩ ⟨*atomic* energy⟩ **2 :** extremely small **:** MINUTE **3 :** existing in the state of separate atoms ⟨*atomic* hydrogen⟩ — **atom·i·cal·ly** \-i-kə-lē, -klē\ *adv*

atomic bomb *n* **1 :** a bomb whose violent explosive power is due to the sudden release of energy resulting from the splitting of nuclei of a heavy chemical element (as plutonium or uranium) by neutrons in a very rapid chain reaction — called also *atom bomb* **2 :** HYDROGEN BOMB

atomic clock *n* **:** a precision clock that depends for its operation on an electrical oscillator regulated by the natural vibration frequencies of an atomic system (as a cesium atom)

atomic mass *n* **:** the mass of any species of atom usually expressed in atomic mass units

atomic mass unit *n* **:** a unit of mass for expressing masses of atoms, molecules, or nuclear particles equal to ¹⁄₁₂ of the atomic mass of the most abundant isotope of carbon

atomic number *n* **:** a number that is characteristic of a chemical element and represents the number of protons in the nucleus

atomic pile *n* **:** REACTOR 2b

atomic reactor *n* **:** REACTOR 2b

atomic theory *n* **1 :** a theory of the nature of matter: all material substances are composed of minute particles or atoms of a comparatively small number of kinds and all the atoms of the same kind are uniform in size, weight, and other properties **2 :** any of several theories of the structure of the atom; *esp* **:** one holding that the atom is composed essentially of a small positively charged comparatively heavy nucleus surrounded by a comparatively large arrangement of electrons

atomic weight *n* **:** the average atomic mass of an element compared to ¹⁄₁₂ the mass of the most abundant isotope of carbon

at·om·ize \ˈat-ə-ˌmīz\ *vt* **1 :** to reduce to minute particles or to a fine spray **2 :** to treat as made up of many individual units **3 :** to subject to nuclear weapons — **at·om·i·za·tion** \ˌat-ə-mə-ˈzā-shən\ *n*

at·om·iz·er \ˈat-ə-ˌmī-zər\ *n* **:** a device for giving a very fine spray of a liquid (as a perfume or disinfectant)

atom smasher *n* **:** ACCELERATOR b

aton·al \ˈā-ˈtōn-l, ˈa-\ *adj* **:** characterized by avoidance of traditional musical tonality — **ato·nal·i·ty** \ˌā-tō-ˈnal-ət-ē\ *n* — **atonal·ly** \ˈā-ˈtōn-l-ē, ˈa-\ *adv*

atone \ə-ˈtōn\ *vb* **:** to do something to make up for a wrong done **:** make amends [Middle English *atonen* "to become reconciled," from *at on* "in harmony," from *at* + *on* "one"]

atone·ment \-mənt\ *n* **1 :** the reconciliation of God and humanity held by Christians to have come through the death of Jesus Christ **2 :** reparation for an offense or injury

¹atop \ə-ˈtäp\ *prep* **:** on top of

²atop *adv or adj* **:** on, to, or at the top

ATP \ˌā-ˌtē-ˈpē, ā-ˈtē-ˌpē\ *n* **:** a nucleotide that is a derivative of adenosine and supplies energy for many processes of living cells by undergoing conversion to ADP and surrendering a phosphate group [*a*denosine *t*ri*p*hosphate]

atri·al \ˈā-trē-əl\ *adj* **:** of or relating to an atrium

atrio·ven·tric·u·lar \ˌā-trē-ō-ven-ˈtrik-yə-lər, -vən-\ *adj* **:** of, relating to, or located between an atrium and ventricle of the heart

atri·um \ˈā-trē-əm\ *n, pl* **atria** \-trē-ə\ *also* **atri·ums 1 :** the central hall of a Roman house **2 :** a rectangular open patio around which a house is built **3 :** an anatomical cavity or passage; *esp* **:** the chamber of the heart receiving blood from the veins and forcing it into a ventricle that in lung-breathing vertebrates (as frogs and human beings) is one of two chambers of which the right receives blood full of carbon dioxide from the body and the left receives oxygen-rich blood from the lungs but in gill-breathing verterates (as fishes) is only a single chamber [Latin]

atro·cious \ə-ˈtrō-shəs\ *adj* **1 :** extremely wicked, brutal, or cruel **2 :** causing horror **:** APPALLING ⟨the *atrocious* weapons of modern war⟩ **3 a :** utterly revolting ⟨*atrocious* working conditions⟩ **b :** of very bad quality ⟨*atrocious* handwriting⟩ [Latin *atroc-, atrox* "gloomy, atrocious," from *ater* "black"] ***synonyms*** see OUTRAGEOUS — **atro·cious·ly** *adv* — **atro·cious·ness** *n*

atroc·i·ty \ə-ˈträs-ət-ē\ *n, pl* **-ties 1 :** the quality or state of being atrocious **2 :** an atrocious act, object, or situation

¹at·ro·phy \ˈa-trə-fē\ *n, pl* **-phies :** decrease in size or wasting away of a body part or tissue [Late Latin *atrophia,* from Greek, from *atrophos* "ill fed," from *a-* + *trephein* "to nourish"] — **atroph·ic** \ā-ˈtrō-fik, ˈā-ˈ\ *adj*

²at·ro·phy \ˈa-trə-fē, -ˌfī\ *vi* **-phied; -phy·ing :** to undergo atrophy

at·ro·pine \ˈa-trə-ˌpēn\ *n* **:** a poisonous white crystalline compound $C_{17}H_{23}NO_3$ from belladonna and related plants used especially to relieve spasms and to dilate the pupil of the eye [New Latin *Atropa,* genus name of belladonna, from Greek *Atropos,* one of the Fates]

at sign *n* **:** the symbol @ especially when used as part of an e-mail address

at·tach \ə-ˈtach\ *vb* **1 :** to take money or property by legal authority especially to secure payment of a debt ⟨*attach* one's salary⟩ **2 a :** to bring (oneself) into an association ⟨*attached* herself to the cause⟩ **b :** to assign (an individual or a unit in the military) temporarily **3 :** to tie or bind by feelings of affection ⟨they were *attached* to their dog⟩ **4 :** to fasten to something (as by tying or gluing) ⟨*attach* a label to a package⟩ **5 :** to think of as belonging to something **:** ATTRIBUTE ⟨*attach* no importance to a remark⟩ **6 :** to be associated or connected ⟨the interest that naturally *attaches* to a statement by the president⟩ [Medieval French *attacher,* alteration of *estachier,* from *estache* "stake," of Germanic origin] — **at·tach·able** \-ə-bəl\ *adj*

at·ta·ché \ˌat-ə-ˈshā, ˌa-ˌta-, ə-ˌta-\ *n* **1 :** a technical expert on the diplomatic staff of a country at a foreign capital ⟨a military *attaché*⟩ **2 :** ATTACHÉ CASE [French, past participle of *attacher*]

at·ta·ché case \ˌat-ə-ˈshā-ˌ, ˌa-ˌta-; ə-ˈtash-ˌā-ˌ\ *n* **:** a small thin suitcase used especially for carrying papers and documents

at·tach·ment \ə-ˈtach-mənt\ *n* **1 :** a seizure by legal process or the writ commanding such seizure **2 :** the state of being personally attached **:** FIDELITY, FONDNESS **3 :** a device that can be attached to a machine or tool ⟨*attachments* for a vacuum cleaner⟩ **4 :** the physical connection by which one thing is attached to another **5 :** the process of physically attaching

¹at·tack \ə-ˈtak\ *vb* **1 :** to set upon forcefully **2 :** to threaten (a piece in chess) with immediate capture **3 :** to use unfriendly or bitter words against **4 :** to begin to affect or to act upon injuriously ⟨*attacked* by fever⟩ **5 :** to set to work on ⟨*attack* a problem⟩ [Middle French *attaquer,* from Italian *attaccare* "to attach, attack," of Germanic origin] — **at·tack·er** *n*

synonyms ATTACK, ASSAIL, ASSAULT, STORM mean to start a fight against. ATTACK implies taking the initiative in a struggle ⟨planned to *attack* the castle at dawn⟩. ASSAIL implies trying to break down resistance by repeated blows or shots ⟨*as-*

sailed the enemy with artillery fire⟩. ASSAULT suggests a direct attempt to overpower by suddenness and violence ⟨troops *assaulted* the building from all sides⟩. STORM implies trying to overrun or capture a defended position by the irresistible weight of rapidly advancing numbers ⟨preparing to *storm* the fortress⟩.

²**attack** *n* **1** : the act of attacking : ASSAULT **2** : the beginning of destructive action (as by a chemical agent) **3** : a setting to work : START **4** : a fit of sickness; *esp* : an active episode of a chronic or recurrent disease **5 a** : an offensive or scoring action in a game **b** : offensive players on a team

attack dog *n* : a dog trained to attack on command or on sight

at·tain \ə-ˈtān\ *vb* **1** : GAIN 1, ACHIEVE ⟨*attain* a goal⟩ **2** : to come into possession of : OBTAIN **3** : to arrive or arrive at ⟨*attain* the top of the mountain⟩ ⟨*attain* to maturity⟩ [Medieval French *ateindre,* "to reach, accomplish, convict," derived from Latin *attingere,* from *ad-* + *tangere* "to touch"] — **at·tain·abil·i·ty** \ə-ˌtā-nə-ˈbil-ət-ē\ *n* — **at·tain·able** \-ˈtā-nə-bəl\ *adj* — **at·tain·able·ness** *n*

at·tain·der \ə-ˈtān-dər\ *n* : the taking away of a person's civil rights when the person has been declared an outlaw or sentenced to death [Medieval French *ateindre* "conviction," from *ateindre* "to convict"]

at·tain·ment \ə-ˈtān-mənt\ *n* **1** : the act of attaining : the state of being attained **2** : something attained : ACCOMPLISHMENT

at·tar \ˈat-ər, ˈa-ˌtär\ *n* : a fragrant essential oil (as from rose petals) used in perfumes or flavorings; *also* : FRAGRANCE [Persian *ʿatir* "perfumed," from Arabic, from *ʿitr* "perfume"]

¹**at·tempt** \ə-ˈtempt\ *vt* : to make an effort to do, accomplish, or solve ⟨*attempt* to swim the river⟩ [Latin *attemptare,* from *ad-* + *temptare* "to touch, try"] ***synonyms*** see TRY

²**attempt** *n* **1** : the act or an instance of attempting; *esp* : an unsuccessful effort **2** : ATTACK, ASSAULT ⟨an *attempt* on the life of the president⟩

at·tend \ə-ˈtend\ *vb* **1** : to look after : take charge of ⟨*attend* to your own work⟩ **2** : to go or stay with as a servant, nurse, or companion **3** : to be present at ⟨*attend* a party⟩ **4** : to be present with : ACCOMPANY ⟨illness *attended* by fever⟩ **5** : to pay attention : HEED [Medieval French *atendre,* from Latin *attendere,* from *ad-* + *tendere* "to stretch"]

at·ten·dance \ə-ˈten-dənts\ *n* **1** : the act of attending ⟨a doctor in *attendance*⟩ **2 a** : the persons or number of persons attending **b** : the number of times a person attends

¹**at·ten·dant** \ə-ˈten-dənt\ *adj* : accompanying or following as a consequence

²**attendant** *n* **1** : a person who goes with or serves another ⟨a bride and her *attendants*⟩ **2** : an employee who waits on customers ⟨a parking lot *attendant*⟩

at·ten·tion \ə-ˈten-chən\ *n* **1** : the act or the power of fixing one's mind upon something : careful listening or watching **2 a** : an instance of noticing : AWARENESS ⟨caught my *attention*⟩ **b** : careful consideration of something with a view to taking action on it ⟨a matter requiring *attention*⟩ **3** : an act of kindness, care, or courtesy **4** : a position taken by a soldier with heels together, body erect, arms at the side, and eyes to the front — often used as a command [Latin *attentio,* from *attendere* "to attend"] — **at·ten·tion·al** \ə-ˈtench-nəl, -ˈten-chən-l\ *adj*

attention deficit disorder *n* : a condition that is characterized by an inability to maintain attention or by hyperactive and impulsive behavior or by a combination of both and that impairs functioning in school, home, work, or social settings

attention span *n* : the length of time during which one is able to concentrate or remain interested

at·ten·tive \ə-ˈtent-iv\ *adj* **1** : paying attention : OBSERVANT **2** : heedful of the comfort of others : COURTEOUS — **at·ten·tive·ly** *adv* — **at·ten·tive·ness** *n*

at·ten·u·ate \ə-ˈten-yə-ˌwāt\ *vb* : to make or become thin or less (as in density, force, value, or vitality) ⟨*attenuate* a virus⟩ ⟨*attenuate* oil by heating⟩ ⟨sorrows *attenuate* with time⟩ [Latin *attenuare,* from *ad-* + *tenuis* "thin"] — **at·ten·u·a·tion** \ə-ˌten-yə-ˈwā-shən\ *n*

at·test \ə-ˈtest\ *vb* **1** : to indicate to be true or genuine especially by signing as a witness ⟨*attest* a will⟩ **2** : to be proof of : SHOW ⟨my conduct *attests* my innocence⟩ **3** : TESTIFY ⟨*attest* to the truth of the statement⟩ [Middle French *attester,* from Latin *attestari,* from *ad-* + *testis* "witness"] — **at·tes·ta·tion** \ˌa-ˌtes-ˈtā-shən\ *n* — **at·test·er** \ə-ˈtes-tər\ *n*

at·tic \ˈat-ik\ *n* **1** : a low story or wall at the top of a classical facade **2** : a room or a space immediately below the roof of a building [French *attique,* from *attique* "of Attica," from Latin *Atticus*]

Word History The ancient Greek city-state of Athens included the whole of the Attic Peninsula, the region called Attica. Typical of the Athenian or Attic style of architecture is the use of rectangular columns projecting from, but attached to, the wall. These take the place of the freestanding and usually rounded pillars common in other architectural styles. Occasionally the large columns at the front of a building are topped by a similar but smaller decorative structure, usually in the Attic style. The French named this structure *attique.* The English borrowed the name, respelling it according to a common pattern. From its originally specialized sense, *attic* was extended to cover the top story, just under the roof, of any building.

At·tic \ˈat-ik\ *adj* **1** : of or relating to Athens **2** : marked by simplicity, purity, and refinement [Latin *Atticus* "of Attica, Athenian," from Greek *Attikos,* from *Attikē* "Attica, Greece"]

¹**at·tire** \ə-ˈtīr\ *vt* : to put clothes on : DRESS; *esp* : to clothe in rich garments [Medieval French *atirer* "to equip, prepare, attire," from *a-* "ad-" + *tire* "order, rank," of Germanic origin]

²**attire** *n* : DRESS, CLOTHES; *esp* : fine clothing

at·ti·tude \ˈat-ə-ˌtüd, -ˌtyüd\ *n* **1** : the arrangement of the body or figure : POSTURE **2** : a way of thinking or feeling about a fact or state **3** : the position of an aircraft or spacecraft in relation to a reference point (as the horizon or a star) **4** : a negative, defiant, or distant state of mind [French, from Italian *attitudine,* literally, "aptitude," from Late Latin *aptitudo*]

at·ti·tu·di·nize \ˌat-ə-ˈtüd-n-ˌīz, -ˈtyüd-\ *vi* : to purposefully take on a mental attitude : POSE

at·to- \ˈat-ō\ *combining form* : one quintillionth (10^{-18}) part of [Danish or Norwegian *atten* "eighteen"]

at·tor·ney \ə-ˈtər-nē\ *n, pl* **-neys** : a person who is legally appointed to transact business for another; *esp* : LAWYER [Medieval French *atorné,* past participle of *atorner* "to prepare, designate, transfer (allegiance of a tenant)," from *a-* "ad-" + *torner* "to turn"]

attorney general *n, pl* **attorneys general** *or* **attorney generals** : the chief law officer of a nation or state who represents the government in legal matters and serves as its principal legal advisor

at·tract \ə-ˈtrakt\ *vb* : to cause to approach or adhere: as **a** : to pull to or toward oneself or itself ⟨a magnet *attracts* iron⟩ **b** : to draw by appealing to interest or feeling ⟨*attract* attention⟩ [Latin *attrahere,* from *ad-* + *trahere* "to draw"]

at·trac·tant \ə-ˈtrak-tənt\ *n* : a substance (as a pheromone) that attracts animals (as insects)

at·trac·tion \ə-ˈtrak-shən\ *n* **1 a** : the act, process, or power of attracting **b** : a feature that attracts; *esp* : personal charm or beauty **2** : a force acting mutually between particles of matter, tending to draw them together, and resisting their separation

at·trac·tive \ə-ˈtrak-tiv\ *adj* : having the power or quality of attracting; *esp* : CHARMING, PLEASING ⟨an *attractive* smile⟩ — **at·trac·tive·ly** *adv* — **at·trac·tive·ness** *n*

¹**at·tri·bute** \ˈa-trə-ˌbyüt\ *n* **1** : a natural or essential characteristic or quality **2** : an object closely associated with a specific person, thing, or office ⟨crown and scepter are *attributes* of royalty⟩ **3** : a word that indicates a quality; *esp* : ADJECTIVE [Latin *attributus,* past participle of *attribuere* "to attribute," from *ad-* + *tribuere* "to bestow"] ***synonyms*** see QUALITY

²**at·trib·ute** \ə-ˈtrib-yət\ *vt* **1** : to explain by indicating a cause ⟨*attribute* their success to hard work⟩ **2 a** : to regard as characteristic of a person or thing ⟨*attributed* the worst motives to them⟩ **b** : to consider to have originated in an indicated fashion ***synonyms*** see ASCRIBE — **at·trib·ut·able** \-yət-ə-bəl\ *adj*

at·tri·bu·tion \ˌa-trə-ˈbyü-shən\ *n* : the act of attributing; *also* : an indicated quality, character, or right

at·trib·u·tive \ə-ˈtrib-yət-iv\ *adj* : relating to or of the nature of an attribute; *esp* : joined directly to a modified noun without a linking verb ⟨*city* in *city streets* is an *attributive* noun⟩ — compare PREDICATE — **attributive** *n* — **at·trib·u·tive·ly** *adv*

at·tri·tion \ə-ˈtrish-ən\ *n* **1** : the act of wearing or grinding down by friction **2** : the act of weakening or exhausting by constant harassment or abuse **3** : gradual reduction of personnel as a result of resignation, retirement, or death [Latin *attritio,* from *atterere* "to rub against," from *ad-* + *terere* "to rub"] — **at·tri·tion·al** \-ˈtrish-nəl, -ən-l\ *adj*

at·tune \ə-ˈtün, -ˈtyün\ *vt* : TUNE — **at·tune·ment** \-mənt\ *n*

ATV \ˌā-ˌtē-ˈvē\ *n* : ALL-TERRAIN VEHICLE

atyp·i·cal \ā-ˈtip-i-kəl, ˈā-ˈ\ *adj* : not typical : IRREGULAR — **atyp·i·cal·ly** \-kə-lē, -klē\ *adv*

au·burn \ˈó-bərn\ *adj* : of a reddish brown color ⟨*auburn* hair⟩ [Middle French *auborne* "blond," from Medieval Latin *alburnus* "whitish," from Latin *albus* "white"]

[1]**auc·tion** \ˈók-shən\ *n* : a sale of property to the highest bidder [Latin *auctio,* from *augēre* "to increase"]

[2]**auction** *vt* **auc·tioned; auc·tion·ing** \-shə-ning, -shning\ : to sell at auction

auction bridge *n* : a bridge game differing from contract bridge only in the scoring

auc·tion·eer \ˌók-shə-ˈniər\ *n* : an agent who sells goods at auction — **auctioneer** *vt*

auc·to·ri·al \ók-ˈtōr-ē-əl, -ˈtór-\ *adj* : of or relating to an author

au·da·cious \ó-ˈdā-shəs\ *adj* **1 a** : FEARLESS, DARING **b** : recklessly bold : RASH **2** : showing a lack of proper respect [Latin *audac-, audax* "bold," from *audēre* "to dare," from *avidus* "eager, avid"] — **au·da·cious·ly** *adv* — **au·da·cious·ness** *n*

au·dac·i·ty \ó-ˈdas-ət-ē\ *n, pl* **-ties** **1** : DARING, BOLDNESS **2** : a disrespectful or arrogant attitude ***synonyms*** see TEMERITY

au·di·ble \ˈód-ə-bəl\ *adj* : loud enough to be heard [Latin *audire* "to hear"] — **au·di·bil·i·ty** \ˌód-ə-ˈbil-ət-ē\ *n* — **au·di·bly** \ˈód-ə-blē\ *adv*

au·di·ence \ˈód-ē-əns\ *n* **1** : an assembled group that listens or watches (as at a play) **2** : an opportunity of being heard; *esp* : a formal interview with a person of high rank **3** : those of the general public who give attention to something said, done, or written ⟨the radio *audience*⟩ ⟨the *audience* for a new novel⟩ [Medieval French, from Latin *audientia,* from *audire* "to hear"]

[1]**au·dio** \ˈód-ē-ˌō\ *adj* **1** : of or relating to electrical or other vibrational frequencies corresponding to normally audible sound waves which are of frequencies approximately from 15 to 20,000 hertz **2 a** : of or relating to sound or its reproduction and especially high-fidelity reproduction **b** : relating to or used in the transmission or reception of sound — compare VIDEO

[2]**audio** *n* **1** : the transmission, reception, or reproduction of sound **2** : the section of television or film equipment that deals with sound

audio- *combining form* **1** : hearing ⟨*audio*meter⟩ **2** : sound ⟨*audio*phile⟩ **3** : auditory and ⟨*audio*visual⟩ [Latin *audire* "to hear"]

au·dio·book \ˈód-ē-ō-ˌbu̇k\ *n* : a recording of a book or magazine being read

au·dio–lin·gual \ˌód-ē-ō-ˈling-gwəl\ *adj* : involving the use of listening and speaking drills in language learning

au·di·ol·o·gist \ˌód-ē-ˈäl-ə-jist\ *n* : a person who specializes in audiology

au·di·ol·o·gy \ˌód-ē-ˈäl-ə-jē\ *n* : a branch of science concerned with hearing and the treatment of people with impaired hearing

au·di·om·e·ter \ˌód-ē-ˈäm-ət-ər\ *n* : an instrument used in measuring acuteness of hearing — **au·dio·met·ric** \ˌód-ē-ə-ˈme-trik\ *adj* — **au·di·om·e·try** \ˌód-ē-ˈäm-ə-trē\ *n*

au·dio·phile \ˈód-ē-ō-ˌfīl\ *n* : one who is enthusiastic about high-fidelity sound reproduction

au·dio·vi·su·al \ˌód-ē-ō-ˈvizh-wəl, -ˈvizh-ə-wəl, -ˈvizh-əl\ *adj* : of, relating to, or making use of both hearing and sight ⟨*audiovisual* teaching aids⟩

au·dio·vi·su·als \-wəlz, -əlz\ *n pl* : audiovisual instructional materials

[1]**aud·it** \ˈód-ət\ *n* **1** : a thorough examination of accounts and account books of a business or individual; *also* : the final report of such an examination **2** : a careful examination or review ⟨an energy *audit* of the house⟩ [Latin *auditus* "act of hearing," from *audire* "to hear"]

[2]**audit** *vt* : to perform an audit of or for ⟨*audit* accounts⟩

[1]**au·di·tion** \ó-ˈdish-ən\ *n* **1** : the power or sense of hearing **2** : a critical hearing **3** : a trial performance for a role or position

[2]**audition** *vb* **-di·tioned; -di·tion·ing** \-ˈdish-ning, -ə-ning\ **1** : to test in an audition ⟨*audition* a new trumpeter⟩ **2** : to give a trial performance ⟨the singers *auditioned* for the choir⟩

au·di·tor \ˈód-ət-ər\ *n* **1** : one that hears or listens; *esp* : a member of an audience **2** : a person authorized to audit accounts

au·di·to·ri·um \ˌód-ə-ˈtōr-ē-əm, -ˈtór-\ *n* **1** : the part of a public building where an audience sits **2** : a room, hall, or building used for public gatherings

au·di·to·ry \ˈód-ə-ˌtōr-ē, -ˌtór-\ *adj* : of or relating to hearing or to the sense or organs of hearing ⟨*auditory* sensation⟩

auditory canal *n* : a narrow tube that leads from the opening of the outer ear to the eardrum and through which sound passes

auditory nerve *n* : either of the 8th pair of cranial nerves that connect the inner ear with the brain and transmit nerve impulses concerned with hearing and balance

Au·ge·an \ó-ˈjē-ən\ *adj* : extremely difficult and sometimes distasteful [from *Augeas,* king of Elis; from the legend that his stable, left neglected for 30 years, was finally cleaned by Hercules]

Augean stable *n* : a condition or place marked by great accumulation of filth or corruption

au·ger \ˈó-gər\ *n* **1** : a tool for boring holes in wood **2** : any of various instruments made like an auger and used for boring (as in soil) [Middle English *nauger* (the phrase *a nauger* being understood as *an auger*), from Old English *nafogār,* from *nafu* "nave" + *gār* "spear"; from its use for boring holes in the naves of wheels]

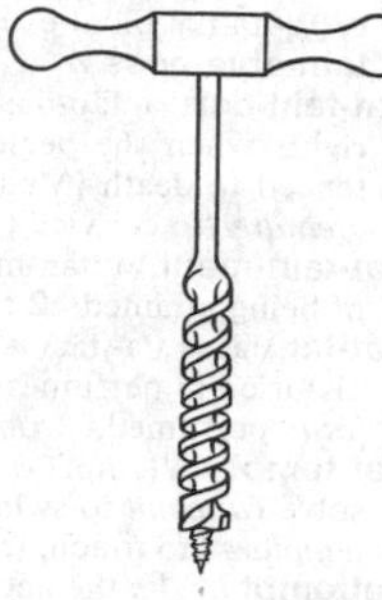

auger 1

Word History Old English *nafela,* "navel," is closely related to Old English *nafu,* "nave." The nave is the central part of a wheel. From it the spokes radiate, and through it a hole is pierced for the axle. (This is not the same word as the *nave* of a church.) The navel is the depression more or less in the center of a person's abdomen. In Old English a compound was formed from *nafu* and *gār,* "spear." *Nafogār* was the "nave spear," the tool used to pierce the hole in the nave of a wheel. The form of the word became *nauger* in Middle English, and in the 15th century *a nauger* began to be divided as *an auger.* Thus we have the modern name of a tool used for boring holes.

[1]**aught** \ˈót, ˈät\ *pron* **1** : ANYTHING **2** : ALL ⟨for *aught* I care, you can stay home⟩ [Old English *āwiht,* from *ā* "ever" + *wiht* "creature, thing"]

[2]**aught** *n* **1** : ZERO 1 **2** : the first decade of a century [*naught,* the phrase *a naught* being understood as *an aught*]

au·gite \ˈó-ˌjīt\ *n* : a black to dark green variety of pyroxene [Latin *augites,* a kind of precious stone, from Greek *augitēs*]

aug·ment \óg-ˈment\ *vb* **1** : to enlarge or increase especially in size, amount, or degree **2** : to add to [Medieval French *augmenter,* from Late Latin *augmentare,* from *augmentum* "increase," from Latin *augēre* "to increase"] — **aug·ment·er** *n*

aug·men·ta·tion \ˌóg-mən-ˈtā-shən, -ˌmen-\ *n* **1** : the act of augmenting **2** : something that augments : INCREASE, ENLARGEMENT

aug·men·ta·tive \óg-ˈment-ət-iv\ *adj* : capable of augmenting or serving to augment

augmented reality *n* : an enhanced version of reality created by the use of technology to overlay digital information on an image of something being viewed through a device (as a smartphone camera); *also* : the technology used to create augmented reality

au gra·tin \ō-ˈgrät-n, ó-, -ˈgrat-\ *adj* : covered with bread crumbs or grated cheese and browned [French, literally, "with the burned scrapings from the pan"]

[1]**au·gur** \ˈó-gər\ *n* : a person (as in ancient Rome) who foretells the future by omens [Latin]

[2]**augur** *vb* **1** : to predict especially from signs or omens **2** : to serve as a sign : INDICATE ⟨the good response *augurs* success⟩

au·gu·ry \ˈó-gyə-rē, -gə-\ *n, pl* **-ries** **1** : telling the future from omens **2** : an indication of the future : OMEN

au·gust \ó-ˈgəst\ *adj* : marked by majestic dignity or grandeur [Latin *augustus*] — **au·gust·ly** *adv* — **au·gust·ness** *n*

Au·gust \ˈó-gəst\ *n* : the 8th month of the year according to the Gregorian calendar [Latin *Augustus,* from Augustus Caesar]

Au·gus·tan \ó-ˈgəs-tən\ *adj* : of, relating to, or characteristic of Augustus Caesar or his time — **Augustan** *n*

[1]**Au·gus·tin·i·an** \ˌó-gə-ˈstin-ē-ən\ *adj* **1** : of or relating to Saint Augustine or his doctrines **2** : of or relating to any of several

religious orders under a rule ascribed to Saint Augustine — **Au·gus·tin·i·an·ism** \-ē-ə-ˌniz-əm\ *n*

[2]Augustinian *n* **1 :** a follower of Saint Augustine **2 :** a member of an Augustinian order; *esp* **:** a friar of the Hermits of Saint Augustine founded in 1256 and devoted to educational, missionary, and parish work

auk \ˈȯk\ *n* **:** any of several black-and-white short-necked diving seabirds that breed in colder parts of the northern hemisphere [Norwegian or Icelandic *alk, alka*]

auk

auld \ˈōl, ˈōld, ˈäl, ˈäld\ *adj, chiefly Scottish* **:** OLD

auld lang syne \ˌōl-ˌang-ˈzīn, -ˌdang-, -ˌlang-, -ˌdlang-, ˌōl-\ *n* **:** the good old times [Scots, literally, "old long ago"]

aunt \ˈant, ˈänt\ *n* **1 :** the sister of one's father or mother **2 :** the wife of one's uncle [Medieval French *ante,* from Latin *amita*]

au·ra \ˈȯr-ə\ *n* **1 :** a distinctive atmosphere or impression surrounding a person or thing ⟨an *aura* of respectability⟩ **2 :** a luminous radiation **:** NIMBUS [Latin, "air, breeze," from Greek]

au·ral \ˈȯr-əl\ *adj* **:** of or relating to the ear or sense of hearing [Latin *auris* "ear"] — **au·ral·ly** \-ə-lē\ *adv*

au·re·ate \ˈȯr-ē-ət\ *adj* **1 :** of a golden color or brilliance **2 :** marked by an overly careful and pompous way of speaking ⟨*aureate* rhetoric⟩ [Medieval Latin *aureatus* "adorned with gold," from Latin *aureus* "golden," from *aurum* "gold"]

au·re·ole \ˈȯr-ē-ˌōl\ *or* **au·re·o·la** \ȯ-ˈrē-ə-lə\ *n* **1 :** a radiant light around the head or body of a representation of a sacred person **2 :** a bright area surrounding a bright light (as the sun) when seen through thin cloud or mist [Medieval Latin *aureola,* from Latin *aureolus* "golden," from *aurum* "gold"]

au re·voir \ˌōr-ə-ˈvwär, ˌȯr-\ *n* **:** GOOD-BYE [French, literally, "till seeing again"]

au·ric \ˈȯr-ik\ *adj* **:** of, relating to, or derived from gold especially when trivalent [Latin *aurum* "gold"]

au·ri·cle \ˈȯr-i-kəl\ *n* **1 :** PINNA 1b **2 :** a small pouch in each atrium of the human heart [Latin *auricula,* from *auris* "ear"]

au·ric·u·lar \ȯ-ˈrik-yə-lər\ *adj* **1 :** of or relating to the ear or the sense of hearing **2 :** told privately ⟨an *auricular* confession⟩ **3 :** known by the sense of hearing **4 :** of or relating to an auricle [Latin *auricula* "little ear," from *auris* "ear"]

au·rif·er·ous \ȯ-ˈrif-rəs, -ə-rəs\ *adj* **:** containing gold [Latin *aurum* "gold"]

Au·ri·ga \ȯ-ˈri-gə\ *n* **:** a constellation between Perseus and Gemini [Latin, literally, "charioteer"]

Au·ri·gna·cian \ˌȯr-ēn-ˈyā-shən\ *adj* **:** of or relating to an Upper Paleolithic culture with finely made stone and bone tools, paintings, and engravings [*Aurignac,* France]

au·rochs \ˈau̇r-ˌäks, ˈȯr-\ *n, pl* **aurochs :** an extinct large long-horned wild ox of Europe that is the wild ancestor of domestic cattle [German]

au·ro·ra \ə-ˈrōr-ə, ȯ-ˈrōr-, -ˈrȯr-\ *n, pl* **auroras** *or* **au·ro·rae** \-ˌē\ **1 :** DAWN 1 **2 :** AURORA BOREALIS **3 :** AURORA AUSTRALIS [Latin] — **au·ro·ral** \-əl\ *adj*

aurora aus·tra·lis \-ȯ-ˈstrā-ləs, -ä-ˈstrā-\ *n* **:** a display of light in the southern hemisphere corresponding to the aurora borealis [New Latin, literally, "southern aurora"]

aurora bo·re·al·is \-ˌbōr-ē-ˈal-əs, -ˌbȯr-\ *n* **:** streamers or arches of light in the sky at night of geomagnetic and electrical origin that appear to best advantage in the arctic regions [New Latin, literally, "northern aurora"]

aus·cul·ta·tion \ˌȯ-skəl-ˈtā-shən\ *n* **:** the act of listening to sounds arising within organs (as the lungs) as an aid to diagnosis and treatment [Latin *auscultatio* "act of listening," from *auscultare* "to listen"] — **aus·cul·tate** \ˈȯ-skəl-ˌtāt\ *vt*

aus·pice \ˈȯ-spəs\ *n, pl* **aus·pic·es** \-spə-səz, -ˌsēz\ **1 :** observation especially of the flight and feeding of birds to discover omens **2 :** OMEN; *esp* **:** a favorable omen **3** *pl* **:** kindly patronage and guidance ⟨a concert given under the *auspices* of the school⟩ [Latin *auspicium,* from *auspex* "diviner by birds," from *avis* "bird" + *specere* "to look at"]

aus·pi·cious \ȯ-ˈspish-əs\ *adj* **1 :** promising success **:** FAVORABLE ⟨an *auspicious* beginning⟩ **2 :** blessed with good auspices **:** HAPPY, FORTUNATE ⟨on this *auspicious* occasion⟩ — **aus·pi·cious·ly** *adv* — **aus·pi·cious·ness** *n*

aus·tere \ȯ-ˈstiər\ *adj* **1 a :** stern and cold in appearance or manner ⟨*austere* Puritans⟩ **b :** SOMBER, GRAVE ⟨an *austere* critic⟩ **2 :** living a harsh life with few pleasures **:** morally strict **:** ASCETIC **3 :** plainly simple and unadorned ⟨an *austere* office⟩ ⟨an *austere* style of writing⟩ ⟨wore *austere* black⟩ **4 :** giving little or no scope for pleasure ⟨an *austere* budget⟩ ⟨*austere* diets⟩ [Medieval French, from Latin *austerus,* from Greek *austēros* "harsh, severe"] ***synonyms*** see SEVERE — **aus·tere·ly** *adv* — **aus·tere·ness** *n*

aus·ter·i·ty \ȯ-ˈster-ət-ē\ *n, pl* **-ties 1 :** the quality or state of being austere **2 :** an austere act, manner, or attitude **3 :** enforced or extreme economy

[1]Austr- *or* **Austro-** *combining form* **1 :** south **:** southern **2 :** Australian and ⟨*Austro*-Malayan⟩ [Latin *Austr-, Auster* "south wind"]

[2]Austr- *or* **Austro-** *combining form* **:** Austrian and ⟨*Austro*-Hungarian⟩

aus·tral \ˈȯs-trəl, ˈäs-\ *adj* **:** of or relating to the southern hemisphere

[1]Aus·tra·lian \ȯ-ˈstrāl-yən, ä-\ *adj* **:** of, relating to, or characteristic of Australia or its people

[2]Australian *n* **1 :** a native or inhabitant of the Australian commonwealth **2 :** a group of about 200 languages spoken by the aboriginal inhabitants of Australia

Australian ballot *n* **:** an official ballot printed at public expense containing the names of all candidates and all proposals, distributed only at the polling place, and marked in secret

Aus·tra·loid \ˈȯs-trə-ˌlȯid, ˈäs-\ *adj* **:** of or relating to a human population group including the Australian aborigines and related peoples — **Australoid** *n*

aus·tra·lo·pith·e·cine \ȯ-ˌstra-lō-ˈpith-ə-ˌsīn, ä-ˌstrā-\ *adj* **:** of or relating to a group of extinct southern and eastern African hominids with humanlike dentition and relatively small brains [Latin *australis* "southern" + Greek *pithēkos* "ape"] — **australopithecine** *n*

Aus·tro·ne·sian \ˌȯs-trə-ˈnē-zhən, ˌäs-\ *n* **:** a family of languages spoken in Indonesia, the Philippines, Madagascar, central and south Pacific island groups, Taiwan, and parts of mainland southeast Asia [*Austronesia,* islands of the southern Pacific] — **Austronesian** *adj*

aut- *or* **auto-** *combining form* **1 :** self **:** same one ⟨*auto*biography⟩ **2 :** automatic **:** self-acting **:** self-regulating [Greek *autos* "same, self"]

aut·ecol·o·gy \ˌȯt-i-ˈkäl-ə-jē\ *n* **:** ecology dealing with individual organisms or individual kinds of organisms — **aut·eco·log·i·cal** \ˌȯt-ˌē-kə-ˈläj-i-kəl, -ek-ə-\ *adj*

au·then·tic \ə-ˈthent-ik, ȯ-\ *adj* **1 :** being really what it seems to be **:** GENUINE ⟨an *authentic* signature of George Washington⟩ **2 :** made to be or look just like an original ⟨an *authentic* copy of an antique table⟩ ⟨*authentic* Mexican food⟩ [Medieval French *autentik,* derived from Greek *authentikos,* from *authentēs* "perpetrator, master"] — **au·then·ti·cal·ly** \-ˈthent-i-kə-lē, -klē\ *adv* — **au·then·tic·i·ty** \ˌȯ-ˌthen-ˈtis-ət-ē, -thən-\ *n*

synonyms AUTHENTIC, GENUINE, BONA FIDE mean being actually and exactly what is claimed. AUTHENTIC implies being fully trustworthy as according with fact or actuality ⟨an *authentic* record of the campaign⟩. GENUINE implies accordance with an original or an accepted type without counterfeiting, admixture, or adulteration ⟨*genuine* maple syrup⟩. BONA FIDE often applies when good faith or sincerity is in question ⟨a *bona fide* proposal⟩.

au·then·ti·cate \ȯ-ˈthent-i-ˌkāt, ə-\ *vt* **:** to prove, establish, or attest to be authentic ***synonyms*** see CONFIRM — **au·then·ti·ca·tion** \ə-ˌthent-i-ˈkā-shən, ȯ-\ *n* — **au·then·ti·ca·tor** \ə-ˈthent-i-ˌkāt-ər, ȯ-\ *n*

au·thor \ˈȯ-thər\ *n* **1 :** a person who writes or composes a literary work (as a book) **2 :** one that originates or makes **:** CREATOR ⟨the *author* of the plan⟩ [Medieval French *auctor, autor,* from Latin *auctor* "promoter, originator, author," from *augēre* "to increase"] — **au·thor** *vt* — **au·tho·ri·al** \ȯ-ˈthōr-ē-əl, -ˈthȯr-\ *adj*

au•thor•ess \'ȯ-thə-rəs, -thrəs\ *n* : a woman or girl who is an author

au•thor•i•tar•i•an \ə-ˌthȯr-ə-'ter-ē-ən, ȯ-, -ˌthär-\ *adj* **1** : relating to or expecting strict obedience to one's authority ⟨*authoritarian* parents⟩ **2** : based on the principle that the leader and not the people have the final authority ⟨an *authoritarian* government⟩ — **authoritarian** *n* — **au•thor•i•tar•i•an•ism** \-ē-ə-ˌniz-əm\ *n*

au•thor•i•ta•tive \ə-'thȯr-ə-ˌtāt-iv, ȯ-, -'thär-\ *adj* **1** : having authority : coming from or based on authority ⟨*authoritative* decisions⟩ **2** : showing reliable authority and expertise ⟨the *authoritative* reference on pirates⟩ — **au•thor•i•ta•tive•ly** *adv* — **au•thor•i•ta•tive•ness** *n*

au•thor•i•ty \ə-'thȯr-ət-ē, ȯ-, -'thär-\ *n, pl* **-ties** **1 a** : a fact, statement, or prior decision used to support a position **b** : a person appealed to as an expert **2** : the right to give commands or to carry out or enforce others' commands **3** : a person or persons having powers of government **4** : the quality of being convincing [Medieval French *auctorité,* from Latin *auctoritas* "opinion, decision, power," from *auctor* "author"]

au•tho•rize \'ȯ-thə-ˌrīz\ *vt* **1** : to give authority to : EMPOWER **2** : to establish by or as if by authority : SANCTION ⟨customs *authorized* by time⟩ ⟨*authorize* a loan⟩ — **au•tho•ri•za•tion** \ˌȯ-thə-rə-'zā-shən, -thrə-'zā-\ *n* — **au•tho•riz•er** \'ȯ-thə-ˌrī-zər\ *n*

Authorized Version *n* : a revision of the English Bible made under James I, published in 1611, and widely used by Protestants — called also *King James Version*

au•thor•ship \'ȯ-thər-ˌship\ *n* **1** : the profession of writing **2** : the origin of a literary or artistic work ⟨a novel of unknown *authorship*⟩

au•tism \'ȯ-ˌtiz-əm\ *n* : a variable disorder that is characterized especially by impaired ability to form normal social relationships and communicate with others and by engagement in repetitive behaviors [*aut-* + *-ism*] — **au•tis•tic** \ȯ-'tis-tik\ *adj*

au•to \'ȯt-ō, 'ät-\ *n, pl* **autos** : AUTOMOBILE

auto- — see AUT-

au•to•bi•og•ra•phy \ˌȯt-ə-bī-'äg-rə-fē, -bē-\ *n* : one's own biography told by oneself — **au•to•bi•og•ra•pher** \-rə-fər\ *n* — **au•to•bio•graph•i•cal** \-'graf-i-kəl\ *also* **au•to•bio•graph•ic** \-'graf-ik\ *adj* — **au•to•bio•graph•i•cal•ly** \-i-kə-lē, -klē\ *adv*

au•toch•tho•nous \ȯ-'täk-thə-nəs\ *adj* : INDIGENOUS, NATIVE ⟨*autochthonous* malaria⟩ [Greek *autochthōn,* from *autos* "same, self" + *chthōn* "earth"]

au•to•clave \'ȯt-ō-ˌklāv\ *n* : an apparatus (as for sterilizing) using steam under pressure [French, from *aut-* + Latin *clavis* "key"] — **autoclave** *vt*

au•toc•ra•cy \ȯ-'täk-rə-sē\ *n, pl* **-cies** **1** : government in which one person possesses unlimited power **2** : a community or state governed by autocracy

au•to•crat \'ȯt-ə-ˌkrat\ *n* : a person having or ruling with unlimited power

au•to•crat•ic \ˌȯt-ə-'krat-ik\ *adj* : of, relating to, characteristic of, or resembling autocracy or an autocrat ⟨*autocratic* rule⟩ — **au•to•crat•i•cal•ly** \-'krat-i-kə-lē, -klē\ *adv*

au•to•cross \'ȯt-ō-ˌkrȯs, 'ät-\ *n* : an automobile contest that tests driving skill [*auto* + moto*cross*]

au•to•erot•i•cism \ˌȯt-ō-i-'rät-ə-ˌsiz-əm\ *n* : sexual gratification without the participation of someone else — **au•to•erot•ic** \-'rät-ik\ *adj*

au•tog•e•nous \ȯ-'täj-ə-nəs\ *also* **au•to•gen•ic** \ˌȯt-ə-'jen-ik\ *adj* : originating within or derived from the same individual ⟨an *autogenous* graft⟩ — **au•tog•e•nous•ly** *adv*

[1]**au•to•graph** \'ȯt-ə-ˌgraf\ *n* : something written with one's own hand; *esp* : a person's handwritten signature

[2]**autograph** *vt* : to write one's signature in or on

au•to•im•mune \ˌȯt-ō-im-'yün\ *adj* : of, relating to, or caused by an abnormal condition in which an organism's immune system attacks and destroys parts of its own cells or tissues ⟨multiple sclerosis is an *autoimmune* disease⟩

au•tol•o•gous \ȯ-'täl-ə-gəs\ *adj* : derived from the same individual; *also* : involving one individual as both donor and recipient ⟨an *autologous* blood transfusion⟩ [*aut-* + *-ologous* (as in *homologous*)]

Au•to•mat \'ȯt-ə-ˌmat\ *service mark* — used for a cafeteria in which food is obtained especially from vending machines

au•to•mate \'ȯt-ə-ˌmāt\ *vb* **1** : to operate by automation **2** : to convert to mainly automatic operation

automated teller machine *n* : ATM

[1]**au•to•mat•ic** \ˌȯt-ə-'mat-ik\ *adj* **1 a** : largely or wholly involuntary; *esp* : REFLEX 2 **b** : acting or done spontaneously or unconsciously **c** : done or produced as if by machine : MECHANICAL **2** : having a self-acting or self-regulating mechanism ⟨*automatic* washer⟩ **3** : firing repeatedly until the trigger is released ⟨an *automatic* rifle⟩ [Greek *automatos* "self-acting"] ***synonyms*** see SPONTANEOUS — **au•to•mat•i•cal•ly** \-'mat-i-kə-lē, -klē\ *adv*

[2]**automatic** *n* : an automatic machine or apparatus; *esp* : an automatic firearm

au•to•ma•tion \ˌȯt-ə-'mā-shən\ *n* **1** : the method of making an apparatus, a process, or a system operate automatically **2** : the state of being operated automatically **3** : automatic operation of an apparatus, process, or system by mechanical or electronic devices that take the place of human operators

au•tom•a•tize \ȯ-'täm-ə-ˌtīz\ *vt* : to make automatic — **au•tom•a•ti•za•tion** \ȯ-ˌtäm-ət-ə-'zā-shən\ *n*

au•tom•a•ton \ȯ-'täm-ət-ən, -'täm-ə-ˌtän\ *n, pl* **-atons** *or* **-a•ta** \-ət-ə\ **1** : a mechanism that is relatively self-operating; *esp* : ROBOT **2** : a person who acts in a mechanical fashion

[1]**au•to•mo•bile** \'ȯt-ə-mō-ˌbēl, ˌȯt-ə-mō-'bēl, ˌȯt-ə-'mō-ˌbēl\ *adj* : AUTOMOTIVE

[2]**automobile** *n* : a usually four-wheeled motor vehicle designed for passenger transportation on streets and roadways and commonly propelled by an internal combustion engine — **automobile** *vi* — **au•to•mo•bil•ist** \-mo-'bē-ləst\ *n*

au•to•mo•tive \ˌȯt-ə-'mōt-iv\ *adj* **1** : SELF-PROPELLED **2** : of, relating to, or concerned with self-propelled vehicles and especially automobiles and motorcycles

au•to•nom•ic \ˌȯt-ə-'näm-ik\ *adj* : of, relating to, controlled by, or being part of the autonomic nervous system — **au•to•nom•i•cal•ly** \-'näm-i-kə-lē, -klē\ *adv*

autonomic nervous system *n* : a part of the vertebrate nervous system that regulates activity (as of glands, cardiac muscle, or smooth muscle) not under voluntary control and that consists of the parasympathetic nervous system and the sympathetic nervous system

au•ton•o•mous \ȯ-'tän-ə-məs\ *adj* : possessing autonomy : SELF-GOVERNING ⟨an *autonomous* country⟩ **2** : existing, responding, reacting, or developing independently of the whole ⟨an *autonomous* growth⟩ [Greek *autonomos* "independent," from *autos* "self" + *nomos* "law"] — **au•ton•o•mous•ly** *adv*

au•ton•o•my \-mē\ *n, pl* **-mies** : the power or right of self-government

au•top•sy \'ȯ-ˌtäp-sē, 'ȯt-əp-\ *n, pl* **-sies** : an examination of a dead body especially to find out the cause of death [Greek *autopsia* "act of seeing with one's own eyes," from *autos* "self" + *opsis* "sight"] — **autopsy** *vt*

au•to•ra•dio•graph \ˌȯt-ō-'rād-ē-ə-ˌgraf\ *or* **au•to•ra•dio•gram** \-ˌgram\ *n* : an image produced on a photographic film or plate by the radiations from a radioactive substance in an object — **au•to•ra•dio•graph•ic** \-ˌrād-ē-ə-'graf-ik\ *adj* — **au•to•ra•di•og•ra•phy** \-ˌrād-ē-'äg-rə-fē\ *n*

au•to•some \'ȯt-ə-ˌsōm\ *n* : a chromosome other than a sex chromosome — **au•to•so•mal** \ˌȯt-ə-'sō-məl\ *adj*

au•to•sug•ges•tion \ˌȯt-ō-səg-'jes-chən, -sə-'jes-, -'jesh-\ *n* : an influencing of one's own attitudes, behavior, or physical condition by mental processes other than conscious thought : SELF-HYPNOSIS

au•tot•o•my \ȯ-'tät-ə-mē\ *n, pl* **-mies** : reflex separation of a part from the body : division of the body into two or more pieces

au•to•troph \'ȯt-ə-ˌtrōf, -ˌträf\ *n* : an organism (as a plant) requiring only carbon from carbon dioxide or carbonates and nitrogen from a simple inorganic compound for the synthesis of organic molecules (as glucose) necessary for life and growth [German, from Greek *autotrophos* "supplying one's own food," from *autos* "self" + *trephein* "to nourish"] — **au•to•tro•phic** \ˌȯt-ə-'trōf-ik\ *adj* — **au•to•tro•phi•cal•ly** \ˌȯt-ə-'träf-i-kə-lē, -klē\ *adv* — **au•to•tro•phy** \ȯ-'tä-trə-fē\ *n*

au•tumn \'ȯt-əm\ *n* **1** : the season between summer and winter comprising in the northern hemisphere usually the months of September, October, and November or, as determined astronomically, extending from the September equinox to the December solstice — called also *fall* **2** : a time of full maturity or beginning decline ⟨in the *autumn* of our lives⟩ [Latin *autumnus*] — **au•tum•nal** \ȯ-'təm-nəl\ *adj*

autumn crocus *n* : an autumn-flowering herb related to the lilies that is a source of colchicine

[1]**aux·il·ia·ry** \óg-ˈzil-yə-rē; -ˈzil-rē, -ə-rē\ *adj* **1 :** offering or providing help : SUPPLEMENTARY ⟨an *auxiliary* engine⟩ **2 :** being a verb that accompanies another verb and typically expresses such things as person, number, mood, or tense [Latin *auxiliaris,* from *auxilium* "help"]

[2]**auxiliary** *n, pl* **-ries** **1 :** an auxiliary person, group, or device **2 :** an auxiliary verb

auxiliary verb *n* : HELPING VERB

aux·in \ˈók-sən\ *n* : a plant hormone (as indoleacetic acid) that stimulates shoot elongation and usually regulates other growth processes (as root formation) in the plant; *also* : PLANT HORMONE [Greek *auxein* "to increase"]

[1]**avail** \ə-ˈvāl\ *vb* : to be of use or advantage : HELP ⟨all our effort *availed* nothing⟩ [Medieval French *availler,* probably from *a-* "ad-" + *valer, valoir* "to be of worth," from Latin *valēre* "to be strong"] — **avail oneself of :** to make use of : take advantage of ⟨we must *avail ourselves of* the facilities we now have⟩

[2]**avail** *n* : help or benefit toward reaching a goal : USE ⟨the effort was of little *avail*⟩

avail·able \ə-ˈvā-lə-bəl\ *adj* **1 :** present or ready for use : at hand ⟨will use any *available* excuse to stay home⟩ **2 :** ACCESSIBLE, OBTAINABLE ⟨the book is *available* at your library⟩ **3 :** qualified or willing to do something ⟨*available* workers⟩ **4 :** present in such chemical or physical form as to be usable (as by a plant) — **avail·abil·i·ty** \ə-ˌvā-lə-ˈbil-ət-ē\ *n* — **avail·able·ness** \ə-ˈvā-lə-bəl-nəs\ *n* — **avail·ably** \-blē\ *adv*

av·a·lanche \ˈav-ə-ˌlanch\ *n* **1 :** a large mass of snow, ice, earth, or rock sliding down a mountainside or over a steep cliff **2 :** a sudden overwhelming rush of something seeming to come down like an avalanche ⟨an *avalanche* of words⟩ [French]

avant–garde \ˌäv-ˌän-ˈgärd, ˌäv-ˌänt-, ˌav-, ˌav-; ə-ˈvänt-\ *n* : people (as artists) who create or use new or experimental ideas [French, "vanguard"] — **avant–garde** *adj*

av·a·rice \ˈav-rəs, -ə-rəs\ *n* : too strong a desire for wealth or gain : GREED [Medieval French, from Latin *avaritia,* from *avarus* "greedy," from *avēre* "to crave"]

av·a·ri·cious \ˌav-ə-ˈrish-əs\ *adj* : greedy especially for money ***synonyms*** see COVETOUS — **av·a·ri·cious·ly** *adv* — **av·a·ri·cious·ness** *n*

avast \ə-ˈvast\ *imperative verb* — used as a nautical command to stop or cease [perhaps from Dutch *houd vast* "hold fast"]

av·a·tar \ˈav-ə-ˌtär\ *n* : an embodiment (as of a concept, philosophy, or tradition) usually in human form [Sanskrit *avatāra* "descent, incarnation of a deity"]

avaunt \ə-ˈvónt, ə-ˈvänt\ *adv* : AWAY, HENCE [Medieval French *avant,* from Latin *abante* "forward, before," from *ab* "from" + *ante* "before"]

Ave Ma·ria \ˌäv-ˌā-mə-ˈrē-ə\ *n* : HAIL MARY [Medieval Latin, "hail, Mary"]

avenge \ə-ˈvenj\ *vt* : to take vengeance for or on behalf of ⟨*avenge* an insult⟩ [Medieval French *avenger,* from *a-* "ad-" + *venger* "to avenge," from Latin *vindicare*] — **aveng·er** *n*

synonyms AVENGE, REVENGE mean getting back at someone for their wrongdoing. AVENGE implies inflicting deserved punishment especially on one who has injured someone other than oneself ⟨*avenged* their leader's death⟩. REVENGE implies getting even or paying back in kind or degree ⟨*revenged* the insult⟩.

av·e·nue \ˈav-ə-ˌnü, -ˌnyü\ *n* **1 :** a way or passage by which a place may be approached or left **2 :** a way or means to an end **3 :** a street especially when broad and attractive [Middle French, from *avenir* "to come to," from Latin *advenire,* from *ad-* + *venire* "to come"]

aver \ə-ˈvər\ *vt* **averred; aver·ring :** to declare positively : ASSERT [Middle French *averer* "to verify," derived from Latin *ad-* + *verus* "true"]

[1]**av·er·age** \ˈav-rij, -ə-rij\ *n* **1 :** a single value that represents a set of other values; *esp* : ARITHMETIC MEAN **2 :** a level typical of a group, class, or series ⟨their work is above the *average*⟩ **3 :** a ratio of successful tries to total tries ⟨batting *average*⟩ [earlier *average* "distribution of costs of damage to ship or cargo," from Middle French *avarie* "damage to ship or cargo," from Italian *avaria,* from Arabic *ʿawārīya* "damaged merchandise"] — **on average** *or* **on the average :** taking the typical example of the group under consideration ⟨prices have increased *on average* by five percent⟩

Word History *Average* came into English from Middle French *avarie,* a derivative (by way of Italian) of Arabic *ʿawārīya,* "damaged merchandise." French *avarie* originally meant damage sustained by a ship or its cargo. It came, by transference, to mean the expenses of such damage and later included other maritime expenses. When the English borrowed the French word, they altered it to conform to the pattern of such English words as *pilotage* and *towage.* When a ship or its cargo was damaged at sea, the owners or insurers of both ship and cargo had to share the expense or average. An average-adjuster determined a fair division of costs among those held accountable. An *average* then became any equal distribution or division, like the determination of an arithmetic mean. Soon the arithmetic mean itself was called an *average.* Now the word may be applied to any mean or middle value or level.

synonyms AVERAGE, MEAN, MEDIAN apply to a value that represents in some way a middle point between extremes. AVERAGE is the result obtained by dividing the sum total of a set of figures by the number of figures in that set ⟨scored an *average* of 85 on tests⟩. MEAN may be the average or it may be the value midway between two extremes ⟨a high of 70° and a low of 50° give a *mean* of 60°⟩. MEDIAN applies to the value above and below which there is an equal number of values ⟨the *average* of a group of persons earning 3, 4, 5, 8, and 10 dollars an hour is 6 dollars an hour, but the *median* is 5 dollars⟩.

[2]**average** *adj* **1 :** equaling or close to an arithmetic mean **2 a :** being about midway between extremes ⟨*average* height⟩ **b :** being not out of the ordinary : COMMON ⟨the *average* person⟩ — **av·er·age·ly** *adv* — **av·er·age·ness** *n*

[3]**average** *vb* **1 :** to do, get, or have on the average ⟨we *average* six calls a day⟩ **2 :** to amount to on the average : be usually ⟨they *average* four feet in height⟩ **3 :** to find the average of **4 :** to divide among a number proportionally ⟨*average* a loss⟩

averse \ə-ˈvərs\ *adj* : having an active feeling of repugnance or distaste ⟨*averse* to strenuous exercise⟩ [Latin *aversus,* past participle of *avertere* "to turn away, avert"] — **averse·ly** *adv* — **averse·ness** *n*

aver·sion \ə-ˈvər-zhən\ *n* **1 :** a strong feeling of dislike ⟨an *aversion* to spiders⟩ **2 :** something disliked ⟨carrots are my *aversion*⟩

avert \ə-ˈvərt\ *vt* **1 :** to turn away ⟨*avert* one's eyes⟩ **2 :** to prevent from happening ⟨barely *averted* an accident⟩ [Middle French *avertir,* from Latin *avertere,* from *ab-* + *vertere* "to turn"] ***synonyms*** see PREVENT

avi·an \ˈā-vē-ən\ *adj* : of, relating to, or derived from birds [Latin *avis* "bird"]

avi·ary \ˈā-vē-ˌer-ē\ *n, pl* **-ar·ies :** a place (as a large cage or a building) where many live birds are kept usually for exhibition

avi·a·tion \ˌā-vē-ˈā-shən, ˌav-ē-\ *n* **1 :** the operation of heavier-than-air aircraft **2 :** military aircraft **3 :** aircraft manufacture, development, and design [French, from Latin *avis* "bird"] — **aviation** *adj*

aviation cadet *n* : a student officer in the air force

avi·a·tor \ˈā-vē-ˌāt-ər, ˈav-ē-\ *n* : the pilot of an aircraft

avi·a·trix \ˌā-vē-ˈā-triks, ˌav-ē-\ *n, pl* **-trix·es** \-trik-səz\ *or* **-tri·ces** \-trə-ˌsēz\ : a woman who is an aviator

av·id \ˈav-əd\ *adj* **1 :** desirous to the point of being greedy : craving very much ⟨*avid* for praise⟩ **2 :** marked by eagerness and enthusiasm ⟨*avid* readers⟩ [Latin *avidus,* from *avēre* "to desire, crave"] — **avid·i·ty** \ə-ˈvid-ət-ē, a-\ *n* — **av·id·ly** \ˈav-əd-lē\ *adv* — **av·id·ness** *n*

avi·on·ics \ˌā-vē-ˈän-iks, ˌav-ē-\ *n* : the development and production of electrical and electronic devices for use in aviation, missilery, and astronautics [*aviation* electronics] — **avi·on·ic** \-ik\ *adj*

avi·ta·min·osis \ˌā-ˌvīt-ə-mə-ˈnō-səs\ *n, pl* **-min·oses** \-ˈnō-ˌsēz\ : disease resulting from a deficiency of one or more vitamins — **avi·ta·min·ot·ic** \-mə-ˈnät-ik\ *adj*

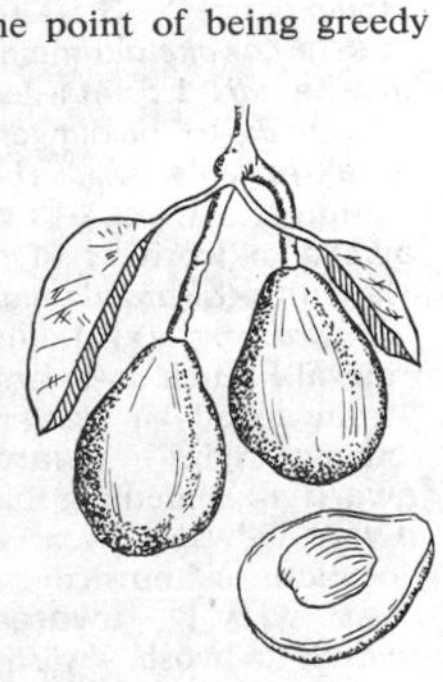

avocado

av·o·ca·do \ˌav-ə-ˈkäd-ō, ˌäv-\ *n, pl*

\ə\ **abut**	\au̇\ **out**	\i\ **tip**	\ȯ\ **saw**	\u̇\ **foot**
\ər\ **further**	\ch\ **chin**	\ī\ **life**	\ȯi\ **coin**	\y\ **yet**
\a\ **mat**	\e\ **pet**	\j\ **job**	\th\ **thin**	\yü\ **few**
\ā\ **take**	\ē\ **easy**	\ng\ **sing**	\t͟h\ **this**	\yu̇\ **cure**
\ä\ **cot, cart**	\g\ **go**	\ō\ **bone**	\ü\ **food**	\zh\ **vision**

-dos *also* **-does** : the usually green or purplish pear-shaped oily edible fruit of a tropical American tree; *also* : the tree that bears this fruit — called also *alligator pear* [Spanish *aguacate,* from Nahuatl *āhuacatl* "avocado, testicle"]

av·o·ca·tion \ˌav-ə-ˈkā-shən, ˈav-ə-ˌ\ *n* **1** : customary employment : VOCATION **2** : an occupation or interest pursued especially for enjoyment : HOBBY [Latin *avocatio,* from *avocare* "to call away," from *ab-* + *vocare* "to call"] — **av·o·ca·tion·al** \-shnəl, -shən-l\ *adj*

av·o·cet \ˈav-ə-ˌset\ *n* : any of several rather large long-legged shorebirds with webbed feet and a slender upward-curving bill [French *avocette,* from Italian *avocetta*]

Avo·ga·dro's number \ˌav-ə-ˈgäd-rōz-\ *n* : the number 6.02 x 10^{23} that equals the number of atoms or molecules in a mole of any substance [after Amedeo *Avogadro,* died 1856, Italian chemist]

avoid \ə-ˈvȯid\ *vt* **1** : to make legally void : ANNUL ⟨*avoid* a contract⟩ **2 a** : to keep away from : SHUN ⟨*avoid* quarrelsome neighbors⟩ **b** : to keep from happening ⟨*avoid* accidents⟩ **c** : to refrain from ⟨*avoid* overeating⟩ [Medieval French *avoider,* from *esvuider,* from *es-* "ex-" + *vuide* "empty, void"] — **avoid·able** \-ə-bəl\ *adj* — **avoid·ably** \-blē\ *adv* — **avoid·er** *n*

avoid·ance \ə-ˈvȯid-ns\ *n* **1** : the act of annulling **2** : the act of keeping away from or clear of

av·oir·du·pois \ˌav-ərd-ə-ˈpȯiz\ *n* **1** : AVOIRDUPOIS WEIGHT **2** : HEAVINESS, WEIGHT [Middle English *avoir de pois* "goods sold by weight," from Medieval French, literally, "goods of weight"]

avoirdupois weight *n* : the series of units of weight based on the pound of 16 ounces and the ounce of 16 drams — see MEASURE table

avouch \ə-ˈvau̇ch\ *vt* **1** : to declare positively : AFFIRM **2** : to vouch for : GUARANTEE ⟨*avouched* her reputation⟩ [Middle English *avouchen* "to cite as authority," from Middle French *avochier* "to summon," from Latin *advocare,* from *ad-* + *vocare* "to call"] — **avouch·ment** \-mənt\ *n*

avow \ə-ˈvau̇\ *vt* : to declare or acknowledge openly and frankly [Medieval French *avuer, avouer,* from Latin *advocare* "to summon," from *ad-* + *vocare* "to call"] ***synonyms*** see ASSERT

avow·al \ə-ˈvau̇-əl, -ˈvau̇l\ *n* : an open declaration or acknowledgment

avowed \ə-ˈvau̇d\ *adj* : openly acknowledged or declared : ADMITTED ⟨an *avowed* bias in the team's favor⟩ — **avowed·ly** \-ˈvau̇-əd-lē, -ˈvau̇d-lē\ *adv*

avun·cu·lar \ə-ˈvəng-kyə-lər\ *adj* : of, relating to, or characteristic of an uncle [Latin *avunculus* "maternal uncle"]

aw \ˈȯ\ *interj* — used to express mild sympathy, entreaty, disbelief, or disgust

await \ə-ˈwāt\ *vb* **1** : to wait for : stay for : EXPECT ⟨*await* a train⟩ **2** : to be ready or waiting for ⟨a reward *awaits* them⟩

[1]**awake** \ə-ˈwāk\ *vb* **awoke** \-ˈwōk\ *also* **awaked** \-ˈwākt\; **awo·ken** \-ˈwō-kən\ *or* **awaked** *also* **awoke; awak·ing 1** : to cease sleeping **2** : to become aware of something ⟨*awoke* to their danger⟩ **3** : AROUSE 1 **4** : to make or become active : STIR ⟨*awoke* old memories⟩

[2]**awake** *adj* **1** : not asleep **2** : fully conscious, alert, and aware ⟨is *awake* to the dangers of skydiving⟩

awak·en \ə-ˈwā-kən\ *vb* **awak·ened; awak·en·ing** \-ˈwāk-ning, -ə-ning\ : AWAKE — **awak·en·er** \-ˈwāk-nər, -ə-nər\ *n*

[1]**award** \ə-ˈwȯrd\ *vt* **1** : to give by judicial decision (as after a lawsuit) ⟨*award* damages⟩ **2** : to give or grant as a reward ⟨*award* a prize⟩ [Middle English *awarden* "to decide," from Medieval French *awarder, agarder* "to look at, examine, resolve," from *a-* "ad-" + *warder, garder* "to look after, guard," of Germanic origin] — **award·able** \-ə-bəl\ *adj* — **award·er** *n*

[2]**award** *n* : something that is conferred or bestowed : PRIZE

aware \ə-ˈwaər, -ˈweər\ *adj* : having or showing realization, perception, or knowledge : CONSCIOUS [Old English *gewær,* from *wær* "wary"] — **aware·ness** *n*

awash \ə-ˈwȯsh, -ˈwäsh\ *adj* **1** : washed by waves or tide **2** : floating in water **3** : overflowed by water **4** : filled or covered as if by a flood ⟨a company *awash* in profits⟩

[1]**away** \ə-ˈwā\ *adv* **1** : on the way : ALONG ⟨get *away* early⟩ **2** : from this or that place ⟨go *away*⟩ **3 a** : in another place ⟨stayed *away*⟩ **b** : in another direction ⟨turn *away*⟩ **4** : out of existence : to an end ⟨echoes dying *away*⟩ **5** : from one's possession ⟨gave *away* a fortune⟩ **6 a** : without stopping : CONTINUOUSLY ⟨clocks ticking *away*⟩ **b** : without hesitation or delay ⟨talk *away*⟩ **7** : by a long distance or interval : FAR ⟨*away* back in 1910⟩

[2]**away** *adj* **1** : absent from a place : GONE ⟨he is *away* from home⟩ **2** : DISTANT ⟨a lake 10 kilometers *away*⟩

[1]**awe** \ˈȯ\ *n* : an emotion of mixed fear, respect, and wonder that is inspired by authority or by the sacred or sublime [Middle English, "terror, awe," from Old Norse *agi* "terror"]

[2]**awe** *vt* : to inspire with awe

aweigh \ə-ˈwā\ *adj* : raised just clear of the bottom — used of an anchor

awe·some \ˈȯ-səm\ *adj* **1** : expressive of awe ⟨an *awesome* silence⟩ **2** : inspiring awe ⟨an *awesome* responsibility⟩ **3** : TERRIFIC, EXTRAORDINARY ⟨had an *awesome* time⟩ — **awe·some·ly** *adv* — **awe·some·ness** *n*

awe·struck \ˈȯ-ˌstrək\ *also* **awe·strick·en** \-ˌstrik-ən\ *adj* : filled with awe ⟨*awestruck* spectators⟩

[1]**aw·ful** \ˈȯ-fəl\ *adj* **1** : inspiring awe **2** : very disagreeable or objectionable **3** : very great ⟨took an *awful* chance⟩ — **aw·ful·ness** *n*

[2]**awful** *adv* : VERY 1, EXTREMELY ⟨*awful* tired⟩

aw·ful·ly *usually* ˈȯ-fə-lē *in sense 1,* ˈȯ-flē *in senses 2 & 3*\ *adv* **1** : in a manner to inspire awe **2** : in a disagreeable or objectionable manner **3** : VERY 2 ⟨an *awfully* cold day⟩

awhile \ə-ˈhwīl, -ˈwīl\ *adv* : for a while : for a short time

awhirl \ə-ˈhwərl, -ˈwərl\ *adj* : being in a whirl

awk·ward \ˈȯ-kwərd\ *adj* **1** : lacking dexterity or skill especially in the use of the hands or of instruments : CLUMSY **2 a** : lacking ease or grace of movement or expression ⟨*awkward* writing⟩ **b** : large and badly proportioned ⟨an *awkward* design⟩ **3** : causing embarrassment ⟨an *awkward* situation⟩ **4** : poorly adapted for use or handling ⟨an *awkward* tool⟩ [Middle English *awke* "turned the wrong way," from Old Norse *ǫfugr*] — **awk·ward·ly** *adv* — **awk·ward·ness** *n*

synonyms AWKWARD, CLUMSY, GAUCHE, INEPT mean not marked by ease especially in performance, movement, or conduct. AWKWARD is widely applicable and may suggest unhandiness or inconvenience of things, lack of muscular coordination or grace of movement, lack of tact, or embarrassment of circumstances or situation ⟨an *awkward* silence⟩. CLUMSY implies stiffness and heaviness and so connotes unwieldiness or lack of ordinary skill ⟨a *clumsy* mechanic⟩. GAUCHE implies the effects of shyness or inexperience ⟨felt *gauche* at formal parties⟩. INEPT is likely to imply a general inadequacy ⟨a hopelessly *inept* lawyer⟩.

awl \ˈȯl\ *n* : a pointed tool for marking surfaces or making small holes (as in leather or wood) [Old English *æl*]

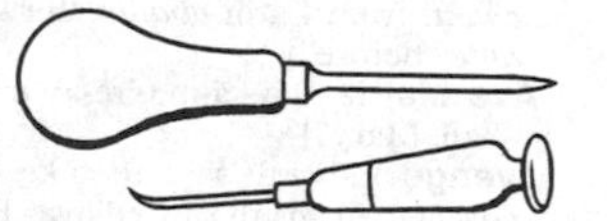
awl

awn \ˈȯn\ *n* : one of the slender bristles that terminate the glumes in some cereal and other grasses [Old Norse *ǫgn*] — **awned** \ˈȯnd\ *adj* — **awn·less** \ˈȯn-ləs\ *adj*

aw·ning \ˈȯn-ing, ˈän-\ *n* : a rooflike cover over or in front of something to provide shade or shelter [origin unknown]

awoke *past of* AWAKE

AWOL \ˈā-ˌwȯl, ˌā-ˌdəb-əl-yü-ˌō-ˈel\ *n* : a person (as a soldier or sailor) who is absent without permission [*a*bsent *w*ith*o*ut *l*eave] — **AWOL** *adv or adj*

awry \ə-ˈrī\ *adv or adj* **1** : turned or twisted toward one side : ASKEW **2** : off the right course : AMISS ⟨their plans went *awry*⟩ ***synonyms*** see CROOKED

ax *or* **axe** \ˈaks\ *n* **1** : a cutting tool that consists of a heavy edged head fixed to a handle and is used for chopping and splitting wood **2** : abrupt discharge or removal (as from a job or a budget) ⟨get the *ax*⟩ [Old English *æcs*] — **ax** *or* **axe** *vt* — **ax to grind** : a usually selfish reason for wanting something done

ax·i·al \ˈak-sē-əl\ *adj* **1** : of, relating to, or functioning as an axis **2** : situated around, in the direction of, on, or along an axis — **ax·i·al·ly** \-sē-ə-lē\ *adv*

axial skeleton *n* : the skeleton of the trunk and head

ax·il \ˈak-səl, -ˌsil\ *n* : the angle between a branch or leaf and the stem from which it arises [Latin *axilla* "armpit"]

ax·il·la \ag-ˈzil-ə, ak-ˈsil-\ *n, pl* **-lae** \-ē, -ˌī\ *or* **-las** : ARMPIT [Latin]

ax·il·lary \ˈak-sə-ˌler-ē\ *adj* **1** : of, relating to, or located near the axilla **2** : situated in or growing from an axil — **axillary** *n*

ax·i·om \'ak-sē-əm\ *n* **1 :** a rule or principle widely accepted as obviously true and not needing to be proved **2 a :** a proposition regarded as a self-evident truth **b :** POSTULATE 1 [Latin *axioma,* from Greek *axiōma,* literally, "honor," from *axioun* "to think worthy," from *axios* "worthy"]

ax·i·om·at·ic \ˌak-sē-ə-'mat-ik\ *adj* **:** taken for granted **:** SELF-EVIDENT — **ax·i·om·at·i·cal·ly** \-'mat-i-kə-lē, -klē\ *adv*

ax·is \'ak-səs\ *n, pl* **ax·es** \'ak-ˌsēz\ **1 a :** a straight line about which a body or a geometric figure rotates or may be supposed to rotate ⟨the earth's *axis*⟩ **b :** a straight line with respect to which a body or figure is symmetrical — called also *axis of symmetry* **c :** one of the reference lines of a coordinate system **2 a :** the second vertebra of the neck on which the head turns as on a pivot **b :** an anatomical structure around which parts are arranged in a symmetrical way **3 :** a plant stem **4 :** a main line of direction, motion, growth, or extension **5 :** ALLIANCE 2a **6 :** a point on which something centers ⟨an *axis* of social power⟩ [Latin, "axis, axle"]

Axis *adj* **:** of or relating to the three powers Germany, Italy, and Japan engaged against the Allies in World War II

ax·le \'ak-səl\ *n* **1 :** a pin or shaft on or with which a wheel or pair of wheels revolves **2 :** AXLETREE [from Old Norse *ǫxull* "axle"]

axle·tree \-ˌtrē\ *n* **:** a fixed bar with bearings at its ends on which wheels (as of a cart) revolve

ax·o·lotl \'ak-sə-ˌlät-l\ *n* **:** any of several salamanders of mountain lakes of Mexico and the western U.S. that ordinarily live and breed in the larval form without metamorphosing [Nahuatl *āxolōtl*]

ax·on \'ak-ˌsän\ *also* **ax·one** \-ˌsōn\ *n* **:** a usually long and single process of a neuron that usually conducts impulses away from the cell body — compare DENDRITE [Greek *axōn* "axis"]

ayah \'ī-ə; 'ä-yə, -ˌyä\ *n* **:** a nurse or maid native to India [Hindi & Urdu *āyā,* from Portuguese *aia,* from Latin *avia* "grandmother"]

aya·tol·lah \ˌī-ə-'tō-lə\ *n* **:** a religious leader among Shiite Muslims — used as a title of respect especially for one who is not an imam [derived from Arabic *āyatallāh,* literally, "sign of God"]

1**aye** *also* **ay** \'ā\ *adv* **:** FOREVER 1, ALWAYS [Old Norse *ei*]

2**aye** *also* **ay** \'ī\ *adv* **:** YES [perhaps from Middle English *ye*]

3**aye** *also* **ay** \'ī\ *n, pl* **ayes :** an affirmative vote or voter

aye–aye \'ī-ˌī\ *n* **:** a nocturnal lemur of Madagascar with large eyes and ears [French, from Malagasy *aiay*]

Ayr·shire \'aər-ˌshiər, 'eər-, -shər\ *n* **:** any of a breed of hardy dairy cattle that vary in color from white to red or brown

aza·lea \ə-'zāl-yə\ *n* **:** any of various rhododendrons with funnel-shaped flowers and usually deciduous leaves that include many grown for ornament [Greek *azaleos* "dry"]

Azer·bai·ja·ni \ˌaz-ər-ˌbī-'jän-ē, ˌäz-\ *n, pl* **Azerbaijanis** *also* **Azerbaijani 1 :** a member of a Turkic-speaking people of Azerbaijan and northwest Iran **2 :** the Turkic language of the Azerbaijanis [Persian *āzarbāyjānī,* from *Azarbāyjān* Azerbaijan] — **Azerbaijani** *adj*

Azeri \ə-'zer-ē, 'ä-zə-rē\ *n* **:** AZERBAIJANI

az·i·do·thy·mi·dine \ə-ˌzid-ō-thī-mə-dēn\ *n* **:** AZT

az·i·muth \'az-məth, -ə-məth\ *n* **:** a measurement in degrees of the distance along the horizon between a fixed point (as true north) and a vertical line that passes from the center of a celestial object to the horizon [Arabic *as-sumūt* "the azimuth," plural of *as-samt* "the way"]

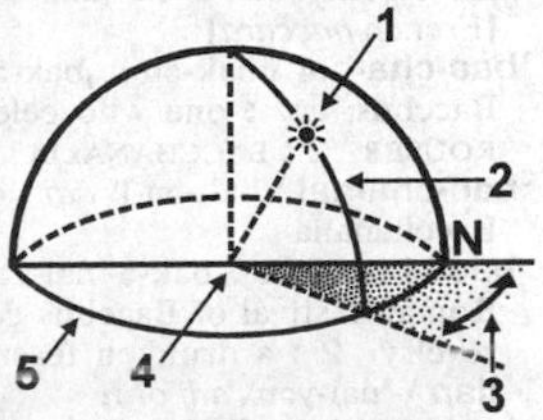

azimuth: *1* object, *2* vertical line, *3* azimuth, *4* observer, *5* horizon, *N* true north

azo \'az-ō\ *adj* **:** relating to or containing the group of nitrogen atoms –N=N– united at both ends to carbon ⟨an *azo* dye⟩ [French *azote* "nitrogen," derived from Greek *a-* + *zōē* "life"]

azon·al \ā-'zōn-l\ *adj* **:** of, relating to, or being a soil or a major soil group lacking well-developed horizons — compare INTRAZONAL

AZT \ˌā-ˌzē-'tē\ *n* **:** an antiviral drug used to treat AIDS

Az·tec \'az-ˌtek\ *n* **1 :** a member of a Nahuatl-speaking people that founded the Mexican empire and were conquered by Cortés in 1519 **2 :** NAHUATL [Spanish *azteca,* from Nahuatl *aztēcah,* plural of *aztēcatl*] — **Az·tec·an** \-ən\ *adj*

azure \'azh-ər\ *n* **:** the blue color of the clear sky [Medieval French *azeure,* derived from Arabic *lāzaward*] — **azure** *adj*

azur·ite \'azh-ə-ˌrīt\ *n* **:** a mineral $Cu_3(OH)_2(CO_3)_2$ that consists of blue basic carbonate of copper and is a copper ore

B

b \'bē\ *n, pl* **b's** *or* **bs** \'bēz\ *often cap* **1 :** the 2nd letter of the English alphabet **2 :** the musical tone B **3 :** a grade rating a student's work as good

baa \'ba, 'bä\ *n* **:** the bleat of a sheep [imitative] — **baa** *vi*

Baal \'bāl, 'bā-əl\ *n, pl* **Baals** *or* **Baa·lim** \'bā-ləm, -ə-ləm\ **:** one of the local gods of ancient Canaan [Hebrew *ba'al* "lord"]

Bab·bitt \'bab-ət\ *n* **:** a person and especially a business or professional man who accepts without thought prevailing middle-class standards [George F. *Babbitt,* character in the novel *Babbitt* (1922) by Sinclair Lewis] — **Bab·bitt·ry** \'bab-ə-trē\ *n*

bab·ble \'bab-əl\ *vb* **bab·bled; bab·bling** \'bab-ling, -ə-ling\ **1 a :** to make meaningless sounds **b :** to talk foolishly or excessively **2 :** to sound as though babbling **3 :** BLAB 1 [Middle English *babelen*] — **babble** *n* — **bab·bler** \'bab-lər, -ə-lər\ *n*

babe \'bāb\ *n* **:** INFANT, BABY

ba·bel \'bā-bəl, 'bab-əl\ *n, often cap* **1 :** a confusion of sounds or voices **2 :** a scene of noise or confusion [Hebrew *Bābhel,* a city where the building of a tower is said in the Book of Genesis to have been interrupted by the confusion of tongues]

ba·boon \ba-'bün\ *n* **:** any of several large African and Asian monkeys having a long squarish muzzle lacking hair and usually a short tail [Middle French *babouin,* from *baboue* "grimace"] — **ba·boon·ish** \-'bü-nish\ *adj*

ba·bush·ka \bə-'büsh-kə, -'bush-\ *n* **:** a kerchief for the head usually folded triangularly [Russian, "grandmother"]

1**ba·by** \'bā-bē\ *n, pl* **babies 1 a :** a very young child; *esp* **:** INFANT **b :** a very young animal **2 :** the youngest of a group **3 :** a childish person [Middle English] — **ba·by·hood** \-ˌhu̇d\ *n* — **ba·by·ish** \-ish\ *adj*

2**baby** *adj* **1 :** of, relating to, or being a baby **2 :** much smaller than the usual ⟨*baby* carrots⟩

3**baby** *vt* **ba·bied; ba·by·ing 1 :** to tend to indulge with often excessive or inappropriate care and solicitude ⟨*babied* their only child⟩ **2 :** to treat or use with care ⟨*babying* a sore knee⟩

baby back ribs *n pl* **:** pork ribs cut from the lower back ribs

baby boom *n* **:** a marked rise in birthrate (as in the U.S. immediately following World War II) — **baby boom·er** \-'bü-mər\ *n*

Bab·y·lon \'bab-ə-lən, -ˌlän\ *n* **:** a city noted for its wealth, luxury, and vice [*Babylon,* ancient capital of Babylonia]

baby oil *n* **:** a usually fragrant mineral oil that is used especially to moisturize and cleanse the skin

baby powder *n* **:** a fine powder composed mainly of talc or cornstarch that is sprinkled or rubbed on the skin especially to absorb moisture and relieve chafing

baby's breath *n* **:** a tall gypsophila with clusters of small white or pink flowers and often used in floral arrangements

\ə\ **abut**	\au̇\ **out**	\i\ **tip**	\ȯ\ **saw**	\u̇\ **foot**
\ər\ **further**	\ch\ **chin**	\ī\ **life**	\ȯi\ **coin**	\y\ **yet**
\a\ **mat**	\e\ **pet**	\j\ **job**	\th\ **thin**	\yü\ **few**
\ā\ **take**	\ē\ **easy**	\ng\ **sing**	\t͟h\ **this**	\yu̇\ **cure**
\ä\ **cot, cart**	\g\ **go**	\ō\ **bone**	\ü\ **food**	\zh\ **vision**

ba·by·sit \ˈbā-bē-ˌsit\ *vi* **-sat** \-ˌsat\; **-sit·ting** : to care for children usually during a short absence of the parents [back-formation from *babysitter*] — **ba·by·sit·ter** *n*

baby talk *n* **1** : the speech used by very young children learning to talk **2** : speech like baby talk sometimes used by adults to speak to very young children

baby tooth *n* : MILK TOOTH

bac·ca·lau·re·ate \ˌbak-ə-ˈlȯr-ē-ət, -ˈlär-\ *n* **1** : the degree of bachelor conferred by universities and colleges **2** : a sermon to a graduating class or the service at which such a sermon is delivered [Medieval Latin *baccalaureatus,* from *baccalaureus* "bachelor"]

bac·ca·rat \ˌbäk-ə-ˈrä, ˌbak-\ *n* : a card game played in casinos [French *baccara*]

[1]**bac·cha·nal** \ˈbak-ən-l; ˌbak-ə-ˈnal, -ˈnäl\ *n* **1 a** : a devotee of Bacchus; *esp* : one who celebrates the Bacchanalia **b** : CAROUSER **2** : BACCHANALIA

[2]**bac·cha·nal** \ˈbak-ən-l\ *adj* : of, relating to, or suggestive of the Bacchanalia

bac·cha·na·lia \ˌbak-ə-ˈnāl-yə\ *n, pl* **bacchanalia** **1** *pl, cap* : a Roman festival of Bacchus celebrated with dancing, song, and revelry **2** : a drunken feast : ORGY [Latin] — **bac·cha·na·lian** \-ˈnāl-yən\ *adj or n*

bac·chant \bə-ˈkant, -ˈkänt; ˈbak-ənt\ *n, pl* **bacchants** *or* **bac·chantes** \bə-ˈkants, -ˈkänts, -ˈkant-ēz, -ˈkänt-ēz\ : BACCHANAL — **bacchant** *adj*

bac·chante \bə-ˈkant, -ˈkänt, -ˈkant-ē, -ˈkänt-ē\ *n* : a priestess or woman follower of Bacchus

bac·chic \ˈbak-ik\ *adj* **1** : of or relating to Bacchus **2** : BACCHANAL

bach·e·lor \ˈbach-lər, -ə-lər\ *n* **1** : a young knight who fights under the banner of another **2** : a person who has received what is usually the lowest degree conferred by a four-year college, university, or professional school ⟨*bachelor* of arts⟩; *also* : the degree itself **3 a** : an unmarried man **b** : an unmated male animal [Medieval French *bacheler*] — **bach·e·lor·dom** \-dəm\ *n* — **bach·e·lor·hood** \-ˌhu̇d\ *n*

bach·e·lor·ette \ˌbach-lə-ˈret, ˌba-chə-\ *n* : an unmarried woman

bachelor's button *n* : a European plant related to the daisies and often grown for its blue, pink, or white flower heads — called also *cornflower*

bac·il·la·ry \ˈbas-ə-ˌler-ē, bə-ˈsil-ə-rē\ *also* **ba·cil·lar** \bə-ˈsil-ər, ˈbas-ə-lər\ *adj* **1** : shaped like a rod; *also* : consisting of small rods **2** : of, relating to, or produced by bacilli

ba·cil·lus \bə-ˈsil-əs\ *n, pl* **-cil·li** \-ˈsil-ˌī, *also* -ē\ : any of a genus of aerobic rod-shaped bacteria usually producing endospores; *also* : a disease-producing bacterium [Medieval Latin, "small staff, rod," from Latin *baculus* "staff, rod"]

[1]**back** \ˈbak\ *n* **1 a** (1) : the rear part of the human body especially from the neck to the end of the spine (2) : the corresponding part of a quadruped or other lower animal **b** (1) : SPINAL COLUMN ⟨break one's *back*⟩ (2) : the muscles and ligaments near the spinal column ⟨strain one's *back*⟩ (3) : the back as considered as the seat of one's awareness of duty or failings ⟨get off my *back*⟩ (4) : the back as considered an area of vulnerability ⟨watched his partner's *back*⟩ **2 a** : the hinder part : REAR; *also* : the farther or reverse side **b** : something at or on the back for support ⟨the *back* of a chair⟩ **3** : a position in some games behind the front line of players; *also* : a player in this position [Old English *bæc*] — **backed** \ˈbakt\ *adj* — **back·less** \ˈbak-ləs\ *adj* — **back of one's mind** : the part of one's mind where thoughts and memories are stored to be drawn on later — **behind one's back** : without one's knowledge

[2]**back** *adv* **1 a** : to, toward, or at the rear **b** : in or into the past : AGO **c** : in or into a reclining position **d** : under restraint ⟨held *back*⟩ **2 a** : to, toward, or in a former place, state, or time ⟨go *back*⟩ **b** : in return or reply ⟨write *back*⟩

[3]**back** *adj* **1 a** : being at or in the back ⟨*back* door⟩ **b** : distant from a central or main area or route : REMOTE ⟨*back* roads⟩ **c** : pronounced with closure or narrowing at or toward the back of the oral passage ⟨the *back* vowels \ä\ and \u̇\⟩ **2** : being in arrears : OVERDUE ⟨*back* rent⟩ **3** : moving or operating backward **4** : not current ⟨*back* issues of a magazine⟩

[4]**back** *vb* **1 a** : to give aid or support to : ASSIST ⟨*backed* the new enterprise by investing in it⟩ **b** : SUBSTANTIATE 2 **2** : to move or cause to move back, backward, or in reverse ⟨*back* a car up⟩ **3 a** : to furnish with a back **b** : to be at the back of **c** : to form a back for — **back·er** *n*

back·ache \ˈbak-ˌāk\ *n* : a pain usually in the lower back

back·beat \-ˌbēt\ *n* : a steady pronounced rhythm stressing the second and fourth beats of a four-beat measure

back·bench·er \-ˈben-chər\ *n* : a rank-and-file member of a British legislature

back·bite \-ˌbīt\ *vb* **-bit** \-ˌbit\; **-bit·ten** \-ˌbit-n\; **-bit·ing** \-ˌbīt-ing\ : to say mean or spiteful things about someone who is absent : SLANDER — **back·bit·er** *n*

back·board \-ˌbōrd, -ˌbȯrd\ *n* : a board or construction placed at the back or serving as a back; *esp* : a rounded or rectangular board behind the basket on a basketball court

back·bone \-ˈbōn, -ˌbōn\ *n* **1** : SPINAL COLUMN **2** : the foundation or sturdiest part of something **3** : firm and resolute character ⟨a coward with no *backbone*⟩ **4** : the longest chain of atoms in a molecule ⟨the carbon *backbone*⟩ **5** : the main high-speed hardware and transmission lines of a network ⟨the Internet *backbone*⟩ — **back·boned** \-ˈbōnd, -ˌbōnd\ *adj*

back·break·ing \-ˌbrāk-ing\ *adj* : demanding all one's strength or endurance ⟨*backbreaking* labor⟩

back·court \-ˌkōrt, -ˌkȯrt\ *n* **1** : a basketball team's defensive half of the court **2** : the positions of the guards on a basketball team; *also* : the guards themselves ⟨a team with a strong *backcourt*⟩

back·cross \ˈbak-ˌkrȯs\ *vt* : to cross (a first-generation hybrid) with one parent or parent strain — **backcross** *n*

back down *vb* : to retreat from a stand one has taken or from a challenge one has accepted

back·drop \ˈbak-ˌdräp\ *n* : an often scenic cloth hung across the back of a stage

back·field \-ˌfēld\ *n* : the football players who line up behind the line of scrimmage

[1]**back·fire** \-ˌfīr\ *n* **1** : a fire started to check an advancing fire by clearing an area **2** : a loud noise caused by the improperly timed explosion of fuel in the cylinder of an internal combustion engine

[2]**backfire** *vi* **1** : to make or undergo a backfire **2** : to have an effect opposite to the one desired or expected

back·fit \-ˌfit\ *vt* : RETROFIT

back·flip \-ˌflip\ *n* : a backward somersault especially in the air

back–formation *n* **1** : a word formed by dropping a real or supposed affix from an already existing longer word (as *pea* from *pease*) **2** : the creation of a back-formation

back·gam·mon \ˈbak-ˌgam-ən, bak-ˈ\ *n* : a game played by two persons on a double board with 12 spaces on each side in which each player has 15 pieces whose movements are determined by throwing dice [perhaps from *back* + Middle English *gamen, game* "game"]

back·ground \ˈbak-ˌgrau̇nd\ *n* **1** : the scenery, ground, or surface behind an object seen or represented (as in a painting) **2** : an inconspicuous position ⟨keeps in the *background*⟩ **3 a** : the setting within which something takes place **b** (1) : the circumstances or events leading up to a situation or development (2) : information essential to understanding a problem or situation **c** : the total of a person's experience, knowledge, and education **4** : sound that interferes with received or recorded electronic signals **5** : a somewhat steady level of radiation in the natural environment (as from cosmic rays or radioactivity) **6** : computer processing time not needed for a primary task that is used to work on an additional task ⟨a program running in the *background*⟩

background radiation *n* : the microwave radiation that exists throughout the universe and is considered to be evidence that supports the big bang theory

[1]**back·hand** \ˈbak-ˌhand\ *n* **1 a** : a stroke made with the back of the hand turned in the direction of movement **b** : a catch made with the arm across the body and the palm turned away from the body **2** : handwriting whose strokes slant downward from left to right

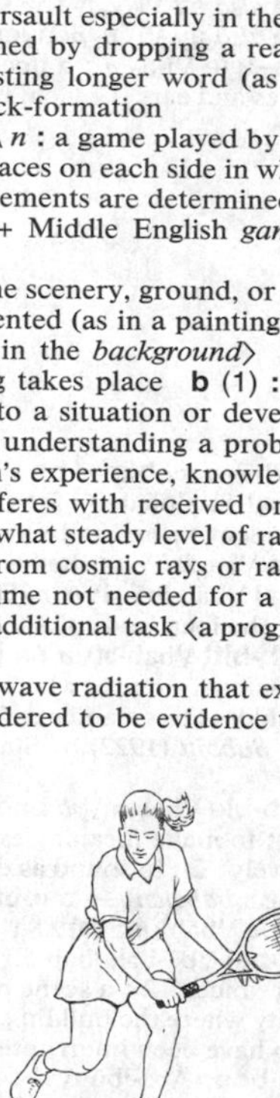
backhand 1a

[2]**backhand** *adj* : using or made with a backhand

[3]**backhand** *vt* : to do, hit, or catch with a backhand

[4]**backhand** *or* **back·hand·ed** \-ˌhan-dəd\ *adv* : with a backhand

back·hand·ed \-ˌhan-dəd\ *adj* **1** : BACKHAND **2 a** : not direct or straightforward **b :** SARCASTIC ⟨a *backhanded* compliment⟩ **3 :** written in backhand

back·hoe \-ˌhō\ *n* **:** an excavating machine having a bucket that is attached to a rigid bar hinged to a boom and that is drawn toward the machine in operation

back·ing \-iŋ\ *n* **1 :** something forming a back **2 a :** SUPPORT, AID **b :** APPROVAL, ENDORSEMENT

back·lash \ˈbak-ˌlash\ *n* **1 :** a sudden violent backward movement or reaction **2 :** a strong adverse reaction (as to a recent social or political development)

back·log \-ˌlȯg, -ˌläg\ *n* **1 :** a large log at the back of a hearth fire **2 :** an accumulation (as of work not done)

back of *prep* **:** BEHIND ⟨out *back of* the barn⟩

back off *vb* **:** BACK DOWN

back order *n* **:** a business order yet to be fulfilled because stock is unavailable

[1]**back·pack** \-ˌpak\ *n* **:** a camping pack worn on the back; *also* **:** KNAPSACK

[2]**backpack** *vb* **1 :** to carry (supplies) in a backpack **2 :** to hike with a backpack — **back·pack·er** *n*

back·rest \ˈbak-ˌrest\ *n* **:** something to support the back

back·side \-ˌsīd\ *n* **:** BUTTOCK 2a

back·slap \-ˌslap\ *vb* **:** to be excessively cordial — **back·slap·per** *n*

back·slash \-ˌslash\ *n* **:** a mark \ used especially in computer programming

back·slide \-ˌslīd\ *vi* **-slid** \-ˌslid\; **-slid** *or* **-slid·den** \-ˌslid-ᵊn\; **-slid·ing** \-ˌslīd-iŋ\ **1 :** to slip back into bad moral or religious practices **2 :** to revert to a worse condition — **back·slide** *n* — **back·slid·er** \-ˌslīd-ər\ *n*

back·space \-ˌspās\ *vi* **:** to move back one space in a text with the press of a key — **backspace** *n*

back·spin \-ˌspin\ *n* **:** a backward rotary motion (as of a ball)

[1]**back·stage** \ˈbak-ˈstāj\ *adv* **1 :** in or to a backstage area **2 :** in secret or private ⟨worked *backstage* to gain support⟩

[2]**backstage** *adj* **1 :** of, relating to, or occurring in the backstage **2 :** SECRET, HIDDEN, COVERT ⟨*backstage* negotiations⟩

back·stay \-ˌstā\ *n* **1 :** a stay extending aft from a masthead **2 :** a strengthening or supporting device at the back

[1]**back·stop** \-ˌstäp\ *n* **:** something serving as a stop behind something else; *esp* **:** a screen or fence used in baseball or other games to keep a ball from leaving the field of play

[2]**backstop** *vt* **:** to back up **:** SUPPORT ⟨found funds to *backstop* the program⟩ — **back·stop·per** *n*

back·stretch \-ˌstrech, -ˈstrech\ *n* **:** the side opposite the homestretch on a racecourse

back·stroke \-ˌstrōk\ *n* **:** a swimming stroke executed by a swimmer lying on his back — **back·strok·er** \-ˌstrō-kər\ *n*

back·swept \-ˌswept\ *adj* **:** swept or slanting backward

back·swim·mer *n* **:** a water bug that swims on its back

back talk *n* **:** an insolent or argumentative reply

back·track \ˈbak-ˌtrak\ *vi* **1 :** to retrace one's course **2 :** to reverse a position or stand

back·up \ˈbak-ˌəp\ *n* **1 :** a person or thing that takes the place of or supports another ⟨has a *backup* in case he gets sick⟩ **2 :** a gathering or piling up because the flow has been stopped ⟨a traffic *backup*⟩ **3 :** a copy of a computer file to protect against loss of data; *also* **:** the act or an instance of making a backup

back up *vb* **1 :** to gather or pile up because the flow has been stopped ⟨traffic *backed up* for miles⟩ **2 :** to make a copy of (as a computer file) to protect against loss of data ⟨*back up* the file⟩ ⟨*back up* the hard drive⟩

[1]**back·ward** \-wərd\ *or* **back·wards** \-wərdz\ *adv* **1 a :** toward the back ⟨look *backward*⟩ **b :** with the back foremost ⟨ride *backward*⟩ **2 a :** in a reverse or opposite direction or way ⟨count *backward*⟩ **b :** toward the past **c :** toward a worse state

[2]**backward** *adj* **1 a :** directed or turned backward ⟨a *backward* glance⟩ **b :** done or executed backward **2 :** DIFFIDENT, SHY **3 :** relatively undeveloped ⟨*backward* nations⟩ — **back·ward·ly** *adv* — **back·ward·ness** *n*

back·wash \-ˌwȯsh, -ˌwäsh\ *n* **1 :** backward movement (as of water or air) produced by a propelling force (as the motion of oars) **2 :** a consequence or by-product of an event

back·wa·ter \ˈbak-ˌwȯt-ər, -ˌwät-\ *n* **1 :** a body of relatively stagnant water formed by the back flow or overflow of a river or sea **2 :** a backward stagnant place or condition

[1]**back·woods** \-ˈwu̇dz, -ˌwu̇dz\ *n pl* **1 :** wooded or partly cleared areas on a frontier **2 :** a remote and culturally backward area — **back·woods·man** \-mən\ *n*

[2]**backwoods** *adj* **:** of, relating to, or suggesting backwoods; *esp* **:** culturally backward or unsophisticated ⟨*backwoods* manner⟩

back·yard \-ˈyärd\ *n* **1 :** an often enclosed area behind a dwelling **2 :** an area that is one's special domain

ba·con \ˈbā-kən\ *n* **1 :** salted and smoked meat from the sides and sometimes the back of a pig **2 :** money gained through employment or legislation — usually used in the phrase *bring home the bacon* [Medieval French, of Germanic origin]

Ba·co·ni·an \bā-ˈkō-nē-ən\ *adj* **:** of, relating to, or characteristic of Francis Bacon or his doctrines

bacteria *plural of* BACTERIUM

bac·te·ri·al \bak-ˈtir-ē-əl\ *adj* **:** of, relating to, or caused by bacteria

bac·te·ri·cid·al \bak-ˌtir-ə-ˈsīd-l\ *adj* **:** destroying bacteria — **bac·te·ri·cide** \-ˈtir-ə-ˌsīd\ *n*

bac·te·rio·chlo·ro·phyll \bak-ˌtir-ē-ō-ˈklōr-ə-ˌfil, -ˈklȯr-\ *n* **:** a substance in photosynthetic bacteria related to the chlorophyll of higher plants

bac·te·ri·ol·o·gy \bak-ˌtir-ē-ˈäl-ə-jē\ *n* **1 :** a science that deals with bacteria and their relations to medicine, industry, and agriculture **2 :** bacterial life and phenomena — **bac·te·ri·o·log·ic** \-ē-ə-ˈläj-ik\ *or* **bac·te·ri·o·log·i·cal** \-ˈläj-i-kəl\ *adj* — **bac·te·ri·o·log·i·cal·ly** \-ˈläj-i-kə-lē, -klē\ *adv* — **bac·te·ri·ol·o·gist** \-ē-ˈäl-ə-jəst\ *n*

bac·te·rio·phage \bak-ˈtir-ē-ə-ˌfāj, -ˌfäzh\ *n* **:** any of various viruses that attack bacteria

bac·te·rio·stat·ic \bak-ˌtir-ē-ō-ˈstat-ik\ *adj* **:** tending to inhibit growth of bacteria without causing their destruction

bac·te·ri·um \bak-ˈtir-ē-əm\ *n, pl* **-ria** \-ē-ə\ **:** any of a group of single-celled microorganisms that are prokaryotes typically living in soil, water, organic matter, or the bodies of plants and animals and are important because of their chemical effects and as causative agents of disease [New Latin, from Greek *baktērion* "staff"]

Bac·tri·an camel \ˈbak-trē-ən-\ *n* **:** CAMEL 1b

[1]**bad** \ˈbad\ *adj* **worse** \ˈwərs\; **worst** \ˈwərst\ **1 a :** below standard **:** POOR ⟨in *bad* repair⟩ **b :** UNFAVORABLE ⟨made a *bad* impression⟩ **c :** ROTTEN 1 ⟨*bad* fish⟩ **2 a :** morally evil ⟨*bad* men⟩ **b :** NAUGHTY 1 ⟨a *bad* dog⟩ **3 :** INADEQUATE ⟨*bad* lighting⟩ **4 :** of a kind to pain or distress ⟨*bad* news⟩ **5 a :** INJURIOUS, HARMFUL ⟨a *bad* influence⟩ **b :** SEVERE ⟨had a *bad* cold⟩ **6 :** INCORRECT, FAULTY ⟨*bad* spelling⟩ **7 :** ILL, SICK ⟨feel *bad*⟩ **8 :** SORRY 1 ⟨felt *bad* about it⟩ **9 :** INVALID, VOID ⟨a *bad* check⟩ [Middle English] — **bad·ness** *n*

[2]**bad** *n* **1 :** something that is bad ⟨take the *bad* with the good⟩ **2 :** an evil or unhappy state

[3]**bad** *adv* **:** BADLY ⟨not doing so *bad*⟩

bad blood *n* **:** ill feeling **:** BITTERNESS ⟨*bad blood* between the two families⟩

bad boy *n* **:** a person who intentionally goes against convention ⟨the *bad boy* of the fashion industry⟩

bad cholesterol *n* **:** LDL

bade *past of* BID

badge \ˈbaj\ *n* **1 :** something worn to show that a person belongs to a certain group, class, or rank ⟨a sheriff's *badge*⟩ **2 :** an outward sign **3 :** an emblem awarded for some achievement ⟨a scout's merit *badge*⟩ [Middle English *bage, bagge*]

[1]**bad·ger** \ˈbaj-ər\ *n* **:** any of several sturdy burrowing carnivorous mammals widely distributed in the northern hemisphere; *also* **:** the pelt or fur of a badger [probably from *badge;* from the white mark on its forehead]

badger

[2]**badger** *vt* **bad·gered; bad·ger·ing** \ˈbaj-riŋ, -ə-riŋ\ **:** to harass persistently [from the practice of baiting badgers]

bad·i·nage \ˌbad-n-ˈäzh\ *n* **:** playful talk back and forth **:** BANTER [French]

\ə\ **abut**	\au̇\ **out**	\i\ **tip**	\ȯ\ **saw**	\u̇\ **foot**
\ər\ **further**	\ch\ **chin**	\ī\ **life**	\ȯi\ **coin**	\y\ **yet**
\a\ **mat**	\e\ **pet**	\j\ **job**	\th\ **thin**	\yü\ **few**
\ā\ **take**	\ē\ **easy**	\ng\ **sing**	\t͟h\ **this**	\yu̇\ **cure**
\ä\ **cot, cart**	\g\ **go**	\ō\ **bone**	\ü\ **food**	\zh\ **vision**

bad·land \ˈbad-ˌland\ *n* **:** a region where erosion has formed the soft rocks into sharp and intricate shapes and where plant life is scarce — usually used in plural

bad·ly \ˈbad-lē\ *adv* **1 :** in a bad manner ⟨played *badly*⟩ **2 :** to a great or intense degree ⟨want something *badly*⟩

bad·min·ton \ˈbad-ˌmit-ⁿn\ *n* **:** a court game played with a light racket and a shuttlecock volleyed over a net [*Badminton,* residence of the Duke of Beaufort, England]

bad–mouth \ˈbad-ˌmau̇th, -ˌmau̇t͟h\ *vt* **:** to criticize severely

[1]**baf·fle** \ˈbaf-əl\ *vt* **baf·fled; baf·fling** \ˈbaf-ling, -ə-ling\ **1 :** to defeat or check by confusing **2 :** to check or break the force or flow of by or as if by a baffle [probably from Middle English (Scots) *bawchillen* "to discredit publicly"] ***synonyms*** see FRUSTRATE — **baf·fle·ment** \-əl-mənt\ *n* — **baf·fler** \ˈbaf-lər, -ə-lər\ *n*

[2]**baffle** *n* **:** a device (as a plate, wall, or screen) to deflect, check, or regulate flow (as of a fluid or of light or sound)

[1]**bag** \ˈbag\ *n* **1 a :** a flexible usually closed container for holding, storing, or carrying something **b :** PURSE; *esp* **:** HANDBAG **c :** SUITCASE **2 :** something resembling a bag: as **a** (1) **:** a pouched or pendulous bodily part or organ; *esp* **:** UDDER (2) **:** a puffy sagging area of loose skin ⟨*bags* under the eyes⟩ **b :** a puffed-out sag or bulge in cloth **c :** a square white canvas container to mark a base in baseball **3 :** the amount contained in a bag **4 :** a quantity of game taken or permitted to be taken **5 :** a slovenly unattractive woman [Old Norse *baggi*] — **in the bag :** SURE, CERTAIN ⟨a win is *in the bag*⟩

[2]**bag** *vb* **bagged; bag·ging 1 a :** to swell out **:** BULGE **b :** to hang loosely **2 :** to put into a bag **3 a :** to take (animals) as game **b :** CAPTURE, SEIZE; *also* **:** to shoot down **:** DESTROY

ba·gasse \bə-ˈgas\ *n* **:** plant residue (as of sugarcane or grapes) left after a product (as juice) has been extracted [French]

bag·a·telle \ˌbag-ə-ˈtel\ *n* **1 :** TRIFLE 1 **2 :** a game played with a cue and balls on an oblong table having cups or cups and arches at one end [French, from Italian *bagattella*]

ba·gel \ˈbā-gəl\ *n* **:** a firm doughnut-shaped roll traditionally made by boiling then baking [Yiddish *beygl*]

[1]**bag·gage** \ˈbag-ij\ *n* **1 :** the traveling bags and personal belongings of a traveler **:** LUGGAGE **2 :** the equipment carried with a military force **3 :** intangible things (as feelings, circumstances, or ideas) that get in the way ⟨emotional *baggage*⟩ [Medieval French *bagage,* from *bague* "bundle"]

[2]**baggage** *n* **:** a contemptible woman; *esp* **:** PROSTITUTE [probably from Middle French *bagasse,* from Old Occitan *bagassa*]

Bag·gies \ˈbag-ēz\ *trademark* — used for transparent plastic bags

bag·gy \ˈbag-ē\ *adj* **bag·gi·er; -est :** loose, puffed out, or hanging like a bag ⟨*baggy* pants⟩ — **bag·gi·ly** \ˈbag-ə-lē\ *adv* — **bag·gi·ness** \ˈbag-ē-nəs\ *n*

bag of waters *n* **:** the double-walled fluid-filled pouch that encloses and protects the fetus in the uterus and that breaks releasing its fluid during the birth process

bag·pipe \ˈbag-ˌpīp\ *n* **:** a wind instrument consisting of a leather bag, a valve-stopped tube, and three or four pipes — often used in plural — **bag·pip·er** \-ˌpī-pər\ *n*

ba·guette \ba-ˈget\ *n* **1 :** a gem having the shape of a long narrow rectangle; *also* **:** the shape itself **2 :** a long thin loaf of French bread [French, literally, "rod"]

bag·worm \ˈbag-ˌwərm\ *n* **:** a moth whose larva lives in a silk case covered with plant debris and is often destructive to the foliage of trees and shrubs

bagworm silk case

bah \ˈbä, ˈba\ *interj* — used to express disdain or contempt

baht \ˈbät\ *n, pl* **baht** *also* **bahts 1 :** the basic monetary unit of Thailand **2 :** a coin or note representing one baht

[1]**bail** \ˈbāl\ *n* **:** a container used to remove water from a boat [Medieval French *baille* "bucket," from Medieval Latin *bajula* "water vessel," from Latin *bajulus* "porter"]

[2]**bail** *vt* **1 :** to remove (water) from a boat by dipping and throwing over the side; *also* **:** to clear (a boat) of water in this way **2 :** BAIL OUT 2 ⟨*bailed* when things got hard⟩

[3]**bail** *n* **1 :** security that guarantees the appearance of a prisoner in court when legally required and that is given in order to obtain his or her release from prison until that time **2 :** the temporary release of a prisoner upon security **3 :** one who provides bail [Medieval French, "custody, bail," literally, "handing over, delivery," from *bailler* "to give, entrust, hand over," from Latin *bajulare* "to carry a burden," from *bajulus* "porter"]

[4]**bail** *vt* **1 :** to entrust (personal property) to another for a specific purpose and a limited time **2 a :** to release under bail **b :** to gain the release of by giving bail — **bail·able** \ˈbā-lə-bəl\ *adj*

[5]**bail** *n* **1 a :** a supporting half hoop **b :** a hinged bar for holding paper against the platen of a typewriter **2 :** the arched handle of a kettle or pail [Middle English *beil, baile*]

bail·ee \bā-ˈlē\ *n* **:** the person to whom property is bailed

bai·ley \ˈbā-lē\ *n* **:** an outer wall of a castle or the space within it [Medieval French *baille, balie* "palisade, bailey"]

bai·liff \ˈbā-ləf\ *n* **1 a :** an official employed by a British sheriff to serve writs and processes and make arrests **b :** a minor officer of some U.S. courts usually serving as a messenger or doorkeeper **2** *chiefly British* **:** one who manages an estate or farm [Medieval French *baillif,* from *bail* "power, authority, office," from *bailler* "to govern, administer," from Medieval Latin *bajulare* "to care for, support," from Latin, "to carry a burden"] — **bai·liff·ship** \-ˌship\ *n*

bai·li·wick \ˈbā-li-ˌwik\ *n* **1 :** the office or jurisdiction of a bailiff **2 :** one's area of special interest or competence [Middle English *baillif* "bailiff" + *wik* "dwelling place, village"]

bail·or \bā-ˈlȯr, ˈbā-lər\ *or* **bail·er** \ˈbā-lər\ *n* **:** one that entrusts personal property to another

bail out *vb* **1 :** to jump with a parachute from an airplane in flight **2 :** to escape or help to escape a difficult situation; *also* **:** LEAVE, DEPART — **bail·out** \ˈbāl-ˌau̇t\ *n*

bails·man \ˈbālz-mən\ *n* **:** one who gives bail for another

bairn \ˈbaərn, ˈbeərn\ *n, chiefly Scottish* **:** CHILD [Middle English *bern, barn,* from Old English *bearn* and Old Norse *barn*]

[1]**bait** \ˈbāt\ *vt* **1 a :** to torment by repeated and usually unfair verbal attacks **b :** to nag at **:** GOAD **2 a :** to torment (an animal) with dogs usually for sport **b :** to attack by biting and tearing **3 a :** to furnish (as a hook) with bait **b :** ENTICE, LURE **4 :** to give food and drink to (an animal) especially on the road [Old Norse *beita*] — **bait·er** *n*

[2]**bait** *n* **1 a :** something (as food) used in luring especially to a hook or trap **b :** a poisonous material placed where it will be eaten by harmful or undesirable animals **2 :** an often treacherous lure

baize \ˈbāz\ *n* **:** a coarse woolen or cotton fabric finished to imitate felt [Middle French *baies,* from *bai* "bay-colored"]

[1]**bake** \ˈbāk\ *vb* **1 :** to cook or be cooked in a dry heat especially in an oven **2 :** to dry or harden by heat ⟨*bake* bricks⟩ **3 :** to prepare baked foods **4 :** to be or become extremely hot ⟨a sidewalk *baking* in the sun⟩ [Old English *bacan*] — **bak·er** *n*

[2]**bake** *n* **1 :** the act or process of baking **2 :** a social gathering at which baked food is served

Ba·ke·lite \ˈbā-kə-ˌlīt, -ˌklīt\ *trademark* — used for any of various synthetic resins and plastics

baker's dozen *n* **:** THIRTEEN

baker's yeast *n* **:** a yeast used or suitable for use as a leaven — compare BREWER'S YEAST

bak·ery \ˈbā-kə-rē, -krē\ *n, pl* **-er·ies :** a place where bread, cakes, and pastry are made or sold

bake sale *n* **:** a fund-raising event at which usually homemade foods (as cakes and cookies) are sold

bake·shop \ˈbāk-ˌshäp\ *n* **:** BAKERY

bake·ware \ˈbāk-waər, -ˌweər\ *n* **:** dishes used for baking and serving food

baking powder *n* **:** a powder that typically consists of sodium bicarbonate, an acidic substance (as cream of tartar), and starch or flour and that makes the dough (as of cake) rise and become light

baking soda *n* **:** SODIUM BICARBONATE

bak·sheesh \ˈbak-ˌshēsh, bak-ˈ\ *n, pl* **baksheesh :** money paid for service especially in the Near East [Persian *bakhshīsh*]

bal·a·lai·ka \ˌbal-ə-ˈlī-kə\ *n* **:** a triangular wooden instrument of Russian origin that is related to the guitar [Russian *balalaĭka*]

[1]**bal·ance** \ˈbal-əns\ *n* **1 :** an instrument for measuring mass or weight (as a beam that is supported freely in the center and has two pans of equal weight suspended from its ends) **2 :** a counterbalancing weight, force, or influence **3 :** a vibrating wheel operating with a hairspring to regulate the movement of a timepiece **4 a :** equilibrium between contrasting or interacting elements ⟨the *balance* of nature⟩ **b :** equality between the totals of the two sides of an account **5 :** an aesthetically pleasing in-

tegration of elements : HARMONY **6** : something left over : REMAINDER; *esp* : the amount by which one side of an account is greater than the other ⟨a *balance* of $10 on the credit side⟩ **7** : mental and emotional steadiness [Medieval French, derived from Latin *bi-* "two" + *lanc-, lanx* "plate"]

synonyms BALANCE, REMAINDER, REST mean that which is left after subtraction or removal of a part. BALANCE strictly involves a comparison of two amounts, where one falls short of the other and must be equalized ⟨a bank *balance* is the amount left in an account after withdrawals and other deductions⟩. REMAINDER refers to what remains after a major or significant part of a group or mass has been taken away or accounted for ⟨a few went ahead, but the *remainder* of the party turned back⟩. REST and REMAINDER are interchangeable although REST often suggests a less precisely measured REMAINDER ⟨the U.S. and the *rest* of the free world⟩.

[2]**balance** *vb* **1 a** (1) : to compute the difference between the debits and credits of an account ⟨*balanced* her checkbook⟩ (2) : to pay the amount due on : SETTLE ⟨sent a payment to *balance* the account⟩ **b** : to arrange so that one set of elements exactly equals another ⟨*balance* an equation⟩ **c** : to complete (a chemical equation) so that the same number of atoms and electric charges of each kind appears on each side **2 a** : to make up for : OFFSET **b** : to equal or equalize in weight, number, or proportion ⟨*balanced* the powers of the three branches of government⟩ **3** : to compare the weight of in or as if in a balance **4 a** : to bring or come to a state or position of equilibrium **b** : to poise in or as if in balance **c** : to bring into harmony or proportion; *also* : to so plan and prepare that all needed elements will be present ⟨*balance* a diet⟩ ⟨a *balanced* aquarium⟩ **5** : to move with a swaying or swinging motion ***synonyms*** see COMPENSATE — **bal·anc·er** *n*

balance beam *n* : a narrow wooden beam supported in a horizontal position above the floor and used for balancing feats in gymnastics

balance of power : an equilibrium of power sufficient to discourage or prevent one nation or party from imposing its will on another

balance of trade : the difference in value over a period of time between a country's imports and exports

balance sheet *n* : a statement of the financial condition of an enterprise at a given date

balance wheel *n* : a wheel that regulates or stabilizes the motion of a mechanism (as in a timepiece or a sewing machine)

balancing act *n* : an attempt to cope with several often conflicting factors or situations at the same time

ba·la·ta \bə-ˈlät-ə\ *n* : the dried latex of a tropical American tree that is related to the sapodilla, similar to gutta-percha, and is used especially in belting and golf balls; *also* : a tree yielding balata [Spanish, from Carib]

bal·brig·gan \bal-ˈbrig-ən\ *n* : a knitted cotton fabric used especially for underwear or hosiery [*Balbriggan,* Ireland]

bal·co·ny \ˈbal-kə-nē\ *n, pl* **-nies** **1** : a platform enclosed by a low wall or a railing and built out from the side of a building **2** : a gallery inside a building (as a theater) extending out over part of the main floor [Italian *balcone,* of Germanic origin]

bald \ˈbȯld\ *adj* **1 a** : lacking a natural or usual covering (as of hair) **b** : having little or no tread ⟨*bald* tires⟩ **2** : UNADORNED, PLAIN ⟨the *bald* truth⟩ **3** : UNDISGUISED ⟨*bald* hate⟩ [Middle English *balled*] — **bald·ly** *adv* — **bald·ness** \ˈbȯld-nəs, ˈbȯl-\ *n*

bal·da·chin \ˈbȯl-də-kən, ˈbal-\ *or* **bal·da·chi·no** \ˌbal-də-ˈkē-nō, ˌbäl-\ *n, pl* **-chins** *or* **-chi·nos** : an ornamental canopy fixed or carried over a dignitary or sacred object as a mark of honor [Italian *baldacchino,* from *Baldacco* "Baghdad"]

bald cypress *n* : either of two large deciduous conifers of the southern U.S. swamps; *also* : the hard red wood of bald cypress

bald eagle *n* : an eagle of North America that is mostly brown when young but has white feathers covering the head and neck and a white tail when mature

bal·der·dash \ˈbȯl-dər-ˌdash\ *n* : NONSENSE 1 [origin unknown]

bald·pate \ˈbȯld-ˌpāt, ˈbȯl-\ *n* : a bald-headed person

bal·dric \ˈbȯl-drik\ *n* : an often ornamented belt worn over one shoulder to support a sword or bugle [Middle English *baudrik*]

[1]**bale** \ˈbāl\ *n* **1** : great evil **2** : mental suffering : WOE [Old English *bealu*]

[2]**bale** *n* : a large bundle of goods; *esp* : one closely pressed, bound together, and often wrapped ⟨a *bale* of hay⟩ [Medieval French, of Germanic origin]

[3]**bale** *vt* : to make up into a bale — **bal·er** *n*

ba·leen \bə-ˈlēn, ˈbā-ˌlēn\ *n* : a horny substance found in two rows of long plates which hang down from the upper jaw of baleen whales — called also *whalebone* [Middle English *baleine* "whale, baleen," from Latin *ballaena* "whale"]

baleen whale *n* : any of various usually large whales lacking teeth but having baleen which is used to filter small marine organisms (as krill) out of large quantities of seawater — compare TOOTHED WHALE

bale·ful \ˈbāl-fəl\ *adj* **1** : deadly or harmful in influence ⟨*baleful* effects⟩ **2** : foreboding or threatening evil ⟨a *baleful* look⟩ — **bale·ful·ly** \-fə-lē\ *adv* — **bale·ful·ness** *n*

[1]**balk** \ˈbȯk\ *n* **1** : a ridge of land left unplowed or missed in plowing **2** : BEAM, RAFTER **3** : something that hinders **4** : failure of a player to complete a motion begun; *esp* : an illegal motion of a baseball pitcher while in position [Old English *balca*]

[2]**balk** *vb* **1** *archaic* : to pass over : fail to grasp **2** : to check or stop by or as if by an obstacle : BLOCK **3** : to stop short and refuse to continue or act ⟨they *balked* at the extra work⟩ **4** : to commit a balk in sports — **balk·er** *n*

bal·kan·ize \ˈbȯl-kə-ˌnīz\ *vt, often cap* **1** : to break up (as a region) into smaller and often hostile units **2** : DIVIDE, COMPARTMENTALIZE [*Balkan* Peninsula] — **bal·kan·i·za·tion** \ˌbȯl-kə-nə-ˈzā-shən\ *n, often cap*

balky \ˈbȯ-kē\ *adj* **balk·i·er; -est** : likely to refuse to proceed, act, or function as directed or expected ⟨a *balky* mule⟩ ⟨a *balky* engine⟩ — **balk·i·ness** *n*

[1]**ball** \ˈbȯl\ *n* **1** : a round or roundish body or mass: as **a** : a usually spherical body used in a game or sport **b** : EARTH, GLOBE **c** : a usually round solid shot for a firearm **d** (1) : the rounded bulge at the base of the thumb (2) : the rounded broad part of the sole of the human foot between the toes and the arch **2** : a game in which a ball is thrown, kicked, or struck; *esp* : BASEBALL **3** : a pitched baseball not struck at by the batter that fails to pass through the strike zone [Middle English *bal*]

[2]**ball** *vb* : to form or gather into a ball

[3]**ball** *n* : a large formal gathering for social dancing [French *bal,* ultimately from Late Latin *ballare* "to dance," from Greek *ballizein*]

bal·lad \ˈbal-əd\ *n* **1** : a narrative poem usually in stanzas of two or four lines and suitable for singing; *esp* : one of unknown authorship handed down orally from generation to generation **2** : a simple song : AIR **3** : a popular song; *esp* : a slow romantic or sentimental dance song [Medieval French *balade,* from Old Occitan *balada* "dance, dancing song," derived from Late Latin *ballare* "to dance"] — **bal·lad·ry** \-ə-drē\ *n*

ball–and–socket joint *n* : a joint (as in the hip) in which a rounded part moves within a socket so as to allow movements in many directions

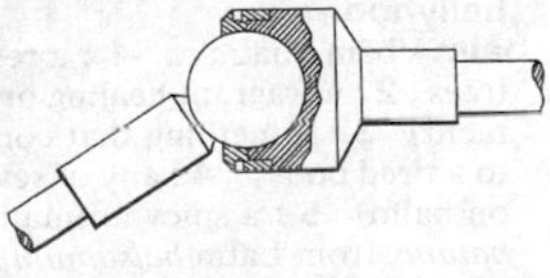

ball-and-socket joint

[1]**bal·last** \ˈbal-əst\ *n* **1** : heavy material used to improve stability and control (as of the draft of a ship or the ascent of a balloon) **2** : gravel, cinders, or crushed stone used in making a roadbed (as of a railroad) or in making concrete [probably from Low German, of Scandinavian origin]

[2]**ballast** *vt* : to provide with ballast

ball bearing *n* **1** : a bearing in which the revolving part turns on steel balls that roll easily in a groove **2** : one of the balls in a ball bearing

ball boy *n* : a male who retrieves balls for players or officials (as in a tennis match or a baseball or basketball game)

ball·car·ri·er \ˈbȯl-ˌkar-ē-ər\ *n* : a football player who carries the ball on offense

bal·le·ri·na \ˌbal-ə-ˈrē-nə\ *n* : a woman ballet dancer [Italian]

bal·let \ˈba-ˌlā, ba-ˈ\ *n* **1 a** : a theatrical art form using dancing to convey a story, theme, or atmosphere **b** : dancing in which conventional poses and steps are combined with light flowing movements (as leaps and turns) **2** : music for a ballet **3** : a

\ə\ abut	\au̇\ **out**	\i\ **tip**	\ȯ\ **saw**	\u̇\ **foot**
\ər\ further	\ch\ **chin**	\ī\ **life**	\ȯi\ **coin**	\y\ **yet**
\a\ mat	\e\ **pet**	\j\ **job**	\th\ **thin**	\yü\ **few**
\ā\ take	\ē\ **easy**	\ng\ **sing**	\t͟h\ **this**	\yu̇\ **cure**
\ä\ cot, cart	\g\ **go**	\ō\ **bone**	\ü\ **food**	\zh\ **vision**

group that performs ballets [French, from Italian *balletto,* derived from Late Latin *ballare* "to dance"]

bal·let·o·mane \ba-ˈlet-ə-ˌmān\ *n* **:** a person who loves ballet [Russian *baletoman,* from *balet* "ballet" + *-o-* "-o-" + *-man,* from *maniya* "mania"]

ball girl *n* **:** a female who retrieves balls for players or officials (as in a tennis match or a baseball or basketball game)

bal·lis·ta \bə-ˈlis-tə\ *n* **:** an ancient military weapon used for hurling large missiles [Latin, derived from Greek *ballein* "to throw"]

bal·lis·tic \bə-ˈlis-tik\ *adj* **1 :** of or relating to ballistics or to a body in motion according to the laws of ballistics **2 :** extremely and usually suddenly excited, upset, or angry **:** WILD ⟨went *ballistic*⟩

ballistic missile *n* **:** a self-propelled missile guided in the ascent of a high-arch path and freely falling in the descent

bal·lis·tics \bə-ˈlis-tiks\ *n sing or pl* **1 a :** the science of the motion of projectiles in flight **b :** the flight characteristics of a projectile **2 :** the firing characteristics of a firearm or cartridge

ball joint *n* **:** BALL-AND-SOCKET JOINT

ball lightning *n* **:** a rare form of lightning consisting of a luminous ball that may move along solid objects or float in the air

[1]**bal·loon** \bə-ˈlün\ *n* **1 :** a nonporous bag filled with heated air or with a gas lighter than air so as to rise and float above the ground and that usually carries a suspended load (as a gondola with passengers) **2 :** a toy or decoration consisting of a bag (as of rubber) that can be inflated with air or gas [French *ballon,* from Italian dialect *ballone,* from *balla* "ball," of Germanic origin] — **bal·loon·ist** \-ˈlü-nəst\ *n*

[2]**balloon** *vb* **1 :** to ascend or travel in or as if in a balloon **2 :** to swell or puff out **3 :** to increase rapidly ⟨costs *ballooned*⟩

balloon catheter *n* **:** a catheter with an inflatable tip that functions especially to hold the catheter in place or to expand an obstructed bodily passage or tube (as an artery)

[1]**bal·lot** \ˈbal-ət\ *n* **1 a :** a small ball used in secret voting **b :** a sheet of paper used to cast a vote **2 a :** the action or a system of secret voting **b :** the right to vote **3 :** the number of votes cast [Italian *ballotta,* from *balla* "ball"]

[2]**ballot** *vi* **:** to vote or decide by ballot — **bal·lot·er** *n*

ball park *n* **:** a park in which ball and especially baseball is played — **in the ball park :** reasonably accurate or acceptable

ball·point \ˈbȯl-ˌpȯint\ *n* **:** a pen having as the writing point a small rotating steel ball that inks itself by contact with an inner ink supply

ball·room \ˈbȯl-ˌrüm, -ˌrụm\ *n* **:** a large room for dances

bal·ly·hoo \ˈbal-ē-ˌhü\ *n, pl* **-hoos 1 :** a noisy attention-getting demonstration or talk **2 :** sensational or exaggerated promotion or publicity **3 :** excited commotion [origin unknown] — **ballyhoo** *vt*

balm \ˈbäm, ˈbälm\ *n* **1 :** a resin from small tropical evergreen trees **2 :** a fragrant healing or soothing preparation (as an ointment) **3 :** something that comforts or refreshes ⟨sleep is *balm* to a tired body⟩ **4 :** any of several spicy fragrant herbs (as lemon balm) **5 :** a spicy aromatic odor [Medieval French *basme, baume,* from Latin *balsamum* "balsam"]

balm of Gil·e·ad \-ˈgil-ē-əd\ **1 a :** a small African and Asian tree with aromatic evergreen leaves; *also* **:** its fragrant oleoresin **b :** any of several poplars (as balsam poplar) having resinous buds **2 :** an agency that soothes, relieves, or heals [*Gilead,* region of ancient Palestine known for its balm]

balmy \ˈbäm-ē, ˈbäl-mē\ *adj* **balm·i·er; -est 1 a :** having the qualities of balm **:** SOOTHING **b :** MILD ⟨*balmy* weather⟩ **2 :** lacking good sense **:** INSANE — **balm·i·ly** \ˈbäm-ə-lē, ˈbäl-mə-\ *adv* — **balm·i·ness** \ˈbäm-ē-nəs, ˈbäl-mē-\ *n*

ba·lo·ney \bə-ˈlō-nē\ *n* **:** silly or absurd talk **:** NONSENSE [alteration of *bologna*]

bal·sa \ˈbȯl-sə\ *n* **1 :** a small raft or boat; *esp* **:** one made of tightly bundled grass or reeds **2 :** a tropical American tree with extremely light strong wood used especially for floats; *also* **:** its wood [Spanish]

bal·sam \ˈbȯl-səm\ *n* **1 a :** an aromatic and usually oily and resinous substance flowing from various plants **b :** a preparation containing or smelling like balsam **2 a :** a tree (as balsam fir) that yields balsam **b :** IMPATIENS; *esp* **:** one grown as an ornamental **3 :** BALM 2 [Latin *balsamum,* from Greek *balsamon*] — **bal·sam·ic** \bȯl-ˈsam-ik\ *adj*

balsam fir *n* **:** a resinous North American fir tree widely used for pulpwood and as a Christmas tree

balsam poplar *n* **:** a North American poplar with resin-coated buds that is often cultivated as a shade tree — called also *tacamahac*

Bal·tic \ˈbȯl-tik\ *adj* **1 :** of or relating to the Baltic Sea or to the states of Lithuania, Latvia, and Estonia **2 :** of or relating to a branch of the Indo-European languages containing Latvian, Lithuanian, and Old Prussian

Bal·ti·more oriole \ˈbȯl-tə-ˌmōr-, -ˌmȯr-, -mər-\ *n* **:** an oriole of the northern and central U.S. that is orange below and in the male mostly black above and in the female mostly greenish-brown above [George Calvert, Lord *Baltimore*]

bal·us·ter \ˈbal-ə-stər\ *n* **:** an upright rounded, square, or vase-shaped support of a rail (as in the railing of a staircase or balcony) [French *balustre,* from Italian *balaustro,* from *balaustra* "pomegranate flower"]

bal·us·trade \ˈbal-ə-ˌstrād\ *n* **:** a row of balusters topped by a rail; *also* **:** a low parapet or barrier

bam·bi·no \bam-ˈbē-nō\ *n, pl* **bambinos** *or* **bam·bi·ni** \-ˈbē-nē\ **1** *pl usually bambini* **:** a representation of the infant Christ **2 :** CHILD 2a; *esp* **:** BABY 1a [Italian]

bam·boo \bam-ˈbü\ *n, pl* **bamboos 1 :** any of various chiefly tropical tall woody grasses including some with strong hollow stems used for building, furniture, or utensils **2 :** the tough woody stem or tissue of a bamboo [Malay *bambu*] — **bamboo** *adj*

bamboo 1

bamboo curtain *n* **:** a political, military, and ideological barrier isolating an area of eastern Asia

bam·boo·zle \bam-ˈbü-zəl\ *vt* **-boo·zled; -boo·zling** \-ˈbüz-ling, -ə-ling\ **1 :** to deceive by trickery **:** HOODWINK **2 :** to confuse, frustrate, or throw off completely [origin unknown] — **bam·boo·zle·ment** \-ˈbü-zəl-mənt\ *n*

[1]**ban** \ˈban\ *vb* **banned; ban·ning 1** *archaic* **:** CURSE 1 **2 :** to prohibit especially by legal means or social pressure **3 :** BAR 4 [Old English *bannan* "to summon"] ***synonyms*** see FORBID

[2]**ban** *n* **1 :** ANATHEMA 1a **2 :** MALEDICTION, CURSE **3 :** an official prohibition **4 :** censure or condemnation especially through public opinion

ba·nal \bə-ˈnal, ba-, -ˈnäl; bā-ˈnal; ˈbān-l\ *adj* **:** lacking originality, freshness, or novelty **:** TRITE, COMMONPLACE [French, from Middle French, "of compulsory feudal service, commonplace," from *ban* "summons to feudal service," of Germanic origin] ***synonyms*** see INSIPID — **ba·nal·i·ty** \bā-ˈnal-ət-ē, bə-\ *n* — **ba·nal·ly** \bə-ˈnal-lē, -ˈnäl-; bān-l-lē, -ē\ *adv*

ba·nana \bə-ˈnan-ə\ *n* **:** any of several widely grown treelike tropical plants with large leaves and with flower clusters that develop into a bunch of finger-shaped fruit which are usually yellow when ripe; *also* **:** its fruit [of African origin]

banana

banana oil *n* **:** a colorless liquid acetate that has a pleasant fruity odor and is used as a solvent

banana republic *n* **:** a small dependent country usually of the tropics; *esp* **:** one run despotically

[1]**band** \ˈband\ *n* **1 :** something (as a fetter or shackle) that confines or constricts **2 :** something that binds or restrains legally, morally, or spiritually ⟨we must break the *bands* of prejudice⟩ **3 :** a strip serving to join or hold things together **4 :** a thin encircling strip that confines, supports, or protects **5 a :** a strip or a stripe with a distinctive characteristic (as color, texture, or composition) ⟨a black beak with a white *band*⟩ **b :** a range of wavelengths or frequencies between two specified limits **c :** a narrow strip serving chiefly as decoration **d** *pl* **:** a pair

of strips hanging at the front of the neck as part of a clerical, legal, or academic dress [partly from Old Norse, "something that constricts" and partly from Medieval French *bende, bande* "strip," of Germanic origin] — **band•ed** \'ban-dəd\ *adj*

[2]**band** *vb* **1 :** to put a band on or fasten with a band **2 :** to finish with a band **3 :** to gather together especially for a common purpose **:** UNITE ⟨*banded* together for protection⟩ — **band•er** *n*

[3]**band** *n* **:** a group of persons, animals, or things; *esp* **:** a group of musicians organized for playing together [Middle French *bande* "troop"]

ban•dage \'ban-dij\ *n* **:** a strip of fabric used especially to cover, dress, and bind up wounds — **bandage** *vt*

Band–Aid \'ban-'dād\ *trademark* — used for a small adhesive strip with a gauze pad for covering minor wounds

ban•dan•na *or* **ban•dana** \ban-'dan-ə\ *n* **:** a large often colorfully patterned handkerchief [Hindi *bā̃dhnū*, cloth dyed by knotting portions so as to leave them undyed, derived from Sanskrit *badhnāti* "he ties"]

band•box \'band-ˌbäks, 'ban-\ *n* **:** a usually cylindrical box for holding light articles of clothing

ban•deau \ban-'dō\ *n, pl* **ban•deaux** *also* **ban•deaus** \-'dōz\ **1 :** a band especially for the hair **2 :** BRASSIERE [French]

ban•de•role *or* **ban•de•rol** \'ban-də-ˌrōl\ *n* **:** a long narrow forked flag or streamer [French *banderole,* from Italian *banderuola,* from *bandiera* "banner," of Germanic origin]

ban•di•coot \'ban-di-ˌküt\ *n* **:** any of various small insect-eating and plant-eating marsupial mammals especially of Australia [Telugu (a Dravidian language of India) *pandikokku*]

ban•dit \'ban-dət\ *n, pl* **ban•dits 1** *pl also* **ban•dit•ti** \ban-'dit-ē\ **:** BRIGAND **2 :** an unethical or criminal person (as a profiteer or gangster) [Italian *bandito,* from *bandire* "to banish," of Germanic origin] — **ban•dit•ry** \'ban-də-trē\ *n*

ban•di•to \ban-ˌdē-tō\ *n, pl* **-tos :** an outlaw especially of Mexican origin [Italian]

band•mas•ter \'band-ˌmas-ter, 'ban-\ *n* **:** a conductor of a musical band

band•mate \'band-ˌmāt\ *n* **:** a fellow member of a band

ban•dog \'ban-ˌdȯg\ *n* **:** a fierce dog formerly kept tied as a watchdog [Middle English *band* + *dogge* "dog"]

ban•do•lier *or* **ban•do•leer** \ˌban-də-'liər\ *n* **:** a belt worn over the shoulder and across the breast to carry something (as cartridges) or as part of an official or ceremonial dress [Middle French *bandoullere,* derived from Spanish *bando* band]

band saw *n* **:** a saw in the form of an endless steel belt running over pulleys

band shell *n* **:** a bandstand backed by a sounding board shaped like a huge concave seashell

bands•man \'banz-mən, 'bandz-\ *n* **:** a member of a musical band

band•stand \'ban-ˌstand, 'band-\ *n* **:** a usually roofed outdoor platform on which a band or orchestra performs

band•wag•on \-ˌwag-ən\ *n* **1 :** a wagon carrying musicians in a parade **2 :** a candidate, side, or cause that attracts increasing support or approval because it seems to be winning or gaining popularity — used in phrases like *jump on the bandwagon*

band•width \'band-ˌwidth\ *n* **1:** a range of frequencies (as of radio waves) **2 :** the capacity for or rate of data transfer ⟨a high *bandwidth* Internet connection⟩

[1]**ban•dy** \'ban-dē\ *vb* **ban•died; ban•dy•ing 1 :** to treat in a careless or high-handed manner **2 a :** EXCHANGE; *esp* **:** to exchange in argument ⟨*bandy* sharp words⟩ **b :** to discuss lightly or glibly or as a subject of gossip ⟨several names were *bandied* about⟩ **3** *archaic* **:** to band together [origin unknown]

[2]**bandy** *adj* **:** curved especially outward **:** BOWED ⟨*bandy* legs⟩ [probably from *bandy* "hockey stick"]

ban•dy–legged \ˌban-dē-'legd, -'leg-əd\ *adj* **:** having bandy legs **:** BOWLEGGED

bane \'bān\ *n* **1 a :** POISON **b :** DEATH, DESTRUCTION **2 :** a source of injury, harm, ruin, or woe [Old English *bana* "killer"]

bane•ful \'bān-fəl\ *adj* **1 :** causing destruction or woe **:** RUINOUS ⟨a *baneful* influence⟩ **2** *archaic* **:** POISONOUS — **bane•ful•ly** \-fə-lē\ *adv*

[1]**bang** \'bang\ *vb* **1 :** to strike against **:** BUMP ⟨*banged* his knee⟩ **2 :** to knock, hit, or thrust with a sharp noise ⟨*banged* the door shut⟩ **3 :** to produce a sharp often explosive noise or series of noises [probably of Scandinavian origin]

[2]**bang** *n* **1 :** a resounding blow **2 :** a sudden loud noise **3 a :** a sudden striking effect **b :** a quick burst of energy ⟨start off with a *bang*⟩ **c :** an emotional thrill ⟨you'll get a *bang* out of this⟩

[3]**bang** *adv* **:** EXACTLY, DIRECTLY ⟨*bang* in the middle⟩

[4]**bang** *n* **:** a fringe of banged hair — usually used in plural [probably from *bangtail* "short tail"]

[5]**bang** *vt* **:** to cut (as front hair) short and squarely across

ban•gle \'bang-gəl\ *n* **1 :** an ornamental circlet worn as a bracelet or anklet **2 :** a small ornament hanging (as from a bracelet) loosely [Hindi *baṅglī*]

bang•tail \'bang-ˌtāl\ *n* **1 :** RACEHORSE **2 :** a wild horse

bang–up \'bang-ˌəp\ *adj* **:** of the best quality **:** FIRST-RATE ⟨had a *bang-up* time⟩

ban•ish \'ban-ish\ *vt* **1 :** to compel by authority to leave a country ⟨the king *banished* the traitors⟩ **2 :** to drive out from or as if from a home **:** EXPEL ⟨*banish* fears⟩ [Medieval French *baniss-,* stem of *banir,* of Germanic origin] — **ban•ish•er** *n* — **ban•ish•ment** \-ish-mənt\ *n*

ban•is•ter *also* **ban•nis•ter** \'ban-ə-stər\ *n* **1 :** one of the upright supports of a handrail alongside a staircase **2 :** a handrail with its supporting posts **3 :** HANDRAIL [alteration of *baluster*]

ban•jo \'ban-ˌjō\ *n, pl* **banjos** *also* **banjoes :** a musical instrument related to the guitar with a long narrow fretted neck and small drum-shaped body [probably of African origin] — **ban•jo•ist** \-ˌjō-əst\ *n*

[1]**bank** \'bangk\ *n* **1 :** a mound, pile, or ridge (as of earth) **2 :** a piled up mass of cloud or fog **3 :** an undersea elevation rising especially from the continental shelf **:** SHOAL **4 :** rising ground bordering a lake, river, or sea or forming the edge of a hollow or cut **5 :** a steep slope (as of a hill) **6 :** the inward tilt of a surface along a curve or of a vehicle (as an airplane) when turning [probably of Scandinavian origin]

[2]**bank** *vb* **1 :** to raise a bank around **2 :** to heap or pile in a bank **3 :** to rise in or form a bank **4 :** to cover (a fire) with fresh fuel so as to reduce the speed of burning **5 :** to build (a curve) with the roadbed or track inclined laterally upward from the inside edge **6 :** to incline an airplane laterally when turning **7 :** to form or group in a tier

[3]**bank** *n* **1 :** a place of business that receives, lends, issues, exchanges, and takes care of money, extends credit, and provides ways of sending funds quickly from place to place **2 :** a small container in which money may be saved **3 a :** a supply of something held in reserve **b** (1) **:** the fund of the banker or dealer in a card or board game (2) **:** a fund of pieces belonging to a game (as dominoes) from which the players draw **4 :** a storage place for a reserve supply ⟨a blood *bank*⟩ [Middle French *banque,* from Italian *banca,* literally, "bench," of Germanic origin]

Word History The literal meaning of Italian *banca* was "bench," but the word was also used for the benchlike counter at which an early money changer transacted business and later for the money changer's shop itself, the bank. When the banking trade spread from Italy to France, and then to England, the Italian word went with it and became our English *bank.* Although they come from different languages, the English homographs of *bank* are all related and are related to the English word *bench* as well.

[4]**bank** *vb* **1 :** to act as a banker **2 :** to have an account in a bank **3 :** to deposit or store in a bank ⟨*banks* $10 every week⟩ — **bank on :** to depend or rely on

[5]**bank** *n* **:** a group or series of objects arranged close together in a row or a tier ⟨a *bank* of seats⟩ [Medieval French *banc* "bench," of Germanic origin]

bank•book \'bangk-ˌbu̇k\ *n* **:** a depositor's book in which a bank records each deposit and withdrawal — called also *passbook*

bank card *n* **:** a card (as a credit card or an ATM card) issued by a bank

bank•er \'bang-kər\ *n* **1 :** one that engages in the business of banking **2 :** the player who keeps the bank in a card or board game

bank holiday *n, British* **:** LEGAL HOLIDAY

bank•ing \'bang-king\ *n* **:** the business of a bank or a banker

\ə\ **abut**	\au̇\ **out**	\i\ **tip**	\ȯ\ **saw**	\u̇\ **foot**
\ər\ **further**	\ch\ **chin**	\ī\ **life**	\ȯi\ **coin**	\y\ **yet**
\a\ **mat**	\e\ **pet**	\j\ **job**	\th\ **thin**	\yü\ **few**
\ā\ **take**	\ē\ **easy**	\ng\ **sing**	\t͟h\ **this**	\yu̇\ **cure**
\ä\ **cot, cart**	\g\ **go**	\ō\ **bone**	\ü\ **food**	\zh\ **vision**

bank note *n* **:** a promissory note issued by a bank, payable to bearer on demand without interest, and acceptable as money

bank·roll \ˈbangk-ˌrōl\ *n* **:** supply of money **:** FUNDS

[1]**bank·rupt** \ˈbang-ˌkrəpt\ *n* **1 :** a person who becomes unable to pay his or her debts; *esp* **:** one whose property is turned over by court order to a trustee to be administered for the benefit of his or her creditors **2 :** a person who lacks completely a specified quality or attribute ⟨a moral *bankrupt*⟩ [Italian *bancarotta* "bankruptcy," literally, "broken bank"]

[2]**bankrupt** *adj* **1 a :** fallen into a state of financial ruin **:** IMPOVERISHED **b :** legally declared bankrupt ⟨the company went *bankrupt*⟩ **2 :** DEPLETED, DESTITUTE 1 — used with *of* or *in* ⟨*bankrupt* of all merciful feelings⟩

[3]**bankrupt** *vt* **:** to make bankrupt

bank·rupt·cy \ˈbang-ˌkrəp-sē, -krəp-\ *n, pl* **-cies :** the condition of being bankrupt

[1]**ban·ner** \ˈban-ər\ *n* **1 a :** a piece of cloth attached by one edge to a staff and used as a standard **b :** [2]FLAG 1 **c :** an ensign displaying a distinctive or symbolic device or inscription **2 :** a headline in large type running across a newspaper page **3 :** a strip of cloth on which a sign is painted **4 :** a name, slogan, or goal associated with a particular group or point of view ⟨crusading under the *banner* of progress⟩ **5 :** an advertisement that runs usually across the top of a World Wide Web page [Medieval French *banere,* of Germanic origin]

[2]**banner** *adj* **:** unusually good ⟨a *banner* year for apple growers⟩

ban·nock \ˈban-ək\ *n* **:** an often unleavened bread of oat or barley flour baked in flat loaves [Old English *bannuc*]

banns \ˈbanz\ *n pl* **:** public announcement especially in church of a proposed marriage [Middle English *bane, ban* "proclamation, ban"]

[1]**ban·quet** \ˈbang-kwət, ˈban-, -ˌkwet\ *n* **:** an elaborate often ceremonious meal for many people frequently in celebration of a special occasion [Middle French, from Italian *banchetto,* from *banca* "bench, bank"]

[2]**banquet** *vb* **1 :** to entertain with a banquet **:** FEAST **2 :** to partake of a banquet — **ban·quet·er** *n*

ban·quette \bang-ˈket, ban-\ *n* **:** a long usually upholstered seat especially along a wall

ban·shee \ˈban-ˌshē, ban-ˈ\ *n* **:** a female spirit in Gaelic folklore whose appearance or wailing warns of approaching death [Irish *bean sídhe* & Scottish Gaelic *bean sìth,* literally, "woman of the fairy mound"]

[1]**ban·tam** \ˈbant-əm\ *n* **1 :** any of numerous small domestic fowls that are often miniatures of members of the standard breeds **2 :** a small and often quarrelsome person [*Bantam,* former territorial unit in Java]

[2]**bantam** *adj* **1 :** SMALL 1, DIMINUTIVE **2 :** pertly quarrelsome

ban·tam·weight \-ˌwāt\ *n* **:** a boxer in a weight division having an upper limit of about 118 pounds

[1]**ban·ter** \ˈbant-ər\ *vb* **1 :** to speak to in a witty and teasing manner **:** RALLY **2 :** to talk or act playfully or wittily [origin unknown] — **ban·ter·er** \-ər-ər\ *n* — **ban·ter·ing·ly** \ˈbant-ə-ring-lē\ *adv*

[2]**banter** *n* **:** good-natured and witty teasing or joking

bant·ling \ˈbant-ling\ *n* **:** a very young child [perhaps from German *Bänkling* "bastard"]

Ban·tu \ˈban-ˌtü, ˈbän-\ *n* **1 :** a group of African languages spoken in central and southern Africa **2 :** a member of any of a group of African peoples who speak Bantu languages — **Bantu** *adj*

ban·yan \ˈban-yən\ *n* **:** a large East Indian tree related to the fig with branches that send out roots which grow downward into the ground and form new supporting trunks [*banyan* "Indian merchant," derived from Sanskrit *vāṇiya* "trader"; from such a tree in Iran under which merchants conducted business]

ban·zai \bän-ˈzī, ˈbän-\ *n* **:** a Japanese cheer or cry of triumph — usually used interjectionally [Japanese]

bao·bab \ˈbau̇-ˌbab, ˈbā-ə-ˌbab\ *n* **:** a tree native to Africa with a broad trunk, an edible acidic fruit resembling a gourd, and bark used in making paper, cloth, and rope [New Latin *bahobab*]

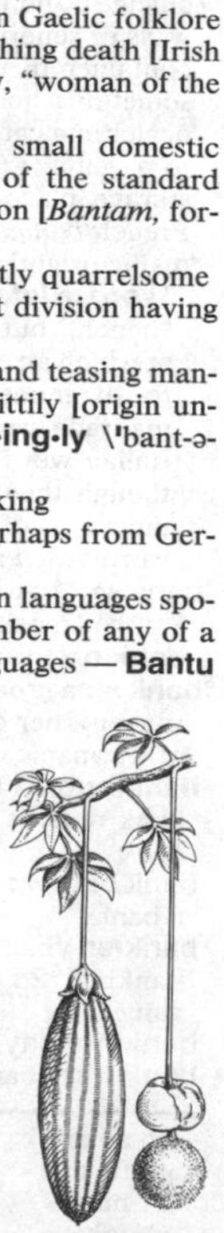

baobab

bap·tism \ˈbap-ˌtiz-əm\ *n* **1 :** a Christian sacrament signifying spiritual rebirth and admitting the recipient to the Christian community through the ritual use of water **2 :** a non-Christian ceremony using water for ritual purification **3 :** an act, experience, or ordeal by which one is named, purified, or initiated into a new life ⟨a soldier's *baptism* of fire⟩ — **bap·tis·mal** \bap-ˈtiz-məl\ *adj* — **bap·tis·mal·ly** \-mə-lē\ *adv*

Bap·tist \ˈbap-təst\ *n* **:** a Protestant of an evangelical denomination practicing congregational government and baptism by immersion for believers — **Baptist** *adj*

bap·tis·tery *or* **bap·tis·try** \ˈbap-tə-strē\ *n, pl* **-ter·ies** *or* **-tries :** a part of a church or formerly a separate building used for baptism

bap·tize \bap-ˈtīz, ˈbap-ˌ\ *vt* **1 :** to administer baptism to **2 a :** to purify spiritually especially by a cleansing experience or ordeal **b :** INITIATE 1 **3 :** to give a name to (as at baptism) **:** CHRISTEN [Greek *baptizein* "to dip, baptize"] — **bap·tiz·er** *n*

[1]**bar** \ˈbär\ *n* **1 a :** a rigid piece (as of wood or metal) that is longer than it is wide and has various uses (as for a lever, barrier, or fastening) **b :** a usually rectangular solid piece or block of material longer than it is wide ⟨*bar* of soap⟩ ⟨candy *bar*⟩ **2 :** something that obstructs or prevents passage, progress, or action **:** IMPEDIMENT: as **a :** any intangible or nonphysical impediment **b :** a submerged or partly submerged bank along a shore or in a river **3 a :** the railing in a courtroom that encloses the place where the business of the court is transacted **b :** a court or system of courts **c :** an authority or tribunal that renders judgment ⟨before the *bar* of public opinion⟩ **d :** the body of lawyers qualified to practice in a jurisdiction ⟨the New York *bar*⟩; *also* **:** the profession of lawyer **4 :** a straight stripe, band, or line much longer than it is wide **5 a :** a counter for serving food or especially alcoholic beverages **b :** BARROOM **6 a :** a vertical line across the musical staff before the initial measure accent **b :** MEASURE 4c **7 :** STANDARD 3a ⟨raise the *bar* for approving new medicines⟩ [Medieval French *barre*] — **behind bars :** in jail

B [1]bar 6a

[2]**bar** *vt* **barred; bar·ring 1 a :** to fasten with a bar **b :** to place bars across to prevent passage **2 :** to mark with bars **:** STRIPE **3 :** to block off **:** OBSTRUCT ⟨*bar* the road to traffic⟩ **4 a :** to keep out **:** EXCLUDE ⟨*bar* reporters from the meeting⟩ **b :** PREVENT, FORBID ⟨the order *bars* discrimination in hiring⟩

[3]**bar** *prep* **:** with the exception of ⟨*bar* none⟩

[4]**bar** *n* **:** a unit of pressure equal to 100,000 pascals [German, from Greek *baros* "weight"]

[1]**barb** \ˈbärb\ *n* **1 a :** a sharp projection extending backward (as from the point of an arrow or fishhook) and preventing easy removal **b :** any of various natural projections (as a hooked plant hair or a side branch of a feather) resembling a barb **2 :** a biting or pointedly critical remark or comment [Medieval French *barbe,* literally, "beard," from Latin *barba*] — **barbless** \-ləs\ *adj*

[2]**barb** *vt* **:** to furnish with a barb

[3]**barb** *n* **:** any of a northern African breed of horses that are noted for speed and endurance [French *barbe,* from Italian *barbero,* from *barbero* "of Barbary"]

bar·bar·i·an \bär-ˈber-ē-ən, bär-ˈbar-\ *adj* **1 :** of, relating to, or being a land, culture, or people foreign to and usually felt to be inferior to one's own **2 :** lacking refinement, learning, or artistic or literary culture [Latin *barbarus,* from Greek *barbaros* "foreign, ignorant"] — **barbarian** *n* — **bar·bar·i·an·ism** \-ē-ə-ˌniz-əm\ *n*

synonyms BARBARIAN, BARBAROUS, BARBARIC, SAVAGE mean characteristic of an uncivilized person. BARBARIAN often implies a state somewhere between tribal savagery and full civilization ⟨the *barbarian* tribes that sacked Rome⟩. BARBAROUS tends to stress the harsher or more brutal side of uncivilized life ⟨tales of the *barbarous* custom are myth⟩. BARBARIC suggests crudeness of taste and fondness for unrestrained display ⟨the *barbaric* use of color and ornament⟩. SAVAGE suggests more primitive culture than BARBARIAN and greater harshness or fierceness than BARBAROUS ⟨a castaway turned nearly *savage*⟩.

bar·bar·ic \bär-ˈbar-ik\ *adj* **1 :** of, relating to, or characteristic of barbarians **2 a :** marked by a lack of restraint **:** WILD **b :** having a bizarre, primitive, or unsophisticated quality ⟨*barbaric* splendor⟩ ***synonyms*** see BARBARIAN

bar·ba·rism \'bär-bə-ˌriz-əm\ *n* **1 a** : a barbarian state of social or intellectual development : BACKWARDNESS **b** : the practice or display of barbarian acts, attitudes, or ideas **2** : an idea, act, word, or expression that offends contemporary standards of good taste or acceptability

bar·bar·i·ty \bär-'bar-ət-ē\ *n, pl* **-ties** **1** : BARBARISM **2 a** : barbarous cruelty : INHUMANITY **b** : an act or instance of barbarous cruelty

bar·ba·rize \'bär-bə-ˌrīz\ *vb* : to make or become barbarian or barbarous — **bar·ba·ri·za·tion** \ˌbär-bə-rə-'zā-shən, -brə-\ *n*

bar·ba·rous \'bär-bə-rəs, -brəs\ *adj* **1** : characterized by the use of barbarisms in speech or writing **2 a** : of or relating to a backward land or people **b** : lacking culture or refinement **3** : mercilessly harsh or cruel ***synonyms*** see BARBARIAN — **bar·ba·rous·ly** *adv* — **bar·ba·rous·ness** *n*

Bar·ba·ry ape \'bär-bə-rē-, -brē-\ *n* : a tailless monkey of North Africa and Gibraltar — called also *Barbary macaque*

[1]**bar·be·cue** \'bär-bi-ˌkyü\ *vt* **1** : to roast or broil on a rack or revolving spit over or before a source of heat (as hot coals) **2** : to cook in a highly seasoned vinegar sauce

[2]**barbecue** *also* **bar·be·que** *n* **1 a** : a large animal (as a hog or steer) roasted or broiled whole or split over an open fire or bed of hot coals **b** : barbecued food ⟨eat *barbecue*⟩ **2** : a social gathering especially outdoors at which barbecued food is eaten **3** : an often portable fireplace over which meat and fish are roasted or broiled [American Spanish *barbacoa* "rack for hanging meat over a fire," from an American Indian language of the Antilles]

barbed \'bärbd\ *adj* **1** : having a barb ⟨a *barbed* hook⟩ **2** : bitingly critical ⟨a *barbed* comment⟩

barbed wire \'bärb-'dwīr, 'bäb-, -'wīr\ *n* : twisted wires armed with sharp points — called also *barbwire*

bar·bel \'bär-bəl\ *n* : a slender tactile process on the lips of certain fishes (as catfishes) [Middle French, derived from Latin *barba* "beard"]

bar·bell \'bär-ˌbel\ *n* : a bar with adjustable weighted disks attached to each end that is used for exercise and in weight lifting

[1]**bar·ber** \'bär-bər\ *n* : one whose business is cutting and dressing hair, shaving and trimming beards, and performing related services [Medieval French *barbour,* from *barbe* "beard," from Latin *barba*]

[2]**barber** *vb* **bar·bered; bar·ber·ing** \-bə-ring, -bring\ : to perform the services of a barber

bar·ber·ry \'bär-ˌber-ē\ *n* : any of a genus of spiny yellow-flowered shrubs with bright red or blackish oblong berries often grown for hedges or ornament [derived from Arabic *barbārīs*]

[1]**bar·ber·shop** \'bär-bər-ˌshäp\ *n* : a barber's place of business

[2]**barbershop** *adj* : having a style of unaccompanied vocal harmonizing of popular songs especially by a quartet

bar·bette \bär-'bet\ *n* : a cylinder of armor protecting a gun turret on a warship [French, "mound from which guns fire over a parapet," probably from *barbe* "headdress"]

bar·bi·can \'bär-bi-kən\ *n* : an outer defensive work; *esp* : a tower at a gate or bridge [Medieval Latin *barbacana*]

bar·bi·tal \'bär-bə-ˌtȯl\ *n* : a white habit-forming drug used especially to induce sleep and sedation

bar·bi·tu·rate \bär-'bich-ə-rət, -ˌrāt\ *n* : any of various derivatives of barbituric acid that are used especially as sedatives or sleep-inducing agents and are often addictive

bar·bi·tu·ric acid \ˌbär-bə-'tyu̇r-ik-, -'tu̇r-\ *n* : a crystalline acid $C_4H_4N_2O_3$ used in making plastics and drugs [German *Barbitursäure,* from the name *Barbara* + New Latin *urea* + German *Säure* "acid"]

bar·bule \'bär-ˌbyül\ *n* : a minute barb; *esp* : one of the processes that project from the barbs of a feather

bar·ca·role *or* **bar·ca·rolle** \'bär-kə-ˌrōl\ *n* **1** : a Venetian boat song characterized by a beat suggesting a rowing rhythm **2** : a piece of music imitating a barcarole [French *barcarolle,* from Italian dialect (Venice) *barcarola,* from *barca* "bark"]

bar chart *n* : BAR GRAPH

bar code *n* : a code made up of variously spaced bars and sometimes numerals that is designed to be scanned and read into computer memory and that contains information (as identification) about the object it labels

bard \'bärd\ *n* **1** : a tribal poet-singer gifted in composing and reciting verses on heroes and their deeds **2** : POET [Irish and Scottish Gaelic] — **bard·ic** \'bärd-ik\ *adj*

[1]**bare** \'baər, 'beər\ *adj* **1 a** : lacking a natural, usual, or appropriate covering ⟨trees *bare* of leaves⟩ **b** : lacking clothing **c** : lacking any tool or weapon ⟨opened the box with his *bare* hands⟩ **2** : open to view : EXPOSED ⟨their guilt was laid *bare*⟩ **3 a** : completely unfurnished or only scantily supplied ⟨the cupboard was *bare*⟩ **b** : DESTITUTE ⟨*bare* of all safeguards⟩ **4 a** : having nothing left over or added : MERE ⟨a *bare* majority⟩ **b** : not adorned or expanded : PLAIN ⟨the *bare* facts⟩ [Old English *bær*] — **bare·ness** *n*

[2]**bare** *vt* : to make or lay bare : UNCOVER, REVEAL

[3]**bare** *archaic past of* BEAR

bare·back \-ˌbak\ *or* **bare·backed** \-'bakt\ *adv or adj* : on the bare back of a horse : without a saddle ⟨learned to ride *bareback*⟩ ⟨a *bareback* rider in the circus⟩

bare·faced \-'fāst\ *adj* **1** : having the face uncovered **2** : SHAMELESS, BOLD ⟨a *barefaced* lie⟩ — **bare·faced·ly** \-'fā-səd-lē, -'fāst-lē\ *adv* — **bare·faced·ness** \-'fā-səd-nəs, -'fāst-nəs\ *n*

bare·foot \-ˌfu̇t\ *or* **bare·foot·ed** \-'fu̇t-əd\ *adv or adj* : with the feet bare : without shoes ⟨went *barefoot* in summer⟩

bare·hand·ed \-'han-dəd\ *adv or adj* **1** : with the hands bare : without gloves or mittens **2** : without tools or weapons

bare·head·ed \-'hed-əd\ *adv or adj* : with the head bare : without a hat

bare·ly *adv* **1** : SCARCELY, HARDLY ⟨*barely* enough money to live on⟩ **2** : in a scanty manner ⟨a *barely* furnished room⟩

barf \'bärf\ *vi* : VOMIT 1 [origin unknown]

[1]**bar·gain** \'bär-gən\ *n* **1** : an agreement between parties settling what each is to give or receive in a transaction **2** : something gained by or as if by bargaining; *esp* : an advantageous purchase ⟨at 35 percent off, the suit was a real *bargain*⟩ **3** : a situation or event with important good or bad results ⟨got the worst of a bad *bargain*⟩ [Medieval French *bargaigne,* from *bargaigner* "to bargain," probably of Germanic origin]

[2]**bargain** *vb* **1** : to talk over the terms of a purchase, agreement, or contract : HAGGLE **2** : to bring to a desired level by bargaining ⟨*bargain* a price down⟩ **3** : to sell or dispose of by bargaining — **bar·gain·er** *n* — **bargain for** : to count on in advance : EXPECT ⟨more trouble than we *bargained for*⟩

[1]**barge** \'bärj\ *n* **1** : a broad flat-bottomed boat used chiefly for the transport of goods on inland waterways **2** : a large motorboat for the use of a naval officer ranking above a captain [Medieval French, "boat, small ship," from Late Latin *barca*]

[2]**barge** *vb* **1** : to carry by barge **2** : to move or thrust oneself clumsily or rudely ⟨they *barged* right in without being invited⟩

barge·man \-mən\ *n* : the master or a deckhand of a barge

bar graph *n* : a graph that shows rectangles with lengths proportional to numbers as a visual way of comparing the numbers — called also *bar chart*

bar·ite \'baər-ˌīt, 'beər-\ *n* : barium sulfate $BaSO_4$ occurring as a mineral

[1]**bari·tone** \'bar-ə-ˌtōn\ *n* **1 a** : a male singing voice of medium range between bass and tenor **b** : a man having such a voice **2** : the saxhorn intermediate in size between althorn and tuba — called also *baritone horn* [derived from Greek *barys* "heavy" + *tonos* "tone"] — **bari·tonal** \ˌbar-ə-'tōn-l\ *adj*

[2]**baritone** *adj* : relating to or having the range or part of a baritone

bar·i·um \'bar-ē-əm, 'ber-\ *n* **1** : a silver-white malleable toxic bivalent metallic chemical element that occurs only in combination — see ELEMENT table **2** : BARIUM SULFATE [New Latin, from Greek *barys* "heavy"]

barium sulfate *n* : a colorless crystalline insoluble compound $BaSO_4$ that is used as a pigment, as a filler, and as a substance opaque to X-rays in medical photography of the digestive tract

[1]**bark** \'bärk\ *vb* **1** : to utter a bark or similar sound **2** : to speak or utter in a sharp loud usually angry tone ⟨*bark* out an order⟩ **3** : to advertise by persistent outcry ⟨vendors *barked* their wares⟩ [Old English *beorcan*] — **bark up the wrong tree** : to speak or act on the basis of a misunderstanding

[2]**bark** *n* : the characteristic short loud cry of a dog

[3]**bark** *n* **1** : the tough exterior covering of a woody root or stem that is made up of tissue outside the cambium **2** : a candy con-

\ə\ abut	\au̇\ **out**	\i\ tip	\ȯ\ saw	\u̇\ foot
\ər\ further	\ch\ **chin**	\ī\ life	\ȯi\ **coin**	\y\ yet
\a\ mat	\e\ pet	\j\ job	\th\ **thin**	\yü\ few
\ā\ take	\ē\ **easy**	\ng\ **sing**	\t͟h\ **this**	\yu̇\ **cure**
\ä\ cot, cart	\g\ go	\ō\ bone	\ü\ **food**	\zh\ vision

taining chocolate and nuts that is made in a sheet and broken into pieces [Old Norse *bǫrkr*]

[4]**bark** *vt* **1 :** to strip the bark from **2 :** to rub off or abrade the skin of ⟨*barked* her knee on the sidewalk⟩

[5]**bark** *or* **barque** *n* **1 a :** a small sailing ship **b :** a 3-masted sailing vessel with foremast and mainmast square-rigged and mizzenmast fore-and-aft rigged **2 :** a craft propelled by sails or oars [Medieval French *barque,* from Occitan *barca,* from Late Latin]

bar·keep \ˈbär-ˌkēp\ *also* **bar·keep·er** \-ˌkē-pər\ *n* **:** a person who owns, operates, or tends a bar

bar·ken·tine *or* **bar·quen·tine** \ˈbär-kən-ˌtēn\ *n* **:** a 3-masted sailing vessel having the foremast square-rigged and the mainmast and mizzenmast fore-and-aft rigged [[5]*bark* + *-entine,* alteration of *-antine* (as in *brigantine*)]

bark·er \ˈbär-kər\ *n* **:** a person who stands at the entrance to a show and tries to attract customers to it with loud fast talk

barky \ˈbär-kē\ *adj* **bark·i·er; -est :** covered with or resembling bark

bar·ley \ˈbär-lē\ *n* **:** a cereal grass with flowers in dense spikes with three spikelets at each joint; *also* **:** its seed used especially in malt beverages, in foods (as soups and cereals), or as livestock feed [Old English *bærlic* "of barley"]

bar·ley·corn \-ˌkȯrn\ *n* **:** a grain of barley

barm \ˈbärm\ *n* **:** yeast formed on fermenting malt liquors [Old English *beorma*]

bar·maid \ˈbär-ˌmād\ *n* **:** a woman who works as a bartender

bar·man \-mən\ *n* **:** a man who works as a bartender

Bar·me·cid·al \ˌbär-mə-ˈsīd-l\ *or* **Bar·me·cide** \ˈbär-mə-ˌsīd\ *adj* **:** providing only an apparent abundance ⟨a *Barmecidal* feast⟩ [*Barmecide,* a wealthy Persian, who, in a tale of *The Arabian Nights,* invited a beggar to a feast of imaginary food]

[1]**bar mitz·vah** \bär-ˈmits-və\ *n, often cap B&M* **1 :** a Jewish boy who reaches his 13th birthday and attains the age of religious duty and responsibility **2 :** the ceremony recognizing a boy as a bar mitzvah [Hebrew *bar miṣwāh,* literally, "son of the law"]

[2]**bar mitzvah** *vt* **bar mitz·vahed; bar mitz·vah·ing :** to administer the ceremony of bar mitzvah to

barn \ˈbärn\ *n* **:** a building used chiefly for storing grain and hay and for housing farm animals (as cows and horses) [Old English *bereærn,* from *bere* "barley" + *ærn* "house, store"]

bar·na·cle \ˈbär-ni-kəl\ *n* **:** any of numerous marine crustaceans with feathery appendages for gathering food that are free-swimming as larvae but fixed (as to rocks or pilings) as adults [Middle English *bernake,* a goose once believed to grow from barnacles] — **bar·na·cled** \-kəld\ *adj*

barn dance *n* **:** an American social dance originally held in a barn and featuring square dances, round dances, and traditional music and calls

barn owl *n* **:** a widely distributed owl that is reddish brown and grey above and mostly white below, is found near barns and other buildings, and preys especially on rodents

barn·storm \ˈbärn-ˌstȯrm\ *vi* **1 :** to tour through rural districts staging theatrical performances usually in one-night stands **2 :** to travel from place to place making brief stops (as in political campaigning) **3 :** to pilot an airplane in sightseeing flights with passengers or in exhibition stunts in an unscheduled course especially in rural districts — **barn·storm·er** *n*

barn swallow *n* **:** a common swallow of both the Old World and the New World that often nests in barns

barn·yard \-ˌyärd\ *n* **:** a usually fenced area adjoining a barn

baro- *combining form* **:** weight **:** pressure ⟨*barometer*⟩ [Greek *baros* "weight"]

baro·graph \ˈbar-ə-ˌgraf\ *n* **:** a barometer that records atmospheric pressure changes on a graph

ba·rom·e·ter \bə-ˈräm-ət-ər\ *n* **1 :** an instrument for determining the pressure of the atmosphere that is used to forecast weather and to determine altitude **2 :** something that registers changes (as in public opinion) — **bar·o·met·ric** \ˌbar-ə-ˈme-trik\ *adj*

barometric pressure *n* **:** the pressure of the atmosphere usually expressed as the height of a column of mercury

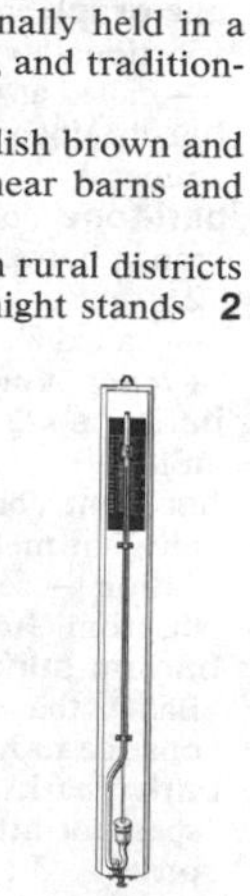

barometer 1: *top* mercury, *bottom* aneroid

bar·on \ˈbar-ən\ *n* **1 a :** a tenant holding rights and title usually by military service directly from a feudal superior (as a king) **b :** a member of the nobility **:** PEER **2 :** a member of the lowest grade of the British peerage **3 :** a person of great or excessive power or influence in some field ⟨cattle *baron*⟩ [Medieval French, of Germanic origin]

bar·on·age \-ə-nij\ *n* **:** the whole body of barons or peers

bar·on·ess \-ə-nəs\ *n* **1 :** the wife or widow of a baron **2 :** a woman who holds a baronial title in her own right

bar·on·et \ˈbar-ə-nət\ *n* **:** a person holding a rank of honor below a baron but above a knight

ba·ro·ni·al \bə-ˈrō-nē-əl\ *adj* **:** of, relating to, or suitable for a baron or the baronage ⟨lives in *baronial* splendor⟩

bar·ony \ˈbar-ə-nē\ *n, pl* **bar·on·ies :** the domain, rank, or dignity of a baron

ba·roque \bə-ˈrōk, ba-, -ˈräk\ *adj* **:** of or relating to a style of artistic expression especially of the 17th century marked by elaborate and sometimes grotesque ornamentation and the use of curved and exaggerated figures in art and architecture, by improvisation, contrast, and tension in music, and by complex form and bizarre, ingenious, and often ambiguous imagery in literature [French, from Middle French *barroque* "irregularly shaped (of a pearl)," from Portuguese *barroco*] — **baroque** *n*

ba·rouche \bə-ˈrüsh\ *n* **:** a four-wheeled carriage with a driver's seat high in front, two double seats inside facing each other, and a folding top [German *Barutsche,* from Italian *biroccio,* derived from Latin *bi-* "two" + *rota* "wheel"]

barque *variant of* BARK

barquentine *variant of* BARKENTINE

bar·rack \ˈbar-ək, -ik\ *n* **1 :** a building or group of buildings in which soldiers are quartered — usually used in plural **2 :** a plain large building — usually used in plural [French *baraque* "hut," from Catalan *barraca*]

bar·ra·cu·da \ˌbar-ə-ˈküd-ə\ *n, pl* **-da** *or* **-das :** any of several large predatory marine fishes of warm seas having sharp teeth and often caught for food or sport [American Spanish]

[1]**bar·rage** \ˈbär-ij\ *n* **:** an artificial dam placed in a watercourse to increase the depth of water or to divert it into a channel for navigation or irrigation [French, from *barrer* "to bar"]

[2]**bar·rage** \bə-ˈräzh, -ˈräj\ *n* **1 :** a barrier of continuous artillery or machine-gun fire directed upon a line close to friendly troops to screen and protect them **2 :** a rapid or concentrated delivery or outpouring (as of speech or writing) — **barrage** *vt*

bar·ra·try \ˈbar-ə-trē\ *n, pl* **-tries 1 :** the purchase or sale of offices of honor or profit in church or state **2 :** a fraudulent breach of duty by the master or crew of a ship intended to harm the owner or cargo **3 :** the practice of inciting lawsuits or quarrels [derived from Medieval French *barater* "to be active, do business, cause strife, deceive"]

Barr body \ˈbär-\ *n* **:** a densely staining inactivated X chromosome present in each somatic cell of most female mammals [after Murray Llewellyn *Barr,* died 1995, Canadian anatomist]

barred \ˈbärd\ *adj* **:** having alternate bands of different color

[1]**bar·rel** \ˈbar-əl\ *n* **1 :** a round bulging container that is longer than it is wide and has flat ends **2 a :** the amount held by a barrel; *esp* **:** the amount (as 42 gallons or 159 liters of petroleum) fixed for a product and used as a unit of measure **b :** a great quantity ⟨a *barrel* of fun⟩ **3 :** a cylindrical or tubular part ⟨gun *barrel*⟩ **4 :** the body proper of a four-footed animal [Medieval French *baril*] — **bar·reled** \-əld\ *adj*

[2]**barrel** *vb* **-reled** *or* **-relled; -rel·ing** *or* **-rel·ling 1 :** to put or pack in a barrel **2 :** to travel at a high speed ⟨*barreling* down the highway⟩

barrel cactus *n* **:** any of various spiny barrel-shaped ridged cacti that are found in Mexico and the adjacent U.S.

bar·rel·ful \ˈbar-əl-ˌfu̇l\ *n, pl* **bar·rel·fuls** \-əl-ˌfu̇lz\ *or* **bar·rels·ful** \-əlz-ˌfu̇l\ **:** as much or as many as a barrel will hold

barrel organ *n* **:** an instrument for producing music by the action of a revolving cylinder studded with pegs that open a series of valves to admit air from a bellows to a set of pipes

[1]**bar·ren** \ˈbar-ən\ *adj* **1 a :** incapable of producing offspring — used especially of females **b :** habitually failing to bear fruit ⟨*barren* apple trees⟩ **2 a :** producing little or no vegetation **:** DESOLATE ⟨*barren* deserts⟩ **b :** producing inferior crops ⟨*barren* soil⟩ **c :** unproductive of results or gain **:** FRUITLESS ⟨a *barren* scheme⟩ **3 :** lacking interest or charm ⟨a *barren* routine⟩ **4 :** lacking inspiration or ideas ⟨a *barren* mind⟩ [Medieval French *barain*] — **bar·ren·ly** *adv* — **bar·ren·ness** \-ən-nəs\ *n*

[2]**barren** *n* **1 :** a tract of barren land **2** *pl* **:** a wide usually level tract with stunted or scrub trees or little vegetation

bar·rette \bä-ˈret, bə-\ *n* **:** a clip or bar for holding the hair in place [French]

[1]**bar·ri·cade** \ˈbar-ə-ˌkād, ˌbar-ə-ˈ\ *vt* **1 :** to block off or stop up with a barricade ⟨*barricade* a street⟩ **2 :** to prevent access to by means of a barricade ⟨*barricaded* himself in his room⟩

[2]**barricade** *n* **:** a hastily made barrier for protecting against attack or for blocking the way [French, derived from Middle French *barrique* "barrel"]

bar·ri·er \ˈbar-ē-ər\ *n* **1 :** a material object or set of objects that serves as a barricade **2 :** something immaterial that impedes or separates ⟨language *barriers* between peoples⟩ **3 :** a factor (as a canyon or lack of food) that keeps organisms from interbreeding or spreading into new territory [Medieval French *barrere,* from *barere* "bar"]

barrier island *n* **:** a long broad sandy island parallel to a shore that is built up by the action of waves, currents, and winds

barrier reef *n* **:** a coral reef roughly parallel to a shore and separated from it by a lagoon

bar·ring \ˈbär-ing\ *prep* **1 :** EXCEPT ⟨*barring* none⟩ **2 :** apart from the possibility of ⟨we'll be there, *barring* accidents⟩

bar·rio \ˈbär-ē-ˌō, ˈbar-\ *n, pl* **-ri·os 1 :** a district of a city or town in a Spanish-speaking country **2 :** a Spanish-speaking section of a city or town in the U.S. [Spanish, from Arabic *barrī* "of the open country"]

bar·ris·ter \ˈbar-ə-stər\ *n* **:** a British lawyer who is permitted to plead cases in court — compare SOLICITOR [from [1]*bar*]

bar·room \ˈbär-ˌrüm, -ˌru̇m\ *n* **:** a room or establishment whose main feature is a bar for the sale of alcoholic beverages

[1]**bar·row** \ˈbar-ō\ *n* **:** a large burial mound of earth or stones [Old English *beorg* "mountain, mound"]

[2]**barrow** *n* **:** a male hog castrated before sexual maturity [Old English *bearg*]

[3]**barrow** *n* **1 a :** HANDBARROW **b :** WHEELBARROW **2 :** a cart with a shallow box body, two wheels, and shafts for pushing it **:** PUSHCART [Old English *bearwe*]

bar·tend·er \ˈbär-ˌten-dər\ *n* **:** a person who serves alcoholic beverages at a bar — **bar·tend** \-ˌtend\ *vi*

[1]**bar·ter** \ˈbärt-ər\ *vb* **:** to trade one commodity directly for another without the use of money [Medieval French *barater* "to do business, exchange"] — **bar·ter·er** \ˈbärt-ər-ər\ *n*

[2]**barter** *n* **:** the exchange of goods without the use of money; *also* **:** something given in such an exchange

bar·ti·zan \ˈbärt-ə-zən\ *n* **:** a small overhanging or projecting structure (as a turret) for lookout or defense [Middle English *bretasinge*]

Ba·ruch \bə-ˈrük, ˈbär-ˌük\ *n* **:** a book of homilies included in the Roman Catholic canon of the Old Testament and in the Protestant Apocrypha — see BIBLE table

bary·on \ˈbar-ē-ˌän\ *n* **:** any of a group of subatomic particles that have a mass equal to or greater than that of the proton and that are composed of three quarks [Greek *barys* "heavy"]

bas·al \ˈbā-səl, -zəl\ *adj* **1 :** relating to, situated at, or forming the base **2 :** of, relating to, or forming a foundation or basis **:** FUNDAMENTAL — **bas·al·ly** \-ē\ *adv*

basal body *n* **:** a minute distinctively staining cell organelle found at the base of a flagellum or cilium and identical to a centriole in structure

basal metabolic rate *n* **:** the rate at which heat is given off by an organism at complete rest

basal metabolism *n* **:** the metabolic activities of a fasting and resting organism in which energy is being used solely to maintain vital cellular activity, respiration, and circulation

ba·salt \bə-ˈsȯlt, ˈbā-ˌ\ *n* **:** a dark fine-grained igneous rock [Latin *basaltes*] — **ba·sal·tic** \bə-ˈsȯl-tik\ *adj*

bas·cule \ˈbas-ˌkyül\ *n* **:** an apparatus or structure (as a bridge) in which one end is counterbalanced by the other on the principle of the seesaw or by weights [French, "seesaw"]

[1]**base** \ˈbās\ *n, pl* **bas·es** \ˈbā-səz\ **1 a :** the bottom of something that serves as its support **:** FOUNDATION **b (1) :** a side or face of a geometrical figure from which an altitude can be constructed; *esp* **:** one on which the figure stands **(2) :** the length of a base **c :** the part of a plant or animal structure by which it is attached to another more central structure ⟨the *base* of the thumb⟩ **2 a :** a main ingredient **b :** an inert ingredient that carries the main ingredient (as of a medicine) **3 :** the fundamental part of something **:** GROUNDWORK **4 a :** the point or line from which a start is made in an action or undertaking **b :** a line in a survey that serves as the origin for calculations of distances or positions **c :** a place where military operations begin **d :** a number (as 5 in $5^{6.44}$ or 5^7) that is raised to a power; *esp* **:** the number that when raised to a power equal to the logarithm of a certain value yields that value ⟨the logarithm of 100 to the *base* 10 is 2 since $10^2 = 100$⟩ **e (1) :** a number equal to the number of units that would be equivalent to one in the next higher place in a given number system **:** a number equal to the number that each place value is an increasing power of ⟨in *base* 10 it takes 10 ones in the units place to equal a one in the tens place⟩ **(2) :** a system of writing numbers using a given base ⟨convert from *base* 10 to *base* 2⟩ **f :** ROOT 5 **5 a :** the starting place or goal in various games **b :** any of the four stations a runner in baseball must touch in order to score **6 a :** any of various compounds that are capable of reacting with an acid to form a salt, that when dissolved in water have a strong somewhat bitter taste, turn litmus blue, and yield hydroxyl ions, that have a molecule or ion which can take up a proton from an acid, or that are substances able to give up to an acid an unshared pair of electrons **b :** any of the five purine or pyrimidine bases of DNA and RNA that include cytosine, guanine, adenine, thymine, and uracil **7 :** a number that is multiplied by a rate or of which a fraction or percentage is calculated ⟨to find the interest on $90 at 10 percent multiply the *base* 90 by .10⟩ [Latin *basis,* from Greek, from *bainein* "to go"] — **based** \ˈbāst\ *adj* — **base·less** \ˈbās-ləs\ *adj* — **off base 1 :** WRONG, MISTAKEN **2 :** by surprise **:** UNAWARES

[2]**base** *vt* **1 :** to make, form, or serve as a base for **2 :** to use as a base or basis for **:** ESTABLISH **3 :** STATION

[3]**base** *adj* **:** constituting or serving as a base

[4]**base** *adj* **1** *archaic* **:** BASEBORN 1 **2 a :** being of comparatively low value and having inferior properties (as resistance to corrosion) ⟨a *base* metal such as iron⟩ **b :** made of or alloyed with a base metal **3 :** morally low **:** MEAN, CONTEMPTIBLE ⟨*base* conduct⟩ [Medieval French *bas* "low," from Late Latin *bassus* "fat, short, low"] — **base·ly** *adv* — **base·ness** *n*

base angle *n* **:** either of the angles of a triangle that have one side in common with the base

base·ball \ˈbās-ˌbȯl\ *n* **:** a game played with a bat and ball between two teams of nine players each on a field with four bases that mark the course a runner must take to score; *also* **:** the ball used in this game

baseball cap *n* **:** a cap of the kind worn by baseball players that has a rounded crown and a long visor

base·board \-ˌbōrd, -ˌbȯrd\ *n* **:** a line of boards or molding covering the joint of a wall and a floor

base·born \-ˈbȯrn\ *adj* **1 :** of humble birth **:** LOWLY **2 :** of illegitimate birth **:** BASTARD

base exchange *n* **:** a post exchange at a naval or air force base

base hit *n* **:** a hit in baseball enabling the batter to reach base safely with no error made and no base runner forced out

base·line \ˈbās-ˌlīn\ *n* **1 :** a line that forms or represents a base **2 a :** either of the lines on a baseball field that lead from home plate to first base and third base and are extended into the outfield as foul lines **b :** BASE PATH

base·ment \ˈbās-mənt\ *n* **1 :** the part of a building that is wholly or partly below ground level **2 :** BASE 1a

ba·sen·ji \bə-ˈsen-jē, -ˈzen-\ *n* **:** any of an African breed of small compact curly-tailed dogs that rarely bark [probably from Lingala (Bantu language of the lower Congo River) *mbwa na basenji,* literally, "dogs of the bush people"]

base on balls : an advance to first base given to a baseball player who receives four balls during a turn at bat

base pair *n* **:** one of the pairs of nucleotide bases on complementary strands of nucleic acid that are linked by bonds of hydrogen and that include adenine linked to thymine in DNA or to uracil in RNA and guanine linked to cytosine in both DNA and RNA

base path *n* **:** the area between the bases of a baseball field used by a base runner

base runner *n* **:** a baseball player of the team at bat who is on base or is attempting to reach a base — **base·run·ning** \ˈbās-ˌrən-ing\ *n*

\ə\ **abut**	\au̇\ **out**	\i\ **tip**	\ȯ\ **saw**	\u̇\ **foot**
\ər\ **further**	\ch\ **chin**	\ī\ **life**	\ȯi\ **coin**	\y\ **yet**
\a\ **mat**	\e\ **pet**	\j\ **job**	\th\ **thin**	\yü\ **few**
\ā\ **take**	\ē\ **easy**	\ng\ **sing**	\t͟h\ **this**	\yu̇\ **cure**
\ä\ **cot, cart**	\g\ **go**	\ō\ **bone**	\ü\ **food**	\zh\ **vision**

[1]bash \ˈbash\ *vb* **1 :** to strike violently : BEAT **2 :** to smash by a blow **3 :** CRASH 1a [origin unknown]

[2]bash *n* **1 :** a forceful blow **2 :** a festive social gathering : PARTY

bash·ful \ˈbash-fəl\ *adj* **1 :** inclined to shrink from public attention : SHY, DIFFIDENT **2 :** characterized by or resulting from extreme sensitiveness or self-consciousness ⟨a *bashful* smile⟩ [Middle English *basshen* "to be abashed"] ***synonyms*** see SHY — **bash·ful·ly** \-fə-lē\ *adv* — **bash·ful·ness** *n*

[1]ba·sic \ˈbā-sik, -zik\ *adj* **1 :** of, relating to, or forming the base or foundation : FUNDAMENTAL ⟨*basic* industries⟩ ⟨the *basic* facts⟩ **2 :** constituting or serving as a basis or starting point ⟨a *basic* course in French⟩ **3 a :** of, relating to, containing, or having the character of a base **b :** having an alkaline reaction **4 :** containing relatively little silica ⟨*basic* rocks⟩ — **ba·si·cal·ly** \-si-klē, -kə-lē\ *adv* — **ba·sic·i·ty** \bā-ˈsis-ət-ē\ *n*

[2]basic *n* **:** something that is basic : FUNDAMENTAL

BA·SIC \ˈbā-sik, -zik\ *n* **:** a simplified language for programming and interacting with a computer [*B*eginner's *A*ll-purpose *S*ymbolic *I*nstruction *C*ode]

basic training *n* **:** the initial period of training a military recruit

ba·sid·io·my·cete \bə-ˌsid-ē-ō-ˈmī-ˌsēt, -ˌmī-ˈsēt\ *n* **:** any of a group of fungi (as rusts, smuts, mushrooms, or puffballs) having septate hyphae and spores borne on a basidium [*basidium* + Greek *mykēt-, mykēs* "fungus"] — **ba·sid·io·my·ce·tous** \-ō-mī-ˈsēt-əs\ *adj*

ba·sid·io·spore \bə-ˈsid-ē-ə-ˌspōr, -ˌspȯr\ *n* **:** a spore produced by a basidium

ba·sid·i·um \bə-ˈsid-ē-əm\ *n, pl* **-ia** \-ē-ə\ **:** a structure of a basidiomycete in which usually four basidiospores are formed [New Latin, from Latin *basis*]

bas·il \ˈbaz-əl, ˈbāz-, ˈbas-, ˈbās-\ *n* **1 :** any of several plants of the mint family; *esp* **:** SWEET BASIL **2 :** the leaves of a basil used for seasoning [derived from Greek *basilikon,* from *basilikos* "royal"]

bas·i·lar \ˈbaz-ə-lər, ˈbas-\ *adj* **:** of, relating to, or situated at a base

ba·sil·i·ca \bə-ˈsil-i-kə, -ˈzil-\ *n* **1 :** an oblong public building of ancient Rome ending in an apse **2 :** an early Christian church building consisting of nave and aisles with clerestory and apse **3 :** a Roman Catholic church with certain ceremonial privileges [Latin, from Greek *basilikē,* literally, "royal (hall)," from *basileus* "king"] — **ba·sil·i·can** \-kən\ *adj*

basilica 2: *1* narthex, *2* nave, *3* aisle, *4* altar

bas·i·lisk \ˈbas-ə-ˌlisk, ˈbaz-\ *n* **1 :** a legendary reptile with fatal breath and glance **2 :** any of several crested tropical American lizards able to run on their hind legs [derived from Greek *basiliskos,* literally, "little king"]

ba·sin \ˈbās-n\ *n* **1 a :** a wide usually round container with sloping or curving sides for holding liquid **b :** the amount that a basin holds **2 a :** a dock built in a tidal river or harbor **b :** an enclosed or partly enclosed water area **3 a :** a large or small depression in the surface of the land or in the ocean floor **b :** the land drained by a river and its branches **c :** a great depression in the surface of the lithosphere occupied by an ocean **4 :** a broad area of the earth beneath which the strata dip from the sides toward the center [Medieval French *bacin,* from Late Latin *bacchinon*]

ba·sis \ˈbā-səs\ *n, pl* **ba·ses** \ˈbā-ˌsēz\ **1 :** the base, foundation, or chief supporting part **2 :** the principal component of something **3 :** something on which something else is constructed or established **4 :** the basic principle [Latin]

bask \ˈbask\ *vi* **:** to lie or relax in a pleasant warmth or atmosphere ⟨*basked* in the sun⟩ ⟨*basking* in their recent success⟩ [Old Norse *bathask* "to bathe oneself"]

bas·ket \ˈbas-kət\ *n* **1 a :** a woven container (as of straw or strips of wood) **b :** the contents of a basket **2 :** something that resembles a basket in shape or use **3 a :** a net open at the bottom and suspended from a metal ring that forms the goal in basketball **b :** a field goal in basketball [Middle English] — **bas·ket·like** \-ˌlīk\ *adj*

bas·ket·ball \-ˌbȯl\ *n* **:** a usually indoor court game between two teams of five players each who score by tossing an inflated ball through a raised goal; *also* **:** the ball used in this game

basket–of–gold *n* **:** a European perennial herb widely cultivated for its grayish foliage and yellow flowers

basket case *n* **1 :** a person who is mentally incapacitated or worn out **2 :** one that is totally disabled or inoperative

bas·ket·ry \ˈbas-kə-trē\ *n* **1 :** BASKETWORK **2 :** the art or craft of making baskets or objects woven like baskets

basket weave *n* **:** a textile weave resembling the checkered pattern of a plaited basket

bas·ket·work \ˈbas-kət-ˌwərk\ *n* **:** objects produced by basketry

basking shark *n* **:** a large shark that feeds on plankton and may reach a length of 45 feet (13.7 meters)

bas·ma·ti rice \ˌbäz-ˈmät-ē, ˌbäs-\ *n* **:** a cultivated aromatic long-grain rice originating in southern Asia [Hindi *bāsmatī,* literally, "something fragrant"]

bas mitzvah *variant of* BAT MITZVAH

ba·so·phil \ˈbā-sə-ˌfil, -zə-\ *also* **ba·so·phile** \-ˌfīl\ *n* **:** a basophilic substance or structure; *esp* **:** a white blood cell with basophilic granules [*base* + *-o-* + [2]*-phil*]

ba·so·phil·ic \ˌbā-sə-ˈfil-ik, -zə-\ *adj* **:** staining readily with basic dyes

Basque \ˈbask\ *n* **1 :** a member of a people inhabiting a region bordering on the Bay of Biscay in northern Spain and southwestern France **2 :** the language of the Basque people [French, derived from Latin *Vasco*] — **Basque** *adj*

bas–re·lief \ˌbä-ri-ˈlēf\ *n* **:** a sculpture in relief in which the design is raised very slightly from the background [French, from *bas* "low" + *relief* "raised work"]

bas-relief

[1]bass \ˈbas\ *n, pl* **bass** *or* **bass·es :** any of various spiny-finned freshwater or marine sport and food fishes [Old English *bærs*]

[2]bass \ˈbās\ *n* **1 :** a deep or low-pitched tone **:** a low-pitched sound **2 a (1) :** the lowest voice part in a 4-part chorus — compare ALTO, SOPRANO, TENOR **(2) :** the lower half of the instrumental tonal range — compare TREBLE **b (1) :** the lowest male singing voice **(2) :** a singer having such a voice **c :** the lowest member in range of a family of instruments; *esp* **:** DOUBLE BASS [Medieval French *bas* "low, base"] — **bass** *adj*

bass clef *n* **1 :** a clef placing the F below middle C on the 4th line of the staff **2 :** the bass staff

bass drum *n* **:** a large drum having two heads and giving a low booming sound

bas·set hound \ˈbas-ət-\ *n* **:** any of an old French breed of short-legged long-eared hunting dogs — called also *basset* [French *basset,* derived from Middle French *bas* "low"]

bass horn *n* **:** TUBA

bas·si·net \ˌbas-ə-ˈnet\ *n* **:** an infant's bed often with a hood over one end [probably from French *barcelonnette,* from *berceau* "cradle"]

bas·so \ˈbas-ō, ˈbäs-\ *n, pl* **bassos** *or* **bas·si** \ˈbäs-ˌē\ **1 :** a bass singer; *esp* **:** an operatic bass **2 :** a low deep voice [Italian, from Late Latin *bassus* "low"]

bas·soon \bə-ˈsün, ba-\ *n* **:** a double-reed woodwind instrument having a long U-shaped conical wooden body connected to the mouthpiece by a thin metal tube sounding usually two octaves lower than the oboe [French *basson,* from Italian *bassone,* from *basso*] — **bas·soon·ist** \-ˈsü-nəst\ *n*

bassoon

bass viol *n* **:** DOUBLE BASS

bass·wood \ˈbas-ˌwu̇d\ *n* **1 :** any of several linden trees; *esp* **:** a tall tree of the central and eastern U.S. **2 :** the pale straight-grained wood of a basswood [*bass* "bast," alteration of *bast*]

bast \ˈbast\ *n* **1 :** PHLOEM **2 :** a strong woody fiber obtained chiefly from the phloem of plants and used especially in cordage, matting, and fabrics [Old English *bæst*]

[1]**bas·tard** \ˈbas-tərd\ *n* **1 :** an illegitimate child **2 :** something that is spurious, irregular, inferior, or of questionable origin [Medieval French] — **bas·tard·ly** *adj*

[2]**bastard** *adj* **1 :** ILLEGITIMATE **2 :** of an inferior or irregular kind, stock, or form **3 :** not genuine or authoritative — **bas·tardy** \-ē\ *n*

[1]**baste** \ˈbāst\ *vt* **:** to sew with long loose temporary stitches [Medieval French *bastir,* of Germanic origin] — **bast·er** *n*

[2]**baste** \ˈbāst\ *vt* **:** to moisten (as roasting meat) with a sauce or fat [Middle English *baisten*] — **bast·er** *n*

Bastille Day *n* **:** July 14 observed in France as a national holiday in commemoration of the fall of the Bastille in 1789

bas·ti·na·do \ˌbas-tə-ˈnād-ō, -ˈnäd-\ *n, pl* **-does :** a punishment consisting of beating the soles of the feet with a stick [Spanish *bastonada,* from *bastón* "stick," from Late Latin *bastum*] — **bastinado** *vt*

bast·ing \ˈbā-sting\ *n* **:** the thread used in loose stitching or the stitching made by this thread

bas·tion \ˈbas-chən\ *n* **1 :** a projecting part of a fortification **2 :** a fortified area or position **3 :** a firmly established place or position [Middle French, from Italian *bastione,* from *bastia* "fortress," from *bastire* "to build," of Germanic origin]

[1]**bat** \ˈbat\ *n* **1 :** a stout solid stick **:** CLUB **2 :** a sharp blow **3 a :** a usually wooden implement used for hitting the ball in various games **b :** a paddle used in various games (as table tennis) **4 :** a turn at batting ⟨at *bat*⟩ **5 :** BATTING 2 **6 :** BINGE 1 [Old English *batt*] — **off the bat :** IMMEDIATELY ⟨recognized him right *off the bat*⟩

[2]**bat** *vb* **bat·ted; bat·ting 1 :** to strike or hit with or as if with a bat **2 a :** to advance (a base runner) by batting **b :** to have a batting average of **3 :** to take one's turn at bat in baseball

[3]**bat** *n* **:** any of an order (Chiroptera) of nocturnal flying mammals with the forelimbs modified to function as wings [alteration of Middle English *bakke,* of Scandinavian origin]

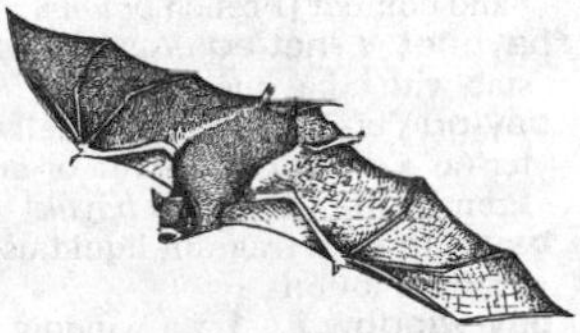

[3]bat

[4]**bat** *vt* **bat·ted; bat·ting :** to wink especially in surprise or emotion ⟨never *batted* an eye⟩; *also* **:** FLUTTER ⟨*batted* his eyelashes⟩ [probably from Middle English *baten* "to beat, flap (wings)"]

bat·boy \ˈbat-ˌbȯi\ *n* **:** a boy who looks after the equipment (as bats) for a baseball team

batch \ˈbach\ *n* **1 :** a quantity baked at one time ⟨the first *batch* of cookies⟩ **2 a :** a quantity of any material for use at one time or produced at one operation ⟨a *batch* of cement⟩ **b :** a group of jobs to be run on a computer at one time with the same program **3 :** a group of persons or things **:** LOT ⟨a *batch* of letters⟩ [Middle English *bache*]

bate \ˈbāt\ *vt* **1 :** to reduce the force or intensity of ⟨listen with *bated* breath⟩ **2 :** to take away **:** DEDUCT [Middle English *baten,* from *abaten* "to abate"]

ba·teau *also* **bat·teau** \ba-ˈtō\ *n, pl* **ba·teaux** *also* **bat·teaux** \-ˈtō, -ˈtōz\ **:** any of various small craft; *esp* **:** a flat-bottomed boat with slanted bow and stern and flaring sides [French *bateau,* derived from Old English *bāt* "boat"]

bat girl *n* **:** a girl or woman who looks after the equipment (as bats) for a baseball team

bath \ˈbath, ˈbȧth\ *n, pl* **baths** \ˈbat͟hz, ˈbaths, ˈbȧt͟hz, ˈbȧths\ **1 :** a washing or soaking (as in water) of all or part of the body ⟨take a *bath*⟩ **2 a :** water used for bathing ⟨drew a *bath*⟩ **b :** a liquid in which objects are placed so that it can act upon them ⟨a dyeing *bath*⟩; *also* **:** the container holding such a liquid **c :** a contained medium for regulating the temperature of something ⟨a hot water *bath*⟩ **3 a :** BATHROOM ⟨a house with two *baths*⟩ **b :** a building containing rooms designed for bathing **c :** SPA — usually used in plural **4 :** a financial setback ⟨took a *bath* when the price of stocks dropped⟩ [Old English *bæth*]

bathe \ˈbāt͟h\ *vb* **bathed; bath·ing 1 :** to take a bath **2 :** to go swimming **3 a :** to wash in a liquid (as water) **b :** MOISTEN, WET **4 :** to apply water or a medicinal liquid to **5 :** to flow along the edge of **:** LAVE **6 :** to surround or cover as a liquid does ⟨trees *bathed* in moonlight⟩ — **bath·er** \ˈbā-t͟hər\ *n*

ba·thet·ic \bə-ˈthet-ik\ *adj* **:** characterized by bathos — **ba·thet·i·cal·ly** \-i-kə-lē, -klē\ *adv*

bath·house \ˈbath-ˌhau̇s, ˈbȧth-\ *n* **1 :** a building equipped for bathing **2 :** a building containing dressing rooms for bathers

bathing suit *n* **:** SWIMSUIT

batho·lith \ˈbath-ə-ˌlith\ *n* **:** a great mass of intrusive igneous rock that stopped in its rise quite a distance below the surface [Greek *bathos* "depth"]

ba·thos \ˈbā-ˌthäs\ *n* **1 a :** the sudden appearance of the commonplace in otherwise elevated matter or style **b :** ANTICLIMAX **2 :** FLATNESS, TRITENESS **3 :** insincere or overdone pathos [Greek, literally, "depth"]

bath·robe \ˈbath-ˌrōb, ˈbȧth-\ *n* **:** a loose usually absorbent robe worn before and after bathing or as a dressing gown

bath·room \ˈbath-ˌrüm, ˈbȧth-, -ˌru̇m\ *n* **:** a room containing a bathtub or shower and usually a sink and toilet

bath·tub \ˈbath-ˌtəb, ˈbȧth-\ *n* **:** a usually fixed tub for bathing

bathy·al \ˈbath-ē-əl\ *adj* **:** DEEP-SEA

bathy·scaphe \ˈbath-i-ˌskaf, -ˌskāf\ *or* **bathy·scaph** \-ˌskaf\ *n* **:** a navigable submersible ship for deep-sea exploration having a spherical watertight cabin attached to its underside [Greek *bathys* "deep" + *skaphē* "light boat"]

bathy·sphere \ˈbath-i-ˌsfiər\ *n* **:** a strongly built sphere-shaped diving apparatus for deep-sea observation

ba·tik \bə-ˈtēk, ˈbat-ik\ *n* **1 a :** an Indonesian method of hand-printing textiles by coating the parts not to be dyed with wax **b :** a design so executed **2 :** a fabric printed by batik [Javanese *baṭik*]

ba·tiste \bə-ˈtēst, ba-\ *n* **:** a fine soft sheer fabric of plain weave [French]

bat·man \ˈbat-mən\ *n* **:** an orderly of a British military officer [French *bât* "packsaddle"]

[1]**bat mitz·vah** \bät-ˈmits-və\ *also* **bas mitz·vah** \bäs-ˈmits-və\ *n, often cap B&M* **1 :** a Jewish girl who at about 12 years of age assumes religious responsibilities **2 :** the ceremony recognizing a girl as a bat mitzvah [Hebrew *bath miṣwāh,* literally, "daughter of the law"]

[2]**bat mitzvah** *also* **bas mitzvah** *vt* **bat mitz·vahed** *also* **bas mitz·vahed; bat mitz·vah·ing** *also* **bas mitz·vah·ing :** to administer the ceremony of bat mitzvah to

ba·ton \bə-ˈtän, ba-, -ˈtōⁿ\ *n* **1 :** a staff borne as a symbol of office **2 :** a slender rod with which a leader directs a band or orchestra **3 :** a hollow cylinder carried by each member of a relay team and passed to the succeeding runner **4 :** a metal rod with a ball at one or both ends carried by a drum major or baton twirler [French *bâton* "stick," derived from Late Latin *bastum*]

ba·tra·chi·an \bə-ˈtrā-kē-ən\ *n* **:** AMPHIBIAN 1; *esp* **:** FROG 1a, TOAD [Greek *batrachos* "frog"] — **batrachian** *adj*

bats·man \ˈbat-smən\ *n* **:** a batter especially in cricket

batt *n* **:** BATTING 2; *also* **:** an often square piece of batting

bat·tal·ion \bə-ˈtal-yən\ *n* **1 :** a large organized body of troops **:** ARMY **2 :** a military unit made up of a headquarters and two or more companies, batteries, or subunits **3 :** a large body of persons organized to act together ⟨labor *battalions*⟩ [derived from Late Latin *battalia* "combat"]

[1]**bat·ten** \ˈbat-n\ *vb* **bat·tened; bat·ten·ing** \ˈbat-ning, -n-ing\ **1 a :** to grow or make fat **:** FATTEN **b :** to feed gluttonously **2 :** to grow prosperous **:** THRIVE [probably from Old Norse *batna* "to improve"]

[2]**batten** *n* **1 :** a thin narrow strip of lumber used especially to seal or reinforce a joint **2 :** a strip, bar, or support like or used like a batten (as in a sail) [Middle English *batent* "finished board," derived from Medieval French *batre* "to beat"]

[3]**batten** *vt* **:** to furnish or fasten with battens — often used with *down* — **batten down the hatches :** to prepare for a difficult or dangerous situation

[1]**bat·ter** \ˈbat-ər\ *vb* **1 :** to beat with successive violent blows ⟨*batter* down the door⟩ **2 :** to wear or damage by blows or hard usage ⟨a *battered* old hat⟩ [Middle English *bateren,* probably from *batten* "to bat"] — **bat·ter·er** *n*

[2]**batter** *n* **:** a mixture that consists chiefly of flour and liquid and

is thin enough to pour or drop from a spoon [Middle English *bater,* probably from *bateren*]

[3]**batter** *n* **:** one that bats; *esp* **:** the baseball player who is batting

battering ram *n* **1 :** a military siege engine used in ancient times to beat down the walls of a besieged place **2 :** a heavy metal bar with handles used to batter down doors and walls

bat•tery \ˈbat-ə-rē, ˈba-trē\ *n, pl* **-ter•ies 1 a :** the act of battering or beating **b :** the unlawful beating or use of force upon a person — compare ASSAULT 2 **2 a :** a tactical grouping of artillery pieces **b :** the guns of a warship **3 :** an artillery unit in the army equivalent to a company **4 a :** a group of two or more electric cells connected together for furnishing electric current; *also* **:** a single electric cell ⟨a flashlight *battery*⟩ **b** *pl* **:** level of energy or enthusiasm ⟨needs a vacation to recharge her *batteries*⟩ **5 a :** a number of similar articles, items, or devices arranged, connected, or used together **:** SET, SERIES ⟨a *battery* of tests⟩ **b :** an impressive group **:** ARRAY **6 :** the pitcher and catcher of a baseball team

battery jar *n* **:** a glass container with straight sides used especially in biology and chemistry laboratories

bat•ting \ˈbat-iŋ\ *n* **1 a :** the action of one who bats **b :** use of or ability with a bat **2 :** layers or sheets of raw cotton or wool used for lining quilts or for stuffing or packaging

batting average *n* **:** a ratio of base hits to official times at bat for a baseball player or team

[1]**bat•tle** \ˈbat-l\ *n* **1 :** a combat between two persons **2 :** a general encounter between armies, ships of war, or aircraft **3 :** an extended contest, struggle, or controversy ⟨a *battle* of wits⟩ [Medieval French *bataille,* from Late Latin *battalia* "combat," derived from Latin *battuere* "to beat"]

[2]**battle** *vb* **bat•tled; bat•tling** \ˈbat-liŋ, -l-iŋ\ **1 :** to engage in battle **:** FIGHT ⟨armies *battling* for a city⟩ **2 :** to struggle using all possible resources (as strength or skill) ⟨*battle* for a cause⟩ **3 :** to fight against ⟨*battle* a fire⟩ — **bat•tler** \-lər, -l-ər\ *n*

bat•tle–ax *or* **bat•tle–axe** \ˈbat-l-ˌaks\ *n* **:** a broadax formerly used as a weapon of war

battle cruiser *n* **:** a large heavily armed warship that is lighter, faster, and more maneuverable than a battleship

battle cry *n* **:** WAR CRY

bat•tle•field \-ˌfēld\ *n* **:** a place where a battle is fought — called also *battleground*

battle group *n* **:** a military unit normally made up of five companies

bat•tle•ment \ˈbat-l-mənt\ *n* **:** a parapet placed at the top of a wall for ornament or defense — **bat•tle•ment•ed** \-ˌment-əd\ *adj*

battlement

battle royal *n, pl* **battles royal** *or* **battle royals 1 a :** a fight involving more than two combatants; *esp* **:** such a contest in which the last one in the ring or standing is declared the winner **b :** a violent struggle **2 :** a heated dispute

bat•tle•ship \ˈbat-l-ˌship\ *n* **:** a warship of the largest and most heavily armed and armored class [short for *line-of-battle ship*]

bat•tle•wag•on \-ˌwag-ən\ *n* **:** BATTLESHIP

bat•ty \ˈbat-ē\ *adj* **bat•ti•er; -est :** CRAZY [[3]*bat*]

bau•ble \ˈbȯ-bəl, ˈbäb-əl\ *n* **1 :** TRINKET 1 **2 :** a jester's scepter **3 :** TRIFLE 1 [Medieval French *babel*]

baud \ˈbȯd, ˈbōd\ *n* **:** a unit of speed (as one bit per second) at which data is sent in communications [after J.M.E. *Baudot,* died 1903, French inventor]

baux•ite \ˈbȯk-ˌsīt, ˈbäk-\ *n* **:** an impure mixture of earthy hydrous aluminum oxides and hydroxides that is the principal ore of aluminum [French, from Les *Baux,* near Arles, France]

baw•bee \ˈbȯ-bē, -ˌbē\ *n* **1 :** any of various Scottish coins of small value **2 :** an English halfpenny [probably from Alexander Orrok, laird of Sille*bawbe,* flourished 1538, Scottish master of the mint]

bawd \ˈbȯd\ *n* **:** one that keeps a house of prostitution; *also* **:** PROSTITUTE [Middle English *bawde*]

bawd•ry \ˈbȯ-drē\ *n, pl* **bawdries :** suggestive or dirty language

bawdy \ˈbȯd-ē\ *adj* **bawd•i•er; -est :** OBSCENE 2a, LEWD — **bawd•i•ly** \ˈbȯd-l-ē\ *adv* — **bawd•i•ness** \ˈbȯd-ē-nəs\ *n*

[1]**bawl** \ˈbȯl\ *vb* **1 :** to cry out loudly and without restraint **:** YELL **2 :** WEEP 1, WAIL [Middle English *baulen*] — **bawl•er** *n*

[2]**bawl** *n* **:** a loud prolonged cry **:** OUTCRY

bawl out *vb* **:** to scold severely

[1]**bay** \ˈbā\ *adj* **:** reddish brown ⟨a *bay* mare⟩ [Medieval French *bai,* from Latin *badius*]

[2]**bay** *n* **1 :** a horse with a bay-colored body and black mane, tail, and points — compare CHESTNUT 3 **2 :** a reddish brown

[3]**bay** *n* **1 :** a main compartment or section of a building **2 :** any of various compartments or sections used for a special purpose (as in an airplane, spacecraft, or gas station) ⟨a bomb *bay*⟩ ⟨a cargo *bay*⟩ **3 :** BAY WINDOW 1 **4 :** a support or housing for electronic equipment [Medieval French *baee* "opening," from *baer* "to be wide open, gape"]

[4]**bay** *vb* **1 a :** to bark or bark at with long deep tones ⟨wolves *baying* at the moon⟩ **b :** to cry out **:** SHOUT **c :** to utter in long deep tones **2 :** to bring (as an animal) to bay [Medieval French *abaier,* of imitative origin]

[5]**bay** *n* **1 :** a deep bark **2 :** the position of one unable to retreat and forced to face danger ⟨brought the fox to *bay*⟩ **3 :** the position of one restrained or held off ⟨kept the infection at *bay*⟩

[6]**bay** *n* **:** an indentation into the land formed by a body of water and usually larger than an inlet and smaller than a gulf [Medieval French *bai,* perhaps from *baier* "to be wide open"]

[7]**bay** *n* **1 a :** LAUREL 1 **b :** any of several shrubs or trees resembling the laurel **2 :** a wreath especially of laurel given as a token of honor for victory or excellence — usually used in plural [Medieval French *baie* "berry, laurel berry," from Latin *baca*]

bay•ber•ry \ˈbā-ˌber-ē\ *n* **1 :** any of several wax myrtles; *esp* **:** a hardy shrub of coastal eastern North America bearing dense clusters of small berries covered with grayish white wax **2 :** the fruit of a bayberry

bay leaf *n* **:** the dried leaf of the European laurel used in cooking

[1]**bay•o•net** \ˈbā-ə-nət, -ˌnet, ˌbā-ə-ˈnet\ *n* **:** a steel blade made to be attached at the muzzle end of a rifle and used in hand-to-hand combat [French *baïonnette,* from *Bayonne,* France]

[2]**bayonet** *vt* **-net•ed** *also* **-net•ted; -net•ing** *also* **-net•ting :** to stab with a bayonet

bay•ou \ˈbī-ü, ˈbī-ō\ *n* **:** a usually marshy or sluggish body of water (as a stream on a delta or an offshoot of a river) [Louisiana French, from Choctaw *bayuk*]

bay rum *n* **:** a fragrant liquid used especially as a cologne or aftershave lotion

bay window *n* **1 :** a window or a set of windows projecting outward from the wall of a building **2 :** POTBELLY 1

ba•zaar \bə-ˈzär\ *n* **1 :** a market (as in the Middle East) that consists of rows of shops or stalls selling miscellaneous goods **2 a :** a place for the sale of goods **b :** DEPARTMENT STORE **3 :** a fair for the sale of articles especially for charitable purposes [Persian *bāzār*]

ba•zoo•ka \bə-ˈzü-kə\ *n* **:** a light portable shoulder weapon that consists of a tube open at both ends and shoots an explosive rocket able to pierce armor [*bazooka,* a crude musical instrument made of pipes and a funnel]

BB \ˈbē-ˌbē\ *n* **:** a small round shot pellet

bcc \ˌbē-ˌsē-ˈsē\ *vb* **bcc'd; bcc'•ing 1 :** to send a blind carbon copy to **2 :** to send as a blind carbon copy [*b*lind *c*arbon *c*opy]

BCD \ˌbē-ˌsē-ˈdē\ *n* **:** a system of writing a decimal number using a binary equivalent ⟨51 in *BCD* is 0101 0001⟩ [*b*inary-*c*oded *d*ecimal]

B cell \ˈbē-ˌsel\ *n* **:** any of the lymphocytes that produce antigen-binding antibodies and that arise and mature in the bone marrow — called also *B lymphocyte*; compare T CELL [*B* probably from *b*ursa-derived (produced by the bursa of Fabricius, a lymphoid organ in birds)]

B complex *n* **:** VITAMIN B COMPLEX

be \bē, ˈbē\ *vb, past 1st and 3rd sing* **was** \wəz, ˈwəz, ˈwäz\; *2nd sing* **were** \wər, ˈwər\; *pl* **were**; *past subjunctive* **were**; *past participle* **been** \bin, ˈbin *chiefly British* bēn *or* ˈbēn\; *present participle* **be•ing** \ˈbē-iŋ\; *present 1st sing* **am** \əm, m, am, ˈam\; *2nd sing* **are** \ər, är, ˈär\; *3rd sing* **is** \iz, ˈiz, əz, z\; *pl* **are**; *present subjunctive* **be 1 a :** to have the same meaning as **:** serve as a sign for ⟨January *is* the first month⟩ ⟨let x *be* 10⟩ **b :** to have identity with ⟨the first person I met *was* my best friend⟩ **c :** to constitute the same class as **d :** to have the quality or character of ⟨the leaves *are* green⟩ **e :** to belong to the class of ⟨the fish *is* a trout⟩ ⟨apes *are* mammals⟩ **2 a :** to have reality **:** EXIST, LIVE ⟨I think, therefore I *am*⟩ ⟨once there *was* a knight⟩ **b :** to have, keep, or occupy a place, situation, or position ⟨the book *is* on the table⟩ **c** : to remain unmolested, undisturbed, or uninterrupted — used only in infinitive form ⟨let it *be*⟩ **d** : to take place : OCCUR ⟨the concert *was* last night⟩ **3** — used with the past participle of transitive verbs as a passive-voice auxiliary ⟨the money *was* found⟩ ⟨the house has *been* built⟩ **4** — used as the auxiliary of the present participle in progressive tenses expressing continuous action ⟨I have *been* sleeping⟩ **5** — used with the past participle of some intransitive verbs as an auxiliary forming archaic perfect tenses **6** — used with the infinitive with *to* to express futurity, arrangement in advance, or obligation ⟨I *am* to interview them today⟩ ⟨they *were* to become famous⟩ [Old English *bēon*]

be- *prefix* **1** : on : around : over ⟨*be*daub⟩ ⟨*be*smear⟩ **2** : to a great or greater degree : thoroughly ⟨*be*fuddle⟩ ⟨*be*rate⟩ **3** : excessively : ostentatiously ⟨*be*deck⟩ **4** : about : to : upon ⟨*be*speak⟩ ⟨*be*stride⟩ **5** : make : cause to be ⟨*be*fool⟩ ⟨*be*little⟩ **6** : affect, provide, or cover with especially excessively ⟨*be*fog⟩ [Old English *bi-, be-*]

[1]**beach** \ˈbēch\ *n* : a shore of a body of water covered by sand, gravel, or larger rock fragments : STRAND [origin unknown]

[2]**beach** *vt* : to run or drive ashore ⟨*beach* a boat⟩

beach buggy *n* : DUNE BUGGY

beach·comb·er \ˈbēch-ˌkō-mər\ *n* **1** : a drifter, loafer, or casual worker along the seacoast **2** : one that searches along a shore (as for salable refuse or for seashells)

beach flea *n* : SAND FLEA 2

beach grass *n* : any of several strongly rooted tough grasses that grow on exposed sandy shores and include some planted to bind the soil on dunes or sandy slopes

beach·head \ˈbēch-ˌhed\ *n* **1** : an area of an enemy-held shore occupied by an advance force of an invading army to protect the later landing of troops or supplies **2** : FOOTHOLD 2

beach plum *n* : a shrubby plum with showy white flowers that grows along the Atlantic coast of the northern U. S. and Canada; *also* : its dark purple fruit often used in preserves

beach towel *n* : a very large usually brightly colored towel designed for use at the beach

[1]**bea·con** \ˈbē-kən\ *n* **1** : a signal fire commonly on a hill, tower, or pole **2 a** : a signal (as a lighthouse) for guidance **b** : a radio transmitter sending out signals for guidance of aircraft **3** : a source of inspiration ⟨a *beacon* of hope⟩ [Old English *bēacen* "sign"]

[2]**beacon** *vb* **1** : to shine as a beacon **2** : to furnish or light up with a beacon

[1]**bead** \ˈbēd\ *n* **1** *pl* : a series of prayers said with a rosary **2** : a small piece of material pierced for threading on a string or wire **3** : a small ball-shaped body: as **a** : a drop of sweat or blood **b** : a bubble formed in or on a beverage **c** : a small metal knob on a firearm used as a front sight **4** : a projecting rim, band, or molding (as on a board or tire) [Middle English *bede* "prayer, prayer bead," from Old English *bed* "prayer"]

Word History Middle English *bede* originally meant "a prayer." The word is related to modern English *bid.* The number and order of a series of prayers are often kept track of with the aid of a string of small round balls. Because each of these balls stands for a prayer, the word *bede,* now *bead* in modern English, was transferred to the balls themselves. Today *bead* is used to refer to any small piece of material pierced for threading on a string or wire. The sense is also extended to refer to any small, round object, such as a drop of sweat.

[2]**bead** *vb* **1** : to adorn or cover with beads or beading **2** : to string together like beads **3** : to form into a bead — **bead·er** *n*

bead·ing \ˈbēd-iŋ\ *n* **1** : material or a part or piece consisting of beads **2** : an open-worked trimming **3** : BEADWORK

bea·dle \ˈbēd-l\ *n* : a minor parish official whose duties include ushering and keeping order in church and sometimes at civic functions [Old English *bydel*]

bead·roll \ˈbēd-ˌrōl\ *n* **1** : a list of names : CATALOG **2** : ROSARY [from the reading in church of a list of names of persons for whom prayers are to be said]

bead·work \ˈbēd-ˌwərk\ *n* : ornamental work of or with beads

beady \ˈbēd-ē\ *adj* **bead·i·er; -est** : resembling beads; *esp* : small, round, and shiny with interest or greed ⟨*beady* eyes⟩

bea·gle \ˈbē-gəl\ *n* : any of a breed of small short-legged smooth-coated hounds [Middle English *begle*]

beak \ˈbēk\ *n* **1 a** : the bill of a bird; *esp* : the bill of a bird of prey adapted for striking and tearing **b** : any of various rigid projecting mouth structures (as of a turtle); *also* : the long sucking mouth of some insects **c** : the human nose **2** : a pointed structure or formation: **a** : a pointed beam projecting from the bow of an ancient galley for piercing an enemy ship **b** : the spout of a vessel [Medieval French *bec,* from Latin *beccus,* of Gaulish origin] ***synonyms*** see BILL — **beaked** \ˈbēkt\ *adj*

bea·ker \ˈbē-kər\ *n* **1** : a large widemouthed drinking cup **2** : a deep widemouthed vessel that often has a projecting lip and is used especially by chemists and pharmacists [Old Norse *bikarr*]

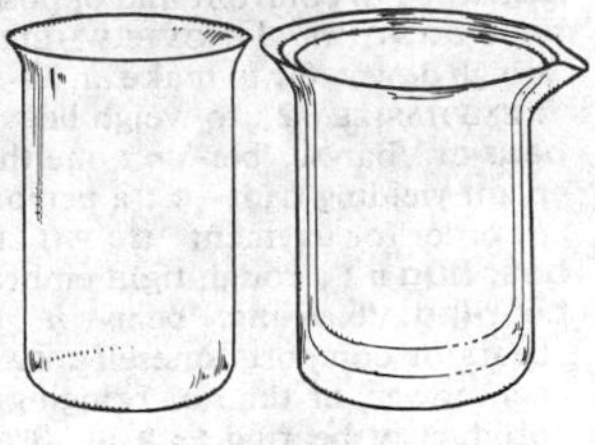
beaker 2

[1]**beam** \ˈbēm\ *n* **1 a** : a long heavy piece of timber or metal used especially as a main horizontal support of a building or a ship **b** : a wood or metal cylinder in a loom on which the warp is wound **2** : the bar of a balance from which the scales hang **3** : the width of a ship at its widest part **4 a** : a ray or shaft of light **b** : a collection of nearly parallel rays (as X-rays) or particles (as electrons) **5** : a constant directional radio signal sent out for the guidance of pilots along a particular course; *also* : the course indicated by this signal [Old English *bēam* "tree, beam"] — **off the beam 1** : on a wrong course **2** : INCORRECT, MISTAKEN — **on the beam 1** : on a right course **2** : exactly correct

[2]**beam** *vb* **1** : to send out in beams or as a beam **2 a** : to transmit especially by satellite **b** : to direct to a particular audience **3** : to send out beams of light **4** : to smile with joy

bean \ˈbēn\ *n* **1 a** : BROAD BEAN **b** : the seed or pod of any of various erect or climbing plants of the legume family **c** : a plant bearing beans **2 a** : a valueless item **b** *pl* : the slightest amount ⟨doesn't know *beans* about it⟩ **3** : a seed or fruit like a bean ⟨coffee *beans*⟩ **4** : HEAD, BRAIN [Old English *bēan*]

bean·bag \ˈbēn-ˌbag\ *n* : a small cloth bag typically filled with beans and used (as for tossing or passing) in many games

bean counter *n* : a person involved in corporate or government financial decisions and especially one reluctant to spend money

bean curd *n* : TOFU

bean·ie \ˈbē-nē\ *n* : a small round tight-fitting skullcap

[1]**bear** \ˈbaər, ˈbeər\ *n, pl* **bears 1** *or pl* **bear** : any of a family of large heavy mammals having long shaggy hair and a rudimentary tail, walking on the soles of its feet, and feeding largely on fruit, plants, and insects as well as on flesh **2** : a surly, uncouth, burly, or clumsy person ⟨is a real *bear* in the morning⟩ ⟨a great *bear* of a man⟩ **3** : one who sells securities or commodities in expectation of a price decline — compare [1]BULL 2 [Old English *bera*]

[2]**bear** *vb* **bore** \ˈbōr, ˈbȯr\; **borne** \ˈbōrn, ˈbȯrn\ *also* **born** \ˈbȯrn\; **bear·ing 1 a** : to move while holding up : CARRY ⟨arrived *bearing* gifts⟩ **b** : to be equipped with ⟨licensed to *bear* arms⟩ **c** : to have as a feature or characteristic ⟨*bears* a good reputation⟩ ⟨*bore* a resemblance to my cousin⟩ **d** : to hold in the mind : HARBOR ⟨*bear* a grudge⟩ **e** : to pass on to others ⟨constantly *bearing* tales⟩ **f** : to bring foward in testifying ⟨*bear* false witness⟩ **g** : BEHAVE 1, CONDUCT ⟨*bore* themselves proudly⟩ **2 a** : to give birth to ⟨*bear* children⟩ ⟨a baby *born* last week⟩ **b** : PRODUCE 2, YIELD **3 a** : to support the weight of : hold up : SUSTAIN ⟨a column *bore* the roof⟩ **b** : to support a burden or strain ⟨*bears* up well in times of grief⟩ **c** : ENDURE 2 ⟨couldn't *bear* the pain⟩ **d** : ASSUME 2a, ACCEPT ⟨*bore* all the costs⟩ ⟨had to *bear* the blame⟩ **e** : to be able to withstand : ALLOW ⟨can't *bear* the suspense⟩ **4** : THRUST 1, PRESS ⟨*borne* along by the crowd⟩ **5 a** : to move, extend, or incline in an indicated direction ⟨*bear* right at the next fork⟩ **b** : to become directed or aimed ⟨brought the guns to *bear* on the target⟩ **6 a** : APPLY 3, PERTAIN ⟨facts *bearing* on the question⟩ **b** : to exert influence or force ⟨brings pressure to *bear* to win votes⟩ [Old English *beran*]

bear·able \ˈbaər-ə-bəl, ˈbeər-\ *adj* : possible to bear

bear·ber·ry \ˈbaər-ˌber-ē, ˈbeər-\ *n* : a trailing evergreen plant of the heath family with glossy red berries

\ə\ **abut**	\au̇\ **out**	\i\ **tip**	\ȯ\ **saw**	\u̇\ **foot**
\ər\ **further**	\ch\ **chin**	\ī\ **life**	\ȯi\ **coin**	\y\ **yet**
\a\ **mat**	\e\ **pet**	\j\ **job**	\th\ **thin**	\yü\ **few**
\ā\ **take**	\ē\ **easy**	\ŋ\ **sing**	\t͟h\ **this**	\yu̇\ **cure**
\ä\ **cot, cart**	\g\ **go**	\ō\ **bone**	\ü\ **food**	\zh\ **vision**

[1]**beard** \ˈbiərd\ *n* **1 :** the hair that grows on a man's face and neck often excluding the mustache **2 :** a hairy or bristly growth or tuft (as on the chin of a goat) [Old English] — **beard·ed** \-əd\ *adj* — **beard·less** \-ləs\ *adj*

[2]**beard** *vt* **:** to confront and oppose daringly **:** DEFY

bear down *vb* **1 :** OVERWHELM, OVERCOME **2 :** to press or weigh down **3 :** to make an all-out effort — **bear down on 1 :** EMPHASIZE **2 :** to weigh heavily on **:** BURDEN

bear·er \ˈbar-ər, ˈber-\ *n* **:** one that bears: as **a :** PORTER **b :** a plant yielding fruit **c :** a person holding a check, draft, bond, or order for payment **d :** PALLBEARER

bear hug *n* **:** a rough tight embrace — **bear–hug** *vt*

bear·ing \ˈbaər-iŋ, ˈbeər-\ *n* **1 :** the manner in which one bears or comports oneself **:** CARRIAGE, BEHAVIOR **2 a :** the act, power, or time of bringing forth offspring or fruit **b :** a product of bearing **:** CROP **3 a :** an object, surface, or point that supports something **b :** a machine part in which one part (as a pivot or pin) turns or slides **4 :** a figure in a coat of arms ⟨armorial *bearings*⟩ **5 a :** PRESSURE 2, THRUST **b :** ENDURANCE 2 **6 a :** the position or direction of one point with respect to another or to the compass **b :** a determination of position ⟨to take a *bearing*⟩ **c** *pl* **:** comprehension of one's position, environment, or situation ⟨lose one's *bearings*⟩ **d :** CONNECTION 2 ⟨the cost had no *bearing* at all on the decision⟩

bear·ish \-ish\ *adj* **1 :** resembling a bear in roughness, gruffness, or surliness **2 :** marked by or expecting a decline in stock prices — **bear·ish·ly** *adv* — **bear·ish·ness** *n*

bear market *n* **:** a market in which stocks are persistently declining in value — compare BULL MARKET

bear out *vt* **:** CONFIRM ⟨research *bore out* the theory⟩

bear·skin \ˈbaər-ˌskin, ˈbeər-\ *n* **:** an article (as a rug or military hat) made of the skin of a bear

beast \ˈbēst\ *n* **1 a :** a four-footed mammal as distinguished from humans and from lower vertebrate and invertebrate animals **b :** a domesticated mammal; *esp* **:** a draft animal **2 :** a cruel person [Medieval French *beste,* from Latin *bestia*]

[1]**beast·ly** \ˈbēst-lē\ *adj* **beast·li·er; -est 1 :** of, relating to, or resembling a beast **:** BESTIAL **2 :** ABOMINABLE 2, NASTY ⟨*beastly* weather⟩ — **beast·li·ness** *n*

[2]**beastly** *adv* **:** VERY ⟨a *beastly* cold day⟩

beast of burden : an animal (as a mule or an ox) used for carrying or pulling heavy loads

[1]**beat** \ˈbēt\ *vb* **beat; beat·en** \ˈbēt-n\ *or* **beat; beat·ing 1 :** to strike repeatedly: **a :** to hit repeatedly so as to inflict pain — often used with *up* **b :** to dash against ⟨rain *beating* on the roof⟩ **c :** to strike at in order to stir up or drive out game **d :** to mix by stirring **:** WHIP **e :** to strike repeatedly to produce music or a signal ⟨*beat* a drum⟩ **2 a :** to drive or force by blows ⟨*beat* off the intruder⟩ **b :** to make by repeated treading or driving over ⟨*beat* a path⟩ **c :** to shape by repeated blows ⟨*beat* swords into plowshares⟩; *esp* **:** to flatten thin by blows **d :** to sound or express especially by a drumbeat **3 :** to cause to strike or flap repeatedly ⟨birds *beating* their wings⟩ **4 a :** OVERCOME 1, DEFEAT; *also* **:** SURPASS 1 **b :** to prevail despite ⟨*beat* the odds⟩ **c :** BEWILDER 2, BAFFLE ⟨it *beats* me how she does it⟩ **d :** EXHAUST 1b, DISPIRIT **e :** CHEAT **5 a** (1) **:** to act ahead of usually so as to forestall (2) **:** to report a news item in advance of **b :** to come or arrive before ⟨*beat* us home⟩ **c :** to evade or offset the effects of **:** CIRCUMVENT ⟨*beat* the system⟩ **6 :** to indicate by beats ⟨*beat* the tempo⟩ **7 a :** DASH 1 **b :** to glare or strike with oppressive intensity ⟨the sun *beats* down⟩ **8 a :** PULSATE **b :** TICK 1 **c :** to sound upon being struck **9 a :** to sail with much tacking **b :** to progress with difficulty [Old English *bēatan*] — **beat about the bush** *or* **beat around the bush :** to fail or refuse to come to the point — **beat it :** to leave immediately **:** SCRAM — **beat the bushes :** to search thoroughly through all possible areas — **beat the pants off :** to defeat overwhelmingly — **beat the rap :** to escape or avoid the penalties connected with an accusation or charge — **beat upon :** to attack physically or verbally

[2]**beat** *n* **1 a :** a single stroke or blow especially in a series; *also* **:** PULSATION, TICK **b :** a sound produced by or as if by beating ⟨the *beat* of waves against the rock⟩ **c :** a driving impact or force **2 :** each of the pulsations of amplitude produced by the union of sound or radio waves or electric currents having different frequencies **3 a :** a metrical or rhythmic stress in poetry or music or the rhythmic effect or pattern produced by such stresses **b :** musical tempo as indicated by the conductor's baton or hand **4 a :** a regularly traversed round ⟨a police officer's *beat*⟩ **b :** a group of news sources that a reporter covers regularly **5 a :** something that excels ⟨I've never seen the *beat* of it⟩ **b :** the reporting of a news story ahead of competitors **6 :** DEADBEAT

[3]**beat** *adj* **1 :** very tired **2 :** sapped of resolution or morale

beat·box \ˈbēt-ˌbäks\ *n* **:** an electronic device that adds a backbeat, manipulates sounds, and mimics musical instruments

beaten *adj* **1 :** hammered into a desired shape ⟨*beaten* gold⟩ **2 :** much trodden and worn smooth; *also* **:** FAMILIAR ⟨a *beaten* path⟩ **3 :** being in a state of exhaustion

beat·er \ˈbēt-ər\ *n* **1 :** one that beats **2 :** a person who flushes game for hunters

be·a·tif·ic \ˌbē-ə-ˈtif-ik\ *adj* **:** giving or expressing great joy or blessedness — **be·a·tif·i·cal·ly** \-ˈtif-i-kə-lē, -klē\ *adv*

beatific vision *n* **:** the direct knowledge of God held to be enjoyed by the blessed in heaven

be·at·i·fy \bē-ˈat-ə-ˌfī\ *vt* **-fied; -fy·ing 1 :** to make supremely happy **2 :** to declare to have attained the blessedness of heaven and authorize the title "Blessed" and limited public religious honor [Late Latin *beatificare,* from Latin *beatus* "blessed, happy"] — **be·at·i·fi·ca·tion** \-ˌat-ə-fə-ˈkā-shən\ *n*

be·at·i·tude \bē-ˈat-ə-ˌtüd, -ˌtyüd\ *n* **1 :** supreme bliss **2 :** a declaration made in the Sermon on the Mount (Matthew 5:3–12) beginning "Blessed are"

beat·nik \ˈbēt-nik\ *n* **:** a person who participated in a social movement of the 1950s and early 1960s which stressed artistic self-expression and rejection of the mores of conventional society; *broadly* **:** a usually young and artistic person who rejects the mores of conventional society

beat–up \ˈbēt-ˌəp\ *adj* **:** worn or damaged by use or neglect

beau \ˈbō\ *n, pl* **beaux** \ˈbōz\ *or* **beaus** \ˈbōz\ **1 :** DANDY 1 **2 :** BOYFRIEND [French, from *beau* "beautiful," derived from Latin *bellus* "pretty"]

Beau Brum·mell \bō-ˈbrəm-əl\ *n* **:** DANDY 1 [nickname of George B. *Brummell,* died 1840, English dandy]

Beau·fort scale \ˈbō-fərt-\ *n* **:** a scale in which the force of the wind is indicated by numbers from 0 for speeds less than about one mile (one kilometer) per hour to 12 for speeds greater than 73 miles (118 kilometers) per hour [Sir Francis *Beaufort,* died 1857, British admiral]

beau geste \bō-ˈzhest\ *n, pl* **beaux gestes** *or* **beau gestes** \bō-ˈzhest\ **:** a gracious or generous act; *esp* **:** one made to please or impress someone else [French, "beautiful gesture"]

beau ide·al \ˌbō-ˌī-ˈdē-əl, -ˈdēl\ *n, pl* **beau ideals :** the perfect type or model [French *beau idéal* "ideal beauty"]

beau monde \bō-ˈmänd\ *n, pl* **beau mondes** *or* **beaux mondes** \bō-ˈmänz\ **:** the world of high society and fashion [French, literally, "beautiful world"]

beau·te·ous \ˈbyüt-ē-əs\ *adj* **:** BEAUTIFUL 1 — **beau·te·ous·ly** *adv* — **beau·te·ous·ness** *n*

beau·ti·cian \byü-ˈtish-ən\ *n* **:** COSMETOLOGIST

beau·ti·ful \ˈbyüt-i-fəl\ *adj* **1 :** having beauty **:** pleasing to the mind, spirit, or senses ⟨a *beautiful* picture⟩ **2 :** generally agreeable **:** FINE ⟨*beautiful* weather⟩ ⟨a *beautiful* dinner⟩ — **beau·ti·ful·ly** \-fə-lē, -flē\ *adv* — **beau·ti·ful·ness** \-fəl-nəs\ *n*

synonyms BEAUTIFUL, LOVELY, FAIR, PRETTY mean giving pleasure to the mind or senses. BEAUTIFUL applies to whatever gives the keenest pleasure and stirs emotion ⟨*beautiful* mountain scenery⟩. LOVELY is close to BEAUTIFUL but applies to things that excite emotions by being graceful, delicate, or exquisite ⟨a *lovely* melody⟩. FAIR suggests beauty because of purity, flawlessness, or freshness ⟨*fair* of face⟩. PRETTY often implies an immediate but superficial or insubstantial impression of attractiveness ⟨a *pretty* dress⟩.

beau·ti·fy \ˈbyüt-ə-ˌfī\ *vt* **-fied; -fy·ing :** to make beautiful or more beautiful — **beau·ti·fi·ca·tion** \ˌbyüt-ə-fə-ˈkā-shən\ *n* — **beau·ti·fi·er** \ˈbyüt-ə-ˌfīr\ *n*

beau·ty \ˈbyüt-ē\ *n, pl* **beauties 1 :** the qualities of a person or a thing that give pleasure to the senses **:** LOVELINESS **2 :** a lovely person or thing; *esp* **:** a beautiful woman **3 :** an outstanding example or instance ⟨that's a *beauty* of a black eye⟩ [Medieval French *beauté, bealté,* from *bel, beau* "beautiful," from Latin *bellus* "pretty"]

beauty mark *n* **:** a small dark mark (as a mole) on the skin especially of the face

beauty shop *n* **:** a shop or department where beauty treatments (as haircuts) are done — called also *beauty parlor, beauty salon*

beaux arts \bō-ˈzär\ *n pl* **:** FINE ARTS [French]

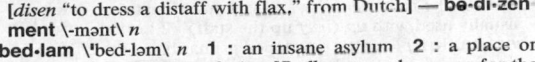

[1]**bea·ver** \ˈbē-vər\ *n, pl* **beavers** **1** *or pl* **beaver** : a large herbivorous rodent with webbed hind feet and a broad flat tail that builds dams and partly submerged houses of mud and branches; *also* : its fur **2** : a hat made of beaver fur or of a fabric imitating it [Old English *beofor*]

[2]**beaver** *n* **1** : a piece of armor protecting the lower part of the face **2** : a helmet visor [Middle French *baviere*]

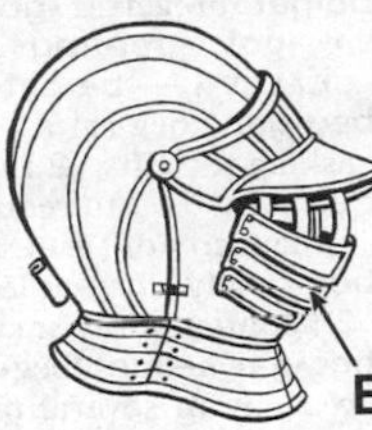
B
B [2]beaver 1

be·calm \bi-ˈkäm, -ˈkälm\ *vt* **1** : to bring to a stop or keep motionless by lack of wind **2** : to make calm : SOOTHE

be·cause \bi-ˈkȯz, -ˈkəz, -kəz\ *conj* : for the reason that

because of *prep* : by reason of : on account of

be·chance \bi-ˈchans\ *vb, archaic* : BEFALL

bêche–de–mer \ˌbāsh-də-ˈmeər\ *n, pl* **bêche–de–mer** *or* **bêches–de–mer** \ˌbāsh-də-, ˌbāsh-əz-də-\ : TREPANG [French]

beck \ˈbek\ *n* **1** : a beckoning gesture **2** : SUMMONS 3, COMMAND ⟨servants at their *beck* and call⟩

beck·et \ˈbek-ət\ *n* : a device for holding something in place; *esp* : a loop of rope with a knot at one end [origin unknown]

beck·on \ˈbek-ən\ *vb* **beck·oned; beck·on·ing** \ˈbek-ning, -ə-ning\ **1** : to summon or signal to a person with a gesture (as a wave or nod) **2** : to appear inviting : ATTRACT ⟨the frontier *beckons*⟩ [Old English *bīecnan,* from *bēacen* "sign"]

be·cloud \bi-ˈklau̇d\ *vt* : to obscure with or as if with a cloud

be·come \bi-ˈkəm\ *vb* **-came** \-ˈkām\; **-come; -com·ing** **1 a** : to come into existence **b** : to come to be ⟨*become* sick⟩ **c** : to undergo change or development ⟨a tadpole *becomes* a frog⟩ ⟨the days *become* shorter in fall⟩ **2** : to look well on : be suitable to : SUIT — **become of** : to happen to ⟨whatever *became of* them⟩

be·com·ing \bi-ˈkəm-ing\ *adj* : SUITABLE; *esp* : attractively suitable ⟨a *becoming* outfit⟩ — **be·com·ing·ly** \-ing-lē\ *adv*

[1]**bed** \ˈbed\ *n* **1 a** : a piece of furniture on or in which one may lie and sleep **b** : SLEEP; *also* : a time for sleeping ⟨took a walk before *bed*⟩ **2** : a flat or level surface: as **a** : a plot of ground prepared for plants **b** : the bottom of a body of water **3** : a supporting surface or structure : FOUNDATION **4** : LAYER 2, STRATUM [Old English *bedd*]

[2]**bed** *vb* **bed·ded; bed·ding** **1 a** : to furnish with a bed or bedding **b** : to put or go to bed ⟨*bedded* down for the night⟩ **2 a** : to fix in a foundation : EMBED ⟨*bedded* on rock⟩ **b** : to plant or arrange in beds **c** : BASE, ESTABLISH **3** : to lay flat or in a layer ⟨*bed* bricks in mortar⟩ **4** : to form a layer

be·daub \bi-ˈdȯb, -ˈdäb\ *vt* : to daub over with something dirty or sticky

be·daz·zle \bi-ˈdaz-əl\ *vt* : DAZZLE — **be·daz·zle·ment** \-əl-mənt\ *n*

bed·bug \ˈbed-ˌbəg\ *n* : a wingless blood-sucking bug sometimes infesting houses and especially beds

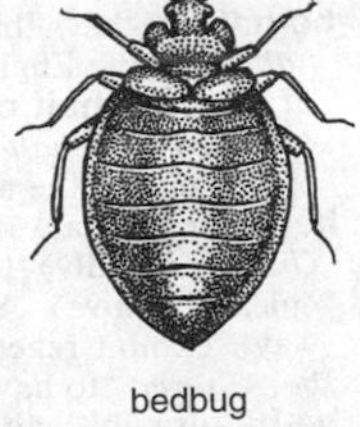
bedbug

bed·clothes \ˈbed-ˌklōz, -ˌklōthz\ *n pl* : the covering (as sheets and blankets) used on a bed

bed·ding \ˈbed-ing\ *n* **1** : BEDCLOTHES **2** : a bottom layer : FOUNDATION **3** : material to provide a bed for livestock **4** : the arrangement of rock in layers

be·deck \bi-ˈdek\ *vt* : to adorn with showy things ⟨*bedecked* with furs and jewels⟩

be·dev·il \bi-ˈdev-əl\ *vt* : to drive frantic : HARASS, TORMENT — **be·dev·il·ment** \-mənt\ *n*

be·dew \bi-ˈdyü, -ˈdü\ *vt* : to wet with or as if with dew

bed·fast \ˈbed-ˌfast\ *adj* : BEDRIDDEN

bed·fel·low \ˈbed-ˌfel-ō\ *n* **1** : one who shares a bed with another **2** : a close associate : ALLY ⟨political *bedfellows*⟩

be·dight \bi-ˈdīt\ *adj, archaic* : ADORNED, DECORATED [Middle English *dighten* "to adorn," from Old English *dihtan* "to arrange, compose," derived from Latin *dictare* "to dictate, compose"]

be·dim \bi-ˈdim\ *vt* : to make dim or obscure

be·di·zen \bi-ˈdīz-n, -ˈdiz-\ *vt* : to dress or adorn in a gaudy way [*disen* "to dress a distaff with flax," from Dutch] — **be·di·zen·ment** \-mənt\ *n*

bed·lam \ˈbed-ləm\ *n* **1** : an insane asylum **2** : a place or scene of uproar and confusion [*Bedlam,* popular name for the Hospital of Saint Mary of Bethlehem, London, an insane asylum, from Middle English *Bedlem* "Bethlehem"]

bed·lam·ite \ˈbed-lə-ˌmīt\ *n* : a crazy person

Bed·ling·ton terrier \ˈbed-ling-tən-\ *n* : any of a breed of swift terriers of light build with a long narrow head, arched back, and usually curly coat [*Bedlington,* parish in Northumberland, England]

bed·ou·in \ˈbed-wən, -ə-wən\ *n, pl* **bedouin** *or* **bedouins** *often cap* : a nomadic Arab of the Arabian, Syrian, or North African deserts [Medieval French *bedoïn,* from Arabic *bidwān,* pl. of *badawi* "desert dweller"]

bed·pan \ˈbed-ˌpan\ *n* : a shallow pan for use as a toilet by a person confined to bed

bed·post \-ˌpōst\ *n* : a usually turned or carved post of a bed

be·drag·gled \bi-ˈdrag-əld\ *adj* **1** : limp, soggy, or dirty from or as if from rain or mud ⟨a wet and *bedraggled* cat⟩ **2** : showing the effect of much use or lack of care : SHABBY, DILAPIDATED ⟨*bedraggled* buildings⟩

bed·rid·den \ˈbed-ˌrid-n\ *adj* : confined to bed especially by illness or weakness [Old English *bedreda* "one confined to bed," literally, "bed rider"]

bed·rock \ˈbed-ˌräk\ *n* **1** : the solid rock underlying surface materials (as soil) **2** : a solid foundation

bed·roll \ˈbed-ˌrōl\ *n* : bedding rolled up for carrying

bed·room \-ˌrüm, -ˌru̇m\ *n* : a room used for sleeping

bed·side \ˈbed-ˌsīd\ *n* : the side of a bed or the place beside a bed especially of a sick or dying person

bedside manner *n* : the often solicitous and sympathetic manner that a physician assumes toward a patient

bed·sore \ˈbed-ˌsōr, -ˌsȯr\ *n* : a sore caused by constant pressure against a bed (as in a long illness)

bed·spread \-ˌspred\ *n* : a decorative cloth cover for a bed

bed·spring \-ˌspring\ *n* : a spring supporting a mattress

bed·stead \-ˌsted\ *n* : the framework of a bed usually including head, foot, and side rails

bed·straw \-ˌstrȯ\ *n* : any of several herbs related to the madder and having squarish stems, opposite or whorled leaves, and small flowers [from its use for mattresses]

bed·time \ˈbed-ˌtīm\ *n* : time to go to bed

bedtime story *n* : a simple story for children at bedtime

bed–wet·ting \-ˌwet-ing\ *n* : the accidental release of urine especially when occurring in bed during sleep — **bed–wet·ter** \-ər\ *n*

[1]**bee** \ˈbē\ *n* **1** : any of numerous insects (as the honeybees and bumblebees) that feed on pollen and nectar and sometimes produce honey and that differ from the wasps especially in the heavier hairier body and in having sucking as well as chewing mouthparts **2** : an eccentric notion : FANCY ⟨a *bee* in one's bonnet⟩ [Old English *bēo*]

[2]**bee** *n* : a gathering of people for a specific purpose ⟨a quilting *bee*⟩ [perhaps from a dialect word *been* "help given by neighbors," derived from Old English *bēn* "prayer"]

bee balm *n* : any of several plants (as Oswego tea) of the mint family attractive to bees

bee·bread \ˈbē-ˌbred\ *n* : a bitter yellowish brown pollen mixture stored in honeycomb cells and used with honey by bees as food

beech \ˈbēch\ *n, pl* **beech·es** *or* **beech** : any of a genus of deciduous trees with smooth gray bark and small edible nuts; *also* : the wood of a beech [Old English *bēce*] — **beech·en** \ˈbē-chən\ *adj*

beech·nut \ˈbēch-ˌnət\ *n* : the edible nut of a beech

[1]**beef** \ˈbēf\ *n, pl* **beefs** \ˈbēfs\ *or* **beeves** \ˈbēvz\ **1** : the flesh of a steer, cow, or bull; *also* : the dressed carcass of a beef animal **2** : a steer, cow, or bull especially when fattened for food **3** : muscular flesh : BRAWN **4** *pl beefs* : COMPLAINT ⟨what's your *beef* with them?⟩ [Medieval French *beof, bef* "ox, beef," from Latin *bov-, bos* "head of cattle"]

[2]**beef** *vb* **1 :** to increase or add weight, strength, or power to — usually used with *up* ⟨*beef* up the staff⟩ **2 :** COMPLAIN

beef cattle *n pl* **:** cattle developed primarily for the efficient production of meat and marked by capacity for rapid growth, heavy well-fleshed body, and stocky build

beef·eat·er \ˈbē-ˌfēt-ər\ *n* **:** YEOMAN OF THE GUARD

beef·steak \ˈbēf-ˌstāk\ *n* **:** a slice of beef suitable for broiling or frying

beefy \ˈbē-fē\ *adj* **beef·i·er; -est** **1 :** THICKSET 2, BRAWNY ⟨a *beefy* bodyguard⟩ **2 :** of or suggesting beef ⟨a *beefy* flavor⟩

[1]**bee·hive** \ˈbē-ˌhīv\ *n* **1 :** [1]HIVE 1 **2 :** something resembling a hive for bees; *esp* **:** a scene of crowded activity

[2]**beehive** *adj* **:** resembling a dome-shaped or conical beehive

bee·keep·er \-ˌkē-pər\ *n* **:** a person who raises bees — **bee·keep·ing** *n*

bee·line \ˈbē-ˌlīn\ *n* **:** a straight direct course [from the belief that nectar-laden bees return to their hives in a direct line]

been *past part of* BE

beep \ˈbēp\ *n* **:** a sound that signals or warns [imitative] — **beep** *vb*

beep·er \ˈbē-pər\ *n* **:** PAGER; *esp* **:** one that beeps

beer \ˈbiər\ *n* **1 :** an alcoholic drink made from malt and flavored with hops **2 :** a nonalcoholic drink made from roots or other parts of plants ⟨birch *beer*⟩ [Old English *bēor*] — **beery** \ˈbiər-ē\ *adj*

beer belly *n* **:** POTBELLY 1 — **beer–bellied** \ˈbir-ˌbel-ēd\ *adj*

bees·wax \ˈbēz-ˌwaks\ *n* **:** [1]WAX 1

beet \ˈbēt\ *n* **:** a biennial garden plant with thick long-stalked edible leaves and usually an enlarged purplish red root used as a vegetable, as a source of sugar, or for forage; *also* **:** this root [Old English *bēte,* from Latin *beta*]

[1]**bee·tle** \ˈbēt-l\ *n* **1 :** any of an order (Coleoptera) of insects having four wings of which the outer pair are modified into stiff cases that protect the inner membranous pair when at rest **2 :** any of various insects resembling a beetle [Old English *bitula*]

[2]**beetle** *n* **:** a heavy tool usually with a wooden head for hammering [Old English *bīetel*]

[3]**beetle** *adj* **:** being prominent and overhanging ⟨*beetle* brows⟩ [Middle English *bitel-browed* "having overhanging brows"]

[4]**beetle** *vi* **bee·tled; bee·tling** \ˈbēt-ling, -l-ing\ **:** to jut out **:** OVERHANG ⟨*beetling* cliffs⟩

be·fall \bi-ˈfȯl\ *vb* **-fell** \-ˈfel\; **-fall·en** \-ˈfȯ-lən\; **-fall·ing** **1 :** to come to pass **:** HAPPEN **2 :** to happen to

be·fit \bi-ˈfit\ *vt* **:** to be suitable to or proper for ⟨words that *befit* the occasion⟩

be·fit·ting \bi-ˈfit-ing\ *adj* **:** SUITABLE 1, 2 — **be·fit·ting·ly** *adv*

be·fog \bi-ˈfȯg, -ˈfäg\ *vt* **1 :** to make foggy **:** OBSCURE **2 :** CONFUSE 2a

be·fool \bi-ˈfül\ *vt* **:** DECEIVE 1

[1]**be·fore** \bi-ˈfōr, -ˈfȯr\ *adv* **1 :** in advance **:** AHEAD ⟨go on *before*⟩ **2 :** at an earlier time **:** PREVIOUSLY ⟨has been here *before*⟩ [Old English *beforan,* from *be-* + *foran* "before"]

[2]**before** *prep* **1 a** (1) **:** forward of **:** in front of ⟨sat *before* the fire⟩ (2) **:** in the presence of ⟨speaking *before* the whole class⟩ **b :** under the consideration of ⟨the case *before* the court⟩ **c :** in store for ⟨many years of life still *before* them⟩ **2 :** earlier than **:** previously to ⟨come *before* six o'clock⟩ **3 :** in a higher or more important position than ⟨put quantity *before* quality⟩

[3]**before** *conj* **1 :** earlier than the time when ⟨think *before* you speak⟩ **2 :** more willingly than ⟨I will starve *before* I will steal⟩

be·fore·hand \-ˌhand\ *adv* **:** in advance **:** ahead of time ⟨think out *beforehand* what you are going to say⟩

before long *adv* **:** in the near future **:** SOON

be·foul \bi-ˈfau̇l\ *vt* **:** to make dirty **:** SOIL

be·friend \bi-ˈfrend\ *vt* **:** to become or act as a friend to

be·fud·dle \bi-ˈfəd-l\ *vt* **1 :** to dull the senses of **:** STUPEFY ⟨the drugs had *befuddled* them⟩ **2 :** to confuse the understanding of **:** PERPLEX ⟨a problem that has *befuddled* the experts⟩ — **be·fud·dle·ment** \-l-mənt\ *n*

beg \ˈbeg\ *vb* **begged; beg·ging** **1 :** to ask for money, food, or help as a charity ⟨*beg* in the streets⟩ **2 :** to ask earnestly or politely ⟨*beg* a favor⟩ [Middle English *beggen*] — **beg the question** **1 :** to pass over or ignore a question by assuming it to be established or settled **2 :** to elicit a question logically as a reaction or response ⟨the quarterback's injury *begs the question* of who will start in his place⟩

synonyms BEG, BESEECH, IMPLORE, ENTREAT mean to ask urgently. BEG suggests earnestness or insistence especially in asking for a favor ⟨children *begging* to stay up late⟩. BESEECH implies great eagerness or anxiety ⟨I *beseech* you to have mercy⟩. IMPLORE adds a suggestion of greater urgency or anguished appeal ⟨*implored* her not to leave him⟩. ENTREAT implies an attempt to persuade or to overcome resistance ⟨*entreated* him to change his mind⟩.

be·get \bi-ˈget\ *vt* **-got** \-ˈgät\ *also* **-gat** \-ˈgat\; **-got·ten** \-ˈgät-n\ *or* **-got; -get·ting** **1 :** to become the father of **:** SIRE **2 :** CAUSE 1 — **be·get·ter** *n*

[1]**beg·gar** \ˈbeg-ər\ *n* **1 :** one that begs; *esp* **:** one that lives by asking for gifts **2 :** PAUPER **3 :** FELLOW 4b

[2]**beggar** *vt* **1 :** to reduce to beggary **2 :** to exceed the resources or capacity of **:** DEFY ⟨the costumes *beggar* description⟩

beg·gar·ly \ˈbeg-ər-lē\ *adj* **1 :** befitting or resembling a beggar **2 :** contemptibly small, poor, or mean — **beg·gar·li·ness** *n*

beg·gar's–lice \ˈbeg-ərz-ˌlīs\ *or* **beg·gar–lice** \-ər-ˌlīs\ *n sing or pl* **:** any of several plants with prickly or adhesive fruits; *also* **:** one of these fruits

beg·gar–ticks *or* **beg·gar's–ticks** \-ˌtiks\ *n sing or pl* **1 :** BUR MARIGOLD; *also* **:** its prickly fruits **2 :** BEGGAR'S-LICE

beg·gary \ˈbeg-ə-rē\ *n* **:** extreme poverty

be·gin \bi-ˈgin\ *vb* **be·gan** \-ˈgan\; **be·gun** \-ˈgən\; **be·gin·ning** **1 a :** to do the first part of an action ⟨please *begin* writing⟩ **b :** to undertake or undergo initial steps **:** COMMENCE ⟨*began* the program with a song⟩ **2 a :** to come into existence **:** ARISE ⟨how the Civil War *began*⟩ **b :** to have a starting point ⟨the road *begins* there⟩ **3 :** to do or succeed in the least degree ⟨does not *begin* to fill our needs⟩ **4 :** to bring into existence **:** FOUND ⟨*begin* a dynasty⟩ **5 :** to come first in ⟨the letter *A begins* the alphabet⟩ [Old English *beginnan*]

be·gin·ner \bi-ˈgin-ər\ *n* **:** one that is beginning something or doing something for the first time

be·gin·ning \bi-ˈgin-ing\ *n* **1 :** the point at which something begins **2 :** the first part **3 :** primary source or cause **:** ORIGIN **4 :** a first stage or early period

be·gone \bi-ˈgȯn, -ˈgän\ *vi* **:** to go away **:** DEPART — usually used in the imperative ⟨*begone* from my sight!⟩

be·go·nia \bi-ˈgō-nyə\ *n* **:** any of a large genus of tropical herbs often grown for their colorful leaves and bright waxy flowers [Michel *Bégon,* died 1710, French governor of Saint Domingue (Haiti)]

be·grime \bi-ˈgrīm\ *vt* **:** to make dirty with grime

be·grudge \bi-ˈgrəj\ *vt* **1 :** to give, do, or allow reluctantly ⟨*begrudge* a person a favor⟩ **2 :** to look upon with disapproval ⟨I don't *begrudge* them their success⟩ — **be·grudg·ing·ly** \-ing-lē\ *adv*

be·guile \bi-ˈgīl\ *vt* **1 :** to deceive by cunning means ⟨was *beguiled* by vague promises⟩ **2 :** to draw notice or interest by wiles or charm ⟨the view *beguiled* them⟩ **3 :** to cause (as time) to pass pleasantly ⟨*beguile* the wait by telling stories⟩ ***synonyms*** see DECEIVE — **be·guile·ment** \-mənt\ *n* — **be·guil·er** *n*

be·guine \bi-ˈgēn\ *n* **:** a vigorous popular dance of the islands of Saint Lucia and Martinique [American French *béguine,* from French *béguin* "flirtation"]

be·gum \ˈbē-gəm\ *n* **:** a Muslim woman of high rank [Hindi & Urdu *begam*]

be·half \bi-ˈhaf, -ˈháf\ *n* **:** useful aid **:** SUPPORT ⟨spoke in my *behalf*⟩ [Middle English, from *by* + *half* "half, side"] — **in behalf of** *or* **on behalf of** **1 :** in the interest of **:** for the benefit of ⟨worked *in behalf of* the government⟩ **2 :** as a representative of ⟨accepting the award *on behalf of* the whole class⟩

be·have \bi-ˈhāv\ *vb* **1 :** to conduct oneself in a particular way ⟨*behaved* badly⟩ **2 :** to conduct oneself in a proper manner ⟨please *behave*⟩ **3 :** to act, function, or react in a particular way **:** exhibit reaction (as to an environment) [Middle English *be-* + *haven* "to have, hold"]

be·hav·ior \bi-ˈhā-vyər\ *n* **1 :** the way in which one behaves **2 :** an observable response by an organism to a stimulus — **be·hav·ior·al** \-vyə-rəl\ *adj* — **be·hav·ior·al·ly** \-rə-lē\ *adv*

be·head \bi-ˈhed\ *vt* **:** to cut off the head of

be·he·moth \bi-ˈhē-məth, ˈbē-ə-ˌmäth\ *n* **1** *often cap* **:** an animal described in the Bible that is probably the hippopotamus **2 :** something of monstrous size or power [Hebrew *bĕhēmōth*]

be·hest \bi-ˈhest\ *n* **:** ORDER 6b, COMMAND ⟨built monuments at the queen's *behest*⟩ [Old English *behǣs* "promise"]

[1]**be·hind** \bi-ˈhīnd\ *adv or adj* **1 a :** in a place, situation, or time that is being or has been departed from ⟨stay *behind*⟩ ⟨leaving years of poverty *behind*⟩ **b :** at, to, or toward the back ⟨look *behind*⟩ **2 a :** in a secondary or inferior position ⟨lag *behind* in

competition⟩ **b** : in a state of failing to keep up to schedule ⟨*behind* in the car payments⟩

[2]**behind** *prep* **1 a** : at, to, or toward the back of ⟨look *behind* you⟩ ⟨a garden *behind* the house⟩ **b** : out of the mind of ⟨they put their worries *behind* them⟩ **2** : inferior to : delayed in relation to ⟨sales *behind* those of last year⟩ ⟨*behind* the rest of the class⟩ **3 a** : in the background of ⟨the conditions *behind* the strike⟩ **b** : in support of ⟨solidly *behind* their candidate⟩

[3]**behind** *n* : BUTTOCK 2a

be·hind·hand \bi-ˈhīnd-ˌhand\ *adv or adj* : not keeping up : LATE ⟨*behindhand* with the rent⟩

be·hold \bi-ˈhōld\ *vb* **1** : to look upon : SEE 1a **2** : to gaze upon : OBSERVE — **be·hold·er** *n*

be·hold·en \bi-ˈhōl-dən\ *adj* : being under obligation for a favor or gift : INDEBTED

be·hoof \bi-ˈhüf\ *n* : BENEFIT 1a, PROFIT [Old English *behōf*]

be·hoove \bi-ˈhüv\ *vt* : to be necessary, fitting, or proper for ⟨it *behooves* a soldier to obey orders⟩ ⟨such behavior ill *behooves* you⟩

be·hove \-ˈhōv\ *chiefly British variant of* BEHOOVE

beige \ˈbāzh\ *n* : a light grayish yellowish brown [French] — **beige** *adj*

be·ing \ˈbē-ing\ *n* **1 a** : the state of having existence **b** : LIFE 1 **c** : one that exists in fact or thought **2** : the qualities that make up an existing thing : ESSENCE; *esp* : PERSONALITY **3** : a living thing; *esp* : PERSON

bel \ˈbel\ *n* : ten decibels [Alexander Graham *Bell*]

be·la·bor \bi-ˈlā-bər\ *vt* **1** : to explain or insist on excessively ⟨*belabor* the obvious⟩ **2** : ASSAIL, ATTACK

be·lat·ed \bi-ˈlāt-əd\ *adj* : delayed beyond the usual time — **be·lat·ed·ly** *adv* — **be·lat·ed·ness** *n*

be·lay \bi-ˈlā\ *vb* **1** : to make fast (as a rope) by turns around a cleat or pin **2** : CEASE, STOP [Old English *belecgan* "to beset," from *be-* + *lecgan* "to lay"]

belch \ˈbelch\ *vb* **1** : to expel gas suddenly from the stomach through the mouth **2** : to give off or issue forth violently ⟨smoke *belched* from the chimney⟩ [Old English *bealcian*] — **belch** *n*

bel·dam *or* **bel·dame** \ˈbel-dəm\ *n* : an old woman [Middle English *beldam* "grandmother," from Medieval French *bel* "beautiful" + Middle English *dam*]

be·lea·guer \bi-ˈlē-gər\ *vt* **-guered; -guer·ing** \-gə-ring, -gring\ **1** : to surround with an army so as to prevent escape : BESIEGE **2** : to subject to troublesome forces : HARASS ⟨the pests that *beleaguer* farmers⟩ [Dutch *belegeren,* from *be-* "be-" + *leger* "camp"]

bel·em·nite \ˈbel-əm-ˌnīt\ *n* : a conical fossil shell of an extinct cephalopod [Greek *belemnon* "dart"] — **bel·em·noid** \ˈbel-əm-ˌnȯid\ *adj or n*

bel·fry \ˈbel-frē\ *n, pl* **belfries** : a tower or a room in a tower for a bell or set of bells [Medieval French *berfroi, belfroi* wheeled tower for besieging fortresses, of Germanic origin]

belfry

Word History In our day *belfry* means "bell tower"; the first syllable is a perfect match with *bell,* whatever *-fry* might mean. But in fact *belfry* does not derive from *bell,* and the original meaning of its medieval French source, *berfroi,* was not "bell tower," but rather "siege tower." A siege tower was a wheeled wooden structure that was pushed up to the walls of a besieged fortress to provide shelter and a base of attack for the besiegers. A variant of French *berfroi* that was also borrowed into English was *belfroi.* The resemblance of this word to Middle English *belle,* "bell," most likely set in motion a shift in meaning that gave *belfry* its current meaning.

Bel·gae \ˈbel-ˌgī, -ˌjē\ *n pl* : a people occupying northern Gaul and Britain in Julius Caesar's time [Latin] — **Bel·gic** \-jik\ *adj*

Bel·gian \ˈbel-jən\ *n* **1** : a native or inhabitant of Belgium **2** : any of a breed of heavy muscular usually roan or chestnut draft horses developed in Belgium — **Belgian** *adj*

Belgian sheepdog *n* : any of a breed of hardy dogs developed in Belgium especially for herding sheep and having a long straight black coat

be·lie \bi-ˈlī\ *vt* **-lied; -ly·ing** **1** : to give a false impression of ⟨a vigor that *belied* their years⟩ **2** : to show to be false ⟨your actions *belie* your promise⟩ — **be·li·er** *n*

be·lief \bə-ˈlēf\ *n* **1** : mental acceptance of something as real or true ⟨a *belief* in your own ability⟩ **2** : the thing that is believed : CONVICTION, OPINION ⟨political *beliefs*⟩ [Middle English *beleave*]

synonyms BELIEF, FAITH, CREDENCE mean the assent to the truth of something offered for acceptance. BELIEF may or may not imply certitude in the believer ⟨my *belief* that I had caught all the errors⟩. FAITH almost always implies trust and confidence even when there is no evidence or proof ⟨had great *faith* in their coach's strategy⟩. CREDENCE implies intellectual acceptance but offers nothing about the soundness of the grounds for acceptance ⟨a theory now given *credence* by scientists⟩. ***synonyms*** see in addition OPINION

be·lieve \bə-ˈlēv\ *vb* **1** : to have a firm religious faith **2** : to have a firm conviction as to the reality or goodness of something ⟨*believe* in fair play⟩ ⟨*believe* in magic⟩ **3** : to accept as true or honest ⟨*believe* the reports⟩ **4** : to hold as an opinion : THINK, SUPPOSE ⟨*believe* it will rain⟩ [Old English *belēfan,* from *be-* + *lēfan* "to allow, believe"] — **be·liev·a·ble** \-ˈlē-və-bəl\ *adj* — **be·liev·a·bly** \-və-blē\ *adv* — **be·liev·er** *n*

be·like \bi-ˈlīk\ *adv, archaic* : most likely : PROBABLY

be·lit·tle \bi-ˈlit-l\ *vt* **-lit·tled; -lit·tling** \-ˈlit-ling, -ˈlit-l-ing\ : to speak of in a slighting way : DISPARAGE ⟨*belittles* her successes⟩ — **be·lit·tle·ment** \-l-mənt\ *n* — **be·lit·tler** \-ˈlit-lər, -l-ər\ *n*

[1]**bell** \ˈbel\ *n* **1** : a hollow usually cup-shaped metallic device that makes a ringing sound when struck **2** : the stroke or sound of a bell that tells the hour especially on shipboard **3 a** : the time indicated by the stroke of a bell **b** : a half hour period of a watch on shipboard **4** : something (as a flower) shaped like a bell [Old English *belle*]

SHIP'S BELLS

NUMBER OF BELLS	HOUR (A.M. OR P.M.)		
1	12:30	4:30	8:30
2	1:00	5:00	9:00
3	1:30	5:30	9:30
4	2:00	6:00	10:00
5	2:30	6:30	10:30
6	3:00	7:00	11:00
7	3:30	7:30	11:30
8	4:00	8:00	12:00

[2]**bell** *vb* **1** : to provide with a bell ⟨*bell* a cat⟩ **2** : to take the form of a bell : FLARE

bel·la·don·na \ˌbel-ə-ˈdän-ə\ *n* **1** : a European poisonous herb of the nightshade family with purple or green bell-shaped flowers, glossy black berries, and root and leaves that yield atropine — called also *deadly nightshade* **2** : a drug or extract from the belladonna plant [Italian, literally, "beautiful lady"]

bell·bird \ˈbel-ˌbərd\ *n* : any of several birds whose notes are likened to the sound of a bell

bell–bot·toms \-ˈbät-əmz\ *n pl* : pants with legs that flare at the bottom — **bell–bottom** *adj*

bell·boy \-ˌbȯi\ *n* : BELLHOP

bell captain *n* : a person in charge of hotel bellhops

belle \ˈbel\ *n* : a popular attractive girl or woman; *esp* : a girl or woman whose charm or beauty make her a favorite ⟨the *belle* of the ball⟩ [French, from the feminine of *beau* "beautiful"]

belles let·tres \bel-letrˈ\ *n pl* : literature of primarily artistic interest and not simply practical or informative [French, literally, "fine letters"] — **bel·le·tris·tic** \ˌbel-ə-ˈtris-tik\ *adj*

bell·flow·er \ˈbel-ˌflau̇-ər, -ˌflau̇r\ *n* : any of a genus of herbs widely cultivated for their showy bell-shaped flowers

bell·hop \ˈbel-ˌhäp\ *n* : a hotel or club employee who escorts guests to rooms, carries luggage, and runs errands [short for *bell-hopper*]

bel·li·cose \ˈbel-ə-ˌkōs\ *adj* : showing a readiness to quarrel or fight [Latin *bellicosus,* derived from *bellum* "war"] ***synonyms*** see BELLIGERENT — **bel·li·cos·i·ty** \ˌbel-ə-ˈkäs-ət-ē\ *n*

\ə\ abut	\au̇\ out	\i\ tip	\ȯ\ saw	\u̇\ foot
\ər\ further	\ch\ chin	\ī\ life	\ȯi\ coin	\y\ yet
\a\ mat	\e\ pet	\j\ job	\th\ thin	\yü\ few
\ā\ take	\ē\ easy	\ng\ sing	\t͟h\ this	\yu̇\ cure
\ä\ cot, cart	\g\ go	\ō\ bone	\ü\ food	\zh\ vision

bel·lig·er·ence \bə-ˈlij-rəns, -ə-rəns\ *n* : a belligerent attitude or disposition

bel·lig·er·en·cy \-rən-sē\ *n* **1** : the status of a nation that is at war **2** : BELLIGERENCE

bel·lig·er·ent \bə-ˈlij-rənt, -ə-rənt\ *adj* **1** : waging war; *esp* : belonging to or recognized as a power at war and protected by and subject to the laws of war ⟨*belligerent* nations⟩ **2** : showing a readiness to fight [Latin *belligerare* "to wage war," from *bellum* "war" + *gerere* "to wage"] — **belligerent** *n* — **bel·lig·er·ent·ly** *adv*

synonyms BELLIGERENT, BELLICOSE, PUGNACIOUS, QUARRELSOME, CONTENTIOUS mean having an aggressive or fighting attitude. BELLIGERENT often implies being actually at war or engaged in hostilities ⟨*belligerent* nations⟩. BELLICOSE suggests a disposition to fight ⟨a drunk in a *bellicose* mood⟩. PUGNACIOUS suggests a disposition that takes pleasure in personal combat ⟨a *pugnacious* gangster⟩. QUARRELSOME stresses an ill-natured readiness to fight without good cause ⟨the heat made us all *quarrelsome*⟩. CONTENTIOUS implies perverse and irritating fondness for arguing and quarreling ⟨wearied by his *contentious* disposition⟩.

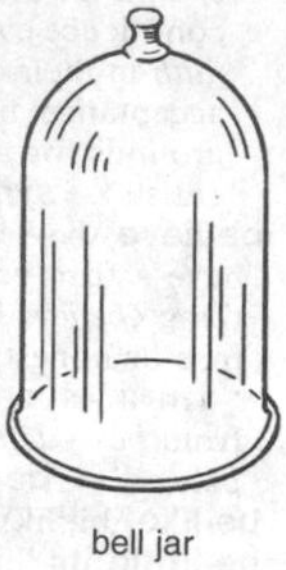

bell jar

bell jar *n* : a bell-shaped usually glass vessel designed to cover objects or to contain gases or a vacuum

bell·man \ˈbel-mən\ *n* **1** : a man (as a town crier) who rings a bell **2** : BELLHOP

bel·low \ˈbel-ō\ *vb* **1** : to make the loud deep roar characteristic of a bull **2** : to shout in a deep voice [Old English *bylgian*] — **bellow** *n*

bel·lows \ˈbel-ōz, -əz\ *n sing or pl* **1** : a device (as for blowing fires or operating an organ) that by alternate expansion and contraction draws in air through a valve and expels it forcibly through a tube; *also* : any of various blowers or enclosures of variable volume **2** : the pleated expandable part of some cameras [Middle English *bely, below* "belly, bellows"]

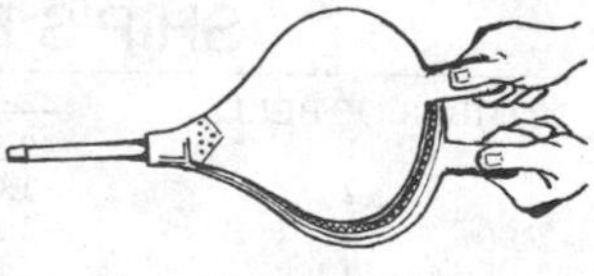

bellows 1

bell pepper *n* : SWEET PEPPER; *esp* : a large bell-shaped sweet pepper

bell·pull \ˈbel-ˌpu̇l\ *n* : a cord or wire with a handle by which one rings a bell

bells and whistles *n pl* : items or features that are useful or decorative but not essential : FRILLS

bell·weth·er \ˈbel-ˈwe<u>th</u>-ər\ *n* : one that takes the lead or initiative; *also* : an indicator of trends ⟨a *bellwether* of fashion⟩ [Middle English, "leading sheep of a flock," from *belle* "bell" + *wether*; from the practice of belling the leading sheep]

[1]**bel·ly** \ˈbel-ē\ *n, pl* **bellies** **1 a** : ABDOMEN 1 **b** : the underside of an animal's body; *also* : hide from this part **c** : UTERUS **d** : STOMACH 1a **2** : an internal cavity : INTERIOR **3** : a surface or object curved or rounded like a human belly ⟨the *belly* of an airplane⟩ **4 a** : the part of a sail that swells out when filled with wind **b** : the enlarged fleshy body of a muscle [Middle English *bely* "bellows, belly," from Old English *belg* "bag, skin"]

[2]**belly** *vb* **bel·lied; bel·ly·ing** : to swell or bulge out

[1]**bel·ly·ache** \ˈbel-ē-ˌāk\ *n* : pain in the abdomen and especially in the stomach : STOMACHACHE

[2]**bellyache** *vi* : to complain in a whining or irritating way ⟨wouldn't stop *bellyaching* about the wait⟩ — **bel·ly·ach·er** *n*

bel·ly·band \ˈbel-ē-ˌband\ *n* : a band around or across the belly: as **a** : GIRTH 1 **b** : a strip of cloth used to protect the navel of a newborn

belly button *n* : the human navel

belly flop *n* : a dive in which the front of the body lands flat against a surface (as of water) — **belly flop** *vb*

bel·ly·ful \ˈbel-ē-ˌfu̇l\ *n* : an excessive amount

bel·ly–land \ˈbe-lē-ˌland\ *vi* : to land an airplane without the use of landing gear — **belly landing** *n*

belly laugh *n* : a deep hearty laugh

be·long \bə-ˈlȯng\ *vi* **1** : to be suitable or appropriate : have a proper place ⟨this *belongs* on the table⟩ **2 a** : to be the property of a person or thing ⟨this book *belongs* to me⟩ **b** : to become attached or bound; *esp* : to be a member of an organization ⟨*belongs* to the club⟩ **3** : to be an attribute, part, adjunct, or function of a person or thing ⟨parts *belonging* to a watch⟩ **4** : to be properly classified ⟨whales *belong* among the mammals⟩ [Middle English *be-* + *longen* "to be suitable"]

be·long·ing \bə-ˈlȯng-ing\ *n* **1** : a thing that belongs to a person : POSSESSION — usually used in plural **2** : close relationship ⟨a sense of *belonging*⟩

be·loved \bi-ˈləvd, -ˈləv-əd\ *adj* : dearly loved — **beloved** *n*

[1]**be·low** \bə-ˈlō\ *adv* **1** : in or to a lower place **2 a** : on earth **b** : in or to Hades or hell **3** : on or to a lower floor or deck **4** : below zero ⟨the temperature was 20 *below*⟩ **5** : lower on the same page or on a following page [Middle English *biloghe*, from *bi-* "by" + *looghe* "low," adjective]

[2]**below** *prep* : lower than in place, rank, or value ⟨*below* sea level⟩ ⟨*below* average⟩

[1]**belt** \ˈbelt\ *n* **1** : a strip of flexible material (as leather or cloth) worn around a person's body for holding in or supporting something (as clothing, tools, or weapons) or for ornament **2 a** : a flexible endless band running around wheels or pulleys and used for moving or carrying something ⟨a fan *belt* on a car⟩ **b** : a band of strong reinforcing material laid beneath the tread of a tire **3** : an area marked by some distinctive feature, product, or activity ⟨the corn *belt*⟩ [Old English, derived from Latin *balteus*] — **belt·ed** \ˈbel-təd\ *adj* — **below the belt** : not fair : in an unfair manner — **under one's belt** : as part of one's experience ⟨100 hours of flying time *under my belt*⟩

[2]**belt** *vt* **1** : to put a belt on or around **2 a** : to beat with or as if with a belt **b** : to hit or strike powerfully ⟨*belted* a home run⟩ **3** : to mark with a band **4** : to sing in a forceful manner ⟨*belt* out a song⟩

[3]**belt** *n* **1** : a jarring blow **2** : DRINK 2 ⟨a *belt* of whiskey⟩

belt·ing \ˈbel-ting\ *n* : material for belts

belt–tight·en·ing \ˈbelt-ˌtīt-ning, -n-ing\ *n* : a reduction in spending

belt·way \ˈbelt-ˌwā\ *n* : a highway going around an urban area — called also *belt highway*

be·lu·ga \bə-ˈlü-gə\ *n* **1** : a sturgeon especially of the Black and Caspian seas **2** : a toothed whale of cold northern waters that attains a length of about 10 to 15 feet (3.0 to 5.0 meters) and is white when adult [sense 1 from Russian *beluga*, from *belyĭ* "white"; sense 2 from Russian *belukha*, from *belyĭ*]

bel·ve·dere \ˈbel-və-ˌdiər\ *n* : a structure (as a gazebo) designed to provide a view of the landscape [Italian, literally, "beautiful view"]

be·mire \bi-ˈmīr\ *vt* **1** : to cover or soil with mud or dirt **2** : to drag through or sink in mire

be·moan \bi-ˈmōn\ *vt* **1** : to express grief over : LAMENT **2** : to look upon with regret or displeasure

be·muse \bi-ˈmyüz\ *vt* **1** : to make confused : BEWILDER **2** : to cause to have feelings of tolerant amusement

[1]**bench** \ˈbench\ *n* **1** : a long seat for two or more persons **2** : a long table for holding work and tools ⟨a carpenter's *bench*⟩ **3 a** : the seat where a judge sits in a court of law **b** : the position or rank of a judge ⟨was appointed to the *bench*⟩ **c** : a person or persons sitting as judge **4** : a seat where the members of a team wait for an opportunity to play **5** : TERRACE 2a, SHELF [Old English *benc*] — **bench·like** \-ˌlīk\ *adj*

[2]**bench** *vt* **1** : to seat on a bench **2** : to remove from or keep out of a game **3** : to seat on a bench **4** : to lift (a weight) in a bench press ⟨*benched* 150 pounds⟩

bench·mark \ˈbench-ˌmärk\ *n* **1** *usually* **bench mark** : a mark on a permanent object indicating elevation and serving as a reference in geological surveys **2** : something that serves as a standard by which others may be measured

bench press *n* : a lift or exercise in which a weight is raised by extending the arms upward while lying on a bench — **bench–press** *vt*

bench·warm·er \ˈbench-ˌwȯr-mər\ *n* : a reserve player on an athletic team

[1]**bend** \ˈbend\ *vb* **bent** \ˈbent\; **bend·ing** **1** : to pull taut or tense ⟨*bend* a bow⟩ **2** : to curve or cause a change of shape ⟨*bend* a wire into a circle⟩ **3** : to turn in a certain direction ⟨*bent* their steps toward town⟩ **4** : to force to yield ⟨*bent* the family to our will⟩ **5** : to apply or apply oneself closely ⟨*bend* your energy to the task⟩ **6** : to curve out of line ⟨the road *bends* to the left⟩ **7** : to curve downward : STOOP ⟨backs *bent* by age⟩ **8** : YIELD, SUBMIT [Old English *bendan*] — **bend**

over backward *or* **bend over backwards :** to make extreme efforts

²bend *n* **1 :** the act or process of bending **:** the state of being bent **2 :** something that is bent; *esp* **:** a curved part of a stream **3** *pl* **:** the painful symptoms (as joint pains) of decompression sickness; *also* **:** DECOMPRESSION SICKNESS

³bend *n* **1 :** a diagonal band in heraldry **2 :** a knot by which one rope is fastened to another or to some object [sense 1 from Middle French *bende, bande* "strip, band," of Germanic origin; sense 2 from Old English *bend* "fetter"]

bend·er \ˈben-dər\ *n* **1 :** one that bends **2 :** SPREE

¹be·neath \bi-ˈnēth\ *adv* **1 :** in or to a lower position **2 :** directly under [Old English *beneothan,* from *be-* + *neothan* "below"]

²beneath *prep* **1 a :** in or to a lower position than **b :** directly under ⟨the ground *beneath* one's feet⟩ **2 :** unworthy of ⟨*beneath* our dignity⟩

Ben·e·dic·tine \ˌben-ə-ˈdik-tən, -ˌtēn\ *n* **:** a monk or a nun of a religious order following the rule of Saint Benedict and devoted especially to scholarship and liturgical worship — **Benedictine** *adj*

bene·dic·tion \ˌben-ə-ˈdik-shən\ *n* **1 :** the saying of a blessing; *esp* **:** a short blessing at the end of a religious service **2 :** an expression of good wishes [Late Latin *benedicere* "to bless," from Latin, "to speak well of," from *bene* "well" + *dicere* "to say"] — **bene·dic·to·ry** \-ˈdik-tə-rē, -trē\ *adj*

Ben·e·dict's solution \ˈben-ə-ˌdiks-, -ˌdikts-\ *n* **:** a blue solution that yields a red, yellow, or orange precipitate upon warming with a sugar (as glucose or maltose) capable of reducing a mild oxidizing agent [Stanley R. *Benedict,* died 1936, American chemist]

Bene·dic·tus \ˌben-ə-ˈdik-təs\ *n* **1 :** a Christian song taken from Matthew 21:9 beginning "Blessed is he that cometh in the name of the Lord" **2 :** a Christian song taken from Luke 1:68 beginning "Blessed be the Lord God of Israel" [Late Latin, "blessed"]

bene·fac·tion \ˈben-ə-ˌfak-shən, ˌben-ə-ˈ\ *n* **1 :** the action of benefiting **2 :** a benefit given; *esp* **:** a charitable donation [Late Latin *benefactio,* from Latin *bene facere* "to do good"]

bene·fac·tor \ˈben-ə-ˌfak-tər\ *n* **:** one that gives help to another especially by giving money

bene·fac·tress \-ˌfak-trəs\ *n* **:** a woman who is a benefactor

ben·e·fice \ˈben-ə-fəs\ *n* **:** a post held by a member of the clergy that gives the right to use certain property and to receive income from stated sources [Medieval French, from Medieval Latin *beneficium,* from Latin, "benefit, favor, promotion"] — **benefice** *vt*

be·nef·i·cence \bə-ˈnef-ə-səns\ *n* **1 :** the quality or state of being beneficent **2 :** BENEFACTION

be·nef·i·cent \-sənt\ *adj* **:** doing or producing good; *esp* **:** performing acts of kindness and charity — **be·nef·i·cent·ly** *adv*

ben·e·fi·cial \ˌben-ə-ˈfish-əl\ *adj* **:** producing good effects **:** HELPFUL, ADVANTAGEOUS [Latin *beneficium* "kindness, benefit," from *beneficus* "conferring benefits," from *bene* "well" + *facere* "to do"] — **ben·e·fi·cial·ly** \-ˈfish-ə-lē\ *adv* — **ben·e·fi·cial·ness** *n*

synonyms BENEFICIAL, ADVANTAGEOUS, PROFITABLE mean bringing good or gain. BENEFICIAL implies promoting health or well-being ⟨the *beneficial* effects of a healthy diet⟩. ADVANTAGEOUS stresses a choice or preference that brings superiority or greater success in attaining an end ⟨discovered a more *advantageous* opportunity⟩. PROFITABLE implies the yielding of useful or lucrative returns ⟨a *profitable* business⟩.

ben·e·fi·cials \-shəlz\ *n pl* **:** organisms (as ladybugs and lacewings) that feed on or parasitize pests of crops, gardens, and turf

ben·e·fi·ci·ary \-ˈfish-ē-ˌer-ē; -ˈfish-rē, -ə-rē\ *n, pl* **-ar·ies :** a person who benefits or is expected to benefit from something ⟨the *beneficiary* of a life insurance policy⟩

¹ben·e·fit \ˈben-ə-ˌfit\ *n* **1 a :** something that promotes well-being **:** ADVANTAGE **b :** useful aid **:** HELP **2 a :** money paid (as by an insurance company or a public agency) at death or when one is sick, retired, or unemployed **b :** a service (as health insurance) or right (as to take vacation time) provided by an employer in addition to wages or salary **3 :** an entertainment or social event to raise funds for a person or cause [Medieval French *benfet* "good deed," from Latin *bene factum,* literally, "thing well done"]

²benefit *vb* **-fit·ed** *also* **-fit·ted; -fit·ing** *also* **-fit·ting 1 :** to be useful or profitable to **2 :** to receive benefit

be·nev·o·lence \bə-ˈnev-ləns, -ə-ləns\ *n* **1 :** disposition to do good **2 a :** an act of kindness **b :** a generous gift

be·nev·o·lent \-lənt\ *adj* **1 :** having or showing goodwill **:** KINDLY ⟨*benevolent* smiles⟩ **2 a :** marked by or disposed to doing good ⟨a *benevolent* donor⟩ **b :** existing or operated to help others and not for profit ⟨*benevolent* institutions⟩ [Latin *benevolens,* from *bene* "well" + *velle* "to wish"] — **be·nev·o·lent·ly** *adv* — **be·nev·o·lent·ness** *n*

Ben·gali \ben-ˈgȯ-lē, beng-\ *n* **1 :** a native or inhabitant of Bengal **2 :** the modern Indo-Aryan language of Bengal — **Bengali** *adj*

ben·ga·line \ˈbeng-gə-ˌlēn\ *n* **:** fabric with a crosswise rib [French, from *Bengal*]

be·night·ed \bi-ˈnīt-əd\ *adj* **1 :** overtaken by night or darkness **2 :** IGNORANT 1a, 2

be·nign \bi-ˈnīn\ *adj* **1 :** of a gentle disposition **:** GRACIOUS **2 a :** showing kindness and gentleness ⟨a *benign* face⟩ **b :** FAVORABLE 2 ⟨a *benign* climate⟩ **3 :** of a mild type or character; *esp* **:** not becoming cancerous ⟨a *benign* tumor⟩ [Latin *benignus* "good-natured," from *bene* "well" + *gignere* "to beget"] — **be·nig·ni·ty** \-ˈnig-nət-ē\ *n* — **be·nign·ly** \-ˈnīn-lē\ *adv*

synonyms BENIGN, BENIGNANT both mean kindly or favorable in appearance. BENIGN suggests actual effect given by action or appearance ⟨the weather remained *benign*⟩ ⟨a frown on a usually *benign* face⟩. BENIGNANT tends to suggest conscious feeling or intention of kindliness ⟨giving out candy with a *benignant* smile for each child⟩.

be·nig·nant \bi-ˈnig-nənt\ *adj* **1 :** serenely mild and kind ⟨a *benignant* face⟩ **2 :** FAVORABLE 2, BENEFICIAL ***synonyms*** see BENIGN — **be·nig·nan·cy** \-nən-sē\ *n* — **be·nig·nant·ly** *adv*

ben·i·son \ˈben-ə-sən, -zən\ *n* **:** BLESSING, BENEDICTION [Medieval French *beneiçon,* from Late Latin *benedictio*]

ben·ny \ˈben-ē\ *n, pl* **bennies** *slang* **:** a tablet of amphetamine [from *Benzadrine*]

¹bent \ˈbent\ *n* **:** BENT GRASS [Middle English]

²bent *adj* **1 :** changed by bending out of a straight or even condition ⟨*bent* twigs⟩ **2 :** strongly inclined **:** DETERMINED ⟨*bent* on winning⟩ — **bent out of shape :** extremely upset or angry

³bent *n* **1 a :** strong inclination or interest **b :** a natural capacity **:** TALENT ⟨a *bent* for languages⟩ **2 :** capacity for endurance [from ²*bend*]

bent grass *n* **:** any of a genus of stiff or velvety grasses that are used especially for pastures and lawns

ben·thic \ˈben-thik, ˈbent-\ *or* **ben·thon·ic** \ben-ˈthän-ik\ *adj* **:** of, relating to, or occurring in the depths of a body of water (as the ocean) or the bottom underlying these depths [Greek *benthos* "depths of the sea"]

ben·thos \ˈben-ˌthäs\ *n* **:** organisms that live on or in the bottom of bodies of water

ben·ton·ite \ˈbent-n-ˌīt\ *n* **:** an absorbent and colloidal clay [Fort *Benton,* Montana]

bent·wood \ˈbent-ˌwu̇d\ *adj* **:** made of wood that is bent rather than cut to shape ⟨*bentwood* furniture⟩

be·numb \bi-ˈnəm\ *vt* **:** to make numb especially by cold

Ben·ze·drine \ˈben-zə-ˌdrēn\ *n* **:** an amphetamine formerly used in medicine [from *Benzedrine,* former trademark]

ben·zene \ˈben-ˌzēn, ben-ˈ\ *n* **:** a colorless volatile flammable toxic liquid hydrocarbon C_6H_6 used as a solvent, a motor fuel, and in making other chemicals (as dyes and drugs) [alteration of *benzine*]

benzene ring *n* **:** an arrangement of atoms in benzene and other aromatic compounds that consists of six carbon atoms linked by alternate single and double bonds in a hexagon

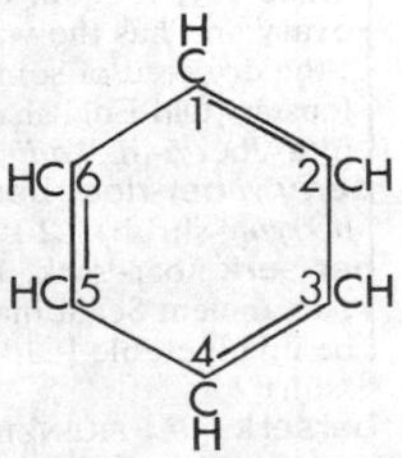

benzene ring

ben·zine \ˈben-ˌzēn, ben-ˈ\ *n* **1 :** BENZENE **2 :** any of various volatile flammable petroleum distillates used especially as solvents for fatty substances or as motor fuels [from *benzoic acid*]

ben·zo·ic acid \ben-ˈzō-ik-\ *n* **:** a white crystalline acid $C_7H_6O_2$ found naturally (as in cranberries) or made syntheti-

\ə\ **abut**	\au̇\ **out**	\i\ **tip**	\ȯ\ **saw**	\u̇\ **foot**
\ər\ **further**	\ch\ **chin**	\ī\ **life**	\ȯi\ **coin**	\y\ **yet**
\a\ **mat**	\e\ **pet**	\j\ **job**	\th\ **thin**	\yü\ **few**
\ā\ **take**	\ē\ **easy**	\ng\ **sing**	\t͟h\ **this**	\yu̇\ **cure**
\ä\ **cot, cart**	\g\ **go**	\ō\ **bone**	\ü\ **food**	\zh\ **vision**

cally and used especially as a preservative, to make other chemicals, and as an antifungal agent [from *benzoin*]
ben·zo·in \'ben-zə-wən, -ˌwēn; -ˌzōin\ *n* **:** a hard fragrant yellowish resin from trees of southeastern Asia used especially as a fixative in perfumes, as incense, and in medicine as an expectorant and skin protectant [Middle French *benjoin,* from Catalan *benjuí,* from Arabic *lubān jāwī,* literally, "frankincense of Java"]
ben·zo·yl peroxide \'ben-zə-ˌwil-, -ˌzōil-\ *n* **:** a white crystalline compound $C_{14}H_{10}O_4$ used in bleaching and in medicine especially in the treatment of acne
be·queath \bi-'kwēth, -'kwēth\ *vt* **1 :** to give or leave (personal property) by will **2 :** to hand down ⟨ideas *bequeathed* by our ancestors⟩ [Old English *becwethan,* from *be-* + *cwethan* "to say"] — **be·queath·al** \-əl\ *n*
be·quest \bi-'kwest\ *n* **1 :** the act of bequeathing **2 :** something bequeathed **:** LEGACY
be·rate \bi-'rāt\ *vt* **:** to scold forcefully
Ber·ber \'bər-bər\ *n* **1 :** a member of a people of northwestern Africa **2 :** any of a group of languages spoken in northwestern Africa [derived from Arabic *Barbar*] — **Berber** *adj*
be·reave \bi-'rēv\ *vt* **-reaved** \-'rēvd\ *or* **-reft** \-'reft\; **-reav·ing** *archaic* **:** to deprive of something [Old English *berēafian,* from *be-* + *rēafian* "to rob"]
1**be·reaved** \bi-'rēvd\ *adj* **:** suffering the death of a loved one ⟨*bereaved* family members⟩
2**bereaved** *n, pl* **bereaved :** one who is bereaved
be·reave·ment \bi-'rēv-mənt\ *n* **:** the state or fact of being bereaved
be·reft \bi-'reft\ *adj* **1 :** not having something needed, wanted, or expected ⟨*bereft* of money⟩ **2 :** BEREAVED
be·ret \bə-'rā\ *n* **:** a soft flat wool cap without a visor [French *béret,* from Gascon (Romance speech of the Gascony region of southwest France) *berret*]
berg \'bərg\ *n* **:** ICEBERG
ber·ga·mot \'bər-gə-ˌmät\ *n* **1 :** a pear-shaped orange whose rind yields an oil used in perfumery; *also* **:** the tree or oil **2 :** any of several mints (as Oswego tea) [French *bergamote*]
beri·beri \ˌber-ē-'ber-ē\ *n* **:** a deficiency disease marked by weakness, wasting, and damage to nerves and caused by a dietary lack of or inability to assimilate thiamine [Sinhalese *bæribæri*]
berke·li·um \'bər-klē-əm\ *n* **:** a radioactive chemical element produced artificially — see ELEMENT table [New Latin, from *Berkeley,* California]
Berk·shire \'bərk-ˌshiər, -shər\ *n* **:** any of a breed of medium-sized black swine with white markings [*Berkshire,* England]
berm \'bərm\ *n* **:** a narrow shelf, path, or ledge typically at the top or bottom of a slope [French *berme,* from Dutch *berm* "strip of ground along a dike"]
Ber·mu·da grass \bər-'myüd-ə-\ *n* **:** a trailing southern European grass widely grown in tropical and subtropical regions as a turf and pasture grass
Bermuda shorts *n pl* **:** knee-length walking shorts
Ber·noul·li's principle \bər-'nü-lēz-\ *n* **:** a principle in hydrodynamics: the pressure in a stream of fluid is reduced as the speed of the flow is increased [Daniel *Bernoulli,* died 1782, Swiss physicist]
1**ber·ry** \'ber-ē\ *n, pl* **berries 1 a :** a small pulpy and usually edible fruit (as a strawberry or raspberry) **b :** a fruit (as a grape, blueberry, tomato, or cucumber) that develops from a single ovary and has the wall of the ripened ovary pulpy or fleshy **c :** the dry seed of some plants (as wheat) **2 :** an egg of a fish or lobster [Old English *berie*] — **ber·ried** \'ber-ēd\ *adj* — **ber·ry·like** \'ber-ē-ˌlīk\ *adj*
2**berry** *vi* **ber·ried; ber·ry·ing 1 :** to bear or produce berries ⟨a *berrying* shrub⟩ **2 :** to gather or seek berries
1**ber·serk** \bər-'sərk, bə-, -'zərk, 'bər-ˌ\ *or* **ber·serk·er** \-ər\ *n* **:** an ancient Scandinavian warrior frenzied in battle and held to be invulnerable [Old Norse *berserkr,* from *bjørn* "bear" + *serkr* "shirt"]
2**berserk** *adj* **:** FRENZIED, CRAZED — usually used in the phrase *go berserk* — **berserk** *adv*
1**berth** \'bərth\ *n* **1 a :** distance sufficient to maneuver a ship **b :** an amount of distance maintained for safety ⟨give the fire a wide *berth*⟩ **2 :** a place where a ship lies at anchor or at a wharf **3 :** a place to sit or sleep on a ship or vehicle **4 :** JOB, POSITION [probably from 2*bear* + *-th*]
2**berth** *vb* **1 :** to bring or come into a berth **2 :** to assign a berth to
ber·tha \'bər-thə\ *n* **:** a wide round collar covering the shoulders [French *berthe,* from *Berthe* (Bertha), died 783, queen of the Franks]

bertha

ber·yl \'ber-əl\ *n* **:** a mineral consisting of a silicate of beryllium and aluminum of great hardness and occurring in prisms of various colors [derived from Greek *bēryllos,* of Indo-Aryan origin]
be·ryl·li·um \bə-'ril-ē-əm\ *n* **:** a steel-gray light strong brittle metallic element used chiefly to harden alloys — see ELEMENT table
be·seech \bi-'sēch\ *vb* **be·sought** \-'sȯt\ *or* **be·seeched; be·seech·ing :** to ask for earnestly **:** IMPLORE [Middle English *besechen,* from *be-* + *sechen* "to seek"] ***synonyms*** see BEG — **be·seech·ing·ly** \-'sē-ching-lē\ *adv*
be·seem \bi-'sēm\ *vb, archaic* **:** to be fitting or becoming **:** BEFIT
be·set \bi-'set\ *vt* **-set; -set·ting 1 :** to set or stud with or as if with ornaments ⟨a pin *beset* with gems⟩ **2 :** to trouble with problems **:** HARASS **3 a :** to set upon **:** ASSAIL **b :** to hem in **:** SURROUND
be·set·ting *adj* **:** constantly present or attacking ⟨a *besetting* sin⟩
be·shrew \bi-'shrü\ *vt, archaic* **:** CURSE
1**be·side** \bi-'sīd\ *adv, archaic* **:** BESIDES
2**beside** *prep* **1 a :** by the side of ⟨walk *beside* me⟩ **b :** in comparison with ⟨the kitten looks tiny *beside* the big dog⟩ **2 :** BESIDES **3 :** not relevant to ⟨*beside* the point⟩ — **beside oneself :** very upset or excited
1**be·sides** \bi-'sīdz\ *prep* **1 :** EXCEPT FOR ⟨no one *besides* us⟩ **2 :** in addition to ⟨*besides* being useful, it looks good⟩
2**besides** *adv* **:** in addition **:** ALSO ⟨the play is excellent, and *besides* the tickets cost very little⟩
be·siege \bi-'sēj\ *vt* **1 :** to surround with or as if with armed forces **:** lay siege to ⟨*besieged* the fortress⟩ ⟨doubts *besieged* him⟩ **2 :** to press especially with questions or requests — **be·sieg·er** *n*
be·smear \bi-'smiər\ *vt* **:** SMEAR
be·smirch \bi-'smərch\ *vt* **:** to reduce the quality or purity of **:** SULLY
be·som \'bē-zəm\ *n* **:** a broom made of twigs [Old English *besma*]
be·sot \bi-'sät\ *vt* **be·sot·ted; be·sot·ting :** to make dull or stupid **:** STUPEFY; *esp* **:** to make stupid with drunkenness
be·spat·ter \bi-'spat-ər\ *vt* **:** SPATTER
be·speak \bi-'spēk\ *vt* **-spoke** \-'spōk\; **-spo·ken** \-'spō-kən\; **-speak·ing 1 a :** to hire or arrange for beforehand **b :** REQUEST **2 a :** to make plain **:** give evidence of ⟨her performance *bespeaks* much practice⟩ **b :** FORETELL
be·spec·ta·cled \bi-'spek-ti-kəld\ *adj* **:** wearing glasses
Bessemer process *n* **:** a process of making steel from pig iron by burning out impurities (as carbon) by means of a blast of air forced through the molten metal
1**best** \'best\ *adj, superlative of* GOOD **1 :** good or useful in the highest degree **:** most excellent **2 :** MOST, LARGEST ⟨rained for the *best* part of their vacation⟩ [Old English *betst*]
2**best** *adv, superlative of* WELL **1 :** in the best way **:** to the greatest advantage ⟨some things are *best* left unsaid⟩ **2 :** to the highest degree **:** MOST ⟨those *best* able to do the work⟩ — **as best :** as well, skillfully, or accurately as ⟨try to do *as best* you can⟩
3**best** *n, pl* **best 1 :** the best state or part **2 :** one that is best ⟨trying to be the *best*⟩ **3 a :** one's maximum effort ⟨do your *best*⟩ **b :** best performance or achievement ⟨ran a new personal *best*⟩ **4 :** best clothes ⟨wear your Sunday *best*⟩ — **at best :** under the most favorable conditions
4**best** *vt* **:** to get the better of **:** OUTDO ⟨*bested* us in every event⟩
bes·tial \'bes-chəl, 'bēs-\ *adj* **1 a :** of or relating to beasts **b :** resembling a beast **2 a :** lacking intelligence or reason **b :** VICIOUS, BRUTAL [Latin *bestia* "beast"] — **bes·tial·ly** \-chə-lē\ *adv*
bes·ti·al·i·ty \ˌbes-chē-'al-ət-ē, ˌbēs-\ *n* **1 :** the condition or status of a lower animal **2 :** display or indulgence of bestial traits or impulses

bes·ti·ary \ˈbes-chē-ˌer-ē, ˈbēs-\ *n, pl* **-ar·ies** : a medieval allegorical or moralizing work on the appearance and habits of animals
be·stir \bi-ˈstər\ *vt* : to stir up : rouse to action
best man *n* : a male friend who stands with the bridegroom at a wedding
be·stow \bi-ˈstō\ *vt* **1** : APPLY 1, USE **2** : QUARTER 2, LODGE **3** : to present as a gift : CONFER ***synonyms*** see PRESENT — **be·stow·al** \-ˈstō-əl\ *n* — **be·stow·er** *n*
be·strew \bi-ˈstrü\ *vt* **-strewed; -strewed** *or* **-strewn; -strew·ing** **1** : STREW 2 **2** : to lie scattered over
be·stride \bi-ˈstrīd\ *vt* **-strode** \-ˈstrōd\; **-strid·den** \-ˈstrid-n\; **-strid·ing** **1** : to ride, sit, or stand with one leg on each side : STRADDLE **2** : to tower over : DOMINATE
best–sell·er \ˈbest-sel-ər\ *n* : an article (as a book) whose sales are among the highest of its class — **best–sell·ing** \-ˈsel-ing\ *adj*
[1]**bet** \ˈbet\ *n* **1 a** : an agreement based on the result of a contest or the outcome of an event requiring the person whose guess proves wrong to give something to a person whose guess proves right **b** : the making of such an agreement : WAGER **2** : the money or thing risked ⟨a *bet* of 10 cents⟩ **3** : a choice made by considering what might happen ⟨your best *bet* is the back road⟩ [origin unknown]
[2]**bet** *vb* **bet** *or* **bet·ted; bet·ting** **1** : to risk in a bet **2** : to make a bet with **3** : to lay a bet **4** : to be certain enough to bet ⟨I *bet* it will rain⟩
be·ta \ˈbāt-ə\ *n* **1** : the 2nd letter of the Greek alphabet — Β or β **2** : the second brightest star of a constellation
be·ta–car·o·tene \-ˈkar-ə-ˌtēn\ *n* : an isomer of carotene found in dark green and dark yellow vegetables and fruits
beta decay *n* : a radioactive nuclear transformation resulting in the emission of a beta particle
be·take \bi-ˈtāk\ *vt* **-took** \-ˈtu̇k\; **-tak·en** \-ˈtā-kən\; **-tak·ing** \-ˈtā-king\ : to cause (oneself) to go
be·ta–lac·ta·mase \ˈbāt-ə-ˈlak-tə-ˌmās\ *n* : an enzyme that inactivates the penicillins and is found especially in staphylococcal bacteria [*lactam,* an amide + *-ase*]
beta particle *n* : an electron or positron ejected from the nucleus of an atom during radioactive decay; *also* : a high-speed electron or positron
beta ray *n* **1** : BETA PARTICLE **2** : a stream of beta particles
beta test *n* : a test of a prototype version of a product — **beta test** *vt* — **beta tester** *n*
be·ta·tron \ˈbāt-ə-ˌträn\ *n* : a device that accelerates electrons by the inductive action of a rapidly varying magnetic field
be·tel \ˈbēt-l\ *n* : a climbing pepper of southeastern Asia whose dried leaves are chewed with betel nut and lime as a stimulant [Portuguese *bétele,* from Tamil *verrilai*]
Be·tel·geuse \ˈbet-l-ˌjüz, ˈbēt-, -ˌju̇z, -ˌjərz\ *n* : a variable red giant star near one shoulder of Orion [French *Bételgeuse,* from Arabic *bayt al-jawzāʾ* "Gemini," literally, "the house of the twins"]
betel nut *n* : the astringent seed of an Asian palm
bête noire \ˌbet-ˈnwär, ˌbāt-\ *n, pl* **bêtes noires** \ˌbet-ˈnwär, ˌbāt-, -nwärz\ : a person or thing strongly detested or avoided [French, literally, "black beast"]
beth·el \ˈbeth-əl\ *n* : a place of worship especially for sailors [Hebrew *bēthʾēl* "house of God"]
be·think \bi-ˈthingk\ *vt* **-thought** \-ˈtho̊t\; **-think·ing** **1 a** : REMEMBER, RECALL **b** : to cause (oneself) to be reminded **2** : to cause (oneself) to consider
be·tide \bi-ˈtīd\ *vb* : to happen or happen to : BEFALL
be·times \bi-tīmz\ *adv* : in good time : EARLY ⟨was up *betimes* this morning⟩
be·to·ken \bi-ˈtō-kən\ *vt* : to be a sign of : INDICATE
be·tray \bi-ˈtrā\ *vt* **1** : to give over to an enemy by treachery or fraud **2** : to be unfaithful or treacherous to : FAIL ⟨*betray* a trust⟩ **3** : to reveal unintentionally ⟨*betray* one's ignorance⟩ **4** : to tell in violation of a trust ⟨*betray* a secret⟩ [Middle English *betrayen,* from *be-* + *trayen* "to betray," from Medieval French *trahir,* from Latin *tradere* "to hand over, betray"] — **be·tray·al** \-ˈtrā-əl, -ˈtrāl\ *n* — **be·tray·er** \-ˈtrā-ər\ *n*
be·troth \bi-ˈtrāth, -ˈtro̊th, -ˈtrōth, *or with* th\ *vt* : to promise to marry or give in marriage
be·troth·al \-ˈtrōth-əl, -ˈtro̊th-, -ˈtrōth-\ *n* **1** : an engagement to be married **2** : the act or ceremony of becoming engaged to be married
be·trothed *n* : the person to whom one is betrothed
bet·ta \ˈbet-ə\ *n* : any of a genus of small brilliantly colored long finned freshwater fishes of southeastern Asia [New Latin, probably from Javanese *wadĕr,* a freshwater fish]

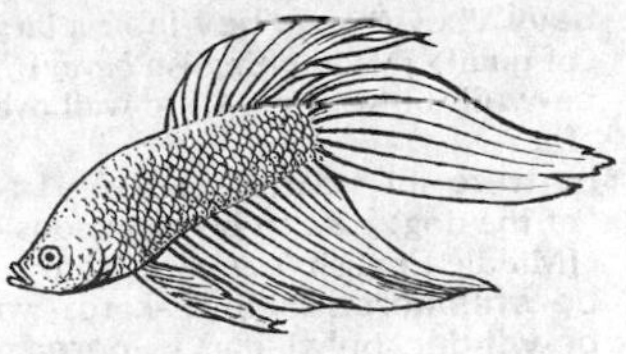
betta

[1]**bet·ter** \ˈbet-ər\ *adj, comparative of* GOOD **1** : more than half ⟨the *better* part of a week⟩ **2** : improved in health **3** : of higher quality [Old English *betera*]
[2]**better** *adv, comparative of* WELL **1** : in a more excellent manner **2 a** : to a higher or greater degree ⟨knows the story *better* than I do⟩ **b** : MORE ⟨*better* than an hour's drive⟩
[3]**better** *n* **1 a** : something better **b** : a superior especially in merit or rank **2** : ADVANTAGE, VICTORY ⟨got the *better* of me⟩
[4]**better** *vt* **1** : to make better **2** : to surpass in excellence : EXCEL
better half *n* : SPOUSE
bet·ter·ment \ˈbet-ər-mənt\ *n* : IMPROVEMENT
bet·tor *or* **bet·ter** \ˈbet-ər\ *n* : one that bets
[1]**be·tween** \bi-ˈtwēn\ *prep* **1 a** : by the common action of ⟨shared the work *between* them⟩ **b** : with shares to each of : AMONG ⟨divided the fortune *between* the heirs⟩ **2** : in the time, space, or interval that separates ⟨*between* nine and ten o'clock⟩ ⟨*between* the desk and the wall⟩ **3** : DISTINGUISHING ⟨the difference *between* soccer and football⟩ **4** : by comparison of ⟨choose *between* the two coats⟩ **5 a** : from one to the other or another of ⟨flew *between* Miami and Chicago⟩ **b** : joining or linking in some relationship ⟨the bond *between* friends⟩ **6** : in confidence restricted to ⟨a secret *between* you and me⟩ **7** : taking together the combined effect of ⟨*between* school and sports, they have little time for television⟩ [Old English *betwēonum,* from *be-* + *-twēonum* "two"]
usage It is often asserted that *between* can be used only of two items and *among* must be used of more than two. It is appropriate, however, to use *between* to denote a one-to-one relationship, regardless of the number of items. It can be used when the number is unspecified ⟨cooperation *between* nations⟩, when more than two are enumerated ⟨*between* you and me and the lamppost⟩, and even when only one item is mentioned but repetition is implied ⟨paused *between* every sentence⟩. *Among* is more appropriate where the emphasis is on distribution rather than individual relationship ⟨discontent *among* the workers⟩.
[2]**between** *adv* : in an intermediate space or interval
be·tween·ness \-nəs\ *n* : the quality or state of being between two others in an ordered set
be·twixt \bi-ˈtwikst\ *adv or prep* : BETWEEN [Old English *betwux*]
betwixt and between *adv or adj* : in an intermediate position or state : neither one thing nor the other
[1]**bev·el** \ˈbev-əl\ *adj* : OBLIQUE 1, BEVELED [derived from Medieval French *baïf* "with open mouth," from *baer* "to yawn"]
[2]**bevel** *n* **1** : an instrument consisting of two rules or arms jointed together and opening to any angle for drawing angles or adjusting surfaces to be cut at an angle **2 a** : the angle that one surface or line makes with another when they are not at right angles **b** : the slant or inclination of such a surface or line

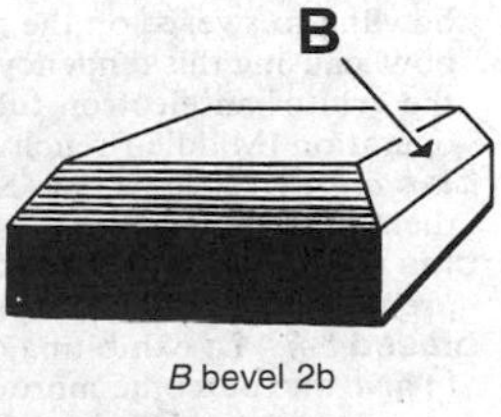

B bevel 2b

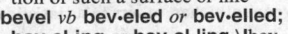

[3]**bevel** *vb* **bev·eled** *or* **bev·elled; bev·el·ing** *or* **bev·el·ling** \ˈbev-ling, -ə-ling\ **1** : to cut or shape (as an edge or surface) to a bevel **2** : INCLINE 3, SLANT
bev·er·age \ˈbev-rij, -ə-rij\ *n* : a liquid for drinking [Medieval French, from *beivre* "to drink," from Latin *bibere*]

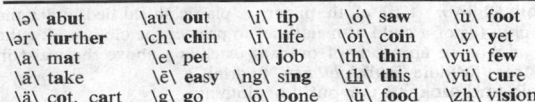

\ə\ **abut**	\au̇\ **out**	\i\ **tip**	\ȯ\ **saw**	\u̇\ **foot**
\ər\ **further**	\ch\ **chin**	\ī\ **life**	\ȯi\ **coin**	\y\ **yet**
\a\ **mat**	\e\ **pet**	\j\ **job**	\th\ **thin**	\yü\ **few**
\ā\ **take**	\ē\ **easy**	\ng\ **sing**	\th\ **this**	\yu̇\ **cure**
\ä\ **cot, cart**	\g\ **go**	\ō\ **bone**	\ü\ **food**	\zh\ **vision**

bevy \ˈbev-ē\ *n, pl* **bev·ies :** a large group or collection ⟨a *bevy* of quail⟩ [Middle English *bevey*]

be·wail \bi-ˈwāl\ *vt* **1 :** to wail over **2 :** to express deep sorrow for

be·ware \bi-ˈwaər, -ˈweər\ *vb* **1 :** to be on one's guard ⟨*beware* of the dog⟩ **2 :** to be suspicious of ⟨*beware* the quick excuse⟩ [Middle English *been war,* from *been* "to be" + *war* "wary"]

be·whis·kered \bi-ˈhwis-kərd, -ˈwis-\ *adj* **:** having whiskers

be·wil·der \bi-ˈwil-dər\ *vt* **-dered; -der·ing** \-də-riŋ, -driŋ\ **1 :** to cause to lose one's bearings **2 :** to perplex or confuse especially by a complex variety or large number of objects or possibilities — **be·wil·der·ing·ly** \-də-riŋ-lē, -driŋ-lē\ *adv* — **be·wil·der·ment** \-dər-mənt\ *n*

be·witch \bi-ˈwich\ *vt* **1 :** to gain an influence over by means of magic or witchcraft **:** put under a spell **2 :** FASCINATE, CHARM — **be·witch·ery** \-ə-rē\ *n* — **be·witch·ment** \-mənt\ *n*

be·wray \bi-ˈrā\ *vt, archaic* **:** DIVULGE, BETRAY, REVEAL [Middle English *bewreyen,* from *be-* + *wreyen* "to accuse," from Old English *wrēgan*]

bey \ˈbā\ *n* **1 :** a provincial governor in the Ottoman Empire **2 :** the former native ruler of Tunis [Turkish, "gentleman, chief"]

¹be·yond \bē-ˈänd\ *adv* **:** on or to the farther side ⟨extending to the river and *beyond*⟩ [Old English *begeondan,* from *be-* "be-" + *geondan* "beyond," from *geond* "yond"]

²beyond *prep* **1 :** on or to the farther side of ⟨*beyond* that tree⟩ **2 a :** out of the reach or sphere of ⟨*beyond* help⟩ **b :** in a degree or amount surpassing ⟨beauty *beyond* measure⟩ **3 :** out of the comprehension of ⟨these ideas are *beyond* me⟩ **4 :** in addition to **:** BESIDES ⟨work *beyond* his usual duties⟩

³beyond *n* **:** HEREAFTER

be·zel \ˈbē-zəl, ˈbez-əl\ *n* **1 :** the top part of a ring setting that holds a stone or ornament; *also* **:** the top including the stone **2 :** the grooved rim that holds the crystal on a watch; *also* **:** a rim that holds a covering (as on a clock dial or headlight) [probably from dialect form of French *biseau* "bezel"]

be·zoar \ˈbē-ˌzōr, -ˌzȯr\ *n* **:** a hard mass of ingested material (as hair) that forms and lodges in the stomach or intestine and was formerly believed to possess magical properties [derived from Persian *pādzahr,* from *pad-* "protecting against" + *zahr* "poison"]

bhang \ˈbaŋ, ˈbäŋ\ *n* **1 :** an intoxicating preparation made from the leaves of hemp; *also* **:** the leaves **2 :** MARIJUANA 2 [Hindi *bhā̃g*]

B horizon *n* **:** a soil layer immediately beneath the A horizon from which it obtains material by leaching and from which it is usually distinguished by less weathering

bi- *combining form* **1 a :** two ⟨*bi*directional⟩ **b :** coming or occurring every two ⟨*bi*monthly⟩ ⟨*bi*weekly⟩ **c :** into two parts ⟨*bi*sect⟩ **2 a :** twice **:** doubly **:** on both sides ⟨*bi*convex⟩ **b :** coming or occurring two times ⟨*bi*monthly⟩ ⟨*bi*weekly⟩ — compare SEMI- [Latin]

bi·an·nu·al \bī-ˈan-yə-wəl, ˈbī-, -ˈan-yəl\ *adj* **1 :** occurring twice a year **2 :** BIENNIAL — **bi·an·nu·al·ly** \-ē\ *adv*

¹bi·as \ˈbī-əs\ *n* **1 :** a line diagonal to the grain of a fabric often utilized in the cutting of garments for smoother fit **2 :** an inclination of temperament or outlook; *esp* **:** such an inclination marked by strong prejudice **3 :** the tendency of a bowl in lawn bowling to swerve on the green; *also* **:** the uneven shape of the bowl causing this tendency **4 :** a voltage applied to a device (as the grid of an electron tube) to establish a reference level for operation [Middle French *biais*] ***synonyms*** see PREJUDICE

²bias *adj* **:** DIAGONAL, SLANTING — used chiefly of fabrics and their cut

³bias *vt* **bi·ased** *or* **bi·assed; bi·as·ing** *or* **bi·as·sing :** to give a prejudiced outlook to ***synonyms*** see INCLINE

biased *adj* **1 :** exhibiting or characterized by bias **2 :** tending to give one outcome more frequently than others in a statistical experiment ⟨a *biased* coin⟩

bias tape *n* **:** a narrow strip of cloth cut on the bias, folded, and used for finishing or decorating clothing

bi·ath·lon \bī-ˈath-lən, -ˌlän\ *n* **:** a contest consisting of cross-country skiing and rifle target shooting [*bi-* + *-athlon* (as in *decathlon*)]

bib \ˈbib\ *n* **1 :** a cloth, paper, or plastic shield tied under the chin (as of a child at mealtime) to protect the clothes **2 :** the part of an apron or of overalls extending above the waist in front [Middle English *bibben* "to drink"]

bib and tucker *n* **:** an outfit of clothing

bib·ber \ˈbib-ər\ *n* **:** a person who regularly drinks alcoholic beverages — **bib·bery** \-ə-rē\ *n*

bi·be·lot \ˈbē-bə-ˌlō\ *n* **:** a small household ornament or decorative object [French]

Bi·ble \ˈbī-bəl\ *n* **1 :** a book made up of the writings accepted by Christians as inspired by God and comprising the Old Testament and the New Testament **2 :** a book containing the sacred writings of another religion (as Judaism) **3** *not cap* **:** a publication that is widely read or outstandingly authoritative ⟨the *bible* of the entertainment industry⟩ [Medieval Latin *biblia,* from Greek, from *biblion* "book," from *byblos* "papyrus, book," from *Byblos,* ancient Phoenician city from which papyrus was exported]

BOOKS OF THE BIBLE

HEBREW BIBLE

Law	Isaiah	Zephaniah	Ruth
Genesis	Jeremiah	Haggai	Lamentations
Exodus	Ezekiel	Zechariah	Ecclesiastes
Leviticus	Hosea	Malachi	Esther
Numbers	Joel	*Writings*	Daniel
Deuteronomy	Amos	Psalms	Ezra
Prophets	Obadiah	Proverbs	Nehemiah
Joshua	Jonah	Job	1 & 2 Chronicles
Judges	Micah	Song of Songs	
1 & 2 Samuel	Nahum		
1 & 2 Kings	Habakkuk		

CHRISTIAN CANON—OLD TESTAMENT

ROMAN CATHOLIC	PROTESTANT	ROMAN CATHOLIC	PROTESTANT
Genesis	Genesis	Wisdom	
Exodus	Exodus	Sirach	
Leviticus	Leviticus	Isaiah	Isaiah
Numbers	Numbers	Jeremiah	Jeremiah
Deuteronomy	Deuteronomy	Lamentations	Lamentations
Joshua	Joshua		
Judges	Judges	Baruch	
Ruth	Ruth	Ezekiel	Ezekiel
1 & 2 Samuel	1 & 2 Samuel	Daniel	Daniel
1 & 2 Kings	1 & 2 Kings	Hosea	Hosea
1 & 2 Chronicles	1 & 2 Chronicles	Joel	Joel
Ezra	Ezra	Amos	Amos
Nehemiah	Nehemiah	Obadiah	Obadiah
Tobit		Jonah	Jonah
Judith		Micah	Micah
Esther	Esther	Nahum	Nahum
Job	Job	Habakkuk	Habakkuk
Psalms	Psalms	Zephaniah	Zephaniah
Proverbs	Proverbs	Haggai	Haggai
Ecclesiastes	Ecclesiastes	Zechariah	Zechariah
Song of Songs	Song of Solomon	Malachi	Malachi
		1 & 2 Maccabees	

PROTESTANT APOCRYPHA

1 & 2 Esdras	Ecclesiasticus or the Wisdom of Jesus Son of Sirach	Prayer of Azariah and the Song of the Three Holy Children	Bel and the Dragon
Tobit	Baruch	Susanna	The Prayer of Manasses
Judith			1 & 2 Maccabees
Additions to Esther			
Wisdom of Solomon			

CHRISTIAN CANON—NEW TESTAMENT

Matthew	Romans	1 & 2 Thessalonians	James
Mark	1 & 2 Corinthians	1 & 2 Timothy	1 & 2 Peter
Luke	Galatians	Titus	1, 2, 3 John
John	Ephesians	Philemon	Jude
Acts of the Apostles	Philippians	Hebrews	Revelation *or* Apocalypse
	Colossians		

bibli- *or* **biblio-** *combining form* **:** book ⟨*biblio*phile⟩ [Greek *biblion*]

bib·li·cal \ˈbib-li-kəl\ *adj* **1 :** of, relating to, or in accord with the Bible **2 :** suggestive of the Bible or Bible times — **bib·li·cal·ly** \-kə-lē, -klē\ *adv*

bib·li·og·ra·pher \ˌbib-lē-ˈäg-rə-fər\ *n* **1 :** an expert in bibliography **2 :** a compiler of bibliographies

bib·li·og·ra·phy \ˌbib-lē-ˈäg-rə-fē\ *n, pl* **-phies** **1 :** the history, identification, or description of writings or publications **2 :** a list often with descriptive or critical notes of writings relating to a particular subject, period, or author; *also* **:** a list of works written by an author or printed by a publishing house **3 :** a list of the works referred to in a text or consulted by the author in its production — **bib·lio·graph·ic** \ˌbib-lē-ə-ˈgraf-ik\ *also* **bib·lio·graph·i·cal** \-ˈgraf-i-kəl\ *adj* — **bib·lio·graph·i·cal·ly** \-kə-lē, -klē\ *adv*

bib·lio·phile \ˈbib-lē-ə-ˌfīl\ *n* **:** a lover of books; *also* **:** a book collector

bib·u·lous \ˈbib-yə-ləs\ *adj* **1 :** highly absorbent **2 a :** fond of alcoholic beverages **b :** of or relating to the drinking of alcoholic beverages [Latin *bibulus,* from *bibere* "to drink"] — **bib·u·lous·ly** *adv* — **bib·u·lous·ness** *n*

bi·cam·er·al \bī-ˈkam-rəl, ˈbī-, -ə-rəl\ *adj* **:** having, consisting of, or based on two legislative chambers ⟨*bicameral* legislatures⟩ [Latin *camera* "room, chamber"] — **bi·cam·er·al·ism** \-rə-ˌliz-əm\ *n*

bi·car·bon·ate \bī-ˈkär-bə-ˌnāt, ˈbī-, -nət\ *n* **:** an acid carbonate

bicarbonate of soda : SODIUM BICARBONATE

bi·cen·te·na·ry \ˌbī-sen-ˈten-ə-rē, -ˈtē-nə-; bī-ˈsent-n-ˌer-ē\ *n* **:** BICENTENNIAL — **bicentenary** *adj*

bi·cen·ten·ni·al \ˌbī-sen-ˈten-ē-əl\ *n* **:** a 200th anniversary or its celebration — **bicentennial** *adj*

bi·ceps \ˈbī-ˌseps\ *n, pl* **biceps :** a muscle having two heads; *esp* **:** a large flexor muscle of the front of the upper arm [Latin *biceps* "two-headed," from *bi-* + *caput* "head"]

bi·chlo·ride \bī-ˈklōr-ˌīd, ˈbī-, -ˈklȯr-\ *n* **:** MERCURIC CHLORIDE — called also *bichloride of mercury*

bi·chon fri·se \bē-ˌshō^{n}-frē-ˈzā\ *n, pl* **bi·chons fri·ses** \-ˌshō^{n}-frē-ˈzā, -ˈzāz\ **:** any of a breed of small dogs of Mediterranean origin having a thick wavy white coat [French *bichon à poil frisé* curly-haired lapdog]

bi·chro·mate \bī-ˈkrō-ˌmāt, ˈbī-\ *n* **:** DICHROMATE

bick·er \ˈbik-ər\ *vi* **bick·ered; bick·er·ing** \ˈbik-ring, -ə-ring\ **:** to engage in an angry and often petty quarrel **:** WRANGLE [Middle English *bikeren*] — **bick·er·er** *n*

bi·col·ored \ˈbī-ˌkəl-ərd\ *adj* **:** two-colored — **bi·col·or** \-ər\ *n*

bi·con·cave \bī-ˌkän-ˈkāv, bī-ˈkän-ˌ, ˈbī-\ *adj* **:** concave on both sides ⟨a *biconcave* lens⟩

bi·con·di·tion·al \ˌbī-kən-ˈdish-nəl, -ən-l\ *n* **:** a statement in logic composed of two propositions each of which is true if and only if the other is true ⟨the statement "*q* if and only if *p*" is a *biconditional*⟩

bi·con·vex \bī-ˌkän-ˈveks, bī-ˈkän-ˌ, ˈbī\ *adj* **:** convex on both sides ⟨a *biconvex* lens⟩

bi·cul·tur·al \bī-ˈkəl-chə-rəl\ *adj* **:** of, relating to, or including two distinct cultures ⟨*bicultural* education⟩ — **bi·cul·tur·al·ism** \-rə-ˌliz-əm\ *n*

^{1}**bi·cus·pid** \bī-ˈkəs-pəd, ˈbī-\ *adj* **:** having or ending in two points [Latin *cuspis* "point, cusp"]

^{2}**bicuspid** *n* **:** a human premolar tooth

bicuspid valve *n* **:** MITRAL VALVE

^{1}**bi·cy·cle** \ˈbī-ˌsik-əl\ *n* **:** a vehicle with two wheels one behind the other, a tubular metal frame, handlebars, a saddle seat, and pedals by which it is propelled [Greek *kyklos* "wheel"]

^{2}**bicycle** *vi* **bi·cy·cled; bi·cy·cling** \-ˌsik-ling, -ə-ling\ **:** to ride a bicycle — **bi·cy·cler** \-ˌsik-lər, -ə-lər\ *n* — **bi·cy·clist** \-ˌsik-ləst, -ə-ləst\ *n*

^{1}**bid** \ˈbid\ *vb* **bade** \ˈbad, ˈbād\ *or* **bid; bid·den** \ˈbid-n\ *or* **bid** *also* **bade; bid·ding** **1 a :** to issue an order to **:** TELL ⟨did as I was *bidden*⟩ **b :** to request to come **:** INVITE **2 :** to give expression to ⟨*bade* me farewell⟩ **3** *past and past part* **bid a :** to offer (a price) for something (as at an auction) **b :** to make a bid of in a card game [partly from Old English *biddan* "to ask, pray"; partly from Old English *bēodan* "to offer, command"] — **bid·der** *n* — **bid fair :** to seem likely

^{2}**bid** *n* **1 :** an offer to pay a stated sum for something or to do something at a stated fee; *also* **:** the price or fee offered **2 :** an opportunity or turn to bid **3 :** INVITATION **4 a :** an announcement of what a card player will attempt to win **b :** the amount of such a bid **5 :** an attempt or effort to win, achieve, or attract

bid·da·ble \ˈbid-ə-bəl\ *adj* **1 :** OBEDIENT, DOCILE **2 :** capable of being bid (as in a card game) — **bid·da·bly** \-blē\ *adv*

bide \ˈbīd\ *vb* **bode** \ˈbōd\ *or* **bid·ed; bided; bid·ing :** to continue in a state or condition; *also* **:** WAIT ⟨*bide* a while⟩ [Old English *bīdan*] — **bid·er** *n* — **bide one's time :** to wait for an appropriate moment before acting

bi·di·rec·tion·al \ˌbī-də-ˈrek-shnel, ˈbī-, -dī-, -shən-l\ *adj* **:** involving, moving, or taking place in two usually opposite directions ⟨*bidirectional* flow⟩

bi·en·ni·al \bī-ˈen-ē-əl, ˈbī-\ *adj* **1 :** occurring every two years **2 :** continuing or lasting for two years; *esp* **:** growing vegetatively during the first year and fruiting and dying during the second — **biennial** *n* — **bi·en·ni·al·ly** \-ē-ə-lē\ *adv*

bi·en·ni·um \bī-ˈen-ē-əm\ *n, pl* **-ni·ums** *or* **-nia** \-ē-ə\ **:** a period of two years [Latin, from *bi-* + *annus* "year"]

bier \ˈbiər\ *n* **:** a stand on which a corpse or coffin is placed; *also* **:** a coffin together with its stand [Old English *bǣr*]

bi·fid \ˈbī-ˌfid, -fəd\ *adj* **:** divided into two equal lobes or parts by a median cleft ⟨a *bifid* leaf⟩ [Latin *bifidus,* from *bi-* + *findere* "to split"]

^{1}**bi·fo·cal** \bī-ˈfō-kəl, ˈbī-\ *adj* **:** having two focal lengths

^{2}**bifocal** *n* **1 :** a bifocal glass or lens **2** *pl* **:** eyeglasses with bifocal lenses that correct for both near and distant vision

bi·fur·cate \ˈbī-fər-ˌkāt, bī-ˈfər-\ *vb* **:** to divide into two branches or parts [Latin *furca* "fork"] — **bi·fur·cate** \bī-ˈfər-kət, ˈbī-, -ˌkāt; ˈbī-fər-ˌkāt\ *adj* — **bi·fur·ca·tion** \ˌbī-fər-ˈkā-shən, -ˌfər-\ *n*

^{1}**big** \ˈbig\ *adj* **big·ger; big·gest** **1 :** of great force ⟨a *big* storm⟩ **2 a :** large in size, bulk, or extent ⟨a *big* house⟩; *also* **:** large in number or amount ⟨*big* money⟩ ⟨a *big* fleet⟩ **b :** conducted on a large scale ⟨*big* government⟩ **c :** ^{1}CAPITAL 2 ⟨*big* letters⟩ **d :** being older ⟨my *big* sister⟩ **3 a :** PREGNANT ⟨*big* with child⟩ **b :** full to overflowing or bursting ⟨eyes *big* with tears⟩ **c :** being full and resonant ⟨a *big* voice⟩ **4 a :** of great importance or significance; *esp* **:** CHIEF, PREDOMINANT ⟨the *big* issue of the campaign⟩ **b :** IMPOSING, PRETENTIOUS; *also* **:** BOASTFUL ⟨*big* talk⟩ **c :** MAGNANIMOUS, GENEROUS ⟨a *big* heart⟩ [Middle English] ***synonyms*** see LARGE — **big·ness** *n* — **big on :** very much in favor of **:** enthusiastic about ⟨*big on* mystery novels⟩

^{2}**big** *adv* **1 :** to a large amount or extent **2 a :** in an outstanding manner ⟨made it *big*⟩ **b :** POMPOUSLY, PRETENTIOUSLY

big·a·mist \ˈbig-ə-məst\ *n* **:** a person who commits bigamy

big·a·my \ˈbig-ə-mē\ *n* **:** the statutory offense of marrying one person while still legally married to another — **big·a·mous** \-məs\ *adj* — **big·a·mous·ly** *adv*

big bang *n* **:** the cosmic explosion that marked the beginning of the universe according to the big bang theory

big bang theory *n* **:** a theory in astronomy: the universe originated billions of years ago in an explosion from a single point of enormous energy — compare STEADY STATE THEORY

big cat *n* **:** a large wild cat (as a leopard or tiger)

Big Dipper *n* **:** DIPPER 3a

big·eye \ˈbig-ˌī\ *n* **:** any or several small widely distributed marine reddish to silvery food fishes of warm seas

big foot *n, often cap* **:** a large hairy humanlike creature reported to exist in the Pacific Northwest — called also *Sasquatch*

big game *n* **:** large animals hunted for sport

big·gish \ˈbig-ish\ *adj* **:** somewhat big **:** comparatively big

big·horn sheep \ˈbig-ˌhȯrn-\ *n* **:** a usually grayish brown wild sheep of mountainous western North America — called also *bighorn, Rocky Mountain sheep*

bighorn sheep

bight \ˈbīt\ *n* **1 :** a bend in a coast or the bay it forms **2 :** a slack part or loop in a rope [Old English *byht* "bend"]

big league *n* **:** the highest level especially in baseball — **big–league** *adj* — **big leaguer** *n*

big·ot \ˈbig-ət\ *n* **:** a person obstinately or intolerantly devoted to his or her own group, beliefs, or opinions; *esp* **:** one who regards or treats the members of a group (as a racial or ethnic

\ə\ **abut**	\au̇\ **out**	\i\ **tip**	\ȯ\ **saw**	\u̇\ **foot**
\ər\ **further**	\ch\ **chin**	\ī\ **life**	\ȯi\ **coin**	\y\ **yet**
\a\ **mat**	\e\ **pet**	\j\ **job**	\th\ **thin**	\yü\ **few**
\ā\ **take**	\ē\ **easy**	\ng\ **sing**	\t͟h\ **this**	\yu̇\ **cure**
\ä\ **cot, cart**	\g\ **go**	\ō\ **bone**	\ü\ **food**	\zh\ **vision**

group) with hatred and intolerance [French, "hypocrite, bigot"] — **big·ot·ed** \-ət-əd\ *adj*

big·ot·ry \ˈbig-ə-trē\ *n, pl* **-ries** : the state of mind of a bigot; *also* : behavior or beliefs arising from such a state of mind

big shot *n* : an important person

big stick *n* : coercive use or threat of military or political intervention [from Theodore Roosevelt's belief that "we must speak softly but carry a big stick"]

big time *n* : the top rank (as of a profession) where income and prestige are greatest

big toe *n* : the innermost and largest toe of the foot

big top *n* **1** : the main tent of a circus **2** : CIRCUS 2

big tree *n* : GIANT SEQUOIA

big·wig \ˈbig-ˌwig\ *n* : an important person

bike \ˈbīk\ *n* **1** : BICYCLE **2** : MOTORCYCLE — **bike** *vi* — **biker** *n*

bi·ki·ni \bə-ˈkē-nē\ *n* : a woman's or girl's scanty two-piece bathing suit [French, from *Bikini,* atoll of the Marshall Islands]

bi·la·bi·al \bī-ˈlā-bē-əl, ˈbī-\ *adj* : of, relating to, or produced with both lips ⟨a *bilabial* consonant⟩

bi·lat·er·al \bī-ˈlat-ə-rəl, ˈbī-, -ˈla-trəl\ *adj* **1** : having or involving two sides; *esp* : affecting two sides or parties mutually ⟨a *bilateral* treaty⟩ **2** : characterized by bilateral symmetry — **bi·lat·er·al·ism** \-ˌiz-əm\ *n* — **bi·lat·er·al·ly** \-ē\ *adv*

bilateral symmetry *n* : a pattern of animal symmetry in which similar parts are arranged on opposite sides of a median axis so that one and only one plane can divide the individual into essentially identical halves — compare RADIAL SYMMETRY

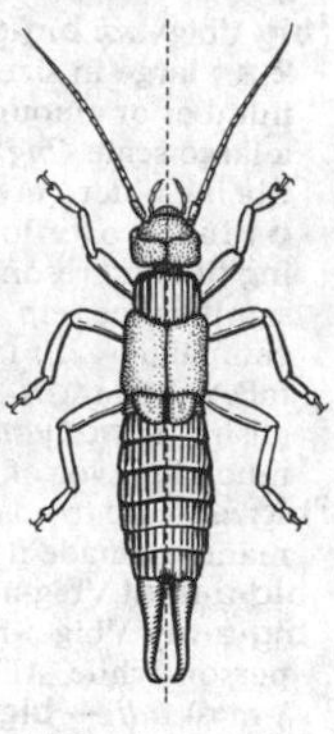
bilateral symmetry

bil·ber·ry \ˈbil-ˌber-ē\ *n* : any of several shrubs of the heath family that resemble blueberries; *also* : the sweet edible bluish fruit [probably of Scandinavian origin]

bile \ˈbīl\ *n* **1** : a thick bitter yellow or greenish fluid secreted by the liver and functioning in the duodenum in the digestion and absorption of fats **2** : tendency toward anger : ILL WILL [Latin *bilis*]

bile duct *n* : a canal by which bile passes from the liver or gallbladder to the duodenum

bile salts *n pl* : a dry mixture of the principal salts of the bile of the ox used as a liver stimulant and as a laxative

[1]**bilge** \ˈbilj\ *n* **1** : the bulging part of a cask or barrel **2 a** : the part of a ship's hull between the flat of the bottom and the vertical topsides **b** : the lowest point of a ship's inner hull **3** : stale or worthless remarks or ideas [probably from Middle French *boulge, bouge* "leather bag, curved part"]

[2]**bilge** *vi* : to become damaged in the bilge

bilge water *n* : water that collects in the bilge of a ship

bil·i·ary \ˈbil-ē-ˌer-ē\ *adj* : of, relating to, or conveying bile

bi·lin·gual \bī-ˈling-gwəl, -gyə-wəl\ *adj* **1** : of, containing, expressed in, or involving the use of two languages ⟨a *bilingual* dictionary⟩ ⟨*bilingual* education⟩ **2** : able to use two languages especially with fluency [Latin *lingua* "tongue, language"] — **bilingual** *n* — **bi·lin·gual·ism** \-ˌiz-əm\ *n*

bil·ious \ˈbil-yəs\ *adj* **1 a** : of or relating to bile **b** : marked by or suffering from disordered liver function **2** : of an irritable ill-natured disposition : PEEVISH — **bil·ious·ly** *adv* — **bil·ious·ness** *n*

bil·i·ru·bin \ˌbil-ə-ˈrü-bən, ˈbil-ə-ˌ\ *n* : a reddish yellow pigment occurring especially in bile and blood [Latin *ruber* "red"]

bil·i·ver·din \-ˈvərd-n, -ˌvərd-\ *n* : a green pigment occurring in bile [obsolete French *verd* "green"]

bilk \ˈbilk\ *vt* : to cheat out of what is due : SWINDLE [perhaps alteration of [2]*balk*]

[1]**bill** \ˈbil\ *n* **1** : the jaws of a bird together with their horny covering **2** : a mouthpart (as the beak of a turtle) resembling a bird's bill **3** : the visor of a cap [Old English *bile*] — **billed** \ˈbild\ *adj*

synonyms BILL, BEAK mean the horny two-parted projection that serves a bird for jaws. In popular usage BEAK is applied especially to the strong triangular pointed or hooked shape associated with striking, tearing, or crushing ⟨an eagle's *beak*⟩ while BILL applies to the structure in any bird ⟨a duck's *bill*⟩.

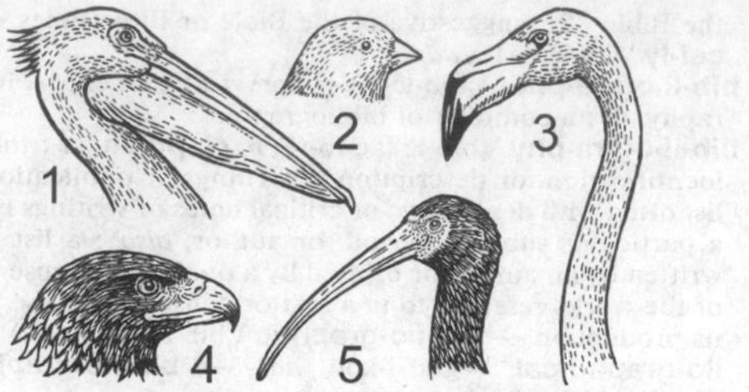

[1]bill 1: *1* pelican, *2* finch, *3* flamingo, *4* eagle, *5* ibis

[2]**bill** *vi* **1** : to touch bill to bill **2** : to caress and kiss affectionately ⟨lovers *billing* and cooing⟩

[3]**bill** *n* : a weapon used up to the 18th century that consists of a long staff with a hook-shaped blade at one end [Old English *bill* "sword"]

[4]**bill** *n* **1** : a draft of a law presented to a legislature for enactment; *also* : the law itself **2** : a written statement of a wrong one person has suffered from another or of a breach of law by some person ⟨a *bill* of complaint⟩ **3** : an itemized list : a detailed statement of items **4** : an itemized account of the cost of goods sold or work done : INVOICE **5 a** : an advertisement posted or distributed to announce an event (as a theatrical entertainment) **b** : an entertainment program or the entertainment presented on it **6** : NOTE 3a; *esp* : a piece of paper money [Medieval Latin *billa* "label, inventory, petition," perhaps alteration of *bulla* "papal seal, bull," from Latin, "bubble, amulet"]

[5]**bill** *vt* **1 a** : to make a bill of ⟨*bill* the goods to my account⟩ **b** : to submit a bill of charges to ⟨*bill* a customer⟩ **2** : to advertise especially by posters or placards — **bill·er** *n*

bill·board \ˈbil-ˌbōrd, -ˌbȯrd\ *n* : a flat surface on which bills are posted; *esp* : a large vertical panel designed to carry outdoor advertising

bill·bug \-ˌbəg\ *n* : a usually small weevil with larvae that eat the roots of grasses

[1]**bil·let** \ˈbil-ət\ *n* **1** : an official order directing that a soldier be lodged (as in a private home) **2** : quarters assigned (as to a soldier) **3** : POSITION, JOB [Middle French *billette* "note, letter," derived from Medieval Latin *billa* "bill"]

[2]**billet** *vt* : to assign lodging to by a billet : QUARTER

[3]**billet** *n* **1** : a short thick piece of wood (as for firewood) **2** : a bar of metal; *esp* : one of iron or steel [Medieval French *billette,* from *bille* "log," of Celtic origin]

bil·let–doux \ˌbil-ā-ˈdü\ *n, pl* **bil·lets–doux** \-ā-ˈdü, -ā-ˈdüz\ : a love letter [French *billet doux,* literally, "sweet note"]

bill·fold \ˈbil-ˌfōld\ *n* : a folding pocketbook for paper money : WALLET

bil·liard \ˈbil-yərd\ *n* — used as an attributive form of *billiards* ⟨a *billiard* ball⟩

bil·liards \ˈbil-yərdz\ *n* : any of several games played on a rectangular table by driving small balls against one another or into pockets with a cue; *esp* : a game in which one scores by causing a cue ball to hit in succession two object balls [Middle French *billard* "billiard cue, billiards," from *bille* "log"]

bil·lings·gate \ˈbil-ingz-ˌgāt\ *n* : coarsely abusive language [*Billingsgate,* a fish market in London, England]

bil·lion \ˈbil-yən\ *n* **1** — see NUMBER table **2** : a very large or indefinitely large number [French, from *bi-* "two" + *-llion* (as in *million*)] — **billion** *adj* — **bil·lionth** \-yənth, -yəntth\ *adj or n*

bil·lion·aire \ˌbil-yə-ˈnaər, -ˈneər, ˈbil-yə-ˌ\ *n* : one whose wealth is a billion or more

bill of exchange : a written order from one individual to another to pay a specified sum of money to a designated person

bill of fare : MENU

bill of health **1** : a certificate given to a ship's master on leaving port that indicates the state of health of the ship's company and of the port with regard to infectious diseases **2** : a usually favorable report following an examination or investigation ⟨gave the restructured business a clean *bill of health*⟩

bill of lad·ing \-ˈlād-ing\ : a document issued by a carrier that lists goods being shipped and specifies the terms of their transport

bill of rights *often cap B&R* : a statement of fundamental rights and privileges guaranteed to a people against violation by the state; *esp* : the first 10 amendments to the U.S. Constitution

bill of sale : a formal document showing transfer of ownership of personal property

[1]**bil·low** \ˈbil-ō\ *n* **1** : WAVE; *esp* : a great wave or surge of water **2** : a rolling mass (as of flame or smoke) like a high wave [probably from Old Norse *bylgja*] — **bil·lowy** \ˈbil-ə-wē\ *adj*

[2]**billow** *vb* **1** : to rise or roll in waves or surges ⟨the *billowing* ocean⟩ **2** : to bulge or swell out (as because of the wind)

bil·ly \ˈbil-ē\ *n, pl* **billies** **1** : BILLY CLUB **2** : BILLY GOAT

billy club *n* : a heavy wooden club; *esp* : a police officer's club

bil·ly goat \ˈbil-ē-\ *n* : a male goat

bi·lobed \ˈbī-ˈlōbd\ *adj* : divided into two lobes

bi·met·al \ˈbī-ˌmet-l\ *adj* : BIMETALLIC

bi·me·tal·lic \ˌbī-mə-ˈtal-ik\ *adj* **1** : of or relating to bimetallism **2** : composed of two different metals — often used of devices having a part in which two metals that expand differently are bonded together — **bimetallic** *n*

bi·met·al·lism \bī-ˈmet-l-ˌiz-əm, ˈbī-\ *n* : the use of two metals (as gold and silver) jointly as a monetary standard — **bi·met·al·list** \-l-əst\ *n* — **bi·met·al·list·ic** \ˌbī-ˌmet-l-ˈis-tik\ *adj*

[1]**bi·month·ly** \bī-ˈmənth-lē, ˈbī-, -ˈməntth-\ *adj* **1** : occurring every two months **2** : occurring twice a month : SEMIMONTHLY

[2]**bimonthly** *n* : a bimonthly publication

[3]**bimonthly** *adv* **1** : once every two months **2** : twice a month

bin \ˈbin\ *n* : an enclosed place (as a box or crib) used for storage [Old English *binn*]

[1]**bi·na·ry** \ˈbī-nə-rē\ *adj* **1** : compounded or consisting of or characterized by two often similar things or parts **2** : relating to, being, or belonging to a system of numbers having two as its base ⟨the *binary* digits 0 and 1⟩ **3** : relating exactly two logical or mathematical elements at a time ⟨addition and multiplication are *binary* operations⟩ [Latin *bini* "two each"]

[2]**binary** *n, pl* **-ries** : something constituted of two things or parts

binary fission *n* : reproduction of a cell by division into two approximately equal parts

binary notation *n* : expression of a number in base 2 that uses either the digit 0 or 1 for each place — compare DECIMAL NOTATION

binary star *n* : a system of two stars that revolve around each other under their mutual gravitation

binary system *n* : a system of two bodies that revolve around each other; *esp* : BINARY STAR

bin·au·ral \bī-ˈnȯr-əl, ˈbī-\ *adj* **1** : of, relating to, or used with two or both ears **2 a** : of, relating to, or constituting a three-dimensional effect of reproduced sound involving the use of two separate recording paths **b** : STEREOPHONIC [Latin *bini* "two each" + *auris* "ear"] — **bin·au·ral·ly** \-ə-lē\ *adv*

[1]**bind** \ˈbīnd\ *vb* **bound** \ˈbau̇nd\; **bind·ing** **1 a** : to tie together or tie securely **b** : to confine, restrain, restrict, or attach by force, obligation, or strong feeling ⟨*bound* by friendship⟩ **c** : to hamper free movement of **2 a** : to wrap around with something so as to enclose, encircle, or cover ⟨a sash *bound* the child's waist⟩ **b** : BANDAGE ⟨*bound* up the wound⟩ **3 a** : to stick together **b** : to form a cohesive mass **c** : to take up and hold by chemical forces **4** : CONSTIPATE **5** : to make firm : ESTABLISH ⟨a deposit *binds* the sale⟩ **6 a** : to protect, strengthen, or decorate by a band or binding **b** : to apply the cover to (a book) **7** : INDENTURE, APPRENTICE [Old English *bindan*]

[2]**bind** *n* : something that binds — **in a bind** : in trouble

bind·er \ˈbīn-dər\ *n* **1** : one that binds something (as books) **2 a** : something used in binding **b** : a detachable cover or device for holding together sheets of paper or similar material **3** : something (as tar or cement) that produces or promotes cohesion in loosely assembled substances **4** : a temporary insurance contract that provides coverage until the policy is issued **5** : something (as money) given to make an agreement binding; *also* : the agreement arrived at

bind·ery \ˈbīn-də-rē, -drē\ *n, pl* **-er·ies** : a place where books are bound

bind·ing \ˈbīn-ding\ *n* **1** : the action of one that binds **2** : a material or device used to bind: as **a** : the cover and fastenings of a book **b** : a narrow fabric used to finish raw edges **c** : a device for securing a boot to a ski

binding energy *n* : the energy required to break up a molecule, atom, or atomic nucleus into its constituent particles

bind over *vt* : to put (a person) under a legal obligation to appear in court or to perform or refrain from some specific action

bind·weed \ˈbīnd-ˌwēd\ *n* : any of various twining plants related especially to the morning glories that grow matted or interlaced with other plants

bine \ˈbīn\ *n* : a twining stem or flexible shoot (as of the hop) [alteration of [2]*bind*]

binge \ˈbinj\ *n* **1** : a period of overindulgence ⟨a buying *binge*⟩ **2** : an act of excessive or compulsive consumption (as of food) [English dialect *binge* "to drink heavily"] — **binge** *vi*

bin·go \ˈbing-gō, -ˌgō\ *n* : a game of chance played with cards having numbered squares corresponding to numbered balls drawn at random and won by the player first covering five squares in a row [earlier *bingo,* interjection used to announce an unexpected event]

bin·na·cle \ˈbin-i-kəl\ *n* : a case, box, or stand containing a ship's compass and a lamp [Middle English *bitakle,* derived from Latin *habitaculum* "habitation"]

[1]**bin·oc·u·lar** \bī-ˈnäk-yə-lər, bə-\ *adj* : of, relating to, using, or adapted to the use of both eyes ⟨*binocular* vision⟩ [Latin *bini* "two each" + *oculus* "eye"] — **bin·oc·u·lar·ly** *adv*

[2]**binocular** *n* **1** : a binocular optical instrument **2** : a handheld magnifying optical instrument that consists of two telescopes, a focusing device, and usually prisms — usually used in plural ⟨a pair of *binoculars*⟩

bi·no·mi·al \bī-ˈnō-mē-əl\ *n* **1** : a mathematical expression consisting of two terms connected by a plus sign or minus sign **2** : a biological species name consisting of two terms according to the system of binomial nomenclature [Latin *bi-* + *nomen* "name, term"] — **binomial** *adj* — **bi·no·mi·al·ly** \-mē-ə-lē\ *adv*

binomial coefficient *n* : a coefficient of a term in the expansion of the binomial $(x + y)^n$ according to the binomial theorem

binomial nomenclature *n* : a system of nomenclature in which each species of animal or plant receives a binomial name of which the first term identifies the genus to which it belongs and the second the species itself

binomial theorem *n* : a theorem that specifies the expansion of a binomial of the form $(x + y)^n$ as the sum of $n + 1$ terms of which the general term is of the form

$$\frac{n!}{(n-k)!\,k!}x^{(n-k)}y^k$$

where k takes on values from 0 to n

bi·nu·cle·ate \bī-ˈnyü-klē-ət, ˈbī-, -ˈnü-\ *adj* : having two nuclei

bio- *combining form* **1** : life ⟨*bio*sphere⟩ **2** : living organisms or tissue ⟨*bio*luminescence⟩ [Greek *bios* "life, mode of life"]

bio·as·say \ˌbī-ō-ˈas-ˌā, -a-ˈsā\ *n* : determination of the relative strength of a substance (as of a drug) by comparing its effect on a test organism with that of a standard preparation — **bio·as·say** \-a-ˈsā, -ˈas-ˌā\ *vt*

bio·avail·abil·i·ty \-ə-ˌvā-lə-ˈbil-ət-ē\ *n* : the degree and rate at which a substance (as a drug) is absorbed into a living system or is made available at the site of physiological activity — **bio·avail·able** \-ˈvā-lə-bəl\ *adj*

bio·chem·is·try \-ˈkem-ə-strē\ *n* : chemistry that deals with the chemical compounds and processes occurring in living things — **bio·chem·i·cal** \ˌbī-ō-ˈkem-i-kəl\ *adj* — **bio·chem·i·cal·ly** \-kə-lē, -klē\ *adv* — **bio·chem·ist** \-ˈkem-əst\ *n*

bio·com·pat·i·bil·i·ty \-kəm-ˌpat-ə-ˈbil-ət-ē\ *n* : compatibility with living tissue or a living system by not being toxic or injurious and not causing immunological rejection — **bio·com·pat·i·ble** \-ˈpat-ə-bəl\ *adj*

bio·con·trol \ˌbī-ō-kən-ˈtrōl\ *n* : BIOLOGICAL CONTROL 1

bio·de·grad·able \-di-ˈgrād-ə-bəl\ *adj* : capable of being broken down especially into relatively harmless products by the action of living things (as microorganisms) — **bio·de·grad·abil·i·ty** \-ˌgrād-ə-ˈbil-ət-ē\ *n* — **bio·de·grade** \-di-ˈgrād\ *vb*

bio·die·sel \ˌbī-ō-ˈdē-zəl, -səl\ *n* : a fuel that is similar to diesel fuel and is derived from usually vegetable sources (as soybean oil)

bio·di·ver·si·ty \-də-ˈvər-sət-ē, -dī-\ *n* : biological diversity in an environment as indicated by numbers of different species of plants and animals

bio·en·er·get·ics \-ˌen-ər-ˈjet-iks\ *n* : the biology of energy transformations and energy exchanges (as in photosynthesis)

\ə\ **abut**	\au̇\ **out**	\i\ **tip**	\ȯ\ **saw**	\u̇\ **foot**
\ər\ **further**	\ch\ **chin**	\ī\ **life**	\ȯi\ **coin**	\y\ **yet**
\a\ **mat**	\e\ **pet**	\j\ **job**	\th\ **thin**	\yü\ **few**
\ā\ **take**	\ē\ **easy**	\ng\ **sing**	\t͟h\ **this**	\yu̇\ **cure**
\ä\ **cot, cart**	\g\ **go**	\ō\ **bone**	\ü\ **food**	\zh\ **vision**

within and between living things and their environments — **bi·o·en·er·get·ic** \-ik\ *adj*

bio·en·gi·neer \-ˌen-jə-ˈnir\ *vt* : to modify or produce by bioengineering — **bioengineer** *n*

bio·en·gi·neer·ing \-ˌen-jə-ˈnir-iŋ\ *n* **1** : the application of engineering principles to medicine and biology — called also *biomedical engineering* **2** : the application of biological techniques (as genetic recombination) to create modified versions of organisms (as crops); *esp* : GENETIC ENGINEERING

bio·feed·back \-ˈfēd-ˌbak\ *n* : the technique of making unconscious or involuntary bodily processes (as heartbeat or brain waves) perceptible to the senses (as by the use of an oscilloscope) in order to manipulate them by conscious mental control

bio·fuel \-ˈfyü-əl\ *n* : a fuel (as wood) composed of or produced from biological raw materials

bio·gas \ˈbī-ō-ˌgas\ *n* : a mixture of methane and carbon dioxide produced by the bacterial decomposition of organic wastes and used as a fuel

bio·gen·e·sis \ˌbī-ō-ˈjen-ə-səs\ *n* : the development of life from preexisting life — **bio·gen·e·sist** \-ə-səst\ *n* — **bio·ge·net·ic** \-jə-ˈnet-ik\ *adj*

biogenetic law *n* : a theory in biology: an organism passes through successive stages in development resembling the series of evolutionary ancestors from which it is descended

bio·ge·og·ra·phy \ˌbī-ō-jē-ˈäg-rə-fē\ *n* : a branch of biology that deals with the geographical distribution of animals and plants — **bio·ge·og·ra·pher** \-jē-ˈäg-rə-fər\ *n* — **bio·geo·graph·ic** \-ˌjē-ə-ˈgraf-ik\ *or* **bio·geo·graph·i·cal** \-ˈgraf-i-kəl\ *adj*

bi·og·ra·pher \bī-ˈäg-rə-fər, bē-\ *n* : a writer of a biography

bio·graph·i·cal \ˌbī-ə-ˈgraf-i-kəl\ *also* **bio·graph·ic** \-ˈgraf-ik\ *adj* **1** : of, relating to, or constituting biography ⟨a *biographical* sketch⟩ **2** : consisting of biographies ⟨a *biographical* dictionary⟩ — **bio·graph·i·cal·ly** \-ˈgraf-i-kə-lē, -klē\ *adv*

bi·og·ra·phy \bī-ˈäg-rə-fē, bē-\ *n, pl* **-phies** **1** : a usually written history of a person's life **2** : biographical writings in general **3** : a life history ⟨the *biography* of a building⟩

bio·haz·ard \ˈbī-ō-ˌhaz-ərd\ *n* : a biological agent or condition that constitutes a hazard to humans or the environment; *also* : the hazard posed by such an agent or condition

bio·in·for·mat·ics \ˌbī-ō-in-fər-ˈmat-iks\ *n* : the collection, organization, storage, and analysis of biochemical and biological data using computers

bi·o·log·ic \ˌbī-ə-ˈläj-ik\ *or* **bi·o·log·i·cal** \-i-kəl\ *n* : a medicinal product of biological origin

bi·o·log·i·cal \ˌbī-ə-ˈläj-i-kəl\ *also* **bi·o·log·ic** \-ˈläj-ik\ *adj* **1** : of or relating to biology, to living things, or to life and living processes ⟨*biological* activity⟩ **2** : connected by direct genetic relationship rather than by adoption or marriage ⟨his *biological* father⟩ — **bi·o·log·i·cal·ly** \-ˈläj-i-kə-lē, -klē\ *adv*

biological clock *n* : an inherent timing mechanism in a living thing responsible for various cyclical physiological and behavioral functions and responses

biological control *n* **1** : elimination or reduction in numbers of pest organisms by interference with their ecology (as by the introduction of parasites or disease) **2** : an agent used in biological control

biological warfare *n* : warfare involving the use of biological weapons

biological weapon *n* : a harmful biological agent (as a pathogenic microorganism or toxin) used as a weapon to cause death or disease usually on a large scale

bi·ol·o·gy \bī-ˈäl-ə-jē\ *n* **1** : a branch of knowledge that deals with living organisms and life processes **2 a** : the plant and animal life of a region or environment **b** : the life processes of an organism or a group — **bi·ol·o·gist** \-jəst\ *n*

bio·lu·mi·nes·cence \ˌbī-ō-ˌlü-mə-ˈnes-nts\ *n* : the emission of light by living organisms — **bio·lu·mi·nes·cent** \-nt\ *adj*

bio·mass \ˈbī-ō-ˌmas\ *n* : the amount of living matter (as in a unit area of a natural habitat or in a unit volume of a liquid culture)

bi·ome \ˈbī-ˌōm\ *n* : a major ecological community type ⟨the grassland *biome*⟩ [*bio-* + Greek *-ōma* "group, mass"]

bio·med·i·cal \ˌbī-ō-ˈmed-i-kəl\ *adj* : of, relating to, or involving biological, medical, and physical science (as in the development of artificial organs or the alteration of human genes)

bi·on·ic \bī-ˈän-ik\ *adj* **1** : of or relating to bionics **2** : having the normal biological ability to perform a physical task improved or increased by special devices

bi·on·ics \bī-ˈän-iks\ *n* : a branch of science concerned with applying facts about the working of biological systems to the solution of engineering problems [*bi-* + *-onics* (as in *electronics*)]

bi·o·nom·ics \ˌbī-ə-ˈnäm-iks\ *n sing or pl* : ECOLOGY [Greek *nomos* "law"] — **bi·o·nom·ic** \-ik\ *adj*

bio·phys·ics \ˌbī-ō-ˈfiz-iks\ *n* : a branch of knowledge concerned with the application of physical principles and methods to biological problems — **bio·phys·i·cal** \ˌbī-ō-ˈfiz-i-kəl\ *adj* — **bio·phys·i·cist** \-ˈfiz-ə-səst\ *n*

bi·op·sy \ˈbī-ˌäp-sē\ *n, pl* **-sies** : the removal and examination of tissue, cells, or fluids from the living body [*bio-* + *-opsy* (as in *autopsy*)]

bio·re·ac·tor \ˌbī-ō-rē-ˈak-tər\ *n* : a device or apparatus in which living organisms and especially bacteria synthesize useful substances or break down harmful ones

bio·rhythm \ˈbī-ō-ˌrith-əm\ *n* : a hypothetical internal rhythm that controls various biological processes or functions

bio·sci·ence \ˌbī-ō-ˈsī-əns\ *n* : BIOLOGY 1; *also* : LIFE SCIENCE

bio·sphere \ˈbī-ə-ˌsfiər\ *n* : the part of the world in which life can exist

bio·sta·tis·tics \ˌbī-ō-stə-ˈtis-tiks\ *n* : statistics applied to the analysis of biological data

bio·syn·the·sis \ˌbī-ō-ˈsin-thə-səs, -ˈsint-\ *n* : the production of a chemical compound by a living organism — **bio·syn·thet·ic** \-sin-ˈthet-ik\ *adj*

bi·o·ta \bī-ˈōt-ə\ *n* : the flora and fauna of a region [New Latin, from Greek *biotē* "life"]

bio·tech·nol·o·gy \ˌbī-ō-tek-ˈnäl-ə-jē\ *n* : the manipulation (as through alteration of genetic material) of living organisms to produce useful products (as pest-resistant crops); *also* : any of various applications of biological science used in such manipulation — **bio·tech·no·log·i·cal** \-ˌtek-nə-ˈläj-ə-kəl\ *adj* — **bio·tech·nol·o·gist** \-ˈnäl-ə-jəst\ *n*

bio·ter·ror·ism \-ˈter-ər-ˌiz-əm\ *n* : terrorism involving the use of biological weapons — **bio·ter·ror·ist** \-ər-əst\ *n or adj*

bi·ot·ic \bī-ˈät-ik\ *adj* : of, relating to, or caused by living organisms ⟨a *biotic* community⟩ [Greek *biōtikos,* from *bioun* "to live," from *bios* "life"]

biotic potential *n* : the inherent capacity of an organism or species to reproduce and survive

bi·o·tin \ˈbī-ə-tən\ *n* : a colorless crystalline growth vitamin of the vitamin B complex found especially in yeast, liver, and egg yolk [Greek *biotos* "life, sustenance"]

bi·o·tite \ˈbī-ə-ˌtīt\ *n* : a generally black or dark green mica containing iron, magnesium, potassium, and aluminum [Jean B. *Biot,* died 1862, French mathematician]

bi·par·ti·san \bī-ˈpärt-ə-zən, ˈbī-\ *adj* : of, relating to, or involving members of two parties ⟨a *bipartisan* foreign policy⟩ — **bi·par·ti·san·ism** \-zə-ˌniz-əm\ *n* — **bi·par·ti·san·ship** \-zən-ˌship\ *n*

bi·par·tite \bī-ˈpär-ˌtīt, ˈbī-\ *adj* **1** : being in two parts **2** : shared by two ⟨a *bipartite* treaty⟩ — **bi·par·tite·ly** *adv* — **bi·par·ti·tion** \ˌbī-ˌpär-ˈtish-ən\ *n*

bi·ped \ˈbī-ˌped\ *n* : a 2-footed animal [Latin *ped-, pes* "foot"] — **bi·ped·al** \bī-ˈped-l, ˈbī-\ *adj*

bi·plane \ˈbī-ˌplān\ *n* : an airplane with two sets of wings usually placed one above the other

biplane

bi·po·lar \bī-ˈpō-lər, ˈbī-\ *adj* **1** : having or involving two poles **2** : having or marked by two mutually repellent forces or wholly opposed natures or views — **bi·po·lar·i·ty** \ˌbī-pō-ˈlar-ət-ē\ *n*

bi·ra·cial \bī-ˈrā-shəl\ *adj* : of, relating to, or involving people from two races ⟨*biracial* communities⟩; *esp* : having biological parents of two different ethnic identities

bi·ra·mous \bī-ˈrā-məs, ˈbī-\ *adj* : having two branches [*bi-* + *ramous* "having branches," from Latin *ramosus,* from *ramus* "branch"]

[1]**birch** \ˈbərch\ *n* **1** : any of a genus of deciduous trees or shrubs having an outer bark that occurs in layers and peels readily; *also* : its hard pale close-grained wood **2** : a birch rod or bun-

dle of twigs for whipping [Old English *beorc*] — **birch** *or* **birch·en** \ˈbər-chən\ *adj*

[2]**birch** *vt* : to beat with or as if with a birch : WHIP

[1]**bird** \ˈbərd\ *n* **1** : any of a class (Aves) of warm-blooded egg-laying vertebrate animals with the body covered with feathers and the forelimbs modified as wings **2** : FELLOW 4a; *esp* : a peculiar person **3** : SHUTTLECOCK [Old English *bridd* "young bird"] — **bird·like** \-ˌlīk\ *adj* — **for the birds** : being worthless or ridiculous

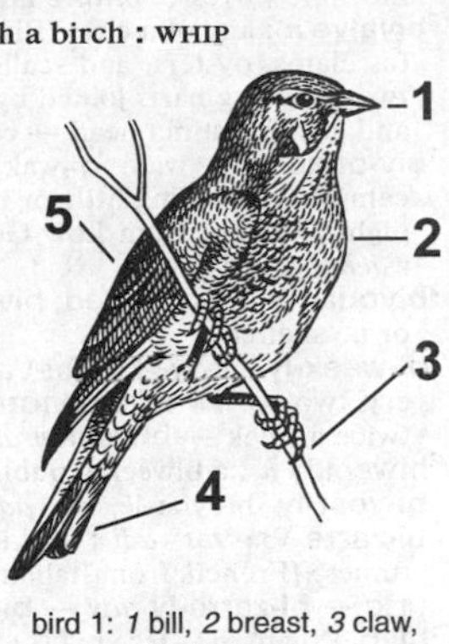

bird 1: *1* bill, *2* breast, *3* claw, *4* tail, *5* wing

[2]**bird** *vi* : to observe or identify wild birds in their natural environment — **bird·er** *n*

bird·bath \ˈbərd-ˌbath, -ˌbáth\ *n* : a basin set up for birds to bathe in

bird·brain \-ˌbrān\ *n* : a flighty thoughtless person : SCATTERBRAIN — **bird·brained** \-ˌbrānd\ *adj*

bird dog *n* : a dog trained to hunt or retrieve birds

bird·house \ˈbərd-ˌhau̇s\ *n* : an artificial nesting place for birds; *also* : AVIARY

[1]**bird·ie** \ˈbərd-ē\ *n* **1** : a little bird **2** : a golf score of one stroke less than par on a hole

[2]**birdie** *vt* **bird·ied; bird·ie·ing** : to shoot (a hole in golf) in one stroke under par

bird·lime \ˈbərd-ˌlīm\ *n* : a sticky substance smeared on twigs to catch and hold small birds

bird·man \ˈbərd-mən *also* -ˌman\ *n* **1** : one who deals with birds **2** : AVIATOR, PILOT

bird–of–paradise *n* : an ornamental southern African plant having a colorful flower head resembling the crested head of a bird

bird of paradise : any of numerous brilliantly colored plumed birds related to the crows and found in the New Guinea area

bird of passage : a migratory bird

bird of prey : a carnivorous bird (as a hawk or owl) that feeds wholly or chiefly on meat taken by hunting

bird·seed \ˈbərd-ˌsēd\ *n* : a mixture of seeds (as of sunflowers and millet) used for feeding birds

bird's–eye \ˈbərd-ˌzī\ *adj* **1** : seen from above as if by a flying bird ⟨a *bird's-eye* view⟩ **2** : marked with spots resembling birds' eyes ⟨*bird's-eye* maple⟩; *also* : made of a bird's-eye wood

bird's–foot trefoil \ˈbərdz-ˌfu̇t-\ *n* : a European herb of the legume family with claw-shaped pods that is widely used for forage and for erosion control

bird–watch·er \ˈbərd-ˌwäch-ər\ *n* : an observer of wild birds — **bird–watch** *vi*

bi·reme \ˈbī-ˌrēm\ *n* : a galley with two banks of oars [Latin *remus* "oar"]

bi·ret·ta \bə-ˈret-ə\ *n* : a square cap with three upright ridges on top worn especially by the Roman Catholic clergy [Italian *berretta,* from Old Occitan *berret* "cap"]

[1]**birth** \ˈbərth\ *n* **1 a** : the emergence of a new individual from the body of its parent **b** : the act or process of bringing forth young from the uterus **2** : a person's descent : LINEAGE ⟨one of noble *birth*⟩ **3** : a coming into existence : BEGINNING ⟨the *birth* of an idea⟩ [Old Norse *byrth*]

[2]**birth** *vb* **1** : to give rise to : ORIGINATE **2** : to bring forth or be brought forth as a child or young

[3]**birth** *adj* : BIOLOGICAL 2 ⟨his *birth* mother⟩

birth canal *n* : the channel formed by the cervix, vagina, and vulva through which the fetus passes during birth

birth control *n* **1** : control of the number of children born especially by preventing or lessening the frequency of conception **2** : contraceptive devices or preparations

birth control pill *n* : any of various preparations that are taken orally especially on a daily basis and act as contraceptives typically preventing ovulation

birth·day \ˈbərth-ˌdā\ *n* **1** : the day of a person's birth **2** : a day of origin or beginning **3** : an anniversary of a birth

birth defect *n* : a serious defect (as in physical or mental function) that is present at birth and may be inherited or environmentally induced

birth·mark \-ˌmärk\ *n* : an unusual mark or blemish on the skin at birth

birth·place \-ˌplās\ *n* : the place where a person was born or something began

birth·rate \-ˌrāt\ *n* : the number of births for every hundred or every thousand persons in a given area or group during a given time

birth·right \-ˌrīt\ *n* : a right, privilege, or possession to which a person is entitled by birth

birth·stone \-ˌstōn\ *n* : a jewel associated symbolically with the month of one's birth

bis·cuit \ˈbis-kət\ *n, pl* **biscuits** *also* **biscuit** **1** : a crisp flat cake; *esp, British* : CRACKER 2 **2** : earthenware or porcelain after the first firing and before glazing **3** : a small quick bread made from dough that has been rolled and cut or dropped from a spoon [Medieval French *bescuit,* from *pain bescuit* "twice-cooked bread"]

Word History In earlier ages the preservation of food was often a great problem, especially on long journeys. One expedient was to preserve flat cakes of bread by baking them a second time in order to dry them out. In Medieval French, this bread was called *pain bescuit* "twice-cooked bread." The second element of the phrase was borrowed into English, and, the notion of cooking twice having been lost, *biscuit* came to be used for any of various hard or crisp, dry baked products, more often called crackers in the U.S. A small quick bread of similar size and shape is also called *biscuit.*

bi·sect \ˈbī-ˌsekt, bī-ˈ\ *vb* **1** : to divide into two usually equal parts ⟨the river *bisects* the town⟩ ⟨*bisect* an angle⟩ **2** : INTERSECT, CROSS [Latin *sect-, secare* "to cut"] — **bi·sec·tion** \ˈbī-sek-shən, bī-ˈ\ *n*

bi·sec·tor \ˈbī-ˌsek-tər, bī-ˈ\ *n* : one that bisects; *esp* : a straight line that bisects an angle or a line segment

bi·sex·u·al \bī-ˈsek-shə-wəl, ˈbī-, -shəl\ *adj* **1** : possessing characters of or having sexual desire for both sexes **2** : of, relating to, or involving two sexes — **bisexual** *n* — **bi·sex·u·al·i·ty** \ˌbī-ˌsek-shə-ˈwal-ət-ē\ *n* — **bi·sex·u·al·ly** \-ē\ *adv*

bish·op \ˈbish-əp\ *n* **1 a** : a high-ranking member of various sects of the Christian clergy typically governing a diocese **b** : a member of the clergy who oversees a church district **2** : a chess piece that can move diagonally across any number of unoccupied squares [Old English *bisceop,* from Late Latin *episcopus,* from Greek *episkopos,* literally, "overseer," from *epi-* "upon" + *skeptesthai* "to look at"]

bish·op·ric \ˈbish-ə-prik\ *n* **1** : DIOCESE **2** : the office of bishop [Old English *bisceop* + *rīce* "realm"]

bis·muth \ˈbiz-məth\ *n* : a heavy brittle grayish white metallic element that is chemically like arsenic and antimony and is used in alloys and pharmaceuticals — see ELEMENT table [German *Wismut, Bismut*]

bi·son \ˈbīs-n, ˈbīz-\ *n, pl* **bison** : any of several large shaggy-maned usually gregarious recent or extinct mammals related to the ox with a large head, short horns, and a large fleshy hump above the shoulders: as **a** : WISENT **b** : BUFFALO c [Latin, of Germanic origin] — **bi·son·tine** \-n-ˌtīn\ *adj*

bisque \ˈbisk\ *n* **1** : a thick cream soup made of shellfish, meat, or vegetables **2** : ice cream containing powdered nuts or macaroons [French]

bis·ter *or* **bis·tre** \ˈbis-tər\ *n* : a grayish to yellowish brown [French *bistre*]

bis·tro \ˈbēs-ˌtrō, ˈbis-\ *n, pl* **bistros** **1** : a small or modest restaurant **2 a** : a small bar or tavern **b** : NIGHTCLUB [French]

bi·sul·fate \bī-ˈsəl-ˌfāt, ˈbī-\ *n* : an acid sulfate

bi·sul·fide \-ˌfīd\ *n* : DISULFIDE

bi·sul·fite \-ˌfīt\ *n* : an acid sulfite

[1]**bit** \ˈbit\ *n* **1** : the part of a bridle inserted in the mouth of a horse **2** : the biting or cutting edge or part of a tool; *also* : a replaceable part

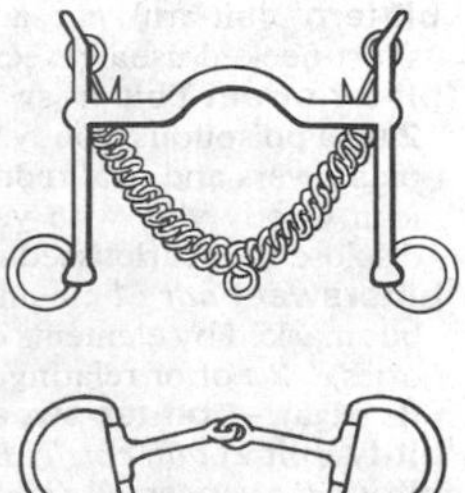
[1]bit 1

\ə\ **abut**	\au̇\ **out**	\i\ **tip**	\ó\ **saw**	\u̇\ **foot**
\ər\ **further**	\ch\ **chin**	\ī\ **life**	\ói\ **coin**	\y\ **yet**
\a\ **mat**	\e\ **pet**	\j\ **job**	\th\ **thin**	\yü\ **few**
\ā\ **take**	\ē\ **easy**	\ng\ **sing**	\th\ **this**	\yu̇\ **cure**
\ä\ **cot, cart**	\g\ **go**	\ō\ **bone**	\ü\ **food**	\zh\ **vision**

of a compound tool that actually performs the function (as drilling or boring) for which the whole tool is designed **3** : something that curbs or restrains [Middle English *bitt,* from Old English *bite* "act of biting"]

²bit *vt* **bit·ted; bit·ting** **1** : to put a bit in the mouth of (a horse) **2** : to control as if with a bit : CURB

³bit *n* **1** : a small piece or amount ⟨a *bit* of cheese⟩ ⟨a little *bit* of luck⟩ **2** : a short time : WHILE ⟨rest a *bit*⟩ [Old English *bita* "piece bitten off"] — **a bit** : SOMEWHAT, RATHER ⟨was *a bit* tired⟩ — **to bits** : TOTALLY, THOROUGHLY ⟨thrilled *to bits*⟩

⁴bit *n* **1** : a unit of computer information equivalent to the result of a choice between two alternatives (as *yes* or *no, on* or *off*) **2** : the physical representation of a bit (as a hole on a card or a magnetized spot on a tape) whose presence or absence stands for data [*bi*nary digi*t*]

bitch \ˈbich\ *n* : a female dog [Old English *bicce*]

¹bite \ˈbīt\ *vb* **bit** \ˈbit\; **bit·ten** \ˈbit-n\; **bit·ing** \ˈbīt-iŋ\ **1** : to seize, grip, or cut into with or as if with teeth ⟨*bite* an apple⟩ ⟨a steam shovel *bites* into the earth⟩ **2** : to wound or pierce with or as if with fangs ⟨*bitten* by a snake⟩ **3** : to make a gash or cut ⟨the sword *bit* into the soldier's arm⟩ **4** : to cause to smart : STING ⟨pepper *bites* the mouth⟩ **5** : to eat into : CORRODE ⟨acid *biting* into metal⟩ **6** : to respond to a lure : take a bait ⟨the fish are really *biting*⟩ [Old English *bītan*] — **bit·er** *n* — **bite the dust** **1** : to fall dead especially in battle **2** : to come to an end

²bite *n* **1** : a seizing of something with the teeth or the mouth **2** **a** : the amount of food taken at a bite **b** : a light informal meal : SNACK **3** : a wound made by biting **4** : a sharp penetrating quality or effect

bite plate *n* : a removable usually plastic device used in orthodontics: as **a** : one worn in the upper or lower jaw especially to reposition the jaw or prevent the habit of grinding one's teeth **b** : ²RETAINER 3

bite·wing \ˈbīt-ˌwiŋ\ *n* : a dental X-ray film designed to show the crowns of the upper and lower teeth simultaneously

bit·ing \ˈbīt-iŋ\ *adj* : causing bodily or mental distress : CUTTING ⟨*biting* remarks⟩ ⟨a *biting* wind⟩ ***synonyms*** see INCISIVE — **bit·ing·ly** *adv*

bit·map \ˈbit-ˌmap\ *n* : an array of computer bits that represents the pixels of an image; *also* : the image represented by a bitmap — **bit·mapped** \-ˌmapt\ *adj*

bitt \ˈbit\ *n* : a post or pair of posts on the deck of a ship for securing mooring lines [probably from Middle French *bitte,* derived from Old Norse *biti* "beam"]

¹bit·ter \ˈbit-ər\ *adj* **1** : being or inducing the one of the four basic taste sensations characterized by a disagreeable acrid taste ⟨*bitter* coffee⟩ **2 a** : hard to bear : PAINFUL ⟨*bitter* disappointment⟩ **b** : being relentlessly determined : VEHEMENT ⟨*bitter* partisans⟩ **c** : sharp and resentful ⟨a *bitter* answer⟩ **d** : unpleasantly cold or raw ⟨a *bitter* wind⟩ **3** : expressing severe pain, grief, or regret ⟨*bitter* tears⟩ [Old English *biter*] — **bit·ter·ish** \ˈbit-ə-rish\ *adj* — **bit·ter·ly** \ˈbit-ər-lē\ *adv* — **bit·ter·ness** *n*

²bitter *adv* : BITTERLY ⟨it's *bitter* cold⟩

³bitter *n* **1** : bitter sensation or quality **2** *pl* : a usually alcoholic solution of bitter and often aromatic plant products used in mixing drinks and as a mild tonic

bit·tern \ˈbit-ərn\ *n* : any of various small or medium-sized short-necked usually secretive herons [Medieval French *butor*]

¹bit·ter·sweet \ˈbit-ər-ˌswēt\ *n* **1** : something that is bittersweet **2 a** : a poisonous woody vine of the nightshade family with purple flowers and oval reddish orange berries **b** : a North American woody vine with yellow capsules that open when ripe to disclose the scarlet seed covers

²bittersweet *adj* **1** : being both bitter and sweet; *esp* : pleasant but marked by elements of suffering or regret ⟨*bittersweet* memories⟩ **2** : of or relating to a prepared chocolate containing little sugar — **bit·ter·sweet·ly** *adv* — **bit·ter·sweet·ness** *n*

¹bit·ty \ˈbit-ē\ *adj, chiefly British* : containing or made up of bits

²bitty *adj* : very small ⟨a little *bitty* dog⟩

bi·tu·men \bə-ˈtyü-mən, bī-, -ˈtü-\ *n* : any of various dark or black mixtures of hydrocarbons (as asphalt, crude petroleum, or tar) [Latin, "asphalt"]

bi·tu·mi·nous \-mə-nəs\ *adj* : resembling, containing, or impregnated with bitumen

bituminous coal *n* : a coal that when heated yields considerable volatile bituminous matter — called also *soft coal*

bi·va·lent \bī-ˈvā-lənt, ˈbī-\ *adj* : having a valence of two

¹bi·valve \ˈbī-ˌvalv\ *adj* : having or being a shell composed of two movable valves ⟨a *bivalve* mollusk⟩

²bivalve *n* : any of a class (Bivalvia) of typically marine mollusks (as clams, oysters, and scallops) that have a shell made up of two opposing parts joined by a hinge, are usually filter feeders, and lack a distinct head — called also *pelecypod*

¹biv·ouac \ˈbiv-ˌwak, -ə-ˌwak\ *n* **1** : a usually temporary encampment offering little or no shelter **2** : a camping out for a night [French, from Low German *biwacht,* from *bi* "by, at" + *wacht* "guard"]

²bivouac *vi* **biv·ouacked; biv·ouack·ing** : to encamp with little or no shelter

¹bi·week·ly \bī-ˈwē-klē, ˈbī-\ *adj* **1** : occurring or produced every two weeks : FORTNIGHTLY **2** : occurring or produced twice a week — **biweekly** *adv*

²biweekly *n* : a biweekly publication

bi·year·ly \bī-ˈyiər-lē, ˈbī-\ *adj* **1** : BIENNIAL 1 **2** : BIANNUAL

bi·zarre \bə-ˈzär\ *adj* : strikingly unusual or odd ⟨*bizarre* costumes⟩ [French, from Italian *bizzarro*] ***synonyms*** see FANTASTIC — **bi·zarre·ly** *adv* — **bi·zarre·ness** *n*

¹blab \ˈblab\ *n* **1** : TATTLETALE **2** : idle or excessive talk : CHATTER [Middle English *blabbe*] — **blab·by** \ˈblab-ē\ *adj*

²blab *vb* **blabbed; blab·bing** **1** : to reveal (secrets) by careless talking **2** : to talk too much : BABBLE

¹blab·ber \ˈblab-ər\ *vb* **blab·bered; blab·ber·ing** \ˈblab-riŋ, -ə-riŋ\ : to talk foolishly or excessively [Middle English *blaberen*]

²blabber *n* : idle talk : BABBLE

³blabber *n* : BLABBERMOUTH

blab·ber·mouth \ˈblab-ər-ˌmau̇th\ *n* : one that talks too much; *esp* : TATTLETALE

¹black \ˈblak\ *adj* **1 a** : of the color black **b** : very dark ⟨a face *black* with rage⟩ **2 a** : having dark skin, hair, and eyes : SWARTHY **b** *often cap* (1) : of or relating to various peoples having dark pigmentation of the skin and especially those of African origin or ancestry (2) : of or relating to African-Americans or their culture ⟨*black* literature⟩ **3** : characterized by the absence of light ⟨a *black* night⟩ **4** : thoroughly sinister or evil : WICKED ⟨a *black* deed⟩ **5** : invoking evil supernatural powers ⟨*black* magic⟩ **6 a** : very sad or gloomy ⟨*black* despair⟩ **b** : marked by disaster ⟨*black* Friday⟩ **7** : characterized by hostility or discontent : SULLEN ⟨*black* resentment⟩ **8** : characterized by grim or distorted satire ⟨*black* humor⟩ [Old English *blæc*] — **black·ish** \-ish\ *adj* — **black·ly** *adv* — **black·ness** *n*

²black *n* **1** : a black pigment or dye; *esp* : one consisting largely of carbon **2** : the color of soot or coal **3** : something that is black: as **a** : black clothing ⟨looks good in *black*⟩ **b** : a black animal (as a horse) **4 a** : a person belonging to any of various population groups having dark pigmentation of the skin and especially one who has African ancestry **b** : AFRICAN-AMERICAN **5** : absence of light : DARKNESS ⟨the *black* of night⟩ **6** : the dark-colored pieces of a board game for two people (as chess) **7** : the condition of making a profit ⟨operating in the *black*⟩

³black *vb* : BLACKEN

black·a·moor \ˈblak-ə-ˌmu̇r\ *n* : a dark-skinned person; *esp* : BLACK 4a [irregularly from *black* + *Moor*]

black–and–blue \ˌblak-ən-ˈblü\ *adj* : darkly discolored as the result of a bruise

Black and Tan *n* : one recruited in England in 1920–21 into the Royal Irish Constabulary to suppress the Irish revolution [from the color of his uniform]

¹black·ball \ˈblak-ˌbȯl\ *n* **1** : a small black ball used to cast a negative vote **2** : an negative vote especially against admitting someone to membership in an organization

²blackball *vt* : to vote against; *esp* : to exclude from membership by casting a negative vote

black bass *n* : any of several freshwater sunfishes (as the largemouth bass) native to eastern and central North America

black bean *n* **1** : a black kidney bean commonly used in Latin American cuisine **2** : a black soybean commonly used usually fermented in Asian cuisine

black bear *n* : the common usually black-furred bear of North America

black belt *n* **1** : an area characterized by rich black soil **2** *often cap both Bs* : an area inhabited by large numbers of blacks

black·ber·ry \ˈblak-ˌber-ē\ *n* **1** : the usually black or dark purple juicy but seedy edible fruit of various brambles **2** : a plant that bears blackberries

black·bird \ˈblak-ˌbərd\ *n* : any of various birds of which the males are largely or entirely black: as **a** : a common European thrush **b** : any of several American birds (as the red-winged blackbird) related to the meadowlarks and orioles

black•board \'blak-ˌbōrd, -ˌbȯrd\ *n* : CHALKBOARD

black•body \'blak-'bäd-ē\ *n* : a body or surface that completely absorbs all radiant energy falling upon it

black book *n* : a book containing a blacklist

black box *n* **1** : a usually electronic device whose components are hidden from or mysterious to the user **2** : a device in aircraft for recording cockpit conversations and flight data and designed to survive a crash

black•cap \'blak-ˌkap\ *n* **1** : any of several black-crowned birds (as the chickadee) **2** : BLACK RASPBERRY

black cod *n* : a large gray to blackish fish of the Pacific coast that is an important food fish with a liver rich in vitamins

black crappie *n* : a silvery black-mottled sunfish of the central and eastern U.S.

black death *n* **1** : PLAGUE 2b **2** : a severe epidemic of plague and especially bubonic plague that occurred in Asia and Europe in the 14th century [from the black patches on the skin of its victims]

black•en \'blak-ən\ *vb* **black•ened; black•en•ing** \'blak-ning, -ə-ning\ **1** : to make or become dark or black **2** : DEFAME ⟨*blackened* his reputation⟩ — **black•en•er** \-nər, -ə-nər\ *n*

black eye *n* : a puffy darkening of the area about an eye caused by bruising (as from a blow)

black–eyed pea \'blak-ˌīd-\ *n* : COWPEA

black–eyed Su•san \-'süz-n\ *n* : a North American daisy with deep yellow or orange ray flowers and a dark conical center

black•face \'blak-ˌfās\ *n* : makeup for a performer playing a black person especially in a minstrel show

black•fish \-ˌfish\ *n* **1** : any of numerous dark-colored fishes: as **a** : TAUTOG **b** : a small food fish of Alaska and Siberia **2** : any of several small toothed whales related to the dolphins; *esp* : PILOT WHALE

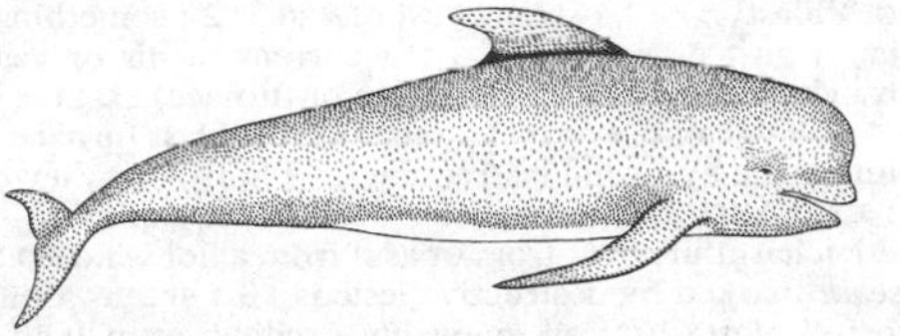

blackfish 2

black flag *n* : JOLLY ROGER

black•fly \'blak-ˌflī\ *n* : any of several small dark-colored insects; *esp* : a two-winged biting fly whose larvae live in flowing streams

Black•foot \-ˌfu̇t\ *n, pl* **Black•feet** \-ˌfēt\ *or* **Blackfoot** : a member of an American Indian people of Montana, Alberta, and Saskatchewan

black–footed ferret *n* : an endangered weasel of western North American prairies having a yellowish coat, black feet and face markings, and a black-tipped tail

black grouse *n* : a large grouse of Europe and western Asia of which the male is black with white wing patches and the female is barred and mottled

[1]**black•guard** \'blag-ərd, -ˌärd; 'blak-ˌgärd\ *n* : a rude or dishonest person — **black•guard•ly** \-lē\ *adj or adv*

[2]**blackguard** *vt* : to abuse with bad language : REVILE

black gum *n* : a tupelo tree of the eastern U.S. with light and soft but tough wood

black hand *n, often cap B&H* : a lawless secret society engaged in crime [*Black Hand,* a Sicilian and Italian-American secret society of the late 19th and 20th centuries] — **black–hand•er** *n*

black•head \'blak-ˌhed\ *n* : a small oily plug blocking the duct of a sebaceous gland especially on the face

black hole *n* : a hypothetical invisible region in space with a small diameter and intense gravitational field that is held to be caused by the collapse of a massive star

black ice *n* : a nearly transparent film of ice on a dark surface (as a paved road or body of water) that is difficult to see

black•ing \'blak-ing\ *n* : a substance that makes things black; *esp* : a paste or liquid used in shining black shoes

black•jack \'blak-ˌjak\ *n* **1** : a small leather-covered club with a flexible handle **2** : an often scrubby oak of the southern U.S. with very dark bark **3** : a card game the object of which is to be dealt cards having a higher count than those of the dealer up to but not exceeding 21 — called also *twenty-one*

black lead \-'led\ *n* : GRAPHITE 1

black•leg \'blak-ˌleg\ *n* : a usually fatal toxemia especially of young cattle caused by a bacterium

black light *n* : invisible ultraviolet or infrared light

black•list \-ˌlist\ *n* : a list of persons who are disapproved of and are to be punished or boycotted — **blacklist** *vt*

black lung *n* : a disease of the lungs caused by habitual inhalation of coal dust — called also *black lung disease*

black•mail \-ˌmāl\ *n* : the forcing of someone to do something or pay money by threatening to reveal a secret that will bring trouble and disgrace; *also* : something (as money) obtained through blackmail [Scots *mail* "payment," from Old English *māl* "agreement, pay," from Old Norse, "agreement"] — **blackmail** *vt* — **black•mail•er** *n*

Black Ma•ria \ˌblak-mə-'rī-ə\ *n* : PATROL WAGON

black market *n* : illicit trade in violation of official regulations; *also* : a place where such trade is carried on — **black–market** *vb* — **black marketer** *or* **black marketeer** *n*

black oak *n* : any of several American oaks having dark bark or foliage; *esp* : a large timber tree of the eastern and central U.S. having a yellow inner bark used for tanning

black•out \'blak-ˌau̇t\ *n* **1** : a period when lights are kept off to guard against enemy airplane attack in war **2** : a period when lights are off as a result of a failure of electrical power **3** : a temporary dulling or loss of vision or consciousness **4** : a blotting out by or as if by censorship ⟨a news *blackout*⟩

black out \blak-'au̇t, 'blak-\ *vb* **1** : to be affected by a blackout ⟨*blacked out* from exhaustion⟩ **2** : to cause a blackout of ⟨an ice storm *blacked* the city *out*⟩ ⟨*black out* the news⟩

black pepper *n* : a pungent seasoning that consists of the fruit of the East Indian pepper ground with the black husk still on

black plague *n* : BLACK DEATH

black power *n, often cap B&P* : the political and economic power of black Americans especially when used to further racial equality

black racer *n* : either of two black snakes of the eastern or southeastern U.S.

black raspberry *n* : a raspberry with a purplish black fruit that is native to eastern North America

black sheep *n* : a disreputable member of an otherwise respectable group ⟨the *black sheep* of the family⟩

Black•shirt \'blak-ˌshərt\ *n* : a member of a fascist group having a black shirt as a distinctive part of its uniform; *esp* : a member of the Italian Fascist party

black•smith \'blak-ˌsmith\ *n* : a worker who shapes iron by heating and then hammering it [from the blacksmith's working with iron, which was known as "black metal" to distinguish it from tin, or "white metal"] — **black•smith•ing** *n*

black smoker *n* : a hydrothermal vent on the ocean floor producing dark clouds of precipitating minerals; *also* : a column of rock built up by such minerals

black•snake \-ˌsnāk\ *n* **1** : any of several snakes largely black or dark in color; *esp* : a black racer or a related harmless snake **2** : a long tapering braided whip

black studies *n pl* : studies (as history and literature) relating to the culture of black Americans

black•thorn \'blak-ˌthȯrn\ *n* : a European spiny plum with hard wood and small white flowers

black tie *n* : semiformal evening clothing

black–tie \blak-'tī, 'blak-\ *adj* : characterized by or requiring the wearing of semiformal evening clothes consisting of a usually black bow tie and tuxedo for men and a formal dress for women ⟨a *black-tie* banquet⟩

black•top \'blak-ˌtäp\ *n* : a bituminous material used especially for surfacing roads; *also* : a surface paved with blacktop — **blacktop** *vt*

black walnut *n* : a walnut of eastern North America with hard strong heavy dark brown wood and oily edible nuts; *also* : its wood or nut

black widow *n* : a poisonous New World spider having the female black with an hourglass-shaped red mark on the underside of the abdomen

blad·der \ˈblad-ər\ *n* **1 :** a membranous sac in an animal in which a liquid or gas is stored; *esp* **:** one in a vertebrate into which urine passes from the kidneys and is stored temporarily until discharged by way of the urethra **2 :** something resembling a bladder; *esp* **:** an inflatable bag or container [Old English *blǣdre*] — **blad·der·like** \-ˌlīk\ *adj*

bladder worm *n* **:** a bladderlike larval tapeworm

blad·der·wort \ˈblad-ər-ˌwərt, -ˌwȯrt\ *n* **:** any of several plants growing in water or on wet shores and having insect-catching bladders on the stem

blade \ˈblād\ *n* **1 a :** a leaf of a plant and especially of a grass **b :** the broad flat part of a leaf as distinguished from its stalk **2 :** something resembling the blade of a leaf: as **a :** the broad flattened part of a paddle **b :** an arm of a propeller, electric fan, or steam turbine **c :** the upper flat part of the tongue immediately behind the tip **3 a :** the cutting part of an implement **b (1) :** SWORD 1 **(2) :** SWORDSMAN **(3) :** a dashing lively man **c :** the runner of an ice skate [Old English *blæd*] — **blad·ed** \ˈblād-əd\ *adj*

blah \ˈblä\ *adj* **:** lacking interest or excitement ⟨a *blah* winter day⟩ [imitative]

blahs \ˈbläz\ *n pl* **:** a feeling of boredom, discomfort, or general dissatisfaction ⟨the post-vacation *blahs*⟩

blain \ˈblān\ *n* **:** an inflammatory swelling or sore [Old English *blegen*]

1**blame** \ˈblām\ *vt* **1 :** to find fault with **:** CENSURE **2 a :** to hold responsible ⟨*blame* them for the failure⟩ **b :** to place responsibility for ⟨*blamed* the error on me⟩ [Medieval French *blamer, blasmer,* from Late Latin *blasphemare* "to blaspheme"] — **blam·able** \ˈblā-mə-bəl\ *adj* — **blam·ably** \-ə-blē\ *adv* — **blam·er** *n*

synonyms BLAME, CENSURE, CONDEMN, CRITICIZE mean to find fault with openly. BLAME may imply simply the opposite of *praise* but often suggests an accusation or the placing of responsibility for something bad or unfortunate ⟨*blamed* careless campers for the fire⟩. CENSURE carries a stronger suggestion of authority and reprimanding than BLAME ⟨officials *censured* the company for bad business practices⟩. CONDEMN usually suggests an unqualified and final unfavorable judgment ⟨a practice *condemned* as unfair⟩. CRITICIZE implies finding fault especially with methods or policies or intentions ⟨members of Congress *criticizing* the President's policy⟩.

2**blame** *n* **1 :** expression of disapproval **2 :** responsibility for something felt to deserve disapproval

blame·less \ˈblām-ləs\ *adj* **:** free from blame or fault — **blame·less·ly** *adv* — **blame·less·ness** *n*

blame·wor·thy \ˈblām-ˌwər-thē\ *adj* **:** deserving blame — **blame·wor·thi·ness** *n*

blanch \ˈblanch\ *vb* **1 :** to take the color out of: **a :** to bleach by excluding light ⟨*blanch* celery⟩ **b :** to scald in order to remove the skin from or whiten ⟨*blanch* almonds⟩ **2 :** to become white or pale [Medieval French *blanchir,* from *blanc* "white"] ***synonyms*** see WHITEN — **blanch·er** *n*

blanc·mange \blə-ˈmänj, -ˈmä^{n}zh\ *n* **:** a dessert made from gelatin or a starchy substance and milk usually sweetened and flavored [Medieval French *blanc manger,* literally, "white food"]

bland \ˈbland\ *adj* **1 :** smooth and soothing in manner **:** GENTLE ⟨a *bland* smile⟩ **2 a :** having soft and soothing qualities **:** not irritating ⟨a *bland* diet⟩ **b :** DULL, UNINTERESTING ⟨a *bland* story⟩ [Latin *blandus*] ***synonyms*** see SUAVE — **bland·ly** *adv* — **bland·ness** \ˈbland-nəs, ˈblan-\ *n*

blan·dish \ˈblan-dish\ *vt* **:** to coax with flattery **:** CAJOLE [Medieval French *blandiss-,* stem of *blandir,* from Latin *blandiri,* from *blandus* "bland"] — **blan·dish·er** *n* — **blan·dish·ment** \-mənt\ *n*

1**blank** \ˈblangk\ *adj* **1 :** free from writing, printing, or marks ⟨*blank* sheets of paper⟩ **2 :** having empty spaces to be filled in ⟨a *blank* form⟩ **3 :** appearing dazed or confused **:** EXPRESSIONLESS ⟨a *blank* look⟩ **4 :** lacking variety, change, or accomplishment **:** EMPTY ⟨a *blank* day⟩ **5 :** without exceptions **:** ABSOLUTE ⟨a *blank* refusal⟩ **6 :** not shaped into finished form ⟨a *blank* key⟩ [Medieval French *blanc* "colorless, white," of Germanic origin] ***synonyms*** see EMPTY — **blank·ly** *adv* — **blank·ness** *n*

2**blank** *n* **1 a :** an empty space (as on a paper) **b :** a paper with spaces for the entry of data **2 :** an empty or featureless place or space ⟨my mind was a *blank* during the test⟩ **3 a :** a piece of material prepared to be made into something (as a key) by a further operation **b :** a cartridge loaded with gunpowder but no bullet

3**blank** *vt* **1 a :** to make obscure **:** OBLITERATE ⟨*blank* out a line⟩ **b :** to stop access to **:** SEAL ⟨*blank* off a tunnel⟩ **2 :** to keep from scoring ⟨were *blanked* for eight innings⟩ **3 :** to become confused ⟨*blanked* out for a moment⟩

blank check *n* **1 :** a signed check with the amount unspecified **2 :** complete freedom of action

1**blan·ket** \ˈblang-kət\ *n* **1 :** a usually heavy woven covering for a bed **2 :** a covering layer ⟨a *blanket* of snow⟩ [Medieval French *blankete,* from *blanc* "white"]

2**blanket** *vt* **:** to cover with or as if with a blanket

3**blanket** *adj* **:** covering all members of a group ⟨*blanket* rules⟩

blank verse *n* **:** unrhymed verse; *esp* **:** unrhymed iambic pentameter verse

1**blare** \ˈblaər, ˈbleər\ *vb* **1 :** to sound loud and harsh **2 :** to utter in a harsh noisy way ⟨radios *blaring* advertisements⟩ [Middle English *bleren*]

2**blare** *n* **:** a harsh loud noise ⟨the *blare* of radios⟩

blar·ney \ˈblär-nē\ *n* **1 :** skillful flattery **:** BLANDISHMENT **2 :** NONSENSE [*Blarney* stone, a stone in *Blarney* Castle near Cork, Ireland, held to make those who kiss it skilled in flattery] — **blarney** *vb*

bla·sé \blä-ˈzā\ *adj* **1 :** indifferent to pleasure or excitement as a result of excessive indulgence **2 :** SOPHISTICATED, WORLDLY-WISE **3 :** not concerned [French]

blas·pheme \blas-ˈfēm, ˈblas-ˌ\ *vb* **1 a :** to speak of or address with irreverence **b :** to utter blasphemy **2 :** ABUSE 1, REVILE [Late Latin *blasphemare,* from Greek *blasphēmein*] — **blas·phem·er** *n*

blas·phe·my \ˈblas-fə-mē\ *n, pl* **-mies :** great disrespect shown to God or to sacred persons or things — **blas·phe·mous** \-məs\ *adj* — **blas·phe·mous·ly** *adv* — **blas·phe·mous·ness** *n*

1**blast** \ˈblast\ *n* **1 :** a strong gust of wind **2 :** something resembling a gust of wind: as **a :** a current of air or gas forced through an opening (as in an organ or furnace) **b :** the blowing that a charge of ore or metal receives in a blast furnace **3 :** the sound made by a wind instrument (as a horn) or by a whistle **4 a :** EXPLOSION **b :** the shock wave of an explosion **5 a :** a sudden harmful effect from or as if from a hot wind **b :** a plant disease marked by destructive lesions **6 :** SPEED, OPERATION ⟨go full *blast*⟩ **7 :** an enjoyably exciting event [Old English *blǣst*]

2**blast** *vb* **1 :** BLARE ⟨music *blasting* from the radio⟩ **2 a :** to use an explosive **b :** SHOOT **3 :** to injure or destroy by or as if by the action of wind ⟨seedlings *blasted* by the hot dry wind⟩ **4 :** to shatter by or as if by an explosive **5 :** to attack vigorously ⟨*blasted* by the local press⟩ **6 :** to cause to blast off ⟨will *blast* themselves from the moon's surface⟩ — **blast·er** *n*

blast- *or* **blasto-** *combining form* **:** bud **:** germ **:** embryo in its early stages ⟨*blasto*coel⟩ [Greek *blastos* "bud, shoot, embryo"]

blast furnace *n* **:** a furnace in which combustion is forced by a current of air under pressure; *esp* **:** one for the reduction of iron ore

blas·to·coel *or* **blas·to·coele** \ˈblas-tə-ˌsēl\ *n* **:** the cavity of a blastula — **blas·to·coe·lic** \ˌblas-tə-ˈsē-lik\ *adj*

blas·to·cyst \ˈblas-tə-ˌsist\ *n* **:** the modified blastula of a placental mammal

blas·to·derm \-tə-ˌdərm\ *n* **:** a discoidal blastula formed especially in an egg (as of birds) with much yolk — **blas·to·der·mic** \-ˈdər-mik\ *adj*

blast off \blas-ˈtȯf, ˈblas-\ *vi* **:** TAKE OFF 5d — used especially of rocket-propelled missiles and vehicles — **blast–off** \ˈblas-ˌtȯf\ *n*

blas·to·mere \ˈblas-tə-ˌmiər\ *n* **:** one of the cells that are produced during cleavage of a zygote and form the morula — **blas·to·mer·ic** \ˌblas-tə-ˈmiər-ik, -ˈmer-\ *adj*

blas·to·pore \ˈblas-tə-ˌpōr, -ˌpȯr\ *n* **:** the opening of the archenteron

blas·tu·la \ˈblas-chə-lə\ *n, pl* **-las** *or* **-lae** \-ˌlē, -ˌlī\ **:** an early metazoan embryo typically having the form of a hollow fluid-filled rounded cavity bounded by a single layer of cells — compare GASTRULA, MORULA [New Latin, from Greek *blastos* "bud, embryo"]

blat \ˈblat\ *vi* **blat·ted; blat·ting :** BLEAT 1 [imitative] — **blat** *n*

bla·tant \ˈblāt-nt\ *adj* **1 :** noisy especially in a vulgar or offensive way **:** CLAMOROUS **2 :** completely obvious or conspicuous especially in an offensive way ⟨a *blatant* disregard for the rules⟩ [perhaps from Latin *blatire* "to chatter"] — **bla·tan·cy** \-n-sē\ *n* — **bla·tant·ly** *adv*

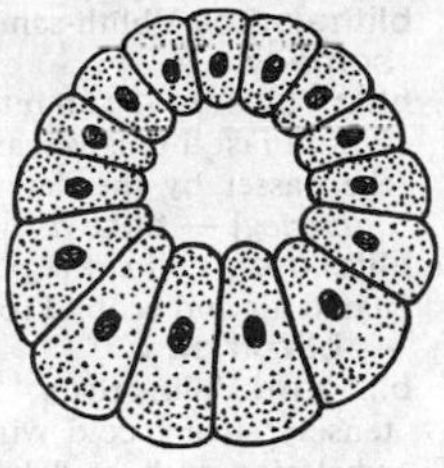
blastula

blath·er \ˈblath-ər\ *vi* **blath·ered; blath·er·ing** \-ring, -ə-ring\ **:** to talk foolishly at length [Old Norse *blathra*] — **blather** *n* — **blath·er·er** \-ər-ər\ *n*

blath·er·skite \ˈblath-ər-ˌskīt\ *n* **:** a person who blathers a lot [*blather* + Scots dialect *skate* "contemptible person"]

[1]**blaze** \ˈblāz\ *n* **1 a :** an intensely burning fire **b :** intense direct light often accompanied by heat ⟨the *blaze* of TV lights⟩ **2 :** a sudden outburst ⟨a *blaze* of flame⟩ ⟨a *blaze* of fury⟩ **3 :** a dazzling display ⟨a *blaze* of color⟩ [Old English *blæse* "torch"]

[2]**blaze** *vi* **1 a :** to burn brightly **b :** to flare up **:** FLAME ⟨suddenly *blazed* with anger⟩ **2 :** to be conspicuously brilliant ⟨fields *blazing* with flowers⟩ **3 :** to shoot rapidly and repeatedly ⟨*blaze* away at a target⟩ **4 :** to proceed very rapidly

[3]**blaze** *vt* **:** to make public **:** PROCLAIM ⟨*blaze* the news abroad⟩ [Middle Dutch *blāsen* "to blow"]

[4]**blaze** *n* **1 :** a usually long white mark down the center of the face of an animal **2 :** a mark made on a tree especially by chipping off a piece of the bark usually to leave a trail [perhaps from Dutch or Low German *bles*]

[5]**blaze** *vt* **:** to mark (as a trail) with blazes

blaz·er \ˈblā-zər\ *n* **:** a sports jacket often with notched collar and patch pockets [[2]*blaze*]

blazing star *n* **:** any of several plants having showy flower clusters; *esp* **:** any of a genus of North American herbs of the composite family with slender grassy leaves and spikes of usually rosy purple flower heads

[1]**bla·zon** \ˈblāz-n\ *n* **1 a :** COAT OF ARMS **b :** the proper description of a coat of arms **2 :** ostentatious display **:** SHOW [Medieval French *blason*]

[2]**blazon** *vt* **bla·zoned; bla·zon·ing** \ˈblāz-ning, -n-ing\ **1 :** to make public **:** PROCLAIM **2 a :** to describe (heraldic or armorial bearings) in technical terms **b :** to represent (armorial bearings) in a drawing or engraving **3 a :** DISPLAY 1 **b :** DECORATE, ADORN ⟨*blazoned* the building with posters⟩ — **bla·zon·er** \ˈblāz-nər, -n-ər\ *n*

bla·zon·ry \ˈblāz-n-rē\ *n, pl* **-ries 1 a :** BLAZON 1b **b :** COAT OF ARMS **2 :** a dazzling display

[1]**bleach** \ˈblēch\ *vb* **1 :** to remove color or stains from **2 :** to make or become whiter or lighter ⟨*bleach* clothing⟩ ⟨hair *bleached* by the sun⟩ [Old English *blǣcean*] ***synonyms*** see WHITEN

[2]**bleach** *n* **1 :** the act or process of bleaching **2 :** a preparation used in bleaching

bleach·er \ˈblē-chər\ *n* **1 :** one that bleaches or is used in bleaching **2 :** a usually uncovered stand of tiered planks providing seats for spectators — usually used in plural

bleaching powder *n* **:** a mixture of calcium hydroxide, chloride, and hypochlorite used as a bleach, disinfectant, or deodorant

bleak \ˈblēk\ *adj* **1 :** exposed to wind or weather ⟨a *bleak* coast⟩ **2 :** COLD 1, RAW ⟨a *bleak* day⟩ **3 a :** lacking warmth or kindliness ⟨a *bleak* personality⟩ **b :** not hopeful or encouraging ⟨a *bleak* outlook⟩ **4 :** severely simple **:** AUSTERE [Middle English *bleke* "pale"] — **bleak·ly** *adv* — **bleak·ness** *n*

[1]**blear** \ˈbliər\ *vt* **1 :** to make (the eyes) sore or watery **2 :** DIM 1, BLUR ⟨*bleared* sight⟩ [Middle English *bleren*]

[2]**blear** *adj* **:** dim with water or tears ⟨*blear* eyes⟩

bleary \ˈbliər-ē\ *adj* **1 :** dull or dimmed especially from fatigue or sleep ⟨*bleary* eyes⟩ **2 :** poorly outlined or defined **:** DIM — **blear·i·ly** \ˈblir-ə-lē\ *adv* — **blear·i·ness** \ˈblir-ē-nəs\ *n*

bleary–eyed \-ˌīd\ *adj* **:** having the eyes dimmed and watery (as from fatigue or emotion)

[1]**bleat** \ˈblēt\ *vb* **1 :** to utter a bleat or similar sound **2 :** to utter in a bleating manner [Old English *blǣtan*]

[2]**bleat** *n* **:** the characteristic cry of a sheep or goat

bleb \ˈbleb\ *n* **:** a small blister [perhaps alteration of *blob*] — **bleb·by** \-ē\ *adj*

bleed \ˈblēd\ *vb* **bled** \ˈbled\; **bleed·ing 1 :** to lose or shed blood ⟨a cut finger *bleeds*⟩ **2 :** to be wounded ⟨fought and *bled* for their country⟩ **3 :** to feel pain or deep sympathy ⟨my heart *bleeds* for them⟩ **4 :** to ooze or flow from or as if from a wounded surface ⟨pitch *bleeding* from the broken bark⟩ **5 a :** to draw fluid (as blood or sap) from ⟨*bleed* a patient⟩ **b :** to run when wetted ⟨dyes that *bleed*⟩ **6 :** to extort money from [Old English *blēdan,* from *blōd* "blood"]

bleed·er \ˈblēd-ər\ *n* **:** one that bleeds; *esp* **:** HEMOPHILIAC

bleeding heart *n* **1 :** a garden plant with drooping spikes of deep pink or white heart-shaped flowers **2 :** a person extravagantly sympathetic toward one felt to be abused

[1]**blem·ish** \ˈblem-ish\ *vt* **:** to spoil by a flaw [Medieval French *blemiss-,* stem of *blemir, blesmir* "to make pale by wounding, damage, sully," of Germanic origin]

[2]**blemish** *n* **:** something (as a mark) that impairs appearance or quality **:** FLAW

synonyms BLEMISH, DEFECT, FLAW mean an imperfection that mars or damages. BLEMISH suggests something that mars the surface or appearance ⟨peaches with *blemishes* are edible⟩. DEFECT implies a lack, often hidden, of something essential to completeness ⟨a *defect* in the organs of vision⟩. FLAW suggests a defect in continuity or cohesion, as a crack, break, or fissure ⟨the beam snapped because of a *flaw*⟩.

[1]**blench** \ˈblench\ *vi* **:** to shrink back out of fear **:** FLINCH [Old English *blencan* "to deceive"]

[2]**blench** *vb* **:** to grow or make pale **:** BLANCH [alteration of *blanch*]

[1]**blend** \ˈblend\ *vb* **1 :** to mix so thoroughly that the separate things mixed cannot be distinguished **2 :** to shade into each other **:** MERGE **3 :** HARMONIZE [probably from Old Norse *blanda*] ***synonyms*** see MIX

[2]**blend** *n* **1 :** a thorough mixture **2 :** a product (as coffee) prepared by blending **3 :** a word produced by combining parts of other words (as *motel* from *motor* and *hotel*)

blend·er \ˈblen-dər\ *n* **:** one that blends; *esp* **:** an appliance for grinding or mixing food

blend·ing inheritance *n* **:** inheritance involving expression in the offspring of characters intermediate between those of the parents due especially to incomplete genetic dominance

blen·ny \ˈblen-ē\ *n, pl* **blennies :** any of numerous usually small and elongated and often scaleless fishes living about rocky seashores [Latin *blennius,* a sea fish, from Greek *blennos*]

bless \ˈbles\ *vt* **blessed** \ˈblest\ *also* **blest** \ˈblest\; **bless·ing 1 :** to consecrate by religious rite or word ⟨*bless* an altar⟩ **2 :** to make the sign of the cross upon or over **3 :** to ask divine care or protection for **4 :** PRAISE 2, GLORIFY **5 :** to make successful or happy **6 :** ENDOW 2 ⟨*blessed* with good health⟩ [Old English *blētsian,* from *blōd* "blood"; from the use of blood in consecration]

bless·ed \ˈbles-əd, ˈblest\ *also* **blest** \ˈblest\ *adj* **1 :** honored in worship ⟨the *blessed* Trinity⟩ **2 a :** bringing or enjoying happiness ⟨a *blessed* relief from pain⟩ **b :** enjoying the bliss of heaven — used as a title for a beatified person — **bless·ed·ly** \ˈbles-əd-lē\ *adv* — **bless·ed·ness** \ˈbles-əd-nəs\ *n*

Bless·ed Sacrament \ˈbles-əd-\ *n* **:** EUCHARIST; *esp* **:** the consecrated Host

bless·ing *n* **1 a :** the act of one that blesses **b :** APPROVAL ⟨gave my *blessing* to the plan⟩ **2 :** something conducive to happiness or welfare **3 :** grace said at a meal

blew *past of* BLOW

[1]**blight** \ˈblīt\ *n* **1 a :** a disease or injury of plants marked by the formation of lesions, withering, and death of parts (as leaves) **b :** an organism that causes blight **2 a :** something that impairs or destroys ⟨the *blight* of totalitarianism⟩ **b :** an impaired or decayed condition ⟨urban *blight*⟩ [origin unknown]

[2]**blight** *vb* **1 :** to affect with blight **2 :** to cause to deteriorate **3 :** to suffer from or become affected with blight

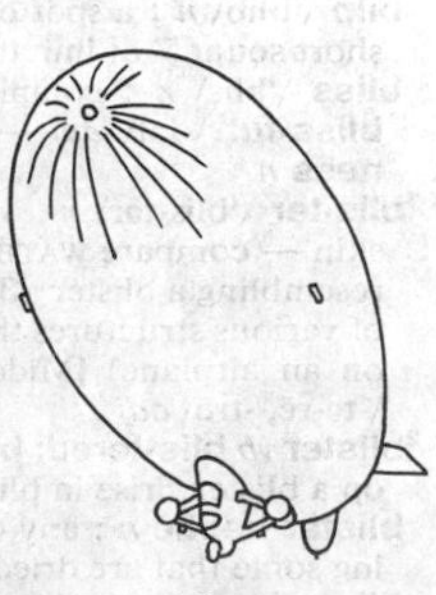
blimp

blimp \ˈblimp\ *n* **:** an airship that maintains its form by the pressure of the gas it is filled with [imitative]

[1]**blind** \ˈblīnd\ *adj* **1 a :** SIGHTLESS **b :** having less than 1⁄10 normal vision in the best eye even with the aid of glasses **2 :** lacking in judgment or understanding **3 :** made or done without the aid of sight or knowledge that could provide guidance or cause bias ⟨a *blind* taste test⟩ **4 a :** closed at one end ⟨a *blind* street⟩ **b :** having no opening ⟨a *blind* wall⟩ [Old English] — **blind·ly** *adv* — **blind·ness** \ˈblīnd-nəs, ˈblīn-\ *n*

[2]**blind** *vt* **1 a :** to make blind **b :** to make temporarily blind ⟨*blinded* by oncoming headlights⟩ **2 :** to deprive of judgment or understanding ⟨*blinded* by love⟩ **3 :** HIDE, CONCEAL

[3]**blind** *n* **1 :** a device to hinder sight or keep out light ⟨window *blinds*⟩ **2 :** a place of concealment for hunters or wildlife observers

[4]**blind** *adv* **1 :** BLINDLY; *esp* **:** to the point of insensibility ⟨*blind* drunk⟩ **2 :** without seeing outside of an airplane ⟨fly *blind*⟩ **3 :** without knowledge of facts that could guide or cause bias

blind carbon copy *n* **:** a copy of a message (as an e-mail) that is sent without the knowledge of the other recipients

blind date *n* **1 :** a date between two persons who have not previously met **2 :** either participant in a blind date

blind·er \ˈblīn-dər\ *n* **:** either of two flaps on a horse's bridle to prevent sight of objects at its sides

blinder

[1]**blind·fold** \ˈblīnd-ˌfōld, ˈblīn-\ *vt* **:** to cover the eyes of with or as if with a piece of material [Middle English *blindfellen,* literally, "to strike blind," from *blind* + *fellen* "to fell"] — **blindfold** *adj*

[2]**blindfold** *n* **:** a piece of material for covering the eyes

blind·man's buff \ˈblīnd-ˌmanz-ˈbəf, ˈblīn-\ *also* **blindman's bluff** \-ˈbləf\ *n* **:** a game in which a blindfolded player tries to catch and identify another

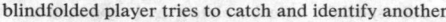

blind spot *n* **1 :** a small area at the back of the retina where the optic nerve enters the eyeball and which lacks rods and cones and is not sensitive to light **2 :** an area of weakness (as in judgment)

bling–bling \ˈbling-ˌbling\ *also* **bling** \ˈbling\ *n* **1 :** flashy jewelry worn especially as an indication of wealth **2 :** expensive and ostentatious possessions [imitative]

[1]**blink** \ˈblingk\ *vb* **1 a :** to look with half-shut eyes **b :** to close and open the eyes involuntarily **2 :** to remove (as tears) from the eye by blinking **3 :** to shine dimly or intermittently **4 a :** IGNORE ⟨*blink* the facts⟩ **b :** to look with surprise or dismay **5 :** YIELD ⟨each side waiting for the other to *blink*⟩ [Middle English *blinken* "to open one's eyes"]

[2]**blink** *n* **1 :** GLIMMER, SPARKLE **2 :** a usually involuntary shutting and opening of the eye — **on the blink :** not functioning properly **:** DISABLED

blink·er \ˈbling-kər\ *n* **1 :** one that blinks; *esp* **:** a light that flashes on and off (as for signaling) **2 :** BLINDER

blin·tze \ˈblin-sə, ˈblint-\ *or* **blintz** \ˈblints\ *n* **:** a thin rolled pancake with a filling usually of cheese [Yiddish *blintse*]

blip \ˈblip\ *n* **:** a spot on a screen ⟨a radar *blip*⟩ [earlier *blip* "a short sound," of imitative origin]

bliss \ˈblis\ *n* **:** complete happiness and joy [Old English] — **bliss·ful** \-fəl\ *adj* — **bliss·ful·ly** \-fə-lē\ *adv* — **bliss·ful·ness** *n*

[1]**blis·ter** \ˈblis-tər\ *n* **1 :** a raised fluid-filled area of the outer skin — compare WATER BLISTER **2 :** a raised spot (as in paint) resembling a blister **3 :** an agent that causes blistering **4 :** any of various structures that bulge out (as a gunner's compartment on an airplane) [Middle English *blister, blester*] — **blis·tery** \-tə-rē, -trē\ *adj*

[2]**blister** *vb* **blis·tered; blis·ter·ing** \-tə-ring, -tring\ **1 :** to develop a blister **:** rise in blisters **2 :** to raise a blister on

blister beetle *n* **:** any of a family of soft-bodied beetles including some that are dried and used medicinally to blister the skin

blistering *adj* **1 :** very intense ⟨*blistering* heat⟩ **2 :** very fast ⟨a *blistering* pace⟩

blister rust *n* **:** any of several diseases of pines caused by rust fungi and marked by external blisters

blithe \ˈblīth, ˈblīth\ *adj* **1 :** of a happy lighthearted character or disposition **2 :** HEEDLESS ⟨*blithe* unconcern⟩ [Old English *blīthe*] ***synonyms*** see MERRY — **blithe·ly** *adv*

blithe·some \ˈblīth-səm, ˈblīth-\ *adj* **:** GAY 1, MERRY — **blithe·some·ly** *adv*

blitz \ˈblits\ *n* **1 :** an intensive series of air raids; *also* **:** AIR RAID **2 a :** a fast intensive campaign ⟨a publicity *blitz*⟩ **b :** a rush of the passer by the defensive linebackers in football [short for *blitzkrieg*] — **blitz** *vt*

blitz·krieg \ˈblits-ˌkrēg\ *n* **:** a swift surprise offensive by coordinated air and ground forces [German, literally, "lightning war"] — **blitzkrieg** *vt*

bliz·zard \ˈbliz-ərd\ *n* **1 :** a long severe snowstorm **2 :** an intensely strong cold wind filled with fine snow **3 :** an overwhelming rush or deluge ⟨a *blizzard* of fan mail⟩ [origin unknown]

[1]**bloat** \ˈblōt\ *vb* **:** to swell by or as if by filling with water or air **:** puff up ⟨a *bloated* stomach⟩ ⟨spending that *bloated* the deficit further⟩ [Middle English *blout* "soft, pliable," from Old Norse *blautr* "soft, weak"]

[2]**bloat** *n* **:** a disorder of cattle marked by accumulation of gas in one or more stomach compartments

bloat·er \ˈblōt-ər\ *n* **:** a large fat herring or mackerel lightly salted and briefly smoked [obsolete *bloat* "to cure"]

blob \ˈbläb\ *n* **:** a small lump or drop of something thick ⟨a *blob* of paste⟩ [Middle English (Scots)]

bloc \ˈbläk\ *n* **1 :** a group of legislators who act together on some issues regardless of party lines ⟨the farm *bloc* in Congress⟩ **2 :** a combination of persons, groups, or nations united by treaty, agreement, or common interest ⟨a *bloc* of voters⟩ [French, literally, "block"]

[1]**block** \ˈbläk\ *n* **1 a :** a solid piece of material (as stone or wood) usually with one or more flat sides ⟨building *blocks*⟩; *also* **:** a hollow rectangular building unit **b :** a piece of wood on which condemned persons are beheaded **c :** a stand for something to be sold at auction **d :** a mold or form on which something is shaped ⟨a hat *block*⟩ **e :** the molded part that contains the cylinders of an internal-combustion engine **2 a :** OBSTACLE **b :** an obstruction of an opponent's play in sports **c** (1) **:** interruption of normal physiological function; *esp* **:** HEART BLOCK (2) **:** interruption or cessation especially of train of thought ⟨a mental *block*⟩ **3 :** a wooden or metal case enclosing one or more pulleys **4 :** a quantity, number, or section of things thought of as forming a group or unit ⟨a *block* of seats⟩ **5 a :** a large building divided into separate houses or shops **:** a number of houses or shops joined ⟨an apartment *block*⟩ **b :** a space enclosed by streets **c :** the length of one of the sides of such a block ⟨three *blocks* south⟩ **6 :** a piece of material having a hand-cut design on its surface from which impressions are to be printed [Middle French *bloc,* from Dutch *blok*]

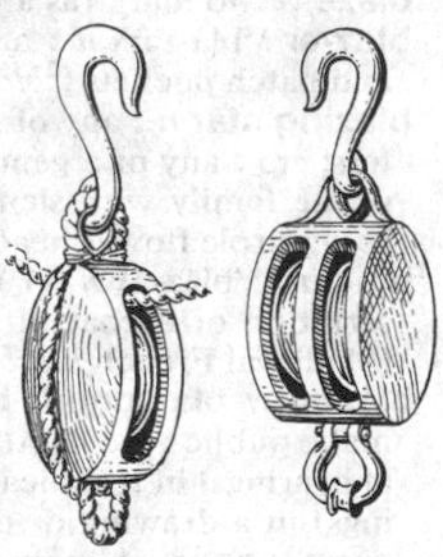
block 3

[2]**block** *vt* **1 a :** to stop up or close off **:** OBSTRUCT ⟨something *blocking* the drain⟩ ⟨a fallen tree *blocking* the road⟩ **b :** to hinder the progress or advance of; *esp* **:** to interfere with an opponent (as in football) **c :** to shut off from view ⟨*block* the sun⟩ **d :** to prevent normal functioning or action of ⟨*block* a nerve with an anesthetic⟩ **2 :** to mark the chief lines of ⟨*block* out a sketch⟩ **3 :** to shape on, with, or as if with a block **4 :** to make (lines of writing or type) flush at the left or at both left and right **5 :** to secure, support, or provide with a block ***synonyms*** see HINDER — **block·er** *n*

block·ade \blä-ˈkād\ *n* **:** the isolation of an area by means of troops or warships to prevent passage of persons or supplies in or out — **blockade** *vt* — **block·ad·er** *n*

block·ade–run·ner \-ˌrən-ər\ *n* **:** a ship or person that runs through a blockade — **block·ade–run·ning** \-ˌrən-ing\ *n*

block·age \ˈbläk-ij\ *n* **:** an act or instance of obstructing **:** the state of being blocked ⟨*blockage* of blood flow in an artery⟩

block and tackle *n* **:** pulley blocks with associated rope or cable for hoisting or hauling

block·bust·er \ˈbläk-ˌbəs-tər\ *n* **1 :** a very large high-explosive demolition bomb **2 :** one that is very successful or extravagant ⟨a *blockbuster* movie⟩

block·head \ˈbläk-ˌhed\ *n* **:** a stupid person

block•house \-ˌhau̇s\ *n* **1 :** a building of heavy timbers or of concrete built with holes in its sides through which persons inside may fire out at an enemy **2 :** a building serving as an observation point for an operation likely to be accompanied by heat, blast, or radiation hazard

block letter *n* **:** a bold simple capital letter composed of strokes of uniform thickness

block printing *n* **:** printing from carved wooden or linoleum blocks

blocky \ˈbläk-ē\ *adj* **block•i•er; -est :** resembling a block **:** solidly built ⟨a *blocky* physique⟩

blog \ˈblȯg, ˈbläg\ *n* **:** a Web site that contains an online personal journal with reflections, comments, and often hyperlinks provided by the writer; *also* **:** the contents of such a site [short for *Weblog*] — **blog** *vb* — **blog•ger** *n* — **blog•ging** *n*

bloke \ˈblōk\ *n, chiefly British* **:** MAN 1a [origin unknown]

[1]**blond** *or* **blonde** \ˈbländ\ *adj* **1 :** of a pale yellowish brown color ⟨*blond* hair⟩; *also* **:** having blond hair ⟨a *blond* man⟩ — spelled *blond* when used of a boy or man and often *blonde* when used of a girl or woman **2 a :** of a light color **b :** of the color blond [Medieval French] — **blond•ish** \ˈblän-dish\ *adj*

[2]**blond** *or* **blonde** *n* **1 :** a blond person — spelled *blond* when used of a boy or man and usually *blonde* when used of a girl or woman **2 :** a light yellowish brown to dark grayish yellow

[1]**blood** \ˈbləd\ *n* **1 a :** the red fluid that circulates in the heart, arteries, capillaries, and veins of a vertebrate animal carrying nourishment and oxygen to and bringing away waste products from all parts of the body **b :** a fluid resembling blood **2 a :** LINEAGE 2, DESCENT; *esp* **:** royal lineage ⟨a prince or princess of the *blood*⟩ **b :** relationship by descent from a common ancestor **:** KINSHIP **c :** descent from parents of superior status or breeding **3 :** blood regarded as the source of emotions [Old English *blōd*]

[2]**blood** *vt* **:** to give experience to ⟨troops *blooded* in battle⟩

blood•bath \-ˌbath, -ˌbäth\ *n* **:** a great slaughter **:** MASSACRE

blood brother *n* **1 :** a brother by birth **2 :** one that is bound in ceremonial blood brotherhood

blood brotherhood *n* **:** a solemn friendship established between men by a ceremonial use of each other's blood

blood cell *n* **:** a cell normally present in blood

blood count *n* **:** the determination of the number of blood cells in a definite volume of blood; *also* **:** the number of cells so determined

blood•cur•dling \ˈbləd-ˌkərd-ling\ *adj* **:** arousing fear or horror **:** TERRIFYING, HORRIBLE ⟨*bloodcurdling* screams⟩

blood•ed \ˈbləd-əd\ *adj* **1 :** having blood of a specified kind — used in combination ⟨cold-*blooded*⟩ **2 :** entirely or largely of pure blood or stock ⟨*blooded* horses⟩

blood feud *n* **:** a feud between different clans or families

blood fluke *n* **:** SCHISTOSOME

blood group *n* **:** one of the classes (as those designated A, B, AB, or O) into which people or their blood can be separated on the basis of the presence or absence of specific antigens in the blood — called also *blood type* — **blood grouping** *n*

blood•hound \ˈbləd-ˌhau̇nd\ *n* **:** any of a breed of large powerful hounds of European origin with a keen sense of smell

blood•less \ˈbləd-ləs\ *adj* **1 :** deficient in blood **2 :** not accompanied by loss of blood or by bloodshed ⟨a *bloodless* revolution⟩ **3 :** lacking in spirit or feeling — **blood•less•ly** *adv* — **blood•less•ness** *n*

blood•let•ting \-ˌlet-ing\ *n* **1 :** the opening of a vein for removing or releasing blood **2 :** BLOODSHED

blood•line \-ˌlīn\ *n* **:** a sequence of direct ancestors especially in a pedigree; *also* **:** FAMILY 1, STRAIN 1a

blood•mo•bile \ˈbləd-mō-ˌbēl\ *n* **:** a motor vehicle staffed and equipped for collecting blood from donors

blood money *n* **1 :** money obtained at the cost of another's life **2 :** money paid to the family of a slain person by the slayer or the slayer's relatives

blood plasma *n* **:** the fluid part of whole blood consisting of water and its dissolved parts (as proteins) — compare BLOOD SERUM

blood platelet *n* **:** PLATELET

blood poisoning *n* **:** invasion of the bloodstream by virulent microorganisms and especially bacteria from a local seat of infection accompanied especially by chills, fever, and prostration — called also *septicemia*; compare SEPSIS

blood pressure *n* **:** pressure of the blood on the walls of blood vessels and especially arteries that varies with physical condition and age

blood•red \ˈbləd-ˈred\ *adj* **:** having the color of blood

blood•root \-ˌrüt, -ˌru̇t\ *n* **:** a plant related to the poppies, having a red root and sap, and bearing a single lobed leaf and white flower in early spring

bloodroot

blood serum *n* **:** blood plasma from which clotting substances (as fibrinogen) have been removed by clot formation

blood•shed \ˈbləd-ˌshed\ *n* **1 :** the shedding of blood **2 :** the taking of life **:** SLAUGHTER

blood•shot \-ˌshät\ *adj* **:** inflamed to redness ⟨*bloodshot* eyes⟩

blood•stain \-ˌstān\ *n* **:** a discoloration caused by blood — **blood•stained** \-ˌstānd\ *adj*

blood•stone \-ˌstōn\ *n* **:** a green quartz speckled with red spots

blood•stream \-ˌstrēm\ *n* **:** the flowing blood in a circulatory system

blood•suck•er \-ˌsək-ər\ *n* **1 :** an animal that sucks blood; *esp* **:** LEECH **2 :** a person who sponges or preys on another — **blood•suck•ing** \-ˌsək-ing\ *adj*

blood sugar *n* **:** the glucose in the blood; *also* **:** its concentration (as in milligrams per 100 milliliters)

blood test *n* **:** a test of the blood; *esp* **:** one to detect the presence of substances which indicate disease or disease-causing agents

blood•thirsty \ˈbləd-ˌthər-stē\ *adj* **:** eager for or marked by the shedding of blood — **blood•thirst•i•ly** \-stə-lē\ *adv* — **blood•thirst•i•ness** \-stē-nəs\ *n*

blood type *n* **:** BLOOD GROUP — **blood–type** *vt*

blood vessel *n* **:** a vessel (as an artery, vein, or capillary) in which blood circulates in the body of an animal

blood•worm \ˈbləd-ˌwərm\ *n* **:** any of various reddish annelid worms often used as bait

bloody \ˈbləd-ē\ *adj* **blood•i•er; -est 1 :** containing, smeared, or stained with blood ⟨a *bloody* handkerchief⟩; *also* **:** BLEEDING ⟨a *bloody* nose⟩ **2 :** causing or accompanied by bloodshed ⟨a *bloody* battle⟩ **3 :** BLOODTHIRSTY, MURDEROUS ⟨a *bloody* deed⟩ — **blood•i•ly** \ˈbləd-l-ē\ *adv* — **blood•i•ness** \ˈbləd-ē-nəs\ *n* — **bloody** *vt*

[1]**bloom** \ˈblüm\ *n* **1 :** a mass of wrought iron from a forge or puddling furnace **2 :** a bar of iron or steel hammered or rolled from an ingot [Old English *blōma*]

[2]**bloom** *n* **1 a :** BLOSSOM 1a **b :** the flowering state ⟨the roses are in *bloom*⟩ **c :** a period of flowering ⟨the spring *bloom*⟩ **d :** a rapid and excessive growth of plankton **2 a :** a state or time of beauty, freshness, and vigor **b :** BLOSSOM 2 **3 :** a surface coating or appearance: as **a :** a delicate powdery coating on some fruits and leaves **b :** a rosy appearance of the cheeks; *also* **:** an outward evidence of freshness or healthy vigor [Old Norse *blōm*] — **bloomy** \ˈblü-mē\ *adj*

[3]**bloom** *vi* **1 :** to produce or yield flowers **2 a :** to achieve one's potential **b :** to be in a state of youthful beauty or freshness **:** FLOURISH **c :** SHINE, GLOW **3 :** to appear unexpectedly in large quantities — **bloom•er** *n*

bloo•mers \ˈblü-mərz\ *n pl* **:** full loose trousers gathered at the knee formerly worn by women (as for athletics); *also* **:** underpants of similar design worn chiefly by girls [Amelia *Bloomer*, died 1894, American pioneer in feminism]

bloop•er \ˈblü-pər\ *n* **:** an embarrassing blunder made in public [*bloop* "an unpleasing sound"]

[1]**blos•som** \ˈbläs-əm\ *n* **1 a :** the flower of a seed plant ⟨apple *blossoms*⟩; *also* **:** the mass of such flowers on a single plant ⟨a light *bloom* on the rose bush⟩ **b :** BLOOM 1b **2 :** a peak period or stage of development [Old English *blōstm*] — **blos•somy** \-ə-mē\ *adj*

[2]**blossom** *vi* **1 :** BLOOM 1 **2 :** to unfold like a blossom: as **a :** to flourish and prosper markedly **b :** DEVELOP 6a, EXPAND **c :** to come into being

[1]**blot** \ˈblät\ *n* **1 :** SPOT, STAIN **2 :** a flaw in morals or reputation [Middle English]

\ə\ **abut**	\au̇\ **out**	\i\ **tip**	\ȯ\ **saw**	\u̇\ **foot**
\ər\ **further**	\ch\ **chin**	\ī\ **life**	\ȯi\ **coin**	\y\ **yet**
\a\ **mat**	\e\ **pet**	\j\ **job**	\th\ **thin**	\yü\ **few**
\ā\ **take**	\ē\ **easy**	\ng\ **sing**	\t͟h\ **this**	\yu̇\ **cure**
\ä\ **cot, cart**	\g\ **go**	\ō\ **bone**	\ü\ **food**	\zh\ **vision**

²blot *vb* **blot·ted; blot·ting** **1 :** to spot, stain, or spatter with a discoloring substance **2 :** to make obscure : DIM **3 :** to bring shame to : DISGRACE **4 :** to dry or remove with or as if with blotting paper **5 :** to mark or become marked with a blot
blotch \ˈbläch\ *n* **1 :** FLAW, BLEMISH **2 :** a spot or mark (as of color or ink) especially when large or irregular [perhaps blend of *blot* and *botch*] — **blotch** *vt* — **blotched** \ˈblächt\ *adj* — **blotchy** \ˈbläch-ē\ *adj*
blot out *vt* **1 a :** to make unimportant or trivial **b :** to make obscure ⟨clouds *blotted out* the sun⟩ **2 :** DESTROY 1, KILL
blot·ter \ˈblät-ər\ *n* **1 :** a piece of blotting paper **2 :** a book in which entries are made temporarily ⟨a police *blotter*⟩
blotting paper *n* **:** a soft spongy paper used to absorb wet ink
blouse \ˈblau̇s *also* ˈblau̇z\ *n, pl* **blous·es** \ˈblau̇-səz, -zəz\ **1 :** a loose overgarment like a shirt or smock varying from hip-length to calf-length **2 :** the jacket of a uniform **3 :** a usually loose-fitting garment especially for woman covering the body from the neck to the waist [French]
¹blow \ˈblō\ *vb* **blew** \ˈblü\; **blown** \ˈblōn\; **blow·ing** **1 :** to move or become moved especially with speed or with power ⟨wind *blowing* from the north⟩ **2 :** to send forth a strong current of air ⟨*blow* on your soup⟩ **3 :** to drive or become driven by a current of air ⟨a tree *blown* down in a storm⟩ **4 :** to make a sound or cause to sound by or as if by blowing ⟨*blow* a horn⟩ ⟨*blew* a tune⟩ **5 a :** to breathe hard or rapidly : PANT **b** *of a whale* **:** to force moisture-filled air out of the lungs through the blowhole **6 a :** to melt when overloaded ⟨the fuse *blew*⟩ **b :** to cause (a fuse) to blow **7 a :** to release suddenly the contained air through a rupture ⟨the tire *blew* out⟩ **b :** to rupture by too much pressure ⟨*blew* a seal⟩ **8 :** to clear of contents by forcing air through ⟨*blow* your nose⟩ **9 a :** to produce or shape by the action of blown or injected air ⟨*blow* bubbles⟩ ⟨*blow* glass⟩ **b :** to project by blowing ⟨*blow* a kiss⟩ **10 :** to shatter or destroy by explosion **11 a :** to put out of breath with exertion **b :** to let (as a horse) pause to catch the breath **12 :** to spend recklessly ⟨*blew* all my money⟩ **13 a :** BUNGLE ⟨*blew* her lines⟩ **b :** to lose or miss (as an opportunity) especially through clumsiness ⟨*blew* my chance⟩ [Old English *blāwan*]
²blow *n* **1 :** a blowing of wind especially when violent : GALE **2 :** a forcing of air from the mouth or nose or through some instrument
³blow *vi* **blew** \ˈblü\; **blown** \ˈblōn\; **blow·ing** **:** FLOWER 1, BLOOM [Old English *blōwan*]
⁴blow *n* **1 :** a display of flowers **2 :** ²BLOOM 1b ⟨lilacs in full *blow*⟩
⁵blow *n* **1 :** a forcible stroke delivered with a part of the body or with an instrument **2 :** a hostile act : COMBAT ⟨come to *blows*⟩ **3 :** a forcible or sudden act or effort : ASSAULT **4 :** a severe and sudden calamity ⟨a heavy *blow* to the nation⟩ [Middle English *blaw*]
synonyms BLOW, STROKE mean a strong physical hit. BLOW implies violence or force ⟨thrown off balance by the *blow*⟩. STROKE suggests suddenness, definiteness, or precision ⟨a *stroke* to the head⟩.
blow away *vt* **1 :** to remove as if with a current of air ⟨*blew away* their doubts⟩ **2 :** to kill by gunfire **3 :** to impress very strongly and usually favorably **4 :** to defeat soundly ⟨*blew away* the opposing team⟩
blow–by–blow \-bī-, -bə-\ *adj* **:** minutely detailed ⟨a *blow-by-blow* account⟩
blow–dry \ˈblō-ˌdrī\ *vb* **:** to dry and usually style (hair) with a blow-dryer
blow–dry·er \ˈblō-ˌdrī-ər, -ˌdrīr\ *n* **:** a handheld hair dryer
blow·er \ˈblō-ər, ˈblōr\ *n* **1 :** one that blows **2 :** a device for producing a current of air or gas
blow·fish \ˈblō-ˌfish\ *n* **:** PUFFER FISH
blow·fly \ˈblō-ˌflī\ *n* **:** any of various two-winged flies (as a bluebottle) that deposit their eggs on meat or in wounds
blow·gun \-ˌgən\ *n* **:** a tube from which an arrow or a dart may be shot by the force of the breath
blow·hard \-ˌhärd\ *n* **1 :** BRAGGART **2 :** WINDBAG
blow·hole \-ˌhōl\ *n* **1 :** a nostril in the top of the head of a whale or related animal **2 :** a hole in the ice to which aquatic mammals (as seals) come to breathe
blown \ˈblōn\ *adj* **1 a :** SWOLLEN **b :** afflicted with bloat **2 :** being out of breath
blow·out \ˈblō-ˌau̇t\ *n* **1 :** a big social affair **2 :** a bursting of a container (as a tire) by pressure of the contents on a weak spot **3 :** an uncontrolled eruption of an oil or gas well
blow out \blō-ˈau̇t, ˈblō-\ *vb* **1 :** to extinguish or become extinguished by a gust **2 :** to dissipate (itself) by blowing — used of a storm **3 :** to defeat easily
blow over *vi* **:** to come to an end without lasting effect ⟨hoped the problem would *blow over* soon⟩
blow·pipe \ˈblō-ˌpīp\ *n* **1 :** a small round tube for blowing a jet of gas (as air) into a flame so as to concentrate and increase the heat **2 :** BLOWGUN
blow·sy *also* **blow·zy** \ˈblau̇-zē\ *adj* **:** DISHEVELED, SLOVENLY; *also* **:** COARSE 3 [English dialect *blowse* "wench"]
blow·torch \ˈblō-ˌtȯrch\ *n* **:** a small portable burner that intensifies combustion by means of a blast of air or oxygen and that usually includes a fuel tank pressurized by a hand pump
blow·up \ˈblō-ˌəp\ *n* **1 :** EXPLOSION **2 :** an outburst of temper **3 :** a photographic enlargement
blow up *vb* **1 a :** to destroy or become destroyed by explosion **b :** to become violently angry **2 :** to build up, expand, or become expanded to unreasonable proportions **3 :** to fill up with a gas ⟨*blow up* a balloon⟩ **4 :** to make a photographic enlargement of
blowy \ˈblō-ē\ *adj* **blow·i·er; -est :** WINDY 1
BLT \ˌbē-ˌel-ˈtē\ *n* **:** a bacon, lettuce, and tomato sandwich
¹blub·ber \ˈbləb-ər\ *n* **1 a :** the fat of whales and other large sea mammals (as whales) **b :** excessive fat on the body **2 :** the action of blubbering [Middle English *bluber* "bubble, foam"]
²blubber *vb* **blub·bered; blub·ber·ing** \ˈbləb-ring, -ə-ring\ **1 :** to weep noisily **2 :** to utter while weeping [Middle English *blubren* "to make a bubbling sound," from *bluber*]
³blub·ber \-ər\ *or* **blub·bery** \ˈbləb-rē, -ə-rē\ *adj* **1 :** having or characterized by blubber **2 :** puffed out : THICK ⟨*blubber* lips⟩
bludg·eon \ˈbləj-ən\ *n* **:** a short club with one end thicker and heavier than the other [origin unknown] — **bludgeon** *vt*
¹blue \ˈblü\ *adj* **1 :** of the color blue **2 a :** BLUISH **b :** LIVID 1 **c :** bluish gray **3 a :** low in spirits : MELANCHOLY **b :** tending to lower the spirits **4 :** PURITANICAL **5 :** INDECENT [Medieval French *blef, blew,* of Germanic origin] — **blue·ly** *adv* — **blue·ness** *n*
²blue *n* **1 :** the color of the clear daytime sky : a color lying between green and violet in the spectrum **2 :** blue clothing or cloth **3 a :** SKY 1 **b :** the far distance ⟨disappeared into the *blue*⟩ **c :** SEA 1a — **out of the blue :** UNEXPECTEDLY ⟨the job came *out of the blue*⟩
³blue *vt* **blued; blue·ing** *or* **blu·ing** **1 :** to make blue **2 :** to add bluing to so as to make white ⟨*blue* the sheets⟩
blue baby *n* **:** an infant with a bluish tint because of insufficient oxygenation of the blood due to a congenital defect of the heart
blue·beard \ˈblü-ˌbiərd\ *n* **:** a man who marries and kills one woman after another [*Bluebeard,* a fairy-tale character]
blue·bell \-ˌbel\ *n* **:** any of various plants (as a harebell) with blue bell-shaped flowers
blue·ber·ry \ˈblü-ˌber-ē, -bə-rē, -brē\ *n* **:** the edible blue or blackish small-seeded berry of any of several North American plants of the heath family; *also* **:** a low or tall shrub producing these berries — compare HUCKLEBERRY
blue·bird \-ˌbərd\ *n* **:** any of three small North American songbirds related to the robin but with blue above and reddish brown or pale blue below
blue blood *n* **1** \ˈblü-ˈbləd\ **:** membership in a noble or socially prominent family **2** \-ˌbləd\ **:** a member of a noble or socially prominent family — **blue–blood·ed** \-ˈbləd-əd\ *adj*
blue·bon·net \ˈblü-ˌbän-ət\ *n* **:** a low-growing annual lupine of Texas with silky foliage and blue flowers
blue·bot·tle \-ˌbät-l\ *n* **:** any of several blowflies with the abdomen or the whole body iridescent blue in color
blue cheese *n* **:** cheese ripened by and marked with greenish blue mold
blue chip *n* **:** a stock issue that commands a high price because of public faith in its worth and stability; *also* **:** a company that offers such stock [from the high value of blue chips in games of chance]
blue–col·lar \ˈblü-ˈkäl-ər\ *adj* **:** of, relating to, or constituting the class of workers whose duties require work clothes
blue crab *n* **:** a largely blue edible crab of the Atlantic and Gulf coasts
blue·fin tuna \ˈblü-ˌfin\ *n* **:** a very large tuna that is dark blue above and lighter colored below and is an important food and game fish — called also *bluefin*

blue·fish \-ˌfish\ *n* : an active saltwater food and sport fish that is bluish above with silvery sides; *also* : any of several bluish food fishes
blue flag *n* : a blue-flowered iris; *esp* : a common iris of the eastern U.S. with a root formerly used medicinally
blue·gill \ˈblü-ˌgil\ *n* : a common food and sport sunfish of the eastern and central U.S.
blue·grass \-ˌgras\ *n* **1** : any of several grasses with usually bluish green stems; *esp* : KENTUCKY BLUEGRASS **2** : country music played on unamplified stringed instruments (as banjos, fiddles, guitars, and mandolins) [sense 2 from the *Blue Grass Boys,* performing group, from the *Bluegrass* state, nickname of Kentucky]
blue–green alga \ˈblü-ˌgrēn-\ *n* : any of a major group of chiefly aquatic photosynthetic microorganisms now usually classified as bacteria or sometimes as plants — called also *cyanobacterium*
blue heron *n* : either of two herons with bluish plumage; *esp* : GREAT BLUE HERON
blue jay \-ˌjā\ *n* : a crested bright blue North American jay

blue jay

blue jeans *n pl* : pants usually made of blue denim
blue law *n* **1** : one of many strict laws regulating morals and conduct in colonial New England **2** : a statute limiting work, commerce, and amusements on Sundays
blue line *n* : either of two wide blue lines that cross an ice hockey rink and divide it approximately into thirds
blue mold *n* : a fungus and especially a penicillium that produces blue or blue-green surface growths
blue moon *n* : a very long period of time ⟨once in a *blue moon*⟩
blue·nose \ˈblü-ˌnōz\ *n* : one who advocates a strict moral code
blue plate \-ˌplāt\ *adj* : being a main course usually offered at a special price in a restaurant
blue·point \-ˌpȯint\ *n* : a small oyster typically from the south shore of Long Island [*Blue Point,* Long Island]
[1]**blue·print** \-ˌprint\ *n* **1** : a photographic print in white on a blue ground used especially for copying mechanical drawings and architects' plans **2** : a detailed plan or program of action
[2]**blueprint** *vt* : to make a blueprint of or for
blue racer *n* : a blue or greenish blue harmless snake occurring chiefly from southern Ontario to Missouri
blue ribbon *n* **1** : a blue ribbon awarded the first-place winner in a competition **2** : an honor or award gained for outstanding performance
blues \ˈblüz\ *n pl* **1** : low spirits : MELANCHOLY **2** : a song sometimes of lamentation characterized by usually three 4-bar phrases and continual occurrence of the flatted third, fifth, and seventh tones of a scale in both the melody and harmony
blue shark *n* : a shark of warm and temperate seas that is blue above and white below and that occasionally attacks humans
blue–sky law \ˈblü-ˈskī-\ *n* : a law providing for the regulation of the sale of securities (as stock) [*blue-sky stock* "worthless stock"; from the emptiness of the sky]
blue spruce *n* : a spruce native to the Rocky Mountains that has sharp usually bluish gray needles and is often planted as an ornamental
blue·stem \ˈblü-ˌstem\ *n* : either of two important hay and forage grasses of North America with bluish leaf sheaths
blue·stock·ing \-ˌstäk-iŋ\ *n* : a woman having intellectual or literary interests [*Bluestocking* society, 18th century literary club]
blue streak *n* **1** : something that moves very fast **2** : a constant stream of words ⟨talked a *blue streak*⟩
blu·et \ˈblü-ət\ *n* : a small North American herb with solitary bluish or white flowers and stems arranged in tufts
blue vitriol *n* : a hydrated copper sulfate $CuSO_4 \cdot 5H_2O$
blue whale *n* : a whale that may reach a weight of 150 tons (135 metric tons) and a length of 100 feet (30 meters) and is generally considered the largest living animal

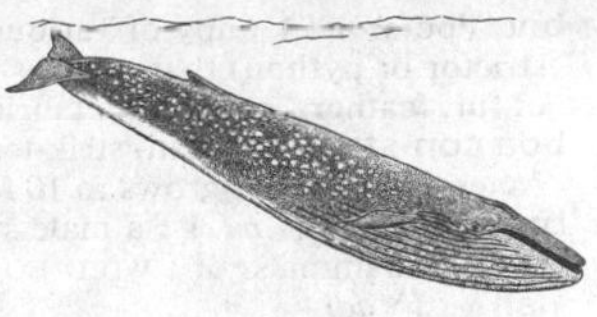
blue whale

[1]**bluff** \ˈbləf\ *adj* **1** : rising steeply with a broad front (as from a plain or shore) ⟨a *bluff* coastline⟩ **2** : blunt and outspoken in a good natured manner [Dutch *blaf* "flat"] — **bluff·ly** *adv* — **bluff·ness** *n*
[2]**bluff** *n* : a high steep bank : CLIFF
[3]**bluff** *vb* : to deceive or frighten by pretending to have strength or confidence that one does not really have [probably from Dutch *bluffen* "to boast"] — **bluff·er** *n*
[4]**bluff** *n* **1 a** : an act or instance of bluffing **b** : the practice of bluffing **2** : one who bluffs
blu·ing *or* **blue·ing** \ˈblü-iŋ\ *n* : a preparation used in washing clothes to prevent yellowing of white fabrics
blu·ish *or* **blue·ish** \ˈblü-ish\ *adj* : somewhat blue
[1]**blun·der** \ˈblən-dər\ *vb* **blun·dered; blun·der·ing** \-də-riŋ, -driŋ\ **1** : to move unsteadily or blindly : STUMBLE **2** : to make a mistake (as through stupidity or carelessness) **3** : to say stupidly or thoughtlessly : BLURT [Middle English *blundren*] — **blun·der·er** \-dər-ər\ *n*
[2]**blunder** *n* : a mistake resulting especially from stupidity or carelessness ***synonyms*** see ERROR
blun·der·buss \ˈblən-dər-ˌbəs\ *n* **1** : a muzzle-loading firearm with a flaring muzzle for ease of loading **2** : a blundering person [obsolete Dutch *donderbus,* literally, "thunder gun"]

blunderbuss 1

[1]**blunt** \ˈblənt\ *adj* **1 a** : lacking in feeling : INSENSITIVE **b** : slow in understanding or in making distinctions : DULL **2** : having an edge or point that is not sharp **3** : abrupt in speech or manner [Middle English] — **blunt·ly** *adv* — **blunt·ness** *n*
synonyms BLUNT, DULL, OBTUSE mean not sharp, keen, or acute. BLUNT suggests an inherent lack of sharpness or quickness of feeling or perception ⟨a person of *blunt* sensitivity⟩. DULL suggests a lack of keenness, zest, or pungency ⟨a *dull* pain⟩ ⟨a *dull* mind⟩. OBTUSE implies bluntness or insensitivity in perception or imagination ⟨too *obtuse* to take a hint⟩.
[2]**blunt** *vb* : to make or become blunt
[1]**blur** \ˈblər\ *n* **1** : a smear or stain that dims but does not completely cover **2** : something vague or indistinct; *esp* : something moving or occurring too quickly to be clearly seen [perhaps related to *blear*] — **blur·ry** \-ē\ *adj*
[2]**blur** *vb* **blurred; blur·ring** **1** : to make indistinct by or as if by smearing **2** : to make (as the senses) dim or confused **3** : to make or become vague, indistinct, or indefinite
blurb \ˈblərb\ *n* : a brief notice (as in advertising) praising a product extravagantly [coined by Gelett Burgess, died 1951, American humorist]
blurt \ˈblərt\ *vt* : to utter suddenly and impulsively ⟨*blurt* out a secret⟩ [probably imitative]
[1]**blush** \ˈbləsh\ *vi* **1** : to become red in the face especially from shame, modesty, or confusion **2** : to feel shame or embarrassment **3** : to have a rosy or fresh color : BLOOM [Old English *blyscan* "to redden"] — **blush·er** *n*
[2]**blush** *n* **1** : outward appearance : VIEW ⟨at first *blush*⟩ **2** : a reddening of the face especially from shame, modesty, or confusion **3** : a red or rosy tint **4** : a cosmetic applied to give a usually pink color to the cheekbone — **blush·ful** \-fəl\ *adj*
[1]**blus·ter** \ˈbləs-tər\ *vi* **blus·tered; blus·ter·ing** \-tə-riŋ, -triŋ\ **1** : to blow violently and noisily **2** : to talk or act in a noisy boastful way [Middle English *blustren*] — **blus·ter·er** \-tər-ər\ *n*
[2]**bluster** *n* **1** : a violent noisy blowing **2** : noisy boisterous activity **3** : loudly boastful or threatening speech — **blus·tery** \-tə-rē, -trē\ *adj*
B lymphocyte *n* : B CELL
BMX \ˌbē-ˌem-ˈeks\ *n* : bicycle racing that is similar to motocross with dirt tracks and jumps and the use of special heavy-duty bicycles [*b*icycle *m*otocross + *x* as symbol for *-cross*]

\ə\ **abut**	\au̇\ **out**	\i\ **tip**	\ȯ\ **saw**	\u̇\ **foot**
\ər\ **further**	\ch\ **chin**	\ī\ **life**	\ȯi\ **coin**	\y\ **yet**
\a\ **mat**	\e\ **pet**	\j\ **job**	\th\ **thin**	\yü\ **few**
\ā\ **take**	\ē\ **easy**	\ŋ\ **sing**	\t͟h\ **this**	\yu̇\ **cure**
\ä\ **cot, cart**	\g\ **go**	\ō\ **bone**	\ü\ **food**	\zh\ **vision**

boa \'bō-ə\ *n* **1 :** any of various large snakes (as the boa constrictor or python) that crushes its prey **2 :** a long fluffy scarf of fur, feathers, or delicate fabric [Latin, a kind of water snake]
boa con·stric·tor \-kən-'strik-tər\ *n* **:** a mottled brown tropical American boa that grows to 10 feet (3 meters) or longer
boar \'bōr, 'bȯr\ *n* **1 :** a male swine; *also* **:** the male of any of several mammals **2 :** WILD BOAR [Old English *bār*] — **boar·ish** \-ish\ *adj*
[1]**board** \'bōrd, 'bȯrd\ *n* **1 :** the side of a ship — often used in combination ⟨star*board*⟩ ⟨over*board*⟩ **2 a :** a thin relatively long piece of lumber **b** *pl* **:** STAGE 2a ⟨trod the *boards* for 40 years⟩ **3 a :** a dining table **b :** regular meals especially when furnished for pay ⟨room and *board*⟩ **c** (1) **:** a group of persons who manage, direct, or investigate ⟨*board* of directors⟩ ⟨school *board*⟩ ⟨*board* of examiners⟩ (2) **:** an examination given by an examining board — often used in plural ⟨pass the medical *boards*⟩ **4 a :** a flat usually rectangular piece of material designed for a special purpose ⟨cutting *board*⟩ ⟨chess *board*⟩: as (1) **:** BACKBOARD (2) **:** SURFBOARD (3) **:** CHALKBOARD (4) **:** a sheet of insulating material carrying circuit elements and terminals that can be inserted in an electronic apparatus **b :** a surface, frame, or device for posting notices or listing market quotations **5 a :** CARDBOARD **b :** a piece of stiff cardboard for the side of a book cover [Old English *bord*] — **across the board :** so as to include all classes or categories ⟨cut spending *across the board*⟩; *also* **:** in all respects ⟨an average player *across the board*⟩ — **by the board 1 :** over the side of a ship **2 :** into a state of discard, neglect, or ruin ⟨all our plans went *by the board*⟩ — **on board :** ABOARD
[2]**board** *vb* **1 :** to go or put aboard **:** get or put on ⟨*boarded* the plane in New York⟩ **2 :** to cover with boards ⟨*boarded* up a window⟩ **3 :** to provide or be provided with regular meals and often lodging usually for pay **4 :** to live at a boarding school
board·er \'bōrd-ər, 'bȯrd-\ *n* **1 :** one that boards; *esp* **:** one who boards at another's house for pay **2 :** a person who rides a snowboard
board foot *n* **:** a unit of quantity for lumber equal to the volume of a board 12 × 12 × 1 inches (about 30.5 × 30.5 × 2.5 centimeters)
board game *n* **:** a game of strategy (as chess, checkers, or backgammon) played by moving pieces on a board
board·ing·house \'bōrd-ing-ˌhau̇s, 'bȯrd-\ *n* **:** a house at which persons are boarded
boarding school *n* **:** a school in which pupils are boarded and lodged as well as taught
board of trade 1 : an organization of business people to promote and protect business interests — compare CHAMBER OF COMMERCE **2 :** a commodities exchange
board·walk \'bōrd-ˌwȯk, 'bȯrd-\ *n* **1 :** a walk constructed of planking **2 :** a walk constructed along a beach
[1]**boast** \'bōst\ *n* **1 :** the act of boasting **:** BRAG **2 :** a cause for pride [Middle English *boost*] — **boast·ful** \'bōst-fəl\ *adj* — **boast·ful·ly** \-fə-lē\ *adv* — **boast·ful·ness** *n*
[2]**boast** *vb* **1 :** to praise oneself **:** BRAG ⟨*boasting* about their money⟩ **2 :** to possess or display proudly ⟨our band *boasted* new uniforms⟩ **3 :** HAVE 1, CONTAIN ⟨a room *boasting* only a bed⟩ — **boast·er** *n*
[1]**boat** \'bōt\ *n* **1 :** a small vessel for travel on water **2 :** SHIP **3 :** a boat-shaped utensil or device ⟨gravy *boat*⟩ [Old English *bāt*] — **in the same boat :** in the same situation
[2]**boat** *vb* **1 :** to place in or bring into a boat ⟨*boated* a large halibut⟩ **2 :** to travel by boat — **boat·er** *n*
boat hook *n* **:** a hook with a point on the back fixed to a pole and used especially to pull or push a boat into place
boat·house \'bōt-ˌhau̇s\ *n* **:** a building to house and protect boats
boat·load \-ˌlōd\ *n* **1 :** a load that fills a boat **2 :** an indefinitely large amount ⟨a *boatload* of money⟩
boat·man \'bōt-mən\ *n* **:** a person who manages, works on, or deals in boats — **boat·man·ship** \-ˌship\ *n*
boat·swain *or* **bo·sun** *also* **bo·s'n** \'bōs-n\ *n* **:** a warrant officer on a warship or a petty officer on a merchant ship in charge of the hull and all related equipment [Middle English *boot* "boat" + *swein* "boy, servant"]
[1]**bob** \'bäb\ *vb* **bobbed; bob·bing 1 a :** to move or cause to move up and down in a short quick movement ⟨a cork *bobbing* in the water⟩ **b :** to emerge or appear suddenly or unexpectedly ⟨this question *bobs* up often⟩ **2 :** to grasp or make a grab with the teeth ⟨*bob* for apples⟩ [Middle English *boben*]
[2]**bob** *n* **:** a short jerky motion ⟨a *bob* of the head⟩
[3]**bob** *n* **1 :** a woman's or child's short haircut **2 :** a weight hanging from a line **3 :** a device (as a cork) buoying the baited end of a fishing line [Middle English *bobbe* "bunch, cluster"]
[4]**bob** *vt* **bobbed; bob·bing 1 :** to cut shorter **:** CROP **2 :** to cut (hair) in the style of a bob
[5]**bob** *n, pl* **bob** *British* **:** SHILLING [perhaps from the name *Bob*]
[6]**bob** *n* **:** BOBSLED
bob·ber \'bäb-ər\ *n* **:** one that bobs
bob·bin \'bäb-ən\ *n* **1 :** a cylinder or spindle on which yarn or thread is wound (as in a sewing machine) **2 :** a coil of insulated wire; *also* **:** the reel it is wound on [origin unknown]
bob·ble \'bäb-əl\ *vb* **bob·bled; bob·bling** \'bäb-ling, -ə-ling\ **1 :** [1]BOB 1a **2 :** FUMBLE 2 [from [1]*bob*] — **bobble** *n*
bob·by \'bäb-ē\ *n, pl* **bobbies** *British* **:** POLICE OFFICER [*Bobby*, nickname for Robert, from Sir Robert Peel, died 1850, organizer of the London police force]
bob·by pin \'bäb-ē-\ *n* **:** a flat wire hairpin with prongs that press close together [perhaps from [3]*bob*]
bobby socks *or* **bobby sox** *n pl* **:** girls' socks reaching above the ankle [perhaps from *bobby* pin]
bob·by–sox·er \'bäb-ē-ˌsäk-sər\ *or* **bob·by–sock·er** \-ˌsäk-ər\ *n* **:** an adolescent girl
bob·cat \'bäb-ˌkat\ *n* **:** a common usually rusty-colored North American lynx with dark markings [[3]*bob;* from the stubby tail]
bob·o·link \'bäb-ə-ˌlingk\ *n* **:** an American migratory songbird related to the blackbirds [imitative]
bob·sled \'bäb-ˌsled\ *n* **1 :** a short sled usually used as one of a joined pair **2 :** a racing sled with two sets of runners in tandem, a seat for two or four riders, a steering device, and a brake — **bobsled** *vi* — **bob·sled·der** *n*
bob·stay \'bäb-ˌstā\ *n* **:** a stay used to hold a ship's bowsprit down
bob·tail \'bäb-ˌtāl\ *n* **1 a :** a bobbed tail **b :** a horse, dog, or cat with a short or bobbed tail **2 :** something shortened or abbreviated — **bobtail** \-ˌtāl\ *or* **bob·tailed** \-ˌtāld\ *adj*
bob·white \bäb-'hwīt, 'bäb-, -'wīt\ *n* **:** any of several American quails; *esp* **:** a gray, white, and reddish game bird of eastern and central North America [imitative]

bobwhite

boc·cie *or* **boc·ci** *or* **boc·ce** \'bäch-ē\ *n* **:** a game similar to lawn bowling played on a long narrow usually dirt court [Italian *bocce* "balls"]
bock \'bäk\ *n* **:** a strong dark rich beer usually sold in the early spring [German]
[1]**bode** \'bōd\ *vb* **1 :** to indicate by signs **2 :** to give promise of something **:** PRESAGE [Old English *bodian*] — **bode·ment** \-mənt\ *n*
[2]**bode** *past of* BIDE
bod·ice \'bäd-əs\ *n* **:** the part of a woman's dress that covers the body from neck to waist

Word History *Bodice* is derived from *body.* One sense of the word *body* is "the part of a garment covering the body or trunk." In the 17th and 18th centuries a woman's corset was often called a "pair of bodies." The plural *bodies,* or *bodice,* was eventually interpreted as a singular. *Bodice* is now most often used to refer to the upper part of a woman's dress.

bod·ied \'bäd-ēd\ *adj* **:** having a body of a specified kind — used in combination ⟨long-*bodied*⟩
bod·i·less \'bäd-i-ləs, 'bäd-l-əs\ *adj* **:** having no body or substance ⟨*bodiless* ghosts⟩ ⟨a *bodiless* rumor⟩
[1]**bod·i·ly** \'bäd-l-ē\ *adj* **1 :** having a body **2 :** of or relating to the body ⟨*bodily* organs⟩ ⟨*bodily* comfort⟩
[2]**bodily** *adv* **1 :** in the flesh **2 :** as a whole **:** ALTOGETHER
bod·ing \'bōd-ing\ *n* **:** FOREBODING
bod·kin \'bäd-kən\ *n* **1 a :** DAGGER 1 **b :** a sharp slender instrument for making holes in cloth **2 :** a blunt needle with a large eye for drawing tape or ribbon through a loop or hem [Middle English]
body \'bäd-ē\ *n, pl* **bod·ies 1 a :** the physical whole of a living or dead organism **b :** the trunk or main part of a plant or animal body as distinguished from the head, appendages, or branches **c :** HUMAN, PERSON **2 :** the main or central part: as **a :** the box of a vehicle on or in which the load is placed **b :** the main part of a document **3 :** the part of a garment covering the body or trunk **4 :** a mass or portion of matter distinct

from other masses ⟨a *body* of water⟩ ⟨a *body* of cold air⟩ **5 a** : a group of individuals united for some purpose ⟨a legislative *body*⟩ **b** : a unit formed of a number of persons or things : a collective whole ⟨a *body* of laws⟩ **6 a** : VISCOSITY ⟨paint with a good *body*⟩ **b** : richness of flavor (as of wine) **c** : denseness or fullness of texture ⟨hair with *body*⟩ [Old English *bodig*]

body·build·ing \ˈ-ˌbil-diŋ\ *n* : the developing of the body through exercise and diet — **body·build·er** \-dər\ *n*

body cavity *n* : a cavity within an animal body; *esp* : COELOM

body clock *n* : the internal mechanisms that schedule periodic bodily functions and activities — usually not used technically

body English *n* : bodily motions made in a usually unconscious effort to influence the progress of a propelled object (as a ball)

body·guard \ˈbäd-ē-ˌgärd\ *n* : a person or group of persons whose duty it is to protect someone

body language *n* : the gestures, movements, and mannerisms by which one communicates with others

body louse *n* : a sucking louse that lives in the clothing and feeds on the human body

body mass index *n* : a measure of body fat that is the ratio of the weight of the body in kilograms to the square of its height in meters

body politic *n* : a group of persons politically organized under a single government

body snatcher *n* : one who steals corpses from graves

body·suit *n* : a close-fitting one-piece garment for the torso

body·surf \ˈbäd-ē-ˌsərf\ *vi* : to ride a wave on the chest and stomach without a surfboard — **body·surf·er** *n*

body·wash \ˈbäd-ē-ˌwȯsh, -ˌwäsh\ *n* : a liquid product for washing the body (as in a shower or bath)

Boer \ˈbōr, ˈbȯr, ˈbu̇r\ *n* : a South African of Dutch or Huguenot descent [Dutch, literally, "farmer"]

[1]**bog** \ˈbäg, ˈbȯg\ *n* : wet spongy ground; *esp* : a poorly drained acid area usually grown over by sedges, heaths, and sphagnum and in which dead plant matter accumulates [of Celtic origin] — **bog·gy** \-ē\ *adj*

[2]**bog** *vb* **bogged; bog·ging** : to sink into or as if into a bog : MIRE — often used with *down* ⟨got *bogged down* in detail⟩

[1]**bo·gey** *or* **bo·gy** *or* **bo·gie** *n, pl* **bogeys** *or* **bogies** **1** \ˈbu̇g-ē, ˈbō-gē, ˈbü-gē\ : GHOST 2, PHANTOM **2** \ˈbō-gē *also* ˈbu̇g-ē *or* ˈbü-gē\ : a source of fear, perplexity, or harassment **3** \ˈbō-gē\ : one golf stroke over par on a hole [probably from English dialect *bogle* "terrifying apparition"]

[2]**bogey** \ˈbō-gē\ *vt* **bo·geyed; bo·gey·ing** : to shoot (a hole in golf) in one over par

bo·gey·man \ˈbu̇g-ē-ˌman, ˈbō-gē-, ˈbü-gē-, ˈbu̇g-ər-\ *n* : a terrifying person or thing : MENACE; *esp* : a monstrous imaginary figure used especially in threatening children

bog·gle \ˈbäg-əl\ *vb* **bog·gled; bog·gling** \ˈbäg-liŋ, -ə-liŋ\ **1** : to be overwhelmed **2** : to hesitate because of doubt, fear, or scruples **3** : to overwhelm with wonder or confusion [perhaps from English dialect *bogle* "terrifying apparition"] — **boggle** *n*

bo·gie *also* **bo·gey** *or* **bo·gy** \ˈbō-gē\ *n, pl* **bogies** *also* **bogeys** **1** : a low strong cart **2** : the driving-wheel assembly of a 6-wheel automotive truck [origin unknown]

bo·gus \ˈbō-gəs\ *adj* : not genuine : COUNTERFEIT, SHAM [obsolete *bogus* "counterfeit money"]

bo·he·mia \bō-ˈhē-mē-ə\ *n, often cap* : a community of bohemians : the world of bohemians

Bo·he·mi·an \bō-ˈhē-mē-ən\ *n* **1 a** : a native or inhabitant of Bohemia **b** : the group of Czech dialects used in Bohemia **2** *often not cap* **a** : one who wanders; *esp* : GYPSY **b** : a writer or artist living an unconventional life — **bohemian** *adj, often cap* — **bo·he·mi·an·ism** \-mē-ə-ˌniz-əm\ *n, often cap*

bohr·i·um \ˈbōr-ē-əm, ˈbȯr-\ *n* : a short-lived radioactive element produced artificially — see ELEMENT table [Niels *Bohr*]

[1]**boil** \ˈbȯil\ *n* : a painful swollen inflamed area of the skin resulting from infection and usually ending with the discharge of pus and a hardened core — compare CARBUNCLE [Old English *bȳl*]

[2]**boil** *vb* **1 a** : to produce bubbles of vapor when heated ⟨the water is *boiling*⟩ **b** : to come or bring to the boiling point **2** : to become agitated : SEETHE ⟨*boiling* flood waters⟩ **3** : to be excited or stirred up ⟨*boiling* with anger⟩ **4** : to subject to the action of a boiling liquid ⟨*boil* eggs⟩ [Medieval French *boillir*, derived from Latin *bulla* "bubble"]

[3]**boil** *n* : the act or state of boiling ⟨bring to a *boil*⟩

boil down *vb* : to reduce or become reduced by or as if by boiling ⟨let the sauce *boil down*⟩ ⟨*boil down* a report⟩

boil·er \ˈbȯi-lər\ *n* **1** : a container in which something is boiled **2** : a tank holding hot water **3** : a strong metal container used in making steam for heating buildings or for driving engines

boil·er·mak·er \-ˌmā-kər\ *n* : a workman who makes, assembles, or repairs boilers

boiling point *n* **1** : the temperature at which a liquid boils **2** : the point at which a person becomes uncontrollably angry **3** : the point of crisis

boil over *vi* : to overflow while boiling or during boiling

bois·ter·ous \ˈbȯi-stə-rəs, -strəs\ *adj* **1 a** : noisily rough : ROWDY ⟨a *boisterous* crowd⟩ **b** : marked by exuberance and high spirits ⟨*boisterous* laughter⟩ **2** : vigorously active : STORMY ⟨*boisterous* winds⟩ [Middle English *boistous* "crude, clumsy"] — **bois·ter·ous·ly** *adv* — **bois·ter·ous·ness** *n*

bok choy \ˈbäk-ˈchȯi\ *n* : a Chinese cabbage with long white stalks and green leaves [Chinese (dialect of Guangzhou and Hong Kong) *baahk-choi*, literally, "white vegetable"]

bo·la \ˈbō-lə\ *or* **bo·las** \-ləs\ *n, pl* **bo·las** \-ləz\ : a cord with weights attached to the ends for throwing at and entangling an animal [American Spanish *bolas*, from Spanish *bola* "ball"]

bold \ˈbōld\ *adj* **1 a** : fearless in meeting danger : DARING **b** : showing a courageous daring spirit ⟨a *bold* plan⟩ **2** : IMPUDENT, PRESUMPTUOUS **3** : very steep : SHEER ⟨*bold* cliffs⟩ **4** : standing out prominently ⟨*bold* colors⟩ [Old English *beald*] — **bold·ly** *adv* — **bold·ness** \ˈbōld-nəs, ˈbōl-\ *n*

bold·face \ˈbōld-ˌfās, ˈbōl-\ *n* : a typeface having thick dark lines; *also* : printing in boldface

bold–faced \-ˈfāst\ *adj* **1** : bold in manner or conduct : FORWARD **2** : set in boldface

bole \ˈbōl\ *n* : the trunk of a tree [Old Norse *bolr*]

bo·le·ro \bə-ˈleər-ō\ *n, pl* **-ros** **1** : a Spanish dance in ¾ time; *also* : the music for it **2** : a short jacket open at the front [Spanish]

bo·lide \ˈbō-ˌlīd, -lid\ *n* : a large bright meteor [derived from Greek *bolid-, bolis*, from *bolē* "throw, stroke"]

bo·li·var \bə-ˈlē-ˌvär, ˈbäl-ə-vər\ *n, pl* **bo·li·vars** *or* **bo·li·va·res** \ˌbäl-ə-ˈvär-ˌās, ˌbō-li-\ **1** : the basic monetary unit of Venezuela **2** : a coin or note representing one bolivar [Simón *Bolívar*]

bo·li·vi·a·no \bə-ˌliv-ē-ˈän-ō\ *n, pl* **-nos** **1** : the basic monetary unit of Bolivia **2** : a coin representing one boliviano [Spanish]

boll \ˈbōl\ *n* : a usually roundish seedpod or capsule of some plants (as cotton and flax) [Middle English]

bol·lard \ˈbäl-ərd\ *n* **1** : a post on a wharf around which to fasten mooring lines **2** : BITT [perhaps from *bole*]

boll weevil *n* : a grayish or brown weevil whose larva lives in and feeds on the buds and bolls of the cotton plant

boll weevil

boll·worm \ˈbōl-wərm\ *n* : CORN EARWORM; *also* : any of several other moths that feed on cotton bolls as larvae

bo·lo \ˈbō-lō\ *n, pl* **bolos** : a long heavy single-edged knife used in the Philippines [Philippine Spanish]

bo·lo·gna \bə-ˈlō-nē *also* -nyə *or* -nə\ *n* : a large smoked sausage of beef, veal, and pork [*Bologna*, Italy]

bo·lom·e·ter \bə-ˈläm-ət-ər\ *n* : a very sensitive thermometer based on varying electrical resistance and used to measure feeble thermal radiation [Greek *bolē* "stroke, beam of light"]

Bol·she·vik \ˈbōl-shə-ˌvik\ *n, pl* **Bolsheviks** *or* **Bol·she·vi·ki** \ˌbōl-shə-ˈvik-ē\ **1** : a member of the radical wing of the Russian Social Democratic party that seized power in Russia by the revolution of November 1917 **2** : COMMUNIST [Russian *bol'shevik*, from *bol'shiĭ* "greater"] — **Bolshevik** *adj*

Bol·she·vism \ˈbōl-shə-ˌviz-əm\ *n* : the doctrine or program of the Bolsheviks calling for violent overthrow of capitalism

Bol·she·vist \-vəst\ *n* : BOLSHEVIK — **Bolshevist** *adj*

[1]**bol·ster** \ˈbōl-stər\ *n* **1** : a long pillow or cushion extending the full width of a bed **2** : a structural part designed to eliminate friction or provide support [Old English]

[2]**bolster** *vt* **bol·stered; bol·ster·ing** \-stə-riŋ, -striŋ\ : to sup-

\ə\ **abut**	\au̇\ **out**	\i\ **tip**	\ȯ\ **saw**	\u̇\ **foot**
\ər\ **further**	\ch\ **chin**	\ī\ **life**	\ȯi\ **coin**	\y\ **yet**
\a\ **mat**	\e\ **pet**	\j\ **job**	\th\ **thin**	\yü\ **few**
\ā\ **take**	\ē\ **easy**	\ng\ **sing**	\t͟h\ **this**	\yu̇\ **cure**
\ä\ **cot, cart**	\g\ **go**	\ō\ **bone**	\ü\ **food**	\zh\ **vision**

port with or as if with a bolster; *also* : REINFORCE ⟨news that *bolstered* my confidence⟩ — **bol·ster·er** \-stər-ər\ *n*

[1]bolt \ˈbōlt\ *n* **1 a** : a shaft or missile for a crossbow or catapult **b** : a lightning stroke : THUNDERBOLT **2** : a sliding bar used to fasten a door **3** : the part of a lock worked by a key **4** : a metal pin or rod usually with a head at one end and a screw thread at the other that is used to hold something in place **5** : a roll of cloth or wallpaper of a specified length **6** : the breech closure of a breech-loading firearm [Old English]

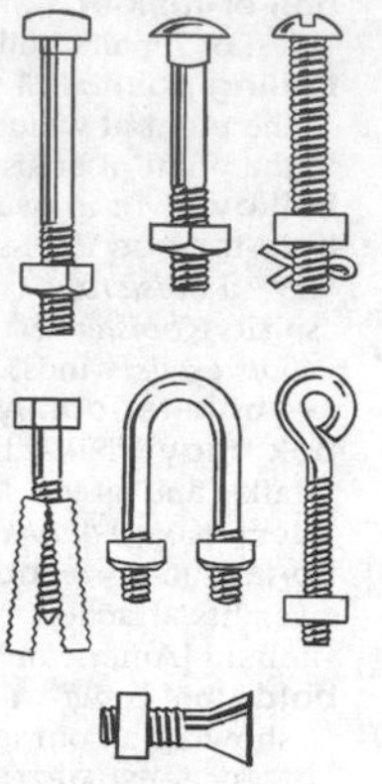
[1]bolt 4

[2]bolt *vb* **1** : to move suddenly or nervously **2** : to move rapidly : DASH ⟨reporters *bolted* for the door⟩ **3** : to run away ⟨the horse shied and *bolted*⟩ **4** : to break away from or oppose a previous affiliation (as one's political party) **5** : to say impulsively : BLURT **6** : to fasten with a bolt **7** : to eat hastily or without chewing ⟨*bolted* down our dinner and rushed out⟩ — **bolt·er** *n*

[3]bolt *adv* : in an erect or straight-backed position ⟨sat *bolt* upright⟩

[4]bolt *n* : an act of bolting

[5]bolt *vt* : to sift (as flour) usually through fine-meshed cloth [Medieval French *buleter,* of Germanic origin] — **bolt·er** *n*

bo·lus \ˈbō-ləs\ *n, pl* **bo·lus·es** : a rounded mass: as **a** : a large pill **b** : a soft mass of chewed food [Greek *bōlos* "lump"]

[1]bomb \ˈbäm\ *n* **1 a** : an explosive device fused to detonate under planned conditions **b** : ATOMIC BOMB; *also* : nuclear weapons in general — usually used with *the* **2 a** : a container for doing chemical reactions under high pressure **b** : a container in which a substance (as an insecticide) is stored under pressure and from which it is released in the form of a fine spray **3** : a rounded mass of lava exploded from a volcano **4** : [2]FLOP 2 [French *bombe,* from Italian *bomba*]

[2]bomb *vb* **1** : to attack with bombs **2** : to fail completely

[1]bom·bard \ˈbäm-ˌbärd\ *n* : a cannon used in late medieval times chiefly to hurl large stones [Middle French *bombarde*]

[2]bom·bard \bäm-ˈbärd, bəm-\ *vt* **1** : to attack with artillery **2** : to attack vigorously or persistently (as with questions) **3** : to subject to the impact of rapidly moving particles (as electrons or alpha rays) — **bom·bard·ment** \-mənt\ *n*

bom·bar·dier \ˌbäm-bə-ˈdiər, -bər-\ *n* : a member of a bomber crew whose duty is to release the bombs

bom·bast \ˈbäm-ˌbast\ *n* : pompous speech or writing [Middle English *bombast* "cotton padding," from Middle French *bombace,* derived from Latin *bombyx* "silkworm, silk," from Greek] — **bom·bas·tic** \bäm-ˈbas-tik\ *adj* — **bom·bas·ti·cal·ly** \-ti-kə-lē, -klē\ *adv*

bom·ba·zine \ˌbäm-bə-ˈzēn\ *n* : a twilled and usually silk fabric usually dyed black [Middle French *bombasin,* derived from Latin *bombyx* "silk"]

bomb bay *n* : a bomb-carrying compartment in the underside of a combat airplane

bomb·er \ˈbäm-ər\ *n* : one that bombs; *esp* : an airplane designed for dropping bombs

bom·bi·nate \ˈbäm-bə-ˌnāt\ *vi* : DRONE, BUZZ [derived from Latin *bombus* "deep hollow sound"] — **bom·bi·na·tion** \ˌbäm-bə-ˈnā-shən\ *n*

bomb·proof \ˈbäm-ˈprüf\ *adj* : safe against the explosive force of bombs

bomb·shell \ˈbäm-ˌshel\ *n* **1** : BOMB 1a **2** : a stunning or upsetting surprise

bomb·sight \-ˌsīt\ *n* : a sighting device on an airplane for aiming bombs

bo·na fide \ˈbō-nə-ˌfīd, ˈbän-ə-; ˌbō-nə-ˈfīd-ē, -ˈfīd-ə\ *adj* **1** : made in good faith without fraud or deceit ⟨a *bona fide* offer⟩ **2** : made with earnest intent : SINCERE **3** : GENUINE 1 ⟨a *bona fide* cowboy⟩ [Latin, "in good faith"] ***synonyms*** see AUTHENTIC

bo·nan·za \bə-ˈnan-zə\ *n* **1** : a large and rich mineral deposit **2** : something that brings a rich return [Spanish, literally, "fair weather," from Medieval Latin *bonacia,* alteration of Latin *malacia* "calm at sea," from Greek *malakia,* literally, "softness," from *malakos* "soft"]

Bo·na·part·ism \ˈbō-nə-ˌpärt-ˌiz-əm\ *n* : a political movement associated chiefly with authoritarian rule [Napoléon *Bonaparte*] — **Bo·na·part·ist** \-ˌpärt-əst\ *n*

bon·bon \ˈbän-ˌbän\ *n* : a candy with chocolate or fondant coating and a soft center with fruits and nuts sometimes added [French, from *bon* "good"]

[1]bond \ˈbänd\ *n* **1** : something that restrains : FETTER **2** : a binding agreement **3 a** : material or a device for binding **b** : an attractive force that acts between atoms, ions, or groups of atoms and holds them together in a molecule or crystal **c** : a cementing material that combines, unites, or strengthens **4** : a tie of loyalty, sentiment, or friendship **5 a** : a pledge to do an act or pay a sum on or before a stated day or to forfeit a sum if the pledge is not fulfilled **b** : one that gives bail or acts as surety **c** : a certificate bearing interest and promising payment of a certain sum on or before a stated day and issued by a government or corporation as an evidence of indebtedness **d** : insurance taken out by a party (as a contractor) to insure another against his failure to perform an obligation **6** : a binding or connection made by overlapping parts of a structure (as in laying brick) **7** : the state of goods manufactured, stored, or transported under the care of bonded agencies until taxes on them are paid [Middle English *band, bond,* from Old Norse *band*]

[2]bond *vb* **1** : to protect or secure by or operate under a bond ⟨*bonded* locksmiths⟩; *esp* : to secure payment of taxes on (goods) by giving a bond **2 a** : to cause to adhere firmly **b** : to embed in a cementing material **c** : to hold together or make solid by or as if by means of a bond or binder **d** : to form a close relationship especially through frequent association ⟨the new mother *bonded* with her child⟩ — **bond·able** \ˈbän-də-bəl\ *adj* — **bond·er** *n*

bond·age \ˈbän-dij\ *n* : involuntary personal servitude (as serfdom or slavery) [Middle English *bonde* "customary tenant" from Old English *bōnda* "householder," from Old Norse *bōndi*]

bond·hold·er \ˈbänd-ˌhōl-dər\ *n* : the owner of a government or corporation bond

bond·man \ˈbänd-mən, ˈbän-\ *n* : SERF, SLAVE

bond paper *n* : a strong durable paper used especially for documents

bond servant *n* : a person bound to service without wages; *also* : SLAVE

[1]bonds·man \ˈbänz-mən\ *n* : BONDMAN

[2]bondsman *n* : SURETY 3

bond·wom·an \ˈbän-ˌdwu̇m-ən\ *n* : a woman who is a slave or serf

[1]bone \ˈbōn\ *n* **1 a** : the hard connective tissue containing chiefly calcium phosphate of which the skeleton of most vertebrate animals is formed; *also* : one of the hard parts in which this tissue occurs ⟨break a *bone*⟩ **b** : a similar hard animal substance (as baleen or ivory) **2 a** *pl* : DIE 1 **b** : STAY 1b **3 a** : CORE 1 ⟨cut costs to the *bone*⟩ **b** : the most deeply ingrained part ⟨felt in her *bones* it was wrong⟩ **4** *pl* : BODY ⟨rest my weary *bones*⟩ **5** : MATTER 1 ⟨a *bone* of contention⟩ [Old English *bān*] — **bone·less** \-ləs\ *adj* — **bone to pick** : a matter to argue or complain about

[2]bone *vb* **1** : to remove the bones from ⟨*bone* a fish⟩ **2** : to provide (a garment) with stays **3** : to study hard ⟨*bone* up on math⟩

bone black *n* : the black chiefly carbon residue of bones heated in a closed vessel that is used especially as a pigment or a decolorizing material — called also *bone char*

bone–dry \ˈbōn-ˈdrī\ *adj* : very dry

bone·fish \ˈbōn-ˌfish\ *n* **1** : a slender silvery small-scaled fish that is a sport and food fish of warm seas **2** : LADYFISH

bone·head \-ˌhed\ *n* : a stupid person : NUMSKULL — **bone·head·ed** \-ˈhed-əd\ *adj*

bone marrow *n* : a soft tissue rich in blood vessels that fills the cavities of most bones and occurs in two forms: **a** : one that is yellowish, consists chiefly of fat cells, and is found especially in long bones (as the femur) **b** : one that is reddish, is the chief site of blood cell formation, and in adults is limited especially to certain flat or short bones (as the ribs)

bone meal *n* : crushed or ground bone used especially as fertilizer or animal feed

bon·er \ˈbō-nər\ *n* **1** : one that bones **2** : a stupid or ridiculous mistake

bon·fire \ˈbän-ˌfīr\ *n* : a large fire built in the open air [Middle English *bonefire* "fire of bones"]

bong \ˈbäŋ, ˈbȯŋ\ *n* **:** a deep resonant sound (as of a bell) [imitative] — **bong** *vb*

bon•go \ˈbäŋ-gō\ *n, pl* **bongos** *also* **bongoes :** one of a pair of small tuned drums played with the hands [American Spanish *bongó*]

bon•ho•mie *also* **bon•hom•mie** \ˌbän-ə-ˈmē, ˌbō-nə-\ *n* **:** good-natured easy friendliness [French *bonhomie,* from *bonhomme* "good-natured man," from *bon* "good" + *homme* "man"]

bon•i•face \ˈbän-ə-fəs, -ˌfās\ *n* **:** the proprietor of a hotel, nightclub, or restaurant [*Boniface,* innkeeper in *The Beaux' Stratagem* (1707), play by George Farquhar]

bo•ni•to \bə-ˈnēt-ō, -ˈnēt-ə\ *n, pl* **bonitos** *or* **bonito :** any of various medium-sized tunas [Spanish, from *bonito* "pretty," from Latin *bonus* "good"]

bon mot \bō^{n}-ˈmō\ *n, pl* **bons mots** \bō^{n}-ˈmō, -ˈmōz\ *or* **bon mots** \-ˈmō, -ˈmōz\ **:** a clever remark **:** WITTICISM [French, literally, "good word"]

bon•net \ˈbän-ət\ *n* **1 :** a child's or woman's hat tied under the chin by ribbons or strings **2 :** a soft woolen cap worn by men in Scotland **3** *British* **:** an automobile hood [Medieval French *bonet*]

bon•ny *also* **bon•nie** \ˈbän-ē\ *adj, chiefly British* **:** having a pleasing look or quality; *also* **:** FINE 4 [Middle English (Scots) *bonie*] — **bon•ni•ly** \ˈbän-l-ē\ *adv*

bon•sai \bōn-ˈsī, ˈbōn-ˌ\ *n, pl* **bonsai :** a potted plant (as a tree) dwarfed by special methods (as by pruning); *also* **:** the art of growing such a plant [Japanese]

bon•spiel \ˈbän-ˌspēl\ *n* **:** a match or tournament between curling clubs [perhaps from Dutch *bond* "league" + *spel* "game"]

bon ton \bän-ˈtän, ˈbän-ˌ\ *n* **1 :** fashionable manner or style **2 :** the fashionable or proper thing [French, literally, "good tone"]

bo•nus \ˈbō-nəs\ *n* **:** something given in addition to what is usual or strictly due; *esp* **:** money given in addition to salary or wages [Latin, "good"]

bon vi•vant \ˌbän-vē-ˈvänt, ˌbō^{n}-vē-ˈvä^{n}\ *n, pl* **bons vivants** \ˌbän-vē-ˈvänts; ˌbō^{n}-vē-ˈvä^{n}, -ˈvä^{n}z\ *or* **bon vivants** *same*\ **:** a person having cultivated or refined tastes especially in food and drink [French, literally, "good liver"]

bon voy•age \ˌbō^{n}v-ˌwī-ˈäzh, -ˌwä-ˈyäzh; ˌbō^{n}-ˌvȯi-ˈäzh, ˌbän-\ *n* **:** FAREWELL 1 — often used interjectionally [French, literally, "good trip"]

bony \ˈbō-nē\ *adj* **bon•i•er; -est 1 :** of or relating to bone ⟨the *bony* structure of the body⟩ **2 :** full of bones **3 :** resembling bone especially in hardness ⟨a *bony* substance⟩ **4 :** having large or prominent bones ⟨a rugged *bony* face⟩ **5 :** SCRAWNY, SKINNY

bony fish *n* **:** any of a class (Osteichthyes) of fishes (as eels, mackerels, and trout) with bony rather than cartilaginous skeletons

[1]**boo** \ˈbü\ *interj* — used to express contempt or disapproval or to startle or frighten [Middle English *bo*]

[2]**boo** *n, pl* **boos 1 :** a shout of disapproval or contempt **2 :** any sound at all ⟨never said *boo*⟩ — **boo** *vb*

boob \ˈbüb\ *n* **1 :** SIMPLETON **2 :** BOOR 2b [short for *booby*]

boo–boo \ˈbü-ˌbü\ *n, pl* **boo–boos 1 :** a usually small bruise or scratch especially on a child **2 :** a foolish mistake [probably alteration of *boohoo,* imitative of the sound of weeping]

boo•by \ˈbü-bē\ *n, pl* **boobies 1 :** a foolish person **:** DOPE **2 :** any of several small tropical seabirds related to the gannets [Spanish *bobo,* from Latin *balbus* "stammering"]

booby prize *n* **:** an award for the poorest performance in a game or competition

booby trap *n* **:** a trap for a careless or unwary person; *esp* **:** a concealed explosive device set to go off when some harmless-looking object is touched — **boo•by–trap** \ˈbü-bē-ˌtrap\ *vt*

boo•dle \ˈbüd-l\ *n* **1 :** a large group of people **:** CROWD **2 :** bribe money [Dutch *boedel* "estate, lot"]

boo•gie–woo•gie \ˌbu̇g-ē-ˈwu̇g-ē, ˌbüg-ē-ˈwüg-ē\ *n* **:** a percussive style of playing blues on the piano characterized by a steady rhythmic bass and a simple often improvised melody — called also *boogie* [origin unknown]

[1]**book** \ˈbu̇k\ *n* **1 a :** a set of written, printed, or blank sheets of paper bound together between a front and back cover **b :** a long written or printed literary composition **c :** a major division of a literary work **d :** a volume of business records (as a ledger) **2** *cap* **:** BIBLE 1 **3 :** something regarded as a source of enlightenment or instruction **4 a :** all the knowledge available about a task or problem ⟨tried every trick in the *book*⟩ **b :** the standards or authority relevant in a situation ⟨plays by the *book*⟩ **5 :** all the charges that can be made against an accused person ⟨threw the *book* at them⟩ **6 a :** LIBRETTO **b :** the script of a play **7 :** a packet of commodities bound together ⟨a *book* of matches⟩ **8 :** the bets registered by a bookmaker **9 :** the tricks a cardplayer must win before scoring [Old English *bōc*] — **in one's book :** in one's opinion — **in one's good books :** in favor with one — **one for the book :** an act or occurrence worth noting

[2]**book** *vb* **1 a :** to engage transportation or reserve lodgings **b :** to schedule engagements for ⟨*book* an entertainer⟩ **2 :** to enter charges against in a police register — **book•er** *n*

[3]**book** *adj* **1 :** derived from books ⟨*book* learning⟩ **2 :** shown by books of account ⟨*book* value⟩

book•bind•ing \ˈbu̇k-ˌbīn-diŋ\ *n* **1 :** the binding of a book **2 :** the art or trade of binding books — **book•bind•er** *n* — **book•bind•ery** \-də-rē, -drē\ *n*

book•case \ˈbu̇k-ˌkās\ *n* **:** a piece of furniture consisting of shelves to hold books

book•end \ˈbu̇k-ˌend\ *n* **:** a support placed at the end of a row of books to hold them up

book•ie \ˈbu̇k-ē\ *n* **:** BOOKMAKER

book•ish \ˈbu̇k-ish\ *adj* **1 :** fond of books and reading **2 :** inclined to rely on knowledge from books rather than practical experience **3 :** resembling or derived from the language of books **:** FORMAL ⟨many English words derived from Latin have a *bookish* tone⟩ — **book•ish•ly** *adv* — **book•ish•ness** *n*

book•keep•er \ˈbu̇k-ˌkē-pər\ *n* **:** a person who keeps accounts (as of a business) — **book•keep•ing** \-piŋ\ *n*

book•let \ˈbu̇k-lət\ *n* **:** a little book; *esp* **:** PAMPHLET

book louse *n* **:** any of several tiny wingless insects (order Corrodentia) injurious especially to books

book lung *n* **:** a specialized breathing organ of spiders and related animals containing numerous thin folds of membrane arranged like the leaves of a book

book•mak•er \ˈbu̇k-ˌmā-kər\ *n* **:** a person who determines odds and receives and pays off bets — **book•mak•ing** \-kiŋ\ *n*

[1]**book•mark** \ˈbu̇k-ˌmärk\ *or* **book•mark•er** \-ˌmär-kər\ *n* **1 :** a marker for keeping one's place in a book **2 :** a computer icon or menu entry that serves as a shortcut (as to a Web site)

[2]**bookmark** *vt* **:** to create a computer bookmark for ⟨*bookmark* a Web site⟩

book•mo•bile \ˈbu̇k-mō-ˌbēl\ *n* **:** a vehicle that serves as a traveling library

Book of Common Prayer : the service book of the Anglican Communion

book•plate \ˈbu̇k-ˌplāt\ *n* **:** a label placed in a book showing who owns it

book review *n* **:** a critical estimate of a book

book•sell•er \ˈbu̇k-ˌsel-ər\ *n* **:** the proprietor of a bookstore

book•stall \-ˌstȯl\ *n* **1 :** a stall where books are sold **2** *chiefly British* **:** NEWSSTAND

book•store \-ˌstōr, -ˌstȯr\ *n* **:** a retail store where books are the main item for sale — called also *bookshop*

book•worm \-ˌwərm\ *n* **1 :** any of various insect larvae that feed on the binding and paste of books **2 :** a person unusually devoted to reading and study

Bool•ean \ˈbü-lē-ən\ *adj* **:** of, relating to, or being Boolean algebra

Boolean algebra *n* **:** a system of algebra that consists of a set and two binary operations (as the taking of unions and intersections) with certain specific rules of combination [George *Boole,* died 1864, English mathematician]

[1]**boom** \ˈbüm\ *vb* **1 :** to make a deep hollow sound **2 a :** to increase in esteem, popularity, or importance **b :** to experience a boom (as in growth) **3 :** to cause to resound — often used with *out* ⟨their voices *boomed* out the song⟩ [Middle English *bomben, bummen,* of imitative origin]

[2]**boom** *n* **1 :** a booming sound or cry — often used interjectionally to indicate suddenness ⟨then *boom,* he was fired⟩ **2 :** a rapid expansion or increase: as **a :** a general movement in support of a candidate for office **b :** rapid settlement and development of a town or district **c :** a rapid widespread expansion of

\ə\ abut	\au̇\ out	\i\ tip	\ȯ\ saw	\u̇\ foot
\ər\ further	\ch\ chin	\ī\ life	\ȯi\ coin	\y\ yet
\a\ mat	\e\ pet	\j\ job	\th\ thin	\yü\ few
\ā\ take	\ē\ easy	\ŋ\ sing	\th\ this	\yu̇\ cure
\ä\ cot, cart	\g\ go	\ō\ bone	\ü\ food	\zh\ vision

business activity **d** : an upsurge in activity, interest, or popularity ⟨a folk music *boom*⟩

[3]**boom** *n* **1** : a long pole; *esp* : one for stretching the bottom of a sail **2 a** : a long beam projecting from the mast of a derrick to support or guide the thing that is being lifted **b** : a long more or less horizontal supporting arm (as for a microphone) **3** : a line of connected floating timbers to hold logs together in a river, lake, or harbor [Dutch, "tree, beam, boom"]

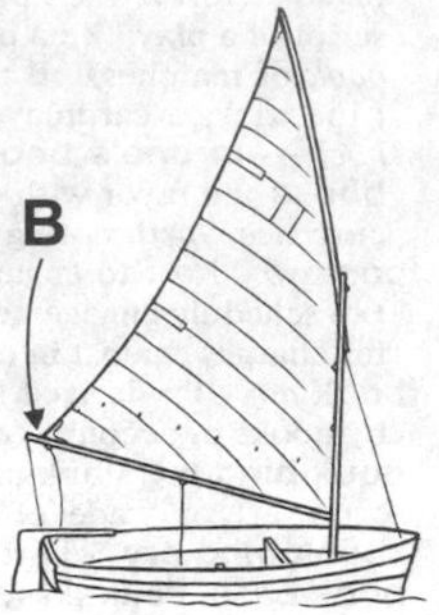

B [3]boom 1

boom box *n* : a large portable radio and often tape or CD player with two attached speakers

boo·mer·ang \ˈbü-mə-ˌrang\ *n* **1** : a curved club or stick usually somewhat flat that can be thrown so as to return near the starting point **2** : an act or utterance that backfires on its originator [from Dharuk (an indigenous language of Australia) *bumariny*] — **boomerang** *vi*

boom·ing \ˈbü-ming\ *adj* **1** : making a deep sound ⟨a *booming* voice⟩ **2** : forcefully or powerfully executed ⟨hit a *booming* serve⟩

boom·town \ˈbüm-ˌtau̇n\ *n* : a town undergoing a sudden growth in business activity and population

[1]**boon** \ˈbün\ *n* : FAVOR 2, KINDNESS: as **a** : one given in answer to a request **b** : a timely benefit : BLESSING [Old Norse *bōn* "request"]

[2]**boon** *adj* : CONVIVIAL, MERRY ⟨a *boon* companion⟩ [Medieval French *bon* "good," from Latin *bonus*]

boon·docks \ˈbün-ˌdäks\ *n pl* **1** : rough country filled with dense brush **2** : a rural area : STICKS [Tagalog *bundok* "mountain"]

boon·dog·gle \ˈbün-ˌdäg-əl, -ˌdȯg-\ *n* : a trivial, useless, or wasteful activity [coined by Robert H. Link, died 1957, American scoutmaster] — **boondoggle** *vi* — **boon·dog·gler** \-lər, -ə-lər\ *n*

boor \ˈbu̇r\ *n* **1** : PEASANT 1 **2 a** : a rough clownish rustic : BUMPKIN **b** : a rude or insensitive person [Dutch *boer*]

boor·ish \ˈbu̇r-ish\ *adj* : resembling a boor : RUDE — **boor·ish·ly** *adv* — **boor·ish·ness** *n*

boos *plural of* BOO

[1]**boost** \ˈbüst\ *vt* **1** : to push or shove up from below **2** : to make greater especially in amount ⟨*boost* prices⟩ ⟨*boost* morale⟩ **3** : to promote enthusiastically the cause or interests of [origin unknown] ***synonyms*** see LIFT

[2]**boost** *n* **1** : a push upward **2** : an increase in amount **3** : an act that brings help or encouragement

boost·er \ˈbü-stər\ *n* : one that boosts: as **a** : an enthusiastic supporter **b** : a device for strengthening radio or television signals **c** : BOOSTER SHOT **d** : the first stage of a multistage rocket providing thrust for the launching and the initial part of the flight

booster shot *n* : a supplementary dose of an immunizing agent given to maintain or revive a previously established immunity

[1]**boot** \ˈbüt\ *n* : something to equalize a trade [Old English *bōt* "advantage, remedy"] — **to boot** : [2]BESIDES

[2]**boot** *vb, archaic* : to be of use : HELP, PROFIT

[3]**boot** *n* **1** : a covering (as of leather or rubber) for the foot and usually reaching above the ankle **2** : a protective sheath or casing **3** : a navy or marine corps recruit undergoing basic training **4** *British* : an automobile trunk **5 a** : a kick with the foot **b** : an abrupt discharge or dismissal — used with *the* ⟨gave him the *boot*⟩ [Medieval French *bote*]

[4]**boot** *vb* **1** : to put boots on **2 a** : KICK **b** : to eject or discharge abruptly — often used with *out* ⟨was *booted* out of office⟩ **3 a** : to load or become loaded into a computer from a disk ⟨*load* a program⟩ ⟨the program *loads* automatically⟩ **b** : to start, make, or become ready for use especially by booting a program ⟨*boot* a microcomputer⟩ ⟨the computer *boots* quickly⟩ — often used with *up*

boot·black \ˈbüt-ˌblak\ *n* : a person who shines boots and shoes

boot camp *n* : a camp for the basic training of navy or marine recruits

boot·ee *or* **boot·ie** \ˈbüt-ē\ *n* : a usually ankle-high boot, slipper, or sock; *esp* : an infant's knitted or crocheted sock

Bo·ö·tes \bō-ˈōt-ēz\ *n* : a northern constellation containing the bright star Arcturus [Greek *Boōtēs*, literally, "plowman," from *bous* "head of cattle"]

booth \ˈbüth\ *n, pl* **booths** \ˈbüt͟hz, ˈbüths\ **1** : a temporary shelter **2 a** : a stall or stand (as at a fair) for the sale or exhibition of goods **b** (1) : a small enclosure affording privacy for one person at a time ⟨voting *booth*⟩ ⟨telephone *booth*⟩ (2) : a small enclosure that separates its occupant from customers or patrons ⟨a ticket *booth*⟩ **c** : a restaurant accommodation consisting of a table between two backed benches [Middle English *bothe*, of Scandinavian origin]

boot·jack \ˈbüt-ˌjak\ *n* : a V-shaped device used in pulling off boots

[1]**boot·leg** \ˈbüt-ˌleg\ *n* : something bootlegged; *esp* : MOONSHINE 3 — **bootleg** *adj*

[2]**boot·leg** *vb* **1** : to make or transport for sale alcoholic liquor contrary to law **2 a** : to produce or sell illicitly ⟨caught *bootlegging* recordings⟩ **b** : SMUGGLE 1 [from the carrying of illicit liquor concealed in the leg of a boot] — **boot·leg·ger** \-ˌleg-ər\ *n*

boot·less \ˈbüt-ləs\ *adj* : FRUITLESS 2 — **boot·less·ly** *adv* — **boot·less·ness** *n*

boot·lick \-ˌlik\ *vb* : to fawn on : curry favor — **boot·lick·er** *n*

boo·ty \ˈbüt-ē\ *n* **1** : SPOIL 1b; *esp* : goods seized from the enemy in war **2** : a rich gain or prize [Middle French *butin*]

[1]**booze** \ˈbüz\ *vi* : to drink intoxicating liquor especially to excess [Middle Dutch *būsen*] — **booz·er** \ˈbü-zər\ *n*

[2]**booze** *n* : intoxicating liquor — **booz·i·ly** \ˈbü-zə-lē\ *adv* — **boozy** \ˈbü-zē\ *adj*

[1]**bop** \ˈbäp\ *vt* **bopped; bop·ping** : HIT, SOCK [imitative]

[2]**bop** *n* : a blow (as from a fist or club) that strikes a person

bor·age \ˈbȯr-ij, ˈbär-\ *n* : a hairy blue-flowered European herb used medicinally and in salads [Medieval French *bourage*]

bo·rate \ˈbōr-ˌāt, ˈbȯr-\ *n* : a salt or ester of a boric acid

bo·rax \ˈbōr-ˌaks, ˈbȯr-\ *n* : a crystalline slightly alkaline compound that is a borate of sodium, occurs as a mineral, and is used as a flux, cleansing agent, and antiseptic [Medieval Latin, from Arabic *būraq*, from Persian *būrah*]

bor·deaux mixture \bȯr-ˈdō-\ *n, often cap B* : a fungicide made by reaction of copper sulfate, lime, and water

[1]**bor·der** \ˈbȯrd-ər\ *n* **1** : an outer part or edge **2** : BOUNDARY **3** : a narrow bed of plants along the edge of a garden or walk **4** : an ornamental design at the edge of a fabric or rug [Medieval French *bordure*, from *border* "to border," from *bort* "border," of Germanic origin] — **bor·dered** \-ərd\ *adj*

synonyms BORDER, EDGE, MARGIN mean a line or narrow space marking the limit or outermost bound of something. A BORDER is that part of a surface lying along its boundary line ⟨lived on the *border* of the plains⟩. EDGE suggests a sharp line marking a fixed limit ⟨the *edge* of the table⟩. MARGIN suggests a border of definite width or distinctive character ⟨do not write in the *margin* of the page⟩.

[2]**border** *vb* **bor·dered; bor·der·ing** \ˈbȯrd-ring, -ə-ring\ **1** : to put a border on **2** : to touch at the edge or boundary : BOUND **3** : to lie on the border of something ⟨the town *borders* on the sea⟩ **4** : to approach the nature of a specified thing : VERGE ⟨*border* on the ridiculous⟩ — **bor·der·er** \-ər-ər\ *n*

bor·der·land \ˈbȯrd-ər-ˌland\ *n* **1** : territory at or near a border : FRONTIER **2** : a vague intermediate state or region ⟨the *borderland* between fantasy and reality⟩

bor·der·line \-ˌlīn\ *adj* **1** : situated at or near a border or boundary **2 a** : situated between two points or states : INTERMEDIATE **b** : not quite average, normal, or acceptable ⟨*borderline* intelligence⟩ ⟨a *borderline* joke⟩

[1]**bore** \ˈbōr, ˈbȯr\ *vb* **1** : to pierce with or as if with a turning or twisting movement of a tool ⟨*bore* a piece of wood⟩ **2** : to make by piercing or drilling ⟨*bore* a well⟩ **3** : to make a hole by boring [Old English *borian*]

[2]**bore** *n* **1** : a hole made by or as if by boring **2** : an interior lengthwise cylindrical cavity; *esp* : the interior cavity of a gun **3 a** : the diameter of a hole or tube; *esp* : the interior diameter of a gun barrel **b** : the diameter of an engine cylinder

[3]**bore** *past of* BEAR

[4]**bore** *n* : a tidal flood with a high abrupt front [Old Norse *bāra* "wave"]

[5]**bore** *n* : one that causes boredom [origin unknown]

[6]**bore** *vt* : to weary by being dull or monotonous

bo·re·al \ˈbōr-ē-əl, ˈbȯr-\ *adj* : of, relating to, or located or growing in northern or mountainous regions ⟨*boreal* coniferous forests⟩ [Greek *Boreas* "north wind, north"]

bore·dom \'bōrd-əm, 'bȯrd-\ *n* : the state of being bored

bor·er \'bōr-ər, 'bȯr-\ *n* : one that bores: as **a** : a tool used for boring **b** (1) : SHIPWORM (2) : an insect that as a larva or an adult bores in the woody parts of plants

bo·ric acid \'bōr-ik-, 'bȯr-\ *n* : a white crystalline weak acid H_3BO_3 easily obtained from its salts and used especially as a mild antiseptic [*boron*]

bor·ing \'bōr-ing, 'bȯr-\ *adj* : causing boredom : TIRESOME

born \'bȯrn\ *adj* **1 a** : brought into life by or as if by birth **b** : NATIVE 2 ⟨American-*born*⟩ **2** : having from birth special natural abilities or character ⟨a *born* leader⟩ **3** : destined from or as if from birth ⟨*born* to succeed⟩ [Old English *boren*, past participle of *beran* "to bear"]

borne *past participle of* BEAR

born·ite \'bȯr-ˌnīt\ *n* : a brittle metallic-looking mineral consisting of a sulfide of copper and iron and constituting a valuable ore of copper [Ignaz von *Born*, died 1791, Austrian mineralogist]

bo·ron \'bōr-ˌän, 'bȯr-\ *n* : a metalloid element found in nature only in combination (as in borax) — see ELEMENT table [*borax* + *-on* (as in *carbon*)]

bor·ough \'bər-ō\ *n* **1 a** : a town or urban constituency in Great Britain that sends a member to Parliament **b** : a self-governing incorporated urban area in Great Britain **2 a** : a municipal corporation in some states corresponding to the incorporated town or village of the other states **b** : one of the five constituent political divisions of New York City **3** : a civil division of the state of Alaska corresponding to a county in most other states [Old English *burg* "fortified town"]

bor·row \'bär-ō\ *vb* **1** : to take or receive something with the promise or intention of returning it **2** : to take for one's own use ⟨*borrow* a phrase⟩ **3** : to take 1 from a digit of the minuend in subtraction and add it as 10 to the digit holding the next lower place [Old English *borgian*] — **bor·row·er** \'bär-ə-wər\ *n*

bor·row·ing \'bär-ə-wing\ *n* : something borrowed; *esp* : a word or phrase adopted from one language into another

borscht \'bȯrsht, 'bȯrsh\ *also* **borsch** \'bȯrsh\ *n* : a soup made largely of beets and served hot or cold often with sour cream [Yiddish *borsht* or Ukrainian & Russian *borshch*]

bor·zoi \'bȯr-ˌzȯi\ *n* : any of a breed of large long-haired dogs developed in Russia especially for pursuing wolves [Russian *borzoĭ*, from *borzoĭ* "swift"]

borzoi

bos·cage *also* **bos·kage** \'bäs-kij\ *n* : a growth of shrubs or trees : THICKET [Medieval French *boscage*, from *bois* "forest"]

bosh \'bäsh\ *n* : foolish talk [Turkish *boş* "empty"]

bosky \'bäs-kē\ *adj* : covered with trees or shrubs [Middle English *bush*, *bosk* "bush"]

bos'n *or* **bosun** *variant of* BOATSWAIN

[1]**bos·om** \'bu̇z-əm\ *n* **1** : the front of the human chest; *esp* : a woman's breasts **2 a** : the chest thought of as the center of emotions and private feelings **b** : a close and comforting relationship ⟨in the *bosom* of her family⟩ **3** : the part of a garment covering the breast [Old English *bōsm*] — **bos·omed** \-əmd\ *adj*

[2]**bosom** *adj* : CLOSE, INTIMATE ⟨*bosom* friends⟩

bo·son \'bō-ˌsän, -ˌzän\ *n* : any of various subatomic particles including the mesons and photons — compare FERMION [Satyendranath *Bose*, died 1974, Indian physicist]

[1]**boss** \'bäs, 'bȯs\ *n* : a projecting and typically rounded part; *also* : a raised or projecting ornament (as on a shield or a ceiling) [Medieval French *boce*]

[2]**boss** *vt* : to ornament with bosses : EMBOSS

[3]**boss** \'bȯs\ *n* **1** : one who has control or authority; *esp* : one who directs or supervises workers **2 a** : a politician who controls votes or dictates appointments or legislative measures **b** : an official having dictatorial authority over an organization [Dutch *baas* "master"] — **boss** *adj* — **boss·ism** \-ˌiz-əm\ *n*

[4]**boss** \'bȯs\ *vt* **1** : to exercise control of : DIRECT **2** : ORDER ⟨refused to be *bossed* around⟩

bos·sa no·va \ˌbäs-ə-'nō-və\ *n* **1** : a Brazilian dance characterized by the step pattern of the samba and a subtle bounce **2** : music influenced by jazz and rhythmically similar to the samba [Portuguese, literally, "new trend"]

[1]**bossy** \'bō-sē\ *n, pl* **boss·ies** : COW 2 [English dialect *buss, boss* "young calf"]

[2]**bossy** *adj* **boss·i·er; -est** : inclined to act like a boss — **boss·i·ness** *n*

Bos·ton cream pie \'bȯ-stən-\ *n* : a rich cake that is usually split, filled with custard or cream, and often topped with icing [*Boston*, Massachusetts]

Boston fern *n* : a fern widely grown for its often drooping much-divided fronds

Boston ivy *n* : a woody Asian vine that is related to the grape, has 3-lobed leaves, and is often grown over walls

Boston terrier *n* : any of a breed of small smooth-coated brindle or black terriers with white markings — called also *Boston bull*

bot \'bät\ *n* : the larva of a botfly [Middle English]

[1]**bo·tan·i·cal** \bə-'tan-i-kəl\ *also* **bo·tan·ic** \-ik\ *adj* **1** : of or relating to plants or botany **2** : made or obtained from plants — **bo·tan·i·cal·ly** \-i-kə-lē, -klē\ *adv*

[2]**botanical** *n* : a usually cosmetic or medicinal product prepared from or containing a plant part or extract; *also* : the plant part or extract used in such a product

bot·a·nize \'bät-n-ˌīz\ *vi* : to collect and study plants

bot·a·ny \'bät-n-ē, 'bät-nē\ *n* **1** : a branch of biology dealing with plant life **2 a** : plant life ⟨the *botany* of a region⟩ **b** : the biology of a plant or plant group [Greek *botanē* "pasture, herb," from *boskein* "to graze"] — **bot·a·nist** \'bät-n-əst, 'bät-nəst\ *n*

[1]**botch** \'bäch\ *vt* **1** : to repair or patch poorly **2** : BUNGLE [Middle English *bocchen*]

[2]**botch** *n* : a botched job : BUNGLE, MESS — **botchy** \-ē\ *adj*

bot·fly \'bät-ˌflī\ *n* : any of various stout two-winged flies whose larvae are parasitic in cavities or tissues of various mammals

[1]**both** \'bōth\ *adj* : being the two : involving the one and the other ⟨*both* feet⟩ [Middle English *bothe*, probably from Old Norse *bāthir*]

[2]**both** *pron, pl in constr* : the one as well as the other ⟨*both* of us⟩ ⟨we are *both* well⟩

[3]**both** *conj* — used as a function word to indicate and stress the inclusion of each of two or more things specified by coordinated words, phrases, or clauses ⟨*both* New York and London⟩

[1]**both·er** \'bät͟h-ər\ *vb* **both·ered; both·er·ing** \'bät͟h-ring, -ə-ring\ **1 a** : to upset with often minor annoyances : TRY **b** : to intrude upon : INTERRUPT **2 a** : to cause to be anxious or concerned : TROUBLE ⟨that cough *bothers* me⟩ **b** : to feel concern or anxiety **3** : to take pains : make an effort ⟨don't *bother* to knock⟩ [origin unknown] ***synonyms*** see ANNOY

[2]**bother** *n* **1 a** : a state of being bothered **b** : something that causes such a state **2** : FUSS 2, DISTURBANCE

both·er·some \'bät͟h-ər-səm\ *adj* : causing bother

[1]**bot·tle** \'bät-l\ *n* **1 a** : a container typically of glass or plastic with a narrow neck and mouth and usually no handle **b** : a bag made of skin for storing a liquid **c** : the quantity held by a bottle **2** : intoxicating drink ⟨hit the *bottle*⟩ **3 a** : a bottle with a rubber or plastic nipple for feeding an infant **b** : liquid food (as milk) that is fed from a bottle [Medieval French *botele*, derived from Late Latin *buttis* "cask"] — **bot·tle·ful** \-ˌfu̇l\ *n*

[2]**bottle** *vt* **bot·tled; bot·tling** \'bät-ling, -l-ing\ **1** : to put into a bottle **2** : to confine or hold back as if in a bottle — usually used with *up* ⟨*bottled* up his anger⟩ — **bot·tler** \'bät-lər, -l-ər\ *n*

bot·tle–feed \'bät-l-ˌfēd\ *vt* **-fed; -feed·ing** : to feed (as an infant) with a bottle

bottled gas *n* : gas under pressure in portable cylinders

bot·tle·neck \'bät-l-ˌnek\ *n* **1** : a narrow passageway **2** : someone or something that holds up progress ⟨a *bottleneck* for traffic⟩ **3** : a style of guitar playing using an object (as a metal bar) pressed against the strings

bot·tle·nose dolphin \'bät-l-ˌnōz-\ *n* : a medium-sized stout-

\ə\ **abut**	\au̇\ **out**	\i\ **tip**	\ȯ\ **saw**	\u̇\ **foot**
\ər\ **further**	\ch\ **chin**	\ī\ **life**	\ȯi\ **coin**	\y\ **yet**
\a\ **mat**	\e\ **pet**	\j\ **job**	\th\ **thin**	\yü\ **few**
\ā\ **take**	\ē\ **easy**	\ng\ **sing**	\t͟h\ **this**	\yu̇\ **cure**
\ä\ **cot, cart**	\g\ **go**	\ō\ **bone**	\ü\ **food**	\zh\ **vision**

bodied toothed whale with a prominent beak and sickle-shaped dorsal fin — called also *bottle-nosed dolphin*

[1]**bot·tom** \ˈbät-əm\ *n* **1 a :** the under surface of something **b :** a supporting surface or part : BASE **c :** BUTTOCK 2a **2 :** the bed of a body of water **3 a :** the part of a ship's hull lying below the water **b :** BOAT, SHIP **4 :** the lowest part, place, or point ⟨the *bottom* of the page⟩ **5 :** low land along a river ⟨the Mississippi River *bottoms*⟩ **6 :** the part of a garment worn on the lower part of the body; *esp* **:** the pants of pajamas — usually used in plural **7 :** BASIS 3, SOURCE ⟨get to the *bottom* of this problem⟩ **8 :** the last half of an inning of baseball **9 :** the main plowing mechanism of a plow [Old English *botm*] — **bot·tomed** \-əmd\ *adj* — **at bottom :** BASICALLY, REALLY

[2]**bottom** *vb* **1 :** to provide with a foundation **2 :** to rest on, bring to, or reach the bottom

bot·tom·land \ˈbät-əm-ˌland\ *n* **:** BOTTOM 5

bot·tom·less \-ləs\ *adj* **1 :** having no bottom **2 :** very deep — **bot·tom·less·ly** *adv* — **bot·tom·less·ness** *n*

bottom line *n* **1 :** the primary or most important point or consideration **2 a :** the line at the bottom of a financial report that shows the net profit or loss **b :** financial considerations (as cost or profit or loss) **c :** the final result

bot·u·lism \ˈbäch-ə-ˌliz-əm\ *n* **:** an acute food poisoning caused by bacterial toxin formed by clostridia in food [from *Clostridium botulinum,* a species of bacterium]

bou·clé *or* **bou·cle** \bü-ˈklā\ *n* **1 :** a yarn made of three plies one of which is looped at intervals **2 :** a fabric made from bouclé yarn [French *bouclé* "curly"]

bou·doir \ˈbüd-ˌwär, ˈbu̇d-\ *n* **:** a dressing room, bedroom, or private sitting room [French, from *bouder* "to pout"]

bouf·fant \bü-ˈfänt, ˈbü-ˌ\ *adj* **:** puffed out ⟨*bouffant* hairdos⟩ [French, from Middle French, from *bouffer* "to puff"]

bough \ˈbau̇\ *n* **:** a branch of a tree; *esp* **:** a main branch [Old English *bōg* "shoulder, bough"] — **boughed** \ˈbau̇d\ *adj*

bought *past of* BUY

bouil·la·baisse \ˌbü-yə-ˈbās\ *n* **:** a highly seasoned fish stew made of at least two kinds of fish [French]

bouil·lon \ˈbu̇l-ˌyän, -yən; ˈbü-ˌyän, ˈbu̇-\ *n* **:** a clear seasoned soup made usually from lean beef; *broadly* **:** BROTH [French, from Medieval French *boillon,* from *boillir* "to boil"]

boul·der *also* **bowl·der** \ˈbōl-dər\ *n* **:** a large detached and rounded or much-worn mass of rock [of Scandinavian origin] — **boul·dery** \-də-rē, -drē\ *adj*

bou·le·vard \ˈbu̇l-ə-ˌvärd, ˈbül-\ *n* **:** a broad often landscaped thoroughfare [French, from Dutch *bolwerc* "bulwark"]

[1]**bounce** \ˈbau̇ns\ *vb* **1 :** to rebound or cause to rebound ⟨*bounce* a ball⟩ **2 a :** DISMISS 2, FIRE **b :** to throw out from a place by force **3 :** to recover quickly from a blow or defeat — usually used with *back* **4** *of a check* **:** to be returned by a bank because of insufficient funds in a checking account **5 :** to leap suddenly : BOUND [Middle English *bounsen*]

[2]**bounce** *n* **1 a :** a sudden leap or bound **b :** a bouncing back : REBOUND **2 :** ENERGY 1, LIVELINESS

bounc·er \ˈbau̇n-sər\ *n* **:** one that bounces; *esp* **:** a person employed in a public place to remove disorderly patrons

bounc·ing \-siŋ\ *adj* **:** enjoying good health : ROBUST ⟨a *bouncing* baby⟩ — **bounc·ing·ly** \-siŋ-lē\ *adv*

bouncing bet \ˌbau̇n-siŋ-ˈbet\ *n, often cap 2nd B* **:** a European perennial herb that is widely naturalized in the U.S. and has pink or white flowers and leaves which yield a detergent when bruised — called also *soapwort* [*Bet,* nickname for Elizabeth]

[1]**bound** \ˈbau̇nd\ *adj* **:** going or intending to go ⟨*bound* for home⟩ ⟨college-*bound*⟩ [Middle English *boun,* from Old Norse *būinn* "ready," from *būa* "to dwell, prepare"]

[2]**bound** *n* **1 :** a boundary line (as of a piece of property) **2 :** a point or a line beyond which one cannot go : LIMIT ⟨out of *bounds*⟩ **3 :** the land within specific bounds — usually used in plural [Medieval French *bounde, bodne,* from Medieval Latin *bodina*]

[3]**bound** *vt* **1 :** to set limits to : CONFINE **2 :** to form a bound or boundary of : ENCLOSE; *also* **:** ADJOIN 2 **3 :** to name the boundaries of ⟨*bound* the state of Ohio⟩

[4]**bound** *adj* **1 a :** fastened by or as if by a band : CONFINED ⟨desk-*bound*⟩ **b :** CERTAIN, SURE ⟨*bound* to rain soon⟩ **2 a :** OBLIGED ⟨duty-*bound*⟩ **b :** RESOLVED, DETERMINED ⟨*bound* to have your own way⟩ **3 :** always occurring in combination with another linguistic form (as *un-* in *unknown, -er* in *speaker*) — compare FREE 14 [from past participle of *bind*]

[5]**bound** *n* **1 :** LEAP 1a, JUMP **2 :** BOUNCE 1b, REBOUND [Middle French *bond,* from *bondir* "to leap"]

[6]**bound** *vi* **1 :** to move by leaping **2 :** REBOUND 1, BOUNCE

bound·a·ry \ˈbau̇n-də-rē, -drē\ *n, pl* **-ries :** a line or strip that marks or shows a limit or end (as of a region or a piece of land) : a line that bounds, divides, or separates

bound·en \ˈbau̇n-dən\ *adj* **:** OBLIGATORY, BINDING ⟨our *bounden* duty⟩

bound·er \ˈbau̇n-dər\ *n* **1 :** one that bounds **2** *chiefly British* **:** a man of objectionable social behavior : CAD, BOOR

bound·less \ˈbau̇nd-ləs\ *adj* **:** having no boundaries or limits : VAST — **bound·less·ly** *adv* — **bound·less·ness** *n*

boun·te·ous \ˈbau̇nt-ē-əs\ *adj* **1 :** BOUNTIFUL 1 **2 :** liberally provided or bestowed : AMPLE — **boun·te·ous·ly** *adv* — **boun·te·ous·ness** *n*

boun·ti·ful \ˈbau̇nt-i-fəl\ *adj* **1 :** giving liberally : GENEROUS ⟨a *bountiful* contributor⟩ **2 :** PLENTIFUL, ABUNDANT ⟨a *bountiful* supply⟩ ***synonyms*** see GENEROUS — **boun·ti·ful·ly** \-fə-lē, -flē\ *adv* — **boun·ti·ful·ness** \-fəl-nəs\ *n*

boun·ty \ˈbau̇nt-ē\ *n, pl* **bounties 1 a :** GENEROSITY 1a **b :** something given generously **2 :** money given as a reward or inducement (as for the killing of vermin) [Medieval French *bunté* "goodness," from Latin *bonitas,* from *bonus* "good"]

bounty hunter *n* **1 :** one who tracks down and captures outlaws for whom a reward is offered **2 :** one who hunts predatory animals for the reward offered

bou·quet \bō-ˈkā, bü-\ *n* **1 :** a bunch of flowers **2 :** FRAGRANCE ⟨the *bouquet* of good wine⟩ [French, from Middle French, "thicket, bunch of flowers"]

bour·bon \ˈbu̇r-bən, *usually* ˈbər- *in sense 3*\ *n* **1** *cap* **:** a member of a French family to which belong many kings of France, Spain, Naples, and the kingdom of the Two Sicilies **2** *often cap* **:** a person who clings firmly to outmoded social and political ideas **3 :** a whiskey distilled from a mash of corn, malt, and rye [from *Bourbon,* seigniory in France; sense 3 from *Bourbon* county, Kentucky] — **bour·bon·ism** \-bə-ˌniz-əm\ *n, often cap*

[1]**bour·geois** \ˈbu̇rzh-ˌwä, bu̇rzh-ˈ\ *n, pl* **bour·geois** \-ˌwä, -ˌwäz, -ˈwä, -ˈwäz\ **1 a :** an inhabitant of a borough or a town **b :** a middle-class person **2 :** a person whose social behavior and political views are held to be influenced by interest in private property; *esp* **:** CAPITALIST **3** *pl* **:** BOURGEOISIE [Middle French, from Medieval French *burgeis,* from *burc, borg* "town," from Latin *burgus* "fortified place"]

[2]**bourgeois** *adj* **1 :** of, relating to, or characteristic of town dwellers or of the middle class **2 :** marked by a concern for material interests and respectability and a leaning toward mediocrity **3 :** controlled by commercial and industrial interests : CAPITALISTIC

bour·geoi·sie \ˌbu̇rzh-ˌwä-ˈzē\ *n* **1 :** the middle class **2 :** a social order controlled by bourgeois [French, from *bourgeois*]

bourn *or* **bourne** \ˈbōrn, ˈbȯrn, ˈbu̇rn\ *n* **:** STREAM 1, BROOK [Middle English *burn, bourne*]

bourne *also* **bourn** \ˈbȯrn, ˈbu̇rn\ *n* **1 :** BOUNDARY, LIMIT **2 :** GOAL, DESTINATION [Middle French *bourne,* from Medieval French *bodne* "bound"]

bour·rée \bu̇-ˈrā\ *n* **:** a lively 17th century French dance [French]

bourse \ˈbu̇rs\ *n* **:** EXCHANGE 5a; *esp* **:** a European stock exchange [Middle French, literally, "purse," from Medieval Latin *bursa*]

bout \ˈbau̇t\ *n* **:** a spell of activity: as **a :** an athletic match (as of boxing) **b :** OUTBREAK, ATTACK ⟨a *bout* of measles⟩ **c :** SESSION 5 ⟨a *bout* of overspending⟩ [English dialect, "a trip going and returning in plowing," from Middle English *bought* "bend"]

bou·tique \bü-ˈtēk\ *n* **:** a small fashionable shop; *also* **:** a small shop within a large department store [French, "shop"]

bou·ton·niere \ˌbüt-n-ˈiər, ˌbü-tən-ˈyeər\ *n* **:** a flower or bouquet worn in a buttonhole [French *boutonnière* "buttonhole," from *bouton* "button"]

[1]**bo·vine** \ˈbō-ˌvīn, -ˌvēn\ *adj* **1 :** of, relating to, or resembling bovines and especially the ox or cow **2 :** both sluggish and patient ⟨a *bovine* disposition⟩ [Late Latin *bovinus,* from Latin *bov-, bos* "ox, cow"]

[2]**bovine** *n* **:** any of a group of ruminant mammals including the oxen, bison, and buffalo that have hollow horns and are related to the sheep and goats

bovine spongiform encephalopathy *n* **:** MAD COW DISEASE

[1]**bow** \ˈbau̇\ *vb* **1 :** to bend the head, body, or knee in greeting, reverence, respect, or submission **2 :** SUBMIT, YIELD ⟨*bow* to

authority⟩ **3** : BEND ⟨*bowed* with age⟩ **4** : to express by bowing ⟨*bow* one's thanks⟩ [Old English *būgan* "to bend, bow"]

[2]**bow** *n* : a bending of the head or body in respect, submission, agreement, or greeting

[3]**bow** \ˈbō\ *n* **1** : RAINBOW 1 **2** : a weapon for shooting arrows that is made of a strip of flexible material (as wood) bent by a cord connecting the two ends **3** : something shaped in a curve like a bow : BEND **4** : a wooden rod with hairs or fibers stretched from end to end used for playing a violin or similar instrument **5** : a knot formed by doubling a ribbon or string into loops [Old English *boga*]

[4]**bow** \ˈbō\ *vb* **1** : to bend into a curve **2** : to play a stringed instrument with a bow

[5]**bow** \ˈbau̇\ *n* : the forward part of a ship [Middle English *bowe, bowgh,* probably from Middle Dutch *boech* bow, shoulder]

bowd·ler·ize \ˈbōd-lə-ˌrīz, ˈbau̇d-\ *vt* : to clean up (as a book) by removing or altering parts considered objectionable [Thomas *Bowdler,* died 1825, English editor of Shakespeare] — **bowd·ler·i·za·tion** \ˌbōd-lə-rə-ˈzā-shən, ˌbau̇d-\ *n*

bow·el \ˈbau̇-əl, ˈbau̇l\ *n* **1 a** : INTESTINE, GUT — usually used in plural **b** : a division of the intestine **2** *archaic* : the seat of pity or tenderness — usually used in plural **3** *pl* : the interior parts ⟨the *bowels* of the earth⟩ [Medieval French *buel, boel,* derived from Latin *botulus* "sausage"]

bowel movement *n* : an act of passing usually solid waste through the rectum and anus; *also* : fecal matter expelled at one passage : STOOL

bow·er \ˈbau̇-ər, ˈbau̇r\ *n* **1** : a place for rest : RETREAT **2** : a pleasant shady place in a garden or forest [Old English *būr* "dwelling"] — **bow·ery** \-ē\ *adj*

bow·er·bird \-ˌbərd\ *n* : any of various birds of Australia and New Guinea of which the male builds a chamber or passage arched over with twigs and grasses

bow·fin \ˈbō-ˌfin\ *n* : a predaceous dull green iridescent North American freshwater fish

bow·ie knife \ˈbü-ē-, ˈbō-ē-\ *n* : a stout straight single-edged hunting knife [James *Bowie,* died 1836, American soldier and pioneer]

bow·knot \ˈbō-ˌnät, -ˈnät\ *n* : a knot with decorative loops

[1]**bowl** \ˈbōl\ *n* **1** : a rounded hollow dish **2** : the contents of a bowl **3** : the bowl-shaped part of something (as a spoon) **4** : a bowl-shaped amphitheater; *esp* : STADIUM 2b [Old English *bolla*] — **bowled** \ˈbōld\ *adj*

[2]**bowl** *n* **1 a** : a ball used in lawn bowling **b** *pl* : the game of lawn bowling **2** : a delivery of the ball in bowling or bowls [Medieval French *boule* "ball," from Latin *bulla* "bubble"]

[3]**bowl** *vb* **1** : to roll a ball or participate in bowling or lawn bowling **2** : to travel smoothly and rapidly

bowlder *variant of* BOULDER

bow·leg \ˈbō-ˌleg, -ˈleg\ *n* : a leg bowed outward at or below the knee — **bow·legged** \ˈbō-ˈleg-əd, -ˈlegd\ *adj*

[1]**bowl·er** \ˈbō-lər\ *n* : a person who bowls

[2]**bow·ler** \ˈbō-lər\ *n* : DERBY 3 [*Bowler,* 19th century family of English hatters]

bowl game *n* : a football game played after the regular season between specially invited teams

bow·line \ˈbō-lən, -ˌlīn\ *n* **1** : a rope used to keep the windward edge of a square sail pulled forward **2** : a knot used for making a loop that will not slip [Middle English *bouline*]

bowl·ing \ˈbō-ling\ *n* **1** : a game played by rolling balls so as to knock down wooden pins set up at the far end of an alley : ninepins or tenpins **2** : LAWN BOWLING

bowl over *vb* **1** : to hit and knock down while quickly moving past **2** : to greatly surprise or impress

bow·man \ˈbō-mən\ *n* : ARCHER

Bow·man's capsule \ˈbō-mənz-\ *n* : a thin membranous double-walled structure enclosing each glomerulus of a vertebrate kidney [Sir William *Bowman,* died 1892, English surgeon]

bow·sprit \ˈbau̇-ˌsprit, ˈbō-\ *n* : a large spar projecting forward from the bow of a ship [Middle English *bouspret*]

bow·string \ˈbō-ˌstring\ *n* : the cord connecting the two ends of a bow

bow tie \ˈbō-\ *n* : a short necktie tied in a bowknot

bow window \ˈbō-\ *n* : a curved bay window

bow·yer \ˈbō-yər\ *n* : one that makes shooting bows

[1]**box** \ˈbäks\ *n, pl* **box** *or* **box·es** : an evergreen shrub or small tree used especially for hedges [Old English, from Latin *buxus,* from Greek *pyxos*]

[2]**box** *n* **1 a** : a usually 4-sided receptacle with a bottom and often a cover **b** : the amount held by a box **2** : a small compartment for a group of spectators in a theater **3** : BOX STALL **4** : the driver's seat on a carriage **5** : a shed that protects ⟨sentry *box*⟩ **6** : a boxlike housing (as for a bearing) **7** : printed matter enclosed by rules or white space **8** : any of the spaces on a baseball diamond where a batter, coach, pitcher, or catcher stands **9** : the limitations of conventionality ⟨thinking outside the *box*⟩ [Old English, from Late Latin *buxis,* from Greek *pyxis,* from *pyxos* "box tree, boxwood"]

[3]**box** *vt* : to enclose in or as if in a box [probably from Spanish *bojar* "to circumnavigate"]

[4]**box** *n* : a punch or slap especially on the ear [Middle English]

[5]**box** *vb* **1** : to strike with the hand **2** : to engage in boxing : fight with the fists

[6]**box** *vt* : to name the 32 points of (the compass) in their order — used figuratively in the phrase *box the compass* to describe making a complete reversal [probably from Spanish *bojar* "to circumnavigate"]

box camera *n* : a camera of simple box shape with a fixed focus and a single shutter speed

box·car \ˈbäk-ˌskär\ *n* : a railroad freight car with a roof and usually with sliding doors in the sides

box cutter *n* : a small cutting tool with a retractable blade used especially for opening cardboard boxes

box elder *n* : a North American maple with compound leaves

[1]**box·er** \ˈbäk-sər\ *n* : one that engages in the sport of boxing

[2]**boxer** *n* : any of a German breed of compact medium-sized short-haired usually fawn or brindle dogs

Box·er \ˈbäk-sər\ *n* : a member of a Chinese secret society that in 1900 attempted by violence to drive foreigners out of China and to force native converts to abandon Christianity [approximate translation of Chinese (Beijing dialect) *yìhé juǎn,* literally, "righteous harmonious fist"]

boxer shorts *n pl* : men's or boys' loose underwear shorts

box·ing *n* : the art of attack and defense with the fists practiced as a sport

Box·ing Day \ˈbäk-sing-\ *n* : the first weekday after Christmas observed as a legal holiday in parts of the Commonwealth of Nations [from the giving of Christmas gifts in boxes on this day to service workers (as postal workers)]

boxing glove *n* : one of a pair of padded leather mittens worn in boxing

box kite *n* : a tailless kite consisting of two or more open-ended connected boxes

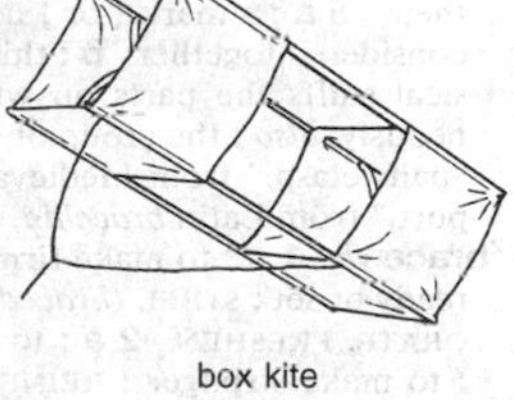
box kite

box·like \ˈbäk-ˌslīk\ *adj* : resembling a box

box office *n* **1** : an office in a public place (as a theater) where tickets of admission are sold **2** : the financial results of an entertainment enterprise; *also* : something affecting these results

box pleat *n* : a pleat made by forming two folded edges one facing right and the other left

box score *n* : a printed summary of a game usually in the form of a table giving essential details of play

box seat *n* : an advantageous position for viewing something

box spring *n* : a bedspring that consists of spiral springs attached to a foundation and enclosed in a cloth-covered frame

box stall *n* : an individual enclosure for an animal

box turtle *n* : any of several North American land turtles able to withdraw completely into the shell

box·wood \ˈbäk-ˌswu̇d\ *n* : the close-grained tough hard wood of the box; *also* : [1]BOX

boy \ˈbȯi\ *n* **1** : a male child from birth to young manhood **2** : SON 1 **3** : a male servant [Middle English] — **boy·hood** \-ˌhu̇d\ *n* — **boy·ish** \-ish\ *adj* — **boy·ish·ly** *adv* — **boy·ish·ness** *n*

bo·yar \bō-ˈyär\ *n* : a member of a Russian aristocratic order next in rank below the ruling princes until its abolition by Peter the Great [Russian *boyarin*]

\ə\ **abut**	\au̇\ **out**	\i\ **tip**	\ȯ\ **saw**	\u̇\ **foot**
\ər\ **further**	\ch\ **chin**	\ī\ **life**	\ȯi\ **coin**	\y\ **yet**
\a\ **mat**	\e\ **pet**	\j\ **job**	\th\ **thin**	\yü\ **few**
\ā\ **take**	\ē\ **easy**	\ng\ **sing**	\th\ **this**	\yu̇\ **cure**
\ä\ **cot, cart**	\g\ **go**	\ō\ **bone**	\ü\ **food**	\zh\ **vision**

[1]**boy·cott** \'bȯi-ˌkät\ *vt* : to jointly refuse to deal with (as a person or country) or use (as a product) usually to express disapproval or force concessions [Charles S. *Boycott,* died 1897, English land agent in Ireland who was ostracized for refusing to reduce rents]

Word History In September 1880 the Irish National Land League, which grew out of unrest following an agricultural depression in Ireland during the 1870s, began a campaign against the eviction of tenants who could not pay their rents. Charles S. Boycott, a retired English army captain who rented a farm in County Mayo and worked as an agent for an absentee landlord, became the first victim of the Land League's campaign. When the landlord's tenants refused to pay their rents unless they received an abatement, Boycott tried to serve eviction notices. As a result, his laborers and servants quit, and the crops on his own farm began to rot. The newly popular tactic of shunning a person to assert a grievance needed a name, and Boycott's name was at hand. The Land League was banned by Parliament in 1881, but the word *boycott* is still part of English.

[2]**boycott** *n* : the process or an instance of boycotting

boy·friend \'bȯi-ˌfrend\ *n* **1** : a male friend **2** : a regular male companion in a romantic relationship

Boyle's law \'bȯilz-\ *n* : a statement in physics: the volume of a gas at constant temperature varies inversely with the pressure exerted on it [Robert *Boyle*]

Boy Scout *n* **1** : a member of any of various national scouting programs (as the Boy Scouts of America) for boys usually 11 to 17 years of age **2** : a person whose values or actions are characteristic of a Boy Scout

boy·sen·ber·ry \'bȯiz-ᵊn-ˌber-ē, 'bȯis-\ *n* : a large berry like a blackberry with the flavor of a raspberry; *also* : the trailing bramble that produces boysenberries and was developed by crossing blackberry and raspberry plants [Rudolph *Boysen,* died 1950, American horticulturist]

bra \'brä\ *n* : BRASSIERE

[1]**brace** \'brās\ *n, pl* **brac·es** *or* **brace** **1** : two of a kind ⟨several *brace* of quail⟩ **2** : something (as a clasp) that connects or fastens **3** : a crank-shaped instrument for turning a wood-boring bit **4 a** : something that transmits, directs, resists, or supports weight or pressure; *esp* : an inclined timber used as a support **b** *pl* : SUSPENDERS **c** : a device for supporting a body part (as the shoulders) **d** *pl* : an orthodontic device usually of wire that is attached to the teeth especially to straighten and reposition them **5 a** : a mark { or } used to connect words or items to be considered together **b** : this mark connecting two or more musical staffs the parts on which are to be performed simultaneously; *also* : the group of staffs so connected [Middle English, "pair, clasp," from Medieval French, "pair of arms, pair, support," from Latin *bracchia,* plural of *bracchium* "arm"]

[2]**brace** *vb* **1 a** : to make firm or taut ⟨*brace* a drum⟩ **b** : to get ready or set : STEEL ⟨*braced* themselves for the test⟩ **c** : INVIGORATE, FRESHEN **2 a** : to furnish or support with a brace **b** : to make stronger : REINFORCE **3** : to plant firmly ⟨*bracing* my feet⟩ **4** : to take heart ⟨*brace* up, all is not lost⟩

brace·let \'brā-slət\ *n* **1** : an ornamental band or chain worn around the wrist **2** : something (as handcuffs) resembling a bracelet [Medieval French, from *bras* "arm," from Latin *bracchium*]

bra·cer \'brā-sər\ *n* : an arm or wrist protector

brace root *n* : PROP ROOT

bra·chi·al \'brā-kē-əl\ *adj* : of or relating to the arm or a comparable structure [Latin *bracchium, brachium* "arm"]

brachial plexus *n* : a network of nerves lying mostly in the armpit and supplying nerves to the chest, shoulder, and arm

bra·chi·ate \'brā-kē-ˌāt\ *vi* : to progress by swinging from one hold to another by the arms ⟨a *brachiating* gibbon⟩ — **bra·chi·a·tion** \ˌbrā-kē-'ā-shən\ *n*

bra·chio·ce·phal·ic artery \ˌbräk-ē-ō-sə-'fal-ik-\ *n* : INNOMINATE ARTERY

brachiocephalic vein *n* : INNOMINATE VEIN

bra·chio·pod \'brā-kē-ə-ˌpäd\ *n* : any of a phylum (Brachiopoda) of marine invertebrate animals with bivalve shells and a pair of arms bearing tentacles — called also *lampshell* [derived from Latin *bracchium* "arm" + Greek *pod-, pous* "foot"] — **brachiopod** *adj*

brachy- *combining form* : short ⟨*brachy*cephalic⟩ [Greek *brachys*]

brachy·ce·phal·ic \ˌbrak-i-sə-'fal-ik\ *adj* : having a head that is relatively short from front to back or relatively wide from side to side — **brachy·ceph·a·ly** \-i-'sef-ə-lē\ *n*

brac·ing \'brā-sing\ *adj* : giving strength or freshness ⟨a *bracing* wind⟩

brack·en \'brak-ən\ *n* : a large coarse branching fern; *also* : a growth of such ferns [Middle English *braken*]

[1]**brack·et** \'brak-ət\ *n* **1** : an overhanging member or fixture that projects from a structure (as a wall) and is usually intended to support a vertical load or to strengthen an angle **2** : a short wall shelf **3 a** : one of a pair of marks [ ] used to enclose matter or in mathematics used as signs indicating that two or more terms are treated as one quantity — called also *square bracket* **b** : one of a pair of marks ⟨ ⟩ used to enclose matter — called also *angle bracket* **4** : a section of a continuously numbered or graded series (as age ranges or income levels) **5** : a pairing of opponents in an elimination tournament [perhaps from Middle French *braguette* "projecting part on breeches," from *brague* "breeches," derived from Latin *braca,* of Celtic origin]

[2]**bracket** *vt* **1** : to place within or as if within brackets **2** : to furnish or fasten with brackets **3** : to put into the same category : ASSOCIATE **4 a** : to get the range on (a target) by firing over and short **b** : to establish the limits of

bracket fungus *n* : a basidiomycete that forms shelflike fruiting bodies

brack·ish \'brak-ish\ *adj* : somewhat salty ⟨*brackish* water⟩ [Dutch *brac* "salty"]

bract \'brakt\ *n* : a small leaf or leaflike structure at the base of a flower or flower cluster [Latin *bractea* "thin metal plate"] — **bract·ed** \'brak-təd\ *adj*

brad \'brad\ *n* : a slender nail with a small often indented head [Old Norse *broddr* "spike"]

brae \'brā\ *n, chiefly Scottish* : a hillside especially along a river [Old Norse *brā* "eyelid"]

[1]**brag** \'brag\ *n* **1** : a pompous or boastful statement **2** : arrogant talk or manner **3** : BRAGGART [Middle English]

[2]**brag** *vb* **bragged; brag·ging** : to talk or assert boastfully — **brag·ger** \'brag-ər\ *n*

brag·ga·do·cio \ˌbrag-ə-'dō-shē-ˌō, -shē-ō, -shō\ *n, pl* **-cios** **1** : BRAGGART, BOASTER **2 a** : empty boasting **b** : COCKINESS [*Braggadochio,* personification of boasting in *Faerie Queene* by Edmund Spenser]

brag·gart \'brag-ərt\ *n* : a loud arrogant boaster — **braggart** *adj*

Brah·ma \'bräm-ə\ *n* : the ultimate ground of all being in Hinduism [Sanskrit *brahman*]

Brah·man *or* **Brah·min** \'bräm-ən; *2 is* 'brām-, 'bräm-, 'bram-\ *n* **1 a** : a Hindu of the highest and traditionally the priestly caste **b** : BRAHMA **2** : ZEBU; *esp* : a large vigorous usually silvery gray animal developed in the southern U.S. from the zebu that is resistant to heat and ticks **3** *usually* **Brahmin** : an aloof intellectually and socially cultivated person; *esp* : such a person from one of the older New England families [Sanskrit *brāhmaṇa*] — **Brahman** *or* **Brah·man·ic** \brä-'man-ik\ *adj*

Brah·man·ism \'bräm-ə-ˌniz-əm\ *n* : orthodox Hinduism that follows the Vedas in accepting the forces and laws of the universe as divine and in practicing ancient rites and ceremonies

[1]**braid** \'brād\ *vt* **1** : to form (three or more strands) into a braid **2** : to ornament especially with ribbon or braid [Old English *bregdan* "to move suddenly, bend, weave"] — **braid·er** *n*

[2]**braid** *n* **1** : a cord or ribbon with usually three or more strands forming a regular diagonal pattern down its length; *esp* : a narrow fabric of intertwined threads used especially for trimming **2** : a length of braided hair

braid·ing \'brād-ing\ *n* : something made of braided material

brail \'brāl\ *n* : a rope fastened to the leech of a sail for hauling the sail up or in [Medieval French *braiel* "strap"] — **brail** *vt*

braille \'brāl\ *n, often cap* : a system of writing for the blind that uses characters made up of raised dots [Louis *Braille*]

[1]**brain** \'brān\ *n* **1 a** : the portion of the vertebrate central nervous system that is the organ of thought and nervous coordination, is made up of neurons and supporting and nutritive structures, is enclosed within the skull, and is continuous with the spinal cord **b** : the main nervous center in an invertebrate animal **2 a** (1) : INTELLECT ⟨has a clever *brain*⟩ (2) : INTELLIGENCE — often used in plural **b** (1) : a very intelligent or intellectual person (2) : the chief planner of an enterprise — usually used in plural ⟨she's the *brains* behind their success⟩ [Old English *brægen*]

[2]**brain** *vt* **1** : to kill by smashing the skull **2** : to hit on the head

brain•case \-ˌkās\ *n* : the cranium enclosing the brain

brain•child \-ˌchīld\ *n* : a product of one's creative imagination

brain death *n* : final cessation of activity in the central nervous system especially as indicated by an electroencephalogram showing no brain waves for a predetermined length of time that is often used as a criterion for human death — **brain–dead** *adj*

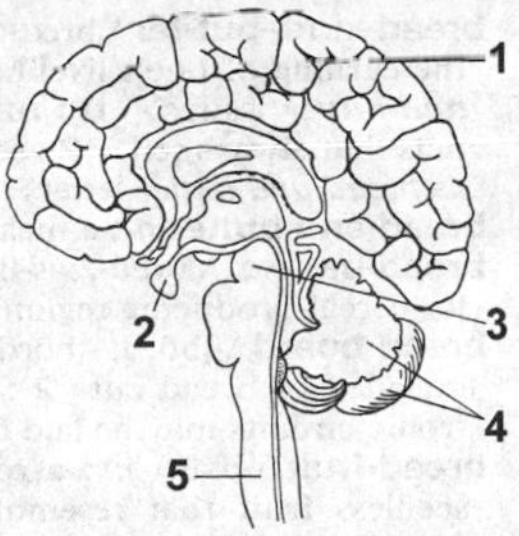

brain 1a: *1* cerebrum, *2* pituitary gland, *3* midbrain, *4* cerebellum, *5* spinal cord

brain freeze *n* : a sudden shooting pain in the head caused by ingesting very cold food (as ice cream) or drink

brain•less \ˈbrān-ləs\ *adj* : UNINTELLIGENT, SILLY — **brain•less•ly** *adv* — **brain•less•ness** *n*

brain stem *n* : the posterior and lower part of the brain including the midbrain, pons, and medulla oblongata

brain•storm \ˈbrān-ˌstȯrm\ *n* **1** : a temporary but violent mental upset or disturbance **2** : a sudden inspiration

brain•storm•ing \ˈbrān-ˌstȯr-miŋ\ *n* : a group problem-solving technique that involves the spontaneous contribution of ideas from all members of the group; *also* : the mulling over of ideas by one or more persons in an attempt to find a solution — **brainstorm** *vb*

brain•teas•er \-ˌtē-zər\ *n* : something (as a puzzle) that demands mental effort and sharpness for its solution

brain trust *n* : a group of official or unofficial advisers dealing especially with planning and strategy — **brain trust•er** \-ˌtrəs-tər\ *n*

brain•wash•ing \ˈbrān-ˌwȯsh-iŋ, -ˌwäsh-\ *n* **1** : a forcible attempt by indoctrination to induce someone to give up basic political, social, or religious beliefs and attitudes and to accept contrasting regimented ideas **2** : persuasion by propaganda or salesmanship — **brain•wash** *vb*

brain wave *n* : rhythmic fluctuations of voltage between parts of the brain resulting in the flow of an electric current

brainy \ˈbrā-nē\ *adj* **brain•i•er; -est** : INTELLIGENT — **brain•i•ness** *n*

braise \ˈbrāz\ *vt* : to cook slowly in fat and then in a little liquid in a closed pot [French *braiser*]

[1]brake \ˈbrāk\ *archaic past of* BREAK

[2]brake *n* : a common bracken fern [Middle English]

[3]brake *n* **1** : a toothed instrument or machine for separating out the fiber of flax or hemp **2** : a machine for bending sheet metal [Low German]

[4]brake *n* : rough or marshy land overgrown usually with one kind of plant [Middle English *-brake*] — **braky** \ˈbrā-kē\ *adj*

[5]brake *n* : a device for slowing or stopping motion (as of a wheel, vehicle, or engine) especially by friction [perhaps from obsolete *brake* "bridle"]

[6]brake *vb* **1** : to slow or stop by or as if by a brake **2** : to operate a brake especially on a vehicle

brake•man \ˈbrāk-mən\ *n* : a freight or passenger train crew member who inspects the train and assists the conductor

bram•ble \ˈbram-bəl\ *n* : any of a large genus of usually prickly shrubs related to the roses and including the raspberries and blackberries [Old English *brēmel*] — **bram•bly** \-bə-lē, -blē\ *adj*

bran \ˈbran\ *n* : the edible broken coat of the seed of cereal grain separated from the flour or meal by sifting or bolting [Medieval French *bren, bran*]

[1]branch \ˈbranch\ *n* **1** : a natural subdivision (as a bough arising from a trunk or a twig from a bough) of a plant stem **2** : something (as a tributary of a river or a secondary road) forming a part of a larger whole in a manner suggesting the relation of a branch to a tree ⟨a *branch* of an antler⟩: as **a** : a division of a family descending from a particular ancestor **b** : a division of an organization ⟨executive *branch* of the government⟩ **c** : a subordinate office or part of a central system ⟨a bank *branch*⟩ **d** : an area of knowledge that may be considered apart from related areas **e** : a part of a mathematical curve separated from others ⟨a *branch* of the hyperbola⟩ [Medieval French *branche,* from Late Latin *branca* "paw"] — **branched** \ˈbrancht\ *adj* — **branch•less** \ˈbranch-ləs\ *adj* — **branchy** \ˈbran-chē\ *adj*

[2]branch *vi* **1** : to develop branches : spread or separate into branches ⟨an elm *branches* over the yard⟩ **2** : to spring out (as from a main stem) : DIVERGE ⟨streets *branching* off the highway⟩ **3** : to extend activities ⟨the business is *branching* out⟩

bran•chi•al \ˈbraŋ-kē-əl\ *adj* : of, relating to, or situated near the gills [Latin *branchia* "gill," from Greek *branchion*]

[1]brand \ˈbrand\ *n* **1** : a charred or burning piece of wood **2** : SWORD **3 a** : a mark made by burning (as on cattle) to show ownership or origin **b** : a printed or stamped mark made for similar purposes **c** : a mark put on criminals with a hot iron **d** : a mark of disgrace : STIGMA **4 a** : a class of goods identified by name as the product of a single firm or manufacturer **b** : a characteristic or distinctive kind : VARIETY ⟨his *brand* of humor⟩ [Old English, "torch, sword"]

[2]brand *vt* **1** : to mark with or as if with a brand **2** : to mark with disapproval : STIGMATIZE ⟨was *branded* a coward⟩ — **brand•er** *n*

bran•dish \ˈbran-dish\ *vt* **1** : to shake or wave (as a weapon) threateningly **2** : to display in a showy or aggressive manner [Medieval French *brandiss-,* stem of *brandir,* from *brand* "sword," of Germanic origin] — **brandish** *n*

brand name *n* : a name that is given by a manufacturer or merchant to an article or service to distinguish it as produced or sold by that manufacturer or merchant and that may be used and protected as a trademark

brand–new \ˈbrand-ˈnü, -ˈnyü\ *adj* : conspicuously new and unused

[1]bran•dy \ˈbran-dē\ *n, pl* **-dies** : an alcoholic liquor distilled from wine or fermented fruit juice (as of apples) [short for *brandywine,* from Dutch *brandewijn,* from *brant* "distilled" + *wijn* "wine"]

[2]brandy *vt* **bran•died; bran•dy•ing** : to flavor, blend, or preserve with brandy ⟨*brandied* cherries⟩

brant \ˈbrant\ *n, pl* **brant** *or* **brants** : a small dark wild goose that breeds in the Arctic [Middle English *brand gos*]

brash \ˈbrash\ *adj* **1** : IMPETUOUS, RASH ⟨a *brash* attack⟩ **2** : aggressively self-assertive : IMPUDENT ⟨a *brash* youth⟩ **3** : piercingly sharp : HARSH ⟨a *brash* squeal of brakes⟩ [origin unknown] — **brash•ly** *adv* — **brash•ness** *n*

brass \ˈbras\ *n* **1** : an alloy consisting essentially of copper and zinc; *also* : the reddish yellow color of this alloy **2 a** : brass musical instruments — often used in plural **b** : a usually brass memorial tablet **c** : bright metal fittings or utensils **3** : brazen self-assurance : GALL **4** : persons in high positions (as in a business or the government) [Old English *bræs*] — **brass** *adj*

brass band *n* : a band consisting chiefly or solely of brass and percussion instruments

brass•bound \ˈbras-ˌbau̇nd, -ˈbau̇nd\ *adj* **1** : having trim made of brass ⟨a *brassbound* trunk⟩ **2** : strictly bound by tradition

brass hat *n* : a person (as a military officer) in a high-ranking position

bras•siere \brə-ˈziər *also* ˌbras-ē-ˈeər\ *n* : a woman's undergarment to cover and support the breasts [obsolete French *brassière* "bodice," from Medieval French *braciere* "arm protector," from *bras* "arm"]

brass instrument *n* : any of a group of wind instruments (as French horn, trombone, trumpet, or tuba) that is usually characterized by a long cylindrical or conical metal tube commonly curved two or more times and ending in a flared bell, that produces tones by the vibrations of the player's lips against a usually cup-shaped mouthpiece, and that usually has valves or a slide by which the player may produce all the tones within the instrument's range

brass knuckles *n pl* : KNUCKLE 3

brass tacks *n pl* : details of immediate practical importance — usually used in the phrase *get down to brass tacks*

brassy \ˈbras-ē\ *adj* **brass•i•er; -est** **1 a** : shamelessly bold **b** : UNRULY **2** : resembling brass especially in color **3** : resembling the sound of a brass instrument — **brass•i•ly** \ˈbras-ə-lē\ *adv* — **brass•i•ness** \ˈbras-ē-nəs\ *n*

brat \ˈbrat\ *n* : CHILD; *esp* : an ill-mannered annoying child [perhaps from English dialect *brat* "coarse garment"] — **brat•tish** \ˈbrat-ish\ *adj* — **brat•ty** \ˈbrat-ē\ *adj*

bra•va•do \brə-ˈväd-ō\ *n, pl* **-does** *or* **-dos** **1** : blustering swag-

\ə\ **abut**	\au̇\ **out**	\i\ **tip**	\ȯ\ **saw**	\u̇\ **foot**
\ər\ **further**	\ch\ **chin**	\ī\ **life**	\ȯi\ **coin**	\y\ **yet**
\a\ **mat**	\e\ **pet**	\j\ **job**	\th\ **thin**	\yü\ **few**
\ā\ **take**	\ē\ **easy**	\ŋ\ **sing**	\t͟h\ **this**	\yu̇\ **cure**
\ä\ **cot, cart**	\g\ **go**	\ō\ **bone**	\ü\ **food**	\zh\ **vision**

gering conduct **2** : a pretense of bravery [Middle French *bravade,* from Italian *bravata,* from *bravare* "to challenge, show off," from *bravo*]

[1]brave \ˈbrāv\ *adj* **1** : COURAGEOUS **2** : making a fine show : COLORFUL ⟨*brave* banners flying in the wind⟩ **3** : SPLENDID ⟨the business collapsed despite a *brave* start⟩ [Middle French, from Italian and Spanish *bravo* "wild, courageous," probably from Latin *barbarus* "barbarous"] — **brave·ly** *adv*

[2]brave *vt* : to face or endure with courage ⟨*braved* the taunts of the mob⟩

[3]brave *n* : one who is brave; *esp* : an American Indian warrior

brav·ery \ˈbrāv-rē, -ə-rē\ *n, pl* **-er·ies** **1** : the quality or state of being brave : FEARLESSNESS **2 a** : fine clothes **b** : showy display ***synonyms*** see COURAGE

[1]bra·vo \ˈbräv-ō\ *n, pl* **bravos** *or* **bravoes** : VILLAIN, DESPERADO; *esp* : a hired assassin [Italian, from *bravo* "wild, courageous"]

[2]bra·vo \ˈbräv-ō, brä-ˈvō\ *n, pl* **bravos** : a shout of approval — often used interjectionally in applauding a performance

[3]bra·vo \ˈbräv-ō, brä-ˈvō\ *vt* **bra·voed; bra·vo·ing** : to applaud by shouts of bravo

bra·vu·ra \brə-ˈvyu̇r-ə, -ˈvu̇r-\ *n* **1** : a florid brilliant musical style **2** : a musical passage requiring agility and skill to perform **3** : a show of daring or brilliance [Italian, literally, "bravery," from *bravare* "to show off"]

braw \ˈbrȯ\ *adj, chiefly Scottish* : GOOD, FINE; *also* : well dressed [Middle French *brave*]

[1]brawl \ˈbrȯl\ *vi* **1** : to quarrel or fight noisily **2** : to make a loud confused noise ⟨the river *brawling* by⟩ [Middle English *brawlen*] — **brawl·er** *n*

[2]brawl *n* : a noisy quarrel or fight

brawn \ˈbrȯn\ *n* **1** : full strong muscles **2** : muscular strength [Medieval French *braon* "flesh, muscle," of Germanic origin]

brawny \ˈbrȯ-nē\ *adj* **brawn·i·er; -est** : having large strong muscles — **brawn·i·ness** *n*

[1]bray \ˈbrā\ *vb* **1** : to utter a bray or similar sound **2** : to utter or play loudly, harshly, or discordantly [Medieval French *braire* "to cry, bellow, roar"]

[2]bray *n* : the characteristic loud harsh cry of a donkey

bray·er \ˈbrā-ər\ *n* : a hand roller for inking something (as a block) to be printed [Middle English *brayen* "to crush to powder," from Medieval French *braier*]

braze \ˈbrāz\ *vb* : to solder with a nonferrous alloy having a relatively high melting point [French *braser,* from Medieval French, "to burn," from *breze* "live coals"]

[1]bra·zen \ˈbrāz-n\ *adj* **1** : made of brass **2 a** : sounding harsh and loud like struck brass **b** : of the color of polished brass **3** : IMPUDENT, SHAMELESS ⟨a *brazen* violation of the rules⟩ [Old English *bræsen,* from *bræs* "brass"] — **bra·zen·ly** *adv* — **bra·zen·ness** \ˈbrāz-n-nəs, -əs\ *n*

[2]brazen *vt* **bra·zened; bra·zen·ing** \ˈbrāz-ning, -n-ing\ : to face with defiance or impudence ⟨would the prisoner *brazen* it out or break down and confess⟩

bra·zen–faced \ˌbrāz-n-ˈfāst\ *adj* : showing insolence and bold disrespect ⟨a *brazen-faced* liar⟩

[1]bra·zier \ˈbrā-zhər\ *n* : one that works in brass [Middle English *brasier,* from *bras* "brass"]

[2]brazier *n* **1** : a pan for holding burning coals **2** : a utensil on which food is exposed to heat (as from burning charcoal) through a grill [French *brasier,* derived from Medieval French *breze* "hot coals"]

Bra·zil nut \brə-ˈzil-\ *n* : a large 3-sided oily edible nut that occurs packed inside the round fruit of a tall tree of tropical South America; *also* : the tree that bears Brazil nuts

[1]breach \ˈbrēch\ *n* **1** : violation of a law, duty, or tie ⟨a *breach* of trust⟩ **2 a** : a broken, ruptured, or torn condition or area **b** : a gap (as in a wall) made by battering **3 a** : a break in accustomed friendly relations **b** : a temporary gap in continuity : HIATUS **4** : a leap especially of a whale out of water [Old English *bræc* "act of breaking"]

[2]breach *vb* **1** : to make a breach in ⟨*breach* the city walls⟩ **2** : BREAK, VIOLATE ⟨*breach* an agreement⟩ **3** : to leap out of water ⟨an otter *breaching*⟩

breach of promise : violation of a promise especially to marry

[1]bread \ˈbred\ *n* **1** : a baked usually leavened food made of a mixture whose basic constituent is flour or meal **2** : FOOD, SUSTENANCE ⟨our daily *bread*⟩ **3 a** : LIVELIHOOD ⟨earn one's *bread* as a laborer⟩ **b** *slang* : MONEY [Old English *brēad*]

[2]bread *vt* : to cover with bread crumbs ⟨*breaded* veal cutlet⟩

bread–and–but·ter \ˌbred-n-ˈbət-ər\ *adj* **1 a** : being as basic as the earning of one's livelihood ⟨unions concerned with *bread-and-butter* issues⟩ **b** : DEPENDABLE ⟨*bread-and-butter* products that always sell⟩ **2** : sent or given as thanks for hospitality ⟨a *bread-and-butter* letter⟩

bread and butter *n* : a means of livelihood

bread·bas·ket \ˈbred-ˌbas-kət\ *n* **1** *slang* : STOMACH **2** : a major cereal-producing region

bread·board \-ˌbōrd, -ˌbȯrd\ *n* **1** : a board on which dough is kneaded or bread cut **2** : a board on which electric or electronic circuits may be laid out

bread·fruit \-ˌfrüt\ *n* : a round usually seedless fruit that resembles bread in color and texture when baked; *also* : a tall tropical tree related to the mulberries that bears this fruit

breadfruit

bread·line \-ˌlīn\ *n* : a line of people waiting to receive free food

bread mold *n* : any of several molds (as a rhizopus) that are found especially on bread

bread·stuff \-ˌstəf\ *n* **1** : a cereal product (as grain or flour) **2** : BREAD

breadth \ˈbredth, ˈbreth, ˈbretth\ *n* **1** : distance from side to side : WIDTH **2 a** : something of full width **b** : a wide expanse **3** : COMPREHENSIVENESS, SCOPE ⟨the remarkable *breadth* of a scholar's learning⟩ [Middle English *breadeth, breth,* from *brede* "breadth," from Old English *brǣdu,* from *brād* "broad"]

bread·win·ner \ˈbred-ˌwin-ər\ *n* : a member of a family whose wages supply its livelihood

[1]break \ˈbrāk\ *vb* **broke** \ˈbrōk\; **bro·ken** \ˈbrō-kən\; **break·ing** **1 a** : to separate suddenly or violently into parts : SHATTER ⟨*break* a dish⟩ **b** : FRACTURE **c** : MAIM **d** : RUPTURE **e** : to curl over and fall apart ⟨waves *breaking* against the shore⟩ **2** : VIOLATE, TRANSGRESS ⟨*broke* the law⟩ **3 a** : to force a way into, out of, or through ⟨burglars *broke* into the house⟩ **b** : to escape with sudden effort ⟨*broke* away from our captors⟩ **c** : to develop, appear, or burst forth with suddenness or force ⟨day *breaks* in the east⟩ ⟨*broke* into laughter⟩ **d** : to become fair ⟨waited for the weather to *break*⟩ **e** : to make a sudden dash ⟨*break* for cover⟩ **f** : to make or effect by cutting, forcing, or pressing ⟨*break* open a package⟩ **g** : PENETRATE, PIERCE **4** : LOOSEN, SUNDER ⟨*break* a hold⟩ **5** : to cut into and turn over the surface of : PLOW ⟨*break* ground for a new school⟩ **6 a** : to disrupt the order or uniformity of ⟨*break* ranks⟩ **b** : to end by or as if by dispersing ⟨police *broke* up the mob⟩ **c** : to give way in disorderly retreat ⟨the soldiers *broke* under fire⟩ **d** : to decline suddenly and sharply in price or value **e** : to end a relationship or accord — usually used with *with* **7 a** : to subdue completely : CRUSH ⟨*broke* the revolt⟩ **b** : to lose or cause to lose health, strength, or spirit ⟨*broke* under the strain⟩ **c** : to become or cause to become inoperative because of damage, wear, or strain ⟨*broke* his watch⟩ ⟨the TV is *broken*⟩ **d** : to ruin financially **e** : to reduce in rank **f** : to force (a strike) to end by measures outside bargaining practices **g** : to ruin the prospects of ⟨could make or *break* my career⟩ **8 a** : to bring to an end suddenly ⟨*break* a deadlock⟩ ⟨*broke* the silence⟩ **b** : INTERRUPT, SUSPEND ⟨*broke* in with a comment⟩ ⟨*broke* their tour for a rest⟩ **9 a** : to make (an animal) fit for use (as by training) **b** : to accustom to an activity or occurrence ⟨*break* in a new worker⟩ **10** : to make known ⟨*break* the news to them⟩ **11** : to halt or lessen the force or intensity of ⟨the bushes *broke* my fall⟩ **12** : EXCEED, SURPASS ⟨*broke* all records⟩ **13** : OPEN ⟨*break* an electric circuit⟩ **14** : to split the surface of ⟨fish *breaking* water⟩ **15** : to cause to discontinue a habit ⟨*broke* the child of thumb-sucking⟩ **16** : SOLVE ⟨*broke* a code⟩ **17 a** : to alter course sharply ⟨*broke* to the left⟩ **b** : to curve, drop, or rise sharply ⟨the pitch *broke* over the plate for a strike⟩ **c** : to alter sharply in tone, pitch, or intensity ⟨a voice *breaking* with emotion⟩ **d** : to shift abruptly from one register to another **18** : HAPPEN, DEVELOP ⟨everything *broke* right for us⟩ [Old English *brecan*] — **break·able** \ˈbrā-kə-bəl\ *adj* — **break camp** : to pack up gear and leave a camp — **break cover** : to start from a covert or lair ⟨the hunted fox *broke cover*⟩ — **break one's heart** : to crush emotionally with sorrow — **break the back** : to subdue the main force ⟨*break the back* of inflation⟩ — **break the ice** **1** : to make a beginning **2** : to get through the first difficulties in starting a conversation — **break wind** : to expel gas from the intestine

[2]**break** *n* **1 a** : an act or action of breaking **b** : the opening shot in a game of pool or billiards **2 a** : a condition produced by breaking ⟨a *break* in the clouds⟩ **b** : a gap in an electric circuit interrupting the flow of current **3** : an interruption in continuity: as **a** : a respite from work or duty **b** : a planned interruption in a radio or television program ⟨a commercial *break*⟩ **c** : a noticeable change (as in a surface, course, movement, or direction) **d** : a notable variation of pitch, intensity, or tone in the voice **e** : an abrupt run : DASH **f** : the act of separating after a boxing or wrestling clinch **4 a** : a rupture in previously friendly relations ⟨a *break* between the two countries⟩ **b** : an abrupt split or difference from something previously followed ⟨a sharp *break* with tradition⟩ **5** : a place or situation at which a break occurs: as **a** : the point where one musical register changes to another **b** : the place at which a word is divided **c** : CAESURA **6** : a stroke of luck ⟨a bad *break*⟩; *esp* : a stroke of good luck ⟨got all the *breaks*⟩ **7 a** : a favorable or opportune situation ⟨a big *break* in show business⟩ **b** : favorable treatment ⟨a tax *break*⟩

break·age \ˈbrā-kij\ *n* **1 a** : the action of breaking **b** : a quantity broken **2** : loss due to or a charge for things broken

break·down \ˈbrāk-ˌdau̇n\ *n* **1 a** : a failure to function properly **b** : a physical, mental, or nervous collapse **2** : DECOMPOSITION **3** : division into categories : CLASSIFICATION

break down \brāk-ˈdau̇n, ˈbrāk-\ *vb* **1 a** : to cause to fall or collapse by breaking or shattering **b** : to make ineffective **c** : to fail in strength or vitality ⟨her health *broke down*⟩ **d** : to succumb to mental or emotional stress ⟨*broke down* and cried⟩ **e** : to lose one's resolve ⟨finally *broke down* and bought a new car⟩ **2 a** : to separate (as a chemical compound) into simpler substances : DECOMPOSE **b** : to undergo decomposition **3** : to become subdivided or separated by analysis

break·er \ˈbrā-kər\ *n* **1** : one that breaks **2** : a wave breaking into foam against the shore

break even *vi* : to end up with neither gain nor loss

break·fast \ˈbrek-fəst\ *n* : the first meal of the day especially when taken in the morning — **breakfast** *vb*

break·neck \ˈbrāk-ˌnek\ *adj* : very fast or dangerous ⟨*breakneck* speed⟩

break·out \ˈbrāk-ˌau̇t\ *n* : a forceful break from restraint

break out \brāk-ˈau̇t, ˈbrāk-\ *vb* **1** : to develop or erupt suddenly and with force ⟨fire *broke out*⟩ ⟨a riot *broke out*⟩ **2** : to be affected with a skin eruption ⟨*broke out* in hives⟩

break·through \ˈbrāk-ˌthrü\ *n* **1** : an act or point of breaking through an obstruction or defensive line **2** : an important advance in knowledge or technique

break·wa·ter \ˈbrāk-ˌwȯt-ər, -ˌwät-\ *n* : an offshore structure (as a wall) to protect a harbor or beach from the force of waves

bream \ˈbrim, ˈbrēm\ *n, pl* **bream** *or* **breams** **1** : any of various freshwater fishes; *esp* : any of several sunfishes (as a bluegill) **2** : any of several marine fishes related to the porgy [Medieval French *breme,* of Germanic origin]

[1]**breast** \ˈbrest\ *n* **1** : either of the pair of mammary glands extending from the front of the chest in the human female and some other mammals; *also* : any mammary gland **2** : the front or ventral part of the body between the neck and the abdomen **3** : the center of emotion and thought : BOSOM [Old English *brēost*] — **breast·ed** \ˈbres-təd\ *adj*

[2]**breast** *vt* : to push against with or as if with the chest

breast·bone \ˈbrest-ˈbōn, ˈbres-, -ˌbōn\ *n* : STERNUM

breast–feed \ˈbrest-ˌfēd\ *vt* **-fed** \-ˌfed\; **-feed·ing** : to feed (a baby) from a mother's breast

breast·plate \ˈbrest-ˌplāt, ˈbres-\ *n* : a metal plate worn as defensive armor for the chest

breast·stroke \ˈbrest-ˌstrōk, ˈbres-\ *n* : a swimming stroke performed by extending the arms in front of the head while drawing the knees forward and outward and then sweeping the arms back with palms out while kicking outward and backward

breast·work \ˈbres-ˌtwərk\ *n* : an improvised or temporary fortification

breath \ˈbreth\ *n* **1** : a slight indication : SUGGESTION **2 a** : the power of breathing **b** : an act of breathing **c** : RESPITE 2, BREATHER **3** : a slight breeze **4 a** : air inhaled and exhaled in breathing **b** : something (as moisture on a cold surface) produced by breathing **5** : a spoken sound : UTTERANCE **6** : expiration of air with the glottis wide open in the formation of speech sounds [Old English *brǣth*] — **out of breath** : breathing very rapidly (as from strenuous exercise)

breathe \ˈbrēth\ *vb* **1** : to draw air into and expel it from the lungs : RESPIRE **2** : LIVE 1 **3** : to blow softly **4** : to pause and rest before continuing **5 a** : to send out by exhaling **b** : to instill by or as if by breathing ⟨*breathe* new life into the movement⟩ **6** : UTTER, EXPRESS ⟨don't *breathe* a word of it⟩ **7** : to allow to rest after exertion ⟨*breathe* a horse⟩ **8** : to take in in breathing ⟨*breathe* the scent of roses⟩ **9** : to allow air or moisture to pass through ⟨a fabric that *breathes*⟩ — **breath·able** \ˈbrē-thə-bəl\ *adj*

breathed \ˈbretht\ *adj* : VOICELESS 2

breath·er \ˈbrē-thər\ *n* **1** : one that breathes **2** : a break in activity for rest

breath·ing \ˈbrē-thing\ *n* : either of the marks ʽ and ʼ used in writing Greek to indicate an initial h-sound or its absence

breath·less \ˈbreth-ləs\ *adj* **1 a** : not breathing **b** : DEAD **2** : gasping for breath : PANTING **b** : BREATHTAKING — **breath·less·ly** *adv* — **breath·less·ness** *n*

breath·tak·ing \ˈbreth-ˌtā-king\ *adj* **1** : making one out of breath ⟨a *breathtaking* climb⟩ **2** : of a kind to excite or thrill ⟨*breathtaking* beauty⟩ — **breath·tak·ing·ly** \-king-lē\ *adv*

brec·cia \ˈbrech-ə, -ē-ə\ *n* : a rock composed of sharp fragments embedded in a fine-grained material [Italian]

[1]**breech** \ˈbrēch; *"breeches" (garment) is usually* ˈbrich-əz\ *n* **1** *pl* **a** : short trousers fitting snugly at or just below the knee **b** : PANTS 1 **2** : BUTTOCK 2a **3** : the part of a firearm at the rear of the bore [Old English *brēc* "breeches," plural of *brōc* "leg covering"]

[2]**breech** *adj* : involving or being a fetus in which the buttocks or legs rather than the head are situated to emerge first through the birth canal ⟨a *breech* delivery⟩ — **breech** *adv*

breech·es buoy \ˈbrē-chəz- *also* ˈbrich-əz-\ *n* : a canvas sling in the form of a pair of short-legged breeches hung from a life buoy running along a rope that is used to take persons off a ship especially in rescue operations

breeches buoy

breech·load·er \ˈbrēch-ˌlōd-ər\ *n* : a firearm that receives its ammunition at the breech

[1]**breed** \ˈbrēd\ *vb* **bred** \ˈbred\; **breed·ing** **1 a** : BEGET 1 **b** : to be the source of ⟨wars *breed* depressions⟩ **2** : to propagate (plants or animals) sexually and usually under controlled conditions **3 a** : to bring up : NURTURE **b** : to instill by training **4** : to mate with **5** : to produce offspring sexually **6** : to produce (a fissionable element) by bombarding a nonfissionable element with neutrons from a radioactive element so that more fissionable material is produced than is used up [Old English *brēdan*] — **breed·er** *n*

[2]**breed** *n* **1** : a group of usually domesticated animals or plants presumably related by descent from common ancestors and visibly similar in most characters **2** : CLASS 3a, KIND

breed·ing *n* **1** : ANCESTRY **2** : training or education especially in manners **3** : the sexual propagation of plants or animals

breeding ground *n* **1** : the place where animals go to breed **2** : a place or situation that helps or allows something to grow or develop ⟨an expanse of warm ocean that is a *breeding ground* for hurricanes⟩

[1]**breeze** \ˈbrēz\ *n* **1 a** : a gentle wind **b** : a wind of from 4 to 31 miles (6 to 50 kilometers) an hour **2** : something easily done : CINCH [probably from Spanish *brisa* "northeast wind"]

[2]**breeze** *vi* : to proceed quickly and easily ⟨*breezed* past the reporters⟩ ⟨*breezed* through the test⟩

breeze·way \ˈbrēz-ˌwā\ *n* : a roofed open passage connecting two buildings (as a house and garage) or parts of a building

breezy \ˈbrē-zē\ *adj* **breez·i·er**; **-est** **1** : swept by breezes **2 a** : both lively and carefree ⟨a *breezy* manner⟩ **b** : NONCHALANT — **breez·i·ly** \-zə-lē\ *adv* — **breez·i·ness** \-zē-nəs\ *n*

\ə\ **abut**	\au̇\ **out**	\i\ **tip**	\ȯ\ **saw**	\u̇\ **foot**
\ər\ **further**	\ch\ **chin**	\ī\ **life**	\ȯi\ **coin**	\y\ **yet**
\a\ **mat**	\e\ **pet**	\j\ **job**	\th\ **thin**	\yü\ **few**
\ā\ **take**	\ē\ **easy**	\ng\ **sing**	\th\ **this**	\yu̇\ **cure**
\ä\ **cot, cart**	\g\ **go**	\ō\ **bone**	\ü\ **food**	\zh\ **vision**

breth·ren \ˈbret͟h-rən, -ərn, -ə-rən\ *plural of* BROTHER — used chiefly in formal or solemn address

Bret·on \ˈbret-ᵊn\ *n* **1 :** a native or inhabitant of Brittany **2 :** the Celtic language of the Bretons — **Breton** *adj*

breve \ˈbrēv, ˈbrev\ *n* **1 :** a mark ˘ placed over a vowel to show that the vowel is short **2 :** a note equivalent to four half notes [Latin, neuter of *brevis* "brief"]

bre·via·ry \ˈbrē-vyə-rē, -və-; -vē-ˌer-ē\ *n, pl* **-ries :** a book containing the prayers, hymns, and readings prescribed especially for priests for each day of the year [Medieval Latin *breviarium,* from Latin, "summary," from *brevis* "brief"]

brev·i·ty \ˈbrev-ət-ē\ *n* **1 :** shortness of duration **2 :** expression in few words : CONCISENESS

[1]**brew** \ˈbrü\ *vb* **1 :** to prepare (as beer or ale) by steeping, boiling, and fermentation **2 :** to form a plot or plan : CONTRIVE **3 :** to prepare (as tea) by steeping in hot water **4 :** to be forming ⟨a storm is *brewing*⟩ [Old English *brēowan*] — **brew·er** \ˈbrü-ər, ˈbru̇-ər, ˈbru̇r\ *n*

[2]**brew** *n* **1 :** a brewed beverage **2 :** a product of brewing

brewer's yeast *n* **:** a yeast used or suitable for use in brewing; *also* **:** the dried pulverized cells of such a yeast used as a source of B-complex vitamins — compare BAKER'S YEAST

brew·ery \ˈbrü-ə-rē, ˈbru̇-ər-ē, ˈbru̇r-ē\ *n, pl* **-er·ies :** a plant where malt liquors are manufactured

[1]**bri·ar** *or* **bri·er** \ˈbrī-ər, ˈbrīr\ *n* **:** a plant (as a blackberry or rose) with a thorny or prickly usually woody stem; *also* **:** a mass or twig of these [Old English *brēr* "thorny plant"] — **briary** *adj*

[2]**briar** *or* **brier** *n* **:** a tobacco pipe made from the root or stem of a European heath [short for *briar pipe,* from *briar* "wood of the European heath," from French *bruyère* "heath"]

[1]**bribe** \ˈbrīb\ *n* **:** money or favor given or promised to influence improperly the judgment or conduct of a person in a position of trust **2 :** something that serves to induce or influence [Middle English, "morsel given to a beggar, bribe," from Medieval French, "morsel"]

[2]**bribe** *vb* **:** to influence by or as if by giving bribes — **brib·able** \ˈbrī-bə-bəl\ *adj* — **brib·er** *n*

brib·ery \ˈbrī-bə-rē, -brē\ *n, pl* **-er·ies :** the act or practice of giving bribes

bric–a–brac \ˈbrik-ə-ˌbrak\ *n* **:** small ornamental articles : KNICKKNACKS [French *bric-à-brac*]

[1]**brick** \ˈbrik\ *n* **1 a** *pl* **bricks** *or* **brick :** a building or paving material made from clay molded into blocks and hardened in the sun or baked **b :** a rectangular block made of brick **2 :** a brick-shaped mass ⟨a *brick* of ice cream⟩ [Middle Dutch *bricke*]

[2]**brick** *vt* **:** to stop up, face, or pave with bricks

brick·bat \ˈbrik-ˌbat\ *n* **1 :** a piece of a broken brick; *esp* **:** one thrown as a missile **2 :** an uncomplimentary remark

brick·lay·er \ˈbrik-ˌlā-ər, -ˌle-ər -ˌler\ *n* **:** a person who builds or paves with bricks — **brick·lay·ing** \-ˌlā-ing\ *n*

brick·work \ˈbrik-ˌwərk\ *n* **:** work of or with brick

brick·yard \-ˌyärd\ *n* **:** a place where bricks are made

[1]**brid·al** \ˈbrīd-ᵊl\ *n* **:** a marriage ceremony : WEDDING [Old English *brȳdealu,* from *brȳd* "bride" + *ealu* "ale"]

[2]**bridal** *adj* **:** of or relating to a bride or a wedding : NUPTIAL

bridal wreath *n* **:** a spirea widely grown for its slender drooping branches and clusters of small white flowers borne in spring

bride \ˈbrīd\ *n* **:** a woman newly married or about to be married [Old English *brȳd*]

bride·groom \-ˌgrüm, -ˌgru̇m\ *n* **:** a man newly married or about to be married [Old English *brȳdguma,* from *brȳd* "bride" + *guma* "man"]

brides·maid \ˈbrīdz-ˌmād\ *n* **:** a woman who attends a bride at her wedding

[1]**bridge** \ˈbrij\ *n* **1 :** a structure built over a depression or an obstacle (as a river or a railroad) to allow passage **2 :** a platform above and across the deck of a ship for the captain or officer in charge **3 :** something resembling a bridge in form or function: as **a :** the upper bony part of the nose **b :** an arch serving to raise the strings of a musical instrument **c :** a musical passage linking two sections of a composition **4 :** something (as a partial denture anchored to adjacent teeth) that fills a gap [Old English *brycg*]

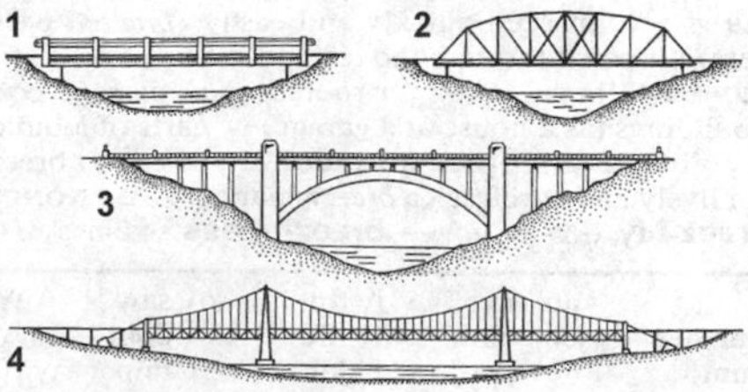

[1]bridge 1: *1* beam, *2* truss, *3* arch, *4* suspension

[2]**bridge** *vt* **:** to make a bridge over or across ⟨*bridge* a gap⟩ — **bridge·able** \-ə-bəl\ *adj*

[3]**bridge** *n* **:** any of various card games for four players developed from whist; *esp* **:** CONTRACT BRIDGE [earlier *biritch,* of unknown origin]

bridge·head \-ˌhed\ *n* **1 :** a fortified position protecting a bridge **2 :** a position seized in enemy territory as a foothold for further advance

bridge·work \-ˌwərk\ *n* **:** the dental bridges in a mouth

[1]**bri·dle** \ˈbrīd-ᵊl\ *n* **1 :** the headgear with which a horse is controlled consisting of a headstall, a bit, and reins **2 :** CURB 2, RESTRAINT [Old English *brīdel*]

[2]**bridle** *vb* **bri·dled; bri·dling** \ˈbrīd-ling, -ᵊl-ing\ **1 :** to put a bridle on **2 :** to restrain with or as if with a bridle **3 :** to show hostility or resentment especially by drawing back the head and chin

bridle path *n* **:** a trail suitable for horseback riding

[1]**brief** \ˈbrēf\ *adj* **1 :** short in duration or extent ⟨a *brief* visit⟩ **2 a :** expressed in few words : CONCISE **b :** CURT, ABRUPT [Medieval French, from Latin *brevis*] — **brief·ly** *adv* — **brief·ness** *n*

[2]**brief** *n* **1 a :** a brief summary of an argument, set of facts, or document **b :** a concise statement of the case a lawyer will present in court **2** *pl* **:** short snug underpants

[3]**brief** *vt* **1 :** to make a summary of **2 a :** to give final instructions to ⟨*brief* a flight crew⟩ **b :** to give essential information to ⟨*brief* reporters⟩

brief·case \-ˌkās\ *n* **:** an often flat flexible case (as of leather) for carrying papers

brier *variant of* BRIAR

[1]**brig** \ˈbrig\ *n* **:** a 2-masted square-rigged sailing vessel [short for *brigantine*]

[2]**brig** *n* **:** a place (as on a ship) for temporary confinement of offenders in the United States Navy [probably from [1]*brig*]

bri·gade \brig-ˈād\ *n* **1 :** a military unit composed of one or more units of infantry or armor with supporting units **2 :** a group of people organized for special activity ⟨fire *brigade*⟩ [French, from Italian *brigata,* from *brigare* "to fight"]

brig·a·dier \ˌbrig-ə-ˈdiər\ *n* **:** BRIGADIER GENERAL

brigadier general *n* **:** an officer rank in the Army, Marine Corps, and Air Force above colonel and below major general

brig·and \ˈbrig-ənd\ *n* **:** a person who lives by plunder usually as a member of a band : BANDIT [Medieval French, from Italian *brigante,* from *brigare* "to fight," from *briga* "strife," of Celtic origin] — **brig·and·age** \-ən-dij\ *n*

brig·an·tine \ˈbrig-ən-ˌtēn\ *n* **:** a 2-masted square-rigged sailing vessel differing from a brig in not carrying a square mainsail [Middle French *brigantin,* from Italian *brigantino,* from *brigante* "brigand"]

bright \ˈbrīt\ *adj* **1 :** shedding much light : SHINING, GLOWING ⟨a *bright* fire⟩ **2 :** very clear or vivid in color ⟨a *bright* red⟩ **3 :** quick in learning : INTELLIGENT **4 :** full of life : CHEERFUL **5 :** promising success ⟨a *bright* future⟩ [Old English *beorht*] — **bright** *adv* — **bright·ly** *adv* — **bright·ness** *n*

bright·en \ˈbrīt-ᵊn\ *vb* **bright·ened; bright·en·ing** \ˈbrīt-ning, -ᵊn-ing\ **:** to make or become bright or brighter

Bright's disease \ˈbrīts-\ *n* **:** kidney disease in which albumin appears in the urine [Richard *Bright,* died 1858, English physician]

brill \ˈbril\ *n, pl* **brill :** a European flatfish related to the turbot [Middle English *brell*]

[1]**bril·liant** \ˈbril-yənt\ *adj* **1 :** very bright : GLITTERING ⟨*brilliant* jewels⟩ **2 a :** outstandingly successful : DISTINGUISHED **b :** unusually keen or alert in mind [French *brillant,* from *briller* "to shine"] — **bril·liance** \-yəns\ *or* **bril·lian·cy** \-yən-sē\ *n* — **bril·liant·ly** *adv* — **bril·liant·ness** *n*

[2]**brilliant** *n* **:** a gem (as a diamond) cut with numerous facets so as to have particular brilliance

bril·lian·tine \ˈbril-yən-ˌtēn\ *n* **1 :** a preparation for making hair glossy **2 :** a light lustrous fabric similar to alpaca

[1]**brim** \ˈbrim\ *n* **1 :** the rim especially of a cup, bowl, or depres-

sion ⟨the *brim* of the crater⟩ **2 :** the projecting rim of a hat [Middle English *brimme*] ***synonyms*** see RIM — **brim·ful** \-ˈfu̇l\ *adj* — **brim·less** \-ləs\ *adj*
[2]**brim** *vb* **brimmed; brim·ming** **1 :** to fill or become filled to overflowing **2 :** to reach or overflow a brim
brim·stone \ˈbrim-ˌstōn\ *n* **:** SULFUR [Middle English *brinston,* probably from *birnen* "to burn" + *ston* "stone"]
brin·dle \ˈbrin-dl\ *n* **:** a brindled color or animal
brin·dled \-dld\ *or* **brin·dle** \-dl\ *adj* **:** having faint dark streaks or flecks on a gray or tawny ground ⟨a *brindled* cow⟩ [Middle English *brended*]
brine \ˈbrīn\ *n* **1 :** water containing a great deal of salt **2 :** the water of a sea or salt lake [Old English *brȳne*]
brine shrimp *n* **:** any of a genus of crustaceans found in salt lakes and the brine of saltworks
bring \ˈbring\ *vt* **brought** \ˈbrȯt\; **bring·ing** \ˈbring-ing\ **1 :** to cause to come with one by carrying or leading ⟨*bring* a lunch⟩ ⟨*bring* a friend⟩ **2 :** to cause to be, act, or move in a special way ⟨their screams *brought* the neighbors⟩ **3 :** to cause to come into a particular state or condition ⟨*bring* water to a boil⟩ **4 :** to cause to exist or occur ⟨winter will *bring* snow⟩ **5 :** to sell for ⟨these apples will *bring* a good price⟩ [Old English *bringan*] — **bring·er** \ˈbring-ər\ *n* — **bring forth :** to give birth to **:** BEAR, PRODUCE — **bring forward** **1 :** INTRODUCE ⟨*brought* new evidence *forward*⟩ **2 :** to carry (a total) forward (as in a checkbook) ⟨what is the balance *brought forward*⟩ — **bring to light :** to make known or visible — **bring to mind :** RECALL — **bring up the rear :** to come last or behind
synonyms BRING, TAKE may denote the same action performed in opposite directions in relation to the speaker. BRING implies carrying, leading, or transporting toward a point where the speaker is or will be. TAKE implies the same action away from the speaker ⟨*take* this message to the superintendent and *bring* back an answer⟩.
bring about *vt* **:** to cause to take place **:** ACCOMPLISH
bring around *vt* **1 :** to cause (someone) to adopt an opinion or a course of action **:** PERSUADE **2 :** to restore to consciousness **:** REVIVE
bring in *vt* **1 :** to produce as profit or return **2 :** INCLUDE 2, INTRODUCE ⟨*bring in* a new topic⟩ **3 :** EARN 2 ⟨*brings in* a good salary⟩
bring off *vt* **:** to carry to a successful conclusion **:** ACHIEVE ⟨I knew you could *bring* it *off*⟩
bring out *vt* **1 :** to develop fully ⟨a challenge seems to *bring out* your best⟩ **2 :** to present to the public ⟨*bring out* a new book⟩
bring to *vt* **:** to restore to consciousness **:** REVIVE
bring up *vb* **1 :** to bring to maturity through care and education ⟨*bring up* a child⟩ **2 :** to stop suddenly **3 :** to bring to attention **:** INTRODUCE
brink \ˈbringk\ *n* **1 :** EDGE; *esp* **:** the edge at the top of a steep place **2 :** the point of onset **:** VERGE ⟨on the *brink* of war⟩ [Middle English]
brink·man·ship \-mən-ˌship\ *also* **brinksmanship** *n* **:** the practice of pushing a dangerous situation to the limit of safety before stopping
briny \ˈbrī-nē\ *adj* **brin·i·er; -est :** of or resembling brine **:** SALTY — **brin·i·ness** *n*
brio \ˈbrē-ō\ *n* **:** VIVACITY, SPIRIT [Italian]
bri·quette *or* **bri·quet** \brik-ˈet\ *n* **:** a compacted often brick-shaped mass of usually fine material ⟨a charcoal *briquette*⟩ [French *briquette,* from *brique* "brick"]
bris *also* **briss** \ˈbris\ *n* **:** the Jewish rite of circumcision
[1]**brisk** \ˈbrisk\ *adj* **1 :** very active or alert **:** LIVELY **2 :** REFRESHING ⟨*brisk* autumn weather⟩ **3 :** full of energy **:** QUICK ⟨a *brisk* pace⟩ [probably from Middle French *brusque*] — **brisk·ly** *adv* — **brisk·ness** *n*
[2]**brisk** *vb* **:** to make or become brisk
bris·ket \ˈbris-kət\ *n* **:** the breast or lower chest of a quadruped animal; *also* **:** a cut of beef from the brisket [Middle English *brusket*]
bris·ling \ˈbriz-ling, ˈbris-\ *n* **:** SPRAT 1 [Norwegian *brisling*]
[1]**bris·tle** \ˈbris-əl\ *n* **:** a short stiff coarse hair or filament [Middle English *bristil,* from *brust* "bristle," from Old English *byrst*] — **bris·tled** \-əld\ *adj* — **bris·tly** \ˈbris-lē, -ə-lē\ *adj*
[2]**bristle** *vi* **bris·tled; bris·tling** \ˈbris-ling, -ə-ling\ **1 :** to rise and stand stiffly erect ⟨quills *bristling* in all directions⟩ **2 :** to show signs of anger or defiance ⟨people who *bristle* at criticism⟩ **3 :** to appear as if covered with bristles ⟨a harbor *bristling* with the masts of ships⟩

bris·tle·cone pine \ˈbris-əl-ˌkōn-\ *n* **:** either of two pines of the western U.S. that include the oldest living trees

bristlecone pine

bris·tle·tail \ˈbris-əl-ˌtāl\ *n* **:** any of various primitive wingless insects with three projecting tail bristles
bris·tol \ˈbris-tl\ *n* **:** cardboard with a smooth surface suitable for writing or printing — called also *bristol board* [*Bristol,* England]
brit *also* **britt** \ˈbrit\ *n* **:** tiny sea animals on which right whales feed [perhaps from Cornish *brȳthel* "mackerel"]
Bri·tan·nia metal \bri-ˈtan-yə-\ *n* **:** a silver-white alloy similar to pewter composed largely of tin, antimony, and copper [Latin *Britannia* "Britain"]
britch·es \ˈbrich-əz\ *n pl* **:** BREECHES, PANTS
Brit·i·cism \ˈbrit-ə-ˌsiz-əm\ *n* **:** a characteristic feature of British English [*Brit*ish + *-icism* (as in *gallicism*)]
[1]**Brit·ish** \ˈbrit-ish\ *n* **1** *pl in constr* **:** the people of Great Britain or their descendants **2 :** the English language characteristic of England
[2]**British** *adj* **1 :** of, relating to, or characteristic of the original inhabitants of Britain **2 a :** of, relating to, or characteristic of Great Britain or the British **b :** ENGLISH
Brit·ish·er \ˈbrit-i-shər\ *n* **:** BRITON 2
British thermal unit *n* **:** the quantity of heat required to raise the temperature of one pound of water one degree Fahrenheit at a specified temperature (as 39°F or 60°F) and equal to about 1055 joules — called also *Btu*
Brit·on \ˈbrit-n\ *n* **1 :** a member of one of the peoples inhabiting Britain previous to the Anglo-Saxon invasions **2 :** a native or subject of Great Britain
Brit·ta·ny spaniel \ˈbrit-n-ē-\ *n* **:** any of a French breed of medium-sized pointers that resemble spaniels in appearance — called also *Brittany*

Brittany spaniel

[1]**brit·tle** \ˈbrit-l\ *adj* **1 a :** easily broken, cracked, or snapped ⟨*brittle* clay⟩ **b :** not firm or substantial **:** FRAIL ⟨a *brittle* promise⟩ **2 :** lacking warmth, depth, or generosity of spirit ⟨a *brittle* selfish person⟩ [Middle English *britil*] — **brit·tle·ness** *n*
synonyms BRITTLE, CRISP, FRIABLE, FRAGILE mean tending to break easily. BRITTLE implies hardness without toughness or elasticity and susceptibility to snapping or fracture ⟨*brittle* bones⟩. CRISP suggests the light firmness and brittleness desirable in some foods as opposed to limpness or sogginess ⟨*crisp* lettuce⟩ ⟨*crisp* crackers⟩. FRIABLE is applied to substances that are readily crumbled or pulverized ⟨*friable* soil⟩. FRAGILE is applicable to anything that must be handled with care and implies delicacy of material or structure ⟨*fragile* china⟩.
[2]**brittle** *n* **:** a hard candy made with sugar and nuts and spread in thin sheets ⟨peanut *brittle*⟩
brittle star *n* **:** any of a group of echinoderms having slender flexible arms distinct from the central disk
bro \ˈbrō\ *n, pl* **bros** **1 :** BROTHER 1 **2 :** BROTHER 2
[1]**broach** \ˈbrōch\ *n* **1 :** any of various pointed or tapered tools, implements, or parts: as **a :** a spit for roasting meat **b :** a tool for tapping casks **c :** a cutting tool with a series of teeth in a straight line used especially for shaping a hole already bored **2**

: BROOCH [Medieval French *broche,* derived from Latin *broccus* "projecting"]

[2]**broach** *vb* **1** : to pierce (as a cask) in order to draw the contents : TAP **2** : to shape or enlarge (a hole) with a broach **3** : to introduce or make known for the first time ⟨*broach* a subject for discussion⟩ **4** : to break the surface from below ⟨saw a submarine *broaching*⟩ — **broach·er** *n*

broad \ˈbrȯd\ *adj* **1** : not narrow : WIDE ⟨a *broad* highway⟩ **2** : extending far and wide : SPACIOUS ⟨*broad* prairies⟩ **3** : being such to a full degree ⟨*broad* daylight⟩ **4** : PLAIN, OBVIOUS ⟨a *broad* hint⟩ **5** : COARSE 3, INDELICATE ⟨*broad* humor⟩ **6** : liberal in thought ⟨*broad* religious views⟩ **7** : not limited : extended in range or amount ⟨a *broad* choice of topics⟩ ⟨education in its *broadest* sense⟩ **8** : being main and essential ⟨*broad* outlines of a problem⟩ **9** : [3]LOW 12 — used specifically of *a* pronounced as in *father* [Old English *brād*] — **broad·ly** *adv* — **broad·ness** *n*

synonyms BROAD, WIDE mean having horizontal extent; they apply to a surface measured or viewed from side to side. BROAD is preferred when full horizontal extent is considered ⟨*broad* shoulders⟩. WIDE is commonly used with units of measure ⟨rugs eight feet *wide*⟩ or is applied to unfilled space between limits ⟨a *wide* view⟩ ⟨*wide* doorways⟩.

broad·ax *or* **broad·axe** \ˈbrȯ-ˌdaks\ *n* : an ax with a broad blade

broad·band \ˈbrȯd-ˌband\ *adj* : of, relating to, or being a high-speed communications network — **broadband** *n*

broad bean *n* : the large flat edible seed of an Old World upright vetch; *also* : this plant widely grown for its seeds and as fodder

[1]**broad·cast** \ˈbrȯd-ˌkast\ *adj* **1** : cast or scattered in all directions **2** : made public by means of radio or television — **broadcast** *adv*

[2]**broadcast** *vb* **-cast** *also* **-cast·ed; -cast·ing** **1** : to scatter or sow (as seed) over a broad area **2** : to make widely known **3 a** : to send out a broadcast from a radio or television transmitting station **b** : to speak or perform on a broadcast program — **broad·cast·er** *n*

[3]**broadcast** *n* **1** : the action of transmitting sound or images by radio or television **2** : a single radio or television program

broad·cloth \ˈbrȯd-ˌklȯth\ *n* **1** : a fine woolen cloth made compact and glossy in finishing **2** : a fine cloth (as of cotton or silk) with plain or ribbed weave

broad·en \ˈbrȯd-n\ *vb* **broad·ened; broad·en·ing** \ˈbrȯd-ning, -n-ing\ : to make or become broad or broader

broad jump *n* : LONG JUMP — **broad jumper** *n*

broad–leaved \-ˈlēvd\ *or* **broad·leaf** \-ˈlēf\ *also* **broad–leafed** \-ˈlēft\ *adj* **1** : having broad leaves; *esp* : having leaves that are not needles ⟨*broad-leaved* evergreens⟩ **2** : composed of broad-leaved plants ⟨*broad-leaved* forests⟩

broad·loom \-ˌlüm\ *adj* : woven on a wide loom ⟨*broadloom* carpets⟩ — **broadloom** *n*

broad–mind·ed \-ˈmīn-dəd\ *adj* **1** : tolerant of differing views **2** : inclined to tolerate minor departures from conventional behavior — **broad–mind·ed·ly** *adv* — **broad–mind·ed·ness** *n*

[1]**broad·side** \ˈbrȯd-ˌsīd\ *n* **1** : the part of a ship's side above the waterline **2 a** : all the guns that can be fired from the same side of a ship **b** : a discharge of all these guns together **3** : a storm of abuse : a strongly worded attack **4** : a sheet of paper printed on one or both sides; *also* : something (as a ballad or an advertisement) printed on a broadside

[2]**broadside** *adv* **1** : with one side forward ⟨turn *broadside*⟩ **2** : from the side ⟨hit the car *broadside*⟩ — **broadside** *adj*

broad–spectrum *adj* : effective against a wide range of organisms ⟨*broad-spectrum* antibiotics⟩

broad·sword \ˈbrȯd-ˌsōrd, -ˌsȯrd\ *n* : a sword with a broad blade for cutting rather than thrusting

broad·tail \-ˌtāl\ *n* : the fur or skin of a premature or newborn karakul lamb characterized by a flat and wavy appearance resembling moiré silk — compare PERSIAN LAMB

Broad·way \ˈbrȯd-ˌwā\ *n* : the world of the theater in New York City : the New York stage ⟨a big star on *Broadway*⟩ [*Broadway,* street in New York City] — **Broadway** *adj*

Brob·ding·nag·ian \ˌbräb-ding-ˈnag-ē-ən, -dig-\ *adj* : very large : TREMENDOUS [*Brobdingnag,* country inhabited by giants in *Gulliver's Travels* by Jonathan Swift]

bro·cade \brō-ˈkād\ *n* : a heavy fabric (as of silk) with raised interwoven patterns [Spanish *brocado,* derived from Italian *broccare* "to spur, weave brocade patterns," from *brocco* "small nail," from Latin *broccus* "projecting"] — **bro·cad·ed** \-ˈkād-əd\ *adj*

broc·co·li \ˈbräk-lē, -ə-lē\ *n* : an open branching form of cauliflower that bears young green flowering shoots used as a vegetable [Italian, derived from *brocco* "small nail, sprout"]

bro·chette \brō-ˈshet\ *n* : a small spit : SKEWER [French, derived from Medieval French *broche* "pointed tool"]

bro·chure \brō-ˈshu̇r\ *n* : PAMPHLET; *esp* : one containing descriptive or advertising material [French, from *brocher* "to sew," derived from Medieval French *broche* "pointed tool"]

bro·gan \ˈbrō-gən, brō-ˈgan\ *n* : a heavy shoe; *esp* : a work shoe reaching to the ankle [Irish *brógán,* from *bróg*]

[1]**brogue** \ˈbrōg\ *n* **1** : a heavy shoe often with a hobnailed sole : BROGAN **2** : a sturdy oxford with an ornamental toe cap [Irish *bróg* and Scottish Gaelic *bròg*]

[2]**brogue** *n* : a dialect or regional pronunciation; *esp* : an Irish accent [Irish *barróg* "accent, speech impediment," literally, "wrestling hold"]

broi·der \ˈbrȯid-ər\ *vt* : EMBROIDER — **broi·dery** \ˈbrȯid-rē, -ə-rē\ *n*

[1]**broil** \ˈbrȯil\ *vb* **1** : to cook or become cooked by direct exposure to radiant heat **2** : to subject to great heat ⟨*broiling* in the sun⟩ [Medieval French *bruiller* "to burn, broil"]

[2]**broil** *vi* : BRAWL 1 [Medieval French *broiller* "to jumble, mix"]

[3]**broil** *n* : a confused or noisy disturbance; *esp* : BRAWL

broil·er \ˈbrȯi-lər\ *n* **1** : a rack and pan or an oven equipped with a rack and pan for broiling meats **2** : a young chicken suitable for broiling

[1]**broke** *past of* BREAK

[2]**broke** \ˈbrōk\ *adj* : having no money : PENNILESS [Middle English, from *broken*]

bro·ken \ˈbrō-kən\ *adj* **1** : shattered into pieces ⟨*broken* glass⟩ **2 a** : RUGGED 1, ROUGH ⟨*broken* terrain⟩ **b** : having gaps or breaks ⟨a *broken* line⟩ **3** : not kept ⟨a *broken* promise⟩ **4** : SUBDUED, CRUSHED ⟨a *broken* spirit⟩ **5 a** : lacking continuity : FRAGMENTARY **b** : imperfectly spoken ⟨*broken* English⟩ **6** : having undergone or been subjected to fracture ⟨a *broken* leg⟩ **7** : having one parent missing (as because of divorce) ⟨children from *broken* homes⟩ [Old English *brocen,* past participle of *brecan* "to break"] — **bro·ken·ly** *adv* — **bro·ken·ness** \-kən-nəs\ *n*

broken–down *adj* : WORN-OUT, WEAK

bro·ken·heart·ed \ˌbrō-kən-ˈhärt-əd\ *adj* : overcome by grief or despair

bro·ker \ˈbrō-kər\ *n* : a person who acts as an agent in the purchase and sale of property [Middle English, "negotiator"]

bro·ker·age \ˈbrō-kə-rij, -krij\ *n* **1** : the business of a broker **2** : the fee or commission charged by a broker

bro·me·li·ad \brō-ˈmē-lē-ˌad\ *n* : any of various chiefly tropical American plants (as the pineapple and Spanish moss) that often grow on the surface of other plants [Olaf *Bromelius,* died 1705, Swedish botanist]

bromeliad

bro·mide \ˈbrō-ˌmīd\ *n* **1** : any of various compounds of bromine with another element or a radical including some (as potassium bromide) used as sedatives **2 a** : a commonplace or tiresome person : BORE **b** : a commonplace or trite expression or idea

Word History The word *bromide* is derived from *bromine.* Several compounds of bromine, especially potassium bromide, are used as sedatives. They can calm a nervous, restless person and help that person to get to sleep. *Bromide* has come to be used too for a boring or tiresome talker, who can often put listeners to sleep as effectively as any drug.

bro·mid·ic \brō-ˈmid-ik\ *adj* : DULL, TRITE ⟨*bromidic* remarks⟩

bro·mine \ˈbrō-ˌmēn\ *n* : an element that is a deep red corrosive toxic liquid giving off an irritating reddish brown vapor of disagreeable odor — see ELEMENT table [derived from Greek *brōmos* "bad smell"]

brom·thy·mol blue \ˌbrōm-ˈthī-ˌmȯl-, -ˌmōl-\ *n* : a dye derived from thymol that is an acid-base indicator — called also *bro·mo·thy·mol blue* \ˌbrō-mō-ˈthī-ˌmȯl-, -ˌmōl-\

bronc \ˈbräŋk\ *n* : BRONCO

bron·chi·al \ˈbräŋ-kē-əl\ *adj* : of, relating to, or involving the bronchi or their branches

bronchial tube *n* : a primary bronchus or any of its branches

bron·chi·ole \ˈbräŋ-kē-ˌōl\ *n* : a tiny thin-walled branch of a bronchial tube

bron·chi·tis \brän-ˈkīt-əs, bräŋ-\ *n* : acute or chronic inflammation of the bronchial tubes or a disease marked by this — **bron·chit·ic** \-ˈkit-ik\ *adj*

bron·cho·pneu·mo·nia \ˌbräŋ-kō-nu̇-ˈmō-nyə, -nü-, ˌbrän-\ *n* : pneumonia involving many relatively small areas of lung tissue — called also *bronchial pneumonia*

bron·chus \ˈbräŋ-kəs\ *n, pl* **bron·chi** \ˈbrän-ˌkī, ˈbräŋ-, -ˌkē\ : either of the main divisions of the trachea each leading to a lung [Greek *bronchos* "windpipe"]

bron·co \ˈbräŋ-kō, ˈbrän-\ *n, pl* **broncos** : an untamed or partly tamed range horse of western North America; *also* : MUSTANG [Mexican Spanish, from Spanish, "rough, wild"]

bron·co·bust·er \-ˌbəs-tər\ *n* : a person who breaks wild horses to the saddle

bron·to·sau·rus \ˌbränt-ə-ˈsȯr-əs\ *also* **bron·to·saur** \ˈbränt-ə-ˌsȯr\ *n* : any of several very large four-footed herbivorous dinosaurs of the Jurassic period — called also *apatosaurus, thunder lizard* [Greek *brontē* "thunder" + *sauros* "lizard"]

Bronx cheer \ˈbräŋks-\ *n* : RASPBERRY 2

[1]**bronze** \ˈbränz\ *vt* : to give the appearance of bronze to

[2]**bronze** *n* **1** : an alloy of copper and tin and sometimes other elements (as zinc) **2** : a work of art (as a statue, bust, or medallion) made of bronze **3** : a moderate yellowish brown **4** : a bronze medal awarded as the third prize in a competition [French, from Italian *bronzo*] — **bronzy** \ˈbrän-zē\ *adj*

Bronze Age *n* : a period of human culture characterized by the use of bronze (as for weapons and tools) that began between 4000 and 3000 B.C.

brooch \ˈbrōch, ˈbrüch\ *n* : an ornamental clasp or pin [Middle English *broche* "pointed tool, brooch"]

[1]**brood** \ˈbrüd\ *n* **1** : a family of young animals or children; *esp* : the young (as of a bird) hatched or cared for at one time **2** : a group having a common nature or origin [Old English *brōd*]

[2]**brood** *vb* **1** : to sit on eggs in order to hatch them **2** : to cover young with the wings **3** : to think anxiously or gloomily upon a subject : PONDER ⟨*brooded* over his mistake⟩ **4** : to hover over : LOOM ⟨*brooding* clouds⟩ — **brood·ing·ly** \-iŋ-lē\ *adv*

[3]**brood** *adj* : kept for breeding ⟨a *brood* mare⟩ ⟨a *brood* flock⟩

brood·er \ˈbrüd-ər\ *n* **1** : one that broods **2** : a heated structure used for raising young fowl

broody \ˈbrüd-ē\ *adj* **1** : physiologically ready to brood eggs **2** : inclined to brood : MOODY — **brood·i·ness** *n*

[1]**brook** \ˈbru̇k\ *vt* : to put up with : BEAR, TOLERATE ⟨*brooks* no interference⟩ [Old English *brūcan* "to use, enjoy"]

[2]**brook** *n* : CREEK 2 [Old English *brōc*]

brook·let \ˈbru̇k-lət\ *n* : a small brook

brook trout *n* : a common speckled cold-water char of eastern North America

broom \ˈbrüm, ˈbru̇m\ *n* **1** : a plant of the legume family with long slender branches along which grow many drooping yellow flowers **2** : a usually long-handled brush used for sweeping and originally made from twigs of broom [Old English *brōm*]

broom·corn \-ˌkȯrn\ *n* : a tall cultivated sorghum whose stiff branched flower clusters are used in brooms and brushes

broom·stick \-ˌstik\ *n* : the handle of a broom

bros *plural of* BRO

broth \ˈbrȯth\ *n, pl* **broths** \ˈbrȯths, ˈbrȯt͟hz\ **1** : liquid in which food has been cooked : STOCK **2** : a fluid culture medium [Old English]

broth·el \ˈbräth-əl, ˈbrȯth-\ *n* : an establishment in which prostitutes are available [Middle English, "worthless fellow, prostitute," derived from Old English *brēothan* "to waste away"]

broth·er \ˈbrət͟h-ər\ *n, pl* **brothers** *also* **breth·ren** \ˈbret͟h-rən, -ərn, -ə-rən\ **1** : a male who has one or both parents in common with another **2** : one related to another by common ties (as of race or interests) **3** : a fellow member — used as a title for ministers in some evangelical denominations ⟨*Brother* Smith⟩ **4** : KINSMAN **5** : a man who is a religious but not a priest ⟨a lay *brother*⟩ [Old English *brōthor*]

broth·er·hood \ˈbrət͟h-ər-ˌhu̇d\ *n* **1** : the state of being brothers or a brother **2** : an association (as a labor union) for a particular purpose **3** : the whole body of persons engaged in a business or profession : FRATERNITY

broth·er–in–law \ˈbrət͟h-rən-ˌlȯ, -ə-rən-, ˈbrət͟h-ərn-ˌlȯ\ *n, pl* **broth·ers–in–law** \ˈbrət͟h-ər-zən-\ **1** : the brother of one's spouse **2** : the husband of one's sister

broth·er·ly \ˈbrət͟h-ər-lē\ *adj* **1** : of or relating to brothers **2** : natural or becoming to brothers : AFFECTIONATE ⟨*brotherly* love⟩ ⟨*brotherly* rivalry⟩ — **broth·er·li·ness** *n*

brougham \ˈbrü-əm, ˈbrüm, ˈbrō-əm\ *n* : a light closed horse-drawn carriage with the driver outside in front [Henry Peter *Brougham*, Baron Brougham and Vaux, died 1868, Scottish jurist]

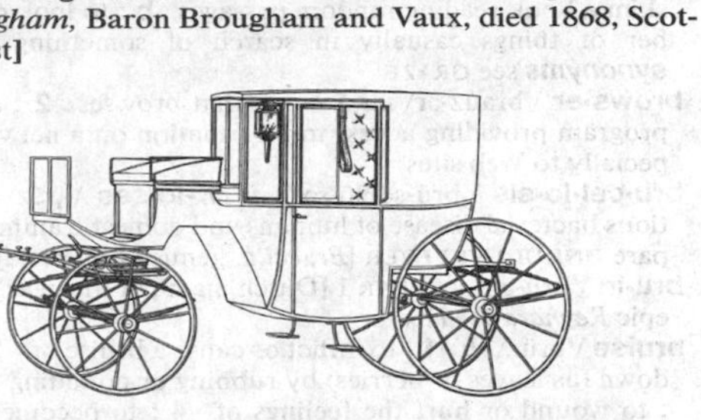

brougham

brought *past and past participle of* BRING

brou·ha·ha \ˈbrü-ˌhä-ˌhä, ˌbrü-ˌhä-ˈhä, brü-ˈhä-ˌhä\ *n* : HUBBUB, UPROAR [French]

brow \ˈbrau̇\ *n* **1 a** : EYEBROW **b** : FOREHEAD 1 **2** : the edge or projecting upper part of a steep slope [Old English *brū*]

brow·beat \ˈbrau̇-ˌbēt\ *vt* **-beat; -beat·en** \-ˌbēt-n\; **-beat·ing** : to frighten by a stern manner or threatening speech

[1]**brown** \ˈbrau̇n\ *adj* : of the color brown; *also* : of dark or tanned complexion [Old English *brūn*]

[2]**brown** *n* : any of a group of dull colors between red and yellow in hue — **brown·ish** \ˈbrau̇-nish\ *adj*

[3]**brown** *vb* : to make or become brown

brown alga *n* : any of a division (Phaeophyta) of mostly marine algae with chlorophyll masked by brown pigment

brown–bag \ˈbrau̇n-ˌbag\ *vb* : to carry one's lunch usually in a brown paper bag ⟨*brown-bagging* it to the game⟩ — **brown–bag** *adj*

brown bear *n* : any of several bears that are mostly brown in color, are usually considered a single species including the grizzly bear, and at one time inhabited much of western North America from Alaska to northern Mexico as well as much of Europe and Asia

brown coal *n* : LIGNITE

brown dwarf *n* : an astronomical object much smaller and dimmer than a normal star

Brown·i·an motion \ˈbrau̇-nē-ən-\ *n* : a random movement of microscopic particles suspended in liquids or gases that results from the impact of molecules of the fluid on the particles — called also *Brownian movement* [Robert *Brown*, died 1858, Scottish botanist]

brown·ie \ˈbrau̇-nē\ *n* **1** : a good-natured sprite who performs helpful services at night **2** : a member of the Girl Scouts of the United States of America from six through eight years of age **3** : a small rectangle of rich usually chocolate cake often containing nuts

brown·out \ˈbrau̇-ˌnau̇t\ *n* : a reduction in the use or availability of electric power; *also* : a period of dimmed lighting resulting from such reduction

brown rat *n* : the common rat found especially about human dwellings that is native to Asia but has spread throughout the world

brown recluse spider *n* : a venomous spider especially of the southern and central U.S. that has a dark violin-shaped mark on the cephalothorax

brown·stone \ˈbrau̇n-ˌstōn\ *n* **1** : a reddish brown sandstone used for building **2** : a dwelling faced with brownstone

brown study *n* : a state of deep absorption in thought

brown sugar *n* : soft sugar whose crystals are covered by a film of refined dark syrup

\ə\ abut	\au̇\ **out**	\i\ tip	\ȯ\ saw	\u̇\ foot
\ər\ further	\ch\ **chin**	\ī\ life	\ȯi\ coin	\y\ yet
\a\ mat	\e\ pet	\j\ job	\th\ **thin**	\yü\ few
\ā\ take	\ē\ easy	\ŋ\ sing	\t͟h\ **this**	\yu̇\ cure
\ä\ cot, cart	\g\ go	\ō\ bone	\ü\ food	\zh\ vision

brown trout *n* : a speckled European trout widely introduced as a game fish

brow·ridge \'braủ-ˌrij\ *n* : a prominent ridge on the bone above the eye caused by sinuses in the skull

¹browse \'braủz\ *n* **1** : tender shoots, twigs, and leaves of trees and shrubs used by animals for food **2** : an act or instance of browsing [probably from Medieval French *brouts* "sprouts"]

²browse *vb* **1** : to nibble or feed on leaves and shoots **2 a** : to skim a book reading random passages **b** : to look over a number of things casually in search of something of interest ***synonyms*** see GRAZE

brows·er \'braủ-zər\ *n* **1** : one that browses **2** : a computer program providing access to information on a network and especially to Web sites

bru·cel·lo·sis \ˌbrü-sə-'lō-səs\ *n, pl* **-lo·ses** \-ˌsēz\ : an infectious bacterial disease of humans and domestic animals — compare UNDULANT FEVER [*Brucella,* genus of bacteria]

bru·in \'brü-ən\ *n* : BEAR 1 [Dutch, name of the bear in the beast epic *Reynard the Fox*]

¹bruise \'brüz\ *vb* **1** : to inflict or cause a bruise on **2** : to break down (as leaves or berries) by rubbing or pounding : CRUSH **3** : to wound or hurt the feelings of **4** : to become bruised or show bruises [partly from Medieval French *bruiser, briser* "to break," of Celtic origin; partly from Old English *brȳsan* "to bruise"]

²bruise *n* **1** : an injury (as from a blow) in which the skin is not broken but is discolored from the breaking of small underlying blood vessels : CONTUSION **2** : an injury to a plant or fruit that resembles a bruise

bruis·er \'brü-zər\ *n* : a big husky person

bruis·ing \'brü-ziŋ\ *adj* : ARDUOUS ⟨a long and *bruising* courtroom battle⟩

¹bruit \'brüt\ *n, archaic* : REPORT, RUMOR [Medieval French, "noise"]

²bruit *vt* : REPORT, RUMOR

brunch \'brənch\ *n* : a late breakfast, an early lunch, or a combination of the two [*breakfast* + *lunch*]

bru·net *or* **bru·nette** \brü-'net\ *adj* : of dark or relatively dark complexion; *esp* : having brown or black hair and eyes [French, derived from Medieval French *brun* "brown," of Germanic origin] — **brunet** *or* **brunette** *n*

brung \'brəŋ\ *chiefly dialect past and past participle of* BRING

brunt \'brənt\ *n* : the main force of a blow or an attack : the heaviest shock, stress, or strain ⟨coastal towns bore the *brunt* of the storm⟩ [Middle English]

bru·schet·ta \brü-'shet-ə; -'sket-\ *n* : thick slices of bread grilled, rubbed with garlic, sprinkled with olive oil, often topped with tomatoes and herbs, and usually served as an appetizer [It]

¹brush \'brəsh\ *n* **1** : BRUSHWOOD **2** : scrubby vegetation; *also* : land covered with this [Medieval French *broce* "brushwood"]

²brush *n* **1** : a device composed of bristles set into a handle and used especially for sweeping, smoothing, scrubbing, or painting **2** : a bushy tail (as of a fox or squirrel) **3** : an electrical conductor that makes sliding contact between a moving and a nonmoving part of an electric motor or generator **4 a** : an act of brushing **b** : a quick light touch or momentary contact [Medieval French *broisse*]

³brush *vb* **1 a** : to apply a brush to **b** : to apply with a brush **2 a** : to remove with or as if with a brush **b** : to dispose of in an offhand way : DISMISS ⟨*brushed* my protest aside⟩ **3** : to pass lightly across : touch gently in passing — **brush·er** *n*

⁴brush *n* : a brief encounter or skirmish ⟨a *brush* with disaster⟩ [*⁵brush*]

⁵brush *vi* : to move quickly or without paying attention ⟨*brushed* past the receptionist⟩ [probably from Medieval French *brosser* "to dash through underbrush," from *broce* "brushwood"]

brush–off \'brəsh-ˌȯf\ *n* : an abrupt or offhand dismissal

brush up *vb* : to refresh one's memory of : renew one's skill in ⟨*brush up* on your Spanish⟩

brush·wood \'brəsh-ˌwủd\ *n* **1** : small branches cut from trees or shrubs **2** : a thicket of shrubs and small trees

¹brushy \'brəsh-ē\ *adj* **brush·i·er; -est** : SHAGGY 1, ROUGH

²brushy *adj* **brush·i·er; -est** : covered with or abounding in brush or brushwood

brusque \'brəsk\ *adj* : unpleasantly curt in manner or speech ⟨spoke in a *brusque* tone⟩ [French, from Italian *brusco,* from Medieval Latin *bruscus,* a kind of plant with stiff branches] — **brusque·ly** *adv* — **brusque·ness** *n*

brus·sels sprout \'brəs-əlz-\ *n, often cap B* : one of the edible small green heads borne on the stem of a plant related to the cabbage; *also* : this plant [*Brussels,* Belgium]

bru·tal \'brüt-l\ *adj* : befitting a brute: as **a** : lacking all mercy ⟨a *brutal* criticism⟩ **b** : causing injury or misery ⟨a *brutal* attack⟩ **c** : HARSH 3, SEVERE ⟨*brutal* weather⟩ **d** : very bad or unpleasant ⟨a *brutal* mistake⟩ — **bru·tal·ly** \-l-ē\ *adv*

synonyms BRUTAL, BRUTE, BRUTISH mean characteristic of an animal in nature, action, or instinct. BRUTAL applies only to human behavior, stresses lack of humanity, and always implies moral condemnation ⟨a senseless and *brutal* war⟩. BRUTE stresses crude force or strength in contrast with skill or intelligence ⟨*brute* forces of nature⟩. BRUTISH stresses likeness to an animal in low intelligence and instinctual appetites and behavior ⟨*brutish* stupidity⟩.

bru·tal·i·ty \brü-'tal-ət-ē\ *n, pl* **-ties** **1** : the quality or state of being brutal **2** : a brutal act or course of action

bru·tal·ize \'brüt-l-ˌīz\ *vt* **1** : to make brutal, unfeeling, or inhuman **2** : to treat brutally — **bru·tal·i·za·tion** \ˌbrüt-l-ə-'zā-shən\ *n*

¹brute \'brüt\ *adj* **1** : of, relating to, or typical of lower animals as distinguished from humans **2** : resembling an animal in quality, action, or instinct: as **a** : irrationally cruel : SAVAGE **b** : not working by reason ⟨*brute* instinct⟩ **c** : wholly physical ⟨*brute* strength⟩ [Medieval French *brut* "rough," from Latin *brutus* "brutish," literally, "heavy"] ***synonyms*** see BRUTAL

²brute *n* **1** : BEAST 1 **2** : a brutal person

brut·ish \'brüt-ish\ *adj* **1** : resembling, befitting, or typical of a brute or beast **2 a** : grossly sensual : ANIMAL 6 ⟨*brutish* gluttony⟩ **b** : UNREASONING, IRRATIONAL ***synonyms*** see BRUTAL — **brut·ish·ly** *adv* — **brut·ish·ness** *n*

bry·ol·o·gy \brī-'äl-ə-jē\ *n* : a branch of botany that deals with mosses and liverworts [Greek *bryon* "moss"]

bry·o·ny \'brī-ə-nē\ *n, pl* **-nies** : any of a genus of tendril-bearing vines of the gourd family with large leaves, red or black fruit, and a cathartic root [Greek *bryōnia*]

bry·o·phyl·lum \ˌbrī-ə-'fil-əm\ *n* : KALANCHOE

bry·o·phyte \'brī-ə-ˌfīt\ *n* : any of a division (Bryophyta) of nonflowering green plants comprising the mosses and liverworts [Greek *bryon* "moss" + *phyton* "plant"] — **bry·o·phyt·ic** \ˌbrī-ə-'fit-ik\ *adj*

bry·o·zo·an \ˌbrī-ə-'zō-ən\ *n* : any of a phylum (Bryozoa) of aquatic mostly marine invertebrate animals that usually form branching or mosslike colonies and reproduce by budding [Greek *bryon* "moss" + *zōion* "animal"] — **bryozoan** *adj*

Btu \ˌbē-ˌtē-'yü\ *n* : BRITISH THERMAL UNIT

¹bub·ble \'bəb-əl\ *n* **1** : a small typically hollow and light globule: as **a** : a small body of gas within a liquid **b** : a thin film of liquid inflated with air or gas ⟨a soap *bubble*⟩ **c** : a globule in a transparent solid ⟨a *bubble* in glass⟩ **2 a** : something that lacks firmness, solidity, or reality **b** : a delusive scheme **3** : a sound like that of bubbling **4** : MAGNETIC BUBBLE [Middle English *bobel*]

²bubble *vb* **bub·bled; bub·bling** \'bəb-liŋ, -ə-liŋ\ **1** : to form bubbles **2** : to flow with a gurgling sound ⟨a brook *bubbling* over rocks⟩ **3 a** : to utter as though giving off bubbles ⟨*bubbling* praise of the new teacher⟩ **b** : to be or become lively ⟨*bubbling* with joy⟩ **4 a** : to cause to bubble **b** : BURP 2

bubble chamber *n* : a chamber of heated liquid in which the path of an ionizing particle is made visible by a string of vapor bubbles

bubble gum *n* : a chewing gum that can be blown into large bubbles

bubble memory *n* : a computer memory that uses magnetic bubbles to store information

bub·bler \'bəb-lər, -ə-lər\ *n* : a drinking fountain from which a stream of water bubbles upward

bub·bly \'bəb-lē, -ə-lē\ *adj* **bub·bli·er; -est** **1** : full of bubbles : EFFERVESCENT ⟨a *bubbly* bottle of soda pop⟩ **2** : full of or showing good spirits : LIVELY **3** : resembling a bubble

bu·bo \'bü-bō, 'byü-\ *n, pl* **buboes** : an inflammatory swelling of a lymph node especially in the groin [Medieval Latin, from Greek *boubōn*] — **bu·bon·ic** \bü-'bän-ik, byü-\ *adj*

bubonic plague *n* : a form of plague spread chiefly from rats to humans by fleas and characterized especially by chills, fever, weakness, and the formation of buboes

buc·cal \'bək-əl\ *adj* : of, relating to, near, or being the surface of a tooth next to the cheek [Latin *bucca* "cheek"] — **buc·cal·ly** \-ē\ *adv*

buc·ca·neer \ˌbək-ə-ˈniər\ *n* : PIRATE [French *boucanier*] — **buccaneer** *vi*

[1]**buck** \ˈbək\ *n, pl* **bucks** **1** *or pl* **buck** : a male animal; *esp* : a male deer or antelope **2 a** : a male human being : MAN **b** : DANDY 1 **3 a** : BUCKSKIN; *also* : an article made of buckskin **b (1)** : DOLLAR 3b **(2)** : a sum of money especially to be gained ‹make a quick *buck*›; *also* : MONEY — usually used in plural **4 a** : a supporting rack or frame **b** : a short thick leather-covered block for gymnastic vaulting [Old English *bucca* "stag, he-goat"]

[2]**buck** *vb* **1 a** : to spring into the air with the back arched ‹a *bucking* horse› **b** : to throw (as a rider) by bucking **2 a** : to move or act forcefully in opposition to ‹*bucking* a storm› **b** : to stand firm in opposition to : RESIST ‹determined to *buck* city hall› **3** : to start, move, or react jerkily **4** : to strive for advancement or promotion ‹*bucking* for sergeant› — **buck·er** *n*

[3]**buck** *n* : an act or instance of bucking

[4]**buck** *n* : RESPONSIBILITY ‹pass the *buck*› ‹the *buck* stops here› [short for *buckhorn knife,* formerly used in poker to mark the next player to deal]

[5]**buck** *adj* : of the lowest grade within a military category ‹*buck* private› [probably from [1]*buck*]

[6]**buck** *adv* : WHOLLY, COMPLETELY ‹*buck* naked› [origin unknown]

buck·a·roo *also* **buck·er·oo** \ˌbək-ə-ˈrü\ *n, pl* **-aroos** *also* **-eroos** **1** : COWBOY **2** : BRONCOBUSTER [Spanish *vaquero,* from *vaca* "cow," from Latin *vacca*]

buck·board \ˈbək-ˌbōrd, -ˌbȯrd\ *n* : a four-wheeled horse-drawn vehicle with a floor made of long springy boards [obsolete English *buck* "body of a wagon"]

[1]**buck·et** \ˈbək-ət\ *n* **1** : a typically round vessel for catching, holding, or carrying liquids or solids **2** : an object resembling a bucket in collecting, scooping, or carrying something: as **a** : the scoop of an excavating machine **b** : one of the vanes of a turbine rotor **3** : BUCKETFUL [Anglo-French *buket,* from Old English *būc* "pitcher"]

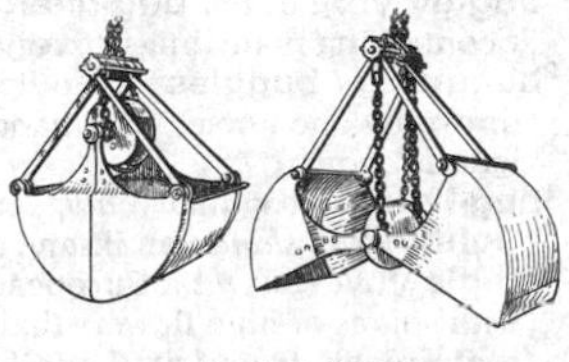

bucket 2a

[2]**bucket** *vb* **1** : to draw or lift in or as if in buckets **2** : HUSTLE 2, HURRY **3 a** : to go about haphazardly or irresponsibly **b** : to move roughly or jerkily

bucket brigade *n* : a chain of persons acting to put out a fire by passing buckets of water from hand to hand

buck·et·ful \ˈbək-ət-ˌfu̇l\ *n, pl* **buck·et·fuls** \-ət-ˌfu̇lz\ *or* **buck·ets·ful** \-əts-ˌfu̇l\ : the amount held by a bucket; *also* : a large quantity

bucket seat *n* : a low individual seat used chiefly in automobiles and airplanes

bucket shop *n* : a dishonest brokerage house [earlier, a saloon in which liquor was sold in buckets or pitchers]

buck·eye \ˈbək-ˌī\ *n* : any of several trees or shrubs related to the horse chestnut; *also* : its large nutlike seed

buck fever *n* : nervous excitement of an inexperienced hunter at the sight of game

[1]**buck·le** \ˈbək-əl\ *n* **1** : a fastening for two loose ends that is attached to one and holds the other by a catch **2** : an ornamental device that suggests a buckle ‹silver shoe *buckles*› [Medieval French *boucle* "boss of a shield, buckle," derived from Latin *bucca* "cheek"]

Word History The literal meaning of Latin *buccula* was "little cheek," but *buccula* was also the name for the part of a helmet that protects the cheek. Its Medieval French descendant, *boucle,* was the word for the boss of a shield, which looks a little like a small cheek on the face of the shield. The use of the word was later extended to belt fasteners. In this sense, the word was borrowed into English.

[2]**buckle** *vb* **buck·led; buck·ling** \ˈbək-ling, -ə-ling\ **1** : to fasten a buckle or with a buckle ‹*buckle* your seat belt› **2** : to apply oneself with vigor ‹*buckle* down to a job› **3** : to bend, warp, or kink usually under the influence of some external agency ‹the pavement *buckled* in the heat› ‹knees *buckling* from fatigue› **4** : to give way : YIELD ‹he *buckled* under pressure›

[3]**buckle** *n* : a product of buckling : BEND, FOLD

buck·ler \ˈbək-lər\ *n* **1** : SHIELD 1; *esp* : a small round shield used to parry blows **2** : one that shields and protects

buck·min·ster·ful·ler·ene \ˈbək-ˌmin-stər-ˌfu̇l-ə-ˈrēn\ *n* : a spherical molecule composed of 60 carbon atoms that is a very stable form of pure carbon [*Buckminster Fuller,* died 1983, American engineer; from the resemblance of the molecules to the geodesic domes designed by Fuller]

buck passer *n* : a person who habitually evades responsibility — **buck–pass·ing** \ˈbək-ˌpas-ing\ *n*

buck·ram \ˈbək-rəm\ *n* : a stiff-finished heavily sized fabric of cotton or linen used in garments, millinery, and bookbindings [Medieval French *bokeram, boquerant,* derived from *Bokhara,* city in central Asia] — **buckram** *adj*

buck·saw \ˈbək-ˌsȯ\ *n* : a saw set in a usually H-shaped frame and used for sawing wood on a sawhorse

buck·shot \-ˌshät\ *n, pl* **buckshot** *or* **buckshots** : coarse lead shot used in shotgun shells

buck·skin \-ˌskin\ *n* **1 a** : the skin of a buck **b** : a soft pliable usually suede-finished leather **2** *pl* : buckskin breeches **3** : a horse of a light yellowish dun color with black mane and tail

buck·thorn \-ˌthȯrn\ *n* : any of a genus of often thorny trees or shrubs some of which yield purgatives or pigments

buck·tooth \-ˈtüth\ *n* : a large protruding front tooth — **buck–toothed** \-ˈtütht\ *adj*

buck up *vb* : to become or cause to become encouraged : cheer up

buck·wheat \ˈbək-ˌhwēt\ *n* : either of two herbs with white or greenish flowers that are grown for their triangular seeds which are used as a cereal grain; *also* : the seeds [Dutch *boekweit*]

[1]**bu·col·ic** \byü-ˈkäl-ik\ *adj* **1** : of or relating to shepherds or herdsmen : PASTORAL **2** : RUSTIC 1 [Latin *bucolicus,* from Greek *boukolikos,* from *boukolos* "cowherd"] — **bu·col·i·cal·ly** \-i-kə-lē, -klē\ *adv*

[2]**bucolic** *n* : a pastoral poem : ECLOGUE

[1]**bud** \ˈbəd\ *n* **1** : a small growth at the tip or on the side of a plant stem that later develops into a flower, leaf, or new shoot **2** : a flower that has not fully opened **3 a** : a part that grows out from the body of an organism and develops into a new organism : GEMMA **b** : an outgrowth having the potential to develop into an organ or part : PRIMORDIUM ‹an embryonic limb *bud*› **4** : a stage of development in which something is not yet fully developed : an early stage or condition ‹trees in *bud*› ‹a plan still in the *bud*› [Middle English *budde*]

[2]**bud** *vb* **bud·ded; bud·ding** **1** : to set or put forth buds **2** : to be or develop like a bud (as in freshness and promise of growth) ‹a *budding* diplomat› **3** : to reproduce asexually especially by the pinching off of a small part of the parent ‹*budding* yeast cells› **4** : to insert a bud from one plant into an opening cut in the bark of (another plant) in order to propagate a desired variety — **bud·der** *n*

Bud·dha \ˈbüd-ə, ˈbu̇d-\ *n* **1** : a person who has attained the perfect spiritual fulfillment sought in Buddhism **2** : a representation of Gautama Buddha [Sanskrit, "enlightened"]

Bud·dhism \ˈbü-ˌdiz-əm, ˈbu̇d-ˌiz-\ *n* : a religion chiefly of eastern and central Asia growing out of the teaching of Gautama Buddha that suffering is inherent in life and that one can be liberated from it by mental and moral self-purification — **Bud·dhist** \ˈbüd-əst, ˈbu̇d-\ *n or adj* — **Bud·dhis·tic** \bü-ˈdis-tik, bu̇-\ *adj*

bud·dy \ˈbəd-ē\ *n, pl* **buddies** : COMPANION 1, PARTNER, PAL [probably baby talk alteration of *brother*]

buddy system *n* : an arrangement in which two individuals are paired for safety (as in swimming)

budge \ˈbəj\ *vb* **1** : MOVE 1 **2** : to give or cause to give way : YIELD ‹wouldn't *budge* on the issue› [Medieval French *bouger,* derived from Latin *bullire* "to boil"]

bud·ger·i·gar \ˈbəj-rē-ˌgär, -ə-rē-\ *n* : a small Australian parrot usually light green with black and yellow markings in the wild but bred under domestication in many colors [from Yuwaalaraay (indigenous language of Australia) *gijirrigaa*]

[1]**bud·get** \ˈbəj-ət\ *n* **1** : a supply available or at hand **2 a** : a statement of estimated expenditures (as of a nation) during a period and of proposals to finance them **b** : a plan for using re-

sources to finance expenditures **c** : the amount of money available for or assigned to some purpose ⟨a low-*budget* operation⟩ [Medieval French *bougette,* from *bouge* "leather bag," from Latin *bulga,* of Celtic origin] — **bud·get·ary** \ˈbəj-ə-ˌter-ē\ *adj*

2budget *vb* **1** : to put in or on a budget ⟨*budget* money for food⟩ **2** : to provide funds for in a budget ⟨*budget* a new car⟩ **3** : to plan or provide for the use of ⟨*budget* your time wisely⟩

bud·gie \ˈbəj-ē\ *n* : BUDGERIGAR

bud scale *n* : one of the leaves resembling scales that form the sheath of a plant bud

1buff \ˈbəf\ *n* **1** : a garment made of buff leather **2** : the state of being nude ⟨sunbathing in the *buff*⟩ **3 a** : a moderate orange yellow **b** : a light to moderate yellow **4** : a device with a soft absorbent surface (as of cloth) for applying polishing material **5** : FAN, ENTHUSIAST ⟨a tennis *buff*⟩ [Middle French *buffle* "wild ox," from Italian *bufalo;* sense 5 from earlier *buff* "one enthusiastic about going to fires," perhaps from the buff overcoats worn by volunteer firemen in New York City about 1820]

2buff *adj* : of the color buff

3buff *vt* : to polish with or as if with a buff

1buf·fa·lo \ˈbəf-ə-ˌlō\ *n, pl* **-lo** *or* **-loes** : any of several wild mammals related to oxen: as **a** : WATER BUFFALO **b** : CAPE BUFFALO **c** : a large shaggy-maned North American mammal that has short horns and heavy forequarters bearing a large muscular hump and that was formerly abundant on the central and western plains — compare WISENT [Italian *bufalo* and Spanish *búfalo,* derived from Greek *boubalos* "African gazelle"]

buffalo c

2buffalo *vt* **-loed; -lo·ing** : BAFFLE 1, BEWILDER; *also* : BAMBOOZLE

buffalo bug *n* : CARPET BEETLE

buffalo grass *n* : a low-growing grass native to the Great Plains

buffalo soldier *n* : an African-American soldier serving in the western U.S. after the American Civil War

buffalo wing *n* : a deep-fried chicken wing coated with a spicy sauce and usually served with a blue cheese dressing [*Buffalo,* NY]

1buff·er \ˈbəf-ər\ *n* : one that buffs

2buffer *n* **1** : a device or material for reducing shock due to contact **2 a** : BUFFER STATE **b** : a person who shields another especially from annoying routine matters **3** : a substance capable in solution of neutralizing both acids and bases and thereby maintaining approximately the original pH of the solution **4** : a temporary storage unit (as for a computer); *esp* : one that accepts information at one rate and delivers it at another [*buff* "to act like a soft body when struck"]

3buffer *vt* **1** : to lessen the shock of : CUSHION **2** : to treat (a solution) with a buffer; *also* : to prepare (aspirin) with an antacid **3** : to collect (as data) in a buffer

buffer state *n* : a small neutral state lying between two larger potentially rival powers

1buf·fet \ˈbəf-ət\ *n* : a blow especially with the hand [Medieval French, from *buffe* "blow"]

2buffet *vb* **1** : STRIKE 2a: as **a** : CUFF, SLAP **b** : to pound repeatedly ⟨waves *buffeted* the cliff⟩ **2 a** : to contend against : STRUGGLE ⟨*buffeting* the wind⟩ **b** : to make one's way by fighting or struggling ⟨*buffeted* on through the storm⟩

3buf·fet \bə-ˈfā, bü-, ˈbü-ˌ\ *n* **1** : SIDEBOARD **2 a** : a counter for refreshments **b** *chiefly British* : a restaurant operated as a public convenience (as in a railway station) **c** : a meal set out on a sideboard, table, or countertop for guests to serve themselves [French]

buff leather *n* : a strong supple oil-tanned leather produced chiefly from cattle hides

buf·fle·head \ˈbəf-əl-ˌhed\ *n* : a small North American diving duck [archaic English *buffle* "buffalo"]

buf·foon \bə-ˈfün, ˌbə-\ *n* **1** : an amusing, absurd, or eccentric person : CLOWN **2** : a crude or stupid person [Middle French *bouffon,* from Italian *buffone*] — **buf·foon·ish** \-ˈfü-nish\ *adj*

buf·foon·ery \-ˈfün-rē, -ə-rē\ *n, pl* **-er·ies** : foolish or playful behavior

1bug \ˈbəg\ *n* **1 a** : an insect (as a beetle) or other creeping or crawling invertebrate (as a centipede) **b** : any of an order (Hemiptera) of insects (as bedbugs and stinkbugs) that are characterized by incomplete metamorphosis, forewings which are usually leathery at the base and membranous at the tip, and sucking mouthparts — called also *true bug* **2** : an unexpected defect, fault, flaw, or imperfection ⟨a *bug* in the software⟩ **3** : a disease-producing germ or a disease caused by it **4 a** : FAD, ENTHUSIASM ⟨got the barbecue *bug*⟩ **b** : ENTHUSIAST ⟨a camera *bug*⟩ **5** : a concealed listening device [origin unknown]

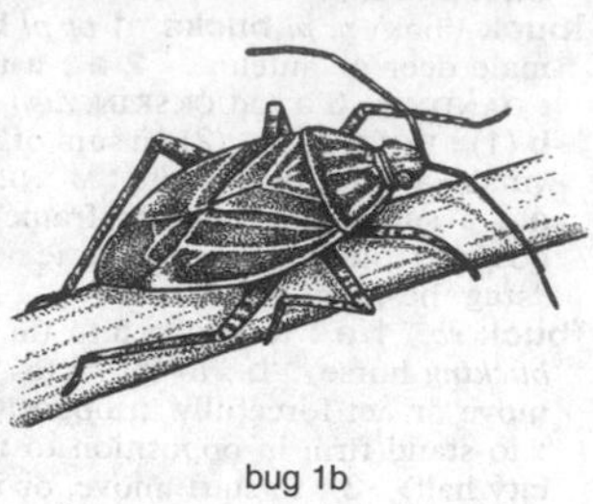
bug 1b

2bug *vt* **bugged; bug·ging** **1** : to plant a concealed microphone in **2** : ANNOY, BOTHER **3** : to lose one's composure — often used with *out*

bug·a·boo \ˈbəg-ə-ˌbü\ *n, pl* **-boos** : BUGBEAR, BOGEY [origin unknown]

bug·bear \ˈbəg-ˌbaər, -ˌbeər\ *n* **1** : an imaginary goblin or specter used to cause fear **2** : an object or source of dread **3** : a source of irritation : PROBLEM

bug–eyed \ˈbəg-ˌīd\ *adj* : having the eyes bulging (as with fright)

1bug·gy \ˈbəg-ē\ *adj* **bug·gi·er; -est** **1** : infested with bugs **2** : containing many bugs ⟨*buggy* software⟩

2buggy *n, pl* **buggies** **1** : a light single-seated carriage usually drawn by one horse **2** : a hand-pushed carriage for a baby [origin unknown]

1bug·house \ˈbəg-ˌhau̇s\ *adj, slang* : mentally deranged : CRAZY

2bughouse *n, slang* : an insane asylum

1bu·gle \ˈbyü-gəl\ *n* : a European annual herb of the mint family with spikes of blue flowers that is naturalized in the U.S. [Medieval French, from Late Latin *bugula*]

2bugle *n* : a brass musical instrument that resembles the trumpet but has no valves [Medieval French, "buffalo, instrument made from a buffalo horn, bugle," from Latin *buculus,* from *bos* "head of cattle"]

3bugle *vb* **bu·gled; bu·gling** \-gə-ling, -gling\ : to sound or summon by or as if by a bugle — **bu·gler** \-glər\ *n*

bu·gloss \ˈbyü-ˌgläs, -ˌglȯs\ *n* : any of several coarse hairy herbs related to the borage [Medieval French *buglosse,* derived from Greek *bous* "head of cattle" + *glōssa* "tongue"]

1build \ˈbild\ *vb* **built** \ˈbilt\; **build·ing** **1** : to make by putting together parts or materials : CONSTRUCT ⟨*build* a bridge⟩ **2** : to produce or create gradually especially by effort ⟨*build* a winning team⟩ ⟨*build* up your strength⟩ **3** : to cause to be constructed ⟨the city *built* a new stadium⟩ **4** : to engage in building **5** : to become greater ⟨costs are *building* up rapidly⟩ **6** : to progress toward a peak ⟨tension *building* up⟩ [Old English *byldan*]

2build *n* : form or style of structure; *esp* : PHYSIQUE

build·ed \ˈbil-dəd\ *dialect past of* BUILD

build·er \ˈbil-dər\ *n* : one that builds; *esp* : a person whose business is the construction of buildings

build in *vt* : to construct as an integral part of something ⟨*build in* a bookcase⟩

build·ing \ˈbil-ding\ *n* **1** : a usually roofed and walled structure built for permanent use (as for a dwelling) **2** : the art, work, or business of assembling materials into a structure ⟨bridge *building*⟩

building block *n* : a unit of construction or composition

build·up \ˈbil-ˌdəp\ *n* **1** : something produced by building up ⟨fluid *buildup* in the lungs⟩ **2** : the act or process of building up

built–in \ˈbil-ˈtin\ *adj* **1 a** : forming an integral part of a structure or object; *esp* : constructed as or in a recess in a wall ⟨*built-in* bookcases⟩ **b** : built into the ground ⟨a *built-in* swimming pool⟩ **2** : INHERENT ⟨a *built-in* advantage⟩

bulb \ˈbəlb\ *n* **1 a** : an underground resting stage of a plant (as an onion or tulip) consisting of a short stem base bearing one or more buds enclosed in thickened storage leaves **b** : a fleshy structure (as a tuber or corm) resembling a bulb in appearance or function **c :** a plant having or developing from a bulb **2 :** a bulb-shaped part; *esp* **:** a glass envelope containing the light source of an electric lamp **3 :** a rounded or swollen anatomical structure [Latin *bulbus,* from Greek *bolbos* "bulbous plant"] — **bulbed** \ˈbəlbd\ *adj*

bul·bar \ˈbəl-bər\ *adj* **:** of or relating to a bulb; *also* **:** involving the medulla oblongata

bul·bil \ˈbəl-bəl, -ˌbil\ *n* **:** BULBLET [French *bulbille,* from *bulbe* "bulb"]

bulb·let \ˈbəlb-lət\ *n* **:** a small or secondary plant bulb; *esp* **:** one produced in a leaf axil or replacing the flowers

bul·bous \ˈbəl-bəs\ *adj* **1 :** having a bulb **:** growing from or bearing bulbs **2 :** resembling a bulb **:** ROUNDED, SWOLLEN ⟨a *bulbous* nose⟩ — **bul·bous·ly** *adv*

bul·bul \ˈbu̇l-ˌbu̇l\ *n* **1 :** a songbird frequently mentioned in Persian poetry that is probably a nightingale **2 :** any of various songbirds of Asia and Africa [Persian, from Arabic]

Bul·gar \ˈbəl-ˌgär, ˈbu̇l-\ *n* **:** BULGARIAN

Bul·gar·i·an \ˌbəl-ˈgar-ē-ən, ˌbu̇l-, -ˈger-\ *n* **1 :** a native or inhabitant of Bulgaria **2 :** the Slavic language of the Bulgarians — **Bulgarian** *adj*

[1]**bulge** \ˈbəlj\ *n* **:** a swelling or distended part or place [Medieval French *boulge, bouge* "leather bag," from Latin *bulga*] ***synonyms*** see PROJECTION — **bulgy** *adj*

[2]**bulge** *vb* **1 :** to become or cause to become bent or swollen outward ⟨*bulging* eyes⟩ **2 :** to be filled to overflowing ⟨a notebook *bulging* with ideas⟩

bul·gur \ˈbəl-gər, ˈbu̇l-\ *n* **:** dried cracked wheat [Turkish]

bu·lim·ia \bü-ˈlē-mē-ə, byü-, -ˈli-\ *n* **:** a serious eating disorder primarily of young women that is characterized by compulsive overeating usually followed by self-induced vomiting or laxative abuse and is often accompanied by depression [Greek *boulimia* "great hunger"] — **bu·lim·ic** \-ˈlē-mik, -ˈli-\ *adj*

[1]**bulk** \ˈbəlk\ *n* **1 :** greatness of size or extent **:** MAGNITUDE, VOLUME **2 :** a large body or mass **3 :** the main or greater part ⟨did the *bulk* of the work⟩ **4 :** FIBER 1c [Old Norse *bulki* "cargo"] — **in bulk 1 :** not divided into parts or packaged in separate units **2 :** in large quantities

synonyms BULK, MASS, VOLUME mean the whole that makes up a body or unit with reference to its size or amount. BULK implies a whole that is large, heavy, or unwieldy ⟨the *bulk* of a skyscraper⟩. MASS suggests a whole made by piling together things of the same kind ⟨a *mass* of boulders⟩. VOLUME applies to a whole without shape or outline and capable of flowing or fluctuating ⟨a large *volume* of water⟩ ⟨the *volume* of traffic⟩.

[2]**bulk** *vb* **1 :** to swell or bulge or cause to swell or bulge **2 :** to appear as a consideration ⟨an issue that *bulks* large in everyone's mind⟩

[3]**bulk** *adj* **:** being in bulk ⟨*bulk* foods⟩

bulk·head \ˈbəlk-ˌhed, ˈbəl-ˌked\ *n* **1 :** an upright partition separating compartments (as on a ship) **2 :** a structure or partition to resist pressure or to shut off water, fire, or gas **3 :** a framework projecting from the outside of a building that has a sloping door giving access to a cellar stairway

bulk up *vb* **:** to gain weight especially by becoming more muscular

bulky \ˈbəl-kē\ *adj* **bulk·i·er; -est :** having bulk: as **a :** large of its kind; *esp* **:** both large and unwieldy **b :** having great volume in proportion to weight ⟨a *bulky* knit sweater⟩ — **bulk·i·ly** \-kə-lē\ *adv* — **bulk·i·ness** \-kē-nəs\ *n*

[1]**bull** \ˈbu̇l\ *n* **1 a :** an adult male bovine animal **b :** a usually adult male of various large animals (as elephants or whales) **2 :** one who buys commodities or securities in expectation of a price rise — compare BEAR 3 **3 :** one that resembles a bull **4 :** BULLDOG **5** *slang* **:** POLICE OFFICER, DETECTIVE [Old English *bula*]

[2]**bull** *adj* **1 a :** MALE ⟨a *bull* calf⟩ **b :** of, relating to, or resembling a bull **2 :** large of its kind

[3]**bull** *vb* **:** to act or act on with the violence of a bull **:** FORCE ⟨*bulling* their way ahead⟩

[4]**bull** *n* **:** a papal pronouncement of the most formal and important kind [Medieval Latin *bulla* "papal seal, papal bull," from Latin, "bubble, amulet"]

[5]**bull** *n* **1 :** a grotesque blunder in language **2** *slang* **a :** empty boastful talk **b :** NONSENSE

[1]**bull·dog** \ˈbu̇l-ˌdȯg\ *n* **:** any of a breed of compact muscular short-haired dogs of a breed developed in England to fight bulls and having forelegs set widely apart and an undershot lower jaw

[2]**bulldog** *adj* **:** suggestive of a bulldog ⟨*bulldog* courage⟩

[3]**bulldog** *vt* **:** to throw (a steer) by seizing the horns and twisting the neck

bull·doze \ˈbu̇l-ˌdōz\ *vt* **1 :** BULLY, INTIMIDATE **2 :** to move, clear, gouge out, or level off with a bulldozer **3 :** to force as if by using a bulldozer ⟨*bulldoze* one's way through brush⟩ [perhaps from [1]*bull* + alteration of *dose*]

bull·doz·er \-ˌdō-zər\ *n* **1 :** one that bulldozes **2 :** a tractor-driven machine having a broad horizontal blade or ram for pushing (as in clearing land or road building)

bul·let \ˈbu̇l-ət\ *n* **1 :** a shaped piece of metal made to be shot from a firearm **2 a :** something suggesting a bullet (as in form or vigor of action) **b :** a large dot placed in printed matter to call attention to a particular passage **3 :** a very fast and accurately thrown or hit object (as a ball) [Middle French *boulet,* from *boule* "ball"] — **bul·let·ed** \-ət-əd\ *adj*

bul·le·tin \ˈbu̇l-ət-n\ *n* **1 :** a brief public notice usually from an authoritative source ⟨a weather *bulletin*⟩ **2 :** a periodical publication; *esp* **:** one issued by an institution or association [French, from Middle French, from *bullette* "seal, notice," from *bulle* "seal," from Medieval Latin *bulla* "papal bull"]

bulletin board *n* **1 :** a board for posting notices **2 :** a place on a computer network (as the Internet) where people can leave or read public messages

bul·let·proof \ˌbu̇l-ət-ˈprüf\ *adj* **1 :** so made as to prevent the passing through of bullets ⟨*bulletproof* glass⟩ **2 :** INVINCIBLE

bullet train *n* **:** a very high-speed passenger train

bull fiddle *n* **:** DOUBLE BASS — **bull fiddler** *n*

bull·fight \ˈbu̇l-ˌfīt\ *n* **:** a spectacle in which persons ceremonially excite, fight with, and usually kill bulls in an arena for public entertainment — **bull·fight·er** *n* — **bull·fight·ing** \-iŋ\ *n*

bull·finch \-ˌfinch\ *n* **:** a thick-billed red-breasted European songbird often kept as a cage bird

bull·frog \-ˌfrȯg, -ˌfräg\ *n* **:** a large heavy frog that makes a booming or bellowing sound

bull·head \-ˌhed\ *n* **:** any of various large-headed fishes; *esp* **:** any of several common freshwater catfishes of the U.S.

bull·head·ed \ˈbu̇l-ˈhed-əd\ *adj* **:** stupidly stubborn **:** HEADSTRONG — **bull·head·ed·ly** *adv* — **bull·head·ed·ness** *n*

bull·horn \ˈbu̇l-ˌhȯrn\ *n* **:** a handheld combined microphone and loudspeaker

bul·lion \ˈbu̇l-yən\ *n* **:** gold or silver especially in bars or ingots [Medieval French *billion, bullion* "melting house, bullion"]

bull·ish \ˈbu̇l-ish\ *adj* **1 :** suggestive of a bull **2 a :** marked by, tending to cause, or hopeful of rising prices (as in a stock market) **b :** OPTIMISTIC — **bull·ish·ly** *adv* — **bull·ish·ness** *n*

bull market *n* **:** a market in which stocks are persistently rising in value — compare BEAR MARKET

bull mastiff *n* **:** any of a breed of large powerful dogs developed in England by crossing bulldogs with mastiffs

Bull Moose \ˈbu̇l-ˈmüs\ *n* **:** a follower of Theodore Roosevelt in the U.S. presidential campaign of 1912 [*bull moose,* emblem of the Progressive party of 1912]

bull neck *n* **:** a thick short powerful neck — **bull-necked** \ˈbu̇l-ˈnekt\ *adj*

bull·ock \ˈbu̇l-ək\ *n* **1 :** a young bull **2 :** a castrated bull **:** STEER — **bull·ocky** \-ə-kē\ *adj*

bull·pen \ˈbu̇l-ˌpen\ *n* **1 :** a large cell where prisoners are held until brought into court **2 a :** a place on a baseball field where relief pitchers warm up **b :** the relief pitchers of a team

bull·ring \ˈbu̇l-ˌriŋ\ *n* **:** an arena for bullfights

bull session *n* **:** an informal group discussion

bull's–eye \ˈbu̇l-ˌzī\ *n* **1 :** a small thick disk of glass inserted (as in a deck) to let in light **2 :** a very hard globular candy **3 a :** the center of a target; *also* **:** something central or critical **b :** a shot that hits a bull's-eye; *also* **:** a complete success **4 :** a simple lens for concentrating rays of light

bull snake *n* **:** any of several large harmless North American snakes feeding chiefly on rodents

bull ter·ri·er \ˈbu̇l-ˈter-ē-ər\ *n* **:** any of a breed of short-haired terriers developed in England by crossing the bulldog with terriers

bull·whip \ˈbu̇l-ˌhwip, -ˌwip\ *n* **:** a rawhide whip with a very long braided lash

[1]**bul·ly** \ˈbu̇l-ē\ *n, pl* **bullies :** a rough browbeating person; *esp* **:** one habitually cruel to others who are weaker [probably from Dutch *boel* "lover"]

Word History The earliest meaning of English *bully* was "sweetheart." The word was probably borrowed from Dutch *boel* "lover." Later *bully* was used for anyone who seemed a good fellow, then for a blustering daredevil. Today, a bully is usually one whose claims to strength and courage are based on the intimidation of those who are weaker.

[2]**bully** *adj* **:** EXCELLENT, FIRST-RATE — often used interjectionally ⟨*bully* for you⟩

[3]**bully** *vb* **bul·lied; bul·ly·ing :** to play the bully toward **:** act like a bully

bul·ly·rag \ˈbu̇l-ē-ˌrag\ *vt* **1 :** to make timid or fearful by bullying **2 :** to annoy by teasing **:** BADGER [origin unknown]

bul·rush \ˈbu̇l-ˌrəsh\ *n* **:** any of several large sedges or rushes growing in wet land or water [Middle English *bulrysche*]

[1]**bul·wark** \ˈbu̇l-wərk, -ˌwərk, -ˌwȯrk; ˈbəl-wərk, -ˌwərk\ *n* **1 a :** a solid wall built for defense **b :** BREAKWATER, SEAWALL **2 :** a strong support or protection **3 :** the side of a ship above the upper deck — usually used in plural [Dutch *bolwerc,* from *bolle* "tree trunk" + *werc* "work"]

[2]**bulwark** *vt* **:** to strengthen or safeguard with a bulwark **:** PROTECT

[1]**bum** \ˈbəm\ *n* **:** BUTTOCK 2a [Middle English *bom*]

[2]**bum** *adj* **1 a :** of poor quality **:** INFERIOR ⟨*bum* advice⟩ **b :** not valid or deserved ⟨a *bum* rap⟩ **c :** not pleasant or enjoyable ⟨a *bum* trip⟩ **2 :** physically disabled ⟨a *bum* knee⟩ [perhaps from [4]*bum*]

[3]**bum** *vb* **bummed; bum·ming 1 :** to go around in the manner of a bum: **a :** LOAF 1 **b :** to wander like a tramp **2 :** to obtain by asking or begging ⟨*bum* a ride⟩ [perhaps back-formation from *bummer* "loafer"]

[4]**bum** *n* **1 :** a person who avoids work and tries to live off others **2 :** TRAMP 1 [probably short for *bummer* "loafer," from German *Bummler*]

[5]**bum** *vt* **:** DEPRESS 3 — often used with *out* ⟨the news really *bummed* me out⟩ [probably from *bummer*]

bum·ble·bee \ˈbəm-bəl-ˌbē\ *n* **:** any of numerous large robust hairy social bees [Middle English *bomblen* "to boom"]

bum·boat \ˈbəm-ˌbōt\ *n* **:** a boat that brings provisions and commodities for sale to ships in port or offshore [probably from Low German *bumboot,* from *bum* "tree" + *boot* "boat"]

bum·mer \ˈbəm-ər\ *n* **1 :** an unpleasant experience (as a bad reaction to a hallucinogenic drug) **2 :** FAILURE, FLOP [[2]*bum*]

[1]**bump** \ˈbəmp\ *n* **1 :** a sudden forceful blow or jolt **2 a :** a rounded projection or bulge; *esp* **:** a swelling of tissue (as from a blow or sting) **b :** an irregularity in a road surface likely to cause a jolt [probably imitative of the sound of a blow]

[2]**bump** *vb* **1 :** to strike or knock against something with force **2 :** to collide with **3 :** to proceed in a series of bumps **:** JOLT — **bump into :** to meet especially by chance

[1]**bump·er** \ˈbəm-pər\ *n* **:** a cup or glass filled to the brim [probably from *bump* "to bulge"]

[2]**bumper** *adj* **:** unusually large or fine ⟨a *bumper* crop⟩

[3]**bumper** *n* **:** a device for absorbing shock or preventing damage (as in collision); *esp* **:** a bar at either end of a motor vehicle [[1]*bump*]

bumper car *n* **:** a small electric car made to be driven around in an enclosure and to be bumped into others (as in an amusement park)

bump·kin \ˈbəm-kən, ˈbəmp-\ *n* **:** an awkward and crude rustic [perhaps from Dutch *bommekijn* "small cask"]

bump·tious \ˈbəm-shəs, ˈbəmp-\ *adj* **:** stupidly and often noisily self-assertive **:** PRESUMPTUOUS [[1]*bump* + *-tious* (as in *fractious*)] — **bump·tious·ly** *adv* — **bump·tious·ness** *n*

bumpy \ˈbəm-pē\ *adj* **bump·i·er; -est :** causing, having, or covered with bumps ⟨a *bumpy* ride⟩ ⟨a *bumpy* surface⟩ — **bump·i·ly** \-pə-lē\ *adv* — **bump·i·ness** \-pē-nəs\ *n*

bum's rush *n* **:** removal by or as if by force

bun \ˈbən\ *n* **1 :** a sweet or plain small bread; *esp* **:** a round roll **2 :** a knot of hair shaped like a bun [Middle English *bunne*]

[1]**bunch** \ˈbənch\ *n* **1 :** BULGE, SWELLING **2 a :** a number of things of the same kind **:** CLUSTER ⟨a *bunch* of grapes⟩ **b :** GROUP 2 ⟨a *bunch* of friends⟩ **c :** a large amount **:** LOT ⟨a *bunch* of money⟩ [Middle English *bunche*] — **bunch·i·ly** \ˈbən-chə-lē\ *adv* — **bunchy** \-chē\ *adj*

[2]**bunch** *vb* **:** to form in or gather into a group or cluster

bunch·ber·ry \ˈbənch-ˌber-ē\ *n* **:** a creeping perennial herb related to the dogwood and bearing clusters of red berries

bunch·grass \-ˌgras\ *n* **:** any of several grasses chiefly of the western U.S. that grow in tufts

bun·co *or* **bun·ko** \ˈbəng-kō\ *n, pl* **buncos** *or* **bunkos :** a swindling game or scheme [perhaps from Spanish *banca* "bench, bank"] — **bunco** *vt*

bund \ˈbu̇nd, ˈbənd\ *n, often cap* **:** a political association; *esp* **:** a pro-Nazi German-American organization of the 1930s [Yiddish *bund* & German *Bund* "league"] — **bund·ist** \-əst\ *n, often cap*

[1]**bun·dle** \ˈbən-dl\ *n* **1 a :** a group of things tied together **b :** PARCEL 4 **c :** a large sum of money **d :** BUNCH 2 **2 a :** a small band of mostly parallel fibers (as of nerve) **b :** VASCULAR BUNDLE [Dutch *bundel*]

[2]**bundle** *vb* **bun·dled; bun·dling** \ˈbən-dling, -dl-ing\ **1 :** to make into a bundle **:** WRAP **2 :** to hurry or send away unceremoniously ⟨*bundled* the children off to school⟩ **3 :** to take part in bundling — **bun·dler** \-dlər, -dl-ər\ *n*

bundle up *vb* **:** to dress warmly

bun·dling \ˈbən-dling, -dl-ing\ *n* **:** a former custom in which a couple during courtship would occupy the same bed without undressing

[1]**bung** \ˈbəng\ *n* **1 :** the stopper in the bunghole of a cask; *also* **:** BUNGHOLE **2 :** the cecum or anus especially of a slaughtered animal [Dutch *bonghe*]

[2]**bung** *vt* **:** to plug with or as if with a bung

bun·ga·low \ˈbəng-gə-ˌlō\ *n* **:** a usually one-storied house with a low-pitched roof; *also* **:** a house having one and a half stories and usually a front porch [Hindi *baṅglā,* literally, (house) "in the Bengal style"]

bun·gee \ˈbən-jē\ *n* **:** BUNGEE CORD

bungee cord *n* **:** an elasticized cord used especially as a fastening device or to absorb shocks — called also *bungee* [origin unknown]

bungee jump *vi* **:** to jump from a height while attached to an elasticized cord — **bungee jumper** *n*

bung·hole \ˈbəng-ˌhōl\ *n* **:** a hole for emptying or filling a cask

bun·gle \ˈbəng-gəl\ *vb* **bun·gled; bun·gling** \-gə-ling, -gling\ **:** to act, make, or work in a clumsy manner [perhaps of Scandinavian origin] — **bungle** *n* — **bun·gler** \-gə-lər, -glər\ *n*

bun·ion \ˈbən-yən\ *n* **:** an inflamed swelling on the first joint of the big toe [probably from *bunny* "swelling"]

[1]**bunk** \ˈbəngk\ *n* **1 :** BUNK BED **2 :** a built-in bed (as on a ship) that is often one of a tier **3 :** a sleeping place [probably short for *bunker*]

[2]**bunk** *vb* **1 :** to occupy a bunk **2 :** to provide with a bunk

[3]**bunk** *n* **:** NONSENSE 1 [short for *bunkum*]

bunk bed *n* **:** one of two single beds usually placed one above the other

bun·ker \ˈbəng-kər\ *n* **1 :** a bin or compartment for storage (as for coal or oil on a ship) **2 a :** a protective dugout; *esp* **:** a fortified chamber mostly below ground **b :** a sand trap on a golf course [Scots *bonker* "chest, box"]

bunk·house \ˈbəngk-ˌhau̇s\ *n* **:** a rough simple building providing sleeping quarters (as for construction workers)

bun·kum *or* **bun·combe** \ˈbəng-kəm\ *n* **:** NONSENSE 1 [*Buncombe* County, North Carolina; from the statement by its congressional representative in defending a seemingly irrelevant speech that he was speaking to Buncombe]

bun·ny \ˈbən-ē\ *n, pl* **bunnies :** RABBIT [English dialect *bun* "rabbit"]

bunny slope *n* **:** a gentle incline for skiing used especially by beginning skiers — called also *bunny hill*

Bun·sen burner \ˈbən-sən-\ *n* **:** a gas burner consisting typically of a tube with small holes at the bottom where air enters and mixes with the gas to produce a very hot blue flame [Robert W. *Bunsen,* died 1899, German chemist]

[1]**bunt** \ˈbənt\ *n* **:** the middle part of a square sail [perhaps from Low German, "bundle"]

[2]**bunt** *n* **:** a destructive smut of wheat in which the grains are replaced by greasy

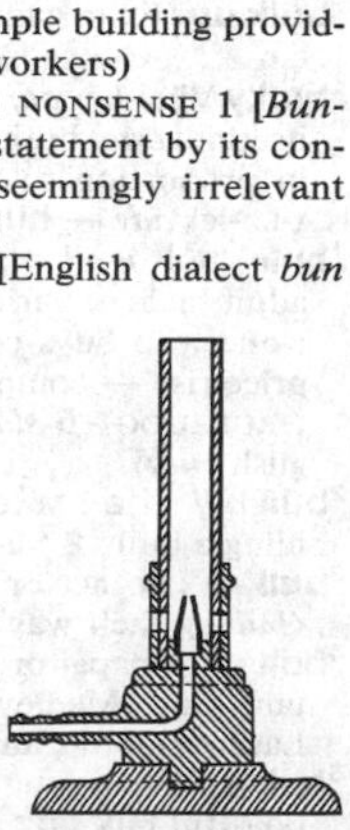

Bunsen burner

masses of dark ill-smelling spores [origin unknown]

[3]**bunt** *vb* **1 :** to strike or push with or as if with the head : BUTT **2 :** to push or tap a baseball lightly without swinging the bat [alteration of [1]*butt*] — **bunt·er** *n*

[4]**bunt** *n* **1 :** an act or instance of bunting **2 :** a bunted ball

[1]**bun·ting** \ˈbənt-iŋ\ *n* **:** any of various stout-billed finches of the size and habits of a sparrow [Middle English]

[2]**bunting** *n* **1 :** a thin cloth used chiefly for making flags and decorations **2 :** flags or decorations made of bunting [perhaps from English dialect *bunt* "to sift"]

bunt·line \ˈbənt-ˌlīn, -lən\ *n* **:** one of the ropes attached to the foot of a square sail to haul the sail up to the yard for furling

[1]**buoy** \ˈbü-ē, ˈbȯi\ *n* **1 :** a floating marker anchored in a body of water to point out a channel or warn of danger **2 :** LIFE BUOY [Middle English *boye,* probably from Dutch *boeye*]

[2]**buoy** *vt* **1 :** to mark by or as if by a buoy **2 a :** to keep afloat **b :** to raise the spirits of : SUSTAIN ⟨*buoyed* up by the news⟩

buoy·an·cy \ˈbȯi-ən-sē, ˈbü-yən-\ *n* **1 a :** the tendency of a body to float or to rise when submerged in a fluid ⟨the *buoyancy* of a cork in water⟩ **b :** the power of a fluid to exert an upward force on a body placed in it ⟨the *buoyancy* of seawater⟩ **2 :** natural lightness of spirit : LIGHTHEARTEDNESS

buoy·ant \ˈbȯi-ənt, ˈbü-yənt\ *adj* **1 :** able to rise and float in the air or on the surface of a liquid **2 :** able to keep a body afloat ⟨hawks gliding in *buoyant* currents of air⟩ **3 :** CHEERFUL ***synonyms*** see ELASTIC — **buoy·ant·ly** *adv*

bur *variant of* BURR

burb \ˈbərb\ *n* **:** SUBURB — usually used in plural

bur·ble \ˈbər-bəl\ *vi* **bur·bled; bur·bling** \ˈbər-bə-liŋ, -bliŋ\ **1 :** to make a bubbling sound : GURGLE **2 :** to talk constantly and enthusiastically : BABBLE [Middle English *burblen*] — **burble** *n* — **bur·bler** \-bə-lər, -blər\ *n* — **bur·bly** \-bə-lē, -blē\ *adj*

bur·bot \ˈbər-bət\ *n, pl* **burbot** *also* **burbots :** a long slender northern freshwater fish related to the cod [Medieval French, from *borbeter* "to stir up mud"]

[1]**bur·den** \ˈbərd-n\ *n* **1 a :** something that is carried : LOAD **b :** something borne as a duty or responsibility often with labor or difficulty ⟨tax *burdens*⟩ **c :** the duty of doing or providing something ⟨*burden* of proof⟩ **2 :** something hard to bear : ENCUMBRANCE **3 a :** the bearing of a load ⟨beasts of *burden*⟩ **b :** capacity for carrying cargo ⟨a ship of 100 tons *burden*⟩ [Old English *byrthen*]

[2]**burden** *vt* **bur·dened; bur·den·ing** \ˈbərd-niŋ, -n-iŋ\ **:** to put a burden on : LOAD, OPPRESS

[3]**burden** *n* **1 :** the refrain or chorus of a song **2 :** a main theme or central idea : GIST [Middle English *burdoun* "bass part," from Medieval French *burdun* "a drone bass"]

bur·den·some \ˈbərd-n-səm\ *adj* **:** difficult to bear : OPPRESSIVE — **bur·den·some·ly** *adv* — **bur·den·some·ness** *n*

bur·dock \ˈbər-ˌdäk\ *n* **:** any of a genus of coarse herbs related to daisies and having globular flower heads with prickly bracts [[1]*burr* + [1]*dock*]

bu·reau \ˈbyu̇r-ō\ *n, pl* **bu·reaus** *also* **bu·reaux** \-ōz\ **1 a** *British* **:** a writing desk; *esp* **:** one with drawers and a slant top **b :** a low chest of drawers for use in a bedroom **2 a :** a subdivision of a governmental department performing a particular function ⟨Federal *Bureau* of Investigation⟩ **b :** a commercial agency providing services for the public or for other businesses ⟨a travel *bureau*⟩ [French, "desk, cloth covering for desks," derived from Late Latin *burra* "shaggy cloth"]

bu·reau·cra·cy \byu̇-ˈräk-rə-sē\ *n, pl* **-cies 1 :** a body of appointed or hired government officials **2 a :** a system of administration characterized by specialization of functions, adherence to fixed rules, and a hierarchy of authority **b :** a system of administration marked by constant strivings for power and by ever increasing inefficiency and red tape

bu·reau·crat \ˈbyu̇r-ə-ˌkrat\ *n* **:** a member of a bureaucracy

bu·reau·crat·ic \ˌbyu̇r-ə-ˈkrat-ik\ *adj* **:** of, relating to, or having the characteristics of a bureaucracy or a bureaucrat ⟨*bureaucratic* government⟩ — **bu·reau·crat·i·cal·ly** \-ˈkrat-i-kə-lē, -klē\ *adv*

bu·rette *or* **bu·ret** \byu̇-ˈret\ *n* **:** a graduated glass tube usually with a small opening at the bottom and a stopcock for delivering measured quantities of liquid or for measuring the liquid or gas received or discharged [French *burette,* from Medieval French *bivrete* "cruet," from *buire* "pitcher"]

burg \ˈbərg\ *n* **1 :** a medieval fortress or walled town **2 :** CITY, TOWN [Old English]

bur·gee \ˌbər-ˈjē\ *n* **:** a swallow-tailed flag used especially by ships for signals or identification [perhaps from French dialect *bourgeais* "shipowner"]

bur·geon \ˈbər-jən\ *vi* **1 a :** to put forth new growth (as buds) **b :** to burst into bloom : BLOSSOM **2 :** to expand rapidly and widely [Middle English *burjon* "bud," from Medieval French, derived from Late Latin *burra* "fluff, shaggy cloth"]

bur·ger \ˈbər-gər\ *n* **1 :** HAMBURGER **2 :** a sandwich similar to a hamburger ⟨veggie *burger*⟩

bur·gess \ˈbər-jəs\ *n* **1 :** a citizen of a British borough **2 :** a representative in the lower house of the legislature of colonial Maryland or Virginia [Middle English *burgeis* "burgher," from Medieval French, from *burc, borg* "town," from Latin *burgus* "fortified place"]

burgh \ˈbər-ō, ˈbə-rō\ *n* **:** BOROUGH; *esp* **:** a Scottish town with certain local lawmaking rights [Old English *burg* "fortified town"]

bur·gher \ˈbər-gər\ *n* **:** an inhabitant of a borough or a town

bur·glar \ˈbər-glər\ *n* **:** a person who commits burglary : THIEF [Anglo-French *burgler,* from Medieval Latin *burglator,* probably alteration of *burgator,* from *burgare* "to commit burglary"]

bur·glar·ize \ˈbər-glə-ˌrīz\ *vt* **:** to break into and steal from

bur·glary \ˈbər-glə-rē\ *n, pl* **-glar·ies :** the act of breaking into a building (as a house) especially at night and for the purpose of committing a crime (as stealing)

bur·go·mas·ter \ˈbər-gə-ˌmas-tər\ *n* **:** the chief magistrate of a town in some European countries [Dutch *burgemeester,* from *burg* "town" + *meester* "master"]

Bur·gun·dy \ˈbər-gən-dē\ *n* **:** a red or white wine from parts of Burgundy; *also* **:** a similar red wine made elsewhere

buri·al \ˈber-ē-əl\ *n* **:** the act of burying

bu·rin \ˈbyu̇r-ən, ˈbər-\ *n* **1 :** a pointed steel cutting tool used by engravers **2 :** a prehistoric flint tool with a point like that of a chisel [French]

bur·ka \ˈbu̇r-kə\ *n* **:** a loose garment that covers the face and body and is worn in public by certain Muslim women [Persian *burqaʿ, burquʿ,* from Arabic *burquʿ*]

[1]**burl** \ˈbərl\ *n* **1 :** a knot or lump in thread or cloth **2 :** a gnarled woody outgrowth on a tree; *also* **:** veneer cut from this [Middle English *burle,* derived from Late Latin *burra* "shaggy cloth"]

[2]**burl** *vt* **:** to finish (cloth) especially by repairing burls — **burl·er** *n*

bur·lap \ˈbər-ˌlap\ *n* **:** a coarse fabric made usually from jute or hemp and used principally for bags and wrappings [origin unknown]

[1]**bur·lesque** \bər-ˈlesk, ˌbər-\ *n* **1 a :** a witty or derisive literary or dramatic imitation **b :** mockery usually by caricature **2 :** theatrical entertainment consisting especially of low comedy skits and dance routines involving displays of partial nudity [*burlesque,* adjective, "comic, droll," from French, from Italian *burlesco,* from *burla* "joke," from Spanish] ***synonyms*** see CARICATURE — **burlesque** *adj*

[2]**burlesque** *vt* **:** to imitate in such a way as to make ridiculous — **bur·lesqu·er** *n*

bur·ly \ˈbər-lē\ *adj* **bur·li·er; -est :** strongly and heavily built : HUSKY [Middle English] — **bur·li·ly** \-lə-lē\ *adv* — **bur·li·ness** *n*

bur marigold *n* **:** any of a genus of coarse herbs related to the daisies with burs that adhere to clothing and fur

Bur·mese \ˌbər-ˈmēz, -ˈmēs\ *n, pl* **Burmese 1 :** a native or inhabitant of Burma **2 :** the language of the Burmese people — **Burmese** *adj*

[1]**burn** \ˈbərn\ *n, British* **:** CREEK 2 [Old English]

[2]**burn** *vb* **burned** \ˈbərnd, ˈbərnt\ *or* **burnt** \ˈbərnt\; **burn·ing 1 a :** BLAZE ⟨the fire *burned* brightly⟩ **b :** to undergo combustion; *also* **:** to undergo nuclear fission or fusion **2 a :** to feel hot ⟨the *burning* sand⟩ **b :** to become affected by or as if by the action of fire or heat; *esp* **:** SCORCH ⟨*burned* the toast⟩ **c :** to give off light : GLOW ⟨left the lights *burning*⟩ **d :** to set on fire; *esp* **:** to destroy by fire ⟨*burn* trash⟩ **e :** to use as fuel ⟨this furnace *burns* gas⟩ **3 a :** to produce by the action of fire or heat ⟨*burned* a hole in my shirt⟩ **b :** to record data or music on an optical disk using a laser ⟨*burn* a CD⟩ **4 :** to injure or alter

by or as if by fire or heat ⟨*burn* out a bearing⟩ **5 :** to suffer sunburn ⟨she *burns* easily⟩ [Old English *byrnan* and *bærnan*] — **burn·able** \ˈbər-nə-bəl\ *adj* — **burn one's bridges :** to cut off all means of retreat — **burn the candle at both ends :** to use one's energy or resources too much — **burn the midnight oil :** to work or study far into the night

[3]**burn** *n* **:** injury, damage, or effect produced by or as if by burning

burned–out \ˈbərnd-ˈau̇t, ˈbərnt-\ *or* **burnt–out** \ˈbərnt-\ *adj* **1 :** very weary **:** WORN-OUT **2 :** destroyed by fire ⟨a *burned-out* building⟩

burn·er \ˈbər-nər\ *n* **:** one that burns: as **a :** the part of a fuel-burning or heat-producing device (as a stove or furnace) where the flame or heat is produced **b :** a device for recording data on an optical disk

burn–in \ˈbər-nin\ *n* **:** the continuous operation of a device (as a computer) as a test for defects or failure prior to putting it to use

burning *adj* **1 a :** being on fire **b :** ARDENT, INTENSE ⟨a *burning* desire⟩ **2 a :** affecting with or as if with heat ⟨a *burning* fever⟩ **b :** resembling that produced by a burn ⟨a *burning* sensation⟩ **3 :** of great importance **:** URGENT ⟨a *burning* issue⟩

[1]**bur·nish** \ˈbər-nish\ *vt* **:** to make shiny or lustrous especially by rubbing **:** POLISH [Medieval French *bruniss-*, stem of *brunir*, literally, "to make brown," from *brun* "brown"] — **bur·nish·er** *n*

[2]**burnish** *n* **:** LUSTER 1

bur·noose *or* **bur·nous** \bər-ˈnüs, ˌbər-\ *n* **:** a hooded cloak worn by Arabs and Berbers [French *burnous*, from Arabic *burnus*]

burnoose

burn·out \ˈbər-ˌnau̇t\ *n* **1 :** the stoppage of a jet or rocket engine; *also* **:** the point at which burnout occurs **2 :** exhaustion of physical or emotional strength usually as a result of prolonged stress or frustration

burn out *vb* **1 :** to drive out or destroy the property of by fire **2 :** to cause to wear out or become exhausted especially from overwork or overuse

burn·sides \ˈbərn-ˌsīdz\ *n pl* **:** SIDE-WHISKERS [Ambrose E. *Burnside*]

[1]**burp** \ˈbərp\ *n* **:** the act or an instance of expelling stomach gas through the mouth **:** BELCH [imitative]

[2]**burp** *vb* **1 :** BELCH 1 **2 :** to help (a baby) expel gas from the stomach especially by patting or rubbing the baby's back

burp gun *n* **:** SUBMACHINE GUN

[1]**burr** \ˈbər\ *n* **1** *usually* **bur a :** a rough or prickly envelope of a fruit **b :** a plant that bears burs **2 :** BURL 2 **3 :** a roughness left by a tool in cutting or shaping metal **4 a :** a trilled uvular \r\ as used by some speakers of English especially in northern England and in Scotland **b :** a tongue-point trill that is the usual Scottish \r\ **5 a :** a small rotary cutting tool **b** *usually* **bur :** a bit used on a dental drill **6 :** a rough humming sound **:** WHIR [Middle English *burre*] — **burred** \ˈbərd\ *adj*

[2]**burr** *vb* **1 :** to speak or pronounce with a burr **2 :** to make a whirring sound **3 a :** to form into a rough edge **b :** to remove burrs from (as a sharp edge) — **burr·er** \ˈbər-ər\ *n*

bur reed *n* **:** any of a genus of plants with globe-shaped fruits resembling burs

bur·ri·to \bə-ˈrēt-ō\ *n, pl* **-tos :** a flour tortilla folded around a filling (as of meat, beans, and cheese) [American Spanish, from Spanish, "little donkey," diminutive of *burro*]

bur·ro \ˈbər-ō, ˈbu̇r-; ˈbə-rō\ *n, pl* **burros :** DONKEY; *esp* **:** a small one used as a pack animal [Spanish, derived from Late Latin *burricus* "small horse"]

[1]**bur·row** \ˈbər-ō, ˈbə-rō\ *n* **:** a hole in the ground made by an animal (as a rabbit) for shelter and habitation [Middle English *borow*]

[2]**burrow** *vb* **1 :** to construct by tunneling **2 :** to conceal oneself in or as if in a burrow **3 a :** to make a burrow **b :** TUNNEL ⟨they *burrowed* under the wall⟩ **4 :** to make a thorough search **:** DELVE ⟨*burrowed* through the files⟩ **5 :** to make a motion suggestive of burrowing **:** NESTLE — **bur·row·er** *n*

bur·ry \ˈbər-ē\ *adj* **:** containing burs

bur·sa \ˈbər-sə\ *n, pl* **bur·sas** *or* **bur·sae** \-ˌsē, -ˌsī\ **:** a bodily pouch or sac; *esp* **:** a small serous sac between a tendon and a bone [Medieval Latin, "bag, purse," from Late Latin, "ox hide," from Greek *byrsa* "animal skin"] — **bur·sal** \-səl\ *adj*

bur·sar \ˈbər-sər, -ˌsär\ *n* **:** a treasurer especially of a college or monastery [Medieval Latin *bursarius*, from *bursa* "bag, purse"]

bur·sa·ry \ˈbərs-rē, -ə-rē\ *n, pl* **-ries :** the treasury of a college or monastery

burse \ˈbərs\ *n* **:** a square cloth case for carrying the corporal in a Communion service [Medieval Latin *bursa* "bag, purse"]

bur·si·tis \bər-ˈsīt-əs\ *n* **:** inflammation of a bursa (as of the shoulder or elbow)

[1]**burst** \ˈbərst\ *vb* **burst; burst·ing 1 a :** to break open, apart, or into pieces from or as if from impact or from or as if from pressure within ⟨buds ready to *burst* open⟩ **b :** to cause to burst ⟨*burst* a balloon⟩ **2 a :** to give way from an excess of emotion ⟨their hearts *burst* with grief⟩ **b :** to give vent suddenly to an emotion ⟨*burst* out laughing⟩ **3 a :** to emerge or spring suddenly ⟨the sun *burst* through the clouds⟩ **b :** LAUNCH, PLUNGE ⟨*burst* into song⟩ **4 :** to be filled to the point of breaking or overflowing ⟨*bursting* with pride⟩ [Old English *berstan*] — **burst at the seams :** to be larger, fuller, or more crowded than expected

[2]**burst** *n* **1 a :** a sudden outbreak or outburst ⟨a *burst* of laughter⟩ **b :** a sudden intense effort or exertion ⟨a *burst* of speed⟩ **c :** a short quick volley of shots ⟨fire a machine gun in *bursts*⟩ **2 :** an act of bursting **3 :** a result of bursting; *esp* **:** a visible puff accompanying the explosion of a shell

bur·then \ˈbər-t͟hən\ *archaic variant of* BURDEN

bur·weed \ˈbər-ˌwēd\ *n* **:** any of various plants with the fruit enclosed in a bur

bury \ˈber-ē\ *vt* **bur·ied; bury·ing 1 :** to deposit (a dead body) in the earth, in a grave, or in the sea especially with funeral ceremonies **2 :** to place in the ground and cover over ⟨*bury* treasure⟩ **3 :** CONCEAL, HIDE ⟨*bury* one's face in one's hands⟩ **4 :** to remove from the world of action ⟨*bury* oneself in a book⟩ [Old English *byrgan*] ***synonyms*** see HIDE — **bur·i·er** *n* — **bury the hatchet :** to settle a disagreement **:** become reconciled

[1]**bus** \ˈbəs\ *n, pl* **bus·es** *also* **bus·ses 1 a :** a large motor vehicle for carrying passengers especially on an established route according to a schedule **b :** AUTOMOBILE **2 :** a conductor for collecting electric currents and distributing them to outgoing feeders — called also *bus bar* [short for *omnibus*]

Word History Latin *omnibus*, the dative plural of *omnis* "all," means "for all." In English, *omnibus* has several meanings. An omnibus may be a public vehicle which carries all or a waiter's assistant who does all odd jobs. The shortening of *omnibus* has given us *bus*, the usual word for the vehicle.

[2]**bus** *vb* **bused** *also* **bussed; bus·ing** *also* **bus·sing :** to travel or transport by bus

bus·boy \ˈbəs-ˌbȯi\ *n* **:** a person employed in a restaurant to remove dirty dishes and reset tables [*omnibus* "busboy"]

bus·by \ˈbəz-bē\ *n, pl* **busbies 1 :** a military full-dress fur hat with a bag hanging down on one side **2 :** the bearskin worn by British guardsmen [probably from the name *Busby*]

bush \ˈbu̇sh\ *n* **1 :** SHRUB; *esp* **:** a low densely branched shrub **2 :** a large sparsely settled area (as in Australia) that is usually scrub-covered or forested — usually used with *the* **3 :** a bushy tuft or mass; *esp* **:** BRUSH 2 [Middle English]

bush baby *n* **:** any of several small African lemurs — called also *galago*

bushed \ˈbu̇sht\ *adj* **:** worn out with fatigue **:** EXHAUSTED

bush·el \ˈbu̇sh-əl\ *n* **1 :** any of various units of dry capacity — see MEASURE table **2 :** a container holding a bushel **3 :** a large quantity **:** LOTS [Medieval French *bussel, buschelle*, from *boisse* "measure of grain," of Celtic origin]

Bu·shi·do \ˈbu̇sh-i-ˌdō, ˈbüsh-\ *n* **:** a Japanese code of feudal chivalry emphasizing loyalty and valuing honor above life [Japanese *bushidō*]

bush·ing \ˈbu̇sh-ing\ *n* **1 :** a usually removable cylindrical lining in an opening of a mechanical part to limit the size of the opening, resist wear, or serve as a guide **2 :** an electrically insulating lining for a hole to protect a conductor [Dutch *bus* "bushing, box," derived from Late Latin *buxis* "box"]

Bush·man \ˈbu̇sh-mən\ *n* **:** a member of a group of peoples of southern Africa who traditionally live by hunting and foraging

bush·mas·ter \-ˌmas-tər\ *n* **:** a tropical American pit viper that is the largest New World venomous snake

bush pilot *n* **:** a pilot who flies a small plane over remote or sparsely settled country where commercial airlines don't go

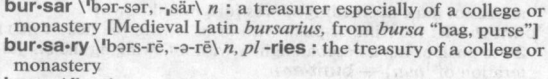

bush·whack \ˈbu̇sh-ˌhwak, -ˌwak\ *vb* **1 :** to clear a path through woods by cutting bushes and low branches **2 :** to live or hide out in the woods **3 :** to attack from a place of hiding **:** AMBUSH — **bush•whack•er** *n* — **bush•whack•ing** *n*

bushy \ˈbu̇sh-ē\ *adj* **bush•i•er; -est** **1 :** full of or overgrown with bushes **2 :** resembling a bush especially in thick spreading form or growth ⟨*bushy* eyebrows⟩ — **bush•i•ness** *n*

busi•ness \ˈbiz-nəs, -nəz\ *n* **1 a :** an activity that takes a major part of the time, attention, or effort of a person or group **b :** a commercial or mercantile activity engaged in as a means of livelihood **2 :** an immediate task or objective **:** MISSION ⟨get down to *business*⟩ **3 a :** a commercial or industrial enterprise **b :** the area of economic activity that usually includes trade, commerce, finance, and industry **c :** transactions of any sort; *esp* **:** PATRONAGE ⟨took their *business* elsewhere⟩ **4 :** AFFAIR, MATTER ⟨a strange *business*⟩ **5 a :** personal concern ⟨none of your *business*⟩ **b :** RIGHT ⟨you had no *business* saying that⟩ [Middle English *bisynesse,* from *bisy* "busy"]

synonyms BUSINESS, COMMERCE, TRADE, INDUSTRY mean activity in supplying commodities. BUSINESS may be an inclusive term but specifically applies to the activities of all engaged in the sale and purchase of commodities or in related financial transactions; COMMERCE and TRADE apply to the exchange and transportation of commodities; INDUSTRY applies to the producing of commodities, especially by manufacturing or processing.

busi•ness•like \ˈbiz-nəs-ˌlīk, -nəz-\ *adj* **1 :** having or showing qualities desirable in business **2 :** SERIOUS, PURPOSEFUL

busi•ness•man \ˈbiz-nə-ˌsman\ *n* **:** a man engaged in business especially on an executive level

busi•ness•peo•ple \-ˌspē-pəl\ *n pl* **:** persons active in business

busi•ness•per•son \-ˌspər-sən\ *n* **:** a businessman or businesswoman

busi•ness•wom•an \-ˌswu̇m-ən\ *n* **:** a woman engaged in business especially on an executive level

bus•kin \ˈbəs-kən\ *n* **1 :** a boot reaching halfway to the knee **2 :** TRAGEDY 1; *esp* **:** tragedy resembling ancient Greek drama [probably from Middle French *brozequin*]

bus•man's holiday \ˈbəs-mənz-\ *n* **:** a holiday spent in doing something similar to one's usual occupation

buss \ˈbəs\ *n* **:** KISS 1 [perhaps from Middle English *bassen* "to kiss"] — **buss** *vt*

¹bust \ˈbəst\ *n* **1 :** a piece of sculpture representing the upper part of the human figure including the head and neck **2 :** the upper portion of the human torso between neck and waist; *esp* **:** the breasts of a woman [French *buste,* from Italian *busto,* from Latin *bustum* "tomb"]

²bust *vb* **bust•ed** *also* **bust; bust•ing** **1 a :** to break or smash especially with force ⟨*busted* my watch⟩ **b :** to break up or apart ⟨*bust* trusts⟩; *also* **:** FRACTURE **c :** to ruin financially **d :** EXHAUST, WEAR OUT — used in phrases like *bust one's butt* to describe making a strenuous effort **e :** to give a hard time to **2 :** TAME ⟨bronco *busting*⟩ **3 :** to demote especially in military rank **4** *slang* **:** ARREST 2 **5 :** HIT, PUNCH **6 :** BURST ⟨laughing fit to *bust*⟩ [alteration of *burst*] — **bust•er** *n*

³bust *n* **1 :** ³PUNCH 2 **2 :** a complete failure **:** FLOP **3 :** SPREE **4** *slang* **:** a police raid or arrest

bus•tard \ˈbəs-tərd\ *n* **:** any of various large Old World and Australian game birds [Middle English, Middle French *bistarde,* derived from Latin *avis tarda,* literally, "slow bird"]

¹bus•tle \ˈbəs-əl\ *vi* **bus•tled; bus•tling** \ˈbəs-ling, -ə-ling\ **1 :** to move about busily and noisily ⟨*bustling* about the house⟩ **2 :** to be busily astir **:** SEETHE ⟨the wharf *bustled* with activity⟩ [probably derived from *busk* "to prepare"]

²bustle *n* **:** noisy or energetic activity

³bustle *n* **:** a pad or a light frame formerly worn by women just below the back waistline to give fullness to the skirt [origin unknown]

bust•line \ˈbəst-ˌlīn\ *n* **:** a line around a woman's body at the bust; *also* **:** the length of this line

¹busy \ˈbiz-ē\ *adj* **bus•i•er; -est** **1 a :** engaged in action **:** OCCUPIED ⟨too *busy* to eat⟩ **b :** being in use ⟨a *busy* telephone⟩ **2 :** full of activity **:** BUSTLING ⟨a *busy* street⟩ **3 :** OFFICIOUS, MEDDLING **4 :** full of distracting detail ⟨a *busy* design⟩ [Old English *bisig*] — **bus•i•ly** \ˈbiz-ə-lē\ *adv* — **busy•ness** \ˈbiz-ē-nəs\ *n*

synonyms BUSY, INDUSTRIOUS, DILIGENT mean seriously involved in doing something. BUSY stresses actively doing something as opposed to idleness ⟨*busy* getting the house ready for guests⟩. INDUSTRIOUS suggests working at something steadily or with determination ⟨*industrious* students working on science projects⟩. DILIGENT suggests working toward a particular goal especially over a long period of time ⟨a *diligent* search for the perfect birthday present⟩.

²busy *vb* **bus•ied; busy•ing :** to make or keep busy **:** OCCUPY

busy•body \ˈbiz-ē-ˌbäd-ē\ *n* **:** a person who meddles in the affairs of others

¹but \bət, ˈbət\ *conj* **1 a :** except that **:** UNLESS ⟨it never rains *but* it pours⟩ **b :** that . . . not ⟨not so stupid *but* you could learn⟩ **c :** THAT — used after a negative ⟨there is no doubt *but* we won⟩ **2 a** (1) **:** on the contrary ⟨not peace *but* a sword⟩ ⟨was called *but* did not answer⟩ (2) **:** despite that fact **:** YET ⟨was poor *but* honest⟩ ⟨we tried *but* we failed⟩ **b :** EXCEPT ⟨no one *but* you may enter⟩ [Old English *būtan* "outside, except, except that"]

²but *prep* **1 :** with the exception of ⟨no one came *but* us⟩ **2 :** other than ⟨this letter is nothing *but* an insult⟩

³but *adv* **1 :** no more than **:** ONLY ⟨we are *but* children⟩ **2 :** otherwise than ⟨who knows *but* that we may succeed⟩

bu•ta•di•ene \ˌbyüt-ə-ˈdī-ˌēn, -ˌdīˈ\ *n* **:** a flammable gaseous hydrocarbon C_4H_6 used in making synthetic rubbers [*butane* + *di-* + *-ene*]

bu•tane \ˈbyü-ˌtān\ *n* **:** either of two flammable gaseous hydrocarbons C_4H_{10} obtained usually from petroleum or natural gas and used as fuels [*butyric* + *-ane*]

¹butch•er \ˈbu̇ch-ər\ *n* **1 a :** a person who slaughters animals or dresses their flesh **b :** a dealer in meat **2 :** one that kills ruthlessly or brutally **3 :** a vendor especially on a train or in theaters [Medieval French *bocher,* from *boc* "he-goat"]

²butcher *vt* **butch•ered; butch•er•ing** \ˈbu̇ch-ring, -ə-ring\ **1 :** to slaughter and dress for market ⟨*butchered* hogs last week⟩ **2 :** to kill in a barbarous manner **3 :** to make a mess of **:** BOTCH ⟨*butchered* the performance⟩

butch•er•bird \ˈbu̇ch-ər-ˌbərd\ *n* **:** any of various shrikes that impale their prey upon thorns

butch•ery \ˈbu̇ch-rē, -ə-rē\ *n, pl* **-er•ies** **1** *chiefly British* **:** SLAUGHTERHOUSE **2 :** the business of a butcher **3 :** brutal murder **:** great slaughter

bu•teo \ˈbyüt-ē-ˌō\ *n, pl* **-te•os :** any of various hawks with broad rounded wings and soaring flight [Latin, a kind of hawk]

but•ler \ˈbət-lər\ *n* **:** the chief male servant of a household [Medieval French *butiller* "servant in charge of wine," from *botele* "bottle"]

butler's pantry *n* **:** a service room between kitchen and dining room

¹butt \ˈbət\ *vb* **:** to strike with the head or horns [Medieval French *boter,* of Germanic origin] — **butt heads :** to come into conflict

²butt *n* **:** a blow or thrust usually with the head or horns

³butt *n* **1 a :** a mound, bank, or structure for stopping missiles shot at a target **b :** TARGET 1a **c** *pl* **:** RANGE 5b **2 :** a target of abuse or ridicule ⟨the *butt* of a joke⟩ [Medieval French *but* "target," of Germanic origin]

⁴butt *vb* **1 :** ABUT 1 **2 :** to place end to end without overlapping

⁵butt *n* **1 :** BUTTOCK 2a — often used in idiomatic expressions ⟨saved our *butts*⟩ ⟨get your *butt* over here⟩ **2 :** the large or thicker end of something; *esp* **:** the thicker or handle end of a tool or weapon **3 :** an unused remainder ⟨a cigarette *butt*⟩ [Middle English]

⁶butt *n* **1 :** a large cask especially for wine, beer, or water **2 :** any of various units of liquid capacity; *esp* **:** a measure equal to 108 imperial gallons (about 491 liters) [Medieval French *but, bout,* from Old Occitan *bota,* from Late Latin *buttis*]

butte \ˈbyüt\ *n* **:** an isolated hill with steep sides usually having a smaller summit area than a mesa [French]

¹but•ter \ˈbət-ər\ *n* **1 :** a solid yellow emulsion of fat, air, and water made by churning milk or cream and used as food **2 :** a substance resembling butter in appearance, texture, or use ⟨apple *butter*⟩ [Old English *butere,* from Latin *butyrum,* from Greek *boutyron,* from *bous* "cow" + *tyros* "cheese"]

²butter *vt* **:** to spread with or as if with butter

but•ter–and–eggs \ˌbət-ə-rə-ˈnegz, -ˈnāgz\ *n sing or pl* **:** a common European herb related to the snapdragons that has showy yellow and orange flowers and is a naturalized weed in much of North America — called also *toadflax*

butter bean *n* **1** : WAX BEAN **2** : LIMA BEAN **3** : a green shell bean especially as opposed to a snap bean

but·ter·cup \ˈbət-ər-ˌkəp\ *n* : any of a genus of herbs having usually cuplike yellow flowers

but·ter·fat \-ˌfat\ *n* : the natural fat of milk and chief constituent of butter

but·ter·fin·gered \ˈbət-ər-ˌfing-gərd\ *adj* : likely to let things fall or slip through the fingers

but·ter·fish \-ˌfish\ *n* : any of numerous fishes with a slippery coating of mucus

but·ter·fly \ˈbət-ər-ˌflī\ *n* **1** : any of numerous slender-bodied day-flying insects (order Lepidoptera) with broad often brightly colored wings — compare MOTH **2** : a person chiefly occupied in the pursuit of pleasure **3** : a swimming stroke performed by moving both arms together in a circular motion while kicking the legs up and down **4** *pl* : a queasy feeling caused by nervousness

butterfly fish *n* : any of various fishes having variegated colors, broad expanded fins, or both

butterfly weed *n* : a showy orange-flowered milkweed of eastern North America

but·ter·milk \ˈbət-ər-ˌmilk\ *n* **1** : the liquid left after the butterfat has been churned from milk or cream **2** : milk from which all or part of the cream has been removed and which has been slightly soured by adding certain bacteria

but·ter·nut \-ˌnət\ *n* : the edible oily nut of a North American tree related to the walnut; *also* : this tree

butternut squash *n* : a smooth buff to yellow winter squash

but·ter·scotch \-ˌskäch\ *n* : a candy made from sugar, corn syrup, and water; *also* : the flavor of such candy

[1]**but·tery** \ˈbət-ə-rē, ˈbə-trē\ *n, pl* **-ter·ies** *chiefly dialect* : PANTRY [Medieval French *boterie* "storeroom for liquors," from *but* "cask, butt"]

[2]**but·tery** \ˈbət-ə-rē\ *adj* **1** : having the qualities (as smoothness or richness) of butter **2** : containing or spread with butter **3** : marked by flattery ⟨*buttery* compliments⟩

butt hinge *n* : a hinge usually set flush into the edge of a door

butt in *vi* : to meddle in the affairs of others

butt joint *n* : a joint made by fastening the parts together end-to-end without overlap and often with reinforcement

but·tock \ˈbət-ək\ *n* **1** : the back of the hip which forms one of the fleshy parts on which a person sits **2 a** *pl* : the seat of the body **b** : RUMP 1a [Middle English *buttok*]

[1]**but·ton** \ˈbət-n\ *n* **1 a** : a small knob or disk used for holding parts of a garment together or as an ornament **b** : a usually round badge bearing a design or slogan ⟨a campaign *button*⟩ **2** : something (as an immature mushroom) that resembles a button **3 a** : PUSH BUTTON; *also* : a computer icon that resembles a push button in appearance and function **b** : something (as a push button) that has the real or symbolic capability of starting a catastrophe (as a nuclear attack) ⟨has his finger on the *button*⟩ **c** : a hidden sensitivity that can be manipulated to produce a desired response ⟨knows how to push my *buttons*⟩ [Medieval French *butun* "rose hip, stud," from *boter* "to thrust, butt"]

[2]**button** *vb* **but·toned; but·ton·ing** \ˈbət-ning, -n-ing\ : to close or fasten with buttons — **but·ton·er** \ˈbət-nər, -n-ər\ *n*

[1]**but·ton·hole** \ˈbət-n-ˌhōl\ *n* : a slit or loop for fastening a button

[2]**buttonhole** *vt* **1** : to furnish with buttonholes **2** : to work with buttonhole stitch — **but·ton·hol·er** *n*

[3]**buttonhole** *vt* : to hold in conversation by or as if by clutching the clothes

buttonhole stitch *n* : a closely worked loop stitch used to make a firm edge (as on a buttonhole)

but·ton·hook \ˈbət-n-ˌhu̇k\ *n* : a hook for drawing small buttons through buttonholes

but·ton·wood \ˈbət-n-ˌwu̇d\ *n* : PLANE TREE

butt out *vi* : to stop meddling in the affairs of others

[1]**but·tress** \ˈbə-trəs\ *n* **1** : a projecting structure (as of masonry) that supports or stabilizes a wall or building **2** : something that supports, props, or strengthens [Medieval French (*arche*) *boteraz* "thrusting (arch)," derived from *boter* "to thrust"]

[2]**buttress** *vt* : to support with or as if with a buttress : PROP, STRENGTHEN ⟨*buttress* an argument with facts⟩

bu·tyl \ˈbyüt-l\ *n* : any of four isomeric radicals C_4H_9– derived from butane [*butyric* acid + *-yl*]

butyl alcohol *n* : any of four flammable alcohols C_4H_9OH derived from butanes and used in organic synthesis and as solvents

bu·tyr·ic acid \byü-ˈtir-ik-\ *n* : an acid $C_4H_8O_2$ of unpleasant odor found in rancid butter and perspiration [Latin *butyrum* "butter"]

bux·om \ˈbək-səm\ *adj* : vigorously or healthily plump; *also* : having a large bosom [Middle English *buxsum* "obedient, tractable," from Old English *būgan* "to bend"] — **bux·om·ly** *adv* — **bux·om·ness** *n*

buttress 1

[1]**buy** \ˈbī\ *vt* **bought** \ˈbȯt\; **buy·ing** **1** : to become owner of by giving money in exchange **2** : to obtain by sacrificing something ⟨*buy* peace at the cost of freedom⟩ **3** : to secure decisive control over by bribery ⟨*buy* votes⟩ **4** : to be sufficient to purchase ⟨$100,000 will *buy* this land⟩ **5** : BELIEVE 3, ACCEPT ⟨I don't *buy* that nonsense⟩ [Old English *bycgan*] — **buy·er** *n* — **buy it** *or* **buy the farm** : to get killed : DIE — **buy time** : to delay an action or decision : STALL

[2]**buy** *n* **1** : an act of buying : PURCHASE **2** : something sold or for sale at a price favorable to a buyer : BARGAIN

buyer's market *n* : a market with many goods at relatively low prices — compare SELLER'S MARKET

buy out *vt* **1** : to purchase the share or interest of **2** : to purchase the entire assets of (a business) — **buy·out** *n*

buy up *vt* : to buy all of the available supply of

[1]**buzz** \ˈbəz\ *vb* **1** : to make a low continuous humming sound like that of a bee **2** : to be filled with a confused murmur ⟨the room *buzzed* with excitement⟩ **3** : to summon or signal with a buzzer; *also* : to let in through an electronically controlled entrance ⟨*buzzed* him in⟩ **4** : to fly low and fast over ⟨planes *buzzed* the crowd⟩ [Middle English *bussen*, of imitative origin]

[2]**buzz** *n* **1** : a persistent sound produced by or as if by rapid vibrations **2** : a confused murmur or flurry of activity **3 a** : a signal conveyed by buzzer **b** : a call on the telephone

buz·zard \ˈbəz-ərd\ *n* **1** *chiefly British* : BUTEO **2** : any of several vultures; *esp* : TURKEY VULTURE [Medieval French *busard*, derived from Latin *buteo*, a kind of hawk]

buzz cut *n* : CREW OUT — **buzz–cut** *adj*

buzz·er \ˈbəz-ər\ *n* : an electric signaling device that makes a buzzing sound

buzz saw *n* : CIRCULAR SAW

B vitamin *n* : any vitamin of the vitamin B complex

[1]**by** \bī, ˈbī, *especially before consonants* bə\ *prep* **1** : close to : NEAR ⟨*by* the sea⟩ **2 a** : ALONG, THROUGH ⟨*by* a different route⟩ ⟨enter *by* the door⟩ **b** : PAST ⟨went right *by* us⟩ **3 a** : during the course of ⟨studied *by* night⟩ **b** : not later than ⟨be there *by* 2 p.m.⟩ **4** : through the agency or instrumentality of ⟨painted *by* a master⟩ ⟨a town taken *by* force⟩ **5** : with the witness or sanction of ⟨swear *by* all that is holy⟩ **6** : in conformity with : ACCORDING TO ⟨*by* the rules⟩ **7** : with respect to ⟨a doctor *by* profession⟩ **8** : in or to the amount or extent of ⟨win *by* a nose⟩ ⟨sold *by* the pound⟩ **9** — used as a function word to indicate a succession of units or groups ⟨walk two *by* two⟩ **10 a** — used as a function word in multiplication, in division, and in measurements ⟨divide 12 *by* 4⟩ ⟨a room 12 feet *by* 15 feet⟩ **b** : plus one point toward ⟨north *by* northeast⟩ **11** : in the opinion of ⟨it's fine *by* me⟩ [Old English *be, bī*] — **by oneself** : ALONE 2

synonyms BY, THROUGH, WITH are used in explaining or accounting for an action or effect. BY names the immediate agent or causative agency ⟨a novel *by* Dickens⟩ ⟨destroyed *by* fire⟩. THROUGH implies intermediateness and names a means or medium ⟨express feelings *through* music⟩ ⟨money lost *through* carelessness⟩. WITH names an instrument or instrumentality used in or accompanying an action ⟨wrote *with* a pen⟩ ⟨amused them *with* a story⟩.

[2]**by** \ˈbī\ *adv* **1 a** : close at hand : NEAR ⟨standing *by*⟩ **b** : at or to another's home ⟨stop *by* for a chat⟩ **2** : PAST ⟨saw them go *by*⟩ **3** : in reserve for future using ⟨putting some money *by*⟩

[3]**by** *or* **bye** \ˈbī\ *n, pl* **byes** \ˈbīz\ : something of secondary importance — **by the by** : by the way : INCIDENTALLY

by–and–by \ˌbī-ən-ˈbī\ *n* : a future time or occasion

by and by \ˌbī-ən-ˈbī\ *adv* : BEFORE LONG, SOON

by and large \ˌbī-ən-ˈlärj\ *adv* : on the whole : in general

by·catch \ˈbī-ˌkach, -ˌkech\ *n* : the portion of a commercial fishing catch that consists of marine animals caught unintentionally

bye–bye *or* **by–by** \'bī-ˌbī, bī-'bī\ *interj* — used to express farewell [from *goodbye*]

by–elec·tion \'bī-ə-ˌlek-shən\ *n* : a special election held between regular elections in order to fill a vacancy

by·gone \'bī-ˌgȯn *also* -ˌgän\ *adj* : gone by : PAST ⟨a *bygone* era⟩ — **bygone** *n*

by·law \'bī-ˌlȯ\ *n* : a rule adopted by an organization (as a club or municipality) for the regulation of its affairs [Middle English *bilawe,* probably from Old Norse *bȳr* "town" + *lǫg* "law"]

by·line \'bī-ˌlīn\ *n* : a line at the head of a newspaper or magazine article giving the writer's name

[1]**by·pass** \'bī-ˌpas\ *n* **1** : a passage to one side or around a congested area **2 a** : a channel through which a fluid passes around a particular part and back to the main stream **b** : SHUNT c; *also* : a surgical procedure for the creation of a shunt

[2]**bypass** *vt* : to make a detour or circuit around ⟨*bypass* a city⟩

by·path \'bī-ˌpath, -ˌpȧth\ *n* : BYWAY 1

by·play \-ˌplā\ *n* : action occurring on the side while the main action proceeds (as in a play)

by–prod·uct \'bī-ˌpräd-əkt, -ˌəkt\ *n* **1** : something produced (as in manufacturing) in addition to the principal product **2** : a secondary and often unexpected or unintended result

byre \'bīr\ *n, chiefly British* : a cow barn [Old English *bȳre*]

by·road \'bī-ˌrōd\ *n* : BYWAY 1

By·ron·ic \bī-'rän-ik\ *adj* : of, relating to, or having the characteristics of the poet Byron or his writings — **By·ron·i·cal·ly** \-'rän-i-kə-lē, -klē\ *adv* — **By·ron·ism** \'bī-rə-ˌniz-əm\ *n*

bys·sus \'bis-əs\ *n* : a tuft of long tough filaments by which some mollusks (as mussels) attach themselves (as to rocks) [Greek *byssos* "flax," of Semitic origin]

by·stand·er \'bī-ˌstan-dər\ *n* : a person present or standing near but taking no part in something going on

by·street \'bī-ˌstrēt\ *n* : a street off a main thoroughfare : a side street

byte \'bīt\ *n* : a group of eight bits that a computer processes as a unit [perhaps alteration of [2]*bite*]

by·way \'bī-ˌwā\ *n* **1** : a little-traveled side road **2** : a secondary or little known aspect or field

by·word \'bī-ˌwərd\ *n* **1** : a proverbial saying **2 a** : one that personifies a type **b** : one that is noteworthy or notorious **3** : EPITHET **4** : a frequently used word or phrase

[1]**Byz·an·tine** \'biz-n-ˌtēn *also* -ˌtīn\ *n* : a native or inhabitant of Byzantium or of the Byzantine Empire

[2]**Byzantine** *adj* **1** : of, relating to, or characteristic of the ancient city of Byzantium or the Eastern Roman Empire **2** : of or relating to a style of architecture developed in the Byzantine Empire especially in the 5th and 6th centuries characterized by a central dome over a square space and by much use of mosaics **3** : of or relating to the Eastern Orthodox Church **4** : intricately involved and often devious ⟨*Byzantine* political maneuvering⟩

C

c \'sē\ *n, pl* **c's** *or* **cs** \'sēz\ *often cap* **1** : the 3rd letter of the English alphabet **2** : one hundred in Roman numerals **3** : a musical tone referred to by the letter C and on which a C-major scale is based **4** : a grade rating a student's work as fair or mediocre **5** : a computer programming language designed especially to be compact and efficient

cab \'kab\ *n* **1 a** : a light closed horse-drawn carriage (as a hansom) **b** : a carriage for hire **2** : TAXICAB **3 a** : the part of a locomotive that houses the engineer and operating controls **b** : a comparable shelter on a truck, tractor, or crane [short for *cabriolet*]

ca·bal \kə-'bal, -'bäl\ *n* : a small group of persons working together to promote their own plans or interests especially by intrigue [French *cabale,* from Medieval Latin *cabbala* "cabala," from Hebrew *qabbālāh,* literally, "received (lore)"]

ca·ba·la *or* **cab·ba·la** *or* **cab·ba·lah** *or* **ka·ba·la** *or* **kab·ba·la** *or* **kab·ba·lah** \'kab-ə-lə, kə-'bäl-ə\ *n, often cap* **1** : a system of Jewish mysticism and magic using a cipher method of interpreting Scripture **2** : a strange and esoteric doctrine or mysterious art [Medieval Latin *cabbala*] — **cab·a·lism** \'kab-ə-ˌliz-əm\ *n* — **ca·ba·list** \'kab-ə-ləst, kə-'bäl-əst\ *adj* — **cab·a·lis·tic** \ˌkab-ə-'lis-tik\ *adj*

ca·bal·le·ro \ˌkab-ə-'leər-ō, -əl-'yeər-, -ə-'yeər-\ *n, pl* **-ros** *chiefly Southwest* : HORSEMAN [Spanish, derived from Latin *caballus* "horse"]

ca·bana \kə-'ban-yə, -'ban-ə\ *n* : a shelter resembling a cabin usually with an open side facing a beach or swimming pool [Spanish *cabaña,* literally, "hut," from Medieval Latin *capanna*]

cab·a·ret \ˌkab-ə-'rā\ *n* : a restaurant serving liquor and providing entertainment (as by singers or dancers) [French]

cab·bage \'kab-ij\ *n* : a short-stemmed garden plant related to the turnips and mustards and producing a dense globular head of usually green leaves used as a vegetable [Middle French dialect *caboche,* literally, "head"]

cabbage butterfly *n* : any of several mostly white butterflies whose green caterpillars feed on cabbages

cabbage palm *n* : a palm with terminal buds eaten as a vegetable

cab·by *or* **cab·bie** \'kab-ē\ *n, pl* **cabbies** : a driver of a cab

cab·driv·er \'kab-ˌdrī-vər\ *n* : a driver of a cab

cab·in \'kab-ən\ *n* **1 a** : a private room on a ship **b** : a compartment below deck on a small boat for passengers or crew **c** : a compartment in a vehicle (as an airplane or spacecraft) for cargo, crew, or passengers **2** : a small one-story dwelling usually of simple construction [Medieval French *cabane,* from Old Occitan *cabana* "hut," from Medieval Latin *capanna*]

cabin boy *n* : a boy working as servant on a ship

cabin class *n* : a class of accommodations on a passenger ship superior to tourist class and inferior to first class

cabin cruiser *n* : CRUISER 3

cab·i·net \'kab-ə-nət, 'kab-nət\ *n* **1 a** : a case or cupboard usually having doors and shelves **b** : CONSOLE 3 **2 a** : a group of ministers acting as advisers to a monarch or chief of state but constituting the real political executive in a cabinet government ⟨the British *cabinet*⟩ **b** : a body of advisers to the president of the United States consisting chiefly of the heads of the executive departments [Middle French, "small room," from Middle French dialect *cabine* "gambling house"]

cabinet government *n* : a government in which the real executive and policy-making power is held by a cabinet of ministers who are responsible to the legislature

cab·i·net·mak·er \-ˌmā-kər\ *n* : a skilled woodworker who makes fine furniture — **cab·i·net·mak·ing** \-king\ *n*

cab·i·net·work \-ˌwərk\ *n* : the finished work of a cabinetmaker

cabin fever *n* : extreme irritability and restlessness that results from living in isolation or in a confined indoor area for a long time

[1]**ca·ble** \'kā-bəl\ *n* **1 a** : a strong rope especially of 10 inches (25 centimeters) or more in circumference **b** : a wire rope or metal chain of great strength **c** : a wire or wire rope by which force is exerted to operate a mechanism ⟨brake *cable*⟩ **2** : CABLE LENGTH **3 a** : a bundle of electrical conductors insulated from each other but held together usually by being twisted around a central core **b** : CABLEGRAM **4** : CABLE TELEVISION [Medieval French, from Medieval Latin *capulum* "lasso," from Latin *capere* "to take"]

[2]**cable** *vb* **ca·bled; ca·bling** \ˈkā-bling, -bə-ling\ **1 :** to fasten or provide with a cable **2 :** to telegraph by submarine cable

cable car *n* **:** a car moved on a railway by an endless cable or along an overhead cableway

ca·ble·gram \ˈkā-bəl-ˌgram\ *n* **:** a message sent by submarine cable

cable length *n* **:** a maritime unit of length variously reckoned as 100 fathoms, 120 fathoms, or 608 feet (about 183, 220, or 185 meters)

cable modem *n* **:** a modem used to connect a computer to a network (as the Internet) over a cable television line

cable television *n* **:** a system of television reception in which signals are picked up by a single antenna and sent by cable to the receivers of paying subscribers — called also *cable TV*

ca·ble·way \ˈkā-bəl-ˌwā\ *n* **:** a suspended cable used as a track along which carriers can be pulled

cab·o·chon \ˈkab-ə-ˌshän\ *n* **:** a gem or bead cut in convex form and highly polished but not faceted; *also* **:** this style of cutting [Middle French, from Middle French dialect *caboche* "head"] — **cabochon** *adv*

ca·boo·dle \kə-ˈbüd-l\ *n* **:** all of a group of things — used in the phrase *the whole caboodle* or *the whole kit and caboodle* [probably from *ca-* (intensive prefix) + *boodle*]

ca·boose \kə-ˈbüs\ *n* **:** a freight-train car attached usually to the rear mainly for the use of the train crew and railroad workers [probably from Dutch *kabuis* "ship's galley"]

cab·ri·ole \ˈkab-rē-ˌōl\ *n* **1 :** a ballet leap in which one leg is extended and the other struck against it **2 :** a curved furniture leg ending in an ornamental foot [French, "caper," from Middle French *capriole* "capriole"]

cab·ri·o·let \ˌkab-rē-ə-ˈlā\ *n* **1 :** a light 2-wheeled one-horse carriage with a folding leather top and upward-curving shafts **2 :** a convertible coupe [French, from *cabriole* "caper"]

cab·stand \ˈkab-ˌstand\ *n* **:** a place for cabs to park while waiting for passengers

ca·cao \kə-ˈkau̇, kə-ˈkā-ō\ *n, pl* **cacaos 1 :** a South American tree with small yellowish flowers followed by fleshy yellow pods with many seeds **2 :** the dried partly fermented fatty seeds of the cacao from which cocoa and chocolate are made — called also *cacao bean, cocoa bean* [Spanish, from Nahuatl *cacahuatl* "cacao beans"]

[1]**cache** \ˈkash\ *n* **1 :** a place for hiding, storing, or safeguarding treasure or food and supplies **2 :** the material hidden or stored in a cache **3 :** a computer memory with very short access time used especially for storage of frequently used instructions or data [French, from *cacher* "to hide"]

[2]**cache** *vt* **:** to place, hide, or store in a cache

ca·chet \ka-ˈshā\ *n* **1 :** a seal especially of official approval **2 :** a characteristic feature or quality conferring prestige [French, from *cacher* "to press, hide"]

ca·chex·ia \kə-ˈkek-sē-ə, ka-\ *n* **:** general physical wasting and malnutrition usually associated with chronic disease [Late Latin, from Greek *kachexia* "bad condition," from *kakos* "bad" + *hexis* "condition"] — **ca·chec·tic** \-ˈkek-tik\ *adj*

ca·cique \kə-ˈsēk\ *n* **:** an Indian chief in Latin America [Spanish, from Taino (American Indian language of the Greater Antilles)]

cack·le \ˈkak-əl\ *vi* **cack·led; cack·ling** \ˈkak-ling, -ə-ling\ **1 :** to make the sharp broken noise or cry characteristic of a hen especially after laying **2 :** to laugh or chatter noisily [Middle English *cakelen,* of imitative origin] — **cackle** *n* — **cack·ler** \ˈkak-lər, -ə-lər\ *n*

ca·coph·o·ny \kə-ˈkäf-ə-nē, ka-\ *n, pl* **-nies :** harsh or discordant sound **:** DISSONANCE [Greek *kakophōnia,* from *kakos* "bad" + *phōnē* "sound"] — **ca·coph·o·nous** \-nəs\ *adj*

cac·tus \ˈkak-təs\ *n, pl* **cac·ti** \-ˌtī, -ˌtē, -tē\ *or* **cac·tus·es** *also* **cactus :** any of a large family of flowering plants able to live in dry regions and having fleshy stems and branches that bear scales or prickles instead of leaves [Latin, "cardoon," from Greek *kaktos*]

cad \ˈkad\ *n* **:** a rude and selfish man [English dialect, "unskilled assistant," from Scots *caddie*]

ca·dav·er \kə-ˈdav-ər\ *n* **:** a dead body especially of a human being **:** CORPSE [Latin, from *cadere* "to fall"] — **ca·dav·er·ic** \-ˈdav-rik, -ə-rik\ *adj*

ca·dav·er·ous \kə-ˈdav-rəs, -ə-rəs\ *adj* **:** of, relating to, or resembling a cadaver: as **a :** GHASTLY 2, PALE **b :** THIN 3, HAGGARD — **ca·dav·er·ous·ly** *adv*

[1]**cad·die** *or* **cad·dy** \ˈkad-ē\ *n, pl* **caddies :** a person who carries a golfer's clubs [Scots *caddie* "one who does odd jobs," from French *cadet* "military cadet"]

[2]**caddie** *or* **caddy** *vi* **-died; -dy·ing :** to work as a caddie

cad·dis fly \ˈkad-əs-\ *n* **:** any of an order (Trichoptera) of 4-winged insects with aquatic larvae that live in and carry around a silken case covered with bits of debris (as of plant matter or gravel) [*caddisworm* "caddis fly larva," probably from obsolete *codworm,* from Middle English *cod* "bag"]

cad·dish \ˈkad-ish\ *adj* **:** of, relating to, or being a cad ⟨*caddish* behavior⟩ — **cad·dish·ly** *adv* — **cad·dish·ness** *n*

cad·dy \ˈkad-ē\ *n, pl* **caddies :** a small box, can, or chest; *esp* **:** one to keep tea in [Malay *kati,* a unit of weight]

ca·dence \ˈkād-ns\ *n* **1 a :** rhythmic flow of sounds in language **b :** the beat, time, or measure of rhythmical motion or activity **2 :** the close of a musical strain; *esp* **:** a musical chord sequence moving to a harmonic close or point of rest [Italian *cadenza,* from *cadere* "to fall," from Latin] — **ca·denced** \-nst\ *adj*

ca·den·za \kə-ˈden-zə\ *n* **1 :** an added flourish in a solo piece (as an aria) commonly just before the end **2 :** a technically brilliant sometimes improvised solo passage toward the close of a movement of a concerto [Italian, "cadence, cadenza"]

ca·det \kə-ˈdet\ *n* **1 a :** a younger brother or son **b :** a younger branch of a family or a member of it **2 :** one in training for a military or naval commission; *esp* **:** a student in a service academy [French, from Gascon (Romance language of Gascony) *capdet* "chief," from Late Latin *capitellum,* from *caput* "head"] — **ca·det·ship** \-ˌship\ *n*

Ca·dette \kə-ˈdet\ *n* **:** a member of a program of the Girl Scouts for girls in the sixth through ninth grades [from *cadet*]

cadge \ˈkaj\ *vb* **:** BEG 1, SPONGE ⟨*cadge* a free cup of coffee⟩ [back-formation from Scots *cadger* "peddler," from Middle English *cadgear*] — **cadg·er** *n*

cad·mi·um \ˈkad-mē-əm\ *n* **:** a bluish white malleable ductile metallic element used especially in protective platings and in bearing metals — see ELEMENT table [Latin *cadmia* "zinc oxide, calamine"; from the occurrence of its ores together with zinc oxide]

cadmium sulfide *n* **:** a yellow-brown poisonous salt CdS used especially in electronic parts, in photoelectric cells, and in medicine

cad·re \ˈkad-rē, ˈkäd-, -ˌrā\ *n* **1 :** a nucleus of trained personnel capable of assuming leadership and control and of training others **2 :** a member of a cadre [French, "frame, framework," from Italian *quadro,* from Latin *quadrum* "square"]

ca·du·ceus \kə-ˈdü-sē-əs, -ˈdyü-, -shəs\ *n, pl* **-cei** \-sē-ˌī\ **1 a :** the symbolic staff of a herald **b :** a representation of a staff with two entwined snakes and two wings at the top **2 :** an insignia bearing a caduceus and symbolizing a physician [Latin, from Greek *karykeion,* from *karyx, kēryx* "herald"] — **ca·du·cean** \-sē-ən, -shən\ *adj*

caduceus

caecal, caecum *variant of* CECAL, CECUM

cae·ci·lian \si-ˈsil-yən, -ˈsēl-\ *n* **:** any of an order (Gymnophiona) of chiefly tropical burrowing limbless amphibians resembling worms [Latin *caecilia,* a species of caecilian, from *caecus* "blind"] — **caecilian** *adj*

Cae·sar \ˈsē-zər\ *n* **1 :** any of the Roman emperors succeeding Augustus Caesar — used as a title **2 a** *often not cap* **:** a powerful ruler: **(1) :** EMPEROR **(2) :** DICTATOR 1b, AUTOCRAT **b :** the civil power **:** a temporal ruler [from Gaius Julius *Caesar;* sense 2b from the reference in Matthew 22:21] — **Cae·sar·e·an** *or* **Cae·sar·i·an** \si-ˈzar-ē-ən, -ˈzer-\ *adj*

caesarean, caesarean section *variant of* CESAREAN, CESAREAN SECTION

cae·si·um *chiefly British variant of* CESIUM

cae·su·ra \si-ˈzu̇r-ə, -ˈzhu̇r-\ *n, pl* **-su·ras** *or* **-su·rae** \-ˈzu̇r-ē, -ˈzhu̇r-\ **:** a break in the flow of sound usually in the middle of a line of verse [Latin, "act of cutting," from *caedere* "to cut"]

ca·fé *also* **ca·fe** \ka-ˈfā, kə-\ *n* **1 :** COFFEEHOUSE **2 :** BARROOM, SALOON **3 :** RESTAURANT; *also* **:** NIGHTCLUB [French *café* "coffee, café," from Turkish *kahve*]

ca·fé au lait \ka-ˌfā-ō-ˈlā\ *n* **:** coffee with usually hot milk in about equal parts [French, "coffee with milk"]
caf·e·te·ria \ˌkaf-ə-ˈtir-ē-ə\ *n* **1 :** a restaurant in which the customers serve themselves or are served at a counter but take the food to tables to eat **2 :** LUNCHROOM [American Spanish *cafetería* "coffeehouse," from *cafetera* "coffeemaker," from French *cafetière,* from *café* "coffee"]
caf·fein·at·ed \ˈkaf-ə-ˌnāt-əd\ *adj* **1 :** stimulated by or as if by caffeine **2 :** containing caffeine ⟨*caffeinated* coffee⟩
caf·feine \ˈka-ˌfēn, ka-ˈfēn\ *n* **:** a bitter stimulating compound $C_8H_{10}N_4O_2$ found especially in coffee, tea, cacao, and kola nuts [German *Kaffein,* from *Kaffee* "coffee," from French *café*]
caf·tan *also* **kaf·tan** \kaf-ˈtan, ˈkaf-ˌ\ *n* **:** an ankle-length garment with long sleeves that is commonly worn in eastern Mediterranean countries [Russian *kaftan,* from Turkish, from Persian *qaftān*]
[1]**cage** \ˈkāj\ *n* **1 :** a largely open-worked enclosure for confining or carrying an animal (as a bird) **2 :** an enclosure like a cage in form or purpose **3 :** a large building with unobstructed interior for practicing outdoor sports and often adapted for indoor events [Medieval French, from Latin *cavea* "cavity, cage," from *cavus* "hollow" — see *Word History* at JAIL] — **cage·ful** \-ˌfu̇l\ *n*
[2]**cage** *vt* **:** to confine or keep in or as if in a cage
cage·ling \ˈkāj-liŋ\ *n* **:** a caged bird
ca·gey *also* **ca·gy** \ˈkā-jē\ *adj* **ca·gi·er; -est :** wary of being trapped or deceived **:** SHREWD, CAUTIOUS [origin unknown] — **ca·gi·ly** \-jə-lē\ *adv* — **ca·gi·ness** \-jē-nəs\ *n*
ca·hoot \kə-ˈhüt\ *n* **:** PARTNERSHIP 1, LEAGUE — usually used in plural ⟨in *cahoots* with the devil⟩ [perhaps from French *cahute* "cabin, hut"]
cai·man *also* **cay·man** \ˈkā-mən; kā-ˈman, kī-\ *n* **:** any of several Central and South American reptiles related to and resembling alligators [Spanish *caimán,* probably from Carib *caymán*]
ca·ïque \kä-ˈēk\ *n* **1 :** a light skiff used on the Bosporus **2 :** a Greek sailing vessel usually equipped with an auxiliary engine [French, from Turkish *kayık*]
cairn \ˈkaərn, ˈkeərn\ *n* **:** a heap of stones piled up as a landmark or as a memorial [Scottish Gaelic *carn*]
cairn terrier *n* **:** any of a breed of small compactly built terriers of Scottish origin with a weather resistant coat of harsh texture [from its use in hunting among cairns]
cais·son \ˈkā-ˌsän, ˈkās-n\ *n* **1 a :** a chest for ammunition **b :** a 2-wheeled vehicle for artillery ammunition **2 a :** a watertight chamber used in construction work underwater or as a foundation **b :** a float for raising a sunken vessel [French, from Middle French, from Old Occitan, from *caissa* "chest," from Latin *capsa* "chest, case"]
caisson disease *n* **:** DECOMPRESSION SICKNESS
cai·tiff \ˈkāt-əf\ *adj* **:** being base, cowardly, or contemptible [Medieval French *caitif* "captive, vile," from Latin *captivus* "captive"] — **caitiff** *n*
ca·jole \kə-ˈjōl\ *vt* **:** to coax or persuade especially by flattery or false promises **:** WHEEDLE [French *cajoler*] — **ca·jol·ery** \-ˈjōl-rē, -ə-rē\ *n*
[1]**Ca·jun** \ˈkā-jən\ *n* **:** a Louisianian descended from French-speaking immigrants from Acadia [alteration of *Acadian*]
[2]**Cajun** *adj* **1 :** of, relating to, or characteristic of the Cajuns **2 :** of, relating to, or prepared in a style of cooking originating with the Cajuns and characterized by the use of hot seasonings (as cayenne)
[1]**cake** \ˈkāk\ *n* **1 :** a small mass of food (as dough, meat, or fish) baked or fried **2 :** a baked food made from a sweet batter or dough **3 :** a substance hardened or molded into a solid mass ⟨a *cake* of soap⟩ **4 :** something easily done ⟨after so much studying, the test was *cake*⟩ [Old Norse *kaka*]
[2]**cake** *vb* **1 :** ENCRUST **2 :** to form or harden into a mass
cal·a·bash \ˈkal-ə-ˌbash\ *n* **1 :** GOURD; *esp* **:** one whose hard shell is used for a utensil (as a bottle) **2 :** a tropical American tree related to the trumpet vine; *also* **:** its hard round fruit **3 :** a utensil made from a calabash shell [Spanish *calabaza*]
cal·a·boose \ˈkal-ə-ˌbüs\ *n* **:** JAIL [Spanish *calabozo* "dungeon"]
ca·la·di·um \kə-ˈläd-ē-əm\ *n* **:** any of a genus of tropical American herbs related to the arums and often grown for their brightly colored leaves [Malay *kĕladi,* a plant of the arum family]
cal·a·mari \ˌkä-lə-ˈmär-ē\ *n* **:** squid used as food [It, plural of *calamaro, calamaio* "squid," from Medieval Latin *calamarium* "ink pot"; from the inky substance the squid secretes]
cal·a·mine \ˈkal-ə-ˌmīn, -mən\ *n* **:** a mixture of zinc oxide and a small amount of ferric oxide used in lotions, liniments, and ointments [Middle English *calamyn* "zinc ore," from Medieval Latin *calamina,* from Latin *cadmia* "zinc oxide," from Greek *kadmeia,* literally, "Theban (earth)," from *kadmeios* "Theban," from *Kadmos* "Cadmus," founder of Thebes]
cal·a·mite \ˈkal-ə-ˌmīt\ *n* **:** a Paleozoic fossil plant resembling a giant horsetail [derived from Latin *calamus* "reed"]
ca·lam·i·ty \kə-ˈlam-ət-ē\ *n, pl* **-ties 1 :** a state of deep distress or misery caused by major misfortune or loss **2 :** a disastrous event marked by great loss and lasting distress and suffering [Latin *calamitas*] ***synonyms*** see DISASTER — **ca·lam·i·tous** \-ət-əs\ *adj* — **ca·lam·i·tous·ly** *adv* — **ca·lam·i·tous·ness** *n*
cal·a·mus \ˈkal-ə-məs\ *n, pl* **-mi** \-ˌmī, -ˌmē\ **1 :** the sweet flag or its aromatic root **2 :** QUILL 2a [Latin, "reed, reed pen," from Greek *kalamos*]
ca·lash \kə-ˈlash\ *n* **1 :** a light small-wheeled 4-passenger carriage with a folding top **2 :** a large hood on a hoop frame worn by women in the 18th century [French *calèche,* from German *Kalesche,* from Czech *kolesa* "wheels, carriage"]
calc- *or* **calci-** *combining form* **:** calcium **:** calcium salt ⟨*calci*fy⟩ [Latin *calc-, calx* "lime"]
cal·ca·ne·us \kal-ˈkā-nē-əs\ *n, pl* **-nei** \-nē-ˌī\ **:** a tarsal bone that in humans is the large bone of the heel [Late Latin, "heel," from Latin *calcaneum,* from *calx* "heel"]
cal·car·e·ous \kal-ˈkar-ē-əs, -ˈker-\ *adj* **1 :** resembling calcite or calcium carbonate especially in hardness **2 :** consisting of or containing calcium carbonate; *also* **:** containing calcium — **cal·car·e·ous·ly** *adv* — **cal·car·e·ous·ness** *n*
cal·cif·er·ol \kal-ˈsif-ə-ˌrȯl, -ˌrōl\ *n* **:** a vitamin D that is used as a dietary supplement and medicinally to treat rickets and related disorders [*calcif*erous + ergoste*rol*]
cal·cif·er·ous \kal-ˈsif-rəs, -ə-rəs\ *adj* **:** producing or containing calcium carbonate
cal·ci·fi·ca·tion \ˌkal-sə-fə-ˈkā-shən\ *n* **1 :** the process of calcifying; *esp* **:** deposition of calcium salts (as in tissue) ⟨bone formation by *calcification* of cartilage⟩ **2 :** a calcified structure
cal·ci·fy \ˈkal-sə-ˌfī\ *vb* **-fied; -fy·ing 1 :** to make calcareous by deposit of calcium salts **2 :** to become calcareous
cal·ci·mine \ˈkal-sə-ˌmīn\ *n* **:** a white or tinted wash of glue, whiting or zinc white, and water used especially on plastered surfaces [alteration of *kalsomine,* of unknown origin] — **calcimine** *vt*
cal·cine \kal-ˈsīn, ˈkal-ˌ\ *vt* **:** to heat to a high temperature but without fusing in order to drive off volatile matter (as carbon dioxide from limestone) [Medieval Latin *calcinare,* from Late Latin *calcina* "lime," from Latin *calx*] — **cal·ci·na·tion** \ˌkal-sə-ˈnā-shən\ *n*
cal·cite \ˈkal-ˌsīt\ *n* **:** a crystalline mineral $CaCO_3$ composed of calcium carbonate and found in numerous forms including limestone, chalk, and marble — **cal·cit·ic** \kal-ˈsit-ik\ *adj*
cal·ci·to·nin \ˌkal-sə-ˈtō-nən\ *n* **:** a protein hormone from the thyroid gland that lowers the level of calcium in the blood plasma [*calc-* + *-tonin* (as in *serotonin*)]
cal·ci·um \ˈkal-sē-əm\ *n* **:** a silver-white bivalent soft metallic element that is found only in combination with other elements (as in limestone) and that is one of the essential parts of the bodies of most plants and animals — see ELEMENT table [New Latin, from Latin *calx* "lime"]
calcium carbide *n* **:** a usually dark gray crystalline compound CaC_2 used especially for the generation of acetylene
calcium carbonate *n* **:** a solid substance $CaCO_3$ found in nature as limestone and marble and in plant ashes, bones, and shells and used especially in making lime and portland cement
calcium chloride *n* **:** a salt $CaCl_2$ that absorbs moisture from the air and that is used as a drying agent and in a hydrated state to control dust and melt ice on roads
calcium cyanamide *n* **:** a substance $CaCN_2$ that is used especially as a fertilizer and weed killer
calcium hydroxide *n* **:** a white crystalline alkali compound $Ca(OH)_2$ that is used especially to make mortar and plaster and to soften water
calcium oxide *n* **:** an oxide of calcium CaO that is white when pure and makes up the major part of lime

calcium phosphate *n* **:** any of various phosphates of calcium: as **a :** the phosphate $Ca_3(PO_4)_2$ used as a fertilizer **b :** a naturally occurring phosphate containing other elements (as fluorine) and occurring as the chief constituent of phosphate rock, bones, and teeth

calcium sulfate *n* **:** a white salt of calcium $CaSO_4$ that is used especially in building materials and as a drying agent

cal·cu·late \ˈkal-kyə-ˌlāt\ *vb* **1 a :** to determine by mathematical processes ⟨*calculate* the average⟩ **b :** to determine by an informed guess **:** ESTIMATE ⟨*calculate* the risk of losing⟩ **2 :** to make a calculation **3 :** to plan by careful thought ⟨a program *calculated* to succeed⟩ **4 :** RELY, DEPEND [Latin *calculare,* from *calculus* "pebble (used in reckoning)"] — **cal·cu·la·ble** \-kyə-lə-bəl\ *adj* — **cal·cu·la·bly** \-blē\ *adv*

cal·cu·lat·ed \-ˌlāt-əd\ *adj* **:** undertaken after estimating the probability of success or failure ⟨a *calculated* risk⟩ — **cal·cu·lat·ed·ly** *adv*

cal·cu·lat·ing \-ˌlāt-iŋ\ *adj* **1 :** designed to make calculations ⟨a *calculating* machine⟩ **2 :** marked by shrewd analysis of one's own self-interest **:** SCHEMING — **cal·cu·lat·ing·ly** \-iŋ-lē\ *adv*

cal·cu·la·tion \ˌkal-kyə-ˈlā-shən\ *n* **1 a :** the process or an act of calculating **b :** the result of an act of calculating **2 :** studied care in analyzing or planning **:** CAUTION — **cal·cu·la·tive** \ˈkal-kyə-ˌlāt-iv\ *adj*

cal·cu·la·tor \ˈkal-kyə-ˌlāt-ər\ *n* **:** one that calculates; *esp* **:** a usually electronic device for performing mathematical calculations

cal·cu·lus \ˈkal-kyə-ləs\ *n, pl* **-li** \-ˌlī, -ˌlē\ *also* **-lus·es** **1 a :** a method of computation or calculation in a special symbolic notation **b :** a branch of mathematics concerned with the theory and applications of integrals and integration (as the determination of lengths, areas, and volumes) and of derivatives and differentiation (as the rate of change of functions with respect to their variables) **2 a :** a mass usually of mineral salts deposited in or around organic material in a hollow organ or bodily duct **b :** TARTAR 2 [Latin, "pebble, stone"]

cal·de·ra \kal-ˈder-ə, kȯl-, -ˈdir-\ *n* **:** a large crater formed by the collapse or explosion of a volcanic cone [Spanish, literally, "cauldron," from Late Latin *caldaria*]

caldron *variant of* CAULDRON

[1]cal·en·dar \ˈkal-ən-dər\ *n* **1 a :** an arrangement of time into days, weeks, months, and years **b :** a record of such an arrangement for a certain period and usually for a year **2 :** an orderly list: as **a :** a list of cases to be tried in court **b :** a list of bills to be considered by a legislative assembly **c :** a schedule of coming events [Medieval Latin *kalendarium,* from Latin *kalendae* "calends"]

[2]calendar *vt* **-dared; -dar·ing** \-də-riŋ, -driŋ\ **:** to enter in a calendar

[1]cal·en·der \ˈkal-ən-dər\ *vt* **-dered; -der·ing** \-də-riŋ, -driŋ\ **:** to press (as cloth or paper) between rollers or plates in order to smooth and glaze or thin into sheets [Middle French *calendrer,* from *calandre* "calender," derived from Greek *kylindros* "cylinder"] — **cal·en·der·er** *n*

[2]calender *n* **:** a machine for calendering cloth or paper

cal·ends *or* **kal·ends** \ˈkal-ənz\ *n pl* **:** the first day of the ancient Roman month [Latin *kalendae*]

ca·len·du·la \kə-ˈlen-jə-lə\ *n* **:** any of a small genus of yellow-rayed herbs related to the daisies — compare POT MARIGOLD [derived from Latin *kalendae* "calends"]

[1]calf \ˈkaf, ˈkȧf\ *n, pl* **calves** \ˈkavz, ˈkȧvz\ **1 a :** the young of the domestic cow **b :** the young of various large animals (as the elephant or whale) **2** *pl* **calfs :** CALFSKIN **3 :** a boy or youth held to be awkward or silly [Old English *cealf*]

[2]calf *n, pl* **calves :** the fleshy or muscular back part of the leg below the knee [Old Norse *kālfi*]

calf·skin \ˈkaf-ˌskin, ˈkȧf-\ *n* **:** leather made of the skin of a calf

cal·i·ber *or* **cal·i·bre** \ˈkal-ə-bər\ *n* **1 a :** mental ability or moral quality **b :** degree of excellence **2 :** the diameter of a bullet or other projectile **3 :** the diameter of the bore of a gun — usually expressed in hundredths or thousandths of an inch and as a decimal fraction ⟨.32 *caliber*⟩ [Middle French *calibre,* from Italian *calibro,* from Arabic *qālib* "shoemaker's last"]

cal·i·brate \ˈkal-ə-ˌbrāt\ *vt* **1 :** to measure the caliber of **2 a :** to determine, correct, or put the measuring marks on (as a thermometer tube) **b :** to make standard (as a measuring instrument) by finding out and correcting for the differences from an accepted or ideal value — **cal·i·bra·tion** \ˌkal-ə-ˈbrā-shən\ *n* — **cal·i·bra·tor** \ˈkal-ə-ˌbrāt-ər\ *n*

cal·i·co \ˈkal-i-ˌkō\ *n, pl* **-coes** *or* **-cos** **1 :** cotton cloth; *esp* **:** cotton cloth with a colored pattern printed on one side **2 :** a blotched or spotted animal ⟨a *calico* cat⟩ [*Calicut,* city in India] — **calico** *adj*

calico bass *n* **:** BLACK CRAPPIE

Cal·i·for·nia condor \ˌkal-ə-ˈfȯr-nyə-\ *n* **:** a large nearly extinct vulture of mountainous southern California that is related to the condor of South America — called also *condor*

California poppy *n* **:** any of a genus of herbs related to the poppies and including one widely grown for its usually yellow or orange flowers

cal·i·for·ni·um \ˌkal-ə-ˈfȯr-nē-əm\ *n* **:** an artificially prepared radioactive element — see ELEMENT table [New Latin, from *California,* U.S.]

cal·i·per \ˈkal-ə-pər\ *n* **:** a measuring instrument with two legs or jaws that can be adjusted to determine thickness, diameter, and distance between surfaces — usually used in plural ⟨a pair of *calipers*⟩ [alteration of *caliber*]

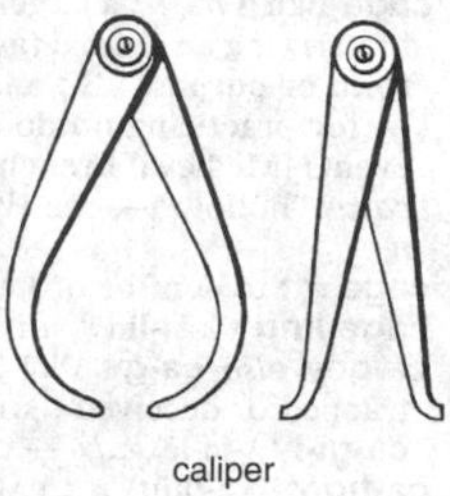

caliper

ca·liph *also* **ca·lif** \ˈkā-ləf, ˈkal-əf\ *n* **:** a successor of Muhammad as temporal and spiritual head of Islam — used as a title [Arabic *khalīfa* "successor"]

ca·liph·ate \ˈkā-lə-ˌfāt, -fət; ˈkal-ə-\ *n* **:** the office or dominion of a caliph

cal·is·then·ics \ˌkal-əs-ˈthen-iks\ *n sing or pl* **1 :** systematic rhythmic bodily exercises performed usually without special equipment **2 :** the art or practice of calisthenics [Greek *kalos* "beautiful" + *sthenos* "strength"] — **cal·is·then·ic** \-ik\ *adj*

[1]calk *variant of* CAULK

[2]calk *or* **caulk** \ˈkȯk\ *n* **:** a cleat on a shoe (as of a horse) to prevent slipping [probably derived from Middle French dialect *calcain* "heel," from Latin *calcaneum,* from *calx* "heel"]

[3]calk *or* **caulk** *vt* **1 :** to furnish with calks **2 :** to wound with a calk

[1]call \ˈkȯl\ *vb* **1 :** to speak in a loud distinct voice so as to be heard at a distance **:** SHOUT **2 :** to utter in a loud clear voice ⟨*call* out a command⟩ **3 a :** to announce with authority **:** PROCLAIM **b :** to announce the action of (as a sports game) **4 a :** to summon with or as if with a shout ⟨*call* the children to dinner⟩ **b :** to cause to come ⟨*call* to mind an old saying⟩ **5 :** to bring into action or discussion ⟨*call* a case into court⟩ **6 :** to make an appeal, request, or demand ⟨*call* on a person's sense of decency⟩ **7 :** to get in touch with by telephone **:** make a telephone call **8 :** SUMMON ⟨*call* a meeting⟩ **9 :** to make a brief visit **10 :** to give a name to **:** address by name **11 :** to regard as being of a certain kind **:** CONSIDER ⟨can hardly be *called* generous⟩ **12 :** to estimate as being ⟨*call* it an even dollar⟩ **13 a :** to utter a characteristic note or cry — used of an animal **b :** to attract (as game) by imitating the characteristic cry **14 :** to make a demand in card games (as for a show of hands) **15 :** to give temporary control of computer processing to a particular set of instructions **16 :** [4]HALT 2, SUSPEND ⟨*call* a game on account of rain⟩ [from Old Norse *kalla*] — **call·able** \ˈkȯ-lə-bəl\ *adj* — **call·er** *n* — **call for** **1 :** to stop (as at one's house) to get ⟨I'll *call for* you later⟩ **2 :** to require as necessary ⟨the job *calls for* computer skills⟩ — **call in question** *or* **call into question :** to challenge the accuracy or truth of — **call it a day :** to stop at least for the present whatever one has been doing — **call it quits :** to call it a day **:** QUIT — **call on** **1 :** to ask or require **:** DEMAND **2 :** to choose (as a student) to respond ⟨the teacher *called on* her first⟩ — **call the shots :** to be in charge or control — **call the tune :** to be in charge or control — **call to account :** to hold responsible — **call upon** **1 :** REQUIRE ⟨*called upon* to do several jobs⟩ **2 :** to make a demand on **:** depend on

[2]call *n* **1 a :** an act of calling with the voice; *also* **:** SHOUT **b :** a cry of an animal (as a bird); *also* **:** an imitation of this or a device used (as in calling game) to make such an imitation **2 a :** a request or command to assemble **b :** a signal on a drum or bugle **c :** an invitation to become the minister of a church or to accept a professional appointment **d :** a divine or inner prompting to a course of action **e :** the attraction or appeal of a particular activity, condition, or place ⟨the *call* of the wild⟩

3 a : DEMAND, CLAIM **b :** NEED, JUSTIFICATION ⟨no *call* to apologize⟩ **c :** REQUEST ⟨many *calls* for the new toy⟩ **d :** a request that control of computer processing temporarily be given to a particular set of instructions **4 :** a short visit **5 :** a name or thing called ⟨the *call* was heads⟩ **6 :** the act of calling in a card game **7 :** the act of calling on the telephone **8 :** a direction or set of directions for a square dance rhythmically called to the dancers **9 :** a decision or ruling made by an official of a sports contest

cal·la lily \ˈkal-ə\ *n* **:** a plant of the arum family often grown for its white showy spathe surrounding a fleshy spike of yellow florets — called also *calla* [Greek *kallaia* "rooster's wattles"]

call·back \ˈkȯl-ˌbak\ *n* **1 :** a return call **2 a :** RECALL 5 **b :** a second or additional audition for a theatrical part

call–board \ˈkȯl-ˌbōrd, -ˌbȯrd\ *n* **:** BULLETIN BOARD 1

call·boy \ˈkȯl-ˌbȯi\ *n* **:** BELLHOP, PAGE

call down *vt* **:** REPRIMAND ⟨*called* me *down* for being late⟩

caller ID \-ˌī-ˈdē\ *n* **:** a telephone service that identifies the phone number of a caller

call forwarding *n* **:** a telephone service that forwards incoming calls to a different phone number

cal·lig·ra·phy \kə-ˈlig-rə-fē\ *n* **1 :** beautiful or elegant handwriting; *also* **:** the art of producing such writing **2 :** PENMANSHIP 2 [Greek *kalligraphia,* from *kallos* "beauty" + *-graphia* "-graphy"] — **cal·lig·ra·pher** \-fər\ *n* — **cal·li·graph·ic** \ˌkal-ə-ˈgraf-ik\ *adj* — **cal·li·graph·i·cal·ly** \-ˈgraf-i-kə-le, -klē\ *adv*

call·ing \ˈkȯ-ling\ *n* **1 :** a strong inner impulse; *esp* **:** one toward the ministry or priesthood **2 :** one's customary profession

cal·li·o·pe \kə-ˈlī-ə-ˌpē, ˈkal-ē-ˌōp\ *n* **:** a keyboard musical instrument resembling an organ and consisting of a series of whistles sounded by steam or compressed air [*Calliope,* a Greek muse]

call letters *n pl* **:** CALL SIGN

call loan *n* **:** a loan payable on demand of either party

call number *n* **:** a combination of characters assigned to a library book to indicate its place on a shelf

call off *vt* **1 :** to draw away **:** DIVERT ⟨*call off* your dog⟩ **2 :** CANCEL ⟨*call off* a meeting⟩

cal·los·i·ty \ka-ˈläs-ət-ē, kə-\ *n, pl* **-ties 1 :** the quality or state of being callous **2 :** CALLUS 1

¹cal·lous \ˈkal-əs\ *adj* **1 a :** being hardened and thickened **b :** having calluses ⟨*callous* hands⟩ **2 :** feeling or showing no sympathy for others **:** UNFEELING ⟨a *callous* disregard for human rights⟩ [Latin *callosus,* from *callus* "callous skin"] — **cal·lous·ly** *adv* — **cal·lous·ness** *n*

²callous *vt* **:** to make callous

cal·low \ˈkal-ō\ *adj* **:** lacking adult sophistication **:** IMMATURE [Old English *calu* "bald"] — **cal·low·ness** *n*

call sign *n* **:** the combination of identifying letters assigned to a radio or television station

call–up \ˈkȯl-ˌəp\ *n* **:** an order to report for military service

¹cal·lus \ˈkal-əs\ *n* **1 :** a thickening of or a hard thickened area on skin or bark **2 :** a mass of exudate and connective tissue that forms around a break in a bone and is converted into bone in the healing of the break **3 :** tissue that forms over an injured plant surface [Latin]

²callus *vi* **:** to form callus or a callus

call–wait·ing \ˈkȯl-wāt-ing\ *n* **:** a telephone service that signals (as by a click) to the user when an incoming call is received while a call is in progress

¹calm \ˈkäm, ˈkälm\ *n* **1 a :** a period or condition of freedom from storm, wind, or rough activity of water **b :** complete lack of wind or the presence of wind of no more than one mile (1.6 kilometers) per hour **2 :** a state of repose and freedom from turmoil or agitation **:** QUIET [probably derived from Spanish *calma,* from Late Latin *cauma* "heat," from Greek *kauma*]

²calm *vb* **1 :** to become calm **2 :** to make calm

³calm *adj* **1 :** marked by calm **:** STILL ⟨a *calm* sea⟩ **2 :** free from agitation, excitement, or disturbance ⟨a *calm* manner⟩ — **calm·ly** *adv* — **calm·ness** *n*

synonyms CALM, TRANQUIL, SERENE, PLACID mean quiet and free from disturbance. CALM implies a contrast with a foregoing or nearby state of agitation or violence ⟨remained *calm* during the fire⟩. TRANQUIL suggests a very deep quietude or composure ⟨the *tranquil* beauty of the garden⟩. SERENE stresses an unclouded and lofty tranquillity ⟨watched the sunset of a *serene* summer's evening⟩. PLACID suggests an undisturbed appearance and often implies complacency ⟨remained *placid* despite the criticism⟩.

ca·ló \ka-ˈlō\ *n* **:** any of several Spanish argots; *esp* **:** one used by Chicano youths in cities of the southwest U.S. [Spanish]

cal·o·mel \ˈkal-ə-məl, -ˌmel\ *n* **:** a white tasteless substance Hg_2Cl_2 that is used especially as a fungicide — called also *mercurous chloride* [probably derived from Greek *kalos* "beautiful" + *melas* "black"]

¹ca·lor·ic \kə-ˈlȯr-ik, -ˈlōr-, -ˈlär-; ˈkal-ə-rik\ *n* **:** a supposed form of matter formerly held responsible for the phenomena of heat and combustion

²caloric *adj* **1 :** of or relating to heat **2 :** relating to or containing calories — **ca·lor·i·cal·ly** \-i-kə-lē, -i-klē\ *adv*

cal·o·rie *also* **cal·o·ry** \ˈkal-rē, -ə-rē\ *n, pl* **-ries 1 :** a unit of heat: **a :** the heat energy required to raise the temperature of one gram of water one degree Celsius and equal to about 4.19 joules — called also *small calorie* **b :** the heat energy required to raise the temperature of one kilogram of water one degree Celsius and equal to 1000 small calories — used especially to indicate the value of foods in the production of heat and energy; called also *large calorie* **2 :** an amount of food having an energy-producing value of one large calorie [French *calorie,* from Latin *calor* "heat," from *calēre* "to be warm"]

cal·o·rif·ic \ˌkal-ə-ˈrif-ik\ *adj* **:** CALORIC

cal·o·rim·e·ter \ˌkal-ə-ˈrim-ət-ər\ *n* **:** an apparatus for measuring quantities of absorbed or evolved heat or for determining specific heats — **cal·o·ri·met·ric** \ˌkal-ə-rə-ˈme-trik\ *adj* — **cal·o·ri·met·ri·cal·ly** \-ˈme-tri-kə-lē, -klē\ *adv* — **cal·o·rim·e·try** \-ˈrim-ə-trē\ *n*

cal·u·met \ˈkal-yə-ˌmet, -mət\ *n* **:** a highly ornamented ceremonial pipe of the American Indians [American French, from French dialect, "pipe stem," derived from Latin *calamus* "reed"]

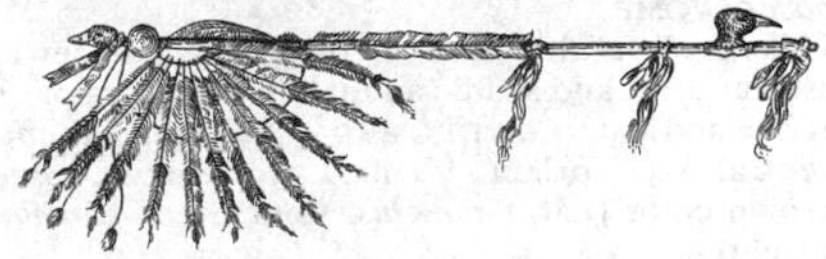

calumet

ca·lum·ni·ate \kə-ˈləm-nē-ˌāt\ *vt* **:** to speak falsely and maliciously about **:** SLANDER ⟨try to *calumniate* the leaders of the opposition⟩ — **ca·lum·ni·a·tion** \-ˌləm-nē-ˈā-shən\ *n* — **ca·lum·ni·a·tor** \-ˈləm-nē-ˌāt-er\ *n*

cal·um·ny \ˈkal-əm-nē\ *n, pl* **-nies :** a false charge made to injure another person's reputation; *also* **:** the uttering of such charges [Latin *calumnia,* from *calvi* "to deceive"] — **ca·lum·ni·ous** \kə-ˈləm-nē-əs\ *adj* — **ca·lum·ni·ous·ly** *adv*

calve \ˈkav, ˈkȧv\ *vb* **1 :** to give birth to a calf; *also* **:** to produce offspring **2** *of an ice mass* **:** to break so that a large part becomes separated ⟨a glacier *calving* icebergs⟩

calves *plural of* CALF

Cal·vin cycle \ˈkal-vən-\ *n* **:** the cycle of enzyme-catalyzed dark reactions of photosynthesis that occurs in the chloroplasts of plants and in many bacteria and that involves the fixation of carbon dioxide and the formation of a 6-carbon sugar [Melvin *Calvin,* died 1997, American chemist]

Cal·vin·ism \ˈkal-və-ˌniz-əm\ *n* **:** the theological system of John Calvin and his followers emphasizing the absolute power of God and especially the doctrine of predestination — **Cal·vin·ist** \-və-nəst\ *n or adj* — **Cal·vin·is·tic** \ˌkal-və-ˈnis-tik\ *adj*

ca·lyp·so \kə-ˈlip-sō\ *n, pl* **-sos :** a ballad of West Indian origin having usually improvised lyrics set to a lively rhythm [Trinidad English] — **ca·lyp·so·ni·an** \kə-ˌlip-ˈsō-nē-ən, ˌkal-ip-\ *adj or n*

ca·lyx \ˈkā-liks *also* ˈkal-iks\ *n, pl* **ca·lyx·es** *or* **ca·ly·ces** \ˈkā-lə-ˌsēz *also* ˈkal-ə-\ **1 :** the external usually green or leafy part of a flower consisting of sepals **2 :** an animal structure shaped like a cup [Latin, from Greek *kalyx*]

cal·zo·ne \kal-ˈzōn, -ˈzō-nē, -zō-nā; käl-ˈzȯn-ā\ *n, pl* **calzone** *or* **calzones :** a baked or fried turnover of pizza dough with various fillings (as cheese) [Italian, from singular of *calzoni* "pants"]

¹cam \ˈkam\ *n* **:** a rotating or sliding mechanical part that trans-

\ə\ **abut**	\au̇\ **out**	\i\ **tip**	\ȯ\ **saw**	\u̇\ **foot**
\ər\ **further**	\ch\ **chin**	\ī\ **life**	\ȯi\ **coin**	\y\ **yet**
\a\ **mat**	\e\ **pet**	\j\ **job**	\th\ **thin**	\yü\ **few**
\ā\ **take**	\ē\ **easy**	\ng\ **sing**	\t͟h\ **this**	\yu̇\ **cure**
\ä\ **cot, cart**	\g\ **go**	\ō\ **bone**	\ü\ **food**	\zh\ **vision**

mits motion to another part (as a rod or lever) and is used especially to transform circular motion into linear motion or vice versa [perhaps from French *came,* from German *Kamm,* literally, "comb"]
[2]**cam** *n* : CAMERA 2
ca·ma·ra·de·rie \ˌkäm-ˈräd-ə-rē, -ə-ˈräd-, ˌkam-, -ˈrad-\ *n* : good feeling existing between comrades [French, from *camarade* "comrade"]
cam·as *also* **cam·ass** \ˈkam-əs\ *n* : any of a genus of plants of the western U.S. that are related to the lilies and have edible bulbs — compare DEATH CAMAS [of American Indian origin]
[1]**cam·ber** \ˈkam-bər\ *vb* **cam·bered; cam·ber·ing** \-bə-ring, -bring\ : to curve upward in the middle : arch slightly [French *cambrer,* derived from Latin *camur* "curved"]
[2]**camber** *n* **1** : a slight convexity, arching, or curvature (as of a beam, deck, or road) **2** : a setting of the wheels of an automotive vehicle closer together at the bottom than at the top
cam·bi·um \ˈkam-bē-əm\ *n, pl* **-bi·ums** *or* **-bia** \-bē-ə\ : a thin cell layer between the xylem and phloem of most vascular plants from which new cells (as of wood and bark) develop [New Latin, from Medieval Latin, "exchange," from Latin *cambiare* "to exchange"] — **cam·bi·al** \-bē-əl\ *adj*
Cam·bri·an \ˈkam-brē-ən\ *n* : the earliest period of the Paleozoic era marked by fossils of nearly every major invertebrate animal group and by scarcely recognizable plant fossils; *also* : the corresponding system of rocks — see GEOLOGIC TIME table [Medieval Latin *Cambria* "Wales"] — **Cambrian** *adj*
cam·bric \ˈkām-brik\ *n* **1** : a fine thin white linen fabric **2** : a cotton fabric that resembles cambric [Dutch *Kamerijk* "Cambrai," city in France]
cam·cord·er \ˈkam-ˌkȯrd-ər\ *n* : a small portable combined camera and VCR [*cam*era + re*corder*]
came *past of* COME
cam·el \ˈkam-əl\ *n* **1** : either of two large cud-chewing mammals used as draft and saddle animals in desert regions especially of Africa and Asia: **a** : DROMEDARY 2 **b** : a 2-humped camel of central Asian origin — called also *Bactrian camel* **2** : a light brown color [Latin *camelus,* from Greek *kamēlos,* of Semitic origin]
cam·el·back \-ˌbak\ *n* : the back of a camel
cam·el·eer \ˌkam-ə-ˈliər\ *n* : a camel driver
camel hair *also* **camel's hair** *n* **1** : the hair of a camel or a substitute for it (as hair from squirrels' tails) **2** : cloth made of camel hair or of camel hair and wool
ca·mel·lia \kə-ˈmēl-yə\ *n* : any of several shrubs or trees related to the tea plant; *esp* : a greenhouse shrub with glossy evergreen leaves and showy roselike flowers [*Camellus* (Georg Josef Kamel), died 1706, Moravian Jesuit missionary]
Ca·mel·o·par·da·lis \kə-ˌmel-ə-ˈpärd-l-əs\ *n* : a northern constellation between Cassiopeia and Ursa Major [Latin, giraffe]
Cam·e·lot \ˈkam-ə-ˌlät\ *n* **1** : the site of King Arthur's palace in Arthurian legend **2** : a time or place of idyllic happiness
Cam·em·bert \ˈkam-əm-ˌbeər\ *n* : a soft cheese with a thin grayish white rind and a yellow interior [*Camembert,* Normandy, France]
cam·eo \ˈkam-ē-ˌō\ *n, pl* **-e·os** **1** : a carved gem in which the design is higher than its background **2** : a small role (as in a movie) performed by a well-known actor and often limited to a single scene [Middle English *camew,* from Middle French *camau, camaheu*]
cam·era \ˈkam-rə, -ə-rə\ *n* **1** : a judge's private office ⟨hearings held in *camera*⟩ **2** : a lightproof box fitted with a lens through the opening of which the image of an object is projected onto a surface that is sensitive to light for recording (as on film) or for conversion into electrical impulses (as for live television broadcast) [Late Latin, "room, chamber"; sense 2 from New Latin *camera obscura,* literally, "dark chamber"] — **off camera** **1** : while not being filmed by a television or movie camera ⟨he's a different person *off camera*⟩ **2** : outside the range of a television or movie camera ⟨sounds of gunfire taking place *off camera*⟩ — **on camera** **1** : before a live television camera; *also* : while being filmed by a television or movie camera ⟨looked relaxed *on camera*⟩ **2** : within the range of a television or movie camera ⟨you can hear the dog but he never appears *on camera*⟩
cam·era·man \-ˌman, -mən\ *n* : a person who operates a camera
cam·era·per·son \-ˌpərs-ᵊn\ *n* : a man or woman who operates a camera
cam·era·wom·an \-ˌwu̇m-ən\ *n* : a woman who operates a camera
cam·i·sole \ˈkam-ə-ˌsōl\ *n* : a short sleeveless undergarment for women [French]
camomile *variant of* CHAMOMILE
cam·ou·flage \ˈkam-ə-ˌfläzh, -ˌfläj\ *n* **1** : the disguising especially of military equipment or installations with paint, nets, or foliage; *also* : the disguise so applied **2 a** : concealment by means of disguise **b** : behavior or a trick intended to deceive or hide [French, from *camoufler* "to disguise"] — **camouflage** *vt*
[1]**camp** \ˈkamp\ *n* **1 a** : a place usually away from cities where tents or simple buildings (as cabins) are erected for shelter or for temporary residence **b** : a group of tents, cabins, or huts **c** : a place usually in the country for recreation or instruction often during the summer ⟨summer *camp*⟩; *also* : a program offering access to recreational or educational facilities for a limited period of time ⟨computer *camp*⟩ ⟨a resort offering boating and hiking *camps*⟩ **2 a** : a body of persons encamped **b** (1) : a group of persons; *esp* : a group engaged in promoting a theory or doctrine ⟨liberal and conservative *camps*⟩ (2) : an ideological position **3** : military service or life [Middle French, derived from Latin *campus* "plain, field"]
[2]**camp** *vi* **1** : to make camp or occupy a camp **2** : to live temporarily in a camp or outdoors ⟨*camp* out overnight⟩
cam·paign \kam-ˈpān\ *n* **1** : a series of military operations forming a distinct phase of a war **2** : a series of operations designed to bring about a particular result ⟨an election *campaign*⟩ [French *campagne,* derived from Late Latin *campania* "level country"] — **campaign** *vi* — **cam·paign·er** *n*
cam·pa·nile \ˌkam-pə-ˈnē-lē, *of United States structures also* -ˈnēl\ *n, pl* **-niles** *or* **-ni·li** \-ˈnē-lē\ : a usually freestanding bell tower [Italian, from *campana* "bell," from Late Latin]

campanile

cam·pan·u·la \kam-ˈpan-yə-lə\ *n* : BELLFLOWER [Late Latin *campana* "bell"]
camp·er \ˈkam-pər\ *n* **1** : one who camps **2** : a portable dwelling (as a specially equipped automotive vehicle) for use during casual travel and camping
cam·pes·tral \kam-ˈpes-trəl\ *adj* : of or relating to fields or open country [Latin *campester,* from *campus* "field"]
camp·fire \ˈkamp-ˌfīr\ *n* : a fire built outdoors (as at a camp)
Camp Fire Girl *n* : a member of a national organization for girls from ages 7 to 18 [*Camp Fire Girls,* Incorporated]
camp·ground \ˈkamp-ˌgrau̇nd\ *n* : the area or place used for a camp or for camping
cam·phor \ˈkam-fər, ˈkamp-\ *n* : a tough gummy volatile fragrant crystalline compound $C_{10}H_{16}O$ obtained especially from the wood and bark of the camphor tree and used as a liniment and topical pain reliever in medicine, as a plasticizer, and as an insect repellent [Medieval Latin *camphora,* from Arabic *kāfūr,* from Malay *kapur*]
cam·phor·ate \-fə-ˌrāt\ *vt* : to impregnate with camphor ⟨*camphorated* oil⟩
camphor tree *n* : a large Asian tree related to the laurels
cam·pi·on \ˈkam-pē-ən\ *n* : any of various plants related to the pinks [probably from obsolete *campion* "champion"]
camp meeting *n* : a series of evangelistic meetings usually held outdoors or in a tent
camp·o·ree \ˌkam-pə-ˈrē\ *n* : a gathering of Boy Scouts or Girl Scouts from a given area [*camp* + *jamboree*]
camp·site \ˈkamp-ˌsīt\ *n* : a place suitable for or used as the site of a camp ⟨a campground with dozens of *campsites*⟩
camp·stool \ˈkamp-ˌstül\ *n* : a folding stool
cam·pus \ˈkam-pəs\ *n* **1** : the grounds and buildings of a school (as a college) **2** : grounds that resemble a campus ⟨a hospital *campus*⟩ [Latin, "field, plain"]
cam·shaft \ˈkam-ˌshaft\ *n* : a shaft to which a cam is fastened or of which a cam forms a part
[1]**can** \kən, kan, ˈkan\ *auxiliary verb, past* **could** \kəd, ku̇d, ˈku̇d\; *present sing & pl* **can** **1 a** : know how to ⟨you *can* read⟩ **b** : be physically or mentally able to ⟨I *can* swim⟩ **c** : be permitted by conscience or feeling to ⟨you *can* hardly blame me⟩ **d** : be inherently able or designed to ⟨all that money *can* buy⟩ **e**

: be enabled by law, agreement, or custom to **2** : have permission to — used interchangeably with *may* ⟨you *can* go now if you like⟩ [Old English, "know, knows, am able, is able"]

usage *Can* and *may* are often interchangeable when used to express possibility or permission. The use of *can* to ask or grant permission has been common since the 19th century, although some people feel *may* is more appropriate in formal contexts.

[2]**can** \ˈkan\ *n* **1** : a usually cylindrical container: **a** : a vessel for holding liquids; *esp* : a drinking vessel **b** : a container (as for milk or garbage) usually with an open top and often with a cover **c** : a container (as of tinplate) in which a perishable product (as food) is hermetically sealed for preservation until use **d** : a jar for packing or preserving fruit or vegetables **2** : the contents of a can [Old English *canne*]

[3]**can** \ˈkan\ *vt* **canned; can·ning** **1** : to put in a can; *esp* : to preserve by sealing in an airtight can or jar **2** : to discharge from a job **3** *slang* : to put a stop or end to — **can·ner** *n*

Can·a·da balsam \ˈkan-əd-ə-\ *n* : a viscid yellowish resin exuded by the balsam fir that solidifies to a transparent mass and is used as a transparent cement especially in microscopy

Canada Day *n* : July 1 observed as a legal holiday in commemoration of the proclamation of dominion status in 1867

Canada goose *n* : a common wild goose of North America that is mostly gray and brownish in color with black head and neck

Ca·na·di·an \kə-ˈnād-ē-ən\ *n* : a native or inhabitant of Canada — **Canadian** *adj*

Canadian bacon *n* : bacon from the loin of a pig that has little fat and is cut into round or oblong slices for cooking

Canadian lynx *or* **Canada lynx** *n* : LYNX c

ca·naille \kə-ˈnī, -ˈnāl\ *n* : RABBLE 2, RIFFRAFF [French, from Italian *canaglia*, from *cane* "dog," from Latin *canis*]

ca·nal \kə-ˈnal\ *n* **1** : a tubular anatomical passage or channel : DUCT **2** : an artificial waterway for navigation or for draining or irrigating land **3** *pl* : faint narrow markings on the planet Mars sometimes seen through telescopes [Latin *canalis* "pipe, channel," from *canna* "reed, cane"]

can·a·lic·u·lus \ˌkan-l-ˈik-yə-ləs\ *n, pl* **-u·li** \-yə-ˌlī, -ˌlē\ : a minute bodily canal (as in bone) [Latin, from *canalis* "canal"]

can·a·li·za·tion \ˌkan-l-ə-ˈzā-shən\ *n* **1** : an act or instance of canalizing **2** : a system of channels

can·a·lize \ˈkan-l-ˌīz\ *vt* **1** : to provide with a canal **2** : to make into or like a canal

can·a·pé \ˈkan-ə-pē, -ˌpā\ *n* : an appetizer consisting of a piece of bread or toast or a cracker topped with a spread (as of fish or cheese) [French, literally, "sofa"]

ca·nard \kə-ˈnärd\ *n* : a false or unfounded report or story; *esp* : one deliberately made up [French, literally, "duck," from Middle French *vendre des canards à moitié* "to cheat," literally, "to half-sell ducks"]

Word History In 16th century France "vendre des canards à moitié" was a colorful way of saying "to cheat." The French phrase means, literally, "to half-sell ducks." Unfortunately, no one now knows just what was meant by "to half-sell"—"vendre à moitié." The proverb was probably based on some story widely known at the time, but the details have not survived. At any rate, the proverbial duck, the *canard*, came to stand for any hoax, especially a made-up report. And French *canard*, in this sense, was borrowed into English.

ca·nary \kə-ˈneər-ē\ *n, pl* **-nar·ies** **1** : a sweet wine made in the Canary Islands **2** : a small usually yellow or greenish finch native to the Canary Islands that is kept as a cage bird [Middle French *canarie*, from Spanish *canario*, from *Islas Canarias* "Canary Islands"]

canary yellow *n* : a light to a moderate yellow

can·can \ˈkan-ˌkan\ *n* : a woman's dance of French origin characterized by high kicking [French]

[1]**can·cel** \ˈkan-səl\ *vb* **-celed** *or* **-celled; -cel·ing** *or* **-cel·ling** \-sə-ling, -sling\ **1 a** : to mark or strike out for deletion **b** : DELETE, OMIT **2 a** : to destroy the force, effectiveness, or validity of : ANNUL ⟨*cancel* a magazine subscription⟩ **b** : to match in force or effect : OFFSET — often used with *out* **c** : to call off usually without expecting to reschedule ⟨*cancel* a party because of bad weather⟩ **3 a** : to remove (a common divisor) from a numerator and denominator **b** : to remove (something equivalent) from both sides of an equation or account **4** : to mark (a postage stamp or check) so as to prevent reuse [Medieval French *canceller*, from Late Latin *cancellare*, from Latin, "to make like a lattice," from *cancelli* "latticework, grating"] ***synonyms*** see ERASE — **can·cel·er** *or* **can·cel·ler** \-sə lər, -slər\ *n*

Word History The original meaning of *cancel* is "to mark out or cross out." The cross-hatchings which sometimes cover a canceled document resemble a lattice. This resemblance was reflected in the formation of the Latin verb *cancellare* from the noun *cancelli* "lattice." *Cancelli* is a diminutive form of *cancer*. This *cancer* is not related to its homonym *cancer*, "crab, disease." Rather it is the word for the type of latticed barrier used to restrain a prisoner. It is an altered form of Latin *carcer*, "prison," the word which has also given us *incarcerate*.

[2]**cancel** *n* : CANCELLATION

can·cel·la·tion *also* **can·cel·ation** \ˌkan-sə-ˈlā-shən\ *n* **1** : an act of canceling **2** : a mark made to cancel something

can·cel·lous \ˈkan-sə-ləs\ *adj* : having a porous structure ⟨*cancellous* bone⟩ [Latin *cancelli* "lattice"]

can·cer \ˈkan-sər\ *n* **1** *cap* **a** : a northern zodiacal constellation between Gemini and Leo **b** : the 4th sign of the zodiac; *also* : one born under this sign **2** : a malignant tumor that tends to spread locally and to other parts of the body; *also* : an abnormal state marked by such tumors **3** : a source of evil or anguish that spreads destructively ⟨the *cancer* of hatred⟩ [Latin, "crab, Cancer, cancer"] — **can·cer·ous** \ˈkans-rəs, -ə-rəs\ *adj*

can·de·la \kan-ˈdē-lə, -ˈdel-ə\ *n* : an international unit of luminous intensity in a given direction of a source that emits radiation only of 540 × 10 hertz and has a radiant intensity in that direction of 1/683 watt per unit of angular measurement in three-dimensional space [Latin, "candle"]

can·de·la·bra \ˌkan-də-ˈläb-rə *sometimes* -ˈlab-\ *n* : CANDELABRUM

can·de·la·brum \-rəm\ *n, pl* **-bra** \-rə\ *also* **-brums** : a candlestick or lamp with several branches holding sockets for several lights [Latin, from *candela* "candle"]

candelabrum

can·des·cent \kan-ˈdes-nt\ *adj* : glowing or dazzling especially from great heat [Latin *candescere* "to grow light or bright," from *candēre* "to shine"] — **can·des·cence** \-ns\ *n*

can·did \ˈkan-dəd\ *adj* **1** : free from prejudice : FAIR **2 a** : marked by honest sincere expression **b** : showing sincere honesty and absence of deception **3** : relating to photography of subjects acting naturally or spontaneously without being posed ⟨a *candid* snapshot⟩ [French *candide*, from Latin *candidus* "shining, white," from *candēre* "to shine"] ***synonyms*** see FRANK — **can·did·ly** *adv* — **can·did·ness** *n*

can·di·da·cy \ˈkan-dəd-ə-sē\ *n, pl* **-cies** : the state of being a candidate ⟨announce one's *candidacy* for office⟩

can·di·date \ˈkan-də-ˌdāt, -ə-, -dət\ *n* : one who offers oneself or is proposed by others for an office, membership, right, or honor ⟨the party's *candidate* for mayor⟩ [Latin *candidatus*, literally, "clothed in white," from *candidus* "white"; from the white toga worn by candidates for office in ancient Rome]

can·di·di·a·sis \ˌkan-də-ˈdī-ə-səs\ *n, pl* **-a·ses** \-ə-ˌsēz\ : infection with a fungus that resembles a yeast

can·died \ˈkan-dēd\ *adj* **1** : encrusted or coated with sugar **2** : baked with sugar or syrup until translucent

[1]**can·dle** \ˈkan-dl\ *n* **1** : a usually cylindrical mass of tallow or wax containing a loosely twisted linen or cotton wick that is burned to give light **2** : CANDELA [Latin *candela*, from *candēre* "to shine"]

[2]**candle** *vt* **can·dled; can·dling** \ˈkan-dling, -dl-ing\ : to examine (an egg) by holding between the eye and a light — **can·dler** \-dlər, -dl-ər\ *n*

can·dle·light \ˈkan-dl-ˌlīt, -ˌīt\ *n* **1 a** : the light of a candle **b** : a soft artificial light **2** : the time when candles are lit : TWILIGHT

Can·dle·mas \ˈkan-dl-məs\ *n* : February 2 observed as a church

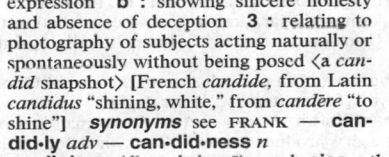

\ə\ **abut**	\au̇\ **out**	\i\ **tip**	\ȯ\ **saw**	\u̇\ **foot**
\ər\ **further**	\ch\ **chin**	\ī\ **life**	\ȯi\ **coin**	\y\ **yet**
\a\ **mat**	\e\ **pet**	\j\ **job**	\th\ **thin**	\yü\ **few**
\ā\ **take**	\ē\ **easy**	\ng\ **sing**	\t͟h\ **this**	\yu̇\ **cure**
\ä\ **cot, cart**	\g\ **go**	\ō\ **bone**	\ü\ **food**	\zh\ **vision**

festival in commemoration of the presentation of Christ in the temple and the purification of the Virgin Mary [Old English *candelmæsse,* from *candel* "candle" + *mæsse* "mass, feast"; from the candles blessed and carried in celebration of the feast]

can·dle·pin \ˈkan-dl-ˌpin\ *n* **1 :** a slender bowling pin tapering toward top and bottom **2** *pl* **:** a bowling game using candlepins and a smaller ball than that used in tenpins

can·dle·pow·er \-ˌpau̇-ər, -ˌpau̇r\ *n* **:** luminous intensity (as of a lightbulb) expressed in candles or candelas

can·dle·stick \-ˌstik\ *n* **:** a holder with a socket for a candle

can·dor \ˈkan-dər\ *n* **1 :** freedom from prejudice **2 :** unreserved, honest, or sincere expression **:** FRANKNESS [Latin, literally, "whiteness," from *candēre* "to shine"]

[1]**can·dy** \ˈkan-dē\ *n, pl* **-dies** **1 :** crystallized sugar formed by boiling down sugar syrup **2 a :** a rich food made largely of sugar often with flavoring and filling **b :** a piece of such food [Medieval French *sucre candi,* from *sucre* "sugar" + Arabic *qandī* "candied," from *qand* "crystallized sugar"]

[2]**candy** *vb* **can·died; can·dy·ing** **1 :** to coat or become coated with sugar; *esp* **:** to cook (fruit or fruit peel) in sugar syrup **2 :** to make seem attractive **:** SWEETEN **3 :** to crystallize into sugar

candy strip·er \-ˈstrī-pər\ *n* **:** a teenage volunteer hospital worker

can·dy·tuft \ˈkan-dē-ˌtəft\ *n* **:** any of a genus of plants related to the mustards and grown for their white, pink, or purple flowers [*Candy* (now *Candia*) "Crete," Greek island + English *tuft*]

[1]**cane** \ˈkān\ *n* **1 a :** a hollow or pithy and usually slender, flexible, and jointed stem (as of a reed or bramble) **b :** any of various tall woody grasses or reeds; *esp* **:** SUGARCANE **2 a :** WALKING STICK 1; *esp* **:** a cane walking stick **b :** a rod for flogging **c :** RATTAN 1b; *esp* **:** split rattan for wickerwork or basketry [Medieval French, derived from Latin *canna,* from Greek *kanna,* of Semitic origin]

[2]**cane** *vt* **1 :** to beat with a cane **2 :** to make or repair with cane ⟨*cane* the seat of a chair⟩

cane·brake \-ˌbrāk\ *n* **:** a thicket of cane

cane sugar *n* **:** sugar from sugarcane commonly used at the dining table and in cooking **:** SUCROSE

[1]**ca·nine** \ˈkā-ˌnīn\ *adj* **1 :** of or relating to dogs or to the family that includes the dogs, wolves, jackals, and foxes **2 :** resembling a dog [Latin *caninus,* from *canis* "dog"]

[2]**canine** *n* **1 :** a conical pointed tooth situated between the outer incisor and the first premolar **2 a :** DOG 1a **b :** DOG 1b

Ca·nis Ma·jor \ˌkā-nəs-ˈmā-jər, ˌkan-əs-\ *n* **:** a constellation to the southeast of Orion containing Sirius [Latin, literally, "greater dog"]

Canis Mi·nor \-ˈmī-nər\ *n* **:** a constellation to the east of Orion containing Procyon [Latin, literally, "lesser dog"]

can·is·ter *also* **can·nis·ter** \ˈkan-ə-stər\ *n* **1 :** a small box or can for holding a dry product (as tea) **2 :** a shell for close-range artillery fire consisting of a number of bullets enclosed in a lightweight case that is burst by the firing charge **3 :** a perforated box for gas masks that contains material to adsorb, filter, or make harmless a poisonous or irritating substance in the air [Latin *canistrum* "basket," from Greek *kanastron,* from *kanna* "reed"]

[1]**can·ker** \ˈkang-kər\ *n* **1 a :** a spreading sore that eats into the tissue **b :** an area of dead tissue in a plant; *also* **:** a plant disease marked by cankers **c :** any of various animal diseases marked by inflammation **2 :** a source of corruption or destruction [Medieval French *cancre, chancre,* from Latin *cancer* "crab, cancer"] — **can·ker·ous** \ˈkang-kə-rəs, -krəs\ *adj*

[2]**canker** *vb* **can·kered; can·ker·ing** \ˈkang-kə-ring, -kring\ **1 :** to become affected by canker **2 :** to become or cause to become corrupted ⟨a mind *cankered* by hate⟩

canker sore *n* **:** a small painful ulcer especially of the mouth

can·ker·worm \ˈkang-kər-ˌwərm\ *n* **:** a moth larva that injures plants especially by feeding on buds and foliage

can·na \ˈkan-ə\ *n* **:** a tall tropical herb with large leaves and bright-colored flowers [Latin, "reed"]

can·na·bis \ˈkan-ə-bəs\ *n* **:** HEMP 1; *also* **:** a psychoactive preparation (as marijuana) or chemical (as THC) derived from hemp [Latin, "hemp," from Greek *kannabis*]

canned \ˈkand\ *adj* **1 :** preserved in a sealed can or jar **2 a :** prepared or recorded in advance; *esp* **:** prepared in one form for ordinary use or wide distribution ⟨*canned* laughter⟩ **b :** lacking originality as if mass-produced ⟨a *canned* speech⟩

can·nel coal \ˈkan-l-\ *n* **:** a bituminous coal containing much volatile matter that burns brightly [probably from English dialect *cannel* "candle"]

can·nery \ˈkan-rē, -ə-rē\ *n, pl* **-ner·ies** **:** a factory for the canning of food

can·ni·bal \ˈkan-ə-bəl\ *n* **:** a human being or an animal that eats its own kind [New Latin *Cannibalis* "Carib," from Spanish *Caníbal,* from Taino (American Indian language of the Greater Antilles) *Caniba,* of Carib origin] — **can·ni·bal·ism** \-bə-ˌliz-əm\ *n* — **can·ni·bal·is·tic** \ˌkan-ə-bə-ˈlis-tik\ *adj*

can·ni·bal·ize \ˈkan-ə-bə-ˌlīz\ *vt* **:** to dismantle (a machine) for parts to be used as replacements in other machines

can·non \ˈkan-ən\ *n, pl* **cannons** *or* **cannon** **1 :** a heavy gun mounted on a carriage and fired from that position **:** a piece of artillery **2 :** a heavy-caliber automatic gun on an airplane [Medieval French *canon,* from Italian *cannone,* literally, "large tube," from *canna* "reed, tube," from Latin, "reed, cane"]

[1]**can·non·ade** \ˌkan-ə-ˈnād\ *n* **:** a heavy firing of artillery

[2]**cannonade** *vb* **:** to attack with artillery

can·non·ball \ˈkan-ən-ˌbȯl\ *n* **:** a round solid missile made for firing from a cannon

cannon bone *n* **:** a bone in hoofed mammals (as horses) that supports the leg from the hock joint to the fetlock

can·non·eer \ˌkan-ə-ˈniər\ *n* **:** an artillery gunner

can·not \ˈkan-ät, -ˌät; kə-ˈnät, ka-\ **:** can not — **cannot but** *or* **cannot help but** *also* **cannot help** **:** to be unable to do otherwise than

can·ny \ˈkan-ē\ *adj* **can·ni·er; -est** **:** being cautious and shrewd **:** watchful of one's own interests ⟨very *canny* with money⟩ [[1]*can*] — **can·ni·ly** \ˈkan-l-ē\ *adv* — **can·ni·ness** \ˈkan-ē-nəs\ *n*

[1]**ca·noe** \kə-ˈnü\ *n* **:** a long light narrow boat with pointed ends and curved sides that is usually paddled by hand [French, from Spanish *canoa,* of American Indian origin]

[2]**canoe** *vb* **ca·noed; ca·noe·ing** **:** to travel or transport in a canoe — **ca·noe·ist** *n*

ca·no·la \kə-ˈnō-lə\ *n* **1 :** a rape plant of an improved variety having seeds that are the source of canola oil **2 :** CANOLA OIL [from *Canola,* former certification mark in Canada]

canola oil *n* **:** an edible vegetable oil obtained from the seeds of canola that is high in monounsaturated fatty acids

[1]**can·on** \ˈkan-ən\ *n* **1 :** a church law or decree **2 :** the fundamental and unvarying part of the Mass including the consecration of the bread and wine **3 :** an official or authoritative list (as of the saints or of the books of the Bible) **4 :** an accepted principle or rule ⟨the *canons* of good taste⟩ **5 :** a musical composition in two or more voice parts in which the melody is imitated exactly and completely by the successive voices [Latin, "ruler, rule, model, standard," from Greek *kanōn*]

[2]**canon** *n* **1 :** a member of the clergy who is on the staff of a cathedral **2 :** CANON REGULAR

cañon *variant of* CANYON

ca·non·i·cal \kə-ˈnän-i-kəl\ *adj* **1 :** of, relating to, or complying with church law **2 :** following a general rule or accepted procedure — **ca·non·i·cal·ly** \-kə-lē; -klē\ *adv*

canonical hour *n* **1 :** a time of day canonically appointed for an office of devotion **2 :** one of the daily offices in the breviary including matins with lauds, prime, terce, sext, none, vespers, and compline

ca·non·i·cals \kə-ˈnän-i-kəlz\ *n pl* **:** the ceremonial garment prescribed by church law for an officiating member of the clergy

can·on·ic·i·ty \ˌkan-ə-ˈnis-ət-ē\ *n* **:** the quality or state of being canonical

can·on·ize \ˈkan-ə-ˌnīz\ *vt* **1 :** to declare to be a saint and worthy of public reverence and respect **2 :** to treat as if holy [Late Latin *canon* "catalog of saints," from Latin, "standard"] — **can·on·i·za·tion** \ˌkan-ə-nə-ˈzā-shən\ *n*

canon law *n* **:** the body of laws governing a church

canon regular *n, pl* **canons regular** **:** a member of one of several Roman Catholic religious institutes of priests living in community

Ca·no·pus \kə-ˈnō-pəs\ *n* **:** a star of the first magnitude not visible north of 37° latitude [Latin, from Greek *Kanōpos*]

[1]**can·o·py** \ˈkan-ə-pē\ *n, pl* **-pies** **1 a :** a covering suspended over a bed, throne, or shrine or carried on poles over a person of high rank or over some sacred object **b :** an overhanging shade or shelter ⟨a *canopy* of chestnut trees⟩ **:** as (1) **:** AWNING (2) **:** the uppermost spreading branchy layer of a forest **2 a :** the transparent covering over an airplane cockpit **b :** the fab-

ric part of a parachute that catches the air [Medieval Latin *canopeum* "mosquito net," from Latin *conopeum,* from Greek *kōnōpion,* from *kōnōps* "mosquito"] — **can·o·py·like** \-ˌlīk\ *adj*

[2]**canopy** *vt* **-pied; -py·ing** : to cover with or as if with a canopy

canst \kənst, kanst, ˈkanst\ *archaic present 2nd singular of* CAN

[1]**cant** \ˈkant\ *n* : a slanting surface or its slope [derived from Middle French dialect *cant* "edge, corner," from Latin *canthus, cantus* "iron tire"]

[2]**cant** *vt* : to give a slant to

[3]**cant** *vi* : to talk hypocritically [probably from Middle French dialect *canter* "to tell," literally, "to sing," from Latin *cantare*]

[4]**cant** *n* **1 a** : ARGOT **b** : JARGON **2** : insincere speech; *esp* : insincerely pious words or statements

can't \ˈkant, ˈkȧnt, *especially South* ˈkānt\ : can not

can·ta·bi·le \kän-ˈtäb-ə-ˌlā, kan-ˈtab-ə-lē\ *adv or adj* : in a singing manner — used as a direction in music [Italian, from Latin *cantare* "to sing"]

Can·ta·bri·gian \ˌkant-ə-ˈbrij-ən, -ē-ən\ *n* : a student or graduate of Cambridge University **2** : a native or resident of Cambridge, Massachusetts [Medieval Latin *Cantabrigia* "Cambridge"] — **Cantabrigian** *adj*

can·ta·loupe *also* **can·ta·loup** \ˈkant-l-ˌōp\ *n* : MUSKMELON; *esp* : a small widely grown muskmelon with a hard ridged rind and reddish orange flesh [*Cantalupo,* former papal villa near Rome, Italy]

can·tan·ker·ous \kan-ˈtang-kə-rəs, kən-, -krəs\ *adj* : difficult or irritating to deal with : ILL-NATURED [perhaps from obsolete *contack* "contention"] — **can·tan·ker·ous·ly** *adv* — **can·tan·ker·ous·ness** *n*

can·ta·ta \kən-ˈtät-ə\ *n* : a poem or narrative set to music to be sung by a chorus and soloists [Italian, from *cantare* "to sing," from Latin]

can·teen \kan-ˈtēn\ *n* **1** : a store (as in a camp or a factory) in which food, drinks, and small supplies are sold **2** : a place of recreation and entertainment for military personnel **3** : a small container for carrying liquid (as drinking water) [French *cantine* "bottle case, sutler's shop," from Italian *cantina* "wine cellar," probably from *canto* "corner," from Latin *canthus* "iron tire"]

[1]**can·ter** \ˈkant-ər\ *vb* : to move or cause to move at or as if at a canter [from *Canterbury,* England; from the supposed gait of pilgrims to Canterbury]

[2]**canter** *n* : a 3-beat gait (as of a horse) resembling but smoother and slower than the gallop

Can·ter·bury bell \ˈkant-ər-ˌber-ē-, -ə-ˌber-ē-\ *n* : a cultivated bellflower

cant hook *n* : a stout wooden lever used especially in handling logs that has a blunt usually metal-clad end and a movable metal arm with a sharp spike [[1]*cant*]

can·ti·cle \ˈkant-i-kəl\ *n* **1** : SONG **2** : any of several liturgical songs taken from the Bible [Latin *canticulum* "little song," from *canticum* "song," from *canere* "to sing"]

Canticle of Canticles : SONG OF SOLOMON

can·ti·le·ver \ˈkant-l-ˌē-vər *also* -ˌev-ər\ *n* **1** : a projecting beam or similar structure fastened (as by being built into a wall or pier) only at one end **2** : either of two beams or structures that project from piers toward each other and when joined form a span in a bridge [perhaps from [1]*cant* + *-i-* + *lever*]

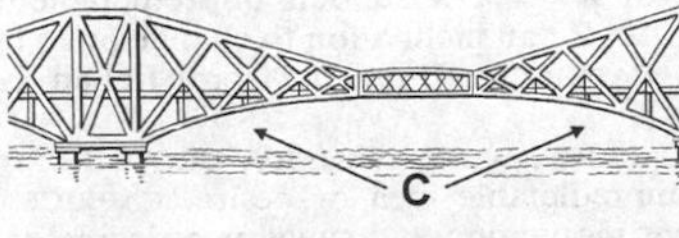

C cantilever 2

can·tle \ˈkant-l\ *n* : the upwardly projecting rear part of a saddle [Medieval French *cantel, chantel* "little corner, part cut off," from *cant* "edge, corner"]

can·to \ˈkan-ˌtō\ *n, pl* **cantos** : one of the major divisions of a long poem [Italian, from Latin *cantus* "song," from *canere* "to sing"]

can·ton \ˈkant-n, ˈkan-ˌtän\ *n* **1** : a small division of a country; *esp* : one of the states of the Swiss confederation **2** : the top inner quarter of a flag [Middle French, from Italian *cantone,* from *canto* "corner," from Latin *canthus* "iron tire"] — **can·ton·al** \ˈkant-n-əl, kan-ˈtän-l\ *adj*

Can·ton·ese \ˌkant-n-ˈēz, -ˈēs\ *n, pl* **Cantonese** **1** : a native or inhabitant of Guangzhou, China **2** : the dialect of Chinese spoken in and around Guangzhou and Hong Kong — **Cantonese** *adj*

can·ton flannel \ˈkan-ˌtän-\ *n, often cap C* : FLANNEL 1b [*Canton,* China]

can·ton·ment \kan-ˈtōn-mənt, -ˈtän-\ *n* **1** : a group of temporary structures for housing troops **2** : a military station in India

can·tor \ˈkant-ər\ *n* **1** : a choir leader **2** : a synagogue official who sings or chants the liturgy and leads the congregation in prayer [Latin, "singer," from *canere* "to sing"]

Ca·nuck \kə-ˈnək\ *n* : a Canadian and especially a French Canadian [origin unknown]

can·vas \ˈkan-vəs\ *n* **1 a** : a strong cloth of hemp, flax, or cotton used for clothing and formerly much used for tents and sails **b** : a piece of cloth used as a surface for painting; *also* : a painting on such a surface **2** : something made of canvas or on canvas **3** : a stiff material (as of coarse cloth or plastic) that has regular meshes for working with a needle (as in needlepoint) **4** : the canvas-covered floor of a boxing or wrestling ring [Medieval French *canevas, chanevaz,* derived from Latin *cannabis* "hemp"]

can·vas·back \-ˌbak\ *n* : a North American wild duck with a reddish brown head and black breast

can·vass \ˈkan-vəs\ *vb* **1 a** : to examine in detail; *esp* : to investigate officially ⟨*canvass* election returns⟩ **b** : DISCUSS, DEBATE ⟨*canvass* a question⟩ **2** : to go through (an area) or to (people) soliciting something (as information, contributions, or votes) ⟨*canvass* faculty members for opinions⟩ [obsolete *canvass* "to toss in a canvas sheet, beat thoroughly"] — **canvass** *n* — **can·vass·er** *n*

can·yon *also* **ca·ñon** \ˈkan-yən\ *n* : a deep valley with high steep slopes and often with a stream flowing through it [American Spanish *cañón*]

caou·tchouc \ˈkau̇-ˌchu̇k, -ˌchük, -ˌchü\ *n* : [1]RUBBER 2a [French, from obsolete Spanish *cauchuc*]

[1]**cap** \ˈkap\ *n* **1** : a head covering; *esp* : one that has a visor and no brim **2** : something that serves as a cover or protection for something ⟨a bottle *cap*⟩ ⟨the *cap* of a fountain pen⟩ **3** : a natural cover or top: as **a** : the umbrella-shaped part that bears the spores of a mushroom — called also *pileus* **b** : the top of a bird's head **4** : a paper or metal container holding an explosive charge (as for a toy pistol) **5** : the symbol $\cap$ indicating the intersection of two sets — compare CUP 7 [OE *cæppe,* from Late Latin *cappa* "head covering, cloak"]

[2]**cap** *vt* **capped; cap·ping** **1** : to cover or provide with a cap **2** : to match with something better ⟨*cap* one story with another⟩ **3** : to prevent from growing or spreading : set an upper limit on ⟨*cap* prices⟩

ca·pa·bil·i·ty \ˌkā-pə-ˈbil-ət-ē\ *n, pl* **-ties** **1** : the quality or state of being capable **2** : a feature or faculty that can be developed : POTENTIALITY

ca·pa·ble \ˈkā-pə-bəl\ *adj* **1** : having the qualities (as physical or mental power) to do or accomplish something ⟨*capable* of better work⟩ **2** : having qualities or features permitting ⟨a room *capable* of holding 50 people⟩ **3** : of such a nature as to make possible : SUSCEPTIBLE ⟨a remark *capable* of being misunderstood⟩ **4** : having general ability ⟨a *capable* performer⟩ [Late Latin *capabilis,* from Latin *capere* "to take"] ***synonyms*** see ABLE — **ca·pa·bly** \-blē\ *adv*

ca·pa·cious \kə-ˈpā-shəs\ *adj* : able to contain a great deal ⟨*capacious* pockets⟩ ⟨students with *capacious* minds⟩ [Latin *capax* "capacious, capable," from *capere* "to take"] — **ca·pa·cious·ly** *adv* — **ca·pa·cious·ness** *n*

ca·pac·i·tance \kə-ˈpas-ət-əns\ *n* : the property of a system of conductors and dielectrics that permits the storage of electrical energy; *also* : a measure of this property — **ca·pac·i·tive** \-ət-iv\ *adj*

ca·pac·i·tor \kə-ˈpas-ət-ər\ *n* : a device giving capacitance and usually consisting of conducting plates separated by layers of dielectric with the plates on opposite sides of the dielectric layers oppositely charged by a source of voltage — called also *condenser*

\ə\ **abut**	\au̇\ **out**	\i\ **tip**	\ȯ\ **saw**	\u̇\ **foot**
\ər\ **further**	\ch\ **chin**	\ī\ **life**	\ȯi\ **coin**	\y\ **yet**
\a\ **mat**	\e\ **pet**	\j\ **job**	\th\ **thin**	\yü\ **few**
\ā\ **take**	\ē\ **easy**	\ng\ **sing**	\t͟h\ **this**	\yu̇\ **cure**
\ä\ **cot, cart**	\g\ **go**	\ō\ **bone**	\ü\ **food**	\zh\ **vision**

ca·pac·i·ty \kə-ˈpas-ət-ē, -ˈpas-tē\ *n, pl* **-ties** **1 a :** the ability to hold or accommodate ⟨the seating *capacity* of a room⟩ **b :** the maximum amount or number that can be contained or accommodated ⟨a jug with a *capacity* of one gallon⟩ **c :** productive ability or potential ⟨a plant with a *capacity* of 50 metric tons a month⟩ **2 :** physical or mental ability ⟨an individual of unknown *capacity*⟩ **3 :** a position or character assigned or assumed ⟨in one's *capacity* as a judge⟩ [Middle French *capacité,* from Latin *capacitas,* from *capax* "capacious"]

[1]**ca·par·i·son** \kə-ˈpar-ə-sən\ *n* **1 a :** an ornamental covering for a horse **b :** decorative trappings and harness **2 :** rich clothing **:** ADORNMENT [Middle French *caparaçon,* from Spanish *caparazón*]

[2]**caparison** *vt* **:** to provide with or as if with a fancy covering

[1]**cape** \ˈkāp\ *n* **:** a point or extension of land jutting out into water either as a peninsula or as a projecting point [Medieval French *cap,* from Old Occitan, from Latin *caput* "head"]

[2]**cape** *n* **:** a sleeveless outer garment or part of a garment that fits closely at the neck and hangs loosely from the shoulders [probably from Spanish *capa,* from Late Latin *cappa* "head covering, cloak"]

Cape buffalo \ˈkāp-\ *n* **:** a large wild buffalo of sub-Saharan Africa [*Cape* of Good Hope, Africa]

cape·lin \ˈkap-lən, -ə-lən\ *n* **:** a small northern sea fish related to the smelts and often used as cod bait [French *capelan* "codfish," derived from Medieval Latin *cappellanus* "chaplain"]

Ca·pel·la \kə-ˈpel-ə\ *n* **:** a bright star in Auriga [Latin, literally, "she-goat," from *caper* "he-goat"]

[1]**ca·per** \ˈkā-pər\ *n* **1 :** any of a genus of low prickly shrubs of the Mediterranean region; *esp* **:** one cultivated for its buds **2 :** one of the flower buds or young berries of the caper pickled for use as a seasoning [Latin *capparis,* from Greek *kapparis*]

[2]**caper** *vi* **ca·pered; ca·per·ing** \-pə-ring, -pring\ **:** to leap about playfully or wildly [probably from *capriole*]

[3]**caper** *n* **1 :** an unrestrained bounding leap **2 :** PRANK, ANTIC **3 :** an illegal act; *esp* **:** THEFT

cap·er·cail·lie \ˌkap-ər-ˈkāl-yē, -ē\ *or* **cap·er·cail·zie** \-yē, -zē\ *n* **:** the largest Old World grouse [Scottish Gaelic *capalcoille,* literally, "horse of the woods"]

cape·skin \ˈkāp-ˌskin\ *n* **:** a leather made from sheepskins with the natural grain retained [*Cape* of Good Hope]

Ca·pe·tian \kə-ˈpē-shən\ *adj* **:** of or relating to the French dynasty that ruled from 987 to 1328 [Hugh *Capet*] — **Capetian** *n*

cap·il·lar·i·ty \ˌkap-ə-ˈlar-ət-ē\ *n* **:** the action by which the surface of a liquid where (as in a slender tube) it is in contact with a solid is raised or lowered depending upon the relative attraction of the molecules of the liquid for each other and for those of the solid

[1]**cap·il·lary** \ˈkap-ə-ˌler-ē\ *adj* **1 :** resembling a hair in having a slender elongated form; *esp* **:** having a very small bore ⟨a *capillary* tube⟩ **2 :** involving, held by, or resulting from surface tension ⟨*capillary* water in the soil⟩ **3 :** of or relating to capillaries or capillarity [Latin *capillaris,* from *capillus* "hair"]

[2]**capillary** *n, pl* **-lar·ies :** a capillary tube; *esp* **:** any of the tiny blood vessels connecting arterioles with venules and forming networks throughout the body

[1]**cap·i·tal** \ˈkap-ət-l, ˈkap-tl\ *adj* **1 a :** punishable by death ⟨a *capital* crime⟩ **b :** resulting in death ⟨*capital* punishment⟩ **2 :** being a letter that belongs to or conforms to the series A, B, C, etc. rather than a, b, c, etc. **3 :** being the seat of government ⟨the *capital* city⟩ **4 :** of or relating to capital ⟨*capital* costs⟩ **5 :** EXCELLENT ⟨a *capital* performance⟩ [Latin *capitalis,* from *caput* "head"]

[2]**capital** *n* **1 a :** accumulated goods on hand at a specified time in contrast to income received over a specified period; *also* **:** the value of such goods **b :** the excess of assets over liabilities **2 a :** capital goods and invested savings used in the process of production **b :** possessions (as money) used to bring in income **c :** persons owning or investing capital **d :** CAPITAL STOCK **3 :** ADVANTAGE, GAIN ⟨make *capital* out of another's weakness⟩ **4 :** a capital letter **5 a :** a capital city ⟨the *capital* of Vermont⟩ **b :** a city that is most important for a particular activity or product ⟨the fashion *capital*⟩ [Italian *capitale,* from *capitale,* adjective, "chief, principal," from Latin *capitalis* "capital"]

[3]**capital** *n* **:** the top part or piece of an architectural column [Medieval French *capitel,* from Late Latin *capitellum* "small head, top of column," from Latin *caput* "head"]

capital goods *n pl* **:** machinery, tools, factories, and commodities used in the production of goods

1 2 3

[3]capital: *1* Doric, *2* Ionic, *3* Corinthian

cap·i·tal·ism \ˈkap-ət-l-ˌiz-əm\ *n* **:** an economic system in which natural resources and means of production are privately owned, investments are determined by private decision rather than by state control, and prices, production, and the distribution of goods are determined mainly by competition in a free market — **cap·i·tal·ist** \-l-əst\ *or* **cap·i·tal·is·tic** \ˌkap-ət-l-ˈis-tik\ *adj* — **cap·i·tal·is·ti·cal·ly** \-ti-kə-lē, -klē\ *adv*

cap·i·tal·ist \ˈkap-ət-l-əst, ˈkap-tl-\ *n* **1 :** a person who has capital; *esp* **:** one who has or controls a great amount of business capital **2 :** a person who favors capitalism

cap·i·tal·i·za·tion \ˌkap-ət-l-ə-ˈzā-shən, ˌkap-tl-\ *n* **1 :** the act or process of capitalizing **2 :** the amount of money used as capital in a business

cap·i·tal·ize \ˈkap-ət-l-ˌīz, ˈkap-tl-\ *vb* **1 :** to write or print with an initial capital or in capitals **2 a :** to charge (an expenditure) to a capital account **b** (1) **:** to supply capital for ⟨*capitalize* an enterprise at $50,000⟩ (2) **:** to use as capital ⟨*capitalize* reserve funds⟩ **3 :** to use to help oneself ⟨*capitalize* on an opponent's mistake⟩

cap·i·tal·ly \ˈkap-ət-l-ē, -tl-ē\ *adv* **:** in a capital manner **:** EXCELLENTLY ⟨got along *capitally* in school⟩

capital stock *n* **:** the amount invested by stockholders in a corporation as holders of its shares; *also* **:** the shares of stock held by these stockholders

cap·i·ta·tion \ˌkap-ə-ˈtā-shən\ *n* **:** POLL TAX [Late Latin *capitatio,* from Latin *caput* "head"]

cap·i·tol \ˈkap-ət-l, ˈkap-tl\ *n* **1 :** a building in which a state legislative body meets **2** *cap* **:** the building in which the United States Congress meets in Washington [Latin *Capitolium,* a temple of Jupiter in Rome on the Capitoline hill]

Cap·i·to·line \ˈkap-ət-l-ˌīn\ *adj* **:** of or relating to the smallest of the seven hills of ancient Rome, the temple on it, or the gods worshiped there [Latin *capitolinus,* from *Capitolium,* a temple of Jupiter]

ca·pit·u·late \kə-ˈpich-ə-ˌlāt\ *vi* **:** to surrender usually on terms agreed upon in advance [Medieval Latin *capitulare* "to draw up by headings or chapters," from Late Latin *capitulum* "chapter," from Latin *caput* "head"]

ca·pit·u·la·tion \kə-ˌpich-ə-ˈlā-shən\ *n* **1 :** a set of terms or articles constituting an agreement between governments **2 :** an act of capitulating **:** a surrender on agreed terms

ca·pit·u·lum \kə-ˈpich-ə-ləm\ *n, pl* **-la** \-lə\ **1 :** a rounded knob (as on a bone) **2 :** HEAD 7a [Latin, "small head," from *caput* "head"]

ca·po \ˈkā-pō\ *n, pl* **capos :** a bar that can be fitted on the fingerboard especially of a guitar to raise the pitch of all the strings [short for *capotasto,* from Italian, literally, "head of fingerboard"]

ca·pon \ˈkā-ˌpän, -pən\ *n* **:** a castrated male chicken [Old English *capūn,* probably from Medieval French *capon, chapun,* from Latin *capo*]

ca·pric·cio \kə-ˈprē-chō, -chē-ˌō\ *n, pl* **-cios :** an instrumental piece in fanciful irregular form usually lively in tempo [Italian, "whim, capriccio"]

ca·price \kə-ˈprēs\ *n* **1 :** a sudden unpredictable turn or change; *esp* **:** WHIM **2 :** an inclination to change one's mind impulsively **3 :** CAPRICCIO [French, from Italian *capriccio* "whim, shudder"]

synonyms CAPRICE, WHIM, VAGARY, CROTCHET mean an irrational or unpredictable idea or desire. CAPRICE stresses lack of apparent motivation and suggests a degree of willfulness ⟨by sheer *caprice* she quit her job⟩. WHIM implies a fantastic, capricious turn or inclination ⟨an odd antique bought on a *whim*⟩. VAGARY stresses the erratic, irresponsible character of the notion or desire ⟨recently he had been prone to strange *vagaries*⟩. CROTCHET implies an eccentric opinion or preference ⟨a serious scientist equally known for her bizarre *crotchets*⟩.

ca·pri·cious \kə-ˈprish-əs, -ˈprē-shəs\ *adj* **:** moved or controlled by caprice **:** apt to change suddenly **:** FICKLE, CHANGEABLE ⟨a *capricious* child⟩ ⟨*capricious* weather⟩ — **ca·pri·cious·ly** *adv* — **ca·pri·cious·ness** *n*

Cap·ri·corn \ˈkap-rə-ˌkȯrn\ *n* **1 :** a southern zodiacal constellation between Sagittarius and Aquarius **2 :** the 10th sign of the zodiac; *also* : one born under this sign [Latin *Capricornus,* from *caper* "goat" + *cornu* "horn"]

cap·ri·ole \ˈkap-rē-ˌōl\ *n* : an upward leap of a horse with a backward kick of the hind legs at the height of the leap [Middle French, from Italian *capriola* "caper," from *capriolo* "roebuck," from Latin *capreolus* "goat, roebuck," from *caper* "he-goat"]

cap·sa·i·cin \kap-ˈsā-ə-sən\ *n* : an irritant substance found in various capsicums that gives hot peppers their pungency [from *capsicum*]

cap·si·cum \ˈkap-si-kəm\ *n* **1** : any of a genus of tropical American herbs and shrubs of the nightshade family widely cultivated for their many-seeded usually fleshy-walled fruits — called also *pepper* **2** : PEPPER 2b [New Latin, genus name, perhaps from Latin *capsa* "case"]

cap·size \ˈkap-ˌsīz, kap-ˈ\ *vb* : to become or cause to become upset or overturned : TURN OVER ⟨canoes *capsize* easily⟩ [perhaps from Spanish *capuzar* or Catalan *cabussar* "to thrust (the head) underwater"]

cap·stan \ˈkap-stən\ *n* : a machine for moving or raising weights that consists of a vertical drum which can be rotated and around which cable is turned [Middle English, probably from Medieval French *cabestant*]

capstan

cap·su·lar \ˈkap-sə-lər\ *adj* : of, relating to, or resembling a capsule

cap·su·lat·ed \-ˌlāt-əd\ *adj* : enclosed in a capsule

[1]**cap·sule** \ˈkap-səl, -ˌsül\ *n* **1** : a membrane or sac enclosing a body part (as a knee joint or kidney) **2** : a closed receptacle containing spores or seeds: as **a** : a dry dehiscent usually many-seeded fruit composed of two or more carpels **b** : the spore sac of a moss **3** : a shell usually of gelatin for packaging something (as a drug); *also* : such a shell together with its contents **4** : an often polysaccharide envelope surrounding a microorganism (as some bacteria) **5** : an extremely brief condensation : OUTLINE **6** : a small pressurized compartment for an aviator or astronaut for flight or emergency escape [French, from Latin *capsula* "small box," from *capsa* "box, case"]

[2]**capsule** *adj* **1** : extremely brief ⟨a *capsule* review of the news⟩ **2** : being small and very compact

[1]**cap·tain** \ˈkap-tən\ *n* **1** : a leader of a group ⟨the *captain* of a team⟩ **2 a** : an officer in the Navy ranking above a commander and below a commodore and in the Coast Guard ranking above commander and below a rear admiral **b** : the commanding officer of a ship **3 a** : the commanding officer of a military unit **b** : an officer in the army, marine corps, and air force ranking above a first lieutenant and below a major **4 a** : a fire or police department officer usually ranking between a chief and a lieutenant **b** : a senior pilot who commands the crew of an airplane **c** : HEADWAITER [Medieval French *capitain,* from Late Latin *capitaneus* "chief," from Latin *caput* "head"] — **captain·ship** \-ˌship\ *n*

[2]**captain** *vt* : to be captain of : LEAD

cap·tain·cy \ˈkap-tən-sē\ *n, pl* **-cies** : a captain's rank or position

[1]**cap·tion** \ˈkap-shən\ *n* **1** : the heading especially of an article or document **2** : the explanation accompanying a pictorial illustration **3** : a motion-picture subtitle [earlier *caption* "part of a legal document that sets out when and where it was taken," probably short for *certificate of caption* ("taking, seizure")]

[2]**caption** *vt* : to furnish with a caption

cap·tious \ˈkap-shəs\ *adj* : quick to find fault especially over trifles [Latin *captiosus* "designed to entrap," from *captio* "deception, quibble," from *capere* "to take"] — **cap·tious·ly** *adv* — **cap·tious·ness** *n*

cap·ti·vate \ˈkap-tə-ˌvāt\ *vt* : to attract and win over : CHARM, FASCINATE ⟨music that *captivated* everybody who heard it⟩ — **cap·ti·va·tion** \ˌkap-tə-ˈvā-shən\ *n* — **cap·ti·va·tor** \ˈkap-tə-ˌvāt-ər\ *n*

cap·tive \ˈkap-tiv\ *adj* **1 a** : taken and held prisoner especially in war **b** : held or confined so as to prevent escape ⟨a *captive* animal⟩ **c** : owned or controlled by a business to meet its own needs rather than to produce for the market ⟨a *captive* mine⟩ **2** : in a situation that makes departure or inattention difficult ⟨a *captive* audience⟩ [Latin *captivus,* from *capere* "to take, capture"] — **captive** *n*

cap·tiv·i·ty \kap-ˈtiv-ət-ē\ *n, pl* **-ties** : the state of being captive

cap·tor \ˈkap-tər\ *n* : one that has captured a person or thing

[1]**cap·ture** \ˈkap-chər\ *n* **1** : the act of catching or gaining control by force or trickery **2** : one that has been taken captive [Middle French, from Latin *captura,* from *capere* "to take"]

[2]**capture** *vt* **cap·tured; cap·tur·ing** \ˈkap-chə-riŋ, ˈkap-shriŋ\ **1 a** : to make captive : take and hold especially by force ⟨*capture* a city⟩ **b** : to preserve in a relatively permanent form ⟨*capture* a smile on film⟩ **c** : to captivate and hold the interest of ⟨*captured* their imagination⟩ **2 a** : to take according to rules of a game (as chess) **b** : to gain or win especially through effort ⟨*captured* first prize⟩ ***synonyms*** see CATCH

capture the flag *n* : a game in which players on each of two teams seek to capture the other team's flag and return it to their side without being captured and imprisoned

ca·pu·chin \ˈkap-yə-shən, -ə-, *sense 2 also* kə-ˈpü-shən, -ˈpyü-\ *n* **1** *cap* : a member of an austere branch of the first order of Saint Francis of Assisi engaged in missionary work and preaching **2** : a South American monkey with the forehead bare and fringed by dark hair [Middle French, from Italian *cappuccino,* from *cappuccio* "hood, cowl," derived from *cappa* "cloak," from Late Latin; from the cowl worn by members of this order]

cap·y·bara \ˌkap-i-ˈbar-ə, -ˈbär-\ *n* : a tailless semiaquatic South American rodent often exceeding four feet (1.2 meters) in length [Portuguese *capivara,* from Tupi *kapiʔiwára,* from *kapíʔi* "grass, brush" + *-wara* "eater"]

capybara

car \ˈkär\ *n* **1** : a vehicle (as a railroad coach or an automobile) that moves on wheels **2** : the compartment of an elevator **3** : the part of a balloon or an airship in which passengers or equipment are carried [Medieval French *carre,* from Latin *carrus,* of Celtic origin]

ca·ra·bao \ˌkar-ə-ˈbaù, ˌkär-\ *n, pl* **-bao** *or* **-baos** : WATER BUFFALO [Philippine Spanish, from Eastern Bisayan (a language of the Visayan Islands, Philippines) *karabáw*]

car·a·bi·neer *or* **car·a·bi·nier** \ˌkar-ə-bə-ˈniər\ *n* : a soldier armed with a carbine [French *carabinier,* from *carabine* "carbine"]

ca·ra·ca·ra \ˌkar-ə-ˈkar-ə, -ə-kə-ˈrä\ *n* : any of various large long-legged hawks related to the falcons and found from the southern U.S. to South America [Portuguese *caracará,* from Tupi *karakará*]

car·a·cole \ˈkar-ə-ˌkōl\ *n* : a half turn to right or left performed by a mounted horse [French, from Spanish *caracol* "snail, spiral stair, caracole"] — **caracole** *vb*

car·a·cul \ˈkar-ə-kəl\ *n* : the pelt of a karakul lamb after the curl begins to loosen [alteration of *karakul*]

ca·rafe \kə-ˈraf, -ˈräf\ *n* : a bottle with a wide base and flaring lip used to hold water or beverages [French, from Italian *caraffa,* from Arabic *gharrāfa*]

car·am·bo·la \ˌkar-əm-ˈbō-lə\ *n* : STAR FRUIT

car·a·mel \ˈkär-məl; ˈkar-ə-mel, -ˌmel\ *n* **1** : a brittle brown and somewhat bitter substance obtained by heating sugar and used as a coloring and flavoring agent **2** : a firm chewy candy [French, from Spanish *caramelo,* from Portuguese, "icicle, caramel," from Late Latin *calamellus* "small reed," from Latin *calamus* "reed"]

car·a·mel·ize \-mə-ˌlīz\ *vb* : to turn into caramel — **car·a·mel·i·za·tion** \ˌkär-mə-lə-ˈzā-shən, ˌkar-ə-mə-\ *n*

car·a·pace \ˈkar-ə-ˌpās\ *n* : a bony or chitinous case or shield covering all or part of the back of an animal (as a turtle or crab) [French, from Spanish *carapacho*]

[1]**carat** *variant of* KARAT

[2]**car·at** \ˈkar-ət\ *n* : a unit of weight for precious stones (as diamonds) equal to 200 milligrams [derived from Arabic *qīrāṭ* "bean pod, a small weight," from Greek *keration,* from *keras* "horn"]

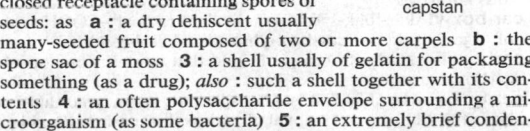

car·a·van \ˈkar-ə-ˌvan\ *n* **1 a :** a company of travelers on a journey through desert or hostile regions **b :** a train of pack animals or of vehicles traveling together **2 :** a covered vehicle: as **a :** one equipped as traveling living quarters **b** *British* **:** TRAILER 2b [Italian *caravana,* from Persian *kārvān*]

car·a·vel \ˈkar-ə-ˌvel, -vəl\ *n* **:** a small 15th and 16th century ship with broad bows, high narrow poop, and usually three masts with lateen or both square and lateen sails [Middle French *caravelle,* from Portuguese *caravela*]

car·a·way \ˈkar-ə-ˌwā\ *n* **1 :** a usually white-flowered aromatic herb related to the carrot **2 :** the aromatic pungent fruit of the caraway used in seasoning and medicine — called also *caraway seed* [probably from Medieval Latin *carvi,* from Arabic *karawyā,* from Greek *karon*]

carb \ˈkärb\ *n* **:** CARBOHYDRATE; *also* **:** a high-carbohydrate food — usually used in plural

carb- *or* **carbo-** *combining form* **:** carbon **:** carbonic **:** carbonyl **:** carboxyl ⟨*carb*ide⟩ ⟨*carbo*hydrate⟩

car·bide \ˈkär-ˌbīd\ *n* **:** a compound of carbon with another element; *esp* **:** CALCIUM CARBIDE

car·bine \ˈkär-ˌbēn, -ˌbīn\ *n* **:** a short light rifle [French *carabine*]

car·bo·hy·drase \ˌkär-bō-ˈhī-ˌdrās, -ˌdrāz\ *n* **:** an enzyme (as amylase) that promotes decomposition or synthesis of a carbohydrate

car·bo·hy·drate \-ˌdrāt\ *n* **:** any of various neutral compounds of carbon, hydrogen, and oxygen (as sugars, starches, or celluloses) most of which are formed by green plants and which constitute a major class of animal foods

car·bol·ic acid \ˌkär-ˈbäl-ik-\ *n* **:** PHENOL 1 [*carb-* + Latin *oleum* "oil"]

car·bon \ˈkär-bən\ *n* **1 :** a nonmetallic chiefly tetravalent chemical element found native (as in the diamond and graphite) or as a constituent of coal, petroleum, and asphalt, of limestone and other carbonates, and of organic compounds or obtained artificially — see ELEMENT table **2 :** a carbon rod used in an arc lamp **3 a :** a sheet of carbon paper **b :** CARBON COPY 1 [French *carbone,* from Latin *carbo* "ember, charcoal"]

car·bo·na·ceous \ˌkär-bə-ˈnā-shəs\ *adj* **:** relating to, containing, or composed of carbon

car·bo·na·do \ˌkär-bə-ˈnād-ō, -ˈnäd-\ *n, pl* **-nados :** an impure opaque dark-colored fine-grained aggregate of diamond particles valuable for its superior toughness [Portuguese, literally, "carbonated"]

[1]**car·bon·ate** \ˈkär-bə-ˌnāt, -nət\ *n* **:** a salt or ester of carbonic acid

[2]**car·bon·ate** \-ˌnāt\ *vt* **1 :** to convert into a carbonate **2 :** to combine or infuse with carbon dioxide ⟨a *carbonated* beverage⟩ — **car·bon·ation** \ˌkär-bə-ˈnā-shən\ *n*

carbon black *n* **:** any of various colloidal black substances consisting wholly or principally of carbon obtained as soot and used especially as pigments

carbon copy *n* **1 :** a copy made by carbon paper **2 :** DUPLICATE 1

carbon cycle *n* **:** the cycle of carbon in living beings in which carbon dioxide fixed by photosynthesis to form organic nutrients is ultimately restored to the inorganic state by respiration, decay, or combustion

carbon dating *n* **:** the determination of age (as of an archaeological find) by means of the content of carbon 14

carbon dioxide *n* **:** a heavy colorless gas CO_2 that does not support combustion, dissolves in water to form carbonic acid, is formed especially by the combustion and decomposition of organic substances (as in animal respiration), is absorbed from the air by plants in photosynthesis, and is used in the carbonation of beverages

carbon disulfide *n* **:** a colorless flammable poisonous liquid CS_2 used as a solvent for rubber — called also *carbon bisulfide*

carbon footprint *n* **:** the amount of greenhouse gases and especially carbon dioxide given off by something (as a person's activities or a product's manufacture and transport) during a given period

carbon 14 *n* **:** a heavy radioactive form of carbon that has mass number 14, is formed especially by the action of cosmic rays on nitrogen in the atmosphere, and is used as a tracer or for determining the age of very old specimens (as bones or charcoal) of formerly living materials

car·bon·ic \kär-ˈbän-ik\ *adj* **:** of, relating to, or derived from carbon, carbonic acid, or carbon dioxide

carbonic acid *n* **:** a weak acid H_2CO_3 that decomposes readily into water and carbon dioxide

carbonic an·hy·drase \-an-ˈhī-ˌdrās, -ˌdrāz\ *n* **:** a zinc-containing enzyme that occurs in living tissues (as red blood cells) and aids carbon-dioxide transport from the tissues and its release from the blood in the lungs

car·bon·if·er·ous \ˌkär-bə-ˈnif-rəs, -ə-rəs\ *adj* **1 :** producing or containing carbon or coal **2** *cap* **:** of, relating to, or being the Carboniferous

Carboniferous *n* **:** the period of the Paleozoic era between the Devonian and the Permian during which reptiles first appeared in the fossil record and tremendous deposits of coal were formed; *also* **:** the corresponding system of rocks

car·bon·ize \ˈkär-bə-ˌnīz\ *vb* **:** to convert or become converted into carbon — **car·bon·i·za·tion** \ˌkär-bə-nə-ˈzā-shən\ *n*

carbon monoxide *n* **:** a colorless odorless very poisonous gas CO formed by the incomplete burning of carbon

carbon paper *n* **:** a thin paper faced with a transferable waxy pigmented coating so that when placed between two sheets of paper the pressure of writing or typing on the top sheet causes reproduction of the graphic material on the bottom sheet

carbon tetrachloride *n* **:** a colorless nonflammable poisonous liquid CCl_4 that has an odor resembling that of chloroform and is used as a solvent especially of grease and as a refrigerant

carbon 12 *n* **:** an isotope of carbon that has a mass number of 12, is the most abundant carbon isotope, and is used as a standard for measurements of atomic weight

car·bon·yl \ˈkär-bə-ˌnil, -ˌnēl\ *n* **:** a bivalent radical CO occurring espicially in aldehydes, ketones, esters, organic acids, and amides

Car·bo·run·dum \ˌkär-bə-ˈrən-dəm\ *trademark* — used for various abrasives

car·box·yl \kär-ˈbäk-səl\ *n* **:** a univalent radical –COOH typical of organic acids — **car·box·yl·ic** \ˌkär-bäk-ˈsil-ik\ *adj*

carboxylic acid *n* **:** an organic acid that contains one or more carboxyl groups

car·box·yl·ase \kär-ˈbäk-sə-ˌlās, -ˌlāz\ *n* **:** an enzyme that catalyzes the addition or removal of carboxyl or carbon dioxide

car·boy \ˈkär-ˌbȯi\ *n* **:** a large container for liquids [Persian *qarāba,* from Arabic *qarrāba* "demijohn"]

car·bun·cle \ˈkär-ˌbəng-kəl\ *n* **1 :** a cut cabochon garnet **2 :** a painful inflammation of the skin and deeper tissues that discharges pus from several openings — compare BOIL [Medieval French, from Latin *carbunculus* "small coal, carbuncle," from *carbo* "charcoal, ember"] — **car·bun·cled** \-kəld\ *adj* — **car·bun·cu·lar** \kär-ˈbəng-kyə-lər\ *adj*

car·bu·re·tor \ˈkär-bə-ˌrāt-ər, -byə-\ *n* **:** a mechanical apparatus for mixing vaporized fuel and air and supplying the mixture to an internal-combustion engine [*carburet* "to combine with carbon," from obsolete *carburet* "carbide"]

car·case \ˈkär-kəs\ *British variant of* CARCASS

car·cass \ˈkär-kəs\ *n* **1 :** a dead body; *esp* **:** the dressed body of a meat animal **2 :** the living body ⟨I hauled my *carcass* out of bed⟩ **3 :** the foundation structure of something (as a tire) [Medieval French *carcas, carkeis*]

car·cin·o·gen \kär-ˈsin-ə-jən, ˈkärs-n-ə-ˌjen\ *n* **:** a substance or agent causing cancer [Greek *karkinos* "ulcerous sore," literally, "crab"] — **car·ci·no·gen·ic** \ˌkärs-n-ō-ˈjen-ik\ *adj* — **car·ci·no·ge·nic·i·ty** \-jə-ˈnis-ət-ē\ *n*

car·ci·no·ma \ˌkärs-n-ˈō-mə\ *n, pl* **-mas** *or* **-ma·ta** \-mət-ə\ **:** a malignant tumor originating in epithelium — **car·ci·no·ma·tous** \ˌkärs-n-ˈō-mət-əs\ *adj*

[1]**card** \ˈkärd\ *vt* **:** to clean and untangle (fibers) by combing with a card before spinning — **card·er** *n*

[2]**card** *n* **:** an instrument usually having bent wire teeth and used for combing fibers (as wool or cotton) [Medieval Latin *cardus, carduus* "thistle, carding instrument," from Latin *carduus* "thistle"]

[3]**card** *n* **1 :** PLAYING CARD **2** *pl* **a :** a game played with cards **b :** card playing **3 :** an amusing person **:** WAG **4 a :** a flat stiff usually small and rectangular piece of paper or thin cardboard (as a postcard) **b :** a sports program ⟨a racing *card*⟩ **c** (1) **:** a wine list (2) **:** MENU 1 **d :** a removable circuit board (as in a microcomputer) **e :** GREETING CARD **f :** CREDIT CARD [Medieval French *carde, carte,* derived from Latin *charta* "leaf of papyrus," from Greek *chartēs* — see *Word History* at CARTEL]

[4]**card** *vt* **1 :** to provide with a card **2 :** to ask for identification (as in a bar)

car·da·mom \ˈkärd-ə-məm, -ˌmäm\ *n* **:** the aromatic capsular fruit of an Indian herb related to ginger with seeds used as a condiment and in medicine; *also* : this plant [Latin *cardamomum,* from Greek *kardamōmon*]

card·board \'kärd-ˌbōrd, -ˌbȯrd\ *n* : a material made from cellulose fiber (as wood pulp) like paper but usually thicker

card catalog *n* : a catalog (as of books) in which the entries are arranged systematically on cards

cardi- *or* **cardio-** *combining form* : heart ⟨*cardio*gram⟩ [Greek *kardia*]

[1]**car·di·ac** \'kärd-ē-ˌak\ *adj* **1** : of, relating to, situated near, or acting on the heart **2** : of, relating to, or being the part of the stomach into which the esophagus opens **3** : of, relating to, or affected with heart disease ⟨*cardiac* patients⟩ [Latin *cardiacus,* from Greek *kardiakos,* from *kardia* "heart"]

[2]**cardiac** *n* : a person with heart disease

cardiac arrest *n* : temporary or permanent stoppage of the heartbeat

cardiac muscle *n* : striated muscle tissue that is found in the heart, is not under voluntary control, and undergoes rhythmic contractions

car·di·gan \'kärd-i-gən\ *n* : a usually collarless sweater opening the full length of the front [James Thomas Brudenell, 7th earl of *Cardigan,* died 1868, English soldier]

Cardigan Welsh corgi *n* : any of a breed of Welsh corgis with rounded ears, slightly bowed forelegs, and a long tail — called also *Cardigan* [*Cardigan* county, Wales]

[1]**car·di·nal** \'kärd-nəl, -n-əl\ *n* **1** : one of the high officials of the Roman Catholic Church who rank next below the pope and who form his advisory and administrative council and elect his successor **2** : CARDINAL NUMBER — usually used in plural **3** : a North American finch of which the male is bright red with a black face and pointed crest [sense 3 from its color, resembling that of a cardinal's robes]

[2]**cardinal** *adj* **1** : of basic importance : MAIN, CHIEF, PRIMARY ⟨a *cardinal* principle⟩ **2** : very serious or grave ⟨a *cardinal* sin⟩ [Medieval French, from Late Latin *cardinalis,* from Latin *cardo* "hinge"] — **car·di·nal·ly** \-ē\ *adv*

car·di·nal·ate \-ət, -ˌāt\ *n* : the office, rank, or dignity of a cardinal

cardinal flower *n* : a North American lobelia that bears a spike of brilliant red flowers

car·di·nal·i·ty \ˌkärd-n-'al-ət-ē\ *n, pl* **-ties** : the numbers of elements in a given mathematical set

cardinal number *n* : a number (as 1, 5, 15) that is used in simple counting and that indicates how many elements there are in a set but not the order in which they are arranged — see NUMBER table; compare ORDINAL NUMBER

cardinal point *n* : one of the four principal points of the compass: north, south, east, or west

car·dio \'kär-dē-ō\ *adj* : CARDIOVASCULAR

car·dio·gram \'kärd-ē-ə-ˌgram\ *n* : the curve or tracing made by a cardiograph

car·dio·graph \-ˌgraf\ *n* : an instrument that graphically records the movements of the heart — **car·dio·graph·ic** \ˌkärd-ē-ə-'graf-ik\ *adj*

car·di·ol·o·gy \ˌkärd-ē-'äl-ə-jē\ *n* : the study of the heart and its action and diseases — **car·di·ol·o·gist** \-jəst\ *n*

car·dio·pul·mo·nary \ˌkär-dē-ō-'pu̇l-mə-ˌner-ē, -'pəl-\ *adj* : of or relating to the heart and lungs

cardiopulmonary resuscitation *n* : a procedure used to restore normal breathing when the heart stops beating that includes clearing the air passages to the lungs, mouth-to-mouth artificial respiration, and applying pressure to the chest to massage the heart

car·dio·vas·cu·lar \-'vas-kyə-lər\ *adj* : of, relating to, or involving the heart and blood vessels

car·doon \kär-'dün\ *n* : a large perennial plant of the Mediterranean region related to the artichoke and sometimes grown for its edible root and leafstalks [French *cardon,* from Late Latin *cardo* "thistle," from Latin *carduus*]

card·play·er \'kärd-ˌplā-ər\ *n* : one that plays cards

card·sharp \-ˌshärp\ *or* **card·sharp·er** \-ˌshär-pər\ *n* : a skilled cheater at cards

card table *n* : a table designed for playing cards; *esp* : a square table with folding legs

[1]**care** \'keər, 'kaər\ *n* **1 a** : an uneasy state of mixed uncertainty, fear, and responsibility : ANXIETY **b** : a cause for such anxiety **2** : painstaking or watchful attention : HEED ⟨take *care* in crossing streets⟩ **3** : SUPERVISION ⟨under a doctor's *care*⟩ **4** : an object of one's watchful attention ⟨the garden was his special *care*⟩ [Old English *caru*]

[2]**care** *vb* **1 a** : to feel trouble or anxiety **b** : to feel interest or concern ⟨*care* about freedom⟩ **2** : to give care ⟨*care* for the sick⟩ **3 a** : to have a liking, fondness, or taste ⟨don't *care* for sweets⟩ **b** : to have an inclination ⟨would you *care* for some pie⟩ **4** : WISH ⟨if you *care* to come⟩ — **car·er** *n* — **care less** : not to care — used positively and negatively with the same meaning ⟨I could *care less* what happens⟩ ⟨I couldn't *care less* what happens⟩

ca·reen \kə-'rēn\ *vb* **1** : to cause a boat to lean or tilt over on one side for cleaning, caulking, or repairing **2** : to sway from side to side : LURCH **3** : CAREER [from *carine* "side of a ship," from Middle French, "submerged part of a hull," from Latin *carina* "hull, half of a nutshell"]

[1]**ca·reer** \kə-'riər\ *n* **1 a** : COURSE 1a **b** : speed in a course ⟨ran at full *career*⟩ **2** : a course of continued progress or activity **3** : a profession for which one trains and which is undertaken as a permanent calling [Middle French *carrière,* from Old Occitan *carriera* "street," from Medieval Latin *carraria* "road for vehicles," from Latin *carrus* "car"]

[2]**career** *vi* : to go at top speed especially in a headlong manner ⟨a car *careering* down the road⟩

care·free \'keər-ˌfrē, 'kaər-\ *adj* : free from care: as **a** : having no worries or troubles **b** : IRRESPONSIBLE ⟨*carefree* with money⟩

care·ful \-fəl\ *adj* **1** : using or taking care ⟨a *careful* driver⟩ **2** : made, done, or said with care ⟨*careful* examination⟩ — **care·ful·ly** \-fə-lē, -flē\ *adv* — **care·ful·ness** \-fəl-nəs\ *n*

synonyms CAREFUL, METICULOUS, SCRUPULOUS, PUNCTILIOUS mean showing close attention to detail. CAREFUL implies attentiveness and cautiousness in avoiding mistakes ⟨a *careful* worker⟩ ⟨*careful* nursing⟩. METICULOUS may imply either commendable extreme carefulness or a hampering finicky caution over small points ⟨a *meticulous* analysis⟩. SCRUPULOUS applies to what is proper, fitting, or ethical ⟨*scrupulous* honesty⟩. PUNCTILIOUS implies close, even excessive attention to fine points ⟨*punctilious* observance of ritual⟩.

care·giv·er \-ˌgiv-ər\ *n* : a person who provides direct care (as for children or the chronically ill)

care·less \'keər-ləs, 'kaər-\ *adj* **1** : CAREFREE **2** : not taking proper care : HEEDLESS ⟨*careless* of danger⟩ **3** : done, made, or said without due care ⟨a *careless* mistake⟩ — **care·less·ly** *adv* — **care·less·ness** *n*

care package *n* : a package of useful or pleasurable items that is sent or given as a gift to another

[1]**ca·ress** \kə-'res\ *n* : a tender or loving touch or embrace [French *caresse,* from Italian *carezza,* from *caro* "dear," from Latin *carus*] — **ca·res·sive** \-'res-iv\ *adj* — **ca·res·sive·ly** *adv*

[2]**caress** *vt* : to touch or stroke lightly in a loving manner — **ca·ress·er** *n*

car·et \'kar-ət\ *n* : a mark ‸ used to show where something is to be inserted in written or printed matter [Latin, "there is lacking," from *carēre* "to lack"]

care·tak·er \'keər-ˌtā-kər, 'kaər-\ *n* : one that takes care of buildings or land often for an absent owner

care·worn \-ˌwōrn, -ˌwȯrn\ *adj* : showing the effect of grief or anxiety ⟨a *careworn* face⟩

car·fare \'kär-ˌfaər, -ˌfeər\ *n* : the fare charged a passenger (as on a bus or streetcar)

car·go \'kär-ˌgō\ *n, pl* **cargoes** *or* **cargos** : the goods or merchandise carried in a ship, airplane, or vehicle : FREIGHT [Spanish, "load, charge," from *cargar* "to load, charge," from Late Latin *carricare*]

cargo pants *n pl* : pants with cargo pockets typically on the sides of the legs at thigh level

cargo pocket *n* : a large pocket usually with a flap and a pleat

car·hop \'kär-ˌhäp\ *n* : one who serves customers at a drive-in restaurant [*car* + *-hop* (as in bellhop)]

Car·ib \'kar-əb\ *n* **1** : a member of an Indian people of northern South America and the Lesser Antilles **2** : the language of the Caribs [Spanish *Caribe,* of Carib origin]

\ə\ **abut**	\au̇\ **out**	\i\ **tip**	\ȯ\ **saw**	\u̇\ **foot**
\ər\ **further**	\ch\ **chin**	\ī\ **life**	\ȯi\ **coin**	\y\ **yet**
\a\ **mat**	\e\ **pet**	\j\ **job**	\th\ **thin**	\yü\ **few**
\ā\ **take**	\ē\ **easy**	\ng\ **sing**	\t͟h\ **this**	\yu̇\ **cure**
\ä\ **cot, cart**	\g\ **go**	\ō\ **bone**	\ü\ **food**	\zh\ **vision**

ca·ri·be \kə-ˈrē-bē\ *n* : PIRANHA [American Spanish, from Spanish, "Carib, cannibal"]

car·i·bou \ˈkar-ə-ˌbü\ *n, pl* **-bou** *or* **-bous** : a large deer of taiga and tundra — used especially for one of the New World; called also *reindeer* [Canadian French, from Micmac *qalipu*]

caribou

car·i·ca·ture \ˈkar-i-kə-ˌchu̇r\ *n* **1** : exaggeration by means of comic distortion of parts or characteristics **2** : a representation especially in literature or art that has the qualities of caricature **3** : something so distorted as to seem like caricature [Italian *caricatura,* literally, "act of loading," from *caricare* "to load," from Late Latin *carricare*] — **caricature** *vt* — **car·i·ca·tur·ist** \-əst\ *n*

synonyms CARICATURE, BURLESQUE, PARODY, TRAVESTY mean a comic or grotesque imitation. CARICATURE implies ludicrous exaggeration of the characteristic features of a subject ⟨*caricatures* of politicians in cartoons⟩. BURLESQUE implies mockery especially through giving a serious or lofty subject a frivolous treatment ⟨the comedy included a *burlesque* of a trial in court⟩. PARODY applies to treatment of a trivial or ludicrous subject in the exactly imitated style of a particular author or work ⟨a witty *parody* of the novel⟩. TRAVESTY implies that the subject remains unaltered but that the style and effect is extravagant or absurd ⟨the movie is a *travesty* of the book⟩.

car·ies \ˈkaər-ēz, ˈkeər-\ *n, pl* **caries** : a progressive destruction of bone or tooth; *esp* : tooth decay [Latin, "decay"] — **car·i·ous** \ˈkar-ē-əs, ˈker-\ *adj*

car·il·lon \ˈkar-ə-ˌlän, -lən\ *n* **1** : a set of bells sounded by hammers controlled by a keyboard **2** : a tune for the carillon [French, from Medieval French *quarregnon,* from Late Latin *quaternio* "set of four"]

car·il·lon·neur \ˌkar-ə-lə-ˈnər, ˌkar-ē-ə-ˈnər\ *n* : a carillon player [French, from *carillon*]

ca·ri·na \kə-ˈrī-nə, -ˈrē-\ *n, pl* **-rinas** *or* **-ri·nae** \-ˈrī-ˌnē, -ˈrē-ˌnī\ : a keel-shaped anatomical part, ridge, or process [Latin, "hull keel"]

car·load \ˈkär-ˈlōd\ *n* : a load (as of passengers) that fills a car

Car·mel·ite \ˈkär-mə-ˌlīt\ *n* : a friar or nun of the Roman Catholic Order of Our Lady of Mount Carmel founded in the 12th century — **Carmelite** *adj*

car·mi·na·tive \kär-ˈmin-ət-iv, ˈkär-mə-ˌnāt-iv\ *adj* : helping to expel gas from the stomach or intestines [French *carminatif,* from Latin *carminare* "to card, comb out knots in"] — **carminative** *n*

car·mine \ˈkär-mən, -ˌmīn\ *n* **1** : a rich crimson or scarlet coloring matter made from cochineal **2** : a vivid red [French *carmin,* from Medieval Latin *carminium,* perhaps derived from Arabic *qirmiz* "kermes" + Latin *minium* "red lead"]

car·nage \ˈkär-nij\ *n* : great and bloody slaughter (as in battle) [Middle French, from Medieval Latin *carnaticum* "tribute of animals or meat," from Latin *caro* "flesh"]

car·nal \ˈkärn-l\ *adj* **1** : of or relating to the body : CORPOREAL **2** : marked by sexuality : SENSUAL ⟨*carnal* love⟩ [Late Latin *carnalis,* from Latin *carn-, caro* "flesh"] — **car·nal·i·ty** \kär-ˈnal-ət-ē\ *n* — **car·nal·ly** \ˈkärn-l-ē\ *adv*

car·nas·si·al \kär-ˈnas-ē-əl\ *adj* : of, relating to, or being a tooth of a carnivore adapted for cutting rather than tearing [French *carnassier* "carnivorous," derived from Latin *caro* "flesh"] — **carnassial** *n*

car·na·tion \kär-ˈnā-shən\ *n* **1** : a moderate red **2** : any of the numerous cultivated usually double-flowered varieties of an Old World pink [Middle French, "color of human flesh," derived from Latin *caro* "flesh"]

car·nau·ba \kär-ˈnȯ-bə, -ˈnau̇; ˌkär-nə-ˈü-bə\ *n* **1** : a Brazilian palm that yields a brittle yellowish wax used especially in polishes — called also *carnauba palm* **2** : the wax produced by the carnauba — called also *carnauba wax* [Brazilian Portuguese *carnaúba,* from Tupi *karanaʔiβa*]

car·ne·lian \kär-ˈnēl-yən\ *n* : a hard tough reddish quartz used as a gem [Medieval French *corneline*]

car·ni·val \ˈkär-nə-vəl\ *n* **1** : a season or festival of merrymaking before Lent **2** : a merrymaking, feasting, or masquerading **3 a** : a traveling enterprise offering amusements **b** : a program of entertainment ⟨a winter *carnival*⟩ [Italian *carnevale,* alteration of earlier *carnelevare,* literally, "removal of meat"]

car·niv·o·ra \kär-ˈniv-rə, -ə-rə\ *n pl* : carnivorous mammals [New Latin]

car·ni·vore \ˈkär-nə-ˌvōr, -ˌvȯr\ *n* **1** : a flesh-eating animal; *esp* : any of an order (Carnivora) of flesh-eating mammals **2** : a plant that traps and digests insects

car·niv·o·rous \kär-ˈniv-rəs, -ə-rəs\ *adj* **1 a** : subsisting or feeding on animal tissues **b** : trapping and digesting insects ⟨a *carnivorous* plant⟩ **2** : of or relating to the carnivores [Latin *carnivorus,* from *carn-, caro* "flesh" + *vorare* "to devour"] — **car·niv·o·rous·ly** *adv* — **car·niv·o·rous·ness** *n*

car·no·tite \ˈkär-nə-ˌtīt\ *n* : a mineral consisting of a radioactive compound of potassium, uranium, vanadium, and oxygen [M. A. *Carnot,* died 1920, French inspector general of mines]

car·ob \ˈkar-əb\ *n* : one of the long pods of a Mediterranean tree of the legume family; *also* : its sweet pulp [Middle French *carobe,* from Medieval Latin *carrubium,* from Arabic *kharrūba*]

[1]**car·ol** \ˈkar-əl\ *n* **1** : an old round dance with singing **2** : a song of joy or mirth **3** : a popular song or ballad of religious joy ⟨Christmas *carols*⟩ [Medieval French *carole,* from Late Latin *choraula* "choral song," from Latin, "choral accompanist," from Greek *choraulēs,* from *choros* "chorus" + *aulein* "to play a reed instrument," from *aulos,* a kind of reed instrument]

[2]**carol** *vb* **-oled** *or* **-olled; -ol·ing** *or* **-ol·ling** **1** : to sing especially in a joyful way **2** : to sing carols — **car·ol·er** *or* **car·ol·ler** *n*

Car·o·line \ˈkar-ə-ˌlin, -lən\ *adj* : of or relating to Charles I or Charles II of England [Medieval Latin *Carolus* "Charles"]

Car·o·lin·gian \ˌkar-ə-ˈlin-jē-ən, -jən\ *adj* : of or relating to a Frankish dynasty dating from about A.D. 613 and ruling France from 751 to 987, Germany from 752 to 911, and Italy from 774 to 961 [French *carolingien,* from Medieval Latin *Karolingi* "Carolingians," from *Karolus* "Charlemagne"] — **Carolingian** *n*

[1]**car·om** \ˈkar-əm\ *n* **1** : a shot in billiards in which the cue ball strikes each of two object balls **2** : a rebounding especially at an angle [Spanish *carambola*]

[2]**carom** *vi* **1** : to make a carom **2** : to strike and rebound at an angle : GLANCE

car·o·tene \ˈkar-ə-ˌtēn\ *n* : any of several orange or red hydrocarbon pigments (as $C_{40}H_{56}$) that occur in plants and in the fatty tissues of plant-eating animals and are convertible to vitamin A [Late Latin *carota* "carrot"]

ca·rot·enoid \kə-ˈrät-n-ˌȯid\ *n* : any of various usually yellow to red pigments (as carotenes) found widely in plants and animals and characterized chemically by a long chain of carbon atoms — **carotenoid** *adj*

ca·rot·id \kə-ˈrät-əd\ *n* : the chief artery or one of the pair of arteries that pass up each side of the neck and supply the head — called also *carotid artery* [Greek *karōtides* "carotid arteries," from *karoun* "to stupefy"] — **carotid** *adj*

ca·rous·al \kə-ˈrau̇-zəl\ *n* : CAROUSE

[1]**ca·rouse** \kə-ˈrau̇z\ *n* : a drunken revel [Middle French *carousse,* from *boire carous* "to empty the cup," from *boire* "to drink" + German *garaus* "all out"]

[2]**carouse** *vi* : to drink liquor freely or excessively — **ca·rous·er** *n*

car·ou·sel *also* **car·rou·sel** \ˌkar-ə-ˈsel *also* -ˈzel\ *n* : MERRY-GO-ROUND 1 [French *carrousel,* from Italian *carosello*]

[1]**carp** \ˈkärp\ *vi* : to find fault : complain fretfully [of Scandinavian origin] — **carp·er** *n*

[2]**carp** *n, pl* **carp** *or* **carps** : a large variable Asian soft-finned freshwater fish often raised for food and widely introduced into U.S. waters; *also* : any of various related or similar fishes [Medieval French *carpe,* from Late Latin *carpa*]

-carp \ˌkärp\ *n combining form* **1** : part of a fruit ⟨meso*carp*⟩ **2** : fruit ⟨schizo*carp*⟩ [Greek *karpos* "fruit"]

[1]**car·pal** \ˈkär-pəl\ *adj* : of or relating to the carpus

[2]**carpal** *n* : a carpal bone or cartilage

car·pel \ˈkär-pəl\ *n* : one of the structures of the innermost whorl of a flower that together form the ovary of a flowering plant [New Latin *carpellum,* from Greek *karpos* "fruit"]

car·pen·ter \ˈkär-pən-tər, ˈkärp-m-tər\ *n* : a worker who builds or repairs wooden structures [Medieval French *carpenter, charpenter,* from Latin *carpentarius* "carriage maker," from *carpentum* "carriage," of Celtic origin] — **carpenter** *vb* — **car·pen·try** \-trē\ *n*

carpenter ant *n* : any of several ants that nest and gnaw passageways in dead or decaying wood

car·pet \ˈkär-pət\ *n* **1 a** : a heavy often tufted fabric used as a floor covering **b** : a floor covering made of this fabric **2** : a surface or layer resembling a carpet ⟨a *carpet* of leaves⟩ [Middle French *carpite,* from Italian *carpita,* from *carpire* "to pluck," from Latin *carpere*] — **carpet** *vt*

[1]**car·pet·bag** \-ˌbag\ *n* : a traveling bag made of carpeting common in the 19th century

[2]**carpetbag** *adj* : of, relating to, or characteristic of carpetbaggers

car·pet·bag·ger \-ˌbag-ər\ *n* : a Northerner in the South after the American Civil War usually seeking private gain by taking advantage of unsettled conditions and political corruption [from their carrying their belongings in *carpetbags*] — **car·pet·bag·gery** \-ˌbag-rē, -ə-rē\ *n*

carpet beetle *n* : a small beetle whose larva damages woolen goods

car·pet·ing \ˈkär-pət-ing\ *n* : material for carpets; *also* : a floor covering made of this material

carp·ing \ˈkär-ping\ *adj* : tending to carp — **carp·ing·ly** \ˈkär-ping-lē\ *adv*

car·port \ˈkär-ˌpōrt, -ˌpȯrt\ *n* : an open-sided automobile shelter usually formed by extension of a roof from the side of a building

car·pus \ˈkär-pəs\ *n, pl* **car·pi** \-ˌpī, -ˌpē\ : the wrist or its bones [New Latin, from Greek *karpos* "wrist"]

car·rack \ˈkar-ək\ *n* : a large armed merchant ship chiefly of the 16th and 17th centuries [Medieval French *carrak,* from Spanish *carraca,* from Arabic *qarāqīr,* plural of *qurqūr* "merchant ship"]

car·ra·geen·an *or* **car·ra·geen·in** \ˌkar-ə-ˈgē-nən\ *n* : a substance obtained from various red algae (as Irish moss) that is used in foods especially to stabilize and thicken them [*carrageen* "Irish moss," from *Carragheen,* near Waterford, Ireland]

car·rel \ˈkar-əl\ *n* : a table that is often partitioned or enclosed for individual study in a library [Middle English *caroll,* from Medieval Latin *carola,* perhaps from *carola* "round dance, something circular," from Late Latin *choraula* "choral song"]

car·riage \ˈkar-ij\ *n* **1** : the act of carrying **2** : manner of bearing the body **3 a** : a wheeled vehicle; *esp* : a horse-drawn vehicle for carrying persons **b** *British* : a railway passenger coach **4** : a wheeled support carrying a load ⟨a gun *carriage*⟩ **5** : a movable part of a machine for supporting or carrying some other movable object or part ⟨a typewriter *carriage*⟩

carriage trade *n* : trade especially from well-to-do people

car·ri·er \ˈkar-ē-ər\ *n* **1** : one that carries **2 a** : a person or firm engaged in transporting passengers or goods **b** : a postal employee who delivers or collects mail **c** : one that delivers newspapers **3 a** : a bearer and transmitter of disease germs; *esp* : one who carries the causative agent of a disease but is asymptomatic or immune to it **b** : one having a specified gene and capable of transmitting it to his offspring but not exhibiting its typical expression **4** : a substance (as a catalyst) by means of which energy, a charged particle, or an ion is transferred from one source to another ⟨ATP is an energy *carrier*⟩ **5** : AIRCRAFT CARRIER **6** : an electromagnetic wave or alternating current whose modulations are used as signals (as in radio, telephonic, or telegraphic transmission)

car·ri·on \ˈkar-ē-ən\ *n* : dead and decaying flesh [Medieval French *caroine, charoine,* derived from Latin *caro* "flesh"]

car·rot \ˈkar-ət\ *n* : a biennial herb with a usually orange spindle-shaped edible root; *also* : its root [Middle French *carotte,* from Late Latin *carota,* from Greek *karōton*]

car·roty \-ət-ē\ *adj* : resembling carrots in color

[1]**car·ry** \ˈkar-ē\ *vb* **car·ried; car·ry·ing** **1 a** : to support and take from one place to another : TRANSPORT, CONVEY ⟨*carry* a package⟩ **b** : to act as a bearer **2** : to influence by mental or emotional appeal : SWAY ⟨the speaker *carried* the audience⟩ **3** : to get possession or control of : CAPTURE ⟨*carry* off a prize⟩ **4** : to transfer from one place (as a column) to another ⟨*carry* a number in addition⟩ **5** : to contain and direct the course of : CONDUCT ⟨a pipe *carries* water⟩ **6 a** : to wear or have on one's person ⟨*carries* a gun⟩ **b** : to bear upon or within one ⟨*carries* a scar⟩ ⟨*carry* an unborn child⟩ **c** : to include as a necessary or natural effect ⟨the crime *carries* a penalty⟩ **7** : to conduct oneself in a specified way **8** : to bear the weight of ⟨pillars *carry* an arch⟩ **9** : to sing in correct pitch ⟨*carry* a tune⟩ **10** : to keep in stock for sale ⟨*carries* three brands of tires⟩ **11** : to provide sustenance for ⟨land *carrying* 10 head of cattle⟩ **12** : to maintain on a list or record ⟨*carry* them on the payroll⟩ **13** : to prolong or maintain in space, time, or degree ⟨*carried* the argument too far⟩ **14 a** : to gain victory for; *esp* : to win adoption or the adoption of ⟨*carry* a bill⟩ **b** : to win a majority of votes in ⟨*carry* a state⟩ **15** : to present for the public ⟨the newspaper *carries* weather reports⟩ **16 a** : to bear the charges of holding (as merchandise) **b** : to keep on one's books as a debtor ⟨a merchant *carries* a customer⟩ **17** : to penetrate to a distance ⟨a voice that *carries* well⟩ [Medieval French *carier* "to transport in a vehicle," from *carre* "vehicle," from Latin *carrus*]

[2]**carry** *n, pl* **carries** **1** : the range of a gun or projectile or of a struck or thrown ball **2 a** : the act or method of carrying ⟨a one-handed *carry*⟩ **b** : PORTAGE 2 **3** : a quantity that is transferred in addition from one number place to the one of next higher place value

car·ry·all \ˈkar-ē-ˌȯl\ *n* **1** : a light covered carriage for four or more persons **2** : a passenger automobile similar to a station wagon but with a higher body often on a truck chassis **3** : a capacious bag or case [by folk etymology from French *carriole,* derived from Latin *carrus* "car"]

carry away *vt* : to arouse to a high and often excessive degree of emotion or enthusiasm

carrying capacity *n* : the maximum population (as of deer) that an area will support without undergoing ecological deterioration

carrying charge *n* : a charge added to the price of merchandise sold on the installment plan

carry on *vb* **1** : to behave in a foolish, excited, or improper manner ⟨embarrassed at the way they *carried on*⟩ **2** : to continue in spite of hindrance or discouragement **3** : to oversee and make decisions about : CONDUCT ⟨*carried on* the business⟩

car·ry·out \ˈkar-ē-ˌau̇t\ *n* : food prepared to be eaten away from its place of sale

carry out *vt* **1** : to bring to a successful conclusion ⟨*carried* out his orders⟩ **2** : to put into execution ⟨*carry out* a plan⟩

car seat *n* : a portable seat for an infant or a small child that attaches to an automobile seat and holds the child safely

car·sick \ˈkär-ˌsik\ *adj* : affected with motion sickness especially in an automobile — **car sickness** *n*

[1]**cart** \ˈkärt\ *n* **1** : a heavy usually horse-drawn 2-wheeled vehicle **2** : a light usually 2-wheeled vehicle drawn by a horse, pony, or dog **3** : a small wheeled vehicle ⟨a garden *cart*⟩ [Middle English, probably from Old Norse *kartr*]

[2]**cart** *vt* : to convey in or as if in a cart — **cart·er** *n*

cart·age \ˈkärt-ij\ *n* : the act of or rate charged for carting

carte blanche \ˈkärt-ˈblä^{n}sh, -ˈblänch\ *n, pl* **cartes blanches** *same*\ : full discretionary power [French, literally, "blank document"]

car·tel \kär-ˈtel\ *n* : a combination of independent commercial enterprises designed to limit competition [Middle French, "letter of defiance," from Italian *cartello,* literally, "placard," from *carta* "leaf of paper"]

Word History The literal meaning of Italian *cartello,* a derivative of *carta,* "leaf of paper," is "placard." The word is also used for a letter of defiance or a challenge. In this sense the Italian word was borrowed into Middle French as *cartel,* and the French word was borrowed into English. In English, a *cartel* was originally a letter of defiance. Later the word came to be used for a written agreement between warring nations to regulate such matters as the treatment and exchange of prisoners. Another type of agreement, a combination of commercial enterprises, is now called a *cartel. Cartel* is ultimately derived from Greek *chartēs* "leaf of papyrus" and is thus a relative of *card* and *chart.*

Car·te·sian \kär-ˈtē-zhən\ *adj* : of or relating to René Descartes, his philosophy, or his mathematical methods [New Latin *Cartesius* "Descartes"]

Cartesian coordinate *n* : either of two coordinates that give the location of a point on a plane by showing its distance from the plane's origin as measured along one of the two usually perpendicular axes

\ə\ **abut**	\au̇\ **out**	\i\ **tip**	\ȯ\ **saw**	\u̇\ **foot**
\ər\ **further**	\ch\ **chin**	\ī\ **life**	\ȯi\ **coin**	\y\ **yet**
\a\ **mat**	\e\ **pet**	\j\ **job**	\th\ **thin**	\yü\ **few**
\ā\ **take**	\ē\ **easy**	\ng\ **sing**	\t͟h\ **this**	\yu̇\ **cure**
\ä\ **cot, cart**	\g\ **go**	\ō\ **bone**	\ü\ **food**	\zh\ **vision**

Cartesian coordinate system *n* **:** a coordinate system based on Cartesian coordinates

Cartesian plane *n* **:** a plane whose points are labeled with Cartesian coordinates

Cartesian product *n* **:** a set that is constructed from two given sets and is made up of all pairs of elements such that the first element of the pair is from the first set and the second is from the second set

Car•thu•sian \kär-ˈthü-zhən, -ˈthyü-\ *n* **:** a member of a religious order founded in 1084 and devoted to prayer and meditation [Medieval Latin *Cartusiensis,* from *Cartusia* Chartreuse, motherhouse of the Carthusian order, near Grenoble, France]

car•ti•lage \ˈkärt-l-ij\ *n* **1 :** a translucent elastic tissue that composes most of the skeleton of vertebrate embryos and except for a small number of parts (as the external ear) becomes converted into bone in the higher vertebrates **2 :** a part or structure composed of cartilage [Latin *cartilago*]

car•ti•lag•i•nous \ˌkärt-l-ˈaj-ə-nəs\ *adj* **:** composed of, relating to, or resembling cartilage

cartilaginous fish *n* **:** any of a class (Chondrichthyes) of fishes (as a shark or ray) having the skeleton wholly or mostly composed of cartilage

car•tog•ra•phy \kär-ˈtäg-rə-fē\ *n* **:** the making of maps [French *cartographie,* from *carte* "card, map"] — **car•tog•ra•pher** \-fər\ *n* — **car•to•graph•ic** \ˌkärt-ə-ˈgraf-ik\ *adj*

car•ton \ˈkärt-n\ *n* **:** a paperboard box or container [French, from Italian *cartone* "pasteboard"]

car•toon \kär-ˈtün\ *n* **1 :** a preparatory design, drawing, or painting **2 a :** a satirical drawing commenting on public and usually political matters **b :** COMIC STRIP **3 :** ANIMATED CARTOON [Italian *cartone* "pasteboard, cartoon," from *carta* "leaf of paper," from Latin *charta* "piece of papyrus"] — **cartoon** *vb* — **car•toon•ist** \-ˈtü-nəst\ *n*

car•tridge \ˈkär-trij\ *n* **:** a case or container that holds a substance or device which is difficult, troublesome, or awkward to handle and that is easily interchangeable: as **a :** a tube containing a complete charge for a firearm **b :** a holder for photographic film **c :** a device on a phonograph that changes vibrations of the needle into electrical signals **d :** a case for holding a magnetic tape or disk **e :** a case for integrated circuitry containing a computer program ⟨a video-game *cartridge*⟩ [Middle French *cartouche* "scroll, cartridge," from Italian *cartoccio,* from *carta* "paper," from Latin *charta* "piece of papyrus"]

cart•wheel \ˈkärt-ˌhwēl, -ˌwēl\ *n* **1 :** a large coin (as a silver dollar) **2 :** a handspring performed to one side with arms and legs extended

carve \ˈkärv\ *vb* **1 :** to cut with care or precision especially artistically ⟨*carve* a statue⟩ **2 :** to make or get by cutting — often used with *out* **3 :** to cut into pieces or slices **4 :** to cut up and serve meat [Old English *ceorfan*] — **car•ver** *n*

carv•en \ˈkär-vən\ *adj* **:** made by carving

carv•ing \ˈkär-ving\ *n* **1 :** the act or art of one who carves **2 :** a carved object, design, or figure

cary•at•id \ˌkar-ē-ˈat-əd\ *n, pl* **-at•ids** *or* **-at•i•des** \-ˈat-ə-ˌdēz\ **:** a statue of a woman in flowing robes used as an architectural column [Latin *caryatides,* plural, from Greek *karyatides* "priestesses of Artemis at Caryae in Laconia, caryatids," from *Karyai* "Caryae"]

caryatid

cary•op•sis \ˌkar-ē-ˈäp-səs\ *n, pl* **-op•ses** \-ˈäp-ˌsēz\ *or* **-op•si•des** \-ˈäp-sə-ˌdēz\ **:** a small one-seeded dry indehiscent fruit in which the fruit and seed fuse in a single grain [Greek *karyon* "nut, kernel" + *opsis* "appearance"]

ca•sa•ba \kə-ˈsäb-ə\ *n* **:** any of several winter melons with usually yellow rind and sweet flesh — called also *casaba melon* [*Kasaba* (now Turgutlu), Turkey]

[1]cas•cade \kas-ˈkād\ *n* **1 :** a steep usually small fall of water; *esp* **:** one of a series **2 :** something arranged or occurring in a series or in a succession of stages so that each stage derives from or acts upon the product of the preceding ⟨a *cascade* amplifier⟩ **3 :** something falling or rushing forth in quantity ⟨a *cascade* of sound⟩ [French, from Italian *cascata,* from *cascare* "to fall"]

[2]cascade *vi* **:** to fall in a cascade

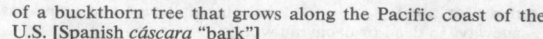

cas•cara \kas-ˈkar-ə\ *n* **:** the dried laxative bark of a buckthorn tree that grows along the Pacific coast of the U.S. [Spanish *cáscara* "bark"]

[1]case \ˈkās\ *n* **1 :** a set of circumstances or conditions ⟨the statement is true in all three *cases*⟩ **2 a :** a situation requiring investigation or action ⟨a *case* for the police⟩ **b :** an object of investigation or consideration **3 a :** a form of a noun, pronoun, or adjective indicating its grammatical relation to other words ⟨the word *child's* in "the child's shirt" is in the possessive *case*⟩ **b :** such a relation whether indicated by inflection or not ⟨the subject of a verb is in the nominative *case*⟩ **4 :** what actually exists or happens **:** FACT ⟨if that's the *case*⟩ **5 a :** a legal suit or action **b** (1) **:** the evidence supporting a conclusion or judgment (2) **:** ARGUMENT; *esp* **:** a convincing argument ⟨made a good *case* for adopting the plan⟩ **6 a :** an instance of disease or injury ⟨a *case* of pneumonia⟩; *also* **:** PATIENT **b :** an instance that calls attention to or exemplifies a situation **:** EXAMPLE ⟨a clear *case* of negligence⟩ [Medieval French *cas,* from Latin *casus* "fall, chance," from *cadere* "to fall"] ***synonyms*** see INSTANCE — **in any case :** without regard to or in spite of other considerations ⟨I'll probably go *in any case*⟩ — **in case 1 :** IF 1 **2 :** as a precaution **3 :** as a precaution against the event that ⟨have extra money *in case* we need it⟩ — **in case of :** in the event of ⟨*in case of* trouble, yell⟩

[2]case *n* **1 a :** a box or receptacle to contain something **b :** a box with its contents **c :** a set of like or related things; *esp* **:** PAIR ⟨a *case* of pistols⟩ **2 :** an outer covering, sheath, or housing ⟨spore *cases*⟩ **3 :** a shallow divided tray for printing type **4 :** the frame of a door or window **:** CASING [Medieval French *casse, chase,* from Latin *capsa* "chest, case," from *capere* "to take"]

[3]case *vt* **:** to enclose in or cover with a case

case hard•en \ˈkās-ˌhärd-n\ *vt* **:** to treat (an iron alloy) so that the outside is harder than the interior — **case–hard•ened** *adj*

case history *n* **:** a record of history, environment, and relevant details (as of individual behavior or condition) especially for use in analysis or illustration

ca•sein \ˈkā-ˌsēn, kā-ˈsēn\ *n* **1 :** a phosphorus-containing protein that is precipitated from milk by heating with an acid or by lactic acid in souring and that is used in making paints and adhesives **2 :** a phosphorus-containing protein that is produced when milk is curdled by rennet, that is one of the chief constituents of cheese, and that is used in making plastics [derived from Latin *caseus* "cheese"]

case in point : a typical or relevant case

case knife *n* **1 :** SHEATH KNIFE **2 :** a table knife

case•mate \ˈkās-ˌmāt\ *n* **:** a fortified position or enclosure from which guns are fired through openings [Middle French, from Italian *casamatta*]

case•ment \ˈkās-mənt\ *n* **:** a window sash opening on hinges like a door; *also* **:** a window with such a sash [Middle English, "hollow molding"]

case•work \ˈkās-ˌwərk\ *n* **:** social work involving direct consideration of the problems, needs, and treatment of the individual case (as of a person or family) — **case•work•er** *n*

[1]cash \ˈkash\ *n* **1 :** ready money **2 :** money or its equivalent (as a check) paid for goods or services at the time of purchase or delivery [Italian *cassa* "money box," from Latin *capsa* "case, chest"]

[2]cash *vt* **:** to pay or obtain cash for ⟨*cash* a check⟩

[3]cash *n, pl* **cash :** any of various coins of small value in China and India; *esp* **:** a Chinese coin with a square hole in the center [Portuguese *caixa,* from Tamil *kācu,* a small copper coin]

cash–and–carry \ˌkash-ən-ˈkar-ē\ *n* **:** the policy of selling for cash and without delivery service

cash•book \ˈkash-ˌbu̇k\ *n* **:** a book in which records are kept of all cash received and paid out

cash•ew \ˈkash-ü, kə-ˈshü\ *n* **:** a tropical American tree related to the sumacs and grown for its edible kidney-shaped nut and for a gum from its bark; *also* **:** its nut [Portuguese *acajú, cajú,* from Tupi *akajú*]

[1]ca•shier \ka-ˈshiər, kə-\ *vt* **:** to discharge in disgrace from a position of responsibility or trust [Dutch *casseren,* from Middle French *casser, quasser* "to discharge, annul," from Latin *quassare* "to shatter"]

[2]cash•ier \ka-ˈshiər\ *n* **1 :** a high officer of a bank responsible for all money received and paid out **2 :** one who receives and records payments ⟨a *cashier* in a supermarket⟩ [Middle French *cassier,* from *casse* "money box," from Italian *cassa*]

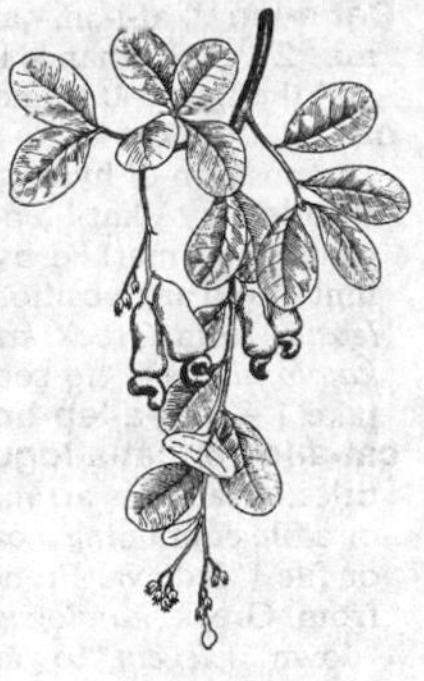

cashew

cashier's check *n* : a check drawn by a bank on its own funds and signed by its cashier

cash•mere \ˈkazh-ˌmiər, ˈkash-\ *n* **1** : fine wool from the undercoat of cashmere goats; *also* : a yarn of this wool **2** : a soft twilled fabric made originally from cashmere wool but now often from sheep's wool [*Cashmere* "Kashmir"]

cashmere goat *n* : an Indian goat whose fine soft undercoat forms cashmere wool

cash register *n* : a business machine that usually has a money drawer, records money received, and shows the amount of each sale

cas•ing \ˈkā-sing\ *n* : something that encases : material for encasing: as **a** : an enclosing frame especially around a door or window opening **b** : TIRE 2b **c** : a membranous case for processed meat (as bologna)

ca•si•no \kə-ˈsē-nō\ *n, pl* **-nos** **1** : a building or room used for social amusements; *esp* : one used for gambling **2** *also* **cas•si•no** : a card game in which players try to match cards in their hands with exposed cards on the table [Italian, from *casa* "house," from Latin, "cottage"]

cask \ˈkask\ *n* : a barrel-shaped container usually for liquids; *also* : the quantity contained in a cask [perhaps from Medieval French *casque* "helmet," from Spanish *casco* "potsherd, skull, helmet"]

cas•ket \ˈkas-kət\ *n* **1** : a small chest or box (as for jewels) **2** : a usually fancy coffin [Middle English, perhaps from Medieval French *cassette* "small chest"]

casque \ˈkask\ *n* : a piece of armor for the head : HELMET [Middle French, from Spanish *casco*]

cas•sa•va \kə-ˈsäv-ə\ *n* : any of several plants of the spurge family grown in the tropics for their fleshy roots which yield a nutritious starch; *also* : the root or its starch — compare TAPIOCA [Spanish *cazabe* "cassava bread," from Taino (American Indian language of the Greater Antilles) *caçábi*]

cas•se•role \ˈkas-ə-ˌrōl\ *n* **1** : a dish in which food can be baked and served **2** : the food cooked and served in a casserole [French, "saucepan," from Middle French *casse* "ladle, dripping pan," perhaps derived from Greek *kyathos* "ladle"]

cas•sette \kə-ˈset\ *n* **1** : a lightproof container for holding film or plates for use in a camera **2** : a small plastic box containing two reels wound with magnetic tape in which the tape on one reel passes to another [French, from Medieval French, "small chest," from *case, chase* "case"]

cas•sia \ˈkash-ə\ *n* **1** : a dried coarse cinnamon bark **2** : any of a genus of herbs, shrubs, and trees of the legume family which grow in warm regions [Latin, from Greek *kassia,* of Semitic origin]

cas•si•mere \ˈkaz-ə-ˌmiər, ˈkas-\ *n* : a smooth twilled usually wool fabric [obsolete *Cassimere* "Kashmir"]

cassino *variant of* CASINO 2

Cas•si•o•pe•ia \ˌkas-ē-ə-ˈpē-ə, -ˈpē-yə\ *n* : a northern constellation between Andromeda and Cepheus [*Cassiopeia,* mythical queen of Ethiopia and mother of Andromeda]

Cassiopeia's Chair *n* : a group of stars in the constellation Cassiopeia

cas•sit•er•ite \kə-ˈsit-ə-ˌrīt\ *n* : a brown or black mineral that consists of tin dioxide and is the chief source of tin [Greek *kassiteros* "tin"]

cas•sock \ˈkas-ək\ *n* : an ankle-length garment worn especially in Roman Catholic and Anglican churches by the clergy and by laypersons assisting at services [Middle French *casaque*]

cas•so•wary \ˈkas-ə-ˌwer-ē\ *n, pl* **-war•ies** : any of several tall swift-running birds of New Guinea and Australia closely related to the emu [Malay *kĕsuari*]

[1]**cast** \ˈkast\ *vb* **cast; cast•ing** **1 a** (1) : THROW 2 ⟨*cast* a stone⟩ (2) : to throw out a lure or line with a fishing rod **b** : DIRECT ⟨*cast* a glance⟩ **c** : to place as if by throwing ⟨*cast* doubt on their integrity⟩ **d** : to deposit (a ballot) formally ⟨*cast* a vote⟩ **e** : to throw off, out, or away ⟨the horse *cast* a shoe⟩: as (1) : to get rid of : DISCARD ⟨*cast* aside all restraint⟩ (2) : SHED, MOLT ⟨a snake *casts* its skin⟩ **2 a** : COMPUTE, FIGURE **b** : to calculate by astrology ⟨*cast* a horoscope⟩ **3 a** : to assign the parts of to actors ⟨*cast* a play⟩ **b** : to assign (an actor) to a part **4 a** : to give shape to (a substance) by pouring in liquid or plastic form into a mold and letting harden without pressure ⟨*cast* steel⟩ **b** : to form by this process ⟨*cast* machine parts⟩ [Old Norse *kasta*] — **cast lots** : to draw lots to determine a matter by chance

cassowary

[2]**cast** *n* **1 a** : an act or instance of casting **b** : something that happens as a result of chance **2 a** : the form in which a thing is constructed **b** : the characters or the actors in a narrative or play **3** : the distance to which a thing can be thrown **4** : a turning of the eye in a particular direction; *also* : EXPRESSION **5** : something thrown or the quantity thrown **6 a** : something formed by casting in a mold or form : CASTING ⟨a bronze *cast* of a statue⟩ **b** : a rigid casing (as of fiberglass or of gauze impregnated with plaster of paris) used for immobilizing a diseased or broken part of the body **7** : a forecast about future events or conditions ⟨to make a long *cast* ahead⟩ **8** : an overspread of a color : SHADE ⟨gray with a greenish *cast*⟩ **9** : physical form or character : APPEARANCE ⟨features of delicate *cast*⟩ **10** : something thrown out or off, shed, or ejected; *esp* : the excrement of an earthworm

cast about *vi* : to look around : SEEK ⟨*cast about* for a seat⟩

cas•ta•net \ˌkas-tə-ˈnet\ *n* : a rhythm instrument that consists of two small ivory, wood, or plastic shells fastened to the thumb and clicked together by the fingers — usually used in plural [Spanish *castañeta,* from *castaña* "chestnut," from Latin *castanea*]

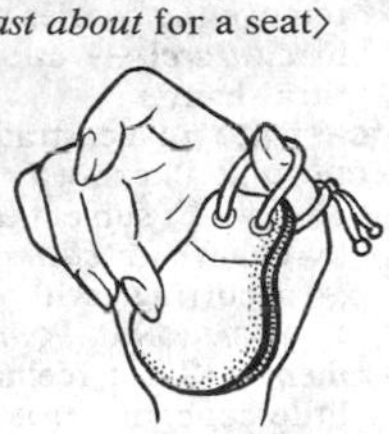

castanet

cast•away \ˈkas-tə-ˌwā\ *adj* **1** : thrown away **2** : cast adrift or ashore as a survivor of a shipwreck — **castaway** *n*

caste \ˈkast\ *n* **1** : one of the hereditary classes formerly dividing Hindu society **2 a** : a division of society based on differences of wealth, inherited rank or privilege, profession, occupation, or race **b** : the position given by caste standing : PRESTIGE **3** : a specialized form that carries out a particular function in the colony of a social insect (as the honeybee) [Portuguese *casta,* literally, "race, lineage," from *casto* "pure, chaste," from Latin *castus*]

cas•tel•lat•ed \ˈkas-tə-ˌlāt-əd\ *adj* : having battlements like a castle [Medieval Latin *castellare* "to fortify," from Latin *castellum* "castle, fortress"]

cast•er \ˈkas-tər\ *n* **1** : one that casts **2** *or* **cas•tor** \ˈkas-tər\ : a small container with a perforated top for sprinkling food seasoning **3** : a small tray for condiment containers **4** : a wheel or set of wheels mounted in a swivel frame used for the support or movement of furniture, trucks, and portable machines

cas•ti•gate \ˈkas-tə-ˌgāt\ *vt* : to punish, reprove, or criticize severely [Latin *castigare* "to correct, chasten, castigate," from *castus* "pure, chaste"] — **cas•ti•ga•tion** \ˌkas-tə-ˈgā-shən\ *n* — **cas•ti•ga•tor** \ˈkas-tə-ˌgāt-ər\ *n*

cas•tile soap \ˌkas-ˈtēl-\ *n, often cap C* : a hard bland soap made from olive oil and sodium hydroxide [*Castile,* region of Spain]

Cas•til•ian \ka-ˈstil-yən\ *n* **1 a** : a native or inhabitant of Castile **b** : SPANIARD **2 a** : the dialect of Castile **b** : the official and literary language of Spain based on this dialect — **Castilian** *adj*

casting *n* **1** : the act of one that casts **2** : something cast in a mold ⟨a bronze *casting*⟩ **3** : something (as skin or excrement) that is cast out or off

casting vote *n* : a deciding vote cast by a presiding officer in case of a tied vote

cast iron *n* : a hard brittle alloy of iron, carbon, and silicon that is cast in a mold

[1]**cas·tle** \ˈkas-əl\ *n* **1 a :** a large fortified building or set of buildings **b :** a massive or imposing house **2 :** [3]ROOK [Medieval French *castel, chastel,* from Latin *castellum* "fortress," from *castrum* "fortified place"]

[2]**castle** *vb* **cas·tled; cas·tling** \ˈkas-ling, -ə-ling\ **1 :** to establish in a castle **2 :** to move a chess king two squares toward a rook and the rook to the square next past the king on a single move

castle in the air : an impracticable project **:** DAYDREAM — called also *castle in Spain*

cast–off \ˈkas-ˌtȯf\ *adj* **:** thrown away or aside — **castoff** *n*

cast off \kas-ˈtȯf\ *vi* **:** to unfasten or untie a boat or a line securing a boat

cas·tor \ˈkas-tər\ *n* **1 :** a bitter strong-smelling orange-brown substance obtained from the beaver and used by perfumers **2 :** a beaver hat [Latin, "beaver," from Greek *kastōr*]

Cas·tor \ˈkas-tər\ *n* **:** the more northern of the two bright stars in Gemini

castor bean *n* **:** the very poisonous seed of the castor-oil plant; *also* **:** CASTOR-OIL PLANT

castor oil *n* **:** a thick yellowish oil extracted from castor beans and used as a lubricant, in soap, and as a laxative [probably from its former use as a substitute for castor in medicine]

castor–oil plant *n* **:** a tropical Old World herb widely grown as an ornamental or for its oil-rich castor beans

castor-oil plant

[1]**cas·trate** \ˈkas-ˌtrāt\ *vt* **a :** to remove the testes of **:** GELD **b :** to remove the ovaries of **:** SPAY [Latin *castrare*] — **cas·tra·tion** \ka-ˈstrā-shən\ *n*

[2]**castrate** *n* **:** a castrated individual

ca·su·al \ˈkazh-wəl, -ə-wəl; ˈkazh-əl\ *adj* **1 :** subject to or occurring by chance ⟨a *casual* meeting⟩ **2 :** occurring without regularity **:** OCCASIONAL ⟨*casual* employment⟩ **3 a :** feeling or showing little concern **:** NONCHALANT ⟨a *casual* approach to cooking⟩ **b :** INFORMAL ⟨*casual* dining⟩ ⟨*casual* clothes⟩ **4 :** done without seriousness or intent for commitment ⟨*casual* sex⟩ [Late Latin *casualis,* from Latin *casus* "fall, chance," from *cadere* "to fall"] ***synonyms*** see ACCIDENTAL, RANDOM — **ca·su·al·ly** \-ē\ *adv* — **ca·su·al·ness** *n*

ca·su·al·ty \ˈkazh-əl-tē; ˈkazh-wəl-, -ə-wəl-\ *n, pl* **-ties 1 :** serious or fatal accident **:** DISASTER **2 a :** a military person lost (as by death or capture) during warfare **b :** a person or thing injured, lost, or destroyed

ca·su·ist·ry \ˈkazh-wə-strē, -ə-wə-\ *n, pl* **-ries 1 :** the study or resolution of questions of right and wrong in conduct **2 :** false reasoning or application of principles especially with regard to morals or law [probably from Spanish *casuista* "casuist," from Latin *casus* "fall, chance," from *cadere* "to fall"] — **ca·su·ist** \ˈkazh-wəst, -ə-wəst\ *n* — **ca·su·is·tic** \ˌkazh-ə-ˈwis-tik\ *adj*

cat \ˈkat\ *n* **1 a :** a small flesh-eating mammal long domesticated and kept by humans as a pet or for catching rats and mice **b :** an animal (as a lion, tiger, leopard, jaguar, cougar, wildcat, lynx, or cheetah) of the same family as the domestic cat **2 :** CAT-O'-NINE-TAILS **3 :** CATFISH [Old English *catt*]

ca·tab·o·lism \kə-ˈtab-ə-ˌliz-əm\ *n* **:** the part of metabolism involving the breakdown of complex materials and the release of energy — compare ANABOLISM [Greek *katabolē* "throwing down," from *kataballein* "to throw down," from *kata* "down" + *ballein* "to throw"] — **cat·a·bol·ic** \ˌkat-ə-ˈbäl-ik\ *adj*

cat·a·clysm \ˈkat-ə-ˌkliz-əm\ *n* **1 :** a great flood **:** DELUGE **2 :** a violent and destructive natural event (as an earthquake) **3 :** a violent social or political upheaval [Greek *kataklysmos,* from *kataklyzein* "to inundate," from *kata* "down" + *klyzein* "to wash"] ***synonyms*** see DISASTER — **cat·a·clys·mal** \ˌkat-ə-ˈkliz-məl\ *adj* — **cat·a·clys·mic** \-ˈkliz-mik\ *adj*

cat·a·comb \ˈkat-ə-ˌkōm\ *n* **:** an underground burying place; *esp* **:** one that has passages with hollowed places in the sides for tombs — usually used in plural [Late Latin *catacumbae* "catacombs"]

ca·tad·ro·mous \kə-ˈtad-rə-məs\ *adj* **:** living in fresh water and going to the sea to spawn ⟨*catadromous* eels⟩ — compare ANADROMOUS [Greek *kata* "down" + *dramein* "to run"]

cat·a·falque \ˈkat-ə-ˌfalk, -ˌfȯlk, -ˌfȯk\ *n* **:** a structure sometimes used in funerals to support the coffin [Italian *catafalco*]

Cat·a·lan \ˈkat-l-ən, -ˌan\ *n* **1 :** a native or inhabitant of Catalonia **2 :** the Romance language of Catalonia, Valencia, Andorra, and the Balearic Islands — **Catalan** *adj*

cat·a·lase \ˈkat-l-ˌās, -ˌāz\ *n* **:** an enzyme that catalyzes the decomposition of hydrogen peroxide into water and oxygen

cat·a·lep·sy \ˈkat-l-ˌep-sē\ *n, pl* **-sies :** a condition resembling a trance and marked by loss of voluntary motion in which the limbs hold any position they are placed in [Medieval Latin *catalepsia,* from Greek *katalēpsis,* literally, "act of seizing," from *katalambanein* "to seize," from *kata* "down" + *lambanein* "to take"] — **cat·a·lep·tic** \ˌkat-l-ˈep-tik\ *adj or n*

[1]**cat·a·log** *or* **cat·a·logue** \ˈkat-l-ˌȯg, -ˌäg\ *n* **1 :** a list of names, titles, or articles arranged according to a system **2 a :** a book or a file containing a catalog **b :** the items listed in such a book or file [Medieval French *catalogue,* from Late Latin *catalogus,* from Greek *katalogos,* from *katalegein* "to list," from *kata* "down" + *legein* "to gather, speak"]

[2]**catalog** *or* **catalogue** *vt* **-loged** *or* **-logued; -log·ing** *or* **logu·ing 1 :** to make a catalog of **2 :** to enter in a catalog; *esp* **:** to classify (books or information) descriptively — **cat·a·log·er** *or* **cat·a·logu·er** *n*

ca·tal·pa \kə-ˈtal-pə, -ˈtȯl-\ *n* **:** any of several trees of North America and Asia with showy flowers and long narrow pods [Creek *katȧlpa,* from *iká* "head" + *tałpa* "wing"]

ca·tal·y·sis \kə-ˈtal-ə-səs\ *n* **:** the change and especially increase in the rate of a chemical reaction brought about by a catalyst [Greek *katalysis* "dissolution," from *katalyein* "to dissolve," from *kata* "down" + *lyein* "to loosen, dissolve"] — **cat·a·lyt·ic** \ˌkat-l-ˈit-ik\ *adj* — **cat·a·lyt·i·cal·ly** \-ˈit-i-kə-lē, -klē\ *adv*

cat·a·lyst \ˈkat-l-əst\ *n* **1 :** a substance (an an enzyme) that speeds up a chemical reaction or enables it to proceed under different conditions (as at a lower temperature) than otherwise possible **2 :** an agent that provokes or speeds significant change or action ⟨a *catalyst* for economic growth⟩

catalytic converter *n* **:** a pollution-control device attached to the exhaust system of an automotive vehicle that contains a chemical catalyst which converts pollutants (as carbon monoxide and unburned hydrocarbons) to other products (as carbon dioxide and water)

cat·a·lyze \ˈkat-l-ˌīz\ *vt* **:** to bring about or produce by chemical catalysis — **cat·a·lyz·er** *n*

cat·a·ma·ran \ˌkat-ə-mə-ˈran, ˈkat-ə-mə-ˌran\ *n* **:** a vessel (as a sailboat) with twin hulls and usually a deck [Tamil *kaṭṭumaram,* from *kaṭṭu* "to tie" + *maram* "tree"]

cat·a·mount \ˈkat-ə-ˌmau̇nt\ *n* **:** any of various wild cats: as **a :** COUGAR **b :** LYNX [Middle English *cat of the mountaine*]

[1]**cat·a·pult** \ˈkat-ə-ˌpəlt, -ˌpu̇lt\ *n* **1 :** an ancient military device for hurling missiles **2 :** a device for launching an airplane at flying speed (as from the deck of an aircraft carrier) [Latin *catapulta,* from Greek *katapaltēs,* from *kata* "down" + *pallein* "to hurl"]

[2]**catapult** *vb* **1 :** to throw or launch by or as if by a catapult **2 :** to become catapulted ⟨he *catapulted* to fame⟩

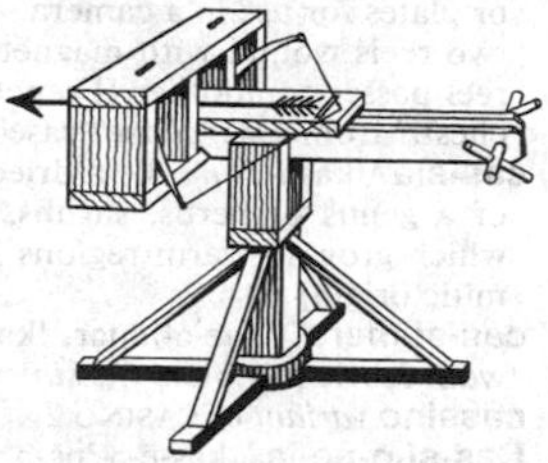

catapult 1

cat·a·ract \ˈkat-ə-ˌrakt\ *n* **1 :** a clouding of the lens of the eye or of its capsule obstructing the passage of light **2 a :** WATERFALL; *esp* **:** a large one over a precipice **b :** steep rapids in a river **c :** FLOOD 3 ⟨a *cataract* of words⟩ [Latin *cataracta* "waterfall, portcullis," from Greek *kataraktēs,* from *katarassein* "to dash down," from *kata* "down" + *arassein* "to strike, dash"]

ca·tarrh \kə-ˈtär\ *n* **:** inflammation of a mucous membrane; *esp* **:** one chronically affecting the human nose and air passages [Late Latin *catarrhus,* from Greek *katarrhous,* from *katarrhein* "to flow down," from *kata* "down" + *rhein* "to flow"] — **ca·tarrh·al** \-ˈtär-əl\ *adj*

ca·tas·tro·phe \kə-ˈtas-trə-fē\ *n* **1 :** the final event of the dramatic action especially of a tragedy **2 :** a momentous tragic event **:** DISASTER **3 :** a violent and sudden change in a feature of the earth **4 :** utter failure or ruin **:** FIASCO [Greek *katastrophē,* from *katastrephein* "to overturn," from *kata* "down" + *strephein* "to turn, twist"] ***synonyms*** see DISASTER — **cat·a·stroph·ic** \ˌkat-ə-ˈsträf-ik\ *adj* — **cat·a·stroph·i·cal·ly** \-ˈsträf-i-kə-lē, -klē\ *adv*

catastrophe theory *n* **:** a branch of mathematics that uses topology to explain events (as an earthquake or a stock market crash) characterized by major abrupt changes

ca·tas·tro·phism \ka-ˈtas-trə-ˌfiz-əm\ *n* **:** a geological doctrine that changes in the earth's crust have in the past been brought about suddenly by physical forces operating in ways that cannot be observed today — compare UNIFORMITARIANISM — **ca·tas·tro·phist** \-fəst\ *n*

cat·bird \ˈkat-ˌbərd\ *n* **:** a dark gray American songbird with black cap and reddish coverts under the tail

cat·boat \-ˌbōt\ *n* **:** a sailboat with a single mast set far forward and a single large sail extended by a long boom

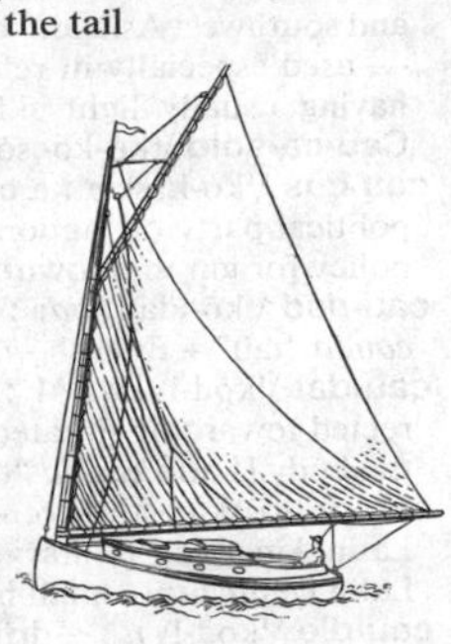

catboat

cat·call \-ˌkȯl\ *n* **:** a loud or raucous cry made to express disapproval (as at a sports event) — **catcall** *vb*

[1]**catch** \ˈkach, ˈkech\ *vb* **caught** \ˈkȯt\; **catch·ing** **1 a :** to capture or seize in flight or motion ⟨*catch* a thief⟩ ⟨*catch* a ball⟩ **b :** TRAP 1a ⟨*caught* in a lie⟩ **c :** DECEIVE 1, MISLEAD **2 a :** to discover unexpectedly **:** FIND ⟨was *caught* in the act⟩ **b :** to check suddenly ⟨*catch* oneself before giving away a secret⟩ **3 a :** to take in and retain ⟨a barrel to *catch* rainwater⟩ **b :** to take in with the mind or senses ⟨*catch* an explanation⟩ ⟨barely *caught* the whisper⟩ **4 a :** to get entangled ⟨*catch* a sleeve on a nail⟩ **b :** to engage firmly ⟨this lock will not *catch*⟩ **c :** to fasten in position **5 :** to become affected by ⟨*catch* a cold⟩ **6 :** to take or get momentarily or quickly ⟨*catch* a glimpse of a friend⟩ **7 a :** to come abreast of **:** OVERTAKE ⟨*catch* the leader in a race⟩ **b :** to get aboard in time ⟨*catch* a bus⟩ **8 :** to play baseball as a catcher [Medieval French *cacher, chacher, chacer* "to hunt," derived from Latin *captare* "to chase," from *capere* "to take"] — **catch·able** \ˈkach-ə-bəl, ˈkech-\ *adj* — **catch fire** **1 :** to begin to burn **2 :** to become excited or exciting — **catch it :** to incur blame, reprimand, or punishment — **catch one's breath :** to pause or rest briefly

synonyms CATCH, CAPTURE, SNARE, TRAP mean to come to possess or control by or as if by seizing. CATCH implies the seizing of something in motion or in flight or in hiding ⟨*catch* that dog⟩. CAPTURE adds an implication of overcoming resistance or difficulty ⟨*captured* the fort after many days⟩. SNARE and TRAP imply using a device that catches by surprise and holds at the mercy of the captor ⟨*trap* animals⟩ ⟨*snared* the butterfly with a net⟩.

[2]**catch** *n* **1 :** something caught; *esp* **:** the total quantity (as of fish) caught at one time **2 a :** the act of catching **b :** a game in which a ball is thrown and caught **3 :** something that checks or holds immovable ⟨a *catch* on a safety pin⟩ **4 :** one worth catching or acquiring **5 :** a round for three or more voices **6 :** FRAGMENT 1 ⟨heard *catches* of a melody⟩ **7 :** a concealed difficulty ⟨there must be a *catch*⟩

catch·all \ˈkach-ˌȯl, ˈkech-\ *n* **:** something to hold odds and ends

catch·er \ˈkach-ər, ˈkech-\ *n* **:** one that catches; *esp* **:** a baseball player positioned behind home plate

catching *adj* **1 :** INFECTIOUS, CONTAGIOUS **2 :** CATCHY 1

catch·ment \ˈkach-mənt, ˈkech-\ *n* **1 :** the action of catching water **2 :** something that catches water

catch on *vi* **1 :** to understand the nature of something ⟨*caught on* to the plot⟩ **2 :** to become popular ⟨a tune that really *caught on*⟩

catch·phrase \ˈkach-ˌfrāz, ˈkech-\ *n* **:** a word or expression that is repeated until it becomes associated with a person, group, idea, or point of view

catchup *variant of* KETCHUP

catch·word \ˈkach-ˌwərd, ˈkech-\ *n* **1 :** GUIDE WORD **2 :** CATCHPHRASE

catchy \ˈkach-ē, ˈkech-ē\ *adj* **catch·i·er; -est** **1 :** likely to attract ⟨a *catchy* tune⟩ **2 :** easily remembered ⟨*catchy* lyrics⟩ **3 :** apt to entangle one **:** TRICKY ⟨a *catchy* question⟩

cat·e·chism \ˈkat-ə-ˌkiz-əm\ *n* **1 :** a summary of religious doctrine often in the form of questions and answers **2 :** a set of formal questions put as a test — **cat·e·chis·mal** \-ˈkiz-məl\ *adj* — **cat·e·chis·tic** \-ˈkis-tik\ *adj*

cat·e·chist \ˈkat-ə-ˌkist, -i-kəst\ *n* **:** one that catechizes

cat·e·chize \ˈkat-ə-ˌkīz\ *vt* **1 :** to instruct systematically especially by questions, answers, and explanations and corrections; *esp* **:** to give religious instruction in this manner **2 :** to question systematically or closely [Late Latin *catechizare,* from Greek *katēchein* "to teach," literally, "to din into," from *kata* "down" + *ēchein* "to resound," from *ēchē* "sound"]

cat·e·chu·men \ˌkat-ə-ˈkyü-mən\ *n* **1 :** a convert to Christianity receiving training in doctrine and discipline before baptism **2 :** one receiving instruction in the basic doctrines of Christianity before being admitted as a member of a church [Greek *katēchoumenos,* from *katēchein* "to teach, catechize"]

cat·e·gor·i·cal \ˌkat-ə-ˈgȯr-i-kəl, -ˈgär-\ *also* **cat·e·gor·ic** \-ik\ *adj* **1 :** involving neither qualification nor reservation **:** ABSOLUTE ⟨a *categorical* denial⟩ **2 :** of, relating to, or being a category [Late Latin *categoricus,* from Greek *katēgorikos,* from *katēgoria* "affirmation, category"] — **cat·e·gor·i·cal·ly** \-i-kə-lē, -klē\ *adv*

cat·e·go·rize \ˈkat-i-gə-ˌrīz\ *vt* **:** to put into a category **:** CLASSIFY — **cat·e·go·ri·za·tion** \ˌkat-i-gə-rə-ˈzā-shən\ *n*

cat·e·go·ry \ˈkat-ə-ˌgōr-ē, -ˌgȯr-\ *n, pl* **-ries** **1 :** a division in a system of classification ⟨courses in the liberal arts *category*⟩ **2 :** a unit of a larger whole made up of members sharing one or more characteristics **:** CLASS ⟨a new *category* of computers⟩ [Late Latin *categoria,* from Greek *katēgoria* "predication, category," from *katēgorein* "to accuse, affirm, predicate," from *kata* "down" + *agora* "public assembly"]

cat·e·nate \ˈkat-ə-ˌnāt\ *vt* **:** to connect in a series **:** LINK [Latin *catenare,* from *catena* "chain"] — **cat·e·na·tion** \ˌkat-ə-ˈnā-shən\ *n*

ca·ter \ˈkāt-ər\ *vi* **1 :** to provide a supply of food ⟨*catered* the party⟩ **2 :** to supply what is required or desired ⟨*catered* to their whims⟩ [obsolete *cater* "buyer of provisions," from Medieval French *acatour,* from *acater, achater* "to buy"]

catercorner *or* **cater–cornered** *variant of* KITTY-CORNER

ca·ter·er \ˈkāt-ər-ər\ *n* **:** one that caters; *esp* **:** one that provides food and service for a social affair

cat·er·pil·lar \ˈkat-ə-ˌpil-ər, ˈkat-ər-ˌ\ *n* **:** the wormlike larva of a butterfly or moth; *also* **:** any of various similar insect larvae (as of a sawfly) [Medieval French dialect *catepelose,* literally, "hairy cat"]

Caterpillar *trademark* — used for a tractor that travels on two endless metal belts for use on rough or soft ground

cat·er·waul \ˈkat-ər-ˌwȯl\ *vi* **:** to make a harsh cry [Middle English *caterwawen*] — **caterwaul** *n*

cat·fish \ˈkat-ˌfish\ *n* **:** any of numerous usually freshwater stout-bodied large-headed fishes with long sensory barbels

cat·gut \-ˌgət\ *n* **:** a tough cord made usually from sheep intestines and used for strings of musical instruments and rackets and for sewing in surgery

ca·thar·sis \kə-ˈthär-səs\ *n, pl* **-thar·ses** \-ˈthär-ˌsēz\ **1 :** the act or result of purging (as of the bowels) **2 :** a purgation or purification that brings about spiritual renewal or release from tension ⟨the *catharsis* of tears⟩ **3 :** release from an emotional problem through expression of its unconscious basis [Greek *katharsis,* from *kathairein* "to purge," from *katharos* "pure"]

[1]**ca·thar·tic** \-ˈthärt-ik\ *adj* **:** of, relating to, or producing catharsis ⟨*cathartic* drugs⟩ ⟨a *cathartic* discussion⟩ — **ca·thar·tic·al·ly** \-i-kə-lē, -i-klē\ *adv*

[2]**cathartic** *n* **:** PURGATIVE, LAXATIVE

ca·the·dra \kə-ˈthē-drə\ *n* **:** a bishop's official throne [Latin, "chair," from Greek *kathedra,* from *kata* "down" + *hedra* "seat"]

[1]**ca·the·dral** \kə-ˈthē-drəl\ *adj* **1 :** of, relating to, or containing a bishop's throne **2 :** something that resembles or suggests a cathedral (as in size or importance) ⟨a *cathedral* of business⟩ ⟨the basketball *cathedral*⟩

[2]**cathedral** *n* **:** a church that contains a bishop's throne and is the principal church of a diocese

ca·thep·sin \kə-ˈthep-sən\ *n* **:** a protease that functions inside the body cells [Greek *kathepsein* "to digest," from *kata* "down" + *hepsein* "to boil"]

cath·e·ter \ˈkath-ət-ər\ *n* **:** a slender tubular medical device for insertion into a bodily passage or cavity usually to permit injec-

\ə\ **abut**	\aủ\ **out**	\i\ **tip**	\ȯ\ **saw**	\ủ\ **foot**
\ər\ **further**	\ch\ **chin**	\ī\ **life**	\ȯi\ **coin**	\y\ **yet**
\a\ **mat**	\e\ **pet**	\j\ **job**	\th\ **thin**	\yü\ **few**
\ā\ **take**	\ē\ **easy**	\ng\ **sing**	\t͟h\ **this**	\yủ\ **cure**
\ä\ **cot, cart**	\g\ **go**	\ō\ **bone**	\ü\ **food**	\zh\ **vision**

tion or withdrawal of fluids or to keep a passage open [Late Latin, from Greek *kathetēr,* from *kathienai* "to send down," from *kata* "down" + *hienai* "to send"]

cath•ode \ˈkath-ˌōd\ *n* **1 :** the negative electrode of an electrolytic cell to which the positive ions are attracted — compare ANODE **2 :** the positive terminal of a primary cell or of a storage battery that is delivering current **3 :** the electron-emitting electrode of an electron tube [Greek *kathodos* "way down," from *kata* "down" + *hodos* "way"] — **ca•thod•ic** \ka-ˈthäd-ik\ *adj*

cathode ray *n* **1 :** one of the high-speed electrons projected in a stream from the heated cathode of a vacuum tube under the propulsion of a strong electric field **2 :** a stream of cathode-ray electrons

cathode–ray tube *n* **:** a vacuum tube in which cathode rays usually in the form of a slender beam are projected upon a fluorescent screen and produce a luminous spot

cath•o•lic \ˈkath-lik, -ə-lik\ *adj* **1 a** *often cap* **:** of, relating to, or forming the church universal **b** *cap* **:** ROMAN CATHOLIC **2 :** COMPREHENSIVE 1, UNIVERSAL; *esp* **:** broad in sympathies, tastes, or interests ⟨a *catholic* taste in music⟩ [Late Latin *catholicus,* from Greek *katholikos* "universal, general," from *katholou* "in general," from *kata* "by" + *holos* "whole"] — **ca•thol•i•cal•ly** \kə-ˈthäl-i-kə-lē, -klē\ *adv* — **Ca•thol•i•cism** \kə-ˈthäl-ə-ˌsiz-əm\ *n* — **ca•thol•i•cize** \kə-ˈthäl-ə-ˌsīz\ *vb*

Catholic *n* **1 :** a person who belongs to the universal Christian church **2 :** a member of a Catholic church; *esp* **:** ROMAN CATHOLIC

cath•o•lic•i•ty \ˌkath-ə-ˈlis-ət-ē\ *n* **1** *cap* **:** the character of being in conformity with a Catholic church **2 a :** liberality of sentiments or views **b :** comprehensive range

cat•ion \ˈkat-ˌī-ən\ *n* **:** the ion in an electrolyzed solution that migrates to the cathode; *also* **:** a positively charged ion [Greek *kation,* from *katienai* "to go down," from *kata* "down" + *ienai* "to go"]

cat•kin \ˈkat-kən\ *n* **:** a flower cluster (as of a birch) in which unisexual flowers lacking petals are arranged along a slender stalk [from its resemblance to a cat's tail]

cat•like \ˈkat-ˌlīk\ *adj or adv* **:** resembling a cat; *esp* **:** STEALTHY

cat•nap \-ˌnap\ *n* **:** a very short light nap — **catnap** *vi*

cat•nip \-ˌnip\ *n* **:** a strong-scented herb of the mint family that contains a substance attractive to cats [*cat* + obsolete *nep* "catnip," from Old English *nepte,* from Latin *nepeta*]

cat–o'–nine–tails \ˌkat-ə-ˈnīn-ˌtālz\ *n, pl* **cat–o'–nine–tails :** a whip made of nine knotted cords fastened to a handle

CAT scan \ˈkat-\ *n* **:** an image made by computed tomography [*c*omputerized *a*xial *t*omography]

cat's cradle *n* **:** a game in which a string looped on the fingers in such a way as to resemble a small cradle is transferred to the hands of another person

cat's–eye \ˈkats-ˌī\ *n* **1 :** any of various gems (as a chrysoberyl or a chalcedony) exhibiting opalescent reflections from within **2 :** a glass playing marble with a colored area that resembles the eye of a cat

cat's–paw \ˈkats-ˌpȯ\ *n* **1 :** a light breeze that ruffles the surface of the water in patches **2 :** a person used by another person for his or her own ends

cat•suit \ˈkat-ˌsüt\ *n* **:** a close-fitting one-piece garment that covers the torso and the legs and sometimes the arms

catsup *variant of* KETCHUP

cat•tail \ˈkat-ˌtāl\ *n* **:** a tall reedy marsh plant with brown furry spikes of very tiny flowers

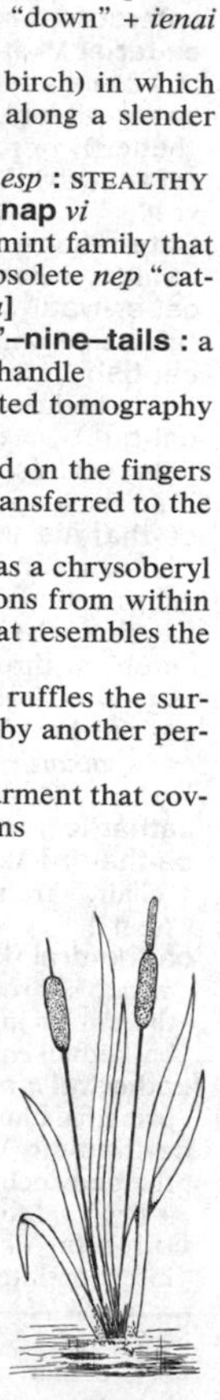

cattail

cat•tle \ˈkat-l\ *n, pl* **cattle 1 :** domesticated four-footed mammals held as property or raised for use; *esp* **:** bovine animals (as cows) kept on a farm or ranch **2 :** people held to be or treated as if of little importance or worth [Medieval French *katil, chatel* "personal property," from Medieval Latin *capitale,* from Latin *capitalis* "of the head, capital"]

cattle egret *n* **:** a small white egret that is native to the Old World but is now found in parts of the eastern U.S.

cattle guard *n* **:** a device that consists of a shallow ditch across which ties or rails are laid far enough apart to prevent livestock from crossing and that is often used instead of a gate at a fence opening

cat•tle•man \-mən, -ˌman\ *n* **:** a person who tends or raises cattle

cat•ty \ˈkat-ē\ *adj* **cat•ti•er; -est :** resembling or held to resemble a cat; *esp* **:** slyly spiteful ⟨a *catty* remark⟩ — **cat•ti•ly** \ˈkat-l-ē\ *adv* — **cat•ti•ness** \ˈkat-ē-nəs\ *n*

catty–corner *or* **catty–cornered** *variant of* KITTY-CORNER

cat•walk \ˈkat-ˌwȯk\ *n* **:** a narrow walk or way (as along a bridge)

Cau•ca•sian \kȯ-ˈkā-zhən, -ˈkazh-ən\ *adj* **1 :** of or relating to the Caucasus or its inhabitants **2 :** of, constituting, or characteristic of a race of humankind native to Europe, North Africa, and southwest Asia and classified according to physical features — used especially in referring to persons of European descent having usually light skin pigmentation — **Caucasian** *n* — **Cau•ca•soid** \ˈkȯ-kə-ˌsȯid\ *adj or n*

cau•cus \ˈkȯ-kəs\ *n* **:** a closed meeting of members of the same political party or faction usually to select candidates or decide policy [origin unknown] — **caucus** *vi*

cau•dad \ˈkȯ-ˌdad\ *adv* **:** toward the tail or posterior end [Latin *cauda* "tail" + English *-ad*]

cau•dal \ˈkȯd-l\ *adj* **1 :** of, relating to, or being a tail **2 :** directed toward or situated in or near the tail or posterior part of the body [Latin *cauda* "tail"] — **cau•dal•ly** \-l-ē\ *adv*

cau•di•llo \kau̇-ˈthē-yō, -ˈthēl-yō\ *n, pl* **-di•llos :** a Spanish or Latin-American military dictator [Spanish, "leader," from Late Latin *capitellum* "small head," from Latin *caput* "head"]

cau•dle \ˈkȯd-l\ *n* **:** a drink usually of warm ale or wine mixed with bread or gruel, eggs, sugar, and spices [Medieval French *caudel, chaudel,* from *caut* "warm," from Latin *calidus*]

caught *past of* CATCH

caul \ˈkȯl\ *n* **1 :** the large fatty omentum covering the intestines (as of a cow or sheep) **2 :** the amnion especially when covering the head at birth [Middle English *calle* "net, omentum," probably from Old English *cawl* "basket"]

caul•dron *also* **cal•dron** \ˈkȯl-drən\ *n* **1 :** a large kettle or boiler **2 :** something resembling a boiling cauldron in intensity or degree of agitation ⟨a *cauldron* of intense emotion⟩ [Medieval French *cauderon,* derived from Latin *caldarius* "used for hot water," from *calidus* "warm"]

cau•li•flow•er \ˈkȯ-li-ˌflau̇-ər, -ˌflau̇r\ *n* **:** a garden plant closely related to the cabbage and grown for its compact edible head of usually white undeveloped flowers; *also* **:** the flower cluster used as a vegetable [Italian *cavolfiore,* from *cavolo* "cabbage" (from Latin *caulis* "stem, cabbage") + *fiore* "flower," from Latin *flor-, flos*]

cauliflower ear *n* **:** an ear deformed from injury and excessive growth of scar tissue

[1]**caulk** *or* **calk** \ˈkȯk\ *vt* **1 :** to waterproof the seams of by filling with a watertight substance **2 :** to make tight against leakage [Medieval French *cauker, calcher* "to trample," from Latin *calcare,* from *calx* "heel"] — **caulk•er** *n*

[2]**caulk** *or* **calk** *also* **caulk•ing** *or* **calk•ing** \ˈkȯ-king\ *n* **:** material used to caulk

[3]**caulk** *variant of* [2]CALK

caus•al \ˈkȯ-zəl\ *adj* **1 :** expressing or indicating cause **2 :** of, relating to, or being a cause ⟨the *causal* agent of the disease⟩ **3 :** involving causation or a cause ⟨a *causal* connection between the economy and unemployment⟩ **4 :** forming from a cause ⟨*causal* development⟩ — **caus•al•ly** \-zə-lē\ *adv*

cau•sal•i•ty \kȯ-ˈzal-ət-ē\ *n, pl* **-ties 1 :** a causal quality or agency **2 :** the relation between a cause and its effect or between regularly related events or facts

cau•sa•tion \kȯ-ˈzā-shən\ *n* **1 a :** the act or process of causing **b :** the act or agency by which an effect is produced **2 :** CAUSALITY

caus•ative \ˈkȯ-zət-iv\ *adj* **1 :** functioning as a cause or agent **2 :** expressing causation — **caus•ative•ly** *adv*

[1]**cause** \ˈkȯz\ *n* **1 :** something or someone that brings about a result **:** one that is the source of an action or state **2 :** a good reason ⟨a *cause* for anxiety⟩ **3 a :** a ground of legal action **b :** CASE 5a **c :** a matter or question to be decided (as by a court) **4 :** a principle or movement strongly defended or supported [Medieval French, from Latin *causa*] — **cause•less** \-ləs\ *adj*

synonyms CAUSE, REASON, OCCASION mean something that produces an effect. CAUSE applies to any event, circumstance, or condition that brings about or helps bring about a result ⟨an icy road was the *cause* of the accident⟩. REASON applies to a traceable or explainable cause of a known effect or action ⟨the storm was the *reason* for the delay⟩. OCCASION applies to a particular time or situation at which underlying causes become effective ⟨the assassination was the *occasion* of the war⟩.

2cause *vt* **1 :** to serve as cause of ⟨fire *caused* the damage⟩ **2 :** to bring about by command, authority, or force ⟨*caused* him to resign⟩ — **caus·er** *n*

cause cé·lè·bre \ˌkōz-sā-ˈlebr, ˌkȯz-\ *n, pl* **causes cé·lè·bres** *same*\ **:** something (as a scandalous affair or a controversial legal case) that attracts great interest [French, literally, "celebrated case"]

cau·se·rie \ˌkōz-ˈrē, -ə-rē\ *n* **1 :** light informal talk **2 :** a short informal composition [French, from *causer* "to chat," from Latin *causari* "to plead, discuss," from *causa* "cause"]

cause·way \ˈkȯz-ˌwā\ *n* **:** a raised way especially across wet ground or water [Middle English *cauciwey,* from *cauci* "causeway" (from Medieval French *causee, chaucee,* from Medieval Latin *calciata* "paved highway," probably from Latin *calx* "limestone") + *wey* "way"]

caus·tic \ˈkȯ-stik\ *adj* **1 :** capable of eating away by chemical action **:** CORROSIVE **2 :** CUTTING 3, INCISIVE ⟨*caustic* wit⟩ [Latin *causticus,* from Greek *kaustikos,* from *kaiein* "to burn"] — **caustic** *n* — **caus·ti·cal·ly** \-sti-kə-lē, -klē\ *adv*

caustic potash *n* **:** POTASSIUM HYDROXIDE

caustic soda *n* **:** SODIUM HYDROXIDE

cau·ter·ize \ˈkȯt-ə-ˌrīz\ *vb* **:** to burn with a hot iron or a caustic substance usually to destroy infected tissue ⟨*cauterize* a wound⟩ [derived from Greek *kaiein* "to burn"] — **cau·ter·iza·tion** \ˌkȯt-ə-rə-ˈzā-shən\ *n*

1cau·tion \ˈkȯ-shən\ *n* **1 :** ADMONITION, WARNING **2 :** careful avoidance of unnecessary risk **3 :** one that astonishes or catches one's attention ⟨that hairstyle is a *caution*⟩ [Latin *cautio* "precaution," from *cavēre* "to be on one's guard"]

2caution *vt* **cau·tioned; cau·tion·ing** \ˈkȯ-shə-ning, ˈkȯsh-ning\ **:** to advise caution to ***synonyms*** see WARN

cau·tion·ary \ˈkȯ-shə-ˌner-ē\ *adj* **:** serving as or offering a warning ⟨a *cautionary* tale⟩

cau·tious \ˈkȯ-shəs\ *adj* **:** marked by or given to caution ⟨a *cautious* driver⟩ — **cau·tious·ly** *adv* — **cau·tious·ness** *n*

cav·al·cade \ˌkav-əl-ˈkād, ˈkav-əl-ˌ\ *n* **1 a :** a procession of riders or carriages **b :** a procession of vehicles or ships **2 :** a sequence of dramatic scenes **:** PAGEANT ⟨a *cavalcade* of American history⟩ [Middle French, "horseback ride," from Italian *cavalcata,* from *cavalcare* "to go on horseback," derived from Latin *caballus* "horse"]

1cav·a·lier \ˌkav-ə-ˈliər\ *n* **1 :** a gentleman trained in arms and horsemanship **2 :** a mounted soldier **:** KNIGHT **3** *cap* **:** an adherent of Charles I of England **4 :** LADIES' MAN [Middle French, from Italian *cavaliere,* derived from Latin *caballus* "horse"]

2cavalier *adj* **1 :** DEBONAIR **2 :** treating important matters or the interests of other people with contemptuous disregard **3 a** *cap* **:** of or relating to the party of Charles I of England in his struggles with the Puritans and Parliament **b :** ARISTOCRATIC — **cav·a·lier·ly** *adv* — **cav·a·lier·ness** *n*

cav·al·ry \ˈkav-əl-rē\ *n, pl* **-ries :** a highly mobile army component mounted on horseback or moving in motor vehicles [Italian *cavalleria* "cavalry, chivalry," from *cavaliere* "cavalier"] — **cav·al·ry·man** \-rē-mən, -ˌman\ *n*

1cave \ˈkāv\ *n* **:** a natural underground chamber or series of chambers open to the surface [Medieval French, from Latin *cava,* from *cavus* "hollow"]

2cave *vb* **1 :** to fall or cause to fall in or down especially from being undermined **:** COLLAPSE ⟨the wall *caved* in⟩ **2 :** to cease to resist **:** SUBMIT ⟨the defenders *caved* in and surrendered⟩

ca·ve·at \ˈkā-vē-ˌat, ˈkav-ē-; ˈkäv-ē-ˌät\ *n* **:** WARNING 2 [Latin, "let him or her beware," from *cavēre* "to be on one's guard"]

caveat emp·tor \-ˈem-tər, -ˈemp-, -ˌtȯr\ *n* **:** a warning that without a warranty the buyer of goods takes the risk of their quality [New Latin, "let the buyer beware"]

cave dweller *n* **:** one (as a prehistoric human) that lives in a cave

cave–in \ˈkā-ˌvin\ *n* **1 :** the action of caving in **2 :** a place where earth has caved in

cave·man \ˈkāv-ˌman\ *n* **1 :** a cave dweller especially of the Stone Age **2 :** a man who acts with rough or violent directness especially toward women

cav·ern \ˈkav-ərn\ *n* **:** a cave often of large size [Medieval French *caverne,* from Latin *caverna,* from *cavus* "hollow"]

cav·ern·ous \-ər-nəs\ *adj* **1 :** having caverns or cavities **2 :** constituting or suggesting a cavern **3 :** composed largely of vascular spaces and capable of filling with blood to bring about the enlargement of a body part — **cav·ern·ous·ly** *adv*

cav·i·ar *also* **cav·i·are** \ˈkav-ē-ˌär *also* ˈkäv-\ *n* **:** processed salted roe of a large fish (as the sturgeon) prepared as an appetizer [obsolete Italian *caviaro,* from Turkish *havyar*]

cav·il \ˈkav-əl\ *vb* **cav·iled** *or* **cav·illed; cav·il·ing** *or* **cav·il·ling** \ˈkav-ling, -ə-ling\ **:** to raise trivial and frivolous objections **:** QUIBBLE [Latin *cavillari* "to jest, cavil," from *cavilla* "raillery"] — **cavil** *n* — **cav·il·er** *or* **cav·il·ler** \-lər, -ə-lər\ *n*

cav·ing \ˈkā-ving\ *n* **:** the sport of exploring caves **:** SPELUNKING

cav·i·ta·tion \ˌkav-ə-ˈtā-shən\ *n* **:** the formation of partial vacuums in a liquid by a swiftly moving body (as a propeller) or by high-frequency sound waves [*cavity* + *-ation*]

cav·i·ty \ˈkav-ət-ē\ *n, pl* **-ties :** an unfilled space within a mass **:** a hollow place **:** HOLE ⟨a *cavity* in a tooth⟩ [Middle French *cavité,* derived from Latin *cavus* "hollow"]

ca·vort \kə-ˈvȯrt\ *vi* **:** to leap or dance about in a lively manner [perhaps alteration of *curvet*]

ca·vy \ˈkā-vē\ *n, pl* **cavies :** any of several short-tailed rough-haired South American rodents; *esp* **:** GUINEA PIG [New Latin *Cavia,* from obsolete Portuguese *çavia* (now *sauiá*), a South American rat, from Tupi *saujá*]

caw \ˈkȯ\ *vi* **:** to utter the characteristic harsh raucous cry of a crow or a similar sound [imitative] — **caw** *n*

cay \ˈkē, ˈkā\ *n* **:** a small low island or emergent reef of sand or coral **:** ISLET, KEY [Spanish *cayo*]

cay·enne \kī-ˈen, kā-\ *n* **1 :** a pungent condiment consisting of the ground dried fruits or seeds of hot peppers **2 :** a hot pepper and especially one with long pungent red fruits; *also* **:** the fruit [by folk etymology from earlier *cayan,* derived from Tupi *kiʔĩnʸá*]

cayenne pepper *n* **:** CAYENNE

cayman *variant of* CAIMAN

Ca·yu·ga \kē-ˈü-gə, kā-ˈyü-, kī-\ *n, pl* **Cayuga** *or* **Cayugas :** a member of an American Indian people of New York

Cay·use \ˈkī-ˌüs, -ˌyüs; kī-ˈ\ *n, pl* **Cayuse** *or* **Cayuses 1 :** a member of an American Indian people of Oregon and Washington **2** *pl cayuses, not cap, Western* **:** a native range horse

CB \ˌsē-ˈbē\ *n* **:** CITIZENS BAND; *also* **:** the radio transmitting and receiving set used for citizens-band communications

CBer \ˌsē-ˈbē-ər, -ˈbir\ *n* **:** one that operates a CB radio

cc \ˌsē-ˈsē\ *vt* **cc'd; cc'·ing :** to send someone a copy of (an e-mail, letter, or memo) ⟨*cc* an e-mail to a coworker⟩ [carbon copy]

CCD \ˌsē-sē-ˈdē\ *n* **:** CHARGE-COUPLED DEVICE

C–clamp \ˈsē-ˌklamp\ *n* **:** a clamp shaped like the letter C

C clef *n* **:** a movable clef indicating middle C by its placement on one of the lines of the staff

CD \ˌsē-ˈdē\ *n* **:** a small plastic disk on which information (as music or computer data) is recorded and read by using a laser

CD–ROM \ˌsē-ˌdē-ˈräm\ *n* **:** a CD containing computer data that cannot be altered [compact *d*isc *r*ead-*o*nly *m*emory]

1cease \ˈsēs\ *vb* **:** to come or bring to an end ⟨ordered the soldiers to *cease* firing⟩ [Medieval French *cesser,* from Latin *cessare* "to delay," from *cedere* "to withdraw, cede"] ***synonyms*** see STOP

2cease *n* **:** CESSATION — usually used with *without*

cease–fire \ˈsēs-ˈfīr\ *n* **1 :** a military order to cease firing **2 :** a suspension of active hostilities

cease·less \ˈsē-sləs\ *adj* **:** continuing without end — **cease·less·ly** *adv* — **cease·less·ness** *n*

ce·cro·pia moth \si-ˈkrō-pē-ə-\ *n* **:** a red and dark brown silkworm moth that is the largest moth of North America [Latin *Cecropius* "Athenian," from Greek *Kekropios,* from *Kekrops* "Cecrops," legendary first king of Athens]

ce·cum *also* **cae·cum** \ˈsē-kəm\ *n, pl* **ce·ca** *also* **cae·ca** \-kə\ **:** a cavity open at one end; *esp* **:** the blind pouch in which the large intestine begins and into which the ileum opens from one side [Latin *intestinum caecum,* literally, "blind intestine"] — **ce·cal** *also* **cae·cal** \-kəl\ *adj*

ce·dar \ˈsēd-ər\ *n* **1 a :** any of a genus of usually tall trees related to the pines and noted for their fragrant durable wood **b :** any of numerous coniferous trees (as some junipers or arborvitaes) resembling the true cedars especially in the fragrance and durability of their wood **2 :** the wood of a cedar [Medieval French *cedre,* from Latin *cedrus,* from Greek *kedros*]

ce·dar·bird \ˈsēd-ər-ˌbərd\ *n* **:** CEDAR WAXWING

cedar waxwing *n* **:** a brown waxwing of temperate North America with a yellow band on the tip of the tail

cede \ˈsēd\ *vt* **1 :** to give up or grant usually by treaty **2 :** ASSIGN 1 ⟨*ceded* the farm to their children⟩ [Latin *cedere* "to go, withdraw, yield"] — **ced·er** *n*

ce·dil·la \si-ˈdil-ə\ *n* **:** a mark placed under the letter *c* (as ç) to show that the *c* is to be pronounced like *s* [Spanish, "the obsolete letter *ç* (actually a medieval form of the letter *z*), cedilla," from *ceda, zeda* "the letter z," from Late Latin *zeta* "zeta," from Greek *zēta*]

cei·ba \ˈsā-bə\ *n* **:** a massive tropical tree related to the silk-cotton tree that bears large pods containing a silky floss which yields the fiber kapok [Spanish, probably from Taino (American Indian language of the Greater Antilles) *ceíba*]

ceil·ing \ˈsē-ling\ *n* **1 :** the overhead inside lining of a room **2 :** something that overhangs like a shelter ⟨a *ceiling* of stars⟩ **3 a :** the greatest height at which an airplane can maintain level flight **b :** the height above the ground of the base of the lowest layer of clouds when over half of the sky is obscured **4 :** an upper usually prescribed limit ⟨a *ceiling* on prices⟩ [Middle English *celen* "to furnish with a ceiling," from Medieval Latin *celare, caelare,* probably from Latin *caelare* "to carve," from *caelum* "chisel"]

cel *also* **cell** \ˈsel\ *n* **:** a transparent sheet of celluloid on which objects are drawn or painted in the making of animated cartoons [from *celluloid*]

cel·an·dine \ˈsel-ən-ˌdīn, -ˌdēn\ *n* **1 :** a yellow-flowered biennial herb related to the poppies **2 :** a perennial tuber-forming buttercup — called also *lesser celandine* [Medieval French *celidoine,* from Latin *chelidonia,* derived from Greek *chelidōn* "swallow"]

cel·e·brant \ˈsel-ə-brənt\ *n* **:** one who celebrates; *esp* **:** the priest who is celebrating a mass

cel·e·brate \ˈsel-ə-ˌbrāt\ *vb* **1 :** to perform publicly and according to rule or form **:** officiate at ⟨*celebrate* a mass⟩ **2 a :** to honor (as a holiday or event) especially with festivities ⟨*celebrate* one's birthday with a party⟩ **b :** to observe a holiday or notable occasion, perform a religious ceremony, or take part in a festival **3 :** to praise or make known publicly ⟨her poetry *celebrates* the glory of nature⟩ [Latin *celebrare* "to frequent, celebrate," from *celeber* "much frequented, famous"] ***synonyms*** see KEEP — **cel·e·bra·tion** \ˌsel-ə-ˈbrā-shən\ *n* — **cel·e·bra·tor** \ˈsel-ə-ˌbrāt-ər\ *n*

cel·e·brat·ed *adj* **:** widely known and often referred to **:** RENOWNED ***synonyms*** see FAMOUS — **cel·e·brat·ed·ness** *n*

ce·leb·ri·ty \sə-ˈleb-rət-ē\ *n, pl* **-ties 1 :** the state of being celebrated **:** FAME ⟨her short-lived *celebrity*⟩ **2 :** a famous or celebrated person ⟨television *celebrities*⟩

ce·le·ri·ac \sə-ˈler-ē-ˌak, -ˈlir-\ *n* **:** a celery grown for its thickened edible root [from *celery*]

ce·ler·i·ty \sə-ˈler-ət-ē\ *n, pl* **-ties :** rapidity of motion or action [Medieval French *celerité,* from Latin *celeritas,* from *celer* "swift"]

synonyms CELERITY, ALACRITY mean quickness of movement or action. CELERITY stresses speed in moving especially so as to accomplish work ⟨got ready with remarkable *celerity*⟩. ALACRITY stresses promptness in responding and often suggests readiness or eagerness ⟨they went with surprising *alacrity*⟩.

cel·ery \ˈsel-rē, -ə-rē\ *n* **:** a European herb related to the carrot and widely grown for its thick edible leafstalks; *also* **:** leafstalks of celery used for food [obsolete French *celeris,* from Italian dialect *seleri,* plural of *selero,* from Late Latin *selinon,* from Greek]

ce·les·ta \sə-ˈles-tə\ *n* **:** a keyboard instrument with hammers that strike steel plates producing a tone similar to that of a glockenspiel [French *célesta,* from *céleste,* literally, "heavenly," from Latin *caelestis*]

ce·les·tial \sə-ˈles-chəl\ *adj* **1 :** of, relating to, or suggesting the spiritual heaven **:** HEAVENLY ⟨*celestial* beings⟩ **2 :** of or relating to the sky or heavens ⟨a star is a *celestial* body⟩ [Medieval French, from Latin *caelestis,* from *caelum* "sky, heaven"] — **ce·les·tial·ly** \-chə-lē\ *adv*

celestial equator *n* **:** the great circle on the celestial sphere midway between the celestial poles

celestial navigation *n* **:** navigation by observation of the positions of celestial bodies

celestial pole *n* **:** one of the two points on the celestial sphere around which the diurnal rotation of the stars appears to take place

celestial sphere *n* **:** an imaginary sphere of infinite radius against which the celestial bodies appear to be projected

ce·li·ac *also* **coe·li·ac** \ˈsē-lē-ˌak\ *adj* **:** of or relating to the abdominal cavity [Latin *coeliacus,* from Greek *koiliakos,* from *koilia* "cavity," from *koilos* "hollow"]

celiac disease *n* **:** a chronic digestive disorder marked by an intolerance to gluten-containing foods (as wheat bread)

cel·i·ba·cy \ˈsel-ə-bə-sē\ *n* **1 :** the state of not being married **2 a :** abstention from sexual intercourse **b :** abstention by vow from marriage

cel·i·bate \ˈsel-ə-bət\ *n* **:** one who practices celibacy [Latin *caelibatus,* from *caelebs* "unmarried"] — **celibate** *adj*

cell \ˈsel\ *n* **1 a :** a one-room dwelling occupied by a solitary person (as a hermit) **b :** a single room (as in a convent or prison) usually for one person **2 :** a small compartment, cavity, or bounded space ⟨the *cells* in a honeycomb often contain honey⟩ **3 :** a tiny mass of protoplasm that includes a nucleus and is enclosed by a semipermeable membrane and that performs all the basic functions of life and is the basic structural element of plants and animals **4 a :** a receptacle (as a jar) containing electrodes and an electrolyte either for generating electricity by chemical action or for use in electrolysis **b :** a single unit in a device for converting radiant energy into electrical energy or for varying the intensity of an electric current in accordance with radiation **5 :** the basic and usually smallest unit of an organization or movement ⟨terrorist *cells*⟩ **6 :** CELL PHONE [derived from Latin *cella* "small room"] — **celled** \ˈseld\ *adj*

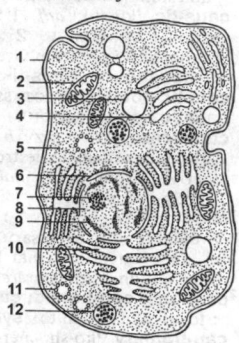

cell 3: *1* cell membrane, *2* mitochondrion, *3* vacuole, *4* Golgi apparatus, *5* cytoplasm, *6* nuclear membrane, *7* nucleolus, *8* nucleus, *9* chromatin, *10* endoplasmic reticulum, *11* centriole, *12* lysosome

cel·lar \ˈsel-ər\ *n* **1 :** BASEMENT 1 **2 :** a stock of wines [Medieval French *celer,* from Latin *cellarium* "storeroom," from *cella* "small room"]

cel·lar·age \ˈsel-ə-rij\ *n* **1 :** a cellar especially for storage **2 :** charge for storage in a cellar

cell body *n* **:** the nucleus-containing central part of a neuron exclusive of its axons and dendrites

cell cycle *n* **:** the complete series of events from one cell division to the next

cell division *n* **:** the process by which cells multiply involving both nuclear and cytoplasmic divisions — compare MEIOSIS, MITOSIS

cel·list \ˈchel-əst\ *n* **:** one that plays the cello

cell membrane *n* **:** a semipermeable outside layer surrounding the contents of a cell and consisting of a phospholipid double layer embedded with proteins — called also *plasma membrane*

cel·lo \ˈchel-ō\ *n, pl* **cellos :** the member of the violin family tuned an octave below the viola [short for *violoncello*]

cel·lo·phane \ˈsel-ə-ˌfān\ *n* **:** a thin transparent usually waterproof material made from cellulose and used especially as a wrapping [French, from *cellulose* + *-phane* (as in *diaphane* "diaphanous")]

cell phone *n* **:** a portable cordless telephone used in a cellular system

cell plate *n* **:** the rudiment of a new cell wall that forms between dividing plant cells

cell sap *n* **:** the liquid consisting of a watery solution of nutrients and wastes that fills the vacuole of most plant cells

cell theory *n* **:** a generally accepted theory in biology that the cell is the fundamental structural and functional unit of living matter and that all cells come from preexisting cells

cel·lu·lar \ˈsel-yə-lər\ *adj* **1 :** of, relating to, or consisting of cells **2 :** containing cavities **:** having a porous texture **3 :** of, relating to, or being a radiotelephone system in which a geographical area (as a city) is divided into small sections each served by a transmitter of limited range ⟨*cellular* phones⟩ — **cel·lu·lar·i·ty** \ˌsel-yə-ˈlar-ət-ē\ *n*

cel·lu·lase \ˈsel-yə-ˌlās, -ˌlāz\ *n* : an enzyme that hydrolyzes cellulose

cel·lu·lite \ˈsel-yə-ˌlīt\ *n* : deposits of lumpy fat within connective tissue (as of the thighs and hips) [French, literally, "accumulation of subcutaneous fat, subcutaneous inflammation"]

cel·lu·loid \ˈsel-yə-ˌlȯid, -ə-\ *n* **1** : a tough flammable thermoplastic composed essentially of nitrocellulose and camphor **2** : a motion-picture film

cel·lu·lose \ˈsel-yə-ˌlōs\ *n* : a complex carbohydrate that constitutes the chief part of the cell walls of plants, is commonly obtained from vegetable matter (as wood or cotton) as a white fibrous substance, and is used in making various products (as rayon and paper) [French, from *cellule* "living cell," from New Latin *cellula,* from Latin *cella* "small room"]

cellulose acetate *n* : any of several compounds formed especially by the action of acetic acid, anhydride of acetic acid, and sulfuric acid on cellulose and used for making textile fibers, packaging sheets, photographic films, and varnishes

cellulose nitrate *n* : NITROCELLULOSE

cel·lu·los·ic \ˌsel-yə-ˈlō-sik, -zik\ *adj* : of, relating to, or made from cellulose ⟨*cellulosic* fibers⟩ — **cellulosic** *n*

cell wall *n* : the firm nonliving permeable wall that encloses and supports the cells of most plants, bacteria, fungi, and algae

Cel·sius \ˈsel-sē-əs, ˈsel-shəs\ *adj* : relating to, conforming to, or having the international thermometer scale on which the interval between the triple point and the boiling point of water is divided into 99.99 degrees with 0.01° representing the triple point and 100.00° the boiling point; *also* : CENTIGRADE ⟨10° *Celsius*⟩ — abbreviation *C* [Anders *Celsius,* died 1744, Swedish astronomer]

Celt \ˈkelt, ˈselt\ *n* **1** : a member of a division of the early Indo-European peoples distributed from the British Isles and Spain to Asia Minor **2** : a modern Gael, Highland Scot, Irishman, Welshman, Cornishman, or Breton [French *Celte,* from Latin *Celtae* "Celts"]

[1]**Celt·ic** \ˈkel-tik, ˈsel-\ *adj* : of, relating to, or characteristic of the Celts or their languages

[2]**Celtic** *n* : a branch of the Indo-European language family containing Irish, Scottish Gaelic, Manx, Welsh, Breton, and Cornish

Celt·i·cist \ˈkel-tə-səst, ˈsel-\ *n* : a person who specializes in Celtic languages or culture

cem·ba·lo \ˈchem-bə-ˌlō\ *n, pl* **-li** \-ˌlē\ *or* **-los** : HARPSICHORD [Italian]

[1]**ce·ment** \si-ˈment\ *n* **1 a** : CONCRETE **b** : a powder of alumina, silica, lime, iron oxide, and magnesia burned together in a kiln and finely pulverized and used as an ingredient of mortar and concrete **2** : a binding element or agency: as **a** : a substance to make objects adhere to each other **b** : a notion or feeling serving to unite firmly **3** : CEMENTUM [Medieval French *ciment,* from Latin *caementum* "stone chips used in making mortar," from *caedere* "to cut"]

[2]**cement** *vb* **1** : to unite by or as if by cement ⟨*cemented* their friendship⟩ **2** : to overlay with concrete — **ce·ment·er** *n*

ce·men·ta·tion \ˌsē-ˌmen-ˈtā-shən\ *n* : the act or process of cementing

ce·ment·ite \si-ˈment-ˌīt\ *n* : a hard brittle carbide of iron Fe_3C in steel, cast iron, and iron-carbon alloys

ce·men·tum \si-ˈment-əm\ *n* : a specialized external bony layer of the part of a tooth normally within the gum

cem·e·tery \ˈsem-ə-ˌter-ē\ *n, pl* **-ter·ies** : a burial ground [Medieval French *cimiterie,* from Late Latin *coemeterium,* from Greek *koimētērion* "sleeping chamber, burial place," from *koiman* "to put to sleep"]

-cene \ˌsēn\ *adj combining form* : recent — in names of geologic periods ⟨Eocene⟩ [Greek *kainos* "new, recent"]

cen·o·bite \ˈsen-ə-ˌbīt\ *also* **coe·no·bite** \ˈsē-nə-\ *n* : a member of a religious group living together [Late Latin *coenobita,* from *coenobium* "monastery," from Late Greek *koinobion,* derived from Greek *koinos* "common" + *bios* "life"] — **cen·o·bit·ic** \ˌsen-ə-ˈbit-ik\ *or* **cen·o·bit·i·cal** \-ˈbit-i-kəl\ *adj*

cen·o·taph \ˈsen-ə-ˌtaf\ *n* : a tomb or a monument erected in honor of a person whose body is elsewhere [French *cénotaphe,* from Latin *cenotaphium,* from Greek *kenotaphion,* from *kenos* "empty" + *taphos* "tomb"]

Ce·no·zo·ic \ˌsē-nə-ˈzō-ik, ˌsen-ə-\ *n* **1** : the most recent of the four eras of geological history that extends to the present time and is marked by a rapid evolution of mammals and birds and of flowering plants and especially grasses — called also *Age of Mammals*; see GEOLOGIC TIME table **2** : the system of rocks corresponding to the Cenozoic [Greek *kainos* "new, recent" + English *-zoic*] — **Cenozoic** *adj*

cen·ser \ˈsen-sər\ *n* : a vessel for burning incense; *esp* : a covered incense burner swung on chains in a religious ritual [Middle English *censen* "to burn incense"]

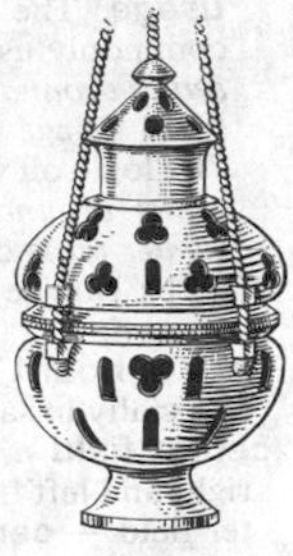
censer

[1]**cen·sor** \ˈsen-sər\ *n* **1** : an official who examines publications or communications for objectionable matter **2** : one of two magistrates of ancient Rome acting as census takers, assessors, and inspectors of morals and conduct [Latin, from *censēre* "to give as one's opinion, assess"] — **cen·so·ri·al** \sen-ˈsōr-ē-əl, -ˈsȯr-\ *adj*

[2]**censor** *vt* **cen·sored; cen·sor·ing** \ˈsens-ring, -ə-ring\ : to examine in order to suppress or delete anything thought to be harmful or dangerous; *also* : to suppress or delete as objectionable

cen·so·ri·ous \sen-ˈsōr-ē-əs, -ˈsȯr-\ *adj* : marked by or given to censure : sternly critical ⟨a *censorious* critic⟩ — **cen·so·ri·ous·ly** *adv* — **cen·so·ri·ous·ness** *n*

cen·sor·ship \ˈsen-sər-ˌship\ *n* : the institution, system, or practice of censoring or of censors

[1]**cen·sure** \ˈsen-chər\ *n* **1** : the act of blaming or condemning sternly **2** : an official reprimand [Latin *censura,* from *censēre* "to give as one's opinion, assess"]

[2]**censure** *vt* **cen·sured; cen·sur·ing** \ˈsench-ring, -ə-ring\ : to find fault with : criticize as blameworthy ***synonyms*** see BLAME — **cen·sur·able** \ˈsench-rə-bəl, -ə-rə-\ *adj* — **cen·sur·er** \ˈsen-chər-ər\ *n*

cen·sus \ˈsen-səs\ *n* **1** : a periodic governmental counting of population and usually gathering of related statistics **2** : COUNT 1, TALLY [Latin, from *censēre* "to give as one's opinion, assess"]

cent \ˈsent\ *n* **1** : a unit of value equal to 1/100 part of a basic monetary unit (as of a dollar or euro) **2** : a coin, token, or note representing one cent [French, "hundred," from Latin *centum*]

cen·taur \ˈsen-ˌtȯr\ *n* : one of a race in Greek mythology who are half human and half horse [Latin *Centaurus,* from Greek *Kentauros*]

cen·ta·vo \sen-ˈtäv-ō\ *n, pl* **-vos** **1** : a unit of value equal to 1/100 part of any of several basic monetary units (as the peso or real) **2** : a coin representing one centavo [Spanish, literally, "hundredth," derived from Latin *centum* "hundred"]

cen·te·nar·i·an \ˌsent-n-ˈer-ē-ən\ *n* : a person who is 100 years old or older — **centenarian** *adj*

cen·ten·a·ry \sen-ˈten-ə-rē, ˈsent-n-ˌer-ē\ *n, pl* **-ries** : CENTENNIAL [Latin *centenarius* "of a hundred," from *centeni* "a hundred each," from *centum* "hundred"] — **centenary** *adj*

cen·ten·ni·al \sen-ˈten-ē-əl\ *n* : a 100th anniversary or its celebration [Latin *centum* "hundred" + English *-ennial* (as in *biennial*)] — **centennial** *adj* — **cen·ten·ni·al·ly** \-ē-ə-lē\ *adv*

[1]**cen·ter** \ˈsent-ər\ *n* **1** : the point inside a circle or sphere that is an equal distance from all the points on the circumference or surface **2 a** : a point, area, person, or thing that is most important in relation to an indicated activity, interest, or condition ⟨the *center* of the controversy⟩ **b** : a group of neurons having a common function ⟨respiratory *center*⟩ **c** : a region of concentrated population ⟨an urban *center*⟩ **d** : a facility providing a place for a particular activity or service ⟨a community *center*⟩ **3 a** : a middle part (as of an army or stage) **b** *often cap* (1) : individuals holding moderate political views especially between those of conservatives and liberals (2) : the views of such individuals **4** : a player occupying a middle position on a team [Middle French *centre,* from Latin *centrum,* from Greek *kentron* "sharp point, center of a circle," from *kentein* "to prick"]

[2]**center** *vb* **cen·tered; cen·ter·ing** \ˈsent-ə-ring, ˈsen-tring\ **1** : to place or fix at or around a center or central area or position

\ə\ **a**but	\au̇\ **ou**t	\i\ t**i**p	\ȯ\ s**aw**	\u̇\ f**oo**t
\ər\ f**ur**ther	\ch\ **ch**in	\ī\ l**i**fe	\ȯi\ c**oi**n	\y\ **y**et
\a\ m**a**t	\e\ p**e**t	\j\ **j**ob	\th\ **th**in	\yü\ f**ew**
\ā\ t**a**ke	\ē\ **ea**sy	\ng\ si**ng**	\t͟h\ **th**is	\yu̇\ c**ure**
\ä\ c**o**t, c**a**rt	\g\ **g**o	\ō\ b**o**ne	\ü\ f**oo**d	\zh\ vi**si**on

2 : to give a central focus or basis : CONCENTRATE ⟨*centers* her hopes on her son⟩ 3 : to adjust (as lenses) so that the axes coincide 4 : to have a center 5 a : to pass (a ball or puck) from either side to or toward the middle of a playing area b : to snap (the ball) in football

usage The verb *center,* in the meaning "to have a center," is commonly used with *in, on, at,* and *around*. The combination *center around* is a standard idiom ⟨the story *centered around* a small village in Maine⟩, but has been objected to as illogical. The logic on which the objections are based is irrelevant, since *center around* is an idiom and idioms have their own logic. *Center on* is currently more common, and *revolve* and similar verbs can be used with *around* if you want to avoid *center around.*

cen·ter·board \ˈsent-ər-ˌbōrd, -ˌbȯrd\ *n* : a retractable keel used especially in sailboats

center field *n* 1 : the part of the baseball outfield between right and left field 2 : the position of the player defending center field — **center fielder** *n*

cen·ter·line \ˈsent-ər-ˈlīn\ *n* : a real or imaginary line that runs down the middle of something ⟨the *centerline* of the highway⟩

center of gravity 1 : CENTER OF MASS 2 : the point at which the entire weight of a body may be considered as concentrated so that if supported at this point the body would remain in equilibrium in any position

center of mass : the point in a body or system of bodies at which the whole mass may be considered as concentrated

cen·ter·piece \ˈsent-ər-ˌpēs\ *n* 1 : an object occupying a central position; *esp* : an adornment in the center of a table 2 : one that is of central importance or interest in a larger whole

cen·tes·i·mal \sen-ˈtes-ə-məl\ *adj* : marked by or relating to division into hundredths [Latin *centesimus* "hundredth," from *centum* "hundred"]

[1]**cen·tes·i·mo** \chen-ˈtez-ə-ˌmō\ *n, pl* **-mi** \-ˌmē\ : a former monetary unit equal to 1/100 Italian lira [Italian]

[2]**cen·tes·i·mo** \sen-ˈtes-ə-ˌmō\ *n, pl* **-mos** : a monetary unit equal to 1/100 Uruguayan peso

centi- *combining form* 1 : hundred ⟨*centi*grade⟩ 2 : one hundredth part of ⟨*centi*meter⟩ [French, from Latin *centum* "hundred"]

cen·ti·grade \ˈsent-ə-ˌgrād, ˈsänt-\ *adj* : relating to, conforming to, or having a thermometer scale on which the interval between the freezing point and the boiling point of water is divided into 100 degrees with 0° representing the freezing point and 100° the boiling point ⟨10° *centigrade*⟩ — abbreviation *C*; compare CELSIUS [French, from Latin *centum* "hundred" + *gradus* "step, degree"]

cen·ti·gram \-ˌgram\ *n* — see METRIC SYSTEM table

cen·ti·li·ter \-ˌlēt-ər\ *n* — see METRIC SYSTEM table

cen·time \ˈsän-ˌtēm, ˈsen-\ *n* 1 : a unit of value equal to 1/100 part of a basic monetary unit (as a franc) 2 : a coin representing one centime [French, from *cent* "hundred," from Latin *centum*]

cen·ti·me·ter \ˈsent-ə-ˌmēt-ər, ˈsänt-\ *n* — see METRIC SYSTEM table

centimeter–gram–second *adj* : of, relating to, or being a system of units based upon the centimeter as the unit of length, the gram as the unit of mass, and the second as the unit of time — abbreviation *cgs*

cen·ti·mo \ˈsent-ə-ˌmō\ *n, pl* **-mos** 1 : a unit of value equal to 1/100 part of a basic monetary unit (as of a bolivar or sol) 2 : a coin representing one centimo [Spanish *céntimo*]

cen·ti·pede \ˈsent-ə-ˌpēd\ *n* : any of a class (Chilopoda) of long flattened many-segmented arthropods with each segment bearing one pair of legs of which the foremost pair is modified into poison fangs — compare MILLIPEDE [Latin *centipeda,* from *centum* "hundred" + *ped-, pes* "foot"]

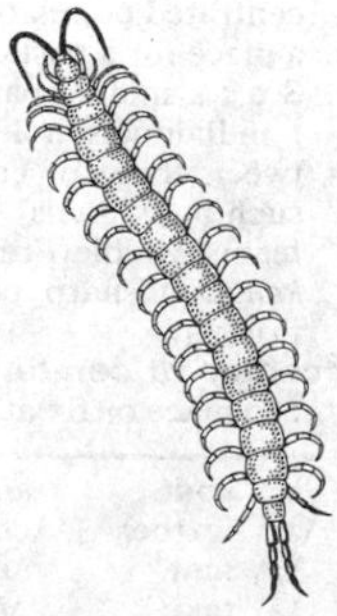

centipede

centr- *or* **centri-** *or* **centro-** *combining form* : center ⟨*centri*fugal⟩ ⟨*centr*oid⟩ [Greek *kentron*]

[1]**cen·tral** \ˈsen-trəl\ *adj* 1 : containing or constituting a center 2 : ESSENTIAL 3, PRINCIPAL ⟨the *central* character⟩ 3 : situated at, in, or near the center ⟨the store is in a *central* location⟩ 4 : controlling or directing local or branch activities ⟨the *central* office⟩ 5 : holding to a middle between extremes : MODERATE 6 : of, relating to, or comprising the brain and spinal cord; *also* : originating within the central nervous system ⟨*central* deafness⟩ — **cen·tral·i·ty** \sen-ˈtral-ət-ē\ *n* — **cen·tral·ly** \ˈsen-trə-lē\ *adv*

[2]**central** *n* 1 : a telephone exchange or operator 2 : a central office or bureau usually controlling others ⟨weather *central*⟩ 3 : a center or hub for a specified activity or group ⟨the family room becomes kid *central*⟩

central angle *n* : an angle with its vertex at the center of a circle and with sides that are radii of the circle

central bank *n* : a national bank that operates to control money supply and interest rates

central committee *n* : a large central executive body of a Communist party that is elected to function between party congresses and that elects in turn from its own membership a powerful executive presidium

cen·tral·ism \ˈsen-trə-ˌliz-əm\ *n* : the concentration of power and control in the central authority especially of a nation — compare FEDERALISM — **cen·tral·ist** \-ləst\ *n or adj* — **cen·tral·is·tic** \ˌsen-trə-ˈlis-tik\ *adj*

cen·tral·ize \ˈsen-trə-ˌlīz\ *vt* : to concentrate (as authority) in a center or central organization — **cen·tral·i·za·tion** \ˌsen-trə-lə-ˈzā-shən\ *n* — **cen·tral·iz·er** \ˈsen-trə-ˌlī-zər\ *n*

central nervous system *n* : the part of the nervous system which in vertebrates consists of the brain and spinal cord, to which sensory impulses are transmitted and from which motor impulses pass out, and which coordinates the activity of the entire nervous system

central processing unit *n* : CPU

central tendency *n* : the extent to which the values of a statistical distribution fall around a middle value ⟨the mean, median, and mode are all used to measure *central tendency*⟩

central time *n, often cap C* : the time of the 6th time zone west of Greenwich that includes the central U.S.

cen·tre \ˈsent-ər\ *chiefly British variant of* CENTER

cen·tric \ˈsen-trik\ *adj* : concentrated about or directed to a center ⟨*centric* activity⟩ — **cen·tri·cal·ly** \-tri-kə-lē, -klē\ *adv* — **cen·tric·i·ty** \sen-ˈtris-ət-ē\ *n*

-cen·tric \ˈsen-trik\ *adj combining form* : having (such) a center or (such or so many) centers : having (something specified) as its center ⟨helio*centric*⟩

cen·trif·u·gal \sen-ˈtrif-yə-gəl, -ˈtrif-i-gəl\ *adj* 1 : proceeding or acting in a direction away from a center or axis 2 : using or acting by centrifugal force ⟨a *centrifugal* pump⟩ [Latin *centrum* "center" + *fugere* "to flee"] — **cen·trif·u·gal·ly** \-gə-lē\ *adv*

centrifugal force *n* : the force that tends to impel a thing or parts of a thing outward from a center of rotation

[1]**cen·tri·fuge** \ˈsen-trə-ˌfyüj, ˈsän-\ *n* : a machine using centrifugal force for separating substances of different densities, for removing moisture, or for simulating gravitational effects — compare SEPARATOR

[2]**centrifuge** *vt* : to subject to centrifugal action especially in a centrifuge — **cen·trif·u·ga·tion** \ˌsen-ˌtrif-yə-ˈgā-shən, -ˌtrif-ə-, ˌsän-\ *n*

cen·tri·ole \ˈsen-trē-ˌōl\ *n* : one of a pair of cellular organelles that are adjacent to the nucleus, function in the formation of the spindle during cell division, and consist of a cylinder with nine tiny tubules arranged peripherally in a circle [German *Zentriol,* from *Zentrum* "center"]

cen·trip·e·tal \sen-ˈtrip-ət-l\ *adj* : proceeding or acting in a direction toward a center or axis [Latin *centrum* "center" + *petere* "to seek"] — **cen·trip·e·tal·ly** \-l-ē\ *adv*

centripetal force *n* : the force that tends to impel a thing or parts of a thing inward toward a center of rotation

cen·troid \ˈsen-ˌtrȯid\ *n* : the point where the medians of a triangle intersect

cen·tro·mere \ˈsen-trə-ˌmiər\ *n* : the point on a chromosome to which the spindle attaches during cell division — **cen·tro·mer·ic** \ˌsen-trə-ˈmer-ik, -ˈmiər-\ *adj*

cen·tro·some \ˈsen-trə-ˌsōm\ *n* 1 : the centriole-containing region of clear cytoplasm adjacent to the cell nucleus 2 : CENTRIOLE

cen·trum \ˈsen-trəm\ *n, pl* **centrums** *or* **cen·tra** \-trə\ 1 : CENTER 2 : the body of a vertebra [Latin, "center"]

cen·tu·ri·on \sen-ˈtu̇r-ē-ən, -ˈtyu̇r-\ *n* : an officer commanding a century in a Roman legion [Latin, from *centuria* "century"]

cen·tu·ry \ˈsench-rē, -ə-rē\ *n, pl* **-ries** 1 : a subdivision of the Roman legion 2 : a group, sequence, or series of 100 like things **3 :** a Roman voting unit based on property qualifications **4 :** a period of 100 years; *esp* **:** one of the 100-year divisions of the Christian era or of the preceding period [Latin *centuria,* from *centum* "hundred"]

century plant *n* **:** a commonly cultivated Mexican agave maturing and flowering only once in many years and then dying

CEO \ˌsē-ˌē-ˈō\ *n* **:** the executive with the chief decision-making authority in an organization or business [chief executive officer]

cephal- *or* **cephalo-** *combining form* **:** head ⟨*cephalo*thorax⟩ [Greek *kephalē*]

ce·phal·ic \sə-ˈfal-ik\ *adj* **1 :** of or relating to the head **2 :** directed toward or situated on or in or near the head — **ce·phal·i·cal·ly** \-i-kə-lē, -klē\ *adv*

ceph·a·lo·pod \ˈsef-ə-lə-ˌpäd\ *n* **:** any of a class (Cephalopoda) of mollusks including the squids, cuttlefishes, and octopuses that move by expelling water from a tubular siphon under the head and have a group of muscular sucker-bearing arms, highly developed eyes, and usually a bag of inky fluid which they can eject for defense — **cephalopod** *adj* — **ceph·a·lop·o·dan** \ˌsef-ə-ˈläp-əd-ən\ *adj or n*

ceph·a·lo·tho·rax \ˌsef-ə-lō-ˈthōr-ˌaks, -ˈthȯr-\ *n* **:** a united head and thorax (as of a spider or crustacean) — **ceph·a·lo·tho·rac·ic** \-thə-ˈras-ik\ *adj*

Ce·phe·id \ˈsē-fē-əd\ *n* **:** one of a class of pulsating stars whose light variations are very regular

Ce·pheus \ˈsē-ˌfyüs, -fē-əs\ *n* **:** a constellation between Cygnus and the north pole [Latin, from Greek *Kēpheus*]

ce·ra·mal \sə-ˈram-əl, ˈser-ə-ˌmal\ *n* **:** CERMET [*ceramic alloy*]

[1]**ce·ram·ic** \sə-ˈram-ik\ *adj* **:** of or relating to a product (as earthenware, porcelain, or brick) made essentially from a nonmetallic mineral by firing at high temperatures [Greek *keramikos,* from *keramos* "potter's clay, pottery"]

[2]**ceramic** *n* **1** *pl* **:** the art of making ceramic articles **2 :** a product of ceramic manufacture

ce·ram·ist \sə-ˈram-əst\ *or* **ce·ram·i·cist** \-ˈram-ə-səst\ *n* **:** one who makes ceramic products or works of art

cer·car·ia \sər-ˈkar-ē-ə, -ˈker-\ *n, pl* **-i·ae** \-ē-ˌē\ **:** a usually tadpole-shaped larval trematode worm that develops in a molluscan host by a redia [Greek *kerkos* "tail"] — **cer·car·i·al** \-ē-əl\ *adj*

cer·cus \ˈsər-kəs\ *n, pl* **cer·ci** \ˈsər-ˌsī\ **:** a many-jointed posterior appendage of an insect [Greek *kerkos* "tail"]

[1]**ce·re·al** \ˈsir-ē-əl\ *adj* **:** relating to grain or to the plants that produce it; *also* **:** made of grain [Latin *cerealis,* literally, "of Ceres," from *Ceres* (name of Roman goddess of grain)]

[2]**cereal** *n* **1 :** a plant (as a grass) yielding starchy grain suitable for food; *also* **:** its grain **2 :** a prepared foodstuff of grain

cer·e·bel·lum \ˌser-ə-ˈbel-əm\ *n, pl* **-bel·lums** *or* **-bel·la** \-ˈbel-ə\ **:** a large part of the brain concerned especially with the coordination of muscles and the maintenance of bodily equilibrium and situated between the brain stem and the back of the cerebrum [Medieval Latin, from Latin *cerebrum* "brain"] — **cer·e·bel·lar** \-ˈbel-ər\ *adj*

cerebr- *or* **cerebro-** *combining form* **1 :** brain **:** cerebrum ⟨*cerebration*⟩ **2 :** cerebral and ⟨*cerebro*spinal⟩ [Latin *cerebrum* "brain"]

ce·re·bral \sə-ˈrē-brəl, ˈser-ə-\ *adj* **1 a :** of or relating to the brain or the intellect **b :** of, relating to, or being the cerebrum **2 :** appealing to the intellect — **ce·re·bral·ly** \-brə-lē\ *adv*

cerebral cortex *n* **:** the surface layer of gray matter of each cerebral hemisphere that functions chiefly in the coordination of sensory and motor information

cerebral hemisphere *n* **:** either of the two hollow convoluted lateral halves of the cerebrum

cerebral palsy *n* **:** a disability resulting from damage to the brain usually before or during birth and outwardly manifested by muscular incoordination and speech disturbances

cer·e·brate \ˈser-ə-ˌbrāt\ *vi* **:** to use the mind **:** THINK — **cer·e·bra·tion** \ˌser-ə-ˈbrā-shən\ *n*

ce·re·bro·spi·nal \sə-ˌrē-brō-ˈspīn-l, ˌser-ə-brō-\ *adj* **:** of or relating to the brain and spinal cord or to these together with the cranial and spinal nerves that innervate voluntary muscles

cerebrospinal fluid *n* **:** a colorless fluid that occupies the cavities of the brain and spinal cord and the space between these and the meninges

ce·re·brum \sə-ˈrē-brəm, ˈser-ə-brəm\ *n, pl* **-brums** *or* **-bra** \-brə\ **1 :** BRAIN 1a **2 :** an enlarged anterior or upper part of the brain; *esp* **:** the expanded anterior portion of the brain that consists of cerebral hemispheres and connecting structures and is held to be the seat of conscious mental processes [Latin]

cere·cloth \ˈsiər-ˌklȯth\ *n* **:** cloth treated with melted wax or gummy matter and formerly used especially for wrapping a dead body [derived from Latin *cera* "wax"]

cere·ment \ˈser-ə-mənt, ˈsiər-mənt\ *n* **:** a shroud for the dead; *esp* **:** CERECLOTH — usually used in plural

[1]**cer·e·mo·ni·al** \ˌser-ə-ˈmō-nē-əl\ *adj* **:** of, relating to, or forming a ceremony — **cer·e·mo·ni·al·ism** \-nē-ə-ˌliz-əm\ *n* — **cer·e·mo·ni·al·ist** \-ləst\ *n* — **cer·e·mo·ni·al·ly** \-nē-ə-lē\ *adj* — **cer·e·mo·ni·al·ness** *n*

synonyms CEREMONIAL, CEREMONIOUS mean marked by attention to or adhering strictly to prescribed forms. CEREMONIAL applies to things that are themselves ceremonies or an essential part of them ⟨*ceremonial* offerings⟩ ⟨a *ceremonial* gown⟩. CEREMONIOUS applies to a person overly careful to observe formalities or to acts performed elaborately or marked by ceremony ⟨the *ceremonious* courtier entered with a flourish⟩ ⟨took *ceremonious* leave⟩.

[2]**ceremonial** *n* **:** a ceremonial act, action, or system

cer·e·mo·ni·ous \ˌser-ə-ˈmō-nē-əs\ *adj* **1 :** CEREMONIAL **2 :** careful to observe forms and ceremony **3 :** according to prescribed usage or procedures ***synonyms*** see CEREMONIAL — **cer·e·mo·ni·ous·ly** *adv* — **cer·e·mo·ni·ous·ness** *n*

cer·e·mo·ny \ˈser-ə-ˌmō-nē\ *n, pl* **-nies** **1 :** a formal act or series of acts prescribed by ritual or custom ⟨graduation *ceremonies*⟩ **2 :** a conventional act of politeness or etiquette ⟨went through the *ceremony* of introductions⟩ **3 :** the social behavior required by strict etiquette **:** FORMALITY ⟨dined without *ceremony*⟩ [Medieval French *ceremonie,* from Latin *caerimonia*]

ce·re·us \ˈsir-ē-əs\ *n* **:** any of various cacti of the western U.S. and tropical America often with showy flowers [Latin, "wax candle," from *cera* "wax"]

ce·rise \sə-ˈrēs, -ˈrēz\ *n* **:** a moderate red [French, literally, "cherry"]

ce·ri·um \ˈsir-ē-əm\ *n* **:** a gray malleable ductile metallic element — see ELEMENT table [*Ceres,* an asteroid]

cer·met \ˈsər-ˌmet\ *n* **:** a strong alloy of a heat-resistant compound (as carbide of titanium) and a metal (as nickel) used especially for turbine blades — called also *ceramal* [*ceramic metal*]

[1]**cer·tain** \ˈsərt-n\ *adj* **1 a :** FIXED 1c, SETTLED ⟨receive a *certain* share of the profits⟩ **b :** proved to be true **2 :** implied as being specific but not named ⟨a *certain* town in Maine⟩ **3 a :** RELIABLE **b :** INDISPUTABLE **4 a :** INEVITABLE ⟨defeat was *certain*⟩ **b :** incapable of failing **:** DESTINED ⟨she is *certain* to do well⟩ **5 :** assured in mind or action [Medieval French, derived from Latin *certus,* from *cernere* "to sift, decide"] ***synonyms*** see SURE — **cer·tain·ly** *adv*

[2]**certain** *pron, pl in constr* **:** certain ones ⟨*certain* of my classmates are absent⟩

cer·tain·ty \-tē\ *n, pl* **-ties** **1 :** something that is certain **2 :** the quality or state of being certain

synonyms CERTAINTY, CERTITUDE, CONVICTION mean a state of being free from doubt. CERTAINTY and CERTITUDE are frequently interchangeable but CERTAINTY may stress objective proof or evidence supporting a belief ⟨scientific *certainty*⟩. CERTITUDE stresses a faith in something not needing or not capable of proof ⟨believes with *certitude* in an afterlife⟩. CONVICTION applies especially to a strong individual belief ⟨has strong *convictions* on the issue⟩.

[1]**cer·tif·i·cate** \sər-ˈtif-i-kət\ *n* **1 :** a document containing a certified statement especially as to the truth of something; *esp* **:** one certifying that a person has fulfilled the requirements of a school or profession ⟨a teaching *certificate*⟩ **2 :** a document showing ownership or debt ⟨stock *certificates*⟩

[2]**cer·tif·i·cate** \-ˈtif-ə-ˌkāt\ *vt* **:** to testify to, furnish with, or authorize by a certificate; *esp* **:** CERTIFY 3 — **cer·tif·i·ca·to·ry** \-ˈtif-i-kə-ˌtōr-ē, -ˌtȯr-\ *adj*

cer·ti·fi·ca·tion \ˌsərt-ə-fə-ˈkā-shən\ *n* **1 :** the act of certifying **:** the state of being certified **2 :** a certified statement

certification mark *n* **:** a mark or device used to identify a product or service that has been certified to conform to a set of standards

certified *adj* **1 :** having earned certification ⟨a *certified* teacher⟩ **2 :** GENUINE, AUTHENTIC ⟨a *certified* big shot⟩

certified check *n* **:** a check drawn on a depositor's account for which the bank guarantees payment

certified mail *n* **:** uninsured first class mail for which the addressee signs a receipt as proof of delivery

certified milk *n* **:** milk of high quality produced under the rules and regulations of an authorized medical milk commission

certified public accountant *n* **:** an accountant who has met the requirements of state law and holds a state certificate

cer·ti·fy \ˈsərt-ə-ˌfī\ *vt* **-fied; -fy·ing** **1 a :** to attest formally or authoritatively **b :** to guarantee to be true or valid or as represented or meeting a standard **2 :** GUARANTEE 1 **3 :** to recognize as having met special qualifications within a field ⟨*certify* a teacher⟩ [Medieval French *certefier,* from Late Latin *certificare,* from Latin *certus* "certain"] — **cer·ti·fi·able** \-ˌfī-ə-bəl\ *adj* — **cer·ti·fi·er** \-ˌfī-ər, -ˌfīr\ *n*

cer·ti·tude \ˈsərt-ə-ˌtüd, -ˌtyüd\ *n* **1 :** the state of being or feeling certain **:** CONFIDENCE **2 :** an end, event, or concept that is certain and unfailing ⟨moral *certitudes*⟩ ***synonyms*** see CERTAINTY — **cer·ti·tu·di·nous** \ˌsərt-ə-ˈtüd-n-əs, -ˈtyüd-\ *adj*

ce·ru·le·an \sə-ˈrü-lē-ən\ *adj* **:** resembling the blue of the sky **:** AZURE [Latin *caeruleus* "dark blue"]

ce·ru·men \sə-ˈrü-mən\ *n* **:** EARWAX [derived from Latin *cera* "wax"] — **ce·ru·mi·nous** \-mə-nəs\ *adj*

cer·vi·cal \ˈsər-vi-kəl\ *adj* **:** of or relating to a neck or cervix

cervical cap *n* **:** a contraceptive device in the form of a thimble-shaped cap that fits over the uterine cervix to block sperm from entering the uterus

cer·vine \ˈsər-ˌvīn\ *adj* **:** of, relating to, or resembling deer [Latin *cervus* "stag, deer"]

cer·vix \ˈsər-viks\ *n, pl* **cer·vi·ces** \ˈsər-və-ˌsēz\ *or* **cer·vix·es** **:** a constricted portion of an organ or part; *esp* **:** the narrow outer end of the uterus [Latin, "neck"]

ce·sar·e·an *or* **cae·sar·e·an** \si-ˈzar-ē-ən, -ˈzer-\ *n, often cap* **:** CESAREAN SECTION — **cesarean** *or* **caesarean** *adj*

cesarean section *or* **caesarean section** *n, often cap C* **:** surgical incision of the walls of the abdomen and uterus for delivery of offspring [from the belief that the original bearer of the Roman cognomen *Caesar* had been cut (Latin *caesus*) from his mother's womb]

ce·si·um \ˈsē-zē-əm\ *n* **:** a silver-white soft ductile element used especially in photoelectric cells — see ELEMENT table [Latin *caesius* "bluish gray"]

ces·sa·tion \se-ˈsā-shən\ *n* **:** a temporary or final ceasing (as of action) **:** STOP [Medieval French, from Latin *cessatio* "delay, idleness," from *cessare* "to delay, be idle"]

ces·sion \ˈsesh-ən\ *n* **:** a giving up (as of territory or rights) to another [Medieval French, from Latin *cessio,* from *cedere* "to withdraw, cede"]

cess·pool \ˈses-ˌpül\ *n* **:** an underground pit or tank for liquid waste (as household sewage) [perhaps by folk etymology from Middle English *suspiral* "vent, tap on a main pipe, settling pool," from Medieval French *suspiral* "vent," from *suspirer* "to sigh, exhale," from Latin *suspirare*]

ces·ta \ˈses-tə\ *n* **:** a narrow curved wicker basket used in jai alai [Spanish, literally, "basket," from Latin *cista* "box, basket"]

ces·tode \ˈses-ˌtōd\ *n* **:** TAPEWORM [derived from Greek *kestos* "girdle"] — **cestode** *adj*

ce·ta·cean \si-ˈtā-shən\ *n* **:** any of an order (Cetacea) of aquatic mostly marine mammals including the whales, dolphins, porpoises, and related forms [Latin *cetus* "whale," from Greek *kētos*] — **cetacean** *adj* — **ce·ta·ceous** \-shəs\ *adj*

Ce·tus \ˈsēt-əs\ *n* **:** an equatorial constellation south of Pisces and Aries [Latin, literally, "whale"]

ce·tyl alcohol \ˈsēt-l-\ *n* **:** a waxy crystalline alcohol $C_{16}H_{34}O$ used especially in drugs, cosmetics, and detergents [*cetyl* from Latin *cetus* "whale" + English *-yl;* from its occurrence in spermaceti]

Chad·ic \ˈchad-ik\ *or* **Chad** \ˈchad\ *n* **:** a branch of the Afro-Asiatic language family comprising numerous languages of northern Nigeria, northern Cameroon, and Chad — **Chadic** *adj*

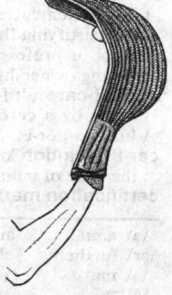

cesta

cha·dor \ˈchəd-ər, ˈchäd-\ *n* **:** a large cloth worn as a combination head covering, veil, and shawl usually by Muslim women [Persian *chaddar, chādar*]

chae·tog·nath \ˈkēt-ˌäg-ˌnath, -əg-, -ə-\ *n* **:** ARROWWORM [Greek *chaitē* "long hair" + *gnathos* "jaw"] — **chaetognath** *adj*

[1]**chafe** \ˈchāf\ *vb* **1 a :** IRRITATE 1, VEX **b :** to feel irritation, discontent, or impatience **2 :** to warm by rubbing **3 a :** to rub so as to wear away **:** ABRADE **b :** to make sore by or as if by rubbing [Medieval French *chaufer* "to warm," derived from Latin *calefacere,* from *calēre* "to be warm" + *facere* "to make"]

[2]**chafe** *n* **1 :** a state of vexation **:** RAGE **2 :** injury or wear caused by friction; *also* **:** FRICTION

cha·fer \ˈchā-fər\ *n* **:** any of various large beetles that feed on plants [Old English *ceafor*]

[1]**chaff** \ˈchaf\ *n* **1 :** the debris (as seed coverings) separated from the seed in threshing grain **2 :** something trivial or worthless [Old English *ceaf*] — **chaffy** \-ē\ *adj*

[2]**chaff** *n* **:** light jesting talk **:** BANTER [probably from [1]*chaff*]

[3]**chaff** *vb* **:** to tease good-naturedly **:** BANTER

chaf·fer \ˈchaf-ər\ *vb* **:** HAGGLE 2, BARGAIN [Middle English *chaffare* "a dispute about price," from *chep* "trade" + *fare* "journey"] — **chaf·fer·er** *n*

chaf·finch \ˈchaf-ˌinch, -inch\ *n* **:** a European finch of which the male has a pinkish brown breast and a cheerful song

chaf·ing dish \ˈchā-fing-\ *n* **:** a utensil for cooking or warming food at the table [Middle English *chafen* "to warm, chafe"]

[1]**cha·grin** \shə-ˈgrin\ *n* **:** a feeling of annoyance caused by failure or disappointment [French, from *chagrin* "sad"]

[2]**chagrin** *vt* **cha·grined** \-ˈgrind\; **cha·grin·ing** \-ˈgrin-ing\ **:** to cause to feel chagrin

chai \ˈchī\ *n* **:** a beverage that is a blend of black tea, honey, spices, and milk [Russian, Persian & Hindi *chay* "tea"]

[1]**chain** \ˈchān\ *n* **1 a :** a series of connected usually metal links or rings **b** (1) **:** a measuring instrument of 100 links used in surveying (2) **:** a unit of length equal to 66 feet (about 20 meters) **2 :** something that confines or restrains **3 a :** a series of things linked, connected, or associated together ⟨a *chain* of events⟩ **b :** a number of atoms or chemical groups united like links in a chain [Medieval French *chaene,* from Latin *catena*]

[2]**chain** *vt* **:** to fasten, bind, or connect with or as if with a chain

chain gang *n* **:** a group of convicts chained together especially as an outside working party

chain mail *n* **:** flexible armor of interlinked metal rings

chain reaction *n* **1 :** a series of events so related to each other that each one initiates the succeeding one **2 :** a chemical or nuclear reaction yielding energy or products that cause further reactions of the same kind — **chain–re·act** \ˌchān-rē-ˈakt\ *vt*

chain saw *n* **:** a portable power saw that has teeth linked together to form an endless chain

chain–smoke \ˈchān-ˈsmōk\ *vb* **:** to smoke cigarettes one right after another — **chain–smok·er** *n*

chain stitch *n* **:** an ornamental stitch like the links of a chain

chain store *n* **:** one of numerous usually retail stores under the same ownership and selling the same lines of goods

chair \ˈcheər, ˈchaər\ *n* **1 :** a seat with legs and a back for use by one person **2 a :** an official seat or a seat of authority or dignity **b :** an office or position of authority or dignity **c :** the presiding officer of a meeting, organization, committee, or event **3 :** any of various devices that hold up or support [Medieval French *chaiere,* from Latin *cathedra,* from Greek *kathedra,* from *kata* "down" + *hedra* "seat"]

chair lift *n* **:** a motor-driven conveyor for skiers consisting of a series of seats suspended from an overhead cable

chair·man \-mən\ *n* **:** CHAIR 2c — **chair·man·ship** \-ˌship\ *n*

chair·per·son \-ˌpərs-n\ *n* **:** CHAIR 2c

chair·wom·an \-ˌwu̇m-ən\ *n* **:** a woman who serves as chairman

chaise \ˈshāz\ *n* **1 :** a 2-wheeled carriage for one or two persons with a folding top **2 :** POST CHAISE [French, "chair, chaise," alteration of Medieval French *chaiere* "chair"]

chaise longue \ˈshāz-ˈlȯng\ *n, pl* **chaise longues** *also* **chaises longues** \ˈshāz-ˈlȯng, -ˈlȯngz\ **:** a long chair for reclining [French, literally, "long chair"]

chaise lounge \ˈshāz-ˈlau̇nj, ˈchās-\ *n* **:** CHAISE LONGUE [by folk etymology from *chaise longue*]

cha·la·za \kə-ˈlā-zə, -ˈlaz-ə\ *n, pl* **-zae** \-ˌzē\ *or* **-zas** **:** either of two twisted bands in the white of a bird's egg that are located at opposite ends of the egg and extend to the yolk [Greek, "hailstone"]

chal·ce·do·ny \kal-ˈsed-n-ē, ˈchal-sə-ˌdän-ē\ *n, pl* **-nies** : a translucent quartz of various colors and with waxy luster [Late Latin *chalcedonius,* a precious stone, from Greek *Chalkēdōn* "Chalcedon" (town in Asia Minor)]

chal·cid \ˈkal-səd\ *n* : any of a large group of mostly tiny wasps parasitic in the larval state on the larvae or pupae of other insects [derived from Greek *chalkos* "copper"] — **chalcid** *adj*

chal·co·cite \ˈkal-kə-ˌsīt\ *n* : a black or gray mineral Cu_2S of metallic luster that is an important ore of copper [derived from Greek *chalkos* "copper"]

chal·co·py·rite \ˌkal-kə-ˈpī-ˌrīt\ *n* : a yellow mineral $CuFeS_2$ consisting of copper-iron sulfide and constituting an important ore of copper

Chal·de·an \kal-ˈdē-ən\ *n* **1** : one of an ancient Semitic people founding the second Babylonian Empire in the 7th century B.C. **2** : the Semitic language of the Chaldeans [*Chaldea,* region of ancient Babylonia] — **Chal·da·ic** \kal-ˈdā-ik\ *adj or n* — **Chaldean** *adj*

Chal·dee \ˈkal-ˌdē\ *n* : CHALDEAN 1

cha·let \sha-ˈlā, ˈshal-ˌā\ *n* **1** : a remote herdsman's hut in the Alps **2 a** : a Swiss dwelling with a wide roof overhang **b** : a cottage in chalet style [French]

chal·ice \ˈchal-əs\ *n* **1** : a drinking cup : GOBLET; *esp* : the liturgical vessel in which wine is consecrated **2** : a flower cup [Medieval French, from Latin *calix*]

[1]**chalk** \ˈchȯk\ *n* **1** : a soft white, gray, or buff limestone chiefly composed of the shells of foraminifers **2** : chalk or a chalky material especially when used as a crayon [Old English *cealc,* from Latin *calx* "lime"] — **chalky** \ˈchȯ-ke\ *adj*

[2]**chalk** *vt* **1** : to rub, mark, write, or draw with chalk **2 a** : to make a rough sketch of ⟨*chalk* out a plan of attack⟩ **b** : to record with or as if with chalk ⟨*chalk* up the totals⟩

chalk·board \-ˌbōrd, -ˌbȯrd\ *n* : a dark smooth surface (as of slate) used for writing or drawing on with chalk

chalk up *vt* **1** : ASCRIBE, CREDIT ⟨*chalk* success *up* to hard work⟩ **2** : ATTAIN 1, ACHIEVE ⟨*chalk up* a victory⟩

[1]**chal·lenge** \ˈchal-ənj\ *vb* **1** : to claim as due or deserved ⟨an act that *challenged* everyone's admiration⟩ **2** : to order to halt and prove identity **3 a** : to take exception to : object to ⟨*challenge* a juror⟩ **b** : to question the legality or legal qualifications of ⟨*challenge* a vote⟩ **4 a** : to call out to duel or combat **b** : to invite into competition **5** : to arouse or stimulate especially by presenting with difficulties ⟨she wants a job that will *challenge* her⟩ [Medieval French *chalenger* "to accuse," from Latin *calumniari* "to accuse falsely," from *calumnia* "calumny"] — **chal·leng·er** *n*

[2]**challenge** *n* **1 a** : an often threatening or provocative summons; *esp* : a summons to a duel **b** : an invitation to compete in a sport **2** : an objection raised to something or someone **3** : a sentry's command to halt and prove identity **4** : a stimulating task or problem ⟨looking for new *challenges*⟩ **5** : a test of immunity by exposure to virulent infective material after specific immunization

chal·lenged \ˈchal-ənjd\ *adj* : having a disability or lacking some necessary quality or element ⟨physically *challenged*⟩

chal·lis \ˈshal-ē\ *n, pl* **chal·lises** \ˈshal-ēz\ : a lightweight soft clothing fabric especially of cotton or wool [probably from the name *Challis*]

cha·lu·pa \chä-ˈlü-pä, chə-ˈlü-pə\ *n* : a fried corn tortilla sometimes shaped like a boat and filled with a savory mixture (as of meat, vegetables, or cheese) [Mexican Spanish, from Spanish, "boat, skiff"]

[1]**cham·ber** \ˈchām-bər\ *n* **1** : ROOM; *esp* : BEDROOM **2** : an enclosed space or compartment **3 a** : a meeting hall of a deliberative, legislative, or judicial body **b** : a room where a judge transacts business out of court **c** : the reception room of a person of rank or authority **4 a** : a legislative or judicial body; *esp* : either of the houses of a bicameral legislature **b** : a voluntary board or council (as of businesspeople) **5 a** : the part of the bore of a gun that holds the cartridge **b** : a compartment in the cartridge cylinder of a revolver [Medieval French *chambre,* from Late Latin *camera,* from Latin, "arched roof," from Greek *kamara*] — **cham·bered** \-bərd\ *adj*

[2]**chamber** *vt* : to place or hold in or as if in a chamber

chambered nautilus *n* : NAUTILUS 1

cham·ber·lain \ˈchām-bər-lən\ *n* **1** : a chief officer in the household of a sovereign or noble **2** : TREASURER [Medieval French *chamberlein,* derived from Late Latin *camera* "chamber"]

cham·ber·maid \ˈchām-bər-ˌmād\ *n* : a maid who makes beds and does general cleaning of bedrooms (as in a hotel)

chamber music *n* : instrumental music intended for performance by a few musicians for a small audience

chamber of commerce : an association of businesspeople to promote commercial and industrial interests

chamber pot *n* : a handled and often lidded bowl for urination and defecation

cham·bray \ˈsham-ˌbrā, -brē\ *n* : a lightweight clothing fabric with colored and white yarns [*Cambrai,* France]

cha·me·leon \kə-ˈmēl-yən\ *n* **1** : any of various lizards having the ability to vary the color of their skin **2 a** : a person given to often quick or frequent change in ideas or character **b** : one that is subject to quick or frequent change in appearance [derived from Greek *chamaileōn,* from *chamai* "on the ground" + *leōn* "lion"]

[1]**cham·fer** \ˈcham-fər, ˈchamp-\ *n* : a beveled edge [Middle French *chanfraindre* "to bevel," from *chant* "edge" (from Latin *canthus* "iron tire") + *fraindre* "to break," from Latin *frangere*]

[2]**chamfer** *vt* **1** : to cut a furrow in (as a column) : GROOVE **2** : to make a chamfer on : BEVEL

cham·ois \ˈsham-ē\ *n, pl* **cham·ois** *also* **cham·oix** \ˈsham-ēz\ **1** : a small goatlike mountain antelope of Europe and the Caucasus **2** *also* **cham·my** *or* **sham·my** \ˈsham-ē\ : a soft pliant leather prepared from the skin of the chamois or from sheepskin [Middle French, from Late Latin *camox*]

cham·o·mile *or* **cam·o·mile** \ˈkam-ə-ˌmīl, -ˌmēl\ *n* **1** : an herb related to the daisies with strong-scented foliage and flower heads **2** : the dried flower heads of chamomile often used in making tea [Medieval Latin *camomilla,* derived from Greek *chamaimēlon,* from *chamai* "on the ground" + *mēlon* "apple"]

chamomile

[1]**champ** \ˈchamp\ *vb* **1** : to bite or chew noisily ⟨a horse *champing* its bit⟩ **2** : to show impatience — usually used in the phrase *champing at the bit* [perhaps imitative]

[2]**champ** *n* : CHAMPION 3

cham·pagne \sham-ˈpān\ *n* : a white sparkling wine made in Champagne, France; *also* : a similar wine made elsewhere

cham·paign \sham-ˈpān\ *n* : an expanse of level open country : PLAIN [Medieval French *champaigne,* from Late Latin *campania* "level country"]

[1]**cham·pi·on** \ˈcham-pē-ən\ *n* **1** : a militant advocate or defender **2** : one that fights for another's rights or honor **3** : the winner of first prize or first place in a competition; *also* : one who shows marked superiority ⟨a *champion* at selling⟩ [Medieval French, "warrior," from Medieval Latin *campio,* of Germanic origin]

[2]**champion** *vt* : to protect or fight for as a champion

cham·pi·on·ship \-ˌship\ *n* **1** : the act of defending as a champion ⟨her *championship* of civil rights⟩ **2 a** : the position or title of champion **b** : a contest held to determine a champion

[1]**chance** \ˈchans\ *n* **1** : the way in which things happen without apparent cause or intent ⟨meet by *chance*⟩ **2** : OPPORTUNITY ⟨had a *chance* to travel⟩ **3** : RISK, GAMBLE ⟨take *chances*⟩ **4 a** : the possibility of a particular outcome in an uncertain situation ⟨a *chance* of failure⟩; *also* : the degree of likelihood of such an outcome ⟨a small *chance* of winning⟩ **b** *pl* : the more likely of possible outcomes ⟨*chances* are they've already left⟩ **5** : a ticket in a raffle [Medieval French, derived from Latin *cadere* "to fall"] — **chance** *adj*

[2]**chance** *vb* **1 a** : to take place, come about, or turn out by chance : HAPPEN **b** : to have good or bad luck ⟨*chanced* to meet⟩ **2** : to come casually and unexpectedly ⟨*chanced* upon a gas station⟩ **3** : to accept the hazard of : RISK ⟨knew the trip

\ə\ **abut**	\au̇\ **out**	\i\ **tip**	\ȯ\ **saw**	\u̇\ **foot**
\ər\ **further**	\ch\ **chin**	\ī\ **life**	\ȯi\ **coin**	\y\ **yet**
\a\ **mat**	\e\ **pet**	\j\ **job**	\th\ **thin**	\yü\ **few**
\ā\ **take**	\ē\ **easy**	\ng\ **sing**	\t͟h\ **this**	\yu̇\ **cure**
\ä\ **cot, cart**	\g\ **go**	\ō\ **bone**	\ü\ **food**	\zh\ **vision**

was dangerous but decided to *chance* it⟩ ***synonyms*** see HAPPEN

chan·cel \ˈchan-səl\ *n* **:** the part of a church containing the altar and seats for the clergy and choir [Medieval French, from Latin *cancelli* "lattice"; from the latticework enclosing it]

chan·cel·lery *or* **chan·cel·lory** \ˈchan-sə-lə-rē, -slə-rē\ *n, pl* **-ler·ies** *or* **-lor·ies** **1 a :** the position or department of a chancellor **b :** the building or room where a chancellor's office is located **2 :** the office or staff of an embassy or consulate

chan·cel·lor \ˈchan-sə-lər, -slər\ *n* **1 :** the head of a university **2 :** a judge in a court of chancery or equity **3 :** the chief minister of state in some European countries [Medieval French *chanceler,* from Late Latin *cancellarius* "doorkeeper, secretary," from Latin *cancelli* "lattice"] — **chan·cel·lor·ship** \-ˌship\ *n*

chancellor of the exchequer : a member of the British cabinet in charge of the public income and expenditure

chan·cery \ˈchans-rē, -ə-rē\ *n, pl* **-cer·ies** **1 :** a record office for public archives **2 :** a court of equity **3 :** CHANCELLERY 2 [Middle English *chancerie,* alteration of *chancellerie* "chancellery"]

chan·cre \ˈshang-kər\ *n* **:** a sore or ulcer at the site of entry of an infective agent (as one causing syphilis) [French, from Latin *cancer*] — **chan·crous** \-kə-rəs, -krəs\ *adj*

chancy \ˈchan-sē\ *adj* **chanc·i·er; -est :** uncertain in outcome or prospect **:** RISKY

chan·de·lier \ˌshan-də-ˈliər\ *n* **:** a branched often ornate lighting fixture usually suspended from a ceiling [French, derived from Latin *candelabrum* "candlestick"]

chan·dler \ˈchan-dlər\ *n* **1 :** a maker or seller of candles **2 :** a dealer in supplies or equipment especially for ships [Medieval French *chandeler,* from *chandele* "candle," from Latin *candela*] — **chan·dlery** \-dlə-rē\ *n*

[1]**change** \ˈchānj\ *vb* **1 :** to make or become different **:** MODIFY **2 a :** to give a different position, course, or direction to **b :** REVERSE ⟨*change* one's vote⟩ **3 a :** to replace with another **:** SWITCH **b :** to exchange for an equivalent sum of money in usually smaller units of value or in a foreign currency ⟨*change* a $20 bill⟩ **c :** to put on fresh clothes or covering ⟨*change* a bed⟩ **4 :** to shift one's means of transportation **:** TRANSFER **5 :** to undergo transformation, transition, or substitution ⟨winter *changed* to spring⟩ **6 :** to give up one thing for something else in return **:** EXCHANGE ⟨*change* places⟩ [Medieval French *changer,* from Latin *cambiare* "to exchange," probably of Celtic origin] — **chang·er** *n* — **change hands :** to pass from the possession of one person to that of another

synonyms CHANGE, ALTER, MODIFY, VARY mean to make or become different. CHANGE implies making either an essential difference amounting to loss of original identity or a substitution of one thing for another ⟨*changed* the shirt for a larger size⟩. ALTER implies a difference in some respect without loss of identity ⟨slightly *altered* the original design⟩. MODIFY suggests a difference that limits, restricts, or adapts to a new purpose ⟨*modified* the building for use by the disabled⟩. VARY stresses a breaking away from exact repetition ⟨*vary* your daily routine⟩.

[2]**change** *n* **1 :** the act, process, or result of changing: as **a :** ALTERATION ⟨a *change* in routine⟩ **b :** TRANSFORMATION ⟨a *change* of seasons⟩ **c :** SUBSTITUTION ⟨a *change* of jobs⟩ **2 :** a fresh set of clothes **3 a :** money in small denominations received in exchange for an equivalent sum in larger denominations **b :** money returned when a payment exceeds the amount due **c :** COINS ⟨a pocketful of *change*⟩ **d :** MONEY 1 ⟨cost a large chunk of *change*⟩

change·able \ˈchān-jə-bəl\ *adj* **1 :** capable of or given to change **:** VARIABLE ⟨*changeable* weather⟩ **2 :** appearing different (as in color) from different points of view — **change·abil·i·ty** \ˌchān-jə-ˈbil-ət-ē\ *n* — **change·able·ness** *n* — **change·ably** \ˈchān-jə-blē\ *adv*

change·ful \ˈchānj-fəl\ *adj* **:** full of or given to change **:** UNCERTAIN ⟨*changeful* times⟩ — **change·ful·ly** \-fə-lē\ *adv* — **change·ful·ness** *n*

change·less \ˈchānj-ləs\ *adj* **:** never changing **:** CONSTANT ⟨*changeless* truths⟩ — **change·less·ly** *adv* — **change·less·ness** *n*

change·ling \ˈchānj-ling\ *n* **:** a child secretly exchanged for another in infancy

change of life : MENOPAUSE; *also* **:** a corresponding period in the male

change ringing *n* **:** the art or practice of ringing a set of tuned bells in continually varying order

[1]**chan·nel** \ˈchan-l\ *n* **1 a :** the bed of a stream **b :** the deeper part of a river, harbor, or strait **c :** a strait or narrow sea between two close landmasses ⟨the English *Channel*⟩ **2 a :** a means aiding communication or exchange ⟨trade *channels*⟩ **b :** a way or course of thought or action ⟨new *channels* of exploration⟩ **3 :** a long gutter, groove, or furrow **4 :** a range of frequencies of sufficient width for a single radio or television transmission [Medieval French *chanel,* from Latin *canalis* "pipe, channel, canal"]

[2]**channel** *vt* **-neled** *or* **-nelled; -nel·ing** *or* **-nel·ling** **1 a :** to form, cut, or wear a channel in **b :** GROOVE ⟨*channel* a chair leg⟩ **2 :** to direct into or through a channel

chan·nel·ize \ˈchan-l-ˌīz\ *vt* **1 :** CHANNEL **2 :** to straighten by means of a channel ⟨*channelize* a stream⟩ — **chan·nel·i·za·tion** \ˌchan-l-ə-ˈzā-shən\ *n*

channel surfing *n* **:** the action or practice of quickly looking at one television channel after another by the use of a remote control — **channel surf** *vi* — **channel surfer** *n*

chan·son \shä^{n}-ˈsō^{n}\ *n, pl* **chan·sons** \-ˈsō^{n}, -ˈsō^{n}z\ **:** SONG; *esp* **:** a music-hall or cabaret song [French]

[1]**chant** \ˈchant\ *vb* **1 :** SING; *esp* **:** to sing a chant **2 :** to recite something in a monotonous repetitive tone [Medieval French *chanter,* from Latin *cantare,* from *canere* "to sing"] — **chant·er** *n*

[2]**chant** *n* **1 :** a melody in which several words or syllables are sung in one tone **2 :** a rhythmic monotonous utterance

chan·te·relle \ˌshant-ə-ˈrel, ˌshänt-\ *n* **:** an edible mushroom of usually yellow to orange color and pleasant aroma [French]

chan·teuse \shä^{n}-ˈtüz, -ˈtərz, shan-ˈtüz\ *n* **:** SONGSTRESS; *esp* **:** a woman who is a concert or nightclub singer [French, from *chanter* "to sing"]

chan·tey *or* **chan·ty** \ˈshant-ē, ˈchant-\ *or* **shanty** \ˈshan-\ *n, pl* **chanteys** *or* **chanties** *or* **shanties :** a song sung by sailors in rhythm with their work [French *chanter* "to sing, chant"]

chan·ti·cleer \ˌchant-ə-ˈkliər, ˌshant-\ *n* **:** ROOSTER [Medieval French *Chantecler,* rooster in the beast epic *Reynard the Fox*]

Chanukah *variant of* HANUKKAH

cha·os \ˈkā-ˌäs\ *n* **:** a state of utter confusion ⟨the blackout caused *chaos*⟩ [Latin, from Greek] ***synonyms*** see ANARCHY — **cha·ot·ic** \kā-ˈät-ik\ *adj* — **cha·ot·i·cal·ly** \-i-kə-lē, -klē\ *adv*

[1]**chap** \ˈchap\ *n* **:** a crack in or a sore roughening of the skin from exposure especially to wind or cold [Middle English *chappes* "cracks in skin," from *chappen*]

[2]**chap** *vb* **chapped; chap·ping :** to open in slits or cracks; *also* **:** to become cracked, roughened, or reddened ⟨*chapped* lips⟩ [Middle English *chappen*]

[3]**chap** \ˈchäp, ˈchap\ *n* **1 :** the fleshy covering of a jaw; *also* **:** JAW — usually used in plural ⟨a wolf's *chaps*⟩ **2 :** the forepart of the face — usually used in plural [origin unknown]

[4]**chap** \ˈchap\ *n, chiefly British* **:** FELLOW 4a [short for *chapman*]

chap·ar·ral \ˌshap-ə-ˈral, -ˈrel\ *n* **1 :** a thicket of dwarf evergreen oaks; *also* **:** a dense impenetrable thicket **2 :** an ecological community composed of shrubby plants adapted to dry summers and moist winters that occurs especially in southern California [Spanish, from *chaparro* "dwarf evergreen oak," from Basque *txapar*]

chap·book \ˈchap-ˌbu̇k\ *n* **:** a small book containing ballads, tales, or tracts [*chap*man + *book*]

cha·peau \sha-ˈpō\ *n, pl* **cha·peaus** \-ˈpōz\ *or* **cha·peaux** \-ˈpō, -ˈpōz\ **:** HAT [French, derived from Medieval Latin *cappellus* "head covering," from Late Latin *cappa*]

chap·el \ˈchap-əl\ *n* **1 :** a place of worship in a residence or institution **2 :** a building or a room or recess for prayer or special religious services **3 :** a service of worship in a school or college [Medieval French *chapele,* from Medieval Latin *cappella,* from Late Latin *cappa* "cloak"; from the preservation of the cloak of Saint Martin of Tours in a chapel built for that purpose]

[1]**chap·er·one** *or* **chap·er·on** \ˈshap-ə-ˌrōn\ *n* **:** a person who accompanies and is responsible for (as at a dance) a young woman or a group of young people [French *chaperon,* literally, "hood," derived from Late Latin *cappa* "head covering, cloak"]

[2]**chaperone** *or* **chaperon** *vb* **:** to act as a chaperone **:** ESCORT — **chap·er·on·age** \-ˌrō-nij\ *n*

chap·fall·en \ˈchap-ˌfȯ-lən, ˈchäp-\ *also* **chop·fall·en** \ˈchäp-\ *adj* **:** cast down in spirits **:** DEPRESSED

chap·lain \'chap-lən\ *n* **1 :** a member of the clergy appointed to serve a dignitary, institution, or military force **2 :** a person chosen to conduct religious exercises for an organization [Medieval French *chapelein* "clergyman in charge of a chapel," from Medieval Latin *cappellanus,* from *cappella* "chapel"] — **chap·lain·cy** \-sē\ *n* — **chap·lain·ship** \-ˌship\ *n*

chap·let \'chap-lət\ *n* **1 :** a wreath worn on the head **2 a :** a string of beads **b :** a part of a rosary comprising five decades [Medieval French *chapelet,* derived from Late Latin *cappa* "head covering, cloak"]

chaplet 1

chap·man \'chap-mən\ *n, British* **:** a traveling merchant [Old English *cēapman,* from *cēap* "trade" + *man*]

chap·pie \'cha-pē\ *n, British* **:** FELLOW 4a

chaps \'shaps, 'chaps\ *n pl* **:** leather leggings resembling trousers without a seat that are worn especially by western ranch hands [Mexican Spanish *chaparreras*]

chap·ter \'chap-tər\ *n* **1 :** a main division of a book or of a law code **2 :** a local branch of a society or fraternity [Medieval French *chapitre, chapitle,* from Late Latin *capitulum,* from Latin *caput* "head"]

[1]**char** *also* **charr** \'chär\ *n, pl* **char** *or* **chars** *also* **charr** *or* **charrs :** any of a genus of small-scaled trouts including the common brook trout [origin unknown]

[2]**char** *vb* **charred; char·ring 1 :** to change to charcoal by burning **2 :** to burn slightly **:** SCORCH **3 :** to burn to a cinder [back-formation from *charcoal*]

[3]**char** *n* **:** a charred substance **:** CHARCOAL

[4]**char** *vi* **charred; char·ring :** to work as a charwoman

char·a·banc \'shar-ə-ˌbang\ *n, British* **:** a sightseeing bus [French *char à bancs,* literally, "wagon with benches"]

char·a·cin \'kar-ə-sən\ *n* **:** any of a family of usually small brightly colored tropical freshwater fishes [derived from Greek *charax* "pointed stake, a kind of fish"] — **characin** *adj*

char·ac·ter \'kar-ik-tər\ *n* **1 a :** a conventional marking indicating origin or ownership **b :** a mark or symbol (as a hieroglyph or a letter of an alphabet) used in writing or printing **c :** a symbol (as a letter or number) that represents information; *also* **:** something standing for such a character that may be accepted by a computer **2 a** (1) **:** a distinguishing feature **:** CHARACTERISTIC (2) **:** the sum total of the distinguishing qualities of a person, group, or thing **:** NATURE **b :** the detectable result of the action of a gene or group of genes **3 :** POSITION, STATUS ⟨his *character* as town official⟩ **4 :** a person having notable traits or characteristics; *esp* **:** an odd or peculiar person **5 :** a person in a story, novel, or play **6 :** REPUTATION 1 **7 :** moral excellence and strength ⟨hard work builds *character*⟩ [Latin *character* "mark, distinctive quality," from Greek *charaktēr,* from *charassein* "to scratch, engrave"] — **char·ac·ter·less** \-ləs\ *adj* — **in character :** in agreement with a person's usual qualities or traits ⟨behaving *in character*⟩ — **out of character :** not in agreement with a person's usual qualities or traits ⟨his rudeness was completely *out of character*⟩

char·ac·ter·i·sa·tion, char·ac·ter·ise *British variant of* CHARACTERIZATION, CHARACTERIZE

[1]**char·ac·ter·is·tic** \ˌkar-ik-tə-'ris-tik\ *n* **1 :** a distinguishing trait, quality, or property **2 :** the part of a common logarithm to the left of the decimal point ⟨the common logarithm of 30 is 1.477, which has the *characteristic* 1⟩

[2]**characteristic** *adj* **:** serving to mark the distinctive character of an individual, group, or class — **char·ac·ter·is·ti·cal·ly** \-ti-kə-lē, -klē\ *adv*

synonyms CHARACTERISTIC, INDIVIDUAL, DISTINCTIVE, PECULIAR mean indicating a special quality or identity. CHARACTERISTIC applies to something that marks a person or thing or a class ⟨feathers are *characteristic* of birds⟩. INDIVIDUAL stresses qualities that distinguish one from all other members of the same kind or class ⟨an *individual* writing style⟩. DISTINCTIVE indicates qualities that are distinguishing and uncommon and often superior or praiseworthy ⟨a *distinctive* singing voice⟩. PECULIAR applies to qualities possessed only by a particular individual or class and stresses rarity or uniqueness ⟨an accent *peculiar* to people from New England⟩.

char·ac·ter·i·za·tion \ˌkar-ik-tə-rə-'zā-shən\ *n* **:** the act of characterizing; *esp* **:** the artistic representation (as in fiction) of human character

char·ac·ter·ize \'kar-ik-tə-ˌrīz\ *vt* **1 :** to indicate the character or characteristics of **:** DESCRIBE ⟨*characterize* him as ambitious⟩ **2 :** to be characteristic of ⟨an era *characterized* by greed⟩

cha·rade \shə-'rād\ *n* **1** *pl* **:** a game in which some of the players try to guess a word or phrase from the actions of another player who may not speak **2 :** an act that is meaningless or is meant to deceive [French]

cha·ras \'chär-əs\ *n* **:** HASHISH [Hindi *caras*]

char·coal \'chär-ˌkōl\ *n* **1 :** a dark or black porous carbon prepared from vegetable or animal substances (as from wood by charring in a kiln from which air is excluded) **2 a :** a piece or pencil of fine charcoal used in drawing **b :** a charcoal drawing [Middle English *charcole*]

chard \'chärd\ *n* **:** SWISS CHARD [French *carde,* from Occitan *cardo* "cardoon," derived from Latin *carduus* "thistle, cardoon"]

[1]**charge** \'chärj\ *n* **1 :** a figure borne on a heraldic field **2 a :** the quantity of material that an apparatus (as a gun or the cylinder of an internal-combustion engine) is intended to receive at one time **b :** a store or accumulation of force **c :** a definite quantity of electricity; *esp* **:** an excess or deficiency of electrons **3 a :** OBLIGATION 2, REQUIREMENT **b :** MANAGEMENT 1, SUPERVISION ⟨has *charge* of the building⟩ **c :** a person or thing committed to the care of another **4 :** INSTRUCTION, COMMAND ⟨a *charge* to a jury⟩ **5 a :** EXPENSE 1, COST **b :** the price of something **c :** a debit to an account **6 a :** a formal accusation of a wrong or offense **b :** an expression of hostile criticism ⟨made a *charge* of racism⟩ **7 a :** a rush to attack an enemy **:** ASSAULT ⟨the *charge* of the brigade⟩ **b :** the signal for attack ⟨sound the *charge*⟩ **c :** a usually illegal rush into an opponent in various sports (as basketball) [Medieval French, from *charger*] — **in charge :** having control of or responsibility for something

[2]**charge** *vb* **1 a :** to place a charge (as of powder) in ⟨*charge* the magazine with three rounds⟩ **b :** to load or fill to capacity **c** (1) **:** to impart an electric charge to (2) **:** to restore the active materials in (a storage battery) by the passage of a direct current through in the opposite direction to that of discharge **2 a :** to impose a task or responsibility on ⟨*charge* him with the job⟩ **b :** to command, instruct, or exhort with right or authority ⟨*charge* a jury⟩ **3 :** ACCUSE, BLAME ⟨*charged* them with murder⟩ **4 :** to rush against or bear down upon a place **:** ASSAULT, ATTACK; *also* **:** to charge an opponent in sports **5 a :** to impose a monetary charge upon a person ⟨*charged* me $50⟩ **b :** to fix or ask as fee or payment ⟨*charge* $10 for a ticket⟩ **c :** to ask or set a price ⟨*charges* too much⟩ [Medieval French *charger* "to load," from Late Latin *carricare,* from Latin *carrus* "wheeled vehicle"] ***synonyms*** see COMMAND — **charge·able** \'chär-jə-bəl\ *adj* — **charge·able·ness** *n*

charge account *n* **:** a customer's account with a creditor (as a merchant) to which the purchase of goods is charged

charge card *n* **:** CREDIT CARD

charge–coupled device *n* **:** a semiconductor device that is used especially as an optical sensor in the formation of images (as in a camera) — called also *CCD*

charged \'chärjd\ *adj* **1 :** having or showing strong emotion ⟨a highly *charged* crowd⟩ **2 :** capable of causing strong emotion ⟨a politically *charged* subject⟩

char·gé d'af·faires \'shär-ˌzhād-ə-'faər, -feər\ *n, pl* **char·gés d'af·faires** \-ˌzhād-ə-, -ˌzhāz-də-\ **1 :** a diplomat who substitutes for an absent ambassador or minister **2 :** a diplomat of inferior rank [French, literally, "one charged with affairs"]

[1]**char·ger** \'chär-jər\ *n* **:** a large flat dish or platter

[2]**charg·er** \'chär-jər\ *n* **1 :** a cavalry horse **2 :** a device for charging storage batteries

char·i·ot \'char-ē-ət\ *n* **:** a 2-wheeled horse-drawn battle car of ancient

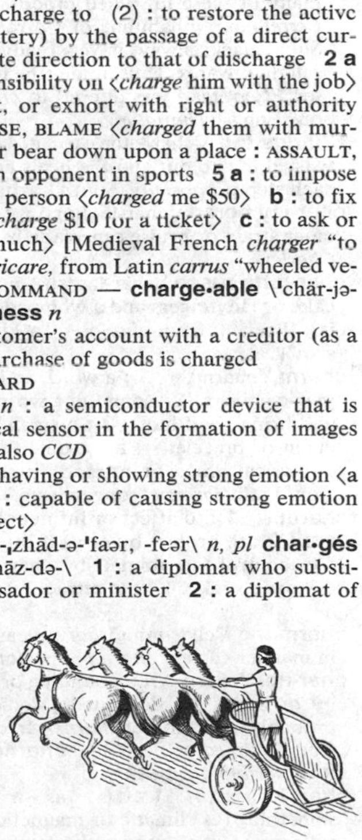
chariot

\ə\ **abut**	\au̇\ **out**	\i\ **tip**	\ȯ\ **saw**	\u̇\ **foot**
\ər\ **further**	\ch\ **chin**	\ī\ **life**	\ȯi\ **coin**	\y\ **yet**
\a\ **mat**	\e\ **pet**	\j\ **job**	\th\ **thin**	\yü\ **few**
\ā\ **take**	\ē\ **easy**	\ng\ **sing**	\t͟h\ **this**	\yu̇\ **cure**
\ä\ **cot, cart**	\g\ **go**	\ō\ **bone**	\ü\ **food**	\zh\ **vision**

times used also in processions and races [Medieval French, from *charrier* "to transport," from *char* "vehicle," from Latin *carrus*]

char·i·o·teer \ˌchar-ē-ə-ˈtiər\ *n* **1** : a driver of a chariot **2** *cap* : the constellation Auriga

char·ism \ˈkar-ˌi-zəm\ *n, pl* **cha·ris·ma·ta** \kə-ˈriz-mə-tə, ˌkar-iz-ˈmä-tə\ *or* **charisms** : an extraordinary power (as of healing) given a Christian by the Holy Spirit for the good of the church [Greek *charisma*]

cha·ris·ma \kə-ˈriz-mə\ *n* **1** : a personal magic of leadership arousing popular loyalty or enthusiasm for a public figure **2** : a special magnetic charm or appeal [Greek, "favor, gift," from *charis* "grace"]

char·is·mat·ic \ˌkar-əz-ˈmat-ik\ *adj* **1** : of or relating to charisma or charism ⟨*charismatic* gifts⟩ **2** : having, showing, or based on charisma or charism ⟨a *charismatic* leader⟩

char·i·ta·ble \ˈchar-ət-ə-bəl\ *adj* **1** : liberal with money or help for poor and needy persons : GENEROUS **2** : given for or serving the needy ⟨*charitable* funds⟩ **3** : generous and kindly in judging other people — **char·i·ta·ble·ness** *n* — **char·i·ta·bly** \-blē\ *adv*

char·i·ty \ˈchar-ət-ē\ *n, pl* **-ties** **1** : love for one's fellow human beings **2** : kindliness in judging others **3 a** : the giving of aid to the poor and suffering **b** : public aid for the poor **c** : an institution or fund for aiding the needy [Medieval French *charité,* from Latin *caritas* "dearness," from *carus* "dear"]

char·la·tan \ˈshär-lə-tən\ *n* : a person who pretends to have a particular knowledge or ability : QUACK [Italian *ciarlatano,* alteration of *cerretano,* literally, "inhabitant of Cerreto, village in Italy"] — **char·la·tan·ism** \-tə-ˌniz-əm\ *n* — **char·la·tan·ry** \-tən-rē\ *n*

Word History In the early 16th century quacks wandered through Italy, peddling medicines and treatments of doubtful value. Because the village of Cerreto seemed to produce so many of these unskilled practitioners of medicine, the name *Cerretano,* "inhabitant of Cerreto," came to mean "quack." Such quacks always have a ready line of glib talk to help them sell their wares. Thus, under the influence of *ciarlare,* "to chatter," *Cerretano* was altered to *ciarlatano,* from which we get our English *charlatan.*

Charles·ton \ˈchärl-stən\ *n* : a dance in which the knees are twisted in and out and the heels are swung sharply outward on each step [*Charleston,* South Carolina]

char·ley horse \ˈchär-lē-ˌhȯrs\ *n* : pain and stiffness from muscular strain or bruise especially in a leg [*Charley,* nickname for *Charles*]

char·lotte russe \ˌshär-lət-ˈrüs\ *n* : a dessert made with sponge cake or ladyfingers and a whipped-cream or custard-gelatin filling [French, from *charlotte,* "a kind of dessert" + *russe* "Russian"]

[1]**charm** \ˈchärm\ *n* **1** : a word, action, or thing believed to have magic powers **2** : something worn or carried to keep away evil and bring good luck **3** : a small decorative object worn on a chain or bracelet **4 a** : a quality that attracts and pleases **b** : physical grace or attractiveness [Medieval French *charme,* from Latin *carmen* "song, charm," from *canere* "to sing"]

[2]**charm** *vt* **1** : to affect or influence by or as if by magic : COMPEL **2** : to protect by or as if by a charm ⟨a *charmed* life⟩ **3** : to control (an animal) by charms (as the playing of music) ⟨*charm* a snake⟩ **4** : to attract by grace or beauty — **charm·er** *n*

charm·ing \ˈchär-ming\ *adj* : pleasant and attractive especially in manner ⟨a very *charming* person⟩

char·nel \ˈchärn-l\ *n* : a building or chamber in which dead bodies or bones are deposited [Medieval French *carnel, charnel,* probably alteration of *charner,* from Medieval Latin *carnarium,* from Latin *caro* "flesh"] — **charnel** *adj*

charr *variant of* [1]CHAR

[1]**chart** \ˈchärt\ *n* **1** : MAP: as **a** : an outline map exhibiting something (as climatic or magnetic variations) in its geographical aspects **b** : a map with specific information for use by navigators **2** : a sheet giving information in the form of a table or of lists or by means of diagrams or graphs; *also* : GRAPH **3** : a sheet of paper ruled and graduated for use in a recording instrument **4** : a record of medical information about a patient [Middle French *charte,* from Latin *charta* "piece of papyrus, document," from Greek *chartēs* "piece of papyrus" — see *Word History* at CARTEL]

[2]**chart** *vt* **1** : to make a chart of ⟨set out to *chart* the coast⟩ **2** : to lay out a plan for ⟨*charting* campaign strategy⟩

[1]**char·ter** \ˈchärt-ər\ *n* **1 a** : an official document granting, guaranteeing, or defining the rights and duties of the body (as a municipality, corporation, or a local society) to which it is issued **b** : CONSTITUTION ⟨the United Nations *Charter*⟩ **2** : a special privilege or immunity **3** : a contract by which the owners of a ship lease it to others **4** : a charter travel arrangement [Medieval French *chartre,* from Medieval Latin *chartula,* from Latin *charta* "document"]

[2]**charter** *vt* **1** : to grant a charter to **2** : to hire (as a ship or a bus) for one's own use — **char·ter·er** \ˈchärt-ər-ər\ *n*

[3]**charter** *adj* : of, relating to, or being a travel arrangement in which transportation (as a bus or plane) is hired by and for a specific group of people ⟨a *charter* flight⟩

charter school *n* : a tax-supported school set up by a charter between an official body (as a state government) and an outside group (as of educators and businesses) which may operate without educational regulations so as to achieve set goals

Char·tism \ˈchärt-ˌiz-əm\ *n* : the principles and practices of a body of 19th century English political reformers advocating better social and industrial conditions for the working classes [Medieval Latin *charta* "charter," from Latin, "document"] — **Char·tist** \ˈchärt-əst\ *adj or n*

char·treuse \shär-ˈtrüz, -ˈtrüs\ *n* : a brilliant yellow green [*Chartreuse,* trademark used for a green or yellow liqueur]

char·wom·an \ˈchär-ˌwu̇m-ən\ *n* : a cleaning woman especially in a large building [Middle English *char* "turn, piece of work," from Old English *cierr*]

chary \ˈchaər-ē, ˈcheər-\ *adj* **char·i·er; -est** **1** : cautious of dangers and risks **2** : slow to give, accept, or spend ⟨*chary* of giving praise⟩ [Old English *cearig* "sorrowful," from *caru* "sorrow, care"] — **char·i·ly** \ˈchar-ə-lē, ˈcher-\ *adv* — **char·i·ness** \ˈchar-ē-nəs, ˈcher-\ *n*

[1]**chase** \ˈchās\ *n* **1 a** : the hunting of wild animals — used with *the* **b** : the act of chasing : PURSUIT **2** : something pursued **3** : a tract of unenclosed land used as a game preserve [Medieval French *chace,* from *chacer* "to chase"]

[2]**chase** *vb* **1** : to follow rapidly : PURSUE **2** : HUNT **3** : to drive away or out ⟨*chase* a dog off the lawn⟩ [Medieval French *chacer,* derived from Latin *captare,* from *capere* "to take"]

synonyms CHASE, PURSUE, FOLLOW, TRAIL mean to go after or on the track of someone or something. CHASE implies going swiftly after and trying to overtake something running ⟨a dog *chasing* a cat⟩. PURSUE may add the suggestion of a continuing effort to overtake ⟨*pursue* a fox⟩. FOLLOW puts less emphasis on speed and may not imply intent to overtake ⟨a stray dog *followed* me home⟩. TRAIL applies to a following of tracks or traces rather than a visible object ⟨*trail* a deer through the snow⟩.

[3]**chase** *vt* : to ornament (metal) by embossing or engraving ⟨*chased* bronze⟩ [Medieval French *enchaser* "to set"]

[4]**chase** *n* : a channel (as in a wall) for something to lie in or pass through [French *chas* "eye of a needle," from Late Latin *capsus* "enclosed space," from Latin *capsa* "box"]

[5]**chase** *n* : a rectangular steel or iron frame into which letterpress matter is locked for printing or plating [probably from French *châsse* "frame," derived from Latin *capsa* "box"]

chas·er \ˈchā-sər\ *n* **1** : one that chases **2** : a mild drink (as water or beer) taken after hard liquor

Chasid *or* **Chassid** *variant of* HASID

chasm \ˈkaz-əm\ *n* **1** : a deep cleft in the earth **2** : a marked division, separation, or difference [Latin *chasma,* from Greek]

chas·seur \sha-ˈsər\ *n* : one of a body of light cavalry or infantry trained for rapid maneuvering [French, from Medieval French *chacer* "to chase"]

chas·sis \ˈshas-ē, ˈchas-ē\ *n, pl* **chas·sis** \-ēz\ : a supporting framework (as that bearing the body of an automobile or airplane or the parts of a radio or television receiving set) [French *châssis,* derived from Latin *capsa* "box"]

chaste \ˈchāst\ *adj* **1 a** : innocent of unlawful sexual intercourse **b** : CELIBATE **2** : pure in thought and act : MODEST **3** : severely simple in design and expression ⟨a *chaste* meal⟩ ⟨*chaste* writing⟩ [Medieval French, from Latin *castus* "pure, chaste"] — **chaste·ly** *adv* — **chaste·ness** \ˈchās-nəs, ˈchāst-\ *n*

synonyms CHASTE, PURE, MODEST mean free from all taint of what is lewd or salacious. CHASTE implies a refraining from acts, thoughts, or desires that are not virginal or not sanctioned by marriage vows ⟨a *chaste* relationship⟩. PURE implies innocence and absence of temptation rather than control of one's impulses ⟨*pure* of heart⟩. MODEST applies especially to behavior and dress as outward signs of inner chastity or purity ⟨a *modest* swimsuit⟩.

chas·ten \ˈchās-n\ *vt* **chas·tened; chas·ten·ing** \ˈchās-ning, -n-ing\ **1 :** to correct by punishment or suffering : DISCIPLINE **2 :** to remove excess, pretense, or falsity from : REFINE [alteration of obsolete *chaste* "to chasten," from Medieval French *chastier,* from Latin *castigare,* from *castus* "pure, chaste"]

chas·tise \chas-ˈtīz\ *vt* **1 :** to inflict punishment on (as by whipping) **2 :** to criticize harshly [Middle English *chastisen,* alteration of *chasten*] ***synonyms*** see PUNISH — **chas·tise·ment** \chas-ˈtīz-mənt, ˈchas-təz-\ *n* — **chas·tis·er** \chas-ˈtī-zər\ *n*

chas·ti·ty \ˈchas-tət-ē\ *n* **:** the quality or state of being chaste; *esp* **:** personal purity and modesty

cha·su·ble \ˈchazh-ə-bəl, ˈchaz-ə-, ˈchas-ə-\ *n* **:** a sleeveless outer vestment worn by the officiating priest at mass [Medieval French, from Late Latin *casubla* "hooded garment"]

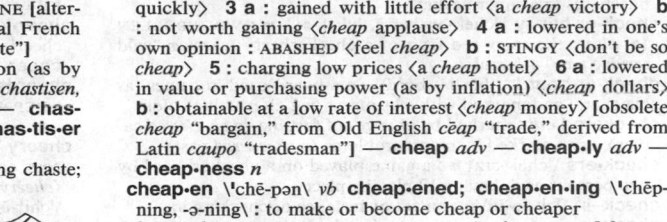

chasuble

1chat \ˈchat\ *vi* **chat·ted; chat·ting** **1 :** CHATTER 2 **2 :** to talk in a light, informal, or familiar manner **3 :** to take part in an online discussion in a chat room [Middle English *chatten,* short for *chatteren* "to chatter"]

2chat *n* **1 a :** light familiar talk **b :** an informal conversation **2 :** a talk held over the Internet by people using a chat room **3 :** any of several songbirds with a chattering call

châ·teau \sha-ˈtō\ *n, pl* **châ·teaus** \-ˈtōz\ *or* **châ·teaux** \-ˈtō, -ˈtōz\ **1 :** a feudal castle in France **2 :** a large country house **3 :** a French vineyard estate [French, from Medieval French *chastel,* from Latin *castellum* "fortress"]

chat·e·laine \ˈshat-l-ˌān\ *n* **1 :** the mistress of a château or a household **2 :** an ornamental clasp or hook for a watch, purse, or bunch of keys [French]

chat room *n* **:** an online interactive discussion group on the Internet

chat·tel \ˈchat-l\ *n* **1 :** SLAVE 1, BONDMAN **2 :** an item of property (as animals, money, or goods) other than real estate [Medieval French *chatel, katil* "property," from Medieval Latin *capitale,* from Latin *capitalis,* literally, "of the head"]

chat·ter \ˈchat-ər\ *vb* **1 :** to utter rapidly succeeding sounds suggesting speech but lacking meaning ⟨squirrels *chattered* angrily⟩ **2 :** to speak idly, continually, or rapidly : JABBER **3 a :** to click repeatedly or uncontrollably ⟨*chattering* teeth⟩ **b :** to vibrate rapidly in cutting ⟨a *chattering* tool⟩ [Middle English *chatteren,* of imitative origin] — **chatter** *n* — **chat·ter·er** \ˈchat-ər-ər\ *n* — **chat·tery** \-ə-rē\ *adj*

chat·ter·box \ˈchat-ər-ˌbäks\ *n* **:** a person who talks a lot

chat·ty \ˈchat-ē\ *adj* **chat·ti·er; -est** **1 :** fond of chatting : TALKATIVE **2 :** having the style and manner of light informal conversation ⟨a *chatty* letter⟩ — **chat·ti·ly** \ˈchat-l-ē\ *adv* — **chat·ti·ness** \ˈchat-ē-nəs\ *n*

1chauf·feur \ˈshō-fər, shō-ˈ\ *n* **:** a person employed to drive a motor vehicle [French, literally, "stoker," from *chauffer* "to heat," derived from Latin *calefacere,* from *calēre* "to be warm" + *facere* "to make"]

Word History The French verb *chauffer* means "to heat," so the literal meaning of the noun *chauffeur* is "one that heats." *Chauffeur* is the French name for the stoker who heats a steam engine and keeps it going. In the early days of the automobile, the French gave the nickname *chauffeur* to motorists. Later, *chauffeur* came to be used especially for people hired to drive for others. This is the sense that was taken into English.

2chauffeur *vb* **1 :** to do the work of a chauffeur **2 :** to transport as or as if as a chauffeur ⟨*chauffeur* children to school⟩

chau·tau·qua \shə-ˈtò-kwə\ *n* **:** any of various traveling shows and local assemblies in the U.S. during the late 19th and early 20th centuries offering educational entertainment in the form of lectures, concerts, and plays [*Chautauqua* Lake, New York]

chau·vin·ism \ˈshō-və-ˌniz-əm\ *n* **1 :** excessive or blind patriotism or devotion to a group to which one belongs **2 :** an attitude of superiority toward members of the opposite sex; *also* **:** behavior expressive of such an attitude [French *chauvinisme,* from Nicolas *Chauvin,* character in a play noted for his excessive devotion to Napoléon and his regime] — **chau·vin·ist** \-və-nəst\ *n or adj* — **chau·vin·is·tic** \ˌshō-və-ˈnis-tik\ *adj* — **chau·vin·is·ti·cal·ly** \-ti-kə-lē, -klē\ *adv*

cheap \ˈchēp\ *adj* **1 :** of low cost or price ⟨a *cheap* watch⟩ **2 :** worth little : of inferior quality ⟨*cheap* material wears out quickly⟩ **3 a :** gained with little effort ⟨a *cheap* victory⟩ **b :** not worth gaining ⟨*cheap* applause⟩ **4 a :** lowered in one's own opinion : ABASHED ⟨feel *cheap*⟩ **b :** STINGY ⟨don't be so *cheap*⟩ **5 :** charging low prices ⟨a *cheap* hotel⟩ **6 a :** lowered in value or purchasing power (as by inflation) ⟨*cheap* dollars⟩ **b :** obtainable at a low rate of interest ⟨*cheap* money⟩ [obsolete *cheap* "bargain," from Old English *cēap* "trade," derived from Latin *caupo* "tradesman"] — **cheap** *adv* — **cheap·ly** *adv* — **cheap·ness** *n*

cheap·en \ˈchē-pən\ *vb* **cheap·ened; cheap·en·ing** \ˈchēp-ning, -ə-ning\ **:** to make or become cheap or cheaper

cheap·skate \-ˌskāt\ *n* **:** a mean or miserly person [*cheap* + *skate* "miserly person"]

1cheat \ˈchēt\ *n* **1 :** an act of cheating : DECEPTION, FRAUD **2 :** one that cheats : DECEIVER [earlier *cheat* "forfeited property," from Middle English *eschete* "escheat"]

2cheat *vb* **1 :** to rob by deceit or fraud ⟨*cheated* them out of a large sum⟩ **2 :** to influence or lead astray by deceit, trick, or artifice **3 :** to elude or thwart by or as if by outwitting ⟨*cheat* death⟩ **4 a :** to practice fraud or trickery **b :** to violate rules dishonestly ⟨*cheating* on the test⟩ **5 :** to be sexually unfaithful ⟨was *cheating* on his wife⟩

synonyms CHEAT, DEFRAUD, SWINDLE mean to get something from another by deception or dishonesty. CHEAT suggests using trickery that escapes observation ⟨*cheat* at cards⟩. DEFRAUD stresses depriving one of his or her rights and connotes deliberate lying or deception ⟨*defrauded* of her inheritance⟩. SWINDLE implies cheating usually on a large scale by abuse of trust ⟨*swindled* of their savings⟩.

cheat sheet *n* **1 :** a sheet containing information (as test answers) used secretly for cheating **2 :** written notes that can be referred to for help in understanding or remembering something complex

1check \ˈchek\ *n* **1 :** exposure of a chess king to an attack **2 a :** a stoppage of progress : ARREST, PAUSE **b :** the checking of an opposing player (as in ice hockey) **3 :** something that arrests, limits, or restrains : RESTRAINT **4 a :** a standard for testing and evaluation : CRITERION **b :** EXAMINATION 1 ⟨a quick *check* of the engine⟩ **c :** INSPECTION, INVESTIGATION ⟨a loyalty *check* on government employees⟩ **d :** the act of testing or verifying; *also* **:** the sample used for testing or verifying **5 :** an order directing a bank to pay out money in accordance with instructions written thereon **6 a :** a ticket or token that shows that the bearer has a claim to property ⟨a baggage *check*⟩ **b :** a slip indicating the amount due : BILL **7 a :** a pattern in squares that resembles a checkerboard **b :** a fabric with such a design **8 :** a mark ✔ placed beside an item to show it has been noted **9 :** CRACK, BREAK ⟨a *check* in wood or steel⟩ [Medieval French *eschec,* from Arabic *shāh,* from Persian, literally, "king"] — **in check :** under restraint or control

2check *vb* **1 :** to put (a chess king) in check **2 a :** to bring to a stop : BRAKE **b :** to halt through caution, uncertainty, or fear : STOP **3 a :** RESTRAIN 1b, CURB **b :** to legally block the progress of (as a hockey player) **4 a :** to make sure of the correctness or satisfactoriness of ⟨*checked* her facts⟩ **b :** to inspect, examine, or look at ⟨*checking* out new cars⟩ ⟨*checked* over the damage⟩ **c :** to mark printing or writing with a check to show that something has been specially noted ⟨*checked* off each item⟩ **5 :** to mark with squares or checks : CHECKER **6 :** to leave or accept for safekeeping in a checkroom or for shipment as baggage **7 :** to correspond point for point : TALLY **8 :** to develop small cracks — **check into** **1 :** to check in at ⟨*check into* a hotel⟩ **2 :** INVESTIGATE ⟨the police are *checking into* his alibi⟩ — **check up on :** INVESTIGATE

check·book \ˈchek-ˌbu̇k\ *n* **:** a book containing blank checks to be drawn on a bank

\ə\ **abut**	\au̇\ **out**	\i\ **tip**	\ȯ\ **saw**	\u̇\ **foot**
\ər\ **further**	\ch\ **chin**	\ī\ **life**	\ȯi\ **coin**	\y\ **yet**
\a\ **mat**	\e\ **pet**	\j\ **job**	\th\ **thin**	\yü\ **few**
\ā\ **take**	\ē\ **easy**	\ng\ **sing**	\th\ **this**	\yu̇\ **cure**
\ä\ **cot, cart**	\g\ **go**	\ō\ **bone**	\ü\ **food**	\zh\ **vision**

[1]**check·er** \'chek-ər\ *n* **1 :** a square or spot resembling the markings on a checkerboard **2 :** a playing piece used in checkers [Medieval French *checker, escheker* "chessboard," from *eschec* "check"]
[2]**checker** *vt* **check·ered; check·er·ing** \'chek-ring, -ə-ring\ **:** to mark with colored squares ⟨a *checkered* tablecloth⟩
[3]**checker** *n* **:** one that checks; *esp* **:** an employee who checks out purchases in a supermarket
check·er·ber·ry \'chek-ər-ˌber-ē, 'chek-ə-ˌ\ *n* **:** WINTERGREEN 1a; *also* **:** the spicy red fruit of a checkerberry [*checker* "wild service tree" + *berry*]
check·er·board \-ˌbōrd, -ˌbȯrd\ *n* **:** a board used in games (as checkers) and marked with 64 squares in 2 alternating colors
checkered *adj* **:** marked by changes of fortune ⟨a *checkered* career⟩; *esp* **:** marked by many problems ⟨a *checkered* past⟩
check·ers \'chek-ərz\ *n* **:** a game played on a checkerboard by two persons each having 12 playing pieces
check–in \'chek-ˌin\ *n* **:** an act or instance of checking in
check in *vb* **1 :** to register at a hotel **2 :** to report one's presence or arrival **3 :** to bring back **:** RETURN ⟨*checked in* the equipment⟩
check·ing account \'chek-ing-\ *n* **:** an account in a bank from which the depositor can draw money by writing checks — compare SAVINGS ACCOUNT
check·list \'chek-ˌlist\ *n* **:** a list of items that may easily be referred to (as for verifying or comparing)
[1]**check·mate** \'chek-ˌmāt\ *vt* **1 :** to arrest or frustrate completely **2 :** to check (a chess opponent's king) so that escape is impossible [Middle English, interjection announcing checkmate, from Medieval French *eschec mat,* from Arabic *shāh māt,* from Persian, literally, "the king is left unable to escape"]
[2]**checkmate** *n* **1 a :** the act of checkmating **b :** the situation of a checkmated king **2 :** a thorough defeat
check·off \'chek-ˌȯf\ *n* **:** an authorized practice of deducting union dues from a worker's paycheck by the employer
check·out \'chek-ˌau̇t\ *n* **1 :** the action or an instance of checking out **2 :** the time at which a lodger must leave a room (as in a hotel) **3 :** a counter or area in a store at which checking out is done
check out *vb* **1 :** to leave and pay for one's room (as at a hotel) **2 :** to satisfy requirements for taking away ⟨*check* a book *out* of the library⟩ **3 :** to total or have totaled the cost of purchases and receive or make payment for them
check·point \'chek-ˌpȯint\ *n* **:** a point at which a check is performed ⟨vehicles were inspected at various *checkpoints*⟩
check·rein \-ˌrān\ *n* **:** a short rein fastened so as to prevent a horse from lowering its head
check·room \-ˌrüm, -ˌru̇m\ *n* **:** a room at which baggage, parcels, or clothing can be left for safekeeping
checks and balances *n pl* **:** a system that allows each branch of a government to amend or veto acts of another branch so as to prevent any one branch from exerting too much power
check·up \'chek-ˌəp\ *n* **:** EXAMINATION; *esp* **:** a general physical examination
ched·dar \'ched-ər\ *n, often cap* **:** a hard pressed cheese of smooth texture [*Cheddar,* England]
cheek \'chēk\ *n* **1 :** the fleshy side of the face below the eye and above and to the side of the mouth **2 a :** something suggesting the human cheek in position or form **b :** a lateral part or side (as of a structure or opening) **3 :** saucy speech or behavior [Old English *cēace*]
cheek·bone \-'bōn, -ˌbōn\ *n* **:** the bone or the bony prominence below the eye
cheek by jowl *adv* **:** beside one another **:** in close proximity
cheek pouch *n* **:** an enlargement of the cheeks in some monkeys and rodents that resembles a sac and is used for holding food
cheek tooth *n* **:** MOLAR
cheeky \'chē-kē\ *adj* **cheek·i·er; -est :** IMPUDENT, SAUCY — **cheek·i·ness** *n*
cheep \'chēp\ *vb* **:** [1]PEEP 1 [imitative] — **cheep** *n*
[1]**cheer** \'chiər\ *n* **1 :** state of mind or heart **:** SPIRIT ⟨be of good *cheer*⟩ **2 :** GAIETY 2, ANIMATION **3 :** food and drink for or fit for a feast **4 :** something that gladdens ⟨words of *cheer*⟩ **5 :** a shout of applause or encouragement ⟨three *cheers* for our side⟩ [Middle English *chere* "face, cheer," from Medieval French, "face"]
[2]**cheer** *vb* **1 :** to give hope to or make happier **:** COMFORT ⟨*cheer* up a sick person⟩ **2 :** to urge on especially with shouts or cheers ⟨*cheer* one's team to victory⟩ **3 :** to shout with joy, approval, or enthusiasm ⟨the students *cheered* loudly⟩ **4 :** to grow or be cheerful **:** REJOICE ⟨*cheer* up—things will get better⟩
cheer·ful \'chiər-fəl\ *adj* **1 a :** full of good spirits **:** HAPPY **b :** WILLING 3 ⟨*cheerful* obedience⟩ **2 :** pleasantly bright **:** likely to dispel gloom or worry ⟨a sunny *cheerful* room⟩ — **cheer·ful·ly** \-fə-lē, -flē\ *adv* — **cheer·ful·ness** \-fəl-nəs\ *n*
cheer·lead·er \'chiər-ˌlēd-ər\ *n* **:** a person who directs organized cheering especially at a sports event — **cheer·lead** \-ˌlēd\ *vt* — **cheer·lead·ing** \-ˌlēd-ing\ *n*
cheer·less \'chiər-ləs\ *adj* **:** lacking in warmth of kindliness **:** DEPRESSING, GLOOMY ⟨a *cheerless* room⟩ — **cheer·less·ly** *adv* — **cheer·less·ness** *n*
cheery \'chiər-ē\ *adj* **cheer·i·er; -est 1 :** marked by cheerfulness or good spirits **2 :** causing or suggesting cheerfulness ⟨*cheery* music⟩ — **cheer·i·ly** \'chir-ə-lē\ *adv* — **cheer·i·ness** \'chir-ē-nəs\ *n*
cheese \'chēz\ *n* **:** a food made from milk especially by separating out the curd and molding or pressing and usually ripening it [Old English *cēse,* derived from Latin *caseus*]
cheese·bur·ger \-ˌbər-gər\ *n* **:** a hamburger with a slice of cheese
cheese·cake \-ˌkāk\ *n* **1 :** a cake made by baking a mixture of cream cheese or cottage cheese, eggs, and sugar in a pastry shell or a mold **2 :** photographs of attractive usually scantily clothed young women
cheese·cloth \-ˌklȯth\ *n* **:** a thin loose-woven cotton cloth [from its use in making cheese]
cheese·steak \'chēz-ˌstāk\ *n* **:** a sandwich consisting of thinly sliced beef topped with melted cheese and usually fried onions or peppers
cheesy \'chē-zē\ *adj* **1 a :** resembling or suggesting cheese (as in texture or odor) **b :** containing cheese **2 :** SHABBY, CHEAP ⟨a *cheesy* movie⟩ — **chees·i·ness** *n*
chee·tah \'chēt-ə\ *n* **:** a long-legged spotted African and formerly Asian cat about the size of a small leopard that is the fastest of all land animals [Hindi *cītā,* from Sanskrit *citraka* "leopard"]
chef \'shef\ *n* **:** COOK; *esp* **:** a head cook [French, short for *chef de cuisine* "head of the kitchen"]
chef d'oeu·vre \shā-'dœvr\ *n, pl* **chefs d'oeuvre** *same*\ **:** a masterpiece especially in art or literature [French *chef-d'oeuvre,* literally, "leading work"]
che·la \'kē-lə\ *n, pl* **che·lae** \-ˌlē\ **:** a pincerlike organ or claw on a limb of a crustacean or arachnid [Greek *chēlē* "claw"]

chela

che·late \'kē-ˌlāt\ *adj* **:** resembling or having chelae
che·lic·era \ki-'lis-ə-rə\ *n, pl* **-er·as** *or* **-er·ae** \-ˌrē\ **:** either of the front pair of appendages of an arachnid often specialized as fangs [New Latin, from French *chélicère,* from Greek *chēlē* "claw" + *keras* "horn"] — **che·lic·er·al** \-ə-rəl\ *adj*
che·li·ped \'kē-lə-ˌped\ *n* **:** either of the pair of legs of a crustacean that bear chelae [Greek *chēlē* "claw" + Latin *ped-, pes* "foot"]
che·lo·ni·an \ki-'lō-nē-ən\ *adj* **:** of, relating to, or being a turtle [Greek *chelōnē* "tortoise"] — **chelonian** *n*
chem- *or* **chemo-** *also* **chemi-** *combining form* **:** chemical **:** chemistry ⟨*chemo*reception⟩
[1]**chem·i·cal** \'kem-i-kəl\ *adj* **1 :** of, relating to, used in, or produced by chemistry or the phenomena of chemistry ⟨*chemical* reactions⟩ **2 :** acting or operated or produced by chemicals ⟨a *chemical* fire extinguisher⟩ [New Latin *chimicus* "alchemist," from Medieval Latin *alchimicus,* from *alchymia* "alchemy"] — **chem·i·cal·ly** \-i-kə-lē, -klē\ *adv*
[2]**chemical** *n* **:** a substance (as an element or compound) obtained by a chemical process or producing a chemical effect
chemical engineering *n* **:** engineering dealing with the industrial application of chemistry
chemical warfare *n* **:** tactical warfare using smoke-producing substances or burning, poisonous, or smothering gases
che·mise \shə-'mēz, -'mēs\ *n* **1 :** a woman's one-piece undergarment **2 :** a loose straight-hanging dress [Medieval French, "shirt," from Late Latin *camisia*]
chem·ist \'kem-əst\ *n* **1 :** one trained or working in chemistry **2** *British* **:** PHARMACIST [New Latin *chimista* "alchemist," from Medieval Latin *alchimista*]

chem·is·try \ˈkem-ə-strē\ *n* **1 :** a science that deals with the composition, structure, and properties of substances and with the changes that they undergo **2 :** chemical composition, properties, or processes ‹the *chemistry* of iron› ‹the *chemistry* of blood›

che·mo·re·cep·tion \ˌkē-mō-ri-ˈsep-shən *also* ˌkem-ō-\ *n* **:** the physiological reception of chemical stimuli — **che·mo·re·cep·tor** \-ˈsep-tər\ *n*

che·mo·syn·the·sis \-ˈsin-thə-səs, -ˈsint-\ *n* **:** formation of organic compounds (as in living cells) using energy derived from chemical reactions — **che·mo·syn·thet·ic** \-sin-ˈthet-ik\ *adj*

che·mo·tax·is \-ˈtak-səs\ *n* **:** orientation or movement of an organism or cell in relation to chemical agents — **che·mo·tac·tic** \-ˈtak-tik\ *adj*

che·mo·ther·a·peu·tic \-ˌther-ə-ˈpyüt-ik\ *adj* **:** of or relating to chemotherapy — **che·mo·ther·a·peu·ti·cal·ly** \-ˈpyüt-i-kə-lē, -klē\ *adv*

che·mo·ther·a·py \-ˈther-ə-pē\ *n* **:** the use of chemical agents in the treatment or control of disease (as cancer)

che·mot·ro·pism \ki-ˈmä-trə-ˌpiz-əm, ke-\ *n* **:** orientation of cells or organisms in relation to chemical stimuli

che·nille \shə-ˈnēl\ *n* **:** a fabric with a deep fuzzy pile often used for bedspreads and rugs [French, literally, "caterpillar," from Latin *canicula* "little dog," from *canis* "dog"]

cheque \ˈchek\ *chiefly British variant of* CHECK 5

cher·ish \ˈcher-ish\ *vt* **1 a :** to hold dear **:** feel or show affection for ‹*cherished* their pet› **b :** to keep with care and affection ‹*cherish* your freedom› **2 :** to harbor in the mind ‹*cherish* a hope› [Medieval French *cheriss-,* stem of *cherir* "to cherish," from *cher* "dear," from Latin *carus*]

cher·no·zem \ˌchər-nə-ˈzhȯm, -ˈzem\ *n* **:** a dark-colored zonal soil with a deep rich humus layer found in temperate to cool climates of rather low humidity [Russian, from *chërnyĭ* "black" + *zemlya* "earth"]

Cher·o·kee \ˈcher-ə-ˌkē\ *n* **:** a member of an American Indian people originally of Tennessee and the Carolinas

Cherokee rose *n* **:** a Chinese climbing rose with fragrant white blossoms that is naturalized in the southern U.S.

cher·ry \ˈcher-ē\ *n, pl* **cherries 1 a :** any of numerous trees and shrubs related to the roses that have rather small pale yellow to deep blackish red smooth-skinned fruits and include several grown for their edible fruits or showy flowers **b :** the fruit of a cherry **c :** the reddish brown wood of a cherry **2 :** a medium red color [Medieval French *cherise* (understood as plural), from Late Latin *ceresia,* from Latin *cerasus* "cherry tree," from Greek *kerasos*] — **cherry** *adj*

chert \ˈchərt, ˈchat\ *n* **:** a rock resembling flint and consisting essentially of fibrous chalcedony and smaller amounts of very fine crystalline quartz and amorphous silica [origin unknown]

cherty \ˈchərt-ē, ˈchat-\ *adj* **chert·i·er; chert·i·est 1 :** resembling flint **2 :** full of flint ‹a *cherty* soil›

cher·ub \ˈcher-əb\ *n* **1** *pl* **cher·u·bim** \ˈcher-yə-ˌbim, ˈker-, -ə-\ **:** an angel of high rank **2** *pl* **cherubs a :** a beautiful usually winged child in fine art **b :** a chubby rosy child [Latin, from Greek *cheroub,* from Hebrew *kĕrūbh*]

cher·vil \ˈchər-vəl\ *n* **:** an aromatic herb related to the carrot with finely divided leaves often used in soups and salads [Old English *cerfille,* derived from Latin *caerefolium*]

Ches·a·peake Bay retriever \ˈches-ˌpēk-ˈbā-, -ə-ˌpēk-\ *n* **:** any of a breed of powerful sporting dogs developed in Maryland and having a dense oily water-shedding brown coat

Chesh·ire cat \ˈchesh-ər-\ *n* **:** a cat with a broad grin in Lewis Carroll's *Alice's Adventures in Wonderland* [*Cheshire,* England]

Cheshire cheese *n* **:** a cheese similar to cheddar made chiefly in Cheshire, England

chess \ˈches\ *n* **:** a game of strategy for 2 players each of whom plays with 16 pieces on a checkerboard [Medieval French *esches,* plural of *eschec* "check"]

chess·board \-ˌbōrd, -ˌbȯrd\ *n* **:** a checkerboard used in the game of chess

chess·man \-ˌman, -mən\ *n* **:** one of the 32 pieces used in chess

chest \ˈchest\ *n* **1 :** a container for storage or shipping; *esp* **:** a box with a lid **2 :** a public fund collected for some purpose **3 :** the part of the body enclosed by the ribs and sternum [Old English *cest,* from Latin *cista* "box, basket," from Greek *kistē* "basket, hamper"] — **chest·ed** \ˈches-təd\ *adj*

ches·ter·field \ˈches-tər-ˌfēld\ *n* **:** an overcoat with a velvet collar [from a 19th century Earl of *Chesterfield*]

Ches·ter White \ˈches-tər-\ *n* **:** any of a breed of large white swine [*Chester* County, Pennsylvania]

[1]**chest·nut** \ˈches-ˌnət, -nət\ *n* **1 a :** an edible nut from several trees or shrubs related to the beeches **b :** a tree or shrub bearing chestnuts; *esp* **:** an American tree that was formerly common and grew to large size in eastern forests but has been largely wiped out by the chestnut blight and now grows only to the size of a shrub or sapling **c :** the wood of a chestnut tree **2 :** HORSE CHESTNUT **3 :** a horse with the body colored pure or reddish brown and the mane, tail, and points of the same or a lighter shade — compare [2]BAY 1, SORREL **4 :** a callosity on the inner side of the leg of the horse **5 :** an old joke or story [Medieval French *chastein, chestain* "chestnut tree," from Latin *castanea,* from Greek *kastanea*]

[2]**chestnut** *adj* **:** of a grayish to reddish brown color

chestnut blight *n* **:** a destructive disease of the American chestnut caused by a fungus

chest of drawers : a piece of furniture containing a set of drawers (as for holding clothing)

che·val–de–frise \shə-ˌval-də-ˈfrēz\ *n, pl* **che·vaux–de–frise** \shə-ˌvōd-ə-\ **:** a defense consisting usually of a timber or barrel covered with projecting spikes and often strung with barbed wire [French, literally, "horse from Friesland"]

che·val glass \shə-ˈval-\ *n* **:** a full-length mirror that may be tilted in a frame [French *cheval* "horse, support"]

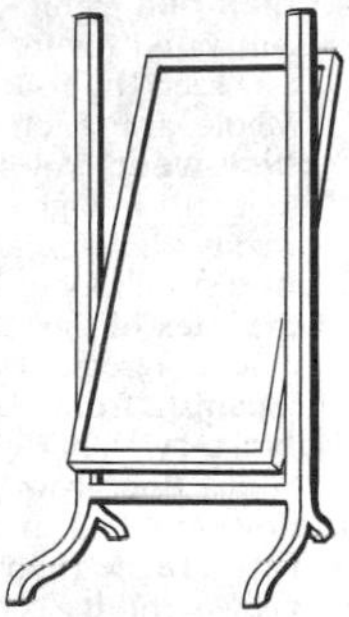
cheval glass

chev·a·lier \ˌshev-ə-ˈliər, *especially for 2 also* shə-ˈval-ˌyā\ *n* **1 :** CAVALIER 2 **2 :** a member of any of various orders of knighthood or of merit (as the French Legion of Honor) [Medieval French, from Late Latin *caballarius* "horseman"]

chev·i·ot \ˈshev-ē-ət, ˈchev-\ *n* **1 :** any of a breed of hardy hornless British sheep **2 a :** a heavy napped woolen or worsted fabric **b :** a sturdy cotton shirting [*Cheviot* hills, England and Scotland]

chev·ron \ˈshev-rən\ *n* **1 :** a figure resembling an upside-down V **2 :** a sleeve badge usually indicating rank or service (as in the armed forces) [Medieval French, "rafter, chevron"]

[1]**chew** \ˈchü\ *vb* **:** to crush or grind with the teeth [Old English *cēowan*] — **chew·able** \-ə-bəl\ *adj* — **chew·er** *n* — **chewy** \ˈchü-ē\ *adj* — **chew on :** to think about **:** PONDER ‹*chewing on* the new plans›

[2]**chew** *n* **1 :** the act of chewing **2 :** something for chewing

chewing gum *n* **:** gum usually of sweetened and flavored chicle prepared for chewing

che·wink \chi-ˈwingk\ *n* **:** TOWHEE [imitative]

chew out *vt* **:** REPRIMAND

chew over *vt* **:** to think about reflectively

Chey·enne \shī-ˈan, -ˈen\ *n, pl* **Cheyenne** *or* **Cheyennes :** a member of an American Indian people of the western plains of the U.S.

chi \ˈkī\ *n* **:** the 22nd letter of the Greek alphabet — X or χ

Chi·an·ti \kē-ˈänt-ē, -ˈant-\ *n* **:** a dry usually red table wine [*Chianti* region, Italy]

chiar·oscu·ro \kē-ˌär-ə-ˈskůr-ō, -ˈskyůr-\ *n* **1 :** pictorial representation in terms of light and shade without regard to color **2 :** the arrangement or treatment of light and dark parts in a pictorial work of art [Italian, from *chiaro* "clear, light" + *oscuro* "obscure, dark"] — **chiar·oscu·rist** \-ˈskůr-əst, -ˈskyůr-\ *n*

chi·as·mus \kī-ˈaz-məs\ *n* **:** reversal in word order between the elements of parallel phrases (as in *we must not live to eat, but eat to live*) [Greek *chiasmos,* from *chiazein* "to mark with a chi"]

Chib·cha \ˈchib-ˌchä\ *n, pl* **Chibcha** *or* **Chibchas :** a member of an Indian people of central Colombia [Spanish]

[1]**chic** \ˈshēk\ *n* **:** STYLE 5 [French]

[2]**chic** *adj* **chic·er; chic·est :** cleverly stylish **:** SMART

chi·cane \shik-ˈān, chik-\ *n* **:** CHICANERY [French]

chi·ca·nery \-ˈān-rē, -ə-rē\ *n, pl* **-ner·ies :** artful trickery

Chi·ca·no \chi-ˈkän-ō, shi-\ *n, pl* **-nos :** an American and especially a man or boy of Mexican descent [Mexican Spanish, alteration of Spanish *mexicano* "Mexican"] — **Chicano** *adj*

chi·chi \ˈshē-ˌshē, ˈchē-ˌchē\ *adj* **1 :** SHOWY **2 :** ARTY ⟨*a chichi* film⟩ **3 :** CHIC ⟨*chichi* nightclubs⟩ [French] — **chichi** *n*

chick \ˈchik\ *n* **1 a :** CHICKEN; *esp* **:** one newly hatched **b :** the young of any bird **2** *slang* **:** GIRL, WOMAN

chick·a·dee \ˈchik-əd-ē\ *n* **:** any of several small North American birds related to the titmice and usually having the crown of the head darker than the body [imitative]

chick·a·ree \ˈchik-ə-ˌrē\ *n* **:** RED SQUIRREL [imitative]

Chick·a·saw \ˈchik-ə-ˌsȯ\ *n, pl* **Chickasaw** *or* **Chickasaws :** a member of an American Indian people of Mississippi and Alabama

chick·en \ˈchik-ən\ *n* **1 :** the common domestic fowl especially when young; *also* **:** its flesh used as food **2 :** any of various birds or their young **3 :** COWARD [Old English *cicen* "young chicken"]

chicken hawk *n* **:** a hawk that preys or is said to prey on chickens

chick·en·heart·ed \ˌchik-ən-ˈhärt-əd\ *adj* **:** TIMID, COWARDLY

chicken pox *n* **:** a contagious virus disease especially of children marked by low fever and watery blisters on the skin

chicken snake *n* **:** any of several rat snakes

chick·pea \ˈchik-ˌpē\ *n* **:** an Asian herb of the legume family cultivated for its short pods with one or two edible seeds; *also* **:** its seed [by folk etymology from Middle English *chiche,* from Medieval French, from Latin *cicer*]

chick·weed \ˈchik-ˌwēd\ *n* **:** any of several low-growing small-leaved weedy plants related to the pinks

chickweed

chi·cle \ˈchik-əl, -lē\ *n* **:** a gum from the latex of the sapodilla used as the chief ingredient of chewing gum [Spanish, from Nahuatl *tzictli*]

chic·o·ry \ˈchik-rē, -ə-rē\ *n, pl* **-ries :** a thick-rooted usually blue-flowered European perennial herb related to the daisies and grown for its roots and as a salad plant; *also* **:** its dried ground roasted root used to flavor or adulterate coffee [Medieval French *cicoree,* from Latin *cichoreum,* from Greek *kichoreia*]

chide \ˈchīd\ *vb* **chid** \ˈchid\ *or* **chid·ed** \ˈchīd-əd\; **chid** *or* **chid·den** \ˈchid-n\ *or* **chided; chid·ing** \ˈchīd-ing\ **:** to speak disapprovingly to **:** SCOLD [Old English *cīdan* "to quarrel, chide," from *cīd* "strife"]

[1]chief \ˈchēf\ *adj* **1 :** highest in rank, office, or authority **2 :** of greatest importance, significance, or influence

[2]chief *n* **1 :** the upper part of a heraldic field **2 :** the head of a group or organization **:** LEADER ⟨*chief* of police⟩ **3 :** the principal part [Medieval French, "head, chief," from Latin *caput* "head"] — **in chief :** in the chief position or place — often used in titles ⟨editor *in chief*⟩

chief executive *n* **:** a principal officer: as **a :** the president of a republic **b :** the governor of a state **c :** CEO

chief justice *n* **:** the principal judge of a court of justice

chief·ly \ˈchē-flē\ *adv* **1 :** most importantly **:** PRINCIPALLY **2 :** for the most part **:** MOSTLY

chief master sergeant *n* **:** an enlisted rank in the air force above senior master sergeant

chief master sergeant of the air force : the ranking noncommissioned officer in the air force serving as advisor to the chief of staff

chief of staff 1 : the ranking officer of a military staff and principal adviser to the commander **2 :** the ranking office of the army or air force

chief of state : the formal head of a national state as distinguished from the head of the government

chief petty officer *n* **:** an enlisted rank in the navy and coast guard above petty officer first class and below senior chief petty officer

chief·tain \ˈchēf-tən\ *n* **:** a chief especially of a band, tribe, or clan [Medieval French *chevetain,* from Late Latin *capitaneus* "chief"] — **chief·tain·cy** \-sē\ *n* — **chief·tain·ship** \-ˌship\ *n*

chief warrant officer *n* **:** a warrant officer of senior rank in the armed forces

[1]chif·fon \shif-ˈän, ˈshif-ˌ\ *n* **:** a sheer usually silk fabric [French, literally, "rag," from Middle French *chipe* "old rag," from Middle English *chip* "chip"]

[2]chiffon *adj* **:** having a light soft texture ⟨a *chiffon* cake⟩

chif·fo·nier \ˌshif-ə-ˈniər\ *n* **:** a high narrow chest of drawers often with a mirror [French *chiffonnier,* from *chiffon*]

chig·ger \ˈchig-ər, ˈjig-\ *n* **:** a 6-legged mite larva that feeds on skin cells and causes itchy red welts [perhaps of African origin]

chi·gnon \ˈshēn-ˌyän\ *n* **:** a knot of hair worn at the back of the head [French]

Chi·hua·hua \chə-ˈwä-ˌwä, shə-, -wə\ *n* **:** any of a breed of very small large-eared dogs of Mexican origin [*Chihuahua,* Mexico]

Chihuahua

chil·blain \ˈchil-ˌblān\ *n* **:** an inflammatory swelling or sore caused by exposure (as of the feet or hands) to cold

child \ˈchīld\ *n, pl* **chil·dren** \ˈchil-drən, -dərn\ **1 :** an unborn or recently born person **2 a :** a young person especially between infancy and youth **b :** a childlike or childish person **c :** a person not yet of legal age **3** *usually* **childe** \ˈchīld\ *archaic* **:** a youth of noble birth **4 a :** a son or daughter of human parents **b :** DESCENDANT 1 **5 :** one strongly influenced by another or by a place or state of affairs ⟨a *child* of the times⟩ [Old English *cild*] — **child·less** \ˈchīl-ləs, -dləs\ *adj* — **with child :** PREGNANT

child·bear·ing \ˈchīl-ˌbar-ing, ˈchīld-, -ˌber-\ *adj* **:** of or relating to the process of conceiving, being pregnant with, and giving birth to children — **childbearing** *n*

child·bed fever \ˈchīl-ˌbed-, ˈchīld-\ *n* **:** PUERPERAL FEVER

child·birth \ˈchīl-ˌbərth, ˈchīld-\ *n* **:** the act or process of giving birth to offspring — called also *parturition*

child·hood \ˈchīld-ˌhu̇d\ *n* **:** the state or time of being a child

child·ish \ˈchīl-dish\ *adj* **1 :** of, resembling, or suitable to a child ⟨*childish* games⟩ **2 :** marked by the less pleasing qualities (as silliness) often felt to be characteristic of the young — **child·ish·ly** *adv* — **child·ish·ness** *n*

child·like \ˈchīl-ˌlīk, -ˌdlīk\ *adj* **1 :** resembling, suggesting, or appropriate to a child or childhood **2 :** marked by the more pleasing qualities (as simplicity, innocence, and trustfulness) often felt to be characteristic of the young — **child·like·ness** *n*

child's play *n* **1 :** an extremely simple task **2 :** something that is unimportant

[1]child·proof \ˈchīld-ˌprüf\ *adj* **1 :** made to prevent tampering or opening by children ⟨a *childproof* bottle⟩ **2 :** made safe for children (as by safe storage of dangerous materials) ⟨a *childproof* home⟩

[2]childproof *vt* **:** to make childproof

child support *n* **:** payment for the support of the children of divorced or separated parents while the children are minors or as otherwise legally required — compare *alimony*

chile re·lle·no \-rā-ˈyā-nō\ *n, pl* **chiles re·lle·nos** *also* **chile rellenos :** a stuffed chili pepper that usually contains cheese or meat and is fried or grilled [Spanish, "stuffed chili pepper"]

Chile saltpeter \ˈchil-ē-\ *n* **:** sodium nitrate especially occurring naturally [*Chile,* South America]

chili *also* **chile** *or* **chil·li** \ˈchil-ē\ *n, pl* **chil·ies** *also* **chil·es** *or* **chilis** *or* **chil·lies 1 :** any of various hot peppers noted for their pungency — called also *chili pepper* **2 :** CHILI CON CARNE [Spanish *chile,* from Nahuatl *chīlli*]

chili con car·ne \ˌchil-ē-ˌkän-ˈkär-nē, -ē-kən-\ *n* **:** a stew of ground beef, hot peppers or chili powder, and usually beans [Spanish *chile con carne* "chili with meat"]

chili dog *n* **:** a hot dog topped with chili

chili powder *n* **:** a seasoning made of ground hot peppers and other spices

chili sauce *n* **:** a spiced tomato sauce usually made with red and green peppers

[1]chill \ˈchil\ *n* **1 :** a sensation of cold accompanied by shivering **2 :** a moderate but unpleasant degree of cold **3 :** a depressing effect on the feelings [Old English *ciele*]

[2]chill *adj* **1 a :** fairly cold ⟨a *chill* night⟩ **b :** COLD 1, RAW ⟨a *chill* wind⟩ **2 :** affected by cold **3 :** cool in manner **:** DISTANT ⟨a *chill* greeting⟩ — **chill·ness** *n*

[3]chill *vb* **1 :** to make or become cold or chilly **2 :** to make cool especially without freezing **3 :** to affect as if with cold ‹we were *chilled* by the ghost story› **4 :** CHILL OUT — **chill•er** *n*

chill•ing \ˈchil-iŋ\ *adj* **:** gravely disturbing or frightening ‹a *chilling* case of abuse› — **chill•ing•ly** *adv*

chill out *vi, slang* **:** to calm down **:** go easy — often used in the imperative

chilly \ˈchil-ē\ *adj* **chill•i•er; -est** **1 :** noticeably cold **2 :** unpleasantly affected by cold **3 :** lacking warmth **:** not friendly — **chill•i•ly** \ˈchil-ə-lē\ *adv* — **chill•i•ness** \ˈchil-ē-nəs\ *n*

[1]chime \ˈchīm\ *n* **1 :** a musically tuned set of bells **2 a :** the sound of a set of bells — usually used in plural **b :** a musical sound suggesting that of bells [Middle English, "cymbal," from Medieval French *chimbe,* from Latin *cymbalum*]

[2]chime *vb* **1 a :** to make a musical and usually harmonious sound **b :** to make the sounds of a chime **c :** to cause to chime **2 :** to be or act in accord **3 :** to call or indicate by chiming ‹a clock *chiming* midnight› **4 :** to utter repetitively — **chim•er** *n*

chime in *vb* **:** to break into or join in a conversation

chi•me•ra \kī-ˈmir-ə, kə-\ *n* **1** *cap* **:** a fire-breathing she-monster in Greek mythology usually with a lion's head, a goat's body, and a serpent's tail **2 :** an often grotesque creation of the imagination **3 :** an individual, organ, or part with tissues of diverse genetic constitution [Latin *chimaera,* from Greek *chimaira* "she-goat, chimera"]

chi•mer•i•cal \kī-ˈmer-i-kəl, kə-, -ˈmir-\ *also* **chi•mer•ic** \-ik\ *adj* **1 :** existing only in the imagination **2 :** inclined to fantastic ideas or schemes — **chi•mer•i•cal•ly** \-i-kə-lē, -klē\ *adv*

chi•mi•chan•ga \ˌchim-ē-ˈchäŋ-gə\ *n* **:** a tortilla wrapped around a filling (as of meat) and deep-fried [Mexican Spanish, "trinket"]

chim•ney \ˈchim-nē\ *n, pl* **chimneys** **1 :** a passage for smoke; *esp* **:** an upright structure (as of brick or stone) extending above the roof of a building **2 :** a glass tube around a lamp flame **3 :** something resembling a chimney [Medieval French *chiminee,* from Late Latin *caminata,* from Latin *caminus* "furnace, fireplace," from Greek *kaminos*]

chim•ney•piece \ˈchim-nē-ˌpēs\ *n* **:** a decorative construction over and around a fireplace that includes the mantel

chimney pot *n* **:** a usually earthenware pipe at the top of a chimney to increase draft and carry off smoke

chimney sweep *n* **:** a person who cleans soot from chimneys

chimney swift *n* **:** a small sooty-gray bird with long narrow wings that often builds its nest inside an unused chimney

chimp \ˈchimp, ˈshimp\ *n* **:** CHIMPANZEE

chim•pan•zee \ˌchim-ˌpan-ˈzē, ˌshim-; chim-ˈpan-zē, shim-\ *n* **:** an African anthropoid ape that is smaller and more arboreal than the gorilla [Kongo (Bantu language of west central Africa) *chimpenzi*]

[1]chin \ˈchin\ *n* **:** the lower portion of the face lying below the lower lip and including the prominence of the lower jaw [Old English *cinn*]

[2]chin *vb* **chinned; chin•ning** **1 :** to raise (oneself) while hanging by the hands until the chin is level with the support **2** *slang* **:** to talk idly **:** CHATTER

chi•na \ˈchī-nə\ *n* **1 :** PORCELAIN **2 :** earthenware or porcelain tableware [Persian *chīnī* "Chinese porcelain"]

chi•na•ber•ry \ˈchī-nə-ˌber-ē\ *n* **:** a small Asian tree related to the mahoganies that is planted in the southern U.S. for shade or ornament

china clay *n* **:** KAOLIN

Chi•na•man \ˈchī-nə-mən\ *n, often offensive* **:** CHINESE 1

Chi•na•town \-ˌtau̇n\ *n* **:** the Chinese quarter of a city

China tree *n* **:** CHINABERRY

chi•na•ware \ˈchī-nə-ˌwaər, -ˌweər\ *n* **:** tableware made of china

chinch \ˈchinch\ *n* **:** BEDBUG [Spanish *chinche,* from Latin *cimex*]

chinch bug *n* **:** a small black-and-white bug that is very destructive to cereal grasses

chin•chil•la \chin-ˈchil-ə\ *n* **1 :** a South American rodent the size of a large squirrel widely bred in captivity for its very soft fur of a pearly gray color; *also* **:** its fur **2 :** a heavy twilled woolen coating [Spanish]

chine \ˈchīn\ *n* **1 :** BACKBONE, SPINE; *also* **:** a cut of meat including the backbone or part of it and the surrounding flesh **2 :** CREST 2, RIDGE **3 :** the intersection of the bottom and sides of a boat [Medieval French *eschine,* of Germanic origin]

Chi•nese \chī-ˈnēz, -ˈnēs\ *n, pl* **Chinese** **1 a :** a native or inhabitant of China **b :** a person of Chinese descent **2 a :** a group of related languages used by the people of China that are often mutually unintelligible in their spoken form but share a single system of writing **b :** MANDARIN 2 — **Chinese** *adj*

Chinese cabbage *n* **:** either of two Asian plants related to the cabbage and widely used as greens

Chinese checkers *n* **:** a game in which each player seeks to be the first to transfer a set of marbles from a home point to the opposite point of a 6-pointed star by means of single moves and jumps

Chinese lantern *n* **:** a collapsible lantern of thin colored paper

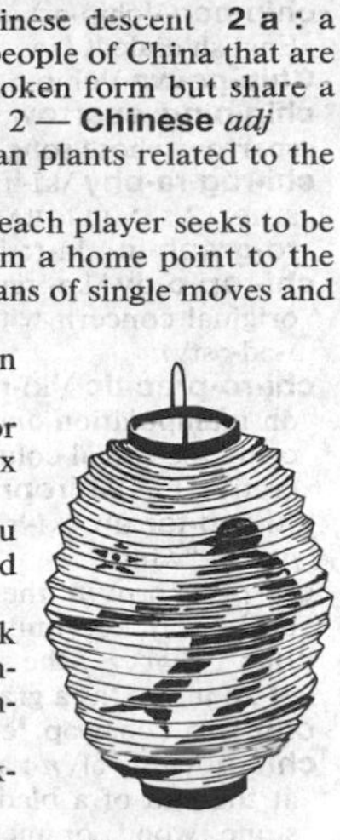

Chinese lantern

Chinese puzzle *n* **1 :** an elaborate or clever puzzle **2 :** something complex and hard to solve

Ching *or* **Ch'ing** \ˈchiŋ\ *n* **:** a Manchu dynasty in China dated 1644–1912 and the last imperial dynasty

[1]chink \ˈchiŋk\ *n* **:** a narrow slit or crack (as in a wall) [probably from Middle English *chin* "crack, fissure," from Old English *cine*]

[2]chink *vt* **:** to fill the chinks of (as by caulking)

[3]chink *n* **:** a short sharp sound [imitative]

[4]chink *vb* **:** to make or cause to make a short sharp sound

chi•no \ˈchē-nō, ˈshē-\ *n, pl* **chinos** **1 :** a usually khaki cotton twill fabric **2** *pl* **:** an article of clothing (as pants) made of chino [origin unknown]

Chi•nook \shə-ˈnu̇k, chə-\ *n, pl* **Chinook** *or* **Chinooks** **1 :** a member of an American Indian people of the north shore of the Columbia River at its mouth **2** *not cap* **a :** a warm moist southwest wind of the coast from Oregon northward **b :** a warm dry wind that descends the eastern slopes of the Rocky Mountains

Chinook salmon *n* **:** a large commercially important salmon of the northern Pacific Ocean with red flesh

chin•qua•pin \ˈchiŋ-ki-ˌpin\ *n* **:** a dwarf chestnut of the U.S.; *also* **:** its edible nut [Virginia Algonquian *chechinquamin*]

chintz \ˈchins\ *n* **1 :** a printed calico from India **2 :** a usually glazed printed cotton fabric [earlier *chints,* plural of *chint,* from Hindi *chı̃ṭ*]

chintzy \ˈchin-sē\ *adj* **chintz•i•er; -est** **1 :** decorated with or as if with chintz **2 a :** GAUDY, CHEAP ‹*chintzy* toys› **b :** STINGY — **chintz•i•ness** *n*

chin–up \ˈchin-ˌəp\ *n* **:** the act or an instance of chinning oneself especially as a conditioning exercise

[1]chip \ˈchip\ *n* **1 a :** a small piece (as of stone) broken off by a sharp blow **:** FLAKE **b :** a small piece of food ‹chocolate *chips*›: as **(1) :** a small thin slice of food; *esp* **:** POTATO CHIP **(2) :** FRENCH FRY **2 a :** a counter used in poker **b** *pl* **:** MONEY ‹in the *chips*› **3 :** a piece of dried dung ‹cow *chip*› **4 :** a flaw left after a small piece has been broken off ‹a cup with a *chip* in it› **5 a :** INTEGRATED CIRCUIT **b :** a small wafer of semiconductor material on which an integrated circuit is placed [Middle English] — **chip off the old block :** a child that resembles his or her parent — **chip on one's shoulder :** a challenging or belligerent attitude

[2]chip *vb* **chipped; chip•ping** **1 a :** to cut with an edged tool ‹*chip* ice from a sidewalk› **b (1) :** to cut or break (a small piece) from something **(2) :** to cut or break a chip from ‹*chip* a cup› **2 :** to break off in small pieces

chip in *vb* **:** CONTRIBUTE ‹everyone *chipped in* to buy the gift›

chip•munk \ˈchip-ˌməŋk\ *n* **:** any of numerous small striped largely terrestrial rodents of North America and Asia related to the squirrels [earlier *chitmunk,* probably from Ojibwa *ačitamo·nʔ* "red squirrel"]

chipped beef \ˈchipt-, ˈchip-\ *n* **:** smoked dried beef sliced thin

Chip•pen•dale \ˈchip-ən-ˌdāl\ *adj* **:** of or relating to a late 18th century English furniture style characterized by graceful outline and often ornate ornamentation [Thomas *Chippendale,* died 1779, English cabinetmaker]

chip·per \ˈchip-ər\ *adj* : SPIRITED, SPRIGHTLY [perhaps from English dialect *kipper* "lively"]
Chip·pe·wa \ˈchip-ə-ˌwȯ, -ˌwä, -ˌwā\ *n* : OJIBWA
chip·ping sparrow \ˈchip-ing-\ *n* : a small North American sparrow whose song is a rapid trill
chi·rog·ra·phy \kī-ˈräg-rə-fē\ *n* **1** : HANDWRITING 1, PENMANSHIP **2** : CALLIGRAPHY 1 — **chi·rog·ra·pher** \-fər\ *n* — **chi·ro·graph·ic** \ˌkī-rə-ˈgraf-ik\ *adj*
chi·rop·o·dy \kə-ˈräp-əd-ē\ *n* : PODIATRY [*chir-* + *-pod,* from its original concern with both hands and feet] — **chi·rop·o·dist** \-əd-əst\ *n*
chi·ro·prac·tic \ˈkī-rə-ˌprak-tik\ *n* : a system of therapy based on manipulation and adjustment of body structures and especially the spinal column [*chir-* + Greek *praktikos* "practical, operative"] — **chiropractic** *adj* — **chi·ro·prac·tor** \-tər\ *n*
chi·rop·ter·an \kī-ˈräp-tə-rən\ *n* : [3]BAT [Greek *cheir* "hand" + *pteron* "wing"]
chirp \ˈchərp\ *n* : the characteristic short sharp sound of a small bird or cricket [imitative] — **chirp** *vi*
chirr \ˈchər\ *n* : the short vibrant or trilled sound characteristic of an insect (as a grasshopper or cicada) [imitative] — **chirr** *vi*
chir·rup \ˈchər-əp, ˈchir-\ *n* : CHIRP [imitative] — **chirrup** *vb*
[1]**chis·el** \ˈchiz-əl\ *n* : a metal tool with a cutting edge at the end of a blade used to shape or chip away stone, wood, or metal [Medieval French, derived from Latin *caedere* "to cut"]

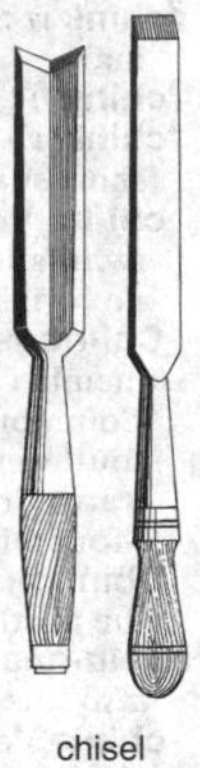
chisel

[2]**chisel** *vb* **-eled** *or* **-elled; -el·ing** *or* **-el·ling** \ˈchiz-ling, -ə-ling\ **1** : to cut or work with or as if with a chisel **2** : to use shrewd or unfair practices — **chis·el·er** \ˈchiz-lər, -ə-lər\ *n*
chis·eled *or* **chis·elled** \ˈchiz-əld\ *adj* : formed or crafted as if with a chisel ⟨a *chiseled* physique⟩ ⟨a *chiseled* essay⟩
chi–square \ˈkī-ˈskwaər, -ˈskweər\ *n* : the sum of a set of quotients each of which is the square of the difference between the observed and theoretical values of a quantity divided by the theoretical value
[1]**chit** \ˈchit\ *n* **1** *archaic* : CHILD 2a **2** : a pert young woman [Middle English *chitte* "kitten, cub"]
[2]**chit** *n* : a small letter or note; *esp* : one serving as a record of a small debt [Hindi & Urdu *ciṭṭhī*]
chit·chat \ˈchit-ˌchat\ *n* : SMALL TALK, GOSSIP [reduplication of *chat*]
chi·tin \ˈkīt-n\ *n* : a horny substance that forms part of the hard outer covering especially of insects, arachnids, and crustaceans [French *chitine,* from Greek *chitōn* "chiton, tunic"] — **chi·tin·ous** \-əs\ *adj*
chi·ton \ˈkīt-n, ˈkī-ˌtän\ *n* **1** : any of a class (Polyplacophora) of bilaterally symmetrical marine mollusks with a dorsal shell of calcareous plates **2** : a tunic worn in ancient Greece [Greek *chitōn* "tunic," of Semitic origin]
chit·ter \ˈchit-ər\ *vi* **1** : TWITTER 1, CHIRP **2** : CHATTER 1 [Middle English *chiteren*]
chit·ter·lings *or* **chit·lins** \ˈchit-lənz\ *n pl* : the intestines of hogs especially when prepared as food [Middle English *chiterling*]
chi·val·ric \shə-ˈval-rik\ *adj* : CHIVALROUS
chiv·al·rous \ˈshiv-əl-rəs\ *adj* **1** : VALIANT **2** : of or relating to chivalry **3** : having or displaying the qualities of an ideal knight of the age of chivalry: as **a** : marked by honor, generosity, and courtesy **b** : marked by especial courtesy and consideration to women — **chiv·al·rous·ly** *adv* — **chiv·al·rous·ness** *n*
chiv·al·ry \-rē\ *n, pl* **-ries** **1** : a body of knights ⟨the *chivalry* of France⟩ **2** : the system, spirit, ways, or customs of medieval knighthood **3** : the qualities of the ideal knight : chivalrous conduct [Medieval French *chevalerie,* from *chevaler* "knight, chevalier"]
chive \ˈchīv\ *n* : a perennial herb related to the onion and having slender leaves used as a seasoning [Medieval French, from Latin *cepa* "onion"]
chivy \ˈchiv-ē\ *vt* **chiv·ied; chivy·ing** : to annoy or bother repeatedly about little things [from *chivy* "hunt, chase"]
chla·myd·ia \klə-ˈmid-ē-ə\ *n, pl* **-i·ae** \-ē-ˌē\ : a bacterium that causes various diseases or infections of the eye and reproductive or excretory organs; *also* : a disease or infection caused by chlamydiae [derived from Greek *chlamys* "cloak, mantle"]
chla·mydo·spore \klə-ˈmid-ə-ˌspōr, -ˌspȯr\ *n* : a thick-walled usually resting spore [Greek *chlamyd-, chlamys* "mantle"]
chlor- *or* **chloro-** *combining form* **1** : green ⟨*chlor*osis⟩ **2** : chlorine ⟨*chlor*tetracycline⟩ [Greek *chlōros* "greenish yellow"]
chlo·ral hydrate \ˈklōr-əl-, ˈklȯr-\ *n* : a bitter white crystalline drug $C_2H_3Cl_3O_2$ used to induce sleep — called also *chloral*
chlor·am·phen·i·col \ˌklōr-ˌam-ˈfen-i-ˌkȯl, ˌklȯr-, -ˌkōl\ *n* : a broad-spectrum antibiotic isolated from cultures of a soil microorganism or prepared synthetically
chlo·rate \ˈklōr-ˌāt, ˈklȯr-\ *n* : a salt of chloric acid
chlor·dane \ˈklōr-ˌdān\ *or* **chlor·dan** \-ˌdan\ *n* : a viscous volatile toxic liquid insecticide $C_{10}H_6Cl_8$ formerly used in the U.S. [*chlor-* + *indane* (C_9H_{10})]
chlor·di·az·epox·ide \ˌklōr-dī-ˌaz-ə-ˈpäk-ˌsīd, ˌklȯr-\ *n* : a compound used especially as a tranquilizer
chlo·rel·la \klə-ˈrel-ə\ *n* : any of a genus of unicellular green algae including some grown as a potential food source [derived from Greek *chlōros* "greenish yellow"]
chlo·ren·chy·ma \klōr-ˈeng-kə-mə, klȯr-\ *n* : chlorophyll-containing plant tissue [*chlor-* + *-enchyma* (as in *parenchyma*)]
chlo·ric acid \ˈklōr-ik-, ˈklȯr-\ *n* : a strong acid $HClO_3$ like nitric acid in oxidizing properties but far less stable
chlo·ride \ˈklōr-ˌīd, ˈklȯr-\ *n* : a chemical compound of chlorine with another element or radical; *esp* : a salt or ester of hydrochloric acid
chloride of lime : BLEACHING POWDER
chlo·ri·nate \ˈklōr-ə-ˌnāt, ˈklȯr-\ *vt* : to treat or cause to combine with chlorine especially for purifying — **chlo·ri·na·tion** \ˌklōr-ə-ˈnā-shən, ˌklȯr-\ *n* — **chlo·ri·na·tor** \ˈklōr-ə-ˌnāt-ər, ˈklȯr-\ *n*
chlorinated lime *n* : BLEACHING POWDER
chlo·rine \ˈklōr-ˌēn, ˈklȯr-, -ən\ *n* : a chemical element that is isolated as a heavy greenish yellow irritating gas of pungent odor used especially as a bleach, an oxidizing agent, and as a disinfectant in water purification — see ELEMENT table
chlo·rite \ˈklōr-ˌīt, ˈklȯr-\ *n* : any of a group of usually green minerals associated with and resembling the micas
chlo·ro·flu·o·ro·car·bon \ˌklōr-ō-ˌflu̇r-ō-ˈkär-bən, ˌklȯr-, -ˌflu̇-ər-\ *n* : any of several gaseous compounds containing carbon, chlorine, fluorine, and sometimes hydrogen that are used as refrigerants, solvents, or aerosol propellants or in the manufacture of plastic foams and are believed to cause ozone loss in the stratosphere
[1]**chlo·ro·form** \ˈklōr-ə-ˌfȯrm, ˈklȯr-\ *n* : a colorless volatile heavy poisonous liquid $CHCl_3$ with anesthetic properties that smells like ether and is used especially as a solvent [*chlor-* + *form*ic acid]
[2]**chloroform** *vt* : to treat with chloroform especially so as to produce anesthesia or death
chlo·ro·phyll \ˈklōr-ə-ˌfil, ˈklȯr-, -fəl\ *n* : the green photosynthetic coloring matter found chiefly in the chloroplasts of plants and occurring especially as a bluish black ester $C_{55}H_{72}MgN_4O_5$ or a dark green ester $C_{55}H_{70}MgN_4O_6$ — called also respectively *chlorophyll a, chlorophyll b* [French *chlorophylle,* from *chlor-* "chlor-" + Greek *phyllon* "leaf"] — **chlo·ro·phyl·lous** \ˌklōr-ə-ˈfil-əs, -ˌklȯr-\ *adj*
chlo·ro·plast \ˈklōr-ə-ˌplast, ˈklȯr-\ *n* : a plastid that contains chlorophyll and is the site of photosynthesis
chlo·ro·quine \ˈklōr-ə-ˌkwēn, ˈklȯr-\ *n* : a drug $C_{18}H_{26}ClN_3$ administered in the form of a phosphate for the treatment of malaria [*chlor-* + *quinine*]
chlo·ro·sis \klə-ˈrō-səs\ *n* **1** : an anemia in which the skin is greenish **2** : a disorder of green plants marked by yellowing or blanching — **chlo·rot·ic** \-ˈrät-ik\ *adj*
chlor·prom·azine \klōr-ˈpräm-ə-ˌzēn, klȯr-, -zən\ *n* : a phenothiazine derivative $C_{17}H_{19}ClN_2S$ used as a tranquilizer in the form of its hydrochloride — compare THORAZINE
chlor·tet·ra·cy·cline \ˌklōr-ˌte-trə-ˈsī-ˌklēn, ˌklȯr-\ *n* : a yellow crystalline antibiotic $C_{22}H_{23}ClN_2O_8$ produced by a soil actinomycete and sometimes added to animal feeds to stimulate growth
[1]**chock** \ˈchäk\ *n* **1** : a wedge or block for steadying a body (as a cask) and holding it motionless, for filling in an unwanted space, or for blocking the movement of a wheel **2** : a metal fitting with two short arms curving inward between which ropes may pass for mooring or towing [origin unknown]
[2]**chock** *vt* : to stop or make fast with or as if with chocks
chock·a·block \ˈchäk-ə-ˌbläk\ *adj* : very full : CROWDED
chock–full *or* **chock·ful** \ˈchək-ˈfu̇l, ˈchäk-\ *adj* : full to the lim-

it ⟨hotels *chock-full* of tourists⟩ [Middle English *chokkefull,* probably from *choken* "to choke" + *full*]

choc·o·hol·ic *also* **choc·a·hol·ic** \ˌchäk-ə-ˈhȯl-ik, ˌchȯk-, -ˈhäl-\ *n* : a person who craves or eats a lot of chocolate [*chocolate* + *-aholic*]

choc·o·late \ˈchäk-lət, ˈchȯk-, -ə-lət\ *n* **1 :** a beverage of chocolate in water or milk **2 :** a food prepared from ground roasted cacao beans **3 :** a candy with a chocolate coating **4 :** a brownish gray color [Spanish, from Nahuatl *chocolātl*] — **chocolate** *adj*

Choc·taw \ˈchäk-ˌtȯ\ *n, pl* **Choctaw** *or* **Choctaws** **1 :** a member of an American Indian people of Mississippi, Alabama, and Louisiana **2 :** the language of the Choctaw people [Choctaw *čahta*]

[1]**choice** \ˈchȯis\ *n* **1 :** the act of choosing : SELECTION ⟨finding it hard to make a *choice*⟩ **2 :** power of choosing : OPTION ⟨you have no *choice*⟩ **3 a :** a person or thing chosen **b :** the best part : CREAM **4 :** a number and variety to choose among ⟨a wide *choice* of options⟩ [Medieval French *chois,* from *choisir* "to choose," of Germanic origin] — **of choice :** to be preferred

synonyms CHOICE, OPTION, ALTERNATIVE, PREFERENCE mean the act or opportunity of choosing or the thing chosen. CHOICE suggests the opportunity or privilege of choosing freely ⟨freedom of *choice*⟩. OPTION implies a power to choose that is specifically granted or guaranteed ⟨the *option* of paying now or later⟩. ALTERNATIVE implies a need to choose one and reject another possibility ⟨equally attractive ALTERNATIVES⟩. PREFERENCE suggests a choice guided by one's judgment or inclinations ⟨a *preference* for cool weather⟩.

[2]**choice** *adj* **1 :** very fine : better than most ⟨*choice* fruits⟩ **2 :** of a grade between prime and good ⟨*choice* meat⟩ — **choice·ly** *adv* — **choice·ness** *n*

choir \ˈkwīr\ *n* **1 :** an organized group of singers especially in a church **2 :** the part of a church assigned to the choir and usually located between the sanctuary and the nave **3 :** any of the nine ranks of angels **4 :** a group of instruments of the same class [Medieval French *queor,* from Latin *chorus* "chorus"]

choir·boy \-ˌbȯi\ *n* : a boy member of a church choir

choir loft *n* : a gallery occupied by a church choir

choir·mas·ter \-ˌmas-tər\ *n* : the director of a choir (as in a church)

[1]**choke** \ˈchōk\ *vb* **1 :** to hinder normal breathing by cutting off the supply of air **2 :** to have the trachea stopped entirely or partly ⟨*choke* on a bone⟩ **3 :** to check the growth or action of : SUPPRESS ⟨*choke* a fire⟩ ⟨*choke* back tears⟩ **4 :** to obstruct by clogging ⟨leaves *choked* the sewer⟩ **5 :** to fill to the limit ⟨a street *choked* with cars⟩ **6 :** to decrease or shut off the air intake of the carburetor of a gasoline engine in order to make the fuel mixture richer **7 :** to grip (as a baseball bat) some distance from the end of the handle — usually used with *up* **8 :** to become or feel constricted in the throat (as from strong emotion) ⟨*choked* up at the wedding⟩ **9 :** to lose composure and perform poorly ⟨*choked* under pressure⟩ [Old English *acēocian*]

[2]**choke** *n* **1 :** the act of choking **2 :** something that chokes: as **a :** a narrowing toward the muzzle in the bore of a gun **b :** a valve for choking a gasoline engine

choke·cher·ry \-ˌcher-ē, -ˈcher-\ *n* : a U.S. and Canadian wild cherry with bitter or astringent fruit; *also* : this fruit

choke hold *n* **1 :** a hold that involves pressure applied to the neck of another **2 :** absolute dominance or control ⟨had a *choke hold* on the city's finances⟩

choky \ˈchō-kē\ *adj* : inclined to choke : having a tendency to choke ⟨grew *choky* with fear⟩

chol- *or* **chole-** *combining form* : bile : gall ⟨*chol*ine⟩ [Greek *cholē*]

cho·le·cys·ti·tis \ˌkō-lə-ˌsis-ˈtīt-əs\ *n* : inflammation of the gallbladder

cho·ler \ˈkäl-ər, ˈkō-lər\ *n* : a tendency toward sudden and often unreasonable irritability : IRASCIBILITY; *also* : ANGER [Medieval French *colere,* from Latin *cholera* "intestinal disorder, cholera," from Greek; taken by later medical authors as a derivative of Greek *cholē* "bile"]

chol·era \ˈkäl-ə-rə\ *n* : any of several diseases usually marked by severe vomiting and dysentery [Latin, from Greek, from *cholē* "bile"] — **chol·e·ra·ic** \ˌkäl-ə-ˈrā-ik\ *adj*

cho·ler·ic \ˈkäl-ə-rik, kə-ˈler-ik\ *adj* **1 :** easily moved to anger : hot-tempered **2 :** showing or expressing anger : IRATE

synonyms see IRASCIBLE

cho·les·ter·ol \kə-ˈles-tə-ˌrȯl, -ˌrōl\ *n* : a waxy substance $C_{27}H_{45}OH$ normally present in cells and tissues, important in many bodily processes, and possibly a contributing factor to arteriosclerosis when deposits in arteries are excessive [derived from *chol-* "chol-" + Greek *stereos* "solid"]

cho·line \ˈkō-ˌlēn\ *n* : a substance $C_5H_{15}NO_2$ that is widely distributed in animal and plant products (as eggs and beans) and is a vitamin of the vitamin B complex essential to liver function

cho·lin·er·gic \ˌkō-lə-ˈnər-jik\ *adj* : liberating or activated by acetylcholine ⟨a *cholinergic* nerve fiber⟩ [acetyl*choline* + Greek *ergon* "work"]

cho·lin·es·ter·ase \ˌkō-lə-ˈnes-tə-ˌrās, -ˌrāz\ *n* : ACETYLCHOLINESTERASE

chomp \ˈchämp, ˈchȯmp\ *vb* **1 :** to chew or bite on noisily or vigorously **2 :** CHAMP 2 — usually used in the phrase *chomping at the bit* [alteration of [1]*champ*] — **chomp** *n*

chon \ˈchän\ *n, pl* **chon** **1 :** a monetary unit equal to 1/100 won **2 :** a coin or note representing one chon [Korean *chŏn*]

choose \ˈchüz\ *vb* **chose** \ˈchōz\; **cho·sen** \ˈchōz-n\; **choos·ing** \ˈchü-zing\ **1 :** to select according to preference especially after consideration **2 a :** DECIDE ⟨*chose* to go by train⟩ **b :** PREFER ⟨*choose* one car over another⟩ **3 :** to see fit : INCLINE ⟨take them if you *choose*⟩ **4 :** to make a choice ⟨finding it hard to *choose*⟩ [Old English *cēosan*] — **choos·er** *n*

choosy *or* **choos·ey** \ˈchü-zē\ *adj* **choos·i·er; -est :** inclined to be very selective : PARTICULAR ⟨*choosy* shoppers⟩

[1]**chop** \ˈchäp\ *vt* **chopped; chop·ping** **1 :** to cut by striking especially repeatedly with something sharp ⟨*chop* down a tree⟩ **2 :** to cut into small pieces : MINCE ⟨*chopped* vegetables⟩ **3 :** to strike (as a ball) with a short quick downward stroke [Middle English *chappen, choppen* "to chop, crack"]

[2]**chop** *n* **1 a :** a forceful sudden stroke with a sharp instrument **b :** a sharp downward blow or stroke especially in sports **2 :** a small cut of meat often including a part of a rib **3 :** a short quick motion (as of a wave)

[3]**chop** *vi* **chopped; chop·ping** **1 :** to change direction **2 :** to veer with or as if with the wind [Old English *cēapian* "to barter"]

chopfallen *variant of* CHAPFALLEN

chop·house \ˈchäp-ˌhau̇s\ *n* : RESTAURANT

chop·per \ˈchäp-ər\ *n* **1 :** one that chops **2 :** HELICOPTER

chop·pi·ness \ˈchäp-ē-nəs\ *n* : the quality or state of being choppy

[1]**chop·py** \ˈchäp-ē\ *adj* **chop·pi·er; -est :** subject to frequent changes : VARIABLE ⟨*choppy* winds⟩

[2]**choppy** *adj* **chop·pi·er; -est** **1 :** rough with small waves ⟨*choppy* seas⟩ **2 a :** JERKY ⟨short *choppy* strides⟩ **b :** DISCONNECTED ⟨*choppy* sentences⟩

chops \ˈchäps\ *n pl* **1 :** MOUTH 1 **2 :** the fleshy covering of the jaws ⟨the dog licked its *chops*⟩ [alteration of [4]*chap*]

chop shop *n* : a place where stolen automobiles are stripped of salable parts

chop·stick \ˈchäp-ˌstik\ *n* : one of a pair of slender sticks used chiefly in Asian countries to lift food to the mouth [Chinese Pidgin English, from *chop* "fast"]

chop su·ey \chäp-ˈsü-ē\ *n* : a dish prepared chiefly from bean sprouts, bamboo shoots, water chestnuts, onions, mushrooms, and meat or fish and served with rice and soy sauce [Chinese (Cantonese) *jaahp-seui* "odds and ends," from *jaahp* "miscellaneous" + *seui* "bits"]

cho·ral \ˈkōr-əl, ˈkȯr-\ *adj* : of, relating to, or performed by a chorus or choir or in chorus — **cho·ral·ly** \-ə-lē\ *adv*

cho·rale \kə-ˈral, -ˈräl\ *n* **1 :** a hymn or psalm sung to a traditional or composed melody; *also* : a hymn tune or a harmonization of a traditional melody **2 :** CHORUS 1c, CHOIR [German *Choral,* short for *Choralgesang* "choral song"]

[1]**chord** \ˈkȯrd\ *n* : a combination of tones that blend harmoniously when sounded together [Middle English *cord,* short for *accord*] — **chord·al** \-l\ *adj*

[2]**chord** *vi* : to play chords especially on a stringed instrument

[3]**chord** *n* **1 :** CORD 3a **2 :** a straight line between two points on a curve **3 :** an individual emotional response ⟨strike a familiar *chord*⟩ [alteration of [1]*cord*]

chor·date \ˈkȯr-ˌdāt, ˈkȯrd-ət\ *n* : any of a phylum (Chordata)

\ə\ **abut**	\au̇\ **out**	\i\ **tip**	\ȯ\ **saw**	\u̇\ **foot**
\ər\ **further**	\ch\ **chin**	\ī\ **life**	\ȯi\ **coin**	\y\ **yet**
\a\ **mat**	\e\ **pet**	\j\ **job**	\th\ **thin**	\yü\ **few**
\ā\ **take**	\ē\ **easy**	\ng\ **sing**	\t͟h\ **this**	\yu̇\ **cure**
\ä\ **cot, cart**	\g\ **go**	\ō\ **bone**	\ü\ **food**	\zh\ **vision**

of animals having at least at some stage of development a notochord, paired gill slits, and a dorsally situated central nervous system and including the vertebrates, lancelets, and tunicates — compare HEMICHORDATE [derived from Latin *chorda* "cord"] — **chordate** *adj*

chore \ˈchōr, ˈchȯr\ *n* **1** *pl* : the routine duties of running a household or farm **2** : a routine task or job **3** : a difficult or disagreeable task ⟨reading should be fun, not a *chore*⟩ [Middle English *char* "turn, piece of work," from Old English *cierr*]

cho·rea \kə-ˈrē-ə\ *n* : a nervous disorder (as of humans or dogs) marked by spasmodic movements and lack of coordination [Latin, "dance," from Greek *choreia*, from *choros* "chorus"]

cho·re·og·ra·phy \ˌkōr-ē-ˈäg-rə-fē, ˌkȯr-\ *n, pl* **-phies** : the art of composing or arranging dances and especially ballets [derived from Greek *choreia* "dance," from *choros* "chorus"] — **cho·reo·graph** \ˈkōr-ē-ə-ˌgraf, ˈkȯr-\ *vt* — **cho·re·og·ra·pher** \ˌkōr-ē-ˈäg-rə-fər, ˌkȯr-\ *n* — **cho·reo·graphic** \-ē-ə-ˈgraf-ik\ *adj* — **cho·reo·graph·i·cal·ly** \-ˈgraf-i-kə-lē, -klē\ *adv*

cho·ric \ˈkōr-ik, ˈkȯr-, ˈkär-\ *adj* : of, relating to, or being in the style of a chorus and especially a Greek chorus

cho·rine \ˈkōr-ˌēn, ˈkȯr-\ *n* : CHORUS GIRL

cho·rio·al·lan·to·is \ˌkōr-ē-ō-ə-ˈlant-ə-wəs, ˌkȯr-\ *n* : a vascular fetal membrane composed of the fused chorion and adjacent wall of the allantois — **cho·rio·al·lan·to·ic** \-ō-ˌal-ən-ˈtō-ik\ *adj*

cho·ri·on \ˈkōr-ē-ˌän, ˈkȯr-\ *n* : the highly vascular outer embryonic membrane of reptiles, birds, and mammals that in placental mammals joins the allantois in the formation of the placenta [Greek] — **cho·ri·on·ic** \ˌkōr-ē-ˈän-ik, ˌkȯr-\ *adj*

cho·ris·ter \ˈkōr-ə-stər, ˈkȯr-, ˈkär-\ *n* : a singer in a choir [Medieval French *cueristre*, from Medieval Latin *chorista*, from Latin *chorus* "chorus"]

C horizon *n* : the layer of a soil lying beneath the B horizon and consisting essentially of more or less weathered parent rock

cho·roid \ˈkōr-ˌȯid, ˈkȯr-\ *also* **cho·ri·oid** \-ē-ˌȯid\ *n* : a vascular pigmented membrane of the vertebrate eye lying between the sclera and the retina [Greek *chorioeidēs*, from *chorion* "chorion"] — **choroid** *adj*

choroid coat *n* : CHOROID

chor·tle \ˈchȯrt-l\ *vi* **chor·tled; chor·tling** \ˈchȯrt-ling, -l-ing\ : to laugh or chuckle especially in satisfaction or exultation [blend of *chuckle* and *snort*] — **chortle** *n* — **chor·tler** \ˈchȯrt-lər, -l-ər\ *n*

[1]**cho·rus** \ˈkōr-əs, ˈkȯr-\ *n* **1 a** : a group of singers and dancers in Greek drama participating in or commenting on the action **b** : a character in Elizabethan drama who speaks the prologue and epilogue and comments on the action **c** : an organized group of singers : CHOIR; *esp* : a body of singers who sing the choral parts of a work (as in opera) **d** : a group of supporting dancers and singers in a musical comedy or revue **2 a** : a recurring part of a song or hymn **b** : the part of a drama sung or spoken by the chorus **c** : a composition to be sung by a chorus **3** : something uttered simultaneously by a number of persons ⟨a *chorus* of boos⟩ [Latin, from Greek *choros*] — **in chorus** : in unison ⟨answering *in chorus*⟩

[2]**chorus** *vb* : to sing or utter in chorus

chorus girl *n* : a young woman who sings or dances in a chorus (as of a musical comedy) — called also *chorine*

chose *past of* CHOOSE

cho·sen \ˈchōz-n\ *adj* : selected or marked for favor or special privilege ⟨privileges granted to a *chosen* few⟩ [Middle English, from past participle of *chosen* "to choose"]

Chou \ˈjō\ *n* : a Chinese dynasty traditionally dated 1122 to about 256 B.C. and marked by the development of the philosophical schools of Confucius and Lao-tzu

chough \ˈchəf\ *n* : an Old World black red-legged bird related to the crows [Middle English]

[1]**chow** \ˈchau̇\ *n* : FOOD, VICTUALS [from *chowchow*]

[2]**chow** *vi* : EAT ⟨*chowing* down on pizza⟩

chow-chow \ˈchau̇-ˌchau̇\ *n* : a relish of chopped mixed pickles in mustard sauce [Chinese Pidgin English, "food"]

chow chow \ˈchau̇-ˌchau̇\ *n* : any of a breed of thick-coated muscular dogs of Chinese origin with a blue-black tongue and a short tail curled close to the back — called also *chow* [perhaps from *chow-chow* "Chinese person," from Chinese Pidgin English *chowchow* "food"]

chow·der \ˈchau̇d-ər\ *n* : a soup or stew of seafood (as clams or fish) usually made with milk or tomatoes, onions, and other vegetables (as potatoes); *also* : a soup resembling chowder ⟨corn *chowder*⟩ [French *chaudière* "kettle," from Late Latin *caldaria*, from Latin *calidus* "warm"]

chow mein \ˈchau̇-ˈmān\ *n* : a seasoned stew of shredded or chopped meat, mushrooms, and vegetables usually served with fried noodles [Chinese (Cantonese) *cháau-mihn* "fried noodles"]

chrism \ˈkriz-əm\ *n* : consecrated oil used especially in baptism, confirmation, and ordination [Late Latin *chrisma*, from Greek, "ointment," from *chriein* "to anoint"]

Christ \ˈkrīst\ *n* **1** : MESSIAH 1 **2** : JESUS [Latin *Christus*, from Greek *Christos*, literally, "anointed," from *chriein* "to anoint"]

chris·ten \ˈkris-n\ *vt* **chris·tened; chris·ten·ing** \ˈkris-ning, -n-ing\ **1 a** : BAPTIZE 1 **b** : to name at baptism ⟨*christened* the baby Sara⟩ **2** : to name or dedicate (as a ship) by a ceremony suggestive of baptism [Old English *cristnian*, from *cristen* "Christian," from Latin *christianus*]

Chris·ten·dom \ˈkris-n-dəm\ *n* **1** : the entire body of Christians **2** : all the countries or peoples that are predominantly Christian

chris·ten·ing *n* : the ceremony of baptizing and naming a child

[1]**Chris·tian** \ˈkris-chən, ˈkrish-\ *n* **1** : a person who believes or professes belief in Jesus Christ and lives according to his teachings **2** : a member of a Christian church **3** : a member of a group (as the Disciples of Christ or the Churches of Christ) seeking a return to New Testament Christianity

[2]**Christian** *adj* **1** : of or relating to Jesus Christ or the religion deriving from him **2** : of or relating to Christians ⟨a *Christian* nation⟩ **3 a** : befitting a Christian ⟨*Christian* charity⟩ **b** : KIND 1, MERCIFUL ⟨has a very *Christian* concern for others⟩

Christian Brother *n* : a member of the Roman Catholic institute of Brothers of the Christian Schools founded in France in 1684 and devoted to education

Christian Era *n* : the period dating from the birth of Christ

chris·ti·ania \ˌkris-chē-ˈan-ē-ə, ˌkrish-chē-, ˌkris-tē-, -ˈän-\ *n* : CHRISTIE [*Christiania*, former name of Oslo, Norway]

Chris·ti·an·i·ty \ˌkris-chē-ˈan-ət-ē, ˌkrish-, -ˈchan-; ˌkris-tē-ˈan-\ *n* **1** : the religion derived from Jesus Christ **2** : the practice of Christianity

Chris·tian·ize \ˈkris-chə-ˌnīz, ˈkrish-\ *vt* : to make Christian — **Chris·tian·i·za·tion** \ˌkris-chə-nə-ˈzā-shən, ˌkrish-\ *n* — **Chris·tian·iz·er** *n*

Christian name *n* : the name given to a person at birth or christening as distinct from the family name

Christian Science *n* : a religion and system of healing founded by Mary Baker Eddy and taught by the Church of Christ, Scientist — **Christian Scientist** *n*

chris·tie *or* **chris·ty** \ˈkris-tē\ *n, pl* **christies** : a skiing turn made by shifting the body weight and skidding into a turn with the skis parallel — called also *christiania* [*Christiania*, former name of Oslo, Norway]

Christ·like \ˈkrīst-ˌlīk\ *adj* : resembling Christ in character or spirit

Christ·mas \ˈkris-məs\ *n* **1** : December 25 celebrated as a church festival in commemoration of the birth of Christ and observed as a legal holiday **2** : CHRISTMASTIDE [Old English *Cristes mæsse*, literally, "Christ's mass"]

Christmas cactus *n* : a branching Brazilian cactus with flat stems and showy flowers

Christmas club *n* : a savings account in which regular deposits are made throughout the year to provide money for Christmas shopping

Christmas fern *n* : a North American evergreen fern often used for winter decorations

Christ·mas·tide \ˈkris-mə-ˌstīd\ *n* : the festival season of Christmas

Christ·mas·time \-ˌstīm\ *n* : CHRISTMASTIDE

Christmas tree *n* : a usually evergreen tree decorated at Christmas

chrom- *or* **chromo-** *combining form* : color : colored ⟨*chromo*sphere⟩ [Greek *chrōma* "color"]

chro·ma \ˈkrō-mə\ *n* : SATURATION 2

chromat- *or* **chromato-** *combining form* : color ⟨*chromat*in⟩ ⟨*chromato*graphy⟩ [Greek *chrōmat-, chrōma*]

chro·mate \ˈkrō-ˌmāt\ *n* : a salt or ester of chromic acid

[1]**chro·mat·ic** \krō-ˈmat-ik\ *adj* **1** : of or relating to color or color phenomena; *esp* : being a shade other than black, gray, or white **2** : of, relating to, or giving all the tones of the chromatic scale — **chro·mat·i·cal·ly** \-ˈmat-i-kə-lē, -klē\ *adv*

[2]**chromatic** *n* : ACCIDENTAL

chromatic aberration *n* : aberration caused by the differences in refraction of the colored rays of the spectrum
chromatic scale *n* : a musical scale that consists entirely of half steps
chro·ma·tid \ˈkrō-mə-təd\ *n* : one of the paired and parallel strands of a duplicated chromosome joined by a single centromere
chro·ma·tin \-tən\ *n* : a complex of DNA and protein (as histone) in a cell's nucleus that condenses during cell division to become visible as a chromosome
chro·mato·gram \krō-ˈmat-ə-ˌgram, krə-\ *n* : the pattern formed on the adsorbent medium by the layers of components separated by chromatography
chro·mato·graph \krō-ˈmat-ə-ˌgraf, krə-\ *n* : an instrument used in chromatography — **chromatograph** *vb*
chro·ma·tog·ra·phy \ˌkrō-mə-ˈtäg-rə-fē\ *n* : a separating especially of closely related compounds by allowing a solution or mixture of them to seep through an adsorbent (as clay or paper) so that each compound becomes adsorbed in a separate often colored layer — **chro·mato·graph·ic** \-ˌmat-ə-ˈgraf-ik\ *adj* — **chro·mato·graph·i·cal·ly** \-i-kə-lē, -klē\ *adv*
chro·mato·phore \krō-ˈmat-ə-ˌfōr, -ˌfȯr\ *n* : a pigment-bearing cell; *esp* : one capable of causing skin color changes in an animal by expanding or contracting
chrome \ˈkrōm\ *n* **1 a** : CHROMIUM **b** : a chromium pigment **2** : something plated with an alloy of chromium [French, from Greek *chrōma* "color"]
-chrome \ˌkrōm\ *n or adj combining form* **1** : colored thing : colored **2** : coloring matter
chrome green *n* : any of various brilliant green pigments containing or consisting of chromium compounds
chrome yellow *n* : any of various bright yellow pigments consisting essentially of a compound $PbCrO_4$ of lead, chromium, and oxygen
chro·mic \ˈkrō-mik\ *adj* : of, relating to, or derived from chromium
chromic acid *n* : an acid H_2CrO_4 analogous to sulfuric acid but known only in solution
chro·mite \ˈkrō-ˌmīt\ *n* : a black mineral that consists of an oxide of iron and chromium and is an important ore of chromium
chro·mi·um \ˈkrō-mē-əm\ *n* : a blue-white metallic element found naturally only in combination and used especially in alloys and in electroplating — see ELEMENT table [New Latin, from French *chrome*]
chro·mo·mere \ˈkrō-mə-ˌmiər\ *n* : one of the small bead-shaped and heavily staining concentrations of chromatin that are linearly arranged along the chromosome
chro·mo·ne·ma \ˌkrō-mə-ˈnē-mə\ *n, pl* **-ne·ma·ta** \-ˈnē-mət-ə\ : the coiled filamentous core of a chromatid [New Latin, from *chrom-* + Greek *nēma* "thread"]
chro·mo·phore \ˈkrō-mə-ˌfōr, -ˌfȯr\ *n* : a group of atoms that gives rise to color in a molecule
chro·mo·plast \-ˌplast\ *n* : a colored plastid usually containing red or yellow pigment
chro·mo·some \ˈkrō-mə-ˌsōm\ *n* : one of the usually rod-shaped or threadlike DNA-containing structures that contain all or most of the genes of an organism and that are located in the nucleus in eukaryotes and are usually ring-shaped in prokaryotes — **chro·mo·som·al** \ˌkrō-mə-ˈsō-məl\ *adj*
chromosome number *n* : the usually constant number of chromosomes characteristic of a particular kind of animal or plant
chro·mo·sphere \ˈkrō-mə-ˌsfiər\ *n* : the part of the atmosphere of the sun or a star between the photosphere and corona
chron- *or* **chrono-** *combining form* : time ⟨*chrono*graph⟩ [Greek *chronos*]
chron·ic \ˈkrän-ik\ *adj* **1 a** : lasting a long time or recurring frequently ⟨*chronic* indigestion⟩ — compare ACUTE 5a **b** : suffering from a chronic disease ⟨*chronic* patients⟩ **2 a** : constantly present or encountered ⟨*chronic* financial difficulties⟩ **b** : being such habitually ⟨a *chronic* complainer⟩ — **chron·i·cal·ly** \-i-kə-lē, -klē\ *adv* — **chro·nic·i·ty** \krä-ˈnis-ət-ē\ *n*
¹chron·i·cle \ˈkrän-i-kəl\ *n* **1** : a historical account of events arranged in order of time without analysis or interpretation **2** : NARRATIVE 1 [Medieval French *chronique,* derived from Greek *chronos* "time"]
²chronicle *vt* **-cled; -cling** \-kəling, -kling\ : to present a record of in or as if in a chronicle — **chron·i·cler** \-kə-lər, -klər\ *n*
Chron·i·cles \ˈkrän-i-kəlz\ *n* : either of two historical books of canonical Jewish and Christian Scriptures — called also *Paralipomenon* — see BIBLE table
chro·no·graph \ˈkrän-ə-ˌgraf, ˈkrō-nə-\ *n* : an instrument for measuring and recording time intervals with accuracy: as **a** : an instrument having a revolving drum on which a stylus makes marks **b** : a watch with a sweep-second hand — **chron·o·graph·ic** \ˌkrän-ə-ˈgraf-ik, ˌkrō-nə-\ *adj* — **chro·nog·ra·phy** \krə-ˈnäg-rə-fē\ *n*
chron·o·log·i·cal \ˌkrän-l-ˈäj-i-kəl, ˌkrōn-\ *adj* : arranged in or according to the order of time ⟨*chronological* tables of American history⟩ — **chron·o·log·i·cal·ly** \-ˈäj-i-kə-lē, -klē\ *adv*
chro·nol·o·gy \krə-ˈnäl-ə-jē\ *n, pl* **-gies** **1** : the science that deals with measuring time by regular divisions and that assigns to events their proper dates **2** : a chronological table or list **3** : an arrangement (as of events) in order of occurrence — **chro·nol·o·gist** \-jəst\ *n*
chro·nom·e·ter \krə-ˈnäm-ət-ər\ *n* : an instrument for measuring time; *esp* : one designed to keep time with great accuracy and used especially in navigation — **chron·o·met·ric** \ˌkrän-ə-ˈme-trik, ˌkrō-nə-\ *adj*
chro·no·scope \ˈkrän-ə-ˌskōp, ˈkrō-nə-\ *n* : an instrument for precise measurement of small time intervals
chrys·a·lid \ˈkris-ə-ləd\ *n* : CHRYSALIS
chrys·a·lis \ˈkris-ə-ləs\ *n, pl* **chry·sal·i·des** \krə-ˈsal-ə-ˌdēz\ *or* **chrys·a·lis·es** \ˈkris-ə-lə-səz\ : the pupa of a butterfly or moth; *also* : the hardened outer layer of such a pupa — compare COCOON [Latin *chrysallis* "gold-colored pupa of butterflies," from Greek, from *chrysos* "gold," of Semitic origin]
chry·san·the·mum \kris-ˈan-thə-məm, -ˈant-\ *n* **1** : any of a genus of plants related to the daisies that include weeds, ornamentals grown for their brightly colored often double flower heads, and sources of medicinals and insecticides **2** : a flower head of an ornamental chrysanthemum [Latin, from Greek *chrysanthemon,* from *chrysos* "gold" + *anthemon* "flower"]
chrys·o·phyte \ˈkris-ə-ˌfīt\ *n* : GOLDEN-BROWN ALGA
chrys·o·prase \ˈkris-ə-ˌprāz\ *n* : a yellowish green chalcedony valued as a gem [derived from Greek *chrysoprasos,* from *chrysos* "gold" + *prason* "leek"]
chrys·o·tile \ˈkris-ə-ˌtīl\ *n* : a fibrous silky serpentine that is one kind of asbestos [derived from Greek *chrysos* "gold" + *-til* "fiber," from *tillein* "to pluck"]
chub \ˈchəb\ *n, pl* **chub** *or* **chubs** : any of several small freshwater fishes related to the carp [Middle English *chubbe*]
chub·by \ˈchəb-ē\ *adj* **chub·bi·er; -est** : PLUMP ⟨a baby's *chubby* cheeks⟩ [*chub*] — **chub·bi·ness** *n*
¹chuck \ˈchək\ *vt* **1** : to give a pat or a tap to ⟨*chuck* a person under the chin⟩ **2** : THROW 2, TOSS ⟨*chuck* a ball back and forth⟩ **3** : DISCARD 2 ⟨*chucked* his old shirt⟩ [origin unknown]
²chuck *n* **1** : a pat or nudge under the chin **2** : THROW 1
³chuck *n* **1** : a portion of a side of dressed beef including most of the neck and the parts about the shoulder blade and the first three ribs **2** *chiefly West* : FOOD **3** : a device for holding work or a tool in a machine (as a drill press or lathe) [English dialect *chuck* "lump"]
chuck·le \ˈchək-əl\ *vi* **chuck·led; chuck·ling** \ˈchək-ling, -ə-ling\ : to laugh inwardly or quietly [probably from Middle English *chukken* "to cluck"] — **chuckle** *n*
chuck·le·head \ˈchək-əl-ˌhed\ *n* : BLOCKHEAD [*chuckle* "lumpish," from English dialect *chuck* "lump"] — **chuck·le·head·ed** \ˌchək-əl-ˈhed-əd\ *adj*
chuck wagon \ˈchək-\ *n* : a wagon carrying a stove and provisions for cooking (as on a ranch)
chuck·wal·la \ˈchək-ˌwäl-ə\ *n* : a large plant-eating lizard of the desert regions of the southwestern U.S. [Mexican Spanish *chacahuala,* of American Indian origin]

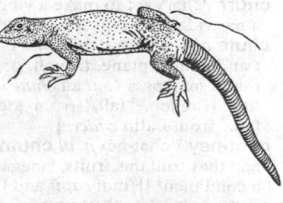

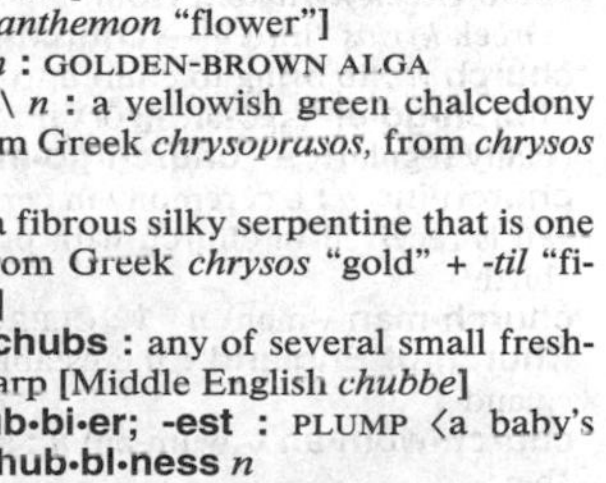
chuckwalla

\ə\ abut	\aů\ out	\i\ tip	\ȯ\ saw	\ů\ foot
\ər\ further	\ch\ chin	\ī\ life	\ȯi\ coin	\y\ yet
\a\ mat	\e\ pet	\j\ job	\th\ thin	\yü\ few
\ā\ take	\ē\ easy	\ng\ sing	\th\ this	\yů\ cure
\ä\ cot, cart	\g\ go	\ō\ bone	\ü\ food	\zh\ vision

chuck–will's–wid•ow \ˌchək-ˌwilz-ˈwid-ō\ *n* **:** a nightjar of the southern U.S. [imitative]

[1]**chug** \ˈchəg\ *n* **:** a dull explosive sound made by or as if by a laboring engine [imitative]

[2]**chug** *vi* **chugged; chug•ging :** to move or go with chugs ⟨a locomotive *chugging* along⟩

chuk•ka \ˈchək-ə\ *n* **:** a short usually ankle-high leather boot with two pairs of eyelets or a buckle and strap [alteration of *chukker;* from a similar polo player's boot]

chuk•ker \ˈchək-ər\ *also* **chuk•ka** \ˈchək-ə\ *n* **:** a playing period of a polo game [Hindi *cakkar* and Urdu *chakkar* "circular course" from Sanskrit *cakra* "wheel"]

[1]**chum** \ˈchəm\ *n* **:** a close friend **:** PAL [perhaps by shortening and alteration from *chamber fellow* "roommate"]

[2]**chum** *vi* **chummed; chum•ming :** to be or become chums

[3]**chum** *n* **:** animal or vegetable matter (as chopped fish or corn) thrown overboard to attract fish [origin unknown]

chum•my \ˈchəm-ē\ *adj* **chum•mi•er; -est :** quite friendly — **chum•mi•ly** \ˈchəm-ə-lē\ *adv* — **chum•mi•ness** \ˈchəm-ē-nəs\ *n*

chump \ˈchəmp\ *n* **:** DUPE [perhaps blend of *chunk* and *lump*]

chunk \ˈchəngk\ *n* **1 :** a short thick piece **:** HUNK ⟨a *chunk* of meat⟩ **2 :** a significant quantity ⟨a *chunk* of money⟩ [perhaps alteration of *chuck* "short piece of wood"]

chunky \ˈchəng-kē\ *adj* **chunk•i•er; -est 1 a :** STOCKY **b :** PLUMP **2 :** filled with chunks ⟨*chunky* peanut butter⟩ — **chunk•i•ly** \-kə-lē\ *adv* — **chunk•i•ness** \-kē-nəs\ *n*

chup•pah *or* **hup•pah** *also* **chup•pa** \ˈk̲u̇-pə\ *n* **:** a canopy under which the bride and groom stand during a Jewish wedding ceremony [Yiddish *khupe,* from Hebrew *ḥuppāh*]

[1]**church** \ˈchərch\ *n* **1 :** a building for public and especially Christian worship **2 a** *often cap* **:** a body or organization of religious believers **b :** the clergy of a religious body **3 :** public worship especially in a church [Old English *cirice,* derived from Late Greek *kyriakon,* from Greek *kyriakos* "of the lord," from Greek *kyrios* "lord"] — **church•ly** \-lē\ *adj*

[2]**church** *vt* **:** to bring to church to receive one of its rites

church•go•er \-ˌgō-ər, -ˌgōr\ *n* **:** one that goes to church especially regularly — **church•go•ing** \-ˌgō-ing\ *adj or n*

church•ing *n* **:** a ceremony in certain churches in which a woman is received in church with prayer and blessings after childbirth

church•man \-mən\ *n* **1 :** CLERGYMAN **2 :** a church member

Church of England : the established episcopal church of England

church•wom•an \-ˌwu̇m-ən\ *n* **:** a woman who is a church member

church•yard \ˈchərch-ˌyärd\ *n* **:** a yard that belongs to a church and is often used as a burial ground

churl \ˈchərl\ *n* **1 :** a medieval peasant **2 :** RUSTIC **3 :** a rude or surly person [Old English *ceorl* "man, freeman of low rank"]

churl•ish \ˈchər-lish\ *adj* **:** offensive in action or manner **:** RUDE, SURLY — **churl•ish•ly** *adv* — **churl•ish•ness** *n*

[1]**churn** \ˈchərn\ *n* **:** a vessel in which cream is agitated in order to separate the butterfat from the other parts [Old English *cyrin*]

[2]**churn** *vb* **1 :** to agitate (milk or cream) in a churn in making butter **:** make (butter) by churning **2 :** to work a churn in making butter **3 a :** to agitate or be agitated violently ⟨the boat's propeller *churning* the water⟩ **b :** to produce, move with, or experience violent motion or agitation ⟨her stomach was *churning*⟩ ⟨*churning* legs⟩

churr \ˈchər\ *vi* **:** to make a vibrant or whirring noise like that of a partridge [imitative] — **churr** *n*

chute *also* **shute** \ˈshüt\ *n* **1 :** a quick drop (as of a river) **2 :** an inclined plane, trough, or passage down or through which things may pass ⟨a mail *chute*⟩ **3 :** PARACHUTE 1 **4 :** SPINNAKER [French, "fall," from Medieval French, from *cheoir* "to fall," from Latin *cadere*]

chut•ney \ˈchət-nē\ *n, pl* **chutneys :** a thick sauce of Indian origin that contains fruits, vinegar, sugar, and spices and is used as a condiment [Hindi *caṭnī* and Urdu *chaṭnī*]

chutz•pah *also* **chutz•pa** *or* **hutz•pah** *or* **hutz•pa** \ˈhu̇t-spə, ˈk̲u̇t-spä\ *n* **:** great self-confidence **:** NERVE 3b [Yiddish *khutspe,* from Hebrew *ḥuṣpāh*]

chyle \ˈkīl\ *n* **:** lymph milky from emulsified fats that is present especially in the lacteals during intestinal absorption of fats [Late Latin *chylus,* from Greek *chylos* "juice, chyle," from *chein* "to pour"]

chyme \ˈkīm\ *n* **:** the semifluid mass of partly digested food that passes from the stomach into the duodenum [Late Latin *chymus* "chyle," from Greek *chymos* "juice"] — **chy•mous** \ˈkī-məs\ *adj*

chy•mo•tryp•sin \ˌkī-mō-ˈtrip-sən\ *n* **:** a pancreatic enzyme that acts on proteins by breaking internal peptide bonds

ci•bo•ri•um \sə-ˈbōr-ē-əm, -ˈbȯr-\ *n, pl* **-ria** \-ē-ə\ *also* **-ri•ums 1 :** a covered goblet-shaped vessel for holding eucharistic bread **2 :** a vaulted canopy supported by four columns over a high altar [Latin, "cup," from Greek *kibōrion*]

ci•ca•da \sə-ˈkād-ə, -ˈkäd-\ *n, pl* **-ca•das** *also* **-ca•dae** \-ˈkād-ˌē, -ˌkäd-ˌē\ **:** any of a family of stout-bodied insects that have a wide blunt head, large transparent wings, and the males of which produce a loud buzzing sound [Latin]

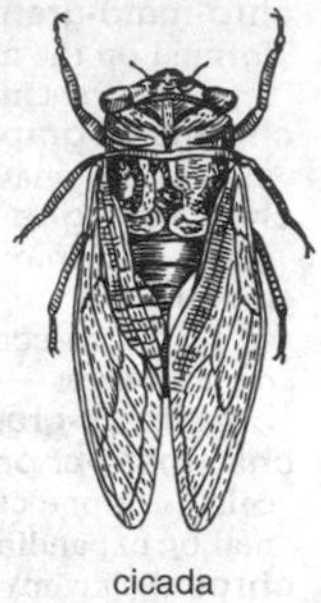

cicada

cic•a•trix \ˈsik-ə-ˌtriks, sə-ˈkā-triks\ *n, pl* **cic•a•tri•ces** \ˌsik-ə-ˈtrī-ˌsēz, sə-ˈkā-trə-ˌsēz\ **1 :** a scar resulting from formation and contraction of fibrous tissue in a flesh wound **2 :** a scar marking the previous point of attachment of a part or organ (as a leaf or seed) [Latin] — **cic•a•tri•cial** \ˌsik-ə-ˈtrish-əl\ *adj*

ci•ce•ro•ne \ˌsis-ə-ˈrō-nē, ˌchich-ə-\ *n, pl* **-ro•ni** \-ˌnē\ **1 :** GUIDE 1b **2 :** MENTOR, TUTOR [Italian, from *Cicerone* "Cicero"]

Cic•ero•nian \ˌsis-ə-ˈrō-nyən, -nē-ən\ *adj* **:** of, relating to, or characteristic of Cicero or his writings

cich•lid \ˈsik-ləd\ *n* **:** any of a family of mostly tropical spiny-finned freshwater fishes including some kept in aquariums [derived from Greek *kichlē* "thrush, kind of fish"] — **cichlid** *adj*

-cide \ˌsīd\ *n combining form* **1 :** killer ⟨insect*icide*⟩ **2 :** killing ⟨geno*cide*⟩ [Latin *-cida,* from *caedere* "to cut, kill"]

ci•der \ˈsīd-ər\ *n* **:** the fresh or fermented juice of fruit (as apples) used as a beverage or for making other products (as vinegar) [Medieval French *sidre,* from Late Latin *sicera* "strong drink," from Greek *sikera,* from Hebrew *shēkhār*]

cig \ˈsig\ *n, slang* **:** CIGARETTE

ci•gar \sig-ˈär\ *n* **:** a roll of tobacco leaves for smoking [Spanish *cigarro*]

cig•a•rette *also* **cig•a•ret** \ˌsig-ə-ˈret, ˈsig-ə-ˌ\ *n* **:** a small roll of cut tobacco wrapped in paper for smoking

cil•i•ary \ˈsil-ē-ˌer-ē\ *adj* **1 :** of or relating to cilia **2 :** of, relating to, or being the muscular body supporting the lens of the eye

cil•i•ate \ˈsil-ē-ət, -ˌāt\ *n* **:** any of a group (Ciliophora) of ciliated protozoans

cil•i•at•ed \-ˌāt-əd\ *or* **ciliate** *adj* **:** possessing cilia

cil•i•um \ˈsil-ē-əm\ *n, pl* **cil•ia** \-ē-ə\ **1 :** one of the tiny filaments of many cells that are capable of lashing movement **2 :** EYELASH [Latin, "eyelid"]

Cim•me•ri•an \sə-ˈmir-ē-ən\ *adj* **:** very dark or gloomy [from *Cimmerians,* a mythical people in Homer dwelling in eternal gloom]

[1]**cinch** \ˈsinch\ *n* **1 :** a strong girth for a pack or saddle **2 :** a tight grip **3 a :** a thing done or gained with ease **b :** a certainty to happen [Spanish *cincha,* from Latin *cingula* "girdle, girth," from *cingere* "to gird"]

[2]**cinch** *vt* **1 :** to put a cinch on **2 :** to make certain **:** ASSURE

cin•cho•na \sing-ˈkō-nə, sin-ˈchō-\ *n* **1 :** any of a genus of South American trees and shrubs **2 :** the dried bark of a cinchona containing alkaloids (as quinine) and formerly used as a malaria remedy — called also *cinchona bark* [countess of *Chinchón,* died 1641, wife of the Peruvian viceroy] — **cin•chon•ic** \sing-ˈkän-ik, sin-ˈchän-\ *adj*

Cinco de Mayo \ˌsing-kō-də-ˈmī-ō, ˌsēng-kō-t̲h̲ā-ˈmä-yō\ *n* **:** a Mexican and Mexican-American celebration held on May 5 in commemoration of the Mexican victory over the French at Puebla in 1862 [Sp, fifth of May]

cinc•ture \ˈsing-chər, ˈsingk-\ *n* **:** BELT 1, GIRDLE [Latin *cinctura,* from *cingere* "to gird"]

cin•der \ˈsin-dər\ *n* **1 :** waste matter from the smelting of metal ores **:** SLAG **2** *pl* **:** a collection of ash after something has been burned **3 a :** a piece of partly burned coal or wood in which fire is extinct **b :** a hot coal without flame **4 :** a fragment of solidified lava from an erupting volcano [Old English *sinder*] — **cin•dery** \-də-rē, -drē\ *adj*

cinder block *n* **:** a building block made of concrete using coal cinders as aggregate

cin•e•ma \'sin-ə-mə\ *n* **1 :** MOTION PICTURE ⟨a *cinema* director⟩ **2 :** a theater for showing movies ⟨went to the *cinema*⟩ **3 a :** the business of making movies ⟨worked in *cinema*⟩ **b :** the art or technique of making movies ⟨a student of French *cinema*⟩ [short for *cinematograph,* derived from Greek *kinēma* "motion," from *kinein* "to move"] — **cin•e•mat•ic** \ˌsin-ə-'mat-ik\ *adj* — **cin•e•mat•i•cal•ly** \-'mat-i-kə-lē, -klē\ *adv*

cin•e•mat•o•graph \ˌsin-ə-'mat-ə-ˌgraf\ *n, chiefly British* **:** a motion-picture camera, projector, theater, or show

cin•e•ma•tog•ra•phy \ˌsin-ə-mə-'täg-rə-fē\ *n* **:** the art or science of motion-picture photography — **cin•e•ma•tog•ra•pher** \-fər\ *n* — **cin•e•mat•o•graph•ic** \ˌsin-ə-ˌmat-ə-'graf-ik\ *adj* — **cin•e•mat•o•graph•i•cal•ly** \-i-kə-lē, -klē\ *adv*

cin•er•ar•ia \ˌsin-ə-'rer-ē-ə, -'rar-\ *n* **:** a potted plant related to the daisies with heart-shaped leaves and clusters of bright flower heads [Latin *cinerarius* "of ashes," from *cinis* "ashes"]

cin•er•ar•i•um \-ē-əm\ *n, pl* **-ar•ia** \-ē-ə\ **:** a place to receive the ashes of the cremated dead [Latin, from *cinis* "ashes"] — **cin•er•ary** \'sin-ə-ˌrer-ē\ *adj*

cin•na•bar \'sin-ə-ˌbär\ *n* **:** a red mineral that consists of a sulfide of mercury HgS and is the only important ore of mercury [Latin *cinnabaris,* from Greek *kinnabari*]

cin•na•mon \'sin-ə-mən\ *n* **1 a :** a spice consisting of the highly aromatic bark of any of several Asian trees related to the laurels; *also* **:** the bark **b :** a tree that yields cinnamon **2 :** a light yellowish brown [Latin, from Greek *kinnamon*] — **cin•na•mony** \-mə-nē\ *adj*

cinque•foil \'singk-ˌfȯil, 'sangk-\ *n* **1 :** any of a genus of plants related to the roses and having 5-lobed leaves **2 :** a design consisting of five joined foils [Medieval French *cincfoille,* from Latin *quinquefolium,* from *quinque* "five" + *folium* "leaf"]

[1]**ci•pher** \'sī-fər\ *n* **1 a :** ZERO 1 — see NUMBER table **b :** an insignificant individual **:** NONENTITY **2 a :** a method of transforming a text in order to conceal its meaning — compare CODE 4 **b :** a message in code **3 :** ARABIC NUMERAL **4 :** a combination of symbolic letters; *esp* **:** the interwoven initials of a name [Medieval Latin *cifra,* from Arabic *ṣifr* "empty, cipher, zero"]

[2]**cipher** *vb* **ci•phered; ci•pher•ing** \-fə-ring, -fring\ **1 :** to use figures in a mathematical process **2 :** ENCIPHER **3 :** to compute arithmetically ⟨a sum *ciphered* out⟩

cir•ca \'sər-kə\ *prep* **:** at, in, or of approximately — used especially with dates ⟨born *circa* 1600⟩ [Latin, from *circum* "around"]

cir•ca•di•an \sər-'kad-ē-ən, -'kad-; sər-kə-'dē-ən, -'dī-\ *adj* **:** being, having, or occurring in approximately 24-hour periods or cycles (as of biological activity or function) ⟨*circadian* rhythms in hatching⟩ [Latin *circa* "about" + *dies* "day" + English *-an*]

Cir•cas•sian walnut \sər-'kash-ən-\ *n* **:** the light brown irregularly black-veined wood of the English walnut much used for veneer and cabinetwork [*Circassia,* Russia]

cir•ci•nate \'sərs-n-ˌāt\ *adj* **:** COILED, ROUNDED; *esp* **:** rolled up on the axis with the apex as a center ⟨*circinate* fronds of ferns⟩ [Latin *circinare* "to round," from *circinus* "pair of compasses," from *circus* "circle, circus"] — **cir•ci•nate•ly** *adv*

[1]**cir•cle** \'sər-kəl\ *n* **1 a :** HALO 1 **b :** a line segment that is curved so that its ends meet and every point on the line is equally far away from a single point inside **c :** the flat surface enclosed by a circle **2 :** something in the form of a circle or section of a circle: as **a :** CIRCLET, DIADEM **b :** a balcony or tier of seats in a theater or opera house **c :** a circle formed on the surface of a sphere by the intersection of a plane that passes through it ⟨*circles* of latitude⟩ — compare GREAT CIRCLE, SMALL CIRCLE **d :** ROTARY 2 **3 :** an area of action or influence **:** REALM **4 a :** CYCLE 2a, ROUND ⟨the wheel has come full *circle*⟩ **b :** fallacious reasoning in which something apparently proved is really taken for granted **5 :** a group bound by a common tie; *esp* **:** COTERIE ⟨a *circle* of friends⟩ [Medieval French *cercle,* from Latin *circulus,* from *circus* "circle, circus"]

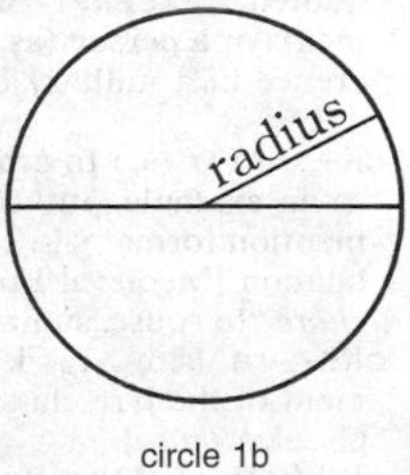

circle 1b

[2]**circle** *vb* **cir•cled; cir•cling** \-kə-ling, -kling\ **1 :** to enclose in or as if in a circle **:** ENCIRCLE **2 :** to move or revolve around ⟨a spacecraft *circling* the earth⟩ **3 :** to move in or as if in a circle — **cir•cler** \-kə-lər, -klər\ *n*

circle graph *n* **:** PIE CHART

cir•clet \'sər-klət\ *n* **:** a little circle; *esp* **:** a circular ornament

cir•cuit \'sər-kət\ *n* **1 :** a boundary line around an area; *also* **:** the space enclosed **2 :** a moving or revolving around (as in a circle or orbit) **:** CIRCLING ⟨the *circuit* of the earth around the sun⟩ **3 a :** a regular tour (as by a judge or preacher) around an assigned territory **b :** the route traveled **4 a :** the complete path of an electric current **b :** an assemblage of electronic elements **:** HOOKUP **5 a :** an association of similar groups **:** LEAGUE **b :** a group of establishments offering similar entertainment or presenting a series of contests; *esp* **:** a number or chain of theaters at which productions are successively presented [Medieval French *circuite,* from Latin *circuitus,* from *circuire* "to go around," from *circum* "around" + *ire* "to go"] — **circuit** *vb* — **cir•cuit•al** \-kət-l\ *adj*

circuit breaker *n* **:** a switch that automatically interrupts the current of an overloaded electric circuit

circuit court *n* **:** a court that sits in two or more places in a judicial district

cir•cu•i•tous \sər-'kyü-ət-əs\ *adj* **1 :** marked by a circular or winding course ⟨a *circuitous* route⟩ **2 :** not being or going straight to the point **:** INDIRECT ⟨a *circuitous* explanation⟩ — **cir•cu•i•tous•ly** *adv* — **cir•cu•i•tous•ness** *n*

cir•cuit•ry \'sər-kə-trē\ *n, pl* **-ries :** the plan or the components of an electric circuit

cir•cu•i•ty \sər-'kyü-ət-ē\ *n* **:** INDIRECTION 1

[1]**cir•cu•lar** \'sər-kyə-lər\ *adj* **1 a :** having the form of a circle **:** ROUND ⟨a *circular* driveway⟩ **b :** having a circular base or bases ⟨a *circular* cone⟩ **2 :** marked by or moving in a circle or spiral **3 :** relating to or forming part of a circle ⟨a *circular* arc⟩ **4 :** CIRCUITOUS **5 :** characterized by reasoning in a circle ⟨*circular* arguments⟩ **6 :** sent around to a number of persons ⟨a *circular* letter⟩ — **cir•cu•lar•i•ty** \ˌsər-kyə-'lar-ət-ē\ *n* — **cir•cu•lar•ly** \'sər-kyə-lər-lē\ *adv* — **cir•cu•lar•ness** *n*

[2]**circular** *n* **:** a paper (as a leaflet containing an advertisement) intended for wide distribution

circular function *n* **:** TRIGONOMETRIC FUNCTION

cir•cu•lar•ize \'sər-kyə-lə-ˌrīz\ *vt* **:** to send circulars to — **cir•cu•lar•i•za•tion** \ˌsər-kyə-lə-rə-'zā-shən\ *n*

circular saw *n* **:** a power saw having a revolving thin steel disk with teeth on its edge

cir•cu•late \'sər-kyə-ˌlāt\ *vb* **1 :** to move or cause to move in a circle, circuit, or orbit; *esp* **:** to follow a course that returns to the starting point ⟨blood *circulates* through the body⟩ **2 :** to pass from person to person or place to place: as **a :** to flow without obstruction ⟨air *circulating* through the house⟩ **b :** to become or cause to become well-known or widespread ⟨*circulate* a rumor⟩ **c :** to come into the hands of readers ⟨a magazine that *circulated* widely⟩ — **cir•cu•la•tor** \-ˌlāt-ər\ *n*

cir•cu•la•tion \ˌsər-kyə-'lā-shən\ *n* **1 :** orderly movement through a circuit; *esp* **:** the movement of blood through the vessels of the body caused by the pumping action of the heart **2 a :** passage or transmission from person to person or place to place; *esp* **:** the interchange of currency ⟨coins in *circulation*⟩ **b :** the extent of dissemination (as of copies of a publication sold over a given period) — **cir•cu•la•tive** \'sər-kyə-ˌlāt-iv\ *adj*

cir•cu•la•to•ry \'sər-kyə-lə-ˌtōr-ē, -ˌtȯr-\ *adj* **:** of or relating to circulation or the circulatory system

circulatory system *n* **:** the system of blood, blood vessels, lymphatics, and heart concerned with the circulation of the blood and lymph

circum- *prefix* **:** around **:** about ⟨*circum*polar⟩ [Latin, from *circus* "circle"]

cir•cum•am•bi•ent \ˌsər-kəm-'am-bē-ənt\ *adj* **:** being on all sides **:** ENCOMPASSING

cir•cum•am•bu•late \-'am-byə-ˌlāt\ *vb* **:** to circle on foot especially as or as if part of a ritual

cir•cum•cen•ter \'sər-kəm-ˌsent-ər\ *n* **:** the point at which the perpendicular bisectors of the sides of a triangle intersect and which is the same distance from each of the three vertices

\ə\ **abut**	\au̇\ **out**	\i\ **tip**	\ȯ\ **saw**	\u̇\ **foot**
\ər\ **further**	\ch\ **chin**	\ī\ **life**	\ȯi\ **coin**	\y\ **yet**
\a\ **mat**	\e\ **pet**	\j\ **job**	\th\ **thin**	\yü\ **few**
\ā\ **take**	\ē\ **easy**	\ng\ **sing**	\th\ **this**	\yu̇\ **cure**
\ä\ **cot, cart**	\g\ **go**	\ō\ **bone**	\ü\ **food**	\zh\ **vision**

cir·cum·cise \ˈsər-kəm-ˌsīz\ *vt* : to cut off the foreskin of [Latin *circumcidere,* from *circum-* + *caedere* "to cut"]

cir·cum·ci·sion \ˌsər-kəm-ˈsizh-ən, ˈsər-kəm-ˌ\ *n* **1** : the act of circumcising or being circumcised; *esp* : a Jewish rite performed on male infants as a sign of inclusion in the covenant between God and Abraham **2** *cap* : January 1 observed as a festival in some churches in commemoration of the circumcision of the infant Jesus

cir·cum·fer·ence \sər-ˈkəm-fərns, sə-, -ˈkəmp-, -fə-rəns, -frəns\ *n* **1** : a line that goes around or encloses a circle **2** : the external boundary or surface of a body : PERIPHERY [Medieval French, from Latin *circumferentia,* from *circumferre* "to carry around," from *circum-* + *ferre* "to carry"] — **cir·cum·fer·en·tial** \-ˌkəm-fə-ˈren-chəl, -ˌkəmp-\ *adj*

[1]**cir·cum·flex** \ˈsər-kəm-ˌfleks\ *adj* **1 a** : having the kind of sound indicated by a circumflex **b** : marked with a circumflex **2** : bending around ⟨a *circumflex* artery⟩ [Latin *circumflexus,* past participle of *circumflectere* "to bend around, mark with a circumflex," from *circum-* + *flectere* "to bend"]

[2]**circumflex** *n* : a mark ˆ, ˆ, or ˜ used chiefly to indicate length, contraction, or a specific vowel quality

cir·cum·lo·cu·tion \ˌsər-kəm-lō-ˈkyü-shən\ *n* : use of many words to express a relatively simple idea or to avoid stating one's position directly or clearly [Latin *circumlocutio,* from *circum-* + *locutio* "speech," from *loqui* "to speak"] — **cir·cum·loc·u·to·ry** \-ˈläk-yə-ˌtōr-ē, -ˌtȯr-\ *adj*

cir·cum·lu·nar \ˌsər-kəm-ˈlü-nər\ *adj* : revolving about or surrounding the moon

cir·cum·nav·i·gate \-ˈnav-ə-ˌgāt\ *vt* : to go completely around (as the earth) especially by water; *also* : to go around instead of through : BYPASS — **cir·cum·nav·i·ga·tion** \-ˌnav-ə-ˈgā-shən\ *n* — **cir·cum·nav·i·ga·tor** \-ˈnav-ə-ˌgāt-ər\ *n*

cir·cum·po·lar \ˌsər-kəm-ˈpō-lər\ *adj* **1** : continually visible above the horizon ⟨a *circumpolar* star⟩ **2** : surrounding or found in the vicinity of the north pole or south pole

cir·cum·scribe \ˈsər-kəm-ˌskrīb\ *vt* **1 a** : to draw a line around **b** : to surround by a boundary **2 a** : to limit the range or activity of definitely and clearly **b** : to define or mark off carefully **3** : to construct or be constructed around (a geometrical figure) so as to touch at as many points as possible ⟨a triangle *circumscribed* about a circle⟩ [Latin *circumscribere,* from *circum-* + *scribere* "to write, draw"] ***synonyms*** see LIMIT

cir·cum·scrip·tion \ˌsər-kəm-ˈskrip-shən\ *n* **1** : something that circumscribes: as **a** : BOUNDARY **b** : RESTRICTION 1 **2** : the act of circumscribing : the state of being circumscribed **3** : a circumscribed area [Latin *circumscriptio,* from *circumscribere* "to circumscribe"]

cir·cum·spect \ˈsər-kəm-ˌspekt\ *adj* : careful to consider all circumstances and possible consequences [Latin *circumspectus,* from *circumspicere* "to look around, be cautious," from *circum-* + *specere* "to look"] — **cir·cum·spec·tion** \ˌsər-kəm-ˈspek-shən\ *n* — **cir·cum·spect·ly** *adv*

cir·cum·stance \ˈsər-kəm-ˌstans\ *n* **1** : a fact or event that must be considered along with another fact or event **2** *pl* : surrounding conditions ⟨under the *circumstances*⟩ **3** *pl* : condition or situation with respect to wealth ⟨in easy *circumstances*⟩ **4** : formal ceremony accompanying an event ⟨pomp and *circumstance*⟩ **5** : a happening or fact in a chain of events : DETAIL **6** : CHANCE 1, FATE ⟨a victim of *circumstance*⟩ [Medieval French, from Latin *circumstantia,* from *circumstare* "to surround," from *circum-* + *stare* "to stand"]

cir·cum·stanced \-ˌstanst\ *adj* : placed in particular circumstances especially in regard to property or income

cir·cum·stan·tial \ˌsər-kəm-ˈstan-chəl\ *adj* **1** : consisting of or relating to circumstances : dependent on circumstances ⟨*circumstantial* evidence⟩ **2** : relating to a matter but not essential to it : INCIDENTAL **3** : containing full details ⟨a *circumstantial* account of what happened⟩ — **cir·cum·stan·tial·ly** \-ˈstanch-lē, -ə-lē\ *adv*

synonyms CIRCUMSTANTIAL, PARTICULAR, MINUTE, DETAILED mean dealing with a matter fully and usually point by point. CIRCUMSTANTIAL implies fullness of details that fixes something described in time and space ⟨a *circumstantial* account of our visit⟩. PARTICULAR implies a precise attention to every detail ⟨a *particular* description of the scene of the crime⟩. MINUTE implies close and searching attention to the smallest details ⟨a *minute* examination of a fossil⟩. DETAILED stresses abundance or completeness of detail ⟨a *detailed* analysis of the event⟩.

cir·cum·vent \ˌsər-kəm-ˈvent\ *vt* **1** : to go around : BYPASS ⟨*circumvent* the town⟩ **2** : to escape from or avoid especially by skill or trickery : get around ⟨*circumvent* the law⟩ ⟨*circumvent* difficulties⟩ [Latin *circumvenire,* from *circum-* + *venire* "to come"] — **cir·cum·ven·tion** \-ˈven-chən\ *n*

cir·cus \ˈsər-kəs\ *n* **1** : a large arena enclosed by tiers of seats and used for spectacles (as athletic contests or horse races) especially in ancient Rome **2 a** : a usually traveling public entertainment that features clowns, acrobats, and animal acts **b** : a performance of a circus **c** : the company of a circus including personnel and livestock **3** : an activity suggesting a circus especially in being a showy public display ⟨turned the campaign into a political *circus*⟩ **4** *British* : a usually circular area at the intersection of streets [Latin, "circle, circus"]

cirque \ˈsərk\ *n* **1** : something round : CIRCLET, CIRCLE **2** : a deep steep-walled hollow on a mountain shaped like half a bowl [French, "circus, amphitheater," from Latin *circus*]

cirque 2

cir·rho·sis \sə-ˈrō-səs\ *n* : fibrosis and hardening of the liver [Greek *kirrhos* "orange-colored"] — **cir·rhot·ic** \-ˈrät-ik\ *adj or n*

cir·ro·cu·mu·lus \ˌsir-ō-ˈkyü-myə-ləs\ *n* : a cloud form of small white rounded masses at a high altitude usually in regular groupings

cir·ro·stra·tus \-ˈstrāt-əs, -ˈstrat-\ *n* : a fairly uniform high thin cloud layer that is darker than cirrus

cir·rus \ˈsir-əs\ *n, pl* **cir·ri** \ˈsiər-ˌī\ **1** : a plant tendril **2** : a slender usually flexible animal appendage **3** : a wispy white cloud usually of minute ice crystals formed at altitudes of about 20,000 to 40,000 feet (6,000 to 12,000 meters) [Latin, "curl, ringlet, tuft, bird's crest, fringe"]

cis \ˈsis\ *adj* : having certain atoms or groups of atoms attached on the same side but opposite ends of a double bond

cis- *prefix* : on this side ⟨*cis*lunar⟩ [Latin]

cis·co \ˈsis-kō\ *n, pl* **ciscoes** : any of various whitefishes; *esp* : LAKE HERRING [Canadian French *ciscoette*]

cis·lu·nar \ˈsis-ˈlü-nər\ *adj* : lying between the earth and the moon or the moon's orbit ⟨*cislunar* space⟩

Cis·ter·cian \sis-ˈtər-shən\ *n* : a member of a monastic order founded at Cîteaux, France, in 1098 under Benedictine rule [Medieval Latin *Cistercium* "Cîteaux"] — **Cistercian** *adj*

cis·tern \ˈsis-tərn\ *n* **1** : an often underground artificial reservoir or tank for storing water and especially rainwater **2** : a fluid-containing sac or cavity in an organism [Latin *cisterna,* from *cista* "box, chest"]

cit·a·del \ˈsit-əd-l, -ə-ˌdel\ *n* **1** : a fortress that commands a city **2** : STRONGHOLD 1 [Middle French *citadelle,* from Italian *cittadella,* from *cittade* "city," from Medieval Latin *civitas*]

ci·ta·tion \sī-ˈtā-shən\ *n* **1** : an official order to appear (as before a court) **2 a** : an act or instance of quoting **b** : a passage quoted : EXCERPT **3 a** : a formal statement of the achievements of a person (as one receiving an award) **b** : specific reference in a military dispatch to praiseworthy performance of duty

cite \ˈsīt\ *vt* **1** : to order to appear before a court **2** : to quote as an example, authority, or proof **3 a** : to refer to; *esp* : to mention formally in commendation or praise **b** : to name in a citation [Medieval French *citer* "to cite, summon," from Latin *citare* "to rouse, summon," from *ciēre* "to stir, move"]

cith·a·ra \ˈsith-ə-rə, ˈkith-\ *n* : an ancient Greek stringed instrument of the lyre class with a wooden soundboard [Latin, from Greek *kithara*]

cit·i·fy \ˈsit-i-ˌfī\ *vt* **-fied; -fy·ing** : to accustom to urban ways

cit·i·zen \ˈsit-ə-zən\ *n* **1** : an inhabitant of a city or town **2 a** : a member of a state **b** : a person who by birth or naturalization owes allegiance to a government and is entitled to protection from it **3** : CIVILIAN [Medieval French *citezein,* alteration of *citeien,* from *cité* "city"] — **cit·i·zen·ly** \-lē\ *adj*

synonyms CITIZEN, SUBJECT, NATIONAL mean a person owing allegiance to and entitled to the protection of a sovereign state. CITIZEN is preferred for one owing allegiance to a state in which sovereign power is retained by the people and sharing in the political rights of those people ⟨the rights of a free *citizen*⟩. SUBJECT implies allegiance to a personal sovereign such as a monarch ⟨the king's *subjects*⟩. NATIONAL designates one who may claim the protection of a state and applies especially to one living or traveling outside that state ⟨American *nationals* working in Europe⟩.

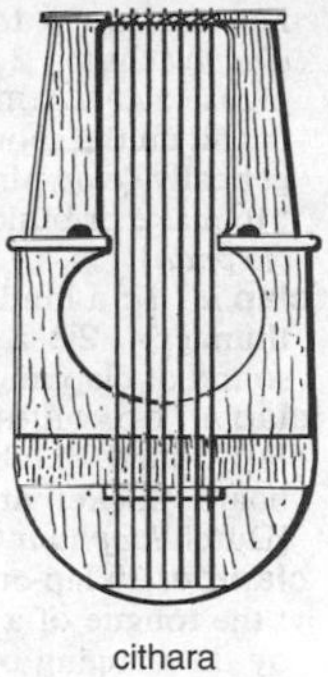
cithara

cit•i•zen•ess \-zə-nəs\ *n* **:** a woman who is a citizen

cit•i•zen•ry \-zən-rē\ *n, pl* **-ries :** the whole body of citizens

citizens band \-zənz-\ *n* **:** one of the frequency bands that in the U.S. is allocated officially for private radio communication

cit•i•zen•ship \-zən-ˌship\ *n* **1 :** possession of the rights and privileges of a citizen **2 :** the quality of a person's response to membership in a community

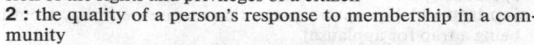

cit•rate \ˈsi-ˌtrāt\ *n* **:** a salt or ester of citric acid

cit•ric acid \ˈsi-trik-\ *n* **:** a pleasantly sour-tasting acid $C_6H_8O_7$ occurring in cellular metabolism and obtained especially from lemon and lime juices or by fermentation of sugars and used as a flavoring

citric acid cycle *n* **:** KREBS CYCLE

cit•rine \ˈsi-ˌtrīn\ *adj* **:** resembling a citron or lemon especially in color [Medieval French *citrin,* from Latin *citrus* "citron tree"]

cit•ron \ˈsi-trən\ *n* **1 a :** a fruit like the lemon in appearance and structure but larger; *also* **:** the citrus tree producing this fruit **b :** the preserved rind of the citron used especially in fruitcake **2 :** a small hard-fleshed watermelon used mostly in pickles and preserves [Middle French, from Latin *citrus* "citron tree"]

cit•ro•nel•la \ˌsi-trə-ˈnel-ə\ *n* **:** a lemon-scented grass of southern Asia that yields an oil used in perfumery and as an insect repellent; *also* **:** its oil [French *citronelle* "lemon balm," from *citron* "citron"]

cit•rul•line \ˈsi-trə-ˌlēn\ *n* **:** an amino acid $C_6H_{13}N_3O_3$ formed especially as an intermediate in the conversion of ornithine to arginine [New Latin *Citrullus,* genus name of the watermelon]

cit•rus \ˈsi-trəs\ *n, pl* **citrus** *or* **cit•rus•es :** any of a genus of often thorny trees and shrubs grown in warm regions for their fruits (as orange, grapefruit, or lemon) with firm usually thick rind and juicy pulp; *also* **:** the fruit of a citrus [Latin, "citron tree"] — **citrus** *adj*

city \ˈsit-ē\ *n, pl* **cit•ies 1 a :** an inhabited place of greater size or importance than a town **b :** a usually large or important place in the U.S. governed under a charter granted by the state **2 :** CITY-STATE **3 :** the people of a city [Medieval French *cité* "large or small town," from Medieval Latin *civitas,* from Latin, "citizenship, state, city of Rome," from *civis* "citizen"]

city hall *n* **1 :** the chief administrative building of a city **2 a :** a municipal government **b :** city officialdom or bureaucracy ⟨you can't fight *city hall*⟩

city manager *n* **:** an official employed by an elected council to administer a city government

city–state \ˈsit-ē-ˈstāt, -ˌstāt\ *n* **:** a self-governing state (as of ancient Greece) consisting of a city and surrounding territory

city•wide \ˈsit-ē-ˌwīd\ *adj* **:** including or involving all parts of a city ⟨a *citywide* blackout⟩

civ•et \ˈsiv-ət\ *n* **1 :** a thick yellowish musky-odored substance obtained from the civet cat and used in perfume **2 :** CIVET CAT [Middle French *civette,* from Italian *zibetto,* from Arabic *zabād* "civet perfume"]

civet cat *n* **1 :** a long-bodied short-legged African mammal that is related to the mongooses and produces most of the civet of commerce **2 :** any of several small spotted skunks of western North America

civ•ic \ˈsiv-ik\ *adj* **:** of or relating to a citizen, a city, or citizenship ⟨*civic* pride⟩ ⟨*civic* duty⟩ [Latin *civicus,* from *civis* "citizen"] — **civ•i•cal•ly** \ˈsiv-i-kə-lē, -klē\ *adv*

civ•ics \ˈsiv-iks\ *n* **:** the study of the rights and duties of citizens

civ•il \ˈsiv-əl\ *adj* **1 :** of or relating to citizens **2 :** of or relating to the state as an organized political body ⟨*civil* institutions⟩ **3 :** of or relating to the general population as distinguished from the military or the church **4 :** marked by courtesy or politeness ⟨gave a *civil* answer⟩ **5 a :** relating to legal proceedings in connection with private rights and obligations ⟨the *civil* code⟩ ⟨a *civil* suit⟩ **b :** of or relating to the civil law [Medieval French, from Latin *civilis,* from *civis* "citizen"]

synonyms CIVIL, POLITE, COURTEOUS mean observant of the forms required by good breeding. CIVIL implies no more than barely meeting the requirements of good breeding and the avoidance of overt rudeness ⟨owed the questioner a *civil* reply⟩. POLITE implies showing good manners and thoughtfulness but may often suggest lack of warmth or cordiality ⟨if you can't be pleasant, at least be *polite*⟩. COURTEOUS implies more actively considerate or dignified politeness ⟨they were *courteous* to their customers⟩.

civil defense *n* **:** organized protective and emergency relief activities by civilians in case of attack or disaster

civil engineering *n* **:** engineering that deals with the designing and construction of public works (as roads or harbors) and of various private works — **civil engineer** *n*

ci•vil•ian \sə-ˈvil-yən\ *n* **:** one not on active duty in the armed services or not on a police or firefighting force — **civilian** *adj*

ci•vil•i•ty \sə-ˈvil-ət-ē\ *n, pl* **-ties 1 :** civilized conduct; *esp* **:** POLITENESS, COURTESY **2 :** a polite act or expression

civ•i•li•za•tion \ˌsiv-ə-lə-ˈzā-shən\ *n* **1 a :** a relatively high level of cultural and technological development **b :** the special culture of a people or a period ⟨Greek *civilization*⟩ ⟨18th century *civilization*⟩ **2 :** the process of becoming civilized **3 a :** refinement of thought, manners, or taste **b :** city life and comforts

civ•i•lize \ˈsiv-ə-ˌlīz\ *vt* **:** to raise out of a savage state; *esp* **:** to bring to an advanced and ordered stage of cultural development — **civ•i•lized** *adj*

civil law *n, often cap C&L* **1 :** a body of law developed from Roman law **2 :** the law of civil or private rights

civil liberty *n* **:** freedom from governmental interference with rights (as of free speech) especially as guaranteed by a bill of rights

civ•il•ly \ˈsiv-ə-lē, -əl-lē\ *adv* **:** in a civil manner **:** POLITELY

civil marriage *n* **:** a marriage performed by a magistrate

civil rights *n pl* **:** the rights of personal liberty guaranteed to U.S. citizens by the 13th and 14th amendments to the Constitution and by acts of Congress

civil servant *n* **:** a member of a civil service

civil service *n* **:** the administrative service of a government exclusive of the armed forces

civil war *n* **:** a war between opposing groups of citizens of the same country or nation

clab•ber \ˈklab-ər\ *n, chiefly dialect* **:** sour milk that has thickened or curdled [short for *bonnyclabber,* from Irish *bainne clabair,* from *bainne* "milk" + *clabar* "sour thick milk"]

clab•bered \ˈklab-ərd\ *adj, of milk or cream* **:** being thickened or curdled

[1]clack \ˈklak\ *vb* **1 :** CHATTER 2, PRATTLE **2 :** to make or cause to make a clatter [Middle English *clacken*] — **clack•er** *n*

[2]clack *n* **1 :** CHATTER ⟨the *clack* of voices⟩ **2 :** a sound of clacking ⟨the *clack* of a typewriter⟩

[1]clad *past and past participle of* CLOTHE

[2]clad \ˈklad\ *adj* **:** CLOTHED, COVERED ⟨ivy-*clad* walls⟩ [past participle of *clothe*]

[1]claim \ˈklām\ *vt* **1 a :** to ask for as one's right or property ⟨*claim* an inheritance⟩ ⟨*claim* one's bags⟩ **b :** to call for **:** REQUIRE ⟨this matter *claims* our attention⟩ **2 a :** to state as a fact **:** MAINTAIN ⟨*claimed* they'd been cheated⟩ **b :** PROFESS ⟨*claimed* to know nothing of the matter⟩ [Medieval French *clamer,* from Latin *clamare* "to cry out"] ***synonyms*** see DEMAND — **claim•able** \ˈklā-mə-bəl\ *adj* — **claim•er** *n*

[2]claim *n* **1 :** a demand for something due or believed to be due ⟨an insurance *claim*⟩ **2 a :** a right to something; *esp* **:** a title to something in the possession of another **b :** an assertion open to challenge ⟨a *claim* of authenticity⟩ **3 :** something claimed; *esp* **:** a tract of land marked out by a settler or prospector

claim•ant \ˈklā-mənt\ *n* **:** a person who asserts a right to something ⟨a *claimant* to an estate⟩

clair•voy•ance \klaar-ˈvȯi-əns, kleər-\ *n* **1 :** the professed power of seeing or knowing about things that are not present to the senses **2 :** sharp insight **:** DISCERNMENT

[1]clair•voy•ant \-ənt\ *adj* **:** of, relating to, or having clairvoyance

⟨claims to be *clairvoyant*⟩ ⟨*clairvoyant* powers⟩ [French, from *clair* "clear" + *voyant,* present participle of *voir* "to see"] — **clair·voy·ant·ly** *adv*

²clairvoyant *n* **:** a person held to have the power of clairvoyance

¹clam \'klam\ *n* **1 :** any of numerous edible marine bivalve mollusks living in sand or mud **2 :** a freshwater mussel [earlier *clam* "clamp," from Old English *clamm* "bond, fetter"; from the clamping action of the shells]

clam 1

²clam *vi* **clammed; clam·ming :** to gather clams especially by digging

clam·bake \'klam-ˌbāk\ *n* **:** a party or outing where food is cooked on heated rocks covered by seaweed; *also* **:** a usually noisy and lively get-together

clam·ber \'klam-bər\ *vi* **clam·bered; clam·ber·ing** \'klam-bə-ring, -bring\ **:** to climb awkwardly (as by scrambling) ⟨*clamber* over steep rocks⟩ [Middle English *clambren*] — **clam·ber·er** \-bər-ər\ *n*

clam·my \'klam-ē\ *adj* **clam·mi·er; -est :** being damp, soft, sticky, and usually cool [Middle English, probably from *clammen* "to smear, stick," from Old English *clǣman*] — **clam·mi·ly** \'klam-ə-lē\ *adv* — **clam·mi·ness** \'klam-ē-nəs\ *n*

¹clam·or \'klam-ər\ *n* **1 a :** noisy shouting **b :** a loud continuous noise **2 :** insistent protest or demand ⟨public *clamor* for a tax cut⟩ [Medieval French *clamour,* from Latin *clamor,* from *clamare* "to cry out"]

²clamor *vb* **clam·ored; clam·or·ing** \'klam-ring, -ə-ring\ **1 :** to make loud noise ⟨gulls *clamored* overhead⟩ **2 :** to express insistently and noisily ⟨*clamoring* that they had been misunderstood⟩

clam·or·ous \'klam-rəs, -ə-rəs\ *adj* **:** full of clamor **:** NOISY — **clam·or·ous·ly** *adv* — **clam·or·ous·ness** *n*

¹clamp \'klamp\ *n* **:** a device that holds or presses two or more parts together firmly [probably from Dutch *klamp*]

²clamp *vt* **1 :** to fasten with or as if with a clamp ⟨*clamp* two boards together⟩ **2 a :** to place by decree **:** IMPOSE — often used with *on* ⟨*clamped* on a curfew after the riots⟩ **b :** to hold tightly

clamp down *vi* **:** to impose restrictions ⟨*clamping down* on speeders⟩

clam·shell \'klam-ˌshel\ *n* **1 :** the shell of a clam **2 :** a bucket or grapple (as on a dredge) having two hinged jaws

clam up *vi* **:** to become silent; *esp* **:** to refuse to talk further ⟨they *clammed up* when asked for details⟩

clam worm *n* **:** any of several large burrowing marine annelid worms often used as bait

clan \'klan\ *n* **1 a :** a group (as in the Scottish Highlands) made up of households whose heads claim descent from a common ancestor **b :** a group of people having a common ancestor **:** FAMILY **2 :** a group united by a common interest ⟨the whole *clan* of actors⟩ [Scottish Gaelic *clann* "offspring, clan," from Irish *cland* "plant, offspring," from Latin *planta* "plant"]

clan·des·tine \klan-'des-tən\ *adj* **:** held in or conducted with secrecy **:** FURTIVE ⟨a *clandestine* meeting⟩ [Latin *clandestinus,* from *clam* "secretly"] ***synonyms*** see SECRET — **clan·des·tine·ly** *adv* — **clan·des·tine·ness** *n*

¹clang \'klang\ *vb* **:** to make or cause to make a clang [Latin *clangere*]

²clang *n* **:** a loud ringing metallic sound ⟨the *clang* of a fire alarm⟩

¹clang·or \'klang-ər, -gər\ *n* **:** a resounding clang or series of clangs ⟨the *clangor* of hammers⟩ [Latin, from *clangere* "to clang"] — **clang·or·ous** \-ə-rəs, -gə-rəs\ *adj* — **clang·or·ous·ly** *adv*

²clangor *vi* **:** to make a clangor

¹clank \'klangk\ *vb* **1 :** to make or cause to make a clank or series of clanks ⟨the radiator hissed and *clanked*⟩ **2 :** to move with a clank ⟨tanks *clanking* through the streets⟩ [probably imitative] — **clank·ing·ly** \'klang-king-lē\ *adv*

²clank *n* **:** a sharp brief metallic ringing sound

clan·nish \'klan-ish\ *adj* **1 :** of or relating to a clan **2 :** tending to associate only with others of similar background or status ⟨a *clannish* clique⟩ — **clan·nish·ly** *adv* — **clan·nish·ness** *n*

clans·man \'klanz-mən\ *n* **:** a member of a clan

¹clap \'klap\ *vb* **clapped; clap·ping 1 :** to strike (as two flat hard surfaces) together to produce a sharp noise ⟨the door *clapped* shut⟩ **2 :** to strike the hands together repeatedly in applause **:** APPLAUD **3 :** to strike with the open hand ⟨*clapped* a friend on the shoulder⟩ **4 :** to place, put, or set especially energetically ⟨*clap* him into jail⟩ ⟨since I first *clapped* eyes on it⟩ **5 :** to make or build hastily ⟨*clap* together a shelter⟩ [Old English *clæppan*]

²clap *n* **1 :** a loud crash made by or as if by clapping ⟨a *clap* of thunder⟩ **2 :** a firm slap ⟨a *clap* on the shoulder⟩ **3 :** the sound of clapping hands; *esp* **:** APPLAUSE

³clap *n* **:** GONORRHEA [Middle French *clapoir* "bubo"]

clap·board \'klab-ərd; 'kla-ˌbōrd, 'klap-, -ˌbȯrd\ *n* **:** a narrow board thicker at one edge than at the other used as siding [Dutch *klaphout* "stave wood"] — **clapboard** *vt*

clap·per \'klap-ər\ *n* **:** one that makes a clapping sound: as **a :** the tongue of a bell **b :** a device that makes noise especially by the banging of one part against another **c :** a person who applauds

clap·trap \'klap-ˌtrap\ *n* **:** pretentious nonsense [¹*clap;* from its being a trap for applause]

claque \'klak\ *n* **1 :** a group hired to applaud at a performance **2 :** a group of self-seeking flatterers [French, from *claquer* "to clap"]

clar·et \'klar-ət\ *n* **1 :** a dry red table wine **2 :** a dark purplish red [Middle French *vin claret* "clear wine"] — **claret** *adj*

clar·i·fy \'klar-ə-ˌfī\ *vb* **-fied; -fy·ing 1 :** to make or become pure or clear ⟨*clarify* a liquid⟩ **2 :** to make or become more readily understandable ⟨*clarify* an explanation⟩ [Medieval French *clarifier,* from Late Latin *clarificare,* from Latin *clarus* "clear"] — **clar·i·fi·ca·tion** \ˌklar-ə-fə-'kā-shən\ *n* — **clar·i·fi·er** \'klar-ə-ˌfī-ər, -fīr\ *n*

clar·i·net \ˌklar-ə-'net, 'klar-ə-nət\ *n* **:** a single-reed woodwind instrument having a cylindrical tube with a moderately flaring end [French *clarinette*] — **clar·i·net·ist** *or* **clar·i·net·tist** \ˌklar-ə-'net-əst\ *n*

clarinet

¹clar·i·on \'klar-ē-ən\ *n* **:** a medieval trumpet with clear shrill tones [Medieval Latin *clario,* from Latin *clarus* "clear"]

²clarion *adj* **:** brilliantly clear ⟨a *clarion* call to action⟩

clar·i·ty \'klar-ət-ē\ *n* **:** CLEARNESS ⟨the *clarity* of the atmosphere⟩ [Latin *claritas,* from *clarus* "clear"]

clary sage \'klaər-ē-, 'kleər-\ *n* **:** an aromatic southern European herb of the mint family grown as an ornamental — called also *clary* [Middle French *sclaree,* from Medieval Latin *sclareia*]

¹clash \'klash\ *vb* **1 :** to make a clash ⟨gears *clashed* as the truck moved on⟩ **2 :** to come into conflict ⟨rebels *clashed* with the police⟩ **3 :** to cause to clash ⟨*clashed* the cymbals together⟩ [imitative] — **clash·er** *n*

²clash *n* **1 :** a noisy usually metallic sound of collision ⟨the *clash* of swords⟩ **2 a :** a hostile encounter ⟨a *clash* between two armies⟩ **b :** a sharp conflict ⟨a *clash* of opinion⟩

¹clasp \'klasp\ *n* **1 :** a device (as a hook) for holding objects or parts together ⟨the *clasp* of a necklace⟩ **2 :** a holding with or as if with the hands **:** EMBRACE, GRASP [Middle English *claspe*]

²clasp *vt* **1 :** to fasten with or as if with a clasp **2 :** to enclose and hold with or as if with the arms; *esp* **:** EMBRACE **3 :** to seize with or as if with the hand **:** GRASP — **clasp·er** *n*

¹class \'klas\ *n* **1 a :** a course of instruction ⟨a *class* in arithmetic⟩ **b :** the group of pupils meeting regularly in a course ⟨a big *class* this year⟩ **c :** the period during which such a group meets **d :** a group of students or alumni whose year of graduation is the same ⟨*class* of '07⟩ **2 a :** a group sharing the same economic or social status ⟨the working *class*⟩ **b :** social rank or level; *esp* **:** high social rank **c :** high quality **:** ELEGANCE ⟨a hotel with *class*⟩ **3 a :** a group or set alike in some way **b :** a major category in biological taxonomy ranking above the order and below the phylum or division **4 :** a division or rating based on grade or quality ⟨a *class* A movie⟩ [French *classe,* from Latin *classis* "group called to military service, fleet, class"] — **class·less** \-ləs\ *adj*

²class *vt* **:** CLASSIFY

class–con·scious \'klas-ˌkän-chəs\ *adj* **1 :** aware of one's common status with others in an economic or social class **2 :** believing in and actively aware of class struggle — **class consciousness** *n*

¹clas·sic \'klas-ik\ *adj* **1 a :** serving as a standard of excellence

b : belonging to the great accomplishments of humanity ⟨*classic* products of the imagination⟩ **c** : characterized by simple tailored lines in fashion year after year ⟨*classic* apparel⟩ **2** : of or relating to the ancient Greeks and Romans or their culture : CLASSICAL 2 **3 a** : AUTHENTIC 1 ⟨a *classic* folk dance⟩ **b** : notable as the most typical instance ⟨a *classic* example⟩ [Latin *classicus* "of the highest class of Roman citizens, of the first rank," from *classis* "class"]

²**classic** *n* **1** : a literary work of ancient Greece or Rome **2** : a work of enduring excellence; *also* : its author **3** : something perfect of its kind : MODEL **4** : a traditional event ⟨a football *classic*⟩

clas·si·cal \ˈklas-i-kəl\ *adj* **1** : having recognized and permanent value : CLASSIC **2** : of or relating to the ancient Greek and Roman world and especially to its literature and art ⟨*classical* studies⟩ ⟨a *classical* scholar⟩ **3** : of, relating to, or being music in established European styles and forms (as the symphony and opera) **4 a** : regarded as of first historical significance : TRADITIONAL **b** : of or relating to the first developed form or system of a science, art, or discipline ⟨the *classical* economists⟩ **c** : conforming to a pattern of usage sanctioned by a body of literature rather than by everyday speech ⟨*classical* Latin⟩ **5** : concerned with a general study of the arts and sciences and not specializing in technical studies ⟨a *classical* high school⟩

clas·si·cal·ly \ˈklas-i-kə-lē, -klē\ *adv* : in a classic or classical manner

clas·si·cism \ˈklas-ə-ˌsiz-əm\ *n* **1 a** : the principles or style embodied in the literature, art, or architecture of ancient Greece and Rome **b** : classical scholarship **c** : a classical idiom or expression **2** : adherence to traditional standards (as of simplicity, restraint, or proportion) that are universally and permanently valid

clas·si·cist \-səst\ *n* **1** : an advocate or follower of classicism **2** : a classical scholar — **clas·si·cis·tic** \ˌklas-ə-ˈsis-tik\ *adj*

clas·si·fi·ca·tion \ˌklas-ə-fə-ˈkā-shən, ˌklas-fə-\ *n* **1** : the act or process of classifying **2 a (1)** : systematic arrangement in groups or categories according to established criteria **(2)** : TAXONOMY 2b **b** : CLASS 3a, CATEGORY — **clas·si·fi·ca·to·ry** \ˈklas-ə-fə-kə-ˌtōr-ē, ˈklas-fə-, -ˌtȯr-\ *adj*

¹**clas·si·fied** \ˈklas-ə-ˌfīd\ *adj* **1** : divided into classes or placed in a class ⟨*classified* ads⟩ **2** : withheld from general circulation for reasons of national security ⟨*classified* information⟩

²**classified** *n* : an advertisement grouped with others according to subject — usually used in plural

clas·si·fy \ˈklas-ə-ˌfī\ *vt* **-fied; -fy·ing** : to arrange in or assign to a class or classes ⟨*classify* books according to subject matter⟩ — **clas·si·fi·able** \-ˌfī-ə-bəl\ *adj* — **clas·si·fi·er** \-ˌfī-ər, -ˌfīr\ *n*

class·mate \ˈklas-ˌmāt\ *n* : a member of the same class in a school or college

class·room \-ˌrüm, -ˌrüm\ *n* : a room in a school or college in which classes meet

classy \ˈklas-ē\ *adj* **class·i·er; -est** : having or showing class: as **a** : ELEGANT, STYLISH **b** : having or showing high standards of personal behavior ⟨a *classy* guy⟩ **c** : admirably skillful and graceful ⟨a *classy* player⟩ — **class·i·ness** *n*

¹**clat·ter** \ˈklat-ər\ *vb* **1** : to make or cause to make a rattling sound ⟨*clattering* the dishes⟩ **2** : to move or go with a clatter ⟨*clatter* down the stairs⟩ **3** : CHATTER 2 [Middle English *clatren*] — **clat·ter·er** \-ər-ər\ *n* — **clat·ter·ing·ly** \ˈklat-ə-ring-lē\ *adv*

²**clatter** *n* **1** : a rattling sound (as of hard bodies striking together) **2** : COMMOTION ⟨the midday *clatter* of the business district⟩ **3** : noisy chatter — **clat·tery** \ˈklat-ə-rē\ *adj*

clause \ˈklȯz\ *n* **1** : a separate section of an article or document ⟨a *clause* in a will⟩ **2** : a group of words having its own subject and predicate but forming only part of a compound or complex sentence (as "when it rained" or "they went inside" in the sentence "when it rained, they went inside") [Medieval French, from Medieval Latin *clausa* "close of a rhetorical period," from Latin *claudere* "to close"] — **claus·al** \ˈklȯ-zəl\ *adj*

claus·tro·pho·bia \ˌklȯ-strə-ˈfō-bē-ə\ *n* : abnormal fear of being in closed or narrow spaces [Latin *claustrum* "bar, bolt," from *claudere* "to close"] — **claus·tro·pho·bic** \-bik\ *adj*

clave *past of* CLEAVE

clav·i·chord \ˈklav-ə-ˌkȯrd\ *n* : an early keyboard instrument in use before the piano [Medieval Latin *clavichordium*, from Latin *clavis* "key" + *chorda* "string"] — **clav·i·chord·ist** \-əst\ *n*

clav·i·cle \ˈklav-i-kəl\ *n* : a bone of the shoulder that joins the breastbone and the shoulder blade — called also *collarbone* [French *clavicule*, derived from Latin *clavis* "key"] — **cla·vic·u·lar** \klə-ˈvik-yə-lər\ *adj*

cla·vier \klə-ˈviər; ˈklāv-ē-ər, ˈklav-\ *n* **1** : the keyboard of a musical instrument **2** : an early keyboard instrument [French, from Medieval French, "key bearer," from Latin *clavis* "key"] — **cla·vier·ist** \-əst\ *n*

¹**claw** \ˈklȯ\ *n* **1 a** : a sharp usually slender and curved nail on the toe of an animal **b** : a sharp curved process especially if at the end of a limb (as of an insect); *also* : one of the pincerlike organs terminating some limbs of an arthropod (as a lobster or scorpion) **2** : something that resembles a claw; *esp* : the forked end of a tool (as a hammer) [Old English *clawu* "hoof, claw"] — **clawed** \ˈklȯd\ *adj* — **claw·like** \-ˌlīk\ *adj*

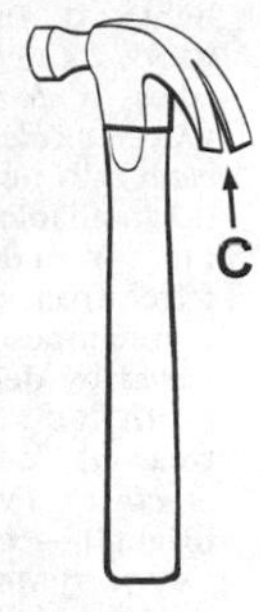

C claw 2

²**claw** *vb* : to rake, seize, or dig with or as if with claws

claw–foot \ˈklȯ-ˌfu̇t\ *n* : a foot (as on a bathtub or piece of furniture) in the shape of a claw

clay \ˈklā\ *n* **1 a** : an earthy material that is plastic when moist but hard when fired, is composed chiefly of silicates of aluminum and water, and is used for brick, tile, and earthenware; *also* : soil composed chiefly of this material having particles less than a specified size **b** : earth especially when moist **2 a** : a plastic substance used for modeling **b** : the human body as distinguished from the spirit [Old English *clǣg*] — **clay·ish** \ˈklā-ish\ *adj* — **clay·like** \-ˌlīk\ *adj*

clay·ey \ˈklā-ē\ *adj* **clay·i·er; -est** : resembling clay or containing much clay ⟨a *clayey* soil⟩

clay loam *n* : a loam consisting of from 20 to 30 percent clay

clay·more \ˈklā-ˌmōr, -ˌmȯr\ *n* : a large 2-edged sword formerly used by Scottish Highlanders [Scottish Gaelic *claidheamh mōr*, literally, "great sword"]

clay pigeon *n* : a saucer-shaped target thrown from a trap in skeet and trapshooting

¹**clean** \ˈklēn\ *adj* **1 a** : free from dirt or pollution ⟨*clean* clothes⟩ ⟨*clean* air⟩ **b** : free from contamination or disease ⟨a *clean* wound⟩ **2** : free from admixture : PURE **3 a** : characterized by moral integrity : HONORABLE ⟨a candidate with a *clean* record⟩; *also* : free from violations ⟨a *clean* driving record⟩ **b** : free from offensive treatment of sexual subjects and from the use of obscenity ⟨a *clean* joke⟩ **4** : ceremonially or spiritually pure **5 a** : so complete as to leave no remainder ⟨made a *clean* sweep⟩ **b** : well done : SKILLFUL ⟨a good *clean* job⟩ **6** : relatively free from error or blemish : CLEAR ⟨a *clean* copy⟩ **7 a** : characterized by clarity and precision : TRIM ⟨a *clean* writing style⟩ ⟨a ship with *clean* lines⟩ **b** : EVEN, SMOOTH ⟨a sharp knife makes a *clean* cut⟩ **8** : habitually neat [Old English *clǣne*] — **clean·ness** \ˈklēn-nəs\ *n*

²**clean** *adv* **1 a** : so as to clean ⟨a new broom sweeps *clean*⟩ **b** : in a clean manner ⟨fight *clean*⟩ **2** : all the way : COMPLETELY ⟨hit the ball *clean* out of the ball park⟩

³**clean** *vb* **1** : to make or become clean ⟨*clean* this room⟩ ⟨*cleaned* up for supper⟩ **2** : to remove or exhaust the contents or resources of ⟨*clean* a fish⟩ ⟨thieves *cleaned* out the safe⟩ — **clean·er** *n* — **clean house** : to get rid of whatever is hampering, wrong, or degrading

synonyms CLEAN, CLEANSE mean to remove dirt or impurities from. CLEAN applies to any removing of dirt, litter, or dust ⟨*clean* up the park⟩. CLEANSE applies chiefly to washing with water or a solvent; it may also apply to figurative purification ⟨*cleansed* from sin⟩.

clean–cut \ˈklēn-ˈkət\ *adj* **1** : CLEAR-CUT ⟨*clean-cut* features⟩ ⟨a *clean-cut* skyline⟩ **2** : of wholesome appearance

¹**clean·ly** \ˈklen-lē\ *adj* **clean·li·er; -est** **1** : careful to keep clean : FASTIDIOUS ⟨a *cleanly* animal⟩ **2** : habitually kept clean ⟨*cleanly* surroundings⟩ — **clean·li·ness** *n*

²**clean·ly** \ˈklēn-lē\ *adv* : in a clean manner

cleanse \ˈklenz\ *vt* : to make clean [Old English *clǣnsian* "to purify," from *clǣne* "clean"] ***synonyms*** see CLEAN

cleans·er \ˈklen-zər\ *n* **1** : one that cleanses **2** : a preparation (as a scouring powder or a skin cream) used for cleaning

\ə\ **abut**	\au̇\ **out**	\i\ **tip**	\ȯ\ **saw**	\u̇\ **foot**
\ər\ **further**	\ch\ **chin**	\ī\ **life**	\ȯi\ **coin**	\y\ **yet**
\a\ **mat**	\e\ **pet**	\j\ **job**	\th\ **thin**	\yü\ **few**
\ā\ **take**	\ē\ **easy**	\ng\ **sing**	\th\ **this**	\yu̇\ **cure**
\ä\ **cot, cart**	\g\ **go**	\ō\ **bone**	\ü\ **food**	\zh\ **vision**

[1]**clean·up** \ˈklē-ˌnəp\ *n* : an act or instance of cleaning
[2]**cleanup** *adj* : being in the fourth position in the batting order of a baseball team ⟨a *cleanup* hitter⟩ — **cleanup** *adv*
clean up \klē-ˈnəp\ *vi* : to make a lot of money ⟨*cleaned up* at the races⟩
[1]**clear** \ˈkliər\ *adj* **1 a** : shining brightly : LUMINOUS ⟨*clear* sunlight⟩ **b** : free from clouds, haze, or mist ⟨a *clear* day⟩ **c** : SERENE 2 ⟨a *clear* gaze⟩ **2** : CLEAN, PURE: as **a** : free of blemishes ⟨a *clear* complexion⟩ **b** : easily seen through : TRANSPARENT ⟨*clear* glass⟩ **3 a** : easily heard ⟨the sound was quite *clear*⟩ **b** : easily visible : PLAIN ⟨a *clear* signal⟩ **c** : easily understandable : UNMISTAKABLE ⟨the meaning was *clear*⟩ **4** : free from doubt : SURE ⟨a *clear* understanding of the issue⟩ **5** : free from guile or guilt : INNOCENT ⟨a *clear* conscience⟩ **6** : unhampered by restriction or limitation: as **a** : unencumbered by debts or charges ⟨a *clear* estate⟩ **b** : NET ⟨a *clear* profit⟩ **c** : free from qualification : ABSOLUTE ⟨a *clear* case of treason⟩ **d** : free from obstruction or entanglement ⟨the coast is *clear*⟩ [Medieval French *cler,* from Latin *clarus* "clear, bright"] — **clear·ly** *adv* — **clear·ness** *n*
synonyms CLEAR, TRANSPARENT, TRANSLUCENT mean capable of being seen through. CLEAR implies absence of cloudiness, haziness, or muddiness ⟨*clear* water⟩. TRANSPARENT implies being so clear that objects can be seen distinctly ⟨a *transparent* sheet of film⟩. TRANSLUCENT usually implies permitting the passage of light but not vision ⟨a *translucent* frosted glass⟩ ⟨*translucent* shades for lamps⟩.
[2]**clear** *adv* **1** : in a clear manner ⟨shout loud and *clear*⟩ **2** : all the way : COMPLETELY ⟨can see *clear* to the mountains⟩
[3]**clear** *vb* **1 a** : to make or become clear or translucent ⟨*clear* the water by filtering⟩ ⟨the sky *cleared*⟩ **b** : to go away : DISPERSE ⟨clouds *cleared* away after the rain⟩ **2 a** : to free from accusation or blame ⟨*clear* one's name⟩ **b** : to certify as trustworthy ⟨*cleared* for top-secret work⟩ **3** : to make intelligible : EXPLAIN ⟨*cleared* the matter up for me⟩ **4** : to free from obstruction: as **a** : to submit for approval ⟨*clear* this with the boss⟩ **b** : to give approval to : AUTHORIZE ⟨*cleared* the article for publication⟩ **c** : to erase stored or displayed data from (as a computer or calculator) **5** : to make free especially from financial obligation : SETTLE ⟨*clear* an account⟩ **6** : to go through (customs) **7** : NET ⟨*cleared* a profit⟩ **8** : to get rid of : REMOVE ⟨*clear* away that trash⟩ **9 a** : to jump or go by without touching ⟨*cleared* the fence⟩ **b** : PASS 7a ⟨the bill *cleared* the legislature⟩ — **clear·able** \ˈklir-ə-bəl\ *adj* — **clear·er** *n* — **clear the air** : to remove tension or confusion ⟨*cleared the air* by discussing their differences⟩
[4]**clear** *n* : a clear space or part — **in the clear** **1** : in inside measurement **2** : free from guilt or suspicion **3** : not in code or cipher ⟨sent the message *in the clear*⟩
clear·ance \ˈklir-əns\ *n* **1** : an act or process of clearing: as **a** : the act of clearing a ship at the customhouse; *also* : the papers showing that a ship has cleared **b** : the passage of checks and claims among banks through a clearinghouse **c** : certification as clear of objection : AUTHORIZATION ⟨was given a security *clearance*⟩ **d** : a sale to clear out stock **2** : the distance by which one object clears another or the clear space between them
clear–cut \ˈkliər-ˈkət\ *adj* **1** : sharply outlined : DISTINCT ⟨a *clear-cut* pattern⟩ **2** : free from uncertainty : DEFINITE ⟨*clear-cut* victory⟩
clear–cut·ting \-ˌkət-ing\ *n* : removal of all the trees in a stand of timber — **clear–cut** \-ˌkət\ *vb*
clear·head·ed \-ˈhed-əd\ *adj* : having a clear understanding — **clear·head·ed·ly** *adv* — **clear·head·ed·ness** *n*
clear·ing \ˈkliər-ing\ *n* **1** : the act or process of making or becoming clear **2** : a tract of land cleared of wood and brush **3 a** : CLEARANCE 1b **b** *pl* : the gross amount of balances adjusted by clearance
clear·ing·house \-ˌhau̇s\ *n* **1** : an establishment maintained by banks for settling mutual claims and accounts **2** : a central agency for collection, classification, and distribution especially of information
clear off *vi, chiefly British* : to go away : DEPART
clear out *vi* : to go away : DEPART
clear–sight·ed \ˈkliər-ˈsīt-əd\ *adj* **1** : having clear vision **2** : DISCERNING ⟨a *clear-sighted* decision⟩ — **clear–sight·ed·ly** *adv* — **clear–sight·ed·ness** *n*
[1]**cleat** \ˈklēt\ *n* **1** : a wedge-shaped piece fastened to something and used as a support or check (as for a rope on the spar of a ship) **2** : a wooden or metal device usually with projecting arms at each end around which a rope may be made fast **3** : a strip or projecting piece fastened on or across something (as a shoe) to give strength, to provide a grip, or to prevent slipping [Middle English *clete* "wedge"]
[2]**cleat** *vt* **1** : to fasten to or by a cleat **2** : to provide with a cleat
cleav·age \ˈklē-vij\ *n* **1** : the quality possessed by a crystallized substance or rock of splitting along definite planes **2** : the action of cleaving : the state of being cleft **3** : cell division; *esp* : the series of mitotic divisions of a fertilized egg that changes the single-celled zygote into a multicellular embryo **4** : the depression between a woman's breasts especially when made visible by a low-cut neckline
[1]**cleave** \ˈklēv\ *vi* **cleaved** \ˈklēvd\ *or* **clove** \ˈklōv\ *also* **clave** \ˈklāv\; **cleav·ing** : to adhere firmly and closely or loyally and unwaveringly ⟨*cleaved* to his family⟩ [Middle English *clevien,* from Old English *clifian*]
[2]**cleave** *vb* **cleaved** \ˈklēvd\ *also* **cleft** \ˈkleft\ *or* **clove** \ˈklōv\; **cleaved** *also* **cleft** *or* **clo·ven** \ˈklō-vən\; **cleav·ing** **1 a** : to split by or as if by a cutting blow ⟨some woods *cleave* along the grain easily⟩ **b** : to cause to separate ⟨the controversy *cleaved* the group into two camps⟩ **2** : to pass through : PENETRATE ⟨a ship's bow *cleaving* the waves⟩ [Middle English *cleven,* from Old English *clēofan*] — **cleav·able** \ˈklē-və-bəl\ *adj*
cleav·er \ˈklē-vər\ *n* : one that cleaves; *esp* : a heavy broad-bladed knife for chopping meat or cutting through bone
cleav·ers \ˈklē-vərz\ *n sing or pl* : an annual bedstraw with prickly stems and white flowers [alteration of Old English *clife* "burdock, cleavers"]
clef \ˈklef\ *n* : a sign placed on the staff in music to show what pitch is represented by each line and space [French, literally, "key," from Latin *clavis*]

clef: *left* treble clef, *right* bass clef

[1]**cleft** \ˈkleft\ *n* **1** : a space or opening made by splitting : FISSURE **2** : a usually V-shaped indentation [Old English *geclyft*]
[2]**cleft** *adj* **1** : partially split or divided ⟨*cleft* wood⟩ **2** : divided about halfway to the midrib ⟨a *cleft* leaf⟩
cleft lip *n* : one or more congenital clefts in the upper lip
cleft palate *n* : congenital fissure of the roof of the mouth
clem·a·tis \ˈklem-ət-əs, kli-ˈmat-əs\ *n* : a vine or herb related to the buttercups that has leaflets with three leaflets and is widely grown for its showy usually white, red, pink, or purple flowers [Latin, from Greek *klēmatis* "brushwood, clematis"]
clem·en·cy \ˈklem-ən-sē\ *n, pl* **-cies** **1 a** : disposition to be merciful **b** : an act or instance of leniency **2** : mildness of weather ***synonyms*** see MERCY
clem·ent \ˈklem-ənt\ *adj* **1** : inclined to be merciful : LENIENT ⟨a *clement* judge⟩ **2** : not harsh or severe ⟨*clement* weather⟩ [Latin *clemens*] — **clem·ent·ly** *adv*
[1]**clench** \ˈklench\ *vb* **1** : CLINCH 1 **2** : to hold fast : CLUTCH **3** : to set or close tightly ⟨*clench* one's teeth⟩ ⟨hands *clenched* together⟩ [Old English *-clencan*]
[2]**clench** *n* **1** : the end of a nail that is turned back in clinching it **2** : an act or instance of clenching
clep·sy·dra \ˈklep-sə-drə\ *n, pl* **-dras** *or* **-drae** \-ˌdrē, -ˌdrī\ : WATER CLOCK [Latin, from Greek *klepsydra,* from *kleptein* "to steal" + *hydōr* "water"]
clere·sto·ry *also* **clear·sto·ry** \ˈkliər-ˌstōr-ē, -ˌstȯr-\ *n, pl* **-ries** : an outside wall of a room or building that rises above an adjoining roof and contains windows [Middle English, from *clere* "clear" + *story*]
cler·gy \ˈklər-jē\ *n, pl* **clergies** **1** : the body of religious officials (as priests, ministers, or rabbis) authorized to conduct services **2** : the official or priestly class of a religion [Medieval French *clergie,* from *clerc* "clergyman"]
cler·gy·man \-ji-mən\ *n* : a member of the clergy
cler·gy·person \-ˌpərs-n\ *n* : a member of the clergy
cler·gy·wom·an \-ˌwu̇m-ən\ *n* : a woman who is a member of the clergy
cler·ic \ˈkler-ik\ *n* **1** : CLERGYMAN **2** : a member of a religious order lower than the priesthood [Late Latin *clericus*]
cler·i·cal \ˈkler-i-kəl\ *adj* **1** : of, relating to, or characteristic of the clergy, a clergyman, or a cleric **2** : of or relating to a clerk or office worker — **cler·i·cal·ly** \ˈkler-i-kə-lē, -klē\ *adv*

clerical collar *n* **:** a narrow stiffly upright white collar buttoned at the back of the neck and worn by clergymen

cler·i·cal·ism \ˈkler-i-kə-ˌliz-əm\ *n* **:** a policy of maintaining or increasing the worldly power of the church — **cler·i·cal·ist** \-list\ *n*

1**clerk** \ˈklərk\ *n* **1 :** CLERIC **2 a :** an official responsible for correspondence, records, and accounts ⟨town *clerk*⟩ **b :** one employed to keep records or accounts or to perform general office work **c :** SALESCLERK [Old English and Medieval French *clerc,* both from Late Latin *clericus,* from Late Greek *klērikos,* from Greek *klēros* "lot, inheritance"; from the statement in Deuteronomy 18:2 that the Lord is the inheritance of the Levite priests]

2**clerk** *vi* **:** to act or work as a clerk

clerk·ly \ˈklər-klē\ *adj* **:** of, relating to, or characteristic of a clerk

clerk·ship \ˈklərk-ˌship\ *n* **:** the position or business of a clerk

clev·er \ˈklev-ər\ *adj* **1 a :** apt and skillful in using the hands or body **:** NIMBLE ⟨*clever* fingers⟩ **b :** quick in learning ⟨a *clever* pupil⟩ **2 :** marked by wit or ingenuity ⟨a *clever* idea⟩ [Middle English *cliver*] — **clev·er·ish** \ˈklev-rish, -ə-rish\ *adj* — **clev·er·ly** \-ər-lē\ *adv* — **clev·er·ness** \-ər-nəs\ *n*

synonyms CLEVER, INTELLIGENT, SMART, ALERT mean mentally quick or keen. CLEVER stresses quickness, deftness, or great aptitude ⟨a person *clever* with horses⟩. INTELLIGENT implies success in understanding and coping with new situations and solving problems ⟨an *intelligent* person could assemble it fast⟩. SMART suggests alertness and quickness to learn, or it may imply pungency of wit tending often toward impudence ⟨a *smart* child who learned to talk early⟩. ALERT stresses quickness in perceiving and understanding ⟨*alert* to new technology⟩.

clev·is \ˈklev-əs\ *n* **:** a usually U-shaped metal shackle with the ends drilled to receive a pin or bolt used for attaching or suspending parts [earlier *clevi,* probably of Scandinavian origin]

1**clew** \ˈklü\ *n* **1 :** a ball of thread, yarn, or cord **2 :** CLUE 1 **3 a :** a lower corner or the after corner of a sail **b :** a metal loop attached to the lower corner of a sail [Old English *cliewen*]

2**clew** *vt* **1 :** to roll into a ball **2 :** CLUE **3 :** to haul (a sail) up or down by ropes through the clews

cli·ché \kli-ˈshā\ *n* **1 :** a trite phrase or expression; *also* **:** the idea expressed by it **2 :** a hackneyed theme or situation [French, literally, "stereotype"] — **cliché** *adj*

1**click** \ˈklik\ *vb* **1 a :** to make or cause to make a click ⟨*click* one's tongue⟩ **b :** to move or strike with a click ⟨high heels *clicking* down the street⟩ ⟨*clicked* on the light⟩ **2 a :** to fit together ⟨they did not *click* as friends⟩ **b :** to work smoothly **3 :** SUCCEED 2 ⟨the idea *clicked*⟩ **4 :** to select by pressing a button on a control device (as a mouse) ⟨*click* on the icon⟩ [probably imitative]

2**click** *n* **1 :** a slight sharp noise **2 :** an instance of clicking ⟨a mouse *click*⟩

click beetle *n* **:** any of a family of elongated tapering beetles that are able when turned over to flip into the air by a sudden thoracic movement that produces a distinct click

click·er \ˈklik-ər\ *n* **:** REMOTE CONTROL 2

cli·ent \ˈklī-ənt\ *n* **1 :** a person under the protection of another **:** DEPENDENT **2 a :** a person who engages the professional services of another **b :** CUSTOMER 1 [Latin *cliens*] — **cli·ent·age** \-ən-tij\ *n* — **cli·en·tal** \klī-ˈent-l, ˈklī-ənt-\ *adj*

cli·en·tele \ˌklī-ən-ˈtel\ *n* **:** a body of clients and especially of customers ⟨a store that caters to an exclusive *clientele*⟩ [French *clientèle,* from Latin *clientela,* from *cliens* "client"]

cliff \ˈklif\ *n* **:** a high steep face of rock [Old English *clif*]

cliff dweller *n, often cap C&D* **:** one of the people of the American Southwest who erected their dwellings on rock ledges or in the recesses of canyon walls and cliffs — **cliff dwelling** *n*

cliff–hang·er \ˈklif-ˌhang-ər\ *n* **1 :** an adventure story or melodrama; *esp* **:** a serial with each installment ending in suspense **2 :** a contest whose outcome is in doubt up to the end

1**cli·mac·ter·ic** \klī-ˈmak-tə-rik, ˌklī-ˌmak-ˈter-ik\ *adj* **1 :** being or relating to a critical period (as of life) **2 :** CRUCIAL [Latin *climactericus,* from Greek *klimaktērikos,* from *klimaktēr* "critical point," literally, "rung of a ladder," from *klimax* "ladder"]

2**climacteric** *n* **1 :** a major turning point or critical stage **2 :** MENOPAUSE; *also* **:** a corresponding period in the male

cli·mac·tic \klī-ˈmak-tik\ *adj* **:** of, relating to, or being a climax — **cli·mac·ti·cal·ly** \-ti-kə-lē, -klē\ *adv*

cli·mate \ˈklī-mət\ *n* **1 a :** a region with specified weather conditions **b :** the average weather conditions of a place or region over a long period **2 :** the prevailing conditions or mood ⟨a favorable financial *climate*⟩ ⟨a *climate* of fear⟩ [Medieval French *climat,* from Late Latin *clima,* from Greek *klima* "inclination, latitude, climate," from *klinein* "to lean"] — **cli·mat·ic** \klī-ˈmat-ik\ *adj* — **cli·mat·i·cal·ly** \-ˈmat-i-kə-lē, -klē\ *adv*

cli·ma·tol·o·gy \ˌklī-mə-ˈtäl-ə-jē\ *n* **:** the science that deals with climates — **cli·ma·to·log·i·cal** \ˌklī-mət-l-ˈäj-i-kəl\ *adj* — **cli·ma·tol·o·gist** \ˌklī-mə-ˈtäl-ə-jəst\ *n*

1**cli·max** \ˈklī-ˌmaks\ *n* **1 a :** a series of ideas or statements so arranged that they increase in force and power from the first to the last **b :** the highest or most forceful in a series **c :** the highest point **:** CULMINATION ⟨the storm had reached its *climax*⟩ **2 :** ORGASM **3 :** a relatively stable ecological stage or community; *esp* **:** the final stage of an ecological succession [Late Latin, from Greek *klimax* "ladder," from *klinein* "to lean"]

2**climax** *vb* **:** to come or bring to a climax

1**climb** \ˈklīm\ *vb* **1 a :** to go up or down by grasping or clutching with hands and feet ⟨*climb* down a ladder⟩ **b :** to ascend in growth (as by twining) ⟨a *climbing* vine⟩ **2 :** to rise gradually to a higher point ⟨*climb* to power⟩ **3 :** to slope upward ⟨the road *climbs* steeply⟩ [Old English *climban*] ***synonyms*** see ASCEND — **climb·able** \ˈklī-mə-bəl\ *adj* — **climb·er** \ˈklī-mər\ *n*

2**climb** *n* **1 :** a place where climbing is necessary **2 :** the act of climbing

climbing iron *n* **:** a steel framework with spikes that may be attached to one's boots for climbing

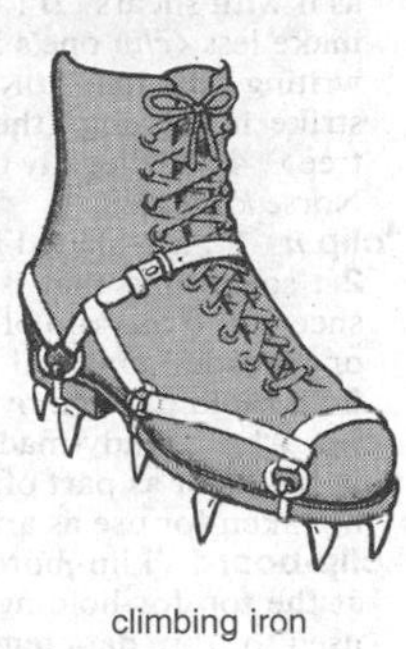
climbing iron

climbing wall *n* **:** a wall specially designed for climbing and often built to be like a rocky surface

clime \ˈklīm\ *n* **:** CLIMATE ⟨travel to warmer *climes*⟩ [Late Latin *clima*]

1**clinch** \ˈklinch\ *vb* **1 a :** to turn over or flatten the protruding end of (as a driven nail) **b :** to fasten by clinching **2 :** CLENCH 2 **3 a :** to make final or irrefutable ⟨*clinch* the deal⟩ **b :** to assure the winning of ⟨a touchdown that *clinched* the game⟩ **4 :** to hold a boxing opponent [probably alteration of 1*clench*]

2**clinch** *n* **1 a :** a fastening by means of a clinched nail, rivet, or bolt **b :** the clinched part of a nail, bolt, or rivet **2 :** an act or instance of clinching in boxing

clinch·er \ˈklin-chər\ *n* **:** one that clinches; *esp* **:** a decisive fact, argument, act, or remark

cline \ˈklīn\ *n* **:** a graded series of differences exhibited by a group of related organisms usually along a line of environmental or geographic change [Greek *klinein* "to lean"]

cling \ˈkling\ *vi* **clung** \ˈkləng\; **cling·ing** \ˈkling-ing\ **1 a :** to adhere firmly as if glued **:** STICK ⟨the burr *clung* to the dog's tail⟩ **b :** to hold or hold on tightly ⟨*clung* desperately to the ladder⟩ **2 :** to have a strong emotional attachment or dependence ⟨*clings* to old friends⟩ [Old English *clingan*] ***synonyms*** see STICK

cling peach *n* **:** a clingstone peach

cling·stone \ˈkling-ˌstōn\ *n* **:** a fruit (as a peach) whose flesh clings to the pit

clin·ic \ˈklin-ik\ *n* **1 :** a class of medical instruction in which patients are examined and discussed **2 :** a group meeting devoted to the analysis and treatment of cases in some special field ⟨writing *clinic*⟩ **3 :** a facility (as of a hospital) in which persons not bedridden are diagnosed or treated [French *clinique,* from Greek *klinikē* "medical practice at the sickbed," from *klinē* "bed," from *klinein* "to lean, recline"]

-clin·ic \ˈklin-ik\ *adj combining form* **1 :** inclining **:** dipping **2 :** having (so many) oblique intersections of the axes ⟨mono*clinic*⟩ ⟨tri*clinic*⟩ [Greek *klinein* "to lean"]

clin·i·cal \ˈklin-i-kəl\ *adj* **1 a :** of, relating to, or conducted in or as if in a clinic ⟨*clinical* examination⟩ **b :** involving or based on direct observation of the patient ⟨*clinical* studies⟩ **2 :** cool-

ly analytical and impersonal ⟨a *clinical* analysis of the program⟩ — **clin·i·cal·ly** \ˈklin-i-kə-lē, -klē\ *adv*
clinical thermometer *n* : a thermometer for measuring body temperature that continues to indicate the maximum temperature reached by a column of liquid until the thermometer is reset by shaking
cli·ni·cian \klin-ˈish-ən\ *n* : a person qualified in clinical practice (as of medicine) as distinguished from a specialist in laboratory or research techniques
¹clink \ˈklingk\ *vb* : to make or cause to make a slight sharp short metallic sound [Middle English *clinken,* of imitative origin]
²clink *n* : a clinking sound
clin·ker \ˈkling-kər\ *n* : stony matter fused together (as in a furnace) : SLAG [obsolete Dutch *klinkaard,* kind of brick]
clin·ker–built \-ˌbilt\ *adj* : having the external planks or plates overlapping like clapboards on a house ⟨a *clinker-built* boat⟩ [*clinker* "clinch," from Middle English *clinken* "to clinch"]
cli·nom·e·ter \klī-ˈnäm-ət-ər\ *n* : an instrument for measuring angles of elevation or inclination [Greek *klinein* "to lean"]
¹clip \ˈklip\ *vb* **clipped; clip·ping** : to clasp, fasten, or secure with a clip ⟨*clip* papers together⟩ [Old English *clyppan*]
²clip *n* **1** : a device that grips, clasps, or hooks **2** : a device to hold cartridges for charging the magazine of a rifle **3** : a piece of jewelry held in position by a spring clip
³clip *vb* **clipped; clip·ping 1 a** : to cut or cut off or out with or as if with shears **b** : to cut off the tip or outer part of **2 a** : to make less ⟨*clip* one's influence⟩ **b** : to abbreviate in speech or writing **3** : HIT, PUNCH 2a ⟨*clipped* him on the chin⟩; *esp* : to strike in passing ⟨the car skidded off the road and *clipped* a tree⟩ **4** : to illegally block (an opposing player) in football [Old Norse *klippa*]
⁴clip *n* **1** : a 2-bladed instrument for cutting especially the nails **2** : something that is clipped: as **a** : the sheared fleece of a sheep; *also* : a crop of wool **b** : a section of filmed, videotaped, or recorded material **3** : an act of clipping **4** : a sharp blow **5** : a rapid pace ⟨move along at a good *clip*⟩
clip art *n* : ready-made usually copyright-free illustrations sold in books or as part of a software package from which they may be taken for use as art in printed matter
clip·board \ˈklip-ˌbōrd, -ˌbȯrd\ *n* **1** : a small board with a clip at the top for holding papers **2** : a part of computer memory used to store data temporarily
clip·per \ˈklip-ər\ *n* **1** : one that clips **2** *pl* : an implement for clipping especially hair, fingernails, or toenails **3** : a fast square-rigged ship with usually three masts, an overhanging bow, and a large sail area
clip·ping \ˈklip-ing\ *n* : a piece clipped or cut out or off of something else ⟨a newspaper *clipping*⟩ ⟨swept up the hair *clippings*⟩
clique \ˈklēk, ˈklik\ *n* : a small exclusive group of people having a shared interest [French] — **cliqu·ey** \-ē\ *adj* — **cliqu·ish** \-ish\ *adj* — **cliqu·ish·ness** *n*
cli·tel·lum \klī-ˈtel-əm\ *n, pl* **-la** : a thickened glandular band about the body of an earthworm that secretes a sticky sac in which the eggs are deposited [Latin *clitellae* "packsaddle"]
cli·to·ris \ˈklit-ə-rəs, kli-ˈtȯr-əs\ *n, pl* **cli·to·ris·es** *also* **cli·to·ri·des** \kli-ˈtȯr-ə-ˌdēz\ : a small organ at the anterior or ventral part of the vulva homologous to the penis [Greek *kleitoris*] — **clit·o·ral** \ˈklit-ə-rəl\ *adj*
clo·a·ca \klō-ˈā-kə\ *n, pl* **-cae** \-ˌkē, -ˌsē\ : a chamber into which the intestinal, urinary, and reproductive canals discharge in birds, reptiles, amphibians, and some fishes; *also* : a comparable chamber of an invertebrate [Latin, "sewer"] — **clo·a·cal** \-ˈā-kəl\ *adj*
¹cloak \ˈklōk\ *n* **1** : a loose outer garment usually longer than a cape **2** : something that conceals or covers ⟨under the *cloak* of darkness⟩ [Old North French *cloque* "bell, cloak," from Medieval Latin *clocca* "bell"; from its shape] ***synonyms*** see DISGUISE
²cloak *vt* : to cover or hide with a cloak
cloak–and–dag·ger \ˌklōk-ən-ˈdag-ər\ *adj* : of or relating to intrigue and spying
cloak·room \ˈklōk-ˌrüm, -ˌru̇m\ *n* : CHECKROOM
clob·ber \ˈkläb-ər\ *vt* **1** : to hit with great force : SMASH **2 a** : to defeat overwhelmingly **b** : to have a strongly negative impact on ⟨businesses *clobbered* by the recession⟩ [origin unknown]
cloche \ˈklōsh\ *n* : a woman's close-fitting hat usually having a deep rounded crown and narrow brim [French, literally, "bell," from Medieval Latin *clocca*]
¹clock \ˈkläk\ *n* **1** : a device to measure or tell time; *esp* : one not intended to be worn or carried about by a person **2** : a registering device usually with a dial; *esp* : ODOMETER **3** : TIME CLOCK **4** : BIOLOGICAL CLOCK **5** : a device (as in a computer) that sends out signals at regular intervals so that other events will happen in the right order [Dutch *clocke* "bell, clock," from Medieval Latin *clocca* "bell," of Celtic origin] — **against the clock 1** : with or within a time constraint ⟨working *against the clock*⟩ **2** : with clocked speed rather than the order of finish to determine placement ⟨trial races *against the clock*⟩ — **around the clock** *also* **round the clock 1** : continuously for 24 hours : day and night continuously **2** : without relaxation and heedless of time — **kill the clock** *or* **run out the clock** : to use up as much as possible of the playing time remaining in a game (as football) while retaining possession of the ball or puck especially to protect a lead
²clock *vt* **1** : to time with a stopwatch or by an electric device **2** : to register on a mechanical recording device : PUNCH IN ⟨he *clocked* in late⟩
clock·wise \-ˌwīz\ *adv* : in the direction in which the hands of a clock rotate — **clockwise** *adj*
clock·work \-ˌwərk\ *n* : machinery (as in a mechanical toy) containing a train of small wheels
clod \ˈkläd\ *n* **1** : a lump or mass especially of earth or clay **2** : a dull or insensitive person : OAF [Old English *clod-* (as in *clodhamer* "field fare"] — **clod·dish** \-ish\ *adj* — **clod·dish·ness** *n* — **clod·dy** \ˈkläd-ē\ *adj*
clod·hop·per \ˈkläd-ˌhäp-ər\ *n* **1** : a clumsy and uncouth person **2** : a large heavy shoe
¹clog \ˈkläg\ *n* **1 a** : a weight attached especially to an animal to hinder motion or prevent escape **b** : something that hinders or restrains ⟨a *clog* in the drain⟩ **2** : a shoe having a thick typically wooden sole [Middle English *clogge* "short thick piece of wood"]
²clog *vb* **clogged; clog·ging 1** : to impede with a clog : HINDER **2 a** : to obstruct passage through by filling beyond capacity ⟨heavy traffic *clogged* the roads⟩ **b** : to cause blockage in ⟨arteries *clogged* up by cholesterol⟩ **3** : to become filled with extraneous matter ⟨pipes *clogged* with grease⟩ **4** : to dance a clog dance
clog dance *n* : a dance in which the performer wears clogs and beats out a clattering rhythm on the floor — **clog dancer** *n* — **clog dancing** *n*
cloi·son·né \ˌklȯiz-n-ˈā, klə-ˌwäz-\ *n* : a decoration made of colored enamels poured into divided areas in a design outlined with bent wire or metal strips [French, from *cloisonner* "to partition"]
¹clois·ter \ˈklȯi-stər\ *n* **1 a** : a place (as a convent or a monastery) of religious seclusion **b** : life in religious seclusion **2** : a covered passage on the side of or around a court usually having one side walled and the other an open arcade or colonnade [Medieval French *cloistre,* from Medieval Latin *claustrum,* from Latin, "bar, bolt," from *claudere* "to close"] — **clois·tral** \-strəl\ *adj*

cloister 2

²cloister *vt* **1** : to shut away from the world in or as if in a cloister **2** : to surround with a cloister ⟨*cloistered* gardens⟩
¹clone \ˈklōn\ *n* **1** : the collection of genetically identical cells or organisms asexually produced by or from a single ancestral cell or organism ⟨used cuttings from fruit trees to produce *clones*⟩ **2** : an individual grown from a single somatic cell or cell nucleus and genetically identical to it ⟨created a sheep *clone*⟩ [Greek *klōn* "twig, slip"] — **clon·al** \ˈklōn-l\ *adj* — **clon·al·ly** \-l-ē\ *adv*
²clone *vt* : to cause to grow as a clone
clop \ˈkläp\ *n* : a sound made by or as if by a hoof or wooden shoe against pavement [imitative] — **clop** *vi*
¹close \ˈklōz\ *vb* **1 a** : to move so as to bar passage through something ⟨*close* the gate⟩ **b** : to block against entry or passage ⟨*close* a street⟩ **2** : to suspend or stop the operations of ⟨*close* school early⟩ **3** : to bring or come to an end : TERMINATE ⟨*close* a meeting⟩ ⟨*close* the computer program⟩ **4 a** : to bring or bind together the parts or edges of ⟨a *closed* fist⟩ ⟨*close*

the book〉 **b** : to fill or stop up 〈*close* a crack with plaster〉 **c** : to make complete by circling or enveloping or by making continuous 〈*close* a circuit〉 **5** : to fold, swing, or slide so as to leave no opening 〈the door *closed*〉 **6 a** : to draw near 〈the ship was *closing* with the island〉 **b** : to engage in a struggle at close quarters : GRAPPLE 〈*close* with the enemy〉 **7** : to reach an agreement on 〈*close* a deal〉 [Medieval French *clos-*, stem of *clore*, from Latin *claudere* "to close"] — **clos•able** \ˈklō-zə-bəl\ *adj* — **clos•er** *n*

synonyms CLOSE, CONCLUDE, TERMINATE, END mean to bring or come to a stopping point or limit. CLOSE implies shutting off from outside forces that could cause further development or change 〈*close* an account〉. CONCLUDE adds a suggestion of formality 〈the church service *concluded* with a prayer〉. TERMINATE implies setting a limit with or without completing 〈your employment *terminates* after three months〉. END stresses finality and usually implies an achievement of progress or concluding of a sequence 〈an armistice *ended* hostilities〉 〈the years *ending* the colonial period〉.

[2]**close** \ˈklōz\ *n* **1 a** : a coming or bringing to a conclusion **b** : CESSATION, END **2** : the last part (as of a speech or play)

[3]**close** \ˈklōs\ *n* : an enclosed area

[4]**close** \ˈklōs\ *adj* **1** : having no openings : CLOSED **2** : confined or carefully guarded 〈*close* arrest〉 **3** : restricted (as in membership) to a privileged group **4 a** : OUT-OF-THE-WAY 1, SECLUDED **b** : SECRETIVE **5** : RIGOROUS 1 〈keep *close* watch〉 **6** : hot and stuffy **7** : reluctant to give up money or possessions **8** : having little space between items or units 〈flying in *close* formation〉 **9 a** : fitting tightly or exactly 〈a *close* gown〉 **b** : very short or near to the surface 〈a *close* haircut〉 **c** : matching or blending without gap 〈ideas in *close* harmony〉 **10** : being near in time, space, effect, or degree 〈at *close* range〉 **11** : intimately associated : FAMILIAR 〈*close* friends〉 **12 a** : very precise and attentive to details 〈a *close* study〉 **b** : marked by faithfulness to an original 〈a *close* copy〉 **13** : having an even or nearly even score 〈a *close* game〉 ***synonyms*** see STINGY — **close•ly** *adv* — **close•ness** *n*

[5]**close** \ˈklōs\ *adv* : in a close position or manner : NEAR

close call \ˈklōs-\ *n* : a narrow escape

closed \ˈklōzd\ *adj* **1 a** : not open : ENCLOSED **b** : composed entirely of closed tubes or vessels 〈a *closed* circulatory system〉 **2 a** : forming a self-contained unit 〈a *closed* association〉 **b** (1) : able to be traced by a moving point that returns to any given starting point 〈a circle is a *closed* curve〉; *also* : having a shape so that an intersection by any plane has the shape of a closed curve 〈a sphere is a *closed* solid〉 (2) : having elements that when a mathematical operation (as addition) is performed on them produce only other elements of the same set 〈the set of whole numbers is *closed* under addition and multiplication〉 (3) : containing its endpoints 〈a *closed* interval〉 **c** : characterized by continuous return or reuse of the working substance 〈a *closed* cooling system〉 **3** : confined to a few 〈a *closed* meeting〉 **4** : ending in a consonant 〈a *closed* syllable〉

closed circuit *n* : a television installation in which the signal is transmitted by wire to a limited number of receivers

closed shop *n* : an establishment in which only union members in good standing are hired

close•fist•ed \ˈklōs-ˈfis-təd\ *adj* : STINGY 1, TIGHTFISTED

close–grained \-ˈgrānd\ *adj* : having a firm smooth texture

close–hauled \-ˈhȯld\ *adj* : having the sails set for sailing as nearly against the wind as the vessel will go

close in \ˈklōz-\ *vi* **1** : to gather in close all around with an oppressing or isolating effect 〈despair *closed in* on her〉 **2** : to approach to close quarters 〈the police *closed in*〉

close•mouthed \-ˈmau̇t͟hd, -ˈmau̇tht\ *adj* : cautious in speaking or disclosing information

close•out \ˈklō-ˌzau̇t\ *n* : a sale of leftover merchandise

close quarters \ˈklōs-\ *n pl* : direct contact or close range 〈fought at *close quarters*〉

close shave *n* : a narrow escape

[1]**clos•et** \ˈkläz-ət\ *n* **1** : an apartment or small room for privacy **2** : a cabinet or recess for china, household utensils, or clothing **3** : WATER CLOSET [Medieval French *closett* "small enclosure," from *clos* "enclosure," from *clore* "to close"]

[2]**closet** *vt* **1** : to shut up in or as if in a closet 〈*closeted* myself in my room〉 **2** : to take into a private room for an interview 〈*closeted* for an hour with the governor〉

closet drama *n* : drama suited primarily for reading

close–up \ˈklōs-ˌəp\ *n* **1** : a photograph or movie shot taken at close range **2** : an intimate view or examination

clos•ing \ˈklō-zing\ *n* **1** : a concluding part (as of a speech) **2** : a closable gap (as in a garment)

clos•trid•i•um \klä-ˈstrid-ē-əm\ *n, pl* **-ia** \-ē-ə\ : any of various spore-forming mostly anaerobic soil or intestinal bacteria including some that produce deadly toxins — compare BOTULISM, TETANUS [derived from Greek *klōstēr* "spindle," from *klōthein* "to spin"]

clo•sure \ˈklō-zhər\ *n* **1** : an act of closing : the condition of being closed **2** : something that closes **3** : CLOTURE **4** : the property that a number system or a set has when it is mathematically closed under an operation 〈the set of whole numbers does not have *closure* under division〉 **5** : an often comforting or satisfying sense of finality; *also* : something (as a satisfying ending) that provides such a sense

[1]**clot** \ˈklät\ *n* : a mass or lump made by a portion of a liquid substance thickening and sticking together 〈a *clot* of blood〉 [Old English *clott*]

[2]**clot** *vb* **clot•ted; clot•ting** : to become thick and partly solid : form clots

cloth \ˈklȯth\ *n, pl* **cloths** \ˈklȯt͟hz, ˈklȯths\ **1** : a material made usually by weaving, felting, or knitting natural or synthetic fibers **2** : a piece of cloth used for a particular purpose; *esp* : TABLECLOTH **3** : distinctive dress of a profession or calling and especially of the clergy; *also* : CLERGY [Old English *clāth*]

clothe \ˈklōt͟h\ *vt* **clothed** *or* **clad** \ˈklad\; **cloth•ing** **1 a** : to cover with or as if with cloth or clothing : DRESS **b** : to provide with clothes **2** : to express by suitable language : COUCH 〈learn to *clothe* your thought effectively〉 **3** : to endow especially with a quality 〈*clothed* with dignity〉 [Old English *clāthian*, from *clāth* "cloth, garment"]

clothes \ˈklōz, ˈklōt͟hz\ *n pl* **1** : CLOTHING **2** : BEDCLOTHES

clothes•horse \-ˌhȯrs\ *n* **1** : a frame on which to hang clothes **2** : one overly concerned with fashion

clothes moth *n* : any of several small dull-colored moths whose larvae eat wool, fur, or feathers

clothes•pin \-ˌpin\ *n* : a forked piece of wood or plastic or a clamp for holding clothes on a line

clothes•press \-ˌpres\ *n* : a receptacle (as a bureau) for clothes

cloth•ier \ˈklōt͟h-yər, ˈklō-t͟hē-ər\ *n* : one who makes or sells cloth or clothing

cloth•ing \ˈklō-t͟hing\ *n* **1** : garments or an outfit of garments **2** : an outer or protective covering 〈the trees' green *clothing*〉

clo•ture \ˈklō-chər\ *n* : the closing or limiting of debate in a legislative body especially by calling for a vote [French *clôture*, literally, "closure"] — **cloture** *vt*

[1]**cloud** \ˈklau̇d\ *n* **1** : a visible mass of particles of water or ice in the form of fog, mist, or haze suspended usually at a considerable height in the air **2** : something resembling or suggesting a cloud: as **a** : a visible mass of minute particles in the air or a mass of obscuring matter in interstellar space **b** : an aggregate of charged particles (as electrons) **c** : a great crowd massed together : SWARM 〈a *cloud* of mosquitoes〉 **3** : something that appears dark or threatening 〈war *clouds*〉 **4** : something that obscures or blemishes 〈worked under a *cloud* of secrecy〉 **5** : a dark vein or spot (as in marble) **6** : the computers and connections that support cloud computing 〈storing files in the *cloud*〉 [Old English *clūd* "rock, hill"] — **cloud•less** \-ləs\ *adj* — **cloudless•ly** *adv* — **cloud•less•ness** *n*

cloud 1: *1* cirrus, *2* cirrostratus, *3* cirrocumulus, *4* altostratus, *5* stratocumulus, *6* nimbostratus, *7* cumulus, *8* cumulonimbus, *9* stratus

[2]**cloud** *vb* **1** : to grow cloudy **2** : to make or become gloomy or ominous 〈her face *clouded* with worry〉 **3** : to envelop or hide with or as if with a cloud 〈smog *clouded* our view〉 **4** : to make

\ə\ **abut**	\au̇\ **out**	\i\ **tip**	\ȯ\ **saw**	\u̇\ **foot**
\ər\ **further**	\ch\ **chin**	\ī\ **life**	\ȯi\ **coin**	\y\ **yet**
\a\ **mat**	\e\ **pet**	\j\ **job**	\th\ **thin**	\yü\ **few**
\ā\ **take**	\ē\ **easy**	\ng\ **sing**	\t͟h\ **this**	\yu̇\ **cure**
\ä\ **cot, cart**	\g\ **go**	\ō\ **bone**	\ü\ **food**	\zh\ **vision**

unclear : OBSCURE ⟨steam *clouded* the windows⟩ **5 :** to make or become soiled or tainted ⟨a *clouded* reputation⟩

cloud·burst \ˌ-bərst\ *n* : a sudden heavy rainfall

cloud chamber *n* : a vessel containing air saturated with water vapor whose sudden expansion reveals the passage of an ionizing particle (as an electron) by a trail of visible droplets

cloud computing *n* : the practice of storing regularly used computer data on multiple servers that can be accessed through the Internet

cloud forest *n* : a wet tropical mountain forest characterized by many plants that are epiphytes and by the presence of clouds even in the dry season

cloud·let \-lət\ *n* : a small cloud

cloudy \ˈklau̇-dē\ *adj* **cloud·i·er; -est** **1 :** of, relating to, or resembling cloud **2 :** darkened by gloom or anxiety ⟨a *cloudy* mood⟩ **3 a :** overcast with clouds ⟨*cloudy* weather⟩ **b :** having a cloudy sky ⟨a *cloudy* day⟩ **4 :** obscure in meaning ⟨*cloudy* issues⟩ **5 :** dimmed or dulled as if by clouds ⟨a *cloudy* mirror⟩ **6 :** uneven in color or texture **7 :** having visible material in suspension ⟨a *cloudy* liquid⟩ — **cloud·i·ly** \ˈklau̇d-l-ē\ *adv* — **cloud·i·ness** \ˈklau̇d-ē-nəs\ *n*

¹clout \ˈklau̇t\ *n* **1 :** a hard hit especially with the hand **2 :** a white cloth used as a target in long-distance archery **3 :** PULL 2b ⟨political *clout*⟩ [Old English *clūt* "cloth, rag"]

²clout *vt* : to hit forcefully

¹clove \ˈklōv\ *n* : one of the small bulbs developed in the axils of the scales of a large bulb ⟨a garlic *clove*⟩ [Old English *clufu*]

²clove *past of* CLEAVE

³clove *n* : the dried flower bud of a tropical tree of the myrtle family that is used as a spice and is the source of an oil; *also* : this tree [Medieval French *clou (de girofle),* literally, "nail (of clove)" from Latin *clavus* "nail"]

cloven *past participle of* CLEAVE

cloven foot *n* **1 :** a foot (as of a sheep) divided into two parts at its outer extremity **2 :** the sign of devilish character [sense 2 from the traditional representation of Satan as cloven-footed] — **clo·ven–foot·ed** \ˌklō-vən-ˈfu̇t-əd\ *adj*

cloven hoof *n* : CLOVEN FOOT — **cloven–hoofed** \ˌklō-vən-ˈhu̇ft, -ˈhu̇vd, -ˈhüft, -ˈhüvd\ *adj*

clo·ver \ˈklō-vər\ *n* : any of a genus of herbs of the legume family having leaves with three leaflets and flowers in dense heads and including many valuable forage and bee plants; *also* : any of various related plants [Old English *clāfre*] — **in clover** *also* **in the clover** : in prosperity or in pleasant circumstances

clo·ver·leaf \-ˌlēf\ *n* : a road plan that in shape resembles a four-leaf clover and that is used for passing one highway over another and routing traffic for turns by turnoffs that lead around to enter the other highway from the right

¹clown \ˈklau̇n\ *n* **1 :** a rude ill-bred person : BOOR **2 a :** a fool, jester, or comedian in an entertainment; *esp* : a grotesquely dressed comedy performer in a circus **b :** one who habitually jokes and plays the buffoon : JOKER [earlier *clown* "countryman, farmer," probably of Low German origin]

²clown *vi* : to act like a clown

clown·ish \ˈklau̇-nish\ *adj* : of or resembling a clown (as in foolishness or ignorance) — **clown·ish·ly** *adv* — **clown·ish·ness** *n*

cloy \ˈklȯi\ *vb* **1 :** to weary or disgust with an excess usually of something once pleasing **2 :** to cause weariness or disgust through being in excess [Middle English "to hinder, lame," from *acloyen* "to harm, maim," from Medieval French *encloer* "to nail, prick a horse with a nail in shoeing," from Medieval Latin *inclavare,* from Latin *in* "in" + *clavus* "nail"] — **cloy·ing·ly** \-ing-lē\ *adv*

¹club \ˈkləb\ *n* **1 a :** a heavy usually tapering staff especially of wood used as a weapon **b :** a stick or bat used for hitting a ball in a game **c :** a black figure resembling a clover leaf used to distinguish a suit of playing cards; *also* : a card of the suit bearing clubs **2 a :** an association of persons for some common object **b :** the meeting place of a club **c :** NIGHTCLUB **3 :** CLUB SANDWICH [Old Norse *klubba*]

²club *vb* **clubbed; club·bing** **1 :** to beat or strike with or as if with a club **2 :** to unite or combine for a common cause — often used with *together* **3 :** to go to nightclubs

club·foot \ˈkləb-ˈfu̇t\ *n* : a misshapen foot twisted out of position from birth; *also* : this deformity — **club·foot·ed** \-əd\ *adj*

club fungus *n* : BASIDIOMYCETE

club·house \-ˌhau̇s\ *n* **1 :** a house occupied by a club or used for club activities **2 :** locker rooms used by an athletic team

club moss *n* : any of an order (Lycopodiales) of low often trailing evergreen vascular plants (as the ground pine) having branching stems covered with small mosslike leaves and reproducing by spores usually borne in club-shaped cones

club sandwich *n* : a sandwich of three slices of bread and two layers of meat and lettuce, tomato, and mayonnaise

club steak *n* : a small steak from just behind the ribs

¹cluck \ˈklək\ *vi* : to utter a cluck or a similar sound [imitative]

²cluck *n* **1 :** the characteristic sound of a hen especially in calling her chicks **2 :** a broody fowl

¹clue \ˈklü\ *n* **1 :** something that guides through a complicated procedure or maze of difficulties; *also* : a piece of evidence that leads toward the solution of a problem **2 :** IDEA, CONCEPTION ⟨had no *clue* what he meant⟩ [alteration of *clew*]

²clue *vt* **clued; clue·ing** *or* **clu·ing** **1 :** to provide with a clue **2 :** to give reliable information to ⟨*clue* me in on what happened⟩

clue·less \ˈklü-ləs\ *adj* **1 :** having or providing no clue ⟨a *clueless* case for the police⟩ **2 :** completely or hopelessly bewildered, unaware, or foolish ⟨*clueless* about what they want⟩

clum·ber spaniel \ˈkləm-bər-\ *n, often cap C* : any of a breed of large heavyset spaniels with a dense silky largely white coat [*Clumber,* estate in Nottinghamshire, England]

¹clump \ˈkləmp\ *n* **1 :** a group of things clustered together ⟨a *clump* of bushes⟩ **2 :** a compact mass : LUMP **3 :** a heavy tramping sound [probably from Low German *klump*] — **clumpy** \ˈkləm-pē\ *adj*

²clump *vb* **1 :** to walk clumsily and noisily **2 :** to form or cause to form clumps

clum·sy \ˈkləm-zē\ *adj* **clum·si·er; -est** **1 a :** lacking dexterity, nimbleness, or grace ⟨*clumsy* fingers⟩ **b :** lacking tact or subtlety ⟨a *clumsy* joke⟩ **2 :** awkwardly or poorly made : UNWIELDY ⟨a *clumsy* tool⟩ [probably from obsolete English *clumse* "benumbed with cold"] ***synonyms*** see AWKWARD — **clum·si·ly** \-zə-lē\ *adv* — **clum·si·ness** \-zē-nəs\ *n*

clung *past of* CLING

¹clus·ter \ˈkləs-tər\ *n* **1 :** a number of similar things growing, collected, or grouped closely together : BUNCH ⟨a *cluster* of houses⟩ ⟨a flower *cluster*⟩ **2 :** two or more consecutive consonants or vowels in a segment of speech [Old English *clyster*]

²cluster *vb* **clus·tered; clus·ter·ing** \-tə-ring, -tring\ : to grow, collect, or assemble in a cluster

¹clutch \ˈkləch\ *vb* **1 :** to grasp or hold with or as if with the hand or claws usually strongly, tightly, or suddenly **2 :** to try to grasp and hold ⟨*clutch* at a railing⟩ [Old English *clyccan*]

²clutch *n* **1 a :** the claws or a hand in the act of grasping or seizing firmly **b :** an often cruel or unrelenting control ⟨had the enemy in their *clutches*⟩ **2 :** a device for gripping an object **3 a :** a coupling used to connect and disconnect a driving and a driven part of a mechanism **b :** a lever operating a clutch **4 :** a tight or critical situation ⟨came through in the *clutch*⟩

³clutch *n* : a nest or batch of eggs or a brood of chicks [alteration of English dialect *cletch* "hatching, brood"]

¹clut·ter \ˈklət-ər\ *vt* : to fill or cover with a disorderly scattering of things ⟨*clutter* up a room⟩ [Middle English *clotteren* "to clot," from *clot*]

²clutter *n* : a crowded or disorderly collection of things

Clydes·dale \ˈklīdz-ˌdāl\ *n* : any of a breed of heavy draft horses originally from Clydesdale, Scotland with long silky hair on the legs

clyp·e·us \ˈklip-ē-əs\ *n, pl* **-ei** \-ē-ˌī, -ē-ˌē\ : a plate on the front central part of an insect's head [Latin, "round shield"]

cni·dar·i·an \nī-ˈder-ē-ən\ *n* : COELENTERATE [derived from Greek *knidē* "nettle"] — **cnidarian** *adj*

co- *prefix* **1 :** with : together : joint : jointly ⟨*co*exist⟩ **2 :** in or to the same degree ⟨*co*extensive⟩ **3 :** fellow : partner ⟨*co*author⟩ [Latin, from *com-*]

coact	**cocomposer**	**cofounder**
coaction	**coconspirator**	**cohead**
coactive	**cocounsel**	**coheir**
coactor	**cocreate**	**coheiress**
coanchor	**cocreator**	**coholder**
coauthor	**codefendant**	**cohost**
cocaptain	**codesign**	**cohostess**
cochair	**coedit**	**coinvent**
cochairman	**coeditor**	**coinventor**
cochairperson	**coexecutor**	**coinvestigator**
cochairwoman	**cofinance**	**coinvestor**
cochampion	**cofound**	**colead**

coleader	**coprincipal**	**coreciplent**
comanage	**coprisoner**	**coresident**
comanagement	**coproduce**	**coresidential**
comanager	**coproducer**	**cosponsor**
co–official	**coproduction**	**costar**
co–organizer	**copromoter**	**cowinner**
co–own	**coproprietor**	**coworker**
co–owner	**copublish**	**cowrite**
copresident	**copublisher**	**cowriter**

co·ac·er·vate \kō-ˈas-ər-ˌvāt\ *n* : an aggregate of colloidal droplets held together by electrostatic forces [Latin *coacervatus,* past participle of *coacervare* "to heap up," from *co-* + *acervus* "heap"] — **co·ac·er·va·tion** \ˌkō-ˌas-ər-ˈvā-shən\ *n*

[1]**coach** \ˈkōch\ *n* **1 a** : a large usually closed four-wheeled carriage having doors in the sides and a raised seat in front for the driver **b** : a railroad passenger car intended primarily for day travel **c** : BUS 1a **d** : an automobile body especially of a closed model **e** : a class of passenger air transportation at a lower fare than first class **2 a** : a private tutor **b** : one who instructs or trains a performer or a team of performers; *esp* : one who instructs players in the fundamentals of a competitive sport and directs team strategy [Middle French *coche,* from German *Kutsche;* sense 2 from the concept that the tutor conveys the student through his examinations]

[2]**coach** *vb* **1** : to go in a horse-drawn coach **2** : to instruct, direct, or prompt as a coach — **coach·er** *n*

coach dog *n* : DALMATIAN

coach·man \ˈkōch-mən\ *n* : a man who drives a coach or carriage

co·ad·ju·tor \ˌkō-ə-ˈjüt-ər, kō-ˈaj-ət-ər\ *n* **1** : one who works together with another : ASSISTANT **2** : a bishop assisting a diocesan bishop and often having the right of succession [Medieval French *coadjuteur,* from Late Latin *coadjutor,* from Latin *co-* + *adjutor* "helper," from *adjuvare* "to help"] — **coadjutor** *adj*

co·ad·ju·trix \ˌkō-ə-ˈjü-triks, kō-ˈaj-ə-triks\ *n, pl* **co·ad·ju·tri·ces** \ˌkō-ə-ˈjü-trə-ˌsēz, kō-ˌaj-ə-ˈtrī-sēz\ : a woman who is a coadjutor [New Latin, feminine of *coadjutor*]

co·ag·u·la·ble \kō-ˈag-yə-lə-bəl\ *adj* : capable of being coagulated — **co·ag·u·la·bil·i·ty** \-ˌag-yə-lə-ˈbil-ət-ē\ *n*

co·ag·u·lant \-ˈag-yə-lənt\ *n* : something that produces coagulation

co·ag·u·lase \-ˌlās, -ˌlāz\ *n* : an enzyme that promotes coagulation (as of the blood)

co·ag·u·late \-ˌlāt\ *vb* : to become or cause to become viscous or thickened into a coherent mass : CLOT [Latin *coagulare* "to curdle," from *coagulum* "curdling agent," from *cogere* "to drive together," from *co-* + *agere* "to drive"] — **co·ag·u·la·tion** \ˌkō-ˌag-yə-ˈlā-shən\ *n*

[1]**coal** \ˈkōl\ *n* **1** : a piece of glowing or charred wood : EMBER **2** : a black or brownish black solid combustible mineral substance formed by the partial decay of vegetable matter under the influence of moisture and often increased pressure and temperature that is widely used as a natural fuel [Old English *col*]

[2]**coal** *vb* **1** : to supply with coal **2** : to take in coal

co·a·lesce \ˌkō-ə-ˈles\ *vi* : to unite by growth into one body [Latin *coalescere,* from *co-* + *alescere* "to grow"] ***synonyms*** see MIX — **co·a·les·cence** \-ˈles-ns\ *n* — **co·a·les·cent** \-nt\ *adj*

coal·field \ˈkōl-ˌfēld\ *n* : a region where deposits of coal occur

coal gas *n* : gas from coal; *esp* : gas made by distilling bituminous coal and used for heating and lighting

co·a·li·tion \ˌkō-ə-ˈlish-ən\ *n* **1** : the union of separate items into a body or group; *also* : a body or group so formed : COMBINATION **2** : a temporary alliance of persons, parties, or countries for joint action [French, from Latin *coalescere* "to coalesce"] — **co·a·li·tion·ist** \-ˈlish-nəst, -ə-nəst\ *n*

coal measures *n pl* : beds of coal with the associated rocks

coal oil *n* **1** : petroleum or a refined oil prepared from petroleum **2** : KEROSENE

coal tar *n* : tar obtained by distilling bituminous coal and used especially in making drugs, dyes, and fuel

coam·ing \ˈkō-ming\ *n* : a raised frame around a hatchway to keep out water [probably derived from *comb*]

coarse \ˈkōrs, ˈkȯrs\ *adj* **1** : of ordinary or inferior quality or appearance : COMMON **2 a** : made up of fairly large parts or particles ⟨*coarse* porous soil⟩ **b** : rough in texture ⟨*coarse* skin⟩ **c** : designed for heavy, fast, or less delicate work ⟨a *coarse* saw with large teeth⟩ **d** : not precise or detailed in adjustment or discrimination **3** : crude in taste, manner, or language **4** : harsh or rough in tone ⟨a *coarse* voice⟩ [Middle English *cors,* perhaps from *course, cors* "course"] — **coarse·ly** *adv* — **coarse·ness** *n*

synonyms COARSE, VULGAR, RIBALD, OBSCENE mean offensive to good taste or morals. COARSE implies roughness, rudeness, or crudeness of spirit, behavior, or language ⟨found the *coarse* humor of coworkers offensive⟩. VULGAR implies actual offensiveness to good taste or decency ⟨a loud *vulgar* burp⟩. RIBALD applies to what is amusingly or picturesquely vulgar or irreverent or mildly indecent ⟨*ribald* folk songs⟩. OBSCENE may apply to whatever strongly offends the sense of decency or propriety but especially implies flagrant violation of taboo in sexual matters ⟨*obscene* language not allowed on T.V.⟩.

coarse–grained \-ˈgrānd\ *adj* **1** : having a coarse grain or texture **2** : lacking in culture : CRUDE

coars·en \ˈkōrs-n, ˈkȯrs-\ *vb* **coars·ened; coars·en·ing** \ˈkōrs-ning, ˈkȯrs-, -n-ing\ : to make or become coarse ⟨hands *coarsened* by hard labor⟩

[1]**coast** \ˈkōst\ *n* **1** : the land near a shore : SEASHORE **2** : a slope suited to sliding (as on a sled) downhill; *also* : a slide down such a slope **3** : the immediate area in view ⟨the *coast* is clear⟩ [Medieval French *coste,* from Latin *costa* "rib, side"]

[2]**coast** *vi* **1** : to sail along a coast **2 a** : to slide, run, or glide (as over snow on a sled) downhill by the force of gravity **b** : to move along (as on a bicycle when not pedaling) without applying power **3** : to proceed easily without special effort ⟨*coasted* through the rest of the term⟩

coast·al \ˈkōst-l\ *adj* : of or relating to a coast : located on, near, or along a coast ⟨*coastal* waters⟩

coast·er \ˈkō-stər\ *n* **1** : one that coasts; *esp* : a ship engaged in coastal trade **2 a** : a tray often on wheels that is used for passing a decanter **b** : a shallow container or a plate or mat to protect a surface ⟨drink *coasters*⟩ **c** : a small vehicle (as a sled) used in coasting

coaster brake *n* : a brake in the hub of the rear wheel of a bicycle operated by reverse pressure on the pedals

coast guard *n* : a military force concerned with enforcing marine laws and traffic regulations, maintaining aids to navigation, and performing rescue service — **coast·guards·man** \ˈkōst-ˌgärdz-mən, ˈkōs-\ *or* **coast·guard·man** \-ˌgärd-mən\ *n*

coast·line \ˈkōst-ˌlīn\ *n* : the outline or shape of a coast

coast·ward \ˈkōs-twərd\ *or* **coast·wards** \-twərdz\ *adv* : toward the coast — **coastward** *adj*

[1]**coat** \ˈkōt\ *n* **1** : an outer garment varying in length and style according to fashion and use **2** : the external growth (as of fur) on an animal **3** : a layer of one substance covering another ⟨a *coat* of paint⟩ [Medieval French *cote,* of Germanic origin] — **coat·ed** \-əd\ *adj*

[2]**coat** *vt* : to cover with a coat and especially with a finishing, protecting, or enclosing layer

co·a·ti \kə-ˈwät-ē, ˌkō-ə-ˈtē\ *n* : a tropical American mammal related to the raccoon but with a longer body and tail and a long flexible snout [Portuguese *coati,* from Tupi *kwáti*]

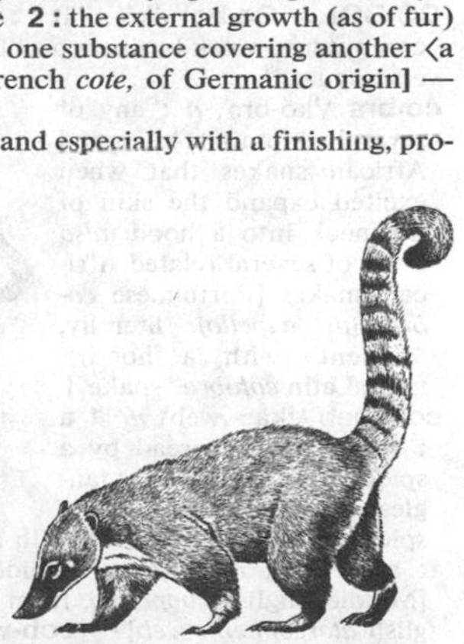
coati

co·a·ti·mun·di \kə-ˌwät-ē-ˈmən-dē, ˌkwä-, -ˈmu̇n-\ *n* : COATI [Portuguese *quatimundé,* from Tupi *kwatimúnde* "older male coati not with a band," from *kwati* "coati" + *múnde* "snare, trap"]

coat·ing \ˈkōt-ing\ *n* **1** : a layer covering a surface : COAT ⟨a *coating* of ice on a pond⟩ **2** : cloth for coats

coat of arms : heraldic arms (as of a person or family) displayed on a shield or surface

coat of mail : a garment of metal scales or rings worn as armor

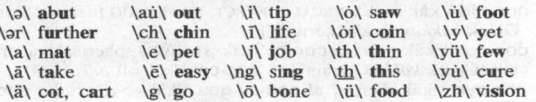

\ə\ **abut**	\au̇\ **out**	\i\ **tip**	\ȯ\ **saw**	\u̇\ **foot**
\ər\ **further**	\ch\ **chin**	\ī\ **life**	\ȯi\ **coin**	\y\ **yet**
\a\ **mat**	\e\ **pet**	\j\ **job**	\th\ **thin**	\yü\ **few**
\ā\ **take**	\ē\ **easy**	\ng\ **sing**	\t͟h\ **this**	\yu̇\ **cure**
\ä\ **cot, cart**	\g\ **go**	\ō\ **bone**	\ü\ **food**	\zh\ **vision**

coat·room \ˈkōt-ˌrüm, -ˌrům\ *n* : CHECKROOM
coat·tail \ˈkōt-ˌtāl\ *n* **1** : the rear flap of a man's coat **2** *pl* : the skirts of a dress coat, cutaway, or frock coat **3** *pl* : the influence or pulling power of a popular movement or person (as a political candidate) ⟨congressmen riding into office on the president's *coattails*⟩
coax \ˈkōks\ *vb* **1** : to influence or gently urge a person by caressing or flattering **2** : to gain by gentle persuasion or flattery ⟨*coax* a dollar from one's father⟩ [obsolete *cokes* "simpleton"] — **coax·er** *n*
co·ax·i·al \kō-ˈak-sē-əl, ˈkō-\ *adj* **1** : having coincident axes **2** : mounted on concentric shafts — **co·ax·i·al·ly** \-sē-ə-lē\ *adv*
coaxial cable *n* : a transmission line that consists of a central conductor surrounded by and insulated from a tube of conducting material and used to transmit telegraph, television, and telephone signals
cob \ˈkäb\ *n* **1** : a male swan **2** : CORNCOB **3** : a stocky short-legged riding horse [Middle English *cobbe* "leader"]
co·bal·a·min \kō-ˈbal-ə-mən\ *n* : VITAMIN B_{12} [*cobalt* + *vitamin*]
co·balt \ˈkō-ˌbȯlt\ *n* : a tough shiny silver-white magnetic metallic element found with iron and nickel and used especially in alloys — see ELEMENT table [German *Kobalt,* from *Kobold* "goblin"; from its occurrence in silver ore, once believed to be due to goblins] — **co·bal·tic** \kō-ˈbȯl-tik\ *adj* — **co·bal·tous** \-təs\ *adj*
cobalt chloride *n* : the dichloride of cobalt $CoCl_2$ that is blue when dehydrated but turns red in the presence of moisture and is used to indicate humidity
co·balt·ite \ˈkō-ˌbȯl-ˌtīt\ *or* **co·balt·ine** \-ˌtēn\ *n* : a grayish to silver-white mineral that consists of cobalt, arsenic, and sulfur
cobalt 60 *n* : a heavy radioactive isotope of cobalt of the mass number 60 produced in nuclear reactors and used as a source of gamma rays
[1]**cob·ble** \ˈkäb-əl\ *vt* **cob·bled; cob·bling** \ˈkäb-ling, -ə-ling\ : to make or put together roughly or hastily ⟨a shed *cobbled* up out of scraps⟩ [Middle English *coblen*]
[2]**cobble** *n* : a naturally rounded stone larger than a pebble and smaller than a boulder; *esp* : such a stone used in paving a street [back-formation from *cobblestone*]
[3]**cobble** *vt* : to pave with cobblestones
cob·bler \ˈkäb-lər\ *n* **1** : one that mends or makes shoes **2** *archaic* : a clumsy worker **3** : a deep-dish fruit pie with a thick top crust [Middle English *cobelere*]
cob·ble·stone \ˈkäb-əl-ˌstōn\ *n* : COBBLE [Middle English, from *cobble-* (probably from *cob*) + *stone*]
CO·BOL *or* **Co·bol** \ˈkō-ˌbȯl\ *n* : a language for programming a computer to work business problems [*co*mmon *b*usiness *o*riented *l*anguage]
co·bra \ˈkō-brə\ *n* : any of several venomous Asian and African snakes that when excited expand the skin of the neck into a hood; *also* : any of several related African snakes [Portuguese *cobra (de capello),* literally, "serpent (with a hood)," from Latin *colubra* "snake"]

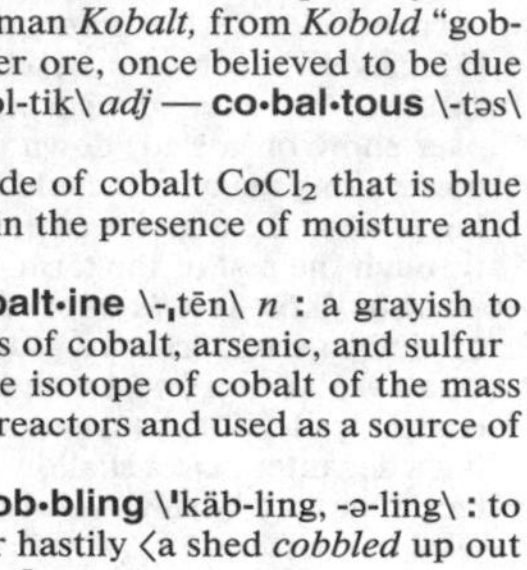
cobra

cob·web \ˈkäb-ˌweb\ *n* **1 a** : the network spread by a spider : SPIDERWEB **b** : tangles of the silken threads of a spiderweb usually covered with accumulated dirt and dust **2** : something resembling a spiderweb ⟨*cobwebs* of intrigue⟩ [Middle English *coppeweb,* from *coppe* "spider" (from Old English *atorcoppe*) + *web*] — **cob·webbed** \-ˌwebd\ *adj* — **cob·web·by** \-ˌweb-ē\ *adj*
co·ca \ˈkō-kə\ *n* : a South American shrub with leaves that are the source of cocaine; *also* : its dried leaves [Spanish, from Quechua *kuka*]
co·caine \kō-ˈkān\ *n* : a bitter habit-forming drug obtained from coca leaves that is used as a local anesthetic and illegally to stimulate the central nervous system
coc·cid \ˈkäk-səd\ *n* : SCALE INSECT, MEALYBUG [derived from Greek *kokkos* "grain, kermes"]
coc·cus \ˈkäk-əs\ *n, pl* **coc·ci** \ˈkäk-ˌsī, -ˌī\ : a spherical bacterium [Greek *kokkos* "grain"] — **coc·cal** \ˈkäk-əl\ *adj*
coc·cyx \ˈkäk-siks\ *n, pl* **coc·cy·ges** \ˈkäk-sə-ˌjēz\ *also* **coc·cyx·es** : the small bone at the end of the spinal column in humans and tailless apes that consists of four reduced fused vertebrae [Greek *kokkyx* "cuckoo, coccyx"; from its resemblance to a cuckoo's beak] — **coc·cyg·eal** \käk-ˈsij-ē-əl, -ˈsij-əl\ *adj*
coch·i·neal \ˈkäch-ə-ˌnēl, ˈkō-chə-\ *n* : a red dyestuff consisting of the dried bodies of female cochineal insects [Spanish *cochinilla* "wood louse, cochineal insect"]
cochineal insect *n* : a small bright red scale insect that feeds on cacti and yields cochineal
co·chlea \ˈkō-klē-ə, ˈkäk-lē-\ *n, pl* **co·chle·as** *or* **co·chle·ae** \ˈkō-klē-ˌē, ˈkäk-lē-, -ˌī\ : a hollow tube in the inner ear of higher vertebrates that is usually coiled like a snail shell and contains the nerve endings which carry information about sound to the brain [Latin, "snail, snail shell," from Greek *kochlias,* from *kochlos* "land snail"] — **co·chle·ar** \ˈkō-klē-ər, ˈkäk-lē-\ *adj*
[1]**cock** \ˈkäk\ *n* **1** : the adult male of a bird and especially the domestic chicken **2** : a device (as a faucet or valve) for regulating the flow of a liquid **3** : the cocked position of the hammer of a firearm [Old English *cocc*]
[2]**cock** *vt* **1 a** : to draw back the hammer of (a firearm) and set for firing **b** : to draw or bend back in preparation to throw or hit ⟨*cock* one's fist⟩ **c** : to set a mechanism (as a camera shutter) for tripping **2** : to turn, tip, or tilt usually to one side ⟨*cock* one's head⟩ **3** : to turn up (as a hat brim)
[3]**cock** *n* : TILT 3a, SLANT ⟨a *cock* of the head⟩
[4]**cock** *n* : a small pile (as of hay) [Middle English *cok*]
[5]**cock** *vt* : to put (as hay) into cocks
cock·ade \kä-ˈkād\ *n* : an ornament (as a rosette) worn on the hat as a badge [French *cocarde,* from *cocard* "vain," from *coq* "cock"] — **cock·ad·ed** \-ˈkād-əd\ *adj*
Cock·aigne \kä-ˈkān\ *n* : an imaginary land of great luxury and ease [Medieval French *pais de cocaigne* "land of plenty"]
cock–and–bull story \ˌkäk-ən-ˈbůl-\ *n* : an absurd, incredible, or highly improbable story told as true
cock·a·tiel \ˌkäk-ə-ˈtēl\ *n* : a crested small gray Australian parrot with a yellow head [Dutch *kaketielje,* from Portuguese *cacatilha,* from *cacatua* "cockatoo"]
cock·a·too \ˈkäk-ə-ˌtü\ *n, pl* **-toos** : any of various large noisy usually showy and crested chiefly Australasian parrots [Dutch *kaketoe,* from Malay *kakatua*]
cock·a·trice \ˈkäk-ə-trəs, -ˌtrīs\ *n* : a legendary serpent with a deadly glance hatched by a reptile from a cock's egg [Medieval French *cocatris* "ichneumon, cockatrice," from Medieval Latin *cocatrix* "ichneumon"]
cock·crow \ˈkäk-ˌkrō\ *n* : DAWN
cocked hat \ˈkäkt-\ *n* : a hat with brim turned up to give a 3-cornered appearance
cock·er·el \ˈkäk-rəl, -ə-rəl\ *n* : a young male domestic chicken [Medieval French *cokerel* "small cock," from *coc* "cock"]
cock·er spaniel \ˈkäk-ər-\ *n* : any of a breed of small spaniels with long ears, square muzzle, and long silky coat [*cocking* "woodcock hunting"]
cock·eye \ˈkäk-ˈī, -ˌī\ *n* : a squinting eye
cock·eyed \ˈkäk-īd\ *adj* **1** : having a cockeye **2 a** : being out of line : ASKEW **b** : slightly foolish or absurd ⟨a *cockeyed* idea⟩ **c** : DRUNK 1, INTOXICATED
cock·fight \ˈkäk-ˌfīt\ *n* : a combat of gamecocks usually fitted with metal spurs — **cock·fight·ing** \-iŋ\ *adj or n*
[1]**cock·le** \ˈkäk-əl\ *n* : any of several weeds mostly of grain fields; *esp* : CORN COCKLE [Old English *coccel*]
[2]**cockle** *n* **1** : an edible mollusk with a ribbed 2-valved shell **2** : COCKLESHELL [Medieval French *coquille* "shell," from Latin *conchylium,* from Greek *konchylion,* from *konchē* "conch"]
cock·le·bur \ˈkäk-əl-ˌbər, ˈkək-\ *n* : any of a genus of prickly-fruited plants related to the thistles; *also* : one of its fruits
cock·le·shell \ˈkäk-əl-ˌshel\ *n* **1 a** : a shell or shell valve of a cockle **b** : a shell (as a scallop) suggesting a cockleshell **2** : a light flimsy boat
cock·les of the heart \ˈkäk-əlz-\ : the deepest part of one's being — usually used in the phrase *warm the cockles of the heart*
cock·ney \ˈkäk-nē\ *n, pl* **cockneys** *often cap* **1** : a native of London and especially of the East End of London **2** : the dialect used by cockneys [Middle English *cokeney* "spoiled child," literally, "cocks' egg," from *cok* "cock" + *ey* "egg"] — **cockney** *adj*
cock·pit \ˈkäk-ˌpit\ *n* **1** : a pit for cockfights **2 a** : an open space aft of a decked area from which a boat or yacht is steered **b** : a space in the fuselage of an airplane for the pilot or the pi-

lot and passengers or in large planes the pilot and crew

cock·roach \'käk-ˌrōch\ *n* **:** any of an order (Blattaria) of mostly nocturnal insects which have flattened bodies and long antennae and some of which are domestic pests [by folk etymology from Spanish *cucaracha*]

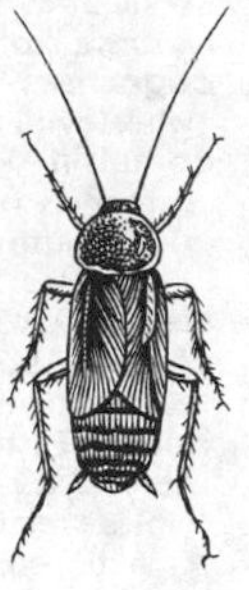

cockroach

cocks·comb \'käk-ˌskōm\ *n* **1 :** COXCOMB **2 :** a garden plant related to the amaranths and grown for its showy flowers

cock·sure \'käk-'shu̇r\ *adj* **1 :** perfectly sure **:** CERTAIN **2 :** marked by overconfidence **:** COCKY — **cock·sure·ly** *adv* — **cock·sure·ness** *n*

cocktail *n* **1 :** an iced drink of distilled liquor mixed with flavoring ingredients **2 :** an appetizer (as tomato juice) served as a first course at a meal

cocky \'käk-ē\ *adj* **cock·i·er; -est 1 :** arrogantly self-confident **2 :** jaunty in behavior or appearance — **cock·i·ly** \'käk-ə-lē\ *adv* — **cock·i·ness** \'käk-ē-nəs\ *n*

co·co \'kō-kō\ *n, pl* **cocos :** the coconut palm or its fruit [Spanish *coco* and Portuguese *côco,* literally, "bogeyman," "grimace"]

co·coa \'kō-kō\ *n* **1 :** a cacao tree **2 a :** powdered ground roasted cacao beans from which a portion of the fat has been removed **b :** a beverage made by heating cocoa with water or milk [Spanish *cacao*]

cocoa bean *n* **:** CACAO 2

cocoa butter *n* **:** a pale fat with a low melting point obtained from cacao beans and used in foods and cosmetics

co·co·nut \'kō-kə-ˌnət, -nət\ *n* **:** the fruit of the coconut palm with an outer fibrous husk yielding coir and a nut containing thick edible meat and coconut milk

coconut oil *n* **:** a nearly colorless oil or soft white fat extracted from coconuts and used in soaps and foods

coconut palm *n* **:** a tall pinnate-leaved palm that grows along tropical coasts and produces coconuts

co·coon \kə-'kün\ *n* **1 a :** an envelope often largely of silk which an insect larva forms about itself and in which it passes the pupa stage — compare CHRYSALIS **b :** any of various other protective coverings produced by animals **2 :** a covering suggesting a cocoon [French *cocon,* from Provençal *coucoun,* from *coco* "shell," from Latin *coccum* "excrescence on a tree," from Greek *kokkos* "grain, seed, kermes berry"]

cod \'käd\ *n, pl* **cod** *also* **cods :** a soft-finned fish of the colder parts of the North Atlantic that is a major food fish; *also* **:** any of several related fishes [Middle English]

co·da \'kōd-ə\ *n* **:** a distinctive formal closing section in a musical composition [Italian, literally, "tail," from Latin *cauda*]

cod·dle \'käd-l\ *vt* **cod·dled; cod·dling** \'käd-ling, -l-ing\ **1 :** to cook slowly in water just below the boiling point ⟨*coddle* eggs⟩ **2 :** to treat with extreme care or kindness **:** PAMPER [perhaps from *caudle*] — **cod·dler** \'käd-lər, -l-ər\ *n*

[1]**code** \'kōd\ *n* **1 :** a systematic statement of a body of law; *esp* **:** one having the force of statute ⟨a criminal *code*⟩ **2 :** a system of principles or rules ⟨moral *codes*⟩ **3 :** a system of signals for communicating **4 :** a system (as of letters or symbols) used to represent assigned and often secret meanings **5 :** GENETIC CODE **6 :** a set of instructions for a computer [Medieval French, from Latin *codex* "tree trunk, document formed originally from wooden tablets"]

[2]**code** *vb* **1 :** to put into the form of a code **2 :** to specify the genetic code ⟨genes that *code* for a protein⟩ — **cod·er** *n*

co·deine \'kō-ˌdēn, 'kōd-ē-ən\ *n* **:** a drug that is obtained from opium, is weaker than morphine, and is used as a pain reliever and in cough remedies [French *codéine,* from Greek *kōdeia* "poppy head"]

co·dex \'kō-ˌdeks\ *n, pl* **co·di·ces** \'kōd-ə-ˌsēz, 'käd-\ **:** a manuscript book (as of the Scriptures) [Latin]

cod·fish \'käd-ˌfish\ *n* **:** COD; *also* **:** its flesh used as food

cod·ger \'käj-ər\ *n* **:** an odd or cranky fellow [probably alteration of *cadger*]

cod·i·cil \'käd-ə-səl, -ˌsil\ *n* **:** a supplementary document that modifies an earlier will [Medieval French *codicille,* from Latin *codex* "book"]

cod·i·fy \'käd-ə-ˌfī, 'kōd-\ *vt* **-fied; -fy·ing 1 :** to reduce (as laws) to a code **2 :** to arrange in a systematic and understandable order — **cod·i·fi·ca·tion** \ˌkäd-ə-fə-'kā-shən, ˌkōd-\ *n*

[1]**cod·ling** \'käd-ling\ *n* **1 :** a young cod **2 :** HAKE

[2]**cod·ling** \'käd-ling\ *or* **cod·lin** \-lən\ *n* **:** a small immature apple; *also* **:** any of several elongated greenish English cooking apples [Middle English *querdlyng*]

codling moth *n* **:** a small moth whose larva lives in apples, pears, quinces, and English walnuts

cod–liver oil *n* **:** an oil obtained from the liver of the cod and related fishes and used as a source of vitamins A and D

co·don \'kō-ˌdän\ *n* **:** a specific sequence of three consecutive nucleotides that is part of the genetic code and that specifies a particular amino acid in a protein or starts or stops protein synthesis

[1]**co·ed** \'kō-ˌed\ *n* **:** a female student in a coeducational school

[2]**coed** *adj* **1 :** of or relating to a coed **2 :** COEDUCATIONAL **3 :** open to or used by both men and women

co·ed·u·ca·tion·al \ˌkō-ej-ə-'kā-shnəl, -shən-l\ *adj* **:** having both male and female students

co·ef·fi·cient \ˌkō-ə-'fish-ənt\ *n* **1 :** a number or symbol by which another number or symbol (as a mathematical variable) is multiplied ⟨in $5xy^2$, 5 is the *coefficient* of xy^2⟩ **2 :** a number that serves as a measure of a property or characteristic (as of a substance or device) ⟨the metal's *coefficient* of expansion⟩

coe·la·canth \'sē-lə-ˌkanth\ *n* **:** a fish or fossil of an order (Coelacanthiformes) of mostly extinct fishes [Greek *koilos* "hollow" + *akantha* "spine"]

-coele *or* **-coel** \ˌsēl\ *n combining form* **:** cavity **:** chamber ⟨blasto*coel*⟩ ⟨entero*coele*⟩ [Greek *koilos,* adjective, "hollow"]

coe·len·ter·ate \si-'lent-ə-ˌrāt, -rət\ *n* **:** any of a phylum (Cnidaria or Coelenterata) of invertebrate animals that include the corals, sea anemones, sea fans, jellyfishes, and hydroids and have a body with radial symmetry — called also *cnidarian* [Greek *koilos* "hollow" + *enteron* "intestine"] — **coelenterate** *adj*

coeliac *variant of* CELIAC

coe·lom \'sē-ləm\ *n, pl* **coe·loms** *or* **coe·lo·ma·ta** \si-'lō-mət-ə\ **:** the usually epithelium-lined body cavity of animals above the lower worms [German, from Greek *koilōma* "cavity," from *koilos* "hollow"] — **coe·lo·mate** \'sē-lə-ˌmāt\ *adj or n* — **coe·lo·mic** \si-'läm-ik, -'lō-mik\ *adj*

coen- *or* **coeno-** *combining form* **:** common **:** general ⟨*coeno*cytic⟩ [Greek *koinos*]

coenobite *variant of* CENOBITE

coe·no·cyt·ic \ˌsē-nə-'sit-ik\ *adj* **:** containing several or many nuclei ⟨a *coenocytic* cell⟩

co·en·zyme \'kō-'en-ˌzīm\ *n* **:** a substance (as a vitamin) closely associated with an enzyme and essential for its normal function

coenzyme A *n* **:** a coenzyme $C_{21}H_{36}N_7O_{16}P_3S$ that occurs in all living cells and is essential to the metabolism of carbohydrates, fats, and some amino acids — compare ACETYL-COA

co·equal \'kō-'ē-kwəl\ *adj* **:** equal with one another — **co·equal·i·ty** \ˌkō-ē-'kwäl-ət-ē\ *n* — **co·equal·ly** \'kō-'ē-kwə-lē\ *adv*

co·erce \kō-'ərs\ *vt* **1 :** to restrain or dominate by force **2 :** to compel to an act or a choice ⟨*coerced* them to agree⟩ **3 :** to enforce by force or threat ⟨*coerce* obedience⟩ [Latin *coercēre,* from *co-* + *arcēre* "to shut up, enclose"] ***synonyms*** see FORCE — **co·erc·ible** \-'ər-sə-bəl\ *adj*

co·er·cion \kō-'ər-zhən, -shən\ *n* **:** the act, process, or power of coercing

co·er·cive \-'ər-siv\ *adj* **:** serving or intended to coerce — **co·er·cive·ly** *adv* — **co·er·cive·ness** *n*

co·eval \kō-'ē-vəl\ *adj* **:** of the same or equal age or duration [Latin *coaevus,* from *co-* + *aevum* "age, lifetime"] — **coeval** *n*

co·evo·lu·tion \ˌkō-ˌev-ə-'lü-shən, -ˌē-və-\ *n* **:** evolution occurring in two interdependent species (as a flowering plant and a pollinator) in which long-term adaptive changes are influenced by their close interactions

co·ex·ist \ˌkō-ig-'zist\ *vi* **1 :** to exist together or at the same time **2 :** to live in peace with each other — **co·ex·is·tence** \-'zis-təns\ *n* — **co·ex·is·tent** \-tənt\ *adj*

co·ex·ten·sive \ˌkō-ik-'sten-siv\ *adj* **:** having the same scope or extent in space or time — **co·ex·ten·sive·ly** *adv*

co·fac·tor \'kō-ˌfak-tər\ *n* **1 :** a substance that acts with another substance to bring about certain effects; *esp* **:** COENZYME **2 :** something (as diet) that acts with or aids another factor in causing disease

\ə\ **abut**	\au̇\ **out**	\i\ **tip**	\ȯ\ **saw**	\u̇\ **foot**
\ər\ **further**	\ch\ **chin**	\ī\ **life**	\ȯi\ **coin**	\y\ **yet**
\a\ **mat**	\e\ **pet**	\j\ **job**	\th\ **thin**	\yü\ **few**
\ā\ **take**	\ē\ **easy**	\ng\ **sing**	\t͟h\ **this**	\yu̇\ **cure**
\ä\ **cot, cart**	\g\ **go**	\ō\ **bone**	\ü\ **food**	\zh\ **vision**

cof•fee \ˈkȯ-fē, ˈkäf-ē\ *n* **1** : a drink made from the roasted and ground or pounded seeds of a tropical tree or shrub of the madder family; *also* : these seeds or a plant producing them **2** : a cup of coffee ⟨two *coffees*⟩ [Italian *caffè,* from Turkish *kahve,* from Arabic *qahwah*]
coffee break *n* : a short period of time for rest and refreshments
cof•fee•house \-ˌhau̇s\ *n* : a place where refreshments (as coffee) are sold
cof•fee•mak•er \-ˌmā-kər\ *n* : a utensil or appliance in which coffee is brewed
cof•fee•pot \-ˌpät\ *n* : a pot for brewing or serving coffee
coffee shop *n* : a small restaurant
coffee table *n* : a low table usually placed in front of a sofa
cof•fer \ˈkȯ-fər, ˈkäf-ər\ *n* **1** : a box or chest usually used for valuables; *esp* : STRONGBOX **2** : monetary funds : TREASURY — usually used in plural **3** : COFFERDAM **4** : a recessed panel in a vault or ceiling [Medieval French *coffre,* from Latin *cophinus* "basket," from Greek *kophinos*]
cof•fer•dam \-ˌdam\ *n* : a watertight enclosure from which water is pumped to expose the bottom of a body of water and permit construction
cof•fin \ˈkȯ-fən\ *n* : a box into which a corpse is placed for burial [Middle English, "basket, receptacle," from Middle French, from Latin *cophinus*]
coffin bone *n* : the bone enclosed within the hoof of the horse
co•func•tion \kō-ˈfəng-shən, -ˈfəngk-, ˈkō-ˌ\ *n* : a trigonometric function whose value for the complement of an angle is equal to the value of a given trigonometric function for the angle itself ⟨the sine is the *cofunction* of the cosine⟩
cog \ˈkäg\ *n* **1** : a tooth on the rim of a wheel or gear **2** : a person whose job is of low rank but still important [Middle English *cogge,* of Scandinavian origin]
co•gent \ˈkō-jənt\ *adj* **1** : having power to compel or constrain ⟨a *cogent* motive⟩ **2** : appealing forcibly to the mind or reason : CONVINCING ⟨*cogent* evidence⟩ [Latin *cogere* "to drive together, compel," from *co-* + *agere* "to drive"] ***synonyms*** see VALID — **co•gen•cy** \-jən-sē\ *n* — **co•gent•ly** *adv*
cog•i•tate \ˈkäj-ə-ˌtāt\ *vb* : to think over carefully or deeply : PONDER [Latin *cogitare* "to think, think about," from *co-* + *agitare* "to drive, agitate"] — **cog•i•ta•tion** \ˌkäj-ə-ˈtā-shən\ *n* — **cog•i•ta•tive** \ˈkäj-ə-ˌtāt-iv\ *adj*
co•gnac \ˈkōn-ˌyak\ *n, often cap* : a French brandy [*Cognac,* district in France]
cog•nate \ˈkäg-ˌnāt\ *adj* **1** : the same or similar nature ⟨illustrated books and *cognate* reference materials⟩ **2** : related by descent from the same ancestral language ⟨Spanish and French are *cognate* languages⟩ ⟨Spanish *madre* meaning "mother" and French *mère* meaning "mother" are *cognate* words⟩ **3 a** : related by processes of derivation within a single language ⟨English *boyish* and *boyhood* are *cognate* words⟩ **b** : related by adoption from one source language into two or more other languages ⟨English *tobacco* and French *tabac* are *cognate* words⟩ **4** : being a substantive that is related usually in derivation to the verb of which it is the object ⟨*song* in "sang the song" is a *cognate* object⟩ [Latin *cognatus* "related by birth," from *co-* + *gnatus, natus,* past participle of *nasci* "to be born"] — **cognate** *n* — **cog•nate•ly** *adv*
cog•ni•tion \käg-ˈnish-ən\ *n* **1** : cognitive mental processes; *also* : something known or produced by these processes **2** : a cognitive activity [Latin *cognitio,* from *cognoscere* "to know, become acquainted with," from *co-* + *gnoscere* "to come to know"] — **cog•ni•tion•al** \-ˈnish-nəl, -ˈnish-ən-l\ *adj*
cog•ni•tive \ˈkäg-nət-iv\ *adj* : of, relating to, or being conscious intellectual activities (as thinking, reasoning, imagining, remembering, or using language) — **cog•ni•tive•ly** *adv*
cog•ni•zance \ˈkäg-nə-zens\ *n* **1 a** : conscious recognition ⟨had no *cognizance* of the crime⟩ **b** : range of understanding or awareness ⟨an idea beyond a child's *cognizance*⟩ **c** : a noting of something : HEED ⟨take *cognizance* of what is happening⟩ **2 a** : the right and power to hear and decide controversies : JURISDICTION **b** : the judicial hearing of a matter [Medieval French *conissance,* from *conoistre* "to know," from Latin *cognoscere*]
cog•ni•zant \-zənt\ *adj* : having cognizance
cog•no•men \käg-ˈnō-mən, ˈkäg-nə-\ *n, pl* **-nomens** *or* **-no•mi•na** \-ˈnäm-ə-nə, -ˈnō-mə-\ **1** : SURNAME; *esp* : the third of the usual three names of an ancient Roman **2** : NAME 1; *esp* : NICKNAME [Latin, from *co-* + *nomen* "name"]
co•gno•scen•te \ˌkän-yə-ˈshent-ē, -ə-; ˌkäg-nə-\ *n, pl* **-scen•ti** \-ˈshent-ē\ : CONNOISSEUR [obsolete Italian, from Latin *cognoscere* "to know"]
cog•wheel \ˈkäg-ˌhwēl, -ˌwēl\ *n* : a wheel with cogs on the rim

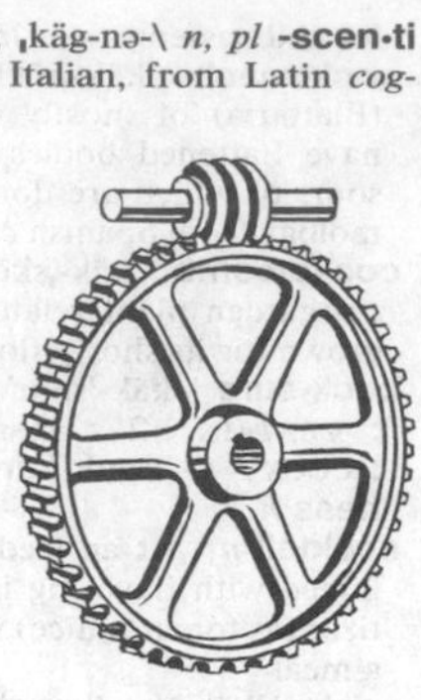
cogwheel

co•hab•it \kō-ˈhab-ət\ *vi* : to live together as or as if husband and wife [Late Latin *cohabitare,* from Latin *co-* + *habitare* "to inhabit"] — **co•hab•i•ta•tion** \ˌkō-ˌhab-ə-ˈtā-shən\ *n*
co•here \kō-ˈhiər\ *vi* **1** : to hold together firmly as parts of the same mass **2** : to consist of parts that cohere **3 a** : to become united in principles, relationships, or interests **b** : to be consistent [Latin *cohaerēre,* from *co-* + *haerēre* "to stick"] ***synonyms*** see STICK — **co•her•ence** \-ˈhir-ənts, -ˈher-\ *or* **co•her•en•cy** \-ən-sē\ *n*
co•her•ent \kō-ˈhir-ənt, -ˈher-\ *adj* **1** : having the quality of cohering **2** : logically consistent — **co•her•ent•ly** *adv*
co•he•sion \kō-ˈhē-zhən\ *n* **1** : the action of sticking together tightly **2** : union between similar plant parts or organs **3** : molecular attraction by which the particles of a body are united throughout the mass [Latin *cohaerēre* "to cohere"]
co•he•sive \kō-ˈhē-siv, -ziv\ *adj* : exhibiting or producing cohesion — **co•he•sive•ly** *adv* — **co•he•sive•ness** *n*
co•ho \ˈkō-ˌhō\ *n, pl* **cohos** *or* **coho** : a small Pacific salmon with light-colored flesh [of American Indian origin]
co•hort \ˈkō-ˌhȯrt\ *n* **1 a** : one of 10 divisions of an ancient Roman legion **b** : a group of warriors or followers **2** : [1]COMPANION 1 [Latin *cohors* "enclosure, throng, cohort"]
co•hous•ing \kō-ˈhau̇-zing\ *n* : housing consisting of a group of private homes and a shared community space (as for cooking)
[1]**coif** \ˈkȯif, *in sense 2 usually* ˈkwäf\ *n* **1** : a close-fitting cap **2** : COIFFURE [Medieval French *coife,* from Late Latin *cofea*]
[2]**coif** \ˈkȯif, ˈkwäf\ *vt* **coiffed** *or* **coifed; coiff•ing** *or* **coif•ing** : to cover or dress with a coif
coif•fure \kwä-ˈfyu̇r\ *n* : a manner of arranging the hair [French, from *coiffer* "to cover with a coif, arrange (hair)," from *coife* "coif"]
coign of van•tage \ˌkȯin-ə-ˈvant-ij\ : an advantageous position [Middle English *coyn, coigne* "projecting corner, coin"]
[1]**coil** \ˈkȯil\ *n* **1** : TUMULT 1 **2** : TROUBLE 1 [origin unknown]
[2]**coil** *vb* **1** : to wind into rings or spirals **2** : to move in a circular, spiral, or winding course **3** : to form or lie in a coil [Middle French *coillir* "to gather," from Latin *colligere* "to collect"]
[3]**coil** *n* **1 a** : a series of loops : SPIRAL **b** : a single loop of a coil **2** : a number of turns of wire especially in spiral form usually for electromagnetic effect or for providing electrical resistance **3** : a series of connected pipes in rows, layers, or windings
[1]**coin** \ˈkȯin\ *n* **1** : a piece of metal issued by governmental authority as money **2** : metal money [Middle English *coyn, coigne* "wedge, corner, coin," from Middle French *coing, coin* "wedge, corner," from Latin *cuneus* "wedge"]
[2]**coin** *vt* **1 a** : to make (a coin) especially by stamping : MINT **b** : to convert (metal) into coins **2** : INVENT ⟨*coin* a phrase⟩ — **coin•er** *n*
[3]**coin** *adj* **1** : of or relating to coins ⟨a *coin* show⟩ **2** : operated by coins ⟨a *coin* washer⟩
coin•age \ˈkȯi-nij\ *n* **1** : the act or process of coining **2 a** : COINS **b** : something (as a word) made up or invented
co•in•cide \ˌkō-ən-ˈsīd\ *vi* **1** : to occupy the same place in space or time **2** : to be the same shape and cover the same area **3** : to correspond or agree exactly ⟨an opinion that *coincides* with my own⟩ [Medieval Latin *coincidere,* from Latin *co-* + *incidere* "to fall on," from *in-* + *cadere* "to fall"]
co•in•ci•dence \kō-ˈin-səd-əns\ *n* **1** : the act or condition of coinciding **2** : two things that happen at the same time by accident but seem to have some connection; *also* : either one of these things
co•in•ci•dent \-səd-ənt\ *adj* **1** : occupying the same space or time ⟨*coincident* events⟩ **2** : of similar nature : HARMONIOUS ***synonyms*** see CONTEMPORARY — **co•in•ci•dent•ly** *adv*
co•in•ci•den•tal \kō-ˌin-sə-ˈdent-l\ *adj* **1** : resulting from a coincidence ⟨a *coincidental* resemblance⟩ **2** : occurring or existing at the same time — **co•in•ci•den•tal•ly** \-ˈdent-l-ē, -ˈdent-lē\ *adv*

coir \ˈkȯir\ *n* : a stiff coarse fiber from the outer husk of the coconut [Tamil *kayiṟu* "rope"]
co·i·tus \ˈkō-ət-əs, kō-ˈēt-\ *n* : SEXUAL INTERCOURSE [Latin, from *coire* "to come together," from *co-* + *ire* "to go"]
[1]**coke** \ˈkōk\ *n* : gray porous lumps of fuel made by heating soft coal in a closed chamber until some of its gases have passed off [perhaps from dialect *coke, colk* "core," from Middle English]
[2]**coke** *vt* : to change into coke
[3]**coke** *n* : COCAINE
Coke *trademark* — used for a cola drink
coke·head \ˈkōk-ˌhed\ *n* : a compulsive user of cocaine
col- — see COM-
co·la \ˈkō-lə\ *n* : a sweet usually caffeinated carbonated soft drink typically colored with caramel and having a flavoring from kola nuts [from *Coca-Cola,* a trademark]
col·an·der \ˈkəl-ən-dər, ˈkäl-\ *n* : a perforated utensil for draining food [Middle English *colyndore,* derived from Latin *colare* "to strain," from *colum* "sieve"]
col·chi·cine \ˈkäl-chə-ˌsēn, ˈkäl-kə-\ *n* : a poisonous substance from the corms or seeds of the autumn crocus used to induce polyploidy in cells and to treat gout
col·chi·cum \ˈkäl-chi-kəm, ˈkäl-ki-\ *n* : AUTUMN CROCUS; *also* : its dried corm or dried ripe seeds containing colchicine [Latin, a kind of plant with a poisonous root, from Greek *kolchikon,* literally, "product of Colchis"]
[1]**cold** \ˈkōld\ *adj* **1** : having a low temperature or one decidedly below normal ⟨a *cold* day⟩ ⟨a *cold* drink⟩ **2** : lacking warmth of feeling : UNFRIENDLY ⟨a *cold* welcome⟩ **3** : suffering or uncomfortable from lack of warmth ⟨feel *cold*⟩ [Old English *ceald, cald*] — **cold·ly** *adv* — **cold·ness** \ˈkōld-nəs, ˈkōl-\ *n* — **in cold blood** : with premeditation : DELIBERATELY
[2]**cold** *n* **1 a** : a condition of low temperature **b** : cold weather **2** : bodily sensation produced by loss or lack of heat : CHILL **3** : a bodily disorder popularly associated with chilling; *esp* : COMMON COLD
cold–blood·ed \ˈkōld-ˈbləd-əd, ˈkōl-\ *adj* **1** : lacking or showing a lack of natural human feelings : not moved by sympathy ⟨a *cold-blooded* criminal⟩ **2** : having cold blood; *esp* : having a body temperature not internally regulated but approximating that of the environment **3** *or* **cold-blood** \-ˈbləd\ : of mixed or inferior breeding **4** : sensitive to cold — **cold–blood·ed·ly** *adv* — **cold–blood·ed·ness** *n*
cold chisel *n* : a strong steel chisel for chipping and cutting cold metal
cold cream *n* : a creamy preparation for cleansing, softening, and soothing the skin
cold cuts *n pl* : sliced assorted cold meats
cold frame *n* : a usually glass- or plastic-covered frame without artificial heat used to protect plants and seedlings
cold front *n* : an advancing edge of a cold air mass
cold shoulder *n* : intentionally cold or unsympathetic treatment — **cold–shoulder** *vt*
cold sore *n* : a group of fluid-filled blisters about or within the mouth that are caused by a common herpes virus and form crusts upon rupturing — called also *fever blister*
cold sweat *n* : perspiration and chill occurring together and usually associated with fear, pain, or shock
cold war *n* : a conflict between nations carried on by methods (as propaganda or economic pressure) short of actual military action and usually without breaking off diplomatic relations
cold wave *n* : a period of unusually cold weather
cole \ˈkōl\ *n* : any of several closely related crop plants (as broccoli, kale, brussels sprouts, and cabbage) related to the mustards [Old English *cāl,* from Latin *caulis* "stem, cabbage"]
cole·man·ite \ˈkōl-mə-ˌnīt\ *n* : a colorless or white crystalline mineral consisting of a hydrous borate of calcium [William T. *Coleman,* died 1893, American mine owner]
co·le·op·tera \ˌkō-lē-ˈäp-tə-rə\ *n pl* : insects that are beetles [Greek *koleon* "sheath" + *pteron* "wing"] — **co·le·op·ter·ist** \-tə-rəst\ *n* — **co·le·op·ter·ous** \-tə-rəs\ *adj*
co·le·op·ter·an \-tə-rən\ *n* : [1]BEETLE 1 — **coleopteran** *adj*
co·le·op·tile \-ˈäp-tl\ *n* : the first leaf of a monocot seedling forming a protective sheath about the plumule [Greek *koleon* "sheath" + *ptilon* "down, feather"]
cole·slaw \ˈkōl-ˌslȯ\ *n* : a salad made of sliced or shredded raw cabbage [Dutch *koolsla,* from *kool* "cabbage" + *sla* "salad"]
co·le·us \ˈkō-lē-əs\ *n* : any of a large genus of herbs of the mint family often grown for their colorful leaves [Greek *koleos, koleon* "sheath"]

col·ic \ˈkäl-ik\ *n* **1** : sharp sudden pain in the abdomen **2** : a condition marked by episodes of prolonged and uncontrollable crying and irritability in an otherwise healthy infant [Medieval Latin *colica passio* "intestinal suffering," from Late Latin *colicus* "colicky," from Greek *kōlikos,* from *kolon* "colon"] — **colicky** \ˈkäl-i-kē\ *adj*
co·li·form \ˈkō-lə-ˌfȯrm\ *adj* : of, relating to, or being bacteria (as E. coli) normally present in the intestine [New Latin *Escherichia coli* "colon bacillus" + English *-form*] — **coliform** *n*
col·i·se·um \ˌkäl-ə-ˈsē-əm\ *n* : a large building, amphitheater, or stadium for sports contests or public entertainments [Medieval Latin *Colosseum, Coliseum* "the Colosseum"]
co·li·tis \kō-ˈlīt-əs, kə-\ *n* : inflammation of the colon
col·lab·o·rate \kə-ˈlab-ə-ˌrāt\ *vi* **1** : to work jointly with others (as in writing a book) **2** : to cooperate with or assist an enemy force occupying one's country — **col·lab·o·ra·tion** \-ˌlab-ə-ˈrā-shən\ *n* — **col·lab·o·ra·tion·ist** \-shə-nəst, -shnəst\ *n* — **col·lab·o·ra·tor** \-ˈlab-ə-ˌrāt-ər\ *n*
col·lage \kə-ˈläzh, kȯ-, kō-\ *n* **1** : an artistic composition of fragments of materials (as printed matter) pasted on a surface **2** : the art of making collages [French, "gluing," from *coller* "to glue," from *colle* "glue," from Greek *kolla*]
col·la·gen \ˈkäl-ə-jən\ *n* : an insoluble fibrous protein that is the chief constituent of connective tissue fibrils and yields gelatin and glue upon boiling with water [Greek *kolla* "glue"] — **collag·e·nous** \kə-ˈlaj-ə-nəs\ *adj*
[1]**col·lapse** \kə-ˈlaps\ *vb* **1** : to break down completely : DISINTEGRATE **2** : to shrink together abruptly and completely ⟨a *collapsed* balloon⟩ **3** : to fall in : give way ⟨the tunnel *collapsed*⟩ **4** : to suddenly lose value or effectiveness ⟨the country's currency *collapsed*⟩ **5** : to break down physically or mentally through exhaustion or disease; *esp* : to fall helpless or unconscious **6** : to fold down into a more compact shape ⟨a chair that *collapses*⟩ [Latin *collabi,* from *com-* + *labi* "to fall, slide"] — **col·laps·ible** \-ˈlap-sə-bəl\ *adj*
[2]**collapse** *n* : the act or an instance of collapsing : BREAKDOWN
[1]**col·lar** \ˈkäl-ər\ *n* **1 a** : a band, strip, or chain worn around the neck or the neckline of a garment **b** : a part of the harness of a draft animal fitted over the shoulders and taking strain when a load is drawn **2** : something resembling a collar (as a ring or round flange to restrain motion or hold something in place) [Medieval French *coler,* from Latin *collare,* from *collum* "neck"] — **col·lared** \-ərd\ *adj* — **col·lar·less** \-ər-ləs\ *adj*
[2]**collar** *vt* **1 a** : to seize by the collar **b** : to take prisoner : NAB **c** : to get control of **2** : to put a collar on
col·lar·bone \ˈkäl-ər-ˌbōn, ˌkäl-ər-ˈ\ *n* : CLAVICLE
collar cell *n* : a flagellated cell that lines the cavity of a sponge
col·lard \ˈkäl-ərd\ *n* : a stalked smooth-leaved kale — usually used in plural [alteration of *colewort* "cole, kale"]
collared lizard *n* : a brightly colored iguana of the south-central U.S. and Mexico
col·late \kə-ˈlāt, kä-, kō-; ˈkäl-ˌāt, ˈkōl-\ *vt* **1** : to collect and compare carefully in order to verify and often to unify or arrange in order **2** : to arrange (as printed sheets) in order for binding [back-formation from *collation*] — **col·la·tor** \-ˈlāt-ər, -ˌāt-\ *n*

collared lizard

[1]**col·lat·er·al** \kə-ˈlat-ə-rəl, -ˈla-trəl\ *adj* **1** : associated but of secondary or supporting importance ⟨a main question and *collateral* questions⟩ **2** : descended from the same ancestors but not in the same line ⟨cousins are *collateral* relatives⟩ **3 a** : of, relating to, or being collateral used as security **b** : secured by collateral [Medieval French, from Medieval Latin *collateralis,* from Latin *com-* + *lateralis* "lateral"] — **collat·er·al·ly** \-ē\ *adv*
[2]**collateral** *n* **1** : property (as stocks, bonds, or a mortgage) handed over or pledged as security for the repayment of a loan **2** : a branch of a bodily part (as a vein)

\ə\ **abut**	\au̇\ **out**	\i\ **tip**	\ȯ\ **saw**	\u̇\ **foot**
\ər\ **further**	\ch\ **chin**	\ī\ **life**	\ȯi\ **coin**	\y\ **yet**
\a\ **mat**	\e\ **pet**	\j\ **job**	\th\ **thin**	\yü\ **few**
\ā\ **take**	\ē\ **easy**	\ng\ **sing**	\th\ **this**	\yu̇\ **cure**
\ä\ **cot, cart**	\g\ **go**	\ō\ **bone**	\ü\ **food**	\zh\ **vision**

collateral damage *n* : injury inflicted on something other than an intended target; *esp* : civilian casualties of a military operation

col·la·tion \kə-ˈlā-shən, kä-, kō-\ *n* **1** : a light meal **2** : the act, process, or result of collating [Medieval French, from Medieval Latin *collatio,* from Late Latin, "conference," from Latin, "bringing together, comparison," from *collatus,* past participle of *conferre* "to bring together," from *com-* + *ferre* "to carry"]

col·league \ˈkäl-ˌēg\ *n* : an associate in a profession or office; *also* : a fellow worker [Middle French *collegue,* from Latin *collega,* from *com-* + *legare* "to appoint, delegate"]

[1]**col·lect** \ˈkäl-ikt, -ˌekt\ *n* : a short prayer consisting of an invocation, petition, and conclusion [Medieval French *collecte,* from Medieval Latin *collecta,* short for *oratio ad collectam* "prayer upon assembly"]

[2]**col·lect** \kə-ˈlekt\ *vb* **1 a** : to bring together into one body or place **b** : to gather from a number of sources ⟨*collect* stamps⟩ **2** : to gain or regain control of ⟨*collect* one's thoughts⟩ **3** : to claim as due and receive payment for ⟨*collect* a bill⟩ **4 a** : ASSEMBLE ⟨a crowd *collected* at the scene of the accident⟩ **b** : ACCUMULATE ⟨dust *collects* on the furniture⟩ [Latin *collectus,* past participle of *colligere* "to collect," from *com-* + *legere* "to gather"] ***synonyms*** see GATHER — **col·lect·able** *or* **col·lect·ible** \-ˈlek-tə-bəl\ *adj*

[3]**col·lect** \kə-ˈlekt\ *adv or adj* : to be paid for by the receiver ⟨we telephoned *collect*⟩ ⟨a *collect* call⟩

col·lect·ed \kə-ˈlek-təd\ *adj* : SELF-POSSESSED, CALM — **col·lect·ed·ly** *adv* — **col·lect·ed·ness** *n*

collecting tubule *n* : the part of a nephron by which urine is collected

col·lec·tion \kə-ˈlek-shən\ *n* **1** : the act or process of collecting **2** : something collected; *esp* : an accumulation of objects gathered for study, comparison, or exhibition or as a hobby **3** : a gathering of money (as for charitable purposes)

[1]**col·lec·tive** \kə-ˈlek-tiv\ *adj* **1** : denoting a number of persons or things considered as one group ⟨"flock" is a *collective* noun⟩ **2** : formed by collecting : AGGREGATED **3** : of, relating to, or involving a group of individuals ⟨*collective* needs⟩ ⟨*collective* legal action⟩ **4** : collectivized or characterized by collectivism **5** : shared or assumed by all members of the group ⟨*collective* leadership⟩ — **col·lec·tive·ly** *adv*

[2]**collective** *n* **1** : a collective body : GROUP **2** : a cooperative unit or organization; *esp* : COLLECTIVE FARM

collective bargaining *n* : negotiation between an employer and union representatives usually on wages, hours, and working conditions

collective farm *n* : a farm in a communist country formed from many small holdings collected into a single unit for joint operation under governmental supervision

collective fruit *n* : MULTIPLE FRUIT

collective mark *n* : a trademark or a service mark of a group (as a cooperative or other association)

col·lec·tiv·ism \kə-ˈlek-ti-ˌviz-əm\ *n* : a political or economic theory advocating collective control especially over production and distribution; *also* : a system marked by such control — **col·lec·tiv·ist** \-vəst\ *adj or n* — **col·lec·tiv·is·tic** \-ˌlek-ti-ˈvis-tik\ *adj*

col·lec·tiv·i·ty \kə-ˌlek-ˈtiv-ət-ē, ˌkäl-ˌek-\ *n, pl* **-ties** : a collective whole

col·lec·tiv·ize \kə-ˈlek-ti-ˌvīz\ *vt* : to organize under collective control — **col·lec·tiv·i·za·tion** \-ˌlek-ti-və-ˈzā-shən\ *n*

col·lec·tor \kə-ˈlek-tər\ *n* : one that collects: as **a** : an official or agent who collects funds or money due ⟨bill *collector*⟩ **b** : one that makes a collection ⟨a stamp *collector*⟩ **c** : an object, device, or substance that collects ⟨the knickknack was a dust *collector*⟩ — **col·lec·tor·ship** \-ˌship\ *n*

col·leen \kä-ˈlēn, ˈkäl-ˌēn\ *n* : an Irish girl [Irish Gaelic *cailín*]

col·lege \ˈkäl-ij\ *n* **1** : a building used for an educational or religious purpose **2 a** : a subordinate school in a university **b** : a school higher than a high school **c** : an independent institution offering a course of general studies leading to a bachelor's degree; *also* : a university division offering this **d** : an institution offering instruction usually in a professional, vocational, or technical field ⟨business *college*⟩ ⟨barber *college*⟩ **3** : an organized body of persons having common interests or duties ⟨the *college* of cardinals⟩ [Medieval French, "body of clergy," from Latin *collegium* "society," from *collega* "colleague"]

col·le·gian \kə-ˈlē-jən, -jē-ən\ *n* : a student or recent graduate of a college

col·le·giate \kə-ˈlē-jət, -jē-ət\ *adj* **1** : of, relating to, or comprising a college **2** : of, relating to, or characteristic of college students ⟨*collegiate* clothes⟩

col·le·gi·um \kə-ˈleg-ē-əm, -ˈlāg-\ *n, pl* **-gia** \-ē-ə\ *or* **-gi·ums** : a governing group in which each member has approximately equal power and authority [Russian *kollegiya,* from Latin *collegium* "society"] — **col·le·gial** \-ˈlē-jē-əl, -jəl; -gē-əl\ *adj*

col·lem·bo·lan \kə-ˈlem-bə-lən\ *n* : SPRINGTAIL [Greek *kolla* "glue" + *embolos* "wedge, stopper"] — **collembolan** *adj*

col·len·chy·ma \kə-ˈleng-kə-mə\ *n* : a plant tissue of living usually elongated cells with thickened walls — compare SCLERENCHYMA [Greek *kolla* "glue" + *-enchyma* (as in *parenchyma*)] — **col·len·chy·ma·tous** \ˌkäl-ən-ˈkim-ət-əs, -ˈkī-mət-\ *adj*

col·lide \kə-ˈlīd\ *vi* **1** : to come together with solid impact ⟨the car *collided* with a tree⟩ **2** : to come into conflict : CLASH ⟨*colliding* cultures⟩ [Latin *collidere,* from *com-* + *laedere* "to injure by striking"]

col·lie \ˈkäl-ē\ *n* : any of a breed of large dogs developed in Scotland especially for herding sheep [probably from English dialect *colly* "black"]

col·lier \ˈkäl-yər\ *n* **1** : a coal miner **2** : a ship for carrying coal [Middle English *colier,* from *col* "coal"]

col·liery \ˈkäl-yə-rē\ *n, pl* **-lier·ies** : a coal mine and the buildings connected with it

col·li·mate \ˈkäl-ə-ˌmāt\ *vt* : to make (as rays of light) parallel [Latin *collimare,* from *collineare* "to make straight," from *com-* + *linea* "line"] — **col·li·ma·tor** \-ˌmāt-ər\ *n*

col·lin·e·ar \kə-ˈlin-ē-ər, kä-\ *adj* : lying on the same straight line — **col·lin·ear·i·ty** \-ˌlin-ē-ˈar-ət-ē\ *n*

col·li·sion \kə-ˈlizh-ən\ *n* : an act or instance of colliding : CRASH [Latin *collisio,* from *collidere* "to collide"]

col·lo·ca·tion \ˌkäl-ə-ˈkā-shən\ *n* : the act or result of placing together

col·lo·di·on \kə-ˈlōd-ē-ən\ *n* : a viscous solution of pyroxylin used especially as a coating for wounds and in cements [Greek *kollōdēs* "glutinous," from *kolla* "glue"]

col·loid \ˈkäl-ˌȯid\ *n* : a very finely divided substance that is scattered throughout another substance; *also* : a mixture (as smoke, gelatine, or marshmallow) consisting of such a substance together with the substance in which it is scattered [Greek *kolla* "glue"] — **col·loi·dal** \kə-ˈlȯid-l, kä-\ *adj* — **col·loi·dal·ly** \-l-ē\ *adv*

col·lo·qui·al \kə-ˈlō-kwē-əl\ *adj* **1** : used in or characteristic of familiar and informal conversation ⟨a *colloquial* word⟩ **2** : using conversational style ⟨a *colloquial* writer⟩ — **col·lo·qui·al·ly** \-kwē-ə-lē\ *adv*

col·lo·qui·al·ism \-kwē-ə-ˌliz-əm\ *n* **1** : a colloquial expression **2** : colloquial style

col·lo·qui·um \kə-ˈlō-kwē-əm\ *n, pl* **-qui·ums** *or* **-quia** \-kwē-ə\ : CONFERENCE; *esp* : a seminar that several lecturers take turns in leading [Latin, "colloquy"]

col·lo·quy \ˈkäl-ə-kwē\ *n, pl* **-quies** : CONVERSATION; *esp* : a formal conversation or conference [Latin *colloquium,* from *colloqui* "to converse," from *com-* + *loqui* "to speak"]

col·lu·sion \kə-ˈlü-zhən\ *n* : secret agreement or cooperation for a deceitful purpose [Medieval French, from Latin *collusio,* from *colludere* "to conspire," from *com-* + *ludere* "to play," from *ludus* "game"] — **col·lu·sive** \-ˈlü-siv, -ziv\ *adj* — **col·lu·sive·ly** *adv*

co·log·a·rithm \ˈkō-ˈlög-ə-ˌrith-əm, -ˈläg-\ *n* : the logarithm of the reciprocal of a number ⟨the *cologarithm* of x equals the logarithm of $^1/_x$⟩

co·logne \kə-ˈlōn\ *n* : a perfumed liquid composed of alcohol and aromatic oils [*Cologne,* Germany]

[1]**co·lon** \ˈkō-lən\ *n* : the part of the large intestine that extends from the cecum to the rectum [Latin, from Greek *kolon*] — **co·lon·ic** \kō-ˈlän-ik\ *adj*

[2]**colon** *n* : a punctuation mark : used chiefly to direct attention to what follows (as a list, explanation, quotation, or amplification) [Latin, "part of a poem," from Greek *kōlon* "limb, clause"]

[3]**co·lon** \kə-ˈlōn\ *n, pl* **co·lo·nes** \-ˈlō-ˌnās\ **1** : the basic monetary unit of Costa Rica **2** : a coin representing one colon [Spanish *colón,* from *Cristóbal Colón* "Christopher Columbus"]

colon bacillus *n* : E. COLI

col·o·nel \ˈkərn-l\ *n* : an officer rank in the Army, Marine Corps, and Air Force above lieutenant colonel and below brigadier general [from earlier *coronel,* from Middle French, from Italian *colonnello* "column of soldiers, colonel," from *colonna* "column," from Latin *columna*] — **col·o·nel·cy** \-l-sē\ *n*

Word History English *colonel* is pronounced the same as *kernel.* A review of the history of *colonel* shows how this difference between spelling and pronunciation came about. In many languages when a word contains two identical or similar sounds, one of these sounds will often change over a period of time. This kind of change is called *dissimilation.* When the Italian word *colonello* was taken into French, it became *coronel;* and the word was borrowed by the English from the French in this form. Later the spelling *colonel* came to be used in order to reflect the Italian origin of the word. But by then the pronunciation with *r* was well established.

[1]**co·lo·nial** \kə-ˈlō-nē-əl, -nyəl\ *adj* **1** : of, relating to, or characteristic of a colony **2** *often cap* : of or relating to the original 13 colonies forming the U.S. **3** : possessing, forming, or composed of colonies ⟨a *colonial* empire⟩ — **co·lo·nial·ize** \-ˌīz\ *vt* — **co·lo·nial·ly** \-ē\ *adv* — **co·lo·nial·ness** *n*

[2]**colonial** *n* : COLONIST 1

co·lo·nial·ism \-nē-ə-ˌliz-əm, -nyə-ˌliz-\ *n* : control by one power over a dependent area or people; *also* : a policy advocating or based on such control — **co·lo·nial·ist** \-ləst\ *n or adj*

col·o·nist \ˈkäl-ə-nəst\ *n* **1** : an inhabitant or member of a colony **2** : a person who takes part in founding a colony

col·o·nize \ˈkäl-ə-ˌnīz\ *vb* **1** : to establish a colony in or on ⟨England *colonized* Australia⟩ **2** : to establish in a colony ⟨the rights of *colonized* people⟩ **3** : to make or establish a colony : SETTLE — **col·o·ni·za·tion** \ˌkäl-ə-nə-ˈzā-shən\ *n* — **col·o·niz·er** *n*

col·on·nade \ˌkäl-ə-ˈnād\ *n* : a row of columns set at regular intervals and usually supporting the base of the roof structure [French, from Italian *colonnato,* from *colonna* "column," from Latin *columna*] — **col·on·nad·ed** \-ˈnād-əd\ *adj*

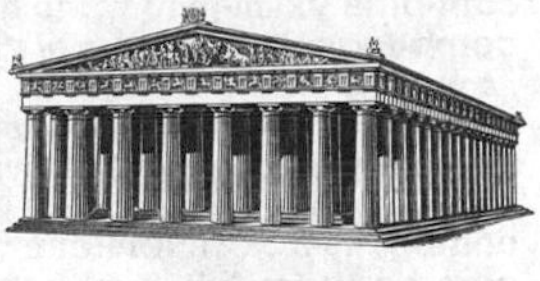
colonnade

co·lo·nos·co·py \ˌkō-lə-ˈnäs-kə-pē\ *n* : examination of the colon using an endoscope

col·o·ny \ˈkäl-ə-nē\ *n, pl* **-nies** **1 a** : a body of people sent out by a state to a new territory **b** : the territory inhabited by people sent to new territory **c** : a distant territory belonging to or under the control of a nation **2 a** : a distinguishable localized population within a species ⟨a *colony* of termites⟩ **b** : a circumscribed mass of microorganisms usually growing in or on a solid medium **c** : the aggregation of zooids of a compound animal **3** : a group of individuals with common characteristics or interests situated in close association; *also* : the section occupied by such a group ⟨an artist *colony*⟩ [Latin *colonia,* from *colonus* "farmer, colonist," from *colere* "to cultivate"]

col·o·phon \ˈkäl-ə-fən, -ˌfän\ *n* **1** : an inscription placed at the end of a book with facts relative to its production **2** : an identifying device, mark, or emblem used by a printer or a publisher [Latin, from Greek *kolophōn* "summit, finishing touch"]

[1]**col·or** \ˈkəl-ər\ *n* **1 a** : a phenomenon of light (as red, brown, pink, gray) or visual perception that enables one to differentiate otherwise identical objects **b** : the aspect of objects and light sources that may be described in terms of hue, lightness, and saturation for objects and hue, brightness, and saturation for light sources ⟨the sky's changing *color*⟩ **c** : a specific combination of hue, lightness or brightness, and saturation ⟨the car comes in six *colors*⟩ **d** : a color other than and contrasted with black, white, or gray **2 a** : an outward often deceptive show : APPEARANCE ⟨the story has the *color* of truth⟩ **b** : a legal claim to or appearance of a right, authority, or office ⟨acting under *color* of law⟩ **c** : an appearance of authenticity : PLAUSIBILITY ⟨this fact gives *color* to his argument⟩ **3 a** : COMPLEXION 2; *esp* : a healthy complexion **b** : BLUSH 2 **4** : vividness or variety of effects of language **5** : the use or combination of colors **6** *pl* **a** : an identifying flag, ensign, or pennant **b** : service in the armed forces ⟨a call to the *colors*⟩ **c** : CHARACTER, NATURE — usually used in plural ⟨showed himself in his true *colors*⟩ **7** : VITALITY 2b, INTEREST ⟨the play had a good deal of *color* to it⟩ **8** : something used to give color : PIGMENT **9** : skin pigmentation other than white characteristic of race ⟨a person of *color*⟩ [Medieval French *colour,* from Latin *color*]

synonyms COLOR, HUE, TINT, SHADE refer to a property of a visible thing recognizable only when rays of light fall upon it. COLOR is the general term for any distinguishable quality of light but specifically implies the property of things seen as red, yellow, blue, and so on as distinguished from white, black, or gray ⟨the green *color* of the foliage⟩. HUE usually implies some modification of or a finer discrimination of a primary color ⟨a reddish orange *hue*⟩. TINT applies especially to a color modified toward white ⟨paint with a bluish *tint*⟩. SHADE applies to a color modified toward black ⟨a dark *shade* of red⟩. All four terms are frequently interchangeable.

[2]**color** *vb* **1 a** : to give color to ⟨the wind *colored* our cheeks⟩ **b** : to change the color of : PAINT **2** : MISREPRESENT, DISTORT ⟨a story *colored* by prejudice⟩ **3** : to take on or change color; *esp* : BLUSH — **col·or·er** \ˈkəl-ər-ər\ *n*

Col·o·ra·do blue spruce \ˌkäl-ə-ˈrad-ō-, -ˈräd-\ *n* : BLUE SPRUCE

Colorado potato beetle *n* : a black-and-yellow striped beetle that feeds on the leaves of the potato — called also *potato beetle, potato bug*

col·or·ation \ˌkəl-ə-ˈrā-shən\ *n* : use or arrangement of colors or shades : COLORING ⟨the *coloration* of a flower⟩

col·or·a·tu·ra \ˌkəl-ə-rə-ˈtu̇r-ə, -ˈtyu̇r-\ *n* **1** : showy style in singing (as in opera) **2** : a soprano specializing in coloratura [obsolete Italian, literally, "coloring," from Latin *colorare* "to color," from *color* "color"]

col·or–blind \ˈkəl-ər-ˌblīnd\ *adj* : affected with partial or total inability to distinguish one or more colors — **color blindness** *n*

col·ored \ˈkəl-ərd\ *adj* **1** : having color ⟨*colored* pictures⟩ **2** : marked by exaggeration or bias : SLANTED **3 a** *sometimes offensive* : of a race other than the white race; *esp* : BLACK 2b **b** *sometimes offensive* : of or relating to persons of a mixed race or a race other than the white race

col·or·fast \ˈkəl-ər-ˌfast\ *adj* : having color that does not fade or run — **col·or·fast·ness** \-ˌfas-nəs, -ˌfast-\ *n*

color filter *n* : FILTER 3b

col·or·ful \ˈkəl-ər-fəl\ *adj* **1** : having striking colors **2** : full of variety or interest ⟨a *colorful* description⟩ — **col·or·ful·ly** \-fə-lē, -flē\ *adv* — **col·or·ful·ness** \-fəl-nəs\ *n*

color guard *n* : an honor guard for the colors of an organization

col·or·im·e·ter \ˌkəl-ə-ˈrim-ət-ər\ *n* : a device for determining colors; *esp* : one used for chemical analysis by comparison of a liquid's color with standard colors — **col·or·i·met·ric** \ˌkəl-ə-rə-ˈme-trik\ *adj* — **col·or·i·met·ri·cal·ly** \-tri-kə-lē, -klē\ *adv* — **col·or·im·e·try** \ˌkəl-ə-ˈrim-ə-trē\ *n*

col·or·ing \ˈkəl-ə-riŋ\ *n* **1** : the act of applying colors **2** : something that produces color **3 a** : the effect produced by applying or combining colors **b** : natural color **c** : COMPLEXION 2, COLORATION **4** : BIAS 2 **5** : COLOR 4 **6** : TIMBRE

coloring book *n* : a book of line drawings for coloring (as with crayons)

col·or·less \ˈkəl-ər-ləs\ *adj* **1** : lacking color **2** : DULL, UNINTERESTING — **col·or·less·ly** *adv* — **col·or·less·ness** *n*

co·los·sal \kə-ˈläs-əl\ *adj* **1** : of, relating to, or resembling a colossus; *esp* : of very great size ⟨a *colossal* office building⟩ **2** : EXCEPTIONAL, ASTONISHING ⟨*colossal* growth⟩ ⟨a *colossal* failure⟩ — **co·los·sal·ly** \-ə-lē\ *adv*

col·os·se·um \ˌkäl-ə-ˈsē-əm\ *n* **1** *cap* : an amphitheater built in Rome in the first century A.D. **2** : COLISEUM [Medieval Latin, from Latin *colosseus* "colossal," from *colossus* "colossus"]

Co·los·sians \kə-ˈläsh-ənz, -ˈläs-ē-ənz\ *n* : a letter written by Saint Paul to the Christians of Colossae and included as a book in the New Testament — see BIBLE table

co·los·sus \kə-ˈläs-əs\ *n, pl* **-los·si** \-ˈläs-ˌī, -ˌē\ **1** : a statue of gigantic size and proportions **2** : a person or thing of great size or power [Latin, from Greek *kolossos*]

co·los·to·my \kə-ˈläs-tə-mē\ *n* : surgical formation of an artificial anus by connecting the colon to an opening in the abdominal wall [Latin *colon* "colon" (from Greek *kolon*) + Greek *stoma* "mouth, opening"]

co·los·trum \kə-ˈläs-trəm\ *n* : milk secreted for a few days after giving birth and characterized by a high content of proteins and antibodies [Latin, "colostrum of a cow"]

col·our \ˈkəl-ər\ *chiefly British variant of* COLOR

\ə\ **abut**	\au̇\ **out**	\i\ **tip**	\ȯ\ **saw**	\u̇\ **foot**
\ər\ **further**	\ch\ **chin**	\ī\ **life**	\ȯi\ **coin**	\y\ **yet**
\a\ **mat**	\e\ **pet**	\j\ **job**	\th\ **thin**	\yü\ **few**
\ā\ **take**	\ē\ **easy**	\ŋ\ **sing**	\t͟h\ **this**	\yu̇\ **cure**
\ä\ **cot, cart**	\g\ **go**	\ō\ **bone**	\ü\ **food**	\zh\ **vision**

colt \ˈkōlt\ *n* **1 :** FOAL; *esp* **:** a young male horse **2 :** a young untried person [Old English]

col·ter \ˈkōl-tər\ *n* **:** a cutter on a plow to cut the turf [Old English *culter* and Medieval French *coltre,* both from Latin *culter* "plowshare"]

colt·ish \ˈkōl-tish\ *adj* **1 :** FRISKY, PLAYFUL **2 :** of, relating to, or resembling a colt — **colt·ish·ly** *adv*

col·um·bine \ˈkäl-əm-ˌbīn\ *n* **:** any of a genus of plants related to the buttercups that have showy flowers with usually five spurred petals [Medieval French, from Medieval Latin *columbina,* from Latin *columba* "dove"]

co·lum·bi·um \kə-ˈləm-bē-əm\ *n* **:** NIOBIUM [New Latin, from *Columbia* "United States," from *Christopher Columbus*]

Co·lum·bus Day \kə-ˈləm-bəs-\ *n* **:** a day, formerly October 12 and now the second Monday in October, observed as a legal holiday in many states of the U.S. in commemoration of the landing of Columbus in the Bahamas in 1492

col·u·mel·la \ˌkäl-yə-ˈmel-ə, ˌkäl-ə-\ *n, pl* **-mel·lae** \-ˈmel-ˌē, -ˌī\ **:** any of various plant or animal parts resembling a column [Latin, "small column," from *columna* "column"]

col·umn \ˈkäl-əm\ *n* **1 a :** a printed or written vertical arrangement of items ⟨a *column* of figures⟩ **b :** one of two or more vertical sections of a printed page **c :** one in a usually regular series of newspaper or magazine articles ⟨a sports *column*⟩ **2 :** a supporting pillar; *esp* **:** one consisting of a usually round shaft, a capital, and a base **3 :** something resembling a column in form, position, or function ⟨a *column* of water⟩ **4 :** a long row (as of soldiers) **5 :** one of the vertical lines of elements of a determinant or matrix [Medieval French *columpne,* from Latin *columna,* from *columen* "top"] — **co·lum·nar** \kə-ˈləm-nər\ *adj* — **col·umned** \ˈkäl-əmd\ *adj*

col·um·nist \ˈkäl-əm-nəst, -əm-əst\ *n* **:** a person who writes a newspaper or magazine column

col·za \ˈkäl-zə, ˈkōl-\ *n* **:** a rape plant or its seed [French, from Dutch *koolzaad,* literally, "cabbage seed"]

com- *or* **col-** *or* **con-** *prefix* **:** with **:** together **:** jointly — usually *com-* before *b, p,* or *m* ⟨*com*mingle⟩, *col-* before *l* ⟨*col*linear⟩, and *con-* before other sounds ⟨*con*centrate⟩ [Medieval French, from Latin, "with, together, thoroughly"]

[1]**co·ma** \ˈkō-mə\ *n* **:** a state of profound unconsciousness caused by disease, injury, or poison [Greek *kōma* "deep sleep"] — **co·ma·tose** \-ˌtōs\ *adj*

[2]**coma** *n, pl* **co·mae** \-ˌmē, -ˌmī\ **:** the head of a comet consisting of a cloud of gas and dust and usually containing a nucleus [Latin, "hair," from Greek *komē*]

Co·man·che \kə-ˈman-chē\ *n, pl* **Comanche** *or* **Comanches** **1 :** a member of an American Indian people ranging from Wyoming and Nebraska south into New Mexico and northwestern Texas **2 :** the Aztec-related language of the Comanche people [American Spanish, of American Indian origin]

[1]**comb** \ˈkōm\ *n* **1 a :** a toothed implement to smooth and arrange the hair or worn in the hair to hold it in place **b :** a toothed instrument for separating fibers (as of wool or flax) **2 :** a fleshy crest on the head of the domestic chicken and some related birds **3 :** HONEYCOMB [Old English *camb*] — **combed** \ˈkōmd\ *adj*

comb 2

[2]**comb** *vb* **1 :** to smooth, arrange, or untangle with a comb ⟨*comb* one's hair⟩ ⟨*comb* wool⟩ **2 :** to go over or through carefully in search of something **:** search thoroughly ⟨*combed* the woods for the lost child⟩

[1]**com·bat** \kəm-ˈbat, ˈkäm-ˌ\ *vb* **-bat·ed** *or* **-bat·ted; bat·ing** *or* **-bat·ting** **1 :** to fight with **:** BATTLE **2 :** to struggle against; *esp* **:** to strive to reduce or eliminate ⟨*combat* disease⟩ [Middle French, from *combatre* "to attack, fight," from Latin *com-* + *battuere* "to beat"]

[2]**com·bat** \ˈkäm-ˌbat\ *n* **1 :** a fight or contest between individuals or groups **2 :** CONFLICT 2a, CONTROVERSY **3 :** active fighting in a war **:** ACTION ⟨soldiers experienced in *combat*⟩

com·bat·ant \kəm-ˈbat-nt, ˈkäm-bət-ənt\ *adj* **:** engaging in or ready to engage in combat — **combatant** *n*

combat fatigue *n* **:** traumatic reaction to intense stress under combat conditions in wartime

com·bat·ive \kəm-ˈbat-iv\ *adj* **:** eager to fight **:** PUGNACIOUS — **com·bat·ive·ly** *adv* — **com·bat·ive·ness** *n*

comb·er \ˈkō-mər\ *n* **1 :** one that combs fibers (as of wool or flax) **2 :** a long curling wave rolling in from the ocean

com·bi·na·tion \ˌkäm-bə-ˈnā-shən\ *n* **1 :** a result or product of combining; *esp* **:** an alliance of persons or groups to achieve some end **2 a :** a sequence of letters or numbers chosen in setting a lock **b :** any of the possible subsets of a set without regard to the order of their elements **3 :** a one-piece undergarment for the upper and lower parts of the body — usually used in plural **4 a :** the act or process of combining; *esp* **:** that of uniting to form a chemical compound **b :** the quality or state of being combined — **com·bi·na·tion·al** \-ˈnā-shnəl, -shən-l\ *adj*

com·bi·na·to·ri·al \ˌkäm-bə-nə-ˈtōr-ē-əl, kəm-ˈbī-nə-, -ˈtȯr-\ *adj* **:** of or relating to the arrangement, operation on, and selection of mathematical elements belonging to finite sets or making up geometric shapes ⟨*combinatorial* mathematics⟩

[1]**com·bine** \kəm-ˈbīn\ *vb* **1 a :** to bring into close relationship **:** UNIFY **b :** to unite or cause to unite into a chemical compound **2 :** to cause to mix together **:** BLEND ⟨*combine* the ingredients⟩ **3 :** to become one **4 :** to act together ⟨many factors *combined* to cause the problem⟩ [Medieval French *combiner,* from Late Latin *combinare,* from Latin *com-* + *bini* "two by two"] ***synonyms*** see JOIN — **com·bin·able** \-ˈbī-nə-bəl\ *adj* — **com·bin·er** *n*

[2]**com·bine** \ˈkäm-ˌbīn\ *n* **1 :** a combination to gain an often illicit end **2 :** a harvesting machine that harvests, threshes, and cleans grain while moving over a field

[3]**com·bine** \ˈkäm-ˌbīn\ *vt* **:** to harvest with a combine

comb·ings \ˈkō-mingz\ *n pl* **:** loose hairs or fibers removed by a comb

com·bin·ing form \kəm-ˈbī-ning-\ *n* **:** a linguistic form that occurs only in compounds or derivatives (as *electro-* in *electromagnetic* or *mal-* in *malodorous*)

comb jelly *n* **:** CTENOPHORE

com·bo \ˈkäm-ˌbō\ *n, pl* **combos** **1 :** a small jazz or dance band **2 :** COMBINATION [alteration of *combination*]

com·bust \kəm-ˈbəst\ *vb* **:** BURN [Latin *combustus,* past participle of *comburere* "to burn up," from *com-* + *urere* "to burn"]

com·bus·ti·ble \kəm-ˈbəs-tə-bəl\ *adj* **1 :** capable of being burned **2 :** catching fire or burning easily — **com·bus·ti·bil·i·ty** \-ˌbəs-tə-ˈbil-ət-ē\ *n* — **combustible** *n* — **com·bus·ti·bly** \-ˈbəs-tə-blē\ *adv*

com·bus·tion \kəm-ˈbəs-chən\ *n* **1 :** the process of burning **2 a :** a chemical process (as an oxidation) accompanied by the evolution of heat and light **b :** a slower oxidation — **com·bus·tive** \-ˈbəs-tiv\ *adj*

com·bus·tor \-ˈbəs-tər\ *n* **:** a chamber (as in a jet engine) in which combustion occurs

come \kəm, ˈkəm\ *vi* **came** \ˈkām\; **come; com·ing** \ˈkəm-ing\ **1 :** to move toward or journey to something **:** APPROACH ⟨*come* here⟩ ⟨*come* see us⟩ **2 :** to arrive at or enter a scene of action ⟨the police *came* to our rescue⟩ **3 a :** to reach the point of being or becoming ⟨the rope *came* untied⟩ **b :** AMOUNT ⟨the bill *came* to 10 dollars⟩ **4 a :** to take place ⟨the holiday *came* on Thursday⟩ **b :** to proceed as a consequence, effect, or conclusion ⟨our plans *came* to naught⟩ **5 a :** ORIGINATE, ARISE ⟨*comes* from a fine family⟩ ⟨honey *comes* from bees⟩ **b :** to issue forth ⟨a sob *came* from her throat⟩ **6 :** to be available ⟨a dress that *comes* in three colors⟩ **7 a :** to reach a particular point in a series ⟨we now *come* to the next chapter⟩ **b :** to arrive in due course ⟨the time has *come*⟩ **8 :** EXTEND, REACH ⟨a coat that *comes* to the knees⟩ **9 a :** to arrive at a particular place, end, result, or conclusion ⟨*came* home tired⟩ **b :** HAPPEN, OCCUR ⟨no harm will *come* to you⟩ **10 :** to fall within a scope ⟨*comes* under the terms of the treaty⟩ **11 :** BECOME ⟨a wish that *came* true⟩ [Old English *cuman*] — **come across** **:** to meet or find by chance — **come into** **:** to acquire as an inheritance — **come into one's own** **:** to approach or reach one's appropriate level of importance, skill, or recognition — **come over** **:** to affect suddenly and strangely ⟨what's *come over* you⟩ — **come to be** **:** to arrive at or attain to being **:** BECOME — **come to pass** **:** HAPPEN — **come upon** **:** to meet or find by chance ⟨*came upon* an old friend⟩ — **to come** **:** existing or arriving in the future ⟨in days *to come*⟩

come about *vi* **1 :** HAPPEN **2 :** to change direction ⟨the wind has *come about* into the north⟩ **3 :** to turn a boat onto a new tack

come along *vi* **1 :** to go with as a companion ⟨asked me to *come along* on the trip⟩ **2 :** to make progress ⟨work is *coming* *along* well⟩ **3 :** to make an appearance ⟨won't take the first job that *comes along*⟩

come around *vi* **:** COME ROUND

come·back \'kəm-ˌbak\ *n* **1 :** [2]RETORT **2 :** a return to a former position or condition (as of health or prosperity) **:** RECOVERY

come by *vb* **1 :** to make a visit ⟨*come by* after dinner⟩ **2 :** ACQUIRE ⟨good jobs are hard to *come by*⟩

co·me·di·an \kə-'mēd-ē-ən\ *n* **1 :** an actor who plays in comedy **2 :** a comical individual; *esp* **:** a professional entertainer who uses various physical or verbal means to be amusing

co·me·di·enne \kə-ˌmēd-ē-'en\ *n* **:** a woman who is a comedian [French *comédienne,* feminine of *comédien* "comedian," from *comédie* "comedy"]

com·e·do \'käm-ə-ˌdō\ *n, pl* **com·e·do·nes** \ˌkäm-ə-'dō-ˌnēz\ **:** BLACKHEAD [Latin, "glutton," from *comedere* "to eat"]

come·down \'kəm-ˌdaün\ *n* **:** a descent in rank or dignity

come down \ˌkəm-'daün\ *vi* **:** to become sick ⟨*came down* with the flu⟩

com·e·dy \'käm-əd-ē\ *n, pl* **-dies 1 a :** a medieval narrative that ends happily ⟨Dante's Divine *Comedy*⟩ **b :** a literary work written in a comic style or treating a comic theme **2 a :** a light amusing play with a happy ending **b :** dramatic literature dealing with the comic or with the serious in a light or satirical manner **3 :** an amusing or ludicrous event [Medieval Latin *comoedia,* from Latin, "drama with a happy ending," from Greek *kōmōidia,* from *kōmos* "revel" + *aidein* "to sing"]

come in *vi* **1 a :** to arrive on a scene ⟨new models *coming in*⟩ **b :** to become available ⟨data began *coming in*⟩ **2 :** to place among those finishing (as a race) ⟨*came in* last⟩ **3 a :** to function in an indicated manner ⟨the tool *came in* handy⟩ **b :** to be received ⟨the radio signal *came in* loud and clear⟩ **4 :** to take on a role or function ⟨that's where you *come in*⟩ **5 :** to attain maturity, fruitfulness, or production — **come in for :** to become subject to ⟨*coming in for* endless criticism⟩

come·ly \'kəm-lē\ *adj* **come·li·er; -est :** pleasing to look at **:** good-looking ⟨*comely* people⟩ [Old English *cȳmlic* "glorious," from *cȳme* "lively, fine"]

come–on \'kəm-ˌȯn, -ˌän\ *n* **:** INDUCEMENT 2, LURE

come out *vi* **1 :** to come into public view **2 :** to declare oneself ⟨*come out* in favor of the proposal⟩ **3 :** to turn out ⟨the cake *came out* splendidly⟩ **4 :** to make one's debut — **come out with 1 :** to give expression to ⟨*come out* with the truth⟩ **2 :** PUBLISH 2a

com·er \'kəm-ər\ *n* **1 :** one that comes ⟨welcomed all *comers*⟩ **2 :** a promising newcomer

come round *vi* **1 :** to return to a former condition; *esp* **:** to regain consciousness **2 :** to change direction or opinion

[1]**co·mes·ti·ble** \kə-'mes-tə-bəl\ *adj* **:** suitable for eating **:** EATABLE, EDIBLE [Medieval Latin *comestibilis,* derived from Latin *comedere* "to eat up," from *com-* + *edere* "to eat"]

[2]**comestible** *n* **:** FOOD 3 — usually used in plural

com·et \'käm-ət\ *n* **:** a celestial body that orbits the sun, that consists of a diffuse head usually surrounding a bright nucleus, and that often develops one or more long tails when near the sun [Latin *cometa,* from Greek *komētēs,* literally, "long-haired," derived from *komē* "hair"]

come to *vi* **:** to recover consciousness

come up *vi* **1 :** RISE 6 **2 :** to come near or approach ⟨*came up* and introduced himself⟩ **3 :** to rise in rank or status **4 :** to come to attention or consideration ⟨the question never *came up*⟩ **5 :** to turn out to be ⟨the coin *came up* tails⟩ — **come up with :** to produce especially in dealing with a problem or challenge ⟨*came up with* a solution⟩

come·up·pance \kə-'məp-əns, ˌkə-\ *n* **:** a deserved rebuke or penalty **:** DESERTS

com·fit \'kəm-fət, 'käm-, 'kəmp-, 'kämp-\ *n* **:** a confection consisting of a piece of fruit, a root (as licorice), or a seed coated and preserved with sugar [Medieval French *confit,* from *confire* "to prepare," from Latin *conficere,* from *com-* + *facere* "to make"]

[1]**com·fort** \'kəm-fərt, 'kəmp-\ *vt* **1 :** to give strength and hope to **:** CHEER **2 :** to ease the grief or trouble of **:** CONSOLE [Medieval French *comforter,* from Late Latin *confortare* "to strengthen greatly," from Latin *com-* + *fortis* "strong"]

[2]**comfort** *n* **1 :** acts or words that comfort **2 :** the feeling of the one that is comforted ⟨find *comfort* in a parent's love⟩ **3 :** something that makes a person comfortable ⟨the *comforts* of home⟩ — **com·fort·less** \-ləs\ *adj*

com·fort·able \'kəm-fərt-ə-bəl, 'kəmp-; 'kəmf-tə-bəl, 'kəmp-, 'kəmpf-, 'kəm-, -tər-\ *adj* **1 :** giving comfort; *esp* **:** providing physical comfort **2 :** more than adequate ⟨a *comfortable* income⟩ **3 :** physically or mentally at ease — **com·fort·able·ness** *n* — **com·fort·ably** \-blē\ *adv*

com·fort·er \'kəm-fərt-ər, 'kəmp-, -fət-\ *n* **1 :** one that gives comfort **2 a :** a long narrow neck scarf **b :** QUILT 1

com·fy \'kəm-fē, 'kəmp-\ *adj* **:** COMFORTABLE [alteration of *comfortable*]

[1]**com·ic** \'käm-ik\ *adj* **1 :** of, relating to, or marked by comedy ⟨a *comic* actor⟩ **2 :** causing laughter or amusement **:** FUNNY ⟨a *comic* monologue⟩ **3 :** of or relating to comic strips [Latin *comicus,* from Greek *kōmikos,* from *kōmos* "revel"]

[2]**comic** *n* **1 :** COMEDIAN 2 **2 a :** COMIC STRIP **b** *pl* **:** the part of a newspaper devoted to comic strips

com·i·cal \'käm-i-kəl\ *adj* **:** provoking spontaneous laughter or amusement **:** DROLL ⟨wearing a *comical* expression⟩ — **com·i·cal·i·ty** \ˌkäm-i-'kal-ət-ē\ *n* — **com·i·cal·ly** \'käm-i-kə-lē, -klē\ *adv*

comic book *n* **:** a magazine made up of a series of comic strips

comic opera *n* **:** a musical dramatic work with spoken dialogue that is usually of light and amusing character

comic strip *n* **:** a sequence of cartoons that tell a story or part of a story

com·ing \'kəm-ing\ *adj* **1 :** APPROACHING, NEXT ⟨the *coming* year⟩ **2 :** gaining importance ⟨a *coming* young star⟩

Com·in·tern \'käm-ən-ˌtərn\ *n* **:** the Communist International established in 1919 in an attempt to supersede the Second International of Socialist organizations [Russian *Komintern,* from *Kom*munisticheskiĭ *Intern*atsional "Communist International"]

co·mi·ty \'käm-ət-ē, 'kō-mət-\ *n, pl* **-ties :** courteous behavior **:** CIVILITY [Latin *comitas,* from *comis* "courteous"]

comity of nations : the code of courtesy and friendship by which nations get along together; *also* **:** the group of nations observing such a code

com·ma \'käm-ə\ *n* **:** a punctuation mark , used chiefly to show separation of words or word groups within a sentence [Latin, "part of a sentence," from Greek *komma* "segment, clause," from *koptein* "to cut"]

[1]**com·mand** \kə-'mand\ *vb* **1 a :** to direct authoritatively **:** ORDER, GOVERN **b :** to have authority and control of a military force or post **:** be commander of **2 a :** to have at one's disposal ⟨*commands* many resources⟩ **b :** to demand as one's due **:** EXACT ⟨*commands* a high fee⟩ **c :** to overlook from a strategic position ⟨the hill *commands* the town⟩ [Medieval French *cumander,* from Latin *commendare* "to commit to one's charge, commend"]

synonyms COMMAND, DIRECT, INSTRUCT, CHARGE mean to issue orders. COMMAND suggests the use of authority and usually some degree of formality ⟨the troops were *commanded* to move forward⟩. DIRECT suggests that obedience is expected and usually applies to specific procedures or methods ⟨we were *directed* to write with pencils only⟩. INSTRUCT is similar to *direct* but sometimes implies greater explicitness or formality ⟨the judge *instructed* the jury to ignore the remark⟩. CHARGE suggests the assigning of a duty or responsibility ⟨the principal is *charged* with keeping the school running smoothly⟩.

[2]**command** *n* **1 :** the act of commanding ⟨march on *command*⟩ **2 :** an order given **3 a :** the ability to control **:** MASTERY ⟨has *command* of the subject⟩ **b :** the authority or right to command **c :** the power to dominate **d :** facility in using ⟨a good *command* of French⟩ **4 :** the personnel, area, or unit under a commander **5 :** a position from which military operations are directed — called also *command post*

[3]**command** *adj* **:** done on command or request ⟨a *command* performance⟩

com·man·dant \'käm-ən-ˌdant, -ˌdänt\ *n* **:** COMMANDING OFFICER

com·man·deer \ˌkäm-ən-'diər\ *vt* **:** to take arbitrary or forcible possession of especially for military purposes [Afrikaans *kommandeer,* from French *commander* "to command"]

com·mand·er \kə-'man-dər\ *n* **1 :** one in official command;

\ə\ **abut**	\aü\ **out**	\i\ **tip**	\ȯ\ **saw**	\ü\ **foot**
\ər\ **further**	\ch\ **chin**	\ī\ **life**	\ȯi\ **coin**	\y\ **yet**
\a\ **mat**	\e\ **pet**	\j\ **job**	\th\ **thin**	\yü\ **few**
\ā\ **take**	\ē\ **easy**	\ng\ **sing**	\th\ **this**	\yu\ **cure**
\ä\ **cot, cart**	\g\ **go**	\ō\ **bone**	\ü\ **food**	\zh\ **vision**

esp : COMMANDING OFFICER **2** : an officer rank in the Navy and Coast Guard above lieutenant commander and below captain — **com·mand·er·ship** \-ˌship\ *n*

commander in chief : one who holds the supreme command of an armed force

commanding officer *n* : a military or naval officer in command of a unit or post

com·mand·ment \kə-ˈman-mənt, -ˈmand-\ *n* : something commanded; *esp* : one of the biblical Ten Commandments

command module *n* : a space vehicle module designed to carry the crew, the chief communication equipment, and the equipment for reentry

com·man·do \kə-ˈman-dō\ *n, pl* **-dos** *or* **-does** **1** : a military unit trained and organized for surprise raids into enemy territory **2** : a member of a specialized raiding unit [Afrikaans *kommando,* from Dutch *commando* "command," from Spanish *comando,* from *comander* "to command," derived from Latin *commendere*]

command sergeant major *n* : an enlisted rank in the Army above first sergeant

comma splice *n* : the unjustified use of a comma between coordinate main clauses not connected by a conjunction — called also *comma fault*

comme il faut \ˌkəm-ˌēl-ˈfō, -ˌē-\ *adj* : conforming to accepted standards : PROPER [French, literally, "as it should be"]

com·mem·o·rate \kə-ˈmem-ə-ˌrāt\ *vt* **1** : to call to remembrance **2** : to mark by a ceremony : OBSERVE **3** : to be a memorial of ⟨a plaque that *commemorates* the battle⟩ [Latin *commemorare,* from *com-* + *memorare* "to remind of," from *memor* "mindful"] ***synonyms*** see KEEP — **com·mem·o·ra·tor** \-ˌrāt-ər\ *n*

com·mem·o·ra·tion \kə-ˌmem-ə-ˈrā-shən\ *n* **1** : the act of commemorating **2** : something (as a ceremony) that commemorates

com·mem·o·ra·tive \kə-ˈmem-ə-ˌrāt-iv, -rət-\ *adj* : intended to commemorate ⟨a *commemorative* stamp⟩ — **commemorative** *n* — **com·mem·o·ra·tive·ly** *adv*

com·mence \kə-ˈmens\ *vb* : to bring or come into activity, being, or operation ⟨*commence* firing⟩ [Medieval French *comencer,* derived from Latin *com-* + *initiare* "to initiate"] — **com·menc·er** *n*

com·mence·ment \-ˈmens-mənt\ *n* **1** : an act, instance, or time of commencing **2 a** : the ceremonies or the day for conferring degrees or diplomas on graduates of a school or college **b** : the period of activities at this time

com·mend \kə-ˈmend\ *vt* **1** : to give into another's care : ENTRUST **2** : to speak of with approval : PRAISE ⟨*commended* her for her honesty⟩ [Latin *commendare,* from *com-* + *mandare* "to entrust"] — **com·mend·able** \-ˈmen-də-bəl\ *adj* — **com·mend·ably** \-də-blē\ *adv*

com·men·da·tion \ˌkäm-ən-ˈdā-shən, -ˌen-\ *n* **1** : an act of commending **2** : something (as a formal citation) that commends — **com·men·da·to·ry** \kə-ˈmen-də-ˌtōr-ē, -ˌtȯr-\ *adj*

com·men·sal \kə-ˈmen-səl\ *adj* : relating to or living in a state of commensalism [Medieval Latin *commensalis* "of those who habitually eat together," from Latin *com-* + *mensa* "table"] — **commensal** *n* — **com·men·sal·ly** \-sə-lē\ *adv*

com·men·sal·ism \-sə-ˌliz-əm\ *n* : a relation between two kinds of organisms in which one obtains a benefit (as food) from the other without either damaging or benefiting it

com·men·su·ra·ble \kə-ˈmens-rə-bəl, -ˈmench-, -ə-rə-\ *adj* : divisible without remainder by a common unit ⟨10 and 25 are *commensurable* because 5 divides them both without remainder⟩ — **com·men·su·ra·bly** \-blē\ *adv*

com·men·su·rate \kə-ˈmens-rət, -ˈmench-, -ə-rət\ *adj* **1** : equal in measure or extent **2** : PROPORTIONATE ⟨a job *commensurate* with one's abilities⟩ [Late Latin *commensuratus,* derived from Latin *com-* + *mensura* "measure"] — **com·men·su·rate·ly** *adv* — **com·men·su·ra·tion** \-ˌmen-sə-ˈrā-shən, -ˌmench-ə-ˈrā-\ *n*

[1]**com·ment** \ˈkäm-ˌent\ *n* **1** : an expression of opinion either in speech or writing **2** : a usually critical or explanatory remark [Late Latin *commentum,* from Latin, "invention," from *commentus,* past participle of *comminisci* "to invent"]

[2]**comment** *vi* : to make a comment : REMARK

com·men·tary \ˈkäm-ən-ˌter-ē\ *n, pl* **-tar·ies** : a series of comments or notes; *also* : a book composed of such material — usually used in plural

com·men·tate \ˈkäm-ən-ˌtāt\ *vb* : to give a commentary on : act as a commentator

com·men·ta·tor \-ˌtāt-ər\ *n* : one that gives a commentary; *esp* : one who reports and discusses news on radio or television

com·merce \ˈkäm-ˌərs, -ərs\ *n* **1** : interchange of ideas, opinions, or sentiments **2** : the exchange or buying and selling of goods on a large scale involving transportation from place to place : TRADE [Middle French, from Latin *commercium,* from *com-* + *merx* "merchandise"] ***synonyms*** see BUSINESS

[1]**com·mer·cial** \kə-ˈmər-shəl\ *adj* **1 a** : of or relating to commerce **b** : engaged in commerce ⟨a *commercial* city⟩ **2 a** : viewed with regard to profit ⟨a *commercial* success⟩ **b** : designed for profit; *esp* : designed for mass appeal ⟨the *commercial* theater⟩ **3** : emphasizing skills and subjects useful in business ⟨*commercial* education⟩ **4** : paid for by advertisers ⟨*commercial* TV⟩ — **com·mer·cial·ly** \-ˈmərsh-lē, -ə-lē\ *adv*

[2]**commercial** *n* : an advertisement broadcast on radio or television

commercial bank *n* : a bank that accepts deposits that can be withdrawn without notice and creates credit through short-term loans mainly to business

com·mer·cial·ism \kə-ˈmər-shə-ˌliz-əm\ *n* : a spirit, method, or practice characteristic of business — **com·mer·cial·is·tic** \-ˌmər-shə-ˈlis-tik\ *adj*

com·mer·cial·ize \kə-ˈmər-shə-ˌlīz\ *vt* **1** : to manage on a business basis for profit **2** : to exploit for profit ⟨*commercialize* Christmas⟩ **3** : to lower in quality for more profit — **com·mer·cial·i·za·tion** \-ˌmər-shə-lə-ˈzā-shən\ *n*

commercial paper *n* : short-term negotiable instruments arising out of commercial transactions

commercial traveler *n* : TRAVELING SALESMAN

com·mi·na·tion \ˌkäm-ə-ˈnā-shən\ *n* : DENUNCIATION [Latin *comminatio,* from *comminari* "to threaten," from *com-* + *minari* "to threaten"] — **com·mi·na·to·ry** \ˈkäm-ə-nə-ˌtōr-ē, -ˌtȯr-; kə-ˈmin-ə-, -ˈmīn-\ *adj*

com·min·gle \kə-ˈming-gəl\ *vb* : MINGLE 1, MIX ⟨*commingle* two liquids⟩

com·mi·nute \ˈkäm-ə-ˌnüt, -nyüt\ *vt* : to reduce to minute particles : PULVERIZE [Latin *comminuere,* from *com-* + *minuere* "to lessen"] — **com·mi·nu·tion** \ˌkäm-ə-ˈnü-shən, -ˈnyü-\ *n*

com·mis·er·ate \kə-ˈmiz-ə-ˌrāt\ *vb* : to feel or express sorrow, compassion, or sympathy for : SYMPATHIZE [Latin *commiserari,* from *com-* + *miserari* "to pity," from *miser* "wretched"] — **com·mis·er·a·tion** \-ˌmiz-ə-ˈrā-shən\ *n* — **com·mis·er·a·tive** \-ˈmiz-ə-ˌrāt-iv\ *adj*

com·mis·sar \ˈkäm-ə-ˌsär\ *n* **1** : a Communist party official assigned to a military unit to teach party principles and policies and to ensure party loyalty **2** : the head of a government department in the U.S.S.R. from 1917 to 1946 [Russian *komissar,* from German *Kommissar* "commissary," from Medieval Latin *commissarius*]

com·mis·sar·i·at \ˌkäm-ə-ˈser-ē-ət, -ˈsar-, *especially for 2* -ˈsär-\ *n* **1** : a system for supplying an army with food **2** : a government department in the U.S.S.R. from 1917 to 1946 [New Latin *commissariatus,* from Medieval Latin *commissarius* "commissary"; sense 2 from Russian *komissariat,* from German *Kommissariat,* from New Latin *commissariatus*]

com·mis·sary \ˈkäm-ə-ˌser-ē\ *n, pl* **-sar·ies** **1** : a person to whom a duty or office is entrusted by a superior **2** : a store supplying provisions especially to military personnel and dependents [Medieval Latin *commissarius,* from Latin *commissus,* past participle of *committere* "to commit"]

[1]**com·mis·sion** \kə-ˈmish-ən\ *n* **1 a** : a formal order granting the power to perform various acts or duties **b** : a certificate conferring military rank and authority; *also* : the rank and authority conferred **2** : an authorization or command to act in a prescribed manner or to perform prescribed acts **3 a** : authority to act as agent for another **b** : a task or matter entrusted to an agent **4 a** : a group of persons directed to perform a duty **b** : a government agency having administrative, legislative, or judicial powers **c** : a city council having legislative and executive functions **5** : an act of committing something ⟨the *commission* of a crime⟩ **6** : a fee paid to an agent or employee for transacting a piece of business or performing a service ⟨a brokerage *commission*⟩ [Middle French, from Latin *commissio* "act of bringing together," from *committere* "to commit"] — **in commission** **1** : ready for active service — used of a ship **2** : in use or ready for use — **out of commission** **1** : out of service or use **2** : out of working order

[2]**commission** *vt* **-mis·sioned; -mis·sion·ing** \-ˈmish-niŋ, -ə-niŋ\ **1 :** to give a commission to ⟨was *commissioned* lieutenant⟩ ⟨*commissioned* to write the biography⟩ **2 :** to order to be made ⟨*commissioned* a portrait⟩ **3 :** to put (a ship) in commission

com·mis·sion·aire \kə-ˌmish-ə-ˈnaər, -ˈneər\ *n, chiefly British* **:** a uniformed attendant [French *commissionnaire,* from *commission* "commission"]

com·mis·sion·er \kə-ˈmish-nər, -ə-nər\ *n* **1 :** a member of a commission **2 :** an official in charge of a government department ⟨*Commissioner* of Public Safety⟩

commission merchant *n* **:** BROKER

com·mis·sure \ˈkäm-ə-ˌshu̇r\ *n* **:** a connecting band of nerve tissue in the brain or spinal cord [Latin *commissura* "a joining," from *committere* "to connect, commit"] — **com·mis·sur·al** \ˌkäm-ə-ˈshu̇r-əl\ *adj*

com·mit \kə-ˈmit\ *vt* **com·mit·ted; com·mit·ting** **1 a :** to give in trust ⟨*commit* power to the legislature⟩ **b :** to place in a prison or mental institution **c :** to consign for preservation, disposal, or safekeeping ⟨*commit* it to memory⟩ **d :** to refer (as a legislative bill) to a committee for consideration and report **2 :** to bring about **:** PERFORM ⟨*commit* a crime⟩ **3 a :** OBLIGATE, BIND ⟨was *committed* to defend them⟩ **b :** to pledge or assign to a particular course or use ⟨*committed* myself to a meeting on Thursday⟩ **c :** to express the opinion of ⟨refused to *commit* themselves on the issue⟩ [Latin *committere* "to connect, entrust," from *com-* + *mittere* "to send"] — **com·mit·ta·ble** \-ˈmit-ə-bəl\ *adj*

com·mit·ment \kə-ˈmit-mənt\ *n* **1 :** an act of committing: as **a :** a consignment to a penal or mental institution **b :** an act of referring a matter to a legislative committee **2 a :** an agreement or pledge to do something in the future **b :** something pledged

com·mit·tal \kə-ˈmit-l\ *n* **:** COMMITMENT 1a

com·mit·tee \kə-ˈmit-ē\ *n* **1 :** a body of persons delegated or elected to consider or take action on some matter **2 :** a self-constituted organization for the promotion of a common goal

com·mit·tee·man \-mən, -ˌman\ *n* **1 :** a member of a committee **2 :** a party leader of a ward or precinct

committee of the whole : the whole membership of a legislative house sitting as a committee and operating under informal rules

com·mit·tee·wom·an \-ˌwu̇m-ən\ *n* **1 :** a woman who is a member of a committee **2 :** a woman who is a party leader of a ward or precinct

com·mix \kə-ˈmiks, kä-\ *vb* **:** to mix or mingle together **:** BLEND

com·mix·ture \-chər\ *n* **:** MIXTURE 2a, COMPOUND

com·mode \kə-ˈmōd\ *n* **1 a :** a low chest of drawers **b :** a movable washstand with a cupboard underneath **2 :** TOILET 2b [French *commode* "suitable, convenient," from Latin *commodus,* from *com-* + *modus* "measure"]

com·mo·di·ous \kə-ˈmōd-ē-əs\ *adj* **1 :** comfortably or conveniently spacious **:** ROOMY ⟨a *commodious* closet⟩ **2** *archaic* **:** HANDY, SERVICEABLE [Medieval Latin *commodosus* "fertile, useful," from Latin *commodum* "convenience," from *commodus* "convenient"] — **com·mo·di·ous·ly** *adv* — **com·mo·di·ous·ness** *n*

com·mod·i·ty \kə-ˈmäd-ət-ē\ *n, pl* **-ties :** an economic good: as **a :** a product of agriculture or mining **b :** an article exchanged in commerce [Medieval French *commoditee* "convenience, advantage," from Latin *commoditas,* from *commodus* "convenient"]

com·mo·dore \ˈkäm-ə-ˌdōr, -ˌdȯr\ *n* **1 :** a commissioned officer in the Navy above captain and below rear admiral **2 :** the senior captain of a line of merchant ships **3 :** the chief officer of a yacht club or boating association [probably from Dutch *commandeur* "commander," from French]

[1]**com·mon** \ˈkäm-ən\ *adj* **1 :** having to do with, belonging to, or used by everybody **:** PUBLIC ⟨work for the *common* good⟩ **2 a :** belonging to or shared by two or more individuals or by the members of a group ⟨a *common* ancestor⟩ **b :** belonging equally to two or more mathematical entities ⟨two angles with a *common* side⟩ **c :** having two or more branches ⟨*common* carotid artery⟩ **3 a :** widely or generally known, met, or seen ⟨facts of *common* knowledge⟩ **b :** satisfying an ordinary standard **:** ADEQUATE ⟨*common* courtesy⟩ ⟨*common* decency⟩ **4 :** FREQUENT, FAMILIAR ⟨a *common* sight⟩ **5 a :** not above the average in rank, merit, or social position ⟨a *common* soldier⟩ ⟨the *common* people⟩ **b :** falling below ordinary standards **:** SECOND-RATE **c :** lacking refinement **:** VULGAR **6 a :** being either masculine or feminine ⟨in French the gender of the word *enfant* is *common*⟩ **b :** being a grammatical case used both for the subject and the object ⟨the word *man* in "the man is tall," "watch the man," and "with the man" is in the *common* case⟩ [Medieval French *commun,* from Latin *communis*] ***synonyms*** see RECIPROCAL — **com·mon·ly** *adv* — **com·mon·ness** \-ən-nəs\ *n*

[2]**common** *n* **1** *pl* **:** the common people **2** *pl* **:** a dining hall **3** *pl, often cap* **a :** the political group or estate comprising the commoners **b :** the parliamentary representatives of the commoners **c :** HOUSE OF COMMONS **4 :** a piece of land subject to common use especially for pasture — often used in plural **5 a :** a religious service suitable for a festival **b :** the ordinary of the Mass — **in common :** shared together ⟨has a lot *in common* with his neighbors⟩

com·mon·al·i·ty \ˌkäm-ə-ˈnal-ət-ē\ *or* **com·mon·al·ty** \ˈkäm-ən-əl-tē\ *n, pl* **-ties :** the common people

common carrier *n* **:** an individual or corporation engaged in transporting persons, goods, or messages for money

common cold *n* **:** a contagious viral illness of the upper respiratory tract marked by congestion and inflammation of mucous membranes and usually accompanied by excessive secretion of mucus and coughing and sneezing

common denominator *n* **1 :** a number or expression that is a multiple of each denominator in a set of fractions ⟨12 is a *common denominator* of ¼ and ⅓⟩ **2 :** a common trait or theme

common difference *n* **:** the difference between two consecutive terms of an arithmetic progression

common divisor *n* **:** a number or expression that divides two or more numbers or expressions without remainder ⟨4 is a *common divisor* of 8 and 12⟩ — called also *common factor*

com·mon·er \ˈkäm-ə-nər\ *n* **:** one of the common people **:** a person not of noble rank

Common Era *n* **:** CHRISTIAN ERA

common fraction *n* **:** a fraction (as ½ or ¾) in which both numerator and denominator are expressed as whole numbers

common law *n* **:** the body of law developed in England primarily from judicial decisions based on custom and precedent, unwritten in statute or code, and forming the basis of the legal system in most jurisdictions of the U.S. and parts of the world under British control or influence

common–law marriage *n* **:** a marriage recognized in some jurisdictions and based on agreement and usually cohabitation but without religious or civil ceremony

common logarithm *n* **:** a logarithm whose base is 10

common market *n* **:** an economic association formed to remove trade barriers among member nations

common multiple *n* **:** a multiple of each of two or more numbers or expressions ⟨20 is a *common multiple* of 5 and 4⟩

common noun *n* **:** a noun (as *car, boy,* or *fear*) that names a general class of persons or things or a unit of such a class

[1]**com·mon·place** \ˈkäm-ən-ˌplās\ *n* **1 :** an obvious or trite remark **2 :** something commonly found or seen

[2]**commonplace** *adj* **:** lacking originality, freshness, or interest

common ratio *n* **:** the ratio of each term of a geometric progression to the term before it

common room *n* **1 :** a lounge available to all members of a residential community **2 :** a room in a college for the use of the faculty

common salt *n* **:** SALT 1a

common school *n* **:** a free public school

common sense *n* **:** sound and prudent judgment based on a simple perception of the situation or facts

common stock *n* **:** stock other than preferred stock

common time *n* **:** four beats to a measure in music

common touch *n* **:** the gift of appealing to or arousing the sympathetic interest of people of all walks of life

com·mon·weal \ˈkäm-ən-ˌwēl\ *n* **1** *archaic* **:** COMMONWEALTH **2 :** the general welfare

com·mon·wealth \-ˌwelth\ *n* **1 :** a political unit whose aim is the common good of all the people **2** *cap* **:** the English state from the death of Charles I in 1649 to the Restoration in 1660 **3** : a state of the U.S. — used officially of Kentucky, Massachusetts, Pennsylvania, and Virginia **4** *cap* : a federal union of states — used officially of Australia **5** *often cap* : an association of self-governing states having a common political and cultural background and united by a common allegiance ⟨the British *Commonwealth*⟩ **6** *often cap* : a political unit having local self-government but voluntarily united with the U.S. — used officially of Puerto Rico and of the Northern Mariana Islands

com·mo·tion \kə-ˈmō-shən\ *n* **1** : disturbed or violent motion : AGITATION **2 a** : noisy excitement and confusion **b** : a confused noisy disturbance : TUMULT [Medieval French *commocion,* from Latin *commotio,* from *commovēre* "to agitate," from *com-* + *movēre* "to move"]

com·mu·nal \kə-ˈmyün-l, ˈkäm-yən-l\ *adj* **1** : of or relating to a commune or community **2 a** : characterized by collective ownership and use of property **b** : shared, participated in, or used in common by members of a group or community

[1]**com·mune** \kə-ˈmyün\ *vi* **1** : to receive Communion **2** : to communicate intimately ⟨went off into the woods to *commune* with nature⟩ [Medieval French *communer* "to share, receive Communion," from Latin *communicare* "to impart, participate," from *communis* "common"]

[2]**com·mune** \ˈkäm-ˌyün; kə-ˈmyün, kä-\ *n* **1** : the smallest administrative district of many countries especially in Europe **2** : COMMUNITY: as **a** : a medieval municipality **b** : a rural community (as the Russian mir) organized on a communal basis [French, from Middle French *comugne,* from Medieval Latin *communia,* from Latin *communis* "common"]

com·mu·ni·ca·ble \kə-ˈmyü-ni-kə-bəl\ *adj* : capable of being communicated : TRANSMITTABLE ⟨*communicable* diseases⟩ — **com·mu·ni·ca·bil·i·ty** \-ˌmyü-ni-kə-ˈbil-ət-ē\ *n* — **com·mu·ni·ca·ble·ness** \-ˈmyü-ni-kə-bəl-nəs\ *n* — **com·mu·ni·ca·bly** \-blē\ *adv*

com·mu·ni·cant \kə-ˈmyü-ni-kənt\ *n* **1 a** : a person who receives Communion **b** : a church member **2** : a person who communicates — **communicant** *adj*

com·mu·ni·cate \kə-ˈmyü-nə-ˌkāt\ *vb* **1 a** : to make known ⟨*communicate* the news⟩ **b** : TRANSFER, TRANSMIT ⟨*communicate* a disease⟩ **2** : to receive Communion **3** : to be in communication **4** : JOIN, CONNECT ⟨the rooms *communicate*⟩ [Latin *communicare* "to impart, participate," from *communis* "common"] — **com·mu·ni·ca·tor** \-ˌkāt-ər\ *n*

com·mu·ni·ca·tion \kə-ˌmyü-nə-ˈkā-shən\ *n* **1** : an act or instance of transmitting **2 a** : information communicated **b** : MESSAGE 1 **3** : an exchange of information **4** *pl* **a** : a system (as of telephones) for communicating **b** : a system of routes for moving troops, supplies, and vehicles **5** *pl* : the business or technology of the transmission of information **6** : the interchange of ideas and opinions

com·mu·ni·ca·tive \kə-ˈmyü-nə-ˌkāt-iv, -ni-kət-\ *adj* **1** : tending to communicate : TALKATIVE **2** : of or relating to communication — **com·mu·ni·ca·tive·ly** *adv* — **com·mu·ni·ca·tive·ness** *n*

com·mu·nion \kə-ˈmyü-nyən\ *n* **1 a** *cap* : a Christian sacrament in which bread and wine are partaken of as a commemoration of the death of Christ **b** : the act of receiving the sacrament **c** *cap* : the part of a religious service in which the sacrament is received **2** : COMMUNICATION 1 **3** : a body of Christians having a common faith [Latin *communio* "mutual participation," from *communis* "common"]

com·mu·ni·qué \kə-ˈmyü-nə-ˌkā, -ˌmyü-nə-ˈ\ *n* : an official communication : BULLETIN [French, from *communiquer* "to communicate," from Latin *communicare*]

com·mu·nism \ˈkäm-yə-ˌniz-əm\ *n* **1** : a social system in which property and goods are owned in common; *also* : a theory advocating such a system **2** *cap* **a** : a doctrine based upon revolutionary Marxian socialism and Marxism-Leninism that was the official ideology of the U.S.S.R. **b** : a totalitarian system of government in which a single party controls state-owned means of production with the professed aim of establishing a stateless society

com·mu·nist \ˈkäm-yə-nəst\ *n* **1** : an adherent or advocate of communism **2** *cap* : a member or adherent of a Communist party or movement — **communist** *adj, often cap* — **com·mu·nis·tic** \ˌkäm-yə-ˈnis-tik\ *adj, often cap* — **com·mu·nis·ti·cal·ly** \-ti-kə-lē, -klē\ *adv*

com·mu·ni·ty \kə-ˈmyü-nət-ē\ *n, pl* **-ties** **1 a** : the people living in an area; *also* : the area itself **b** : an interacting population of various kinds of individuals (as species) in a common location **c** : a group of people with common interests living together within a larger society ⟨a *community* of artists⟩ **d** : a body of persons or nations having a common history or common social, economic, and political interests **2 a** : joint ownership or participation ⟨*community* of goods⟩ **b** : LIKENESS ⟨a *community* of interests⟩ **c** : shared activity **d** : a social state or condition [Medieval French *communité,* from Latin *communitas,* from *communis* "common"]

community center *n* : a building or group of buildings for a community's educational and recreational activities

community chest *n* : a general fund made up of individual subscriptions in a community to provide public aid

community college *n* : a 2-year government-supported college that offers an associate degree

com·mu·nize \ˈkäm-yə-ˌnīz\ *vb* **1** : to place under common ownership **2** : to organize according to Communist principles — **com·mu·ni·za·tion** \ˌkäm-yə-nə-ˈzā-shən\ *n*

com·mu·ta·tion \ˌkäm-yə-ˈtā-shən\ *n* **1** : EXCHANGE 2; *esp* : a substitution of one form of payment for another **2** : a reduction of a legal penalty **3** : an act of commuting **4** : the process of reversing the direction of an electric circuit

com·mu·ta·tive \kə-ˈmyüt-ət-iv, ˈkäm-yə-ˌtāt-iv\ *adj* : of, relating to, or having the property of giving the same mathematical result no matter in which order two numbers are used with an operation ⟨addition of positive numbers is *commutative* but subtraction is not⟩ — **com·mu·ta·tiv·i·ty** \kə-ˌmyüt-ə-ˈtiv-ət-ē\ *n*

com·mu·ta·tor \ˈkäm-yə-ˌtāt-ər\ *n* : a device for reversing the direction of an electric current so that the alternating currents generated in the armature of a dynamo are converted to direct current

[1]**com·mute** \kə-ˈmyüt\ *vb* **1 a** : INTERCHANGE, SUBSTITUTE **b** : CHANGE 1, ALTER **2** : to substitute one form of obligation for another **3** : to change a penalty to another one that is less severe ⟨*commute* a death sentence to life imprisonment⟩ **4** : to travel back and forth regularly [Latin *commutare* "to change, exchange," from *com-* + *mutare* "to change"] — **com·mut·able** \-ˈmyüt-ə-bəl\ *adj* — **com·mut·er** *n*

[2]**commute** *n* **1** : an act or instance of commuting ⟨the morning *commute*⟩ **2** : the distance covered in commuting ⟨a long *commute*⟩

[1]**com·pact** \kəm-ˈpakt, ˈkäm-ˌ\ *adj* **1** : closely united, collected, or packed **2** : arranged or designed so as to save space ⟨a *compact* house⟩ **3** : not wordy : CONCISE **4** : short-bodied, solid, and without excess flesh [Latin *compactus* "firmly put together," from past participle of *compingere* "to put together," from *com-* + *pangere* "to fasten"] — **com·pact·ly** *adv* — **com·pact·ness** \-ˈpakt-nəs, -ˈpak-; -ˌpakt-, -ˌpak-\ *n*

[2]**compact** *vb* **1** : to make up by connecting or combining : COMPOSE **2** : to knit or draw together : COMBINE **3** : to make or become compact : COMPRESS — **com·pac·tor** *also* **com·pact·er** *n*

[3]**com·pact** \ˈkäm-ˌpakt\ *n* **1** : a small case for cosmetics **2** : a relatively small automobile

[4]**com·pact** \ˈkäm-ˌpakt\ *n* : an agreement (as a treaty) between two or more parties [Latin *compactum,* from *compacisci* "to make an agreement," from *com-* + *pacisci* "to contract"]

compact disc *n* : CD

com·pac·tion \kəm-ˈpak-shən\ *n* : the act or process of compacting : the state of being compacted

com·pa·dre \kəm-ˈpäd-rā\ *n* : a close friend [Spanish, literally, "godfather"]

[1]**com·pan·ion** \kəm-ˈpan-yən\ *n* **1** : one that accompanies another : COMRADE **2 a** : one of a pair of matching things **b** : one employed to live with and serve another [Medieval French *cumpaing, cumpaignun,* from Late Latin *companio,* from Latin *com-* + *panis* "bread, food"]

[2]**companion** *n* **1** : a covering at the top of a companionway **2** : COMPANIONWAY [by folk etymology from Dutch *kampanje* "poop deck"]

com·pan·ion·able \kəm-ˈpan-yə-nə-bəl\ *adj* : fitted to be a companion : SOCIABLE — **com·pan·ion·ably** \-blē\ *adv*

companion cell *n* : a living nucleated cell adjacent to a sieve tube of a vascular plant

com·pan·ion·ship \kəm-ˈpan-yən-ˌship\ *n* : FELLOWSHIP

com·pan·ion·way \-ˌwā\ *n* : a ship's stairway from one deck to another

com·pa·ny \ˈkəmp-nē, -ə-nē\ *n, pl* **-nies** **1 a** : association with another : FELLOWSHIP ⟨enjoy a person's *company*⟩ **b** : persons with whom one regularly associates ⟨known by the *company* you keep⟩ **c** : VISITORS **2 a** : a group of persons or things **b** : a body of soldiers; *esp* : a unit especially of infantry consisting usually of a headquarters and two or more platoons **c** : an organization of musical or dramatic performers ⟨an opera *company*⟩ **d** : the officers and crew of a ship **e** : a firefighting unit **3 a** : an association of persons carrying on a commercial or industrial enterprise **b** : those members of a partnership whose names do not appear in the firm name ⟨Doe and *Company*⟩ [Medieval French *cumpaingnie,* from *cumpaing* "companion," from Late Latin *companio*]

company union *n* : an unaffiliated labor union of the employees of a single firm; *esp* : one dominated by the employer

com·pa·ra·ble \ˈkäm-pə-rə-bəl, -prə-\ *adj* **1** : capable of being compared **2** : EQUIVALENT, SIMILAR ⟨fabrics of *comparable* quality⟩ — **com·pa·ra·bly** \-blē\ *adv*

1**com·par·a·tive** \kəm-ˈpar-ət-iv\ *adj* **1** : of, relating to, or constituting the degree of grammatical comparison that denotes increase in the quality, quantity, or relation expressed by an adjective or adverb **2** : measured by comparison : RELATIVE ⟨a *comparative* stranger⟩ **3** : involving systematic study of comparable elements ⟨*comparative* anatomy⟩ — **com·par·ative·ly** *adv* — **com·par·a·tive·ness** *n*

2**comparative** *n* : the comparative degree or a comparative form in a language ⟨"taller" is the *comparative* of "tall"⟩

com·par·a·tor \kəm-ˈpar-ət-ər, ˈkäm-pə-ˌrāt-\ *n* : an instrument for comparing something with a like thing or with a standard measure

1**com·pare** \kəm-ˈpaər, -ˈpeər\ *vb* **1** : to represent as similar : LIKEN ⟨*compare* an anthill to a town⟩ **2** : to examine in order to discover likenesses or differences ⟨*compare* two bicycles⟩ **3** : to be worthy of comparison ⟨roller-skating does not *compare* with ice-skating⟩ **4** : to inflect or modify (an adjective or adverb) according to the degrees of comparison [Medieval French *comparer,* from Latin *comparare* "to couple, compare," from *compar* "like," from *com-* + *par* "equal"]

synonyms COMPARE, CONTRAST mean to set side by side in order to show differences and likenesses. COMPARE implies an aim of showing relative values by observing characteristic qualities whether similar or divergent ⟨*compared* the business programs of the two colleges⟩. CONTRAST implies an emphasis on differences or opposite qualities ⟨*contrast* his rudeness with his brother's polite manners⟩.

2**compare** *n* : the possibility of comparing ⟨beauty beyond *compare*⟩

com·par·i·son \kəm-ˈpar-ə-sən\ *n* **1** : the act of comparing : the state of being compared **2** : an examination of two or more objects to find the likenesses and differences between them **3** : change in the form of an adjective or an adverb (as by having *-er* or *-est* added or *more* or *most* prefixed) to show different levels of quality, quantity, or relation

comparison shop *vi* : to compare prices in order to find the best value — **comparison shopper** *n*

com·part·ment \kəm-ˈpärt-mənt\ *n* **1** : one of the parts into which an enclosed space is divided **2** : a separate division or section [Middle French *compartiment,* from Italian *compartimento,* from *compartire* "to mark out in parts," from Late Latin *compartiri* "to share," from Latin *com-* + *partiri* "to share," from *pars* "part, share"] — **com·part·ment·ed** \-ˌment-əd\ *adj*

com·part·men·tal·ize \kəm-ˌpärt-ˈment-l-ˌīz\ *vt* : to separate into compartments — **com·part·men·tal·i·za·tion** \-ˌment-l-ə-ˈzā-shən\ *n*

1**com·pass** \ˈkəm-pəs, ˈkäm-\ *vt* **1** : to travel entirely around ⟨*compass* the earth⟩ **2 a** : to bring about : ACHIEVE **b** : to get into one's power or possession : OBTAIN **3** : to understand fully : COMPREHEND [Medieval French *cumpasser* "to measure," derived from Latin *com-* + *passus* "pace"]

2**compass** *n* **1 a** : an often rounded or curved boundary limit : CIRCUMFERENCE **b** : an enclosed space **c** : RANGE, SCOPE ⟨the *compass* of a voice⟩ **2 a** : a device for determining directions by means of a magnetic needle turning freely on a pivot and pointing to the magnetic north **b** : any of various nonmagnetic devices that indicate direction **c** : an instrument for making circles or transferring measurements that consists of two pointed branches joined at the top by a pivot — usually used in plural; called also *pair of compasses*

compass card *n* : the circular card attached to the needles of a mariner's compass on which are marked the 360° of the circle and 32 equidistant points

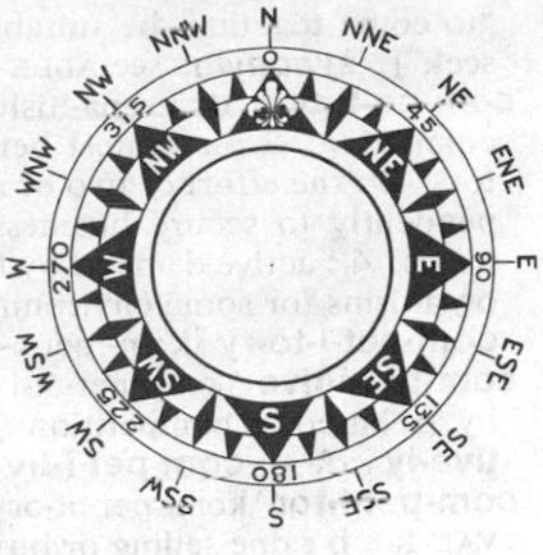

compass card

com·pas·sion \kəm-ˈpash-ən\ *n* : sorrow or pity aroused by the suffering or misfortune of another : SYMPATHY, MERCY [Late Latin *compassio,* from *compati* "to sympathize," from Latin *com-* + *pati* "to suffer"]

com·pas·sion·ate \kəm-ˈpash-nət, -ə-nət\ *adj* : having or showing compassion : SYMPATHETIC — **com·pas·sion·ate·ly** *adv*

com·pat·i·ble \kəm-ˈpat-ə-bəl\ *adj* **1** : capable of existing together in harmony ⟨*compatible* colors⟩ **2** : able to cross-fertilize freely ⟨*compatible* plants⟩ **3** : free from adverse or unwanted effects when present together ⟨*compatible* drugs⟩ [Medieval Latin *compatibilis* "sympathetic," from Latin *compati* "to sympathize"] — **com·pat·i·bil·i·ty** \-ˌpat-ə-ˈbil-ət-ē\ *n* — **com·pat·i·bly** \-ˈpat-ə-blē\ *adv*

com·pa·tri·ot \kəm-ˈpā-trē-ət, -ˌät\ *n* **1** : a fellow countryman **2** : COLLEAGUE, COMPANION

com·pel \kəm-ˈpel\ *vt* **com·pelled; com·pel·ling** **1** : to drive or urge forcefully or irresistibly : CONSTRAIN **2** : to cause to do or occur by overwhelming pressure ⟨*compel* obedience⟩ [Medieval French *compeller,* from Latin *compellere,* from *com-* + *pellere* "to drive"] ***synonyms*** see FORCE — **com·pel·ler** *n*

com·pend \ˈkäm-ˌpend\ *n* : COMPENDIUM

com·pen·di·ous \kəm-ˈpen-dē-əs\ *adj* : marked by brief expression of a comprehensive matter : CONCISE ⟨a *compendious* book⟩ — **com·pen·di·ous·ly** *adv* — **com·pen·di·ous·ness** *n*

com·pen·di·um \-dē-əm\ *n, pl* **-di·ums** *or* **-dia** \-dē-ə\ : a brief summary of a larger work or of a field of knowledge : ABSTRACT [Latin, "saving, shortcut," from *compendere* "to weigh together," from *com-* + *pendere* "to weigh"]

com·pen·sate \ˈkäm-pən-ˌsāt\ *vb* **1** : to be equivalent to in value or effect : make up for : COUNTERBALANCE **2** : to make amends or amends to ⟨nothing can *compensate* for the loss of reputation⟩ **3** : to make equal return to : PAY ⟨*compensate* workers for their labor⟩ [Latin *compensare,* from *compendere* "to weigh together"] — **com·pen·sa·tor** \ˈkäm-pən-ˌsāt-ər\ *n* — **com·pen·sa·to·ry** \kəm-ˈpen-sə-ˌtōr-ē, -ˌtȯr-\ *adj*

synonyms COMPENSATE, BALANCE, OFFSET mean to make up in one thing what is deficient or excessive in another. COMPENSATE implies making up a lack or making amends for loss or injury ⟨*compensated* for his lack of physical strength with dexterity⟩. BALANCE suggests the equalizing or adjusting of two things so that neither outweighs the other in effect ⟨the profits *balanced* the losses⟩. OFFSET implies neutralizing one thing's good or bad effect by something exerting an opposite effect ⟨his grumpiness was *offset* by a kind heart⟩. ***synonyms*** see in addition PAY

com·pen·sa·tion \ˌkäm-pən-ˈsā-shən\ *n* **1** : the act of compensating : the state of being compensated **2 a** : something that compensates; *esp* : payment to an unemployed or injured workers or their dependents **b** : SALARY, WAGES — **com·pen·sa·tion·al** \-shnəl, -shən-l\ *adj*

com·pete \kəm-ˈpēt\ *vi* : to strive for something (as position, profit, or a prize) for which another is also striving [Late Latin *competere* "to seek together," derived from Latin *com-* + *petere* "to go to, seek"]

com·pe·tence \ˈkäm-pət-əns\ *n* **1** : means sufficient for the necessities of life **2** : the quality or state of being competent

com·pe·ten·cy \-ən-sē\ *n* : COMPETENCE

com·pe·tent \ˈkäm-pət-ənt\ *adj* **1** : having the necessary ability or qualities : FIT ⟨a *competent* musician⟩ **2** : legally qualified ⟨a *competent* witness⟩ [Latin *competens,* from *competere* "to come together, be suitable," from *com-* + *petere* "to go to, seek"] ***synonyms*** see ABLE — **com•pe•tent•ly** *adv*

com•pe•ti•tion \ˌkäm-pə-ˈtish-ən\ *n* **1 :** the act or process of competing **2 :** a contest between rivals; *also* **:** one's competitors **3 :** the effort of two or more persons or firms acting independently to secure business by offering the most favorable terms **4 :** active demand by two or more organisms or kinds of organisms for some environmental resource in short supply — **com•pet•i•to•ry** \kəm-ˈpet-ə-ˌtōr-ē, -ˌtȯr-\ *adj*

com•pet•i•tive \kəm-ˈpet-ət-iv\ *adj* **:** relating to, characterized by, or based on competition ⟨*competitive* sports⟩ — **com•pet•i•tive•ly** *adv* — **com•pet•i•tive•ness** *n*

com•pet•i•tor \kəm-ˈpet-ət-ər\ *n* **:** one that competes: as **a :** RIVAL 1a **b :** one selling or buying goods or services in the same market as another **c :** an organism that lives in competition with another

com•pi•la•tion \ˌkäm-pə-ˈlā-shən\ *n* **1 :** the act or process of compiling **2 :** something compiled; *esp* **:** a book composed of materials gathered from other books or documents

com•pile \kəm-ˈpīl\ *vt* **1 :** to collect into a volume **2 :** to compose out of materials from other documents **3 :** to translate (as a computer program) with a compiler [Medieval French *compiler,* from Latin *compilare* "to plunder"]

com•pil•er \kəm-ˈpī-lər\ *n* **1 :** one that compiles **2 :** a computer program that automatically translates an entire set of instructions written in a computer language (as BASIC) into machine language

com•pla•cence \kəm-ˈplās-ns\ *n* **:** SELF-SATISFACTION

com•pla•cen•cy \-n-sē\ *n* **:** COMPLACENCE

com•pla•cent \kəm-ˈplās-nt\ *adj* **1 :** marked by complacence **:** SELF-SATISFIED ⟨a *complacent* smile⟩ **2 :** feeling or showing complaisance **3 :** UNCONCERNED [Latin *complacēre* "to please greatly," from *com-* + *placēre* "to please"] — **com•pla•cent•ly** *adv*

com•plain \kəm-ˈplān\ *vi* **1 :** to express grief, pain, or discontent **2 :** to make a formal accusation or charge [Medieval French *compleindre,* derived from Latin *com-* + *plangere* "to lament"] — **com•plain•er** *n* — **com•plain•ing•ly** \-ˈplā-ning-lē\ *adv*

com•plain•ant \kəm-ˈplā-nənt\ *n* **1 :** one that makes a complaint in a legal action or proceeding **2 :** one who complains

com•plaint \kəm-ˈplānt\ *n* **1 :** expression of grief, pain, or resentment **2 a :** a cause or reason for complaining **b :** a bodily ailment or disease **3 :** a formal charge against a person

com•plai•sance \kəm-ˈplās-ns, -ˈplāz-; ˌkäm-plā-ˈzans\ *n* **:** inclination to please or oblige

com•plai•sant \-nt; -ˈzant\ *adj* **:** marked by an inclination to please or oblige or consent to others' wishes [French, from Middle French *complaire* "to gratify, acquiesce," from Latin *complacēre* "to please greatly"] — **com•plai•sant•ly** *adv*

¹com•ple•ment \ˈkäm-plə-mənt\ *n* **1 :** something that fills up, completes, or makes perfect **2 :** full quantity, number, or amount ⟨a ship's *complement* of officers and crew⟩ **3 a :** an angle or arc that when added to a given angle or arc equals a right angle **b :** a subset that contains all the elements of a set that are not contained in a particular one of its subsets **4 :** an added word or group of words by which the predicate of a sentence is made complete ⟨*president* in "they elected me president" and *good* in "that is good" are different kinds of *complements*⟩ **5 :** a heat-sensitive substance in normal blood that in combination with antibodies destroys antigens [Latin *complementum,* from *complēre* "to complete"]

usage COMPLEMENT and COMPLIMENT are not synonyms but are easily confused. COMPLEMENT applies to a thing, quantity, or part required to make something complete or full ⟨fast baserunning is a fine *complement* to good hitting⟩. COMPLIMENT is an often formal expression of approval, praise, or greeting ⟨offered their *compliments* to the chef for the wonderful meal⟩.

²com•ple•ment \-ˌment\ *vt* **:** to be complementary to

com•ple•men•tal \ˌkäm-plə-ˈment-l\ *adj* **:** relating to or being a complement **:** COMPLEMENTARY

com•ple•men•ta•ry \ˌkäm-plə-ˈment-ə-rē, -ˈmen-trē\ *adj* **1 :** forming or serving as a complement **2 :** of or relating to the precise pairing of purine to pyrimidine bases between strands of DNA and sometimes RNA through which the structure of one strand determines the other — **complementary** *n*

complementary angles *n pl* **:** two angles whose sum is 90 degrees

complementary colors *n pl* **:** a pair of colors that when mixed in proper proportions produce a neutral color

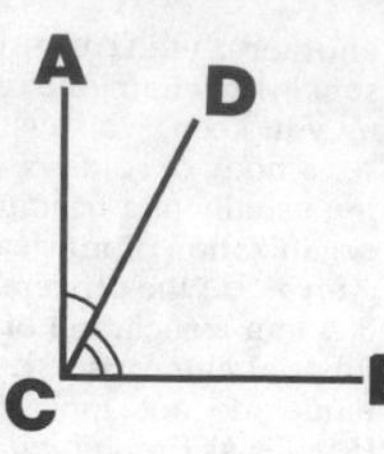

complementary angles: ACD and DCB

¹com•plete \kəm-ˈplēt\ *adj* **1 a :** possessing all necessary parts **:** ENTIRE **b :** having all four sets of floral organs **2 :** brought to an end **:** CONCLUDED **3 :** highly proficient ⟨a *complete* artist⟩ **4 a :** fully carried out **:** THOROUGH **b :** TOTAL, ABSOLUTE ⟨*complete* silence⟩ **c** *of a football pass* **:** legally caught [Latin *completus,* from *complēre* "to complete," from *com-* + *plēre* "to fill"] — **com•plete•ly** *adv* — **com•plete•ness** *n*

²complete *vt* **1 :** to bring to an end **:** accomplish or achieve fully ⟨*complete* a job⟩ **2 :** to make whole or perfect ⟨the shoes *complete* the outfit⟩ ***synonyms*** see FINISH

complete metamorphosis *n* **:** insect metamorphosis (as of a butterfly) in which there is a pupal stage between the immature stage and the adult and in which the young insect is very different in form from the adult — compare INCOMPLETE METAMORPHOSIS

complete protein *n* **:** protein (as in meat, fish, milk, and eggs) supplying all the amino acids that are needed by the human body but cannot be made by it

com•ple•tion \kəm-ˈplē-shən\ *n* **:** the act or process of completing **:** the state of being complete ⟨a job near *completion*⟩

¹com•plex \ˈkäm-ˌpleks\ *n* **1 :** a whole made up of complicated or interrelated parts ⟨the military-industrial *complex*⟩ **2 a :** a group of culture traits usually associated with a particular activity or process **b :** a system of repressed desires and memories that exerts a dominating influence upon the personality; *also* **:** an exaggerated reaction to or preoccupation with a subject or situation **c :** a group of obviously related units of which the degree and nature of the relationship is imperfectly known **3 :** a building or group of buildings housing related units ⟨an apartment *complex*⟩ [Late Latin *complexus* "totality," from Latin, "embrace," from *complecti* "to embrace, comprise," from *com-* + *plectere* "to braid"]

²com•plex \käm-ˈpleks, kəm-ˈ, ˈkäm-ˌ\ *adj* **1 :** composed of two or more parts ⟨a *complex* mixture⟩: as **a :** consisting of a main clause and one or more subordinate clauses ⟨*complex* sentence⟩ **b :** formed by union of simpler substances ⟨a *complex* protein⟩ **2 :** having many interrelated parts, patterns, or elements that are hard to separate, analyze, or solve **3 :** of or relating to complex numbers [Latin *complexus,* past participle of *complecti* "to embrace, comprise"] — **com•plex•ly** *adv* — **com•plex•ness** *n*

synonyms COMPLEX, COMPLICATED, INTRICATE, INVOLVED mean having confusingly interrelated parts. COMPLEX suggests an unavoidable and necessary lack of simplicity and does not imply a fault or failure in designing or arranging ⟨a *complex* recipe⟩. COMPLICATED applies to what offers difficulty in understanding, explaining, or solving ⟨a *complicated* math problem⟩. INTRICATE implies an interlacing of parts that can scarcely be grasped or traced separately ⟨an *intricate* web of deceit⟩. INVOLVED implies extreme complication and often suggests disorder ⟨a rambling, *involved* explanation⟩.

complex carbohydrate *n* **:** a polysaccharide (as starch) consisting of usually hundreds or thousands of monosaccharide units; *also* **:** a food (as rice or pasta) composed primarily of such polysaccharides

complex fraction *n* **:** a fraction with a fraction or mixed number in the numerator or denominator or both — compare SIMPLE FRACTION

com•plex•ion \kəm-ˈplek-shən\ *n* **1 :** natural disposition **:** TEMPERAMENT **2 :** the hue or appearance of the skin especially of the face ⟨a dark *complexion*⟩ **3 :** general appearance or impression **:** CHARACTER [Medieval Latin *complexio* "combination of qualities that determines temperament," from Latin, "combination," from *complecti* "to comprise"] — **com•plex•ioned** \-shənd\ *adj*

com•plex•i•ty \kəm-ˈplek-sət-ē, käm-\ *n, pl* **-ties** **1 :** something complex ⟨the *complexities* of the English language⟩ **2 :** the quality or state of being complex

complex number *n* **:** a number of the form $a + b\sqrt{-1}$ where a and b are real numbers

complex plane *n* : a coordinate plane on which complex numbers are represented as points

com·pli·ance \kəm-ˈplī-əns\ *n* **1** : the act or process of complying **2** : a readiness or disposition to yield to others — **in compliance with** : in agreement with : in obedience to

com·pli·an·cy \-ən-sē\ *n* : COMPLIANCE

com·pli·ant \-ənt\ *adj* : ready or disposed to comply : SUBMISSIVE — **com·pli·ant·ly** *adv*

com·pli·cate \ˈkäm-plə-ˌkāt\ *vb* : to make or become complex, intricate, or difficult [Latin *complicare* "to fold together," from *com-* + *plicare* "to fold"]

com·pli·cat·ed *adj* **1** : consisting of parts intricately combined **2** : difficult to analyze, understand, or explain ***synonyms*** see COMPLEX — **com·pli·cat·ed·ly** *adv* — **com·pli·cat·ed·ness** *n*

com·pli·ca·tion \ˌkäm-plə-ˈkā-shən\ *n* **1 a** : a situation or a detail of character complicating the main thread of a plot **b** : a making difficult, involved, or intricate **c** : a complex or intricate feature or element **d** : something that makes a situation more complicated or difficult **2** : a secondary disease or condition developing in the course of a primary disease

com·plic·i·ty \kəm-ˈplis-ət-ē\ *n, pl* **-ties** : association or participation in a wrongful act [French *complicité,* from *complice* "associate, accomplice," from Late Latin *complex* "partner," from Latin *complicare* "to fold together"]

[1]**com·pli·ment** \ˈkäm-plə-mənt\ *n* **1** : an expression of esteem, respect, affection, or admiration; *esp* : a flattering remark **2** *pl* : best wishes : REGARDS [Middle French, from Italian *complimento,* from Spanish *cumplimiento,* from *cumplir* "to comply, be courteous"] ***usage*** see COMPLEMENT

[2]**com·pli·ment** \-ˌment\ *vt* : to pay a compliment to

com·pli·men·ta·ry \ˌkäm-plə-ˈment-ə-rē, -ˈmen-trē\ *adj* **1** : expressing or containing a compliment ⟨a *complimentary* remark⟩ **2** : given free as a courtesy or favor ⟨a *complimentary* ticket⟩ — **com·pli·men·tar·i·ly** \-ˌmen-ˈter-ə-lē\ *adv*

com·pline \ˈkäm-plən, -ˌplīn\ *n* : the last of the canonical hours [Medieval French *cumplie,* from Late Latin *completa,* from Latin *completus* "complete"]

com·ply \kəm-ˈplī\ *vi* **com·plied; com·ply·ing** : to conform, submit, or adapt (as to a regulation or to another's wishes) as required or requested ⟨*comply* with federal law⟩ ⟨*comply* with a request⟩ [Italian *complire,* from Spanish *cumplir* "to perform what is due, comply, be courteous," from Latin *complēre* "to complete"] — **com·pli·er** \-ˈplī-ər, -ˈplīr\ *n*

[1]**com·po·nent** \kəm-ˈpō-nənt, ˈkäm-ˌ, käm-ˈ\ *n* **1** : a constituent part : INGREDIENT ⟨the *components* of a solution⟩ **2 a** : any one of the vector terms added to form a vector sum or resultant **b** : a coordinate of a vector [Latin *componere* "to put together," from *com-* + *ponere* "to put"] ***synonyms*** see ELEMENT — **com·po·nen·tial** \ˌkäm-pə-ˈnen-chəl\ *adj*

[2]**component** *adj* : being or forming a part : CONSTITUENT ⟨the *component* parts of a machine⟩

com·port \kəm-ˈpōrt, -ˈpȯrt\ *vb* **1** : to be fitting : ACCORD ⟨actions that *comport* with the rules⟩ **2** : CONDUCT ⟨*comport* oneself with dignity⟩ [Middle French *comporter* "to bear, conduct," from Latin *comportare* "to bring together," from *com-* + *portare* "to carry"]

com·port·ment \kəm-ˈpōrt-mənt, -ˈpȯrt-\ *n* : BEHAVIOR, BEARING

com·pose \kəm-ˈpōz\ *vb* **1 a** : to form by putting together : FASHION **b** : to make up : CONSTITUTE ⟨a cake *composed* of many ingredients⟩ **c** : to assemble the characters of (text) in order for printing : SET **2** : to create by mental or artistic labor ⟨*compose* a song⟩ **3** : to reduce to a minimum ⟨*compose* their differences⟩ **4** : to arrange in proper form **5** : to free from agitation : CALM ⟨*composed* herself⟩ [Medieval French *composer,* from Latin *componere,* from *com-* + *ponere* "to put"]

com·posed \-ˈpōzd\ *adj* : free from agitation : CALM; *esp* : SELF-POSSESSED — **com·pos·ed·ly** \-ˈpō-zəd-lē\ *adv* — **com·pos·ed·ness** \-ˈpō-zəd-nəs\ *n*

com·pos·er \kəm-ˈpō-zər\ *n* : one that composes; *esp* : a person who writes music

[1]**com·pos·ite** \käm-ˈpäz-ət, kəm-\ *adj* **1** : made up of various distinct parts or elements ⟨a *composite* photograph⟩ **2** : of or relating to a large family (Compositae) of dicotyledonous trees, shrubs, and herbs (as the dandelion, sunflower, and zinnia) characterized by florets arranged in dense heads that resemble single flowers ⟨the daisy and other *composite* plants⟩ **3** : able to be factored into two or more prime factors other than 1 and itself ⟨12 is a *composite* number since 2 × 2 × 3 = 12⟩ [Latin *compositus,* past participle of *componere* "to compose"] — **com·pos·ite·ly** *adv*

[2]**composite** *n* **1** : something that is made up of different parts : COMPOUND **2** : a composite plant **3** : a structural material made of plastic and an embedded fibrous material

com·po·si·tion \ˌkäm-pə-ˈzish-ən\ *n* **1 a** : the act or process of composing **b** : the composing of matter to be printed **2** : the manner in which the parts of a thing are put together : MAKEUP ⟨the *composition* of a painting⟩ **3** : the makeup of a compound or mixture ⟨the *composition* of rubber⟩ **4** : a product of combining various ingredients : COMBINATION ⟨a *composition* made of several different metals⟩ **5** : a literary, musical, or artistic production; *esp* : a short piece of writing done as an educational exercise ⟨must write one *composition* each week⟩ — **com·po·si·tion·al** \-ˈzish-nəl, -ən-l\ *adj*

com·pos·i·tor \kəm-ˈpäz-ət-ər\ *n* : one who sets type

[1]**com·post** \ˈkäm-ˌpōst\ *n* : a mixture largely of decayed organic matter (as leaves or grass clippings) used for fertilizing and conditioning land [Medieval Latin *compostum,* from Latin *componere* "to put together"]

[2]**compost** *vt* : to convert (as plant debris) to compost

com·po·sure \kəm-ˈpō-zhər\ *n* : calmness or repose especially of mind, bearing, or appearance : SELF-POSSESSION

com·pote \ˈkäm-ˌpōt\ *n* **1** : fruits cooked in syrup **2** : a bowl usually with a base and stem from which compotes, fruits, nuts, or sweets are served [French, from Medieval French *composte,* derived from Latin *componere* "to put together, compose"]

[1]**com·pound** \käm-ˈpau̇nd, kəm-ˈ, ˈkäm-ˌ\ *vb* **1** : to put together or be joined to form a whole : COMBINE **2** : to form by combining parts ⟨*compound* a medicine⟩ **3** : to settle peaceably : COMPROMISE **4 a** : to pay (interest) on both the accrued interest and the principal ⟨*compound* interest quarterly⟩ **b** : to add to **5** : to agree for a consideration not to prosecute (an offense) ⟨*compound* a felony⟩ [Medieval French *compondre,* from Latin *componere* "to put together, compose"] — **com·pound·able** \-ə-bəl\ *adj* — **com·pound·er** *n*

[2]**com·pound** \ˈkäm-ˌpau̇nd, käm-ˈ, kəm-ˈ\ *adj* **1 a** : made up of or by the union of separate elements or parts ⟨a *compound* substance⟩ **b** : composed of united similar elements especially of a kind usually independent ⟨a *compound* fruit⟩ **c** : having the blade divided to the midrib and forming two or more leaflets on a common axis ⟨a *compound* leaf⟩ **2** : involving or used in a combination : COMPOSITE **3 a** : being a word that is a compound ⟨the *compound* noun *steamboat*⟩ **b** : consisting of two or more main clauses ⟨a *compound* sentence⟩

[3]**com·pound** \ˈkäm-ˌpau̇nd\ *n* **1 a** : a word consisting of components that are words ⟨*rowboat, high school,* and *light-year* are *compounds*⟩ **b** : a word consisting of any of various combinations of words, word elements, or affixes ⟨*anthropology, kilocycle,* and *builder* are *compounds*⟩ **2** : something formed by a union of elements, ingredients, or parts; *esp* : a distinct substance formed by the union of two or more chemical elements in definite proportion by weight

[4]**com·pound** \ˈkäm-ˌpau̇nd\ *n* : a large fenced or walled-in area [by folk etymology from Malay *kampung* "group of buildings, village"]

compound–complex *adj* : having two or more main clauses and one or more subordinate clauses ⟨*compound-complex* sentence⟩

compound eye *n* : an eye (as of an insect) made up of many separate visual units

compound fracture *n* : a breaking of a bone in such a way as to produce an open wound through which bone fragments stick out — compare SIMPLE FRACTURE

compound interest *n* : interest paid or to be paid both on the principal and on accumulated interest

compound microscope *n* : a microscope consisting of an objective and an eyepiece mounted in a drawtube

com·pre·hend \ˌkäm-pri-ˈhend\ *vt* **1** : to grasp the meaning of : UNDERSTAND **2** : to take in : EMBRACE [Latin *comprehendere,* from *com-* + *prehendere* "to grasp"] ***synonyms*** see COMPRISE, INCLUDE — **com·pre·hend·ible** \-ˈhen-də-bəl\ *adj*

com·pre·hen·si·ble \-ˈhen-sə-bəl\ *adj* : capable of being comprehended : INTELLIGIBLE — **com·pre·hen·si·bil·i·ty** \-ˌhen-sə-ˈbil-ət-ē\ *n* — **com·pre·hen·si·bly** \-ˈhen-sə-blē\ *adv*

com·pre·hen·sion \ˌkäm-pri-ˈhen-chən\ *n* **1 a** : the act or process of including or comprising **b** : COMPREHENSIVENESS **2 a** : the act or action of grasping with the intellect **b** : knowledge gained by comprehending **c** : the capacity for understanding [Latin *comprehensio,* from *comprehendere* "to comprehend"]

com·pre·hen·sive \-ˈhen-siv\ *adj* **1** : covering broadly or completely : INCLUSIVE ⟨*comprehensive* insurance⟩ ⟨a *comprehensive* examination⟩ **2** : having or showing wide mental comprehension ⟨*comprehensive* knowledge⟩ — **com·pre·hen·sive·ly** *adv* — **com·pre·hen·sive·ness** *n*

[1]**com·press** \kəm-ˈpres\ *vb* **1** : to press or become pressed together **2** : to reduce the size, quantity, or volume of by or as if by pressure [Late Latin *compressare* "to press hard," from *comprimere* "to compress," from *com-* + *premere* "to press"] ***synonyms*** see CONDENSE

[2]**com·press** \ˈkäm-ˌpres\ *n* **1** : a folded cloth or pad applied so as to press upon a body part ⟨a cold *compress*⟩ **2** : a machine for compressing cotton into bales

com·pressed \kəm-ˈprest, ˈkäm-ˌ\ *adj* : flattened as though subjected to compression: **a** : flattened laterally ⟨stems *compressed*⟩ **b** : narrow from side to side and deep in a dorsoventral direction ⟨a *compressed* fish⟩

compressed air *n* : air under pressure greater than that of the atmosphere

com·press·ible \kəm-ˈpres-ə-bəl\ *adj* : capable of being compressed — **com·press·ibil·i·ty** \-ˌpres-ə-ˈbil-ət-ē\ *n*

com·pres·sion \kəm-ˈpresh-ən\ *n* **1** : the act or process of compressing : the state of being compressed **2** : the process of compressing the fuel mixture in the cylinders of an internal-combustion engine (as of an automobile) — **com·pres·sion·al** \-ˈpresh-nəl, -ən-l\ *adj* — **com·pres·sive** \-ˈpres-iv\ *adj*

com·pres·sor \-ˈpres-ər\ *n* **1** : one that compresses **2** : a machine that compresses gases and especially air

com·prise \kəm-ˈprīz\ *vt* **1** : to include especially within a particular scope : CONTAIN ⟨the test *comprised* two essay questions⟩ **2** : to be made up of ⟨the play *comprises* three acts⟩ **3** : to make up : CONSTITUTE ⟨nine players *comprise* a baseball team⟩ [Medieval French *compris,* past participle of *comprendre* "to include, comprehend," from Latin *comprehendere*]

synonyms COMPRISE, INCLUDE, COMPREHEND, EMBRACE mean to take in or contain within one unit or boundary. COMPRISE implies that the list of parts or members is complete ⟨New York City *comprises* the boroughs Manhattan, Brooklyn, Queens, Staten Island, and the Bronx⟩. INCLUDE suggests that something is part of a larger whole, but does not imply that all constituent members are presently specified ⟨the price of dinner *includes* dessert⟩. COMPREHEND implies that something falls within the scope of a whole ⟨a view *comprehending* parts of three states⟩. EMBRACE implies a gathering of several items into a whole ⟨their philosophy *embraced* several schools of thought⟩.

[1]**com·pro·mise** \ˈkäm-prə-ˌmīz\ *n* **1** : a settlement of a dispute by each party giving up some demands **2** : a giving up to something that is wrong or degrading ⟨a *compromise* of one's principles⟩ **3** : an agreement reached as a result of a compromise ⟨the Missouri *Compromise*⟩ [Medieval French *compromisse,* from Latin *compromissum,* from *compromittere* "to promise mutually," from *com-* + *promittere* "to promise"]

[2]**compromise** *vb* **1** : to adjust or settle differences by means of a compromise **2** : to expose to discredit, suspicion, or danger ⟨*compromised* his reputation⟩ **3** : to make unworthy compromises ⟨wouldn't *compromise* with their principles⟩ — **com·pro·mis·er** *n*

comp·trol·ler \kən-ˈtrō-lər, ˈkäm-ˌ, ˈkämp-ˌ, käm-ˈ, kämp-ˈ\ *n* **1** : a public official who audits government accounts and sometimes certifies expenditures **2** : CONTROLLER 1b [Middle English, alteration of *conterroller* "controller"] — **comp·trol·ler·ship** \-ˌship\ *n*

com·pul·sion \kəm-ˈpəl-shən\ *n* **1 a** : an act of compelling : the state of being compelled **b** : a force or agency that compels **2** : an irresistible persistent impulse to do something (as wash the hands) [Late Latin *compulsio,* from Latin *compellere* "to compel"]

com·pul·sive \-ˈpəl-siv\ *adj* **1** : having power to compel **2** : of, relating to, or caused by compulsion ⟨*compulsive* behavior⟩ — **com·pul·sive·ly** *adv* — **com·pul·sive·ness** *n*

com·pul·so·ry \-ˈpəls-rē, -ə-rē\ *adj* **1** : required by authority ⟨*compulsory* education⟩ **2** : having the power of compelling ⟨a *compulsory* law⟩

com·punc·tion \kəm-ˈpəng-shən, -ˈpəngk-\ *n* **1** : anxiety caused by a sense of guilt **2** : a passing feeling of regret for some slight wrong [Late Latin *compunctio,* from Latin *compungere* "to prick hard, sting," from *com-* + *pungere* "to prick"] ***synonyms*** see QUALM — **com·punc·tious** \-shəs\ *adj*

com·pu·ta·tion \ˌkäm-pyu̇-ˈtā-shən\ *n* **1** : the act or action of computing : CALCULATION **2** : a system of calculating especially by mathematical means **3** : an amount computed — **com·pu·ta·tion·al** \-shnəl, -shən-l\ *adj*

com·pute \kəm-ˈpyüt\ *vb* : to determine or calculate especially by mathematical means; *also* : to determine or calculate by means of a computer [Latin *computare,* from *com-* + *putare* "to consider"] — **com·put·able** \-ˈpyüt-ə-bəl\ *adj*

computed to·mog·ra·phy \-tō-ˈmäg-rə-fē\ *n* : radiography in which a three-dimensional image of a body structure is constructed by computer from a series of cross-sectional images made along an axis — called also *computerized tomography*

com·put·er \-ˈpyüt-ər\ *n* : one that computes; *esp* : an automatic electronic machine that can store, retrieve, and process data

com·put·er·ize \-ə-ˌrīz\ *vt* **1** : to carry out, control, or conduct by means of a computer **2** : to equip with computers **3 a** : to store in a computer **b** : to put into a form a computer can use — **com·put·er·i·za·tion** \-ˌpyüt-ə-rə-ˈzā-shən\ *n*

computer science *n* : a branch of science that deals with the theory of computing or the design of computers

com·rade \ˈkäm-ˌrad, -rəd\ *n* **1 a** : an intimate friend or associate : COMPANION **b** : a fellow soldier **2** : COMMUNIST [Middle French *camarade* "group sleeping in one room, companion," from Spanish *camarada,* from *cámara* "room," from Late Latin *camera;* sense 2 from its use as a form of address by Communists]

com·rade·ship \-ˌship\ *n* : FELLOWSHIP 1, FRIENDSHIP

[1]**con** \ˈkän\ *vt* **conned; con·ning** **1** : to study carefully : PERUSE **2** : MEMORIZE [Middle English *connen* "to know, study," alteration of *cunnen* "to know," infinitive of *can*]

[2]**con** *adv* : on the negative side : in opposition [short for *contra*]

[3]**con** *n* **1** : an opposing argument, person, or position **2** : the negative position or one holding it

[4]**con** *adj* : CONFIDENCE ⟨a *con* game⟩

[5]**con** *vt* **conned; con·ning** **1** : SWINDLE **2** : COAX, CAJOLE

[6]**con** *n* : CONVICT

con- — see COM-

con amo·re \ˌkän-ə-ˈmōr-ē, ˌkō-nə-ˈmōr-ˌā, -ˈmȯr-\ *adv* **1** : with love, devotion, or zest **2** : TENDERLY — used as a direction in music [Italian, "with love"]

con·cat·e·nate \kän-ˈkat-ə-ˌnāt\ *vt* : to link together in a series or chain [Late Latin *concatenare,* from Latin *com-* + *catena* "chain"] — **con·cat·e·na·tion** \ˌkän-ˌkat-ə-ˈnā-shən\ *n*

con·cave \kän-ˈkāv, ˈkän-ˌ\ *adj* : hollowed or rounded inward like the inside of a bowl [Latin *concavus,* from *com-* + *cavus* "hollow"] — **con·cave·ly** *adv* — **con·cave·ness** *n*

con·cav·i·ty \kän-ˈkav-ət-ē\ *n, pl* **-ties** **1** : a concave surface or space : HOLLOW **2** : the quality or state of being concave

con·cavo–con·vex \kän-ˌkā-vō-kän-ˈveks, -kən-, -ˈkän-ˌveks\ *adj* **1** : concave on one side and convex on the other **2** : having the concave side of greater curvature than the convex

con·ceal \kən-ˈsēl\ *vt* **1** : to keep secret ⟨*conceal* the truth⟩ **2** : to hide from sight ⟨a *concealed* weapon⟩ [Medieval French *conceler,* from Latin *concelare,* from *com-* + *celare* "to hide"] ***synonyms*** see HIDE — **con·ceal·able** \-ə-bəl\ *adj* — **con·ceal·er** *n*

con·ceal·ment \-mənt\ *n* **1** : the act of hiding : the state of being hidden **2** : a hiding place

con·cede \kən-ˈsēd\ *vb* **1** : to grant as a right or privilege **2** : to acknowledge or admit grudgingly : YIELD [Latin *concedere,* from *com-* + *cedere* "to yield, cede"] ***synonyms*** see GRANT — **con·ced·ed·ly** \-ˈsēd-əd-lē\ *adv* — **con·ced·er** *n*

con·ceit \kən-ˈsēt\ *n* **1** : excessive pride in one's own worth or virtue **2 a** : a fanciful idea **b** : an elaborate metaphor [Medieval French *conceite* "idea," from *conceivre* "to conceive"]

con·ceit·ed \-ˈsēt-əd\ *adj* : having or showing a very high opinion of oneself — **con·ceit·ed·ly** *adv* — **con·ceit·ed·ness** *n*

con·ceiv·able \kən-ˈsē-və-bəl\ *adj* : capable of being conceived : IMAGINABLE — **con·ceiv·ably** \-blē\ *adv*

con·ceive \kən-ˈsēv\ *vb* **1 :** to become pregnant or pregnant with ‹*conceive* a child› **2 a :** to take into the mind ‹*conceived* a liking for the singer› **b :** to form an idea of : IMAGINE ‹*conceive* a new design› **3 :** to have as an opinion : THINK ‹not likely to *conceive* of me as a genius› [Middle English *conceiven,* from Medieval French *conceivre,* from Latin *concipere,* from *com-* + *capere* "to take"] — **con·ceiv·er** *n*

1**con·cen·trate** \ˈkän-sən-ˌtrāt\ *vb* **1 a :** to bring, direct, or come toward a common center or objective ‹*concentrate* one's efforts› **b :** to gather into one body, mass, or force **2 :** to make stronger by removing something unwanted ‹*concentrate* ore› **3 :** to fix one's powers, efforts, or attention on one thing ‹*concentrate* on a problem› [*com-* + Latin *centrum* "center"] — **con·cen·tra·tor** \-ˌtrāt-ər\ *n*

2**concentrate** *n* **:** something concentrated ‹frozen orange juice *concentrate*›

con·cen·tra·tion \ˌkän-sən-ˈtrā-shən\ *n* **1 :** the act or process of concentrating : the state of being concentrated; *esp* : direction of attention on a single object **2 :** a concentrated mass **3 :** the relative amount of an ingredient : STRENGTH ‹the *concentration* of salt in a solution›

concentration camp *n* **:** a camp where persons (as prisoners of war or political prisoners) are detained or confined

con·cen·tric \kən-ˈsen-trik, ˈkän-\ *adj* **:** having a common center ‹*concentric* circles› [Medieval Latin *concentricus,* from Latin *com-* + *centrum* "center"] — **con·cen·tri·cal·ly** \-tri-kə-lē, -klē\ *adv* — **con·cen·tric·i·ty** \ˌkän-ˌsen-ˈtris-ət-ē\ *n*

con·cept \ˈkän-ˌsept\ *n* **1 :** something conceived in the mind : THOUGHT, NOTION **2 :** an abstract idea generalized from particular instances [Latin *conceptum,* neuter of *conceptus,* past participle of *concipere* "to conceive"] ***synonyms*** see IDEA

con·cep·tion \kən-ˈsep-shən\ *n* **1 :** the beginning of pregnancy : the formation of a zygote **2 a :** the function or process of forming or understanding ideas or abstractions or their symbols **b :** a general idea : CONCEPT **3 :** the originating of something (as a plan) in the mind ***synonyms*** see IDEA — **con·cep·tion·al** \-shnəl, -shən-l\ *adj* — **con·cep·tive** \-ˈsep-tiv\ *adj*

con·cep·tu·al \kən-ˈsep-chə-wəl, -chəl\ *adj* **:** of, relating to, or consisting of concepts — **con·cep·tu·al·ly** \-ē\ *adv*

1**con·cern** \kən-ˈsərn\ *vt* **1 :** to relate to : be about ‹the novel *concerns* three soldiers› **2 :** to be the business or affair of : AFFECT ‹the problem *concerns* us all› **3 :** to make anxious or worried ‹our mother's illness *concerns* us› **4 :** INVOLVE, OCCUPY ‹*concerned* himself in the matter› [Medieval Latin *concernere,* from Late Latin, "to sift together, mingle," from Latin *com-* + *cernere* "to sift"]

2**concern** *n* **1 :** a state of interest and uncertainty : ANXIETY ‹showed deep *concern* for their friend's welfare› ‹public *concern* over the threat of war› **2 :** something that relates to or involves one : AFFAIR ‹the usual *concerns* of the day› **3 :** a business or manufacturing establishment

con·cerned \-ˈsərnd\ *adj* **1 :** ANXIOUS 1 ‹*concerned* for their safety› **2 :** interestedly engaged

con·cern·ing \-ˈsər-niŋ\ *prep* **:** relating to ‹news *concerning* friends›

con·cern·ment \-ˈsərn-mənt\ *n* **1 :** something in which one is concerned **2 :** IMPORTANCE 1

1**con·cert** \ˈkän-ˌsərt, -sərt\ *n* **1 :** agreement in design or plan ‹work in *concert*› **2 :** a musical performance of some length by several voices or instruments or both [Middle French, from Italian, from *concertare* "to concert"] — **concert** *adj* — **in concert :** TOGETHER

2**con·cert** \kən-ˈsərt\ *vb* **:** to plan or arrange together : settle by agreement ‹the allies *concerted* their tactics› [Middle French *concerter,* from Italian *concertare,* perhaps from *com-* + *certo* "certain, decided," from Latin *certus*]

con·cert·ed \kən-ˈsərt-əd\ *adj* **1 a :** mutually planned or agreed on ‹*concerted* effort› **b :** performed in unison ‹*concerted* artillery fire› **2 :** arranged in parts for several voices ‹*concerted* music›

con·cer·ti·na \ˌkän-sər-ˈtē-nə\ *n* **:** a musical instrument of the accordion family

con·cer·ti·no \ˌkän-chər-ˈtē-nō\ *n, pl* **-nos :** a short concerto [It]

con·cert·mas·ter \ˈkän-sərt-ˌmas-tər\ *or* **con·cert·meis·ter** \-ˌmī-stər\ *n* **:** the leader of the first violins and assistant conductor

con·cer·to \kən-ˈchert-ō\ *n, pl* **-tos** *or* **-ti** \-ē\ **:** a piece for one or more soloists and orchestra usually in symphonic form with three contrasting movements [Italian, from *concerto* "concert"]

concertina

con·ces·sion \kən-ˈsesh-ən\ *n* **1 :** the act or an instance of conceding **2 :** something conceded: **a :** ACKNOWLEDGMENT, ADMISSION ‹a *concession* of guilt› **b :** a grant of property or of a right by a government ‹a mining *concession*› **c :** a lease of a part of premises for some purpose ‹a *concession* to sell souvenirs›; *also* : the part leased or the activities carried on [Latin *concessio,* from *concedere* "to concede"]

con·ces·sion·aire \kən-ˌsesh-ə-ˈnaər, -ˈneər\ *n* **:** one that owns or operates a concession [French *concessionnaire,* from *concession* "concession"]

con·ces·sive \kən-ˈses-iv\ *adj* **:** tending toward, expressing, or being a concession — **con·ces·sive·ly** *adv*

conch \ˈkäŋk, ˈkänch\ *n, pl* **conchs** \ˈkäŋks\ *or* **conch·es** \ˈkän-chəz\ **1 :** a large spiral-shelled marine gastropod mollusk; *also* : its shell used especially for cameos **2 :** 1CONCHA [Latin *concha* "mussel, mussel shell," from Greek *konchē*]

1**con·cha** \ˈkäŋ-kə\ *n, pl* **con·chae** \-ˌkē, -ˌkī\ **:** the largest and deepest concavity of the external ear [Latin, "shell"]

2**con·cha** \ˈkän-chə\ *also* **con·cho** \-chōl\ *n* **:** an ornamental disk (as on clothing) of American Indian origin featuring a shell or flower design [American Spanish *concha,* from Spanish, "shell," derived from Latin *concha*]

con·chol·o·gy \käŋ-ˈkäl-ə-jē\ *n* **:** a branch of zoology that deals with shells

con·cierge \kōⁿ-ˈsyerzh\ *n* **:** an attendant at the entrance of a building especially in France who oversees people coming or going, handles mail, and acts as a janitor or porter [French, from Medieval French, probably derived from Latin *conservus* "fellow slave," from *com-* + *servus* "slave"]

con·cil·i·ate \kən-ˈsil-ē-ˌāt\ *vt* **1 :** to bring into agreement or harmony : RECONCILE **2 :** to gain the goodwill or favor of [Latin *conciliare* "to assemble, unite, win over," from *concilium* "assembly, council"] — **con·cil·i·a·tion** \-ˌsil-ē-ˈā-shən\ *n* — **con·cil·i·a·tor** \-ˈsil-ē-ˌāt-ər\ *n* — **con·cil·ia·to·ry** \-ˈsil-yə-ˌtōr-ē, -ˈsil-ē-ə-, -ˌtȯr-\ *adj*

con·cise \kən-ˈsīs\ *adj* **:** marked by brevity of expression or statement ‹a *concise* summary› [Latin *concisus,* from *concidere* "to cut up," from *com-* + *caedere* "to cut"] — **con·cise·ly** *adv* — **con·cise·ness** *n*

con·clave \ˈkän-ˌklāv\ *n* **1 :** a private meeting or secret assembly; *esp* : a meeting of Roman Catholic cardinals to choose a pope **2 :** a gathering of a group : CONVENTION [Medieval Latin, from Latin, "room that can be locked up," from *com-* + *clavis* "key"] — **con·clav·ist** \-ˌklā-vəst\ *n*

con·clude \kən-ˈklüd\ *vb* **1 :** to bring or come to an end : FINISH ‹*conclude* a speech› **2 :** to form an opinion : decide by reasoning ‹*conclude* that a statement is true› **3 :** to bring about as a result : ARRANGE ‹*conclude* an agreement› [Latin *concludere* "to shut up, end, infer," from *com-* + *claudere* "to shut"] ***synonyms*** see CLOSE — **con·clud·er** *n*

con·clu·sion \kən-ˈklü-zhən\ *n* **1 a :** a reasoned judgment : INFERENCE **b :** the necessary consequence of two or more propositions taken as premises **2 :** the last part of something: as **a :** a final result : OUTCOME **b :** a final summing up **3 :** an act or instance of concluding [Latin *conclusio,* from *concludere* "to conclude"]

con·clu·sive \kən-ˈklü-siv, -ziv\ *adj* **:** involving a conclusion or decision : DECISIVE, FINAL ‹*conclusive* proof› — **con·clu·sive·ly** *adv* — **con·clu·sive·ness** *n*

con·coct \kən-ˈkäkt, kän-\ *vt* **1 :** to prepare by combining various ingredients ‹*concoct* a stew› **2 :** to make up : INVENT ‹*concoct* a likely story› [Latin *concoquere* "to cook together," from *com-* + *coquere* "to cook"] — **con·coct·er** *n* — **con·coc·tion** \-ˈkäk-shən\ *n* — **con·coc·tive** \-ˈkäk-tiv\ *adj*

con·com·i·tant \kən-ˈkäm-ət-ənt, kän-\ *adj* **:** accompanying es-

\ə\ abut	\au̇\ out	\i\ tip	\ȯ\ saw	\u̇\ foot
\ər\ further	\ch\ chin	\ī\ life	\ȯi\ coin	\y\ yet
\a\ mat	\e\ pet	\j\ job	\th\ thin	\yü\ few
\ā\ take	\ē\ easy	\ŋ\ sing	\t͟h\ this	\yu̇\ cure
\ä\ cot, cart	\g\ go	\ō\ bone	\ü\ food	\zh\ vision

pecially in a subordinate or incidental way [Latin *concomitari* "to accompany," from *com-* + *comit-, comes* "companion"] — concomitant *n* — **con·com·i·tant·ly** *adv*

con·cord \'kän-ˌkȯrd, 'käng-\ *n* **1 a** : a state of agreement : HARMONY **b** : a harmonious combination of tones heard together **2** : agreement by covenant or treaty [Medieval French *concorde,* from Latin *concordia,* from *concord-, concors* "agreeing," from *com-* + *cord-, cor* "heart"]

con·cor·dance \kən-'kȯrd-ns\ *n* **1** : an alphabetical index of the principal words in a book or in the works of an author with their contexts **2** : CONCORD

con·cor·dant \-nt\ *adj* : marked by harmony : CONSONANT — **con·cor·dant·ly** *adv*

con·cor·dat \kən-'kȯr-ˌdat\ *n* : a compact or covenant especially between a pope and a government about church affairs [French, derived from Latin *concors* "agreeing"]

con·course \'kän-ˌkōrs, 'käng-, -ˌkȯrs\ *n* **1** : a gathering together ⟨a great *concourse* of people⟩ **2** : a place (as a boulevard, open area, or hall) where many people pass or congregate ⟨met in the *concourse* of the bus terminal⟩ [Latin *concursus,* from *concurrere* "to run together, concur"]

con·cres·cence \kən-'kres-ns, kän-\ *n* : a growing together : COALESCENCE [Latin *concrescentia,* from *concrescere* "to grow together"] — **con·cres·cent** \-nt\ *adj*

[1]**con·crete** \kän-'krēt, 'kän-ˌ\ *adj* **1** : naming a real thing or class of things : not abstract ⟨a *concrete* noun⟩ **2 a** : belonging to or derived from actual experience ⟨*concrete* examples⟩ **b** : existing in fact : REAL ⟨*concrete* evidence⟩ **3** \'kän-ˌ, kän-'\ : relating to or made of concrete ⟨a *concrete* mixer⟩ [Latin *concretus* "formed by coalition of particles, concrete," from *concrescere* "to grow together," from *com-* + *crescere* "to grow"] — **con·crete·ly** *adv* — **con·crete·ness** *n*

[2]**con·crete** \'kän-ˌkrēt, kän-'\ *n* : a hard strong building material made by mixing cement, sand, and gravel with sufficient water to cause the cement to set and bind the entire mass

[3]**con·crete** \'kän-ˌkrēt, kän-'\ *vb* **1** : to form into a solid mass : SOLIDIFY **2** : to cover with, form of, or set in concrete

con·cre·tion \kän-'krē-shən, kən-\ *n* **1** : the act or process of solidifying **2** : something solidified; *esp* : a hard usually inorganic mass formed in a living body — **con·cre·tion·ary** \-shə-ˌner-ē\ *adj*

con·cu·bine \'käng-kyə-ˌbīn, 'kän-\ *n* : a woman who lives with a man and among some peoples has a legally recognized position in his household less than that of a wife [Latin *concubina,* from *com-* + *cubare* "to lie"] — **con·cu·bi·nage** \kän-'kyü-bə-nij, kən-\ *n*

con·cu·pis·cence \kän-'kyü-pə-səns, kən-\ *n* : ardent desire; *esp* : sexual desire [derived from Latin *concupiscere* "to desire ardently," from *com-* + *cupere* "to desire"] — **con·cu·pis·cent** \-sənt\ *adj*

con·cur \kən-'kər, kän-\ *vi* **con·curred; con·cur·ring** **1** : to act together to a common end or single effect **2** : to be in agreement : ACCORD ⟨four justices *concurred* in the decision⟩ **3** : to happen together : COINCIDE [Latin *concurrere,* from *com-* + *currere* "to run"]

con·cur·rence \kən-'kər-əns, -'kə-rəns\ *n* **1 a** : agreement in action, opinion, or intent : COOPERATION **b** : CONSENT **2** : a coming together : CONJUNCTION

con·cur·rent \-'kər-ənt, -'kə-rənt\ *adj* **1** : operating at the same time ⟨*concurrent* expeditions to the Antarctic⟩ **2 a** : running parallel **b** : coming together; *esp* : meeting in a point ⟨*concurrent* lines⟩ **3** : acting in conjunction **4** : exercised over the same matter or area by two different authorities ⟨*concurrent* jurisdiction⟩ ***synonyms*** see CONTEMPORARY — **concurrent** *n* — **con·cur·rent·ly** *adv*

concurrent resolution *n* : a resolution that is passed by both houses of a legislative body and lacks the force of law

con·cuss \kən-'kəs\ *vt* : to affect with concussion

con·cus·sion \kən-'kəsh-ən\ *n* **1** : a violent irregular motion **2** : a smart or hard blow or collision **3** : bodily injury especially of the brain resulting from a sudden sharp jar (as from a blow) [Latin *concussio,* from *concutere* "to shake violently," from *com-* + *quatere* "to shake"] — **con·cus·sive** \-'kəs-iv\ *adj*

con·demn \kən-'dem\ *vt* **1** : to declare to be wrong : CENSURE ⟨*condemned* their behavior⟩ **2 a** : to pronounce guilty : CONVICT **b** : SENTENCE 1a ⟨*condemn* a prisoner to die⟩ **3** : to declare officially to be unfit for use or consumption ⟨a *condemned* building⟩ **4** : to take for public use under the right of eminent domain [Latin *condemnare,* from *com-* + *damnare* "to damn"] ***synonyms*** see BLAME — **con·dem·nable** \-'dem-nə-bəl, -'dem-ə-bəl\ *adj* — **con·dem·na·to·ry** \kən-'dem-nə-ˌtōr-ē, -ˌtȯr-\ *adj* — **con·demn·er** *or* **con·dem·nor** \-'dem-ər\ *n*

con·dem·na·tion \ˌkän-ˌdem-'nā-shən, -dəm-\ *n* **1** : CENSURE 1 **2** : the act of judicially condemning **3** : the state of being condemned **4** : a reason for condemning

con·den·sa·tion \ˌkän-ˌden-'sā-shən, -dən-\ *n* **1** : the act or process of condensing **2** : a chemical reaction involving union between molecules often with elimination of a simple molecule (as water) to form a new and more complex compound **3** : the quality or state of being condensed **4** : a product of condensing; *esp* : an abridgment of a literary work — **con·den·sa·tion·al** \-shnəl, -shən-l\ *adj*

con·dense \kən-'dens\ *vb* **1** : to make or become more close, compact, concise, or dense : CONCENTRATE, COMPRESS ⟨*condense* a paragraph into a sentence⟩ **2** : to change from a less dense to a denser form ⟨steam *condenses* into water⟩ **3** : to subject to or undergo condensation ⟨a chemical that *condenses* to form a plastic⟩ [Latin *condensare,* from *com-* + *densus* "dense"] — **con·dens·able** \-'den-sə-bəl\ *adj*

synonyms CONDENSE, CONTRACT, CONSTRICT, COMPRESS mean to decrease in bulk or volume. CONDENSE implies reduction of something to greater compactness usually without significant loss of material ⟨*condense* gas into liquid⟩. CONTRACT applies to the drawing together of surfaces or particles or a reduction of area or length ⟨molten iron *contracts* as it cools⟩. CONSTRICT implies a tightening that reduces diameter ⟨a *constricted* throat⟩. COMPRESS implies reduction by pressure from without ⟨*compress* a bale of cotton⟩.

condensed milk *n* : evaporated milk with sugar added

con·dens·er \kən-'den-sər\ *n* **1** : one that condenses: as **a** : a lens or mirror used to concentrate light on an object **b** : an apparatus in which gas or vapor is condensed **2** : CAPACITOR

con·de·scend \ˌkän-di-'send\ *vi* **1** : to descend to a level considered less dignified or humbler than one's own **2** : to grant favors with a superior air [Late Latin *condescendere,* from Latin *com-* + *descendere* "to descend"] ***synonyms*** see STOOP

con·de·scend·ing *adj* : showing or characterized by condescension : PATRONIZING — **con·de·scend·ing·ly** \-'sen-ding-lē\ *adv*

con·de·scen·sion \ˌkän-di-'sen-chən\ *n* : a patronizing attitude

con·dign \kən-'dīn, 'kän-ˌ\ *adj* : especially deserved or appropriate ⟨*condign* punishment⟩ [Medieval French *condigne,* from Latin *condignus* "very worthy," from *com-* + *dignus* "worthy"] — **con·dign·ly** *adv*

con·di·ment \'kän-də-mənt\ *n* : something used to give an appetizing taste to food; *esp* : a pungent seasoning [Latin *condimentum,* from *condire* "to season"]

[1]**con·di·tion** \kən-'dish-ən\ *n* **1** : a provision upon which the carrying out of an agreement depends : STIPULATION ⟨*conditions* of employment⟩ **2** : something essential to another : PREREQUISITE **3** : a restricting factor : LIMITATION **4 a** : a state of being ⟨the human *condition*⟩ **b** : social status : RANK **c** *pl* : attendant circumstances ⟨poor living *conditions*⟩ **5 a** : a usually defective state of health ⟨a serious heart *condition*⟩ **b** : physical fitness or readiness for use ⟨the car was in good *condition*⟩ ⟨exercised to get in *condition*⟩ [Latin *condicio* "items of agreement, condition," from *condicere* "to agree," from *com-* + *dicere* "to say"]

[2]**condition** *vt* **-di·tioned; -di·tion·ing** \-'dish-ning, -ə-ning\ **1** : to put into a proper or desired condition **2 a** : to adapt, modify, or mold to respond in a particular way **b** : to modify the behavior of so that a response previously associated with one stimulus becomes associated with another ⟨*condition* dogs to salivate when a bell rings⟩

[1]**con·di·tion·al** \kən-'dish-nəl, -ən-l\ *adj* **1** : subject to, implying, or dependent upon a condition ⟨a *conditional* promise⟩ **2** : expressing, containing, or implying a supposition ⟨a *conditional* clause⟩ — **con·di·tion·al·ly** \-ē\ *adv*

[2]**conditional** *n* : IMPLICATION 3

conditioned *adj* **1** : CONDITIONAL 1 **2** : brought or put into a specified state **3** : determined or established by conditioning ⟨a *conditioned* reflex⟩ ⟨a conditioned response⟩

con·di·tion·er \-'dish-nər, -ə-nər\ *n* : something that conditions; *esp* : a preparation used to improve the condition of hair

con·do \'kän-dō\ *n, pl* **condos** : CONDOMINIUM 3

con·dole \kən-'dōl\ *vi* : to express sympathetic sorrow ⟨*condole* with them in their grief⟩ [Late Latin *condolēre* "to suffer with," from Latin *com-* + *dolēre* "to feel pain"]

con·do·lence \kən-ˈdō-ləns, ˈkän-də-\ *n* : expression of sympathy with another in sorrow or grief ⟨sent our *condolences* to the family⟩
con·dom \ˈkän-dəm, ˈkən-\ *n* : a usually rubber sheath worn over the penis during sexual intercourse to prevent pregnancy or venereal disease [origin unknown]
con·do·min·i·um \ˌkän-də-ˈmin-ē-əm\ *n* **1** : joint sovereignty by two or more nations **2** : a politically dependent territory under condominium **3** : individual ownership of a unit in a multi-unit structure (as an apartment building); *also* : a unit so owned [Latin *com-* + *dominium* "domain"]
con·done \kən-ˈdōn\ *vt* : to regard or treat (something bad or blameworthy) as acceptable, forgivable, or harmless ⟨*condone* a friend's faults⟩ [Latin *condonare* "to forgive," from *com-* + *donare* "to give"] ***synonyms*** see EXCUSE — **con·do·na·tion** \ˌkän-dō-ˈnā-shən, -də-\ *n* — **con·don·er** \kən-ˈdō-nər\ *n*
con·dor \ˈkän-dər, -ˌdȯr\ *n* **1** : a very large South American vulture having the head and neck bare and the plumage dull black with a downy white neck ruff **2** : CALIFORNIA CONDOR [Spanish *cóndor,* from Quechua *kuntur*]

condor 1

con·duce \kən-ˈdüs, -ˈdyüs\ *vi* : to lead or tend to a usually desirable result [Latin *conducere* "to conduct, conduce," from *com-* + *ducere* "to lead"]
con·du·cive \kən-ˈdü-siv, -ˈdyü-\ *adj* : tending to promote or aid : CONTRIBUTING ⟨action *conducive* to success⟩ — **con·du·cive·ness** *n*
[1]**con·duct** \ˈkän-ˈdəkt, -dəkt\ *n* **1** : the act, manner, or process of carrying on : MANAGEMENT ⟨the *conduct* of foreign affairs⟩ **2** : personal behavior ⟨scolded for bad *conduct*⟩ [derived from Medieval Latin *conductus* "act of leading," from Latin *conducere* "to conduct, conduce"]
[2]**con·duct** \kən-ˈdəkt\ *vb* **1** : GUIDE 1b, ESCORT ⟨*conducted* tourists through the museum⟩ **2** : to carry on or out usually from a position of command or control ⟨*conduct* a business⟩ **3** **a** : to convey in a channel **b** : to act as a medium for conveying ⟨copper *conducts* electricity⟩ **4** : to cause (oneself) to act in an indicated manner ⟨*conducted* themselves badly⟩ **5** : to act as leader or director ⟨*conduct* an orchestra⟩ **6** : to have the quality of transmitting light, heat, sound, or electricity — **con·duct·i·bil·i·ty** \-ˌdək-tə-ˈbil-ət-ē\ *n* — **con·duct·ible** \-ˈdək-tə-bəl\ *adj*
synonyms CONDUCT, MANAGE, CONTROL, DIRECT mean to use one's powers to lead, guide, or dominate. CONDUCT implies guiding or leading in person ⟨selected to *conduct* negotiations⟩. MANAGE implies handling of details and maneuvering toward a desired result ⟨*manages* the store⟩. CONTROL implies a regulating or restraining so as to keep on a desired course ⟨*controlling* his appetite⟩. DIRECT implies constant guiding and regulating so as to achieve smooth operation ⟨*directs* the company's day-to-day expenses⟩.
con·duc·tance \kən-ˈdək-təns\ *n* **1** : conducting power **2** : the readiness with which a conductor transmits an electric current expressed as the reciprocal of electrical resistance
con·duc·tion \kən-ˈdək-shən\ *n* **1** : the act of conducting or conveying **2 a** : transmission through a conductor **b** : CONDUCTIVITY **3** : the transmission of excitation through living and especially nervous tissue
con·duc·tive \kən-ˈdək-tiv\ *adj* : having conductivity
con·duc·tiv·i·ty \ˌkän-ˌdək-ˈtiv-ət-ē\ *n, pl* **-ties** : the quality or power of conducting or transmitting
con·duc·tor \kən-ˈdək-tər\ *n* : one that conducts: as **a** : a person who collects fares in a public means of transportation (as a bus or railroad train) **b** : the leader of a musical ensemble **c** : a substance or body capable of readily transmitting electricity, heat, or sound — **con·duc·to·ri·al** \ˌkän-ˌdək-ˈtōr-ē-əl, -ˈtȯr-\ *adj*
con·duc·tress \kən-ˈdək-trəs\ *n* : a woman who is a conductor
con·duit \ˈkän-ˌdü-ət, -ˌdyü-ət, -dət\ *n* **1** : a natural or artificial channel through which water or other fluid is conveyed **2** *archaic* : FOUNTAIN **3** : a pipe or tube for protecting electric wires or cables [Medieval French *cunduit* "pipe, passage, conduct," in part from *cunduire* "to lead," from Latin *conducere,* in part Medieval Latin *conductus*]
con·dy·larth \ˈkän-də-ˌlärth\ *n* : any of an order (Condylarthra) of primitive extinct ungulate mammals [derived from Greek *kondylos* "knuckle, joint" + *arthron* "joint"]
con·dyle \ˈkän-ˌdīl, -dl\ *n* : a prominence at the end of a bone that forms part of a joint; *esp* : one resembling a pair of knuckles [Latin *condylus* "knuckle," from Greek *kondylos*]
cone \ˈkōn\ *n* **1** : a mass of overlapping woody scales that especially in the pines and other conifers are arranged on an axis and bear seeds between them; *also* : any of several flower or fruit clusters resembling such cones **2 a** : a solid figure formed by rotating a right triangle about one of its legs — called also *right circular cone* **b** : a solid figure that slopes evenly to a point from a usually circular base **3** : something that resembles a cone in shape: as **a** : any of the light-sensitive cells of the retina that function in color vision **b** : a crisp cone-shaped wafer for holding ice cream [Latin *conus,* from Greek *kōnos*]
cone·nose \ˈkōn-ˌnōz\ *n* : KISSING BUG
Con·es·to·ga \ˌkän-ə-ˈstō-gə\ *n* : a broad-wheeled covered wagon used by American pioneers especially for transporting freight across the prairies — called also *Conestoga wagon* [*Conestoga,* Pennsylvania]

Conestoga

co·ney *or* **co·ny** \ˈkō-nē\ *n, pl* **coneys** *or* **conies** **1 a** (1) : RABBIT; *esp* : the common European rabbit (2) : PIKA **b** : HYRAX **c** : rabbit fur **2** : any of several fishes; *esp* : a dusky reddish-finned grouper of the tropical Atlantic [Medieval French *conil,* from Latin *cuniculus*]
con·fab \ˈkän-ˌfab, kən-ˈ\ *n* **1** : CHAT 1 **2** : DISCUSSION, CONFERENCE — **con·fab** \kən-ˈfab, ˈkän-ˌ\ *vi*
con·fab·u·late \kən-ˈfab-yə-ˌlāt\ *vi* **1** : CHAT 2 **2** : CONFER 1 [Latin *confabulari,* from *com-* + *fabulari* "to talk," from *fabula* "story"] — **con·fab·u·la·tion** \-ˌfab-yə-ˈlā-shən\ *n* — **con·fab·u·la·tor** \-ˈfab-yə-ˌlāt-ər\ *n*
con·fect \kən-ˈfekt\ *vt* : to put together from varied material : PREPARE [Latin *confectus,* past participle of *conficere* "to prepare," from *com-* + *facere* "to make"]
con·fec·tion \kən-ˈfek-shən\ *n* **1** : the act or process of confecting **2** : something confected: as **a** : a fancy dish or sweetmeat **b** : a work of fine or elaborate craftsmanship
con·fec·tion·er \-shə-nər, -shnər\ *n* : a manufacturer of or dealer in confections
con·fec·tion·ery \-shə-ˌner-ē\ *n, pl* **-er·ies** **1** : the confectioner's art or business **2** : sweet edibles (as candy) **3** : a confectioner's shop
con·fed·er·a·cy \kən-ˈfed-rə-sē, -ə-rə-\ *n, pl* **-cies** **1** : a league of persons, parties, or states : ALLIANCE, CONFEDERATION **2** : a group united in a league; *esp, cap* : the Confederate States of America composed of the 11 southern states that seceded from the U.S. in 1860 and 1861 — **con·fed·er·al** \-ˈfed-rəl, -ə-rəl\ *adj*
[1]**con·fed·er·ate** \kən-ˈfed-rət, -ə-rət\ *adj* **1** : united in a league : ALLIED **2** *cap* : of or relating to the Confederate States of America [Late Latin *confoederare* "to unite by a league," from Latin *com-* + *foedus* "compact"]
[2]**confederate** *n* **1** : ALLY 2a, ACCOMPLICE **2** *cap* : a soldier, citizen, or supporter of the Confederate States of America or their cause
[3]**con·fed·er·ate** \-ˈfed-ə-ˌrāt\ *vb* : to unite in a confederacy
Confederate Memorial Day *n* : any of several days appointed for the commemoration of servicemen of the Confederacy
con·fed·er·a·tion \kən-ˌfed-ə-ˈrā-shən\ *n* **1** : an act of confederating : a state of being confederated **2** : LEAGUE 1
con·fer \kən-ˈfər\ *vb* **con·ferred; con·fer·ring** **1** : to compare views : CONSULT ⟨*confer* with the committee⟩ **2** : to grant from or as if from a position of superiority [Latin *conferre* "to bring together," from *com-* + *ferre* "to carry"] ***synonyms*** see PRESENT — **con·fer·ral** \-ˈfər-əl\ *n* — **con·fer·rer** \-ˈfər-ər\ *n*
con·fer·ee \ˌkän-fə-ˈrē\ *n* : one taking part in a conference ⟨the *conferees* met to elect new officers⟩
con·fer·ence \ˈkän-fə-rəns, -frəns, -fərns\ *n* **1** : a meeting for

formal discussion or exchange of opinions; *also* : the discussion itself **2** : a meeting of members of the two branches of a legislature to adjust differences **3** : an association of athletic teams ⟨a football *conference*⟩

con·fess \kən-ˈfes\ *vb* **1** : to tell of or make known (as something wrong) ⟨*confess* a crime⟩ **2 a** : to acknowledge one's sins to God or to a priest **b** : to receive the confession of ⟨the priest *confessed* the penitents⟩ **3** : to declare faith in : PROFESS [Medieval French *confesser,* from *confés* "having confessed," from Latin *confessus,* past participle of *confitēri* "to confess," from *com-* + *fatēri* "to confess"] ***synonyms*** see ACKNOWLEDGE

con·fess·ed·ly \-ˈfes-əd-lē, -ˈfest-lē\ *adv* : by confession : ADMITTEDLY

con·fes·sion \kən-ˈfesh-ən\ *n* **1 a** : an act of confessing; *esp* : a disclosure of one's sins in the sacrament of penance **b** : a meeting for the confessing of sins ⟨go to *confession*⟩ **2** : a statement of something confessed: as **a** : a written or oral acknowledgment of guilt by one accused of an offense **b** : a formal statement of religious beliefs : CREED **3** : an organized religious body having a common creed — **con·fes·sion·al** \-ˈfesh-nəl, -ən-l\ *adj*

con·fes·sion·al \-ˈfesh-nəl, -ən-l\ *n* **1** : a place where a priest hears confessions **2** : the practice of confessing to a priest

con·fes·sor \kən-ˈfes-ər\ *n* **1** : one that confesses **2** : a Christian who gives heroic evidence of faith but does not suffer martyrdom **3** : a priest who hears confessions

con·fet·ti \kən-ˈfet-ē\ *n* : small bits of brightly colored paper made for throwing (as at weddings) [Italian, plural of *confetto* "sweetmeat," from Medieval Latin *confectum,* from Latin *conficere* "to prepare"]

con·fi·dant \ˈkän-fə-ˌdant, -ˌdänt\ *n* : one to whom secrets are entrusted; *esp* : INTIMATE [French *confident,* derived from Latin *confidere* "to confide"]

con·fi·dante \ˈkän-fə-ˌdant, -ˌdänt\ *n* : CONFIDANT; *esp* : one who is a woman [French *confidente,* feminine of *confident* "confidant"]

con·fide \kən-ˈfīd\ *vb* **1** : to have confidence : TRUST ⟨*confide* in a doctor's skill⟩ **2** : to show confidence by imparting secrets ⟨*confided* in one's mother⟩ **3** : to tell confidentially ⟨*confide* a secret to a friend⟩ **4** : ENTRUST 1 ⟨*confide* one's safety to the police⟩ [Latin *confidere,* from *com-* + *fidere* "to trust"] — **con·fid·er** *n*

[1]**con·fi·dence** \ˈkan-fəd-əns, -fə-ˌdens\ *n* **1** : FAITH, TRUST ⟨had *confidence* in the leader⟩ **2** : consciousness of feeling sure : ASSURANCE ⟨spoke with great *confidence*⟩ **3 a** : reliance on another's discretion ⟨told a friend in *confidence*⟩ **b** : legislative support ⟨a vote of *confidence*⟩ **4** : a communication made in confidence : SECRET ⟨*confidences* between friends⟩

[2]**confidence** *adj* : of, relating to, or skilled at swindling by false promises ⟨a *confidence* game⟩ ⟨a *confidence* man⟩

con·fi·dent \ˈkän-fəd-ənt, -fə-ˌdent\ *adj* : having or showing confidence; *esp* : SELF-ASSURED ⟨*confident* of winning⟩ — **con·fi·dent·ly** *adv*

con·fi·den·tial \ˌkän-fə-ˈden-chəl\ *adj* **1** : known only to a few people : PRIVATE ⟨*confidential* information⟩ **2** : marked by intimacy : FAMILIAR ⟨a *confidential* tone of voice⟩ **3** : trusted with secret matters ⟨a *confidential* secretary⟩ — **con·fi·den·ti·al·i·ty** \-ˌden-chē-ˈal-ə-tē\ *n* — **con·fi·den·tial·ly** \-ˈdench-lē, -ə-lē\ *adv*

con·fid·ing \kən-ˈfīd-ing\ *adj* : tending to confide : TRUSTFUL ⟨a *confiding* friend⟩ — **con·fid·ing·ly** \-ing-lē\ *adv*

con·fig·u·ra·tion \kən-ˌfig-yə-ˈrā-shən, -ˌfig-ə-\ *n* : relative arrangement of parts; *also* : something (as a figure, contour, or pattern) produced by such arrangement [Late Latin *configuratio* "similar formation," from Latin *configurare* "to form from or after," from *com-* + *figurare* "to form," from *figura* "figure"] — **con·fig·u·ra·tion·al** \-shnəl, -shən-l\ *adj* — **con·fig·u·ra·tion·al·ly** \-ē\ *adv* — **con·fig·u·ra·tive** \-ˈfig-yə-ˌrāt-iv, -ˈfig-ə-, -rət-\ *adj*

con·fig·ure \kən-ˈfig-yər\ *vt* : to set up for operation especially in a particular way ⟨ships *configured* for battle⟩

con·fine \kən-ˈfīn\ *vt* **1** : to keep within limits : RESTRICT ⟨*confined* the message to twenty words⟩ **2 a** : to shut up : IMPRISON ⟨*confined* for life⟩ **b** : to keep indoors ⟨*confined* with a cold⟩ ***synonyms*** see LIMIT — **con·fin·er** *n*

con·fine·ment \kən-ˈfīn-mənt\ *n* : an act of confining : the state of being confined ⟨solitary *confinement*⟩; *esp* : LYING-IN

con·fines \ˈkän-ˌfīnz\ *n pl* : something that encloses or restrains ⟨within the *confines* of the city⟩ ⟨the *confines* of poverty⟩ [Latin *confine* "border," from *confinis* "adjacent," from *com-* + *finis* "end"]

con·firm \kən-ˈfərm\ *vt* **1** : to make firm or firmer (as in habit, faith, or intention) **2** : to give approval to : RATIFY ⟨*confirm* a treaty⟩ **3** : to administer the rite of confirmation to **4** : to make sure of the truth of : VERIFY ⟨*confirm* a suspicion⟩ [Latin *confirmare,* from *com-* + *firmus* "firm"] — **con·firm·able** \-ˈfər-mə-bəl\ *adj*

synonyms CONFIRM, CORROBORATE, AUTHENTICATE, VERIFY mean to support the truth or validity of something. CONFIRM implies removing doubts by an authoritative statement or an indisputable fact ⟨*confirmed* the reports⟩. CORROBORATE suggests the strengthening of what is already partly established ⟨witnesses *corroborated* his story⟩. AUTHENTICATE implies establishing genuineness by showing legal or official documents or presenting expert opinion ⟨handwriting experts *authenticated* the diaries⟩. VERIFY implies the authentication of something supposed or presumed with appropriate facts or events ⟨*validated* the hypothesis by experiments⟩.

con·fir·ma·tion \ˌkän-fər-ˈmā-shən\ *n* **1** : an act or process of confirming: as **a** : a Christian rite or sacrament conferring the gifts of the Holy Spirit and also entitling the recipient to full church privileges **b** : a ceremony confirming Jewish youths in their ancestral faith **c** : the ratification of an executive act by a legislative body **2** : something that confirms : PROOF — **con·fir·ma·to·ry** \kən-ˈfər-mə-ˌtōr-ē, -ˌtȯr-\ *adj*

con·firmed \kən-ˈfərmd\ *adj* **1 a** : deeply established ⟨a *confirmed* habit⟩ **b** : HABITUAL, CHRONIC ⟨a *confirmed* do-gooder⟩ **2** : having received the rite of confirmation — **con·firm·ed·ly** \-ˈfər-məd-lē\ *adv*

con·fis·cate \ˈkän-fə-ˌskāt\ *vt* : to seize by or as if by authority ⟨smuggled goods may be *confiscated*⟩ [Latin *confiscare,* from *com-* + *fiscus* "treasury"] — **con·fis·ca·tion** \ˌkän-fə-ˈskā-shən\ *n* — **con·fis·ca·tor** \ˈkän-fə-ˌskāt-ər\ *n* — **con·fis·ca·to·ry** \kən-ˈfis-kə-ˌtōr-ē, -ˌtȯr-\ *adj*

con·fi·te·or \kən-ˈfēt-ē-ər\ *n* : a confession of fault or error; *esp* : a liturgical form in the Mass in which sinfulness is admitted [Latin, "I confess," from *confitēri* "to confess"]

con·fla·gra·tion \ˌkän-flə-ˈgrā-shən\ *n* : FIRE; *esp* : a large disastrous fire [Latin *conflagratio,* from *conflagrare* "to burn up," from *com-* + *flagrare* "to burn"]

[1]**con·flict** \ˈkän-ˌflikt\ *n* **1** : a hostile encounter : FIGHT, BATTLE **2 a** : a clashing or sharp disagreement (as between ideas, interests, or purposes) **b** : mental struggle resulting from incompatible or opposing needs, drives, wishes, or demands [Latin *conflictus* "act of striking together," from *confligere* "to strike together," from *com-* + *fligere* "to strike"]

[2]**con·flict** \kən-ˈflikt, ˈkän-ˌ\ *vi* : to show antagonism : CLASH ⟨duty and desire often *conflict*⟩

con·flict·ed \kən-ˈflik-təd\ *adj* : experiencing or marked by ambivalence or a conflict especially of emotions ⟨*conflicted* feelings⟩

con·flu·ence \ˈkän-ˌflü-əns\ *n* **1** : a coming or flowing together at one point ⟨the *confluence* of scholarship that produced the atomic bomb⟩ **2** : a flowing together or place of meeting especially of two or more streams

con·flu·ent \ˈkän-ˌflü-ənt, kən-ˈ\ *adj* **1** : flowing or coming together ⟨*confluent* rivers⟩ **2** : run together ⟨a *confluent* rash⟩ [Latin *confluere* "to flow together," from *com-* + *fluere* "to flow"]

con·form \kən-ˈfȯrm\ *vb* **1** : to bring into harmony ⟨*conform* one's behavior to the circumstances⟩ **2** : to be similar or identical ⟨the data *conforms* to the pattern⟩ **3** : to be obedient or compliant; *esp* : to adapt oneself to prevailing standards or customs ⟨found it easier to *conform* than rebel⟩ [Latin *conformare,* from *com-* + *forma* "form"] ***synonyms*** see ADAPT — **con·form·er** *n* — **con·form·ism** \-ˈfȯr-ˌmiz-əm\ *n* — **con·form·ist** \-məst\ *n*

con·form·able \kən-ˈfȯr-mə-bəl\ *adj* **1** : corresponding or consistent in form or character : SIMILAR ⟨*conformable* to established practices⟩ **2** : giving compliance : SUBMISSIVE — **con·form·ably** \-blē\ *adv*

con·for·mal \kən-ˈfȯr-məl, kän-\ *adj* **1** : leaving the size of the angle between corresponding curves unchanged **2** : representing small areas in their true shape ⟨a *conformal* map⟩

con·form·ance \kən-ˈfȯr-məns\ *n* : CONFORMITY 2, 3

con·for·ma·tion \ˌkän-fȯr-ˈmā-shən, -fər-\ *n* **1** : the act of conforming or producing conformity : ADAPTATION **2** : formation of something by an assembling into a whole **3 a** : STRUCTURE ‹the *conformation* of the ocean bed› **b :** the proportionate shape or contour especially of an animal

con·for·mi·ty \kən-ˈfȯr-mət-ē\ *n, pl* **-ties** **1 :** correspondence in form, manner, or character **:** AGREEMENT ‹behaved in *conformity* with his beliefs› **2 :** an act or instance of conforming **3 :** action in accordance with some standard or authority **:** OBEDIENCE ‹*conformity* to social custom›

con·found \kən-ˈfau̇nd, kän-\ *vt* **1** *archaic* **:** to bring to ruin **:** DESTROY **2 :** to put to shame **:** DISCOMFIT **3 :** to swear at **:** DAMN, CURSE **4 :** to throw into disorder **:** mix up **:** CONFUSE [Medieval French *confundre,* from Latin *confundere* "to pour together, mingle, confuse," from *com-* + *fundere* "to pour"]

con·found·ed \kən-ˈfau̇n-dəd, ˈkän-ˌfau̇n-\ *adj* **1 :** filled with confusion **:** PERPLEXED **2 :** DAMNED 1 — **con·found·ed·ly** *adv*

con·fra·ter·ni·ty \ˌkän-frə-ˈtər-nət-ē\ *n, pl* **-ties :** a society devoted to a religious or charitable cause

con·frere \ˈkōⁿ-ˌfreər, ˈkän-\ *n* **:** COLLEAGUE, COMRADE [Medieval French, translation of Medieval Latin *confrater* "fellow, brother," from Latin *com-* + *frater* "brother"]

con·front \kən-ˈfrənt\ *vt* **1 :** to face especially in challenge **:** OPPOSE ‹*confront* an enemy› **2 :** to bring face-to-face **:** cause to meet ‹*confronted* with a problem› [Middle French *confronter* "to border on, confront," derived from Latin *com-* + *frons* "forehead, front"] — **con·fron·ta·tion** \ˌkän-frən-ˈtā-shən, -ˌfrən-\ *n* — **con·fron·ta·tion·al** \-shnəl, -shə-nl\ *adj*

Con·fu·cian \kən-ˈfyü-shən\ *adj* **:** of or relating to the Chinese philosopher Confucius or his teachings or followers — **Confucian** *n* — **Con·fu·cian·ism** \-shə-ˌniz-əm\ *n* — **Con·fu·cian·ist** \-shə-nəst\ *n or adj*

con·fuse \kən-ˈfyüz\ *vt* **1 a :** to make embarrassed **b :** to disturb in mind or purpose **:** throw off ‹the complicated problem *confused* me› **2 a :** to make indistinct **:** BLUR ‹stop *confusing* the issue› **b :** to mix up **:** JUMBLE ‹their motives were hopelessly *confused*› **c :** to fail to distinguish between ‹teachers always *confused* the twins› [back-formation from Middle English *confused* "frustrated, ruined," from Medieval French *confus,* from Latin *confusus,* past participle of *confundere* "to mingle, confuse"] — **con·fused·ly** \-ˈfyüz-əd-lē\ *adv* — **con·fus·ing·ly** \-ˈfyü-zing-lē\ *adv*

con·fu·sion \kən-ˈfyü-zhən\ *n* **1 :** an act or instance of confusing **2 :** the quality or state of being confused — **con·fu·sion·al** \-ˈfyüzh-nəl, -ˈfyü-zhən-l\ *adj*

con·fute \kən-ˈfyüt\ *vt* **:** to overwhelm in argument **:** refute conclusively [Latin *confutare* "to restrain, silence"] — **con·fu·ta·tion** \ˌkän-fyü-ˈtā-shən\ *n* — **con·fu·ta·tive** \kən-ˈfyüt-ət-iv\ *adj* — **con·fut·er** \kən-ˈfyüt-ər\ *n*

con·ga \ˈkäng-gə\ *n* **1 :** a Cuban dance of African origin performed by a group usually in single file **2 :** a tall narrow bass drum played with the hands [American Spanish]

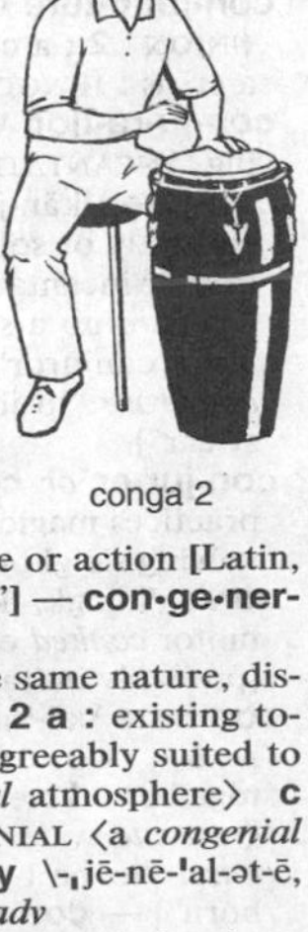
conga 2

con·gé \kōⁿ-ˈzhā, ˈkän-ˌjā\ *also* **con·gee** \ˈkän-jē, -zhē\ *n* **1 :** DISMISSAL **2 :** FAREWELL 2 [French]

con·geal \kən-ˈjēl\ *vb* **1 :** to change from a fluid to a solid state by or as if by cold **2 :** to make or become viscid or curdled **:** COAGULATE **3 :** to make or become rigid or inflexible [Middle French *congeler,* from Latin *congelare,* from *com-* + *gelare* "to freeze"] — **con·geal·ment** \-mənt\ *n*

con·ge·ner \ˈkän-jə-nər, kən-ˈjē-\ *n* **1 :** a member of the same taxonomic genus as another plant or animal **2 :** a person, organism, or thing resembling another in nature or action [Latin, "of the same kind," from *com-* + *genus* "kind"] — **con·ge·ner·ic** \ˌkän-jə-ˈner-ik\ *adj*

con·ge·nial \kən-ˈjē-nyəl\ *adj* **1 :** having the same nature, disposition, or tastes ‹*congenial* companions› **2 a :** existing together harmoniously **b :** PLEASANT; *esp* **:** agreeably suited to one's nature, tastes, or outlook ‹a *congenial* atmosphere› **c :** characterized by friendly sociability **:** GENIAL ‹a *congenial* host› [*com-* + *genius*] — **con·ge·nial·i·ty** \-ˌjē-nē-ˈal-ət-ē, -ˌjēn-ˈyal-\ *n* — **con·ge·nial·ly** \-ˈjē-nyə-lē\ *adv*

con·gen·i·tal \kən-ˈjen-ə-tl\ *adj* **1 :** existing at or dating from birth ‹*congenital* heart disease› **2 :** being such by nature **:** INHERENT ‹a *congenital* liar› [Latin *congenitus,* from *com-* + *genitus,* past participle of *gignere* "to bring forth"] ***synonyms*** see INNATE — **con·gen·i·tal·ly** \-tl-ē\ *adv*

con·ger eel \ˈkäng-gər-\ *n* **:** a scaleless saltwater eel that may reach a length of over eight feet (2.4 meters) and is sometimes used as food [Medieval French *congre,* from Latin *conger,* probably from Greek *gongros*]

con·ge·ries \ˈkän-jə-rēz, -ˌrēz\ *n, pl* **congeries** *same*\ **:** COLLECTION, AGGREGATION [Latin, from *congerere* "to bring together"]

con·gest \kən-ˈjest\ *vb* **1 :** to cause an excessive accumulation especially of blood or mucus in blood vessels of (as an organ or part) **2 :** CLOG 2 ‹traffic *congested* the streets› **3 :** to concentrate in a small or narrow space [Latin *congestus,* past participle of *congerere* "to bring together," from *com-* + *gerere* "to carry"] — **con·ges·tion** \-ˈjes-chən\ *n* — **con·ges·tive** \-ˈjes-tiv\ *adj*

congestive heart failure *n* **:** heart failure in which the heart is unable to maintain an adequate circulation of blood in the bodily tissues or to pump out the blood returned to it by the veins

¹con·glom·er·ate \kən-ˈgläm-rət, -ə-rət\ *adj* **:** made up of parts from various sources or of various kinds ‹an ethnically *conglomerate* culture› [Latin *conglomerare* "to roll together," from *com-* + *glomus* "ball"]

²con·glom·er·ate \-ˈgläm-ə-ˌrāt\ *vb* **:** to gather into a mass

³con·glom·er·ate \-ˈgläm-rət, -ə-rət\ *n* **1 :** a composite mass or mixture; *esp* **:** rock composed of rounded fragments varying from small pebbles to large boulders in a cement (as of hardened clay) **2 :** a widely diversified corporation

con·glom·er·a·tion \kən-ˌgläm-ə-ˈrā-shən, ˌkän-\ *n* **1 :** the act of conglomerating **:** the state of being conglomerated **2 :** something that is conglomerated

Con·go red \ˈkäng-ˌgō-\ *n* **:** an azo dye red in alkaline and blue in acid solution [*Congo,* region in Africa]

con·grat·u·late \kən-ˈgrach-ə-ˌlāt\ *vt* **:** to express pleasure to on account of success or good fortune ‹*congratulated* the winner› [Latin *congratulari* "to wish joy," from *com-* + *gratus* "pleasing"] — **con·grat·u·la·to·ry** \-ˈgrach-lə-ˌtōr-ē, -ə-lə-, -ˌtȯr-\ *adj*

con·grat·u·la·tion \-ˌgrach-ə-ˈlā-shən\ *n* **1 :** the act of congratulating **2 :** an expression of pleasure at another's success, happiness, or good fortune — usually used in plural

con·gre·gate \ˈkäng-gri-ˌgāt\ *vb* **:** to collect into a group or crowd **:** ASSEMBLE [Latin *congregare,* from *com-* + *greg-, grex* "flock"] ***synonyms*** see GATHER — **con·gre·ga·tor** \-ˌgāt-ər\ *n*

con·gre·ga·tion \ˌkäng-gri-ˈgā-shən\ *n* **1 a :** an assembly of persons; *esp* **:** one gathered for religious worship **b :** a religious community: as **(1) :** an organized body of believers in a particular locality **(2) :** a Roman Catholic religious society with only simple vows **2 :** the action of congregation **:** the state of being congregated; *also* **:** a collection of separate things **3 :** a body of cardinals and officials forming an administrative division of the papal curia

con·gre·ga·tion·al \-ˈgā-shnəl, -shən-l\ *adj* **1 :** of or relating to a congregation **2** *cap* **:** of or relating to a body of Protestant churches affirming the essential importance and the autonomy of the local congregation **3 :** of or relating to church government placing final authority in the assembly of the local congregation — **con·gre·ga·tion·al·ism** \-ˌiz-əm\ *n, often cap* — **con·gre·ga·tion·al·ist** \-əst\ *n or adj, often cap*

con·gress \ˈkäng-grəs\ *n* **1 a :** the act or action of coming together and meeting **b :** COITUS **2 :** a formal meeting of delegates for discussion and action **3 :** the supreme legislative body of a nation and especially of a republic **4 :** an association of constituent organizations **5 :** a single meeting or session of a group [Latin *congressus,* from *congredi* "to come together," from *com-* + *gradi* "to step, go"] — **con·gres·sion·al** \kən-ˈgresh-nəl, -ən-l\ *adj* — **con·gres·sion·al·ly** \-ē\ *adv*

con·gress·man \ˈkäng-grəs-mən\ *n* **:** a member of a congress; *esp* **:** a member of the U.S. House of Representatives

con·gress·wom·an \-ˌwu̇m-ən\ *n* **:** a woman who is a member of a congress; *esp* **:** a woman who is a member of the U.S. House of Representatives

con·gru·ence \kən-ˈgrü-əns, ˈkäng-grə-wəns\ *n* **1 :** the quality or state of agreeing, coinciding, or being congruent **2 :** a statement that two numbers are congruent with respect to a modulus

con·gru·en·cy \-ən-sē, -wən-sē\ *n* : CONGRUENCE

con·gru·ent \kən-ˈgrü-ənt, ˈkäng-grə-wənt\ *adj* **1** : being in agreement ⟨the report proved to be *congruent* with the facts⟩ **2** : having the same size and shape : capable of being placed over one another and exactly matching ⟨*congruent* triangles⟩ **3** : having a difference that is divisible by a given modulus ⟨12 is *congruent* to 2 with respect to a modulus of 5 since 12 – 2 = 10 and 10 is divisible by 5⟩ [Latin *congruere* "to come together, agree"] — **con·gru·ent·ly** *adv*

con·gru·i·ty \kən-ˈgrü-ət-ē, kän-\ *n, pl* **-i·ties** **1** : the quality or state of being congruent or congruous : AGREEMENT **2** : a point of agreement

con·gru·ous \ˈkäng-grə-wəs\ *adj* **1 a** : being in agreement, harmony, or correspondence **b** : conforming to the circumstances of a situation : APPROPRIATE **2** : marked by harmony among parts [Latin *congruus,* from *congruere* "to come together, agree"] — **con·gru·ous·ly** *adv* — **con·gru·ous·ness** *n*

[1]**con·ic** \ˈkän-ik\ *adj* **1** : CONICAL **2** : of or relating to a cone

[2]**conic** *n* : CONIC SECTION

con·i·cal \ˈkän-i-kəl\ *adj* : resembling a cone especially in shape ⟨*conical* roots⟩ — **con·i·cal·ly** \-i-kə-lē, -klē\ *adv*

conic section *n* : a curve formed by the intersection of a plane and a cone : a curve (as an ellipse, parabola, hyperbola, or circle) generated by a point which always moves so that the ratio of its distance from a fixed point to its distance from a fixed line is constant

conidia *plural of* CONIDIUM

co·nid·io·phore \kə-ˈnid-ē-ə-ˌfōr, -ˌfȯr\ *n* : a specialized hypha of some fungi that bears conidia

co·nid·i·um \kə-ˈnid-ē-əm\ *n, pl* **-ia** \-ē-ə\ : an asexual spore produced on a conidiophore [Greek *konis* "dust"] — **co·nid·i·al** \-ē-əl\ *adj*

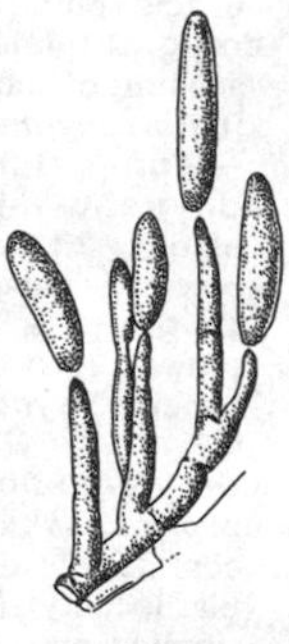
conidium

co·ni·fer \ˈkän-ə-fər *also* ˈkō-nə-\ *n* : any of an order (Coniferales) of mostly evergreen trees and shrubs that are gymnosperms having usually needle-shaped or scalelike leaves and include forms (as pines) with true cones [Latin *conifer* "cone-bearing," from *conus* "cone"] — **co·nif·er·ous** \kō-ˈnif-rəs, kə-, -ə-rəs\ *adj*

con·jec·tur·al \kən-ˈjek-chə-rəl, -ˈjeksh-rəl\ *adj* **1** : of the nature of, involving, or based on conjecture **2** : given to conjectures — **con·jec·tur·al·ly** \-ē\ *adv*

[1]**con·jec·ture** \kən-ˈjek-chər\ *n* **1** : inference from inadequate evidence **2** : a conclusion reached by surmise or guesswork ⟨a mistaken *conjecture*⟩ [Latin *conjectura,* from *conjectus,* past participle of *conicere* "to throw together, form a conclusion about," from *com-* + *jacere* "to throw"]

[2]**conjecture** *vb* **-jec·tured; -jec·tur·ing** \-ˈjek-chə-ring, -ˈjek-shring\ **1** : to arrive at by conjecture : GUESS **2** : to make conjectures as to : SURMISE ⟨*conjecture* the meaning of a statement⟩ — **con·jec·tur·er** \-ˈjek-chər-ər\ *n*

synonyms CONJECTURE, SURMISE, GUESS mean the forming of an opinion or the arriving at a conclusion without full supporting evidence. CONJECTURE implies forming an opinion on the basis of some evidence that is recognized as insufficient ⟨scientists *conjecture* that the disease is caused by a defective gene⟩. SURMISE implies even slighter evidence and suggests the influence of suspicion or imagination ⟨could only *surmise* that they had traveled by plane, since they arrived so quickly⟩. GUESS stresses hitting on a conclusion at random or from very uncertain evidence ⟨asked them to *guess* what number he was thinking of⟩.

con·join \kən-ˈjȯin, kän-\ *vb* : to join together for a common purpose

con·joint \-ˈjȯint\ *adj* **1** : being or coming together so as to unite **2** : related to, made up of, or carried on by two or more in combination : JOINT — **con·joint·ly** *adv*

con·ju·gal \ˈkän-ji-gəl, kən-ˈjü-\ *adj* : of or relating to the married state or to married persons and their relations : CONNUBIAL [Latin *conjugalis,* from *conjux* "spouse," from *conjungere* "to join, unite in marriage," from *com-* + *jungere* "to join"] — **con·ju·gal·ly** *adv*

con·ju·gant \ˈkän-ji-gənt\ *n* : either of a pair of conjugating gametes or organisms

[1]**con·ju·gate** \ˈkän-ji-gət, -jə-ˌgāt\ *adj* **1 a** : joined together especially in pairs **b** : acting or operating as if joined **2** : having features in common but opposite or inverse in some particular; *esp* : being complex numbers that are conjugates [Latin *conjugare* "to unite," from *com-* + *jugum* "yoke"] — **con·ju·gate·ly** *adv* — **con·ju·gate·ness** *n*

[2]**con·ju·gate** \ˈkän-jə-ˌgāt\ *vb* **1** : to give the various inflectional forms of (a verb) in a prescribed order **2** : to join together : COUPLE **3** : to pair and fuse in conjugation

[3]**con·ju·gate** \-gət, -ˌgāt\ *n* **1** : something conjugate : a product of conjugating **2** : one of two complex numbers (as *a* + *bi* and *a* – *bi*) differing only in the sign of the imaginary part

conjugated protein *n* : a compound of a protein with a nonprotein

con·ju·ga·tion \ˌkän-jə-ˈgā-shən\ *n* **1** : the act of conjugating : the state of being conjugated **2 a** : an orderly arrangement of the inflectional forms of a verb **b** : verb inflection **c** : a class of verbs having the same type of inflectional forms ⟨the weak *conjugation*⟩ **3 a** : fusion of usually similar gametes that in most fungi and some algae serves as a simple form of sexual reproduction **b** : temporary cytoplasmic union with exchange of nuclear material that is the usual sexual process in ciliated protozoans **c** : the transfer of DNA from one bacterium to another when in direct contact — **con·ju·ga·tion·al** \-shnəl, -shən-l\ *adj* — **con·ju·ga·tion·al·ly** \-ē\ *adv* — **con·ju·ga·tive** \ˈkän-jə-ˌgāt-iv\ *adj*

con·junct \kən-ˈjəngt, kän-, -ˈjəngkt\ *adj* : bound together : JOINED, UNITED [Latin *conjunctus,* past participle of *conjungere* "to join," from *com-* + *jungere* "to join"]

con·junc·tion \kən-ˈjəng-shən, -ˈjəngk-\ *n* **1** : the act or an instance of conjoining : the state of being conjoined **2** : occurrence together in time or space : CONCURRENCE **3** : the apparent meeting or passing of two or more celestial bodies in the same degree of the zodiac **4** : an uninflected word or expression that joins together sentences, clauses, phrases, or words **5** : a statement formed by joining two or more statements together with the word *and* that is true only if all its components are true — **con·junc·tion·al** \-shnəl, -shən-l\ *adj* — **con·junc·tion·al·ly** \-ē\ *adv*

con·junc·ti·va \ˌkän-ˌjəngk-ˈtī-və, -ˈtē-\ *n, pl* **-tivas** *or* **-ti·vae** \-ˈtī-ˌvē, -ˈtē-ˌvī\ : the mucous membrane that lines the inner surface of the eyelids and is continued over the front part of the eyeball [derived from Latin *conjungere* "to join"] — **con·junc·ti·val** \-vəl\ *adj*

con·junc·tive \kən-ˈjəng-tiv, -ˈjəngk-\ *adj* **1** : CONNECTIVE **2** : done or existing in conjunction : CONJUNCT **3** : being or functioning like a conjunction ⟨*conjunctive* adverbs such as *hence, however,* and *therefore*⟩ — **conjunctive** *n* — **con·junc·tive·ly** *adv*

con·junc·ti·vi·tis \kən-ˌjəng-ti-ˈvīt-əs, -ˌjəngk-\ *n* : inflammation of the conjunctiva

con·junc·ture \kən-ˈjəng-chər, -ˈjəngk-\ *n* **1** : CONJUNCTION 1, UNION **2** : a combination of circumstances usually producing a crisis : JUNCTURE

con·ju·ra·tion \ˌkän-jə-ˈrā-shən, ˌkən-\ *n* **1** : the act of conjuring : INCANTATION **2** : an expression or trick used in conjuring

con·jure \ˈkän-jər, ˈkən-; *in sense 1* kən-ˈju̇r\ *vb* **1** : to entreat earnestly or solemnly : BESEECH **2 a** : to summon by invocation or incantation **b** : to create or bring about as if by magic ⟨*conjure* up a scheme⟩ **3 a** : to practice magical arts **b** : to use a conjuror's tricks [Medieval French *conjurer,* from Latin *conjurare* "to join in taking an oath," from *com-* + *jurare* "to swear"]

con·jur·er *or* **con·ju·ror** \ˈkän-jər-ər, ˈkən-\ *n* **1** : one that practices magic arts : WIZARD **2** : one that performs tricks involving sleight of hand and illusion : MAGICIAN

conk \ˈkängk, ˈkȯngk\ *vi* **1** : to break down; *esp* : STALL ⟨the motor *conked* out⟩ **2** : to go to sleep ⟨*conked* out after lunch⟩ [probably imitative]

con·nate \kä-ˈnāt, ˈkän-ˌāt\ *adj* **1** : INNATE 1 **2** : agreeing in nature : CONGENIAL ⟨*connate* spirits⟩ **3** : born or originated together **4** : entrapped in sediments at the time of deposition ⟨*connate* water⟩ [Late Latin *connatus,* past participle of *connasci* "to be born together," from Latin *com-* + *nasci* "to be born"] — **con·nate·ly** *adv*

con·nect \kə-ˈnekt\ *vb* **1** : to join or link together directly or by something coming between ⟨*connect* two wires⟩ ⟨towns *connected* by a railroad⟩ **2** : to join by personal relationship or association ⟨*connected* by marriage⟩ **3** : to associate in the mind ⟨*connect* two ideas⟩ **4** : to be related (as by cause or logic) ⟨an event *connected* with the fire⟩ **5 :** to establish a means of communication ⟨*connect* to the Internet⟩ [Latin *connectere,* from *com-* + *nectere* "to bind"] ***synonyms*** see JOIN — **con·nec·tor** *also* **con·nect·er** \-ˈnek-tər\ *n*

connecting rod *n* **:** a rod that transmits motion between a rotating part of a machine and a reciprocating part

con·nec·tion \kə-ˈnek-shən\ *n* **1 :** the act of connecting **2 :** the fact or condition of being connected **:** RELATIONSHIP ⟨the *connection* between two ideas⟩ **3 a :** a thing that connects **:** BOND, LINK ⟨a loose *connection* in a radio⟩ **b :** a means of communication ⟨a telephone *connection*⟩ **4 a :** a person connected with others especially by marriage or kinship ⟨an uncle and some family *connections*⟩ **b :** a social, professional, or commercial relationship ⟨business *connections* in the city⟩ **5 :** a means of continuing a journey by transferring to another conveyance ⟨make a *connection* for New York at Chicago⟩ **6 :** a set of persons associated together: as **a :** DENOMINATION 3 **b :** a large family **:** CLAN — **con·nec·tion·al** \-shnəl, -shən-l\ *adj*

[1]**con·nec·tive** \kə-ˈnek-tiv\ *adj* **:** connecting or tending to connect — **con·nec·tive·ly** *adv* — **con·nec·tiv·i·ty** \ˌkä-ˌnek-ˈtiv-ət-ē\ *n*

[2]**connective** *n* **:** something that connects; *esp* **:** a word or expression (as a conjunction or a relative pronoun) that connects words or word groups

connective tissue *n* **:** a tissue (as bone, cartilage, or tendon) of mesodermal origin that consists of various cells and interlacing protein fibers in a carbohydrate matrix and that supports, covers, or binds together other tissues in the body

con·ning tower \ˈkän-ing-\ *n* **1 :** an armored pilothouse (as on a battleship) **2 :** a raised structure on the deck of a submarine that contains observation and communications equipment for use when the submarine is on the surface [*conn* "to direct the steering of a ship," from Middle English *condien* "to conduct," from Medieval French *conduire,* from Latin *conducere*]

conning tower 2

con·nip·tion \kə-ˈnip-shən\ *n* **:** a fit of rage, hysteria, or alarm [origin unknown]

con·niv·ance \kə-ˈnī-vəns\ *n* **:** the act of conniving; *esp* **:** knowledge of and active or passive consent to wrongdoing

con·nive \kə-ˈnīv\ *vi* **1 :** to pretend ignorance of something that one ought to oppose or stop **2 :** to cooperate secretly or have a secret understanding **3 :** PLOT 3, CONSPIRE [Latin *conivēre, connivēre* "to close the eyes, connive"] — **con·niv·er** *n*

con·nois·seur \ˌkän-ə-ˈsər *also* -ˈsu̇r\ *n* **:** a person qualified to act as a judge in matters involving taste and appreciation **:** EXPERT ⟨a *connoisseur* of French painting⟩ [obsolete French, from Medieval French *connoistre* "to know," from Latin *cognoscere,* from *com-* + *gnoscere, noscere* "to know"] — **connois·seur·ship** \-ˌship\ *n*

con·no·ta·tion \ˌkän-ə-ˈtā-shən\ *n* **1 :** a meaning or significance suggested by a word apart from and in addition to the thing it explicitly names or describes ⟨the word *home* with all its heart-warming *connotations*⟩ — compare DENOTATION 2 **2 :** something implied **:** IMPLICATION ⟨a speech with political *connotations*⟩ — **con·no·ta·tion·al** \-shnəl, -shən-l\ *adj*

con·no·ta·tive \ˈkän-ə-ˌtāt-iv, kə-ˈnōt-ət-iv\ *adj* **1 :** connoting or tending to connote **2 :** relating to connotation — **con·no·ta·tive·ly** *adv*

con·note \kə-ˈnōt\ *vt* **:** to suggest or mean along with or in addition to the explicit meaning ⟨the word *home* usually *connotes* comfort and security⟩ [Medieval Latin *connotare,* from Latin *com-* + *notare* "to note"] ***synonyms*** see DENOTE

con·nu·bi·al \kə-ˈnü-bē-əl, -ˈnyü-\ *adj* **:** of or relating to marriage **:** CONJUGAL [Latin *connubium* "marriage," from *com-* + *nubere* "to marry"] — **con·nu·bi·al·ly** \-bē-ə-lē\ *adv*

co·noid \ˈkō-ˌnȯid\ *or* **co·noi·dal** \kō-ˈnȯid-l\ *adj* **:** shaped like or nearly like a cone — **conoid** *n*

con·quer \ˈkäng-kər\ *vb* **con·quered; con·quer·ing** \-kə-ring, -kring\ **1 :** to gain or acquire by force of arms **:** SUBJUGATE ⟨*conquer* a country⟩ **2 :** to overcome by force of arms **:** VANQUISH ⟨*conquered* all their enemies⟩ **3 :** to master or win by overcoming obstacles or opposition ⟨*conquered* the mountain⟩ **4 :** to overcome by mental or moral power ⟨*conquer* one's fear⟩ **5 :** to be victorious [Medieval French *conquerre,* derived from Latin *conquirere* "to search for, collect," from *com-* + *quaerere* "to seek, ask"] — **con·quer·or** *n*

synonyms CONQUER, SUBDUE, SUBJUGATE, VANQUISH mean to defeat by force or strategy. CONQUER implies gaining mastery of after a prolonged effort and with more or less permanent result ⟨ancient Rome *conquered* most of southern Europe⟩. SUBDUE implies overpowering and suppressing ⟨*subdued* the rebel forces after years of fighting⟩. SUBJUGATE stresses a bringing under oppressive or humiliating rule or control ⟨the dictator used military force to *subjugate* his people⟩. VANQUISH implies a complete or final overpowering ⟨*vanquished* the enemy and ended the war⟩.

con·quest \ˈkän-ˌkwest, ˈkäng-\ *n* **1 :** the act or process of conquering **2 a :** something conquered; *esp* **:** territory seized in war **b :** a person whose affections have been won [Medieval French, derived from Latin *conquisitus,* past participle of *conquirere* "to search for, collect"] ***synonyms*** see VICTORY

con·quis·ta·dor \kȯng-ˈkēs-tə-ˌdȯr; kän-ˈkis-, -ˈkwis-; kən-\ *n, pl* **con·quis·ta·do·res** \kȯng-ˌkēs-tə-ˈdȯr-ēz, -ˈdȯr-ˌās, -ˈdōr-; kän-ˌkis-, -kwis-; kən-\ *or* **con·quis·ta·dors :** one that conquers; *esp* **:** a leader in the Spanish conquest of America and especially of Mexico and Peru in the 16th century [Spanish, from *conquista* "conquest"]

con·san·guin·e·ous \ˌkän-ˌsan-ˈgwin-ē-əs, -ˌsang-\ *adj* **:** of the same blood or origin; *esp* **:** descended from the same ancestor [Latin *consanguineus,* from *com-* + *sanguin-, sanguis* "blood"] — **con·san·guin·e·ous·ly** *adv* — **con·san·guin·i·ty** \-ˈgwin-ət-ē\ *n*

con·science \ˈkän-chəns\ *n* **:** the sense or consciousness of the moral goodness or badness of one's own conduct, intentions, or character together with a feeling of obligation to do right or be good [Medieval French, from Latin *conscientia,* from *conscire* "to be conscious, be conscious of guilt," from *com-* + *scire* "to know"] — **in all conscience** *or* **in conscience :** in all fairness

conscience money *n* **:** money paid to relieve the conscience by restoring what has been wrongfully acquired

con·sci·en·tious \ˌkän-chē-ˈen-chəs\ *adj* **1 :** governed by or in accordance with one's conscience **:** SCRUPULOUS ⟨a *conscientious* public servant⟩ **2 :** marked by or done with exactness and thought **:** CAREFUL ⟨*conscientious* workmanship⟩ — **con·sci·en·tious·ly** *adv* — **con·sci·en·tious·ness** *n*

conscientious objector *n* **:** a person who refuses to serve in the armed forces or bear arms on the grounds of moral or religious principles

con·scious \ˈkän-chəs\ *adj* **1 :** perceiving or noticing facts or feelings **2 :** personally felt ⟨*conscious* guilt⟩ **3 :** capable of or marked by thought, will, design, or perception **4 :** SELF-CONSCIOUS **5 :** mentally alert or active **:** AWAKE **6 :** done or acting with critical awareness ⟨a *conscious* effort⟩ [Latin *conscius,* from *com-* + *scire* "to know"] — **con·scious·ly** *adv*

con·scious·ness \ˈkän-chəs-nəs\ *n* **1 :** awareness of something ⟨*consciousness* of evil⟩ **2 :** the condition of having ability to feel, think, and react **:** MIND **3 :** the normal state of conscious life as distinguished from sleep or insensibility **4 :** the part of mental life that is characterized by conscious thought and awareness

[1]**con·script** \ˈkän-ˌskript\ *adj* **1 :** enrolled into service by compulsion **:** DRAFTED **2 :** made up of conscripted persons ⟨a *conscript* army⟩ [French *conscrit,* from Latin *conscriptus,* past participle of Latin *conscribere* "to enroll, enlist," from *com-* + *scribere* "to write"]

[2]**conscript** *n* **:** a person who has been conscripted

[3]**con·script** \kən-ˈskript\ *vt* **:** to enroll into service by compulsion **:** DRAFT

con·scrip·tion \kən-ˈskrip-shən\ *n* **1 :** compulsory enrollment of persons especially for military service **:** DRAFT **2 :** a forced contribution (as of money) imposed by a government in time of emergency (as war)

\ə\ **abut**	\au̇\ **out**	\i\ **tip**	\ȯ\ **saw**	\u̇\ **foot**
\ər\ **further**	\ch\ **chin**	\ī\ **life**	\ȯi\ **coin**	\y\ **yet**
\a\ **mat**	\e\ **pet**	\j\ **job**	\th\ **thin**	\yü\ **few**
\ā\ **take**	\ē\ **easy**	\ng\ **sing**	\t͟h\ **this**	\yu̇\ **cure**
\ä\ **cot, cart**	\g\ **go**	\ō\ **bone**	\ü\ **food**	\zh\ **vision**

[1]**con·se·crate** \ˈkän-sə-ˌkrāt\ *adj* : dedicated to a sacred purpose

[2]**consecrate** *vb* **1** : to induct into a permanent office with a religious rite; *esp* : to ordain to the office of bishop **2** : to make or declare sacred : set apart for the service of God **3** : to devote to a purpose with deep solemnity or dedication **4** : to make inviolate or venerable ⟨rules *consecrated* by time⟩ [Latin *consecrare,* from *com-* + *sacrare* "to consecrate," from *sacer* "sacred"] ***synonyms*** see DEVOTE — **con·se·cra·tor** \-ˌkrāt-ər\ *n*

con·se·cra·tion \ˌkän-sə-ˈkrā-shən\ *n* **1** : the act or ceremony of consecrating **2** : the state of being consecrated **3** *often cap* : the part of a Communion rite in which the bread and wine are consecrated

con·sec·u·tive \kən-ˈsek-yət-iv, -ət-\ *adj* : following one after the other in order without gaps [Latin *consecutus,* past participle of *consequi* "to follow along"] — **con·sec·u·tive·ly** *adv* — **con·sec·u·tive·ness** *n*

synonyms CONSECUTIVE, SUCCESSIVE mean following one after the other. CONSECUTIVE stresses immediacy in following and implies that no interruption or interval occurs in the series ⟨three *consecutive* terms in office⟩. SUCCESSIVE may apply to things of the same kind that follow each other regardless of length of interval between ⟨rain fell on three *successive* weekends⟩.

con·sen·su·al \kən-ˈsench-wəl, -ə-wəl; -ˈsen-shəl\ *adj* : involving, made by, or based on shared consent ⟨a *consensual* contract⟩

con·sen·sus \kən-ˈsen-səs\ *n* **1** : general agreement (as in opinion or testimony) : ACCORD **2** : the trend of opinion [Latin, from *consentire* "to agree in feeling"]

[1]**con·sent** \kən-ˈsent\ *vi* : to give assent or approval : AGREE ⟨*consent* to being tested⟩ [Latin *consentire* "to agree in feeling," from *com-* + *sentire* "to feel"]

[2]**consent** *n* : compliance in or approval of what is asked or proposed : ACQUIESCENCE

con·se·quence \ˈkän-sə-ˌkwens, -si-kwəns\ *n* **1** : something produced by a cause or necessarily following from a set of conditions **2** : a conclusion that results from reason or argument **3 a** : importance with respect to power to produce an effect : MOMENT ⟨a mistake of no *consequence*⟩ **b** : social importance ⟨a person of *consequence*⟩ ***synonyms*** see EFFECT

[1]**con·se·quent** \-si-kwənt, -sə-ˌkwent\ *n* **1** : the conclusion of a conditional sentence **2** : the second term of a ratio

[2]**consequent** *adj* **1** : following as a result or effect **2** : observing logical sequence : RATIONAL [Latin *consequi* "to follow along," from *com-* + *sequi* "to follow"]

con·se·quen·tial \ˌkän-sə-ˈkwen-chəl\ *adj* **1** : of the nature of a consequence or result : following as a consequence **2** : having significant consequences **3** : having or displaying self-importance — **con·se·quen·tial·ly** \-ˈkwench-lē, -ə-lē\ *adv* — **con·se·quen·tial·ness** \-ˈkwen-chəl-nəs\ *n*

con·se·quen·tial·ism \-chə-ˌliz-əm\ *n* : the theory that the value and especially the moral value of an act should be judged by the value of its consequences — **con·se·quen·tial·ist** \-list\ *adj or n*

con·se·quent·ly \ˈkän-sə-ˌkwent-lē, -kwənt-\ *adv* : as a result : ACCORDINGLY

con·ser·van·cy \kən-ˈsər-vən-sē\ *n, pl* **-cies** : an organization or area designated to conserve and protect natural resources

con·ser·va·tion \ˌkän-sər-ˈvā-shən\ *n* : a careful preservation and protection of something; *esp* : planned management of a natural resource to prevent exploitation, destruction, or neglect — **con·ser·va·tion·al** \-shnəl, -shən-l\ *adj*

con·ser·va·tion·ist \-ˈvā-shə-nəst, -shnəst\ *n* : one who advocates conservation especially of natural resources

conservation of energy : a principle in physics: the total energy of an isolated system remains constant irrespective of whatever internal changes may take place

conservation of mass : a principle in classical physics: the total mass of any material system is neither increased nor diminished by reactions between the parts — called also *conservation of matter*

con·ser·va·tism \kən-ˈsər-və-ˌtiz-əm\ *n* **1 a** : disposition in politics to preserve what is established **b** : a political philosophy supporting tradition, social stability, and established institutions and preferring gradual development to abrupt change **2** : the tendency to prefer an existing situation and to be suspicious of change

[1]**con·ser·va·tive** \kən-ˈsər-vət-iv\ *adj* **1** : tending to conserve or preserve **2 a** : of or relating to conservatism **b** *often cap* : of or constituting a political party professing conservatism **3 a** : tending or disposed to maintain existing views, conditions, or institutions : TRADITIONAL **b** : MODERATE, CAUTIOUS ⟨a *conservative* investment⟩ **c** : marked by traditional standards of taste, elegance, or manners ⟨a *conservative* suit⟩ — **con·ser·va·tive·ly** *adv* — **con·ser·va·tive·ness** *n*

[2]**conservative** *n* **1 a** : an adherent or advocate of conservatism **b** *often cap* : a member or supporter of a conservative political party **2** : a cautious or discreet person

Conservative Judaism *n* : a movement in Judaism that holds sacred the Torah and Talmud but makes allowance for some changes suitable for different times and circumstances

con·ser·va·tor \kən-ˈsər-vət-ər, -və-ˌtȯr; ˈkän-sər-ˌvāt-ər\ *n* **1** : one that preserves or guards : PROTECTOR **2** : one designated to take over and protect the interests of an incompetent **3** : an official charged with the protection of something affecting public welfare and interests

con·ser·va·to·ry \kən-ˈsər-və-ˌtōr-ē, -ˌtȯr-\ *n, pl* **-ries** **1** : a greenhouse for growing or displaying plants **2** : a school specializing in one of the fine arts ⟨a music *conservatory*⟩

[1]**con·serve** \kən-ˈsərv\ *vt* **1** : to keep in a safe or sound state : PRESERVE ⟨*conserve* natural resources⟩ **2** : to preserve with sugar **3** : to maintain (a quantity) constant during a process of chemical, physical, or evolutionary change [Medieval French *conserver,* from Latin *conservare,* from *com-* + *servare* "to keep, guard, observe"] — **con·serv·er** *n*

[2]**con·serve** \ˈkän-ˌsərv\ *n* **1** : CONFECTION; *esp* : a candied fruit **2** : PRESERVE; *esp* : one prepared from a mixture of fruits

con·sid·er \kən-ˈsid-ər\ *vb* **-sid·ered; -sid·er·ing** \-ˈsid-ring, -ə-ring\ **1 a** : to think over carefully **b** : to think about with the idea of taking some action ⟨we are *considering* you for the job⟩ **2** : to regard or treat in a kind or thoughtful way ⟨he *considered* her every wish⟩ **3** : to think of in a certain way : regard as being ⟨*consider* the price too high⟩ [Medieval French *considerer,* from Latin *considerare* "to observe, think about," from *com-* + *sider-, sidus* "heavenly body"]

con·sid·er·able \kən-ˈsid-ər-bəl, -ər-ə-bəl, -ˈsid-rə-bəl\ *adj* **1** : worth consideration : IMPORTANT ⟨a *considerable* artist⟩ **2** : large in extent or degree ⟨a *considerable* area⟩ ⟨a *considerable* number⟩ — **con·sid·er·ably** \-blē\ *adv*

con·sid·er·ate \kən-ˈsid-rət, -ə-rət\ *adj* **1** : marked by or given to careful consideration : CIRCUMSPECT **2** : thoughtful of the rights and feelings of others ***synonyms*** see THOUGHTFUL — **con·sid·er·ate·ly** *adv* — **con·sid·er·ate·ness** *n*

con·sid·er·ation \kən-ˌsid-ə-ˈrā-shən\ *n* **1** : careful thought : DELIBERATION **2** : something considered as a ground : REASON **3** : thoughtfulness for other people **4** : RESPECT 3a, REGARD ⟨a person of *consideration* in that field⟩ **5** : a payment made in return for something : COMPENSATION

con·sid·er·ing \-ˈsid-ring, -ə-ring\ *prep* : in view of : taking into account ⟨he did well *considering* his limitations⟩

con·sign \kən-ˈsīn\ *vt* **1** : to give over to another's care : ENTRUST **2** : to give, transfer, or deliver formally ⟨*consign* a body to the grave⟩ **3** : to send or address to an agent to be cared for or sold [Latin *consignare,* from *com-* + *signum* "sign, mark, seal"] — **con·sign·able** \-ˈsī-nə-bəl\ *adj* — **con·sign·ee** \kən-ˌsī-ˈnē, ˌkän-ˌsī-, ˌkän-sə-\ *n* — **con·sign·or** \kən-ˈsī-nər; kən-ˌsī-ˈnȯr, ˌkän-ˌsī-, ˌkän-sə-\ *n*

con·sign·ment \kən-ˈsīn-mənt\ *n* **1** : the act or process of consigning **2** : something consigned especially in a single shipment

con·sist \kən-ˈsist\ *vi* **1** : to be contained : LIE, RESIDE — used with *in* ⟨happiness *consists* in good health and fortune⟩ **2** : to be composed or made up — used with *of* ⟨breakfast *consisted* of bacon and eggs⟩ [Latin *consistere,* literally, "to stop, stand still," from *com-* + *sistere* "to take a stand"]

con·sis·tence \kən-ˈsis-təns\ *n* : CONSISTENCY

con·sis·ten·cy \kən-ˈsis-tən-sē\ *n, pl* **-cies** **1** : the degree of density, firmness, viscosity, or resistance to movement or separation of constituent particles ⟨mud with the *consistency* of glue⟩ **2 a** : agreement or harmony of parts or features to one another or a whole **b** : harmony of conduct or practice with past performance or stated aims

con·sis·tent \kən-ˈsis-tənt\ *adj* **1** : marked by harmony, regularity, or steady continuity ⟨*consistent* statements⟩ **2** : marked by agreement : COMPATIBLE ⟨statements not *consistent* with the truth⟩ **3** : conforming steadily to one's own belief, profession, or character ⟨were *consistent* in their opposition⟩ — **con·sis·tent·ly** *adv*

con·sis·to·ry \kən-ˈsis-tə-rē, -trē\ *n, pl* **-ries** : a solemn meeting of Roman Catholic cardinals presided over by the pope [Medieval Latin *consistorium* "church tribunal," from Latin *consistere* "to stand still, remain, consist of"] — **con·sis·to·ri·al** \ˌkän-ˌsis-ˈtōr-ē-əl, -ˈtȯr-, kən-\ *adj*

con·so·la·tion \ˌkän-sə-ˈlā-shən\ *n* **1 :** the act or an instance of consoling : the state of being consoled : COMFORT **2 :** a contest held for those who have lost early in a tournament — **con·sol·a·to·ry** \kən-ˈsō-lə-ˌtōr-ē, -ˈsäl-ə-, -ˌtȯr-\ *adj*

consolation prize *n* **:** a prize given to a runner-up or a loser in a contest

1**con·sole** \kən-ˈsōl\ *vt* **:** to lessen the grief or sense of loss of [French *consoler,* from Latin *consolari,* from *com-* + *solari* "to console"] — **con·sol·able** \-ˈsō-lə-bəl\ *adj*

2**con·sole** \ˈkän-ˌsōl\ *n* **1 :** an architectural bracket used for ornament or support **2 a :** the desk from which an organ is played and which contains the keyboards, pedal board, and controls **b :** a panel or cabinet on which are mounted dials and switches used in controlling an electronic or mechanical device or system **3 :** a cabinet (as for a radio or television set) designed to rest directly on the floor **4 :** an electronic system that connects to a display (as a television set) and is used primarily to play video games [French]

console 1

con·sol·i·date \kən-ˈsäl-ə-ˌdāt\ *vb* **1 :** MERGE 2 **2 :** to make firm or secure : STRENGTHEN ⟨*consolidate* a beachhead⟩ **3 :** to form into a compact mass [Latin *consolidare* "to make solid," from *com-* + *solidus* "solid"]

consolidated school *n* **:** a public school formed by merging other schools

con·sol·i·da·tion \kən-ˌsäl-ə-ˈdā-shən\ *n* **1 :** the act or process of consolidating : the state of being consolidated **2 :** the merger of two or more corporations into one

con·som·mé \ˌkän-sə-ˈmā\ *n* **:** a clear soup chiefly of meat stock [French, from *consommer* "to complete, boil down," from Latin *consummare* "to complete"]

con·so·nance \ˈkän-sə-nəns, -snəns\ *n* **1 :** harmony or agreement of parts **2 a :** an agreeable combination or correspondence of musical tones or speech sounds **b :** a musical interval included in a major or minor triad and its inversions

1**con·so·nant** \ˈkän-sə-nənt, -snənt\ *n* **1 :** a speech sound (as \p\, \n\, or \s\) characterized by narrowing or stoppage at one or more points in the breath channel **2 :** a letter representing a consonant; *esp* **:** any letter of the English alphabet except *a, e, i, o,* and *u* [Latin *consonans,* from *consonare* "to sound together, agree," from *com-* + *sonare* "to sound"]

2**consonant** *adj* **1 :** being in agreement or harmony ⟨*consonant* with the truth⟩ **2 :** marked by musical consonances **3 :** having like sounds ⟨*consonant* words⟩ — **con·so·nant·ly** *adv*

con·so·nan·tal \ˌkän-sə-ˈnant-l\ *adj* **:** relating to, being, or marked by a consonant or group of consonants

1**con·sort** \ˈkän-ˌsȯrt\ *n* **1 :** ASSOCIATE **2 :** a ship sailing in company with another ship **3 :** SPOUSE [Middle French, "associate," from Latin *consors* "partner, sharer," from *com-* + *sors* "lot, share"]

2**con·sort** \kən-ˈsȯrt\ *vb* **1 :** to keep company : ASSOCIATE ⟨*consorting* with criminals⟩ **2 :** ACCORD 2, HARMONIZE

consortia *plural of* CONSORTIUM

con·sor·tium \kən-ˈsȯr-shē-əm, -shəm\ *n, pl* **-tia** \-shē-ə, -shə\ **:** an international business or banking agreement or combination [Latin, "fellowship," from *consors* "partner"]

con·spe·cif·ic \ˌkän-spi-ˈsif-ik\ *adj* **:** of the same species

con·spec·tus \kən-ˈspek-təs\ *n* **1 :** a brief survey or summary **2 :** a condensed version of a larger work : SYNOPSIS [Latin, "sight," from *conspicere* "to catch sight of"]

con·spic·u·ous \kən-ˈspik-yə-wəs\ *adj* **1 :** obvious to the eye or mind **2 :** attracting attention : STRIKING **3 :** noticeably violating good taste [Latin *conspicuus,* from *conspicere* "to catch sight of, notice," from *com-* + *specere* "to look"] ***synonyms*** see NOTICEABLE — **con·spic·u·ous·ly** *adv* — **con·spic·u·ous·ness** *n*

con·spir·a·cist \kən-ˈspir-ə-sist\ *n* **:** one who believes or promotes a conspiracy theory

con·spir·a·cy \kən-ˈspir-ə-sē\ *n, pl* **-cies** **1 :** the act of conspiring together **2 a :** an agreement among conspirators **b :** a group of conspirators ***synonyms*** see PLOT

conspiracy theory *n* **:** a theory that explains an event or situation as being the result of a secret plot — **conspiracy theorist** *n*

con·spir·a·tor \kən-ˈspir-ət-ər\ *n* **:** one who conspires : PLOTTER

con·spir·a·to·ri·al \kən-ˌspir-ə-ˈtōr-ē-əl, -ˈtȯr-\ *adj* **:** of, relating to, or characteristic of a conspiracy — **con·spir·a·to·ri·al·ly** \-ē\ *adv*

con·spire \kən-ˈspīr\ *vi* **1 :** to join in a secret agreement to do an unlawful or wrongful act or an act which becomes unlawful as a result of the secret agreement ⟨*conspire* against the state⟩ **2 :** to act in harmony ⟨events *conspired* to defeat their efforts⟩ [Medieval French *conspirer,* from Latin *conspirare* "to be in harmony, conspire," from *com-* + *spirare* "to breathe"]

con·sta·ble \ˈkän-stə-bəl, ˈkən-\ *n* **1 :** a high officer of a royal court or noble household especially in the Middle Ages **2 :** the warden of a royal castle or a fortified town **3 a :** a public officer responsible for keeping the peace **b** *chiefly British* **:** POLICE OFFICER [Medieval French *conestable,* from Late Latin *comes stabuli,* literally, "officer of the stable"]

Word History When the word *constable* first came into English from French in the Middle Ages, a *conestable* was the chief officer of a king's household. His office was one of great power: he could be commander of an army or governor of a domain, subordinate only to the king himself. Latin *comes stabuli,* which is the ancestor of *constable,* means literally "officer of the stable." The title was transferred from stable to court, but without great increase in prestige. All the king's horses were scarcely less valuable to the king than all his men, and being in charge of them was a very important duty.

con·stab·u·lary \kən-ˈstab-yə-ˌler-ē\ *n, pl* **-lar·ies** **1 :** an organized body of police **2 :** an armed police force organized on military lines but distinct from the regular army

con·stan·cy \ˈkän-stən-sē\ *n* **1 a :** firmness in one's beliefs : STEADFASTNESS **b :** steadiness in attachments : LOYALTY **2 :** freedom from change : STABILITY

1**con·stant** \ˈkän-stənt\ *adj* **1 :** marked by firm resolution or faithfulness : STEADFAST ⟨a *constant* friend⟩ **2 :** remaining unchanged : UNIFORM ⟨a *constant* flow⟩ **3 :** continually occurring or recurring : REGULAR ⟨a *constant* annoyance⟩ [Middle French, from Latin *constans,* from *constare* "to stand firm," from *com-* + *stare* "to stand"] ***synonyms*** see CONTINUAL, FAITHFUL — **con·stant·ly** *adv*

2**constant** *n* **:** something invariable or unchanging: as **a :** a number that has a fixed value (as the velocity of light) in a given situation or universally or that is a characteristic (as the refractive index of glass) of some substance or instrument **b :** a quantity whose value does not change under given mathematical conditions — compare VARIABLE 1

con·stan·tan \ˈkän-stən-ˌtan\ *n* **:** an alloy of copper and nickel used especially for electrical resistors and in thermocouples [from the fact that its resistance remains constant under change of temperature]

con·stel·la·tion \ˌkän-stə-ˈlā-shən\ *n* **1 :** any of 88 groups of stars forming patterns (as the Big Dipper) or an area of the heavens covering one of these groups **2 :** an assemblage, collection, or group of usually related persons, qualities, or things ⟨a *constellation* of symptoms⟩ [Medieval French, from Late Latin *constellatio,* from Latin *com-* + *stella* "star"]

con·ster·nate \ˈkän-stər-ˌnāt\ *vt* **:** to fill with consternation

con·ster·na·tion \ˌkän-stər-ˈnā-shən\ *n* **:** amazement or dismay that hinders or throws into confusion [Latin *consternatio,* from *consternare* "to throw into confusion"]

con·sti·pate \ˈkän-stə-ˌpāt\ *vt* **:** to cause constipation in [Medieval Latin *constipare,* from Latin, "to crowd together," from *com-* + *stipare* "to pack tight"]

con·sti·pat·ed \-ˌpāt-əd\ *adj* **:** affected with constipation

con·sti·pa·tion \ˌkän-stə-ˈpā-shən\ *n* **:** abnormally delayed or infrequent passage of dry hardened feces

con·stit·u·en·cy \kən-ˈstich-wən-sē, -ə-wən-\ *n, pl* **-cies** **1 :** a body of citizens entitled to elect a representative to a legislative or other public body **2 a :** the residents in an electoral district **b :** an electoral district **3 :** a group of supporters

\ə\ **abut**	\au̇\ **out**	\i\ **tip**	\ȯ\ **saw**	\u̇\ **foot**
\ər\ **further**	\ch\ **chin**	\ī\ **life**	\ȯi\ **coin**	\y\ **yet**
\a\ **mat**	\e\ **pet**	\j\ **job**	\th\ **thin**	\yü\ **few**
\ā\ **take**	\ē\ **easy**	\ng\ **sing**	\t͟h\ **this**	\yu̇\ **cure**
\ä\ **cot, cart**	\g\ **go**	\ō\ **bone**	\ü\ **food**	\zh\ **vision**

[1]**con·stit·u·ent** \kən-ˈstich-wənt, -ə-wənt\ *n* **1 :** an essential part **:** COMPONENT, ELEMENT ⟨flour is the chief *constituent* of bread⟩ **2 a :** one of a group who elects another as a representative in public office **b :** a resident in a constituency [French *constituant,* from Middle French *constituer* "to constitute," from Latin *constituere*] ***synonyms*** see ELEMENT

[2]**constituent** *adj* **1 :** forming a part of a whole **:** COMPONENT **2 :** having the power to create a government or to frame or amend a constitution ⟨a *constituent* assembly⟩ — **con·stit·u·ent·ly** *adv*

con·sti·tute \ˈkän-stə-ˌtüt, -tyüt\ *vt* **1 :** to appoint to an office or duty ⟨a duly *constituted* representative⟩ **2 :** to set up **:** ESTABLISH ⟨a fund was *constituted* to help needy students⟩ **3 :** to make up **:** FORM ⟨twelve months *constitute* a year⟩ [Latin *constituere* "to set up, constitute," from *com-* + *statuere* "to set, fix," from *status* "position, state"]

con·sti·tu·tion \ˌkän-stə-ˈtü-shən, -ˈtyü-\ *n* **1 :** the act of establishing, making, or setting up **2 a :** the physical makeup of an individual especially with respect to the health, strength, and appearance of the body **b :** the structure, composition, or nature of something **3 a :** the basic principles and laws of a nation, state, or social group that determine the powers and duties of the government and guarantee certain rights to the people in it **b :** a document containing a constitution

[1]**con·sti·tu·tion·al** \-shnəl, -shən-l\ *adj* **1 :** of, relating to, or affecting a person's physical or mental makeup **2 :** of, relating to, or entering into the fundamental makeup of something **:** ESSENTIAL **3 :** of, relating to, or in accordance with the constitution of a nation or state ⟨a *constitutional* amendment⟩ ⟨*constitutional* rights⟩ — **con·sti·tu·tion·al·ly** \-ē\ *adv*

[2]**constitutional** *n* **:** a walk taken for one's health

con·sti·tu·tion·al·ism \-ˌiz-əm\ *n* **:** adherence to or government according to constitutional principles — **con·sti·tu·tion·al·ist** \-əst\ *n*

con·sti·tu·tion·al·i·ty \ˌkän-stə-ˌtü-shə-ˈnal-ət-ē, -ˌtyü-\ *n* **:** the quality or state of being in accordance with the provisions of a constitution

con·sti·tu·tive \ˈkän-stə-ˌtüt-iv, -ˌtyüt-; kən-ˈstich-ət-iv\ *adj* **:** forming part of the structure of a thing **:** CONSTITUENT, ESSENTIAL — **con·sti·tu·tive·ly** *adv*

con·strain \kən-ˈstrān\ *vt* **1 :** to force by imposed restriction or limitation **2 :** to force or produce in an unnatural or strained manner ⟨a *constrained* smile⟩ **3 :** to secure by or as if by bond **:** CONFINE **4 :** to hold back by force **:** RESTRAIN [Medieval French *constraindre,* from Latin *constringere* "to constrict, constrain," from *com-* + *stringere* "to draw tight"] ***synonyms*** see FORCE — **con·strained·ly** \-ˈstrān-əd-lē, -ˈstrān-dlē\ *adv*

con·straint \kən-ˈstrānt\ *n* **1 a :** the act of constraining **:** the state of being constrained **b :** a constraining agency or force **:** CHECK ⟨legal *constraints*⟩ **2 a :** a holding back of one's feelings, behavior, or actions **b :** a sense of being constrained **:** EMBARRASSMENT

con·strict \kən-ˈstrikt\ *vb* **1 a :** to make or become smaller in bulk or volume by means of compression; *also* **:** SQUEEZE 1a, COMPRESS ⟨snakes that kill by *constricting* their prey⟩ **b :** to make or become narrow or narrower ⟨the pupil of the eye *constricts* in bright light⟩ **2 :** to slow down, stop, or cause to falter **:** INHIBIT ⟨a lack of funds *constricted* construction⟩ [Latin *constrictus,* past participle of *constringere* "to constrict, constrain"] — **con·stric·tive** \-ˈstrik-tiv\ *adj*

con·stric·tion \kən-ˈstrik-shən\ *n* **1 :** an act of constricting **:** the state of being constricted **2 :** something that constricts **:** a part that is constricted

con·stric·tor \kən-ˈstrik-tər\ *n* **1 :** one that constricts **2 :** a snake that kills prey by coiling around and compressing it

con·struct \kən-ˈstrəkt\ *vt* **1 :** to make or form by combining parts **2 :** to draw (a geometrical figure) with suitable instruments and under specified conditions [Latin *constructus,* past participle of *construere* "to construct," from *com-* + *struere* "to build"] — **con·struct·able** *or* **con·struct·ible** \-ˈstrək-tə-bəl\ *adj* — **con·struc·tor** \-ˈstrək-tər\ *n*

con·struc·tion \kən-ˈstrək-shən\ *n* **1 :** the act or result of construing, interpreting, or explaining ⟨strict *construction* of the law⟩ **2 :** the process, art, or manner of constructing; *also* **:** a thing constructed **:** STRUCTURE **3 :** the arrangement and connection of words or groups of words in a sentence — **con·struc·tion·al** \-shnəl, -shən-l\ *adj* — **con·struc·tion·al·ly** \-ē\ *adv*

con·struc·tion·ist \kən-ˈstrək-shə-nəst, -shnəst\ *n* **:** one who construes a legal document (as the U.S. Constitution) in a specific way ⟨a strict *constructionist*⟩

construction paper *n* **:** a thick colored paper used especially for school art work

con·struc·tive \kən-ˈstrək-tiv\ *adj* **1 :** fitted for or given to constructing ⟨Edison was a *constructive* genius⟩ **2 :** helping to develop or improve something ⟨*constructive* criticism⟩ — **con·struc·tive·ly** *adv* — **con·struc·tive·ness** *n*

con·strue \kən-ˈstrü\ *vb* **1 :** to explain the grammatical relationships of the words in a sentence, clause, or phrase **2 :** to understand or explain the sense or intention of **:** INTERPRET [Late Latin *construere,* from Latin, "to construct"] — **con·stru·able** \-ˈstrü-ə-bəl\ *adj*

con·sul \ˈkän-səl\ *n* **1 :** either of two chief magistrates of the Roman republic **2 :** an official appointed by a government to live in a foreign country to represent the commercial interests of citizens of the appointing country [Latin] — **con·sul·ar** \-sə-lər, -slər\ *adj* — **con·sul·ship** \-səl-ˌship\ *n*

con·sul·ate \ˈkän-sə-lət, -slət\ *n* **1 :** a government by consuls **2 :** the office, term of office, or jurisdiction of a consul **3 :** the residence or official premises of a consul

con·sult \kən-ˈsəlt\ *vb* **1 :** to ask the advice or opinion of ⟨*consult* a doctor⟩ **2 :** to seek information from ⟨*consult* a dictionary⟩ **3 :** to have regard to **:** CONSIDER ⟨*consult* one's best interests⟩ **4 :** to deliberate together **:** CONFER [Latin *consultare,* from *consulere* "to deliberate, counsel, consult"] — **con·sult·er** *n*

con·sult·ant \kən-ˈsəlt-nt\ *n* **1 :** one who consults another **2 :** one who gives professional advice or services

con·sul·ta·tion \ˌkän-səl-ˈtā-shən\ *n* **1 :** CONFERENCE 1, COUNCIL; *esp* **:** a deliberation between physicians on a case or its treatment **2 :** the act of consulting or conferring

con·sul·ta·tive \kən-ˈsəl-tət-iv\ *adj* **:** of, relating to, or intended for consultation **:** ADVISORY

con·sul·tor \kən-ˈsəl-tər\ *n* **:** one who consults or advises; *esp* **:** a member of a Roman Catholic diocesan advisory council

con·sume \kən-ˈsüm\ *vb* **1 :** to destroy or be destroyed by or as if by fire **2 a :** to spend wastefully **:** SQUANDER **b :** to use up **:** EXPEND ⟨the search *consumed* most of our time⟩ **3 :** to eat or drink up **4 :** to engage one's interest or attention ⟨*consumed* with curiosity⟩ **5 :** to use as a customer ⟨*consume* goods and services⟩ [Latin *consumere,* from *com-* + *sumere* "to take up, take," from *sub-* "up" + *emere* "to take"] — **con·sum·able** \-ˈsü-mə-bəl\ *adj*

con·sum·er \kən-ˈsü-mər\ *n* **:** one that consumes: as **a :** one that buys and uses economic goods **b :** an organism requiring complex organic compounds for food which it obtains by preying on other organisms or by eating particles of organic matter — compare PRODUCER 3

consumer credit *n* **:** credit granted to an individual especially to finance purchase of consumer goods or defray personal expenses

consumer goods *n pl* **:** goods that directly satisfy human wants

con·sum·er·ism \kən-ˈsü-mə-ˌriz-əm\ *n* **:** concern for or protection of the consumer's welfare — **con·sum·er·ist** \-rəst\ *n or adj*

[1]**con·sum·mate** \kən-ˈsəm-ət, ˈkän-sə-mət\ *adj* **1 :** complete in every detail **:** PERFECT **2 :** of the highest degree or quality ⟨*consummate* skill⟩ [Latin *consummare* "to sum up, finish," from *com-* + *summa* "sum"] — **con·sum·mate·ly** *adv*

[2]**con·sum·mate** \ˈkän-sə-ˌmāt\ *vt* **1 a :** to bring to completion **:** FINISH ⟨*consummate* a deal⟩ **b :** to make perfect **2 :** to make (marital union) complete by sexual intercourse — **con·sum·ma·tion** \ˌkän-sə-ˈmā-shən\ *n*

con·sump·tion \kən-ˈsəm-shən, -ˈsəmp-\ *n* **1 a :** the act or process of consuming **b :** the amount consumed ⟨yearly fuel *consumption*⟩ **2 a :** a progressive wasting away of the body especially from pulmonary tuberculosis **b :** TUBERCULOSIS [Latin *consumptio,* from *consumere* "to consume"]

[1]**con·sump·tive** \kən-ˈsəm-tiv, -ˈsəmp-\ *adj* **1 :** tending to consume **2 :** of, relating to, or affected with consumption — **con·sump·tive·ly** *adv*

[2]**consumptive** *n* **:** a person affected with consumption

[1]**con·tact** \ˈkän-ˌtakt\ *n* **1 a :** union or junction of surfaces **b (1) :** the junction of two electrical conductors through which a current passes **(2) :** a special part made for such a junction or connection **2 a :** a social or business connection ⟨has *contacts* in the government⟩ **b :** a condition or instance of meeting, connecting, or communicating ⟨let's keep in *contact*⟩ **c :** di-

rect visual observation of the earth's surface made from an airplane especially as an aid to navigation **d** : an establishing of communication with someone or an observing or receiving of a significant signal from a person or object ⟨radar *contact* with Mars⟩ [Latin *contactus,* from *contingere* "to have contact with," from *com-* + *tangere* "to touch"]

[2]**con·tact** \ˈkän-ˌtakt, kən-ˈ\ *vb* : to bring or come into contact

[3]**con·tact** \ˈkän-ˌtakt\ *adj* : maintaining, involving, or caused by contact ⟨*contact* sports⟩

contact lens *n* : a thin lens designed to fit over the cornea and usually worn to correct defects in vision

contact print *n* : a photographic print made with the negative in contact with the sensitized paper, plate, or film

con·ta·gion \kən-ˈtā-jən\ *n* **1** : the passing of a disease from one individual to another by direct or indirect contact **2** : a contagious disease or its causative agent **3 a** : rapid communication of an influence (as an idea or doctrine) **b** : an influence that spreads rapidly [Latin *contagio,* from *contingere* "to have contact with"]

con·ta·gious \kən-ˈtā-jəs\ *adj* **1** : communicable by contact : CATCHING ⟨*contagious* diseases⟩ **2** : bearing contagion ⟨a person who is *contagious*⟩ **3** : used for contagious diseases ⟨a *contagious* ward⟩ **4** : exciting similar emotions or behavior in others ⟨*contagious* enthusiasm⟩ — **con·ta·gious·ly** *adv* — **con·ta·gious·ness** *n*

con·tain \kən-ˈtān\ *vt* **1** : to keep within limits : hold back : RESTRAIN ⟨*contain* one's anger⟩ **2 a** : to have within : HOLD **b** : COMPRISE, INCLUDE ⟨a gallon *contains* four quarts⟩ **3** : to be divisible by especially without a remainder ⟨12 *contains* 3⟩ [Medieval French *cuntenir,* from Latin *continēre* "to hold together, hold in, contain," from *com-* + *tenēre* "to hold"] — **con·tain·able** \-ˈtā-nə-bəl\ *adj*

synonyms CONTAIN, HOLD, ACCOMMODATE mean to have or be capable of having within. CONTAIN implies the actual presence of a specified substance or quantity within something ⟨the can *contains* a quart of oil⟩. HOLD may imply only the capacity or usual function of containing or keeping ⟨the bookcase will *hold* all my books⟩. ACCOMMODATE stresses capacity to hold without crowding or inconvenience ⟨the hall can *accommodate* 500 people⟩.

con·tain·er \kən-ˈtā-nər\ *n* : one that contains; *esp* : RECEPTACLE

con·tain·er·ship \-ˌship\ *n* : a ship designed or equipped to carry very large containers of cargo

con·tain·ment \kən-ˈtān-mənt\ *n* **1** : the act or process of containing **2** : the policy, process, or result of preventing the expansion of a hostile power or ideology

con·tam·i·nant \kən-ˈtam-ə-nənt\ *n* : something that contaminates

con·tam·i·nate \kən-ˈtam-ə-ˌnāt\ *vt* **1** : to soil, stain, or infect by contact or association **2** : to make unfit for use by introduction of unwholesome or undesirable elements [Latin *contaminare*] — **con·tam·i·na·tion** \-ˌtam-ə-ˈnā-shən\ *n* — **con·tam·i·na·tive** \-ˌnāt-iv\ *adj* — **con·tam·i·na·tor** \-ˈtam-ə-ˌnāt-ər\ *n*

con·temn \kən-ˈtem\ *vt* : to view or treat with contempt : SCORN [Medieval French *contempner,* from Latin *contemnere,* from *com-* + *temnere* "to despise"] ***synonyms*** see DESPISE — **con·tem·ner** *also* **con·tem·nor** \-ˈtem-ər, -ˈtem-nər\ *n*

con·tem·plate \ˈkänt-əm-ˌplāt, ˈkän-ˌtem-\ *vb* **1** : to consider long and carefully : MEDITATE **2** : to look forward to : have in mind : INTEND ⟨*contemplating* a trip to Europe⟩ [Latin *contemplari,* from *com-* + *templum* "temple, space marked out for observation of auguries"] — **con·tem·pla·tor** \-ˌplāt-ər\ *n*

con·tem·pla·tion \ˌkänt-əm-ˈplā-shən, ˌkän-ˌtem-\ *n* **1** : concentration on spiritual things as a form of private devotion **2** : an act of considering with attention : STUDY **3** : the act of regarding steadily **4** : the act of considering a future event : EXPECTATION

con·tem·pla·tive \kən-ˈtem-plət-iv; ˈkänt-əm-ˌplāt-, ˈkän-ˌtem-\ *adj* **1** : marked by or given to contemplation **2** : of or relating to a religious order devoted to prayer and penance — **con·tem·pla·tive·ly** *adv* — **con·tem·pla·tive·ness** *n*

con·tem·po·ra·ne·ous \kən-ˌtem-pə-ˈrā-nē-əs\ *adj* : existing, occurring, or originating during the same time [Latin *contemporaneus,* from *com-* + *tempor-, tempus* "time"] — **con·tem·po·ra·ne·ous·ly** *adv* — **con·tem·po·ra·ne·ous·ness** *n*

[1]**con·tem·po·rary** \kən-ˈtem-pə-ˌrer-ē\ *adj* **1** : living or occurring during the same time : CONTEMPORANEOUS ⟨*contemporary* events in different countries⟩ **2** : of the same age **3** : existing in the present : CURRENT ⟨our *contemporary* writers⟩ [*com-* + Latin *tempor-, tempus* "time"]

synonyms CONTEMPORARY, SIMULTANEOUS, CONCURRENT, COINCIDENT mean existing or occurring at the same time. CONTEMPORARY applies chiefly to people and what relates to them and suggests indefinite lengths of time ⟨playwrights *contemporary* with Shakespeare⟩. SIMULTANEOUS implies correspondence in a moment of time ⟨the two shots were almost *simultaneous*⟩. CONCURRENT implies beginning and ending together ⟨*concurrent* prison sentences⟩. COINCIDENT stresses simultaneousness of events and may emphasize lack of causal relation ⟨found that their birthdays were *coincident*⟩.

[2]**contemporary** *n, pl* **-rar·ies** **1** : one that is contemporary with another **2** : one of about the same age as another

con·tempt \kən-ˈtemt, -ˈtempt\ *n* **1 a** : the act of despising **b** : the state of mind of one who despises : DISDAIN **2** : the state of being despised **3** : disobedience to or open disrespect for a court, judge, or legislative body [Latin *contemptus,* from *contemnere* "to contemn"]

con·tempt·ible \kən-ˈtem-tə-bəl, -ˈtemp-\ *adj* : deserving contempt ⟨a *contemptible* lie⟩ — **con·tempt·ibly** \-blē\ *adv*

synonyms CONTEMPTIBLE, DESPICABLE, SCURVY mean arousing or deserving scorn. CONTEMPTIBLE may apply to whatever is worthy of contempt ⟨a *contemptible* liar⟩. DESPICABLE implies utter worthlessness and usually suggests arousing an attitude of indignant moral disapproval ⟨a *despicable* criminal⟩. SCURVY implies extreme meanness and the arousing of disgust ⟨*scurvy* bandits⟩.

con·temp·tu·ous \kən-ˈtem-chə-wəs, -ˈtemp-, -chəs; -ˈtemsh-wəs, -ˈtempsh-\ *adj* : feeling or showing contempt ⟨a *contemptuous* sneer⟩ — **con·temp·tu·ous·ly** *adv* — **con·temp·tu·ous·ness** *n*

con·tend \kən-ˈtend\ *vb* **1** : to strive in opposition to someone or something ⟨*contending* against temptation⟩ **2** : MAINTAIN 2, ARGUE ⟨*contend* that their opinions are right⟩ **3** : RIVAL 2, COMPETE ⟨*contend* for a prize⟩ [Latin *contendere,* from *com-* + *tendere* "to stretch"] — **con·tend·er** *n*

[1]**con·tent** \kən-ˈtent\ *adj* : being satisfied ⟨*content* to wait⟩ [Middle French, from Latin *contentus,* from *continēre* "to hold in, contain"]

[2]**content** *vt* : to appease the desires of : SATISFY

[3]**content** *n* : CONTENTMENT; *esp* : freedom from care of discomfort

[4]**con·tent** \ˈkän-ˌtent\ *n* **1** : something contained — usually used in plural ⟨the *contents* of a jar⟩ **2 a** : the topics or matter treated in a written work ⟨table of *contents*⟩ **b** : essential meaning or significance **3** : the amount of specified material contained : PROPORTION ⟨the sulfur *content* in a coal sample⟩ [Latin *contentus,* past participle of *continēre* "to contain"]

con·tent·ed \kən-ˈtent-əd\ *adj* : satisfied or showing satisfaction with one's possessions, status, or situation ⟨a *contented* smile⟩ — **con·tent·ed·ly** *adv* — **con·tent·ed·ness** *n*

con·ten·tion \kən-ˈten-chən\ *n* **1** : an act or instance of contending : STRIFE, DISPUTE **2** : a point advanced or maintained in a debate or argument [Medieval French *cuntenciun,* from Latin *contentio,* from *contendere* "to contend"]

con·ten·tious \kən-ˈten-chəs\ *adj* : inclined to quarrels and disputes often over unimportant matters ***synonyms*** see BELLIGERENT — **con·ten·tious·ly** *adv* — **con·ten·tious·ness** *n*

con·tent·ment \kən-ˈtent-mənt\ *n* : the state of being contented : peaceful satisfaction

con·ter·mi·nous \kən-ˈtər-mə-nəs, kän-\ *adj* **1** : having the same or a common boundary **2** : enclosed within one common boundary ⟨the 48 *conterminous* states of the U.S.⟩ [Latin *conterminus,* from *com-* + *terminus* "boundary"] — **con·ter·mi·nous·ly** *adv*

[1]**con·test** \kən-ˈtest, ˈkän-ˌ\ *vb* **1** : to make the subject of dispute or litigation; *esp* : CHALLENGE 3b ⟨*contest* a claim⟩ **2** : to struggle over or for ⟨a *contested* territory⟩ **3** : RIVAL 2, VIE ⟨*contested* for the prize⟩ [Middle French *contester,* from Latin *contestari* "to call to witness, contest (a lawsuit)," from *com-* + *testis* "witness"] — **con·test·able** \-ə-bəl\ *adj* — **con·test·er** *n*

\ə\ **abut**	\au̇\ **out**	\i\ **tip**	\ȯ\ **saw**	\u̇\ **foot**
\ər\ **further**	\ch\ **chin**	\ī\ **life**	\ȯi\ **coin**	\y\ **yet**
\a\ **mat**	\e\ **pet**	\j\ **job**	\th\ **thin**	\yü\ **few**
\ā\ **take**	\ē\ **easy**	\ng\ **sing**	\th\ **this**	\yu̇\ **cure**
\ä\ **cot, cart**	\g\ **go**	\ō\ **bone**	\ü\ **food**	\zh\ **vision**

[2]**con·test** \ˈkän-ˌtest\ *n* : a struggle for victory or superiority : COMPETITION

con·tes·tant \kən-ˈtes-tənt, ˈkän-ˌtes-\ *n* : one that takes part in a contest

con·text \ˈkän-ˌtekst\ *n* **1** : the parts of a written or spoken passage that are near a certain word or group of words and that help to explain its meaning **2** : the circumstances surrounding an act or event [Latin *contextus* "connection of words, coherence," from *contexere* "to weave together," from *com-* + *texere* "to weave"] — **con·tex·tu·al** \kän-ˈteks-chə-wəl, -chəl\ *adj* — **con·tex·tu·al·ly** \-ē\ *adv*

con·ti·gu·i·ty \ˌkänt-ə-ˈgyü-ət-ē\ *n, pl* **-ties** : the quality or state of being contiguous : PROXIMITY

con·tig·u·ous \kən-ˈtig-yə-wəs\ *adj* **1** : being in contact : TOUCHING **2** : very near though not in actual contact : NEIGHBORING **3** : CONTERMINOUS 2 [Latin *contiguus,* from *contingere* "to have contact with"] — **con·tig·u·ous·ly** *adv* — **con·tig·u·ous·ness** *n*

con·ti·nence \ˈkänt-n-əns\ *n* **1** : self-restraint especially from engaging in sexual intercourse **2** : the ability to retain a bodily discharge voluntarily

[1]**con·ti·nent** \ˈkänt-n-ənt\ *adj* : exercising continence [Medieval French, from Latin *continens,* from *continēre* "to hold together, hold in, contain"] — **con·ti·nent·ly** *adv*

[2]**con·ti·nent** \ˈkänt-n-ənt, ˈkänt-nənt\ *n* **1** : a continuous mass of land **2 a** : one of the great divisions of land (as North America, South America, Europe, Asia, Africa, Australia, or Antarctica) on the globe **b** *often cap* : the continent of Europe

[1]**con·ti·nen·tal** \ˌkänt-n-ˈent-l\ *adj* **1** : of, relating to, or characteristic of a continent ⟨*continental* waters⟩; *esp* : of or relating to the continent of Europe **2** *often cap* : of or relating to the colonies later forming the U.S. ⟨*Continental* Congress⟩ — **con·ti·nen·tal·ly** \-l-ē\ *adv*

[2]**continental** *n* **1 a** *often cap* : an American soldier of the Revolution in the Continental army **b** : a piece of paper currency issued by the Continental Congress **c** : the least bit ⟨not worth a *continental*⟩ **2** : an inhabitant of a continent and especially the continent of Europe [sense 1c from the doubtful value of Continental currency]

continental breakfast *n, often cap C* : a light breakfast (as of rolls or toast and coffee)

continental drift *n* : a slow movement of the continents on a deep viscous zone within the earth

continental shelf *n* : a shallow submarine plain of varying width forming a border to a continent and typically ending in a steep slope to the depths of the ocean

continental slope *n* : a steep slope from the continental shelf to the ocean floor

con·tin·gen·cy \kən-ˈtin-jən-sē\ *n, pl* **-cies** **1** : the state of being contingent **2** : a chance happening or event **3** : a possible event or one foreseen as possible if another occurs

[1]**con·tin·gent** \-jənt\ *adj* **1** : likely but not certain to happen : POSSIBLE **2 a** : happening by chance or unforeseen causes **b** : intended for use in circumstances not completely foreseen ⟨*contingent* funds⟩ **3** : dependent on or conditioned by something else ⟨plans *contingent* on the weather⟩ [Medieval French, from Latin *contingere* "to have contact with, happen to"] — **con·tin·gent·ly** *adv*

[2]**contingent** *n* **1** : a chance occurrence : CONTINGENCY **2** : a number of persons representing or drawn from an area or group ⟨a *contingent* of troops from each regiment⟩

con·tin·u·al \kən-ˈtin-yə-wəl, -ˈtin-yəl\ *adj* **1** : continuing indefinitely without interruption ⟨*continual* fear⟩ **2** : recurring in steady and usually rapid succession ⟨*continual* interruptions⟩ — **con·tin·u·al·ly** \-ē\ *adv*

synonyms CONTINUAL, CONTINUOUS, INCESSANT, CONSTANT mean marked by continued occurrence or recurrence. CONTINUAL implies prolonged succession or recurrence ⟨*continual* rain showers⟩. CONTINUOUS implies uninterrupted flow ⟨the *continuous* roar of the falls⟩. INCESSANT implies ceaseless activity of varying intensity ⟨*incessant* quarreling⟩. CONSTANT implies uniform or persistent occurrence or recurrence ⟨a *constant* supply of work⟩.

con·tin·u·ance \kən-ˈtin-yə-wəns\ *n* **1** : the act of continuing in a state, condition, or course of action ⟨during the *continuance* of the illness⟩ **2** : unbroken succession : CONTINUATION **3** : postponement of court proceedings to a specified day

con·tin·u·a·tion \kən-ˌtin-yə-ˈwā-shən\ *n* **1** : continuance in or extension of a state or activity **2** : resumption after an interruption **3** : something that continues, increases, or adds ⟨a *continuation* of last week's story⟩

con·tin·ue \kən-ˈtin-yü\ *vb* **1** : to remain in a place or a condition : STAY ⟨*continue* in one's present job⟩ **2** : ENDURE, LAST ⟨rain *continued*⟩ **3** : to go on or carry forward in a course ⟨*continue* to study hard⟩ **4** : to go on or carry on after an interruption : RESUME ⟨play *continued* after a time-out⟩ **5** : to postpone a legal proceeding to a later date **6** : to allow or cause to remain especially in a position ⟨the town officials were *continued* in office⟩ [Medieval French *continuer,* from Latin *continuare,* from *continuus* "continuous"] — **con·tin·u·er** *n*

continued fraction *n* : a fraction whose numerator is a whole number and whose denominator is a whole number plus a fraction whose numerator is a whole number and whose denominator is a whole number plus a fraction and so on

con·ti·nu·i·ty \ˌkänt-n-ˈü-ət-ē, -ˈyü-\ *n, pl* **-ties** **1 a** : uninterrupted connection, succession, or union **b** : persistence without change **2 a** : a motion-picture, radio, or television script **b** : transitional spoken or musical matter for a radio or television program

con·tin·u·ous \kən-ˈtin-yə-wəs\ *adj* : being without break or interruption : UNBROKEN ⟨a *continuous* line⟩ [Latin *continuus,* from *continēre* "to hold together, contain"] ***synonyms*** see CONTINUAL — **con·tin·u·ous·ly** *adv* — **con·tin·u·ous·ness** *n*

con·tin·u·um \-yə-wəm\ *n, pl* **-ua** \-wə\ *also* **-u·ums** : a coherent whole thought of as a collection, sequence, or progression of values or elements varying by minute degrees ⟨"light" and "dark" stand at opposite ends of a *continuum*⟩ [Latin, neuter of *continuus* "continuous"]

con·tort \kən-ˈtȯrt\ *vb* : to twist into an unusual appearance or unnatural shape : DEFORM, DISTORT [Latin *contortus,* past participle of *contorquēre* "to contort," from *com-* + *torquēre* "to twist"] — **con·tor·tion** \-ˈtȯr-shən\ *n*

con·tor·tion·ist \-shə-nəst, -shnəst\ *n* : one that contorts; *esp* : an acrobat who specializes in contortion of the body — **con·tor·tion·is·tic** \-ˌtȯr-shə-ˈnis-tik\ *adj*

con·tour \ˈkän-ˌtu̇r\ *n* **1** : the outline of a figure or body; *also* : a line or a drawing representing such an outline ⟨sketch the *contour* of a coast⟩ **2** : SHAPE, FORM ⟨*contour* of the land⟩ [French, from Italian *contorno,* from *contornare* "to round off," from Latin *com-* + *tornare* "to turn in a lathe," from *tornus* "lathe"]

[2]**contour** *vt* **1** : to shape the contour of **2** : to shape to fit contours

[3]**contour** *adj* : following or fitted to the contour of something ⟨*contour* farming⟩ ⟨*contour* flooding⟩

contour feather *n* : one of the medium-sized feathers that form the general covering of a bird and determine the external contour

contour line *n* : a line (as on a map) connecting the points on a land surface that have the same elevation

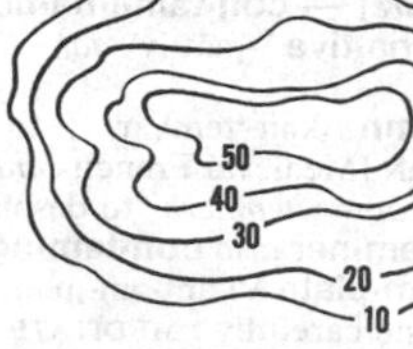

contour line

contour map *n* : a map having contour lines

contra- *prefix* **1** : against : contrary : contrasting ⟨*contra*distinction⟩ **2** : pitched below normal bass ⟨*contra*bassoon⟩ [Latin, from *contra* "against, opposite"]

con·tra·band \ˈkän-trə-ˌband\ *n* **1** : goods or merchandise whose importation, exportation, or possession is forbidden **2** : smuggled goods [Italian *contrabbando,* from Medieval Latin *contrabannum,* from *contra-* + *bannum* "decree, ban"] — **contraband** *adj*

con·tra·bass \ˈkän-trə-ˌbās\ *n* : DOUBLE BASS

con·tra·bas·soon \ˌkän-trə-bə-ˈsün, -ba-\ *n* : the largest member of the oboe family an octave lower in pitch than the bassoon

con·tra·cep·tion \ˌkän-trə-ˈsep-shən\ *n* : deliberate prevention of conception or impregnation [*contra-* + *conception*]

[1]**con·tra·cep·tive** \-ˈsep-tiv\ *adj* : relating to or used for contraception

[2]**contraceptive** *n* : a contraceptive agent or device

[1]**con·tract** \ˈkän-ˌtrakt\ *n* **1 a** : a legally binding agreement between two or more persons or parties : COVENANT **b** : a docu-

ment containing the terms and conditions of a contract **2 :** an undertaking to win a specified number of tricks or points in bridge [Latin *contractus,* from *contrahere* "to draw together, make a contract, reduce in size," from *com-* + *trahere* "to draw"]

^{2}**con·tract** \kən-ˈtrakt, *usually for 2* ˈkän-ˌ\ *vb* **1 a :** to bring on oneself especially inadvertently ⟨*contract* debts⟩ **b :** to become affected with ⟨*contract* a cold⟩ **2 :** to enter into or undertake by contract ⟨*contract* to build a bridge⟩ **3 a :** to draw together or draw up so as to make or become shorter and broader ⟨*contract* a muscle⟩ ⟨brows *contracting* in puzzlement⟩ **b :** to make or become smaller ⟨metal *contracts* on cooling⟩ **4 :** to make a contraction of (as a word) by omitting one or more sounds or letters ***synonyms*** see CONDENSE — **con·tract·ibil·i·ty** \kən-ˌtrak-tə-ˈbil-ət-ē, ˌkän-\ *n* — **con·tract·ible** \kən-ˈtrak-tə-bəl, ˈkän-ˌ\ *adj*

contract bridge \ˈkän-ˌtrakt-, -ˌtrak-\ *n* : a card game for four players in two partnerships in which players bid for the right to name a trump suit and contract to win a specific number of tricks

con·trac·tile \kən-ˈtrak-tl\ *adj* : having the power or property of contracting ⟨*contractile* fibers⟩ — **con·trac·til·i·ty** \ˌkän-ˌtrak-ˈtil-ət-ē\ *n*

contractile vacuole *n* : a vacuole in a unicellular organism that contracts regularly to discharge water from the cell

con·trac·tion \kən-ˈtrak-shən\ *n* **1 a :** the act or process of contracting : the state of being contracted **b :** the shortening and thickening of a functioning muscle or muscle fiber **2 :** a shortening of a word, syllable, or word group by omission of a sound or letter; *also* : a form produced by such shortening ⟨"aren't" is a *contraction* of "are not"⟩ — **con·trac·tion·al** \-ˈtrak-shnəl, -shən-l\ *adj* — **con·trac·tive** \-ˈtrak-tiv\ *adj*

con·trac·tor \ˈkän-ˌtrak-tər, kən-ˈ\ *n* : one that enters into a contract; *esp* : one that agrees to perform work or provide supplies at a given price or within a given time ⟨a building *contractor*⟩

con·trac·tu·al \kən-ˈtrak-chə-wəl, kän-, -chəl\ *adj* : of, relating to, or constituting a contract ⟨*contractual* agreements⟩ — **con·trac·tu·al·ly** \-ē\ *adv*

con·tra dance *or* **con·tre·danse** \ˈkän-trə-ˌdans\ *n* **1 :** a folk dance in which couples face each other in two lines or in a square **2 :** a piece of music for a contra dance [French *contredanse,* by folk etymology from English *country-dance*]

con·tra·dict \ˌkän-trə-ˈdikt\ *vt* **1 :** to state the opposite of what another has said : deny the truth of ⟨*contradict* a story⟩ **2 :** to imply the opposite or a denial of ⟨your actions *contradict* your words⟩ [Latin *contradicere,* from *contra-* + *dicere* "to say"] — **con·tra·dict·able** \-ˈdik-tə-bəl\ *adj* — **con·tra·dic·tor** \-tər\ *n*

con·tra·dic·tion \-ˈdik-shən\ *n* **1 a :** a statement that contradicts another **b :** denial of the truth of something said **2 :** opposition between things ⟨a *contradiction* between desire and reality⟩

con·tra·dic·to·ry \ˌkän-trə-ˈdik-tə-rē, -trē\ *adj* **1 :** tending to contradict **2 :** involving contradiction : OPPOSED ⟨*contradictory* statements⟩ ***synonyms*** see CONTRARY — **con·tra·dic·to·ri·ly** \-tə-rə-lē, -trə-lē\ *adv* — **con·tra·dic·to·ri·ness** \-tə-rē-nəs, -trē-\ *n*

con·tra·dis·tinc·tion \ˌkän-trə-dis-ˈting-shən, -ˈtingk-\ *n* : distinction by contrast ⟨painting in *contradistinction* to sculpture⟩ — **con·tra·dis·tinc·tive** \-ˈting-tiv, -ˈtingk-\ *adj* — **con·tra·dis·tinc·tive·ly** *adv*

con·tra·dis·tin·guish \-ˈting-gwish\ *vt* : to distinguish by contrast of qualities

con·trail \ˈkän-ˌtrāl\ *n* : streaks of condensed water vapor created in the air by an airplane or rocket at high altitudes [*con*densation *trail*]

con·tra·in·di·ca·tion \ˌkän-trə-ˌin-də-ˈkā-shən\ *n* : something (as a preexisting condition) that makes a particular treatment or procedure inadvisable

con·tral·to \kən-ˈtral-tō\ *n, pl* **-tos** **1 a :** the lowest female singing voice **b :** a singer having such a voice **2 :** the part sung by a contralto [Italian, from *contra-* + *alto* "high"]

con·tra·pos·i·tive \ˌkän-trə-ˈpäz-ət-iv, -ˈpäz-tiv\ *n* : the statement obtained by interchanging the hypothesis and conclusion of a conditional statement and denying both clauses ⟨the *contrapositive* of "if A, then B" is "if not B, then not A"⟩

con·trap·tion \kən-ˈtrap-shən\ *n* : CONTRIVANCE 2, GADGET [perhaps blend of *contrivance, trap,* and *invention*]

con·tra·pun·tal \ˌkän-trə-ˈpənt-l\ *adj* **1 :** of or relating to counterpoint **2 :** consisting of or relating to two or more melodies combined into a unified musical composition : POLYPHONIC [Italian *contrappunto* "counterpoint," from Medieval Latin *contrapunctus*] — **con·tra·pun·tal·ly** \-l-ē\ *adv*

con·tra·pun·tist \-ˈpənt-əst\ *n* : one who writes counterpoint

con·trari·wise \ˈkän-ˌtrer-ē-ˌwīz, kən-ˈ\ *adv* **1 :** on the contrary **2 :** vice versa : CONVERSELY **3 :** in a contrary manner : PERVERSELY

^{1}**con·trary** \ˈkän-ˌtrer-ē\ *n, pl* **-trar·ies** **1 :** a fact or condition incompatible with another : OPPOSITE **2 :** one of a pair of opposites **3 :** a proposition in logic related to another in such a way that though both may be false they cannot both be true

^{2}**con·trary** \ˈkän-ˌtrer-ē, *4 is often* kən-ˈtreər-ē\ *adj* **1 :** exactly opposite : wholly different ⟨*contrary* opinions⟩ **2 :** OPPOSED ⟨an act *contrary* to law⟩ **3 :** UNFAVORABLE ⟨a *contrary* wind⟩ **4 :** inclined to oppose or resist : WAYWARD ⟨a *contrary* child⟩ [Medieval French *contraire,* from Latin *contrarius,* from *contra* "opposite, adverse"] — **con·trar·i·ly** \-ˌtrer-ə-lē, -ˈtrer-\ *adv* — **con·trar·i·ness** \-ˌtrer-ē-nəs, -ˈtrer-\ *n*

synonyms CONTRARY, OPPOSITE, CONTRADICTORY mean being so far apart or different as to be or seem irreconcilable. CONTRARY implies extreme divergence and often antagonism ⟨*contrary* evidence⟩. OPPOSITE applies to things in sharp contrast or reversed positions ⟨*opposite* points of view⟩. CONTRADICTORY implies the impossibility of two things being true or valid at the same time ⟨*contradictory* test results⟩.

^{3}**con·trary** *\like* ^{2}\ *adv* : in a contrary manner : CONTRARILY

^{1}**con·trast** \ˈkän-ˌtrast\ *n* **1 :** the act or process of contrasting : the state of being contrasted **2 :** a person or thing that exhibits differences when contrasted **3 :** difference especially when sharp or striking between associated things ⟨the *contrast* between light and dark⟩

^{2}**con·trast** \kən-ˈtrast, ˈkän-ˌ\ *vb* **1 :** to show noticeable differences ⟨black and gold *contrast* sharply⟩ **2 :** to compare especially so as to show differences ⟨*contrast* winter and summer⟩ [French *contraster,* derived from Latin *contra-* + *stare* "to stand"] ***synonyms*** see COMPARE — **con·trast·able** \-ə-bəl\ *adj* — **con·trast·ing·ly** \-ing-lē\ *adv*

con·tra·vene \ˌkän-trə-ˈvēn\ *vt* **1 :** to go or act contrary to ⟨*contravene* a law⟩ **2 :** to oppose in argument : CONTRADICT ⟨*contravene* a proposition⟩ [Late Latin *contravenire,* from Latin *contra-* + *venire* "to come"] — **con·tra·ven·er** *n*

con·tra·ven·tion \ˌkän-trə-ˈven-chən\ *n* : the act of contravening : VIOLATION [Middle French, from Late Latin *contravenire* "to contravene"]

con·tre·temps \ˈkän-trə-ˌtä^{n}\ *n, pl* **con·tre·temps** \-ˌtä^{n}, -ˌtä^{n}z\ **1 :** an untimely and embarrassing occurrence : MISHAP **2 :** DISPUTE, ARGUMENT [French, from *contre-* "counter-" + *temps* "time"]

con·trib·ute \kən-ˈtrib-yət, -ˌyüt\ *vb* **1 :** to give along with others ⟨*contribute* to charities⟩ **2 :** to have a share in something ⟨factors *contributing* to an accident⟩ **3 :** to supply for publication ⟨*contributed* a poem to the school paper⟩ [Latin *contribuere,* from *com-* + *tribuere* "to grant"] — **con·trib·u·tive** \-yət-iv\ *adj* — **con·trib·u·tor** \-yət-ər\ *n*

con·tri·bu·tion \ˌkän-trə-ˈbyü-shən\ *n* **1 :** LEVY 1, TAX **2 a :** the act of contributing **b :** the sum or thing contributed

con·trib·u·to·ry \kən-ˈtrib-yə-ˌtōr-ē, -ˌtȯr-ē\ *adj* **1 :** contributing or serving to contribute; *esp* : helping to accomplish a result ⟨carelessness *contributory* to an accident⟩ **2 a :** of, relating to, or forming a contribution **b :** supported by contributions ⟨a *contributory* pension plan⟩

con·trite \ˈkän-ˌtrīt, kən-ˈ\ *adj* : feeling or showing sorrow and remorse for a wrong that one has done ⟨a *contrite* criminal⟩ ⟨*contrite* tears⟩ [Medieval French *contrit,* from Medieval Latin *contritus,* from Latin *conterere* "to bruise," from *com-* + *terere* "to rub"] — **con·trite·ly** *adv* — **con·trite·ness** *n*

con·tri·tion \kən-ˈtrish-ən\ *n* : the state of being contrite ***synonyms*** see PENITENCE

con·triv·ance \kən-ˈtrī-vəns\ *n* **1 :** the act or faculty of contriving : the state of being contrived **2 :** something contrived; *esp* : a mechanical device

con·trive \kən-ˈtrīv\ *vb* **1 :** PLAN, SCHEME ⟨*contrive* a means of

\ə\ **abut**	\au̇\ **out**	\i\ **tip**	\ȯ\ **saw**	\u̇\ **foot**
\ər\ **further**	\ch\ **chin**	\ī\ **life**	\ȯi\ **coin**	\y\ **yet**
\a\ **mat**	\e\ **pet**	\j\ **job**	\th\ **thin**	\yü\ **few**
\ā\ **take**	\ē\ **easy**	\ng\ **sing**	\th\ **this**	\yu̇\ **cure**
\ä\ **cot, cart**	\g\ **go**	\ō\ **bone**	\ü\ **food**	\zh\ **vision**

escape⟩ **2 :** to form or make in a skillful or ingenious way : INVENT **3 :** BRING ABOUT, MANAGE ⟨*contriving* to make ends meet⟩ [Middle English *controven, contreven,* from Medieval French *controver,* from Late Latin *contropare* "to compare"] — **con·triv·er** *n*

con·trived *adj* **:** ARTIFICIAL 3, UNNATURAL ⟨the *contrived* ending of a play⟩

[1]con·trol \kən-ˈtrōl\ *vt* **con·trolled; con·trol·ling** **1 :** to incorporate suitable controls ⟨a *controlled* experiment⟩ **2 a :** to exercise restraining or directing influence over : REGULATE ⟨*control* one's temper⟩ **b :** to have power over : RULE ⟨*control* a territory⟩ **c :** to reduce the incidence or severity of especially to harmless levels ⟨*control* insects⟩ ⟨*control* a disease⟩ [Middle French *contrerouler,* from *contreroule* "audit," derived from Latin *contra-* "counter-" + Medieval Latin *rotulus* "roll, account"] ***synonyms*** see CONDUCT — **con·trol·la·bil·i·ty** \-ˌtrō-lə-ˈbil-ət-ē\ *n* — **con·trol·la·ble** \-ˈtrō-lə-bəl\ *adj*

[2]control *n* **1 :** the power or authority to control or command ⟨children under their parents' *control*⟩ **2 :** ability to control ⟨lose *control* of a car⟩ **3 :** a means or method of controlling : one that controls: as **a :** a mechanism used to regulate or guide the operation of a machine, apparatus, or system ⟨the *controls* of an airplane⟩ ⟨price *controls*⟩ **b :** an organization that directs a spaceflight ⟨mission *control*⟩ **c :** a personality or spirit believed to actuate the utterances or performances of a spiritualist medium **4 a :** CONTROLLED EXPERIMENT **b :** an individual or group in a controlled experiment that is not subject to the factor being tested and functions as a standard of comparison

controlled experiment *n* **:** an experiment in which all the variables in a control group and an experimental group are the same except for one — called also *control, control experiment*

control freak *n* **:** a person whose behavior shows a powerful need to control people or circumstances in everyday matters

con·trolled \kən-ˈtrōld\ *adj* **1 :** RESTRAINED **2 :** regulated by law with regard to possession and use ⟨*controlled* drugs⟩

con·trol·ler \kən-ˈtrō-lər, ˈkän-ˌ\ *n* **1 a :** COMPTROLLER 1 **b :** the chief accounting officer of a business or institution **2 :** one that controls ⟨air traffic *controller*⟩ — **con·trol·ler·ship** \-ˌship\ *n*

controlling *adj* **:** inclined to control the behavior of other people : DOMINEERING

con·tro·ver·sial \ˌkän-trə-ˈvər-shəl, -ˈvər-sē-əl\ *adj* **1 :** of, relating to, or arousing controversy ⟨a *controversial* public figure⟩ **2 :** fond of controversy : ARGUMENTATIVE — **con·tro·ver·sial·ist** \-əst\ *n* — **con·tro·ver·sial·ly** \-ē\ *adv*

con·tro·ver·sy \ˈkän-trə-ˌvər-sē\ *n, pl* **-sies** **1 :** a discussion marked especially by expression of opposing views : DISPUTE **2 :** QUARREL 2, STRIFE [Latin *controversia,* from *controversus* "disputable," literally, "turned against," from *contro-* "opposite" + *versus,* past participle of *vertere* "to turn"]

con·tro·vert \ˈkän-trə-ˌvərt, ˌkän-trə-ˈ\ *vt* **:** to dispute or oppose by reasoning ⟨*controvert* a point in a discussion⟩ [derived from *controversy*] — **con·tro·vert·er** *n* — **con·tro·vert·ible** \-ə-bəl\ *adj*

con·tume·ly \kän-ˈtyü-mə-lē, kən-, -ˈtü-; ˈkän-tyə-ˌmē-lē, -tə-; ˈkän-tyüm-lē\ *n, pl* **-lies :** rude language or treatment arising from arrogance and contempt; *also* **:** an instance of such language or treatment [Medieval French *contumelie,* from Latin *contumelia*]

con·tu·sion \kən-ˈtü-zhən, -ˈtyü-\ *n* **:** injury to tissue usually without breaking the skin : BRUISE [Latin *contusio,* from *contundere* "to crush, bruise," from *com-* + *tundere* "to beat"] — **con·tuse** \-ˈtüz, -ˈtyüz\ *vt*

co·nun·drum \kə-ˈnən-drəm\ *n* **1 :** a riddle whose answer is or involves a pun **2 :** an intricate and difficult problem [origin unknown]

con·ur·ba·tion \ˌkän-ər-ˈbā-shən\ *n* **:** a continuous network of urban communities [*com-* + Latin *urbs* "city"]

co·nus ar·te·ri·o·sus \ˈkō-nəs-är-ˌtir-ē-ˈō-səs\ *n* **1 :** an extension of the ventricle of amphibians and some fishes that has a spiral valve separating venous blood going to the respiratory arteries from blood going to the aorta and systemic arteries **2 :** a conical extension of the right ventricle in mammals from which the pulmonary arteries emerge — called also *conus* [New Latin, literally, "arterial cone"]

con·va·lesce \ˌkän-və-ˈles\ *vi* **:** to recover health and strength gradually after illness or weakness [Latin *convalescere,* from *com-* + *valescere* "to grow strong," from *valēre* "to be strong, be well"]

con·va·les·cence \ˌkän-və-ˈles-ns\ *n* **:** the process or period of convalescing — **con·va·les·cent** \-nt\ *adj or n*

con·vec·tion \kən-ˈvek-shən\ *n* **:** the circulatory motion that occurs in a gas or liquid at a nonuniform temperature owing to currents caused by differences in density with the warmer portions rising and the colder denser portions sinking; *also* **:** the transfer of heat by this automatic circulation of a fluid [Late Latin *convectio,* from Latin *convehere* "to bring together," from *com-* + *vehere* "to carry"] — **con·vec·tion·al** \-shnəl, -shən-l\ *adj* — **con·vec·tive** \-ˈvek-tiv\ *adj*

convection oven *n* **:** an oven with a fan that circulates hot air evenly and continuously around the food as it cooks

con·vec·tor \-ˈvek-tər\ *n* **:** a heating unit in which air heated by contact with a heating device in a casing circulates by convection

con·vene \kən-ˈvēn\ *vb* **1 :** to come together in a body : MEET ⟨the legislature *convened* Tuesday⟩ **2 :** to cause to assemble : call together ⟨the chairman *convened* the meeting⟩ [Medieval Latin *convenire,* from Latin *com-* + *venire* "to come"] — **con·ven·er** *n*

[1]con·ve·nience \kən-ˈvē-nyəns\ *n* **1 :** fitness or suitability for meeting a requirement **2 :** personal comfort : EASE **3 :** a suitable time : OPPORTUNITY ⟨come at your earliest *convenience*⟩ **4 :** something (as a device or a service) that gives comfort or advantage ⟨a house with all modern *conveniences*⟩

[2]convenience *adj* **:** designed for quick easy preparation or use

convenience store *n* **:** a small market that is open long hours

con·ve·nient \kən-ˈvē-nyənt\ *adj* **1 a :** suited to personal comfort or to easy use ⟨a *convenient* location⟩ ⟨a *convenient* time⟩ **b :** suited to a particular situation ⟨found it *convenient* to ignore the remark⟩ **2 :** near at hand : CLOSE ⟨*convenient* parking⟩ [Latin *conveniens,* from *convenire* "to come together, agree, be suitable"] — **con·ve·nient·ly** *adv*

con·vent \ˈkän-vənt, -ˌvent\ *n* **:** a local community or house of a religious order or congregation; *esp* **:** an establishment of nuns [Medieval French *covent,* from Medieval Latin *conventus,* from Latin, "assembly," from *convenire* "to convene"] — **con·ven·tu·al** \kən-ˈvench-ə-wəl, kän-\ *adj*

con·ven·tion \kən-ˈven-chən\ *n* **1 :** AGREEMENT 2, COVENANT ⟨an international *convention* for treatment of prisoners of war⟩ **2 :** generally accepted custom, practice, or belief; *also* **:** something accepted by convention as true, useful, or convenient ⟨the *convention* of driving on the right⟩ **3 :** an assembly of persons met for a common purpose ⟨a constitutional *convention*⟩ **4 :** a practice in bidding or playing that conveys information between partners in a card game (as bridge) [Latin *conventio,* from *convenire* "to convene, be suitable"]

con·ven·tion·al \kən-ˈvench-nəl, -ˈven-chən-l\ *adj* **1 :** behaving according to convention ⟨a very *conventional* person⟩ **2 :** settled or prescribed by convention : CUSTOMARY ⟨*conventional* methods⟩ **3 a :** ORDINARY 1, COMMONPLACE ⟨*conventional* remarks⟩ **b :** conforming to established rules or traditions : not showing originality — **con·ven·tion·al·ly** \-ē\ *adv*

con·ven·tion·al·i·ty \kən-ˌven-chə-ˈnal-ət-ē\ *n, pl* **-ties** **1 :** the quality or state of being conventional especially in social behavior **2 :** a conventional practice, custom, or rule

con·ven·tion·al·ize \kən-ˈvench-nə-ˌlīz, -ˈven-chən-l-ˌīz\ *vt* **:** to make conventional — **con·ven·tion·al·i·za·tion** \-ˌvench-nə-lə-ˈzā-shən, -ˌven-chən-l-ə-ˈzā-\ *n*

con·verge \kən-ˈvərj\ *vb* **1 :** to tend or move toward one point or one another : MEET ⟨*converging* paths⟩ **2 :** to come together and unite in a common interest or focus **3 :** to cause to come together [Late Latin *convergere,* from Latin *com-* + *vergere* "to bend, incline"]

con·ver·gence \kən-ˈvər-jəns\ *n* **1 :** the act or condition of converging especially toward union or uniformity **2 :** independent development of similar characters (as of bodily structure of unrelated organisms or cultural traits) often associated with similarity of habits or environment — **con·ver·gent** \-jənt\ *adj*

convergent evolution *n* **:** convergence of two or more unrelated biological species

con·verg·ing lens \kən-ˈvərj-ing-\ *n* **:** a lens that causes parallel rays (as of light) to come to a focus

con·ver·sant \kən-ˈvərs-nt\ *adj* **:** having knowledge or experience : FAMILIAR ⟨they were *conversant* with the facts⟩ — **con·ver·sant·ly** *adv*

con·ver·sa·tion \ˌkän-vər-ˈsā-shən\ *n* **:** oral exchange of sentiments, observations, opinions, or ideas; *also* **:** an instance of such exchange : TALK ⟨a quiet *conversation*⟩

con·ver·sa·tion·al \ˌkän-vər-ˈsā-shnəl, -shən-l\ *adj* **1 :** of, relating to, or suitable for informal friendly talk ⟨written in *conversational* style⟩ **2 :** fond of or given to conversation — **con·ver·sa·tion·al·ly** \-ē\ *adv*

con·ver·sa·tion·al·ist \-shnə-ləst, -shən-l-əst\ *n* **:** a person who is fond of or good at conversation

[1]**con·verse** \kən-ˈvərs\ *vi* **:** to exchange thoughts and opinions in speech **:** TALK [Medieval French *converser* "to live with," from Latin *conversari,* from *convertere* "to turn around, convert"] — **con·vers·er** *n*

[2]**con·verse** \ˈkän-ˌvərs\ *n* **:** CONVERSATION

[3]**con·verse** \ˈkän-ˌvərs\ *n* **:** something that is the opposite of something else: as **a :** a theorem formed by the interchange of the hypothesis and the conclusion in a given theorem **b :** the statement obtained by interchanging the subject and predicate of a logical proposition ⟨"no *P* is *S*" is the *converse* of "no *S* is *P*"⟩ [Latin *conversus,* past participle of *convertere* "to turn around"]

[4]**con·verse** \kən-ˈvərs, ˈkän-ˌ\ *adj* **:** reversed in order, relation, or action; *also* **:** being a converse ⟨a *converse* theorem in geometry⟩ — **con·verse·ly** *adv*

con·ver·sion \kən-ˈvər-zhən\ *n* **1 :** the act of converting **:** the state of being converted **2 :** a change in the nature or form of a thing ⟨the *conversion* of water into steam by boiling⟩ **3 :** a spiritual change in a person associated with a change of religious belief or with the adoption of religion **4 :** the taking and using of another's property without right as one's own **5 :** a successful attempt for a point or points especially after a touchdown or for a first down — **con·ver·sion·al** \-ˈvərzh-nəl, -ən-l\ *adj*

[1]**con·vert** \kən-ˈvərt\ *vb* **1 :** to bring over from one belief, view, or party to another **2 a :** to change from one form or function to another **:** TRANSFORM ⟨*convert* starch into sugar⟩ **b :** to exchange for an equivalent ⟨*convert* diamonds into cash⟩ **3 :** to take over without right **4 :** to undergo conversion **5 :** to succeed in an attempt for a point, field goal, or free throw [Medieval French *convertir,* from Latin *convertere* "to turn around, convert," from *com-* + *vertere* "to turn"]

[2]**con·vert** \ˈkän-ˌvərt\ *n* **:** one that is converted

con·vert·ed rice \kən-ˈvərt-əd-\ *n* **:** rice that has been soaked and briefly steamed under pressure in order to retain vitamins and minerals, improve texture, and extend shelf life

con·vert·er \kən-ˈvərt-ər\ *n* **:** one that converts: as **a :** the furnace used in the Bessemer process **b** *or* **con·ver·tor** \-ˈvərt-ər\ **:** a device employing mechanical rotation for changing alternating current to direct current **c :** CATALYTIC CONVERTER

[1]**con·vert·ible** \kən-ˈvərt-ə-bəl\ *adj* **1 :** capable of being converted **2 :** having a top that may be lowered or removed ⟨a *convertible* coupe⟩ — **con·vert·ibil·i·ty** \-ˌvərt-ə-ˈbil-ət-ē\ *n* — **con·vert·ibly** \-ˈvərt-ə-blē\ *adv*

[2]**convertible** *n* **:** something convertible; *esp* **:** a convertible automobile

con·vex \kän-ˈveks, ˈkän-ˌ, kən-ˈ\ *adj* **1 :** curved or rounded like the outside of a sphere or circle **2 :** being a set that contains every straight line joining two points in that set; *also* **:** having the property that the union of its perimeter and its interior is a convex set ⟨a *convex* polygon⟩ [Latin *convexus*] — **con·vex·ly** *adv* — **con·vex·ness** *n*

con·vex·i·ty \kən-ˈvek-sət-ē, kän-\ *n, pl* **-ties 1 :** the quality or state of being convex **2 :** a convex surface or part

con·vexo–con·cave \kən-ˌvek-sō-kän-ˈkāv, -ˈkän-ˌ\ *adj* **:** having the convex side of greater curvature than the concave

con·vey \kən-ˈvā\ *vt* **con·veyed; con·vey·ing 1 :** to carry from one place to another **:** TRANSPORT ⟨*convey* passengers by bus⟩ **2 :** to serve as a means of transferring ⟨an infection *conveyed* by insects⟩ **3 :** to communicate or serve as a means of communicating ⟨a red light *conveys* a warning⟩ **4 :** to transfer or deliver to another; *esp* **:** to transfer title to real estate by a legal document [Medieval French *conveer* "to accompany, escort," from Latin *com-* + *via* "way"]

con·vey·ance \kən-ˈvā-əns\ *n* **1 :** the act of conveying **2 :** a means or way of conveying: as **a :** a legal document by which title to property is conveyed **b :** a means of transport **:** VEHICLE

con·vey·or *also* **conveyer** \kən-ˈvā-ər\ *n* **1 :** one that conveys **2** *usually conveyor* **:** a mechanical apparatus for carrying (as by an endless moving belt or a chain of receptacles) packages or bulk material from place to place

[1]**con·vict** \kən-ˈvikt\ *vb* **:** to find or prove to be guilty [Latin *convictus,* past participle of *convincere* "to refute, convict," from *com-* + *vincere* "to conquer"]

[2]**con·vict** \ˈkän-ˌvikt\ *n* **1 :** a person convicted of a crime **2 :** a person serving a prison sentence usually for a long term

con·vic·tion \kən-ˈvik-shən\ *n* **1 :** the act or process of convicting especially of a crime in a court of law **:** the state of being convicted **2 :** the state of being convinced **:** CERTITUDE ⟨speaks with *conviction*⟩ **3 :** a strong belief or opinion ⟨a person with firm *convictions*⟩ ***synonyms*** see CERTAINTY, OPINION

con·vince \kən-ˈvins\ *vt* **:** to bring by argument or evidence to agreement or belief **:** overcome the disbelief or objections of ⟨*convinced* me that they were qualified⟩ [Latin *convincere* "to refute, convict, prove"] — **con·vinc·er** *n*

con·vinc·ing \-ˈvin-siŋ\ *adj* **:** having the power or the effect of overcoming objection or disbelief **:** strongly persuasive ⟨a *convincing* argument⟩ — **con·vinc·ing·ly** \-siŋ-lē\ *adv* — **con·vinc·ing·ness** *n*

con·viv·ial \kən-ˈviv-yəl, -ˈviv-ē-əl\ *adj* **:** relating to, occupied with, or fond of good company and festivity [Late Latin *convivialis,* from Latin *convivium* "banquet," from *com-* + *vivere* "to live"] — **con·viv·i·al·i·ty** \-ˌviv-ē-ˈal-ət-ē\ *n* — **con·viv·ial·ly** \-ē\ *adv*

con·vo·ca·tion \ˌkän-və-ˈkā-shən\ *n* **1 :** ASSEMBLY 1, MEETING **2 :** the act or process of convoking — **con·vo·ca·tion·al** \-shnəl, -shən-l\ *adj*

con·voke \kən-ˈvōk\ *vt* **:** to call together to a meeting [Middle French *convoquer,* from Latin *convocare,* from *com-* + *vocare* "to call"]

con·vo·lute \ˈkän-və-ˌlüt\ *vb* **:** COIL 1, TWIST [Latin *convolutus,* past participle of *convolvere* "to roll up, enfold," from *com-* + *volvere* "to roll"]

con·vo·lut·ed *adj* **1 :** having elaborately curved or twisted windings; *esp* **:** having convolutions **2 :** INTRICATE, INVOLVED ⟨a *convoluted* argument⟩

con·vo·lu·tion \ˌkän-və-ˈlü-shən\ *n* **1 :** one of the irregular ridges on the surface of the brain and especially of the cerebrum of higher mammals **2 :** a convoluted form or structure — **con·vo·lu·tion·al** \-shnəl, -shən-l\ *adj*

con·vol·vu·lus \kən-ˈväl-vyə-ləs, -ˈvȯl-\ *n, pl* **-lus·es** *or* **-li** \-ˌlī, -ˌlē\ **:** any of a genus of erect, trailing, or twining herbs and shrubs related to the morning glories [Latin *convolvere* "to roll up, enfold"]

[1]**con·voy** \ˈkän-ˌvȯi, kən-ˈ\ *vt* **:** ACCOMPANY; *esp* **:** to escort for protection ⟨a destroyer *convoying* merchant ships⟩ [Medieval French *convoier,* from Latin *com-* + *via* "way"]

[2]**con·voy** \ˈkän-ˌvȯi\ *n* **1 :** one that convoys; *esp* **:** a protective escort (as for ships) **2 :** the act of convoying **:** the state of being convoyed ⟨ships traveling in *convoy*⟩ **3 :** a group convoyed ⟨a *convoy* of freighters⟩

con·vulse \kən-ˈvəls\ *vt* **:** to shake or agitate violently; *esp* **:** to shake with or as if with irregular spasms ⟨*convulsed* with laughter⟩ ⟨land *convulsed* by an earthquake⟩ [Latin *convulsus,* past participle of *convellere* "to pluck up, convulse," from *com-* + *vellere* "to pluck"] ***synonyms*** see SHAKE

con·vul·sion \-ˈvəl-shən\ *n* **1 :** an abnormal violent and involuntary contraction or series of contractions of the muscles **2 a :** a violent disturbance **b :** an uncontrolled fit **:** PAROXYSM — **con·vul·sion·ary** \-shə-ˌner-ē\ *adj*

con·vul·sive \-ˈvəl-siv\ *adj* **1 :** constituting or producing a convulsion **2 :** caused by or affected with convulsions — **con·vul·sive·ly** *adv* — **con·vul·sive·ness** *n*

cony *variant of* CONEY

coo \ˈkü\ *vi* **1 :** to utter the low soft cry characteristic of a dove or pigeon or a similar sound **2 :** to talk fondly or amorously [imitative] — **coo** *n*

[1]**cook** \ˈku̇k\ *n* **:** one who prepares food for eating [Old English *cōc,* from Latin *coquus,* from *coquere* "to cook"]

[2]**cook** *vb* **1 :** to prepare food for eating especially by a heating process **2 :** to undergo cooking ⟨the rice is *cooking* now⟩ **3 a :** to go on **:** HAPPEN ⟨what's *cooking*⟩ **b :** CONCOCT, DEVISE ⟨*cook* up a scheme⟩ **4 :** to subject to the action of heat or fire

\ə\ **abut**	\au̇\ **out**	\i\ **tip**	\ȯ\ **saw**	\u̇\ **foot**
\ər\ **further**	\ch\ **chin**	\ī\ **life**	\ȯi\ **coin**	\y\ **yet**
\a\ **mat**	\e\ **pet**	\j\ **job**	\th\ **thin**	\yü\ **few**
\ā\ **take**	\ē\ **easy**	\ng\ **sing**	\t͟h\ **this**	\yu̇\ **cure**
\ä\ **cot, cart**	\g\ **go**	\ō\ **bone**	\ü\ **food**	\zh\ **vision**

— **cook·er** *n* — **cook one's goose** : to make one's failure or ruin certain

cook·book \ˈku̇k-ˌbu̇k\ *n* : a book of cooking directions and recipes

cook·ery \ˈku̇k-rē, -ə-rē\ *n* : the art or practice of cooking

cook·ie *or* **cooky** \ˈku̇k-ē\ *n, pl* **cook·ies** **1** : any of various small sweet crisp or slightly raised cakes **2** *cookie* : a small computer file that contains information relating to Web sites a person has visited [Dutch *koekje* "small cake," from *koek* "cake"]

cooking spray *n* : an aerosol that contains vegetable oil and that is sprayed on cookware (as frying pans) to prevent food from sticking

cook·out \ˈku̇k-ˌau̇t\ *n* : an outdoor gathering at which a meal is cooked and served; *also* : such a meal

cook·stove \ˈku̇k-ˌstōv\ *n* : a stove for cooking : RANGE

cook·ware \ˈku̇k-ˌwaər, -ˌweər\ *n* : utensils used in cooking

[1]**cool** \ˈkül\ *adj* **1** : somewhat cold **2 a** : marked by steady calmness and self-control **b** : restrained in emotion **3** — used as an intensive ⟨a *cool* million dollars⟩ **4** : marked by unfriendliness or lack of due respect ⟨a *cool* reply⟩ **5** : not letting in or keeping in heat ⟨*cool* clothes⟩ **6** : producing an impression of coolness ⟨blue is a *cool* color⟩ **7** *slang* **a** : very good : EXCELLENT **b** : FASHIONABLE [Old English *cōl*] — **cool·ish** \ˈkü-lish\ *adj* — **cool·ly** \ˈkül-lē, -ē\ *adv* — **cool·ness** \ˈkül-nəs\ *n*

[2]**cool** *vb* **1** : to make or become cool **2** : to moderate or calm especially in emotional intensity ⟨allow tempers to *cool*⟩ — **cool it** : to calm down

[3]**cool** *n* **1** : a cool time or place ⟨the *cool* of the night⟩ **2** : COMPOSURE ⟨he lost his *cool*⟩

cool·ant \ˈkü-lənt\ *n* : a usually fluid cooling agent

cool·er \ˈkü-lər\ *n* **1** : one that cools: as **a** : a container for cooling liquids **b** : REFRIGERATOR **2** : LOCKUP, JAIL

cool·head·ed \ˈkül-ˈhed-əd\ *adj* : not easily excited : CALM

coo·lie \ˈkü-lē\ *n, offensive* : an unskilled Asian worker who is paid low wages [Hindi & Urdu *qulī*]

cool·ing tower \ˈkü-ling-\ *n* : a structure over which water is trickled to reduce its temperature by partial evaporation

coon \ˈkün\ *n* : RACCOON

coon·hound \ˈkün-ˌhau̇nd\ *n* : a dog trained to hunt raccoons

coon·skin \-ˌskin\ *n* : the fur or pelt of the raccoon

[1]**coop** \ˈküp, ˈku̇p\ *n* **1** : a cage or small enclosure or building for housing poultry or small animals **2** : a confined place [Middle English *cupe*]

[2]**coop** *vt* : to place or keep in or as if in a coop : PEN

co–op \ˈkō-ˌäp, kō-ˈäp\ *n* : COOPERATIVE

coo·per \ˈkü-pər, ˈku̇p-ər\ *n* : one that makes or repairs wooden casks or tubs [derived from Latin *cupa* "cask"]

coo·per·age \ˈkü-pə-rij, -prij; ˈku̇p-ə-rij, -ə-rij\ *n* **1** : a cooper's place of business **2** : a cooper's work or products

co·op·er·ate \kō-ˈäp-ˌrāt, -ə-ˌrāt\ *vi* : to act, work, or associate with others especially for mutual benefit [Late Latin *cooperari,* from Latin *co-* + *operari* "to work"]

co·op·er·a·tion \kō-ˌäp-ə-ˈrā-shən\ *n* **1** : the act or process of cooperating **2** : association of individuals or groups for mutual benefit

[1]**co·op·er·a·tive** \kō-ˈäp-rət-iv, -ə-rət-, -ə-ˌrāt-\ *adj* **1** : marked by cooperation or a willingness to cooperate **2** : of, relating to, or organized as a cooperative ⟨a *cooperative* store⟩ — **co·op·er·a·tive·ly** *adv* — **co·op·er·a·tive·ness** *n*

[2]**cooperative** *n* : an association owned by and operated for the benefit of those using its services

Coo·per's hawk \ˈkü-pərz-, ˈku̇p-ərz-\ *n* : an American hawk that has a rounded tail and is slightly smaller than a crow [William *Cooper,* died 1864, American naturalist]

co–opt \kō-ˈäpt\ *vt* **1** : to choose or elect as a fellow member or colleague **2** : ASSIMILATE 1a ⟨protesters were *co-opted* by the establishment⟩ **3** : TAKE OVER, APPROPRIATE 3 [Latin *cooptare,* from *co-* + *optare* "to choose"] — **co–op·ta·tion** \ˌkō-ˌäp-ˈtā-shən\ *n* — **co–op·tion** \-ˈäp-shən\ *n*

[1]**co·or·di·nate** \kō-ˈȯrd-nət, -n-ət\ *adj* **1** : equal in rank or order ⟨*coordinate* branches of government⟩ **2 a** : being of equal rank in a compound sentence ⟨*coordinate* clauses⟩ **b** : joining words or word groups of the same grammatical rank ⟨the word "and" is a *coordinate* conjunction⟩ [back-formation from *coordination*] — **co·or·di·nate·ly** *adv* — **co·or·di·nate·ness** *n*

[2]**coordinate** *n* **1** : one who has the same rank, authority, or importance as another **2** : any of a set of numbers used to locate a point on a line or surface or in space — compare ABSCISSA, ORDINATE

[3]**co·or·di·nate** \kō-ˈȯrd-n-ˌāt\ *vb* **1** : to make or become coordinate **2** : to bring into a common action, movement, or condition ⟨*coordinated* the efforts of all three agencies⟩ — **co·or·di·na·tor** \-ˌāt-ər\ *n*

coordinate axis *n* : a line in a coordinate system along which coordinates are measured — compare X-AXIS, Y-AXIS

coordinate geometry *n* : ANALYTIC GEOMETRY

coordinate system *n* : any of various systems for locating points with coordinates and coordinate axes; *esp* : CARTESIAN COORDINATE SYSTEM

co·or·di·nat·ing *adj* : COORDINATE 2b

co·or·di·na·tion \kō-ˌȯrd-n-ˈā-shən\ *n* **1** : the act of coordinating **2** : the state of being coordinate : harmonious working together ⟨muscular *coordination*⟩ [Late Latin *coordinatio,* from Latin *co-* + *ordinatio* "arrangement," from *ordo* "order"]

coot \ˈküt\ *n* **1** : any of various slaty-black birds of the rail family that somewhat resemble ducks **2** : a North American scoter **3** : a strange usually old man [Middle English *coote*]

coo·tie \ˈküt-ē\ *n* : BODY LOUSE [perhaps from Malay *kutu*]

[1]**cop** \ˈkäp\ *vt* **copped; cop·ping** **1** *slang* : to get hold of : CATCH **2** *slang* : STEAL **3** : ADOPT 2 ⟨*cop* an attitude⟩ [perhaps from Dutch *kapen* "to steal"] — **cop a plea** : to plead guilty to a lesser charge in order to avoid a more serious one

[2]**cop** *n* : POLICE OFFICER [short for [3]*copper*]

co·pa·ce·tic *also* **co·pa·se·tic** *or* **co·pe·se·tic** \ˌkō-pə-ˈset-ik\ *adj* : very satisfactory [origin unknown]

co·pal \ˈkō-pəl, -ˌpal; kō-ˈpal\ *n* : a recent or fossil resin from various tropical trees used in making varnishes [Spanish, from Nahuatl *copalli* "resin"]

[1]**cope** \ˈkōp\ *n* **1** : a long loose ecclesiastical vestment **2** : something resembling a cope (as by covering) [Old English *-cāp,* from Late Latin *cappa* "head covering, cloak"]

[2]**cope** *vt* : to cover or furnish with a cope or coping

[3]**cope** *vi* : to struggle or contend especially with some success ⟨a difficult situation to *cope* with⟩ [Middle English *copen* "to strike, fight with," from Medieval French *couper* "to strike," from *cop* "blow, coup"]

co·pe·pod \ˈkō-pə-ˌpäd\ *n* : any of a large group (Copepoda) of usually tiny freshwater and marine crustaceans [Greek *kōpē* "oar" + *pod-, pous* "foot"]

Co·per·ni·can \kō-ˈpər-ni-kən\ *adj* : of or relating to Copernicus or his theory that the earth rotates daily on its axis and the planets revolve in orbits round the sun

co·per·nic·i·um \ˌkō-pər-ˈnis-ē-əm\ *n* : a short-lived artificially produced radioactive element that has 112 protons — see ELEMENT table [New Latin, from Nikolaus *Copernicus*]

copi·er \ˈkäp-ē-ər\ *n* : one that copies; *esp* : a machine for making copies of printing, drawings, or pictures

co·pi·lot \ˈkō-ˌpī-lət\ *n* : a pilot who assists or relieves the pilot but is not in command

cop·ing \ˈkō-ping\ *n* : the covering course of a wall usually with a sloping top [[1]*cope*]

coping saw *n* : a handsaw with a very narrow blade held in a U-shaped frame for cutting curves in wood [from *cope* "to notch," probably from French *couper* "to cut"]

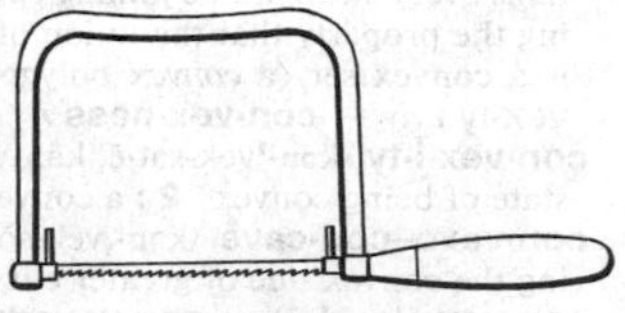
coping saw

co·pi·ous \ˈkō-pē-əs\ *adj* **1 a** : full of thought, information, or matter **b** : profuse or exuberant in words, expression, or style ⟨a *copious* talker⟩ **2** : very plentiful : ABUNDANT [Latin *copiosus,* from *copia* "abundance," from *co-* + *ops* "wealth"] ***synonyms*** see PLENTIFUL — **co·pi·ous·ly** *adv* — **co·pi·ous·ness** *n*

co·pla·nar \ˈkō-ˈplā-nər\ *adj* : lying in the same plane ⟨*coplanar* lines⟩

co·pol·y·mer \ˈkō-ˈpäl-ə-mər\ *n* : a product of copolymerization

co·po·ly·mer·i·za·tion \ˌkō-pə-ˌlim-ə-rə-ˈzā-shən, ˌkō-ˌpäl-ə-mə-rə-\ *n* : the polymerization of two substances (as two different monomers) together — **co·po·ly·mer·ize** \ˌkō-pə-ˈlim-ə-ˌrīz, ˈkō-ˈpäl-ə-mə-\ *vb*

cop–out \ˈkäp-ˌau̇t\ *n* **1** : the act or an instance of copping out **2** : an excuse or means for copping out **3** : a person who cops out

cop out \käp-ˈau̇t, ˈkäp-\ *vi* **1** : to withdraw from unwanted responsibility ⟨*cop out* on jury duty⟩ **2** : to avoid or take the easy way out of something one ought to do ⟨*cop out* on a promise⟩

[1]**cop·per** \ˈkäp-ər\ *n* **1** : a reddish chiefly univalent and bivalent metallic element that is ductile and malleable and one of the best conductors of heat and electricity — see ELEMENT table **2** : a copper or bronze coin **3** : any of various small butterflies usually with copper-colored wings [Old English *coper,* from Late Latin *cuprum,* from Latin *aes Cyprium,* literally, "metal of Cyprus"] — **cop·pery** \ˈkäp-rē, -ə-rē\ *adj*

[2]**copper** *vt* : to cover with copper

[3]**copper** *n* : POLICE OFFICER [[1]*cop*]

cop·per·as \ˈkäp-rəs, -ə-rəs\ *n* : FERROUS SULFATE [Medieval French *coperose,* from Medieval Latin *cuprosa,* probably from *aqua cuprosa,* literally, "copper water," from Late Latin *cuprum* "copper"]

cop·per·head \ˈkäp-ər-ˌhed\ *n* **1** : a common largely coppery brown pit viper of the eastern and central U.S. **2** : a person in the northern states who sympathized with the South during the American Civil War

cop·per·plate \ˌkäp-ər-ˈplāt\ *n* : an engraved or etched copper printing plate; *also* : a print made from such a plate

cop·per·smith \ˈkäp-ər-ˌsmith\ *n* : a worker in copper

copper sulfate *n* : a crystalline compound $CuSO_4$ that is white when anhydrous but that is usually encountered in the blue hydrated form $CuSO_4 \cdot 5H_2O$ and that is used especially in solutions to destroy algae and fungi, in dyeing and printing, and in electric batteries

cop·pice \ˈkäp-əs\ *n* **1** : a thicket, grove, or growth of small trees **2** : forest originating mainly from sprouts or root suckers rather than seed [Middle French *copeis,* derived from Medieval Latin *colpare* "to cut wood"]

co·pra \ˈkō-prə\ *n* : dried coconut meat yielding coconut oil [Portuguese, from Malayalam (a Dravidian language of India) *koppara*]

co·pro·ces·sor \ˌkō-ˈpräs-ˌes-ər, ˈkō-, -ˈprōs-\ *n* : an extra processor in a computer that is designed to perform specialized tasks

cop·ro·lite \ˈkäp-rə-ˌlīt\ *n* : fossil excrement [derived from Greek *kopros* "dung"]

copse \ˈkäps\ *n* : COPPICE 1 [by alteration]

Copt \ˈkäpt\ *n* **1** : a member of the ancient Christian church of Egypt **2** : a member of a people descended from the ancient Egyptians [Arabic *qubt* "Copts," from Coptic *gyptios* "Egyptian," from Greek *Aigyptios*] — **Cop·tic** \ˈkäp-tik\ *adj*

cop·u·la \ˈkäp-yə-lə\ *n* **1** : a word or expression in the form of the verb *to be* that links a subject with its predicate (as in "he is a shoemaker" instead of "he makes shoes") **2** : LINKING VERB [Latin, "bond"]

cop·u·late \ˈkäp-yə-ˌlāt\ *vi* : to engage in sexual intercourse — **cop·u·la·tion** \ˌkäp-yə-ˈlā-shən\ *n* — **cop·u·la·to·ry** \ˈkäp-yə-lə-ˌtōr-ē, -ˌtȯr-\ *adj*

[1]**cop·u·la·tive** \ˈkäp-yə-lət-iv, -ˌlāt-\ *adj* **1** : joining together coordinate words or word groups and indicating that their meanings are to be added ⟨*copulative* conjunctions⟩ ⟨"and" in "bread and meat" is *copulative*⟩ **2** : being a copula ⟨a *copulative* verb⟩ — **cop·u·la·tive·ly** *adv*

[2]**copulative** *n* : a copulative word or expression

[1]**copy** \ˈkäp-ē\ *n, pl* **cop·ies** **1** : an imitation, transcript, or reproduction of an original work **2** : one of the printed reproductions of an original text, engraving, or photograph **3** : text to be composed for printing [Medieval French *copie,* from Medieval Latin *copia,* from Latin, "abundance"] ***synonyms*** see DUPLICATE

[2]**copy** *vb* **cop·ied; copy·ing** **1** : to make a copy : DUPLICATE **2** : to model oneself on : IMITATE

copy·book \-ˌbu̇k\ *n* : a book containing copies especially of penmanship for learners to imitate

copy·boy \-ˌbȯi\ *n* : one that carries copy and runs errands (as in a newspaper office)

copy·cat \-ˌkat\ *n* : a person who imitates the behavior or work of another

copy·desk \-ˌdesk\ *n* : the desk at which newspaper copy is edited

copy editor *n* **1** : one that reads and corrects manuscript copy in a publishing house for the typesetter **2** : one that edits and writes headlines for newspaper copy — **copy·edit** \ˈkäp-ē-ˌed-ət\ *vt*

copy·ist \ˈkäp-ē-əst\ *n* **1** : a person who makes copies **2** : IMITATOR

copy·read·er \ˈkäp-ē-ˌrēd-ər\ *n* : COPY EDITOR — **copy·read** \-ˌrēd\ *vt*

[1]**copy·right** \-ˌrīt\ *n* : the sole legal right to reproduce, publish, sell, or distribute the matter and form of a literary, musical, or artistic work — **copyright** *adj*

[2]**copyright** *vt* : to secure a copyright on

copy·writ·er \-ˌrīt-ər\ *n* : a writer of advertising or publicity copy

co·quet *or* **co·quette** \kō-ˈket\ *vi* **co·quet·ted; co·quet·ting** : FLIRT 2a [French *coquet* "man who flirts," from *coq* "cock"]

co·que·try \ˈkō-kə-trē, kō-ˈke-trē\ *n, pl* **-tries** : a flirtatious act or attitude

co·quette \kō-ˈket\ *n* : FLIRT 2 — **co·quett·ish** \-ˈket-ish\ *adj* — **co·quett·ish·ly** *adv* — **co·quett·ish·ness** *n*

co·qui·na \kō-ˈkē-nə\ *n* **1** : a small marine clam used for broth or chowder **2** : a soft whitish limestone formed of broken shells and corals used for building [Spanish]

cor·a·cle \ˈkȯr-ə-kəl, ˈkär-\ *n* : a boat made of horsehide or tarpaulin stretched over a wicker frame [Welsh *corwgl*]

cor·a·coid \ˈkȯr-ə-ˌkȯid, ˈkär-\ *adj* : of, relating to, or being a short process of the scapula in most mammals or a bone of other vertebrates (as reptiles) that extends from the scapula to or toward the sternum [Greek *korax* "raven"] — **coracoid** *n*

cor·al \ˈkȯr-əl, ˈkär-\ *n* **1 a** : the stony or horny skeletal deposit produced by chiefly anthozoan polyps; *esp* : a richly red coral used in jewelry **b** : a polyp or polyp colony together with its membranes and skeleton **2** : a deep pink [Medieval French, from Latin *corallium,* from Greek *korallion*] — **coral** *adj*

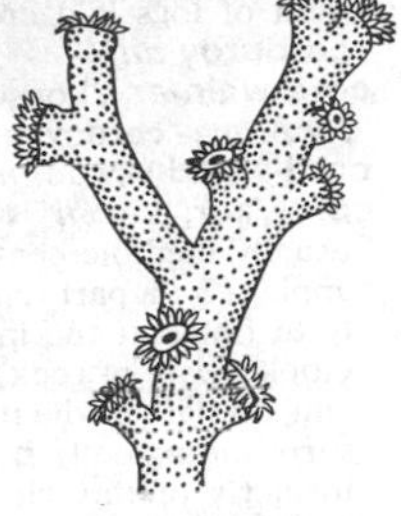

coral 1b

[1]**cor·al·line** \ˈkȯr-ə-ˌlīn, ˈkär-\ *adj* : of, relating to, or resembling coral or a coralline

[2]**coralline** *n* : any of various plants or animals (as some red algae and bryozoans) that resemble corals

coral reef *n* : a reef made up of corals, other organic deposits, and the solid limestone resulting from their fusion

coral snake *n* : any of several poisonous chiefly tropical New World snakes brilliantly banded in red, black, and yellow or white; *also* : any of several harmless snakes resembling the coral snakes

[1]**cor·bel** \ˈkȯr-bəl\ *n* : a bracket-shaped architectural member that projects from a wall and supports a weight [Medieval French, from *corp* "raven," from Latin *corvus*]

[2]**corbel** *vt* **-beled** *or* **-belled; -bel·ing** *or* **-bel·ling** : to furnish with or make into a corbel

[1]**cord** \ˈkȯrd\ *n* **1** : a string or small rope consisting of several strands woven or twisted together **2** : a moral, spiritual, or emotional bond **3 a** : an anatomical structure (as a tendon or nerve) resembling a cord; *esp* : UMBILICAL CORD **b** : a small flexible insulated electrical cable with fittings for connecting an appliance (as a lamp) with a receptacle **4** : a unit of wood cut for fuel equal to a stack 4×4×8 feet or 128 cubic feet (about 3.6 cubic meters) **5 a** : a rib like a cord on a textile; *also* : a fabric with such ribs **b** *pl* : trousers made of this fabric [Medieval French *corde,* from Latin *chorda* "string," from Greek *chordē*] — **cord·like** \-ˌlīk\ *adj*

[2]**cord** *vt* **1** : to furnish, bind, or connect with a cord **2** : to pile up (wood) in cords — **cord·er** *n*

cord·age \ˈkȯrd-ij\ *n* **1** : ropes or cords; *esp* : the ropes in the rigging of a ship **2** : the number of cords (as of wood) on a given area

cord·ed \ˈkȯrd-əd\ *adj* **1 a** : having ridges or cords ⟨*corded* fabric⟩ **b** : having muscles protruding in ridges ⟨a *corded* neck⟩ **c** *of a muscle* : TENSE, TAUT ⟨a thick *corded* muscle⟩ **2** : bound or wound about with cords

[1]**cor·dial** \ˈkȯr-jəl\ *adj* **1** : tending to revive, cheer, or invigorate

2 : HEARTFELT, HEARTY ⟨a *cordial* greeting⟩ [Medieval Latin *cordialis* "of the heart, hearty," from Latin *cord-, cor* "heart"] — **cor·di·al·i·ty** \ˌkȯr-jē-ˈal-ət-ē\ *n* — **cor·dial·ly** \ˈkȯrj-lē, -ə-lē\ *adv* — **cor·dial·ness** \ˈkȯr-jəl-nəs\ *n*

[2]**cordial** *n* **1** : a stimulating medicine or drink **2** : LIQUEUR

cor·dil·le·ra \ˌkȯrd-l-ˈyer-ə, -ˈer-; kȯr-ˈdil-ə-rə\ *n* : a system of mountain ranges often consisting of a number of more or less parallel chains [Spanish] — **cor·dil·le·ran** \-ˈyer-ən, -ˈer-ən; -ə-rən\ *adj*

cord·ite \ˈkȯr-ˌdīt\ *n* : a smokeless gunpowder composed of nitroglycerin, guncotton, and a stabilizing jelly

cord·less \ˈkȯrd-ləs\ *adj* : having no cord; *esp* : powered by a battery ⟨a *cordless* telephone⟩ — **cordless** *n*

cor·do·ba \ˈkȯrd-ə-bə, -ə-və\ *n* **1** : the basic monetary unit of Nicaragua **2** : a coin or note representing one cordoba [Spanish *córdoba,* from Francisco Fernández de *Córdoba,* died 1526, Spanish explorer]

cor·don \ˈkȯrd-n, ˈkȯr-ˌdän\ *n* **1 a** : an ornamental cord used especially on costumes **b** : a cord or ribbon worn as a badge or decoration **2** : a line of persons or things around a person or place ⟨a *cordon* of police⟩ [French, from *corde* "cord"]

cor·do·van \ˈkȯrd-ə-vən\ *n* **1** : a fine-grained colored leather **2** : thick leather tanned from the inner layer of horsehide [Spanish *Córdova* (now *Córdoba*), Spain] — **cordovan** *adj*

cor·du·roy \ˈkȯrd-ə-ˌrȯi\ *n, pl* **-roys** **1 a** : a durable ribbed usually cotton fabric **b** *pl* : trousers of corduroy **2** : a road built of logs laid crosswise side by side [origin unknown] — **corduroy** *adj*

cord·wain·er \ˈkȯr-ˌdwā-nər\ *n* : SHOEMAKER [Middle English *cordwane* "cordovan leather"]

cord·wood \-ˌwu̇d\ *n* : wood cut for fuel and sold by the cord

[1]**core** \ˈkōr, ˈkȯr\ *n* **1** : a central or most important part **2** : the usually inedible central part of some fruits (as a pineapple or apple) **3** : a part removed from the interior of a mass especially to find out the interior composition or a hidden condition ⟨took a *core* of rock⟩ **4 a** : a mass of iron used to concentrate and strengthen the magnetic field resulting from a current in a surrounding coil **b** : a computer memory made up especially formerly of tiny rings of magnetic material **c** : the internal memory of a computer **5** : the central part of the earth having different properties from those of the surrounding parts; *also* : the central part of a heavenly body **6** : a system of studies that brings together material from subjects that are usually taught separately **7** : the place in a nuclear reactor where fission takes place [Middle English]

[2]**core** *vt* : to remove the core from — **cor·er** *n*

co·re·li·gion·ist \ˌkō-ri-ˈlij-nəst, -ə-nəst\ *n* : a person of the same religion

co·re·op·sis \ˌkōr-ē-ˈäpsəs, ˌkȯr-\ *n* : any of a genus of herbs related to the daisies and widely grown for their showy flower heads [Greek *koris* "bedbug" + *opsis* "appearance"]

co·re·spon·dent \ˌkō-ri-ˈspän-dənt\ *n* : a person named as guilty of adultery with the defendant in a divorce suit

co·ri·an·der \ˈkōr-ē-ˌan-dər, ˈkȯr-\ *n* : an Old World herb related to the carrot with tiny aromatic fruits; *also* : its dried ripened fruit used as a flavoring [Medieval French *coriandre,* from Latin *coriandrum,* from Greek *koriandron*]

Co·rin·thi·an \kə-ˈrin-thē-ən\ *adj* : of or relating to the lightest and most ornate of the three Greek types of architecture characterized especially by its bell-shaped capital decorated with acanthuses [*Corinth,* Greece]

Cor·in·thi·ans \-ənz\ *n* : either of two letters written by Saint Paul to the Christians of Corinth and included as books of the New Testament — see BIBLE table

Co·ri·o·lis effect \ˌkōr-ē-ˌō-ləs-, ˌkȯr-\ *n* : the deflection of a moving object that is a result of the Coriolis force

Coriolis force *n* : an apparent force that as a result of the earth's rotation deflects moving objects (as projectiles) or air currents to the right in the northern hemisphere and to the left in the southern hemisphere [Gaspard G. *Coriolis,* died 1843, French civil engineer]

co·ri·um \ˈkōr-ē-əm, ˈkȯr-\ *n, pl* **-ria** \-ē-ə\ : DERMIS [Latin, "leather"]

[1]**cork** \ˈkȯrk\ *n* **1 a** : the elastic tough outer tissue of the cork oak used especially for stoppers and insulation **b** : the tissue of a woody plant making up most of the bark and arising from an inner cambium — called also *phellem* **2** : a usually cork stopper for a bottle or jug [Middle English, probably from Arabic *qurq,* from Latin *quercus* "oak"]

[2]**cork** *vt* **1** : to furnish, fit, or seal with a cork ⟨*cork* a bottle⟩ **2** : to blacken with burnt cork ⟨*corked* faces⟩

cork cambium *n* : PHELLOGEN

cork·er \ˈkȯr-kər\ *n* **1** : one that corks containers (as bottles) **2** : an outstanding person or thing

cork·ing \ˈkȯr-king\ *adj* : extremely fine

cork oak *n* : an oak of southern Europe and northern Africa that is the source of the cork of commerce

[1]**cork·screw** \ˈkȯrk-ˌskrü\ *n* : a pointed spiral piece of metal with a handle that is used to draw corks from bottles

[2]**corkscrew** *adj* : resembling a corkscrew : SPIRAL

corky \ˈkȯr-kē\ *adj* **cork·i·er; -est** : resembling cork

corm \ˈkȯrm\ *n* : a thick fleshy underground stem (as of the crocus or gladiolus) that resembles a bulb and bears membranous or scaly leaves and buds — compare BULB, TUBER [Greek *kormos* "tree trunk"]

cor·mo·rant \ˈkȯrm-rənt, -ə-rənt\ *n* **1** : any of various dark-colored web-footed seabirds with a long neck, a wedge-shaped tail, a hooked bill, and a patch of bare often brightly colored skin under the mouth **2** : a greedy or gluttonous person [Medieval French, from earlier *cormareng,* from *corp* "raven" + *marenc* "of the sea," from Latin *marinus*]

cormorant 1

[1]**corn** \ˈkȯrn\ *n* **1 a** : a tall American cereal grass plant widely grown for its large elongated ears of starchy grain which come in many varieties **2** : the seeds of a corn plant that are used especially as food for humans and livestock and are typically yellow or whitish **3** : an ear of corn with or without its leafy outer covering **4** : corny actions or speech [Old English]

[2]**corn** *vb* : to preserve by packing with salt or by soaking in brine ⟨*corned* beef⟩

[3]**corn** *n* : a local hardening and thickening of skin (as on a toe) [Medieval French *corne* "horn," from Latin *cornu* "horn, point"]

corn belt *n* : an area (as the central portion of the U.S.) in which more land is used for growing corn than any other single crop

corn borer *n* : any of several insects that bore chiefly in corn; *esp* : EUROPEAN CORN BORER

corn bread *n* : bread made with cornmeal

corn chip *n* : a piece of a dry crisp snack food prepared from a seasoned cornmeal batter

corn·cob \ˈkȯrn-ˌkäb\ *n* : the woody core on which the kernels of corn are arranged

corncob pipe *n* : a tobacco pipe with a bowl made from a hollowed-out piece of corncob

corn cockle *n* : an annual hairy weed with purplish red flowers found in grain fields

corn·crib \ˈkȯrn-ˌkrib\ *n* : a crib for storing ears of corn

corn dog *n* : a frankfurter dipped in cornmeal batter, fried, and served on a stick

cor·nea \ˈkȯr-nē-ə\ *n* : the transparent part of the coat of the eyeball that covers the iris and pupil and admits light to the interior [Medieval Latin, from Latin *corneus* "horny," from *cornu* "horn"] — **cor·ne·al** \-nē-əl\ *adj*

corn earworm *n* : a moth whose large striped yellow-headed larva is especially destructive to corn, tomatoes, and cotton

cor·nel \ˈkȯrn-l\ *n* : any of several dogwoods [derived from Latin *cornus,* a kind of dogwood]

[1]**cor·ner** \ˈkȯr-nər\ *n* **1 a** : the point or place where converging lines, edges, or sides meet : ANGLE **b** : the place of intersection of two streets or roads **c** : a piece designed to form, mark, or protect a corner **2** : a usually remote area, region, or part ⟨a quiet *corner* of the town⟩ **3** : a position from which escape or retreat is difficult or impossible ⟨was backed into a *corner*⟩ **4** : control or ownership of enough of the available supply of something to control its price [Medieval French *cornere,* from *corne* "horn, corner," from Latin *cornu* "horn"] — **cor·nered** \-nərd\ *adj* — **around the corner** : being about to happen : at hand ⟨good times are just *around the corner*⟩

[2]**corner** *vb* **1** : to force into a corner ⟨the police *cornered* the

criminal〉 **2 :** to get a corner on 〈*corner* the wheat market〉 **3 :** to turn a corner 〈a car that *corners* well〉

[3]**corner** *adj* **1 :** situated at a corner 〈the *corner* drugstore〉 **2 :** used or fitted for use in or on a corner 〈a *corner* cupboard〉

cor·ner·back \-ˌbak\ *n* **:** a defensive halfback in football who defends the flank

corner kick *n* **:** a free kick in soccer from the corner of the field awarded to an offensive player after the defending team drives the ball out of bounds over the end line

cor·ner·stone \-ˌstōn\ *n* **1 :** a stone forming part of a corner in a wall; *esp* **:** such a stone laid at the formal beginning of the erection of a building **2 :** something of basic importance 〈a *cornerstone* of foreign policy〉

cor·net \kȯr-ˈnet\ *n* **1 :** a brass instrument resembling the trumpet but having a shorter tube and a more mellow tone **2 :** something (as a piece of paper twisted for use as a container) shaped like a cone [Middle French, from *corn* "horn," from Latin *cornu*]

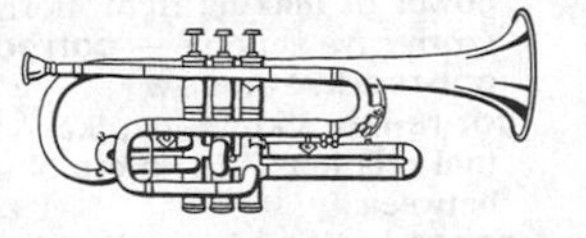
cornet 1

cor·net·ist *or* **cor·net·tist** \kȯr-ˈnet-əst\ *n* **:** one that plays the cornet

corn·field \ˈkȯrn-ˌfēld\ *n* **:** a field in which corn is grown

corn·flow·er \ˈkȯrn-ˌflau̇-ər, -ˌflau̇r\ *n* **1 :** CORN COCKLE **2 :** BACHELOR'S BUTTON

cor·nice \ˈkȯr-nəs\ *n* **1 :** the ornamental projecting piece that forms the top edge of a building or pillar **2 :** an ornamental molding placed where the walls meet the ceiling of a room **3 :** a decorative band of metal or wood to conceal curtain fixtures [Middle French, from Italian]

[1]**Cor·nish** \ˈkȯr-nish\ *adj* **:** of, relating to, or characteristic of Cornwall, Cornishmen, or Cornish

[2]**Cornish** *n* **1 :** the Celtic language of Cornwall **2 :** any of an English breed of domestic chickens much used in crossbreeding for meat production

Cor·nish·man \-mən\ *n* **:** a native or inhabitant of Cornwall, England

corn·meal \ˈkȯrn-ˈmēl, -ˌmēl\ *n* **:** meal ground from corn

corn oil *n* **:** a yellow fatty oil obtained from the germ of corn kernels and used chiefly in salad oil, in soft soap, and in margarine

corn pone *n, Southern & Midland* **:** corn bread often made without milk or eggs and baked or fried

corn smut *n* **:** a smut of corn that is characterized by grayish white swellings that rupture to expose a black mass of spores

corn snow *n* **:** granular snow formed by alternate thawing and freezing

corn·stalk \ˈkȯrn-ˌstȯk\ *n* **:** a stalk of corn

corn·starch \-ˌstärch\ *n* **:** a fine starch made from corn and used in cooking as a thickening agent, in making corn syrup and sugars, and in making adhesives and sizes for papers and textiles

corn sugar *n* **:** sugar made by hydrolysis of cornstarch

corn syrup *n* **:** a syrup made from cornstarch and used in baked goods and candy

cor·nu·co·pia \ˌkȯr-nyə-ˈkō-pē-ə, -nə-\ *n* **1 :** a horn-shaped container overflowing with fruits and flowers used as a symbol of abundance **2 :** a great abundance **3 :** a container shaped like a horn or a cone [Late Latin, from Latin *cornu copiae* "horn of plenty"]

corn whiskey *n* **:** whiskey distilled from a mash made up of not less than 80 percent corn

corny \ˈkȯr-nē\ *adj* **corn·i·er; -est :** tastelessly old-fashioned **:** tiresomely simple or sentimental 〈*corny* jokes〉

co·rol·la \kə-ˈräl-ə\ *n* **:** the inner floral envelope of a flower consisting of petals and enclosing the stamens and pistil [Latin, "small crown, garland," from *corona* "crown"] — **co·rol·late** \-ˈräl-ət\ *adj*

cor·ol·lary \ˈkȯr-ə-ˌler-ē, ˈkär-\ *n, pl* **-lar·ies 1 :** something that follows directly from something that has been proved **2 :** something that naturally follows **:** RESULT 〈enjoyed his newfound fame but not its *corollary,* a lack of privacy〉 [Late Latin *corollarium,* from Latin, "money paid for a garland, gratuity," from *corolla* "crown, garland"] — **corollary** *adj*

co·ro·na \kə-ˈrō-nə\ *n* **1 :** a usually colored circle often seen around and close to a luminous body (as the sun or moon) **2 :** the tenuous outermost part of the atmosphere of a star (as the sun) **3 :** the upper portion of a body part (as a tooth or the skull) **4 :** an appendage on the inner side of the corolla in some flowers (as the daffodil) **5 :** a discharge of electricity seen as a faint glow adjacent to the surface of an electrical conductor at high voltage [Latin, "garland, crown"]

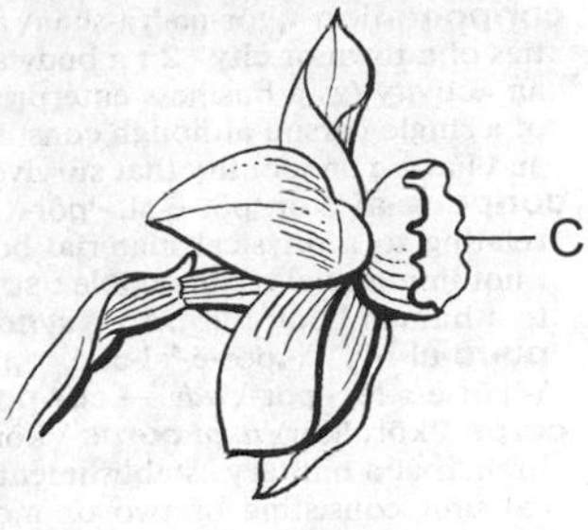

C corona 4

Corona Bo·re·al·is \-ˌbōr-ē-ˈal-əs, -ˌbȯr-\ *n* **:** a northern constellation between Hercules and Boötes [Latin, literally, "northern crown"]

cor·o·nach \ˈkȯr-ə-nək, ˈkär-\ *n* **:** DIRGE [Scottish Gaelic *corranach* and Irish Gaelic *coránach*]

[1]**cor·o·nal** \ˈkȯr-ən-l, ˈkär-\ *n* **:** a circlet for the head

[2]**cor·o·nal** \ˈkȯr-ən-l, ˈkär-; kə-ˈrōn-\ *adj* **:** of or relating to a corona or crown

[1]**cor·o·nary** \ˈkȯr-ə-ˌner-ē, ˈkär-\ *adj* **:** of, relating to, or being the arteries or veins that carry blood to or away from the heart; *also* **:** of or relating to the heart

[2]**coronary** *n, pl* **-nar·ies 1 :** a coronary artery or vein **2 :** CORONARY THROMBOSIS; *also* **:** HEART ATTACK

coronary artery *n* **:** either of the two arteries that arise one from the left and one from the right side of the aorta and supply the tissues of the heart

coronary heart disease *n* **:** a condition and especially one caused by atherosclerosis that reduces blood flow through the coronary arteries to the heart and typically results in chest pain or heart damage — called also *coronary artery disease*

coronary occlusion *n* **:** the partial or complete blocking (as by a thrombus, by spasm, or by sclerosis) of a coronary artery

coronary sclerosis *n* **:** hardening of the coronary arteries of the heart

coronary thrombosis *n* **:** the blocking of a coronary artery by a thrombus

coronary vein *n* **:** any of several veins that drain the tissues of the heart

cor·o·na·tion \ˌkȯr-ə-ˈnā-shən, ˌkär-\ *n* **:** the act or ceremony of crowning

cor·o·ner \ˈkȯr-ə-nər, ˈkär-\ *n* **:** an elected public officer that is typically not required to have specific medical qualifications and whose chief duty is to discover the causes of any death possibly not due to natural causes — compare MEDICAL EXAMINER [Middle English, "officer of the crown," from Medieval French *corone* "crown," from Latin *corona*]

cor·o·net \ˌkȯr-ə-ˈnet, ˌkär-\ *n* **1 :** a small crown worn by a person of noble but not of royal rank **2 :** an ornamental wreath or band worn around the head

[1]**cor·po·ral** \ˈkȯr-pə-rəl, -prəl\ *n* **:** a linen cloth on which the eucharistic elements are placed at mass [Medieval French, derived from Latin *corporalis* "of the body"; from the doctrine that the bread of the Eucharist becomes or represents the body of Christ]

[2]**corporal** *adj* **:** of or relating to the body 〈whipping and other *corporal* punishments〉 [Middle French, from Latin *corporalis,* from *corpor-, corpus* "body"] — **cor·po·ral·ly** \-pə-rə-lē, -prə-lē\ *adv*

[3]**corporal** *n* **:** an enlisted rank in the Army above private first class and below sergeant and in the Marine Corps above lance corporal and below sergeant [Middle French, alteration of *caporal,* from Italian *caporale,* from *capo* "head," from Latin *caput*]

cor·po·rate \ˈkȯr-pə-rət, -prət\ *adj* **1 a :** INCORPORATED **b :** of or relating to a corporation **2 :** of or relating to a whole composed of individuals **:** COLLECTIVE [Latin *corporare* "to form into a body," from *corpus* "body"] — **cor·po·rate·ly** *adv*

cor·po·rate–wide \-ˌwīd\ *adj* **:** extending throughout or involving an entire corporation 〈a *corporate-wide* smoking ban〉

\ə\ abut	\au̇\ out	\i\ tip	\ȯ\ saw	\u̇\ foot
\ər\ further	\ch\ chin	\ī\ life	\ȯi\ coin	\y\ yet
\a\ mat	\e\ pet	\j\ job	\th\ thin	\yü\ few
\ā\ take	\ē\ easy	\ng\ sing	\t͟h\ this	\yu̇\ cure
\ä\ cot, cart	\g\ go	\ō\ bone	\ü\ food	\zh\ vision

cor·po·ra·tion \ˌkȯr-pə-ˈrā-shən\ *n* **1 :** the municipal authorities of a town or city **2 :** a body authorized by law to carry on an activity (as a business enterprise) with the rights and duties of a single person although constituted by one or more persons and having an identity that survives its incorporators

cor·po·re·al \kȯr-ˈpōr-ē-əl, -ˈpȯr-\ *adj* **:** having, consisting of, or relating to a physical material body: as **a :** not spiritual **b :** not immaterial or intangible : SUBSTANTIAL **c :** of or relating to a human body : BODILY ***synonyms*** see MATERIAL — **cor·po·re·al·i·ty** \-ˌpōr-ē-ˈal-ət-ē, -ˌpȯr-\ *n* — **cor·po·re·al·ly** \-ˈpōr-ē-ə-lē, -ˈpȯr-\ *adv* — **cor·po·re·al·ness** *n*

corps \ˈkōr, ˈkȯr\ *n, pl* **corps** \ˈkōrz, ˈkȯrz\ **1 a :** an organized branch of a military establishment ⟨Marine *Corps*⟩ **b :** a tactical unit consisting of two or more divisions and supporting forces **2 :** a group of persons associated together or acting under common direction ⟨diplomatic *corps*⟩ [French, from Latin *corpus* "body"]

corps de bal·let \ˌkōrd-ə-ba-ˈlā, ˌkȯrd-\ *n, pl* **corps de ballet** *same*\ **:** the chorus of a ballet company [French]

corpse \ˈkȯrps\ *n* **:** a dead body especially of a human being [Medieval French *corps* "body," from Latin *corpus*]

corps·man \ˈkōr-mən, ˈkȯr-, ˈkōrz-, ˈkȯrz-\ *n* **:** an enlisted man trained to give first aid

cor·pu·lent \ˈkȯr-pyə-lənt\ *adj* **:** having a large bulky body : OBESE [Latin *corpulentus,* from *corpus* "body"] — **cor·pu·lence** \-ləns\ *n* — **cor·pu·len·cy** \-lən-sē\ *n* — **cor·pu·lent·ly** *adv*

cor·pus \ˈkȯr-pəs\ *n, pl* **cor·po·ra** \-pə-rə, -prə\ **1 :** the main or central part of a bodily structure ⟨the *corpus* of the jaw⟩ **2 :** the main body or principal substance of a thing **3 a :** all the works on a particular subject or by a particular author **b :** a collection or body of knowledge or evidence [Latin, "body"]

Cor·pus Chris·ti \ˌkȯr-pəs-ˈkris-tē\ *n* **:** the Thursday after Trinity Sunday observed as a Roman Catholic festival in honor of the Eucharist [Medieval Latin, literally, "body of Christ"]

cor·pus·cle \ˈkȯr-ˌpəs-əl\ *n* **1 :** a minute particle **2 :** a living cell; *esp* **:** one (as a red blood cell) not aggregated into continuous tissues [Latin *corpusculum* "small body," from *corpus* "body"] — **cor·pus·cu·lar** \kȯr-ˈpəs-kyə-lər\ *adj*

cor·pus de·lic·ti \ˌkȯr-pəs-di-ˈlik-ˌtī, -ˌtē\ *n, pl* **cor·po·ra delic·ti** \ˌkȯr-pə-rə-, -prə-\ **1 :** the substantial fact necessary to prove the commission of a crime **2 :** the material substance (as the body of a murder victim) upon which a crime has been committed [New Latin, literally, "body of the crime"]

cor·pus lu·te·um \ˌkȯr-pəs-ˈlüt-ē-əm\ *n, pl* **cor·po·ra lu·tea** \ˌkȯr-pə-rə-ˈlüt-ē-ə, -prə-\ **:** a yellowish mass of endocrine tissue formed in a graafian follicle after the egg is released [New Latin, literally, "yellowish body"]

[1]**cor·ral** \kə-ˈral\ *n* **1 :** a pen or enclosure for confining or capturing livestock **2 :** an enclosure made with wagons for defense of an encampment [Spanish, derived from Latin *currus* "cart," from *currere* "to run"]

[2]**corral** *vt* **cor·ralled; cor·ral·ling 1 :** to confine in or as if in a corral **2 :** to arrange (as wagons) so as to form a corral **3 :** to round up : GATHER ⟨*corralling* votes for the election⟩

[1]**cor·rect** \kə-ˈrekt\ *vt* **1 a :** to make or set right : AMEND **b :** COUNTERACT, NEUTRALIZE **c :** to alter or adjust so as to bring to some standard or required condition **2 a :** REBUKE, PUNISH **b :** to point out the errors or faults of ⟨*correct* a student's composition⟩ [Latin *correctus,* past participle of *corrigere* "to correct," from *com-* + *regere* "to lead straight"] — **cor·rect·able** \-ˈrek-tə-bəl\ *adj* — **cor·rec·tor** \-ˈrek-tər\ *n*

synonyms CORRECT, RECTIFY, AMEND, EMEND mean to make right what is wrong. CORRECT implies taking action to remove errors, faults, or deviations ⟨*correct* your spelling⟩. RECTIFY implies a more essential changing to make something right, just, or proper ⟨*rectify* a misguided policy⟩. AMEND implies improving or restoring by making slight changes ⟨*amend* a law⟩. EMEND especially applies to the correction of a text ⟨*emend* the manuscript⟩.

[2]**correct** *adj* **1 :** conforming to an approved or conventional standard ⟨*correct* behavior⟩ **2 :** agreeing with fact, logic, or known truth : ACCURATE ⟨the *correct* answer⟩ — **cor·rect·ly** *adv* — **cor·rect·ness** \-ˈrek-nəs, -ˈrekt-\ *n*

synonyms CORRECT, ACCURATE, EXACT, PRECISE mean conforming to fact, truth, or standard. CORRECT implies freedom from fault or error ⟨the *correct* dress for the occasion⟩. ACCURATE implies greater fidelity to truth or fact attained by exercise of care ⟨an *accurate* description of a situation⟩. EXACT stresses a very strict agreement with fact or truth ⟨a suit tailored to *exact* measurements⟩. PRECISE adds to EXACT an emphasis on sharpness of definition or delimitation ⟨the *precise* terms of a contract⟩.

cor·rec·tion \kə-ˈrek-shən\ *n* **1 :** the action or an instance of correcting **2 :** a change that corrects something **3 :** punishment or discipline intended to correct faults of character or behavior **4 :** the treatment of offenders through a program involving penal custody, parole, and probation — **cor·rec·tion·al** \-shnəl, -shən-l\ *adj*

correction fluid *n* **:** a liquid used to paint over typing or writing errors

cor·rec·tive \kə-ˈrek-tiv\ *adj* **:** serving to correct : having the power of making right, normal, or regular ⟨*corrective* lenses⟩ ⟨*corrective* action⟩ — **corrective** *n* — **cor·rec·tive·ly** *adv* — **cor·rec·tive·ness** *n*

cor·re·late \ˈkȯr-ə-ˌlāt, ˈkär-\ *vb* **1 :** to have reciprocal or mutual relations **2 :** to establish a mutual or reciprocal relation between

cor·re·la·tion \ˌkȯr-ə-ˈlā-shən, ˌkär-\ *n* **1 :** the act or process of correlating **2 :** the state of being correlated; *esp* **:** a mutual relation existing between things ⟨the apparent *correlation* between the degree of poverty in a society and the crime rate⟩ [Medieval Latin *correlatio,* from Latin *com-* + *relatio* "relation"] — **cor·re·la·tion·al** \-shnəl, -shən-l\ *adj*

[1]**cor·rel·a·tive** \kə-ˈrel-ət-iv\ *adj* **1 :** mutually related **2 :** having a mutual grammatical relation and regularly used together ⟨*either* and *or* are *correlative* conjunctions⟩ — **cor·rel·a·tive·ly** *adv*

[2]**correlative** *n* **:** either of two correlative things

cor·re·spond \ˌkȯr-ə-ˈspänd, ˌkär-\ *vi* **1 a :** to be in conformity or agreement : SUIT **b :** to compare closely : MATCH **c :** to be equivalent or parallel **2 :** to communicate with a person by exchange of letters [Medieval Latin *correspondēre,* from Latin *com-* + *respondēre* "to respond"]

cor·re·spon·dence \-ˈspän-dəns\ *n* **1 a :** the agreement of things with one another **b :** a particular similarity **c :** a relation between sets in which each member of one set is associated with one or more members of the other ⟨a one-to-one *correspondence*⟩ **2 :** communication by letters; *also* **:** the letters exchanged

correspondence school *n* **:** a school that teaches non-resident students by mailing them lessons and exercises which upon completion are returned to the school for grading

[1]**cor·re·spon·dent** \ˌkȯr-ə-ˈspän-dənt, ˌkär-\ *adj* **1 :** SIMILAR 1 **2 :** being in agreement : FITTING

[2]**correspondent** *n* **1 :** something that corresponds or conforms to something else **2 a :** one who communicates with another by letter **b :** one who has regular commercial relations with another **c :** one who contributes news or comment to a newspaper often from a distant place

corresponding *adj* **:** having the same relationship (as kind, degree, position, or function) with regard to the same or like wholes (as a geometric figure) ⟨*corresponding* parts of similar triangles⟩

corresponding angles *n pl* **:** any pair of angles each of which is on the same side of one of two lines cut by another line and on the same side of that other line

cor·re·spond·ing·ly \-ˈspän-ding-lē\ *adv* **:** in a corresponding manner : in such a way as to correspond

cor·ri·da \kȯ-ˈrē-t͟hə\ *n* **:** BULLFIGHT [Spanish, literally, "act of running"]

cor·ri·dor \ˈkȯr-əd-ər, ˈkär-, -ə-ˌdȯr\ *n* **1 :** a passageway into which compartments or rooms open (as in a hotel or school) **2 :** a narrow strip of land especially through foreign-held territory **3 :** an air route (as over a foreign country) to which aircraft are restricted [Middle French, from Italian *corridore,* from *correre* "to run," from Latin *currere*]

cor·ri·gen·dum \ˌkȯr-ə-ˈjen-dəm, ˌkär-\ *n, pl* **-da** \-də\ **:** an error in a printed work discovered after printing and shown with its correction on a separate sheet [Latin, "thing to be corrected," from *corrigere* "to correct"]

cor·ri·gi·ble \ˈkȯr-ə-jə-bəl, ˈkär-\ *adj* **:** capable of being set right [Middle French, derived from Latin *corrigere* "to correct"] — **cor·ri·gi·bil·i·ty** \ˌkȯr-ə-jə-ˈbil-ət-ē, ˌkär-\ *n* — **cor·ri·gi·bly** \ˈkȯr-ə-jə-blē, ˈkär-\ *adv*

cor·rob·o·rate \kə-ˈräb-ə-ˌrāt\ *vt* **:** to support with evidence or authority : make more certain [Latin *corroborare* "to strengthen," from *com-* + *robur* "strength"] ***synonyms*** see CONFIRM

— **cor·rob·o·ra·tion** \-ˌräb-ə-ˈrā-shən\ *n* — **cor·rob·o·ra·tive** \-ˈräb-ə-ˌrāt-iv, -ˈräb-rət-, -ə-rət-\ *adj* — **cor·rob·o·ra·tor** \-ˌrāt-ər\ *n* — **cor·rob·o·ra·to·ry** \-ˈräb-rə-ˌtōr-ē, -ə-rə-, -ˌtȯr-\ *adj*

cor·rode \kə-ˈrōd\ *vb* : to destroy or be destroyed gradually as if by gnawing; *esp* : to wear away gradually usually by chemical action ⟨the metal was *corroded* beyond repair⟩ [Latin *corrodere* "to gnaw to pieces," from *com-* + *rodere* "to gnaw"] — **cor·rod·ible** \-ˈrōd-ə-bəl\ *adj*

cor·ro·sion \kə-ˈrō-zhən\ *n* : the action, process, or effect of corroding [Late Latin *corrosio* "act of gnawing," from Latin *corrodere* "to gnaw"]

[1]**cor·ro·sive** \-ˈrō-siv, -ziv\ *adj* : tending or having the power to corrode ⟨*corrosive* acids⟩ — **cor·ro·sive·ly** *adv* — **cor·ro·sive·ness** *n*

[2]**corrosive** *n* : something corrosive

corrosive sublimate *n* : MERCURIC CHLORIDE

cor·ru·gate \ˈkȯr-ə-ˌgāt, ˈkär-\ *vb* : to form or shape into parallel wrinkles or folds or ridges and grooves ⟨*corrugated* paper⟩ [Latin *corrugare,* from *com-* + *ruga* "wrinkle"]

cor·ru·ga·tion \ˌkȯr-ə-ˈgā-shən, ˌkär-\ *n* **1 :** the act of corrugating : the state of being corrugated **2 :** a ridge or groove of a corrugated surface

[1]**cor·rupt** \kə-ˈrəpt\ *vb* **1 a :** to change from good to bad in morals, manners, or actions **b :** to influence a public official improperly : BRIBE **2 :** TAINT 2, ROT **3 :** to alter from an original or correct form or version ⟨*corrupt* a text⟩ **4 :** to become debased [Latin *corruptus,* past participle of *corrumpere* "to corrupt," from *com-* + *rumpere* "to break"] ***synonyms*** see DEBASE — **cor·rupt·er** *also* **cor·rup·tor** \-ˈrəp-tər\ *n*

[2]**corrupt** *adj* **1 :** morally debased : DEPRAVED **2 :** characterized by improper conduct (as bribery or the selling of political favors) ⟨a *corrupt* administration⟩ — **cor·rupt·ly** *adv* — **cor·rupt·ness** \-ˈrəpt-nəs, -ˈrəp-\ *n*

cor·rupt·ible \kə-ˈrəp-tə-bəl\ *adj* : capable of being corrupted — **cor·rupt·ibil·i·ty** \-ˌrəp-tə-ˈbil-ət-ē\ *n*

cor·rup·tion \kə-ˈrəp-shən\ *n* **1 a :** physical decay or rotting **b :** moral debasement : DEPRAVITY **c :** inducement to do wrong by unlawful or improper means (as bribery) **d :** a departure from the original or from what is pure or correct **2** *archaic* : an agency or influence that corrupts

cor·rup·tive \kə-ˈrəp-tiv\ *adj* : producing corruption

cor·sage \kȯr-ˈsäzh, -ˈsäj, ˈkȯr-ˌ\ *n* **1 :** the waist or bodice of a woman's dress **2 :** an arrangement of flowers to be worn by a woman [French, "bust, bodice," from Medieval French, "bust," from *cors* "body," from Latin *corpus*]

cor·sair \ˈkȯr-ˌsaər, -ˌseər\ *n* : PIRATE; *esp* : a privateer of the Barbary coast [Middle French *corsaire,* derived from Medieval Latin *cursarius,* from Latin *cursus* "course"]

corse \ˈkȯrs\ *n, archaic* : CORPSE [Medieval French *cors* "body"]

corse·let *n* **1** *or* **cors·let** \ˈkȯr-slət\ : armor worn on the upper part of the body **2** *or* **cor·se·lette** \ˌkȯr-sə-ˈlet\ : a woman's undergarment somewhat like a corset [Middle French, from *cors* "body, bodice"]

corselet 1

[1]**cor·set** \ˈkȯr-sət\ *n* : a tight-fitting stiffened undergarment worn to support or give shape to waist and hips [Medieval French, a kind of jacket, from *cors* "body"]

[2]**corset** *vt* : to dress in or fit with a corset

cor·tege *also* **cor·tège** \kȯr-ˈtezh, ˈkȯr-ˌ\ *n* **1 :** a train of attendants : RETINUE **2 :** PROCESSION; *esp* : a funeral procession [French *cortège,* from Italian *corteggio,* from *corte* "court," from Latin *cohors* "enclosure"]

cor·tex \ˈkȯr-ˌteks\ *n, pl* **cor·ti·ces** \ˈkȯrt-ə-ˌsēz\ *or* **cor·tex·es** **1 :** an outer or surrounding layer of an organ or part ⟨the *cortex* of the kidney⟩; *esp* : CEREBRAL CORTEX **2 :** the layer of tissue outside the vascular tissue and inside the corky or epidermal tissues of a vascular plant; *also* : all tissues external to the xylem [Latin *cortic-, cortex* "bark"] — **cor·ti·cal** \ˈkȯrt-i-kəl\ *adj* — **cor·ti·cal·ly** \-i-kə-lē, -klē\ *adv*

cor·ti·co·tro·pin \ˌkȯrt-i-kō-ˈtrō-pən\ *n* : ACTH; *also* : a preparation of ACTH that is used especially in the treatment of rheumatoid arthritis and rheumatic fever

cor·ti·sol \ˈkȯrt-ə-ˌsȯl, -ˌzȯl, -ˌsōl, -ˌzōl\ *n* : a hormone of the adrenal cortex that is derived from cortisone and has a similar use and whose levels in the blood may rise in response to stress — called also *hydrocortisone*

cor·ti·sone \-ˌsōn, -ˌzōn\ *n* : a steroid hormone of the adrenal cortex used in synthetic form especially to reduce inflammation (as in the treatment of rheumatoid arthritis)

co·run·dum \kə-ˈrən-dəm\ *n* : a very hard mineral that consists of aluminum oxide and is used as an abrasive or in some crystalline forms as a gem (as ruby or sapphire) [Tamil *kuruntam*]

cor·us·cate \ˈkȯr-ə-ˌskāt, ˈkär-\ *vi* : to give off flashes of light : SPARKLE [Latin *coruscare*] — **cor·us·ca·tion** \ˌkȯr-ə-ˈskā-shən, ˌkär-\ *n*

cor·vette \kȯr-ˈvet\ *n* **1 :** a warship of the old sailing navies smaller than a frigate **2 :** a highly maneuverable armed escort ship smaller than a destroyer [French]

Cor·vus \ˈkȯr-vəs\ *n* : a small constellation adjoining Virgo on the south [Latin, literally, "raven"]

Cor·y·bant \ˈkȯr-ə-ˌbant, ˈkär-\ *n, pl* **Cor·y·bants** *or* **Cor·y·ban·tes** \ˌkȯr-ə-ˈban-ˌtēz, ˌkär-\ : one of the attendants or priests of the ancient goddess Cybele noted for their orgiastic rites [French *Corybante,* from Latin *Corybas,* from Greek *Korybas*] — **cor·y·ban·tic** \ˌkȯr-ə-ˈbant-ik, ˌkär-\ *adj*

co·rymb \ˈkȯr-ˌim, ˈkär-\ *n* : a flat-topped inflorescence in which the flower stalks arise at different levels on the main axis and reach about the same height and in which the outer flowers open first [French *corymbe,* from Latin *corymbus* "cluster of fruit or flowers," from Greek *korymbos*]

co·se·cant \ˈkō-ˈsē-ˌkant, kō-, -kənt\ *n* **1 :** the trigonometric function that for an acute angle is the ratio between the hypotenuse of a right triangle of which the angle is considered part and the side opposite the angle — abbreviation *csc* **2 :** a trigonometric function csc θ that is the reciprocal of the sine for all real numbers θ for which the sine is not zero and that is exactly equal to the cosecant of an angle of measure θ in radians

co·sig·na·to·ry \ˈkō-ˈsig-nə-ˌtōr-ē, -ˌtȯr-\ *n, pl* **-ries :** a joint signer

co·sign·er \ˈkō-ˌsī-nər\ *n* : COSIGNATORY — **co·sign** \-ˌsīn\ *vb*

cosily, cosiness *chiefly British variant of* COZILY, COZINESS

co·sine \ˈkō-ˌsīn\ *n* **1 :** the trigonometric function that for an acute angle is the ratio between the side adjacent to the angle when it is considered part of a right triangle and the hypotenuse — abbreviation *cos* **2 :** a trigonometric function cos θ that for all real numbers θ is given by the sum of the alternating series

$$\cos\theta = 1 - \frac{\theta^2}{2!} + \frac{\theta^4}{4!} - \frac{\theta^6}{6!} + \frac{\theta^8}{8!} - \ldots$$

and that is exactly equal to the cosine of an angle of measure θ in radians

[1]**cos·met·ic** \käz-ˈmet-ik\ *n* : a cosmetic preparation (as a cream, lotion, or powder) for external use

[2]**cosmetic** *adj* **1 :** intended to beautify the hair or complexion **2 :** correcting defects especially of the face ⟨*cosmetic* surgery⟩ [Greek *kosmētikos* "skilled in adornment," from *kosmein* "to arrange, adorn," from *kosmos* "order"]

cos·me·tol·o·gist \ˌkäz-mə-ˈtäl-ə-jəst\ *n* : a person who gives beauty treatments (as to skin and hair) — **cos·me·tol·o·gy** \-jē\ *n*

cos·mic \ˈkäz-mik\ *adj* **1 :** of or relating to the cosmos ⟨*cosmic* theories⟩ **2 :** extremely vast : GRAND ⟨a topic of *cosmic* proportions⟩ — **cos·mi·cal·ly** \-mi-kə-lē, -klē\ *adv*

cosmic dust *n* : very fine particles of solid matter in any part of the universe and especially in interstellar space

cosmic microwave background *n* : BACKGROUND RADIATION

cosmic ray *n* : a stream of atomic nuclei of extremely penetrating character that enter the earth's atmosphere from outer space at speeds approaching that of light

cosmic string *n* : any of a class of hypothetical astronomical objects of very high mass that are very thin but are millions of light years long

cos·mog·o·ny \käz-ˈmäg-ə-nē\ *n, pl* **-nies** **1 :** a theory of the origin of the universe **2 :** the creation or origination of the world or universe [Greek *kosmogonia,* from *kosmos* "order, universe" + *gonos* "offspring"] — **cos·mog·o·nist** \-nəst\ *n*

cos·mog·ra·phy \käz-ˈmäg-rə-fē\ *n, pl* **-phies** **1 :** a general de-

\ə\ **abut**	\au̇\ **out**	\i\ **tip**	\ȯ\ **saw**	\u̇\ **foot**
\ər\ **further**	\ch\ **chin**	\ī\ **life**	\ȯi\ **coin**	\y\ **yet**
\a\ **mat**	\e\ **pet**	\j\ **job**	\th\ **thin**	\yü\ **few**
\ā\ **take**	\ē\ **easy**	\ng\ **sing**	\th̲\ **this**	\yu̇\ **cure**
\ä\ **cot, cart**	\g\ **go**	\ō\ **bone**	\ü\ **food**	\zh\ **vision**

scription of the world or of the universe **2** : the science that deals with the constitution of the whole order of nature — **cos·mog·ra·pher** \-fər\ *n* — **cos·mo·graph·ic** \ˌkäz-mə-ˈgraf-ik\ *adj*

cos·mol·o·gy \käz-ˈmäl-ə-jē\ *n, pl* **-gies** : a study that deals with the origin, structure, and space-time relationships of the universe — **cos·mo·log·i·cal** \ˌkäz-mə-ˈläj-i-kəl\ *adj* — **cos·mol·o·gist** \käz-ˈmäl-ə-jəst\ *n*

cos·mo·naut \ˈkäz-mə-ˌnȯt, -ˌnät\ *n* : a Soviet or Russian astronaut [Russian *kosmonavt,* from Greek *kosmos* "universe" + Russian *-navt* (as in *aeronavt* "aeronaut")]

cos·mo·pol·i·tan \ˌkäz-mə-ˈpäl-ət-n\ *adj* **1** : having a worldwide scope or outlook : not limited or narrow ⟨*cosmopolitan* world travelers⟩ **2** : composed of persons or elements from many parts of the world ⟨a *cosmopolitan* city⟩ **3** : found in most parts of the world and under varied ecological conditions ⟨a *cosmopolitan* herb⟩ [derived from Greek *kosmos* "world, cosmos" + *politēs* "citizen," from *polis* "city, state"] — **cosmopolitan** *n* — **cos·mo·pol·i·tan·ism** \-n-ˌiz-əm\ *n*

cos·mop·o·lite \käz-ˈmäp-ə-ˌlīt\ *n* : a cosmopolitan person or organism

cos·mos \ˈkäz-məs, *1 & 2 also* -ˌmōs, -ˌmäs\ *n* **1** : the orderly systematic universe **2** : a complex harmonious system **3** : a tall garden plant that is related to the daisies and has showy white, pink, or rose-colored flower heads with usually yellow centers [Greek *kosmos* "order, adornment, universe"]

Cos·sack \ˈkäs-ˌak, -ək\ *n* **1** : a member of any of the groups that formed in Ukraine, southern Russia, the Caucasus, and Siberia after 1400 and were included in czarist Russia during the 18th and 19th centuries **2** : a mounted soldier serving in a unit drafted from Cossack communities [Polish and Ukrainian *kozak,* of Turkic origin]

[1]**cos·set** \ˈkäs-ət\ *n* : a pet lamb; *also* : PET [origin unknown]

[2]**cosset** *vt* : to treat as a pet : PAMPER

[1]**cost** \ˈkȯst\ *n* **1 a** : the amount paid or charged for something : PRICE **b** : the effort made or loss suffered to achieve an object ⟨won the battle at the *cost* of many lives⟩ **2** *pl* : legal expenses especially expenses awarded to the winning party against the losing party ⟨fined $50 and *costs*⟩ — **at all costs** : regardless of the cost or consequences ⟨wanted to win *at all costs*⟩

[2]**cost** *vb* **cost; cost·ing** **1** : to have a price of : require payment ⟨each ticket *costs* one dollar⟩ ⟨the best tickets *cost* more⟩ **2** : to cause one to pay, spend, or lose ⟨selfishness *cost* them many friends⟩ [Medieval French *custer, couster,* from Latin *constare* "to stand firm, cost," from *com-* + *stare* "to stand"]

cos·ta \ˈkäs-tə\ *n, pl* **cos·tae** \-ˌtē, -ˌtī\ : RIB 1a; *also* : a part (as the midrib of a leaf) resembling a rib [Latin, "rib, side"] — **cos·tal** \ˈkäst-l\ *adj*

cos·tard \ˈkäs-tərd\ *n* **1** : any of several large English cooking apples **2** *archaic* : HEAD, NODDLE [Middle English]

cos·ter \ˈkäs-tər\ *n, British* : COSTERMONGER

cos·ter·mon·ger \ˈkäs-tər-ˌməng-gər, -ˌmäng-\ *n, British* : a person who sells fruit or vegetables in the street from a stand or cart [*costard,* a kind of apple + *monger*]

cos·tive \ˈkäs-tiv, ˈkȯs-\ *adj* **1** : affected with constipation **2** : causing constipation ⟨a *costive* diet⟩ [Medieval French *costiver* "to constipate," from Latin *constipare*] — **cos·tive·ly** *adv* — **cos·tive·ness** *n*

cost·ly \ˈkȯst-lē\ *adj* **cost·li·er; -est** **1** : very expensive or valuable ⟨*costly* furs⟩ **2** : gained at great cost or sacrifice ⟨a *costly* victory⟩ — **cost·li·ness** *n*

synonyms COSTLY, EXPENSIVE, VALUABLE, DEAR mean having a great price or value. COSTLY implies high price and may suggest luxury or rarity ⟨*costly* jewels⟩. EXPENSIVE may imply a price beyond the thing's value or the buyer's means ⟨*expensive* concert tickets⟩. VALUABLE suggests worth measured in usefulness as well as price ⟨oil is a *valuable* resource⟩. DEAR implies a relatively high or excessive price often due to factors other than the thing's intrinsic value ⟨poor growing conditions making vegetables *dear*⟩.

cost·mary \ˈkȯst-ˌmer-ē\ *n, pl* **-mar·ies** : an aromatic herb related to the daisies and used as a potherb and in flavoring [Middle English *coste* "costmary" + *Marie,* the Virgin Mary]

[1]**cos·tume** \ˈkäs-ˌtüm, -ˌtyüm *also* -təm *or* -chəm\ *n* **1** : the prevailing fashion in hair style, jewelry, and apparel of a period, country, or class **2** : an outfit worn to create the appearance characteristic of a particular period, person, place, or thing ⟨Halloween *costumes*⟩ **3** : a person's ensemble of outer garments; *esp* : a woman's ensemble of dress with coat or jacket [French, from Italian, "custom, dress," from Latin *consuetudo* "custom"]

[2]**cos·tume** \käs-ˈtüm, -ˈtyüm *also* -ˈchüm; *or like* [1]\ *vt* **1** : to provide with a costume **2** : to design costumes for

[3]**cos·tume** *like* [1]\ *adj* **1** : characterized by use of costumes ⟨a *costume* ball⟩ **2** : suitable for or enhancing the effect of a particular costume ⟨a *costume* handbag⟩

cos·tum·er \ˈkäs-ˌtü-mər, -ˌtyü-\ *n* : one that makes, sells, or rents costumes

cos·tu·mi·er \käs-ˈtü-mē-ˌā, -ˈtyü-\ *n, chiefly British* : COSTUMER

co·sy *chiefly British variant of* COZY

[1]**cot** \ˈkät\ *n* : a small house : COTTAGE [Old English]

[2]**cot** *n* : a small often collapsible bed usually of fabric stretched on a frame [Hindi & Urdu *khāṭ* "bedstead"]

co·tan·gent \ˈkō-ˈtan-jənt, kō-\ *n* **1** : the trigonometric function that for an acute angle is the ratio between the side adjacent to the angle and the side opposite when the angle is considered part of a right triangle — abbreviation *cot* **2** : a trigonometric function cot θ that is equal to the cosine divided by the sine for all real numbers θ for which the sine is not equal to zero and is exactly equal to the cotangent of an angle of measure θ in radians

cote \ˈkōt, ˈkät\ *n* : a shed or coop for small domestic animals (as pigeons) [Old English]

co·te·rie \ˈkōt-ə-rē, ˌkōt-ə-ˈ\ *n* : a small close group of persons with a shared interest or purpose [French, from Middle French, "tenants," from Medieval Latin *cotarius* "cotter"]

co·ter·mi·nous \ˈkō-ˈtər-mə-nəs, kō-\ *adj* **1** : having the same boundaries **2** : having the same scope or duration — **co·ter·mi·nous·ly** *adv*

co·til·lion *also* **co·til·lon** \kō-ˈtil-yən, kə-\ *n* **1** : an elaborate dance with frequent changing of partners led by one couple at formal balls **2** : a formal ball [French *cotillon,* literally, "petticoat," from Medieval French, from *cote* "coat"]

co·to·neas·ter \kə-ˈtō-nē-ˌas-tər, ˈkät-n-ˌēs-\ *n* : any of a genus of Old World flowering shrubs related to the rose [derived from Latin *cotoneum* "quince"]

cot·ta \ˈkät-ə\ *n* : a waist-length surplice [Medieval Latin, of Germanic origin]

cot·tage \ˈkät-ij\ *n* **1** : a usually small frame one-family house **2** : a small house for vacation use [Middle English *cotage,* from Medieval French, from Middle English *cot*]

cottage cheese *n* : a soft uncured cheese made from soured skim milk

cottage pudding *n* : plain cake covered with a hot sweet sauce

cot·tag·er \ˈkät-ij-ər\ *n* : one who lives in a cottage; *esp* : one occupying a private house at a vacation resort

cot·tar *or* **cot·ter** \ˈkät-ər\ *n* : a peasant or rural laborer occupying a small holding [Medieval Latin *cotarius,* from Middle English *cot* "cottage"]

cot·ter \ˈkät-ər\ *n* : a wedge-shaped or tapered piece used to fasten together parts of a structure [origin unknown]

cotter pin *n* : a half-round metal strip bent into a pin whose ends can be flared after insertion through a slot or hole

[1]**cot·ton** \ˈkät-n\ *n* **1 a** : a soft usually white fibrous substance composed of the hairs surrounding the seeds of various erect freely branching tropical plants related to the mallows **b** : a plant producing cotton **c** : a crop of cotton **2 a** : fabric made of cotton **b** : yarn spun from cotton [Medieval French *coton,* from Italian *cotone,* from Arabic *quṭn*] — **cotton** *adj*

[2]**cotton** *vi* **cot·toned; cot·ton·ing** \ˈkät-ning, -n-ing\ : to take a liking ⟨*cottoned* to them at first sight⟩

cotton candy *n* : a candy made of spun sugar

cotton gin *n* : a machine that separates the seeds, hulls, and foreign material from cotton

cot·ton·mouth \ˈkät-n-ˌmau̇th\ *n* : WATER MOCCASIN — called also *cottonmouth moccasin*

cot·ton·seed \-ˌsēd\ *n* : the seed of the cotton plant

cottonseed oil *n* : a pale yellow oil obtained from cottonseed and used chiefly in salad and cooking oils and in shortenings and margarine

cot·ton·tail \-ˌtāl\ *n* : any of several small brownish gray rabbits with a fluffy tail that is white on the underside

cot·ton·wood \-ˌwu̇d\ *n* : a poplar that produces a tuft of cottony hairs on the seed; *esp* : one of the eastern and central U.S. noted for its rapid growth and luxuriant foliage

cotton wool *n* : raw cotton; *esp* : cotton batting

cot·tony \ˈkät-nē, -n-ē\ *adj* **:** resembling cotton in appearance or character: as **a :** covered with soft hairs **:** DOWNY **b :** SOFT 1e

-cotyl \ˌkät-ᵊl\ *n combining form* **:** cotyledon ⟨*epicotyl*⟩

cot·y·le·don \ˌkät-ᵊl-ˈēd-ᵊn\ *n* **1 :** a small lobe of the mammalian placenta **2 :** the first leaf or one of the first pair or whorl of leaves developed by the embryo of a seed plant — called also *seed leaf* [Greek *kotylēdōn* "cup-shaped hollow," from *kotylē* "cup"] — **cot·y·le·don·ary** \-ˈēd-ᵊn-ˌer-ē\ *adj*

cot·y·lo·saur \ˈkät-ᵊl-ō-ˌsȯr\ *n* **:** any of an order (Cotylosauria) of ancient extinct primitive reptiles that were probably the earliest truly terrestrial vertebrate animals [Greek *kotylē* "cup" + *sauros* "lizard"]

1**couch** \ˈkau̇ch\ *vb* **1 :** to recline for rest or sleep **2 :** to bring down **:** LOWER ⟨a knight charging with *couched* lance⟩ **3 :** to phrase in a specified manner ⟨a letter *couched* in polite terms⟩ **4 :** to lie in ambush [Medieval French *coucher,* from Latin *collocare* "to set in place," from *com-* + *locus* "place"]

2**couch** *n* **:** a piece of furniture (as a sofa) for sitting or reclining

couch·ant \ˈkau̇-chənt\ *adj* **:** lying down especially with the head up ⟨a heraldic lion *couchant*⟩

couch grass \ˈkau̇ch-, ˈküch-\ *n* **:** QUACK GRASS [*couch,* alteration of *quitch* "couch grass" from Old English *cwice*]

couch potato *n* **:** someone who spends a lot of time sitting and watching television

cou·gar \ˈkü-gər, -ˌgär\ *n, pl* **cougars** *also* **cougar** **:** a large powerful tawny brown cat formerly widespread in the Americas but now reduced in number or extinct in many areas — called also *catamount, mountain lion, panther, puma* [French *couguar,* derived from Tupi *siwasuarána,* from *siwásu* "deer" + *rana* "resembling"]

cougar

1**cough** \ˈkȯf\ *vb* **1 :** to force air from the lungs with a sharp short noise or series of noises **2 :** to make a noise like that of coughing ⟨an engine *coughing* and sputtering⟩ [Medieval English *coughen*]

2**cough** *n* **1 :** a condition marked by repeated or frequent coughing **2 :** an act or sound of coughing

cough drop *n* **:** a medicated tablet or candy used to relieve coughing

cough syrup *n* **:** any of various sweet usually medicated liquids used to relieve coughing

cough up *vt* **1 :** to get rid of by coughing ⟨*cough up* mucus⟩ **2 :** DELIVER, PAY ⟨*cough up* the money⟩

could \kəd, ˈku̇d\ *past of* CAN — used as an auxiliary verb in the past ⟨we found we *could* go⟩ ⟨we said we would go if we *could*⟩ and as a polite or less forceful alternative to *can* ⟨*could* you do this for me⟩ [Old English *cūthe*]

could·est \ˈku̇d-əst\ *archaic past 2nd singular of* CAN

couldn't \ˈku̇d-ᵊnt\ **:** could not

couldst \kədst, ˈku̇dst\ *archaic past 2nd singular of* CAN

cou·lee \ˈkü-lē\ *n* **1 a :** a dry creek bed **b :** a steep-walled valley **2 :** a thick sheet or stream of lava [Canadian French *coulée,* from French, "flowing, flow of lava," from *couler* "to flow," from Latin *colare* "to strain," from *colum* "sieve"]

cou·lomb \ˈkü-ˌläm, -ˌlōm, kü-ˈ\ *n* **:** a unit of electric charge equal to the quantity of electricity transferred by a current of one ampere in one second [Charles A. de *Coulomb,* died 1806, French physicist]

Cou·lomb's law \ˈkü-ˌlämz-, -ˌlōmz-\ *n* **:** a statement in physics: the force of attraction or repulsion between two electric charges is proportional to the product of the charges and inversely proportional to the square of the distance between them

coun·cil \ˈkau̇n-səl\ *n* **1 :** a meeting for consultation, advice, or discussion **2 :** an advisory or legislative body ⟨the governor's *council*⟩ **3 :** an administrative body (as of a town) **4 :** deliberation in a council **5 a :** a federation of or a central body uniting a group of organizations or other bodies **b :** a local chapter of an organization **c :** CLUB 2a, SOCIETY [Medieval French *cuncile,* from Latin *concilium,* from *com-* + *calare* "to call"]

coun·cil·lor *or* **coun·cil·or** \ˈkau̇n-sə-lər, -slər\ *n* **:** a member of a council — **coun·cil·lor·ship** \-ˌship\ *n*

coun·cil·man \ˈkau̇n-səl-mən\ *n* **:** a member of a council especially in a city government

coun·cil·wom·an \ˈkau̇n-səl-ˌwu̇-mən\ *n* **:** a woman who is a member of a council

1**coun·sel** \ˈkau̇n-səl\ *n* **1 a :** advice given especially as a result of consultation **b :** a policy or plan of action or behavior **2 :** DELIBERATION, CONSULTATION ⟨take *counsel* together⟩ **3** *pl* **counsel :** a lawyer who gives advice in law or manages cases for clients in court [Medieval French *cunseil,* from Latin *consilium,* from *com-* + *calare* "to call"]

2**counsel** *vb* **-seled** *or* **-selled; -sel·ing** *or* **-sel·ling** \-sə-liŋ, -sliŋ\ **1 :** to give advice to ⟨*counsel* a student on a choice of studies⟩ **2 :** to suggest or recommend (something)

coun·sel·or *or* **coun·sel·lor** \ˈkau̇n-sə-lər, -slər\ *n* **1 :** ADVISER **2 :** LAWYER; *esp* **:** one that manages cases for clients in court **3 :** a supervisor of campers or activities at a summer camp — **coun·sel·or·ship** \-ˌship\ *n*

1**count** \ˈkau̇nt\ *vb* **1 a :** to find the total number of by naming units or groups ⟨*count* the apples in a box⟩ **b :** to name the consecutive numbers up to and including ⟨*count* ten⟩ **c :** to recite the numbers in order by units or groups ⟨*count* to one hundred by fives⟩ **d :** to include in a tally ⟨40 present, *counting* children⟩ **2 a :** CONSIDER ⟨*count* oneself lucky⟩ **b :** to include or exclude by or as if by counting ⟨*counted* themselves out⟩ **3 a :** to have value, significance, or importance ⟨every vote *counts*⟩ **b :** to deserve to be regarded or considered ⟨a job so easy it hardly *counts* as work⟩ [Medieval French *counter,* from Latin *computare,* from *com-* + *putare* "to consider"] — **and counting :** with more to come ⟨in business for 50 years *and counting*⟩ — **count on 1 :** to look forward to as certain **:** ANTICIPATE ⟨*counted on* winning⟩ **2 :** to rely or depend on (someone)

2**count** *n* **1 :** the act or process of counting; *also* **:** a total number counted **2 :** ALLEGATION, CHARGE; *esp* **:** one stating a separate cause of action in a legal declaration or indictment ⟨guilty on all *counts*⟩ **3 a :** the calling off of the seconds from one to ten when a boxer has been knocked down **b :** the number of balls and strikes called on a baseball batter during one turn

3**count** *n* **:** a European nobleman whose rank corresponds to that of a British earl [Medieval French *cunte,* from Late Latin *comes,* from Latin, "companion, one of the imperial court," from *com-* + *ire* "to go"]

count·able \-ə-bəl\ *adj* **:** capable of being counted; *esp* **:** capable of being put into one-to-one correspondence with the positive integers

count·down \ˈkau̇nt-ˌdau̇n\ *n* **:** an audible backward counting off in fixed units (as seconds) to mark the time remaining before an event (as the launching of a rocket)

1**coun·te·nance** \ˈkau̇nt-ᵊn-əns, ˈkau̇nt-nəns\ *n* **1 a :** calm expression **b :** mental composure **c :** LOOK 2a, EXPRESSION **2 :** FACE, VISAGE; *esp* **:** facial expression as an indication of mood, emotion, or character **3 :** a show of approval [Medieval French *contenance* "demeanor, bearing," from Latin *continentia* "restraint," from *continens* "continent"]

2**countenance** *vt* **:** TOLERATE 1, SANCTION

1**count·er** \ˈkau̇nt-ər\ *n* **1 :** a piece (as of metal or plastic) used in counting or in games **2 :** a level surface (as a table or board) over which transactions are conducted or food is served or on which goods are displayed or work is done — **over the counter :** without a prescription ⟨drugs available *over the counter*⟩

2**count·er** *n* **:** one that counts; *esp* **:** a device for indicating a number or amount

3**coun·ter** \ˈkau̇nt-ər\ *vb* **coun·tered; coun·ter·ing** \ˈkau̇nt-ə-riŋ, ˈkau̇n-triŋ\ **1 :** to act in opposition to **:** OPPOSE ⟨*countering* the charges⟩ **2 :** RETALIATE ⟨*countered* with a left hook⟩

4**coun·ter** *adv* **:** in a contrary manner or direction ⟨acted *counter* to our orders⟩ [Middle French *contre,* from Latin *contra* "against, opposite"]

5**coun·ter** *n* **1 :** the after portion of a boat from the waterline to the extreme outward swell or overhang **2 :** the act of giving a retaliatory blow; *also* **:** the blow given

6**coun·ter** *adj* **1 :** moving in an opposite direction ⟨ships slowed by *counter* tides⟩ **2 :** designed to oppose

counter- *prefix* **1 a :** contrary **:** opposite ⟨*counter*clockwise⟩ **b :** opposing **:** retaliatory ⟨*counter*offensive⟩ **2 :** complementa-

\ə\ **abut**	\au̇\ **out**	\i\ **tip**	\ȯ\ **saw**	\u̇\ **foot**
\ər\ **further**	\ch\ **chin**	\ī\ **life**	\ȯi\ **coin**	\y\ **yet**
\a\ **mat**	\e\ **pet**	\j\ **job**	\th\ **thin**	\yü\ **few**
\ā\ **take**	\ē\ **easy**	\ŋ\ **sing**	\t͟h\ **this**	\yu̇\ **cure**
\ä\ **cot, cart**	\g\ **go**	\ō\ **bone**	\ü\ **food**	\zh\ **vision**

ry : corresponding ⟨*counter*weight⟩ **3** : duplicate : substitute ⟨*counter*foil⟩ [Medieval French *cuntre*]

counteraccusation
counteradvertising
counteraggression
counterargue
counterargument
counterassault
counterbid
counterblockade
counterblow
countercampaign
countercharge
countercomplaint
countercoup
countercriticism
counterdemand
counterdemonstrate
counterdemonstration
counterdemonstrator
countereffort
counterevidence
counterfire
counterforce
counterimage
counterinflation
counterinflationary
counterinfluence
counterinvasion
countermove
countermovement
counterpetition
counterplay
counterploy
counterpower
counterpressure
counterpropaganda
counterprotest
counterprotester
counterquestion
counterraid
counterrally
counterreaction
counterreform
counterreformer
counterresponse
counterretaliation
countershot
counterstate
counterstatement
counterstep
counterstrategist
counterstrategy
counterstrike
counterstroke
counterstyle
countersue
countersuggestion
countersuit
countertactics
countertendency
counterterror
counterterrorism
counterterrorist
counterthreat
counterthrust
countertradition
countertrend
counterviolence

coun·ter·act \ˌkau̇nt-ər-ˈakt\ *vt* : to lessen the force, action, or influence of : OFFSET ⟨a drug that *counteracts* the effect of a poison⟩ ⟨*counteract* an evil influence⟩ — **coun·ter·ac·tion** \-ˈak-shən\ *n* — **coun·ter·ac·tive** \-ˈrak-tiv\ *adj*

coun·ter·at·tack \ˈkau̇nt-ər-ə-ˌtak\ *n* : an attack made against an enemy's attack — **counterattack** *vb*

1**coun·ter·bal·ance** \ˈkau̇nt-ər-ˌbal-əns, ˌkau̇nt-ər-ˈ\ *n* **1** : a weight that balances another **2** : a force or influence that offsets or checks an opposing force

2**counterbalance** \ˌkau̇nt-ər-ˈ, ˈkau̇nt-ər-ˌ\ *vt* : to oppose with an equal weight or force

1**coun·ter·check** \ˈkau̇nt-ər-ˌchek\ *n* : a check or restraint often operating against something that is itself a check

2**countercheck** *vt* : to check a second time for verification

counter check *n* : a blank check obtainable at a bank; *esp* : one to be cashed at the bank by the drawer

coun·ter·claim \ˈkau̇nt-ər-ˌklām\ *n* : an opposing claim especially in law — **counterclaim** *vb*

coun·ter·clock·wise \ˌkau̇nt-ər-ˈkläk-ˌwīz\ *adv* : in a direction opposite to that in which the hands of a clock rotate — **counterclockwise** *adj*

coun·ter·cur·rent \ˈkau̇nt-ər-ˌkər-ənt, -ˌkə-rənt\ *n* : a current flowing in a direction opposite to that of another one

coun·ter·es·pi·o·nage \ˌkau̇nt-ər-ˈes-pē-ə-ˌnäzh, -nij, -ˌnäj\ *n* : activities intended to discover and defeat enemy espionage

coun·ter·ex·am·ple \ˈkau̇nt-ər-ig-ˌzam-pəl\ *n* : an example that refutes or disproves a theorem or proposition

1**coun·ter·feit** \ˈkau̇nt-ər-ˌfit\ *adj* **1** : made in imitation of something else with intent to deceive ⟨*counterfeit* money⟩ **2** : not real : SHAM ⟨showing a *counterfeit* interest⟩ [Medieval French *cuntrefait,* from *contrefaire* "to imitate," from *cuntre-* "counter-" + *faire* "to make," from Latin *facere*]

2**counterfeit** *vb* **1** : to imitate or copy especially with intent to deceive ⟨*counterfeiting* money⟩ **2** : PRETEND 2 ⟨*counterfeiting* concern⟩ ***synonyms*** see ASSUME — **coun·ter·feit·er** *n*

3**counterfeit** *n* **1** : something counterfeit : FORGERY **2** : something that is likely to be confused with the genuine thing

coun·ter·foil \ˈkau̇nt-ər-ˌfȯil\ *n* : a detachable stub usually serving as a record or receipt

coun·ter·in·tel·li·gence \ˌkau̇nt-ər-in-ˈtel-ə-jəns\ *n* : organized activities of an intelligence service intended to foil the activities of an enemy's intelligence service by blocking its sources of information and by deceiving the enemy through tricks and misinformation

coun·ter·ir·ri·tant \ˌkau̇nt-ər-ˈir-ə-tənt\ *n* : something (as wintergreen oil) used to produce surface inflammation in order to reduce inflammation in deeper nearby structures — **counterirritant** *adj*

count·er·man \ˈkau̇nt-ər-ˌman, -mən\ *n* : one who tends a counter (as in a lunchroom)

coun·ter·mand \ˈkau̇nt-ər-ˌmand, ˌkau̇nt-ər-ˈ\ *vt* **1** : to cancel (a command) by a contrary order **2** : to recall or order back by a contrary order [Medieval French *cuntremander,* from *cuntre-* "counter-" + *mander* "to command," from Latin *mandare*] — **countermand** *n*

coun·ter·march \ˈkau̇nt-ər-ˌmärch\ *n* : a marching back; *esp* : a maneuver by which a unit of troops reverses direction but keeps the same order — **countermarch** *vi*

coun·ter·mea·sure \-ˌmezh-ər, -ˌmāzh-\ *n* : an action or device designed to negate or offset another

coun·ter·of·fen·sive \ˈkau̇nt-ər-ə-ˌfen-siv\ *n* : a large-scale counterattack

coun·ter·of·fer \-ˌȯf-ər, -ˌäf-\ *n* : a return offer made by one who has rejected an offer

coun·ter·pane \ˈkau̇nt-ər-ˌpān\ *n* : BEDSPREAD [Middle English *countrepointe,* from Medieval French *coute pointe,* literally, "embroidered quilt"]

coun·ter·part \ˈkau̇nt-ər-ˌpärt\ *n* **1** : a part or thing corresponding to another ⟨the left arm is the *counterpart* of the right arm⟩ **2** : something that serves to complete something else : COMPLEMENT **3** : one closely resembling another ⟨the twins were *counterparts* of each other⟩

coun·ter·party \ˈkau̇nt-ər-ˌpärt-ē\ *n* : a party to a financial transaction

1**coun·ter·plot** \-ˌplät\ *vb* : to plot against (a plot or plotter) : INTRIGUE

2**counterplot** *n* : a plot in opposition to another plot

coun·ter·point \ˈkau̇nt-ər-ˌpȯint\ *n* **1** : one or more melodies added above or below a given melody **2** : combination of two or more melodies into a single harmonic texture [Medieval French *contrepoint,* from Medieval Latin *contrapunctus,* from Latin *contra-* "counter-" + Medieval Latin *punctus* "musical note, melody"]

1**coun·ter·poise** \-ˌpȯiz\ *vt* : COUNTERBALANCE

2**counterpoise** *n* **1** : COUNTERBALANCE **2** : a state of balance

coun·ter·pro·pos·al \-prə-ˌpō-zəl\ *n* : a return proposal made by one who has rejected a proposal

Coun·ter–Ref·or·ma·tion \ˌkau̇nt-ər-ˌref-ər-ˈmā-shən\ *n* : the reform movement in the Roman Catholic Church following the Reformation

coun·ter·rev·o·lu·tion \-ˌrev-ə-ˈlü-shən\ *n* : a revolution intended to undo a current or earlier one — **coun·ter·rev·o·lu·tion·ary** \-shə-ˌner-ē\ *adj or n* — **coun·ter·rev·o·lu·tion·ist** \-shə-nəst, -shnəst\ *n*

coun·ter·shaft \ˈkau̇nt-ər-ˌshaft\ *n* : a shaft that receives motion from a main shaft and transmits it to a working part

coun·ter·sign \-ˌsīn\ *n* **1** : a signature confirming the authenticity of a document already signed by another **2** : a sign used in reply to another; *esp* : a secret signal that must be given by one wishing to pass a guard — **countersign** *vt* — **coun·ter·sig·na·ture** \ˌkau̇nt-ər-ˈsig-nə-ˌchu̇r, -chər\ *n*

1**coun·ter·sink** \ˈkau̇nt-ər-ˌsingk\ *vt* **-sunk** \-ˌsəngk\; **-sink·ing** **1** : to make a countersink on (a hole) **2** : to set the head of (as a screw, bolt, or nail) at or below the surface

2**countersink** *n* **1** : a bit or drill for making a countersink **2** : a funnel-shaped enlargement at the outer end of a drilled hole

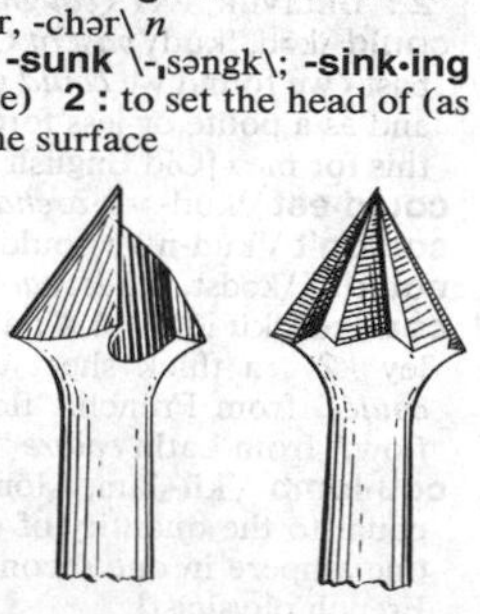

countersink 1

coun·ter·spy \-ˌspī\ *n* : a spy employed in counterintelligence

coun·ter·ten·or \-ˌten-ər\ *n* : a tenor with an unusually high range

coun·ter·top \ˈkau̇nt-ər-ˌtäp\ *n* : the flat working surface on top of waist-level kitchen cabinets

coun·ter·weight \-ˌwāt\ *n* : COUNTERBALANCE 1 — **counterweight** *vt*

count·ess \ˈkau̇nt-əs\ *n* **1** : the wife or widow of a count or an earl **2** : a woman who holds the rank of a count or an earl in her own right

count·ing·house \ˈkau̇nt-ing-ˌhau̇s\ *n* : a building, room, or office used for keeping books and transacting business

counting number *n* : NATURAL NUMBER

counting room *n* : COUNTINGHOUSE

count·less \ˈkau̇nt-ləs\ *adj* : too numerous to be counted : INNUMERABLE ***synonyms*** see MANY

coun·tri·fied *also* **coun·try·fied** \ˈkən-tri-ˌfīd\ *adj* : looking or acting as if from the country : RUSTIC

1**coun·try** \ˈkən-trē\ *n, pl* **countries** **1** : an indefinite usually large or open stretch of land : REGION ⟨hill *country*⟩ **2 a** : the land of a person's birth, residence, or citizenship **b** : a political state or nation or its territory **3** : the people of a state or district : POPULACE **4** : rural as distinguished from urban areas ⟨lives out in the *country*⟩ [Medieval French *cuntree, contré,* from Medieval Latin *contrata,* from Latin *contra* "against, on the opposite side"]

Word History English *country* is derived from Latin *contra,* which means "against" or "on the opposite side." In Medieval Latin the noun *contrata* was formed from *contra. Contrata* was literally "that which is situated opposite the beholder." But that which is opposite the beholder is just what he or she sees. So *contrata* meant "landscape." It also came to mean "expanse of land, region." This was the original meaning of English *country,* which over the years has itself developed a number of new meanings.

[2]**country** *adj* : of, relating to, or characteristic of the country

country club *n* : a suburban club for social life and recreation

coun·try–dance \ˈkən-trē-ˌdans\ *n* : an English dance in which partners face each other especially in rows

coun·try·man \ˈkən-trē-mən, *3 is often* -ˌman\ *n* **1** : an inhabitant or native of a specified country ⟨a north *countryman*⟩ **2** : COMPATRIOT 1 **3** : one living in the country or marked by country ways : RUSTIC

country music *n* : music derived from or imitating the folk style of the southern U.S. or of the Western cowboy

coun·try·seat \ˌkən-trē-ˈsēt\ *n* : a mansion or estate in the country

coun·try·side \ˈkən-trē-ˌsīd\ *n* : a rural area or its people

coun·try·wom·an \ˈkən-trē-ˌwu̇m-ən\ *n* **1** : a woman who is a compatriot **2** : a woman who is a resident of the country

coun·ty \ˈkau̇nt-ē\ *n, pl* **counties** **1** : the domain of a count **2 a** : one of the chief territorial divisions of England and Wales and formerly also of Scotland and Northern Ireland for administrative, judicial, and political purposes **b** : the largest territorial division for local government within a state of the U.S. [Medieval French *cunté, counté,* from Medieval Latin *comitatus,* from Late Latin, "office of a count," from *comit-, comes* "count"]

county agent *n* : a government agent employed to provide information about agriculture and home economics in rural areas

county seat *n* : a town that is the seat of county administration

coup \ˈkü\ *n, pl* **coups** \ˈküz\ **1** : a brilliant, sudden, and usually highly successful act **2** : COUP D'ETAT [French, "blow, stroke," from Late Latin *colpus,* from Latin *colaphus,* from Greek *kolaphos* "slap"]

coup de grâce \ˌküd-ə-ˈgräs\ *n, pl* **coups de grâce** \ˌküd-ə-\ **1** : a death blow or shot administered to end the suffering of one mortally wounded **2** : a decisive finishing blow or event [French *coup de grâce,* literally, "stroke of mercy"]

coup d'e·tat \ˌküd-ə-ˈtä, ˌküd-ā-\ *n, pl* **coups d'e·tat** \-ˈtä, -ˈtäz\ : a sudden decisive political move; *esp* : the overthrow of an existing government by a small group [French *coup d'état,* literally, "stroke of state"]

cou·pé *or* **coupe** \kü-ˈpā, *2 is often* ˈküp\ *n* **1** : a four-wheeled closed horse-drawn carriage for two persons inside with an outside seat for the driver in front **2** *usually* **coupe** **a** : a closed 2-door automobile for usually two persons **b** : a usually closed 2-door automobile with a full-width rear seat [French *coupé,* from *couper* "to cut, strike," from *coup* "blow, coup"]

[1]**cou·ple** \ˈkəp-əl\ *n* **1 a** : two persons married, engaged, or otherwise romantically paired **b** : two persons paired together **2** : BRACE 1, PAIR **3** : two equal and opposite forces that act along parallel lines **4** : an indefinite small number ⟨a *couple* of days ago⟩ [Medieval French *cuple* "pair, bond," from Latin *copula* "bond"]

[2]**couple** *vb* **cou·pled; cou·pling** \ˈkəp-ling, -ə-ling\ **1** : to join together : CONNECT ⟨freight cars *coupled* end to end⟩ **2** : COPULATE **3** : to bring (two electric circuits) into such close proximity as to permit mutual influence

[3]**couple** *adj* : TWO; *also* : SEVERAL 2 ⟨a *couple* days ago⟩

cou·pler \ˈkəp-lər, -ə-lər\ *n* **1** : one that couples **2** : a device on a keyboard instrument by which keyboards or keys are connected to play together

cou·plet \ˈkəp-lət\ *n* : two successive lines of verse forming a unit; *esp* : two rhyming lines of the same length — compare HEROIC COUPLET

cou·pling \ˈkəp-ling (usual for 2), -ə-ling\ *n* **1** : the act of bringing or coming together : PAIRING **2** : something that joins or connects two parts or things ⟨a car *coupling*⟩ ⟨a pipe *coupling*⟩ **3** : the joining of or the part of the body that joins the hindquarters to the forequarters of a quadruped

cou·pon \ˈkü-ˌpän, ˈkyü-\ *n* **1** : a statement of due interest to be cut from a bond and presented for payment on a stated date **2 a** : one of a series of attached tickets to be detached and presented as needed **b** : a ticket or form authorizing purchases of rationed commodities **c** : a certificate or similar evidence of a purchase redeemable in premiums **d** : a part of a printed advertisement to be cut out or off for use as an order blank or inquiry form or to obtain a discount on goods or services [French, from *couper* "to cut"]

cour·age \ˈkər-ij, ˈkə-rij\ *n* : mental or moral strength to venture, persevere, and withstand danger, fear, or difficulty [Medieval French *curage,* from *quer, coer* "heart," from Latin *cor*]

synonyms COURAGE, BRAVERY, VALOR, HEROISM mean greatness of heart in facing danger or difficulty. COURAGE implies strength in overcoming fear and in persisting against odds or difficulties ⟨the *courage* of pioneers⟩. BRAVERY stresses bold and daring defiance of danger ⟨the *bravery* shown by the firefighters⟩. VALOR applies especially to bravery in fighting a dangerous enemy ⟨honored for *valor* in battle⟩. HEROISM suggests bravery and boldness in accepting risk or sacrifice for a noble or generous purpose ⟨the *heroism* of early feminists⟩.

cou·ra·geous \kə-ˈrā-jəs\ *adj* : having or characterized by courage : BRAVE — **cou·ra·geous·ly** *adv* — **cou·ra·geous·ness** *n*

cou·ri·er \ˈku̇r-ē-ər, ˈkər-ē-, ˈkə-rē-\ *n* : MESSENGER: as **a** : a member of a diplomatic service entrusted with bearing messages **b** : a member of the armed services who carries mail, information, or supplies [Middle French *courrier,* from Italian *corriere,* from *correre* "to run," from Latin *currere*]

[1]**course** \ˈkōrs, ˈkȯrs\ *n* **1 a** : the act or action of moving in a path from point to point **b** : LIFE HISTORY 2, CAREER **2** : the path over which something moves: as **a** : RACECOURSE **b** : the direction of flight of an airplane **c** : WATERCOURSE **d** : land laid out for golf **3 a** : accustomed procedure or action ⟨the law taking its *course*⟩ **b** : a manner of conducting oneself : BEHAVIOR ⟨the wisest *course* is to retreat⟩ **c** : progression through a series of acts or events or a development or period ⟨in the *course* of one's career⟩ **4 a** : an ordered process or succession **b** : a series of lectures or discussions dealing with a subject; *also* : a number of such courses constituting a curriculum **5 a** : a part of a meal served at one time **b** : ROW, LAYER; *esp* : a continuous level range of brick or masonry throughout a wall [Medieval French, from Latin *cursus,* from *currere* "to run"] — **of course** **1** : following the ordinary way or procedure ⟨did it as a matter *of course*⟩ **2** : as might be expected

[2]**course** *vb* **1 a** : to hunt or pursue (game) with hounds **b** : to cause (dogs) to run (as after game) **2** : to run through or over ⟨when buffalo *coursed* the plains⟩ **3** : to move rapidly : RACE ⟨blood *coursing* through the veins⟩

cours·er \ˈkōr-sər, ˈkȯr-\ *n* : a swift or spirited horse

[1]**court** \ˈkōrt, ˈkȯrt\ *n* **1 a** : the residence of a dignitary and especially a sovereign **b** : a sovereign's formal assembly of councillors and officers **c** : the sovereign and officials who constitute the governing power **d** : the family and retinue of a sovereign **e** : a reception held by a sovereign **2 a** : an open space wholly or partly surrounded by buildings **b** : a space arranged for playing any of various games with a ball ⟨a tennis *court*⟩ **c** : a short street or lane **3 a** : an assembly for the transaction of judicial business **b** : a session of a judicial assembly ⟨*court* is now adjourned⟩ **c** : a place (as a chamber) for the administration of justice **d** : a judge in session **e** : a faculty or agency of judgment or evaluation **4 a** : an assembly or board with legislative or administrative powers **b** : LEGISLATURE, PARLIAMENT **5** : attention designed to win favor or dispel hostility ⟨pay *court* to the king⟩ [Medieval French, from Latin *cohors* "enclosure, throng, cohort"]

[2]**court** *vb* **1 a** : to try to gain ⟨*courting* favor with the higher-ups⟩ **b** : to act so as to provoke ⟨was *courting* disaster⟩ **2** : to seek the affections of **3** : to try to get the support of ⟨both candidates *courted* the independent voters⟩ **4 a** : to engage in a social relationship and activities usually leading to marriage **b**

\ə\ **abut**	\au̇\ **out**	\i\ **tip**	\ȯ\ **saw**	\u̇\ **foot**
\ər\ **further**	\ch\ **chin**	\ī\ **life**	\ȯi\ **coin**	\y\ **yet**
\a\ **mat**	\e\ **pet**	\j\ **job**	\th\ **thin**	\yü\ **few**
\ā\ **take**	\ē\ **easy**	\ng\ **sing**	\t͟h\ **this**	\yu̇\ **cure**
\ä\ **cot, cart**	\g\ **go**	\ō\ **bone**	\ü\ **food**	\zh\ **vision**

: to engage in activity leading to mating ⟨a pair of robins *courting*⟩

cour·te·ous \ˈkərt-ē-əs\ *adj* **1** : marked by polished manners, gallantry, or ceremonial usage of a court **2** : marked by respect for and consideration of others ***synonyms*** see CIVIL — **cour·te·ous·ly** *adv* — **cour·te·ous·ness** *n*

cour·te·san \ˈkōrt-ə-zən, ˈkȯrt- *also* ˈkərt-\ *n* : a prostitute with an upper-class clientele [Middle French *courtisane,* from Italian *cortigiana* "female courtier," from *corte* "court," from Latin *cohors* "throng"]

cour·te·sy \ˈkərt-ə-sē\ *n, pl* **-sies** **1** : courtly politeness **2** : a favor courteously performed **3** : consideration and generosity in providing something ⟨flowers given through the *courtesy* of a florist⟩

courtesy title *n* : a title (as "Professor" for any teacher) taken by the user and commonly accepted without consideration of official right

court·house \ˈkōrt-ˌhau̇s, ˈkȯrt-\ *n* **1 a** : a building in which courts of law are held **b** : a building in which county offices are housed **2** : COUNTY SEAT

court·ier \ˈkōrt-ē-ər, ˈkȯrt-\ *n* **1** : a person in attendance at a royal court **2** : a person who practices flattery

court·ly \ˈkōrt-lē, ˈkȯrt-\ *adj* **court·li·er; -est** **1 a** : of a quality befitting a royal court : ELEGANT ⟨*courtly* manners⟩ **b** : insincerely flattering **2** : favoring the policy or party of the court — **court·li·ness** *n*

[1]**court–mar·tial** \ˈkōrt-ˌmär-shəl, ˈkȯrt-\ *n, pl* **courts–martial** *also* **court–martials** **1** : a military court for the trial of members of the armed forces or others within its jurisdiction **2** : a trial by court-martial

[2]**court–martial** *vt* **-mar·tialed** *also* **-mar·tialled; -mar·tial·ing** *also* **-mar·tial·ling** \-ˌmärsh-ling, -ə-ling\ : to subject to trial by court-martial

Court of St. James's \-sānt-ˈjāmz, -sənt-\ : the British royal court [from *Saint James's Palace,* London, former seat of the British court]

court plaster *n* : an adhesive plaster especially of silk coated with isinglass and glycerin [from its use for beauty spots by ladies at royal courts]

court·room \ˈkōrt-ˌrüm, ˈkȯrt-, -ˌru̇m\ *n* : a room in which a court of law is held

court·ship \-ˌship\ *n* : the act, process, or period of courting

court tennis *n* : a game similar to tennis played with a ball and racket in an enclosed court

court·yard \ˈkōrt-ˌyärd, ˈkȯrt-\ *n* : a court or enclosure attached to a building

cous·in \ˈkəz-n\ *n* **1 a** : a child of one's uncle or aunt **b** : a relative descended from a common ancestor in a different line **2** : a person belonging to an ethnically or culturally related group ⟨our English *cousins*⟩ [Medieval French *cusin, cosin,* from Latin *consobrinus,* from *com-* + *sobrinus* "second cousin," from *soror* "sister"]

co·va·lence \kō-ˈvā-ləns, kō-\ *or* **co·va·len·cy** \-lən-sē\ *n* : valence characterized by the sharing of electrons in pairs by two atoms in a chemical compound; *also* : the number of pairs of electrons an atom can share with its neighbors — **co·va·lent** \-lənt\ *adj* — **co·va·lent·ly** *adv*

cove \ˈkōv\ *n* **1 a** : an architectural member with a concave cross section **b** : a trough for concealed lighting at the upper part of a wall **2** : a small sheltered inlet or bay **3** : a level area sheltered by hills or mountains [Old English *cofa* "den, cave"]

cov·en \ˈkəv-ən\ *n* : a meeting or band of witches [Middle French *covin* "band," derived from Latin *convenire* "to come together"]

[1]**cov·e·nant** \ˈkəv-nənt, -ə-nənt\ *n* **1** : a solemn and binding agreement : COMPACT **2 a** : a written agreement or promise usually under seal between parties **b** : a promise incidental to and contained in an agreement (as a deed) [Medieval French, from *covenir,* from Latin *convenire* "to come together, agree," from *com-* + *venire* "to come"] — **cov·e·nan·tal** \ˌkəv-ə-ˈnant-l\ *adj*

[2]**cov·e·nant** \ˈkəv-nənt, -ə-nənt, -ə-nant\ *vb* **1** : to promise by a covenant : PLEDGE **2** : to enter into a covenant : CONTRACT — **cov·e·nant·er** \-ə-ˌnant-ər\ *n*

Cov·en·try \ˈkəv-ən-trē, ˈkäv-\ *n* : a state of ostracism or exclusion ⟨sent to *Coventry*⟩ [*Coventry,* England]

[1]**cov·er** \ˈkəv-ər\ *vb* **cov·ered; cov·er·ing** \ˈkəv-ring, -ə-ring\ **1 a** : to guard from attack **b** : to have within gunshot range **c** (1) : to provide protection or security to : INSURE ⟨this insurance *covers* the traveler in any accident⟩ (2) : to provide protection against or compensation for ⟨the policy *covered* all water damage⟩ **d** : to maintain a check on especially by patrolling ⟨state police *covering* the highways⟩ **2 a** : to hide from sight or knowledge ⟨*cover* up a scandal⟩ **b** : to conceal something illicit, blameworthy, or embarrassing from notice ⟨*cover* for a friend in an investigation⟩ **c** : to act as a substitute or replacement during an absence ⟨*covered* for me during my vacation⟩ **3** : to overlay so as to protect or shelter ⟨*cover* the plants with mulch⟩ **4 a** : to spread or lie over or on ⟨water *covered* the floor⟩ ⟨snow *covering* the hills⟩ **b** : to appear here and there on the surface of ⟨a resort area *covered* with lakes⟩ **5** : to put something protective or concealing over ⟨*cover* your head⟩ **6** : to sit on and incubate (eggs) **7** : to have sufficient scope to include or take into account ⟨an exam *covering* a semester's work⟩ **8** : to deal with ⟨material *covered* in the first chapter⟩ **9** : to have as one's territory or field of activity ⟨one salesperson *covers* the whole state⟩ **10** : to report news about **11** : to pass over or through ⟨*covering* 500 kilometers a day⟩ **12** : to pay or provide for the payment of ⟨*cover* expenses⟩ **13** : to accept an offered bet **14** : to buy securities or commodities for delivery against (an earlier short sale) [Medieval French *covrir,* from Latin *cooperire,* from *co-* + *operire* "to close, cover"] — **cov·er·able** \ˈkəv-rə-bəl, -ə-rə-\ *adj* — **cov·er·er** \-ər-ər\ *n*

[2]**cover** *n* **1** : something that protects, shelters, or guards: as **a** : natural shelter for an animal or the factors that provide such shelter **b** : a position or situation affording protection from enemy fire **2** : something that is placed over or about another thing: **a** : LID 1, TOP **b** : a binding or case for a book; *also* : the front or back of such a binding **c** : an overlay or outer layer especially for protection ⟨a mattress *cover*⟩ **d** : tableware laid out for one person **e** : ROOF **f** : a cloth (as a blanket or bedspread) used on a bed for warmth or for decoration ⟨lying under the *covers*⟩ **g** : something (as vegetation or snow) that covers the ground **3** : something that conceals or obscures ⟨under *cover* of darkness⟩ **4** : an envelope or wrapper for mail — **under cover** : under concealment : in secret

cov·er·age \ˈkəv-rij, -ə-rij\ *n* **1** : the act or fact of covering or something that covers: as **a** : inclusion within the scope of protection (as of an insurance policy) **b** : inclusion within the scope of discussion or reporting ⟨*coverage* of a political convention⟩ **2 a** : the number or amount covered : SCOPE **b** : all the risks covered by the terms of an insurance contract ⟨a policy with an extensive *coverage*⟩

cov·er·all \ˈkəv-ər-ˌȯl\ *n* : a one-piece outer garment worn to protect one's clothes — usually used in plural

cover charge *n* : a charge made by a restaurant or nightclub in addition to the charge for food and drink

cover crop *n* : a crop planted to prevent soil erosion and to provide humus

covered wagon *n* : a wagon with a canvas top supported by bows

cover glass *n* : a piece of very thin glass or plastic used to cover material mounted on a microscope slide

cov·er·ing \ˈkəv-ring, -ə-ring\ *n* : something that covers or conceals

cov·er·let \ˈkəv-ər-lət\ *n* : BEDSPREAD [Middle English, alteration of *coverlite,* from Medieval French *covrir* "to cover" + *lit* "bed"]

cov·er·slip \ˈkəv-ər-ˌslip\ *n* : COVER GLASS

[1]**co·vert** \ˈkō-ˌvərt, -vərt, kō-ˈ; ˈkəv-ərt\ *adj* **1** : not openly shown, engaged in, or avowed ⟨a *covert* alliance⟩ **2** : covered over : SHELTERED ⟨a *covert* nook⟩ [Medieval French, past participle of *covrir* "to cover"] ***synonyms*** see SECRET — **co·vert·ly** *adv* — **co·vert·ness** *n*

[2]**co·vert** \ˈkəv-ər, -ərt; ˈkō-vərt\ *n* **1 a** : hiding place : SHELTER **b** : a thicket affording cover for game **2** : a feather covering the bases of the quills of the wings and tail of a bird **3** : a firm durable twilled sometimes waterproofed cloth

cov·et \ˈkəv-ət\ *vb* : to wish earnestly especially for what belongs to another [Medieval French *coveiter,* derived from Latin *cupiditas* "desire, cupidity"] — **cov·et·able** \-ə-bəl\ *adj* — **cov·et·er** \-ər\ *n* — **cov·et·ing·ly** \-ing-lē\ *adv*

cov·et·ous \ˈkəv-ət-əs\ *adj* : marked by a too eager desire for wealth or possessions or for another's possessions — **cov·et·ous·ly** *adv* — **cov·et·ous·ness** *n*

synonyms COVETOUS, AVARICIOUS, GREEDY, GRASPING mean having or showing a strong desire for especially material possessions. COVETOUS implies excessive desire especially for what belongs to another ⟨*covetous* of his brother's house⟩. AVARICIOUS implies a strong desire to gain and keep money ⟨an *avaricious* miser⟩. GREEDY stresses lack of restraint and often of discrimination in desire ⟨a leader *greedy* for absolute power⟩. GRASPING adds the implications of selfishness and ruthlessness ⟨a hard *grasping* trader who cheated the natives⟩.

cov•ey \ˈkəv-ē\ *n, pl* **coveys** **1 :** a mature bird or pair of birds with a brood of young; *also* **:** a small flock **2 :** COMPANY 2a, GROUP [Medieval French *covee,* "sitting (of a hen)," from *cover* "to sit on, brood over," from Latin *cubare* "to lie"]

[1]**cow** \ˈkau̇\ *n* **1 :** the mature female of cattle or of any various usually large animals (as elephants or whales) **2 :** a domestic bovine animal regardless of sex or age [Old English *cū*] — **cowy** \-ē\ *adj*

[2]**cow** *vt* **:** to subdue the spirits or courage of **:** INTIMIDATE ⟨*cowed* by threats⟩ [probably of Scandinavian origin]

cow•ard \ˈkau̇-ərd, ˈkau̇rd\ *n* **:** one who shows disgraceful fear or timidity [Medieval French *cuard,* from *coe, cue* "tail," from Latin *cauda*] — **coward** *adj*

Word History A frightened animal may draw its tail between its hind legs, or it may simply turn its tail and run. In such an animal as the hare, the white flash of the fleeing tail is especially remarkable. But even a tailless animal like a human being can turn tail and flee when afraid. And unless an army is in retreat, it is in the tail of the army that you can expect to find the cowards. Whether it is the idea of an animal's tail or an army's that is responsible, it is certain that Medieval French *cuard,* from which we get our *coward,* is a derivative of *coe,* "tail."

cow•ard•ice \-əs\ *n* **:** lack of courage or resolution

[1]**cow•ard•ly** \-lē\ *adv* **:** in a cowardly manner

[2]**cowardly** *adj* **1 :** disgracefully timid ⟨a *cowardly* rascal⟩ **2 :** resembling or befitting a coward ⟨a *cowardly* retreat⟩ — **cow•ard•li•ness** *n*

cow•bane \ˈkau̇-ˌbān\ *n* **:** any of several poisonous plants (as a water hemlock) related to the carrot

cow•bell \-ˌbel\ *n* **:** a bell hung about the neck of a cow to indicate its whereabouts

cow•bird \-ˌbərd\ *n* **:** a small North American blackbird that lays its eggs in the nests of other birds

cow•boy \-ˌbȯi\ *n* **1 :** one who tends or drives cattle; *esp* **:** a usually mounted cattle ranch hand **2 :** a participant in rodeos

cow•catch•er \-ˌkach-ər, -ˌkech-\ *n* **:** an inclined frame on the front of a railroad locomotive for throwing obstacles off the track

cow•er \ˈkau̇-ər, ˈkau̇r\ *vi* **:** to shrink away or cringe (as from fear) ⟨*cowered* at the sight of a whip⟩ [Middle English *couren*]

cow•fish \ˈkau̇-ˌfish\ *n* **:** any of various small brightly colored fishes with projections resembling horns over the eyes

cow•girl \-ˌgərl\ *n* **:** a girl or woman who works as a cowboy

cow•hand \-ˌhand\ *n* **:** COWBOY

cow•herd \-ˌhərd\ *n* **:** one who tends cows

[1]**cow•hide** \-ˌhīd\ *n* **1 :** the hide of a cow or leather made from it **2 :** a coarse whip of rawhide or braided leather

[2]**cowhide** *vt* **:** to flog with a cowhide whip

cowl \ˈkau̇l\ *n* **1 :** a hood or long hooded cloak especially of a monk **2 a :** a chimney covering for improving the draft **b :** the top portion of the front part of an automobile body forward of the two front doors to which are attached the windshield and instrument panel **c :** COWLING [Old English *cugele,* from Late Latin *cuculla* "monk's hood," from Latin *cucullus* "hood"] — **cowled** \ˈkau̇ld\ *adj*

cow•lick \ˈkau̇-ˌlik\ *n* **:** a turned-up tuft of hair growing in a direction different from the rest of the hair [from its appearance of having been licked by a cow]

cowl•ing \ˈkau̇-ling\ *n* **:** a removable metal covering for the engine and sometimes a portion of the fuselage or nacelle of an airplane; *also* **:** a metallic cover for any engine

cow•man \ˈkau̇-mən, -ˌman\ *n* **1 :** COWHERD, COWBOY **2 :** a cattle owner or rancher

cow•pea \ˈkau̇-ˌpē\ *n* **:** a sprawling herb related to the bean and grown in the southern U.S. especially for forage and green manure; *also* **:** its edible seed — called also *black-eyed pea, field pea*

Cow•per's gland \ˈkau̇-pərz-, ˈkü-pərz-, ˈku̇p-ərz-\ *n* **:** either of two small glands discharging a secretion into the semen [William *Cowper,* died 1709, English surgeon]

cow•poke \ˈkau̇-ˌpōk\ *n* **:** COWBOY [*cow* + *poke* "to punch"]

cow pony *n* **:** a light saddle horse trained for herding cattle

cow•pox \ˈkau̇-ˌpäks\ *n* **:** a mild rash-producing virus disease of the cow that when passed on to a human protects against smallpox

cow•punch•er \-ˌpən-chər\ *n* **:** COWBOY

cow•rie *also* **cow•ry** \ˈkau̇r-ē\ *n, pl* **cowries :** any of numerous usually small snails of warm seas with glossy often brightly colored shells; *also* **:** the shell of a cowrie [Hindi *kauṛī*]

cow•slip \ˈkau̇-ˌslip\ *n* **1 :** a common European primrose with fragrant yellow flowers **2 :** MARSH MARIGOLD [Old English *cūslyppe,* literally, "cow dung"]

cox \ˈkäks\ *n* **:** COXSWAIN 2 — **cox** *vb*

coxa \ˈkäk-sə\ *n, pl* **cox•ae** \-ˌsē, -ˌsī\ **:** the segment of an arthropod limb nearest the body [Latin, "hip"] — **cox•al** \-səl\ *adj*

cox•comb \ˈkäk-ˌskōm\ *n* **:** a conceited foppish person [Middle English *cokkes comb,* literally, "cock's comb"] — **cox•comb•i•cal** \käk-ˈskō-mi-kəl, -ˈkäm-i-\ *adj*

cox•swain \ˈkäk-sən, -ˌswān\ *n* **1 :** a sailor who has charge of a ship's boat and its crew **2 :** one who steers a racing shell [Middle English *cokswayne,* from *cok* "small boat" + *swain* "servant"]

coy \ˈkȯi\ *adj* **1 a :** BASHFUL 1 **b :** marked by cute or artful playfulness ⟨using *coy* tricks to attract attention⟩ **2 :** showing reluctance to make a definite commitment ⟨politicians *coy* about their plans⟩ [Medieval French *quoi, quei, coi* "quiet, calm," from Latin *quietus*] ***synonyms*** see SHY — **coy•ly** *adv* — **coy•ness** *n*

coy•ote \kī-ˈōt-ē, ˈkī-ˌōt\ *n, pl* **coyotes** *or* **coyote :** a tannish gray to reddish gray North American mammal that is related to but smaller than the wolf [Mexican Spanish, from Nahuatl *coyōtl*]

coyote

coy•pu \ˈkȯi-ˌpü\ *n* **:** NUTRIA [American Spanish *coipú,* from Mapuche (American Indian language of Chile) *coipu*]

coz•en \ˈkəz-n\ *vb* **:** to deceive by artful coaxing ⟨tried to *cozen* their opponent's supporters⟩ [perhaps from obsolete Italian *cozzonare,* from Italian *cozzone* "horse trader," from Latin *cocio* "trader"] — **coz•en•age** \-n-ij\ *n* — **coz•en•er** *n*

[1]**co•zy** \ˈkō-zē\ *adj* **co•zi•er; -est 1 :** enjoying or affording warmth and ease **:** SNUG **2 :** marked by a cautious attitude ⟨a *cozy* waiting game⟩ [probably of Scandinavian origin] — **co•zi•ly** \-zə-lē\ *adv* — **co•zi•ness** \-zē-nəs\ *n*

[2]**cozy** *adv* **:** in a cautious manner ⟨play it *cozy*⟩

[3]**cozy** *n, pl* **coz•ies :** a padded covering for a vessel (as a teapot) used to keep the contents hot

cpu \ˌsē-ˌpē-ˈyü\ *n, often cap C&P&U* **:** the component of a computer that performs most of the data processing and that controls the operation of the other parts of the computer [*c*entral *p*rocessing *u*nit]

[1]**crab** \ˈkrab\ *n* **1 :** any of various crustaceans with a short broad usually flattened shell of chitin, a small abdomen curled forward beneath the body, and a front pair of limbs with strong pincers; *also* **:** any of various other crustaceans resembling true crabs in having a small abdomen **2 :** any of various machines for raising or hauling heavy weights **3** *pl* **:** infestation with crab lice [Middle English *crabbe,* from Old English *crabba*]

[1]crab 1

[2]**crab** *vi* **crabbed; crab•bing :** to fish for crabs — **crab•ber** *n*

[3]**crab** *n* **:** CRAB APPLE [Middle English *crabbe,* perhaps from *crabbe* "[1]crab"]

\ə\ **abut**	\au̇\ **out**	\i\ **tip**	\ȯ\ **saw**	\u̇\ **foot**
\ər\ **further**	\ch\ **chin**	\ī\ **life**	\ȯi\ **coin**	\y\ **yet**
\a\ **mat**	\e\ **pet**	\j\ **job**	\th\ **thin**	\yü\ **few**
\ā\ **take**	\ē\ **easy**	\ng\ **sing**	\t͟h\ **this**	\yu̇\ **cure**
\ä\ **cot, cart**	\g\ **go**	\ō\ **bone**	\ü\ **food**	\zh\ **vision**

[4]**crab** *vb* **crabbed; crab·bing :** to find fault : COMPLAIN [Middle English *crabben,* probably back-formation from *crabbed*]

[5]**crab** *n* : a disagreeable ill-natured person

crab apple *n* : any of several cultivated or wild trees related to the apple tree and producing a small sour fruit; *also* : the fruit

crab·bed \ˈkrab-əd\ *adj* **1 :** CROSS 3 **2 :** difficult to read or understand ⟨*crabbed* writing⟩ [Middle English, "perverse, ill- tempered," probably partly from *crabbe* "crustacean," partly from *crabbe* "crab apple"] — **crab·bed·ly** *adv* — **crab·bed·ness** *n*

crab·by \ˈkrab-ē\ *adj* **crab·bi·er; -est :** ILL-NATURED ⟨a *crabby* disposition⟩

crab·grass \ˈkrab-ˌgras\ *n* **:** a weedy grass with creeping or sprawling stems that root freely at the nodes

crab louse *n* : a louse infesting the human pubic region

[1]**crack** \ˈkrak\ *vb* **1 a :** to break or cause to break with a sudden sharp sound : SNAP **b :** to make or cause to make such a sound ⟨*crack* a whip⟩ **2 :** to break with or without total separation of parts ⟨the ice *cracked* in several places⟩ **3 :** to tell especially in a clever or witty way ⟨*crack* jokes⟩ **4 a :** to lose control under pressure — often used with *up* **b :** to fail in tone ⟨their voices *cracked*⟩ **c :** to give or receive a sharp blow ⟨*crack* one's head⟩ **5 a :** to puzzle out and solve or discover the secret of ⟨*crack* a code⟩ **b :** to break into ⟨*crack* a safe⟩ **c :** to open slightly ⟨*crack* the window⟩ **d :** to break through (as a barrier) **e :** to show or begin showing especially reluctantly or uncharacteristically ⟨*crack* a smile⟩ **6 a :** to subject (hydrocarbons) to cracking ⟨*crack* petroleum⟩ **b :** to produce by cracking ⟨*cracked* gasoline⟩ [Old English *cracian*]

[2]**crack** *n* **1 :** a sudden sharp noise **2 :** a sharp witty remark : QUIP **3 a :** a narrow break **b :** a narrow opening ⟨open the window a *crack*⟩ **4 a :** a weakness or flaw caused by decay, age, or shortcoming **b :** a broken tone of the voice **5 :** MOMENT ⟨the *crack* of dawn⟩ **6 :** a sharp resounding blow **7 :** an attempt or opportunity to do something ⟨take a *crack* at it⟩ **8 :** highly purified cocaine in small chips used illicitly usually for smoking

[3]**crack** *adj* : of superior quality ⟨*crack* troops⟩

crack·brain \ˈkrak-ˌbrān\ *n* : an erratic or unbalanced person — **crack·brained** \-ˈbrānd\ *adj*

crack·down \ˈkrak-ˌdau̇n\ *n* : an act or instance of cracking down ⟨a *crackdown* on gambling⟩

crack down \ˈkrak-ˈdau̇n\ *vi* : to take strong action especially to control or put down ⟨*crack down* on crime⟩

cracked \ˈkrakt\ *adj* **1 :** broken into coarse pieces ⟨*cracked* wheat⟩ **2 :** mentally disturbed

crack·er \ˈkrak-ər\ *n* **1 :** something (as a firecracker) that makes a cracking noise **2 :** a dry thin crisp baked food made of flour and water **3 :** the equipment in which cracking is carried out

crack·er·jack \ˈkrak-ər-ˌjak\ *n* : something very excellent — **crackerjack** *adj*

Cracker Jack *trademark* — used for a candied popcorn confection

crack·ing *n* : a process in which relatively heavy hydrocarbons (as oils from petroleum) are broken up by heat into lighter products (as gasoline)

[1]**crack·le** \ˈkrak-əl\ *vi* **crack·led; crack·ling** \ˈkrak-ling, -ə-ling\ **1 a :** to make small sharp sudden repeated noises **b :** to show spirit : SPARKLE **2 :** to develop a surface network of fine cracks [derived from [1]*crack*]

[2]**crackle** *n* **1 :** the noise of repeated small cracks **2 :** a network of fine cracks on an otherwise smooth surface

crack·ling *n* **1** \ˈkrak-ling, -ə-ling\ : a series of small sharp crackling sounds **2** \ˈkrak-lən, -ling\ : the crisp remainder left after the fat has been separated from the fibrous tissue (as in frying the skin of pork) — usually used in plural

crack·ly \ˈkrak-lē, -ə-lē\ *adj* : inclined to crackle : CRISP

crack·nel \ˈkrak-nl\ *n* **1 :** a hard brittle biscuit **2 :** CRACKLING 2 — usually used in plural [Middle English *krakenelle*]

crack·pot \ˈkrak-ˌpät\ *n* : a crazy or peculiar person — **crackpot** *adj*

cracks·man \ˈkrak-smən\ *n* : BURGLAR; *also* : SAFECRACKER

crack–up \ˈkrak-ˌəp\ *n* : WRECK ⟨an automobile *crack-up*⟩

crack up *vb* **1 :** to assert the excellence of : PRAISE ⟨it's not all it's *cracked up* to be⟩ **2 :** to damage or destroy by crashing ⟨*crack up* a car⟩ **3 :** to damage or destroy a vehicle (as by losing control) ⟨*cracked up* on a curve⟩

-c·ra·cy \k-rə-sē\ *n combining form* **1 :** form of government; *also* : state having such a government ⟨demo*cracy*⟩ **2 :** social or political class (as of powerful persons) ⟨mobo*cracy*⟩ [Middle French *-cratie,* from Greek *-kratia,* from *kratos* "strength, power"]

[1]**cra·dle** \ˈkrād-l\ *n* **1 :** a bed for a baby usually on rockers **2 a :** the earliest period of life **b :** a place of origin ⟨the *cradle* of civilization⟩ **3 :** something serving as a framework or support: as **a :** the support for a telephone receiver or handset **b :** an implement with rods like fingers attached to a scythe and used formerly for harvesting grain **4 :** a rocking device used in panning for gold [Old English *cradol*]

[2]**cradle** *vt* **cra·dled; cra·dling** \ˈkrād-ling, -l-ing\ **1 a :** to place or keep in or as if in a cradle **b :** to shelter in childhood : REAR **c :** to protect and cherish lovingly **2 :** to cut (grain) with a cradle scythe **3 :** to place, raise, support, or transport on a cradle **4 :** to wash in a miner's cradle

cra·dle·song \ˈkrād-l-ˌsȯng\ *n* : LULLABY

[1]**craft** \ˈkraft\ *n* **1 :** skill in planning, making, or executing **2 a :** an occupation or trade requiring artistic skill or ease in using the hands **b** *pl* : articles made by craftspeople ⟨a store selling *crafts*⟩ **3 :** skill in deceiving to gain an end ⟨used *craft* and guile to close the deal⟩ **4 :** the members of a trade or trade association **5** *pl usually* **craft a :** a boat especially of small size **b :** AIRCRAFT [Old English *cræft* "strength, skill"] ***synonyms*** see ART

[2]**craft** *vt* : to make or produce with care, skill, or ingenuity ⟨is *crafting* a new sculpture⟩ ⟨a carefully *crafted* story⟩ — **craft·er** \ˈkraf-tər\ *n*

crafts·man \ˈkraf-smən, ˈkraft-\ *n* **1 :** a worker who practices a trade or handicraft **2 :** a highly skilled worker in any field — **crafts·man·ship** \-ˌship\ *n*

crafts·peo·ple \-ˌspē-pəl\ *n* : workers who practice a trade or craft

crafts·per·son \-ˌspər-sn\ *n* : a craftsman or craftswoman

crafts·wom·an \-ˌswu̇m-ən\ *n* **1 :** a woman who is an artisan **2 :** a woman who is skilled in a craft

craft union *n* : a labor union with membership limited to workers of the same craft — compare INDUSTRIAL UNION

crafty \ˈkraf-tē\ *adj* **craft·i·er; -est :** skillful at deceiving others : CUNNING ***synonyms*** see SLY — **craft·i·ly** \-tə-lē\ *adv* — **craft·i·ness** \-tē-nəs\ *n*

crag \ˈkrag\ *n* : a steep rugged rock or cliff [Middle English, of Celtic origin] — **crag·gy** \-ē\ *adj*

crake \ˈkrāk\ *n* : any of various rails; *esp* : one with a short bill [Middle English, probably from Old Norse *krāka* "crow" or *krākr* "raven"]

cram \ˈkram\ *vb* **crammed; cram·ming 1 :** to stuff or crowd in ⟨*cram* clothes into a bag⟩ **2 :** to fill full ⟨barns *crammed* with hay⟩ **3 :** to eat greedily : STUFF **4 :** to study a subject intensively especially in preparation for an examination to be taken soon [Old English *crammian*] — **cram·mer** *n*

[1]**cramp** \ˈkramp\ *n* **1 :** a sudden painful involuntary contraction of muscle **2 :** a temporary paralysis of muscles from overuse — compare WRITER'S CRAMP **3 :** sharp abdominal pain — usually used in plural [Medieval French *crampe,* of Germanic origin] — **crampy** \ˈkram-pē\ *adj*

[2]**cramp** *n* **1 :** a usually iron device bent at the ends and used to hold timbers or blocks of stone together **2 :** [1]CLAMP [Middle Dutch *krampe* "hook"] — **cramp** *adj*

[3]**cramp** *vt* **1 :** to affect with or as if with cramp **2 a :** CONFINE ⟨felt *cramped* in the tiny room⟩ **b :** HAMPER — used in the phrase *cramp one's style* **3 :** to fasten or hold with a cramp

cram·pon \ˈkram-ˌpän\ *n* **1 :** a hooked clutch or dog for raising heavy objects — usually used in plural **2 :** a set of steel spikes that fit on the bottom of a climbing boot to give better grip on slopes of hard ice or snow — usually used in plural [Medieval French *crampon,* of Germanic origin]

cran·ber·ry \ˈkran-ˌber-ē, -bə-rē, -brē\ *n* : the bright red sour berry of any of several trailing plants of the heath family; *also* : a plant producing these [Low German *kraanbere,* from *kraan* "crane" + *bere* "berry"]

cranberry bush *n* : a viburnum that has leaves with three lobes and bears red fruit

[1]**crane** \ˈkrān\ *n* **1 :** any of a family of tall wading birds related to the rails **2 :** any of several herons **3 a :** a machine for raising, shifting, and lowering heavy weights by means of a projecting swinging arm or with the hoisting apparatus supported on an overhead track **b :** an iron arm in a fireplace for supporting

kettles **c** : a long movable support for a motion-picture or television camera [Old English *cran*]

[2]**crane** *vb* **1** : to raise or lift by a crane **2** : to stretch one's neck forward to see better

crane fly *n* : any of numerous long-legged slender two-winged flies that resemble large mosquitoes but do not bite

cranes•bill \ˈkrānz-ˌbil\ *n* : GERANIUM 1

cra•ni•al \ˈkrā-nē-əl\ *adj* **1** : of or relating to the cranium **2** : CEPHALIC — **cra•ni•al•ly** \-ə-lē\ *adv*

cranial nerve *n* : any of the paired nerves that arise from the lower surface of the brain and pass through openings in the skull

cra•ni•um \ˈkrā-nē-əm\ *n, pl* **-ni•ums** *or* **-nia** \-nē-ə\ : SKULL; *esp* : the part that encloses the brain [Medieval Latin, from Greek *kranion*]

[1]**crank** \ˈkrangk\ *n* **1** : a bent part of an axle or shaft or an arm at right angles to the end of a shaft by which circular motion is imparted to or received from the axle or shaft **2 a** : WHIM **b** : an eccentric person **c** : a bad-tempered person : GROUCH [Old English *cranc-* (as in *crancstæf,* a weaving instrument)]

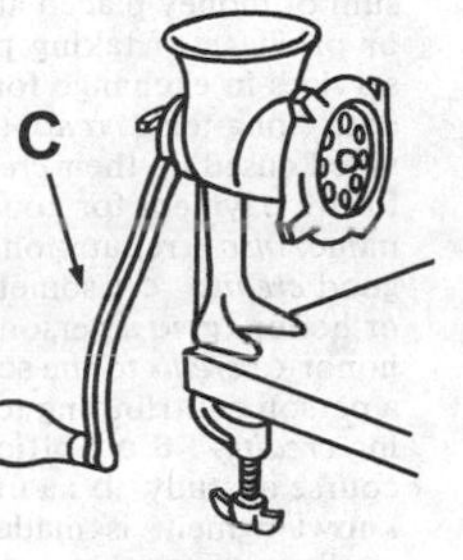

C crank 1

[2]**crank** *vb* **1** : to move with a winding course : ZIGZAG **2** : to bend into the shape of a crank **3** : to start or operate by or as if by the turning of a crank **4** : TURN UP 2 ⟨*crank* up the volume⟩

crank•case \ˈkrangk-ˌkās\ *n* : the housing of a crankshaft

crank•pin \-ˌpin\ *n* : the cylindrical piece which forms the handle of a crank or to which the connecting rod is attached

crank•shaft \-ˌshaft\ *n* : a shaft turning or driven by a crank or consisting of a series of cranks

cranky \ˈkrang-kē\ *adj* **crank•i•er; -est** **1** : IRRITABLE 1 **2** : not in good working order ⟨a *cranky* old tractor⟩ — **crank•i•ness** *n*

cran•ny \ˈkran-ē\ *n, pl* **crannies** : a small break or slit [Medieval French *cren, cran* "notch"]

crape \ˈkrāp\ *n* **1** : CREPE 1 **2** : a band of crepe worn on a hat or sleeve as a sign of mourning [alteration of French *crêpe*]

crape myrtle *n* : an Asian shrub related to the loosestrifes and widely grown in warm regions for its showy flowers

crap•pie \ˈkräp-ē\ *n* **1** : BLACK CRAPPIE **2** : WHITE CRAPPIE [Canadian French *crapet*]

craps \ˈkraps\ *n pl* : a gambling game played with two dice [French, from English *crabs* "lowest throw at hazard," from [1]*crab*]

crap•shoot•er \ˈkrap-ˌshüt-ər\ *n* : a person who plays craps — **crap•shoot•ing** \-ˌshüt-ing\ *n*

[1]**crash** \ˈkrash\ *vb* **1 a** : to break violently and noisily : SMASH **b** : to damage an airplane in landing **2 a** : to make or cause to make a loud noise **b** : to force through with loud crashing noises **3** : to enter or attend without invitation or without paying ⟨*crash* a party⟩ **4** : to move toward aggressively ⟨hockey players *crashing* the net⟩ **5** : to decline, fail, or cause to fail suddenly ⟨the computer *crashed*⟩ **6** *slang* : to go to bed or fall asleep; *also* : to reside temporarily ⟨*crashed* with friends for a week⟩ [Middle English *crasschen*] — **crash•er** *n*

[2]**crash** *n* **1** : a loud sound (as of things smashing) **2 a** : a breaking to pieces by or as if by collision **b** : an instance of crashing ⟨a computer *crash*⟩ **3** : a sudden decline or failure (as of a business or prices) ⟨a stock-market *crash*⟩

[3]**crash** *adj* : effected in the shortest possible time especially to meet emergency conditions ⟨a *crash* renovation program⟩

[4]**crash** *n* : a coarse fabric used for draperies, toweling, and clothing [probably from Russian *krashenina* "colored linen"]

crash course *n* : a rapid and intense course of study; *also* : an experience that resembles such a course ⟨given a *crash course* in foreign policy in his first weeks in office⟩

crash dive *n* : a dive made by a submarine in the least possible time — **crash–dive** \ˈkrash-ˈdīv\ *vi*

crash helmet *n* : a padded helmet that is worn (as by motorcyclists) as protection against head injury

crash–land \ˈkrash-ˈland\ *vb* : to land an aircraft under emergency conditions usually with damage to the craft — **crash landing** *n*

crass \ˈkras\ *adj* : GROSS, INSENSITIVE ⟨*crass* ignorance⟩ [Latin *crassus* "thick, gross"] — **crass•ly** *adv* — **crass•ness** *n*

-crat \ˌkrat\ *n combining form* **1** : advocate or partisan of a (specified) form of government ⟨demo*crat*⟩ **2** : member of a (specified) dominant class ⟨pluto*crat*⟩ [French *-crate,* back-formation from *-cratie* "-cracy"]

[1]**crate** \ˈkrāt\ *n* **1** : a box usually ventilated and made of thin wooden slats for packing fruit or vegetables **2** : an enclosing framework for protecting something (as in shipment) [Latin *cratis* "wickerwork, hurdle"]

[2]**crate** *vt* : to pack in a crate

cra•ter \ˈkrāt-ər\ *n* : a bowl-shaped depression: as **a** : one around the opening of a volcano **b** : one formed by the impact of a meteorite **c** : a hole in the ground made by the explosion of a bomb or shell [Latin, "mixing bowl, crater," from Greek *kratēr,* from *kerannynai* "to mix"]

cra•vat \krə-ˈvat\ *n* : NECKTIE [French *cravate,* from *Cravate* "Croatian"]

crave \ˈkrāv\ *vb* **1** : to ask for earnestly : BEG **2** : to have a strong desire or need for [Old English *crafian*]

[1]**cra•ven** \ˈkrā-vən\ *adj* : COWARDLY [Middle English *cravant*] — **cra•ven•ly** *adv* — **cra•ven•ness** \-vən-nəs\ *n*

[2]**craven** *n* : COWARD

crav•ing \ˈkrā-ving\ *n* : a great desire or longing; *esp* : an abnormal desire (as for a habit-forming drug)

craw \ˈkrȯ\ *n* **1** : the crop of a bird or insect **2** : the stomach especially of a lower animal [Middle English *crawe*]

craw•dad \ˈkrȯ-ˌdad\ *n* : CRAYFISH 1 [alteration of *crawfish*]

craw•fish \ˈkrȯ-ˌfish\ *n* **1** : CRAYFISH 1 **2** : SPINY LOBSTER [by folk etymology from Middle English *crevis*]

[1]**crawl** \ˈkrȯl\ *vb* **1** : to move slowly with the body close to the ground : CREEP **2** : to move or progress slowly or laboriously ⟨the traffic *crawled* along⟩ **3** : to advance by cunning or servility ⟨*crawling* into favor by obeying without complaint⟩ **4** : to be swarming with or have the sensation of swarming with creeping things ⟨the floor was *crawling* with ants⟩ [Old Norse *krafla*] — **crawl•er** *n*

[2]**crawl** *n* **1** : the act or motion of crawling **2** : a fast stroke in which a swimmer lies facing down in the water and moves forward by overarm strokes and a flutter kick

crawly \ˈkrȯ-lē\ *adj* **crawl•i•er; -est** **1** : CREEPY **2** : marked by crawling or slow motion ⟨*crawly* creatures⟩

cray•fish \ˈkrā-ˌfish\ *n* **1** : any of numerous freshwater crustaceans resembling but usually much smaller than the lobster **2** : SPINY LOBSTER [by folk etymology from Middle English *crevis,* from Medieval French *creveis, escreveice,* of Germanic origin]

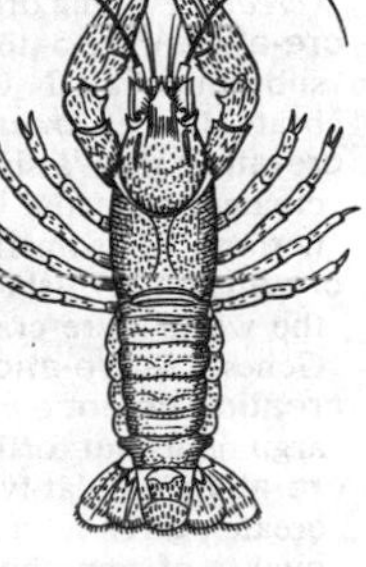
crayfish 1

[1]**cray•on** \ˈkrā-ˌän, -ən; ˈkran\ *n* **1** : a stick of white or colored chalk or of colored wax used for writing or drawing **2** : a crayon drawing [French, "crayon, pencil," from *craie* "chalk," from Medieval French *croie,* from Latin *creta*]

[2]**crayon** *vt* : to draw or color with a crayon — **cray•on•ist** \ˈkrā-ə-nəst\ *n*

[1]**craze** \ˈkrāz\ *vb* **1** : to make or become insane **2** : to develop a network of fine cracks ⟨*crazed* glass⟩ [Middle English *crasen* "to crush, craze," of Scandinavian origin]

[2]**craze** \ˈkrāz\ *n* **1** : a strong but temporary interest in something or the object of such an interest : FAD ⟨the latest *craze* among high school students⟩ **2** : a fine crack in glaze or enamel or on a painted surface

[1]**cra•zy** \ˈkrā-zē\ *adj* **cra•zi•er; -est** **1 a** : full of cracks or flaws : UNSOUND **b** : CROOKED 1 **2 a** : mentally disordered : INSANE **b (1)** : wildly impractical ⟨a *crazy* plan⟩ **(2)** : ERRATIC 1 ⟨*crazy* drivers⟩ **3** : distracted with desire or excitement ⟨a *crazy* audience⟩ **4 a** : filled with infatuation ⟨*crazy* about the girl⟩ **b** : passionately preoccupied ⟨*crazy* about boats⟩ ***synonyms*** see INSANE — **cra•zi•ly** \-zə-lē\ *adv* — **cra•zi•ness**

\ə\ **abut**	\au̇\ **out**	\i\ **tip**	\ȯ\ **saw**	\u̇\ **foot**
\ər\ **further**	\ch\ **chin**	\ī\ **life**	\ȯi\ **coin**	\y\ **yet**
\a\ **mat**	\e\ **pet**	\j\ **job**	\th\ **thin**	\yü\ **few**
\ā\ **take**	\ē\ **easy**	\ng\ **sing**	\t͟h\ **this**	\yu̇\ **cure**
\ä\ **cot, cart**	\g\ **go**	\ō\ **bone**	\ü\ **food**	\zh\ **vision**

\-zē-nəs\ *n* — **crazy** *n* — **like crazy** : to an extreme degree ⟨working *like crazy*⟩

[2]**crazy** *adv* : to an extreme degree ⟨*crazy* good⟩

crazy bone *n* : FUNNY BONE 1

crazy quilt *n* : a patchwork quilt without a design

[1]**creak** \ˈkrēk\ *vi* : to make a prolonged grating or squeaking sound [Middle English *creken* "to croak"]

[2]**creak** *n* : a rasping or grating noise — **creak•i•ly** \ˈkrē-kə-lē\ *adv* — **creaky** \ˈkrē-kē\ *adj*

[1]**cream** \ˈkrēm\ *n* **1** : the yellowish part of milk containing butterfat **2 a** : a food prepared with cream **b** : something (as a medicinal or cosmetic preparation) having the consistency of cream **3** : the choicest part ⟨the *cream* of the crop⟩ **4** : a pale yellow [Medieval French *creme, cresme,* from Late Latin *cramum,* of Celtic origin]

[2]**cream** *vb* **1** : to form cream **2 a** : SKIM 1b **b** : to take the choicest part of something **3** : to furnish, prepare, or treat with cream **4 a** : to beat into a creamy froth **b** : to work or blend to the consistency of cream

cream cheese *n* : an unripened soft white cheese made from whole milk enriched with cream

cream•er \ˈkrē-mər\ *n* **1** : a device for separating cream from milk **2** : a small pitcher or jug for serving cream

cream•ery \ˈkrēm-rē, -ə-rē\ *n, pl* **-er•ies** : an establishment where butter and cheese are made or where milk and cream are sold or prepared

cream of tartar : a white crystalline salt $C_4H_5KO_6$ used especially in baking powder and in galvanic tinning of metals

cream puff *n* : a round shell of light pastry filled with whipped cream or a cream filling

cream sauce *n* : WHITE SAUCE

creamy \ˈkrē-mē\ *adj* **cream•i•er; -est 1** : containing cream **2** : resembling cream (as in color, texture, or taste) — **cream•i•ly** \-mə-lē\ *adv* — **cream•i•ness** \-mē-nəs\ *n*

[1]**crease** \ˈkrēs\ *n* **1** : a line or mark made by or as if by folding **2** : a specially marked area around a goal (as in hockey) [probably from Middle English *creste* "crest"]

[2]**crease** *vb* **1** : to make a crease in or on **2** : to wound slightly especially by grazing **3** : to become creased — **creas•er** *n*

cre•ate \krē-ˈāt, ˈkrē-ˌ\ *vt* **1** : to bring into existence **2 a** : to install in a new office or rank ⟨was *created* a lieutenant⟩ **b** : to produce or bring about ⟨*create* a disturbance⟩ **3 a** : to produce through imaginative skill ⟨*create* a painting⟩ **b** : DESIGN ⟨*creates* evening dresses⟩ [Latin *creare*]

cre•atine \ˈkrē-ə-ˌtēn, -ət-n\ *n* : a white crystalline nitrogenous substance $C_4H_9N_3O_2$ found especially in the muscles of vertebrates [Greek *kreat-, kreas* "flesh"]

cre•ation \krē-ˈā-shən\ *n* **1** : the act of creating or fact of being created; *esp* : the bringing of the world into existence out of nothing **2** : something created **3** : all created things : WORLD

cre•ation•ism \-shə-ˌniz-əm\ *n* : a theory that matter, life, and the world were created by God from nothing as described in Genesis — **cre•ation•ist** \-shə-nəst, -shnəst\ *n or adj*

creation science *n* : CREATIONISM; *also* : scientific evidence or arguments put forth in support of creationism

cre•ative \krē-ˈāt-iv\ *adj* **1** : marked by the ability or power to create : given to creating ⟨the *creative* impulse⟩ **2** : having the quality of something created rather than imitated : IMAGINATIVE ⟨*creative* writing⟩ — **cre•ative•ly** *adv* — **cre•ative•ness** *n*

cre•ativ•i•ty \ˌkrē-ā-ˈtiv-ət-ē, ˌkrē-ə-\ *n* : ability to create

cre•ator \krē-ˈāt-ər\ *n* **1** : one that creates or produces : MAKER **2** *cap* : GOD 1

crea•ture \ˈkrē-chər\ *n* **1** : a created being **2 a** : a lower animal; *esp* : a farm animal **b** : a human being **c** : a being of abnormal or uncertain nature ⟨*creatures* of fantasy⟩ **3** : one that is servile to or the obedient tool of another [Late Latin *creatura,* from Latin *creare* "to create"] — **crea•tur•al** \ˈkrēch-rəl, -ə-rəl\ *adj*

creature comfort *n* : something (as food or warmth) that gives bodily comfort

crèche \ˈkresh\ *n* **1** : a representation of the Nativity scene in the stable at Bethlehem **2** : a day nursery or foundling home [French, from Medieval French *creche* "manger, crib," of Germanic origin]

cre•dence \ˈkrēd-ns\ *n* **1** : mental acceptance as true or real : BELIEF ⟨give *credence* to gossip⟩ **2** : a small table where the bread and wine rest before consecration [Medieval Latin *credentia,* from Latin *credere* "to believe, trust"]

cre•den•tial \kri-ˈden-chəl\ *n* **1** : something that gives a title to credit or confidence; *also* : QUALIFICATION 2a **2** *pl* : documents showing that a person is entitled to confidence or has a right to exercise official power

cre•den•za \kri-ˈden-zə\ *n* : a sideboard, buffet, or bookcase; *esp* : one without legs [Italian, literally, "belief, confidence," from Medieval Latin *credentia*]

cred•i•ble \ˈkred-ə-bəl\ *adj* : capable of being believed : deserving to be believed ⟨a *credible* story⟩ [Latin *credibilis,* from *credere* "to believe"] ***synonyms*** see PLAUSIBLE — **cred•i•bil•i•ty** \ˌkred-ə-ˈbil-ət-ē\ *n* — **cred•i•bly** \ˈkred-ə-blē\ *adv*

[1]**cred•it** \ˈkred-ət\ *n* **1** : reliance on the truth or reality of something ⟨a story that deserves little *credit*⟩ **2 a** : a favorable balance in a bank account **b** : an entry in an account representing an addition of income or net worth ⟨debits and *credits*⟩ **c** : a sum of money placed at one's disposal by a bank **d** : the right or privilege of taking present possession of money, goods, or services in exchange for a promise to pay for them at a future date ⟨long-term *credit*⟩; *also* : money, goods, or services so provided ⟨used up their *credit*⟩ **3 a** : trust given to a customer for future payment for goods purchased ⟨buy on *credit*⟩ **b** : good name; *also* : reputation for fulfilling financial obligations ⟨has good *credit*⟩ **c** : something that adds to a person's reputation or honor ⟨give a person *credit* for a discovery⟩ **4** : a source of honor ⟨a *credit* to the school⟩ **5** : acknowledgment by name of a person contributing to a performance (as a movie) ⟨the opening *credits*⟩ **6 a** : official certification of the completion of a course of study **b** : a unit of academic work for which such acknowledgment is made [Middle French, derived from Latin *creditum* "something entrusted to another, loan," from *credere* "to believe, trust"]

[2]**credit** *vt* **1** : to trust in the truth of : BELIEVE **2** : to enter upon the credit side of ⟨we'll *credit* your account with $10⟩ **3 a** : to think of usually favorably as the source, agent, or performer of an action or the possessor of a trait ⟨*credits* him with an excellent sense of humor⟩ **b** : to attribute to some person ⟨they *credit* the invention to him⟩ ***synonyms*** see ASCRIBE

cred•it•able \ˈkred-ət-ə-bəl\ *adj* **1** : worthy of belief **2** : worthy of praise — **cred•it•abil•i•ty** \ˌkred-ət-ə-ˈbil-ət-ē\ *n* — **cred•it•ably** \ˈkred-ət-ə-blē\ *adv*

credit card *n* : a card authorizing purchases on credit

cred•i•tor \ˈkred-ət-ər\ *n* : a person to whom a debt is owed; *esp* : a person to whom money or goods are due

credit union *n* : a cooperative association that makes small loans to its members at low rates and offers other banking services (as savings and checking accounts)

cre•do \ˈkrēd-ō, ˈkrād-\ *n, pl* **credos** : CREED [Latin, "I believe"]

cre•du•li•ty \kri-ˈdü-lət-ē, -ˈdyü-\ *n* : a willingness to believe especially on little or no evidence

cred•u•lous \ˈkrej-ə-ləs\ *adj* : ready to believe especially on slight or uncertain evidence [Latin *credulus,* from *credere* "to believe"] — **cred•u•lous•ly** *adv* — **cred•u•lous•ness** *n*

Cree \ˈkrē\ *n, pl* **Cree** *or* **Crees 1** : a member of an American Indian people of Quebec, Ontario, Manitoba, and Saskatchewan **2** : the Algonquian language of the Cree [Canadian French *Cris* "Crees," short for *Cristinaux,* from an Ojibwa name for a Cree band]

creed \ˈkrēd\ *n* **1** : a statement of the essential beliefs of a religious faith **2** : a set of guiding principles or beliefs [Old English *crēda,* from Latin *credo* "I believe" (first word of the Apostles' and Nicene creeds), from *credere* "to believe"] — **creed•al** *or* **cre•dal** \ˈkrēd-l\ *adj*

creek \ˈkrēk, ˈkrik\ *n* **1** *chiefly British* : a small narrow inlet extending farther inland than a cove **2** : a natural stream of water usually smaller than a river [Middle English *crike, creke,* from Old Norse *-kriki* "bend"]

Creek \ˈkrēk\ *n* : a member of a confederacy of American Indian peoples formerly occupying most of Alabama and Georgia

creel \ˈkrēl\ *n* : a wicker basket (as for carrying newly caught fish) [Middle English *creille, crele*]

[1]**creep** \ˈkrēp\ *vi* **crept** \ˈkrept\; **creep•ing 1** : to move along with the body prone and close to the ground; *also* : to move slowly on hands and knees **2** : to go slowly ⟨the hours *crept* by⟩ **3** : to have the sensation of being covered with creeping things ⟨the scream made my skin *creep*⟩ **4** : to spread or grow over a surface usually rooting at intervals ⟨*creeping* vines⟩ **5** : to slip or gradually shift position [Old English *crēopan*]

[2]**creep** *n* **1** : a creeping movement **2 a** : a distressing sensation

like that of insects creeping over one's flesh **b :** a feeling of horror — usually used in plural with *the* ⟨that gives me the *creeps*⟩ **3 :** a feed trough accessible only by young animals (as calves) that is used to supply special feed

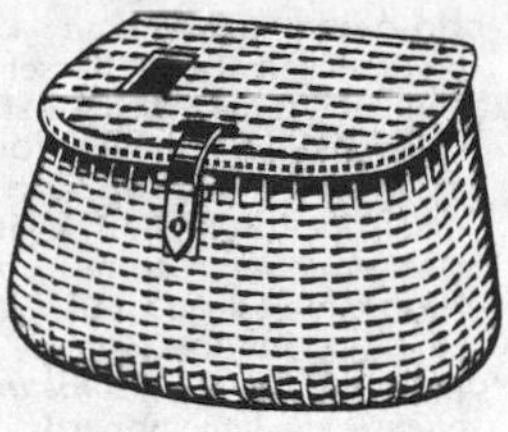

creel

creep·er \ˈkrē-pər\ *n* **1 :** one that creeps: as **a :** a creeping plant **b :** a bird that creeps about on trees or bushes searching for insects **2 :** a device with iron points worn on a shoe to prevent slipping

creepy \ˈkrē-pē\ *adj* **creep·i·er; -est :** feeling or producing nervous shivery apprehension ⟨a *creepy* horror story⟩; *also* : EERIE — **creep·i·ly** \-pə-lē\ *adv* — **creep·i·ness** \-pē-nəs\ *n*

cre·mate \ˈkrē-ˌmāt, kri-ˈ\ *vt* : to reduce (a corpse) to ashes by burning [Latin *cremare*] — **cre·ma·tion** \kri-ˈmā-shən\ *n*

cre·ma·to·ri·um \ˌkrē-mə-ˈtōr-ē-əm, ˌkrem-ə-, -ˈtȯr-\ *n, pl* **-riums** *or* **-ria** \-ē-ə\ : CREMATORY

cre·ma·to·ry \ˈkrē-mə-ˌtōr-ē, ˈkrem-ə-, -ˌtȯr-\ *n, pl* **-ries :** a furnace for cremating; *also* : a structure containing such a furnace — **crematory** *adj*

crème de ca·cao \ˌkrēm-də-ˈkō-kō, ˌkrem-də-kə-ˈkau̇, -kə-ˈkā-ō\ *n* : a sweet liqueur flavored with cacao beans and vanilla [French, literally, "cream of cacao"]

crème de menthe \ˌkrem-də-ˈmenth, ˌkrēm-, -ˈmint\ *n* : a sweet mint-flavored liqueur [French, literally, "cream of mint"]

cre·nate \ˈkrē-ˌnāt, ˈkren-ˌāt\ *or* **cre·nat·ed** \-əd\ *adj* : having the margin (as of a leaf) cut into rounded scallops [Medieval Latin *crena* "notch"] — **cre·na·tion** \kri-ˈnā-shən\ *n*

cren·el·lat·ed *or* **cren·el·at·ed** \ˈkren-l-ˌāt-əd\ *adj* : having battlements ⟨a *crenellated* tower⟩ [French *créneler* "to furnish with embrasures," from Medieval French *querneler,* from *kernel, crenel* "embrasure," from *cren* "notch"] — **cren·el·la·tion** *also* **cren·el·a·tion** \ˌkren-l-ˈā-shən\ *n*

cre·o·dont \ˈkrē-ə-ˌdänt\ *n* : any of a group (Creodonta) of extinct primitive carnivorous mammals [Greek *kreas* "flesh" + *odont-, odous* "tooth"] — **creodont** *adj*

cre·ole \ˈkrē-ˌōl\ *adj* **1** *often cap* : of or relating to Creoles or their language **2** *often cap* : relating to or being highly seasoned food typically made with rice, okra, tomatoes, and peppers ⟨shrimp *creole*⟩

Cre·ole \ˈkre-ˌol\ *n* **1 :** a person of European descent born especially in the West Indies or Spanish America **2 :** a white person descended from early French or Spanish settlers in the U.S. Gulf states and preserving their speech and culture **3 :** a person of mixed French or Spanish and black descent speaking a dialect of French or Spanish **4 a :** a language evolved from a pidgin based on French that is spoken by blacks in southern Louisiana **b** *not cap* : a language that has evolved from a pidgin and serves as the native language of a speech community [French *créole,* from Spanish *criollo,* from Portuguese *crioulo* "white person born in the colonies"]

[1]**cre·o·sote** \ˈkrē-ə-ˌsōt\ *n* **1 :** a clear or yellowish oily liquid mixture of compounds obtained by the distillation of tar derived from wood and especially from beech wood **2 :** a brownish oily liquid obtained by distillation of coal tar and used especially as a wood preservative **3 :** a dark flammable tar deposited in a chimney especially from wood smoke **4 :** CREOSOTE BUSH [German *Kreosot,* from Greek *kreas* "flesh" + *sōtēr* "preserver," from *sōzein* "to preserve," from *sōs* "safe"]

[2]**creosote** *vt* : to treat with creosote

creosote bush *n* : a desert shrub of the southwestern U.S. and Mexico with aromatic foliage and small yellow flowers

crepe *or* **crêpe** \ˈkrāp\ *n* **1 :** a thin crinkled fabric (as of silk, wool, or cotton) **2 :** a small very thin pancake [French *crêpe,* from Middle French *crespe* "curly," from Latin *crispus*] — **crepe** *adj*

crepe de chine \ˌkrāp-də-ˈshēn\ *n, often cap 2nd C* : a soft fine clothing crepe [French *crêpe de Chine,* literally, "crepe of China"]

crepe paper *n* : paper with a crinkled or puckered texture

crepe su·zette \ˌkrāp-sü-ˈzet\ *n, pl* **crepes suzette** \ˌkrāp-sü-, ˌkrāps-\ *or* **crepe suzettes** \ˌkrāp-sü-ˈzets\ : a thin folded or rolled pancake in a hot orange-butter sauce that is sprinkled with a liqueur and set ablaze for serving [French *crêpe Suzette,* from *crêpe* "pancake" + *Suzette* "Susy"]

crept *past of* CREEP

cre·pus·cu·lar \kri-ˈpəs-kyə-lər\ *adj* **1 :** of, relating to, or resembling twilight : DIM **2 :** occurring or active during twilight ⟨*crepuscular* insects⟩ [Latin *crepusculum* "twilight"]

cre·scen·do \kri-ˈshen-dō\ *n, pl* **-dos** *or* **-does** **1 :** a gradual increase in volume of sound in music; *also* : a passage so performed **2 :** a gradual increase (as in physical or emotional force); *also* : the peak of such an increase [Italian, from *crescendo* "increasing," from *crescere* "to increase," from Latin] — **crescendo** *adv or adj*

cres·cent \ˈkres-nt\ *n* **1 a :** the moon at any stage between new moon and first quarter and between last quarter and the succeeding new moon **b :** the figure of the moon defined by a convex and a concave edge **2 :** an object shaped like a crescent [Medieval French *cressant,* from *crestre* "to grow, increase," from Latin *crescere*] — **cres·cen·tic** \kre-ˈsent-ik\ *adj*

cre·sol \ˈkrē-ˌsȯl, -ˌsōl\ *n* : any of three isomeric poisonous colorless crystalline or liquid organic substances C_7H_8O obtained from coal tar and used as disinfectants or in making resins [derived from *creosote*]

cress \ˈkres\ *n* : any of various plants related to the mustards with leaves used especially in salads [Old English *cressa*]

[1]**crest** \ˈkrest\ *n* **1 a :** a showy tuft or process on the head of an animal (as a bird) **b :** a plume worn on a knight's helmet **c :** a heraldic design above the escutcheon in a coat of arms **2 :** an upper part, edge, or limit ⟨the *crest* of a hill⟩ **3 :** a high point of an action or process : CLIMAX, CULMINATION ⟨at the *crest* of their fame⟩ [Middle French *creste,* from Latin *crista*] — **crest·less** *adj*

C crest 1a

[2]**crest** *vb* **1 :** to furnish with a crest : CROWN **2 :** to reach the crest of ⟨*crest* the hill⟩ **3 :** to rise to a crest ⟨waves *cresting* in the storm⟩

crest·ed \ˈkres-təd\ *adj* : having a crest ⟨a *crested* bird⟩

crest·fall·en \ˈkrest-ˌfȯ-lən, ˈkres-\ *adj* : feeling shame or humiliation : DEJECTED — **crest·fall·en·ness** *n*

Cre·ta·ceous \kri-ˈtā-shəs\ *n* : the 3rd and last period of the Mesozoic era during which chalk and most of the coal of the U.S. west of the Great Plains were formed and at the end of which dinosaurs became extinct; *also* : the corresponding system of rocks — see GEOLOGIC TIME table [Latin *cretaceus* "chalky," from *creta* "chalk"] — **Cretaceous** *adj*

cre·tin \ˈkrēt-n\ *n* **1 :** one affected with cretinism **2 :** a stupid, vulgar, or insensitive person : CLOD [French *crétin,* from French dialect *cretin,* literally, "wretch, innocent victim," from Latin *christianus* "Christian"] — **cre·tin·ous** \-əs\ *adj*

Word History Chronic iodine deficiencies in diet can result in malfunctions of the thyroid gland, which produces hormones necessary for normal human development. Some mountainous regions, such as parts of the Alps, cannot naturally provide their inhabitants with a diet rich enough in iodine, and the resultant hyperthyroidism causes dwarfism and severe mental retardation. In Franco-Provençal (the Romance speech of French Switzerland and adjacent areas of France), a person malformed due to hyperthyroidism was called a *cretin,* literally, "wretch, innocent victim," a word that in origin meant simply "Christian" and emphasized the hyperthyroid victim's basic humanity.

cre·tin·ism \-ˌiz-əm\ *n* : a usually congenital abnormal condition marked by physical stunting and mental retardation and caused by deficient functioning of the thyroid gland

cre·tonne \ˈkrē-ˌtän, kri-ˈ\ *n* : a strong cotton or linen cloth used especially for curtains and upholstery [French, from *Creton,* Normandy]

cre·vasse \kri-ˈvas\ *n* **1 :** a deep crevice or fissure (as in a glacier) **2 :** a breach in a levee [French, from Medieval French *crevace*]

\ə\ **abut**	\au̇\ **out**	\i\ **tip**	\ȯ\ **saw**	\u̇\ **foot**
\ər\ **further**	\ch\ **chin**	\ī\ **life**	\ȯi\ **coin**	\y\ **yet**
\a\ **mat**	\e\ **pet**	\j\ **job**	\th\ **thin**	\yü\ **few**
\ā\ **take**	\ē\ **easy**	\ng\ **sing**	\t͟h\ **this**	\yu̇\ **cure**
\ä\ **cot, cart**	\g\ **go**	\ō\ **bone**	\ü\ **food**	\zh\ **vision**

crev•ice \ˈkrev-əs\ *n* : a narrow opening that results from a split or crack : FISSURE, CLEFT ⟨a *crevice* in a rock⟩ [Middle French *crevace,* from *crever* "to split," from Latin *crepare* "to crack"]

[1]**crew** \ˈkrü\ *chiefly British past of* CROW

[2]**crew** \ˈkrü\ *n* **1** : a group of people associated together in a common activity or by common traits or interests **2 a** : a group of people working together **b** : the group of persons who operate a ship **c** : the persons who operate an aircraft in flight **d** : the rowers and coxswain of a racing shell [Middle English *crue,* literally, "reinforcement," from Medieval French *creue,* literally, "increase," from *creistre* "to increase," from Latin *crescere*]

crew cut *n* : a very short haircut in which the hair resembles the bristles of a brush

crew•el \ˈkrü-əl\ *n* : loosely twisted worsted yarn used for embroidery [Middle English *crule*]

[1]**crib** \ˈkrib\ *n* **1** : a manger for feeding animals **2** : a small child's bedstead with high enclosing usually slatted sides **3** : a building for storage **4** : the cards discarded in cribbage for the dealer to use in scoring **5 a** : a literal translation; *esp* : PONY 3 **b** : a device used for cheating in an examination **6** : CRÈCHE 2 [Old English *cribb*]

[2]**crib** *vb* **cribbed; crib•bing 1** : to copy (as an idea or passage) and use as one's own : PLAGIARIZE **2** : to make use of a translation or notes dishonestly — **crib•ber** *n*

crib•bage \ˈkrib-ij\ *n* : a card game for two players in which each player attempts to form various counting combinations of the cards [[1]*crib*]

crick \ˈkrik\ *n* : a painful spasm of muscles (as of the neck or back) [Middle English *cryk*] — **crick** *vt*

[1]**crick•et** \ˈkrik-ət\ *n* : any of a family of leaping insects that are related to the grasshoppers and have leathery forewings used by the males to produce a chirping sound especially to attract a mate [Medieval French *criket,* of imitative origin]

[2]**cricket** *n* **1** : a game played with a ball and bat by two sides of 11 players each on a large field centering upon 2 wickets **2** : fair and honorable behavior [Middle French *criquet* "goal stake in a bowling game"] — **crick•et•er** *n*

cri•er \ˈkrī-ər, ˈkrīr\ *n* : one that cries; *esp* : one who proclaims orders or announcements

crime \ˈkrīm\ *n* **1** : the doing of an act forbidden by law or the failure to do an act required by law **2** : a serious offense especially against morality **3** : criminal activity ⟨led a life of *crime*⟩ **4** : something shameful, foolish, or regrettable ⟨a *crime* to waste food⟩ [Medieval French, from Latin *crimen* "accusation, fault, crime"]

[1]**crim•i•nal** \ˈkrim-ən-l\ *adj* **1** : involving or being a crime ⟨a *criminal* act⟩ **2** : relating to crime ⟨*criminal* courts⟩ **3** : guilty of crime; *also* : of or suitable to a criminal ⟨a *criminal* mind⟩ [Late Latin *criminalis,* from Latin *crimen* "crime"] — **crim•i•nal•i•ty** \ˌkrim-ə-ˈnal-ət-ē\ *n* — **crim•i•nal•ly** \ˈkrim-ən-l-ē\ *adv*

[2]**criminal** *n* : one that has committed or has been convicted of a crime

crim•i•nol•o•gy \ˌkrim-ə-ˈnäl-ə-jē\ *n* : a scientific study of crime, criminals, and their punishment or correction — **crim•i•no•log•i•cal** \ˌkrim-ən-l-ˈäj-i-kəl\ *adj* — **crim•i•nol•o•gist** \ˌkrim-ə-ˈnäl-ə-jəst\ *n*

[1]**crimp** \ˈkrimp\ *vt* **1** : to make wavy, bent, or warped **2** : to put a crimp in : INHIBIT [Dutch or Low German *krimpen* "to shrivel"] — **crimp•er** *n*

[2]**crimp** *n* **1** : something produced by or as if by crimping **2** : something that cramps or inhibits

[1]**crim•son** \ˈkrim-zən\ *n* : deep purplish red [Spanish *cremesín,* from Arabic *qirmizī,* from *qirmiz* "kermes"] — **crimson** *adj*

[2]**crimson** *vb* : to make or become crimson

[1]**cringe** \ˈkrinj\ *vi* **cringed; cring•ing 1** : to draw in or contract one's muscles involuntarily **2** : to shrink in fear or distaste : COWER **3** : to behave in a servile way [Middle English *crengen*] — **cring•er** *n*

[2]**cringe** *n* : an act of cringing

[1]**crin•kle** \ˈkring-kəl\ *vb* **crin•kled; crin•kling** \-kə-ling, -kling\ **1 a** : to form many short bends or ripples ⟨don't *crinkle* the paper⟩ **b** : WRINKLE **2** : to emit a thin crackling sound : RUSTLE ⟨*crinkling* silk⟩ [Middle English *crynkelen*]

[2]**crinkle** *n* : CREASE 1, WRINKLE ⟨*crinkles* around the eyes⟩ — **crin•kly** \-kə-lē, -klē\ *adj*

cri•noid \ˈkrī-ˌnȯid\ *n* : any of a large class (Crinoidea) of echinoderms usually having a cup-shaped body with five or more feathery arms [Greek *krinon* "lily"] — **crinoid** *adj*

crinoid

crin•o•line \ˈkrin-l-ən\ *n* **1** : a cloth originally of horsehair and linen thread used for stiffening and lining **2 a** : HOOPSKIRT **b** : a full stiff skirt or underskirt [French, from Italian *crinolino,* from *crino* "horsehair" + *lino* "flax, linen"] — **crinoline** *adj*

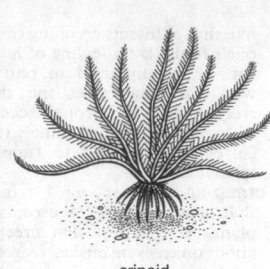

[1]**crip•ple** \ˈkrip-əl\ *n, sometimes offensive* : a lame or partly disabled individual [Old English *crypel*]

[2]**cripple** *vt* **crip•pled; crip•pling** \ˈkrip-ling, -ə-ling\ **1** : to deprive of the use of a limb and especially a leg ⟨was *crippled* by the accident⟩ **2** : to deprive of strength, efficiency, wholeness, or capability for service ⟨the loss of power *crippled* the city⟩ — **crip•pler** \-lər\ *n*

cri•sis \ˈkrī-səs\ *n, pl* **cri•ses** \ˈkrī-ˌsēz\ **1** : the turning point for better or worse in an acute disease or fever **2** : a decisive moment (as in the plot of a story) **3** : an unstable or crucial time or state of affairs ⟨a political *crisis*⟩ [Latin, from Greek *krisis,* literally, "decision," from *krinein* "to judge, decide"] ***synonyms*** see JUNCTURE

[1]**crisp** \ˈkrisp\ *adj* **1** : CURLY, WAVY ⟨*crisp* hair⟩ **2** : easily crumbled : FLAKY ⟨*crisp* pastry⟩ **3** : being desirably firm and crunchy ⟨*crisp* lettuce⟩ **4 a** : being notably sharp, clean, and concise ⟨a *crisp* photo⟩ **b** : noticeably neat ⟨a *crisp* new suit⟩ **c** : keenly alert and lively : INCISIVE ⟨a *crisp* performance⟩ **d** : briskly cold ⟨*crisp* weather⟩ [Old English, from Latin *crispus*] ***synonyms*** see BRITTLE — **crisp•ly** *adv* — **crisp•ness** *n*

[2]**crisp** *vb* : to make or become crisp — **crisp•er** *n*

[3]**crisp** *n* : something crisp or brittle ⟨dinner burned to a *crisp*⟩

crispy \ˈkris-pē\ *adj* **crisp•i•er; -est 1** : CURLY, WAVY **2** : appealingly crunchy : CRISP ⟨*crispy* fried chicken⟩ — **crisp•i•ness** *n*

[1]**criss•cross** \ˈkris-ˌkrȯs\ *vb* **1** : to mark with intersecting lines **2** : to go or pass back and forth

[2]**crisscross** *n* : a pattern formed by or as if by crossed lines [obsolete *christcross* "mark of a cross," from *Christ* + *cross*] — **crisscross** *adj or adv*

cris•ta \ˈkris-tə\ *n, pl* **cris•tae** \-ˌtē, -ˌtī\ : any of the inwardly projecting folds of the inner membrane of a mitochondrion [Latin, "crest"]

cri•te•ri•on \krī-ˈtir-ē-ən\ *n, pl* **-ria** \-ē-ə\ *also* **-ri•ons** : a standard on which a judgment or decision may be based [Greek *kritērion,* from *krinein* "to judge, decide"] ***synonyms*** see STANDARD

crit•ic \ˈkrit-ik\ *n* **1** : a person who judges the value, worth, beauty, or excellence of something; *esp* : one whose profession is to express trained judgment on work in art, music, drama, or literature **2** : one inclined to harsh or unfair criticism : FAULTFINDER [Latin *criticus,* from Greek *kritikos,* from *krinein* "to judge"]

crit•i•cal \ˈkrit-i-kəl\ *adj* **1 a** : inclined to criticize harshly and unfavorably **b** : consisting of or involving criticism ⟨*critical* writings⟩ **c** : using or involving careful judgment **2 a (1)** : of, relating to, or being a turning point ⟨the *critical* phase of a fever⟩ **(2)** : critically ill **b** : relating to or being a state in which or a measurement or point at which a quality, property, or phenomenon suffers a definite change ⟨the *critical* temperature⟩ **c** : CRUCIAL ⟨a *critical* test⟩ **3 a** : of sufficient size to sustain a chain reaction — used of a mass of fissionable material **b** : sustaining a chain reaction — used of a nuclear reactor — **crit•i•cal•ly** \-i-kə-lē, -klē\ *adv* — **crit•i•cal•ness** \-kəl-nəs\ *n*

critical angle *n* : the least angle of incidence at which total reflection takes place

crit•i•cism \ˈkrit-ə-ˌsiz-əm\ *n* **1 a** : the act of criticizing; *esp* : FAULTFINDING **b** : a critical remark or observation **c** : CRITIQUE **2** : the art of judging expertly the merits and faults of works of art or literature

crit•i•cize \ˈkrit-ə-ˌsīz\ *vb* **1** : to examine and judge as a critic : EVALUATE **2** : to express criticism especially of an unfavorable kind **3** : to find fault or find fault with ⟨some people are too quick to *criticize*⟩ — **crit•i•ciz•er** *n*

[1]**cri•tique** \krə-ˈtēk\ *n* : an act or instance of criticizing; *esp* : a critical estimate or discussion

[2]**critique** *vt* **cri•tiqued; cri•tiqu•ing** : to examine critically : REVIEW ⟨*critique* the plan⟩

[1]**croak** \'krōk\ *vb* **1 a :** to make a deep harsh sound **b :** to speak in a hoarse throaty voice **2 :** to grumble dourly : COMPLAIN **3** *slang* **a :** DIE 1 **b :** KILL 1 [Middle English *croken*]

[2]**croak** *n* : a hoarse harsh cry or sound (as of a frog)

croak·er \'krō-kər\ *n* **1 :** an animal (as a frog) that croaks **2 :** any of various fishes that produce croaking or grunting noises

Croat \'krōt, 'krō-ˌat\ *n* : CROATIAN — **Croat** *adj*

Cro·a·tian \krō-'ā-shən\ *n* **1 :** a native or inhabitant of Croatia **2 :** a south Slavic language spoken by the Croatian people — **Croatian** *adj*

[1]**cro·chet** \krō-'shā\ *n* : needlework consisting of interlocked looped stitches formed with a single thread and a hooked needle [French, from Medieval French, from *croche* "hook," of Scandinavian origin]

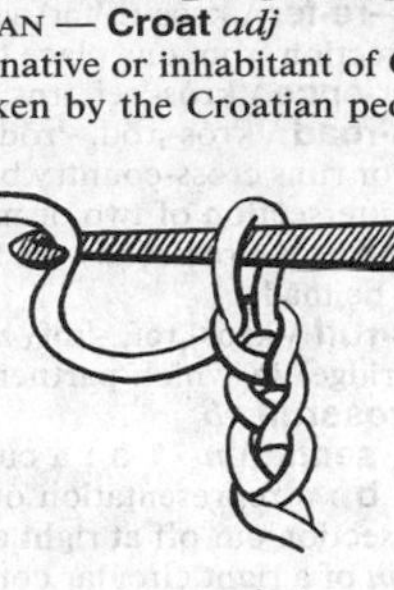
crochet

[2]**crochet** *vb* : to make of or work with crochet — **cro·chet·er** \-'shā-ər\ *n*

[1]**crock** \'kräk\ *n* : a thick earthenware pot or jar [Old English *crocc*]

[2]**crock** *n* : one that is broken down, disabled, or impaired [Middle English *crok,* perhaps of Low German origin]

crock·ery \'kräk-rē, -ə-rē\ *n* : EARTHENWARE

Crock–Pot \'kräk-ˌpät\ *trademark* — used for an electric cooking pot

croc·o·dile \'kräk-ə-ˌdīl\ *n* **1 :** any of several large thick-skinned long-bodied aquatic reptiles of tropical and subtropical waters; *also* : CROCODILIAN — compare ALLIGATOR **2 :** the skin or hide of a crocodile [Latin *crocodilus,* from Greek *krokodilos* "lizard, crocodile," from *krokē* "pebble" + *drilos* "worm"]

crocodile tears *n pl* : false or pretended tears : insincere sorrow [from the ancient belief that crocodiles weep in sympathy for their victims]

croc·o·dil·ian \ˌkräk-ə-'dil-ē-ən, -'dil-yən\ *n* : any of an order (Crocodylia) of reptiles including the crocodiles, alligators, caimans, and related extinct forms — **crocodilian** *adj*

cro·cus \'krō-kəs\ *n, pl* **cro·cus·es 1** *pl also* **crocus** *or* **cro·ci** \-ˌkē, -ˌkī, -ˌsī\ : any of a genus of small herbs related to the irises with showy solitary long-tubed flowers and slender linear leaves **2 :** SAFFRON 1b [Latin, "saffron," from Greek *krokos,* of Semitic origin]

croft \'krȯft\ *n* **1** *chiefly British* : a small enclosed field **2** *chiefly British* : a small farm worked by a tenant [Old English] — **croft·er** *n, chiefly British*

crois·sant \krə-ˌwä-'sän, ˌkwä-\ *n, pl* **croissants** \-'sän, -'sänz\ : a flaky rich crescent-shaped roll [French, literally, "crescent," from Medieval French *creissant*]

Cro–Mag·non \krō-'mag-nən, -'man-yən\ *n* : any of a race of tall erect people that lived approximately 35,000 to 10,000 years ago and are often placed in the same species as present-day human beings [*Cro-Magnon,* a cave near Les Eyzies, France] — **Cro–Magnon** *adj*

crom·lech \'kräm-ˌlek\ *n* **1 :** DOLMEN **2 :** a circle of monoliths enclosing a dolmen [Welsh, literally, "bent stone"]

crone \'krōn\ *n* : HAG 1 [Middle English, a term of abuse, from Medieval French *caroine,* literally, "carrion"]

cro·ny \'krō-nē\ *n, pl* **cronies :** a close friend especially of long standing : PAL [perhaps from Greek *chronios* "long-lasting," from *chronos* "time"]

[1]**crook** \'krůk\ *n* **1 :** an implement having a bent or hooked form: as **a :** a shepherd's staff **b :** CROSIER **2 :** a dishonest person; *esp* : CRIMINAL **3 :** BEND 2, CURVE **4 :** a hook-shaped, curved, or bent part [Old Norse *krōkr* "hook"]

[2]**crook** *vb* : to turn from a straight line : BEND, CURVE

crook·ed \'krůk-əd\ *adj* **1 :** having a crook or curve : BENT **2 :** DISHONEST — **crook·ed·ly** *adv* — **crook·ed·ness** *n*

synonyms CROOKED, AWRY, ASKEW mean not straight. CROOKED applies to what is itself not straight but curving, bent, or twisted ⟨a *crooked* road⟩. AWRY applies to what is out of a straight line in relation to something else ⟨the picture on the wall is *awry*⟩. ASKEW implies having a decided slant away from a straight course ⟨his tie is *askew*⟩.

crook·neck \'krůk-ˌnek\ *n* : a squash with a long curved neck

croon \'krün\ *vb* : to hum or sing in a gentle murmuring way ⟨*croon* a lullaby⟩ [Dutch *cronen* "to bellow"] — **croon** *n* — **croon·er** *n*

[1]**crop** \'kräp\ *n* **1 :** the stock or handle of a whip; *also* : a riding whip with a short straight stock and a loop **2 :** a pouched enlargement of the gullet of a bird or insect that receives food and prepares it for digestion **3 a :** an earmark on an animal; *esp* : one made by removing the upper part of the ear **b :** a close haircut **4 a :** a plant or animal or plant or animal product that can be grown and harvested **b :** the product or yield especially of a harvested crop **c :** BATCH 3, LOT ⟨a new *crop* of students⟩ [Old English *cropp* "craw, cluster, head of a plant"]

[2]**crop** *vb* **cropped; crop·ping 1 a :** to remove the upper or outer parts of ⟨*crop* a hedge⟩ ⟨*crop* a dog's ears⟩ **b :** to cut off short : CLIP ⟨*crop* a photograph⟩ **2 a :** to cause (land) to bear a crop; *also* : to grow as a crop **b :** HARVEST ⟨*crop* trout⟩ **3 :** to feed by cropping something ⟨sheep *cropping* in the meadow⟩ **4 :** to yield or make a crop **5 :** to appear unexpectedly or casually ⟨problems *crop* up daily⟩

crop duster *n* : a person who sprays crops from an airplane especially with insecticide or fungicide; *also* : the airplane used for such spraying

crop·land \'kräp-ˌland\ *n* : land that is suited to or used for the production of plant crops

[1]**crop·per** \'kräp-ər\ *n* : one that raises crops; *esp* : SHARECROPPER

[2]**cropper** *n* **1 :** a severe fall **2 :** a sudden or violent failure or collapse [probably from English dialect *crop* "neck," from [1]*crop*]

crop rotation *n* : the practice of growing different crops in succession on the same land chiefly to preserve the capacity of the soil to produce crops

cro·quet \krō-'kā\ *n* : a game in which the players use mallets to drive wooden balls through a series of hoops set in the ground [probably from obsolete French, "sharp blow," from *croquer*]

cro·quette \krō-'ket\ *n* : a small roll or ball of minced meat, fish, or vegetables fried in deep fat [French, from *croquer* "to crunch"]

cro·sier *or* **cro·zier** \'krō-zhər\ *n* : a staff resembling a shepherd's crook carried by bishops and abbots as a symbol of office [Medieval French *crosser* "crosier bearer," from *crosse* "crosier," of Germanic origin]

[1]**cross** \'krȯs\ *n* **1 a :** a structure consisting of an upright beam and a crossbar used especially by the ancient Romans for execution **b** *often cap* : the cross on which Jesus was crucified **2 :** an affliction that tries one's virtue, steadfastness, or patience **3 :** a cruciform sign made to invoke the blessing of Christ especially by touching the forehead, breast, and shoulders **4 :** a cross-shaped mark or structure; *esp* : one used as a Christian emblem **5 :** the intersection of two ways or lines : CROSSING **6 a :** an act of crossing unlike individuals **b :** a crossbred individual or kind **7 :** a punch thrown over an opponent's lead in boxing [Old English, derived from Latin *crux*]

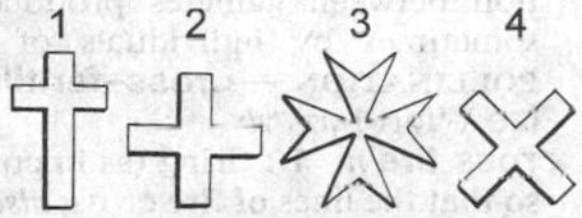

cross 4: *1* Latin, *2* Greek, *3* Maltese, *4* Saint Andrew's

[2]**cross** *vb* **1 a :** to lie or be located across **b :** INTERSECT ⟨where two roads *cross*⟩ **2 :** to make the sign of the cross on or over **3 :** to cancel by marking a cross on or drawing a line through **4 :** to place or fold crosswise one over the other ⟨*cross* the arms⟩ **5 a :** to run counter to : OPPOSE ⟨gets angry when *crossed*⟩ **b :** to turn against : BETRAY **6 a :** to extend across : TRAVERSE ⟨a highway *crossing* the state⟩ **b :** to go from one side to the other of **7 :** to draw a line across ⟨*cross* a *t*⟩ **8 :** INTERBREED **9 :** to meet and pass on the way — **cross paths** : to meet especially by chance

[3]**cross** *adj* **1 :** lying or moving across ⟨*cross* traffic⟩ **2 :** running counter : OPPOSITE ⟨*cross* winds⟩ **3 :** marked by bad temper : GRUMPY — **cross·ly** *adv* — **cross·ness** *n*

cross·bar \'krȯs-ˌbär\ *n* : a transverse bar or stripe

cross·bill \-ˌbil\ *n* : any of a genus of finches with curved mandibles that cross each other when the bill is closed

\ə\ **abut**	\au̇\ **out**	\i\ **tip**	\ȯ\ **saw**	\u̇\ **foot**
\ər\ **further**	\ch\ **chin**	\ī\ **life**	\ȯi\ **coin**	\y\ **yet**
\a\ **mat**	\e\ **pet**	\j\ **job**	\th\ **thin**	\yü\ **few**
\ā\ **take**	\ē\ **easy**	\ng\ **sing**	\th\ **this**	\yu̇\ **cure**
\ä\ **cot, cart**	\g\ **go**	\ō\ **bone**	\ü\ **food**	\zh\ **vision**

cross·bones \-ˌbōnz\ *n pl* : two leg or arm bones placed or depicted crosswise — compare SKULL AND CROSSBONES

cross·bow \-ˌbō\ *n* : a weapon that consists of a short bow mounted crosswise near the end of a wooden stock and that shoots stones or short arrows

cross·bow·man \-mən\ *n, pl* **-men** \-mən\ : a person who uses a crossbow

cross·bred \ˈkrȯs-ˈbred\ *adj* : HYBRID; *esp* : produced by interbreeding two pure but different breeds, strains, or varieties — **cross·bred** \-ˌbred\ *n*

[1]**cross·breed** \-ˌbrēd, -ˈbrēd\ *vb* **1** : HYBRIDIZE; *esp* : to interbreed two varieties or breeds of the same species **2** : to engage in or undergo crossbreeding

[2]**cross·breed** \-ˌbrēd\ *n* : HYBRID 1

cross–coun·try \-ˈkən-trē\ *adj* **1** : extending across a country ⟨a *cross-country* tour⟩ **2** : proceeding over countryside and not by roads **3** : of or relating to racing over the countryside — **cross–country** *adv*

cross·cur·rent \-ˈkər-ənt, -ˈkə-rənt\ *n* **1** : a current running counter to another **2** : a conflicting tendency

[1]**cross·cut** \-ˌkət, -ˈkət\ *vt* **-cut; -cut·ting** **1** : to cut with a crosscut saw **2** : to cut, go, or move across or through

[2]**crosscut** *adj* **1** : made or used for crosscutting ⟨a saw with *crosscut* teeth⟩ **2** : cut across or transversely ⟨a *crosscut* incision⟩

[3]**cross·cut** \-ˌkət\ *n* : something (as a walk) that cuts across or through ⟨took a *crosscut* through the park⟩

crosscut saw *n* : a saw designed chiefly to cut across the grain of wood

cross–dress·ing \ˈkrȯs-ˌdres-iŋ\ *n* : the wearing of clothes designed for the opposite sex — **cross–dress·er** \-ˌdres-ər\ *n*

crosse \ˈkrȯs\ *n* : the stick with a small net at one end that is used in lacrosse [French, literally, "crosier"]

cross–ex·am·i·na·tion \ˌkrȯs-ig-ˌzam-ə-ˈnā-shən\ *n* : the questioning of a witness called by the opposing party to a legal action in order to check or discredit his or her testimony — **cross–ex·am·ine** \-ˈzam-ən\ *vt* — **cross–ex·am·in·er** *n*

cross–eye \ˈkrȯs-ˌī\ *n* **1** : an abnormality in which the eye turns inward toward the nose **2** *pl* : eyes affected with cross-eye — **cross–eyed** \-ˈīd\ *adj*

cross–fer·til·i·za·tion \ˈkrȯs-ˌfərt-l-ə-ˈzā-shən\ *n* **1** : fertilization between gametes produced by separate individuals or sometimes by individuals of different kinds **2** : CROSS-POLLINATION — **cross–fer·tile** \-ˈfərt-l\ *adj* — **cross–fer·til·ize** \-ˈfərt-l-ˌīz\ *vb*

cross fire *n* **1** : firing (as in combat) from two or more points so that the lines of fire cross; *also* : a situation in which forces of opposing factions meet, cross, or clash **2** : rapid or heated interchange (as of words)

cross–grained \ˈkrȯs-ˈgrānd\ *adj* **1** : having the grain or fibers running diagonally, transversely, or irregularly **2** : difficult to deal with : CONTRARY

cross hair *n* : one of the fine wires or threads in the focus of the eyepiece of an optical instrument used as a reference line

cross·hatch \ˈkrȯs-ˌhach\ *vt* : to mark with a series of parallel lines that cross — **crosshatch** *n* — **cross–hatch·ing** *n*

cross·ing \ˈkrȯ-siŋ\ *n* **1 a** : the act or action of one that crosses **b** : a traversing or going across ⟨a channel *crossing*⟩ **c** : the act or process of interbreeding or hybridizing **2** : a place or structure (as on a street or over a river) where pedestrians or vehicles cross **3** : a point of intersection (as of streets)

cross·ing–over \ˌkrȯ-siŋ-ˈō-vər\ *n* : an exchange of genes or segments between associated parts of homologous chromosomes in synapsis during meiosis

cross–legged \ˈkrȯs-ˈleg-əd, -ˈlegd\ *adv or adj* **1** : with legs crossed and knees spread wide **2** : with one leg placed over and across the other

cross multiply *vb* : to multiply the numerator of each side of a proportion by the denominator of the other side — **cross multiplication** *n*

cross·over \ˈkrȯs-ˌō-vər\ *n* **1** : CROSSING 2 **2** : an instance or product of genetic crossing-over

cross·piece \ˈkrȯs-ˌpēs\ *n* : a horizontal member (as of a structure)

cross–pol·li·nate \-ˈpäl-ə-ˌnāt\ *vt* : to subject to cross-pollination

cross–pol·li·na·tion \ˌkrȯs-ˌpäl-ə-ˈnā-shən\ *n* : the transfer of pollen from one flower to the stigma of another

cross product *n* : either of the two products obtained by multiplying together the two means or the two extremes of a proportion

cross–pur·pose \ˈkrȯs-ˈpər-pəs\ *n* : an opposing or conflicting purpose ⟨working at *cross-purposes*⟩

cross–ques·tion \-ˈkwes-chən\ *vt* : to subject to close questioning; *esp* : CROSS-EXAMINE — **cross–question** *n*

cross–re·fer \ˌkrȯs-ri-ˈfər\ *vt* : to refer (a reader) by a notation or direction from one place to another (as in a book) — **cross–ref·er·ence** \ˈkrȯs-ˈref-ərns, -ˈref-rəns, -ə-rəns\ *n*

cross·road \ˈkrȯs-ˌrōd, -ˈrōd\ *n* **1** : a road that crosses a main road or runs cross-country between main roads **2** *usually pl* **a** : an intersection of two or more roads **b** : a small community located at a crossroads **3** : a crucial point where a decision must be made

cross·ruff \ˈkrȯs-ˌrəf, -ˈrəf\ *n* : a series of plays in a card game (as bridge) in which partners alternately trump different suits — **crossruff** *vb*

cross section *n* **1 a** : a cutting made across something (as a log) **b** : a representation of a cutting made across something **c** : a section cut off at right angles to an axis by a plane ⟨a *cross section* of a right circular cone is a circle⟩ **2** : a number of persons or things selected to represent the general nature of a group ⟨a *cross section* of society⟩ — **cross–sec·tion·al** \ˈkrȯs-ˈsek-shnəl, -shən-l\ *adj*

cross–stitch \ˈkrȯs-ˌstich\ *n* **1** : a needlework stitch that forms an X **2** : work done with cross-stitch — **cross–stitch** *vb*

cross·town \ˈkrȯs-ˌtau̇n, -ˈtau̇n\ *adj* **1** : situated at opposite points of a town **2** : extending or running across a town ⟨a *crosstown* street⟩ — **crosstown** *adv*

cross–train \ˈkrȯs-ˌtrān\ *vb* **1** : to engage in various sports or exercises especially for well-rounded health and muscular development **2** : to train (an employee) to do more than one specific job — **cross–train·ing** *n*

cross–train·er \ˈkrȯs-ˌtrā-nər\ *n* : a sports shoe designed for cross-training

cross·trees \ˈkrȯs-ˌtrēz\ *n pl* : two horizontal crosspieces near the top of a ship's mast to spread apart the upper ropes that support the mast

cross·walk \ˈkrȯs-ˌwȯk\ *n* : a specially paved or marked path for pedestrians crossing a street or road

cross·way \-ˌwā\ *n* : CROSSROAD 2a — often used in plural

cross·ways \-ˌwāz\ *adv* : CROSSWISE 2, DIAGONALLY

[1]**cross·wise** \-ˌwīz\ *adv* **1** *archaic* : in the form of a cross **2** : so as to cross something : ACROSS

[2]**crosswise** *adj* : extended or lying across

cross·word puzzle \ˈkrȯs-ˌwərd-\ *n* : a puzzle in which words are filled into a pattern of numbered squares in answer to similarly numbered clues and in such a way that they read across and down

crotch \ˈkräch\ *n* **1** : an angle formed by the parting of two branches or parts **2** : the region of the human body between the legs where the legs join the trunk [probably alteration of *crutch*]

crotch·et \ˈkräch-ət\ *n* : a peculiar opinion or habit [Medieval French *crochet* "small hook," from *croche* "hook"] ***synonyms*** see CAPRICE

crotch·ety \ˈkräch-ət-ē\ *adj* : marked by or given to whims or ill temper — **crotch·et·i·ness** *n*

cro·ton \ˈkrōt-n\ *n* : any of several herbs and shrubs of the spurge family; *esp* : an Asian plant yielding an oil used as a strong purgative [Greek *krotōn* "castor-oil plant"]

crouch \ˈkrau̇ch\ *vb* **1** : to lower the body especially by bending the legs **2** : to bend or bow servilely : CRINGE [Middle English *crouchen*] — **crouch** *n*

[1]**croup** \ˈkrüp\ *n* : the rump of a four-footed animal [Medieval French *croupe,* of Germanic origin]

[2]**croup** *n* : a laryngitis especially of infants marked by episodes of difficult breathing and a hoarse metallic cough [English dialect *croup* "to cry hoarsely, cough"] — **croupy** \-pē\ *adj*

crou·pi·er \ˈkrü-pē-ər, -pē-ˌā\ *n* : an employee of a gambling casino who collects and pays bets at a gaming table [French, literally, "rider on the croup of a horse"]

crou·ton \ˈkrü-ˌtän, krü-ˈ\ *n* : a small crisp cube of bread [French *croûton* "small crust," from *croûte* "crust"]

[1]**crow** \ˈkrō\ *n* **1** : any of various large usually entirely glossy black birds related to the jays **2** : CROWBAR **3** : a member of an American Indian people of southeastern Montana **4** : HUMBLE PIE ⟨the braggart was forced to eat *crow*⟩ [Old English *crāwe*] — **as the crow flies** : in a straight line

1crow 1

2crow *vi* **crowed** \ˈkrōd\ *also in sense 1 chiefly British* **crew** \ˈkrü\; **crow·ing** **1 :** to utter the characteristic loud shrill cry of a cock or a similar sound **2 :** to utter a sound expressive of pleasure **3 a :** to exult gloatingly especially over the distress of another **b :** to brag exultantly or blatantly [Old English *crāwan*]

3crow *n* **1 :** the cry of a cock or a similar loud shrill sound **2 :** a triumphant cry

crow·bar \ˈkrō-ˌbär\ *n* **:** a metal bar usually wedge-shaped at the working end for use as a pry or lever

crow·ber·ry \ˈkrō-ˌber-ē\ *n* **1 :** an evergreen shrub of arctic and alpine regions with an edible tasteless black berry **2 :** the fruit of a crowberry

1crowd \ˈkrau̇d\ *vb* **1 :** to press onward **:** HURRY **2 :** to press close ⟨*crowd* around the speaker⟩ **3 :** to collect in numbers **4 :** to fill by pressing or thronging together **:** PACK ⟨*crowd* a room⟩ ⟨*crowd* children into a bus⟩ [Old English *crūdan*]

2crowd *n* **1 :** a large number of persons collected into a body without order **2 :** the great body of the people **:** POPULACE ⟨books that appeal to the *crowd*⟩ **3 :** a large number of things close together **4 :** a group of people having a common interest ⟨in with the wrong *crowd*⟩ ***synonyms*** see MULTITUDE

crow·foot \ˈkrō-ˌfu̇t\ *n, pl* **crow·feet** \-ˌfēt\ **1** *pl usually* **crowfoots :** any of numerous plants having leaves with cleft lobes; *esp* **:** BUTTERCUP **2 :** CROW'S-FOOT 1 — usually used in plural

1crown \ˈkrau̇n\ *n* **1 :** a wreath or band for the head; *esp* **:** one worn as a mark of victory or honor **2 :** a royal headdress **:** DIADEM **3 :** the highest part: as **a :** the topmost part of the skull or head **b :** the summit of a mountain **c :** the head of foliage of a tree or shrub **d :** the part of a hat covering the crown of the head **e :** the part of a tooth external to the gum or an artificial substitute for this **4 :** something (as the corona of a flower) resembling a crown **5** *often cap* **a** (1) **:** imperial or regal power **:** SOVEREIGNTY (2) **:** the government under a constitutional monarchy **b :** MONARCH 1 **6 :** the highest point of development **:** CULMINATION **7 a :** a former British monetary unit equal to five shillings **b :** any of several coins representing this unit **8 a :** the region of a seed plant in which stem and root merge **b :** the thick arching end of the shank of an anchor where the arms join it [Medieval French *corone,* from Latin *corona* "wreath, crown," from Greek *korōnē* "culmination, something curved like a crow's beak," literally, "crow"] — **crown** *adj, often cap* — **crowned** \ˈkrau̇nd\ *adj*

2crown *vt* **1 a :** to place a crown on; *esp* **:** to invest with regal dignity and power **b :** to recognize officially as ⟨was *crowned* champion⟩ **2 :** IMBUE 1, ENDOW ⟨*crowned* with wisdom⟩ **3 :** SURMOUNT 1, TOP; *esp* **:** to top (a checker) with a checker to make a king **4 :** to bring to a successful conclusion **5 :** to put an artificial crown upon (a tooth) **6** *of a forest fire* **:** to burn rapidly through the tops of trees

crown colony *n, often cap both Cs* **:** a British colony

crown glass *n* **:** a very clear glass with a low refractive index that is used for optical instruments

crown prince *n* **:** the heir apparent to a crown or throne

crown princess *n* **1 :** the wife of a crown prince **2 :** a woman who is an heir apparent to a crown or throne

crow's–foot \ˈkrōz-ˌfu̇t\ *n, pl* **crow's–feet** \-ˌfēt\ **1 :** any of the wrinkles around the outer corners of the eyes — usually used in plural **2 :** CROWFOOT 1

crow's nest *n* **:** a partly enclosed platform high on a ship's mast for a lookout; *also* **:** any similar lookout

crozier *variant of* CROSIER

CRT \ˌsē-ˌär-ˈtē\ *n, pl* **CRTs** *or* **CRT's :** CATHODE-RAY TUBE; *also* **:** the display device containing a cathode-ray tube

cruces *plural of* CRUX

cru·cial \ˈkrü-shəl\ *adj* **:** of the utmost importance ⟨a *crucial* moment in the game⟩; *esp* **:** DECISIVE 1 ⟨this experiment would be *crucial*⟩ [French, literally, "cruciform," from Latin *cruc-, crux* "cross"] — **cru·cial·ly** *adv*

cru·ci·ble \ˈkrü-sə-bəl\ *n* **1 :** a pot made of a heat-resistant material and used for holding a substance for treatment in a process that requires high temperature **2 :** a severe test [Medieval Latin *crucibulum,* "earthen pot for melting metals"]

cru·ci·fer \ˈkrü-sə-fər\ *n* **1 :** one who carries a cross especially at the head of a church procession **2 :** any of a family of plants that produce flowers with four petals in the shape of a cross and includes the cabbage, turnip, and mustard [Late Latin, from Latin *crux* "cross" + *-fer* "-fer"] — **cru·cif·er·ous** \krü-ˈsif-rəs, -ə-rəs\ *adj*

cru·ci·fix \ˈkrü-sə-ˌfiks\ *n* **:** a representation of Christ on the cross [Late Latin *crucifixus* "the crucified Christ," from *crucifigere* "to crucify," from Latin *cruc-, crux* "cross" + *figere* "to fasten, fix"]

cru·ci·fix·ion \ˌkrü-sə-ˈfik-shən\ *n* **:** an act of crucifying; *esp, cap* **:** the crucifying of Christ

cru·ci·form \ˈkrü-sə-ˌfȯrm\ *adj* **:** forming or arranged in a cross — **cru·ci·form·ly** *adv*

cru·ci·fy \ˈkrü-sə-ˌfī\ *vt* **-fied; -fy·ing** **1 :** to put to death by nailing or binding the hands and feet to a cross **2 :** to treat cruelly **:** TORTURE, PERSECUTE — **cru·ci·fi·er** \-ˌfī-ər\ *n*

crud \ˈkrəd\ *n* **1 :** a deposit of something filthy, greasy, or sticky ⟨machinery covered with *crud*⟩ **2 :** something disagreeable or contemptible [Middle English *curd, crudd* "curd"]

1crude \ˈkrüd\ *adj* **1 :** existing in a natural state and unaltered by processing **:** not refined ⟨*crude* oil⟩ **2 :** lacking refinement, good manners, or tact; *esp* **:** marked by grossness or vulgarity **3 :** rough in plan or execution **:** RUDE ⟨a *crude* shelter⟩ **4 :** not concealed or glossed over **:** BARE ⟨the *crude* facts⟩ [Latin *crudus* "raw"] — **crude·ly** *adv* — **crude·ness** *n* — **cru·di·ty** \ˈkrüd-ət-ē\ *n*

2crude *n* **:** a substance in its natural unprocessed state; *esp* **:** unrefined petroleum

cru·el \ˈkrü-el\ *adj* **cru·el·er** *or* **cru·el·ler; cru·el·est** *or* **cru·el·lest** **1 :** disposed to inflict pain **2 a :** causing or helping to cause injury, grief, or pain **b :** devoid of leniency **:** MERCILESS [Medieval French, from Latin *crudelis,* from *crudus* "raw"] — **cru·el·ly** \ˈkrü-ə-lē\ *adv* — **cru·el·ness** *n*

cru·el·ty \ˈkrü-əl-tē\ *n, pl* **-ties** **1 :** the quality or state of being cruel **2 a :** a cruel action **b :** inhuman treatment

cru·el·ty–free \-ˈfrē\ *adj* **:** developed or produced without inhumane testing on animals ⟨*cruelty-free* cosmetics⟩

cru·et \ˈkrü-ət\ *n* **:** a small glass bottle for holding vinegar, oil, or sauce [Medieval French, from *crue* "pitcher," of Germanic origin]

1cruise \ˈkrüz\ *vb* **1 :** to sail about touching at a series of ports **2 :** to travel for the sake of traveling **3 :** to go about the streets at random but on the lookout for possible developments **4 :** to travel at an efficient operating speed ⟨the *cruising* speed of an airplane⟩ **5 :** to travel over or about [Dutch *kruisen* "to make a cross, cruise," derived from Latin *crux* "cross"]

2cruise *n* **:** an act or an instance of cruising

cruis·er \ˈkrü-zər\ *n* **1 :** a boat or vehicle that cruises; *esp* **:** SQUAD CAR **2 :** a warship intermediate in size between a battleship and a destroyer **3 :** a motorboat with arrangements necessary for living aboard — called also *cabin cruiser*

crul·ler \ˈkrəl-ər\ *n* **1 :** a small sweet cake formed in a twisted strip and fried in deep fat **2** *Northern & Midland* **:** a doughnut made without yeast [Dutch *krulle,* a twisted cake, from *krul* "curly"]

1crumb \ˈkrəm\ *n* **1 :** a small fragment especially of something baked (as bread) **2 :** PARTICLE 2 [Old English *cruma*]

2crumb *vt* **1 :** to break into crumbs **:** CRUMBLE **2 :** to cover or thicken with crumbs ⟨*crumb* a chicken leg⟩ **3 :** to remove crumbs from ⟨*crumb* a table⟩

crum·ble \ˈkrəm-bəl\ *vb* **crum·bled; crum·bling** \-bə-ling, -bling\ **1 :** to break into small pieces **:** DISINTEGRATE ⟨*crumble* bread⟩ ⟨the wall *crumbled*⟩ **2 :** to break down completely **:** COLLAPSE ⟨relationships *crumble*⟩ [derived from Old English *cruma* "crumb"]

crum·bly \-bə-lē, -blē\ *adj* **crum·bli·er; -est :** easily crumbled

crum·my \ˈkrəm-ē\ *adj* **crum·mi·er; -est :** very poor or inferior **:** LOUSY [Middle English *crumme* "crumbly"]

crum·pet \ˈkrəm-pət\ *n* **:** a small round cake made of unsweetened batter cooked on a griddle [perhaps from Middle English *crompid cake,* "wafer," literally, "curled-up cake"]

1crum·ple \ˈkrem-pəl\ *vb* **crum·pled; crum·pling** \-pə-ling,

\ə\ **abut**	\au̇\ **out**	\i\ **tip**	\ȯ\ **saw**	\u̇\ **foot**
\ər\ **further**	\ch\ **chin**	\ī\ **life**	\ȯi\ **coin**	\y\ **yet**
\a\ **mat**	\e\ **pet**	\j\ **job**	\th\ **thin**	\yü\ **few**
\ā\ **take**	\ē\ **easy**	\ng\ **sing**	\t͟h\ **this**	\yu̇\ **cure**
\ä\ **cot, cart**	\g\ **go**	\ō\ **bone**	\ü\ **food**	\zh\ **vision**

-pling\ **1 :** to press, bend, or crush out of shape **2 :** to become crumpled **3 :** to cause the collapse of or undergo collapse [Middle English *crumpen* "to curve, curl up," from *crump* "crooked," from Old English]

[2]**crumple** *n* **:** a wrinkle or crease made by crumpling

[1]**crunch** \'krənch\ *vb* **1 :** to chew, grind, or press with a crushing or grinding noise **2 a :** CRISIS 3 **b :** SHORTAGE ⟨an energy *crunch*⟩ **3 :** a conditioning exercise performed in a supine position by raising and lowering the trunk without reaching a sitting position and without lifting the feet [probably of imitative origin]

[2]**crunch** *n* **1 :** an act or sound of crunching **2 :** to make one's way with a crushing sound — **crunchy** \'krən-chē\ *adj*

crup·per \'krəp-ər, 'krůp-\ *n* **1 :** a leather loop passing under a horse's tail and buckled to the saddle of the harness **2 :** the rump of a horse **:** CROUP [Medieval French *cruper,* from *croupe* "croup"]

[1]**cru·sade** \krü-'sād\ *n* **1** *cap* **:** any of the military expeditions undertaken by Christian powers in the 11th, 12th, and 13th centuries to win the Holy Land from the Muslims **2 :** a campaign undertaken with zeal and enthusiasm ⟨a *crusade* against corruption⟩ [Middle French *croisade* and Spanish *cruzada,* both derived from Latin *crux* "cross"]

[2]**crusade** *vi* **:** to engage in a crusade — **cru·sad·er** *n*

cruse \'krüz, 'krüs\ *n* **:** a small vessel (as a jar or pot) for holding a liquid (as water or oil) [Middle English]

[1]**crush** \'krəsh\ *vb* **1 a :** to squeeze or force by pressure so as to alter or destroy structure **b :** to squeeze together into a mass **2 :** to embrace strongly **:** HUG **3 :** to reduce to particles by pounding or grinding **4 a :** SUPPRESS 1 ⟨*crush* a rebellion⟩ **b :** to oppress or burden seriously ⟨a *crushing* burden of guilt⟩ **c :** to subdue completely **:** DEFEAT **5 :** CROWD 4, PUSH ⟨people *crushed* into an elevator⟩ **6 :** to become crushed [Medieval French *croissir, croistre,* of Germanic origin] — **crush·er** *n*

[2]**crush** *n* **1 :** an act of crushing **2 :** a tightly packed crowd **3 :** an intense infatuation; *also* **:** the object of infatuation

crust \'krəst\ *n* **1 a :** the hardened exterior surface of bread **b :** a piece of dry hard bread **2 :** the pastry portion of a pie **3 a :** a hard external covering or surface layer ⟨a *crust* of snow⟩ **b :** the outer part of the earth composed essentially of crystalline rocks **c :** a deposit of dried secretions or exudate ⟨wiped the *crust* from the corner of her eye⟩; *also* **:** SCAB 2 [Latin *crusta*] — **crust** *vb*

crus·ta·cea \ˌkrəs-'tā-shē-ə, -shə\ *n pl* **:** arthropods that are crustaceans

crus·ta·cean \ˌkrəs-'tā-shən\ *n* **:** any of a large class (Crustacea) of mostly aquatic arthropods (as lobsters, shrimps, crabs, wood lice, water fleas, and barnacles) that have an exoskeleton of chitin or of a compound of chitin and calcium [derived from Latin *crusta* "crust, shell"] — **crustacean** *adj*

crust·al \'krəst-l\ *adj* **:** relating to a crust and especially to that of the earth or the moon

crust·ose \'krəs-ˌtōs\ *adj* **:** forming a firm thin crust ⟨*crustose* lichens⟩ — compare FOLIOSE, FRUTICOSE

crusty \'krəs-tē\ *adj* **crust·i·er; -est 1 :** having or being a crust ⟨*crusty* bread⟩ **2 :** giving an effect of surly incivility — **crust·i·ly** \-tə-lē\ *adv* — **crust·i·ness** \-tē-nəs\ *n*

crutch \'krəch\ *n* **1 :** a support typically fitting under the armpit for use by a disabled or injured person in walking **2 :** a usually forked support [Old English *crycc*]

crux \'krəks, 'krůks\ *n, pl* **crux·es** *also* **cru·ces** \'krü-ˌsēz\ **1 a :** a puzzling or difficult problem **:** an unsolved question **b :** a crucial or critical point ⟨the *crux* of the problem⟩ **2 :** a main or central feature (as of an argument) [Latin, "cross, torture"]

cru·zei·ro \krü-'zeər-ō, -ü\ *n, pl* **-ros :** a former basic monetary unit of Brazil [Portuguese]

[1]**cry** \'krī\ *vb* **cried; cry·ing 1 :** to call loudly **:** SHOUT **2 :** WEEP 1, SOB **3 :** to utter a characteristic sound or call **4 :** BESEECH, BEG **5 :** to proclaim publicly **:** call out [Medieval French *crier,* from Latin *quiritare* "to make a public outcry," perhaps from *Quirit-, Quiris* "Roman citizen"] — **cry havoc :** to sound an alarm — **cry over spilled milk :** to express vain regrets over something that cannot be recovered or undone — **cry wolf :** to give alarm unnecessarily

[2]**cry** *n, pl* **cries 1 :** a loud call or shout (as of pain, fear, or joy) **2 :** APPEAL ⟨the *cries* of the poor⟩ **3 :** a fit of weeping **4 :** the characteristic sound uttered by an animal (as a bird) **5 :** SLOGAN, WATCHWORD **6 a :** a pack of hounds **b** (1) **:** PURSUIT — used in the phrase *in full cry* ⟨hounds in full *cry*⟩ (2) **:** a peak of activity or excitement ⟨a campaign in full *cry*⟩

cry·ba·by \'krī-ˌbā-bē\ *n* **:** one who cries or complains easily or often

cry down *vt* **:** BELITTLE, DISPARAGE

cry·ing \'krī-ing\ *adj* **1 :** calling for attention and correction ⟨a *crying* need⟩ **2 :** NOTORIOUS ⟨a *crying* shame⟩

cryo·gen·ic \ˌkrī-ə-'jen-ik\ *adj* **1 :** of, relating to, being, or producing extremely low temperatures **2 :** requiring or involving the use of a cryogenic temperature

cryo·gen·ics \ˌkrī-ə-'jen-iks\ *n* **:** a branch of physics that relates to the production and effects of very low temperatures [Greek *kryos* "cold, freezing"]

cryo·lite \'krī-ə-ˌlīt\ *n* **:** a mineral consisting of sodium, aluminum, and fluorine found especially in Greenland and used in making aluminum

cry·on·ics \krī-'än-iks\ *n* **:** the practice of freezing a person who has died of a disease in the hopes of restoring life at some future time when a cure has been developed [Greek *kryos* cold + *-onics* (as in *byonics*)]

crypt \'kript\ *n* **1 :** an underground vault or room; *esp* **:** one under the floor of a church used as a burial place **2 :** a simple gland, glandular pit, or recess **:** FOLLICLE [Latin *crypta,* from Greek *kryptē,* from *kryptos* "hidden," from *kryptein* "to hide"]

cryp·tic \'krip-tik\ *adj* **1 :** SECRET 1a, OCCULT **2 :** having or seeming to have a hidden meaning ⟨a *cryptic* remark⟩ **3 :** serving to conceal ⟨*cryptic* coloration in animals⟩ **4 :** employing cipher or code ⟨*cryptic* writing⟩ ***synonyms*** see OBSCURE — **cryp·ti·cal·ly** \-ti-kə-lē, -klē\ *adv*

cryp·to·gam \'krip-tə-ˌgam\ *n* **:** a plant or plantlike organism (as a fern, moss, alga, or fungus) reproducing by spores and not producing flowers or seed [derived from Greek *kryptos* "hidden" + *-gamia* "-gamy"] — **cryp·to·gam·ic** \ˌkrip-tə-'gam-ik\ *adj*

cryp·to·gram \'krip-tə-ˌgram\ *n* **:** a writing in cipher or code

cryp·to·graph \-ˌgraf\ *n* **:** CRYPTOGRAM — **cryp·to·graph·ic** \ˌkrip-tə-'graf-ik\ *adj* — **cryp·to·graph·i·cal·ly** \-'graf-i-kə-lē, -klē\ *adv*

cryp·tog·ra·phy \krip-'täg-rə-fē\ *n* **:** the enciphering and deciphering of messages in secret code — **cryp·tog·ra·pher** \-fər\ *n*

[1]**crys·tal** \'kris-tl\ *n* **1 :** quartz that is transparent or nearly so and that is either colorless or only slightly tinged **2 :** something resembling crystal in transparency and colorlessness **3 :** a body that is formed by the solidification of a substance or mixture and has a regularly repeating internal arrangement of its atoms and often external plane faces ⟨a *crystal* of quartz⟩ ⟨a snow *crystal*⟩ **4 :** a clear colorless glass of superior quality **5 :** the transparent cover over a watch or clock dial **6 :** methamphetamine in powdered and especially crystal form when used illegally **7 :** a crystalline material used in electronics (as in a radio receiver) [Medieval French *cristal,* from Latin *crystallum,* from Greek *krystallos* "ice, crystal"]

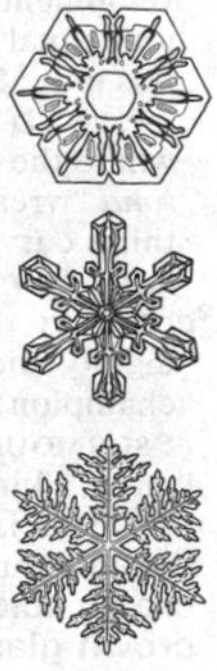

crystal 3

[2]**crystal** *adj* **1 :** consisting of or resembling crystal **:** CLEAR **2 :** relating to or using a crystal ⟨a *crystal* radio receiver⟩

crystal clear *adj* **:** perfectly or transparently clear ⟨*crystal clear* water⟩ ⟨her directions were *crystal clear*⟩

crys·tal·line \'kris-tə-lən\ *adj* **1 :** strikingly clear or sparkling **2 :** made of crystal or composed of crystals **3 :** of or relating to a crystal — **crys·tal·lin·i·ty** \ˌkris-tə-'lin-ət-ē\ *n*

crystalline lens *n* **:** the lens of the vertebrate eye

crys·tal·lize \'kris-tə-ˌlīz\ *vb* **1 :** to cause to form crystals or assume crystalline form **2 :** to give a definite form to ⟨try to *crystallize* your thoughts⟩ **3 :** to become crystallized — **crys·tal·liz·able** \-ˌlī-zə-bəl\ *adj* — **crys·tal·li·za·tion** \ˌkris-tə-lə-'zā-shən\ *n* — **crys·tal·liz·er** *n*

crys·tal·log·ra·phy \ˌkris-tə-'läg-rə-fē\ *n* **:** a science that deals with the form and structure of crystals — **crys·tal·log·ra·pher** \-fər\ *n* — **crys·tal·lo·graph·ic** \-tə-lō-'graf-ik\ *adj*

crys·tal·loid \'kris-tə-ˌlȯid\ *n* **:** a substance that forms a true solution and is capable of being crystallized

crystal set *n* **:** a radio receiver having a crystal for a detector and no vacuum tubes

C–sec·tion \'sē-ˌsek-shən\ *n* **:** CESAREAN SECTION

cteno·phore \'ten-ə-ˌfōr, -ˌfȯr\ *n* **:** any of a phylum (Ctenophora) of nearly globe-shaped marine animals that superficially resemble jellyfishes but swim by means of eight bands of ciliated plates — called also *comb jelly* [derived from Greek *kten-, kteis* "comb" + *pherein* "to carry"] — **cte·noph·o·ran** \tl-ˈnäf-ə-rən\ *adj or n*

CT scan \ˌsē-ˈtē-\ *n* : CAT SCAN

cub \ˈkəb\ *n* **1 a** : a young flesh-eating mammal (as a bear, fox, or lion) **b** : a young shark **2** : a young person **3** : APPRENTICE; *esp* : an inexperienced newspaper reporter [probably akin to *cob* ("lump, head, corncob")]

cub·by·hole \ˈkəb-ē-ˌhōl\ *n* : a snug or confined place (as for hiding or storing things) [obsolete English *cub* "pen," from Dutch *kub* "thatched roof"]

[1]**cube** \ˈkyüb\ *n* **1** : a regular solid that has six equal square sides **2** : the result of raising a number or expression to the third power ⟨the *cube* of 2 is 8⟩ [Latin *cubus,* from Greek *kybos*]

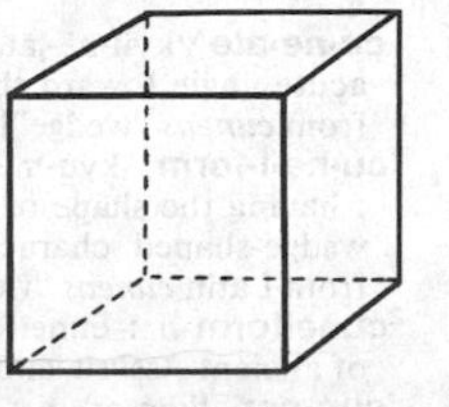
cube 1

[2]**cube** *vt* **1** : to raise to the third power ⟨2 *cubed* is 8⟩ **2** : to form or cut into cubes

cu·beb \ˈkyü-ˌbeb\ *n* : the dried unripe berry of a tropical shrub that is used as a spice [Medieval French *cubibe,* from Medieval Latin *cubeba,* from Arabic *kubāba*]

cube root *n* : a number whose cube is a given number ⟨the *cube root* of 27 is 3⟩

cu·bic \ˈkyü-bik\ *also* **cu·bi·cal** \ˈkyü-bi-kəl\ *adj* **1** : having the shape of a cube **2 a** : THREE-DIMENSIONAL **b** : having, being, or relating to volume; *esp* : being the volume of a cube whose edge is a specified unit ⟨a *cubic* centimeter⟩

cubic equation *n* : a polynomial equation in which the sum of the exponents of the variables in any term is no greater than three ⟨$x^3 + 2x^2y + 5xy^2 + 10y^3 + 6 = 0$ is a *cubic equation*⟩ — called also *cubic*

cu·bi·cle \ˈkyü-bi-kəl\ *n* **1** : a small partitioned compartment especially for sleeping **2** : a small partitioned space with a desk used for work in a business office or for studying [Latin *cubiculum,* from *cubare* "to lie, recline"]

cubic measure *n* : a unit (as a cubic inch or cubic centimeter) for measuring volume — see MEASURE table, METRIC SYSTEM table

cub·ism \ˈkyü-ˌbiz-əm\ *n* : an art form characterized by the abstraction of natural forms into fragmented geometric shapes — **cub·ist** \-bəst\ *adj or n*

cu·bit \ˈkyü-bət\ *n* : a unit of length based on the length of the forearm from the elbow to the tip of the middle finger and usually equal to about 18 inches (46 centimeters) [Latin *cubitum* "elbow, cubit"]

cu·boi·dal \kyü-ˈbȯid-l\ *adj* : somewhat cubical : made up of nearly cubical elements ⟨*cuboidal* epithelium⟩

Cub Scout *n* : a member of the Boy Scouts of America program for boys in the first through fifth grades of school

[1]**cuck·old** \ˈkək-əld, -ōld\ *n* : a man whose wife is unfaithful [Middle English *cokewold*] — **cuck·old·ry** \-əl-drē\ *n*

[2]**cuckold** *vt* : to make a cuckold of

[1]**cuck·oo** \ˈkük-ü, ˈkuk-\ *n, pl* **cuckoos** **1** : a largely grayish brown European bird that lays its eggs in the nests of other birds for them to hatch; *also* : any of various related birds **2** : the call of a cuckoo [Middle English *cuccu*]

[2]**cuckoo** *adj* **1** : of or resembling the cuckoo **2** : SILLY 1, CRAZY

cuckoo spit *n* **1** : a frothy secretion exuded upon plants by the nymphs of spittlebugs **2** : SPITTLEBUG

cu·cum·ber \ˈkyü-ˌkəm-bər, -kəm-\ *n* : the long fleshy usually many-seeded green-skinned fruit of a vine of the gourd family grown as a garden vegetable; *also* : this vine [Medieval French *cucumbre,* from Latin *cucumis*]

cu·cur·bit \kyü-ˈkər-bət\ *n* : a plant of the gourd family [Medieval French *cucurbite,* from Latin *cucurbita* "gourd"]

cud \ˈkəd, ˈkud\ *n* : food brought up into the mouth by a ruminating animal (as a cow) from its rumen to be chewed again [Old English *cwudu*]

cud·dle \ˈkəd-l\ *vb* **cud·dled; cud·dling** \ˈkəd-ling, -l-ing\ **1** : to hold close for warmth or comfort or in affection **2** : to lie close : SNUGGLE [origin unknown] — **cuddle** *n* — **cud·dly** \ˈkəd-lē, -l-ē\ *adj*

[1]**cud·gel** \ˈkəj-əl\ *n* : a short heavy club [Old English *cycgel*]

[2]**cudgel** *vt* **-geled** *or* **-gelled; -gel·ing** *or* **-gel·ling** : to beat with or as if with a cudgel

[1]**cue** \ˈkyü\ *n* **1** : a word, phrase, or action in a play serving as a signal for the next actor to speak or act **2** : something serving as a signal or suggestion : HINT [probably from *qu,* abbreviation (used as a direction in actors' copies of plays) of Latin *quando* "when"]

[2]**cue** *n* **1** : QUEUE 2 **2 a** : a tapering rod for striking a ball in games (as billiards or pool) **b** : a long-handled stick with a concave head for shoving disks in shuffleboard [French *queue* "tail, line of people," from Medieval French *cue, coe* "tail," from Latin *cauda*]

cue ball *n* : the ball a player strikes with the cue in billiards and pool

[1]**cuff** \ˈkəf\ *n* **1** : something (as a part of a sleeve) encircling the wrist **2** : the turned-back hem of a trouser leg **3** : an inflatable band that is wrapped around an extremity to control the flow of blood through the part when recording blood pressure with a sphygmomanometer [Middle English]

[2]**cuff** *vt* : to strike with or as if with the palm of the hand : SLAP [perhaps from obsolete English, "glove," from Middle English]

[3]**cuff** *n* : a blow with the hand especially when open : SLAP

cuff link *n* : a usually decorative device worn by a man consisting of two parts joined by a shank, chain, or bar for passing through buttonholes to fasten shirt cuffs — usually used in plural

cui·rass \kwi-ˈras, kyu̇-\ *n* **1** : a piece of armor covering the body from neck to waist; *also* : the breastplate of such a piece **2** : something (as a plaster cast on the trunk and neck) resembling a cuirass [Medieval French *cuirasse,* derived from Late Latin *coreaceus* "leathern," from Latin *corium* "skin, leather"]

cuir·as·sier \ˌkwir-ə-ˈsiər, ˌkyu̇r-\ *n* : a mounted soldier wearing a cuirass

cui·sine \kwi-ˈzēn\ *n* : manner of preparing food ⟨Mexican *cuisine*⟩; *also* : the food prepared [French, literally, "kitchen," from Medieval French, from Late Latin *coquina,* from Latin *coquere* "to cook"]

cu·lex \ˈkyü-ˌleks\ *n* : any of a large widespread genus of mosquitoes that includes the mosquito commonly found in or about buildings in Europe and North America [Latin, "gnat"]

cu·li·nary \ˈkəl-ə-ˌner-ē, ˈkyü-lə-\ *adj* : of or relating to the kitchen or cookery [Latin *culina* "kitchen," from *coquere* "to cook"]

[1]**cull** \ˈkəl\ *vt* **1** : to select from a group : CHOOSE **2** : to reduce or control the size of (as a herd) by removal of usually weaker animals ⟨a hunt to *cull* the growing deer population⟩ [Medieval French *culier, coillir,* from Latin *colligere* "to bind together, collect"] — **cull·er** *n*

[2]**cull** *n* : something rejected as inferior or worthless

[1]**culm** \ˈkəlm\ *n* : refuse coal screenings : SLACK [Middle English]

[2]**culm** *n* : the stem of a monocotyledonous plant (as a grass) [Latin *culmus* "stalk"]

cul·mi·nate \ˈkəl-mə-ˌnāt\ *vi* : to reach the highest or climactic point [Medieval Latin *culminare,* from Latin *culmen* "top, summit"]

cul·mi·na·tion \ˌkəl-mə-ˈnā-shən\ *n* **1** : the action of culminating **2** : the culminating position : CLIMAX

cu·lotte \ˈkü-ˌlät, ˈkyü-; kü-ˈ, kyü-ˈ\ *n* : a divided skirt or a garment with a divided skirt — often used in plural [French, "breeches," from *cul* "backside"]

cul·pa·ble \ˈkəl-pə-bəl\ *adj* : deserving condemnation or blame ⟨*culpable* negligence⟩ [Medieval French, from Latin *culpabilis,* from *culpare* "to blame," from *culpa* "fault, guilt"] — **cul·pa·bil·i·ty** \ˌkəl-pə-ˈbil-ət-ē\ *n* — **cul·pa·ble·ness** \ˈkəl-pə-bəl-nəs\ *n* — **cul·pa·bly** \-pə-blē\ *adv*

cul·prit \ˈkəl-prət, -ˌprit\ *n* **1** : one accused of or charged with a crime **2** : one guilty of a crime or fault [Medieval French *cul.* (abbreviation of *culpable* "guilty") + *prest, prit* "ready" (that is, to prove it), from Latin *praestus*]

cult \ˈkəlt\ *n* **1** : formal religious veneration : WORSHIP **2** : a system of religious beliefs and ritual; *also* : the body of people practicing it **3 a** : enthusiastic and usually temporary devotion to a person, idea, or thing **b** : the object of such devotion **c**

: a group of persons showing such devotion [Latin *cultus* "care, adoration," from *colere* "to cultivate, worship"] — **cult·ist** \ˈkəl-təst\ *n*

cul·ti·gen \ˈkəl-tə-jən\ *n* : a cultivated organism (as the kidney bean) of a variety or species for which a wild ancestor is unknown or uncertain [*culti*vated + *-gen*]

cul·ti·va·ble \ˈkəl-tə-və-bəl\ *adj* : capable of being cultivated

cul·ti·var \ˈkəl-tə-ˌvär\ *n* : an organism and especially a plant (as an apple tree) originating and persisting under cultivation [*culti*vated + *var*iety]

cul·ti·vate \ˈkəl-tə-ˌvāt\ *vt* **1 a** : to prepare or prepare and use for the raising of crops : TILL **b** : to loosen or break up the soil about (growing plants) **2 a** : to foster the growth of ⟨*cultivate* vegetables⟩ ⟨*cultivate* oysters⟩ **b** : CULTURE 2 **c** : REFINE, IMPROVE ⟨*cultivate* the mind⟩ **3** : FURTHER, ENCOURAGE ⟨*cultivate* the arts⟩ **4** : to seek the society of [Medieval Latin *cultivare,* from *cultivus* "cultivated," derived from Latin *colere* "to cultivate"] — **cul·ti·vat·able** \-ˌvāt-ə-bəl\ *adj*

cul·ti·vat·ed \-ˌvāt-əd\ *adj* **1** : subjected to or produced under cultivation ⟨*cultivated* farms⟩ ⟨*cultivated* fruits⟩ **2** : having or showing good education and elegant taste, speech, and manners : REFINED, EDUCATED ⟨*cultivated* speech⟩

cul·ti·va·tion \ˌkəl-tə-ˈvā-shən\ *n* **1** : the act or art of cultivating; *esp* : TILLAGE **2** : CULTURE 3, REFINEMENT

cul·ti·va·tor \ˈkəl-tə-ˌvāt-ər\ *n* : one that cultivates; *esp* : an implement to loosen the soil while crops are growing

cul·tur·al \ˈkəlch-rəl, -ə-rəl\ *adj* **1** : of or relating to culture **2** : produced by breeding — **cul·tur·al·ly** \-ē\ *adv*

cultural anthropology *n* : a division of anthropology that deals with human culture — compare PHYSICAL ANTHROPOLOGY

[1]**cul·ture** \ˈkəl-chər\ *n* **1** : CULTIVATION 1, TILLAGE **2 a** : the rearing or development of a particular product, stock, or crop ⟨bee *culture*⟩ ⟨the *culture* of grapes⟩ **b** : professional or expert care and training ⟨voice *culture*⟩ **3** : the state of being cultivated; *esp* : refinement in manners, taste, and thought **4 a** : the characteristic features of a civilization including its beliefs, its artistic and material products, and its social institutions ⟨ancient Greek *culture*⟩ **b** : the beliefs, material traits, and social practices of a racial, religious, or social group **c** : the characteristic features of everyday life shared by people in a particular place or time ⟨southern *culture*⟩ ⟨popular *culture*⟩ **d** : the set of values, conventions, or social practices that characterizes an institution or organization ⟨a corporate *culture* focused on profits⟩ **5** : cultivation of living material (as bacteria) in prepared nutrient media; *also* : a product of such cultivation [Medieval French, from Latin *cultura,* derived from *colere* "to cultivate"]

[2]**culture** *vt* **cul·tured; cul·tur·ing** \ˈkəlch-ring, -ə-ring\ **1** : CULTIVATE 1 **2** : to grow in a prepared medium

cul·tured \ˈkəl-chərd\ *adj* **1** : CULTIVATED ⟨*cultured* fields⟩ ⟨*cultured* speech⟩ **2** : produced under artificial conditions ⟨*cultured* pearls⟩

cul·vert \ˈkəl-vərt\ *n* **1** : a drain crossing under a road or railroad **2** : a conduit for a culvert **3** : a bridge over a culvert [origin unknown]

cum·ber \ˈkəm-bər\ *vt* **cum·bered; cum·ber·ing** \-bə-ring, -bring\ **1** : to hinder by being in the way **2** : to clutter up ⟨rocks *cumbering* the yard⟩ [Medieval French *acumbrer, encumbrer* "to encumber"]

cum·ber·some \ˈkəm-bər-səm\ *adj* **1** : unwieldy because of heaviness and bulk **2** : slow-moving : LUMBERING — **cum·ber·some·ly** *adv* — **cum·ber·some·ness** *n*

cum·brous \ˈkəm-brəs\ *adj* : CUMBERSOME — **cum·brous·ly** *adv* — **cum·brous·ness** *n*

cum·in \ˈkəm-ən\ *n* : a small annual herb related to the carrot and grown for its aromatic seedlike fruits used as a spice; *also* : the fruits [Old English *cymen,* from Latin *cuminum,* from Greek *kyminon,* of Semitic origin]

cum lau·de \ku̇m-ˈlau̇d-ə, -ē; ˌkəm-ˈlȯd-ē\ *adv or adj* : with academic distinction ⟨graduated *cum laude*⟩ [New Latin, "with praise"]

cum·mer·bund \ˈkəm-ər-ˌbənd\ *n* : a broad sash worn as a waistband [Hindi & Urdu *kamarband,* from Persian, from *kamar* "waist" + *band* "band"]

cu·mu·late \ˈkyü-myə-ˌlāt\ *vb* : ACCUMULATE [Latin *cumulare,* from *cumulus* "mass, heap"] — **cu·mu·la·tion** \ˌkyü-myə-ˈlā-shən\ *n*

cu·mu·la·tive \ˈkyü-myə-lət-iv, -ˌlāt-\ *adj* **1** : increasing (as in force, strength, or amount) by successive additions **2** : tending to prove the same point ⟨*cumulative* evidence⟩ **3 a** : taking effect upon completion of another penal sentence ⟨a *cumulative* prison sentence⟩ **b** : increasing in severity with repetition of the offense ⟨*cumulative* penalty⟩ **4** : formed by addition of new material of the same kind ⟨a *cumulative* book index⟩ — **cu·mu·la·tive·ly** *adv* — **cu·mu·la·tive·ness** *n*

cu·mu·lo·nim·bus \ˌkyü-myə-lō-ˈnim-bəs\ *n* : a cumulus cloud that has a low base and that is often spread out in the shape of an anvil extending to great heights

cu·mu·lous \ˈkyü-myə-ləs\ *adj* : resembling a cumulus

cu·mu·lus \-ləs\ *n, pl* **cu·mu·li** \-ˌlī, -ˌlē\ **1** : HEAP 2, ACCUMULATION **2** : a dense puffy cloud form having a flat base and rounded outlines often piled up like a mountain [Latin, "heap, mass"]

cu·ne·ate \ˈkyü-nē-ˌāt, -nē-ət\ *adj* : narrowly triangular with the acute angle toward the base ⟨a *cuneate* leaf⟩ [Latin *cuneatus,* from *cuneus* "wedge"]

[1]**cu·ne·i·form** \kyu̇-ˈnē-ə-ˌfȯrm; ˈkyü-nə-ˌfȯrm, -nē-ə-ˌ\ *adj* **1** : having the shape of a wedge **2** : composed of or written in wedge-shaped characters ⟨the *cuneiform* alphabet⟩ [derived from Latin *cuneus* "wedge"]

[2]**cuneiform** *n* : cuneiform writing (as of ancient Assyria and Babylonia)

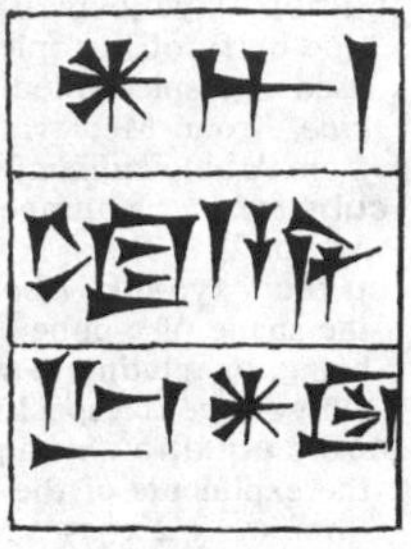
cuneiform

cun·ner \ˈkən-ər\ *n* : a small American food fish that is common on the rocky shores of New England [origin unknown]

[1]**cun·ning** \ˈkən-ing\ *adj* **1** : dexterous or crafty in the use of resources (as skill or knowledge) ⟨*cunning* schemers⟩ **2** : marked by wily artfulness ⟨a *cunning* plot⟩ **3** : prettily appealing : CUTE [Middle English, from *can* "know, can"] — **cun·ning·ly** \-ing-lē\ *adv*

[2]**cunning** *n* **1** : SKILL 1, DEXTERITY **2** : SLYNESS, CRAFTINESS

[1]**cup** \ˈkəp\ *n* **1** : an open bowl-shaped drinking vessel usually with a handle **2 a** : the contents of a cup : CUPFUL **b** : the consecrated wine of the Communion **3** : a large ornamental cup offered as a prize **4 a** : something (as the corolla of a flower) resembling a cup **b** : a usually plastic-reinforced athletic supporter **c** : either of two parts of a brassiere that are shaped like and fit over the breasts **d** : the metal case inside a hole in golf; *also* : the hole itself **5** : a half pint : eight fluid ounces **6** : a food served in a cup-shaped vessel ⟨fruit *cup*⟩ **7** : the symbol ∪ indicating the union of two sets — compare CAP 5 [Old English *cuppe,* from Late Latin *cuppa,* from Latin *cupa* "tub"] — **cup·like** \ˈkəp-ˌlīk\ *adj*

[2]**cup** *vt* **cupped; cup·ping** **1** : to treat by cupping **2 a** : to curve into the shape of a cup ⟨*cupped* my hands⟩ **b** : to place in or as if in a cup — **cup·per** *n*

cup·bearer \ˈkəp-ˌbar-ər, -ˌber-\ *n* : one who has the duty of filling and handing around cups of wine

cup·board \ˈkəb-ərd\ *n* **1** : a closet with shelves for cups, dishes, or food **2** : a small closet

cup·cake \ˈkəp-ˌkāk\ *n* : a small cake baked in a cuplike mold

cu·pel \kyü-ˈpel, ˈkyü-pəl\ *n* : a small shallow porous cup especially of bone ash used in assaying to separate precious metals from lead [French *coupelle* "small cup," from *coupe* "cup," from Late Latin *cuppa*]

cup·ful \ˈkəp-ˌfu̇l\ *n, pl* **cup·fuls** \-ˌfu̇lz\ *also* **cups·ful** \ˈkəps-ˌfu̇l\ **1** : the amount held by a cup **2** : CUP 5

cup fungus *n* : any of an order of mostly saprophytic fungi bearing a cuplike fleshy or horny spore-bearing structure that is often colored

cu·pid \ˈkyü-pəd\ *n* : a winged naked figure of an infant often with a bow and arrow that represents the Roman god of love

cu·pid·i·ty \kyu̇-ˈpid-ət-ē\ *n* : excessive desire especially for wealth : GREED [Medieval French *cupidité,* from Latin *cupiditas,* from *cupidus* "desirous," from *cupere* "to desire"]

cu·po·la \ˈkyü-pə-lə\ *n* **1** : a rounded vault forming a roof or ceiling **2** : a small structure built on top of a roof [Italian, from Latin *cupula* "small tub," from *cupa* "tub"]

cupping *n* : a technique formerly used for drawing blood to the surface of the body by application of a glass vessel from which air had been evacuated by heat forming a partial vacuum

cu·pric \ˈkü-prik, ˈkyü-\ *adj* : of, relating to, or containing bivalent copper [Late Latin *cuprum* "copper"]

cu·prite \ˈkü-ˌprīt, ˈkyü-\ *n* : a red mineral that consists of an oxide of copper and is an ore of copper
cu·prous \-prəs\ *adj* : of, relating to, or containing univalent copper
cur \ˈkər\ *n* **1** : a mongrel dog **2** : a low contemptible person [Middle English]
cur·able \ˈkyu̇r-ə-bəl\ *adj* : capable of being cured
cu·ra·cy \ˈkyu̇r-ə-sē\ *n, pl* **-cies** : the office or term of office of a curate
cu·ra·re \kyu̇-ˈrär-ē, ku̇-\ *n* : a dried aqueous extract especially of a tropical American vine used in native arrow poisons and in medicine to produce muscular relaxation [Portuguese and Spanish, from Carib *kurari*]
cu·rate \ˈkyu̇r-ət\ *n* **1** : a clergyman in charge of a parish **2** : a clergyman serving as assistant (as to a rector) in a parish [Medieval Latin *curatus,* from *cura* "cure of souls," from Latin, "care"]
cu·ra·tive \ˈkyu̇r-ət-iv\ *adj* : relating to or used in the cure of diseases ⟨*curative* treatments⟩
cu·ra·tor \kyu̇-ˈrāt-ər, ˈkyu̇r-ˌāt-\ *n* : one who has the care and supervision of something; *esp* : one in charge of a museum or zoo [Latin, from *curare* "to care," from *cura* "care"] — **cu·ra·to·ri·al** \ˌkyu̇r-ə-ˈtōr-ē-əl, -ˈtȯr-\ *adj* — **cu·ra·tor·ship** \kyu̇-ˈrāt-ər-ˌship, ˈkyu̇r-ət-\ *n*
[1]**curb** \ˈkərb\ *n* **1** : a chain or strap on a bit used to restrain a horse **2** : RESTRAINT 2a, CHECK ⟨price *curbs*⟩ **3** : a frame or a raised edge or margin to strengthen or confine ⟨the *curb* of a well⟩ **4** : an edging built along a street to form part of a gutter [Middle French *courbe* "curve, curved piece of wood or iron," from Latin *curvus* "curved"]
[2]**curb** *vt* **1** : to furnish with a curb **2** : to check or control with or as if with a curb ⟨*curb* your appetite⟩ **3** : to lead (a dog) to a suitable place (as a gutter) for defecation
curb·ing \ˈkər-biŋ\ *n* **1** : material for a curb **2** : CURB
curb·stone \ˈkərb-ˌstōn\ *n* : a stone forming a curb
cur·cu·lio \kər-ˈkyü-lē-ˌō\ *n, pl* **-li·os** : any of various weevils; *esp* : one that injures fruit [Latin, "grain weevil"]
[1]**curd** \ˈkərd\ *n* **1** : the thick casein-rich part of coagulated milk — compare WHEY **2** : something resembling the curd of milk [Middle English *crud, curd*] — **curdy** \-ē\ *adj*
[2]**curd** *vb* : COAGULATE, CURDLE
cur·dle \ˈkərd-l\ *vb* **cur·dled; cur·dling** \ˈkərd-liŋ, -l-iŋ\ **1** : to form curds : COAGULATE **2** : to cause curds to form in **3** : SOUR, SPOIL **4** — used in expressions such as *make one's blood curdle* to indicate a feeling of terror
[1]**cure** \ˈkyu̇r\ *n* **1 a** : spiritual charge **b** : pastoral charge of a parish **2 a** : recovery or relief from a disease **b** : something (as a drug or treatment) that cures a disease **c** : a course, system, or period of treatment **3** : a process or method of curing ⟨a brine *cure* for meat⟩ [Medieval French, from Medieval Latin *cura* "cure of souls," from Latin, "care"] — **cure·less** \-ləs\ *adj*
[2]**cure** *vb* **1 a** : to restore to health, soundness, or normality **b** : to bring about recovery from **2** : to eliminate or free from something objectionable or harmful **3** : to prepare by or undergo chemical or physical processing for keeping or use ⟨*cure* bacon⟩ ⟨hay *curing* in the sun⟩ — **cur·er** \ˈkyu̇r-ər\ *n*
synonyms CURE, HEAL, REMEDY mean to rectify an unhealthy or undesirable condition. CURE applies to causing recovery from a disease ⟨*cure* pneumonia⟩. HEAL may also apply to this but more commonly suggests restoring a wounded or sore part to soundness ⟨*heal* a scrape on the knee⟩. REMEDY in extended use suggests correction or relief of a morbid or evil condition ⟨*remedy* a skin condition⟩.
cu·ré \kyu̇-ˈrā, ˈkyu̇r-ˌā\ *n* : a parish priest [French, from Medieval French, from Medieval Latin *curatus*]
cure–all \ˈkyu̇r-ˌȯl\ *n* : a remedy for all ills : PANACEA
cur·et·tage \ˌkyu̇r-ə-ˈtäzh\ *n* : a surgical cleaning or scraping of a body part (as the uterus) [French, from *curette,* a surgical instrument]
cur·few \ˈkər-ˌfyü\ *n* **1** : a regulation requiring persons of a usually specified kind to be off the streets at a stated time **2** : a signal (as the ringing of a bell) to announce the beginning of a curfew **3 a** : the time when a curfew begins **b** : the period during which a curfew is in effect [Medieval French *coverfeu* "signal given to bank the hearth fire, curfew," from *covrir* "to cover" + *feu* "fire"]
Word History In Europe in the Middle Ages people were required to put out or cover their hearth fires by a certain time in the evening. A hearth fire left unattended overnight might spread and destroy the house or even the town. A bell was rung to let people know they must cover their fires. In Medieval French this signal was called *coverfeu,* a compound of *covrir,* "to cover," and *feu,* "fire." Even when hearth fires were no longer regulated, many towns had other rules that called for the ringing of an evening bell, and this signal was still called *coverfeu.* A common *coverfeu* regulation required that certain people be off the streets by a given time. The English borrowed *curfew* from French *coverfeu.*
cu·ria \ˈkyu̇r-ē-ə, ˈku̇r-\ *n, pl* **cu·ri·ae** \ˈkyu̇r-ē-ˌē, ˈku̇r-ē-ˌī\ **1** : a division of an ancient Roman tribe **2** : a medieval royal court or court of justice **3** *often cap* : the group of administrative and judicial bodies through which the pope governs the Roman Catholic Church [Latin] — **cu·ri·al** \ˈkyu̇r-ē-əl\ *adj*
cu·rie \ˈkyu̇r-ˌē, kyu̇-ˈrē\ *n* **1** : a unit quantity of any radioactive element in which 37 billion disintegrations occur per second **2** : a unit of radioactivity equal to 37 billion disintegrations per second [Marie *Curie*]
cu·rio \ˈkyu̇r-ē-ˌō\ *n, pl* **-ri·os** : something (as a decorative object) considered novel, rare, or bizarre; *also* : an unusual or bizarre person [short for *curiosity*]
cu·ri·os·i·ty \ˌkyu̇r-ē-ˈäs-ət-ē\ *n, pl* **-ties** **1** : an eager desire to learn and often to learn what does not concern one : INQUISITIVENESS **2 a** : something strange or unusual **b** : CURIO
cu·ri·ous \ˈkyu̇r-ē-əs\ *adj* **1** : eager to learn **2** : overly eager to learn about others' concerns **3** : exciting attention as strange or novel ⟨a *curious* insect⟩ ⟨*curious* notions⟩ [Medieval French *curios,* from Latin *curiosus* "careful, inquisitive," from *cura* "care"] — **cu·ri·ous·ly** *adv* — **cu·ri·ous·ness** *n*
synonyms CURIOUS, INQUISITIVE, PRYING mean interested in what is not one's own business. CURIOUS, a neutral term, in general suggests an active desire to learn or to know ⟨children are *curious* about everything⟩. INQUISITIVE implies habitual curiosity especially about the personal affairs of others ⟨dreaded the visits of their *inquisitive* relatives⟩. PRYING implies officious, active meddling ⟨*prying* neighbors who refuse to mind their own business⟩.
cu·ri·um \ˈkyu̇r-ē-əm\ *n* : a metallic radioactive element artificially produced — see ELEMENT table [New Latin, from Marie and Pierre *Curie*]
[1]**curl** \ˈkərl\ *vb* **1** : to form into coils or ringlets **2** : to form into a curved shape : TWIST **3 a** : to grow in coils or spirals **b** : to move in curves or spirals **4** : to play the game of curling [Middle English *curlen,* from *crul* "curly"]
[2]**curl** *n* **1** : a lock of hair that coils : RINGLET **2** : something having a spiral or winding form : COIL **3** : the action of curling : the state of being curled **4** : an abnormal rolling or curling of leaves
curl·er \ˈkər-lər\ *n* **1** : one that curls; *esp* : a device for putting a curl into hair **2** : a player in the game of curling
cur·lew \ˈkər-ˌlü, ˈkərl-ˌyü\ *n, pl* **curlews** *or* **curlew** : any of various largely brownish mostly migratory birds related to the woodcocks and distinguished by long legs and a long slender down-curved bill [Medieval French *curleu*]

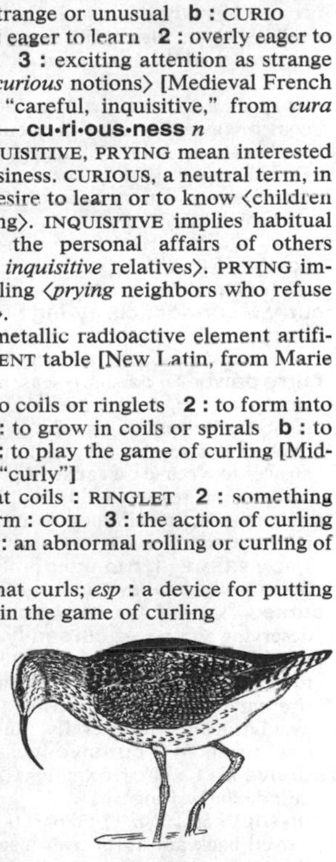
curlew

curli·cue *also* **curly·cue** \ˈkər-li-ˌkyü\ *n* : a fancifully curved or spiral figure (as a flourish in handwriting) [*curly* + *cue* "braid of hair"]
curl·ing \ˈkər-liŋ\ *n* : a game in which two teams of four players each slide special stones over ice toward a target circle
curly \ˈkər-lē\ *adj* **curl·i·er; -est** **1** : tending to curl; *also* : having curls **2** : having the grain composed of wavy fibers that do not cross and that often form alternating light and dark lines ⟨*curly* maple⟩ — **curl·i·ness** *n*
curly endive *n* : FRISÉE
cur·mudg·eon \kər-ˈməj-ən\ *n* : a bad-tempered and often old man [origin unknown] — **cur·mudg·eon·ly** *adj*
cur·rant \ˈkər-ənt, ˈkə-rənt\ *n* **1** : a small seedless raisin grown

\ə\ **abut**	\au̇\ **out**	\i\ **tip**	\ȯ\ **saw**	\u̇\ **foot**
\ər\ **further**	\ch\ **chin**	\ī\ **life**	\ȯi\ **coin**	\y\ **yet**
\a\ **mat**	\e\ **pet**	\j\ **job**	\th\ **thin**	\yü\ **few**
\ā\ **take**	\ē\ **easy**	\ŋ\ **sing**	\t͟h\ **this**	\yu̇\ **cure**
\ä\ **cot, cart**	\g\ **go**	\ō\ **bone**	\ü\ **food**	\zh\ **vision**

chiefly in the Levant **2 :** the acid edible fruit of any of several shrubs related to the gooseberries; *also* **:** a plant bearing currants [Middle English *raison of Coraunte,* literally, "raisin of Corinth"]

cur·ren·cy \ˈkər-ən-sē, ˈkə-rən-\ *n, pl* **-cies 1 :** general use or acceptance ⟨a story that gained wide *currency*⟩ **2 :** coins, government notes, and bank notes circulating as a medium of exchange **:** money in circulation

[1]**cur·rent** \ˈkər-ənt, ˈkə-rənt\ *adj* **1 a :** presently elapsing ⟨the *current* month⟩ **b :** occurring in or belonging to the present time ⟨the *current* crisis⟩ **2 :** generally accepted, used, or practiced ⟨*current* customs⟩ [derived from Latin *currere* "to run"] ***synonyms*** see PREVAILING — **cur·rent·ly** *adv* — **cur·rent·ness** *n*

[2]**current** *n* **1 a :** the part of a fluid body moving continuously in a certain direction **b :** the swiftest part of a stream **c :** a strong or forceful flow **2 :** general course or movement **:** TREND ⟨changed the *current* of our lives⟩ **3 :** a movement of electricity analogous to the flow of a stream of water; *also* **:** the rate of such movement

cur·ri·cle \ˈkər-i-kəl, ˈkə-ri-\ *n* **:** a 2-wheeled chaise usually drawn by two horses [Latin *curriculum* "running, chariot"]

cur·ric·u·lum \kə-ˈrik-yə-ləm\ *n, pl* **-la** \-lə\ *also* **-lums :** a course of study; *esp* **:** the body of courses offered in a school or college or in one of its departments [Latin, "running, racecourse, chariot," from *currere* "to run"] — **cur·ric·u·lar** \-lər\ *adj*

[1]**cur·ry** \ˈkər-ē, ˈkə-rē\ *vt* **cur·ried; cur·ry·ing 1 :** to dress the coat of (as a horse) with a currycomb **2 :** to treat (tanned leather) especially by incorporating oil or grease [Medieval French *correier* "to prepare, curry," of Germanic origin] — **cur·ri·er** *n* — **curry fa·vor** \-ˈfā-vər\ **:** to seek to gain favor by flattery or attentions

[2]**cur·ry** *also* **cur·rie** \ˈkər-ē, ˈkə-rē\ *n, pl* **curries 1 :** CURRY POWDER **2 :** a food seasoned with curry powder ⟨shrimp *curry*⟩ [of Dravidian origin]

[3]**curry** *vt* **cur·ried; cur·ry·ing :** to flavor or cook with curry

cur·ry·comb \-ˌkōm\ *n* **:** a comb with rows of metallic teeth or ridges used especially to curry horses — **currycomb** *vt*

curry powder *n* **:** a sharp seasoning consisting of ground spices

[1]**curse** \ˈkərs\ *n* **1 :** a prayer that harm or injury may come upon someone or something **2 :** a word or an expression used in cursing or swearing **3 :** evil or misfortune that comes as if in answer to a curse **:** a cause of great harm or evil ⟨floods are the *curse* of this region⟩ [Old English *curs*]

[2]**curse** *vb* **1 :** to call upon divine or supernatural power to send injury upon **2 a :** to use profanely insolent language against **:** BLASPHEME **b :** to utter profane or obscene words **:** SWEAR **3 :** to bring great evil upon **:** AFFLICT

cursed \ˈkər-səd, ˈkərst\ *also* **curst** \ˈkərst\ *adj* **:** being under or deserving a curse — **cursed·ly** *adv* — **cursed·ness** *n*

[1]**cur·sive** \ˈkər-siv\ *adj* **1 :** written or formed with the strokes of the letters joined together and most of the angles rounded ⟨*cursive* handwriting⟩ **2 :** having a flowing easy character [Medieval Latin *cursivus,* literally, "running," derived from Latin *currere* "to run"] — **cur·sive·ly** *adv* — **cur·sive·ness** *n*

[2]**cursive** *n* **1 :** cursive writing **2 :** a style of printed letter imitating handwriting

cur·sor \ˈkər-sər\ *n* **1 :** a part (as a transparent slide with a line) moved back and forth over a surface (as of a slide rule) to enable accurate readings to be made **2 :** a mark (as a bright blinking spot) on a computer display screen that shows the place where the user is working [Latin, "runner," from *currere* "to run"]

cur·so·ry \ˈkərs-rē, -ə-rē\ *adj* **:** rapidly and often superficially performed **:** HASTY ⟨a *cursory* reading of the book⟩ [Late Latin *cursorius* "of running," from Latin *currere* "to run"] ***synonyms*** see SUPERFICIAL — **cur·so·ri·ly** \ˈkərs-rə-lē, -ə-rə-\ *adv* — **cur·so·ri·ness** \ˈkərs-rē-nəs, -ə-rē-\ *n*

curt \ˈkərt\ *adj* **:** rudely abrupt or brief ⟨a *curt* reply⟩ [Latin *curtus* "mutilated, curtailed"] — **curt·ly** *adv* — **curt·ness** *n*

cur·tail \kər-ˈtāl\ *vt* **:** to shorten or reduce by cutting away the end or another part of [derived from Latin *curtus* "mutilated, curtailed"] ***synonyms*** see SHORTEN — **cur·tail·er** *n* — **cur·tail·ment** \-ˈtāl-mənt\ *n*

[1]**cur·tain** \ˈkərt-n\ *n* **1 a :** a piece of material hung (as at a window) for decoration, privacy, or control of light and drafts **b :** the screen separating the stage from the auditorium of a theater **2 a :** the ascent or descent of a theater curtain **b :** the time at which a theatrical performance begins **3 :** something that covers, conceals, or separates like a curtain **4 :** CURTAIN WALL [Medieval French *curtine,* from Late Latin *cortina,* from Latin *cohors* "enclosure, court"] — **curtain** *vt*

curtain call *n* **:** an appearance by a performer usually at a final curtain (as of a play) in response to the applause of the audience

curtain raiser *n* **1 :** a short play used to open a performance **2 :** a usually short and unimportant preliminary to a main event

curtain wall *n* **:** an exterior enclosing wall (as of a skyscraper) that does not support any weight but its own

[1]**curt·sy** *also* **curt·sey** \ˈkərt-sē\ *n, pl* **curtsies** *also* **curtseys :** a gesture of respect made chiefly by women that consists of a slight lowering of the body and bending of the knees [alteration of *courtesy*]

[2]**curtsy** *also* **curtsey** *vi* **curt·sied** *also* **curt·seyed; curt·sy·ing** *also* **curt·sey·ing :** to make a curtsy

cur·va·ceous \ˌkər-ˈvā-shəs\ *adj* **:** having or suggesting the curves of a well-proportioned feminine figure; *also* **:** having a smoothly curving shape ⟨a *curvaceous* coastline⟩

cur·va·ture \ˈkər-və-ˌchu̇r, -chər\ *n* **1 :** the act of curving **:** the state of being curved **2 :** a measure of the amount of curving of a curved line or surface **3 a :** an abnormal curving (as of a bodily structure) ⟨*curvature* of the spine⟩ **b :** a curved surface (as of an organ)

[1]**curve** \ˈkərv\ *vb* **1 :** to turn, change, or deviate gradually from a straight line **2 :** to cause to curve **:** BEND [Latin *curvare,* from *curvus* "curved"]

[2]**curve** *n* **1 :** a line especially when curved **:** BEND **2 :** something curved ⟨a *curve* in the road⟩ **3 :** a ball thrown so that it swerves from its normal course — called also *curve ball* **4 :** the path of a moving point **5 a :** a line determined by an equation **b :** the graph of a variable — **curved** \ˈkərvd\ *adj*

[1]**cur·vet** \ˌkər-ˈvet\ *n* **:** a prancing leap of a horse in which first the forelegs and then the hind are raised so that for an instant all the legs are in the air [Italian *corvetta,* from Middle French *courbette,* from *courber* "to curve," from Latin *curvare*]

[2]**curvet** *vi* **cur·vet·ted** *or* **cur·vet·ed; cur·vet·ting** *or* **cur·vet·ing :** to make a curvet; *also* **:** CAPER, PRANCE

cur·vi·lin·ear \ˌkər-və-ˈlin-ē-ər\ *adj* **:** consisting of, characterized by, or bounded by curved lines

[1]**cush·ion** \ˈku̇sh-ən\ *n* **1 :** a soft pillow or pad to rest on or against **2 :** something resembling a cushion in use, shape, or softness **3 :** a pad of springy rubber along the inside of the rim of a billiard table **4 :** something serving to lighten the effects of disturbances or disorders ⟨saved money as a *cushion* against hard times⟩ [Medieval French *cussin, quissin,* derived from Latin *coxa* "hip"]

[2]**cushion** *vt* **cush·ioned; cush·ion·ing** \ˈku̇sh-ning, -ə-ning\ **1 :** to seat or place on a cushion **2 :** to furnish with a cushion ⟨*cushion* the bench⟩ **3 a :** to lighten the effects of ⟨tried to *cushion* the blow⟩ **b :** to shield from harm or injury **:** PROTECT ⟨*cushioned* the children from harsh realities⟩

Cush·it·ic \ˌkəsh-ˈit-ik, ku̇sh-\ *n* **:** a subfamily of the Afro-Asiatic language family comprising various languages spoken in eastern Africa and especially in Ethiopia, Djibouti, Somalia, and Kenya [*Cush* (Kush), ancient country in the Nile valley] — **Cushitic** *adj*

cushy \ˈku̇sh-ē\ *adj* **cushi·er; cushi·est :** EASY ⟨a *cushy* job⟩ [Hindi & Urdu *khush* "pleasant," from Persian *khūsh*] — **cushi·ly** \ˈku̇sh-ə-lē\ *adv*

cusk \ˈkəsk\ *n, pl* **cusk** *or* **cusks :** a large edible marine fish related to the cod [probably alteration of *tusk,* a kind of codfish]

cusp \ˈkəsp\ *n* **:** APEX 1, POINT: as **a :** either of the pointed ends of a crescent moon **b :** a point on a mathematical curve where the curve exactly reverses its direction **c :** a point on the grinding surface of a tooth **d :** a fold or flap of a cardiac valve [Latin *cuspis* "point"]

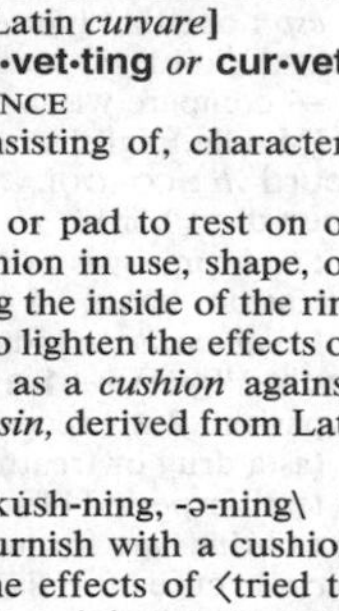

C cusp b

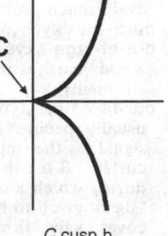

cus·pid \ˈkəs-pəd\ *n* **:** CANINE 1 [back-formation from *bicuspid*]

cus·pi·dor \ˈkəs-pə-ˌdȯr\ *n* **:** SPITTOON [Portuguese *cuspidouro,* from *cuspir* "to spit," from Latin *conspuere,* from *com-* + *spuere* "to spit"]

[1]**cuss** \ˈkəs\ *n* **1 :** CURSE **2 :** FELLOW ⟨an obstinate *cuss*⟩ [alteration of *curse*]

[2]**cuss** *vb* **:** CURSE — **cuss·er** *n*

cuss·ed \ˈkəs-əd\ *adj* **1 :** CURSED **2 :** difficult to deal with **:** OBSTINATE — **cuss·ed·ly** *adv* — **cuss·ed·ness** \-əd-nəs\ *n*

cus·tard \ˈkəs-tərd\ *n* **:** a usually sweetened mixture of milk and eggs baked, boiled, or frozen [Middle English, a kind of pie]

custard apple *n* **1 :** any of several chiefly tropical American soft-fleshed edible fruits; *also* **:** a tree or shrub bearing such fruit **2 :** PAWPAW 2

cus·to·di·al \ˌkə-ˈstōd-ē-əl\ *adj* **1 a :** relating to guardianship **b :** having sole or primary custody of a child ⟨the *custodial* parent⟩ **2 :** relating to, providing, or being protective care or services for basic needs ⟨nursing and *custodial* care⟩

cus·to·di·an \ˌkə-ˈstōd-ē-ən\ *n* **:** one that guards and protects or maintains: as **a :** one entrusted with guarding prisoners or inmates **b :** one entrusted with guarding and keeping property or records — **cus·to·di·an·ship** \-ˌship\ *n*

cus·to·dy \ˈkəs-təd-ē\ *n* **:** immediate charge and control (as of a ward or suspect) exercised by a person or an authority [Latin *custodia* "guarding," from *custos* "guardian"]

[1]**cus·tom** \ˈkəs-təm\ *n* **1 a :** a usage or practice common to many or habitual with an individual **b :** long-established practice considered as unwritten law **2** *pl* **:** duties, tolls, or imposts imposed by the law of a country on imports or exports **3 :** support given to a business by its customers **:** CUSTOMERS [Medieval French *custume,* from Latin *consuetudo,* from *consuescere* "to accustom" from *com-* + *suescere* "to accustom"] ***synonyms*** see HABIT

[2]**custom** *adj* **1 :** made or performed according to personal order ⟨*custom* clothes⟩ **2 :** specializing in custom work or operation

cus·tom·ary \ˈkəs-tə-ˌmer-ē\ *adj* **1 :** based on or established by custom ⟨*customary* rent⟩ **2 :** commonly practiced or observed **:** HABITUAL ⟨*customary* courtesy⟩ ***synonyms*** see USUAL — **cus·tom·ar·i·ly** \ˌkəs-tə-ˈmer-ə-lē\ *adv* — **cus·tom·ar·i·ness** \ˈkəs-tə-ˌmer-ē-nəs\ *n*

cus·tom–built \ˌkəs-təm-ˈbilt\ *adj* **:** built to individual order

cus·tom·er \ˈkəs-tə-mər\ *n* **1 :** one that buys from or patronizes a business especially on a regular basis **2 :** PERSON, FELLOW ⟨a real tough *customer*⟩

cus·tom·house \ˈkəs-təm-ˌhau̇s\ *also* **cus·toms·house** \-təmz-\ *n* **:** a building where customs are collected and where ships are entered and cleared at a port

cus·tom–made \ˌkəs-təm-ˈmād, -ˈād\ *adj* **:** made to individual order

[1]**cut** \ˈkət\ *vb* **cut; cut·ting 1 a :** to penetrate with or as if with an edged instrument **:** GASH **b :** to function as or like an edged tool ⟨the knife *cuts* well⟩ **c :** to allow being shaped, penetrated, or divided with an edged tool ⟨cheese *cuts* easily⟩ **d :** to work with or as if with an edged tool ⟨a tailor busy *cutting*⟩ **e :** to experience the growth of (a tooth) through the gum **2 a :** to hurt emotionally ⟨the remark *cut* me⟩ **b** (1) **:** to strike sharply (2) **:** to strike or strike at (as a ball) with a glancing stroke **c :** to have validity or effect ⟨that argument *cuts* both ways⟩ **3 a :** to make less in amount ⟨*cut* costs⟩ **b :** to shorten by omissions ⟨*cut* a manuscript⟩ **c :** DILUTE ⟨*cut* whiskey with water⟩ **4 a :** TRIM 3a, PARE ⟨*cut* your hair⟩ **b :** MOW, REAP ⟨*cut* hay⟩ **c :** to divide into parts with an edged tool ⟨*cut* the pie⟩ **d :** FELL, HEW ⟨*cut* timber⟩ **5 :** to remove or separate from a group ⟨*cut* two players from the team⟩ **6 a :** to turn sharply ⟨*cut* right to avoid a collision⟩ ⟨*cut* the wheels⟩ **b :** to move fast ⟨*cut* along the road⟩ **c :** to take a short or direct route ⟨*cut* across the campus⟩ **d :** INTERSECT, CROSS ⟨lines *cutting* other lines⟩ **e :** BREAK, INTERRUPT ⟨they *cut* our supply line⟩ **f :** to divide a deck of cards **g :** to divide (as money) into shares **:** SPLIT **h :** to make a sudden transition from one sound or image to another in motion pictures, radio, or television **7 a :** CEASE, STOP ⟨*cut* the nonsense⟩ **b :** to refuse to recognize (an acquaintance) **c :** to fail to attend (as a meeting or class) **d :** to stop (a motor) by opening a switch **e :** to stop filming a motion picture **8 a :** to make or give shape to with or as if with an edged tool ⟨*cut* a hole in the wall⟩ ⟨the floodwaters *cut* new channels⟩ ⟨*cut* a diamond⟩ **b :** to sing, play, or act for the recording of ⟨*cut* an album⟩ **9 a :** to engage in **:** PERFORM ⟨*cut* a caper⟩ **b :** to give the appearance of ⟨*cuts* a fine figure⟩ **10 :** to advance by skipping or going around another ⟨*cut* to the front of the line⟩ [Middle English *cutten*] — **cut a deal :** to negotiate an agreement — **cut both ways :** to have good and bad implications — **cut corners :** to reduce cost, time, or difficulty often at the expense of quality — **cut ice :** to be important ⟨his opinion *cuts* no *ice* with me⟩ — **cut it :** to cut the mustard — **cut the mustard :** to meet the standard of performance necessary for success — **cut to the chase :** to get to the point

[2]**cut** *n* **1 :** something cut or cut off: as **a :** a yield of products cut especially during one harvest **b :** a part of a meat carcass ⟨a rib *cut*⟩ **c :** an allotted part **:** SHARE ⟨took our *cut* and left⟩ **2 :** an effect produced by or as if by cutting: as **a :** a wound made by something sharp **:** GASH **b :** a surface or outline made by cutting ⟨a smooth *cut* in a board⟩ **c :** a passage made by cutting ⟨a railroad *cut*⟩ **d :** a grade or step especially in a social scale ⟨a *cut* above the neighbors⟩ **e :** a pictorial illustration **3 :** the act or an instance of cutting: as **a :** a gesture or expression that wounds the feelings of another ⟨an unkind *cut*⟩ **b :** a straight path or course **c :** STROKE, BLOW ⟨took a *cut* at the ball⟩ **d :** the act of reducing or removing a part ⟨a *cut* in pay⟩ **e :** the act of or a turn at cutting cards ⟨it's your *cut*⟩ **f :** the elimination of participants from further consideration or competition ⟨played well and made the *cut*⟩ **4 :** a voluntary absence from a class **5 :** an abrupt transition from one sound or image to another in motion pictures, radio, or television **6 :** the shape and style in which a thing is cut, formed, or made ⟨clothes of the latest *cut*⟩ **7 :** BAND 5e

cut–and–dried \ˌkət-n-ˈdrīd\ *also* **cut–and–dry** \-ˈdrī\ *adj* **:** being or done according to a plan, set procedure, or formula **:** ROUTINE ⟨a *cut-and-dried* presentation⟩

cu·ta·ne·ous \kyu̇-ˈtā-nē-əs\ *adj* **:** of, relating to, or affecting the skin ⟨a *cutaneous* infection⟩ [Latin *cutis* "skin"] — **cu·ta·ne·ous·ly** *adv*

[1]**cut·away** \ˈkət-ə-ˌwā\ *adj* **:** having or showing parts removed ⟨a *cutaway* model of a beehive showing its inner structure⟩

[2]**cutaway** *n* **1 :** a coat with skirts tapering from the front waistline to form tails at the back **2 :** a cutaway picture or representation

cut·back \ˈkət-ˌbak\ *n* **1 :** something cut back **2 :** DECREASE ⟨a *cutback* in employment⟩

cut back \ˈkət-ˈbak, ˌkət-\ *vb* **1 :** to shorten by cutting **:** PRUNE **2 :** DECREASE, REDUCE ⟨*cut back* production⟩ **3 :** to interrupt the sequence of a plot (as of a movie) by introducing events prior to those last presented

cut down *vb* **1 :** to strike down and kill or wound **2 :** to remake in a smaller size ⟨*cut down* the dress⟩ **3 a :** REDUCE 1b ⟨*cut down* the accident rate⟩ **b :** to reduce or curtail volume or activity ⟨*cut down* on smoking⟩

cute \ˈkyüt\ *adj* **1 :** SHREWD, WILY **2 :** attractive or pretty especially in a childish, youthful, or delicate way **3 :** obviously straining for effect [short for *acute*] — **cute·ly** *adv* — **cute·ness** *n*

cute·sy \ˈkyüt-sē\ *adj* **cute·si·er; -est :** self-consciously cute ⟨*cutesy* mannerisms⟩ — **cute·si·ness** *n*

cut glass *n* **:** glass ornamented with patterns cut into its surface and polished

cu·ti·cle \ˈkyüt-i-kəl\ *n* **1 :** an outer covering layer: as **a :** an external envelope (as of an insect) secreted usually by epidermal cells **b :** the epidermis when it is the outermost layer **c :** a thin continuous fatty film on the external surface of many higher plants **2 :** dead or horny epidermis (as around a fingernail) [Latin *cuticula,* from *cutis* "skin"] — **cu·tic·u·lar** \kyu̇-ˈtik-yə-lər\ *adj*

cut·ie *or* **cut·ey** \ˈkyüt-ē\ *n, pl* **cuties** *or* **cuteys :** an attractive person; *esp* **:** a pretty girl

cut·ie–pie \-ˌpī\ *n* **:** a cute person

cu·tin \ˈkyüt-n\ *n* **:** an insoluble substance containing waxes, fatty acids, soaps, and resinous matter that forms a continuous layer on the outer epidermal wall of a plant [Latin *cutis* "skin"] — **cu·tin·ized** \-n-ˌīzd\ *adj*

cut in *vb* **1 :** to thrust oneself into a position between others or belonging to another **2 :** to join in something suddenly ⟨*cut in* on the conversation⟩ **3 :** to interrupt a dancing couple and take one of them as a partner **4 :** INCLUDE ⟨*cut* me *in* on the profits⟩

cut·lass \ˈkət-ləs\ *n* **:** a short curved sword formerly used by sailors on warships [Middle French *coutelas,* from *coutel* "knife," from Latin *cultellus,* from *culter* "knife, plowshare"]

cut·ler \ˈkət-lər\ *n* **:** one who makes, deals in, or repairs cutlery

[Medieval French *cuteler,* from Late Latin *cultellarius,* from Latin *cultellus* "knife"]

cut·lery \ˈkət-lə-rē\ *n* **1 :** the business of a cutler **2 :** edged or cutting tools; *esp* **:** implements for cutting and eating food

cut·let \ˈkət-lət\ *n* **1 :** a small slice of meat ⟨a veal *cutlet*⟩ **2 :** a piece of food shaped like a cutlet [French *côtelette,* from Medieval French *costelette,* from *coste* "rib, side," from Latin *costa*]

cut·off \ˈkət-ˌȯf\ *n* **1 :** the action of cutting off **2 a :** the channel formed when a stream cuts through the neck of an oxbow **b :** SHORTCUT 1 **3 :** DEADLINE — **cutoff** *adj*

cut off \ˌkət-ˈȯf, ˈkət-\ *vt* **1 :** to bring to an untimely end **2 :** to stop the passage of ⟨*cut off* our supplies⟩ **3 :** DISCONTINUE ⟨*cut off* negotiations⟩ **4 :** SEPARATE, ISOLATE ⟨*cut off* from friends⟩ **5 :** DISINHERIT ⟨threatened to *cut* him *off* without a penny⟩ **6 a :** to stop the operation of ⟨*cut off* a motor⟩ **b :** to stop (someone) from talking **:** INTERRUPT

cut·out \ˈkət-ˌau̇t\ *n* **:** something cut out or meant for cutting out (as from paper) ⟨animal *cutouts*⟩ — **cutout** *adj*

[1]**cut out** \ˌkət-ˈau̇t, ˈkət-\ *vb* **1 :** to assign through necessity ⟨you have your work *cut out* for you⟩ **2 :** SUPPLANT 1 ⟨*cut out* a competitor⟩ **3 :** to put an end to ⟨*cut out* wasteful spending⟩ **4 :** to remove from a series or circuit **:** DISCONNECT **5 :** to cease operating ⟨the engine *cut out*⟩

[2]**cut out** *adj* **:** fitted by nature ⟨not *cut out* to be a lawyer⟩

cut·over \ˈkət-ˈō-vər\ *adj* **:** having most of its salable timber cut

cut·purse \ˈkət-ˌpərs\ *n* **:** PICKPOCKET

cut–rate \ˈkət-ˈrāt\ *adj* **1 :** marked by, offering, or making use of a reduced rate or price ⟨a *cut-rate* store⟩ **2 :** SECOND-RATE

cut·ter \ˈkət-ər\ *n* **1 :** one that cuts ⟨a diamond *cutter*⟩ ⟨a cookie *cutter*⟩ **2 a :** a boat used by warships for carrying passengers and stores to and from the shore **b :** a small one-masted sailing boat that usually carries two headsails **c :** a small armed boat in the coast guard **3 :** a small sleigh

[1]**cut·throat** \ˈkət-ˌthrōt\ *n* **:** a murderous person **:** MURDERER

[2]**cutthroat** *adj* **1 :** MURDEROUS, CRUEL ⟨a *cutthroat* rogue⟩ **2 :** MERCILESS, RUTHLESS ⟨*cutthroat* competition⟩

cut time *n* **:** ALLA BREVE

[1]**cutting** *n* **1 :** something cut or cut off or out: as **a :** a section of a plant capable of developing into a new plant **b :** HARVEST 2 **2 :** something made by cutting; *esp* **:** RECORD 4

[2]**cutting** *adj* **1 :** designed for cutting **:** SHARP ⟨the *cutting* edge of a knife⟩ **2 :** piercingly cold ⟨a *cutting* wind⟩ **3 :** SARCASTIC ***synonyms*** see INCISIVE — **cut·ting·ly** \-iŋ-lē\ *adv*

cutting board *n* **:** a board on which something (as food or cloth) is placed for cutting

cutting edge *n* **1 :** the sharp edge of a cutting tool **2 :** the newest and most advanced area of an activity — **cutting–edge** *adj*

cut·tle·bone \ˈkət-l-ˌbōn\ *n* **:** the hard internal shell of a cuttlefish used for making polishing powder or for supplying birds housed in cages with lime and salts [Middle English *cotul* "cuttlefish"]

cut·tle·fish \-ˌfish\ *n* **:** a marine mollusk having eight short arms and two longer tentacles and differing from the related squid in having an internal shell composed of compounds of calcium [Middle English *cotul* "cuttlefish," from Old English *cudele*]

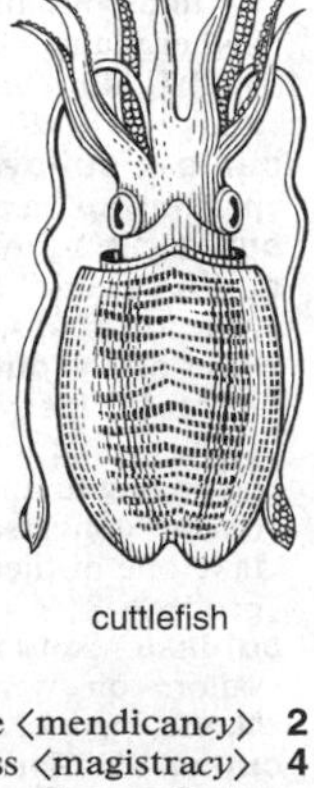

cuttlefish

cut·up \ˈkət-ˌəp\ *n* **:** one who clowns or acts boisterously

cut up \ˌkət-ˈəp, ˈkət-\ *vb* **1 a :** to cut or be cut into parts or pieces **b :** to distress deeply ⟨*cut up* by the criticism⟩ **2 :** to damage by or as if by cutting ⟨the truck *cut up* the lawn⟩ **3 :** to clown or act boisterously

cut·wa·ter \ˈkət-ˌwȯt-ər, -ˌwät-\ *n* **:** the forepart of a ship's stem

cut·worm \-ˌwərm\ *n* **:** any of various smooth-bodied moth caterpillars that hide by day and feed especially on young plant stems near ground level at night

-cy \sē\ *n suffix, pl* **-cies 1 :** action **:** practice ⟨mendican*cy*⟩ **2 :** rank **:** office ⟨chaplain*cy*⟩ **3 :** body **:** class ⟨magistra*cy*⟩ **4 :** state **:** quality ⟨accura*cy*⟩ ⟨bankrupt*cy*⟩ — often replacing a final *-t* or *-te* of the base word [Medieval French *-cie,* from Latin *-tia*]

cy·an \ˈsī-ˌan; -ən\ *n* **:** a greenish blue color — used in photography and color printing of one of the primary colors

cyan- *or* **cyano-** *combining form* **1 :** dark blue **:** blue ⟨*cyano*sis⟩ **2 :** cyanogen ⟨*cyan*ide⟩ **3 :** cyanide [Greek *kyanos* "dark blue enamel"]

cy·an·a·mide \sī-ˈan-ə-məd\ *n* **1 :** a caustic acidic compound CH_2N_2 **2 :** CALCIUM CYANAMIDE

cy·a·nide \ˈsī-ə-ˌnīd, -nəd\ *n* **1 :** a compound of cyanogen with an element or another radical: as **a :** POTASSIUM CYANIDE **b :** SODIUM CYANIDE **2 :** CYANOGEN 1

cy·a·no·bac·te·ri·um \ˌsī-ə-nō-bak-ˈtir-ē-əm; sī-ˌan-ō-\ *n* **:** BLUE-GREEN ALGA

cy·an·o·gen \sī-ˈan-ə-jən\ *n* **1 :** a univalent radical –CN that consists of carbon and nitrogen and is present in cyanides **2 :** a colorless flammable poisonous gas $(CN)_2$

cy·a·no·sis \ˌsī-ə-ˈnō-səs\ *n* **:** a bluish or purplish discoloration (as of skin) due to lack of oxygen in the blood — **cy·a·not·ic** \ˌsī-ə-ˈnät-ik\ *adj*

cy·ber \ˈsī-bər\ *adj* **:** relating to computers or computer networks

cyber- \ˈsī-bər\ *combining form* **:** computer **:** computer network ⟨*cyber*space⟩ [*cybernetic*]

cy·ber·net·ics \ˌsī-bər-ˈnet-iks\ *n* **:** the science of communication and control theory that is concerned especially with the comparative study of automatic control systems (as the nervous system and brain and mechanical-electrical communication systems) [Greek *kybernētēs* "pilot, governor," from *kybernan* "to steer, govern"] — **cy·ber·net·ic** \-ik\ *adj*

cy·ber·space \ˈsī-bər-ˌspās\ *n* **:** the online world of computer networks

cy·cad \ˈsī-kəd\ *n* **:** any of a family of tropical palmlike evergreen plants that are gymnosperms [New Latin *Cycad-, Cycas,* genus name]

cycl- *or* **cyclo-** *combining form* **:** circle ⟨*cyclo*meter⟩ [Greek *kyklos*]

cy·cla·men \ˈsī-klə-mən, ˈsik-lə-\ *n* **:** any of a genus of plants related to the primroses and grown as potted plants for their showy nodding flowers [Greek *kyklaminos*]

[1]**cy·cle** \ˈsī-kəl, *6 is also* ˈsik-əl\ *n* **1 :** a period of time taken up by a series of events or actions that repeat themselves regularly and in the same order ⟨the *cycle* of the seasons⟩ **2 a :** a course or series of events or activities that recur regularly and usually lead back to the starting point ⟨the *cycle* of the blood from the heart, through the blood vessels, and back again⟩ **b :** one complete performance of a series of recurring events; *esp* **:** one complete series of changes in voltage and current direction of an alternating electric current **3 :** a circular or spiral arrangement; *esp* **:** a whorl of floral leaves **4 :** a long period of time **:** AGE **5 a :** a group of poems, plays, novels, or songs treating the same theme **b :** a series of narratives dealing typically with the exploits of a legendary hero **6 a :** BICYCLE **b :** TRICYCLE **c :** MOTORCYCLE [Late Latin *cyclus,* from Greek *kyklos* "circle, wheel, cycle"] — **cy·clic** \ˈsī-klik, ˈsik-lik\ *or* **cy·cli·cal** \ˈsī-kli-kəl, ˈsik-li-\ *adj* — **cy·cli·cal·ly** \-kə-lē, -klē\ *adv*

[2]**cy·cle** \ˈsī-kəl, *2 is also* ˈsik-əl\ *vb* **cy·cled; cy·cling** \ˈsī-kə-liŋ, -kliŋ; ˈsik-liŋ, -ə-liŋ\ **1 a :** to pass or cause to go through a cycle **b :** to recur in cycles **2 :** to ride a cycle — **cy·cler** \ˈsī-kə-lər, -klər; ˈsik-lər, -ə-lər\ *n*

cyclic AMP *n* **:** a nucleotide formed from ATP that initiates biological activities within a cell by relaying signals brought to the cell's surface by hormones

cycling *n* **:** the sport of bicycling and especially bicycle racing

cy·clist \ˈsī-kə-ləst, -kləst; ˈsik-ləst, -ə-ləst\ *n* **:** one who rides a cycle and especially a bicycle

cy·cloid \ˈsī-ˌklȯid\ *n* **:** a curve traced out by a point on the circumference of a circle that is rolling along a straight line — **cy·cloi·dal** \sī-ˈklȯid-l\ *adj*

cy·clom·e·ter \sī-ˈkläm-ət-ər\ *n* **:** a device designed to record revolutions of a wheel and often used to register distance traversed by a wheeled vehicle

cy·clone \ˈsī-ˌklōn\ *n* **1 :** a storm or system of winds that rotates about a center of low atmospheric pressure counterclockwise in the northern hemisphere, advances at a speed of 20 to 30 miles (about 30 to 50 kilometers) an hour, and often brings abundant rain **2 :** TORNADO [Greek *kyklōma* "wheel, coil," from *kykloun* "to go around," from *kyklos* "circle"] — **cy·clon·ic** \sī-ˈklän-ik\ *adj* — **cy·clon·i·cal·ly** \-ˈklän-i-kə-lē, -klē\ *adv*

cy·clo·pe·an \ˌsī-klə-ˈpē-ən, sī-ˈklō-pē-\ *adj* **1** *often cap* **:** of, relating to, or characteristic of a Cyclops **2 :** HUGE a, MASSIVE

cy·clo·pe·dia *also* **cy·clo·pae·dia** \ˌsī-klə-ˈpēd-ē-ə\ *n* **:** ENCYCLOPEDIA — **cy·clo·pe·dic** \-ˈpēd-ik\ *adj*

cy·clops \ˈsī-ˌkläps\ *n* **1** *pl* **cy·clo·pes** \sī-ˈklō-ˌpēz\ *cap* **:** any of a race of giants in Greek mythology with a single eye in the middle of the forehead **2** *pl* **cyclops** : any of a genus of small pear-shaped water fleas with a single eye [Greek *Kyklōps,* from *kyklos* "circle" + *ōps* "eye"]

cy•clo•ra•ma \ˌsī-klə-ˈram-ə, -ˈräm-\ *n* : a large pictorial representation encircling the spectator and often having real objects as a foreground [*cycl-* + *-orama* (as in *panorama*)]

cy•clo•sis \sī-ˈklō-səs\ *n* : the streaming of cytoplasm within a cell

cy•clo•stome \ˈsī-klə-ˌstōm\ *n* : any of a class (Cyclostomata) of jawless fishes (as lampreys) with a large sucking mouth [Greek *kyklos* "circle" + *stoma* "mouth"]

cy•clo•thy•mic \ˌsī-klə-ˈthī-mik\ *adj* : having a temperament marked by alternating lively and depressed moods [derived from Greek *kyklos* "circle" + *thymos* "mind"]

cy•clo•tron \ˈsī-klə-ˌträn\ *n* : an accelerator in which charged particles (as protons or ions) are propelled by an alternating electric field in a constant magnetic field

cyg•net \ˈsig-nət\ *n* : a young swan [Medieval French *cignet,* from *cigne* "swan," from Latin *cygnus,* from Greek *kyknos*]

Cyg•nus \ˈsig-nəs\ *n* : a northern constellation between Lyra and Pegasus in the Milky Way [Latin, literally, "swan"]

cyl•in•der \ˈsil-ən-dər\ *n* **1** : a geometric shape composed of two parallel faces of identical size and shape (as circles) and a curved surface that completely connects their borders **2** : a long round solid or hollow body (as the piston chamber of an engine, the barrel of a pump, or the part of a revolver which turns and holds the cartridges) [Latin *cylindrus,* from Greek *kylindros,* from *kylindein* "to roll"] — **cyl•in•dered** \-dərd\ *adj*

cy•lin•dri•cal \sə-ˈlin-dri-kəl\ *also* **cy•lin•dric** \-drik\ *adj* : of, relating to, or having the form or properties of a cylinder — **cy•lin•dri•cal•ly** \-dri-kə-lē, -klē\ *adv*

cym•bal \ˈsim-bəl\ *n* : a brass plate that is struck with a drumstick or is used in pairs struck glancingly together to make a clashing sound [Medieval French *cymbele,* from Latin *cymbalum,* from Greek *kymbalon,* from *kymbē* "bowl"]

cym•bid•i•um \sim-ˈbid-ē-əm\ *n* : any of a genus of tropical Old World orchids with showy boat-shaped flowers [Latin *cymba* "boat," from Greek *kymbē* "bowl, boat"]

cyme \ˈsīm\ *n* : a broad branching often flat-topped cluster of flowers with a single flower at the end of each branch and with the individual flowers opening in sequence from the center toward the margin of the cluster [Latin *cyma* "cabbage sprout," from Greek *kyma* "swell, cabbage sprout," from *kyein* "to be pregnant"] — **cy•mose** \ˈsī-ˌmos\ *adj*

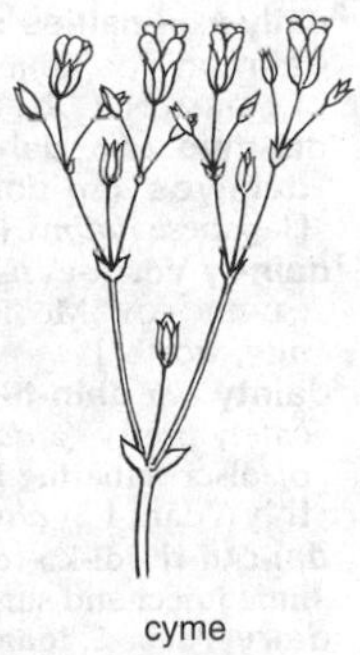

cyme

[1]Cym•ric \ˈkəm-rik, ˈkim-\ *adj* **1** : of, relating to, or characteristic of the non-Gaelic Celtic people of Britain or their language **2** : WELSH [Welsh *Cymry* "Welshmen"]

[2]Cymric *n* **1** : the non-Gaelic Celtic languages **2** : WELSH 2

cyn•ic \ˈsin-ik\ *n* **1** *cap* : an adherent of the view held by some ancient Greek philosophers that virtue is the only good and that its essence lies in self-control and independence **2** : one who believes that human conduct is motivated wholly by self-interest [Latin *cynicus,* a member of a school of ancient Greek philosophers, from Greek *kynikos,* from *kynikos* "like a dog," from *kyōn* "dog"] — **cynic** *adj*

Word History The ancient Greek philosopher Antisthenes taught that virtue is the only goal worth striving for. He and his followers were devoted to an ascetic life and made great show of their contempt for wealth and pleasure. Such a philosopher was called *kynikos,* which means literally "doglike." It is likely that one reason for the name was that Antisthenes taught in a school outside Athens which was called *Kynosarges.* It is likely, however, that most Greeks who applied *kynikos* to these philosophers had been offended by their surly reproaches. *Cynic* has been used in English since the 16th century as a word for a philosopher of this school. The word had not been long in English before it was applied to any faultfinding critic, especially to one who doubts the sincerity of all human motives except self-interest.

cyn•i•cal \ˈsin-i-kəl\ *adj* : having the attitude or temper of a cynic; *esp* : contemptuously distrustful of human nature and motives — **cyn•i•cal•ly** \-kə-lē, -klē\ *adv*

cyn•i•cism \ˈsin-ə-ˌsiz-əm\ *n* **1** : cynical character, attitude, or quality **2** : a cynical remark

cy•no•sure \ˈsī-nə-ˌshu̇r, ˈsin-ə-\ *n* **1** *cap* : the northern constellation Ursa Minor; *also* : NORTH STAR **2** : a center of attraction or attention ⟨the *cynosure* of all eyes⟩ [Latin *cynosura,* from Greek *kynosoura,* from *kynos oura* "dog's tail"]

cy•pher *chiefly British variant of* CIPHER

cy•press \ˈsī-prəs\ *n* **1** : any of a genus of evergreen trees and shrubs having overlapping scalelike leaves **2** : BALD CYPRESS **3** : the wood of a cypress tree [Medieval French *ciprès,* from Latin *cyparissus,* from Greek *kyparissos*]

cyp•ri•pe•di•um \ˌsip-rə-ˈpēd-ē-əm\ *n* : any of a genus of leafy-stemmed terrestrial orchids that have large usually showy drooping flowers in the form of a pouch [Late Latin *Cypris,* a name for Venus + Greek *pedilon* "sandal"]

Cy•ril•lic \sə-ˈril-ik\ *adj* : of, relating to, or constituting an alphabet used for Russian and various other languages of eastern Europe and Asia [Saint *Cyril,* died 869, apostle of the Slavs, reputed inventor of the Cyrillic alphabet]

cyst \ˈsist\ *n* **1** : a closed sac of fluid or semisolid material developing abnormally in a cavity or structure of the body **2** : a covering (as of a parasite) resembling a cyst; *also* : a body (as a spore) with such a covering [Greek *kystis* "bladder, pouch"]

cyst- *or* **cysti-** *or* **cysto-** *combining form* : bladder ⟨*cyst*itis⟩: sac [Greek *kystis*]

-cyst \ˌsist\ *n combining form* : bladder : sac ⟨blasto*cyst*⟩

cys•te•ine \ˈsis-tə-ˌēn\ *n* : a sulfur-containing amino acid $C_3H_7NO_2S$ that is readily oxidized to cystine [derived from *cystine*]

cys•tic \ˈsis-tik\ *adj* **1** : of, relating to, or containing cysts **2** : of or relating to the urinary bladder or the gallbladder

cys•ti•cer•cus \ˌsis-tə-ˈsər-kəs\ *n, pl* **-cer•ci** \-ˈsər-ˌsī\ : a tapeworm larva consisting of a head in a fluid-filled sac [*cyst-* + Greek *kerkos* "tail"]

cystic fibrosis *n* : a hereditary glandular disease that appears usually in early childhood and is marked especially by defective functioning of the pancreas, difficult breathing from mucus in the airways, and excessive loss of salt in the sweat

cys•tine \ˈsis-ˌtēn\ *n* : an amino acid $C_6H_{12}N_2O_4S_2$ widespread in proteins (as keratins) [from its discovery in bladder stones]

cys•ti•tis \sis-ˈtīt-əs\ *n* : inflammation of the urinary bladder

cyt- *or* **cyto-** *combining form* : cell ⟨*cyto*logy⟩ [Greek *kytos* "hollow vessel"]

-cyte \ˌsīt\ *n combining form* : cell ⟨leuko*cyte*⟩

cy•to•chrome \ˈsīt-ə-ˌkrōm\ *n* : any of several iron-containing enzymes that function in the transport of electrons to molecular oxygen in the living cell by undergoing alternate oxidation and reduction

cy•to•kine \ˈsīt-ə-ˌkīn\ *n* : any of a group of proteins that regulate the immune system [*cyt-* + Greek *kinein* "to move about"]

cy•to•ki•ne•sis \ˌsīt-ō-kə-ˈnē-səs, -kī-\ *n* : the division of cytoplasm into daughter cells following mitosis or meiosis [*cyt-* + *-kinesis*]

cy•to•ki•nin \ˌsīt-ə-ˈkī-nən\ *n* : any of various substances that promote growth in plants [*cyt-* + *kinin,* a plant growth factor, from Greek *kinein* "to move, stimulate"]

cy•tol•o•gy \sī-ˈtäl-ə-jē\ *n* : a branch of biology dealing with cells — **cy•to•log•i•cal** \ˌsīt-l-ˈäj-i-kəl\ *or* **cy•to•log•ic** \-ˈäj-ik\ *adj* — **cy•to•log•i•cal•ly** \-ˈäj-i-kə-lē, -klē\ *adv* — **cy•tol•o•gist** \sī-ˈtäl-ə-jəst\ *n*

cy•to•plasm \ˈsīt-ə-ˌplaz-əm\ *n* : the part of a cell outside the nucleus and its membrane that includes a fluidlike substance and membrane-bound organelles — **cy•to•plas•mic** \ˌsīt-ə-ˈplaz-mik\ *adj* — **cy•to•plas•mi•cal•ly** \-mi-kə-lē, -klē\ *adv*

cy•to•sine \ˈsīt-ə-ˌsēn\ *n* : a pyrimidine base $C_4H_5N_3O$ that codes genetic information in the polynucleotide chain of DNA and RNA — compare ADENINE, GUANINE, THYMINE, URACIL

cy•to•skel•e•ton \ˌsīt-ə-ˈskel-ət-n\ *n* : the network of protein filaments and microtubules in the cytoplasm that controls cell shape, maintains organization, and is involved in cell movement — **cy•to•skel•e•tal** \-l\ *adj*

cy•to•tox•ic T cell \ˌsīt-ə-ˈtäk-sik-\ *n* : KILLER T CELL

czar *also* **tsar** *or* **tzar** \ˈzär\ *n* **1** : the ruler of Russia until the

\ə\ **abut**	\au̇\ **out**	\i\ **tip**	\ȯ\ **saw**	\u̇\ **foot**
\ər\ **further**	\ch\ **chin**	\ī\ **life**	\ȯi\ **coin**	\y\ **yet**
\a\ **mat**	\e\ **pet**	\j\ **job**	\th\ **thin**	\yü\ **few**
\ā\ **take**	\ē\ **easy**	\ng\ **sing**	\t͟h\ **this**	\yu̇\ **cure**
\ä\ **cot, cart**	\g\ **go**	\ō\ **bone**	\ü\ **food**	\zh\ **vision**

1917 revolution **2** : one having great power or authority ⟨a baseball *czar*⟩ [Russian *tsar′*, from Old Russian Gothic *kaisar* "emperor," from Latin *Caesar*] — **czar·dom** *also* **tsar·dom** *or* **tzar·dom** \ˈzärd-əm\ *n*

czar·e·vitch *also* **tsar·e·vitch** *or* **tzar·e·vitch** \ˈzär-ə-ˌvich\ *n* : an heir of a Russian czar

cza·ri·na *also* **tsa·ri·na** *or* **tza·ri·na** \zä-ˈrē-nə\ *n* : the wife of a czar

czar·ism *also* **tsar·ism** *or* **tzar·ism** \ˈzär-ˌiz-əm\ *n* **1** : the government of Russia under the czars **2** : autocratic rule — **czar·ist** *also* **tsar·ist** *or* **tzar·ist** \ˈzär-əst\ *n or adj*

Czech \ˈchek\ *n* **1** : a native or inhabitant of western Czechoslovakia (including Bohemia and Moravia) or the Czech Republic **2** : the Slavic language of the Czechs — **Czech** *adj* — **Czech·ish** \-ish\ *adj*

D

d \ˈdē\ *n, pl* **d's** *or* **ds** \ˈdēz\ *often cap* **1** : the 4th letter of the English alphabet **2** : five hundred in Roman numerals — see NUMBER table **3** : the musical tone D : the 2nd tone of the C-major scale **4** : a grade rating a student's work as poor

-d *symbol* — used after the figure 2 or 3 to indicate the ordinal number second or third ⟨*2d*⟩ ⟨*23d*⟩

'd \d, əd\ *vb* **1** : HAD ⟨they'*d* gone⟩ **2** : WOULD ⟨we'*d* go⟩ **3** : DID ⟨where'*d* they go?⟩

[1]**dab** \ˈdab\ *n* **1** : a sudden blow or thrust : POKE **2** : a gentle touch or stroke : PAT [Middle English *dabbe*]

[2]**dab** *vb* **dabbed; dab·bing** **1** : to strike or touch lightly ⟨*dabbed* at her eyes with a handkerchief⟩ **2** : to apply lightly or irregularly : DAUB — **dab·ber** *n*

[3]**dab** *n* **1** : DAUB 1 **2** : a small amount

[4]**dab** *n* : FLATFISH; *esp* : any of several flounders [Anglo-French *dabbe*]

dab·ble \ˈdab-əl\ *vb* **dab·bled; dab·bling** \ˈdab-ling, -ə-ling\ **1** : to wet by splashing : SPATTER **2 a** : to paddle or play in or as if in water **b** : to reach with the bill to the bottom of shallow water to obtain food ⟨*dabbling* ducks⟩ **3** : to work or concern oneself lightly or superficially ⟨*dabbles* in poetry⟩ [perhaps from [2]*dab*] — **dab·bler** \ˈdab-lər, -ə-lər\ *n*

da ca·po \dä-ˈkäp-ō\ *adv or adj* : from the beginning — used as a direction in music to repeat [Italian]

dace \ˈdās\ *n, pl* **dace** : any of various small North American freshwater fishes related to the carp [Medieval French *dars*, from Medieval Latin *darsus*]

da·cha \ˈdäch-ə\ *n* : a Russian country house [Russian]

dachs·hund \ˈdäks-ˌhu̇nt, ˈdäk-sənt\ *n, pl* **dachs·hunds** : any of a breed of dogs of German origin with a long body, short legs, and long drooping ears [German, from *Dachs* "badger" + *Hund* "dog"]

dachshund

Da·cron \ˈdā-ˌkrän, ˈdak-ˌrän\ *trademark* — used for a synthetic polyester textile fiber

dac·tyl \ˈdak-tl\ *n* : a metrical foot consisting of one accented syllable followed by two unaccented syllables (as in *tenderly*) [Latin *dactylus* "foot of one long syllable followed by two short syllables," from Greek *daktylos*, literally, "finger"; from the fact that the first of three syllables is the longest, like the joints of the finger] — **dac·tyl·ic** \dak-ˈtil-ik\ *adj*

dad \ˈdad\ *n* : FATHER 1a [probably baby talk]

dad·dy \ˈdad-ē\ *n, pl* **daddies** : FATHER 1a

dad·dy long·legs \ˌdad-ē-ˈlȯng-ˌlegz\ *n* **1** : CRANE FLY **2** : any of an order (Opiliones) of arachnids that have slender usually long legs and that resemble spiders but have an oval body lacking a constriction — called also *harvestman*

da·do \ˈdād-ō\ *n, pl* **dadoes** **1** : the part of the pedestal of a column above the base **2** : the lower part of an interior wall when specially decorated or faced [Italian, "die, plinth"]

daemon *variant of* DEMON

daf·fo·dil \ˈdaf-ə-ˌdil\ *n* : any of various bulbous herbs with long slender leaves and flowers borne in spring; *esp* : one with flowers whose inner parts are arranged to form a trumpet-shaped tube — compare JONQUIL, NARCISSUS [probably from Dutch *de affodil* "the asphodel"]

daf·fy \ˈdaf-ē\ *adj* **daf·fi·er; -est** : CRAZY 2a, FOOLISH [obsolete English *daff* "fool"]

daft \ˈdaft\ *adj* **1** : SILLY, FOOLISH **2** : CRAZY 2a, INSANE [Middle English *dafte* "gentle, stupid"] — **daft·ly** *adv* — **daft·ness** \ˈdaft-nəs, ˈdaf-\ *n*

dag·ger \ˈdag-ər\ *n* **1** : a short weapon for stabbing **2** : a character † used as a reference mark or to indicate a death date [Middle English]

da·guerre·o·type \də-ˈger-ō-ˌtīp, -ˈger-ē-ō-ˌ\ *n* : an early photograph produced on a plate of silver or silver-covered copper; *also* : the process of producing such pictures [French *daguerréotype*, from L. J. M. *Daguerre*, died 1851, French painter]

dahl·ia \ˈdal-yə, ˈdäl-\ *n* : any of a genus of American tuberous-rooted herbs related to the daisies that have flower heads with brightly colored rays [Anders *Dahl*, died 1789, Swedish botanist]

[1]**dai·ly** \ˈdā-lē\ *adj* **1 a** : occurring, done, produced, or used every day or every weekday ⟨a *daily* newspaper⟩ **b** : of or relating to every day ⟨a *daily* visitor⟩ **2** : computed in terms of one day ⟨*daily* wages⟩ — **daily** *adv*

[2]**daily** *n, pl* **dailies** : a newspaper published every weekday

dai·mon \ˈdī-ˌmōn\ *n, pl* **dai·mo·nes** \ˈdī-mə-ˌnēz\ *or* **daimons** **1** : DEMON 2 **2** : DEMON 3 [Greek *daimōn*]

dai·myo *also* **dai·mio** \ˈdī-mē-ˌō, dī-ˈmyō\ *n, pl* **daimyo** *or* **daimyos** *also* **daimio** *or* **daimios** : a Japanese feudal baron [Japanese *daimyō*]

[1]**dain·ty** \ˈdānt-ē\ *n, pl* **dainties** : something that tastes delicious : DELICACY [Medieval French *deintié*, from Latin *dignitas* "dignity, worth"]

[2]**dainty** *adj* **dain·ti·er; -est** **1** : TASTY 1, DELICIOUS **2** : delicately pretty ⟨a *dainty* flower⟩ **3** : having or showing delicate or discriminating taste : FASTIDIOUS ⟨a *dainty* eater⟩ — **dain·ti·ly** \ˈdānt-l-ē\ *adv* — **dain·ti·ness** \ˈdānt-ē-nəs\ *n*

dai·qui·ri \ˈdī-kə-rē, ˈdak-ə-\ *n* : a cocktail made usually of rum, lime juice, and sugar [*Daiquirí*, Cuba]

dairy \ˈdeər-ē, ˈdaər-\ *n, pl* **dair·ies** **1** : a place where milk is kept and butter or cheese is made **2** : a farm devoted to the production of milk **3** : a company that sells milk and milk products **4** : milk from a cow or other domestic animal (as a goat) ; *also* : food (as ice cream, cheese, or yogurt) made primarily of or from milk [Middle English *deye* "dairymaid," from Old English *dǣge* "kneader of dough"]

Word History *Dairy* is related to *dough.* Old English *dǣge*, a relative of Old English *dāg*, "dough," meant "a kneader of bread" or "a maid." The Middle English form *deye* meant "maid" or, more specifically, "dairymaid." A dairy, then, is the place where the (dairy)maid works.

dairy cattle *n* : cattle kept for milk production

dairy·ing \ˈder-ē-ing\ *n* : the business of operating a dairy

dairy·maid \-ē-ˌmād\ *n* : a woman employed in a dairy

dairy·man \-ē-mən, -ˌman\ *n* : one who operates a dairy farm or works in a dairy

da·is \ˈdā-əs\ *n* : a raised platform in a hall or large room [Medieval French *deis*, from Late Latin *discus* "high table," from Latin *discus* "dish, quoit"]

dai·sy \ˈdā-zē\ *n, pl* **daisies** **1** : any of numerous plants of the composite family having flower heads with well-developed ray flowers usually in one or a few whorls: as **a** : a low-growing European herb with white or pink ray flowers — called also *En-*

glish *daisy* **b** : a tall leafy-stemmed European wildflower with a yellow center and long white ray flowers that is naturalized in the U.S. — called also *oxeye daisy* **2** : the flower head of a daisy **3** *cap* : a member of the Girl Scouts of the United States of America program for girls in kindergarten and first grade [Old English *dægesēage,* from *dæg* "day" + *ēage* "eye"]

daisy 1b

daisy–chain *vt* : to link together in series

daisy chain *n* : an interlinked series ⟨a *daisy chain* of devices⟩ ⟨a *daisy chain* of toddlers⟩

daisy wheel *n* : a disk with spokes bearing type that serves as the printing element of an electric typewriter or printer; *also* : a printer that uses such a disk [from its resemblance to the flower]

Da•ko•ta \də-ˈkōt-ə\ *n, pl* **Dakotas** *also* **Dakota** : a member of an American Indian people of the northern Mississippi valley

Da•lai La•ma \ˌdäl-ˌī-ˈläm-ə\ *n* : the spiritual head of Tibetan Buddhism [Mongolian *dalai* "ocean"]

dale \ˈdāl\ *n* : VALLEY 1 [Old English *dæl*]

dal•li•ance \ˈdal-ē-əns\ *n* : an act of dallying: as **a** : amorous play (as flirting or caressing) **b** : frivolous wasting of time : TRIFLING ⟨a short *dalliance* with radical ideas⟩

dal•ly \ˈdal-ē\ *vi* **dal•lied; dal•ly•ing** **1 a** : to act playfully; *esp* : to play amorously **b** : to deal lightly : TOY ⟨*dally* with a problem⟩ **2 a** : to waste time ⟨*dally* at one's work⟩ **b** : DAWDLE 2 ⟨*dally* on the way home⟩ [Anglo-French *dalier*] — **dal•li•er** *n*

dal•ma•tian \dal-ˈmā-shən\ *n, often cap* : any of a breed of medium-sized dogs having a white short-haired coat with many black or brown spots [from the supposed origin of the breed in Dalmatia]

dal•mat•ic \dal-ˈmat-ik\ *n* : a wide-sleeved robe with slit sides worn by a deacon or prelate [Late Latin *dalmatica,* from Latin *dalmaticus* "of Dalmatia"]

dal se•gno \däl-ˈsān-yō\ *adv* — used as a direction in music to return to the sign that marks the beginning of a repeat [Italian, "from the sign"]

dal•ton \ˈdȯlt-ⁿn\ *n* : ATOMIC MASS UNIT [John Dalton, died 1844, English chemist]

1**dam** \ˈdam\ *n* : the female parent of an animal and especially of a domestic animal [Middle English *dam, dame* "lady, dam"]

2**dam** *n* **1** : a barrier preventing the flow of water or of loose solid materials (as soil); *esp* : a barrier built across a watercourse **2** : a body of water confined by a dam [Middle English]

3**dam** *vt* **dammed; dam•ming** **1** : to provide or restrain with a dam ⟨*dam* a stream⟩ **2** : to stop up ⟨*dam* up an emotion⟩

1**dam•age** \ˈdam-ij\ *n* **1** : a loss or harm resulting from injury to person, property, or reputation **2** *pl* : compensation in money imposed by law for loss or injury [Medieval French, from *dan* "damage," from Latin *damnum*] ***synonyms*** see INJURY

2**damage** *vt* : to cause damage to

dam•ar *or* **dam•mar** \ˈdam-ər\ *n* : a clear to yellow resin obtained from Malayan and Indonesian trees and used in varnishes and inks [Malay]

dam•a•scene \ˈdam-ə-ˌsēn\ *vt* : to ornament (as iron or steel) with wavy patterns or with inlaid work of precious metals [Middle French *damasquiner,* from *damasquin* "of Damascus"]

dam•ask \ˈdam-əsk\ *n* **1** : a firm lustrous reversible patterned fabric used especially for household linen **2** : a tough steel having decorative wavy lines **3** : a grayish red [Medieval Latin *damascus,* from *Damascus*] — **damask** *adj*

damask rose *n* : a hardy rose introduced from Asia Minor and having large fragrant pink or white flowers that are the source of attar of roses [obsolete *Damask* "of Damascus"]

dame \ˈdām\ *n* **1** : a woman of rank, station, or authority: as **a** *archaic* : the mistress of a household **b** : the wife or daughter of a lord **c** : a woman who is a member of an order of knighthood — used as a title before a given name **2 a** : an elderly woman **b** : WOMAN 1 [Middle English, from Medieval French, from Latin *domina,* feminine of *dominus* "master"]

1**damn** \ˈdam\ *vb* **1** : to condemn to a punishment or fate; *esp* : to condemn to hell **2** : to condemn as bad or as a failure **3** : to swear at : CURSE [Medieval French *dampner,* from Latin *damnare,* from *damnum* "damage, penalty"]

2**damn** *n* **1** : the utterance of the word *damn* as a curse **2** : the least bit ⟨not worth a *damn*⟩

3**damn** *adj or adv* : DAMNED

dam•na•ble \ˈdam-nə-bəl\ *adj* **1** : liable to or deserving condemnation ⟨*damnable* conduct⟩ **2** : very bad : DETESTABLE ⟨*damnable* weather⟩ — **dam•na•bly** \-blē\ *adv*

dam•na•tion \dam-ˈnā-shən\ *n* **1** : the act of damning **2** : the state of being damned

1**damned** \ˈdamd\ *adj* **damned•er** \ˈdam-dər\; **damned•est** *or* **damnd•est** \ˈdam-dəst\ **1** : DAMNABLE ⟨this *damned* smog⟩ **2** : COMPLETE, UTTER ⟨*damned* nonsense⟩ **3** : EXTRAORDINARY 1b — used in the superlative ⟨the *damnedest* thing I ever saw⟩

2**damned** \ˈdamd, ˈdam\ *adv* : VERY 2, EXTREMELY ⟨a *damned* good job⟩

1**damp** \ˈdamp\ *n* **1** : a harmful gas especially in a coal mine **2** : slight or moderate wetness : HUMIDITY **3** : DAMPER 2, DISCOURAGEMENT [Dutch or Low German, "vapor"]

2**damp** *vb* **1 a** : to lessen the activity or intensity of — often used with *down* ⟨failure *damped* their enthusiasm⟩ ⟨*damp* down a furnace⟩ **b** : to check the vibration or oscillation of **2** : DAMPEN 2

3**damp** *adj* **1** : lacking in vigor or spirit : DEPRESSED **2** : slightly or moderately wet : MOIST ⟨a *damp* cellar⟩ — **damp•ly** *adv* — **damp•ness** *n*

damp•en \ˈdam-pən\ *vb* **damp•ened; damp•en•ing** \ˈdamp-ning, -ə-ning\ **1** : to check or diminish in activity or vigor : DEADEN **2** : to make or become damp — **damp•en•er** \ˈdamp-nər, -ə-nər\ *n*

damp•er \ˈdam-pər\ *n* **1** : a device that damps: as **a** : a valve or plate (as in the flue of a furnace) for regulating the draft **b** : a small felted block to stop the vibration of a piano string **c** : a device for checking oscillation **2** : a dulling or deadening influence ⟨put a *damper* on the celebration⟩

dam•sel \ˈdam-zəl\ *n* : a young woman [Medieval French *dameisele,* derived from Latin *domina* "lady"]

dam•sel•fish \ˈdam-zəl-ˌfish\ *n* : any of numerous often brilliantly colored marine fishes that live especially along coral reefs

dam•sel•fly \ˈdam-zəl-ˌflī\ *n* : any of numerous insects that are closely related to the dragonflies but have laterally projecting eyes and fold the wings above the body when at rest

dam•son \ˈdam-zən\ *n* : an Asian plum grown for its small tart purple fruit; *also* : this fruit [Latin *prunum damascenum,* literally, "plum of Damascus"]

1**dance** \ˈdans\ *vb* **1** : to perform a rhythmic and patterned succession of bodily movements usually to music **2** : to move quickly up and down or about **3** : to perform or take part in as a dancer **4** : to cause to dance [Medieval French *dancer*] — **danc•er** *n*

2**dance** *n* **1** : an act or instance of dancing **2** : a social gathering for dancing **3** : a piece of music by which dancing may be guided **4** : the art of dancing

dan•de•li•on \ˈdan-dl-ˌī-ən\ *n* : any of a genus of yellow-flowered herbs related to the daisies; *esp* : one with long deeply toothed stemless leaves sometimes grown as a potherb [Medieval French *dent de lion,* literally, "lion's tooth"]

dan•der \ˈdan-dər\ *n* **1** : minute scales from hair, feathers, or skin that may cause allergy **2** : TEMPER 4d, ANGER ⟨get one's *dander* up⟩ [alteration of *dandruff*]

dan•di•fy \ˈdan-di-ˌfī\ *vt* **-fied; -fy•ing** : to cause to resemble a dandy — **dan•di•fi•ca•tion** \ˌdan-di-fə-ˈkā-shən\ *n*

dan•dle \ˈdan-dl\ *vt* **dan•dled; dan•dling** \-dling, -dl-ing\ **1** : to move (as a baby) up and down in one's arms or on one's knee **2** : PAMPER, PET [origin unknown]

dan•druff \ˈdan-drəf\ *n* : scaly white or grayish flakes of dead skin cells especially of the scalp; *also* : the condition marked by the excessive shedding of such flakes [origin unknown]

1**dan•dy** \ˈdan-dē\ *n, pl* **dandies** **1** : a man who gives much attention to dress **2** : something excellent in its class [origin unknown] — **dan•dy•ish** \-dē-ish\ *adj* — **dan•dy•ish•ly** *adv*

2**dandy** *adj* **dan•di•er; -est** : very good : FIRST-RATE

Dane \ˈdān\ *n* **1** : a native or inhabitant of Denmark **2** : a person of Danish descent [Old Norse *Danr*]

dane•geld \ˈdān-ˌgeld\ *n, often cap* : an annual tax once imposed in England supposedly to buy off Danish invaders or to maintain forces to oppose them but continued as a land tax [Middle English, from *Dan* "Dane" + *geld* "tribute, payment," from Old English *gield*]

Dane·law \'dān-ˌlȯ\ *n* **1** : the law in force in the part of England held by the Danes before the Norman Conquest **2** : the part of England under the Danelaw

dan·ger \'dān-jər\ *n* **1** : exposure or liability to injury, harm, or evil ⟨their lives were in *danger*⟩ **2** : a case or cause of danger ⟨the *dangers* of mining⟩ [Middle English *daunger* "jurisdiction, liability," from Medieval French *dongier, dangier* "jurisdiction," derived from Latin *dominium* "dominion, ownership"]

synonyms DANGER, PERIL, HAZARD, RISK mean a threat of loss, injury, or death. DANGER implies possible but not necessarily inescapable harm ⟨an animal in *danger* of becoming extinct⟩. PERIL suggests impending danger and cause for fear ⟨during the tornado our lives were in *peril*⟩. HAZARD implies danger from chance or something beyond one's control ⟨the *hazards* of mining coal⟩. RISK implies danger following on a chance voluntarily taken ⟨accepts the *risks* that come with flying a plane⟩.

dan·ger·ous \'dānj-rəs, -ə-rəs\ *adj* **1** : exposing to or involving danger ⟨a *dangerous* mission⟩ **2** : able or likely to inflict injury ⟨*dangerous* weapons⟩ — **dan·ger·ous·ly** *adv* — **dan·ger·ous·ness** *n*

dan·gle \'dang-gəl\ *vb* **dan·gled; dan·gling** \-gə-ling, -gling\ **1** : to hang loosely especially with a swinging motion **2** : to be a hanger-on or dependent **3** : to be left without proper grammatical connection in a sentence ⟨a *dangling* participle⟩ **4** : to cause to dangle : SWING **5** : to keep hanging uncertainly : hold suspended [probably of Scandinavian origin] — **dan·gler** \-gə-lər, -glər\ *n*

Dan·iel \'dan-yəl\ *n* : a book of narratives, visions, and prophecies in canonical Jewish and Christian Scriptures — see BIBLE table

[1]**Dan·ish** \'dā-nish\ *adj* : of, relating to, or characteristic of Denmark, the Danes, or the Danish language

[2]**Danish** *n* : the Germanic language of the Danes

Danish pastry *n* : a pastry made of rich yeast-raised dough

dank \'dangk\ *adj* : unpleasantly moist or wet [Middle English *danke*] — **dank·ly** *adv* — **dank·ness** *n*

dan·seur \dänⁿ-'sər, dän-\ *n* : a male ballet dancer [French, from *danser* "to dance"]

dan·seuse \dänⁿ-'süz, -'sərz; dän-'süz\ *n* : a female ballet dancer [French, feminine of *danseur*]

daph·nia \'daf-nē-ə\ *n* : any of a genus of tiny water fleas with antennae used for movement [New Latin, genus name]

dap·per \'dap-ər\ *adj* **1** : being neat and trim in dress or appearance : SPRUCE **2** : being alert and lively in movement and manners [Dutch, "quick, strong"] — **dap·per·ly** *adv* — **dap·per·ness** *n*

[1]**dap·ple** \'dap-əl\ *n* **1** : any spot or patch of a dappled pattern **2** : a dappled state **3** : a dappled animal (as a horse) [Middle English *dappel-gray* "gray with spots of a different color"]

[2]**dapple** *vb* **dap·pled; dap·pling** \'dap-ling, -ə-ling\ : to mark or become marked with a dappled pattern

dappled *also* **dapple** *adj* : marked with small spots or patches of a color or shade different from their background ⟨a *dappled* horse⟩

[1]**dare** \'daər, 'deər\ *vb* **1 a** : to have sufficient courage : be bold enough to ⟨try it if you *dare*⟩ **b** — used as an auxiliary verb ⟨no one *dared* say a word⟩ **2** : to confront boldly ⟨*dared* the dangerous crossing⟩ **3** : to challenge to perform an action especially as proof of courage ⟨I *dare* you⟩ [Old English *dear* "I dare, he dares"]

[2]**dare** *n* : an act or instance of daring : CHALLENGE ⟨dived from the bridge on a *dare*⟩

dare·dev·il \'daər-ˌdev-əl, 'deər-\ *n* : a recklessly bold person — **daredevil** *adj*

[1]**dar·ing** \'daər-ing, 'deər-\ *adj* : fearlessly ready to take risks — **dar·ing·ly** \-ing-lē\ *adv* — **dar·ing·ness** *n*

synonyms DARING, RASH, RECKLESS, FOOLHARDY mean exposing oneself to danger more than is sensible. DARING stresses fearlessness ⟨*daring* mountain climbers⟩. RASH implies imprudent hastiness ⟨a *rash* decision⟩. RECKLESS implies complete heedlessness of likely consequences ⟨a *reckless* driver⟩. FOOLHARDY suggests recklessness and foolish daring ⟨a *foolhardy* dive into shallow water⟩. ***synonyms*** see in addition ADVENTUROUS

[2]**daring** *n* : venturesome boldness

[1]**dark** \'därk\ *adj* **1 a** : being without light or without much light ⟨in winter it gets *dark* early⟩ **b** : not giving off light ⟨the *dark* side of the moon⟩ **2** : not light in color ⟨a *dark* suit⟩; *esp* : of low or very low lightness ⟨*dark* blue⟩ **3** : not bright and cheerful : GLOOMY ⟨look on the *dark* side of things⟩ **4** : lacking knowledge and culture ⟨a *dark* period in history⟩ **5 a** : not clear to the understanding ⟨*dark* sayings⟩ **b** : not known or explored because of remoteness ⟨the *darkest* reaches of the forest⟩ **6** : not fair in complexion : SWARTHY ⟨their *dark* good looks⟩ **7** : SECRET 1a ⟨kept their plans *dark*⟩ [Old English *deorc*] ***synonyms*** see OBSCURE — **dark·ish** \'där-kish\ *adj* — **dark·ly** \-klē\ *adv* — **dark·ness** \'därk-nəs\ *n*

[2]**dark** *n* **1** : absence of light : DARKNESS **2 a** : a place or time of little or no light **b** : NIGHT, NIGHTFALL ⟨get home before *dark*⟩ **3** : a dark or deep color — **in the dark 1** : in secrecy **2** : in ignorance

dark adaptation *n* : the process by which the eye adapts to seeing in weak light — **dark–adapt·ed** \ˌdärk-ə-'dap-təd\ *adj*

dark age *n* **1** *pl, cap D&A* : the period in European history from about A.D. 476 to about 1000; *also* : MIDDLE AGES **2** *often pl, often cap D&A* : the primitive period in the development of something ⟨the *dark ages* of computers⟩

dark·en \'där-kən\ *vb* **dark·ened; dark·en·ing** \'därk-ning, -ə-ning\ **1** : to make or grow dark or darker ⟨*darken* a room⟩ ⟨the sky is *darkening*⟩ **2** : to make less clear : OBSCURE ⟨ignorance *darkens* the understanding⟩ **3** : TAINT, TARNISH ⟨*darken* a reputation⟩ **4** : to make or become gloomy or forbidding ⟨*darkened* their hopes⟩ ⟨a face *darkened* in anger⟩ — **dark·en·er** \'därk-ner, -ə-nər\ *n*

dark horse *n* : a contestant or a political figure whose abilities and chances as a contender are not known ⟨the convention nominated a *dark horse*⟩

Word History Sometimes in a horse race a horse whose name and ability are not widely known puts on a surprisingly good show and defeats his more famous rivals. Such a horse is called *dark,* not because of his color (which might be anything), but because of his obscurity. The use of the term *dark horse* has been extended from racehorses to obscure competitors who do unexpectedly well in contests of other kinds. It is most often used to refer to a little known political candidate who will surprise people if he or she wins.

dark lantern *n* : a lantern that can be closed to conceal the light

dark·ling \'där-kling\ *adj* **1** : DARK **2** : done or taking place in the dark

dark matter *n* : unseen matter that is thought to exist in the universe but has not yet been directly detected or observed

dark reaction *n* : the part of photosynthesis that does not require light and that uses carbon dioxide in the formation of carbohydrate; *esp* : CALVIN CYCLE

dark·room \'därk-ˌrüm, -ˌru̇m\ *n* : a lightproof room used in developing sensitive photographic materials (as film or prints)

dark·some \'därk-səm\ *adj* : gloomily somber : DARK

[1]**dar·ling** \'där-ling\ *n* **1** : a dearly loved person **2** : FAVORITE [Old English *dēorling,* from *dēore* "dear"]

[2]**darling** *adj* **1** : dearly loved : FAVORITE **2** : very pleasing : CHARMING — **dar·ling·ly** \-ling-lē\ *adv*

darm·stadt·i·um \ˌdärm-'stat-ē-əm\ *n* : a short-lived radioactive element produced artificially — see ELEMENT table [New Latin, from *Darmstadt,* Germany]

[1]**darn** \'därn\ *vb* : to mend with interlacing stitches ⟨*darn* socks⟩ [probably from French dialect *darner*]

[2]**darn** *n* : a place (as in a sock) that has been darned

[3]**darn** *vb* : DAMN 3 [euphemism] — **darn** \'därn\ *or* **darned** \'därnd, 'därn\ *adj or adv*

[4]**darn** *n* : [2]DAMN 2 ⟨don't give a *darn*⟩

dar·nel \'därn-l\ *n* : any of several usually weedy grasses with bristly flower clusters [Middle English]

darning needle *n* **1** : a long needle with a large eye for use in darning **2** : DRAGONFLY, DAMSELFLY

[1]**dart** \'därt\ *n* **1 a** : a small missile usually pointed at one end and feathered on the other **b** *pl* : a game in which darts are thrown at a target **2 a** : something projected with sudden speed; *esp* : a sharp glance **b** : a sudden pain or distress **3** : a stitched tapering fold in a garment **4** : a quick movement ⟨made a *dart* for the door⟩ [Medieval French, of Germanic origin]

[2]**dart** *vb* **1** : to throw with a sudden movement ⟨*dart* a javelin⟩ **2** : to thrust or move suddenly or rapidly

dart·er \'därt ər\ *n* **:** any of numerous small North American freshwater fishes closely related to the perches

Dar·win·ian \där-'win-ē-ən\ *adj* **:** of or relating to Charles Darwin, his theories especially of evolution, or his followers — **Darwinian** *n*

Dar·win·ism \'där-wə-ˌniz-əm\ *n* **1 :** a theory of evolution that explains how species of plants and animals arose and continue to arise by variation among offspring of a given plant or animal, by the survival of well-adapted variations in the process of natural selection, and by the gradual accumulation of differences over time **2 :** a theory that unchangeable forces allow only the fittest persons or organizations to prosper in a competitive environment or situation ⟨economic *Darwinism*⟩ — **Dar·win·ist** \-wə-nəst\ *n or adj*

Dar·win's finches \ˌdär-wənz-\ *n, pl* **:** finches of the Galápagos Islands having great variation in bill shape among the various species

[1]**dash** \'dash\ *vb* **1 :** to knock, hurl, or thrust violently ⟨the storm *dashed* the boat against a reef⟩ **2 :** to break by striking or knocking ⟨the statue was *dashed* to pieces when it fell⟩ **3 :** SPLASH 1b, SPATTER ⟨clothes *dashed* with mud⟩ **4 a :** DESTROY 1, RUIN ⟨our hopes were *dashed* every time⟩ **b :** to lower in spirit or mood **:** DEPRESS **5 :** to affect by mixing in something different ⟨oil *dashed* with vinegar⟩ **6 :** to perform or finish hastily ⟨*dash* off a letter⟩ **7 :** to move with sudden speed [Middle English *dasshen*] — **dash·er** *n*

[2]**dash** *n* **1 :** a sudden burst or splash **2 a :** a short stroke of a pen **b :** a punctuation mark — used chiefly to indicate a break in the thought or structure of a sentence **3 :** a small usually distinctive addition ⟨a *dash* of salt⟩ **4 :** a flashy display **5 :** animation in style and action **6 a :** a sudden rush or attempt **b :** a short fast race **7 :** a long click or buzz forming a letter or part of a letter (as in Morse code) **8 :** DASHBOARD 2

dash·board \'dash-ˌbōrd, -ˌbȯrd\ *n* **1 :** a screen on the front of a usually horse-drawn vehicle to keep out water, mud, or snow **2 :** a panel extending across an automobile or aircraft below the windshield and usually containing dials and controls

dashed \'dasht\ *adj* **:** made up of a series of dashes

da·shi·ki \də-'shē-kē\ *n* **:** a usually brightly colored loose-fitting pullover garment [Yoruba (a language of western Africa) *dàńṣíkí*]

dashiki

dash·ing \'dash-ing\ *adj* **1 :** marked by vigorous action ⟨a *dashing* attack⟩ **2 :** marked by smartness especially in dress and manners ⟨made a *dashing* appearance⟩ — **dash·ing·ly** *adv*

das·tard \'das-tərd\ *n* **:** COWARD; *esp* **:** one who commits treacherous acts [Middle English]

das·tard·ly \-lē\ *adj* **:** mean and treacherously cowardly — **das·tard·li·ness** *n*

da·ta \'dāt-ə, 'dat- *also* 'dät-\ *n sing or pl* **1 :** factual information (as measurements or statistics) used as a basis for reasoning, discussion, or calculation **2 :** information in numerical form for use especially in a computer [plural of *datum*]

data bank *n* **:** DATABASE

da·ta·base \'dāt-ə-ˌbās, 'dat- *also* 'dät-\ *n* **:** a collection of data that is organized especially to be used by a computer

data processing *n* **:** the process of turning raw data into a form that a computer can use and then having the computer perform useful operations on the data

data structure *n* **:** any of the various ways of organizing computer data (as in an array or file)

[1]**date** \'dāt\ *n* **1 :** the oblong edible fruit of a tall Old World palm **2 :** the palm that produces dates — called also *date palm* [Medieval French, derived from Latin *dactylus,* from Greek *daktylos,* literally, "finger"]

Word History The *date* that means "the fruit of the date palm" is not related to the *date* that means "a time." The earlier *date* is descended from Greek *daktylos.* The primary meaning of *daktylos* is "finger," but the word was also used for the fruit. The reason for this extension of meaning is debated. Some suggest that the pinnately divided leaves of the date palm look rather like fingers and that this fact gave the fruit its name. This account would be more convincing if the tree, rather than its fruit, had been named *daktylos.* It is more likely that the clustered dates themselves were felt to resemble fingers.

[2]**date** *n* **1 a :** the time at which an event occurs **b :** a statement giving the time of execution or making ⟨the *date* on the check⟩ **2 :** DURATION 2 **3 :** the period of time to which something belongs ⟨sculptures of an early *date*⟩ **4 a :** APPOINTMENT 3; *esp* **:** a social engagement between two persons that often has a romantic character **b :** a person with whom one has a social engagement [Medieval French, from Late Latin *data,* from *data* "given" (as in *data Romae* "given at Rome"), from Latin *dare* "to give"] — **to date :** up to the present moment ⟨have received no complaints *to date*⟩

Word History The English word *date* has nothing to do etymologically with *day* but is descended from Latin *dare,* "to give." In ancient Rome, the date of a letter was written in this manner: "Datam Romae Kal. Aprilis." (I gave [this letter] at Rome April 1—the calends of April.) A later formula used *data Romae,* "given at Rome," instead of *datam Romae,* "I gave at Rome." By the 6th century A.D., *data* had become a noun used for the date on a letter. In French its descendant *date* was used not only for the date on a letter, but also for the actual time that such a date indicated or indeed for any given point in time.

[3]**date** *vb* **1 :** to determine the date of ⟨*date* an antique⟩ **2 :** to record the date of or on ⟨*date* a letter⟩ **3 :** to mark with characteristics typical of a particular period ⟨the architecture *dates* the house⟩ **4 a :** to make or have a date with **b :** to go out on usually romantic dates **5 a :** ORIGINATE 2 ⟨that chair *dates* from the 16th century⟩ **b :** to go as far back **:** EXTEND ⟨*dating* back to childhood⟩ — **dat·able** *also* **date·able** \'dāt-ə-bəl\ *adj* — **dat·er** *n*

dat·ed \'dāt-əd\ *adj* **1 :** having a date **2 :** OLD-FASHIONED 1 ⟨*dated* formalities⟩ — **dat·ed·ly** *adv* — **dat·ed·ness** *n*

date·less \'dāt-ləs\ *adj* **1 :** ENDLESS 1 **2 :** having no date **3 :** too ancient to be dated **4 :** not restricted to a particular time or date

date·line \'dāt-ˌlīn\ *n* **1 :** a line in a publication giving the date and place of composition or issue **2** *usually* **date line :** INTERNATIONAL DATE LINE — **dateline** *vt*

date rape *n* **:** rape committed by the victim's date

da·tive \'dāt-iv\ *adj* **:** of, relating to, or being the grammatical case that marks typically the indirect object of a verb or the object of some prepositions [Latin *dativus,* from *dare* "to give"] — **dative** *n*

da·tum \'dāt-əm, 'dat-, 'dät-\ *n, pl* **da·ta** \-ə\ *or* **datums :** something used as a basis for reasoning or inference or for calculating or measuring [Latin, "something given," from *datus,* past participle of *dare* "to give"]

[1]**daub** \'dȯb, 'däb\ *vb* **1 :** to cover with soft adhesive matter **:** PLASTER **2 :** to coat with a dirty substance **3 :** to apply (as paint) crudely [Medieval French *dauber*] — **daub·er** *n*

[2]**daub** *n* **1 :** something daubed on **2 :** a crudely painted picture

[1]**daugh·ter** \'dȯt-ər\ *n* **1 a :** a female offspring especially of human parents **b :** a female adopted child **c :** a human female descendant **2 :** something considered as a daughter **3 :** an isotope that is the product of the radioactive decay of a given element [Old English *dohtor*] — **daugh·ter·ly** \-lē\ *adj*

[2]**daughter** *adj* **1 :** having the characteristics or relationship of a daughter ⟨*daughter* cities⟩ **2 :** belonging to the first generation of offspring, cells, parts of cells, or molecules produced by reproduction, division, or formation of replicas ⟨*daughter* cells⟩ ⟨*daughter* DNA molecules⟩

daugh·ter–in–law \'dȯt-ə-rən-ˌlȯ, -ərn-ˌlȯ\ *n, pl* **daugh·ters–in–law** \-ər-zən-\ **:** the wife of one's son

daunt \'dȯnt, 'dänt\ *vt* **:** to lessen the courage of **:** make afraid [Medieval French *danter, daunter,* from Latin *domitare* "to tame," from *domare* "to tame"]

daunt·ing \'dȯnt-ing\ *adj* **:** tending to overwhelm or intimidate ⟨a *daunting* task⟩ — **daunt·ing·ly** *adv*

daunt·less \-ləs\ *adj* **:** FEARLESS, UNDAUNTED ⟨a *dauntless* hero⟩ — **daunt·less·ly** *adv* — **daunt·less·ness** *n*

dau·phin \'dō-fən\ *n, often cap* **:** the eldest son of a king of

France [Medieval French *dolphyn,* from earlier *dalfin,* title of lords of the Dauphiné, from *Dalfin,* a surname]

dav·en·port \ˈdav-ən-ˌpōrt, ˈdav-m-, -ˌpȯrt\ *n* : a large upholstered sofa [probably from the name *Davenport*]

da·vit \ˈdā-vət, ˈdav-ət\ *n* : one of a pair of crane arms used for carrying small boats (as lifeboats or dinghies) aboard ships or yachts and for raising and lowering them to the water; *also* : a similar hoist (as over a hatchway) [Medieval French *daviet* "joiner's cramp," probably from the name *David*]

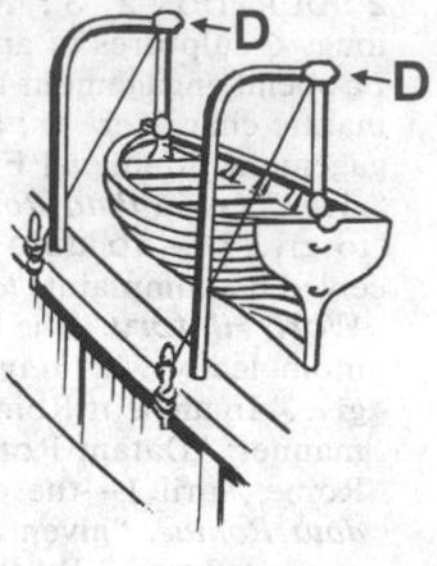

D davit

Da·vy Jones's locker \ˈdā-vē-ˌjōnz, -ˌjōnz-əz-\ *n* : the bottom of the sea [*Davy Jones,* legendary spirit of the sea]

daw \ˈdȯ\ *n* : JACKDAW [Middle English *dawe*]

daw·dle \ˈdȯd-l\ *vb* **daw·dled; daw·dling** \ˈdȯd-ling, -l-ing\ **1** : to spend time wastefully or idly : LINGER ⟨*dawdle* over homework⟩ **2** : to move lackadaisically : LOITER ⟨*dawdles* on the way back⟩ **3** : IDLE 3 ⟨*dawdle* the time away⟩ [origin unknown] — **daw·dler** \ˈdȯd-lər, -l-ər\ *n*

1**dawn** \ˈdȯn, ˈdän\ *vi* **1** : to become dawn : begin to grow light as the sun rises **2** : to begin to appear or develop ⟨a smile *dawned* on her face⟩ **3** : to begin to be perceived or understood ⟨the truth *dawned* on them⟩ [Middle English *dawnen,* from *dawning* "daybreak"]

2**dawn** *n* **1** : the first appearance of light in the morning **2** : a first appearance : BEGINNING ⟨the *dawn* of a new era⟩

day \ˈdā\ *n* **1 a** : the time of light between one night and the next **b** : DAYLIGHT 1 **2** : the period of rotation of a planet (as earth) or a moon on its axis **3** : a period of 24 hours beginning at midnight **4** : a specified day or date ⟨the *day* of the picnic⟩ **5** : a specified time or period : AGE ⟨in our parents' *day*⟩ **6** : the conflict or contention of the day ⟨played hard and won the *day*⟩ **7** : the time set apart by usage or law for work ⟨the 8-hour *day*⟩ [Old English *dæg*]

day·bed \ˈdā-ˌbed\ *n* : a couch that can be converted into a bed

day·book \-ˌbu̇k\ *n* : JOURNAL 1b, DIARY

day·break \-ˌbrāk\ *n* : DAWN 1

day care *n* **1** : supervision of and care for children or disabled adults that is provided during the day by a person or organization **2** : a program, facility, or organization offering day care

1**day·dream** \-ˌdrēm\ *n* : a dreamy sequence of usually happy or pleasant imaginings

2**daydream** *vi* : to have a daydream — **day·dream·er** *n*

day laborer *n* : one who works for daily wages especially as an unskilled laborer

day letter *n* : a telegram sent during the day that has a lower priority than a regular telegram — compare NIGHT LETTER

day·light \ˈdā-ˌlīt\ *n* **1** : the light of day **2** : DAYTIME **3** : DAWN 1 **4** : understanding of something that has been unclear ⟨began to see *daylight* on the problem⟩ **5** *pl* : mental soundness or stability : WITS ⟨scared the *daylights* out of them⟩

daylight saving time *n* : time usually one hour ahead of standard time — called also *daylight saving, daylight savings, daylight savings time, daylight time*

day·lily \ˈdā-ˌlil-ē\ *n* : any of various Eurasian plants related to the lilies with short-lived flowers that are widespread in cultivation and naturalized in the wild

day–neutral *adj* : flowering or developing to maturity regardless of relative length of alternating light and dark periods — compare LONG-DAY, SHORT-DAY

day nursery *n* : a public center for the care and training of young children; *also* : NURSERY SCHOOL

Day of Atonement : YOM KIPPUR

days \ˈdāz\ *adv* : in the daytime repeatedly ⟨work *days*⟩

day school *n* : an elementary or secondary school held on weekdays; *esp* : a private school without boarding facilities

day·star \ˈdā-ˌstär\ *n* **1** : MORNING STAR **2** : SUN 1a

day·time \ˈdā-ˌtīm\ *n* : the time during which there is daylight

day–to–day \ˈdāt-ə-ˌdā\ *adj* **1** : taking place, made, or done in the course of days ⟨*day-to-day* operations⟩; *also* : EVERYDAY ⟨*day-to-day* life⟩ **2** : providing for a day at a time with little thought for the future ⟨an aimless *day-to-day* existence⟩

daze \ˈdāz\ *vt* **1** : to stupefy especially by a blow : STUN **2** : to dazzle with light [Middle English *dasen*] — **daze** *n*

daz·zle \ˈdaz-əl\ *vb* **daz·zled; daz·zling** \ˈdaz-ling, -ə-ling\ **1 a** : to shine brightly ⟨a *dazzling* jewel⟩ **b** : to overpower with light ⟨the desert sunlight *dazzled* them⟩ **2** : to impress greatly or confound with brilliance ⟨*dazzled* the crowd with their performances⟩ [from *daze*] — **dazzle** *n* — **daz·zler** \ˈdaz-lər, -ə-lər\ *n* — **daz·zling·ly** \ˈdaz-ling-lē, -ə-ling-\ *adv*

D–day *n* : a day set for launching an operation [*D,* abbreviation for *day*]

DDT \ˌdēd-ˌē-ˈtē\ *n* : a colorless odorless water-insoluble compound formerly used widely as an insecticide that tends to accumulate in the environment and has toxic effects on many vertebrates [from the initial letters of its chemical components]

de- *prefix* **1 a** : do the opposite of ⟨*de*vitalize⟩ **b** : reverse of **2** : remove (a specified thing) from ⟨*de*louse⟩: remove from (a specified thing) ⟨*de*throne⟩ **3** : reduce ⟨*de*value⟩ **4** : something derived from (a specified thing) : derived from something (of a specified nature) ⟨*de*nominative⟩ **5** : get off of (a specified thing) ⟨*de*plane⟩ [Latin *de-* "down, away, from"]

dea·con \ˈdē-kən\ *n* : a subordinate officer in a Christian church: as **a** : a clergyman next below a priest **b** : a layman with particular duties in various Christian churches [Old English *dēacon,* from Late Latin *diaconus,* from Greek *diakonos,* literally, "servant"]

dea·con·ess \ˈdē-kə-nəs\ *n* : a laywoman chosen to assist in the church ministry; *esp* : one in a Protestant order

de·ac·ti·vate \dē-ˈak-tə-ˌvāt\ *vt* : to make inactive or ineffective — **de·ac·ti·va·tion** \ˌdē-ˌak-tə-ˈvā-shən\ *n*

1**dead** \ˈded\ *adj* **1** : deprived of life : having died : LIFELESS **2 a** : having the appearance of death : DEATHLY ⟨in a *dead* faint⟩ **b** : lacking the power to move, feel, or respond : NUMB **c** : very tired **d** : UNRESPONSIVE ⟨*dead* to pity⟩ **e** : grown cold : burned out ⟨*dead* coals⟩ **3 a** : not naturally endowed with life : INANIMATE ⟨*dead* matter⟩ **b** : no longer producing or functioning ⟨a *dead* battery⟩ **4 a** : lacking power, significance, or effect ⟨a *dead* law⟩ **b** : no longer in use : OBSOLETE ⟨a *dead* language⟩ **c** : no longer active : EXTINCT ⟨a *dead* volcano⟩ **d** : lacking in fun or activity ⟨a *dead* party⟩ **e** (1) : lacking in commercial activity : QUIET (2) : commercially idle or unproductive ⟨*dead* capital⟩ **f** : lacking elasticity ⟨a *dead* tennis ball⟩ **g** : being out of action or out of use; *esp* : free from any connection to a source of voltage and free from electric charges ⟨a *dead* telephone line⟩ **h** : being out of play ⟨a *dead* ball⟩ ⟨*dead* cards⟩ **5 a** : not circulating : STAGNANT ⟨*dead* air⟩ **b** : lacking warmth, vigor, or taste ⟨a *dead* wine⟩ **6 a** : absolutely uniform ⟨the *dead* level of the prairie⟩ **b** : UNERRING, EXACT ⟨a *dead* shot⟩ ⟨*dead* center of the target⟩ **c** : SUDDEN 1a ⟨a *dead* stop⟩ **d** : ABSOLUTE 4, TOTAL ⟨a *dead* loss⟩ [Old English *dēad*] — **dead·ness** *n* — **over one's dead body** : only by overcoming one's utter and determined resistance

2**dead** *n, pl* **dead** **1** : one that is dead — usually used collectively ⟨the living and the *dead*⟩ **2** : the time of greatest quiet ⟨the *dead* of night⟩

3**dead** *adv* **1** : ABSOLUTELY, UTTERLY ⟨*dead* certain⟩ **2** : suddenly and completely ⟨stopped *dead*⟩ **3** : DIRECTLY ⟨*dead* ahead⟩

dead·beat \ˈded-ˌbēt\ *n* : one who persistently fails to pay debts

dead bolt *n* : a lock bolt that is moved by turning a knob or key

dead·en \ˈded-n\ *vt* **dead·ened; dead·en·ing** \ˈded-ning, -n-ing\ **1** : to impair in vigor or sensation : BLUNT ⟨*deaden* pain with drugs⟩ **2 a** : to deprive of brilliance or spirit **b** : to make (as a wall) soundproof — **dead·en·er** \ˈded-nər, -n-ər\ *n* — **dead·en·ing·ly** \-ning-lē, -n-ing-lē\ *adv*

dead–end \ˈded-ˈend\ *adj* **1 a** : having no opportunities for advancement ⟨a *dead-end* job⟩ **b** : lacking an exit ⟨a *dead-end* street⟩ **2** : UNRULY ⟨*dead-end* kids⟩

dead end *n* **1** : an end (as of a street) without an exit **2** : a position, situation, or course of action that leads to nothing further

dead·eye \ˈded-ˌī\ *n* : an expert marksman

dead heat *n* : a contest in which two or more contestants tie

dead letter *n* **1** : something that has lost its force or authority without being formally abolished **2** : a letter that is undeliverable and unreturnable by the post office

dead·line \ˈded-ˌlīn\ *n* : a date or time before which something must be done

dead·lock \ˈded-ˌläk\ *n* : a stoppage of action because both sides in a struggle are equally powerful and neither will give in — **deadlock** *vb*

1**dead·ly** \ˈded-lē\ *adj* **dead·li·er; -est** **1** : likely to cause or capable of causing death ⟨a *deadly* disease⟩ **2 a** : aiming to kill or destroy : IMPLACABLE ⟨a *deadly* enemy⟩ **b** : very accurate : UNERRING ⟨a *deadly* marksman⟩ **3 a** : tending to deprive of force or vitality ⟨a *deadly* habit⟩ **b** : suggestive of death especially in dullness or lack of animation ⟨a *deadly* conversation⟩ **4** : very great : EXTREME ⟨a *deadly* bore⟩ — **dead·li·ness** *n*

synonyms DEADLY, MORTAL, FATAL, LETHAL mean causing or capable of causing death. DEADLY applies to an established or very likely cause of death ⟨a *deadly* disease⟩. MORTAL implies that death has occurred or is inevitable ⟨a *mortal* wound⟩. FATAL stresses the inevitability of what has in fact resulted in death or destruction ⟨*fatal* consequences⟩. LETHAL applies to something that is bound to cause death or exists for the destruction of life ⟨*lethal* gas⟩.

[2]**deadly** *adv* **1** : in a manner suggesting death ⟨*deadly* pale⟩ **2** : EXTREMELY, VERY ⟨*deadly* dull⟩

deadly nightshade *n* : BELLADONNA 1

deadly sin *n* : one of seven sins of pride, covetousness, lust, anger, gluttony, envy, and sloth believed by Christians to be fatal to spiritual progress

dead man's float *n* : a floating position in which a person lies face down in the water with the arms extended forward

dead march *n* : a solemn march for a funeral

[1]**dead·pan** \ˈded-ˌpan\ *adj* : marked by an impassive manner, style, or expression [English slang *pan* "face," from [1]*pan*] — **deadpan** *adv*

[2]**deadpan** *n* : a completely expressionless face

dead reckoning *n* : the determination without the aid of celestial observations of the position of a ship or aircraft from the record of the courses sailed or flown and the distance made from the last known position

dead·weight \ˈded-ˈwāt\ *n* : the unrelieved weight of an inert mass

dead·wood \ˈded-ˌwu̇d\ *n* **1** : wood dead on the tree : dead branches **2** : useless personnel or material

deaf \ˈdef\ *adj* **1** : wholly or partly unable to hear **2** : unwilling to hear or listen ⟨*deaf* to all suggestions⟩ [Old English *dēaf*] — **deaf·ness** *n*

deaf·en \ˈdef-ən\ *vb* **deaf·ened; deaf·en·ing** \ˈdef-ning, -ə-ning\ : to make deaf — **deaf·en·ing·ly** \-lē\ *adv*

deaf–mute \ˈdef-ˌmyüt\ *n, often offensive* : a deaf person who cannot speak — **deaf–mute** *adj, often offensive*

[1]**deal** \ˈdēl\ *n* **1** : a usually large or indefinite quantity or degree ⟨means a great *deal*⟩ ⟨a good *deal* faster⟩ **2 a** : the act or right of distributing cards to players in a card game **b** : HAND 11b [Old English *dǣl* "part, quantity"]

[2]**deal** *vb* **dealt** \ˈdelt\; **deal·ing** \ˈdē-ling\ **1** : to give as one's portion : DISTRIBUTE ⟨*deal* out sandwiches⟩ ⟨*deal* the cards⟩ **2** : DELIVER 5, BESTOW ⟨*dealt* the dog a blow⟩ **3** : to have to do ⟨the book *deals* with art⟩ **4** : to take action ⟨*deal* with offenders⟩ **5 a** : to engage in bargaining : TRADE **b** : to sell or distribute something as a business ⟨*deals* in books⟩ — **deal·er** *n*

[3]**deal** *n* **1 a** : an act of dealing : BARGAINING **b** : the result of bargaining : a mutual agreement ⟨make a *deal* for a used car⟩ **2** : treatment received ⟨a dirty *deal*⟩ **3** : an arrangement for mutual advantage

[4]**deal** *n* : wood or a board of fir or pine [Dutch or Low German *dele* "plank"] — **deal** *adj*

dealing *n* **1** *pl* : social or business interactions ⟨it's foolish to have *dealings* with such people⟩ **2** : a way of acting or of doing business ⟨believed in fair *dealing*⟩

de·am·i·nase \dē-ˈam-ə-ˌnās\ *n* : an enzyme that promotes removal of amino groups

de·am·i·nate \-ˌnāt\ *vt* : to remove the amino group from (a compound) — **de·am·i·na·tion** \ˌdē-ˌam-ə-ˈnā-shən\ *n*

dean \ˈdēn\ *n* **1 a** : the head of the chapter of a collegiate or cathedral church **b** : a Roman Catholic priest who supervises one district of a diocese **2 a** : the head of a division, faculty, college, or school of a university **b** : a college or secondary school administrator in charge of counseling and disciplining students **3** : the senior member of a group ⟨the *dean* of the diplomatic corps⟩ [Medieval French *deien*, from Late Latin *decanus*, literally, "chief of ten," from Greek *dekanos*, from *deka* "ten"] — **dean·ship** \-ˌship\ *n*

dean·ery \ˈdēn-rē, -ə-rē\ *n, pl* **-er·ies** : the office, jurisdiction, or official residence of a clerical dean

[1]**dear** \ˈdiər\ *adj* **1** : highly valued : PRECIOUS ⟨a *dear* memory⟩ — often used in a salutation ⟨*Dear* Ms. Smith⟩ **2** : feeling or expressing love : AFFECTIONATE **3** : EXPENSIVE **4** : HEARTFELT ⟨my *dearest* wish⟩ [Old English *dēore*] ***synonyms*** see COSTLY — **dear** *adv* — **dear·ly** *adv* — **dear·ness** *n*

[2]**dear** *n* **1** : a loved one : DARLING **2** : a lovable person

dearth \ˈdərth\ *n* **1** : scarcity that makes dear; *esp* : FAMINE **2** : inadequate supply : LACK

death \ˈdeth\ *n* **1** : a permanent cessation of all vital functions : the end of life — compare BRAIN DEATH **2** : the cause of loss of life **3** *cap* : the destroyer of life represented usually as a skeleton with a scythe **4** : the state of being dead **5** : the passing or destruction of something inanimate or intangible ⟨the *death* of feudalism⟩ [Old English *dēath*] — **death·like** \-ˌlīk\ *adj*

death·bed \ˈdeth-ˌbed\ *n* **1** : the bed in which a person dies **2** : the last hours of life — **on one's deathbed** : near death

death·blow \-ˌblō\ *n* : a destructive or killing stroke or event

death camas *n* : any of several plants related to the lilies that cause poisoning of livestock in the western U.S.

death cap *n* : a very poisonous mushroom of North America and Europe that varies in color from pure white to olive or yellow — called also *death cup*

death·less \ˈdeth-ləs\ *adj* : IMMORTAL 3 ⟨*deathless* fame⟩ — **death·less·ly** *adv* — **death·less·ness** *n*

death·ly \ˈdeth-lē\ *adj* **1** : DEADLY 1, FATAL **2** : of, relating to, or suggestive of death ⟨a *deathly* pallor⟩ — **deathly** *adv*

death mask *n* : a cast taken from the face of a dead person

death rate *n* : the proportion of deaths in a population that is often expressed as the number of individuals that die in a year per thousand individuals in the population at the beginning of the year

death rattle *n* : a rattling or gurgling sound produced by air passing through mucus in the lungs and air passages of a dying person

death ray *n* : a weapon that generates an intense beam of particles or radiation by which it destroys its target

death's–head \ˈdeths-ˌhed\ *n* : a human skull symbolizing death

death trap *n* : a structure or situation that is potentially very dangerous to life

[1]**death·watch** \ˈdeth-ˌwäch\ *n* : any of several small insects that make a ticking sound [*death* + *watch* (timepiece); from the superstition that its ticking presages death]

[2]**deathwatch** *n* : a vigil kept over the dead or dying [*death* + *watch* (vigil)]

death wish *n* : the conscious or unconscious desire for the death of oneself

deb \ˈdeb\ *n* : DEBUTANTE

de·ba·cle \di-ˈbäk-əl, -ˈbak-\ *also* **dé·bâ·cle** *same, also* dā-ˈbäk, -ˈbäk-lə\ *n* **1** : a tumultuous breaking up of ice in a river **2** : a violent disruption (as of an army) : ROUT **3 a** : a great disaster ⟨the stock market *debacle*⟩ **b** : a complete failure : FIASCO [French *débâcle*, from *débâcler* "to clear"]

de·bar \di-ˈbär\ *vt* : to bar from having or doing something : PRECLUDE — **de·bar·ment** \-mənt\ *n*

de·bark \di-ˈbärk\ *vb* : DISEMBARK [Middle French *debarquer*, from *de-* "de-" + *barque* "bark" (ship)] — **de·bar·ka·tion** \ˌdē-ˌbär-ˈkā-shən\ *n*

de·base \di-ˈbās\ *vt* : to lower in status, dignity, value, quality, or character — **de·base·ment** \-mənt\ *n* — **de·bas·er** *n*

synonyms DEBASE, CORRUPT, DEPRAVE, PERVERT mean to cause deterioration or lowering in quality or character. DEBASE implies loss of worth, value, or dignity ⟨excess commercialism has *debased* the holiday⟩. CORRUPT implies loss of soundness, purity, or integrity through forces that break down, pollute, or destroy ⟨believes that slang is *corrupting* the language⟩. DEPRAVE implies moral deterioration ⟨a *depraved* disregard for human rights⟩. PERVERT implies a distorting from what is natural or normal ⟨*perverted* the peaceful protest into a violent riot⟩.

de·bat·able \di-ˈbāt-ə-bəl\ *adj* **1** : open to debate : QUESTIONABLE ⟨a *debatable* conclusion⟩ **2** : capable of being debated — **de·bat·ably** \-blē\ *adv*

[1]**de·bate** \di-ˈbāt\ *n* : a verbal argument: as **a** : the formal dis-

\ə\ **abut**	\au̇\ **out**	\i\ **tip**	\ȯ\ **saw**	\u̇\ **foot**
\ər\ **further**	\ch\ **chin**	\ī\ **life**	\ȯi\ **coin**	\y\ **yet**
\a\ **mat**	\e\ **pet**	\j\ **job**	\th\ **thin**	\yü\ **few**
\ā\ **take**	\ē\ **easy**	\ng\ **sing**	\t͟h\ **this**	\yu̇\ **cure**
\ä\ **cot, cart**	\g\ **go**	\ō\ **bone**	\ü\ **food**	\zh\ **vision**

cussion of a motion before a deliberative body **b :** a regulated discussion of a proposition between two matched sides

[2]**debate** *vb* **1 :** to discuss or examine a question by presenting and considering arguments on both sides **2 :** to take part in a debate **3 :** to present or consider the reasons for and against **:** CONSIDER [Medieval French *debatre* "to fight, contend," from *de-* "de-" + *batre* "to beat," from Latin *battuere*] ***synonyms*** see DISCUSS — **de·bat·er** *n*

[1]**de·bauch** \di-ˈbȯch, -ˈbäch\ *vt* **:** to lead away from virtue or morality **:** CORRUPT [Medieval French *debaucher* "to make disloyal"] — **de·bauch·er** *n*

[2]**debauch** *n* **1 :** an act or occasion of debauchery **2 :** ORGY 2

de·bauch·ee \di-ˌbȯch-ˈē, -ˌbäch-\ *n* **:** one given to debauchery

de·bauch·ery \di-ˈbȯch-rē, -ˈbäch-, -ə-rē\ *n, pl* **-er·ies :** extreme indulgence in sensual pleasure

de·ben·ture \di-ˈben-chər\ *n* **:** a bond secured only by the general assets of the issuing government or corporation [Latin *debentur* "they are due," from *debēre* "to owe"]

de·bil·i·tate \di-ˈbil-ə-ˌtāt\ *vt* **:** to impair the strength of **:** WEAKEN — **de·bil·i·ta·tion** \di-ˌbil-ə-ˈtā-shən\ *n*

de·bil·i·ty \di-ˈbil-ət-ē\ *n, pl* **-ties :** an infirm or weakened state [Medieval French *debilité,* from Latin *debilitas,* from *debilis* "weak"]

[1]**deb·it** \ˈdeb-ət\ *n* **1 :** an entry in an account representing amount paid out or owed **2 :** something regarded as unfavorable **:** DRAWBACK [Latin *debitum* "debt"]

[2]**debit** *vt* **:** to enter as a debit **:** charge with or as a debt

debit card *n* **:** a card like a credit card but by which money is withdrawn from the holder's bank account immediately at the time of a transaction (as a purchase)

deb·o·nair \ˌdeb-ə-ˈnaər, -ˈneər\ *adj* **:** gracefully charming ⟨a *debonair* manner⟩ [Medieval French *deboneire,* from *de bon aire* "of good family or nature"] — **deb·o·nair·ly** *adv* — **deb·o·nair·ness** *n*

de·bouch \di-ˈbüsh\ *vi* **:** to come out (as from a narrow passage) into an open area ⟨crowds *debouched* from side streets into the square⟩ [French *déboucher,* from *dé-* "de-" + *bouche* "mouth," from Latin *bucca* "cheek"] — **de·bouch·ment** \-mənt\ *n*

de·brief \di-ˈbrēf, ˈdē-\ *vt* **:** to interrogate (as an astronaut back from a mission) in order to obtain useful information

de·bris \də-ˈbrē, ˈdā-ˌbrē\ *n, pl* **de·bris** \-ˈbrēz, -ˌbrēz\ **1 :** the remains of something broken down or destroyed **2 :** an accumulation of fragments of rock **3 :** something discarded **:** RUBBISH [French *débris,* from Medieval French *debrisier* "to break to pieces," from *de-* "de-" + *brisier* "to break"]

debt \ˈdet\ *n* **1 :** SIN 1, TRESPASS **2 :** a state of owing ⟨hopelessly in *debt*⟩ **3 :** something owed **:** OBLIGATION ⟨pay a *debt* of $10⟩ [Medieval French *dette* "something owed," derived from Latin *debitum,* from *debēre* "to owe," from *de-* + *habēre* "to have"]

debt·or \ˈdet-ər\ *n* **1 :** SINNER **2 :** one that owes a debt

de·bug \ˈdē-ˈbəg, dē-\ *vt* **:** to eliminate errors or malfunctions in ⟨*debug* a computer program⟩

de·bunk \dē-ˈbəngk, ˈdē-\ *vt* **:** to expose the sham or falseness of ⟨*debunk* a hero legend⟩ — **de·bunk·er** *n*

[1]**de·but** \ˈdā-ˌbyü, dā-ˈ\ *n* **1 :** a first public appearance ⟨made his singing *debut*⟩ **2 :** a formal entrance into society ⟨sixteen is the usual age for making one's *debut*⟩ [French *début,* from *débuter* "to begin"]

[2]**debut** *vb* **1 :** to make a debut **2 :** to present to society for the first time ⟨*debut* a new product⟩

deb·u·tante \ˈdeb-yu̇-ˌtänt\ *n* **:** a young woman making her formal entrance into society [French *débutante,* from *débuter* "to begin"]

deca- *or* **dec-** *or* **deka-** *or* **dek-** *combining form* **:** ten [Latin *deca,* from Greek *deka*]

de·cade \ˈdek-ˌād, -əd; de-ˈkād; *3 is usually* ˈdek-əd\ *n* **1 :** a group or set of 10 **2 :** a period of 10 years **3 :** a division of the rosary that is made up primarily of 10 Hail Marys

dec·a·dence \ˈdek-əd-əns, di-ˈkād-ns\ *n* **1 :** the process of becoming decadent **:** the quality or state of being decadent **2 :** a period of decline [Medieval French, from Medieval Latin *decadentia,* from Late Latin *decadere* "to fall, sink," from Latin *de-* + *cadere* "to fall"]

dec·a·dent \ˈdek-əd-ənt, di-ˈkād-nt\ *adj* **1 :** marked by decay or decline **2 :** characterized by or appealing to self-indulgence ⟨a *decadent* meal⟩ — **decadent** *n* — **dec·a·dent·ly** *adv*

de·caf \ˈdē-ˌkaf\ *n* **:** decaffeinated coffee

de·caf·fein·at·ed \dē-ˈkaf-ə-ˌnāt-əd\ *adj* **:** having the caffeine removed ⟨*decaffeinated* coffee⟩

deca·gon \ˈdek-ə-ˌgän\ *n* **:** a polygon of 10 angles and 10 sides

deca·gram \ˈdek-ə-ˌgram\ *n* **:** DEKAGRAM

de·cal \ˈdē-ˌkal, di-ˈkal; *Canadian usually* ˈdek-əl\ *n* **:** a picture or design made to be transferred (as to glass) from specially prepared paper [short for *decalcomania*]

de·cal·co·ma·nia \di-ˌkal-kə-ˈmā-nē-ə\ *n* **1 :** the art or process of transferring or ornamenting with decals **2 :** DECAL [French *décalcomanie,* from *décalquer* "to copy by tracing" + *manie* "mania"]

deca·li·ter \ˈdek-ə-ˌlēt-ər\ *n* **:** DEKALITER

deca·logue \ˈdek-ə-ˌlȯg, -ˌläg\ *n* **1** *cap* **:** TEN COMMANDMENTS **2 :** a basic set of rules carrying binding authority [Late Latin *decalogus,* from Greek *dekalogos,* from *deka* "ten" + *logos* "speech, word"]

deca·me·ter \ˈdek-ə-ˌmēt-ər\ *n* **:** DEKAMETER

de·camp \di-ˈkamp\ *vi* **1 :** to break up a camp **2 :** to depart suddenly **:** ABSCOND ⟨*decamped* with the funds⟩ — **de·camp·ment** \-mənt\ *n*

de·cant \di-ˈkant\ *vt* **1 :** to pour from one vessel into another **2 :** to draw off without disturbing any sediment ⟨*decant* wine⟩ [New Latin *decantare,* from Latin *de-* + Medieval Latin *cantus* "side," from Latin, "iron tire"] — **de·can·ta·tion** \ˌdē-ˌkan-ˈtā-shən\ *n*

de·cant·er \di-ˈkant-ər\ *n* **:** a special glass bottle used to decant liquids or to receive and serve decanted liquids (as wine)

de·cap·i·tate \di-ˈkap-ə-ˌtāt\ *vt* **:** to cut off the head of **:** BEHEAD [Late Latin *decapitare,* from Latin *de-* + *caput* "head"] — **de·cap·i·ta·tion** \di-ˌkap-ə-ˈtā-shən\ *n*

deca·pod \ˈdek-ə-ˌpäd\ *n* **1 :** any of an order (Decapoda) of crustaceans (as shrimps, lobsters, and crabs) with five pairs of appendages attached to the thorax one or more of which are modified into pincers **2 :** any of the cephalopod mollusks (as the cuttlefishes and squids) with 10 arms — **decapod** *adj* — **de·cap·o·dan** \di-ˈkap-əd-ən\ *adj or n*

deca·syl·lab·ic \ˌdek-ə-sə-ˈlab-ik\ *adj* **:** having 10 syllables or composed of verses of 10 syllables — **decasyllabic** *n*

de·cath·lon \di-ˈkath-lən, -ˌlän\ *n* **:** an athletic contest in which each competitor participates in each of a series of 10 track-and-field events [French *décathlon,* from *déca-* "deca-" + Greek *athlon* "contest"]

[1]**de·cay** \di-ˈkā\ *vb* **1 :** to decline from a sound or prosperous condition **2 :** to decrease gradually in size, quantity, activity, or force **3 :** to fall into ruin **4 :** to decline in health, strength, or vigor **5 :** to undergo or cause to undergo decomposition ⟨*decaying* fruit⟩ [Medieval French *decaïr,* from Late Latin *decadere* "to fall, sink," from Latin *de-* + *cadere* "to fall"]

synonyms DECAY, DECOMPOSE, ROT, SPOIL mean to undergo disintegration or dissolution. DECAY implies a slow deterioration from a state of soundness or perfection ⟨a *decaying* mansion⟩. DECOMPOSE stresses a breaking down into components or dissolution through corruption ⟨the strong odor of *decomposing* vegetation⟩. ROT implies decay with corruption and often suggests foulness ⟨fruit left to *rot* in the warehouse⟩. SPOIL applies chiefly to the decomposition of foods ⟨keep the ham from *spoiling*⟩.

[2]**decay** *n* **1 :** gradual decline in strength, soundness, prosperity, excellence, or value **2 :** ROT; *esp* **:** decomposition of proteins in the presence of oxygen chiefly by bacteria **3 :** a decline in health or vigor **4 a :** spontaneous decrease in the number of radioactive atoms in radioactive material **b :** spontaneous disintegration (as of an atom or a meson)

de·cease \di-ˈsēs\ *n* **:** DEATH 1 [Medieval French *deces,* from Latin *decessus* "departure, death," from *decedere* "to depart, die," from *de-* + *cedere* "to go"] — **decease** *vi*

[1]**de·ceased** \-ˈsēst\ *n, pl* **deceased :** a dead person

[2]**deceased** *adj* **:** no longer living

de·ce·dent \di-ˈsēd-nt\ *n* **:** a deceased person — used chiefly in law

de·ceit \di-ˈsēt\ *n* **1 :** the act or practice of deceiving **:** DECEPTION **2 :** an attempt or scheme to deceive **:** TRICK **3 :** the quality of being deceitful **:** DECEITFULNESS [Medieval French *deceite,* derived from Latin *decipere* "to deceive"]

de·ceit·ful \-fəl\ *adj* **1 :** using or tending to use trickery **2 :** marked by deceit **:** MISLEADING ⟨a *deceitful* answer⟩ — **de·ceit·ful·ly** \-fə-lē\ *adv* — **de·ceit·ful·ness** *n*

de·ceive \di-ˈsēv\ *vb* **1 :** to cause to believe what is untrue **:** MISLEAD **2 :** to use trickery [Medieval French *deceivre,* from

Latin *decipere,* from *de-* + *capere* "to take"] — **de·ceiv·er** *n* — **de·ceiv·ing·ly** \-ˈsē-viŋ-lē\ *adv*

synonyms DECEIVE, MISLEAD, DELUDE, BEGUILE mean to lead astray or frustrate usually by underhandedness. DECEIVE implies imposing a false idea or belief that causes ignorance, bewilderment, or helplessness ⟨tried to *deceive* me about the cost⟩. MISLEAD implies a leading astray that may or may not be intentional ⟨the confusing sign *misled* him⟩. DELUDE implies deceiving so thoroughly that the truth is obscured ⟨we were *deluded* into thinking we were invincible⟩. BEGUILE stresses the use of charm and persuasion in deceiving ⟨was *beguiled* by false promises⟩.

de·cel·er·ate \dē-ˈsel-ə-ˌrāt\ *vb* **:** to slow down or cause to slow down [*de-* + *accelerate*] — **de·cel·er·a·tion** \ˌdē-ˌsel-ə-ˈrā-shən\ *n* — **de·cel·er·a·tor** \dē-ˈsel-ə-ˌrāt-ər\ *n*

De·cem·ber \di-ˈsem-bər\ *n* **:** the 12th month of the year according to the Gregorian calendar [Medieval French *Decembre,* from Latin *December,* from *decem* "ten"; from its having been originally the tenth month of the Roman calendar]

de·cem·vir \di-ˈsem-vər\ *n* **:** one of a body of 10 magistrates in ancient Rome [Latin, from *decem* "ten" + *vir* "man"] — **de·cem·vi·rate** \-və-rət\ *n*

de·cen·cy \ˈdēs-n-sē\ *n, pl* **-cies** **1 a :** the quality or state of being decent **b :** conformity to standards of taste, propriety, or quality **2 :** standard of propriety — usually used in plural

de·cen·ni·al \di-ˈsen-ē-əl\ *adj* **1 :** consisting of or lasting for 10 years **2 :** happening every 10 years ⟨*decennial* census⟩ [Latin *decennium* "period of 10 years," from *decem* "ten" + *annus* "year"] — **decennial** *n* — **de·cen·ni·al·ly** \-ē-ə-lē\ *adv*

de·cent \ˈdēs-nt\ *adj* **1 a :** conforming to standards of propriety, good taste, or morality **b :** modestly clothed **2 :** free from immodesty or obscenity **3 :** fairly good **:** ADEQUATE ⟨*decent* housing⟩ **4 :** marked by moral integrity, kindness, and goodwill ⟨hardworking and *decent* folks⟩ [Latin *decens,* present participle of *decēre* "to be fitting"] — **de·cent·ly** *adv*

de·cen·tral·ize \dē-ˈsen-trə-ˌlīz\ *vt* **1 :** to disperse or distribute among various regional or local authorities ⟨*decentralize* the administration of flood relief⟩ **2 :** to cause to withdraw from urban centers to outlying areas ⟨*decentralize* industries⟩ — **de·cen·tral·i·za·tion** \ˌdē-ˌsen-trə-lə-ˈzā-shən\ *n*

de·cep·tion \di-ˈsep-shən\ *n* **1 a :** the act of deceiving **b :** the fact or condition of being deceived **2 :** something that deceives **:** TRICK [Medieval French, from Late Latin *deceptio,* from Latin *decipere* "to deceive"] — **de·cep·tion·al** \-shə-nəl\ *adj*

synonyms DECEPTION, FRAUD, TRICKERY mean the acts or practices of one who deliberately deceives. DECEPTION may suggest cheating or merely legitimate indirection ⟨magicians are masters of *deception*⟩. FRAUD always implies guilt and often criminality ⟨suspected of *fraud*⟩. TRICKERY implies ingenious ways of fooling or cheating ⟨resorted to *trickery* to win the game⟩.

de·cep·tive \di-ˈsep-tiv\ *adj* **:** tending or having power to deceive **:** MISLEADING ⟨a *deceptive* appearance⟩ — **de·cep·tive·ly** *adv* — **de·cep·tive·ness** *n*

deci- *combining form* **:** tenth part [Latin *decimus* "tenth," from *decem* "ten"]

deci·bel \ˈdes-ə-ˌbel, -bəl\ *n* **1 :** a unit for expressing the ratio of two amounts of electric or acoustic signal power equal to 10 times the common logarithm of this ratio **2 :** a unit for measuring the relative intensity of sounds on a scale from zero for the average least perceptible sound to about 130 for the average pain level

de·cide \di-ˈsīd\ *vb* **1 :** to arrive at a solution that ends uncertainty or dispute about ⟨*decided* the case in favor of the defendant⟩ **2 :** to bring to a definitive end ⟨one blow *decided* the fight⟩ **3 :** to induce to come to a choice ⟨what *decided* your mind⟩ **4 :** to make a choice or judgment ⟨*decided* to go⟩ [Latin *decidere,* literally, "to cut off," from *de-* + *caedere* "to cut"] — **de·cid·able** \-ˈsīd-ə-bəl\ *adj* — **de·cid·er** *n*

de·cid·ed \-ˈsīd-əd\ *adj* **1 :** free from ambiguity **:** CLEAR, UNMISTAKABLE ⟨a *decided* advantage⟩ **2 :** free from doubt or wavering **:** DETERMINED ⟨a *decided* tone of voice⟩ — **de·cid·ed·ly** *adv* — **de·cid·ed·ness** *n*

de·cid·u·ous \di-ˈsij-ə-wəs\ *adj* **1 :** falling off or shed (as at the end of a growing period or stage of development) ⟨antlers are *deciduous*⟩ ⟨*deciduous* leaves⟩ **2 :** having deciduous parts or members with deciduous parts ⟨*deciduous* trees⟩ ⟨*deciduous* forests are typical of the temperate zones⟩ — compare EVERGREEN **3 :** of only passing interest or importance [Latin *deciduus,* from *decidere* "to fall off," from *de-* + *cadere* "to fall"] — **de·cid·u·ous·ly** *adv* — **de·cid·u·ous·ness** *n*

deciduous tooth *n* **:** MILK TOOTH

deci·gram \ˈdes-ə-ˌgram\ *n* — see METRIC SYSTEM table

deci·li·ter \ˈdes-ə-ˌlēt-ər\ *n* — see METRIC SYSTEM table

de·cil·lion \di-ˈsil-yən\ *n* — see NUMBER table [Latin *decem* "ten" + English *-illion* (as in *million*)]

[1]**dec·i·mal** \ˈdes-məl, -ə-məl\ *adj* **1 :** based on the number 10; *esp* **:** expressed in or using a number system with a base of 10 especially with a decimal point ⟨¼ in *decimal* form is .25⟩ **2 :** divided into 10th or 100th units ⟨switched to a *decimal* money system⟩ [derived from Latin *decimus* "tenth," from *decem* "ten"] — **dec·i·mal·ly** \-mə-lē\ *adv*

[2]**decimal** *n* **1 :** any real number expressed in base 10 **2 :** a fraction in which the denominator is a power of 10 and that is expressed in decimal form ⟨the *decimal* .25 is equivalent to the common fraction $^{25}/_{100}$⟩ — called also *decimal fraction*

decimal fraction *n* **:** DECIMAL 2

decimal notation *n* **:** expression of a number in base 10 that uses one of the digits from 0 to 9 in each place — compare BINARY NOTATION

decimal place *n* **:** any of the places to the right of the decimal point in a number expressed in decimal notation ⟨5.732 has three *decimal places*⟩

decimal point *n* **:** the dot at the left of a decimal fraction (as .678) or between the decimal and whole parts of a mixed number (as 3.678)

decimal system *n* **1 :** a system of numbers that uses a base of 10 **2 :** a system of measurement or money in which the basic units increase by powers of 10 ⟨the metric system is a *decimal system*⟩

dec·i·mate \ˈdes-ə-ˌmāt\ *vt* **1 :** to select by lot and kill every tenth man of **2 :** to destroy a large part of ⟨disease *decimated* the population of the city⟩ [Latin *decimare,* from *decimus* "tenth"] — **dec·i·ma·tion** \ˌdes-ə-ˈmā-shən\ *n*

deci·me·ter \ˈdes-ə-ˌmēt-ər\ *n* — see METRIC SYSTEM table

de·ci·pher \dē-ˈsī-fər\ *vt* **1 a :** to convert into intelligible form **b :** DECODE ⟨*decipher* a message⟩ **2 :** to make out the meaning of despite indistinctness or obscurity ⟨*decipher* bad handwriting⟩ — **de·ci·pher·a·ble** \-fə-rə-bəl, -frə-\ *adj* — **de·ci·pher·ment** \-fər-mənt\ *n*

de·ci·sion \di-ˈsizh-ən\ *n* **1 :** the act or result of deciding especially by giving judgment ⟨the *decision* of the court⟩ **2 :** promptness and firmness in deciding **:** DETERMINATION ⟨people of courage and *decision*⟩ [Medieval French, from Latin *decisio,* from *decidere* "to decide"]

de·ci·sive \di-ˈsī-siv\ *adj* **1 :** having the power or quality of deciding ⟨a *decisive* battle⟩ **2 :** UNMISTAKABLE, UNQUESTIONABLE ⟨a *decisive* break from tradition⟩ **3 :** marked by or showing decision ⟨a *decisive* manner⟩ — **de·ci·sive·ly** *adv* — **de·ci·sive·ness** *n*

[1]**deck** \ˈdek\ *n* **1 :** a platform in a ship serving as a structural element and as a floor or a covering (as for a cabin) **2 :** something resembling the deck of a ship: as **a :** the roadway of a bridge **b :** a flat floored roofless area adjoining a house **3 :** a pack of playing cards [Middle English *dekke* "covering of a ship," probably derived from Low German *decken* "to cover"] — **on deck :** next in line

[2]**deck** *vt* **1 a :** to clothe elegantly **:** ARRAY ⟨*decked* out in a new suit⟩ **b :** DECORATE 1 **2 :** to furnish with a deck **3 :** to knock down forcibly [Dutch *dekken* "to cover"]

deck chair *n* **:** a folding chair often having an adjustable leg rest

deck chair

deck·er \ˈdek-ər\ *n* **:** something having a deck or a specified number of levels, floors, or layers — used in combination ⟨the buses are double-*deckers*⟩

deck·hand \ˈdek-ˌhand\ *n* **:** a

\ə\ **a**but	\au̇\ **ou**t	\i\ t**i**p	\ȯ\ s**aw**	\u̇\ f**oo**t
\ər\ furth**er**	\ch\ **ch**in	\ī\ l**i**fe	\ȯi\ c**oi**n	\y\ **y**et
\a\ m**a**t	\e\ p**e**t	\j\ **j**ob	\th\ **th**in	\yü\ f**ew**
\ā\ t**a**ke	\ē\ **ea**sy	\ŋ\ si**ng**	\t͟h\ **th**is	\yu̇\ c**u**re
\ä\ c**o**t, c**a**rt	\g\ **g**o	\ō\ b**o**ne	\ü\ f**oo**d	\zh\ vi**s**ion

sailor who performs manual duties

deck·le edge \ˈdek-əl-\ *n* : the rough untrimmed edge of paper [derived from German *decken* "to cover"] — **deck·le–edged** \-ˈejd\ *adj*

de·claim \di-ˈklām\ *vb* : to speak or deliver in the manner of a formal oration [Latin *declamare,* from *de-* + *clamare* "to cry out"] — **de·claim·er** *n* — **dec·la·ma·tion** \ˌdek-lə-ˈmā-shən\ *n*

de·clam·a·to·ry \di-ˈklam-ə-ˌtōr-ē, -ˌtȯr-\ *adj* : of, relating to, or marked by declamation or rhetorical display

dec·la·ra·tion \ˌdek-lə-ˈrā-shən\ *n* **1** : the act of declaring : ANNOUNCEMENT **2 a** : something declared **b** : a document containing such a declaration ⟨the *Declaration* of Independence⟩

de·clar·a·tive \di-ˈklar-ət-iv\ *adj* : making a declaration or statement ⟨a *declarative* sentence⟩

de·clar·a·to·ry \di-ˈklar-ə-ˌtōr-ē, -ˌtȯr-\ *adj* : serving to declare or explain

de·clare \di-ˈklaər, -ˈkleər\ *vb* **1** : to make known formally or explicitly ⟨*declare* war⟩ **2** : to state emphatically : AFFIRM ⟨*declare* one's innocence⟩ **3** : to make a full statement of (taxable or dutiable property) **4** : to announce one's intentions (as to run for political office) ⟨*declared* for mayor⟩ [Medieval French *declarer* "to make clear," from Latin *declarare,* derived from *de-* + *clarus* "clear"]

synonyms DECLARE, ANNOUNCE, PUBLISH, PROCLAIM mean to make known publicly or openly. DECLARE suggests a plainness and formality of statement ⟨the referee *declared* the contest a draw⟩. ANNOUNCE implies a declaration for the first time of something of interest or intended to satisfy curiosity ⟨*announced* the engagement⟩ ⟨*announced* the winner⟩. PUBLISH denotes a making public especially through print ⟨*published* the results of the study⟩. PROCLAIM suggests a clear, forceful, and authoritative declaration ⟨the president *proclaimed* a national holiday⟩. ***synonyms*** see in addition ASSERT

de·clar·er \-ˈklar-ər, -ˈkler-\ *n* **1** : one that declares **2** : the bridge player who plays both his or her own hand and that of the dummy

de·clas·si·fy \dē-ˈklas-ə-ˌfī, ˈdē-\ *vt* : to remove or reduce the security classification of ⟨*declassify* a secret document⟩

de·clen·sion \di-ˈklen-chən\ *n* **1 a** : inflection of a noun, adjective, or pronoun especially in some prescribed order of the forms **b** : a class of nouns or adjectives having the same inflectional forms **2** : a falling off or away : DETERIORATION **3** : a downward slope [derived from Latin *declinare* "to inflect, turn aside"] — **de·clen·sion·al** \-ˈklench-nəl, -ən-l\ *adj*

dec·li·na·tion \ˌdek-lə-ˈnā-shən\ *n* **1** : angular distance north or south from the celestial equator measured along a great circle passing through the celestial poles ⟨the *declination* of a star⟩ **2** : DETERIORATION ⟨moral *declination*⟩ **3** : a bending downward : INCLINATION **4** : a formal refusal **5** : the angle that the magnetic needle makes with a true north and south line — **dec·li·na·tion·al** \-ˈnā-shnəl, -shən-l\ *adj*

[1]**de·cline** \di-ˈklīn\ *vb* **1 a** : to slope downward : DESCEND **b** : to bend down : DROOP ⟨*decline* one's head⟩ **2** : to reach or pass toward a lower level or state ⟨his health *declined*⟩ ⟨their enthusiasm *declined*⟩ **3** : to draw toward a close : WANE ⟨the day *declined*⟩ **4** : to withhold consent **5** : to become less in amount ⟨prices *declined*⟩ **6 a** : to refuse to undertake, engage in, or comply with ⟨*decline* battle⟩ **b** : to decide not to accept especially courteously ⟨*decline* an invitation⟩ **7** : to give in a prescribed order the inflectional forms of a noun, pronoun, or adjective [derived from Latin *declinare* "to turn aside, inflect," from *de-* + *clinare* "to incline"] — **de·clin·able** \-ˈklī-nə-bəl\ *adj*

[2]**decline** *n* **1** : the process of declining: **a** : a gradual wasting away **b** : a change to a lower state or level ⟨business activity showed a sharp *decline* last month⟩ **2** : the time when something is approaching its end **3** : a downward slope : DECLIVITY **4** : a disease characterized by gradual loss of strength and health; *esp* : pulmonary tuberculosis

de·cliv·i·ty \di-ˈkliv-ət-ē\ *n, pl* **-ties** **1** : downward inclination **2** : a descending slope [Latin *declivitas,* from *declivis* "sloping down," from *de-* + *clivus* "slope"]

de·coc·tion \di-ˈkäk-shən\ *n* : an extracting (as of a flavor or active principle) by boiling in water; *also* : a product of this process [Late Latin *decoctio,* from Latin *decoquere* "to cook down," from *de-* + *coquere* "to cook"]

de·code \dē-ˈkōd, ˈdē-\ *vt* : to change (a coded message) into ordinary language — **de·cod·er** *n*

dé·col·le·tage \ˌdā-ˌkäl-ə-ˈtäzh, ˌdek-lə-\ *n* **1** : the low-cut neckline of a dress **2** : a décolleté dress [French]

dé·col·le·té \ˌdā-ˌkäl-ə-ˈtā, ˌdek-lə-\ *adj* **1** : wearing a strapless or low-necked dress **2** : having a low-cut neckline [French]

de·col·or·ize \dē-ˈkəl-ə-ˌrīz, ˈdē-\ *vt* : to remove color from — **de·col·or·i·za·tion** \ˌdē-ˌkəl-ə-rə-ˈzā-shən\ *n* — **de·col·or·iz·er** *n*

de·com·mis·sion \ˌdē-kə-ˈmish-ən\ *vt* : to take out of commission ⟨a *decommissioned* battleship⟩

de·com·pose \ˌdē-kəm-ˈpōz\ *vb* **1** : to separate into parts or elements or into simpler compounds **2** : to break down through or as if through chemical change : ROT ***synonyms*** see DECAY — **de·com·pos·able** \-ˈpō-zə-bəl\ *adj* — **de·com·po·si·tion** \ˌdē-ˌkäm-pə-ˈzish-ən\ *n*

de·com·pos·er \ˌdē-kəm-ˈpō-zər\ *n* : an organism (as a bacterium or a fungus) that feeds on and breaks down dead animal or plant tissue

de·com·press \ˌdē-kəm-ˈpres\ *vt* **1** : to release from pressure or compression **2** : to convert (as a computer file) from a compressed form to an expanded or original size — **de·com·pres·sion** \-ˈpresh-ən\ *n*

decompression sickness *n* : a sometimes fatal disorder that is marked by pain and paralysis, difficulty in breathing, and often collapse, and that is caused by the release of gas bubbles (as of nitrogen) in tissue upon too rapid a change from an atmosphere of high pressure to one of lower pressure — called also *bends, caisson disease*

de·con·ges·tant \ˌdē-kən-ˈjes-tənt\ *n* : an agent (as a medicine) that relieves congestion (as of the mucous membranes of the nose)

de·con·tam·i·nate \ˌdē-kən-ˈtam-ə-ˌnāt\ *vt* : to free from contamination — **de·con·tam·i·na·tion** \-ˌtam-ə-ˈnā-shən\ *n*

de·cor *or* **dé·cor** \dā-ˈkȯr, ˈdā-ˌ\ *n* : DECORATION; *esp* : the arrangement of accessories in interior decoration [French *décor,* from *décorer* "to decorate," from Latin *decorare*]

dec·o·rate \ˈdek-ə-ˌrāt\ *vt* **1** : to make more attractive by adding something beautiful or becoming ⟨*decorate* a room⟩ **2** : to award a decoration of honor to [Latin *decorare,* from *decor-, decus* "ornament"] ***synonyms*** see ADORN

dec·o·ra·tion \ˌdek-ə-ˈrā-shən\ *n* **1** : the act or process of decorating **2** : something that adorns or beautifies **3** : a badge of honor (as a medal)

Decoration Day *n* : MEMORIAL DAY

dec·o·ra·tive \ˈdek-rət-iv, -ə-rət-; ˈdek-ə-ˌrāt-\ *adj* : serving to decorate; *esp* : purely ornamental — **dec·o·ra·tive·ly** *adv* — **dec·o·ra·tive·ness** *n*

dec·o·ra·tor \ˈdek-ə-ˌrāt-ər\ *n* : one that decorates; *esp* : a person who designs or executes the interiors of buildings and their furnishings

dec·o·rous \ˈdek-ə-rəs; di-ˈkōr-əs, -ˈkȯr-\ *adj* : marked by propriety and good taste : CORRECT ⟨*decorous* conduct⟩ [Latin *decorus,* from *decor* "beauty, grace"] — **dec·o·rous·ly** *adv* — **dec·o·rous·ness** *n*

de·co·rum \di-ˈkōr-əm, -ˈkȯr-\ *n* **1** : conformity to accepted standards of conduct : proper behavior ⟨social *decorum*⟩ **2** : ORDERLINESS [Latin, from *decorus* "decorous"]

synonyms DECORUM, PROPRIETY, DIGNITY mean socially acceptable behavior or standards. DECORUM suggests conduct according with good taste often formally prescribed ⟨the *decorum* of the courtroom⟩. PROPRIETY suggests an artificial standard of what is correct in conduct or speech ⟨only a sense of *propriety* stopped her from telling the secret⟩. DIGNITY implies reserve or restraint in conduct prompted by a sense of personal integrity or social importance ⟨approached his challenger with *dignity*⟩.

[1]**de·coy** \ˈdē-ˌkoi, di-ˈ\ *n* **1** : something intended to lure into a trap; *esp* : an artificial bird used to attract live birds within shooting range **2** : a person used to lead another into a trap [probably from Dutch *de kooi,* literally, "the cage"]

[2]**decoy** *vt* : to lure by or as if by a decoy : ENTICE ***synonyms*** see LURE

[1]**de·crease** \di-ˈkrēs, ˈdē-ˌ\ *vb* : to become or cause to become less [derived from Latin *decrescere,* from *de-* + *crescere* "to grow"]

synonyms DECREASE, LESSEN, DIMINISH, DWINDLE mean to grow or make less. DECREASE suggests progressive reduction in size, amount, or number ⟨slowly *decreased* the amount of pressure⟩. LESSEN suggests a decline in amount rather than in number ⟨unable to *lessen* her debt⟩. DIMINISH stresses loss, as in numbers or amount, and implies subtraction from the whole ⟨the deer population *diminished*⟩. DWINDLE implies progressive lessening, especially of things growing visibly smaller ⟨their supplies *dwindled* slowly⟩.

[2]**de·crease** \ˈdē-ˌkrēs, di-ˈ\ *n* **1 :** a process of decreasing ⟨a *decrease* in automobile accidents⟩ **2 :** the amount by which a thing decreases : REDUCTION ⟨a *decrease* of three dollars in wages⟩

[1]**decree** \di-ˈkrē\ *n* **1 :** an order usually having the force of law : EDICT **2 a :** a religious ordinance enacted by a church assembly or head **b :** the will of the Deity **c :** something allotted by fate **3 :** a judicial decision especially in an equity or probate court ⟨a divorce *decree*⟩ [Medieval French *decré,* from Latin *decretum,* from *decernere* "to decide," from *de-* + *cernere* "to sift, decide"]

[2]**decree** *vb* **de·creed; de·cree·ing** **1 :** to order authoritatively ⟨*decree* an amnesty⟩ **2 :** to determine or order judicially ⟨*decree* a punishment⟩ — **de·cre·er** \-ˈkrē-ər\ *n*

dec·re·ment \ˈdek-rə-mənt\ *n* : DECREASE [Latin *decrementum,* from *decrescere* "to decrease"]

de·crep·it \di-ˈkrep-ət\ *adj* : broken down or weakened by age [Medieval French, from Latin *decrepitus*] — **de·crep·it·ly** *adv* — **de·crep·it·ness** *n*

de·crep·i·tude \di-ˈkrep-ə-ˌtüd, -ˌtyüd\ *n* : the quality or state of being decrepit : infirmity especially from old age

[1]**de·cre·scen·do** \ˌdā-krə-ˈshen-dō\ *n, pl* **-dos** **1 :** a lessening in volume of sound **2 :** a decrescendo musical passage [Italian, literally, "decreasing," derived from Latin *decrescere* "to decrease"]

[2]**decrescendo** *adv or adj* : with diminishing volume — used as a direction in music

de·cry \di-ˈkrī\ *vt* **1 :** to speak slightingly of : belittle publicly ⟨*decry* a hero's deeds⟩ **2 :** to find fault with : express strong disapproval of ⟨*decried* the waste of natural resources⟩ [French *décrier,* from Medieval French *decrier,* from *de-* "de-" + *crier* "to cry"] — **de·cri·er** \-ˈkrī-ər, -ˈkrīr\ *n*

de·cum·bent \di-ˈkəm-bənt\ *adj* : lying down [Latin *decumbere* "to lie down," from *de-* + *-cumbere* "to lie down"] — **de·cum·ben·cy** \-bən-sē\ *n*

ded·i·cate \ˈded-i-ˌkāt\ *vt* **1 :** to set apart for some purpose and especially a sacred or serious purpose ⟨*dedicate* one's life to medicine⟩ **2 :** to address or inscribe as a compliment ⟨*dedicate* a book to a friend⟩ [Latin *dedicare,* from *de-* + *dicare* "to proclaim, dedicate"] ***synonyms*** see DEVOTE — **ded·i·ca·tor** \-ˌkāt-ər\ *n*

ded·i·ca·tion \ˌded-i-ˈkā-shən\ *n* **1 a :** an act or rite of dedicating to a divine being or to a sacred use **b :** a setting aside for a particular purpose **2 :** an inscription dedicating a literary, musical, or artistic work to a person or cause **3 :** self-sacrificing devotion — **ded·i·ca·tive** \ˈded-i-ˌkāt-iv\ *adj* — **ded·i·ca·to·ry** \ˈded-i-kə-ˌtōr-ē, -ˌtȯr-\ *adj*

de·duce \di-ˈdüs, -ˈdyüs\ *vt* **1 :** to draw a conclusion about particulars by applying them to a general principle or rule; *also* : to determine by reasoning from a general principle or rule **2 :** to trace the course of [Latin *deducere,* literally, "to lead away," from *de-* + *ducere* "to lead"] — **de·duc·i·ble** \-ˈdü-sə-bəl, -ˈdyü-\ *adj*

de·duct \di-ˈdəkt\ *vt* : to take away (an amount) from a total : SUBTRACT [Latin *deductus,* past participle of *deducere* "to deduce, lead away"]

de·duct·ible \di-ˈdək-tə-bəl\ *adj* : capable of being deducted : allowable as a deduction — **de·duct·ibil·i·ty** \di-ˌdək-tə-ˈbil-ət-ē\ *n*

de·duc·tion \di-ˈdək-shən\ *n* **1 a :** an act of taking away **b :** something that is or may be subtracted ⟨*deductions* from taxable income⟩ **2 a :** the forming of a conclusion by reasoning; *esp* : inference in which the conclusion about particulars follows necessarily from a general principle or rule **b :** a conclusion reached by logical deduction — **de·duc·tive** \-ˈdək-tiv\ *adj* — **de·duc·tive·ly** *adv*

[1]**deed** \ˈdēd\ *n* **1 :** something that is done : ACT; *esp* : a brave or noteworthy act ⟨judge them by their *deeds*⟩ **2 :** a legal document by which one person transfers an interest in land or buildings to another [Old English *dǣd*] — **deed·less** \-ləs\ *adj*

[2]**deed** *vt* : to convey or transfer by legal deed

dee·jay \ˈdē-ˌjā\ *n* : DISC JOCKEY [*d*isc *j*ockey]

deem \ˈdēm\ *vb* : to come to think or judge : have an opinion : BELIEVE, SUPPOSE [Old English *dēman*]

[1]**deep** \ˈdēp\ *adj* **1 a :** extending far downward ⟨a *deep* well⟩ **b :** having a great distance between the top and bottom surfaces : not shallow ⟨*deep* water⟩ **c :** extending well inward from an outer surface ⟨a *deep* gash⟩ **d :** extending well back from a front surface ⟨a *deep* closet⟩ **e :** extending far outward from a center ⟨*deep* borders of lace⟩ **f :** occurring or located near the outer limits ⟨*deep* right field⟩ **2 :** having a specified extension downward, inward, or backward ⟨a shelf 40 centimeters *deep*⟩ **3 a :** difficult to understand ⟨a *deep* book⟩ **b :** MYSTERIOUS, OBSCURE ⟨a *deep* dark secret⟩ **c :** WISE ⟨a *deep* thinker⟩ **d :** completely absorbed or engrossed ⟨*deep* in thought⟩ **e :** of great intensity : PROFOUND ⟨*deep* sleep⟩ **4 a :** high in saturation and low in lightness ⟨a *deep* red⟩ **b :** having a low musical pitch or range ⟨a *deep* voice⟩ **5 a :** coming from or situated well within ⟨a *deep* sigh⟩ **b :** covered, enclosed, or filled often to a specified degree ⟨knee-*deep* in water⟩ [Old English *dēop*] — **deep·ly** *adv*

[2]**deep** *adv* **1 :** to a great depth : DEEPLY ⟨still waters run *deep*⟩ **2 :** far on : LATE ⟨read *deep* into the night⟩

[3]**deep** *n* **1 :** an extremely deep place or part; *esp* : OCEAN **2 :** the middle or most intense part ⟨the *deep* of winter⟩

deep–dish *adj* : baked in a deep dish ⟨a *deep-dish* pizza⟩; *esp* : baked in a deep dish with usually a fruit filling and no bottom crust ⟨a *deep-dish* apple pie⟩

deep·en \ˈdē-pən\ *vb* **deep·ened; deep·en·ing** \ˈdēp-ning, -ə-ning\ : to make or become deep or deeper

deep fat *n* : hot fat or oil deep enough in a cooking utensil to cover the food to be fried

deep–fry \ˈdēp-ˈfrī\ *vt* : to cook in deep fat

deep–root·ed \ˈdēp-ˈrüt-əd, -ˈru̇t-\ *adj* : deeply implanted or established ⟨a *deep-rooted* loyalty⟩

deep–sea \ˈdēp-ˈsē\ *adj* : of, relating to, or occurring in the deeper parts of the sea ⟨*deep-sea* fishing⟩

deep–seat·ed \ˈdēp-ˈsēt-əd\ *adj* **1 :** situated far below the surface **2 :** firmly established ⟨a *deep-seated* tradition⟩

deep–set \ˈdēp-ˈset\ *adj* : set far in ⟨*deep-set* eyes⟩

deep–sky \ˈdēp-ˌskī\ *adj* : relating to or existing in space outside the solar system ⟨*deep-sky* objects⟩

deep space *n* : space well outside the earth's atmosphere and especially that part lying beyond the earth-moon system

deep·wa·ter \ˈdēp-ˌwȯt-ər; -ˌwät-\ *adj* : of or relating to water of great depth; *esp* : DEEP-SEA ⟨*deepwater* sailors⟩

deer \ˈdiər\ *n, pl* **deer** : any of a family of cloven-hoofed cud-chewing mammals with antlers borne by the males of nearly all and by the females of a few forms [Old English *dēor* "wild animal, beast"] — **deer·like** \-ˌlīk\ *adj*

Word History The development of a word's meaning is often from the general to the specific. For instance, *deer* is used in modern English to denote numerous species, including white-tailed deer, reindeer, caribou, elk, and moose, all belonging to the same natural family. The Old English *dēor,* however, could refer to any beast or wild animal, or to wild animals in general. In time, *deer* came to be restricted to the animal that was the primary object of the hunt in England. From that usage the term has spread to other members of the same family and become somewhat more general again though not so general as once.

deer fly *n* : any of various small horseflies having a painful bite

deer·hound \-ˌhau̇nd\ *n* : SCOTTISH DEERHOUND

deer mouse *n* : any of numerous North American mice occurring in fields and woods

deer·skin \ˈdiər-ˌskin\ *n* : leather made from the skin of a deer; *also* : a garment of such leather

deer tick *n* : a tick that transmits the bacterium causing Lyme disease

deer mouse

\ə\ **abut**	\au̇\ **out**	\i\ **tip**	\ȯ\ **saw**	\u̇\ **foot**
\ər\ **further**	\ch\ **chin**	\ī\ **life**	\ȯi\ **coin**	\y\ **yet**
\a\ **mat**	\e\ **pet**	\j\ **job**	\th\ **thin**	\yü\ **few**
\ā\ **take**	\ē\ **easy**	\ng\ **sing**	\t͟h\ **this**	\yu̇\ **cure**
\ä\ **cot, cart**	\g\ **go**	\ō\ **bone**	\ü\ **food**	\zh\ **vision**

de–es·ca·late \dē-ˈes-kə-ˌlāt, ˈdē-\ *vb* : to make less (as in extent or scope) — **de–es·ca·la·tion** \ˌdē-ˌes-kə-ˈlā-shən\ *n*

de·face \di-ˈfās\ *vt* : to destroy or mar the face or surface of [Medieval French *desfacer,* from *des-* "de-" + *face* "face"] — **de·face·ment** \-ˈfās-mənt\ *n* — **de·fac·er** *n*

synonyms DEFACE, DISFIGURE mean to mar the appearance of. DEFACE suggests superficial injuries or the removal of some part or detail 〈*defaced* the wall with graffiti〉. DISFIGURE implies deeper or more permanent injury that impairs beauty or attractiveness 〈a face *disfigured* by smallpox〉.

de fac·to \di-ˈfak-ˌtō, dā-\ *adj or adv* **1** : ACTUAL 1a; *esp* : being such in effect though not formally recognized 〈a *de facto* state of war〉 **2** : exercising power as if legally constituted 〈a *de facto* government〉 **3** : resulting from economic or social factors rather than from laws or actions of the state 〈*de facto* segregation〉 — compare DE JURE [New Latin, adverb, "in fact"]

de·fal·ca·tion \ˌdē-ˌfal-ˈkā-shən, -ˌfȯl-; ˌdef-əl-\ *n* : a misuse or theft of money placed in one's keeping [Medieval Latin *defalcatio* "deduction," from *defalcare* "to deduct," from Latin *de-* + *falx* "sickle"] — **de·fal·cate** \di-ˈfal-ˌkāt, -ˈfȯl-, ˈdef-əl-\ *vi* — **de·fal·ca·tor** \-ˌkāt-ər\ *n*

def·a·ma·tion \ˌdef-ə-ˈmā-shən\ *n* : the act of defaming : SLANDER, LIBEL — **de·fam·a·to·ry** \di-ˈfam-ə-ˌtōr-ē, -ˌtȯr-\ *adj*

de·fame \di-ˈfām\ *vt* : to injure or destroy the good name of : speak evil of ***synonyms*** see SLANDER — **de·fam·er** *n*

¹de·fault \di-ˈfȯlt\ *n* **1** : failure to do something required by law or duty **2** : a failure to pay financial debts **3** : a failure to compete in or to finish a contest 〈lost the game by *default*〉 **4 a** : a selection made usually automatically or without active consideration due to lack of an alternative 〈remained the club's president by *default*〉 **b** : a selection to be made automatically according to a computer program when the user does not specify a choice [Medieval French *defaute,* derived from Latin *de-* + *fallere* "to deceive"]

²default *vb* **1** : to fail to carry out a contract, obligation, or duty; *also* : to forfeit something by such failure **2** : to make a default selection 〈the software *defaults* to a standard font〉 — **de·fault·er** *n*

¹de·feat \di-ˈfēt\ *vt* **1 a** : NULLIFY 〈*defeat* a will〉 **b** : FRUSTRATE 2 〈*defeat* a hope〉 **2** : to win victory over : BEAT [Medieval French *defait,* past participle of *defaire* "to destroy," from Medieval Latin *disfacere,* from Latin *dis-* + *facere* "to do"] — **de·feat·able** \-ˈfēt-ə-bəl\ *adj*

²defeat *n* **1** : frustration by prevention of success 〈the *defeat* of our plans〉 **2 a** : an overthrow of an army in battle **b** : loss of a contest (as by a team)

de·feat·ism \-ˌiz-əm\ *n* : an attitude of expecting defeat or of accepting defeat on the ground that further effort would be useless or unwise — **de·feat·ist** \-əst\ *n or adj*

def·e·cate \ˈdef-i-ˌkāt\ *vb* **1** : to free from impurity or corruption : REFINE **2** : to discharge feces from the bowels [Latin *defaecare,* from *de-* + *faex* "dregs, lees"] — **def·e·ca·tion** \ˌdef-i-ˈkā-shən\ *n*

¹de·fect \ˈdē-ˌfekt, di-ˈ\ *n* : a lack of something necessary for completeness or perfection [Latin *defectus* "lack," from *deficere* "to desert, fail," from *de-* + *facere* "to do"] ***synonyms*** see BLEMISH

²de·fect \di-ˈfekt\ *vi* : to desert a cause or party often in order to take up another — **de·fec·tion** \-ˈfek-shən\ *n* — **de·fec·tor** \-ˈfek-tər\ *n*

¹de·fec·tive \di-ˈfek-tiv\ *adj* **1** : lacking something essential : FAULTY **2** : lacking one or more of the usual forms of grammatical inflection 〈*must* is a *defective* verb〉 — **de·fec·tive·ly** *adv* — **de·fec·tive·ness** *n*

²defective *n* : a person who is subnormal physically or mentally

de·fence, de·fence·man *chiefly British variant of* DEFENSE, DEFENSEMAN

de·fend \di-ˈfend\ *vb* **1** : to repel danger or attack **2** : to act as attorney for **3** : to oppose the claim of another in a lawsuit : CONTEST **4** : to uphold against opposition 〈*defend* a theory〉 [Medieval French *defendre,* from Latin *defendere,* from *de-* + *-fendere* "to strike"]

synonyms DEFEND, PROTECT, SHIELD, GUARD mean to keep secure from danger or against attack. DEFEND denotes warding off actual or threatened attack 〈*defending* their country〉. PROTECT implies something, as a covering, that serves as a bar to the admission or impact of that which may attack or injure 〈*protect* one's eyes with safety goggles〉 〈a bird sanctuary *protected* by state law〉. SHIELD suggests protective intervention in imminent danger or actual attack 〈*shielded* her eyes from the sun with her hand〉. GUARD implies protecting with vigilance and force against expected danger 〈the base was well *guarded*〉.

de·fend·ant \di-ˈfen-dənt\ *n* : a person against whom an accusation or claim is made in a legal action — compare PLAINTIFF

de·fend·er \di-ˈfend-ər\ *n* **1** : one that defends **2** : a player in a sport (as football) assigned to a defensive position

de·fense \di-ˈfens\ *n* **1** : the act of defending : resistance against attack **2** : capability of resisting attack **3 a** : means or method of defending **b** : an argument in support or justification **4 a** : a defending party or group (as in a court of law) **b** : a defensive team **5** : the answer made by the defendant in a legal action [Medieval French, derived from Latin *defendere* "to defend"] — **de·fense·less** \-ləs\ *adj* — **de·fense·less·ly** *adv* — **de·fense·less·ness** *n*

de·fense·man \-mən, -ˌman\ *n* : a player in a sport who is assigned to a defensive zone or position

defense mechanism *n* **1** : a defensive reaction by an organism **2** : a mental process (as rationalization or repression) by which one avoids becoming aware of or confronting unpleasant thoughts, feelings, or emotions

de·fen·si·ble \di-ˈfen-sə-bəl\ *adj* : capable of being defended 〈a *defensible* hill〉 — **de·fen·si·bil·i·ty** \-ˌfen-sə-ˈbil-ət-ē\ *n* — **de·fen·si·bly** \-ˈfen-sə-blē\ *adv*

¹de·fen·sive \di-ˈfen-siv\ *adj* **1** : serving or intended to defend or protect 〈a *defensive* move〉 **2 a** : devoted to resisting or preventing attack 〈*defensive* behavior〉 **b** : of or relating to the attempt to keep an opponent from scoring in a game or contest 〈a player with good *defensive* skills〉 — **de·fen·sive·ly** *adv* — **de·fen·sive·ness** *n*

²defensive *n* : a defensive position — **on the defensive** : in a state of readiness to oppose attack or criticism

¹de·fer \di-ˈfər\ *vt* **de·ferred; de·fer·ring** : to put off : DELAY 〈*defer* payment for goods〉 [Medieval French *differer,* from Latin *differre* "to postpone, be different"] — **de·fer·ra·ble** \-ˈfər-ə-bəl\ *adj* — **de·fer·rer** *n*

synonyms DEFER, POSTPONE mean to delay an action or proceeding. DEFER may imply a deliberate putting off until a later usually indefinite time or may imply a delay in fulfillment 〈*defer* college plans〉. POSTPONE implies an intentional deferring usually to a definite time 〈*postpone* the meeting until Monday〉.

²defer *vi* **de·ferred; de·fer·ring** : to yield to another's wish or opinion [Middle French *deferer,* from Latin *deferre* "to bring down," from *de-* + *ferre* "to carry"]

def·er·ence \ˈdef-rəns, -ə-rəns\ *n* : courteous respectful regard for another or another's wishes — **in deference to** : in consideration of or out of respect for 〈returned early *in deference to* her parents' wishes〉

synonyms DEFERENCE, RESPECT, REVERENCE, HONOR mean esteem shown to another. DEFERENCE implies a courteous yielding of one's own opinion or preference to that of another 〈showed *deference* to their elders〉. RESPECT implies regard for a person or quality or achievement as worthy of honor or confidence 〈they *respect* her opinion〉. REVERENCE implies profound respect mingled with awe or devotion 〈great *reverence* for my father〉. HONOR implies that the recognition shown is entirely due 〈the nomination was an *honor*〉.

def·er·en·tial \ˌdef-ə-ˈren-chəl\ *adj* : showing or expressing deference — **def·er·en·tial·ly** \-ˈrench-lē, -ə-lə\ *adv*

de·fer·ment \di-ˈfər-mənt\ *n* : the act of delaying or postponing; *esp* : official postponement of military service

de·fi·ance \di-ˈfī-əns\ *n* **1** : the act or an instance of defying : CHALLENGE **2** : disposition to resist : contempt of opposition — **in defiance of** : contrary to : DESPITE 〈worked *in defiance of* doctor's orders〉

de·fi·ant \-ənt\ *adj* : full of or showing defiance : BOLD, IMPUDENT 〈a *defiant* refusal〉 — **de·fi·ant·ly** *adv*

de·fi·cien·cy \di-ˈfish-ən-sē\ *n, pl* **-cies** **1** : the quality or state of being deficient **2** : shortage of something needed; *esp* : a shortage of substances necessary to health

deficiency disease *n* : a disease (as scurvy) caused by a lack of essential dietary elements and especially a vitamin or mineral

¹de·fi·cient \di-ˈfish-ənt\ *adj* : lacking something necessary for completeness : DEFECTIVE 〈a diet *deficient* in proteins〉 [Latin *deficiens,* present participle of *deficere* "to be wanting, fail," from *de-* + *facere* "to do"] — **de·fi·cient·ly** *adv*

²deficient *n* : one that is deficient 〈a mental *deficient*〉

def·i·cit \ˈdef-ə-sət\ *n* : a deficiency in amount; *esp* : an excess of expenses over income [French *déficit,* from Latin *deficit* "it is wanting," from *deficere* "to be wanting"]

[1]**de·file** \di-ˈfīl\ *vt* : to make unclean or impure: as **a** : to corrupt the purity or perfection of : DEBASE ⟨*defile* buildings with posters⟩ **b** : RAPE 2, VIOLATE **c** : DESECRATE ⟨invaders *defiled* the shrine⟩ **d** : TARNISH, ABASE ⟨*defile* a hero's record with lies⟩ [alteration of Middle English *defoilen* "to trample, defile," from Medieval French *defoiller, defuler* "to trample," from *de-* "de-" + *fuller* "to trample"] — **de·file·ment** \-mənt\ *n* — **de·fil·er** *n*

[2]**de·file** \di-ˈfīl, ˈdē-ˌ\ *vi* : to march off in a single line [French *défiler,* from *dé-* "de-" + *filer* "to move in a column"]

[3]**de·file** \di-ˈfīl, ˈdē-ˌ\ *n* : a narrow passage or gorge

de·fine \di-ˈfīn\ *vt* **1 a** : to fix or mark the limits of ⟨the boundary was clearly *defined*⟩ **b** : to make distinct, clear, or detailed especially in outline ⟨your argument is not sufficiently *defined*⟩ **2 a** : to determine the essential qualities of ⟨*define* the concept of loyalty⟩ **b** : to discover and set forth the meaning of ⟨*define* a word⟩ **c** : CHARACTERIZE, DISTINGUISH 3 ⟨*defined* himself as a great writer⟩ **d** : to specify (as a programming task) for a computer to use ⟨*define* a procedure⟩ [Latin *definire,* from *de-* + *finis* "boundary, end"] — **de·fin·able** \-ˈfī-nə-bəl\ *adj* — **de·fin·er** *n*

def·i·nite \ˈdef-nət, -ə-nət\ *adj* **1** : having certain or distinct limits : FIXED ⟨a *definite* period of time⟩ **2** : clear in meaning : EXACT, EXPLICIT ⟨a *definite* answer⟩ **3** : typically designating an identified or immediately identifiable person or thing ⟨the *definite* article *the*⟩ [Latin *definitus,* past participle of *definire* "to define"] — **def·i·nite·ly** *adv* — **def·i·nite·ness** *n*

synonyms DEFINITE, DEFINITIVE are sometimes confused. DEFINITE denotes that which has limits so clearly fixed, defined, or stated there can be no doubt about the range or meaning ⟨a *definite* sum of money⟩. DEFINITIVE denotes supplying an answer as final and serving to end dispute and doubt ⟨a *definitive* statement of political belief⟩. ***synonyms*** see in addition EXPLICIT

def·i·ni·tion \ˌdef-ə-ˈnish-ən\ *n* **1** : an act of determining or settling the limits **2 a** : a statement of the meaning of a word or word group or of a sign or symbol **b** : the action or process of defining **3 a** : the action or the power of making definite and clear **b** : the state of being clear ⟨the *definition* of the hills⟩ — **def·i·ni·tion·al** \-ˈnish-nəl, -ˈnish-ən-l\ *adj*

de·fin·i·tive \di-ˈfin-ət-iv\ *adj* **1** : providing a final solution : CONCLUSIVE ⟨a *definitive* victory⟩ **2** : authoritative and apparently completely informative ⟨the *definitive* book on the subject⟩ **3** : defining or limiting precisely ⟨*definitive* laws⟩ ***synonyms*** see DEFINITE — **de·fin·i·tive·ly** *adv* — **de·fin·i·tive·ness** *n*

de·flate \di-ˈflāt, ˈdē-\ *vb* **1** : to release air or gas from **2** : to reduce in size, importance, or effectiveness ⟨the scandal *deflated* his reputation⟩ **3** : to reduce from a state of inflation ⟨*deflate* the currency⟩ **4** : to become deflated : COLLAPSE [*de-* + *-flate* (as in *inflate*)] — **de·fla·tor** \-ˈflāt-ər\ *n*

de·fla·tion \di-ˈflā-shən, ˈdē-\ *n* **1** : an act or instance of deflating : the state of being deflated **2** : a reduction in the volume of available money or credit that results in a decline of the general price level — **de·fla·tion·ary** \-shə-ˌner-ē\ *adj*

de·flect \di-ˈflekt\ *vb* : to take or cause to take a new course : turn aside ⟨*deflect* a stream from its bed⟩ ⟨the ball *deflected* off the wall⟩ [Latin *deflectere* "to bend down, turn aside," from *de-* + *flectere* "to bend"] — **de·flec·tion** \-ˈflek-shən\ *n*

de·fog \dē-ˈfȯg, -ˈfäg\ *vt* : to remove fog or condensed moisture from ⟨*defog* a windshield⟩ — **de·fog·ger** *n*

de·fo·li·ant \ˈdē-ˈfō-lē-ənt\ *n* : a chemical applied to plants to cause the leaves to drop off prematurely

de·fo·li·ate \ˈde-ˈfō-lē-ˌāt\ *vt* : to deprive of leaves especially prematurely [Latin *defoliare,* from *de-* + *folium* "leaf"] — **de·fo·li·a·tion** \ˌdē-ˌfō-lē-ˈā-shən\ *n* — **de·fo·li·a·tor** \ˈdē-ˈfō-lē-ˌāt-ər\ *n*

de·for·est \ˈdē-ˈfȯr-əst, -ˈfär-\ *vt* : to clear of forests — **de·for·es·ta·tion** \ˌdē-ˌfȯr-ə-ˈstā-shən, -ˌfär-\ *n*

de·form \di-ˈfȯrm, ˈdē-\ *vb* **1** : to spoil the form or natural appearance of : DISFIGURE ⟨a leg *deformed* by an injury⟩ ⟨a face *deformed* by grief⟩ **2** : to become misshapen or changed in shape — **de·for·ma·tion** \ˌdē-ˌfȯr-ˈmā-shən, ˌdef-ər-\ *n*

de·for·mi·ty \di-ˈfȯr-mət-ē\ *n, pl* **-ties** **1** : the state of being deformed **2** : a physical blemish or distortion **3** : a moral or aesthetic flaw

de·frag \dē-ˈfrag\ *vt* **de·fragged; de·frag·ging** : DEFRAGMENT

de·frag·ment \dē-ˈfrag-mənt\ *vt* : to reorganize fragments of related data on (a computer disk) into a continuous arrangement — **de·frag·men·ta·tion** \-ˌfrag-mən-ˈtā-shən\ *n*

de·fraud \di-ˈfrȯd\ *vt* : to deprive of something by trickery, deception, or fraud ⟨*defrauded* of their money⟩ ***synonyms*** see CHEAT — **de·fraud·er** \di-ˈfrȯd-ər\ *n*

de·fray \di-ˈfrā\ *vt* : to pay or provide for the payment of ⟨needs more money to *defray* expenses⟩ [Middle French *deffroyer,* from *des-* "de-" + *frayer* "to expend," derived from Latin *frangere* "to break"] — **de·fray·able** \-ˈfrā-ə-bəl\ *adj* — **de·fray·al** \-ˈfrā-əl, -ˈfrāl\ *n*

de·frost \di-ˈfrȯst, ˈdē-\ *vb* **1** : to free from ice or a frozen state ⟨*defrost* meat⟩ ⟨*defrost* a refrigerator⟩ **2** : to remove fog or condensed moisture from ⟨*defrost* the windshield⟩ — **de·frost·er** *n*

deft \ˈdeft\ *adj* : quick and skillful in action ⟨knitting with *deft* fingers⟩ [Middle English *defte* "gentle"] ***synonyms*** see DEXTEROUS — **deft·ly** *adv* — **deft·ness** *n*

de·funct \di-ˈfəngt, -ˈfəngkt\ *adj* : no longer living or existing ⟨a *defunct* factory⟩ [Latin *defunctus,* from *defungi* "to finish, die," from *de-* + *fungi* "to perform"]

de·fy \di-ˈfī\ *vt* **de·fied; de·fy·ing** **1** : to challenge to do something considered impossible : DARE ⟨the magician *defied* the audience to explain the trick⟩ **2** : to refuse boldly to yield or conform to ⟨*defy* public opinion⟩ ⟨*defy* the law⟩ **3** : to resist attempts at ⟨a scene that *defies* description⟩ [Medieval French *defier* "to renounce faith in, challenge," from *de-* "de-" + *fier* "to entrust," from Latin *fidere* "to trust"] — **de·fi·er** \-ˈfī-ər, -ˈfīr\ *n*

de·gas \ˈdē-ˈgas\ *vt* : to free from gas

de·gauss \ˈdē-ˈgau̇s\ *vt* : DEMAGNETIZE

de·gen·er·a·cy \di-ˈjen-rə-sē, -ə-rə-\ *n, pl* **-cies** **1** : the state of being or process of becoming degenerate **2** : sexual perversion

[1]**de·gen·er·ate** \di-ˈjen-rət, -ə-rət\ *adj* : having sunk to a lower state or level: as **a** : having declined or become less specialized (as in structure or function) from an ancestral or earlier state ⟨a *degenerate* eye⟩ **b** : fallen below what is normal or desirable; *esp* : fallen to a corrupt, evil, or vicious state [Latin *degeneratus,* past participle of *degenerare* "to deteriorate," from *de-* + *genus* "race, kind"]

[2]**de·gen·er·ate** \di-ˈjen-ə-ˌrāt\ *vi* **1** : to pass from a higher to a lower type or condition : DETERIORATE ⟨the road *degenerated* into a rough track⟩ **2** : to undergo evolution toward an earlier or less highly organized biological type

[3]**de·gen·er·ate** \di-ˈjen-rət; -ə-rət\ *n* : a degenerate person; *esp* : a sexual pervert

de·gen·er·a·tion \di-ˌjen-ə-ˈrā-shən, ˌdē-\ *n* **1** : a lowering (as of power, vitality, or quality) to a feebler and poorer kind or state **2 a** : a change in a tissue or an organ resulting in lessened activity or usefulness ⟨fatty *degeneration* of the heart⟩ **b** : a condition marked by progressive deterioration of physical characters or parts (as organs) present in related or earlier forms ⟨tapeworms exhibit extreme *degeneration*⟩

de·gen·er·a·tive \di-ˈjen-ə-ˌrāt-iv\ *adj* : of, relating to, or tending to cause degeneration ⟨a *degenerative* disease⟩

de·gla·ci·a·tion \dē-ˌglā-shē-ˈā-shən, -sē-\ *n* : the melting of a glacier or ice cap

deg·ra·da·tion \ˌdeg-rə-ˈdā-shən\ *n* **1** : a reduction in rank, dignity, or standing **b** : removal from office **2** : loss of honor or reputation : HUMILIATION **3** : moral or intellectual decline : DEGENERATION

de·grade \di-ˈgrād\ *vb* **1** : DEMOTE; *also* : DEPOSE 1 **2** : to drag down in moral or intellectual character : CORRUPT ⟨*degraded* by a life of crime⟩ **3** : to reduce the complexity of : DECOMPOSE — **de·grad·er** *n*

de·gree \di-ˈgrē\ *n* **1** : a step or stage in a process, course, or order of classification ⟨advance by *degrees*⟩ **2 a** : the extent,

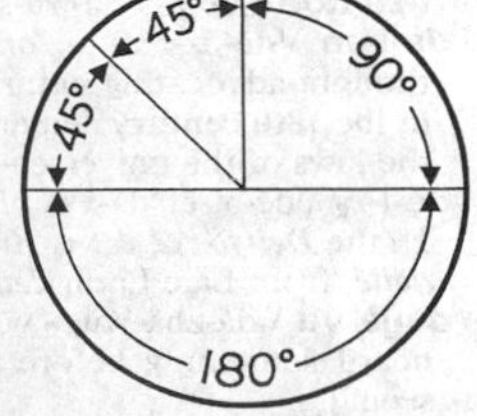

degree 6

\ə\ **abut**	\au̇\ **out**	\i\ **tip**	\ȯ\ **saw**	\u̇\ **foot**
\ər\ **further**	\ch\ **chin**	\ī\ **life**	\ȯi\ **coin**	\y\ **yet**
\a\ **mat**	\e\ **pet**	\j\ **job**	\th\ **thin**	\yü\ **few**
\ā\ **take**	\ē\ **easy**	\ng\ **sing**	\th\ **this**	\yu̇\ **cure**
\ä\ **cot, cart**	\g\ **go**	\ō\ **bone**	\ü\ **food**	\zh\ **vision**

intensity, or scope of something especially as measured by a graded series ⟨murder in the first *degree*⟩ **b** : one of the forms or sets of forms used in the comparison of an adjective or adverb **3 a** : a rank or grade of official or social position **b** : the civil condition or status of a person **4 a** : a grade of membership attained in a ritualistic order or society **b** : the formal ceremonies observed in the awarding of a ritualistic distinction **c** : a title conferred upon students by a college, university, or professional school upon completion of a program of study **d** : an academic title conferred honorarily **5** : one of the divisions or intervals marked on a scale of a measuring instrument — symbol ° **6** : a unit of measure for angles and arcs that for angles is equal to an angle with its vertex at the center of a circle and its sides cutting off 1/360 of the circumference and that for an arc is equal to 1/360 of the circumference **7 a** : the sum of the exponents of the variables in the term with highest degree in a polynomial ⟨the *degree* of $3x^3 + 2x^2y + 5x$ is 3⟩ **b** : the sum of the exponents of the variables in a single term mathematical expression ⟨the *degree* of $3x^2y$ is 3⟩ **8 a** : a line or space of the musical staff **b** : a step, note, or tone of a musical scale [Medieval French *degré* "step, stair," from Latin *de-* + *gradus* "step, grade"] — **to a degree 1** : to a remarkable extent : EXCEEDINGLY **2** : in a small way

degree–day *n* : a unit that represents one degree of departure from a given point (as 65°F or 18°C) in the mean daily outdoor temperature and is usually used to measure heat requirements

de·hisce \di-ˈhis\ *vi* : to split open along a natural line especially with discharge of contents ⟨seedpods *dehiscing* at maturity⟩ [Latin *dehiscere* "to split open," from *de-* + *hiscere* "to gape"] — **de·his·cence** \-ˈhis-ns\ *n* — **de·his·cent** \-nt\ *adj*

de·horn \dē-ˈhȯrn, ˈdē-\ *vt* : to deprive of horns — **de·horn·er** *n*

de·hu·man·ize \dē-ˈhyü-mə-ˌnīz, dē-ˈyü-, ˈdē-\ *vt* : to strip of human qualities or personality — **de·hu·man·i·za·tion** \dē-ˌhyü-mə-nə-ˈzā-shən, dē-ˌyü-, ˈdē-\ *n*

de·hu·mid·i·fy \ˌdē-hyü-ˈmid-ə-ˌfī, ˌdē-yü-\ *vt* : to remove moisture from (as the air) — **de·hu·mid·i·fi·ca·tion** \-ˌmid-ə-fə-ˈkā-shən\ *n* — **de·hu·mid·i·fi·er** \-ˈmid-ə-ˌfī-ər, -ˌfīr\ *n*

de·hy·drate \dē-ˈhī-ˌdrāt, ˈdē-\ *vb* **1** : to remove water from (as foods) **2** : to lose water or body fluids — **de·hy·dra·tion** \ˌdē-ˌhī-ˈdrā-shən\ *n*

de·hy·drog·e·nase \ˌdē-ˌhī-ˈdräj-ə-ˌnās, dē-ˈhī-drə-jə-\ *n* : an enzyme that accelerates the removal and transfer of hydrogen

de·hy·dro·ge·nate \ˌdē-ˌhī-ˈdräj-ə-ˌnāt, dē-ˈhī-drə-jə-\ *vt* : to remove hydrogen from — **de·hy·dro·ge·na·tion** \ˌdē-ˌhī-ˌdräj-ə-ˈnā-shən, ˌdē-ˌhī-drə-jə-\ *n*

de·ice \dē-ˈīs, ˈdē-\ *vt* : to keep free or rid of ice — **de·ic·er** *n*

de·i·fy \ˈdē-ə-ˌfī\ *vt* **-fied; -fy·ing 1 a** : to make a god of **b** : to take as an object of worship **2** : to treat as an object of supreme regard ⟨*deify* money⟩ [Medieval French *deifier,* from Late Latin *deificare,* from Latin *deus* "god" + *-ficare* "-fy"] — **de·i·fi·ca·tion** \ˌdē-ə-fə-ˈkā-shən\ *n*

deign \ˈdān\ *vi* : to condescend reluctantly ⟨would not even *deign* to talk to him⟩ [Medieval French *deignier,* from Latin *dignare,* from *dignus* "worthy"] ***synonyms*** see STOOP

dei·non·y·chus \dī-ˈnän-i-kəs\ *n* : a small flesh-eating dinosaur of the Cretaceous period having small forelegs and walking on sharp-clawed hind legs [New Latin, from Greek *deinos* "terrifying" + *-onychos* "clawed" (from *onyx* "claw, nail")]

de·ion·ize \dē-ˈī-ə-ˌnīz, ˈdē-\ *vt* : to remove ions from — **de·ion·i·za·tion** \ˌdē-ˌī-ə-nə-ˈzā-shən\ *n*

de·ism \ˈdē-ˌiz-əm\ *n, often cap* : a movement or system of thought advocating natural religion, emphasizing morality, and in the 18th century denying the interference of the Creator with the laws of the universe — **de·ist** \ˈdē-əst\ *n, often cap*

de·i·ty \ˈdē-ət-ē, ˈdā-\ *n, pl* **-ties 1 a** : DIVINITY 1 **b** *cap* : GOD 1 ⟨the *Deity*⟩ **2 a** : GOD 2 **b** : GODDESS 1 [Medieval French *deité,* from Late Latin *deitas,* from Latin *deus* "god"]

dé·jà vu \ˌdā-zhä-ˈvü, -ˈvue-\ *n* : a feeling that one has seen or heard something before [French, adjective, literally, "already seen"]

de·ject·ed \di-ˈjek-təd\ *adj* : cast down in spirits : DEPRESSED ⟨*dejected* over her failure⟩ [Latin *dejectus,* past participle of *deicere* "to cast down," from *de-* + *jacere* "to throw"] — **de·ject·ed·ly** *adv* — **de·ject·ed·ness** *n*

de·jec·tion \di-ˈjek-shən\ *n* : lowness of spirits : SADNESS ***synonyms*** see MELANCHOLY

de ju·re \dē-ˈju̇r-ē, dā-ˈyu̇r-\ *adj or adv* **1** : existing or exercising power by legal right ⟨*de jure* government⟩ **2** : based on laws or actions of the state ⟨*de jure* segregation⟩ — compare DE FACTO [Medieval Latin, "by right"]

deka- *or* **dek-** — see DECA-

deka·gram \ˈdek-ə-ˌgram\ *n* — see METRIC SYSTEM table

deka·li·ter \-ˌlēt-ər\ *n* — see METRIC SYSTEM table

deka·me·ter \-ˌmēt-ər\ *n* — see METRIC SYSTEM table

deke \ˈdēk\ *vb* **deked; deke·ing** : to fake an opponent out of position (as in ice hockey) [short for [2]*decoy*] — **deke** *n*

de·lam·i·na·tion \ˌdē-ˌlam-ə-ˈnā-shən\ *n* : separation or splitting into distinct layers — **de·lam·i·nate** \dē-ˈlam-ə-ˌnāt\ *vi*

Del·a·ware \ˈdel-ə-ˌwaər, -ˌweər, -wər\ *n, pl* **Delaware** *or* **Delawares** : a member of an American Indian people of the Delaware valley

[1]**de·lay** \di-ˈlā\ *n* **1** : the act of delaying : the state of being delayed ⟨start without *delay*⟩ **2** : the time during which something is delayed ⟨a *delay* of 30 minutes⟩

[2]**delay** *vb* **1** : to put off : POSTPONE **2** : to stop, detain, or hinder for a time ⟨*delayed* by a storm⟩ **3** : to cause to be slower or to occur more slowly than normal ⟨*delay* a child's development⟩ **4** : to move or act slowly [Medieval French *delaier,* from *de-* + *laier* "to leave," alteration of *laissier,* from Latin *laxare* "to slacken"] — **de·lay·er** *n*

de·lec·ta·ble \di-ˈlek-tə-bəl\ *adj* **1** : highly pleasing : DELIGHTFUL **2** : DELICIOUS ⟨a *delectable* meal⟩ [Medieval French, from Latin *delectabilis,* from *delectare* "to delight"] — **de·lec·ta·bly** \-blē\ *adv*

de·lec·ta·tion \ˌdē-ˌlek-ˈta-shən, di-; ˌdel-ək-\ *n* **1** : DELIGHT 1 **2** : something that gives pleasure

[1]**del·e·gate** \ˈdel-i-gət, -ˌgāt\ *n* : a person sent with power to act for another: as **a** : a representative to a convention, conference, or assembly **b** : a representative of a U.S. territory in the House of Representatives **c** : a member of the lower house of the legislature of Maryland, Virginia, or West Virginia [derived from Latin *delegare* "to delegate," from *de-* + *legare* "to send"]

[2]**del·e·gate** \-ˌgāt\ *vt* **1** : to entrust to another ⟨*delegate* responsibility⟩ **2** : to appoint as one's delegate

del·e·ga·tion \ˌdel-i-ˈgā-shən\ *n* **1** : the act of delegating (as power or authority) to another **2** : one or more persons chosen to represent others

de·lete \di-ˈlēt\ *vt* : to eliminate especially by blotting out, cutting out, or erasing ⟨*delete* a passage of the story⟩ ⟨*delete* a computer file⟩ [Latin *delēre* "to wipe out, destroy"]

del·e·te·ri·ous \ˌdel-ə-ˈtir-ē-əs\ *adj* : having a harmful effect [Greek *dēlētērios,* from *dēleisthai* "to hurt"] — **del·e·te·ri·ous·ly** *adv* — **del·e·te·ri·ous·ness** *n*

de·le·tion \di-ˈlē-shən\ *n* **1** : an act of deleting **2** : something deleted

delft \ˈdelft\ *n* **1** : a Dutch pottery covered with an opaque white glaze upon which a predominantly blue decoration is painted **2** : glazed pottery especially when blue and white [*Delft,* Netherlands]

delft·ware \ˈdelf-ˌtwaər, -ˌtweər\ *n* : DELFT

deli \ˈdel-ē\ *n, pl* **del·is** : DELICATESSEN

[1]**de·lib·er·ate** \di-ˈlib-rət, -ə-rət\ *adj* **1** : marked by or resulting from thorough and careful consideration ⟨a *deliberate* judgment⟩ **2** : showing awareness of the significance or nature of the thing done or said ⟨a *deliberate* lie⟩ **3** : slow, unhurried, and steady as though allowing time for decision on each individual action involved ⟨*deliberate* movements⟩ [Latin *deliberatus,* past participle of *deliberare* "to weigh in the mind," from *de-* + *libra* "scale, pound"] ***synonyms*** see VOLUNTARY — **de·lib·er·ate·ly** *adv* — **de·lib·er·ate·ness** *n*

[2]**de·lib·er·ate** \di-ˈlib-ə-ˌrāt\ *vb* : to think about deliberately : CONSIDER ⟨*deliberate* before answering⟩

de·lib·er·a·tion \di-ˌlib-ə-ˈrā-shən\ *n* **1** : the act of deliberating **2** : a discussion and consideration of the reasons for and against a measure or question **3** : the quality of being deliberate : DELIBERATENESS

de·lib·er·a·tive \di-ˈlib-ə-ˌrāt-iv; -ˈlib-rət-, -ə-rət-\ *adj* : of or relating to deliberation : engaged in or devoted to deliberation ⟨the legislature is a *deliberative* body of government⟩ — **de·lib·er·a·tive·ly** *adv* — **de·lib·er·a·tive·ness** *n*

del·i·ca·cy \ˈdel-i-kə-sē\ *n, pl* **-cies 1** : something pleasing to eat because it is rare or luxurious **2 a** : FINENESS, DAINTINESS ⟨lace of great *delicacy*⟩ **b** : FRAILTY 1 **3** : nicety or subtle expressiveness of touch (as in painting or music) **4 a** : precise and refined perception and discrimination **b** : extreme sensitivity : PRECISION **5** : SQUEAMISHNESS **6** : the quality or state of requiring delicate treatment ⟨the *delicacy* of a situation⟩

del·i·cate \ˈdel-i-kət\ *adj* **1 :** pleasing to the senses ⟨a *delicate* breeze⟩ ⟨a *delicate* aroma⟩ **2 :** marked by fineness of structure, workmanship, or texture ⟨*delicate* lace⟩ **3 a :** marked by keen sensitivity or fine discrimination ⟨a *delicate* interpretation⟩ **b :** FASTIDIOUS, SQUEAMISH ⟨a person of *delicate* tastes⟩ **4 :** easily torn or hurt ⟨a *delicate* butterfly wing⟩; *also* **:** WEAK 1a, SICKLY **5 :** calling for or involving extremely careful treatment ⟨a *delicate* balance of power⟩ **6 :** requiring skill or tact ⟨*delicate* negotiations⟩ **7 :** marked by great precision and sensitivity ⟨a *delicate* instrument⟩ [Latin *delicatus*] — **del·i·cate·ly** *adv* — **del·i·cate·ness** *n*

del·i·ca·tes·sen \ˌdel-i-kə-ˈtes-n\ *n pl* **1 :** ready-to-eat food products (as cooked meats and prepared salads) **2** *sing, pl* **delicatessens :** a store where delicatessen are sold [obsolete German (now *Delikatessen),* plural of *Delicatesse* "delicacy," from French *délicatesse,* derived from Latin *delicatus* "delicate"]

Word History Near the end of the 19th century, the word *delicatessen* began to appear in English. Its earliest sense is "delicacies" or "ready-to-eat food products." In this sense *delicatessen* is a plural noun, reflecting its origin in a German word now spelled *Delikatessen,* the plural of *Delikatesse.* The German is a borrowing from French *délicatesse,* meaning "delicacy." In English a second sense of *delicatessen* developed when the word was understood as a singular noun used for a store where delicacies are sold. In spite of the widespread popular belief to the contrary, *delicatessen* has no etymological connection with the German verb *essen,* "to eat."

de·li·cious \di-ˈlish-əs\ *adj* **:** giving great pleasure **:** DELIGHTFUL; *esp* **:** very pleasing to the taste or smell [Medieval French, derived from Latin *delicere* "to allure"] — **de·li·cious·ly** *adv* — **de·li·cious·ness** *n*

Delicious *n, pl* **De·li·cious·es** *or* **Delicious :** a sweet red or yellow apple of U.S. origin with five bumps arranged around the end opposite the stem

¹de·light \di-ˈlīt\ *n* **1 :** extreme pleasure or satisfaction **:** JOY **2 :** something that gives great pleasure

²delight *vb* **1 :** to take great pleasure ⟨*delighted* in playing guitar⟩ **2 :** to give joy or satisfaction to **:** please greatly ⟨a book sure to *delight*⟩ [Medieval French *deliter,* from Latin *delectare,* from *delicere* "to allure," from *de-* + *lacere* "to allure"]

de·light·ed *adj* **:** highly pleased **:** GRATIFIED — **de·light·ed·ly** *adv* — **de·light·ed·ness** *n*

de·light·ful \di-ˈlīt-fəl\ *adj* **:** highly pleasing **:** giving delight ⟨a *delightful* vacation⟩ — **de·light·ful·ly** \-fə-lē\ *adv* — **de·light·ful·ness** *n*

de·lim·it \di-ˈlim-ət\ *vt* **:** to fix the limits of **:** BOUND — **de·lim·i·ta·tion** \-ˌlim-ə-ˈtā-shən\ *n*

de·lin·eate \di-ˈlin-ē-ˌāt\ *vt* **1 :** to indicate by lines drawn in the form or figure of **:** PORTRAY **2 :** to describe in usually sharp or vivid detail ⟨*delineate* the characters in a story⟩ [Latin *delineare,* from *de-* + *linea* "line"] — **de·lin·ea·tion** \di-ˌlin-ē-ˈā-shən\ *n* — **de·lin·ea·tor** \-ē-ˌāt-ər\ *n*

de·lin·quen·cy \di-ˈling-kwən-sē\ *n, pl* **-cies :** the quality or state of being delinquent

¹de·lin·quent \-kwənt\ *n* **:** a delinquent person

²delinquent *adj* **1 :** offending by neglect or violation of duty or of law **2 :** overdue for payment ⟨a *delinquent* charge account⟩ [Latin *delinquere* "to fail, offend," from *de-* + *linquere* "to leave"] — **de·lin·quent·ly** *adv*

del·i·quesce \ˌdel-ə-ˈkwes\ *vi* **:** to melt away: **a :** to dissolve gradually by absorbing moisture from the air ⟨a *deliquescing* substance⟩ **b :** to become soft or liquid ⟨*deliquescing* mushrooms⟩ [Latin *deliquescere,* from *de-* + *liquēre* "to be fluid"] — **del·i·ques·cence** \-ˈkwes-ns\ *n*

del·i·ques·cent \-ˈkwes-nt\ *adj* **1 :** marked by or undergoing deliquescence **2 :** having repeated division into branches ⟨elms are *deliquescent* trees⟩ — compare EXCURRENT

de·lir·i·ous \di-ˈlir-ē-əs\ *adj* **1 :** of or relating to delirium **2 :** affected with or marked by delirium; *also* **:** wildly excited — **de·lir·i·ous·ly** *adv* — **de·lir·i·ous·ness** *n*

de·lir·i·um \-ˈlir-ē-əm\ *n* **1 :** a mental disturbance characterized by confusion, disordered speech, and hallucinations **2 :** frenzied excitement [Latin, from *delirare* "to be crazy," literally, "to leave the furrow (in plowing)," from *de-* + *lira* "furrow"]

delirium tre·mens \-ˈtrē-mənz, -ˈtrem-ənz\ *n* **:** a violent delirium with tremors that is induced by excessive and prolonged use of alcoholic liquors — called also *D.T.'s* [New Latin, literally, "trembling delirium"]

de·liv·er \di-ˈliv-ər\ *vb* **-liv·ered; -liv·er·ing** \-ˈliv-ring, -ə-ring\ **1 :** to set free **:** SAVE **2 :** to hand over **:** CONVEY, TRANSFER ⟨*deliver* a letter⟩ **3 a :** to assist in giving birth; *also* **:** to aid in the birth of ⟨a doctor *delivered* the baby⟩ **b :** to give birth to ⟨*delivered* her only child late in life⟩ **4 :** UTTER, COMMUNICATE ⟨*deliver* a speech⟩ **5 :** to send to an intended target or destination ⟨*deliver* a pitch⟩ **6 :** to produce the promised, desired, or expected result ⟨*deliver* on a promise⟩ [Medieval French *delivrer,* from Late Latin *deliberare,* from Latin *de-* + *liberare* "to liberate"] ***synonyms*** see RESCUE — **de·liv·er·able** \-ˈliv-rə-bəl, -ə-rə-\ *adj* — **de·liv·er·er** \-ˈliv-ər-ər\ *n*

de·liv·er·ance \di-ˈliv-rəns, -ə-rəns\ *n* **1 :** the act of delivering someone or something **:** the state of being delivered; *esp* **:** RESCUE **2 :** something delivered or communicated; *esp* **:** a publicly expressed opinion or decision

de·liv·ery \di-ˈliv-rē, -ə-rē\ *n, pl* **-er·ies 1 :** a delivering from something that restricts or burdens **2 a :** the act of handing over **b :** a legal transfer of right or title **c :** something delivered at one time or in one unit **3 :** the act of giving birth **4 :** a delivering especially of a speech; *also* **:** manner or style of uttering in speech or song **5 :** the act or manner of sending forth or throwing

dell \ˈdel\ *n* **:** a secluded small valley usually covered with trees or turf [Middle English *delle*]

de·louse \dē-ˈlau̇s, ˈdē-, -ˈlau̇z\ *vt* **:** to remove lice from

Del·phi·an \ˈdel-fē-ən\ *or* **Del·phic** \-fik\ *adj* **1 :** of or relating to ancient Delphi or its oracle **2 :** AMBIGUOUS, OBSCURE

del·phin·i·um \del-ˈfin-ē-əm\ *n* **:** any of a large genus of chiefly perennial herbs related to the buttercups and widely grown for their flowers in showy spikes — compare LARKSPUR [Greek *delphinion* "larkspur," from *delphis* "dolphin"]

Del·phi·nus \del-ˈfī-nəs, -ˈfē-\ *n* **:** a northern constellation nearly west of Pegasus [Latin, literally, "dolphin"]

del·ta \ˈdel-tə\ *n* **1 :** the 4th letter of the Greek alphabet — Δ or δ **2 :** something shaped like a capital Δ; *esp* **:** the triangular or fan-shaped piece of land made by deposits of mud and sand at the mouth of a river — **del·ta·ic** \del-ˈtā-ik\ *adj*

del·toid \ˈdel-ˌtȯid\ *n* **:** a large triangular muscle that covers the shoulder joint and serves to raise the arm laterally [Greek *deltoeidēs* "shaped like a delta"]

del·toi·de·us \del-ˈtȯid-ē-əs\ *n, pl* **del·toi·dei** \-ē-ˌī\ **:** DELTOID [New Latin, from Greek *deltoeidēs* "shaped like a delta"]

de·lude \di-ˈlüd\ *vt* **:** to mislead the mind or judgment of ⟨*deluded* by false promises⟩ [Latin *deludere,* from *de-* + *ludere* "to play"] ***synonyms*** see DECEIVE — **de·lud·er** *n* — **de·lud·ing·ly** \-ˈlüd-ing-lē\ *adv*

¹del·uge \ˈdel-ˌyüj\ *n* **1 a :** an overflowing of the land by water **:** FLOOD **b :** a drenching rain **2 :** an overwhelming amount or number ⟨a *deluge* of Christmas mail⟩ [Medieval French *deluje,* from Latin *diluvium,* from *diluere* "to wash away," from *dis-* + *lavere* "to wash"]

²deluge *vt* **1 :** to overflow with water **:** INUNDATE, FLOOD **2 :** to overwhelm as if with a deluge ⟨was *deluged* with inquiries⟩

de·lu·sion \di-ˈlü-zhən\ *n* **1 :** the act of deluding **:** the state of being deluded **2 a :** something that is falsely or delusively believed **b :** a false belief regarding the self or persons or objects outside the self that persists despite evidence to the contrary and is common in some abnormal mental states [Latin *delusio,* from *deludere* "to delude"] — **de·lu·sion·al** \-ˈlüzh-nəl, -ˈlü-zhən-l\ *adj*

synonyms DELUSION, ILLUSION mean something accepted as true or real that is actually false or unreal. DELUSION implies persistent self-deception concerning facts or situations and usually suggests a disordered state of mind ⟨an illness that causes *delusions*⟩. ILLUSION implies an attributing of truth or reality to something that seems to normal perception to be true and real but in fact is not ⟨a picture that presented an optical *illusion*⟩.

de·lu·sive \-ˈlü-siv, -ˈlü-ziv\ *adj* **:** deluding or apt to delude — **de·lu·sive·ly** *adv* — **de·lu·sive·ness** *n*

de·luxe \di-ˈlüks, -ˈləks, -ˈlüks\ *adj* **:** notably luxurious or elegant ⟨a *deluxe* edition⟩ [French *de luxe,* literally, "of luxury"]

delve \ˈdelv\ *vi* **1 :** to dig or labor with a spade **2 a :** to make a careful or detailed search for information ⟨*delve* into the past⟩

\ə\ **abut**	\au̇\ **out**	\i\ **tip**	\ȯ\ **saw**	\u̇\ **foot**
\ər\ **further**	\ch\ **chin**	\ī\ **life**	\ȯi\ **coin**	\y\ **yet**
\a\ **mat**	\e\ **pet**	\j\ **job**	\th\ **thin**	\yü\ **few**
\ā\ **take**	\ē\ **easy**	\ng\ **sing**	\t͟h\ **this**	\yu̇\ **cure**
\ä\ **cot, cart**	\g\ **go**	\ō\ **bone**	\ü\ **food**	\zh\ **vision**

b : to examine a subject in detail ⟨the book *delves* into the latest research⟩ [Old English *delfan*] — **delv·er** *n*

Dem \ˈdem\ *n* **:** DEMOCRAT 2

de·mag·ne·tize \dē-ˈmag-nə-ˌtīz\ *vt* **:** to deprive of magnetic properties — **de·mag·ne·ti·za·tion** \ˌdē-ˌmag-nət-ə-ˈzā-shən\ *n* — **de·mag·ne·tiz·er** \dē-ˈmag-nə-ˌtī-zər\ *n*

dem·a·gogue *also* **dem·a·gog** \ˈdem-ə-ˌgäg\ *n* **:** a person who appeals to the emotions and prejudices of people in order to arouse discontent and advance personal political ends [Greek *dēmagōgos,* from *dēmos* "people" + *agein* "to lead"] — **dem·a·gog·ic** \ˌdem-ə-ˈgäj-ik, -ˈgäg-\ *adj* — **dem·a·gogu·ery** \ˈdem-ə-ˌgäg-rē, -ə-rē\ *n* — **dem·a·gogy** \-ˌgäj-ē, -ˌgäg-ē\ *n*

[1]**de·mand** \di-ˈmand\ *n* **1 a :** an act of demanding or asking especially with authority ⟨a *demand* for obedience⟩ **b :** something claimed as due ⟨a list of *demands*⟩ **2 a :** the ability and need or desire to purchase goods or services at a specified time and price ⟨the *demand* for housing⟩ ⟨the *demand* for new cars⟩ **b :** the quantity of an article or service that is wanted at a specified time and price ⟨supply and *demand*⟩ **3 :** a seeking or state of being sought after ⟨tickets are in great *demand*⟩ **4 :** a pressing need or requirement ⟨the *demands* of the job⟩ — **on demand :** upon request for payment; *also* **:** when requested or needed

[2]**demand** *vb* **1 :** to ask or call for with authority **:** claim as one's right ⟨*demand* payment of a debt⟩ **2 :** to ask earnestly or in the manner of a command ⟨the sentry *demanded* the password⟩ **3 :** to call for as useful or necessary ⟨the job *demands* a lot of time⟩ [Medieval French *demander,* from Medieval Latin *demandare,* from Latin, "to entrust," from *de-* + *mandare* "to enjoin"] — **de·mand·able** \-ˈman-də-bəl\ *adj* — **de·mand·er** *n*

synonyms DEMAND, CLAIM, REQUIRE, EXACT mean to ask or call for something as due or as necessary. DEMAND carries a suggestion of authoritativeness, insistence, and a right to make a request that is to be regarded as a command ⟨*demanded* to see the manager⟩. CLAIM implies a demand for the concession of something due as one's own or one's right ⟨the company *claimed* the right to the trademark⟩. REQUIRE strictly implies imperativeness arising from inner necessity or the compulsion of law or the urgency of the case ⟨the patient *requires* constant attention⟩. EXACT implies not only demanding but getting what one demands ⟨*exact* payment of an overdue debt⟩.

de·mand·ing *adj* **:** requiring much time, effort, or attention **:** EXACTING ⟨*demanding* teachers⟩ — **de·mand·ing·ly** \-ˈman-ding-lē\ *adv*

de·mar·cate \di-ˈmär-ˌkāt, ˈdē-ˌmär-\ *vt* **1 :** to mark the limits of **2 :** to set apart **:** DISTINGUISH [back-formation from *demarcation,* derived from Spanish *demarcación,* from *demarcar* "to delimit," from *de-* "de-" + *marcar* "to mark"] — **de·mar·ca·tion** \ˌdē-ˌmär-ˈkā-shən\ *n*

deme \ˈdēm\ *n* **:** a unit of local government in ancient Attica [Greek *dēmos,* "people, deme"]

[1]**de·mean** \di-ˈmēn\ *vt* **de·meaned; de·mean·ing :** to conduct or behave (oneself) usually in a proper manner [Medieval French *demener* "to conduct," from *de-* "de-" + *mener* "to lead," from Latin *minare* "to drive," from *minari* "to threaten"]

[2]**demean** *vt* **de·meaned; de·mean·ing :** DEGRADE, DEBASE ⟨refused to *demean* themselves by cheating⟩ [*de-* + [1]*mean*]

de·mean·or \di-ˈmē-nər\ *n* **:** outward manner or behavior **:** CONDUCT, BEARING

de·ment·ed \di-ˈment-əd\ *adj* **1 :** mentally disordered **:** INSANE **2 :** suffering from cognitive dementia — **de·ment·ed·ly** *adv* — **de·ment·ed·ness** *n*

de·men·tia \di-ˈmen-chə\ *n* **1 :** a condition of deteriorated cognitive functioning **2 :** INSANITY 3a ⟨the *dementia* of racial hatred⟩ [Latin, from *demens* "mad," from *de-* + *mens* "mind"]

de·mer·it \di-ˈmer-ət\ *n* **1 :** a quality that deserves blame **:** FAULT **2 :** a mark placed against a person's record for some fault or offense

de·mesne \di-ˈmān, -ˈmēn\ *n* **1 :** manorial land possessed by the lord and not held by free tenants **2 a :** the land attached to a mansion **b :** landed property **:** ESTATE **c :** a geographical area **:** REGION **3 :** realm or range especially of interests or activity [Medieval French *demesne, demeine,* from Latin *dominium* "domain"]

demi- *prefix* **1 :** half **2 :** one that partly belongs to (a specified type or class) ⟨*demi*god⟩ [Medieval French *demi,* derived from Latin *dimidius,* from *dis-* + *medius* "mid"]

demi·god \ˈdem-ē-ˌgäd\ *n* **1 :** a mythological being with more power than a mortal but less than a god **2 :** an outstanding person who seems godlike

demi·john \-ˌjän\ *n* **:** a large bottle of glass or stoneware enclosed in wickerwork [by folk etymology from French *dame-jeanne,* literally, "Lady Jane"]

demijohn

de·mil·i·ta·rize \dē-ˈmil-ə-tə-ˌrīz\ *vt* **:** to strip of military forces, weapons, or fortification ⟨a *demilitarized* zone⟩ — **de·mil·i·ta·ri·za·tion** \ˌdē-ˌmil-ə-tə-rə-ˈzā-shən\ *n*

demi·mon·daine \ˌdem-ē-ˌmän-ˈdān\ *n* **1 :** a woman of the demimonde **2 :** a woman supported by a wealthy lover [French *demi-mondaine,* from *demi-monde*]

demi·monde \ˈdem-ē-ˌmänd\ *n* **1 :** a class of women on the fringes of respectable society supported by wealthy lovers; *also* **:** their world **2 :** a group engaged in activity of doubtful legality or propriety [French *demi-monde,* from *demi-* + *monde* "world," from Latin *mundus*]

de·mise \di-ˈmīz\ *n* **1 :** a letting of property **:** LEASE **2 :** transfer of sovereignty to a successor ⟨the *demise* of the crown⟩ **3 a :** DEATH 1 **b :** an end of existence or activity ⟨the *demise* of Roman domination⟩ [Medieval French *demise,* feminine of *demis,* past participle of *demettre* "to dismiss," from Latin *demittere* "to send down," from *de-* + *mittere* "to send"]

demi·tasse \ˈdem-ē-ˌtas, -ˌtäs\ *n* **:** a small cup of black coffee; *also* **:** the cup used to serve it [French *demi-tasse,* from *demi-* + *tasse* "cup," from Arabic *ṭass,* from Persian *tasht*]

demo \ˈdem-ō\ *n pl* **dem·os 1 :** an example of a product that is not yet ready to be sold **2 :** an act of showing how something is used or done [short for *demonstration*]

de·mo·bi·lize \di-ˈmō-bə-ˌlīz\ *vt* **:** to discharge from military service ⟨*demobilize* an army⟩ — **de·mo·bi·li·za·tion** \-ˌmō-bə-lə-ˈzā-shən\ *n*

de·moc·ra·cy \di-ˈmäk-rə-sē\ *n, pl* **-cies 1 a :** government by the people; *esp* **:** rule of the majority **b :** government in which the supreme power is vested in the people and exercised by them directly or indirectly through representation **2 :** a political unit that has a democratic government **3 a :** the absence of hereditary or arbitrary class distinctions or privileges **b :** belief in or practice of social or economic equality for all people [Middle French *democratie,* derived from Greek *dēmokratia,* from *dēmos* "people" + *-kratia* "-cracy"]

dem·o·crat \ˈdem-ə-ˌkrat\ *n* **1 a :** an adherent of democracy **b :** one who practices social equality **2** *cap* **:** a member of the Democratic party of the U.S.

dem·o·crat·ic \ˌdem-ə-ˈkrat-ik\ *adj* **1 :** of, relating to, or favoring political, social, or economic democracy **2** *often cap* **:** of or relating to a major U.S. political party evolving from the anti-federalists and the Democratic-Republican party and associated with policies of broad social reform and internationalism **3 :** of, relating to, or appealing to the broad masses of the people ⟨*democratic* art⟩ **4 :** favoring social equality **:** not snobbish — **dem·o·crat·i·cal·ly** \-i-kə-lē, -klē\ *adv*

Democratic–Republican *adj* **:** of or relating to an early 19th century American political party favoring strict interpretation of the constitution and emphasizing states' rights

de·moc·ra·tize \di-ˈmäk-rə-ˌtīz\ *vt* **:** to make democratic — **de·moc·ra·ti·za·tion** \-ˌmäk-rət-ə-ˈzā-shən\ *n*

de·mod·u·late \dē-ˈmäj-ə-ˌlāt\ *vt* **:** to extract the information from (a modulated signal) — **de·mod·u·la·tion** \ˌdē-ˌmäj-ə-ˈlā-shən\ *n* — **de·mod·u·la·tor** \-ˈmäj-ə-ˌlāt-ər\ *n*

de·mog·ra·phy \di-ˈmäg-rə-fē\ *n* **:** the statistical study of human populations and especially their size and distribution and the number of births and deaths [French *démographie,* from Greek *dēmos* "people" + French *-graphie* "-graphy"] — **de·mog·ra·pher** \-fər\ *n* — **de·mo·graph·ic** \ˌdem-ə-ˈgraf-ik, ˌdē-mə-\ *adj* — **de·mo·graph·i·cal·ly** \-ˈgraf-i-kə-lē, -klē\ *adv*

dem·oi·selle \ˌdem-wə-ˈzel, -ə-\ *n* **:** a young lady [French]

de·mol·ish \di-ˈmäl-ish\ *vt* **1 a :** to tear down **:** RAZE **b :** to break to pieces **:** SMASH **2 :** to do away with **:** put an end to [Middle French *demoliss-,* stem of *demolir,* from Latin *demoliri,* from *de-* + *moliri* "to construct," from *moles* "mass"] ***synonyms*** see DESTROY — **de·mol·ish·er** *n* — **de·mol·ish·ment** \-ish-mənt\ *n*

dem·o·li·tion \ˌdem-ə-ˈlish-ən, ˌdē-mə-\ *n* **:** the act of demolishing; *esp* **:** destruction by means of explosives — **dem·o·li·tion·ist** \-ˈlish-nəst, -ə-nəst\ *n*

de·mon *or* **dae·mon** \ˈdē-mən\ *n* **1 a :** an evil spirit **b :** a source or agent of harm, distress, or ruin **2** *usually daemon* **:** an attendant power or spirit **:** GENIUS **3** *usually daemon* **:** a demigod of Greek mythology **4 :** one that has exceptional enthusiasm, drive, or effectiveness ⟨a *demon* for work⟩ [Latin *daemon* "divinity, spirit," from Greek *daimōn*]

de·mon·e·tize \dē-ˈmän-ə-ˌtīz, -ˈmən-\ *vt* **:** to stop using as money or as a monetary standard ⟨*demonetize* silver⟩ [French *démonétiser,* from *dé-* "de-" + Latin *moneta* "coin"] — **de·mon·e·ti·za·tion** \ˌdē-ˌmän-ət-ə-ˈzā-shən, -ˌmən-\ *n*

[1]**de·mo·ni·ac** \di-ˈmō-nē-ˌak\ *also* **de·mo·ni·a·cal** \ˌdē-mə-ˈnī-ə-kəl\ *adj* **1 :** possessed or influenced by a demon **2 :** DEMONIC — **de·mo·ni·a·cal·ly** \ˌdē-mə-ˈnī-ə-kə-lē, -klē\ *adv*

[2]**demoniac** *n* **:** one held to be possessed by a demon

de·mon·ic \di-ˈmän-ik\ *adj* **:** of, relating to, or suggestive of a demon **:** FIENDISH

de·mon·ol·o·gy \ˌdē-mə-ˈnäl-ə-jē\ *n* **1 :** the study of demons **2 :** belief in demons

de·mon·stra·ble \di-ˈmän-strə-bəl, ˈdem-ən-strə-\ *adj* **1 :** capable of being demonstrated or proved **2 :** APPARENT 2, EVIDENT — **de·mon·stra·bil·i·ty** \di-ˌmän-strə-ˈbil-ət-ē, ˌdem-ən-strə-\ *n* — **de·mon·stra·ble·ness** \di-ˈmän-strə-bəl-nəs, ˈdem-ən-strə-\ *n* — **de·mon·stra·bly** \-blē\ *adv*

dem·on·strate \ˈdem-ən-ˌstrāt\ *vb* **1 :** to show clearly **2 a :** to prove or make clear by reasoning or evidence **b :** to illustrate and explain especially with many examples **3 :** to show publicly the good qualities of a product ⟨*demonstrate* a new car⟩ **4 :** to make a demonstration ⟨citizens *demonstrated* in protest⟩ [Latin *demonstrare,* from *de-* + *monstrare* "to show," from *monstrum* "portent, monster"]

dem·on·stra·tion \ˌdem-ən-ˈstrā-shən\ *n* **1 :** an outward expression or display ⟨a *demonstration* of joy⟩ **2 :** an act, process, or means of demonstrating to the intelligence: **a :** convincing evidence **:** PROOF **b :** an explanation (as of a theory) by experiment **c :** a course of reasoning intended to prove that a conclusion must follow when certain conditions are accepted **d :** a showing of the merits of a product or service to a prospective buyer **3 :** a show of armed force **4 :** a public display of group feelings toward a person or cause — **dem·on·stra·tion·al** \-shnəl, -shən-l\ *adj*

[1]**de·mon·stra·tive** \di-ˈmän-strət-iv\ *adj* **1 a :** demonstrating as real or true **b :** characterized or established by demonstration ⟨*demonstrative* reasoning⟩ **2 :** pointing out the one referred to and distinguishing it from others of the same class ⟨the *demonstrative* pronoun *this* in "this is my hat"⟩ ⟨the *demonstrative* adjective *that* in "that chair"⟩ **3 :** marked by display of feeling ⟨a *demonstrative* greeting⟩ — **de·mon·stra·tive·ly** *adv* — **de·mon·stra·tive·ness** *n*

[2]**demonstrative** *n* **:** a demonstrative word; *esp* **:** a demonstrative pronoun

dem·on·stra·tor \ˈdem-ən-ˌstrāt-ər\ *n* **1 :** a person who makes or takes part in a demonstration **2 :** a product (as an automobile) used for purposes of demonstration

de·mor·al·ize \di-ˈmȯr-ə-ˌlīz, -ˈmär-\ *vb* **1 :** to corrupt in morals **:** make bad **2 :** to destroy the morale of **:** weaken in discipline or spirit ⟨fear *demoralized* the army⟩ — **de·mor·al·i·za·tion** \di-ˌmȯr-ə-lə-ˈzā-shən, -ˌmär-\ *n* — **de·mor·al·iz·er** \-ˈmȯr-ə-ˌlī-zər, -ˈmär-\ *n*

de·mote \di-ˈmōt, ˈdē-\ *vt* **:** to reduce to a lower grade or rank [*de-* + *-mote* (as in *promote*)] — **de·mo·tion** \-ˈmō-shən\ *n*

de·mot·ic \di-ˈmät-ik\ *adj* **1 :** of or relating to the general public **:** POPULAR, COMMON **2 :** of, relating to, or written in a simplified form of the ancient Egyptian writing **3 :** of or relating to the form of Modern Greek that is based on conversational use [Greek *dēmotikos,* from *dēmotēs* "commoner," from *dēmos* "people"]

de·mount \dē-ˈmau̇nt\ *vt* **1 :** to remove from a mounted position **2 :** DISASSEMBLE — **de·mount·able** \-ə-bəl\ *adj*

[1]**de·mul·cent** \di-ˈməl-sənt\ *adj* **:** SOOTHING [Latin *demulcēre* "to soothe," from *de-* + *mulcēre* "to soothe"]

[2]**demulcent** *n* **:** a usually oily or somewhat thick and jellylike preparation used to soothe or protect an abraded mucous membrane

[1]**de·mur** \di-ˈmər\ *vi* **de·murred; de·mur·ring 1 :** to enter a demurrer **2 :** to take exception **:** OBJECT **3** *archaic* **:** DELAY 1, HESITATE [Medieval French *demurer, demoerer* "to linger," from Latin *demorari,* from *de-* + *morari* "to linger," from *mora* "delay"]

[2]**demur** *n* **1 :** HESITATION **2 :** the act of objecting **:** PROTEST ⟨accepted without *demur*⟩

de·mure \di-ˈmyu̇r\ *adj* **1 :** marked by quiet modesty **2 :** affectedly modest, reserved, or serious [Middle English] — **de·mure·ly** *adv* — **de·mure·ness** *n*

de·mur·rage \di-ˈmər-ij, -ˈmə-rij\ *n* **1 :** the detention of a ship by the shipper or receiver beyond a time specified for loading, unloading, or sailing **2 :** a charge for detaining a ship, freight car, or truck beyond a time specified for loading or unloading

[1]**de·mur·rer** \di-ˈmər-ər, -ˈmə-rər\ *n* **1 :** a claim by the defendant in a legal action that the pleadings of the plaintiff are insufficient or defective **2 :** OBJECTION

[2]**de·mur·rer** \-ˈmər-ər\ *n* **:** one that demurs

[1]**den** \ˈden\ *n* **1 :** the shelter or resting place of a wild animal **2 a :** a hiding place (as for thieves) **b :** a center of secret activity ⟨a gambling *den*⟩ **3 :** a small usually squalid dwelling ⟨*dens* of misery⟩ **4 :** a comfortable room set apart usually for reading and relaxation **5 :** a subdivision of a cub-scout pack [Old English *denn*]

[2]**den** *vb* **denned; den·ning 1 :** to live in or retire to a den **2 :** to drive into a den

de·nar·i·us \di-ˈnar-ē-əs, -ˈner-\ *n, pl* **de·nar·ii** \-ē-ˌī, -ē-ˌē\ **:** a small silver coin of ancient Rome; *also* **:** a gold coin equal to 25 silver denarii [Latin, a coin worth ten asses, derived from *deni* "ten each," from *decem* "ten"]

de·na·tion·al·ize \dē-ˈnash-nə-ˌlīz, -ˈnash-ən-l-ˌīz\ *vt* **1 :** to strip of national character or rights **2 :** to remove from ownership or control by the national government

de·nat·u·ral·ize \dē-ˈnach-rə-ˌlīz, -ə-rə-\ *vt* **1 :** to make unnatural **2 :** to deprive of the rights and duties of a citizen

de·na·tur·ant \dē-ˈnāch-rənt, -ə-rənt\ *n* **:** a denaturing agent

de·na·ture \dē-ˈnā-chər\ *vt* **de·na·tured; de·na·tur·ing** \-ˈnāch-ring, -ə-ring\ **:** to deprive of natural qualities: as **a :** to make (alcohol) unfit for drinking without impairing usefulness for other purposes **b :** to modify (as a protein) so as to diminish or destroy some of the original properties — **de·na·tur·ation** \ˌdē-ˌnā-chə-ˈrā-shən\ *n*

dendr- *or* **dendro-** *combining form* **:** tree ⟨*dendro*chronology⟩: resembling a tree ⟨*dendr*ite⟩ [Greek *dendron* "tree"]

den·drite \ˈden-ˌdrīt\ *n* **1 :** a branching figure (as in a mineral or stone) resembling a tree **2 :** any of the usually branching processes of a neuron that conduct impulses toward the cell body — compare AXON — **den·drit·ic** \den-ˈdrit-ik\ *adj*

den·dro·chro·nol·o·gy \ˌden-drō-krə-ˈnäl-ə-jē\ *n* **:** the science of dating events by comparative study of growth rings in trees and aged wood — **den·dro·chron·o·log·i·cal** \-ˌkrän-l-ˈäj-i-kəl, -ˌkrōn-\ *adj*

den·drol·o·gy \den-ˈdräl-ə-jē\ *n* **:** the study of trees — **den·dro·log·i·cal** \ˌden-drə-ˈläj-i-kəl\ *adj*

Den·eb \ˈden-ˌeb, -əb\ *n* **:** the brightest star in the constellation Cygnus [Arabic *dhanab al-dajāja,* literally, "tail of the hen"]

den·gue \ˈdeng-gē, -ˌgā\ *n* **:** an acute virus disease transmitted by mosquitoes and characterized by headache, severe joint pain, and rash [American Spanish]

de·ni·al \di-ˈnī-əl, -ˈnīl\ *n* **1 :** a refusal to grant something asked for **2 :** a refusal to admit the truth of a statement ⟨a flat *denial* of the charges⟩ **3 :** a refusal to acknowledge something; *esp* **:** a statement of disbelief or rejection **4 :** a cutting down or limiting **:** RESTRICTION ⟨*denial* of one's appetite⟩ — **in denial :** refusing to admit the truth or reality of something bad ⟨a patient *in denial* about his health problems⟩

[1]**de·ni·er** \di-ˈnī-ər, -ˈnīr\ *n* **:** one who denies

[2]**de·nier** *n* **1** \də-ˈniər, dən-ˈyā\ **:** a small originally silver coin formerly used in western Europe **2** \ˈden-yər\ **:** a unit of fineness for yarn equal to the fineness of a yarn weighing one gram for each 9000 meters [Medieval French, from Latin *denarius* "denarius"]

den·i·grate \ˈden-i-ˌgrāt\ *vt* **:** to attack the reputation of **:** DEFAME ⟨*denigrate* one's opponents⟩ [Latin *denigrare,* from *de-* + *nigrare* "to blacken," from *niger* "black"] — **den·i·gra·tion** \ˌden-i-ˈgrā-shən\ *n* — **den·i·gra·tive** \ˈde-ni-ˌgrāt-iv\ *adj* — **den·i·gra·tor** \ˈden-i-ˌgrāt-ər\ *n* — **den·i·gra·to·ry** \-grə-ˌtōr-ē, -ˌtȯr-\ *adj*

den·im \ˈden-əm\ *n* **1 :** a firm durable twilled usually cotton fabric **2** *pl* **:** overalls or trousers of usually blue denim [French *serge de Nîmes,* "serge of Nîmes, France"] — **den·imed** \-nəmd\ *adj*

Word History Many fabrics have been named for the places where they originated or were manufactured. *Denim* comes from the French *de Nîmes,* meaning "of Nîmes." It was originally used in the phrase *serge de Nîmes,* which appeared in English in the 17th century as *serge denim. Serge,* from the Latin adjective *sericus,* "of silk," is a durable twilled fabric, and Nîmes is a city of southern France where textiles are still an important industry.

de·ni·tri·fy \dē-ˈnī-trə-ˌfī\ *vt* **1 :** to remove nitrogen or its compound from **2 :** to convert (a nitrate or a nitrite) into free nitrogen or to a different state especially as a step in the nitrogen cycle — **de·ni·tri·fi·ca·tion** \ˌdē-ˌnī-trə-fə-ˈkā-shən\ *n* — **de·ni·tri·fi·er** \ˌdē-ˈnī-trə-ˌfī-ər, -ˌfīr\ *n*

den·i·zen \ˈden-ə-zən\ *n* **:** INHABITANT; *esp* **:** a person, animal, or plant found or naturalized in a particular region or environment ⟨*denizens* of the forest⟩ [Medieval French *denisein, denzein,* from *denz* "within," from Late Latin *deintus,* from Latin *de-* + *intus* "within"]

de·nom·i·nate \di-ˈnäm-ə-ˌnāt\ *vt* **:** to give a name to

de·nom·i·nate number \di-ˈnäm-ə-nət-\ *n* **:** a number (as *7* in *7 meters*) that specifies a quantity in terms of a unit of measurement

de·nom·i·na·tion \di-ˌnäm-ə-ˈnā-shən\ *n* **1 :** an act of denominating **2 :** NAME, DESIGNATION; *esp* **:** a general name for a class of things **3 :** a religious body comprising a number of congregations with similar beliefs **4 :** one of a series of related values each having a special name ⟨bills in $5 and $10 *denominations*⟩ — **de·nom·i·na·tion·al** \-shnəl, -shən-l\ *adj* — **de·nom·i·na·tion·al·ly** \-ē\ *adv*

de·nom·i·na·tion·al·ism \-shnəl-ˌiz-əm, -shən-l-ˌiz-\ *n* **:** devotion to the principles or interests of a denomination

de·nom·i·na·tive \di-ˈnäm-nət-iv, -ə-nət-\ *adj* **:** derived from a noun or adjective ⟨*denominative* verbs⟩ — **denominative** *n*

de·nom·i·na·tor \di-ˈnäm-ə-ˌnāt-ər\ *n* **:** the part of a fraction that is below the line and that functions as the divisor of the numerator

de·no·ta·tion \ˌdē-nō-ˈtā-shən\ *n* **1 :** an act or process of denoting **2 :** MEANING; *esp* **:** a direct specific meaning as distinct from connotations **3 :** a denoting term or label **:** NAME, SIGN

de·no·ta·tive \ˈdē-nō-ˌtāt-iv, di-ˈnōt-ət-iv\ *adj* **1 :** denoting or tending to denote **2 :** relating to denotation

de·note \di-ˈnōt\ *vt* **1 :** to serve as an indication of ⟨red flares *denoting* danger⟩ **2 :** to make known **:** ANNOUNCE **3 :** to have the meaning of **:** MEAN, NAME ⟨in England the word "lift" *denotes* an elevator⟩

synonyms DENOTE and CONNOTE, when used of words, refer to conveying meaning. DENOTE implies all that strictly belongs to the definition of the word; CONNOTE implies all the ideas or emotions suggested by the word ⟨"home" *denotes* the place where one lives, but it *connotes* the comforts, the privacy, and a whole range of experience one enjoys there⟩.

de·noue·ment \ˌdā-ˌnü-ˈmäⁿ, -ˈnü-ˌ\ *n* **1 :** the final untangling of the conflicts or difficulties that make up the plot of a literary work **2 :** a solution or working out especially of a complex or difficult situation [French *dénouement,* literally, "untying," derived from Medieval French *desnoer* "to untie," from *des-* "de-" + *noer* "to tie," from Latin *nodare,* from *nodus* "knot"]

de·nounce \di-ˈnau̇ns\ *vt* **1 :** to point out as deserving blame or punishment **2 :** to inform against **:** ACCUSE **3 :** to announce formally the ending of (as a treaty) [Medieval French *denuncier* "to proclaim," from Latin *denuntiare,* from *de-* + *nuntiare* "to report"] — **de·nounce·ment** \-mənt\ *n* — **de·nounc·er** *n*

de no·vo \di-ˈnō-vō, dā-\ *adv* **:** over again **:** ANEW [Latin]

dense \ˈdens\ *adj* **1 a :** marked by compactness or crowding together of parts ⟨a *dense* forest⟩ **b :** having a high mass per unit volume ⟨a *dense* metal⟩ **2 :** slow to understand **:** STUPID, THICKHEADED **3 :** having high opacity ⟨*dense* fog⟩ **4 :** having between any two mathematical elements at least one element ⟨the set of rational numbers is *dense*⟩ [Latin *densus*]

synonyms see STUPID — **dense·ly** *adv* — **dense·ness** *n*

den·si·ty \ˈden-sət-ē\ *n, pl* **-ties** **1 :** the quality or state of being dense **2 :** the quantity of something per unit volume, unit area, or unit length: as **a :** the mass of a substance per unit volume ⟨*density* expressed in grams per cubic centimeter⟩ **b :** the average number of individuals or units in a unit of area or volume ⟨a population *density* of 500 per square mile⟩ **3 :** STUPIDITY 1 **4 :** the degree of opacity of a translucent medium

[1]**dent** \ˈdent\ *n* **1 :** a hollow made by a blow or by pressure **2 a :** an impression or effect often made against resistance ⟨hasn't made a *dent* in the problem⟩ **b :** a weakening or lessening effect ⟨costs that have made a *dent* in the budget⟩ [Middle English, "blow," alteration of *dint*]

[2]**dent** *vb* **1 :** to make a dent in or on **2 :** to become marked by a dent

dent- *or* **denti-** *or* **dento-** *combining form* **:** tooth **:** teeth [Latin *dent-, dens* "tooth"]

[1]**den·tal** \ˈdent-l\ *adj* **1 :** of or relating to the teeth or to dentistry **2 :** pronounced with the tip or blade of the tongue against or near the upper front teeth — **den·tal·ly** \-l-ē\ *adv*

[2]**dental** *n* **:** a dental consonant

dental floss *n* **:** a thread used to clean between the teeth

dental hygienist *n* **:** a licensed dental professional who cleans and examines teeth

den·tate \ˈden-ˌtāt\ *adj* **:** having pointed conical projections ⟨a *dentate* margin of a leaf⟩

dent corn *n* **:** corn having kernels that contain both hard and soft starch and that become indented at maturity

den·ti·cle \ˈdent-i-kəl\ *n* **:** a small conical pointed projection (as a tooth) [Latin *denticulus* "small tooth," from *dens* "tooth"]

den·ti·frice \ˈdent-ə-frəs\ *n* **:** a powder, paste, or liquid for cleaning the teeth [Latin *dentifricium,* from *dens* "tooth" + *fricare* "to rub"]

den·til \ˈdent-l\ *n* **:** one of a series of small projecting rectangular blocks especially under a cornice [obsolete French *dentille,* from *dent* "tooth"]

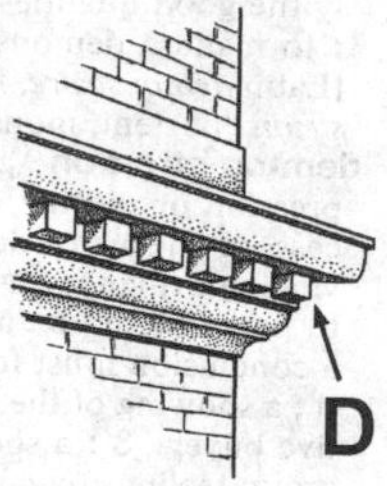

D dentil

den·tin \ˈdent-n\ *or* **den·tine** \ˈden-ˌtēn, den-ˈ\ *n* **:** a calcium-containing material like bone but harder and denser that composes the principal mass of a tooth — **den·tin·al** \den-ˈtēn-l, ˈdent-n-əl\ *adj*

den·tist \ˈdent-əst\ *n* **:** one whose profession is the care and treatment of the teeth and gums and the fitting of false teeth

den·tist·ry \ˈdent-ə-strē\ *n* **:** the profession or practice of a dentist

den·ti·tion \den-ˈtish-ən\ *n* **1 :** the development and cutting of teeth **2 :** the number, kind, and arrangement of teeth (as of a person)

den·ture \ˈden-chər\ *n* **1 :** a set of teeth **2 :** an artificial replacement for one or more teeth; *esp* **:** a set of false teeth

de·nude \di-ˈnüd, -ˈnyüd\ *vt* **:** to strip of covering **:** lay bare ⟨erosion that *denudes* the rocks of soil⟩ — **de·nu·da·tion** \ˌdē-ˌnü-ˈdā-shən, -ˌnyü-; ˌden-yu̇-ˈdā-\ *n* — **de·nu·da·tion·al** \-shnəl, -shən-l\ *adj* — **de·nud·er** \di-ˈnüd-ər, -ˈnyüd-\ *n*

de·nu·mer·a·ble \di-ˈnüm-rə-bəl, -ˈnyüm-, -ə-rə-\ *adj* **:** COUNTABLE — **de·nu·mer·a·bly** \-rə-blē\ *adv*

de·nun·ci·a·tion \di-ˌnən-sē-ˈā-shən\ *n* **:** the act of denouncing; *esp* **:** a public accusation — **de·nun·ci·a·to·ry** \-ˈnən-sē-ə-ˌtōr-ē, -ˌtȯr-\ *adj*

de·ny \di-ˈnī\ *vt* **de·nied; de·ny·ing** **1 :** to declare not to be true **:** CONTRADICT ⟨*deny* a report⟩ **2 :** to refuse to acknowledge **:** DISOWN ⟨*deny* one's faith⟩ **3 :** to refuse to grant ⟨*deny* a request⟩ **4 :** to reject as false ⟨*deny* a theory⟩ [Medieval French *deneier, denier,* from Latin *denegare,* from *de-* + *negare* "to deny"] — **de·ny·ing·ly** \-ˈnī-ing-lē\ *adv*

de·o·dar \ˈdē-ə-ˌdär\ *n* **:** an East Indian cedar valued as an ornamental and timber tree [Hindi and Urdu *devadār, deodār,* from Sanskrit *devadāru,* literally, "timber of the gods"]

de·odor·ant \dē-ˈōd-ə-rənt\ *n* **:** a preparation that eliminates or masks unpleasant odors — **deodorant** *adj*

de·odor·ize \dē-ˈōd-ə-ˌrīz\ *vt* **:** to eliminate or prevent offensive odor of or in ⟨*deodorize* a room⟩ — **de·odor·i·za·tion** \ˌdē-ˌōd-ə-rə-ˈzā-shən\ *n* — **de·odor·iz·er** \dē-ˈōd-ə-ˌrī-zər\ *n*

Deo vo·len·te \ˌdā-ō-və-ˈlent-ē, ˌdē-\ **:** God being willing [Latin]

de·ox·i·dize \dē-ˈäk-sə-ˌdīz, ˈdē-\ *vt* **:** to remove oxygen from — **de·ox·i·diz·er** *n*

de·oxy·gen·at·ed \-ˈäk-si-jə-ˌnāt-əd\ *adj* **:** having the hemoglobin in the reduced state

de·oxy·ri·bo·nu·cle·ic acid \ˌdē-ˌäk-sē-ˈrī-bō-nu̇-ˌklē-ik-, -nyu̇-, -ˌklā-\ *n* **:** DNA

de·oxy·ri·bose \dē-ˌäk-sē-ˈrī-ˌbōs\ *n* **:** a sugar $C_5H_{10}O_4$ that is a constituent of DNA

de·part \di-ˈpärt\ *vb* **1 a :** to go away or go away from **:** LEAVE

b : DIE **2 :** to turn aside **:** DEVIATE [Medieval French *departir* "to divide, part company," from *de-* "de-" + *partir* "to divide," from Latin *partire,* from *pars* "part"]

de·part·ed *adj* **1 :** BYGONE ⟨*departed* days⟩ **2 :** no longer living

de·part·ment \di-ˈpärt-mənt\ *n* **1 :** a distinct sphere **:** PROVINCE **2 a :** a major administrative division of a government or business **b :** a major territorial administrative division **c :** a division of a college or school giving instruction in a particular subject **d :** a section of a department store [French *département,* from Medieval French, "act of dividing," from *departir* "to divide"] — **de·part·men·tal** \di-ˌpärt-ˈment-l, ˌdē-\ *adj* — **de·part·men·tal·ly** *adv*

de·part·men·tal·ize \di-ˌpärt-ˈment-l-ˌīz, ˌdē-\ *vt* **:** to divide into departments — **de·part·men·tal·i·za·tion** \-ˌment-l-ə-ˈzā-shən\ *n*

department store *n* **:** a store having separate sections for different kinds of goods

de·par·ture \di-ˈpär-chər\ *n* **1 a :** the act of going away **b** *archaic* **:** DEATH **2 :** a setting out (as on a new course) **3 :** DIVERGENCE 3

de·pend \di-ˈpend\ *vi* **1 :** to be determined by or based on some action, condition, or variable ⟨success of the picnic will *depend* on the weather⟩ ⟨the value of the polynomial $x^2 + 2x + 2$ *depends* on the value of x⟩ **2 :** to place reliance or trust ⟨you can *depend* on me⟩ **3 :** to rely for support ⟨children *depend* on their parents⟩ **4 :** to hang down ⟨a vine *depending* from a tree⟩ [Medieval French *dependre,* from Latin *dependēre,* from *de-* + *pendere* "to hang"]

de·pend·able \di-ˈpen-də-bəl\ *adj* **:** capable of being depended on **:** TRUSTWORTHY, RELIABLE — **de·pend·abil·i·ty** \-ˌpen-də-ˈbil-ət-ē\ *n* — **de·pend·ably** \-ˈpen-də-blē\ *adv*

de·pen·dence \di-ˈpen-dəns\ *n* **1 :** the quality or state of being dependent; *esp* **:** the quality or state of being influenced by or subject to another **2 :** RELIANCE, TRUST ⟨*dependence* on friends⟩ **3 :** something on which one relies **4 a :** drug addiction **b :** HABITUATION 2

de·pen·den·cy \-dən-sē\ *n, pl* **-cies 1 :** DEPENDENCE 1 **2 :** something that is dependent on something else; *esp* **:** a territory under the jurisdiction of a nation but not formally annexed by it

[1]**de·pen·dent** \di-ˈpen-dənt\ *adj* **1 :** hanging down **2 a :** determined or conditioned by another **b (1) :** relying on another for support ⟨*dependent* children⟩ **(2) :** affected with a drug dependence **c :** subject to another's jurisdiction ⟨a *dependent* territory⟩ **3 :** SUBORDINATE 3a ⟨a *dependent* clause⟩ — **de·pen·dent·ly** *adv*

[2]**dependent** *also* **de·pend·ant** *n* **:** one that is dependent; *esp* **:** a person who relies on another for support

dependent variable *n* **:** a mathematical variable whose value is determined by that of one or more other variables in a function — compare INDEPENDENT VARIABLE

de·pict \di-ˈpikt\ *vt* **1 :** to represent by a picture **2 :** to describe in words [Latin *depictus,* past participle of *depingere* "to depict," from *de-* + *pingere* "to paint"] — **de·pic·tion** \-ˈpik-shən\ *n*

dep·i·la·tion \ˌdep-ə-ˈlā-shən\ *n* **:** the removal of hair, wool, or bristles by chemical or mechanical methods [derived from Latin *depilare* "to remove hair from," from *de-* + *pilus* "hair"] — **dep·i·late** \ˈdep-ə-ˌlāt\ *vt*

de·pil·a·to·ry \di-ˈpil-ə-ˌtōr-ē, -ˌtȯr-\ *n, pl* **-ries :** a preparation for removing hair, wool, or bristles — **depilatory** *adj*

de·plane \ˈdē-ˈplān\ *vi* **:** to get off an airplane

de·plete \di-ˈplēt\ *vt* **:** to reduce in amount by using up **:** exhaust especially of strength or resources ⟨soil *depleted* of minerals⟩ ⟨a *depleted* treasury⟩ [Latin *deplēre,* from *de-* + *plēre* "to fill"] — **de·plet·able** \-ˈplēt-ə-bəl\ *adj* — **de·plet·er** \-ˈplēt-ər\ *n* — **de·ple·tion** \-ˈplē-shən\ *n* — **de·ple·tive** \-ˈplēt-iv\ *adj*

de·plor·able \di-ˈplōr-ə-bəl, -ˈplȯr-\ *adj* **1 :** deserving to be deplored **:** LAMENTABLE ⟨a *deplorable* accident⟩ **2 :** very bad **:** WRETCHED ⟨*deplorable* conditions⟩ — **de·plor·able·ness** *n* — **de·plor·ably** \-blē\ *adv*

de·plore \di-ˈplōr, -ˈplȯr\ *vt* **1 a :** to feel or express grief for **b :** to regret strongly **2 :** to consider unfortunate or deserving of disapproval [Latin *deplorare,* from *de-* + *plorare* "to wail"] — **de·plor·er** *n* — **de·plor·ing·ly** \-ing-lē\ *adv*

de·ploy \di-ˈplȯi\ *vb* **:** to move, spread out, or place in position for some purpose ⟨troops *deployed* for battle⟩ [French *déployer,* from Latin *displicare* "to scatter," from *dis-* + *plicare* "to fold"] — **de·ploy·ment** \-mənt\ *n*

de·po·lar·ize \dē-ˈpō-lə-ˌrīz, ˈdē-\ *vt* **:** to prevent, reduce, or remove polarization of (as a dry cell or the membrane of a neuron) — **de·po·lar·i·za·tion** \ˌdē-ˌpō-lə-rə-ˈzā-shən\ *n* — **de·po·lar·iz·er** \dē-ˈpō-lə-ˌrī-zər, ˈdē-\ *n*

[1]**de·po·nent** \di-ˈpō-nənt\ *adj* **:** occurring with passive or middle voice forms but with active voice meaning ⟨*deponent* verbs in Latin and Greek⟩ [Late Latin *deponens,* from Latin *deponere* "to put down," from *de-* + *ponere* "to put"]

[2]**deponent** *n* **1 :** a deponent verb **2 :** one who gives evidence

de·pop·u·late \dē-ˈpäp-yə-ˌlāt, ˈdē-\ *vt* **:** to reduce greatly the population of (as a city or region) by destroying or driving away the inhabitants ⟨*depopulated* by a plague⟩ — **de·pop·u·la·tion** \ˌdē-ˌpäp-yə-ˈlā-shən\ *n*

de·port \di-ˈpōrt, -ˈpȯrt\ *vt* **1 :** to cause (oneself) to act in a certain way **:** CONDUCT ⟨*deported* themselves with dignity⟩ **2 :** to send out of the country by legal deportation [Middle French *deporter,* from Latin *deportare* "to carry away," from *de-* + *portare* "to carry"]

de·por·ta·tion \ˌdē-ˌpōr-ˈtā-shən, -ˌpȯr-\ *n* **1 :** an act or instance of deporting **2 :** the removal from a country of an alien whose presence is determined to be unlawful or harmful to the public

de·por·tee \ˌdē-ˌpōr-ˈtē, -ˌpȯr-\ *n* **:** one who has been deported or is under sentence of deportation

de·port·ment \di-ˈpōrt-mənt, -ˈpȯrt-\ *n* **:** manner of conducting oneself **:** BEHAVIOR

de·pose \di-ˈpōz\ *vb* **1 :** to remove from a throne or other high position **2 :** to testify under oath or by affidavit [Medieval French *deposer,* derived from Latin *deponere* "to put down," from *de-* + *ponere* "to put"]

[1]**de·pos·it** \di-ˈpäz-ət\ *vb* **1 :** to place for safekeeping; *esp* **:** to put money in a bank **2 :** to give as a pledge that a purchase will be made or a service used ⟨*deposit* $10 on a new bicycle⟩ **3 :** to lay down **:** PLACE, PUT ⟨*deposit* a parcel on a table⟩ **4 :** to let fall or sink ⟨sand and silt *deposited* by a flood⟩ **5 :** to become deposited **:** SETTLE [Latin *depositus,* past participle of *deponere* "to put down"] — **de·pos·i·tor** \-ˈpäz-ət-ər, -ˈpäz-tər\ *n*

[2]**deposit** *n* **1 :** the state of being deposited ⟨money on *deposit*⟩ **2 a :** something placed for safekeeping; *esp* **:** money deposited in a bank **b :** money given as a pledge **3 :** an act of depositing **4 :** something laid or thrown down ⟨a *deposit* of silt left by the flood⟩ **5 :** an accumulation of mineral matter (as iron ore, oil, or gas) in nature

de·pos·i·tary \di-ˈpäz-ə-ˌter-ē\ *n, pl* **-tar·ies 1 :** a person to whom something is entrusted **2 :** DEPOSITORY 2

dep·o·si·tion \ˌdep-ə-ˈzish-ən, ˌdē-pə-\ *n* **1 :** the act of deposing a person from a position of authority ⟨the *deposition* of the dictator⟩ **2 :** a statement especially in writing made under oath **3 :** the action or process of depositing ⟨the *deposition* of silt by a stream⟩ **4 :** material deposited **:** SEDIMENT 2 — **dep·o·si·tion·al** \-ˈzish-nəl, -ˈzish-ən-l\ *adj*

de·pos·i·to·ry \di-ˈpäz-ə-ˌtōr-ē, -ˌtȯr-\ *n, pl* **-ries 1 :** DEPOSITARY 1 **2 :** a place where something is deposited especially for safekeeping

de·pot *1 & 2 are* ˈdep-ˌō *also* ˈdē-ˌpō, *3 is* ˈdē-ˌpō *sometimes* ˈdep-ˌō\ *n* **1 :** a place where military supplies are kept or where troops are assembled and trained **2 :** a place of deposit for goods **:** STOREHOUSE **3 :** a building for railroad or bus passengers or freight **:** STATION [French *dépôt,* derived from Latin *deponere* "to put down"]

de·prave \di-ˈprāv\ *vt* **:** to make bad **:** corrupt the morals of **:** PERVERT [Medieval French *depraver* "to speak ill of," from Latin *depravare* "to pervert," from *de-* + *pravus* "crooked, bad"] ***synonyms*** see DEBASE — **de·pra·va·tion** \ˌdep-rə-ˈvā-shən\ *n* — **de·prave·ment** \di-ˈprāv-mənt\ *n* — **de·prav·er** \-ˈprā-vər\ *n*

de·praved \-ˈprāvd\ *adj* **:** marked by corruption, unwholesomeness, or evil — **de·praved·ly** \-ˈprā-vəd-lē, -ˈprāv-dlē\ *adv* — **de·praved·ness** \-ˈprā-vəd-nəs, -ˈprāvd-nəs\ *n*

de·prav·i·ty \di-ˈprav-ət-ē\ *n, pl* **-ties 1 :** a corrupt act or practice **2 :** the quality or state of being depraved

\ə\ **abut**	\au̇\ **out**	\i\ **tip**	\ȯ\ **saw**	\u̇\ **foot**
\ər\ **further**	\ch\ **chin**	\ī\ **life**	\ȯi\ **coin**	\y\ **yet**
\a\ **mat**	\e\ **pet**	\j\ **job**	\th\ **thin**	\yü\ **few**
\ā\ **take**	\ē\ **easy**	\ng\ **sing**	\t͟h\ **this**	\yu̇\ **cure**
\ä\ **cot, cart**	\g\ **go**	\ō\ **bone**	\ü\ **food**	\zh\ **vision**

dep•re•cate \ˈdep-ri-ˌkāt\ *vt* **1** : to express disapproval of **2** : DEPRECIATE 2 [Latin *deprecari* "to avert by prayer," from *de-* + *precari* "to pray"] — **dep•re•cat•ing•ly** \-ˌkāt-ing-lē\ *adv* — **dep•re•ca•tion** \ˌdep-ri-ˈkā-shən\ *n*

dep•re•ca•to•ry \ˈdep-ri-kə-ˌtōr-ē, -ˌtȯr-\ *adj* **1** : seeking to avert disapproval : APOLOGETIC **2** : serving to deprecate

de•pre•ci•ate \di-ˈprē-shē-ˌāt\ *vb* **1** : to lower the price or value of **2** : to represent as of little value : DISPARAGE **3** : to fall in value [Late Latin *depretiare,* from Latin *de-* + *pretium* "price"] — **de•pre•cia•tive** \-shē-ˌāt-iv, -shē-ət-, -shət-\ *adj* — **de•pre•cia•to•ry** \-shē-ə-ˌtōr-ē, -shə-ˌ, -ˌtȯr-\ *adj*

de•pre•ci•a•tion \di-ˌprē-shē-ˈā-shən\ *n* **1** : a decline in the purchasing power or exchange value of money **2** : the act of belittling : DISPARAGEMENT **3** : a decline (as from age or wear and tear) in the value of something

dep•re•da•tion \ˌdep-rə-ˈdā-shən\ *n* : the action or an act of plundering or laying waste : RAVAGING, PILLAGING [Late Latin *depraedatio,* from *depraedari* "to plunder," from Latin *de-* + *praedari* "to plunder"] — **dep•re•date** \ˈdep-rə-ˌdāt\ *vb*

de•press \di-ˈpres\ *vt* **1 a** : to press down **b** : to cause to sink to a lower position **2** : to lessen the activity or strength of **3** : to make sad or downcast : DISCOURAGE **4** : to lessen in price or value : DEPRECIATE [Middle French *depresser* "to repress," from Latin *depressus,* past participle of *deprimere* "to press down," from *de-* + *premere* "to press"] — **de•press•ible** \-ə-bəl\ *adj* — **de•press•ing•ly** \-ing-lē\ *adv*

synonyms DEPRESS, OPPRESS mean to lower in spirit or mood. DEPRESS stresses the resulting state of inactivity or dullness or dejection ⟨*depressed* by failure⟩. OPPRESS emphasizes the burden imposed that may or may not be successfully borne or withstood ⟨*oppressed* by unending obstacles⟩.

de•pres•sant \di-ˈpres-nt\ *n* : one that depresses; *esp* : an agent (as alcohol) that reduces activity of bodily functions — **depressant** *adj*

de•pressed *adj* **1 a** : low in spirits : SAD **b** : affected with psychological depression **2** : FLATTENED; *esp* : lying flat or prostrate **3** : suffering from economic depression

de•pres•sion \di-ˈpresh-ən\ *n* **1** : an act of depressing : a state of being depressed: as **a** : a pressing down : LOWERING **b** : DEJECTION; *also* : a psychological disorder marked by sadness, inactivity, difficulty in thinking and concentration, and feelings of dejection and hopelessness **c** (1) : a reduction in activity, amount, quality, or force (2) : a lowering of vitality or functional activity **2** : a depressed place or part : HOLLOW **3** : a region of low barometric pressure **4** : a period of low general economic activity with widespread unemployment ***synonyms*** see MELANCHOLY

de•pres•sive \-ˈpres-iv\ *adj* : of , relating to, marked by, or affected by psychological depression

de•pres•sor \-ˈpres-ər\ *n* : one that depresses: as **a** : a muscle that draws down a part — compare LEVATOR **b** : a device for pressing a part (as the tongue) down or aside

de•pres•sur•ize \dē-ˈpresh-ə-ˌrīz, ˈdē-\ *vt* : to release (as a pressurized aircraft) from pressure

de•prive \di-ˈprīv\ *vt* **1** : to take something away from ⟨*deprive* a ruler of power⟩ **2** : to stop from having something ⟨*deprived* a citizen of her rights⟩ [Medieval French *depriver,* from Medieval Latin *deprivare,* from Latin *de-* + *privare* "to deprive"] — **de•pri•va•tion** \ˌdep-rə-ˈvā-shən, ˌdē-ˌprī-\ *n*

de•pro•gram \dē-ˈprō-ˌgram, -grəm\ *vt* : to dissuade from strongly held convictions or indoctrinated beliefs

depth \ˈdepth\ *n, pl* **depths** \ˈdepts, ˈdeps, ˈdepths\ **1 a** (1) : something that is deep : a deep place or part (2) : ABYSS **b** : a part that is far from the outside or surface ⟨the *depths* of the woods⟩ **c** (1) : the middle of a time ⟨the *depth* of winter⟩ (2) : an extreme state (as of despair) (3) : the worst part **2** : the distance from top to bottom or from front to back **3** : the quality of being deep **4** : degree of intensity ⟨the *depth* of a color⟩ [Middle English, from *dep* "deep"] — **depth•less** \ˈdepth-ləs\ *adj*

depth charge *n* : an explosive device for underwater use especially against submarines that is designed to explode at a predetermined depth — called also *depth bomb*

dep•u•ta•tion \ˌdep-yə-ˈtā-shən\ *n* **1** : the act of appointing a deputy **2** : a group of people appointed to represent others

de•pute \di-ˈpyüt\ *vt* : DELEGATE [Medieval French *deputer* "to appoint," from Late Latin *deputare* "to assign," derived from Latin *de-* + *putare* "to consider"]

dep•u•tize \ˈdep-yə-ˌtīz\ *vb* **1** : to appoint as deputy **2** : to act as deputy

dep•u•ty \ˈdep-yət-ē\ *n, pl* **-ties** **1** : a person appointed to act for or in place of another **2** : an assistant empowered to act as a substitute in the absence of his or her superior **3** : a member of a lower house of a legislative assembly — **deputy** *adj*

de•rail \di-ˈrāl\ *vb* : to leave or cause to leave the rails — **derail•ment** \-mənt\ *n*

de•rail•leur \di-ˈrā-lər\ *n* : a mechanism for shifting gears on a bicycle that operates by moving the chain from one set of exposed gears to another [French *dérailleur,* from *dérailler* "to throw off the track," from *dé-* "de-" + *rail* "rail," from English]

de•range \di-ˈrānj\ *vt* **1** : DISARRANGE **2** : to disturb the operation or functions of **3** : to make insane [French *déranger,* derived from Medieval French *de-* "de-" + *reng* "line, row," of Germanic origin] — **de•range•ment** \-mənt\ *n*

der•by \ˈdər-bē, *especially British* ˈdär-\ *n, pl* **derbies** **1** : any of several horse races held annually and usually restricted to 3-year-olds **2** : a race or contest open to all comers ⟨a fishing *derby*⟩ **3** : a man's stiff felt hat with dome-shaped crown and narrow brim [Edward Stanley, died 1834, 12th earl of *Derby*]

de•re•cho \də-ˈrā-chō\ *n, pl* **de•re•chos** : a large fast-moving complex of thunderstorms with powerful winds that move in a straight line and that cause widespread destruction [Spanish, "straight" (contrasted with *tornado,* taken to mean "turned"), from Latin *directus* "direct"]

[1]**der•e•lict** \ˈder-ə-ˌlikt\ *adj* **1** : abandoned by the owner or occupant ⟨a *derelict* ship⟩ **2** : NEGLECTFUL, NEGLIGENT [Latin *derelictus,* past participle of *derelinquere* "to abandon," from *de-* + *relinquere* "to leave"]

[2]**derelict** *n* **1** : something voluntarily abandoned; *esp* : a ship abandoned on the high seas **2** : a person without apparent means of support : VAGRANT

der•e•lic•tion \ˌder-ə-ˈlik-shən\ *n* **1** : the act of abandoning : the state of being abandoned ⟨the *dereliction* of a cause by its leaders⟩ **2** : neglect of one's duty : DELINQUENCY

de•ride \di-ˈrīd\ *vt* : to laugh at scornfully : make fun of [Latin *deridēre,* from *de-* + *ridēre* "to laugh"] ***synonyms*** see RIDICULE — **de•rid•er** *n* — **de•rid•ing•ly** \-ˈrīd-ing-lē\ *adv*

de ri•gueur \də-ˌrē-ˈgər\ *adj* : prescribed or required by fashion, etiquette, or custom : PROPER [French]

de•ri•sion \di-ˈrizh-ən\ *n* **1** : scornful or contemptuous ridicule **2** : an object of ridicule [Medieval French, from Late Latin *derisio,* from Latin *deridēre* "to deride"]

de•ri•sive \di-ˈrī-siv\ *adj* : expressing or characterized by derision ⟨*derisive* laughter⟩ — **de•ri•sive•ly** *adv* — **de•ri•sive•ness** *n*

de•ri•so•ry \di-ˈrī-sə-rē, -zə-\ *adj* : DERISIVE

der•i•va•tion \ˌder-ə-ˈvā-shən\ *n* **1 a** : the formation (as by the addition of an affix) of a word from another word or root **b** : ETYMOLOGY 1 **2 a** : a point of origin : SOURCE **b** : development from a source : DESCENT **c** : an act or process of deriving — **der•i•va•tion•al** \-shnəl, -shən-l\ *adj*

[1]**de•riv•a•tive** \di-ˈriv-ət-iv\ *adj* **1** : formed by derivation **2** : made up of or characterized by elements derived from something else ⟨*derivative* poetry⟩ — **de•riv•a•tive•ly** *adv*

[2]**derivative** *n* **1** : a word formed by derivation **2** : something derived **3** : the limit of the ratio of the change in a function's value to the corresponding change in its indpendent variable as the change of that variable approaches zero **4** : a substance that can be made from another substance in one or more steps

de•rive \di-ˈrīv\ *vb* **de•rived; de•riv•ing** **1 a** : to receive or obtain from a source **b** : to obtain (as a chemical substance) from a parent substance **2** : to trace the origin, descent, or derivation of **3** : to come from a certain source **4** : INFER 1, DEDUCE [Medieval French *deriver,* from Latin *derivare,* literally, "to draw off (water)," from *de-* + *rivus* "stream"] — **de•riv•able** \di-ˈrī-və-bəl\ *adj*

-derm \ˌdərm\ *n combining form* : skin : covering : layer ⟨ecto*derm*⟩ [Greek *derma* "skin," from *derein* "to skin"]

der•mal \ˈdər-məl\ *adj* : of or relating to the dermis or epidermis

dermat- *or* **dermato-** *combining form* : skin ⟨*dermato*logy⟩ [Greek *dermat-, derma*]

der•ma•ti•tis \ˌdər-mə-ˈtīt-əs\ *n, pl* **der•ma•tit•i•des** \-ˈtit-ə-ˌdēz\ *or* **dermatitises** : inflammation of the skin

der•ma•tol•o•gy \ˌdər-mə-ˈtäl-ə-jē\ *n* : a branch of medicine dealing with the structure, functions, and diseases of the skin — **der•ma•to•log•ic** \-mət-l-ˈäj-ik\ *or* **der•ma•to•log•i•cal** \-i-kəl\ *adj* — **der•ma•tol•o•gist** \ˌdər-mə-ˈtäl-ə-jəst\ *n*

der·mes·tid \dər-ˈmes-təd\ *n* **:** any of a family of beetles that are very destructive to material of animal origin (as dried meat, fur, or wool) [derived from Greek *dermēstēs,* a leather-eating worm, literally, "skin-eater"] — **dermestid** *adj*

der·mis \ˈdər-məs\ *n* **:** the sensitive vascular inner layer of the skin below the epidermis — called also *corium* [New Latin, from Greek *derma* "skin"]

der·o·gate \ˈder-ə-ˌgāt\ *vb* **1 :** to cause to seem inferior **:** BELITTLE **2 :** to take away a part so as to impair **:** DETRACT [Late Latin *derogare,* from Latin, "to annul (a law), detract," from *de-* + *rogare* "to ask, propose (a law)"] — **der·o·ga·tion** \ˌder-ə-ˈgā-shən\ *n* — **de·rog·a·tive** \di-ˈräg-ət-iv, ˈder-ə-ˌgāt-\ *adj*

de·rog·a·to·ry \di-ˈräg-ə-ˌtōr-ē, -ˌtȯr-\ *adj* **:** intended to lower the reputation of a person or thing **:** DISPARAGING — **de·rog·a·to·ri·ly** \-ˌräg-ə-ˈtōr-ə-lē, -ˈtȯr-\ *adv*

der·rick \ˈder-ik\ *n* **1 :** any of various machines for moving or hoisting heavy weights by means of a long beam fitted with pulleys and ropes or cables **2 :** a framework or tower built over a deep drill hole (as of an oil well) for supporting machinery [obsolete *derrick* "hangman, gallows," from *Derick,* name of a 17th century English hangman]

Word History In the reign of Queen Elizabeth I of England an executioner named *Derick* achieved some notoriety because of his position. The common people therefore named the gallows at London after Derick the hangman. This usage spread, and throughout the 17th century *derrick* was a term for both a hangman and a gallows. These senses eventually died out, but in the next century *derrick* began to be used for a hoisting apparatus resembling a gallows. Subsequently, *derrick* has become a term for a framework or tower over an oil well.

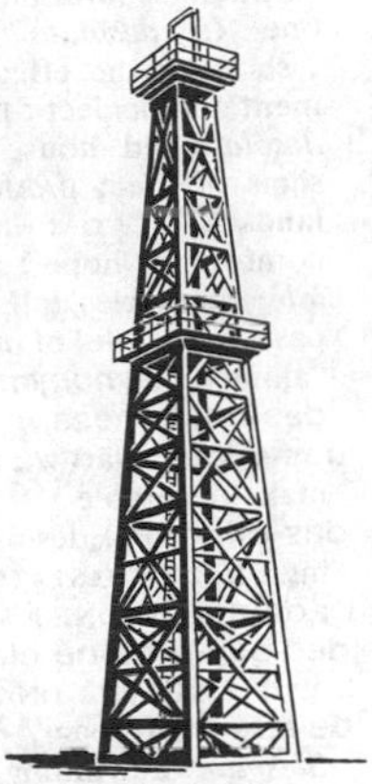
derrick 2

der·ri·ere *or* **der·ri·ère** \ˌder-ē-ˈeər\ *n* **:** BUTTOCK 2a [French *derrière,* derived from Latin *de retro* "behind"]

der·ring–do \ˌder-ing-ˈdü\ *n* **:** daring action **:** DARING [Middle English *dorring don* "daring to do"]

der·rin·ger \ˈder-ən-jər\ *n* **:** a short-barreled pocket pistol [Henry *Deringer,* 19th century American inventor]

der·ris \ˈder-əs\ *n* **:** any of a large genus of tropical Eurasian shrubs and woody vines of the legume family including commercial sources of rotenone; *also* **:** an insecticide prepared from the roots of a derris [Greek, "skin"]

der·vish \ˈdər-vish\ *n* **:** a member of a Muslim religious order noted for devotional exercises (as bodily movements leading to a trance) [Turkish *derviş,* literally, "beggar," from Persian *darvīsh*]

de·sa·li·nate \dē-ˈsal-ə-ˌnāt\ *vt* **:** DESALT — **de·sa·li·na·tion** \ˌdē-ˌsal-ə-ˈnā-shən\ *n* — **de·sa·li·na·tor** \dē-ˈsal-ə-ˌnāt-ər\ *n*

de·sa·li·nize \dē-ˈsal-ə-ˌnīz\ *vt* **:** DESALT — **de·sa·li·ni·za·tion** \-ˌsal-ə-nə-ˈzā-shən\ *n*

de·salt \dē-ˈsȯlt, ˈdē-\ *vt* **:** to remove salt from — **de·salt·er** *n*

¹des·cant \ˈdes-ˌkant\ *n* **1 :** a melody sung above a principal melody **2 :** the art of composing or singing part music; *also* **:** a piece of music so composed **3 :** a strain of melody **:** SONG **4 :** a discourse or comment on a subject [Medieval Latin *discantus,* from Latin *dis-* + *cantus* "song"]

²des·cant \ˈdes-ˌkant, des-ˈ\ *vi* **1 :** to sing or play a descant **2 :** to talk or write at length

de·scend \di-ˈsend\ *vb* **1 a :** to pass from a higher to a lower place or level **b :** to pass, move, or climb down or down along **2 a :** to originate or come from an ancestral stock or source **:** DERIVE **b :** to pass by inheritance **c :** to pass by transmission **3 :** to incline, lead, or extend downward **4 :** to swoop down in a sudden attack **5 :** to sink in status or condition [Medieval French *descendre,* from Latin *descendere,* from *de-* + *scandere* "to climb"] — **de·scend·ible** \-ˈsen-də-bəl\ *adj*

¹de·scen·dant *also* **de·scen·dent** \di-ˈsen-dənt\ *adj* **1 :** moving or directed downward **2 :** proceeding from an ancestor or source

²descendant *also* **descendent** *n* **1 :** one descended from another or from a common stock **2 :** one deriving directly from a precursor or prototype

de·scent \di-ˈsent\ *n* **1 :** the act or process of descending **2 :** a downward step (as in status or value) **:** DECLINE **3 :** derivation from an ancestor **:** BIRTH, LINEAGE **4 a :** an inclination downward **:** SLOPE **b :** a descending way (as a downgrade or stairway) **5 :** a sudden hostile raid or assault

de·scram·ble \dē-ˈskram-bəl\ *vt* **:** UNSCRAMBLE 2 — **de·scram·bler** \-bə-lər, -blər\ *n*

de·scribe \di-ˈskrīb\ *vt* **1 :** to represent or give an account of in words **2 :** to trace or traverse the outline of ⟨*describe* a circle⟩ [Latin *describere,* from *de-* + *scribere* "to write"] — **de·scrib·able** \-ˈskrī-bə-bəl\ *adj* — **de·scrib·er** *n*

de·scrip·tion \di-ˈskrip-shən\ *n* **1 a :** an act or instance of describing **b :** an account that presents a picture to a person who reads or hears it **2 :** KIND, SORT ⟨people of every *description*⟩ [Latin *descriptio,* from *describere* "to describe"]

de·scrip·tive \-ˈskrip-tiv\ *adj* **:** serving to describe — **de·scrip·tive·ly** *adv* — **de·scrip·tive·ness** *n*

de·scry \di-ˈskrī\ *vt* **de·scried; de·scry·ing 1 :** to catch sight of **2 :** EXPOSE 2 **3 :** FIND OUT [Medieval French *decrier* "to proclaim, reveal," from *de-* "de-" + *crier* "to cry"]

des·e·crate \ˈdes-i-ˌkrāt\ *vt* **:** to violate the sanctity of [*de-* + *-secrate* (as in *consecrate*)] — **des·e·crat·er** *or* **des·e·cra·tor** \-ˌkrāt-ər\ *n* — **des·e·cra·tion** \ˌdes-i-ˈkrā-shən\ *n*

de·seg·re·gate \dē-ˈseg-ri-ˌgāt, ˈdē-\ *vb* **:** to eliminate segregation in or from — **de·seg·re·ga·tion** \dē-ˌseg-ri-ˈgā-shən\ *n*

de·se·lect \ˌdē-sə-ˈlekt\ *vt* **de·se·lect·ed; de·se·lect·ing 1 :** DISMISS 3, REJECT **2 :** to cause (something previously selected) to no longer be selected in a software interface ⟨*deselect* the songs you don't want⟩

de·sen·si·tize \dē-ˈsen-sə-ˌtīz, ˈdē-\ *vt* **1 :** to make (an individual) insensitive or nonreactive to a sensitizing agent (as pollen) **2 :** to make emotionally insensitive or callous; *esp* **:** to eliminate or reduce an emotional response (as fear or guilt) to stimuli that formerly induced it — **de·sen·si·ti·za·tion** \dē-ˌsen-sət-ə-ˈzā-shən\ *n* — **de·sen·si·tiz·er** *n*

¹des·ert \ˈdez-ərt\ *n* **:** arid land with usually little vegetation that is incapable of supporting a considerable population without an artificial water supply [Medieval French, from Late Latin *desertum,* from Latin *deserere* "to desert"] — **des·ert·like** \-ˌlīk\ *adj*

²des·ert \ˈdez-ərt\ *adj* **:** of, relating to, or resembling a desert; *esp* **:** being barren and uninhabited ⟨a *desert* island⟩

³de·sert \di-ˈzərt\ *n* **1 :** worthiness of reward or punishment ⟨rewarded according to their *deserts*⟩ **2 :** deserved reward or punishment ⟨got their just *deserts*⟩ [Medieval French *deserte,* from *deservir* "to deserve"]

⁴de·sert \di-ˈzərt\ *vb* **1 :** to withdraw from **:** LEAVE **2 :** to leave in a helpless or unsupported position **:** FORSAKE ⟨*desert* a friend in trouble⟩ **3 :** to fail one in time of need ⟨my courage *deserted* me⟩ **4 :** to quit one's post without permission especially with the intent to remain away permanently [French *déserter,* derived from Latin *deserere* "to desert," from *de-* + *serere* "to join together"] ***synonyms*** see ABANDON — **de·sert·er** *n*

de·ser·tion \di-ˈzər-shən\ *n* **1 :** an act of deserting; *esp* **:** the abandonment of a person (as a wife or child) to whom one has legal and moral duties and obligations **2 :** a state of being deserted or forsaken **:** DESOLATION

de·serve \di-ˈzərv\ *vb* **:** to be worthy of **:** MERIT ⟨*deserves* another chance⟩ [Medieval French *deservir,* from Latin *deservire* "to devote oneself to," from *de-* + *servire* "to serve"]

de·served \-ˈzərvd\ *adj* **:** of, relating to, or being that which one deserves ⟨a *deserved* punishment⟩ — **de·serv·ed·ly** \-ˈzər-vəd-lē\ *adv* — **de·serv·ed·ness** \-ˈzər-vəd-nəs\ *n*

de·serv·ing *adj* **:** MERITORIOUS, WORTHY

de·sex \dē-ˈseks\ *vt* **:** CASTRATE, SPAY

deshabille *variant of* DISHABILLE

des·ic·cant \ˈdes-i-kənt\ *n* **:** a drying agent

des·ic·cate \-ˌkāt\ *vb* **1 :** to dry up or become dried up **2 :** to preserve (a food) by drying **:** DEHYDRATE [Latin *desiccare,* from *de-* + *siccare* "to dry," from *siccus* "dry"] — **des·ic·ca·tion** \ˌdes-i-ˈkā-shən\ *n* — **des·ic·ca·tor** \ˈdes-i-ˌkāt-ər\ *n*

\ə\ **abut**	\au̇\ **out**	\i\ **tip**	\ȯ\ **saw**	\u̇\ **foot**
\ər\ **further**	\ch\ **chin**	\ī\ **life**	\ȯi\ **coin**	\y\ **yet**
\a\ **mat**	\e\ **pet**	\j\ **job**	\th\ **thin**	\yü\ **few**
\ā\ **take**	\ē\ **easy**	\ng\ **sing**	\t͟h\ **this**	\yu̇\ **cure**
\ä\ **cot, cart**	\g\ **go**	\ō\ **bone**	\ü\ **food**	\zh\ **vision**

de·sid·er·a·tum \di-ˌsid-ə-ˈrät-əm, -ˌzid-, -ˈrāt-\ *n, pl* **-ta** \-ə\ : something sought for or aimed at [Latin]

[1]**de·sign** \di-ˈzīn\ *vt* **1** : to conceive and plan out in the mind ⟨*designed* the perfect crime⟩ **2 a** : to have as a purpose : INTEND ⟨*designed* to go to law school⟩ **b** : to devise for a specific function or end ⟨a dictionary *designed* for older students⟩ **3 a** : to make a pattern or sketch of **b** : to conceive and draw the plans for ⟨*design* an airplane⟩ [Middle English, "to outline, indicate, mean," from Medieval French *designer* "to designate," from Medieval Latin *designare,* from Latin, "to mark out," from *de-* + *signare* "to mark, mark out"]

[2]**design** *n* **1** : a project or scheme in which means to an end are laid down **2** : a planned purpose or intention ⟨happened by accident rather than by *design*⟩ **3 a** : a secret project or scheme : PLOT **b** *pl* : aggressive or evil intent — used with *on* or *against* ⟨he has *designs* on the money⟩ **4** : a sketch or plan showing the main features of something to be done **5** : the arrangement of elements that make up a structure or a work of art **6** : a decorative pattern ***synonyms*** see INTENTION, PLAN

[1]**des·ig·nate** \ˈdez-ig-ˌnāt, -nət\ *adj* : chosen for an office but not yet installed ⟨ambassador *designate*⟩

[2]**des·ig·nate** \-ˌnāt\ *vt* **1** : to mark or point out : INDICATE **2** : to appoint or choose by name for a special purpose ⟨*designate* someone as supervisor⟩ **3** : to call by a name or title [Latin *designare* "to design, designate"] — **des·ig·na·tive** \-ˌnāt-iv\ *adj* — **des·ig·na·tor** \-ˌnāt-ər\ *n* — **des·ig·na·to·ry** \-nə-ˌtōr-ē, -ˌtȯr-\ *adj*

designated driver *n* : a person chosen to abstain from intoxicants (as alcohol) so as to transport others safely who are not abstaining

designated hitter *n* **1** : a baseball player designated at the start of a game to bat in place of the pitcher without causing the pitcher to be removed from the game **2** : REPRESENTATIVE 2a, SUBSTITUTE

des·ig·na·tion \ˌdez-ig-ˈnā-shən\ *n* **1** : the act of designating or identifying **2** : a distinguishing name, sign, or title **3** : appointment to or selection for an office, post, or service

[1]**de·sign·er** \di-ˈzī-nər\ *n* : one that designs: as **a** : one who creates and often carries out plans for a project or structure **b** : one who creates and manufactures a new product style or design; *esp* : one who designs and manufactures high-fashion clothing

[2]**designer** *adj* : of, relating to, or produced by a designer; *also* : displaying the name, signature, or logo of a designer or manufacturer ⟨*designer* jeans⟩

designer drug *n* : a synthetic version of a drug (as heroin) that is produced with a slightly altered molecular structure to avoid having it classified as an illicit drug

de·sign·ing *adj* : CRAFTY, SCHEMING

de·sir·able \di-ˈzī-rə-bəl\ *adj* **1** : having pleasing qualities or properties : ATTRACTIVE ⟨a *desirable* location⟩ **2** : worth seeking or doing as advantageous, beneficial, or wise ⟨*desirable* legislation⟩ — **de·sir·abil·i·ty** \-ˌzī-rə-ˈbil-ət-ē\ *n* — **de·sir·able·ness** \-ˈzī-rə-bəl-nəs\ *n* — **de·sir·ably** \-blē\ *adv*

[1]**de·sire** \di-ˈzīr\ *vb* **1** : to long for : wish for earnestly ⟨*desire* peace⟩ **2** : to express a wish for : REQUEST ⟨they *desire* an answer right away⟩ **3** : to have desire ⟨you can, if you *desire,* stay here⟩ [Medieval French *desirer,* from Latin *desiderare,* from *de-* + *sider-, sidus* "heavenly body"]

synonyms DESIRE, WISH, WANT mean to have a longing for. DESIRE stresses the strength of feeling and often implies strong intention or aim ⟨*desires* to start a new life⟩. WISH sometimes implies a general or transient longing for the unattainable ⟨*wishes* for world peace⟩. WANT specifically suggests a felt need or lack ⟨*wants* to have children⟩.

[2]**desire** *n* **1** : a strong wish : LONGING **2** : an expressed wish : REQUEST **3** : something desired

de·sir·ous \di-ˈzīr-əs\ *adj* : eagerly wishing : DESIRING ⟨*desirous* of an invitation⟩ — **de·sir·ous·ly** *adv*

de·sist \di-ˈzist, -ˈsist\ *vi* : to cease to proceed or act [Medieval French *desister,* from Latin *desistere,* from *de-* + *sistere* "to stand, stop"] ***synonyms*** see STOP

desk \ˈdesk\ *n* **1 a** : a table, frame, or case with a flat or sloping surface especially for writing and reading **b** : a counter at which a person works **2 a** : a specialized division of an organization (as a newspaper) ⟨city *desk*⟩ **b** : a seating position according to rank in an orchestra [Medieval Latin *desca,* from Italian *desco* "table," from Latin *discus* "dish, disc"]

[1]**desk·top** \ˈdesk-ˌtäp\ *n* **1 a** : the top of a desk **b** : an area on a computer screen in which icons are arranged like objects on top of a desk **2** : a desktop computer

[2]**desktop** *adj* : of a size that can be conveniently used on a desk or table ⟨*desktop* computers⟩

desktop publishing *n* : the production of printed matter using a desktop computer with a layout program that integrates text and graphics

des·mid \ˈdez-məd\ *n* : any of numerous one-celled or colonial green algae (order Zygnematales) [Greek *desmos* "bond, ligature"]

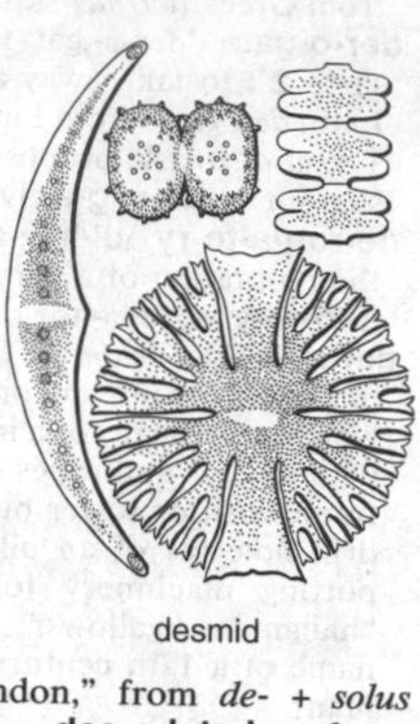

desmid

[1]**des·o·late** \ˈdes-ə-lət, ˈdez-\ *adj* **1** : lacking inhabitants and visitors : DESERTED **2** : joyless, disconsolate, and sorrowful through or as if through separation from a loved one ⟨a *desolate* widow⟩ **3 a** : showing the effects of abandonment and neglect : DILAPIDATED ⟨a *desolate* old house⟩ **b** : lacking signs of life : BARREN ⟨a *desolate* landscape⟩ **c** : lacking warmth, comfort, or hope : GLOOMY ⟨*desolate* memories⟩ [Latin *desolatus,* past participle of *desolare* "to abandon," from *de-* + *solus* "alone"] ***synonyms*** see SOLITARY — **des·o·late·ly** *adv* — **des·o·late·ness** *n*

[2]**des·o·late** \-ˌlāt\ *vt* : to make desolate : **a** : to lay waste **b** : to make miserable

des·o·la·tion \ˌdes-ə-ˈlā-shən, ˌdez-\ *n* **1** : the action of desolating **2** : DEVASTATION, RUIN **3** : a barren wasteland **4 a** : GRIEF 1, SADNESS **b** : LONELINESS

des·oxy·ri·bo·nu·cle·ic acid \de-ˌzäk-sē-ˈrī-bō-nu̇-ˌklē-ik-, -nyu̇-, -ˌklā-\ *n* : DNA

[1]**de·spair** \di-ˈspaər, -ˈspeər\ *vi* : to lose all hope or confidence ⟨*despair* of winning⟩ [Medieval French *desperer,* from Latin *desperare,* from *de-* + *sperare* "to hope"]

[2]**despair** *n* **1** : utter loss of hope ⟨a cry of *despair*⟩ **2** : a cause of hopelessness ***synonyms*** see DESPONDENCY

de·spair·ing *adj* : given to, arising from, or marked by despair : devoid of hope ***synonyms*** see DESPONDENT — **de·spair·ing·ly** \-ing-lē\ *adv*

des·patch *chiefly British variant of* DISPATCH

des·per·a·do \ˌdes-pə-ˈräd-ō, -ˈrād-\ *n, pl* **-does** *or* **-dos** : a bold or reckless criminal [probably from *desperate*]

des·per·ate \ˈdes-pə-rət, -prət\ *adj* **1** : being beyond or almost beyond hope ⟨a *desperate* illness⟩ **2** : reckless because of despair : RASH ⟨a *desperate* attempt⟩ **3** : extremely intense : OVERPOWERING ⟨*desperate* poverty⟩ [Latin *desperatus,* past participle of *desperare* "to despair"] ***synonyms*** see DESPONDENT — **des·per·ate·ly** *adv* — **des·per·ate·ness** *n*

des·per·a·tion \ˌdes-pə-ˈrā-shən\ *n* **1** : a loss of hope and surrender to misery or dread **2** : a state of hopelessness leading to extreme recklessness

de·spi·ca·ble \di-ˈspik-ə-bəl, ˈdes-ˌpik-\ *adj* : deserving to be despised ⟨a *despicable* traitor⟩ [Late Latin *despicabilis,* from Latin *despicari* "to despise"] ***synonyms*** see CONTEMPTIBLE — **de·spi·ca·ble·ness** *n* — **de·spi·ca·bly** \-blē\ *adv*

de·spise \di-ˈspīz\ *vt* **1** : to look down on with contempt or scorn ⟨*despised* liars⟩ **2** : to regard as negligible, worthless, or distasteful [Medieval French *despis-,* stem of *despire* "to despise," from Latin *despicere,* from *de-* + *specere* "to look"] — **de·spise·ment** \-mənt\ *n* — **de·spis·er** *n*

synonyms DESPISE, SCORN, DISDAIN, CONTEMN mean to regard as unworthy of one's notice or consideration. DESPISE may cover a range of feeling from strong dislike to loathing ⟨*despises* cowards⟩. SCORN suggests a ready or indignant contempt ⟨*scorns* the very thought of retirement⟩. DISDAIN implies an arrogant or haughty aversion to what is regarded as unworthy ⟨*disdained* popular music⟩. CONTEMN suggests vehement condemnation of a person or thing ⟨*contemns* their racist behavior⟩.

[1]**de·spite** \di-ˈspīt\ *n* **1** : the feeling or attitude of despising : CONTEMPT **2** : MALICE, SPITE **3 a** : an act of contempt or defiance **b** : HARM 1, INJURY [Medieval French *despit,* from Latin *despectus,* from *despicere* "to despise"] — **in despite of** : in spite of

[2]**despite** *prep* : in spite of ⟨walked to town *despite* the rain⟩

de·spite·ful \di-ˈspīt-fəl\ *adj* : expressing malice or hate — **de·spite·ful·ly** \-fə-lē\ *adv* — **de·spite·ful·ness** *n*

de·spoil \di-ˈspȯil\ *vt* : to strip of belongings, possessions, or value : PLUNDER, PILLAGE — **de·spoil·er** *n* — **de·spoil·ment** \-ˈspȯil-mənt\ *n*

de·spo·li·a·tion \di-ˌspō-lē-ˈā-shən\ *n* : the action or process of despoiling

[1]**de·spond** \di-ˈspänd\ *vi* : to become discouraged or disheartened [Latin *despondēre* "to give up, despond," from *de-* + *spondēre* "to promise solemnly"]

[2]**despond** *n* : DESPONDENCY

de·spon·den·cy \di-ˈspän-dən-sē\ *n* : the state of being despondent : DEJECTION, DISCOURAGEMENT

de·spon·dent \-dənt\ *adj* : feeling extreme discouragement, dejection, or depression — **de·spon·dent·ly** *adv*

synonyms DESPONDENT, DESPARING, DESPERATE, HOPELESS mean having lost all or nearly all hope. DESPONDENT implies a deep dejection arising from a conviction of the uselessness of further effort ⟨*despondent* about yet another rejection⟩. DESPAIRING suggests the slipping away of all hope and often despondency ⟨*despairing* appeals for the return of the lost dog.⟩ DESPERATE implies despair that prompts reckless action or violence in the face of defeat or frustration ⟨one last *desperate* attempt to turn the tide of battle⟩. HOPELESS suggests despair and the cessation of effort or resistance and often implies acceptance or resignation ⟨the situation of the beached whale is *hopeless*⟩.

des·pot \ˈdes-pət, -ˌpät\ *n* **1** : a ruler with absolute power and authority **2** : a person exercising power abusively, oppressively, or tyrannously [Greek *despotēs* "master, lord"] — **des·pot·ic** \des-ˈpät-ik\ *adj* — **des·pot·i·cal·ly** \-i-kə-lē, -klē\ *adv*

des·po·tism \ˈdes-pə-ˌtiz-əm\ *n* **1 a** : rule by a despot : TYRANNY **b** : despotic exercise of power **2** : a state or a system of government in which the ruler has unlimited power

des·sert \di-ˈzərt\ *n* : a course of usually sweet food, fruit, or cheese usually served at the end of a meal [Middle French, from *desservir* "to clear the table," from *des-* "de-" + *servir* "to serve"]

de·stig·ma·tize \dē-ˈstig-mə-ˌtīz\ *vt* : to remove associations of shame or disgrace from ⟨*destigmatize* mental illness⟩

des·ti·na·tion \ˌdes-tə-ˈnā-shən\ *n* **1** : an act of appointing, setting aside for a purpose, or predetermining **2** : the purpose for which something is destined **3** : a place which is the goal of a journey or to which something is sent

des·tine \ˈdes-tən\ *vt* **1** : to determine the fate of in advance ⟨a plan *destined* to fail⟩ **2** : to designate, assign, or dedicate in advance ⟨*destined* their children for college⟩ **3** : to be bound or directed ⟨a ship *destined* for New York⟩ [Medieval French *destiner*, from Latin *destinare*]

des·ti·ny \ˈdes-tə-nē\ *n, pl* **-nies** **1** : something to which a person or thing is destined : FORTUNE **2** : a predetermined course of events often held to be an irresistible power or agency ***synonyms*** see FATE

des·ti·tute \ˈdes-tə-ˌtüt, -ˌtyüt\ *adj* **1** : lacking something needed or desirable ⟨a lake *destitute* of fish⟩ **2** : extremely poor : suffering great want ⟨a *destitute* family⟩ [Latin *destitutus*, past participle of *destituere* "to abandon, deprive," from *de-* + *statuere* "to set up"] — **des·ti·tute·ness** *n*

des·ti·tu·tion \ˌdes-tə-ˈtü-shən, -ˈtyü-\ *n* : the state of being destitute; *esp* : extreme poverty

de–stress \ˈdē-ˈstres\ *vi* : UNWIND 2

de·stroy \di-ˈstrȯi\ *vb* **1** : to ruin the structure, organic existence, or condition of ⟨a house *destroyed* by fire⟩ **2** : KILL ⟨have a sick animal *destroyed*⟩ [Medieval French *destruire*, derived from Latin *destruere*, from *de-* + *struere* "to build"]

synonyms DESTROY, DEMOLISH, ANNIHILATE mean to bring to ruin. DESTROY implies any force that wrecks, kills, annihilates, or tears down or apart ⟨*destroy* a friendship by deceit⟩. DEMOLISH implies a pulling or smashing to pieces or a tearing down to the point of ruin ⟨*demolish* a building⟩. ANNIHILATE suggests destruction so complete as to make any restoration impossible ⟨*annihilate* a city by nuclear attack⟩.

de·stroy·er \-ˈstrȯi-ər, -ˈstrȯir\ *n* **1** : a destroying agent or agency **2** : a small fast warship armed with guns, depth charges, torpedoes, and often guided missiles

destroyer escort *n* : a warship similar to but smaller than a destroyer

de·struct \di-ˈstrəkt\ *n* : the deliberate destruction of a rocket after launching

de·struc·ti·ble \di-ˈstrək-tə-bəl\ *adj* : capable of being destroyed — **de·struc·ti·bil·i·ty** \-ˌstrək-tə-ˈbil-ət-ē\ *n*

de·struc·tion \di-ˈstrək-shən\ *n* **1** : the action or process of destroying something **2** : the state or fact of being destroyed : RUIN **3** : something that destroys [Medieval French, from Latin *destructio*, from *destruere* "to destroy"]

de·struc·tive \di-ˈstrək-tiv\ *adj* **1** : causing destruction : RUINOUS ⟨*destructive* storms⟩ **2** : designed or tending to destroy or harm ⟨*destructive* criticism⟩ — **de·struc·tive·ly** *adv* — **de·struc·tive·ness** *n*

destructive distillation *n* : decomposition of a substance (as coal or oil) by heat in a closed container and collection of the volatile products produced

de·struc·tor \di-ˈstrək-tər\ *n* **1** : a furnace for burning refuse : INCINERATOR **2** : a device for destroying a missile in flight

des·ue·tude \ˈdes-wi-ˌtüd, -ˌtyüd, di-ˈsü-ə-ˌ\ *n* : discontinuance from use or exercise : DISUSE [Latin *desuetudo*, from *desuescere* "to become unaccustomed," from *de-* + *suescere* "to become accustomed"]

des·ul·to·ry \ˈdes-əl-ˌtōr-ē, -ˌtȯr-\ *adj* : marked by lack of definite plan, regularity, or purpose : AIMLESS ⟨*desultory* reading⟩ [Latin *desultorius*, literally, "of a circus rider who leaps from horse to horse," from *desilire* "to leap down," from *de-* + *salire* "to leap"] — **des·ul·to·ri·ly** \ˌdes-əl-ˈtōr-ə-lē, -ˈtȯr-\ *adv* — **des·ul·to·ri·ness** \ˈdes-əl-ˌtōr-ē-nəs, -ˌtȯr-\ *n*

de·tach \di-ˈtach\ *vt* **1** : to separate especially from a larger mass and usually without violence or damage **2** : DISENGAGE, WITHDRAW [French *détacher*, from Medieval French *destachier*, from *des-* "de-" + *-tachier* (as in *atachier* "to attach")] — **de·tach·able** \-ə-bəl\ *adj* — **de·tach·ably** \-blē\ *adv*

de·tached \-ˈtacht\ *adj* **1** : not joined or connected : SEPARATE ⟨a *detached* house⟩ **2** : UNBIASED, IMPARTIAL ⟨a *detached* appraisal⟩ **3** : ALOOF, UNCONCERNED ⟨a *detached* observer⟩ — **de·tached·ly** \-ˈtach-əd-lē, -ˈtach-tlē\ *adv* — **de·tached·ness** \-ˈtach-əd-nəs; -ˈtacht-nəs, -ˈtach-\ *n*

de·tach·ment \di-ˈtach-mənt\ *n* **1** : the action or process of detaching : SEPARATION **2 a** : the dispatching of a body of troops or part of a fleet from the main body for a special service **b** : the part so dispatched **c** : a small permanent military unit having a special task or function **3 a** : indifference to worldly concerns : UNWORLDLINESS **b** : freedom from bias or prejudice

[1]**de·tail** \di-ˈtāl, ˈdē-ˌ\ *n* **1 a** : thorough treatment of or attention to particular items ⟨go into *detail* about an adventure⟩ **b** : a small part : ITEM ⟨the *details* of the party preparations⟩ **2 a** : selection (as of a group of soldiers) for some special service **b** : a soldier or group of soldiers appointed for special duty [French *détail*, from Medieval French *detail* "slice, piece," from *detaillier* "to cut in pieces"] ***synonyms*** see ITEM — **in detail** : with all the particulars : THOROUGHLY ⟨told the story *in detail*⟩

[2]**detail** *vt* **1** : to report in detail **2** : ENUMERATE 2, SPECIFY **3** : to assign to a task — **de·tail·er** *n*

de·tailed \di-ˈtāld, ˈdē-ˌ\ *adj* **1 a** : including many details **b** : marked by careful attention to details **2** : furnished with finely finished details ⟨beautifully *detailed* clothes⟩ ***synonyms*** see CIRCUMSTANTIAL — **de·tailed·ly** \di-ˈtāl-əd-lē, -ˈtāld-lē, ˈdē-ˌ\ *adv* — **de·tailed·ness** \di-ˈtā-ləd-nəs, -ˈtāld-nəs, -ˈtāl-nəs-, ˈdē-ˌ\ *n*

de·tail·ing \ˈdē-ˌtāl-ing\ *n* : the act or process of thoroughly cleaning an automobile

de·tain \di-ˈtān\ *vt* **1** : to hold or keep in or as if in custody **2** : to keep back (as something due) : WITHHOLD **3** : to restrain especially from proceeding : STOP ⟨was *detained* by a flat tire⟩ [Medieval French *detenir*, from Latin *detinēre*, from *de-* + *tenēre* "to hold"] — **de·tain·ment** \-mənt\ *n*

de·tect \di-ˈtekt\ *vt* **1** : to discover the nature, existence, presence, or fact of ⟨*detect* smoke⟩ **2** : DEMODULATE [Latin *detectus*, past participle of *detegere* "to uncover," from *de-* "de-" + *tegere* "to cover"] — **de·tect·able** \-ˈtek-tə-bəl\ *adj*

de·tec·tion \di-ˈtek-shən\ *n* **1** : the act of detecting : the state or fact of being detected : DISCOVERY **2** : the extraction of information from a radio, laser, or computer signal

\ə\ **abut**	\au̇\ **out**	\i\ **tip**	\ȯ\ **saw**	\u̇\ **foot**
\ər\ **further**	\ch\ **chin**	\ī\ **life**	\ȯi\ **coin**	\y\ **yet**
\a\ **mat**	\e\ **pet**	\j\ **job**	\th\ **thin**	\yü\ **few**
\ā\ **take**	\ē\ **easy**	\ng\ **sing**	\t͟h\ **this**	\yu̇\ **cure**
\ä\ **cot, cart**	\g\ **go**	\ō\ **bone**	\ü\ **food**	\zh\ **vision**

[1]**de·tec·tive** \di-ˈtek-tiv\ *adj* **1 :** fitted for or used in detecting something ‹a *detective* device for coal gas› **2 :** of or relating to detectives or their work ‹a *detective* story›

[2]**detective** *n* **:** one employed or engaged in catching criminals or gathering information that is not readily or publicly accessible

de·tec·tor \di-ˈtek-tər\ *n* **1 :** one that detects **2 :** a device for demodulating a radio signal

de·tent \ˈdē-ˌtent, di-ˈ\ *n* **:** a mechanism that locks or unlocks a movement **:** PAWL [French *détente,* from Medieval French *destendre* "to slacken," from *des-* "de-" + *tendre* "to stretch," from Latin *tendere*]

dé·tente \dā-ˈtänt, -ˈtäⁿt\ *n* **:** a relaxation of strained relations or tensions (as between nations) [French]

de·ten·tion \di-ˈten-chən\ *n* **:** the act of detaining **:** the state of being detained: as **a :** CONFINEMENT; *esp* **:** temporary custody preceding trial **b :** the punishment of being kept in after school [Latin *detentio,* from *detinēre* "to detain"]

de·ter \di-ˈtər\ *vt* **de·terred; de·ter·ring :** to turn aside, discourage, or prevent from acting (as by fear) [Latin *deterrēre,* from *de-* + *terrēre* "to frighten"] — **de·ter·ment** \-ˈtər-mənt\ *n*

de·ter·gen·cy \di-ˈtər-jən-sē\ *n* **:** cleansing quality or power

[1]**de·ter·gent** \-jənt\ *adj* **:** CLEANSING ‹*detergent* oil for engines› [Latin *detergēre* "to wash off," from *de-* + *tergēre* "to wipe"]

[2]**detergent** *n* **:** a cleansing agent; *esp* **:** any of numerous synthetic organic preparations that are chemically different from soaps but resemble them in the ability to emulsify oils and hold dirt in suspension

de·te·ri·o·rate \di-ˈtir-ē-ə-ˌrāt\ *vb* **1 :** to make or become worse or of less value **:** DEGENERATE **2 :** DISINTEGRATE 1 [Late Latin *deteriorare,* from Latin *deterior* "worse"] — **de·te·ri·o·ra·tion** \-ˌtir-ē-ə-ˈrā-shən\ *n* — **de·te·ri·o·ra·tive** \-ˈtir-ē-ə-ˌrāt-iv\ *adj*

de·ter·min·able \di-ˈtərm-ə-nə-bəl, -ˈtərm-nə-\ *adj* **:** capable of being determined or ascertained — **de·ter·min·able·ness** *n* — **de·ter·min·ably** \-blē\ *adv*

de·ter·mi·nant \di-ˈtərm-ə-nənt, -ˈtərm-nənt\ *n* **1 :** something that determines or conditions **2 :** a group of mathematical elements arranged in a square of rows and columns that is bordered on either side by a straight line and that has a value calculated from the values of its elements **3 :** GENE

de·ter·mi·nate \-mə-nət\ *adj* **1 :** having fixed limits **:** DEFINITE **2 :** definitely settled ‹arranged in a *determinate* order› **3 :** having a single flower terminating the main stalk and opening before those below or around it ‹a *determinate* inflorescence› — **de·ter·mi·nate·ly** *adv* — **de·ter·mi·nate·ness** *n*

de·ter·mi·na·tion \di-ˌtər-mə-ˈnā-shən\ *n* **1 :** the act of coming to a decision; *also* **:** the decision or conclusion reached **2 :** the act of fixing the extent, position, or character of something ‹*determination* of the position of a ship› **3 :** accurate measurement (as of length or volume) **4 :** firm or fixed purpose or intention to achieve a desired end **5 :** an identification of the taxonomic position of a plant or animal

de·ter·mi·na·tive \-ˈtər-mə-ˌnāt-iv\ *adj* **:** having power or tendency to determine — **determinative** *n*

de·ter·mine \di-ˈtər-mən\ *vb* **1 a :** to fix conclusively or authoritatively ‹two points *determine* a straight line› **b :** to bring about as a result ‹demand *determines* the price› **2 :** to find out or come to a decision ‹*determine* the answer to the problem› ‹she *determined* to do better› **3 :** to be the cause of or reason for ‹the quality of your work *determines* your grade› **4 :** to discover the taxonomic position or the generic and specific names of [Medieval French *determiner,* from Latin *determinare,* from *de-* + *terminare* "to limit, terminate"] ***synonyms*** see DISCOVER

de·ter·mined \-mənd\ *adj* **1 :** having reached a decision **:** firmly resolved ‹*determined* to be a pilot› ‹*determined* to succeed› **2 :** showing or characterized by determination ‹a *determined* attack› — **de·ter·mined·ly** \-mən-dlē, -mə-nəd-lē\ *adv* — **de·ter·mined·ness** \-mənd-nəs, -mən-\ *n*

de·ter·min·er \-mə-nər\ *n* **:** one that determines: as **a :** GENE, DETERMINANT **b :** a word belonging to a group of noun modifiers characterized by occurrence before descriptive adjectives modifying the same noun ‹*my* in "my new car" is a *determiner*›

de·ter·min·ism \-mə-ˌniz-əm\ *n* **:** a doctrine that acts of the will, natural events, or social changes are determined by preceding causes — **de·ter·min·ist** \-mə-nəst\ *n or adj* — **de·ter·min·is·tic** \-ˌtər-mə-ˈnis-tik\ *adj*

de·ter·rence \di-ˈtər-əns, -ˈter-\ *n* **:** the act, process, or capacity of deterring

de·ter·rent \-ənt\ *adj* **1 :** serving to deter **2 :** relating to deterrence — **deterrent** *n* — **de·ter·rent·ly** *adv*

de·test \di-ˈtest\ *vt* **:** to dislike intensely **:** LOATHE, ABHOR [Latin *detestari* "to curse while calling a deity to witness, detest," from *de-* + *testari* "to call to witness"] ***synonyms*** see HATE — **de·test·er** *n*

de·test·able \di-ˈtes-tə-bəl\ *adj* **:** arousing or deserving intense dislike — **de·test·able·ness** *n* — **de·test·ably** \-blē\ *adv*

de·tes·ta·tion \ˌdē-ˌtes-ˈtā-shən\ *n* **1 :** intense hatred or dislike **:** LOATHING **2 :** an object of hatred or contempt

de·throne \di-ˈthrōn\ *vt* **:** to remove from a throne **:** DEPOSE — **de·throne·ment** \-mənt\ *n* — **de·thron·er** *n*

det·o·nate \ˈdet-n-ˌāt, ˈdet-ə-ˌnāt\ *vb* **:** to explode or cause to explode with sudden violence [French *détoner* "to explode," from Latin *detonare* "to expend thunder," from *de-* + *tonare* "to thunder"] — **det·o·na·tion** \ˌdet-n-ˈā-shən, ˌdet-ə-ˈnā-shən\ *n*

det·o·na·tor \ˈdet-n-ˌāt-ər, ˈdet-ə-ˌnāt-\ *n* **:** a device or small quantity of explosive used for detonating a high explosive

[1]**de·tour** \ˈdē-ˌtu̇r, di-ˈ\ *n* **:** a deviation from a direct course or the usual procedure; *esp* **:** a roundabout way temporarily replacing part of a regular route [French *détour,* derived from Medieval French *destorner* "to divert," from *des-* "de-" + *torner* "to turn"]

[2]**detour** *vb* **1 :** to send or proceed by a detour ‹*detour* traffic around an accident› **2 :** to avoid by going around **:** BYPASS

de·tox \ˈdē-ˌtäks, di-ˈtäks\ *n* **1 :** detoxification from an intoxicating or addictive substance **2 :** a program or facility for detoxification ‹spent a week in *detox*› — **detox** *vb*

de·tox·i·fy \dē-ˈtäk-sə-ˌfī\ *vt* **-fied; -fy·ing 1 :** to remove a harmful substance (as a poison or toxin) or the effect of such from **2 :** to free (as a drug user or an alcoholic) from an intoxicating or an addictive substance in the body or from dependence on or addiction to such a substance — **de·tox·i·fi·ca·tion** \ˌdē-ˌtäk-sə-fə-ˈkā-shən\ *n*

de·tract \di-ˈtrakt\ *vb* **1 :** to lessen in importance, value, or praiseworthiness ‹*detract* from a person's reputation› **2 :** DISTRACT 1 ‹*detract* attention› [Latin *detractus,* past participle of *detrahere* "to pull down, disparage," from *de-* + *trahere* "to draw"] — **de·trac·tor** \-ˈtrak-tər\ *n*

de·trac·tion \di-ˈtrak-shən\ *n* **:** a lessening of reputation or esteem especially by malicious or petty criticism **:** BELITTLING — **de·trac·tive** \-ˈtrak-tiv\ *adj* — **de·trac·tive·ly** *adv*

de·train \dē-ˈtrān, ˈdē-\ *vb* **:** to get off or remove from a railroad train — **de·train·ment** \-mənt\ *n*

det·ri·ment \ˈde-trə-mənt\ *n* **:** injury or damage or its cause **:** HURT [Latin *detrimentum,* from *deterere* "to wear away, impair," from *de-* + *terere* "to rub"]

det·ri·men·tal \ˌde-trə-ˈment-l\ *adj* **:** causing detriment **:** DAMAGING — **det·ri·men·tal·ly** \-l-ē\ *adv*

de·tri·tus \di-ˈtrīt-əs\ *n* **1 :** loose material that results directly from rock disintegration or abrasion **2 :** a product of disintegration or wearing away [French *détritus,* from Latin *detritus,* past participle of *deterere* "to wear away"] — **de·tri·tal** \-ˈtrīt-l\ *adj*

[1]**deuce** \ˈdüs, ˈdyüs\ *n* **1 a** (1) **:** the face of a die that bears two spots (2) **:** a playing card bearing the number two **b :** a cast of dice yielding a point of two **2 :** a tie in tennis with each side having a score of 40 **3 :** DEVIL 1, DICKENS — used chiefly as a mild oath [Medieval French *deus* "two," derived from Latin *duo;* sense 3 from obsolete English *deuce* "bad luck"]

[2]**deuce** *vt* **:** to bring the score of (a tennis game or set) to deuce

deuc·ed \ˈdü-səd, ˈdyü-\ *adj* **:** DAMNED, CONFOUNDED ‹in a *deuced* fix› — **deuced** *or* **deuc·ed·ly** *adv*

deu·te·ri·um \dü-ˈtir-ē-əm, dyü-\ *n* **:** the hydrogen isotope that is of approximately twice the mass of ordinary hydrogen and that occurs in water — called also *heavy hydrogen;* symbol *D* [New Latin, from Greek *deuteros* "second"]

deuterium oxide *n* **:** heavy water D_2O composed of deuterium and oxygen

deu·ter·on \ˈdüt-ə-ˌrän, ˈdyüt-\ *n* **:** the nucleus of the deuterium atom that consists of one proton and one neutron

Deu·ter·on·o·my \ˌdüt-ə-ˈrän-ə-mē, ˌdyüt-\ *n* **:** the fifth book of canonical Jewish and Christian Scriptures containing narrative and laws — see BIBLE table [Greek *Deuteronomion,* from *deuteros* "second" + *nomos* "law"]

deut·sche mark \ˈdȯi-chə-ˌmärk, ˈdȯich-\ *also* **deutsch·mark** \ˈdȯich-\ *n* **:** the basic monetary unit of West Germany from 1948 to 1990 and of reunified Germany from 1990 to 2001 [German, "German mark"]

de·val·ue \dē-ˈval-yü, ˈdē-\ *vb* **1 :** to reduce the international exchange value of a currency **2 :** to lessen the value of — **de·val·u·a·tion** \ˌdē-ˌval-yə-ˈwā-shən\ *n*

dev·as·tate \ˈdev-ə-ˌstāt\ *vt* **1 :** to reduce to ruin : lay waste ⟨a country *devastated* by war⟩ **2 :** OVERPOWER, OVERWHELM ⟨*devastated* by grief⟩ [Latin *devastare,* from *de-* + *vastare* "to lay waste"] ***synonyms*** see RAVAGE — **dev·as·tat·ing·ly** \-ˌstāt-ing-lē\ *adv* — **dev·as·ta·tor** \-ˌstāt-ər\ *n*

dev·as·ta·tion \ˌdev-ə-ˈstā-shən\ *n* **:** the action of devastating : the state of being devastated : DESOLATION

de·vel·op \di-ˈvel-əp\ *vb* **1 a :** to make known gradually or in detail ⟨*developed* his argument⟩ **b :** to subject (exposed photographic material) especially to a chemical treatment to produce a visible image ⟨*develop* film⟩; *also* **:** to make visible by such a method ⟨*develop* pictures⟩ **c :** to elaborate (a musical theme) by working out rhythmic and harmonic changes **2 :** to bring to a more advanced or more nearly perfect state ⟨study to *develop* the mind⟩ **3 a :** to work out the possibilities of ⟨*develop* an idea⟩ **b :** to create or produce by effort over time ⟨*develop* new ways of doing business⟩ **4 :** to make more available or usable ⟨*develop* land⟩ **5 :** to acquire gradually ⟨*develop* a taste for olives⟩ **6 a :** to go through a process of natural growth, differentiation, or evolution ⟨a blossom *develops* from a bud⟩ **b :** to acquire secondary sex characteristics **7 :** to become apparent [French *développer,* from Medieval French *desvoluper,* from *des-* "de-" + *voloper* "to wrap"] — **de·vel·op·able** \-ˈvel-ə-pə-bəl\ *adj*

de·vel·oped \di-ˈvel-əpt\ *adj* **:** having a relatively high level of industrialization and standard of living ⟨a *developed* country⟩

de·vel·op·er \-ˈvel-ə-pər\ *n* **:** one that develops; as **a :** a chemical used to develop exposed photographic materials **b :** a person who develops real estate

de·vel·op·ment \di-ˈvel-əp-mənt\ *n* **1 :** the act, process, or result of developing **2 :** the state of being developed **3 :** a developed piece of land; *esp* **:** one with houses built on it

de·vel·op·men·tal \-ˌvel-əp-ˈment-l\ *adj* **:** of or relating to development ⟨*developmental* processes⟩ ⟨a *developmental* disability⟩ — **de·vel·op·men·tal·ly** \-l-ē\ *adv*

developmentally disabled *adj* **:** having a physical or mental disability (as mental retardation) that hampers or prevents normal development

de·vi·ant \ˈdē-vē-ənt\ *adj* **:** deviating especially from an accepted norm — **de·vi·ance** \-əns\ *n* — **deviant** *n*

[1]**de·vi·ate** \ˈdē-vē-ˌāt\ *vb* **:** to turn aside especially from a standard, principle, or topic [Late Latin *deviare,* from Latin *de* + *via* "way"]

[2]**de·vi·ate** \-vē-ət, -vē-ˌāt\ *adj* **:** DEVIANT — **deviate** *n*

de·vi·a·tion \ˌdē-vē-ˈā-shən\ *n* **:** an act or instance of deviating: as **a :** the difference found by subtracting some fixed number (as the arithmetic mean of a series of statistical data) from any item of the series **b :** departure from an established ideology or party line **c :** noticeable departure from accepted norms (as of behavior) — **de·vi·a·tion·ism** \-shə-ˌniz-əm\ *n* — **de·vi·a·tion·ist** \-shə-nəst, -shnəst\ *n*

de·vice \di-ˈvīs\ *n* **1 a :** a scheme to deceive : STRATAGEM **b :** a piece of equipment or a mechanism designed to serve a special purpose **2** *pl* **:** a way of doing or acting : unsupervised activities ⟨left to their own *devices*⟩ **3 :** an emblematic design used especially as a heraldic bearing [Medieval French *devis* "division, plan," from *deviser* "to divide, regulate, tell," derived from Latin *dividere* "to divide"]

[1]**dev·il** \ˈdev-əl\ *n* **1** *often cap* **:** the personified supreme spirit of evil often represented in Jewish and Christian belief as the ruler of hell — often used with *the* as a mild imprecation or expression of surprise, vexation, or emphasis **2 :** DEMON 1 **3 :** an extremely wicked person **4 :** a person of notable energy, recklessness, and dashing spirit; *also* **:** one who is mischievous **5 :** INDIVIDUAL 2 ⟨you lucky *devil*⟩ ⟨lost his job, the poor *devil*⟩ [Old English *dēofol,* from Late Latin *diabolus,* from Greek *diabolos,* literally, "slanderer," from *diaballein* "to throw across, slander," from *dia-* + *ballein* "to throw"]

[2]**devil** *vt* **dev·iled** *or* **dev·illed; dev·il·ing** *or* **dev·il·ling** \ˈdev-ling, -ə-ling\ **1 :** to season highly ⟨*deviled* eggs⟩ **2 :** ANNOY; *esp* **:** to press, beg, or urge persistently

dev·il·fish \ˈdev-əl-ˌfish\ *n* **1 :** MANTA RAY **2 :** OCTOPUS 1

dev·il·ish \ˈdev-lish, -ə-lish\ *adj* **1 :** characteristic of or resembling the devil ⟨*devilish* tricks⟩ **2 :** EXTREME 1, EXCESSIVE ⟨in a *devilish* hurry⟩ — **devilish** *adv* — **dev·il·ish·ly** *adv* — **dev·il·ish·ness** *n*

dev·il–may–care \ˌdev-əl-ˌmā-ˈkeər, -ˈkaər\ *adj* **:** heedless of authority : RECKLESS

dev·il·ment \ˈdev-əl-mənt, -ˌment\ *n* **:** reckless mischief

devil ray *n* **:** MANTA RAY

dev·il·ry \ˈdev-əl-rē\ *or* **dev·il·try** \-əl-trē\ *n, pl* **-ries** *or* **-tries** **1 :** action performed with the help of the devil : WITCHCRAFT **2 a :** wicked or cruel behavior **b :** reckless unrestrained conduct : MISCHIEF

devil's advocate *n* **1 :** a Roman Catholic official whose duty is to examine critically the evidence on which a demand for beatification or canonization rests **2 :** a person who supports a less accepted or approved cause for the sake of argument

devil's darning needle *n* **1 :** DRAGONFLY **2 :** DAMSELFLY

dev·il's food cake \ˈdev-əlz-ˌfüd-ˌkāk\ *n* **:** a rich chocolate cake

devil's paintbrush *n* **:** any of various hawkweeds found in the eastern U.S.; *esp* **:** ORANGE HAWKWEED

de·vi·ous \ˈdē-vē-əs\ *adj* **1 :** deviating from a straight line : ROUNDABOUT ⟨a *devious* path⟩ **2 a :** straying from a right or accepted course : ERRANT 2b ⟨*devious* conduct⟩ **b :** SNEAKY, DECEPTIVE ⟨a *devious* plan⟩ [Latin *devius,* from *de-* + *via* "way"] — **de·vi·ous·ly** *adv* — **de·vi·ous·ness** *n*

de·vise \di-ˈvīz\ *vt* **1 a :** to form in the mind by new combinations or applications of ideas or principles : INVENT ⟨*devise* a new strategy⟩ **b :** to plan to obtain or bring about : PLOT ⟨*devise* the death of an enemy⟩ **2 :** to give (real estate) by will ⟨*devised* the property to his daughter⟩ [Medieval French *deviser* "to divide, distinguish, invent," derived from Latin *dividere* "to divide"] — **de·vis·er** *n*

de·vi·tal·ize \dē-ˈvīt-l-ˌīz\ *vt* **:** to deprive of life or vitality ⟨the seeds were *devitalized* by the heat⟩ — **de·vi·tal·i·za·tion** \-ˌvīt-l-ə-ˈzā-shən\ *n*

de·void \di-ˈvȯid\ *adj* **:** being without a usual, typical, or expected quality or accompaniment ⟨a book *devoid* of interest⟩

de·voir \dəv-ˈwär, ˈdev-ˌ\ *n* **1 :** DUTY, RESPONSIBILITY **2 :** a usually formal act of respect [Medieval French *deveir,* from *devoir, deveir* "to owe, be obliged," from Latin *debēre*]

dev·o·lu·tion \ˌdev-ə-ˈlü-shən, ˌdē-və-\ *n* **:** transference (as of rights or powers) from one individual to another [Medieval Latin *devolutio,* from Latin *devolvere* "to roll down"] — **dev·o·lu·tion·ary** \-shə-ˌner-ē\ *adj* — **dev·o·lu·tion·ist** \-shə-nəst, -shnəst\ *n*

de·volve \di-ˈvälv, -ˈvȯlv\ *vb* **:** to pass by transmission or succession from one person to another [Latin *devolvere* "to roll down, fall to," from *de-* + *volvere* "to roll"]

dev·on \ˈdev-ən\ *n, often cap* **:** any of an English breed of vigorous red cattle used for meat and milk [*Devon,* England]

De·vo·ni·an \di-ˈvō-nē-ən\ *n* **1 :** the period of the Paleozoic era between the Silurian and Mississippian — called also *Age of Fishes*; see GEOLOGIC TIME table **2 :** the system of rocks corresponding to the Devonian period [*Devon,* England] — **Devonian** *adj*

de·vote \di-ˈvōt\ *vt* **1 :** to set apart for a special use ⟨*devote* land to farming⟩ **2 :** to center the attention or activities of (oneself) ⟨*devoted* themselves to restoring the house⟩ [Latin *devotus,* past participle of *devovēre* "to dedicate, devote," from *de-* + *vovēre* "to vow"]

synonyms DEVOTE, DEDICATE, CONSECRATE mean to set apart for a special and often higher purpose. DEVOTE is likely to suggest strong reasons and often a long-term goal ⟨*devoted* her evenings to studying law⟩. DEDICATE suggests a solemn devotion to a serious or sacred purpose ⟨*dedicated* his life to helping the poor⟩. CONSECRATE suggests the giving of a solemn or sacred quality to something ⟨*consecrate* a church to the worship of God⟩.

de·vot·ed *adj* **:** having strong loyalty, affection, or dedication ⟨*devoted* admirers⟩ — **de·vot·ed·ly** *adv* — **de·vot·ed·ness** *n*

dev·o·tee \ˌdev-ə-ˈtē, -ˈtā\ *n* **:** an ardent or zealous follower, supporter, or enthusiast ⟨a *devotee* of sports⟩ ⟨a religious *devotee*⟩

de·vo·tion \di-ˈvō-shən\ *n* **1 a :** religious fervor : PIETY **b :** an act of prayer — usually used in plural **c :** a religious exercise or practice other than the regular worship of a congregation **2 a :** the act of devoting or the quality of being devoted **b :** intense love, affection, or dedication — **de·vo·tion·al** \-shnəl, -shən-l\ *adj* — **de·vo·tion·al·ly** \-ē\ *adv*

de·vo·tion·al \-shnəl, -shən-l\ *n* : a short worship service

de·vour \di-ˈvau̇r\ *vt* **1** : to eat up greedily or hungrily **2** : to use up or destroy as if by eating ⟨fire *devoured* the building⟩ **3** : to enjoy avidly ⟨*devour* a book⟩ [Medieval French *devorer,* from Latin *devorare,* from *de-* + *vorare* "to devour"]

de·vout \di-ˈvau̇t\ *adj* **1** : devoted to religion or to religious duties or exercises **2** : expressing devotion or piety ⟨a *devout* attitude⟩ **3 a** : devoted to a pursuit, belief, or type of behavior ⟨a *devout* baseball fan⟩ **b** : warmly sincere ⟨*devout* thanks⟩ [Medieval French *devot,* from Late Latin *devotus,* from Latin *devovēre* "to devote"] — **de·vout·ly** *adv* — **de·vout·ness** *n*

dew \ˈdü, ˈdyü\ *n* **1** : moisture condensed upon cool surfaces at night **2** : something resembling dew in purity, freshness, or power to refresh **3** : moisture especially when appearing in minute droplets [Old English *dēaw*] — **dew** *vt* — **dew·less** *adj*

dew·ar \ˈdü-ər\ *n, often cap* : a container similar to a thermos that is used especially to store liquefied gases [James *Dewar,* died 1923, Scottish chemist]

dew·ber·ry \-ˌber-ē\ *n* : any of several sweet edible berries related to and resembling blackberries; *also* : a trailing bramble that bears dewberries

dew·claw \-ˌklȯ\ *n* : a vestigial digit on the foot of a mammal or a claw or hoof on such a digit — **dew·clawed** \-ˌklȯd\ *adj*

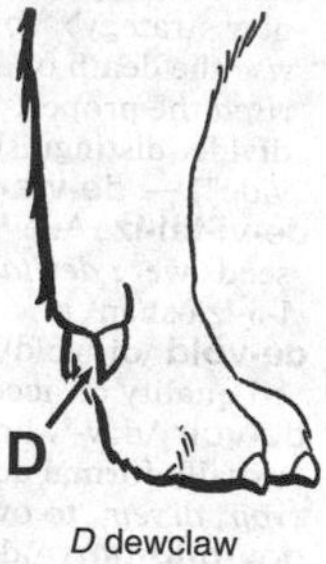

D dewclaw

dew·drop \-ˌdräp\ *n* : a drop of dew

Dew·ey decimal classification \ˈdü-ē-, ˈdyü-\ *n* : a system of classifying books and other publications whereby main classes are designated by a 3-digit number and subdivisions are shown by numbers after a decimal point — called also *Dewey decimal system* [Melvil *Dewey,* died 1931, American librarian]

dew·fall \ˈdü-ˌfȯl, ˈdyü-\ *n* : formation of dew; *also* : the time when dew begins to form

dew·lap \-ˌlap\ *n* : a fold or flap of skin on the neck of some animals as: **a** : loose skin hanging under the neck of dogs and cattle of some breeds **b** : a usually brightly colored extensible flap of skin on the throat of a lizard (as an anole) — **dew·lapped** \-ˌlapt\ *adj*

dew point *n* : the temperature at which the moisture in the air begins or would begin to condense

dewy \ˈdü-ē, ˈdyü-\ *adj* **dew·i·er; -est** : moist with, affected by, or suggestive of dew ⟨eyes *dewy* with tears⟩ — **dew·i·ly** \ˈdü-ə-lē, ˈdyü-\ *adv* — **dew·i·ness** \-ē-nəs\ *n*

Dex·e·drine \ˈdek-sə-ˌdrēn, -drən\ *trademark* — used for dextroamphetamine

dex·ter \ˈdek-stər\ *adj* **1** : relating to or situated on the right **2** : being or related to the side of a heraldic shield at the right of the person bearing it [Latin, "on the right side, skillful"] — **dexter** *adv*

dex·ter·i·ty \dek-ˈster-ət-ē\ *n, pl* **-ties** **1** : readiness and grace in physical activity; *esp* : skill and ease in using the hands **2** : mental skill or quickness

dex·ter·ous *also* **dex·trous** \ˈdek-stə-rəs, -strəs\ *adj* **1** : mentally quick and skillful : EXPERT ⟨her *dexterous* negotiating⟩ **2** : done with skillfulness ⟨a *dexterous* maneuver⟩ **3** : skillful and competent with the hands — **dex·ter·ous·ly** *adv*

synonyms DEXTEROUS, ADROIT, DEFT mean ready and skilled in physical or mental movement. DEXTEROUS implies expertness with ease and quickness in manipulation or movement ⟨unrolled the sleeping bag with a *dexterous* toss⟩. ADROIT adds artfulness and resourcefulness to dexterity ⟨an *adroit* magician⟩. DEFT stresses lightness, neatness, and sureness of touch ⟨a surgeon's *deft* use of the scalpel⟩.

dextr- *or* **dextro-** *combining form* **1** : right : on or toward the right **2** *usually* **dextro-** : turning the plane of polarization of light to the right ⟨*dextrose*⟩ [Latin *dextr-, dexter*]

dex·tral \ˈdek-strəl\ *adj* : of, relating to, or inclined to the right; *esp* : RIGHT-HANDED

dex·trin \ˈdek-strən\ *also* **dex·trine** \-ˌstrēn, -strən\ *n* : any of various water-soluble gummy substances obtained from starch by the action of heat, acids, or enzymes

dex·tro·am·phet·amine \ˈdek-ˌstrō-am-ˈfet-ə-ˌmēn, -mən\ *n* : a stimulant of the central nervous system that is a derivative of amphetamine — compare DEXEDRINE

dex·trose \ˈdek-ˌstrōs\ *n* : a sugar $C_6H_{12}O_6$ that is a kind of glucose, occurs in plants, fruits, and blood, is a source of energy for living things, may be obtained by hydrolysis of starch in acid solution, and is used in making candy [from the fact that it turns the plane of polarization of light to the right]

dey \ˈdā\ *n* : a ruling official of the Ottoman Empire in northern Africa [French, from Turkish *dayı,* literally, "maternal uncle"]

¹DH \ˌdē-ˈāch\ *n, pl* **DHs** : DESIGNATED HITTER

²DH \ˌdē-ˈāch, ˈdē-ˌāch\ *vi* **DHed; DHing** : to play as a designated hitter in a baseball game

dhar·ma \ˈdər-mə\ *n* **1** : custom or law regarded as duty in Hinduism **2 a** : the basic principles of cosmic or individual existence in Hinduism and Buddhism **b** : conformity to one's duty and nature in Hinduism and Buddhism [Sanskrit, from *dhārayati* "he holds"]

dhow \ˈdau̇\ *n* : any of a number of typically lateen-rigged Arab sailing vessels [Arabic *dāwa*]

dhow

di- *combining form* **1** : twice : twofold : double ⟨*di*chromatic⟩ **2** : containing two atoms, radicals, or groups ⟨*di*chromate⟩ [Greek]

dia- *also* **di-** *prefix* : through : across [Greek, "through, apart," from *dia*]

di·a·be·tes \ˌdī-ə-ˈbēt-ēz, -ˈbēt-əs\ *n* : any of various abnormal conditions characterized by the secretion and excretion of excessive amounts of urine; *esp* : DIABETES MELLITUS [Latin, from Greek *diabētēs,* from *diabainein* "to walk with the legs apart, cross over," from *dia-* + *bainein* "to go"] — **di·a·bet·ic** \ˌdī-ə-ˈbet-ik\ *adj or n*

diabetes in·sip·i·dus \-in-ˈsip-əd-əs\ *n* : a disorder of the pituitary gland characterized by intense thirst and by the excretion of large amounts of urine [New Latin, literally, "bland diabetes"]

diabetes mel·li·tus \-ˈmel-ət-əs\ *n* : an endocrine disorder characterized by inadequate secretion or utilization of insulin, by the discharge of abnormal amounts of urine, by large amounts of sugar in the blood and urine, and by thirst, hunger, and loss of weight [New Latin, literally, "honey-sweet diabetes"]

di·a·bol·i·cal \ˌdī-ə-ˈbäl-i-kəl\ *or* **di·a·bol·ic** \-ˈbäl-ik\ *adj* : of, relating to, or characteristic of the devil : FIENDISH [Middle French *diabolique,* from Late Latin *diabolicus,* from *diabolus* "devil"] — **di·a·bol·i·cal·ly** \-i-kə-lē, -klē\ *adv* — **di·a·bol·i·cal·ness** \-i-kəl-nəs\ *n*

di·ac·o·nate \dī-ˈak-ə-nət, dē-, -ˌnāt\ *n* **1** : the office or period of office of a deacon or deaconess **2** : an official body of deacons [Late Latin *diaconatus,* from *diaconus* "deacon"]

di·a·crit·ic \ˌdī-ə-ˈkrit-ik\ *n* : a mark used with a letter or group of letters and indicating a sound value different from that given the unmarked or otherwise marked letter or combination of letters

di·a·crit·i·cal \ˌdī-ə-ˈkrit-i-kəl\ *also* **di·a·crit·ic** \-ˈkrit-ik\ *adj* : serving as a diacritic ⟨a *diacritical* mark⟩ [Greek *diakritikos* "separative," from *diakrinein* "to distinguish," from *dia-* + *krinein* "to separate"]

di·a·dem \ˈdī-ə-ˌdem, -əd-əm\ *n* **1** : CROWN 2; *esp* : an ornamental headband worn as a badge of royalty **2** : CROWN 5a(1) [Medieval French *diademe,* derived from Greek *diadēma,* from *diadein* "to bind around," from *dia-* + *dein* "to bind"]

di·aer·e·sis *or* **di·er·e·sis** \dī-ˈer-ə-səs\ *n, pl* **-e·ses** \-ˌsēz\ : a mark ¨ placed over a vowel to show that it is pronounced in a separate syllable (as in *naïve* or *Brontë*) [Late Latin, from Greek *diairesis,* literally, "division," from *diairein* "to divide," from *dia-* + *hairein* "to take"]

di·ag·nose \ˈdī-ig-ˌnōs, -ˌnōz, ˌdī-ig-ˈ\ *vb* : to recognize (as a disease) by signs and symptoms : make a diagnosis ⟨*diagnose* a play in football⟩ [back-formation from *diagnosis*] — **di·ag·nos·able** \ˌdī-ig-ˈnō-sə-bəl, -zə-\ *adj*

di·ag·no·sis \ˌdī-ig-ˈnō-səs\ *n, pl* **-no·ses** \-ˈnō-ˌsēz\ **1 a** : the art or act of identifying a disease from its signs and symptoms **b** : the conclusion reached by diagnosis **2** : a concise technical description of a taxonomic group or entity **3 a** : a careful critical study of something especially to determine its nature or importance **b** : the conclusion reached after a critical study [Greek *diagnōsis,* from *diagignōskein* "to distinguish," from *dia-*

+ *gignōskein* "to know"] — **di·ag·nos·tic** \-ˈnäs-tik\ *adj* — **di·ag·nos·ti·cal·ly** \-ˈnäs-ti-kə-lē, -klē\ *adv*

di·ag·nos·ti·cian \ˌdī-ig-ˌnäs-ˈtish-ən\ *n* **:** a person who makes diagnoses; *esp* **:** a specialist in making medical diagnoses

1di·ag·o·nal \dī-ˈag-ən-l\ *adj* **1 :** joining two nonadjacent corners of a two-dimensional shape whose edges are all straight lines or of a three-dimensional solid whose surface is made up of all flat faces **2 a :** running in a slanting direction **b :** having diagonal markings or parts ⟨a *diagonal* weave⟩ [Latin *diagonalis,* from Greek *diagōnios* "from angle to angle," from *dia-* + *gōnia* "angle"] — **di·ag·o·nal·ly** \-ˈag-ən-l-ē, -ˈag-nə-lē\ *adv*

2diagonal *n* **1 :** a diagonal line or plane **2 a :** a diagonal direction **b :** a diagonal row, arrangement, or pattern **3 :** 2SLASH 4

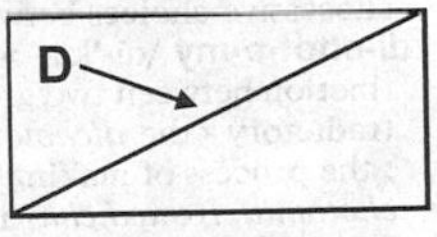

D diagonal 1

1di·a·gram \ˈdī-ə-ˌgram\ *n* **:** a drawing, sketch, plan, or chart that makes something clearer or easier to understand [Greek *diagramma,* from *diagraphein* "to mark out by lines," from *dia-* + *graphein* "to write"] — **di·a·gram·mat·ic** \ˌdī-ə-grə-ˈmat-ik\ *also* **di·a·gram·mat·i·cal** \-ˈmat-i-kəl\ *adj* — **di·a·gram·mat·i·cal·ly** \-ˈmat-i-kə-lē, -klē\ *adv*

2diagram *vt* **-grammed** *or* **-gramed** \-ˌgramd\; **-gram·ming** *or* **-gram·ing** \-ˌgram-ing\ **:** to represent by or put into the form of a diagram ⟨*diagram* a sentence⟩ ⟨*diagrammed* a football play⟩

1di·al \ˈdī-əl, ˈdīl\ *n* **1 a :** the face of a watch or clock **b :** SUNDIAL **2 a :** a face or scale upon which some measurement or other number is registered or indicated usually by means of numbers and a pointer ⟨the *dial* of a pressure gauge⟩ **b :** a disk usually with a knob or slots that may be turned to make electrical connections (as on a telephone) or to regulate the operation of a device (as a radio) [Medieval Latin *dialis* "clock wheel revolving daily," from Latin *dies* "day"]

2dial *vb* **di·aled** *or* **di·alled; di·al·ing** *or* **di·al·ling** **1 :** to manipulate a dial so as to operate, regulate, or select **2 :** to make a telephone call or connection

di·a·lect \ˈdī-ə-ˌlekt\ *n* **1 :** a regional variety of a language usually transmitted orally and differing distinctively from the standard language ⟨the Lancashire *dialect* of English⟩ **2 :** a variety of language whose identity is fixed by a factor (as social class or occupation) other than geography [Middle French *dialecte,* from Latin *dialectus,* from Greek *dialektos* "conversation, dialect," from *dialegesthai* "to converse," from *dia-* + *legein* "to speak"] — **di·a·lec·tal** \ˌdī-ə-ˈlek-tl\ *adj* — **di·a·lec·tal·ly** \ˌdī-ə-ˈlek-tl-ē\ *adv*

synonyms DIALECT, LINGO, JARGON, SLANG mean language not recognized as standard. DIALECT applies to a form of language used regionally ⟨the *dialects* of Texas⟩. LINGO is mildly contemptuous for any language not readily understood ⟨computer *lingo*⟩. JARGON applies to a specialized or technical language ⟨the *jargon* of football⟩ ⟨medical *jargon*⟩. SLANG designates a class of mostly recently coined and often short-lived terms or usages informally preferred to standard usage as being forceful, novel, or fashionable ⟨used *slang* her parents didn't understand⟩.

di·a·lec·tic \ˌdī-ə-ˈlek-tik\ *n* **:** a process of reasoning based on the clash of one idea with its opposite leading to a resolution of these ideas in the form of a truer or more comprehensive concept [Latin *dialectica* "art of reasoning, logic," from Greek *dialektikē,* from *dialektikos* "of conversation," from *dialektos*]

di·a·lec·ti·cal \ˌdī-ə-ˈlek-ti-kəl\ *also* **di·a·lec·tic** \-tik\ *adj* **1 :** of, relating to, or in accordance with dialectic ⟨*dialectical* method⟩ **2 :** of, relating to, or characteristic of a dialect **:** DIALECTAL — **di·a·lec·ti·cal·ly** \-ti-kə-lē, -klē\ *adv*

di·a·lec·tol·o·gy \ˌdī-ə-ˌlek-ˈtäl-ə-jē\ *n* **:** the systematic study of dialect — **di·a·lec·tol·o·gist** \-jəst\ *n*

dialog box *n* **:** a box of text on a computer screen displaying options to choose from or providing space for inputting information

di·a·logue *also* **di·a·log** \ˈdī-ə-ˌlȯg\ *n* **1 a :** a conversation between two or more persons **b :** an exchange of ideas and opinions **2 :** the parts of a literary or dramatic composition that represent conversation [Medieval French, from Latin *dialogus,* from Greek *dialogos,* from *dialegesthai* "to converse," from *dia-* + *legein* "to speak"]

di·al–up \ˈdī-əl-ˌəp, ˈdīl-\ *adj* **:** relating to or done using an ordinary telephone line ⟨*dial-up* Internet access⟩

di·al·y·sis \dī-ˈal-ə-səs\ *n, pl* **-y·ses** \-ə-ˌsēz\ **1 :** the separation of substances in solution by means of their unequal diffusion through semipermeable membranes; *esp* **:** such a separation of colloids from soluble substances **2 :** the process of removing blood from an artery (as of a patient with failing kidneys), purifying it by dialysis, and returning it to a vein [Greek, "separation," from *dialyein* "to dissolve," from *dia-* + *lyein* "to loosen"]

di·a·lyze \ˈdī-ə-ˌlīz\ *vt* **:** to subject to dialysis

dia·mag·net·ic \ˌdī-ə-ˌmag-ˈnet-ik\ *adj* **:** slightly repelled by a magnet — **dia·mag·ne·tism** \-ˈmag-nə-ˌtiz-əm\ *n*

di·am·e·ter \dī-ˈam-ət-ər\ *n* **1 :** a straight line passing through the center of a figure or body; *esp* **:** a line segment passing through the center of a circle and having its ends on the circle's circumference **2 :** the length of a diameter [Medieval French *diametre,* from Latin *diametros,* from Greek, from *dia-* + *metron* "measure"] — **di·am·e·tral** \-ˈam-ə-trəl\ *adj*

di·a·met·ric \ˌdī-ə-ˈme-trik\ *or* **di·a·met·ri·cal** \-tri-kəl\ *adj* **1 :** of, relating to, or being a diameter **2 :** completely opposed or opposite ⟨a *diametric* contradiction⟩ — **di·a·met·ri·cal·ly** \-tri-kə-lē, -klē\ *adv*

di·a·mond \ˈdī-ə-mənd, ˈdī-mənd\ *n* **1 a :** native crystalline carbon that is usually nearly colorless, that when transparent and free from flaws is highly valued as a precious stone, and that is used industrially as an abrasive; *also* **:** a piece of this substance especially when cut and polished **b :** crystallized carbon produced artificially **2 :** a shape formed by four equal straight lines and having two opposite acute angles and two opposite obtuse angles **3 a :** a playing card marked with a red diamond-shaped figure **b** *pl* **:** the suit made up of cards marked with diamonds **4 a :** INFIELD 1 **b :** the entire playing field in baseball or softball [Medieval French *diamant,* from Late Latin *diamas,* alteration of Latin *adamas* "hardest metal, diamond," from Greek]

di·a·mond·back \ˈdī-mənd-ˌbak, -ə-mənd-, -mən-\ *adj* **:** having marks like diamonds on the back

diamondback rattlesnake *n* **:** either of two large and deadly rattlesnakes of the southern U.S. — called also *diamondback, diamondback rattler*

diamondback terrapin *n* **:** any of several edible terrapins of coastal salt marshes of the southeastern U.S.

di·a·pa·son \ˌdī-ə-ˈpāz-n, -ˈpās-\ *n* **1 :** a burst of sound ⟨*diapasons* of laughter⟩ **2 :** the principal stop in an organ extending through the complete scale of the instrument **3 :** the full range of musical tones [Latin, from Greek *(hē) dia pasōn (chordōn symphōnia)* "(the concord) through all (the notes)"]

dia·pause \ˈdī-ə-ˌpȯz\ *n* **:** a period of dormancy (as in some insects) in which development slows down or in which activity decreases

1di·a·per \ˈdī-pər, -ə-pər\ *n* **1 :** a usually white linen or cotton fabric woven in a pattern formed by the repetition of a simple usually geometric design; *also* **:** the design on such cloth **2 :** a basic garment for infants comprising a piece of absorbent material drawn up between the legs and fastened at the waist [Medieval French *diaspre,* from Medieval Latin *diasprum*]

diaper 1

2diaper *vt* **1 :** to ornament with diaper designs **2 :** to put a diaper on ⟨*diaper* a baby⟩

di·aph·a·nous \dī-ˈaf-ə-nəs\ *adj* **:** characterized by such a delicate texture as to permit seeing through **:** SHEER ⟨*diaphanous* chiffon⟩ [Medieval Latin *diaphanus,* from Greek *diaphanēs,* from *diaphainein* "to show through," from *dia-* + *phainein* "to show"] — **di·aph·a·nous·ly** *adv* — **di·aph·a·nous·ness** *n*

di·a·phragm \ˈdī-ə-ˌfram\ *n* **1 :** a body partition of muscle and connective tissue; *esp* **:** the partition separating the chest and abdominal cavities in mammals **2 :** a dividing membrane or thin partition (as in a tube) **3 :** a device that limits the aperture of a lens or optical system (as of a camera) **4 :** a thin flexible disk that vibrates (as in a microphone) **5 :** a molded cap usually of thin rubber fitted over the cervix of the uterus to act as a

\ə\ **abut**	\au̇\ **out**	\i\ **tip**	\ȯ\ **saw**	\u̇\ **foot**
\ər\ **further**	\ch\ **chin**	\ī\ **life**	\ȯi\ **coin**	\y\ **yet**
\a\ **mat**	\e\ **pet**	\j\ **job**	\th\ **thin**	\yü\ **few**
\ā\ **take**	\ē\ **easy**	\ng\ **sing**	\th\ **this**	\yu̇\ **cure**
\ä\ **cot, cart**	\g\ **go**	\ō\ **bone**	\ü\ **food**	\zh\ **vision**

contraceptive barrier [Late Latin *diaphragma,* from Greek, from *diaphrassein* "to barricade," from *dia-* + *phrassein* "to enclose"] — **di·a·phrag·mat·ic** \ˌdī-ə-ˌfrag-ˈmat-ik\ *adj* — **di·a·phrag·mat·i·cal·ly** \-ˈmat-i-kə-lē, -klē\ *adv*

di·a·rist \ˈdī-ə-rəst\ *n* : one who keeps a diary

di·ar·rhea \ˌdī-ə-ˈrē-ə\ *n* : an abnormally frequent or abundant discharge of loose or fluid material from the bowels [Late Latin *diarrhoea,* from Greek *diarrhoia,* from *diarrhein* "to flow through," from *dia-* + *rhein* "to flow"] — **di·ar·rhe·al** \-ˈrē-əl\ *also* **di·ar·rhe·ic** \-ˈrē-ik\ *adj*

di·a·ry \ˈdī-ə-rē, ˈdī-rē\ *n, pl* **-ries** : a daily record especially of personal experiences, observations, and thoughts; *also* : a book intended or used as a diary [Latin *diarium,* from *dies* "day"]

di·as·po·ra \dī-ˈas-pə-rə, -prə\ *n* **1** *cap* **a** : the settling of scattered colonies of Jews outside Palestine after the Babylonian exile **b** : the Jews living outside Palestine or modern Israel **2 a** : the movement, migration, or scattering of a people away from an established or ancestral homeland **b** : people settled far from their ancestral homeland ⟨the African *diaspora*⟩ [Greek, "dispersion," from *diaspeirein* "to scatter," from *dia-* + *speirein* "to sow"]

di·a·stase \ˈdī-ə-ˌstās\ *n* : AMYLASE; *esp* : a mixture of amylases from malt [French, from Greek *diastasis* "separation," from *distanai* "to separate," from *dia-* + *histanai* "to cause to stand"] — **di·a·stat·ic** \ˌdī-ə-ˈstat-ik\ *adj*

di·as·to·le \dī-ˈas-tə-ˌlē\ *n* : the relaxation of the heart during which its cavities expand and fill with blood — compare SYSTOLE [Greek *diastolē* "expansion," from *diastellein* "to dilate, expand," from *dia-* + *stellein* "to send"]

di·a·stol·ic \ˌdī-ə-ˈstäl-ik\ *adj* : of, relating to, caused by, or occurring during diastole ⟨*diastolic* blood pressure is lower than systolic blood pressure⟩

di·as·tro·phism \dī-ˈas-trə-ˌfiz-əm\ *n* : TECTONISM [Greek *diastrophē* "twisting," from *diastrephein* "to distort," from *dia-* + *strephein* "to twist"] — **di·a·stroph·ic** \ˌdī-ə-ˈsträf-ik\ *adj*

dia·ther·my \ˈdī-ə-ˌthər-mē\ *n* : the production of heat in tissue by electric currents for medical or surgical purposes — **dia·ther·mic** \ˌdī-ə-ˈthər-mik\ *adj*

di·ath·e·sis \dī-ˈath-ə-səs\ *n, pl* **-e·ses** \-ə-ˌsēz\ : a constitutional predisposition toward an abnormality or disease [Greek, literally, "arrangement," from *diatithenai* "to arrange," from *dia-* + *tithenai* "to set"]

di·a·tom \ˈdī-ə-ˌtäm\ *n* : any of a class (Bacillariophyceae) of minute floating single-celled or colonial algae that are abundant in fresh and salt water and have a cell wall of silica that persists as a skeleton after death [derived from Greek *diatomos* "cut in half," from *diatemnein* "to cut through," from *dia-* + *temnein* "to cut"] — **di·a·to·ma·ceous** \ˌdī-ət-ə-ˈmā-shəs\ *adj*

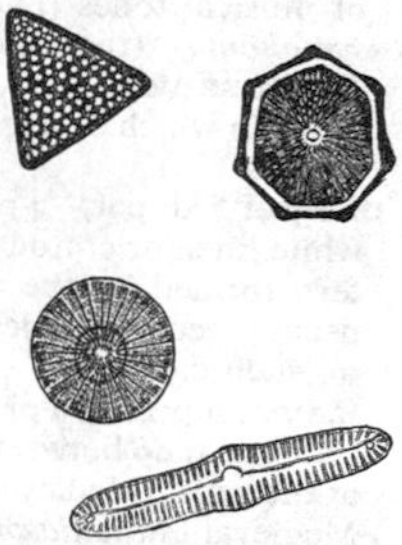
diatom

diatomaceous earth *n* : a light crumbly silica-containing material derived chiefly from diatom remains and used especially as a filter

di·atom·ic \ˌdī-ə-ˈtäm-ik\ *adj* : having two atoms in the molecule

di·at·o·mite \dī-ˈat-ə-ˌmīt\ *n* : DIATOMACEOUS EARTH

dia·ton·ic \ˌdī-ə-ˈtän-ik\ *adj* : relating to or being a standard major or minor scale of eight tones to the octave [Late Latin *diatonicus,* from Greek *diatonikos,* from *diatonos* "stretching," from *diateinein* "to stretch out," from *dia-* + *teinein* "to stretch"] — **dia·ton·i·cal·ly** \-ˈtän-i-kə-lē, -klē\ *adv*

di·a·tribe \ˈdī-ə-ˌtrīb\ *n* : a bitter and abusive speech or writing [Latin *diatriba* "discourse," from Greek *diatribē* "pastime, discourse," from *diatribein* "to spend (time), wear away," from *dia-* + *tribein* "to rub"]

di·az·e·pam \dī-ˈaz-ə-ˌpam\ *n* : a tranquilizer $C_{16}H_{13}ClN_2O$ used especially to relieve anxiety and tension and to relax muscles — compare VALIUM

di·ba·sic \dī-ˈbā-sik, ˈdī-\ *adj* : having two replaceable hydrogen atoms — used of acids

1**dib·ble** \ˈdib-əl\ *n* : a small hand tool for making holes in the ground for plants, seeds, or bulbs [Middle English *debylle*]

2**dibble** *vt* **dib·bled; dib·bling** \ˈdib-ling, -ə-ling\ **1** : to plant with a dibble **2** : to make holes in (soil) with or as if with a dibble

1**dice** \ˈdīs\ *n, pl* **dice** **1** : DIE 1 **2** : a gambling game played with dice [Middle English *dees, dyce,* pl. of *dee* "die"] — **no dice** : by no means; *also* : of no use

2**dice** *vb* **1** : to cut into small cubes ⟨*dice* carrots⟩ **2** : to play games with dice — **dic·er** *n*

di·chlo·ride \dī-ˈklōr-ˌīd, -ˈklȯr-\ *n* : a binary compound containing two atoms of chlorine combined with an element or radical

di·chot·o·mous \dī-ˈkät-ə-məs\ *adj* **1** : dividing into two parts **2** : relating to, involving, or proceeding from dichotomy — **di·chot·o·mous·ly** *adv*

dichotomous key *n* : a key to biological classification based on successive choices between pairs of alternate characters

di·chot·o·my \dī-ˈkät-ə-mē\ *n, pl* **-mies** : a division into or distinction between two groups that are mutually exclusive or contradictory ⟨the *dichotomy* between theory and practice⟩; *also* : the process of making such a division or distinction [Greek *dichotomia,* from *dicha* "in two" + *temnein* "to cut"]

di·chro·ic \dī-ˈkrō-ik\ *adj* : having the property of dichroism [Greek *dichroos* "two-colored," from *di-* + *chrōs* "color"]

di·chro·ism \ˈdī-krə-ˌwiz-əm\ *n* **1** : the property according to which the colors are unlike when a crystal is viewed in the direction of two different axes **2** : the property of a surface of reflecting light of one color and transmitting light of other colors

di·chro·mate \dī-ˈkrō-ˌmāt, ˈdī-\ *n* : a usually orange to red chromium salt containing the radical Cr_2O_7 — called also *bichromate*

di·chro·mat·ic \ˌdī-krō-ˈmat-ik\ *adj* : having or exhibiting two colors

dick·cis·sel \dik-ˈsis-əl\ *n* : a common migratory black-throated finch of the central U.S. [imitative]

dickcissel

dick·ens \ˈdik-ənz\ *n* : DEVIL 1, DEUCE — used chiefly as a mild oath ⟨what the *dickens* do you mean?⟩ [euphemism]

Dick·en·si·an \dik-ˈen-zē-ən, -sē-\ *adj* : of, relating to, or characteristic of Charles Dickens or his writings

dick·er \ˈdik-ər\ *vi* **dick·ered; dick·er·ing** \ˈdik-ring, -ə-ring\ : HAGGLE 2, BARGAIN ⟨buyers *dickering* for lower prices⟩ [origin unknown] — **dicker** *n*

dick·ey *or* **dicky** \ˈdik-ē\ *n, pl* **dick·eys** *or* **dick·ies** **1** : any of various articles of clothing: as **a** : a separate or detachable shirtfront **b** : a small cloth insert worn to fill in a neckline **2** : a small bird [*Dicky,* nickname for *Richard*]

di·cli·nous \dī-ˈklī-nəs, ˈdī-\ *adj* : having the stamens and pistils in separate flowers [*di-* + Greek *klinē* "bed"]

di·cot \ˈdī-ˌkät\ *n* : DICOTYLEDON — **dicot** *adj*

di·cot·y·le·don \ˌdī-ˌkät-l-ˈēd-n\ *n* : any of a group (Dicotyledoneae) of flowering plants (as an aster, an oak, or a bean) having an embryo with two cotyledons and usually net-veined leaves and flower parts that occur in groups of four or five — compare MONOCOTYLEDON — **di·cot·y·le·don·ous** \-n-əs\ *adj*

Dic·ta·phone \ˈdik-tə-ˌfōn\ *trademark* — used for a dictating machine

1**dic·tate** \ˈdik-ˌtāt\ *vb* **1** : to speak or read for a person to transcribe or for a machine to record ⟨*dictate* a letter⟩ **2** : to say or state with authority : give orders ⟨*dictate* terms of surrender⟩ [Latin *dictare* "to assert, dictate," from *dicere* "to say"]

2**dictate** *n* : an authoritative rule, prescription, or injunction ⟨the *dictates* of conscience⟩ ⟨the *dictates* of good taste⟩

dictating machine *n* : a machine used especially for the recording of human speech for transcription

dic·ta·tion \dik-ˈtā-shən\ *n* **1** : the act or process of giving arbitrary commands **2 a** : the dictating of words ⟨write from *dictation*⟩ **b** : something that is dictated or is taken down as dictated ⟨take *dictation*⟩

dic·ta·tor \ˈdik-ˌtāt-ər, dik-ˈ\ *n* **1 a** : a person given absolute emergency power by the ancient Roman senate **b** : one holding complete autocratic and often oppressive control **2** : one that dictates

dic·ta·to·ri·al \ˌdik-tə-ˈtōr-ē-əl, -ˈtȯr-\ *adj* **1** : of, relating to, or characteristic of a dictator or a dictatorship ⟨a *dictatorial* manner⟩ ⟨a *dictatorial* regime⟩ **2** : oppressive to or contemptuously overbearing toward others — **dic·ta·to·ri·al·ly** \-ē-ə-lē\ *adv* — **dic·ta·to·ri·al·ness** *n*

synonyms DICTATORIAL, DOGMATIC, DOCTRINAIRE mean imposing one's will or opinions on others. DICTATORIAL stresses autocratic, high-handed methods and a domineering manner ⟨exercised *dictatorial* control over the office⟩. DOGMATIC implies being unduly and offensively positive in laying down principles and expressing opinions ⟨*dogmatic* about what is and what is not art⟩. DOCTRINAIRE implies a disposition to follow abstract theories in framing laws or policies affecting people ⟨a *doctrinaire* approach to improving the economy⟩.

dic·ta·tor·ship \dik-ˈtāt-ər-ˌship\ *n* **1 :** the office or term of office of a dictator **2 :** autocratic rule, control, or leadership **3 :** a government, form of government, or country in which absolute power is held by a dictator or a small clique

dic·tion \ˈdik-shən\ *n* **1 :** choice of words especially as to correctness, clearness, or effectiveness : WORDING ⟨careless *diction* in the essay⟩ **2 :** quality of vocal expression : ENUNCIATION ⟨a singer with excellent *diction*⟩ [Latin *dictio* "speaking, style," from *dicere* "to say"]

synonyms DICTION, STYLE mean the manner in which one expresses oneself with words. DICTION applies to choice of words in reference to their effectiveness in expressing ideas or emotions ⟨poetic *diction*⟩. STYLE refers to a manner of expression characteristic of its author and having artistic distinction ⟨Hemingway's terse *style*⟩.

dic·tio·nary \ˈdik-shə-ˌner-ē\ *n, pl* **-nar·ies** **1 :** a reference source in print or electronic form containing words usually alphabetically arranged along with information about their forms, pronunciations, functions, etymologies, meanings, and syntactical and idiomatic uses **2 :** a reference book listing alphabetically terms or names important to a particular subject or activity along with discussion of their meanings and applications ⟨a law *dictionary*⟩ **3 :** a reference book giving for words of one language equivalents in another ⟨an English-French *dictionary*⟩ [Medieval Latin *dictionarium,* from Late Latin *dictio* "word," from Latin, "speaking"]

dic·tum \ˈdik-təm\ *n, pl* **dic·ta** \-tə\ *also* **dic·tums :** a formal authoritative statement : PRONOUNCEMENT [Latin, from *dictus,* past participle of *dicere* "to say"]

did *past of* DO

di·dac·tic \dī-ˈdak-tik\ *adj* **:** intended primarily to instruct rather than to entertain ⟨a *didactic* story with a moral lesson⟩ [Greek *didaktikos,* from *didaskein* "to teach"] — **di·dac·ti·cal** \-ti-kəl\ *adj* — **di·dac·ti·cal·ly** \-ti-kə-lē, -klē\ *adv* — **di·dac·ti·cism** \-tə-ˌsiz-əm\ *n*

di·dac·tics \-tiks\ *n sing or pl* **:** systematic instruction : PEDAGOGY

didn't \ˈdid-nt\ **:** did not

di·do \ˈdīd-ō\ *n, pl* **didoes** *or* **didos** **1 :** a foolish or mischievous act ⟨cutting *didoes*⟩ **2 :** something frivolous or showy [origin unknown]

didst \didst, ˈdidst\ *archaic past 2nd singular of* DO

[1]**die** \ˈdī\ *vi* **died; dy·ing** \ˈdī-ing\ **1 :** to stop living : EXPIRE ⟨*died* of old age⟩ **2 a :** to pass out of existence : CEASE ⟨their anger was *dying* down⟩ **b :** to disappear or subside gradually ⟨the wind *died* down⟩ **3 a :** to long keenly or desperately ⟨*dying* to go⟩ **b :** to be overwhelmed by emotion ⟨almost *died* of embarrassment⟩ **4 :** to stop functioning ⟨the motor *died*⟩ [Middle English *dien,* from or akin to Old Norse *deyja* "to die"]

[2]**die** \ˈdī\ *n, pl* **dice** \ˈdīs\ *or* **dies** \ˈdīz\ **1** *pl dice* **:** a small cube marked on each face with from one to six spots and used usually in pairs in various games — often used figuratively in expressions concerning chance or the absence of possible change in a course of action ⟨the *die* was cast⟩ **2** *pl dies* **:** any of various tools or devices for imparting a desired shape, form, or finish to a material or for impressing an object or material: as **a :** the larger of a pair of cutting or shaping tools that when moved toward each other produce a certain desired form in or impress a desired device on an object **b :** a hollow screw-cutting tool for forming screw threads **c :** a perforated block through which metal or plastic is drawn or forced [Middle English *dee,* from Medieval French *dé*]

die–hard \ˈdī-ˌhärd\ *adj* **:** strongly or fanatically determined or devoted ⟨*die-hard* fans⟩; *esp* **:** strongly resisting change ⟨a *die-hard* conservative⟩ — **die·hard** *n*

diel·drin \ˈdēl-drən\ *n* **:** a white crystalline toxic chlorine-containing compound used formerly as an insecticide [*Diels-Alder* reaction, from Otto *Diels,* died 1954, and Kurt *Alder,* died 1958, German chemists]

di·elec·tric \ˌdī-ə-ˈlek-trik\ *n* **:** a nonconductor of direct electric current [*dia-* + *electric*] — **dielectric** *adj*

di·en·ceph·a·lon \ˌdī-ˌen-ˈsef-ə-ˌlän\ *n* **:** the posterior subdivision of the forebrain [*dia-* + *encephalon*] — **di·en·ce·phal·ic** \ˌdī-ˌen-sə-ˈfal-ik\ *adj*

die–off \ˈdī-ˌȯf\ *n* **:** a sudden sharp decline of an animal or plant population

dieresis *variant of* DIAERESIS

die·sel \ˈdē-zəl, -səl\ *n* **1 :** DIESEL ENGINE **2 :** a vehicle driven by a diesel engine **3 :** a fuel designed for use in diesel engines [Rudolf *Diesel,* died 1913, German engineer]

diesel engine *n* **:** an internal-combustion engine in which air is compressed to a temperature sufficiently high to ignite fuel injected into the cylinder

Di·es Irae \ˌdē-ˌās-ˈē-ˌrā\ *n* **:** a medieval Latin hymn on the Day of Judgment sung in requiem masses [Medieval Latin, "day of wrath"; from the first words of the hymn]

[1]**di·et** \ˈdī-ət\ *n* **1 a :** the food and drink that a person, animal, or group usually takes : customary nourishment **b :** the kind and amount of food selected for a person or animal for a special reason (as improving health) ⟨a high-protein *diet*⟩ **c :** a regimen of eating and drinking sparingly so as to reduce one's weight ⟨going on a *diet*⟩ **2 :** something provided or experienced repeatedly (as for enjoyment) ⟨a steady *diet* of television⟩ [Medieval French *diete,* from Latin *diaeta* "prescribed diet," from Greek *diaita,* literally, "manner of living," from *diaitasthai* "to lead one's life"]

[2]**diet** *vb* **:** to eat or cause to eat less or according to set rules — **di·et·er** *n*

[3]**diet** *n* **:** a formal deliberative assembly; *esp* **:** any of various national or provincial legislatures [Middle English *diete* "day's journey, day set for a meeting," from Medieval Latin *dieta,* literally, "daily regimen, diet" (associated with Latin *dies* "day"), from Latin *diaeta*]

[4]**diet** *adj* **1 :** reduced in calories ⟨a *diet* soft drink⟩ **2 :** promoting weight loss (as by lessening appetite) ⟨*diet* pills⟩

di·e·tary \ˈdī-ə-ˌter-ē\ *adj* **:** of or relating to a diet or to the rules of diet

di·e·tet·ic \ˌdī-ə-ˈtet-ik\ *adj* **:** of or relating to diet or dietetics — **di·e·tet·i·cal·ly** \-ˈtet-i-kə-lē, -klē\ *adv*

di·e·tet·ics \-ˈtet-iks\ *n* **:** the science or art of applying the principles of nutrition to feeding

di·e·ti·tian *or* **di·e·ti·cian** \ˌdī-ə-ˈtish-ən\ *n* **:** a person qualified in or practicing dietetics ⟨a hospital *dietitian*⟩

diff \ˈdif\ *n, slang* **:** DIFFERENCE

dif·fer \ˈdif-ər\ *vi* **dif·fered; dif·fer·ing** \ˈdif-ring, -ə-ring\ **1 :** to be not the same : be unlike ⟨children who *differ* in looks⟩ **2 :** DISAGREE 2 ⟨they *differ* about what should be done⟩ [Latin *differre* "to postpone, be different," from *dis-* + *ferre* "to carry"]

dif·fer·ence \ˈdif-ərns, ˈdif-rəns, -ə-rəns\ *n* **1 :** unlikeness between persons or things ⟨the striking *difference* in the children's looks⟩ **2 :** the degree or amount by which things differ in quantity or measure; *esp* **:** the number left after a subtraction ⟨the *difference* between 4 and 6 is 2⟩ **3 :** a disagreement in opinion : DISSENSION ⟨we tried to settle our *differences*⟩ **4 :** a significant change in or effect on a situation ⟨makes no *difference* to me⟩

dif·fer·ent \ˈdif-ərnt, ˈdif-rənt, -ə-rənt\ *adj* **1 :** partly or totally unlike another in nature, form, or quality ⟨this apple is *different* from the others⟩ **2 :** not the same: as **a :** DISTINCT ⟨*different* age groups⟩ **b :** VARIOUS ⟨*different* members of the class⟩ **c :** ANOTHER ⟨switch to a *different* channel⟩

synonyms DIFFERENT, DIVERSE, DISPARATE, DIVERGENT mean unlike in kind or character. DIFFERENT often implies little more than separateness but may also suggest contrast or contrariness ⟨*different* foods⟩. DIVERSE implies both distinctness and marked contrast ⟨a person of *diverse* interests⟩. DISPARATE stresses incongruity or incompatibility ⟨*disparate* notions of freedom⟩. DIVERGENT implies movement apart or along different courses with little chance for an ultimate meeting ⟨*divergent* paths⟩.

dif·fer·en·tia \ˌdif-ə-ˈren-chē-ə, -chə\ *n, pl* **-ti·ae** \-chē-ˌē, -chē-ˌī\ : the element, feature, or factor that distinguishes one thing, state, or class from another [Latin, "difference," from *differre* "to differ"]

[1]**dif·fer·en·tial** \ˌdif-ə-ˈren-chəl\ *adj* **1 a :** of, relating to, or constituting a distinction : DISTINGUISHING **b :** making a distinction between individuals or classes ⟨*differential* legislation⟩ **c :** based upon or resulting from a differential ⟨*differential* freight charges⟩ **d :** functioning or proceeding differently or at a different rate ⟨*differential* melting in a glacier⟩ **2 :** relating to quantitative differences ⟨*differential* readings on a scale⟩ — **dif·fer·en·tial·ly** \-ˈrench-lē, -ə-lē\ *adv*

[2]**differential** *n* **1 :** the product of the derivative of a function of one variable by the amount of change of the independent variable **2 :** an amount or degree of difference between comparable individuals or classes **3 :** an arrangement of gears in an automobile that allows one of the driving wheels to turn (as in going around a curve) faster than the other

differential calculus *n* : a branch of mathematics concerned chiefly with the study of the rate of change of functions with respect to their variables especially through the use of derivatives and differentials — compare INTEGRAL CALCULUS

differential gear *n* : DIFFERENTIAL 3

dif·fer·en·ti·ate \ˌdif-ə-ˈren-chē-ˌāt\ *vb* **1 :** to obtain the mathematical derivative of ⟨*differentiate* the function⟩ **2 :** to make or become different in some way ⟨the color of their eyes *differentiates* the twins⟩ **3 :** to undergo or cause differentiation in the course of development **4 :** to recognize or state the difference or differences ⟨*differentiate* between two plants⟩

dif·fer·en·ti·a·tion \-ˌren-chē-ˈā-shən\ *n* **1 :** the act or process of differentiating **2 :** development from the one to the many, the simple to the complex, or the homogeneous to the heterogeneous **3 :** the developmental processes by which cells, tissues, and structures attain their specialized adult form and function; *also* : the result of these processes

dif·fer·ent·ly \ˈdif-ərnt-lē, ˈdif-rənt-, -ə-rənt-\ *adv* **1 :** in a different manner ⟨they talk *differently* from us⟩ **2 :** to the contrary ⟨thought they would win but learned *differently*⟩

dif·fi·cult \ˈdif-i-ˌkəlt, -kəlt\ *adj* **1 :** hard to do, make, or carry out ⟨a *difficult* climb⟩ **2 a :** hard to deal with, manage, or overcome ⟨a *difficult* child⟩ **b :** hard to understand ⟨*difficult* reading⟩ [back-formation from *difficulty*] — **dif·fi·cult·ly** *adv*

dif·fi·cul·ty \-ˌkəl-tē, -kəl-\ *n, pl* **-ties** **1 :** the quality or state of being difficult ⟨the *difficulty* of the climb⟩ **2 :** great effort ⟨accomplish a task with *difficulty*⟩ **3 :** a disagreement in opinion ⟨the partners ironed out their *difficulties*⟩ **4 :** something difficult ⟨overcame great *difficulties*⟩ **5 :** a difficult or distressing situation : TROUBLE ⟨in financial *difficulties*⟩ [Latin *difficultas,* from *difficilis* "difficult," from *dis-* + *facilis* "easy"]

dif·fi·dent \-əd-ənt, -ə-ˌdent\ *adj* **1 :** lacking confidence : TIMID **2 :** RESERVED 1, UNASSERTIVE [Latin *diffidens,* present participle of *diffidere* "to distrust," from *dis-* + *fidere* "to trust"] — **dif·fi·dence** \-əd-əns, -ə-ˌdens\ *n* — **dif·fi·dent·ly** *adv*

dif·fract \dif-ˈrakt\ *vt* : to cause to undergo diffraction ⟨*diffract* light⟩ [back-formation from *diffraction*]

dif·frac·tion \dif-ˈrak-shən\ *n* : a modification which light undergoes especially in passing by the edges of opaque bodies or through narrow slits and in which the rays appear to be deflected and typically produce a series of parallel light and dark or colored bands; *also* : a similar modification of other waves [New Latin *diffractio,* from Latin *diffringere* "to break apart," from *dis-* + *frangere* "to break"]

diffraction grating *n* : GRATING 2

[1]**dif·fuse** \dif-ˈyüs\ *adj* **1 :** poured or spread out : SCATTERED **2 :** marked by wordiness : VERBOSE ⟨a *diffuse* writer⟩ [Latin *diffusus,* past participle of *diffundere* "to spread out," from *dis-* + *fundere* "to pour"] — **dif·fuse·ly** *adv* — **dif·fuse·ness** *n*

[2]**dif·fuse** \dif-ˈyüz\ *vb* **1 :** to pour out and spread freely **2 :** to subject to or undergo diffusion — **dif·fus·er** \-ˈyü-zər\ *n*

dif·fus·ible \dif-ˈyü-zə-bəl\ *adj* : capable of diffusing or of being diffused

dif·fu·sion \dif-ˈyü-zhən\ *n* **1 :** a diffusing or a being diffused; *also* : the state of being diffused **2 :** the intermingling of the particles of liquids, gases, or solids as a result of their spontaneous movement so that in dissolved substances they move from a region of higher to one of lower concentration **3 :** the scattering of light from a rough surface or by passage through a translucent material (as frosted glass) — **dif·fu·sion·al** \-ˈyüzh-nəl, -ˈyü-zhən-l\ *adj*

dif·fu·sive \dif-ˈyü-siv, -ziv\ *adj* : tending to diffuse : characterized by diffusion — **dif·fu·sive·ly** *adv* — **dif·fu·sive·ness** *n*

[1]**dig** \ˈdig\ *vb* **dug** \ˈdəg\; **dig·ging** **1 a :** to turn up the soil (as with a spade) **b :** to hollow out or form by removing earth ⟨*dig* a hole⟩ ⟨*dig* a cellar⟩ **2 :** to uncover or seek by or as if by turning up earth ⟨*dig* potatoes⟩ ⟨*dig* for gold⟩ ⟨*dig* through books for information⟩ **3 :** to bring to light : DISCOVER ⟨*dig* up information⟩ **4 :** JAB ⟨*dig* a person in the ribs⟩ **5 :** to work hard **6 a :** to pay attention to : NOTICE ⟨*dig* those shoes⟩ **b :** UNDERSTAND 1, GRASP ⟨you *dig* me?⟩ **c :** LIKE 1 ⟨really *digs* music⟩ [Middle English *diggen*] — **dig·ger** *n*

[2]**dig** *n* **1 :** POKE 1 **2 :** a cutting remark **3 :** a place where an excavation is made for ancient relics; *also* : the excavation itself

[1]**di·gest** \ˈdī-ˌjest\ *n* : a summary or condensation of a body of information or of a literary work ⟨a *digest* of the laws⟩ [Latin *digesta* "systematic arrangement of laws," from *digerere* "to distribute, arrange, digest," from *dis-* + *gerere* "to carry"]

[2]**di·gest** \dī-ˈjest, də-\ *vb* **1 :** to think over and arrange in the mind : take in mentally **2 :** to convert food into simpler forms that can be taken in and used by the body **3 :** to soften or decompose or to extract soluble ingredients from by heat and moisture or chemical action **4 :** to condense into a short summary **5 :** to become digested — **di·gest·er** *n* — **di·gest·ible** \-ˈjes-tə-bəl\ *adj* — **di·gest·ibil·i·ty** \-ˌjes-tə-ˈbil-ət-ē\ *n*

di·ges·tion \dī-ˈjes-chən, də-, -ˈjesh-\ *n* : the process by which food is broken down into simpler forms in the body by mechanical and enzymatic means

[1]**di·ges·tive** \-ˈjes-tiv\ *n* : something that aids digestion

[2]**digestive** *adj* **1 :** of or relating to digestion ⟨*digestive* processes⟩ **2 :** having the power to cause or promote digestion ⟨*digestive* enzymes⟩ — **di·ges·tive·ly** *adv*

digestive system *n* : the bodily system concerned with the intake, breakdown, and absorption of food and the discharge of wastes and that includes the mouth, pharynx, esophagus, stomach, intestine, anus, and glands (as the salivary glands)

digger wasp *n* : a burrowing wasp; *esp* : one that digs nest burrows in the soil and provisions them with insects or spiders paralyzed by stinging

dig·gings \ˈdig-ingz\ *n pl* **1 :** a place where ore, metals, or precious stones are dug **2 :** LODGING 2

dight \ˈdīt\ *vt* **dight·ed** *or* **dight; dight·ing** *archaic* : DRESS, ADORN [Old English *dihtan* "to arrange, compose," from Latin *dictare* "to dictate, compose"]

dig in *vi* **1 :** to dig and take position in defensive trenches **2 :** to go to work **3 :** to begin eating

dig·it \ˈdij-ət\ *n* **1 a :** any of the arabic numerals 1 to 9 and usually the symbol 0 **b :** one of the elements that combine to form numbers in a system other than the decimal system **2 :** a finger or toe [Latin *digitus* "finger, toe"]

dig·i·tal \ˈdij-ət-l\ *adj* **1 :** of or relating to the fingers or toes **2 :** done with a finger **3 :** of, relating to, or using calculation by numerical methods or by discrete units **4 :** of or relating to data in the form of numerical digits ⟨*digital* images⟩ ⟨*digital* broadcasting⟩ **5 :** providing a readout in numerical digits ⟨a *digital* watch⟩ **6 :** relating to an audio recording method in which sound waves are represented digitally (as on magnetic tape) **7 :** characterized by electronic and computerized technology ⟨the *digital* age⟩ — **dig·i·tal·ly** \-l-ē\ *adv*

digital camera *n* : a camera that records images as digital data instead of on film

digital computer *n* : a computer that operates with numbers in the form of digits — compare ANALOG COMPUTER

dig·i·tal·is \ˌdij-ə-ˈtal-əs\ *n* **1 :** FOXGLOVE **2 :** a powerful drug used as a heart stimulant and prepared from the dried leaves of the common foxglove [Latin, "of a finger," from *digitus* "finger, toe"; from its finger-shaped corolla]

digital versatile disc *n* : DVD

digital video disc *n* : DVD

dig·i·tate \ˈdij-ə-ˌtāt\ *adj* : having divisions arranged like those of a bird's foot ⟨*digitate* leaves⟩

dig·i·ti·grade \ˈdij-ət-ə-ˌgrād\ *adj* : walking on the toes with the back part of the foot raised [French, from Latin *digitus* "finger, toe" + *gradi* "to step, go"]

dig·i·tize \ˈdij-ə-ˌtīz\ *vt* : to convert (as data or an image) to digital form — **dig·i·tiz·er** *n*

dig·ni·fied \ˈdig-nə-ˌfīd\ *adj* : showing or expressing dignity

dig·ni·fy \-ˌfī\ *vt* **-fied; -fy·ing** : to give dignity or distinction to : HONOR [Medieval French *dignifier,* from Late Latin *dignificare,* from Latin *dignus* "worthy"]

dig·ni·tary \ˈdig-nə-ˌter-ē\ *n, pl* **-tar·ies** : a person of high position or honor ⟨*dignitaries* of the church⟩

dig·ni·ty \ˈdig-nət-ē\ *n, pl* **-ties** **1** : the quality or state of being worthy, honored, or esteemed **2** : high rank, office, or position **3** : formal reserve of manner or language [Medieval French *digneté,* from Latin *dignitas,* from *dignus* "worthy"] ***synonyms*** see DECORUM

di·graph \ˈdī-ˌgraf\ *n* : a group of two successive letters representing a single sound or a complex sound which is not a combination of the sounds ordinarily represented by each in other occurrences ⟨*ea* in *bread* and *ch* in *chin* are *digraphs*⟩ — **di·graph·ic** \dī-ˈgraf-ik\ *adj*

di·gress \dī-ˈgres, də-\ *vi* : to turn aside especially from the main subject in writing or speaking [Latin *digressus,* past participle of *digredi* "to go off, digress," from *dis-* + *gradi* "to step, go"] — **di·gres·sion** \-ˈgresh-ən\ *n*

di·gres·sive \-ˈgres-iv\ *adj* : characterized by digressions ⟨a *digressive* book⟩ — **di·gres·sive·ly** *adv* — **di·gres·sive·ness** *n*

di·he·dral angle \dī-ˈhē-drəl-\ *n* : the figure formed by two intersecting planes

di·hy·brid \dī-ˈhī-brəd, ˈdī-\ *adj* : heterozygous with respect to two pairs of genes — **dihybrid** *n*

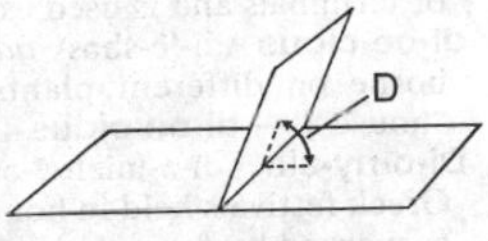

D dihedral angle

[1]dike \ˈdīk\ *n* **1** : an artificial watercourse : DITCH **2** : a bank of earth constructed to control or confine water : LEVEE **3** : a long usually vertical body of igneous rock that has been forced while molten into a fissure [Middle English, probably from Old Norse *dīk* "ditch" and Middle Low German *dīk* "dam"]

[2]dike *vt* **1** : to surround or protect with a dike **2** : to drain by a dike — **dik·er** *n*

di·lap·i·dat·ed \də-ˈlap-ə-ˌdāt-əd\ *adj* : partly ruined or decayed especially through neglect or misuse ⟨a *dilapidated* old house⟩ [Latin *dilapidare* "to squander, destroy," from *dis-* + *lapidare* "to pelt with stones," from *lapis* "stone"]

di·lap·i·da·tion \də-ˌlap-ə-ˈdā-shən\ *n* : partial ruin (as from neglect)

di·la·ta·tion \ˌdil-ə-ˈtā-shən, ˌdī-lə-\ *n* **1** : the condition of being stretched beyond normal dimensions especially as a result of overwork or disease ⟨*dilatation* of the heart⟩ **2** : DILATION 2 **3** : a dilated part or formation — **di·la·ta·tion·al** \-shnəl, -shən-l\ *adj*

di·late \dī-ˈlāt, ˈdī-ˌ\ *vb* : to make or grow larger or wider ⟨eyes *dilated* with fear⟩ ⟨lungs *dilated* with air⟩ [Medieval French *dilater,* from Latin *dilatare,* literally, "to spread wide," from *dis-* + *latus* "wide"] ***synonyms*** see EXPAND — **di·lat·able** \dī-ˈlāt-ə-bəl\ *adj* — **di·la·tor** \dī-ˈlāt-ər, ˈdī-ˌ\ *n*

di·la·tion \dī-ˈlā-shən\ *n* **1** : the act of dilating : the state of being dilated : EXPANSION ⟨*dilation* of the pupils of the eyes⟩ **2** : the action of stretching or enlarging an organ or part of the body

dil·a·to·ry \ˈdil-ə-ˌtōr-ē, -ˌtȯr-\ *adj* **1** : tending or intended to cause delay ⟨*dilatory* tactics⟩ **2** : characterized by dawdling or delay ⟨*dilatory* in paying her bills⟩ [Late Latin *dilatorius,* from Latin *differre* (past participle *dilatus*) "to postpone, differ," from *dis-* + *ferre* "to carry"] — **dil·a·to·ri·ly** \ˌdil-ə-ˈtōr-ə-lē, -ˈtȯr-\ *adv* — **dil·a·to·ri·ness** \ˈdil-ə-ˌtōr-ē-nəs, -ˌtȯr-\ *n*

di·lem·ma \də-ˈlem-ə *also* dī-\ *n* : a choice or a situation in which one has to choose between two or more things, ways, or plans that are equally unsatisfactory : a difficult choice [Late Latin, from Late Greek *dilēmma,* from Greek *di-* + *lēmma* "assumption"] ***synonyms*** see PREDICAMENT

dil·et·tante \ˈdil-ə-ˌtänt, -ˌtant; ˌdil-ə-ˈ; -ˈtänt-ē, -ˈtant-ē\ *n, pl* **-tantes** *or* **-tan·ti** \-ˈtänt-ē, -ˈtant-ē\ **1** : an admirer or lover of the arts **2** : a person who engages usually superficially in an art or branch of knowledge as a pastime [Italian, from *dilettare* "to delight," from Latin *dilectare*] — **dilettante** *adj* — **dil·et·tan·tism** \-ˌtän-ˌtiz-əm, -ˌtan-, -ˈtän-, -ˈtan-\ *n*

[1]dil·i·gence \ˈdil-ə-jəns\ *n* : careful and continued work : conscientious effort : INDUSTRY

[2]dil·i·gence \ˈdil-ə-ˌzhäⁿs, ˈdil-ə-jəns\ *n* : STAGECOACH [French, "industry, haste, stagecoach"]

dil·i·gent \ˈdil-ə-jənt\ *adj* : characterized by steady, earnest, and energetic application and effort : PAINSTAKING ⟨a *diligent* worker⟩ ⟨a *diligent* search⟩ [Medieval French, from Latin *diligens,* from *diligere* "to esteem, love," from *di-* (from *dis-* "apart") + *legere* "to select"] ***synonyms*** see BUSY — **dil·i·gent·ly** *adv*

dill \ˈdil\ *n* : any of several plants related to the carrot; *esp* : a European herb with aromatic foliage and seeds used in flavoring foods and especially pickles [Old English *dile*]

dill pickle *n* : a pickle seasoned with dill

dil·ly·dal·ly \ˈdil-ē-ˌdal-ē\ *vi* : to waste time by loitering or delay : DAWDLE ⟨*dillydallied* too long before making a decision⟩ [reduplication of *dally*]

dil·u·ent \ˈdil-yə-wənt\ *n* : a diluting agent

[1]di·lute \dī-ˈlüt, də-\ *vt* **1** : to make more liquid by admixture (as with water) ⟨*dilute* the thickened paint⟩ **2** : to lessen the strength, flavor, or quality of by admixture ⟨*dilute* a medicine⟩ [Latin *diluere* "to wash away, dilute," from *dis-* + *lavere* "to wash"] — **di·lut·er** *or* **di·lu·tor** *n*

[2]dilute *adj* : that has been diluted ⟨a *dilute* acid⟩ — **di·lute·ness** *n*

di·lu·tion \dī-ˈlü-shən, də-\ *n* **1** : the action of diluting : the state of being diluted **2** : something (as a solution) that is diluted

di·lu·vi·al \də-ˈlü-vē-əl, dī-\ *or* **di·lu·vi·an** \-vē-ən\ *adj* : of, relating to, or brought about by a flood [Latin *diluvium* "deluge"]

[1]dim \ˈdim\ *adj* **dim·mer; dim·mest** **1** : not bright or distinct : OBSCURE, FAINT ⟨a *dim* light⟩ **2** : being without luster : DULL ⟨*dim* colors⟩ **3 a** : not seen or understood clearly ⟨had only a *dim* notion of what was going on⟩ **b** : characterized by a skeptical or unfavorable attitude ⟨took a *dim* view of the proceedings⟩ **4** : not seeing or understanding clearly ⟨*dim* eyes⟩ [Old English] — **dim·ly** *adv* — **dim·ness** *n*

[2]dim *vb* **dimmed; dim·ming** **1** : to make or become dim **2** : to reduce the light from

dime \ˈdīm\ *n* : a United States coin worth 1/10 dollar [Medieval French, "tenth part," from Latin *decima,* from *decimus* "tenth," from *decem* "ten"] — **a dime a dozen** : so plentiful or commonplace as to be of little value

[1]di·men·sion \də-ˈmen-chən *also* dī-\ *n* **1 a** : measure in one direction; *esp* : one of three coordinates determining a position in space or four coordinates determining a position in space and time **b** : measure of extension in one direction or in all directions **2** : the range over which something extends : SCOPE — usually used in plural [Medieval French, from Latin *dimensio* "measurement, dimension," from *dimetiri* "to measure out," from *dis-* + *metiri* "to measure"] — **di·men·sion·al** \-ˈmench-nəl, -ˈmen-chən-l\ *adj* — **di·men·sion·al·i·ty** \-ˌmen-chə-ˈnal-ət-ē\ *n* — **di·men·sion·al·ly** \-ˈmench-nə-lē, -ˈmen-chən-l-ē\ *adv* — **di·men·sion·less** \-ˈmen-chən-ləs\ *adj*

[2]dimension *vt* **1** : to form to the required dimensions **2** : to indicate the dimensions of (as on a drawing)

dime store *n* : a store that sells mainly inexpensive goods

dim·e·ter \ˈdim-ət-ər\ *n* : a line of verse consisting of two metrical feet [Late Latin, from Greek *dimetros* "being a dimeter," from *di-* + *metron* "measure"]

di·min·ish \də-ˈmin-ish\ *vb* **1** : to make less or cause to appear less **2** : to lessen the authority, dignity, or reputation of : BELITTLE **3** : to become gradually less (as in size or importance) : DWINDLE ⟨interest in the project was *diminishing*⟩ [Middle English *deminishen,* alteration of *diminuen,* from Medieval French *diminuer,* derived from Latin *deminuere,* from *de-* + *minuere* "to lessen"] ***synonyms*** see DECREASE — **di·min·ish·able** \-ish-ə-bəl\ *adj* — **di·min·ish·ment** \-ish-mənt\ *n*

di·min·ished *adj* : made one half step less than perfect or minor ⟨the musical interval of a *diminished* fifth⟩

di·min·u·en·do \də-ˌmin-yə-ˈwen-dō, -ˌmin-ə-\ *adv or adj* : DECRESCENDO [Italian, literally, "diminishing," derived from Latin *deminuere* "to diminish"] — **diminuendo** *n*

dim·i·nu·tion \ˌdim-ə-ˈnü-shən, -ˈnyü-\ *n* : the act, process, or an instance of diminishing : DECREASE

[1]di·min·u·tive \də-ˈmin-yət-iv\ *n* **1** : a diminutive word, name, or affix **2** : a diminutive individual

[2]diminutive *adj* **1** : indicating small size and sometimes the state or quality of being lovable, pitiable, or contemptible ⟨the *diminutive* suffixes *-ette* and *-ling*⟩ ⟨the *diminutive* nouns *kitchenette* and *duckling*⟩ **2** : extremely small : TINY — **di·min·u·tive·ly** *adv* — **di·min·u·tive·ness** *n*

dim·i·ty \ˈdim-ət-ē\ *n, pl* **-ties** : a sheer usually corded cotton

\ə\ **abut**	\au̇\ **out**	\i\ **tip**	\ȯ\ **saw**	\u̇\ **foot**
\ər\ **further**	\ch\ **chin**	\ī\ **life**	\ȯi\ **coin**	\y\ **yet**
\a\ **mat**	\e\ **pet**	\j\ **job**	\th\ **thin**	\yü\ **few**
\ā\ **take**	\ē\ **easy**	\ng\ **sing**	\t͟h\ **this**	\yu̇\ **cure**
\ä\ **cot, cart**	\g\ **go**	\ō\ **bone**	\ü\ **food**	\zh\ **vision**

fabric of plain weave in checks or stripes [Middle English *demyt,* from Medieval Latin *dimitum,* from Middle Greek *dimitos* "of two threads"]

dim·mer \'dim-ər\ *n* **1 :** a device for regulating the intensity of an electric lighting unit **2 :** LOW BEAM

di·mor·phic \dī-'mȯr-fik\ *adj* **1 :** DIMORPHOUS 1 **2 :** occuring in two distinct forms ⟨a *dimorphic* butterfly⟩

di·mor·phism \-ˌfiz-əm\ *n* **:** the condition or property of being dimorphic or dimorphous; *esp* **:** occurrence of individuals of a species in two distinguishable forms (as of color or size) ⟨sexual *dimorphism* in birds⟩

di·mor·phous \-fəs\ *adj* **1 :** crystallizing in two distinct forms **2 :** DIMORPHIC 2

[1]**dim·ple** \'dim-pəl\ *n* **1 :** a slight natural indentation in the surface of some part of the human body (as the chin) **2 :** a slight hollow ⟨*dimples* on a golf ball⟩ [Middle English *dympull*]

[2]**dimple** *vb* **dim·pled; dim·pling** \-pə-ling, -pling\ **:** to mark with or form dimples ⟨you *dimple* when you smile⟩

dim sum \'dim-'səm\ *n* **:** traditional Chinese food consisting of a variety of items (as dumplings, pieces of chicken, and meat-filled buns) served in small portions [Chinese (dialect of Guangzhou & Hong Kong) *dímsām,* from *dím* "dot, speck" + *sām* "heart, center"]

[1]**din** \'din\ *n* **:** a loud noise; *esp* **:** a jumble of confused or discordant sounds [Old English *dyne*]

[2]**din** *vb* **dinned; din·ning 1 a :** to make a loud noise **b :** to deafen with loud noise **2 :** to impress by insistent repetition ⟨*dinning* the lesson into their heads⟩

di·nar \di-'när, 'dē-ˌ\ *n* **1 :** a gold coin formerly used in countries of southwest Asia and north Africa **2 a :** a basic monetary unit (as of Bahrain, Jordan, and Kuwait) **b :** a coin or note representing one dinar **3 :** an Irani monetary unit equal to 1/100 rial [Arabic *dīnār,* from Greek *dēnarion* "denarius," from Latin *denarius*]

dine \'dīn\ *vb* **1 :** to eat dinner **2 :** to give a dinner to **:** FEED ⟨wined and *dined* their friends⟩ [Medieval French *disner, diner,* derived from Latin *dis-* + *jejunus* "fasting"]

din·er \'dī-nər\ *n* **1 :** one that dines **2 a :** DINING CAR **b :** a restaurant usually in the shape of a railroad car

di·nette \dī-'net\ *n* **:** a small space usually off a kitchen used for dining

ding \'ding\ *vi* **:** to make a ringing sound [imitative]

ding–dong \'ding-ˌdȯng, -ˌdäng\ *n* **:** the sound of repeated strokes especially on a bell [imitative]

din·ghy \'ding-ē, -gē\ *n, pl* **dinghies 1 :** an East Indian rowboat or sailboat **2 a :** a small boat carried on or towed behind a larger boat as a tender or a lifeboat **b :** a small sailboat **3 :** a rubber life raft [Bengali *ḍiṅgi* and Hindi & Urdu *ḍiṅgī*]

din·gle \'ding-gəl\ *n* **:** a small narrow wooded valley [Middle English, "abyss"]

din·go \'ding-ˌgō\ *n, pl* **dingoes :** a reddish brown bushy-tailed wild dog of Australia [from Dharuk (an indigenous language of Australia)]

dingo

din·gus \'ding-gəs, -əs\ *n* **:** something whose common name is unknown or forgotten **:** THINGAMAJIG [Dutch *dinges*]

din·gy \'din-jē\ *adj* **din·gi·er; -est :** not fresh or clean **:** GRIMY ⟨a *dingy* room⟩ [origin unknown] — **din·gi·ly** \-jə-lē\ *adv* — **din·gi·ness** \-jē-nəs\ *n*

dining car *n* **:** a railroad car in which meals are served

dining room *n* **:** a room used for eating meals

din·key *or* **din·ky** \'ding-kē\ *n, pl* **dinkeys** *or* **dinkies :** a small locomotive used especially for hauling freight, logging, and shunting [probably from *dinky* "small"]

din·ky \'ding-kē\ *adj* **din·ki·er; -est :** overly or unattractively small ⟨a *dinky* two-room apartment⟩ [Scottish *dink* "neat"]

din·ner \'din-ər\ *n* **1 a :** the main meal of the day **b :** the food provided for a dinner **2 :** a formal banquet [Medieval French *diner,* from *disner, diner* "to dine"]

dinner jacket *n* **:** a jacket for formal evening wear

din·ner·time \'din-ər-ˌtīm\ *n* **:** the customary time for dinner

din·ner·ware \'din-ər-ˌwaər, -ˌweər\ *n* **:** utensils (as dishes and glasses) used at the dinner table

di·no·flag·el·late \ˌdī-nō-'flaj-ə-lət, -ˌlāt\ *n* **:** any of an order (Dinoflagellata) of chiefly marine unicellular floating organisms that resemble both algae and protozoa and are important in marine food chains [Greek *dinos* "rotation, eddy"]

di·no·saur \'dī-nə-ˌsȯr\ *n* **:** any of a group (Dinosauria) of extinct often very large chiefly land-dwelling long-tailed reptiles of the Mesozoic era [Greek *deinos* "terrible" + *sauros* "lizard"] — **di·no·sau·ri·an** \ˌdī-nə-'sȯr-ē-ən\ *adj or n*

[1]**dint** \'dint\ *n* **1 :** FORCE, POWER — used chiefly in the phrase *by dint of* ⟨succeeded by *dint* of hardwork⟩ **2 :** a mark left by a blow **:** DENT [Old English *dynt*]

[2]**dint** *vt* **:** DENT 1

di·oc·e·san \dī-'äs-ə-sən\ *n* **:** a bishop having jurisdiction over a diocese

di·o·cese \'dī-ə-səs, -ˌsēz, -ˌsēs\ *n, pl* **di·o·ces·es** \-sə-səz, -ˌsē-zəz, -ˌsē-səz; 'dī-ə-ˌsēz\ **:** the district over which a bishop has authority [Medieval French *diocise,* derived from Greek *dioikēsis* "administration, administrative division," from *dioikein* "to keep house, govern," from *dia-* + *oikein* "to dwell, manage," from *oikos* "house"] — **di·oc·e·san** \dī-'äs-ə-sən\ *adj*

di·ode \'dī-ˌōd\ *n* **:** an electronic device that has two electrodes or terminals and is used especially as a rectifier

di·oe·cious \dī-'ē-shəs\ *adj* **:** having male and female flowers borne on different plants [derived from Greek *di-* + *oikos* "house"] — **di·oe·cious·ly** *adv* — **di·oe·cism** \-'ē-ˌsiz-əm\ *n*

Di·o·ny·sia \ˌdī-ə-'nizh-ē-ə, -'niz-, -'nish-, -'nis-\ *n pl* **:** ancient Greek festivals held in honor of Dionysus; *esp* **:** such observances marked by dramatic performances

di·o·rama \ˌdī-ə-'ram-ə, -'räm-\ *n* **:** a scenic representation in which a partly transparent painting is seen from a distance through an opening or in which lifelike sculptured figures and surrounding details are displayed against a painted background [French, from *dia-* "dia-" + *-orama* (as in *panorama,* from English)]

di·o·rite \'dī-ə-ˌrīt\ *n* **:** a granular crystalline igneous rock [French, from Greek *diorizein* "to distinguish," from *dia-* + *horizein* "to define"]

di·ox·ide \dī-'äk-ˌsīd\ *n* **:** an oxide containing two atoms of oxygen in the molecule

di·ox·in \dī-'äk-sin\ *n* **:** any of several toxic compounds of carbon, hydrogen, and usually chlorine and oxygen that occur especially as by-products of various industrial processes and waste incineration

[1]**dip** \'dip\ *vb* **dipped; dip·ping 1 a :** to plunge momentarily or partially under the surface (as of a liquid) so as to moisten, cool, or coat **b :** to thrust in a way to suggest immersion **2 :** to lift a portion of by reaching below the surface with something shaped to hold liquid **:** LADLE ⟨*dip* water from a pail⟩ **3 :** to lower and then raise again ⟨*dip* a flag in salute⟩ **4 a :** to plunge into a liquid and quickly emerge ⟨oars *dipping* rhythmically⟩ **b :** to immerse something for treatment into a liquid preparation **5 a :** to suddenly drop down or out of sight ⟨the road *dipped* below the crest⟩ **b :** to decrease moderately and usually temporarily ⟨prices *dipped*⟩ **6 :** to reach down inside or as if inside or below a surface especially to withdraw a part of the contents ⟨*dipped* into their savings⟩ **7 :** to examine or read something casually or tentatively ⟨*dip* into a book⟩ [Old English *dyppan*]

[2]**dip** *n* **1 :** an act of dipping; *esp* **:** a brief plunge into the water for sport or exercise **2 a :** inclination downward **b :** a sharp or slight downward course **:** DROP ⟨a *dip* in prices⟩ **3 :** the angle formed with the horizon by a magnetic needle free to rotate in a vertical plane **4 :** something obtained by or used in dipping ⟨a *dip* of ice cream⟩ **5 a :** a sauce or soft mixture into which food (as raw vegetables) may be dipped **b :** a liquid preparation into which something may be dipped (as for cleansing or coloring) ⟨an insecticidal sheep *dip*⟩

di·pep·tide \dī-'pep-ˌtīd\ *n* **:** a peptide composed of two molecules of amino acid

di·phos·pho·gly·cer·ic acid \dī-'fäs-fō-glis-ˌer-ik-\ *n* **:** a phosphate of glyceric acid that is important in photosynthesis and in glycolysis and fermentation

diph·the·ria \dif-'thir-ē-ə, dip-\ *n* **:** a contagious bacterial disease with fever in which the air passages become coated with a membranous layer that often obstructs breathing [French *diphthérie,* from Greek *diphthera* "leather"; from the toughness of the membranous layer] — **diph·the·rit·ic** \ˌdif-thə-'rit-ik, ˌdip-\ *adj*

diph·thong \'dif-ˌthȯng, 'dip-\ *n* **1 :** a 2-element speech sound that begins with the tongue position for one vowel and ends with the tongue position for another all within one syllable ⟨the sounds of *ou* in *out* and of *oy* in *boy* are *diphthongs*⟩ **2 :** DIGRAPH [Medieval French *diptongue,* from Late Latin *diphthongus,* from Greek *diphthongos,* from *di-* + *phthongos* "voice, sound"] — **diph·thon·gal** \dif-ˈthȯŋ-gəl, dip-, -gəl\ *adj*

diph·thong·ize \-ˌthȯŋ-ˌīz\ *vb* **:** to change into or pronounce as a diphthong — **diph·thong·i·za·tion** \ˌdif-thȯŋ-ə-ˈzā-shən, ˌdip-\ *n*

dipl- *or* **diplo-** *combining form* **:** double **:** twofold ⟨*diploid*⟩ [Greek *diploos,* from *di-* + *-ploos* "-fold"]

dip·lo·blas·tic \ˌdip-lō-ˈblas-tik\ *adj* **:** being an embryo or an invertebrate (as a hydra or a sponge) that has only two germ layers and lacks a true mesoderm

dip·lo·coc·cus \ˌdip-lō-ˈkäk-əs\ *n, pl* **-coc·ci** \-ˈkäk-ˌsī, -ˌī, -ˌsē, -ˌē\ **:** any of various parasitic bacteria that occur usually in pairs in a capsule and include serious disease-causing agents

di·plod·o·cus \də-ˈpläd-ə-kəs, dī-\ *n* **:** any of a genus of very large plant-eating dinosaurs known from fossils found in several western U.S. states [Greek *dipl-* + *dokos* "beam"]

dip·loid \ˈdip-ˌlȯid\ *adj* **:** having two haploid sets of homologous chromosomes ⟨a *diploid* cell⟩ — **diploid** *n* — **dip·loi·dy** \-ˌlȯid-ē\ *n*

di·plo·ma \də-ˈplō-mə\ *n* **1 :** a document conferring a privilege or honor **2 :** an official paper bearing record of graduation from or of a degree conferred by an educational institution [Latin, "passport, diploma," from Greek *diplōma* "folded paper, passport," from *diploun* "to double," from *diploos* "double"]

di·plo·ma·cy \də-ˈplō-mə-sē\ *n* **1 :** the art and practice of conducting negotiations between nations **2 :** skill in handling affairs without arousing hostility **:** TACT

dip·lo·mat \ˈdip-lə-ˌmat\ *n* **:** a person employed or skilled in diplomacy

dip·lo·mat·ic \ˌdip-lə-ˈmat-ik\ *adj* **1 :** of, relating to, or concerned with diplomacy or diplomats ⟨*diplomatic* relations⟩ **2 :** TACTFUL ⟨found a *diplomatic* way to say it⟩ [French *diplomatique* "connected with documents regulating international relations," derived from Latin *diploma* "document, diploma"] — **dip·lo·mat·i·cal·ly** \-ˈmat-i-kə-lē, -klē\ *adv*

di·plo·ma·tist \də-ˈplō-mət-əst\ *n* **:** DIPLOMAT

dip·lo·pod \ˈdip-lə-ˌpäd\ *n* **:** MILLIPEDE [derived from Greek *dipl-* + *pod-, pous* "foot"]

dip net *n* **:** a small bag-shaped net with a handle that is used especially to scoop small fish from the water

di·pole \ˈdī-ˌpōl\ *n* **1 a :** a pair of equal and opposite electric charges or magnetic poles of opposite sign separated by a small distance **b :** a body (as a molecule) having such charges or poles **2 :** a radio antenna consisting of two horizontal rods in line with each other with their ends slightly separated — **di·polar** \dī-ˈpō-lər, ˈdī-\ *adj*

dip·per \ˈdip-ər\ *n* **1 :** one that dips; *esp* **:** something (as a long-handled cup) used for dipping **2 :** any of several birds that dive into streams in search of food — called also *water ouzel* **3** *cap* **a :** the seven principal stars in the constellation of Ursa Major arranged in a form resembling a dipper — called also *Big Dipper* **b :** the seven principal stars in Ursa Minor similarly arranged with the North Star forming the outer end of the handle — called also *Little Dipper*

dipper 1

dip·so·ma·nia \ˌdip-sə-ˈmā-nē-ə, -nyə\ *n* **:** an uncontrollable craving for alcoholic liquors [Greek *dipsa* "thirst"] — **dip·so·ma·ni·ac** \-nē-ˌak\ *n* — **dip·so·ma·ni·a·cal** \ˌdip-sō-mə-ˈnī-ə-kəl\ *adj*

dip·stick \ˈdip-ˌstik\ *n* **:** a graduated rod for indicating depth (as of oil in a crankcase)

dip·tera \ˈdip-tə-rə\ *n pl* **:** insects that are two-winged flies

dip·ter·an \ˈdip-tə-rən\ *adj* **:** of, relating to, or being a two-winged fly — **dipteran** *n*

dip·ter·ous \-rəs\ *adj* **:** DIPTERAN [Greek *dipteros* "two-winged," from *di-* + *pteron* "wing"]

dip·tych \ˈdip-tik\ *n* **1 :** a picture or series of pictures (as an altarpiece) painted on two hinged tablets **2 :** a work made up of two matching parts [derived from Greek *di-* + *ptychē* "fold"]

dire \ˈdīr\ *adj* **1 :** exciting horror **:** DREADFUL ⟨*dire* suffering⟩ **2 :** warning of disaster ⟨a *dire* forecast⟩ **3 :** EXTREME ⟨*dire* poverty⟩ ⟨*dire* need⟩ [Latin *dirus*] — **dire·ly** *adv* — **dire·ness** *n*

[1]**di·rect** \də-ˈrekt, dī-\ *vt* **1 :** to mark with a name and address ⟨*direct* a letter⟩ **2 :** to cause to turn, move, or point or to follow a straight course **3 :** to point, extend, or project in a specified line, course, or direction **4 :** to show or point out the way for **5 a :** to regulate the activities or course of ⟨*directed* the project⟩ **b :** to guide the organizing, supervising, or performance of ⟨*direct* a play⟩ ⟨*direct* an orchestra⟩ **6 :** to request or instruct with authority ⟨use only as *directed*⟩ [Medieval French *directer,* from Latin *directus* "straight," from past participle of *dirigere* "to set straight, direct," from *dis-* + *regere* "to lead straight"] ***synonyms*** see COMMAND, CONDUCT

[2]**direct** *adj* **1 :** proceeding from one point to another in time or space without deviation or interruption **2 a :** stemming immediately from a source ⟨a *direct* result⟩ **b :** being or passing in a straight line of descent from parent to offspring **:** LINEAL ⟨a *direct* ancestor⟩ **3 :** NATURAL, STRAIGHTFORWARD ⟨a *direct* manner⟩ **4 :** operating without an intervening agency or step ⟨*direct* action⟩ **5 a :** effected by the action of the people or the electorate and not by representatives **b :** consisting of or reproducing the exact words of a speaker or writer ⟨a *direct* quotation⟩ — **direct** *adv* — **di·rect·ness** \-ˈrekt-nəs, -ˈrek-\ *n*

direct current *n* **:** an electric current flowing in one direction only — abbreviation *DC*

di·rect·ed *adj* **:** proceeding or measured in a direction designated as positive or negative ⟨a *directed* line segment⟩

di·rec·tion \də-ˈrek-shən, dī-\ *n* **1 :** guidance or supervision of action or conduct ⟨working under her *direction*⟩ **2 :** an authoritative instruction, indication, or order ⟨follow *directions*⟩ **3 :** the line or course along which something moves, lies, points, or is measured ⟨heading in a northerly *direction*⟩ **4 :** a course of progress or development **:** TREND ⟨a new *direction* in literature⟩ **5 :** the art and technique of directing an orchestra or a theatrical production

di·rec·tion·al \-shnəl, -shən-l\ *adj* **1 :** relating to or indicating direction in space ⟨the *directional* signal lights on an automobile⟩: **a :** suitable for sending out or receiving radio signals in one direction only ⟨a *directional* antenna⟩ **b :** operating in a particular direction ⟨a *directional* microphone⟩ **2 :** relating to direction or guidance especially of thought or effort

[1]**di·rec·tive** \də-ˈrek-tiv, dī-\ *adj* **:** serving to direct, guide, or influence ⟨the *directive* power of conscience⟩

[2]**directive** *n* **:** something that serves to direct, guide, and usually impel toward an action or goal; *esp* **:** an authoritative instruction issued by a high-level body or official

di·rec·tiv·i·ty \də-ˌrek-ˈtiv-ət-ē, ˌdī-\ *n* **:** the property of being directional

di·rect·ly \də-ˈrek-tlē, dī-, -lē, *in sense 2 also* ˈdrek-lē\ *adv* **1 a :** in a direct manner ⟨spoke *directly*⟩ **b :** most closely situated ⟨the person *directly* to my left⟩ **2 :** without delay **:** IMMEDIATELY ⟨go *directly* home⟩ **3 :** in the manner of direct variation ⟨the perimeter of a square varies *directly* with the length of a side⟩

directly proportional *adj* **:** related by direct variation ⟨our earnings are *directly proportional* to the number of magazines we sell⟩ — compare INVERSELY PROPORTIONAL

direct object *n* **:** a grammatical object representing the primary goal or the result of the action of a verb ⟨"me" in "you called me" and "house" in "we built a house" are *direct objects*⟩

di·rec·tor \də-ˈrek-tər, dī-\ *n* **:** one that directs: as **a :** the head of an organized group or administrative unit (as a school) **b :** one of a group of persons who direct the affairs of a corporation **c :** one that supervises the production of a show **d :** CONDUCTOR b — **di·rec·to·ri·al** \də-ˌrek-ˈtōr-ē-əl, ˌdī-, -ˈtȯr-\ *adj* — **di·rec·tor·ship** \də-ˈrek-tər-ˌship, dī-\ *n*

di·rec·tor·ate \də-ˈrek-tə-rət, dī-, -trət\ *n* **1 :** the office of director **2 :** a board of directors (as of a corporation)

di·rec·to·ry \-tə-rē, -trē\ *n, pl* **-ries 1 :** an alphabetical or classified list containing names and addresses **2 :** a body of directors (as of a government)

direct primary *n* **:** a primary in which nominations of candidates for office are made by direct vote

di·rec·trix \də-ˈrek-triks, dī-\ *n* **:** a straight line whose distance from any point on a conic section is in fixed ratio to the distance from the same point to the focus

direct variation *n* **1** : mathematical relationship between two variables which can be expressed by an equation in which one variable is equal to a constant times the other **2** : an equation or function expressing direct variation — compare INVERSE VARIATION

dire·ful \'dīr-fəl\ *adj* **1** : causing great fear : DREADFUL **2** : foretelling bad things to come : OMINOUS — **dire·ful·ly** \-fə-lē\ *adv*

dire wolf *n* : a large extinct wolflike mammal whose remains are found in Pleistocene deposits of North America

dirge \'dərj\ *n* : a song or hymn of grief; *esp* : one intended for funeral or memorial rites [Latin *dirige* (the first word of a Late Latin antiphon), imperative of *dirigere* "to direct"]

Word History The meaning of English *dirge* is not directly related to the meaning of the Latin word it comes from. *Dirge* and its earlier form *dirige* come from the first word of a Latin chant used in the church service for the dead: "Dirige, Domine deus meus, in conspectu tuo viam meam" (Direct, O Lord my God, my way in thy sight). The first word of the Latin chant became the English term for a song or hymn of grief.

dir·ham \'dir-həm\ *n* **1** : the basic monetary unit of Morocco and the United Arab Emirates **2** : a coin or note representing one dirham

¹di·ri·gi·ble \'dir-ə-jə-bəl, də-'rij-ə-\ *adj* : capable of being steered [Latin *dirigere* "to direct"]

²dirigible *n* : AIRSHIP

dirk \'dərk\ *n* : a long straight-bladed dagger [Scots *durk*] — **dirk** *vt*

dirndl \'dərn-dl\ *n* **1** : a dress with tight bodice and gathered skirt **2** : a full skirt with a tight waistband [short for German *Dirndlkleid,* from German dialect *Dirndl* "girl" + German *Kleid* "dress"]

dirt \'dərt\ *n* **1 a** : a filthy or soiling substance (as mud, dust, or grime) **b** : a contemptible person ⟨treated me like *dirt*⟩ **2** : loose or packed earth : SOIL ⟨a mound of *dirt*⟩ **3 a** : CORRUPTION 1c ⟨cleaned up the government's *dirt*⟩ **b** : obscene language or theme **4** : scandalous gossip ⟨spread *dirt* about him⟩ [Old Norse *drit* "excrement"]

dirt bike *n* : a lightweight motorcycle designed to be used off the road

¹dirty \'dərt-ē\ *adj* **dirt·i·er; -est** **1** : not clean : FILTHY, SOILED ⟨*dirty* clothes⟩ **2** : characterized by unfairness : DISHONORABLE ⟨a *dirty* trick⟩ **3** : OBSCENE 2a, SMUTTY ⟨*dirty* language⟩ **4** : disagreeable or objectionable but usually necessary (as in achieving a desired result) ⟨had to scrub the floor and do other *dirty* work⟩ **5** : STORMY 1 ⟨*dirty* weather⟩ **6** : not clear in color : DULL ⟨a *dirty* red⟩ **7** : conveying ill-natured resentment ⟨gave them a *dirty* look⟩ — **dirt·i·ly** \'dərt-l-ē\ *adv* — **dirt·i·ness** \'dərt-ē-nəs\ *n*

synonyms DIRTY, FILTHY, FOUL, NASTY mean conspicuously unclean or impure, literally or figuratively. DIRTY applies generally to whatever is soiled by dirt of any kind ⟨*dirty* hands⟩ or is capable of soiling ⟨*dirty* jokes⟩. FILTHY suggests offensiveness and a cluttered state ⟨*filthy* rags⟩. FOUL adds to the offensiveness an implication of rottenness or loathsomeness ⟨*foul* sewers⟩. NASTY applies to something that is unpleasant or repugnant to one who is fastidious about cleanliness, sweetness, or freshness ⟨a *nasty* smell⟩ or it may imply mere disagreeableness ⟨received a *nasty* shock⟩.

²dirty *vb* **dirt·ied; dirty·ing** **1** : to make or become dirty **2** : to stain with dishonor : SULLY

dirty rice *n* : a Cajun dish of white rice cooked with chopped or ground giblets

dis \'dis\ *vt* **dissed; dis·sing** **1** *slang* : to treat with disrespect or contempt : INSULT **2** *slang* : to find fault with : CRITICIZE [short for *disrespect*]

dis- *prefix* **1 a** : do the opposite of ⟨*dis*establish⟩ **b** : deprive of (a specified quality, rank, or object) ⟨*dis*able⟩ ⟨*dis*mast⟩ **c** : exclude or expel from ⟨*dis*bar⟩ **2** : opposite or absence of ⟨*dis*union⟩ **3** : not ⟨*dis*agreeable⟩ **4** : DYS- [Latin, literally, "apart"; sense 4 by folk etymology from *dys-*]

dis·abil·i·ty \ˌdis-ə-'bil-ət-ē\ *n, pl* **-ties** **1 a** : the condition of being disabled **b** : inability to pursue an occupation because of physical or mental impairment **2** : lack of legal qualification to do something **3** : a disqualification, restriction, or disadvantage

dis·able \dis-'ā-bəl\ *vt* **dis·abled; dis·abling** \-bə-ling, -bling\ **1** : to disqualify legally **2** : to make incapable or ineffective ⟨*disable* a computer key⟩; *esp* : to deprive of physical, moral, or intellectual strength ⟨a *disabling* illness⟩ — **dis·able·ment** \-bəl-mənt\ *n*

disabled *adj* : incapacitated by illness or injury; *also* : physically or mentally impaired in a way that limits or interferes with activity especially in relation to education or employment

dis·abuse \ˌdis-ə-'byüz\ *vt* : to free from error (as in reasoning or judgment) : UNDECEIVE ⟨*disabused* us of our misconceptions⟩ [French *désabuser,* from *dés-* "dis-" + *abuser* "to abuse"]

di·sac·cha·ride \dī-'sak-ə-ˌrīd\ *n* : any of a class of sugars (as sucrose) that yield on hydrolysis two monosaccharide molecules

¹dis·ad·van·tage \ˌdis-əd-'vant-ij\ *n* **1** : loss or damage especially to reputation or finances ⟨the deal worked to our *disadvantage*⟩ **2 a** : an unfavorable or prejudicial condition ⟨was at a *disadvantage* in educated company⟩ **b** : a cause of difficulty : HANDICAP ⟨the machine has two serious *disadvantages*⟩

²disadvantage *vt* : to place at a disadvantage : HARM

dis·ad·van·taged *adj* : lacking essentials (as standard housing or civil rights) held to be necessary for an equal position in society

dis·ad·van·ta·geous \ˌdis-ˌad-ˌvan-'tā-jəs, -vən-\ *adj* : constituting a disadvantage ⟨in a *disadvantageous* position⟩ — **dis·ad·van·ta·geous·ly** *adv* — **dis·ad·van·ta·geous·ness** *n*

dis·af·fect \ˌdis-ə-'fekt\ *vt* : to alienate the affection or loyalty of : cause discontent in ⟨the troops were *disaffected*⟩ — **dis·af·fec·tion** \ˌdis-ə-'fek-shən\ *n*

dis·agree \ˌdis-ə-'grē\ *vi* **1** : to fail to agree ⟨the two accounts *disagree*⟩ **2** : to differ in opinion ⟨*disagree* over the price⟩ **3** : to cause discomfort or distress ⟨fried foods *disagree* with me⟩

dis·agree·able \-'grē-ə-bəl\ *adj* **1** : causing discomfort : UNPLEASANT ⟨a *disagreeable* taste⟩ **2** : marked by ill temper — **dis·agree·able·ness** *n* — **dis·agree·ably** \-blē\ *adv*

dis·agree·ment \ˌdis-ə-'grē-mənt\ *n* **1** : the act of disagreeing **2 a** : the state of being different or at odds **b** : QUARREL 2

dis·al·low \ˌdis-ə-'laù\ *vt* : to refuse to admit or recognize : REJECT ⟨*disallow* a claim⟩ — **dis·al·low·ance** \-'laù-əns\ *n*

dis·ap·pear \ˌdis-ə-'piər\ *vi* **1** : to pass from view ⟨the moon *disappeared* behind a cloud⟩ **2** : to pass from existence ⟨dinosaurs *disappeared* ages ago⟩ — **dis·ap·pear·ance** \-'pir-əns\ *n*

dis·ap·point \ˌdis-ə-'pòint\ *vt* : to fail to meet the expectation or hope of ⟨the team *disappointed* its fans⟩ [Medieval French *desapointer,* from *des-* "dis-" + *appointer* "to arrange"]

dis·ap·point·ed *adj* : defeated in expectation or hope ⟨we were *disappointed* he said no⟩

dis·ap·point·ment \ˌdis-ə-'pòint-mənt\ *n* **1** : the act or an instance of disappointing : the state of being disappointed **2** : one that disappoints ⟨the play was a *disappointment*⟩

dis·ap·pro·ba·tion \ˌdis-ˌap-rə-'bā-shən\ *n* : DISAPPROVAL

dis·ap·prov·al \ˌdis-ə-'prü-vəl\ *n* **1** : the act of disapproving : the state of being disapproved ⟨frowned in *disapproval*⟩ **2** : unfavorable opinion or judgment : CENSURE ⟨the plan met with *disapproval*⟩

dis·ap·prove \-'prüv\ *vb* **1** : to pass unfavorable judgment on : CONDEMN ⟨I *disapprove* your conduct⟩ **2** : to refuse approval to : REJECT ⟨*disapproved* the architect's plans⟩ **3** : to feel or express disapproval ⟨*disapproves* of smoking⟩ — **dis·ap·prov·ing·ly** \-'prü-ving-lē\ *adv*

dis·arm \dis-'ärm\ *vb* **1** : to deprive of arms : take arms or weapons from **2** : to disband or reduce the size and strength of the armed forces of a country **3** : to make harmless, peaceable, or friendly : remove dislike or suspicion ⟨a *disarming* smile⟩ — **dis·ar·ma·ment** \-'är-mə-mənt\ *n*

dis·ar·range \ˌdis-ə-'rānj\ *vt* : to disturb the arrangement or order of ⟨hair *disarranged* by the wind⟩ — **dis·ar·range·ment** \-mənt\ *n*

¹dis·ar·ray \ˌdis-ə-'rā\ *n* **1** : a lack of order or sequence : CONFUSION ⟨the room was in *disarray*⟩ **2** : disorderly dress

²disarray *vt* : to throw into disorder

dis·as·sem·ble \ˌdis-ə-'sem-bəl\ *vt* : to take apart ⟨*disassemble* an engine⟩ — **dis·as·sem·bly** \-blē\ *n*

dis·as·so·ci·ate \ˌdis-ə-'sō-shē-ˌāt, -sē-\ *vt* : to detach from association : DISSOCIATE — **dis·as·so·ci·a·tion** \-ˌsō-sē-'ā-shən, -ˌsō-shē-\ *n*

di·sas·ter \diz-'as-tər, dis-\ *n* : a sudden great misfortune; *esp* : one bringing with it destruction of life or property or causing complete ruin [Middle French *desastre* "unfavorable aspect of a star," from Italian *disastro,* from *dis-* "dis-" + *astro* "star," from Latin *astrum*]

synonyms DISASTER, CATASTROPHE, CALAMITY, CATACLYSM mean an event or situation that is a terrible misfortune. DISASTER is an unforeseen, ruinous, and often sudden misfortune that happens either through lack of foresight or through some hostile external agency ⟨a natural *disaster*⟩. CATASTROPHE implies a disastrous conclusion, emphasizing finality ⟨the *catastrophe* of war⟩. CALAMITY heightens the personal reaction to a great public loss ⟨an economic *calamity*⟩. CATACLYSM, originally a deluge or geological convulsion, applies to an event or situation that produces an upheaval or complete reversal ⟨the *cataclysm* that killed the dinosaurs⟩.

di·sas·trous \-ˈas-trəs\ *adj* : accompanied by or producing suffering or disaster : CALAMITOUS — **di·sas·trous·ly** *adv*

dis·avow \ˌdis-ə-ˈvau̇\ *vt* : to refuse to acknowledge : deny responsibility for — **dis·avow·al** \-ˈvau̇-əl, -ˈvau̇l\ *n*

dis·band \dis-ˈband\ *vb* : to break up the organization of : DISPERSE ⟨*disband* an army⟩ — **dis·band·ment** \-ˈband-mənt, -ˈban-\ *n*

dis·bar \dis-ˈbär\ *vt* **dis·barred; dis·bar·ring** : to deprive (a lawyer) of the rights and privileges of membership in the legal profession — **dis·bar·ment** \-ˈbär-mənt\ *n*

dis·be·lief \ˌdis-bə-ˈlēf\ *n* : the act of disbelieving : mental rejection of something as untrue ***synonyms*** see UNBELIEF

dis·be·lieve \-ˈlēv\ *vb* **1 :** to hold not to be true or real **2 :** to withhold or reject belief — **dis·be·liev·er** *n*

dis·bud \dis-ˈbəd, ˈdis-\ *vt* : to remove some flower buds from in order to improve the remaining flowers

dis·bur·den \dis-ˈbərd-n\ *vt* : UNBURDEN — **dis·bur·den·ment** \-mənt\ *n*

dis·burse \dis-ˈbərs\ *vt* : to pay out : EXPEND ⟨*disburse* money⟩ [Medieval French *desbourser,* from *des-* "dis-" + *bourse* "purse," from Medieval Latin *bursa*] — **dis·burs·er** *n*

dis·burse·ment \-ˈbər-smənt\ *n* : the act of disbursing; *also* : funds paid out

disc *variant of* DISK

[1]**dis·card** \dis-ˈkärd, ˈdis-ˌ\ *vb* **1 a :** to remove a playing card from one's hand **b :** to play (a card) from a suit other than trump but different from the one led **2 :** to get rid of as useless or unwanted ⟨*discard* old shoes⟩ — **dis·card·able** \-ə-bəl\ *adj*

[2]**dis·card** \ˈdis-ˌkärd\ *n* **1 :** the act of discarding in a card game **2 :** a person or thing cast off or rejected

disc brake *n* : a brake that operates by the friction of two plates pressing against the sides of a rotating disc

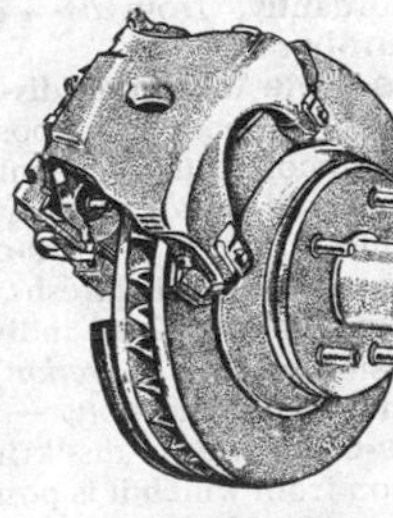
disc brake

dis·cern \dis-ˈərn, diz-\ *vt* **1 :** to detect with the eyes : DISTINGUISH ⟨*discern* an airplane in the clouds⟩ **2 :** to come to know, recognize, or discriminate mentally ⟨*discern* the basic issue⟩ [Medieval French *discerner,* from Latin *discernere* "to distinguish between," from *dis-* + *cernere* "to sift"] — **dis·cern·ible** \-ˈər-nə-bəl\ *adj* — **dis·cern·ibly** \-blē\ *adv*

dis·cern·ing *adj* : revealing insight and understanding : PERCEPTIVE ⟨a *discerning* critic⟩ — **dis·cern·ing·ly** \-ˈər-ning-lē\ *adv*

dis·cern·ment \dis-ˈərn-mənt, diz-\ *n* : skill in discerning or discriminating : keenness of insight

[1]**dis·charge** \dis-ˈchärj, ˈdis-ˌ\ *vb* **1 :** to relieve of a charge, load, or burden : UNLOAD ⟨*discharge* a ship⟩ **2 :** SHOOT 1, FIRE ⟨*discharge* a gun⟩ **3 :** to release from confinement or care ⟨*discharge* a prisoner⟩ ⟨*discharge* a patient⟩ **4 :** to dismiss from service or employment ⟨*discharge* a soldier⟩ **5 :** to let go or let off ⟨*discharge* passengers⟩ **6 :** to give forth fluid or other contents ⟨this river *discharges* into the ocean⟩ **7 :** to get rid of by paying or doing ⟨*discharge* a debt⟩ ***synonyms*** see FREE — **dis·charg·er** *n*

[2]**dis·charge** \ˈdis-ˌchärj, dis-ˈ\ *n* **1 a :** the act of discharging, unloading, or releasing **b :** something that discharges; *esp* : a certification of release or payment **2 :** a firing off of a weapon or missile **3 a :** a flowing or issuing out; *also* : a rate of flow **b :** something that is emitted **4 a :** release or dismissal especially from an office or employment **b :** complete separation from military service **5 a :** the equalization of electric potential between two points by a flow of electricity **b :** the conversion of the chemical energy of a battery into electrical energy

discharge tube *n* : an electron tube which contains gas or vapor at low pressure and through which electrical conduction takes place when a high voltage is applied

dis·ci·ple \dis-ˈī-pəl\ *n* **1 :** a pupil or follower who accepts and helps to spread the teachings of another: as **a :** APOSTLE 1a **b :** a convinced adherent **2** *cap* **:** a member of the Disciples of Christ founded in the U.S. in 1809 [derived from Latin *discipulus* "pupil"] — **dis·ci·ple·ship** \-ˌship\ *n*

dis·ci·pli·nar·i·an \ˌdis-ə-plə-ˈner-ē-ən\ *n* : one that disciplines or enforces order — **disciplinarian** *adj*

dis·ci·plin·ary \ˈdis-ə-plə-ˌner-ē\ *adj* : of or relating to discipline : CORRECTIVE ⟨take *disciplinary* action⟩

[1]**dis·ci·pline** \ˈdis-ə-plən\ *n* **1 :** a field of study : SUBJECT **2 :** training that corrects, molds, or perfects mental ability or moral character **3 :** PUNISHMENT 1 **4 :** control gained by obedience or order ⟨tried to maintain *discipline*⟩ **5 :** a system of rules governing conduct or activity [Latin *disciplina* "teaching, learning," from *discipulus* "pupil"]

[2]**discipline** *vt* **1 :** to punish or penalize for the sake of discipline **2 :** to train or develop by instruction and exercise especially in self-control **3 :** to bring (a group) under control ⟨*discipline* troops⟩ ***synonyms*** see PUNISH — **dis·ci·plin·er** *n*

disc jockey *or* **disk jockey** *n* : an announcer of a radio show of popular recorded music; *also* : a person who plays recorded music for dancing (as at a party)

dis·claim \dis-ˈklām\ *vt* : to deny having a connection with or responsibility for ⟨*disclaimed* taking part in the prank⟩

dis·claim·er \-ˈklā-mər\ *n* : an act of disclaiming : a statement that denies responsibility : DENIAL

dis·close \dis-ˈklōz\ *vt* : to expose to view : make known : REVEAL ⟨*disclose* secrets⟩ — **dis·clos·er** *n*

dis·clos·ing \-ˈklō-zing\ *adj* : being a substance (as a tablet or liquid) containing a usually red dye that is used to stain and make visible dental plaque

dis·clo·sure \-ˈklō-zhər\ *n* **1 :** the act or an instance of disclosing : EXPOSURE **2 :** something disclosed : REVELATION

dis·co \ˈdis-kō\ *n, pl* **discos 1 :** a nightclub for dancing to live and recorded music **2 :** popular dance music characterized by strong steady rhythms, repetitive lyrics, and electronically produced sounds [short for *discotheque*]

dis·cog·ra·phy \dis-ˈkäg-rə-fē\ *n, pl* **-phies :** a descriptive list of musical recordings

dis·coid \ˈdis-ˌkȯid\ *adj* **1 :** resembling a disk especially in being flat and circular **2 :** relating to, forming, or being part of a disk or disk flower

dis·coi·dal \dis-ˈkȯid-l\ *adj* : of, resembling, or producing a disk

dis·col·or \dis-ˈkəl-ər\ *vb* : to alter or change in color especially for the worse ⟨the stain *discolored* the rug⟩ — **dis·col·or·a·tion** \ˌdis-ˌkəl-ə-ˈrā-shən\ *n*

dis·com·bob·u·late \ˌdis-kəm-ˈbäb-yə-ˌlāt, -ə-\ *vt* : UPSET 4a, CONFUSE [probably alteration of *discompose*]

dis·com·fit \dis-ˈkəm-fət, -ˈkəmp-, *especially in the South* ˌdis-kəm-ˈfit\ *vt* : to put into a state of perplexity and embarrassment ⟨hecklers *discomfited* the speaker⟩ [Medieval French *descumfit,* past participle of *descumfire* "to destroy, defeat," from *des-* "dis-" + *cumfire* "to prepare"] ***synonyms*** see EMBARRASS — **dis·com·fi·ture** \dis-ˈkəm-fə-ˌchu̇r, -ˈkəmp-, -fə-chər\ *n*

[1]**dis·com·fort** \dis-ˈkəm-fərt, -ˈkəmp-\ *vt* : to make uncomfortable or uneasy

[2]**discomfort** *n* : physical or mental uneasiness : DISTRESS

dis·com·mode \ˌdis-kə-ˈmōd\ *vt* : to cause inconvenience to : TROUBLE [French *discommoder,* from *dis-* "dis-" + *commode* "convenient"]

dis·com·pose \ˌdis-kəm-ˈpōz\ *vt* **1 :** to disturb the calmness or peace of : AGITATE ⟨*discomposed* by the bad news⟩ **2 :** DISARRANGE ⟨hair *discomposed* by the wind⟩ — **dis·com·po·sure** \-ˈpō-zhər\ *n*

dis·con·cert \ˌdis-kən-ˈsərt\ *vt* **1 :** to throw into confusion ⟨the unexpected event *disconcerted* their plans⟩ **2 :** to disturb the composure of ⟨the verdict *disconcerted* the defendant⟩ ***synonyms*** see EMBARRASS — **dis·con·cert·ing·ly** *adv*

\ə\ **abut**	\au̇\ **out**	\i\ **tip**	\ȯ\ **saw**	\u̇\ **foot**
\ər\ **further**	\ch\ **chin**	\ī\ **life**	\ȯi\ **coin**	\y\ **yet**
\a\ **mat**	\e\ **pet**	\j\ **job**	\th\ **thin**	\yü\ **few**
\ā\ **take**	\ē\ **easy**	\ng\ **sing**	\t͟h\ **this**	\yu̇\ **cure**
\ä\ **cot, cart**	\g\ **go**	\ō\ **bone**	\ü\ **food**	\zh\ **vision**

dis·con·nect \ˌdis-kə-ˈnekt\ *vt* **:** to undo or break the connection of ⟨*disconnect* two pipes⟩ ⟨*disconnect* a telephone⟩ — **dis·con·nec·tion** \-ˈnek-shən\ *n*

dis·con·nect·ed *adj* **1 :** not connected **:** SEPARATE **2 :** impossible to understand **:** INCOHERENT ⟨a *disconnected* speech⟩ — **dis·con·nect·ed·ly** *adv* — **dis·con·nect·ed·ness** *n*

dis·con·so·late \dis-ˈkän-sə-lət\ *adj* **1 :** DEJECTED, DOWNCAST ⟨the team was *disconsolate* after three straight losses⟩ **2 :** causing or suggestive of dejection **:** CHEERLESS ⟨a *disconsolate* row of empty houses⟩ [Medieval Latin *disconsolatus,* from Latin *dis-* + *consolari* "to console"] — **dis·con·so·late·ly** *adv* — **dis·con·so·late·ness** *n*

¹dis·con·tent \ˌdis-kən-ˈtent\ *adj* **:** DISCONTENTED

²discontent *vt* **:** to make discontented — **dis·con·tent·ment** \-mənt\ *n*

³discontent *n* **1 :** lack of contentment **:** UNEASINESS **2 :** a yearning for improvement or perfection

dis·con·tent·ed *adj* **:** not satisfied **:** MALCONTENT — **dis·con·tent·ed·ly** *adv* — **dis·con·tent·ed·ness** *n*

dis·con·tin·u·ance \ˌdis-kən-ˈtin-yə-wəns\ *n* **:** the act or an instance of discontinuing

dis·con·tin·ue \ˌdis-kən-ˈtin-yü\ *vb* **1 :** to break the continuity of **:** cease to operate, use, produce, or take ⟨will *discontinue* that product⟩ **2 :** to come or bring to an end **:** STOP ⟨*discontinued* broadcast of my favorite show⟩

dis·con·tin·u·ous \ˌdis-kən-ˈtin-yə-wəs\ *adj* **:** not continuous **:** having interruptions or gaps **:** BROKEN ⟨*discontinuous* sleep⟩ — **dis·con·ti·nu·i·ty** \ˌdis-ˌkänt-n-ˈü-ət-ē, -ˈyü-\ *n* — **dis·con·tin·u·ous·ly** \ˌdis-kən-ˈtin-yə-wəs-lē\ *adv*

dis·cord \ˈdis-ˌkȯrd\ *n* **1 :** lack of agreement or harmony (as between persons, things, or ideas) **:** CONFLICT **2 a :** a harsh combination of musical sounds **b :** a harsh or unpleasant sound [derived from Latin *discordia,* from *discors* "discordant," from *dis-* + *cor* "heart"]

dis·cor·dance \dis-ˈkȯrd-ns\ *n* **1 :** the state or an instance of being discordant **2 :** discordant sound or noises

dis·cor·dant \-nt\ *adj* **1 a :** being at variance **:** DISAGREEING ⟨*discordant* opinions⟩ **b :** QUARRELSOME ⟨a *discordant* family⟩ **2 :** relating to or producing a discord **:** JARRING ⟨*discordant* music⟩ — **dis·cor·dant·ly** *adv*

dis·co·theque \ˈdis-kə-ˌtek, ˌdis-kə-ˈ\ *n* **:** DISCO 1 [French *discothèque,* from *disque* "disk, record" + *-othèque* (as in *bibliothèque* "library")]

¹dis·count \ˈdis-ˌkau̇nt\ *n* **1 :** a reduction made from a regular or list price ⟨a ten percent *discount* for employees⟩ **2 :** a deduction of interest in advance when lending money

²dis·count \ˈdis-ˌkau̇nt, dis-ˈ\ *vt* **1 a :** to reduce or deduct from the amount of a bill, debt, or charge **b :** to sell or offer for sale at a discount **2 :** to lend money on (a note) after deducting the discount **3 a :** MINIMIZE 2b ⟨*discounted* the value of experience⟩ **b :** to believe only partly **:** to view with doubt ⟨*discount* a rumor⟩ **c :** to take into account (as a future event) in present calculations ⟨the stock market has already *discounted* the company's better prospects for next year⟩ — **dis·count·able** \-ə-bəl\ *adj*

dis·coun·te·nance \dis-ˈkau̇nt-n-əns, -ˈkau̇nt-nəns\ *vt* **1 :** DISCONCERT 2, EMBARRASS **2 :** to look with disfavor on

dis·cour·age \dis-ˈkər-ij, -ˈkə-rij\ *vt* **1 :** to lessen the courage or confidence of ⟨*discouraged* by a single failure⟩ **2 a :** to hinder by inspiring fear of consequences **:** DETER ⟨laws that *discourage* speeding⟩ **b :** to attempt to dissuade ⟨*discouraged* students from dropping out of school⟩ — **dis·cour·ag·ing·ly** \-ˈkər-i-jing-lē, -ˈkə-ri-\ *adv*

dis·cour·age·ment \-ˈkər-ij-mənt, -ˈkə-rij-\ *n* **1 :** an act of discouraging **:** the state of being discouraged **2 :** something that discourages

¹dis·course \ˈdis-ˌkōrs, -ˌkȯrs, dis-ˈ\ *n* **1 :** verbal interchange of ideas **:** CONVERSATION **2 :** formal and orderly and usually extended expression of thought on a subject [Late Latin *discursus* "conversation," from Latin *discurrere* "to run about," from *dis-* + *currere* "to run"]

²dis·course \dis-ˈkōrs, -ˈkȯrs, ˈdis-ˌ\ *vi* **1 :** to express oneself especially in oral discourse **2 :** TALK 5, CONVERSE

dis·cour·te·ous \dis-ˈkərt-ē-əs\ *adj* **:** lacking courtesy **:** RUDE — **dis·cour·te·ous·ly** *adv* — **dis·cour·te·ous·ness** *n*

dis·cour·te·sy \-ˈkərt-ə-sē\ *n* **1 :** rudeness of behavior or language **2 :** a rude act

dis·cov·er \dis-ˈkəv-ər\ *vt* **dis·cov·ered; dis·cov·er·ing** \-ˈkəv-ring, -ə-ring\ **1 :** to make known or visible (as something secret or hidden) **2 a :** to obtain sight or knowledge of for the first time ⟨*discover* the solution⟩ ⟨*discover* an uncharted island⟩ **b :** to detect the presence of **:** FIND ⟨*discovered* a present waiting on the table⟩ **c :** FIND OUT ⟨*discovered* my keys were lost⟩ — **dis·cov·er·able** \-ˈkəv-rə-bəl, -ə-rə-\ *adj* — **dis·cov·er·er** \-ˈkəv-ər-ər\ *n*

synonyms DISCOVER, ASCERTAIN, DETERMINE, UNEARTH, LEARN mean to find out what one did not previously know. DISCOVER may apply to something requiring exploration or investigation or to a chance encounter ⟨*discovered* the source of the river⟩. ASCERTAIN implies effort to find the facts or the truth proceeding from awareness of ignorance or uncertainty ⟨attempts to *ascertain* the population of the region⟩. DETERMINE emphasizes the intent to establish the facts definitely or precisely ⟨unable to *determine* the origin of the word⟩. UNEARTH implies bringing to light something forgotten or hidden ⟨*unearth* old records⟩. LEARN may imply acquiring knowledge with little effort or conscious intention (as by simply being told) or it may imply study and practice ⟨I *learned* her name only today⟩ ⟨*learning* French⟩.

dis·cov·ery \dis-ˈkəv-rē, -ə-rē\ *n, pl* **-er·ies 1 :** the act or process of discovering **2 :** something discovered

¹dis·cred·it \dis-ˈkred-ət\ *vt* **1 :** to refuse to accept as true or accurate **:** DISBELIEVE ⟨*discredit* a rumor⟩ **2 :** to cause disbelief in the accuracy or authority of ⟨*discredit* a witness⟩ **3 :** to destroy the reputation of **:** DISGRACE ⟨involvement in the scandal *discredited* them⟩

²discredit *n* **1 :** loss of credit or reputation ⟨brought *discredit* on their family⟩ **2 :** lack or loss of belief or confidence **:** DOUBT ⟨bring a story into *discredit*⟩

dis·cred·it·able \-ə-bəl\ *adj* **:** injurious to reputation — **dis·cred·it·ably** \-blē\ *adv*

dis·creet \dis-ˈkrēt\ *adj* **:** having or showing good judgment in conduct and especially in speech **:** PRUDENT; *esp* **:** capable of observing cautious silence [Medieval French *discret,* from Latin *discretus,* past participle of *discernere* "to distinguish, discern"] — **dis·creet·ly** *adv* — **dis·creet·ness** *n*

dis·crep·an·cy \dis-ˈkrep-ən-sē\ *n, pl* **-cies 1 :** the quality or state of disagreeing **:** DIFFERENCE ⟨the extent of *discrepancy* between two reports⟩ **2 :** an instance of being different or disagreeing ⟨*discrepancies* in the firm's financial statements⟩

dis·crep·ant \-ənt\ *adj* **:** not being the same **:** DISAGREEING ⟨widely *discrepant* conclusions⟩ [Latin *discrepare* "to sound discordantly," from *dis-* + *crepare* "to rattle, creak"] — **dis·crep·ant·ly** *adv*

dis·crete \dis-ˈkrēt, ˈdis-ˌ\ *adj* **1 :** individually distinct **:** SEPARATE ⟨radiation composed of *discrete* particles⟩ **2 :** consisting of unconnected elements **:** DISCONTINUOUS ⟨a *discrete* series⟩ [Latin *discretus,* past participle of *discernere* "to separate, distinguish, discern"] — **dis·crete·ly** *adv* — **dis·crete·ness** *n*

dis·cre·tion \dis-ˈkresh-ən\ *n* **1 :** the quality of being discreet **:** PRUDENCE **2 a :** individual choice or judgment ⟨left the decision to your *discretion*⟩ **b :** power of free decision ⟨reached the age of *discretion*⟩ — **dis·cre·tion·ary** \-ˈkresh-ə-ˌner-ē\ *adj*

dis·crim·i·nant \dis-ˈkrim-ə-nənt\ *n* **:** a mathematical expression from which it is possible to make statements about the value of another more complicated expression, relation, or set of relations

dis·crim·i·nate \dis-ˈkrim-ə-ˌnāt\ *vb* **1 a :** to perceive the distinguishing features of ⟨*discriminate* the geological features of a terrain⟩ **b :** DIFFERENTIATE 4, DISTINGUISH ⟨*discriminate* hundreds of colors⟩ **2 :** to see and note the differences ⟨*discriminate* among values⟩; *esp* **:** to distinguish one like object from another ⟨*discriminate* between a maple and an oak⟩ **3 :** to treat differently on a basis other than individual merit ⟨*discriminated* against because of their race⟩ [Latin *discriminare,* from *discrimen* "distinction," from *discernere* "to distinguish, discern"] — **dis·crim·i·na·ble** \-ˈkrim-nə-bəl, -ə-nə-\ *adj*

dis·crim·i·nat·ing *adj* **1 :** showing careful judgment **:** DISCERNING ⟨*discriminating* taste⟩ **2 :** DISCRIMINATORY ⟨accused of *discriminating* practices⟩ — **dis·crim·i·nat·ing·ly** \-ˌnāt-ing-lē\ *adv*

dis·crim·i·na·tion \dis-ˌkrim-ə-ˈnā-shən\ *n* **1 :** the act of perceiving distinctions **2 :** the ability to make fine distinctions **3 :** the act or practice of discriminating unfairly **:** prejudiced treatment, outlook, or action ⟨racial *discrimination*⟩ — **dis·crim·i·na·tion·al** \-shnəl, -shən-l\ *adj*

dis·crim·i·na·tive \dis-ˈkrim-ə-ˌnāt-iv\ *adj* **1 :** making distinctions **2 :** DISCRIMINATORY — **dis·crim·i·na·tive·ly** *adv*

dis·crim·i·na·to·ry \dis-ˈkrim-nə-ˌtōr-ē, -ə-nə-, -ˌtȯr-\ *adj* : marked by unjust discrimination ⟨*discriminatory* treatment⟩

dis·cur·sive \dis-ˈkər-siv\ *adj* : passing from one topic to another : RAMBLING [Medieval Latin *discursivus,* from Latin *discurrere* "to run about," from *dis-* + *currere* "to run"] — **dis·cur·sive·ly** *adv* — **dis·cur·sive·ness** *n*

dis·cus \ˈdis-kəs\ *n, pl* **dis·cus·es** : a heavy disk (as of wood or plastic) thicker in the center than at the edge that is hurled for distance in track-and-field competition; *also* : the event [Latin, "disk, dish"]

discus

dis·cuss \dis-ˈkəs\ *vt* **1** : to investigate or consider carefully by reasoning or argument ⟨*discuss* a proposal⟩ **2** : to talk about ⟨*discuss* the weather⟩ [Latin *discussus,* past participle of *discutere* "to shake apart, scatter," from *dis-* + *quatere* "to shake"]

synonyms DISCUSS, ARGUE, DEBATE, DISPUTE mean to talk about in order to reach conclusions or to convince others. DISCUSS implies a presentation of considerations pro and con and suggests an interchange of opinion for the sake of clarifying issues ⟨*discuss* the need for a new highway⟩. ARGUE implies the offering of evidence and reasons to support a proposition or proposal ⟨*argued* over who was to blame⟩. DEBATE stresses formal or public argument between opposing parties ⟨*debated* the merits of the new regulations⟩. DISPUTE implies quarrelsome or heated argument ⟨*disputed* the victory⟩.

dis·cus·sion \dis-ˈkəsh-ən\ *n* **1** : consideration of a question in open and usually informal debate **2** : a formal treatment of a topic in speech or writing

[1]**dis·dain** \dis-ˈdān\ *n* : a feeling of contempt for something or someone regarded as beneath one : SCORN

[2]**disdain** *vt* **1** : to look with scorn on ⟨*disdained* us as cowards⟩ **2** : to reject or refrain from because of disdain ⟨*disdained* to answer⟩ [Medieval French *desdeigner,* derived from Latin *dis-* + *dignare* "to deign"] ***synonyms*** see DESPISE

dis·dain·ful \-fəl\ *adj* : full of or expressing disdain : SCORNFUL ***synonyms*** see PROUD — **dis·dain·ful·ly** \-fə-lē\ *adv* — **dis·dain·ful·ness** *n*

dis·ease \diz-ˈēz\ *n* **1** : a condition of the living animal or plant body that impairs normal functioning and can usually be recognized by signs and symptoms : ILLNESS **2** : a harmful development [Medieval French *desaise* "trouble," from *des-* "dis-" + *aise* "ease"] — **dis·eased** \-ˈēzd\ *adj*

dis·em·bark \ˌdis-əm-ˈbärk\ *vb* **1** : to put ashore (as cargo) from a ship **2** : to leave a vehicle (as a ship or plane) — **dis·em·bar·ka·tion** \ˌdis-ˌem-ˌbär-ˈkā-shən, -bər-\ *n*

dis·em·bar·rass \ˌdis-əm-ˈbar-əs\ *vt* : to free from something troublesome or unnecessary

dis·em·body \ˌdis-əm-ˈbäd-ē\ *vt* : to deprive of bodily existence

dis·em·bow·el \ˌdis-əm-ˈbau̇-əl, -ˈbau̇l\ *vt* **-eled** *or* **-elled; -el·ing** *or* **-el·ling** : to take out the bowels of — **dis·em·bow·el·ment** \-mənt\ *n*

dis·em·pow·er \dis-im-ˈpau̇-ər, -ˈpau̇r\ *vt* : to deprive of authority, power, or influence : make weak, ineffectual, or unimportant — **dis·em·pow·er·ment** \-mənt\ *n*

dis·en·chant \ˌdis-n-ˈchant\ *vt* : to free from illusion — **dis·en·chant·ment** \-mənt\ *n*

dis·en·cum·ber \ˌdis-n-ˈkəm-bər\ *vt* : to free from something that burdens or obstructs

dis·en·fran·chise \ˌdis-n-ˈfran-ˌchīz\ *vt* : to deprive of a franchise, a legal right, or a privilege or immunity; *esp* : to deprive of the right to vote — **dis·en·fran·chise·ment** \-ˌchīz-mənt, -chəz-\ *n*

dis·en·gage \ˌdis-n-ˈgāj\ *vb* : to free, release, or become detached from an engagement, entanglement, or encumbrance ⟨*disengage* an automobile clutch⟩ — **dis·en·gage·ment** \-ˈgāj-mənt\ *n*

dis·en·tan·gle \ˌdis-n-ˈtang-gəl\ *vb* : to free or become free from entanglement ***synonyms*** see EXTRICATE — **dis·en·tan·gle·ment** \-mənt\ *n*

dis·equi·lib·ri·um \ˌdis-ˌē-kwə-ˈlib-rē-əm, -ˌek-wə-\ *n* : loss or lack of equilibrium

dis·es·tab·lish \ˌdis-ə-ˈstab-lish\ *vt* : to deprive of an established status; *esp* : to deprive of the status and privileges of an established church — **dis·es·tab·lish·ment** \-mənt\ *n*

[1]**dis·es·teem** \ˌdis-ə-ˈstēm\ *vt* : to regard with disfavor

[2]**disesteem** *n* : lack of esteem : DISFAVOR, DISREPUTE

[1]**dis·fa·vor** \dis-ˈfā-vər, ˈdis-\ *n* **1** : DISAPPROVAL, DISLIKE ⟨practices looked on with *disfavor*⟩ **2** : the state or fact of being deprived of favor ⟨in *disfavor* at school⟩

[2]**disfavor** *vt* : to regard with disfavor

dis·fig·ure \dis-ˈfig-yər, *especially British* -ˈfig-ər\ *vt* : to spoil the appearance of ⟨*disfigured* by a scar⟩ ***synonyms*** see DEFACE — **dis·fig·ure·ment** \-mənt\ *n*

dis·fran·chise \dis-ˈfran-ˌchīz\ *vt* : DISENFRANCHISE — **dis·fran·chise·ment** \-ˌchīz-mənt, -chəz-\ *n*

dis·gorge \dis-ˈgȯrj, ˈdis-\ *vb* **1** : VOMIT 1 **2** : to discharge violently or forcefully ⟨a volcano *disgorging* lava⟩ **3** : to discharge contents ⟨the river *disgorges* into the sea⟩

[1]**dis·grace** \dis-ˈgrās\ *vt* : to bring reproach or shame to — **dis·grac·er** *n*

[2]**disgrace** *n* **1** : the condition of being out of favor : loss of respect ⟨in *disgrace* with one's schoolmates⟩ **2** : SHAME, DISHONOR ⟨the *disgrace* of being a coward⟩ **3** : a cause of shame ⟨that child's manners are a *disgrace*⟩

dis·grace·ful \-fəl\ *adj* : bringing or involving disgrace — **dis·grace·ful·ly** \-fə-lē\ *adv* — **dis·grace·ful·ness** *n*

dis·grun·tle \dis-ˈgrənt-l\ *vt* **dis·grun·tled; dis·grun·tling** \-ˈgrənt-ling, -l-ing\ : to put in bad humor [*dis-* + Middle English *gruntlen* "to grumble," from *grunten* "to grunt"] — **dis·grun·tle·ment** \-l-mənt\ *n*

[1]**dis·guise** \dis-ˈgīz\ *vt* **1** : to change the dress or looks of so as to conceal the identity or so as to resemble another ⟨*disguised* themselves with wigs⟩ **2** : to conceal or hide the existence or true nature of ⟨*disguised* their true feelings⟩ ⟨tried to *disguise* my voice⟩ — **dis·guised·ly** \-ˈgīz-əd-lē, -ˈgīzd-lē\ *adv* — **dis·guis·er** \-ˈgī-zər\ *n*

[2]**disguise** *n* **1** : clothing put on to conceal one's identity or imitate another's **2 a** : an outward form hiding or misrepresenting the true nature or identity of something ⟨a blessing in *disguise*⟩ **b** : an artificial manner : PRETENSE **3** : the act of disguising

synonyms DISGUISE, CLOAK, MASK mean an appearance that hides one's true identity or nature. DISGUISE implies a change in appearance or behavior that misleads by presenting a different apparent identity ⟨spies in *disguise* as tourists⟩. CLOAK suggests a means of hiding a movement or an intention completely ⟨used ambition as a *cloak* for her greed⟩. MASK suggests some usually obvious means of preventing recognition and does not always imply deception or pretense ⟨a *mask* of happiness⟩.

[1]**dis·gust** \dis-ˈgəst\ *n* : marked aversion to something distasteful or loathsome : REPUGNANCE

[2]**disgust** *vt* : to provoke to loathing, repugnance, or aversion : be offensive to [Middle French *desgouster,* from *des-* "dis-" + *goust* "taste," from Latin *gustus*] — **dis·gust·ed** *adj* — **dis·gust·ed·ly** *adv* — **dis·gust·ing** \-ˈgəs-ting\ *adj* — **dis·gust·ing·ly** \-ting-lē\ *adv*

[1]**dish** \ˈdish\ *n* **1 a** : a usually concave vessel from which food is served **b** : the contents of a dish ⟨ate a *dish* of strawberries⟩ **2** : food prepared in a particular way **3 a** : something resembling a dish especially in being shallow and concave **b** : a directional receiver having a concave usually parabolic reflector; *esp* : one used as a microwave antenna [Old English *disc* "plate," from Latin *discus* "quoit, disk, dish," from Greek *diskos,* from *dikein* "to throw"]

[2]**dish** *vt* **1** : to put into a dish or set of dishes **2** : to make concave like a dish ⟨a *dished* metal disk⟩

dis·ha·bille *or* **des·ha·bille** \ˌdis-ə-ˈbēl\ *n* : the state of being dressed in a casual or careless style [French *déshabillé,* from *déshabiller* "to undress," from *dés-* "dis-" + *habiller* "to dress"]

dis·har·mo·ny \dis-ˈhär-mə-nē\ *n* : lack of harmony : DISCORD — **dis·har·mon·ic** \-här-ˈmän-ik\ *adj* — **dis·har·mo·ni·ous** \-här-ˈmō-nē-əs\ *adj*

dish·cloth \ˈdish-ˌklȯth\ *n* : a cloth for washing dishes

dis·heart·en \dis-ˈhärt-n\ *vt* : to deprive of courage and hope : DISCOURAGE — **dis·heart·en·ing** \-ˈhärt-ning, -n-ing\ *adj* —

\ə\ **abut**	\au̇\ **out**	\i\ **tip**	\ȯ\ **saw**	\u̇\ **foot**
\ər\ **further**	\ch\ **chin**	\ī\ **life**	\ȯi\ **coin**	\y\ **yet**
\a\ **mat**	\e\ **pet**	\j\ **job**	\th\ **thin**	\yü\ **few**
\ā\ **take**	\ē\ **easy**	\ng\ **sing**	\t͟h\ **this**	\yu̇\ **cure**
\ä\ **cot, cart**	\g\ **go**	\ō\ **bone**	\ü\ **food**	\zh\ **vision**

dis·heart·en·ing·ly \-ning-lē, -n-ing-lē\ *adv* — **dis·heart·en·ment** \-ˈhärt-n-mənt\ *n*

di·shev·el \dish-ˈev-əl\ *vt* **di·shev·eled** *or* **di·shev·elled; di·shev·el·ing** *or* **di·shev·el·ling** \-ˈev-ling, -ə-ling\ : to put into disorder or disarray ⟨the wind *disheveled* her clothes⟩ [Medieval French *deschevelé* "bare-headed, with disordered hair," from *des-* "dis-" + *chevel* "hair," from Latin *capillus*] — **di·shev·el·ment** \-əl-mənt\ *n*

di·shev·eled *or* **di·shev·elled** *adj* : marked by disorder ⟨*disheveled* hair⟩

dis·hon·est \dis-ˈän-əst, ˈdis-\ *adj* : not honest or trustworthy : DECEITFUL ⟨*dishonest* dealings⟩ ⟨*dishonest* people⟩ — **dis·hon·est·ly** *adv*

dis·hon·es·ty \-ə-stē\ *n* : lack of honesty or integrity : disposition to defraud or deceive

1dis·hon·or \dis-ˈän-ər, ˈdis-\ *n* **1 a** : loss of honor or reputation **b** : the state of one who has lost honor or prestige **c** : a cause of disgrace **2** : the refusal to accept or pay (as a bill or check)

2dishonor *vt* **1** : to bring shame on : DISGRACE **2** : to refuse to accept or pay (as a bill or check) — **dis·hon·or·er** *n*

dis·hon·or·able \dis-ˈän-rə-bəl, -ˈän-ə-rə-bəl, -ˈän-ər-bəl\ *adj* : not honorable : SHAMEFUL ⟨*dishonorable* conduct⟩ — **dis·hon·or·ably** \-blē\ *adv*

dish out *vt* : to give out freely ⟨*dish out* advice⟩

dish·rag \ˈdish-ˌrag\ *n* : DISHCLOTH

dish·wash·er \ˈdish-ˌwȯsh-ər, -ˌwäsh-\ *n* : a person or a machine that washes dishes

dish·wa·ter \-ˌwȯt-ər, -ˌwät-\ *n* : water in which dishes have been or are to be washed

1dis·il·lu·sion \ˌdis-ə-ˈlü-zhən\ *n* : the loss of illusions or hopes

2disillusion *vt* **-lu·sioned; -lu·sion·ing** \-ˈlüzh-ning, -ə-ning\ : to free from mistaken beliefs or foolish hopes ⟨a loss that *disillusioned* the fans⟩ — **dis·il·lu·sion·ment** \-ˈlü-zhən-mənt\ *n*

dis·in·cline \ˌdis-n-ˈklīn\ *vb* : to make or be unwilling — **dis·in·cli·na·tion** \ˌdis-ˌin-klə-ˈnā-shən, -ˌing-\ *n*

dis·in·fect \ˌdis-n-ˈfekt\ *vt* : to free from infection especially by destroying harmful germs; *also* : CLEANSE — **dis·in·fec·tion** \-ˈfek-shən\ *n*

dis·in·fec·tant \-ˈfek-tənt\ *n* : a substance that destroys harmful germs (as bacteria and fungi) but not ordinarily spores — **disinfectant** *adj*

dis·in·gen·u·ous \ˌdis-n-ˈjen-yə-wəs\ *adj* : lacking in candor : giving a false appearance of frankness ⟨a *disingenuous* expression of concern⟩ — **dis·in·gen·u·ous·ly** *adv* — **dis·in·gen·u·ous·ness** *n*

dis·in·her·it \ˌdis-n-ˈher-ət\ *vt* : to deprive of the right to inherit

dis·in·te·grate \dis-ˈint-ə-ˌgrāt\ *vb* **1** : to break or decompose into constituent elements, parts, or particles **2 a** : to destroy the unity or integrity of **b** : to lose unity or integrity by or as if by breaking into parts **3** : to undergo a change in composition ⟨an atomic nucleus that *disintegrates* because of radioactivity⟩ — **dis·in·te·gra·tion** \ˌdis-ˌint-ə-ˈgrā-shən\ *n* — **dis·in·te·gra·tor** \dis-ˈint-ə-ˌgrāt-ər\ *n*

dis·in·ter \ˌdis-n-ˈtər\ *vt* **1** : to take out of the grave or tomb **2** : to bring to light : UNEARTH — **dis·in·ter·ment** \-mənt\ *n*

dis·in·ter·est·ed \dis-ˈint-ə-ˌres-təd, ˈdis-; -ˈin-trəs-, -ˌtres-; -ˈint-ərs-, -ˈint-ə-rəs-\ *adj* **1** : not interested **2** : free from selfish motive or interest : UNBIASED ⟨a *disinterested* decision⟩ ***usage*** see UNINTERESTED — **dis·in·ter·est·ed·ly** *adv* — **dis·in·ter·est·ed·ness** *n*

dis·join \dis-ˈjȯin, ˈdis-\ *vb* : to end the union of or become separated ⟨chromosome pairs *disjoin* in meiosis⟩

1dis·joint \dis-ˈjȯint, ˈdis-\ *adj* : having no elements in common ⟨*disjoint* mathematical sets⟩

2disjoint *vb* **1** : to separate the parts of **2** : to take or come apart at the joints

dis·joint·ed *adj* **1** : separated at or as if at the joint **2** : lacking coherence or orderly sequence ⟨*disjointed* conversation⟩ — **dis·joint·ed·ly** *adv* — **dis·joint·ed·ness** *n*

dis·junc·tion \dis-ˈjəng-shən, -ˈjəngk-\ *n* **1** : DISUNION, SEPARATION ⟨a *disjunction* between theory and practice⟩ **2** : a proposition in logic composed of two or more statements joined by the connective *or*; *esp* : one in which one and only one of the statements is true at a time

1dis·junc·tive \-ˈjəng-tiv, -ˈjəngk-\ *n* : a disjunctive conjunction

2disjunctive *adj* **1** : marked by breaks or separations **2** : expressing an alternative between the meanings of the words connected ⟨the *disjunctive* conjunction *or*⟩

1disk *or* **disc** \ˈdisk\ *n* **1** : the seemingly flat figure of a celestial body ⟨solar *disk*⟩ **2 a** : the central part of the flower head of a typical plant (as a daisy) of the composite family made up of closely packed tubular flowers **b** : any of various rounded and flattened animal anatomical structures; *esp* : INTERVERTEBRAL DISK **3** : a thin circular object: as **a** *usually disc* : a phonograph record **b** : a round flat plate coated with a magnetic substance on which data for a computer may be stored **c** : CD **4** *usually disc* : a tilling implement (as a harrow or plow) with sharp-edged circular concave cutting blades; *also* : one of these blades [Latin *discus* "dish, disk"] — **disk·like** \-ˌlīk\ *adj*

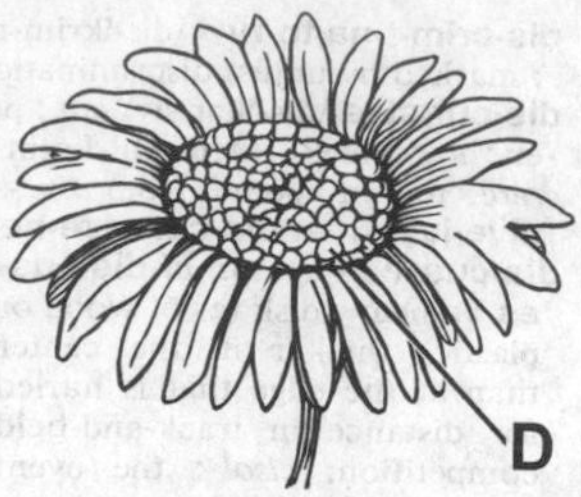

D disk 2a

2disk *or* **disc** *vt* : to cultivate (land) with a disc

disk·ette \ˈdis-ˌket, ˌdis-ˈ\ *n* : FLOPPY DISK

disk drive *n* : a device for reading and writing computer data on a magnetic disk

disk flower *n* : one of the tubular flowers in the disk of a plant (as a daisy) of the composite family — called also *disk floret*; compare RAY FLOWER

disk jockey *variant of* DISC JOCKEY

1dis·like \dis-ˈlīk, ˈdis-\ *n* : a feeling of aversion or disapproval

2dislike *vt* : to regard with dislike : DISAPPROVE

dis·lo·cate \ˈdis-lō-ˌkāt, dis-ˈlō-\ *vt* **1** : to put out of place; *esp* : to displace (a bone) from normal connections with another bone **2** : DISRUPT 2 — **dis·lo·ca·tion** \ˌdis-ˌlō-ˈkā-shən\ *n*

dis·lodge \dis-ˈläj, ˈdis-\ *vt* **1** : to force out of a resting place **2** : to drive from a place of hiding or defense

dis·loy·al \dis-ˈlȯi-əl, -ˈlȯil\ *adj* : lacking in loyalty ***synonyms*** see FAITHLESS — **dis·loy·al·ly** \-ˈlȯi-ə-lē\ *adv*

dis·loy·al·ty \-ˈlȯi-əl-tē, -ˈlȯil-\ *n* : lack of loyalty

dis·mal \ˈdiz-məl\ *adj* : showing or causing gloom or depression ⟨a *dismal* voice⟩ ⟨*dismal* winter afternoons⟩ [derived from Medieval Latin *dies mali* "evil days"] — **dis·mal·ly** \-mə-lē\ *adv*

Word History In late antiquity, certain days of each month, called in Latin *dies Aegyptiaci*, "Egyptian days," were regarded as unlucky times, when new enterprises of any sort were not to be undertaken. These days of ill omen were probably a relic of ancient Egyptian astrological traditions, but their source had been forgotten by the Middle Ages. People then took them to be anniversaries of the plagues visited on Egypt in Moses' time—despite the fact that there were 24 Egyptian days in a year and only ten Biblical plagues. In a 13th century Anglo-French calendar, the Egyptian days were called collectively *dismal* (from Latin *dies mali*, "evil days"), and this word was borrowed into Middle English. Any day of the 24 was a *dismal day*, but the original sense "evil days" was forgotten, and *dismal* in the phrase was taken as an adjective meaning "disastrous." In Modern English this sense has been weakened to "causing gloom," perhaps by association with *dismay*.

dis·man·tle \dis-ˈmant-l\ *vt* **dis·man·tled; dis·man·tling** \-ˈmant-ling, -l-ing\ **1** : to strip of furniture and equipment **2** : to take apart ⟨*dismantled* the engine to repair it⟩ [Middle French *desmanteler* "to strip of dress," from *des-* "dis-" + *mantel* "mantle"] — **dis·man·tle·ment** \-ˈmant-l-mənt\ *n*

dis·mast \dis-ˈmast, ˈdis-\ *vt* : to remove or break off the mast of ⟨a ship *dismasted* in a storm⟩

1dis·may \dis-ˈmā, diz-\ *vt* **1** : to cause to lose courage or resolution (as because of alarm or fear) : DAUNT ⟨*dismayed* by the task before us⟩ **2** : UPSET 3a, PERTURB ⟨*dismayed* by the poor turnout⟩ [Medieval French *desmaier*, from *des-* "dis-" + *-maiier* "to enable," of Germanic origin] — **dis·may·ing·ly** \-ing-lē\ *adv*

2dismay *n* **1** : sudden loss of courage or resolution from alarm or fear **2** : a feeling of alarm or disappointment

dis·mem·ber \dis-ˈmem-bər, ˈdis-\ *vt* **dis·mem·bered; dis·mem·ber·ing** \-bə-ring, -bring\ **1** : to cut off or separate the limbs, members, or parts of **2** : to break up or tear into pieces — **dis·mem·ber·ment** \-bər-mənt\ *n*

dis·miss \dis-ˈmis\ *vt* **1** : to permit or cause to leave ⟨*dismiss* the class⟩ **2** : to discharge from office, service, or employment **3** : to put aside or out of mind ⟨*dismiss* the thought⟩ **4** : to refuse further judicial consideration to ⟨the judge *dismissed* the charge⟩ [Latin *dimissus,* past participle of *dimittere* "to dismiss," from *dis-* "apart" + *mittere* "to send"] — **dis·mis·sive** \-ˈmi-siv\ *adj* — **dis·mis·sive·ly** *adv*

dis·miss·al \-ˈmis-əl\ *n* **:** the act of dismissing **:** the fact or state of being dismissed

dis·mount \dis-ˈmau̇nt, ˈdis-\ *vb* **1 :** to get down from something (as a horse or bicycle) **2 :** to remove or throw down especially from a horse **:** UNHORSE

dis·obe·di·ence \ˌdis-ə-ˈbēd-ē-əns\ *n* **:** neglect or refusal to obey — **dis·obe·di·ent** \-ənt\ *adj* — **dis·obe·di·ent·ly** *adv*

dis·obey \ˌdis-ə-ˈbā\ *vb* **:** to fail to obey **:** be disobedient

dis·oblige \ˌdis-ə-ˈblīj\ *vt* **1 :** to go counter to the wishes of **2 :** to cause inconvenience to

¹dis·or·der \dis-ˈȯrd-ər, ˈdis-\ *vt* **1 :** to disturb the order of **2 :** to disturb the regular or normal functions of

²disorder *n* **1 a :** lack of order ⟨clothes in *disorder*⟩ **b :** breach of the peace or public order **2 :** an abnormal physical or mental condition **:** AILMENT — **dis·or·dered** \-ˈȯrd-ərd\ *adj*

dis·or·der·ly \-ər-lē\ *adj* **1 :** engaged in or being conduct offensive to public order or decency ⟨*disorderly* behavior⟩ ⟨*disorderly* persons⟩ **2 :** not in an orderly condition **:** characterized by disorder ⟨a *disorderly* mass of papers⟩ — **dis·or·der·li·ness** *n*

dis·or·ga·nize \ˈdis-ˈȯr-gə-ˌnīz\ *vt* **:** to break up the regular arrangement or system of **:** throw into disorder **:** CONFUSE — **dis·or·ga·ni·za·tion** \ˌdis-ˌȯrg-ə-nə-ˈzā-shən, -ˌȯrg-nə-\ *n*

dis·ori·ent \dis-ˈōr-ē-ˌent, -ˈȯr-\ *vt* **1 :** to cause to lose bearings **:** deprive of the normal sense of position, place, or time **2 :** to cause to be confused — **dis·ori·en·ta·tion** \ˌdis-ˌōr-ē-ən-ˈtā-shən, -ˌȯr-\ *n*

dis·own \dis-ˈōn, ˈdis-\ *vt* **:** to refuse to acknowledge as one's own **:** REPUDIATE

dis·par·age \dis-ˈpar-ij\ *vt* **1 :** to lower in rank or reputation **:** DEGRADE **2 :** to speak slightingly of **:** BELITTLE ⟨*disparaged* their achievements⟩ [Middle French *desparagier* "to marry below one's class," from *des-* "dis-" + *parage* "lineage," from *per* "peer"] — **dis·par·age·ment** \-mənt\ *n* — **dis·par·ag·ing** \-ij-ing\ *adj* — **dis·par·ag·ing·ly** \-lē\ *adv*

dis·par·ate \dis-ˈpar-ət; ˈdis-pə-rət, -prət\ *adj* **:** markedly distinct in quality or character [Latin *disparatus,* past participle of *disparare* "to separate," from *dis-* + *parare* "to prepare"] ***synonyms*** see DIFFERENT — **dis·par·ate·ly** *adv* — **dis·par·ate·ness** *n* — **dis·par·i·ty** \dis-ˈpar-ət-ē\ *n*

dis·pas·sion·ate \dis-ˈpash-nət, -ə-nət\ *adj* **:** not influenced by strong feeling **:** IMPARTIAL — **dis·pas·sion·ate·ly** *adv*

¹dis·patch \dis-ˈpach\ *vt* **1 :** to send away promptly or rapidly to a particular place or for a particular purpose ⟨*dispatch* a messenger⟩ ⟨*dispatch* a train⟩ **2 :** KILL 1 **3 :** to attend to or dispose of speedily ⟨*dispatch* business⟩ [Spanish *despachar* or Italian *dispacciare,* from Provençal *despachar* "to get rid of," from Medieval French *despeechier* "to set free"] — **dis·patch·er** *n*

²dispatch *n* **1 a :** the sending of a message or messenger **b :** the shipment of goods **2 :** MESSAGE; *esp* **:** an important official message **3 :** the act of killing **4 :** a news item sent in by a correspondent to a newspaper **5 :** promptness and efficiency in performing a task

dis·pel \dis-ˈpel\ *vt* **dis·pelled; dis·pel·ling :** to drive away by or as if by scattering **:** DISSIPATE [Latin *dispellere,* from *dis-* + *pellere* "to drive, beat"] ***synonyms*** see SCATTER

dis·pens·able \dis-ˈpen-sə-bəl\ *adj* **:** capable of being dispensed with — **dis·pens·abil·i·ty** \-ˌpen-sə-ˈbil-ət-ē\ *n*

dis·pen·sa·ry \dis-ˈpens-rē, -ə-rē\ *n, pl* **-ries :** a place where medical or dental aid is dispensed

dis·pen·sa·tion \ˌdis-pən-ˈsā-shən, -ˌpen-\ *n* **1 a :** a system of rules for ordering affairs **b :** a particular arrangement or provision especially of nature **2 :** an exemption from a rule or from a vow or oath **3 a :** the act of dispensing **b :** something dispensed or distributed — **dis·pen·sa·tion·al** \-shnəl, -shən-l\ *adj*

dis·pen·sa·to·ry \dis-ˈpen-sə-ˌtōr-ē, -ˌtȯr-\ *n, pl* **-ries :** a book containing descriptions of medicines

dis·pense \dis-ˈpens\ *vt* **1 a :** to deal out in portions **b :** ADMINISTER ⟨*dispense* justice⟩ **2 :** to prepare and distribute (medication) [Latin *dispensare* "to distribute," from *dis-* + *pensare* "to weigh," from *pendere* "to weigh, pay out," from *dis-* + *pendere* "to weigh"] — **dispense with 1 :** to set aside **:** DISCARD **2 :** to do without

dis·pens·er \dis-ˈpen-sər\ *n* **:** one that dispenses; *esp* **:** a container that releases its contents in convenient amounts ⟨a soap *dispenser*⟩

dis·pers·al \dis-ˈpər-səl\ *n* **:** the act or result of dispersing

dis·perse \dis-ˈpərs\ *vb* **1 a :** to cause to break up and go in different ways ⟨police *dispersed* the crowd⟩ **b :** to cause to become spread widely especially to the point of vanishing **c :** to cause to evaporate or vanish ⟨the sun *dispersing* the dew⟩ **2 a :** to subject (as light) to dispersion **b :** to distribute more or less evenly throughout a medium ⟨*disperse* particles in water⟩ **3 :** DISSIPATE 3 ⟨the clouds *dispersed*⟩ [Latin *dispersus,* past participle of *dispergere* "to scatter," from *dis-* + *spargere* "to scatter"] ***synonyms*** see SCATTER — **dis·pers·ible** \-ˈpər-sə-bəl\ *adj*

dis·per·sion \dis-ˈpər-zhən\ *n* **1 :** the act or process of dispersing **:** the state of being dispersed **2 :** the separation of light into colors by refraction or diffraction with formation of a spectrum **3 a :** a result or product of dispersing **:** something dispersed **b :** a system consisting of a dispersed substance and the medium in which it is dispersed ⟨a *dispersion* of fine particles in water⟩ — **dis·per·sive** \-ˈpər-siv, -ziv\ *adj* — **dis·per·sive·ly** *adv* — **dis·per·sive·ness** *n*

dis·pir·it \dis-ˈpir-ət, ˈdis-\ *vt* **:** to deprive of morale or enthusiasm **:** DISHEARTEN [*dis-* + *spirit*] — **dis·pir·it·ed** *adj* — **dis·pir·it·ed·ly** *adv* — **dis·pir·it·ed·ness** *n*

dis·place \dis-ˈplās, ˈdis-\ *vt* **1 :** to remove from a usual or proper place; *esp* **:** to expel or force to flee from home or homeland ⟨*displaced* persons⟩ **2 a :** to remove physically out of position ⟨water *displaced* by a floating object⟩ **b :** to take the place of **:** REPLACE — **dis·place·able** \-ə-bəl\ *adj*

dis·place·ment \-ˈplās-mənt\ *n* **1 :** the act of displacing **:** the state of being displaced **2 a :** the volume or weight of a fluid (as water) displaced by a floating body (as a ship) with the weight of the displaced fluid being equal to that of the displacing body ⟨a ship of 3000 tons *displacement*⟩ **b :** the difference between the initial position of an object and any later position **c :** the volume displaced by a piston (as in a pump or engine) in a single stroke; *also* **:** the total volume displaced in this way by all the pistons in an internal-combustion engine (as of an automobile)

¹dis·play \dis-ˈplā\ *vb* **1 a :** to put in plain view ⟨*display* the flag⟩ **b :** to make evident ⟨*displayed* great skill⟩ **2 :** to make a display of ⟨liked to *display* his new car⟩ [Medieval French *desplaier, desploier,* literally, "to unfold," from *des-* "dis-" + *ploier, plier* "to fold," from Latin *plicare* "to fold"] ***synonyms*** see SHOW

²display *n* **1 a :** a displaying of something ⟨a fireworks *display*⟩ **b :** unnecessary show especially for effect **c :** an eye-catching exhibition ⟨a *display* of artifacts⟩ ⟨her early paintings are currently on *display*⟩ **d :** an electronic device (as a cathode-ray tube in a computer or radar receiver) that presents information in visual form; *also* **:** the information presented **2 :** a pattern of behavior exhibited especially by male birds in the breeding season

dis·please \dis-ˈplēz, ˈdis-\ *vb* **1 :** to arouse the disapproval and dislike of **2 :** to be offensive to **3 :** to give displeasure

dis·plea·sure \dis-ˈplezh-ər, ˈdis-, -ˈplāzh-\ *n* **:** the feeling of one who is displeased **:** DISSATISFACTION

dis·port \dis-ˈpōrt, -ˈpȯrt\ *vb* **1 a :** DIVERT, AMUSE ⟨*disporting* themselves on the beach⟩ **b :** FROLIC **2 :** DISPLAY 1b [Medieval French *desporter* "to carry away, comfort, entertain," from *des-* "dis-" + *porter* "to carry"] — **dis·port·ment** \-mənt\ *n*

dis·pos·able \dis-ˈpō-zə-bəl\ *adj* **:** made to be used once and then thrown away ⟨*disposable* diapers⟩

dis·pos·al \dis-ˈpō-zəl\ *n* **1 :** the power or authority to dispose of or make use of as one chooses ⟨the car was at my *disposal*⟩ **2 :** an orderly distribution **:** ARRANGEMENT **3 :** MANAGEMENT 1, ADMINISTRATION **4 :** the transfer of something into new hands **5 :** a discarding or destroying especially in a systematic way **6 :** a device used to reduce waste matter (as by grinding)

dis·pose \dis-ˈpōz\ *vt* **1 :** to give a tendency to **:** INCLINE ⟨they were *disposed* to refuse⟩ **2 :** to put in place **:** set in readiness **:** ARRANGE [Medieval French *desposer,* from Latin *disponere* "to arrange," from *dis-* + *ponere* "to put"] ***synonyms*** see IN-

CLINE — **dis·pos·er** *n* — **dispose of** **1** : to settle or determine the fate, condition, or use of : deal with conclusively ⟨has the right to *dispose of* the personal property⟩ **2** : to transfer to the control of another ⟨we had to *dispose of* the house before we moved⟩ **3** : to get rid of ⟨*dispose of* rubbish⟩

dis·po·si·tion \ˌdis-pə-ˈzish-ən\ *n* **1 a** : the act or power of disposing : DISPOSAL **b** : a final settlement **2** : the giving up or transferring of something **3** : ARRANGEMENT **4 a** : TENDENCY, INCLINATION **b** : one's usual attitude toward things

dis·pos·sess \ˌdis-pə-ˈzes\ *vt* : to deprive of possession or occupancy (as of land or houses) — **dis·pos·ses·sion** \-ˈzesh-ən\ *n*

dis·praise \dis-ˈprāz, ˈdis-\ *vt* : to comment on with disapproval or censure — **dispraise** *n* — **dis·prais·er** *n* — **dis·prais·ing·ly** \-ˈprā-zing-lē\ *adv*

dis·proof \dis-ˈprüf, ˈdis-\ *n* **1** : the action of disproving **2** : evidence that disproves

dis·pro·por·tion \ˌdis-prə-ˈpōr-shən, -ˈpȯr-\ *n* : lack of proportion, symmetry, or proper relation : DISPARITY; *also* : an instance of this — **disproportion** *vt* — **dis·pro·por·tion·al** \-shnəl, -shən-l\ *adj* — **dis·pro·por·tion·ate** \-shə-nət, -shnət\ *adj* — **dis·pro·por·tion·ate·ly** *adv*

dis·prove \dis-ˈprüv\ *vt* : to prove to be false : REFUTE — **dis·prov·able** \-ˈprü-və-bəl\ *adj*

dis·pu·ta·tion \ˌdis-pyu̇-ˈtā-shən\ *n* **1** : the act of disputing : DEBATE **2** : an oral defense of an academic thesis

dis·pu·ta·tious \ˌdis-pyu̇-ˈtā-shəs\ *adj* : inclined to dispute : ARGUMENTATIVE — **dis·pu·ta·tious·ly** *adv* — **dis·pu·ta·tious·ness** *n*

[1]**dis·pute** \dis-ˈpyüt\ *vb* **1** : to engage in argument : DEBATE; *esp* : to argue irritably or with irritating persistence **2** : WRANGLE 1 **3 a** : to engage in controversy over : argue about **b** : to deny the truth or rightness of : QUESTION **4 a** : to struggle against : OPPOSE **b** : to struggle over : CONTEST [Medieval French *desputer,* from Latin *disputare* "to discuss," from *dis-* + *putare* "to think"] ***synonyms*** see DISCUSS — **dis·put·able** \dis-ˈpyüt-ə-bəl, ˈdis-pyət-\ *adj* — **dis·put·ably** \-blē\ *adv* — **dis·pu·tant** \dis-ˈpyüt-nt, ˈdis-pyət-ənt\ *n* — **dis·put·er** *n*

[2]**dispute** *n* **1** : verbal controversy : DEBATE **2** : QUARREL 2

dis·qual·i·fy \dis-ˈkwäl-ə-ˌfī, ˈdis-\ *vt* **1** : to deprive of necessary qualifications : make unfit ⟨*disqualified* for military service by poor vision⟩ **2** : to make or declare ineligible ⟨*disqualify* voters who cannot read and write⟩ — **dis·qual·i·fi·ca·tion** \ˌdis-ˌkwäl-ə-fə-ˈkā-shən\ *n*

[1]**dis·qui·et** \dis-ˈkwī-ət\ *vt* : to make uneasy or restless : DISTURB — **dis·qui·et·ing** \-ing\ *adj* — **dis·qui·et·ing·ly** \-ing-lē\ *adv*

[2]**disquiet** *n* : DISQUIETUDE

dis·qui·etude \dis-ˈkwī-ə-ˌtüd, -ˌtyüd\ *n* : lack of peace and tranquillity : a state of unrest or anxiety

dis·qui·si·tion \ˌdis-kwə-ˈzish-ən\ *n* : a formal inquiry or discussion : DISCOURSE [Latin *disquisitio,* from *disquirere* "to investigate," from *dis-* + *quaerere* "to seek"]

[1]**dis·re·gard** \ˌdis-ri-ˈgärd\ *vt* : to pay no attention to : treat as unworthy of regard or notice ***synonyms*** see NEGLECT

[2]**disregard** *n* : the act of disregarding : the state of being disregarded — **dis·re·gard·ful** \-fəl\ *adj*

dis·re·pair \ˌdis-ri-ˈpaər, -ˈpeər\ *n* : the state of being in need of repair

dis·rep·u·ta·ble \dis-ˈrep-yət-ə-bəl, ˈdis-\ *adj* : not reputable; *esp* : having a bad reputation — **dis·rep·u·ta·ble·ness** *n* — **dis·rep·u·ta·bly** \-blē\ *adv*

dis·re·pute \ˌdis-ri-ˈpyüt\ *n* : loss or lack of esteem or reputation : DISCREDIT

[1]**dis·re·spect** \ˌdis-ri-ˈspekt\ *vt* **1** : to have disrespect for **2** : to show or express disrespect or contempt for : INSULT

[2]**disrespect** *n* : lack of respect : DISCOURTESY — **dis·re·spect·ful** \-fəl\ *adj* — **dis·re·spect·ful·ly** \-fə-lē\ *adv* — **dis·re·spect·ful·ness** *n*

dis·re·spect·able \-ˈspek-tə-bəl\ *adj* : not respectable — **dis·re·spect·abil·i·ty** \-ˌspek-tə-ˈbil-ət-ē\ *n*

dis·robe \dis-ˈrōb, ˈdis-\ *vb* : UNDRESS

dis·rupt \dis-ˈrəpt\ *vt* **1** : to break apart : RUPTURE **2** : to throw into disorder : break up ⟨his outburst *disrupted* the class⟩ **3** : to interrupt the unity or continuity of ⟨the storm *disrupted* communications⟩ [Latin *disruptus,* past participle of *disrumpere* "to break apart," from *dis-* + *rumpere* "to break"] — **dis·rupt·er** *n* — **dis·rup·tion** \-ˈrəp-shən\ *n* — **dis·rup·tive** \-ˈrəp-tiv\ *adj* — **dis·rup·tive·ly** *adv* — **dis·rup·tive·ness** *n*

dis·sat·is·fac·tion \ˌdis-ˌsat-əs-ˈfak-shən, ˌdis-ˌat-\ *n* : the quality or state of being dissatisfied : DISCONTENT

dis·sat·is·fac·to·ry \-ˈfak-tə-rē, -trē\ *adj* : causing dissatisfaction

dis·sat·is·fied \dis-ˈsat-əs-ˌfīd, ˈdis-, -ˈat-\ *adj* : expressing or showing lack of satisfaction : not pleased or satisfied ⟨a *dissatisfied* look⟩ ⟨*dissatisfied* customers⟩

dis·sat·is·fy \dis-ˈsat-əs-ˌfī, ˈdis-, -ˈat-\ *vt* : to fail to satisfy

dis·sect \dī-ˈsekt, di-; ˈdī-ˌsekt\ *vt* **1** : to divide (as a plant or an animal) into separate parts for examination and study **2** : to analyze thoroughly ⟨*dissect* a proposed plan⟩ [Latin *dissecare* "to cut apart," from *dis-* + *secare* "to cut"] — **dis·sec·tor** \-ər\ *n*

dis·sect·ed *adj* : cut deeply into fine lobes ⟨a *dissected* leaf⟩

dis·sec·tion \-ˈsek-shən, -ˌsek-\ *n* **1** : the act or process of dissecting : the state of being dissected **2** : an anatomical specimen prepared by dissecting

dis·sem·ble \dis-ˈem-bəl\ *vb* **-bled; -bling** \-bə-ling, -bling\ **1** : to hide under or put on a false appearance : conceal facts, intentions, or feelings under some pretense **2** : to put on the appearance of : SIMULATE [Medieval French *dissimuler,* from Latin *dissimulare* "to dissimulate"] — **dis·sem·bler** \-bə-lər, -blər\ *n*

dis·sem·i·nate \dis-ˈem-ə-ˌnāt\ *vt* : to spread abroad as though sowing seed ⟨*disseminate* ideas⟩ [Latin *disseminare,* from *dis-* + *seminare* "to sow," from *semen* "seed"] — **dis·sem·i·na·tion** \-ˌem-ə-ˈnā-shən\ *n* — **dis·sem·i·na·tor** \-ˈem-ə-ˌnāt-ər\ *n*

dis·sen·sion \dis-ˈen-chən\ *n* : disagreement in opinion : DISCORD, QUARRELING [Medieval French *discension,* from Latin *dissensio,* from *dissentire* "to dissent"]

[1]**dis·sent** \dis-ˈent\ *vi* **1** : to withhold assent **2** : to differ in opinion [Latin *dissentire,* from *dis-* + *sentire* "to feel"]

[2]**dissent** *n* **1** : difference of opinion; *esp* : religious nonconformity **2** : a written statement in which a justice disagrees with the opinion of the majority — called also *dissenting opinion* **3** : political opposition to a government or its policies

dis·sent·er \dis-ˈent-ər\ *n* **1** : one that dissents **2** *cap* : an English Nonconformist

dis·ser·ta·tion \ˌdis-ər-ˈtā-shən\ *n* : an extended usually written treatment of a subject; *esp* : one submitted for a doctorate [Latin *dissertatio* "discussion," derived from *disserere* "to discourse," from *dis-* + *serere* "to join, arrange"]

dis·ser·vice \dis-ˈsər-vəs, -ˈər-\ *n* : ill service : HARM; *also* : an unhelpful, unkind, or harmful act ⟨misinformation that does a *disservice* to readers⟩

dis·si·dence \ˈdis-əd-əns\ *n* : DISSENT 1, DISAGREEMENT

dis·si·dent \-ənt\ *adj* : openly differing with an opinion or a group : expressing dissent [Latin *dissidēre* "to sit apart, disagree," from *dis-* + *sedēre* "to sit"] — **dissident** *n*

dis·sim·i·lar \dis-ˈsim-ə-lər, -ˈim-\ *adj* : UNLIKE — **dis·sim·i·lar·i·ty** \ˌdis-ˌsim-ə-ˈlar-ət-ē, -ˌim-\ *n* — **dis·sim·i·lar·ly** \dis-ˈsim-ə-lər-lē, -ˈim-\ *adv*

dis·sim·i·la·tion \ˌdis-ˌim-ə-ˈlā-shən\ *n* : the change or omission of one of two identical or closely related sounds in a word — **dis·sim·i·la·tive** \dis-ˈim-ə-ˌlāt-iv\ *adj*

dis·si·mil·i·tude \ˌdis-sə-ˈmil-ə-ˌtüd, ˌdis-ə-, -ˌtyüd\ *n* : lack of resemblance

dis·sim·u·late \dis-ˈim-yə-ˌlāt\ *vb* : to hide under a false appearance : DISSEMBLE [Latin *dissimulare,* from *dis-* + *simulare* "to simulate"] — **dis·sim·u·la·tion** \ˌdis-ˌim-yə-ˈlā-shən\ *n* — **dis·sim·u·la·tor** \dis-ˈim-yə-ˌlāt-ər\ *n*

dis·si·pate \ˈdis-ə-ˌpāt\ *vb* **1 a** : to break up and drive off (as a crowd) **b** : to cause to spread out to the point of vanishing : DISSOLVE ⟨the breeze *dissipated* the fog⟩ **2 a** : to expend aimlessly or foolishly ⟨*dissipate* our energies⟩ **b** : SQUANDER ⟨*dissipated* a fortune in gambling⟩ **3** : to separate into parts and scatter or vanish **4** : to be extravagant or uncontrolled in the pursuit of pleasure; *esp* : to drink to excess [Latin *dissipare,* from *dis-* + *supare* "to throw"] ***synonyms*** see SCATTER

dis·si·pat·ed *adj* : given to or marked by dissipation — **dis·si·pat·ed·ly** *adv* — **dis·si·pat·ed·ness** *n*

dis·si·pa·tion \ˌdis-ə-ˈpā-shən\ *n* : the act of dissipating : the state of being dissipated: **a** : DISPERSION 1 **b** : wasteful expenditure **c** : intemperate living; *esp* : excessive drinking

dis·so·ci·ate \dis-ˈō-sē-ˌāt, -shē-ˌāt\ *vb* **1** : to separate from association or union with another : DISCONNECT **2** : DISUNITE; *esp* : to subject to chemical dissociation **3** : to undergo dissociation ⟨salts and acids *dissociate* in water⟩ [Latin *dissociare,* from *dis-* + *sociare* "to join," from *socius* "companion"]

dis·so·ci·a·tion \ˌdis-ˌō-sē-ˈā-shən, -ˌō-shē-\ *n* : the act or process of dissociating : the state of being dissociated; *esp* : the process by which a chemical combination breaks up into simpler constituents — **dis·so·cia·tive** \dis-ˈō-sē-ˌāt-iv, -sē-ˌāt-, -shət-iv\ *adj*

dis·so·lute \ˈdis-ə-ˌlüt\ *adj* **:** lacking restraint; *esp* **:** loose in morals or conduct [Latin *dissolutus,* from *dissolvere* "to loosen, dissolve"] — **dis·so·lute·ly** *adv* — **dis·so·lute·ness** *n*

dis·so·lu·tion \ˌdis-ə-ˈlü-shən\ *n* **1 :** the action or process of dissolving: as **a :** separation into component parts **b :** DECAY 1 **2 :** the termination or breaking up of an assembly or a partnership or corporation

1**dis·solve** \diz-ˈälv, -ˈölv\ *vb* **1 :** to break up into component parts **2 :** to pass or cause to pass into solution ⟨sugar *dissolves* in water⟩ **3 :** to bring to an end **:** TERMINATE ⟨*dissolve* parliament⟩ **4 :** to waste or fade away as if by breaking up or melting ⟨their courage *dissolved* in the face of danger⟩ **5 :** to fade out (a motion-picture shot) in a dissolve **6 :** to be overcome emotionally ⟨*dissolved* into tears⟩ [Latin *dissolvere,* from *dis-* + *solvere* "to loosen"] — **dis·solv·able** \-ə-bəl\ *adj* — **dis·solv·er** *n*

2**dissolve** *n* **:** a gradual superimposing of one motion-picture or television shot upon another on a screen

dis·so·nance \ˈdis-ə-nəns\ *n* **1 :** a harsh or unpleasant sound or combination of sounds **2 :** lack of agreement **:** DISCORD **3 :** an unresolved musical interval or chord

dis·so·nant \ˈdis-ə-nənt\ *adj* **1 :** marked by dissonance in sound **2 :** not being in harmony or agreement ⟨*dissonant* viewpoints⟩ [Latin *dissonare* "to be discordant," from *dis-* + *sonare* "to sound"] — **dis·so·nant·ly** *adv*

dis·suade \dis-ˈwād\ *vt* **:** to advise against a course of action **:** persuade or try to persuade not to do something [Latin *dissuadēre,* from *dis-* + *suadēre* "to urge"] — **dis·sua·sion** \-ˈwā-zhən\ *n* — **dis·sua·sive** \-ˈwā-siv, -ziv\ *adj* — **dis·sua·sive·ly** *adv* — **dis·sua·sive·ness** *n*

1**dis·taff** \ˈdis-ˌtaf\ *n, pl* **dis·taffs** \-ˌtafs, -ˌtavz\ **1 :** a staff for holding the flax, tow, or wool in spinning **2 :** the female branch or side of a family [Old English *distæf*]

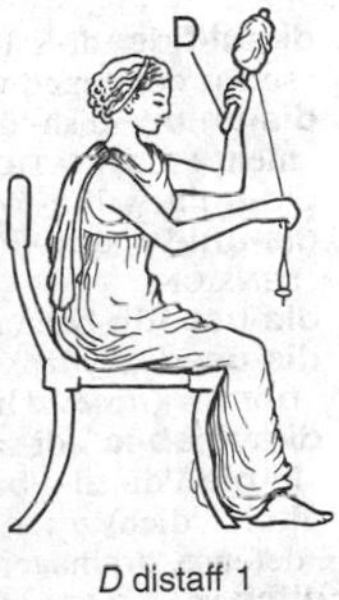

D distaff 1

Word History A *distaff* is a small staff used in spinning yarn or thread. Because spinning was in former times an important activity of most women, the *distaff* became a symbol for women's work. Activity that was felt to be proper to men rather than to women was symbolized by the spear, and the male side of a family was known as the "spear side." This term is now used very rarely, if at all, but the female side of a family is still commonly called the "distaff side" or simply the "distaff."

2**distaff** *adj* **1 :** MATERNAL 2 **2 :** FEMALE 1a

dis·tal \ˈdist-l\ *adj* **1 :** away or far from the point of attachment or origin (as of a bone or limb) — compare PROXIMAL **2 :** of, relating to, or being the surface of a tooth that is most distant from the middle of the front of the jaw and is usually next to the tooth behind it [*distant* + *-al*] — **dis·tal·ly** \-l-ē\ *adv*

1**dis·tance** \ˈdis-təns\ *n* **1 :** separation in time **2 :** separation in space **:** the amount of space between two points, lines, surfaces, or objects ⟨the *distance* from the earth to the moon⟩ **3 a :** a measurable advance along a route or course ⟨walked a *distance* of five kilometers⟩ **b :** an amount or degree of progress ⟨have come quite a *distance* toward achieving peace⟩ **c :** a full course or extent ⟨go the *distance*⟩ **4 :** the quality or state of being distant: **a :** remoteness in space ⟨their parents sought to keep them at a *distance*⟩ **b :** COLDNESS, RESERVE ⟨they keep their *distance*⟩ **5 :** a distant point or region ⟨saw a car off in the *distance*⟩

2**distance** *vt* **:** to leave far behind **:** OUTSTRIP

dis·tant \ˈdis-tənt\ *adj* **1 a :** separated in space **:** AWAY ⟨a point 100 meters *distant*⟩ **b :** situated at a great distance **:** FAR-OFF ⟨travel to *distant* lands⟩ **2 :** not close in relationship ⟨a *distant* cousin⟩ **3 :** reserved or aloof in personal relationship **:** COLD ⟨they have recently been very *distant* toward me⟩ **4 :** coming from or going to a distance ⟨*distant* voyages⟩ [Medieval French, from Latin *distare* "to stand apart, be distant," from *dis-* + *stare* "to stand"] — **dis·tant·ly** *adv* — **dis·tant·ness** *n*

synonyms DISTANT, FAR, REMOTE, REMOVED mean not close or near in space, time, or relationship. DISTANT is the opposite of *close* and implies separation in space or time ⟨in the *distant* future⟩. FAR is the opposite of *near* and implies a relatively long distance away ⟨England is *far* from China⟩. REMOTE applies to what is far removed especially from what is regarded as a center of interest ⟨a *remote* corner of the world⟩. REMOVED implies separateness and often a contrast in character or quality as well as time or space ⟨lives in a small town well *removed* from the city⟩.

dis·taste \dis-ˈtāst, ˈdis-\ *n* **:** DISLIKE ⟨a *distaste* for work⟩

dis·taste·ful \-fəl\ *adj* **:** disagreeable or unpleasant especially because in poor taste, inappropriate, or unethical — **dis·taste·ful·ly** \-fə-lē\ *adv* — **dis·taste·ful·ness** *n*

1**dis·tem·per** \dis-ˈtem-pər\ *n* **1 :** a bad humor or temper **2 :** a disordered or abnormal bodily state especially of four-footed mammals: as **a :** a highly contagious virus disease especially of dogs marked by fever and by respiratory and sometimes nervous symptoms **b :** PANLEUKOPENIA

2**distemper** *n* **:** a water-based paint in which the pigments are usually mixed with size or a casein binder and which is used for scene painting and mural decoration [Medieval French *destemprer* "to dilute," from Latin *dis-* + *temperare* "to temper"]

dis·tend \dis-ˈtend\ *vb* **:** to stretch out or bulge out in all directions **:** SWELL [Latin *distendere,* from *dis-* + *tendere* "to stretch"] ***synonyms*** see EXPAND

dis·ten·sion *or* **dis·ten·tion** \dis-ˈten-chən\ *n* **:** the act of distending **:** the state of being distended especially unduly or abnormally

dis·till *also* **dis·til** \dis-ˈtil\ *vb* **dis·tilled; dis·till·ing 1 :** to fall or let fall in drops **2 a :** to subject to or transform by distillation ⟨*distill* water⟩ **b :** to obtain by distillation ⟨*distill* brandy from wine⟩ **3 :** to extract the essence of **:** CONCENTRATE ⟨*distilled* the information in the report⟩ **4 :** to undergo distillation **:** condense from a still after distillation [Medieval French *distiller,* derived from Latin *destillare,* derived from *de-* + *stilla* "drop"]

dis·til·late \ˈdis-tə-ˌlāt, dis-ˈtil-ət\ *n* **:** a liquid product condensed from vapor during distillation

dis·til·la·tion \ˌdis-tə-ˈlā-shən\ *n* **1 :** a process that consists of driving gas or vapor from liquids or solids by heating and condensing to liquid products and that is used especially for purification, separation, or the formation of new substances **2 :** something obtained by or as if by a process of distilling **:** ESSENCE

dis·till·er \dis-ˈtil-ər\ *n* **:** one that distills especially alcoholic liquors

dis·till·ery \dis-ˈtil-rē, -ə-rē\ *n, pl* **-er·ies :** a place where distilling especially of alcoholic liquors is done

dis·tinct \dis-ˈtingt, -tingkt\ *adj* **1 :** distinguished from others **:** SEPARATE ⟨guilty of three *distinct* crimes⟩ **2 :** clearly seen, heard, or understood **:** UNMISTAKABLE ⟨*distinct* footprints⟩; *also* **:** NOTABLE ⟨a *distinct* improvement⟩ [Medieval French, from Latin *distinctus,* from *distinguere* "to distinguish"] — **distinct·ly** *adv* — **dis·tinct·ness** *n*

dis·tinc·tion \dis-ˈting-shən, -ˈtingk-\ *n* **1 :** the act of distinguishing a difference **2 :** the quality or state of being different or distinct **:** DIFFERENCE ⟨the *distinction* between good and evil⟩ **3 :** something that makes a difference **:** a distinguishing quality or mark ⟨the *distinction* of being the tallest building in town⟩ **4 :** SIGNIFICANCE, EMINENCE ⟨a speaker of *distinction*⟩ **5 :** special honor or recognition ⟨graduated with *distinction*⟩

dis·tinc·tive \dis-ˈting-tiv, -ˈtingk-\ *adj* **:** clearly marking a person or a thing as different from others ⟨a *distinctive* way of speaking⟩ ***synonyms*** see CHARACTERISTIC — **dis·tinc·tive·ly** *adv* — **dis·tinc·tive·ness** *n*

dis·tin·guish \dis-ˈting-gwish, -wish\ *vb* **1 :** to recognize as different by some mark or quality ⟨*distinguish* the sound of a piano in an orchestra⟩ **2 :** to make distinctions ⟨*distinguish* between right and wrong⟩ **3 :** to mark as different or distinct **:** set apart ⟨a church *distinguished* by the absence of a steeple⟩ **4 :** to perceive clearly **:** make out ⟨*distinguish* a light in the distance⟩ **5 :** to separate from others by a mark of honor **:** single out; *also* **:** to make (oneself) prominent ⟨*distinguished* themselves in Congress⟩ [Medieval French *distinguer,* from Latin *distinguere,* literally, "to separate by pricking"] — **dis·tin·guish·able** \-ə-bəl\ *adj* — **dis·tin·guish·ably** \-ə-blē\ *adv*

\ə\ abut	\au̇\ out	\i\ tip	\ȯ\ saw	\u̇\ foot
\ər\ further	\ch\ chin	\ī\ life	\ȯi\ coin	\y\ yet
\a\ mat	\e\ pet	\j\ job	\th\ thin	\yü\ few
\ā\ take	\ē\ easy	\ng\ sing	\th\ this	\yu̇\ cure
\ä\ cot, cart	\g\ go	\ō\ bone	\ü\ food	\zh\ vision

dis·tin·guished *adj* **1** : marked by eminence, distinction, or excellence **2** : befitting an eminent person
dis·tort \dis-ˈtȯrt\ *vt* **1** : to twist out of the true meaning : MISREPRESENT **2** : to twist out of a natural, normal, or original shape or condition [Latin *distortus,* past participle of *distorquēre* "to distort," from *dis-* + *torquēre* "to twist"] — **dis·tort·er** *n*
dis·tor·tion \dis-ˈtȯr-shən\ *n* **1** : the act of distorting **2** : the condition of being distorted or a product of distortion: as **a** : a misshapen condition of an image caused by defects in a lens **b** : falsified reproduction of a sound or of a video image — **dis·tor·tion·al** \-shnəl, -shən-l\ *adj*
dis·tract \dis-ˈtrakt\ *vt* **1** : to turn aside : DIVERT; *esp* : to draw (the attention or mind) to a different object **2** : to stir up or confuse with conflicting emotions or motives [Latin *distractus,* past participle of *distrahere,* literally, "to draw apart," from *dis-* + *trahere* "to draw"] — **dis·trac·tible** *also* **dis·tract·able** \-ˈtrak-tə-bəl\ *adj* — **dis·tract·ing·ly** \-ting-lē\ *adv*
dis·trac·tion \dis-ˈtrak-shən\ *n* **1** : the act of distracting or the state of being distracted; *esp* : mental confusion ⟨driven to *distraction*⟩ **2** : something that distracts; *esp* : AMUSEMENT ⟨a harmless *distraction*⟩ — **dis·trac·tive** \-ˈtrak-tiv\ *adj*
dis·traught \dis-ˈtrȯt\ *adj* **1** : troubled with doubt or mental conflict or pain **2** : being or acting insane : CRAZED [Middle English, from Latin *distractus* "distracted"]
¹dis·tress \dis-ˈtres\ *n* **1** : great suffering of body or mind : PAIN, ANGUISH ⟨suffer *distress* from loss of a friend⟩ **2** : MISFORTUNE, TROUBLE ⟨unemployment and economic *distress*⟩ **3** : a condition of danger or desperate need ⟨a ship in *distress*⟩ [Medieval French *destresce,* derived from Latin *distringere* "to draw apart, detain"]
synonyms DISTRESS, SUFFERING, MISERY, AGONY mean the state of being in physical or mental anguish. DISTRESS implies a usually temporary cause of physical or mental stress or strain ⟨the hurricane put everyone in great *distress*⟩. SUFFERING connotes conscious awareness and endurance of pain ⟨the *suffering* of victims burned in the fire⟩. MISERY stresses the unhappy or wretched conditions attending distress or suffering ⟨the *misery* of the homeless⟩. AGONY suggests suffering too intense to be borne ⟨in *agony* over the death of their child⟩.
²distress *vt* **1** : to subject to great strain or difficulties **2** : to cause to worry or be troubled : UPSET ⟨the news *distressed* her⟩ — **dis·tress·ing·ly** \-ing-lē\ *adv*
dis·tress·ful \-fəl\ *adj* : causing distress : full of distress — **dis·tress·ful·ly** \-fə-lē\ *adv* — **dis·tress·ful·ness** *n*
dis·trib·u·tary \dis-ˈtrib-yə-ˌter-ē\ *n, pl* **-taries** : a river branch flowing away from the main stream
dis·trib·ute \dis-ˈtrib-yət\ *vt* **1** : to divide among several or many : APPORTION ⟨*distribute* food packages to the needy⟩ **2 a** : to spread out so as to cover something : SCATTER ⟨*distribute* grass seed over a lawn⟩ **b** : to hand out : DELIVER ⟨*distributing* fliers to customers⟩ **3** : to divide or separate especially into kinds **4** : to market (a line of goods) in a particular area usually as a wholesaler [Latin *distribuere,* from *dis-* + *tribuere* "to allot"] — **dis·trib·ut·able** \-yət-ə-bəl\ *adj*
dis·tri·bu·tion \ˌdis-trə-ˈbyü-shən\ *n* **1** : the act or process of distributing **2 a** : the position, arrangement, or frequency of occurrence (as of the members of a group) over an area or throughout a space or unit of time ⟨the *distribution* of iron ore in the U.S.⟩ **b** : the natural geographic range of an organism **3 a** : something distributed **b** : FREQUENCY DISTRIBUTION **4** : the marketing or merchandising of commodities — **dis·tri·bu·tion·al** \-shnəl, -shən-l\ *adj*
dis·trib·u·tive \dis-ˈtrib-yət-iv\ *adj* **1** : of or relating to distribution **2** : referring singly and without exception to the members of a group ⟨the *distributive* adjectives *each* and *every*⟩ **3** : of, having, or being the property of producing the same mathematical result when an operation is carried out on a whole expression and when it is carried out on each part of an expression with the results then collected together ⟨the *distributive* property of multiplication means that $a(b + c) = ab + ac$⟩ — **dis·trib·u·tive·ly** *adv* — **dis·trib·u·tive·ness** *n*
dis·trib·u·tor \dis-ˈtrib-yət-ər\ *n* **1** : one that distributes **2** : an agent or agency for marketing goods **3** : a device for distributing electric current to the spark plugs of an engine in the proper firing order
¹dis·trict \ˈdis-trikt\ *n* **1** : a territorial division marked off or defined (as for administrative or electoral purposes) ⟨school *districts*⟩ ⟨a judicial *district*⟩ **2** : a distinctive area or region ⟨the residential *district*⟩ [French, from Medieval Latin *districtus* "jurisdiction, district," from *distringere* "to force to satisfy an obligation by means of seizing property," from Latin, "to draw apart, detain"]
²district *vt* : to divide or organize into districts
district attorney *n* : a public official who is the prosecuting officer for a judicial district
district court *n* : a trial court with jurisdiction over certain cases within a specified judicial district
¹dis·trust \dis-ˈtrəst, ˈdis-\ *vt* : to have no confidence in : SUSPECT
²distrust *n* : a lack of trust or confidence : SUSPICION, WARINESS ***synonyms*** see DOUBT — **dis·trust·ful** \-fəl\ *adj* — **dis·trust·ful·ly** \-fə-lē\ *adv* — **dis·trust·ful·ness** *n*
dis·turb \dis-ˈtərb\ *vt* **1 a** : to interfere with : INTERRUPT **b** : to alter the position, arrangement, or stability of **2 a** : to destroy the tranquillity or composure of : make uneasy ⟨the noise *disturbed* my sleep⟩ **b** : to throw into disorder **c** : to put to inconvenience ⟨sorry to *disturb* you so late⟩ [Latin *disturbare,* from *dis-* + *turbare* "to throw into disorder"] — **dis·turb·er** *n*
synonyms DISTURB, PERTURB, AGITATE, FLUSTER mean to destroy capacity for collected thought or decisive action. DISTURB implies interference with one's mental processes caused by worry, perplexity, or interruption ⟨the discrepancy in accounts *disturbed* me⟩. PERTURB implies deep disturbance of mind and emotions ⟨*perturbed* by her husband's strange behavior⟩. AGITATE suggests obvious external signs of nervous or emotional excitement ⟨we could see he was unable to work in his *agitated* state⟩. FLUSTER suggests bewildered agitation ⟨his declaration of love completely *flustered* her⟩.
dis·tur·bance \dis-ˈtər-bəns\ *n* **1** : the act of disturbing : the state of being disturbed **2** : mental confusion : UPSET ⟨an emotional *disturbance*⟩ **3** : public disorder : COMMOTION
dis·turbed *adj* : showing symptoms of mental or emotional illness
di·sul·fide \dī-ˈsəl-ˌfīd\ *n* : a compound containing two atoms of sulfur combined with an element or radical
dis·union \dish-ˈü-nyən, dis-, -ˈyü-\ *n* : lack of union or agreement : SEPARATION
dis·unite \ˌdish-ü-ˈnīt, ˌdis-, -yü-\ *vt* : DIVIDE 1, SEPARATE
dis·uni·ty \dish-ˈü-nət-ē, dis-, -ˈyü-\ *n* : lack of unity; *esp* : DISSENSION
dis·use \dis-ˈyüs\ *n* : cessation of use or practice
dis·used \-ˈyüzd\ *adj* : no longer used or occupied : ABANDONED ⟨*disused* buildings⟩
di·syl·lab·ic \ˌdī-sə-ˈlab-ik\ *adj* : having two syllables — **di·syl·la·ble** \ˈdī-ˌsil-ə-bəl, dī-ˈ\ *n*
¹ditch \ˈdich\ *n* : a long narrow excavation dug in the earth for defense, drainage, or irrigation [Old English *dīc* "dike, ditch"]
²ditch *vt* **1 a** : to enclose with a ditch **b** : to provide with ditches (as for drainage or irrigation) **2 a** : to get rid of : DISCARD ⟨*ditch* an old car⟩ **b** : to end association with : LEAVE ⟨his girlfriend *ditched* him⟩ **3** : to make a forced landing of (an airplane) on water
dith·er \ˈdith-ər\ *n* : a highly nervous, excited, or agitated state [Middle English *didderen*] — **dith·ery** \-ə-rē\ *adj*
dith·y·ramb \ˈdith-i-ˌram\ *n* **1** : a usually short poem in an inspired wild irregular strain **2** : an exalted or impassioned statement or writing [Greek *dithyrambos*] — **dith·y·ram·bic** \ˌdith-i-ˈram-bik\ *adj*
dit·to \ˈdit-ō\ *n, pl* **dittos** **1** : another of the same thing mentioned before or above — used to avoid repeating a word ⟨lost: one shirt (white); *ditto* (blue)⟩ **2** : a mark composed of a pair of inverted commas or apostrophes used as a symbol for the word *ditto* [Italian *ditto, detto,* past participle of *dire* "to say," from Latin *dicere*]
dit·ty \ˈdit-ē\ *n, pl* **ditties** : SONG; *esp* : a short simple song [Medieval French *dité* "story, song," from *ditier* "to compose," from Latin *dictare* "to dictate, compose"]
dit·ty bag \ˈdit-ē-\ *n* : a small bag used especially by sailors to hold odds and ends of gear (as thread, needles, or tape) [origin unknown]
dit·zy *or* **dit·sy** \ˈdit-sē\ *adj* **ditz·i·er** *or* **dits·i·er; -est** : unusually silly or giddy [origin unknown] — **dit·zi·ness** *or* **dit·si·ness** \-nəs\ *n*
di·uret·ic \ˌdī-yü-ˈret-ik\ *adj* : tending to increase the excretion of urine ⟨*diuretic* drugs⟩ [Late Latin *diureticus,* from Greek *diourētikos,* from *diourein* "to urinate," from *dia-* + *ourein* "to urinate"] — **diuretic** *n*
di·ur·nal \dī-ˈərn-l\ *adj* **1 a** : recurring every day ⟨a *diurnal* task⟩ **b** : having a daily cycle ⟨*diurnal* tides⟩ **2 a** : of, relating

to, occurring in, or active during the daytime ⟨a *diurnal* organism⟩ **b :** opening during the day and closing at night ⟨*diurnal* flowers⟩ [Latin *diurnalis,* from *diurnus* "of the day," from *dies* "day"] — **di·ur·nal·ly** \-l-ē\ *adv*

di·va \'dē-və\ *n, pl* **di·vas** *or* **di·ve** \-ˌvā\ **1 a :** PRIMA DONNA 1 **b :** PRIMA DONNA 2 **2 :** a usually glamorous and successful female performer or celebrity ⟨a fashion *diva*⟩; *esp* **:** a popular female singer ⟨pop *divas*⟩ [Italian, literally, "goddess," from Latin, feminine of *divus* "divine, god"]

di·va·gate \'dī-və-ˌgāt, 'div-ə-\ *vi* **:** to wander about **:** STRAY [Late Latin *divagari,* from Latin *dis-* + *vagari* "to wander"] — **di·va·ga·tion** \ˌdī-və-'gā-shən, ˌdiv-ə-\ *n*

di·va·lent \dī-'vā-lənt, 'dī-\ *adj* **:** BIVALENT

di·van \di-'van, 'dī-ˌvan\ *n* **:** a large couch or sofa usually without back or arms and often designed for use as a bed [Turkish, "council," from Persian *dīvān* "account book"]

[1]**dive** \'dīv\ *vi* **dived** \'dīvd\ *or* **dove** \'dōv\; **div·ing** **1 a :** to plunge into water headfirst; *esp* **:** to execute a dive **b :** SUBMERGE **2 a :** PLUNGE 3b **b :** to descend in a dive **3 :** to plunge into some matter or activity **4 :** DART, LUNGE ⟨*dived* for cover⟩ [Old English *dȳfan* "to dip" and *dūfan* "to dive"]

[2]**dive** *n* **1 :** the act or an instance of diving: as **a :** a plunge into water executed in a prescribed manner **b :** a submerging of a submarine **c :** a steep descent of an airplane with or without power **2 :** a sharp decline **3 :** a shabby and disreputable establishment (as a bar or nightclub)

dive–bomb \'dīv-ˌbäm\ *vt* **:** to bomb from an airplane by making a steep dive toward the target before releasing the bomb — **dive–bomb·er** *n*

div·er \'dī-vər\ *n* **1 :** one that dives **2 a :** a person who stays underwater for long periods by having air supplied from the surface or by carrying a supply of compressed air **b :** any of various diving birds; *esp* **:** LOON

di·verge \də-'vərj, dī-\ *vi* **1 a :** to move or extend in different directions from a common point **:** draw apart ⟨*diverging* rays of light⟩ **b :** to differ in character, form, or opinion **2 :** to turn aside from a path or course **:** DEVIATE [Medieval Latin *divergere,* from Latin *dis-* + *vergere* "to incline"]

di·ver·gence \-'vər-jəns\ *n* **1 :** a drawing apart (as of lines extending from a common center) **2 :** DIFFERENCE 3, DISAGREEMENT **3 :** a deviation from a course or standard

di·ver·gent \-jənt\ *adj* **1 :** drawing apart from each other **:** SPREADING **2 :** differing from each other or from a standard **:** DEVIANT ***synonyms*** see DIFFERENT — **di·ver·gent·ly** *adv*

di·vers \'dī-vərz\ *adj* **:** VARIOUS 3 [Middle English *divers, diverse*]

di·verse \dī-'vərs, də-, 'dī-ˌ\ *adj* **1 :** differing from one another **:** UNLIKE **2 :** having distinct or unlike elements or qualities ⟨a *diverse* personality⟩ [Middle English, from Latin *diversus,* from *divertere* "to divert"] ***synonyms*** see DIFFERENT — **di·verse·ly** *adv* — **di·verse·ness** *n*

di·ver·si·fy \də-'vər-sə-ˌfī, dī-\ *vb* **-fied; -fy·ing** **1 :** to make diverse **:** give variety to ⟨*diversify* an educational program by adding new subjects⟩ **2 :** to increase the variety of the products of ⟨*diversify* a business⟩ **3 :** to produce variety; *esp* **:** to engage in a variety of operations ⟨manufacturers *diversifying* into new fields⟩ — **di·ver·si·fi·ca·tion** \də-ˌvər-sə-fə-'kā-shən, ˌdī-\ *n*

di·ver·sion \də-'vər-zhən, dī-\ *n* **1 :** the act or an instance of diverting from a course, activity, or use **:** DEVIATION **2 :** something that diverts or amuses **:** PASTIME **3 :** an attack made to draw the attention of an enemy from the point of a principal operation — **di·ver·sion·ary** \-zhə-ˌner-ē\ *adj*

di·ver·si·ty \də-'vər-sət-ē, dī-\ *n, pl* **-ties** **1 a :** the condition of being different or having differences **b :** having diverse people (as people of different races or cultures) in a group or organization ⟨*diversity* in schools⟩ **2 :** an instance or a point of difference **3 :** VARIETY ⟨*diversity* of opinion⟩

di·vert \də-'vərt, dī-\ *vb* **1 a :** to turn from one course or use to another **:** DEFLECT **b :** DISTRACT ⟨trying to *divert* her attention⟩ **2 :** to give pleasure to by causing the time to pass pleasantly [Latin *divertere* "to turn in opposite directions," from *dis-* + *vertere* "to turn"] ***synonyms*** see AMUSE

di·ver·tic·u·lum \ˌdī-vər-'tik-yə-ləm\ *n, pl* **-la** \-lə\ **:** a pocket or closed branch opening off a main passage ⟨intestinal *diverticula*⟩ [Latin, "bypath," probably derived from *devertere* "to turn aside," from *de-* + *vertere* "to turn"]

di·ver·ti·men·to \di-ˌvərt-ə-'ment-ō, -ˌvert-\ *n, pl* **-men·ti** \-'ment-ē\ *or* **-men·tos :** a light instrumental musical work in several movements [Italian, literally, "diversion"]

di·vest \dī-'vest, də-\ *vt* **1 :** to strip especially of clothing, ornament, or equipment **2 :** to deprive especially of a right [Middle French *desvestir,* derived from Latin *dis-* + *vestire* "to clothe"] — **di·vest·ment** \-mənt\ *n*

[1]**di·vide** \də-'vīd\ *vb* **1 a :** to separate into two or more parts, areas, or groups **b :** to separate into classes, categories, or divisions **2 a :** to give out in shares **:** DISTRIBUTE **b :** to possess or make use of in common **:** SHARE ⟨*divide* the blame⟩ **3 :** to cause to be separate, distinct, or apart from one another **4 a :** to subject (a number or quantity) to the operation of finding how many times it contains another number or quantity ⟨*divide* 42 by 14⟩ **b :** to use as a divisor ⟨*divide* 14 into 42⟩ **5 a :** to undergo cell division **b :** to branch out **:** DIVERGE [Latin *dividere,* from *dis-* + *-videre* "to separate"] ***synonyms*** see SEPARATE

[2]**divide** *n* **:** a dividing ridge between drainage areas **:** WATERSHED

di·vid·ed *adj* **1 a :** separated into parts or pieces ⟨finely *divided* particles of iron⟩ **b :** cut into distinct parts by incisions extending to the base or to the midrib ⟨a *divided* leaf⟩ **c :** having a barrier (as a guardrail) to separate lanes of traffic going in opposite directions ⟨a 4-lane *divided* highway⟩ **2 a :** disagreeing with each other **:** DISUNITED ⟨sharply *divided* over the issue⟩ **b :** directed or moved toward conflicting goals ⟨*divided* loyalties⟩

div·i·dend \'div-ə-ˌdend, -əd-ənd\ *n* **1 :** a sum or amount to be distributed or an individual share of such a sum: as **a :** a share of profits distributed to stockholders or of surplus to an insurance policyholder **b :** interest paid on a bank account **2 :** BONUS **3 :** a number to be divided by another

di·vid·er \də-'vīd-ər\ *n* **1 :** one that divides or separates ⟨a room *divider*⟩ **2** *pl* **:** an instrument that consists of two pointed branches joined at a pivot for measuring or marking (as in dividing lines and transferring dimensions)

div·i·na·tion \ˌdiv-ə-'nā-shən\ *n* **1 :** the art or practice that seeks to foresee or foretell future events or discover hidden knowledge usually by interpreting omens or by means of supernatural powers **2 :** unusual insight or intuitive perception

[1]**di·vine** \də-'vīn\ *adj* **1 a :** of, relating to, or proceeding directly from God or a god ⟨*divine* law⟩ **b :** being deity ⟨the *divine* Savior⟩ **c :** directed to a deity ⟨*divine* worship⟩ **2 a :** supremely good **:** SUPERB ⟨this pie is *divine*⟩ **b :** HEAVENLY, GODLIKE ⟨*divine* beauty⟩ [Medieval French *divin,* from Latin *divinus,* from *divus* "god"] — **di·vine·ly** *adv*

[2]**divine** *n* **1 :** CLERGYMAN **2 :** THEOLOGIAN

[3]**divine** *vb* **1 :** to discover or perceive by intuition or insight **:** INFER ⟨*divine* the truth⟩ **2 :** to practice divination [Latin *divinare,* from *divinus* "soothsayer," from *divinus,* adjective, "divine"] — **di·vin·er** *n*

Divine Liturgy *n* **:** the eucharistic rite of Eastern churches

Divine Office *n* **:** the daily devotional readings prescribed for priests

divine right *n* **:** a theory that a monarch receives his right to rule from God and not from the people

diving bell *n* **:** a diving apparatus consisting of a container open only at the bottom and supplied with compressed air by a hose

diving board *n* **:** a flexible board secured at one end and extending over water (as at a swimming pool) that is used to gain height in diving

diving duck *n* **:** any of various ducks that frequent deep waters and obtain their food by diving

diving suit *n* **:** a waterproof suit with a helmet that is worn for underwater work by a person who is supplied with air through a tube from the surface

divining rod *n* **:** a forked rod believed to indicate the presence of water or minerals by dipping downward when held over a vein

di·vin·i·ty \də-'vin-ət-ē\ *n, pl* **-ties** **1 :** THEOLOGY **2 :** the quality or state of being divine **3** *often cap* **a :** GOD 1 **b (1) :** GOD 2 **(2) :** GODDESS 1 **c :** DEMIGOD

di·vis·i·ble \də-'viz-ə-bəl\ *adj* **:** capable of being separated or divided — **di·vis·i·bil·i·ty** \-ˌviz-ə-'bil-ət-ē\ *n*

di·vi·sion \də-'vizh-ən\ *n* **1 a :** the act, process, or operation of dividing **:** the state of being divided **b :** DISTRIBUTION ⟨agreed on the *division* of profits⟩ **c** : CELL DIVISION **2** : one of the parts, sections, or groupings into which a whole is divided: as **a** : a large self-contained military unit capable of independent action **b** : an administrative or operating unit of a governmental, business, or educational organization **3** : a group of organisms forming part of a larger group; *esp* : a primary category in biological classification of the plant kingdom that is typically equivalent to a phylum **4** : something that divides, separates, or marks off ⟨the *divisions* of the compass⟩ **5** : difference in opinion or interest : DISAGREEMENT **6** : the mathematical operation of dividing something [Medieval French, from Latin *divisio,* from *dividere* "to divide"] — **di·vi·sion·al** \-ˈvizh-nəl, -ən-l\ *adj*

division of labor : the distribution of tasks among members of a group or to different areas to increase efficiency

di·vi·sive \də-ˈvī-siv *also* -ˈviz-iv\ *adj* : creating disunity or dissension — **di·vi·sive·ly** *adv* — **di·vi·sive·ness** *n*

di·vi·sor \də-ˈvī-zər\ *n* : the number by which a dividend is divided

[1]**di·vorce** \də-ˈvōrs, -ˈvȯrs\ *n* **1** : a complete legal dissolution of a marriage **2** : complete separation [Medieval French *divorse,* from Latin *divortium,* from *divertere, divortere* "to divert, leave one's husband"]

[2]**divorce** *vt* **1 a** : to obtain a divorce from (one's spouse) **b** : to dissolve the marriage between (two spouses) **2** : to make or keep separate : SEPARATE ⟨*divorce* church from state⟩ — **di·vorce·ment** \-mənt\ *n*

di·vor·cé \də-ˌvōr-ˈsā, -ˌvȯr-, -ˈsē\ *n* : a divorced man [French]

di·vor·cée \də-ˌvōr-ˈsā, -ˌvȯr-, -ˈsē\ *n* : a divorced woman [French]

div·ot \ˈdiv-ət\ *n* : a piece of turf dug from a golf fairway in making a stroke [Scottish, "a square of turf or sod," from earlier *devat,* from Middle English *duvat*]

di·vulge \də-ˈvəlj, dī-\ *vt* : to make known : DISCLOSE, REVEAL ⟨*divulge* a secret⟩ [Latin *divulgare,* from *dis-* + *vulgare* "to make known," from *vulgus* "mob"] — **di·vul·gence** \-ˈvəl-jəns\ *n*

Dix·ie·crat \-ˌkrat\ *n* : a dissident Southern Democrat; *esp* : a supporter of a 1948 presidential ticket opposing the civil rights stand of the regular Democrats — **Dix·ie·crat·ic** \ˌdik-sē-ˈkrat-ik\ *adj*

Dix·ie·land \-ˌland\ *n* : jazz music usually played by a small band and characterized by ensemble and solo improvisation [probably from the *Original Dixieland Jazz Band*]

DIY \ˌdē-ˌī-ˈwī\ *adj* : DO-IT-YOURSELF

[1]**diz·zy** \ˈdiz-ē\ *adj* **diz·zi·er; -est** **1 a** : having a whirling sensation in the head : GIDDY **b** : mentally confused **2 a** : causing or associated with a whirling sensation or a feeling of falling ⟨a *dizzy* height⟩ **b** : extremely rapid ⟨works at a *dizzy* pace⟩ [Old English *dysig* "stupid"] — **diz·zi·ly** \ˈdiz-ə-lē\ *adv* — **diz·zi·ness** \ˈdiz-ē-nəs\ *n*

[2]**dizzy** *vt* **diz·zied; diz·zy·ing** : to cause to feel dizzy

DJ \ˈdē-ˌjā\ *n, often not cap* : DISC JOCKEY

D layer *n* : a layer or region of the lower ionosphere

DNA \ˌdē-ˌen-ˈā\ *n* : any of various nucleic acids that are found especially in cell nuclei, are usually the molecular basis of heredity, and differ from RNA especially in containing a deoxyribose sugar and being constructed of a double helix composed of two nucleotide chains held together by hydrogen bonds in a pattern much like a flexible ladder twisted on its base — compare RNA [*d*eoxyribo*n*ucleic *a*cid]

DNA fingerprinting *n* : a method of identification (as for forensic purposes) by determining the unique pattern in an individual's DNA — **DNA fingerprint** *n*

[1]**do** \dü, ˈdü\ *vb* **did** \did, ˈdid, dəd\; **done** \ˈdən\; **do·ing** \ˈdü-iŋ\; **does** \dəz, ˈdəz\ **1 a** : to carry out : PERFORM ⟨*do* some work⟩ ⟨*do* me a favor⟩ **b** : to work on ⟨*doing* a puzzle⟩ **2** : ACT, BEHAVE ⟨*do* as I say, not as I *do*⟩ **3 a** : to affect in a usually specified way ⟨it might *do* you good⟩ **b** : to act so as to cause or create a feeling or sense of ⟨*do* honor to a soldier's memory⟩ **4 a** : to be successful : get along : FLOURISH ⟨not *doing* very well in school⟩ **b** : to be in regard to health : FEEL ⟨*doing* well after the operation⟩ **5** : to carry on in one's affairs : MANAGE ⟨can *do* without your help⟩ **6** : to take place : HAPPEN ⟨see what's *doing* tonight⟩ **7** : to come or bring to an end : FINISH — used in the past participle ⟨the work is finally *done*⟩ **8** : to put forth (as an effort) ⟨*do* your best to win⟩ **9** : to be about one's work or duty ⟨up and *doing*⟩ **10** : to produce by creative effort ⟨*do* a sketch⟩ **11 a** : to take suitable action on ⟨*did* the dishes⟩ **b** : SET 12 ⟨must *do* my hair⟩ **12** : DECORATE, FURNISH ⟨*did* the bedroom in blue⟩ **13** : to work at as a vocation ⟨what one *does* for a living⟩ **14 a** : to travel at a speed of ⟨*doing* 55 miles per hour⟩ **b** : to visit and explore as or as if sightseeing : enjoy the sights and attractions of ⟨*did* Europe last fall⟩ ⟨*doing* the town⟩ **15** : to be suitable to the needs of : SERVE ⟨worms will *do* us for bait⟩ **16** : to serve out (a period of imprisonment) ⟨*doing* 20 years for armed robbery⟩ **17** : to be approved of especially by custom, propriety, or opinion : be fitting or appropriate — usually used in the negative ⟨it just won't *do* to be late⟩ **18** — used as a substitute verb to avoid repetition ⟨wanted to run and play as children *do*⟩ **19** — used as an auxiliary verb (1) before the subject of an interrogative sentence ⟨*do* you work?⟩ and after certain adverbs ⟨rarely *do* I go out⟩ ⟨they work and so *do* I⟩, (2) in a negative statement ⟨you *don't* look well⟩, (3) for emphasis ⟨*do* be careful⟩, and (4) as a substitute for a preceding verb or verb phrase ⟨this looks better than that *does*⟩ [Old English *dōn*] — **do away with** **1** : to put an end to : ABOLISH **2** : to put to death : KILL — **do by** : to deal with : TREAT ⟨*did* well *by* us⟩ — **do justice** **1** : to act justly **2** : to treat fairly **3** : to show proper appreciation for — **do proud** : to give cause for pride or gratification — **do the trick** : to produce the desired result — **do with** : to make good use of : benefit by ⟨could *do with* a snack⟩

[2]**do** \ˈdō\ *n* : the 1st note of the diatonic scale [Italian]

do·able \ˈdü-ə-bəl\ *adj* : capable of being done

dob·bin \ˈdäb-ən\ *n* **1** : a farm horse **2** : a quiet plodding horse [*Dobbin,* nickname for *Robert*]

Do·ber·man pin·scher \ˌdō-bər-mən-ˈpin-chər\ *n* : any of a breed of short-haired medium-sized dogs of German origin [Friedrich Ludwig *Dobermann,* 19th century German dog breeder]

dob·son·fly \ˈdäb-sən-ˌflī\ *n* : a large-eyed winged insect with a large carnivorous aquatic larva — compare HELLGRAMMITE

do·cent \ˈdōs-nt; dō-ˈsent, dōt-\ *n* : TEACHER, LECTURER [obsolete German, derived from Latin *docēre* "to teach"]

doc·ile \ˈdäs-əl\ *adj* : easily taught, led, or managed : TRACTABLE ⟨a *docile* pony⟩ [Latin *docilis,* from *docēre* "to teach"] — **doc·ile·ly** \ˈdäs-əl-lē, -ə-lē\ *adv* — **do·cil·i·ty** \dä-ˈsil-ət-ē, dō-\ *n*

[1]**dock** \ˈdäk\ *n* : any of a genus of coarse weedy plants which are related to buckwheat and some of which are cooked for use as vegetables [Old English *docce*]

[2]**dock** *n* : the solid part of an animal's tail as distinguished from the hair [probably from Old English *-docca* (as in *fingirdocca* "finger muscle")]

[3]**dock** *vt* **1** : to cut off the end of : cut short ⟨a *docked* tail⟩ **2** : to take away a part of : make a deduction from ⟨*dock* one's wages⟩ **3** : to penalize by depriving of something due; *esp* : to fine by a deduction of wages ⟨*docked* him for being late⟩

[4]**dock** *n* **1** : an artificial basin for the reception of ships that has gates to keep the water in or out **2** : a slip or waterway usually between two piers to receive ships **3** : a wharf or platform for the loading or unloading of materials **4** : a usually wooden pier used as a landing place or moorage [probably from Dutch *docke* "dock, ditch"]

[5]**dock** *vb* **1** : to haul or guide into or alongside a dock **2** : to come or go into or alongside a dock **3** : to join (as two spacecraft) mechanically while in space

[6]**dock** *n* : the place in a criminal court where a defendant stands or sits during trial [Flemish *docke* "cage"]

dock·age \ˈdäk-ij\ *n* **1** : a charge for the use of a dock **2** : docking facilities **3** : the docking of ships

[1]**dock·et** \ˈdäk-ət\ *n* **1 a** : a formal abridged record of the proceedings in a legal action **b** : a register of such records **2** : a list of legal causes to be tried **3** : a calendar of matters to be acted on : AGENDA [Middle English *doggette* "brief summary, abstract"]

[2]**docket** *vt* **1** : to mark with an identifying statement : LABEL **2** : to make a brief abstract of (as a legal matter) and enter it in a list **3** : to place on the docket for legal action

dock·hand \ˈdäk-ˌhand\ *n* : LONGSHOREMAN

dock·yard \ˈdäk-ˌyärd\ *n* : SHIPYARD

[1]**doc·tor** \ˈdäk-tər\ *n* **1 a** : an eminent theologian declared a sound expounder of doctrine by the Roman Catholic Church — called also *doctor of the church* **b** : a learned or authoritative teacher **c** : a person holding one of the highest academic degrees (as a PhD) conferred by a university **2 a** : a person skilled or specializing in healing; *esp* : one (as a physician, dentist, or veterinarian) licensed to practice **b** : MEDICINE MAN

[Medieval Latin, from Latin, "teacher," from *docēre* "to teach"] — **doc·tor·al** \-tə-rəl, -trəl\ *adj*

[2]**doctor** *vb* **doc·tored; doc·tor·ing** \-tə-riŋ, -triŋ\ **1 a :** to give medical treatment to **b :** to practice medicine **c :** to restore to good condition : REPAIR ⟨*doctor* an old clock⟩ **2 a :** to adapt or modify for a desired end ⟨*doctored* the play by abridging the last act⟩ **b :** to alter deceptively ⟨*doctored* the election returns⟩

doc·tor·ate \ˈdäk-tə-rət, -trət\ *n* **:** the degree, title, or rank of a doctor

doc·tri·naire \ˌdäk-trə-ˈnaər, -ˈneər\ *n* **:** one who attempts to put an abstract theory into effect without regard to practical difficulties [French, from *doctrine* "doctrine"] ***synonyms*** see DICTATORIAL — **doctrinaire** *adj*

doc·trine \ˈdäk-trən\ *n* **1 :** something that is taught **2 :** a principle or position or the body of principles in a branch of knowledge or system of belief **3 :** a principle of law established through past decisions [Latin *doctrina* "teaching, instruction," from *doctor* "teacher"] — **doc·tri·nal** \-trən-l\ *adj* — **doc·tri·nal·ly** \-l-ē\ *adv*

synonyms DOCTRINE, DOGMA, TENET mean a principle accepted as authoritative. DOCTRINE implies authoritative teaching accepted by a body of believers or adherents of a philosophy or school ⟨Christian *doctrine*⟩ ⟨the economic *doctrine* that governments should not interfere with free markets⟩. DOGMA implies a doctrine laid down as true and beyond dispute or doubt ⟨ideological *dogma*⟩. TENET stresses a principle widely accepted and believed by a body of adherents ⟨freedom of speech and other *tenets* of democracy⟩.

docu·dra·ma \ˈdäk-yə-ˌdräm-ə, -ˌdram-\ *n* **:** a drama made for television, motion pictures, or theater dealing freely with historical events especially of a recent or controversial nature [*documentary* + *drama*]

[1]**doc·u·ment** \ˈdäk-yə-mənt\ *n* **1 :** a usually original or official paper furnishing information or used as proof of something **2 :** a computer file usually created with an application program (as a word processor) [Medieval French, "precept, teaching," from Late Latin *documentum* "official paper," from Latin, "lesson, proof," from *docēre* "to teach"] — **doc·u·men·tal** \ˌdäk-yə-ˈment-l\ *adj*

[2]**doc·u·ment** \ˈdäk-yə-ˌment\ *vt* **:** to furnish documentary evidence of — **doc·u·ment·able** \-ə-bəl, ˌdäk-yə-ˈment-\ *adj*

[1]**doc·u·men·ta·ry** \ˌdäk-yə-ˈment-ə-rē, -ˈmen-trē\ *adj* **1 :** consisting of or being documents; *also* **:** contained or certified in writing ⟨*documentary* proof⟩ **2 :** giving factual material in artistic form ⟨a *documentary* film⟩ — **doc·u·men·tar·i·ly** \-mən-ˈter-ə-lē, -ˌmen-\ *adv*

[2]**documentary** *n, pl* **-ries :** a documentary presentation (as a film)

doc·u·men·ta·tion \ˌdäk-yə-mən-ˈtā-shən, -ˌmen-\ *n* **1 :** the providing or the using of documents in proof of something **2 :** evidence in the form of documents or references (as in footnotes) to documents **3 :** written instructions for using a computer or computer program

[1]**dod·der** \ˈdäd-ər\ *n* **:** any of a genus of leafless herbs related to the morning glories that are deficient in chlorophyll and parasitic on other plants [Middle English *doder*]

[2]**dodder** *vi* **dod·dered; dod·der·ing** \ˈdäd-riŋ, -ə-riŋ\ **1 :** to tremble from weakness or age **2 :** to progress feebly [Middle English *dadiren*]

dod·der·ing *adj* **:** feeble and dull especially from age

do·deca·gon \dō-ˈdek-ə-ˌgän\ *n* **:** a polygon of 12 angles and 12 sides [Greek *dōdekagōnon,* from *dōdeka* "twelve" + *-gōnon* "-gon"]

do·deca·he·dron \ˌdō-ˌdek-ə-ˈhē-drən\ *n, pl* **-drons** *or* **-dra** \-drə\ **:** a polyhedron having 12 faces

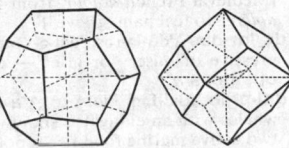

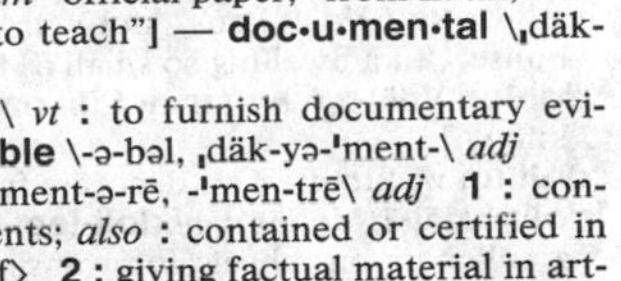
dodecahedron

[1]**dodge** \ˈdäj\ *n* **1 :** an act of evading by sudden bodily movement **2 a :** an artful device to evade, deceive, or trick ⟨crafty legal *dodges*⟩ **b :** EXPEDIENT 2 [origin unknown]

[2]**dodge** *vb* **1 a :** to move suddenly aside or to and fro ⟨*dodged* through the crowd⟩ **b :** to avoid by moving quickly aside ⟨*dodge* a batted ball⟩ **2 :** to avoid by trickery or evasion ⟨*dodge* work⟩ — **dodge a bullet** *also* **dodge the bullet :** to barely avoid an unwelcome, harmful, or disastrous outcome or occurrence

dodge·ball \ˈdäj-ˌbȯl\ *n* **:** a game in which players stand in a circle and attempt to hit a player within the circle with a large inflated ball

dodg·er \ˈdäj-ər\ *n* **1 :** one that dodges; *esp* **:** one who uses trickery **2 :** a small handbill

do·do \ˈdōd-ō\ *n, pl* **dodoes** *or* **dodos 1 :** a large heavy flightless extinct bird related to the pigeons and formerly found on the island of Mauritius; *also* **:** a related extinct bird formerly found on the island of Réunion **2 a :** a person hopelessly behind the times **b :** a stupid person [Portuguese *doudo,* from *doudo* "silly, stupid"]

doe \ˈdō\ *n, pl* **does** *or* **doe :** an adult female deer; *also* **:** the female especially when adult of any mammal (as an antelope or hare) of which the male is called buck [Old English *dā*]

do·er \ˈdü-ər\ *n* **:** one that does; *esp* **:** a person who gets things done

does *present 3rd singular of* DO

doe·skin \ˈdō-ˌskin\ *n* **1 :** the skin of does or leather made of it; *also* **:** soft leather from sheepskins or lambskins **2 :** a soft firm cloth

doesn't \ˈdəz-nt\ **:** does not

do·est \ˈdü-əst\ *archaic present 2nd singular of* DO

do·eth \ˈdü-əth\ *archaic present 3rd singular of* DO

doff \ˈdäf, ˈdȯf\ *vt* **1 a :** to remove (an article of clothing) from the body **b :** to take off (the hat) in greeting or as a sign of respect **2 :** to rid oneself of **:** put aside [Middle English *doffen,* from *don* "to do" + *of* "off"]

[1]**dog** \ˈdȯg\ *n* **1 a :** a variable carnivorous domesticated mammal closely related to the gray wolf **b :** an animal of the family to which the domesticated dog belongs **c :** a male dog **2 a :** a worthless or contemptible fellow **b :** FELLOW, CHAP ⟨a lazy *dog*⟩ **3 :** any of various devices for holding, gripping, or fastening that consist of a spike, rod, or bar **4 :** affected stylishness or dignity ⟨put on the *dog*⟩ **5** *pl, slang* **:** FEET **6** *pl* **:** RUIN ⟨go to the *dogs*⟩ [Old English *docga*] — **dog·like** \-ˌlīk\ *adj*

[2]**dog** *vt* **dogged; dog·ging 1 :** to hunt, track, or follow like a hound **2 :** HOUND ⟨*dogged* by bad luck⟩

dog·bane \ˈdȯg-ˌbān\ *n* **:** any of a genus of often poisonous plants with milky juice and fibrous bark

dog·cart \-ˌkärt\ *n* **1 :** a cart drawn by a dog **2 :** a light one-horse carriage with two seats back to back

dog·catch·er \-ˌkach-ər, -ˌkech-\ *n* **:** a community official assigned to catch and dispose of stray dogs

dog days *n pl* **:** the hot sultry period of summer between early July and early September [from their beginning at the date when the Dog Star (Sirius) rises just before the sun]

doge \ˈdōj\ *n* **:** the chief magistrate in the republics of Venice and Genoa [Italian dialect, from Latin *dux* "leader"]

dog–ear \ˈdȯg-ˌiər\ *n* **:** the turned-down corner of a page of a book — **dog–ear** *vt*

dog–eared \-ˌiərd\ *adj* **1 :** having dog-ears ⟨a *dog-eared* book⟩ **2 :** SHABBY 2, TIMEWORN

dog–eat–dog \ˌdȯg-ˌēt-ˈdȯg\ *adj* **:** marked by ruthless self-interest ⟨a *dog-eat-dog* business⟩

dog·face \ˈdȯg-ˌfās\ *n* **:** SOLDIER; *esp* **:** INFANTRYMAN

dog·fight \-ˌfīt\ *n* **1 :** a fight between dogs **2 :** a fiercely fought contest **3 :** a fight between two or more fighter planes usually at close quarters — **dog·fight** *vi* — **dog·fight·er** \-ˌfīt-ər\ *n*

dog·fish \-ˌfish\ *n* **:** any of various small sharks that often appear in schools near shore

dog·ged \ˈdȯ-gəd\ *adj* **:** stubbornly determined **:** TENACIOUS ⟨*dogged* persistence⟩ ***synonyms*** see OBSTINATE — **dog·ged·ly** *adv* — **dog·ged·ness** *n*

[1]**dog·ger·el** \ˈdȯg-rəl, ˈdäg-, -ə-rəl\

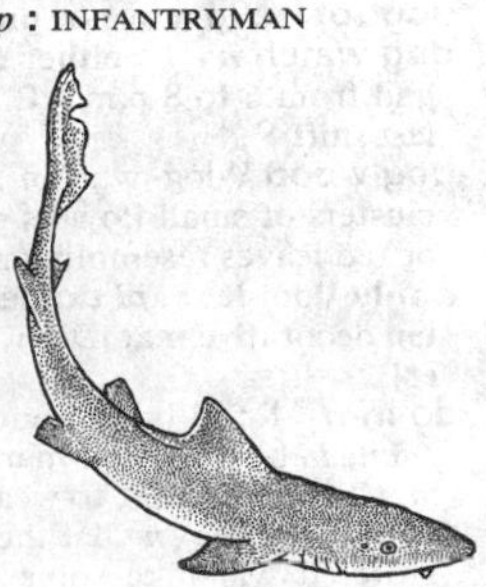
dogfish

\ə\ **abut**	\au̇\ **out**	\i\ **tip**	\ȯ\ **saw**	\u̇\ **foot**
\ər\ **further**	\ch\ **chin**	\ī\ **life**	\ȯi\ **coin**	\y\ **yet**
\a\ **mat**	\e\ **pet**	\j\ **job**	\th\ **thin**	\yü\ **few**
\ā\ **take**	\ē\ **easy**	\ŋ\ **sing**	\th\ **this**	\yu̇\ **cure**
\ä\ **cot, cart**	\g\ **go**	\ō\ **bone**	\ü\ **food**	\zh\ **vision**

adj : loose in style and irregular in meter ⟨comic *doggerel* verse⟩ [Middle English *dogerel*]

[2]**doggerel** *n* : doggerel verse

doggie bag *or* **doggy bag** *n* : a container for leftover food to be carried home from a meal eaten at a restaurant [[1]*doggy;* from the presumption that such leftovers are intended for a pet dog]

[1]**dog·gone** \ˈdäg-ˈgän, ˈdȯg-ˈgȯn\ *vb* : DAMN 3 [euphemism for *God damn*]

[2]**dog·gone** *or* **dog·goned** \ˈdäg-ˈgän, -ˈgänd; ˈdȯg-ˈgȯn, -ˈgȯnd\ *adj or adv* : DAMNED

[3]**doggone** *n* : DAMN 2

[1]**dog·gy** *or* **dog·gie** \ˈdȯ-gē\ *n, pl* **doggies** : a small dog

[2]**dog·gy** \ˈdȯ-gē\ *adj* **dog·gi·er; -est** **1** : resembling or suggestive of a dog ⟨*doggy* odor⟩ **2** : STYLISH, SHOWY

dog·house \ˈdȯg-ˌhau̇s\ *n* : a shelter for a dog — **in the doghouse** : in a state of disfavor

do·gie \ˈdō-gē\ *n, chiefly Western* : a motherless calf in a range herd [origin unknown]

dog in the manger : a person who selfishly withholds from others something useless to himself or herself [from the fable of the dog who prevented an ox from eating hay which he did not want himself]

dog·ma \ˈdȯg-mə, ˈdäg-\ *n, pl* **dog·mas** *also* **dog·ma·ta** \-mət-ə\ **1 a** : something held as an established opinion; *esp* : a tenet set forth as authoritative **b** : a point of view or opinion set forth as authoritative without adequate grounds **2** : a doctrine or body of doctrines concerning faith or morals laid down by a church [Latin *dogmat-, dogma,* from Greek, from *dokein* "to seem"] ***synonyms*** see DOCTRINE

dog·mat·ic \dȯg-ˈmat-ik, däg-\ *adj* **1** : characterized by or given to the expression of opinions very strongly or positively as if they were facts ⟨a *dogmatic* critic⟩ **2** : of or relating to dogma ***synonyms*** see DICTATORIAL — **dog·mat·i·cal·ly** \-ˈmat-i-kə-lē, -klē\ *adv*

dog·ma·tism \ˈdȯg-mə-ˌtiz-əm, ˈdäg-\ *n* **1** : positiveness in assertion of opinion especially when unwarranted or arrogant **2** : a viewpoint or system of ideas based on inadequate study or knowledge

dog·ma·tist \-mət-əst\ *n* : one who dogmatizes

dog·ma·tize \-mə-ˌtīz\ *vb* : to speak or write dogmatically — **dog·ma·ti·za·tion** \-mət-ə-ˈzā-shən\ *n* — **dog·ma·tiz·er** *n*

do–good·er \ˈdü-ˌgu̇d-ər\ *n* : an earnest often naive humanitarian or reformer

dog paddle *n* : an elementary form of swimming in which the head is kept out of the water and the arms paddle in the water while the legs maintain a kicking motion

dog·sled \ˈdȯg-ˌsled\ *n* : a sled drawn by dogs — **dogsled** *vi*

Dog Star *n* : SIRIUS

dog tag *n* : an identification tag (as for military personnel or pets)

dog tick *n* : a common North American tick especially of dogs and humans that may transmit the bacterium causing Rocky Mountain spotted fever and tularemia

dog·tooth violet \ˈdȯg-ˌtüth-\ *n* : any of a genus of small spring-flowering bulbous herbs related to the lilies

[1]**dog·trot** \ˈdȯg-ˌträt\ *n* : an easy gait suggesting that of a dog

[2]**dogtrot** *vi* : to move or progress at a dogtrot

dog watch *n* **1** : either of two shipboard watches from 4 to 6 and from 6 to 8 p.m. **2** : any of various night shifts; *esp* : the last shift

dog·wood \ˈdȯg-ˌwu̇d\ *n* : any of various trees and shrubs with clusters of small flowers often surrounded by four white, pink, or red leaves resembling petals

doi·ly \ˈdȯi-lē\ *n, pl* **doilies** **1** : a small napkin **2** : a small often decorative mat [*Doily* or *Doyley,* 18th century London draper]

do in *vt* **1** : to bring about the defeat or destruction of : RUIN ⟨*done in* by the stock-market crash⟩ **2** : KILL ⟨tried to *do* them *in* with a club⟩ **3** : to wear out : EXHAUST ⟨*done in* after work⟩

do·ing \ˈdü-ing\ *n* **1** : the act of performing or executing : ACTION ⟨it will take some *doing* to beat this record⟩ **2** *pl* **a** : things that are done or that occur ⟨everyday *doings*⟩ **b** : social activities ⟨big *doings* tonight⟩

doit \ˈdȯit\ *also* **duit** \ˈdȯit, ˈdīt\ *n* **1** : an old Dutch coin equal to about ¼ cent **2** : TRIFLE 1 [Dutch *duit*]

do–it–your·self \ˌdü-ə-chər-ˈself\ *adj* : of, relating to, or designed for use in construction, repair, or artistic work done by an amateur or hobbyist ⟨*do-it-yourself* tools⟩

dol·ce \ˈdōl-chā\ *adv or adj* : SOFT 1b, SMOOTH — used as a direction in music [Italian, literally, "sweet," from Latin *dulcis*]

dol·drums \ˈdōl-drəmz, ˈdäl-\ *n pl* **1** : a spell of listlessness or despondency **2** : a part of the ocean near the equator abounding in calms and light shifting winds **3** : a state of inactivity, stagnation, or slump [probably related to Old English *dol* "foolish"]

[1]**dole** \ˈdōl\ *n* **1 a** (1) : a giving out of food, money, or clothing to the needy (2) : money, food, or clothing so given **b** : a grant of government funds to the unemployed **2** : something portioned out and distributed [Old English *dāl* "portion"]

[2]**dole** *vt* **1** : to distribute as charity ⟨*doled* out blankets and clothing to the flood victims⟩ **2** : to give out in small portions or gradually ⟨*dole* out stories each evening⟩

[3]**dole** *n, archaic* : GRIEF 1, SORROW [Medieval French *dol,* derived from Latin *dolor*]

dole·ful \ˈdōl-fəl\ *adj* : full of grief : SAD — **dole·ful·ly** \-fə-lē\ *adv* — **dole·ful·ness** *n*

doll \ˈdäl, ˈdȯl\ *n* **1** : a small-scale figure of a human being used especially as a child's plaything **2 a** : a pretty but often scatterbrained young woman **b** : WOMAN 1 **c** : DARLING 1, SWEETHEART **d** : an attractive person [probably from *Doll,* nickname for *Dorothy*]

dol·lar \ˈdäl-ər\ *n* **1** : TALER **2** : a coin (as a Spanish peso) patterned after the taler **3 a** : a basic monetary unit (as of the U.S. and Canada) **b** : a coin, note, or token representing one dollar [Dutch or Low German *daler,* from German *Taler*]

Word History In the mountains of northwestern Bohemia is the small town of Jáchymov. In the early 16th century the town was known by its German name, Sankt Joachimstal. At that time a silver mine was opened nearby, and coins were minted to which the name *joachimstaler* was applied. In German this was shortened to *Taler.* Shortly afterward the Dutch or Low German form *daler* was borrowed into English to refer to the Taler and other coins that were patterned after it. Our modern word *dollar* is a different spelling of this daler.

dollar diplomacy *n* : diplomacy held to be designed primarily to further private financial and commercial interests

doll·house \ˈdäl-ˌhau̇s, ˈdȯl-\ *n* **1** : a child's small-scale toy house **2** : a dwelling so small as to suggest a house for dolls

dol·lop \ˈdäl-əp\ *n* : LUMP 1, BLOB ⟨a *dollop* of jelly⟩ [origin unknown]

doll up *vb* : to dress or decorate formally or elegantly

[1]**dolly** \ˈdäl-ē, ˈdȯ-lē\ *n, pl* **doll·ies** **1** : DOLL 1 **2** : a platform on a roller or on wheels for transporting heavy objects; *esp* : a wheeled platform for a television or motion-picture camera

[2]**dolly** *vi* **doll·ied; doll·y·ing** : to move a motion-picture or television dolly about while shooting a scene

dolman sleeve *n* : a sleeve that is very wide at the armhole and tight at the wrist

dol·men \ˈdōl-mən, ˈdȯl-, ˈdäl-\ *n* : a prehistoric monument consisting of two or more upright stones supporting a horizontal stone slab [French, probably from Cornish *tolmen,* from *tol* "hole" + *men* "stone"]

dolmen

do·lo·mite \ˈdō-lə-ˌmīt, ˈdäl-ə-\ *n* : a mineral consisting of a calcium magnesium carbonate found in crystals and in extensive beds as a compact limestone [Déodat de *Dolomieu,* died 1801, French geologist] — **do·lo·mit·ic** \ˌdō-lə-ˈmit-ik, ˌdäl-ə-\ *adj*

do·lor \ˈdō-lər, ˈdäl-ər\ *n* : mental suffering or grief : SORROW [Medieval French *dolour,* from Latin *dolor* "pain, grief," from *dolēre* "to feel pain, grieve"]

do·lor·ous \ˈdō-lə-rəs, ˈdäl-ə-\ *adj* : causing, marked by, or expressive of misery or grief — **do·lor·ous·ly** *adv* — **do·lor·ous·ness** *n*

dol·phin \ˈdäl-fən, ˈdȯl-\ *n* **1 a** : any of various small toothed whales with an elongated snout **b** : PORPOISE 1 **2** : either of two active marine food fishes noted for their brilliant colors **3** *cap* : DELPHINUS [Medieval French *delphin,* derived from Latin *delphinus,* from Greek *delphis*]

dolt \ˈdōlt\ *n* : a stupid person [probably related to Old English *dol* "foolish"] — **dolt·ish** \ˈdōl-tish\ *adj* — **dolt·ish·ly** *adv* — **dolt·ish·ness** *n*

Dom *n* **1** \ˌdäm\ — used as a title prefixed to the name of some monks and canons regular **2** \ˌdō^{n}\ — used as a title prefixed to the Christian name of a Portuguese or Brazilian man of rank [Latin *dominus* "master"]

-dom \dəm\ *n suffix* **1 a :** dignity : office ⟨duke*dom*⟩ **b :** realm : jurisdiction ⟨king*dom*⟩ **2 :** state or fact of being ⟨free*dom*⟩ **3 :** those having a (specified) office, occupation, interest, or character ⟨official*dom*⟩ [Old English *-dōm*]

do·main \dō-ˈmān, də-\ *n* **1 a :** complete and absolute ownership of land — compare EMINENT DOMAIN **b :** land completely owned **2 :** a territory over which dominion is exercised **3 :** a sphere of influence or activity ⟨the widening *domain* of science⟩ **4 :** the set of values to which a mathematical variable is limited; *esp* **:** the set of values that an independent variable may take on — compare RANGE 8 **5 :** a small region of a magnetic substance that contains a group of atoms all aligned in the same direction so that each group has the effect of a tiny magnet pointing in one direction **6 :** the highest category in biological classification ranking above the kingdom **7 :** a main subdivision of the Internet denoted by an abbreviation (as *com* or *gov*); *also* **:** DOMAIN NAME [Medieval French *demaine,* from Latin *dominium,* from *dominus* "master"]

domain name *n* **:** an identifying name (as Merriam-Webster.com) that includes a domain abbreviation and that serves as the primary Internet address for a Web site

[1]**dome** \ˈdōm\ *n* **1** *archaic* **:** a stately building : MANSION **2 :** a large hemispherical roof or ceiling **3 :** a natural formation that resembles the dome or cupola of a building ⟨elevated rock *domes*⟩ **4 :** a roofed sports stadium [Medieval Latin *domus* "church," from Latin, "house"]

[2]**dome** *vb* **1 :** to cover with or as if with a dome **2 :** to form into or swell upward or outward like a dome

[1]**do·mes·tic** \də-ˈmes-tik\ *adj* **1 :** of or relating to the household or the family ⟨*domestic* life⟩ **2 :** of, relating to, produced, or carried on within one country ⟨*domestic* trade⟩ **3 a :** living near or about human habitations ⟨*domestic* vermin⟩ **b :** adapted to life with and to the advantage of humans : TAME ⟨a *domestic* cat⟩ **4 :** devoted to home duties and pleasures ⟨living a quietly *domestic* life⟩ [Medieval French *domestique,* from Latin *domesticus,* from *domus* "house, home"] — **do·mes·ti·cal·ly** \-ti-kə-lē, -klē\ *adv*

[2]**domestic** *n* **:** a household servant

domestic animal *n* **:** any of various animals (as the horse or sheep) adapted by humans to live and breed in domestication

do·mes·ti·cate \də-ˈmes-ti-ˌkāt\ *vt* **1 :** to bring into domestic use : ADOPT ⟨European customs *domesticated* in America⟩ **2 :** to fit for domestic life **3 :** to adapt (an animal or plant) to life in intimate association with and to the advantage of human beings — **do·mes·ti·ca·tion** \də-ˌmes-ti-ˈkā-shən\ *n*

do·mes·tic·i·ty \ˌdō-ˌmes-ˈtis-ət-ē, də-\ *n, pl* **-ties 1 :** the quality or state of being domestic or domesticated **2 :** domestic activities or life **3** *pl* **:** domestic affairs

domestic prelate *n* **:** a priest having permanent honorary membership in the papal household

domestic science *n* **:** instruction in domestic management and the household arts (as cooking and sewing)

domestic system *n* **:** a system of manufacturing in the home with raw materials supplied by an employer

domestic violence *n* **:** the inflicting of physical injury by one family or household member on another; *also* **:** a repeated or habitual pattern of such behavior

dom·i·cal \ˈdō-mi-kəl, ˈdäm-i-\ *adj* **:** relating to, shaped like, or having a dome

[1]**do·mi·cile** \ˈdäm-ə-ˌsīl, ˈdō-mə-; ˈdäm-ə-səl\ *n* **1 :** a dwelling place : place of residence : HOME **2 :** a person's fixed, permanent, and principal home for legal purposes [Medieval French, from Latin *domicilium,* from *domus* "house"] — **do·mi·cil·i·ary** \ˌdäm-ə-ˈsil-ē-ˌer-ē, ˌdō-mə-\ *adj*

[2]**domicile** *vt* **:** to establish in or provide with a domicile

dom·i·nance \ˈdäm-nəns, -ə-nəns\ *n* **:** the fact or state of being dominant: as **a :** a dominant position especially in a social hierarchy **b :** the property of one of a pair of alternate forms of a gene or trait that prevents or masks expression of the other when both are present in the heterozygous condition **c :** the influence or control exerted over an ecological community by a dominant **d :** greater activity and usage of one of a pair of body parts (as the right hand compared to the left hand)

[1]**dom·i·nant** \-nənt\ *adj* **1 a :** commanding, controlling, or prevailing over all others ⟨a *dominant* political figure⟩ **b :** very important, powerful, or successful ⟨a *dominant* theme⟩ ⟨a *dominant* industry⟩ **2 :** overlooking from a higher elevation ⟨a *dominant* hill⟩ **3 :** being the more effective or predominant in action of a pair of bodily structures ⟨*dominant* eye⟩ **4 :** exhibiting or exerting genetic dominance — compare RECESSIVE 2 **5 :** of, relating to, or being an ecological dominant — **dom·i·nant·ly** *adv*

[2]**dominant** *n* **1 a :** a dominant gene or genetic trait **b :** a kind of organism (as a species) that exerts a controlling influence on an ecological community **2 :** the 5th note of a major or minor scale

dom·i·nate \ˈdäm-ə-ˌnāt\ *vb* **1 :** to exert dominance over : be dominant ⟨refused to be *dominated* by friends⟩ **2 :** to have a commanding position or controlling power over ⟨the rock of Gibraltar *dominates* the straits⟩ **3 :** to rise high above ⟨the mountain range was *dominated* by a single snow-capped peak⟩ [Latin *dominari,* from *dominus* "master"] — **dom·i·na·tive** \-ˌnāt-iv\ *adj* — **dom·i·na·tor** \-ˌnāt-ər\ *n*

dom·i·na·tion \ˌdäm-ə-ˈnā-shən\ *n* **1 :** supremacy over another **2 :** exercise of authority or power

dom·i·neer \ˌdäm-ə-ˈniər\ *vb* **1 :** to rule in a haughty manner **2 :** to be overbearing

dom·i·neer·ing *adj* **:** inclined to domineer ***synonyms*** see MASTERFUL — **dom·i·neer·ing·ly** \-iŋ-lē\ *adv* — **dom·i·neer·ing·ness** *n*

Do·min·i·can \də-ˈmin-i-kən\ *n* **:** a member of a mendicant Order of Preachers founded in 1215 [Saint *Dominic*] — **Dominican** *adj*

do·mi·nie *1 usually* ˈdäm-ə-nē, *2 usually* ˈdō-mə-\ *n* **1** *chiefly Scottish* **:** SCHOOLMASTER **2 :** CLERGYMAN [derived from Latin *dominus* "master"]

do·min·ion \də-ˈmin-yən\ *n* **1 :** supreme authority **2 :** DOMAIN 2 **3** *often cap* **:** a self-governing nation of the Commonwealth of Nations other than the United Kingdom that acknowledges the British monarch as chief of state [Medieval French, from Latin *dominium,* from *dominus* "master"]

Dominion Day *n* **:** CANADA DAY

dom·i·no \ˈdäm-ə-ˌnō\ *n, pl* **-noes** *or* **-nos 1 :** a long loose hooded cloak usually worn with a half mask as a masquerade costume **2 a :** a small rectangular block (as of wood or plastic) whose face is divided into two equal parts that are blank or bear from one to usually six dots arranged as on dice faces **b** *pl* **:** any of several games played with a set of usually 28 dominoes [French, probably derived from Latin *dominus* "master"]

Word History English *domino* was borrowed from French but is ultimately derived from Latin *dominus,* which means "lord" or "master." The hooded cape worn in masquerades was given its French name of *domino* because it looks rather like the hooded capes worn by members of some religious orders. The name of the garment was probably derived from the Latin phrase "Benedicamus Domino" (Let us bless the Lord), used in prayers. Another meaning of *domino* is "a rectangular block used in games." This *domino* came into our language from Italian, by way of French. Formerly, the winner of a game of dominoes would exclaim "Domino!" It is likely that this Italian exclamation originally meant "(I am) master!" Italian *domino,* meaning "master" or "lord," was derived from Latin *dominus.*

[1]**don** \ˈdän\ *n* **1 :** a Spanish nobleman or gentleman — used as a title prefixed to the Christian name **2 :** a head, tutor, or fellow in a college of Oxford or Cambridge University; *also* **:** a college or university professor [Spanish, from Latin *dominus* "master"]

[2]**don** *vt* **donned; don·ning :** to put on : dress oneself in ⟨*don* an apron for washing dishes⟩ [*do + on*]

do·ña \ˌdō-nyə\ *n* **:** a Spanish woman of rank — used as a title prefixed to the Christian name [Spanish, from Latin *domina* "lady," from *dominus* "master"]

do·nate \ˈdō-ˌnāt, dō-ˈ\ *vb* **:** to make a gift of; *esp* **:** to contribute to a public or charitable cause ⟨*donate* a site for a park⟩ ⟨*donate* to the scholarship fund⟩ [back-formation from *donation*] ***synonyms*** see GIVE — **do·na·tor** \-ˌnāt-ər, -ˈnāt-\ *n*

do·na·tion \dō-ˈnā-shən\ *n* **1 :** the action of donating something **2 :** a free contribution : GIFT [Latin *donatio,* from *donare* "to present," from *donum* "gift"]

[1]**done** \ˈdən\ *past participle of* DO

[2]**done** *adj* **1 :** socially acceptable ⟨that's not the *done* thing⟩ **2 :** physically exhausted : SPENT ⟨felt completely *done* at the end of the hike⟩ **3 :** gone by : FINISHED **4 :** doomed to failure, defeat, or death **5 :** cooked sufficiently
done deal *n* **:** FAIT ACCOMPLI
do·nee \dō-ˈnē\ *n* **:** one that receives a gift [*don*or + *-ee*]
done for \ˈdən-ˌfȯr\ *adj* **:** having no hope of overcoming : WASHED-UP ⟨that blunder means you are *done for* as a politician⟩
don·jon \ˈdän-jən, ˈdən-\ *n* **:** a massive inner tower in a medieval castle [Medieval French, derived from Latin *dominus* "lord"]

D donjon

Don Juan \ˈdän-ˈwän, -ˈhwän; dän-ˈjü-ən\ *n* **:** [5]RAKE [*Don Juan,* unprincipled nobleman of Spanish legend]
don·key \ˈdäng-kē, ˈdəng-, ˈdȯng-\ *n, pl* **donkeys 1 :** the domestic ass **2 :** a stupid or stubborn person [origin unknown]
donkey engine *n* **1 :** a small usually portable auxiliary engine **2 :** a small locomotive used in switching
don·na \ˌdän-ə\ *n, pl* **don·ne** \-ā\ **:** an Italian woman usually of rank — used as a title prefixed to the Christian name [Italian, from Latin *domina* "lady"]
don·nish \ˈdän-ish\ *adj* **:** suggestive of a university don ⟨a prim *donnish* greeting⟩ — **don·nish·ly** *adv* — **don·nish·ness** *n*
don·ny·brook \ˈdän-ē-ˌbru̇k\ *n, often cap* **:** an uproarious brawl [*Donnybrook* Fair, annual Irish event known for its brawls]
do·nor \ˈdō-nər, -ˌnȯr\ *n* **1 :** one that donates **2 :** one used as a source of biological material ⟨a blood *donor*⟩ ⟨a kidney *donor*⟩ [Medieval French *doneur,* from Latin *donator,* from *donare* "to present"] — **do·nor·ship** \-ˌship\ *n*
[1]**do–noth·ing** \ˈdü-ˌnəth-ing\ *n* **:** a shiftless or lazy person
[2]**do–nothing** *adj* **:** marked by inactivity; *esp* **:** marked by lack of ambition, unwillingness to disturb the existing state of affairs, or failure to make positive progress ⟨a *do-nothing* government⟩ — **do–noth·ing·ism** \-ing-ˌiz-əm\ *n*
don't \dōnt, ˈdōnt\ **:** do not
donut *variant of* DOUGHNUT
doo·dad \ˈdü-ˌdad\ *n* **:** a small article whose common name is unknown or forgotten [origin unknown]
[1]**doo·dle** \ˈdüd-l\ *vb* **doo·dled; doo·dling** \ˈdüd-ling, -l-ing\ **:** to draw or scribble aimlessly while occupied with something else [perhaps from earlier *doodle* "to ridicule," from *doodle* "fool"] — **doo·dler** \ˈdüd-lər, -l-ər\ *n*
[2]**doodle** *n* **:** something produced by doodling
doo·dle·bug \ˈdüd-l-ˌbəg\ *n* **1 :** the larva of an ant lion **2 :** a device (as a divining rod) used in attempting to locate underground gas, water, oil, or ores [probably from *doodle* "fool"]
doo·hick·ey \ˈdü-ˌhik-ē\ *n* **:** DOODAD [probably from *doo*dad + *hickey* "gadget," of unknown origin]
[1]**doom** \ˈdüm\ *n* **1 a :** a judicial decision; *esp* **:** a judicial sentence **b** (1) **:** a final determining of what is just (2) **:** JUDGMENT DAY **2 a :** an inevitable and usually calamitous state or end **b :** DEATH 2, RUIN [Old English *dōm* "law, judgment"] ***synonyms*** see FATE
[2]**doom** *vt* **1 :** to give judgment against : CONDEMN **2 a :** to fix the fate of : DESTINE **b :** to ensure the failure or destruction of
dooms·day \ˈdümz-ˌdā\ *n* **:** JUDGMENT DAY
door \ˈdōr, ˈdȯr\ *n* **1 a :** a usually swinging or sliding barrier by which an entry (as in a building) is closed and opened **b :** a similar part of a piece of furniture **2 :** DOORWAY **3 :** a means of access ⟨the *door* to success⟩ [Old English *duru* "door" and *dor* "gate"]
door·bell \ˈdōr-ˌbel, ˈdȯr-\ *n* **:** a bell, gong, or set of chimes to be rung usually by a push button at an outside door
door·jamb \-ˌjam\ *n* **:** an upright piece forming the side of a door opening
door·keep·er \-ˌkē-pər\ *n* **:** a person who tends a door
door·knob \-ˌnäb\ *n* **:** a knob that when turned releases a door latch
door·man \-ˌman, -mən\ *n* **1 :** DOORKEEPER **2 :** a person who tends a door (as of a hotel) and assists people by calling taxis and helping them in and out of cars
door·mat \-ˌmat\ *n* **:** a mat placed before or inside a door for wiping dirt from the shoes
door·nail \-ˌnāl, -ˈnāl\ *n* **:** a large-headed nail — used chiefly in the phrase *dead as a doornail*
door·plate \-ˌplāt\ *n* **:** a nameplate on a door
door·post \-ˌpōst\ *n* **:** DOORJAMB
door·sill \-ˌsil\ *n* **:** SILL 1b
door·step \-ˌstep\ *n* **:** a step or series of steps before an outer door
door–to–door \ˌdōrt-ə-ˈdōr, ˌdȯrt-ə-ˈdȯr\ *adj* **:** going or made by going to each house in a neighborhood — **door–to–door** *adv*
door·way \-ˌwā\ *n* **1 :** the opening that a door closes **2 :** a means of gaining access
door·yard \-ˌyärd\ *n* **:** a yard outside the door of a house
do·pa·mine \ˈdō-pə-ˌmēn\ *n* **:** a substance $C_8H_{11}NO_2$ that occurs especially as a neurotransmitter in the brain [*dopa* (*di-* + hydroxyl + *p*henyl*a*lanine) + *amine*]
[1]**dope** \ˈdōp\ *n* **1 a :** a thick liquid or pasty preparation **b :** a preparation for giving a desired quality to a substance or surface; *esp* **:** an antiknock added to gasoline **2 a :** an illicit, habit-forming, or narcotic drug; *esp* **:** MARIJUANA **b :** a stupid person **3 :** information especially from a reliable source [Dutch *doop* "sauce," from *dopen* "to dip"]
[2]**dope** *vt* **1 :** to treat or affect with dope; *esp* **:** to give a narcotic to **2 :** to guess the result of : predict (an outcome) especially by means of special information or skill ⟨*dope* out which team will win⟩ — **dop·er** *n*
[3]**dope** *adj, slang* **:** GREAT, EXCELLENT
dope·ster \ˈdōp-stər\ *n* **:** a forecaster of the outcome of future events (as sports contests or elections)
dop·ey \ˈdō-pē\ *adj* **dop·i·er; -est 1 a :** dulled by or as if by alcohol or a narcotic **b :** SLUGGISH **2 :** STUPID, SILLY ⟨a *dopey* TV show⟩ — **dop·i·ness** *n*
Dopp·ler effect \ˈdäp-lər-\ *n* **:** a change in the frequency with which waves (as of sound or light) from a given source reach an observer when the source and observer are moving rapidly toward or away from each other [Christian J. *Doppler,* died 1853, Austrian physicist and mathematician]
Doppler radar *n* **:** a radar system using the Doppler effect for measuring velocity
do–rag \ˈdü-ˌrag\ *n* **:** a kerchief worn to cover the hair [hair*do*]
Do·ri·an \ˈdōr-ē-ən, ˈdȯr-\ *n* **:** one of a Hellenic race that completed the overthrow of Mycenaean civilization and settled especially in the Peloponnese and Crete [*Doris,* region of ancient Greece] — **Dorian** *adj*
Dor·ic \ˈdȯr-ik, ˈdär-\ *adj* **1 :** of, relating to, or characteristic of the Dorians **2 :** belonging to the oldest and simplest Greek architectural order
dork \ˈdȯrk\ *n, slang* **:** JERK 3
dorky \ˈdȯr-kē\ *adj* **dork·i·er; -est** *slang* **:** foolishly stupid
dorm \ˈdȯrm\ *n* **:** DORMITORY 2
dor·mant \ˈdȯr-mənt\ *adj* **1 :** not active but capable of resuming activity ⟨a *dormant* volcano⟩ **2 a :** sleeping or appearing to be asleep : SLUGGISH **b :** having growth or other biological activity much reduced or suspended ⟨a *dormant* bud⟩ **3 :** of, relating to, or used during a period of inactivity or lack of growth ⟨a *dormant* condition⟩ ⟨*dormant* sprays⟩ [Middle French, "stationary," from *dormir* "to sleep," from Latin *dormire*] ***synonyms*** see LATENT — **dor·man·cy** \-mən-sē\ *n*
dor·mer \ˈdȯr-mər\ *n* **:** a window placed upright in a sloping roof; *also* **:** a roofed structure containing such a window [Middle French *dormeor* "dormitory," from Latin *dormitorium*]
dor·mi·to·ry \ˈdȯr-mə-ˌtōr-ē, -ˌtȯr-\ *n, pl* **-ries 1 :** a room for sleeping; *esp* **:** a large room containing a number of beds **2 :** a residence hall providing sleeping rooms [Latin *dormitorium,* from *dormire* "to sleep"]
dor·mouse \ˈdȯr-ˌmau̇s\ *n, pl* **dor·mice** \-ˌmīs\ **:** any of numerous Old World rodents that resemble small squirrels [perhaps from Medieval French *dormir* "to sleep"]
dors- *or* **dorsi-** *or* **dorso-** *combining form* **1 :** back ⟨*dors*ad⟩ **2 :** dorsal and ⟨*dorso*ventral⟩ [Latin *dorsum*]
dor·sad \ˈdȯr-ˌsad\ *adv* **:** toward the back : DORSALLY
dor·sal \ˈdȯr-səl\ *adj* **:** relating to or situated near or on the back (as of an animal) — **dor·sal·ly** \-sə-lē\ *adv*
dorsal fin *n* **:** a fin on the ridge along the middle of the back of a fish or an aquatic mammal (as a whale)
dorsal lip *n* **:** the dorsal margin of the blastopore of a gastrula

dor·so·ven·tral \ˌdȯr-sō-ˈven-trəl\ *adj* : extending from the dorsal toward the ventral side — **dor·so·ven·tral·ly** \-trə-lē\ *adv*

dor·sum \ˈdȯr-səm\ *n, pl* **dor·sa** \-sə\ : the dorsal surface (as of an animal or one of its parts) [Latin, "back"]

do·ry \ˈdōr-ē, ˈdȯr-\ *n, pl* **dories** : a flat-bottomed boat with a sharp bow and high sides that curve upward and outward [Miskito (a Central American Indian language) *dóri* "dugout"]

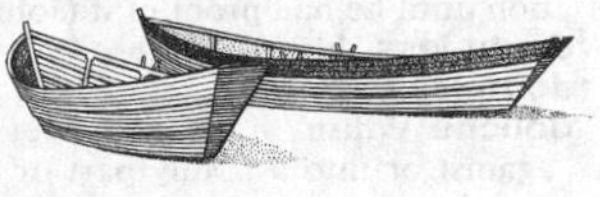
dory

dos·age \ˈdō-sij\ *n* **1 a** : the giving of medicine in doses **b** : the amount of a single dose **2 a** : the addition of a substance or the application of an agent in a measured dose **b** : the presence and relative representation or strength of a factor or agent

[1]**dose** \ˈdōs\ *n* **1 a** : the measured amount of a medicine to be taken at one time **b** : the quantity of radiation administered or absorbed **2** : a portion of a substance added during a process **3** : an experience to which one is exposed ⟨a *dose* of defeat⟩ [Medieval French, from Late Latin *dosis,* from Greek, literally, "act of giving," from *didonai* "to give"]

[2]**dose** *vt* **1** : to give medicine to **2** : to divide (as a medicine) into doses **3** : to treat with an application or agent

do·sim·e·ter \dō-ˈsim-ət-ər\ *n* : an instrument for measuring doses of X-rays or of radioactivity

dos·sier \ˈdȯs-ˌyā, ˈdȯs-ē-ˌā, ˈdäs-\ *n* : a file of papers containing a detailed report or detailed information [French, "bundle of documents labeled on the back, dossier," from *dos* "back," from Latin *dorsum*]

dost \dəst, ˈdəst\ *archaic present 2nd singular of* DO

[1]**dot** \ˈdät\ *n* **1** : a small spot : SPECK **2 a** : a small point made with or as if with a pen **b** (1) : a point after a note or rest in music indicating increase of the time value by one half (2) : a point over or under a note indicating staccato **c** : a centered point · used as a multiplication sign **3** : a precise point in time or space ⟨arrived at six on the *dot*⟩ **4** : a short click or buzz forming a letter or part of a letter (as in the Morse code) [Old English *dott* "head of a boil"]

[2]**dot** *vt* **dot·ted; dot·ting** **1** : to mark with a dot ⟨*dot* an i⟩ **2** : to cover with or as if with dots ⟨a lake *dotted* with boats⟩ — **dot·ter** *n*

dot·age \ˈdōt-ij\ *n* : SECOND CHILDHOOD, SENILITY

dot·ard \ˈdōt-ərd\ *n* : a person in his or her dotage

dot–com \ˈdät-ˌkäm\ *n* : a company that markets its products or services primarily online using a Web site [from the use of *.com* in the URLs of such companies]

dote \ˈdōt\ *vi* **1** : to be feebleminded especially from old age **2** : to show excessive or foolish affection or fondness ⟨*doted* on their grandchildren⟩ [Middle English *doten*] — **dot·er** *n* — **dot·ing·ly** \-ing-lē\ *adv*

doth \dəth, ˈdəth\ *archaic present 3rd singular of* DO

dot matrix *n* : a rectangular arrangement of dots from which letters, numbers, and symbols can be formed (as by a computer printer or on a display screen)

dotted swiss *n* : a sheer light muslin ornamented with evenly spaced raised dots

dot·ter·el \ˈdät-ə-rəl, ˈdä-trəl\ *n* : a Eurasian plover formerly common in England; *also* : any of several related birds [Middle English *dotrelle,* from *doten* "to dote"]

dot·tle \ˈdät-l\ *n* : unburned and partly burned tobacco caked in the bowl of a pipe [Middle English *dottel* "plug"]

dot·ty \ˈdät-ē\ *adj* **dot·ti·er; -est** : mentally unbalanced : CRAZY [Middle English *doten* "to dote"]

[1]**dou·ble** \ˈdəb-əl\ *adj* **1** : TWOFOLD, DUAL ⟨serving a *double* function⟩ **2** : consisting of two members or parts ⟨an egg with a *double* yolk⟩ **3** : being twice as great or as many ⟨had *double* the number of expected sales⟩ **4** : DECEITFUL 1 **5** : folded in two **6** : having more than the usual number of floral leaves ⟨*double* roses⟩ **7** : designed for the use of two persons ⟨a *double* bed⟩ [Medieval French, from Latin *duplus,* from *duo* "two" + *-plus* "multiplied by"] — **dou·ble·ness** *n*

[2]**double** *n* **1 a** : something twice another ⟨12 is the *double* of 6⟩ **b** : a base hit in baseball that enables the batter to reach second base **2** : COUNTERPART; *esp* : a person who closely resembles another **3** : a sharp turn : REVERSAL **4** : something that is folded in two **5** *pl* : a game between two pairs of players **6** : an act of doubling in a card game — **on the double** : very quickly : RIGHT AWAY

[3]**double** *adv* **1** : to twice the extent or amount : DOUBLY **2** : two together ⟨sleep *double*⟩ **3** : downward and forward from the usual position ⟨he was bent *double* with pain⟩

[4]**double** *vb* **dou·bled; dou·bling** \ˈdəb-ling, -ə-ling\ **1 a** : to make, be, or become twice as great or as many **b** : to make a call in bridge that increases the value of tricks over or less than (an opponent's bid) **2 a** : to bend or fold (as a sheet of paper) usually in the middle so that one part lies directly against the other part **b** : CLENCH 3 ⟨*doubled* his fist⟩ **c** : to cause to stoop **d** : to become bent or folded usually in the middle ⟨she *doubled* up in pain⟩ **3** : to have an additional use or job ⟨the cook *doubles* as dishwasher⟩ **4** : to make a double in baseball **5** : to turn sharply and go back on one's course — **dou·bler** \ˈdəb-lər, -ə-lər\ *n*

double bar *n* : two vertical lines or a heavy single line separating principal sections of a musical composition

double bass *n* : the largest instrument of the viol family

double bassoon *n* : CONTRABASSOON

double boiler *n* : a cooking utensil consisting of two saucepans fitting into each other so that the contents of the upper can be cooked or heated by boiling water in the lower

double bond *n* : a chemical bond in which two pairs of electrons are shared by two atoms in a molecule — compare SINGLE BOND, TRIPLE BOND

dou·ble–breast·ed \ˌdəb-əl-ˈbres-təd\ *adj* : having one half of the front lapped over the other and usually two rows of buttons ⟨a *double-breasted* jacket⟩

dou·ble–check \ˌdəb-əl-ˈchek, ˈdəb-əl-ˌ\ *vb* : to make or subject to a double check

double check *n* : a careful checking to determine accuracy, condition, or progress especially of something already checked

double chin *n* : a fleshy or fatty fold under the chin — **dou·ble–chinned** \ˌdəb-əl-ˈchind\ *adj*

double cross *n* **1** : an act of betraying or cheating especially an associate **2** : a cross between first-generation hybrids of four separate inbred lines — **dou·ble–cross** \ˌdəb-əl-ˈkrȯs\ *vt* — **dou·ble–cross·er** *n*

double dagger *n* : a character ‡ used as a reference mark

dou·ble–deal·ing \ˌdəb-əl-ˈdē-ling\ *n* : DUPLICITY — **dou·ble–deal·er** *n* — **double–dealing** *adj*

dou·ble–deck \-ˈdek\ *or* **dou·ble–decked** \-ˈdekt\ *adj* : having two decks, levels, or layers ⟨a *double-deck* bus⟩ ⟨a *double-deck* bridge⟩

dou·ble–deck·er \-ˈdek-ər\ *n* : something (as a bus or sandwich) having two decks, levels, or layers

double dribble *n* : an illegal action in basketball that occurs when a player resumes a dribble after stopping or dribbles the ball with both hands simultaneously

dou·ble entendre \ˌdüb-ˌlä^{n}-ˈtä^{n}dr, ˌdəb-, -ə-ˌlä^{n}-\ *n, pl* **double entendres** \-ˈtä^{n}dr, -ˈtä^{n}d-rəz\ : a word or expression capable of two interpretations one of which is usually improper or indecent [obsolete French, literally, "double meaning"]

double entry *n* : a method of bookkeeping that debits the amount of a business transaction to one account and credits it to another so that the total debits equal the total credits

double fertilization *n* : fertilization characteristic of seed plants in which one of the two sperm nuclei fuses with the egg nucleus to form an embryo and the other fuses with the two separate or fused polar nuclei to form endosperm

dou·ble·head·er \ˌdəb-əl-ˈhed-ər\ *n* **1** : a train pulled by two locomotives **2** : two games, contests, or events held consecutively on the same program

double helix *n* : the arrangement in space of DNA that resembles a spirally twisted ladder with the sides made up of the sugar and phosphate units of the two nucleotide strands and the rungs made up of the pyrimidine and purine bases extending into the center and joined by hydrogen bonds

double–hung \ˌdə-bəl-ˈhəŋ\ *adj* : being a window that has an upper and lower sash that can slide past each other

double hyphen *n* : a punctuation mark ⸗ used in place of a hyphen at the end of a line to indicate that the word so divided is normally hyphenated

dou·ble–joint·ed \ˌdəb-əl-ˈjȯint-əd\ *adj* : having a joint that permits an exceptional degree of freedom of motion of the parts joined

double knit *n* **:** a knitted fabric made with a double set of needles to produce a double thickness of fabric with each thickness joined by interlocking stitches

double negative *n* **:** a now nonstandard syntactic construction that contains two negatives and has a negative meaning (as in "I didn't hear nothing" instead of "I didn't hear anything")

dou·ble–park \ˌdəb-əl-ˈpärk\ *vb* **:** to park beside a row of vehicles already parked parallel to the curb

double play *n* **:** a play in baseball by which two players are put out

double pneumonia *n* **:** pneumonia involving both lungs

dou·ble–quick \ˈdəb-əl-ˌkwik\ *n* **:** DOUBLE TIME — **double–quick** *vi*

double reed *n* **:** two reeds bound together with a slight separation between them so that air passing through them causes them to beat against one another and that are used as a sound-producing device in certain woodwind instruments (as an oboe)

dou·ble–space \ˌdəb-əl-ˈspās\ *vb* **1 :** to type (copy) leaving every other line blank **2 :** to type on every second line

double standard *n* **:** a set of standards that applies differently and usually more harshly to one group of people or circumstances than to another

double star *n* **:** two stars that appear very near each other; *esp* **:** BINARY STAR

double sugar *n* **:** DISACCHARIDE

dou·blet \ˈdəb-lət\ *n* **1 :** a close-fitting jacket worn by men of western Europe chiefly in the 16th century **2 :** one of two similar or identical things **3 :** one of two or more words in the same language derived by different routes from the same source ⟨"dish" and "disk" are *doublets*⟩ [Medieval French *dublet,* from *duble* "double"]

D doublet 1

dou·ble–talk \ˈdəb-əl-ˌtȯk\ *n* **1 :** language that appears to be meaningful but in fact is a mixture of sense and nonsense **2 :** deliberately ambiguous language — **double–talk** *vi* — **dou·ble–talk·er** *n*

dou·ble–time \ˈdəb-əl-ˌtīm\ *vi* **:** to move at double time

double time *n* **1 :** a marching cadence of 180 30-inch steps per minute **2 :** payment of a worker at twice the regular wage rate

double vision *n* **:** vision in which an object is seen as double (as from unequal action of the eye muscles)

dou·bloon \ˌdə-ˈblün\ *n* **:** an old gold coin of Spain and Spanish America [Spanish *doblón,* derived from Latin *duplus* "double"]

dou·bly \ˈdəb-lē\ *adv* **1 :** to twice the degree ⟨*doubly* glad⟩ **2 :** in a twofold manner

[1]doubt \ˈdau̇t\ *vb* **1 :** to be uncertain about ⟨*doubts* her sincerity⟩ **2 :** to lack confidence in **:** DISTRUST **3 :** to consider unlikely ⟨I *doubt* if I'll be able to go⟩ [Medieval French *duter, douter,* from Latin *dubitare*] — **doubt·able** \-ə-bəl\ *adj* — **doubt·er** *n* — **doubt·ing·ly** \-ing-lē\ *adv*

[2]doubt *n* **1 :** uncertainty of belief or opinion **2 :** a state of affairs that causes uncertainty or suspense ⟨the outcome is in *doubt*⟩ **3 a :** a lack of confidence **:** DISTRUST ⟨has *doubts* about his abilities⟩ **b :** an inclination not to believe or accept ⟨a theory met with *doubt*⟩

synonyms DOUBT, UNCERTAINTY, DISTRUST, SUSPICION mean lack of sureness about someone or something. DOUBT implies uncertainty about the truth or reality of something and an inability to make a decision ⟨so filled with *doubt* that she didn't know what to do⟩. UNCERTAINTY may range from a falling short of certainty to an almost complete lack of knowledge about an outcome or result ⟨there is still *uncertainty* about what caused the accident⟩. DISTRUST implies lack of trust or confidence on vague or general grounds ⟨a long-standing *distrust* of strangers⟩. SUSPICION stresses lack of faith in the truth or reality of someone or something and implies an often unfounded charge of wrongdoing ⟨my *suspicion* is that he is lying⟩.

doubt·ful \ˈdau̇t-fəl\ *adj* **1 :** not clear or certain as to fact ⟨a *doubtful* claim⟩ **2 :** questionable in character ⟨*doubtful* intentions⟩ **3 :** not settled in opinion **:** UNDECIDED ⟨*doubtful* about what to do⟩ **4 :** not certain in outcome ⟨a *doubtful* battle⟩ — **doubt·ful·ly** \-fə-lē\ *adv* — **doubt·ful·ness** *n*

doubting Thom·as \-ˈtäm-əs\ *n* **:** an incredulous or habitually doubtful person [*Thomas,* apostle who doubted Jesus' resurrection until he had proof of it (John 20:24–29)]

[1]doubt·less \ˈdau̇t-ləs\ *adv* **1 :** without doubt **2 :** PROBABLY

[2]doubtless *adj* **:** free from doubt **:** CERTAIN

douche \ˈdüsh\ *n* **1 a :** a jet of liquid (as water) directed against or into a bodily part or cavity **b :** a cleansing with a douche **2 :** a device for giving douches [French] — **douche** *vb*

dough \ˈdō\ *n* **1 a :** a soft mass of moistened flour or meal thick enough to knead or roll **b :** something resembling dough especially in consistency **2 a :** MONEY 1 **b :** MONEY 2 [Old English *dāg*] — **doughy** \ˈdō-ē\ *adj*

dough·boy \ˈdō-ˌbȯi\ *n* **:** an American infantryman especially in World War I

dough·nut *also* **do·nut** \ˈdō-nət, -ˌnət\ *n* **:** a small usually ring-shaped cake fried in fat

dough·ty \ˈdau̇t-ē\ *adj* **dough·ti·er; -est :** being strong and valiant **:** BOLD [Old English *dohtig*] — **dough·ti·ly** \ˈdau̇t-l-ē\ *adv* — **dough·ti·ness** \ˈdau̇t-ē-nəs\ *n*

Doug·las fir \ˈdəg-ləs-\ *n* **:** a tall evergreen cone-bearing timber tree of the western United States; *also* **:** its wood [David *Douglas,* died 1834, Scottish botanist]

do up *vt* **1 :** to put in order; *also* **:** REPAIR ⟨planned to *do up* the house⟩ **2 :** WRAP 1b ⟨*do up* holiday packages⟩ **3 :** ARRAY 2, CLOTHE ⟨all *done up* in a pirate costume⟩ **4 :** FASTEN 2 ⟨*do up* the buttons of your shirt⟩

dour \ˈdu̇r, ˈdau̇r\ *adj* **1 :** STERN 3, HARSH **2 :** MOROSE 1 [Latin *durus* "hard"] — **dour·ly** *adv* — **dour·ness** *n*

[1]douse \ˈdau̇s\ *vt* **:** to take in ⟨*douse* a sail⟩ [earlier *douse* "blow, stroke"]

[2]douse *also* **dowse** \ˈdau̇s, ˈdau̇z\ *vt* **doused** *also* **dowsed; dous·ing** *also* **dows·ing 1 a :** to plunge into water **b :** to throw a liquid on **:** DRENCH **2 :** to put out **:** EXTINGUISH ⟨*douse* the lights⟩ [probably from obsolete English *douse* "to smite"]

[1]dove \ˈdəv\ *n* **1 :** any of numerous pigeons; *esp* **:** a small wild pigeon **2 :** a person who advocates negotiations and compromise in a dispute; *esp* **:** an opponent of war — compare HAWK [Middle English] — **dov·ish** \ˈdəv-ish\ *adj*

dove 1

[2]dove \ˈdōv\ *past of* DIVE

dove·cote \ˈdəv-ˌkōt, -ˌkät\ *also* **dove·cot** \-ˌkät\ *n* **:** a small raised house or box with compartments for domestic pigeons

dove·kie \ˈdəv-kē\ *n* **:** a small short-billed auk breeding on arctic coasts and ranging south in winter [from *dove*]

[1]dove·tail \ˈdəv-ˌtāl\ *n* **:** something resembling a dove's tail; *esp* **:** a flaring projection on a board and a slot into which it fits tightly making an interlocking joint between two pieces

[2]dovetail *vb* **1 a :** to join by means of dovetails **b :** to cut to a dovetail **2 :** to fit skillfully together to form a whole

dow·a·ger \ˈdau̇-i-jər\ *n* **1 :** a widow holding property or a title received from her deceased husband **2 :** a dignified elderly woman [Middle French *douagiere,* from *douage* "dower," from *douer* "to endow," from Latin *dotare,* from *dot-, dos* "gift, dower"]

[1]dowdy \ˈdau̇d-ē\ *n, pl* **dowd·ies :** a dowdy woman [Middle English *doude*]

[2]dowdy *adj* **dowd·i·er; -est :** not neatly or becomingly dressed or cared for **:** SHABBY; *also* **:** lacking in smartness or taste — **dowd·i·ly** \ˈdau̇d-l-ē\ *adv* — **dowd·i·ness** \ˈdau̇d-ē-nəs\ *n*

[1]dow·el \ˈdau̇-əl, ˈdau̇l\ *n* **:** a pin or peg projecting from one of two parts or surfaces (as of wood) to be fastened together and fitting into a hole prepared in the other part; *also* **:** a rod for cutting up into dowels [Middle English *dowle*]

[2]dowel *vt* **-elled** *also* **-eled; -el·ling** *also* **-el·ing :** to fasten by or furnish with dowels

[1]dow·er \ˈdau̇-ər, ˈdau̇r\ *n* **1 :** the part of or interest in the real estate of a deceased husband given by law to his widow during her life **2 :** DOWRY

[2]**dower** *vt* : to supply with a dower or dowry : ENDOW
[1]**down** \'dau̇n\ *n* : an undulating usually treeless upland with sparse soil — usually used in plural [Old English *dūn* "hill"]
[2]**down** *adv* **1 a** (1) : toward or in a lower physical position (2) : to a lying or sitting position (3) : toward or to the ground, floor, or bottom **b** : as a down payment ⟨paid $10 *down*⟩ **2** : in a direction that is the opposite of up: as **a** : SOUTH **b** : away from a center (as of activity) ⟨went *down* to the country⟩ **c** : in or into the stomach ⟨can't keep food *down*⟩ **3** : to or in a lower or worse condition, level, or status **4** : from a past time ⟨heirlooms handed *down*⟩ **5** : to or in a state of less activity ⟨excitement *died* down⟩ **6** : to a concentrated state ⟨got a report *down* to three pages⟩ [Old English *dūne,* short for *adūne,* from *a-* "off, from" + *dūn* "hill"]
[3]**down** *adj* **1 a** : occupying a low position; *esp* : lying on the ground **b** : directed or going downward ⟨a *down* escalator⟩ **c** : being at a lower level ⟨sales were *down*⟩ **2 a** : being in a state of reduced or low activity ⟨a *down* economy⟩ **b** (1) : DEJECTED, DEPRESSED ⟨felt *down* after losing the game⟩ (2) : SICK ⟨*down* with flu⟩ (3) : having a low opinion or dislike ⟨was *down* on me for not helping⟩ **3** : DONE 3, FINISHED ⟨eight *down* and two to go⟩ — **down on** : having a low opinion of or dislike for — **down on one's luck** : experiencing misfortune and especially financial trouble
[4]**down** *prep* : down along : down through : down toward : down in : down into : down on ⟨*down* the road⟩
[5]**down** *n* **1** : a low or falling period (as in activity, emotional life, or fortunes) ⟨have their ups and *downs*⟩ **2 a** : a complete play to advance the ball in football **b** : one of a series of four attempts to advance a football 10 yards
[6]**down** *vb* **1 a** : to go or cause to go or come down **b** : CONSUME 3 ⟨*downing* slices of pizza⟩ **2** : to cause (a football) to be out of play **3** : DEFEAT 1a ⟨*downed* a proposal⟩
[7]**down** *n* **1** : a covering of soft fluffy feathers **2** : something soft and fluffy like down [Old Norse *dūnn*]
down•beat \'dau̇n-ˌbēt\ *n* : the downward stroke of a conductor indicating the principally accented note of a measure of music
down•burst \-ˌbərst\ *n* : a powerful downdraft
down•cast \-ˌkast\ *adj* **1** : low in spirit : DISCOURAGED ⟨a *downcast* manner⟩ **2** : directed down ⟨*downcast* eyes⟩
down•draft \-ˌdraft\ *n* : a downward current of gas (as air in a chimney or during a thunderstorm)
down•er \'dau̇-nər\ *n* **1** : a depressant drug; *esp* : BARBITURATE **2** : someone or something depressing, disagreeable, or unsatisfactory
down•fall \'dau̇n-ˌfȯl\ *n* **1** : FALL 2c; *esp* : a sudden or heavy fall (as of rain) **2** : a sudden descent (as from a high position) : RUIN ⟨the *downfall* of a champion⟩ **3** : the cause of a downfall ⟨gambling was his *downfall*⟩ — **down•fall•en** \-ˌfȯ-lən\ *adj*
[1]**down•grade** \-ˌgrād\ *n* **1** : a downward grade or slope **2** : a decline toward a worse condition ⟨a neighborhood on the *downgrade*⟩ — **down•grade** \-'grād\ *adv*
[2]**down•grade** \-ˌgrād\ *vt* : to lower in grade, rank, position, or status
down•heart•ed \'dau̇n-'härt-əd\ *adj* : DEJECTED, DOWNCAST — **down•heart•ed•ly** *adv* — **down•heart•ed•ness** *n*
[1]**down•hill** \'dau̇n-'hil\ *adv* **1** : toward the bottom of a hill ⟨sleds traveling *downhill* at high speeds⟩ **2** : toward a worsened or inferior state or level ⟨the town has gone *downhill* since the mill closed⟩
[2]**down•hill** \-ˌhil\ *adj* : sloping downhill ⟨a *downhill* path⟩
[3]**downhill** *n* **1** : a descending slope **2 a** : the sport of skiing on downhill trails ⟨*downhill* skiing⟩ **b** : a skiing race against time down a trail ⟨finished second in the *downhill*⟩
[1]**down•load** \'dau̇n-ˌlōd\ *n* : an instance of downloading; *also* : the item downloaded
[2]**download** *vt* : to transfer (data) from a usually large computer to the memory of another device (as a smaller computer) — **down•load•able** \-ˌlōd-ə-bəl\ *adj*
down payment *n* : a part of the full price paid at the time of purchase with the balance to be paid later
down•pour \'dau̇n-ˌpōr, -ˌpȯr\ *n* : a heavy rain
down•range \-'rānj\ *adv* : away from a launching site ⟨a missile landing 5000 kilometers *downrange*⟩ — **down•range** *adj*
[1]**down•right** \-ˌrīt\ *adv* : OUTRIGHT 1 ⟨*downright* mean⟩
[2]**downright** *adj* **1** : ABSOLUTE 4, UTTER ⟨a *downright* lie⟩ **2** : PLAIN 4b, BLUNT ⟨a straightforward *downright* person⟩ — **down•right•ly** *adv* — **down•right•ness** *n*
down•size \'dau̇n-ˌsīz\ *vb* : to reduce in size ⟨*downsizing* staff to cut costs⟩
Down syndrome \'dau̇n-\ *or* **Down's syndrome** \'dau̇nz-\ *n* : a genetic disorder marked by moderate to severe mental retardation, by distinctive physical characteristics (as slanting eyes and broad hands with short fingers), and by the presence of three chromosomes of the chromosome pair numbered 21 in human beings [J.L.H. *Down,* died 1896, English physician]
down•stage \-'stāj\ *adv or adj* : toward or at the front of a theatrical stage
[1]**down•stairs** \'dau̇n-'staərz, -'steərz\ *adv* : down the stairs : on or to a lower floor
[2]**down•stairs** \-ˌstaərz, -ˌsteərz\ *adj* : located on the main, lower, or ground floor of a building
[3]**down•stairs** \'dau̇n-', 'dau̇n-ˌ\ *n* : the lower floor of a building
down•stream \'dau̇n-'strēm\ *adv or adj* : in the direction of flow of a stream
down•stroke \-ˌstrōk\ *n* : a stroke made in a downward direction
down•swing \-ˌswiŋ\ *n* **1** : a downward swing **2** : DOWNTURN 2
down–to–earth \ˌdau̇n-tə-'ərth, -'wərth\ *adj* **1** : PRACTICAL 3 ⟨*down-to-earth* advice⟩ **2** : UNPRETENTIOUS ⟨a *down-to-earth* person⟩ — **down–to–earthness** *n*
[1]**down•town** \'dau̇n-'tau̇n\ *adv* : to, toward, or in the lower part or business center of a town or city — **downtown** *adj*
[2]**down•town** \-ˌtau̇n\ *n* : an urban business center
down•trod•den \'dau̇n-'träd-n\ *adj* : crushed by superior power : OPPRESSED
down•turn \-ˌtərn\ *n* **1** : a turning downward **2** : a decline especially in business and economic activity
[1]**down•ward** \'dau̇n-wərd\ *or* **down•wards** \-wərdz\ *adv* **1** : from a higher to a lower place or condition **2 a** : from an earlier time **b** : from an ancestor or predecessor
[2]**downward** *adj* **1** : moving or extending downward **2** : descending from a head, origin, or source — **down•ward•ly** *adv*
down•wind \'dau̇n-'wind\ *adv or adj* : in the direction that the wind is blowing
downy \'dau̇-nē\ *adj* **down•i•er; -est** **1** : suggesting a bird's down (as in softness or lightness) **2** : covered with or made of down
downy mildew *n* : a parasitic mold that bears whitish masses of spore-producing bodies on the undersurface of the leaves of the host; *also* : a plant disease caused by a downy mildew
downy woodpecker *n* : a small black-and-white woodpecker of North America that has a white back
dow•ry \'dau̇r-ē\ *n, pl* **dowries** **1** : the property that a woman brings to her husband in marriage **2** : a gift of money or property by a man to or for his bride [Medieval French *dowarie,* derived from Medieval Latin *dotarium,* from Latin *dot-, dos* "gift, dower"]
[1]**dowse** *variant of* DOUSE
[2]**dowse** \'dau̇z\ *vb* : to use a divining rod especially to find water [origin unknown] — **dows•er** *n*
dox•ol•o•gy \däk-'säl-ə-jē\ *n, pl* **-gies** : a usually liturgical expression of praise to God [Medieval Latin *doxologia,* from Late Greek, from Greek *doxa* "opinion, glory" (from Greek *dokein* "to seem, seem good") + *-logia* "-logy"]
doze \'dōz\ *vi* : to sleep lightly [probably of Scandinavian origin] — **doze** *n* — **doz•er** *n*
doz•en \'dəz-n\ *n, pl* **dozens** *or* **dozen** : a group of twelve [Medieval French *duzeine, dozeyne,* from *duze* "twelve," from Latin *duodecim,* from *duo* "two" + *decem* "ten"] — **dozen** *adj* — **doz•enth** \-nth, -ntth\ *adj*
doz•er \'dō-zər\ *n* : BULLDOZER 2
DP \'dē-'pē\ *n, pl* **DP's** *or* **DPs** **1** : a displaced person **2** : DOUBLE PLAY
[1]**drab** \'drab\ *n* : a light olive brown [Middle French *drap* "cloth," from Late Latin *drappus*]
[2]**drab** *adj* **drab•ber; drab•best** **1** : of the color drab **2** : characterized by dullness and monotony : CHEERLESS ⟨they lead *drab* lives⟩ — **drab•ly** *adv* — **drab•ness** *n*

\ə\ **abut**	\au̇\ **out**	\i\ **tip**	\ȯ\ **saw**	\u̇\ **foot**
\ər\ **further**	\ch\ **chin**	\ī\ **life**	\ȯi\ **coin**	\y\ **yet**
\a\ **mat**	\e\ **pet**	\j\ **job**	\th\ **thin**	\yü\ **few**
\ā\ **take**	\ē\ **easy**	\ng\ **sing**	\th\ **this**	\yu̇\ **cure**
\ä\ **cot, cart**	\g\ **go**	\ō\ **bone**	\ü\ **food**	\zh\ **vision**

drachm \'dram\ *n* **1** : DRACHMA 2a **2** *chiefly British* **a** : DRAM 1 **b** : DRAM 2b [from Middle English *dragme*]

drach•ma \'drak-mə\ *n, pl* **drach•mas** *or* **drach•mai** \-ˌmī\ *or* **drach•mae** \-ˌmē, -ˌmī\ **1 a** : any of various ancient Greek units of weight **b** : any of various modern units of weight; *esp* : DRAM 1 **2 a** : an ancient Greek silver coin equivalent to 6 obols **b** : the basic monetary unit of modern Greece until 2002; *also* : a coin representing this unit [Latin, "drachma, dram," from Greek *drachmē*]

Dra•co \'drā-kō\ *n* : a northern circumpolar constellation between the Big Dipper and Little Dipper [Latin, literally, "dragon"]

[1]**draft** \'draft, 'draft\ *n* **1** : the act of drawing a net; *also* : HAUL 2b **2** : the act of moving loads by drawing or pulling **3 a** : the force required to pull an implement **b** : load-pulling capacity **4 a** : the act or an instance of drinking or inhaling; *also* : the portion drunk or inhaled **b** : a potion prepared for drinking : DOSE **5 a** : DELINEATION, REPRESENTATION; *esp* : a construction plan ⟨the *draft* of a future building⟩ **b** : a preliminary sketch, outline, or version ⟨a rough *draft* of the essay⟩ **6** : the act or result of drawing out or stretching **7** : the act of drawing (as from a cask); *also* : a portion of liquid so drawn **8** : the depth of water a ship draws especially when loaded **9 a** : the selection of a person especially for compulsory military service **b** : a group of persons selected especially by military draft **10 a** : an order (as a check) issued by one party to another (as a bank) to pay money to a third party **b** : a heavy demand : STRAIN ⟨a *draft* on natural resources⟩ **11 a** : a current of air in an enclosed space **b** : a device for regulating the flow of air (as in a fireplace) **12** : a narrow border along the edge of a stone or across its face serving as a stonecutter's guide **13** : a system whereby exclusive rights to selected new players are apportioned among professional teams [Middle English *draght*] — **on draft** : ready to be drawn from a receptacle ⟨beer *on draft*⟩

[2]**draft** *adj* **1** : used for drawing loads ⟨*draft* animals⟩ **2** : constituting a preliminary or tentative version, sketch, or outline ⟨a *draft* treaty⟩ **3** : being or having been on draft ⟨*draft* beer⟩

[3]**draft** *vt* **1** : to select usually on a compulsory basis; *esp* : to conscript for military service **2 a** : to draw up a preliminary sketch, version, or plan of ⟨*draft* a constitution⟩ **b** : to put into written form ⟨*draft* an essay⟩ **3** : to draw off or away ⟨water *drafted* by pumps⟩ — **draft•er** *n*

draft•ee \draf-'tē, draf-\ *n* : a person who is drafted especially into the armed forces

drafts•man \'draf-smən, 'draf-, 'draft-, 'draft-\ *n* : a person who draws plans and sketches (as for machinery) — **drafts•man•ship** \-ˌship\ *n*

drafty \'draf-tē, 'draf-\ *adj* **draf•ti•er; -est** : having or exposed to a draft ⟨a *drafty* hall⟩ — **draft•i•ly** \-tə-lē\ *adv* — **draft•i•ness** \-tē-nəs\ *n*

[1]**drag** \'drag\ *n* **1** : something used to drag with; *esp* : a device for dragging under water to detect or obtain objects **2** : something that is dragged, pulled, or drawn along or over a surface: as **a** : HARROW **b** : a sledge for carrying heavy loads **3 a** : something that retards motion **b** : the retarding force acting on a body (as an airplane) moving through a fluid (as air) **c** : friction between engine parts **d** : something that hinders or obstructs progress **4 a** : the act or an instance of dragging or drawing **b** : a drawing along or over a surface with effort or pressure **c** : motion achieved with slowness or difficulty; *also* : the condition of having or seeming to have such motion **d** : a draw on a pipe, cigarette, or cigar : PUFF; *also* : a draft of liquid **5** : a movement, inclination, or retardation caused by or as if by dragging **6** *slang* : influence securing special favor **7** : STREET 1, ROAD ⟨the main *drag*⟩ **8** : one that is boring ⟨the movie was a *drag*⟩ [Middle English *dragge*]

[2]**drag** *vb* **dragged; drag•ging** **1 a** : to draw slowly or heavily : HAUL **b** : to move or cause to move with slowness or difficulty ⟨*dragged* myself up the stairs⟩ **c** : to bring by or as if by force or compulsion ⟨*dragged* them to the theater⟩ **d** : to pass (time) laboriously or tediously ⟨the day *dragged* on⟩ **e** : PROTRACT ⟨*drag* a story out⟩ **2** : to hang or lag behind **3** : to trail along a surface **4** : to explore, search, or fish with a drag **5** : to inhale deeply ⟨*drag* on a cigarette⟩ **6** : to participate in a drag race **7** : to move (an item on a computer screen) using a mouse — **drag•ging•ly** \'dra-ging-lē\ *adv* — **drag one's feet** *also* **drag one's heels** : to act in a slow manner or in a manner intended to cause delay

drag•ger \'drag-ər\ *n* : one that drags; *esp* : a fishing boat operating a trawl or dragnet

drag•gle \'drag-əl\ *vb* **drag•gled; drag•gling** \'drag-ling, -ə-ling\ **1** : to make or become wet and dirty by dragging **2 a** : to follow slowly : STRAGGLE **b** : to move along slowly [derived from *drag*]

drag•gy \'drag-ē\ *adj* **drag•gi•er; -est** **1** : DULL 3 **2** : TEDIOUS

drag•net \'drag-ˌnet\ *n* **1 a** : a net drawn along the bottom of a body of water : TRAWL **b** : a net used (as to capture small game) on the ground **2** : a network of planned actions for pursuing and catching a criminal

drag•o•man \'drag-ə-mən\ *n, pl* **-mans** *or* **-men** \-mən\ : an interpreter chiefly of Arabic, Turkish, or Persian employed especially in the Near East [Medieval French *drugeman,* from Italian *dragomanno,* from Middle Greek *dragomanos,* from Arabic *tarjumān,* from Aramaic *tūrgĕmānā*]

drag•on \'drag-ən\ *n* **1** : an imaginary animal usually represented as a huge winged and scaly serpent or lizard with a crested head and enormous claws **2** *cap* : DRACO **3** : a fierce or very strict person [Medieval French, from Latin *draco* "serpent, dragon," from Greek *drakōn* "serpent"]

drag•on•fly \-ˌflī\ *n* : any of a group (Anisoptera) of large harmless insects that have four long wings held horizontally when at rest and feed especially on flies, gnats, and mosquitoes — compare DAMSELFLY

[1]**dra•goon** \drə-'gün, dra-\ *n* : a cavalry soldier [French *dragon* "dragon, dragoon"]

[2]**dragoon** *vt* : to force into submission by violent measures

drag race *n* : an acceleration contest between motor vehicles — **drag racer** *n* — **drag racing** *n*

drag•ster \'drag-stər\ *n* **1** : a vehicle made for drag racing **2** : one who participates in a drag race

drag strip *n* : a place for drag races that is paved and at least a quarter mile long

[1]**drain** \'drān\ *vb* **1 a** : to draw off or flow off gradually or completely ⟨*drain* water from a tank⟩ **b** : to cause the gradual disappearance of ⟨*drain* the city's funds⟩ **c** : to exhaust physically or emotionally **2 a** : to make or become gradually dry or empty ⟨*drain* a swamp⟩ ⟨*drained* the country of its resources⟩ **b** : to carry away the surface water of : discharge surface or surplus water ⟨the river *drains* the valley⟩ [Old English *drēahnian*] — **drain•er** *n*

[2]**drain** *n* **1** : a means by which usually liquid matter is drained **2 a** : the act of draining **b** : a gradual outflow or withdrawal : DEPLETION **3** : something that causes depletion : BURDEN ⟨a *drain* on one's resources⟩ — **down the drain** : to a state of being wasted or completely lost

drain•age \'drā-nij\ *n* **1** : the act, process, or mode of draining; *also* : something drained off **2** : a means for draining; *also* : a system of drains **3** : an area drained

drain•pipe \'drān-ˌpīp\ *n* : a pipe for drainage

drake *n* : a male duck [Middle English]

dram \'dram\ *n* **1 a** — see MEASURE table **b** : FLUID DRAM **2 a** : a small portion of something to drink **b** : a small amount [Late Latin *dragma* "dram, drachma," from Latin *drachma,* from Greek *drachmē,* literally, "handful," from *drassesthai* "to grasp"]

DRAM \'dram *also* 'dē-ˌram\ *n* : a computer memory chip that must be continuously supplied with power in order to retain data [*d*ynamic + *RAM* (*r*andom-*a*ccess *m*emory)]

dra•ma \'dräm-ə, 'dram-\ *n* **1 a** : a composition telling a story through action and dialogue and designed for theatrical performance : PLAY **b** : a play, movie, or television production with a serious tone or subject **2** : dramatic art, literature, or affairs **3 a** : a situation or series of events involving interesting or intense conflict of forces ⟨the *drama* of the courtroom proceedings⟩ **b** : dramatic state, effect, or quality ⟨used colored lighting and music for *drama*⟩ [Late Latin *dramat-, drama,* from Greek, "deed, drama," from *dran* "to do, act"]

Dram•a•mine \'dram-ə-ˌmēn\ *trademark* — used for a crystalline compound used to prevent or treat motion sickness

dra•mat•ic \drə-'mat-ik\ *adj* **1** : of or relating to drama ⟨a *dramatic* actor⟩ **2 a** : suitable to or characteristic of drama ⟨a *dramatic* escape⟩ **b** : striking in appearance or effect ⟨a *dramatic* pause⟩ — **dra•mat•i•cal•ly** \-'mat-i-kə-lē, -klē\ *adv*

synonyms DRAMATIC, THEATRICAL, HISTRIONIC, MELODRAMATIC mean having a character or an effect like that of acted plays. DRAMATIC applies to situations in life and literature that stir the imagination and emotions deeply ⟨a *dramatic* meeting of world leaders⟩. THEATRICAL implies a crude appeal through artificiality or exaggeration in gesture or vocal expression ⟨a *theatrical* oration⟩. HISTRIONIC applies to tones, gestures, and motions and suggests a deliberate affectation or staginess ⟨a *histrionic* show of grief⟩. MELODRAMATIC suggests an exaggerated emotionalism or an inappropriate theatricalism ⟨made a *melodramatic* plea⟩.

dra•mat•ics \-iks\ *n sing or pl* **1 :** the study or practice of theatrical arts (as acting and stagecraft) **2 :** dramatic behavior or expression

dra•ma•tis per•so•nae \ˌdram-ət-əs-pər-ˈsō-ˌnē, ˌdräm-, -ˌnī\ *n pl* **:** the characters or actors in a drama [New Latin]

dra•ma•tist \ˈdram-ət-əst, ˈdräm-\ *n* **:** PLAYWRIGHT

dra•ma•tize \ˈdram-ə-ˌtīz, ˈdräm-\ *vt* **1 :** to adapt for theatrical presentation **2 :** to present or represent in a dramatic manner — **dra•ma•ti•za•tion** \ˌdram-ət-ə-ˈzā-shən, ˌdräm-\ *n*

dra•ma•tur•gy \ˈdram-ə-ˌtər-jē, ˈdräm-\ *n* **:** the art or technique of dramatic composition and theatrical representation [German *Dramaturgie,* from Greek *dramatourgia* "dramatic composition," derived from *drama* "drama" + *ergon* "work"] — **dra•ma•tur•gic** \ˌdram-ə-ˈtər-jik, ˌdräm-\ *adj*

drank *past of* DRINK

[1]**drape** \ˈdrāp\ *vb* **1 :** to cover or adorn with or as if with folds of cloth **2 :** to cause to hang or stretch out loosely or carelessly ⟨*drape* oneself over a chair⟩ **3 :** to arrange or become arranged in flowing lines or folds ⟨a beautifully *draped* satin dress⟩ [probably from *drapery*]

[2]**drape** *n* **1 :** a drapery especially for a window **:** CURTAIN **2 :** arrangement in or of folds **3 :** the cut or hang of clothing ⟨the *drape* of a jacket⟩

drap•er \ˈdrā-pər\ *n, chiefly British* **:** a dealer in cloth and sometimes also in clothing and dry goods

drap•ery \ˈdrā-pə-rē, -prē\ *n, pl* **-er•ies** **1** *British* **:** DRY GOODS **2 a :** a decorative fabric usually hung in loose folds and arranged in a graceful design **b :** a hanging of heavy fabric used as a curtain **3 :** the draping or arranging of materials [Medieval French *draperie,* from *drap* "cloth" + *-erie* "-ery"]

dras•tic \ˈdras-tik\ *adj* **1 :** acting rapidly or violently ⟨a *drastic* purgative⟩ **2 :** extreme in effect **:** SEVERE ⟨*drastic* changes in the law⟩ [Greek *drastikos,* from *dran* "to do"] — **dras•ti•cal•ly** \-ti-kə-lē, -klē\ *adv*

draught \ˈdraft, ˈdråft\ *chiefly British variant of* DRAFT

draughts \ˈdrafs, ˈdråfs, ˈdrafts, ˈdråfts\ *n, British* **:** CHECKERS [Middle English *draghtes,* from *draght* "draft, move in chess"]

Dra•vid•i•an \drə-ˈvid-ē-ən\ *n* **1 :** a member of an ancient people of southern India **2 :** any of several languages of India, Sri Lanka, and Pakistan constituting a language family [Sanskrit *Draviḍa*] — **Dravidian** *adj*

[1]**draw** \ˈdrȯ\ *vb* **drew** \ˈdrü\; **drawn** \ˈdrȯn\; **draw•ing** **1 :** to cause to move continuously toward or after a force applied in advance **:** PULL ⟨*draw* your chair up by the fire⟩: as **a :** to move (as a covering) over or to one side ⟨*draw* the curtains⟩ **b :** to pull up or out of a receptacle or place where carried ⟨*draw* water from the well⟩ ⟨*drew* a gun⟩; *also* **:** to cause to come out of a container or source ⟨*draw* water for a bath⟩ ⟨the nurse *drew* a blood sample⟩ **2 a :** to cause to go in a certain direction (as by leading) ⟨*drew* us aside⟩ **b :** to move or go steadily or gradually ⟨night *draws* near⟩ **3 a :** ATTRACT, ENTICE ⟨honey *draws* flies⟩ **b :** to bring on oneself **:** PROVOKE ⟨*drew* enemy fire⟩ **4 :** INHALE ⟨*drew* a deep breath⟩ **5 a :** to extract the essence from ⟨*draw* tea⟩ **b :** EVISCERATE ⟨a *drawn* and plucked hen⟩ **6 :** to require (a specified depth) to float in ⟨a ship that *draws* four meters of water⟩ **7 a :** ACCUMULATE, GAIN ⟨*drawing* interest⟩ **b :** to take (money) from a place of deposit **:** WITHDRAW **c :** to receive regularly from a source ⟨*draw* a salary⟩ **8 a :** to take (cards) from a stack or the dealer **b :** to receive or take at random ⟨*drew* a winning number⟩ **9 :** to bend (a bow) by pulling back the string **10 a :** to cause to shrink or tighten **b :** to change shape by or as if by pulling or stretching ⟨a face *drawn* with fatigue⟩ **11 :** to strike (a ball) so as to impart a backward spin **12 :** to leave (a contest) undecided **:** TIE **13 a :** to produce a likeness of by or as if by making lines on a surface **:** DELINEATE ⟨*draw* a picture⟩ **b :** to write out in proper form **:** DRAFT ⟨*draw* up a will⟩ **c :** express in detail **:** FORMULATE ⟨*draw* comparisons⟩ **14 :** to infer from evidence or premises ⟨*draw* a conclusion⟩ **15 :** to spread or elongate (metal) by hammering or by pulling through dies **16 a :** to produce or allow a draft or current of air ⟨the furnace *draws* well⟩ **b :** to swell out in a wind ⟨all sails *drawing*⟩ [Old English *dragan*] — **draw•able** \-ə-bəl\ *adj* — **draw a bead on :** to take aim at — **draw a blank :** to fail to gain a desired object (as information sought); *also* **:** to be unable to think of something — **draw on** *or* **draw upon :** to use as a source of supply ⟨*drawing* on the whole community for support⟩ — **draw straws :** to decide or assign something by lottery in which straws of unequal length are used — **draw the line** *or* **draw a line** **1 :** to fix a boundary between things that tend to intermingle **2 :** to set a limit that points out what one will not tolerate or do

[2]**draw** *n* **1 :** the act, process, or result of drawing **2 :** a lot or chance drawn at random ⟨a win at the first *draw*⟩ **3 :** the movable part of a drawbridge **4 :** a contest left undecided or deadlocked **:** TIE **5 :** something that draws attention or patronage **6 :** a gully shallower than a ravine

draw away *vi* **:** to move ahead (as of an opponent in a race) ⟨the brown horse soon *drew away* from the others⟩

draw•back \ˈdrȯ-ˌbak\ *n* **:** an objectionable feature **:** DISADVANTAGE

draw•bar \-ˌbär\ *n* **:** a beam across the rear of a tractor to which implements are hitched

draw•bridge \-ˌbrij\ *n* **:** a bridge made to be raised up, let down, or drawn aside so as to permit or hinder passage

drawbridge

draw•ee \drȯ-ˈē\ *n* **:** the party (as a bank) ordered to pay a draft

draw•er \ˈdrȯ-ər, ˈdrȯr\ *n* **1 :** one that draws: as **a :** a person who draws liquor **b :** DRAFTSMAN **c :** one who executes a draft or makes a promissory note **2 :** a sliding box or receptacle (as in a table or desk) opened by pulling out and closed by pushing in **3** *pl* **:** an undergarment for the lower part of the body

draw•ing \ˈdrȯ-iŋ\ *n* **1 a :** an act or instance of drawing **b :** the deciding of something by drawing lots **2 :** the act, art, or technique of representing an object by means of lines **3 :** something drawn or capable of being drawn; *esp* **:** a representation formed by drawing

drawing board *n* **1 :** a board on which paper to be drawn on is fastened **2 :** a planning stage ⟨a project still on the *drawing board*⟩

drawing card *n* **:** one that attracts attention or patronage ⟨the store's low prices continue to be a *drawing card* for shoppers⟩

drawing room *n* **1 a :** a formal reception room **b :** a private room on a railroad passenger car with three berths and an enclosed toilet **2 :** a formal reception ⟨at the queen's *drawing room*⟩ [short for *withdrawing room*]

draw•knife \ˈdrȯ-ˌnīf\ *n* **:** a woodworker's tool having a blade with a handle at each end used to shave off surfaces

[1]**drawl** \ˈdrȯl\ *vb* **:** to speak slowly with vowels greatly prolonged **:** utter in a slow lengthened tone [probably from *draw*] — **drawl•er** *n* — **drawl•ing•ly** \ˈdrȯ-liŋ-lē\ *adv*

[2]**drawl** *n* **:** a drawling manner of speaking — **drawly** \ˈdrȯ-lē\ *adj*

drawn butter *n* **:** melted butter

drawn•work \ˈdrȯn-ˌwərk\ *n* **:** decoration on cloth made by drawing out threads according to a pattern

draw on *vb* **1 a :** APPROACH 1a ⟨night *draws on*⟩ **b :** to bring on **:** CAUSE **2 :** to take funds from ⟨*draw on* a bank account⟩

draw out *vt* **1 :** EXTRACT 1 ⟨*draw out* a confession⟩ **2 :** to cause to speak freely ⟨tried to *draw* them *out* on the subject⟩ **3 :** PROLONG 1 ⟨refused to *draw out* the interview⟩

draw•shave \ˈdrȯ-ˌshāv\ *n* **:** DRAWKNIFE

draw•string \-ˌstriŋ\ *n* **:** a string, cord, or tape run through a hem, a casing, or eyelets and used to close a bag or to control fullness in garments and curtains

draw•tube \-ˌtüb, -ˌtyüb\ *n* **:** a telescoping tube (as for the eyepiece of a microscope)

draw up *vb* **1 :** to arrange (as troops) in order **2 :** to prepare a draft or version of ⟨*draw up* plans⟩ **3 :** to straighten (oneself) to an erect posture especially as an assertion of dignity or resentment **4 :** to bring or come to a halt ⟨the car *drew up* at the door⟩

[1]**dray** \ˈdrā\ *n* **:** a vehicle used to haul goods; *esp* **:** a strong low cart or wagon without sides [Middle English *draye,* a wheelless vehicle]

[2]**dray** *vt* **:** to carry or transport on a dray

dray·age \ˈdrā-ij\ *n* **:** the work or cost of draying

dray·man \ˈdrā-mən\ *n* **:** one whose work is draying

[1]**dread** \ˈdred\ *vb* **1 a :** to fear greatly **:** be apprehensive or fearful **b** *archaic* **:** to regard with awe **2 :** to feel extreme reluctance to meet or face [Old English *drǣdan*]

[2]**dread** *n* **1 a :** great fear especially in the face of impending evil or harm **b** *archaic* **:** AWE **2 :** one causing fear or awe **3 a :** DREADLOCK 1 **b** *pl* **:** DREADLOCK 2 ***synonyms*** see FEAR

[3]**dread** *adj* **:** causing dread **:** DREADFUL

dread·ful \ˈdred-fəl\ *adj* **1 :** inspiring dread or awe **:** FRIGHTENING **2 :** extremely distasteful, unpleasant, or shocking — **dread·ful·ly** \-fə-lē, -flē\ *adv* — **dread·ful·ness** \-fəl-nəs\ *n*

dread·lock \ˈdred-ˌläk\ *n* **1 :** a narrow ropelike strand of hair formed by matting and braiding **2** *pl* **:** a hairstyle consisting of dreadlocks — **dread·locked** \-läkt\ *adj*

dread·nought \ˈdred-ˌnȯt, -ˌnät\ *n* **:** BATTLESHIP [*Dreadnought,* a British battleship]

[1]**dream** \ˈdrēm\ *n* **1 :** a series of thoughts, images, or emotions occurring during sleep **2 a :** a visionary creation of the imagination **:** DAYDREAM **b :** a state of mind in which a person is lost in fancies or reveries **c :** an object seen in a dreamlike state **:** VISION **3 :** something notable for its beauty, excellence, or enjoyable quality **4 :** a goal or purpose strongly desired [Old English *drēam* "noise, joy"] — **dream·like** \-ˌlīk\ *adj*

Word History Not until the 13th century was our word *dream* used in the sense of "a series of thoughts, images, or emotions occurring during sleep." But the word itself is considerably older. In Old English *dream* means "joy," "noise," or "music." Yet the shift in sense did not come simply from the development of a more specialized sense. Rather it appears that after many Scandinavian conflicts, conquests, and settlements in Britain the Old Norse *draumr,* meaning "a dream during sleep," influenced the meaning of the similar and probably related English word. By the end of the 14th century the earlier meanings had been entirely replaced.

[2]**dream** \ˈdrēm\ *vb* **dreamed** \ˈdremt, ˈdrēmd\ *or* **dreamt** \ˈdremt\; **dream·ing** \ˈdrē-ming\ **1 :** to have a dream ⟨*dreamed* of taking a trip⟩ **2 :** to indulge in daydreams or fantasies ⟨*dreaming* of world peace⟩ **3 :** to consider as a possibility **:** IMAGINE ⟨never *dreamed* that I would win⟩ **4 :** to pass (time) in reverie or inaction ⟨*dreaming* the hours away⟩ — **dream of :** to consider possible or fitting ⟨wouldn't *dream of* disturbing you⟩

dream·er \ˈdrē-mər\ *n* **1 :** one that dreams **2 a :** one that lives in a world of fancy and imagination **b :** one that constantly conceives of impractical projects

dream·land \ˈdrēm-ˌland\ *n* **:** an unreal delightful country existing only in imagination or in dreams

dream·world \-ˌwərld\ *n* **:** DREAMLAND; *also* **:** a world of illusion or fantasy

dreamy \ˈdrē-mē\ *adj* **dream·i·er; -est 1 :** full of dreams ⟨*dreamy* sleep⟩ **2 :** given to or marked by dreaming or fantasy **3 a :** having the quality or characteristics of a dream **b :** quiet and soothing ⟨*dreamy* music⟩ **c :** DELIGHTFUL ⟨a *dreamy* car⟩ — **dream·i·ly** \-mə-lē\ *adv* — **dream·i·ness** \-mē-nəs\ *n*

drea·ry \ˈdriər-ē\ *adj* **drea·ri·er** \ˈdrir-ē-ər\; **-est :** causing feelings of cheerlessness **:** GLOOMY ⟨a *dreary* landscape⟩ [Old English *drēorig* "sad, bloody," from *drēor* "gore"] — **drea·ri·ly** \ˈdrir-ə-lē\ *adv* — **drea·ri·ness** \ˈdrir-ē-nəs\ *n*

[1]**dredge** \ˈdrej\ *vb* **1 a :** to dig, gather, or pull out with or as if with a dredge ⟨*dredged* up scallops from the sea bottom⟩ **b :** to deepen (as a waterway) with a dredge **2 :** to bring to light by deep searching ⟨*dredging* up memories⟩ [probably related to Old English *dragan* "to draw"] — **dredg·er** *n*

[2]**dredge** *n* **1 :** an oblong iron frame with an attached bag net used especially for gathering fish and shellfish **2 :** a machine for removing earth usually by buckets on an endless chain or by a suction tube **3 :** a barge used in dredging

[3]**dredge** *vt* **:** to coat (food) by sprinkling (as with flour) [Middle English *drage, drege* "sweetmeat," from Medieval French *dragee,* from Latin *tragemata* "sweetmeats," from Greek *tragēmata,* pl. of *tragēma* "sweetmeat," from *trōgein* "to gnaw"] — **dredger** *n*

dreg \ˈdreg\ *n* **1 :** sediment contained in a liquid or precipitated from it **:** LEES — usually used in plural **2 :** the most undesirable part — usually used in plural ⟨the *dregs* of society⟩ **3 :** the last remaining part **:** VESTIGE — usually used in plural ⟨the last *dregs* of fuel⟩ [Old Norse *dregg*]

[1]**drench** \ˈdrench\ *n* **1 :** a medicinal potion for a domestic animal **2 a :** something that drenches **b :** a quantity sufficient to drench or saturate

[2]**drench** *vt* **1 a** *archaic* **:** to force to drink **b :** to administer a drench to (an animal) **2 :** to wet thoroughly **:** SATURATE [Old English *drencan*] ***synonyms*** see SOAK

[1]**dress** \ˈdres\ *vb* **1 :** to make or set straight **2 a :** to put clothes on **b :** to provide with clothing **c :** to put on or wear formal or fancy clothes **3 :** to add decorative details to **:** EMBELLISH ⟨*dress* a store window⟩ **4 :** to prepare for use or service **5 a :** to apply dressings or medication to ⟨*dress* a wound⟩ **b :** to arrange (as the hair) by combing, brushing, or curling **c :** to prepare (an animal) by grooming **d :** to kill and prepare for market ⟨*dress* a chicken⟩ **e :** CULTIVATE, TEND; *esp* **:** to apply manure or fertilizer to **6 :** SMOOTH, FINISH ⟨*dress* timber⟩ [Medieval French *drescer, dresser* "to direct, put right," derived from Latin *directus* "straight, direct"]

[2]**dress** *n* **1 :** APPAREL, CLOTHING **2 :** an outer garment with a skirt used by women or girls **3 :** covering, adornment, or appearance appropriate or peculiar to a particular time **4 :** the particular style in which something is presented **:** GUISE

[3]**dress** *adj* **1 :** relating to or used for a dress ⟨*dress* fabric⟩ **2 :** suitable for a formal occasion ⟨*dress* clothes⟩ **3 :** requiring or permitting formal dress ⟨a *dress* affair⟩

dres·sage \drə-ˈsäzh, dre-\ *n* **:** the execution by a horse of complex maneuvers in response to barely perceptible movements of a rider's hands, legs, and weight

dress circle *n* **:** the first or lowest curved tier of seats above the main floor in a theater

dress down *vt* **1 :** to reprimand severely **2 :** to dress casually

[1]**dress·er** \ˈdres-ər\ *n* **1** *obsolete* **:** a table or sideboard for preparing and serving food **2 :** a cupboard to hold dishes and cooking utensils **3 :** a chest of drawers or bureau with a mirror

[2]**dresser** *n* **:** one that dresses ⟨a fashionable *dresser*⟩

dress·ing *n* **1 a :** the act or process of one that dresses **b :** an instance of dressing **2 a :** a sauce for adding to a dish **b :** a seasoned mixture usually used as a stuffing (as for poultry) **3 a :** material used to cover an injury **b :** fertilizing material

dres·sing–down \ˌdres-ing-ˈdau̇n\ *n* **:** a severe reprimand

dressing gown *n* **:** a loose robe worn especially while dressing or resting

dressing room *n* **:** a room used chiefly for dressing; *esp* **:** a room in a theater for changing costumes and makeup

dressing station *n* **:** a station for giving first aid to the wounded

dressing table *n* **:** a low table with a mirror at which one sits while dressing

dress·mak·er \ˈdres-ˌmā-kər\ *n* **:** one that does dressmaking

dress·mak·ing \-king\ *n* **:** the process or occupation of making dresses

dress rehearsal *n* **:** a full rehearsal of a play in costume and with stage properties shortly before the first performance

dress shirt *n* **:** a man's shirt especially for wear with evening dress

dress uniform *n* **:** a uniform for formal wear

dress up *vb* **1 :** to make more attractive, glamorous, or fancy ⟨*dress up* a plain dessert with chocolate sauce⟩ **2 a :** to put on one's best or formal clothes **b :** to put on clothes suited to a particular role ⟨*dress up* for Halloween⟩

dressy \ˈdres-ē\ *adj* **dress·i·er; -est 1 :** showy in dress **2 :** SMART 6a, STYLISH ⟨*dressy* clothes⟩ **3 :** requiring or characterized by fancy or formal dress ⟨a *dressy* event⟩

drew *past of* DRAW

[1]**drib·ble** \ˈdrib-əl\ *vb* **drib·bled; drib·bling** \ˈdrib-ling, -ə-ling\ **1 :** to fall or flow or let fall in drops **:** TRICKLE **2 :** DROOL 1, SLOBBER **3 :** to come or issue little by little ⟨replies *dribbled* in⟩ **4 :** to propel by tapping, bouncing, or kicking ⟨*dribble* a basketball⟩ ⟨*dribble* a puck⟩ [from *drib* "to dribble"] — **dribbler** \ˈdrib-lər, -ə-lər\ *n*

[2]**dribble** *n* **1 :** a small trickling stream or flow **2 :** a tiny or insignificant quantity **3 :** an act or instance of dribbling a ball or puck

drib·let \ˈdrib-lət\ *n* **1 :** a small amount **2 :** a drop of liquid

dri·er *or* **dry·er** \ˈdrī-ər, ˈdrīr\ *n* **1 :** something that extracts or absorbs moisture **2 :** a substance that accelerates drying (as of oils, paints, and printing inks) **3** *usually dryer* **:** a device for drying (as clothes) by heat or air

[1]drift \ˈdrift\ *n* **1 a :** the act of driving something along **b :** the flow of a river or ocean stream **2 a :** wind-driven snow, rain, or smoke usually near the ground surface **b :** a mass of matter (as sand) deposited together by or as if by wind or water **c :** a deposit of clay, sand, gravel, and boulders transported by a glacier or by running water from a glacier **3 a :** a general underlying design or tendency ⟨understanding the *drift* of the government's policies⟩ **b :** the underlying meaning of what is spoken or written ⟨the *drift* of a conversation⟩ **4 a :** a ship's deviation from its course caused by currents **b :** the lateral motion of an airplane due to air currents **5 a :** a gradual shift in attitude, opinion, or position **b :** an aimless course [Middle English] ***synonyms*** see TENDENCY

[2]drift *vb* **1 a :** to be or cause to be driven or carried along by a current (as of water or air) **b :** to move or float smoothly and effortlessly **2 a :** to move along a line of least resistance **b :** to move in a random or casual way **c :** to become carried along subject to no guidance or control ⟨the conversation *drifted* from one topic to another⟩ **3 a :** to accumulate or cause to accumulate in a mass ⟨*drifting* snow blocked the road⟩ **b :** to cover or become covered with a drift ⟨the road was *drifted* shut⟩ **4 :** to vary or deviate from a set course or adjustment — **drift·er** *n* — **drift·ing·ly** \ˈdrif-ting-lē\ *adv*

drift·age \ˈdrif-tij\ *n* **1 :** a drifting of some object especially through action of wind or water **2 :** deviation from a set course due to drifting **3 :** something that drifts

drift·wood \ˈdrift-ˌwu̇d\ *n* **1 :** wood drifted or floated by water **2 :** someone or something that drifts aimlessly

[1]drill \ˈdril\ *vb* **1 :** to pierce or bore with or as if with a drill ⟨*drill* a tooth⟩ ⟨*drill* a hole⟩ **2 a :** to instruct by repetition ⟨*drill* a class in multiplication⟩ **b :** to impart or communicate by repetition ⟨impossible to *drill* the simplest idea into some people⟩ **c :** to train or exercise in military skill and discipline ⟨*drill* soldiers⟩ [Dutch *drillen*] — **drill·er** *n*

[2]drill *n* **1 :** a tool for making holes in hard substances by revolving or by a succession of blows **2 :** the training of soldiers in military skill and discipline **3 :** a physical or mental exercise regularly and repeatedly practiced **4 :** a marine snail that destroys oysters by boring through their shells and feeding on the soft parts

[3]drill *n* **:** a west African baboon closely related to the mandrills [origin unknown]

[4]drill *n* **1 :** a shallow furrow or trench into which seed is sown **2 :** a planting implement that makes holes or furrows, drops in seed, and covers it with earth [perhaps from earlier *drill* "small brook"]

[2]drill 1

[5]drill *vt* **:** to sow with or as if with a drill

[6]drill *n* **:** a durable cotton fabric in twill weave [derived from German *Drillich,* from Middle High German *drilich* "fabric woven with a threefold thread," from Latin *trilix* "made up of three threads," from *tri-* + *licium* "thread"]

drill·mas·ter \ˈdril-ˌmas-tər\ *n* **:** an instructor in military drill

drill press *n* **:** an upright drilling machine in which the drill is pressed to the work by a hand lever or by power

[1]drink \ˈdringk\ *vb* **drank** \ˈdrangk\; **drunk** \ˈdrəngk\ *or* **drank; drink·ing 1 a :** to swallow liquid **:** IMBIBE **b :** to take in or suck up **c :** to take in or receive avidly ⟨*drink* in the scenery⟩ **2 :** to give or join in a toast ⟨*drink* to success⟩ **3 a :** to drink alcoholic beverages **b :** to spend in or waste on consumption of alcoholic beverages ⟨*drank* the day away⟩ **c :** to bring to a specified state by taking drink [Old English *drincan*]

[2]drink *n* **1 a :** liquid suitable for swallowing **:** BEVERAGE **b :** alcoholic liquor **2 :** a draft or portion of liquid **3 :** excessive consumption of alcoholic beverages

[1]drink·able \ˈdring-kə-bəl\ *adj* **:** suitable or safe for drinking

[2]drinkable *n* **:** a liquid suitable for drinking **:** BEVERAGE

drink–driv·ing \ˈdringk-ˈdrī-ving\ *n, British* **:** driving a vehicle while drunk

drink·er \ˈdring-kər\ *n* **1 :** one that drinks **2 :** a person who drinks alcoholic beverages especially to excess

[1]drip \ˈdrip\ *vb* **dripped; drip·ping 1 :** to fall or let fall in drops **2 a :** to let fall drops of moisture or liquid ⟨a *dripping* faucet⟩ **b :** to overflow with or as if with moisture [Old English *dryppan*] — **drip·per** *n*

[2]drip *n* **1 a :** a falling in drops **b :** liquid that falls, overflows, or is extruded in drops **2 :** the sound made by or as if by falling drops **3 :** a part of a cornice or other member that projects to throw off rainwater; *also* **:** an overlapping metal strip serving the same purpose **4 :** a dull or unattractive person

drip–dry \ˈdrip-ˈdrī\ *vi* **:** to dry with few or no wrinkles when hung dripping wet — **drip–dry** \-ˌdrī\ *adj*

drip·ping \ˈdrip-ing\ *n* **:** fat and juices that drip from meat during cooking — often used in plural

[1]drive \ˈdrīv\ *vb* **drove** \ˈdrōv\; **driv·en** \ˈdriv-ən\; **driv·ing** \ˈdrī-ving\ **1 a :** to urge, push, or force onward ⟨*drive* cattle⟩ ⟨waves *drove* the boat ashore⟩ **b :** to cause to penetrate with force ⟨*drive* a nail⟩ **2 a (1) :** to direct the movement or course of ⟨*drive* a car⟩ **(2) :** to operate a vehicle ⟨learn how to *drive*⟩ **b :** to convey or transport in a vehicle ⟨*drove* us to the airport⟩ **c :** to ride in a vehicle ⟨we *drove* into town⟩ **3 :** to set or keep in motion ⟨*drive* machinery by electricity⟩ **4 :** to carry through strongly ⟨*drive* a hard bargain⟩ **5 a :** to force to act ⟨*driven* by hunger to steal⟩ **b :** to project, inject, or impress forcefully ⟨his last example *drove* the lesson home⟩ **6 :** to bring into a specified condition ⟨the noise is *driving* me crazy⟩ **7 :** to produce by opening a way (as by drilling) ⟨*drive* a well⟩ **8 :** to move ahead rapidly or with great force ⟨the rain was *driving* hard⟩ **9 a :** to hit (a ball or puck) swiftly or forcefully **b :** to hit a golf ball from the tee **c :** to cause (a run or runner) to be scored in baseball — usually used with *in* ⟨*drove* in two runs with a double⟩ [Old English *drīfan*] ***synonyms*** see MOVE

[2]drive *n* **1 :** an act of driving or being driven: as **a :** a trip in a vehicle (as an automobile) **b :** a driving together of animals **c :** the guiding of logs downstream to a mill **d :** the act of driving a ball **e :** the flight of a ball **2 a :** DRIVEWAY 2 **b :** a public road for driving **3 a :** an offensive or aggressive move; *esp* **:** a strong sustained military attack **b :** an intensive group effort ⟨a charity *drive*⟩ **4 :** the state of being hurried and under pressure **5 a :** an urgent, basic, or instinctual need or longing ⟨the sex *drive*⟩ **b :** dynamic quality ⟨full of *drive*⟩ **6 a :** the means for giving motion to a machine or machine part ⟨a chain *drive*⟩ **b :** the means by which the motive power of an automotive vehicle is applied to the road ⟨front wheel *drive*⟩ **7 :** a device for reading or writing data (as on magnetic tape or disks)

[1]drive–by \ˈdrīv-ˈbī\ *adj* **:** carried out from a moving vehicle ⟨a *drive-by* shooting⟩

[2]drive–by \ˈdrīv-ˌbī\ *n, pl* **drive–bys :** a drive-by shooting

drive–in \ˈdrīv-ˌin\ *adj* **:** arranged and equipped to accommodate patrons while they remain in their vehicles ⟨a *drive-in* theater⟩ — **drive–in** *n*

[1]driv·el \ˈdriv-əl\ *vb* **driv·eled** *or* **driv·elled; driv·el·ing** *or* **driv·el·ling** \ˈdriv-ling, -ə-ling\ **1 :** to let saliva dribble from the mouth **:** SLAVER **2 :** to talk stupidly and carelessly [Old English *dreflian*] — **driv·el·er** *or* **driv·el·ler** \ˈdriv-lər, -ə-lər\ *n*

[2]drivel *n* **:** NONSENSE 1

driv·er \ˈdrī-vər\ *n* **:** one that drives: as **a :** the operator of a motor vehicle **b :** a golf club having a usually wooden head with a nearly straight face used in driving

driver ant *n* **:** ARMY ANT

driver's seat *n* **:** the position of top authority or dominance

drive shaft *n* **:** a shaft that transmits mechanical power

drive–through \ˈdrīv-ˌthrü\ *adj* **:** DRIVE-UP

drive–up \ˈdrīv-ˌəp\ *adj* **:** designed to allow patrons or customers to be served while remaining in their automobiles ⟨a bank's *drive-up* window⟩

drive·way \ˈdrīv-ˌwā\ *n* **1 :** a road or way along which animals are driven **2 :** a short private road leading from a public street to a house, barn, garage, or parking lot

driving range *n* **:** an area equipped with markers, clubs, balls, and tees for practicing golf shots

[1]driz·zle \ˈdriz-əl\ *vb* **driz·zled; driz·zling** \ˈdriz-ling, -ə-ling\ **1 :** to rain in very small drops **:** SPRINKLE **2 :** to shed in minute drops or particles **3 :** to make wet with minute drops ⟨vegeta-

\ə\ **abut**	\au̇\ **out**	\i\ **tip**	\ȯ\ **saw**	\u̇\ **foot**
\ər\ **further**	\ch\ **chin**	\ī\ **life**	\ȯi\ **coin**	\y\ **yet**
\a\ **mat**	\e\ **pet**	\j\ **job**	\th\ **thin**	\yü\ **few**
\ā\ **take**	\ē\ **easy**	\ng\ **sing**	\t͟h\ **this**	\yu̇\ **cure**
\ä\ **cot, cart**	\g\ **go**	\ō\ **bone**	\ü\ **food**	\zh\ **vision**

bles *drizzled* with olive oil⟩ [perhaps from Middle English *drysnen* "to fall"]

[2]**drizzle** *n* **1 :** a fine misty rain **2 :** something that is drizzled ⟨a *drizzle* of syrup⟩ — **driz·zly** \ˈdriz-lē, -ə-lē\ *adj*

drogue \ˈdrōg\ *n* **:** a small parachute for slowing down or stabilizing something (as an astronaut's capsule) or for pulling out a larger parachute [probably alteration of [1]*drag*]

droll \ˈdrōl\ *adj* **:** having a humorous, whimsical, or odd quality ⟨a *droll* expression⟩ [French *drôle*] — **droll·ness** \ˈdrōl-nəs\ *n* — **drol·ly** \ˈdrōl-lē\ *adv*

droll·ery \ˈdrōl-rē, -ə-rē\ *n, pl* **-er·ies 1 :** something droll; *esp* **:** an amusing story or gesture **2 :** droll behavior **3 :** whimsical humor

-drome \ˌdrōm\ *n combining form* **1 :** racecourse **2 :** large specially prepared place ⟨aero*drome*⟩ [hippo*drome*]

drom·e·dary \ˈdräm-ə-ˌder-ē *also* ˈdrəm-\ *n, pl* **-dar·ies 1 :** a camel of unusual speed bred and trained especially for riding **2 :** the one-humped camel of western Asia and northern Africa [Medieval French *dromedarie,* from Late Latin *dromedarius,* from Latin *dromas,* from Greek, "running"]

dromedary 2

[1]**drone** \ˈdrōn\ *n* **1 :** a stingless male bee (as of the honeybee) whose only function is to mate with the queen bee **2 :** one that lives on the labors of others **:** PARASITE **3 :** a pilotless aircraft or ship controlled by radio signals [Old English *drān*]

[2]**drone** *vb* **:** to make or speak with a low dull monotonous humming sound

[3]**drone** *n* **1 :** one of the pipes on a bagpipe that sound fixed continuous tones **2 :** a deep monotonous sound **:** HUM

drone fly *n* **:** a large two-winged fly resembling a honeybee

drool \ˈdrül\ *vb* **1 a :** to secrete saliva in anticipation of food **b :** to let saliva or some other substance flow from the mouth **:** DRIVEL **2 a :** to talk foolishly **b :** to make a sentimental or effusive show of pleasure or often envious or covetous appreciation [perhaps alteration of *drivel*]

[1]**droop** \ˈdrüp\ *vb* **1 :** to hang or incline downward **2 :** to sink gradually **3 :** to become depressed or weakened **4 :** to let droop [Old Norse *drūpa*] — **droop·ing·ly** \ˈdrü-ping-lē\ *adv*

[2]**droop** *n* **:** the condition or appearance of drooping

droopy \ˈdrü-pē\ *adj* **droop·i·er; -est 1 :** drooping or tending to droop **2 :** GLOOMY 2, DOWNCAST

[1]**drop** \ˈdräp\ *n* **1 a** (1) **:** the quantity of fluid that falls in one spherical mass (2) *pl* **:** a dose of medicine measured by drops ⟨eye *drops*⟩ **b :** a small quantity of drink **c :** the smallest practical unit of liquid measure **2 :** something (as a hanging ornament on jewelry) shaped like a drop **3 a :** the act or an instance of dropping **:** FALL **b :** a decline in quantity or quality **c :** a descent by parachute; *also* **:** the persons or equipment dropped by parachute **4 :** the distance through which something drops **5 :** a slot into which something is to be dropped **6 :** an unframed piece of cloth scenery in a theater **7 :** ADVANTAGE 1 ⟨we've got the *drop* on them⟩ [Old English *dropa*]

[2]**drop** *vb* **dropped; drop·ping 1 :** to fall or let fall in drops **2 a :** to let fall **:** cause to fall ⟨*drop* a book⟩ **b :** to let fall gradually **:** LOWER ⟨*drop* one's voice⟩ **3 :** SEND ⟨*drop* me a letter⟩ **4 :** to let go **:** DISMISS ⟨*drop* the subject⟩ ⟨*drop* a failing student⟩ **5 :** to bring down with a shot or a blow ⟨*drop* an opponent in a fight⟩ **6 :** to go lower ⟨prices *dropped*⟩ **7 :** to come or go unexpectedly or informally ⟨*drop* in for a chat⟩ **8 :** to pass into a less active state ⟨*drop* off to sleep⟩ **9 :** to move downward or with a current **10 :** to leave (a letter representing a speech sound) unsounded ⟨*drop* the first *r* in *surprise*⟩ **11 :** to give birth to ⟨the cow *dropped* a fine calf⟩ **12 :** to draw from an external point (as from a point to a line or plane) ⟨*drop* a perpendicular to a plane⟩

drop–down \ˈdräp-ˌdau̇n\ *adj* **:** PULL-DOWN

drop–forge \ˈdräp-ˈfōrj, -ˈfȯrj\ *vt* **:** to forge between dies by a drop hammer or punch press — **drop forger** *n*

drop hammer *n* **:** a power hammer raised and then released to drop (as on metal resting on an anvil or die)

drop·kick \ˈdräp-ˈkik\ *n* **:** a kick made by dropping a ball to the ground and kicking it at the moment it starts to rebound — **drop–kick** *vb* — **drop–kick·er** *n*

drop leaf *n* **:** a hinged leaf on a table that can be folded down

drop·let \ˈdräp-lət\ *n* **:** a very small drop

droplet infection *n* **:** infection transmitted by airborne droplets of sputum containing infectious organisms

drop·out \ˈdräp-ˌau̇t\ *n* **:** one who drops out (as from school)

drop out *vi* **:** to withdraw from participation or membership **:** QUIT ⟨*dropped out* of school⟩

dropped egg *n* **:** a poached egg

drop·per \ˈdräp-ər\ *n* **1 :** one that drops **2 :** a short glass or plastic tube with a rubber bulb used to measure out liquids by drops — called also *eyedropper, medicine dropper*

drop·pings \ˈdräp-ingz\ *n pl* **:** animal dung

drop·sy \ˈdräp-sē\ *n* **:** EDEMA [Medieval French *ydropesie,* from Latin *hydropisis,* from Greek *hydrōps,* from *hydōr* "water"] — **drop·si·cal** \-si-kəl\ *adj*

dro·soph·i·la \drō-ˈsäf-ə-lə\ *n* **:** any of a genus of fruit flies used in the study of inheritance and in genetic research [Greek *drosos* "dew" + *-philos* "-phil"]

dross \ˈdräs, ˈdrȯs\ *n* **1 :** the scum that forms on the surface of molten metal **2 :** waste or foreign matter **:** IMPURITY [Old English *drōs* "dregs"]

drought *also* **drouth** \ˈdrau̇th, ˈdrau̇t\ *n* **:** a long period of dry weather [Old English *drūgath,* from *drūgian* "to dry up"] — **droughty** \-ē\ *adj*

drove \ˈdrōv\ *n* **1 :** a group of animals driven or moving in a body **2 :** a crowd of people moving or acting together [Old English *drāf,* from *drīfan* "to drive"]

drov·er \ˈdrō-vər\ *n* **:** one who drives cattle or sheep

drown \ˈdrau̇n\ *vb* **1 a :** to suffocate by submersion especially in water **b :** to become drowned **2 :** to cover with water **:** INUNDATE **3 :** to engage (oneself) deeply and strenuously ⟨*drowned* himself in work⟩ **4 :** to cause (a sound) not to be heard by making a loud noise — usually used with *out* ⟨the music was *drowned* out by shouting⟩ **5 a :** to drive out (as a sensation or an idea) ⟨*drowned* his sorrows in hot fudge sundaes⟩ **b :** to reduce to insignificance **:** OVERWHELM ⟨a personality that *drowned* all who stood by her⟩ [Middle English *drounen*]

drowse \ˈdrau̇z\ *vi* **:** to sleep lightly **:** DOZE [probably related to Gothic *driusan* "to fall"] — **drowse** *n*

drowsy \ˈdrau̇-zē\ *adj* **drows·i·er; -est 1 :** ready to fall asleep **2 :** making one sleepy ⟨*drowsy* music⟩ — **drows·i·ly** \-zə-lē\ *adv* — **drows·i·ness** \-zē-nəs\ *n*

drub \ˈdrəb\ *vt* **drubbed; drub·bing 1 :** to beat severely **2 :** to defeat decisively ⟨*drubbed* her opponent in the tennis match⟩ [perhaps from Arabic *ḍaraba*]

[1]**drudge** \ˈdrəj\ *vi* **:** to do hard, menial, or monotonous work [Middle English *druggen*] — **drudg·er** *n*

[2]**drudge** *n* **:** one engaged in drudgery

drudg·ery \ˈdrəj-rē, -ə-rē\ *n, pl* **-er·ies :** tiresome or menial work

[1]**drug** \ˈdrəg\ *n* **1 :** a substance used as a medicine or in making medicines **2 :** something for which there is little demand — used in the phrase *drug on the market* **3 :** a usually illegal substance or preparation that causes addiction, psychological dependence, or a marked change in consciousness [ME *drogge*]

[2]**drug** *vb* **drugged; drug·ging 1 :** to affect or treat with a drug; *esp* **:** to stupefy by a narcotic drug **2 :** to lull or stupefy as if with a drug

drug·gist \ˈdrəg-əst\ *n* **:** a person who sells or dispenses drugs and medicines: as **a :** PHARMACIST **b :** an owner or manager of a drugstore

drug·store \ˈdrəg-ˌstōr, -ˌstȯr\ *n* **:** a retail shop where medicines and miscellaneous articles are sold — called also *pharmacy*

dru·id \ˈdrü-əd\ *n, often cap* **:** one of an ancient Celtic priesthood appearing in sagas and legends as magicians and wizards [Latin *druides,* from Gaulish] — **dru·id·ic** \drü-ˈid-ik\ *or* **dru·id·i·cal** \-i-kəl\ *adj, often cap* — **dru·id·ism** \ˈdrü-ə-ˌdiz-əm\ *n, often cap*

[1]**drum** \ˈdrəm\ *n* **1 :** a musical percussion instrument consisting of a hollow cylinder with a thin layer of material (as animal skin or plastic) stretched over one or both ends that is beaten with the hands or with a stick **2 :** EARDRUM **3 :** the sound of a drum; *also* **:** a similar sound **4 :** a drum-shaped object: as **a :** a cylindrical machine or mechanical device or part **b :** a cylindrical container **c :** a disk-shaped magazine for an automatic weapon **5 :** any of various chiefly marine fishes that make a drumming or croaking noise [probably from Dutch *trom*]

[2]**drum** *vb* **drummed; drum·ming 1 :** to beat or play on or as if on a drum **2 :** to throb or sound rhythmically **3 :** to stir up in-

terest : SOLICIT ⟨*drum* up customers⟩ **4 :** to dismiss dishonorably : EXPEL ⟨*drummed* out of the army⟩ **5 :** to drive or force by steady effort or reiteration ⟨*drum* a lesson into their heads⟩ **6 :** to strike or tap repeatedly so as to produce rhythmic sounds ⟨*drummed* the table with his fingers⟩

drum•beat \ˈdrəm-ˌbēt\ *n* **:** a stroke on a drum or its sound

drum brake *n* **:** a brake that operates by the friction of a shoe pressed against a rotating drum

drum•lin \ˈdrəm-lən\ *n* **:** a long or oval hill of glacial drift [Irish Gaelic *druim* "back, ridge"]

drum major *n* **:** the leader of a marching band

drum ma•jor•ette \ˈdrəm-ˌmā-jə-ˈret\ *n* **:** a girl or woman who leads a marching band

drum•mer \ˈdrəm-ər\ *n* **1 :** one that plays a drum **2 :** TRAVELING SALESMAN

drum•stick \ˈdrəm-ˌstik\ *n* **1 :** a stick for beating a drum **2 :** the lower segment of a fowl's leg

[1]**drunk** \ˈdrəngk\ *adj* **1 :** having the faculties impaired by alcohol **2 :** controlled by an intense feeling ⟨*drunk* with power⟩ **3 a :** DRUNKEN 2a **b :** occurring while drunk ⟨*drunk* driving⟩ [Middle English *drunke,* alteration of *drunken*]

[2]**drunk** *n* **1 a :** a person who is drunk **b :** DRUNKARD **2 :** a period of excessive drinking : SPREE

drunk•ard \ˈdrəng-kərd\ *n* **:** one who is habitually drunk

drunk•en \ˈdrəng-kən\ *adj* **1 a :** DRUNK 1 **b :** given to habitual excessive use of alcohol **2 a :** of, relating to, or resulting from intoxication ⟨a *drunken* brawl⟩ **b :** DRUNK 3b **3 :** unsteady or lurching as if from intoxication [Old English *druncen,* from past participle of *drincan* "to drink"] — **drunk•en•ly** *adv* — **drunk•en•ness** \-kən-nəs\ *n*

drupe \ˈdrüp\ *n* **:** a fruit (as the plum, cherry, or peach) having one seed enclosed in hard stony material that is usually surrounded by pulpy flesh with a firm skin [Latin *drupa* "overripe olive," from Greek *dryppa* "olive"] — **dru•pa•ceous** \drü-ˈpā-shəs\ *adj*

drupe•let \ˈdrüp-lət\ *n* **:** a small drupe; *esp* **:** one of the individual parts of an aggregate fruit (as the raspberry)

[1]**dry** \ˈdrī\ *adj* **dri•er** \ˈdrī-ər, ˈdrīr\; **dri•est** \ˈdrī-əst\ **1 :** free or freed from water or liquid **2 :** characterized by loss or lack of water: as **a :** lacking precipitation and humidity ⟨a *dry* climate⟩ **b :** lacking freshness : STALE **c :** low in or deprived of tissue moisture ⟨*dry* hay⟩ ⟨*dry* fruits⟩ **3 :** not being in or under water ⟨*dry* land⟩ **4 a :** THIRSTY 1 **b :** marked by the absence of alcoholic beverages ⟨a *dry* party⟩ **c :** no longer liquid or sticky ⟨the ink is *dry*⟩ **5 :** containing or employing no liquid (as water) ⟨a *dry* creek⟩ ⟨*dry* heat⟩ **6 :** not giving milk ⟨a *dry* cow⟩ **7 :** lacking natural lubrication ⟨a *dry* cough⟩ **8 :** solid as opposed to liquid ⟨*dry* groceries⟩ **9 :** not productive ⟨a writer going through a *dry* spell⟩ **10 :** marked by a matter-of-fact, ironic, or terse manner of expression ⟨*dry* humor⟩ **11 :** UNINTERESTING, WEARISOME ⟨*dry* reading⟩ **12 :** not sweet ⟨*dry* wines⟩ **13 :** relating to, favoring, or practicing prohibition of alcoholic beverages ⟨a *dry* state⟩ [Old English *drȳge*] — **dri•ly** *or* **dry•ly** *adv* — **dry•ness** *n*

[2]**dry** *vb* **dried; dry•ing :** to make or become dry

[3]**dry** *n, pl* **drys :** PROHIBITIONIST

dry•ad \ˈdrī-əd, -ˌad\ *n* **:** WOOD NYMPH [Latin *dryas,* from Greek, from *drys* "tree"]

dry cell *n* **:** a small battery whose contents are not spillable

dry–clean \ˈdrī-ˌklēn\ *vt* **:** to subject to dry cleaning — **dry–clean•able** \-ˌklē-nə-bəl\ *adj* — **dry clean•er** \-ˌklē-nər\ *n*

dry clean•ing \-ˌklē-ning\ *n* **:** the cleansing of fabrics with organic solvents (as naphtha)

dry dock \ˈdrī-ˌdäk\ *n* **:** a dock that can be kept dry for use during the construction or repairing of ships

dryer *variant of* DRIER

dry–erase board *n* **:** WHITEBOARD

dry farm \ˈdrī-ˈfärm\ *n* **:** a farm on dry land operated without irrigation on the basis of moisture-conserving tillage and drought-resistant crops — **dry–farm** *vt* — **dry farmer** *n* — **dry farming** *n*

dry fly *n* **:** an artificial angling fly designed to float upon the surface of the water

dry goods \ˈdrī-ˌgu̇dz\ *n pl* **:** textiles, ready-to-wear clothing, and notions as distinguished from other goods (as hardware and groceries)

dry heaves *n pl* **:** repeated involuntary retching unaccompanied by vomit

dry ice *n* **:** solidified carbon dioxide

drying oil *n* **:** an oil (as linseed oil) that changes readily to a hard tough elastic substance when exposed in a thin film to air

dry measure *n* **:** a series of units of capacity for dry commodities — see MEASURE table, METRIC SYSTEM table

dry•point \ˈdrī-ˌpȯint\ *n* **:** an engraving made with a pointed instrument on the metal plate without the use of acid

dry rot *n* **:** a fungal decay of seasoned timber in which the cellulose of wood is consumed leaving a soft skeleton readily reduced to powder — **dry–rot** *vb*

dry run *n* **1 :** a practice firing without ammunition **2 :** a practice exercise : REHEARSAL

dry•wall \ˈdrī-ˌwȯl\ *n* **:** a wallboard made of several layers of fiberboard, paper, or felt bonded to a gypsum plaster core

dry wash *n, West* **:** WASH 3d

d.t.'s \dē-ˈtēz\ *n pl, often cap D&T* **:** DELIRIUM TREMENS

du•al \ˈdü-əl, ˈdyü-\ *adj* **1 :** having two parts or elements ⟨*dual* air bags⟩ **2 :** having a double character or nature ⟨a *dual* function⟩ [Latin *dualis,* from *duo* "two"] — **du•al•i•ty** \dü-ˈal-ət-ē, dyü-\ *n* — **du•al•ly** \ˈdü-ə-lē, ˈdyü-\ *adv*

du•al•ism \ˈdü-ə-ˌliz-əm, ˈdyü-\ *n* **:** a doctrine that the universe is made up of or governed by two opposing principles (as good and evil) — **du•al•ist** \-ləst\ *n*

du•al–pur•pose \ˌdü-əl-ˈpər-pəs, ˌdyü-\ *adj* **:** intended for or serving two purposes ⟨*dual-purpose* cattle⟩

[1]**dub** \ˈdəb\ *vt* **dubbed; dub•bing 1 :** to confer knighthood upon **2 :** to call by a descriptive name [Old English *dubbian*]

[2]**dub** *vt* **dubbed; dub•bing 1 :** to provide (a motion-picture film) with a new sound track **2 :** to add (sound effects) to a film or broadcast [from *double*]

du•bi•ous \ˈdü-bē-əs, ˈdyü-\ *adj* **1 :** causing doubt : UNCERTAIN ⟨a *dubious* honor⟩ **2 :** feeling doubt : UNDECIDED **3 :** of doubtful promise or uncertain outcome ⟨a *dubious* battle⟩ **4 :** of questionable value, quality, or propriety ⟨a *dubious* bargain⟩ ⟨won by *dubious* means⟩ [Latin *dubius,* from *dubare* "to vacillate"] — **du•bi•ous•ly** *adv* — **du•bi•ous•ness** *n*

du•bi•ta•ble \ˈdü-bət-ə-bəl, ˈdyü-\ *adj* **:** open to doubt or question

dub•ni•um \ˈdüb-nē-əm, ˈdəb-\ *n* **:** a short-lived radioactive element produced artificially — see ELEMENT table [*Dubna,* city in Russia where the element is produced and studied]

du•cal \ˈdü-kəl, ˈdyü-\ *adj* **:** of or relating to a duke or duchy

duc•at \ˈdək-ət\ *n* **:** a former usually gold coin of various European countries [Medieval French, from Italian *ducato* "coin with the doge's portrait on it," from *duca* "doge," from Late Greek *doux* "leader," from Latin *dux*]

duch•ess \ˈdəch-əs\ *n* **1 :** the wife or widow of a duke **2 :** a woman who is sovereign ruler of a duchy [Medieval French *duchesse,* from *duc* "duke"]

duchy \ˈdəch-ē\ *n, pl* **duch•ies :** the territory of a duke or duchess : DUKEDOM [Medieval French *duché,* from *duc* "duke"]

[1]**duck** \ˈdək\ *n, pl* **duck** *or* **ducks 1 :** any of various typically web-footed swimming birds with the neck and legs short, the body heavy, the bill often broad and flat, and the sexes usually differing in color; *also* **:** the flesh of a duck used as food **2 :** a female duck — compare DRAKE [Old English *dūce*]

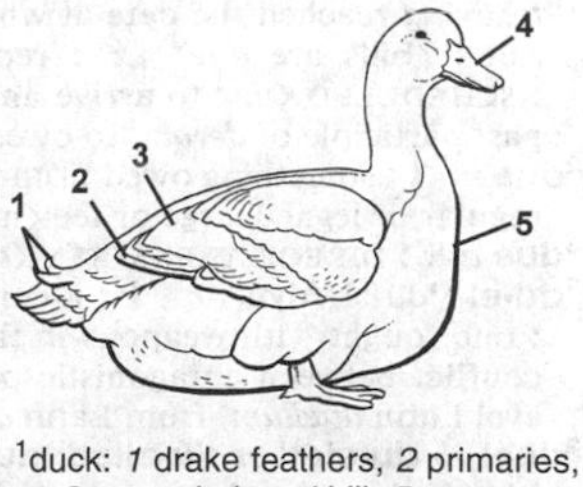

[1]duck: *1* drake feathers, *2* primaries, *3* secondaries, *4* bill, *5* coverts

[2]**duck** *vb* **1 :** to thrust or plunge underwater **2 :** to lower the head or body suddenly **3 a :** to move quickly : disappear suddenly ⟨he *ducked* around the corner to escape detection⟩ **b :** to evade a duty, question, or responsibility : DODGE ⟨*duck* the issue⟩ [Middle English *douken*] — **duck•er** *n*

[3]**duck** *n* **:** an instance of ducking

[4]**duck** *n* **1 :** a durable closely woven usually cotton fabric **2** *pl* **:** clothes made of duck [Dutch *doek* "cloth"]

\ə\ **abut**	\au̇\ **out**	\i\ **tip**	\ȯ\ **saw**	\u̇\ **foot**
\ər\ **further**	\ch\ **chin**	\ī\ **life**	\ȯi\ **coin**	\y\ **yet**
\a\ **mat**	\e\ **pet**	\j\ **job**	\th\ **thin**	\yü\ **few**
\ā\ **take**	\ē\ **easy**	\ng\ **sing**	\th\ **this**	\yu̇\ **cure**
\ä\ **cot, cart**	\g\ **go**	\ō\ **bone**	\ü\ **food**	\zh\ **vision**

duck·bill \ˈdək-ˌbil\ *n* **1 :** PLATYPUS **2 :** DUCK-BILLED DINOSAUR

duck–billed dinosaur \ˈdək-ˈbild-\ *also* **duckbill dinosaur** *n* **:** any of numerous plant-eating dinosaurs with a long flat snout and often a crested skull

duckbilled platypus *n* **:** PLATYPUS

duck·board \ˈdək-ˌbōrd, -ˌbȯrd\ *n* **:** a boardwalk or slatted flooring laid on a wet, muddy, or cold surface — usually used in plural

duck·ling \ˈdək-ling\ *n* **:** a young duck

duck·pin \ˈdək-ˌpin\ *n* **1 :** a small bowling pin shorter and wider in the middle than a tenpin **2** *pl* **:** a bowling game using duckpins

ducks and drakes *n* **:** the pastime of skimming flat stones or shells along the surface of calm water

duck sauce *n* **:** a thick sweet sauce made chiefly of fruits (as plums or apricots), sweeteners, and vinegar and used especially with Chinese food

duck soup *n* **:** something easy to do

duck·weed \-ˌwēd\ *n* **:** a tiny free-floating stemless plant that grows on the surface of bodies of still water (as a pond)

duct \ˈdəkt\ *n* **1 :** a tube or vessel carrying a bodily fluid (as the secretion of a gland) **2 a :** a pipe, tube, or channel that conveys a fluid (as air or water) **b :** a pipe or tubular passage for conductors (as an electric power line or telephone cables) [New Latin *ductus,* from Medieval Latin, "aqueduct," from Latin, "act of leading," from *ducere* "to lead"] — **duct·less** \ˈdəkt-ləs\ *adj*

duc·tile \ˈdək-tl, -ˌtīl\ *adj* **1 :** capable of being drawn out (as into a wire) or hammered thin ⟨*ductile* metal⟩ **2 :** easily led or influenced — **duc·til·i·ty** \ˌdək-ˈtil-ət-ē\ *n*

ductless gland *n* **:** ENDOCRINE GLAND

duct tape *n* **:** a wide cloth adhesive tape

duc·tus ar·te·ri·o·sus \ˈdək-təs-är-ˌtir-ē-ˈō-səs\ *n* **:** a short broad vessel in the fetus that conducts most of the blood directly from the right ventricle to the aorta bypassing the lungs [New Latin, literally, "arterial duct"]

dud \ˈdəd\ *n* **1** *pl* **a :** CLOTHES 1 **b :** personal belongings **2 :** one that fails completely **3 :** a missile (as a bomb or shell) that fails to explode [Middle English *dudde*]

dude \ˈdüd, ˈdyüd\ *n* **1 :** an extremely fastidious man **:** DANDY **2 :** a city man; *esp* **:** an Easterner in the West **3 :** FELLOW 4a, MAN [origin unknown] — **dud·ish** \ˈdüd-ish, ˈdyüd-\ *adj* — **dud·ish·ly** *adv*

dude ranch *n* **:** a vacation resort offering horseback riding and other activities typical of Western ranches

[1]**due** \ˈdü, ˈdyü\ *adj* **1 :** owed or owing as a debt or right ⟨respect *due* to the court⟩ **2 :** according to accepted notions or procedures **:** APPROPRIATE ⟨treat the judge with *due* respect⟩ **3 a :** SUFFICIENT, ADEQUATE ⟨arrived in *due* time⟩ **b :** REGULAR 2a, LAWFUL ⟨*due* process of law⟩ **4 :** being a result **:** ATTRIBUTABLE — used with *to* ⟨an accident *due* to negligence⟩ **5 :** having reached the date at which payment is required **:** PAYABLE ⟨bills are *due*⟩ **6 :** required or expected to happen **:** SCHEDULED ⟨*due* to arrive any time⟩ [Medieval French *deu,* past participle of *devoir* "to owe," from Latin *debēre*]

[2]**due** *n* **1 :** something owed **:** DEBT ⟨pay them their *due*⟩ **2** *pl* **:** a regular or legal charge or fee ⟨membership *dues*⟩

[3]**due** *adv* **:** DIRECTLY, EXACTLY ⟨*due* north⟩

[1]**du·el** \ˈdü-əl, ˈdyü-\ *n* **1 :** a combat between two persons; *esp* **:** one fought with weapons in the presence of witnesses **2 :** a conflict between antagonistic persons, ideas, or forces [Medieval Latin *duellum,* from Latin *duellum, bellum* "war"]

[2]**duel** *vb* **du·eled** *or* **du·elled; du·el·ing** *or* **du·el·ling :** to fight in a duel — **du·el·er** *or* **du·el·ler** *n* — **du·el·ist** *or* **du·el·list** \ˈdü-ə-ləst, ˈdyü-\ *n*

du·en·na \dü-ˈen-ə, dyü-\ *n* **1 :** an elderly woman in charge of the younger ladies in a Spanish or Portuguese family **2 :** GOVERNESS, CHAPERONE [Spanish *dueña,* from Latin *domina* "mistress, lady"]

du·et \dü-ˈet, dyü-\ *n* **:** a composition for or performance by two performers [Italian *duetto,* from *duo,* from Latin, "two"]

due to *prep* **:** because of

duff \ˈdəf\ *n* **1 :** a steamed pudding usually containing raisins and currants **2 :** partly decayed organic matter on the forest floor [English dialect, alteration of *dough*]

duf·fel \ˈdəf-əl\ *n* **:** an outfit of supplies (as for camping) **:** KIT [Dutch *duffel,* a kind of cloth, from *Duffel,* Belgium]

duffel bag *n* **:** a soft oblong bag for personal belongings

duf·fer \ˈdəf-ər\ *n* **:** an incompetent or clumsy person [perhaps from *duff* "something worthless"]

[1]**dug** *past of* DIG

[2]**dug** \ˈdəg\ *n* **:** UDDER 1, BREAST; *also* **:** TEAT 1, NIPPLE [perhaps of Scandinavian origin]

du·gong \ˈdü-ˌgäng, -ˌgȯng\ *n* **:** an aquatic plant-eating mammal related to the manatees but having a 2-lobed tail and tusks in the male — compare SIRENIAN [probably from *dugung* in Cebuano or a related language of the central Philippines]

dug·out \ˈdəg-ˌau̇t\ *n* **1 :** a boat made by hollowing out a large log **2 :** a shelter dug in a hillside, in the ground, or in the side of a trench **3 :** a low shelter facing a baseball diamond and containing the players' bench

DUI \ˌdē-ˌyü-ˈī\ *n* **:** the act or crime of driving while affected by alcohol [*d*riving *u*nder the *i*nfluence]

dui·ker \ˈdī-kər\ *n* **:** any of several small African antelopes [Afrikaans, literally, "diver"]

duit *variant of* DOIT

duke \ˈdük, ˈdyük\ *n* **1 :** a sovereign ruler of a duchy **2 :** a noble of the highest rank; *esp* **:** a member of the highest grade of the British peerage **3** *slang* **:** FIST 1, HAND — usually used in plural [Medieval French *duc,* from Latin *duc-, dux* "leader," from *ducere* "to lead"] — **duke·dom** \-dəm\ *n*

dul·cet \ˈdəl-sət\ *adj* **:** sweet to the ear **:** MELODIOUS ⟨*dulcet* tones⟩ [Middle French *doucet* "sweet to the taste," from *douz* "sweet," from Latin *dulcis*]

dul·ci·mer \ˈdəl-sə-mər\ *n* **1 :** a wire-stringed instrument played with light hammers held in the hands **2** *or* **dul·ci·more** \-ˌmōr, -ˌmȯr\ **:** an American folk instrument with three or four strings stretched over an elongate fretted sound box held on the lap and played by strumming or plucking [Medieval French *doulcemer,* from Italian *dolcimelo*]

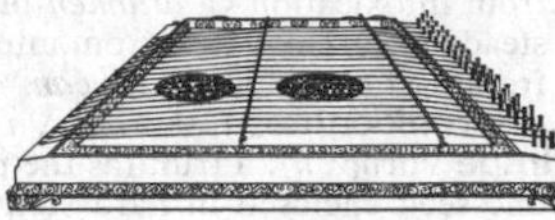

dulcimer 1

[1]**dull** \ˈdəl\ *adj* **1 :** mentally slow **:** STUPID **2 a :** slow in perception or sensibility ⟨were *dull* to what went on around them⟩ **b :** lacking zest or vivacity **:** LISTLESS **3 :** slow in action **:** SLUGGISH ⟨a *dull* market⟩ **4 :** lacking sharpness of edge or point **5 :** lacking brilliance or luster **6 :** not resonant or ringing **7 :** CLOUDY 3a, OVERCAST **8 :** TEDIOUS, UNINTERESTING ⟨*dull* sermons⟩ **9 :** low in saturation and lightness ⟨a *dull* shade of blue⟩ [Middle English *dul*] ***synonyms*** see BLUNT, STUPID — **dull·ness** *also* **dul·ness** \ˈdəl-nəs\ *n* — **dul·ly** \ˈdəl-lē, -ē\ *adv*

[2]**dull** *vb* **:** to make or become dull

dull·ard \ˈdəl-ərd\ *n* **:** a stupid person

dulse \ˈdəls\ *n* **:** any of several coarse red seaweeds especially of northern seas that are used as food [Scottish Gaelic and Irish Gaelic *duileasg*]

du·ly \ˈdü-lē, ˈdyü-\ *adv* **:** in a due manner, time, or degree ⟨*duly* authorized⟩ ⟨will be *duly* considered⟩

du·ma \ˈdü-mə\ *n* **:** a representative council in Russia; *esp, often cap* **:** the principal legislative assembly in Russia from 1906 to 1917 and since 1993 [Russian]

dumb \ˈdəm\ *adj* **1 a :** lacking the human power of speech ⟨*dumb* animals⟩ **b** *of a person, often offensive* **:** lacking the ability to speak **2 :** not willing to speak **3 :** STUPID 1, FOOLISH [Old English] — **dumb·ly** \ˈdəm-lē\ *adv* — **dumb·ness** *n*

dumb·bell \ˈdəm-ˌbel\ *n* **1 :** a weight consisting of a short bar with a sphere or weighted disk at each end and used usually in pairs for exercise or building strength **2 :** a stupid person **:** DUMMY

dumb down *vt* **:** to lower the level of difficulty and the intellectual content of (as a textbook)

dumb·found *also* **dum·found** \ˌdəm-ˈfau̇nd\ *vt* **:** to confuse briefly and usually with astonishment [*dumb* + *-found* (as in confound)] — **dumb·found·ing·ly** \-ˈfau̇n-ding-lē\ *adv*

dumb show *n* **:** signs and gestures without words

dumb·wait·er \ˈdəm-ˈwāt-ər\ *n* **1 :** a portable serving table **2 :** a small elevator for conveying food and dishes or small goods from one story of a building to another

dum·dum \ˈdəm-ˌdəm\ *n* **:** a soft-nosed bullet that expands when it hits [*Dum-Dum,* arsenal near Kolkata, India]

[1]**dum·my** \ˈdəm-ē\ *n, pl* **dum·mies** **1 :** a person who lacks or seems to lack the power of speech **2 :** a stupid person **3 :** an imitation, copy, or likeness of something used as a substitute: as **a :** MANNEQUIN 1b **b :** a large puppet usually having movable

features (as mouth and arms) controlled by a ventriloquist **4 a** : an exposed hand in bridge played by one of the players in addition to his own hand **b** : a bridge player whose hand is a dummy **5** : one seeming to act independently but actually acting for another usually with little or no freedom of action **6** : a set of pages (as for a magazine) with the position of text and artwork indicated for the printer

[2]**dummy** *adj* : resembling a dummy; *esp* : having the appearance of being real but lacking ability to function ⟨*dummy* wooden guns⟩

[1]**dump** \ˈdəmp\ *vb* **1 a** : to let fall in a heap or mass : UNLOAD ⟨*dumped* his clothes on the bed⟩ **b** : to get rid of quickly or unceremoniously ⟨got *dumped* by his girlfriend⟩ **c** : to dump refuse **2** : to sell in quantity at a very low price **3** : to copy (data in a computer's internal storage) to an external storage device or to an output device [perhaps from Dutch *dompen* "to immerse, topple"] — **dump·er** *n*

[2]**dump** *n* **1** : a place where discarded materials are dumped **2** : a place where reserve military supplies are stored ⟨an ammunition *dump*⟩ **3** : a disorderly, slovenly, or objectionable place **4** : an instance of dumping data stored in a computer

dump·ling \ˈdəm-pliŋ\ *n* **1** : a small mass of dough cooked by boiling or steaming **2** : a dessert of fruit baked in biscuit dough [perhaps alteration of *lump*]

dumps \ˈdəmps\ *n pl* : a dull gloomy state of mind : low spirits ⟨in the *dumps*⟩ [probably from Dutch *domp* "haze"]

dump truck *n* : a truck for transporting and dumping loose materials

dumpy \ˈdəm-pē\ *adj* **dump·i·er; -est** **1** : short and thick in build : SQUAT **2** : SHABBY, DINGY [English dialect *dump* "lump"] — **dump·i·ness** *n*

[1]**dun** \ˈdən\ *adj* **1 a** : having a dun color **b** : having a grayish yellow coat with black mane and tail ⟨*dun* horses⟩ **2** : marked by dullness and drabness [Old English *dunn*] — **dun·ness** \ˈdən-nəs\ *n*

[2]**dun** *n* **1** : a dun horse **2** : a nearly neutral slightly brownish dark gray **3** : an immature winged mayfly

[3]**dun** *vt* **dunned; dun·ning** **1** : to make persistent demands upon for payment **2** : to plague or pester constantly ⟨*dunned* by financial problems⟩ [origin unknown]

[4]**dun** *n* **1** : a person who duns another **2** : an urgent request; *esp* : a demand for payment

dunce \ˈdəns\ *n* : a dull-witted or stupid person [John *Duns* Scotus, died about 1308, Scottish scholastic theologian, whose once accepted writings were ridiculed in the 16th century]

dun·der·head \ˈdən-dər-ˌhed\ *n* : DUNCE, BLOCKHEAD [perhaps from Dutch *donder* "thunder"] — **dun·der·head·ed** \ˌdən-dər-ˈhed-əd\ *adj*

dune \ˈdün, ˈdyün\ *n* : a hill or ridge of sand piled up by the wind [French, from Medieval French, from Middle Dutch]

dune buggy *n* : a motor vehicle with oversize tires for use on sand

[1]**dung** \ˈdəŋ\ *n* : the feces of an animal : MANURE [Old English] — **dungy** \ˈdəŋ-ē\ *adj*

[2]**dung** *vt* : to fertilize or dress with manure

dun·ga·ree \ˌdəŋ-gə-ˈrē\ *n* **1** : blue denim **2** *pl* : clothing made of blue denim [Hindi *dũgrī* and Urdu *dungrī*]

dung beetle *n* : a beetle (as a tumblebug) that rolls balls of dung in which it lays eggs and on which the larvae feed

dun·geon \ˈdən-jən\ *n* **1** : DONJON **2** : a dark usually underground prison or vault [Medieval French *donjun*, derived from Latin *dominus* "lord, master"]

dung·hill \ˈdəŋ-ˌhil\ *n* : a manure pile

dunk \ˈdəŋk\ *vb* **1** : to dip (as bread or cake) into liquid while eating **2** : to dip or submerge temporarily in liquid **3** : to submerge oneself in water [Pennsylvania German *dunke*, derived from Old High German *dunkōn*]

dunk shot *n* : a shot in basketball made by leaping high into the air and throwing the ball down through the basket

dun·lin \ˈdən-lən\ *n, pl* **dunlins** *or* **dunlin** : a widely distributed small sandpiper largely brown above and white below with a black patch on the belly [[1]*dun* + *-lin* (alteration of *-ling*)]

dun·nage \ˈdən-ij\ *n* **1** : loose materials used around a cargo to prevent damage; *also* : padding in a shipping container **2** : [1]BAGGAGE 1 [origin unknown]

duo \ˈdü-ō, ˈdyü-\ *n, pl* **du·os** **1** : DUET **2** : a group of two : PAIR [Italian, from Latin, "two"]

duo·dec·i·mal \ˌdü-ə-ˈdes-ə-məl, ˌdyü-\ *adj* **1** : of, relating to, or proceeding by 12 **2** : relating to, expressed in, or being a number system with a base of 12 [Latin *duodecim* "twelve"] — **duodecimal** *n*

du·o·de·num \ˌdü-ə-ˈdē-nəm, ˌdyü-; dü-ˈäd-n-əm, dyü-\ *n, pl* **-de·na** \-ˈdē-nə, -n-ə\ *or* **-denums** : the first part of the small intestine extending from the pylorus to the jejunum [Medieval Latin, from Latin *duodeni* "twelve each," from *duodecim* "twelve"; from its length, about 12 fingers' breadth] — **du·o·de·nal** \-ˈdēn-l, -n-əl\ *adj*

duo·logue \ˈdü-ə-ˌlȯg, ˈdyü-\ *n* : a dialogue between two persons

[1]**dupe** \ˈdüp, ˈdyüp\ *n* : one who is easily deceived or cheated [French]

[2]**dupe** *vt* : to make a dupe of : DECEIVE — **dup·er** *n*

du·ple \ˈdü-pəl, ˈdyü-\ *adj* **1** : taken by twos : TWOFOLD **2** : having two beats or a multiple of two beats per measure of music ⟨*duple* time⟩ [Latin *duplus* "double"]

[1]**du·plex** \ˈdü-ˌpleks, ˈdyü-\ *adj* **1** : DOUBLE 2, TWOFOLD; *esp* : having two parts that act at the same time or in the same way **2** : allowing telecommunication in opposite directions at the same time [Latin, from *duo* "two" + *-plex* "-fold"]

[2]**duplex** *n* : something duplex; *esp* : a 2-family house

duplex apartment *n* : an apartment having rooms on two floors

[1]**du·pli·cate** \ˈdü-pli-kət, ˈdyü-\ *adj* **1** : having or being two corresponding or identical parts or examples **2** : being the same as another **3** : of or relating to a card game in which players play identical hands in order to compare scores ⟨*duplicate* bridge⟩ [Latin *duplicare* "to double," from *duplex* "double"]

[2]**duplicate** *n* **1** : a thing that exactly resembles another in appearance, pattern, or content : COPY **2** : two copies both alike ⟨typed in *duplicate*⟩

synonyms DUPLICATE, COPY, FACSIMILE, REPRODUCTION mean a thing made to closely resemble another. DUPLICATE suggests exact sameness of pattern and usually of material ⟨the baseball cards are *duplicates*⟩. COPY applies to anything reproduced mechanically or without intentional changes ⟨made 20 *copies* of the test⟩. FACSIMILE implies exact and detailed reproduction of pattern that may differ in scale or material ⟨sold *facsimiles* of the statue⟩. REPRODUCTION implies an exact or very close imitation of an original in all respects ⟨printed *reproductions* of Shakespeare's plays⟩.

[3]**du·pli·cate** \ˈdü-pli-ˌkāt, ˈdyü-\ *vt* **1** : to make double **2** : to make a duplicate of — **du·pli·ca·tive** \-ˌkāt-iv\ *adj*

du·pli·ca·tion \ˌdü-pli-ˈkā-shən, ˌdyü-\ *n* **1 a** : an act or process of duplicating **b** : the quality or state of being duplicated **2** : DUPLICATE, COUNTERPART

du·pli·ca·tor \ˈdü-pli-ˌkāt-ər, ˈdyü-\ *n* : one that duplicates; *esp* : a machine for making copies of graphic matter

du·plic·i·ty \dü-ˈplis-ət-ē, dyü-\ *n, pl* **-ties** : deception by pretending to feel and act one way while feeling and acting another

du·ra·ble \ˈdür-ə-bəl\ *adj* : able to last a long time ⟨*durable* clothing⟩ [Medieval French, derived from Latin *durare* "to last"] ***synonyms*** see LASTING — **du·ra·bil·i·ty** \ˌdür-ə-ˈbil-ət-ē, ˌdyür-\ *n* — **du·ra·ble·ness** *n* — **du·ra·bly** \ˈdür-ə-blē, ˈdyür-\ *adv*

du·ral·u·min \dü-ˈral-yə-mən, dyü-; ˌdür-ə-ˈlü-mən, ˌdyür-\ *n* : a light strong alloy of aluminum, copper, manganese, and magnesium [from *Duralumin*, a trademark]

du·ra ma·ter \ˈdür-ə-ˌmät-ər, ˈdyür-, -ˌmät-\ *n* : the outermost and tough fibrous membrane that envelops the brain and spinal cord [Medieval Latin, literally, "hard mother"]

du·rance \ˈdür-əns, ˈdyür-\ *n* : IMPRISONMENT [Medieval French, "endurance," from *durer* "to endure"]

du·ra·tion \dü-ˈrā-shən, dyü-\ *n* **1** : continuance in time ⟨a storm of short *duration*⟩ **2** : the time during which something lasts ⟨the *duration* of the war⟩ [Medieval Latin *duratio*, from Latin *durare* "to last"]

du·ress \dü-ˈres, dyü-\ *n* **1** : forcible restraint **2** : compulsion by threat ⟨a confession obtained under *duress*⟩ [Medieval French *duresce* "hardness, severity," from Latin *duritia*, from *durus* "hard"]

Dur·ham \ˈdər-əm, ˈdə-rəm, ˈdür-əm\ *n* : SHORTHORN [County *Durham*, England]

du·ri·an \ˈdür-ē-ən, ˈdyür-\ *n* : a large oval tasty but foul-smelling fruit with a prickly rind and soft pulp; *also* : the East Indian tree that bears durians [Malay]

dur·ing \ˈdu̇r-ing, ˈdyu̇r-\ *prep* **1** : throughout the duration of ⟨*during* their whole lifetimes⟩ **2** : at some time or times in the course of ⟨occasional showers *during* the day⟩ [Middle English, from *duren* "to last," from Medieval French *durer,* from Latin *durare,* from *durus* "hard"]

dur·ra \ˈdu̇r-ə\ *n* : any of several sorghums grown for their grain in warm dry regions [Arabic *dhurah*]

du·rum wheat \ˈdu̇r-əm-, ˈdyu̇r-\ *n* : a wheat that yields a flour that is rich in gluten and is used especially in pasta — called also *durum* [Latin *durum,* neuter of *durus* "hard"]

[1]**dusk** \ˈdəsk\ *vb* : to make or become dark or gloomy [Middle English *dosk* "dusky," alteration of Old English *dox*]

[2]**dusk** *n* **1** : the darker part of twilight especially at night **2** : GLOOM

dusky \ˈdəs-kē\ *adj* **dusk·i·er; -est** **1** : somewhat dark in color; *esp* : having dark skin **2** : marked by slight or deficient light : DIM ⟨a *dusky* room⟩ — **dusk·i·ly** \-kə-lē\ *adv* — **dusk·i·ness** \-kē-nəs\ *n*

[1]**dust** \ˈdəst\ *n* **1** : fine particles (as of earth or in space); *also* : a fine powder **2** : the earthy remains of bodies once alive; *esp* : the human corpse **3 a** : a place (as in the earth) of burial **b** : the surface of the ground **4 a** : something worthless **b** : a low or miserable condition : state of humiliation [Old English *dūst*] — **dust·less** \ˈdəst-ləs\ *adj*

[2]**dust** *vb* **1** : to make free of dust : brush or wipe away dust ⟨*dusted* the living room⟩ **2** : to sprinkle with fine particles or in the form of dust ⟨*dust* a pan with flour⟩ ⟨*dust* an insecticide on plants⟩

dust·bin \ˈdəst-ˌbin, ˈdəs-\ *n, British* : a trash or garbage can

dust bowl *n* : a region that suffers from prolonged droughts and dust storms

dust devil *n* : a small whirlwind containing sand or dust

dust·er \ˈdəs-tər\ *n* **1** : one that removes dust **2 a** : a light outer garment to protect clothing from dust **b** : a loose-fitting usually lightweight long coat — called also *duster coat* **c** : a dress-length housecoat **3** : one that scatters fine particles; *esp* : a device for applying insecticidal or fungicidal dusts to crops — compare CROP DUSTER

dust jacket *n* : a removable usually decorative paper cover for a book

dust·man \ˈdəst-mən, ˈdəs-\ *n, British* : a trash or garbage collector

dust mite *n* : any of various mites that are commonly found in house dust and often cause allergic responses

dust·pan \-ˌpan\ *n* : a shovel-shaped pan for sweepings

dust storm *n* : strong turbulent winds bearing clouds of dust across a dry region

dusty \ˈdəs-tē\ *adj* **dust·i·er; -est** **1** : filled or covered with dust ⟨a *dusty* table⟩ ⟨*dusty* streets⟩ **2** : consisting of or resembling dust : POWDERY ⟨*dusty* soil⟩ — **dust·i·ly** \-tə-lē\ *adv* — **dust·i·ness** \-tē-nəs\ *n*

dutch \ˈdəch\ *adv, often cap* : with each person paying his or her own way ⟨went *dutch* to the movies⟩

[1]**Dutch** \ˈdəch\ *adj* **1** : GERMAN **2** : of or relating to the Netherlands, its inhabitants, or their language [Middle English *Duch,* from Dutch *duutsch*]

[2]**Dutch** *n* **1** : the Germanic language of the Netherlands **2** *pl in constr* : the people of the Netherlands **3** : DISFAVOR, TROUBLE ⟨was in *Dutch* with the teacher⟩

Dutch clover *n* : WHITE CLOVER

Dutch door *n* : a door divided horizontally so that the lower part can be shut while the upper part remains open

Dutch elm disease *n* : a fungal disease of elms characterized by yellowing of the foliage, loss of leaves, and death

Dutch·man \ˈdəch-mən\ *n* **1 a** : a native or inhabitant of the Netherlands **b** : a person of Dutch descent **2** : GERMAN

Dutch·man's–breech·es \ˈdəch-mənz-ˈbrich-əz\ *n pl* : a delicate spring-flowering herb of the eastern U.S. resembling the related bleeding heart but having white double-spurred flowers

Dutch oven *n* **1** : a metal shield for roasting before an open fire **2** : a brick oven in which cooking is done by the preheated walls **3 a** : a cast-iron kettle with a tight cover used for baking in an open fire **b** : a heavy pot with a tight-fitting domed cover

Dutch treat *n* : something (as a meal) for which each participant pays his or her own way

Dutch uncle *n* : one who admonishes sternly and bluntly

Dutchman's-breeches

du·te·ous \ˈdüt-ē-əs, ˈdyüt-\ *adj* : DUTIFUL, OBEDIENT — **du·te·ous·ly** *adv* — **du·te·ous·ness** *n*

du·ti·able \ˈdüt-ē-ə-bəl, ˈdyüt-\ *adj* : subject to a duty ⟨*dutiable* imports⟩

du·ti·ful \ˈdüt-i-fəl, ˈdyüt-\ *adj* **1** : motivated by a sense of duty **2** : coming from or showing a sense of duty ⟨*dutiful* affection⟩ — **du·ti·ful·ly** \-fə-lē\ *adv* — **du·ti·ful·ness** *n*

du·ty \ˈdüt-ē, ˈdyüt-\ *n, pl* **duties** **1** : conduct due to parents and superiors : RESPECT **2 a** : the action required by one's position or occupation **b** : assigned service or business; *esp* : active military service **3 a** : a moral or legal obligation **b** : the force of moral obligation ⟨obey the call of *duty*⟩ **4** : TAX; *esp* : a tax on imports **5** : the service required (as of a machine) : USE ⟨heavy *duty*⟩ [Medieval French *dueté,* from *deu* "due"] ***synonyms*** see TASK

du·um·vir \du̇-ˈəm-vər, dyu̇-\ *n* : either of two Roman officers or magistrates jointly constituting a board or court [Latin, from *duum* (genitive of *duo* "two") + *vir* "man"]

du·um·vi·rate \-və-rət\ *n* **1** : two people associated in high office **2** : government or control by two people

DVD \ˌdē-ˌvē-ˈdē\ *n* : a high-capacity plastic disk on which information (as computer data or a movie) is recorded digitally and read by using a laser [*d*igital *v*ideo *d*isc]

[1]**dwarf** \ˈdwȯrf\ *n, pl* **dwarfs** \ˈdwȯrfs\ *also* **dwarves** \ˈdwȯrvz\ **1** : a person, animal, or plant much below normal size **2** : a small legendary humanlike being usually misshapen and ugly and skilled as a craftsman **3** : a star (as the sun) that gives off a relatively ordinary or small amount of energy and has relatively small mass and size [Old English *dweorg, dweorh*] — **dwarf** *adj* — **dwarf·ish** \ˈdwȯr-fish\ *adj* — **dwarf·ness** *n*

[2]**dwarf** *vb* **1** : to restrict the growth or development of : STUNT ⟨*dwarf* a tree⟩ **2** : to cause to appear smaller

dwarf·ism \ˈdwȯr-ˌfiz-əm\ *n* : a condition of stunted growth

dwarf planet *n* : a celestial body that orbits the sun and has a spherical shape but is too small to disturb other objects from its orbit

dwell \ˈdwel\ *vi* **dwelled** \ˈdweld, ˈdwelt\ *or* **dwelt** \ˈdwelt\; **dwell·ing** **1** : to remain for a time **2** : to live as a resident : RESIDE **3 a** : to linger over something (as with the eyes or mind) : keep the attention directed ⟨*dwelled* on their mistakes⟩ **b** : to write or speak at length or insistently [Old English *dwellan* "to go astray, hinder"] — **dwell·er** *n*

dwell·ing \ˈdwel-ing\ *n* : a building or other shelter in which people live : HOUSE

DWI \ˌdē-ˌdəb-əl-ˌyu-ˈī\ *n* : DUI [*d*riving *w*hile *i*ntoxicated]

dwin·dle \ˈdwin-dl\ *vb* **dwin·dled; dwin·dling** \ˈdwin-dling, -dl-ing\ : to make or become gradually less [probably from *dwine* "to waste away"] ***synonyms*** see DECREASE

dyb·buk \ˈdib-ək\ *n* : a wandering soul believed in Jewish folklore to enter and control a person [Yiddish *dibek,* from Hebrew *dibbūq*]

[1]**dye** \ˈdī\ *n* **1** : color from dyeing **2** : a material used for dyeing or staining [Old English *dēah, dēag*]

[2]**dye** *vb* **dyed; dye·ing** **1** : to stain or color usually permanently **2** : to impart (a color) by dyeing **3** : to take up or impart color in dyeing — **dy·er** \ˈdī-ər, ˈdīr\ *n*

dyed–in–the–wool \ˌdīd-n-t͟hə-ˈwu̇l\ *adj* : THOROUGHGOING, UNCOMPROMISING ⟨a *dyed-in-the-wool* conservative⟩

dye·stuff \ˈdī-ˌstəf\ *n* : DYE 2

dy·ing *present participle of* DIE

dy·nam·ic \dī-ˈnam-ik\ *adj* **1** *also* **dy·nam·i·cal** \-i-kəl\ **a** : of or relating to physical force or energy **b** : of or relating to dynamics **2 a** : marked by continuous activity or change ⟨a *dynamic* city⟩ **b** : marked by energy ⟨a *dynamic* personality⟩ **3** : being a computer memory that requires connection to a power source in order to retain data ⟨*dynamic* RAM⟩ [French *dynamique,* derived from Greek *dynamis* "power," from *dynasthai* "to be able"] — **dy·nam·i·cal·ly** \-i-kə-lē, -klē\ *adv*

dy·nam·ics \dī-ˈnam-iks\ *n sing or pl* **1** : a branch of mechanics that deals with the motion of bodies and the action of forces in producing or changing their motion **2** : physical, moral, or intellectual forces or the laws relating to them **3** : the pattern of change or growth typical of something **4 :** variation and contrast in force or intensity (as in music)

dy·na·mism \ˈdī-nə-ˌmiz-əm\ *n* **1 a :** a theory that explains the universe in terms of forces and their interplay **b :** DYNAMICS 3 **2 :** a dynamic quality

[1]**dy·na·mite** \ˈdī-nə-ˌmīt\ *n* **:** a blasting explosive that is made chiefly of nitroglycerin absorbed in a porous material; *also* **:** any of various blasting explosives that contain no nitroglycerin

[2]**dynamite** *vt* **:** to blow up with dynamite — **dy·na·mit·er** *n*

dy·na·mo \ˈdī-nə-ˌmō\ *n, pl* **-mos** **1 :** GENERATOR 3 **2 :** a forceful energetic person [short for *dynamoelectric machine*]

dy·na·mom·e·ter \ˌdī-nə-ˈmäm-ət-ər\ *n* **:** an apparatus for measuring mechanical power (as of an engine) — **dy·na·mo·met·ric** \ˌdī-nə-mō-ˈme-trik\ *adj* — **dy·na·mom·e·try** \ˌdī-nə-ˈmäm-ə-trē\ *n*

dy·na·mo·tor \ˈdī-nə-ˌmōt-ər\ *n* **:** a motor generator combining the electric motor and generator

dy·nas·ty \ˈdī-nə-stē, -ˌnas-tē\ *n, pl* **-ties** **1 :** a succession of rulers of the same line of descent **2 :** a powerful group or family that maintains its position for a considerable time [Greek *dynasteia* "power, lordship," from *dynastēs* "ruler," from *dynasthai* "to be able"] — **dy·nas·tic** \dī-ˈnas-tik\ *adj* — **dy·nas·ti·cal·ly** \-ti-kə-lē, -klē\ *adv*

dyne \ˈdīn\ *n* **:** the unit of force in the centimeter-gram-second system equal to the force that would give a free mass of one gram an acceleration of one centimeter per second per second that is equivalent to 10^{-5} newton [French, from Greek *dynamis* "power"]

dys- *prefix* **1 :** abnormal **2 :** difficult ⟨*dys*menorrhea⟩ — compare EU- **3 :** impaired ⟨*dys*function⟩ [Greek, "bad, difficult"]

dys·en·tery \ˈdis-n-ˌter-ē\ *n* **1 :** a disease characterized by severe diarrhea with passage of mucus and blood and usually caused by infection **2 :** DIARRHEA [Latin *dysenteria,* from Greek, from *dys-* + *enteron* "intestine"] — **dys·en·ter·ic** \ˌdis-n-ˈter-ik\ *adj*

dys·func·tion \dis-ˈfəng-shən, -ˈfəngk-\ *n* **1 :** impaired or abnormal functioning ⟨liver *dysfunction*⟩ **2 :** abnormal or unhealthy interpersonal behavior or interaction within a group — **dys·func·tion·al** \-shnəl, -shən-l\ *adj*

dys·lex·ia \dis-ˈlek-sē-ə\ *n* **:** a learning disability in which difficulties in acquiring and processing language usually result in a lack of proficiency in reading, spelling, and writing [*dys-* + Greek *lexis* "word, speech"] — **dys·lex·ic** \-sik\ *adj*

dys·men·or·rhea \ˌdis-ˌmen-ə-ˈrē-ə\ *n* **:** painful menstruation [*dys-* + *meno-* "menstruation" + *-rrhea*] — **dys·men·or·rhe·ic** \-ˈrē-ik\ *adj*

dys·pnea \ˈdis-nē-ə\ *n* **:** difficult or labored breathing [Latin *dyspnoea,* from *dyspnoia,* from *dyspnoos* "short of breath," from *dys-* "dys-" + *pnein* "to breathe"]

dys·pep·sia \dis-ˈpep-shə, -sē-ə\ *n* **:** INDIGESTION [Latin, from Greek, from *dys-* + *pepsis* "digestion," from *peptein, pessein* "to cook, digest"]

dys·pep·tic \-ˈpep-tik\ *adj* **1 :** relating to or having dyspepsia **2 :** GLOOMY 2, CROSS — **dys·pep·ti·cal·ly** \-ti-kə-lē, -klē\ *adv*

dys·pro·si·um \dis-ˈprō-zē-əm\ *n* **:** a chemical element that forms highly magnetic compounds — see ELEMENT table [New Latin, from Greek *dysprositos* "hard to get at," from *dys-* + *prositos* "approachable"]

dys·tro·phy \ˈdis-trə-fē\ *n, pl* **-phies** **:** any of several disorders of nerves and muscles; *esp* **:** MUSCULAR DYSTROPHY — **dys·tro·phic** \dis-ˈtrō-fik\ *adj*

E

e \ˈē\ *n, pl* **e's** *or* **es** \ˈēz\ *often cap* **1 :** the 5th letter of the English alphabet **2 :** the musical tone E **:** the 3rd tone of a C-major scale **3 :** a transcendental number with the approximate value of 2.71828 that is the base of natural logarithms **4 :** a grade rating a student's work as poor or failing

[1]**e-** \ē, ˈē, i\ *prefix* **1 :** missing **:** absent **2 :** out, forth, away [Latin, "out, forth, away," from *ex-*]

[2]**e-** *combining form* **:** electronic ⟨*e*-mail⟩

[1]**each** \ˈēch\ *adj* **:** being one of two or more distinct individuals [Old English *ǣlc*]

[2]**each** *pron* **:** each one ⟨*each* of us had a twin⟩

[3]**each** *adv* **:** to or for each **:** APIECE ⟨cost a dollar *each*⟩

each other *pron* **:** each of two or more in reciprocal action or relation ⟨looked at *each other*⟩

ea·ger \ˈē-gər\ *adj* **:** marked by enthusiastic or impatient desire or interest [Medieval French *aigre* "sharp, sour, keen," from Latin *acer*] — **ea·ger·ly** *adv* — **ea·ger·ness** *n*

synonyms ANXIOUS, EAGER mean moved by urgent desire or interest. EAGER implies ardor and enthusiasm and suggests impatience at delay or restraint. ANXIOUS stresses fear of frustration or failure or disappointment.

eager beaver *n* **:** one who is extremely enthusiastic in performing duties and in volunteering for more

[1]**ea·gle** \ˈē-gəl\ *n* **1 :** any of various large day-flying sharp-eyed birds of prey that have a powerful flight and are related to the hawks **2 :** a seal, standard, or insignia shaped like or bearing an eagle **3 :** a 10-dollar gold coin of the United States bearing an eagle on the reverse **4 :** a golf score of two strokes less than par on a hole [Medieval French *aigle,* from Latin *aquila*]

[2]**eagle** *vt* **:** to score an eagle on (a golf hole)

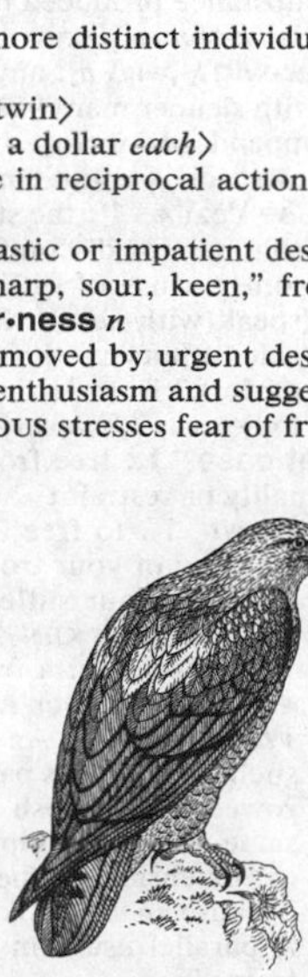

eagle 1

Eagle Scout *n* **:** a Boy Scout who has reached the highest level of achievement in scouting

ea·glet \ˈē-glət\ *n* **:** a young eagle

-ean — see -AN

[1]**ear** \ˈiər\ *n* **1 a :** the vertebrate organ of hearing and balance consisting in the typical mammal of a sound-collecting outer ear separated by an eardrum from a sound-transmitting middle ear that in turn is separated from a sensory inner ear **b :** the outer ear **c :** any of various organs (as of a fish) capable of detecting vibrations **2 a :** the sense or act of hearing **b :** an ability to understand and appreciate something heard ⟨a good *ear* for music⟩ ⟨an *ear* for languages⟩ **3 :** willing or sympathetic attention ⟨lend an *ear*⟩ ⟨give *ear* to a request⟩ **4 :** something resembling an ear in shape or position [Old English *ēare*] — **eared** \ˈiərd\ *adj* — **ear·less** \ˈiər-ləs\ *adj* — **all ears :** eagerly

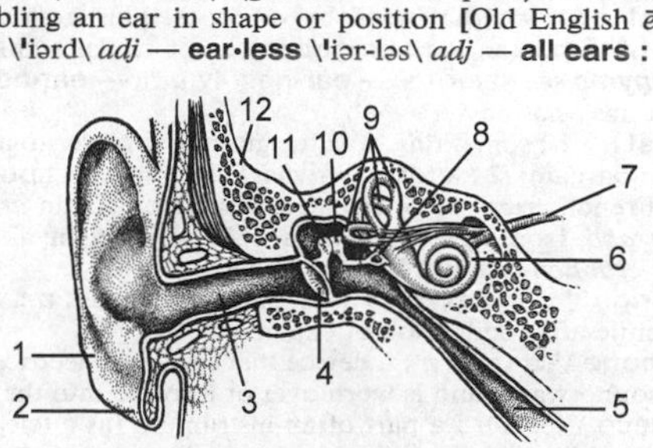

[1]ear 1a: *1* pinna, *2* lobe, *3* auditory canal, *4* eardrum, *5* eustachian tube, *6* cochlea, *7* auditory nerve, *8* stapes, *9* semicircular canals, *10* incus, *11* malleus, *12* bones of skull

listening ⟨was *all ears* when her friends spoke⟩ — **by ear** : relying on what one has heard rather than reading music ⟨play a song *by ear*⟩

[2]**ear** *n* : the fruiting spike of a cereal (as corn) including both the seeds and protective structures [Old English *ēar*] — **ear** *vi*

ear·ache \ˈiər-ˌāk\ *n* : an ache or pain in the ear

ear·bud \ˈiər-ˌbəd\ *n* : a small earphone inserted into the ear

ear canal *n* : AUDITORY CANAL

ear·drum \-ˌdrəm\ *n* : the thin membrane that separates the outer and middle ear and transmits sound waves as vibrations to the chain of tiny bones in the middle ear — called also *tympanic membrane, tympanum*

eared seal *n* : any of a family of seals including the sea lions and fur seals and having small well-developed external ears — compare HAIR SEAL

ear·ful \-ˌfu̇l\ *n* **1** : an outpouring of news or gossip **2** : a sharp reprimand

earl \ˈərl\ *n* : a member of the British nobility ranking below a marquess and above a viscount [Old English *eorl* "warrior, nobleman"] — **earl·dom** \-dəm\ *n*

earless seal *n* : HAIR SEAL

ear·lobe \ˈiər-ˌlōb\ *n* : the pendent part of the ear of human beings or some domestic chickens

[1]**ear·ly** \ˈər-lē\ *adv* **ear·li·er; -est** **1** : near the beginning of a period of time or of a process or series ⟨woke up *early* in the morning⟩ **2** : before the usual or expected time ⟨arrived *early*⟩ [Old English *ǣrlīce,* from *ǣr* "early, soon"]

[2]**early** *adj* **ear·li·er; -est** **1 a** : of, relating to, or occurring near the beginning of a period of time, a development, or a series ⟨in the *early* evening⟩ **b** : PRIMITIVE ⟨*early* art forms⟩ **2 a** : occurring before the usual or expected time ⟨spring was *early* this year⟩ **b** : occurring in the near future ⟨finish up as *early* as possible⟩ **c** : maturing or producing sooner than related forms ⟨an *early* peach⟩ — **ear·li·ness** *n*

early on *adv* : at or during an early point on stage ⟨had decided *early on* not to accept⟩

[1]**ear·mark** \ˈiər-ˌmärk\ *n* **1** : a mark of identification on the ear of an animal **2** : a distinguishing characteristic ⟨all the *earmarks* of poverty⟩

[2]**earmark** *vt* **1** : to mark with or as if with an earmark **2** : to set aside (as funds) for a specific use ⟨money *earmarked* for college⟩

ear·muff \ˈiər-ˌməf\ *n* : one of a pair of ear coverings connected by a flexible band and worn as protection against cold or noises

earn \ˈərn\ *vt* **1 a** : to get for services given ⟨*earn* a good salary⟩ **b** : to yield as a profit of business or investment : RETURN ⟨investments *earning* 8%⟩ **2** : to deserve as a result of labor or service ⟨you *earned* your grades⟩ [Old English *earnian*] — **earn·er** *n*

earned run *n* : a run in baseball that scores without benefit of an error

earned run average *n* : the average number of earned runs per game scored against a pitcher in baseball

[1]**ear·nest** \ˈər-nəst\ *n* : a serious and intent state of mind ⟨a promise made in *earnest*⟩ [Old English *eornost*]

[2]**earnest** *adj* : characterized by or proceeding from a serious state of mind ⟨an *earnest* request⟩ : not trivial : IMPORTANT ***synonyms*** see SERIOUS — **ear·nest·ly** *adv* — **ear·nest·ness** \-nəst-nəs, -nəs-nəs\ *n*

[3]**earnest** *n* **1** : something of value given by a buyer to a seller to bind a bargain **2** : a token of what is to come : PLEDGE [Medieval French *erres,* pl. of *erre* "earnest," from Latin *arra,* short for *arrabo,* from Greek *arrhabōn,* of Semitic origin; akin to Hebrew *ʽērābhōn* "pledge"]

earn·ings \ˈər-ningz\ *n pl* : something earned: as **a** : WAGE **b** : revenue after deduction of expenses

ear·phone \ˈiər-ˌfōn\ *n* : a device that converts electrical energy into sound waves and is worn over or inserted into the ear

ear·piece \-ˌpēs\ *n* : a part of an instrument (as a telephone or hearing aid) that is placed against or in the ear; *esp* : EARPHONE

ear·ring \ˈiər-ˌring\ *n* : an ornament for the earlobe

ear·shot \ˈiər-ˌshät\ *n* : the range within which one may hear a person's unaided voice ⟨waited until she was out of *earshot*⟩

ear·split·ting \-ˌsplit-ing\ *adj* : intolerably loud or shrill ⟨an *earsplitting* scream⟩

[1]**earth** \ˈərth\ *n* **1** : the soft or granular material composing part of the surface of the globe; *esp* : cultivable soil **2** : the sphere of mortal life as distinguished from heaven and hell **3** : areas of land as distinguished from sea and air : GROUND **4** *often cap* : the planet on which we live and which is 3rd in order of distance from the sun — see PLANET table **5** : the lair of a burrowing animal [Old English *eorthe*] — **earth·like** \-ˌlīk\ *adj*

synonyms EARTH, WORLD, UNIVERSE mean the entire area in which humanity thinks of itself as living. EARTH denotes the material global body, the planet of the sun, but often means the immediate sphere of human action in contrast to the religious concepts of heaven and hell. WORLD often equals EARTH but may apply to space, earth, and all visible celestial bodies within our present range of knowledge. UNIVERSE denotes the entire system of created things and physical phenomena regarded as a unit in its arrangement and operation.

[2]**earth** *vt* : to draw soil about (plants) — often used with *up*

earth·en \ˈər-thən, -t͟hən\ *adj* : made of earth or of baked clay ⟨an *earthen* floor⟩ ⟨*earthen* dishes⟩

earth·en·ware \-ˌwaər, -ˌweər\ *n* : articles (as dishes or ornaments) made of baked clay

earth·light \ˈərth-ˌlīt\ *n* : EARTHSHINE

earth·ling \ˈərth-ling\ *n* : an inhabitant of the earth

earth·ly \ˈərth-lē\ *adj* **1 a** : of, relating to, or characteristic of the earth **b** : relating to human life on the earth ⟨*earthly* joys⟩ **2** : POSSIBLE, IMAGINABLE ⟨that tool is of no *earthly* use⟩ — **earth·li·ness** *n*

synonyms EARTHLY, WORLDLY, MUNDANE mean belonging to or characteristic of the earth. EARTHLY often implies contrast with what is heavenly or spiritual ⟨abandoned *earthly* concerns and entered a convent⟩. WORLDLY and MUNDANE both imply a relation to the immediate concerns and activities of human beings, WORLDLY suggesting tangible personal gain or gratification ⟨*worldly* goods⟩ and MUNDANE suggesting reference to the immediate and practical ⟨a *mundane* discussion of finances⟩.

earth·quake \ˈərth-ˌkwāk\ *n* : a shaking or trembling of a portion of the earth caused by movement of rock masses or by volcanic shocks

earth science *n* : any of the sciences (as geology, meteorology, or oceanography) that deal with the earth or with one or more of its parts

earth·shine \-ˌshīn\ *n* : sunlight reflected by the earth that illuminates the dark part of the moon — called also *earthlight*

earth·work \-ˌwərk\ *n* : an embankment or other construction made of earth; *esp* : one made as a fortification

earth·worm \-ˌwərm\ *n* : a long slender annelid worm that lives in damp earth, moves with the aid of setae, and feeds on decaying matter

earthy \ˈər-thē, -t͟hē\ *adj* **earth·i·er; -est** **1** : consisting of or resembling earth ⟨an *earthy* flavor⟩ **2 a** : PRACTICAL **b** : not polite : CRUDE ⟨*earthy* humor⟩ — **earth·i·ness** *n*

ear·wax \ˈiər-ˌwaks\ *n* : a brownish yellow or orange waxlike substance produced by the glands of the external ear — called also *cerumen, wax*

ear·wig \-ˌwig\ *n* : any of numerous insects (order Dermaptera) with slender many-jointed antennae and a pair of large terminal appendages arranged like forceps [Old English *ēarwicga,* from *ēare* "ear" + *wicga* "insect"]

[1]**ease** \ˈēz\ *n* **1** : the state of being comfortable: as **a** : freedom from pain or discomfort **b** : freedom from care **c** : freedom from a sense of difficulty or embarrassment : NATURALNESS ⟨speak with *ease*⟩ **2** : a lack of exertion : EFFORTLESSNESS ⟨rides a horse with *ease*⟩ [Medieval French *aise* "convenience, comfort," from Latin *adjacens* "neighborhood," from *adjacēre* "to lie near," from *ad-* + *jacēre* "to lie"] — **ease·ful** \-fəl\ *adj* — **at ease** **1** : free from pain or discomfort **2** : free from formality or restraint

[2]**ease** *vb* **1** : to free from something that disquiets or burdens ⟨*ease* you of your troubles⟩ **2** : to make less painful : ALLEVIATE ⟨*ease* your suffering⟩ **3** : to make less tight or difficult : LOOSEN, SLACKEN ⟨*ease* credit⟩ ⟨*ease* up on a rope⟩

ea·sel \ˈē-zəl\ *n* : a frame for supporting something (as an artist's canvas) [Dutch *ezel* "ass"]

Word History An *easel* is a frame for supporting something, such as an artist's painting or a blackboard. The word was borrowed into English from Dutch *ezel,* which was used for the same piece of equipment. This sense of *ezel* was a metaphorical extension of the literal meaning "ass, donkey," probably because an *easel,* like a beast of burden, is used to hold things. A parallel usage in English is *horse* in the sense "supporting frame."

eas·i·ly \ˈēz-lē, -ə-lē\ *adv* **1** : without difficulty ⟨won the game

easily⟩ **2 a :** by far ⟨*easily* the best candidate⟩ **b :** at least ⟨costs *easily* twice as much⟩
[1]**east** \ˈēst\ *adv* **:** to, toward, or in the east ⟨traveling *east*⟩ [Old English *ēast*]
[2]**east** *adj* **1 :** situated toward or at the east ⟨the *east* window of the school⟩ **2 :** coming from the east ⟨an *east* wind⟩
[3]**east** *n* **1 a :** the general direction of sunrise **b :** the compass point directly opposite to west **2** *cap* **:** regions or countries east of a specified or implied point **3 :** the altar end of a church
east•bound \ˈēst-ˌbau̇nd, ˈēs-\ *adj* **:** headed east
Eas•ter \ˈē-stər\ *n* **:** a Christian holiday that commemorates Jesus' resurrection and is observed on the first Sunday after the full moon on or next after March 21 or one week later if the full moon falls on Sunday [Old English *ēastre*]
Easter lily *n* **:** any of several white cultivated lilies that bloom in early spring
east•er•ly \ˈē-stər-lē\ *adv or adj* **1 :** toward the east ⟨the *easterly* shore⟩ **2 :** from the east ⟨an *easterly* wind⟩
east•ern \ˈē-stərn\ *adj* **1** *cap* **:** of, relating to, or characteristic of a region conventionally designated East ⟨*Eastern* religion⟩ **2** *cap* **a :** of, relating to, or being the Christian churches originating in the church of the Eastern Roman Empire **b :** EASTERN ORTHODOX **3 :** lying toward or coming from the east [Old English *ēasterne*] — **east•ern•most** \-ˌmōst\ *adj*
East•ern•er \ˈē-stər-nər, -stə-nər\ *n* **:** a native or inhabitant of the East (as of the United States)
eastern hemisphere *n, often cap E&H* **:** the half of the earth to the east of the Atlantic ocean including Europe, Asia, Australia, and Africa
Eastern Orthodox *adj* **:** of or consisting of the Eastern churches that form a loose federation honoring the patriarch of Constantinople
eastern time *n, often cap E* **:** the time of the 5th time zone west of Greenwich that includes the eastern United States
east•ing \ˈē-sting\ *n* **1 :** easterly progress ⟨made a lot of *easting*⟩ **2 :** difference in longitude to the east from the last noted point
east–northeast *n* **:** the compass point that is two points north of east **:** N67°30′E
east–southeast *n* **:** the compass point that is two points south of east **:** S67°30′E
[1]**east•ward** \ˈēs-twərd\ *adv or adj* **:** toward the east — **eastwards** \-twərdz\ *adv*
[2]**eastward** *n* **:** eastward direction or part
[1]**easy** \ˈē-zē\ *adj* **eas•i•er; -est 1 :** not hard to do ⟨an *easy* lesson⟩ **2 a :** not severe **:** LENIENT ⟨an *easy* teacher⟩ **b :** not steep or abrupt ⟨*easy* slopes⟩ **3 a :** marked by peace and comfort ⟨an *easy* life⟩ **b :** not hurried ⟨an *easy* pace⟩ **4 a :** free from pain, trouble, or worry ⟨a comforting voice that made him *easier*⟩ **b :** not false or strained **:** NATURAL ⟨an *easy* manner⟩ **5 a :** giving comfort or relaxation ⟨an *easy* chair⟩ **b :** not imposing hardship ⟨buying on *easy* terms⟩ ***synonyms*** see SIMPLE — **eas•i•ness** *n*
[2]**easy** *adv* **easier; -est 1 :** EASILY 1 ⟨promises come *easy*⟩ **2 :** without undue speed or excitement ⟨take it *easy*⟩ **3 a :** without worry or care ⟨told him to rest *easy*⟩ **b :** without severe penalty ⟨got off *easy*⟩
easy•go•ing \ˌē-zē-ˈgō-ing\ *adj* **:** taking life easily **:** CAREFREE — **easy•go•ing•ness** *n*
easy street *n* **:** a situation with no worries
eat \ˈēt\ *vb* **ate** \ˈāt\; **eat•en** \ˈēt-n\; **eat•ing 1 :** to take into the mouth as food **:** chew and swallow in turn **2 :** to take a meal ⟨*eat* at home⟩ **3 :** to destroy, use up, or waste by or as if by eating ⟨costs *ate* up the profits⟩ **4 a :** to affect something by gradual destruction or consumption ⟨acid *ate* into the metal⟩ **b :** BOTHER ⟨what's *eating* you⟩ **5 :** to enjoy with excitement ⟨the audience *ate* the show up⟩ [Old English *etan*] — **eat•er** *n* — **eat alive :** to defeat or conquer completely ⟨was *eaten alive* by the competition⟩ — **eat one's heart out :** to suffer deep distress (as from grief or envy) — **eat one's words :** to take back what one has said
[1]**eat•able** \ˈēt-ə-bəl\ *adj* **:** fit to be eaten
[2]**eatable** *n* **1 :** something to eat **2** *pl* **:** FOOD
eating disorder *n* **:** any of several disorders (as anorexia nervosa and bulimia) marked by abnormal eating behaviors
eau de cologne \ˌōd-ə-kə-ˈlōn\ *n, pl* **eaux de cologne** \ˌōd-ə-, ˌōzd-ə-\ **:** COLOGNE [French, literally, "water from Cologne"]
eave \ˈēv\ *n* **:** the overhanging lower edge of a roof projecting beyond the wall of a building — usually used in plural [Old English *efes*, singular]

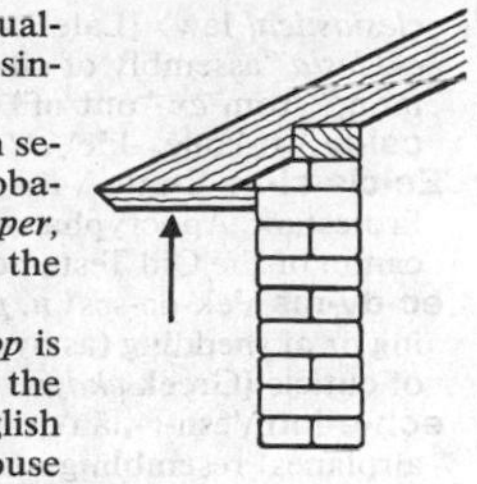
eaves

eaves•drop \ˈēvz-ˌdräp\ *vi* **:** to listen secretly to what is said in private [probably back-formation from *eavesdropper*, literally, "one standing under the eaves"] — **eaves•drop•per** *n*
Word History The verb *eavesdrop* is probably a back-formation from the noun *eavesdropper*. In Middle English the ground below the eaves of a house on which rainwater drips was called *evesdrop*, spelled *eavesdrop* in modern English (the noun is now very rare). *Eavesdropper* was originally used for a person who stood on the eavesdrop in order to overhear what was going on inside.
eaves trough *n* **:** GUTTER 1a
[1]**ebb** \ˈeb\ *n* **1 :** the recession of the tide toward the sea **2 a :** a passing from a high to a low point **b :** a period or state of decline ⟨relations were at a low *ebb*⟩ [Old English *ebba*]
[2]**ebb** *vi* **1 :** to recede from the flood **2 :** to decline from a higher level or a better state ⟨her popularity *ebbed*⟩
ebb tide *n* **1 :** the tide while ebbing **2 :** EBB 2b
EBCDIC \ˈeps-ə-ˌdik, ˈebs-\ *n* **:** a computer code for representing letters, numerals, and symbols [*e*xtended *b*inary *c*oded *d*ecimal *i*nterchange *c*ode]
Ebo•la \ē-ˈbō-lə\ *n* **:** a serious often fatal disease that is caused by a virus of African origin and is marked by fever, muscle aches, and internal hemorrhage; *also* **:** the virus causing Ebola [*Ebola* River, Democratic Republic of the Congo]
eb•o•nite \ˈeb-ə-ˌnīt\ *n* **:** hard rubber especially when black
[1]**eb•o•ny** \ˈeb-ə-nē\ *n, pl* **-nies :** a hard heavy blackish wood yielded by various tropical chiefly southeast Asian trees related to the persimmon; *also* **:** a tree yielding ebony [derived from Greek *ebenos*, from Egyptian *hbnj*]
[2]**ebony** *adj* **1 :** made of or resembling ebony **2 :** BLACK 1, DARK
e–book \ˈē-ˌbu̇k\ *n* **:** a book composed in or converted to digital format for display on a computer screen or handheld device
ebul•lient \i-ˈbu̇l-yənt\ *adj* **1 :** intensely agitated **2 :** having or showing liveliness and enthusiasm ⟨*ebullient* performers⟩ ⟨*ebullient* charm⟩ [Latin *ebullire* "to bubble out," from *e-* + *bullire* "to bubble, boil"] — **ebul•lience** \-yəns\ *n* — **ebullient•ly** *adv*
eb•ul•li•tion \ˌeb-ə-ˈlish-ən\ *n* **1 :** a sudden or violent outburst or display **2 :** the process or state of boiling or bubbling up
[1]**ec•cen•tric** \ik-ˈsen-trik, ek-\ *adj* **1 :** deviating from some established pattern or from accepted usage or conduct **2 a :** not following a truly circular path ⟨an *eccentric* orbit⟩ **b :** located somewhere other than at the geometrical center ⟨an *eccentric* center of gravity⟩ [Medieval Latin *eccentricus*, from Greek *ekkentros*, from *ex* "out of" + *kentron* "center"] — **ec•cen•tri•cal•ly** \-tri-kə-lē, -klē\ *adv*
[2]**eccentric** *n* **1 :** a disklike device that turns around a shaft not at its center and is used in machinery for changing circular motion into back-and-forth motion **2 :** a strange person
ec•cen•tric•i•ty \ˌek-ˌsen-ˈtris-ət-ē\ *n, pl* **-ties 1 a :** the quality or state of being eccentric **b :** deviation from an established pattern, rule, or norm; *esp* **:** odd behavior **2 :** the amount by which a nearly circular path is eccentric ⟨the orbit's *eccentricity*⟩
synonyms ECCENTRICITY, IDIOSYNCRASY mean a peculiar trait or habit. ECCENTRICITY stresses divergence from the usual or customary and suggests whimsicality or oddness ⟨was fond of her father's *eccentricities*⟩. IDIOSYNCRASY stresses the following of one's particular bent or temperament and connotes strong individuality and independence of action ⟨the painting reflects the *idiosyncrasies* of the artist⟩.
Ec•cle•si•as•tes \ik-ˌlē-zē-ˈas-ˌtēz\ *n* **:** a book of wisdom literature in canonical Jewish and Christian Scriptures — see BIBLE table [Greek *Ekklēsiastēs*, literally, "preacher"]
ec•cle•si•as•tic \-ˈas-tik\ *n* **:** a member of the clergy
ec•cle•si•as•ti•cal \-ti-kəl\ *or* **ec•cle•si•as•tic** \-tik\ *adj* **:** of or relating to a church especially as an established institution ⟨ec-

\ə\ **abut**	\au̇\ **out**	\i\ **tip**	\ȯ\ **saw**	\u̇\ **foot**
\ər\ **further**	\ch\ **chin**	\ī\ **life**	\ȯi\ **coin**	\y\ **yet**
\a\ **mat**	\e\ **pet**	\j\ **job**	\th\ **thin**	\yü\ **few**
\ā\ **take**	\ē\ **easy**	\ng\ **sing**	\th\ **this**	\yu̇\ **cure**
\ä\ **cot, cart**	\g\ **go**	\ō\ **bone**	\ü\ **food**	\zh\ **vision**

clesiastical law⟩ [Late Latin *ecclesiasticus,* derived from Greek *ekklēsia* "assembly of citizens, church," from *ekkalein* "to summon," from *ex* "out of" + *kalein* "to call"] — **ec·cle·si·as·ti·cal·ly** \-ti-kə-lē, -klē\ *adv*

Ec·cle·si·as·ti·cus \-ti-kəs\ *n* : a didactic book included in the Protestant Apocrypha and as Sirach in the Roman Catholic canon of the Old Testament — see BIBLE table

ec·dy·sis \ˈek-də-səs\ *n, pl* **-dy·ses** \-də-ˌsēz\ : the act of molting or of shedding (as by insects and crustaceans) an outer layer of cuticle [Greek *ekdysis* "act of getting out"]

ech·e·lon \ˈesh-ə-ˌlän\ *n* **1 a** : a formation of units (as troops or airplanes) resembling a series of steps **b** : any of several military units in echelon formation **2 a** : one of a series of levels or grades especially of authority ⟨involved employees at every *echelon*⟩ **b** : the individuals at such a level ⟨the upper *echelons* of society⟩ [French *échelon,* literally, "rung of a ladder"]

echid·na \i-ˈkid-nə\ *n* : a spiny-coated toothless burrowing egg-laying mammal of Australia with a tapering snout and long tongue for eating ants [Latin, "viper," from Greek]

echi·no·derm \i-ˈkī-nə-ˌdərm\ *n* : any of a phylum (Echinodermata) of marine invertebrate animals (as starfishes, sea cucumbers, sea urchins, and crinoids) that have true coeloms, similar body parts (as the arms of a starfish) arranged symmetrically around a central axis, a calcium-containing endoskeleton, and a water-vascular system [*echin-* "prickle" (from Greek *echinos* "sea urchin") + Greek *derma* "skin"] — **echi·no·der·ma·tous** \i-ˌkī-nə-ˈdər-mət-əs\ *adj*

echi·noid \i-ˈkī-ˌnȯid, ˈek-ə-ˌnȯid\ *n* : SEA URCHIN

echi·nus \i-ˈkī-nəs\ *n, pl* **-ni** \-ˌnī\ : SEA URCHIN [Latin, from Greek *echinos* "hedgehog, sea urchin"]

[1]**echo** \ˈek-ō\ *n, pl* **ech·oes** **1** : the repetition of a sound caused by reflection of sound waves **2 a** : a repetition or imitation of another **b** : REPERCUSSION, RESULT ⟨the economic collapse had political *echoes*⟩ **3** : one who closely imitates or repeats another **4 a** : the repetition of a received radio signal due especially to reflection off the atmosphere **b** (1) : the reflection of transmitted radar signals by an object (2) : the visual indication of this reflection on a radarscope [Latin, from Greek *ēchō*] — **echo·ic** \i-ˈkō-ik, e-\ *adj*

[2]**echo** *vb* **ech·oed; echo·ing** **1** : to resound with echoes ⟨a stadium *echoing* with cheers⟩ **2** : to produce an echo : send back or repeat a sound **3 a** : REPEAT, IMITATE ⟨*echoing* the words of the teacher⟩ **b** : to restate in support or agreement **c** : to be reminiscent of ⟨music that *echoes* an earlier time⟩

echo·lo·ca·tion \ˌek-ō-lō-ˈkā-shən\ *n* : a process for locating distant or invisible objects by means of sound waves reflected back to the sender from the objects

echo sounder *n* : an instrument for determining the depth of a body of water or of an object below the surface by means of sound waves

éclair \ā-ˈklaər, -ˈkleər, ˈā-ˌ\ *n* : an oblong pastry with whipped cream or custard filling [French, literally, "lightning"]

eclamp·sia \e-ˈklam-sē-ə, -ˈklamp-\ *n* : a convulsive state; *esp* : an attack of convulsions during pregnancy or during the process of giving birth [Greek *eklampsis* "sudden flashing," from *eklampein* "to shine forth," from *ex* "out" + *lampein* "to shine"]

éclat \ā-ˈklä\ *n* **1** : brilliant or conspicuous success **2** : PRAISE 1 [French, "splinter, burst, éclat"]

eclec·tic \e-ˈklek-tik, i-\ *adj* **1** : selecting what appears to be best from various doctrines, methods, or styles ⟨*eclectic* taste in music⟩ **2** : composed of elements drawn from various sources ⟨an *eclectic* group of speakers⟩ [Greek *eklektikos,* from *eklegein* "to select," from *ex* "out" + *legein* "to gather"] — **eclectic** *n* — **eclec·ti·cal·ly** \-ti-kə-lē, -klē\ *adv* — **eclec·ti·cism** \-tə-ˌsiz-əm\ *n*

[1]**eclipse** \i-ˈklips\ *n* **1 a** : a complete or partial hiding or darkening of one celestial body by another **b** : the passing into the shadow of a heavenly body **2** : a falling into obscurity or decline [Greek *ekleipsis,* from *ekleipein* "to omit, suffer eclipse," from *ex-* "out" + *leipein* "to leave"]

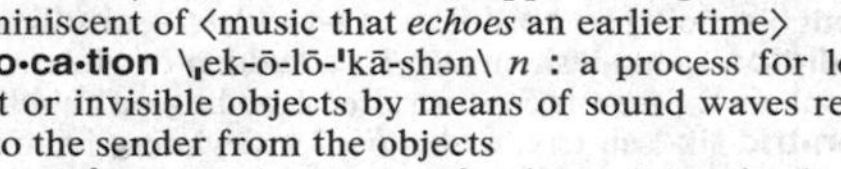

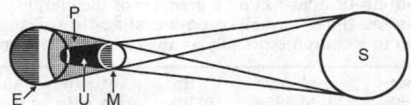

eclipse 1a: *E* earth, *M* moon in solar eclipse, *P* penumbra, *S* sun, *U* umbra

[2]**eclipse** *vt* **1** : to cause an eclipse of **2** : to reduce in fame **3** : to surpass greatly : OUTSHINE

[1]**eclip·tic** \i-ˈklip-tik\ *n* : the great circle of the celestial sphere that is the apparent path of the sun among the stars [Late Latin *ecliptica linea,* literally, "line of eclipses"]

[2]**ecliptic** *adj* : of or relating to the ecliptic or an eclipse

ec·logue \ˈek-ˌlȯg\ *n* : a poem in which shepherds converse [Latin *Eclogae,* title of Virgil's pastorals, literally, "selections"]

eco- *combining form* **1** : habitat or environment ⟨*eco*system⟩ **2** : ecology [Greek *oikos* "house"]

E. coli \ˌē-ˈkō-ˌlī\ *n, pl* **E. coli** : a rod-shaped bacterium with various strains including one that produces intestinal illness and others that live harmlessly in the intestine [short for *Escherichia coli,* the Latin taxonomic name]

eco·log·i·cal \ˌē-kə-ˈläj-i-kəl, ˌek-ə-\ *also* **eco·log·ic** \-ik\ *adj* : of, relating to, concerned with, or affecting ecology or the ecology of a particular group of organisms or an environment — **eco·log·i·cal·ly** \-i-kə-lē, -klē\ *adv*

ecol·o·gist \i-ˈkäl-ə-jist; e-\ *n* : a person who specializes in ecology

ecol·o·gy \i-ˈkäl-ə-jē, e-\ *n* **1** : a branch of science concerned with the interrelationship of organisms and their environments **2** : the pattern of relations between one or more organisms and the environment

e–com·merce \ˈē-ˌkäm-ˌərs, -ərs\ *n* : the buying and selling of goods over the Internet [*e*lectronic]

ec·o·nom·ic \ˌek-ə-ˈnäm-ik, ˌē-kə-\ *adj* **1 a** : of or relating to the science of economics ⟨*economic* theories⟩ **b** : of, relating to, or based on the production, distribution, and consumption of goods and services ⟨*economic* growth⟩ **c** : of or relating to an economy ⟨an *economic* advisor⟩ **2** : having practical or industrial significance or uses : affecting material resources ⟨*economic* pests⟩

ec·o·nom·i·cal \-ˈnäm-i-kəl\ *adj* **1** : marked by careful and efficient use of resources : THRIFTY **2** : operating with little waste or at a saving ⟨an *economical* car⟩ — **ec·o·nom·i·cal·ly** \-ˈnäm-i-kə-lē, -klē\ *adv*

ec·o·nom·ics \ˌek-ə-ˈnäm-iks, ˌē-kə-\ *n sing or pl* **1** : a social science concerned chiefly with description and analysis of the production, distribution, and consumption of goods and services **2** : financial aspect or significance ⟨the *economics* of buying a car⟩ **3** : economic conditions ⟨current *economics*⟩ — **econ·o·mist** \i-ˈkän-ə-məst\ *n*

econ·o·mize \i-ˈkän-ə-ˌmīz\ *vb* **1** : to practice economy : be frugal ⟨*economize* on groceries⟩ **2** : to use more economically : SAVE ⟨*economize* fuel⟩ — **econ·o·miz·er** *n*

[1]**econ·o·my** \i-ˈkän-ə-mē\ *n, pl* **-mies** **1 a** : thrifty use of material resources : frugality in expenditures; *also* : an act of economizing **b** : efficient and sparing use of nonmaterial resources (as effort or language) **2** : systematic arrangement of something : ORGANIZATION **3** : the structure of economic life in a country, area, or period; *also* : an economic system [derived from Greek *oikonomos* "household manager," from *oikos* "house" + *nemein* "to manage"]

[2]**economy** *adj* : designed to save money ⟨*economy* cars⟩

eco·sys·tem \ˈē-kō-ˌsis-təm, ˈek-ō-\ *n* : a complex system composed of an ecological community of organisms interacting with their environment especially under natural conditions

ec·ru \ˈek-rü, ˈā-krü\ *n* : BEIGE [French *écru* "unbleached"]

ec·sta·sy \ˈek-stə-sē\ *n, pl* **-sies** **1** : a state of being beyond reason and self-control **2** : a state of overwhelming emotion; *esp* : rapturous delight **3** : a synthetic drug $C_{11}H_{15}NO_2$ used unlawfully for its stimulant and hallucinogenic properties [derived from Greek *ekstasis,* from *existanai* "to derange," from *ex* "out" + *histanai* "to cause to stand"]

ec·stat·ic \ek-ˈstat-ik\ *adj* : of, relating to, or marked by ecstasy — **ec·stat·i·cal·ly** \-i-kə-lē, -klē\ *adv*

ect- *or* **ecto-** *combining form* : outside : external ⟨*ecto*derm⟩ — compare END-, EXO- [Greek *ektos,* from *ex* "out, out of"]

ec·to·derm \ˈek-tə-ˌdərm\ *n* **1** : the outer cellular layer of a 2-layered animal (as a jellyfish) **2** : the outermost of the three primary germ layers of an embryo from which skin, nerves, and certain other structures develop; *also* : a tissue (as skin or nerve) derived from this — **ec·to·der·mal** \ˌek-tə-ˈdər-məl\ *adj*

ec·to·mor·phic \ˌek-tə-ˈmȯr-fik\ *adj* : having a lean slender body build — **ec·to·morph** \ˈek-tə-ˌmȯrf\ *n* — **ec·to·mor·phy** \ˈek-tə-ˌmȯr-fē\ *n*

-ec·to·my \ˈek-tə-mē\ *n combining form, pl* **-mies** : surgical removal ⟨tonsil*lectomy*⟩ [Greek *ektemnein* "to cut out," from *ex-* "out" + *temnein* "to cut"]

ec·to·plasm \ˈek-tə-ˌplaz-əm\ *n* **1 :** the outer relatively rigid layer of the cytoplasm usually held to be reversibly convertible from a gel to a sol — compare ENDOPLASM **2 :** a substance held to be the material form of a ghost — **ec·to·plas·mic** \ˌek-tə-ˈplaz-mik\ *adj*

ec·to·therm \ˈek-tə-ˌthərm\ *n* **:** a cold-blooded animal **:** POIKILOTHERM [*ecto-* + Greek *thermē* "heat"] — **ec·to·ther·mic** \ˌek-tə-ˈthər-mik\ *adj*

ec·u·men·i·cal \ˌek-yə-ˈmen-i-kəl\ *adj* **1 :** worldwide or general in extent, influence, or application **2 :** of, relating to, or representing the whole of a body of churches **3 :** promoting Christian unity or cooperation [Late Latin *oecumenicus,* derived from Greek *oikoumenē* "the inhabited world," from *oikein* "to inhabit," from *oikos* "house"] — **ec·u·men·i·cal·ly** \-i-kə-lē, -klē\ *adv* — **ec·u·me·nic·i·ty** \-mə-ˈnis-ət-ē\ *n*

ec·ze·ma \ig-ˈzē-mə, ˈek-sə-mə, ˈeg-zə-\ *n* **:** a skin inflammation marked by redness, itching, and scaly or crusted lesions [Greek *ekzema,* from *ekzein* "to erupt," from *ex* "out" + *zein* "to boil"] — **ec·zem·a·tous** \ig-ˈzem-ət-əs\ *adj*

ed \ˈed\ *n* **:** EDUCATION ⟨driver's *ed*⟩

[1]**-ed** \d *after a vowel or* b, g, j, l, m, n, ng, r, th, v, z, zh; əd, id *after* d, t; t *after other sounds; exceptions are pronounced at their subentries or entries*\ *vb suffix or adj suffix* **1** — used to form the past participle of regular weak verbs ⟨end*ed*⟩ ⟨fad*ed*⟩ ⟨tri*ed*⟩ ⟨patt*ed*⟩ **2** — used to form adjectives of identical meaning from Latin-derived adjectives ending in *-ate* ⟨umbilicat*ed*⟩ **3 a :** having **:** characterized by ⟨cultur*ed*⟩ ⟨two-fac*ed*⟩ **b :** having the characteristics of ⟨bigot*ed*⟩ [Old English *-ed, -od, -ad*]

[2]**-ed** *vb suffix* — used to form the past tense of regular weak verbs ⟨judg*ed*⟩ ⟨deni*ed*⟩ ⟨dropp*ed*⟩ [Old English *-de, -ede, -ode, -ade*]

Edam \ˈēd-əm, ˈē-ˌdam\ *n* **:** a Dutch pressed cheese of yellow color and mild flavor [*Edam,* Netherlands]

ed·a·ma·me \ˌed-ə-ˈmäm-ā\ *n* **:** immature green soybeans usually in the pod [Japanese]

edaph·ic \i-ˈdaf-ik\ *adj* **:** of, relating to, or resulting from the soil [Greek *edaphos* "bottom, ground"] — **edaph·i·cal·ly** \-ˈdaf-i-kə-lē, -klē\ *adv*

Ed·dic \ˈed-ik\ *adj* **:** of, relating to, or resembling the Old Norse Edda which is a 13th century collection of chiefly mythological poems in alliterative verse

[1]**ed·dy** \ˈed-ē\ *n, pl* **eddies** **1 :** a current of air or water running contrary to the main current; *esp* **:** a current moving in a circle like a whirlpool **2 :** a substance moving like an eddy ⟨*eddies* of dust⟩ [Middle English (Scots) *ydy*]

[2]**eddy** *vb* **ed·died; ed·dy·ing :** to move in an eddy or in a way that forms an eddy ⟨the stream *eddied* about a large rock⟩

eddy current *n* **:** an electric current induced by an alternating magnetic field

edel·weiss \ˈād-l-ˌwīs\ *n* **:** a small perennial woolly herb that is related to the thistles and grows high in the Alps [German, from *edel* "noble" + *weiss* "white"]

edelweiss

ede·ma \i-ˈdē-mə\ *n* **:** abnormal accumulation of watery fluid in a bodily tissue or cavity [Greek *oidēma* "swelling," from *oidein* "to swell"] — **edem·a·tous** \i-ˈdem-ət-əs\ *adj*

Eden \ˈēd-n\ *n* **:** PARADISE 3 [from *Eden,* the garden where Adam and Eve are held to have lived first, from Late Latin, from Hebrew *'Ēdhen*] — **Eden·ic** \i-ˈden-ik\ *adj*

eden·tate \ē-ˈden-ˌtāt\ *n* **:** any of an order (Edentata) of mammals having few or no teeth and including the sloths, armadillos, and New World anteaters — **edentate** *adj*

[1]**edge** \ˈej\ *n* **1 a :** the cutting side of a blade ⟨a knife's *edge*⟩ **b :** the sharpness of a blade ⟨a razor with no *edge*⟩ **c :** a harsh or sharp quality ⟨a voice with a sarcastic *edge*⟩ **2 a :** the line where an object or surface begins or ends; *also* **:** the narrow part next to it ⟨the *edge* of the deck⟩ **b :** a line or line segment where two planes or plane faces of a solid meet ⟨an *edge* of the cube⟩ **3 :** ADVANTAGE 3 [Old English *ecg*] ***synonyms*** see BORDER — **edged** \ˈejd\ *adj* — **on edge :** ANXIOUS 1, NERVOUS

[2]**edge** *vb* **1 :** to give an edge to ⟨*edge* an axe⟩ ⟨a voice *edged* with anger⟩ **2 :** to move or advance slowly or by short moves ⟨the crowd *edged* along⟩ **3 :** to incline (a ski) sideways

edge tool *n* **:** a tool (as a chisel, knife, plane, or gouge) with a sharp cutting edge

edge·ways \ˈej-ˌwāz\ *adv, chiefly British* **:** SIDEWAYS

edge·wise \-ˌwīz\ *adv* **1 :** with the edge in front **:** SIDEWAYS **2 :** as if by an edge **:** BARELY ⟨couldn't get a word in *edgewise*⟩

edg·ing \ˈej-ing\ *n* **:** something that forms an edge or border ⟨a lace *edging*⟩

edgy \ˈej-ē\ *adj* **edg·i·er; -est** **1 :** having an edge **:** SHARP ⟨an *edgy* tone⟩ **2 :** being on edge **:** TENSE — **edg·i·ly** \ˈej-ə-lē\ *adv* — **edg·i·ness** \ˈej-ē-nəs\ *n*

ed·i·ble \ˈed-ə-bəl\ *adj* **:** fit or safe to be eaten [Late Latin *edibilis,* from Latin *edere* "to eat"] — **ed·i·bil·i·ty** \ˌed-ə-ˈbil-ət-ē\ *n* — **edible** *n* — **ed·i·ble·ness** *n*

edict \ˈē-ˌdikt\ *n* **:** a decree or order proclaimed by an authority (as a sovereign) that has the force of law [Latin *edictum,* from *edicere* "to decree," from *e-* + *dicere* "to say"] — **edic·tal** \i-ˈdik-tl\ *adj*

ed·i·fice \ˈed-ə-fəs\ *n* **:** BUILDING; *esp* **:** a large or impressive building (as a church) [derived from Latin *aedificium,* from *aedificare* "to erect a house"]

ed·i·fy \ˈed-ə-ˌfī\ *vt* **-fied; -fy·ing :** to instruct and improve especially in moral and religious knowledge ⟨plays that *edify* the audience⟩ [derived from Late Latin *aedificare* "to instruct spiritually," from Latin, "to erect a house," from *aedes* "temple, house"] — **ed·i·fi·ca·tion** \ˌed-ə-fə-ˈkā-shən\ *n*

ed·it \ˈed-ət\ *vt* **ed·it·ed; ed·it·ing** **1 a :** to correct, revise, and prepare especially for publication ⟨*edit* Poe's works⟩ **b :** to assemble (as a motion-picture or tape recording) by cutting and rearranging **2 :** to supervise the publication of [back-formation from *editor*]

edi·tion \i-ˈdish-ən\ *n* **1 :** the form in which a text (as a printed book) is published ⟨the paperback *edition*⟩ **2 :** the whole number of copies printed or published at one time ⟨a third *edition*⟩ **3 :** one of the several issues of a newspaper for a single day ⟨the late *edition*⟩ [Latin *editio* "publication, edition," from *edere* "to bring forth, publish"]

ed·i·tor \ˈed-ət-ər\ *n* **1 :** a person who edits **2 :** a computer program that permits the user to create or change data (as text or graphics) in a computer system [Late Latin, "publisher," from Latin *edere* "to bring forth, publish"] — **ed·i·tor·ship** \-ˌship\ *n*

[1]**ed·i·to·ri·al** \ˌed-ə-ˈtōr-ē-əl, -ˈtȯr-\ *adj* **1 :** of or relating to an editor or editing **2 :** being or resembling an editorial ⟨an *editorial* statement⟩ — **ed·i·to·ri·al·ly** \-ē-ə-lē\ *adv*

[2]**editorial** *n* **:** a newspaper or magazine article that gives the opinions of its editors or publishers

ed·i·to·ri·al·ist \-ē-ə-ləst\ *n* **:** a writer of editorials

ed·i·to·ri·al·ize \ˌed-ə-ˈtōr-ē-ə-ˌlīz, -ˈtȯr-\ *vi* **1 :** to express an opinion in the form of an editorial **2 :** to introduce opinion into the reporting of facts — **ed·i·to·ri·al·i·za·tion** \-ˌtōr-ē-ə-lə-ˈzā-shən, -ˌtȯr-\ *n* — **ed·i·to·ri·al·iz·er** \-ˈtōr-ē-ə-ˌlī-zər, -ˈtȯr-\ *n*

ed·u·ca·ble \ˈej-ə-kə-bəl\ *also* **ed·u·cat·able** \-ˌkāt-ə-bəl\ *adj* **:** capable of being educated

ed·u·cate \ˈej-ə-ˌkāt\ *vt* **1 :** to provide schooling for **2 a :** to develop mentally and morally especially by formal instruction **b :** TRAIN [Latin *educare* "to rear, educate"] ***synonyms*** see TEACH — **ed·u·ca·tor** \-ˌkāt-ər\ *n*

ed·u·cat·ed \ˈej-ə-ˌkāt-əd\ *adj* **1 :** having an education; *esp* **:** having an education beyond the average **2 :** giving evidence of education ⟨*educated* speech⟩ **3 :** based on some knowledge of fact ⟨an *educated* guess⟩

ed·u·ca·tion \ˌej-ə-ˈkā-shən\ *n* **1 a :** the action or process of educating or of being educated **b :** the knowledge and development resulting from an educational process ⟨a person of little *education*⟩ **2 :** the field of study that deals mainly with methods and problems of teaching — **ed·u·ca·tion·al** \-shnəl, -shən-l\ *adj* — **ed·u·ca·tion·al·ly** \-ē\ *adv*

synonyms EDUCATION, TRAINING mean the process of being taught. EDUCATION is the general term for institutional

\ə\ **abut**	\au̇\ **out**	\i\ **tip**	\ȯ\ **saw**	\u̇\ **foot**
\ər\ **further**	\ch\ **chin**	\ī\ **life**	\ȯi\ **coin**	\y\ **yet**
\a\ **mat**	\e\ **pet**	\j\ **job**	\th\ **thin**	\yü\ **few**
\ā\ **take**	\ē\ **easy**	\ng\ **sing**	\th\ **this**	\yu̇\ **cure**
\ä\ **cot, cart**	\g\ **go**	\ō\ **bone**	\ü\ **food**	\zh\ **vision**

learning and implies the guidance and training intended to develop a person's full capacities and intelligence ⟨a high school *education*⟩. TRAINING suggests exercise or practice to gain skill, endurance, or facility in a specific field ⟨*training* in self-defense⟩.

ed•u•ca•tive \ˈej-ə-ˌkāt-iv\ *adj* **1 :** tending to educate **:** INSTRUCTIVE ⟨an *educative* experience⟩ **2 :** of or relating to education ⟨improvements in *educative* procedures⟩

educe \i-ˈdüs, -ˈdyüs\ *vt* **1 :** to draw forth **:** BRING OUT, ELICIT ⟨*educe* a response⟩ **2 :** to arrive at (as a solution or conclusion) [Latin *educere* "to draw out," from *e-* + *ducere* "to lead"] — **educ•ible** \-ˈdü-sə-bəl, -ˈdyü-\ *adj* — **educ•tion** \-ˈdək-shən\ *n* — **educ•tor** \-ˈdək-tər\ *n*

Ed•war•di•an \ed-ˈwärd-ē-ən\ *adj* **:** of, relating to, or characteristic of Edward VII of England or his age — **Edwardian** *n*

-ee \ˈē, ˌē, ē\ *n suffix* **1 :** recipient or beneficiary of (a specified action or thing) ⟨appoint*ee*⟩ ⟨grant*ee*⟩ ⟨patent*ee*⟩ **2 :** one who performs (a specified action) ⟨escap*ee*⟩ [Medieval French *-é,* from *-é,* past participle ending, from Latin *-atus*]

eel \ˈēl\ *n, pl* **eels** *or* **eel** **1 :** any of numerous long snakelike fishes with smooth slimy skin, no pelvic fins, and the fins in the middle of the back and bottom continuous around the tail **2 :** EELWORM [Old English *ǣl*] — **eel•like** \ˈēl-ˌlīk\ *adj* — **eely** \ˈē-lē\ *adj*

eel•grass \ˈēl-ˌgras\ *n* **:** a marine plant that is a monocotyledon, grows underwater, and has long narrow leaves

eel•pout \-ˌpau̇t\ *n* **1 :** any of various marine fishes resembling blennies **2 :** BURBOT

eel•worm \-ˌwərm\ *n* **:** a nematode worm; *esp* **:** one living in soil or parasitic on plants

e'en \ēn, ˈēn\ *adv* **:** EVEN

-eer \ˈiər\ *n suffix* **:** one that is concerned with professionally, conducts, or produces ⟨auction*eer*⟩ ⟨pamphlet*eer*⟩ — often in words with derogatory meaning ⟨profit*eer*⟩ [Middle French *-ier,* from Latin *-arius*]

e'er \eər, ˈeər, aər, ˈaər\ *adv* **:** EVER

ee•rie *also* **ee•ry** \ˈiər-ē\ *adj* **ee•ri•er; -est :** causing fear or uneasiness because of strangeness or gloominess ⟨*eerie* lights shone from the swamp⟩ [Old English *earg* "cowardly, wretched"] ***synonyms*** see WEIRD — **ee•ri•ly** \ˈir-ə-lē\ *adv* — **ee•ri•ness** \ˈir-ē-nəs\ *n*

ef•face \i-ˈfās, e-\ *vt* **1 a :** WIPE OUT, OBLITERATE **b :** to make indistinct by or as if by rubbing out **:** ERASE ⟨*efface* an inscription⟩ **2 :** to make (oneself) inconspicuous or modestly unnoticeable [Medieval French *effacer,* from *ex-* "ex-" + *face* "face"] — **ef•face•able** \-ˈfā-sə-bəl\ *adj* — **ef•face•ment** \-ˈfās-mənt\ *n* — **ef•fac•er** *n*

[1]ef•fect \i-ˈfekt\ *n* **1 :** an event, condition, or state of affairs that is produced by a cause **2 :** INFLUENCE ⟨the *effect* of climate on growth⟩ **3** *pl* **:** GOODS, POSSESSIONS ⟨household *effects*⟩ **4 a :** the act of making a particular impression ⟨talked merely for *effect*⟩ **b (1) :** something designed to produce a distinctive or desired impression — usually used in plural **(2)** *pl* **:** SPECIAL EFFECTS ⟨blown away by the movie's *effects*⟩ **5 :** EXECUTION, OPERATION ⟨the law went into *effect* today⟩ [Latin *effectus,* from *efficere* "to bring about," from *ex-* + *facere* "to make, do"] — **in effect :** in reality ⟨the suggestion was *in effect* an order⟩

synonyms EFFECT, CONSEQUENCE, RESULT mean a condition or occurrence traceable to a cause. EFFECT designates something that necessarily and directly follows or occurs by reason of a cause ⟨the *effect* of the medicine was drowsiness⟩. CONSEQUENCE implies a looser or remoter connection with a cause that may no longer be operating ⟨the loss of prestige was a *consequence* of this ill-advised action⟩. RESULT often applies to the last in a series of effects.

[2]effect *vt* **:** BRING ABOUT, ACCOMPLISH — **ef•fect•er** *n*

usage *Effect* and *affect* are often confused because of their similar spelling and pronunciation. The verb [2]*affect* usually has to do with pretense ⟨she *affected* a cheery disposition despite feeling down⟩. The more common [3]*affect* denotes having an effect or influence ⟨the weather *affected* everyone's mood⟩. The verb *effect* goes beyond mere influence; it refers to actual achievement of a final result ⟨the new adminstration hopes to *effect* a peace settlement⟩. The uncommon noun *affect,* which has a meaning relating to psychology, is also sometimes mistakenly used for the very common *effect.* In ordinary use, the noun you will want is *effect* ⟨waiting for the new law to take *effect*⟩ ⟨the weather had an *effect* on everyone's mood⟩.

[1]ef•fec•tive \i-ˈfek-tiv\ *adj* **1 a :** producing a decided, decisive, or desired effect ⟨*effective* treatment of a disease⟩ **b :** IMPRESSIVE, STRIKING ⟨an *effective* window display⟩ **2 :** ready for service or action ⟨one hundred *effective* soldiers at the fort⟩ **3 :** being in effect **:** OPERATIVE ⟨the law becomes *effective* next year⟩ **4 :** equal to the rate of simple interest paid once at the end of the interest period that yields the same amount as a given rate of compound interest over the same period ⟨an interest rate of 7 percent per year compounded daily has an *effective* rate of about 7.25 percent⟩ — **ef•fec•tive•ly** *adv* — **ef•fec•tive•ness** *n*

synonyms EFFECTIVE, EFFECTUAL, EFFICIENT, EFFICACIOUS mean producing or capable of producing a result. EFFECTIVE stresses the actual production of an effect when in use or force ⟨the law becomes *effective* immediately⟩. EFFECTUAL suggests the decisive accomplishment of a result or fulfillment of an intention ⟨*effectual* methods of pest control⟩. EFFICIENT suggests having given proof of power to produce maximum results with minimum effort ⟨an *efficient* worker⟩ ⟨an *efficient* machine⟩. EFFICACIOUS implies possession of special qualities giving effective power ⟨this fluid is *efficacious* in removing ink spots⟩.

[2]effective *n* **:** one that is effective; *esp* **:** a soldier equipped for duty

ef•fec•tor \i-ˈfek-tər\ *n* **:** a bodily part (as a gland or muscle) that becomes active in response to stimulation (as by a nerve)

ef•fec•tu•al \i-ˈfek-chə-wəl, -ˈfek-chəl, -ˈfeksh-wəl\ *adj* **:** producing or capable of producing a desired effect ⟨an *effectual* remedy⟩ ***synonyms*** see EFFECTIVE — **ef•fec•tu•al•ly** \-ē\ *adv* — **ef•fec•tu•al•ness** *n*

ef•fec•tu•ate \i-ˈfek-chə-ˌwāt\ *vt* **:** BRING ABOUT, EFFECT

ef•fem•i•na•cy \ə-ˈfem-ə-nə-sē\ *n* **:** the quality of being effeminate

ef•fem•i•nate \ə-ˈfem-ə-nət\ *adj* **1 :** having feminine qualities not typical of a man **:** not manly **2 :** marked by overrefinement and love of ease ⟨an *effeminate* civilization⟩ [Latin *effeminatus,* from *effeminare* "to make effeminate," from *ex-* + *femina* "woman"] — **ef•fem•i•nate•ly** *adv* — **ef•fem•i•nate•ness** *n*

ef•fer•ent \ˈef-ə-rənt; ˈef-ˌer-ənt, ˈē-ˌfer-\ *adj* **:** conducting outward from a part or organ; *esp* **:** conveying nerve impulses to an effector ⟨*efferent* nerve fibers⟩ — compare AFFERENT [French *efférent,* from Latin *efferre* "to carry outward," from *ex-* + *ferre* "to carry"] — **efferent** *n*

ef•fer•vesce \ˌef-ər-ˈves\ *vi* **1 :** to bubble, hiss, and foam as gas escapes ⟨ginger ale *effervesces*⟩ **2 :** to show liveliness or exhilaration ⟨*effervesced* with excitement⟩ [Latin *effervescere,* from *ex-* + *fervescere* "to begin to boil," from *fervēre* "to boil"] — **ef•fer•ves•cence** \-ˈves-nts\ *n* — **ef•fer•ves•cent** \-nt\ *adj* — **ef•fer•ves•cent•ly** *adv*

ef•fete \e-ˈfēt, i-\ *adj* **1 :** no longer productive **2 :** WORN-OUT, EXHAUSTED; *also* **:** marked by weakness or decadence ⟨an *effete* civilization⟩ [Latin *effetus,* from *ex-* + *fetus* "fruitful"] — **ef•fete•ly** *adv* — **ef•fete•ness** *n*

ef•fi•ca•cious \ˌef-ə-ˈkā-shəs\ *adj* **:** having the power to produce a desired effect ⟨an *efficacious* remedy⟩ [Latin *efficax,* from *efficere* "to bring about"] ***synonyms*** see EFFECTIVE — **ef•fi•ca•cious•ly** *adv* — **ef•fi•ca•cious•ness** *n*

ef•fi•ca•cy \ˈef-i-kə-sē\ *n, pl* **-cies :** the power to produce effects **:** EFFECTIVENESS ⟨a medicine of tested *efficacy*⟩

ef•fi•cien•cy \i-ˈfish-ən-sē\ *n, pl* **-cies** **1 :** the quality or degree of being efficient **2 a :** efficient operation **b :** effective operation as measured by a comparison of production with cost (as in energy, time, and money) **3 :** the ratio of the useful energy delivered by a dynamic system (as a machine) to the energy supplied to it

efficiency expert *n* **:** one who analyzes methods, procedures, and jobs in order to secure maximum efficiency — called also *efficiency engineer*

ef•fi•cient \i-ˈfish-ənt\ *adj* **:** capable of producing desired effects; *esp* **:** productive without waste ⟨*efficient* machinery⟩ [Latin *efficiens,* from *efficere* "to bring about"] ***synonyms*** see EFFECTIVE — **ef•fi•cient•ly** *adv*

ef•fi•gy \ˈef-ə-jē\ *n, pl* **-gies :** an image or likeness especially of a person; *esp* **:** a crude figure representing a hated person [Latin *effigies,* from *effingere* "to form," from *ex-* + *fingere* "to shape"]

ef•flo•resce \ˌef-lə-ˈres\ *vi* **1 :** to burst forth or appear as if by flowering **2 a :** to change to a powder from loss of water of crystallization ⟨a salt that *effloresces*⟩ **b :** to form or become covered with a powdery crust ⟨a brick that *effloresces*⟩ [Latin *efflorescere,* from *ex-* + *florescere* "to begin to blossom"]

ef·flo·res·cence \-ˈres-ⁿs\ *n* **1 :** the act, process, period, or result of developing or unfolding **2 :** fullness of manifestation : CULMINATION **3 :** the process or product of efflorescing chemically — **ef·flo·res·cent** \-ⁿt\ *adj*

ef·flu·ence \ˈef-ˌlü-əns; e-ˈflü-, ə-ˈ\ *n* **1 :** something that flows out **2 :** an action or process of flowing out [Latin *effluere* "to flow out," from *ex-* + *fluere* "to flow"]

ef·flu·ent \ˈef-ˌlü-ənt; e-ˈflü-, ə-ˈ\ *n* **:** EFFLUENCE 1; *esp* **:** waste material (as sewage or liquid industrial by-products) discharged into the environment — **effluent** *adj*

ef·flu·vi·um \e-ˈflü-vē-əm\ *n, pl* **-via** \-vē-ə\ *also* **-vi·ums :** an invisible emission; *esp* **:** an offensive exhalation or smell [Latin, "act of flowing out," from *effluere* "to flow out"]

ef·fort \ˈef-ərt, -ˌȯrt\ *n* **1 :** conscious exertion of power ⟨requires time and *effort*⟩ **2 :** a serious attempt : TRY ⟨made a good *effort*⟩ **3 :** something produced by work ⟨the novel was her best *effort*⟩ **4 :** the force applied to a simple machine (as a lever) in contrast to the force applied by it against a load **5 :** the total work done to achieve a particular end ⟨the war *effort*⟩ [Medieval French *esfort,* from *esforcier* "to force," from *ex-* "ex-" + *forcier* "to force"]

synonyms EFFORT, EXERTION, PAINS, TROUBLE mean the active use of energy in producing a result. EFFORT stresses the calling up or directing of energy by the conscious will and suggests a single action or attempt ⟨made an *effort* to arrive on time⟩. EXERTION suggests sustained, laborious, or exhausting effort ⟨sore from the *exertion* of moving furniture⟩. PAINS implies toilsome or solicitous effort ⟨took *pains* to ensure her guests' comfort⟩. TROUBLE suggests that the effort inconveniences one ⟨went to the *trouble* of daily visits⟩.

ef·fort·less \ˈef-ərt-ləs\ *adj* **:** showing or requiring little or no effort : EASY — **ef·fort·less·ly** *adv* — **ef·fort·less·ness** *n*

ef·fron·tery \i-ˈfrənt-ə-rē, e-\ *n, pl* **-ter·ies :** shameless boldness : NERVE ⟨had the *effrontery* to deny all guilt⟩ [French *effronterie,* derived from Late Latin *effrons* "shameless," from Latin *ex-* + *frons* "forehead"]

ef·ful·gence \i-ˈfu̇l-jəns, e-, -ˈfəl-\ *n* **:** radiant splendor : BRILLIANCE [Late Latin *effulgentia,* from Latin *effulgēre* "to shine forth," from *ex-* + *fulgēre* "to shine"] — **ef·ful·gent** \-jənt\ *adj*

¹ef·fuse \i-ˈfyüz, e-\ *vb* **1 :** to pour out (a liquid) **2 :** to flow out : EMANATE **3 :** to display great enthusiasm ⟨*effused* about his success⟩ [Latin *effusus,* past participle of *effundere* "to pour out," from *ex-* + *fundere* "to pour"]

²ef·fuse \-ˈfyüs\ *adj* **:** spread or poured out freely

ef·fu·sion \i-ˈfyü-zhən, e-\ *n* **1 :** an act of effusing **2 :** unrestrained expression of words or feelings **3 a :** escape of a fluid from containing vessels (as a blood vessel) **b :** the fluid that escapes

ef·fu·sive \i-ˈfyü-siv, e-, -ziv\ *adj* **1 :** expressing or showing great emotion or enthusiasm ⟨*effusive* thanks⟩ **2 :** characterized or formed by a nonexplosive outpouring of lava — **ef·fu·sive·ly** *adv* — **ef·fu·sive·ness** *n*

eft \ˈeft\ *n* **:** NEWT [Old English *efete*]

egad \i-ˈgad\ *interj* — used as a mild oath [probably euphemism for *oh God*]

egal·i·tar·i·an \i-ˌgal-ə-ˈter-ē-ən\ *adj* **:** asserting, promoting, or marked by egalitarianism [French *égalitaire,* from *égalité* "equality," from Latin *aequalitas,* from *aequalis* "equal"] — **egalitarian** *n*

egal·i·tar·i·an·ism \-ē-ə-ˌniz-əm\ *n* **1 :** a belief in human equality especially in social, political, and economic affairs **2 :** a social philosophy advocating the removal of social, political and economic inequalities

egest \i-ˈjest\ *vt* **:** to rid the body of (waste); *esp* **:** DEFECATE [Latin *egestus,* past participle of *egerere* "to carry outside, discharge," from *e-* + *gerere* "to carry"] — **eges·tion** \-ˈjes-chən\ *n* — **eges·tive** \-ˈjes-tiv\ *adj*

¹egg \ˈeg\ *vt* **:** to incite to action : URGE — usually used with *on* ⟨bystanders *egged* them on to fight⟩ [Old Norse *eggja*]

²egg *n* **1 a :** the hard-shelled reproductive body produced by a bird and especially by domestic poultry; *also* **:** its contents used as food **b :** an animal reproductive body consisting of an ovum with its nutritive and protective envelopes and being capable of development into a new individual **c :** OVUM **2 :** something resembling an egg **3 :** PERSON, INDIVIDUAL ⟨a good *egg*⟩ [Old Norse]

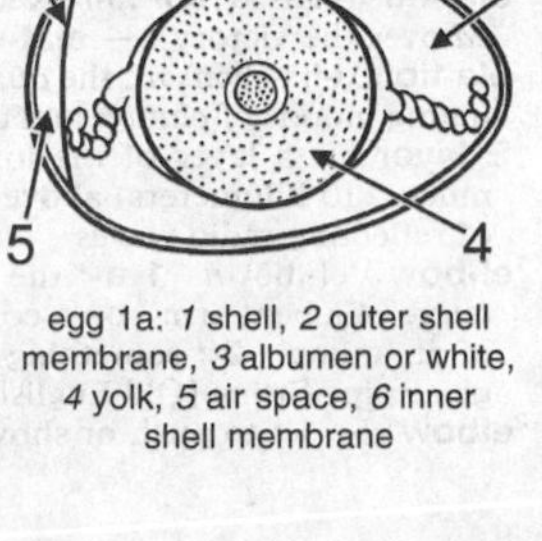

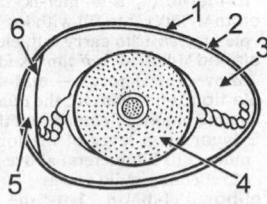

egg 1a: *1* shell, *2* outer shell membrane, *3* albumen or white, *4* yolk, *5* air space, *6* inner shell membrane

egg·beat·er \ˈeg-ˌbēt-ər\ *n* **:** a rotary beater operated by hand for beating eggs or liquids (as cream)

egg case *n* **:** a case that encloses and protects eggs (as of an insect)

egg cell *n* **:** OVUM

egg·head \ˈeg-ˌhed\ *n* **:** INTELLECTUAL, HIGHBROW

egg·nog \-ˌnäg\ *n* **:** a drink consisting of eggs beaten with sugar, milk or cream, and often alcoholic liquor

egg·plant \-ˌplant\ *n* **:** a widely cultivated perennial Asian herb that is related to the potato and yields edible fruit; *also* **:** its usually smooth and blackish purple ovoid fruit

egg roll *n* **:** a thin egg-dough casing filled with minced vegetables and often bits of meat (as shrimp or pork) and usually deep-fried

¹egg·shell \-ˌshel\ *n* **:** the hard exterior covering of an egg

²eggshell *adj* **1 :** being thin and fragile ⟨*eggshell* china⟩ **2 :** slightly glossy ⟨paint with an *eggshell* finish⟩

egg tooth *n* **:** a hard sharp prominence on the beak of an unhatched bird or the nose of an unhatched reptile that is used to break through the eggshell

eg·lan·tine \ˈeg-lən-ˌtīn, -ˌtēn\ *n* **:** SWEETBRIER [Middle French *aiglent*]

ego \ˈē-gō\ *n, pl* **egos 1 :** the self especially as contrasted with another self or the world **2 a :** EGOTISM 2 ⟨has a big *ego*⟩ **b :** SELF-ESTEEM 1 ⟨winning boosted her *ego*⟩ **3 :** the one of the three divisions of the mind in psychoanalytic theory that acts as a go-between between demands of the outside world and basic inner drives — compare ID, SUPEREGO [Latin, "I"]

ego·cen·tric \ˌē-gō-ˈsen-trik\ *adj* **:** overly concerned with the self; *esp* **:** SELF-CENTERED, SELFISH — **egocentric** *n*

ego·ism \ˈē-gə-ˌwiz-əm\ *n* **:** excessive interest in oneself **:** a self-centered attitude

ego·ist \ˈē-gə-wəst\ *n* **:** a self-centered person — **ego·is·tic** \ˌē-gə-ˈwis-tik\ *adj* — **ego·is·ti·cal·ly** \-ˈwis-ti-kə-lē, -klē\ *adv*

ego·tism \ˈē-gə-ˌtiz-əm\ *n* **1 :** too frequent reference (as by use of the word *I*) to oneself **2 :** an exaggerated sense of self-importance : CONCEIT [Latin *ego* "I" + English *-tism* (as in *idiotism* "idiocy," from *idiot* + *-ism*)]

ego·tist \ˈē-gə-təst\ *n* **:** a conceited person ***synonyms*** see EGOIST — **ego·tis·tic** \ˌē-gə-ˈtis-tik\ *or* **ego·tis·ti·cal** \-ˈtis-ti-kəl\ *adj* — **ego·tis·ti·cal·ly** \-ˈtis-ti-kə-lē, -klē\ *adv*

ego trip *n* **:** an act that satisfies one's ego

egre·gious \i-ˈgrē-jəs\ *adj* **:** very noticeable; *esp* **:** conspicuously bad : FLAGRANT ⟨*egregious* errors⟩ [Latin *egregius* "distinguished," from *e-* + *greg-, grex* "herd"] — **egre·gious·ly** *adv* — **egre·gious·ness** *n*

Word History English *egregious* comes from Latin *egregius,* which means "distinguished" or "eminent." The Latin word was derived from *e-,* "out of," and *grex* "herd, flock." An egregious person, then, has some quality that sets him or her apart from others. Originally this was a remarkably good quality that placed one above others. In 16th century English, however, *egregious* began to be used for one that was conspicuously bad. This shift to a pejorative sense may have resulted from the ironic use of the original sense. In any case, the pejorative meaning is the one that persists in common use today.

egress \ˈē-ˌgres\ *n* **1 :** the act or right of going or coming out **2 :** a place or means of going out : EXIT [Latin *egressus,* from *egredi* "to go out," from *e-* + *gradi* "to go"]

egret \ˈē-grət, i-ˈgret, ˈē-ˌgret, ˈeg-rət\ *n* **:** any of var-

egret

\ə\ **abut**	\au̇\ **out**	\i\ **tip**	\ȯ\ **saw**	\u̇\ **foot**
\ər\ **further**	\ch\ **chin**	\ī\ **life**	\ȯi\ **coin**	\y\ **yet**
\a\ **mat**	\e\ **pet**	\j\ **job**	\th\ **thin**	\yü\ **few**
\ā\ **take**	\ē\ **easy**	\ng\ **sing**	\t͟h\ **this**	\yu̇\ **cure**
\ä\ **cot, cart**	\g\ **go**	\ō\ **bone**	\ü\ **food**	\zh\ **vision**

ious herons that bear long plumes during the breeding season [Medieval French]

Egyp·tian \i-ˈjip-shən\ *n* **1 :** a native or inhabitant of Egypt **2 :** the language spoken by the ancient Egyptians from earliest times to about the 3rd century A.D. — **Egyptian** *adj*

Egyptian cotton *n* **:** a fine often somewhat brownish cotton with relatively long fibers that is grown chiefly in Egypt

Egyp·tol·o·gy \ˌē-jip-ˈtäl-ə-jē\ *n* **:** the study of Egyptian antiquities — **Egyp·tol·o·gist** \-jəst\ *n*

eh \ˈā, ˈe, ˈa, *also with* h *preceding and/or with nasalization*\ *interj* — used to ask for confirmation or to express inquiry [Middle English *ey*]

ei·der \ˈī-dər\ *n* **1 :** any of several large northern sea ducks having fine soft down that is used by the female for lining the nest — called also *eider duck* **2 :** EIDERDOWN 1 [derived from Icelandic *æthur*]

ei·der·down \-ˌdau̇n\ *n* **1 :** the down of the eider **2 :** a comforter filled with eiderdown

ei·det·ic \ī-ˈdet-ik\ *adj* **:** marked by or involving peculiarly vivid recall especially of visual images ⟨an *eidetic* memory⟩ [Greek *eidētikos* "of a form," from *eidos* "form"]

eight \ˈāt\ *n* **1** — see NUMBER table **2 :** the eighth in a set or series **3 :** something having eight units or members: as **a :** an 8-oared racing boat or crew **b :** an 8-cylinder engine or automobile [Old English *eahta*] — **eight** *adj or pron*

eight ball *n* **1 :** a black pool ball numbered 8 **2 :** MISFIT — **behind the eight ball :** in a highly disadvantageous position

eigh·teen \ā-ˈtēn, āt-, ˈā-, ˈāt-\ *n* — see NUMBER table [Old English *eahtatīene*] — **eighteen** *adj or pron* — **eigh·teenth** \-ˈtēnth, -ˈtēntth\ *adj or n*

eighth \ˈātth\ *n, pl* **eighths** \ˈāts, ˈātths\ **:** number eight in a countable series — see NUMBER table — **eighth** *adj or adv*

eighth note *n* **:** a musical note with the time value of 1/8 of a whole note

eighth rest *n* **:** a musical rest equal in time value to an eighth note

eighty \ˈāt-ē\ *n, pl* **eight·ies** — see NUMBER table [Old English *eahtatig*] — **eighty** *adj or pron* — **eight·i·eth** \ˈāt-ē-əth\ *adj or n*

ein·stei·ni·um \īn-ˈstī-nē-əm\ *n* **:** a radioactive element produced artificially — see ELEMENT table [New Latin, from Albert *Einstein*]

1ei·ther \ˈē-t͟hər *also* ˈī-\ *adj* **1 :** being the one and the other of two **:** EACH ⟨flowers blooming on *either* side of the walk⟩ **2 :** being the one or the other of two ⟨take *either* road⟩ [Old English *ǣghwæther* "both, each"]

2either *pron* **:** the one or the other ⟨tell *either* of my sisters⟩

3either *conj* — used before the first of two or more words or word groups of which the last is preceded by *or* to indicate that they represent alternatives ⟨a statement is *either* true or false⟩

4either *adv* **1 :** LIKEWISE 2, MOREOVER — used for emphasis after a negative ⟨not wise or handsome *either*⟩ **2 :** as far as that is concerned — used for emphasis after an alternative following a question or conditional clause especially where negation is implied ⟨if their father had come or their mother *either* all would have gone well⟩

ejac·u·late \i-ˈjak-yə-ˌlāt\ *vb* **1 :** to eject a fluid and especially semen **2 :** to utter suddenly and vigorously [Latin *ejaculari* "to throw out," from *e-* + *jaculari* "to throw," from *jaculum* "dart," from *jacere* "to throw"] — **ejac·u·la·to·ry** \-yə-lə-ˌtōr-ē, -ˌtȯr-\ *adj*

ejac·u·la·tion \i-ˌjak-yə-ˈlā-shən\ *n* **1 :** an act or process of ejaculating; *esp* **:** a sudden discharging of a fluid from a duct **2 :** something ejaculated; *esp* **:** a short sudden emotional utterance (as an exclamation)

eject \i-ˈjekt\ *vt* **1 a :** to throw out especially by physical force or authority ⟨*ejected* from the club⟩ **b :** to evict from property **2 :** to throw out or off from within ⟨*ejects* the cassette⟩ [Latin *ejectus*, past participle of *eicere* "to eject," from *e-* + *jacere* "to throw"] — **ejec·tion** \-ˈjek-shən\ *n* — **ejec·tor** \-ˈjek-tər\ *n*

synonyms EJECT, EXPEL, EVICT, OUST mean to drive or force out. EJECT carries a strong implication of throwing or thrusting out from within as a physical action ⟨hot lava *ejected* from a volcano⟩. EXPEL stresses a thrusting out or driving away especially permanently ⟨*expelled* from school⟩. EVICT chiefly applies to turning out of house and home ⟨*evicted* for nonpayment of rent⟩. OUST implies removal or dispossession by power of the law or by compulsion of necessity ⟨got the sheriff to *oust* the squatters⟩.

ejection seat *n* **:** an emergency escape seat for propelling an occupant out and away from an airplane by means of an explosive charge

eke out \ˈēk-\ *vt* **1 a :** SUPPLEMENT ⟨*eked out* a small income by getting a second job⟩ **b :** to make (a supply) last by careful use **2 :** to get with great difficulty ⟨*eke out* a living⟩ [Old English *īecan, ēcan* "to increase, lengthen"]

el \ˈel\ *n, often cap* **:** a city railroad operating chiefly on elevated tracks

1elab·o·rate \i-ˈlab-rət, -ə-rət\ *adj* **1 :** planned or carried out with great care ⟨*elaborate* preparations⟩ **2 :** marked by complexity, fullness of detail, or ornateness ⟨an *elaborate* design⟩ [Latin *elaboratus*, from *elaborare* "to work out," from *e-* + *laborare* "to work"] — **elab·o·rate·ly** *adv* — **elab·o·rate·ness** *n*

2elab·o·rate \i-ˈlab-ə-ˌrāt\ *vb* **1 :** to build up (complex organic compounds) from simple ingredients ⟨a substance *elaborated* by a gland⟩ **2 :** to work out in detail **:** DEVELOP ⟨*elaborate* an idea⟩ **3 :** to expand something in detail ⟨*elaborate* on a story⟩ — **elab·o·ra·tion** \-ˌlab-ə-ˈrā-shən\ *n* — **elab·o·ra·tive** \-ˈlab-ə-ˌrāt-iv\ *adj*

élan \ā-ˈlä^{n}\ *n* **:** vigorous spirit or enthusiasm [French]

eland \ˈē-lənd\ *n* **:** either of two large African antelopes resembling oxen and having short spirally twisted horns in both sexes [Afrikaans, from Dutch, "elk"]

elapse \i-ˈlaps\ *vi* **:** to slip or glide away **:** PASS ⟨years *elapsed*⟩ [Latin *elapsus*, past participle of *elabi* "to slip by," from *e-* + *labi* "to slip"]

elas·mo·branch \i-ˈlaz-mə-ˌbrangk\ *n, pl* **-branchs :** any of a class (Chondrichthyes) of fishes (as a shark or ray) with skeletons of cartilage and with platelike gills [Greek *elasmos* "metal plate" + Latin *branchia* "gill"] — **elasmobranch** *adj*

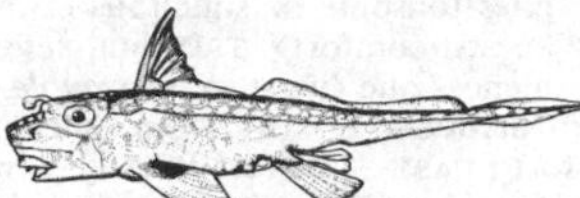
elasmobranch

1elas·tic \i-ˈlas-tik\ *adj* **1 a :** capable of recovering shape or size after being stretched, pressed, or squeezed together **:** SPRINGY ⟨sponges are *elastic*⟩ **b :** capable of indefinite expansion — used of a gas **2 :** able to recover quickly especially from depression or fatigue ⟨a youthful, *elastic* spirit⟩ **3 :** FLEXIBLE, ADAPTABLE ⟨a plan *elastic* enough to be changed at any time⟩ [Late Greek *elastos* "ductile, beaten," from Greek *elaunein* "to beat out"] — **elas·ti·cal·ly** \-ti-kə-lē, -klē\ *adv*

synonyms ELASTIC, RESILIENT, BUOYANT mean quick to recover from depression or a setback. ELASTIC may indicate an ability to recover quickly from discouragement or dejection ⟨an *elastic* power of forgetting bad times⟩. RESILIENT may stress speed of return to usual good or high spirits after strain or setback ⟨the *resilient* energy of the storm-wracked villagers⟩. BUOYANT may stress a lightness of spirit incapable of lasting dejection ⟨a team *buoyant* despite the loss⟩.

2elastic *n* **1 :** easily stretched rubber; *esp* **:** RUBBER BAND **2 a :** an elastic fabric usually made of yarns containing rubber **b :** something made from elastic fabric

elas·tic·i·ty \i-ˌlas-ˈtis-ət-ē, ˌē-ˌlas-\ *n, pl* **-ties :** the quality or state of being elastic **:** RESILIENCE, ADAPTABILITY

elas·ti·cized \i-ˈlas-tə-ˌsīzd\ *adj* **:** made with elastic thread or inserts

elas·tin \i-ˈlas-tən\ *n* **:** a protein that is similar to collagen and is the chief constituent of the elastic fibers of connective tissue

elas·to·mer \i-ˈlas-tə-mər\ *n* **:** any of various elastic substances resembling rubber [*elastic* + *-o-* + Greek *meros* "part"] — **elas·to·mer·ic** \i-ˌlas-tə-ˈmer-ik\ *adj*

elate \i-ˈlāt\ *vt* **:** to fill with joy or pride [Latin *elatus*, past participle of *efferre* "to carry out, elevate," from *ex-* + *ferre* "to carry"]

elat·ed \i-ˈlāt-əd\ *adj* **:** marked by high spirits **:** EXULTANT ⟨*elated* over the victory⟩ — **elat·ed·ly** *adv* — **elat·ed·ness** *n*

ela·tion \i-ˈlā-shən\ *n* **:** the quality or state of being elated ⟨alternating moods of *elation* and despair⟩

E layer *n* **:** a layer of the ionosphere that occurs at about 65 miles (110 kilometers) above the earth's surface and is capable of reflecting radio waves

1el·bow \ˈel-ˌbō\ *n* **1 a :** the joint of the arm; *also* **:** the outer curve of a bent arm **b :** a corresponding joint in the front limb of an animal **2 :** something resembling an elbow; *esp* **:** an angular pipe fitting [Old English *elboga*]

2elbow *vb* **1 :** to push or shove with the elbow **:** JOSTLE **2 :** to

force or advance by or as if by pushing with the elbow ⟨*elbowed* their way through the crowd⟩
elbow grease *n* : physical effort : hard work
el·bow·room \-ˌrüm, -ˌru̇m\ *n* **1** : room for moving the elbows freely **2** : enough space for work or operation
eld \ˈeld\ *n* **1** : old age **2** *archaic* : ancient times : ANTIQUITY [Old English *ieldo*]
[1]**el·der** \ˈel-dər\ *n* : any of a genus of shrubs or trees related to the honeysuckles with flat clusters of small white or pink flowers and black or red drupes resembling berries [Old English *ellærn*]
[2]**elder** *adj* : of earlier birth or greater age : OLDER [Old English *ieldra,* comparative of *eald* "old"]
[3]**elder** *n* **1** : one who is older : SENIOR **2** : a person having authority by virtue of age and experience ⟨the village *elders*⟩ **3** : any of various church officers — **el·der·ship** \-ˌship\ *n*
el·der·ber·ry \ˈel-dər-ˌber-ē, -də-\ *n* **1** : the edible fruit of an elder **2** : [1]ELDER
el·der·ly \ˈel-dər-lē\ *adj* **1** : rather old; *esp* : past middle age **2** : of, relating to, or characteristic of later life or elderly persons ⟨*elderly* pursuits⟩ — **el·der·li·ness** *n*
elder statesman *n* : a prominent senior member of a group or organization; *esp* : a retired statesman who unofficially advises current leaders
el·dest \ˈel-dəst\ *adj* : OLDEST
El Dorado \ˌel-də-ˈräd-ō, -ˈrād-\ *n* **1** : a city or country of fabulous riches held by 16th century explorers to exist in South America **2** : a place of great wealth, abundance, or opportunity [Spanish, literally, "the gilded one"]
ele·cam·pane \ˌel-i-ˌkam-ˈpān\ *n* : a coarse yellow-flowered composite herb of Eurasia naturalized in the United States [Medieval Latin *enula campana,* literally, "field elecampane"]
[1]**elect** \i-ˈlekt\ *adj* **1** : carefully selected : CHOSEN **2** : chosen for salvation through divine mercy **3** : chosen for office or position but not yet installed ⟨president-*elect*⟩ [Latin *electus,* from *eligere* "to select," from *e-* + *legere* "to choose"]
[2]**elect** *n pl* : a carefully chosen group — usually used with *the*
[3]**elect** *vb* **1** : to select usually by vote for an office, position, or membership **2** : to choose especially by preference
elec·tion \i-ˈlek-shən\ *n* **1 a** : an act or process of electing; *esp* : the process of voting to choose a person for office **b** : the fact of being elected **2** : predestination to salvation **3** : the power or privilege of making a choice
elec·tion·eer \i-ˌlek-shə-ˈniər\ *vi* : to work for the election of a candidate or party
[1]**elec·tive** \i-ˈlek-tiv\ *adj* **1** : chosen by election ⟨an *elective* official⟩ **2** : of, relating to, or based on elections ⟨an *elective* government⟩ **3** : filled by a person who is elected ⟨the presidency is an *elective* office⟩ **4** : followed or taken by choice : not required ⟨an *elective* course in school⟩ — **elec·tive·ly** *adv* — **elec·tive·ness** *n*
[2]**elective** *n* : an elective course or subject in school
elec·tor \i-ˈlek-tər, -ˌtȯr\ *n* **1** : one qualified to vote in an election **2 a** : one of the German princes entitled to take part in choosing the Holy Roman emperor **b** : a member of the electoral college in the United States
elec·tor·al \i-ˈlek-tə-rəl, -trəl\ *adj* : of or relating to an election or electors
electoral college *n* : a body of electors; *esp* : one that elects the president and vice president of the United States
elec·tor·ate \i-ˈlek-tə-rət, -trət\ *n* : a body of people entitled to vote
electr- *or* **electro-** *combining form* **1 a** : electricity ⟨*electro*meter⟩ **b** : electric ⟨*electr*ode⟩ **c** : electric and ⟨*electro*chemical⟩ **2** : electron ⟨*electro*valence⟩
[1]**elec·tric** \i-ˈlek-trik\ *adj* **1** *or* **elec·tri·cal** \-tri-kəl\ : of, relating to, operated by, or produced by electricity ⟨an *electric* current⟩ **2** : EXCITING, THRILLING ⟨an *electric* performance⟩ [New Latin *electricus* "produced from amber by friction, electric," from Latin *electrum* "amber," from Greek *ēlektron*] — **elec·tri·cal·ly** \-tri-kə-lē, -klē\ *adv*

Word History We think of electricity as a modern discovery, but some electrical phenomena have been known since ancient times. Philosophers of ancient Greece found that, by rubbing amber with a piece of cloth, they could enable the amber to pick up light objects, such as feathers. In the 17th century, students of natural science began to discover that other natural phenomena were related to the effect of friction on amber. The word *electric,* used to refer to such phenomena, is derived from the Greek word for amber, *ēlektron.*

[2]**electric** *n* : something (as a light, automobile, or train) operated by electricity
electrical engineering *n* : engineering that deals with the practical applications of electricity — **electrical engineer** *n*
electrical storm *n* : THUNDERSTORM — called also *electric storm*
electric chair *n* **1** : a chair used in legal electrocution **2** : the penalty of death by electrocution
electric eel *n* : a large South American eel-shaped fish able to give a severe electric shock

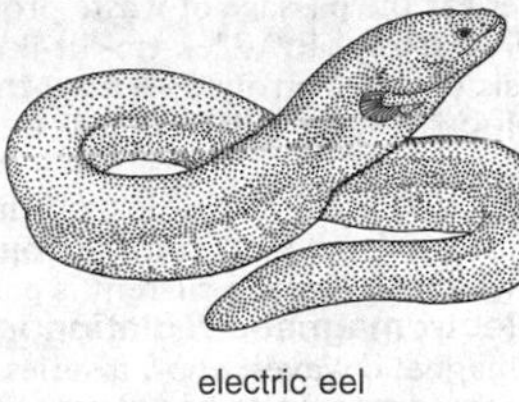
electric eel

electric eye *n* : PHOTOELECTRIC CELL
electric field *n* : a region associated with a distribution of electric charge or a varying magnetic field in which forces due to that charge or field act upon other electric charges
elec·tri·cian \i-ˌlek-ˈtrish-ən\ *n* : a person who installs, operates, or repairs electrical equipment
elec·tric·i·ty \i-ˌlek-ˈtris-ət-ē, -ˈtris-tē\ *n* **1 a** : a fundamental phenomenon of nature consisting of negative and positive kinds composed respectively of electrons and protons, observable in the attractions and repulsions of bodies electrified by friction and in natural phenomena (as lightning), and usually utilized as a source of energy in the form of electric currents **b** : electric current **2** : a science that deals with the phenomena and laws of electricity **3** : a feeling of excitement or tension
electric ray *n* : any of various round-bodied short-tailed rays of warm seas able to give a severe electric shock
elec·tri·fy \i-ˈlek-trə-ˌfī\ *vt* **-fied; -fy·ing** **1 a** : to charge with electricity **b** (1) : to equip for use of electric power (2) : to supply with electric power **2** : to excite intensely or suddenly : THRILL — **elec·tri·fi·ca·tion** \i-ˌlek-trə-fə-ˈkā-shən\ *n*
elec·tro·car·dio·gram \i-ˌlek-trō-ˈkärd-ē-ə-ˌgram\ *n* : the tracing made by an electrocardiograph; *also* : the procedure for producing such a tracing
elec·tro·car·dio·graph \-ˌgraf\ *n* : an instrument for recording the changes of electrical potential occurring during the heartbeat — **elec·tro·car·dio·graph·ic** \-ˌkärd-ē-ə-ˈgraf-ik\ *adj* — **elec·tro·car·dio·graph·i·cal·ly** \-ˈgraf-i-kə-lē, -klē\ *adv* — **elec·tro·car·di·og·ra·phy** \-ē-ˈäg-rə-fē\ *n*
elec·tro·chem·is·try \i-ˌlek-trō-ˈkem-ə-strē\ *n* : a science that deals with the relation of electricity to chemical changes and with the mutual conversion of chemical and electrical energy — **elec·tro·chem·i·cal** \-ˈkem-i-kəl\ *adj* — **elec·tro·chem·i·cal·ly** \-i-kə-lē, -klē\ *adv* — **elec·tro·chem·ist** \-ist\ *n*
elec·tro·con·vul·sive therapy \i-ˌlek-trō-kən-ˈvəl-siv-\ *n* : ELECTROSHOCK THERAPY
elec·tro·cute \i-ˈlek-trə-ˌkyüt\ *vt* : to kill by electric shock; *esp* : to execute (a criminal) in this way [*electr-* + *-cute* (as in *execute*)] — **elec·tro·cu·tion** \i-ˌlek-trə-ˈkyü-shən\ *n*
elec·trode \i-ˈlek-ˌtrōd\ *n* : a conductor (as a metal or carbon) used to establish electrical contact with a nonmetallic part of a circuit (as in a storage battery, electron tube, or arc lamp)
elec·tro·de·pos·it \i-ˌlek-trō-di-ˈpäz-ət\ *vt* : to deposit (as metal or rubber) by electrolysis — **elec·tro·dep·o·si·tion** \-ˌdep-ə-ˈzish-ən, -ˌdē-pə-\ *n*
elec·tro·dy·nam·ics \-dī-ˈnam-iks\ *n* : physics that deals with the effects arising from the interactions of electric currents with magnets, with other currents, or with themselves — **elec·tro·dy·nam·ic** \-ik\ *adj*
elec·tro·en·ceph·a·lo·gram \-en-ˈsef-ə-lō-ˌgram\ *n* : the tracing of brain waves that is made by an electroencephalograph
elec·tro·en·ceph·a·lo·graph \-ˌgraf\ *n* : an apparatus for detecting and recording brain waves — **elec·tro·en·ceph·a·lo·graph·ic** \-en-ˌsef-ə-lō-ˈgraf-ik\ *adj* — **elec·tro·en·ceph·a·log·ra·phy** \-ˌsef-ə-ˈläg-rə-fē\ *n*
elec·trol·y·sis \i-ˌlek-ˈträl-ə-səs\ *n* **1 a** : the producing of chemical changes by passage of an electric current through an electrolyte with the ions carrying the current by migrating to

the electrodes where they may form new substances that are given off as gases or deposited as solids **b :** subjection to this action **2 :** the destruction of hair roots with an electric current

elec•tro•lyte \i-ˈlek-trə-ˌlīt\ *n* **1 :** a nonmetallic electric conductor in which current is carried by the movement of ions **2 a :** a substance that when dissolved in a suitable solvent or when fused becomes an ionic conductor **b :** any of the ions (as of sodium or calcium) that regulate or affect metabolic processes (as the passage of waste products out of a cell)

elec•tro•lyt•ic \i-ˌlek-trə-ˈlit-ik\ *adj* **:** of or relating to electrolysis or an electrolyte — **elec•tro•lyt•i•cal•ly** \-i-kə-lē, -klē\ *adv*

elec•tro•lyze \i-ˈlek-trə-ˌlīz\ *vt* **:** to subject to chemical electrolysis

elec•tro•mag•net \i-ˌlek-trō-ˈmag-nət\ *n* **:** a core of magnetic material (as soft iron) surrounded by a coil of wire through which an electric current is passed to magnetize the core

electromagnetic radiation *n* **:** energy in the form of electromagnetic waves; *also* **:** a series of electromagnetic waves

electromagnetic spectrum *n* **:** the entire range of wavelengths or frequencies of electromagnetic waves extending from gamma rays to the longest radio waves and including visible light

electromagnetic wave *n* **:** a wave (as a radio wave, infrared wave, wave of visible light, or X-ray) that travels at the speed of light and that consists of an associated magnetic and electric effect

elec•tro•mag•ne•tism \i-ˌlek-trō-ˈmag-nə-ˌtiz-əm\ *n* **1 :** magnetism developed by a current of electricity **2 a :** a fundamental force in nature responsible for interactions between charged particles which result from their charge **b :** physical science that deals with the physical relations between electricity and magnetism — **elec•tro•mag•net•ic** \-mag-ˈnet-ik\ *adj* — **elec•tro•mag•net•i•cal•ly** \-ˈnet-i-kə-lē, -klē\ *adv*

elec•tro•me•chan•i•cal \i-ˌlek-trō-mə-ˈkan-i-kəl\ *adj* **:** of, relating to, or being a mechanical process or device put into motion or controlled electrically

elec•trom•e•ter \i-ˌlek-ˈträm-ət-ər\ *n* **:** an instrument for detecting or measuring potential differences or ionizing radiations

elec•tro•mo•tive force \i-ˌlek-trə-ˈmōt-iv-\ *n* **:** the work per unit charge required to carry a positive charge around a closed path (as a complete circuit) in an electric field — abbreviation *emf*

elec•tron \i-ˈlek-ˌträn\ *n* **:** a negatively charged elementary particle that travels around the nucleus of an atom and that is of the kind of particle that makes up an electric current

elec•tro•neg•a•tive \i-ˌlek-trō-ˈneg-ət-iv\ *adj* **1 :** charged with negative electricity **2 :** capable of acting as the negative electrode of a voltaic cell **3 :** having a tendency to attract electrons — **elec•tro•neg•a•tiv•i•ty** \-ˌneg-ə-ˈtiv-ət-ē\ *n*

electron gun *n* **:** the part of a cathode-ray tube that produces, accelerates, and focuses a stream of electrons

elec•tron•ic \i-ˌlek-ˈträn-ik\ *adj* **1 :** of or relating to electrons **2 a :** of, relating to, or utilizing devices constructed or working by principles of electronics **b :** involving or done on or by a computer ⟨*electronic* banking⟩ — **elec•tron•i•cal•ly** \-ˈträn-i-kə-lē, -klē\ *adv*

electronic mail *n* **:** E-MAIL

elec•tron•ics \-ˈträn-iks\ *n* **1 :** a branch of physics that deals with the emission, behavior, and effects of electrons (as in electron tubes and transistors) and with electronic devices **2 :** electronic circuits, devices, or equipment

electron micrograph *n* **:** a micrograph made with an electron microscope

electron microscope *n* **:** an instrument in which a beam of electrons is used to produce an enlarged image of a tiny object

electron tube *n* **:** a device in which a controlled electron current flows through a vacuum or a gas within a sealed glass or metal container and which has various common uses (as in radio and television)

electron volt *n* **:** a unit of energy equal to the energy gained by an electron in passing from a point of low potential to a point one volt higher in potential that is equivalent to 1.60×10^{-19} joule

elec•tro•pho•re•sis \i-ˌlek-trə-fə-ˈrē-səs\ *n* **:** the movement of suspended particles through a fluid under the action of an electromotive force applied to electrodes in contact with the suspension [Greek *phorein* "to carry"] — **elec•tro•pho•ret•ic** \-ˈret-ik\ *adj*

elec•tro•plate \i-ˈlek-trə-ˌplāt\ *vt* **:** to cover with a coating (as of metal or rubber) by means of electrolysis

elec•tro•pos•i•tive \i-ˌlek-trō-ˈpäz-ət-iv, -ˈpäz-tiv\ *adj* **1 a :** charged with positive electricity **b :** capable of acting as the positive electrode of a voltaic cell **2 :** having a tendency to release electrons ⟨an *electropositive* atom⟩

elec•tro•scope \i-ˈlek-trə-ˌskōp\ *n* **:** any of various instruments for detecting the presence of an electric charge on a body, for determining whether the charge is positive or negative, or for indicating and measuring intensity of radiation

elec•tro•shock therapy \-ˌshäk-\ *n* **:** the treatment of mental disorder by the induction of unconsciousness and convulsive seizures in the brain with an electric current applied to the head — called also *electroconvulsive therapy, electroshock*

elec•tro•stat•ic \i-ˌlek-trə-ˈstat-ik\ *adj* **:** of or relating to static electricity or electrostatics — **elec•tro•stat•i•cal•ly** \-ˈstat-i-kə-lē, -klē\ *adv*

electrostatic generator *n* **:** VAN DE GRAAFF GENERATOR

electrostatic precipitator *n* **:** an electrostatic device in a chimney flue that removes particles from escaping gases

elec•tro•stat•ics \i-ˌlek-trə-ˈstat-iks\ *n* **:** physics that deals with phenomena due to attractions or repulsions of electric charges but not dependent upon their motion

elec•tro•ther•mal \-ˈthər-məl\ *or* **elec•tro•ther•mic** \-mik\ *adj* **:** relating to the generation of heat by electricity

elec•tro•type \i-ˈlek-trə-ˌtīp\ *n* **:** a plate for use in printing made by electroplating — **elec•tro•typ•er** \-ˌtī-pər\ *n*

elec•tro•va•lence \i-ˌlek-trō-ˈvā-ləns\ *or* **elec•tro•va•len•cy** \-lən-sē\ *n* **:** valence characterized by the transfer of electrons from one atom to another with the formation of ions; *also* **:** the number of charges acquired by an atom by the loss or gain of electrons — **elec•tro•va•lent** \-lənt\ *adj*

elec•tro•weak \i-ˈlek-trō-ˌwēk\ *adj* **:** relating to or being a combination of electromagnetism and the weak force

elec•trum \i-ˈlek-trəm\ *n* **:** a naturally occurring pale yellow alloy of gold and silver [Latin, "amber, electrum," from Greek *ēlektron*]

elec•tu•ary \i-ˈlek-chə-ˌwer-ē\ *n, pl* **-ar•ies :** a medicinal preparation made with honey or syrup [Latin *electuarium*]

el•ee•mos•y•nary \ˌel-i-ˈmäs-n-ˌer-ē, -ˈmäz-\ *adj* **:** of, relating to, or supported by charity [Late Latin *eleemosyna* "alms," from Greek *eleēmosynē* "pity, alms," from *eleēmōn* "merciful," from *eleos* "pity"]

el•e•gance \ˈel-i-gəns\ *n* **1 :** refined gracefulness **2 :** tasteful richness of design or decoration

el•e•gan•cy \-gən-sē\ *n, pl* **-cies :** ELEGANCE

el•e•gant \ˈel-i-gənt\ *adj* **1 :** marked by elegance ⟨*elegant* clothes⟩ **2 :** EXCELLENT, FIRST-RATE ⟨*elegant* gems⟩ [Latin *elegans*] — **el•e•gant•ly** *adv*

el•e•gy \ˈel-ə-jē\ *n, pl* **-gies :** a poem or song expressing sorrow especially for one who is dead [Latin *elegia,* from Greek *elegeia,* from *elegos* "song of mourning"] — **el•e•gi•ac** \ˌel-ə-ˈjī-ək, i-ˈlē-jē-ˌak\ *adj* — **el•e•gize** \ˈel-ə-ˌjīz\ *vb*

el•e•ment \ˈel-ə-mənt\ *n* **1 a :** one of the four substances air, water, fire, or earth formerly believed to compose the physical universe **b** *pl* **:** forces of nature; *esp* **:** stormy or cold weather **c :** the state or sphere natural or suited to a person or thing ⟨in her *element* at school⟩ **2 :** a constituent part: as **a** *pl* **:** the simplest principles of a subject of study **:** RUDIMENTS **b (1) :** a point, line, or surface whose motion traces out a geometric figure **(2) :** one of the basic individual things that belong to a mathematical set **(3) :** one of the numbers or expressions that make up a matrix or determinant **c :** any of more than 100 fundamental substances that consist of atoms of only one kind ⟨gold and carbon are *elements*⟩ **d :** a distinct part of a composite device **e :** a subdivision of a military unit **3** *pl* **:** the bread and wine used in the sacrament of Communion [Latin *elementum*]

synonyms ELEMENT, COMPONENT, CONSTITUENT, INGREDIENT mean one of the parts of a compound or complex whole. ELEMENT applies to any such part and often connotes irreducible simplicity ⟨the basic *elements* of geometry⟩. COMPONENT and CONSTITUENT may designate any of the substances or qualities that enter into the makeup of a complex product; COMPONENT stresses its separate entity ⟨the *components* of a stereo system⟩ while CONSTITUENT stresses its essential or formative character ⟨the *constituents* of a chemical compound⟩. INGREDIENT applies to any substance that combines with others to form something else ⟨*ingredients* of a sauce⟩.

el•e•men•tal \ˌel-ə-ˈment-l\ *adj* **1 a :** of, relating to, or being an element; *esp* **:** existing as an uncombined chemical element **b**

CHEMICAL ELEMENTS

ELEMENT	SYMBOL	ATOMIC NUMBER	ATOMIC WEIGHT[1]
actinium	Ac	89	227.0277
aluminum	Al	13	26.98154
americium	Am	95	(243)
antimony	Sb	51	121.760
argon	Ar	18	39.948
arsenic	As	33	74.92160
astatine	At	85	(210)
barium	Ba	56	137.33
berkelium	Bk	97	(247)
beryllium	Be	4	9.012182
bismuth	Bi	83	208.98038
bohrium	Bh	107	(264)
boron	B	5	10.81
bromine	Br	35	79.904
cadmium	Cd	48	112.41
calcium	Ca	20	40.078
californium	Cf	98	(251)
carbon	C	6	12.011
cerium	Ce	58	140.116
cesium	Cs	55	132.90545
chlorine	Cl	17	35.453
chromium	Cr	24	51.996
cobalt	Co	27	58.93320
copernicium	Cn	112	(285)
copper	Cu	29	63.546
curium	Cm	96	(247)
darmstadtium	Ds	110	(269)
dubnium	Db	105	(262)
dysprosium	Dy	66	162.50
einsteinium	Es	99	(252)
erbium	Er	68	167.259
europium	Eu	63	151.964
fermium	Fm	100	(257)
fluorine	F	9	18.998403
francium	Fr	87	(223)
gadolinium	Gd	64	157.25
gallium	Ga	31	69.723
germanium	Ge	32	72.64
gold	Au	79	196.96655
hafnium	Hf	72	178.49
hassium	Hs	108	(277)
helium	He	2	4.002602
holmium	Ho	67	164.93032
hydrogen	H	1	1.0079
indium	In	49	114.818
iodine	I	53	126.90447
iridium	Ir	77	192.217
iron	Fe	26	55.845
krypton	Kr	36	83.80
lanthanum	La	57	138.9055
lawrencium	Lr	103	(262)
lead	Pb	82	207.2
lithium	Li	3	6.941
lutetium	Lu	71	174.967
magnesium	Mg	12	24.305
manganese	Mn	25	54.93805
meitnerium	Mt	109	(268)
mendelevium	Md	101	(258)
mercury	Hg	80	200.59
molybdenum	Mo	42	95.94
neodymium	Nd	60	144.24
neon	Ne	10	20.180
neptunium	Np	93	(237)
nickel	Ni	28	58.6934
niobium	Nb	41	92.90638
nitrogen	N	7	14.0067
nobelium	No	102	(259)
osmium	Os	76	190.23
oxygen	O	8	15.9994
palladium	Pd	46	106.42
phosphorus	P	15	30.973761
platinum	Pt	78	195.078
plutonium	Pu	94	(244)
polonium	Po	84	(209)
potassium	K	19	39.0983
praseodymium	Pr	59	140.90765
promethium	Pm	61	(145)
protactinium	Pa	91	(231)
radium	Ra	88	(226)
radon	Rn	86	(222)
rhenium	Re	75	186.207
rhodium	Rh	45	102.90550
roentgenium	Rg	111	(280)
rubidium	Rb	37	85.4678
ruthenium	Ru	44	101.07
rutherfordium	Rf	104	(261)
samarium	Sm	62	150.36
scandium	Sc	21	44.95591
seaborgium	Sg	106	(266)
selenium	Se	34	78.96
silicon	Si	14	28.0855
silver	Ag	47	107.8682
sodium	Na	11	22.989770
strontium	Sr	38	87.62
sulfur	S	16	32.07
tantalum	Ta	73	180.9479
technetium	Tc	43	(98)
tellurium	Te	52	127.60
terbium	Tb	65	158.92534
thallium	Tl	81	204.3833
thorium	Th	90	232.0381
thulium	Tm	69	168.93421
tin	Sn	50	118.71
titanium	Ti	22	47.867
tungsten	W	74	183.84
uranium	U	92	(238)
vanadium	V	23	50.9415
xenon	Xe	54	131.29
ytterbium	Yb	70	173.04
yttrium	Y	39	88.90585
zinc	Zn	30	65.39
zirconium	Zr	40	91.224

[1]Weights are based on the naturally occurring isotope compositions and scaled to $^{12}C = 12$. For elements lacking stable isotopes, the mass number of the most stable nuclide is shown in parentheses.

: of, relating to, or being a basic or essential part : FUNDAMENTAL **c :** ELEMENTARY 1a **d :** forming an integral part : INHERENT **2 :** of, relating to, or resembling a great force of nature — **el·e·men·tal·ly** \-l-ē\ *adv*

el·e·men·ta·ry \ˌel-ə-ˈment-ə-rē, -ˈmen-trē\ *adj* **1 a :** of or relating to the simplest principles of something (as a subject) **b :** of or relating to an elementary school **2 :** ELEMENTAL 1a

elementary particle *n* **:** any of the ultimate constituents (as the electron, proton, or neutron) of matter

elementary school *n* **:** a school usually including the first six or sometimes the first four or eight grades

el·e·phant \ˈel-ə-fənt\ *n* **:** any of a family of huge thickset nearly hairless mammals having the snout prolonged as a trunk and two incisors in the upper jaw developed into long outward-curving pointed ivory tusks and including two living forms: **a :** one with large ears that occurs in tropical Africa **b :** one with relatively small ears that occurs in forests of southeastern Asia [Latin *elephantus,* from Greek *elephas*]

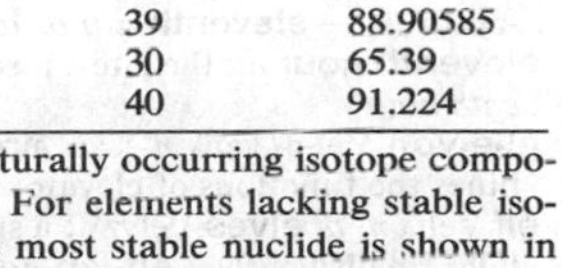

elephant: *left* African, *right* Asian

elephant bird *n* **:** a huge extinct flightless bird of Madagascar

\ə\ **abut**	\au̇\ **out**	\i\ **tip**	\ȯ\ **saw**	\u̇\ **foot**
\ər\ **further**	\ch\ **chin**	\ī\ **life**	\ȯi\ **coin**	\y\ **yet**
\a\ **mat**	\e\ **pet**	\j\ **job**	\th\ **thin**	\yü\ **few**
\ā\ **take**	\ē\ **easy**	\ng\ **sing**	\th\ **this**	\yu̇\ **cure**
\ä\ **cot, cart**	\g\ **go**	\ō\ **bone**	\ü\ **food**	\zh\ **vision**

elephant grass *n* : an Old World cattail used especially in making baskets

el·e·phan·ti·a·sis \ˌel-ə-fən-ˈtī-ə-səs, -ˌfan-\ *n, pl* **-a·ses** \-ə-ˌsēz\ : extreme enlargement and thickening of tissues of a limb or the scrotum caused by obstruction by filarial worms of vessels that carry lymph [Latin, a kind of leprosy, from Greek, from *elephas* "elephant"]

el·e·phan·tine \ˌel-ə-ˈfan-ˌtēn, -ˌtīn, ˈel-ə-fən-\ *adj* **1 a** : IMMENSE, HUGE ⟨an *elephantine* task⟩ **b** : lacking grace or ease : CLUMSY **2** : of or relating to an elephant

el·e·vate \ˈel-ə-ˌvāt\ *vt* **1** : to lift up or make higher : RAISE **2** : to raise in rank or status **3** : to improve morally, intellectually, or culturally **4** : to raise the spirits of : ELATE [Latin *elevare,* from *e-* + *levare* "to raise"]

[1]**el·e·vat·ed** \-ˌvāt-əd\ *adj* **1** : raised especially above the ground ⟨an *elevated* freeway⟩ **2 a** : being on a high plane morally or intellectually ⟨an *elevated* mind⟩ **b** : FORMAL, DIGNIFIED ⟨*elevated* diction⟩

[2]**elevated** *n* : EL

el·e·va·tion \ˌel-ə-ˈvā-shən\ *n* **1** : the height to which something is raised: as **a** : the angular distance of a celestial object above the horizon **b** : the degree to which a gun is aimed above the horizon **c** : the height above sea level : ALTITUDE **2** : an act or instance of elevating **3 a** : something that is elevated **b** : an elevated place or station **4** : the quality or state of being elevated **5** : a scale drawing showing a vertical section (as of a building) ***synonyms*** see HEIGHT

el·e·va·tor \ˈel-ə-ˌvāt-ər\ *n* **1 a** : a continuous belt or chain conveyor with cleats, scoops, or buckets for raising material **b** : a cage or platform and its hoisting machinery for conveying things or people to different levels **c** : a building for elevating, storing, discharging, and sometimes processing grain — called also *grain elevator* **2** : a movable airfoil usually attached to the tail plane of an airplane for producing motion up or down

elev·en \i-ˈlev-ən\ *n* **1** — see NUMBER table **2** : the 11th in a set or series **3** : something having 11 units or members [Old English *endleofan*] — **eleven** *adj or pron* — **elev·enth** \-ənth, -əntth\ *n* — **eleventh** *adj or adv*

eleventh hour *n* : the latest possible time ⟨was saved at the *eleventh hour*⟩

el·e·von \ˈel-ə-ˌvän\ *n* : an airplane control surface that combines the functions of elevator and aileron [*elev*ator + aileron]

elf \ˈelf\ *n, pl* **elves** \ˈelvz\ : a small and often mischievous fairy [Old English *ælf*] — **elf·ish** *adj* — **elf·ish·ly** \ˈel-fish-lē\ *adv*

elf·in \ˈel-fən\ *adj* **1** : of or relating to an elf or elves **2** : resembling an elf; *esp* : having a strange beauty or charm

elf owl *n* : a very small insectivorous owl of the southwestern U.S. and northern Mexico that roosts and nests in the cavities of trees and saguaro cacti

elic·it \i-ˈlis-ət\ *vt* : to draw forth or bring out often by skillful questioning or discussion ⟨*elicit* the truth from an unwilling witness⟩ [Latin *elicitus,* past participle of *elicere* "to elicit," from *e-* + *lacere* "to allure"] — **elic·i·ta·tion** \i-ˌlis-ə-ˈtā-shən\ *n* — **elic·i·tor** \i-ˈlis-ət-ər\ *n*

elide \i-ˈlīd\ *vt* **1** : to suppress or alter (as a vowel) by elision **2** : to leave out of consideration : IGNORE ⟨*elided* important differences⟩ [Latin *elidere* "to strike out," from *e-* + *laedere* "to injure by striking"]

el·i·gi·ble \ˈel-ə-jə-bəl\ *adj* : qualified to be chosen or to participate : ENTITLED ⟨*eligible* candidates for office⟩ ⟨*eligible* for benefits⟩ [Late Latin *eligibilis,* from Latin *eligere* "to choose"] — **el·i·gi·bil·i·ty** \ˌel-i-jə-ˈbil-ət-ē\ *n* — **eligible** *n* — **el·i·gi·bly** \ˈel-i-jə-blē\ *adv*

elim·i·nate \i-ˈlim-ə-ˌnāt\ *vt* **1 a** : to put an end to or get rid of : REMOVE ⟨*eliminate* errors⟩ **b** : to remove from consideration ⟨*eliminated* her as a suspect⟩ **c** : to remove from further competition by defeating ⟨a team *eliminated* in the first round⟩ **2** : to expel (as waste) from the living body **3** : to cause (a variable) to disappear by combining two or more equations [Latin *eliminare,* from *e-* + *limen* "threshold"] — **elim·i·na·tion** \i-ˌlim-ə-ˈnā-shən\ *n* — **elim·i·na·tive** \i-ˈlim-ə-ˌnāt-iv\ *adj* — **elim·i·na·tor** \-ˌnāt-ər\ *n*

ELISA \ē-ˈlī-sə, -zə\ *n* : ENZYME-LINKED IMMUNOSORBENT ASSAY

eli·sion \i-ˈlizh-ən\ *n* **1 a** : the omission of a final or initial sound of a word ⟨*is* has become *'s* in *there's* by *elision*⟩ **b** : the omission of an unstressed vowel or syllable in a verse to achieve a uniform rhythm **2** : the act or an instance of dropping out or omitting something [Late Latin *elisio,* from Latin *elidere* "to strike out"]

elite \ā-ˈlēt, i-\ *n* : the choice part ⟨the *elite* of the entertainment world⟩; *esp* : a socially superior group ⟨a store catering to the *elite*⟩ [French *élite,* from Medieval French *eslite,* from *eslire* "to choose," from Latin *eligere*] — **elite** *adj*

elix·ir \i-ˈlik-sər\ *n* **1 a** : a substance held to be capable of changing metals into gold **b** : a substance held to be capable of prolonging life indefinitely **c** : CURE-ALL **2** : a sweetened usually alcoholic liquid containing medicinal ingredients [Medieval Latin, from Arabic *al-iksīr* "the elixir"]

Eliz·a·be·than \i-ˌliz-ə-ˈbē-thən\ *adj* : of, relating to, or characteristic of Elizabeth I of England or her age — **Elizabethan** *n*

elk \ˈelk\ *n, pl* **elk** *or* **elks** **1 a** : MOOSE — used for one of the Old World **b** : a large deer of North America, Europe, Asia, and northwestern Africa that has large curved antlers with many branches and that lives in herds — called also *red deer, wapiti* **c** : any of various large Asian deer **2** *cap* : a member of a major benevolent and fraternal order [Middle English]

elk 1b

[1]**ell** \ˈel\ *n* : a former English unit of length for cloth equal to 45 inches (about 1.14 meters) [Old English *eln*]

[2]**ell** *n* : an extension at right angles to a building [from the resulting shape like the letter *L*]

el·lipse \i-ˈlips, e-\ *n* **1** : an elongated circle : OVAL **2** : an oval shape generated by a point moving in such a way that the sums of its distances from two fixed points is a constant : a conic section that is a closed curve but not a circle [Greek *elleipsis*]

el·lip·sis \i-ˈlip-səs, e-\ *n, pl* **-lip·ses** \-ˈlip-ˌsēz\ **1** : the omission of one or more words from a phrase when such omission does not affect its meaning ⟨"fire when ready" for "fire when you are ready" is an example of *ellipsis*⟩ **2** : marks or a mark (as . . .) used to show the omission especially of letters or words [Latin, from Greek *elleipsis* "ellipsis, ellipse," from *elleipein* "to leave out, fall short," from *en-* "in-" + *leipein* "to leave"]

el·lip·soid \i-ˈlip-ˌsȯid, e-\ *n* : a surface whose intersection by any plane has the shape of an ellipse or a circle; *esp* : SPHEROID — **ellipsoid** *or* **el·lip·soi·dal** \i-ˌlip-ˈsȯid-l\ *adj*

el·lip·tic \i-ˈlip-tik, e-\ *or* **el·lip·ti·cal** \-ti-kəl\ *adj* **1** : of, relating to, or shaped like an ellipse **2** : of, relating to, or marked by ellipsis — **el·lip·ti·cal·ly** \-ti-kə-lē, -klē\ *adv*

elm \ˈelm\ *n* **1** : any of a genus of large deciduous trees that have alternate toothed leaves and a fruit that is a nearly circular samara and are often grown as shade trees; *esp* : AMERICAN ELM **2** : the wood of an elm [Old English]

El Ni·ño \el-ˈnē-nyō\ *n, pl* **El Niños** : an irregularly occurring flow of unusually warm surface water along the western coast of South America that disrupts the normal regional and global weather patterns — compare LA NIÑA [Spanish, literally, "the child" (i.e., the Christ child); from the appearance of the flow at the Christmas season]

el·o·cu·tion \ˌel-ə-ˈkyü-shən\ *n* **1** : a style of speaking especially in public **2** : the art of effective public speaking [Latin *elocutio,* from *eloqui* "to speak out"] — **el·o·cu·tion·ary** \-shə-ˌner-ē\ *adj* — **el·o·cu·tion·ist** \-shə-nəst, -shnəst\ *n*

elo·dea \i-ˈlōd-ē-ə\ *n* : any of a small American genus of submerged aquatic herbs that are monocotyledons [Greek *helōdēs* "marshy," from *helos* "marsh"]

[1]**elon·gate** \i-ˈlȯng-ˌgāt\ *vb* **1** : to extend the length of **2** : to grow in length — **elon·ga·tion** \ˌē-ˌlȯng-ˈgā-shən\ *n*

[2]**elongate** *or* **elon·gat·ed** \i-ˈlȯng-ˌgāt-əd\ *adj* **1** : stretched out **2** : SLENDER

elope \i-ˈlōp\ *vi* **1** : to slip away : ESCAPE **2** : to run away secretly with the intention of getting married usually without parental consent [Anglo-French *aloper*] — **elope·ment** \-mənt\ *n* — **elop·er** *n*

el·o·quence \ˈel-ə-kwəns\ *n* : speech or writing marked by force and persuasiveness; *also* : the art or power of using such speech or writing

el·o·quent \-kwənt\ *adj* **1** : marked by forceful and fluent expression ⟨an *eloquent* speaker⟩ **2** : vividly or movingly expressive or revealing ⟨an *eloquent* monument⟩ [Middle French, from Latin *eloquens,* from *eloqui* "to speak out," from *e-* + *loqui* "to speak"] — **el·o·quent·ly** *adv*

[1]**else** \ˈels\ *adv* **1 a :** in a different manner or place or at a different time ⟨how *else* can we act⟩ ⟨when *else* can they come⟩ **b :** in an additional place or manner or at an additional time **2 :** if not : OTHERWISE ⟨leave or *else* you'll be sorry⟩ [Old English *elles*]

[2]**else** *adj* : OTHER: as **a :** being different in identity ⟨somebody *else*⟩ **b :** being in addition ⟨what *else*⟩

else·where \-ˌhweər, -ˌhwaər, -ˌweər, -ˌwaər\ *adv* : in or to another place ⟨took my business *elsewhere*⟩

elu·ci·date \i-ˈlü-sə-ˌdāt\ *vt* : to make clear or plain : EXPLAIN [Late Latin *elucidare,* from Latin *e-* + *lucidus* "lucid"] — **elu·ci·da·tion** \i-ˌlü-sə-ˈdā-shən\ *n* — **elu·ci·da·tive** \i-ˈlü-sə-ˌdāt-iv\ *adj* — **elu·ci·da·tor** \-ˌdāt-ər\ *n*

elude \ē-ˈlüd\ *vt* **1 :** to skillfully avoid or escape ⟨the identity of the disease *eluded* researchers⟩ **2 :** to escape the understanding or grasp of [Latin *eludere,* from *e-* + *ludere* "to play"] ***synonyms*** see EVADE

elu·sive \ē-ˈlü-siv, -ziv\ *adj* **1 :** hard to find or capture : EVASIVE ⟨*elusive* prey⟩ **2 :** hard to comprehend or define ⟨an *elusive* idea⟩ — **elu·sive·ly** *adv* — **elu·sive·ness** *n*

elute \ē-ˈlüt\ *vt* : to extract especially by means of a solvent [Latin *eluere* "to wash out," from *e-* + *lavere* "to wash"]

elu·vi·al \ē-ˈlü-vē-əl\ *adj* : of or relating to eluvium

elu·vi·um \-vē-əm\ *n* **1 :** fine material produced where found by weathering of rock **2 :** fine soil material deposited by wind [New Latin, from Latin *eluere* "to wash out"]

el·ver \ˈel-vər\ *n* : a young eel [alteration of *eelfare* "migration of eels"]

elves *plural of* ELF

elv·ish \ˈel-vish\ *adj* : MISCHIEVOUS 2, 3

Ely·si·um \i-ˈlizh-ē-əm, -ˈliz-\ *n* **1 :** the abode of the good after death in classical mythology **2 :** a place or condition of ideal happiness : PARADISE 3 [Latin, from Greek *Elysion*] — **Ely·sian** \i-ˈlizh-ən\ *adj*

el·y·tron \ˈel-ə-ˌträn\ *also* **el·y·trum** \-trəm\ *n, pl* **-tra** \-trə\ : one of the thick modified front wings in beetles and some other insects that protect the pair of functional hind wings [Greek *elytron* "sheath, wing cover," from *eilyein* "to roll, wrap"]

E elytron

em \ˈem\ *n* : the width of a piece of type about as wide as it is tall used as a unit of measure of printed matter [from the size of the quad used for the letter *m*]

em- — see EN-

ema·ci·ate \i-ˈmā-shē-ˌāt\ *vt* **1 :** to cause to lose flesh so as to become very thin **2 :** to make feeble [Latin *emaciare,* from *e-* + *macies* "leanness," from *macer* "lean"] — **ema·ci·a·tion** \i-ˌmā-shē-ˈā-shən, -sē-ˈā-\ *n*

e–mail \ˈē-ˌmāl\ *n* **1 :** a system for transmitting messages electronically (as between computers) **2 :** messages sent through an e-mail system ⟨a lot of *e-mail*⟩; *also* : one such message ⟨sent her an *e-mail*⟩ [electronic] — **e–mail** *vb* — **e–mail·er** \-ˌmāl-ər\ *n*

em·a·nate \ˈem-ə-ˌnāt\ *vb* **1 :** to come out from a source ⟨a scent *emanating* from the flowers⟩ **2 :** EMIT, EXUDE ⟨seems to *emanate* confidence⟩ [Latin *emanare,* from *e-* + *manare* "to flow"]

em·a·na·tion \ˌem-ə-ˈnā-shən\ *n* **1 :** the action of emanating **2 :** something that emanates or is produced by emanation — **em·a·na·tion·al** \-shnəl, -shən-l\ *adj* — **em·a·na·tive** \ˈem-ə-ˌnāt-iv\ *adj*

eman·ci·pate \i-ˈman-sə-ˌpāt\ *vt* : to free from restraint, control, or the power of another; *esp* : to free from slavery [Latin *emancipare,* from *e-* + *mancipare* "to transfer ownership of," from *manceps* "purchaser," from *manus* "hand" + *capere* "to take"] — **eman·ci·pa·tion** \i-ˌman-sə-ˈpā-shən\ *n* — **eman·ci·pa·tor** \i-ˈman-sə-ˌpāt-ər\ *n* — **eman·ci·pa·tory** \-pə-ˌtōr-ē, -ˌtȯr-\ *adj*

emas·cu·late \i-ˈmas-kyə-ˌlāt\ *vt* **1 :** to deprive of vigor or spirit : WEAKEN **2 :** CASTRATE [Latin *emasculare,* from *e-* + *masculus* "male"] — **emas·cu·la·tion** \i-ˌmas-kyə-ˈlā-shən\ *n* — **emas·cu·la·tor** \i-ˈmas-kyə-ˌlāt-ər\ *n*

em·balm \im-ˈbäm, -ˈbälm\ *vb* **1 :** to treat a corpse with special preparations to preserve it from decay **2 :** to preserve as if by embalming ⟨*embalm* a hero's memory⟩ [Medieval French *embasmer,* from *en-* + *basme* "balm"] — **em·balm·er** *n* — **em·balm·ment** \-ˈbäm-mənt, -ˈbälm-\ *n*

em·bank \im-ˈbangk\ *vt* : to enclose or confine by an embankment

em·bank·ment \-mənt\ *n* **1 :** a raised bank or wall to carry a roadway or to hold back water **2 :** the action of embanking

em·bar·go \im-ˈbär-gō\ *n, pl* **-goes** **1 :** an order of a government prohibiting the departure of commercial ships from its ports **2 :** legal prohibition or restriction of commerce **3 :** an informal or unofficial stoppage : IMPEDIMENT; *esp* : PROHIBITION 2 [Spanish, from *embargar* "to bar"] — **embargo** *vt*

em·bark \im-ˈbärk\ *vb* **1 :** to go or put on board a ship or airplane **2 :** to enter into an enterprise or undertaking ⟨*embark* on a career⟩ [Middle French *embarquer,* from Provençal *embarcar,* from *em-* "en-" + *barca* "bark"] — **em·bar·ka·tion** \ˌem-ˌbär-ˈkā-shən\ *n* — **em·bark·ment** \im-ˈbärk-mənt\ *n*

em·bar·rass \im-ˈbar-əs\ *vt* **1 :** to cause to feel self-consciously confused or distressed **2 :** to hinder the freedom of movement of : IMPEDE ⟨soldiers *embarrassed* by heavy packs⟩ **3 :** to involve in financial difficulties ⟨unexpected laughter *embarrassed* the speaker⟩ [derived from Portuguese *embaraçar,* from *em-* in- + *baraça* noose] — **em·bar·rass·ing·ly** \-ə-sing-lē\ *adv*

synonyms EMBARRASS, ABASH, DISCONCERT, DISCOMFIT mean to distress by confusing or confounding. EMBARRASS implies an influence that impedes thought, speech, or action ⟨*embarrassed* to admit she liked the movie⟩. ABASH suggests producing feelings of shame, shyness, or unworthiness by suddenly destroying self-confidence ⟨*abashed* by his sharp and sudden rebuke⟩. DISCONCERT implies producing uncertainty or hesitancy ⟨*disconcerted* by her unexpectedly large audience⟩. DISCOMFIT implies a hampering or frustrating accompanied by confusion ⟨hecklers *discomfited* the speaker⟩.

em·bar·rass·ment \im-ˈbar-ə-smənt\ *n* **1 :** the state of being embarrassed: as **a :** confusion or discomposure of mind **b :** difficulty arising from a lack of money to pay debts **2 a :** something that embarrasses : IMPEDIMENT **b :** an excessive quantity from which to select — used especially in the phrase *embarrassment of riches*

em·bas·sy \ˈem-bə-sē\ *n, pl* **-sies** **1 :** a body of diplomatic representatives **2 a :** the function or position of an ambassador **b :** a mission abroad undertaken by an ambassador **3 :** the official residence or office of an ambassador [Medieval French *ambassee,* of Germanic origin]

em·bat·tle \im-ˈbat-l\ *vt* **1 :** to arrange in battle order : prepare for battle **2 :** FORTIFY a

em·bat·tled \im-ˈbat-ld\ *adj* : engaged in battle or conflict

em·bed *also* **im·bed** \im-ˈbed\ *vb* **em·bed·ded** *also* **im·bed·ded; em·bed·ding** *also* **im·bed·ding** **1 :** to enclose closely in or as if in a surrounding mass : set solidly in or as if in a bed ⟨*embed* a post in concrete⟩ **2 :** to become embedded **3 :** to prepare (a microscopy specimen) for cutting by infiltrating with and enclosing in a supporting substance (as paraffin)

em·bel·lish \im-ˈbel-ish\ *vt* **1 :** to make beautiful with ornamentation : DECORATE ⟨a book *embellished* with pictures⟩ **2 :** to heighten the attractiveness of by adding decorative or fanciful details ⟨*embellishes* stories⟩ [Medieval French *embeliss-,* stem of *embelir* "to embellish," from *en-* + *bel* "beautiful"] ***synonyms*** see ADORN — **em·bel·lish·ment** \-mənt\ *n*

em·ber \ˈem-bər\ *n* **1 :** a glowing piece of coal or wood from a fire; *esp* : such a piece smoldering in ashes **2** *pl* **:** smoldering remains (as of a fire or a romance) [Old Norse *eimyrja*]

em·ber day \ˈem-bər-\ *n* : a Wednesday, Friday, or Saturday following the first Sunday in Lent, Whitsunday, September 14, or December 13 and set apart for fasting and prayer in Western churches [Old English *ymbrendæg,* from *ymbrene* "anniversary" + *dæg* "day"]

em·bez·zle \im-ˈbez-əl\ *vt* **em·bez·zled; em·bez·zling** \-ˈbez-ling, -ə-ling\ : to take (property entrusted to one's care) dishonestly for one's own use ⟨*embezzled* thousands of dollars⟩ [Medieval French *embesiller* to make away with, from *en-* + *besiller* to steal, plunder] — **em·bez·zle·ment** \-ˈbez-əl-mənt\ *n* — **em·bez·zler** \-ˈbez-lər, -ə-lər\ *n*

\ə\ **abut**	\au̇\ **out**	\i\ **tip**	\ȯ\ **saw**	\u̇\ **foot**
\ər\ **further**	\ch\ **chin**	\ī\ **life**	\ȯi\ **coin**	\y\ **yet**
\a\ **mat**	\e\ **pet**	\j\ **job**	\th\ **thin**	\yü\ **few**
\ā\ **take**	\ē\ **easy**	\ng\ **sing**	\t͟h\ **this**	\yu̇\ **cure**
\ä\ **cot, cart**	\g\ **go**	\ō\ **bone**	\ü\ **food**	\zh\ **vision**

em·bit·ter \im-ˈbit-ər\ *vt* **:** to make bitter or more bitter; *esp* **:** to arouse bitter feeling in — **em·bit·ter·ment** \-mənt\ *n*

em·bla·zon \im-ˈblāz-n\ *vt* **1 :** to inscribe or ornament with markings or emblems used in heraldry **2 :** CELEBRATE 3, EXTOL ⟨a name *emblazoned* in history⟩

em·blem \ˈem-bləm\ *n* **1 :** an object or the figure of an object symbolizing and suggesting another object or an idea ⟨the flag is the *emblem* of one's country⟩ **2 :** a device, symbol, or figure used as an identifying mark [Latin *emblema* "inlaid work," from Greek *emblēma,* from *emballein* "to insert," from *en-* + *ballein* "to throw"]

em·blem·at·ic \ˌem-blə-ˈmat-ik\ *also* **em·blem·at·i·cal** \-ˈmat-i-kəl\ *adj* **:** of, relating to, or constituting an emblem **:** SYMBOLIC

em·bod·i·ment \im-ˈbäd-i-mənt\ *n* **1 :** the act of embodying **:** the state of being embodied **2 :** one that embodies something

em·body \im-ˈbäd-ē\ *vt* **-bod·ied; -body·ing 1 :** to make a part of a body or system **:** INCORPORATE ⟨*embodied* a tax provision in the new law⟩ **2 :** to express in a concrete or definite form ⟨*embody* one's ideas in words⟩ **3 :** to represent in visible form ⟨a person who *embodies* courage⟩ — **em·bod·i·er** *n*

em·bold·en \im-ˈbōl-dən\ *vt* **:** to make bold

em·bo·lism \ˈem-bə-ˌliz-əm\ *n* **1 :** the sudden obstruction of a blood vessel by an embolus **2 :** EMBOLUS — **em·bol·ic** \em-ˈbäl-ik\ *adj*

em·bo·lus \ˈem-bə-ləs\ *n, pl* **-li** \-ˌlī, -ˌlē\ **:** an abnormal particle (as an air bubble) circulating in the blood — compare THROMBUS [Greek *embolos* "wedge-shaped object, stopper," from *emballein* "to insert, intercalate"]

em·bos·om \im-ˈbu̇z-əm\ *vt* **:** to shelter closely **:** ENCLOSE

em·boss \im-ˈbäs, -ˈbȯs\ *vt* **:** to ornament with a raised pattern or design [Middle French *embocer,* from *en-* + *boce* "boss"] — **em·boss·er** *n* — **em·boss·ment** \-mənt\ *n*

em·bou·chure \ˌäm-bu̇-ˈshu̇r\ *n* **1 :** the position and use of the lips, tongue, and teeth in producing a musical tone on a wind instrument **2 :** the mouthpiece of a musical instrument [French, from *(s')emboucher* "to flow into," from *en-* + *bouche* "mouth"]

em·bow·er \im-ˈbau̇-ər, -ˈbau̇r\ *vt* **:** to shelter or enclose in or as if in a shelter of tree branches

[1]**em·brace** \im-ˈbrās\ *vb* **1 :** to clasp in the arms **:** HUG **2 :** ENCIRCLE 1, ENCLOSE **3 a :** to take up readily or gladly ⟨*embrace* a cause⟩ **b :** to avail oneself of **:** WELCOME ⟨*embrace* an opportunity⟩ **4 :** TAKE IN, INCLUDE [Medieval French *embracer,* from *en-* + *brace* "two arms," from Latin *bracchia,* plural of *bracchium* "arm"] ***synonyms*** see COMPRISE — **em·brace·able** \-ˈbrā-sə-bəl\ *adj* — **em·brace·ment** \-ˈbrās-mənt\ *n* — **em·brac·er** *n*

[2]**embrace** *n* **:** a gathering into one's arms and holding close **:** HUG

em·bra·sure \im-ˈbrā-zhər\ *n* **1 :** an opening with sides flaring outward in a wall or parapet usually for allowing the firing of cannon **2 :** a recess of a door or window [French]

E

embrasure 2

em·bro·ca·tion \ˌem-brə-ˈkā-shən\ *n* **:** LINIMENT [Late Latin *embrocare* "to rub with a lotion," from Greek *embrochē* "lotion"]

em·broi·der \im-ˈbrȯid-ər\ *vb* **em·broi·dered; em·broi·der·ing** \-ˈbrȯid-ring, -ə-ring\ **1 :** to make or fill in a design with needlework **2 :** to ornament with needlework **3 :** to elaborate with often fictitious details **:** EXAGGERATE [derived from Medieval French *embrouder*] — **em·broi·der·er** \-ˈbrȯid-ər-ər\ *n*

em·broi·dery \im-ˈbrȯid-rē, -ə-rē\ *n, pl* **-der·ies 1 a :** the process or art of embroidering **b :** decorative needlework **2 :** elaboration in details

em·broil \im-ˈbrȯil\ *vt* **1 :** to throw into disorder or confusion **2 :** to involve in conflict or difficulties ⟨*embroiled* in a lawsuit⟩ [French *embrouiller,* from *en-* + *brouiller* "to jumble"] — **em·broil·ment** \-mənt\ *n*

em·bryo \ˈem-brē-ˌō\ *n, pl* **em·bry·os 1 :** an animal in the early stages of development that are characterized by cleavage, the laying down of fundamental tissues, and the formation of primitive organs and organ systems — compare FETUS **2 :** a rudimentary plant within a seed **3 :** a beginning or undeveloped stage — used especially in the phrase *in embryo* [Medieval Latin, from Greek *embryon,* from *en-* + *bryein* "to swell"]

em·bry·ol·o·gy \ˌem-brē-ˈäl-ə-jē\ *n* **1 :** a branch of biology dealing with embryos and their development **2 :** the events and processes involved in the formation and development of an embryo — **em·bry·o·log·ic** \ˌem-brē-ə-ˈläj-ik\ *or* **em·bry·o·log·i·cal** \-ˈläj-i-kəl\ *adj* — **em·bry·o·log·i·cal·ly** \-i-kə-lē, -klē\ *adv* — **em·bry·ol·o·gist** \ˌem-brē-ˈäl-ə-jəst\ *n*

em·bry·on·ic \ˌem-brē-ˈän-ik\ *adj* **1 :** of or relating to an embryo **2 :** being in an early or undeveloped stage **:** being in embryo ⟨an *embryonic* idea⟩ — **em·bry·on·i·cal·ly** \-i-kə-lē, -klē\ *adv*

embryo sac *n* **:** the individual that produces female germ cells in the sexually reproducing generation of a seed plant and that consists of a thin-walled sac containing the egg nucleus and other nuclei which form nutritive tissue upon fertilization

[1]**em·cee** \ˈem-ˈsē\ *n* **:** MASTER OF CEREMONIES [*M.C.*]

[2]**emcee** *vb* **em·ceed; em·cee·ing :** to act as master of ceremonies **:** HOST ⟨*emcee* an awards show⟩

emend \ē-ˈmend\ *vt* **:** to correct usually by textual changes ⟨*emend* a manuscript⟩ [Latin *emendare* "to emend, amend"] ***synonyms*** see CORRECT — **emend·able** \-ˈmen-də-bəl\ *adj*

emen·da·tion \ˌē-ˌmen-ˈdā-shən, ˌem-ən-\ *n* **1 :** the act of emending **2 :** a change designed to correct or improve

[1]**em·er·ald** \ˈem-rəld, -ə-rəld\ *n* **1 :** a rich green beryl prized as a gemstone **2 :** a green gemstone (as synthetic corundum) [Medieval French *esmeralde,* from Latin *smaragdus,* from Greek *smaragdos*]

[2]**emerald** *adj* **:** brightly or richly green

emerald green *n* **1 :** a clear bright green resembling that of the emerald **2 :** a strong green

emerge \i-ˈmərj\ *vi* **1 :** to become known or apparent ⟨new problems *emerged*⟩ **2 :** to rise from or as if from an enveloping fluid **:** come out into view ⟨a diver *emerging* from the ocean⟩ **3 :** to rise from an obscure or inferior condition ⟨*emerged* as the leader⟩ [Latin *emergere,* from *e-* + *mergere* "to plunge"]

emer·gence \i-ˈmər-jəns\ *n* **:** the act or an instance of emerging

emer·gen·cy \i-ˈmər-jən-sē\ *n, pl* **-cies 1 :** an unforeseen circumstance or the resulting state that calls for immediate action **2 :** a pressing need ***synonyms*** see JUNCTURE

emergency medical technician *n* **:** EMT

emergency room *n* **:** a hospital room or area with medical personnel and equipment for treating persons requiring immediate medical care

[1]**emer·gent** \i-ˈmər-jənt\ *adj* **1 :** rising out of or as if out of a fluid **2 :** rooted in shallow water and having most of its growth above water ⟨cattails are *emergent* plants⟩

[2]**emergent** *n* **:** an emergent plant

emer·i·tus \i-ˈmer-ət-əs\ *adj* **1 :** holding after retirement an honorary title corresponding to that held last during active service ⟨professor *emeritus*⟩ **2 :** retired from an office or position [Latin, past participle of *emereri* "to serve out one's term," from *e-* + *mereri, merēre* "to earn, serve"] — **emeritus** *n*

emer·sion \ē-ˈmər-zhən\ *n* **:** an act or instance of emerging [Latin *emersus,* past participle of *emergere* "to emerge"]

em·ery \ˈem-rē, -ə-rē\ *n, pl* **em·er·ies :** a dark corundum used especially in the form of powder or grains for grinding and polishing [Medieval French *esmeril,* from Italian *smiriglio,* from Medieval Latin *smiriglum,* from Greek *smyris*]

emet·ic \i-ˈmet-ik\ *n* **:** an agent that induces vomiting [Latin *emetica,* from Greek *emetikē,* from *emein* "to vomit"] — **emetic** *adj* — **emet·i·cal·ly** \-ˈmet-i-kə-lē, -klē\ *adv*

emf \ˌē-ˌem-ˈef\ *n* **:** POTENTIAL DIFFERENCE [*e*lectro*m*otive *f*orce]

-emia \ˈē-mē-ə\ *n combining form* **1 :** condition of having (such) blood ⟨septic*emia*⟩ **2 :** condition of having (a specified thing) in the blood ⟨ur*emia*⟩ [Greek *haima* "blood"]

em·i·grant \ˈem-i-grənt\ *n* **1 :** one that emigrates **2 :** a migrant plant or animal — **emigrant** *adj*

synonyms EMIGRANT, IMMIGRANT mean one who leaves his or her country to settle in another. EMIGRANT applies to the person leaving a country; IMMIGRANT applies to the same person entering and settling in another country.

em·i·grate \ˈem-ə-ˌgrāt\ *vi* **:** to leave one's residence or country to live or reside elsewhere [Latin *emigrare,* from *e* + *migrare* "to migrate"] — **em·i·gra·tion** \ˌem-ə-ˈgrā-shən\ *n*

émi·gré *also* **em·i·gré** \ˈem-i-ˌgrā, ˌem-i-ˈ\ *n* **:** EMIGRANT; *esp* **:** a person forced to emigrate for political reasons [French *émigré,* from *émigrer* "to emigrate," from Latin *emigrare*]

em·i·nence \ˈem-ə-nəns\ *n* **1 :** a condition or station of prominence or superiority **2 a :** a person of high rank or achievement — often used as a title for a cardinal **b :** a natural elevation : HEIGHT

em·i·nent \-nənt\ *adj* : standing above all others especially in rank, merit, or virtue : NOTABLE ⟨an *eminent* physician⟩ [Latin *eminens,* from *eminēre* "to stand out"] — **em·i·nent·ly** *adv*

eminent domain *n* : a right of a government to buy private property for public use even if the owner is unwilling to sell

emir *or* **amir** \ə-ˈmir, ā-\ *n* : a ruler, chief, or commander in Islamic countries [Arabic *amīr* "commander" — see *Word History* at ADMIRAL]

emir·ate \ˈe-mə-rət, -ˌrāt\ *n* : the state or jurisdiction of an emir

em·is·sary \ˈem-ə-ˌser-ē\ *n, pl* **-sar·ies** **1 :** one sent on a mission as the agent of another **2 :** a secret agent [Latin *emissarius,* from *emittere* "to send out"]

emis·sion \ē-ˈmish-ən\ *n* **1 :** an act or instance of emitting **2 :** something emitted or discharged — **emis·sive** \ē-ˈmis-iv\ *adj*

emit \ē-ˈmit\ *vt* **emit·ted; emit·ting** **1 a :** to throw or give off or out (as light or heat) **b :** to send out : EJECT **2 :** to issue (as a decree) with authority **3 :** to give voice to : EXPRESS ⟨*emitted* a groan⟩ [Latin *emittere* "to send out," from *e* + *mittere* "to send"] — **emit·ter** *n*

em·mer \ˈem-ər\ *n* : an ancient wheat having spikelets with two hard red kernels [German]

Em·my \ˈem-ē\ *n, pl* **Emmys** : a statuette awarded annually for notable achievement in television [from *Immy,* nickname for *image orthicon,* a camera tube used in television]

[1]**emol·lient** \i-ˈmäl-yənt\ *adj* : making soft or supple; *also* : soothing especially to the skin or mucous membrane [Latin *emollire* "to soften," from *e-* + *mollis* "soft"]

[2]**emollient** *n* : something that softens or soothes

emol·u·ment \i-ˈmäl-yə-mənt\ *n* : profit from one's employment or from an office held : SALARY, WAGES [Latin *emolumentum,* literally, "miller's fee," from *emolere* "to grind up," from *e-* + *molere* "to grind"]

emote \i-ˈmōt\ *vi* : to express emotion in or as if in a play [back-formation from *emotion*] — **emot·er** *n*

emo·ti·con \i-ˈmō-ti-ˌkän\ *n* : a group of characters (as :-)) that suggests an attitude or facial expression [*emotion* + *icon*]

emo·tion \i-ˈmō-shən\ *n* **1 :** strong feeling : EXCITEMENT ⟨spoke with *emotion*⟩ **2 :** a mental reaction (as anger or fear) experienced as a strong feeling and usually accompanied by physiological and behavioral changes in the body [Middle French, from *emouvoir* "to stir up," from Latin *exmovēre* "to move away, disturb," from *ex-* + *movēre* "to move"] ***synonyms*** see FEELING

emo·tion·al \i-ˈmō-shnəl, -shən-l\ *adj* **1 :** of or relating to the emotions ⟨an *emotional* upset⟩ **2 :** inclined to show or express emotion : easily moved ⟨an *emotional* person⟩ **3 :** appealing to or arousing emotion ⟨an *emotional* speech⟩ — **emo·tion·al·ly** \-ē\ *adv*

emo·tive \i-ˈmōt-iv\ *adj* **1 :** EMOTIONAL 1 **2 :** EMOTIONAL 3 — **emo·tive·ly** *adv*

empanel *variant of* IMPANEL

em·pa·thy \ˈem-pə-thē\ *n* : the capacity for experiencing as one's own the feelings of another [Greek *empatheia,* literally, "passion," from *empathēs* "emotional," from *en-* + *pathos* "feeling, emotion"] — **em·path·ic** \em-ˈpath-ik\ *adj* — **em·pa·thize** \ˈem-pə-ˌthīz\ *vi*

em·pen·nage \ˌäm-pə-ˈnäzh, ˌem-\ *n* : the tail assembly of an airplane [French, "feathers of an arrow, empennage"]

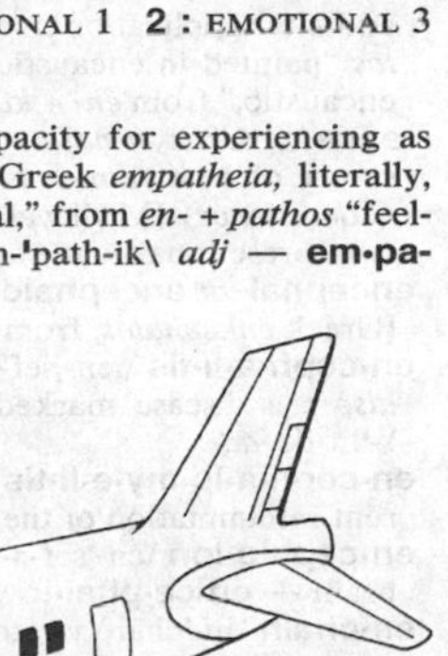

empennage

em·per·or \ˈem-pər-ər, -prər\ *n* : the sovereign ruler of an empire — compare MONARCH [Medieval French *emperur,* from Latin *imperator,* literally, "commander," from *imperare* "to command," from *in-* + *parare* "to prepare, arrange"]

em·pery \ˈem-pə-rē, -prē\ *n* : wide dominion : EMPIRE

em·pha·sis \ˈem-fə-səs, ˈemp-\ *n, pl* **-pha·ses** \-fə-ˌsēz\ **1 a :** forcefulness of expression ⟨spoke with *emphasis*⟩ **b :** prominence given to a word or syllable in reading or speaking **2 :** special stress or insistence on something ⟨put great *emphasis* on cleanliness⟩ [Latin, from Greek, "exposition, emphasis," from *emphainein* "to indicate," from *en-* + *phainein* "to show"]

em·pha·size \ˈem-fə-ˌsīz, ˈemp-\ *vt* : to place emphasis on : STRESS

em·phat·ic \im-ˈfat-ik, em-\ *adj* **1 :** uttered with or marked by emphasis **2 :** tending to express oneself in forceful speech or action **3 :** attracting special attention ⟨an *emphatic* contrast⟩ **4 :** constituting or belonging to a set of verb forms in English that have the auxiliary *do* and are used rarely for emphasis and regularly to take the place of a simple verb form in questions or negative statements ⟨the *emphatic* form "do know" or "do . . . know" in "but I tell you I do know him," "do you know him?," and "I do not know him"⟩ — **em·phat·i·cal·ly** \-ˈfat-i-kə-lē, -klē\ *adv*

em·phy·se·ma \ˌem-fə-ˈsē-mə, ˌemp-, -ˈzē-\ *n* : a disorder marked by abnormal enlargement of the alveoli and shortness of breath and that may lead to impaired heart action [Greek *emphysēma* "bodily inflation"] — **em·phy·se·ma·tous** \-mət-əs\ *adj*

em·pire \ˈem-ˌpīr\ *n* **1 a** (1) **:** a major political unit with a great extent of territory or a number of territories or peoples under one sovereign authority; *esp* : one having an emperor as chief of state (2) **:** the territory of such a unit **b :** something held to resemble a political empire; *esp* : an extensive territory or enterprise under one control **2 :** imperial sovereignty, rule, or dominion [Medieval French, from Latin *imperium,* from *imperare* "to command"]

Em·pire \ˈäm-ˌpiər, ˈem-ˌpīr\ *adj* : of or relating to an early 19th century French style (as of clothing or furniture) characterized by elaborateness and formality [French, from *le premier Empire* "the first Empire (of France)"]

em·pir·ic \im-ˈpir-ik, em-\ *n* : one who relies on practical experience [Greek *empeirikos* "doctor relying on experience alone," from *empeiria* "experience," from *en-* + *peiran* "to attempt"]

em·pir·i·cal \-ˈpir-i-kəl\ *also* **em·pir·ic** \-ˈpir-ik\ *adj* **1 :** relying on experience or observation usually without due regard for system and theory ⟨*empirical* medicine⟩ **2 :** originating in or based on observation or experience **3 :** capable of being verified or disproved by observation or experiment ⟨*empirical* laws of nature⟩ — **em·pir·i·cal·ly** \-ˈpir-i-kə-lē, -klē\ *adv*

empirical formula *n* : a chemical formula showing the simplest ratio of elements in a compound

em·pir·i·cism \im-ˈpir-ə-ˌsiz-əm, em-\ *n* **1 :** reliance on observation and experiment especially in the natural sciences **2 :** a theory that knowledge originates in experience — **em·pir·i·cist** \-səst\ *n or adj*

em·place \im-ˈplās\ *vt* : to put into place

em·place·ment \im-ˈplā-smənt\ *n* **1 :** a prepared position for weapons or military equipment **2 :** a putting into position : PLACEMENT

[1]**em·ploy** \im-ˈplȯi\ *vt* **1 a :** to make use of **b :** to use (as time) advantageously ⟨a job that *employed* her skills⟩ **2 a :** to use or engage the services of **b :** to provide with a job that pays wages or a salary ⟨a company that *employs* fifty⟩ **3 :** to devote (as time or energy) to or direct toward a particular activity or person ⟨*employed* all her energies to help the poor⟩ [Medieval French *emploier,* from Latin *implicare* "to enfold, involve, implicate"] ***synonyms*** see USE — **em·ploy·able** \-ə-bəl\ *adj*

[2]**employ** *n* : the state of being employed especially for wages or a salary ⟨generous to workers in their *employ*⟩

em·ploy·ee \im-ˌplȯi-ˈē, ˌem-; im-ˈplȯi-ˌē\ *n* : one employed by another usually for wages or a salary

em·ploy·er \im-ˈplȯi-ər, -ˈplȯir\ *n* : one that employs others

em·ploy·ment \im-ˈplȯi-mənt\ *n* **1 :** USE 1a, PURPOSE; *also* : the act of using **2 a :** the act of engaging a person for work : HIRING **b :** the work at which one is employed : OCCUPATION, JOB **c :** the state of being employed ⟨*employment* in the machine trade⟩ **d :** the extent or degree to which a labor force is employed ⟨*employment* is high⟩

em·po·ri·um \im-ˈpōr-ē-əm, em-, -ˈpȯr-\ *n, pl* **-ri·ums** *or* **-ria** \-ē-ə\ **1 :** a place of trade : MARKETPLACE; *esp* : a commercial center **2 :** a store carrying a wide variety of merchandise [Latin, from Greek *emporion,* from *emporos* "traveler, trader," from *en* "in" + *poros* "passage"]

\ə\ **abut**	\au̇\ **out**	\i\ **tip**	\ȯ\ **saw**	\u̇\ **foot**
\ər\ **further**	\ch\ **chin**	\ī\ **life**	\ȯi\ **coin**	\y\ **yet**
\a\ **mat**	\e\ **pet**	\j\ **job**	\th\ **thin**	\yü\ **few**
\ā\ **take**	\ē\ **easy**	\ng\ **sing**	\t͟h\ **this**	\yu̇\ **cure**
\ä\ **cot, cart**	\g\ **go**	\ō\ **bone**	\ü\ **food**	\zh\ **vision**

em·pow·er \im-ˈpau̇-ər, -ˈpau̇r\ *vt* **:** to give official authority or legal power to ***synonyms*** see ENABLE

em·press \ˈem-prəs\ *n* **1 :** the wife or widow of an emperor **2 :** a woman who holds an imperial title in her own right

em·prise \em-ˈprīz\ *n* **:** an adventurous, daring, or chivalrous enterprise [Medieval French, from *emprendre* "to undertake"]

[1]emp·ty \ˈem-tē, ˈemp-\ *adj* **emp·ti·er; -est** **1 :** containing nothing ⟨an *empty* box⟩ **2 :** UNOCCUPIED, VACANT ⟨an *empty* house⟩ **3 :** being without reality or substance ⟨*empty* dreams⟩ **4 :** lacking in value, sense, or effect ⟨an *empty* threat⟩ ⟨*empty* pleasures⟩ **5 :** HUNGRY ⟨feel *empty* before dinner⟩ **6 :** having no elements ⟨*empty* set⟩ [Old English *ǣmettig* "unoccupied," from *ǣmetta* "leisure"] — **emp·ti·ly** \-tə-lē\ *adv* — **emp·ti·ness** \-tē-nəs\ *n*

synonyms EMPTY, VACANT, VOID, BLANK mean lacking contents which could or should be present. EMPTY implies a complete absence of contents ⟨*empty* jars⟩. VACANT implies lack of what is considered as or intended to be the usual occupant, tenant, or attribute ⟨a *vacant* store⟩ ⟨a *vacant* look⟩. VOID intensifies emptiness ⟨*void* of compassion⟩. BLANK stresses what is free from writing or marking and implies lack of signs of expression, comprehension, or meaning ⟨a *blank* page⟩ ⟨a *blank* face⟩.

[2]empty *vb* **emp·tied; emp·ty·ing** **1 :** to make or become empty by removal of contents ⟨*empty* a barrel⟩ ⟨the theater *emptied* quickly⟩ **2 :** to remove from what holds or encloses ⟨*empty* the trash⟩ **3 :** to discharge its contents ⟨the river *empties* into the ocean⟩

[3]empty *n, pl* **empties :** an empty container

emp·ty–hand·ed \ˌem-tē-ˈhan-dəd, ˌemp-\ *adj* **1 :** having nothing in the hands **2 :** having acquired or gained nothing ⟨came back *empty-handed*⟩

em·pur·ple \im-ˈpər-pəl\ *vb* **em·pur·pled; em·pur·pling** \-ˈpər-pə-ling, -pling\ **:** to tinge or color purple

em·py·re·an \ˌem-ˌpī-ˈrē-ən, -pə-; em-ˈpir-ē-ən, -ˈpī-rē-\ *n* **1 :** the highest heaven or heavenly sphere **2 :** FIRMAMENT, HEAVENS [Late Latin *empyreus* "celestial," from Late Greek *empyrios,* from Greek *en* "in" + *pyr* "fire"] — **em·py·re·al** \-əl\ *adj* — **empyrean** *adj*

EMT \ˌē-ˌem-ˈtē\ *n* **:** a specially trained medical technician certified to provide basic emergency medical services before and during transport to a hospital [*e*mergency *m*edical *t*echnician]

emu \ˈē-ˌmyü, -ˌmü\ *n* **:** a swift-running Australian bird with undeveloped wings that is related to but smaller than the ostrich [Portuguese *ema* "cassowary"]

emu

em·u·late \ˈem-yə-ˌlāt\ *vt* **1 :** to strive to equal or excel **2 :** to equal or approach equality with **:** RIVAL [Latin *aemulari,* from *aemulus* "rivaling"] — **em·u·la·tor** \-ˌlāt-ər\ *n*

em·u·la·tion \ˌem-yə-ˈlā-shən\ *n* **:** effort or desire to equal or excel — **em·u·la·tive** \ˈem-yə-ˌlāt-iv\ *adj*

em·u·lous \ˈem-yə-ləs\ *adj* **:** eager or ambitious to equal or excel another — **em·u·lous·ly** *adv* — **em·u·lous·ness** *n*

emul·si·fi·er \i-ˈməl-sə-ˌfī-ər, -ˈfīr\ *n* **:** an agent (as a soap) promoting the formation and stabilization of an emulsion

emul·si·fy \-ˌfī\ *vt* **-fied; -fy·ing :** to convert (as an oil) into an emulsion — **emul·si·fi·able** \-ˌfī-ə-bəl\ *adj* — **emul·si·fi·ca·tion** \i-ˌməl-sə-fə-ˈkā-shən\ *n*

emul·sion \i-ˈməl-shən\ *n* **1 :** a material consisting of a mixture of liquids that do not dissolve in each other and having droplets of one liquid dispersed throughout the other ⟨an *emulsion* of oil in water⟩ **2 :** a light-sensitive coating on photographic plates, film, or paper consisting of particles of a silver salt suspended in a thick substance (as a gelatin solution) [New Latin *emulsio,* from Latin *emulgēre* "to milk out," from *e-* + *mulgēre* "to milk"] — **emul·sive** \-siv\ *adj*

en \ˈen\ *n* **:** one half of an em [from the size of the quad used for the letter *n*]

[1]en- *also* **em-** \e *also occurs in these prefixes although only* i *may be shown as in "engage"*\ *prefix* **1 :** put into or onto ⟨*en*throne⟩: go into or onto ⟨*en*train⟩ — in verbs formed from nouns **2 :** cause to be ⟨*en*able⟩ ⟨*en*slave⟩ — in verbs formed from adjectives or nouns **3 :** provide with ⟨*em*power⟩ — in verbs formed from nouns **4 :** so as to cover ⟨*en*wrap⟩: thoroughly ⟨*en*tangle⟩ — in verbs formed from verbs; in all senses usually *em-* before *b, m,* or *p* [Medieval French, from Latin *in-*]

[2]en- *also* **em-** *prefix* **:** in **:** within ⟨*em*pathy⟩ — usually *em-* before *b, m,* or *p* [Greek, from *en* "in"]

[1]-en \ən, ᵊn\ *also* **-n** \n\ *adj suffix* **:** made of **:** consisting of ⟨earth*en*⟩ ⟨silver*n*⟩ ⟨wool*en*⟩ [Old English]

[2]-en *vb suffix* **1 :** become or cause to be ⟨sharp*en*⟩ **2 :** cause or come to have ⟨strength*en*⟩ [Old English *-nian*]

en·able \in-ˈā-bəl\ *vt* **en·abled; en·abling** \-bə-ling, -bling\ **1 a :** to make able ⟨glasses *enable* me to read⟩ **b :** to make possible, practical, or easy **2 :** to give a legal power or right to

synonyms ENABLE, EMPOWER mean to make one able to do something. ENABLE implies providing the means or opportunity for doing ⟨training that *enables* people to earn a living⟩. EMPOWER implies the granting of power or delegation of authority to do ⟨*empowered* her attorney to act on her behalf⟩.

en·act \in-ˈakt\ *vt* **1 :** to make (as a bill) into law **2 :** to act out **:** REPRESENT — **en·ac·tor** \-ˈak-tər\ *n*

en·act·ment \-ˈakt-mənt, -ˈak-\ *n* **1 :** the act of enacting **:** the state of being enacted **2 :** something (as a law) that has been enacted

[1]enam·el \in-ˈam-əl\ *vt* **enam·eled** *or* **enam·elled; enam·el·ing** *or* **enam·el·ling** \-ˈam-ling, -ə-ling\ **1 :** to cover or inlay with enamel **2 :** to form a glossy surface on [Medieval French *enameller,* from *en-* + *esmal, asmal* "enamel," of Germanic origin]

[2]enamel *n* **1 :** a usually opaque glassy composition applied by fusion to the surface of metal, glass, or pottery **2 :** a surface that resembles enamel **3 :** a usually glossy paint that turns to a smooth hard coat when applied **4 :** a very hard outer layer covering the crown of a tooth

enam·el·ware \-ˌwaər, -ˌweər\ *n* **:** metal utensils (as pots and pans) coated with enamel

en·am·or \in-ˈam-ər\ *vt* **:** to fill with love, delight, or fascination ⟨*enamored* of his new neighbor⟩ ⟨baseball fans *enamored* with statistics⟩ [Medieval French *enamourer,* from *en-* + *amour* "love"]

en bloc \ä^{n}-ˈbläk\ *adv or adj* **:** as a whole **:** in a mass [French]

en·camp \in-ˈkamp\ *vb* **1 :** to set up and occupy a camp **:** CAMP **2 :** to place or establish in a camp ⟨*encamp* troops⟩

en·camp·ment \-mənt\ *n* **1 :** the place where a group is encamped; *also* **:** the group encamped **2 :** the act of encamping **:** the state of being encamped

en·cap·su·late \in-ˈkap-sə-ˌlāt\ *vb* **1 :** to encase in a capsule **2 :** to become encapsulated ⟨parasites that *encapsulate* in muscle⟩ **3 :** EPITOMIZE 1 — **en·cap·su·la·tion** \-ˌkap-sə-ˈlā-shən\ *n*

en·case \in-ˈkās\ *vt* **:** to enclose in or as if in a case — **en·case·ment** \-ˈkā-smənt\ *n*

en·caus·tic \in-ˈkȯ-stik\ *n* **:** a paint mixed with melted beeswax and after application fixed by heat [derived from Greek *enkaustos* "painted in encaustic," from *enkaiein* "to burn in, paint in encaustic," from *en-* + *kaiein* "to burn"]

-ence \əns, ᵊns\ *n suffix* **1 :** action or process ⟨emerg*ence*⟩ **:** instance of an action or process ⟨refer*ence*⟩ **2 :** quality or state ⟨coexist*ence*⟩ [Medieval French, from Latin *-entia,* from *-ent-, -ens,* present participle ending + *-ia* "-y"]

encephal- *or* **encephalo-** *combining form* **:** brain ⟨*encephal*itis⟩ [Greek *enkephalos,* from *en* "in" + *kephalē* "head"]

en·ceph·a·li·tis \ˌen-ˌsef-ə-ˈlīt-əs\ *n* **:** inflammation of the brain; *also* **:** a disease marked by encephalitis — **en·ceph·a·lit·ic** \-ˈlit-ik\ *adj*

en·ceph·a·lo·my·e·li·tis \en-ˌsef-ə-lō-ˌmī-ə-ˈlīt-əs\ *n* **:** concurrent inflammation of the brain and spinal cord

en·ceph·a·lon \en-ˈsef-ə-ˌlän, -lən\ *n, pl* **-la** \-lə\ **:** the vertebrate brain — **en·ce·phal·ic** \ˌen-sə-ˈfal-ik\ *adj*

en·chain \in-ˈchān\ *vt* **:** to bind or hold with or as if with chains — **en·chain·ment** \-mənt\ *n*

en·chant \in-ˈchant\ *vt* **1 :** to influence by charms and incantation **:** BEWITCH **2 :** to attract and move deeply [Medieval French *enchanter,* from Latin *incantare,* from *in-* + *cantare* "to sing"]

en·chant·er \-ər\ *n* **:** one that enchants; *esp* **:** SORCERER

en·chant·ing *adj* **:** ATTRACTIVE, CHARMING — **en·chant·ing·ly** \-ing-lē\ *adv*

en·chant·ment \in-ˈchant-mənt\ *n* **1 :** the act or art of enchanting **:** the state of being enchanted **2 :** something that enchants **:** SPELL, CHARM

en·chant·ress \in-ˈchan-trəs\ *n* **1 :** a woman who practices magic : SORCERESS **2 :** a fascinating or beautiful woman

enchase \in-ˈchās\ *vt* **1 :** ORNAMENT: as **a :** to cut or carve in relief **b :** INLAY **2 :** SET ⟨*enchase* a gem⟩ [Medieval French *enchaser* "to set (gems)," from *en-* + *case, chase* "case, box," from Latin *capsa* "case"]

en·chi·la·da \ˌen-chə-ˈläd-ə\ *n* **:** a tortilla rolled around a meat or cheese filling and covered with chili sauce [American Spanish, from *enchilar* "to season with chilies"]

en·ci·pher \in-ˈsī-fər, en-\ *vt* **:** to convert (a message) into cipher

en·cir·cle \in-ˈsər-kəl\ *vt* **1 :** to form a circle around : SURROUND **2 :** to pass completely around — **en·cir·cle·ment** \-kəl-mənt\ *n*

en·clave \ˈen-ˌklāv, ˈän-, ˈäng-\ *n* **:** a distinct territorial, cultural, or social group enclosed within or as if within foreign territory ⟨ethnic *enclaves*⟩ [French, from Medieval French *enclaver* "to enclose," from Latin *in-* + *clavis* "key"]

en·clit·ic \en-ˈklit-ik\ *adj* **:** being without independent accent and treated in pronunciation as forming a part of the preceding word ⟨*thee* in *prithee* and *not* in *cannot* are *enclitic*⟩ [Late Latin *encliticus,* from Greek *enklitikos,* from *enklinesthai* "to lean on," from *en-* + *klinein* "to lean"] — **enclitic** *n*

en·close *also* **in·close** \in-ˈklōz\ *vt* **1 a :** to close in : SURROUND; *esp* **:** to mark off (land) by or as if by a fence **b :** to hold in : CONFINE **2 :** to place in a parcel or envelope

en·clo·sure *also* **in·clo·sure** \in-ˈklō-zhər\ *n* **1 :** the act of enclosing : the state of being enclosed **2 :** an enclosed space **3 :** something (as a fence) that encloses **4 :** something enclosed ⟨a letter with two *enclosures*⟩

en·code \in-ˈkōd\ *vt* **:** to transfer from one system of communication into another; *esp* **:** to convert (a message) into code

en·co·mi·ast \en-ˈkō-mē-ˌast, -mē-əst\ *n* **:** one that praises : EULOGIST — **en·co·mi·as·tic** \-ˌkō-mē-ˈas-tik\ *adj*

en·co·mi·um \en-ˈkō-mē-əm\ *n, pl* **-mi·ums** *also* **-mia** \-mē-ə\ **:** warm or high praise especially when formally expressed [Latin, from Greek *enkōmion,* from *en* "in" + *kōmos* "celebration"]

en·com·pass \in-ˈkəm-pəs, -ˈkäm-\ *vt* **1 :** to form a circle about : ENCLOSE **2 a :** ENVELOP **b :** INCLUDE ⟨a plan that *encompasses* a number of aims⟩ — **en·com·pass·ment** \-mənt\ *n*

en·core \ˈän-ˌkōr, -ˌkòr\ *n* **:** a demand made by an audience for a repeat or an additional performance; *also* **:** a further performance in response to such a demand [French, "again"] — **encore** *vb*

[1]**en·coun·ter** \in-ˈkaůnt-ər\ *vt* **en·coun·tered; en·coun·ter·ing** \-ˈkaůnt-ə-ring, -ˈkaůn-tring\ **1 :** to meet as an enemy : engage in conflict with **2 :** to come upon face-to-face **3 :** to come upon or experience unexpectedly ⟨*encounter* difficulties⟩ [Medieval French *encuntrer,* derived from Latin *in-* + *contra* "against"]

[2]**encounter** *n* **1 a :** a meeting between unfriendly factions or persons **b :** a sudden often violent clash : COMBAT **2 a :** a chance meeting **b :** a meeting face-to-face

en·cour·age \in-ˈkər-ij, -ˈkə-rij\ *vt* **1 a :** to inspire with courage, spirit, or hope : HEARTEN **b :** to try to persuade ⟨*encouraged* him to try again⟩ **2 :** to spur on : STIMULATE ⟨moisture *encourages* plant growth⟩ **3 :** to give help to : FOSTER — **en·cour·ag·ing·ly** \-ing-lē\ *adv*

en·cour·age·ment \-mənt\ *n* **1 :** the act of encouraging : the state of being encouraged **2 :** something that encourages

en·croach \in-ˈkrōch\ *vi* **1 :** to enter or force oneself gradually upon another's property or rights **2 :** to advance beyond the usual or proper limits ⟨the gradually *encroaching* sea⟩ [Medieval French *encrocher* "to get, seize," from *en-* + *croche* "hook"] — **en·croach·ment** \-mənt\ *n*

en·crust *also* **in·crust** \in-ˈkrəst\ *vb* **1 :** to cover with or as if with a crust **2 :** to form a crust

encrustation *variant of* INCRUSTATION

en·cum·ber \in-ˈkəm-bər\ *vt* **en·cum·bered; en·cum·ber·ing** \-bə-ring, -bring\ **1 :** to weigh down : BURDEN **2 :** to hamper the function or activity of : HINDER **3 :** to burden with a legal claim (as a mortgage) ⟨*encumber* an estate⟩ [Medieval French *encumbrer,* from *en-* + *combre* "dam, weir"]

en·cum·brance \in-ˈkəm-brəns\ *n* **1 :** something that encumbers : LOAD, BURDEN **2 :** a legal claim (as a mortgage) against property

-en·cy \ən-sē, ᵊn-sē\ *n suffix* **:** quality or state ⟨despond*ency*⟩ [Latin *-entia* "-ency, -ence"]

[1]**en·cyc·li·cal** \in-ˈsik-li-kəl, en-\ *adj* **:** addressed to all the individuals of a group : GENERAL [Late Latin *encyclicus,* from Greek *enkyklios* "circular, general," from *en* "in" + *kyklos* "circle"]

[2]**encyclical** *n* **:** an encyclical letter; *esp* **:** a papal letter to the bishops of the church as a whole or to those in one country

en·cy·clo·pe·dia *also* **en·cy·clo·pae·dia** \in-ˌsī-klə-ˈpēd-ē-ə\ *n* **:** a work that contains information on all branches of knowledge or treats comprehensively a particular branch of knowledge usually in articles arranged alphabetically by subject [Medieval Latin *encyclopaedia* "course of general education," from Greek *enkyklios paideia* "general education"]

en·cy·clo·pe·dic *also* **en·cy·clo·pae·dic** \-ˈpēd-ik\ *adj* **1 :** of or relating to an encyclopedia **2 :** covering a wide range of subjects ⟨*encyclopedic* knowledge⟩ — **en·cy·clo·pe·di·cal·ly** \-ˈpēd-i-kə-lē, -klē\ *adv*

en·cyst \in-ˈsist, en-\ *vi* **:** to form or become enclosed in a cyst — **en·cyst·ment** \-ˈsist-mənt, -ˈsis-\ *n*

[1]**end** \ˈend\ *n* **1 a :** the part of an area that lies at the boundary **b :** a point that marks the extent or limit of something ⟨no *end* to their generosity⟩ **c :** the point where something ceases to exist ⟨world without *end*⟩ **d :** the extreme or last part lengthwise : TIP **e :** a football lineman whose position is at the farthest part of the line **2 a :** cessation of a course of action or activity **b :** DEATH, DESTRUCTION ⟨meet one's *end* bravely⟩ **c** (1) **:** the final state (2) **:** the result of an activity ⟨the *end* of the talks was an agreement⟩ **3 :** something left over **4 :** the goal toward which an agent acts or should act : PURPOSE **5 :** a particular part or phase of an undertaking ⟨the sales *end* of the business⟩ [Old English *ende*] — **end·ed** \ˈen-dəd\ *adj* — **in the end :** AFTER ALL, ULTIMATELY ⟨will surely succeed *in the end*⟩ — **on end :** without interruption ⟨it rained for days *on end*⟩

synonyms END, TERMINATION, ENDING mean the point or line beyond which a thing does not or cannot go. END implies the final limit in time, space, extent, influence, or range of possibility ⟨the *end* of his endurance⟩. TERMINATION applies to the end of something complete or finished or having a set limit ⟨the *termination* of the treaty⟩. ENDING also includes the portion leading to the actual final point ⟨the *ending* of a play⟩ ⟨a long *ending* to a symphony⟩.

[2]**end** *vb* **1 a :** to bring or come to an end : STOP **b :** DESTROY 1 **2 :** to make up the end of ***synonyms*** see CLOSE

end- *or* **endo-** *combining form* **1 :** within : inside ⟨*endo*skeleton⟩ — compare ECT-, EXO- **2 :** taking in ⟨*endo*thermal⟩ [Greek *endon* "within"]

en·dan·ger \in-ˈdān-jər\ *vt* **en·dan·gered; en·dan·ger·ing** \-ˈdānj-ring, -ə-ring\ **:** to bring into danger or peril

endangered *adj* **:** threatened with extinction ⟨an *endangered* species of bird⟩

end brush *n* **:** END PLATE

en·dear \in-ˈdiər\ *vt* **:** to cause to become dear or beloved ⟨her generosity *endeared* her to the public⟩

en·dear·ment \-mənt\ *n* **:** a word or an act (as a caress) showing love or affection

[1]**en·deav·or** \in-ˈdev-ər\ *vb* **en·deav·ored; en·deav·or·ing** \-ˈdev-ring, -ə-ring\ **:** to make an effort : work for a particular end : TRY ⟨*endeavor* to do better⟩ [Middle English *en-* + *dever* "duty," from Medieval French, from *deveir* "to owe," from Latin *debēre*]

[2]**endeavor** *n* **:** a serious determined effort

[1]**en·dem·ic** \en-ˈdem-ik\ *adj* **:** restricted or peculiar to a locality or region ⟨*endemic* diseases⟩ ⟨an *endemic* plant⟩ [derived from Greek *endēmos* "belonging to a particular people or country," from *en* "in" + *dēmos* "people, populace"] ***synonyms*** see NATIVE — **en·dem·i·cal·ly** \-ˈdem-i-kə-lē, -klē\ *adv* — **en·de·mic·i·ty** \ˌen-ˌdem-ˈis-ət-ē, -də-ˈmis-\ *n*

[2]**endemic** *n* **:** NATIVE 2b

end·er·gon·ic \ˌen-dər-ˈgän-ik\ *adj* **:** ENDOTHERMIC ⟨an *endergonic* biochemical reaction⟩ [*end-* + Greek *ergon* "work"]

end·ing \ˈen-ding\ *n* **:** something that constitutes an end: as **a :** CONCLUSION, END ⟨a novel with a happy *ending*⟩ **b :** one or more sounds or letters added at the end of a word especially in inflection ***synonyms*** see END

en·dive \ˈen-ˌdīv\ *n* **1 :** an annual or biennial herb closely related to chicory and widely grown as a salad plant — called also *escarole* **2** : the developing crown of chicory when blanched for use as a vegetable and in salads by growing in darkness [Medieval French, from Late Latin *endivia,* from Late Greek *entybion,* from Latin *intubus*]

end·less \ˈen-dləs, -ləs\ *adj* **1** : being or seeming to be without end **2** : joined at the ends ⟨an *endless* belt⟩ ***synonyms*** see ETERNAL — **end·less·ly** *adv* — **end·less·ness** *n*

end line *n* : a line at each end of a playing area (as a court or field) perpendicular to the sidelines marking a boundary

end man *n* : a comedian at either end of the line of performers in a minstrel show

end·most \ˈend-ˌmōst, ˈen-\ *adj* : situated at the very end

en·do·car·di·tis \ˌen-dō-kär-ˈdīt-əs\ *n* : inflammation of the lining of the heart and its valves

en·do·car·di·um \ˌen-dō-ˈkärd-ē-əm\ *n* : a thin membrane lining the cavities of the heart [New Latin, from *end-* + Greek *kardia* "heart"]

en·do·carp \ˈen-də-ˌkärp\ *n* : the inner layer of the pericarp of a fruit (as the stony wall enclosing the seed of a peach) — compare EXOCARP, MESOCARP

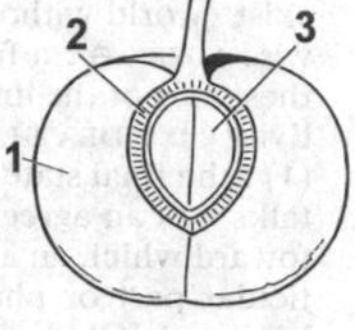

endocarp (cross section of a cherry): *1* mesocarp, *2* endocarp, *3* seed

1en·do·crine \ˈen-də-krən, -ˌkrīn, -ˌkrēn\ *adj* **1** : producing secretions that are distributed in the body by way of the bloodstream or lymph **2** : of, relating to, being, or resembling an endocrine gland or secretion [*end-* + Greek *krinein* "to separate"]

2endocrine *n* **1** : HORMONE **2** : ENDOCRINE GLAND

endocrine gland *n* : any of various glands (as the thyroid) that have no duct and release their secretions directly into the blood or lymph — called also *ductless gland*

endocrine system *n* : the bodily system of glands and cells that release their secretions and especially hormones directly into the bloodstream or lymph and include the thyroid, pituitary gland, adrenal glands, and islets of Langerhans

en·do·cri·nol·o·gy \ˌen-də-kri-ˈnäl-ə-jē, -krī-\ *n* : a branch of medicine dealing with the endocrine glands — **en·do·cri·no·log·i·cal** \-ˌkrin-l-ˈäj-i-kəl, -ˌkrīn-\ *adj* — **en·do·cri·nol·o·gist** \-kri-ˈnäl-ə-jəst, -krī-\ *n*

en·do·cy·to·sis \ˌen-də-sī-ˈtō-səs\ *n* : the process by which a cell takes in materials by phagocytosis or pinocytosis — compare EXOCYTOSIS [New Latin, from *end-* + *-cytosis* (as in *phagocytosis*)]

en·do·derm \ˈen-də-ˌdərm\ *n* **1** : the innermost of the three primary germ layers of an embryo giving rise to the epithelium of the digestive tract and its derivatives and of the lower respiratory tract; *also* : a tissue derived from this layer **2** : the inner layers of cells of an animal (as a jellyfish or hydra) whose body is composed of two layers of cells

en·do·der·mal \ˌen-də-ˈdər-məl\ *adj* : of or derived from endoderm or from endodermis

en·do·der·mis \ˌen-də-ˈdər-məs\ *n* : the innermost tissue of the cortex in many roots and stems

en·dog·a·my \en-ˈdäg-ə-mē\ *n* : mating between members of a social group or population usually consisting of genetically related individuals — **en·dog·a·mous** \-məs\ *adj*

en·dog·e·nous \en-ˈdäj-ə-nəs\ *adj* : developing or originating within the cell or body — **en·dog·e·nous·ly** *adv*

en·do·lymph \ˈen-də-ˌlimf, -ˌlimpf\ *n* : the watery fluid in the inner ear

en·do·me·tri·um \ˌen-dō-ˈmē-trē-əm\ *n, pl* **-tria** \-trē-ə\ : the mucous membrane lining the uterus [New Latin, from *end-* + Greek *mētra* uterus]

en·do·mor·phic \ˌen-də-ˈmȯr-fik\ *adj* : broad and heavy in build [*endo*derm + *-morphic;* from the predominance in such people of structures developed from the endoderm] — **en·do·morph** \ˈen-də-ˌmȯrf\ *n* — **en·do·mor·phy** \-ˌmȯr-fē\ *n*

en·do·plasm \ˈen-də-ˌplaz-əm\ *n* : the inner relatively fluid part of the cytoplasm — compare ECTOPLASM — **en·do·plas·mic** \ˌen-də-ˈplaz-mik\ *adj*

endoplasmic reticulum *n* : a system of cavities and minute connecting canals that occupy much of the cytoplasm of the cell, are studded with ribosomes in some places, and function especially in the transport of materials within the cell

end organ *n* : a structure forming the end of a path of nerve conduction and consisting of an effector or a receptor with its associated nerve terminations

en·dor·phin \en-ˈdȯr-fən\ *n* : any of a group of peptides found especially in the brain that are able to relieve pain [*end*ogenous + m*orphine*]

en·dorse *also* **in·dorse** \in-ˈdȯrs\ *vt* **1** : to sign the back of (a financial document) for some special purpose (as to receive payment or transfer to another) ⟨*endorse* a check⟩ **2** : to express support or approval of publicly ⟨*endorse* a candidate⟩ [Medieval French *endosser* "to put on, don, write on the back of," from *en-* + *dos* "back," from Latin *dorsum*] ***synonyms*** see APPROVE — **en·dors·ee** \in-ˌdȯr-ˈsē, ˌen-\ *n* — **en·dors·er** \in-ˈdȯr-sər\ *n*

en·dorse·ment *also* **in·dorse·ment** \in-ˈdȯr-smənt\ *n* **1** : the act or process of endorsing **2** : something written in the process of endorsing **3** : APPROVAL ⟨*endorsement* of a plan⟩

en·do·scope \ˈen-də-ˌskōp\ *n* : a lighted tubular medical instrument for viewing the interior of a hollow organ or body part that typically has one or more channels to enable passage of instruments (as forceps) — **en·do·scop·ic** \ˌen-də-ˈskäp-ik\ *adj*

en·do·skel·e·ton \ˌen-dō-ˈskel-ət-n\ *n* : an internal skeleton or supporting framework in an animal — compare EXOSKELETON — **en·do·skel·e·tal** \-ət-l\ *adj*

en·do·sperm \ˈen-də-ˌspərm\ *n* : a nutritive tissue in seed plants formed within the embryo sac

en·do·spore \ˈen-də-ˌspōr, -ˌspȯr\ *n* : an asexual spore developed within the cell especially in bacteria

en·do·the·li·um \ˌen-də-ˈthē-lē-əm\ *n, pl* **-lia** \-lē-ə\ : an inner layer (as of epithelium or of a seed coat) [*end-* + epi*thelium*] — **en·do·the·li·al** \-lē-əl\ *adj*

en·do·therm \ˈen-dō-ˌthərm\ *n* : a warm-blooded animal [*end-* + Greek *thermē* heat]

en·do·ther·mic \ˌen-də-ˈthər-mik\ *adj* **1** : characterized by or formed with absorption of heat ⟨*endothermic* chemical reactions⟩ **2** : WARM-BLOODED 1

en·do·tox·in \ˌen-dō-ˈtäk-sən\ *n* : a poisonous substance of a bacterium (as one causing typhoid fever) that is released from the cell only on its disintegration

en·dow \in-ˈdau̇\ *vt* **1** : to furnish with money for support or maintenance ⟨*endow* a hospital⟩ **2** : to furnish with something freely or naturally ⟨humans are *endowed* with reason⟩ [Medieval French *endouer,* from *en-* + *douer* "to endow," from Latin *dotare,* from *dot-, dos* "gift"]

en·dow·ment \-mənt\ *n* **1** : the providing of a permanent fund for support; *also* : the fund provided ⟨a college with a large *endowment*⟩ **2** : natural ability or talent

end·pa·per \ˈend-ˌpā-pər, ˈen-\ *n* : a sheet of paper folded once with one half pasted flat against the inside of the front or back cover of a book and the other pasted to the base of the front or last page

end plate *n* : a treelike ending of a motor nerve fiber

end·point \ˈend-ˌpȯint, ˈen-\ *n* **1** : a point marking the end of a process or a stage in a process **2** : either of two points that mark the ends of a line segment; *also* : a point that marks the end of a ray

end run *n* : a football play in which the ballcarrier attempts to run wide around the end

end table *n* : a small table used beside a larger piece of furniture

en·due *or* **in·due** \in-ˈdü, -ˈdyü\ *vt* : to provide with a quality or power ⟨*endued* with grace⟩ [Medieval French *enduire* "to bring in, introduce," from Latin *inducere,* from *in-* + *ducere* "to lead"]

en·dur·ance \in-ˈdu̇r-əns, -ˈdyu̇r-\ *n* **1** : PERMANENCE, DURATION **2** : the ability to withstand hardship, misfortune, or stress **3** : TRIAL 3, SUFFERING

en·dure \in-ˈdu̇r, -ˈdyu̇r\ *vb* **1** : to continue in the same state : LAST **2 a** : to remain firm under suffering or misfortune without yielding **b** : to bear patiently : SUFFER **3** : to put up with : TOLERATE [Medieval French *endurer,* from Latin *indurare* "to harden," from *in-* + *durare* "to harden, endure"] — **en·dur·able** \-ə-bəl\ *adj* — **en·dur·ably** \-ə-blē\ *adv*

en·dur·ing \in-ˈdu̇r-ing, -ˈdyu̇r-\ *adj* : LASTING, DURABLE — **en·dur·ing·ly** \-ing-lē\ *adv* — **en·dur·ing·ness** *n*

end user *n* : the ultimate consumer of a finished product

end·ways \ˈen-ˌdwāz\ *adv or adj* **1** : with the end forward **2** : in or toward the direction of the ends : LENGTHWISE **3** : on end : UPRIGHT

end·wise \-ˌdwīz\ *adv or adj* : ENDWAYS

end zone *n* : the area at each end of a football field bounded by the end line, the goal line, and the sidelines

-ene \ˌēn\ *n suffix* **:** unsaturated carbon compound ⟨benz*ene*⟩; *esp* **:** carbon compound with one double bond ⟨ethyl*ene*⟩ [Greek *-ēnē* feminine of *-ēnos* adj. suffix]

en·e·ma \ˈen-ə-mə\ *n* **:** the injection of liquid into the rectum by way of the anus usually to cause the intestines to empty; *also* **:** the material injected [Late Latin, from Greek, from *enienai* "to inject," from *en-* + *hienai* "to send"]

en·e·my \ˈen-ə-mē\ *n, pl* **-mies** **1 :** one that hates another **:** one that attacks or tries to harm another **2 :** something that harms **3 a :** a nation with which a country is at war **b :** a hostile unit or force [Medieval French *enemi,* from Latin *inimicus,* from *in-* "[1]in-" + *amicus* "friend"]

synonyms ENEMY, FOE mean one who shows hostility or ill will. ENEMY stresses antagonism showing itself in hatred or destructive attitude or action ⟨defeating the *enemy* at both fronts⟩. FOE stresses active fighting or struggle and is used poetically for an enemy in war ⟨bravely met their *foe*⟩.

en·er·get·ic \ˌen-ər-ˈjet-ik\ *adj* **:** having or showing energy **:** ACTIVE, FORCEFUL [Greek *energētikos,* from *energein* "to be active," from *energos* "active"] ***synonyms*** see VIGOROUS — **en·er·get·i·cal·ly** \-ˈjet-i-kə-lē, -klē\ *adv*

en·er·gize \ˈen-ər-ˌjīz\ *vb* **1 :** to put forth energy **:** ACT **2 a :** to impart energy to ⟨sunlight *energizes* the chemical reactions⟩ **b :** to make energetic or vigorous ⟨the pep talk *energized* the team⟩ **3 :** to apply voltage to — **en·er·giz·er** *n*

en·er·gy \ˈen-ər-jē\ *n, pl* **-gies** **1 :** power or capacity to be active **:** strength of body or mind to do things or to work ⟨a person of great intellectual *energy*⟩ **2 :** natural power vigorously exerted **:** vigorous action ⟨work with *energy*⟩ **3 :** the capacity for performing work **4 :** usable power; *also* **:** the resources for producing such power — compare KINETIC ENERGY, POTENTIAL ENERGY [Late Latin *energia,* from Greek *energeia* "activity," from *energos* "active," from *en* "in" + *ergon* "work"] ***synonyms*** see POWER

energy level *n* **:** one of the stable states of constant energy that may be assumed by a physical system — used especially of electrons in atoms

energy pyramid *n* **:** a triangle-shaped diagram that represents the amount of energy in an ecosystem that is transferred from one trophic level of a food chain or food web to the next

en·er·vate \ˈen-ər-ˌvāt\ *vt* **:** to cause to lose strength or vigor **:** WEAKEN [Latin *enervare,* from *e-* + *nervus* "sinew"] — **en·er·va·tion** \ˌen-ər-ˈvā-shən\ *n*

en·fant ter·ri·ble \äⁿ-ˌfäⁿ-te-ˈrēbl\ *n* **:** a person whose remarks or actions cause embarrassment [French, literally, "terrifying child"]

en·fee·ble \in-ˈfē-bəl\ *vt* **en·fee·bled; en·fee·bling** \-bə-ling, -bling\ **:** to make feeble — **en·fee·ble·ment** \-bəl-mənt\ *n*

[1]en·fi·lade \ˈen-fə-ˌlād, -ˌläd\ *n* **:** gunfire directed along the length of an enemy battle line [French, from *enfiler* "to thread, enfilade," from *en-* + *fil* "thread"]

[2]enfilade *vt* **:** to rake or be in a position to rake with gunfire in a lengthwise direction

en·fold \in-ˈfōld\ *vt* **1 a :** to cover with or as if with folds **:** ENVELOP **b :** to surround with a covering **:** CONTAIN **2 :** to clasp within the arms **:** EMBRACE

en·force \in-ˈfōrs,-ˈfȯrs\ *vt* **1 :** FORCE, COMPEL ⟨*enforce* obedience⟩ **2 :** to carry out effectively ⟨*enforce* the law⟩ — **en·force·able** \-ə-bəl\ *adj* — **en·force·ment** \-mənt\ *n* — **en·forc·er** *n*

en·fran·chise \in-ˈfran-ˌchīz\ *vt* **1 :** to set free (as from slavery) **2 :** to grant the privileges of a citizen to; *esp* **:** to grant the right to vote to [Medieval French *enfranchiss-,* stem of *enfranchir* "to enfranchise," from *en-* + *franc* "free"] — **en·fran·chise·ment** \-ˌchīz-mənt, -chəz-\ *n*

en·gage \in-ˈgāj\ *vb* **1 :** to interlock with **:** MESH; *also* **:** to cause to mesh **2 :** to bind oneself to do something; *esp* **:** to bind by a pledge to marry **3 a :** to arrange to obtain the use or services of **:** HIRE **b :** ENGROSS, OCCUPY ⟨the task *engaged* my attention⟩ **4 :** to enter into contest or battle with **5 a :** to begin and carry on an enterprise ⟨he *engaged* in sales⟩ **b :** PARTICIPATE [Medieval French *engager,* from *en-* + *gage* "[1]gage"]

en·gaged \in-ˈgājd\ *adj* **1 :** OCCUPIED, EMPLOYED, BUSY ⟨*engaged* in conversation⟩ **2 :** pledged to be married

en·gage·ment \in-ˈgāj-mənt\ *n* **1 a :** a promise to be present at a specified time and place **b :** employment especially for a stated time **2 :** PLEDGE 3b, OBLIGATION ⟨financial *engagements* to fulfill⟩ **3 a :** the act of engaging **:** the state of being engaged **b :** an agreement to marry **4 :** the state of being in gear **5 :** a hostile encounter between military forces

en·gag·ing \in-ˈgā-jing\ *adj* **:** ATTRACTIVE, PLEASING — **en·gag·ing·ly** \-jing-lē\ *adv*

en·gen·der \in-ˈjen-dər\ *vt* **en·gen·dered; en·gen·der·ing** \-də-ring, -dring\ **1 :** BEGET 1 **2 :** to cause to exist **:** PRODUCE ⟨angry words *engender* strife⟩ [Medieval French *engendrer,* from Latin *ingenerare,* from *in-* + *generare* "to generate"]

en·gine \ˈen-jən\ *n* **1 :** something used to bring about an effect or result ⟨*engines* of economic growth⟩ **2 a :** a mechanical tool (as an instrument of war) **b :** a mechanical appliance — often used in combination ⟨fire *engine*⟩ **3 :** a machine for converting energy into mechanical force and motion **4 :** a railroad locomotive [Medieval French *engin* "ingenuity, contrivance, engine of war," from Latin *ingenium* "natural disposition, talent," from *in-* + *gignere* "to beget"]

[1]en·gi·neer \ˌen-jə-ˈniər\ *n* **1 :** a member of a military group devoted to engineering work **2 a :** a designer or builder of engines **b :** a person who is trained in or follows as a profession a branch of engineering **c :** a person who skillfully carries out an enterprise **3 :** a person who runs or supervises an engine or an apparatus

[2]engineer *vt* **1 :** to plan, build, or manage as an engineer **2 :** to guide the course of ⟨*engineer* a fund-raising campaign⟩

en·gi·neer·ing \ˌen-jə-ˈniər-ing\ *n* **1 :** the art or profession of an engineer **2 :** the application of science and mathematics by which the properties of matter and the sources of energy in nature are made useful to human beings

[1]En·glish \ˈing-glish *also* ˈing-lish\ *adj* **:** of, relating to, or characteristic of England, the English people, or the English language [Old English *englisc,* from *Engle* "Angles"] — **En·glish·man** \-mən\ *n* — **En·glish·wom·an** \-ˌwu̇m-ən\ *n*

[2]English *n* **1 a :** the language of the people of England, the U.S., and many areas now or formerly under British control **b :** English language, literature, or composition as a subject of study **2** *pl in constr* **:** the people of England **3 :** a sideways spin given to a ball

[3]English *vt* **1 :** to translate into English **2 :** to adopt into English

English daisy *n* **:** DAISY 1a

English horn *n* **:** a double-reed woodwind instrument similar to the oboe but a fifth lower in pitch

English ivy *n* **:** IVY 1

English setter *n* **:** any of a breed of bird dogs with a long flat silky coat of white or white with flecks of color

English shepherd *n* **:** any of a breed of medium-sized dogs with a long glossy black coat and usually tan to brown markings

English sonnet *n* **:** a sonnet consisting of three quatrains and a couplet with a rhyme scheme of *abab cdcd efef gg*

English sparrow *n* **:** HOUSE SPARROW

English walnut *n* **:** a Eurasian walnut with large edible nuts and hard richly figured wood; *also* **:** its nut

en·gorge \in-ˈgȯrj\ *vb* **1 :** GORGE, GLUT **2 :** to fill with blood **:** CONGEST — **en·gorge·ment** \-mənt\ *n*

English horn

en·grave \in-ˈgrāv\ *vt* **1 a :** to impress deeply ⟨the incident was *engraved* in my memory⟩ **b :** to form (as letters or devices) by cutting into a surface **2 a :** to cut figures, letters, or devices upon especially for printing; *also* **:** to print from an engraved plate **b :** PHOTOENGRAVE — **en·grav·er** *n*

en·grav·ing \in-ˈgrā-ving\ *n* **1 :** the art of cutting figures, letters, or devices in wood, stone, or metal **2 :** something engraved: as **a :** an engraved printing surface **b :** engraved work **3 :** a print made from an engraved surface

en·gross \in-ˈgrōs\ *vt* **1 a :** to copy or write in a large hand **b :** to prepare the usually final handwritten or printed text of (an

\ə\ **abut**	\au̇\ **out**	\i\ **tip**	\ȯ\ **saw**	\u̇\ **foot**
\ər\ **further**	\ch\ **chin**	\ī\ **life**	\ȯi\ **coin**	\y\ **yet**
\a\ **mat**	\e\ **pet**	\j\ **job**	\th\ **thin**	\yü\ **few**
\ā\ **take**	\ē\ **easy**	\ng\ **sing**	\th\ **this**	\yu̇\ **cure**
\ä\ **cot, cart**	\g\ **go**	\ō\ **bone**	\ü\ **food**	\zh\ **vision**

official document) **2** : to take up the whole interest of : occupy fully : ABSORB ⟨*engrossed* in the project⟩ [sense 1 from Medieval French *engrosser* "to put (a legal document) in final form," from Medieval Latin *ingrossare,* from *in grossam* "(put) into final form," literally, "(written) in large (letter)"; sense 2 from Medieval French *engrosser* "to buy large quantitites of, amass," from *en gros* "wholesale, in quantity"] — **en·gross·er** *n* — **en·gross·ment** \-ˈgrō-smənt\ *n*

en·gulf \in-ˈgəlf\ *vt* **1** : to flow over and enclose : OVERWHELM **2** : to take in (food) by flowing over and enclosing — **en·gulf·ment** \-mənt\ *n*

en·hance \in-ˈhans\ *vt* : to increase or improve as in value, desirability, or attractiveness : HEIGHTEN [Medieval French *enhaucer,* derived from Latin *in* "in" + *altus* "high"] ***synonyms*** see INTENSIFY — **en·hance·ment** \-mənt\ *n* — **en·hanc·er** *n*

enig·ma \i-ˈnig-mə\ *n* : something hard to understand or explain : PUZZLE [Latin *aenigma,* from Greek *ainigmat-, ainigma,* from *ainissesthai* "to speak in riddles," from *ainos* "fable, riddle"] ***synonyms*** see MYSTERY — **enig·mat·ic** \ˌen-ig-ˈmat-ik *also* ˌē-nig-\ *or* **enig·mat·i·cal** \-ˈmat-i-kəl\ *adj* — **enig·mat·i·cal·ly** \-i-kə-lē, -klē\ *adv*

en·jamb·ment *also* **en·jambe·ment** \in-ˈjam-mənt\ *n* : the running over of a sentence from one verse or couplet into another so that closely related words fall in different lines [French *enjambement,* from *enjamber* "to straddle," from *en-* + *jambe* "leg"]

en·join \in-ˈjȯin\ *vt* **1** : to direct or impose by authoritative order **2** : FORBID 1, PROHIBIT

en·joy \in-ˈjȯi\ *vt* **1** : to take pleasure or satisfaction in ⟨*enjoy* the nice weather⟩ **2** : to have for one's use, benefit, or lot ⟨*enjoyed* great success⟩ ⟨*enjoying* the freedom to pursue his goals⟩ — **en·joy·able** \-ə-bəl\ *adj* — **en·joy·able·ness** *n* — **en·joy·ably** \-ə-blē\ *adv*

en·joy·ment \in-ˈjȯi-mənt\ *n* **1** : the condition of enjoying something : possession and use of something that gives satisfaction ⟨the *enjoyment* of good health⟩ **2** : PLEASURE, SATISFACTION ⟨find *enjoyment* in skating⟩ **3** : something that gives pleasure

en·kin·dle \in-ˈkin-dl\ *vb* **1** : KINDLE 1 **2** : KINDLE 2

en·lace \in-ˈlās\ *vt* **1** : ENCIRCLE, ENFOLD **2** : ENTWINE, INTERLACE

en·large \in-ˈlärj\ *vb* **1** : to make or grow larger **2** : ELABORATE ⟨*enlarge* on a story⟩ — **en·larg·er** *n*

en·large·ment \in-ˈlärj-mənt\ *n* **1** : an act or instance of enlarging : the state of being enlarged **2** : a photographic print that is larger than the negative and is made by projecting an image of the negative upon a photographic printing surface

en·light·en \in-ˈlīt-n\ *vt* **en·light·ened; en·light·en·ing** \-ˈlīt-ning, -n-ing\ **1** : to furnish knowledge to : INSTRUCT **2** : to give spiritual insight to — **en·light·en·ment** \-ˈlīt-n-mənt\ *n*

en·list \in-ˈlist\ *vb* **1** : to enroll for military or naval service; *esp* : to join one of the armed services voluntarily **2** : to obtain the aid or support of ⟨*enlisted* our help⟩; *also* : to participate heartily (as in a cause) — **en·list·ment** \-ˈlist-mənt, -ˈlis-\ *n*

en·list·ed \in-ˈlist-əd\ *adj* : of, relating to, or constituting the part of a military or naval force below commissioned or warrant officers

en·liv·en \in-ˈlī-vən\ *vt* : to give life, action, or spirit to : ANIMATE

en masse \än-ˈmas, äⁿ-\ *adv* : in a body : as a whole [French]

en·mesh \in-ˈmesh\ *vt* : to entangle in or as if in meshes ⟨was *enmeshed* in disputes with his neighbors⟩

en·mi·ty \ˈen-mət-ē\ *n, pl* **-ties** : positive, active, and typically mutual hatred or ill will [Medieval French *enemité,* from *enemi* "enemy"]

synonyms ENMITY, HOSTILITY, ANIMOSITY, ANTAGONISM mean deep-seated dislike or ill will. ENMITY suggests positive hatred which may be open or concealed ⟨an unspoken *enmity*⟩. HOSTILITY suggests enmity showing itself in attacks or aggression ⟨*hostility* between the two nations⟩. ANIMOSITY implies intense ill will and vindictiveness that threaten to kindle hostility ⟨*animosity* that led to revenge⟩. ANTAGONISM suggests a clash of temperaments leading readily to hostility ⟨*antagonism* between the brothers⟩.

en·no·ble \in-ˈō-bəl\ *vt* **-bled; -bling** \-bə-ling, -bling\ **1** : to make noble : ELEVATE ⟨seemed *ennobled* by suffering⟩ **2** : to raise to the rank of nobility — **en·no·ble·ment** \-bəl-mənt\ *n*

en·nui \ˈän-ˈwē\ *n* : a feeling of weariness and dissatisfaction : BOREDOM [French, from Medieval French *enui* "annoyance," from *enuier* "to vex," from Late Latin *inodiare* "to make loathsome"]

enor·mi·ty \i-ˈnȯr-mət-ē\ *n, pl* **-ties** **1** : great wickedness : OUTRAGEOUSNESS ⟨the *enormity* of the offense⟩ **2** : an outrageous or immoral act or offense **3** : very large size **4** : the quality of momentous importance or impact

enor·mous \i-ˈnȯr-məs\ *adj* **1** *archaic* **a** : ABNORMAL, INORDINATE **b** : exceedingly wicked : OUTRAGEOUS **2** : very great in size, number, or degree [Latin *enormis,* from *e, ex* "out of" + *norma* "norm"] — **enor·mous·ly** *adv* — **enor·mous·ness** *n*

synonyms ENORMOUS, IMMENSE, HUGE, VAST mean exceedingly large. ENORMOUS implies exceeding ordinary bounds in size, amount, or degree ⟨*enormous* expenditures⟩. IMMENSE suggests size far in excess of ordinary measurements or concepts ⟨an *immense* waste of resources⟩. HUGE suggests immensity of bulk, size, or capacity ⟨*huge* barrels of oil⟩. VAST usually suggests immensity of extent ⟨*vast* stretches of grassland⟩.

[1]**enough** \i-ˈnəf; *after* t, d, s, z *often* n-ˈəf\ *adj* : occurring in such quantity, quality, or scope as to fully satisfy demands or needs [Middle English *ynough,* from Old English *genōg*] ***synonyms*** see SUFFICIENT

[2]**enough** *adv* **1** : in or to a sufficient amount or degree : SUFFICIENTLY ⟨ran fast *enough*⟩ **2** : FULLY, QUITE ⟨ready *enough* to admit it⟩ **3** : in a tolerable degree ⟨sang well *enough*⟩

[3]**enough** *n* : a sufficient quantity ⟨we have *enough* to eat⟩

enow \i-ˈnau̇\ *adv or adj, archaic* : ENOUGH [Middle English *inow,* from Old English *genōg*]

en·plane \in-ˈplān\ *vi* : to board an airplane

en·quire, en·qui·ry *chiefly British variant of* INQUIRE, INQUIRY

en·rage \in-ˈrāj\ *vt* : to fill with rage : MADDEN

en·rapt \in-ˈrapt\ *adj* : RAPT 1, ENRAPTURED

en·rap·ture \in-ˈrap-chər\ *vt* **-rap·tured; -rap·tur·ing** \-ˈrap-chə-ring, -ˈrap-shring\ : to fill with delight

en·rich \in-ˈrich\ *vt* **1** : to make rich or richer ⟨*enrich* the mind⟩ **2** : ADORN, ORNAMENT **3 a** : to make (soil) more fertile **b** : to improve (a food) in nutritive value by adding vitamins and minerals in processing — **en·rich·ment** \-mənt\ *n*

en·robe \in-ˈrōb\ *vt* : to cover with or as if with a robe

en·roll *also* **en·rol** \in-ˈrōl\ *vb* **en·rolled; en·roll·ing** **1** : to enter in a list, catalog, or roll **2** : ENTER, JOIN ⟨*enroll* in school⟩ — **en·roll·ment** \-ˈrōl-mənt\ *n*

en route \än-ˈrüt, en-, in-\ *adv* : on or along the way [French]

en·sconce \in-ˈskäns\ *vt* **1** : to place or hide securely : CONCEAL **2** : to establish comfortably : settle snugly

en·sem·ble \än-ˈsäm-bəl, äⁿ-\ *n* : a group constituting a whole or producing a single effect: as **a** : concerted music of two or more parts; *also* : the musicians that perform it **b** : a complete costume of matching clothes **c** : a group of supporting performers [French, from *ensemble* "together," from Medieval French, from Latin *insimul* "at the same time," from *in-* + *simul* "at the same time"]

en·sheathe \in-ˈshē<u>th</u>\ *vt* : to cover with or as if with a sheath

en·shrine \in-ˈshrīn\ *vt* **1** : to enclose in or as if in a shrine **2** : to preserve or cherish as sacred

en·shroud \in-ˈshrau̇d\ *vt* : to cover or enclose with or as if with a shroud

en·sign \ˈen-sən, *in senses 1 & 2 also* ˈen-ˌsīn\ *n* **1** : a flag flown as the symbol of nationality **2** : a badge of office, rank, or power **3** : an officer rank in the Navy and Coast Guard below lieutenant junior grade [Medieval French *enseigne,* from Latin *insignia* "insignia, flags"]

en·si·lage \ˈen-sə-lij\ *n* : the process of converting feed crops into silage; *also* : SILAGE

en·sile \en-ˈsīl, in-\ *vt* : to prepare and store (fodder) so as to induce conversion to silage [French *ensiler,* from *en-* + *silo* "silo," from Spanish]

en·slave \in-ˈslāv\ *vt* : to reduce to slavery : SUBJUGATE — **en·slave·ment** \-mənt\ *n* — **en·slav·er** *n*

en·snare \in-ˈsnaər, -ˈsneər\ *vt* : SNARE 1, ENTRAP

en·sue \in-ˈsü\ *vi* : to come after in time or as a result ⟨*ensuing* effects⟩ [Medieval French *ensivre,* from *en-* + *sivre* "to follow"] ***synonyms*** see FOLLOW

en·sure \in-ˈshu̇r\ *vt* : to make sure, certain, or safe : GUARANTEE [Medieval French *enseurer*]

en·tab·la·ture \in-ˈtab-lə-ˌchu̇r, -chər\ *n* : the upper section of a wall or story usually supported on columns or pilasters and in classical orders consisting of architrave, frieze, and cornice [obsolete French, derived from Latin *in-* + *tabula* "board, table"]

1**en·tail** \in-ˈtāl\ *vt* **1 :** to limit the inheritance of (property) to the owner's direct descendants or to a class of these **2 :** to impose, involve, or imply as a necessary accompaniment or result ⟨the project will *entail* great expense⟩ [derived from Medieval French *taille* "limitation," from *tailler* "to cut, limit"] — **en·tail·ment** \-mənt\ *n*

2**en·tail** \ˈen-ˌtāl, in-ˈtāl\ *n* **1 a :** an entailing of property **b :** an entailed estate **2 :** the rule by which the descent of property is fixed

en·tan·gle \in-ˈtang-gəl\ *vt* **1 :** to make tangled, complicated, or confused **2 :** to involve in or as if in a tangle — **en·tan·gle·ment** \-gəl-mənt\ *n*

en·tente \än-ˈtänt\ *n* **1 :** an international understanding providing for a common course of action **2 :** a coalition of parties to an entente [French, from Medieval French, "intent, understanding"]

en·ter \ˈent-ər\ *vb* **en·tered; en·ter·ing** \ˈent-ə-ring, ˈen-tring\ **1 :** to go or come in or into ⟨*enter* a room⟩ ⟨*enter* by the back door⟩ **2 :** to pass into or through usually by overcoming resistance : PIERCE ⟨the needle *entered* the vein⟩ **3 :** to cause to be admitted to : ENROLL ⟨*enter* a child in kindergarten⟩ **4 :** to become a member of or participant in : JOIN ⟨*enter* the club⟩ ⟨*enter* into a discussion⟩ **5 :** to make a beginning ⟨*enter* into business⟩ **6 :** to play a part : be a factor ⟨other considerations *enter* when money is involved⟩ **7 :** to take possession ⟨*entered* upon their inheritance⟩ **8 :** to put in : INSERT ⟨*enter* the new data into the computer⟩ **9 :** to make a report to customs officials of (a ship or its cargo) upon arrival in port **10 :** to put formally on record ⟨*enter* a complaint⟩ [Medieval French *entrer,* from Latin *intrare,* from *intra* "within"] — **en·ter·able** \ˈent-ə-rə-bəl\ *adj*

synonyms ENTER, PENETRATE, PIERCE mean to make way into something. ENTER is the general term and may imply going in or forcing a way in ⟨firefighters *entered* the burning building⟩. PENETRATE carries a strong implication of an impelling force or compelling power that achieves entrance ⟨the enemy *penetrated* the fortress⟩. PIERCE means entering or cutting through with a sharp-pointed instrument ⟨*pierced* the boil with a lancet⟩.

enter- *or* **entero-** *combining form* : intestine ⟨*enter*itis⟩ [Greek *enteron*]

en·ter·ic \en-ˈter-ik\ *adj* : of or relating to the alimentary canal : INTESTINAL

en·ter·i·tis \ˌent-ə-ˈrīt-əs\ *n* : inflammation of the intestine; *also* : a disease marked by this

en·tero·coc·cus \ˌent-ə-rō-ˈkäk-əs\ *n* : any of a genus of bacteria that resemble streptococci; *esp* : one normally present in the intestine — **en·tero·coc·cal** \-ˈkäk-əl\ *adj*

en·tero·coele *or* **en·tero·coel** \ˈent-ə-rō-ˌsēl\ *n* : a coelom originating by outgrowth from the cavity of the gastrula — **en·tero·coe·lic** \ˌent-ə-rō-ˈsē-lik\ *adj* — **en·tero·coe·lous** \-ləs\ *adj*

en·tero·ki·nase \ˌent-ə-rō-ˈkīn-ˌās, -ˌnāz\ *n* : an intestinal enzyme that converts trypsinogen to trypsin [*enter-* + *kin*etic + *-ase*]

en·ter·on \ˈent-ə-ˌrän, -rən\ *n* : an embryonic alimentary canal

en·ter·prise \ˈent-ər-ˌprīz, ˈent-ə-ˌ\ *n* **1 :** a difficult, complicated, or risky project or undertaking **2 :** readiness to engage in daring or difficult action : INITIATIVE **3 :** a business organization [Medieval French, from *entreprendre* "to undertake," from *entre-* "inter-" + *prendre* "to take," from Latin *prehendere* "to seize"] — **en·ter·pris·er** \-ˌprī-zər\ *n*

en·ter·pris·ing \-ˌprī-zing\ *adj* : marked by an independent energetic spirit and by readiness to act ⟨an *enterprising* young reporter⟩

en·ter·tain \ˌent-ər-ˈtān\ *vb* **1 :** to receive and provide for as host : have as a guest ⟨*entertain* friends over the weekend⟩ **2 :** to provide entertainment especially for guests **3 :** to have in mind : CONSIDER ⟨*entertained* thoughts of quitting⟩ **4 :** to provide entertainment for ⟨*entertained* us with stories⟩ [Medieval French *entretenir,* from *entre-* "inter-" + *tenir* "to hold," from Latin *tenēre*] ***synonyms*** see AMUSE — **en·ter·tain·er** *n*

en·ter·tain·ing \ˌen-tər-ˈtā-ning\ *adj* : providing entertainment ⟨an *entertaining* book⟩

en·ter·tain·ment \-ˈtān-mənt\ *n* **1 :** the act of providing pleasure, recreation, or amusement especially for guests **2 :** a means of amusement or diversion; *esp* : a public performance

en·thrall *or* **en·thral** \in-ˈthrȯl\ *vt* **en·thralled; en·thrall·ing** **1** : ENSLAVE **2 :** to hold spellbound : CHARM — **en·thrall·ment** \-ˈthrȯl-mənt\ *n*

en·throne \in-ˈthrōn\ *vt* **1 a :** to install in a position of authority or influence **b :** to install ceremonially on a throne **2 :** to regard as having supreme virtue or value : EXALT — **en·throne·ment** \-mənt\ *n*

en·thuse \in-ˈthüz, -ˈthyüz\ *vb* **1 :** to make or grow enthusiastic **2 :** to show enthusiasm [back-formation from *enthusiasm*]

en·thu·si·asm \in-ˈthü-zē-ˌaz-əm, -ˈthyü-\ *n* **1 :** strong excitement of feeling : FERVOR **2 :** something inspiring zeal or fervor [Greek *enthousiasmos,* from *enthousiazein* "to be inspired," from *entheos* "inspired," from *en-* + *theos* "god"] ***synonyms*** see ZEAL

en·thu·si·ast \-zē-ˌast, -əst\ *n* : a person filled with enthusiasm

en·thu·si·as·tic \in-ˌthü-zē-ˈas-tik, -ˌthyü-\ *adj* : filled with or marked by enthusiasm ⟨an *enthusiastic* welcome⟩ — **en·thu·si·as·ti·cal·ly** \-ti-kə-lē, -klē\ *adv*

en·tice \in-ˈtīs\ *vt* : to attract by arousing hope or desire : TEMPT [Medieval French *enticer*] — **en·tice·ment** \-mənt\ *n* ***synonyms*** see LURE

en·tire \in-ˈtīr, ˈen-ˌ\ *adj* **1 :** having no element or part left out **2 :** COMPLETE, TOTAL ⟨an *entire* regiment was lost⟩ **3 :** having the margin continuous and free from indentations ⟨an *entire* leaf⟩ [Medieval French *entier,* from Latin *integer,* literally, "untouched," from *in-* + *tangere* "to touch"] ***synonyms*** see WHOLE — **entire** *adv* — **en·tire·ly** *adv* — **en·tire·ness** *n*

en·tire·ty \in-ˈtī-rət-ē, -ˈtīrt-ē\ *n* **1 :** the state of being entire or complete **2 :** sum total : WHOLE

en·ti·tle \in-ˈtīt-l\ *vt* **en·ti·tled; en·ti·tling** \-ˈtīt-ling, -l-ing\ **1 :** to give a title to : DESIGNATE **2 a :** to give a legal right to **b :** to qualify for something ⟨this ticket *entitles* me to a free ride⟩ — **en·ti·tle·ment** \-ˈtīt-l-mənt\ *n*

en·ti·ty \ˈent-ət-ē\ *n, pl* **-ties** : something existing or thought of as existing : BEING [Medieval Latin *entitas,* from Latin *ent-, ens* "existing thing," from coined present participle of *esse* "to be"]

en·tomb \in-ˈtüm\ *vt* : to place in a tomb : BURY — **en·tomb·ment** \-ˈtüm-mənt\ *n*

en·to·mol·o·gy \ˌent-ə-ˈmäl-ə-jē\ *n* : a branch of zoology that deals with insects [French *entomologie,* from Greek *entomon* "insect," from *entomos* "cut up," from *en-* + *temnein* "to cut" — see *Word History* at INSECT] — **en·to·mo·log·i·cal** \ˌent-ə-mə-ˈläj-i-kəl\ *adj* — **en·to·mo·log·i·cal·ly** \-i-kə-lē, -klē\ *adv* — **en·to·mol·o·gist** \ˌent-ə-ˈmäl-ə-jəst\ *n*

en·tou·rage \ˌän-tu̇-ˈräzh\ *n* : one's attendants or associates : RETINUE [French]

en·tr'acte \ˈän-ˌtrakt, ˈä^{n}-; än-ˈ, ä^{n}-ˈ\ *n* **1 :** the interval between two acts of a play **2 :** a dance, piece of music, or interlude performed between two acts of a play [French, from *entre-* "inter-" + *acte* "act"]

en·trails \ˈen-trəlz, -ˌtrālz\ *n pl* : internal parts : VISCERA; *esp* : INTESTINES [Medieval French *entrailles,* from Medieval Latin *intralia,* alteration of Latin *interanea,* from *interaneus* "interior"]

en·train \in-ˈtrān\ *vb* : to put or go aboard a train

1**en·trance** \ˈen-trəns\ *n* **1 :** the right to enter : ADMISSION **2 :** the act of entering **3 :** the means or place of entry **4 :** the point at which a voice or instrument part begins in ensemble music **5 :** the first appearance of an actor in a scene

2**en·trance** \in-ˈtrans\ *vt* **1 :** to put into a trance **2 :** to fill with delight, wonder, or rapture — **en·trance·ment** \-mənt\ *n*

en·trant \ˈen-trənt\ *n* : one that enters; *esp* : one that enters a contest

en·trap \in-ˈtrap\ *vt* **1 :** to catch in or as if in a trap **2 :** to lure into a compromising statement or act — **en·trap·ment** \-mənt\ *n*

en·treat \in-ˈtrēt\ *vb* : to ask earnestly or urgently : PLEAD [Medieval French *entreter* "to treat," from *en-* + *treter* "to treat"] ***synonyms*** see BEG — **en·treat·ing·ly** \-ing-lē\ *adv*

en·treaty \in-ˈtrēt-ē\ *n, pl* **-treat·ies** : an earnest request : PLEA

en·trée *or* **en·tree** \ˈän-ˌtrā\ *n* **1 a :** the act or manner of entering : ENTRANCE **b :** freedom of entry or access **2 :** the main dish of a meal in the U.S. [French *entrée*]

\ə\ **abut**	\au̇\ **out**	\i\ **tip**	\ȯ\ **saw**	\u̇\ **foot**
\ər\ **further**	\ch\ **chin**	\ī\ **life**	\ȯi\ **coin**	\y\ **yet**
\a\ **mat**	\e\ **pet**	\j\ **job**	\th\ **thin**	\yü\ **few**
\ā\ **take**	\ē\ **easy**	\ng\ **sing**	\t͟h\ **this**	\yu̇\ **cure**
\ä\ **cot, cart**	\g\ **go**	\ō\ **bone**	\ü\ **food**	\zh\ **vision**

en·trench *also* **in·trench** \in-ˈtrench\ *vb* **1 a :** to dig, place within, surround with, or occupy a trench especially for defense **b :** to establish solidly **2 :** to cut into **:** FURROW; *esp* **:** to erode downward so as to form a trench **3 :** ENCROACH 1 — used with *on* or *upon* — **en·trench·ment** \in-ˈtrench-mənt\ *n*

en·tre·pre·neur \ˌän-trə-prə-ˈnər, -pə-, -ˈnu̇r, -ˈnyu̇r\ *n* **:** one who organizes, manages, and assumes the risks of a business or enterprise [French]

en·tro·py \ˈen-trə-pē\ *n* **1 :** a measure of the unavailable energy in a closed thermodynamic system that is usually considered to be a measure of the system's disorder **2 :** the degradation of the matter and energy in the universe to an ultimate state of inert uniformity [German *Entropie,* from Greek *en-* + *trepein* "to turn, change"]

en·trust *also* **in·trust** \in-ˈtrəst\ *vt* **1 :** to give into the care of another (as for safekeeping) **2 :** to give custody, care, or charge of something to as a trust ⟨*entrusted* a bank with their savings⟩ — **en·trust·ment** \-ˈtrəst-mənt, -ˈtrəs-\ *n*

en·try \ˈen-trē\ *n, pl* **entries** **1 :** the act of entering **:** ENTRANCE **2 :** a place through which entrance is made **:** HALL 3a, VESTIBULE **3 a :** the act of making (as in a book or list) a written record of something **b :** the thing thus recorded: as (1) **:** HEADWORD (2) **:** a headword with its definition or identification (3) **:** VOCABULARY ENTRY **4 :** a person, thing, or group entered into something (as a contest or market)

en·twine \in-ˈtwīn\ *vb* **:** to twine together or around

enu·mer·ate \i-ˈnü-mə-ˌrāt, -ˈnyü-\ *vt* **1 :** to ascertain the number of **:** COUNT **2 :** to specify one after another **:** LIST [Latin *enumerare,* from *e-* + *numerare* "to count," from *numerus* "number"] — **enu·mer·a·ble** \-ˈnüm-rə-bəl, ˈnyüm-, -ə-rə-\ *adj* — **enu·mer·a·tion** \-ˌnü-mə-ˈrā-shən, -ˌnyü-\ *n* — **enu·mer·a·tive** \-ˈnü-mə-ˌrā-tiv, -ˈnyü, -rə-tiv\ *adj* — **enu·mer·a·tor** \-ˈnü-mə-ˌrāt-ər, -ˈnyü-\ *n*

enun·ci·ate \ē-ˈnən-sē-ˌāt\ *vt* **1 :** to make known publicly **:** PROCLAIM ⟨*enunciate* the aims of a program⟩ **2 :** to utter distinctly **:** PRONOUNCE ⟨*enunciate* your words clearly⟩ [Latin *enuntiare* "to report, declare," from *e-* + *nuntiare* "to report," from *nuntius* "messenger"] — **enun·cia·ble** \-ˈnən-sē-ə-bəl\ *adj* — **enun·ci·a·tion** \-ˌnən-sē-ˈā-shən\ *n* — **enun·ci·a·tor** \-ˈnən-sē-ˌāt-ər\ *n*

en·ure·sis \ˌen-yu̇-ˈrē-səs\ *n* **:** involuntary discharge of urine **:** bed wetting [New Latin, from Greek *enourein* "to urinate in, wet the bed," from *en-* + *ourein* "to urinate"] — **en·uret·ic** \-ˈret-ik\ *adj or n*

en·vel·op \in-ˈvel-əp\ *vt* **:** to enclose or enfold completely with or as if with a covering [Medieval French *envoluper,* from *en-* + *voluper* "to wrap"] — **en·vel·op·ment** \-mənt\ *n*

en·ve·lope \ˈen-və-ˌlōp, ˈän-\ *n* **1 :** a flat usually paper container (as for a letter) **2 :** something that envelops **3 :** the bag containing the gas in a balloon or airship **4 :** a natural enclosing covering (as a membrane)

en·ven·om \in-ˈven-əm\ *vt* **1 :** to taint or fill with poison **2 :** EMBITTER

en·vi·a·ble \ˈen-vē-ə-bəl\ *adj* **:** highly desirable — **en·vi·a·ble·ness** *n* — **en·vi·a·bly** \-blē\ *adv*

en·vi·ous \ˈen-vē-əs\ *adj* **:** feeling or showing envy ⟨*envious* of a friend's wealth⟩ — **en·vi·ous·ly** *adv* — **en·vi·ous·ness** *n*

synonyms ENVIOUS, JEALOUS mean feeling spiteful malice and resentment over another's advantage. ENVIOUS suggests malicious begrudging of another's possessions and accomplishments ⟨*envious* of his rival's talent⟩. JEALOUS implies a begrudging of something regarded as properly belonging to oneself; it may also indicate a vigilant guarding ⟨*jealous* of her good name⟩.

en·vi·ron·ment \in-ˈvī-rən-mənt, -ˈvī-ərn-, -ˈvīrn-\ *n* **1 :** the circumstances, objects, or conditions by which one is surrounded **2 :** surrounding conditions or forces that influence or change: as **a :** the whole complex of factors (as soil, climate, and living things) that determine the form and survival of an organism or ecological community **b :** the social and cultural conditions that influence the life of a person or human community [*environ* "to surround," from Medieval French *enviruner,* from *envirun* "around," from *en-* "in" + *virun* "circle"] — **en·vi·ron·men·tal** \in-ˌvī-rən-ˈment-l, -ˌvī-ərn-, -ˌvīrn-\ *adj* — **en·vi·ron·men·tal·ly** \-l-ē\ *adv*

en·vi·ron·men·tal·ism \in-ˌvī-rən-ˈment-l-ˌiz-əm\ *n* **:** the act or process of preserving, restoring, or improving the natural environment

en·vi·ron·men·tal·ist \-ˌvī-rən-ˈment-l-əst, -ˌvī-ərn-, -ˌvīrn-\ *n* **:** a person who practices environmentalism; *also* **:** a person concerned about environmental quality especially of the human environment with respect to the control of pollution

en·vi·rons \in-ˈvī-rənz, -ˈvī-ərnz, -ˈvīrnz\ *n pl* **1 :** the districts around a city **2 :** ENVIRONMENT 1, SURROUNDINGS

en·vis·age \in-ˈviz-ij\ *vt* **:** to have a mental picture of especially in advance of realization **:** VISUALIZE

en·vi·sion \in-ˈvizh-ən\ *vt* **:** to picture to oneself **:** IMAGINE

en·voy \ˈen-ˌvȯi, ˈän-\ *n* **1 a :** a diplomatic representative who ranks between an ambassador and a minister **b :** a representative sent by one government to another **2 :** REPRESENTATIVE, MESSENGER [French *envoyé,* from *envoyer* "to send," from Latin *in-* + *via* "way"]

¹en·vy \ˈen-vē\ *n, pl* **envies** **1 :** painful or resentful awareness of an advantage enjoyed by another joined with a desire to possess the same advantage **2 :** an object of envy ⟨their new car was the *envy* of the neighborhood⟩ [Medieval French *envie,* from Latin *invidia,* from *invidus* "envious," from *invidēre* "to look askance at, envy," from *in-* + *vidēre* "to see"]

²envy *vt* **en·vied; en·vy·ing :** to feel envy toward or on account of — **en·vi·er** *n* — **en·vy·ing·ly** \-ing-lē\ *adv*

en·wrap \in-ˈrap\ *vt* **1 :** to wrap in a covering **:** ENFOLD **2 :** to hold one's interest **:** ENGROSS

en·zy·mat·ic \ˌen-zə-ˈmat-ik\ *adj* **:** of, relating to, or produced by an enzyme — **en·zy·mat·i·cal·ly** \-i-kə-lē, -klē\ *adv*

en·zyme \ˈen-ˌzīm\ *n* **:** any of various complex proteins produced by living cells that bring about or accelerate reactions (as in the digestion of food) without being permanently altered [German *enzym,* derived from Greek *en-* + *zymē* "leaven"]

enzyme–linked im·mu·no·sor·bent assay \-ˌim-yə-nō-ˈsȯr-bənt-\ *n* **:** an in vitro test for quantifying an antibody or antigen concentration by exposing the test material to an enzyme-antigen or enzyme-antibody complex — called also *ELISA*

en·zy·mic \en-ˈzī-mik\ *adj* **:** ENZYMATIC — **en·zy·mi·cal·ly** \-mi-kə-lē, -klē\ *adv*

eo- *combining form* **:** earliest **:** oldest ⟨*Eocene*⟩ [Greek *ēōs* "dawn"]

Eo·cene \ˈē-ə-ˌsēn\ *n* **:** the epoch of the Tertiary between the Paleocene and the Oligocene; *also* **:** the corresponding series of rocks — **Eocene** *adj*

eo·hip·pus \ˌē-ō-ˈhip-əs\ *n* **:** any of a genus of small primitive horses from the Lower Eocene of the western U.S. and Europe with four toes on each forelimb and three toes on each hind limb [Greek *hippos* "horse"]

eo·lian *also* **ae·o·lian** \ē-ˈō-lē-ən, -ˈōl-yən\ *adj* **:** borne, deposited, produced, or eroded by the wind ⟨*eolian* sand⟩ [Latin *Aeolus,* god of the winds]

eo·lith \ˈē-ə-ˌlith\ *n* **:** a very crudely chipped flint from the earliest phase of human culture

eon *variant of* AEON

eo·sin \ˈē-ə-sən\ *also* **eo·sine** \-sən, -ˌsēn\ *n* **:** a red synthetic fluorescent dye used especially in cosmetics and as a toner; *also* **:** a salt of this dye used chiefly in red pigments and as a stain for biological tissue [Greek *ēōs* "dawn"]

eo·sin·o·phil \ˌē-ə-ˈsin-ə-ˌfil\ *n* **:** a white blood cell with granule-containing cytoplasm that is present in the body at sites of allergic reactions and parasitic infections

-eous *adj suffix* **:** like **:** resembling [Latin *-eus*]

ep·au·let *also* **ep·au·lette** \ˌep-ə-ˈlet\ *n* **:** a shoulder ornament on a uniform especially of a military or naval officer [French *épaulette,* from *épaule* "shoulder," from Medieval French *espalle,* from Late Latin *spatula* "shoulder blade, spoon," from Latin *spatha* "spoon, sword"]

épée \ˈep-ˌā, ā-ˈpā\ *n* **:** a fencing or dueling sword having a bowl-shaped guard and a tapering rigid blade with no cutting edge [French, from Medieval French *espee,* from Latin *spatha* "spoon, sword"]

ephah \ˈē-fə, ˈef-ə\ *n* **:** an ancient Hebrew unit of dry measure equal to a little more than a bushel (about 35 liters) [Hebrew *ēphāh,* from Egyptian *ˀpt*]

épée

ephed·rine \i-ˈfed-rən\ *n* **:** a crystalline basic substance extracted from Chinese woody plants or synthesized and used as a salt in relieving hay fever, asthma, and nasal congestion [New Latin *Ephedra,* genus of shrubs]

ephem·era \i-ˈfem-rə, -ə-rə\ *n pl* **:** ephemeral things
ephem·er·al \i-ˈfem-rəl, -ə-rəl\ *adj* **1 :** lasting one day only ‹an *ephemeral* fever› **2 :** lasting a very short time ‹*ephemeral* pleasures› [Greek *ephēmeros* "lasting a day, daily," from *epi-* + *hēmera* "day"] ***synonyms*** see TRANSIENT — **ephem·er·al·i·ty** \-ˌfem-ə-ˈral-ət-ē\ *n* — **ephem·er·al·ly** \-ˈfem-rə-lē, -ə-rə-lē\ *adv*
ephem·er·is \-rəs\ *n, pl* **eph·e·mer·i·des** \ˌef-ə-ˈmer-ə-ˌdēz\ **:** a tabular statement of the assigned places of a celestial body for regular intervals [Latin, "diary, ephemeris," from Greek *ephēmeris,* from *ephēmeros* "daily"]
Ephe·sians \i-ˈfē-zhənz\ *n* **:** a letter addressed to early Christians and included as a book in the New Testament — see BIBLE table
eph·or \ˈef-ər, -ˌȯr\ *n* **:** one of five ancient Spartan magistrates having power over the king [Latin *ephorus,* from Greek *ephoros,* from *ephoran* "to oversee," from *epi-* + *horan* "to see"]
epi- *prefix* **:** upon ‹*epi*phyte›**:** attached to ‹*epi*didymis› **:** over ‹*epi*center›**:** outer ‹*epi*carp›**:** after ‹*epi*genesis› [Greek, from *epi* "on"]
¹ep·ic \ˈep-ik\ *adj* **1 :** of, relating to, or having the characteristics of an epic **2 :** unusually long especially in size or scope [Latin *epicus,* from Greek *epikos,* from *epos* "word, speech, poem"]
²epic *n* **1 :** a long serious narrative poem in a dignified style relating the deeds of a legendary or historical hero **2 :** a work of art that resembles or suggests an epic **3 :** a series of events or body of tradition held to form the proper subject of an epic
epi·carp \ˈep-ə-ˌkärp\ *n* **:** EXOCARP
epi·cen·ter \ˈep-ə-ˌsent-ər\ *n* **1 :** the part of the earth's surface directly above the focus of an earthquake **2 :** CENTER 2a ‹the *epicenter* of cultural activity›
ep·i·cot·yl \ˈep-ə-ˌkät-l\ *n* **:** the part of a plant embryo or seedling above the cotyledons
ep·i·cure \ˈep-i-ˌkyu̇r\ *n* **:** a person with discriminating tastes in food or wine [*Epicurus,* died 270 B.C., Greek philosopher]
¹ep·i·cu·re·an \ˌep-i-kyu̇-ˈrē-ən, -ˈkyu̇r-ē-\ *adj* **1** *cap* **:** of or relating to Epicurus or Epicureanism **2 :** of, relating to, or suited to an epicure
²epicurean *n* **1** *cap* **:** a follower of Epicurus **2 :** EPICURE
Ep·i·cu·re·an·ism \-ə-ˌniz-əm\ *n* **:** the philosophy of Epicurus that pleasure is the only good and the pleasures of wise, just, and moderate living are the best
¹ep·i·dem·ic \ˌep-ə-ˈdem-ik\ *adj* **1 :** affecting many individuals at one time ‹an *epidemic* disease› **2 :** widespread especially to an excessive degree ‹crime was *epidemic*› [derived from Greek *epidēmia* "visit, epidemic," from *epidēmos* "visiting, epidemic," from *epi-* + *dēmos* "people"] — **ep·i·dem·i·cal·ly** \-ˈdem-i-kə-lē, -klē\ *adv* — **ep·i·de·mic·i·ty** \-ˌdem-ˈis-ət-ē\ *n*
²epidemic *n* **1 :** an outbreak of epidemic disease **2 :** a sudden rapidly spreading outbreak ‹a crime *epidemic*›
ep·i·de·mi·ol·o·gy \ˌep-ə-ˌdē-mē-ˈäl-ə-jē\ *n* **1 :** a branch of medical science that deals with the rate of occurrence, distribution, and control of disease in a population **2 :** the sum of the factors controlling the presence or absence of a particular disease — **ep·i·de·mi·o·log·i·cal** \-ˈläj-i-kəl\ *also* **ep·i·de·mi·o·log·ic** \-mē-ə-ˈläj-ik\ *adj* — **ep·i·de·mi·o·log·i·cal·ly** \-i-kə-lē, -klē\ *adv* — **ep·i·de·mi·ol·o·gist** \-mē-ˈäl-ə-jəst\ *n*
epi·der·mis \ˌep-ə-ˈdər-məs\ *n* **1 :** the thin outer layer of the animal body that in vertebrates forms an insensitive covering over the dermis **2 :** a thin surface layer of protecting cells in seed plants and ferns **3 :** any of various covering layers resembling the epidermis of the skin [Late Latin, from Greek, from *epi-* + *derma* "skin"] — **epi·der·mal** \-məl\ *adj*
ep·i·did·y·mis \ˌep-ə-ˈdid-ə-məs\ *n, pl* **-mi·des** \-mə-ˌdēz\ **:** a mass at the back of the testis composed of coiled tubes in which sperms are stored [Greek, from *epi-* + *didymos* "testicle," from *dyo* "two"] — **epi·did·y·mal** \-ˈdid-ə-məl\ *adj*
epi·du·ral \ˌep-i-ˈdu̇r-əl; -ˈdyu̇r-\ *n* **:** an injection of an anesthetic into the space outside the dura mater of the spinal cord in the lower back region to produce loss of feeling especially in the abdomen or pelvic region [*epi-* + *dura* mater]
epi·gen·e·sis \ˌep-ə-ˈjen-ə-səs\ *n, pl* **-e·ses** \-ˌsēz\ **:** development in which an initially unspecialized entity (as a spore) gradually develops specialized characters (as of a whole plant) — **ep·i·ge·net·ic** \-jə-ˈnet-ik\ *adj*
epi·glot·tis \ˌep-ə-ˈglät-əs\ *n* **:** a thin plate of flexible cartilage in front of the glottis that folds back over and protects the glottis during swallowing — **epi·glot·tal** \-ˈglät-l\ *adj*
ep·i·gram \ˈep-ə-ˌgram\ *n* **1 :** a short often satirical poem ending with a clever or witty turn of thought **2 :** a brief witty saying [Latin *epigramma,* from Greek, from *epigraphein* "to write on, inscribe," from *epi-* + *graphein* "to write"] — **ep·i·gram·ma·tist** \ˌep-ə-ˈgram-ət-əst\ *n*
ep·i·gram·mat·ic \ˌep-i-grə-ˈmat-ik\ *adj* **1 :** of, relating to, or resembling an epigram **2 :** marked by or given to the use of epigrams — **ep·i·gram·mat·i·cal** \-ˈmat-i-kəl\ *adj* — **ep·i·gram·mat·i·cal·ly** \-i-kə-lē, -klē\ *adv*
epig·ra·phy \i-ˈpig-rə-fē, e-\ *n* **:** the study of inscriptions and especially of ancient inscriptions [Greek *epigraphein* "to inscribe," from *epi-* + *graphein* "to write"]
epig·y·nous \i-ˈpij-ə-nəs, e-\ *adj* **1 :** grown to and appearing to arise from the top of a plant ovary ‹*epigynous* stamens› **2 :** having epigynous floral organs
ep·i·lep·sy \ˈep-ə-ˌlep-sē\ *n* **:** a disorder marked by abnormal electrical discharges in the brain and characterized by brief episodes of convulsions, involuntary movements, and loss of consciousness [derived from Greek *epilēpsia,* from *epilambanein* "to seize," from *epi-* + *lambanein* "to take, seize"] — **ep·i·lep·tic** \ˌep-ə-ˈlep-tik\ *adj or n*
ep·i·logue \ˈep-ə-ˌlȯg, -ˌläg\ *n* **1 :** a concluding section that brings to an end and summarizes or comments on the design of a literary work **2 :** a speech often in verse addressed to the audience by an actor at the end of a play **3 :** a concluding event or development [derived from Greek *epilogos,* from *epilegein* "to say in addition," from *epi-* + *legein* "to say"]
epi·neph·rine *also* **epi·neph·rin** \ˌep-ə-ˈnef-rən\ *n* **:** a hormone of the adrenal gland acting especially on smooth muscle, causing narrowing of blood vessels, and raising blood pressure — called also *adrenaline* [derived from Greek *epi-* + *nephros* "kidney"]
epiph·a·ny \i-ˈpif-ə-nē\ *n, pl* **-nies** **1** *cap* **:** January 6 observed as a church festival in commemoration of the coming of the three wise men to Jesus at Bethlehem or in the Eastern Church in commemoration of Jesus' baptism **2 :** an appearance or manifestation especially of a divine being **3 :** an intuitive discovery or realization [derived from Late Latin *epiphania,* from Late Greek, plural, probably from Greek *epiphaneia* "appearance, manifestation," from *epi-* + *phainein* "to show"]
epiph·y·sis \i-ˈpif-ə-səs\ *n, pl* **-y·ses** \-ə-ˌsēz\ **:** the end of a long bone [Greek, "growth," from *epi-* + *physesthai* "to grow"] — **epiph·y·se·al** \i-ˌpif-ə-ˈsē-əl\ *adj*
ep·i·phyte \ˈep-ə-ˌfīt\ *n* **:** a plant that derives its moisture and nutrients from the air and rain and usually grows on another plant

epiphyte

ep·i·phyt·ic \ˌep-ə-ˈfit-ik\ *adj* **1 :** of, relating to, or being an epiphyte **2 :** living on the surface of plants ‹*epiphytic* algae on kelps› — **ep·i·phyt·i·cal·ly** \-ˈfit-i-kə-lē, -klē\ *adv*
epis·co·pa·cy \i-ˈpis-kə-pə-sē\ *n, pl* **-cies** **1 :** government of the church by bishops **2 :** EPISCOPATE 2
epis·co·pal \i-ˈpis-kə-pəl\ *adj* **1 :** of or relating to a bishop or episcopacy **2** *cap* **:** of or relating to the Protestant Episcopal Church [Late Latin *episcopalis,* from *episcopus* "bishop," from Greek *episkopos,* literally, "overseer," from *epi-* + *skeptesthai* "to look at"] — **epis·co·pal·ly** \-pə-lē, -plē\ *adv*
Epis·co·pa·lian \i-ˌpis-kə-ˈpāl-yən\ *n* **1 :** an adherent of episcopacy **2 :** a member of the Protestant Episcopal Church — **Episcopalian** *adj* — **Epis·co·pa·lian·ism** \-yə-ˌniz-əm\ *n*
epis·co·pate \i-ˈpis-kə-pət\ *n* **1 :** the rank or office of or term of as a bishop **2 :** the whole body of bishops
epi·si·ot·o·my \i-ˌpi-zē-ˈät-ə-mē, -ˌpē-\ *n* **:** a surgical procedure to enlarge the opening of the vagina during the birth process to make delivery easier [*episio-* "vulva" (from Greek *epision* "pubic area") + *-tomy*]
ep·i·sode \ˈep-ə-ˌsōd\ *n* **1 a :** a developed situation integral to but separable from a continuous narrative **:** INCIDENT **b :** one of a series of loosely connected stories or scenes **2 :** an event

\ə\ **abut**	\au̇\ **out**	\i\ **tip**	\ȯ\ **saw**	\u̇\ **foot**
\ər\ **further**	\ch\ **chin**	\ī\ **life**	\ȯi\ **coin**	\y\ **yet**
\a\ **mat**	\e\ **pet**	\j\ **job**	\th\ **thin**	\yü\ **few**
\ā\ **take**	\ē\ **easy**	\ng\ **sing**	\th̲\ **this**	\yu̇\ **cure**
\ä\ **cot, cart**	\g\ **go**	\ō\ **bone**	\ü\ **food**	\zh\ **vision**

that is distinctive and separate especially in history or in a life ⟨an *episode* of the war⟩ ⟨an *episode* of coughing⟩ **3 :** a digressive subdivision in a musical composition [Greek *epeisodion,* from *epeisodios* "coming in besides," from *epi-* + *eisodios* "coming in," from *eis* "into" + *hodos* "road"] ***synonyms*** see OCCURRENCE — **ep·i·sod·ic** \ˌep-ə-ˈsäd-ik\ *also* **ep·i·sod·i·cal** \-ˈsäd-i-kəl\ *adj* — **ep·i·sod·i·cal·ly** \-i-kə-lē, -klē\ *adv*

epis·tle \i-ˈpis-əl\ *n* **1** *cap* **a :** any of the letters of the New Testament **b :** a liturgical reading usually from one of the New Testament Epistles **2 :** LETTER 2; *esp* **:** a formal or elegant letter [Medieval French, literally, "letter," from Latin *epistula, epistola,* from Greek *epistolē,* from *epi-* + *stellein* "to send"]

epis·to·lary \i-ˈpis-tə-ˌler-ē\ *adj* **1 :** of, relating to, or suitable to a letter **2 :** contained in or carried on by letters ⟨*epistolary* friendships⟩ **3 :** written in the form of a series of letters ⟨an *epistolary* novel⟩

ep·i·taph \ˈep-ə-ˌtaf\ *n* **:** an inscription (as on a tombstone) in memory of a dead person [Medieval Latin *epitaphium,* from Latin, "funeral oration," from Greek *epitaphion,* from *epi-* + *taphos* "tomb, funeral"]

ep·i·the·li·um \ˌep-ə-ˈthē-lē-əm\ *n, pl* **-lia** \-lē-ə\ **1 :** a membranous cellular tissue that covers a free surface or lines a tube or cavity of an animal body and usually encloses parts of the body, produces secretions and excretions, or functions in assimilation **2 :** a usually thin layer of parenchyma that lines a cavity or tube of a plant [*epi-* + Greek *thēlē* "nipple"] — **ep·i·the·li·al** \-lē-əl\ *adj* — **ep·i·the·li·oid** \-lē-ˌȯid\ *adj*

ep·i·thet \ˈep-ə-ˌthet\ *n* **1 :** a word or phrase (as *Lion-Hearted* in "Richard the Lion-Hearted") that expresses a quality held to be characteristic of a person or thing **2 :** a disparaging or abusive word or phrase **3 :** the part of a taxonomic name identifying a subunit (as a species or variety) within a genus [Latin *epitheton,* from Greek, from *epitithenai* "to put on, add," from *epi-* + *tithenai* "to put"] — **ep·i·thet·ic** \ˌep-ə-ˈthet-ik\ *or* **ep·i·thet·i·cal** \-ˈthet-i-kəl\ *adj*

epit·o·me \i-ˈpit-ə-mē\ *n* **1 :** a summary of a written work **2 :** a typical or ideal example **:** EMBODIMENT ⟨the *epitome* of good taste⟩ [Latin, from Greek *epitomē,* from *epitemnein* "to cut short," from *epi-* + *temnein* "to cut"]

epit·o·mize \i-ˈpit-ə-ˌmīz\ *vt* **1 :** to form or give an epitome of **:** SUMMARIZE **2 :** TYPIFY 2, EXEMPLIFY

[1]**epi·zo·ot·ic** \ˌep-ə-zə-ˈwät-ik\ *adj* **:** of, relating to, or being a disease that affects many animals of one kind at the same time

[2]**epizootic** *n* **:** an epizootic disease

e plu·ri·bus unum \ˌē-ˌplu̇r-ə-bəs-ˈyü-nəm; ˌā-ˌplu̇r-, -bə-ˈsü-\ **:** one composed of many — used on the seal of the U.S. and on several U.S. coins [Latin, "one out of many"]

ep·och \ˈep-ək, -ˌäk\ *n* **1 :** an instant of time selected as a point of reference in astronomy **2 a :** an event or a time that begins a new period or development **b :** a memorable event or date **3 a :** an extended period of time characterized by a distinctive development or by a memorable series of events **b :** a division of geologic time less than a period and greater than an age [Medieval Latin *epocha,* from Greek *epochē* "cessation, fixed point," from *epechein* "to pause, hold back," from *epi-* + *echein* "to hold"] ***synonyms*** see PERIOD — **ep·och·al** \-əl\ *adj* — **ep·och·al·ly** \-ə-lē\ *adv*

epon·y·mous \i-ˈpän-ə-məs, e-\ *adj* **:** of, relating to, or being the person for whom something is named or is believed to be named [Greek *epōnymos,* from *epi-* + *onyma* "name"]

epoxy \ˌep-ˈäk-sē\ *vt* **ep·ox·ied** *or* **ep·oxyed; ep·oxy·ing :** to glue, fill, or coat with epoxy resin

epoxy resin *n* **:** a flexible usually thermosetting resin made by polymerization of an oxygen-containing compound and used chiefly in coatings and adhesives — called also *epoxy* [*epi-* + *oxygen*]

ep·si·lon \ˈep-sə-ˌlän, -lən\ *n* **:** the 5th letter of the Greek alphabet — Ε or ϵ

Ep·som salt \ˈep-səm-\ *n* **:** a bitter colorless or white crystalline salt $MgSO_4·7H_2O$ that is a hydrated sulfate of magnesium and is used especially as a strong laxative — usually used in plural [*Epsom,* England]

eq·ua·ble \ˈek-wə-bəl, ˈē-kwə-\ *adj* **1 :** marked by lack of variation or change **:** UNIFORM ⟨an *equable* distance apart⟩ **2 :** free from extremes or sudden or harsh changes ⟨an *equable* temper⟩ ⟨an *equable* climate⟩ [Latin *aequabilis,* from *aequare* "to make level or equal," from *aequus* "level, equal"] — **eq·ua·bly** \-blē\ *adv*

[1]**equal** \ˈē-kwəl\ *adj* **1 a (1) :** of the same measure, quantity, amount, or number as another **:** LIKE **(2) :** identical in mathematical value **:** EQUIVALENT **b :** like in quality, nature, or status **c :** like for each member; *esp* **:** not restricted to a particular ethnic, social, or sexual group ⟨*equal* job opportunities⟩ **d :** not varying **:** UNIFORM ⟨*equal* pressure throughout⟩ **2 :** FAIR 5a, IMPARTIAL ⟨*equal* laws⟩ **3 a :** free from extremes **b :** tranquil of mind or mood **4 :** capable of meeting requirements ⟨was *equal* to the task⟩ [Latin *aequalis,* from *aequus* "level, equal"]

[2]**equal** *n* **1 :** one that is equal ⟨has no *equal* at chess⟩ **2 :** an equal quantity

[3]**equal** *vt* **equaled** *or* **equalled; equal·ing** *or* **equal·ling 1 :** to be equal to; *esp* **:** to be identical in value to **2 :** to produce something equal to **:** MATCH

equal–area *adj* **:** preserving the true extent of area of the forms represented although with distortion of shape ⟨*equal-area* maps⟩

equal·i·ty \i-ˈkwäl-ət-ē\ *n, pl* **-ties 1 :** the quality or state of being equal **2 :** EQUATION 2a

equal·ize \ˈē-kwə-ˌlīz\ *vt* **1 :** to make equal **2 :** to make uniform; *esp* **:** to distribute evenly or uniformly **:** BALANCE — **equal·i·za·tion** \ˌē-kwə-lə-ˈzā-shən\ *n* — **equal·iz·er** \ˈē-kwə-ˌlī-zər\ *n*

equal·ly \ˈē-kwə-lē\ *adv* **1 :** in an equal manner **:** EVENLY ⟨sharing the money *equally*⟩ **2 :** to an equal degree **:** ALIKE ⟨respected *equally* by young and old⟩

equal protection *n* **:** a guarantee under the 14th Amendment to the U.S. Constitution that a state must treat an individual or class of individuals the same as it treats other individuals or classes in like circumstances

equal sign *n* **:** a sign = indicating mathematical or logical equivalence — called also *equals sign*

equa·nim·i·ty \ˌē-kwə-ˈnim-ət-ē, ˌek-wə-\ *n* **:** evenness of emotion or temper ⟨accept misfortunes with *equanimity*⟩ [Latin *aequanimitas,* from *aequo animo* "with even mind"]

equate \i-ˈkwāt\ *vt* **:** to make or treat as equal **:** represent or express as equal or equivalent

equa·tion \i-ˈkwā-zhən, -shən\ *n* **1 a :** the act or process of equating **b :** a state of being equated; *esp* **:** the regarding of two or more things as identical or similar **2 a :** a statement of the equality of two mathematical expressions ⟨solve the *equation* $x^2 - 6x + 9 = 0$ for x⟩ **b :** an expression representing a chemical reaction by means of chemical symbols

equa·tion·al \i-ˈkwāzh-nəl, -ˈkwāsh-, -ən-l\ *adj* **:** of, using, or involving equations or the equating of elements

equa·tor \i-ˈkwāt-ər, ˈē-ˌkwāt-\ *n* **1 :** the great circle of the celestial sphere whose plane is perpendicular to the axis of the earth **2 :** a great circle of the earth that is everywhere equally distant from the two poles and divides the earth's surface into the northern and southern hemispheres **3 :** a circle or roughly circular cross section dividing a body into two usually equal and symmetrical parts ⟨chromosomes move to the *equator* of a dividing cell⟩ [Medieval Latin *aequator,* literally, "equalizer," from Latin *aequare* "to make equal"; from its containing the equinoxes]

equa·to·ri·al \ˌē-kwə-ˈtōr-ē-əl, ˌek-wə-, -ˈtȯr-\ *adj* **1 :** of, relating to, or located at the equator or an equator **2 :** of, originating in, or suggesting the region around the geographic equator ⟨*equatorial* heat⟩

equatorial plate *n* **:** METAPHASE PLATE

eq·uer·ry \ˈek-wə-rē, i-ˈkwer-ē\ *n, pl* **-ries 1 :** an officer in charge of the horses of a prince or noble **2 :** a personal attendant of a member of the British royal family [Medieval French *escurie* "squires, duties of a squire," from *escuier* "squire"]

[1]**eques·tri·an** \i-ˈkwes-trē-ən\ *adj* **1 :** of, relating to, or featuring horseback riding **2 :** representing a person on horseback ⟨an *equestrian* statue⟩ [Latin *equester* "of a horseman," from *eques* "horseman," from *equus* "horse"]

[2]**equestrian** *n* **:** one who rides on horseback

eques·tri·enne \i-ˌkwes-trē-ˈen\ *n* **:** a girl or woman who rides on horseback

equi- *combining form* **:** equal ⟨*equi*potential⟩ **:** equally ⟨*equi*distant⟩ [Latin *aequus* "equal"]

equi·an·gu·lar \ˌē-kwi-ˈang-gyə-lər, ˌek-wi-\ *adj* **:** having all or corresponding angles equal ⟨an *equiangular* triangle⟩

equi·ca·lor·ic \ˌē-kwa-ka-ˈlȯr-ik, ˌek-wa-, -ˈlär-\ *adj* **:** capable of yielding equal amounts of energy in the body ⟨*equicaloric* diets⟩

equi·dis·tant \ˌē-kwə-ˈdis-tənt, ˌek-wə-\ *adj* **:** equally distant ⟨two points *equidistant* from a line⟩

equi·lat·er·al \ˌē-kwə-ˈlat-ə-rəl, ˌek-wə-, -ˈla-trəl\ *adj* **:** having all sides or all faces equal ⟨an *equilateral* triangle⟩
equil·i·brate \i-ˈkwil-ə-ˌbrāt\ *vb* **1 :** to bring into or keep in equilibrium **2 :** to bring about, come to, or be in equilibrium — **equil·i·bra·tion** \i-ˌkwil-ə-ˈbrā-shən\ *n*
equi·lib·ri·um \ˌē-kwə-ˈlib-rē-əm, ˌek-wə-\ *n, pl* **-ri·ums** *or* **-ria** \-rē-ə\ **1 :** a static or dynamic state of balance between opposing forces or actions **2 :** a state of intellectual or emotional balance **:** POISE **3 :** the normal oriented state of the animal body in respect to the ground beneath it [Latin *aequilibrium,* from *aequi-* "equi-" + *libra* "weight, balance"]
equine \ˈē-ˌkwīn, ˈek-ˌwīn\ *adj* **:** of, relating to, or resembling a horse or the horse family [Latin *equinus,* from *equus* "horse"] — **equine** *n*
[1]**equi·noc·tial** \ˌē-kwə-ˈnäk-shəl, ˌek-wə-\ *adj* **1 :** of, relating to, or occurring at or near an equinox ⟨*equinoctial* storms⟩ **2 :** of or relating to the regions or climate of the equator ⟨*equinoctial* lands⟩ ⟨*equinoctial* heat⟩
[2]**equinoctial** *n* **1 :** EQUATOR 1 **2 :** an equinoctial storm
equi·nox \ˈē-kwə-ˌnäks, ˈek-wə-\ *n* **1 :** either of the two points on the celestial sphere where the celestial equator intersects the ecliptic **2 :** either of the two times each year (as about March 21 and September 23) when the sun crosses the equator and day and night are everywhere of equal length [Medieval Latin *equinoxium,* alteration of Latin *aequinoctium,* from *aequi-* "equi-" + *noct-, nox* "night"]
equip \i-ˈkwip\ *vt* **equipped; equip·ping :** to provide with what is necessary for service or action [Medieval French *eskiper, eschiper* "to load on board a ship, outfit, man," of Germanic origin]
eq·ui·page \ˈek-wə-pij\ *n* **1 :** material or articles used in equipment **:** OUTFIT **2 :** a horse-drawn carriage with its attendants or the carriage alone
equip·ment \i-ˈkwip-mənt\ *n* **1 a :** the equipping of a person or thing **b :** the state of being equipped **2 :** the articles or resources serving to equip a person or thing; *also* **:** the implements used in an operation or activity **:** APPARATUS
eq·ui·poise \ˈek-wə-ˌpȯiz, ˈē-kwə-\ *n* **1 :** a state of balance **:** EQUILIBRIUM **2 :** a weight used to balance another weight
equi·pon·der·ate \ˌē-kwə-ˈpän-də-ˌrāt\ *vb* **:** to be or make equal in weight or force
equi·po·ten·tial \-pə-ˈten-chəl\ *adj* **:** having the same electrical potential **:** of uniform potential throughout ⟨*equipotential* points⟩
equi·prob·a·ble \-ˈpräb-ə-bəl, -ˈpräb-bəl\ *adj* **:** having the same degree of logical or mathematical probability ⟨*equiprobable* outcomes⟩
eq·ui·se·tum \ˌek-wə-ˈsēt-əm\ *n* **:** HORSETAIL [Latin *equisaetum,* from *equus* "horse" + *saeta* "bristle"]
eq·ui·ta·ble \ˈek-wət-ə-bəl\ *adj* **:** having or exhibiting equity **:** JUST ***synonyms*** see FAIR — **eq·ui·ta·ble·ness** *n* — **eq·ui·ta·bly** \-blē\ *adv*
eq·ui·ta·tion \ˌek-wə-ˈtā-shən\ *n* **:** the act or art of riding on horseback [Latin *equitare* "to ride on horseback," from *eques* "horseman," from *equus* "horse"]
eq·ui·ty \ˈek-wət-ē\ *n, pl* **-ties 1 :** fairness or justice in dealings between persons **2 :** a system of law that is a more flexible supplement to common and statute law and is intended to protect legal rights and enforce legal duties **3 :** the value of an owner's interest in a property in excess of claims or liens against it (as the amount of a mortgage)
equivalence relation *n* **:** a relation (as equality) that for a given set (as the real numbers) is symmetric, reflexive, and transitive and for any two elements may or may not hold
equiv·a·lent \i-ˈkwiv-lənt, -ə-lənt\ *adj* **1 a :** alike or equal in number, numerical value, or meaning ⟨*equivalent* fractions⟩ ⟨*equivalent* statements⟩ **b :** having the same solution set ⟨*equivalent* equations⟩ **c :** equal in area or volume but not capable of superposition ⟨a square *equivalent* to a triangle⟩ **2 :** corresponding or virtually identical in effect or function ⟨*equivalent* methods⟩ **3 :** having the same chemical combining capacity [Late Latin *aequivalēre* "to have equal power," from Latin *aequi-* "equi-" + *valēre* "to be strong"] — **equiv·a·lence** \-ləns\ *n* — **equivalent** *n* — **equiv·a·lent·ly** *adv*
equiv·o·cal \i-ˈkwiv-ə-kəl\ *adj* **1 :** having two or more possible meanings **:** AMBIGUOUS ⟨an *equivocal* answer⟩ **2 :** uncertain as an indication or sign **:** DOUBTFUL ⟨an *equivocal* result⟩ **3 :** QUESTIONABLE 2, SUSPICIOUS ⟨*equivocal* behavior⟩ [Late Latin *aequivocus,* from Latin *aequi-* "equi-" + *voc-, vox* "voice"] — **equiv·o·cal·ly** \-kə-lē, -klē\ *adv* — **equiv·o·cal·ness** \-kəl-nəs\ *n*
equiv·o·cate \i-ˈkwiv-ə-ˌkāt\ *vi* **1 :** to use unclear language especially with intent to deceive **2 :** to avoid committing oneself in speaking ***synonyms*** see [3]LIE — **equiv·o·ca·tion** \i-ˌkwiv-ə-ˈkā-shən\ *n* — **equiv·o·ca·tor** \i-ˈkwiv-ə-ˌkāt-ər\ *n*
[1]**-er** \ər; *after some vowels, often* r; *after* ng, *usually* gər\ *adj suffix or adv suffix* — used to form the comparative degree of adjectives and adverbs of one syllable ⟨hott*er*⟩ ⟨dri*er*⟩ and of some adjectives and adverbs of two or more syllables ⟨kindli*er*⟩ [Old English *-ra* (in adjectives), *-or* (in adverbs)]
[2]**-er** \ər; *after some vowels, often* r\ *also* **-ier** \ē-ər, yər\ *or* **-yer** \yər\ *n suffix* **1 a :** a person occupationally connected with ⟨furri*er*⟩ ⟨hatt*er*⟩ ⟨lawy*er*⟩ **b :** person or thing belonging to or associated with ⟨old-tim*er*⟩ **c :** native of ⟨New York*er*⟩ **:** resident of ⟨cottag*er*⟩ **d :** one that has ⟨three-deck*er*⟩ **e :** one that produces or yields ⟨pork*er*⟩ **2 a :** one that does or performs (a specified action) ⟨report*er*⟩ — sometimes added to both elements of a compound ⟨build*er*-upp*er*⟩ **b :** one that is a suitable object of (a specified action) ⟨fry*er*⟩ **3 :** one that is ⟨foreign*er*⟩ [Middle English, partly from Old English *-ere,* partly from Medieval French *-er, -ier,* both from Latin *-arius* "-ary"]
era \ˈir-ə, ˈer-ə, ˈē-rə\ *n* **1 :** a period of time reckoned from a special date or event ⟨the Christian *era*⟩ **2 :** an important or distinctive period of history ⟨the Revolutionary *era*⟩ **3 :** one of the five major divisions of geologic time [Late Latin *aera,* from Latin, "counters," plural of *aer-, aes* "copper, money"] ***synonyms*** see PERIOD
erad·i·cate \i-ˈrad-ə-ˌkāt\ *vt* **1 :** to remove by uprooting ⟨*eradicate* weeds⟩ **2 :** to do away with completely ⟨a plan to *eradicate* illiteracy⟩ [Latin *eradicare,* from *e-* + *radix* "root"] — **erad·i·ca·ble** \-ˈrad-i-kə-bəl\ *adj* — **erad·i·ca·tion** \-ˌrad-ə-ˈkā-shən\ *n* — **erad·i·ca·tor** \-ˈrad-ə-ˌkāt-ər\ *n*
erase \i-ˈrās\ *vb* **1 a :** to rub or scrape out (as something written) **b :** to remove written or drawn marks from ⟨*erase* a chalkboard⟩ **c :** to erase recorded matter from **d :** to delete from a computer storage device ⟨*erase* a file⟩ **2 :** to remove as if by erasing ⟨*erased* the event from their memories⟩ **3 :** to yield to being erased ⟨the ink *erases*⟩ [Latin *erasus,* past participle of *eradere* "to erase," from *e-* + *radere* "to scratch, scrape"] — **eras·abil·i·ty** \-ˌrā-sə-ˈbil-ət-ē\ *n* — **eras·able** \-ˈrā-sə-bəl\ *adj*

synonyms ERASE, CANCEL, OBLITERATE, EXPUNGE mean to remove by deletion. ERASE implies rubbing or wiping out symbols or impressions often for correction or insertion of new matter ⟨*erased* the misspelled word⟩. CANCEL implies an action (as marking, revoking, or neutralizing) that makes a thing no longer effective or usable ⟨*cancelled* the ticket with a hole puncher⟩. OBLITERATE implies a covering up or defacing that removes all distinct traces of a thing's existence ⟨hieroglyphs *obliterated* by years of wind and sand⟩. EXPUNGE stresses a removal or destruction that leaves no trace ⟨all mention of the incident was *expunged* from the records⟩.

eras·er \i-ˈrā-sər\ *n* **:** one that erases; *esp* **:** a device (as a piece of rubber or a felt pad) used to erase marks (as of chalk or ink)
era·sure \i-ˈrā-shər, -zhər\ *n* **:** an act or instance of erasing
er·bi·um \ˈər-bē-əm\ *n* **:** a soft metallic rare earth element — see ELEMENT table [New Latin, from *Ytterby,* Sweden]
[1]**ere** \ˌeər, ˌaər\ *prep* **:** [2]BEFORE 2 [Old English *ǣr* "early, soon"]
[2]**ere** *conj* **:** [3]BEFORE 2
e–read·er \ˈē-ˌrēd-ər\ *n* **:** a handheld electronic device designed to be used for reading e-books and similar material
[1]**erect** \i-ˈrekt\ *adj* **1 a :** vertical in position **:** UPRIGHT ⟨an *erect* pole⟩ **b :** straight in posture ⟨*erect* bearing⟩ **c :** standing up or out from the body ⟨a porcupine with quills *erect*⟩ **2 :** directed upward ⟨a tree with *erect* branches⟩ **3 :** being in a state of physiological erection [Latin *erectus,* past participle of *erigere* "to erect," from *e-* + *regere* "to lead straight"] — **erect·ly** *adv* — **erect·ness** \-ˈrekt-nəs, -ˈrek-\ *n*
[2]**erect** *vt* **1 a :** to put up by the fitting together of materials **:** BUILD ⟨*erect* a building⟩ **b :** to fix in an upright position ⟨*erect* a flagpole⟩ **c :** to cause to stand up or out **2 :** to elevate in status **3 :** to set up **:** ESTABLISH ⟨*erect* social barriers⟩ **4**

\ə\ **a**but	\au̇\ **ou**t	\i\ t**i**p	\ȯ\ s**aw**	\u̇\ f**oo**t
\ər\ f**ur**ther	\ch\ **ch**in	\ī\ l**i**fe	\ȯi\ c**oi**n	\y\ **y**et
\a\ m**a**t	\e\ p**e**t	\j\ **j**ob	\th\ **th**in	\yü\ f**ew**
\ā\ t**a**ke	\ē\ **ea**sy	\ng\ si**ng**	\t͟h\ **th**is	\yu̇\ c**u**re
\ä\ c**o**t, c**a**rt	\g\ **g**o	\ō\ b**o**ne	\ü\ f**oo**d	\zh\ vi**si**on

: to construct (as a perpendicular) upon a given base — **erec·tor** \-ˈrek-tər\ *n*

erec·tile \i-ˈrek-tl, -ˌtīl\ *adj* : capable of becoming erect ⟨*erectile* tissue⟩ ⟨*erectile* feathers of a bird⟩

erec·tion \i-ˈrek-shən\ *n* **1** : the process of erecting : the state of being erected **2 a** : a state marked by firm swollen form and erect position of a previously limp or flabby bodily part whose tissue becomes dilated with blood **b** : an occurrence of such a state (as in the penis) **3** : something erected

ere·long \eər-ˈlȯŋ, aər-\ *adv* : before long : SOON

erep·sin \i-ˈrep-sən\ *n* : a mixture of peptidases from the intestinal juice [*er-* (probably from Latin *eripere* "to sweep away") + *pepsin*]

erg \ˈərg\ *n* : a centimeter-gram-second unit of work equal to the work done by a force of one dyne acting through a distance of one centimeter and equivalent to 10^{-7} joule [Greek *ergon* "work"]

er·go· \ˈeər-ˌgō, ˈər-\ *adv* : THEREFORE, HENCE [Latin]

ergo- *combining form* : work ⟨*ergometer*⟩ [Greek, from *ergon* "work"]

er·gom·e·ter \ər-ˈgäm-ə-tər\ *n* : an apparatus for measuring the work performed (as by a person exercising); *also* : an exercise machine equipped with an ergometer

er·go·nom·ics \ˌər-gə-ˈnäm-iks\ *n sing or pl* **1** : a science concerned with designing and arranging things people use so that the people and things interact most efficiently and safely **2** : the design characteristics of an object (as a chair) resulting especially from the application of the science of ergonomics [*ergo-* + *-nomics* (as in *economics*)] — **er·go·nom·ic** \-ik\ *adj* — **er·go·nom·i·cal·ly** \-i-k(ə-)lē\ *adv*

er·gos·ter·ol \ˌər-ˈgäs-tə-ˌrȯl, -ˌrōl\ *n* : a steroid alcohol that occurs especially in yeast, molds, and ergot and is converted by ultraviolet irradiation into vitamin D [*ergot* + *sterol*]

er·got \ˈər-gət, -ˌgät\ *n* **1 a** : the dark club-shaped fruiting body of several fungi that replaces the seed of a grass (as rye) **b** : a disease of cereals (as rye) caused by ergot-producing fungi **2** : dried ergots that are used medicinally for their contractile effect on smooth muscle [French, literally, "cock's spur"]

er·got·ism \ˈər-gət-ˌiz-əm\ *n* : a toxic condition caused by consumption of ergot (as in grain or bread)

Erie \ˈiər-ē\ *n* : a member of an Iroquoian people of the Lake Erie region

Er·len·mey·er flask \ˈər-lən-ˌmī-ər-, ˈer-lən-, -ˌmīr-\ *n* : a flat-bottomed conical laboratory flask [Emil *Erlenmeyer*, died 1909, German chemist]

Erlenmeyer flask

er·mine \ˈər-mən\ *n, pl* **ermines** **1** *or pl* **ermine** **a** : any of several weasels with black on the tail and a brown coat of fur which usually becomes white in the winter **b** : the white fur of an ermine **2** : a rank or office whose robe is ornamented with ermine [Medieval French *hermin*, of Germanic origin]

ermined \-mənd\ *adj* : clothed or adorned with ermine

erne \ˈərn, ˈeərn\ *n* : EAGLE; *esp* : a white-tailed sea eagle [Old English *earn*]

erode \i-ˈrōd\ *vb* **1** : to diminish or destroy by degrees: **a** : to eat into or away by slow destruction of substance : CORRODE **b** : to wear away by or as if by the action of water, wind, or glacial ice ⟨corruption that *eroded* confidence in government⟩ **2** : to undergo erosion [Latin *erodere* "to eat away," from *e-* + *rodere* "to gnaw"] — **erod·ible** *also* **erod·able** \-ˈrōd-ə-bəl\ *adj*

ero·sion \i-ˈrō-zhən\ *n* : the process of eroding : the state of being eroded [Latin *erosio*, from *erodere* "to erode"] — **ero·sion·al** \-ˈrōzh-nəl, -ˈrō-zhən-l\ *adj*

ero·sive \i-ˈrō-siv, -ziv\ *adj* : eating or wearing away ⟨the *erosive* effect of water⟩ ⟨an *erosive* ulcer⟩ — **ero·sive·ness** *n* — **ero·siv·i·ty** \i-ˌrō-ˈsiv-ət-ē\ *n*

erot·ic \i-ˈrät-ik\ *adj* **1** : of, devoted to, or tending to arouse sexual love or desire ⟨*erotic* art⟩ **2** : strongly marked or affected by sexual love or desire [Greek *erōtikos*, from *erōt-*, *erōs* "love"] — **erot·i·cal·ly** \-i-kə-lē, -klē\ *adv* — **erot·i·cism** \-ˈrät-ə-ˌsiz-əm\ *n*

err \ˈeər, ˈər\ *vi* **1** : to make a mistake ⟨*err* in one's calculations⟩ **2** : to violate an accepted standard of conduct [Medieval French *errer* "to stray," from Latin *errare*]

er·ran·cy \ˈer-ən-sē\ *n, pl* **-cies** : the state or an instance of erring

er·rand \ˈer-ənd\ *n* : a short trip taken to do or get something often for another; *also* : the object or purpose of such a trip [Old English *ǣrend* "message, business"]

er·rant \ˈer-ənt\ *adj* **1** : wandering especially in search of adventure ⟨an *errant* knight⟩ **2 a** : straying outside the proper bounds ⟨an *errant* calf⟩ **b** : behaving wrongly ⟨an *errant* child⟩ — **er·rant·ry** \-ən-trē\ *n*

er·ra·ta \e-ˈrät-ə, -ˈrāt-, -ˈrat-\ *n* : a list of corrigenda [from plural of *erratum*]

er·rat·ic \ir-ˈat-ik\ *adj* **1** : having no fixed course : WANDERING ⟨an *erratic* comet⟩ **2 a** : marked by lack of consistency or regularity ⟨*erratic* dieting⟩ **b** : deviating from what is ordinary or standard : ECCENTRIC ⟨*erratic* behavior⟩ [Latin *erraticus*, from *errare* "to stray"] — **er·rat·i·cal·ly** \-i-kə-lē, -klē\ *adv*

er·ra·tum \e-ˈrät-əm, -ˈrāt-, -ˈrat-\ *n, pl* **-ta** \-ə\ : CORRIGENDUM [Latin, from *errare* "to stray"]

er·ro·ne·ous \ir-ˈō-nē-əs, e-ˈrō-\ *adj* : containing or characterized by error [Latin *erroneus* "wandering," from *erro* "wanderer," from *errare* "to stray"] — **er·ro·ne·ous·ly** *adv* — **er·ro·ne·ous·ness** *n*

er·ror \ˈer-ər\ *n* **1 a** : deviation from a code of behavior ⟨saw the *error* of their ways⟩ **b** : an act involving an unintentional deviation from truth or accuracy ⟨an arithmetic *error*⟩ **c** : an act that through ignorance, deficiency, or accident fails to achieve what should be done ⟨an *error* in judgment⟩ **d** : a defensive misplay made by a baseball player **2** : the quality or state of erring **3** : a false belief or a set of false beliefs **4** : something produced by mistake **5** : the difference between an observed or calculated value and the true value; *esp* : variation in measurements, calculations, or observations of a quantity due to mistakes or to uncontrollable factors [Medieval French *errour*, from Latin *error*, from *errare* "to stray"] — **er·ror·less** \-ləs\ *adj*

synonyms ERROR, MISTAKE, BLUNDER, SLIP mean a departure from what is true, right, or proper. ERROR is a deviation from what is right, correct, or sanctioned ⟨an *error* in reasoning⟩ ⟨an *error* in addition⟩. MISTAKE implies misunderstanding or an oversight or unintentional wrongdoing and connotes less severe judgment than ERROR ⟨took someone else's coat by *mistake*⟩. BLUNDER suggests ignorance, stupidity, carelessness, or lack of foresight and sometimes implies blame ⟨a diplomatic *blunder*⟩. SLIP carries a strong implication of inadvertence or accident producing trivial mistakes ⟨a *slip* of the tongue⟩.

er·satz \ˈer-ˌzäts, er-ˈ\ *adj* : being a usually artificial and inferior substitute ⟨*ersatz* cream⟩ [German, noun, "substitute"]
synonyms see ARTIFICIAL

Erse \ˈərs\ *n* **1** : SCOTTISH GAELIC **2** : IRISH 2 [Middle English (Scots) *Erisch* "Irish"] — **Erse** *adj*

[1]**erst·while** \ˈərst-ˌhwīl, -ˌwīl\ *adv* : in the past : FORMERLY [Old English *ǣrest*, superlative of *ǣr* "early"]

[2]**erstwhile** *adj* : FORMER 4, PREVIOUS ⟨*erstwhile* enemies⟩

eruct \i-ˈrəkt\ *vb* : BELCH [Latin *eructare*, from *e-* + *ructare* "to belch"] — **eruc·ta·tion** \i-ˌrək-ˈtā-shən, ˌē-ˌrək-\ *n*

er·u·dite \ˈer-yə-ˌdīt, -ə-\ *adj* : characterized by erudition : LEARNED [Latin *eruditus*, from *erudire* "to instruct," from *e-* + *rudis* "rude, ignorant"] — **er·u·dite·ly** *adv*

er·u·di·tion \ˌer-yə-ˈdish-ən, -ə-\ *n* : extensive knowledge gained chiefly from books : LEARNING

erupt \i-ˈrəpt\ *vi* **1 a** (1) : to burst from limits or restraint (2) : to break through a surface ⟨teeth *erupting* from the gum⟩ **b** : to force out or release suddenly and often violently something pent up ⟨the volcano *erupted*⟩ **c** : to become active or violent : EXPLODE ⟨riots *erupted*⟩ **2** : to break out with or as if with a skin eruption [Latin *eruptus*, past participle of *erumpere* "to burst forth," from *e-* + *rumpere* "to break"]

erup·tion \i-ˈrəp-shən\ *n* **1 a** : an act, process, or instance of erupting **b** : the breaking out of a rash on the skin **2** : a product (as a skin rash) of erupting — **erup·tive** \-ˈrəp-tiv\ *adj*

-ery \ə-rē, -rē\ *n suffix, pl* **-eries** **1** : qualities collectively : character : -NESS ⟨snobb*ery*⟩ **2** : art : practice ⟨cook*ery*⟩ **3** : place of doing, keeping, producing, or selling (a specified thing) ⟨bak*ery*⟩ ⟨fish*ery*⟩ **4** : collection : aggregate ⟨fin*ery*⟩ **5** : state or condition ⟨slav*ery*⟩ [Medieval French *-erie*, from *-er* "-er" + *-ie* "-y"]

er·y·sip·e·las \ˌer-ə-ˈsip-ləs, ˌir-, -ə-ləs\ *n* : an acute disease marked by fever and intense local inflammation of the skin and underlying tissues and caused by a streptococcus [Latin, from Greek]

eryth·ro·blas·to·sis fe·tal·is \i-ˌrith-rə-ˌblas-ˈtō-səs-fi-ˈtal-əs\ *n* : a disease of fetuses and newborn babies that occurs when the system of an Rh-negative mother produces antibodies which destroy the red blood cells of an Rh-positive fetus and that is marked by an increase in immature red blood cells and by jaundice and anemia [New Latin, "fetal erythroblastosis" (abnormal presence of red bone marrow cells in blood)]

eryth·ro·cyte \i-ˈrith-rə-ˌsīt\ *n* : RED BLOOD CELL [Greek *erythros* "red"] — **eryth·ro·cyt·ic** \-ˌrith-rə-ˈsit-ik\ *adj*

eryth·ro·my·cin \i-ˌrith-rə-ˈmīs-n\ *n* : an antibiotic produced by a streptomyces and active against various bacteria

eryth·ro·poi·e·tin \i-ˌrith-rō-ˈpȯi-ət-n\ *n* : a hormone that stimulates red blood cell formation and is formed especially in the kidney [*erythropoiesis* "production of red blood cells," from Greek *erythro-* "red" + *poiēsis* "creation"]

1**-es** \əz, iz *after* s, z, sh, ch; z *after* v *or a vowel*\ *n pl suffix* **1** — used to form the plural of most nouns that end in *s* ⟨glass*es*⟩, *z* ⟨fuzz*es*⟩, *sh* ⟨bush*es*⟩, *ch* ⟨peach*es*⟩, or a final *y* that changes to *i* ⟨ladi*es*⟩ and of some nouns ending in *f* that changes to *v* ⟨loav*es*⟩; compare 1-s 1 **2** : 1-s 2 [Old English *-as,* nominative and accusative plural ending of some masculine nouns]

2**-es** *vb suffix* — used to form the third person singular present of most verbs that end in *s* ⟨bless*es*⟩, *z* ⟨fizz*es*⟩, *sh* ⟨hush*es*⟩, *ch* ⟨catch*es*⟩, or a final *y* that changes to *i* ⟨defi*es*⟩; compare 3-s [Old English *-es, -as*]

es·ca·drille \ˈes-kə-ˌdril, -ˌdrē\ *n* : a European air command unit with usually six airplanes [French, "flotilla, escadrille," from Spanish *escuadrilla,* from *escuadra* "squadron, squad"]

es·ca·late \ˈes-kə-ˌlāt\ *vb* : to increase or be increased in extent, number, intensity, or scope [back-formation from *escalator*] — **es·ca·la·tion** \ˌes-kə-ˈlā-shən\ *n*

1**es·ca·la·tor** \ˈes-kə-ˌlāt-ər\ *n* : a power-driven set of stairs arranged like an endless belt that ascend or descend continuously [from *Escalator,* a former trademark]

2**escalator** *adj* : providing for a periodic proportional upward or downward adjustment (as of prices or wages)

es·ca·pade \ˈes-kə-ˌpād\ *n* : an exciting, foolish, or dangerous adventure or experience

1**es·cape** \is-ˈkāp\ *vb* **1 a** : to get away (as by flight) ⟨*escape* from prison⟩ **b** : to leak out ⟨gas is *escaping*⟩ **c** : to run wild from cultivation **2** : AVOID ⟨*escaped* punishment⟩ **3** : to fail to be noticed or recalled by ⟨the name *escapes* me⟩ **4** : to issue from or be uttered involuntarily by ⟨a sigh *escaped* me⟩ [Medieval French *escaper, eschaper,* derived from Latin *ex-* + Late Latin *cappa* "head covering, cloak"] — **es·cap·er** *n*

Word History If you were being held captive by someone gripping your coat or cloak, you might be able to get away by slipping out of it and leaving the would-be captor holding an empty garment. This is the idea behind the word *escape. Escape* is derived from Latin *ex,* which means "out of," and Late Latin *cappa,* which means "head covering" or "cloak." This *cappa* is also the ancestor of English *cap* and *cape.*

2**escape** *n* **1** : an act or instance of escaping **2** : a means of escaping **3** : a cultivated plant run wild

es·cap·ee \ˌes-ˌkā-ˈpē, is-ˌkā-, ˌes-kə-\ *n* : one that has escaped; *esp* : an escaped prisoner

escape mechanism *n* : a mode of behavior or thinking adopted to evade unpleasant facts or responsibilities

es·cape·ment \is-ˈkāp-mənt\ *n* **1** : a device in a timepiece through which the energy of the weight or spring is transmitted to the pendulum or balance by means of impulses that permit one tooth on a wheel to escape from a projecting part at regular intervals **2** : a device that permits motion in one direction only and in equal steps

escapement 1

escape velocity *n* : the minimum velocity that a moving body (as a rocket) must have to escape from the gravitational field of the earth or of a celestial body and move outward into space

es·cap·ism \is-ˈkā-ˌpiz-əm\ *n* : habitual thinking about imaginary or entertaining things in order to escape from reality or routine — **es·cap·ist** \-pəst\ *adj or n*

es·car·got \ˌes-ˌkär-ˈgō\ *n, pl* **-gots** \-ˈgō(z)\ : a snail prepared for use as food [French, "snail"]

es·ca·role \ˈes-kə-ˌrōl\ *n* : endive with broad flat leaves used especially cooked as a vegetable [French]

es·carp·ment \is-ˈkärp-mənt\ *n* **1** : a steep slope in front of a fortification **2** : a long cliff [French *escarpement,* from *escarper* "to cut so as to form a scarp"]

-escent \ˈes-nt\ *adj suffix* **1** : beginning : beginning to be : slightly ⟨irid*escent*⟩ **2** : reflecting or emitting light (in a specified way) ⟨opal*escent*⟩ ⟨phosphor*escent*⟩ [Latin *-escent-, -escens,* present participle ending of verbs in *-escere*]

1**es·cheat** \is-ˈchēt\ *n* : the reversion of property to the state upon the death of the owner when there are no heirs; *also* : the property that reverts [Medieval French *eschete,* from *escheir* "to fall, devolve," derived from Latin *ex-* + *cadere* "to fall"]

2**escheat** *vb* : to revert or cause to revert by escheat — **es·cheat·able** \-ə-bəl\ *adj*

es·chew \is-ˈchü, ish-\ *vt* : to abstain or refrain from : SHUN, AVOID [Medieval French *eschiuver,* of Germanic origin]

1**es·cort** \ˈes-ˌkȯrt\ *n* **1 a** : a person or group of persons accompanying another to give protection or show courtesy **b** : the man who goes on a date with a woman **c** : a protective screen of vehicles, warships, or airplanes ⟨motorcycle *escort*⟩ **2** : accompaniment by a person or an armed protector [French *escorte,* from Italian *scorta,* from *scorgere* "to guide," derived from Latin *ex-* + *corrigere* "to make straight, correct"]

2**es·cort** \is-ˈkȯrt, es-ˈ, ˈes-ˌ\ *vt* : to accompany as an escort

es·crow \ˈes-ˌkrō, es-ˈ\ *n* : something (as a deed or a sum of money) delivered by one person to another to be delivered by the second to a third party only upon the fulfillment of a condition [Medieval French *escroue* "scroll"] — **in escrow** : in trust as an escrow ⟨held $500 *in escrow* to pay taxes⟩

es·cu·do \is-ˈküd-ō\ *n, pl* **-dos** **1** : any of various former gold or silver coins of Hispanic countries **2 a** : the basic monetary unit of Portugal until 2002 **b** : a coin representing this unit [Spanish and Portuguese, literally, "shield"]

es·cu·lent \ˈes-kyə-lənt\ *adj* : fit to be eaten : EDIBLE [Latin *esculentus,* from *esca* "food," from *edere* "to eat"] — **esculent** *n*

es·cutch·eon \is-ˈkəch-ən\ *n* : the usually shield-shaped surface on which a coat of arms is shown [Medieval French *escuchoun,* derived from Latin *scutum* "shield"]

escutcheon

Es·dras \ˈez-drəs\ *n* : either of two uncanonical books of Scripture included in the Protestant Apocrypha — see BIBLE table

1**-ese** \ˈēz, ˈēs\ *adj suffix* : of, relating to, or originating in (a specified place or country) ⟨Japan*ese*⟩ [Portuguese *-ês* and Italian *-ese,* from Latin *-ensis*]

2**-ese** *n suffix, pl* **-ese** **1** : native or resident of (a specified place or country) ⟨Chin*ese*⟩ **2 a** : language of (a specified place, country, or nationality) ⟨Japan*ese*⟩ **b** : speech, literary style, or diction peculiar to (a specified place, person, group, discipline, subject, or activity) — usually in words applied in depreciation ⟨journal*ese*⟩

es·ker \ˈes-kər\ *n* : a long narrow mound of material deposited by a stream flowing on, within, or beneath a stagnant glacier [Irish *eiscir* "ridge"]

Es·ki·mo \ˈes-kə-ˌmō\ *n, pl* **Eskimo** *or* **Eskimos** **1** : a member of a group of peoples of northern Canada, Greenland, Alaska, and eastern Siberia **2** : any of the languages of the Eskimo peoples [of American Indian origin]

Es·ki·mo–Aleut \-ˈal-ē-ˌüt\ *n* : a language family including Eskimo and Aleut languages

Eskimo dog *n* : any of an American breed of spitz dogs with a thick white coat; *also* : any of a breed of Canadian sled dogs

esoph·a·gus \i-ˈsäf-ə-gəs\ *n, pl* **-gi** \-ˌgī, -ˌjī, -ˌgē\ : a muscular tube that leads from the pharynx to the stomach in vertebrates; *also* : a part of the muscular tube between the mouth and the stomach in some invertebrates [Greek *oisophagos,* from *oisein* "to be going to carry" + *phagein* "to eat"] — **esoph·a·ge·al** \i-ˌsäf-ə-ˈjē-əl\ *adj*

es·o·ter·ic \ˌes-ə-ˈter-ik\ *adj* **1 a** : designed for or understood by the specially initiated alone ⟨an *esoteric* ritual⟩ **b** : requir-

\ə\ **abut**	\au̇\ **out**	\i\ **tip**	\ȯ\ **saw**	\u̇\ **foot**
\ər\ **further**	\ch\ **chin**	\ī\ **life**	\ȯi\ **coin**	\y\ **yet**
\a\ **mat**	\e\ **pet**	\j\ **job**	\th\ **thin**	\yü\ **few**
\ā\ **take**	\ē\ **easy**	\ng\ **sing**	\th\ **this**	\yu̇\ **cure**
\ä\ **cot, cart**	\g\ **go**	\ō\ **bone**	\ü\ **food**	\zh\ **vision**

ing or exhibiting knowledge that is restricted to a small group : RECONDITE ⟨*esoteric* terminology⟩ ⟨*esoteric* strategies⟩ **2 a** : limited to a small group ⟨engaging in *esoteric* pursuits⟩ **b** : PRIVATE 2b, CONFIDENTIAL ⟨an *esoteric* purpose⟩ **3** : of special or unusual interest ⟨*esoteric* building materials⟩ [Late Latin *esotericus,* from Greek *esōterikos,* from *esōterō,* comparative of *eisō, esō* "within"] — **es·o·ter·i·cal·ly** \-ˈter-i-kə-lē, -klē\ *adv*

ESP \ˌē-ˌes-ˈpē\ *n* : EXTRASENSORY PERCEPTION

es·pa·drille \ˈes-pə-ˌdril\ *n* : a flat sandal usually having a fabric upper and a flexible sole [French]

es·pal·ier \is-ˈpal-yər, -ˌyā\ *n* : a plant (as a fruit tree) trained to grow flat against a support (as a wall or trellis) [French] — **espalier** *vt*

es·par·to \is-ˈpärt-ō\ *n, pl* **-tos** : either of two Spanish and Algerian grasses from which cordage, shoes, baskets, and paper are made — called also *esparto grass* [Spanish]

es·pe·cial \is-ˈpesh-əl\ *adj* **1 a** : directed toward a particular individual, group, or end ⟨took *especial* care to speak clearly⟩ **b** : unusually great or significant ⟨a decision of *especial* importance⟩ **2** : PARTICULAR 3 ⟨had no *especial* destination in mind⟩ [Medieval French, "special"] — **es·pe·cial·ly** \-ˈpesh-lē, -ə-lē\ *adv*

Es·pe·ran·to \ˌes-pə-ˈrant-ō, -ˈränt-\ *n* : an artificial international language based as far as possible on words common to the chief European languages [Dr. *Esperanto,* pseudonym of L. L. Zamenhof, died 1917, Polish oculist, its inventor]

es·pi·al \is-ˈpī-əl, -ˈpīl\ *n* **1** : an act of spying or watching **2** : an act of noticing

es·pi·o·nage \ˈes-pē-ə-ˌnäzh, -nij, -ˌnäj\ *n* : the practice of spying or the use of spies to obtain information about the plans and activities especially of a foreign government or a business competitor [French *espionnage,* from Medieval French *espionner* "to spy," from *espion* "spy," from Italian *spione,* from *spia* "spy," of Germanic origin]

es·pla·nade \ˈes-plə-ˌnäd, -ˌnād\ *n* : a level open stretch or area; *esp* : one designed for walking or driving along a shore [French]

es·pous·al \is-ˈpau̇-zəl *also* -səl\ *n* **1 a** : BETROTHAL **b** : WEDDING 1 **c** : MARRIAGE 2a **2** : a taking up of a cause or belief

es·pouse \is-ˈpau̇z *also* -ˈpau̇s\ *vt* **1** : MARRY **2** : to take up the cause of : SUPPORT — **es·pous·er** *n*

espres·so \e-ˈspres-ō\ *also* **ex·pres·so** *n* : coffee brewed by forcing steam or hot water through finely ground darkly roasted coffee beans [Italian *caffè espresso,* literally, "coffee made on the spot"]

es·prit \is-ˈprē\ *n* : lively cleverness or wit [French, from Medieval French *espirit,* Latin *spiritus* "spirit"]

es·prit de corps \is-ˌprēd-ə-ˈkōr, -ˈkȯr\ *n* : the common spirit existing in the members of a group and inspiring enthusiasm, devotion, and strong regard for the honor of the group [French]

es·py \is-ˈpī\ *vt* **es·pied** \-ˈpīd\; **es·py·ing** : to catch sight of [Medieval French *espier* "to spy," of Germanic origin]

-esque \ˈesk\ *adj suffix* : in the manner or style of : like ⟨Roman*esque*⟩ ⟨statu*esque*⟩ [French, from Italian *-esco,* of Germanic origin]

es·quire \ˈes-ˌkwīr, is-ˈ\ *n* **1** : a member of the English gentry ranking immediately below a knight **2** : a candidate for knighthood serving as attendant to a knight **3** *often cap* — used as a courtesy title usually placed in its abbreviated form after a surname (as of an attorney) ⟨John M. Doe, *Esq.*⟩ [Medieval French *esquier* "squire"]

-ess \əs, is *also* ˌes\ *n suffix* : female ⟨poet*ess*⟩ [Medieval French *-esse,* from Late Latin *-issa,* from Greek]

[1]**es·say** \e-ˈsā, ˈes-ˌā\ *vt* : to make an often tentative effort to perform : TRY ⟨*essayed* the role of mediator⟩

[2]**es·say** \ˈes-ˌā, *in sense 1 also* e-ˈsā\ *n* **1** : ATTEMPT; *esp* : an initial tentative effort **2** : a usually short analytic or interpretative literary composition dealing with its subject from a limited or personal point of view [Middle French *essai,* derived from Late Latin *exagium* "act of weighing," from Latin *ex-* + *agere* "to drive"]

es·say·ist \ˈes-ˌā-əst\ *n* : a writer of essays

es·sence \ˈes-ns\ *n* **1** : the basic nature of a thing : the quality or qualities that make a thing what it is ⟨the *essence* of honesty is truthfulness⟩ **2** : a substance extracted (as from a plant or drug) that retains the special qualities of its source ⟨*essence* of peppermint⟩ **3** : PERFUME 1, SCENT [Latin *essentia,* from *esse* "to be"]

Es·sene \is-ˈēn, ˈes-ˌ\ *n* : a member of a monastic brotherhood of Jews in Palestine from the 2nd century B.C. to the 2nd century A.D. [Greek *Essēnos*]

[1]**es·sen·tial** \i-ˈsen-chəl\ *adj* **1** : forming or belonging to the fundamental nature of a thing ⟨free speech is an *essential* right of citizenship⟩ **2** : containing or having the character of a volatile essence ⟨*essential* oils⟩ **3** : important in the highest degree : NECESSARY ⟨food is *essential* to life⟩ — **es·sen·ti·al·i·ty** \-ˌsen-chē-ˈal-ət-ē\ *n* — **es·sen·tial·ly** \-ˈsench-lē, -ə-lē\ *adv* — **es·sen·tial·ness** \-əl-nəs\ *n*

synonyms ESSENTIAL, FUNDAMENTAL, VITAL mean so important as to be indispensable. ESSENTIAL implies belonging to the very nature of a thing and therefore being incapable of removal without destroying the thing itself or its character ⟨conflict is *essential* to drama⟩. FUNDAMENTAL suggests something that is of the nature of a foundation without which an entire system or complex whole would collapse ⟨the *fundamental* principles of a democracy⟩. VITAL suggests that which is as necessary to continuance as air, food, and water are to living things ⟨resources *vital* to security⟩. ***synonyms*** see in addition NECESSARY

[2]**essential** *n* : something basic, necessary, or indispensable ⟨the *essentials* for success⟩

essential amino acid *n* : an amino acid that is necessary for proper growth of the animal body and that cannot be manufactured by the body in sufficient quantity but must be obtained from protein food

[1]**-est** \əst, ist\ *adj suffix or adv suffix* — used to form the superlative degree of adjectives and adverbs of one syllable ⟨fatt*est*⟩ ⟨lat*est*⟩ and of some adjectives and adverbs of two or more syllables ⟨lucki*est*⟩ ⟨beggarli*est*⟩ [Old English]

[2]**-est** \əst, ist\ *or* **-st** \st\ *vb suffix* — used to form the archaic second person singular of verbs (with *thou*) ⟨gett*est*⟩ ⟨did*st*⟩ ⟨can*st*⟩ [Old English]

es·tab·lish \is-ˈtab-lish\ *vb* **1** : to enact permanently ⟨*establish* a constitution⟩ **2** : to make firm or stable ⟨*establish* a statue on its base⟩ **3 a** : to bring into existence : FOUND ⟨*establish* a republic⟩ **b** : to bring about : EFFECT ⟨*establish* a good relationship⟩ **4 a** : to set on a firm basis : SET UP ⟨*established* their children in business⟩ **b** : to put into a favorable position ⟨the *established* order⟩ **c** : to gain full recognition or acceptance of ⟨*establish* a claim⟩ **5** : to put beyond doubt : PROVE ⟨*establish* one's innocence⟩ **6** : to become naturalized ⟨a grass that *establishes* on poor soil⟩ [Medieval French *establiss-,* stem of *establir* "to establish," from Latin *stabilire,* from *stabilis* "stable"] — **es·tab·lish·er** *n*

established church *n* : a church recognized by law as the official church of a nation

es·tab·lish·ment \is-ˈtab-lish-mənt\ *n* **1 a** : the act of establishing : the state or fact of being established **b** : the granting of a privileged position ⟨*establishment* of a church⟩ **2** : a permanent civil or military organization **3** : a place of business or residence with its furnishings and staff ⟨a dry-cleaning *establishment*⟩ **4** : an established order of society; *also, often cap* : the social, economic, and political leaders of such an order

es·tan·cia \es-ˈtäns-yä\ *n* : a South American cattle ranch or stock farm [American Spanish, from Spanish, "stay, room"]

[1]**es·tate** \is-ˈtāt\ *n* **1** : STATE 1a, CONDITION **2** : social standing or rank especially of a high order **3** : a social or political class; *esp* : one of the great classes (as the nobility, clergy, and commons) formerly having distinct political powers **4 a** : the nature and extent of one's interest in property **b** : POSSESSIONS, PROPERTY; *esp* : a person's property in land and tenements **c** : the assets and liabilities left by a person at death **5** : a usually extensive landed property often with a large house **6** : FARM 1, PLANTATION; *also* : VINEYARD [Medieval French *estat,* from Latin *status* "state"]

[2]**estate** *adj* : previously owned by another and usually of high quality ⟨*estate* jewelry⟩

[1]**es·teem** \is-ˈtēm\ *n* : the regard in which someone or something is held; *esp* : high regard

[2]**esteem** *vt* **1 a** : to view as : CONSIDER ⟨*esteem* it a privilege⟩ **b** : THINK 3a, BELIEVE **2** : to set a high value on : PRIZE [Medieval French *estimer* "to estimate," from Latin *aestimare*] ***synonyms*** see REGARD

es·ter \ˈes-tər\ *n* : an organic compound formed by the reaction between an acid and an alcohol [German, from *Essigäther* "ethyl acetate," from *Essig* "vinegar" + *Äther* "ether"]

es·ter·ase \ˈes-tə-ˌrās\ *n* : an enzyme that accelerates the breakdown or synthesis of esters

es·ter·i·fy \e-ˈster-ə-ˌfī\ *vt* **-fied; -fy·ing :** to convert into an ester — **es·ter·i·fi·ca·tion** \-ˌster-ə-fə-ˈkā-shən\ *n*

Es·ther \ˈes-tər\ *n* **:** a canonical book of Jewish and Christian Scriptures — see BIBLE table

esthete, esthetic, estheticism, esthetics *variant of* AESTHETE, AESTHETIC, AESTHETICISM, AESTHETICS

es·ti·ma·ble \ˈes-tə-mə-bəl\ *adj* **:** worthy of esteem — **es·ti·ma·ble·ness** *n*

[1]**es·ti·mate** \ˈes-tə-ˌmāt\ *vt* **1 :** to judge or determine tentatively or approximately the value, size, or cost of ⟨*estimate* a painting job⟩ **2 :** to form an opinion of **:** JUDGE, CONCLUDE [Latin *aestimare* "to value, estimate"] — **es·ti·ma·tor** \-ˌmāt-ər\ *n*

synonyms ESTIMATE, APPRAISE, EVALUATE, ASSESS mean to judge a thing with respect to its worth. ESTIMATE implies a judgment that precedes or takes the place of actual measuring, counting, or testing ⟨*estimated* the crowd at two hundred⟩. APPRAISE implies the fixing of the monetary worth of a thing by an expert ⟨had their house *appraised*⟩. EVALUATE suggests an attempt to determine the relative or intrinsic worth of something in terms other than of money ⟨*evaluate* a student's work⟩. ASSESS implies a critical appraisal for the purpose of understanding or interpreting or as a guide in taking action ⟨officials are *assessing* the damage⟩.

[2]**es·ti·mate** \ˈes-tə-mət\ *n* **1 :** the act of appraising or valuing **2 :** an opinion or judgment of the nature, character, or quality of a thing **3 :** a rough or approximate calculation **4 :** a statement of the cost of a job

es·ti·ma·tion \ˌes-tə-ˈmā-shən\ *n* **1 :** an opinion formed or expressed **2 a :** the act of estimating **b :** the value, amount, or size determined by an estimate **3 :** ESTEEM, HONOR

es·ti·vate *also* **aes·ti·vate** \ˈes-tə-ˌvāt\ *vi* **:** to pass the summer in an inactive or resting state [Latin *aestivare* "to spend the summer," from *aestivus* "of summer," from *aestas* "summer"] — **es·ti·va·tion** \ˌes-tə-ˈvā-shən\ *n*

Es·to·nian \e-ˈstō-nē-ən, -nyən\ *n* **1 :** a native or inhabitant of Estonia **2 :** the Finno-Ugric language of the Estonian people — **Estonian** *adj*

estr- *or* **estro-** *combining form* **:** estrus ⟨*estro*gen⟩

es·tra·di·ol \ˌes-trə-ˈdī-ˌȯl, -ˌōl\ *n* **:** a powerful estrogenic hormone administered in its natural or synthesized form for medicinal use

es·trange \is-ˈtrānj\ *vt* **1 :** to remove from customary environment or associations **2 :** to arouse especially mutual hate or indifference in where there had once been love, affection, or friendliness **:** ALIENATE ⟨friends *estranged* by gossip⟩ [Medieval French *estranger,* from Medieval Latin *extraneare,* from Latin *extraneus* "strange"] — **es·trange·ment** \-mənt\ *n*

es·tri·ol \ˈes-ˌtrī-ˌȯl, e-ˈstrī-, -ˌōl\ *n* **:** a natural estrogenic hormone usually obtained from the urine of pregnant women

es·tro·gen \ˈes-trə-jən\ *n* **:** a substance (as estradiol) tending to stimulate the development of secondary sex characteristics in the female and promote the growth and normal functioning of the female reproductive system — **es·tro·gen·ic** \ˌes-trə-ˈjen-ik\ *adj*

es·trone \ˈes-ˌtrōn\ *n* **:** a natural estrogenic hormone used to treat medical conditions involving estrogen defeciency

estrous cycle *n* **:** the series of physiological changes of the endocrine and reproductive systems of a female mammal from the beginning of one period of estrus to the beginning of the next

es·trus \ˈes-trəs\ *n* **1 :** a regularly recurrent state of sexual receptiveness during which the female of most mammals is willing to mate with the male and is capable of conceiving **:** HEAT **2 :** ESTROUS CYCLE [Latin *oestrus* "gadfly, frenzy," from Greek *oistros*] — **es·trous** \-trəs\ *adj*

es·tu·a·rine \ˈes-chə-wə-ˌrīn\ *adj* **:** of, relating to, or formed in an estuary

es·tu·ary \ˈes-chə-ˌwer-ē\ *n, pl* **-ar·ies :** a water passage where the tide meets a river current; *esp* **:** an arm of the sea at the lower end of a river [Latin *aestuarium,* from *aestus* "boiling, tide"]

[1]**-et** \ˈet, ˌet, ət, it\ *n suffix* **:** small one **:** lesser one ⟨baron*et*⟩ ⟨isl*et*⟩ [Medieval French, from Latin *-itus*]

[2]**-et** *n suffix* **:** group ⟨oct*et*⟩

eta \ˈāt-ə\ *n* **:** the 7th letter of the Greek alphabet — Η or η

et cetera \et-ˈset-ə-rə, -ˈse-trə\ **:** and others especially of the same kind **:** and so forth [Latin]

etch \ˈech\ *vt* **1 a :** to produce (as a design) on a hard material by eating into the material's surface (as by acid or laser beam) **b :** to subject to such etching **2 :** to impress (as on the mind) sharply or clearly [Dutch *etsen,* from German *ätzen,* "to corrode, etch"] — **etch·er** *n*

etch·ing \ˈech-ing\ *n* **1 :** the art of producing pictures or designs by printing from an etched metal plate **2 :** an impression from an etched plate

eter·nal \i-ˈtərn-l\ *adj* **1 :** having no beginning and no end **:** lasting forever ⟨*eternal* bliss⟩ **2 :** continuing without interruption **:** UNCEASING ⟨that dog's *eternal* barking⟩ [Late Latin *aeternalis,* from Latin *aeternus* "eternal"] — **eter·nal·ly** \-l-ē\ *adv* — **eter·nal·ness** *n*

synonyms ETERNAL, EVERLASTING, ENDLESS mean continuing on and on without end. ETERNAL implies being without either beginning or end and so unaffected by time or change ⟨*eternal* truths⟩. EVERLASTING and ENDLESS apply to what exists and endures in time without end or limit; EVERLASTING stresses the quality of permanence or the fact of duration ⟨*everlasting* fame⟩ and ENDLESS frequently suggests a wearisome stretching out without conclusion or final rest ⟨*endless* arguments about money⟩.

Eternal *n* **:** GOD 1 — used with *the*

eter·ni·ty \i-ˈtər-nət-ē\ *n, pl* **-ties 1 :** the quality or state of being eternal **2 :** infinite time **3 :** the state after death **:** IMMORTALITY **4 :** a seemingly endless time **:** AGE [Medieval French *eternité,* from Latin *aeternitas,* from *aeternus* "eternal"]

[1]**-eth** \əth, ith\ *or* **-th** \th\ *vb suffix* — used to form the archaic 3rd person singular present of verbs ⟨go*eth*⟩ ⟨do*th*⟩ [Old English]

[2]**-eth** — see [2]-TH

eth·ane \ˈeth-ˌān\ *n* **:** a colorless odorless gas C_2H_6 that consists of carbon and hydrogen, is found in natural gas, and is used especially as a fuel [*eth*yl + *-ane*]

eth·a·nol \ˈeth-ə-ˌnȯl, -ˌnōl\ *n* **:** a colorless volatile flammable liquid C_2H_5OH that is the intoxicating agent in liquors and that is also used as a solvent and in fuel — called also *ethyl alcohol, grain alcohol*

eth·ene \ˈeth-ˌēn\ *n* **:** ETHYLENE

ether \ˈē-thər\ *n* **1 :** the upper regions of space **:** HEAVENS **2 a :** a medium formerly held to permeate all space and transmit transverse waves (as light) **b :** the medium that transmits radio waves **3 a :** a light volatile flammable liquid $C_4H_{10}O$ obtained by the distillation of alcohol with sulfuric acid and used chiefly as a solvent especially of fats and especially formerly as an anesthetic **b :** any of various organic compounds characterized by an oxygen atom attached to two carbon atoms [Latin *aether,* from Greek *aithēr,* from *aithein* "to ignite"]

ethe·re·al \i-ˈthir-ē-əl\ *adj* **1 :** of or relating to the heavens **:** HEAVENLY ⟨*ethereal* spirits⟩ **2 :** being light and airy **:** DELICATE ⟨*ethereal* music⟩ — **ethe·re·al·i·ty** \i-ˌthir-ē-ˈal-ət-ē\ *n* — **ethe·re·al·ly** \-ˈthir-ē-ə-lē\ *adv* — **ethe·re·al·ness** *n*

ether·ize \ˈē-thə-ˌrīz\ *vt* **:** to treat or anesthetize with ether — **ether·i·za·tion** \ˌē-thə-rə-ˈzā-shən\ *n* — **ether·iz·er** *n*

Ether·net \ˈē-thər-ˌnet\ *n* **:** a type of computer network used especially in local area networks [former trademark]

eth·i·cal \ˈeth-i-kəl\ *also* **eth·ic** \-ik\ *adj* **1 :** of or relating to ethics **2 :** conforming to accepted and especially professional standards of conduct ⟨*ethical* practices⟩ **3 :** sold only on a doctor's prescription ⟨*ethical* drugs⟩ [Latin *ethicus,* from Greek *ēthikos,* from *ēthos* "character"] ***synonyms*** see MORAL — **eth·i·cal·ly** \ˈeth-i-kə-lē, -klē\ *adv*

eth·ics \ˈeth-iks\ *n sing or pl* **1 :** a branch of philosophy dealing with what is good and bad and with moral duty and obligation **2 a** *or* **ethic :** a set of moral principles ⟨an old-fashioned work *ethic*⟩ ⟨humanist *ethics*⟩ **b :** the principles of moral conduct governing an individual or a group **3 :** a set of moral issues or aspects ⟨debated the *ethics* of human cloning⟩

Ethi·o·pi·an \ˌē-thē-ˈō-pē-ən\ *n* **1 :** a member of any of the mythical or actual peoples usually described by the ancient Greeks as dark-skinned and living far to the south **2 :** a native or inhabitant of Ethiopia — **Ethiopian** *adj*

Ethi·op·ic \-ˈäp-ik, -ˈō-pik\ *n* **:** a Semitic language formerly spoken in Ethiopia and still used in church services there

eth·moid \ˈeth-ˌmȯid\ *or* **eth·moi·dal** \eth-ˈmȯid-l\ *adj* **:** of, relating to, adjoining, or being one or more bones of the walls of the nasal cavity [French *ethmoïde,* from Greek *ēthmoeidēs,* literally, "like a strainer," from *ēthmos* "strainer"] — **ethmoid** *n*

[1]**eth·nic** \'eth-nik\ *adj* : of or relating to groups of people classed according to common traits and customs ⟨*ethnic* minorities⟩ [Late Latin *ethnicus* "heathen," from Greek *ethnikos* "national, gentile," from *ethnos* "nation, people"] — **eth·ni·cal·ly** \-ni-kə-lē, -klē\ *adv*

[2]**ethnic** *n* : a member of an ethnic group; *esp* : one retaining traditional customs, language, and a sense of shared identity

ethno- *combining form* : race : people : cultural group ⟨*ethnocentric*⟩ [Greek *ethnos* "nation, people"]

eth·no·cen·tric \ˌeth-nō-'sen-trik\ *adj* : favoring especially one's own ethnic group ⟨*ethnocentric* views⟩

eth·nog·ra·phy \eth-'näg-rə-fē\ *n* : the study and systematic recording of human cultures; *also* : a descriptive work produced from such research — **eth·nog·ra·pher** \-fər\ *n* — **eth·no·graph·ic** \ˌeth-nə-'graf-ik\ *or* **eth·no·graph·i·cal** \-i-kəl\ *adj* — **eth·no·graph·i·cal·ly** \-i-kə-lē, -klē\ *adv*

eth·nol·o·gy \eth-'näl-ə-jē\ *n* : anthropology dealing chiefly with the comparative and analytical study of cultures — **eth·no·log·i·cal** \-i-kəl\ *also* **eth·no·log·ic** \ˌeth-nə-'läj-ik\ *adj* — **eth·nol·o·gist** \eth-'näl-ə-jəst\ *n*

ethol·o·gy \ē-'thäl-ə-jē\ *n* : the scientific study of animal behavior [Latin *ethologia* "art of depicting character," from Greek *ēthologia,* from *ēthos* "character" + *-logia* "-logy"] — **etho·log·i·cal** \ˌē-thə-'läj-i-kəl, ˌeth-ə-\ *adj* — **ethol·o·gist** \ē-'thäl-ə-jəst\ *n*

eth·yl \'eth-əl\ *n* : a chemical radical C_2H_5 consisting of carbon and hydrogen [*eth*er + *-yl*]

ethyl alcohol *n* : ETHANOL

ethyl cellulose *n* : any of various thermoplastic substances used especially in plastics and lacquers

eth·yl·ene \'eth-ə-ˌlēn\ *n* **1** : a colorless flammable gas C_2H_4 found in coal gas or obtained from petroleum hydrocarbons and used to ripen fruits or as an anesthetic **2** : a bivalent hydrocarbon radical C_2H_4 derived from ethane — **eth·yl·enic** \ˌeth-ə-'lē-nik\ *adj*

ethylene gly·col \-'glī-ˌkȯl, -ˌkōl\ *n* : a thick liquid alcohol $C_2H_6O_2$ used especially as an antifreeze

eth·yne \'eth-ˌīn, eth-'\ *n* : ACETYLENE

-et·ic \'et-ik\ *adj suffix* : -IC ⟨limn*etic*⟩ — often in adjectives corresponding to nouns ending in *-esis* ⟨gen*etic*⟩ [Greek *-etikos, -ētikos,* from *-etos, -ētos,* ending of certain verbals]

eti·o·late \'ēt-ē-ə-ˌlāt\ *vt* **1** : to make (a green plant) pale and spindly by lack of light **2** : to make pale and sickly [French *étioler*] — **eti·o·la·tion** \ˌēt-ē-ə-'lā-shən\ *n*

eti·ol·o·gy \ˌēt-ē-'äl-ə-jē\ *n* : the cause or origin especially of a disease [Medieval Latin *aetiologia* "statement of causes," from Greek *aitiologia,* from *aitia* "cause"] — **eti·o·log·ic** \ˌēt-ē-ə-'läj-ik\ *or* — **eti·o·log·i·cal** \-i-kəl\ *adj* — **eti·o·log·i·cal·ly** \-i-kə-lē, -i-klē\ *adv*

et·i·quette \'et-i-kət, -ˌket\ *n* : the body of rules governing the way in which people behave socially, ceremonially, or in public life [French *étiquette,* literally, "ticket"]

Word History The primary meaning of French *étiquette* is "ticket, label attached to something for description or identification." In 16th century Spain, the French word was borrowed as *etiqueta* and used to denote the written protocols describing order of precedence and other aspects of correct courtly behavior. The *etiqueta* eventually became the court ceremonies themselves as well as the documents that described them. Under the influence of Spanish, French *étiquette* also acquired the meaning "proper court behavior." English borrowed both word and meaning from French in the 18th century.

Eton jacket *n* : a short black jacket with long sleeves, wide lapels, and an open front [*Eton* College, English public school]

Etrus·can \i-'trəs-kən\ *n* **1** : a native or inhabitant of ancient Etruria **2** : the language of the Etruscans — **Etruscan** *adj*

-ette \'et, ˌet, ət, it\ *n suffix* **1** : little one ⟨kitchen*ette*⟩ **2** : female ⟨drum major*ette*⟩ [French, feminine of *-et*]

étude \'ā-ˌtüd, -ˌtyüd\ *n* **1** : a piece of music for practice to develop technical skill **2** : a composition built on a technical motif but played for its artistic value [French, literally, "study," from Medieval French *estude, estudie*]

et·y·mol·o·gy \ˌet-ə-'mäl-ə-jē\ *n, pl* **-gies** **1** : the history of a word as shown by identifying its related forms in other languages and tracing these to their origin in a common form in an earlier parent language or by tracing the transmission of a word from one language to another **2** : a branch of language study concerned with etymologies [Latin *etymologia,* from Greek, from *etymon* "the literal meaning of a word according to its origin," from *etymos* "true"] — **et·y·mo·log·i·cal** \-mə-'läj-i-kəl\ *adj* — **et·y·mo·log·i·cal·ly** \-'läj-i-kə-lē, -klē\ *adv* — **et·y·mol·o·gist** \ˌet-ə-'mäl-ə-jəst\ *n*

eu- *combining form* **1** : well : easily : good — compare DYS- **2** : true, truly ⟨*eu*caryote⟩ [Greek, "well, good"]

eu·bac·te·ri·um \ˌyü-bak-'tir-ē-əm\ *n* : any of the bacteria excluding those that are archaebacteria

eu·ca·lypt \'yü-kə-ˌlipt\ *n* : EUCALYPTUS

eu·ca·lyp·tus \ˌyü-kə-'lip-təs\ *n, pl* **-ti** \-ˌtī, -ˌtē\ *or* **-tus·es** : any of a genus of mostly Australian evergreen trees of the myrtle family including many that are widely cultivated for their gums, resins, oils, and useful woods [*eu-* + Greek *kalyptos* "covered," from *kalyptein* "to conceal"; from the conical covering of the buds]

Eu·cha·rist \'yü-kə-rəst, -krəst\ *n* : COMMUNION 1a; *esp* : a Roman Catholic sacrament renewing Christ's sacrifice of his body and blood [Late Latin *eucharistia,* from Greek, "gratitude, Eucharist," from *eu-* + *charis* "favor, grace, gratitude"] — **eu·cha·ris·tic** \ˌyü-kə-'ris-tik\ *adj, often cap*

eu·chre \'yü-kər\ *n* : a card game in which each player is dealt five cards and the player making trump must take three tricks to win a hand [origin unknown]

Eu·clid·e·an \yu̇-'klid-ē-ən\ *adj* : of or relating to the geometry of Euclid

Euclidean algorithm *n* : a method of finding the greatest common divisor of two numbers by dividing the larger by the smaller, the smaller by the remainder, the first remainder by the second remainder, and so on until division without a remainder occurs and the greatest common divisor is the divisor leaving no remainder

eu·gen·ic \yu̇-'jen-ik\ *adj* **1** : relating to or fitted for the production of good offspring **2** : of or relating to eugenics — **eu·gen·i·cal·ly** \-'jen-i-kə-lē, -klē\ *adv*

eu·gen·ics \yu̇-'jen-iks\ *n* : a science that deals with the improvement of hereditary qualities of a race or breed and especially of human beings

eu·gle·na \yu̇-'glē-nə\ *n* : any of a large genus of green freshwater flagellates often classified as algae [*eu-* + Greek *glēnē* "eyeball"]

eu·gle·noid \yu̇-'glē-ˌnȯid\ *n* : any of a group of varied flagellates that are typically green or colorless, solitary, and have one or two flagella emerging from the gullet — **euglenoid** *adj*

euglenoid movement *n* : writhing protoplasmic movement typical of some euglenoid flagellates

eu·kary·ote *also* **eu·cary·ote** \yü-'kar-ē-ˌōt, -ē-ət\ *n* : an organism composed of one or more cells with visibly evident nuclei and organelles — compare PROKARYOTE [*eu-* + *kary-* + *-ote* (as in *zygote*)] — **eu·kary·ot·ic** \ˌyü-ˌkar-ē-'ät-ik\ *adj*

eu·lo·gize \'yü-lə-ˌjīz\ *vt* : to speak or write in high praise of : EXTOL — **eu·lo·gist** \-jəst\ *n* — **eu·lo·gis·tic** \ˌyü-lə-'jis-tik\ *adj* — **eu·lo·gis·ti·cal·ly** \-ti-kə-lē, -klē\ *adv*

eu·lo·gy \'yü-lə-jē\ *n, pl* **-gies** **1** : a speech or a writing in honor of a person or thing; *esp* : a formal speech in honor of a dead person **2** : high praise

eu·nuch \'yü-nək\ *n* : a castrated man; *esp* : one placed in charge of a harem or employed as a court official [Latin *eunuchus,* from Greek *eunouchos,* from *eunē* "bed" + *echein* "to have, have charge of"]

eu·on·y·mus \yu̇-'än-ə-məs\ *n* : any of a genus of shrubs and small trees often grown as ornamentals [Latin *euonymos,* from Greek *euōnymos,* literally, "having an auspicious name," from *eu-* + *onyma* "name"]

eu·phe·mism \'yü-fə-ˌmiz-əm\ *n* : the substitution of an agreeable or inoffensive expression for one that may offend or suggest something unpleasant; *also* : an expression so substituted ⟨pass away is a widely used *euphemism* for die⟩ [Greek *euphēmismos,* from *eu-* + *phēmē* "speech," from *phanai* "to speak"] — **eu·phe·mis·tic** \ˌyü-fə-'mis-tik\ *adj* — **eu·phe·mis·ti·cal·ly** \-ti-kə-lē, -klē\ *adv*

eu·pho·ni·ous \yu̇-'fō-nē-əs\ *adj* : pleasing to the ear — **eu·pho·ni·ous·ly** *adv* — **eu·pho·ni·ous·ness** *n*

eu·pho·ni·um \-nē-əm\ *n* : a tenor tuba like a baritone but mellower in tone

eu·pho·ny \'yü-fə-nē\ *n, pl* **-nies** : pleasing or sweet sound; *esp* : the effect of words so combined as to please the ear [French *euphonie,* from Late Latin *euphonia,* from Greek *euphōnia,* from *eu-* + *phōnē* "voice"] — **eu·phon·ic** \yu̇-ˈfän-ik\ *adj* — **eu·phon·i·cal·ly** \-ˈfän-i-kə-lē, -klē\ *adv*

eu·phor·bia \yu̇-ˈfȯr-bē-ə\ *n* : any of a genus of herbs, shrubs, and trees of the spurge family that have milky juice and flowers without a calyx [Latin *euphorbea,* from *Euphorbus,* 1st century A.D. physician]

eu·pho·ria \yu̇-ˈfōr-ē-ə, -ˈfȯr-\ *n* : a strong feeling of well-being or elation [Greek, from *euphoros* "healthy," from *eu-* + *pherein* "to bear"] — **eu·phor·ic** \-ˈfȯr-ik, -ˈfär-\ *adj*

Eur- *or* **Euro-** *combining form* : European and ⟨*Eur*asian⟩ : European ⟨*Euro*currency⟩

Eur·asian \yu̇-ˈrā-zhən, -shən\ *adj* **1** : of or relating to Eurasia **2** : of mixed European and Asian origin — **Eurasian** *n*

eu·re·ka \yu̇-ˈrē-kə\ *interj* — used to express triumph on a discovery [Greek *heurēka* "I have found," from *heuriskein* "to find"; from the exclamation attributed to Archimedes on his discovering a method for determining the purity of gold]

eu·ro \ˈyu̇r-ō\ *n, pl* **euros** *also* **euro** **1** : the common basic monetary unit of most countries of the European Union **2** : a coin representing one euro

Eu·ro–Amer·i·can \ˌyu̇r-ō-ə-ˈmər-ə-kən\ *adj* **1** : of or relating to Europe and America **2** : of mixed European and American origin — **Euro–American** *n*

Eu·ro·cur·ren·cy \ˌyu̇r-ō-ˈkər-ən-sē, -ˈkə-rən-\ *n* : moneys (as of the U.S. and Japan) held outside their countries of origin and used in the money markets of Europe

Eu·ro·dol·lar \ˈyu̇r-ō-ˌdäl-ər\ *n* : a U.S. dollar held as Eurocurrency

[1]**Eu·ro·pe·an** \ˌyu̇r-ə-ˈpē-ən\ *adj* : of or relating to Europe or its inhabitants

[2]**European** *n* **1** : a native or inhabitant of Europe **2** : a person of European descent

European corn borer *n* : an Old World moth whose larva is a major pest in eastern North America in the stems, crowns, and fruits of crop plants and especially corn

Eu·ro·pe·an·ism \ˌyu̇r-ə-ˈpē-ə-ni-zəm\ *n* : attachment or loyalty to the traditions, interests, or ideals of Europeans

Eu·ro·pe·an·ize \yu̇r-ə-ˈpē-ə-ˌnīz\ *vb* : to make or become European — **Eu·ro·pe·an·i·za·tion** \-ˌpē-ə-nə-ˈzā-shən\ *n*

European plan *n* : a hotel plan whereby the daily rate covers only the cost of the room — compare AMERICAN PLAN

eu·ro·pi·um \yu̇-ˈrō-pē-əm\ *n* : a soft metallic rare earth element — see ELEMENT table [New Latin, from *Europa* "Europe"]

eu·ro·zone \ˈyu̇r-ō-ˌzōn\ *n* : the geographical area comprising the countries that use the euro as the official currency

eury- *combining form* : broad : wide ⟨*eury*haline⟩ [Greek *eurys*]

eu·ry·ha·line \ˌyu̇r-i-ˈhā-ˌlīn, -ˈhal-ˌīn\ *adj* : able to live in waters of a wide range of salinity ⟨*euryhaline* crabs⟩

eu·ryp·ter·id \yu̇-ˈrip-tə-rəd\ *n* : any of an order (Eurypterida) of usually large aquatic Paleozoic arthropods resembling scorpions and related to the horseshoe crabs [derived from Greek *eurys* "broad" + *pteron* "wing"] — **eurypterid** *adj*

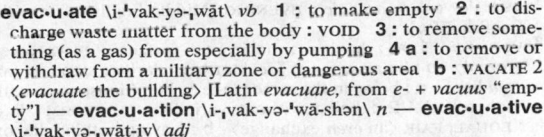

eurypterid

eu·so·cial \ˌyü-ˈsō-shəl\ *adj* : living in a cooperative group (as of termites or ants) in which usually one female and several males are involved in the production of young and the other members of the group care for the young or protect and provide for the group

eu·sta·chian tube \yu̇-ˈstā-shən- *also* -ˈstā-kē-ən-\ *n, often cap E* : a tube connecting the middle ear with the nasopharynx and equalizing air pressure on both sides of the eardrum [Bartolomeo *Eustachio,* died 1574, Italian anatomist]

eu·stat·ic \yu̇-ˈstat-ik\ *adj* : relating to or characterized by worldwide change of sea level

eu·tha·na·sia \ˌyü-thə-ˈnā-zhə, -zhē-ə\ *n* : the act or practice of killing or permitting the death of hopelessly sick or injured persons or animals for reasons of mercy — called also *mercy killing* [Greek, "easy death," from *eu-* + *thanatos* "death"]

eu·tro·phic \yu̇-ˈtrō-fik\ *adj* : being a body of water rich in dissolved nutrients (as phosphates) but often shallow and seasonally deficient in oxygen [derived from Greek *eutrophos* "well nourished, nourishing," from *eu-* + *trephein* "to nourish"] — **eu·tro·phi·ca·tion** \-ˌtrō-fə-ˈkā-shən\ *n*

evac·u·ate \i-ˈvak-yə-ˌwāt\ *vb* **1** : to make empty **2** : to discharge waste matter from the body : VOID **3** : to remove something (as a gas) from especially by pumping **4 a** : to remove or withdraw from a military zone or dangerous area **b** : VACATE 2 ⟨*evacuate* the building⟩ [Latin *evacuare,* from *e-* + *vacuus* "empty"] — **evac·u·a·tion** \i-ˌvak-yə-ˈwā-shən\ *n* — **evac·u·a·tive** \i-ˈvak-yə-ˌwāt-iv\ *adj*

evac·u·ee \i-ˌvak-yə-ˈwē\ *n* : an evacuated person

evade \i-ˈvād\ *vb* **1** : to get away or avoid by skill or trickery ⟨*evade* a question⟩ **2** : to avoid facing up to ⟨*evade* responsibility⟩ **3** : BAFFLE, FOIL ⟨the problem *evades* all efforts at solution⟩ [Latin *evadere,* from *e-* + *vadere* "to go, walk"] — **evad·able** \i-ˈvād-ə-bəl\ *adj* — **evad·er** *n*

synonyms EVADE, ELUDE mean to get away or keep away from something. EVADE implies adroitness, ingenuity, or lack of scruple in escaping or avoiding ⟨changed the subject to *evade* the question⟩. ELUDE implies a slippery or baffling quality in the person or thing that escapes ⟨what she sees in him *eludes* me⟩.

eval·u·ate \i-ˈval-yə-ˌwāt\ *vt* **1** : to determine or fix the value of **2** : determine the value or condition of usually by careful study ***synonyms*** see ESTIMATE — **eval·u·a·tion** \-ˌval-yə-ˈwā-shən\ *n* — **eval·u·a·tive** \-ˈval-yə-ˌwāt-iv\ *adj*

ev·a·nesce \ˌev-ə-ˈnes\ *vi* : to dissipate like vapor [Latin *evanescere,* from *e-* + *vanus* "empty"]

ev·a·nes·cence \ˌev-ə-ˈnes-ns\ *n* **1** : the process or fact of evanescing **2** : evanescent quality

ev·a·nes·cent \-nt\ *adj* : tending to vanish like vapor : not lasting : quickly passing ⟨*evanescent* pleasures⟩ ***synonyms*** see TRANSIENT

[1]**evan·gel·i·cal** \ˌē-ˌvan-ˈjel-i-kəl, ˌev-ən-\ *also* **evan·gel·ic** \-ˈjel-ik\ *adj* **1** : of, relating to, or in agreement with the Christian gospel especially as it is presented in the four Gospels **2** : PROTESTANT 1b **3** : emphasizing salvation by faith in the atoning death of Jesus Christ through personal conversion, the authority of Scripture, and the importance of preaching as contrasted with ritual **4** *often cap* **a** : FUNDAMENTALIST **b** : LOW CHURCH **5** : marked by militant or crusading zeal ⟨*evangelical* propaganda⟩ [Late Latin *evangelicus,* from *evangelium* "Gospel," from Greek *euangelion,* literally, "good news," from *eu-* + *angelos* "messenger"] — **Evan·gel·i·cal·ism** \-i-kə-ˌliz-əm\ *n* — **evan·gel·i·cal·ly** \-i-kə-lē, -klē\ *adv*

[2]**evangelical** *n, often cap* : one holding evangelical principles or belonging to an evangelical party or church

evan·ge·lism \i-ˈvan-jə-ˌliz-əm\ *n* **1** : the winning or revival of personal commitments to Christ **2** : militant or crusading zeal — **evan·ge·lis·tic** \i-ˌvan-jə-ˈlis-tik\ *adj* — **evan·ge·lis·ti·cal·ly** \-ti-kə-lē\ *adv*

evan·ge·list \i-ˈvan-jə-ləst\ *n* **1** *often cap* : a writer of any of the four Gospels **2** : a person who evangelizes

evan·ge·lize \i-ˈvan-jə-ˌlīz\ *vb* **1** : to preach the gospel **2** : to convert to Christianity — **evan·ge·li·za·tion** \-ˌvan-jə-lə-ˈzā-shən\ *n* — **evan·ge·liz·er** \-ˈvan-jə-ˌlī-zər\ *n*

evap·o·rate \i-ˈvap-ə-ˌrāt\ *vb* **1** : to change into vapor ⟨ether *evaporates* rapidly in air⟩; *also* : to pass off or cause to pass off in vapor or minute particles **2 a** : to pass off or away : DISAPPEAR **b** : to diminish quickly **3** : to expel moisture from (as by heat) [Latin *evaporare,* from *e-* + *vapor* "steam, vapor"] — **evap·o·ra·tion** \-ˌvap-ə-ˈrā-shən\ *n* — **evap·o·ra·tive** \-ˈvap-ə-ˌrāt-iv\ *adj* — **evap·o·ra·tor** \-ˌrāt-ər\ *n*

evaporated milk *n* : unsweetened canned milk concentrated by partial evaporation

evap·o·rite \i-ˈvap-ə-ˌrīt\ *n* : a sedimentary rock (as gypsum) that originates by evaporation of seawater in an enclosed basin

eva·sion \i-ˈvā-zhən\ *n* **1** : a means of evading **2** : the act or an instance of evading : ESCAPE ⟨tax *evasion*⟩ [Late Latin *evasio,* from Latin *evadere* "to evade"]

eva·sive \i-ˈvā-siv, -ziv\ *adj* : tending or intended to evade : EQUIVOCAL ⟨*evasive* answers⟩ — **eva·sive·ly** *adv* — **eva·sive·ness** *n*

eve \ˈēv\ *n* **1** : EVENING **2** : the evening or the day before a special day ⟨Christmas *Eve*⟩ **3** : the period immediately preceding an event [Middle English *even, eve*]

\ə\ **abut**	\au̇\ **out**	\i\ **tip**	\ȯ\ **saw**	\u̇\ **foot**
\ər\ **further**	\ch\ **chin**	\ī\ **life**	\ȯi\ **coin**	\y\ **yet**
\a\ **mat**	\e\ **pet**	\j\ **job**	\th\ **thin**	\yü\ **few**
\ā\ **take**	\ē\ **easy**	\ng\ **sing**	\t͟h\ **this**	\yu̇\ **cure**
\ä\ **cot, cart**	\g\ **go**	\ō\ **bone**	\ü\ **food**	\zh\ **vision**

[1]even \ˈē-vən\ *n, archaic* : EVENING [Middle English, from Old English *ǣfen*]

[2]even *adj* **1 a** : having a horizontal surface : FLAT ⟨*even* ground⟩ **b** : being without break or irregularity : SMOOTH ⟨an *even* line⟩ **c** : being in the same plane or line ⟨houses *even* with each other⟩ **2** : being without variation : UNIFORM **3 a** : EQUAL, FAIR ⟨an *even* exchange⟩ **b** : leaving nothing due on either side : SQUARE ⟨now we're *even*⟩ **c** : BALANCED; *esp* : showing neither profit nor loss **4 a** : being any number (as –2, 0, and +2) that is exactly divisible by 2 **b** : marked by an even number ⟨an *even* page of the book⟩ **5** : EXACT, PRECISE ⟨an *even* dozen⟩ **6** : as likely as not : FIFTY-FIFTY 2 ⟨an *even* chance of winning⟩ [Old English *efen*] ***synonyms*** see STEADY — **even·ly** *adv* — **even·ness** \-vən-nəs\ *n*

[3]even *adv* **1 a** : PRECISELY, EXACTLY ⟨believes *even* as you and I⟩ **b** : to a degree that extends : FULLY, QUITE ⟨faithful *even* unto death⟩ **c** : at the very time ⟨*even* as the clock struck⟩ **2 a** — used as an intensive to emphasize the identity or character of something ⟨he looked content, *even* happy⟩ ⟨forgot his car keys and *even* left the engine running⟩ **b** — used as an intensive to stress an extreme or highly unlikely condition or instance ⟨so simple *even* a child can do it⟩ **c** — used as an intensive to stress the comparative degree ⟨she did *even* better⟩ **d** — used as an intensive to indicate a small or minimum amount ⟨didn't *even* try⟩

[4]even *vb* **evened; even·ing** \ˈēv-ning, -ə-ning\ : to make or become even — **even·er** \ˈēv-nər, -ə-nər\ *n*

even·hand·ed \ˌē-vən-ˈhan-dəd\ *adj* : FAIR 5a, IMPARTIAL

[1]eve·ning \ˈēv-ning\ *n* **1** : the latter part and end of the day and early part of the night **2** : the latter part ⟨the *evening* of life⟩ [derived from Old English *ǣfen* "evening"]

[2]evening *adj* : suitable for formal or semiformal evening social occasions ⟨*evening* dress⟩ ⟨*evening* clothes⟩

evening prayer *n, often cap E&P* : the daily evening service of the Anglican liturgy

evening primrose *n* : a coarse biennial herb of North America with yellow flowers that open in the evening; *also* : any of several related plants

eve·nings \ˈēv-ningz\ *adv* : in the evening repeatedly ⟨goes bowling *evenings*⟩

evening star *n* : a bright planet (as Venus) seen in the western sky at or after sunset

even·song \ˈē-vən-ˌsȯng\ *n, often cap* **1** : VESPERS 1 **2** : EVENING PRAYER

event \i-ˈvent\ *n* **1 a** : something that happens : OCCURRENCE **b** : a noteworthy happening **c** : a social occasion or activity **2** : EVENTUALITY ⟨in the *event* of rain the picnic will be postponed⟩ **3** : any of the contests in a program of sports **4** : a subset of the possible outcomes of an experiment in probability or statistics ⟨rolling a 7 is an *event* in the throwing of two dice⟩ [Latin *eventus,* from *evenire* "to happen," from *e-* + *venire* "to come"] ***synonyms*** see OCCURRENCE — **at all events** : in any case — **in any event** : in any case

event·ful \-fəl\ *adj* **1** : full of or rich in events ⟨an *eventful* day⟩ **2** : MOMENTOUS — **event·ful·ly** \-fə-lē\ *adv* — **event·ful·ness** *n*

event horizon *n* : the boundary of a black hole

even·tide \ˈē-vən-ˌtīd\ *n* : EVENING

even·tu·al \i-ˈvench-wəl, -ə-wəl; -ˈven-chəl\ *adj* : taking place at an unspecified later time : ULTIMATE ⟨*eventual* success⟩ — **even·tu·al·ly** \-ē\ *adv*

even·tu·al·i·ty \i-ˌven-chə-ˈwal-ət-ē\ *n, pl* **-ties** : something that may happen : POSSIBILITY

even·tu·ate \i-ˈven-chə-ˌwāt\ *vi* : to come out finally : RESULT

ev·er \ˈev-ər\ *adv* **1** : ALWAYS ⟨*ever* faithful⟩ **2 a** : at any time ⟨seldom if *ever* home⟩ **b** : in any way ⟨how can I *ever* repay you⟩ **3** — used as an intensive especially with *so* ⟨*ever* so angry⟩ [Old English *ǣfre*]

ev·er·bloom·ing \ˌev-ər-ˈblü-ming\ *adj* : blooming more or less continuously throughout the growing season

ev·er·glade \ˈev-ər-ˌglād\ *n* : a swampy grassland especially in southern Florida usually containing saw grass and at least seasonally covered by slowly moving water [the *Everglades,* Florida]

[1]ev·er·green \ˈev-ər-ˌgrēn\ *adj* : having foliage that remains green and functional through more than one growing season ⟨most conifers are *evergreen* trees⟩ — compare DECIDUOUS

[2]evergreen *n* **1** : an evergreen plant; *also* : CONIFER **2** *pl* : twigs and branches of evergreen plants used for decoration

[1]ev·er·last·ing \ˌev-ər-ˈlas-ting\ *adj* **1** : lasting or enduring through all time : ETERNAL **2 a** (1) : continuing for a long time or indefinitely : PERPETUAL ⟨*everlasting* natural resources⟩ (2) : retaining form or color when dried ⟨*everlasting* flowers⟩ **b** : tediously persistent ⟨*everlasting* demands⟩ **3** : wearing indefinitely : DURABLE ⟨*everlasting* jeans⟩ ***synonyms*** see ETERNAL — **ev·er·last·ing·ly** \-ting-lē\ *adv* — **ev·er·last·ing·ness** *n*

[2]everlasting *n* **1** *cap* : GOD 1 — used with *the* **2** : ETERNITY ⟨from *everlasting*⟩ **3 a** : a plant especially of the daisy family with everlasting flowers **b** : an everlasting flower

ev·er·more \ˌev-ər-ˈmōr, -ˈmȯr\ *adv* : at all times : FOREVER

ever·sion \i-ˈvər-zhən, -shən\ *n* **1** : the act of turning inside out : the state of being turned inside out ⟨*eversion* of the bladder⟩ **2** : the condition (as of the foot) of being turned or rotated outward — **ever·si·ble** \-sə-bəl\ *adj*

evert \i-ˈvərt\ *vt* **1** : OVERTURN 1, UPSET **2** : to cause to undergo eversion [Latin *evertere,* from *e-* + *vertere* "to turn"]

ev·ery \ˈev-rē\ *adj* **1** : being each individual or part of a group without exception **2** : COMPLETE, ENTIRE ⟨I have *every* confidence in you⟩ [Middle English *everich, every,* from Old English *ǣfre ǣlc,* from *ǣfre* "ever" + *ǣlc* "each"]

ev·ery·body \ˈev-ri-ˌbäd-ē, -bəd-\ *pron* : EVERYONE

ev·ery·day \ˈev-rē-ˈdā\ *adj* : encountered or used routinely or typically : ORDINARY ⟨*everyday* clothes⟩

ev·ery·one \ˈev-rē-wən, -ˌwən\ *pron* : every person : EVERYBODY

ev·ery·thing \ˈev-rē-ˌthing\ *pron* **1 a** : all that exists **b** : all that relates to the subject ⟨tell *everything*⟩ **2** : something that is most important : all that counts ⟨money isn't *everything*⟩

ev·ery·where \-ˌhweər, -ˌhwaər\ *adv* : in every place or part

evict \i-ˈvikt\ *vt* : to put (an occupant) out from property by legal process [Late Latin *evictus,* past participle of *evincere* "to evict," from Latin, "to vanquish," from *e-* + *vincere* "to conquer"] ***synonyms*** see EJECT — **evic·tion** \-ˈvik-shən\ *n* — **evic·tor** \-ˈvik-tər\ *n*

[1]ev·i·dence \ˈev-əd-əns, -ə-ˌdens\ *n* **1 a** : an outward sign : INDICATION **b** : something that provides proof : TESTIMONY; *esp* : material legally submitted to a tribunal to determine the truth of a matter **2** : one who bears witness; *esp* : one who voluntarily confesses a crime and testifies for the prosecution against his or her accomplices — **ev·i·den·tial** \ˌev-ə-ˈden-chəl\ *adj* — **in evidence** : to be seen : CONSPICUOUS

[2]evidence *vt* : to offer evidence of : PROVE

ev·i·dent \ˈev-əd-ənt, -ə-ˌdent\ *adj* : clear to the sight or understanding : PLAIN ⟨was *evident* that they were twins⟩ [Medieval French, from Latin *evidens,* from *e-* + *videns,* present participle of *vidēre* "to see"] ***synonyms*** see APPARENT

evi·dent·ly \ˈev-əd-ənt-lē; -ə-ˌdent-; ˌev-ə-ˈdent-lē\ *adv* **1** : in an evident manner : CLEARLY, OBVIOUSLY ⟨a document *evidently* forged⟩ **2** : according to available evidence ⟨she was *evidently* born in Poland⟩

[1]evil \ˈē-vəl\ *adj* **evil·er** *or* **evil·ler; evil·est** *or* **evil·lest** **1 a** : morally bad : WICKED, SINFUL **b** : arising from bad character or conduct ⟨a person of *evil* reputation⟩ **2 a** : causing discomfort or repulsion : OFFENSIVE ⟨an *evil* odor⟩ **b** : DISAGREEABLE ⟨in an *evil* mood⟩ **3 a** : causing harm : PERNICIOUS **b** : marked by misfortune : UNLUCKY ⟨an *evil* day⟩ [Old English *yfel*] — **evil·ly** \-vəl-lē, -və-lē\ *adv*

[2]evil *n* **1** : the fact of suffering, misfortune, and wrongdoing **2** : something that brings sorrow, distress, or calamity — **evil·do·er** \ˌē-vəl-ˈdü-ər\ *n* — **evil·do·ing** \-ˈdü-ing\ *n*

evil eye *n* : an eye or glance held to be capable of inflicting harm

evil–mind·ed \ˌē-vəl-ˈmīn-dəd\ *adj* : having an evil disposition or evil thoughts

evince \i-ˈvins\ *vt* **1** : to be evidence of : SHOW ⟨the child's bare feet *evincing* poverty⟩ **2** : to display clearly : REVEAL ⟨her musical talent *evinced* at an early age⟩ [Latin *evincere* "to vanquish, win a point," from *e-* + *vincere* "to conquer"] — **evinc·i·ble** \i-ˈvin-sə-bəl\ *adj*

evis·cer·ate \i-ˈvis-ə-ˌrāt\ *vt* **1** : to take out the entrails of : DISEMBOWEL **2** : to deprive of vital content or force — **evis·cer·a·tion** \i-ˌvis-ə-ˈrā-shən\ *n*

evo·ca·tion \ˌē-vō-ˈkā-shən, ˌev-ə-\ *n* : the act or fact of evoking

evoc·a·tive \i-ˈväk-ət-iv\ *adj* : evoking or tending to evoke an especially emotional response ⟨an *evocative* song reminiscent of childhood⟩ — **evoc·a·tive·ly** *adv* — **evoc·a·tive·ness** *n*

evoke \i-ˈvōk\ *vt* **1** : to call forth or up: as **a** : CONJURE 2a

⟨*evoke* evil spirits⟩ **b** : to cite especially with approval : INVOKE **c** : to bring to mind ⟨this place *evokes* happy memories⟩ **2** : to re-create imaginatively [French *évoquer,* from Latin *evocare,* from *e-* + *vocare* "to call"] ***usage*** see INVOKE — **ev•o•ca•ble** \ˈev-ə-kə-bəl, i-ˈvō-kə-\ *adj* — **evo•ca•tor** \ˈē-vō-ˌkāt-ər, ˈev-ə-\ *n*

ev•o•lu•tion \ˌev-ə-ˈlü-shən, ˌē-və-\ *n* **1** : one of a set of prescribed movements (as of a dancer) **2 a** : a process of evolving or emitting ⟨*evolution* of a gas⟩ **b** : a process of change especially from a lower to a higher state : GROWTH **c** : something evolved **3** : the process of working out or developing something (as an idea) **4** : the calculation of a mathematical root **5 a** : PHYLOGENY **b** : a theory that the various types of animals and plants have their origin in other preexisting types and that the distinguishable differences are due to changes in successive generations; *also* : the process described by this theory **6** : a process in which the whole universe is a progression of interrelated phenomena [Latin *evolutio* "unrolling," from *evolvere* "to unroll"] — **ev•o•lu•tion•ary** \-shə-ˌner-ē\ *adj* — **ev•o•lu•tion•ism** \-shə-ˌniz-əm\ *n* — **ev•o•lu•tion•ist** \-shə-nəst, -shnəst\ *n or adj*

evolve \i-ˈvälv, -ˈvȯlv\ *vb* **1** : to give off : EMIT **2 a** : to arrive at through thought or study : work out ⟨*evolve* a plan⟩ **b** : to produce by natural evolutionary processes ⟨insects *evolved* wings⟩ **3** : to undergo evolutionary change ⟨species *evolve* continuously⟩ [Latin *evolvere* "to unroll," from *e-* + *volvere* "to roll"] — **evolv•able** \i-ˈväl-və-bəl; -ˈvȯl-\ *adj* — **evolve•ment** \-mənt\ *n*

ewe \ˈyü, ˈyō\ *n* : the female of the sheep or a related animal especially when mature [Old English *ēowu*]

ew•er \ˈyü-ər, ˈyu̇-ər, ˈyu̇r\ *n* : a vase-shaped pitcher or jug [Medieval French *ewer, ewter,* derived from Latin *aquarius* "of water," from *aqua* "water"]

ewer

ex \eks, ˌeks\ *prep* **1 a** : out of : FROM ⟨goods supplied *ex* stock⟩ **b** : from a specified dam ⟨a promising colt by Ranger *ex* Margot⟩ **2** : without an indicated value or right — used especially of securities ⟨*ex* dividend⟩ [Latin]

¹ex- *prefix* **1** \e *also occurs in this prefix where only* i *is shown in entries below and* ks *sometimes occurs where only* gz *is shown*\ : out of : outside ⟨exurb⟩ **2** \eks, ˌeks, ˈeks\ : former ⟨ex-president⟩ [Latin, "out, out of, thoroughly," from *ex* "out of, from"]

²ex- — see EXO-

ex•ac•er•bate \ig-ˈzas-ər-ˌbāt, ek-ˈsas-\ *vt* : to make more violent, bitter, or severe [Latin *exacerbare,* from *ex-* + *acerbus* "harsh, bitter," from *acer* "sharp"] — **ex•ac•er•ba•tion** \ig-ˌzas-ər-ˈbā-shən, ek-ˌsas-\ *n*

¹ex•act \ig-ˈzakt\ *vt* **1** : to call for forcibly or urgently and obtain ⟨*exact* burdensome concessions⟩ **2** : to call for as necessary, appropriate, or desirable ⟨*exact* a high price⟩ [Latin *exactus,* past participle of *exigere* "to drive out, demand," from *ex-* + *agere* "to drive"] ***synonyms*** see DEMAND — **ex•act•able** \-ˈzak-tə-bəl\ *adj*

²exact *adj* **1** : showing strict, particular, and complete accordance with fact ⟨*exact* knowledge⟩ **2 a** : marked by thorough consideration or minute measurement of small factual details ⟨build an *exact* replica⟩ **b** : not incomplete or approximate ⟨*exact* measurements⟩ ***synonyms*** see CORRECT — **exact•ness** \-ˈzakt-nəs -ˈzak-\ *n*

ex•act•ing \ig-ˈzak-ting\ *adj* **1** : making severe demands upon a person : TRYING ⟨an *exacting* teacher⟩ **2** : requiring precise accuracy ⟨*exacting* work⟩ — **ex•act•ing•ly** \-ting-lē\ *adv* — **ex•act•ing•ness** *n*

ex•ac•tion \ig-ˈzak-shən\ *n* **1** : the act or process of exacting especially by way of extortion **2** : something exacted; *esp* : something demanded with compelling force

ex•ac•ti•tude \ig-ˈzak-tə-ˌtüd, -ˌtyüd\ *n* : the quality or an instance of being exact

ex•act•ly \ig-ˈzak-tlē, -lē\ *adv* **1 a** : in an exact manner : PRECISELY ⟨copy the quotation *exactly*⟩ **b** : ALTOGETHER, ENTIRELY ⟨not *exactly* what I had in mind⟩ **2** : quite so — used to express agreement

exact science *n* : a science (as physics, chemistry, or astronomy) whose laws are capable of expression in accurately measured quantities

ex•ag•ger•ate \ig-ˈzaj-ə-ˌrāt\ *vb* **1** : to enlarge a fact beyond what is actual or true : OVERSTATE **2** : to enlarge or increase especially beyond the normal : OVEREMPHASIZE [Latin *exaggerare,* literally, "to heap up," from *ex-* + *agger* "heap"] — **ex•ag•ger•at•ed•ly** \-ˌrāt-əd-lē\ *adv* — **ex•ag•ger•at•ed•ness** \-nəs\ *n* — **ex•ag•ger•a•tion** \-ˌzaj-ə-ˈrā-shən\ *n* — **ex•ag•ger•a•tor** \-ˈzaj-ə-ˌrāt-ər\ *n*

ex•alt \ig-ˈzȯlt\ *vt* **1** : to raise in rank, power, or character **2** : to elevate by praise or in estimation : GLORIFY **3** : to raise high : ELEVATE [Latin *exaltare,* from *ex-* + *altus* "high"] — **ex•alt•ed•ly** \ig-ˈzȯlt-əd-lē\ *adv* — **ex•alt•er** *n*

ex•al•ta•tion \ˌeg-ˌzȯl-ˈtā-shən\ *n* **1** : the act of exalting : the state of being exalted **2** : a greatly heightened sense of well-being, power, or importance

ex•am \ig-ˈzam\ *n* : EXAMINATION

ex•am•i•na•tion \ig-ˌzam-ə-ˈnā-shən\ *n* **1** : the act or process of examining : the state of being examined **2** : an exercise designed to examine progress or test qualification or knowledge **3** : a formal interrogation — **ex•am•i•na•tion•al** \-shnəl, -shən-l\ *adj*

ex•am•ine \ig-ˈzam ən\ *vb* **1 a** : to inspect closely ⟨*examine* rock specimens⟩ **b** : to test the condition of ⟨have your eyes *examined*⟩ **c** : to inquire into carefully : INVESTIGATE **2** : to question closely in order to determine progress, fitness, or knowledge ⟨*examine* the students⟩ ⟨*examine* the witness⟩ [Medieval French *examiner,* from Latin *examinare,* from *examen* "tongue of a balance, examination," from *exigere* "to drive out, measure"] ***synonyms*** see SCRUTINIZE — **ex•am•in•er** *n*

ex•am•ple \ig-ˈzam-pəl\ *n* **1** : something to be imitated or not to be imitated : MODEL ⟨a good *example*⟩ ⟨a bad *example*⟩ **2 a** : punishment inflicted on someone as a warning to others **b** : the person so punished **3** : a sample of something taken to show what the whole is like ⟨a striking *example* of scientific method⟩ **4** : a problem to be solved in order to show how a rule works ⟨an *example* in arithmetic⟩ [Medieval French, from Latin *exemplum,* from *eximere* "to take out," from *ex-* + *emere* "to take"] ***synonyms*** see INSTANCE

ex•arch \ˈek-ˌsärk\ *n* : an Eastern bishop ranking below a patriarch and above a metropolitan; *esp* : the head of an independent church [Late Latin *exarchus,* from Greek *exarchos* "leader," from *ex-* "ex-" + *archein* "to begin, rule"] — **ex•ar•chal** \ek-ˈsär-kəl\ *adj* — **ex•arch•ate** \ˈek-ˌsär-kət\ *n* — **ex•ar•chy** \ˈek-ˌsär-kē\ *n*

ex•as•per•ate \ig-ˈzas-pə-ˌrāt\ *vt* **1** : to make angry : ENRAGE **2** : to cause irritation or annoyance to [Latin *exasperare,* from *ex-* + *asper* "rough"] ***synonyms*** see IRRITATE

ex•as•per•a•tion \ig-ˌzas-pə-ˈrā-shən\ *n* **1** : the state of being exasperated **2** : the act or an instance of exasperating

Ex•cal•i•bur \ek-ˈskal-ə-bər\ *n* : the legendary sword of King Arthur [Medieval French *Escalibor,* from Medieval Latin *Caliburnus*]

ex ca•the•dra \ˌeks-kə-ˈthē-drə\ *adv or adj* : officially and with authority ⟨*ex cathedra* pronouncements⟩ [New Latin, literally, "from the chair"]

ex•ca•vate \ˈek-skə-ˌvāt\ *vt* **1** : to hollow out : form a hole in ⟨*excavate* a hillside⟩ **2** : to make by hollowing out ⟨*excavate* a tunnel⟩ **3** : to dig out and remove ⟨*excavate* sand⟩ **4** : to uncover by digging away covering earth [Latin *excavare,* from *ex-* + *cavare* "to make hollow," from *cavus* "hollow"] — **ex•ca•va•tor** \-ˌvāt-ər\ *n*

ex•ca•va•tion \ˌek-skə-ˈvā-shən\ *n* **1** : the act or process of excavating **2** : a hollowed-out place formed by excavating

ex•ceed \ik-ˈsēd\ *vt* **1** : to extend outside of ⟨the river will *exceed* its banks⟩ **2** : to be greater than or superior to : SURPASS ⟨the cost *exceeded* our funds⟩ **3** : to go beyond a limit set by ⟨*exceed* one's authority⟩ [Medieval French *exceder,* from Latin *excedere,* from *ex-* + *cedere* "to go"]

synonyms EXCEED, EXCEL, SURPASS, TRANSCEND mean to go or be beyond a stated or implied limit, measure, or degree. EXCEED implies going beyond a limit or standard set by authority, custom, or previous achievement ⟨*exceed* last year's

\ə\ **abut**	\au̇\ **out**	\i\ **tip**	\ȯ\ **saw**	\u̇\ **foot**
\ər\ **further**	\ch\ **chin**	\ī\ **life**	\ȯi\ **coin**	\y\ **yet**
\a\ **mat**	\e\ **pet**	\j\ **job**	\th\ **thin**	\yü\ **few**
\ā\ **take**	\ē\ **easy**	\ng\ **sing**	\t͟h\ **this**	\yu̇\ **cure**
\ä\ **cot, cart**	\g\ **go**	\ō\ **bone**	\ü\ **food**	\zh\ **vision**

production⟩. EXCEL implies preeminence in achievement or quality ⟨*excelling* in athletics⟩. SURPASS suggests superiority in quality, merit, or skill ⟨the book *surpassed* our expectations⟩. TRANSCEND implies a rising or extending notably above or beyond ordinary limits ⟨*transcended* the values of their culture⟩.

ex·ceed·ing \ik-ˈsēd-ing\ *adj* : exceptional in amount, quality, or degree ⟨*exceeding* darkness⟩

ex·ceed·ing·ly \ik-ˈsēd-ing-lē\ *also* **exceeding** *adv* : to an extreme degree : EXTREMELY ⟨an *exceedingly* fine job⟩

ex·cel \ik-ˈsel\ *vb* **ex·celled; ex·cel·ling** : to be superior : surpass in accomplishment or achievement ⟨*excels* in mathematics⟩ ⟨*excelled* her classmates⟩ [Latin *excellere,* from *ex-* + *-cellere* "to rise, project"] ***synonyms*** see EXCEED

ex·cel·lence \ˈek-sə-ləns, -sləns\ *n* **1** : the quality of being excellent **2** : an excellent or valuable quality : VIRTUE **3** : EXCELLENCY 2

ex·cel·len·cy \-sə-lən-sē, -slən-\ *n, pl* **-cies** **1** : outstanding or valuable quality — usually used in plural **2** — used as a form of address for a high dignitary of state (as a foreign ambassador) or church (as a Roman Catholic bishop) ⟨Your *Excellency*⟩

ex·cel·lent \ˈek-sə-lənt, -slənt\ *adj* : very good of its kind : FIRST-CLASS — **ex·cel·lent·ly** *adv*

ex·cel·si·or \ik-ˈsel-sē-ər\ *n* : fine curled wood shavings used especially for packing fragile items [trade name, from Latin, "higher," from *excelsus* "high," from *excellere* "to excel"]

[1]**except** *also* **ex·cept·ing** *prep* : with the exclusion or exception of ⟨everybody *except* you⟩ ⟨open daily *except* Sundays⟩

[2]**ex·cept** \ik-ˈsept\ *vt* : to take or leave out from a number or a whole : EXCLUDE, OMIT [Medieval French *excepter,* from Latin *exceptare,* from *excipere* "to take out, except," from *ex-* + *capere* "to take"]

[3]**except** *also* **excepting** *conj* **1** : UNLESS ⟨*except* you repent⟩ **2** : with this exception, namely ⟨was inaccessible *except* by boat⟩ **3** : [3]ONLY 2 ⟨I would go *except* it's too far⟩

except for *prep* : with the exception of : but for ⟨all A's *except for* a B in Latin⟩

ex·cep·tion \ik-ˈsep-shən\ *n* **1** : the act of excepting : EXCLUSION **2** : one that is excepted; *esp* : a case where a rule does not apply ⟨we'll make an *exception* this time⟩ **3** : an objection or a ground for objection ⟨took *exception* to the remark⟩

ex·cep·tion·able \ik-ˈsep-shə-nə-bəl, -shnə-\ *adj* : likely to cause objection : OBJECTIONABLE — **ex·cep·tion·ably** \-blē\ *adv*

ex·cep·tion·al \ik-ˈsep-shnəl, -shən-l\ *adj* **1** : forming an exception : UNUSUAL ⟨an *exceptional* number of rainy days⟩ **2** : better than average : SUPERIOR ⟨*exceptional* skill⟩ **3** : deviating from the norm; *esp* : having above or below average intelligence — **ex·cep·tion·al·ly** \-ē\ *adv* — **ex·cep·tion·al·ness** *n*

[1]**ex·cerpt** \ek-ˈsərpt, eg-ˈzərpt, ˈek-ˌ, ˈeg-ˌ\ *vt* : to select (a passage) for quoting : EXTRACT [Latin *excerpere,* from *ex-* + *carpere* "to gather, pluck"]

[2]**ex·cerpt** \ˈek-ˌsərpt, ˈeg-ˌzərpt\ *n* : a passage selected or copied : EXTRACT ⟨read an *excerpt* from the play⟩

[1]**ex·cess** \ik-ˈses, ˈek-ˌ\ *n* **1 a** : the state or an instance of surpassing usual limits : SUPERFLUITY **b** : the amount or degree by which one thing or quantity exceeds another **2** : INTEMPERANCE [Late Latin *excessus,* from Latin *excedere* "to exceed"] — **in excess of** : to an amount or degree beyond : OVER

[2]**excess** *adj* : being more than the usual, proper, or specified amount ⟨*excess* baggage⟩

ex·ces·sive \ik-ˈses-iv\ *adj* : exceeding what is usual, proper, or normal — **ex·ces·sive·ly** *adv* — **ex·ces·sive·ness** *n*

synonyms EXCESSIVE, EXORBITANT, INORDINATE, EXTRAVAGANT mean going beyond a normal limit. EXCESSIVE implies an amount or degree too great to be reasonable or acceptable ⟨*excessive* punishment⟩. EXORBITANT applies to what is grossly excessive ⟨*exorbitant* demands⟩. INORDINATE implies an exceeding of the limits dictated by reason or good judgment ⟨an *inordinate* appetite⟩ ⟨*inordinate* desire for power⟩. EXTRAVAGANT implies an indifference to restraints imposed by truth, prudence, or good taste ⟨*extravagant* purchases⟩.

[1]**ex·change** \iks-ˈchānj, ˈeks-ˌ\ *n* **1** : a giving or taking one thing in return for another : TRADE **2** : the act of substituting one thing for another **3** : something offered, given, or received in an exchange **4 a** : funds payable currently at a distant point (as in another country) in foreign or domestic currency **b** (1) : interchange of two kinds of money (as money of two different countries) with allowance for difference in value (2) : the amount of one currency that will buy a given amount of another **5** : a place where things or services are exchanged: as **a** : an organized market or center for trading in securities or commodities ⟨stock *exchange*⟩ **b** : a central office in which telephone lines are connected to permit communication

[2]**exchange** *vt* **1 a** : to give in exchange : TRADE, SWAP **b** : to replace by other merchandise ⟨*exchange* this shirt for one in a larger size⟩ **2** : to part with for a substitute ⟨*exchange* future security for immediate pleasure⟩ — **ex·change·able** \-ə-bəl\ *adj* — **ex·chang·er** *n*

exchange rate *n* : the ratio at which the principal units of two currencies may be traded

exchange student *n* : a student from one country received into a school in another country in exchange for one sent to a school in the home country of the first student

ex·che·quer \ˈeks-ˌchek-ər, iks-ˈ\ *n* **1** : the department of the British government concerned with the receipt and care of the national revenue **2** : TREASURY; *esp* : a national or royal treasury **3** : money available : FUNDS [Medieval French *escheker* "chessboard, counting table, exchequer," from *eschec* "check"]

[1]**ex·cise** \ˈek-ˌsīz, -ˌsīs\ *n* : an internal tax levied on the manufacture, sale, or consumption of a commodity within a country [obsolete Dutch *excijs*]

[2]**ex·cise** \ek-ˈsīz\ *vt* : to remove by cutting out ⟨*excise* a tumor⟩ [Latin *excisus,* past participle of *excidere* "to excise," from *ex-* + *caedere* "to cut"] — **ex·ci·sion** \-ˈsizh-ən\ *n*

ex·cit·able \ik-ˈsīt-ə-bəl\ *adj* : readily roused into action or an active state; *esp* : capable of activation by and reaction to stimuli — **ex·cit·abil·i·ty** \-ˌsīt-ə-ˈbil-ət-ē\ *n*

ex·ci·ta·tion \ˌek-ˌsī-ˈtā-shən, ˌek-sə-\ *n* : EXCITEMENT; *esp* : the activity or change in condition resulting from stimulation of an individual, organ, tissue, or cell

ex·cit·ato·ry \ik-ˈsīt-ə-ˌtōr-ē, -ˌtȯr-\ *adj* : tending to produce or marked by usually physiological excitation

ex·cite \ik-ˈsīt\ *vt* **1 a** : to call to activity **b** : to rouse to an emotional response **c** : to arouse (as an emotional response) by appropriate stimuli **2 a** : ENERGIZE **b** : to produce a magnetic field in **3** : to increase the activity of (as nervous tissue) **4** : to raise (as an atom) to a higher energy level [Medieval French *exciter,* from Latin *excitare,* from *ex-* + *citare* "to rouse"] ***synonyms*** see PROVOKE — **ex·cit·er** \-ˈsīt-ər\ *n*

ex·cit·ed \-ˈsīt-əd\ *adj* : having or showing strong feeling : worked up ⟨*excited* about the trip⟩ — **ex·cit·ed·ly** *adv*

ex·cite·ment \ik-ˈsīt-mənt\ *n* **1** : the act of exciting : the state of being excited **2** : something that excites

ex·cit·ing \-ˈsīt-ing\ *adj* : causing excitement : STIRRING ⟨*exciting* news⟩ — **ex·cit·ing·ly** \-ing-lē\ *adv*

ex·claim \iks-ˈklām\ *vb* **1** : to speak or cry out in strong or sudden emotion **2** : to speak loudly or forcefully [Middle French *exclamer,* from Latin *exclamare,* from *ex-* + *clamare* "to cry out"]

ex·cla·ma·tion \ˌeks-klə-ˈmā-shən\ *n* **1** : a sharp or sudden utterance : OUTCRY **2** : forceful expression of protest or complaint

exclamation point *n* : a punctuation mark ! used chiefly after an exclamation to show forceful utterance or strong feeling

ex·clam·a·to·ry \iks-ˈklam-ə-ˌtōr-ē, -ˌtȯr-\ *adj* : containing, expressing, using, or relating to exclamation ⟨an *exclamatory* sentence⟩

ex·clude \iks-ˈklüd\ *vt* **1 a** : to shut or keep out **b** : to bar from participation, consideration, or inclusion **2** : to put out : EXPEL [Latin *excludere* (past participle *exclusus*), from *ex-* + *claudere* "to close"] — **ex·clud·able** \-ˈklüd-ə-bəl\ *adj* — **ex·clud·er** *n* — **ex·clu·sion** \-ˈklü-zhən\ *n*

[1]**ex·clu·sive** \iks-ˈklü-siv, -ziv\ *adj* **1 a** : excluding or having the power to exclude **b** : limiting or limited to certain persons or classes (as in ownership, membership, or privileges) **2** : catering to a distinct and especially a fashionable class ⟨an *exclusive* neighborhood⟩ **3** : SOLE, SINGLE ⟨*exclusive* use of a beach⟩ **4** : COMPLETE, UNDIVIDED ⟨give me your *exclusive* attention⟩ — **ex·clu·sive·ly** *adv* — **ex·clu·sive·ness** *n*

[2]**exclusive** *n* **1** : something exclusive **2** : a news story at first released to or reported by only one source

exclusive of *prep* : not taking into account ⟨for five days *exclusive of* today⟩

ex·cog·i·tate \eks-ˈkäj-ə-ˌtāt\ *vt* : to think out : DEVISE — **ex·cog·i·ta·tion** \ˌeks-ˌkäj-ə-ˈtā-shən\ *n* — **ex·cog·i·ta·tive** \eks-ˈkäj-ə-ˌtāt-iv\ *adj*

ex·com·mu·ni·cate \ˌeks-kə-ˈmyü-nə-ˌkāt\ *vt* : to deprive officially of the rights of church membership — **ex·com·mu·ni-**

cation \-ˌmyü-nə-ˈkā-shən\ *n* — **ex·com·mu·ni·ca·tor** \-ˈmyü-nə-ˌkāt-ər\ *n*

ex·co·ri·ate \ek-ˈskōr-ē-ˌāt, -ˈskȯr-\ *vt* **1** : to wear off the skin of : ABRADE **2** : to censure very severely [Late Latin *excoriare,* from Latin *ex-* + *corium* "skin, hide"] — **ex·co·ri·a·tion** \ek-ˌskōr-ē-ˈā-shən, -ˌskȯr-\ *n*

ex·cre·ment \ˈek-skrə-mənt\ *n* : waste matter discharged from the body; *esp* : FECES [Latin *excrementum,* from *excernere* "to discharge"] — **ex·cre·men·tal** \ˌek-skrə-ˈment-l\ *adj*

ex·cres·cence \ek-ˈskres-ns\ *n* : OUTGROWTH; *esp* : an abnormal outgrowth (as a wart) on the body

ex·cres·cent \-nt\ *adj* : being or forming an excrescence [Latin *excrescere* "to grow out," from *ex-* + *crescere* "to grow"] — **ex·cres·cent·ly** *adv*

ex·cre·ta \ek-ˈskrēt-ə\ *n pl* : waste matter (as feces) eliminated or separated from the body

ex·crete \ek-ˈskrēt\ *vt* : to separate and eliminate (waste) from the blood or tissues or from the active protoplasm usually in the form of sweat or urine [Latin *excretus,* past participle of *excernere* "to sift out, discharge," from *ex-* + *cernere* "to sift"] — **ex·cret·er** *n*

ex·cre·tion \ek-ˈskrē-shən\ *n* **1** : the act or process of excreting **2** : excreted matter

ex·cre·to·ry \ˈek-skrə-ˌtōr-ē, -ˌtȯr-\ *adj* : of, relating to, or functioning in excretion

ex·cru·ci·ate \ik-ˈskrü-shē-ˌāt\ *vt* : to subject to intense pain or mental distress [Latin *excruciare,* from *ex-* + *cruciare* "to crucify," from *cruc-, crux* "cross"] — **ex·cru·ci·a·tion** \-ˌskrü-shē-ˈā-shən, -sē-ˈā-\ *n*

ex·cru·ci·at·ing \-ˈskrü-shē-ˌāt-ing\ *adj* **1** : causing great pain or mental distress : AGONIZING ⟨an *excruciating* problem⟩ **2** : very intense : EXTREME ⟨*excruciating* pain⟩ — **ex·cru·ci·at·ing·ly** \-ing-lē\ *adv*

ex·cul·pate \ˈek-skəl-ˌpāt, -ˌskəl-, ek-ˈ\ *vt* : to clear from alleged fault or guilt [derived from Latin *ex-* + *culpa* "blame"] — **ex·cul·pa·tion** \ˌek-skəl-ˈpā-shən, -ˌskəl-\ *n* — **ex·cul·pa·to·ry** \ek-ˈskəl-pə-ˌtōr-ē, -ˌtȯr-\ *adj*

ex·cur·rent \ek-ˈskər-ənt, -ˈskə-rənt\ *adj* **1** : characterized by a current that flows outward ⟨the *excurrent* siphon of a clam⟩ **2** : having a straight main stem that extends without forking to the top ⟨the spruce is an *excurrent* tree⟩ — compare DELIQUESCENT

ex·cur·sion \ik-ˈskər-zhən\ *n* **1 a** : a going out or forth : EXPEDITION **b** : a usually brief pleasure trip; *esp* : such a trip at special reduced rates **2** : departure from a direct or proper course; *esp* : DIGRESSION [Latin *excursio,* from *excurrere* "to run out, extend," from *ex-* + *currere* "to run"]

ex·cur·sion·ist \ik-ˈskərzh-nəst, -ə-nəst\ *n* : a person who goes on an excursion

ex·cur·sive \ik-ˈskər-siv\ *adj* : constituting a digression : characterized by digression — **ex·cur·sive·ly** *adv* — **ex·cur·sive·ness** *n*

ex·cur·sus \ik-ˈskər-səs\ *n, pl* **ex·cur·sus·es** *also* **ex·cur·sus** \-səs, -ˌsüs\ : an appendix or a digression containing further exposition of some point or topic [Latin, "digression," from *excurrere* "to run out, extend"]

[1]**ex·cuse** \ik-ˈskyüz\ *vt* **1** : to make apology for : try to remove blame from ⟨*excuse* oneself for being late⟩ **2** : to forgive entirely or disregard as of little importance ⟨*excused* the student's tardiness⟩ **3** : EXEMPT, RELEASE ⟨*excuse* a person from a debt⟩ **4** : to serve as an acceptable reason or explanation for (something said or done) : JUSTIFY ⟨nothing can *excuse* dishonesty⟩ [Medieval French *excuser,* from Latin *excusare,* from *ex-* + *causa* "cause, explanation"] — **ex·cus·able** \-ˈskyü-zə-bəl\ *adj* — **ex·cus·ably** \-blē\ *adv* — **ex·cus·er** *n*

synonyms EXCUSE, CONDONE, PARDON, FORGIVE mean to exact neither punishment nor redress. EXCUSE implies an overlooking of a fault, omission, or failure without censure or due punishment ⟨*excused* the interruption⟩. CONDONE suggests accepting without protest or censure a reprehensible act or condition ⟨does not *condone* cheating on taxes⟩. PARDON implies freeing from penalty due for admitted or proved offense ⟨*pardon* a criminal⟩. FORGIVE implies a sincere change of feeling that makes no claim to retaliation and gives up resentment or desire for revenge ⟨*forgave* their insensitivity⟩.

[2]**ex·cuse** \ik-ˈskyüs\ *n* **1** : the act of excusing **2 a** : something offered as justification or as grounds for being excused **b** : a note of explanation of an absence **3** : JUSTIFICATION 2, REASON ***synonyms*** see APOLOGY

ex·ec \ig-ˈzek\ *n* **1** : EXECUTIVE OFFICER **2** : EXECUTIVE 2 **3** : EXECUTIVE 3

ex·e·cra·ble \ˈek-si-krə-bəl\ *adj* **1** : DETESTABLE ⟨*execrable* crimes⟩ **2** : very bad : WRETCHED ⟨*execrable* cafeteria food⟩ — **ex·e·cra·ble·ness** *n* — **ex·e·cra·bly** \-blē\ *adv*

ex·e·crate \ˈek-sə-ˌkrāt\ *vt* **1** : to declare to be evil or detestable **2** : to dislike utterly : ABHOR [Latin *exsecrari* "to put under a curse," from *ex-* + *sacer* "sacred"] — **ex·e·cra·tion** \ˌek-sə-ˈkrā-shən\ *n* — **ex·e·cra·tor** \ˈek-sə-ˌkrāt-ər\ *n*

ex·e·cute \ˈek-sə-ˌkyüt\ *vt* **1** : to put into effect : carry out : PERFORM ⟨*execute* the plan⟩ **2** : to do what is provided or required by ⟨*execute* a decree⟩ **3** : to put to death according to legal orders **4** : to make or produce especially by carrying out a design ⟨a statue *executed* in bronze⟩ **5** : to perform what is required (as signing) to give legal force to ⟨*execute* a deed⟩ [Medieval French *executer,* derived from Latin *exsequi,* from *ex-* + *sequi* "to follow"]

ex·e·cu·tion \ˌek-sə-ˈkyü-shən\ *n* **1** : the act or process of executing : PERFORMANCE ⟨put a plan into *execution*⟩ **2** : a putting to death as a legal penalty **3** : a judicial writ empowering an officer to carry out a judgment (as against a debtor) **4** : the act or mode or result of performance in something requiring special skill **5** *archaic* : effective or destructive action

ex·e·cu·tion·er \-ˈkyü-shə-nər, -shnər\ *n* : one that executes; *esp* : one who carries out a sentence of death

[1]**ex·ec·u·tive** \ig-ˈzek-yət-iv, -ˈzek-ət-\ *adj* **1** : of or relating to the execution of the laws and the conduct of public and national affairs ⟨the *executive* branch⟩ **2** : designed for or relating to the execution of affairs ⟨*executive* board⟩ ⟨*executive* skills⟩ **3** : of or relating to an executive ⟨the *executive* offices⟩

[2]**executive** *n* **1** : the executive branch of a government **2** : an individual or group that directs an organization **3** : one who holds a position of administrative or managerial responsibility

executive officer *n* : the officer second in command of a military or naval unit or vessel

executive session *n* : a usually closed session (as of a legislative body)

ex·ec·u·tor \ig-ˈzek-yət-ər, -ˈzek-ət-, *in sense 1 also* ˈek-sə-ˌkyüt-\ *n* **1** : one that executes something **2** : the person named in a will to carry out its provisions

ex·ec·u·trix \ig-ˈzek-yə-ˌtriks, -ˈzek-ə-\ *n, pl* **ex·ec·u·tri·ces** *or* **ex·ec·u·trix·es** \-ˌzek-yə-ˈtrī-ˌsēz, -ˌzek-ə-\ : a woman who is an executor

ex·e·ge·sis \ˌek-sə-ˈjē-səs\ *n, pl* **-ge·ses** \-ˈjē-ˌsēz\ : explanation or critical interpretation of a text [Greek *exēgēsis,* from *exēgeisthai* "to explain, interpret," from *ex-* "ex-" + *hēgeisthai* "to lead"] — **ex·e·get·i·cal** \-ˈjet-i-kəl\ *also* **ex·e·get·ic** \-ˈjet-ik\ *adj* — **ex·e·get·i·cal·ly** \-i-kə-lē, -klē\ *adv*

ex·e·gete \ˈek-sə-ˌjēt\ *n* : one who practices exegesis

ex·em·plar \ig-ˈzem-ˌplär, -plər\ *n* : one that serves as a model or an example: as **a** : an ideal model **b** : a typical or standard specimen [Latin, from *exemplum* "example"]

ex·em·pla·ry \ig-ˈzem-plə-rē\ *adj* **1 a** : serving as a pattern **b** : deserving imitation ⟨*exemplary* behavior⟩ **2** : serving as a warning ⟨given an *exemplary* punishment⟩ **3** : serving as an example, instance, or illustration — **ex·em·plar·i·ly** \ˌeg-zəm-ˈpler-ə-lē\ *adv* — **ex·em·pla·ri·ness** \ig-ˈzem-plə-rē-nəs\ *n*

ex·em·pli·fy \ig-ˈzem-plə-ˌfī\ *vt* **-fied; -fy·ing** **1** : to show or illustrate by example ⟨stories that *exemplify* virtues⟩ **2** : to serve as an example of ⟨she *exemplifies* a good leader⟩ — **ex·em·pli·fi·ca·tion** \-ˌzem-plə-fə-ˈkā-shən\ *n*

ex·em·pli gra·tia \ig-ˌzem-plē-ˈgrät-ē-ˌä\ *adv* : for example [Latin]

[1]**ex·empt** \ig-ˈzempt\ *adj* : free or released from an obligation or requirement to which others are subject ⟨was *exempt* from jury duty⟩ [Latin *exemptus,* past participle of *eximere* "to take out," from *ex-* + *emere* "to take"]

[2]**exempt** *vt* : to make exempt

ex·emp·tion \ig-ˈzem-shən, -ˈzemp-\ *n* **1** : the act of exempting : the state of being exempt **2** : something exempted; *esp* : a source or an amount of income exempted from taxation

ex·e·quy \ˈek-sə-kwē\ *n, pl* **-quies** : a funeral rite — usually

\ə\ **abut**	\au̇\ **out**	\i\ **tip**	\ȯ\ **saw**	\u̇\ **foot**
\ər\ **further**	\ch\ **chin**	\ī\ **life**	\ȯi\ **coin**	\y\ **yet**
\a\ **mat**	\e\ **pet**	\j\ **job**	\th\ **thin**	\yü\ **few**
\ā\ **take**	\ē\ **easy**	\ng\ **sing**	\t͟h\ **this**	\yu̇\ **cure**
\ä\ **cot, cart**	\g\ **go**	\ō\ **bone**	\ü\ **food**	\zh\ **vision**

used in plural [Latin *exsequiae,* plural, from *exsequi* "to follow out"]

[1]**ex·er·cise** \ˈek-sər-ˌsīz\ *n* **1 :** the act of putting into use, action, or practice ⟨the *exercise* of self-control⟩ **2 a :** regular or repeated use of a mental faculty or bodily organ **b :** bodily exertion for the sake of physical fitness **3 :** something performed or practiced in order to develop, improve, or display a specific capability or skill : EXAMPLE ⟨10 *exercises* for math homework⟩ **4 a :** a drill carried out for training and discipline ⟨naval *exercises*⟩ **b** *pl* **:** a program including speeches, announcements of awards and honors, and various traditional practices ⟨graduation *exercises*⟩ [Middle French *exercice,* from Latin *exercitium,* from *exercēre* "to drive on, keep busy," from *ex-* + *arcēre* "to hold off"]

[2]**exercise** *vb* **1 :** put into use : EXERT ⟨*exercise* patience⟩ **2 a :** to use repeatedly in order to strengthen or develop ⟨*exercise* a muscle⟩ **b :** to train (as troops) by drills **c :** to go or put through exercises ⟨*exercise* a dog⟩ **3 a :** to engage the attention and effort of ⟨a riddle that *exercises* the mind⟩ **b :** to cause anxiety, alarm, or indignation in ⟨citizens *exercised* about pollution⟩ — **ex·er·cis·able** \-ˈsī-zə-bəl\ *adj* — **ex·er·cis·er** *n*

ex·ert \ig-ˈzərt\ *vt* **1 :** to put forth (as strength, force or power) : bring into play ⟨*exert* influence⟩ **2 :** to put (oneself) into action or to tiring effort [Latin *exsertus,* past participle of *exserere* "to thrust out," from *ex-* + *serere* "to join"]

ex·er·tion \ig-ˈzər-shən\ *n* **:** the act or an instance of exerting; *esp* **:** laborious or perceptible effort ***synonyms*** see EFFORT

ex·e·unt \ˈek-sē-ənt, -sē-ˌənt\ — used as a stage direction to specify that all or certain named characters leave the stage [Latin, "they go out," from *exire* "to go out," from *ex-* + *ire* "to go"]

ex·fo·liant \eks-ˈfō-lē-ənt\ *n* **:** a mechanical or chemical agent (as an abrasive skin wash or salicylic acid) that is applied to the skin to remove dead cells from the surface

ex·fo·li·ate \eks-ˈfō-lē-ˌāt, ˈeks-\ *vb* **:** to shed or remove in thin layers or scales [Late Latin *exfoliare* "to strip of leaves," from Latin *ex-* + *folium* "leaf"] — **ex·fo·li·a·tion** \ˌeks-ˌfō-lē-ˈā-shən\ *n* — **ex·fo·li·a·tive** \eks-ˈfō-lē-ˌāt-iv\ *adj*

ex·fo·li·a·tor \eks-ˈfō-lē-ˌāt-ər\ *n* **:** EXFOLIANT

ex·hal·ant \eks-ˈhā-lənt\ *adj* **:** bearing out or outward : EXCURRENT 1

ex·ha·la·tion \ˌeks-ə-ˈlā-shən, -hə-ˈlā-\ *n* **1 :** something exhaled or given off : EMANATION **2 :** an act of exhaling

ex·hale \eks-ˈhāl\ *vb* **1 :** to rise or be given off as vapor **2 :** to breathe out **3 :** to send forth (as gas or odor) : EMIT ⟨the fragrance that flowers *exhale*⟩ [Latin *exhalare,* from *ex-* + *halare* "to breathe"]

[1]**ex·haust** \ig-ˈzȯst\ *vb* **1 a :** to use up the whole supply of ⟨*exhausted* our funds for the week⟩ **b :** to use up all of the mental or physical energy of : TIRE, WEAR OUT ⟨*exhausted* by the long hike⟩ **2 :** to destroy the fertility of (soil) **3 a :** to draw off or let out completely ⟨*exhaust* the air from the jar⟩ **b :** to empty by drawing something from; *esp* **:** to create a vacuum in **4 a :** to think about or discuss (a subject) completely **b :** to try out the whole number of ⟨had *exhausted* all possibilities⟩ **5 :** to pass or flow out : EMPTY [Latin *exhaustus,* past participle of *exhaurire* "to exhaust," from *ex-* + *haurire* "to draw"] — **exhaust·er** *n* — **ex·haust·ibil·i·ty** \-ˌzȯ-stə-ˈbil-ət-ē\ *n* — **exhaust·ible** \-ˈzȯ-stə-bəl\ *adj*

[2]**exhaust** *n* **1 a :** the escape of used steam or gas from an engine **b :** the gas thus escaping **2 a :** a conduit through which used gases escape **b :** an arrangement for withdrawing fumes, dusts, or odors from an enclosure

ex·haus·tion \ig-ˈzȯs-chən\ *n* **1 :** the act or process of exhausting **2 :** the state of being exhausted; *esp* **:** extreme weariness or fatigue

ex·haus·tive \ig-ˈzȯ-stiv\ *adj* **1 :** serving or tending to exhaust **2 :** THOROUGH 1, COMPLETE ⟨an *exhaustive* discussion⟩ — **exhaus·tive·ly** *adv* — **ex·haus·tive·ness** *n*

ex·haust·less \ig-ˈzȯst-ləs\ *adj* **:** INEXHAUSTIBLE

[1]**ex·hib·it** \ig-ˈzib-ət\ *vt* **1 :** to present in legal form (as to a court) **2 :** to show outwardly ⟨*exhibit* an interest in music⟩ **3 :** to put on display ⟨*exhibit* a collection of paintings⟩ [Latin *exhibitus,* past participle of *exhibēre* "to exhibit," from *ex-* + *habēre* "to have, hold"] ***synonyms*** see SHOW — **ex·hib·i·tive** \-ət-iv\ *adj* — **ex·hib·i·tor** \-ət-ər\ *n*

[2]**exhibit** *n* **1 :** a document or material object produced and identified in a court for use as evidence **2 :** something exhibited **3 :** an act or instance of exhibiting : EXHIBITION 3

ex·hi·bi·tion \ˌek-sə-ˈbish-ən\ *n* **1 :** an act or instance of exhibiting **2** *British* **:** a grant drawn from the funds of a school or university to help support a student **3 :** a public showing (as of works of art, objects of manufacture, or athletic skill)

ex·hi·bi·tion·er \-ˈbish-nər, -ə-nər\ *n, British* **:** one who holds a grant from a school or university

ex·hi·bi·tion·ism \-ˈbish-ə-ˌniz-əm\ *n* **1 a :** a compulsive tendency to expose one's body and especially the genitals in a public place where such exposure is regarded as indecent **b :** an act of such exposure **2 :** the act or practice of behaving so as to attract attention to oneself — **ex·hi·bi·tion·ist** \-ˈbish-nəst, -ə-nəst\ *n or adj* — **ex·hi·bi·tion·is·tic** \-ˌbish-ə-ˈnis-tik\ *adj*

ex·hil·a·rate \ig-ˈzil-ə-ˌrāt\ *vt* **1 :** to make cheerful and excited **2 :** to fill with a lively sense of well-being ⟨was *exhilarated* by the fresh air⟩ [Latin *exhilarare,* from *ex-* + *hilarare* "to gladden," from *ex-* + *hilarus* "cheerful"] — **ex·hil·a·rat·ingly** \-ˌrāt-ing-lē\ *adv* — **ex·hil·a·ra·tive** \-ˌrāt-iv\ *adj*

ex·hil·a·ra·tion \ig-ˌzil-ə-ˈrā-shən\ *n* **1 :** the action of exhilarating **2 :** the state or the feeling of being exhilarated : high spirits

ex·hort \ig-ˈzȯrt\ *vb* **:** to arouse by argument or advice : urge strongly ⟨*exhorting* people to vote⟩ [Medieval French *exorter,* from Latin *exhortari,* from *ex-* + *hortari* "to incite"] — **ex·hort·er** *n*

ex·hor·ta·tion \ˌeks-ˌȯr-ˈtā-shən, ˌegz-\ *n* **1 :** an act or instance of exhorting **2 :** a speech intended to exhort : earnestly spoken words of urgent advice or warning

ex·hor·ta·tive \ig-ˈzȯrt-ət-iv\ *adj* **:** serving to exhort

ex·hor·ta·to·ry \-ə-ˌtōr-ē, -ˌtȯr-\ *adj* **:** using exhortation : EXHORTATIVE ⟨an *exhortatory* appeal⟩

ex·hume \igz-ˈüm,-ˈyüm; iks-ˈyüm, -ˈhyüm\ *vt* **1 :** to uncover and take out of a place of burial : DISINTER 1 **2 :** to bring back from neglect or obscurity ⟨*exhumed* the works of the forgotten author⟩ [Medieval Latin *exhumare,* from Latin *ex* "out of" + *humus* "earth"] — **ex·hu·ma·tion** \ˌeks-yü-ˈmā-shən, -hyü-; ˌegz-ü-, -yü-\ *n* — **ex·hum·er** *n*

ex·i·gence \ˈek-sə-jəns\ *n* **:** EXIGENCY

ex·i·gen·cy \ˈek-sə-jən-sē, ig-ˈzij-ən-\ *n, pl* **-cies :** a case or a state of affairs demanding immediate action or remedy ***synonyms*** see NEED

ex·i·gent \ˈek-sə-jənt\ *adj* **1 :** requiring immediate aid or action : URGENT ⟨*exigent* circumstances⟩ **2 :** requiring or calling for much : DEMANDING, EXACTING ⟨an *exigent* client⟩ [Latin *exigere* "to demand," from *ex-* + *agere* "to drive"] — **ex·i·gent·ly** *adv*

ex·ig·u·ous \eg-ˈzig-yə-wəs\ *adj* **:** scanty in amount ⟨*exiguous* evidence⟩ [Latin *exiguus,* from *exigere* "to demand"] — **ex·i·gu·ity** \ˌek-sə-ˈgyü-ət-ē\ *n* — **ex·ig·u·ous·ly** \eg-ˈzig-yə-wəs-lē\ *adv* — **ex·ig·u·ous·ness** *n*

[1]**ex·ile** \ˈeg-ˌzīl, ˈek-ˌsīl\ *n* **1 a :** forced removal or voluntary absence from one's country or home **b :** the state of one so absent **2 :** a person who is in exile [Medieval French *exil,* from Latin *exilium,* from *exul* "an exile"]

[2]**exile** *vt* **:** to banish or expel from one's own country or home

ex·ist \ig-ˈzist\ *vi* **1 :** to have actuality or reality : be real : BE ⟨do unicorns *exist*?⟩ **2 :** to continue to live : stay alive ⟨earn hardly enough to *exist* on⟩ **3 :** to be found : OCCUR ⟨a disease that no longer *exists*⟩ [Latin *exsistere* "to come into being, exist," from *ex-* + *sistere* "to stand"]

ex·ist·ence \ig-ˈzis-təns\ *n* **1 :** the fact or the state of having being or of being real ⟨the largest animal in *existence*⟩ **2 a :** the sum total of existing things **b :** a particular being **3 :** continuance in living or way of living : LIFE ⟨a happy *existence*⟩ **4 :** actual or present occurrence ⟨the *existence* of war⟩

ex·ist·ent \-tənt\ *adj* **1 :** having being : EXISTING **2 :** existing now : PRESENT

ex·is·ten·tial \ˌeg-zis-ˈten-chəl, ˌek-sis-\ *adj* **1 :** of, relating to, or dealing with existence **2 a :** grounded in existence or the experience of existence **b :** having being in time and space **3 :** concerned with or involving human existence or its nature

[1]**ex·it** \ˈeg-zət, ˈek-sət\ — used as a stage direction to specify who goes off stage [Latin, "he, she, or it goes out," from *exire* "to go out," from *ex-* + *ire* "to go"]

[2]**exit** *n* **1 :** a departure from a stage **2 :** the act of going out or away **3 :** a way out of an enclosed place or space

[3]**exit** *vi* **:** to go out : LEAVE, DEPART

exo- *or* **ex-** *combining form* **:** outside ⟨*exogamy*⟩: outer ⟨*exoskeleton*⟩ — compare ECT-, END- [Greek *exō* "out, outside," from *ex* "out of"]

exo·bi·ol·o·gy \ˌek-sō-bī-ˈäl-ə-jē\ *n* **:** a branch of biology concerned with the search for life outside the earth and with effects of extraterrestrial environments on living organisms — **exo·bi·o·log·i·cal** \ˌbī-ə-ˈläj-i-kəl\ *adj* — **exo·bi·ol·o·gist** \-bī-ˈäl-ə-jəst\ *n*

exo·carp \ˈek-sō-ˌkärp\ *n* **:** the usually thin membranous outermost layer of the pericarp of a fruit (as the skin of a peach) — compare ENDOCARP, MESOCARP

exo·crine \ˈek-sə-krən, -ˌkrīn, -ˌkrēn\ *adj* **:** producing, being, or relating to a secretion that is released outside its source ⟨*exocrine* cells⟩ [*exo-* + Greek *krinein* "to separate"]

exocrine gland *n* **:** a gland (as a salivary gland, a sweat gland, or a pancreas) that releases a secretion outside of or at the surface of an organ or part by means of a duct or canal

exo·cy·to·sis \ˌek-sō-sī-ˈtō-səs\ *n* **:** the process by which a cell packages materials in vesicles and secretes them to the exterior — compare ENDOCYTOSIS [*exo-* + *cyt-* + *-osis*]

ex·o·dus \ˈek-səd-əs\ *n* **1** *cap* **:** the mainly narrative second book of canonical Jewish and Christian Scriptures — see BIBLE table **2 :** a mass departure [Latin, from Greek *Exodos,* literally, "road out," from *ex-* + *hodos* "road"]

ex of·fi·cio \ˌeks-ə-ˈfish-ē-ˌō\ *adv or adj* **:** because of an office ⟨the Vice President serves *ex officio* as president of the Senate⟩ [Late Latin]

ex·og·a·my \ek-ˈsäg-ə-mē\ *n* **:** marriage outside a specific group especially as required by custom or law — **ex·og·a·mous** \-məs\ *adj*

ex·og·e·nous \ek-ˈsäj-ə-nəs\ *adj* **:** developing or originating outside the cell or body — **ex·og·e·nous·ly** *adv*

ex·on \ˈek-ˌsän\ *n* **:** a DNA sequence in a gene that codes information for protein synthesis and that is copied and spliced together with other such sequences to form messenger RNA — compare INTRON [*ex*pressed sequence + *-on*]

ex·on·er·ate \ig-ˈzän-ə-ˌrāt\ *vt* **:** to clear from a charge of wrongdoing or from blame **:** declare innocent [Latin *exonerare* "to unburden," from *ex-* + *oner-, onus* "load"] — **ex·on·er·a·tion** \ig-ˌzän-ə-ˈrā-shən\ *n* — **ex·on·er·a·tive** \ig-ˈzän-ə-ˌrāt-iv\ *adj*

ex·or·bi·tant \ig-ˈzȯr-bət-ənt\ *adj* **:** going beyond the limits of what is fair, reasonable, or expected ⟨*exorbitant* prices⟩ [Late Latin *exorbitare* "to deviate," from Latin *ex-* + *orbita* "track, rut"] ***synonyms*** see EXCESSIVE — **ex·or·bi·tance** \-bət-əns\ *n* — **ex·or·bi·tant·ly** *adv*

ex·or·cise \ˈek-ˌsȯr-ˌsīz, -sər-\ *vt* **1 a :** to drive (an evil spirit) off or out by religious exercises or by spells **b :** to get rid of (something that troubles or menaces) **2 :** to free (as a person or place) from an evil spirit [Medieval French *exorciser,* from Late Latin *exorcizare,* from Greek *exorkizein,* from *ex-* + *horkizein* "to bind by oath," from *horkos* "oath"] — **ex·or·cis·er** *n*

ex·or·cism \-ˌsiz-əm\ *n* **1 :** the act or practice of exorcising **2 :** a spell or formula used in exorcising — **ex·or·cist** \-ˌsist, -səst\ *n*

exo·skel·e·ton \ˌek-sō-ˈskel-ət-n\ *n* **:** a hard supporting or protective structure (as of a crustacean or insect) developed on the outside of the body — compare ENDOSKELETON — **exo·skel·e·tal** \-ət-l\ *adj*

exo·sphere \ˈek-sō-ˌsfiər\ *n* **:** the outermost region of the atmosphere of the earth or a planet

exo·ther·mic \ˌek-sō-ˈthər-mik\ *adj* **:** characterized by or formed by the giving off of heat ⟨an *exothermic* chemical reaction⟩

[1]**ex·ot·ic** \ig-ˈzät-ik\ *adj* **1 :** introduced from another country ⟨*exotic* plants⟩ **2 :** strikingly or excitingly different or unusual ⟨*exotic* colors⟩ [Latin *exoticus,* from Greek *exōtikos,* from *exō* "outside," from *ex* "out of"] — **ex·ot·i·cal·ly** \-ˈzät-i-kə-lē, -klē\ *adv* — **ex·ot·ic·ness** \-ik-nəs\ *n*

[2]**exotic** *n* **:** something (as a plant) that is exotic

exo·tox·in \ˌek-sō-ˈtäk-sən\ *n* **:** a soluble poisonous substance given off by a microorganism

ex·pand \ik-ˈspand\ *vb* **1 :** to open wide **:** UNFOLD ⟨a bird with wings *expanded*⟩ **2 :** to increase in size, number, or amount **:** ENLARGE ⟨metals *expand* under heat⟩ **3 :** to develop more fully ⟨*expand* an argument⟩ **4 a :** to perform the indicated mathematical operations of **:** write out in full ⟨*expand* both sides of an equation⟩ **b :** to express (a function) in the form of a series [Latin *expandere,* from *ex-* + *pandere* "to spread"] — **ex·pand·able** \-ˈspan-də-bəl\ *adj* — **ex·pand·er** *n*

synonyms EXPAND, DILATE, DISTEND, INFLATE mean to increase in size or volume. EXPAND applies to any enlarging that comes from within or without and regardless of manner (as growth, unfolding, or addition of parts) ⟨a business that *expands* every year⟩. DILATE suggests expansion of diameter or circumference ⟨the pupil of the eye *dilates* in dim light⟩. DISTEND implies outward extension caused by pressure from within ⟨a *distended* stomach⟩. INFLATE implies expanding by the introduction of air or something insubstantial and suggests a vulnerability and liability to sudden collapse ⟨an *inflated* balloon⟩ ⟨*inflated* currency⟩.

expanded notation *n* **:** the writing of a number in terms of powers of the base in which it is expressed ⟨123 in base 10 when written in *expanded notation* is $1(10^2) + 2(10^1) + 3(10^0)$⟩

ex·panse \ik-ˈspans\ *n* **:** a wide space, area, or stretch ⟨the vast *expanse* of the ocean⟩ [Latin *expansus,* past participle of *expandere* "to expand"]

ex·pan·si·ble \ik-ˈspan-sə-bəl\ *adj* **:** capable of being expanded — **ex·pan·si·bil·i·ty** \-ˌspan-sə-ˈbil-ət-ē\ *n*

ex·pan·sion \ik-ˈspan-chən\ *n* **1 :** the act or process of expanding **2 :** the quality or state of being expanded **3 a :** an expanded part **b :** something that results from an act of expanding **4 :** the result of carrying out the indicated mathematical operations ⟨write out the *expansion* of the equation⟩ **:** the expression of a function in the form of a series

ex·pan·sive \ik-ˈspan-siv\ *adj* **1 :** having a capacity or a tendency to expand ⟨gases are *expansive*⟩ **2 :** causing or tending to cause expansion ⟨an *expansive* force⟩ **3 :** characterized by high spirits, generosity, or readiness to talk ⟨in an *expansive* mood⟩ **4 :** having considerable extent **:** BROAD ⟨the topic is too *expansive* for brief treatment⟩ — **ex·pan·sive·ly** *adv* — **ex·pan·sive·ness** *n*

ex par·te \ek-ˈspärt-ē, ˈek-\ *adv or adj* **:** from a one-sided or partisan point of view [Medieval Latin, "on behalf"]

ex·pa·ti·ate \ek-ˈspā-shē-ˌāt\ *vi* **:** to speak or write at length or in detail [Latin *exspatiari* "to wander, digress," from *ex-* + *spatium* "space, course"] — **ex·pa·ti·a·tion** \ek-ˌspā-shē-ˈā-shən\ *n*

[1]**ex·pa·tri·ate** \ek-ˈspā-trē-ˌāt\ *vb* **1 :** to drive into exile **:** BANISH **2 :** to leave one's native country; *esp* **:** to renounce allegiance to one's native country [Medieval Latin *expatriare* "to leave one's country," from Latin *ex-* + *patria* "native country," from *pater* "father"] — **ex·pa·tri·a·tion** \ek-ˌspā-trē-ˈā-shən\ *n*

[2]**ex·pa·tri·ate** \ek-ˈspā-trē-ˌāt, -trē-ət\ *adj* **:** living in a foreign country **:** EXPATRIATED

[3]**expatriate** *n* **:** a person living in a foreign country; *esp* **:** one who has renounced his or her native country

ex·pect \ik-ˈspekt\ *vb* **1 :** to be pregnant **2 :** to anticipate or look forward to the coming or occurrence of ⟨*expect* rain⟩ ⟨*expect* a phone call⟩ **3 :** THINK, SUPPOSE ⟨who do you *expect* will win?⟩ **4 a :** to consider probable or certain ⟨*expect* to be forgiven⟩ **b :** to consider reasonable, due, or necessary ⟨*expect* an honest day's work⟩ **c :** to consider obligated ⟨*expect* you to pay your dues⟩ [Latin *exspectare* "to look forward to," from *ex-* + *spectare* "to look at," from *specere* "to look"] — **ex·pect·able** \-ˈspek-tə-bəl\ *adj* — **ex·pect·ably** \-blē\ *adv* — **ex·pect·ed·ly** \-təd-lē\ *adv* — **ex·pect·ed·ness** \-nəs\ *n*

ex·pect·ance \ik-ˈspek-təns\ *n* **:** EXPECTATION

ex·pect·an·cy \ik-ˈspek-tən-sē\ *n, pl* **-cies 1 :** EXPECTATION 1 **2 a :** EXPECTATION 3 **b :** the expected amount (as of years of life) based on statistical probability ⟨life *expectancy*⟩

ex·pect·ant \-tənt\ *adj* **1 :** characterized by or being in a state of expectation **2 :** expecting the birth of a child ⟨*expectant* parents⟩ — **expectant** *n* — **ex·pect·ant·ly** *adv*

ex·pec·ta·tion \ˌek-ˌspek-ˈtā-shən, ik-\ *n* **1 :** the act or state of expecting **:** a looking forward to or waiting for something **2 :** prospect of good or bad fortune; *esp* **:** prospects of inheriting — usually used in plural **3 :** something expected

ex·pec·to·rant \ik-ˈspek-tə-rənt\ *n* **:** an agent that promotes the discharge of mucus from the respiratory tract — **expectorant** *adj*

ex·pec·to·rate \ik-ˈspek-tə-ˌrāt\ *vb* **1 :** to discharge (as phlegm) from the throat or lungs by coughing and spitting **2 :** [3]SPIT 1a [Latin *expectorare* "to cast out of the mind," from *ex-* + *pector, pectus* "breast, soul"] — **ex·pec·to·ra·tion** \-ˌspek-tə-ˈrā-shən\ *n*

ex·pe·di·ence \ik-ˈspēd-ē-əns\ *n* **:** EXPEDIENCY

ex·pe·di·en·cy \ik-ˈspēd-ē-ən-sē\ *n, pl* **-cies 1 :** the quality or state of being suited to the end in view : SUITABILITY **2** : the use of expedient means

¹ex·pe·di·ent \ik-ˈspēd-ē-ənt\ *adj* **1** : appropriate to and efficient in attaining an end **2** : concerned with immediate advantage rather than with what is just or right [Latin *expediens,* present participle of *expedire* "to extricate, be useful," from *ex-* + *ped-, pes* "foot"] — **ex·pe·di·ent·ly** *adv*

synonyms EXPEDIENT, POLITIC, ADVISABLE mean dictated by practical or prudent motives. EXPEDIENT usually applies to what is immediately advantageous often without regard for ethics ⟨a politically *expedient* decision⟩. POLITIC stresses judiciousness and tactical value but usually implies some lack of sincerity ⟨a *politic* show of interest⟩. ADVISABLE applies to what is practical, prudent, or advantageous without derogatory implication ⟨*advisable* to drive carefully⟩.

²expedient *n* **1** : something expedient **2** : a means to accomplish an end; *esp* : one used in place of a better means that is not available ***synonyms*** see RESOURCE

ex·pe·dite \ˈek-spə-ˌdīt\ *vt* **1** : to carry out rapidly : execute promptly **2** : to accelerate the process or progress of : speed up **3** : to send out : DISPATCH [Latin *expedire* "to extricate, prepare, be useful"]

ex·pe·dit·er *also* **ex·pe·di·tor** \-ˌdīt-ər\ *n* : one that expedites; *esp* : one employed to ensure adequate supplies of raw materials and equipment or to coordinate the flow of materials, tools, parts, and processed goods within a plant

ex·pe·di·tion \ˌek-spə-ˈdish-ən\ *n* **1 a** : a journey or trip undertaken for a specific purpose (as war or exploring) **b** : a group making such a journey **2** : efficient promptness : SPEED — **ex·pe·di·tion·er** \-dish-(ə-)nər\ *n*

ex·pe·di·tion·ary \-ˈdish-ə-ˌner-ē\ *adj* : of, relating to, or constituting an expedition; *esp* : sent on military service abroad ⟨an *expeditionary* force⟩

ex·pe·di·tious \ˌek-spə-ˈdish-əs\ *adj* : characterized by or acting with promptness and efficiency : SPEEDY ⟨*expeditious* service⟩ — **ex·pe·di·tious·ly** *adv* — **ex·pe·di·tious·ness** *n*

ex·pel \ik-ˈspel\ *vt* **ex·pelled; ex·pel·ling** **1** : to drive or force out ⟨*expel* air from the lungs⟩ **2** : to force to leave usually by official action ⟨*expelled* from college⟩ [Latin *expellere,* from *ex-* + *pellere* "to drive"] ***synonyms*** see EJECT — **ex·pel·la·ble** \-ˈspel-ə-bəl\ *adj*

ex·pend \ik-ˈspend\ *vt* **1** : to pay out : SPEND **2** : to consume by use : use up ⟨*expend* hours on the study⟩ [Latin *expendere* "to weigh out, expend," from *ex-* + *pendere* "to weigh, pay"]

ex·pend·able \ik-ˈspen-də-bəl\ *adj* : that may be normally used up in service ⟨*expendable* supplies like pencils and paper⟩ — **ex·pend·abil·i·ty** \-ˌpen-də-ˈbil-ət-ē\ *n* — **expendable** *n* — **ex·pend·ably** \-ˈpen-də-blē\ *adv*

ex·pen·di·ture \ik-ˈspen-di-chər, -də-ˌchu̇r\ *n* **1** : the act or process of expending **2** : an amount (as of money or time) expended

ex·pense \ik-ˈspens\ *n* **1 a** : something expended to secure a benefit or bring about a result **b** : financial burden or outlay : COST ⟨went to college at his own *expense*⟩ **2** : a cause of expenditure ⟨a car is a great *expense*⟩ **3** : SACRIFICE 3 — usually used in the phrase *at the expense of* ⟨achieved success at the *expense* of his personal life⟩ : a loss, injury, or embarrassment that results from some action or gain [Late Latin *expensa,* from Latin *expendere* "to expend"]

expense account *n* : an account of expenses reimbursable to an employee

ex·pen·sive \ik-ˈspen-siv\ *adj* **1** : involving high cost or sacrifice ⟨an *expensive* hobby⟩ **2 a** : having a high price ⟨*expensive* gifts⟩ **b** : marked by high prices ⟨*expensive* shops⟩ ***synonyms*** see COSTLY — **ex·pen·sive·ly** *adv* — **ex·pen·sive·ness** *n*

¹ex·pe·ri·ence \ik-ˈspir-ē-əns\ *n* **1** : the actual living through an event or series of events ⟨learn by *experience*⟩ **2 a** : the skill or knowledge gained by actually doing or feeling a thing ⟨a job that requires *experience*⟩ **b** : the amount of work one has done and the skill or knowledge gained ⟨a person with five years' *experience*⟩ **3 a** : the usually conscious perception or understanding of reality or of an event **b** : the sum total of the conscious events that make up an individual life or the past of a community, nation, or humankind generally **4** : something that one has actually done or lived through ⟨a soldier's *experiences* in war⟩ [Medieval French, from Latin *experientia* "act of trying," from *experiri* "to try"] — **ex·pe·ri·en·tial** \-ˌspir-ē-ˈen-chəl\ *adj*

²experience *vt* **1** : to learn by experience **2** : to have experience of : UNDERGO ⟨*experienced* severe hardships as a child⟩

ex·pe·ri·enced \ik-ˈspir-ē-ənst\ *adj* : having experience : made skillful or wise through experience ⟨an *experienced* pilot⟩

¹ex·per·i·ment \ik-ˈsper-ə-mənt\ *n* **1 a** : TEST 1a, TRIAL **b** : a tentative procedure or policy **c** : an operation or procedure carried out under controlled conditions in order to discover an unknown effect or law, to test or establish a hypothesis, or to illustrate a known law **2** : the process of testing : EXPERIMENTATION [Medieval French, from Latin *experimentum,* from *experiri* "to try"]

²ex·per·i·ment \-ˌment\ *vi* : to conduct experiments : try out a new method, idea, or activity — **ex·per·i·men·ta·tion** \ik-ˌsper-ə-mən-ˈtā-shən, -ˌmen-\ *n* — **ex·per·i·ment·er** \-ˈsper-ə-ˌment-ər\ *n*

ex·per·i·men·tal \ik-ˌsper-ə-ˈment-l\ *adj* **1** : of, relating to, or based on experience **2** : founded on or derived from experiment ⟨an *experimental* finding⟩ **3** : serving the ends of or used for experimentation ⟨*experimental* apparatus⟩ **4** : relating to or having the characteristics of experiment : TENTATIVE ⟨*experimental* flights⟩ — **ex·per·i·men·tal·ly** \-l-ē\ *adv*

experiment station *n* : an establishment for scientific research (as in agriculture) where experiments and studies of practical application are made and information is given out

¹ex·pert \ˈek-ˌspərt, ik-ˈ\ *adj* : having, involving, or displaying special skill or knowledge derived from training or experience [Latin *expertus,* from *experiri* "to try"] ***synonyms*** see PROFICIENT — **ex·pert·ly** *adv* — **ex·pert·ness** *n*

²ex·pert \ˈek-ˌspərt\ *n* : one who has acquired special skill in or knowledge of a subject

ex·per·tise \ˌek-spər-ˈtēz, -ˌspər-, *also* -ˈtēs\ *n* **1** : expert opinion or commentary **2** : the skill of an expert : KNOW-HOW [French, from *expert* "expert"]

expert system *n* : computer software that attempts to mimic the reasoning of a human specialist

ex·pi·ate \ˈek-spē-ˌāt\ *vt* **1** : to extinguish the guilt incurred by **2** : to make amends for : ATONE [Latin *expiare* "to atone for," from *ex-* + *piare* "to appease"] — **ex·pi·a·ble** \-spē-ə-bəl\ *adj* — **ex·pi·a·tor** \-ˌāt-ər\ *n*

ex·pi·a·tion \ˌek-spē-ˈā-shən\ *n* **1** : the act of making atonement **2** : the means by which atonement is made

ex·pi·a·to·ry \ˈek-spē-ə-ˌtōr-ē, -ˌtȯr-\ *adj* : serving to expiate

ex·pi·ra·tion \ˌek-spə-ˈrā-shən\ *n* **1 a** : the expelling of air from the lungs in breathing **b** : air or vapor expelled from the lungs **2** : the fact of coming to an end : TERMINATION

expiration date *n* **1** : the date on which something expires ⟨the *expiration date* of a credit card⟩ **2** : the last date on which a product can be safely used ⟨the *expiration date* on a box of cereal⟩

ex·pi·ra·to·ry \ek-ˈspī-rə-ˌtōr-ē, -ˌtȯr-\ *adj* : of, relating to, or used in respiratory expiration

ex·pire \ik-ˈspīr, *usually for 3* ek-\ *vb* **1** : DIE 1 **2** : to come to an end : STOP **3 a** : to emit the breath **b** : to breathe out from or as if from the lungs [Latin *exspirare,* from *ex-* + *spirare* "to breathe"]

ex·pi·ry \ik-ˈspīr-ē, ˈek-spə-rē\ *n, pl* **-ries** **1** : DEATH 1 **2** : TERMINATION; *esp* : the termination of a time or period fixed by law, contract, or agreement

ex·plain \ik-ˈsplān\ *vb* **1** : to make plain or understandable ⟨footnotes that *explain* the terms⟩ **2** : to give the reason for or cause of ⟨unable to *explain* her behavior⟩ **3** : to show the logical development or relationships of ⟨*explained* the new theory⟩ [Latin *explanare,* literally, "to make level," from *ex-* + *planus* "level"] — **ex·plain·able** \-ˈsplā-nə-bəl\ *adj* — **ex·plain·er** *n*

synonyms EXPLAIN, EXPOUND, EXPLICATE, INTERPRET mean to make something clear or understandable. EXPLAIN implies making plain or intelligible ⟨*explain* the rules⟩. EXPOUND implies a careful often elaborate explanation ⟨*expounding* one's philosophy of life⟩. EXPLICATE adds the idea of a developed or detailed analysis ⟨*explicate* the plot of a novel⟩. INTERPRET adds the use of the imagination, sympathy, or special knowledge in dealing with something ⟨*interpret* a poem⟩ ⟨*interpret* the law⟩.

ex·pla·na·tion \ˌek-splə-ˈnā-shən\ *n* **1** : the act or process of explaining **2** : something that explains; *esp* : a statement that makes something clear

ex·plan·a·to·ry \ik-ˈsplan-ə-ˌtōr-ē, -ˌtȯr-\ *adj* : serving to explain ⟨*explanatory* notes⟩ — **ex·plan·a·to·ri·ly** \-ˌsplan-ə-ˈtōr-ə-lē, -ˈtȯr-\ *adv*

ex·plant \ek-ˈsplant, ˈek-\ *vt* **:** to remove (living tissue) especially to a tissue culture medium

ex·ple·tive \ˈek-splət-iv\ *n* **1 :** a syllable, word, or phrase inserted to fill a vacancy (as in a sentence or a line of verse) without adding to the sense; *esp* **:** a word that occupies the position of the subject or object of a verb in normal English word order and anticipates a subsequent word or phrase that supplies the needed meaningful content ⟨*it* in "it is easy to say so" and in "make it clear which you prefer" is an *expletive*⟩ **2 :** an exclamatory word or phrase; *esp* **:** one that is obscene or profane [Late Latin *expletivus* "serving to fill up," from Latin *explēre* "to fill out," from *ex-* + *plēre* "to fill"] — **expletive** *adj*

ex·pli·cate \ˈek-splə-ˌkāt\ *vt* **:** to give a detailed explanation of [Latin *explicare,* literally, "to unfold," from *ex-* + *plicare* "to fold"] ***synonyms*** see EXPLAIN — **ex·pli·ca·ble** \ek-ˈsplik-ə-bəl, ˈek-splik-\ *adj* — **ex·pli·ca·tion** \ˌek-splə-ˈkā-shən\ *n* — **ex·pli·ca·tive** \ek-ˈsplik-ət-iv, ˈek-splə-ˌkāt-\ *adj* — **ex·pli·ca·tor** \ˈek-splə-ˌkāt-ər\ *n* — **ex·pli·ca·to·ry** \ek-ˈsplik-ə-ˌtōr-ē, ˈek-splik-, -ˌtȯr-\ *adj*

ex·plic·it \ik-ˈsplis-ət\ *adj* **1 :** so clear in statement that there is no doubt about the meaning **:** fully stated ⟨*explicit* instructions⟩ — compare IMPLICIT **2 :** containing nudity or sexuality ⟨*explicit* books and films⟩ [Medieval Latin *explicitus,* from Latin *explicare* "to explicate"] — **ex·plic·it·ly** *adv* — **ex·plic·it·ness** *n*

synonyms EXPLICIT, DEFINITE, EXPRESS, SPECIFIC mean perfectly clear in meaning. EXPLICIT implies such verbal plainness and distinctness that there is no room for doubt or difficulty in understanding ⟨*explicit* directions⟩. DEFINITE stresses precise, clear statement or arrangement that leaves no doubt or indecision ⟨*definite* plans⟩. EXPRESS implies explicitness and direct and positive utterance ⟨*express* denial of the charges⟩. SPECIFIC applies to what is precisely and fully treated in detail or particular ⟨two *specific* theories⟩.

ex·plode \ik-ˈsplōd\ *vb* **1 :** to cause to be given up or rejected **:** DISCREDIT ⟨science has *exploded* many old ideas⟩ **2 :** to burst or cause to burst violently and noisily; *esp* **:** to undergo a rapid chemical or nuclear reaction with the production of noise, heat, and violent expansion of gases **3 :** to give forth a sudden noisy outburst of emotion ⟨*exploded* in anger⟩ **4 :** to move with sudden speed and force ⟨*exploded* from the starting gate⟩ **5 :** to increase rapidly ⟨the population of the city *exploded*⟩ [Latin *explodere* "to drive off the stage by clapping," from *ex-* + *plaudere* "to clap"]

Word History When the ancient Romans disapproved of a theatrical performance, they drove the performers from the stage by prolonged, loud clapping. The Latin word for this was *explodere,* a compound of *ex-,* "out of, from," and *plaudere,* "to clap," meaning "to drive off by clapping." The Latin verb was borrowed into English with the meaning "to drive from the stage by noisy disapproval." From this sense developed the now current senses "to reject or discredit" and "to burst noisily." *Explode* is no longer used in its original sense.

ex·plod·ed *adj* **:** showing the parts separated but in correct relationship to each other ⟨an *exploded* view of a carburetor⟩

[1]**ex·ploit** \ˈek-ˌsplȯit, ik-ˈ\ *n* **:** a deed notable especially for heroism [Medieval French, "outcome, success," derived from Latin *explicare* "to explicate, unfold"] ***synonyms*** see FEAT

[2]**ex·ploit** \ik-ˈsplȯit, ˈek-ˌ\ *vt* **1 :** to make productive use of **:** UTILIZE ⟨*exploiting* your talents⟩ ⟨*exploit* your opponent's weakness⟩ **2 :** to make use of unfairly for one's own advantage ⟨*exploiting* migrant farm workers⟩ — **ex·ploit·abil·i·ty** \-ˌsplȯit-ə-ˈbil-ət-ē\ *n* — **ex·ploit·able** \-ik-ˈsplȯit-ə-bəl; ˈek-ˌ\ *adj* — **ex·ploi·ta·tion** \ˌek-ˌsplȯi-ˈtā-shən\ *n* — **ex·ploit·er** \ik-ˈsplȯit-ər, ˈek-ˌ\ *n*

ex·plo·ra·tion \ˌek-splə-ˈrā-shən\ *n* **:** the act or an instance of exploring — **ex·plor·ative** \ik-ˈsplōr-ət-iv, -ˈsplȯr-\ *adj* — **ex·plor·ato·ry** \-ə-ˌtōr-ē, -ˌtȯr-\ *adj*

ex·plore \ik-ˈsplōr, -ˈsplȯr\ *vb* **1 :** to investigate, study, or analyze **:** look into **2 :** to go into or travel over for purposes of adventure or discovery ⟨*explore* an uncharted sea⟩ **3 :** to examine carefully and in detail especially for diagnostic purposes ⟨*explore* a wound⟩ **4 :** to make or conduct a systematic search ⟨*explore* for oil⟩ [Latin *explorare* "to seek for," from *ex-* + *plorare* "to cry out"; probably from the outcry of hunters on sighting game]

ex·plor·er \ik-ˈsplōr-ər, -ˈsplȯr-\ *n* **1 :** one that explores; *esp* **:** a person who travels in search of geographical or scientific information **2** *cap* **:** a member of the scouting program of the Boy Scouts of America for young people 14 to 20 years of age

ex·plo·sion \ik-ˈsplō-zhən\ *n* **1 :** the act or an instance of exploding **2 :** a large-scale, rapid, and spectacular expansion or bursting out or forth ⟨the *explosion* of suburban neighborhoods⟩ **3 :** a violent outburst of feeling [Latin *explosio* "act of driving off by clapping," from *explodere* "to drive off by clapping"]

[1]**ex·plo·sive** \ik-ˈsplō-siv, -ziv\ *adj* **1 :** relating to, characterized by, or operated by explosion **2 :** likely to explode ⟨an *explosive* temper⟩ — **ex·plo·sive·ly** *adv* — **ex·plo·sive·ness** *n*

[2]**explosive** *n* **:** an explosive substance

ex·po·nent \ik-ˈspō-nənt, ˈek-ˌ\ *n* **1 :** a symbol written above and to the right of a mathematical expression to indicate the operation of raising to a power ⟨in the expression a^3, the *exponent* 3 indicates that *a* is to be raised to the third power⟩ **2 a :** one that expounds or interprets **b :** one that champions or advocates [Latin *exponere* "to set forth, explain," from *ex-* + *ponere* "to put"]

ex·po·nen·tial \ˌek-spə-ˈnen-chəl\ *adj* **1 a :** of or relating to an exponent **b :** expressed in a form using exponents **2 :** involving a variable exponent ⟨a function of the form $y=10^x$ is an *exponential* function⟩ — **ex·po·nen·tial·ly** \-ˈnench-lē, -ə-lē\ *adv*

ex·po·nen·ti·a·tion \ˌek-spə-ˌnen-shē-ˈā-shən\ *n* **:** the mathematical operation of raising a quantity to a power — called also *involution*

[1]**ex·port** \ek-ˈspōrt, -ˈspȯrt, ˈek-ˌ\ *vt* **:** to carry or send (as a commodity) to another country or place especially for sale [Latin *exportare,* from *ex-* + *portare* "to carry"] — **ex·port·able** \-ə-bəl\ *adj* — **ex·por·ta·tion** \ˌek-ˌspōr-ˈtā-shən, -ˌspȯr-, -spər-\ *n* — **ex·port·er** \ek-ˈspōrt-ər, -ˈspȯrt-, ˈek-ˌ\ *n*

[2]**ex·port** \ˈek-ˌspōrt, -ˌspȯrt\ *n* **1 :** something exported; *esp* **:** a commodity conveyed from one country or region to another for purposes of trade **2 :** an act of exporting **:** EXPORTATION

[3]**export** \ˈek-ˌ\ *adj* **1 :** of or relating to exportation or exports ⟨*export* duties⟩ **2 :** intended for export ⟨*export* goods⟩

ex·pose \ik-ˈspōz\ *vt* **1 a :** to deprive of shelter, protection, or care ⟨*expose* troops needlessly⟩ **b :** to submit or subject to an action or influence ⟨*expose* students to good books⟩ ⟨had been *exposed* to measles⟩; *esp* **:** to subject (a sensitive photographic film, plate, or paper) to the action of radiant energy (as light) **c :** to abandon (an infant) especially in the open **2 :** to make known **:** to bring to light ⟨*expose* a murderer⟩ **3 :** to cause to be open to view **:** DISPLAY [Medieval French *exposer,* from Latin *exponere* "to set forth, explain," from *ex-* + *ponere* "to put, place"] — **ex·pos·er** *n*

ex·po·sé \ˌek-spō-ˈzā\ *n* **:** an exposure of something discreditable ⟨a newspaper *exposé* of illegal gambling⟩ [French, from *exposer* "to expose"]

ex·po·si·tion \ˌek-spə-ˈzish-ən\ *n* **1 :** an explanation of the meaning or purpose of something (as a piece of writing) **2 :** a composition that explains something **3 :** the first part of a musical composition in sonata form in which the thematic material of the movement is presented **4 :** a public exhibition or show — **ex·pos·i·to·ry** \ik-ˈspäz-ə-ˌtōr-ē, -ˌtȯr-\ *adj*

ex·pos·i·tor \ik-ˈspäz-ət-ər\ *n* **:** one that expounds or explains [Medieval French *expositur,* from Late Latin *expositor,* from Latin *exponere* "to set forth, explain"]

[1]**ex post fac·to** \ˌeks-ˌpōst-ˈfak-tō\ *adv* **:** after the fact ⟨a rationale given *ex post facto*⟩ [Late Latin, "from a thing done afterward"]

[2]**ex post facto** *adj* **:** made, done, or formulated after the fact ⟨*ex post facto* approval⟩

ex·pos·tu·late \ik-ˈspäs-chə-ˌlāt\ *vi* **:** to reason earnestly with a person for purposes of dissuasion or protest [Latin *expostulare* "to demand, dispute," from *ex-* + *postulare* "to ask for"] — **ex·pos·tu·la·tion** \-ˌspäs-chə-ˈlā-shən\ *n* — **ex·pos·tu·la·to·ry** \-ˈspäs-chə-lə-ˌtōr-ē, -ˌtȯr-\ *adj*

ex·po·sure \ik-ˈspō-zhər\ *n* **1 :** the fact or condition of being exposed: as **a :** the condition of being presented to view or made known ⟨a politician seeking *exposure*⟩ **b :** the condition of being unprotected especially from severe weather ⟨died of *exposure*⟩ **c :** the condition of being subject to some condition or influence ⟨risk *exposure* to the flu⟩ **2 :** the act or instance of exposing: as **a :** disclosure of something **b :** the treating of sensitive material (as film) to amounts of radiant energy (as light); *also* **:** the length of time of such treatment **3 :** a position with respect to direction or to weather conditions ⟨a southern *exposure*⟩ **4 :** a section of a film for a single picture ⟨36 *exposures* per roll⟩

ex·pound \ik-ˈspau̇nd\ *vt* **1 a :** to set forth **:** STATE **b :** to defend (as a theory) with argument **2 :** to make clear the meaning of **:** INTERPRET ⟨*expound* a law⟩ [Medieval French *espundre,* from Latin *exponere* "to explain"] ***synonyms*** see EXPLAIN — **ex·pound·er** *n*

[1]**ex·press** \ik-ˈspres\ *adj* **1 a :** directly and distinctly stated **:** EXPLICIT ⟨*express* consent⟩ **b :** exactly represented **:** PRECISE **2 :** of a particular sort **:** SPECIFIC ⟨for that *express* purpose⟩ **3 a :** sent or traveling at high speed ⟨*express* mail⟩; *esp* **:** traveling with few or no stops ⟨an *express* train⟩ **b :** adapted or suitable for travel at high speed ⟨an *express* highway⟩ [Medieval French *expres,* from Latin *expressus,* past participle of *exprimere* "to press out," from *ex-* + *premere* "to press"] ***synonyms*** see EXPLICIT

[2]**express** *adv* **:** by express ⟨send a package *express*⟩

[3]**express** *n* **1 a :** a system for the prompt transportation of goods at an extra charge **b :** a company operating such a service **c :** the goods or shipments so transported **2 :** an express vehicle

[4]**express** *vt* **1 a :** to represent especially in words or symbols **b :** to give expression to the opinions, feelings, or abilities of (oneself) **c :** SYMBOLIZE ⟨the sign = *expresses* equality⟩ **2 :** to press or squeeze out ⟨*express* juice from a lemon⟩ **3 :** to send by express **4 :** to cause (a gene) to manifest its effects in the phenotype; *also* **:** to manifest or produce (a character, molecule, or effect) by a genetic process — **ex·press·er** *n* — **ex·press·ible** \-ə-bəl\ *adj*

ex·pres·sion \ik-ˈspresh-ən\ *n* **1 :** the act or process of expressing especially in words or symbols **2 a :** a word, phrase, or sign that expresses a thought, feeling, or quality; *esp* **:** a significant word or phrase **b :** a mathematical symbol or a combination of symbols and signs representing a quantity or operation **3 :** a way of speaking or singing or of playing an instrument so as to show mood or feeling **4 :** the way one's face looks or one's voice sounds that shows one's feelings **5 :** the detectable effect of a gene **6 :** an act or product of pressing out — **ex·pres·sion·less** \-ləs\ *adj* — **ex·pres·sion·less·ly** *adv* — **ex·pres·sion·less·ness** *n*

ex·pres·sion·ism \ik-ˈspresh-ə-ˌniz-əm\ *n* **:** a theory or practice in art of trying to depict the artist's personal responses to objects and events — **ex·pres·sion·ist** \-ˈspresh-nəst, -ə-nəst\ *n or adj* — **ex·pres·sion·is·tic** \-ˌspresh-ə-ˈnis-tik\ *adj*

ex·pres·sive \ik-ˈspres-iv\ *adj* **1 :** of or relating to expression **2 :** serving to express **3 :** effectively showing meaning or feeling ⟨an *expressive* face⟩ — **ex·pres·sive·ly** *adv* — **ex·pres·sive·ness** *n*

ex·press·ly \ik-ˈspres-lē\ *adv* **1 :** in an express manner **:** EXPLICITLY ⟨was *expressly* forbidden to smoke⟩ **2 :** for the express purpose **:** PARTICULARLY ⟨made *expressly* for me⟩

expresso *variant of* ESPRESSO

ex·press·way \ik-ˈspres-ˌwā\ *n* **:** a high-speed divided highway with controlled access

ex·pro·pri·ate \ek-ˈsprō-prē-ˌāt\ *vt* **:** to take away from a person the possession of or right to (property) [Medieval Latin *expropriare,* from Latin *ex-* + *proprius* "own"] — **ex·pro·pri·a·tion** \ˌek-ˌsprō-prē-ˈā-shən\ *n* — **ex·pro·pri·a·tor** \ek-ˈsprō-prē-ˌāt-ər\ *n*

ex·pul·sion \ik-ˈspəl-shən\ *n* **:** the act of expelling **:** the state of being expelled [Latin *expulsio,* from *expellere* "to expel"] — **ex·pul·sive** \-ˈspəl-siv\ *adj*

ex·punge \ik-ˈspənj\ *vt* **1 :** to strike out, obliterate, or mark for deletion **2 :** to efface completely **:** DESTROY [Latin *expungere* "to mark for deletion by dots," from *ex-* + *pungere* "to prick"] ***synonyms*** see ERASE — **ex·pung·er** *n*

ex·pur·gate \ˈek-spər-ˌgāt\ *vt* **:** to clear of something wrong or objectionable; *esp* **:** to clear (as a book) of objectionable words or passages [Latin *expurgare,* from *ex-* + *purgare* "to purge"] — **ex·pur·ga·tion** \ˌek-spər-ˈgā-shən\ *n* — **ex·pur·ga·tor** \ˈek-spər-ˌgāt-ər\ *n*

ex·quis·ite \ek-ˈskwiz-ət; ˈek-skwiz-, -ˌskwiz-\ *adj* **1 :** marked by flawless craftsmanship or delicate execution **2 :** keenly appreciative **:** DISCRIMINATING ⟨*exquisite* taste⟩ **3 :** pleasing through beauty or excellence **4 :** ACUTE 3, INTENSE ⟨*exquisite* pain⟩ [Latin *exquisitus,* from *exquirere* "to search out," from *ex-* + *quaerere* "to seek"] — **ex·quis·ite·ly** *adv* — **ex·quis·ite·ness** *n*

ex·tant \ˈek-stənt, ek-ˈstant\ *adj* **:** currently existing **:** not destroyed or lost [Latin *exstare* "to stand out, be in existence," from *ex-* + *stare* "to stand"]

ex·tem·po·ra·ne·ous \ek-ˌstem-pə-ˈrā-nē-əs\ *adj* **1 :** composed, performed, or uttered on the spur of the moment **:** IMPROMPTU **2 :** carefully prepared but delivered without notes or text **3 :** provided, made, or put to use as an expedient **:** MAKESHIFT ⟨an *extemporaneous* shelter⟩ [Late Latin *extemporaneus,* from Latin *ex tempore* "on the spur of the moment"] — **ex·tem·po·ra·ne·ous·ly** *adv* — **ex·tem·po·ra·ne·ous·ness** *n*

ex·tem·po·rary \ik-ˈstem-pə-ˌrer-ē\ *adj* **:** EXTEMPORANEOUS — **ex·tem·po·rar·i·ly** \-ˌstem-pə-ˈrer-ə-lē\ *adv*

ex·tem·po·re \ik-ˈstem-pə-rē\ *adv or adj* **:** in an extemporaneous manner ⟨speaking *extempore*⟩

ex·tem·po·rize \ik-ˈstem-pə-ˌrīz\ *vb* **:** to do, make, or utter extemporaneously **:** IMPROVISE — **ex·tem·po·ri·za·tion** \ik-ˌstem-pə-rə-ˈzā-shən\ *n* — **ex·tem·po·riz·er** \-ˈstem-pə-ˌrī-zər\ *n*

ex·tend \ik-ˈstend\ *vb* **1 :** to spread out or stretch forth ⟨*extend* one's arm⟩ **2 :** to exert (oneself) to full capacity ⟨*extended* themselves to meet the deadline⟩ **3 :** to increase the bulk of (a product) by the addition of a cheaper substance **4 a :** to make the offer of **:** PROFFER ⟨*extend* an apology⟩ **b :** to make available ⟨*extend* credit⟩ **5 :** to cause to be longer; *esp* **:** to prolong in time ⟨*extend* a visit⟩ **6 a :** to cause to be of greater area or volume **:** ENLARGE **b :** to increase the scope, meaning, or application of **:** BROADEN ⟨an *extended* metaphor⟩ **7 :** to stretch out in distance, space, or time **:** REACH ⟨the bridge *extends* across the river⟩ [Latin *extendere,* from *ex-* + *tendere* "to stretch"] — **ex·tend·abil·i·ty** *n* — **ex·tend·able** *also* **ex·tend·ible** \-ˈsten-də-bəl\ *adj*

synonyms EXTEND, LENGTHEN, PROLONG, PROTRACT mean to draw out or add to so as to increase in length. EXTEND and LENGTHEN imply a drawing out in space or time ⟨*extend* a vacation⟩ ⟨*lengthen* a skirt⟩ ⟨*lengthen* the work week⟩. EXTEND may also imply increase in width, scope, area, or range ⟨*extend* services⟩. PROLONG suggests chiefly increase in duration especially beyond usual limits ⟨*prolonged* illness⟩. PROTRACT adds to PROLONG implications of needlessness, vexation, or indefiniteness ⟨*protracted* litigation⟩.

ex·tend·ed family \ik-ˈsten-dəd-\ *n* **:** a family that includes parents and children and other relatives (as grandparents, aunts, or uncles) in the same household

ex·tend·er \ik-ˈsten-dər\ *n* **:** something added to another thing usually to dilute or modify or increase bulk

ex·ten·si·ble \ik-ˈsten-sə-bəl\ *adj* **:** capable of being extended — **ex·ten·si·bil·i·ty** \-ˌsten-sə-ˈbil-ət-ē\ *n*

ex·ten·sion \ik-ˈsten-chən\ *n* **1 a :** the act of extending **:** the state of being extended **b :** something extended **2 :** the total range over which something extends **3 :** the property of occupying space **4 :** an increase in time; *esp* **:** a granting of extra time to fulfill an obligation **5 :** an educational program with special arrangements for persons unable to attend a school **6 a :** a part constituting an addition **b :** a section forming an additional length **c :** an extra telephone connected to the principal line [Late Latin *extensio,* from Latin *extendere* "to extend"]

extension cord *n* **:** an electric cord fitted with a plug at one end and a receptacle at the other

ex·ten·sive \ik-ˈsten-siv\ *adj* **:** having wide or considerable extent — **ex·ten·sive·ly** *adv* — **ex·ten·sive·ness** *n*

ex·ten·sor \ik-ˈsten-sər\ *n* **:** a muscle serving to extend a bodily part (as a limb) — compare FLEXOR

ex·tent \ik-ˈstent\ *n* **1 a :** the range, distance, or space over which something extends **:** SCOPE **b :** the point, degree, or limit to which something extends ⟨using talents to the greatest *extent*⟩ **2 :** an extended tract or region [Medieval French *estente* "land valuation," from *estendre* "to survey, evaluate," literally, "to extend," from Latin *extendere*]

ex·ten·u·ate \ik-ˈsten-yə-ˌwāt\ *vt* **:** to lessen or try to lessen the seriousness or extent of by making partial excuses ⟨*extenuating* circumstances⟩ [Latin *extenuare,* from *ex-* + *tenuis* "thin"] — **ex·ten·u·a·tion** \-ˌsten-yə-ˈwā-shən\ *n* — **ex·ten·u·a·tor** \-ˈsten-yə-ˌwāt-ər\ *n* — **ex·ten·u·a·to·ry** \-wə-ˌtōr-ē, -ˌtȯr-\ *adj*

[1]**ex·te·ri·or** \ek-ˈstir-ē-ər\ *adj* **1 :** situated on the outside ⟨an *ex-*

terior surface⟩ **2 :** [1]EXTERNAL 1a **3 :** suitable for outside surfaces ⟨*exterior* paint⟩ [Latin, comparative of *exter, exterus* "being on the outside," from *ex* "out of"] — **ex·te·ri·or·ly** *adv*

[2]**exterior** *n* **1 a :** an exterior part or surface : OUTSIDE **b :** outward manner or appearance **2 :** a representation of an outdoor scene

exterior angle *n* **1 :** the angle between a side of a polygon and an extended adjacent side **2 :** an angle formed by a line cutting across two other lines and that lies outside of those lines

ex·ter·mi·nate \ik-ˈstər-mə-ˌnāt\ *vt* **:** to get rid of completely usually by killing off : ANNIHILATE [Latin *exterminare,* from *ex-* + *terminus* "boundary"] — **ex·ter·mi·na·tion** \-ˌstər-mə-ˈnā-shən\ *n* — **ex·ter·mi·na·tor** \-ˈstər-mə-ˌnāt-ər\ *n*

[1]**ex·ter·nal** \ek-ˈstərn-l\ *adj* **1 a :** outwardly visible ⟨*external* signs⟩ **b :** having only the outward appearance of : SUPERFICIAL **2 a :** of, relating to, or connected with the outside or an outer part ⟨the building's *external* features⟩ **b :** applied or applicable to the outside **3 a** (1) **:** situated outside, apart, or beyond (2) **:** arising or acting from outside ⟨*external* force⟩ **b :** of or relating to relationships with foreign countries ⟨*external* affairs⟩ [Latin *externus,* from *exter* "being on the outside"] — **ex·ter·nal·ly** \-l-ē\ *adv*

[2]**external** *n* **:** an external feature or aspect — usually used in plural

external–combustion engine *n* **:** a heat engine (as a steam engine) that derives its heat from fuel consumed outside the engine cylinder

external ear *n* **:** the outer part of the ear consisting of the sound-collecting pinna and the canal leading from this to the eardrum

external respiration *n* **:** exchange of gases between the external environment and a distributing system of the animal body (as gills or lungs) or between the alveoli of the lungs and the blood — compare INTERNAL RESPIRATION

ex·tinct \ik-ˈstingt, ˈek-ˌ, -ˈstingkt\ *adj* **1 :** no longer burning : EXTINGUISHED **2 :** no longer active ⟨an *extinct* volcano⟩ **3 :** no longer existing ⟨an *extinct* animal⟩ [Latin *extinctus,* past participle of *extinguere* "to extinguish"]

ex·tinc·tion \ik-ˈsting-shən; -ˈstingk-\ *n* **1 :** an act of making extinct or causing to be extinguished **2 :** the state of being extinct; *also* **:** the process of becoming extinct **3 :** the process of eliminating or reducing a conditioned response by not reinforcing it

ex·tin·guish \ik-ˈsting-gwish\ *vt* **1 a :** to bring to an end **b :** to put out (as a fire or a light) **c :** to cause extinction of (a conditioned response) **d :** to dim the brightness of : ECLIPSE **2 :** to cause to be void : NULLIFY ⟨*extinguish* a claim⟩ [Latin *extinguere* (from *ex-* + *stinguere* "to extinguish") + English *-ish* (as in *abolish*)] — **ex·tin·guish·able** \-ə-bəl\ *adj* — **ex·tin·guish·er** \-ər\ *n* — **ex·tin·guish·ment** \-mənt\ *n*

ex·tir·pate \ˈek-stər-ˌpāt, ek-ˈ\ *vt* **1 a :** to pull up by the roots **b :** to destroy completely **2 :** to cut out by surgery [Latin *exstirpare,* from *ex-* + *stirps* "trunk, root"]

ex·tol *also* **ex·toll** \ik-ˈstōl\ *vt* **ex·tolled; ex·tol·ling :** to praise highly : GLORIFY [Latin *extollere,* from *ex-* + *tollere* "to lift up"] — **ex·tol·ler** *n* — **ex·tol·ment** \-ˈstōl-mənt\ *n*

ex·tort \ik-ˈstȯrt\ *vt* **:** to obtain (as money or a confession) from a person by force or threats [Latin *extortus,* past participle of *extorquēre* "to wrench out, extort," from *ex-* + *torquēre* "to twist"] — **ex·tort·er** *n* — **ex·tor·tive** \-ˈstȯrt-iv\ *adj*

ex·tor·tion \ik-ˈstȯr-shən\ *n* **1 :** the act or practice of extorting; *esp* **:** the offense committed by an official engaging in this practice **2 :** something extorted; *esp* **:** a gross overcharge — **ex·tor·tion·er** \-ˈstȯr-shə-nər, -shnər\ *n* — **ex·tor·tion·ist** \-shə-nəst, -shnəst\ *n*

ex·tor·tion·ate \ik-ˈstȯr-shə-nət, -shnət\ *adj* **1 :** characterized by extortion **2 :** EXCESSIVE, EXORBITANT ⟨*extortionate* prices⟩ — **ex·tor·tion·ate·ly** *adv*

[1]**ex·tra** \ˈek-strə\ *adj* **1 a :** more than is due, usual, or necessary : ADDITIONAL ⟨*extra* work⟩ **b :** subject to an additional charge ⟨room service is *extra*⟩ **2 :** SUPERIOR ⟨*extra* quality⟩ [probably short for *extraordinary*]

[2]**extra** *n* **:** something extra or additional: as **a :** an added charge **b :** a special edition of a newspaper **c :** an additional worker; *esp* **:** one hired to act in a group scene in a motion picture or stage production

[3]**extra** *adv* **:** beyond the usual size, extent, or degree ⟨*extra* long⟩

extra- *prefix* **:** outside **:** beyond ⟨*extra*curricular⟩ [Latin, from *extra* "outside, except, beyond"]

extra–base hit *n* **:** a base hit in baseball that enables the batter to take more than one base

ex·tra·cel·lu·lar \ˌek-strə-ˈsel-yə-lər\ *adj* **:** situated, acting, or occurring outside a cell or the cells of the body ⟨*extracellular* digestion⟩ — **ex·tra·cel·lu·lar·ly** *adv*

[1]**ex·tract** \ik-ˈstrakt, *usually in sense 5* ˈek-ˌ\ *vt* **1 a :** to draw forth ⟨the magician *extracted* a rabbit from the hat⟩ **b :** to pull out forcibly ⟨*extract* a tooth⟩ **c :** to obtain by effort from someone unwilling ⟨*extract* a confession⟩ **2 :** to separate or otherwise obtain (as a juice or a constituent element) by physical or chemical process **3 :** to separate (a metal) from an ore **4 :** to determine (a mathematical root) by calculation **5 :** to select (excerpts) and copy out or cite [Latin *extractus,* past participle of *extrahere* "to extract," from *ex-* + *trahere* "to draw"] — **ex·tract·able** \-ə-bəl\ *adj* — **ex·trac·tor** \-ər\ *n*

[2]**ex·tract** \ˈek-ˌstrakt\ *n* **1 :** a selection from a writing or discourse : EXCERPT **2 :** a product (as a concentrate) prepared by extracting; *esp* **:** a solution of essential constituents of a complex material (as meat or an aromatic plant)

ex·trac·tion \ik-ˈstrak-shən\ *n* **1 :** the act or process of extracting ⟨a tooth *extraction*⟩ **2 :** ANCESTRY 1, LINEAGE ⟨a family of French *extraction*⟩ **3 :** something extracted

[1]**ex·trac·tive** \ik-ˈstrak-tiv\ *adj* **1 a :** of, relating to, or involving extraction ⟨*extractive* processes⟩ **b :** capable of being extracted ⟨*extractive* by-products of coal tar⟩ **2 :** drawing on natural and especially irreplaceable resources ⟨*extractive* industries such as mining and lumbering⟩

[2]**extractive** *n* **:** an extractive substance

ex·tra·cur·ric·u·lar \ˌek-strə-kə-ˈrik-yə-lər\ *adj* **1 :** not falling within a regular curriculum; *esp* **:** of, relating to, or being those activities (as athletics) connected with school but usually not carrying academic credit **2 :** being outside one's regular duties or routine

ex·tra·dite \ˈek-strə-ˌdīt\ *vt* **1 :** to deliver up to extradition **2 :** to obtain the extradition of [back-formation from *extradition*] — **ex·tra·dit·able** \-ˌdīt-ə-bəl\ *adj*

ex·tra·di·tion \ˌek-strə-ˈdish-ən\ *n* **:** the surrender of an alleged criminal by one authority (as a state) to another for trial [French, from *ex-* "ex-" + Latin *traditio* "act of handing over"]

ex·tra·dos \ˈek-strə-ˌdäs, -ˌdō; ek-ˈstrā-ˌdäs\ *n, pl* **extrados** \-ˌdōz, -ˌdäs\ *or* **ex·tra·dos·es** \-ˌdäs-əz\ **:** the exterior curve of an arch [French, from Latin *extra* "outside" + French *dos* "back"]

E extrados

ex·tra·em·bry·on·ic \ˌek-strə-ˌem-brē-ˈän-ik\ *adj* **:** situated outside the embryo; *esp* **:** developed from the fertilized egg but not part of the embryo ⟨*extraembryonic* membranes⟩

ex·tra·le·gal \ˌek-strə-ˈlē-gəl\ *adj* **:** not regulated or sanctioned by law — **ex·tra·le·gal·ly** *adv*

ex·tra·mar·i·tal \ˌek-strə-ˈmar-ət-l\ *adj* **:** of or relating to sexual intercourse between a married person and someone other than his or her spouse

ex·tra·ne·ous \ek-ˈstrā-nē-əs\ *adj* **1 :** existing or coming from the outside **2 a :** not forming an essential or vital part **b :** having no relevance [Latin *extraneus* "external, strange," from *extra* "outside"] — **ex·tra·ne·ous·ly** *adv* — **ex·tra·ne·ous·ness** *n*

ex·traor·di·nary \ik-ˈstrȯrd-n-ˌer-ē, ˌek-strə-ˈȯrd-\ *adj* **1 a :** going beyond what is usual, regular, or customary ⟨*extraordinary* powers⟩ **b :** very exceptional : REMARKABLE ⟨*extraordinary* beauty⟩ **2 :** employed for or sent on a special function or service ⟨an ambassador *extraordinary*⟩ — **ex·traor·di·nar·i·ly** \ik-ˌstrȯrd-n-ˈer-ə-lē, ˌek-strə-ˌȯrd-\ *adv* — **ex·traor·di·nar·i·ness** \ik-ˈstrȯrd-n-ˌer-ē-nəs, ˌek-strə-ˈȯrd-\ *n*

extra point *n* **:** a point scored in football after a touchdown by kicking the ball between the goalposts or advancing it a short distance into the end zone

ex·trap·o·late \ik-ˈstrap-ə-ˌlāt\ *vb* **:** to infer facts and data from

\ə\ **abut**	\au̇\ **out**	\i\ **tip**	\ȯ\ **saw**	\u̇\ **foot**
\ər\ **further**	\ch\ **chin**	\ī\ **life**	\ȯi\ **coin**	\y\ **yet**
\a\ **mat**	\e\ **pet**	\j\ **job**	\th\ **thin**	\yü\ **few**
\ā\ **take**	\ē\ **easy**	\ng\ **sing**	\t͟h\ **this**	\yu̇\ **cure**
\ä\ **cot, cart**	\g\ **go**	\ō\ **bone**	\ü\ **food**	\zh\ **vision**

known facts and data [Latin *extra* "outside" + English *-polate* (as in *interpolate*)] — **ex·trap·o·la·tion** \-ˌstrap-ə-ˈlā-shən\ *n*

ex·tra·sen·so·ry \ˌek-strə-ˈsens-rē; -ə-rē\ *adj* : not acting or occurring through use of the known senses

extrasensory perception *n* : an awareness of events or facts held to involve communication outside all the known senses

ex·tra·ter·res·tri·al \ˌek-strə-tə-ˈres-trē-əl, -ˈresh-chəl\ *adj* : originating, existing, or taking place outside the earth or its atmosphere ‹*extraterrestrial* life› — **extraterrestrial** *n*

ex·tra·ter·ri·to·ri·al \-ˌter-ə-ˈtōr-ē-əl, -ˈtȯr-\ *adj* : located outside the territorial limits of a jurisdiction — **ex·tra·ter·ri·to·ri·al·ly** \-ē-ə-lē\ *adv*

ex·tra·ter·ri·to·ri·al·i·ty \-ˌtōr-ē-ˈal-ət-ē, -ˌtȯr-\ *n* : exemption from the application or jurisdiction of local law or tribunals

ex·trav·a·gance \ik-ˈstrav-i-gəns\ *n* **1 a** : an extravagant act; *esp* : excessive spending of money **b** : something extravagant **2** : the quality or fact of being extravagant

ex·trav·a·gant \-gənt\ *adj* **1** : going beyond what is reasonable or suitable ‹*extravagant* praise› **2** : wasteful especially of money ‹*extravagant* spending› **3** : too high in price ‹an *extravagant* purchase› [Medieval French, from Medieval Latin *extravagans,* from Latin *extra-* + *vagari* "to wander about"] ***synonyms*** see EXCESSIVE — **ex·trav·a·gant·ly** *adv*

Word History *Extravagant* is derived from Medieval Latin *extravagans,* formed from the prefix *extra-,* meaning "outside" or "beyond," and the verb *vagari,* "to wander about." Something that is *extravagant,* then, wanders beyond the borders of its usual home. Developing from its literal sense, "wandering," *extravagant* came to mean "exceeding the limits of reason or necessity" and "lacking in moderation, balance, and restraint." From these is derived the related wasteful sense of *extravagant,* that is, "spending much more than necessary."

ex·trav·a·gan·za \ik-ˌstrav-ə-ˈgan-zə\ *n* **1** : a literary or musical work marked by extreme freedom of style and structure **2** : a spectacular show [Italian *estravaganza,* literally, "extravagance"]

ex·tra·ve·hic·u·lar \ˌek-strə-vē-ˈhik-yə-lər\ *adj* : taking place outside a vehicle (as a spacecraft)

[1]**ex·treme** \ik-ˈstrēm\ *adj* **1 a** : existing in a very high degree ‹*extreme* poverty› **b** : going to great or exaggerated lengths **c** : exceeding the ordinary, usual, or expected ‹*extreme* measures› **2** : most distant from a center ‹the country's *extreme* north› **3** : farthest advanced : UTMOST ‹the *extreme* edge of the cliff› **4** : of, relating to, or being an outdoor activity or sport that involves an unusually high degree of risk [Medieval French, from Latin *extremus,* superlative of *exter, exterus* "being on the outside"] — **ex·treme·ly** *adv* — **ex·treme·ness** *n*

[2]**extreme** *n* **1 a** : something situated at or marking one end or the other of a range ‹*extremes* of heat and cold› **b** : the first term or the last term of a mathematical proportion **2 a** : a very high degree **b** : highest degree : MAXIMUM **3** : an extreme measure or expedient ‹go to *extremes*›

extremely high frequency *n* : a ratio frequency in the range between 30,000 and 300,000 megahertz — abbreviation *EHF*

extreme unction *n* : ANOINTING OF THE SICK

ex·trem·ism \ik-ˈstrē-ˌmiz-əm\ *n* **1** : the quality or state of being extreme **2** : advocacy of extreme measures or views especially in politics; *esp* : RADICALISM — **ex·trem·ist** \-məst\ *n or adj*

ex·trem·i·ty \ik-ˈstrem-ət-ē\ *n, pl* **-ties** **1 a** : the farthest or most remote part, section, or point **b** : a limb of the body; *esp* : a human hand or foot **2 a** : extreme danger or critical need **b** : a moment of such danger or need **3** : the utmost degree (as of emotion or pain) **4** : a drastic or desperate act or measure

ex·tri·cate \ˈek-strə-ˌkāt\ *vt* : to free or remove from an entanglement or difficulty [Latin *extricare,* from *ex-* + *tricae* "trifles, perplexities"] — **ex·tri·ca·ble** \ek-ˈstrik-ə-bəl, ˈek-strik-\ *adj* — **ex·tri·ca·tion** \ˌek-strə-ˈkā-shən\ *n*

synonyms EXTRICATE, DISENTANGLE, UNTANGLE mean to free from what binds or holds back. EXTRICATE implies the use of care or ingenuity in freeing from a difficult position or situation ‹*extricate* himself from financial trouble›. DISENTANGLE and UNTANGLE suggest a painstaking separation of two or more things that are confused together or closely interrelated ‹*disentangling* fact from fiction› ‹*untangles* a web of deceit›.

ex·trin·sic \ek-ˈstrin-zik, -ˈstrin-sik\ *adj* **1 a** : not forming part of or belonging to a thing : EXTRANEOUS **b** : originating from or on the outside **2** : EXTERNAL [Latin *extrinsecus* "from without"] — **ex·trin·si·cal·ly** \-zi-kə-lē, -si, -klē\ *adv*

ex·tro·vert *also* **ex·tra·vert** \ˈek-strə-ˌvərt\ *n* **1** : a person whose attention and interests are directed wholly or predominantly toward what is outside the self **2** : a gregarious and unreserved person — **ex·tro·ver·sion** \ˌek-strə-ˈvər-zhən, -shən\ *n* — **extrovert** *adj* — **ex·tro·vert·ed** \ˈek-strə-ˌvərt-əd\ *adj*

ex·trude \ik-ˈstrüd\ *vb* **1** : to force, press, or push out ‹volcanoes *extrude* lava› **2** : to shape (as metal) by forcing through a die **3** : to become extruded [Latin *extrudere,* from *ex-* + *trudere* "to thrust"] — **ex·trud·er** *n*

ex·tru·sion \ik-ˈstrü-zhən\ *n* : the act or process of extruding; *also* : a form or product produced by this process [Medieval Latin *extrusio,* from Latin *extrudere* "to extrude"]

ex·tru·sive \-ˈstrü-siv, -ziv\ *adj* : formed by crystallization of lava poured out on the earth's surface ‹*extrusive* rock›

ex·u·ber·ant \ig-ˈzü-bə-rənt, -brənt\ *adj* **1** : extreme or excessive in degree, size, or extent ‹*exuberant* wealth› **2** : joyously unrestrained and enthusiastic ‹*exuberant* praise› **3** : produced in great abundance : PLENTIFUL ‹*exuberant* vegetation› [Medieval French, from Latin *exuberare* "to be abundant," from *ex-* + *uber* "fruitful," from *uber* "udder"] — **ex·u·ber·ance** \-bə-rəns, -brənts\ *n* — **ex·u·ber·ant·ly** *adv*

ex·u·date \ˈeks-ə-ˌdāt, ˈegz-\ *n* : exuded matter

ex·ude \ig-ˈzüd\ *vb* **1** : to discharge slowly through pores or cuts : OOZE ‹sap *exuding* from a cut stem› **2** : to give off or out conspicuously or abundantly ‹*exudes* charm› [Latin *exsudare,* from *ex-* + *sudare* "to sweat"] — **ex·u·da·tion** \ˌek-sü-ˈdā-shən, -syü-, -shü-\ *n* — **ex·u·da·tive** \ig-ˈzüd-ət-iv\ *adj*

ex·ult \ig-ˈzəlt\ *vi* : to be extremely and often triumphantly joyful ‹the team *exulted* in their victory› [Middle French *exulter,* from Latin *exsultare,* literally, "to leap up," from *ex-* + *saltare* "to leap"] — **ex·ult·ing·ly** \-ˈzəl-ting-lē\ *adv*

ex·ult·ant \ig-ˈzəlt-nt\ *adj* : filled with or expressing great joy : JUBILANT ‹*exultant* cheer› — **ex·ult·ant·ly** *adv*

ex·ul·ta·tion \ˌeks-əl-ˈtā-shən, ˌegz-, -ˌəl-\ *n* : the act of exulting : the state of being exultant

ex·urb \ˈek-ˌsərb, ˈeg-ˌzərb\ *n* : a region or district outside a city and usually beyond its suburbs and that often is inhabited chiefly by well-to-do families [*ex-* + *-urb* (as in suburb)] — **ex·ur·bia** \ek-ˈsər-bē-ə, eg-ˈzər-\ *n*

ex·ur·ban·ite \ek-ˈsər-bə-ˌnīt, eg-ˈzər-\ *n* : one who lives in an exurb

-ey — see -Y

[1]**eye** \ˈī\ *n* **1 a** : a specialized light-sensitive organ of sight; *esp* : a rounded hollow organ that is filled with a jellylike material, is lined with a photosensitive retina, and is lodged in a bony orbit in the vertebrate skull **b** : all the visible structures and parts (as the eyelids) within and surrounding the bony orbit **c** : the ability to see with the eyes **d** : the ability to perceive or appreciate ‹an *eye* for beauty› **e** : LOOK, GLANCE ‹gave them the *eye*› **f** : very close attention or observation ‹kept an *eye* on them› **g** : POINT OF VIEW, JUDGMENT — often used in plural ‹guilty in the *eyes* of the law› **2** : something suggestive of an eye: as **a** : the hole through the head of a needle **b** : a loop to receive a hook **c** : an undeveloped bud (as on a potato) **3** : something central : CENTER ‹the *eye* of a hurricane› [Old English *ēage*] — **eyed** \ˈīd\ *adj* — **eye·less** \ˈī-ləs\ *adj* — **eye·like** \ˈī-ˌlīk\ *adj*

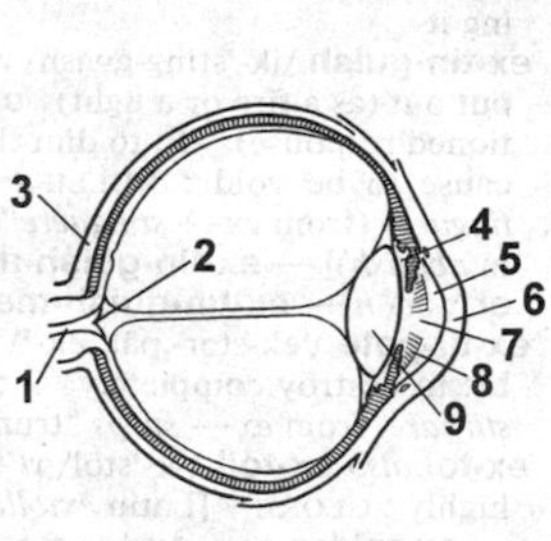

eye 1a: *1* optic nerve, *2* blind spot, *3* sclera, *4* posterior chamber, *5* anterior chamber, *6* cornea, *7* pupil, *8* iris, *9* lens

[2]**eye** *vt* **eyed; eye·ing** *or* **ey·ing** : to watch or study closely

eye·ball \ˈī-ˌbȯl\ *n* : the vertebrate eye

eye·brow \ˈī-ˌbrau̇\ *n* : the ridge over the eye or the hair growing in a line or arch on the skin over it

eye–catch·er \ˈī-ˌkach-ər, -ˌkech-\ *n* : something that strongly attracts the eye — **eye–catch·ing** \-ing\ *adj*

eye chart *n* : a chart with rows of letters or objects of decreasing size that is read at a fixed distance for purposes of testing sight

eye·cup \ˈī-ˌkəp\ *n* : a small oval cup with a rim curved to fit the orbit of the eye used for applying liquid remedies to the eyes

eye·drop·per \ˈī-ˌdräp-ər\ *n* : DROPPER 2

eye·ful \ˈī-ˌfu̇l\ *n* **1 :** a satisfying view **2 :** one that is visually attractive

eye·glass \ˈī-ˌglas\ *n* **1 a :** a glass lens used to improve faulty eyesight **b** *pl* **:** GLASS 2c **2 :** EYEPIECE

eye·lash \ˈī-ˌlash\ *n* **1** *pl* **:** the fringe of hair edging the eyelid **2 :** a single hair of the eyelashes

eye lens *n* **:** the lens nearest the eye in an eyepiece

eye·let \ˈī-lət\ *n* **1 :** a small hole designed to receive a cord or used for decoration (as in embroidery) **2 :** GROMMET 2

eye·lid \ˈī-ˌlid\ *n* **:** one of the movable lids of skin and muscle that can be closed over the eyeball

eye·lin·er \ˈī-ˌlī-nər\ *n* **:** makeup applied in a line around the eyes

eye–open·er \ˈī-ˌōp-nər, -ə-nər\ *n* **:** something startling or surprising — **eye–open·ing** \-ning\ *adj*

eye·piece \ˈī-ˌpēs\ *n* **:** the lens or combination of lenses at the eye end of an optical instrument

eye shadow *n* **:** tinted makeup applied to the eyelids

eye·sight \ˈī-ˌsīt\ *n* **:** SIGHT, VISION ⟨keen *eyesight*⟩

eye socket *n* **:** ORBIT 1

eye·sore \ˈī-ˌsōr, -ˌsȯr\ *n* **:** something displeasing to the sight

eye·spot \ˈī-ˌspät\ *n* **1 :** a spot of color (as on the wing of a butterfly) that resembles an eye **2 a :** a simple or primitive visual organ **:** OCELLUS **b :** a small pigmented body of various unicellular algae

eye·stalk \ˈī-ˌstȯk\ *n* **:** a movable stalk bearing an eye at the tip in a crustacean

eye·strain \ˈī-ˌstrān\ *n* **:** weariness or a strained state of the eye

eye·tooth \ˈī-ˈtüth\ *n* **:** a canine tooth of the upper jaw

eye·wash \ˈī-ˌwȯsh, -ˌwäsh\ *n* **1 :** an eye lotion **2 :** misleading or deceptive statements, actions, or procedures

eye·wear \ˈī-ˌwaər; -ˌweər\ *n* **:** corrective or protective devices (as glasses) for the eyes

eye·wit·ness \ˈī-ˈwit-nəs\ *n* **:** a person who sees an occurrence and is able to give a firsthand account of it

ey·rie *chiefly British variant of* AERIE

Eze·kiel \i-ˈzē-kyəl, -kē-əl\ *n* **:** a prophetic book of canonical Jewish and Christian Scriptures written by a Hebrew priest and prophet of the sixth century B.C. — see BIBLE TABLE

Ez·ra \ˈez-rə\ *n* **:** a narrative book of canonical Jewish and Christian Scriptures — see BIBLE table

F

f \ˈef\ *n, pl* **f's** *or* **fs** \ˈefs\ *often cap* **1 :** the 6th letter of the English alphabet **2 :** the musical note F **:** the 4th tone of a C-major scale **3 :** a grade rating a student's work as failing

fa \ˈfä\ *n* **:** the 4th note of the diatonic scale [Medieval Latin]

Fa·bi·an \ˈfā-bē-ən\ *adj* **:** of, relating to, or being a society of socialists organized in England in 1884 to spread socialist principles gradually [the *Fabian* Society, from Quintus *Fabius* Maximus, died 203 B.C., Roman general] — **Fabian** *n* — **Fa·bi·an·ism** \-ə-ˌniz-əm\ *n*

¹fa·ble \ˈfā-bəl\ *n* **:** a fictitious narrative or statement: as **a :** a legendary story of supernatural happenings **b :** a story meant to teach a lesson; *esp* **:** one in which animals speak and act like human beings **c :** FALSEHOOD 1, LIE [Medieval French, from Latin *fabula* "conversation, story," from *fari* "to speak"] ***synonyms*** see MYTH

²fable *vt* **fa·bled; fa·bling** \-bə-ling, -bling\ **:** to talk or write about as if true — **fa·bler** \-bə-lər, -blər\ *n*

fa·bled \ˈfā-bəld\ *adj* **1 :** FICTITIOUS **2 :** told or mentioned in fables **:** LEGENDARY

fab·ric \ˈfab-rik\ *n* **1 :** underlying structure **:** FRAMEWORK ⟨the *fabric* of society⟩ **2 a :** CLOTH 1 **b :** a material that resembles cloth [Middle French *fabrique,* from Latin *fabrica* "workshop, structure," from *faber* "artisan, smith"]

fab·ri·cate \ˈfab-ri-ˌkāt\ *vt* **1 a :** INVENT, CREATE **b :** to make up in order to deceive ⟨*fabricate* evidence⟩ **2 :** to construct especially from standardized parts ***synonyms*** see FICTION — **fab·ri·ca·tion** \ˌfab-ri-ˈkā-shən\ *n* — **fab·ri·ca·tor** \ˈfab-ri-ˌkāt-ər\ *n*

fab·u·list \ˈfab-yə-ləst\ *n* **:** a creator or teller of fables

fab·u·lous \ˈfab-yə-ləs\ *adj* **1 :** resembling a fable especially in incredible, marvelous, or exaggerated quality ⟨the *fabulous* adventures of an explorer⟩ **2 :** WONDERFUL, MARVELOUS ⟨had a *fabulous* meal⟩ **3 :** told about in fable ⟨*fabulous* animals⟩ — **fab·u·lous·ly** *adv* — **fab·u·lous·ness** *n*

synonyms FABULOUS, LEGENDARY, MYTHICAL mean having the character of what is invented or imagined. FABULOUS stresses marvelousness or incredibility often without implying actual nonexistence or impossibility ⟨the company made *fabulous* profits⟩. LEGENDARY suggests having a fabulous character created by the distortions or exaggerations of historical fact by popular tradition ⟨*legendary* deeds of Robin Hood⟩. MYTHICAL applies to what is or has been popularly believed but does not in fact exist ⟨*mythical* wood nymphs⟩.

fa·cade *also* **fa·çade** \fə-ˈsäd\ *n* **1 :** the front of a building especially when given special architectural treatment **2 :** a false, superficial, or artificial appearance ⟨a *facade* of wealth⟩ [French *façade*]

facade 1

¹face \ˈfās\ *n* **1 :** the front part of the head including the chin, mouth, nose, cheeks, eyes, and usually the forehead **2 a :** LOOK 2a, EXPRESSION **b :** GRIMACE ⟨made a *face* in disgust⟩ **3 a :** outward appearance ⟨suspicious on the *face* of it⟩ **b :** ASSURANCE 2, CONFIDENCE ⟨maintained a firm *face* despite opposition⟩ **c :** DIGNITY, PRESTIGE ⟨afraid to lose *face*⟩ **4 :** SURFACE: **a :** a front, upper, or outer surface; *esp* **:** an exposed surface of rock **b :** any of the flat surfaces that bound a geometric solid ⟨every cube has six *faces*⟩ **c :** a surface or side that is marked or specially prepared ⟨the *face* of a clock⟩ **5 :** an end or wall (as of a mine tunnel) at which work is progressing **6 :** PERSON ⟨a lot of new *faces* around here⟩ [Medieval French, derived from Latin *facies* "make, form, face," from *facere* "to make"] — **in one's face :** directly and aggressively ⟨dunked the ball *in her face*⟩ — **in the face of :** face-to-face with **:** DESPITE ⟨brave *in the face of* danger⟩

²face *vb* **1 :** to confront brazenly ⟨*face* out a compromising situation⟩ **2 a :** to line near the edge especially with a different material ⟨*face* a hem⟩ **b :** to cover the front or surface of ⟨*faced* the building with marble⟩ **3 :** to meet face to face or in competition ⟨*faced* the opposing team⟩ ⟨*face* one's accusers⟩ **4 a :** to stand or sit with the face toward ⟨*face* the class⟩ **b :** to have the front oriented toward ⟨a house *facing* the park⟩ **5 a :** to recognize and deal with firmly ⟨*faces* danger bravely⟩ **b :** to master by confronting with determination ⟨*faced* down the critics of their policy⟩ **6 :** to turn or cause to turn the face or body in a specified direction ⟨quickly *faced* to the right⟩ — **face the music :** to meet a danger or an unpleasant situation

face card *n* **:** a playing card that is a king, queen, or jack

-faced \ˈfāst\ *adj combining form* **:** having (such) a face or (so many) faces ⟨rosy-*faced*⟩ ⟨two-*faced*⟩

face·down \ˈfās-ˈdau̇n\ *adv* **:** with the face downward ⟨fell *facedown*⟩

\ə\ **abut**	\au̇\ **out**	\i\ **tip**	\ȯ\ **saw**	\u̇\ **foot**
\ər\ **further**	\ch\ **chin**	\ī\ **life**	\ȯi\ **coin**	\y\ **yet**
\a\ **mat**	\e\ **pet**	\j\ **job**	\th\ **thin**	\yü\ **few**
\ā\ **take**	\ē\ **easy**	\ng\ **sing**	\t͟h\ **this**	\yu̇\ **cure**
\ä\ **cot, cart**	\g\ **go**	\ō\ **bone**	\ü\ **food**	\zh\ **vision**

face–first \ˌfās-ˈfərst\ *adv* : with the face leading the body ⟨hit the ground *face–first*⟩ — **face–first** *adj*

face·less \ˈfās-ləs\ *adj* **1 a** : lacking character or individuality ⟨the *faceless* masses⟩ **b** : not identified ⟨a *faceless* accuser⟩ **2** : lacking a face — **face·less·ness** *n*

face–lift \ˈfās-ˌlift\ *n* **1** : plastic surgery on the face and neck to remove defects and imperfections (as wrinkles or sagging skin) typical of aging **2** : an alteration, restoration, or remodeling (as of a building) intended especially to modernize — **face–lift** *vt*

face off *vi* : to be in or come into opposition or competition ⟨politicians *facing off* against each other in a debate⟩

face–off \ˈfā-ˌsȯf\ *n* : a method of putting the puck in play in ice hockey by dropping it between two opposing players

face·plate \ˈfā-ˌsplāt\ *n* **1** : a disk fixed with its face at right angles to the live spindle of a lathe for the attachment of the work **2** : a protective plate or cover

fac·et \ˈfas-ət\ *n* **1** : a small plane surface (as on a cut gem) **2** : a definable aspect of something being considered ⟨explained all *facets* of the company⟩ **3** : the external surface of a unit of a compound eye (as of an insect) [French *facette,* from *face* "face"] — **fac·et·ed** \ˈfas-ət-əd\ *adj*

fa·ce·tious \fə-ˈsē-shəs\ *adj* **1** : joking or jesting often inappropriately ⟨just being *facetious*⟩ **2** : meant to be humorous or funny : not serious ⟨a *facetious* remark⟩ [Middle French *facetieux,* from *facetie* "jest," from Latin *facetia*] ***synonyms*** see WITTY — **fa·ce·tious·ly** *adv* — **fa·ce·tious·ness** *n*

face–to–face *adv or adj* **1** : being within each other's sight or presence ⟨a *face–to–face* interview⟩ **2** : in or into direct contact or confrontation ⟨*face–to–face* with an emergency⟩

face·up \ˈfā-ˈsəp\ *adv* : with the face up ⟨the card fell *faceup*⟩

face value *n* **1** : the value indicated on the face (as of a bill or a stock certificate) **2** : the apparent worth ⟨can't take what he says at *face value*⟩

[1]**fa·cial** \ˈfā-shəl\ *adj* : of or relating to the face — **fa·cial·ly** \-shə-lē\ *adv*

[2]**facial** *n* : a treatment to improve the condition of the facial skin

facial nerve *n* : either of the 7th pair of cranial nerves that control facial and ear movements and transmit sensations of taste

fa·cies \ˈfā-shēz, -shē-ˌēz\ *n, pl* **facies** : a particular form or appearance ⟨a plant species with a distinct *facies*⟩; *esp* : a rock or group of rocks that can be distinguished (as by composition) in a single rock mass [Latin, "face"]

fac·ile \ˈfas-əl\ *adj* **1 a** : easily accomplished or attained ⟨a *facile* success⟩ **b** : SIMPLISTIC 2, SHALLOW ⟨too *facile* a solution to a complex problem⟩ **c** : easily produced or displayed and often insincere ⟨*facile* tears⟩ **2** : working, moving, or performing with skill and ease : FLUENT ⟨a *facile* writer⟩ [Medieval French, from Latin *facilis,* from *facere* "to do, make"] — **fac·ile·ly** \-əl-lē, -ə-lē\ *adv* — **fac·ile·ness** \-əl-nəs\ *n*

fa·cil·i·tate \fə-ˈsil-ə-ˌtāt\ *vt* : to make easier — **fa·cil·i·ta·tion** \-ˌsil-ə-ˈtā-shən\ *n*

fa·cil·i·ta·tor \fə-ˈsil-ə-ˌtāt-ər\ *n* : one who facilitates; *esp* : a person who guides or supervises a group working to accomplish a task (as learning or communication) ⟨the *facilitator* of a workshop⟩

fa·cil·i·ty \fə-ˈsil-ət-ē\ *n, pl* **-ties** **1** : the quality of being easily performed **2** : ease in performance : APTITUDE **3** : readiness to be influenced : PLIANCY **4 a** : something that makes an action, operation, or course of conduct easier — usually used in plural ⟨*facilities* for graduate study⟩ **b** : something built, installed, or established to serve a particular purpose ⟨a hospital *facility*⟩

fac·ing \ˈfā-sing\ *n* **1 a** : a lining along an edge (as of a garment) **b** *pl* : the collar, cuffs, and trimmings of a uniform coat **2** : an ornamental or protective layer ⟨a house with brick *facing*⟩ **3** : material for facing

fac·sim·i·le \fak-ˈsim-ə-lē\ *n* **1** : an exact copy **2** : a system of transmitting and reproducing graphic matter by means of signals sent over telephone lines [Latin *fac simile* "make similar"] ***synonyms*** see DUPLICATE

fact \ˈfakt\ *n* **1 a** : a thing done : DEED **b** : CRIME 1 ⟨accessory after the *fact*⟩ **2** : the quality of being actual **3** : something that actually exists or occurs ⟨space travel is now a *fact*⟩ **4** : information or an item of information that is accurate and true ⟨they do not know *fact* from fancy⟩ [Latin *factum,* from *facere* "to make, do"] — **in fact** : in truth : ACTUALLY

fac·tion \ˈfak-shən\ *n* **1** : a group or party acting together within and usually against a larger body (as in a state, political party, or church) : CLIQUE **2** : dissension within a group [Latin *factio* "act of making, faction," from *facere* "to make, do"] — **fac·tion·al** \-shnəl, -shən-l\ *adj* — **fac·tion·al·ism** \-ˌiz-əm\ *n* — **fac·tion·al·ist** \-shnəl-əst, -shən-l-\ *n*

fac·tious \ˈfak-shəs\ *adj* **1** : of, relating to, or caused by faction ⟨*factious* disputes⟩ **2** : inclined to faction or the formation of factions ⟨*factious* politicians⟩ — **fac·tious·ly** *adv* — **fac·tious·ness** *n*

fac·ti·tious \fak-ˈtish-əs\ *adj* : not natural or genuine : ARTIFICIAL ⟨a *factitious* display of grief⟩ [Latin *facticius,* from *facere* "to make, do"] ***synonyms*** see FICTITIOUS — **fac·ti·tious·ly** *adv* — **fac·ti·tious·ness** *n*

fact of life *n* **1** : something that exists and must be taken into consideration ⟨tests are a *fact of life* for students⟩ **2** *pl* : the fundamental physiological processes and behavior involved in sex and reproduction

fac·toid \ˈfak-ˌtoid\ *n* **1** : an invented fact thought to be true due to its appearance in print **2** : a brief often trivial news item

[1]**fac·tor** \ˈfak-tər\ *n* **1 a** : one that buys or sells property for another **b** : an agent in charge of a trading post **2** : something that actively contributes to the production of a result ⟨hard work was a *factor* in their success⟩ **3** : GENE **4** : any of the numbers or symbols in mathematics that when multiplied together form a product; *esp* : a number that divides another number without leaving a remainder ⟨the *factors* of 6 are 1, 2, 3, and 6⟩ [Medieval French *facteur,* from Latin *factor* "doer," from *facere* "to do, make"] — **fac·tor·ship** \-ˌship\ *n*

[2]**factor** *vb* **fac·tored; fac·tor·ing** \-tə-ring, -tring\ **1** : to find the mathematical factors of and especially the prime mathematical factors **2** : to act as a factor ⟨class participation will *factor* into your grade⟩ — **fac·tor·able** \-tə-rə-bəl, -trə-\ *adj*

factor VIII \-ˈāt\ *n* : a protein of blood that is essential for blood clotting and is absent or inactive in hemophilia

[1]**fac·to·ri·al** \fak-ˈtōr-ē-əl, -ˈtȯr-\ *n* **1** : the product of all the positive whole numbers from 1 to the number given — symbol ! **2** : the quantity 0! that is defined as equal to 1

[2]**factorial** *adj* : of or relating to factors, factoring, or factorials

fac·tor·i·za·tion \ˌfak-tə-rə-ˈzā-shən\ *n* : the act or process or an instance or result of factoring

factor tree *n* : a branching diagram that shows the prime factors of a number by successively showing the factors of each composite factor

fac·to·ry \ˈfak-tə-rē, -trē\ *n, pl* **-ries** **1** : a trading station where factors trade ⟨a colonial *factory*⟩ **2** : a building or set of buildings used or suitable for manufacturing

factory system *n* : a system of manufacturing based on concentration of industry into large establishments that began with the Industrial Revolution

fac·to·tum \fak-ˈtōt-əm\ *n* : an employee with numerous varied duties [Latin *fac* "do" + *totum* "everything"]

fac·tu·al \ˈfak-chə-wəl, -chəl\ *adj* **1** : of or relating to fact or facts ⟨*factual* evidence⟩ **2** : restricted to or based on fact ⟨little *factual* knowledge of ancient civilizations⟩ — **fac·tu·al·i·ty** \ˌfak-chə-ˈwal-ət-ē\ *n* — **fac·tu·al·ly** \ˈfak-chə-wə-lē, -chə-lē\ *adv* — **fac·tu·al·ness** *n*

fac·u·la \ˈfak-yə-lə\ *n, pl* **-lae** \-ˌlē, -ˌlī\ : any of the brighter regions of the sun's photosphere [New Latin, from Latin *fac-, fax* "torch"]

fac·ul·ta·tive \ˈfak-əl-ˌtāt-iv\ *adj* **1** : taking place under some conditions but not under others ⟨*facultative* diapause⟩ **2** : showing the typical mode of life under some environmental conditions but not under others ⟨*facultative* anaerobes⟩ — **fac·ul·ta·tive·ly** *adv*

fac·ul·ty \ˈfak-əl-tē\ *n, pl* **-ties** **1** : ability to do something : TALENT ⟨a *faculty* for making friends⟩ **2** : one of the powers of the mind or body ⟨the *faculty* of hearing⟩ **3 a** : the members of a profession **b** : the teachers in a school or college or in one of its departments [Medieval French *faculté,* from Latin *facultas,* from *facilis* "facile"]

fad \ˈfad\ *n* : a practice or interest followed for a time with great zeal : CRAZE [origin unknown] — **fad·dish** \ˈfad-ish\ *adj* — **fad·dist** \ˈfad-əst\ *n* — **fad·dy** \-ē\ *adj*

[1]**fade** \ˈfād\ *vb* **1** : to lose freshness, strength, or vitality : WITHER **2** : to lose or cause to lose freshness or brilliance of color **3** : to grow dim or disappear gradually ⟨their hopes *faded*⟩ **4** : to change gradually in loudness or visibility — used of a motion-picture image or of an electronics signal and usually with *in* or *out* [Medieval French *fader,* from *fade* "feeble, insipid," derived from Latin *fatuus* "fatuous, insipid"]

²fade *n* : a gradual changing of one picture to another in a motion-picture or television sequence

fae·cal, fae·ces *chiefly British variant of* FECAL, FECES

fa·er·ie *also* **fa·ery** \ˈfā-rē, ˈfā-ə-rē, ˈfaər-ē, ˈfeər-ē\ *n, pl* **fa·er·ies** **1** : FAIRYLAND **2** : FAIRY — **faery** *adj*

¹fag \ˈfag\ *vb* **fagged; fag·ging** **1** : to work hard **2** : to act as servant to a fellow student in an English public school **3** : to tire by strenuous activity [obsolete *fag* "to droop"]

²fag *n* **1** : an English public-school boy who acts as servant to another **2** : MENIAL, DRUDGE

³fag *n* : CIGARETTE [*fag end*]

fag end *n* **1 a** : a poor or worn-out end **b** : the extreme end **2 a** : the last part or coarser end of a piece of cloth **b** : the untwisted end of a rope [Middle English *fagge* "flap"]

fag·ot *or* **fag·got** \ˈfag-ət\ *n* : a bundle of sticks or twigs used especially for fuel [Medieval French *fagot*]

fag·ot·ing *or* **fag·got·ing** \ˈfag-ət-ing\ *n* : an embroidery produced by tying threads in hourglass-shaped clusters

Fahr·en·heit \ˈfar-ən-ˌhīt\ *adj* : relating or conforming to a temperature scale on which under standard atmospheric pressure the boiling point of water is at 212 degrees above the zero of the scale and the freezing point is at 32 degrees above zero — abbreviation *F* [Gabriel D. *Fahrenheit*]

fa·ience *or* **fa·ïence** \fā-ˈäns\ *n* : earthenware decorated with opaque colored glazes [French, from *Faenza,* Italy]

¹fail \ˈfāl\ *vb* **1 a** : to lose strength ⟨her health was *failing*⟩ **b** : to stop working ⟨the engine *failed*⟩ **2 a** : to fall short ⟨*failed* in their duty⟩ **b** : to be or become absent or lacking ⟨the power *failed*⟩ **c** : to be unsuccessful ⟨the marriage *failed*⟩ **d** (1) : to be unsuccessful in passing ⟨*failed* the exam⟩ (2) : to grade as not passing ⟨*fail* a student⟩ **e** : to become bankrupt ⟨the bank *failed*⟩ **3** : DISAPPOINT, DESERT ⟨*fail* a friend⟩ **4** : to leave undone : NEGLECT ⟨*failed* to lock the door⟩ [Medieval French *faillir,* from Latin *fallere* "to deceive, disappoint"]

²fail *n* : FAILURE — usually used in the phrase *without fail*

¹fail·ing \ˈfā-ling\ *n* : a slight defect in character or conduct ***synonyms*** see FAULT

²failing *prep* : in the absence or lack of ⟨*failing* specific instructions, use your own judgment⟩

faille \ˈfīl\ *n* : a lustrous closely woven ribbed fabric [French]

¹fail–safe \ˈfāl-ˌsāf\ *adj* : having some feature for counteracting the effect of an anticipated possible failure

²fail–safe *n* : a device or measure that makes something fail-safe

fail·ure \ˈfāl-yər\ *n* **1 a** : a failing to do or perform ⟨their *failure* to appear⟩ **b** : a state of inability to perform a normal function adequately ⟨heart *failure*⟩ **2 a** : lack of satisfactory performance or effect ⟨our *failure* in the campaign⟩ **b** : a lack of commercial or financial success ⟨a business *failure*⟩ **3 a** : a falling short : DEFICIENCY ⟨crop *failure*⟩ **b** : DETERIORATION, BREAKDOWN ⟨a *failure* of memory⟩ **4** : one that has failed ⟨a plan that was a complete *failure*⟩

¹fain \ˈfān\ *adj* **1** *archaic* : GLAD, HAPPY **2** *archaic* : INCLINED 1 **3** : OBLIGED [Old English *fægen*]

²fain *adv* **1** *archaic* : WILLINGLY **2** *archaic* : RATHER 4

¹faint \ˈfānt\ *adj* **1** : lacking courage and spirit : COWARDLY ⟨*faint* heart⟩ **2** : being weak, dizzy, and likely to faint ⟨feel *faint* at the sight of blood⟩ **3** : lacking strength : FEEBLE ⟨a *faint* attempt⟩ **4 a** : lacking distinctness : barely perceptible ⟨a *faint* sound⟩ **b** : VAGUE 2 ⟨haven't the *faintest* idea⟩ [Medieval French *feint, faint,* from *feindre, faindre* "to feign, shirk"] — **faint·ly** *adv* — **faint·ness** *n*

²faint *vi* **1** *archaic* : to lose courage or spirit **2** : to lose consciousness because of a temporary decrease in the blood supply to the brain

³faint *n* : an act or condition of fainting

faint·heart·ed \ˈfānt-ˈhärt-əd\ *adj* : lacking courage or resolution — **faint·heart·ed·ly** *adv* — **faint·heart·ed·ness** *n*

¹fair \ˈfaər, ˈfeər\ *adj* **1** : attractive in appearance : BEAUTIFUL ⟨our *fair* city⟩ **2** : deceptively agreeable ⟨*fair* promises⟩ **3 a** : CLEAN, PURE ⟨*fair* sparkling water⟩ **b** : CLEAR, LEGIBLE ⟨a *fair* copy⟩ **4** : not stormy or cloudy ⟨*fair* weather⟩ **5 a** : marked by impartiality and honesty : JUST ⟨a *fair* trial⟩ **b** : conforming with the rules : ALLOWED ⟨*fair* play⟩ **c** : open to legitimate pursuit or attack ⟨*fair* game⟩ **6 a** : PROMISING, LIKELY ⟨a *fair* chance of winning⟩ **b** : favorable to a ship's course ⟨a *fair* wind⟩ **7** : not dark ⟨*fair* skin⟩ **8** : moderately good ⟨got *fair* grades⟩ [Old English *fæger*] — **fair·ness** *n*

synonyms FAIR, JUST, EQUITABLE, IMPARTIAL, UNBIASED mean free from favor toward either or any side. FAIR implies eliminating one's own feelings, prejudices, or desires so as to achieve a proper balance of conflicting interests ⟨a *fair* decision⟩. JUST implies an exact following of a standard of what is right and proper ⟨a *just* settlement of claims⟩. EQUITABLE stresses equal treatment of all concerned ⟨*equitable* sharing in the profits⟩. IMPARTIAL implies absence of favor or prejudice ⟨an *impartial* referee⟩. UNBIASED stresses more definitely complete absence of prejudice or predisposition ⟨your *unbiased* opinion⟩. ***synonyms*** see in addition BEAUTIFUL

²fair *adv* : in a fair way ⟨play *fair*⟩

³fair *n* **1** : a gathering of buyers and sellers at a particular place and time for trade **2 a** : a competitive exhibition (as of farm products) usually with accompanying entertainment and amusements **b** : an exhibition that promotes the availability of services or opportunities ⟨a job *fair*⟩ **3** : a sale of collected articles usually for charity [Medieval French *feire,* from Medieval Latin *feria,* from Latin *feriae* (plural) "holidays"]

fair ball *n* : a batted baseball that settles within the foul lines in the infield, that first touches the ground within the foul lines in the outfield, or that is within the foul lines when bounding to the outfield past first or third base or when going beyond the outfield for a home run

fair catch *n* : a catch of a kicked football by a player who gives a signal, may not advance the ball, and may not be tackled

fair·ground \ˈfaər-ˌgrau̇nd, ˈfeər-\ *n* : an area set aside for fairs, circuses, and exhibitions

¹fair·ing \ˈfaər-ing, ˈfeər-\ *n, British* : GIFT; *esp* : a present bought or given at a fair

²fairing *n* : a structure (as on an aircraft or missile) whose function is to produce a smooth outline and reduce resistance to motion through the air

fair·ish \ˈfaər-ish, ˈfeər-\ *adj* : fairly good ⟨a *fairish* wage⟩

fair·lead \ˈfaər-ˌlēd, ˈfeər-\ *n* : a block or ring that guides a rope on board a boat or ship to prevent it from chafing

fair·ly \ˈfaər-lē, ˈfeər-\ *adv* **1** : HANDSOMELY, FAVORABLY ⟨*fairly* situated⟩ **2** : so to speak : NEARLY ⟨*fairly* bursting with pride⟩ **3** : in a fair manner : JUSTLY ⟨treat each person *fairly*⟩ **4** : MODERATELY ⟨a *fairly* easy job⟩

fair–spo·ken \ˈfaər-ˌspō-kən, ˈfeər-\ *adj* : pleasant and courteous in speech

fair trade *n* **1** : trade in conformity with a fair-trade agreement **2** : a movement that aims to help producers in developing countries get a fair price for their products so as to reduce poverty, provide for the ethical treatment of workers and farmers, and promote environmentally sustainable practices — **fair–trade** *vt*

fair–trade agreement *n* : an agreement between a producer and a seller that commodities bearing a trademark, label, or brand name belonging to a producer be sold at or above a specified price

fair·way \-ˌwā\ *n* **1** : a navigable part of a river, bay, or harbor **2** : an open path or space **3** : the mowed part of a golf course between a tee and a green

fair–weather *adj* : loyal only when things are going well ⟨a *fair-weather* friend⟩

fairy \ˈfaər-ē, ˈfeər-\ *n, pl* **fairies** : a usually small humanlike being of folklore and romance endowed with magical powers [Medieval French *faerie* "fairyland, fairy people," from *feie, fee* "fairy," from Latin *Fata,* goddess of fate, from *fatum* "fate"] — **fairy** *adj* — **fairy·like** \-ˌlīk\ *adj*

fairy·land \-ˌland\ *n* **1** : a land of fairies **2** : a place of delicate beauty or magical charm

fairy ring *n* : a ring of mushrooms in a lawn or meadow that is produced at the edge of a mass of mycelium which is growing outward from a central point

fairy shrimp *n* : any of several very small translucent freshwater crustaceans (order Anostraca)

fairy tale *n* **1** : a simple children's story about supernatural beings — called also *fairy story* **2** : a made-up story usually meant to mislead

fait ac·com·pli \ˈfāt-ˌak-ˌōⁿ-ˈplē, ˌfe-ˌtak-, -ˌōⁿm-\ *n, pl* **faits accomplis** *same, or* -ˈplēz\ : a thing accomplished and presumably irreversible [French, "accomplished fact"]

\ə\ **abut**	\au̇\ **out**	\i\ **tip**	\ȯ\ **saw**	\u̇\ **foot**
\ər\ **further**	\ch\ **chin**	\ī\ **life**	\ȯi\ **coin**	\y\ **yet**
\a\ **mat**	\e\ **pet**	\j\ **job**	\th\ **thin**	\yü\ **few**
\ā\ **take**	\ē\ **easy**	\ng\ **sing**	\t͟h\ **this**	\yu̇\ **cure**
\ä\ **cot, cart**	\g\ **go**	\ō\ **bone**	\ü\ **food**	\zh\ **vision**

faith \ˈfāth\ *n* **1 a :** allegiance to duty or a person : LOYALTY **b :** the quality of keeping one's promises **2 a** (1) **:** belief and trust in and loyalty to God (2) **:** belief in the traditional doctrines of a religion **b** (1) **:** firm belief in something for which there is no proof (2) **:** complete confidence **3 :** something that is believed especially with strong conviction; *also* **:** a system of religious beliefs [Medieval French *feid, foi,* from Latin *fides*] ***synonyms*** see BELIEF — **in faith :** by my faith : TRULY

[1]**faith·ful** \ˈfāth-fəl\ *adj* **1 :** steady, firm, and dependable in allegiance or devotion : LOYAL ⟨a *faithful* friend⟩ **2 :** consistent in keeping promises or in fulfilling duties ⟨a *faithful* worker⟩ **3 :** true to the facts : ACCURATE ⟨a *faithful* copy⟩ — **faith·ful·ly** \-fə-lē\ *adv* — **faith·ful·ness** *n*

synonyms FAITHFUL, LOYAL, CONSTANT, STEADFAST mean firm in adherence to whatever one owes allegiance. FAITHFUL implies unswerving adherence to a person or to an oath or promise ⟨*faithful* to her promise⟩. LOYAL implies a firm resistance to any temptation to desert or betray ⟨remained *loyal* to the king⟩. CONSTANT implies continuing firmness of emotional attachment ⟨a *constant* friend⟩. STEADFAST stresses a steady and unwavering adherence ⟨a *steadfast* fighter for civil rights⟩.

[2]**faithful** *n* **1** *pl in constr* **a :** church members in full communion and in good standing — used with *the* **b :** the body of believers in Islam — used with *the* **2** *pl* **faithful** *or* **faithfuls :** one who is faithful; *esp* **:** a loyal follower, member, or fan ⟨party *faithfuls*⟩

faith·less \ˈfāth-ləs\ *adj* **1 :** not true to allegiance or duty : DISLOYAL **2 :** not worthy of trust or reliance : UNTRUSTWORTHY — **faith·less·ly** *adv* — **faith·less·ness** *n*

synonyms FAITHLESS, FALSE, DISLOYAL, PERFIDIOUS mean untrue to what should command one's fidelity or allegiance. FAITHLESS may apply to any failure to keep a promise or pledge or to any breach of allegiance or loyalty ⟨*faithless* allies⟩. FALSE often implies a degree of premeditation and deception in betrayal or treachery ⟨*false* friends⟩. DISLOYAL implies a lack of complete faithfulness to a friend, cause, leader, or country ⟨*disloyal* officers⟩. PERFIDIOUS implies an inability to be faithful or reliable ⟨a *perfidious* double-crosser⟩.

[1]**fake** \ˈfāk\ *adj* **:** COUNTERFEIT, PHONY

[2]**fake** *n* **1 :** an imitation that is passed off as genuine : FRAUD, COUNTERFEIT ⟨the supposed antique was a *fake*⟩ **2 :** a person passing herself or himself off as something she or he is not : IMPOSTOR ⟨a medical *fake*⟩

[3]**fake** *vt* **1 :** to treat so as to falsify ⟨*faked* the statistics to prove a point⟩ **2 :** COUNTERFEIT ⟨*fake* a rare edition⟩ **3 :** PRETEND, SIMULATE ⟨*fake* surprise⟩ [origin unknown] — **fak·er** \ˈfā-kər\ *n* — **fak·ery** \-kə-rē, -krē\ *n*

fa·kir \fə-ˈkiər, fä-, fa-, ˈfā-kər\ *n* **1 :** a Muslim beggar : DERVISH **2 :** a wandering Hindu ascetic or wonder-worker [Arabic *faqīr,* literally, "poor man"]

fal·chion \ˈfȯl-chən\ *n* **:** a broad-bladed slightly curved medieval sword [Medieval French *fauchun,* "to mow," from Latin *falc-, falx* "sickle, scythe"]

fal·con \ˈfal-kən *also* ˈfȯl- *sometimes* ˈfȯ-kən\ *n* **1 :** a hawk trained for use in falconry; *esp* **:** a female peregrine falcon — compare TIERCEL **2 :** any of various swift hawks with long pointed wings and a notch on the upper half of the beak for killing prey [Medieval French, from Late Latin *falco*]

fal·con·er \-kə-nər\ *n* **:** a person who breeds, trains, or hunts with hawks

fal·con·ry \ˈfal-kən-rē *also* ˈfȯl- *sometimes* ˈfȯ-kən-\ *n* **1 :** the art of training hawks to hunt in cooperation with a person **2 :** the sport of hunting with hawks

falderal *variant of* FOLDEROL

[1]**fall** \ˈfȯl\ *vi* **fell** \ˈfel\; **fall·en** \ˈfȯ-lən\; **fall·ing** **1 a :** to descend freely by the force of gravity **b :** to hang freely ⟨the drapes *fall* quite gracefully⟩ **c :** to drop oneself to a lower position ⟨*fall* to one's knees⟩ **d :** to come as if by descending ⟨darkness *falls* early in winter⟩ **2 a :** to become lower in degree or level ⟨the temperature *fell* 10 degrees⟩ **b :** to drop in pitch or volume **c :** to become uttered ⟨as the words *fell* from my lips⟩ **d :** to become lowered ⟨her eyes *fell*⟩ **3 a :** to tip over from an upright position ⟨the lamp *fell* on its side⟩ **b :** to enter as if unawares : STUMBLE ⟨*fell* into error⟩ **c :** to drop down wounded or dead; *esp* **:** to die in battle **d :** to become captured or defeated ⟨the fortress *fell*⟩ **e :** to suffer ruin or failure ⟨our plans *fell* through⟩ **4 :** to commit a wrong or immoral act **5 a :** to move or extend in a downward direction ⟨the ground *falls* away to the east⟩ **b :** to become less in amount or degree : SUBSIDE ⟨the tide is *falling*⟩ **c :** to decline in quality, activity, quantity, or value ⟨prices *fell*⟩ **d :** to lose weight — used with *off* or *away* **e :** to assume a look of shame or dejection ⟨his face *fell* when he lost⟩ **6 a :** to occur at a certain time ⟨my birthday *falls* on a Tuesday⟩ **b :** to come by chance ⟨*fell* in with a bad crowd⟩ **c :** to come by assignment or inheritance : DEVOLVE ⟨it *fell* to us to break the news⟩ **d :** to have the proper place or station ⟨the accent *falls* on the second syllable⟩ **7 :** to come within the scope of something ⟨*falls* under her job description⟩ **8 :** to pass from one condition of body or mind to another ⟨*fall* ill⟩ ⟨*fall* asleep⟩ **9 :** to set about heartily or actively ⟨*fell* to work⟩ [Old English *feallan*] — **fall all over oneself** *or* **fall over oneself :** to display excessive eagerness — **fall flat :** to produce no response or result : FAIL — **fall for 1 :** to fall in love with **2 :** to become a victim of ⟨we *fell* for the trick⟩ — **fall from grace :** to lapse morally : SIN, BACKSLIDE — **fall into line :** to comply with a certain course of action — **fall short 1 :** to be deficient **2 :** to fail to attain

[2]**fall** *n* **1 :** the act of falling by the force of gravity ⟨a *fall* from a horse⟩ **2 a :** a falling out, off, or away : DROPPING ⟨the *fall* of the leaves⟩ **b :** AUTUMN **c :** a thing or quantity that falls or has fallen ⟨a heavy *fall* of snow⟩ **3 a :** loss of greatness : COLLAPSE ⟨the *fall* of the Roman Empire⟩ **b :** the surrender or capture of a place under attack **c :** lapse or departure from innocence or goodness **d :** loss of a woman's chastity **4 a :** the downward slope of a hill **b :** WATERFALL — usually used in plural **5 :** a decrease in size, quantity, degree, activity, or value **6 :** the distance which something falls **7 a :** an act of forcing a wrestler's shoulders to the mat **b :** a bout of wrestling

fal·la·cious \fə-ˈlā-shəs\ *adj* **1 :** embodying a fallacy ⟨a *fallacious* argument⟩ **2 :** tending to deceive or mislead ⟨cherish a *fallacious* hope⟩ — **fal·la·cious·ly** *adv* — **fal·la·cious·ness** *n*

fal·la·cy \ˈfal-ə-sē\ *n, pl* **-cies** **1 a :** a false or mistaken idea ⟨the popular *fallacy* that kids are impractical⟩ **b :** the quality or state of being false **2 :** false or illogical reasoning or an instance of this [Latin *fallacia,* from *fallac-, fallax* "deceptive," from *fallere* "to deceive"]

fall back *vi* **:** RETREAT 1, RECEDE — **fall back on** *or* **fall back upon :** to turn to for help ⟨*fell back on* their reserves⟩ ⟨can always *fall back on* her friends⟩

fall·er \ˈfȯ-lər\ *n* **:** a logger who cuts down trees

fall guy *n* **:** a person on whom something is blamed : SCAPEGOAT 2

fal·li·ble \ˈfal-ə-bəl\ *adj* **:** capable of making a mistake or being wrong ⟨even experts are *fallible*⟩ ⟨a *fallible* generalization⟩ [Medieval Latin *fallibilis,* from Latin *fallere* "to deceive"] — **fal·li·bil·i·ty** \ˌfal-ə-ˈbil-ət-ē\ *n* — **fal·li·bly** \ˈfal-ə-blē\ *adv*

fall in *vi* **:** to take one's proper place in a military formation

fall·ing–out \ˌfȯ-ling-ˈau̇t\ *n, pl* **fallings–out** *or* **falling–outs :** QUARREL 2 ⟨had a *falling-out* with his parents⟩

falling star *n* **:** METEOR

fal·lo·pi·an tube \fə-ˈlō-pē-ən-\ *n, often cap F* **:** either of the pair of tubes that carry the egg from the ovary to the uterus [Gabriel *Fallopius,* died 1562, Italian anatomist]

fall·out \ˈfȯ-ˌlau̇t\ *n* **:** the often radioactive particles resulting from a nuclear explosion and descending through the atmosphere

fall out \ˌfȯ-ˈlau̇t, fȯ-\ *vi* **1 :** to have a quarrel **2 :** TURN OUT, HAPPEN ⟨everything *fell out* well⟩ **3 a :** to leave one's place in the ranks **b :** to leave a building to take one's place in a military formation

[1]**fal·low** \ˈfal-ō\ *adj* **:** of a light yellowish brown [Old English *fealu*]

[2]**fallow** *n* **1 :** land for crops allowed to lie idle during the growing season **2 :** the state or period of being fallow ⟨fields in summer *fallow*⟩ **3 :** the tilling of land without sowing it for a season [Old English *fealg* "plowed land"]

[3]**fallow** *vt* **:** to till (land) without seeding

[4]**fallow** *adj* **1 :** left untilled or if tilled left unsown **2 :** DORMANT 1, INACTIVE — **fal·low·ness** *n*

fallow deer *n* **:** a small European deer with broad antlers and a pale yellow coat spotted white in the summer

fall to *vi* **:** to begin doing something (as working or eating) especially vigorously

[1]**false** \ˈfȯls\ *adj* **1 :** not genuine : ARTIFICIAL ⟨*false* teeth⟩ **2 a :** intentionally untrue ⟨*false* testimony⟩ **b :** adjusted or made so as to deceive ⟨*false* scales⟩ **c :** tending to mislead ⟨a *false* promise⟩ **3 :** not true ⟨*false* statements⟩ **4 a :** not faithful or loyal : TREACHEROUS **b :** not natural or sincere ⟨*false* modes-

ty⟩ **5 :** not essential to structure ⟨a *false* ceiling⟩ **6 :** inaccurate in pitch ⟨a *false* note⟩ **7 a :** based on mistaken ideas ⟨*false* pride⟩ **b :** inconsistent with the true facts ⟨a *false* sense of security⟩ [Latin *falsus,* from *fallere* "to deceive"] ***synonyms*** see FAITHLESS — **false·ly** *adv* — **false·ness** *n*

[2]false *adv* **:** in a false or faithless manner **:** TREACHEROUSLY ⟨they played us *false*⟩

false·hood \ˈfȯls-ˌhu̇d\ *n* **1 :** an untrue statement **:** LIE **2 :** absence of truth or accuracy **3 :** the practice of lying

false rib *n* **:** a rib whose cartilages unite indirectly or not at all with the sternum — compare FLOATING RIB

[1]fal·set·to \fȯl-ˈset-ō\ *n, pl* **-tos 1 :** an artifically high voice; *esp* **:** an artificial singing voice that extends above the range of the full voice especially of a tenor **2 :** a singer who uses falsetto [Italian, from *falso* "false," from Latin *falsus*]

[2]falsetto *adv* **:** in falsetto ⟨sang the song *falsetto*⟩

fal·si·fy \ˈfȯl-sə-ˌfī\ *vb* **-fied; -fy·ing 1 :** to prove to be false ⟨promises *falsified* by events⟩ **2 :** to make false **:** change so as to deceive ⟨*falsify* financial accounts⟩ **3 a :** to tell lies **:** LIE **b :** MISREPRESENT — **fal·si·fi·ca·tion** \ˌfȯl-sə-fə-ˈkā-shən\ *n* — **fal·si·fi·er** \ˈfȯl-sə-ˌfī-ər, -ˌfīr\ *n*

fal·si·ty \ˈfȯl-sət-ē, -stē\ *n, pl* **-ties 1 :** something false **:** LIE **2 :** the quality or state of being false

[1]fal·ter \ˈfȯl-tər\ *vb* **fal·tered; fal·ter·ing** \ˈfȯl-tə-ring, -tring\ **1 :** to move unsteadily **:** WAVER **2 :** to stumble or hesitate in speech **:** STAMMER ⟨her voice *faltered*⟩ **3 :** to hesitate in purpose or action ⟨courage that never *falters*⟩ [Middle English *falteren*] ***synonyms*** see HESITATE — **fal·ter·er** \-tər-ər\ *n* — **fal·ter·ing·ly** \-tə-ring-lē, -tring-\ *adv*

[2]falter *n* **:** an act or instance of faltering

fame \ˈfām\ *n* **:** the fact or condition of being known to the public **:** RENOWN [Medieval French, from Latin *fama* "report, fame"]

famed \ˈfāmd\ *adj* **:** known widely and well **:** FAMOUS

fa·mil·ial \fə-ˈmil-yəl\ *adj* **:** of, relating to, or characteristic of a family

[1]fa·mil·iar \fə-ˈmil-yər\ *n* **1 :** an intimate associate **:** COMPANION **2 :** a spirit held to attend and serve or guard a person — called also *familiar spirit* **3 :** one that frequents a place

[2]familiar *adj* **1 :** closely acquainted **:** INTIMATE ⟨*familiar* friends⟩ **2 :** INFORMAL 1, CASUAL ⟨spoke in a *familiar* manner⟩ **3 :** overly free and unrestrained **:** FORWARD **4 a :** frequently seen or experienced **b :** of everyday occurrence **5 :** having a good knowledge ⟨*familiar* with the rules of soccer⟩ [Medieval French *familier,* from Latin *familiaris,* from *familia* "family"] — **fa·mil·iar·ly** *adv*

fa·mil·iar·i·ty \fə-ˌmil-ˈyar-ət-e, -ˌmil-e-ˈar-\ *n, pl* **-ties 1 :** close friendship **:** INTIMACY **2 :** lack of formality **:** freedom and ease in personal relations **3 :** close acquaintance with or knowledge of something ⟨acquire a *familiarity* with French⟩ **4 :** an unduly informal or forward act or expression

fa·mil·iar·ize \fə-ˈmil-yə-ˌrīz\ *vt* **1 :** to make well-known ⟨advertising *familiarizes* the name of a product⟩ **2 :** to make thoroughly acquainted **:** ACCUSTOM ⟨*familiarize* oneself with a new job⟩ — **fa·mil·iar·i·za·tion** \-ˌmil-yə-rə-ˈzā-shən\ *n*

fam·i·ly \ˈfam-lē, -ə-lē\ *n, pl* **-lies 1 :** a group of individuals living under one roof and usually under one head **:** HOUSEHOLD **2 :** a group of persons of common ancestry **:** CLAN **3 :** a group of things having common characteristics or properties; *esp* **:** a closely related series of chemical elements or compounds **4 a :** a social group composed of one or two parents and their children **b :** any of various social units different from but regarded as equivalent to the traditional family **5 :** a group of related plants or animals ranking in biological classification above a genus and below an order [Latin *familia* "household (including servants as well as kin of the householder)," from *famulus* "servant"]

family name *n* **:** SURNAME 2

family planning *n* **:** planning intended to determine the number and spacing of one's children through birth control

family tree *n* **1 :** GENEALOGY 1 **2 :** a diagram showing family relationships

fam·ine \ˈfam-ən\ *n* **1 :** an extreme general scarcity of food **2 :** a great shortage [Medieval French, from *feim* "hunger," from Latin *fames*]

fam·ish \ˈfam-ish\ *vb* **1 :** to suffer or cause to suffer from extreme hunger **2 :** to suffer for lack of something necessary ⟨*famished* for news from home⟩ — **fam·ish·ment** \-mənt\ *n*

fa·mous \ˈfā-məs\ *adj* **1 :** widely and favorably known ⟨a *famous* explorer⟩ **2 :** EXCELLENT ⟨*famous* weather for a picnic⟩

synonyms FAMOUS, RENOWNED, CELEBRATED, NOTED, NOTORIOUS mean known far and wide. FAMOUS may imply no more than being widely and favorably known for any reason and any length of time ⟨a *famous* singer⟩. RENOWNED implies glory and praise ⟨heroes *renowned* in song and story⟩. CELEBRATED stresses frequent public notice and mention especially in print ⟨the most *celebrated* actress of all time⟩. NOTED suggests well-deserved public attention ⟨the *noted* mystery writer⟩. NOTORIOUS implies fame for usually questionable acts or qualities ⟨a *notorious* gangster⟩.

fa·mous·ly \ˈfā-məs-lē\ *adv* **:** very well ⟨got along *famously* together⟩

[1]fan \ˈfan\ *n* **1 :** any of various devices for winnowing grain **2 :** a device for producing a current of air: as **a :** a device that consists of material (as paper or silk) often in the shape of a segment of a circle and is waved to and fro by hand **b :** a device with a set of rotating blades driven by a motor **3 :** something shaped like or suggesting a hand fan [Old English *fann,* from Latin *vannus*] — **fan·like** \-ˌlīk\ *adj*

[2]fan *vb* **fanned; fan·ning 1 :** to drive away the chaff from grain by winnowing **2 :** to move or impel air with a fan **3 a :** to direct a current of air upon with a fan **b :** to stir up to activity as if by fanning **:** STIMULATE **4 :** to spread out or move like a fan **5 :** to strike out in baseball **6 :** to fire a gun by squeezing the trigger and striking the hammer to the rear with the free hand — **fan·ner** *n*

[3]fan *n* **1 :** an enthusiastic follower of a sport or entertainment **2 :** an enthusiastic admirer (as of an athlete or movie star) [probably short for *fanatic*]

fa·nat·ic \fə-ˈnat-ik\ *adj* **:** marked or moved by excessive enthusiasm and intense uncritical devotion [Latin *fanaticus* "inspired by a deity, frenzied," from *fanum* "temple"] — **fanatic** *n* — **fa·nat·i·cal** \-i-kəl\ *adj* — **fa·nat·i·cal·ly** \-i-kə-lē, -klē\ *adv* — **fa·nat·i·cism** \-ˈnat-ə-ˌsiz-əm\ *n*

Word History The Latin adjective *fanaticus,* a derivative of the noun *fanum,* "temple," originally meant "of or relating to a temple." It was later used to refer to those pious individuals who were thought to have been inspired by a god or goddess. In time the sense "frantic, frenzied, mad" arose because it was thought that persons behaving in such a manner were possessed by a deity. This was the first meaning of the English word *fanatic.* This sense is now obsolete, but it led to the development of the sense "excessively enthusiastic, especially about religious matters." The word later became less specific, meaning simply "excessively enthusiastic or unreasonable." The noun *fan,* meaning "enthusiast," is probably a shortening of *fanatic.*

fan·ci·er \ˈfan-sē-ər\ *n* **1 :** one with a special liking or interest ⟨a *fancier* of cheese⟩ **2 :** a person who breeds or grows a particular animal or plant especially to meet some standard of excellence ⟨a cat *fancier*⟩

fan·ci·ful \ˈfan-si-fəl\ *adj* **1 :** marked by or showing unrestrained imagination rather than reason and experience ⟨a *fanciful* tale⟩ **2 :** existing in fancy only ⟨a *fanciful* notion⟩ **3 :** marked by or as if by fancy or whim ⟨gave their children *fanciful* names⟩ ⟨a *fanciful* impractical person⟩ — **fan·ci·ful·ly** \-fə-lē, -flē\ *adv* — **fan·ci·ful·ness** \-fəl-nəs\ *n*

[1]fan·cy \ˈfan-sē\ *vt* **fan·cied; fan·cy·ing 1 :** to have a fancy for **:** LIKE **2 :** to form a mental image of **:** IMAGINE **3 :** to believe without evidence

[2]fancy *n, pl* **fancies 1 :** LIKING ⟨take a *fancy* to a person⟩ **2 :** WHIM, NOTION ⟨changed plans at the slightest *fancy*⟩ **3 :** IMAGINATION **4 :** taste or judgment especially in art, literature, or decoration **5 :** enthusiasts over something (as an art or pursuit) **:** FANCIERS [Middle English *fantasie, fantsy* "fantasy, fancy," from Medieval French *fantasie*]

[3]fancy *adj* **fan·ci·er; -est 1 :** based on fancy **:** UNPREDICTABLE **2 a :** not plain **:** SHOWY **b :** of particular excellence **c :** bred primarily for showiness ⟨a *fancy* goldfish⟩ **3 :** executed with technical skill and superior grace ⟨*fancy* footwork⟩ — **fan·ci·ly** \ˈfan-sə-lē\ *adv* — **fan·ci·ness** \-sē-nəs\ *n*

\ə\ **abut**	\au̇\ **out**	\i\ **tip**	\ȯ\ **saw**	\u̇\ **foot**
\ər\ **further**	\ch\ **chin**	\ī\ **life**	\ȯi\ **coin**	\y\ **yet**
\a\ **mat**	\e\ **pet**	\j\ **job**	\th\ **thin**	\yü\ **few**
\ā\ **take**	\ē\ **easy**	\ng\ **sing**	\th\ **this**	\yu̇\ **cure**
\ä\ **cot, cart**	\g\ **go**	\ō\ **bone**	\ü\ **food**	\zh\ **vision**

fan·cy–free \ˈfan-sē-ˈfrē\ *adj* **1 :** not in love **2 :** free to imagine

fan·cy·work \-ˌwərk\ *n* **:** ornamental needlework (as embroidery)

fan·dan·go \fan-ˈdang-gō\ *n, pl* **-gos :** a lively Spanish or Spanish-American dance [Spanish]

fane \ˈfān\ *n* **:** a place of worship [Latin *fanum*]

fan·fare \ˈfan-ˌfaər, -ˌfeər\ *n* **1 :** a short lively sounding of trumpets **2 :** a showy outward display [French]

fang \ˈfang\ *n* **:** a long sharp tooth: as **a :** one by which an animal's prey is seized and held or torn **b :** one of the long hollow or grooved poison-injecting teeth of a venomous snake [Old English] — **fanged** \ˈfangd\ *adj*

fan–jet \ˈfan-ˌjet\ *n* **1 :** a jet engine having a fan that operates in a duct and draws in extra air whose compression and expulsion provide extra thrust **2 :** an airplane powered by a fan-jet engine

fan·light \ˈfan-ˌlīt\ *n* **:** a semicircular window having bars extending from the center that is placed over a door or window

fanlight

fan mail *n* **:** letters sent to a public figure by admirers

fan·ny \ˈfan-ē\ *n, pl* **fannies :** BUTTOCKS

fanny pack *n* **:** a pack for carrying personal articles that straps to the waist

fan·tail \ˈfan-ˌtāl\ *n* **1 :** a fan-shaped tail or end **2 a :** a domestic pigeon having a broad rounded tail **b :** a fancy goldfish with the tail fins double **3 :** an architectural part resembling a fan **4 :** the part of the stern of a ship that overhangs the water

fan–tan \ˈfan-ˌtan\ *n* **1 :** a Chinese gambling game **2 :** a card game in which players play in sequence upon sevens [Chinese (Guangzhou dialect) *fāantāan*]

fan·ta·sia \fan-ˈtā-zhə, ˌfant-ə-ˈzē-ə\ *n* **:** an instrumental composition written without following a particular style [Italian *fantasia,* literally, "fancy"]

fan·ta·size \ˈfant-ə-ˌsīz\ *vb* **:** to create mental images by daydreaming

fan·tas·tic \fan-ˈtas-tik, fən-\ *also* **fan·tas·ti·cal** \-ti-kəl\ *adj* **1 :** produced or seemingly produced by unrestrained imagination ⟨*fantastic* dreams⟩ ⟨a *fantastic* scheme⟩ **2 :** going beyond belief **:** incredible or hardly credible ⟨airplanes now travel at *fantastic* speeds⟩ **3 :** extremely individual or eccentric ⟨*fantastic* behavior⟩ **4 :** GREAT, EXCELLENT ⟨a *fantastic* meal⟩ [Late Latin *phantasticus,* from Greek *phantastikos* "producing mental images," from *phantazein* "to present to the mind"] — **fan·tas·ti·cal·ly** \-ti-kə-lē, -klē\ *adv* — **fan·tas·ti·cal·ness** *n*

synonyms FANTASTIC, BIZARRE, GROTESQUE mean conceived or produced without reference to reality, truth, or common sense. FANTASTIC may imply unrestrained extravagance in invention ⟨a *fantastic* theory⟩ ⟨*fantastic* prices⟩ or merely elaborateness of decorative invention ⟨makes up *fantastic* stories⟩. BIZARRE implies strangeness produced by a strikingly strange combination ⟨*bizarre* architecture of an amusement park⟩. GROTESQUE implies extreme distortion of what is natural or expected with a comic, startling, or sad result ⟨*grotesque* masks⟩ ⟨made *grotesque* attempts at operatic roles⟩.

fan·ta·sy *also* **phan·ta·sy** \ˈfant-ə-sē, -ə-zē\ *n, pl* **-sies 1 :** IMAGINATION 1, FANCY **2 :** something produced by a person's imagination: as **a :** ILLUSION 2 **b :** FANTASIA **c :** fiction set in an unreal world often with superhuman characters and monsters **3 :** a mental image produced to fill a psychological need **:** DAYDREAM [Medieval French *fantasie* "fancy," from Latin *phantasia,* from Greek, "imagination," from *phantazein* "to present to the mind," from *phainein* "to show"]

[1]**far** \ˈfär\ *adv* **far·ther** \-t͟hər\ *or* **fur·ther** \ˈfər-\; **far·thest** *or* **fur·thest** \-t͟həst\ **1 :** at or to a considerable distance in space or time ⟨*far* from home⟩ ⟨*far* in the future⟩ **2 :** to a great extent **:** MUCH ⟨this is *far* better⟩ **3 :** to or at a definite distance, point, or degree ⟨as *far* as I know⟩ **4 :** to an advanced point or extent **:** a long way ⟨a field in which one can go *far*⟩ [Middle English *fer,* from Old English *feorr*] — **by far :** FAR AND AWAY, GREATLY ⟨*by far* our best runner⟩

[2]**far** *adj* **farther** *or* **further; farthest** *or* **furthest 1 :** remote in space or time **2 :** LONG 1 ⟨a *far* journey⟩ **3 :** the more distant of two ⟨on the *far* side of the lake⟩ ***synonyms*** see DISTANT

far·ad \ˈfar-ˌad, -əd\ *n* **:** the unit of capacitance equal to the capacitance of a capacitor between whose plates there appears a potential of one volt when it is charged by one coulomb of electricity [Michael *Faraday*]

far and away *adv* **:** by a great extent or degree ⟨was *far and away* the better team⟩

far and wide *adv* **:** in every direction **:** EVERYWHERE ⟨searched *far and wide*⟩

far·away \ˈfär-ə-ˌwā\ *adj* **1 :** DISTANT 1 ⟨*faraway* lands⟩ **2 :** PREOCCUPIED, DREAMY ⟨a *faraway* look⟩

farce \ˈfärs\ *n* **1 :** a play about ridiculous and absurd situations intended to make people laugh **2 :** humor characteristic of a farce **3 :** a ridiculous action, display, or pretense [Medieval French, "stuffing, farce," from Latin *farcire* "to stuff"] — **far·ci·cal** \ˈfär-si-kəl\ *adj*

far·ceur \fär-ˈsər\ *n* **:** a writer or actor of farce [French]

far cry *n* **1 :** a long distance **2 :** something notably different ⟨her completed project was a *far cry* from what she had envisioned⟩

[1]**fare** \ˈfaər, ˈfeər\ *vi* **1 :** GO, TRAVEL ⟨*fare* forth on a journey⟩ **2 :** to progress toward a goal **:** SUCCEED ⟨how did you *fare*?⟩ **3 :** EAT 2, DINE [Old English *faran*]

[2]**fare** *n* **1 :** range of food **:** DIET ⟨a restaurant that serves American *fare*⟩ **2 a :** the money a person pays to travel on a public conveyance **b :** a person paying a fare

[1]**fare·well** \faər-ˈwel, feər-\ *imperative verb* **:** get along well — used interjectionally to or by one departing

[2]**farewell** *n* **1 :** a wish of welfare at parting **:** GOOD-BYE **2 :** an act of departure **:** LEAVE-TAKING

[3]**fare·well** \ˈfaər-ˈwel, ˈfeər-\ *adj* **:** of or relating to a time or act of leaving **:** FINAL ⟨a *farewell* concert⟩

far–fetched \ˈfär-ˈfecht\ *adj* **:** not easily or naturally thought of **:** IMPROBABLE ⟨some *far-fetched* excuse⟩

far–flung \ˈfär-ˈfləng\ *adj* **:** covering a great area ⟨a *far-flung* empire⟩

fa·ri·na \fə-ˈrē-nə\ *n* **:** a fine meal (as of nuts or a cereal grain) used especially as a breakfast cereal [Latin, "meal, flour," from *far* "spelt"]

far·i·na·ceous \ˌfar-ə-ˈnā-shəs\ *adj* **1 :** having a mealy texture or surface **2 :** containing or rich in starch

[1]**farm** \ˈfärm\ *n* **1 a :** a tract of land devoted to raising crops or livestock **b :** a tract of water used for the cultivation of aquatic animals ⟨oyster *farms*⟩ **2 :** a minor-league baseball team connected with a major-league team to which recruits are assigned for training [Middle English *ferme* "privilege of collecting revenues, lease," from Medieval French, from *fermer* "to make a contract," from Latin *firmare* "to make firm," from *firmus* "firm"]

[2]**farm** *vb* **1 :** to turn over to another usually for an agreed payment — usually used with *out* ⟨*farm out* the electrical work⟩ **2 a :** to devote to agriculture ⟨*farm* 60 acres⟩ **b :** to engage in raising crops or animals — **farm·er** *n*

farm·hand \ˈfärm-ˌhand\ *n* **:** a farm laborer

farm·house \-ˌhau̇s\ *n* **:** a dwelling on a farm

farm·ing \ˈfär-ming\ *n* **:** the occupation or business of a person who farms **:** AGRICULTURE

farm·land \ˈfärm-ˌland\ *n* **:** land used or suitable for farming [Middle English *fermelond* "rented or leased land"]

farm·stead \-ˌsted\ *n* **:** the building and adjacent service areas of a farm

farm·yard \-ˌyärd\ *n* **:** space around or enclosed by farm buildings

faro \ˈfaər-ō, ˈfeər-\ *n, pl* **far·os :** a gambling game in which players bet on cards drawn from a dealing box [probably alteration of earlier *pharaoh*]

far–off \ˈfär-ˈȯf\ *adj* **:** remote in time or space

fa·rouche \fə-ˈrüsh\ *adj* **:** marked by shyness and lack of polish; *also* **:** UNRESTRAINED 1, WILD [French, "wild, shy," from Medieval French *forasche,* from Late Latin *forasticus* "belonging outside," from Latin *foras* "outdoors"]

far–out \ˈfär-ˈau̇t\ *adj* **:** departing considerably from the conventional or traditional ⟨*far-out* clothes⟩

far·ra·go \fə-ˈräg-ō, -ˈrā-gō\ *n, pl* **-goes :** a confused collection **:** MIXTURE [Latin, "mixed fodder, mixture," from *far* "spelt"]

far–reach·ing \ˈfär-ˈrē-ching\ *adj* **:** having a wide range, influence, or effect ⟨a *far-reaching* decision⟩

far·ri·er \'far-ē-ər\ *n* : a blacksmith who shoes horses [Medieval French *ferrour,* derived from Latin *ferrum* iron]

[1]**far·row** \'far-ō\ *vb* : to give birth to pigs [Middle English *farwen,* derived from Old English *fearh* "young pig"]

[2]**farrow** *n* : a litter of pigs

far·see·ing \'fär-'sē-ing\ *adj* : FARSIGHTED 1

Far·si \'fär-sē\ *n* : PERSIAN 2b

far·sight·ed \-'sīt-əd\ *adj* **1 a :** seeing or able to see to a great distance **b :** able to judge how something will work out in the future **2 :** affected with hyperopia — **far·sight·ed·ly** *adv* — **far·sight·ed·ness** *n*

[1]**far·ther** \'fär-t͟hər\ *adv* **1 :** at or to a greater distance or more advanced point **2 :** more completely [Middle English *ferther,* alteration of *further*]

usage *Farther* and *further* have been used more or less interchangeably throughout most of their history, but currently they are showing signs of going in different directions. As adverbs, they continue to be used interchangeably whenever distance in space or time is involved, or when the distance is metaphorical. But when there is no notion of distance, *further* is used ⟨our techniques can be *further* refined⟩. *Further* is also used as a sentence modifier ⟨*further,* the new students were highly motivated⟩, but *farther* is not. A difference is also appearing in their adjective use. *Farther* is taking over the meaning of distance ⟨the *farther* shore⟩ and *further* the meaning of addition ⟨needs no *further* improvement⟩.

[2]**farther** *adj* **1 :** more distant : REMOTER **2 :** [3]FURTHER 2, ADDITIONAL

far·ther·most \-ˌmōst\ *adj* : most distant : FARTHEST

[1]**far·thest** \'fär-t͟həst\ *adj* : most distant in space or time

[2]**farthest** *adv* **1 :** to or at the greatest distance in space or time : REMOTEST **2 :** to the most advanced point **3 :** by the greatest degree or extent : MOST

far·thing \'fär-t͟hing\ *n* : a former British monetary unit equal to ¼ of a penny; *also* : a coin representing this unit [Old English *fēorthung*]

far·thin·gale \'fär-t͟hən-ˌgāl, -t͟hing-\ *n* : a support (as of hoops) worn especially in the 16th century to swell out a skirt [Middle French *verdugale,* from Spanish *verdugado,* from *verdugo* "young shoot of a tree," from *verde* "green," from Latin *viridis*]

fas·ces \'fas-ˌēz\ *n sing or pl* : a bundle of rods surrounding an ax with projecting blade carried in front of ancient Roman magistrates as a badge of authority [Latin, from plural of *fascis* "bundle"]

fasces

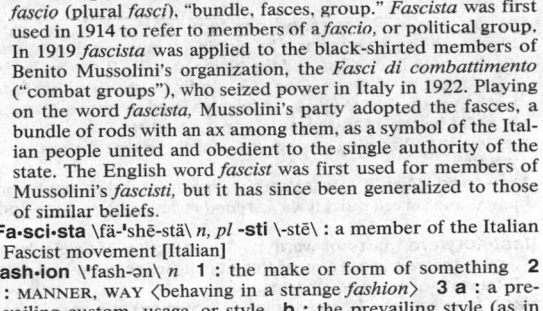

fas·cia \'fash-ə, 'fash-ē-ə, 'fāsh-\ *n, pl* **fas·ci·ae** \-ē-ˌē\ *or* **fas·cias :** a sheet of connective tissue covering or binding together body structures (as muscles) [Latin, "band, bandage"]

fas·ci·cle \'fas-i-kəl\ *n* **1 :** a small slender bundle (as of pine needles) **2 :** one of the divisions of a book published in parts [Latin *fasciculus,* from *fascis* "bundle"] — **fas·ci·cled** \-kəld\ *adj* — **fas·cic·u·lar** \fə-'sik-yə-lər, fa-\ *adj* — **fas·cic·u·late** \-lət\ *adj*

fas·ci·nate \'fas-n-ˌāt\ *vb* **1 :** to grip the attention of especially so as to take away the power to move, act, or think for oneself **2 :** to allure and hold by charming qualities : CAPTIVATE [Latin *fascinare,* from *fascinum* "evil spell"] — **fas·ci·na·tion** \ˌfas-n-'ā-shən\ *n*

fas·ci·nat·ing \'fas-n-ˌāt-ing\ *adj* : extremely interesting or charming — **fas·ci·nat·ing·ly** *adv*

fas·ci·na·tor \'fas-n-ˌāt-ər\ *n* **1 :** one that fascinates **2 :** a crocheted head covering for women

fas·cine \fa-'sēn, fə-\ *n* : a long bundle of sticks of wood bound together and used for such purposes as filling ditches and making short, protective walls [French, from Latin *fascina,* from *fascis* "bundle"]

fas·cism \'fash-ˌiz-əm\ *n, often cap* : a political philosophy, movement, or regime that promotes nation and often race above individual worth and that supports a centralized autocratic government headed by a dictator, severe economic and social regimentation, and forcible suppression of opposition [Italian *fascismo,* from *fascio* "bundle, fasces, group," from Latin *fascis* "bundle" and *fasces* "fasces"] — **fas·cist** \'fash-əst\ *n or adj, often cap* — **fas·cis·tic** \fa-'shis-tik\ *adj, often cap*

Word History The English words *fascism* and *fascist* are borrowings from Italian *fascismo* and *fascista,* derivatives of *fascio* (plural *fasci*), "bundle, fasces, group." *Fascista* was first used in 1914 to refer to members of a *fascio,* or political group. In 1919 *fascista* was applied to the black-shirted members of Benito Mussolini's organization, the *Fasci di combattimento* ("combat groups"), who seized power in Italy in 1922. Playing on the word *fascista,* Mussolini's party adopted the fasces, a bundle of rods with an ax among them, as a symbol of the Italian people united and obedient to the single authority of the state. The English word *fascist* was first used for members of Mussolini's *fascisti,* but it has since been generalized to those of similar beliefs.

Fa·sci·sta \fä-'shē-stä\ *n, pl* **-sti** \-stē\ : a member of the Italian Fascist movement [Italian]

[1]**fash·ion** \'fash-ən\ *n* **1 :** the make or form of something **2 :** MANNER, WAY ⟨behaving in a strange *fashion*⟩ **3 a :** a prevailing custom, usage, or style **b :** the prevailing style (as in dress) during a particular time or among a particular group ⟨*fashions* in women's hats⟩ [Medieval French *façun, fauschoun,* "shape, manner," from Latin *factio* "act of making, faction"] — **after a fashion :** in a rough or approximate way ⟨did the job *after a fashion*⟩

synonyms FASHION, STYLE, MODE, VOGUE mean the usage accepted by those who want to be up-to-date. FASHION may apply to any way of dressing, behaving, writing, or performing that is favored at any one time or place ⟨the current *fashion*⟩. STYLE often implies the fashion approved by the wealthy or socially prominent ⟨a superstar used to traveling in *style*⟩. MODE suggests the fashion among those anxious to appear elegant and sophisticated ⟨muscled bodies are the *mode* at this resort⟩. VOGUE applies to a temporary widespread style ⟨long skirts are back in *vogue*⟩.

[2]**fashion** *vt* **fash·ioned; fash·ion·ing** \'fash-ning, -ə-ning\ : to give shape or form to : MOLD, CONSTRUCT — **fash·ion·er** \'fash-nər, -ə-nər\ *n*

fash·ion·able \'fash-nə-bəl, -ə-nə-\ *adj* **1 :** following the fashion or established style : STYLISH ⟨*fashionable* clothes⟩ **2 :** of or relating to the world of fashion : popular among those who conform to fashion ⟨*fashionable* stores⟩ — **fash·ion·able·ness** *n* — **fash·ion·ably** \-blē\ *adj*

[1]**fast** \'fast\ *adj* **1 a :** firmly fixed or bound **b :** tightly shut **c :** adhering firmly **2 :** firmly loyal ⟨became *fast* friends⟩ **3 a :** characterized by quick motion, operation, or effect: (1) : moving or able to move rapidly : SWIFT (2) : taking a comparatively short time ⟨a *fast* trip⟩ (3) : giving quickness of motion ⟨a *fast* bowler⟩ **b :** favorable to quickness of play or action ⟨the *faster* route⟩ **c** (1) : indicating ahead of the correct time ⟨my watch is *fast*⟩ (2) : according to daylight saving time **d :** contributing to a shortening of photographic exposure time ⟨a *fast* lens⟩ **e :** gotten by or involving shady or dishonest methods ⟨schemes to make a *fast* dollar⟩ ⟨pulled a *fast* one⟩ **4 :** not easily loosened or disturbed ⟨a *fast* hold on her purse⟩ **5 :** not likely to fade ⟨*fast* colors⟩ **6 a :** INTEMPERATE b, WILD ⟨a *fast* crowd⟩ **b :** daringly unconventional especially in sexual matters [Old English *fæst*]

synonyms FAST, RAPID, SWIFT, FLEET mean moving, proceeding, or acting with speed. FAST and RAPID are very close in meaning but FAST applies especially to the thing that moves ⟨a *fast* horse⟩ and RAPID to the movement ⟨a series of *rapid* blows⟩. SWIFT suggests great rapidity together with ease of movement ⟨*swift* play of the imagination⟩. FLEET adds an implication of lightness and nimbleness ⟨*fleet* little ponies⟩.

[2]**fast** *adv* **1 :** in a fast or fixed manner ⟨stuck *fast* in the mud⟩ **2 :** SOUNDLY, DEEPLY ⟨*fast* asleep⟩ **3 a :** in a rapid manner **b :** in quick succession **4 :** in a reckless manner

[3]**fast** *vi* **1 :** to eat no food **2 :** to eat sparingly or avoid some foods [Old English *fæstan*]

[4]**fast** *n* **1 :** the act or practice of fasting **2 :** a time of fasting

fast·back \'fast-ˌbak, 'fas-\ *n* : an automobile roof with a long curving downward slope to the rear; *also* : an automobile with such a roof

fast·ball *n* : a baseball pitch thrown at full speed

\ə\ **abut**	\au̇\ **out**	\i\ **tip**	\ȯ\ **saw**	\u̇\ **foot**
\ər\ **further**	\ch\ **chin**	\ī\ **life**	\ȯi\ **coin**	\y\ **yet**
\a\ **mat**	\e\ **pet**	\j\ **job**	\th\ **thin**	\yü\ **few**
\ā\ **take**	\ē\ **easy**	\ng\ **sing**	\t͟h\ **this**	\yu̇\ **cure**
\ä\ **cot, cart**	\g\ **go**	\ō\ **bone**	\ü\ **food**	\zh\ **vision**

fast break *n* : a quick offensive move toward a goal (as in basketball) in an attempt to score before the defense can get into position

fas·ten \ˈfas-n\ *vb* **fas·tened; fas·ten·ing** \ˈfas-ning, -n-ing\ **1** : to attach or join by or as if by pinning, tying, or nailing ⟨*fasten* clothes on a line⟩ ⟨*fastened* the blame on us⟩ **2** : to make fast : fix securely ⟨*fasten* a door⟩ **3** : to fix or set steadily ⟨*fasten* one's eyes on the view⟩ **4** : to become fixed or joined ⟨*fastened* her seat belt⟩ — **fas·ten·er** \ˈfas-nər, -n-ər\ *n*

fas·ten·ing \ˈfas-ning, -n-ing\ *n* : something that fastens : FASTENER

fast–food \ˈfast-ˌfüd\ *adj* : specializing in food that can be prepared and served quickly ⟨a *fast-food* restaurant⟩ — **fast–food** *n*

1fast–forward \ˌfast-ˈfȯr-wərd\ *n* **1** : a function of an electronic device that advances a recording at a higher than normal speed **2** : a state of rapid advancement

2fast–forward *vb* **1** : to advance (a recording) at a speed that is higher than normal **2** : to proceed rapidly especially in time ⟨*fast-forward* to the future⟩

fas·tid·i·ous \fa-ˈstid-ē-əs\ *adj* : very difficult to please : very particular [Latin *fastidiosus* "disgusted, fastidious," from *fastidium* "disgust"] — **fas·tid·i·ous·ly** *adv* — **fas·tid·i·ous·ness** *n*

fast lane *n* **1** : a traffic lane used by vehicles moving at higher speeds **2** : a way of life marked by a fast pace and the pursuit of immediate gratification **3** : FAST TRACK — **fast–lane** *adj*

fast·ness \ˈfast-nəs, ˈfas-\ *n* **1** : the quality or state of being fast **2** : a fortified or secure place : STRONGHOLD

1fast–track \ˈfast-ˌtrak, ˈfas-\ *adj* : of, relating to, or moving along a fast track

2fast–track *vb* : to speed up the processing or production of in order to meet a goal — **fast–track·er** \-ˌtrak-ər\ *n*

fast track *n* : a course leading to rapid advancement or success

1fat \ˈfat\ *adj* **fat·ter; fat·test 1 a** : PLUMP, FLESHY **b** : OILY 2a, GREASY **2 a** : THICK, BIG **b** : well stocked : ABUNDANT ⟨a *fat* purse⟩ **3** : richly rewarding : PROFITABLE **4** : PRODUCTIVE, FERTILE **5** : being swollen ⟨got a *fat* lip in the fight⟩ [Old English *fǣtt*, from *fǣtan* "to cram"] — **fat·ness** *n*

2fat *vt* **fat·ted; fat·ting** : to make fat : FATTEN

3fat *n* **1** : animal tissue consisting chiefly of cells containing much greasy or oily matter **2 a** : any of numerous compounds of carbon, hydrogen, and oxygen that are esters of glycerol and fatty acids, the chief constituents of plant and animal fat, a major class of energy-rich food, and that are soluble in organic solvents but not in water **b** : a solid or semisolid fat (as lard) as distinguished from an oil **3** : the best or richest part ⟨lived on the *fat* of the land⟩ **4** : the amount beyond what is usual or needed : EXCESS

fa·tal \ˈfāt-l\ *adj* **1** : determining one's fate : FATEFUL ⟨a *fatal* day in our lives⟩ **2** : causing death or ruin ⟨a *fatal* accident⟩ [Latin *fatalis*, from *fatum* "fate"] ***synonyms*** see DEADLY — **fa·tal·ly** \-l-ē\ *adv*

fa·tal·ism \ˈfāt-l-ˌiz-əm\ *n* : the belief that events are determined in advance by powers beyond human control; *also* : the attitude of mind of a person holding this belief — **fa·tal·ist** \-l-əst\ *n* — **fa·tal·is·tic** \ˌfāt-l-ˈis-tik\ *adj* — **fa·tal·is·ti·cal·ly** \-ˈis-ti-kə-lē, -klē\ *adv*

fa·tal·i·ty \fā-ˈtal-ət-ē, fə-\ *n, pl* **-ties 1 a** : the quality or state of causing death : DEADLINESS **b** : the quality or condition of being destined for disaster **2** : FATE 1, DESTINY **3** : a death resulting from a disaster or accident

fat·back \ˈfat-ˌbak\ *n* : a fatty strip from the back of the hog usually cured by salting and drying

fat body *n* : a mass of fatty tissue especially of nearly mature insect larvae that serves as a food reserve

fat cell *n* : one of the fat-laden cells making up adipose tissue

1fate \ˈfāt\ *n* **1** : a power beyond human control that is held to determine what happens : DESTINY ⟨blamed the failure on *fate*⟩ **2** : something that happens as though determined by fate : FORTUNE ⟨it was their *fate* to meet again⟩ **3** : an unavoidable and often unpleasant outcome, condition, or end ⟨awaited news of the *fate* of the polar expedition⟩ **4** : DISASTER; *esp* : DEATH **5** : a final result ⟨determined the *fate* of the research⟩ **6** *pl, cap* : three goddesses of classical mythology who determine the course of human life [Latin *fatum*, literally, "what has been spoken," from *fari* "to speak"]

synonyms FATE, DESTINY, LOT, DOOM mean a predetermined state or end. FATE implies an inevitable and usually adverse outcome or end ⟨the *fate* of the ship is unknown⟩. DESTINY implies something foreordained and usually suggests a great or notable course or end ⟨the country's *destiny* to be a model of liberty⟩. LOT implies a distribution of success or happiness by fate or destiny according to blind chance ⟨was his *lot* to remain childless⟩. DOOM implies a grim or disastrous fate ⟨if caught, his *doom* is certain⟩.

2fate *vt* : DESTINE 1; *also* : DOOM

fate·ful \ˈfāt-fəl\ *adj* **1** : foretelling usually bad things to come : OMINOUS, PROPHETIC ⟨the *fateful* circling of the vultures overhead⟩ **2** : having or marked by serious consequences : IMPORTANT ⟨a *fateful* decision⟩ ⟨that *fateful* day⟩ — **fate·ful·ly** \-fə-lē\ *adv* — **fate·ful·ness** *n*

1fa·ther \ˈfäth-ər, ˈfȧth-\ *n* **1 a** : a male parent **b** *cap* (1) : GOD 1 (2) : the first person of the Christian Trinity **2** : ANCESTOR **3** : one who cares for another as a father might **4** *often cap* : a pre-Scholastic Christian writer accepted by the church as an authoritative witness to its teaching and practice **5** : a person who invents or begins something ⟨the *father* of modern art⟩ **6** : PRIEST — used especially as a title ⟨*Father* Smith⟩ **7** : one of the leading men (as of a city) — usually used in plural [Old English *fæder*] — **fa·ther·hood** \-ˌhu̇d\ *n* — **fa·ther·less** \-ləs\ *adj*

2father *vb* **fa·thered; fa·ther·ing** \ˈfäth-ring, ˈfȧth-, -ə-ring\ **1 a** : BEGET **b** : to be the founder, producer, or author of **2** : to treat or care for someone as a father

fa·ther–in–law \ˈfäth-rən-ˌlȯ, ˈfȧth-, -ə-rən-ˌlȯ, -ərn-ˌlȯ\ *n, pl* **fathers–in–law** \ˈfäth-ər-zən-\ : the father of one's spouse

fa·ther·land \ˈfäth-ər-ˌland, ˈfȧth-\ *n* **1** : the native land of one's ancestors **2** : one's native land

fa·ther·ly \-lē\ *adj* **1** : of or resembling a father ⟨a *fatherly* old man⟩ **2** : showing the affection or concern of a father ⟨*fatherly* advice⟩ — **fa·ther·li·ness** *n*

Father's Day *n* : the 3rd Sunday in June appointed for the honoring of fathers

1fath·om \ˈfath-əm\ *n* : a unit of length equal to 6 feet (about 1.83 meters) that is used especially for measuring the depth of water [Old English *fæthm* "outstretched arms, length of the outstretched arms"]

2fathom *vb* **1** : to measure by a sounding line : take soundings; *also* : PROBE **2** : to come to understand ⟨failed to *fathom* the problem⟩ — **fath·om·able** \ˈfath-ə-mə-bəl\ *adj*

Fa·thom·e·ter \fa-ˈthäm-ət-ər; ˈfath-əm-ˌmēt-, ˈfath-ə-ˌ\ *trademark* — used for a sonic depth finder

fath·om·less \ˈfath-əm-ləs\ *adj* : incapable of being understood

1fa·tigue \fə-ˈtēg\ *n* **1 a** : manual or menial work performed by military personnel **b** *pl* : the uniform or work clothing worn on fatigue and in the field **2 a** : weariness from labor or exertion **b** : temporary loss of power to respond (as of a sense organ) after prolonged stimulation **3** : the tendency of a material (as metal) to break under repeated stress (as bending) [French, from *fatiguer* "to fatigue," from Latin *fatigare*]

2fatigue *vb* **1** : to weary or become weary with labor or exertion ⟨pulling weeds *fatigues* me⟩ **2** : to induce a condition of fatigue in ⟨running *fatigues* my legs⟩

fat·ling \ˈfat-ling\ *n* : a young animal fattened for slaughter

fat·ten \ˈfat-n\ *vb* **fat·tened; fat·ten·ing** \ˈfat-ning, -n-ing\ **1 a** : to make or become fat or fatter ⟨cattle *fattening* on the range⟩ **b** : to make larger ⟨*fatten* profits⟩ **2** : to make (as land) fertile : ENRICH — **fat·ten·er** \ˈfat-nər, -n-ər\ *n*

fat·ty \ˈfat-ē\ *adj* **fat·ti·er; -est 1** : containing fat especially in unusual amounts; *also* : unduly stout **2** : GREASY — **fat·ti·ly** \ˈfat-l-ē\ *adv* — **fat·ti·ness** \ˈfat-ē-nəs\ *n*

fatty acid *n* : any of numerous acids that contain only carbon, hydrogen, and oxygen and that occur naturally in the form of glycerides in fats and various oils

fa·tu·ity \fə-ˈtü-ət-ē, fa-, -ˈtyü-\ *n, pl* **-ities 1** : something stupid or foolish **2** : FOOLISHNESS, STUPIDITY ⟨the *fatuity* of such a remark⟩

fat·u·ous \ˈfach-wəs, -ə-wəs\ *adj* : FOOLISH, SILLY [Latin *fatuus*] — **fat·u·ous·ly** *adv* — **fat·u·ous·ness** *n*

fat·wa \ˈfət-wə, ˈfät-wä\ *n* : a legal opinion or decree handed down by an Islamic religious leader [Arabic *fatwā*]

fau·bourg \fō-ˈbu̇r\ *n* **1** : SUBURB 1; *esp* : a suburb of a French city **2** : a city quarter [Medieval French *fauxbourg*, alteration of earlier *forsbourg, forsborc*, from *fors* "outside" + *borc* "town"]

fau·ces \ˈfȯ-ˌsēz\ *n pl* : the narrow passage between the soft palate and the base of the tongue that joins the mouth to the pharynx [Latin, "throat, fauces"] — **fau·cial** \ˈfȯ-shəl\ *adj*

fau·cet \ˈfȯ-sət, ˈfäs-ət\ *n* : a fixture for controlling the flow of a liquid (as from a pipe) [Medieval French *fausset* "bung"]

[1]**fault** \ˈfȯlt\ *n* **1 a** : a weakness in character : FAILING; *esp* : a moral weakness less serious than a vice **b** : a physical or intellectual imperfection or impairment **c** : an error especially in a service in a racket game (as tennis) **2 a** : a trivial wrongful act **b** : MISTAKE 2 **3** : responsibility for wrongdoing or failure ⟨it's all my *fault*⟩ **4** : a fracture in the earth's crust accompanied by a displacement of rock masses in a direction parallel to the fracture [Medieval French *faute, falte,* derived from Latin *fallere* "to deceive, disappoint"] — **at fault** : deserving of blame : RESPONSIBLE — **to a fault** : to an excessive degree ⟨generous *to a fault*⟩

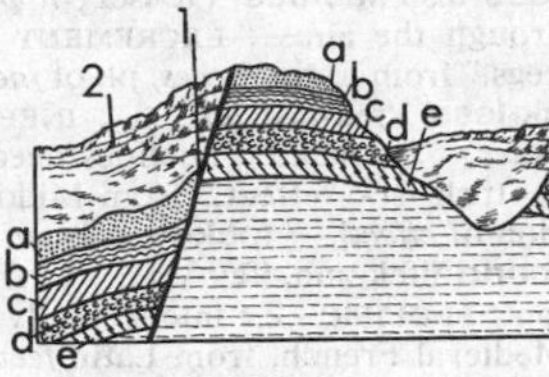

fault 4: *1* fault with displaced strata *a, b, c, d, e;* *2* scarp

synonyms FAULT, FAILING, FOIBLE, FRAILTY mean a weakness or imperfection of character. FAULT applies to any failure, serious or trivial, to attain a standard of perfection in action, disposition, or habit ⟨has many virtues and few *faults*⟩. FAILING suggests a minor shortcoming in character ⟨tardiness is a *failing* of mine⟩. FOIBLE implies a harmless or even endearing weakness ⟨the eccentric's charming *foibles*⟩. FRAILTY implies weakness in the face of temptation ⟨human *frailties*⟩.

[2]**fault** *vb* **1** : to commit a fault : ERR **2** : to fracture so as to produce a geologic fault **3** : to find a fault in ⟨could not *fault* that argument⟩

fault·find·er \ˈfȯlt-ˌfīn-dər\ *n* : a person who is inclined to complain or criticize — **fault·find·ing** \-diŋ\ *n or adj*

fault·less \ˈfȯlt-ləs\ *adj* : free from fault : including no error or imperfection — **fault·less·ly** *adv* — **fault·less·ness** *n*

faulty \ˈfȯl-tē\ *adj* **fault·i·er; -est** : marked by fault or defect : IMPERFECT — **fault·i·ly** \-tə-lē\ *adv* — **fault·i·ness** \-tē-nəs\ *n*

faun \ˈfȯn, ˈfän\ *n* : a figure in Roman mythology dwelling in fields and forests and represented as part goat and part man [Latin *faunus,* from *Faunus,* god of animals]

fau·na \ˈfȯn-ə, ˈfän-\ *n, pl* **faunas** *also* **fau·nae** \-ˌē, -ˌī\ : animals or animal life especially of a region, period, or environment — compare FLORA [New Latin, from Latin *Fauna,* sister of Faunus, god of animals] — **fau·nal** \ˈfȯn-l, ˈfän-\ *adj* — **fau·nal·ly** \-l-ē\ *adv*

fau·vism \ˈfō-ˌviz-əm\ *n, often cap* : a movement in painting typified by the work of Matisse and characterized by vivid colors, free treatment of form, and a resulting vibrant and decorative effect [French *fauvisme,* from *fauve* "wild animal"] — **fau·vist** \-vəst\ *n or adj, often cap*

faux \ˈfō\ *adj* : IMITATION ⟨*faux* marble⟩ [French, "false"]

faux pas \fō-ˈpä\ *n, pl* **faux pas** \-ˈpä, -ˈpäz\ : BLUNDER; *esp* : a social blunder [French, literally, "false step"]

fa·va bean \ˈfäv-ə-\ *n* : BROAD BEAN [Italian *fava,* from Latin *faba* "bean"]

fav·ism \ˈfäv-ˌiz-əm\ *n* : a hereditary condition especially of males of Mediterranean descent that causes a severe allergic reaction to the broad bean or its pollen

[1]**fa·vor** \ˈfā-vər\ *n* **1 a** : friendly regard shown toward another especially by a superior ⟨enjoyed the *favor* of the king⟩ **b** : APPROVAL, APPROBATION ⟨look with *favor* on a project⟩ **c** : PARTIALITY, PREFERENCE ⟨the judge showed *favor* to the defendant⟩ **d** : POPULARITY ⟨a fad loses *favor* quickly⟩ **2** : gracious kindness ⟨treated the child with *favor*⟩; *also* : an act of such kindness ⟨do me a *favor*⟩ **3 a** : a token of love (as a ribbon) usually worn conspicuously **b** : a small gift or decorative item given out at a party **4** : a special privilege or right granted or conceded **5** *archaic* : LETTER **6** : BEHALF, INTEREST [Medieval French, "friendly regard," from Latin, from *favēre* "to be favorable"] — **in favor of 1** : in agreement or sympathy with **2** : in support of — **out of favor** : not now popular : DISLIKED ⟨study seems *out of favor* today⟩

[2]**favor** *vt* **fa·vored; fa·vor·ing** \ˈfāv-riŋ, -ə-riŋ\ **1 a** : to regard or treat with favor **b** (1) : to do a kindness for : OBLIGE (2) : ENDOW ⟨*favored* by nature⟩ **c** : to treat gently or carefully : SPARE ⟨*favor* an injured leg⟩ **2** : PREFER 1 **3 a** : to give support to : SUSTAIN **b** : to offer chances for success to : FACILITATE ⟨darkness *favors* attack⟩ **4** : to bear a resemblance to ⟨children who *favor* their parents⟩ — **fa·vor·er** \ˈfā-vər-ər\ *n*

fa·vor·able \ˈfāv-rə-bəl, -ə-rə-; ˈfā-vər-bəl\ *adj* **1** : showing favor : APPROVING ⟨a *favorable* opinion⟩ **2** : tending to promote or advance something : ADVANTAGEOUS ⟨*favorable* weather for the fair⟩ — **fa·vor·able·ness** *n* — **fa·vor·ably** \-blē\ *adv*

[1]**fa·vor·ite** \ˈfāv-rət, -ə-rət\ *n* **1** : a person or a thing that is favored above others **2** : the contestant regarded as having the best chance to win [Italian *favorito,* past participle of *favorire* "to favor," from *favore* "favor," from Latin *favor*]

[2]**favorite** *adj* : being a favorite ⟨our *favorite* show⟩

favorite son *n* : a candidate supported by the delegates of his state at a presidential nominating convention

fa·vor·it·ism \ˈfāv-rət-ˌiz-əm, -ə-rət-\ *n* : unfairly favorable treatment of one or some while neglecting others : PARTIALITY

[1]**fawn** \ˈfȯn, ˈfän\ *vi* **1** : to show affection — used especially of a dog **2** : to try to win favor by behavior that shows lack of self-respect [Old English *fagnian* "to rejoice," from *fægen* "glad, fain"] — **fawn·er** *n* — **fawn·ing·ly** \-iŋ-lē\ *adv*

[2]**fawn** *n* **1** : a young deer; *esp* : one in its first year **2** : a light grayish brown [Medieval French *feun, foon* "young of an animal," derived from Latin *fetus* "offspring"]

fax \ˈfaks\ *n* **1** : FACSIMILE 2 **2** : a machine used to send or receive facsimile communications **3** : a facsimile communication — **fax** *vb*

[1]**fay** \ˈfā\ *n* : FAIRY, ELF [Medieval French *fee*]

[2]**fay** *adj* : ELFIN 2

faze \ˈfāz\ *vt* : to disturb the composure or courage of : DAUNT ⟨didn't *faze* her⟩ [Old English *fēsian* "to drive away"]

F clef *n* : BASS CLEF

fe·al·ty \ˈfē-əl-tē, ˈfēl-\ *n* **1** : the loyalty of a feudal vassal to his or her lord **2** : ALLEGIANCE 2, LOYALTY [Medieval French *feelté, fealté,* from Latin *fidelitas* "fidelity"] ***synonyms*** see FIDELITY

[1]**fear** \ˈfiər\ *n* **1 a** : an unpleasant often strong emotion caused by expectation or awareness of danger **b** : an instance of fear or a state marked by fear **2** : anxious concern : WORRY **3** : reverential awe especially toward God [Old English *fǣr* "sudden danger"]

synonyms FEAR, DREAD, FRIGHT, PANIC mean a painful emotion experienced in the presence or expectation of danger. FEAR is the general term and implies great anxiety and usually loss of courage ⟨*fear* of the unknown⟩. DREAD adds the idea of intense aversion and reluctance to face something ⟨faced the exam with *dread*⟩. FRIGHT suggests the shock of sudden, startling appearance of danger or threat ⟨*fright* at the sudden banging⟩. PANIC implies completely dominating fear that causes hysterical activity ⟨the news caused widespread *panic*⟩.

[2]**fear** *vb* **1** : to have a reverential awe of ⟨*fear* God⟩ **2** : to be afraid of : have fear **3** : to be worried or anxious ⟨*feared* they would miss the train⟩ — **fear·er** *n*

fear·ful \ˈfiər-fəl\ *adj* **1** : causing fear ⟨the *fearful* roar of a lion⟩ **2** : filled with fear ⟨*fearful* of danger⟩ **3** : showing or caused by fear ⟨a *fearful* glance⟩ **4** : extremely bad, large, or intense ⟨*fearful* cold⟩ — **fear·ful·ly** \-fə-lē\ *adv* — **fear·ful·ness** *n*

fear·less \ˈfiər-ləs\ *adj* : free from fear : BRAVE — **fear·less·ly** *adv* — **fear·less·ness** *n*

fear·some \ˈfiər-səm\ *adj* **1** : causing fear **2** : TIMID — **fear·some·ly** *adv* — **fear·some·ness** *n*

fea·si·ble \ˈfē-zə-bəl\ *adj* **1** : capable of being done or carried out ⟨a *feasible* plan⟩ **2** : capable of being used or dealt with successfully : SUITABLE ⟨a *feasible* new energy source⟩ **3** : REASONABLE, LIKELY ⟨a *feasible* story⟩ [Medieval French *faisable,* from *fais-,* stem of *faire* "to make, do," from Latin *facere*] ***synonyms*** see POSSIBLE — **fea·si·bil·i·ty** \ˌfē-zə-ˈbil-ət-ē\ *n* — **fea·si·ble·ness** \ˈfē-zə-bəl-nəs\ *n* — **fea·si·bly** \-blē\ *adv*

[1]**feast** \ˈfēst\ *n* **1 a** : an elaborate meal : BANQUET **b** : something that gives great enjoyment ⟨a *feast* of wit⟩ **2** : a religious festival : HOLY DAY [Medieval French *feste* "festival," from Latin *festum,* from *festus* "solemn, festal"]

[2]**feast** *vb* **1** : to eat plentifully : participate in a feast **2** : to en-

\ə\ **abut**	\au̇\ **out**	\i\ **tip**	\ȯ\ **saw**	\u̇\ **foot**
\ər\ **further**	\ch\ **chin**	\ī\ **life**	\ȯi\ **coin**	\y\ **yet**
\a\ **mat**	\e\ **pet**	\j\ **job**	\th\ **thin**	\yü\ **few**
\ā\ **take**	\ē\ **easy**	\ŋ\ **sing**	\t͟h\ **this**	\yu̇\ **cure**
\ä\ **cot, cart**	\g\ **go**	\ō\ **bone**	\ü\ **food**	\zh\ **vision**

tertain with rich and plentiful food **3 :** DELIGHT 2 ⟨*feasted* our eyes on the beautiful view⟩ — **feast•er** *n*

[1]**feat** *n* **1 :** ACT 1, DEED **2 a :** a deed notable especially for courage **b :** an act or product of skill, endurance, or cleverness [Medieval French *fait, fet,* from Latin *factum,* from *facere* "to make, do"]

synonyms FEAT, EXPLOIT, ACHIEVEMENT mean a remarkable deed. FEAT implies strength or dexterity or daring in achieving ⟨an acrobatic *feat*⟩. EXPLOIT applies to an adventurous or heroic act that brings fame ⟨his *exploits* as a spy⟩. ACHIEVEMENT implies hard-won success in the face of difficulty or opposition ⟨her *achievements* as a chemist⟩.

[2]**feat** \ˈfēt\ *adj* **1** *archaic* **:** BECOMING, NEAT **2** *archaic* **:** SKILLFUL, DEXTEROUS [Medieval French *fait,* past participle of *faire* "to make, do"]

[1]**feath•er** \ˈfe<u>th</u>-ər\ *n* **1 a :** one of the light horny outgrowths that form the external covering of the body of a bird **b :** the vane of an arrow **2 a :** KIND 1b, SORT ⟨birds of a *feather*⟩ **b :** CLOTHING, DRESS ⟨in full *feather*⟩ **c :** CONDITION 5b, MOOD ⟨in fine *feather*⟩ **d** *pl* **:** COMPOSURE ⟨some *feathers* had been ruffled⟩ **3 :** a feathery tuft or fringe of hair **4 :** a projecting strip, rib, or fin **5 :** the act of feathering an oar [Old English *fether*] — **feath•ered** \-ərd\ *adj* — **feath•er•less** \ˈfe<u>th</u>-ər-ləs\ *adj* — **a feather in one's cap :** a mark of distinction **:** HONOR

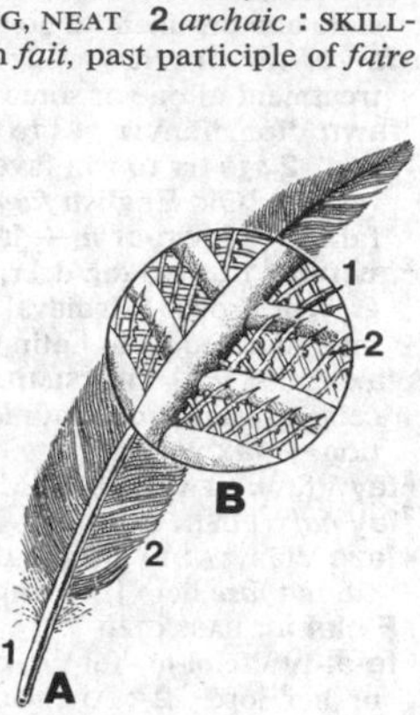

feather 1a: *A: 1* quill, *2* vane; *B: 1* barb, *2* barbule

[2]**feather** *vb* **feath•ered; feath•er•ing** \ˈfe<u>th</u>-ring, -ə-ring\ **1 a :** to furnish (as an arrow) with feathers **b :** to cover, clothe, or adorn with feathers **2 a :** to turn (an oar blade) almost horizontal when lifting from the water at the end of a stroke in order to reduce air resistance **b :** to change the angle of (the blades of an aircraft propeller) in order to decrease wind resistance **3 :** to grow or form feathers **4 :** to move, spread, or grow like feathers — **feather one's nest :** to provide for oneself especially by taking advantage of a position of trust

feath•er bed \ˈfe<u>th</u>-ər-ˌbed\ *n* **:** a mattress filled with feathers; *also* **:** a bed with such a mattress

feath•er•bed•ding \-ˌbed-ing\ *n* **:** the requiring of an employer usually under a union rule or safety statute to employ more workers than are needed or to limit production

feath•er•brain \ˈfe<u>th</u>-ər-ˌbrān\ *n* **:** a foolish scatterbrained person — **feath•er•brained** \ˌfe<u>th</u>-ər-ˈbrānd\ *adj*

feath•er•edge \ˈfe<u>th</u>-ə-ˌrej, ˌfe<u>th</u>-ə-ˈ\ *n* **:** a very thin sharp edge; *esp* **:** one that is easily broken or bent — **featheredge** *vt*

feath•er•weight \-ər-ˌwāt\ *n* **1 :** one that is very light in weight; *esp* **:** a boxer in a weight division having an upper limit of about 126 pounds **2 :** a person of limited intelligence or effectiveness ⟨a political *featherweight*⟩

feath•ery \ˈfe<u>th</u>-re, -ə-rē\ *adj* **:** resembling, suggesting, or covered with feathers; *esp* **:** extremely light

[1]**fea•ture** \ˈfē-chər\ *n* **1 a :** the shape or appearance of the face ⟨stern of *feature*⟩ **b :** a single part of the face (as the nose or the mouth) **2 :** a prominent part or detail **:** CHARACTERISTIC ⟨such earth *features* as mountains⟩ **3 :** a main or outstanding attraction: as **a :** the main movie presented **b :** a special column or section in a newspaper or magazine [Medieval French *feture,* from Latin *factura* "act of making," from *facere* "to make, do"]

[2]**feature** *vb* **fea•tured; fea•tur•ing** \ˈfēch-ring, -ə-ring\ **1 :** to picture in the mind **:** IMAGINE ⟨*feature* wearing such a hat⟩ **2 :** to give special prominence to ⟨*feature* a story in a newspaper⟩ **3 :** to play an important part

fea•ture•less \ˈfē-chər-ləs\ *adj* **:** having no distinctive features

feb•ri•fuge \ˈfeb-rə-ˌfyüj\ *n* **:** ANTIPYRETIC [French *fébrifuge,* derived from Latin *febris* "fever" + *fugare* "to put to flight"] — **febrifuge** *adj*

fe•brile \ˈfeb-ˌrīl *also* ˈfēb-\ *adj* **:** affected with or as if with fever **:** FEVERISH [Medieval Latin *febrilis,* from Latin *febris* "fever"]

Feb•ru•ary \ˈfeb-yə-ˌwer-ē, ˈfeb-ə-, ˈfeb-rə-\ *n* **:** the 2nd month of the year according to the Gregorian calendar [Latin *Februarius,* from *Februa,* a festival held during the month]

fe•ces *also* **fae•ces** \ˈfē-ˌsēz\ *n pl* **:** bodily waste discharged through the anus **:** EXCREMENT [Middle English, "sediment, dregs," from Latin *faeces,* pl. of *faex*] — **fe•cal** \ˈfē-kəl\ *adj*

feck•less \ˈfek-ləs\ *adj* **1 :** INEFFECTUAL, WEAK ⟨a *feckless* leader⟩ **2 :** lacking qualities needed for efficiency or success [Scottish *feck* "effect," from Middle English (Scots) *fek,* alteration of *effect*] — **feck•less•ly** *adv* — **feck•less•ness** *n*

fe•cund \ˈfek-ənd, ˈfēk-\ *adj* **1 :** fruitful in offspring or vegetation **:** PROLIFIC **2 :** intellectually creative to a marked degree [Medieval French, from Latin *fecundus*] ***synonyms*** see FERTILE — **fe•cun•di•ty** \fi-ˈkən-dət-ē\ *n*

fe•cun•date \ˈfek-ən-ˌdāt, ˈfē-kən-\ *vt* **:** FERTILIZE — **fe•cun•da•tion** \ˌfek-ən-ˈdā-shən, ˌfē-kən-\ *n*

fed•er•al \ˈfed-rəl, -ə-rəl\ *adj* **1 a :** formed by an agreement between political units that give up individual sovereignty to a central authority but retain certain limited powers of government **b :** of or being a form of government in which power is distributed between a central authority and constituent territorial units **c :** of or relating to the central government of a federation **2** *cap* **:** supporting the principle of a federal government with strong centralized powers; *esp* **:** FEDERALIST 1 **3** *often cap* **:** of, relating to, or loyal to the federal government or the Union armies of the U.S. in the American Civil War [Latin *foeder-, foedus* "compact, league"] — **fed•er•al•ly** \-ē\ *adv*

Federal *n* **1 :** a supporter of the government of the U.S. in the American Civil War; *esp* **:** a soldier in the federal armies **2 :** a federal agent or officer

federal district *n* **:** a district (as the District of Columbia) set apart as the seat of the central government of a federation

fed•er•al•ism \ˈfed-rə-ˌliz-əm, -ə-rə-\ *n* **1 a** *often cap* **:** the federal principle of organization **b :** support or advocacy of this principle **2** *cap* **:** the principles of the Federalists

fed•er•al•ist \-ləst\ *n* **1 :** an advocate of federalism; *esp, often cap* **:** an advocate of a federal union between the American colonies after the Revolution and of the adoption of the United States Constitution **2** *cap* **:** a member of a major political party in the early years of the United States favoring a strong centralized national government — **federalist** *adj, often cap*

fed•er•al•ize \ˈfed-rə-ˌliz, -ə-rə-\ *vt* **1 :** to unite in or under a federal system **2 :** to bring under the jurisdiction of a federal government — **fed•er•al•i•za•tion** \ˌfed-rə-lə-ˈzā-shən, -ə-rə-\ *n*

Federal Reserve bank *n* **:** a bank of the Federal Reserve System

Federal Reserve System *n* **:** the central banking system of the U.S. consisting of 12 districts with a Federal Reserve bank in the principal commercial city of each district

fed•er•ate \ˈfed-ə-ˌrāt\ *vt* **:** to join in a federation

fed•er•a•tion \ˌfed-ə-ˈrā-shən\ *n* **1 :** a political or societal entity formed by uniting smaller entities: as **a :** a federal government **b :** a union of organizations **2 :** the act of creating or becoming a federation; *esp* **:** the forming of a federal union

fed•er•a•tive \ˈfed-ə-ˌrāt-iv; ˈfed-rət-, -ə-rət-\ *adj* **:** involving or arising from federation ⟨a *federative* republic⟩

fe•do•ra \fi-ˈdōr-ə, -ˈdór-\ *n* **:** a low soft felt hat with the crown creased lengthwise [*Fédora* (1882), drama by V. Sardou]

fed up *adj* **:** utterly worn out and disgusted ⟨*fed up* with their mistakes⟩

fee \ˈfē\ *n* **1 a :** an estate in land held from a feudal lord in return for homage and service paid him **b :** an inherited or inheritable estate in land **2 a :** a fixed charge ⟨an admission *fee*⟩ ⟨license *fees*⟩ **b :** a charge for a professional service ⟨a doctor's *fees*⟩ **c :** GRATUITY, TIP [Medieval French *fé, fief,* of Germanic origin]

fee•ble \ˈfē-bəl\ *adj* **fee•bler** \-bə-lər, -blər\; **-blest** \-bə-ləst, -bləst\ **1 a :** greatly deficient in physical strength ⟨a *feeble* patient⟩ **b :** showing weakness ⟨*feeble* steps⟩ **2 :** not strong or effective (as in quality, character, or mind) **:** INADEQUATE ⟨*feeble* imagery⟩ ⟨a *feeble* attempt⟩ [Medieval French *feble,* from Latin *flebilis* "lamentable, wretched," from *flēre* "to weep"] — **fee•ble•ness** \-bəl-nəs\ *n* — **fee•bly** \-blē\ *adv*

fee•ble•mind•ed \ˌfē-bəl-ˈmīn-dəd\ *adj* **:** lacking normal intelligence **:** mentally deficient — **fee•ble•mind•ed•ly** *adv* — **fee•ble•mind•ed•ness** *n*

[1]**feed** \ˈfēd\ *vb* **fed** \ˈfed\; **feed•ing 1 a :** to give food to **b :** to give as food **c :** to consume food **:** EAT ⟨cattle *feeding* in the barn⟩ **d :** PREY — used with *on, upon,* or *off* ⟨*feeds* on insects⟩ **2 a :** to furnish with something essential to growth, sustenance,

or operation **b :** to become nourished or satisfied as if by food **3 :** to give satisfaction to : GRATIFY ⟨praise only *fed* their vanity⟩ **4 a :** to supply for use or consumption **b :** to supply (a signal) to an electronic circuit **c :** to send (a signal) to a transmitting station for broadcast **5 :** to supply (a performer) with cues and situations that make a role more effective [Old English *fēdan*]

²feed *n* **1 a :** an act of eating **b :** MEAL; *esp* : a large meal **2 a :** food for livestock **b :** the amount given at one feeding **3 a :** material supplied (as to a furnace or machine) **b :** a mechanism by which the action of feeding is carried out **c :** the motion or process of carrying forward the material to be operated on (as in a machine) **d :** the signal fed to a transmitting station ⟨a live video *feed*⟩

feed·back \ˈfēd-ˌbak\ *n* **1 :** the return to the input of a part of the output of a machine, system, or process **2 :** transmission to the original or controlling source of information about an action or process ⟨asked for student *feedback* about course content⟩; *also* : the information so transmitted **3 :** a rumbling, whining, or whistling sound that results from an amplified or broadcast signal that has been returned as input

feed·er \ˈfēd-ər\ *n* **1 :** one that feeds: as **a :** a device or apparatus for supplying food **b :** TRIBUTARY **2 :** one that eats; *esp* : an animal being fattened or suitable for fattening — **feeder** *adj*

feed·lot \ˈfēd-ˌlät\ *n* : a plot of land on which livestock are fattened for market

feed·stuff \-ˌstəf\ *n* : FEED 2a; *also* : any of the nutrients in an animal ration

¹feel \ˈfēl\ *vb* **felt** \ˈfelt\; **feel·ing 1 a :** to perceive as a result of physical contact ⟨*feel* a blow⟩ **b :** to examine or test by touching : HANDLE ⟨*feel* a fabric with one's fingers⟩ **2 a :** EXPERIENCE ⟨*felt* their scorn⟩ **b :** to suffer from ⟨*feel* the heat⟩ **3 :** to discover by trying cautiously — often used with *out* **4 a :** to be aware or aware of ⟨*feel* the joy of victory⟩ **b :** to be conscious of a physical or mental state ⟨*feel* happy⟩ ⟨*feel* sick⟩ **c :** BELIEVE 4, THINK ⟨say what you really *feel*⟩ **5 :** to search for something with the fingers **6 :** to seem especially to the sense of touch ⟨*feels* like wool⟩ **7 :** to have sympathy or pity ⟨I *feel* for you⟩ [Old English *fēlan*] — **feel in one's bones :** to be sure for no evident reason — **feel like :** to have an inclination for ⟨*feel like* a walk?⟩

²feel *n* **1 :** the sense of touch **2 :** SENSATION, FEELING ⟨success brought them a *feel* of power⟩ **3 :** the quality of a thing as learned through touch **4 :** intuitive knowledge or ability ⟨has a *feel* for animals⟩

feel·er \ˈfē-lər\ *n* **1 :** one that feels; *esp* : a movable organ (as an antenna) of an animal that usually functions for touch **2 :** a proposal or remark made to find out the views of other people

feel–good \ˈfēl-ˌgu̇d\ *adj* **1 :** relating to or promoting an often false sense of satisfaction or well-being **2 :** cheerfully sentimental : LIGHTHEARTED ⟨a *feel-good* movie⟩

¹feel·ing \ˈfē-ling\ *n* **1 a :** a sense whose receptors are chiefly in the skin and by which the hardness or softness, hotness or coldness, or heaviness or lightness of things is determined; *esp* : TOUCH 3 **b :** a sensation experienced through this sense **2 a :** a state of mind ⟨a *feeling* of loneliness⟩ **b** *pl* : general emotional condition : SENSIBILITIES ⟨hurt one's *feelings*⟩ **3 a :** OPINION, BELIEF ⟨it's my *feeling* we will win⟩ **b :** unreasoned attitude : SENTIMENT ⟨public *feeling* was aroused by the crime⟩ **4 :** capacity to respond emotionally especially with the higher emotions : SYMPATHY ⟨saw how much *feeling* his mother had⟩ **5 :** the quality of a work of art that conveys the emotion of the artist ⟨sang with *feeling*⟩

synonyms FEELING, EMOTION, SENTIMENT, PASSION mean a subjective response to a person, thing, or situation. FEELING applies to any response or awareness marked by pleasure, pain, attraction, or repulsion; it may suggest the existence of a response without implying anything definite about its nature or intensity ⟨no longer has any *feelings* for it⟩. EMOTION implies a clearly defined feeling and usually greater excitement or agitation ⟨a movie about the *emotions* of youth⟩. SENTIMENT may imply emotion inspired by an idea or belief ⟨argued more from grounds of moral *sentiment* than cold logic⟩. PASSION suggests a very powerful or controlling emotion ⟨revenge became his ruling *passion*⟩.

²feeling *adj* : SENSITIVE 1; *esp* : easily moved emotionally — **feel·ing·ly** \ˈfē-ling-lē\ *adv* — **feel·ing·ness** *n*

feet *plural of* FOOT

feet·first \ˈfēt-ˈfərst\ *adv* : with the feet foremost ⟨jumped into the water *feetfirst*⟩

feign \ˈfān\ *vb* **1 :** to give a false appearance of : FAKE ⟨*feign* illness⟩ **2 :** to assert as if true ⟨*feign* an excuse⟩ [Medieval French *feindre,* from Latin *fingere* "to shape, feign"] ***synonyms*** see ASSUME — **feign·er** *n*

feint \ˈfānt\ *n* : something feigned; *esp* : a mock blow or attack at one point in order to distract attention from the point one really intends to attack [French *feinte,* from *feindre* "to feign"] — **feint** *vi*

feisty \ˈfī-stē\ *adj* **feist·i·er; -est :** having an excited aggressiveness : SCRAPPY

feld·spar \ˈfeld-ˌspär, ˈfel-\ *n* : any of a group of crystalline minerals that consist of silicates of aluminum with either potassium, sodium, calcium, or barium and that are an essential constituent of nearly all crystalline rocks [German *Feldspat,* from *Feld* "field" + *Spat* "spar"]

fe·lic·i·tate \fi-ˈlis-ə-ˌtāt\ *vt* : to offer congratulations to — **fe·lic·i·ta·tion** \-ˌlis-ə-ˈtā-shən\ *n* — **fe·lic·i·ta·tor** \-ˈlis-ə-ˌtāt-ər\ *n*

fe·lic·i·tous \fi-ˈlis-ət-əs\ *adj* **1 :** suitably expressed : APT ⟨*felicitous* wording⟩ **2 :** PLEASANT, DELIGHTFUL ⟨*felicitous* weather⟩ — **fe·lic·i·tous·ly** *adv* — **fe·lic·i·tous·ness** *n*

fe·lic·i·ty \fi-ˈlis-ət-ē\ *n, pl* **-ties 1 :** the quality or state of being happy; *esp* : great happiness **2 :** something that causes happiness **3 a :** a talent for apt expression **b :** an apt expression [Medieval French *felicité,* from Latin *felicitas,* from *felix* "fruitful, happy"]

fe·line \ˈfē-ˌlīn\ *adj* **1 a :** belonging to the family of soft-furred flesh-eating mammals that includes the cats, lions, tigers, leopards, pumas, and lynxes **b :** of or resembling a cat : characteristic of cats **2 a :** SLY 1, TREACHEROUS **b :** STEALTHY 1 [Latin *felinus,* from *felis* "cat"] — **feline** *n*

¹fell \ˈfel\ *n* : ²HIDE, SKIN [Old English]

²fell *vt* **1 a :** to cut, beat, or knock down ⟨*fell* trees for lumber⟩ **b :** KILL 1 **2 :** to sew (a seam) by folding one edge under the other [Old English *fellan*] — **fell·able** \-ə-bəl\ *adj*

³fell *past of* FALL

⁴fell *adj* : FIERCE 1, CRUEL; *also* : DEADLY [Medieval French *fel, felon* "villain, felon"]

fel·lah \ˈfel-ə, fə-ˈlä\ *n, pl* **fel·la·hin** \ˌfel-ə-ˈhēn, fə-ˌlä-ˈhēn\ : a peasant or agricultural laborer in Arab countries (as Egypt or Syria) [Arabic *fallāḥ*]

fel·low \ˈfel-ō\ *n* **1 :** COMRADE 1a, ASSOCIATE **2 a :** an equal in rank, power, or character : PEER **b :** one of a pair : MATE **3 :** a member of an incorporated literary or scientific society **4 a :** a male human being ⟨played cards with the *fellows*⟩ **b :** INDIVIDUAL 2, PERSON ⟨won't give a *fellow* a chance⟩ **c :** BOYFRIEND ⟨on a date with her *fellow*⟩ **5 :** a person granted funds for advanced study [Old English *fēolaga,* from Old Norse *fēlagi,* from *fēlag* "partnership," from *fē* "cattle, money" + *lag* "act of laying"] — **fellow** *adj*

Word History The Old Norse word for a partner, *fēlagi,* means literally "one who puts down property." Such people were those who laid together their property for some common purpose. Old English borrowed *fēlagi* from Old Norse and called a partner a *fēolaga.* This word has come down to us, through several centuries and the development of a number of senses, as modern English *fellow.* Perhaps its most common use today is its very general one, in which it is applied to any boy or man.

fel·low·man \ˌfel-ō-ˈman\ *n* : a human being of similar nature

fel·low·ship \ˈfel-ō-ˌship\ *n* **1 :** the condition of friendly relationship existing among persons **2 :** a community of interest, activity, or feeling **3 :** a group with similar interests **4 a :** the position of a fellow (as of a university) **b :** the funds granted a fellow

fellow traveler *n* : a sympathetic supporter of another's cause; *esp* : a person who sympathizes with and often furthers the ideals and program of an organized group (as the Communist party) without joining it or regularly participating in its activities [translation of Russian *poputchik*]

fel·ly \ˈfel-ē\ *or* **fel·loe** \-ō\ *n, pl* **fellies** *or* **felloes :** the outside rim or a part of the rim of a wheel supported by the spokes [Old English *felg*]

fel·on \ˈfel-ən\ *n* **1** : one who has committed a felony **2** : WHITLOW [Medieval French *felon, fel* "villain, inflammation"]

fel·o·ny \ˈfel-ə-nē\ *n, pl* **-nies** : a serious crime usually punishable by a sentence heavier than that for a misdemeanor — **fe·lo·ni·ous** \fə-ˈlō-nē-əs\ *adj* — **fe·lo·ni·ous·ly** *adv*

[1]felt \ˈfelt\ *n* **1** : an unwoven cloth (as of wool and fur) made by matting the fibers with heat, moisture, and pressure **2** : an article made of felt **3** : a material resembling felt [Old English]

[2]felt *vt* **1** : to make into felt **2** : to cause to adhere and mat together **3** : to cover with felt

[3]felt *past of* FEEL

felt·ing \ˈfel-tiŋ\ *n* **1** : the process by which felt is made **2** : FELT 1

fe·luc·ca \fə-ˈlü-kə, -ˈlək-ə\ *n* : a narrow fast sailing vessel with a triangular sail used in the Mediterranean [Italian *feluca*]

[1]fe·male \ˈfē-ˌmāl\ *n* : a female plant or animal [Middle English *femelle,* from Medieval French, from Medieval Latin *femella,* from Latin, "girl," from *femina* "woman"]

Word History In the 14th century *female* appeared in English with spellings such as *femel, femelle,* and *female.* It is derived from Latin *femella,* "young woman, girl," which is a diminutive of *femina,* "woman." In English the similarity in form and pronunciation between the words *female* and *male* led to the retention only of the spelling *female.* It also gave rise to the popular belief that *female* is derived from or somehow related to male. Apart from the influence on the spelling, however, there is no etymological connection between them.

[2]female *adj* **1 a** : of, relating to, or being the sex that bears young or produces eggs **b** : having only seed-producing flowers : PISTILLATE ⟨a *female* holly⟩ **2 a** : of, relating to, or characteristic of the female sex **b** : made up of females ⟨the *female* population⟩ **3** : designed with a hollow into which a corresponding male part fits ⟨a *female* hose coupling⟩ — **fe·male·ness** *n*

[1]fem·i·nine \ˈfem-ə-nən\ *adj* **1** : of the female sex **2** : characteristic of or belonging to women : WOMANLY **3** : of, relating to, or constituting the class of words that ordinarily includes most of those referring to females ⟨a *feminine* noun⟩ ⟨the *feminine* gender⟩ **4** : having or occurring in an unstressed extra final syllable ⟨*feminine* rhyme⟩ [Medieval French *feminin,* from Latin *femininus,* from *femina* "woman"] — **fem·i·nine·ly** *adv* — **fem·i·nine·ness** *n*

[2]feminine *n* **1** : a word or form of the feminine gender **2** : the feminine gender

fem·i·nin·i·ty \ˌfem-ə-ˈnin-ət-ē\ *n* **1** : the quality or nature of the female sex **2** : EFFEMINACY **3** : female human beings : WOMANKIND

fem·i·nism \ˈfem-ə-ˌniz-əm\ *n* **1** : a theory advocating political, economic, and social equality of the sexes **2** : organized activity on behalf of women's rights and interests — **fem·i·nist** \-nəst\ *n or adj* — **fem·i·nis·tic** \ˌfem-ə-ˈnis-tik\ *adj*

fem·o·ral \ˈfem-rəl, -ə-rəl\ *adj* : of, relating to, or situated in or near the femur or thigh ⟨*femoral* artery⟩

femto- \ˌfem-tō\ *combining form* : one quadrillionth (10^{-15}) part of [Danish or Norwegian *femten* "fifteen"]

fem·to·sec·ond \ˈfem-tə-ˌsek-ənd *also* -ənt\ *n* : one quadrillionth of a second

fe·mur \ˈfē-mər\ *n, pl* **fe·murs** *or* **fem·o·ra** \ˈfem-rə, -ə-rə\ **1** : the long bone of the hind or lower limb extending from the hip to the knee — called also *thighbone* **2** : the segment of an insect's leg that is third from the body [Latin *femor-, femur* "thigh"]

[1]fen \ˈfen\ *n* : low land covered naturally in whole or in part with water [Old English *fenn*]

[2]fen \ˈfən\ *n, pl* **fen** **1** : a monetary unit equal to 1/100 yuan **2** : a coin representing one fen [Chinese (Beijing dialect) *fēn*]

[1]fence \ˈfens\ *n* **1** : a barrier intended to prevent escape or intrusion or to mark a boundary **2** : a person who receives stolen goods or a shop where stolen goods are disposed of [Middle English *fens* "defense," short for *defens*] — **fence·less** \-ləs\ *adj* — **on the fence** : being neutral or undecided

[2]fence *vb* **1 a** : to enclose with a fence **b** : to keep in or out with a fence **2** : to engage in fencing **3** : to sell (stolen property) to a fence — **fenc·er** *n*

fence·row \ˈfens-ˌrō\ *n* : the land occupied by a fence including the uncultivated land on each side

fenc·ing *n* **1** : the art or sport of attack and defense with a sword **2 a** : the fences of a property or region **b** : material used for building fences

fend \ˈfend\ *vb* **1** : to keep or ward off : REPEL **2** : to try to get along without help ⟨*fend* for yourself⟩ [Middle English *fenden,* short for *defenden*]

fend·er \ˈfen-dər\ *n* : a device that protects: as **a** : a cushion hung over the side of a boat to protect it when two boats are together or when alongside a dock **b** : RAILING **c** : a device in front of a locomotive or streetcar to lessen injury to animals or pedestrians in case of collision **d** : a guard over the wheel of a motor vehicle **e** : a screen or a low metal frame before an open fireplace

fe·nes·tra \fi-ˈnes-trə\ *n, pl* **-trae** \-ˌtrē, -ˌtrī\ : a small opening; *esp* : either of two membrane-covered apertures in the bone between the middle and inner ear [Latin, "window"] — **fe·nes·tral** \-trəl\ *adj*

fen·es·tra·tion \ˌfen-əs-ˈtrā-shən\ *n* : the arrangement, proportioning, and design of windows and doors in a building

feng shui \ˈfəŋ-ˈshwē, -ˈshwā\ *n* : a Chinese practice in which a structure or place is chosen or arranged so that it harmonizes with the spiritual forces there [Chinese (Beijing dialect) *fēng-shuǐ,* literally, "wind-water"]

Fe·ni·an \ˈfē-nē-ən\ *n* **1** : one of a legendary band of Irish warriors of the 2nd and 3rd centuries A.D. **2** : a member of a secret 19th century Irish and Irish-American organization dedicated to the overthrow of British rule in Ireland [Irish *fiann* (genitive singular *féinne)* "band of warriors"] — **Fenian** *adj*

fen·nec \ˈfen-ik\ *n* : a small large-eared African fox [Arabic *fanak*]

fen·nel \ˈfen-l\ *n* : a perennial European herb of the carrot family grown for its aromatic seeds and leaves; *also* : its seed [Old English *finugl,* from Latin *feniculum,* from *fenum* "hay"]

fen·ny \ˈfen-ē\ *adj* **1** : characteristic of a fen : BOGGY **2** : peculiar to or found in a fen

fen·u·greek \ˈfen-yə-ˌgrēk\ *n* : a white-flowered Old World legume with aromatic seeds [Medieval French *fenugrec,* from Latin *fenum Graecum,* literally, "Greek hay"]

-fer \fər\ *n combining form* : one that bears ⟨aqui*fer*⟩ [Latin, from *ferre* "to carry, bear"]

fe·ral \ˈfir-əl, ˈfer-\ *adj* **1** : of, relating to, or suggestive of a wild beast : SAVAGE **2** : having escaped from domestication and become wild [Medieval Latin *feralis,* from Latin *fera* "wild animal," from *ferus* "wild"]

fer–de–lance \ˌferd-l-ˈans, -ˈäns\ *n, pl* **fer–de–lance** : a large extremely poisonous pit viper of Central and South America [French, literally, "lance iron"]

fer-de-lance

fe·ria \ˈfir-ē-ə, ˈfer-\ *n* : a weekday of a church calendar on which no feast is celebrated [Medieval Latin, "weekday, fair"] — **fe·ri·al** \-ē-əl\ *adj*

[1]fer·ment \fər-ˈment\ *vb* **1** : to undergo or cause to undergo fermentation **2** : to be or cause to be in a state of unrest or excitement — **fer·ment·able** \-ə-bəl\ *adj* — **fer·ment·er** *n*

[2]fer·ment \ˈfər-ˌment\ *n* **1** : an agent (as an enzyme or a yeast) capable of bringing about fermentation **2 a** : FERMENTATION 1 **b** : a state of intense activity or unrest : AGITATION [Latin *fermentum* "yeast"]

fer·men·ta·tion \ˌfər-mən-ˈtā-shən, -ˌmen-\ *n* **1** : chemical breakdown of an organic substance (as in the souring of milk or the formation of alcohol from sugar) produced by an enzyme and often accompanied by the formation of a gas; *esp* : such an energy-yielding reaction occuring without the aid of free oxygen **2** : FERMENT 2b — **fer·men·ta·tive** \fər-ˈment-ət-iv\ *adj*

fer·mi·on \ˈfer-mē-ˌän, ˈfər-\ *n* : any of various subatomic particles including the electron, proton, and neutron — compare BOSON [Enrico *Fermi* + *-on*]

fer·mi·um \ˈfer-mē-əm, ˈfər-\ *n* : a radioactive metallic element artificially produced (as by bombardment of plutonium with neutrons) — see ELEMENT table [Enrico *Fermi*]

fern \ˈfərn\ *n* : any of a division (Filicophyta) or class (Filicopsida) of flowerless spore-producing vascular plants; *esp* : any of an order (Filicales) resembling seed plants in having root, stem, and leaflike fronds [Old English *fearn*] — **fern·like** \-ˌlīk\ *adj* — **ferny** \ˈfər-nē\ *adj*

fern·ery \ˈfərn-rē, -ə-rē\ *n, pl* **-er·ies** **1** : a place for growing ferns **2** : a collection of growing ferns

fe·ro·cious \fə-ˈrō-shəs\ *adj* **1** : showing or given to extreme fierceness, violence, and brutality **2** : unbearably intense ⟨*ferocious* heat⟩ [Latin *feroc-, ferox*] ***synonyms*** see FIERCE — **fe·ro·cious·ly** *adv* — **fe·ro·cious·ness** *n*

fe·roc·i·ty \fə-ˈräs-ət-ē\ *n, pl* **-ties** : the quality or state of being ferocious

-ferous *adj combining form* : bearing : producing ⟨carboni*ferous*⟩

fer·re·dox·in \ˌfer-ə-ˈdäk-sən\ *n* : an iron-containing plant protein that functions as an electron carrier especially in photosynthesis [Latin *ferrum* "iron" + English *redox* + *-in*]

[1]**fer·ret** \ˈfer-ət\ *n* **1** : a domesticated usually albino, brownish, or silver-gray mammal closely related to the European polecat **2** : BLACK-FOOTED FERRET [Medieval French *furet,* derived from Latin *fur* "thief"]

[2]**ferret** *vb* **1** : to hunt game with ferrets **2 a** : to drive out of a hiding place **b** : to find and bring to light by searching — usually used with *out* — **fer·ret·er** *n*

fer·ric \ˈfer-ik\ *adj* **1** : of, relating to, or containing iron **2** : being or containing iron usually with a valence of three [Latin *ferrum* "iron"]

ferric oxide *n* : the red or black oxide of iron Fe_2O_3 that is found in nature as hematite and as rust, is obtained synthetically, and is used especially as a pigment and for polishing

Fer·ris wheel \ˈfer-əs-\ *n* : an amusement ride consisting of a large upright power-driven wheel carrying seats around its rim [G. W. G. *Ferris,* died 1896, American engineer]

fer·rite \ˈfer-ˌīt\ *n* : any of several magnetic substances consisting of ferric oxide combined with the oxides of one or more other metals

ferro- *combining form* : iron : iron and ⟨*ferro*magnetic⟩ [Latin *ferrum*]

fer·ro·mag·net·ic \ˌfer-ō-mag-ˈnet-ik\ *adj* : of or relating to substances (as iron and nickel) that are easily magnetized

fer·ro·type \ˈfer-ə-ˌtīp\ *vt* : to give a gloss to (a photographic print) by pressing with the face down while wet on a metal plate and allowing to dry

fer·rous \ˈfer-əs\ *adj* **1** : of, relating to, or containing iron **2** : being or containing bivalent iron

ferrous sulfate *n* : a salt $FeSO_4$ that consists of iron, sulfur, and oxygen and is used in making pigments and ink, in treating industrial wastes, and in medicine

fer·ru·gi·nous \fə-ˈrü-jə-nəs, fe-\ *adj* **1** : of, relating to, or containing iron **2** : resembling iron rust in color [Latin *ferruginus,* from *ferrugo* "iron rust," from *ferrum* "iron"]

fer·rule \ˈfer-əl\ *n* : a metal ring or cap placed around the end of a slender shaft of wood (as a cane) or around a tool handle to prevent splitting or to provide a strong well-fitting joint [Middle English *virole,* from Medieval French, from Latin *viriola* "little bracelet," from *viria* "bracelet," of Celtic origin]

[1]**fer·ry** \ˈfer-ē\ *vb* **fer·ried; fer·ry·ing** **1 a** : to carry by boat over a body of water (as a river) **b** : to cross by a ferry **2 a** : to carry (as by aircraft or motor vehicle) from one place to another **b** : to deliver (an airplane) by flying it to its destination [Old English *ferian* "to carry, convey"]

[2]**ferry** *n, pl* **ferries** **1** : a place where persons or things are carried across a body of water in a boat **2** : FERRYBOAT **3** : an organized service and route for flying airplanes — **fer·ry·man** \-mən\ *n*

fer·ry·boat \-ˌbōt\ *n* : a boat used to ferry passengers, vehicles, or goods

fer·tile \ˈfərt-l\ *adj* **1 a** : producing or bearing fruit in great quantities : PRODUCTIVE **b** : producing abundant thoughts and ideas ⟨a *fertile* mind⟩ **2 a** (1) : favorable to plant growth ⟨*fertile* soil⟩ (2) : affording abundant possibilities for development ⟨a *fertile* area for research⟩ **b** : capable of growing or developing ⟨a *fertile* egg⟩ **c** : capable of reproducing or of producing reproductive cells ⟨a *fertile* bull⟩ ⟨*fertile* fungal hyphae⟩ [Latin *fertilis,* from *ferre* "to bear"] — **fer·tile·ly** \-l-lē, -l-ē\ *adv* — **fer·tile·ness** \-l-nəs\ *n* — **fer·til·i·ty** \fər-ˈtil-ət-ē\ *n*

synonyms FERTILE, FRUITFUL, PROLIFIC, FECUND mean producing or capable of producing offspring or fruit. FERTILE implies having the inherent power to reproduce in kind or to assist in reproduction and growth ⟨*fertile* soil⟩. FRUITFUL adds the implication of actually producing desirable and useful results ⟨*fruitful* methods⟩. PROLIFIC stresses the power of multiplying and spreading rapidly ⟨*prolific* rabbits⟩ or of creating freely ⟨a *prolific* writer⟩. FECUND emphasizes abundance or rapidity in bearing fruit or offspring ⟨a *fecund* herd⟩.

fer·til·i·za·tion \ˌfərt-l-ə-ˈzā-shən\ *n* : an act or process of making fertile: as **a** : the application of fertilizer **b** : union of male and female germ cells to form a zygote

fer·til·ize \ˈfərt-l-ˌīz\ *vt* : to make fertile: as **a** : to cause the fertilization of; *also* : to unite with in the process of fertilization ⟨a sperm *fertilizes* an egg⟩ **b** : to apply a fertilizer to ⟨*fertilize* land⟩ — **fer·til·iz·able** \-ˌī-zə-bəl\ *adj*

fer·til·iz·er \-ˌī-zər\ *n* : one that fertilizes; *esp* : a substance (as manure or a chemical mixture) used to make soil more fertile

fer·ule \ˈfer-əl\ *n* : a rod or ruler used in punishing children [Latin *ferula*]

fer·ven·cy \ˈfər-vən-sē\ *n* : FERVOR 2

fer·vent \ˈfər-vənt\ *adj* **1** : very hot : GLOWING **2** : marked by great intensity of feeling : ARDENT [Latin *fervens,* present participle of *fervēre* "to boil, be hot"] ***synonyms*** see IMPASSIONED — **fer·vent·ly** *adv*

fer·vid \ˈfər-vəd\ *adj* : FERVENT [Latin *fervidus,* from *fervēre* "to boil, be hot"] — **fer·vid·ly** *adv* — **fer·vid·ness** *n*

fer·vor \ˈfər-vər\ *n* **1** : intense heat **2** : intensity of feeling or expression [Latin, from *fervēre* "to boil, be hot"] ***synonyms*** see PASSION

fes·cue \ˈfes-kyü\ *n* : any of various tufted perennial grasses [Medieval French *festu* "stalk, straw," derived from Latin *festuca*]

fest \ˌfest\ *n* : a gathering, event, or show having a specified focus ⟨a music *fest*⟩ — often used in combination ⟨gab*fest*⟩ [German *Fest* "celebration," from Latin *festum*]

fes·tal \ˈfest-l\ *adj* : of or relating to a feast or festival : FESTIVE [Latin *festum* "feast, festival"] — **fes·tal·ly** \-l-ē\ *adv*

[1]**fes·ter** \ˈfes-tər\ *n* : a pus-filled sore : PUSTULE [Medieval French *festre,* from Latin *fistula* "pipe, fistula"]

[2]**fester** *vb* **fes·tered; fes·ter·ing** \-tə-riŋ, -triŋ\ **1** : to form pus **2** : PUTREFY, ROT **3** : to grow or cause to grow increasingly more irritating ⟨let her resentment *fester*⟩

fes·ti·val \ˈfes-tə-vəl\ *n* **1** : a time of celebration marked by special observances **2** : a periodic celebration or program of events or entertainment ⟨a music *festival*⟩ — **festival** *adj*

fes·tive \ˈfes-tiv\ *adj* **1** : of, relating to, or suitable for a feast or festival **2** : JOYFUL, MERRY — **fes·tive·ly** *adv* — **fes·tive·ness** *n*

fes·tiv·i·ty \fe-ˈstiv-ət-ē\ *n, pl* **-ties** **1** : FESTIVAL 1 **2** : the quality or state of being festive : GAIETY **3** : festive activity

[1]**fes·toon** \fe-ˈstün\ *n* **1** : a decorative chain or strip hanging between two points **2** : a carved, molded, or painted ornament representing a decorative chain [French *feston,* from Italian *festone,* from *festa* "festival," from Latin *festum*]

festoon 1

[2]**festoon** *vt* **1** : to hang or form festoons on **2** : to shape into festoons **3** : DECORATE, ADORN

fe·ta \ˈfet-ə\ *n* : a white Greek cheese made from sheep's or goat's milk and cured in salt water [Modern Greek *pheta* "slice (of cheese)"]

fe·tal \ˈfēt-l\ *adj* : of, relating to, or being a fetus

fetal alcohol syndrome *n* : a variable group of birth defects including mental retardation and deficient growth that tend to occur in the offspring of women who drink large amounts of alcohol during pregnancy

fetal position *n* : a position (as of a sleeping person) in which the body lies on one side curled up with the arms and legs drawn toward the chest

[1]**fetch** \ˈfech\ *vb* **1** : to go after and bring back ⟨*fetch* a glass of water⟩ **2** : to cause to come ⟨*fetch* tears to one's eyes⟩ **3** : to

\ə\ **abut**	\au̇\ **out**	\i\ **tip**	\ȯ\ **saw**	\u̇\ **foot**
\ər\ **further**	\ch\ **chin**	\ī\ **life**	\ȯi\ **coin**	\y\ **yet**
\a\ **mat**	\e\ **pet**	\j\ **job**	\th\ **thin**	\yü\ **few**
\ā\ **take**	\ē\ **easy**	\ŋ\ **sing**	\t͟h\ **this**	\yu̇\ **cure**
\ä\ **cot, cart**	\g\ **go**	\ō\ **bone**	\ü\ **food**	\zh\ **vision**

bring as a price : sell for **4** : to arrive at [Old English *feccan*] — **fetch·er** *n*

[2]**fetch** *n* : an act or instance of fetching

fetch·ing *adj* : ATTRACTIVE, PLEASING ⟨a *fetching* smile⟩ — **fetch·ing·ly** \-ing-lē\ *adv*

fetch up *vb* **1** : to bring up or out : PRODUCE **2** : to make up (as lost time) **3** : to come to or bring to a stop

[1]**fete** *or* **fête** \ˈfāt, ˈfet\ *n* **1** : FESTIVAL 1 **2** : a lavish entertainment or party [French *fête,* from Medieval French *feste*]

[2]**fete** *or* **fête** *vt* **1** : to honor or commemorate with a fete **2** : to pay high honor to

fet·id \ˈfet-əd\ *adj* : having an offensive smell [Latin *foetidus,* from *foetēre* "stink"] — **fet·id·ly** *adv* — **fet·id·ness** *n*

fet·ish *also* **fet·ich** \ˈfet-ish, ˈfēt-\ *n* **1** : an object (as an idol or image) believed to have supernatural or magical powers **2** : an object of unreasoning devotion or concern ⟨make a *fetish* of secrecy⟩ [French *fétiche,* from Portuguese *feitiço,* from *feitiço* "artificial," from Latin *facticius* "factitious"] — **fet·ish·ism** \-ˌiz-əm\ *n*

fet·lock \ˈfet-ˌläk\ *n* **1** : a projection with a tuft of hair on the back of a horse's leg above the hoof **2** : the tuft of hair growing out of the fetlock [Middle English *fitlok*]

[1]**fet·ter** \ˈfet-ər\ *n* **1** : a chain or shackle for the feet **2** : something that confines : RESTRAINT [Old English *feter*]

[2]**fetter** *vt* **1** : to put fetters on : SHACKLE **2** : to restrain from motion or action : CONFINE ***synonyms*** see HAMPER

fet·tle \ˈfet-l\ *n* : a state of fitness or order : CONDITION ⟨in fine *fettle*⟩ [Middle English *fetlen* "to shape, prepare"]

fe·tus \ˈfēt-əs\ *n* : a young animal while in the body of its mother or in the egg especially in the later stages of development; *esp* : a developing human in the uterus from usually two months after conception to birth — compare EMBRYO 1 [Latin, "act of bearing young, offspring"]

[1]**feud** \ˈfyüd\ *n* : a prolonged quarrel; *esp* : a lasting conflict between families or clans marked by violent attacks undertaken for revenge [Medieval French *feide,* of Germanic origin] — **feud** *vi*

[2]**feud** *n* : FEE 1a [Medieval Latin *feodum, feudum,* of Germanic origin]

feu·dal \ˈfyüd-l\ *adj* **1** : of, relating to, or having the characteristics of a medieval fee **2** : of, relating to, or characteristic of feudalism — **feu·dal·ly** \-l-ē\ *adv*

feu·dal·ism \-ˌiz-əm\ *n* : a system of political organization in medieval Europe in which a vassal gave service to a lord and received protection and land in return; *also* : any of various similar political or social systems — **feu·dal·is·tic** \ˌfyüd-l-ˈis-tik\ *adj*

[1]**feu·da·to·ry** \ˈfyüd-ə-ˌtōr-ē, -ˌtȯr-\ *adj* : owing feudal allegiance

[2]**feudatory** *n, pl* **-ries** **1** : one who holds lands by feudal law or usage **2** : FIEF

fe·ver \ˈfē-vər\ *n* **1 a** : a rise of body temperature above the normal **b** : a disease of which fever is a prominent symptom **2 a** : a state of heightened or intense emotion or activity **b** : CRAZE 1 [Old English *fēfer,* from Latin *febris*] — **fe·vered** \-vərd\ *adj*

fever blister *n* : COLD SORE

fe·ver·few \ˈfē-vər-ˌfyü\ *n* : a perennial European herb related to the daisies [Late Latin *febrifugia,* a plant related to the gentians]

fe·ver·ish \ˈfēv-rish, -ə-rish\ *adj* **1 a** : having a fever **b** : relating to or indicative of fever **c** : tending to cause fever **2** : marked by intense emotion, activity, or instability ⟨*feverish* excitement⟩ — **fe·ver·ish·ly** *adv* — **fe·ver·ish·ness** *n*

[1]**few** \ˈfyü\ *pron, pl in constr* : not many persons or things ⟨*few* were present⟩ ⟨*few* cars on the road⟩ [Old English *fēawa*]

[2]**few** *adj* **1** : consisting of or amounting to a small number ⟨one of the *few* sports I play⟩ **2** : not many but some ⟨caught a *few* fish⟩ — **few·ness** *n*

[3]**few** *n pl* **1** : a small number of units or individuals ⟨a *few* of them⟩ **2** : a special limited number ⟨the select *few*⟩

[1]**few·er** \ˈfyü-ər\ *pron, pl in constr* : a smaller number of persons or things ⟨*fewer* came than were expected⟩

[2]**fewer** *adj, comparative of* FEW

usage The traditional view is that *fewer* applies to matters of number and modifies plural nouns, while *less* applies to matters of degree, value, or amount and modifies collective nouns, mass nouns, or nouns denoting an abstract whole. *Less* has been used to modify plural nouns since the 9th century, and the usage, though criticized, appears to be increasing. *Less* is more likely than *fewer* to modify plural nouns when distances, sums of money, and a few fixed phrases are involved ⟨*less* than 100 miles⟩ ⟨an investment of *less* than $2000⟩ ⟨in 25 words or *less*⟩ and as likely as *fewer* to modify periods of time ⟨in *less* (or *fewer*) than four hours⟩.

fey \ˈfā\ *adj* **1** *chiefly Scottish* : fated to die; *also* : marked by a foreboding of death or calamity **2** : CRAZY 2, MAD **3** : having an unworldly air : ELFIN [Old English *fǣge*]

fez \ˈfez\ *n, pl* **fez·zes** : a brimless flat-crowned hat that usually has a tassel, is made of red felt, and is worn especially by men in eastern Mediterranean countries [French, from *Fez,* Morocco]

fi·an·cé \ˌfē-ˌän-ˈsā, fē-ˈän-ˌsā\ *n* : a man engaged to be married [French, from *fiancer* "to betroth"]

fi·an·cée \ˌfē-ˌän-ˈsā, fē-ˈän-ˌsā\ *n* : a woman engaged to be married [French, feminine of *fiancé*]

fi·as·co \fē-ˈas-kō\ *n, pl* **-coes** : a complete failure [French, from Italian, literally, "bottle"]

fi·at \ˈfē-ət, -ˌat, -ˌät; ˈfī-ət, -ˌat\ *n* : an authoritative often arbitrary order or decree [Latin, "let it be done," from *fieri* "to be done, become"]

[1]**fib** \ˈfib\ *n* : a trivial or harmless lie [perhaps from *fable*]

[2]**fib** *vi* **fibbed; fib·bing** : to tell a fib ***synonyms*** see [3]LIE — **fib·ber** *n*

fi·ber \ˈfī-bər\ *n* **1** : a thread or a structure or object resembling a thread: as **a** : a slender root (as of a grass) **b** : a long tapering thick-walled plant cell especially of vascular tissue **c** (1) : a strand of nerve tissue : AXON, DENDRITE (2) : a muscle cell **d** : a slender and greatly elongated natural or synthetic unit of material (as wool, cotton, glass, or rayon) typically capable of being spun into yarn **e** : mostly indigestible material in food that stimulates the intestine to peristalsis — called also *bulk, roughage* **2** : material made of fibers **3 a** : an element that gives texture or substance **b** : basic toughness : STRENGTH [French *fibre,* from Latin *fibra*]

fi·ber·board \ˈfī-bər-ˌbōrd, -ˌbȯrd\ *n* : a material made by compressing fibers (as of wood) into stiff sheets; *also* : CARDBOARD

fi·ber·fill \ˈfī-bər-ˌfil\ *n* : synthetic fibers used as a filling material (as for pillows)

fi·ber·glass \ˈfī-bər-ˌglas\ *n* : glass in fibrous form used in making various products (as yarn and insulation)

fi·ber–op·tic \ˈfī-bər-ˌäp-tik\ *adj* : of or relating to fiber optics

fiber optics *n* **1** *pl* : thin transparent enclosed fibers of glass or plastic that carry light by internal reflections; *also* : a bundle of such fibers used in an instrument **2** : the technique of the use of fiber optics

Fi·bo·nac·ci number \ˌfē-bə-ˈnäch-ē-, ˌfib-ə-\ *n* : any of the integers in the infinite sequence 1, 1, 2, 3, 5, 8, 13 . . . of which the first two terms are 1 and 1 and each following term is the sum of the two just before it [Leonardo *Fibonacci,* died about 1250, Italian mathematician]

Fibonacci sequence *n* : a mathematical sequence composed of the Fibonacci numbers in order

fibr- *or* **fibro-** *combining form* : fiber : fibrous tissue : fibrous and ⟨*fibroid*⟩ [Latin *fibra*]

fi·bre *chiefly British variant of* FIBER

fi·bril \ˈfīb-rəl, ˈfib-\ *n* : a small filament or fiber (as a root hair) — **fi·bril·lar** \-rə-lər\ *adj*

fi·bril·la·tion \ˌfib-rə-ˈlā-shən, ˌfīb-\ *n* : rapid irregular contractions of muscle fibers of the heart

fi·brin \ˈfī-brən\ *n* : a white insoluble fibrous protein formed in the clotting of blood — **fi·brin·ous** \ˈfib-rə-nəs, ˈfīb-\ *adj*

fi·brin·o·gen \fī-ˈbrin-ə-jən\ *n* : a soluble protein produced in the liver, present especially in blood plasma, and converted into fibrin during clotting of blood

fi·bro·blast \ˈfī-brə-ˌblast\ *n* : a cell giving rise to connective tissue [Greek *blastos* "bud, shoot"] — **fi·bro·blas·tic** \ˌfī-brə-ˈblas-tik\ *adj*

fi·broid \ˈfī-ˌbrȯid\ *adj* : resembling, forming, or consisting of fibrous tissue ⟨*fibroid* tumors⟩

fi·bro·my·al·gia \ˌfī-brō-ˌmī-ˈal-jē-ə\ *n* : a disorder characterized especially by pain, tenderness, and stiffness of the muscles and associated connective tissue [*fibr-* + *myalgia* "muscle pain," from *my-* + *-algia*]

fi·bro·sis \fī-ˈbrō-səs\ *n* : an abnormal condition in which increased amounts of fibrous tissue form in other tissues — **fi·brot·ic** \-ˈbrät-ik\ *adj*

fi·brous \ˈfī-brəs\ *adj* **1** : containing, consisting of, or resembling fibers **2** : TOUGH 1, STRINGY

fibrous root *n* : one of many slender roots (as in most grasses) branching directly from the base of the stem of a plant — compare TAPROOT

fibrous tissue *n* : a connective tissue rich in fibers that forms in and supports body structures and is prominent in healing wounds

fi·bro·vas·cu·lar bundle \ˌfī-brō-ˈvas-kyə-lər-\ *n* : VASCULAR BUNDLE

fib·u·la \ˈfib-yə-lə\ *n, pl* **-lae** \-ˌlē, -ˌlī\ *or* **-las** : the outer and usually the smaller of the two bones between the knee and ankle of the hind or lower limb [Latin, "clasp, brace"] — **fib·u·lar** \-lər\ *adj*

-fic \fik\ *adj suffix* : making : causing ⟨sudori*fic*⟩ [Latin *-ficus*, from *facere* "to make, do"]

-fication \fə-ˈkā-shən\ *n suffix* : making : production ⟨syllabi*fication*⟩ [Latin *-fication-, -ficatio*, from *-ficare* "-fy"]

fichu \ˈfish-ü\ *n* : a woman's light triangular scarf draped over the shoulders and fastened in front [French]

fick·le \ˈfik-əl\ *adj* : not firm or stable in attitude or character : INCONSTANT ⟨*fickle* friends⟩ [Old English *ficol* "deceitful"] — **fick·le·ness** *n* — **fick·ly** \ˈfik-lē, ˈfik-ə-lē\ *adv*

fic·tion \ˈfik-shən\ *n* **1** : something told or written that is not fact : something made up **2** : a made-up story; *also* : such stories as a category of literature [Medieval French, from Latin *fictio* "act of fashioning, fiction," from *fingere* "to shape, fashion, feign"] — **fic·tion·al** \ˈfik-shnəl, -shən-l\ *adj* — **fic·tion·al·ly** \-ē\ *adv*

synonyms FICTION, FIGMENT, FABRICATION mean something that is an invention of the human mind. FICTION implies imaginative creation of events, characters, or circumstances with or more often without intent to deceive ⟨King Arthur belongs to *fiction* rather than to history⟩. FIGMENT suggests a creation of the imagination that deceives its own creator ⟨this *figment* of a fevered brain⟩. FABRICATION implies something deliberately made up to deceive or mislead ⟨their story of being robbed was pure *fabrication*⟩.

fic·tion·al·ize \ˈfik-shnəl-ˌīz, -shən-l-\ *vt* : to make into fiction ⟨*fictionalize* a war diary⟩ — **fic·tion·al·i·za·tion** \ˌfik-shnəl-ə-ˈzā-shən, -shən-l-\ *n*

fic·tion·ize \ˈfik-shə-ˌnīz\ *vt* : FICTIONALIZE — **fic·tion·i·za·tion** \ˌfik-shə-nə-ˈzā-shən\ *n*

fic·ti·tious \fik-ˈtish-əs\ *adj* **1** : of, relating to, or suggestive of fiction : IMAGINARY ⟨*fictitious* stories⟩ **2** : not genuinely felt or expressed : SIMULATED [Latin *ficticius* "artificial, feigned," from *fingere* "to feign"] — **fic·ti·tious·ly** *adv* — **fic·ti·tious·ness** *n*

fic·tive \ˈfik-tiv\ *adj* **1** : not genuine : FAKE **2** : of , relating to, or capable of imaginative creation **3** : of, relating to, or having the characteristics of fiction : FICTIONAL

fid \ˈfid\ *n* : a pin usually of hard wood that tapers to a point and is used in opening the strands of a rope [origin unknown]

[1]fid·dle \ˈfid-l\ *n* : VIOLIN [Middle English *fithele*]

[2]fiddle *vb* **fid·dled; fid·dling** \ˈfid-ling, -l-ing\ **1** : to play on a fiddle **2 a** : to move the hands or fingers restlessly **b** : to spend time in aimless activity : PUTTER **c** : TAMPER 2, MEDDLE — usually used with *with* — **fid·dler** \ˈfid-lər, -l-ər\ *n*

fid·dle·head \ˈfid-l-ˌhed\ *n* : one of the young coiled fronds of some ferns that are often eaten as greens

fiddler crab *n* : any of various burrowing crabs with one claw much larger than the other in the male

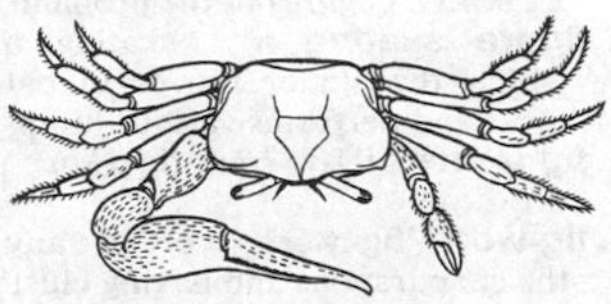
fiddler crab

fid·dle·stick \ˈfid-l-ˌstik\ *n* **1** : a violin bow **2** *pl* : NONSENSE — used as an interjection

fi·del·i·ty \fə-ˈdel-ət-ē, fī-\ *n, pl* **-ties** **1 a** : the quality or state of being faithful **b** : accuracy in details : EXACTNESS **2** : the degree to which an electronic device (as a radio or phonograph) accurately reproduces its effect (as sound) [Medieval French *fidelité*, from Latin *fidelitas*, from *fidelis* "faithful," from *fides* "faith"]

synonyms FIDELITY, ALLEGIANCE, FEALTY, LOYALTY mean faithfulness to something to which one is bound by promise or duty. FIDELITY implies strict and continuous faithfulness to an obligation, trust, or duty ⟨marital *fidelity*⟩. ALLEGIANCE implies the formal obedient adherence of a subject to a sovereign or a citizen to a state ⟨pledging *allegiance*⟩. FEALTY implies a fidelity acknowledged by the individual and as compelling as a sworn vow ⟨*fealty* to the truth⟩. LOYALTY implies a faithfulness that is steadfast in the face of any temptation to renounce, desert, or betray ⟨valued the *loyalty* of her friends⟩.

[1]fidg·et \ˈfij-ət\ *n* **1** *pl* : uneasiness or restlessness as shown by nervous movements **2** : one that fidgets [Scots *fidge* "to fidget"] — **fidg·ety** \-ət-ē\ *adj*

[2]fidget *vb* : to move or cause to move or act nervously or restlessly

[1]fi·du·cia·ry \fə-ˈdü-shē-ˌer-ē, fī-, -ˈdyü-, -shə-rē\ *n, pl* **-ries** **1** : one that acts as a trustee for another **2** : one that acts in a confidential capacity

[2]fiduciary *adj* **1** : involving a confidence or trust ⟨employed in a *fiduciary* capacity⟩ **2** : held or holding in trust for another ⟨*fiduciary* accounts⟩ [Latin *fiduciarius*, from *fiducia* "confidence, trust," from *fidere* "to trust"]

fie \ˈfī\ *interj* — used to express mild disapproval or disgust [Medieval French *fi*]

fief \ˈfēf\ *n* : a feudal estate : FEE [French, from Medieval French *fief, fé*, of Germanic origin]

[1]field \ˈfēld\ *n* **1 a** : an open land area free of woods and buildings **b** : an area of cleared land used especially for cultivating a crop **c** : a piece of land put to a special use or yielding a special product ⟨an athletic *field*⟩ ⟨a gas *field*⟩ **d** : a place where a battle is fought : the region in which military operations are carried on **e** : an open space or expanse ⟨a *field* of ice⟩ **2 a** : a sphere or range of activity or influence ⟨the *field* of science⟩ **b** : the area of practical activity outside a laboratory, office, or factory ⟨geologists working in the *field*⟩ **3** : a background on which something is drawn, painted, or mounted ⟨painted white stars on a blue *field*⟩ **4** : the individuals that make up all or part of a contest **5** : a region or space in which a given effect (as gravity, electricity, or magnetism) exists **6** : the area visible through the lens of an optical instrument [Old English *feld*]

[2]field *vb* **1 a** : to catch or pick up (as a batted ball) and usually throw to a teammate ⟨*field* a ground ball⟩ **b** : to take care of or respond to (as a telephone call) **c** : to give an impromptu answer or solution to ⟨*fielding* reporters' questions⟩ **2** : to put into the field ⟨*field* an army⟩ ⟨*field* a team⟩

[3]field *adj* : of or relating to a field: as **a** : growing or living in open country ⟨*field* flowers⟩ **b** : made, conducted, used, or operating in the field ⟨*field* notes⟩

field artillery *n* : artillery other than antiaircraft artillery used with armies in the field

field corn *n* : a corn with starchy kernels grown for feeding livestock or for market grain

field day *n* **1** : a day devoted to outdoor sports and athletic competition **2** : a time of unusual pleasure or unexpected opportunity ⟨the newspaper had a *field day* with the scandal⟩

field·er \ˈfēl-dər\ *n* : one that fields; *esp* : a baseball player stationed in the outfield

field event *n* : an event in a track meet other than a race

field glasses *n pl* : a hand-held magnifying instrument consisting of two telescopes, a focusing device, and no prisms

field goal *n* **1** : a score of three points in football made by drop-kicking or place-kicking the ball over the crossbar from ordinary play **2** : a goal in basketball made while the ball is in play

field guide *n* : a manual with descriptions and pictures for identifying plants, animals, or natural objects (as rocks) found in nature

field hockey *n* : a game played on a field between two teams of 11 players whose object is to knock a ball into the opponent's goal with a curved stick

field magnet *n* : a magnet for producing and maintaining a magnetic field especially in a generator or electric motor

field marshal *n* : an officer (as in the British army) of the highest rank

field mouse *n* : any of various mice that inhabit fields

field of view : [1]FIELD 6

field of vision : VISUAL FIELD

\ə\ **abut**	\aù\ **out**	\i\ **tip**	\ò\ **saw**	\ù\ **foot**
\ər\ **further**	\ch\ **chin**	\ī\ **life**	\òi\ **coin**	\y\ **yet**
\a\ **mat**	\e\ **pet**	\j\ **job**	\th\ **thin**	\yü\ **few**
\ā\ **take**	\ē\ **easy**	\ng\ **sing**	\t͟h\ **this**	\yù\ **cure**
\ä\ **cot, cart**	\g\ **go**	\ō\ **bone**	\ü\ **food**	\zh\ **vision**

field pea *n* **1 :** a small-seeded pea grown for forage, food, or green manure; *also* **:** its green or yellow seed **2 :** COWPEA

field piece \ˈfēld-ˌpēs\ *n* **:** a gun or howitzer for use in the field

field•stone \ˈfēld-ˌstōn\ *n* **:** stone used in building in usually unchanged form as taken from nature

field trial *n* **1 :** a trial of sporting dogs in actual performance **2 :** a trial of a new product in actual situations for which it was designed

field trip *n* **:** a visit (as to a factory, farm, or museum) made by students and usually a teacher for purposes of firsthand observation

fiend \ˈfēnd\ *n* **1 a :** DEVIL 1 **b :** DEMON 1a **2 :** an extremely wicked or cruel person **3 a :** a person excessively devoted to a pursuit **:** FANATIC ⟨a golf *fiend*⟩ **b :** a person who uses very large quantities of something **:** ADDICT ⟨a dope *fiend*⟩ [Old English *fiend*]

fiend•ish \ˈfēn-dish\ *adj* **:** extremely cruel or wicked **:** DIABOLICAL — **fiend•ish•ly** *adv* — **fiend•ish•ness** *n*

fierce \ˈfiərs\ *adj* **1 a :** violently hostile or aggressive in temperament **b :** given to fighting or killing **:** PUGNACIOUS **2 :** marked by unrestrained zeal or vehemence **:** INTENSE **3 :** furiously active or determined **4 :** wild or menacing in appearance [Medieval French *fiers,* from Latin *ferus* "wild, savage"] — **fierce•ly** *adv* — **fierce•ness** *n*

synonyms FIERCE, FEROCIOUS mean showing fury or malice in looks or actions. FIERCE implies inspiring fear because of a wild and menacing aspect or display of fury in attack ⟨*fierce* mountain tribes⟩. FEROCIOUS implies extreme fierceness and unrestrained violence and brutality ⟨a *ferocious* predator⟩.

fi•ery \ˈfī-rē, -ə-rē\ *adj* **fi•eri•er; -est 1 a :** consisting of fire **b :** BURNING, BLAZING ⟨a *fiery* furnace⟩ **c :** FLAMMABLE ⟨a *fiery* vapor⟩ **2 a :** hot like fire **b** (1) **:** INFLAMED ⟨a *fiery* sore⟩ (2) **:** feverish and flushed ⟨a *fiery* forehead⟩ **3 :** of the color of fire **:** RED **4 a :** full of emotion or spirit **b :** easily provoked **:** IRRITABLE ⟨a *fiery* temper⟩ — **fi•eri•ness** *n*

fi•es•ta \fē-ˈes-tə\ *n* **:** FESTIVAL; *esp* **:** a saint's day celebrated in Spain and Latin America with processions and dances [Spanish, from Latin *festa,* pl. of *festum*]

fife \ˈfīf\ *n* **:** a small shrill musical instrument resembling a flute [German *Pfeife* "pipe, fife"]

fif•teen \fif-ˈtēn, ˈfif-\ *n* **1** — see NUMBER table **2 :** the 1st point scored by a side in a game of tennis — called also *five* [Old English *fiftēne*] — **fifteen** *adj or pron* — **fif•teenth** \-ˈtēnth, -ˈtēntth\ *adj or n*

fifth \ˈfifth, ˈfiftth\ *n, pl* **fifths** \ˈfifths, ˈfiftths, ˈfifts, ˈfifs\ **1** — see NUMBER table **2 a :** the musical interval embracing five diatonic degrees **b :** a tone at this interval **c :** the harmonic combination of two tones at this interval **3 :** a unit of measure for liquor equal to one fifth of a U.S. gallon (about .757 liter) **4** *cap* **:** the right given by the Fifth Amendment to the U.S. Constitution to refuse to testify against oneself ⟨took the *Fifth* in court⟩ — **fifth** *adj or adv* — **fifth•ly** *adv*

fifth column *n* **:** a group of secret sympathizers or supporters of a nation's enemy that engage in espionage or sabotage within the country [name applied to rebel sympathizers in Madrid in 1936 when four rebel columns were advancing on the city] — **fifth columnist** *n*

fifth wheel *n* **:** one that is unnecessary or superfluous

fif•ty \ˈfif-tē\ *n, pl* **fifties** — see NUMBER table [Old English *fiftig*] — **fifty** *adj or pron* — **fif•ti•eth** \-tē-əth\ *adj or n*

fif•ty–fif•ty \ˌfif-tē-ˈfif-tē\ *adj* **1 :** shared equally ⟨a *fifty-fifty* proposition⟩ **2 :** half favorable and half unfavorable ⟨a *fifty-fifty* chance⟩ — **fifty–fifty** *adv*

fig \ˈfig\ *n* **1 :** the usually edible oblong or pear-shaped fruit of a tree of the mulberry family; *also* **:** a tree bearing figs **2 :** TRIFLE 1 [Medieval French *fige, figue,* derived from Latin *ficus* "fig tree, fig"]

[1]fight \ˈfīt\ *vb* **fought** \ˈfȯt\; **fight•ing 1 a :** to contend against another in battle or physical combat **b :** to engage in boxing **:** BOX **2 :** to try hard **3 a :** to act in opposition **:** STRUGGLE ⟨*fight* for the right⟩ **b :** to attempt to prevent the success or effectiveness of ⟨*fight* off a cold⟩ **4 :** to carry on **:** WAGE ⟨*fight* a war⟩ **5 :** to gain by struggle ⟨*fought* our way through⟩ [Old English *feohtan*]

[2]fight *n* **1 a :** a hostile encounter **:** BATTLE **b :** a boxing match **c :** a verbal disagreement **2 :** a struggle for a goal or an objective **3 :** strength or disposition for fighting ⟨full of *fight*⟩

fight•er \ˈfīt-ər\ *n* **:** one that fights: **a :** SOLDIER 1, WARRIOR **b :** [1]BOXER **c :** an airplane of high speed and maneuverability with weapons for destroying enemy aircraft

fight–or–flight *adj* **:** relating to, being, or causing physiological changes in the body (as an increase in heart rate) in response to stress ⟨a *fight-or-flight* reaction⟩

fig•ment \ˈfig-mənt\ *n* **:** something imagined or made up ⟨a *figment* of a fevered imagination⟩ [Latin *figmentum,* from *fingere* "to shape, feign"] ***synonyms*** see FICTION

fig•u•ra•tion \ˌfig-yə-ˈrā-shən, ˌfig-ə-ˈ\ *n* **1 :** OUTLINE 1, FORM **2 :** an act or instance of representation in figures and shapes

fig•u•ra•tive \ˈfig-yə-rət-iv, ˈfig-ə-; ˈfig-yərt-iv, -ərt-\ *adj* **1 :** representing by a figure **:** EMBLEMATIC **2 a :** expressing one thing in terms normally denoting another **:** METAPHORICAL **b :** characterized by figures of speech — **fig•u•ra•tive•ly** *adv* — **fig•u•ra•tive•ness** *n*

[1]fig•ure \ˈfig-yər, *especially British* ˈfig-ər\ *n* **1 a :** a number symbol **:** NUMERAL **b** *pl* **:** ARITHMETIC 2 **c :** a written or printed character (as a letter or number) **d :** value especially as expressed in numbers **:** PRICE **2 a :** the shape or outline of something **b :** bodily shape especially of a person **c :** an object noticeable only as a shape ⟨*figures* moving in the dusk⟩ **3 a :** the graphic representation of a form especially of a person **b :** a diagram or pictorial illustration of a text **c :** a combination of points, lines, or surfaces in geometry ⟨a circle is a closed plane *figure*⟩ **4 :** FIGURE OF SPEECH **5 :** an often repetitive pattern or design ⟨a polka-dot *figure*⟩ **6 :** impression produced ⟨the couple cut quite a *figure*⟩ **7 a :** a series of movements in a dance **b :** an outline representation of a form traced by a series of movements (as with skates on ice) **8 :** a prominent personality **:** PERSONAGE [Medieval French, from Latin *figura,* from *fingere* "to shape, feign"] ***synonyms*** see FORM

[2]figure *vb* **1 :** to represent by or as if by a figure or outline **:** PORTRAY **2 :** to decorate with a pattern **3 :** to indicate or represent by numerals **4 a :** CONCLUDE, DECIDE ⟨*figured* there was no use⟩ **b :** REGARD, CONSIDER ⟨*figure* oneself a good candidate⟩ **5 :** to be or appear important or conspicuous ⟨*figure* in the news⟩ **6 :** COMPUTE, CALCULATE **7 :** to seem rational, normal, or expected ⟨that *figures*⟩ — **fig•ur•er** \-yər-ər, -ər-ər\ *n* — **figure on 1 :** to take into consideration **2 :** to rely on **3 :** PLAN 2 ⟨I *figure on* going into town⟩

fig•ured *adj* **1 :** being represented **:** PORTRAYED **2 :** adorned with, formed into, or marked with a figure **3 :** indicated by figures

figure eight *n* **:** something (as a skating figure) resembling the Arabic numeral 8 in shape

fig•ure•head \ˈfig-yər-ˌhed, -ər-\ *n* **1 :** a figure, statue, or bust on the bow of a ship **2 :** a head or chief in name only

figurehead 1

figure of speech : a form of expression (as a simile or metaphor) in which words are intentionally used in other than a plain or literal way so as to produce fresh, vivid, or poetic effects

figure out *vt* **1 :** FIND, OUT, DISCOVER ⟨*figured out* a way to do it⟩ **2 :** SOLVE ⟨*figure out* the problem⟩

figure skating *n* **:** skating in which the skater moves in patterns and performs various jumps and turns

fig•u•rine \ˌfig-yə-ˈrēn, fig-ə-\ *n* **:** a small carved or molded figure

fig•wort \ˈfig-ˌwərt, -ˌwȯrt\ *n* **:** any of a genus of herbs related to the snapdragons and having clusters of small flowers

fil•a•ment \ˈfil-ə-mənt\ *n* **:** a single thread or a thin flexible threadlike object, process, or appendage: as **a :** a wire (as in an electric lamp) made incandescent by the passage of an electric current; *esp* **:** a cathode in the form of a metal wire in an electron tube **b :** a long chain of cells (as of some bacteria or algae) **c :** the anther-bearing stalk of a stamen [Middle French, from Medieval Latin *filamentum,* from Late Latin *filare* "to spin," from Latin *filum* "thread"] — **fil•a•men•tous** \ˌfil-ə-ˈment-əs\ *adj*

fi•lar•ia \fə-ˈlar-ē-ə, -ˈler-\ *n, pl* **-i•ae** \-ē-ˌē, -ē-ˌī\ **:** any of numerous slender threadlike nematodes that as adults are parasites in the blood or tissues of mammals and as larvae usually develop in biting insects [derived from Latin *filum* "thread"] — **fi•lar•i•al** \-ē-əl\ *adj*

fil·a·ri·a·sis \ˌfil-ə-ˈrī-ə-səs\ *n, pl* **-a·ses** \-ˌsēz\ **:** infestation with or disease caused by filariae

fil·bert \ˈfil-bərt\ *n* **1 :** either of two hazels of Europe and Asia **2 :** the sweet thick-shelled nut of a filbert; *also* **:** HAZELNUT [Anglo-French *philber,* from Saint *Philibert,* died 684, Frankish abbot whose feast day falls in the nutting season]

filch \ˈfilch\ *vt* **:** to steal slyly **:** PILFER [Middle English *filchen*]

1file \ˈfīl\ *n* **:** a usually steel tool with cutting ridges for forming or smoothing hard surfaces (as metal) [Old English *fēol*]

2file *vt* **:** to rub, smooth, or cut away with a file

3file *vb* **1 :** to arrange in order for preservation or reference **2 a :** to enter or record as prescribed by law ⟨*file* a mortgage⟩ **b :** to send (copy) to a newspaper ⟨*file* a story⟩ **3 :** to register as a candidate especially in a primary election [Medieval Latin *filare* "to string documents on a string or wire," from *filum* "file of documents," literally, "thread," from Latin]

4file *n* **1 :** a device (as a folder, case, or cabinet) in which records are kept in order **2 a :** a collection of material kept in a file **b :** a collection of data considered as a unit (as for a computer)

5file *n* **:** a row of persons, animals, or things arranged one behind the other [Medieval French, derived from Latin *filum* "thread"]

6file *vi* **:** to march or proceed in file

file·fish \ˈfīl-ˌfish\ *n* **:** any of various fishes with rough granular leathery skin

fi·let \fi-ˈlā\ *n* **:** a lace with a square mesh and geometric designs [French, literally, "net"]

fi·let mi·gnon \ˌfil-ˌā-mēn-ˈyō^{n}, fi-ˌlā-\ *n, pl* **filets mignons** *same or* -ˈyō^{n}z\ **:** a thick slice of beef cut from the narrow end of a beef tenderloin [French, literally, "dainty fillet"]

fil·ial \ˈfil-ē-əl, ˈfil-yəl\ *adj* **1 :** of, relating to, or befitting a son or daughter **2 :** having or assuming the relation of a child or offspring ⟨*filial* obedience⟩ [Late Latin *filialis,* from Latin *filius* "son"] — **fil·ial·ly** \-ē\ *adv*

filial generation *n* **:** a generation of offspring in a breeding experiment that is produced by the parents in the original cross or by their offspring

1fil·i·bus·ter \ˈfil-ə-ˌbəs-tər\ *n* **1 :** an irregular military adventurer; *esp* **:** an American engaged in stirring up rebellions in Latin America in the mid-19th century **2 a :** the use of delaying tactics (as extremely long speeches) in an attempt to delay or prevent action in a legislative assembly **b :** an instance of this practice [Spanish *filibustero,* derived from English *freebooter*]

Word History The Dutch word *vrijbuiter,* "plunderer," has left its mark on the English vocabulary not once but twice. It first appeared in the 16th century as *freebooter.* Though the spelling had changed, the meaning remained the same. From English it passed into Spanish and became *filibustero.* In the middle of the 19th century bands of adventurers organized in the United States were active in Central America and the West Indies stirring up revolutions. Such an adventurer came to be called in English a *filibuster,* from Spanish *filibustero,* and so *vrijbuiter* made its second appearance in a very different guise. Later in the 19th century, the use of delaying tactics became very common in the United States Senate. Senators who practiced such tactics were compared with the troublesome *filibusters* and were said to be *filibustering.*

2filibuster *vb* **fil·i·bus·tered; fil·i·bus·ter·ing** \-tə-ring, -tring\ **1 :** to carry out revolutionary activities in a foreign country **2 :** to engage in a legislative filibuster — **fil·i·bus·ter·er** \-tər-ər\ *n*

fil·i·form \ˈfil-ə-ˌfȯrm, ˈfī-lə-\ *adj* **:** shaped like a thread

fil·i·gree \ˈfil-ə-ˌgrē\ *n* **1 :** ornamental work especially of fine wire applied chiefly to gold and silver surfaces **2 a :** ornamental work of delicate or intricate design done so as to show openings through the material **b :** a pattern or design resembling this openwork [French *filigrane,* from Italian *filigrana,* from Latin *filum* "thread" + *granum* "grain"]

fil·ing \ˈfī-ling\ *n* **1 :** the act of one who files **2 :** a small piece scraped off by a file ⟨iron *filings*⟩

Fil·i·pi·na \ˌfil-ə-ˈpē-nə\ *n* **:** a Filipino girl or woman

Fil·i·pi·no \ˌfil-ə-ˈpē-nō\ *n, pl* **-nos :** a native or inhabitant of the Philippines [Spanish] — **Filipino** *adj*

1fill \ˈfil\ *vb* **1 :** to put into as much as can be held or conveniently contained **2 :** to become full ⟨puddles *filling* with rain⟩ **3 :** FULFILL 2 ⟨*fill* all requirements⟩ **4 :** to take up whatever space there is **5 :** to spread through ⟨laughter *filled* the room⟩ **6 :** to stop up (as crevices or holes) **:** PLUG ⟨*fill* a tooth⟩ **7 a :** to have and perform the duties of **:** OCCUPY ⟨*fill* the office of president⟩ **b :** to put a person in ⟨*filled* several vacancies⟩ **8 :** to supply according to directions ⟨*fill* an order⟩ [Old English *fyllan*] — **fill one's shoes :** to take one's place or position

2fill *n* **1 :** a full supply; *esp* **:** a quantity that satisfies or satiates **2 :** material used especially for filling a ditch or hollow in the ground

fill·er \ˈfil-ər\ *n* **:** one that fills: as **a :** a substance added to a product (as to increase bulk, weight, opacity, or strength) **b :** a material used for filling cracks and pores in wood before painting **c :** a pack of paper for insertion in a binder **d :** a sound, word, or phrase used to fill pauses in speaking

1fil·let \ˈfil-ət\ *also* **fi·let** \fi-ˈlā, ˈfil-ā\ *n* **1 :** a narrow strip of material (as a ribbon) used as a headband **2 a :** a thin narrow strip of material **b :** a piece or slice of boneless meat or fish **3 a :** a flat molding separating other moldings **b :** the space between two flutings in a shaft [Medieval French *filet,* from *fil* "thread," from Latin *filum*]

fillet 1

2fillet *vt* **1 :** to bind or adorn with or as if with a fillet **2 :** to cut into fillets

fill in *vb* **1 :** to furnish with specified information ⟨*fill in* an application⟩ **2 :** to fill a vacancy usually temporarily **:** SUBSTITUTE ⟨*filled in* while he was out⟩

fill·ing \ˈfil-ing\ *n* **1 :** material that is used to fill something ⟨a *filling* for a tooth⟩ **2 :** something that completes: as **a :** the yarn interlacing the warp in a fabric **b :** a food mixture used to fill pastry or sandwiches

filling station *n* **:** GAS STATION

1fil·lip \ˈfil-əp\ *n* **1 :** a blow or gesture made by the sudden forcible straightening of a finger curled up against the thumb **2 :** something tending to arouse or excite [probably imitative]

2fillip *vt* **1 :** to tap with the finger by flicking the fingernail outward across the end of the thumb **2 :** to urge on **:** STIMULATE

fill out *vi* **:** to put on flesh

fil·ly \ˈfil-ē\ *n, pl* **fillies :** a young female horse usually less than four years old [Old Norse *fylja*]

1film \ˈfilm\ *n* **1 :** a thin skin or membrane **2 :** a thin coating or layer **3 :** a roll or strip of thin flexible transparent material coated with a chemical substance sensitive to light and used in taking pictures **4 :** MOVIE [Old English *filmen*]

2film *vb* **1 :** to cover or become covered with film ⟨eyes *filmed* with tears⟩ **2 :** to make a motion picture of ⟨*film* a battle scene⟩

film·ic \ˈfil-mik\ *adj* **:** of, relating to, or resembling motion pictures

film noir \-ˈnwär\ *n, pl* **film noirs** \-ˈnwär, -nwärz\ *or* **films noir** *or* **films noirs** \-ˈnwär\ **:** a type of crime film featuring cynical malevolent characters in a sleazy setting and an ominous atmosphere that is conveyed by shadowy photography and foreboding background music; *also* **:** a film of this type [French, literally, "black film"]

film·og·ra·phy \fil-ˈmäg-rə-fē\ *n, pl* **-phies :** a list of motion pictures featuring the work of a prominent film figure or relating to a particular topic [*film* + *-ography* (as in *bibliography*)]

film·strip \ˈfilm-ˌstrip\ *n* **:** a strip of film bearing images for projection as still pictures

filmy \ˈfil-mē\ *adj* **film·i·er; -est 1 :** of, resembling, or composed of film **2 :** covered with a haze or film — **film·i·ness** *n*

1fil·ter \ˈfil-tər\ *n* **1 :** a porous article or mass through which a gas or liquid is passed to separate out matter in suspension **2 :** an apparatus containing a filter medium **3 a :** a device or material for suppressing or minimizing waves or oscillations of certain frequencies (as of electricity, light, or sound) **b :** a transparent material (as colored glass) that absorbs light of certain colors and is used for modifying the light which reaches a sensitized photographic material **4 :** software for sorting or blocking access to certain online material [Medieval Latin *filtrum* "piece of felt used as a filter," of Germanic origin]

2filter *vb* **fil·tered; fil·ter·ing** \-tə-ring, -tring\ **1 :** to subject to the action of a filter **2 :** to remove by means of a filter **3 :** to pass through or as if through a filter

fil·ter·able *also* **fil·tra·ble** \ˈfil-tə-rə-bəl, -trə-bəl\ *adj* **:** capable of being separated by or of passing through a filter ⟨*filterable* microorganisms⟩ ⟨a *filterable* liquid⟩ — **fil·ter·abil·i·ty** \ˌfil-tə-rə-ˈbil-ət-ē, -trə-ˈ\ *n*

filterable virus *n* **:** any of the infectious agents that remain infectious after passing through a filter with pores too fine for a bacterium to pass through

filter bed *n* **:** a bed of sand or gravel for filtering water or sewage

filter feeder *n* **:** an animal (as a clam or baleen whale) that obtains its food by filtering organic matter or minute organisms from a current of water that passes through some part of its body

filter paper *n* **:** porous paper used for filtering

filter tip *n* **:** a cigar or cigarette with a tip designed to filter the smoke before it enters the smoker's mouth

filth \ˈfilth\ *n* **1 :** foul or putrid matter; *esp* **:** disgusting dirt or refuse **2 a :** moral corruption **b :** something that tends to corrupt or disgust [Old English *fȳlth,* from *fūl* "foul"]

filthy \ˈfil-thē\ *adj* **filth·i·er; -est 1 :** covered with or containing filth **:** disgustingly dirty **2 a :** morally polluted **:** EVIL ⟨*filthy* politics⟩ **b :** OBSCENE ***synonyms*** see DIRTY — **filth·i·ly** \-thə-lē\ *adv* — **filth·i·ness** \-thē-nəs\ *n*

fil·trate \ˈfil-ˌtrāt\ *n* **:** fluid that has passed through a filter

fil·tra·tion \fil-ˈtrā-shən\ *n* **:** the act or process of filtering

fin \ˈfin\ *n* **1 :** a thin external process of an aquatic animal (as a fish or whale) used in propelling or guiding the body **2 a :** a fin-shaped part (as on an airplane, boat, or automobile) **b :** FLIPPER 2 **c :** a projecting rib on a radiator or an engine cylinder [Old English *finn*] — **fin·like** \-ˌlīk\ *adj* — **finned** \ˈfind\ *adj*

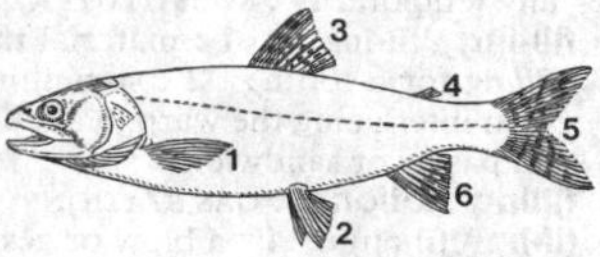

fin 1: *1* pectoral, *2* pelvic, *3, 4* dorsal, *5* caudal, *6* anal

fi·na·gle \fə-ˈnā-gəl\ *vb* **fi·na·gled; fi·na·gling** \-ˈnā-gə-ling, -gling\ **1 :** to obtain by indirect or involved means **2 :** to obtain by trickery [perhaps from *fainaigue* "to renege"] — **fi·na·gler** \-gə-lər, -glər\ *n*

[1]fi·nal \ˈfīn-l\ *adj* **1 a :** not to be altered or undone ⟨reached a *final* decision⟩ ⟨all sales are *final*⟩ **b :** of or relating to a concluding court action ⟨*final* decree⟩ **2 :** coming at the end **:** being the last in a series or process ⟨the *final* chapter⟩ **3 :** being or relating to an end or purpose ⟨our *final* goal⟩ [Medieval French, from Latin *finalis,* from *finis* "end, boundary"] ***synonyms*** see LAST — **fi·nal·ly** \ˈfīn-l-ē, ˈfīn-lē\ *adv*

[2]final *n* **:** something final: as **a :** a deciding match, game, or trial — usually used in plural **b :** the last examination in a course — often used in plural

fi·na·le \fə-ˈnal-ē, fi-ˈnäl-\ *n* **:** the close or termination of something; *esp* **:** the last section of an instrumental musical composition [Italian, from Latin *finalis* "final"]

fi·nal·ist \ˈfīn-l-əst\ *n* **:** a contestant in the finals of a competition

fi·nal·i·ty \fī-ˈnal-ət-ē, fə-\ *n, pl* **-ties 1 :** the character or condition of being final, settled, or complete **2 :** something final

fi·nal·ize \ˈfīn-l-ˌīz\ *vt* **:** to put in final or finished form

[1]fi·nance \fə-ˈnans, ˈfī-ˌ, fī-ˈ\ *n* **1** *pl* **:** liquid resources (as money) available to a government, business, group, or individual **2 :** the system that includes the circulation of money, the granting of credit, the making of investments, and the provision of banking facilities **3 :** the obtaining of funds or capital **:** FINANCING [Middle English, "ending, payment," from Medieval French, from *finer* "to end, pay," from *fin* "end," from Latin *finis*]

[2]finance *vt* **1 :** to raise or provide funds or capital for ⟨*finance* a new car⟩ **2 :** to sell to or supply on credit ⟨*finance* farmers until harvest⟩

finance charge *n* **:** a charge for credit that is generally a percentage of the amount of credit given

finance company *n* **:** a company that specializes in making small loans usually to individuals

fi·nan·cial \fə-ˈnan-chəl, fī-\ *adj* **:** having to do with finance or with finances — **fi·nan·cial·ly** \-ˈnanch-lē, -ə-lē\ *adv*

synonyms FINANCIAL, MONETARY, PECUNIARY, FISCAL mean having to do with money. FINANCIAL implies money matters involving a large scale or some degree of complexity ⟨*financial* aspects of a business⟩. MONETARY refers to money as coined, distributed, or circulating ⟨*monetary* reform⟩. PECUNIARY implies reference to money matters affecting the individual ⟨*pecuniary* rewards of an office⟩. FISCAL applies to the financial affairs of a corporation, institution, or state ⟨*fiscal* policy⟩.

fi·nan·cier \ˌfin-ən-ˈsiər, fə-ˌnan-, ˌfī-ˌnan-\ *n* **:** a person who deals with finance and investment on a large scale

fin·back \ˈfin-ˌbak\ *n* **:** FIN WHALE

finch \ˈfinch\ *n* **:** any of numerous songbirds (as sparrows, grosbeaks, crossbills, goldfinches, and buntings) having a short stout conical bill adapted for crushing seeds [Old English *finc*]

[1]find \ˈfīnd\ *vb* **found** \ˈfau̇nd\; **find·ing 1 :** to encounter someone or something by chance ⟨*found* a penny⟩ **2 :** to come upon by searching or study **:** DISCOVER ⟨*found* the answer⟩ **3 :** to obtain by effort or management ⟨*find* time to do it⟩ **4 :** to arrive at **:** REACH ⟨*find* one's place in the world⟩ **5 :** to make a decision and declare it ⟨*find* a verdict⟩ **6 :** to know by experience ⟨people *found* them honest⟩ **7 :** to gain or regain the use of ⟨*find* one's feet after an illness⟩ **8 :** PROVIDE, SUPPLY ⟨*find* room for a guest⟩ [Old English *findan*] — **find fault :** to criticize unfavorably

[2]find *n* **1 :** an act or instance of finding **2 :** something found; *esp* **:** a valuable discovery

find·er \ˈfīn-dər\ *n* **:** one that finds: as **a :** a small telescope attached to a larger one for finding an object **b :** a device on a camera that shows the view being photographed by the camera — called also *viewfinder*

fin de siè·cle \ˌfa^{n}-də-sē-ˈekl\ *adj* **1 :** of, relating to, or characteristic of the close of the 19th century **2 :** of or relating to the end of a century [French, "end of the century"] — **fin de siècle** *n*

finding *n* **1 a :** the act of one that finds **b :** FIND 2 **2 :** the result of a judicial proceeding or investigation

find out *vt* **1 :** to learn by study or observation **2 :** to catch doing something bad ⟨the criminal was *found out*⟩

[1]fine \ˈfīn\ *n* **:** a sum of money to be paid as punishment for an offense [Medieval French *fin* "end, fine," from Latin *finis* "end, limit, boundary"]

[2]fine *vt* **:** to impose a fine on **:** punish by a fine

[3]fine *adj* **1 a :** free from impurity **b :** having a stated proportion of pure metal in the composition ⟨silver 800/1000 *fine*⟩ **2 a :** very thin in gauge or texture ⟨*fine* thread⟩ **b :** not coarse ⟨*fine* sand⟩ **c :** very small ⟨*fine* print⟩ **d :** very accurate or precise ⟨*fine* adjustments⟩ **3 :** subtle or sensitive in perception or discrimination ⟨a *fine* distinction⟩ **4 :** superior in quality, conception, or appearance **:** EXCELLENT ⟨a *fine* musician⟩ **5 :** marked by or affecting elegance or refinement ⟨*fine* manners⟩ **6 :** to one's liking **:** AGREEABLE ⟨that's *fine* with me⟩ **7 :** very well ⟨feel *fine*⟩ [Medieval French *fin,* from Latin *finis* "end, limit"] — **fine·ly** *adv* — **fine·ness** \ˈfīn-nəs\ *n*

[4]fine *adv* **:** very well **:** FINELY ⟨did *fine* on the test⟩

[5]fi·ne \ˈfē-ˌnā\ *n* **:** END — used as a direction in music to mark the closing point after a repeat [Italian, from Latin *finis* "end"]

fine art *n* **:** art (as sculpture or music) concerned primarily with the creation of beautiful objects — usually used in plural

fin·ery \ˈfīn-rē, -ə-rē\ *n, pl* **-er·ies :** ORNAMENT 1a, DECORATION; *esp* **:** showy clothing and jewels

fines \ˈfīnz\ *n pl* **:** finely crushed or powdered material (as ore or coal)

[1]fi·nesse \fə-ˈnes\ *n* **1 :** refinement or delicacy of workmanship or composition ⟨a painting done with *finesse*⟩ **2 :** skillful handling of a situation **3 :** the withholding of one's highest card or trump in the hope that a lower card will take the trick because the only opposing higher card is in the hand of an opponent who has already played [Middle French, from *fin* "fine"]

[2]finesse *vb* **1 a :** to make a finesse in playing cards **b :** to play (a card) as a finesse **2 a :** to bring about by shrewd maneuvering **b :** to avoid skillfully **:** SKIRT ⟨*finessed* the hard issues⟩

fin·fish \ˈfin-ˌfish\ *n* **:** FISH 1b

[1]fin·ger \ˈfing-gər\ *n* **1 :** one of the five divisions of the end of the hand; *esp* **:** one other than the thumb **2 a :** something that resembles or does the work of a finger **b :** a part of a glove into which a finger is inserted **3 :** the width of a finger [Old English] — **fin·gered** *adj* — **fin·ger·like** \-ˌlīk\ *adj*

[2]finger *vb* **fin·gered; fin·ger·ing** \ˈfing-gə-ring, -gring\ **1 :** to touch with the fingers **:** HANDLE **2 :** to perform with the fingers or with a certain fingering **3 :** to mark the notes of a piece of music to show what fingers are to be used **4 :** to point out **:** IDENTIFY ⟨*fingered* the culprit⟩

fin·ger·board \ˈfiŋ-gər-ˌbōrd, -ˌbȯrd\ *n* **:** the part of a stringed instrument against which the fingers press the strings to vary the pitch

finger bowl *n* **:** a small bowl to hold water for rinsing the fingers at the table

finger food *n* **:** a food that is meant to be picked up with the fingers and eaten

finger hole *n* **:** a hole in a wind instrument by means of which the pitch of the tone is changed when it is left open or closed by the finger

fingering *n* **1 :** the act or method of using the fingers in playing an instrument **b :** the marking on a musical score of the method of fingering **2 :** the act or process of handling or touching with the fingers

fin·ger·ling \ˈfiŋ-gər-liŋ\ *n* **:** a young fish especially up to one year of age

fin·ger·nail \ˈfiŋ-gər-ˌnāl, ˌfiŋ-gər-ˈ\ *n* **:** the nail of a finger

finger painting *n* **1 :** a technique of spreading pigment on paper with the fingertips **2 :** a picture produced by finger painting

fin·ger·post \ˈfiŋ-gər-ˌpōst\ *n* **:** a post bearing one or more signs often ending in a pointing finger

fin·ger·print \ˈfiŋ-gər-ˌprint\ *n* **1 :** the pattern of marks made by pressing the tip of a finger or thumb on a surface; *esp* **:** an ink impression of the lines on the tip of a finger or thumb taken for the purpose of identification **2 :** the sequence of base pairs in an individual's DNA that is obtained by DNA fingerprinting — **fingerprint** *vt* — **fin·ger·print·ing** *n*

fin·ger·tip \-ˌtip\ *n* **:** the tip of a finger

fin·i·al \ˈfin-ē-əl\ *n* **:** an ornamental projection or end (as on a spire or topping a lamp shade) [Middle English, from *final, finial* "final"]

finial

fin·icky \ˈfin-i-kē\ *adj* **:** very particular or exacting in taste or standards **:** FUSSY ⟨a *finicky* eater⟩ [probably derived from [3]*fine*] — **fin·ick·i·ness** *n*

fi·nis \ˈfin-əs, ˈfī-nəs\ *n* **:** END 1b, CONCLUSION [Latin]

[1]**fin·ish** \ˈfin-ish\ *vb* **1 a :** to bring or come to an end **:** TERMINATE **b :** to use or dispose of entirely ⟨her sandwich *finished* the loaf⟩ **2 :** to come to the end of a course, task, or undertaking **3 a :** to bring to completion ⟨*finished* their new home before winter⟩ **b :** to put a final coat or surface on **4 :** to end a competition in a specified manner or position ⟨*finished* third in the race⟩ **5 :** to bring about the death of [Medieval French *finiss-*, stem of *finir* "to finish," from Latin *finire,* from *finis* "end"] — **fin·ish·er** *n*

synonyms FINISH, COMPLETE mean to bring to an end. FINISH implies accomplishing the final act or stage in producing, performing, or perfecting something ⟨needed more paint to *finish* the job⟩. COMPLETE stresses a bringing of something to a state of wholeness, fullness, or soundness ⟨one more link was needed to *complete* the circle⟩.

[2]**finish** *n* **1 :** END 1b, CONCLUSION ⟨a close *finish* in a race⟩ **2 :** the final treatment or coating of a surface **3 :** the result or product of a finishing process ⟨a glossy *finish*⟩

finishing school *n* **:** a private school for girls that emphasizes cultural studies and prepares students especially for social activities

finish line *n* **:** a line marking the end of a racecourse

fi·nite \ˈfī-ˌnīt\ *adj* **1 :** having definite or definable limits **:** limited in scope or nature **2 :** not infinite but limited in number or extent; *esp* **:** having the number of elements or terms equal to zero or some positive integer ⟨a *finite* set⟩ **3 :** showing distinction of grammatical person and number ⟨a *finite* verb⟩ [Latin *finitus,* past participle of *finire* "to limit, finish"] — **fi·nite·ly** *adv* — **fi·nite·ness** *n*

Finn \ˈfin\ *n* **1 :** a member of a people speaking Finnish or a related language **2 a :** a native or inhabitant of Finland **b :** a person of Finnish descent [Swedish *Finne*]

[1]**Finn·ish** \ˈfin-ish\ *adj* **:** of, relating to, or characteristic of Finland, the Finns, or Finnish

[2]**Finnish** *n* **:** the Finno-Ugric language of the Finns

Fin·no–Ugric \ˌfin-ō-ˈyü-grik, -ˈü-\ *adj* **1 :** of, relating to, or constituting a subfamily of the Uralic family of languages comprising various languages spoken in Hungary, Lapland, Finland, Estonia, and parts of western Russia **2 :** of or relating to any of the peoples speaking Finno-Ugric languages [derived from *Finn* + Old Russian *Ugre* "Hungarians"] — **Finno–Ugric** *n*

fin·ny \ˈfin-ē\ *adj* **1 :** resembling or having fins **2 :** relating to or being fish

fin whale *n* **:** a baleen whale that may attain a length of over 70 feet (21 meters)

fiord *variant of* FJORD

fip·ple flute \ˈfip-əl-\ *n* **:** a wind instrument (as the recorder) having a straight tubelike shape, a mouthpiece, and finger holes [origin unknown]

fir \ˈfər\ *n* **1 :** any of various usually large symmetrical evergreen trees of the pine family which have cones growing upward on the branches and some of which yield useful lumber or resins **2 :** the wood of a fir [Old English *fyrh*]

[1]**fire** \ˈfīr\ *n* **1 :** the light and heat and especially the flame produced by burning **2 :** ardent liveliness **:** ENTHUSIASM **3 :** fuel that is burning (as in a fireplace or stove) **4 :** the destructive burning of something (as a building or a forest) **5 :** the discharge of firearms [Old English *fȳr*] — **on fire 1 a :** in a state of combustion **b :** very hot **2 :** EAGER — **under fire 1 :** exposed to the firing of enemy guns **2 :** under attack

[2]**fire** *vb* **1 a :** to set on fire **:** KINDLE, IGNITE **b :** STIR, ENLIVEN ⟨*fire* the imagination⟩ **2 :** to dismiss from employment **3 :** to cause to explode ⟨*fire* dynamite⟩ **4 a :** to propel from or as if from a gun **:** LAUNCH ⟨*fire* an arrow⟩ ⟨*fire* a rocket⟩ **b :** DISCHARGE ⟨*fire* a gun⟩ **c :** to throw with speed **:** HURL ⟨*fired* the ball to first base⟩ **5 a :** to subject to intense heat ⟨*fire* pottery⟩ **b :** to feed or serve the fire of ⟨*fire* a furnace⟩ **6 a :** to take fire **:** KINDLE **b :** to have the explosive charge ignite at the proper time ⟨a cylinder that does not *fire* right⟩ **7 :** to emit or let fly an object **8 :** to transmit a nerve impulse ⟨the neuron *fired*⟩ — **fir·er** *n*

fire ant *n* **:** any of a genus of fiercely stinging ants; *esp* **:** IMPORTED FIRE ANT

fire·arm \ˈfīr-ˌärm\ *n* **:** a weapon from which a shot is discharged by gunpowder — usually used of small arms

fire·ball \-ˌbȯl\ *n* **1 :** a ball of fire **2 :** a brilliant meteor **3 :** the highly luminous cloud of vapor and dust created by a nuclear explosion (as of an atomic bomb)

fire blight *n* **:** a destructive highly infectious disease especially of apples and pears that is caused by a bacterium

fire·boat \ˈfīr-ˌbōt\ *n* **:** a boat or ship equipped with apparatus (as pumps) for fighting fire

fire·bomb \-ˌbäm\ *n* **:** an incendiary bomb — **firebomb** *vt*

fire·box \-ˌbäks\ *n* **1 :** a chamber (as of a furnace or steam boiler) that contains a fire **2 :** a box containing an apparatus for transmitting an alarm to a fire station

fire·brand \-ˌbrand\ *n* **1 :** a piece of burning wood **2 :** a person who creates unrest or strife **:** AGITATOR

fire·break \-ˌbrāk\ *n* **:** a barrier of cleared or plowed land intended to stop the spread of a forest or grass fire

fire·brick \-ˌbrik\ *n* **:** a brick capable of withstanding great heat and used for lining furnaces or fireplaces

fire·bug \-ˌbəg\ *n* **:** a person who deliberately sets destructive fires **:** ARSONIST

fire·clay \-ˌklā\ *n* **:** clay capable of withstanding high temperatures and used especially for firebrick and crucibles

fire·crack·er \-ˌkrak-ər\ *n* **:** a paper cylinder containing an explosive and a fuse and set off to make a noise

fired \ˈfīrd\ *adj* **:** using a specified fuel ⟨an oil-*fired* power plant⟩

fire·damp \-ˌdamp\ *n* **:** a combustible mine gas that consists chiefly of methane; *also* **:** the explosive mixture of this gas with air

fire·dog \-ˌdȯg\ *n, chiefly Southern & Midland* **:** ANDIRON

fire drill *n* **:** a practice drill in extinguishing fires or in the conduct and manner of exit in case of fire

fire engine *n* **:** a mobile apparatus for directing water or an extinguishing chemical on fires; *esp* **:** FIRE TRUCK

\ə\ abut	\au̇\ out	\i\ tip	\ȯ\ saw	\u̇\ foot
\ər\ further	\ch\ chin	\ī\ life	\ȯi\ coin	\y\ yet
\a\ mat	\e\ pet	\j\ job	\th\ thin	\yü\ few
\ā\ take	\ē\ easy	\ŋ\ sing	\th\ this	\yu̇\ cure
\ä\ cot, cart	\g\ go	\ō\ bone	\ü\ food	\zh\ vision

fire escape *n* : a stairway or ladder for escape from a burning building
fire extinguisher *n* : something used to put out a fire; *esp* : a portable apparatus for ejecting fire-extinguishing chemicals
firefighter *n* : one that fights fires : FIREMAN — **firefighting** *n*
fire•fly \'fīr-ˌflī\ *n* : any of numerous nocturnal beetles producing a bright soft flashing light for courtship purposes — called also *lightning bug*
fire•house \-ˌhau̇s\ *n* : FIRE STATION
fire irons *n pl* : tools for tending a fire especially in a fireplace
fire•light \'fīr-ˌlīt\ *n* : the light of a fire (as in a fireplace)
fire line *n* : FIREBREAK
fire•man \-mən\ *n* **1** : a member of a company organized to fight fires **2** : one who tends or feeds fires : STOKER
fire•place \-ˌplās\ *n* **1** : a framed opening made in a chimney to hold an open fire : HEARTH **2** : an outdoor structure of brick, stone, or metal for an open fire
fire•plug \-ˌpləg\ *n* : HYDRANT
fire•pow•er \-ˌpau̇-ər, -ˌpau̇r\ *n* : the ability (as of a military unit) to deliver gunfire or missiles on a target
[1]**fire•proof** \-'prüf\ *adj* : proof against or resistant to fire
[2]**fireproof** *vt* : to make fireproof
fire sale *n* : a sale of merchandise damaged by fire
fire screen *n* : a protective screen before a fireplace
fire•side \'fīr-ˌsīd\ *n* **1** : a place near the fire or hearth **2** : HOME 1a
fire station *n* : a building housing fire apparatus and usually firefighters
fire tower *n* : a tower (as in a forest) from which a watch for fires is kept
fire•trap \'fīr-ˌtrap\ *n* : a place (as a building) apt to catch on fire or difficult to escape from in case of fire
fire truck *n* : an automotive vehicle equipped with apparatus (as pumps) for fighting fire
fire wall *n* **1** : a wall for preventing the spread of fire **2** *usu* **fire•wall** \'fīr-ˌwȯl\ : computer hardware or software that limits access by outside users on a network
fire•wa•ter \-ˌwȯt-ər, -ˌwät\ *n* : intoxicating liquor
fire•weed \-ˌwēd\ *n* **1** : a tall perennial with long spikes of pinkish purple flowers that is related to the evening primrose and tends to spring up in clearings or burned areas **2** : any of several plants similar or related to the fireweed
fire•wood \-ˌwu̇d\ *n* : wood cut for fuel
fire•work \-ˌwərk\ *n* **1** : a device for producing a striking display (as of light or noise) by the combustion of explosive or flammable compositions **2** *pl* : a display of fireworks **3** *pl* : a display of temper or hostility
firing line *n* **1** : a line from which gunfire is directed at a target **2** : the forefront of an activity
firing pin *n* : a pin that strikes the cartridge primer in the breech mechanism of a firearm
firing squad *n* **1** : a detachment detailed to fire volleys over the grave of one buried with military honors **2** : a detachment detailed to carry out a death sentence by shooting
fir•kin \'fər-kən\ *n* **1** : a small wooden vessel or cask **2** : any of various British units of capacity usually equal to ¼ barrel [derived from Dutch *veerdel* "fourth"]

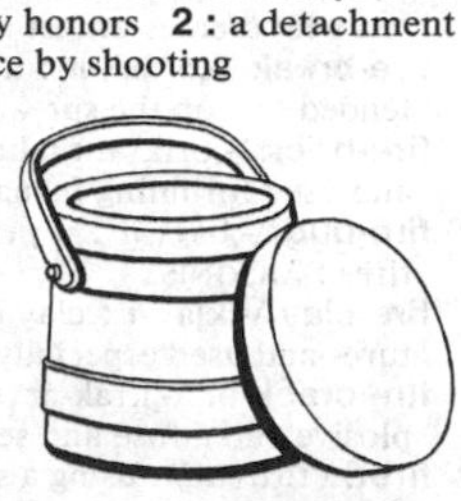
firkin 1

[1]**firm** \'fərm\ *adj* **1 a** : securely or solidly fixed in place **b** : not weak or uncertain : VIGOROUS **c** : having a solid or compact texture **2 a** : not subject to change or fluctuation ⟨a *firm* price⟩ **b** : not easily moved or disturbed : STEADFAST **c** : WELL-FOUNDED ⟨a *firm* argument⟩ **3** : indicating firmness or resolution ⟨a *firm* mouth⟩ [Medieval French *ferm,* from Latin *firmus*] — **firm•ly** *adv* — **firm•ness** *n*
[2]**firm** *vb* **1 a** : to make secure ⟨*firm* your grip on the racket⟩ **b** : to make solid or compact ⟨*firm* the soil⟩ **2** : to become firm
[3]**firm** *n* **1** : the name under which a company does business **2** : a business partnership of two or more persons **3** : a business enterprise [German *Firma,* from Italian, "signature," derived from Latin *firmare* "to make firm, confirm," from *firmus* "firm"]
fir•ma•ment \'fər-mə-mənt\ *n* : the arch of the sky : HEAVENS [Latin *firmamentum* "support," from *firmare* "to make firm"]
firm•ware \'fərm-ˌwaər, -ˌweər\ *n* : computer programs contained permanently in a hardware device (as a read-only memory)
firn \'firn\ *n* : NÉVÉ [German]
[1]**first** \'fərst\ *adj* **1** : being number one in a countable series ⟨the *first* day of spring⟩ **2** : preceding all others (as in time, order, or importance) **3** : being the lowest forward gear or speed of a motor vehicle **4** : highest or most prominent in carrying the melody ⟨*first* violin⟩ [Old English *fyrst*]
[2]**first** *adv* **1** : before any other ⟨we got there *first*⟩ **2** : for the first time **3** : before doing other things
[3]**first** *n* **1** — see NUMBER table **2** : something that is first: as **a** : the lowest gear or speed of a motor vehicle **b** : the winning place in a competition or contest **3** : FIRST BASE — **at first** : in the beginning : INITIALLY
first aid *n* : emergency care or treatment given to an ill or injured person
first base *n* **1** : the base that must be touched first by a base runner in baseball **2** : the position of the player defending the area around first base **3** : the first step or stage in a course of action ⟨the plan never got to *first base*⟩
first base•man \-'bā-smən\ *n* : the player defending the area around first base
first•born \'fərst-'bȯrn, 'fərs-\ *adj* : born first : ELDEST — **firstborn** *n*
first–class *adj* **1** : of or relating to first class **2** : of the highest quality ⟨a *first-class* meal⟩ — **first–class** *adv*
first class *n* : the best or highest group in a classification: as **a** : the highest class of travel accommodations **b** : a class of mail that comprises letters, postcards, or matter sealed against inspection
first–degree burn *n* : a mild burn marked by heat, pain, and reddening of the burned surface but not showing blistering or charring of tissues
first down *n* **1** : the first of a series of four downs in football in which a team must make a net gain of 10 yards **2** : the right to start a new series of downs after a gain of 10 or more yards
first•hand \'fərst-'hand\ *adj* : coming directly from the original source ⟨a *firsthand* account⟩ — **firsthand** *adv*
first lady *n, often cap F&L* **1** : the wife or hostess of a male chief executive of a country or jurisdiction **2** : the leading woman of an art or profession
first lieutenant *n* : an officer rank in the Army, Marine Corps, and Air Force above second lieutenant and below captain
first•ling \'fərst-ling\ *n* : one that comes or is produced first
first•ly \-lē\ *adv* : in the first place
first offender *n* : one convicted of an offense for the first time
first person *n* **1** : a set of words or forms (as pronouns or verb forms) referring to the speaker or writer of the utterance in which they occur; *also* : a word or form belonging to such a set **2** : a writing style marked by general use of the first person
first–rate \'fərst-'rāt\ *adj* : of the first order of size, importance, or quality — **first–rate** *adv* — **first–rat•er** \-'rāt-ər\ *n*
first responder *n* : a person (as a police officer or an EMT) who is among those responsible for going immediately to the scene of an accident or emergency to provide assistance
first sergeant *n* **1** : a noncommissioned officer serving as chief enlisted assistant to the commander (as of a company) **2** : an enlisted rank in the Army above a platoon sergeant and below command sergeant major and in the Marine Corps above gunnery sergeant and below sergeant major
first–string \'fərst-'string, 'fərs-\ *adj* : being a regular as distinguished from a substitute (as on a football team) — **first–stringer** \-'string-ər\ *n*
first water *n* **1** : the purest luster — used of gems **2** : the highest grade, degree, or quality ⟨a novel of the *first water*⟩
firth \'fərth\ *n* : a narrow arm of the sea; *also* : ESTUARY [Old Norse *fjǫrthr*]
fis•cal \'fis-kəl\ *adj* **1** : of or relating to taxation, public revenues, or public debt **2** : of or relating to financial matters [Latin *fiscalis,* from *fiscus* "basket, treasury"] ***synonyms*** see FINANCIAL — **fis•cal•ly** \-kə-lē\ *adv*
[1]**fish** \'fish\ *n, pl* **fish** *or* **fish•es** **1 a** : an aquatic animal — usually used in combination ⟨star*fish*⟩ ⟨cuttle*fish*⟩ **b** : any of numerous cold-blooded aquatic water-breathing vertebrates with a usually long scaly tapering body, limbs developed as fins, and a vertical tail fin **2** : the flesh of fish used as food **3** : INDIVIDUAL 2 ⟨an odd *fish*⟩ **4** : a piece of wood or iron fastened along-

side another member to strengthen it [Old English *fisc*] — **fish·like** \ˈfish-ˌlīk\ *adj*

fish 1b: *1* operculum, *2* scales, *3* lateral line

²fish *vb* **1 :** to catch or try to catch fish **2 :** to seek something by roundabout means ⟨*fishing* for a compliment⟩ **3 :** to catch or try to catch fish in ⟨*fish* the stream⟩ **4 :** to search for something underwater ⟨*fish* for pearls⟩ **5 :** to seek something by or as if by groping ⟨*fishing* around in her purse for her keys⟩

fish–and–chips \ˌfish-ən-ˈchips\ *n pl* **:** fried fish and french fried potatoes

fish cake *n* **:** a round fried cake made of shredded fish and mashed potato — called also *fish ball*

fish·er \ˈfish-ər\ *n* **1 :** one that fishes **2 :** a dark brown North American carnivorous mammal related to the weasels; *also* **:** its valuable fur or pelt

fish·er·man \-mən\ *n* **1 :** one who engages in fishing as an occupation or for pleasure **2 :** a ship used in commercial fishing

fish·ery \ˈfish-rē, -ə-rē\ *n, pl* **-er·ies** **1 :** the activity or business of taking fish or other aquatic animals **:** FISHING **2 :** a place or establishment for catching fish or other aquatic animals

fish hawk *n* **:** OSPREY

fish·hook \ˈfish-ˌhu̇k\ *n* **:** a usually barbed hook for catching fish

fish·ing \ˈfish-ing\ *n* **:** the sport or business of catching fish

fish ladder *n* **:** a series of pools arranged like steps by which fishes can pass over or around a dam in going upstream

fish meal *n* **:** ground dried fish and fish waste used as fertilizer and animal food

fish·mon·ger \ˈfish-ˌməng-gər, -ˌmäng-\ *n, chiefly British* **:** a fish dealer

fish·net \-ˌnet\ *n* **:** netting fitted with floats and weights or a supporting frame for catching fish

fish·plate \-ˌplāt\ *n* **:** a steel plate used to lap a butt joint

fish·pond \-ˌpänd\ *n* **:** a pond stocked with fish

fish stick *n* **:** a small elongated breaded fillet of fish

fish story *n* **:** an extravagant or incredible story

fish·wife \ˈfish-ˌwīf\ *n* **1 :** a woman who sells fish **2 :** a coarsely abusive woman

fishy \ˈfish-ē\ *adj* **fish·i·er; -est** **1 :** of, relating to, or resembling fish ⟨a *fishy* odor⟩ **2 :** creating doubt or suspicion **:** QUESTIONABLE ⟨that story sounds *fishy* to me⟩

fis·sile \ˈfis-əl, -ˌīl\ *adj* **1 :** capable of being split or divided along the grain or along planes ⟨a *fissile* crystal⟩ **2 :** FISSIONABLE

¹fis·sion \ˈfish-ən *also* ˈfizh-\ *n* **1 :** a splitting or breaking up into parts **2 :** reproduction by spontaneous division of a body or a cell into two or more parts each of which grows into a complete individual **3 :** the splitting of an atomic nucleus resulting in the release of large amounts of energy [Latin *fissio,* from *findere* "to split"]

²fission *vb* **:** to undergo or cause to undergo fission

fis·sion·able \ˈfish-nə-bəl, ˈfizh, -ə-nə-\ *adj* **:** capable of undergoing fission ⟨*fissionable* material⟩

fis·sip·a·rous \fis-ˈip-ə-rəs\ *adj* **:** tending to break something up into parts **:** DIVISIVE ⟨*fissiparous* opposition within a political party⟩ [Latin *fissus,* past participle of *findere* "to split" + *parere* "to give birth to, produce"]

¹fis·sure \ˈfish-ər\ *n* **1 :** a narrow opening or crack of some length and depth ⟨a *fissure* in rock⟩ **2 :** a narrow natural space between body parts (as bones of the skull) or in the substance of an organ **3 :** a separation or disagreement in thought or point of view [Latin *fissura,* from *fissus*]

²fissure *vb* **1 :** to break into fissures **:** CLEAVE **2 :** CRACK 2, DIVIDE

fist \ˈfist\ *n* **1 :** the hand clenched with fingers doubled into the palm **2 :** CLUTCH 1a, GRASP **3 :** INDEX 3 [Old English *fȳst*]

fist·ic \ˈfis-tik\ *adj* **:** of or relating to boxing or to fist fighting

fist·i·cuffs \ˈfis-ti-ˌkəfs\ *n pl* **:** a fight with the fists [alteration of *fisty cuff,* from *fisty* "fistic" + *cuff*]

fis·tu·la \ˈfis-chə-lə\ *n, pl* **-las** *or* **-lae** \-ˌlē, -ˌlī\ **:** an abnormal passage leading from an abscess or hollow organ to the body surface or from one hollow organ to another [Latin, "reed, pipe, fistula"] — **fis·tu·lous** \-ləs\ *adj*

¹fit \ˈfit\ *adj* **fit·ter; fit·test** **1 a :** adapted to an end or design **:** APPROPRIATE ⟨water *fit* for drinking⟩ **b :** adapted to the environment so as to be capable of surviving **2 :** SEEMLY 3, PROPER ⟨a movie *fit* for the whole family⟩ **3 :** put into a suitable state ⟨a house *fit* to live in⟩ **4 :** QUALIFIED 1, COMPETENT **5 :** sound physically and mentally **:** HEALTHY [Middle English] — **fit·ly** *adv* — **fit·ness** *n*

synonyms FIT, SUITABLE, PROPER, APPROPRIATE mean right with respect to the nature, condition, or use of the thing qualified. FIT stresses adaptability to the end in view or special readiness for a particular activity ⟨*fit* to teach young children⟩. SUITABLE implies answering the demands or requirements of an occasion ⟨*suitable* clothes for the reception⟩. PROPER suggests a suitability through essential nature ⟨a *proper* diet⟩ or in accordance with custom ⟨a request made in *proper* form⟩. APPROPRIATE implies a marked or distinctive fitness or suitability ⟨*appropriate* words of congratulation⟩.

²fit *n* **1 :** a sudden violent attack of a disorder (as epilepsy) especially when marked by convulsions or loss of consciousness **2 :** a sudden flurry (as of activity) ⟨completed the assignment in a *fit* of efficiency⟩ **3 :** an emotional outburst ⟨a *fit* of anger⟩ [Old English *fitt* "strife"] — **by fits** *or* **by fits and starts** *or* **in fits and starts :** in an impulsive and irregular manner

³fit *vb* **fit·ted; fit·ting** **1 :** to be suitable for or to **:** BEFIT **2 a :** to be the right size or shape ⟨the suit *fits*⟩ **b :** to insert or adjust until correctly in place **c :** to make a place or room for **3 :** to be in agreement or accord with ⟨the theory *fits* the facts⟩ **4 a :** to make ready **:** PREPARE **b :** to bring to a required form and size **:** ADJUST **c :** to cause to conform to or suit something else **5 :** SUPPLY, EQUIP ⟨*fit* her with new shoes⟩ **6 :** to be in harmony or accord **:** BELONG — often used with *in* [Middle English *fitten*] — **fit·ter** \ˈfit-ər\ *n*

⁴fit *n* **1 :** the quality, state, or manner of being fitted **2 :** the manner in which clothing fits the wearer **3 :** the degree of closeness with which surfaces are brought together in an assembly of parts

fitch \ˈfich\ *or* **fitch·ew** \ˈfich-ü\ *n* **:** POLECAT 1; *also* **:** its fur or pelt [Medieval French *fichau,* from Dutch *vitsau*]

fit·ful \ˈfit-fəl\ *adj* **:** not regular **:** INTERMITTENT ⟨a *fitful* breeze⟩ — **fit·ful·ly** \-fə-lē\ *adv* — **fit·ful·ness** *n*

¹fitting *adj* **:** of a kind appropriate to the situation **:** SUITABLE — **fit·ting·ly** \-ing-lē\ *adv* — **fit·ting·ness** *n*

²fitting *n* **1 a :** the action or act of one that fits **b :** a trying on of clothes being made or altered **2 :** a small often standardized accessory ⟨an electrical *fitting*⟩

five \ˈfīv\ *n* **1** — see NUMBER table **2 :** the fifth in a set or series **3 :** something having five units or members; *esp* **:** a basketball team **4 :** a 5-dollar bill **5 :** FIFTEEN 2 **6 :** a slapping of extended hands by two people (as in greeting or celebration) ⟨I slapped him *five* after he scored⟩ [Old English *fīf*] — **five** *adj or pron*

five–and–ten \ˌfī-vən-ˈten\ *n* **:** a variety store that carries chiefly inexpensive items — called also *five-and-dime*

¹fix \ˈfiks\ *vb* **1 a :** to make firm, stable, or fast **b :** to give a permanent or final form to: as **(1) :** to change into a stable or available form ⟨bacteria that *fix* nitrogen⟩ **(2) :** to kill, harden, and preserve for microscopic study **(3) :** to make the image of (a photographic film or print) permanent by chemical treatment **c :** AFFIX 1, ATTACH **2 :** to hold or direct steadily ⟨*fixed* their eyes on the horizon⟩ **3 a :** to set or place definitely **:** ESTABLISH ⟨*fix* the date of a meeting⟩ **b :** ASSIGN ⟨*fix* blame⟩ **4 :** to set in order **:** ADJUST **5 :** to get ready **:** PREPARE ⟨*fix* lunch⟩ **6 a :** to make sound or whole again: **(1) :** REPAIR, MEND ⟨*fix* the clock⟩ **(2) :** RESTORE, CURE ⟨the doctor *fixed* me up⟩ **b :** SPAY, CASTRATE **7 :** to get even with **8 :** to influence the actions, outcome, or effect of by improper or illegal methods ⟨*fix* a horse race⟩ **9 :** get set **:** be on the verge ⟨*fixing* to leave⟩ [Latin *fixus,* past participle of *figere* "to fasten"] ***synonyms*** see MEND — **fix·able** \ˈfik-sə-bəl\ *adj*

²fix *n* **1 :** a position of difficulty or embarrassment **:** PREDICAMENT **2 :** the position (as of a ship) determined by bearings, observations, or radio; *also* **:** a precise determination of one's position **3 :** a dose of something strongly desired or craved ⟨a coffee *fix*⟩; *esp* : a shot of a narcotic **4 :** something that fixes or restores ⟨an easy *fix*⟩

fix·ate \ˈfik-ˌsāt\ *vb* **1 :** to make unchanging : FIX **2 a :** to focus one's eyes upon **b :** to concentrate one's attention

fix·a·tion \fik-ˈsā-shən\ *n* **1 :** the act, process, or result of fixing or fixating ⟨*fixation* of nitrogen⟩ **2 :** an unhealthy or abnormally persistent state of concern or attachment

fix·a·tive \ˈfik-sət-iv\ *n* **:** something that stabilizes or sets: as **a :** a substance added to a perfume especially to prevent too rapid evaporation **b :** a varnish used especially for the protection of pencil or charcoal drawings — **fixative** *adj*

fixed \ˈfikst\ *adj* **1 a :** securely placed or fastened : STATIONARY **b** (1) **:** NONVOLATILE ⟨*fixed* oil⟩ (2) **:** COMBINED ⟨*fixed* nitrogen⟩ **c :** not subject to change or fluctuation : SETTLED ⟨a *fixed* income⟩ **d :** recurring on the same date from year to year ⟨*fixed* holidays⟩ **e :** INTENT ⟨a *fixed* stare⟩ **2 :** supplied with something (as money) needed or desirable ⟨comfortably *fixed*⟩ — **fix·ed·ly** \ˈfix-səd-lē\ *adv* — **fix·ed·ness** \ˈfik-səd-nəs\ *n*

fixed–point *adj* **:** involving or being a system of representing numbers (as in computer programming) in which each number is written using the same number of digits and the point separating the whole and the fractional part of a number is always in the same place — compare FLOATING-POINT

fixed star *n* **:** a star so distant that its motion can be measured only by very precise long-term observations

fix·er \ˈfik-sər\ *n* **1 :** one that fixes **2 :** SODIUM THIOSULFATE; *also* **:** a solution of sodium thiosulfate

fix·er–up·per \ˈfik-sər-ˌəp-ər\ *n* **:** something (as a house or car) that needs fixing up

fix·ing \ˈfik-sing, *2 is often* -sənz\ *n* **1 :** a putting in permanent form **2** *pl* **:** TRIMMINGS ⟨a turkey dinner with all the *fixings*⟩

fix·i·ty \ˈfik-sət-ē\ *n* **:** the quality or state of being fixed or stable

fix·ture \ˈfiks-chər\ *n* **1 :** the act of fixing : the state of being fixed **2 :** something attached to another thing as a permanent part ⟨bathroom *fixtures*⟩ **3 :** one firmly established in a place

fix up *vt* **1 :** RENOVATE **2 :** to set right : SETTLE **3 :** to provide with something needed or wanted; *esp* : to arrange a date for

[1]**fizz** \ˈfiz\ *vi* **:** to make a hissing or sputtering sound [probably imitative]

[2]**fizz** *n* **1 :** a hissing sound **2 :** an effervescent beverage — **fizzy** \ˈfiz-ē\ *adj*

[1]**fiz·zle** \ˈfiz-əl\ *vi* **fiz·zled; fiz·zling** \ˈfiz-ling, -ə-ling\ **1 :** FIZZ **2 :** to fail or end feebly especially after a promising start — often used with *out* [probably alteration of *fist* "to break wind"]

[2]**fizzle** *n* **:** an abortive effort : FAILURE

fjord *also* **fiord** \fē-ˈȯrd\ *n* **:** a narrow inlet of the sea between cliffs or steep slopes [Norwegian, from Old Norse *fjǫrthr*]

fjord

flab·ber·gast \ˈflab-ər-ˌgast\ *vt* **:** to overwhelm with shock, surprise, or wonder : ASTOUND [origin unknown]

flab·by \ˈflab-ē\ *adj* **flab·bi·er; -est 1 :** lacking resilience or firmness ⟨*flabby* muscles⟩ **2 :** being weak and ineffective : FEEBLE ⟨*flabby* writing⟩ [alteration of *flappy* "tending to flap"] ***synonyms*** see LIMP — **flab·bi·ly** \ˈflab-ə-lē\ *adv* — **flab·bi·ness** \ˈflab-ē-nəs\ *n*

flac·cid \ˈflas-əd, ˈflak-səd\ *adj* **:** FLABBY ⟨a *flaccid* muscle⟩; *also* **:** deficient in turgor ⟨*flaccid* stems⟩ [Latin *flaccidus*] ***synonyms*** see LIMP — **flac·cid·i·ty** \flak-ˈsid-ət-ē, fla-\ *n* — **flac·cid·ly** \ˈflak-səd-lē, ˈflas-əd-\ *adv*

flac·on \ˈflak-ən, -ˌän; fla-ˈkōⁿ\ *n* **:** a small usually ornamental bottle with a tight cap [French]

[1]**flag** \ˈflag\ *n* **:** any of various plants with long narrow leaves: as **a :** IRIS; *esp* : a wild iris **b :** SWEET FLAG [Middle English *flagge* "reed, rush"]

[2]**flag** *n* **1 :** a usually rectangular piece of fabric of distinctive design that is used as a symbol (as of a nation) or as a signaling device **2 a :** something used like a flag to attract attention **b :** one of the cross strokes of a musical note less than a quarter note in value [probably akin to *fag* "end of cloth"]

[3]**flag** *vt* **flagged; flag·ging 1 :** to signal with or as if with a flag; *esp* : to signal to stop ⟨*flag* a taxi⟩ **2 :** to mark or identify with or as if with a flag ⟨*flagged* the important pages with red tabs⟩

[4]**flag** *vi* **flagged; flag·ging 1 :** to hang loose without stiffness; *also* **:** to droop especially from lack of water ⟨plants *flagging* under the summer sun⟩ **2 a :** to become weak ⟨our interest *flagged*⟩ **b :** to decline in interest, attraction, or value ⟨the topic *flagged*⟩ [probably from [2]*flag*]

[5]**flag** *n* **1 :** a hard stone that is composed of even layers and splits into flat pieces suitable for paving **2 :** a thin piece of flag used for paving [perhaps from Old Norse *flaga* "slab"]

[6]**flag** *vt* **flagged; flag·ging :** to pave (as a walk) with flags

Flag Day *n* **:** June 14 observed in various states in commemoration of the adoption in 1777 of the official United States flag

fla·gel·lant \ˈflaj-ə-lənt, flə-ˈjel-ənt\ *n* **:** one that whips; *esp* **:** a person who scourges himself or herself as a public penance

[1]**flag·el·late** \ˈflaj-ə-ˌlāt\ *vt* **:** to punish by whipping : WHIP [Latin *flagellare,* from *flagellum* "small whip," from *flagrum* "whip"] — **flag·el·la·tion** \ˌflaj-ə-ˈlā-shən\ *n*

[2]**fla·gel·late** \ˈflaj-ə-lət, -ˌlāt; flə-ˈjel-ət\ *adj* **1 a** *or* **flag·el·lat·ed** \ˈflaj-ə-ˌlāt-əd\ **:** having flagella **b :** resembling a flagellum **2 :** of, relating to, or caused by flagellates

[3]**flagellate** *like* [2]\ *n* **:** a protozoan or alga having flagella

fla·gel·lum \flə-ˈjel-əm\ *n, pl* **-gel·la** \-ˈjel-ə\ *also* **-gel·lums :** a tapering process that projects singly or in groups from a cell and is the primary organ of motion of many microorganisms [Latin, "whip, shoot of a plant"] — **fla·gel·lar** \-ˈjel-ər\ *adj*

fla·geo·let \ˌflaj-ə-ˈlet\ *n* **:** a small woodwind instrument belonging to the flute class [French]

flag football *n* **:** a variation of football in which a player pulls a flag from the ballcarrier's clothing to stop play instead of tackling

flag·ging \ˈflag-ing\ *n* **:** a pavement of flagstones

fla·gi·tious \flə-ˈjish-əs\ *adj* **:** marked by outrageous or scandalous crime or vice : VILLAINOUS [Latin *flagitiosus,* from *flagitium* "shameful thing"] — **fla·gi·tious·ly** *adv* — **fla·gi·tious·ness** *n*

flag·man \ˈflag-mən\ *n* **:** one who signals with or as if with a flag

flag officer *n* **:** any of the officers in the navy or coast guard above captain

flag of truce : a white flag carried or displayed to an enemy to signal a desire to negotiate or surrender

flag·on \ˈflag-ən\ *n* **:** a container for liquids that has a handle, spout, and often a lid [Medieval French *flascon, flacon* "bottle," from Late Latin *flasco*]

flag·pole \ˈflag-ˌpōl\ *n* **:** a pole on which to display a flag

flag rank *n* **:** a rank of a flag officer

fla·grant \ˈflā-grənt\ *adj* **:** conspicuously bad or objectionable : OUTRAGEOUS ⟨*flagrant* abuse of power⟩ [Latin *flagrare* "to blaze, burn"] — **fla·gran·cy** \-grən-sē\ *n* — **fla·grant·ly** *adv*

synonyms FLAGRANT, GLARING, GROSS, RANK mean conspicuously bad or objectionable. FLAGRANT applies to behavior, errors, or offenses so bad that they cannot escape notice or be excused ⟨*flagrant* disobedience⟩. GLARING suggests painful or damaging obtrusiveness ⟨*glaring* imperfection⟩. GROSS applies to utterly inexcusable faults or offenses ⟨*gross* dishonesty⟩ ⟨*gross* carelessness⟩. RANK applies to what is openly and extremely objectionable and utterly condemned ⟨*rank* corruption in politics⟩.

fla·gran·te de·lic·to \flə-ˌgrant-ē-di-ˈlik-ˌtō\ *adv* **:** IN FLAGRANTE DELICTO

flag·ship \ˈflag-ˌship\ *n* **1 :** the ship that carries the commander of a fleet or subdivision of a fleet and flies the commander's flag **2 :** the finest, largest, or most important of a series or group

flag·staff \-ˌstaf\ *n* **:** FLAGPOLE

flag·stone \-ˌstōn\ *n* **:** [5]FLAG

flag–wav·ing \ˈflag-ˌwā-ving\ *n* **:** passionate appeal to patriotic or partisan sentiment : political chauvinism — **flag–wav·er** \-ər\ *n*

[1]**flail** \ˈflāl\ *n* **:** a hand threshing tool consisting of a wooden handle with a free-swinging stout short stick at the end [Medieval French *flael,* from Latin *flagellum* "whip"]

[2]**flail** *vb* **1 :** to strike with or as if with a flail **2 :** to move or wave about as if swinging a flail ⟨*flailed* their arms at the insects⟩

flair \ˈflaər, ˈfleər\ *n* **1 :** instinctive discernment ⟨relying on *flair* more than careful study⟩ **2 :** natural aptitude : BENT **3 :** a uniquely attractive quality : STYLE ⟨a car with real *flair*⟩

[French, literally, "sense of smell," from Medieval French, "odor," from *flairier* "to give off an odor," from Late Latin *flagrare,* alteration of Latin *fragrare*] ***synonyms*** see PENCHANT

flak *also* **flack** \ˈflak\ *n, pl* **flak** *also* **flack** **1 :** antiaircraft guns or the bursting shells fired from them **2 :** severe criticism [German, from *Fl*ieger*ab*wehr*k*anonen, from *Flieger* "flier" + *Abwehr* "defense" + *Kanonen* "cannons"]

[1]**flake** \ˈflāk\ *n* **:** a thin flattened usually loose piece ⟨a *flake* of snow⟩ ⟨soap *flakes*⟩ [Middle English, of Scandinavian origin]

[2]**flake** *vb* **:** to form or separate into flakes ⟨this paint *flakes* badly⟩

flaky \ˈflā-kē\ *adj* **flak•i•er; -est** **1 :** consisting of flakes **2 :** tending to flake ⟨pie with a crisp *flaky* crust⟩ **3 :** odd or strange in behavior — **flakily** *adv* — **flak•i•ness** *n*

flam•beau \ˈflam-ˌbō\ *n, pl* **flam•beaux** \-ˌbōz\ *or* **flambeaus** **:** a flaming torch [French]

flam•boy•ant \flam-ˈbȯi-ənt\ *adj* **1** *often cap* **:** characterized by waving curves suggesting flames ⟨*flamboyant* window tracery⟩ ⟨*flamboyant* architecture⟩ **2 :** FLORID 1, ORNATE ⟨*flamboyant* writing⟩ **3 :** marked by or given to strikingly elaborate or colorful display or behavior **:** SHOWY ⟨a *flamboyant* dress⟩ [French, from *flamboyer* "to flame," from Medieval French, from *flambe* "flame"] — **flam•boy•ance** \-əns\ *also* **flam•boy•an•cy** \-ən-sē\ *n* — **flam•boy•ant•ly** *adv*

[1]**flame** \ˈflām\ *n* **1 :** the glowing gaseous part of a fire **2 a :** a state of blazing combustion ⟨the car burst into *flame*⟩ **b :** a condition or appearance suggesting a flame **3 :** burning zeal or passion **4 :** SWEETHEART ⟨an old *flame*⟩ **5 :** a hostile or abusive electronic message ⟨sent me a *flame* via e-mail⟩ [Medieval French *flamme, flambe,* derived from Latin *flamma*]

[2]**flame** *vb* **1 :** to burn with a flame **:** BLAZE **2 :** to burst or break out violently or passionately ⟨*flaming* with anger⟩ **3 :** to shine brightly **:** GLOW **4 :** to treat or affect with flame **5 :** to send a hostile or abusive electronic message to or about — **flam•er** *n*

flame cell *n* **:** a hollow excretory cell of various lower invertebrates that has a tuft of cilia

fla•men•co \flə-ˈmeng-kō\ *n, pl* **-cos** **:** a vigorous rhythmic dance style of the Andalusian Gypsies [Spanish, "Flemish, like a Gypsy," from Dutch *Vlaminc* "Fleming"]

flame•out \ˈflā-ˌmau̇t\ *n* **:** the unintentional cessation of operation of a jet airplane engine

flame•proof \ˈflām-ˈprüf\ *adj* **:** resistant to damage or burning on contact with flame — **flameproof** *vt* — **flame•proof•er** *n*

flame•throw•er \-ˌthrō-ər, -ˌthrōr\ *n* **:** a device that shoots a burning stream of liquid or semiliquid fuel under pressure

flam•ing \ˈflā-ming\ *adj* **1 :** producing flames **2 :** suggesting a flame in brilliance or wavy outline **3 :** ARDENT 1, PASSIONATE — **flam•ing•ly** \-ming-lē\ *adv*

fla•min•go \flə-ˈming-gō\ *n, pl* **-gos** *also* **-goes** **:** any of several aquatic long-legged and long-necked birds with a broad bill bent downward at the end and usually rosy-white plumage with scarlet on the wings [obsolete Spanish *flamengo*]

flamingo

flam•ma•ble \ˈflam-ə-bəl\ *adj* **:** capable of being easily ignited and of burning with extreme rapidity — **flam•ma•bil•i•ty** \ˌflam-ə-ˈbil-ət-ē\ *n* — **flam•mable** *n*

fla•neur *also* **flâ•neur** \flä-ˈnər\ *n* **:** an idle man-about-town [French *flâneur*]

[1]**flange** \ˈflanj\ *n* **:** a rib or rim used for strength, for guiding, or for attachment to another object ⟨a *flange* on a pipe⟩ [perhaps from *flanch* "a curving charge on a heraldic shield"]

[2]**flange** *vt* **:** to furnish with a flange

[1]**flank** \ˈflangk\ *n* **1 a :** the fleshy part of the side between the ribs and the hip; *also* **:** the side of a four-footed animal **b :** a cut of meat from this part of an animal **2 a :** SIDE 2 **b :** the right or left of a formation [Medieval French *flanc,* of Germanic origin]

[2]**flank** *vt* **1 :** to be situated at the side of **:** BORDER **2 :** to protect a flank of **3 :** to attack or threaten the flank of

flank•er \ˈflang-kər\ *n* **1 :** one that flanks **2 :** a football player stationed wide of the formation; *esp* **:** an offensive halfback who lines up on the flank and serves chiefly as a pass receiver — called also *flanker back*

flan•nel \ˈflan-l\ *n* **1 a :** a soft twilled wool or worsted fabric with a napped surface **b :** a stout cotton fabric napped on one side **2** *pl* **:** flannel underwear or trousers [Middle English *flaunneol* "woolen cloth or garment"]

flan•nel•ette \ˌflan-l-ˈet\ *n* **:** a cotton flannel napped on one or both sides

[1]**flap** \ˈflap\ *n* **1 :** a stroke with something broad **:** SLAP **2 :** something broad, limber, or flat and usually thin that hangs loose: as **a :** a piece on a garment that hangs free **b :** an extended part forming the closure (as of an envelope) **3 :** the motion of something broad and limber (as a sail or wing) **4 :** a movable auxiliary airfoil attached to the trailing edge of an airplane wing permitting a steeper gliding angle in landing **5 :** a state of excitement or agitation **:** UPROAR ⟨created a *flap* by denying the workers their raises⟩ [Middle English *flappe*]

[2]**flap** *vb* **flapped; flap•ping** **1 :** to beat with something broad and flat **2 :** to move or cause to move with a beating motion ⟨birds *flapping* their wings⟩ **3 :** to sway loosely usually with a noise of striking ⟨the flag *flapped* in the wind⟩ **4 :** to talk foolishly and persistently

flap•jack \ˈflap-ˌjak\ *n* **:** PANCAKE

flap•per \ˈflap-ər\ *n* **1 :** one that flaps **2 :** a young woman of the 1920s who dressed and behaved in a way that was considered very modern

[1]**flare** \ˈflaər, ˈfleər\ *n* **1 a :** a fire or blaze of light used to signal, illuminate, or attract attention; *also* **:** a device or composition used to produce such a flare **b :** a temporary outburst of energy from a small area of the sun's surface **2 :** an unsteady glaring light **3 :** a sudden outburst (as of sound, excitement, or anger) **4 :** a spreading outward; *also* **:** a place or part that spreads ⟨the *flare* of a skirt⟩ ⟨the *flare* of a trumpet⟩

[2]**flare** *vb* **1 :** to burn with an unsteady flame **2 a :** to shine with a sudden light **b :** to become suddenly excited or angry ⟨*flare* up⟩ **3 :** to open or spread outward [origin unknown]

flare–up \-ˌəp\ *n* **:** a sudden burst (as of flame or anger)

[1]**flash** \ˈflash\ *vb* **1 :** to shine in or like a sudden flame ⟨lightning *flashed*⟩ **2 :** to send out in or as if in flashes ⟨*flash* a message⟩ **3 :** to appear or pass very suddenly ⟨a car *flashed* by⟩ **4 :** to make a sudden display (as of brilliance or feeling) ⟨their eyes *flashed* with excitement⟩ **5 :** to give off light suddenly or in brief bursts **6 :** to expose to view usually suddenly and briefly ⟨*flash* a badge⟩ [Middle English *flaschen*]

Word History The origin of the word *flash* is uncertain, though it rhymes with a number of other verbs that also connote forceful, often violent movement that may come to a quick end: *dash, lash, crash, slash, clash, gash, bash, splash, smash.* These words turn up in English over a fairly long period of time, from *dash*—the only word in the group with a likely foreign source—in the 14th century to *smash* in the 18th century. The element *-ash* has thus provided a kind of template for new coinages. The initial *fl-* that is added to *-ash* to make *flash* is also echoed in words denoting quick movement, as *flee, fly, flicker,* and *flutter*.

synonyms FLASH, GLANCE, GLINT, SPARKLE mean to send forth light. FLASH implies a sudden burst of bright light ⟨lightning *flashed*⟩. GLANCE suggests a light reflected from a quickly moving surface ⟨sunlight *glancing* from the ripples⟩. GLINT suggests a cold glancing light ⟨*glinting* steel⟩. SPARKLE implies many moving points of bright light ⟨*sparkling* jewels⟩.

[2]**flash** *n* **1 a :** a sudden burst of light **b :** a movement of a flag in signaling **2 :** a sudden and brilliant burst (as of wit) **3 :** a brief time **4 a :** SHOW 2, DISPLAY **b :** one that attracts notice; *esp* **:** an outstanding athlete **5 :** something flashed: as **a :** GLIMPSE 1, LOOK **b :** a first brief news report **c :** a device for producing a brief and very bright flash of light for taking photographs **d :** a quick-spreading flame or momentary intense outburst of radiant heat

[3]**flash** *adj* **1 :** FLASHY SHOWY **2 :** of sudden origin and short duration ⟨a *flash* fire⟩ **3 :** having or using a solid-state data storage technology that retains data even without a connection to a power source

flash•back \ˈflash-ˌbak\ *n* **1 :** interruption of chronological sequence (as in a motion picture or literary work) by introduction

\ə\ **abut**	\au̇\ **out**	\i\ **tip**	\ȯ\ **saw**	\u̇\ **foot**
\ər\ **further**	\ch\ **chin**	\ī\ **life**	\ȯi\ **coin**	\y\ **yet**
\a\ **mat**	\e\ **pet**	\j\ **job**	\th\ **thin**	\yü\ **few**
\ā\ **take**	\ē\ **easy**	\ng\ **sing**	\t͟h\ **this**	\yu̇\ **cure**
\ä\ **cot, cart**	\g\ **go**	\ō\ **bone**	\ü\ **food**	\zh\ **vision**

of events of earlier occurrence; *also* : an instance of flashback **2** : a past incident recurring vividly in the mind

flash back *vi* **1** : to focus one's mind on or vividly remember a past time or incident — usually used with *to* **2** : to use a flashback (as in a film) — usually used with *to*

flash·bulb \-ˌbəlb\ *n* : an electric bulb that produces a brief and very bright flash for taking photographs

flash card *n* : a card bearing words, numbers, or pictures briefly displayed by a teacher to a class during drills (as in reading, spelling, or arithmetic)

flash drive *n* : a data storage device that uses flash memory; *specif* : a small rectangular device that is designed to be plugged into a USB port on a computer and is often used for transferring files from one computer to another — called also *jump drive, thumb drive*

flash·er \ˈflash-ər\ *n* : one that flashes; *esp* : BLINKER

flash flood *n* : a local flood of short duration generally resulting from nearby heavy rainfall

flash·gun \ˈflash-ˌgən\ *n* : a device for operating a flashbulb

flash·ing \ˈflash-ing\ *n* : sheet metal used in waterproofing roof valleys or the angle between a chimney or wall and a roof

flash lamp *n* : a lamp for producing a brief but intense flash of light for taking photographs

flash·light \ˈflash-ˌlīt\ *n* **1** : a flash of light or a light that flashes **2** : a small battery-operated portable electric light

flash memory *n* : a computer memory chip that retains its data even without a connection to a power source

flash·over \-ˌō-vər\ *n* : an abnormal electrical discharge (as through the air to the ground) from a high potential source

flash point *n* : the lowest temperature at which vapors above a volatile combustible substance ignite in air when exposed to flame

flash·tube \ˈflash-ˌtüb, -ˌtyüb\ *n* : a gas discharge tube that produces very brief intense flashes of light and is used especially in photography

flashy \ˈflash-ē\ *adj* **flash·i·er; -est** **1** : momentarily dazzling **2 a** : superficially attractive : BRIGHT **b** : tastelessly showy ***synonyms*** see GAUDY — **flash·i·ly** \ˈflash-ə-lē\ *adv* — **flash·i·ness** \ˈflash-ē-nəs\ *n*

flask \ˈflask\ *n* : a container often somewhat narrowed toward the outlet and often fitted with a closure: **a** : a broad flat container (as for liquor) sometimes curved to fit a hip pocket **b** : a round or conical glass container with a narrow opening used in a laboratory [Middle French *flasque* "powder flask," derived from Late Latin *flasco* "bottle," of Germanic origin]

[1]**flat** \ˈflat\ *adj* **flat·ter; flat·test** **1** : having a smooth level horizontal surface ⟨*flat* ground⟩ **2** : being smooth and even or having a smooth even surface ⟨a *flat* rock⟩ **3** : spread out on or along a surface ⟨was *flat* on the ground⟩ **4** : having opposite major surfaces essentially parallel ⟨a *flat* board⟩ **5** : clearly unmistakable : DOWNRIGHT ⟨a *flat* refusal⟩ **6** : FIXED, UNCHANGING ⟨charge a *flat* rate⟩ **7** : EXACT ⟨a *flat* four minutes⟩ **8 a** : lacking in interest or flavor : DULL, INSIPID ⟨a *flat* story⟩ ⟨the stew tastes *flat*⟩ **b** : lacking effervescence ⟨*flat* ginger ale⟩ **c** : commercially inactive ⟨sales were *flat*⟩ **9** : DEFLATED — used of tires **10 a** : lower than the true pitch **b** : lower by a half step ⟨tone of A *flat*⟩ **c** : having a flat in the signature ⟨key of B *flat*⟩ **11** : pronounced like the vowel of *hat* ⟨a *flat* a⟩ **12 a** : having little or no illusion of depth ⟨a *flat* painting⟩ **b** : lacking contrast ⟨a *flat* photographic negative⟩ **c** : free from gloss ⟨*flat* paint⟩ [Old Norse *flatr*] — **flat·ly** *adv* — **flat·ness** *n*

[2]**flat** *n* **1** : a level surface of land with little or no relief : PLAIN **2** : a flat part or surface **3 a** : a musical note or tone one half step lower than a specified note or tone **b** : a character ♭ on a line or space of the staff indicating such a note or tone **4** : something flat: as **a** : a shallow box in which seedlings are started **b** : a flat piece of theatrical scenery **c** : a shoe or slipper having a flat heel or no heel **5** *chiefly British* : an apartment on one floor **6** : a deflated tire **7** : the area to either side of an offensive football formation

[3]**flat** *adv* **1** : in a flat manner : DIRECTLY **2** : in a complete manner : ABSOLUTELY ⟨*flat* broke⟩ **3** : EXACTLY ⟨four minutes *flat*⟩ **4** : below the true musical pitch ⟨sang *flat*⟩

[4]**flat** *vb* **flat·ted; flat·ting** **1** : FLATTEN **2 a** : to lower in pitch especially by a half step **b** : to sing or play below the true pitch

[1]**flat·bed** \ˈflat-ˌbed\ *adj* : having a horizontal bed on which material rests ⟨a *flatbed* scanner⟩

[2]**flatbed** *n* : a truck or trailer with a body shaped like a platform or shallow box

flat·boat \-ˌbōt\ *n* : a boat with a flat bottom and square ends used for transporting heavy freight on rivers

flat·car \-ˌkär\ *n* : a railroad freight car without permanent sides, ends, or covering

flat·fish \-ˌfish\ *n* : any of an order (Heterosomata) of marine usually bottom-dwelling fishes (as halibuts, flounders, or soles) that as adults swim on one side of the laterally compressed body and have both eyes on the upper side

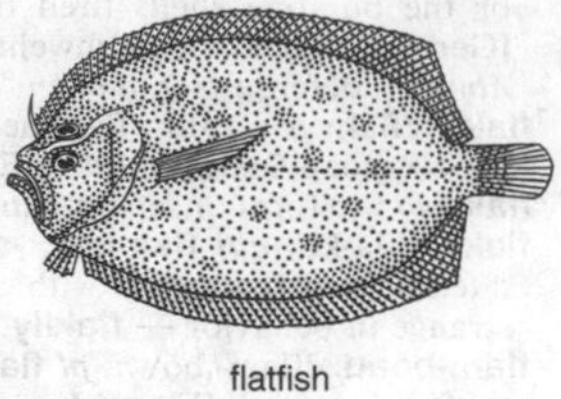
flatfish

flat·foot \-ˌfu̇t, *1,2 also* -ˈfu̇t\ *n, pl* **flat·feet** **1** : a condition in which the main arch of the foot is so flattened that the entire sole rests upon the ground **2** : a foot affected with flatfoot **3** *or pl* **flatfoots** *slang* : POLICE OFFICER; *esp* : PATROLMAN — **flat–foot·ed** \-ˈfu̇t-əd\ *adj*

flat·iron \ˈflat-ˌī-ərn, -ˌīrn\ *n* : an iron for pressing clothes

flat–pan·el \ˈflat-ˈpan-l\ *adj* : relating to or being a thin flat video display

flat·ten \ˈflat-n\ *vb* **flat·tened; flat·ten·ing** \ˈflat-ning, -n-ing\ : to make or become flat

flat·ter \ˈflat-ər\ *vt* **1** : to praise too much or without sincerity especially out of self-interest **2** : to judge (oneself) favorably or too favorably especially in respect to an accomplishment or ability ⟨I *flatter* myself on my skill as a swimmer⟩ **3** : to represent too favorably ⟨the picture *flatters* us⟩ [Middle English *flateren*, from Medieval French *flater* "to lap, flatter," of Germanic origin] — **flat·ter·er** \ˈflat-ər-ər\ *n* — **flat·ter·ing·ly** \ˈflat-ə-ring-lē\ *adv*

flat·tery \ˈflat-ə-rē\ *n, pl* **-ter·ies** **1** : the act of flattering **2** : flattering speech or attentions : insincere or excessive praise

flat·top \ˈflat-ˌtäp\ *n* : AIRCRAFT CARRIER

flat·u·lent \ˈflach-ə-lənt\ *adj* **1 a** : marked by or affected with gases formed in the intestine or stomach **b** : likely to cause such gases to form **2** : pretentious without real worth or substance : POMPOUS [Middle French, from Latin *flatus* "act of blowing, wind," from *flare* "to blow"] — **flat·u·lence** \-ləns\ *n* — **flat·u·lent·ly** *adv*

fla·tus \ˈflāt-əs\ *n* : gas formed in the intestine or stomach

flat·ware \ˈflat-ˌwaər, -ˌweər\ *n* **1** : relatively flat tableware (as plates or saucers) **2** : eating and serving utensils (as forks, spoons, and knives)

flat·ways \-ˌwāz\ *adv* : FLATWISE

flat·wise \-ˌwīz\ *adv* : with the flat side downward or next to another object

flat·worm \-ˌwərm\ *n* : any of a phylum (Platyhelminthes) of flat bilaterally symmetrical unsegmented worms (as planarians, liver flukes, or tapeworms) that lack a body cavity

flaunt \ˈflȯnt, ˈflänt\ *vb* **1** : to wave or flutter showily ⟨the flag *flaunts* in the breeze⟩ **2** : to call public attention to oneself **3** : to display ostentatiously or boldly : PARADE ⟨he *flaunted* his victory⟩ [perhaps of Scandinavian origin] — **flaunt** *n* — **flaunt·ing·ly** \-ing-lē\ *adv*

flau·ta \ˈflau̇t-ə\ *n* : a usually corn tortilla rolled tightly around a filling (as of meat) and deep-fried [American Spanish, literally, "flute"]

flau·tist \ˈflȯt-əst, ˈflau̇t-\ *n* : FLUTIST [Italian *flautista*, from *flauto* "flute"]

fla·vo·pro·tein \ˌflā-vō-ˈprō-ˌtēn, -ˈprōt-ē-ən\ *n* : an enzyme that serves in the removal and transport of hydrogen and plays a major role in biological oxidations [derived from Latin *flavus* "yellow"]

[1]**fla·vor** \ˈflā-vər\ *n* **1 a** : the quality of something that affects the sense of taste : SAVOR **b** : the blend of taste and smell sensations evoked by a substance in the mouth **2** : a substance that flavors ⟨artificial *flavors*⟩ **3** : characteristic or predominant quality ⟨the ethnic *flavor* of the neighborhood⟩ **4** : an appealing or enlivening quality ⟨a character that adds *flavor* to the story⟩ [Middle English *flavour*, from Medieval French *flaur, flour*, derived from Latin *flare* "to blow"] — **fla·vored** \-vərd\ *adj* — **fla·vor·ful** \-vər-fəl\ *adj* — **fla·vor·less** \-ləs\ *adj*

[2]**flavor** *vt* **fla·vored; fla·vor·ing** \ˈflāv-ring, -ə-ring\ : to give or add flavor to

flavoring *n* : FLAVOR 2

fla·vour *chiefly British variant of* FLAVOR

[1]**flaw** \ˈflȯ\ *n* **1** : an often hidden defect that may cause failure ⟨a

flaw in a plan⟩ **2 :** a marred or imperfect part ⟨a diamond with a *flaw*⟩ [Middle English, "flake," from Old Norse *flaga* "stone slab"] ***synonyms*** see BLEMISH — **flaw·less** \-ləs\ *adj* — **flaw·less·ly** *adv* — **flaw·less·ness** *n*

[2]**flaw** *vb* **:** to make or become defective

flax \ˈflaks\ *n* **:** a slender erect blue-flowered plant grown for its fiber and seeds; *also* **:** its fiber especially prepared for spinning — compare LINEN [Old English *fleax*]

flax·en \ˈflak-sən\ *adj* **1 :** made of flax **2 :** resembling flax especially in pale soft strawy color ⟨*flaxen* hair⟩

flax·seed \ˈflak-ˌsēd\ *n* **:** the small seed of flax used as a source of linseed oil and medicinal preparations

flay \ˈflā\ *vt* **1 :** to strip off the skin or surface of **:** SKIN **2 :** to criticize harshly **:** SCOLD [Old English *flean*]

F layer *n* **:** the highest and most densely ionized regular layer of the ionosphere

flea \ˈflē\ *n* **:** any of an order (Siphonaptera) of small wingless blood-sucking insects with a hard laterally compressed body and legs adapted to leaping [Old English *flēa*]

flea·bane \-ˌbān\ *n* **:** any of various plants related to the daisies

flea beetle *n* **:** any of various small beetles that leap like fleas, feed on foliage, and include some that are agricultural pests

flea–bit·ten \ˈflē-ˌbit-n\ *adj* **:** bitten by or infested with fleas

flea collar *n* **:** a collar for an animal (as a dog or a cat) that contains insecticide for killing fleas

flea market *n* **:** a usually open-air market for secondhand articles and antiques [translation of French *Marché aux Puces,* a market in Paris]

[1]**fleck** \ˈflek\ *vt* **:** STREAK, SPOT ⟨hair *flecked* with gray⟩ [back-formation from *flecked* "spotted," from Middle English]

[2]**fleck** *n* **1 :** SPOT 2a, MARK **2 :** FLAKE, PARTICLE

flec·tion \ˈflek-shən\ *n* **:** FLEXION — **flec·tion·al** \-shnəl, -shən-l\ *adj*

fledge \ˈflej\ *vb* **1 :** to develop the feathers necessary for flying; *also* **:** to leave the nest after developing such feathers **2 :** to furnish with feathers ⟨*fledge* an arrow⟩ [Old English *-flycge* "capable of flying"]

fledg·ling \ˈflej-ling\ *n* **1 :** a young bird just fledged **2 :** an immature or inexperienced person

flee \ˈflē\ *vb* **fled** \ˈfled\; **flee·ing** **1 a :** to run away from danger or evil **:** FLY **b :** to run away from **:** SHUN **2 :** to pass away swiftly **:** VANISH [Old English *flēon*]

[1]**fleece** \ˈflēs\ *n* **1 :** the coat of wool covering an animal (as a sheep) **2 :** a soft or woolly covering **3 :** a soft bulky deep-piled knitted or woven fabric used chiefly for clothing [Old English *flēos*]

[2]**fleece** *vt* **1 :** to rob by fraud or extortion **2 :** to remove the fleece from **:** SHEAR

fleecy \ˈflē-sē\ *adj* **fleec·i·er; -est :** covered with, made of, or resembling fleece — **fleec·i·ness** *n*

[1]**fleet** \ˈflēt\ *vb* **1 :** to fly swiftly **2 :** to pass or cause to pass rapidly ⟨time is *fleeting*⟩ [Old English *flēotan* "to float, flow"]

[2]**fleet** *n* **1 :** a group of warships under one command **2 :** a group of ships or vehicles that move together or are operated under one management ⟨a *fleet* of trucks⟩ ⟨a *fleet* of airplanes⟩ [Old English *flēot* "ship," from *flēotan* "to float"]

[3]**fleet** *adj* **1 :** swift in motion **:** NIMBLE **2 :** not enduring **:** MOMENTARY [probably from [1]*fleet*] ***synonyms*** see FAST — **fleet·ly** *adv* — **fleet·ness** *n*

Fleet Admiral *n* **:** a commissioned officer of highest rank in the Navy whose insignia is five stars

fleet–foot·ed \ˈflēt-ˌfu̇t-əd\ *adj* **:** swift of foot — **fleet–foot·ed·ness** *n*

fleeting *adj* **:** passing swiftly ⟨a *fleeting* glimpse⟩ ***synonyms*** see TRANSIENT

Flem·ing \ˈflem-ing\ *n* **:** a member of the Germanic people inhabiting northern Belgium and a small section of northern France bordering on Belgium [Dutch *Vlaminc*]

Flem·ish \ˈflem-ish\ *n* **1 :** the Germanic language of the Flemings that is made up of dialects of Dutch **2** *pl in constr* **:** FLEMINGS — **Flemish** *adj*

[1]**flesh** \ˈflesh\ *n* **1 a :** the soft parts of the body of an animal; *esp* **:** skeletal muscle of a vertebrate **b :** the condition of having ample fat on the body ⟨cattle in good *flesh*⟩ **2 :** parts of an animal used as food **3 :** the physical being of a person as distinguished from the soul **4 a :** human beings **:** HUMANKIND **b :** living beings **c :** STOCK 5b, KINDRED **5 :** a fleshy plant part used as food; *esp* **:** the fleshy part of a fruit [Old English *flǣsc*] — **fleshed** \ˈflesht\ *adj* — **in the flesh :** in person and alive

[2]**flesh** *vb* **1 :** to give substance to ⟨*flesh* out a story with details⟩ **2 :** to remove flesh from **3 :** to become fleshy — often used with *up* or *out*

flesh fly *n* **:** a two-winged fly whose maggots feed on flesh

flesh·ly \ˈflesh-lē\ *adj* **1 :** CORPOREAL c, BODILY **2 a :** CARNAL, SENSUAL ⟨*fleshly* desires⟩ **b :** not spiritual **:** WORLDLY

flesh wound *n* **:** an injury involving penetration of body muscles without damage to bones or internal organs

fleshy \ˈflesh-ē\ *adj* **flesh·i·er; -est** **1 a :** resembling or consisting of flesh **b :** having abundant flesh; *esp* **:** FAT **2 :** having or being soft juicy tissue **:** PULPY ⟨*fleshy* fruits⟩ — **flesh·i·ness** *n*

fleur–de–lis *or* **fleur–de–lys** \ˌflərd-l-ˈē, ˌflu̇rd-\ *n, pl* **fleurs–de–lis** *or* **fleur–de–lis** *or* **fleurs–de–lys** *or* **fleur–de–lys** *same or* -ˈēz\ **1 :** IRIS 3 **2 :** a conventionalized iris in art and heraldry [Medieval French *flur de lis,* literally, "lily flower"]

fleur-de-lis 2

flew *past of* FLY

flews \ˈflüz\ *n pl* **:** the drooping lateral parts of a dog's upper lip [origin unknown]

flex \ˈfleks\ *vb* **1 :** to bend especially repeatedly **2 a :** to move muscles so as to cause flexion of (a joint) **b :** to move or tense (a muscle) by contraction **3 :** USE 1, DEMONSTRATE ⟨*flexing* her skills as a singer⟩ [Latin *flexus,* past participle of *flectere* "to bend, flex"]

flex·i·ble \ˈflek-sə-bəl\ *adj* **1 :** capable of being flexed **:** PLIANT **2 :** readily changed or changing **:** ADAPTABLE — **flex·i·bil·i·ty** \ˌflek-sə-ˈbil-ət-ē\ *n* — **flex·i·bly** \ˈflek-sə-blē\ *adv*

flex·ion \ˈflek-shən\ *n* **:** a bending movement around a joint (as the knee or elbow) in an arm or leg that decreases the angle between the bones of the arm or leg at the joint; *also* **:** the resulting state

flex·or \ˈflek-sər\ *n* **:** a muscle that produces flexion — compare EXTENSOR — **flexor** *adj*

flex·ure \ˈflek-shər\ *n* **1 :** the quality or state of being flexed **2 :** TURN, FOLD — **flex·ur·al** \-shə-rəl, -shrəl\ *adj*

[1]**flick** \ˈflik\ *n* **1 :** a light sharp jerky stroke or movement ⟨a *flick* of the wrist⟩ **2 :** a sound produced by a flick [imitative]

[2]**flick** *vb* **1 :** to strike lightly with a quick sharp motion ⟨*flicked* a speck off the table⟩ **2 :** FLICKER 1

[3]**flick** *n, slang* **:** MOVIE [short for [2]*flicker*]

[1]**flick·er** \ˈflik-ər\ *vb* **flick·ered; flick·er·ing** \ˈflik-ring, -ə-ring\ **1 :** to move irregularly or unsteadily **:** FLUTTER **2 :** to burn irregularly or with a fluctuating light ⟨a *flickering* candle⟩ [Old English *flicorian*]

[2]**flicker** *n* **1 :** an act of flickering **2 :** a brief stirring ⟨a *flicker* of interest⟩ **3 :** a flickering light — **flick·ery** \ˈflik-rē, -ə-rē\ *adj*

[3]**flicker** *n* **:** a large insect-eating No. American woodpecker with a black crescent on the breast and yellow or red on the underside of the wings and tail — compare RED-SHAFTED FLICKER, YELLOW-SHAFTED FLICKER [imitative]

flied *past of* [3]FLY

fli·er *also* **fly·er** \ˈflī-ər, ˈflīr\ *n* **1 :** one that flies; *esp* **:** AVIATOR **2 :** a speculative undertaking **3 :** an advertising circular

[1]**flight** \ˈflīt\ *n* **1 :** an act or instance of passing through the air by the use of wings ⟨a *flight* in a plane⟩ ⟨the *flight* of birds⟩ **2 a :** a passing through the air or through space outside the earth's atmosphere ⟨the *flight* of a bullet⟩ ⟨a moon *flight*⟩ **b :** the distance covered in a flight **c :** swift movement **3 :** an airplane making a scheduled flight **4 :** a group of similar things flying through the air together ⟨a *flight* of ducks⟩ ⟨a *flight* of bombers⟩ **5 :** a brilliant, imaginative, or unrestrained exercise or display ⟨a *flight* of fancy⟩ **6 :** a continuous series of stairs from one landing or floor to another [Old English *flyht*]

[2]**flight** *n* **:** an act or instance of fleeing [Middle English *fliht*]

flight attendant *n* **:** a person who attends passengers on an airplane

flight control *n* **:** the control from a ground station of an airplane or spacecraft especially by radio

flight engineer *n* **:** a member of a flight crew responsible for mechanical operation

flight feather *n* : one of the quills of a bird's wing or tail that support it in flight
flight·less \ˈflīt-ləs\ *adj* : unable to fly ⟨*flightless* birds⟩
flight line *n* : a parking and servicing area for airplanes
flight path *n* : the path made or followed by something (as a spacecraft, airplane, or particle) in flight
flighty \ˈflīt-ē\ *adj* **flight·i·er; -est** **1** : easily upset : VOLATILE ⟨a *flighty* temper⟩ **2** : easily excited : SKITTISH ⟨a *flighty* horse⟩ **3** : CAPRICIOUS, SILLY — **flight·i·ly** \ˈflīt-l-ē\ *adv* — **flight·i·ness** \ˈflīt-ē-nəs\ *n*
flim·flam \ˈflim-ˌflam\ *n* **1** : deceptive nonsense **2** : DECEPTION 1, FRAUD [perhaps of Scandinavian origin] — **flimflam** *vb*
flim·sy \ˈflim-zē\ *adj* **flim·si·er; -est** **1 a** : lacking strength or substance ⟨a *flimsy* car⟩ **b** : of inferior materials and workmanship ⟨a *flimsy* house⟩ **2** : having little worth or plausibility ⟨a *flimsy* excuse⟩ [perhaps derived from [1]*film*] — **flim·si·ly** \-zə-lē\ *adv* — **flim·si·ness** \-zē-nəs\ *n*
flinch \ˈflinch\ *vi* : to shrink from or as if from physical pain : WINCE [Middle French *flenchir* "to bend"] — **flinch** *n* — **flinch·er** *n*
[1]**fling** \ˈfling\ *vb* **flung** \ˈfləng\; **fling·ing** \ˈfling-ing\ **1** : to move in a brusque or headlong manner ⟨*flung* out of the room⟩ **2** : to kick or plunge vigorously ⟨the horse *flung* out at him⟩ **3 a** : to throw or swing with force or recklessness ⟨*flung* herself down on the sofa⟩ **b** : to cast aside : DISCARD **4** : to place or put suddenly and unexpectedly into a state or condition ⟨*flung* the troops into confusion⟩ [Middle English *flingen,* perhaps of Scandinavian origin] ***synonyms*** see THROW — **fling·er** \ˈfling-ər\ *n*
[2]**fling** *n* **1** : an act or instance of flinging **2 a** : a casual try : ATTEMPT **b** : a casual or brief love affair **3** : a period of self-indulgence
flint \ˈflint\ *n* **1** : a hard dark quartz that produces a spark when struck by steel **2 a** : a piece of flint **b** : an alloy (as of iron and cerium) used for producing a spark in cigarette lighters **3** : something resembling flint in hardness ⟨a heart of *flint*⟩ [Old English]
flint glass *n* : heavy glass that contains an oxide of lead and is used in lenses and prisms
flint·lock \ˈflint-ˌläk\ *n* **1** : a lock for a gun using a flint to ignite the charge **2** : a firearm fitted with a flintlock

flintlock 2

flinty \ˈflint-ē\ *adj* **flint·i·er; -est** **1** : composed of or covered with flint **2 a** : notably hard ⟨*flinty* seeds⟩ **b** : UNYIELDING, STERN ⟨a strong *flinty* character⟩ — **flint·i·ly** \ˈflint-l-ē\ *adv* — **flint·i·ness** \ˈflint-ē-nəs\ *n*
[1]**flip** \ˈflip\ *vb* **flipped; flip·ping** **1** : to turn by tossing ⟨*flip* a coin⟩ **2** : to turn quickly ⟨*flip* the pages of a book⟩ **3** : FLICK ⟨*flip* a light switch⟩ **4** : to lose self-control [probably imitative]
[2]**flip** *n* **1** : an act or instance of flipping : TOSS, FLICK **2** : a somersault performed in the air
[3]**flip** *adj* : FLIPPANT
flip·pant \ˈflip-ənt\ *adj* : treating lightly something serious or worthy of respect : lacking earnestness [probably from [1]*flip*] — **flip·pan·cy** \-ən-sē\ *n* — **flip·pant·ly** *adv*
flip·per \ˈflip-ər\ *n* **1** : a broad flat limb (as of a seal or whale) adapted for swimming **2** : a flat rubber shoe with the front expanded into a paddle used in skin diving
[1]**flirt** \ˈflərt\ *vi* **1** : to move erratically : FLIT **2 a** : to behave amorously without serious intent **b** : TOY ⟨*flirted* with the idea of getting a job⟩ [origin unknown] — **flir·ta·tion** \ˌflər-ˈtā-shən\ *n* — **flir·ta·tious** \-shəs\ *adj* — **flir·ta·tious·ness** *n* — **flirt·er** \ˈflərt-ər\ *n*
[2]**flirt** *n* **1** : an act or instance of flirting **2** : a person who flirts
flit \ˈflit\ *vi* **flit·ted; flit·ting** : to move in a quick erratic manner [Middle English *flitten,* of Scandinavian origin] — **flit** *n*
flit·ter \ˈflit-ər\ *vi* : FLUTTER 1, FLICKER [derived from *flit*]
fliv·ver \ˈfliv-ər\ *n* : a small cheap usually old automobile [origin unknown]
[1]**float** \ˈflōt\ *n* **1** : an act or instance of floating **2** : something that floats in or on the surface of a fluid: as **a** : [3]BOB 3 **b** : a floating platform anchored near a shoreline for use by swimmers or boats **c** : a hollow ball that controls the flow or level of the liquid it floats on (as in a tank or cistern) **d** : a watertight structure giving an airplane buoyancy on water **3** : a vehicle carrying an exhibit in a parade; *also* : the vehicle and exhibit together **4 a** : an amount of money represented by checks outstanding and in the process of collection **b** : the time between a transaction and the withdrawal of funds to cover it **c** : the volume of a company's shares available for trading **5** : a drink consisting of ice cream floating in a beverage [Middle English *flote* "boat, float," from Old English *flota* "ship"]
[2]**float** *vb* **1** : to rest or cause to rest in or on the surface of a fluid **2 a** : to drift or cause to drift on or through or as if on or through a fluid ⟨dust *floating* through the air⟩ ⟨*float* logs down a river⟩ **b** : WANDER ⟨*floating* from town to town⟩ **3 a** : to put forth (a proposal) for acceptance **b** : to offer (an issue of stocks or bonds) in order to finance an enterprise **c** : to finance (an enterprise) by floating an issue of stocks or bonds **d** : to arrange for ⟨*float* a loan⟩
float·er \ˈflōt-ər\ *n* **1 a** : one that floats **b** : a person who floats something **2** : a person without a permanent home or job : VAGRANT
float·ing \ˈflōt-ing\ *adj* **1** : buoyed on or in a fluid **2 a** : not settled or committed : not established ⟨*floating* capital⟩ ⟨a *floating* population⟩ **b** : short-term and usually not funded ⟨a *floating* debt⟩ **3** : connected or constructed so as to operate and adjust smoothly ⟨a *floating* axle⟩
floating–point *adj* : involving or being a system of representing numbers (as in computer programming) in which a quantity is written as a number multiplied by a power of that number's base ⟨999.9 can be expressed in a *floating-point* system as 9.999 x 10^2⟩ — compare FIXED-POINT
floating rib *n* : a rib (as one of the last two pairs in human beings) that has no attachment to the sternum — compare FALSE RIB
floc·cu·late \ˈfläk-yə-ˌlāt\ *vb* : to collect or cause to collect into a flocculent mass — **floc·cu·la·tion** \ˌfläk-yə-ˈlā-shən\ *n*
floc·cu·lent \ˈfläk-yə-lənt\ *adj* : resembling wool especially in loose fluffy texture [Latin *floccus* "flock of wool"]
[1]**flock** \ˈfläk\ *n* **1** : a group of animals (as birds or sheep) assembled or herded together **2** : a group under the guidance of a leader **3** : a large number [Old English *flocc* "crowd, band"]
[2]**flock** *vi* : to gather or move in a crowd ⟨they *flocked* to the beach⟩
[3]**flock** *n* **1** : a tuft of wool or cotton fiber **2** : woolen or cotton refuse used for stuffing furniture and mattresses **3** : very short or pulverized fiber used to form a pattern on cloth or paper or a protective covering on metal [Middle English *flok,* from Medieval French, from Latin *floccus*]
[4]**flock** *vt* **1** : to fill with flock **2** : to decorate with flock
flock·ing \ˈfläk-ing\ *n* : a design in flock
floe \ˈflō\ *n* : a sheet or mass of floating ice [probably from Norwegian *flo* "flat layer"]
flog \ˈfläg\ *vt* **flogged; flog·ging** : to beat severely with a rod or whip [perhaps from Latin *flagellare* "to whip"] — **flog·ger** *n*
[1]**flood** \ˈfləd\ *n* **1 a** : a great flow of water that rises and spreads over the land; *also* : a condition of overflowing ⟨rivers in *flood*⟩ **b** *cap* : a flood described in the Bible as covering the earth in the time of Noah **2** : the flowing in of the tide **3** : an overwhelming quantity or volume ⟨a *flood* of mail⟩ [Old English *flōd*]
[2]**flood** *vb* **1** : to cover or become filled with a flood ⟨the river *flooded* the lowlands⟩ ⟨the cellar *floods* after a rain⟩ **2** : to fill abundantly or excessively ⟨a room *flooded* with light⟩ **3** : to pour forth in a flood **4** : to supply excess fuel to so that operation is hampered ⟨*flooded* the engine⟩
flood·gate \ˈfləd-ˌgāt\ *n* **1** : a gate (as in a canal) for shutting out, admitting, or releasing a body of water : SLUICE **2** : something serving to restrain an outburst ⟨opened the *floodgates* of criticism⟩
flood·light \-ˌlīt\ *n* **1** : artificial illumination in a broad beam **2** : a lighting unit for projecting a beam of light — **floodlight** *vt*
flood·plain \-ˌplān\ *n* **1** : low flat land along a stream that may flood **2** : a plain built up by deposits of earth from floodwaters
flood tide *n* **1** : the tide while rising or at its greatest height **2 a** : an overwhelming quantity **b** : a high point : PEAK ⟨our success was at *flood tide*⟩
flood·wa·ter \ˈfləd-ˌwȯt-ər, -ˌwät-\ *n* : the water of a flood
flood·way \-ˌwā\ *n* : a channel for diverting floodwaters
[1]**floor** \ˈflōr, ˈflȯr\ *n* **1** : the part of a room on which one stands **2 a** : the lower inside surface of a hollow structure **b** : a ground surface ⟨the ocean *floor*⟩ ⟨the *floor* of a forest⟩ **3 a** : a structure dividing a building into stories **b** : STORY ⟨they live

on the first *floor*⟩ **c** : the occupants of a story **4** : the surface of a structure on which one travels ⟨the *floor* of a bridge⟩ **5 a** : a main level space (as in a legislative chamber) distinguished from a platform or gallery **b** : the right to speak from one's place in an assembly ⟨the senator has the *floor*⟩ **6** : a lower limit (as of prices) [Old English *flōr*]

[2]**floor** *vt* **1** : to cover with a floor or flooring **2 a** : to knock to the floor **b** : SHOCK, OVERWHELM ⟨the news *floored* us⟩

floor·board \ˈflōr-ˌbōrd, ˈflȯr-ˌbȯrd\ *n* **1** : a board in a floor **2** : the floor of an automobile

floor exercise *n* : a gymnastic event in which participants perform various ballet and tumbling feats on a floor mat

floor·ing \ˈflōr-ing, ˈflȯr-\ *n* **1** : FLOOR 1 **2** : material for floors

floor lamp *n* : a tall lamp that stands on the floor

floor leader *n* : a member of a legislative body chosen by a party to have charge of its organization and strategy on the floor

floor show *n* : a series of acts presented in a nightclub

floor·walk·er \ˈflōr-ˌwȯ-kər, ˈflȯr-\ *n* : a person employed in a retail store to oversee the salespeople and aid customers

floo·zy \ˈflü-zē\ *n, pl* **floozies** : a woman of loose morals [origin unknown]

[1]**flop** \ˈfläp\ *vb* **flopped; flop·ping** **1** : to swing or bounce loosely : flap about ⟨a hat brim *flopping* in the wind⟩ **2 a** : to throw oneself down heavily, clumsily, or in a completely relaxed manner ⟨*flop* into the chair⟩ **b** : to throw or drop suddenly and usually heavily or noisily ⟨*flopped* the bundles onto the table⟩ **3** : to fail completely ⟨the play *flopped*⟩ [alteration of [2]*flap*]

[2]**flop** *n* **1** : an act or sound of flopping **2** : a complete failure : DUD ⟨the play was a *flop*⟩

[3]**flop** *adv* : RIGHT, SQUARELY ⟨fall *flop* on my face⟩

flop·house \-ˌhau̇s\ *n* : a cheap rooming house or hotel

flop·py \ˈfläp-ē\ *adj* **flop·pi·er; -est** : tending to flop; *esp* : being soft and flexible ⟨a hat with a *floppy* brim⟩

floppy disk *n* : a thin flexible disk with a magnetic coating on which data for a computer can be stored

flo·ra \ˈflōr-ə, ˈflȯr-\ *n, pl* **floras** *also* **flo·rae** \-ˌē, -ˌī\ : plant or bacterial life especially of a region, period, or environment ⟨studied the *flora* of Hawaii⟩ ⟨the intestinal *flora*⟩ — compare FAUNA [Latin *Flora,* Roman goddess of flowers]

flo·ral \ˈflōr-əl, ˈflȯr-\ *adj* : of or relating to flowers or a flora [Latin *flor-, flos* "flower"] — **flo·ral·ly** \-ə-lē\ *adv*

Flor·ence flask \ˈflȯr-əns-, ˈflär-\ *n* : a round usually flat-bottomed glass laboratory vessel with a long neck [*Florence,* Italy; from the use of flasks of this shape for Italian wines]

flo·res·cence \flȯ-ˈres-ns, flə-\ *n* : a state or period of being in bloom or flourishing ⟨the highest *florescence* of a civilization⟩ [Latin *florescere* "to begin to bloom," from *florēre* "to blossom, flourish"] — **flo·res·cent** \-nt\ *adj*

flo·ret \ˈflōr-ət, ˈflȯr-\ *n* : a small flower; *esp* : one of the small flowers forming the head of a plant of the composite family

flori- *combining form* : flower or flowers ⟨*florigen*⟩ [Latin *flor-, flos* "flower"]

flor·id \ˈflȯr-əd, ˈflär-\ *adj* **1** : excessively flowery in style : ORNATE ⟨*florid* writing⟩ **2** : tinged with red : RUDDY ⟨a *florid* complexion⟩ [Latin *floridus* "blooming, flowery," from *florēre* "to blossom, flourish"] — **flo·rid·i·ty** \flə-ˈrid-ət-ē, flȯ-\ *n* — **flor·id·ly** \ˈflȯr-əd-lē, ˈflär-\ *adv* — **flor·id·ness** *n*

flo·rif·er·ous \flȯ-ˈrif-rəs, -ə-rəs\ *adj* : bearing flowers; *esp* : blooming freely — **flo·rif·er·ous·ness** *n*

flo·ri·gen \ˈflōr-ə-jən, ˈflȯr-, ˈflär-\ *n* : a plant hormone that promotes flowering

flor·in \ˈflȯr-ən, ˈflär-, ˈflōr-\ *n* **1 a** : an old gold coin first struck at Florence in 1252 **b** : any of various former gold coins of European countries patterned after the Florentine florin **2 a** : a former British silver coin worth two shillings **b** : any of several similar coins issued in parts of the Commonwealth of Nations **3** : GULDEN [Medieval French, from Italian *fiorino,* from *fiore* "flower," from Latin *flor-, flos;* from the lily on the first florins]

flo·rist \ˈflōr-əst, ˈflȯr-, ˈflär-\ *n* : a person who sells flowers and ornamental plants

flo·ris·tic \flȯ-ˈris-tik\ *adj* : FLORAL — **flo·ris·ti·cal·ly** \-ti-kə-lē, -klē\ *adv*

[1]**floss** \ˈfläs, ˈflȯs\ *n* **1 a** : soft thread of silk or mercerized cotton for embroidery **b** : DENTAL FLOSS **2** : fluffy fibrous material; *esp* : SILK COTTON [probably from French *floche* "soft, weak (of silk fibers)"]

[2]**floss** *vb* : to use or clean with dental floss ⟨*floss* daily⟩

flossy \ˈfläs-ē, ˈflȯs-\ *adj* **floss·i·er; -est** **1 a** : of, relating to, or having the characteristics of floss **b** : DOWNY 2 **2** : stylish or glamorous especially at first impression ⟨slick *flossy* writing⟩

flo·ta·tion *also* **floa·ta·tion** \flō-ˈtā-shən\ *n* **1** : the act, process, or state of floating **2** : the separation of the particles of a mass of pulverized ore according to their relative capacity for floating on a given liquid

flo·til·la \flō-ˈtil-ə\ *n* **1** : a fleet of ships; *esp* : a navy unit consisting of two or more squadrons of small warships [Spanish, from *flota* "fleet," from Medieval French *flote,* from Old Norse *floti*]

flot·sam \ˈflät-səm\ *n* : floating wreckage of a ship or its cargo [Medieval French *floteson,* from *floter* "to float," of Germanic origin]

[1]**flounce** \ˈflau̇ns\ *vi* **1** : to move with exaggerated jerky motions **2** : to go with sudden determination ⟨*flounced* out of the room in anger⟩ [perhaps of Scandinavian origin]

[2]**flounce** *n* : an act or instance of flouncing

[3]**flounce** *vt* : to trim or finish with a flounce

[4]**flounce** *n* : a strip of fabric attached by the upper edge ⟨a wide *flounce* at the bottom of the skirt⟩ [alteration of Middle English *frouncen* "to curl"]

[1]**floun·der** \ˈflau̇n-dər\ *n, pl* **flounder** *or* **flounders** : FLATFISH; *esp* : any of various important marine food fishes [Middle English, of Scandinavian origin]

[2]**flounder** *vi* **floun·dered; floun·der·ing** \-də-ring, -dring\ : to struggle or proceed clumsily ⟨*flounder* in the deep snow⟩ [probably alteration of *founder*]

[1]**flour** \ˈflau̇r\ *n* **1 a** : finely ground powdery meal of wheat usually largely freed from bran **b** : a similar meal of any cereal grain or edible seed **2** : a fine soft powder [Middle English, "flower, best of anything, flour"]

[2]**flour** *vt* : to coat with flour

flour beetle *n* : any of several usually elongated flattened brown beetles that typically feed on and lay eggs in grain products (as flour)

[1]**flour·ish** \ˈflər-ish, ˈflə-rish\ *vb* **1** : to grow luxuriantly : THRIVE **2 a** : to achieve success : PROSPER **b** : to be active or prominent ⟨*flourished* around 1850⟩ **3** : to make bold and sweeping gestures **4** : to wield with dramatic gestures : BRANDISH ⟨*flourish* a sword⟩ [Medieval French *floriss-,* stem of *florir* "to flourish," from Latin *florēre,* from *flor-, flos* "flower"]

[2]**flourish** *n* **1** : an act or instance of brandishing or waving **2 a** : a flowery bit of speech or writing **b** : an ornamental stroke in writing **c** : a decorative or finishing detail ⟨a house with clever little *flourishes*⟩ **3** : FANFARE **4** : a period of thriving **5** : dramatic action ⟨introduced them with a *flourish*⟩ **6** : a sudden burst ⟨a *flourish* of activity⟩

floury \ˈflau̇r-ē\ *adj* **1** : of, relating to, or resembling flour **2** : covered with flour

flout \ˈflau̇t\ *vb* **1** : to treat with contemptuous disregard : SCORN ⟨*flouting* their parents' advice⟩ **2** : to indulge in scornful behavior [probably from Middle English *flouten* "to play the flute," from *floute* "flute"] ***synonyms*** see FLAUNT — **flout·er** *n*

[1]**flow** \ˈflō\ *vi* **1 a** : to issue or move in a stream **b** : to move with a continual shifting of the constituent particles ⟨the molasses *flowed* slowly⟩ **2** : RISE ⟨the tide ebbs and *flows*⟩ **3** : ABOUND ⟨a land that *flows* with milk and honey⟩ **4 a** : to proceed smoothly and readily ⟨the words *flowed* from my mouth⟩ **b** : to have a smooth uninterrupted continuity **5** : to hang loose and billowing ⟨a flag *flowing* in the breeze⟩ **6** : to come from as a source **7** : MENSTRUATE [Old English *flōwan*] — **flow·ing·ly** \-ing-lē\ *adv*

[2]**flow** *n* **1** : an act of flowing **2 a** : FLOOD 1a **b** : the flowing in of the tide ⟨the tide's ebb and *flow*⟩ **3 a** : a smooth uninterrupted movement or progress ⟨a *flow* of information⟩ **b** : a stream of fluid; *also* : a mass of matter which has flowed when molten ⟨a lava *flow*⟩ **4 a** : the quantity that flows in a certain time ⟨the *flow* of water over a dam⟩ **b** : OUTPUT 1a, YIELD **5** : MENSTRUATION **6** : a continuous transfer of energy ⟨a *flow* of electricity⟩

\ə\ **abut**	\au̇\ **out**	\i\ **tip**	\ȯ\ **saw**	\u̇\ **foot**
\ər\ **further**	\ch\ **chin**	\ī\ **life**	\ȯi\ **coin**	\y\ **yet**
\a\ **mat**	\e\ **pet**	\j\ **job**	\th\ **thin**	\yü\ **few**
\ā\ **take**	\ē\ **easy**	\ng\ **sing**	\t͟h\ **this**	\yu̇\ **cure**
\ä\ **cot, cart**	\g\ **go**	\ō\ **bone**	\ü\ **food**	\zh\ **vision**

flow chart *n* : a diagram showing step-by-step progression through a procedure or system

flow cy·tom·e·try \-sī-ˈtäm-ə-trē\ *n* : a technique for identifying and sorting cells and their components (as DNA) by staining with a fluorescent dye and detecting the fluorescence usually by laser beam illumination

[1]**flow·er** \ˈflau̇-ər, ˈflau̇r\ *n* 1 a : BLOSSOM, INFLORESCENCE b : a shoot of the spore-producing generation of a higher plant that is specialized for reproduction and consists of a shortened axis bearing modified leaves (as petals and sporophylls) c : a plant cultivated or valued for its blossoms 2 a : the best part or example ⟨the *flower* of the family⟩ b : the finest most vigorous period c : a state of blooming or flourishing ⟨when knighthood was in *flower*⟩ 3 *pl* : a finely divided powder produced especially by condensation or sublimation ⟨*flowers* of sulfur⟩ [Middle English *flour,* from Medieval French, from Latin *flor-, flos*] — **flow·er·less** \-ləs\ *adj* — **flow·er·like** \-ˌlīk\ *adj*

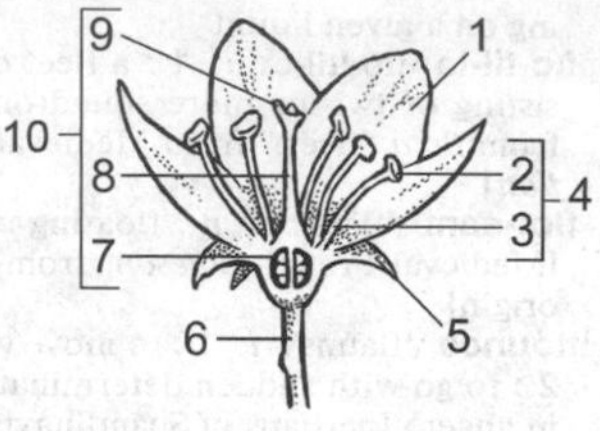

flower 1a: *1* petal, *2* anther, *3* filament, *4* stamen, *5* sepal, *6* pedicel, *7* ovary, *8* style, *9* stigma, *10* pistil

[2]**flower** *vb* 1 : to produce flowers : BLOOM 2 a : DEVELOP ⟨*flowered* into a real scholar⟩ b : FLOURISH 2 3 : to decorate with floral designs

flow·ered \ˈflau̇-ərd, ˈflau̇rd\ *adj* 1 : having or bearing flowers 2 : decorated with flowers or flowerlike figures ⟨*flowered* silk⟩

flow·er·et \ˈflau̇-ər-ət, ˈflau̇r-ət\ *n* : FLORET

flower girl *n* : a young girl who carries flowers at a wedding

flower head *n* : a tight cluster of small stemless flowers that looks like a single flower

flowering plant *n* : any of a major group (Angiospermae) of higher plants that comprises those which produce flowers, fruits, and seeds with the seeds in a closed ovary — called also *angiosperm*; compare SEED PLANT

flow·er·pot \ˈflau̇-ər-ˌpät, ˈflau̇r-\ *n* : a pot in which to grow plants

flow·ery \ˈflau̇-ər-ē, flau̇r-\ *adj* **flow·er·i·er; -est** 1 : full of or covered with flowers 2 : full of fine words or phrases : FLORID ⟨*flowery* language⟩ — **flow·er·i·ness** *n*

flown *past participle of* FLY

flu \ˈflü\ *n* 1 : INFLUENZA 1 2 : any of several virus diseases marked especially by respiratory or intestinal symptoms — **flu-like** \-ˌlīk\ *adj*

flub \ˈfləb\ *vb* **flubbed; flub·bing** 1 : BOTCH ⟨the actor *flubbed* the line⟩ 2 : BLUNDER 2 [origin unknown] — **flub** *n*

fluc·tu·ate \ˈflək-chə-ˌwāt\ *vi* 1 : to move up and down or back and forth like a wave 2 : to be changing constantly and irregularly (as between points, levels, or conditions) ⟨the market *fluctuated* wildly⟩ ⟨one's health may *fluctuate* with the weather⟩ [Latin *fluctuare,* from *fluctus* "flow, wave," from *fluere* "to flow"] — **fluc·tu·a·tion** \ˌflək-chə-ˈwā-shən\ *n*

flue \ˈflü\ *n* : an enclosed passageway for directing a current: as a : a channel in a chimney for conveying flame and smoke to the outer air b : a pipe for conveying flame and hot gases around or through water in a steam boiler c : FLUE PIPE [origin unknown]

flu·en·cy \ˈflü-ən-sē\ *n* : the quality or state of being fluent especially in speech

flu·ent \ˈflü-ənt\ *adj* 1 : capable of flowing : FLUID 2 a : capable of using a language easily and accurately ⟨*fluent* in Spanish⟩ b : effortlessly smooth and flowing : POLISHED ⟨*fluent* speech⟩ [Latin *fluere* "to flow"] — **flu·ent·ly** *adv*

flue pipe *n* : an organ pipe whose tone is produced by an air current striking the lip and causing the air within to vibrate

flue stop *n* : an organ stop made up of flue pipes

[1]**fluff** \ˈfləf\ *n* 1 : [3]NAP, DOWN ⟨soft *fluff* from a pillow⟩ 2 : something fluffy 3 : something unimportant 4 : BLUNDER; *esp* : an actor's lapse of memory [perhaps blend of *flue* "fluff," and *puff*]

[2]**fluff** *vb* 1 : to make or become fluffy ⟨*fluff* up a pillow⟩ 2 : to spoil by or make a mistake : BOTCH 3 : to deliver badly or fail to remember (one's lines in a play)

fluffy \ˈfləf-ē\ *adj* **fluff·i·er; -est** 1 a : having, covered with, or resembling fluff or down ⟨*fluffy* fur⟩ b : being light and soft or airy : puffed up ⟨a *fluffy* omelet⟩ 2 : SILLY 3 — **fluff·i·ness** *n*

[1]**flu·id** \ˈflü-əd\ *adj* 1 a : capable of flowing like a liquid or gas b : likely or tending to change or move ⟨boundaries became *fluid*⟩ 2 : characterized by or employing a smooth easy style ⟨a *fluid* performance⟩ 3 a : available for various uses ⟨a *fluid* computer program⟩ b : easily converted into cash ⟨*fluid* assets⟩ [Latin *fluidus,* from *fluere* "to flow"] — **flu·id·i·ty** \flü-ˈid-ət-ē\ *n* — **flu·id·like** \ˈflü-əd-ˌlīk\ *adj* — **flu·id·ly** \ˈflü-əd-lē\ *adv* — **flu·id·ness** *n*

[2]**fluid** *n* : a substance tending to flow or conform to the outline of its container ⟨liquids and gases are *fluids*⟩

fluid dram *or* **flu·i·dram** \ˌflü-əd-ˈdram\ *n* : a unit of liquid capacity equal to 1/8 fluid ounce (about 3.7 milliliters) — see MEASURE table

fluid mechanics *n sing or pl* : a branch of mechanics that deals with the properties of liquids and gases

fluid ounce *n* : a unit of liquid capacity equal to 1/16 pint (about 29.6 milliliters) — see MEASURE table

[1]**fluke** \ˈflük\ *n* 1 : FLATFISH 2 : any of various trematodes — compare LIVER FLUKE [Old English *flōc*]

[2]**fluke** *n* 1 : the part of an anchor that digs into the ground 2 : a barbed head (as of a harpoon) 3 : one of the lobes of a whale's tail [perhaps from [1]*fluke*]

[3]**fluke** *n* : a stroke of luck ⟨won by a *fluke*⟩ [origin unknown]

fluky \ˈflü-kē\ *adj* **fluk·i·er; -est** 1 : happening by or depending on chance 2 : being unsteady or uncertain : CHANGEABLE ⟨a *fluky* wind⟩

flume \ˈflüm\ *n* 1 : an inclined channel for conveying water (as for power) 2 : a ravine or gorge with a stream running through it [probably from Middle English *flum* "river," from Medieval French, from Latin *flumen,* from *fluere* "to flow"]

flum·mery \ˈfləm-rē, -ə-rē\ *n, pl* **-mer·ies** 1 a : a soft jelly or porridge made with flour or meal b : any of several sweet desserts 2 a : something trashy b : empty compliment : HUMBUG [Welsh *llymru*]

flum·mox \ˈfləm-əks, -iks\ *vt* : CONFUSE 1 [origin unknown]

flung *past of* FLING

flunk \ˈfləngk\ *vb* 1 : to fail an examination or course 2 : to give a failing grade to [perhaps blend of *flinch* and *funk*] — **flunk** *n*

flunk out *vb* : to dismiss or be dismissed from a school or college for failure

flun·ky *also* **flun·key** *or* **flun·kie** \ˈfləng-kē\ *n, pl* **flunkies** *also* **flunkeys** 1 a : a servant in livery b : one doing menial duties 2 : TOADY, YES-MAN [Scots]

fluor- *or* **fluoro-** *combining form* 1 : fluorine ⟨*fluor*ide⟩ 2 *also* **fluori-** : fluorescence ⟨*fluoro*scope⟩

flu·o·resce \flu̇r-ˈes, ˌflü-ər-\ *vi* : to produce, undergo, or exhibit fluorescence [back-formation from *fluorescence*]

flu·o·res·ce·in \-ˈes-ē-ən\ *n* : a yellow or red crystalline dye with a bright yellow-green fluorescence in alkaline solution

flu·o·res·cence \-ˈes-ns\ *n* : the property of a substance of emitting radiation usually as visible light when exposed to radiation from another source; *also* : the radiation emitted

flu·o·res·cent \-ˈes-nt\ *adj* 1 : having or relating to fluorescence 2 a : bright and glowing as a result of fluorescence ⟨*fluorescent* inks⟩ b : very bright in color — **fluorescent** *n* — **flu·o·res·cent·ly** *adv*

fluorescent lamp *n* : an electric lamp in which light is produced on the inside fluorescent coating of a glass tube by the action of ultraviolet light

flu·o·ri·date \ˈflu̇r-ə-ˌdāt\ *vt* : to add a fluoride to ⟨*fluoridate* drinking water⟩ — **flu·o·ri·da·tion** \ˌflu̇r-ə-ˈdā-shən\ *n*

flu·o·ride \ˈflu̇-ər-ˌīd, ˈflu̇r-ˌ\ *n* : a compound of fluorine with another chemical element or a radical

flu·o·ri·nate \ˈflu̇r-ə-ˌnāt\ *vt* : to treat or cause to combine with fluorine or a compound of fluorine — **flu·o·ri·na·tion** \ˌflu̇r-ə-ˈnā-shən\ *n*

flu·o·rine \ˈflu̇r-ˌēn, ˈflu̇-ər-\ *n* : a nonmetallic univalent chemical element that is normally a pale yellowish flammable irritating toxic gas — see ELEMENT table [French, from New Latin *fluor* "mineral belonging to a group including fluorite and used as fluxes," from Latin, "flow," from *fluere* "to flow"]

flu·o·rite \ˈflu̇r-ˌīt, ˈflu̇-ər-\ *n* : a transparent or translucent mineral CaF_2 of different colors that consists of a fluoride of calcium and is used as a flux and in making glass

flu·o·ro·car·bon \ˈflu̇r-ō-ˌkär-bən, ˈflü-ər-\ *n* **:** any of various inert compounds of carbon and fluorine used chiefly as lubricants, refrigerants, nonstick coatings, and formerly propellants for aerosols and in making resins and plastics; *also* **:** CHLOROFLUOROCARBON

1**flu·o·ro·scope** \ˈflu̇r-ə-ˌskōp\ *n* **:** an instrument that is used especially in examining inner parts of the body (as the lungs) by observing light and dark shadows produced on a screen by the action of X-rays — **flu·o·ro·scop·ic** \ˌflu̇r-ə-ˈskäp-ik\ *adj* — **flu·o·ros·co·py** \ˌflu̇r-ˈäs-kə-pē, ˌflu̇-ər-ˈ\ *n*

2**fluoroscope** *vt* **:** to examine by a fluoroscope

flu·or·spar \ˈflu̇r-ˌspär, ˈflü-ər-\ *n* **:** FLUORITE

1**flur·ry** \ˈflər-ē, ˈflə-rē\ *n, pl* **flurries** **1 a :** a gust of wind **b :** a brief light snowfall **2 :** nervous commotion **3 :** a brief outburst of activity ⟨a *flurry* of trading in the stock exchange⟩ [probably from *flurr* "to strew"]

2**flurry** *vb* **flur·ried; flur·ry·ing :** to become or cause to become agitated and confused

1**flush** \ˈfləsh\ *vb* **:** to take flight or cause to take flight suddenly ⟨*flushed* a covey of quail⟩ [Middle English *flusshen*]

2**flush** *n* **:** a hand of playing cards all of the same suit [Middle French *flus,* from Latin *fluxus* "flow"]

3**flush** *n* **1 :** a sudden flow (as of water) **2 a :** a sudden increase (as of growth) ⟨a spring *flush* of grass⟩ **b :** a surge of emotion ⟨a *flush* of anger⟩ **3 a :** a tinge of red **:** BLUSH **b :** a fresh and vigorous state ⟨in the *flush* of youth⟩ **4 :** a brief sensation of extreme heat [perhaps from Latin *fluxus* "flow"]

4**flush** *vb* **1 :** to flow and spread suddenly and freely **2 a :** to glow brightly **b :** BLUSH 1 **c :** to have a rosy or fresh color **3 :** to pour liquid over or through; *esp* **:** to wash out with a rush of liquid ⟨*flush* a toilet⟩ **4 :** INFLAME, EXCITE ⟨troops *flushed* with victory⟩ **5 :** to make red or hot ⟨a face *flushed* with fever⟩

5**flush** *adj* **1 a :** of a ruddy healthy color **b :** full of life and vigor **:** LUSTY **2 a :** filled to overflowing **b :** fully supplied especially with money ⟨he had just got paid and was feeling *flush*⟩ **3 :** readily available **:** ABUNDANT **4 a :** having an unbroken continuous surface ⟨*flush* paneling⟩ **b :** directly abutting or immediately adjacent **c :** set even with an edge of a type page or column — **flush·ness** *n*

6**flush** *adv* **1 :** in a flush manner **2 :** SQUARELY ⟨was hit *flush* on the chin⟩

7**flush** *vt* **:** to make flush ⟨*flush* the headings on a page⟩

1**flus·ter** \ˈfləs-tər\ *vt* **flus·tered; flus·ter·ing** \-tə-riŋ, -triŋ\ **1 :** BEFUDDLE 1 **2 :** to make nervous and unsure **:** UPSET ⟨*flustered* by their rudeness⟩ [probably of Scandinavian origin] ***synonyms*** see DISTURB

2**fluster** *n* **:** a state of agitated confusion

1**flute** \ˈflüt\ *n* **1 a :** RECORDER 3 **b :** a woodwind instrument consisting of a tube with keys that is played by blowing across a hole near the closed end **2 a :** a grooved pleat **b :** a rounded groove; *esp* **:** one of the vertical parallel grooves on a classical architectural column [Middle English *floute,* from Medieval French *floute, flaüte*] — **flute·like** \-ˌlīk\ *adj*

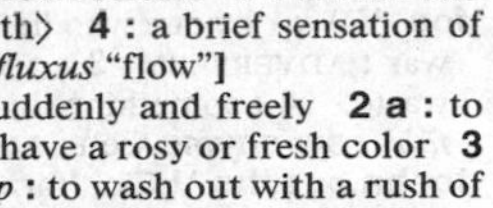
flute 1b

2**flute** *vb* **1 :** to play a flute **2 :** to make a sound like that of a flute **3 :** to form flutes in ⟨*fluted* columns⟩

flut·ing \ˈflüt-iŋ\ *n* **:** fluted decoration

flut·ist \ˈflüt-əst\ *n* **:** a flute player

1**flut·ter** \ˈflət-ər\ *vb* **1 :** to move or cause the wings to move rapidly without flying or in short flights ⟨butterflies *flutter*⟩ **2 a :** to move with quick wavering or flapping motions ⟨flags *fluttered* in the breeze⟩ **b :** to vibrate in irregular spasms ⟨a *fluttering* pulse⟩ **3 :** to move about or behave in an agitated aimless way [Old English *floterian,* from *flotian* "to float"] — **flut·ter·er** *n* — **flut·tery** \ˈflət-ə-rē\ *adj*

2**flutter** *n* **1 :** an act of fluttering **2 a :** a state of nervous confusion or excitement **b :** FLURRY 3 **3 :** a distortion in reproduced sound similar to but of a higher pitch than wow

flutter kick *n* **:** an alternating whipping motion of the legs used in various swimming strokes (as the crawl)

flu·vi·al \ˈflü-vē-əl\ *adj* **:** produced by the action of a stream ⟨a *fluvial* plain⟩ [Latin *fluvialis,* from *fluvius* "river," from *fluere* "to flow"]

1**flux** \ˈfləks\ *n* **1 :** an excessive fluid discharge from the body and especially the bowels **2 a :** a flowing in ⟨*flux* of the tide⟩ **b :** a series of changes **:** a state of continuous change **3 :** a substance used to promote fusion especially of metals or minerals **4 :** the rate of flow of fluid, particles, or energy across a given surface [Latin *fluxus* "flow," from *fluere* "to flow"]

2**flux** *vb* **1 :** to become or cause to become fluid **:** FUSE **2 :** to treat with a flux

1**fly** \ˈflī\ *vb* **flew** \ˈflü\; **flown** \ˈflōn\; **fly·ing** **1 a :** to move in or pass through the air with wings **b :** to move through the air or before the wind or through outer space **c :** to float or cause to float, wave, or soar in the air ⟨flags *flying*⟩ **2 a :** to take flight **:** FLEE **b :** to fade and disappear **:** VANISH **3 :** to move, pass, or spread swiftly ⟨time *flies*⟩ ⟨rumors were *flying*⟩ **4 :** to become spent or wasted rapidly ⟨our money just *flew*⟩ **5 a :** to operate or travel in an aircraft **b :** to journey over by flying ⟨to *fly* the Atlantic⟩ **c :** to transport by aircraft ⟨to *fly* passengers⟩ [Old English *flēogan*] — **fly at :** to attack suddenly and violently — **fly blind :** to fly an airplane solely by instruments — **fly contact :** to fly an airplane with the aid of visible landmarks or reference points — **fly high :** to be elated — **fly in the face of** *or* **fly in the teeth of :** to act forthrightly or brazenly in defiance or disobedience of

2**fly** *n, pl* **flies** **1 :** the action or process of flying **:** FLIGHT **2 :** a horse-drawn public coach or delivery wagon **3** *pl* **:** the space over a theater stage **4 :** something attached by one edge: as **a :** a garment closing concealed by a fold of cloth extending over the fastener **b :** the outer fabric of a tent with a double top **c :** the length of an extended flag from its staff or support; *also* **:** the outer or loose end of a flag **5 :** a baseball hit high into the air — **on the fly** **1 :** continuously active **:** very busy **2 :** while still in the air ⟨the home run carried 450 feet *on the fly*⟩ **3 :** in a hurry and often without preparation **:** HASTILY ⟨making decisions *on the fly*⟩; *also* **:** SPONTANEOUSLY

3**fly** *vi* **flied; flying :** to hit a fly in baseball

4**fly** *n, pl* **flies** **1 :** a winged insect — usually used in combination ⟨may*fly*⟩ **2 :** a winged or rarely wingless insect (order Diptera) **:** TWO-WINGED FLY; *esp* **:** one (as a housefly or horsefly) that is relatively large and stout-bodied — compare GNAT **3 :** a fishhook dressed to suggest an insect [Old English *flēoge*] — **fly in the ointment :** a detracting factor or element

fly·able \ˈflī-ə-bəl\ *adj* **:** suitable for flying or being flown

fly agaric *n* **:** a poisonous amanita mushroom with a usually bright red cap

fly ash *n* **:** fine solid particles of noncombustible ash carried out of a bed of burning solid fuel by the draft

fly ball *n* **:** 2FLY 5

fly·blown \ˈflī-ˌblōn\ *adj* **1 :** infested with the eggs or young larvae of a flesh fly or blowfly **2 :** not pure **:** TAINTED, CORRUPT

fly·by \-ˌbī\ *n, pl* **flybys** **1 :** a usually low-altitude flight past a chosen place by one or more aircraft **2 a :** a flight of a spacecraft past a heavenly body (as Mars) close enough to obtain scientific data **b :** a spacecraft that makes a flyby

fly–by–night \ˈflī-bə-ˌnīt\ *adj* **1 :** given to making quick profits by shady or irresponsible acts **2 :** SHORT-LIVED, TRANSITORY ⟨*fly-by-night* fashions⟩

fly–by–wire *adj* **:** controlled or operated by electrical signals rather than mechanically ⟨a *fly-by-wire* jet⟩

fly casting *n* **:** the casting of artificial flies (as in fly-fishing)

fly·catch·er \ˈflī-ˌkach-ər, -ˌkech-\ *n* **:** a small bird that feeds on insects that it captures in the air

flyer *variant of* FLIER

fly–fishing \ˈflī-ˌfish-iŋ\ *n* **:** fishing with artificial flies cast by means of a large flexible pole and a relatively heavy line — **fly–fish** \-ˌfish\ *vi*

1**fly·ing** \ˈflī-iŋ\ *adj* **1 a :** moving or made by moving rapidly ⟨a *flying* leap⟩ **b :** HASTY 1a ⟨a *flying* visit⟩ **2 :** ready to move or act quickly **:** MOBILE ⟨a *flying* squad car⟩

2**flying** *n* **1 :** travel by air **2 :** the operation of an aircraft or spacecraft

flying boat *n* **:** a seaplane with a hull adapted for floating

\ə\ **abut**	\au̇\ **out**	\i\ **tip**	\ȯ\ **saw**	\u̇\ **foot**
\ər\ **further**	\ch\ **chin**	\ī\ **life**	\ȯi\ **coin**	\y\ **yet**
\a\ **mat**	\e\ **pet**	\j\ **job**	\th\ **thin**	\yü\ **few**
\ā\ **take**	\ē\ **easy**	\ng\ **sing**	\th\ **this**	\yu̇\ **cure**
\ä\ **cot, cart**	\g\ **go**	\ō\ **bone**	\ü\ **food**	\zh\ **vision**

flying buttress *n* : a projecting arched structure to support a wall or building

flying buttress

flying colors *n pl* : complete success ⟨passed the exam with *flying colors*⟩
flying fish *n* : any of numerous sea fishes that have long fins suggesting wings and are able to glide for a distance through the air
flying fox *n* : FRUIT BAT
flying jib *n* : a sail forward of the jib set on an extension of the jibboom
flying machine *n* : AIRCRAFT
flying saucer *n* : any of various unidentified flying objects and usually described as being saucer-shaped or disk-shaped
flying squirrel *n* : a squirrel with folds of skin connecting the forelegs and hind legs that enable it to make long gliding leaps
flying start *n* : a start in racing in which the participants are moving when they receive the starting signal
fly·leaf \ˈflī-ˌlēf\ *n* : the half of the endpaper of a book that is not pasted down to the cover
fly·pa·per \-ˌpā-pər\ *n* : paper poisoned or coated with a sticky substance for killing or catching flies
fly·speck \-ˌspek\ *n* **1** : a speck of fly dung **2** : something small and insignificant — **flyspeck** *vt*
fly·swat·ter \-ˌswät-ər\ *n* : a device for killing insects that consists of a flat piece of perforated rubber or plastic or fine-mesh wire netting attached to a handle
fly·way \-ˌwā\ *n* : an established air route of migratory birds
fly·weight \-ˌwāt\ *n* : a boxer in a weight division having an upper limit of 112 pounds
fly·wheel \-ˌhwēl, -ˌwēl\ *n* : a heavy wheel attached to the shaft of a revolving machine that reduces fluctuation in shaft speed through its inertia
FM \ˈef-ˌem\ *n* : a system of broadcasting using frequency modulation; *also* : a receiver of radio waves broadcast by such a system [*f*requency *m*odulation] — **FM** *adj*
f–number \ˈef-ˌnəm-bər\ *n* : a number following the symbol f/ that expresses the ratio of the focal length of a camera or telescope lens to the aperture and that determines the range of sharpness and the brightness of the image so that the smaller the number the brighter the image but the larger the number the greater the range of sharpness [*f*ocal length]
[1]foal \ˈfōl\ *n* : a young animal of the horse family; *esp* : one under one year [Old English *fola*]
[2]foal *vb* : to give birth to a foal
[1]foam \ˈfōm\ *n* **1** : a light frothy mass of fine bubbles formed in or on a liquid **2** : a froth formed (as by a horse) in salivating or sweating **3** : a stabilized froth produced chemically and used especially in fighting oil fires **4** : a material (as rubber) in a lightweight cellular form resulting from introduction of gas bubbles during manufacture [Old English *fām*]
[2]foam *vb* **1 a** : to produce or form foam **b** : to froth at the mouth especially in anger; *also* : to be angry **2** : to gush out in foam **3** : to cause to form foam; *esp* : to cause air bubbles to form in **4** : to convert (as a plastic) into a foam
foam rubber *n* : spongy rubber of fine texture made from latex by foaming before vulcanization
foamy \ˈfō-mē\ *adj* **foam·i·er; -est** **1** : covered with foam : FROTHY **2** : full of, consisting of, or resembling foam — **foam·i·ly** \-mə-lē\ *adv* — **foam·i·ness** \-mē-nəs\ *n*
fob \ˈfäb\ *n* **1** : a short strap, chain, or ribbon attached especially to a pocket watch **2** : a small ornament worn on a watch chain [perhaps akin to German dialect *Fuppe* "pocket"]
fob off *vt* **1** : to put off with a trick or excuse **2** : to offer as genuine **3** : to put aside [Middle English *fobben* "to cheat"]
fo·cal \ˈfō-kəl\ *adj* : of, relating to, or having a focus — **fo·cal·ly** \-kə-lē\ *adv*
focal infection *n* : a persistent localized infection especially when causing symptoms elsewhere in the body
focal length *n* : the distance of the focus from the surface of a lens or concave mirror
focal point *n* : [1]FOCUS 1, 4
fo'c'sle *variant of* FORECASTLE
[1]fo·cus \ˈfō-kəs\ *n, pl* **fo·ci** \-ˌsī\ *also* **fo·cus·es** **1** : a point at which rays (as of light, heat, or sound) converge or from which they diverge or appear to diverge; *esp* : the point at which an image is formed by a mirror, lens, or optical system **2 a** : FOCAL LENGTH **b** : adjustment (as of the eye or binoculars) for clear vision; *also* : the area that may be seen distinctly or resolved into a clear image **3** : a point or one of a pair of points whose location is used in defining a circle, ellipse, parabola, or hyperbola **4** : a center of activity, attraction, or attention **5** : the place of origin of an earthquake [Latin, "hearth"]
Word History The Latin word *focus* meant "hearth, fireplace." In the scientific Latin of the 17th century the word is used to refer to the point at which rays of light refracted by a lens converge. Because rays of sunlight when directed by a magnifying glass can produce enough heat to ignite paper, a word meaning "fireplace" is quite appropriate as a metaphor to describe their convergence point. From this sense of *focus* have arisen extended senses such as "center of activity."
[2]focus *vb* **fo·cused** *also* **fo·cussed; fo·cus·ing** *also* **fo·cus·sing** **1 a** : to bring into focus **b** : to adjust the focus of ⟨*focus* the eyes⟩ ⟨*focus* a telescope⟩ **2** : to cause to be concentrated ⟨*focus* public attention on a problem⟩ **3** : to bring to a focus ⟨*focus* rays of light⟩ **4** : to come to a focus **5** : to adjust one's eye or a camera to a particular range ⟨*focus* at 3 meters⟩
fod·der \ˈfäd-ər\ *n* : coarse dry food (as cornstalks) for livestock [Old English *fōdor*] — **fodder** *vt*
foe \ˈfō\ *n* **1** : one who hates another : ENEMY **2** : an enemy in war : ADVERSARY **3** : one who opposes on principle ⟨a *foe* to waste⟩ **4** : something injurious ⟨a *foe* to health⟩ [Old English *fāh*] ***synonyms*** see ENEMY
foehn *or* **föhn** \ˈfœn, ˈfərn, ˈfān\ *n* : a warm dry wind blowing down the side of a mountain [German *Föhn*]
foe·tal, foe·tus *chiefly British variant of* FETAL, FETUS
[1]fog \ˈfȯg, ˈfäg\ *n* **1 a** : fine particles of water suspended in the lower atmosphere that differ from cloud only in being near the ground **b** : a fine spray or a foam for firefighting **2** : a murky condition of the atmosphere or a substance causing it **3** : a state of mental confusion **4** : cloudiness in a developed photographic image [probably back-formation from *foggy*]
[2]fog *vb* **fogged; fog·ging** **1** : to cover or become covered with or as if with fog **2** : to make obscure or confusing **3** : to make confused
fog·bound \ˈfȯg-ˌbau̇nd, ˈfäg-\ *adj* **1** : unable to move because of fog ⟨*fogbound* ships⟩ **2** : covered by fog ⟨a *fogbound* coast⟩
fog·gy \ˈfȯg-ē, ˈfäg-\ *adj* **fog·gi·er; -est** **1 a** : filled or abounding with fog **b** : covered or made opaque by moisture or grime **2** : VAGUE 2 [earlier, "spongy, marshy, thick," from *fog* "second growth of grass," from Middle English *fogge*] — **fog·gi·ly** \-ə-lē\ *adv* — **fog·gi·ness** \-ē-nəs\ *n*
fog·horn \ˈfȯg-ˌhȯrn, ˈfäg-\ *n* : a horn (as on a ship) sounded in foggy weather to give warning
fo·gy *also* **fo·gey** \ˈfō-gē\ *n, pl* **fogies** *also* **fogeys** : a person with old-fashioned ideas — usually used with *old* [origin unknown] — **fo·gy·ish** *or* **fo·gey·ish** \-gē-ish\ *adj* — **fo·gy·ism** *or* **fo·gey·ism** \-gē-ˌiz-əm\ *n*
foi·ble \ˈfȯi-bəl\ *n* : a minor flaw or shortcoming in personal character or behavior : WEAKNESS [obsolete French, from Medieval French *feble* "feeble"] ***synonyms*** see FAULT
[1]foil \ˈfȯil\ *vt* : to prevent from attaining an end : DEFEAT ⟨*foil* a plot⟩ [Middle English *foilen* "to trample," alteration of *fullen* "to full (cloth)"] ***synonyms*** see FRUSTRATE
[2]foil *n* **1** : a very thin sheet of metal ⟨tin or aluminum *foil*⟩ **2** : a thin leaf of polished and colored metal placed under an inferior or paste gem to add color and brilliance **3** : one that serves as a contrast to another ⟨acted as a *foil* for a comedian⟩ **4** : a leaf-shaped architectural ornamentation or one of the arcs or rounded spaces between its projections [Medieval French *fuille, foille* "leaf," derived from Latin *folium*]
[3]foil *n* **1** : a fencing weapon with a flat guard and a light flexible blade tapering to a blunt point **2** : the art or practice of fencing with foils — often used in plural [origin unknown]
foils·man \ˈfȯilz-mən\ *n* : one that fences with a foil
foist \ˈfȯist\ *vt* : to pass off as genuine or worthy [probably from Dutch *vuisten* "to take into one's hand," from *vuist* "fist"]
[1]fold \ˈfōld\ *n* **1** : an enclosure for sheep **2 a** : a flock of sheep **b** : a group of people with a common faith, belief, or interest [Old English *falod, fald*]
[2]fold *vt* : to pen up or confine (as sheep) in a fold
[3]fold *vb* **1** : to lay one part over or against another part ⟨*fold* a blanket⟩ **2** : to clasp together ⟨*fold* one's hands⟩ **3** : EM-

BRACE 1 **4 :** to incorporate (a food ingredient) into a mixture by overturning repeatedly without stirring or beating **5 :** to become doubled or pleated ⟨the map *folds* into its case⟩ **6 :** to fail completely ⟨the business *folded*⟩ [Old English *fealdan*]

[4]**fold** *n* **1 :** a doubling or folding over **2 :** a part doubled or laid over another part

-fold \ˌfōld, ˈfōld\ *suffix* **1 :** multiplied by (a specified number) : times — in adjectives ⟨a twelve*fold* increase⟩ and adverbs ⟨repay you ten*fold*⟩ **2 :** having (so many) parts ⟨three*fold* solution to the problem⟩ [Old English *-feald*]

fold·boat \ˈfōld-ˌbōt, ˈfōl-\ *n* **:** a collapsible kayak made of rubberized fabric stretched over a framework

fold·er \ˈfōl-dər\ *n* **1 :** one that folds **2 :** a printed circular of folded sheets **3 a :** a folded cover or large envelope for holding loose papers **b :** an element of a computer operating system used to group and organize files

fol·de·rol *also* **fal·de·ral** \ˈfäl-də-ˌräl\ *n* **1 :** a useless trifle **2 :** NONSENSE 1 [*fol-de-rol,* a nonsense refrain in songs]

fo·li·a·ceous \ˌfō-lē-ˈā-shəs\ *adj* **:** of, relating to, or resembling a plant leaf

fo·li·age \ˈfō-lē-ij, -lyij, -lij\ *n* **:** the mass of leaves of a plant : LEAFAGE [Middle French *fuellage,* from *foille* "leaf," derived from Latin *folium*] — **fo·li·aged** \-lē-ijd, -lyjd, -lijd\ *adj*

foliage plant *n* **:** a plant grown for its decorative foliage

fo·li·ar \ˈfō-lē-ər\ *adj* **:** consisting of or relating to leaves

fo·li·ate \ˈfō-lē-ət\ *adj* **1 :** shaped like a leaf ⟨a *foliate* sponge⟩ **2 :** FOLIATED

fo·li·at·ed \ˈfō-lē-ˌāt-əd\ *adj* **1 :** composed of or separable into layers ⟨a *foliated* rock⟩ **2 :** ornamented with foils or a leaf design

fo·li·a·tion \ˌfō-lē-ˈā-shən\ *n* **1 :** the leafing out of a plant : the state of being in leaf **2 :** the act of numbering the leaves of a book; *also* **:** the total count of leaves numbered **3 :** a decoration resembling a leaf **4 :** foliated texture

foliation 3

fo·lic acid \ˈfō-lik-\ *n* **:** a vitamin of the B complex used especially in the treatment of nutritional anemias [Latin *folium* "leaf"]

fo·lio \ˈfō-lē-ˌō\ *n, pl* **fo·li·os** **1 :** a leaf of a manuscript or book **2 a :** a book made of sheets of paper each folded once to make two leaves or four pages **b :** a very large book [Latin, ablative of *folium* "leaf"]

fo·li·ose \ˈfo-le-ˌos\ *adj* **:** suggesting a leaf or an arrangement of leaves ⟨*foliose* lichens⟩ — compare CRUSTOSE, FRUTICOSE

[1]**folk** \ˈfōk\ *n, pl* **folk** *or* **folks** **1 :** a group of people forming a tribe or nation; *also* **:** the largest number or most characteristic part of such a group **2** *pl* **:** people of a specified kind or class ⟨country *folk*⟩ ⟨old *folks*⟩ **3** *pl* **:** people generally **4** *folks pl* **:** the persons of one's own family; *esp* **:** PARENTS ⟨visit your *folks*⟩ **5 :** folk music [Old English *folc*]

[2]**folk** *adj* **:** of, relating to, or originating among the common people ⟨*folk* dances⟩ ⟨*folk* music⟩

folk art *n* **:** the traditional typically anonymous art of usually untrained people

folk etymology *n* **:** the transformation of words so as to give them an apparent relationship to other better-known or better-understood words (as the change of *chaise longue* to *chaise lounge*)

folk·lore \ˈfōk-ˌlōr, -ˌlȯr\ *n* **:** customs, beliefs, stories, and sayings of a people handed down from generation to generation — **folk·lor·ist** \-ˌlōr-əst, -ˌlȯr-\ *n*

folk medicine *n* **:** traditional medicine involving especially the empirical and nonprofessional use of plant-derived remedies

folk·sing·er \ˈfōk-ˌsing-ər\ *n* **:** one who sings folk songs — **folk·sing·ing** \-ing\ *n*

folk song *n* **:** a traditional or composed song typically characterized by stanzaic form, refrain, and simplicity of melody

folksy \ˈfōk-sē\ *adj* **folks·i·er; -est** **1 :** SOCIABLE 1, FRIENDLY **2 :** informal, casual, or familiar in manner or style ⟨*folksy* humor⟩ — **folks·i·ly** \-sə-lē\ *adv* — **folks·i·ness** \-sē-nəs\ *n*

folk·tale \ˈfōk-ˌtāl\ *n* **:** an anonymous tale circulated orally among a people

folk·way \ˈfōk-ˌwā\ *n* **:** a way of thinking, feeling, or acting common to a people or to a social group

fol·li·cle \ˈfäl-i-kəl\ *n* **1 a :** a small anatomical cavity or deep narrow-mouthed depression (as from which a hair grows) **b :** GRAAFIAN FOLLICLE **2 :** a dry one-celled fruit (as in the peony, larkspur, or milkweed) that splits open by only one seam when ripe [Latin *folliculus* "small bag," from *follis* "bellows, bag"] — **fol·lic·u·lar** \fə-ˈlik-yə-lər, fä-\ *adj*

follicle–stimulating hormone *n* **:** a hormone from the pituitary gland that stimulates the growth of graafian follicles in females and activates sperm-forming cells in males

[1]**fol·low** \ˈfäl-ō\ *vb* **1 :** to go or come after or behind **2 :** to accept as authority : OBEY ⟨*follow* your conscience⟩ ⟨*follow* instructions⟩ **3 :** to go after or on the track of ⟨*follow* that car⟩ **4 :** to proceed along ⟨*follow* a path⟩ **5 :** to engage in as a calling or a way of life ⟨*follow* the sea⟩ **6 :** to come after in order of rank or natural sequence ⟨two *follows* one⟩ **7 :** to result from something ⟨disaster *followed* the blunder⟩ **8 :** to keep one's eyes or attention fixed on ⟨*follow* a lesson⟩ [Old English *folgian*] — **follow one's nose** **1 :** to go in a straight or obvious course **2 :** to proceed without plan or reflection : obey one's instincts — **follow suit** **1 :** to play a card of the same suit as the card led **2 :** to follow an example set

synonyms FOLLOW, SUCCEED, ENSUE mean to come after or later than something or someone. FOLLOW may apply to a coming after in time, position, or logical sequence ⟨continue the sentence on the *following* page⟩ ⟨the punishment that *follows* crime⟩. SUCCEED may add a stronger implication of displacing or replacing ⟨hoped to *succeed* the president in office⟩. ENSUE commonly suggests a logical consequence or naturally expected development ⟨after the talk a lively debate *ensued*⟩. ***synonyms*** see in addition CHASE

[2]**follow** *n* **:** the act or process of following

fol·low·er \ˈfäl-ə-wər\ *n* **1 :** one in the service of another : RETAINER **2 :** one that follows the opinions or teachings of another **3 :** one that imitates another

[1]**fol·low·ing** \ˈfäl-ə-wing\ *adj* **1 :** being next in order or time ⟨the *following* day⟩ **2 :** listed or shown next ⟨trains will leave at the *following* times⟩

[2]**following** *n* **:** a group of followers, adherents, or partisans

[3]**following** *prep* **:** immediately after : subsequent to

follow out *vt* **1 :** to follow to the end or to a conclusion **2 :** to carry out : EXECUTE ⟨*followed out* their orders⟩

fol·low–through \ˈfäl-ō-ˌthrü, ˌfäl-ō-ˈ, -ə-\ *n* **1 :** the part of a stroke or swing following the striking of an object **2 :** the act or an instance of following through

follow through *vi* **1 :** to continue a stroke or swing to the end of its arc **2 :** to press on in an activity to a conclusion

fol·low–up \ˈfäl-ə-ˌwəp\ *n* **1 :** the act or an instance of following up **2 :** something that follows up — **follow–up** *adj*

follow up \ˌfäl-ə-ˈwəp\ *vt* **1 :** to follow with something similar, related, or additional ⟨*follow up* an idea with action⟩ **2 :** to pursue in an effort to take further action ⟨the police are *following up* leads⟩

fol·ly \ˈfäl-ē\ *n, pl* **follies** **1 :** lack of good sense or normal prudence and foresight **2 :** foolish actions or conduct **3 :** a foolish act or idea **4 :** an excessively costly or unprofitable undertaking [Medieval French *folie,* from *fol* "fool"]

Fol·som \ˈfōl-səm\ *adj* **:** of or relating to a prehistoric culture of North America on the east side of the Rocky Mountains characterized especially by a leaf-shaped flint projectile point [*Folsom,* New Mexico]

fo·ment \fō-ˈment\ *vt* **:** to stir up : ROUSE, INSTIGATE ⟨*foment* rebellion⟩ [Middle English *fomenten* "to apply a warm substance to," from Late Latin *fomentare,* from Latin *fomentum* "fomentation," from *fovēre* "to heat, soothe"] ***synonyms*** see INCITE — **fo·ment·er** \fō-ˈment-ər\ *n*

fo·men·ta·tion \ˌfō-mən-ˈtā-shən, -ˌmen-\ *n* **1 :** a warm or hot moist material (as a hot damp cloth) applied to the body to ease pain **2 :** the act of fomenting : INSTIGATION

fond \ˈfänd\ *adj* **1 :** FOOLISH, SILLY ⟨*fond* pride⟩ **2 a :** prizing highly : DESIROUS ⟨*fond* of praise⟩ **b :** having an affection or liking ⟨*fond* of music⟩ **3 :** LOVING, AFFECTIONATE **4 :** doted on : DEAR ⟨their *fondest* hopes⟩ [Middle English, from *fonne* "fool"] — **fond·ly** *adv* — **fond·ness** \ˈfänd-nəs, ˈfän-\ *n*

\ə\ **abut**	\au̇\ **out**	\i\ **tip**	\ȯ\ **saw**	\u̇\ **foot**
\ər\ **further**	\ch\ **chin**	\ī\ **life**	\ȯi\ **coin**	\y\ **yet**
\a\ **mat**	\e\ **pet**	\j\ **job**	\th\ **thin**	\yü\ **few**
\ā\ **take**	\ē\ **easy**	\ng\ **sing**	\th\ **this**	\yu̇\ **cure**
\ä\ **cot, cart**	\g\ **go**	\ō\ **bone**	\ü\ **food**	\zh\ **vision**

fon·dant \ˈfän-dənt\ *n* **1 :** a creamy preparation of sugar used as a basis for candies or icings **2 :** a candy consisting chiefly of fondant [French, from *fondre* "to melt"]

fon·dle \ˈfän-dl\ *vt* **fon·dled; fon·dling** \-dliŋ, -dl-iŋ\ **:** to touch or handle in a tender or loving manner **:** CARESS [derived from *fond*] — **fon·dler** \-dlər, -dl-ər\ *n*

fon·due \fän-ˈdü, -ˈdyü\ *n* **1 :** a preparation of melted cheese flavored with wine or brandy **2 :** a dish consisting of small pieces of food (as meat or fruit) cooked in or dipped into a hot liquid [French, from *fondre* "to melt"]

[1]**font** \ˈfänt\ *n* **1 :** a basin for baptismal or holy water **2 :** a point from which something originates **:** SOURCE ⟨a *font* of wisdom⟩ [Old English, from Latin *font-, fons* "fountain"]

[2]**font** *n* **:** an assortment of type or characters all of one size and style [Medieval French *fonte* "act of founding," derived from Latin *fundere* "to found, pour"]

fon·ta·nel *or* **fon·ta·nelle** \ˌfänt-n-ˈel\ *n* **:** a membrane-covered opening in bone or between bones; *esp* **:** one between the bones of a fetal or young skull [Middle English *fontinelle* "bodily hollow or pit," from Medieval French *funtainele*, from *funtaine* "fountain"]

food \ˈfüd\ *n* **1 a :** material containing or consisting of carbohydrates, fats, proteins, and supplementary substances (as minerals) used in the body of an animal to sustain growth, repair, and vital processes and to furnish energy **b** (1) **:** inorganic substances absorbed by plants in gaseous form or in water solution (2) **:** organic material produced by green plants and used by them as building material and as a source of energy **2 :** nourishment in solid form **3 :** something that nourishes, sustains, or supplies ⟨*food* for thought⟩ [Old English *fōda*] — **food·less** \-ləs\ *adj* — **food·less·ness** *n*

food chain *n* **1 :** a series of the organisms of an ecological community in which each uses the next usually lower member of the series as a food source **2 :** a hierarchy based on power of importance ⟨at the top of the corporate *food chain*⟩

food·ie \ˈfüd-ē\ *n* **:** a person having an avid interest in the latest food fads

food poisoning *n* **:** an acute digestive disorder caused by bacteria or their toxic products or by chemicals in food

food pyramid *n* **:** a system of ecological food relationships arranged by levels in which a chief predator is at the top, each level preys on the next lower level, and usually green plants are at the bottom

food stamp *n* **:** a government-issued coupon that can be used as currency to buy food

food·stuff \ˈfüd-ˌstəf\ *n* **:** a substance with food value; *esp* **:** a specific nutrient (as protein or fat)

food vacuole *n* **:** a vacuole (as in an amoeba) in which ingested food is digested

food web *n* **:** the totality of interacting food chains in an ecological community

[1]**fool** \ˈfül\ *n* **1 :** a person who lacks sense or judgment **2 a :** a person formerly kept in a noble or royal household for casual entertainment — called also *jester* **b :** DUPE **3 a :** a person lacking in common powers of understanding **b :** a person with a deep liking for something ⟨a *fool* for candy⟩ [Medieval French *fol*, derived from Latin *follis* "bellows, bag"]

[2]**fool** *vb* **1 a :** to spend time idly or aimlessly ⟨just *fooling* around⟩ **b :** to meddle or tamper thoughtlessly or ignorantly ⟨don't *fool* with that gun⟩ **2 :** to speak or act in jest **:** JOKE ⟨I was only *fooling*⟩ **3 :** to make a fool of **:** DECEIVE ⟨I *fooled* you⟩ **4 :** to spend on trifles or without advantage **:** FRITTER — used with *away* ⟨*fooled* away his allowance⟩

fool·ery \ˈfül-rē, -ə-rē\ *n, pl* **-er·ies** **1 :** a foolish act, utterance, or belief **2 :** foolish behavior

fool·har·dy \ˈfül-ˌhärd-ē\ *adj* **:** foolishly adventurous and bold **:** RASH ***synonyms*** see DARING — **fool·har·di·ly** \-ˌhärd-l-ē\ *adv* — **fool·har·di·ness** \-ˌhärd-ē-nəs\ *n*

fool·ish \ˈfü-lish\ *adj* **1 :** lacking in sense, judgment, or discretion **2 :** amusingly absurd or ridiculous ⟨a *foolish* little hat⟩ — **fool·ish·ly** *adv* — **fool·ish·ness** *n*

fool·proof \ˈfül-ˈprüf\ *adj* **:** so simple, plain, or reliable as to leave no opportunity for error, misuse, or failure ⟨a *foolproof* plan⟩

fool's gold *n* **1 :** PYRITE **2 :** CHALCOPYRITE

fool's paradise *n* **:** a state of delusory happiness

foos·ball \ˈfüz-ˌbȯl\ *n, often cap* **:** a table game resembling soccer in which the ball is moved by manipulating rods to which small figures of players are attached — called also *table soccer* [probably from German *Tischfussball*, from *Tisch* table + *Fussball* soccer]

[1]**foot** \ˈfu̇t\ *n, pl* **feet** \ˈfēt\ *also* **foot** **1 a :** the terminal part of the vertebrate leg upon which an individual stands **b :** an invertebrate organ of locomotion or attachment; *esp* **:** a ventral muscular part of a mollusk **2 :** any of various units of length based on the length of the human foot; *esp* **:** a unit equal to ⅓ yard and comprising 12 inches (.3048 meter) ⟨a 10-*foot* pole⟩ ⟨6 *feet* tall⟩ — see MEASURE table **3 :** the basic unit of verse meter consisting of a group of accented and unaccented syllables **4 :** something resembling an animal's foot in position or use or in being opposite to the head ⟨the *foot* of a mountain⟩ ⟨the *foot* of a bed⟩ **5 :** the lower edge (as of a sail) **6 foots** *pl* **:** material deposited especially on aging or refining **:** DREGS [Old English *fōt*] — **footlike** \ˈfu̇t-ˌlīk\ *adj* — **on foot** **1 :** by walking ⟨went *on foot*⟩ **2 :** under way **:** in progress ⟨an investigation was set *on foot*⟩ — **on one's feet** **1 :** in a standing position **2 :** in an established position or state **:** in a recovered condition (as from illness) ⟨back *on my feet*⟩ **3 :** while in action ⟨good debaters can think *on their feet*⟩

[2]**foot** *vb* **1 :** DANCE 1 — often used with *it* **2 :** to go on foot **3 a :** to add up **b :** to pay or provide for paying ⟨*foot* the bill⟩

foot·age \ˈfu̇t-ij\ *n* **:** length expressed in feet

foot–and–mouth disease *n* **:** an acute virus disease especially of cattle marked by fever and by ulcers in the mouth, about the hooves, and on the udder — called also *hoof-and-mouth disease*

foot·ball \ˈfu̇t-ˌbȯl\ *n* **1 :** any of several games that are played with an inflated ball on a rectangular field having two goalposts at each end by two teams whose object is to get the ball over a goal line or between goalposts by running, passing, or kicking: as **a** *British* **:** SOCCER **b** *British* **:** RUGBY **c :** an American game played between two teams of 11 players each in which the ball is advanced by running or passing **2 :** the ball used in football **3 :** something treated roughly especially as the subject of a prolonged dispute ⟨the issue became a political *football*⟩

foot·board \ˈfu̇t-ˌbōrd, -ˌbȯrd\ *n* **1 :** a narrow platform on which to stand or brace the feet **2 :** a board at the foot of a bed

foot·bridge \-ˌbrij\ *n* **:** a bridge for pedestrians

foot–can·dle \ˈfu̇t-ˈkan-dl\ *n* **:** a unit for measuring illumination that equals the illumination on a surface all parts of which are one foot from a light having an intensity of one candle and equal to one lumen per square foot

foot·ed \ˈfu̇t-əd\ *adj* **:** having a foot or feet especially of a specified kind or number ⟨flat-*footed*⟩ ⟨a four-*footed* animal⟩

foot·fall \ˈfu̇t-ˌfȯl\ *n* **:** FOOTSTEP 1a; *also* **:** the sound of a footstep

foot·gear \-ˌgiər\ *n* **:** FOOTWEAR

foot·hill \-ˌhil\ *n* **:** a hill at the foot of higher hills or mountains

foot·hold \-ˌhōld\ *n* **1 :** a hold for the feet **:** FOOTING **2 :** a position usable as a base for further advance

foot·ing \ˈfu̇t-iŋ\ *n* **1 :** the placing of one's feet in a stable position **2 :** the act of moving on foot **3 a :** a place or position for providing a base of operations **:** FOOTHOLD ⟨gained a *footing* in the capital for advancement into the country⟩ **b :** position with respect to one another **:** STATUS ⟨all started off on an equal *footing*⟩ **c :** BASIS ⟨put the enterprise on a firm *footing*⟩ **4 :** the sum of a column of figures

foot·lights \ˈfu̇t-ˌlīts\ *n pl* **1 :** a row of lights set across the front of a stage floor **2 :** the stage as a profession ⟨the lure of the *footlights*⟩

foot·ling \-liŋ\ *adj* **1 :** INEPT ⟨*footling* amateurs⟩ **2 :** TRIVIAL 2 ⟨*footling* matters⟩ [*footle* "to trifle"]

foot·lock·er \-ˌläk-ər\ *n* **:** a small trunk designed to be placed at the foot of a bed (as in barracks)

foot·loose \-ˌlüs\ *adj* **:** having no ties **:** free to roam

foot·man \ˈfu̇t-mən\ *n* **:** a male servant who attends a carriage, waits on table, admits visitors, and runs errands

foot·mark \-ˌmärk\ *n* **:** FOOTPRINT

foot·note \-ˌnōt\ *n* **1 :** a note of reference, explanation, or comment often placed below the text on a printed page **2 :** one that is a relatively subordinate or minor part (as of an event, work, or field) — **footnote** *vt*

foot·pad \-ˌpad\ *n* **:** a flattish foot on the leg of a spacecraft to minimize sinking into a surface

foot·path \-ˌpath, -ˌpȧth\ *n* **:** a narrow path for pedestrians

foot–pound \-ˈpau̇nd\ *n, pl* **foot–pounds** **:** a unit of work that equals the work done by a force of one pound acting through a distance of one foot and that amounts to about 1.36 joules

foot–pound–second *adj* **:** being or relating to a system of units based upon the foot as the unit of length, the pound as the unit of weight, and the second as the unit of time — abbreviation *fps*

foot·print \ˈfu̇t-ˌprint\ *n* : an impression left by a foot

foot·race \-ˌrās\ *n* : a race run by humans on foot

foot·rest \-ˌrest\ *n* : a support for the feet

foot soldier *n* : INFANTRYMAN

foot·sore \ˈfu̇t-ˌsōr, -ˌsȯr\ *adj* : having sore or tender feet (as from much walking)

foot·step \-ˌstep\ *n* **1 a** : a step of the foot **b** : distance covered by a step : PACE **2** : the mark of the foot : TRACK **3** : a step on which to ascend or descend **4** : a way of life, conduct, or action ⟨followed in his father's *footsteps*⟩

foot·stone \-ˌstōn\ *n* : a stone placed at the foot of a grave

foot·stool \-ˌstül\ *n* : a low stool to support the feet

foot·way \-ˌwā\ *n* : a narrow way or path for pedestrians

foot·wear \-ˌwaər, -ˌweər\ *n* : covering (as shoes) for the feet

foot·work \-ˌwərk\ *n* : the movement of the feet (as in boxing)

foo·zle \ˈfü-zəl\ *vt* **foo·zled; foo·zling** \ˈfüz-ling, -ə-ling\ : to manage or play awkwardly : BUNGLE [perhaps from German dialect *fuseln* "to work carelessly"] — **foozle** *n*

fop \ˈfäp\ *n* : a man who is vain about his dress or appearance : DANDY [Middle English *foppe* foolish or silly person] — **fop·pish** \ˈfäp-ish\ *adj* — **fop·pish·ly** *adv* — **fop·pish·ness** *n*

fop·pery \ˈfäp-rē, -ə-re\ *n, pl* **-per·ies** **1** : foolish character or action : FOLLY **2** : the behavior or dress of a fop

¹for \fər, fȯr, ˈfȯr\ *prep* **1** — used as a function word to indicate purpose ⟨money *for* college⟩, intended destination ⟨left *for* home⟩, or an object of one's desire ⟨now *for* a good rest⟩ **2** : as being ⟨do you take me *for* a fool⟩ **3** : because of ⟨cried *for* joy⟩ **4 a** : in support of ⟨fighting *for* their country⟩ **b** — used as a function word to indicate suitability or fitness ⟨medicine *for* a cold⟩ ⟨ready *for* action⟩ **c** : so as to bring about a certain state ⟨shouted the news *for* all to hear⟩ **5 a** : in place of ⟨go to the store *for* me⟩ **b** : as the equal or equivalent of ⟨paid $10 *for* a hat⟩ **6** : in spite of ⟨unconvinced *for* all the clever arguments⟩ **7** : with respect to : CONCERNING ⟨a stickler *for* detail⟩ **8** — used as a function word to indicate equality or proportion ⟨point *for* point⟩ ⟨tall *for* their age⟩ **9** — used as a function word to indicate duration of time or extent of space ⟨waited *for* several hours⟩ **10** : ²AFTER 3b ⟨named *for* my grandfather⟩ [Old English]

²for *conj* : for this reason : on this ground : BECAUSE

for- *prefix* **1** : so as to involve prohibition, exclusion, omission, failure, neglect, or refusal ⟨*for*bid⟩ **2** : destructively or detrimentally ⟨*for*do⟩ **3** : completely : excessively : to exhaustion : to pieces ⟨*for*lorn⟩ [Old English]

fora *plural of* FORUM

¹for·age \ˈfȯr-ij, ˈfär-\ *n* **1** : food for animals especially when taken by browsing or grazing **2** : the act of foraging : search for provisions [Medieval French, from *fuerre, foer* "fodder," of Germanic origin]

²forage *vb* **1** : to collect forage from **2** : to get by foraging ⟨*forage* a chicken⟩ **3** : to seek forage or provisions **4** : RUMMAGE 1 ⟨*forage* through the refrigerator⟩ — **for·ag·er** *n*

fo·ram \ˈfōr-əm, ˈfȯr-\ *n* : FORAMINIFER

fo·ra·men \fə-ˈrā-mən\ *n, pl* **-ram·i·na** \-ˈram-ə-nə\ *or* **-ra·mens** \-ˈrā-mənz\ : a small opening, perforation, or orifice [Latin *foramin-, foramen,* from *forare* "to bore"]

fo·ra·men mag·num \fə-ˌrā-mən-ˈmag-nəm\ *n* : the opening in the skull through which the spinal cord joins the brain [New Latin, literally, "great opening"]

foramen ova·le \-ō-ˈval-ē, -ˈväl-, -ˈvāl-\ *n* : a small opening between the two atria of the heart that is normally present only in the fetus [New Latin, literally, "oval opening"]

for·a·min·i·fer \ˌfȯr-ə-ˈmin-ə-fər, ˌfär-\ *n* : any of an order (Foraminifera) of large chiefly marine amoeboid protozoans that usually have perforated shells containing calcium and whose remains form a large part of chalk and limestone deposits [New Latin *Foraminifera,* derived from *foramen* + *-i* + *-ferum* "-fer"] — **fo·ra·mi·nif·er·al** \-rəl\ *adj*

fo·ra·mi·nif·era \fə-ˌram-ə-ˈnif-rə, -ə-rə; ˌfȯr-ə-mə-ˈnif-, ˌfär-\ *n pl* : protozoans that are foraminifers

fo·ra·mi·nif·er·an \-rən\ *n* : FORAMINIFER

for·as·much as \ˈfȯr-əz-ˌməch-əz\ *conj* : in view of the fact that : SINCE

for·ay \ˈfȯr-ˌā\ *vb* : to raid often in search of plunder : PILLAGE [Medieval French *forreyer,* derived from *fuerre, foer* "fodder"] — **foray** *n*

forb \ˈfȯrb\ *n* : an herb other than a grass [Greek *phorbē* "fodder, food," from *pherbein* "to graze"]

¹for·bear \fȯr-ˈbaər, fər-, -ˈbeər\ *vb* **-bore** \-ˈbōr, -ˈbȯr\; **-borne** \-ˈbōrn, -ˈbȯrn\; **-bear·ing** **1** : to refrain or desist from : ABSTAIN **2** : to control oneself when provoked : be patient [Old English *forberan* "to endure, do without," from *for-* + *beran* "to bear"] ***synonyms*** see REFRAIN — **for·bear·er** *n*

²forbear *variant of* FOREBEAR

for·bear·ance \fȯr-ˈbar-əns, fər-, -ˈber-\ *n* **1** : the act of forbearing **2** : the quality of being forbearing : PATIENCE

for·bid \fər-ˈbid, fȯr-\ *vt* **-bade** \-ˈbad, -ˈbād\ *also* **-bad** \-ˈbad\; **-bid·den** \-ˈbid-n\; **-bid·ding** **1** : to order not to do something or not to be done or used : PROHIBIT ⟨they *forbade* us to leave⟩ ⟨loitering is *forbidden*⟩ **2** : to hinder or prevent as if by command ⟨space *forbids* quoting in full⟩ [Old English *forbēodan,* from *for-* + *bēodan* "to bid"] — **for·bid·der** *n*

synonyms FORBID, PROHIBIT, INHIBIT mean to keep one from doing something or to order that something not be done. FORBID implies that the order is from one in authority and that obedience is expected ⟨smoking is *forbidden* in the building⟩. PROHIBIT suggests the issuing of laws, statutes, or regulations ⟨*prohibited* the sale of liquor⟩. INHIBIT implies hampering or restricting by authority or more often by circumstances out of one's control ⟨high tariffs *inhibited* trade⟩.

forbidding *adj* **1** : REPELLENT, UNPLEASANT ⟨a stern *forbidding* manner⟩ ⟨a *forbidding* task⟩ **2** : GRIM, MENACING ⟨a dark *forbidding* sky⟩ — **for·bid·ding·ly** \-ing-lē\ *adv*

forbode *variant of* FOREBODE

¹force \ˈfōrs, ˈfȯrs\ *n* **1 a** : strength or energy exerted : active power ⟨*forces* of nature⟩ **b** : moral or mental strength **c** (1) : capacity to persuade or convince ⟨the *force* of this argument⟩ (2) : legal effectiveness ⟨that law is still in *force*⟩ **2 a** : military strength **b** (1) : a body (as of troops or ships) assigned to a military purpose (2) *pl* : ARMED FORCES **c** : a body of persons available for a particular end ⟨the labor *force*⟩ ⟨a police *force*⟩ **3** : violence, compulsion, or constraint exerted on or against a person or thing **4** : an influence (as a push or pull) that if applied to a free body results chiefly in an acceleration of the body and sometimes in other effects (as deformation) [Medieval French, derived from Latin *fortis* "strong"] ***synonyms*** see POWER — **force·less** \-ləs\ *adj* — **in force** **1** : in great numbers ⟨picnickers were out *in force*⟩ **2** : VALID, OPERATIVE ⟨the ban remains *in force*⟩

²force *vt* **1** : to compel by force : COERCE ⟨*forced* them to quit⟩ **2** : to make or cause through natural or logical necessity ⟨*forced* to admit I am wrong⟩ **3** : to pass or effect against resistance ⟨*force* a bill through the legislature⟩ **4 a** : to gain by struggle or violence ⟨*force* one's way in⟩ **b** : to break open or through ⟨*force* a lock⟩ **5 a** : to raise or accelerate to the utmost ⟨*forcing* the pace⟩ **b** : to produce with unnatural effort ⟨*forced* a laugh⟩ **6 a** : to hasten the rate of progress or growth of **b** : to bring (as plants) to maturity out of the normal season ⟨*forcing* lilies for Easter⟩ — **forc·er** *n*

synonyms FORCE, COMPEL, COERCE, CONSTRAIN mean to make someone or something yield. FORCE implies the use of physical power to overcome resistance of persons or things ⟨*forced* them to submit⟩ ⟨*forced* the door with a crowbar⟩. COMPEL and COERCE take only personal objects, COMPEL implying the working of an irresistible force ⟨hunger *compelled* them to surrender⟩ and COERCE suggesting the use of threatened violence or injury ⟨*coerced* into signing over the rights to the house⟩. CONSTRAIN suggests the effect of a force or circumstance that limits action or choice ⟨*constrained* by conscience⟩.

forced \ˈfōrst, ˈfȯrst\ *adj* **1** : compelled by force : INVOLUNTARY ⟨a *forced* landing⟩ **2** : done or produced with effort, exertion, or pressure ⟨*forced* laughter⟩ — **forc·ed·ly** \ˈfōr-səd-lē, ˈfȯr-\ *adv*

force–feed \ˈfōrs-ˌfēd, ˈfȯrs-\ *vt* **-fed** \-ˌfed\; **-feed·ing** **1** : to feed (an animal or person) by forcible administration of food **2** : to force to take in ⟨*forcefeed* students the classics⟩ ⟨*forcefed* rules to her children⟩

\ə\ **abut**	\au̇\ **out**	\i\ **tip**	\ȯ\ **saw**	\u̇\ **foot**
\ər\ **further**	\ch\ **chin**	\ī\ **life**	\ȯi\ **coin**	\y\ **yet**
\a\ **mat**	\e\ **pet**	\j\ **job**	\th\ **thin**	\yü\ **few**
\ā\ **take**	\ē\ **easy**	\ng\ **sing**	\t͟h\ **this**	\yu̇\ **cure**
\ä\ **cot, cart**	\g\ **go**	\ō\ **bone**	\ü\ **food**	\zh\ **vision**

force·ful \ˈfōrs-fəl, ˈfȯrs-\ *adj* : possessing much force : VIGOROUS — **force·ful·ly** \-fə-lē\ *adv* — **force·ful·ness** *n*
force·meat \ˈfōrs-ˌmēt, ˈfȯrs-\ *n* : chopped and seasoned meat or fish served alone or used as a stuffing [*force* (alteration of *farce* "stuffing") + *meat*]
for·ceps \ˈfȯr-səps, -ˌseps\ *n, pl* **forceps** : an instrument for grasping, holding, or moving objects especially for delicate operations (as by jewelers or surgeons) [Latin, perhaps from *formus* "warm" + *capere* "to take"] — **for·ceps·like** \-ˌlīk\ *adj*

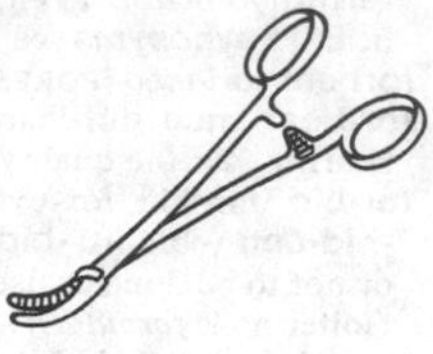
forceps

forc·ible \ˈfōr-sə-bəl, ˈfȯr-\ *adj* **1** : got, made, or done by force or violence ⟨a *forcible* entrance⟩ **2** : showing force or energy : POWERFUL — **forc·ibly** \-blē\ *adv*
[1]**ford** \ˈfōrd, ˈfȯrd\ *n* : a shallow part of a body of water that may be crossed by wading [Old English]
[2]**ford** *vt* : to cross (a body of water) by wading — **ford·able** \-ə-bəl\ *adj*
for·do *also* **fore·do** \fȯr-ˈdü, fōr-\ *vt* **-did** \-did\; **-done** \-ˈdən\; **-do·ing** : to overcome with fatigue : EXHAUST [Old English *fordōn* "to destroy," from *for-* + *dōn* "to do"]
[1]**fore** \ˈfōr, ˈfȯr\ *adv* : in, toward, or near the front : FORWARD ⟨the shell hit *fore* of the mast⟩ [Old English]
[2]**fore** *adj* : being or coming before in time, order, or space
[3]**fore** *n* : something that occupies a front position — **to the fore** : in or into a prominent position
[4]**fore** *interj* — used by a golfer to warn anyone within range of the probable line of flight of the ball [probably short for *before*]
fore- *combining form* **1 a** : earlier : beforehand ⟨*fore*named⟩ **b** : occurring earlier : occurring beforehand ⟨*fore*thought⟩ ⟨*fore*see⟩ **2 a** : situated at the front : in front ⟨*fore*leg⟩ **b** : front part of (something specified) ⟨*fore*brain⟩ [Old English, from *fore,* adv.]
fore–and–aft \ˌfōr-ə-ˈnaft, ˌfȯr-\ *adj* **1** : lying, running, or acting in the general line of the length of a construction (as a ship) ⟨*fore-and-aft* sails⟩ **2** : having no square sails
fore and aft *adv* : lengthwise of a ship : from stem to stern
fore–and–aft·er \-ˈnaf-tər\ *n* : a ship with a fore-and-aft rig; *esp* : SCHOONER
fore–and–aft rig *n* : a sailing-ship rig in which most or all of the sails are not attached to yards but are bent to gaffs or set on the masts or on stays in a fore-and-aft line — **fore–and–aft rigged** *adj*
[1]**fore·arm** \fōr-ˈärm, ˈfōr-, ˈfȯr-\ *vt* : to arm in advance : PREPARE
[2]**fore·arm** \ˈfōr-ˌärm, ˈfȯr-\ *n* : the part of the human arm between the elbow and the wrist
fore·bear *also* **for·bear** \ˈfōr-ˌbaər, ˈfȯr-, -ˌbeər\ *n* : ANCESTOR 1, FOREFATHER [Middle English (Scots) *forebear,* from *fore-* + *-bear* "one that is," from *been* "to be"]
fore·bear·er \-ər\ *n* : ANCESTOR 1, FOREFATHER
fore·bode *also* **for·bode** \fōr-ˈbōd, fȯr-\ *vb* **1** : to have a premonition of (as misfortune) **2** : FORETELL, PORTEND ⟨such heavy air *forebodes* a storm⟩ — **fore·bod·er** *n*
[1]**fore·bod·ing** \fōr-ˈbōd-ing, fȯr-\ *n* : an omen, prediction, or presentiment especially of coming evil : PORTENT
[2]**foreboding** *adj* : indicative of or marked by foreboding — **fore·bod·ing·ly** \-ing-lē\ *adv* — **fore·bod·ing·ness** *n*
fore·brain \ˈfōr-ˌbrān, ˈfȯr-\ *n* : the front division of the embryonic vertebrate brain or the parts (as the cerebrum and olfactory lobes) developed from it
[1]**fore·cast** \ˈfōr-ˌkast, ˈfȯr-\ *vb* **forecast** *also* **fore·cast·ed; fore·cast·ing** **1** : to calculate or predict (a future event or condition) usually as a result of study and analysis of data; *esp* : to predict (weather conditions) on the basis of meteorological observations **2** : to indicate as likely to occur ⟨*forecast* an easy victory at the polls⟩ ***synonyms*** see FORETELL — **fore·cast·er** *n*
[2]**forecast** *n* : a prophecy, estimate, or prediction of a future happening or condition ⟨weather *forecasts*⟩
fore·cas·tle \ˈfōk-səl; ˈfōr-ˌkas-əl, ˈfȯr-\ *or* **fo'·c'sle** \ˈfōk-səl\ *n* **1** : the forward part of the upper deck of a ship **2** : the part of a ship where the crew is housed
fore·close \fōr-ˈklōz, fȯr-\ *vb* **1** : to rule out ⟨didn't *foreclose* the possibility of a second term⟩ **2** : to take legal measures to end a mortgage and take possession of the mortgaged property because the conditions of the mortgage have not been met by the mortgagor [Medieval French *forclore,* from *fors* "outside" + *clore* "to close"]
fore·clo·sure \-ˈklō-zhər\ *n* : the act of foreclosing; *esp* : the legal procedure of foreclosing a mortgage
fore·deck \ˈfōr-ˌdek, ˈfȯr-\ *n* : the forepart of a ship's main deck
foredo *variant of* FORDO
fore·doom \fōr-ˈdüm, fȯr-\ *vt* : to doom beforehand ⟨efforts *foredoomed* to failure⟩
fore·fa·ther \ˈfōr-ˌfäth-ər, ˈfȯr-, -ˌfäth-\ *n* **1** : ANCESTOR 1 **2** : a person of an earlier period and common heritage
fore·fin·ger \ˈfōr-ˌfing-gər, ˈfȯr-\ *n* : INDEX FINGER
fore·foot \-ˌfu̇t\ *n* **1** : one of the front feet of a four-footed animal **2** : the forward part of a ship where the stem and keel meet
fore·front \-ˌfrənt\ *n* : the foremost part or place : the place of greatest activity or interest ⟨an event in the *forefront* of the news⟩
foregather *variant of* FORGATHER
[1]**fore·go** \fōr-ˈgō, fȯr-\ *vb* **-went** \-ˈwent\; **-gone** \-ˈgȯn, -ˈgän\; **-go·ing** \-ˈgō-ing\ : to go before : PRECEDE — **fore·go·er** \-ˈgō-ər, -ˈgōr\ *n*
[2]**forego** *variant of* FORGO
fore·go·ing \fōr-ˈgō-ing, fȯr-\ *adj* : going before; *esp* : said, written, or listed before or above ***synonyms*** see PRECEDING
fore·gone \ˈfōr-ˌgȯn, ˈfȯr-, -ˌgän\ *adj* : determined or settled in advance ⟨success was a *foregone* conclusion⟩
fore·ground \ˈfōr-ˌgrau̇nd, ˈfȯr-\ *n* **1** : the part of a scene or representation that is nearest to and in front of the spectator **2** : a position of prominence : FOREFRONT
fore·gut \-ˌgət\ *n* : the part of the alimentary canal of a vertebrate embryo that develops into the pharynx, esophagus, stomach, and first part of the intestine
[1]**fore·hand** \ˈfōr-ˌhand, ˈfȯr-\ *n* : a stroke made with the palm of the hand turned in the direction of movement
[2]**forehand** *adv* : with a forehand
[3]**forehand** *adj* : using or made with a forehand
fore·hand·ed \ˈfōr-ˈhan-dəd, ˈfȯr-\ *adj* **1** : mindful of the future : THRIFTY, PRUDENT **2** : FOREHAND — **fore·hand·ed·ly** *adv* — **fore·hand·ed·ness** *n*
fore·head \ˈfȯr-əd, ˈfär-; ˈfōr-ˌhed, ˈfȯr-\ *n* **1** : the part of the face above the eyes **2** : the front or forepart of something
for·eign \ˈfȯr-ən, ˈfär-\ *adj* **1** : situated outside a place or country; *esp* : situated outside one's own country ⟨*foreign* nations⟩ **2** : born in, belonging to, or characteristic of some place or country other than the one under consideration ⟨a *foreign* language⟩ **3** : alien in character : not connected or pertinent ⟨material *foreign* to the topic under discussion⟩ **4** : related to or dealing with other nations ⟨*foreign* affairs⟩ **5** : occurring in an abnormal situation in the living body and commonly introduced from outside ⟨a *foreign* body in the eye⟩ [Medieval French *forein,* from Late Latin *foranus* "on the outside," from Latin *foris* "outside"] — **for·eign·ness** \-ən-nəs\ *n*
for·eign·er \ˈfȯr-ə-nər, ˈfär-\ *n* : a person belonging to or owing allegiance to a foreign country : ALIEN
foreign exchange *n* **1** : a process of settling accounts or debts between persons living in different countries **2** : foreign currency or current short-term credit instruments payable in such currency
for·eign·ism \ˈfȯr-ə-ˌniz-əm, ˈfär-\ *n* : something peculiar to a foreign language or people; *esp* : a foreign idiom or custom
foreign minister *n* : a governmental minister for foreign affairs
fore·know \fōr-ˈnō, fȯr-, ˈfōr-, ˈfȯr-\ *vt* **-knew** \-ˈnu, -ˈnyu\; **-known** \-ˈnōn\; **-know·ing** : to have previous knowledge of : know beforehand ***synonyms*** see FORESEE — **fore·knowl·edge** \-ˈnäl-ij\ *n*
fore·la·dy \ˈfōr-ˌlād-ē, ˈfȯr-\ *n* : FOREWOMAN
fore·land \-lənd\ *n* : PROMONTORY, HEADLAND
fore·leg \-ˌleg\ *n* : a front leg
fore·limb \-ˌlim\ *n* : an arm, fin, wing, or leg that is one of a front pair of limbs
fore·lock \-ˌläk\ *n* : a lock of hair growing from the front of the head
fore·man \ˈfōr-mən, ˈfȯr-\ *n* **1** : a member of a jury who acts as chairperson and spokesperson **2** : a person in charge of a group of workers
fore·mast \-ˌmast, -məst\ *n* : the mast nearest the bow of a ship
[1]**fore·most** \ˈfōr-ˌmōst, ˈfȯr-\ *adj* : first in time, place, or order; *also* : most important [Old English *formest,* superlative of *forma* "first"]

²foremost *adv* **1** : in the first place **2** : most importantly ⟨first and *foremost*⟩
fore·name \-ˌnām\ *n* : a first name
fore·named \-ˌnāmd\ *adj* : previously named : AFORESAID
fore·noon \ˈfōr-ˌnün, ˈfȯr-\ *n* : the early part of the day ending with noon : MORNING
¹fo·ren·sic \fə-ˈren-sik, -ˈren-zik\ *adj* **1** : belonging to, used in, or suitable to courts of law or to public discussion and debate **2** : RHETORICAL 1 **3** : relating to or dealing with the application of scientific knowledge to legal problems ⟨*forensic* medicine⟩ [Latin *forensis,* from *forum* "forum"] — **fo·ren·si·cal·ly** \-si-kə-lē, -zi-, -klē\ *adv*
²forensic *n* **1** : an argumentative exercise **2** *pl* : the art or study of argumentative discourse
fore·or·dain \ˌfōr-ȯr-ˈdān, ˌfȯr-\ *vt* : to ordain or decree in advance : PREDESTINE ⟨a *foreordained* course of events⟩ — **fore·or·di·na·tion** \-ˌȯrd-n-ˈā-shən\ *n*
fore·part \ˈfōr-ˌpärt, ˈfȯr-\ *n* : the part most advanced or first in place or in time ⟨the *forepart* of the day⟩
fore·paw \-ˌpȯ\ *n* : the paw of a foreleg
fore·quar·ter \-ˌkwȯrt-ər, -ˌkwȯt-\ *n* : the left or right half of the front half of the body or carcass of a four-footed animal ⟨a *forequarter* of beef⟩
fore·reach \fōr-ˈrēch, fȯr-\ *vb* **1** : to gain ground in tacking **2** : to gain on or overhaul and go ahead of (a ship) when close-hauled
fore·run·ner \ˈfōr-ˌrən-ər, ˈfȯr-\ *n* **1** : one that precedes and indicates the approach of another ⟨the dark clouds were *forerunners* of a storm⟩ **2** : one that precedes another (as in office or an activity) : PREDECESSOR ⟨*forerunners* of the modern cartoon⟩
fore·sail \ˈfōr-ˌsāl, ˈfȯr-, -səl\ *n* **1** : the lowest sail on the foremast of a square-rigged ship **2** : the lower sail set on the foremast of a schooner

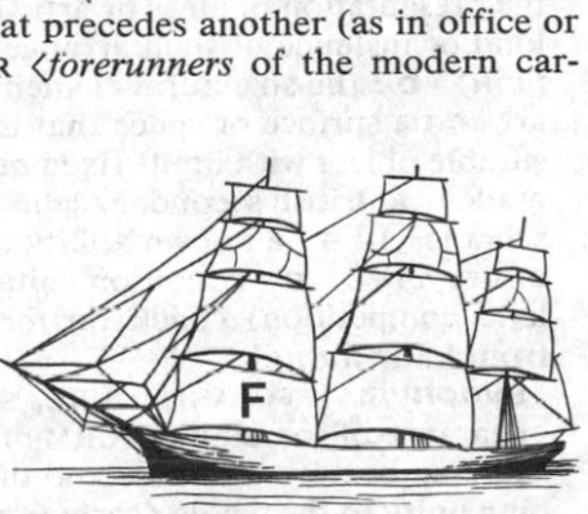

F foresail 1

fore·see \fōr-ˈsē, fȯr-\ *vt* **-saw** \-ˈsȯ\; **-seen** \-ˈsēn\; **-see·ing** : to see or realize (as a development) beforehand : EXPECT — **fore·see·able** \-ə-bəl\ *adj* — **fore·se·er** \-ˈsē-ər\ *n*
synonyms FORESEE, FOREKNOW, ANTICIPATE mean to know beforehand. FORESEE implies nothing about how the knowledge is derived and may apply to ordinary reasoning and experience ⟨economists should have *foreseen* the recession⟩. FOREKNOW usually implies the involvement of supernatural forces ⟨*foreknow* our destinies⟩. ANTICIPATE implies responding emotionally to or taking action about something before it happens ⟨the waiter *anticipated* our every need⟩.
fore·shad·ow \-ˈshad-ō\ *vt* : to represent or indicate beforehand : PREFIGURE ⟨clouds *foreshadowed* rain⟩ — **fore·shad·ow·er** *n*
fore·sheet \-ˌshēt\ *n* **1** : one of the sheets of a foresail **2** *pl* : the forward part of an open boat
fore·shock \-ˌshäk\ *n* : a minor tremor preceding an earthquake
fore·shore \-ˌshōr, -ˌshȯr\ *n* : the part of a seashore between high-water and low-water marks
fore·short·en \fōr-ˈshȯrt-n, fȯr-\ *vt* : to shorten (a detail) in a drawing or painting so that the composition appears to have depth
fore·side \ˈfōr-ˌsīd, ˈfōr-\ *n* : the front side or part : FRONT
fore·sight \ˈfōr-ˌsīt, ˈfȯr-\ *n* **1** : the act or power of foreseeing; *also* : knowledge of something before it happens **2** : care or provision for the future : PRUDENCE **3** : the act of looking forward; *also* : a view forward — **fore·sight·ed** \-ˌsīt-əd\ *adj* — **fore·sight·ed·ly** *adv* — **fore·sight·ed·ness** *n* — **foresight·ful** *adj*
fore·skin \-ˌskin\ *n* : a fold of skin that covers the end of the penis — called also *prepuce*
for·est \ˈfȯr-əst, ˈfär-\ *n* **1** : a dense growth of trees and underbrush covering a large tract; *also* : an area covered by forest **2** : something resembling a forest especially in profusion or lushness ⟨a *forest* of masts⟩ ⟨a kelp *forest*⟩ [Medieval French, "forest, hunting preserve," from Medieval Latin *forestis,* from Latin *foris* "outside"] — **for·est·ed** \ˈfȯr-ə-stəd, ˈfär-\ *adj*
fore·stage \ˈfōr-ˌstāj, ˈfȯr-\ *n* : APRON 2a
fore·stall \fōr-ˈstȯl, fȯr-\ *vt* : to keep out, hinder, or prevent by measures taken in advance ⟨*forestall* unnecessary questions by giving careful directions⟩ ***synonyms*** see PREVENT — **fore·stall·er** *n* — **fore·stall·ment** \-ˈstȯl-mənt\ *n*
for·es·ta·tion \ˌfȯr-ə-ˈstā-shən, ˌfär-\ *n* : the planting and care of a forest
fore·stay \ˈfōr-ˌstā, ˈfȯr-\ *n* : a stay from the top of a ship's foremast to the deck
for·est·er \ˈfȯr-ə-stər, ˈfär-\ *n* : a person who practices or is trained in forestry
forest floor *n* : the upper layer of mixed soil and organic debris typical of forested land
forest green *n* : a dark yellowish or moderate olive green
forest ranger *n* : an officer in charge of forest protection (as by preventing, detecting, and fighting fires) and management (as supervision of lumbering and recreation)
for·est·ry \ˈfȯr-ə-strē, ˈfär-\ *n* : scientific management of forests including development, care, and often economic harvesting
foreswear *variant of* FORSWEAR
¹fore·taste \ˈfōr-ˌtāst, ˈfȯr-\ *n* : a preliminary or partial experience of something that will not be fully experienced until later ⟨through maneuvers a soldier gets a *foretaste* of war⟩
²fore·taste \fōr-ˈtāst, fȯr-ˈ, ˈfōr-ˌ, ˈfȯr-ˌ\ *vt* : to have a foretaste of
fore·tell \fōr-ˈtel, fȯr-\ *vt* **-told** \-ˈtōld\; **-tell·ing** : to tell of or describe beforehand — **fore·tell·er** *n*
synonyms FORETELL, PREDICT, FORECAST, PROPHESY mean to tell beforehand. FORETELL applies to the telling of the coming of a future event by any procedure or any source of information ⟨a sorcerer *foretold* their evil end⟩. PREDICT implies often exact foretelling through scientific methods ⟨*predict* an eclipse⟩. FORECAST commonly deals in probabilities and eventualities rather than certainties ⟨*forecasting* the week's weather⟩. PROPHESY suggests the presence of inspired or mystic knowledge of the future ⟨*prophesying* the end of the world⟩.
fore·thought \ˈfōr-ˌthȯt, ˈfȯr-\ *n* **1** : a thinking or planning out in advance : PREMEDITATION **2** : thoughtful care or consideration for the future — **fore·thought·ful** \-fəl\ *adj*
¹fore·to·ken \ˈfōr-ˌtō-kən, ˈfȯr-\ *n* : a premonitory sign
²fore·to·ken \fōr-ˈtō-kən, fȯr-\ *vt* **-to·kened**; **-to·ken·ing** \-ˈtōk-ning, -ə-ning\ : to indicate in advance ⟨the bright sunset *foretokened* good weather⟩
fore·top \ˈfōr-ˌtäp, ˈfȯr-; -təp\ *n* : the platform at the head of the ship's foremast
for·ev·er \fə-ˈrev-ər, fȯ-\ *adv* **1** : for a limitless time : EVERLASTINGLY ⟨wants to live *forever*⟩ **2** : at all times : CONSTANTLY ⟨a dog that was *forever* chasing cars⟩
for·ev·er·more \-ˌrev-ər-ˈmōr, -ˌrev-ə-ˈ, -ˈmȯr\ *adv* : FOREVER 1
fore·warn \fōr-ˈwȯrn, fȯr-\ *vt* : to warn in advance ⟨*forewarned* of danger⟩
fore·wing \ˈfōr-ˌwing, ˈfȯr-\ *n* : either of the front wings of a 4-winged insect
fore·wom·an \ˈfōr-ˌwu̇m-ən, ˈfȯr-\ *n* : a woman who is a foreman
fore·word \ˈfōr-wərd, ˈfȯr-, -ˌwərd\ *n* : PREFACE 2
¹for·feit \ˈfȯr-fət\ *n* **1** : something lost by or taken away from a person because of an offense or error committed : PENALTY, FINE **2** *pl* : a game in which the players redeem personal articles by paying amusing or embarrassing penalties [Medieval French *forfait,* from *forfaire* "to commit a crime, forfeit"]
²forfeit *vt* : to lose or lose the right to especially by some error, offense, or crime — **for·feit·er** *n*
³forfeit *adj* : forfeited or subject to forfeiture
for·fei·ture \ˈfȯr-fə-ˌchu̇r, -chər\ *n* **1** : the act of forfeiting **2** : something forfeited : PENALTY
for·fend \fȯr-ˈfend\ *vt* **1 a** *archaic* : FORBID 1 **b** : to ward off : PREVENT **2** : PRESERVE 1, PROTECT
for·gath·er *or* **fore·gath·er** \fȯr-ˈgath-ər, fōr-\ *vi* **1** : to come together : ASSEMBLE **2** : to meet someone usually by chance
¹forge \ˈfōrj, ˈfȯrj\ *n* **1** : a furnace or a shop with its furnace

\ə\ **abut**	\au̇\ **out**	\i\ **tip**	\ȯ\ **saw**	\u̇\ **foot**
\ər\ **further**	\ch\ **chin**	\ī\ **life**	\ȯi\ **coin**	\y\ **yet**
\a\ **mat**	\e\ **pet**	\j\ **job**	\th\ **thin**	\yü\ **few**
\ā\ **take**	\ē\ **easy**	\ng\ **sing**	\th\ **this**	\yu̇\ **cure**
\ä\ **cot, cart**	\g\ **go**	\ō\ **bone**	\ü\ **food**	\zh\ **vision**

where metal is heated and worked **2 :** a workshop where wrought iron is produced or where iron is made malleable [Medieval French, from Latin *fabrica* "workshop," from *faber* "artisan, smith"]

[2]**forge** *vt* **1 a :** to form (as metal) by heating and hammering **b :** to form (metal) by a mechanical or hydraulic press **2 :** to make or imitate falsely especially with intent to defraud : COUNTERFEIT ⟨*forge* a check⟩ **3 :** to form or shape in any way : FASHION ⟨*forge* ties of friendship⟩

[3]**forge** *vi* **:** to move forward steadily but gradually ⟨the ship *forged* ahead through heavy seas⟩

forg·er \ˈfōr-jər, ˈfȯr-\ *n* : one that forges; *esp* : a person guilty of forgery

forg·ery \ˈfōrj-rē, ˈfȯrj-, -ə-rē\ *n, pl* **-er·ies 1 :** something (as a signature) that has been forged **2 :** the crime of falsely making or changing a written paper or signing someone else's name

for·get \fər-ˈget, fȯr-\ *vb* **-got** \-ˈgät\; **-got·ten** \-ˈgät-n\ *or* **-got; -get·ting 1 :** to be unable to think of or recall ⟨*forgot* the address⟩ **2 a :** to fail to recall at the proper time ⟨*forgot* about paying the bill⟩ **b :** NEGLECT ⟨*forget* old friends⟩ **3 a :** to disregard intentionally : OVERLOOK ⟨I shouldn't have said that, so just *forget* it⟩ **b :** to give up hope for ⟨as for prompt service, *forget* it⟩ **4 :** to stop remembering or noticing ⟨forgive and *forget*⟩ [Old English *forgietan*] ***synonyms*** see NEGLECT — **for·get·ter** *n* — **forget oneself :** to lose one's dignity, temper, or self-control

for·get·ful \-ˈget-fəl\ *adj* **1 :** likely to forget ⟨became more *forgetful* with age⟩ **2 :** CARELESS, NEGLECTFUL ⟨*forgetful* of responsibilities⟩ — **for·get·ful·ly** \-ˈget-fə-lē\ *adv* — **for·get·ful·ness** *n*

for·get–me–not \fər-ˈget-mē-ˌnät, fȯr-\ *n* **:** any of a genus of small herbs with bright blue or white flowers usually in a curved spike

forget-me-not

for·get·ta·ble \-ˈget-ə-bəl\ *adj* **:** likely to be forgotten

forg·ing \ˈfōr-jing, ˈfȯr-\ *n* **:** a piece of forged work ⟨aluminum *forgings*⟩

for·give \fər-ˈgiv, fȯr-\ *vb* **-gave** \-ˈgāv\; **-giv·en** \-ˈgiv-ən\; **-giv·ing 1 a :** to give up resentment of or claim to requital for ⟨*forgive* an insult⟩ **b :** to grant relief from payment of ⟨*forgive* a debt⟩ **2 :** to cease to feel resentment against (an offender) : PARDON ⟨*forgive* your enemies⟩ [Old English *forgifan,* from *for-* + *gifan* "to give"] ***synonyms*** see EXCUSE — **for·giv·able** \-ˈgiv-ə-bəl\ *adj* — **for·giv·ably** \-blē\ *adv* — **for·giv·er** *n*

for·give·ness \-ˈgiv-nəs\ *n* **:** the act of forgiving : PARDON

for·giv·ing \-ˈgiv-ing\ *adj* **1 :** showing forgiveness : inclined or ready to forgive ⟨a person with a *forgiving* nature⟩ **2 :** allowing room for error or weakness ⟨designed to be a *forgiving* tennis racquet⟩ — **for·giv·ing·ly** \-ing-lē\ *adv* — **for·giv·ing·ness** *n*

for·go *also* **fore·go** \fȯr-ˈgō, fōr-\ *vt* **-went** \-ˈwent\; **-gone** \-ˈgȯn, -ˈgän\; **-go·ing** \-ˈgō-ing\ **:** to give up : let pass : go without ⟨*forgo* lunch⟩ ⟨*forgo* an opportunity⟩ [Old English *forgān* "to pass by, forgo," from *for-* + *gān* "to go"]

fo·rint \ˈfȯr-ˌint\ *n, pl* **forints** *also* **forint 1 :** the basic monetary unit of Hungary **2 :** a coin representing one forint [Hungarian]

[1]**fork** \ˈfȯrk\ *n* **1 :** an implement with two or more prongs used especially for taking up (as in eating), pitching, or digging **2 :** a forked part, tool, or piece of equipment **3 a :** a dividing into branches or the place where something divides into branches ⟨a *fork* in the road⟩ **b :** a branch of a fork ⟨take the left *fork* at the crossroads⟩ [Old English *forca* and Medieval French *furke,* both from Latin *furca*]

[2]**fork** *vb* **1 :** to divide into two or more branches ⟨the road *forks*⟩ **2 :** to give the form of a fork to ⟨*fork* one's fingers⟩ **3 :** to raise or pitch with a fork ⟨*fork* hay⟩ **4 :** PAY 1 ⟨had to *fork* over $100⟩ — **fork·er** *n*

forked \ˈfȯrkt, ˈfȯr-kəd\ *adj* **1 :** shaped like a fork ⟨a *forked* road⟩ **2 :** resembling a fork ⟨*forked* lightning⟩

fork·ful \ˈfȯrk-ˌfu̇l\ *n, pl* **forkfuls** \ˈfȯrk-ˌfu̇lz\ *also* **forks·ful** \ˈfȯrks-ˌfu̇l\ **:** as much as a fork will hold

fork·lift \ˈfȯrk-ˌlift\ *n* **:** a machine for hoisting and transporting heavy objects by means of steel fingers inserted under the load

for·lorn \fər-ˈlȯrn\ *adj* **1 :** seeming sad and lonely especially because of isolation or desertion : DESOLATE ⟨a *forlorn* landscape⟩ **2 :** being or feeling deserted or neglected : WRETCHED ⟨a *forlorn* shack in the woods⟩ **3 :** nearly hopeless ⟨a *forlorn* cause⟩ [Old English *forloren,* past participle of *forlēosan* "to lose, abandon," from *for-* + *lēosan* "to lose"] ***synonyms*** see SOLITARY — **for·lorn·ly** *adv* — **for·lorn·ness** \-ˈlȯrn-nəs\ *n*

forlorn hope *n* **1 :** a body of men selected to perform a perilous service **2 :** a desperate or extremely difficult enterprise [by folk etymology from Dutch *verloren hoop,* literally, "lost band"]

[1]**form** \ˈfȯrm\ *n* **1 a :** the shape and structure of something as distinguished from its material **b :** a body (as of a person) especially in its external appearance or as distinguished from the face **2 :** the essential nature of a thing as distinguished from its matter **3 a :** an established manner of doing or saying something ⟨the *forms* of worship⟩ **b :** a standard or expectation based on past experience : PRECEDENT ⟨true to *form,* the champions won again⟩ **4 :** a printed or typed document with blank spaces for insertion of required information ⟨a tax *form*⟩ **5 a :** conduct regulated by custom or etiquette : CEREMONY, CONVENTION; *also* : display without substance ⟨outward *forms* of mourning⟩ **b :** manner of performing according to recognized standards ⟨such behavior is bad *form*⟩ **6 :** a long seat : BENCH **7 a :** a supporting frame model of the human figure used for displaying clothes **b :** a mold in which concrete is placed to set **8 :** printing type or matter arranged and secured ready for printing **9 :** one of the different varieties of a particular thing or substance : KIND 1 ⟨coal is a *form* of carbon⟩ **10 a :** a meaningful unit of speech (as a morpheme, word, or sentence) **b :** any of the different pronunciations or spellings a word may take in inflection or compounding **11 :** a mathematical expression of a particular type ⟨the number 2.5 can be written in fractional *form* as 5/2⟩ **12 a :** orderly method of arrangement (as in the presentation of ideas or artistic elements); *also* : a particular kind or instance of such arrangement ⟨the sonnet is a poetical *form*⟩ **b :** the structural element, plan, or design of a work of art **c :** a surface or space that is bounded : a visible and measurable object with limits fixed or marked by an outline **13 :** a grade in a British secondary school or in some American private schools **14 a :** a known ability to perform ⟨a singer at the top of her *form*⟩ **b :** condition suitable for performing (as in athletic competition) ⟨back on *form*⟩ [Medieval French *forme,* from Latin *forma*]

synonyms FORM, FIGURE, SHAPE mean the outward appearance of something. FORM may refer both to internal structure and external outline and often suggests the principle giving unity to the whole ⟨early *forms* of animal life⟩. FIGURE applies chiefly to the bounding or enclosing lines of a form ⟨cutting doll *figures* out of paper⟩. SHAPE may also suggest an outline, but carries a stronger implication of a three-dimensional body ⟨the *shape* of the monument was pyramidal⟩.

[2]**form** *vb* **1 :** to give form or shape to : FASHION, MAKE ⟨*form* a letter of the alphabet⟩ **2 :** TRAIN, INSTRUCT ⟨education *forms* the mind⟩ **3 :** to make up : CONSTITUTE ⟨a hat *formed* of straw⟩ **4 :** DEVELOP, ACQUIRE ⟨*form* a habit⟩ **5 :** to arrange themselves in ⟨the customers *formed* a line⟩ **6 :** to take form : ARISE ⟨fog *forms* in the valleys⟩ **7 :** to take a definite form, shape, or arrangement ⟨the dancers *formed* in circles⟩ — **form·er** *n*

-form \ˌfȯrm\ *adj combining form* **:** in the form or shape of : resembling ⟨reni*form*⟩ [Latin *-formis,* from *forma* "form"]

[1]**for·mal** \ˈfȯr-məl\ *adj* **1 :** relating to, concerned with, or constituting the outward form of something as distinguished from its content **2 a :** following or according with established form, custom, or rule ⟨*formal* dress⟩ ⟨paying *formal* attention to his hostess⟩ ⟨a *formal* dinner⟩ **b :** done in due or lawful form ⟨a *formal* contract⟩ **3 :** characterized by punctilious respect for form : METHODICAL ⟨very *formal* in all their dealings⟩ **4 :** having the appearance without the substance ⟨*formal* Christians who go to church only at Easter⟩ ⟨a purely *formal* requirement⟩ — **for·mal·ly** \-mə-lē\ *adv*

[2]**formal** *n* **:** something (as a social event) formal in character

form·al·de·hyde \fȯr-ˈmal-də-ˌhīd, fər-\ *n* **:** a colorless gas CH_2O that has a sharp irritating odor and is used as a disinfectant and preservative [*form*ic acid + *aldehyde*]

for·ma·lin \ˈfȯr-mə-lən, -ˌlēn\ *n* **:** a clear water solution of formaldehyde containing a small amount of methanol that is used especially as a preservative

for·mal·ism \ˈfȯr-mə-ˌliz-əm\ *n* **:** the strict observance of forms or conventions (as in religion or art) — **for·mal·ist** \-ləst\ *n* — **for·mal·is·tic** \ˌfȯr-mə-ˈlis-tik\ *adj* — **for·mal·is·ti·cal·ly** \-ti-kə-lē, -klē\ *adv*

for·mal·i·ty \fȯr-ˈmal-ət-ē\ *n, pl* **-ties 1 :** compliance with formal or conventional rules : CEREMONY **2** : the quality or state of being formal **3** : an established form that is required or conventional ⟨the interview was just a *formality*⟩

for·mal·ize \ˈfȯr-mə-ˌlīz\ *vt* **1** : to make formal **2** : to give formal status or approval to — **for·mal·i·za·tion** \ˌfȯr-mə-lə-ˈzā-shən\ *n* — **for·mal·iz·er** *n*

[1]**for·mat** \ˈfȯr-ˌmat\ *n* **1** : the shape, size, and general makeup of a publication **2** : the general plan of organization or arrangement of something **3** : a method of organizing computer data ⟨common file *formats*⟩ [German, from Latin *formare* "to form," from *forma* "form"]

[2]**format** *vb* **1** : to produce in a particular format **2** : to prepare for storing data ⟨*format* the disk⟩

for·ma·tion \fȯr-ˈmā-shən\ *n* **1** : a forming of something ⟨the *formation* of good habits during childhood⟩ **2** : something that is formed ⟨new word *formations*⟩ **3** : the manner in which a thing is formed : STRUCTURE, SHAPE ⟨an abnormal *formation* of the jaw⟩ **4** : a bed of rocks or series of beds recognizable as a unit **5** : an arrangement or grouping of persons, ships, or airplanes ⟨battle *formation*⟩ ⟨planes flying in *formation*⟩ — **for·ma·tion·al** \-shnəl, -shən-l\ *adj*

for·ma·tive \ˈfȯr-mət-iv\ *adj* **1** : giving or capable of giving form : CONSTRUCTIVE ⟨a *formative* influence⟩ **2** : of, relating to, or characterized by important growth or formation ⟨*formative* years⟩ — **for·ma·tive·ly** *adv* — **for·ma·tive·ness** *n*

form class *n* : a class of linguistic forms that can be used in the same position in a construction and that have one or more morphological or syntactical features in common

for·mer \ˈfȯr-mər\ *adj* **1** : coming before in time; *esp* : of, relating to, or occurring in the past ⟨our *former* correspondence⟩ **2** : preceding in place or arrangement : FOREGOING ⟨the *former* part of the chapter⟩ **3** : first in order of two things mentioned or understood ⟨of these two spellings, the *former* is more common⟩ **4** : having been previously ⟨*former* classmates⟩ [Middle English, from *forme* "first," from Old English *forma*]

for·mer·ly \-mər-lē, -mə-lē\ *adv* : at an earlier time : PREVIOUSLY

form·fit·ting \ˈfȯrm-ˌfit-ing\ *adj* : conforming to the outline of the body ⟨a *formfitting* sweater⟩

For·mi·ca \fȯr-ˈmī-kə, fər-\ *trademark* — used for any of various laminated plastic products used especially for surface finish

for·mic acid \ˈfȯr-mik-\ *n* : a colorless strong-smelling liquid acid CH_2O_2 that irritates the skin, is found in insects (as ants) and in many plants, and is used chiefly in dyeing and finishing textiles [Latin *formica* "ant"]

for·mi·cary \ˈfȯr-mə-ˌker-ē\ *n, pl* **-car·ies** : an ant nest

for·mi·da·ble \ˈfȯr-məd-ə-bəl, fȯr-ˈmid-\ *adj* **1** : arousing fear ⟨a *formidable* foe⟩ **2** : imposing serious difficulties or hardships ⟨the mountains were a *formidable* barrier⟩ **3** : tending to inspire awe or wonder : IMPRESSIVE ⟨the *formidable* accomplishments of science⟩ [Latin *formidabilis,* from *formidare* "to fear," from *formido* "terror, bogey"] — **for·mi·da·bil·i·ty** \ˌfȯr-məd-ə-ˈbil-ət-ē, fȯr-ˌmid-\ *n* — **for·mi·da·ble·ness** *n* — **for·mi·da·bly** \-blē\ *adv*

form·less \ˈfȯrm-ləs\ *adj* : having no regular form or shape — **form·less·ly** *adv* — **form·less·ness** *n*

for·mu·la \ˈfȯr-myə-lə\ *n, pl* **-las** *or* **-lae** \-ˌlē, -ˌlī\ **1** : a set form of words for use in a ceremony or ritual **2 a** : RECIPE, PRESCRIPTION ⟨our *formula* for happiness⟩ **b** : a milk mixture or substitute for a baby **3 a** : a symbolic expression of the composition or constitution of a substance ⟨the *formula* for water is H_2O⟩ **b** : a general fact, rule, or principle expressed in usually mathematical symbols **4** : a prescribed or set form or method [Latin, "small form," from *forma* "form"] — **for·mu·la·ic** \ˌfȯr-myə-ˈlā-ik\ *adj* — **for·mu·la·ical·ly** \-ˈlā-ə-kə-lē, -klē\ *adv*

for·mu·la·rize \ˈfȯr-myə-lə-ˌrīz\ *vt* : to state in or reduce to a formula : FORMULATE — **for·mu·la·ri·za·tion** \ˌfȯr-myə-lə-rə-ˈzā-shən\ *n* — **for·mu·la·riz·er** *n*

for·mu·lary \ˈfȯr-myə-ˌler-ē\ *n, pl* **-lar·ies** **1** : a book or collection of stated and prescribed forms (as prayers) **2** : a prescribed form or model : FORMULA **3** : a book containing a list of medicinal substances and formulas — **formulary** *adj*

for·mu·late \ˈfȯr-myə-ˌlāt\ *vt* **1** : to express in a formula **2** : to put in systematic form : state definitely and clearly ⟨*formulate* a plan⟩ — **for·mu·la·tion** \ˌfȯr-myə-ˈlā-shən\ *n* — **for·mu·la·tor** \ˈfȯr-myə-ˌlāt-ər\ *n*

for·ni·cate \ˈfȯr-nə-ˌkāt\ *vi* : to commit fornication [Late Latin *fornicare,* "to have intercourse with prostitutes," from Latin *fornix* "arch, vault, brothel"] — **for·ni·ca·tor** \-ˌkāt-ər\ *n*

for·ni·ca·tion \ˌfȯr-nə-ˈkā-shən\ *n* : human sexual intercourse between two persons not married to each other — compare ADULTERY

for·nix \ˈfȯr-niks\ *n, pl* **for·ni·ces** \-nə-ˌsēz\ : an anatomical arch or fold [Latin, "arch"]

for–prof·it \ˈfȯr-ˈpräf-ət\ *adj* : conducted or maintained for the purpose of profit ⟨*for-profit* businesses⟩

for·sake \fər-ˈsāk, fȯr-\ *vt* **for·sook** \-ˈsu̇k\; **for·sak·en** \-ˈsā-kən\; **for·sak·ing** : to give up or leave entirely : withdraw from ⟨*forsook* the theater for other work⟩ ⟨*forsaken* by false friends⟩ [Old English *forsacan,* from *for-* + *sacan* "to dispute"]
synonyms see ABANDON

for·sooth \fər-ˈsüth\ *adv* : in truth : INDEED

for·swear *also* **fore·swear** \fȯr-ˈswaər, fōr-, -ˈsweər\ *vb* **-swore** \-ˈswōr, -ˈswȯr\; **-sworn** \-ˈswōrn, -ˈswȯrn\; **-swear·ing** **1** : to make a liar of (oneself) under or as if under oath **2 a** : to reject or renounce under oath **b** : to deny under oath **3** : to swear falsely : commit perjury **4** : to pledge oneself to give up ⟨*forswear* gambling⟩

for·syth·ia \fər-ˈsith-ē-ə\ *n, pl* **-ias** *also* **-ia** : any of a genus of shrubs related to the olive and widely grown for their yellow bell-shaped flowers appearing before the leaves in early spring [William *Forsyth,* died 1804, British botanist]

fort \ˈfōrt, ˈfȯrt\ *n* **1** : a strong or fortified place; *esp* : a place surrounded with defenses and occupied by soldiers **2** : a permanent army post [Medieval French, from *fort* "strong," from Latin *fortis*]

[1]**forte** \ˈfōrt, ˈfȯrt, ˈfȯr-ˌtā\ *n* : something in which a person shows special ability : a strong point ⟨music was always your *forte*⟩ [French *fort,* from *fort* "strong"]

usage In *forte* we have a word derived from French that in its "strong point" sense has no entirely satisfactory pronunciation. Usage writers have criticized \ˈfȯr-ˌtā\ and \ˈfȯr-tē\ because they reflect the influence of the Italian-derived [2]*forte.* Their recommended pronunciation \ˈfōrt\, however, does not exactly reflect French either: the French would write the word *le fort* and would rhyme it with English *for.* So you can take your choice, knowing that someone somewhere will dislike whichever variant you choose. All are standard, however. In American English, \ˈfȯr-ˌtā\ and \fȯr-ˈtā\ appear to be the most frequent pronunciations.

[2]**for·te** \ˈfȯr-ˌtā, ˈfȯrt-ē\ *adv or adj* : LOUD — used as a direction in music [Italian, from *forte* "strong," from Latin *fortis*]

forth \ˈfōrth, ˈfȯrth\ *adv* **1** : FORWARD, ONWARD ⟨from that time *forth*⟩ ⟨back and *forth*⟩ **2** : out into view : OUT ⟨plants putting *forth* leaves⟩ [Old English]

forth·com·ing \fōrth-ˈkəm-ing, fȯrth-\ *adj* **1 a** : being about to appear : APPROACHING ⟨the *forthcoming* holidays⟩ ⟨your *forthcoming* novel⟩ **b** : readily available ⟨the needed supplies were *forthcoming*⟩ **2 a** : RESPONSIVE 2, FRIENDLY ⟨a *forthcoming* and courteous man⟩ **b** : characterized by openness and candidness ⟨not *forthcoming* about her past⟩

forth·right \ˈfōrth-ˌrīt, ˈfȯrth-\ *adj* : STRAIGHTFORWARD, DIRECT ⟨a *forthright* answer⟩ — **forth·right·ly** *adv* — **forth·right·ness** *n*

forth·with \fōrth-ˈwith, fȯrth-, -ˈwith\ *adv* : IMMEDIATELY ⟨expect an answer *forthwith*⟩

for·ti·fi·ca·tion \ˌfȯrt-ə-fə-ˈkā-shən\ *n* **1** : the act of fortifying **2 a** : a construction built for the defense of a place : FORT **b** *pl* : works built to defend a place or position

for·ti·fy \ˈfȯrt-ə-ˌfī\ *vt* **-fied; -fy·ing** : to make strong: as **a** : to strengthen and secure by military defenses ⟨*fortify* a town⟩ **b** : to give physical strength, courage, or endurance to ⟨*fortify* the body against illness⟩ **c** : to add mental or moral strength to : ENCOURAGE ⟨*fortified* by prayer⟩ **d** : to add material to for strengthening or improving : ENRICH ⟨*fortify* a soil with fertilizer⟩ [Medieval French *fortifier,* from Late Latin *fortificare,* from Latin *fortis* "strong"] — **for·ti·fi·er** \-ˌfī-ər, -ˌfīr\ *n*

for·tis·si·mo \fȯr-ˈtis-ə-ˌmō\ *adv or adj* : very loud — used as a direction in music [Italian, superlative of *forte* "strong"]

for·ti·tude \ˈfȯrt-ə-ˌtüd, -ˌtyüd\ *n* : strength of mind that enables a person to meet danger or bear pain or adversity with courage [Latin *fortitudo* "strength," from *fortis* "strong"]

\ə\ **abut**	\au̇\ **out**	\i\ **tip**	\ȯ\ **saw**	\u̇\ **foot**
\ər\ **further**	\ch\ **chin**	\ī\ **life**	\ȯi\ **coin**	\y\ **yet**
\a\ **mat**	\e\ **pet**	\j\ **job**	\th\ **thin**	\yü\ **few**
\ā\ **take**	\ē\ **easy**	\ng\ **sing**	\t͟h\ **this**	\yu̇\ **cure**
\ä\ **cot, cart**	\g\ **go**	\ō\ **bone**	\ü\ **food**	\zh\ **vision**

fort·night \ˈfȯrt-ˌnīt, ˈfȯrt-\ *n* : a period of 14 days : two weeks [Middle English *fourtenight,* alteration of *fourtene night* "fourteen nights"]

¹fort·night·ly \-lē\ *adj* : occurring or appearing once in a fortnight

²fortnightly *adv* : once in a fortnight : every fortnight

³fortnightly *n, pl* **-lies** : a publication issued fortnightly

FOR·TRAN *or* **For·tran** \ˈfȯr-ˌtran\ *n* : an algebraic and logical language for programming a computer [*for*mula *tran*slation]

for·tress \ˈfȯr-trəs\ *n* : a fortified place; *esp* : a large and permanent fortification sometimes including a town [Medieval French *fortelesce, forteresse,* from Medieval Latin *fortalitia,* from Latin *fortis* "strong"]

for·tu·i·tous \fȯr-ˈtü-ət-əs, fər-, -ˈtyü-\ *adj* **1** : occurring by chance **2** : FORTUNATE, LUCKY [Latin *fortuitus*] ***synonyms*** see ACCIDENTAL — **for·tu·i·tous·ly** *adv* — **for·tu·i·tous·ness** *n*

for·tu·i·ty \-ət-ē\ *n, pl* **-ties** **1** : the quality or state of being fortuitous **2** : a chance event or occurrence

for·tu·nate \ˈfȯrch-nət, -ə-nət\ *adj* **1** : coming or happening by good luck **2** : receiving some unexpected good : LUCKY ***synonyms*** see LUCKY — **for·tu·nate·ly** *adv*

for·tune \ˈfȯr-chən\ *n* **1 a** : favorable results that come partly by chance : SUCCESS **b** : the cause of something that happens to one suddenly and unexpectedly : CHANCE, LUCK **2** : what happens to a person : good or bad luck ‹her *fortunes* varied but she never gave up› **3** : a person's destiny or fate ‹tell one's *fortune*›; *also* : a prediction of fortune **4 a** : possession of material goods : WEALTH ‹people of *fortune*› **b** : a store of material possessions : RICHES ‹the family *fortune*› [Medieval French, from Latin *fortuna*]

fortune cookie *n* : a folded cookie containing a slip of paper on which is printed a fortune, proverb, or humorous statement

fortune hunter *n* : a person who seeks wealth especially by marriage

for·tune–tell·er \-ˌtel-ər\ *n* : a person who professes to foretell future events — **for·tune–tell·ing** \-ˌtel-ing\ *n or adj*

for·ty \ˈfȯrt-ē\ *n, pl* **forties** **1** — see NUMBER table **2** : the 3rd point scored by a side in a game of tennis [Old English *fēowertig*] — **for·ti·eth** \-ē-əth\ *adj or n* — **forty** *adj or pron* — **for·ty·ish** \-ē-ish\ *adj*

for·ty–five \ˌfȯrt-ē-ˈfīv\ *n* **1** : a .45 caliber pistol — usually written .45 **2** : a phonograph record for play at 45 revolutions per minute

Forty Hours *n sing or pl* : a Roman Catholic devotion in which the churches of a diocese in two-day turns maintain continuous daytime prayer before the exposed Blessed Sacrament

for·ty–nin·er \ˌfȯrt-ē-ˈnī-nər\ *n* : a person in California in the gold rush of 1849

forty winks *n sing or pl* : a short sleep : NAP

fo·rum \ˈfōr-əm, ˈfȯr-\ *n, pl* **forums** *also* **fo·ra** \-ə\ **1 a** : the marketplace or public place of an ancient Roman city serving as the center of judicial and public business **b** : a medium (as a newspaper or online service) of open discussion or expression of ideas **2** : a judicial body or assembly : COURT **3 a** : a public meeting or lecture involving audience discussion **b** : a program (as on radio or television) involving discussion of a problem usually by several authorities [Latin]

¹for·ward \ˈfȯr-wərd\ *adj* **1** : near, being at, or belonging to the front **2 a** : strongly inclined : READY **b** : tending to push oneself : BRASH **3** : notably advanced or developed **4** : moving, tending, or leading toward a position in front ‹*forward* movement› **5** : of, relating to, or getting ready for the future ‹*forward* buying of produce› [Old English *foreweard,* from *fore-* + *-weard* "-ward"] — **for·ward·ly** *adv* — **for·ward·ness** *n*

²forward *adv* : to or toward what is ahead or in front

³forward *vt* **1** : to help onward : ADVANCE ‹*forward* a friend's career› **2 a** : to send forward : TRANSMIT ‹will *forward* the goods on receipt of your check› **b** : to send or ship onward from an intermediate post or station in transit ‹*forward* a letter›

⁴forward *n* : a player who plays at the front of the team near the opponent's goal

for·ward·er \ˈfȯr-wərd-ər\ *n* : one that forwards; *esp* : an agent who forwards goods ‹a freight *forwarder*›

for·ward·ing \-wərd-ing\ *n* : the act of one that forwards; *esp* : the business of a forwarder of goods

forward pass *n* : a pass in football thrown in the direction of the opponent's goal

for·wards \ˈfȯr-wərdz\ *adv* : FORWARD

¹fos·sa \ˈfäs-ə\ *n, pl* **fos·sae** \ˈfäs-ˌē, -ˌī\ : an anatomical pit or depression [Latin, "ditch"]

²fossa *n* : a slender long-tailed meat-eating mammal of Madagascar that has usually reddish brown short thick fur and is an excellent climber [Malagasy *fosa*]

fosse *or* **foss** \ˈfäs\ *n* : DITCH, MOAT [Medieval French *fosse,* from Latin *fossa,* from *fodere* "to dig"]

¹fos·sil \ˈfäs-əl\ *adj* **1** : preserved from a past geologic age ‹*fossil* plants› **2** : being or resembling a fossil **3** : of or relating to fossil fuel

²fossil *n* **1** : a trace or impression or the remains of a plant or animal of a past age preserved in the earth's crust **2 a** : a person whose ideas are out-of-date **b** : something that has become rigidly fixed [Latin *fossilis* "obtained by digging," from *fodere* "to dig"]

fossil fuel *n* : a fuel (as coal, oil, or natural gas) that is formed in the earth from plant or animal remains

fos·sil·if·er·ous \ˌfäs-ə-ˈlif-rəs, -ə-rəs\ *adj* : containing fossils

fos·sil·ize \ˈfäs-ə-ˌlīz\ *vb* **1** : to convert or become converted into a fossil **2** : to make outmoded, rigid, or fixed — **fos·sil·i·za·tion** \ˌfäs-ə-lə-ˈzā-shən\ *n*

fos·so·ri·al \fä-ˈsōr-ē-əl, -ˈsȯr-\ *adj* : adapted to or occupied in digging ‹a *fossorial* foot› ‹*fossorial* animals›

¹fos·ter \ˈfȯs-tər, ˈfäs-\ *adj* : affording, receiving, or sharing nurture or parental care though not related by blood or legal ties ‹*foster* parent› ‹*foster* child› [Old English *fōstor-,* from *fōstor* "food, feeding"]

²foster *vt* **fos·tered; fos·ter·ing** \-tə-ring, -tring\ **1** : to give parental care to : NURTURE **2** : to promote the growth or development of : ENCOURAGE — **fos·ter·er** \-tər-ər\ *n*

fos·ter·age \ˈfȯs-tə-rij, ˈfäs-\ *n* : the act of fostering

foster home *n* : a household in which an orphaned, neglected, or delinquent child is placed for care

fos·ter·ling \-tər-ling\ *n* : a foster child

Fou·cault pendulum \ˌfü-ˈkō-\ *n* : a pendulum that consists of a heavy weight hung by a long wire and that swings in a constant direction which appears to change showing that the earth rotates [J. B. L. *Foucault,* died 1868, French physicist]

fought *past of* FIGHT

¹foul \ˈfau̇l\ *adj* **1 a** : offensive to the senses ‹a *foul* sewer› **b** : clogged or covered with dirt ‹*foul* clothes› **2 a** : morally or spiritually odious : DETESTABLE ‹*foul* crimes› **b** : notably unpleasant or distressing ‹a *foul* mood› **3** : OBSCENE, ABUSIVE ‹*foul* language› **4** : being wet and stormy ‹*foul* weather› **5 a** : grossly unfair : DISHONORABLE ‹by fair means or *foul*› **b** : violating a rule in a game or sport ‹a *foul* blow in boxing› **6** : being outside the foul lines in baseball ‹a *foul* grounder› [Old English *fūl*] ***synonyms*** see DIRTY — **foul·ly** \ˈfau̇l-lē, fau̇-\ *adv* — **foul·ness** *n*

²foul *n* **1** : an entanglement or collision especially in fishing or sailing **2** : an infringement of the rules in a game or sport **3** : FOUL BALL

³foul *vb* **1** : to make or become foul or filthy ‹*foul* the air› ‹*foul* a stream› **2** : DISGRACE ‹*foul* one's good name› **3 a** : to commit a violation of the rules in a sport or game **b** : to hit a foul ball **4** : to entangle or become entangled ‹*foul* a rope› **5** : to collide with ‹*foul* a launch in moving away from the dock›

⁴foul *adv* : FOULLY

fou·lard \fü-ˈlärd\ *n* **1** : a lightweight plain-woven or twilled silk usually decorated with a printed pattern **2** : an article of clothing (as a scarf) made of foulard [French]

foul ball *n* : a baseball hit into foul territory

foul line *n* **1** : either of two straight lines extending from the rear corner of home plate through the outer corners of first and third bases and continued to the boundary of a baseball field **2** : a line across a bowling alley that a player must not step over when delivering the ball **3** : either of 2 lines on a basketball court behind which a player stands to shoot a free throw

foul·mouthed \ˈfau̇l-ˈmau̇thd, -ˈmau̇tht\ *adj* : inclined to use dirty, profane, or abusive language

foul of *prep* : AFOUL OF

foul play *n* : unfair play or dealing : dishonest conduct; *esp* : VIOLENCE ‹a victim of *foul play*›

foul shot *n* : a free throw in basketball

foul tip *n* : a pitched baseball that is slightly deflected by the bat

foul–up \ˈfau̇-ˌləp\ *n* **1** : a state of confusion caused by bungling, carelessness, or mismanagement **2** : a mechanical difficulty

foul up \fau̇-ˈləp, ˈfau̇-\ *vb* **1** : to make dirty **2** : to spoil by making mistakes or using poor judgment : CONFUSE **3** : to become confused : get into difficulty : BUNGLE

[1]found \ˈfau̇nd\ *past of* FIND

[2]found *vt* **1** : to take the first steps in building : ESTABLISH ⟨*found* a colony⟩ **2** : to set or ground on something solid : BASE ⟨a house *founded* on rock⟩ **3** : to establish and often to provide for the future maintenance of ⟨*found* a college⟩ [Medieval French *funder,* from Latin *fundare,* from *fundus* "bottom"]

[3]found *vt* : to melt (metal) and pour into a mold [Middle French *fondre* "to pour, melt," from Latin *fundere*]

foun·da·tion \fau̇n-ˈdā-shən\ *n* **1** : the act of founding **2** : the base or basis upon which something stands or is supported ⟨a house with a cinder-block *foundation*⟩ ⟨suspicions with no *foundation* in fact⟩ **3** : funds given for the permanent support of an institution : ENDOWMENT; *also* : an organization or institution so endowed — **foun·da·tion·al** \-shnəl, -shən-l\ *adj*

[1]found·er \ˈfau̇n-dər\ *n* : one that founds or establishes something ⟨the *founders* of the town⟩

[2]foun·der \ˈfau̇n-dər\ *vb* **foun·dered; foun·der·ing** \-də-ring, -dring\ **1** : to go or cause to go lame ⟨the horse *foundered*⟩ **2** : to give way ⟨the building *foundered* in the fire⟩ **3** : to sink or cause to sink below the surface of the water ⟨a *foundering* ship⟩ **4** : to come or cause to come to grief : FAIL ⟨their efforts all *foundered*⟩ [Medieval French *fondrer* "to fall to the ground, sink," alteration of *fondre,* from Latin *fundere* "to pour, cast, disperse, lay low"]

[3]found·er *n* : one that founds metal

founder effect *n* : the effect on the resulting gene pool that occurs when a new isolated population is founded by a small number of individuals possessing limited genetic variation relative to the larger population from which they have migrated

found·ing father \ˈfau̇n-ding-\ *n* **1** : an originator of an institution or movement : FOUNDER **2** *often cap both Fs* : a leading figure in the founding of the U.S.

found·ling \ˈfau̇n-dling\ *n* : an infant found after its unknown parents have abandoned it

foundry \ˈfau̇n-drē\ *n, pl* **foundries** **1** : an establishment where founding is carried on **2** : the act, process, or art of casting metals

fount \ˈfau̇nt\ *n* : SOURCE 1b ⟨a *fount* of information⟩

foun·tain \ˈfau̇nt-n\ *n* **1** : a spring of water issuing from the earth **2** : SOURCE 1b **3** : an artificially produced jet of water; *also* : the structure from which it rises **4** : a reservoir containing a liquid that can be drawn off as needed [Medieval French *funtaine,* from Late Latin *fontana,* derived from Latin *font-, fons*]

foun·tain·head \-ˌhed\ *n* **1** : a spring that is the source of a stream **2** : a primary source : ORIGIN ⟨the *fountainhead* of our liberties⟩

fountain pen *n* : a pen with a reservoir that automatically feeds the writing point with ink

four \ˈfōr, ˈfȯr\ *n* **1** — see NUMBER table **2** : the 4th in a set or series **3** : something having four units or members [Old English *fēower*] — **four** *adj or pron*

4x4 \ˈfōr-bī-ˌfōr, ˈfȯr-bī-ˌfȯr\ *also* **four–by–four** *n* : a four-wheel automotive vehicle with four-wheel drive

four–dimensional *adj* : relating to or having four dimensions; *esp* : consisting of or relating to mathematical elements requiring four coordinates to determine them

four·fold \-ˌfōld, -ˈfōld\ *adj* **1** : having four units or members **2** : being four times as great or as many — **fourfold** *adv*

four–foot·ed \-ˈfu̇t-əd\ *adj* : having four feet : QUADRUPED

4–H \-ˈāch\ *adj* : of or relating to a program set up by the U.S. Department of Agriculture to help young people become productive citizens by instructing them in useful skills (as in agriculture), community service, and personal development ⟨*4-H* club⟩ [from the fourfold aim of improving the head, heart, hands, and health] — **4–H'er** \-ˈā-chər\ *n*

four–hand \ˈfōr-ˌhand, ˈfȯr-\ *adj* : FOUR-HANDED

four–hand·ed \-ˈhan-dəd\ *adj* **1** : designed for four hands **2** : engaged in by four persons ⟨a *four-handed* card game⟩

Four Horsemen *n pl* : war, famine, pestilence, and death personified as the four major plagues of humankind [from the apocalyptic vision in Revelation 6:2–8]

Four Hundred *or* **400** *n* : the exclusive social set of a community — used with *the* [from the idea that a social elite must necessarily be small in number]

four–in–hand \ˈfōr-ən-ˌhand, ˈfȯr-\ *n* **1 a** : a vehicle drawn by a team of four horses driven by one person **b** : such a team of four horses **2** : a necktie tied in a slipknot with long ends overlapping vertically in front

four–letter word *n* **1** : any of a group of dirty or abusive words typically made up of four letters **2** : a taboo word or topic ⟨homework is a *four-letter word* to him⟩

four–o'clock \-ə-ˌkläk\ *n* : an American garden plant with fragrant yellow, red, or white flowers opening late in the afternoon

four–post·er \-ˈpō-stər\ *n* : a bed with tall corner posts originally designed to support curtains or a canopy

four·ra·gère \ˌfu̇r-ə-ˈzheər\ *n* : a braided cord worn (as by a soldier in uniform) usually around the left shoulder [French]

four·score \ˈfōr-ˌskōr, ˈfȯr-ˌskȯr\ *adj* : being four times twenty : EIGHTY

four·some \ˈfōr-səm, ˈfȯr-\ *n* **1** : a group of four persons or things **2** : a golf match in which two players compete against two others with players on each side taking turns playing one ball; *broadly* : any golf match involving four players

four·square \-ˈskwaər, -ˈskwər\ *adj* **1** : SQUARE 1a **2** : marked by boldness and conviction : FORTHRIGHT — **four-square** *adv*

four·teen \fōr-ˈtēn, fȯr-, fōrt-, fȯrt-, ˈfōr-, ˈfȯr-, ˈfōrt-, ˈfȯrt-\ *n* — see NUMBER table [Old English *fēowertīene*] — **fourteen** *adj or pron* — **fourteenth** \-ˈtēnth, -ˈtēntth\ *adj or n*

four·teen·er \-ˈtē-nər\ *n* : a verse consisting of 14 syllables or especially of 7 iambic feet

fourth \ˈfōrth, ˈfȯrth\ *n* **1** — see NUMBER table **2 a** : the musical interval embracing four tones of the diatonic scale **b** : a tone at this interval **c** : the harmonic combination of two tones a fourth apart **3** : the 4th forward gear or speed of a motor vehicle — **fourth** *adj or adv* — **fourth·ly** *adv*

fourth dimension *n* **1** : a dimension in addition to length, width, and depth; *esp* : a coordinate in addition to three rectangular coordinates **2** : something outside the range of ordinary experience

fourth estate *n, often cap F&E* : the public press

Word History In Europe, in earlier days, the people who participated in the government of a country were generally divided into three classes or estates. In England the three traditional estates were the nobility, the clergy, and the commons. Occasionally the term *fourth estate* was used for some other group, like the mob or the public press, that had unofficial but often great influence on government. In time *fourth estate* came to refer exclusively to the press.

Fourth of July : INDEPENDENCE DAY

four–wheel \ˈfōr-ˌhwēl, ˈfȯr-, -ˌwēl\ *or* **four–wheeled** \-ˈhwēld, -ˈwēld\ *adj* **1** : having four wheels **2** : acting on or by means of four wheels of an automotive vehicle ⟨*four-wheel* drive⟩

fo·vea \ˈfō-vē-ə\ *n, pl* **-ve·ae** \-vē-ˌē, -vē-ˌī\ : an area in the center of the retina containing only cones and providing the sharpest vision and most acute color discrimination of any part of the retina [Latin, "pit"] — **fo·ve·al** \-vē-əl\ *adj* — **fo·ve·ate** \-vē-ˌāt\ *adj*

[1]fowl \ˈfau̇l\ *n, pl* **fowl** *or* **fowls** **1** : BIRD 1: as **a** : a domestic cock or hen; *esp* : an adult hen **b** : any of several domesticated or wild birds related to the common domestic cock and hen **2** : the meat of fowls used as food [Middle English *foul,* from Old English *fugel*]

[2]fowl *vi* : to seek, catch, or kill wildfowl — **fowl·er** *n*

fowling piece *n* : a light gun for shooting birds or small animals

[1]fox \ˈfäks\ *n, pl* **fox·es** *also* **fox** **1 a** : any of various carnivorous mammals related to the wolves but smaller and with shorter legs and more pointed muzzle **b** : the fur of a fox **2** : a clever crafty person **3** : an attractive young person [Old English]

[2]fox *vt* : to trick by cleverness or cunning : OUTWIT

foxed \ˈfäkst\ *adj* : discolored with foxing ⟨the *foxed* pages of an old book⟩

fox fire *n* : an eerie phosphorescent light (as of decaying wood); *also* : a luminous fungus that causes decaying wood to glow

fox·glove \ˈfäks-ˌgləv\ *n* : any of a genus of erect herbs related to the snapdragons; *esp* : a common biennial or perennial plant that bears showy spikes of dotted white or purple tubular flowers and is a source of digitalis

fox grape *n* : any of several native grapes of eastern North America with sour or musky fruit

fox·hole \ˈfäks-ˌhōl\ *n* : a pit dug hastily during combat for individual cover against enemy fire

fox·hound \-ˌhau̇nd\ *n* : a large swift powerful hound of any of several breeds often trained to hunt foxes

foxhound

fox·ing \ˈfäk-siŋ\ *n* : brownish spots on old paper

fox·tail \ˈfäks-ˌtāl\ *n* : any of several grasses with spikes resembling brushes

foxtail millet *n* : a coarse drought-resistant but frost-sensitive annual grass grown for grain, hay, and forage

fox terrier *n* : a small lively terrier formerly used to dig out foxes and known in smooth-haired and wire-haired varieties

fox–trot \ˈfäks-ˌträt\ *n* **1** : a short broken slow trotting gait of the horse **2** : a ballroom dance in duple time that includes slow walking steps, quick running steps, and the step of the two-step — **fox–trot** *vi*

foxy \ˈfäk-sē\ *adj* **fox·i·er; -est** **1 a** : resembling or suggestive of a fox ⟨a narrow *foxy* face⟩ **b** : being alert and knowing : CLEVER, SHREWD **2** : having the color of a fox **3** : physically attractive — **fox·i·ly** \-sə-lē\ *adv* — **fox·i·ness** \-sē-nəs\ *n*

foy·er \ˈfȯiər, ˈfȯir; ˈfȯi-ˌā, -ˌyā\ *n* : an anteroom or lobby especially of a theater; *also* : an entrance hallway [French, literally, "fireplace," derived from Latin *focus* "hearth"]

fra·cas \ˈfrā-kəs, ˈfrak-əs\ *n* : a noisy quarrel : BRAWL [French]

frack·ing \ˈfrak-iŋ\ *n* : the injection of fluid into shale beds at high pressure in order to free up petroleum resources (such as oil or natural gas) [shortened from *(hydraulic) fracturing*] — **frack** \ˈfrak\ *vb*

frac·tal \ˈfrak-tl\ *n* : an irregular shape that looks the same at any scale on which it is examined [French *fractale,* from Latin *fractus* "broken, uneven," from *frangere* "to break"]

frac·tion \ˈfrak-shən\ *n* **1** : a number (as ½, ¾, or 3.323) that indicates a number of equal parts of a whole or the division of one number by another **2 a** : a piece broken off : FRAGMENT **b** : PORTION, SECTION ⟨a small *fraction* of the voters⟩ [Late Latin *fractio* "act of breaking," from Latin *frangere* "to break"]

frac·tion·al \-shnəl, -shən-l\ *adj* **1** : of, relating to, or being a fraction **2** : relatively small : INCONSIDERABLE **3** : of, relating to, or involving a separating of components from a mixture through differences in physical or chemical properties ⟨*fractional* distillation⟩ — **frac·tion·al·ly** \-ē\ *adv*

fractional equation *n* : an equation in which the unknown is in the denominator of one or more terms ⟨a/x + b/x + 1 = c is a *fractional equation*⟩

frac·tion·ate \ˈfrak-shə-ˌnāt\ *vt* : to separate into different portions especially by a fractional process — **frac·tion·ation** \ˌfrak-shə-ˈnā-shən\ *n*

frac·tious \ˈfrak-shəs\ *adj* **1** : hard to handle or control ⟨a *fractious* horse⟩ **2** : QUARRELSOME [*fraction* ("discord") + *-ous*] — **frac·tious·ly** *adv* — **frac·tious·ness** *n*

[1]**frac·ture** \ˈfrak-chər\ *n* **1** : the act or process of breaking or the state of being broken; *esp* : the breaking of a bone — compare SIMPLE FRACTURE, COMPOUND FRACTURE **2** : the result of fracturing; *esp* : an injury resulting from the fracture of a bone [Latin *fractura,* from *frangere* "to break"]

synonyms FRACTURE, RUPTURE mean a break in tissue. FRACTURE applies to the cracking of a hard substance ⟨*fractured* bones⟩. RUPTURE applies to the tearing or bursting of soft tissues ⟨a *ruptured* blood vessel⟩.

[2]**fracture** *vb* **frac·tured; frac·tur·ing** \-chə-riŋ, -shriŋ\ **1** : to cause a fracture in : BREAK **2** : to damage or destroy as if by breaking ⟨*fractured* families⟩ **3** : to undergo fracture

frag·ile \ˈfraj-əl, -ˌīl\ *adj* **1** : easily broken or destroyed : DELICATE **2** : TENUOUS, SLIGHT ⟨*fragile* evidence⟩ [Middle French, from Latin *fragilis,* from *frangere* "to break"] ***synonyms*** see BRITTLE — **fra·gil·i·ty** \frə-ˈjil-ət-ē\ *n*

[1]**frag·ment** \ˈfrag-mənt\ *n* **1** : a part broken off, detached, or incomplete **2** : SENTENCE FRAGMENT [Latin *fragmentum,* from *frangere* "to break"]

[2]**frag·ment** \-ˌment\ *vb* **frag·ment·ed; frag·ment·ing** : to break or cause to break into pieces ⟨a coalition *fragmenting*⟩

frag·men·tal \frag-ˈment-l\ *adj* : FRAGMENTARY

frag·men·tary \ˈfrag-mən-ˌter-ē\ *adj* : consisting of fragments ⟨*fragmentary* evidence⟩

frag·men·tate \ˈfrag-mən-ˌtāt\ *vb* : FRAGMENT [back-formation from *fragmentation*] — **frag·men·ta·tion** \ˌfrag-mən-ˈtā-shən, -ˌmen-\ *n*

frag·men·tize \ˈfrag-mən-ˌtīz\ *vb* : FRAGMENT

fra·grance \ˈfrā-grəns\ *n* **1** : a sweet, pleasing, and often flowery or fruity odor — compare AROMA **2** : something (as a perfume) made to give off a sweet or pleasant odor

fra·grant \-grənt\ *adj* : having a sweet or pleasant smell [Latin *fragrans,* from *fragrare* "to be fragrant"] — **fra·grant·ly** *adv*

frail \ˈfrāl\ *adj* **1** : morally weak **2** : FRAGILE 1 **3** : physically weak ⟨a *frail* child⟩ ⟨a *frail* voice⟩ [Medieval French *fraile,* from Latin *fragilis* "fragile"] — **frail·ly** \ˈfrāl-lē\ *adv* — **frail·ness** *n*

frail·ty \ˈfrā-əl-tē, ˈfrāl-\ *n, pl* **frailties** **1** : the quality or state of being frail **2** : a fault due to weakness especially of moral character ***synonyms*** see FAULT

[1]**frame** \ˈfrām\ *vt* **1** : to construct by fitting and uniting the parts of the skeleton of (a structure) **2 a** : PLAN 1, CONTRIVE ⟨*frame* a new method⟩ **b** : SHAPE 1, CONSTRUCT ⟨*frame* a figure out of clay⟩ **c** : to give expression to : FORMULATE ⟨*frame* your reply⟩ **d** : to draw up (as a document) **3** : to make (an innocent person) appear guilty **4** : to fit or adjust for a purpose : ARRANGE **5** : to enclose in a frame ⟨*frame* a picture⟩ [Old English *framian* "to benefit, make progress"] — **fram·er** *n*

[2]**frame** *n* **1 a** : something composed of parts fitted together and united **b** : the physical makeup of an animal and especially a human body : PHYSIQUE **2** : an arrangement of structural parts that gives form or support to something ⟨the *frame* of a car⟩ ⟨the bony *frame* of the body⟩; *esp* : one (as of girders, beams, and joists) that forms the main support of a structure (as a building) **3 a** : a machine built on or in a frame ⟨a spinning *frame*⟩ **b** : a supporting or enclosing border or open case (as for a window or a picture) **c** : a part of a pair of glasses that holds the lenses **4 a** : an enclosing border **b** : matter or an area enclosed by a border: as (1) : one of the squares in which scores for each round are recorded (as in bowling); *also* : a turn in bowling (2) : one of the drawings in a comic strip (3) : one picture of the series on a length of film (4) : a complete image being transmitted by television **5** : a particular state of mind

[3]**frame** *adj* : having a wood frame ⟨*frame* houses⟩

frame of reference : a set or system (as of facts or ideas) serving to orient or give particular meaning

frame–up \ˈfrā-ˌməp\ *n* : a scheme to cause an innocent person to be accused of a crime; *also* : the result of such a scheme

frame·work \ˈfrām-ˌwərk\ *n* **1** : a structural or skeletal frame **2** : a basic structure (as of ideas)

fram·ing \ˈfrā-miŋ\ *n* : FRAME 2, FRAMEWORK

franc \ˈfraŋk\ *n* **1 a** : any of various former basic monetary units (as in France, Belgium, or Luxembourg) **b** : the basic monetary unit of any of several countries (as Switzerland) **2** : a coin or note representing one franc [Medieval French]

fran·chise \ˈfran-ˌchīz\ *n* **1 a** : a special privilege or exemption granted (as by a government); *esp* : the right to exist and function as a corporation **b** : a right or license to market a company's goods or services in a particular territory; *also* : the territory covered by such a right or license **2** : a legal right or privilege; *esp* : the right to vote [Medieval French, "freedom from a restriction," from *franchir* "to free," from *franc* "free, frank"]

[1]**Fran·cis·can** \fran-ˈsis-kən\ *adj* : of or relating to Saint Francis of Assisi or one of the orders under his monastic rule [Medieval Latin *Franciscus* "Francis"]

[2]**Franciscan** *n* : a member of a religious order established by Saint Francis of Assisi and engaging chiefly in preaching and in missionary and charitable work

fran·ci·um \ˈfran-sē-əm\ *n* : a short-lived radioactive chemical element — see ELEMENT table [New Latin, from *France*]

Franco- *combining form* **1** : French and ⟨*Franco*-American⟩ **2** : French ⟨*Franco*phile⟩ [Medieval Latin *Francus* "Frenchman," from Late Latin, "Frank"]

fran·co·lin \ˈfraŋ-kə-lən\ *n* : any of various African or Asian partridges [French, from Italian *francolino*]

Fran·co·phile \ˈfraŋ-kə-ˌfīl\ *adj* : admiring or favoring France or French culture — **Francophile** *n*

fran·gi·ble \ˈfran-jə-bəl\ *adj* : easily broken : FRAGILE [Medieval Latin *frangibilis,* from Latin *frangere* "to break"]

fran·gi·pani *also* **fran·gi·pan·ni** \ˌfran-jə-ˈpan-ē\ *n, pl* **-pani** *also* **-pan·ni** : any of several ornamental shrubs or small trees of the American tropics with milky sap and large fragrant waxy white, yellow, red, or pink flowers; *also* : a perfume derived from or imitating the odor of the flower [Italian *frangipane,* from Marquis Muzio *Frangipane,* 16th century Italian nobleman]

[1]frank \ˈfrangk\ *adj* **1** : free and forthright in expressing one's feelings and opinions : OUTSPOKEN **2** : unmistakably evident : DOWNRIGHT ⟨*frank* treason⟩ [Medieval French *franc* "free, frank," from Medieval Latin *francus,* from Late Latin *Francus* "Frank"] — **frank·ly** *adv* — **frank·ness** *n*

Word History The word *frank* comes from the name of the Franks, a West Germanic people who lived long ago. In the early Middle Ages the Franks were in power in France. (It was from them that the country got its name, in Latin *Francia*.) The Franks eventually merged with the earlier Gaulish and Roman inhabitants, and their name (*Francus* in Latin) lost its ethnic sense and referred to any inhabitant of *Francia* who was free, that is, not a slave or bondman. As an adjective, *francus* came to mean simply "free." From the English adjective *frank,* which means "free" or "forthright," we get the verb *frank,* which means "to mark mail with an official sign so that it may be mailed free."

synonyms FRANK, CANDID, OPEN, PLAIN mean showing willingness to tell one's thoughts or feelings. FRANK implies absence of the evasiveness that springs from considerations of tact or of expedience ⟨a *frank* declaration of selfish motives⟩. CANDID stresses sincerity and honesty of expression especially in offering unwelcome criticism or opinion ⟨gave a *candid* appraisal of my faults⟩. OPEN implies frankness but suggests more indiscretion than FRANK and less earnestness than CANDID ⟨*open* betrayal of a friend⟩. PLAIN suggests outspokenness and freedom from affectation or subtlety in expression ⟨*plain* talk⟩.

[2]frank *vt* : to mark (a piece of mail) with an official signature, sign, stamp, or mark indicating the right of the sender to free mailing or that the sender has paid postage; *also* : to mail in this manner

[3]frank *n* **1** : a signature, mark, or stamp on a piece of mail indicating that it can be mailed free **2** : the privilege of sending mail free of charge

Frank \ˈfrangk\ *n* : a member of a West Germanic tribal confederacy that entered the Roman provinces in A.D. 253 and established themselves in the Netherlands, in Gaul, and along the Rhine [Medieval French *Franc,* from Late Latin *Francus,* of Germanic origin] — **Frank·ish** \ˈfrang-kish\ *adj*

Fran·ken·stein \ˈfrang-kən-ˌstīn, -ˌstēn\ *n* **1** : a monster in the shape of a man **2 a** : a monstrous creation **b** : a work or agency that ruins its originator [from *Frankenstein,* a student of physiology in Mary W. Shelley's novel *Frankenstein* whose life is ruined by a monster he creates]

frank·furt·er \ˈfrangk-fərt-ər, -fət-ər\ *or* **frank·furt** \-fərt\ *n* : a seasoned beef or beef and pork sausage that may be skinless or stuffed in casing [German *frankfurter* "of Frankfurt," from *Frankfurt am Main,* Germany]

frank·in·cense \ˈfrang-kən-ˌsens\ *n* : a fragrant gum resin from African or Arabian trees that is burned as incense [Middle English *frank* "frank, free, pure" + *incense*]

frank·lin \ˈfrang-klən\ *n* : a medieval English landowner of free but not noble birth [Medieval French *frauncleín,* from *franc* "free"]

Frank·lin stove \ˈfrang-klən-\ *n* : a metal heating stove resembling an open fireplace but designed to be set out in a room [Benjamin *Franklin,* its inventor]

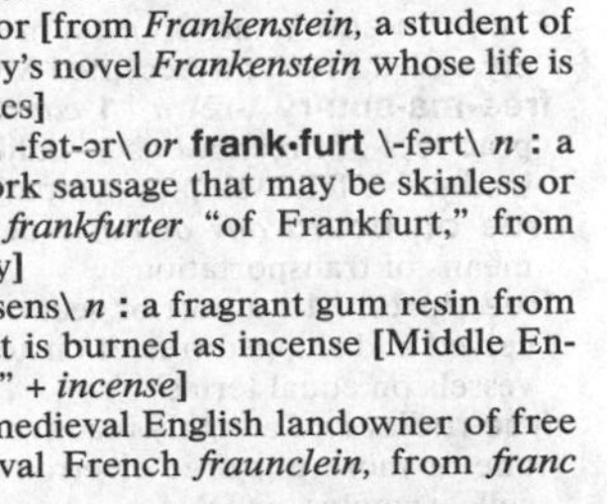

Franklin stove

fran·tic \ˈfrant-ik\ *adj* **1** : wildly or uncontrollably excited ⟨*frantic* with pain⟩ ⟨*frantic* cries for help⟩ **2** : marked by fast and nervous or disordered activity ⟨made a *frantic* search for the lost child⟩ [Middle English *frenetik, frantik* "insane," from Medieval French *frenetik,* from Latin *phreneticus,* from Greek *phrenitikos,* from *phrenitis* "inflammation of the brain," from *phrēn* "mind"] — **fran·ti·cal·ly** \-i-kə-lē, -klē\ *adv* — **fran·tic·ly** \-i-klē\ *adv* — **fran·tic·ness** *n*

frap·pé \fra-ˈpā\ *or* **frappe** \ˈfrap, fra-ˈpā\ *n* **1** : an iced or frozen mixture or drink **2** : a thick milk shake [French *frappé* "iced, chilled," from *frapper* "to strike, chill"] — **frappé** *adj*

fra·ter·nal \frə-ˈtərn-l\ *adj* **1 a** : of, relating to, or involving brothers **b** : of, relating to, or being a fraternity or society **2** : BROTHERLY 2, FRIENDLY [Medieval Latin *fraternalis,* from Latin *fraternus,* from *frater* "brother"] — **fra·ter·nal·ism** \-l-ˌiz-əm\ *n* — **fra·ter·nal·ly** \-l-ē\ *adv*

fraternal twin *n* : either member of a pair of twins that are produced from different fertilized egg cells, usually differ in some or many genes, and are often not physically similar

fra·ter·ni·ty \frə-ˈtər-nət-ē\ *n, pl* **-ties** **1** : a social, honorary, or professional organization; *esp* : a social club of male college students **2** : BROTHERHOOD 1, BROTHERLINESS **3** : persons of the same class, profession, character, or tastes ⟨the legal *fraternity*⟩

frat·er·nize \ˈfrat-ər-ˌnīz\ *vi* **1** : to associate or mingle as brothers or friends **2** : to associate on friendly terms with citizens or troops of a hostile nation — **frat·er·ni·za·tion** \ˌfrat-ər-nə-ˈzā-shən\ *n* — **frat·er·niz·er** \ˈfrat-ər-ˌnī-zər\ *n*

frat·ri·cide \ˈfra-trə-ˌsīd\ *n* **1** : one who murders his or her own brother or sister **2** : the act of a fratricide [derived from Latin *fratr-, frater* "brother"] — **frat·ri·cid·al** \ˌfra-trə-ˈsīd-l\ *adj*

Frau \ˈfrau̇\ *n, pl* **Frau·en** \ˈfrau̇-ən\ — used by German-speaking people as a courtesy title equivalent to *Mrs.* [German]

fraud \ˈfrȯd\ *n* **1 a** : DECEIT; *esp* : misrepresentation intended to induce another to part with something of value or to surrender a legal right **b** : an act of deceiving or misrepresenting : TRICK **2 a** : one who is not what he pretends to be : IMPOSTOR **b** : one who defrauds : CHEAT [Medieval French *fraude,* from Latin *fraus*] ***synonyms*** see DECEPTION

fraud·ster \ˈfrȯd-stər\ *n, chiefly British* : a person who engages in fraud : CHEAT

fraud·u·lent \ˈfrȯ-jə-lənt\ *adj* : characterized by, based on, or done by fraud : DECEITFUL ⟨*fraudulent* claims of injury⟩ — **fraud·u·lence** \-ləns\ *n* — **fraud·u·lent·ly** *adv* — **fraud·u·lent·ness** *n*

fraught \ˈfrȯt\ *adj* : full of or accompanied by something specified ⟨a situation *fraught* with danger⟩ [Middle English, "laden," from *fraughten* "to load," from *fraught* "freight, load," from Dutch or Low German *vracht, vrecht*]

Fräu·lein \ˈfrȯi-ˌlīn\ *n* — used by German-speaking people as a courtesy title equivalent to *Miss* [German]

[1]fray \ˈfrā\ *n* **1** : a noisy quarrel or fight : BRAWL **2** : a heated dispute [Middle English, short for *affray*]

[2]fray *vb* **1 a** : to wear (as an edge of cloth) by rubbing **b** : to separate the threads at the edge of ⟨cutoff jeans with *frayed* edges⟩ **c** : to wear out or into shreds **2 a** : STRAIN, IRRITATE ⟨tempers were *frayed*⟩ **b** : to show signs of strain ⟨nerves were beginning to *fray*⟩ [Medieval French *freier, froier* "to rub," from Latin *fricare*]

fraz·zle \ˈfraz-əl\ *vb* **fraz·zled; fraz·zling** \ˈfraz-ling, -ə-ling\ **1** : FRAY 1 **2** : to exhaust physically or emotionally ⟨*frazzled* by hard work⟩ [alteration of English dialect *fazle* "to tangle, fray"] — **frazzle** *n*

[1]freak \ˈfrēk\ *n* **1 a** : WHIM **b** : a seemingly capricious action or event **2** : one that is very unusual or abnormal; *esp* : a person or animal having a physical oddity and appearing in a circus sideshow **3** *slang* : a person who uses an illicit drug **4 a** : an ardent enthusiast ⟨movie *freaks*⟩ **b** : a person who is obsessed with something ⟨a control *freak*⟩ [origin unknown] — **freak·ish** \ˈfrē-kish\ *adj* — **freak·ish·ly** *adv* — **freak·ish·ness** *n*

[2]freak *adj* : having the character of a freak; *esp* : very unusual ⟨a *freak* accident⟩

[3]freak *vb* **1** : to experience nightmarish hallucinations as a result of taking drugs — often used with *out* **2 a** : to behave irrationally under the influence of drugs — often used with *out* **b** : to react with extreme or irrational distress or discomposure — often used with *out* ⟨saw the spider and *freaked* out⟩ **3** : to dis-

\ə\ **abut**	\au̇\ **out**	\i\ **tip**	\ȯ\ **saw**	\u̇\ **foot**
\ər\ **further**	\ch\ **chin**	\ī\ **life**	\ȯi\ **coin**	\y\ **yet**
\a\ **mat**	\e\ **pet**	\j\ **job**	\th\ **thin**	\yü\ **few**
\ā\ **take**	\ē\ **easy**	\ng\ **sing**	\t͟h\ **this**	\yu̇\ **cure**
\ä\ **cot, cart**	\g\ **go**	\ō\ **bone**	\ü\ **food**	\zh\ **vision**

turb the composure of — often used with *out* ⟨the bad news *freaked* them out⟩ — **freaked** \'frēkt\ *adj* — **freaked–out** \-'au̇t\ *adj*

freak–out \'frē-ˌau̇t\ *n* : an act or instance of freaking out

freaky \'frē-kē\ *adj* **freak·i·er; -est** **1** : CAPRICIOUS **2** : markedly strange or abnormal ⟨a *freaky* coincidence⟩ ⟨a *freaky* appearance⟩

1**freck·le** \'frek-əl\ *n* : a small brownish spot in the skin usually due to precipitation of pigment on exposure to sunlight [Middle English *freken, frekel,* of Scandinavian origin] — **freck·ly** \'frek-lē, -ə-lē\ *adj*

2**freckle** *vb* **freck·led; freck·ling** \'frek-ling, -ə-ling\ : to mark or become marked with freckles or small spots

1**free** \'frē\ *adj* **fre·er** \'frē-ər\; **fre·est** \'frē-əst\ **1 a** : having liberty : not being a slave or prisoner **b** : not controlled by others : INDEPENDENT ⟨a *free* state⟩ **2** : made or done voluntarily or spontaneously ⟨a *free* choice⟩ **3** : relieved from or lacking something and especially something unpleasant or burdensome ⟨*free* from worry⟩ ⟨a speech *free* of hyperbole⟩ **4** : not subject to government regulation ⟨*free* trade⟩ **5** : having no obligations ⟨I'll be *free* this evening⟩ **6 a** : not obstructed : CLEAR ⟨a road *free* of ice⟩ ⟨a *free* kick⟩ **b** : not being used or occupied ⟨*free* time⟩ ⟨a *free* seat⟩ **c** : not fastened or bound : able to act, move, or turn **d** : not restricted or impeded ⟨*free* to leave⟩ **7** : LAVISH ⟨a *free* spender⟩ **8** : not held back by fear or distrust : OPEN, FRANK ⟨*free* expression of opinion⟩ **9** : given without charge ⟨*free* tickets⟩ **10** : chemically uncombined ⟨*free* oxygen⟩ **11** : capable of being used meaningfully apart from another linguistic form ⟨the word "hats" is a *free* form⟩ **12** : not literal or exact ⟨a *free* translation⟩ **13** : not restricted by conventional forms ⟨*free* verse⟩ [Old English *frēo*] — **free·ly** *adv*

synonyms FREE, INDEPENDENT, SOVEREIGN mean not subject to the rule or control of another. FREE stresses the complete absence of external rule and the full right to make decisions ⟨a *free* society of equals⟩. INDEPENDENT implies standing alone; applied to a state it implies that no other state has power to interfere with its citizens, laws, or policies ⟨the colony's struggle to become *independent*⟩. SOVEREIGN stresses supremacy within one's own domain or sphere and implies the absence of any superior power ⟨separate and *sovereign* armed services⟩.

2**free** *vt* **freed; free·ing** **1** : to cause to be free : set free ⟨*free* a prisoner⟩ **2** : to relieve or rid of what restrains, confines, restricts, or embarrasses ⟨*free* a person from debt⟩ — often used with *up* ⟨*free* up space on the hard drive⟩ **3** : to clear of obstacles ⟨*free* a road of debris⟩

synonyms FREE, RELEASE, LIBERATE, DISCHARGE mean to set loose from restraint or constraint. FREE implies usually permanent removal from whatever binds, entangles, or oppresses ⟨*freed* the animals from their cages⟩. RELEASE suggests a setting loose from confinement or from a state of pressure or tension ⟨*release* anger⟩. LIBERATE stresses the state resulting from freeing or releasing ⟨*liberate* their country from the tyrant⟩. DISCHARGE may imply removing from a lighter degree of restraint or constraint ⟨*discharge* the prisoner⟩.

3**free** *adv* **1** : in a free manner **2** : without charge ⟨was admitted *free*⟩

free association *n* **1** : expression of thoughts as they come to mind without control or censorship **2** : the reporting of the first thought that comes to mind in response to a given stimulus and especially a word

1**free·base** \'frē-ˌbās\ *vb* : to prepare or use cocaine as freebase

2**freebase** *n* : purified solid cocaine that can be heated to produce vapors for inhalation or smoked as crack

free·bie *or* **free·bee** \'frē-bē\ *n* : something given without charge [alteration of obsolete *freeby* "gratis," from *free*]

free·board \'fre-ˌbōrd, -ˌbȯrd\ *n* : the vertical distance between the waterline and the deck of a ship or the upper edge of the side of a boat

free·boo·ter \'frē-ˌbüt-ər\ *n* : PIRATE, PLUNDERER [Dutch *vrijbuiter,* from *vrijbuit* "plundering," from *vrij* "free" + *buit* "booty" — see *Word History* at FILIBUSTER]

free·born \'frē-'bȯrn\ *adj* **1** : not born in vassalage or slavery **2** : relating to or befitting one that is freeborn

freed·man \'frēd-mən\ *n* : a person freed from slavery

free·dom \'frēd-əm\ *n* **1** : the quality or state of being free: as **a** : the absence of necessity, coercion, or constraint in choice or action **b** : liberation from slavery or restraint or from the power of another : INDEPENDENCE **c** : EXEMPTION, RELEASE ⟨*freedom* from care⟩ **d** : EASE, FACILITY ⟨*freedom* of movement⟩ **e** : the quality of being outspoken ⟨answered with *freedom*⟩ **f** : unrestricted use ⟨the dog had the *freedom* of the yard⟩ **2** : PRIVILEGE, RIGHT; *esp* : one guaranteed by fundamental law

synonyms FREEDOM, LIBERTY, LICENSE mean the power or condition of acting without compulsion. FREEDOM has a broad range of application from total absence of restraint to merely a sense of not being unduly hampered or frustrated ⟨*freedom* of the press⟩. LIBERTY suggests release from former restraint or compulsion ⟨the released prisoner had difficulty adjusting to his new *liberty*⟩. LICENSE implies freedom specially granted or conceded and may connote an abuse of freedom ⟨freedom without responsibility may degenerate into *license*⟩.

freedom fighter *n* : a person who takes part in a resistance movement against an oppressive political or social establishment

freed·wom·an \'frēd-ˌwu̇m-ən\ *n* : a woman freed from slavery

free enterprise *n* : freedom of private business to organize and operate for profit in competition with other businesses with a minimum of interference by the government; *also* : an economic system providing this freedom

free–fire zone \'frē-ˌfīr-\ *n* : a combat area in which any moving thing is a legitimate target

free–for–all \'frē-fə-ˌrȯl\ *n* : a competition, dispute, or fight open to all comers and usually with no rules

free·hand \'frē-ˌhand\ *adj* : done without mechanical aids or devices ⟨*freehand* drawing⟩ — **freehand** *adv*

free hand \-'hand\ *n* : freedom of action or decision ⟨given a *free hand* to get the job done⟩

free·hand·ed \-'han-dəd\ *adj* : OPENHANDED, GENEROUS

free·hold \'frē-ˌhōld\ *n* : ownership of real estate for life usually with the right of leaving it to one's heirs; *also* : an estate so owned — **free·hold·er** \-ˌhōl-dər\ *n*

freelance \'frē-ˌlans\ *n* **1** *usually* **free lance** : a knight whose services could be bought by any ruler or state **2** : one who pursues a profession (as writing, art, or acting) without being committed to work for one employer for a long period — **freelance** *adj* — **freelance** *vb* — **freelancer** *n*

free–liv·ing \'frē-'liv-ing\ *adj* : being neither parasitic nor symbiotic

free·load \-'lōd\ *vi* : SPONGE 3 — **free·load·er** *n*

free·man \'frē-mən\ *n* **1** : a person enjoying civil or political liberty **2** : one having the full rights of a citizen

free market *n* : an economic market operating by free competition

free·mar·tin \-ˌmärt-n\ *n* : a sexually imperfect usually sterile female calf born in the same birth with a male [origin unknown]

Free·ma·son \-'mās-n\ *n* : a member of a secret fraternal society called Free and Accepted Masons

free·ma·son·ry \-rē\ *n* **1** *cap* : the principles, institutions, or practices of Freemasons — called also *Masonry* **2** : natural or instinctive fellowship or sympathy

free on board *adv or adj* : delivered without charge onto a means of transportation

free port *n* **1** : a port or section of a port where goods are received and shipped free of customs duty **2** : a port open to all vessels on equal terms

free radical *n* : a highly reactive atom or group of atoms having one or more unpaired electrons; *esp* : one that is damaging to cells, proteins, or DNA

free–range \'frē-ˌrānj\ *adj* : allowed to roam and forage freely ⟨*free-range* chickens⟩; *also* : of, relating to, or produced by free-range animals ⟨*free-range* eggs⟩

free·sia \'frē-zhə, -zhē-ə\ *n* : any of a genus of sweet-scented African herbs with showy usually red, white, or yellow flowers [F.H.T. *Freese,* died 1876, German physician]

free silver *n* : the free coinage of silver often at a fixed ratio with gold

free–soil *adj* **1** : characterized by free soil **2** *cap F&S* : of, relating to, or constituting a minor United States political party prior to the American Civil War opposing the extension of slavery into United States territories and the admission of slave states into the Union — **Free–Soil·er** \-ˌsȯi-lər\ *n*

free soil *n* : United States territory where slavery was prohibited before the American Civil War

free speech *n* : speech that is protected by the First Amendment to the U.S. Constitution; *also* : the right to such speech

free spirit *n* : NONCONFORMIST 2
free–spo·ken \ˈfrē-ˈspō-kən\ *adj* : OUTSPOKEN
free·stand·ing \-ˈstan-diŋ\ *adj* : standing alone or on its own foundation free of attachment or support
free·stone \ˈfrē-ˌstōn\ *n* **1** : a stone that may be cut without splitting **2 a** : a fruit stone to which the flesh does not cling **b** : a fruit (as a peach or cherry) having a freestone
free·style \-ˌstīl\ *n* : competition in which each competitor is free to use a style, method, or performance of his or her choice
free·think·er \-ˈthiŋ-kər\ *n* : one who forms opinions independently and on the basis of reason; *esp* : one who doubts or denies religious dogma — **free·think·ing** \-kiŋ\ *n or adj*
free throw *n* : an unhindered shot in basketball made from behind a fixed line and awarded because of a foul by an opponent
free trade *n* : trade based on the unrestricted international exchange of goods without high tariffs
free·ware \ˈfree-ˌwaər, -ˌweər\ *n* : software available at no cost
free·way \ˈfrē-ˌwā\ *n* **1** : an expressway with fully controlled access **2** : a toll-free highway
free·wheel \ˈfrē-ˈhwēl, -ˈwēl\ *vi* : to move or live freely or irresponsibly — **free·wheel·er** *n*
free·wheel·ing \ˌfrē-ˈhwē-liŋ, -ˈwē-\ *adj* : free and loose in form or manner; *esp* : not bound by formal rules, procedures, or guidelines ⟨led a *freewheeling* life in the big city⟩
free·will \ˌfrē-ˌwil\ *adj* : VOLUNTARY ⟨a *freewill* offering⟩
free will *n* : the power of directing one's own actions without restraint by necessity or fate
free world *n* : the part of the world where political democracy and capitalism or moderate socialism rather than totalitarian or Communist political and economic systems prevail
free·writ·ing \ˈfrē-ˈrīt-iŋ\ *n* : automatic writing done especially as a classroom exercise — **free·write** \-ˌrīt\ *vi*
¹freeze \ˈfrēz\ *vb* **froze** \ˈfrōz\; **fro·zen** \ˈfrōz-n\; **freez·ing** **1** : to harden into or be hardened into ice or a like solid by loss of heat ⟨the river *froze* over⟩ ⟨*freeze* the stew for dinner next week⟩ **2** : to chill or become chilled with cold ⟨almost *froze* to death⟩ **3 a** : to act on usually destructively by frost ⟨*froze* the tomato plants⟩ **b** : to anesthetize by cold **4 a** : to adhere solidly by freezing **b** : to cause to grip tightly or remain in immovable contact ⟨fear *froze* the driver to the wheel⟩ **5** : to clog or become clogged with ice ⟨the water pipes *froze*⟩ **6** : to become fixed or motionless; *esp* : to make or become incapable of acting or speaking ⟨fear *froze* them in their tracks⟩ **7** : to fix at a certain stage or level ⟨*freeze* prices⟩ [Old English *frēosan*]
²freeze *n* **1** : a state of weather marked by low temperature **2 a** : an act or instance of freezing **b** : the state of being frozen
freeze–dry \ˈfrēz-ˌdrī\ *vt* : to dry in a frozen state under high vacuum especially for preservation ⟨*freeze-dried* foods⟩
freez·er \ˈfrē-zər\ *n* : one that freezes or keeps cool; *esp* : an insulated compartment or room for keeping food at a temperature below freezing or for freezing perishable food rapidly
freezer burn *n* : a dried-out spot on food (as meat) that has been frozen as a result of improper packaging or wrapping
freezing point *n* : the temperature at which a liquid solidifies ⟨the *freezing point* of water is 0°C or 32°F⟩
F region *n* : the highest region of the atmosphere occurring from 140 to more than 400 kilometers above the earth
¹freight \ˈfrāt\ *n* **1** : the amount paid to a common carrier for carrying goods **2** : goods or cargo carried by a common carrier **3 a** : the ordinary carrying of goods from one place to another by a common carrier especially as distinguished from express **b** : a train that carries freight [Dutch or Low German *vracht, vrecht*]
²freight *vt* **1 a** : to load with goods for transportation **b** : to weigh down : BURDEN ⟨*freighted* with fear⟩ **2** : to transport or ship by freight
freight·er \ˈfrāt-ər\ *n* **1** : one that loads or charters and loads a ship **2** : SHIPPER **3** : a ship or airplane used chiefly to carry freight
¹French \ˈfrench\ *adj* : of, relating to, or characteristic of France, its people, or their language [Old English *frencisc,* from *Franca* "Frank"] — **French·man** \-mən\ *n* — **French·wom·an** \-ˌwu̇m-ən\ *n*
²French *n* **1** : a Romance language developed out of the Vulgar Latin of Transalpine Gaul and that became the literary and official language of France **2** *pl in constr* : the French people
French Canadian *n* : one of the descendants of French settlers in Lower Canada — **French–Canadian** *adj*
French cuff *n* : a shirt cuff that is made by turning back part of a wide cuff and is fastened with a cuff link
French door *n* : a door with glass rectangular panels extending the full length; *also* : one of a pair of such doors in a single frame
French dressing *n* **1** : a salad dressing made with oil and vinegar or lemon juice and spices **2** : a creamy salad dressing flavored with tomatoes
¹french fry *n, often cap 1st F* : a strip of potato fried in deep fat — usually used in plural
²french fry *vt, often cap 1st F* : to fry (as strips of potato) in deep fat until brown
French horn *n* : a brass wind instrument consisting of a long curved conical tube with a narrow funnel-shaped mouthpiece at one end and a flaring bell at the other

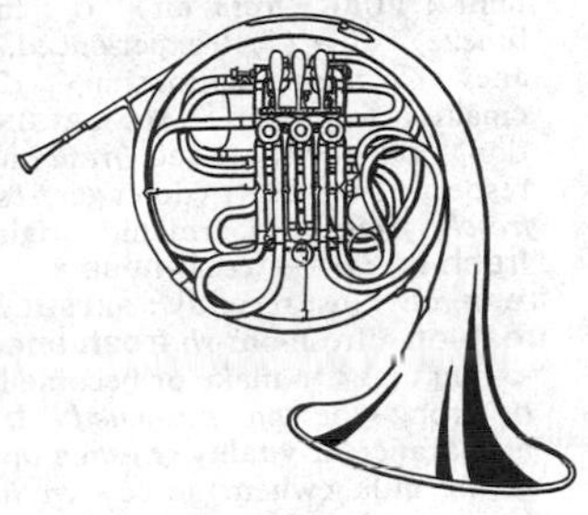
French horn

French kiss *n* : an open-mouth kiss usually involving tongue-to-tongue contact — **French–kiss** *vb*
French leave *n* : an informal, hasty, or secret departure [from an 18th century French custom of leaving a reception without taking leave of the host or hostess]
French toast *n* : bread dipped in a mixture of egg and milk and then fried
French twist *n* : a woman's hairstyle in which the hair is coiled in the back and secured in place
French window *n* : a pair of windows that reaches to the floor, opens in the middle, and is placed in an outside wall
fre·net·ic \fri-ˈnet-ik\ *adj* : HECTIC 4, FRANTIC 1 [Medieval French *frenetique* "insane," from Latin *phreneticus* "insane, frantic"] — **fre·net·i·cal·ly** \-ˈnet-i-kə-lē, -klē\ *adv*
fren·u·lum \ˈfren-yə-ləm\ *n* : FRENUM
fre·num \ˈfrē-nəm\ *n, pl* **frenums** *or* **fre·na** \-nə\ : a fold of membrane (as beneath the tongue) that supports or restrains [Latin, literally, "bridle"]
fren·zied \ˈfren-zēd\ *adj* : feeling or showing great excitement or emotional disturbance ⟨had a *frenzied* look in his eye⟩ — **fren·zied·ly** *adv*
fren·zy \ˈfren-zē\ *n, pl* **frenzies** **1** : a temporary madness or violent agitation **2** : intense and usually wild activity [Medieval French *frenesie,* derived from Latin *phrenesis,* from *phreneticus* "insane, frantic"] — **frenzy** *vt*
Fre·on \ˈfrē-ˌän\ *trademark* — used for any of various nonflammable gaseous and liquid fluorocarbons used as refrigerants
fre·quen·cy \ˈfrē-kwən-sē\ *n, pl* **-cies** **1** : the fact or condition of occurring frequently **2** : the number, proportion, or percentage of one kind of item in a set of data ⟨the *frequency* of twin births at the hospital⟩ **3** : the number of repetitions of a periodic process in a unit of time: as **a** : the number of times per second that an electric current flowing in one direction changes direction then changes back ⟨a current having a *frequency* of 60 hertz⟩ **b** : the number of waves (as of sound or electromagnetic energy) that pass a fixed point each second ⟨a sound having a *frequency* of 1500 hertz⟩ ⟨the *frequency* of a radio wave⟩ ⟨the *frequency* of yellow light⟩
frequency distribution *n* : a diagram that shows the frequency of different values of a variable in statistics
frequency modulation *n* : modulation of the frequency of a carrier wave in accordance with speech or a signal; *esp* : a system of broadcasting using this method of modulation
¹fre·quent \ˈfrē-kwənt\ *adj* **1** : happening often or at short intervals ⟨made *frequent* trips to town⟩ **2** : HABITUAL, CONSTANT ⟨a *frequent* visitor⟩ [Latin *frequens* "crowded, frequent"] — **fre·quent·ly** *adv* — **fre·quent·ness** *n*
²fre·quent \frē-ˈkwent, ˈfrē-kwənt\ *vt* : to visit often : associate

\ə\ **abut**	\au̇\ **out**	\i\ **tip**	\ȯ\ **saw**	\u̇\ **foot**
\ər\ **further**	\ch\ **chin**	\ī\ **life**	\ȯi\ **coin**	\y\ **yet**
\a\ **mat**	\e\ **pet**	\j\ **job**	\th\ **thin**	\yü\ **few**
\ā\ **take**	\ē\ **easy**	\ŋ\ **sing**	\t͟h\ **this**	\yu̇\ **cure**
\ä\ **cot, cart**	\g\ **go**	\ō\ **bone**	\ü\ **food**	\zh\ **vision**

with, be in, or resort to habitually ⟨*frequented* the library⟩ — **fre·quent·er** *n*

fres·co \'fres-ˌkō\ *n, pl* **frescoes** **1 :** the art of painting on freshly spread moist lime plaster with pigments suspended in water **2 :** a painting done in fresco [Italian, from *fresco* "fresh," of Germanic origin] — **fresco** *vt*

1fresh \'fresh\ *adj* **1 a :** not stored, cured, or preserved ⟨*fresh* vegetables⟩ **b :** having its original qualities unimpaired: as (1) **:** full of or renewed in vigor **:** REFRESHED ⟨felt *fresh* after the nap⟩ (2) **:** not stale, sour, or decayed ⟨*fresh* bread⟩ (3) **:** not faded ⟨the lesson is *fresh* in my mind⟩ (4) **:** not worn or wrinkled ⟨a *fresh* shirt⟩ **2 a :** not salt ⟨*fresh* water⟩ **b :** free from taint **:** PURE ⟨*fresh* air⟩ **c :** fairly strong **:** BRISK ⟨a *fresh* breeze⟩ **3 a** (1) **:** experienced, made, or received newly or anew ⟨a *fresh* relationship⟩ (2) **:** ADDITIONAL, ANOTHER ⟨make a *fresh* start⟩ **b :** ORIGINAL, NEW ⟨a *fresh* interpretation⟩ **c :** newly arrived ⟨*fresh* out of college⟩ **4 :** showing disrespect **:** IMPUDENT ⟨don't get *fresh* with me⟩ [Medieval French *fresch, freis,* of Germanic origin] ***synonyms*** see NEW — **fresh·ly** *adv* — **fresh·ness** *n*

2fresh *adv* **:** just recently **:** FRESHLY ⟨a *fresh* laid egg⟩

fresh·en \'fresh-ən\ *vb* **fresh·ened; fresh·en·ing** \'fresh-ning, -ə-ning\ **1 :** to make or become fresh: as **a :** to become brisk or strong ⟨the wind *freshened*⟩ **b :** to make or become fresh in appearance or vitality ⟨*freshen* up with a shower⟩ **2 :** to begin giving milk ⟨when the cow *freshens*⟩ — **fresh·en·er** \'fresh-nər, -ə-nər\ *n*

fresh·et \'fresh-ət\ *n* **:** a great rise or overflowing of a stream caused by heavy rains or melted snow [from *fresh* "increased flow, freshet, stream of fresh water," from 1*fresh*]

fresh·man \'fresh-mən\ *n* **1 :** a newcomer to an occupation or activity **:** NOVICE **2 :** a student in the first year (as of high school or college)

fresh·wa·ter \'fresh-'wȯt-ər, -'wät-\ *adj* **1 :** of, relating to, or living in fresh water ⟨a *freshwater* fish⟩ **2 :** accustomed to navigating only in inland waters ⟨a *freshwater* sailor⟩

1fret \'fret\ *vb* **fret·ted; fret·ting** **1 :** to suffer or cause to suffer emotional strain **:** WORRY, VEX ⟨*fretted* over petty problems⟩ **2 a :** to eat into or wear away ⟨rock *fretted* by rainwater⟩ **b :** FRAY 1a **c :** to cause by wearing away ⟨the stream *fretted* a channel⟩ **3 :** to affect something as if by gnawing or biting **:** GRATE ⟨the siren *fretted* at their nerves⟩ **4 :** to cause (water) to ripple [Old English *fretan* "to devour"]

2fret *n* **:** an irritated or worried state ⟨be in a *fret*⟩

3fret *vt* **fret·ted; fret·ting** **:** to decorate with interlaced designs [Middle English, back-formation from *fret, fretted* "adorned, interwoven," from Medieval French *fretté,* from fretter "to tie"]

4fret *n* **:** ornamental work consisting of small straight intersecting bars

5fret *n* **:** one of a series of ridges fixed across the fingerboard of a stringed musical instrument [probably from Medieval French *frete* "ferrule"] — **fret·less** *adj* — **fret·ted** \'fret-əd\ *adj*

6fret *vt* **fret·ted; fret·ting** **:** to press (the strings of a stringed instrument) against the frets

fret·ful \'fret-fəl\ *adj* **1 :** inclined to worry ⟨a *fretful* child⟩ **2 :** not relaxing or restful ⟨a *fretful* sleep⟩ — **fret·ful·ly** \-fə-lē\ *adv* — **fret·ful·ness** *n*

fret·saw \'fret-ˌsȯ\ *n* **:** a narrow-bladed fine-toothed saw for cutting curved outlines

fret·work \-ˌwərk\ *n* **1 :** decoration consisting of work adorned with frets **2 :** ornamental openwork or work in relief

Freud·ian \'frȯid-ē-ən\ *adj* **:** of, relating to, or according with the psychoanalytic theories or practices of Sigmund Freud — **Freudian** *n* — **Freud·ian·ism** \-ē-ə-ˌniz-əm\ *n*

fri·a·ble \'frī-ə-bəl\ *adj* **:** easily crumbled or pulverized [Latin *friabilis,* from *friare* "to crumble"] ***synonyms*** see BRITTLE — **fri·a·bil·i·ty** \ˌfrī-ə-'bil-ət-ē\ *n* — **fri·a·ble·ness** \'frī-ə-bəl-nəs\ *n*

fri·ar \'frī-ər, 'frīr\ *n* **:** a member of one of several Roman Catholic religious orders for men in which monastic life is combined with preaching and other priestly duties — compare MONK [Medieval French *frere,* literally, "brother," from Latin *frater*]

fri·ary \'frī-ə-rē, 'frī-rē\ *n, pl* **-ar·ies** **:** a monastery of friars

1fric·as·see *also* **fric·as·sée** \'frik-ə-ˌsē, ˌfrik-ə-'\ *n* **:** a dish of meat (as chicken) or vegetables cut into pieces and stewed in a white sauce [Middle French]

2fricassee *vt* **-seed; -see·ing** **:** to cook as a fricassee

fric·a·tive \'frik-ət-iv\ *n* **:** a consonant characterized by frictional passage of the expired breath through a narrowing at some point in the mouth or throat ⟨\f v th th s z sh zh h\ are *fricatives*⟩ [Latin *fricare* "to rub"] — **fricative** *adj*

fric·tion \'frik-shən\ *n* **1 a :** the rubbing of one body against another **b :** the force that resists motion between two bodies in contact ⟨the *friction* of a box sliding along the floor⟩ **2 :** discord between two persons or parties **3 :** sound produced by the movement of air through a narrow constriction in the mouth or glottis [Latin *frictio,* from *fricare* "to rub"] — **fric·tion·less** \-ləs\ *adj* — **fric·tion·less·ly** *adv*

fric·tion·al \'frik-shnəl, -shən-l\ *adj* **1 :** of or relating to friction **2 :** moved or produced by friction — **fric·tion·al·ly** \-ē\ *adv*

friction tape *n* **:** a usually cloth tape impregnated with insulating material and an adhesive and used especially to protect and insulate electrical conductors

Fri·day \'frīd-ā, -ē\ *n* **:** the 6th day of the week [Old English *frīgedæg,* derived from a translation of Latin *Veneris dies* "day of Venus"; from the fact that Frig, or Fria, was the Germanic goddess of love]

fried rice *n* **:** a dish of rice that is cooked and then stir-fried with soy sauce and meat, vegetables, or beaten eggs

1friend \'frend\ *n* **1 a :** one attached to another by affection or esteem **b :** ACQUAINTANCE 2 **2 :** one who is not hostile ⟨are you *friend* or foe⟩ **3 :** one who supports or favors something ⟨a *friend* of liberal education⟩ **4** *cap* **:** a member of a Christian group that stresses Inner Light, rejects sacraments and an ordained ministry, and opposes war — called also *Quaker* [Old English *frēond*] — **friend·less** \'fren-dləs\ *adj* — **friend·less·ness** *n*

2friend *vb* **friend·ed; friend·ing** **1 :** to act as the friend of **:** BEFRIEND **2 :** to include (a name) in a list of designated friends on a person's social networking site

friend·ly \'fren-dlē, -lē\ *adj* **friend·li·er; -est** **1 :** of, relating to, or befitting a friend: as **a :** showing kindly interest and goodwill ⟨a *friendly* gesture⟩ **b :** not hostile ⟨*friendly* natives⟩ **c :** COMFORTING, CHEERFUL ⟨the *friendly* glow of the fire⟩ **2 :** serving a beneficial or helpful purpose **:** FAVORABLE ⟨a *friendly* breeze⟩ **3 :** easy to use or understand ⟨*friendly* computer software⟩ — often used in combination ⟨a reader-*friendly* layout⟩ **4 :** COMPATIBLE 1, ACCOMMODATING — often used in combination ⟨a kid-*friendly* restaurant⟩ — **friend·li·ness** *n*

friend·ship \'frend-ˌship, 'fren-\ *n* **1 :** the state of being friends **2 :** a friendly feeling **:** FRIENDLINESS

frier *variant of* FRYER

1frieze \'frēz, frē-'zā\ *n* **:** a woolen cloth with a rough surface [Medieval French *frise,* from Dutch *vriese*]

2frieze \'frēz\ *n* **1 :** the part of an entablature between the architrave and the cornice **2 :** a sculptured or richly ornamented band (as around a building) [Middle French *frise,* perhaps derived from Latin *Phrygius* "Phrygian"]

frig·ate \'frig-ət\ *n* **1 :** a square-rigged warship intermediate between a corvette and a ship of the line **2 :** a modern warship that is smaller than a destroyer and that is used for escort, antisubmarine, and patrol duties [Middle French, from Italian *fregata*]

frigate bird *n* **:** any of several chiefly tropical seabirds noted for their power of flight and the habit of robbing other birds of fish — called also *man-o'-war bird*

frigate bird

1fright \'frīt\ *n* **1 :** fear or alarm caused by sudden danger ⟨cry out in *fright*⟩ **2 :** something that is strange, ugly, or shocking ⟨you look a *fright*⟩ [Old English *fyrhto, fryhto*] ***synonyms*** see FEAR

2fright *vt* **:** to alarm suddenly **:** FRIGHTEN

fright·en \'frīt-n\ *vb* **fright·ened; fright·en·ing** \'frīt-ning, -n-ing\ **1 :** to make afraid **:** TERRIFY **2 :** to drive away or out by frightening **3 :** to become frightened — **fright·en·ing·ly** \-ning-lē, -n-ing-\ *adv*

fright·ful \'frīt-fəl\ *adj* **1 :** causing fear or alarm **:** TERRIFYING **2 :** causing shock or horror **:** STARTLING ⟨a *frightful* novel⟩ **3 :** EXTREME ⟨a *frightful* thirst⟩ — **fright·ful·ly** \-fə-lē\ *adv* — **fright·ful·ness** *n*

frig·id \'frij-əd\ *adj* **1 :** intensely cold **2 :** lacking warmth or ardor **:** INDIFFERENT ⟨a *frigid* stare⟩ [Latin *frigidus,* from *frig-*

ēre "to be cold"] — **fri·gid·i·ty** \frij-ˈid-ət-ē\ *n* — **frig·id·ly** \ˈfrij-əd-lē\ *adv* — **frig·id·ness** *n*

frigid zone *n* : the area or region between the arctic circle and the north pole or between the antarctic circle and the south pole

fri·jo·le \frē-ˈhō-lē\ *also* **fri·jol** \frē-ˈhōl\ *n, pl* **fri·jo·les** \-ˈhō-lēz\ : BEAN 1b [Spanish *frijol*]

1**frill** \ˈfril\ *vt* : to provide or decorate with a frill

2**frill** *n* **1** : a gathered, pleated, or ruffled edging (as of lace) **2** : a ruff of hair or feathers or a bony or cartilaginous projection about the neck of an animal **3** : something decorative but not essential [perhaps from Dutch dialect *frul*] — **frilly** \ˈfril-ē\ *adj*

1**fringe** \ˈfrinj\ *n* **1** : an ornamental border consisting of short straight or twisted threads or strips hanging from cut or raveled edges or from a separate band **2** : something resembling a fringe : BORDER — often used in plural ⟨lived on the *fringes* of the city⟩ **3 a** : something that is secondary or additional to some activity, process, or subject ⟨a *fringe* sport⟩ **b** : a group with marginal or extremist views [Medieval French *frenge,* from Latin *fimbriae* (pl.) "fibers, fringe"]

2**fringe** *vt* **1** : to furnish or adorn with a fringe **2** : to serve as a fringe for : BORDER

fringe area *n* : a region in which reception from a broadcasting station is weak or subject to serious distortion

fringe benefit *n* : an employment benefit (as health insurance) paid for by an employer without affecting basic wage rates

frip·pery \ˈfrip-rē, -ə-rē\ *n, pl* **-per·ies** **1** : cheap showy finery **2** : affected elegance : pretentious display [Middle French *friperie* "cast-off clothes," derived from Medieval French *frepe* "old garment"] — **frippery** *adj*

Fris·bee \ˈfriz-bē\ *trademark* — used for a plastic disk for tossing between players

fri·sée \frē-ˈzā\ *n* : curly leaves of endive (sense 1) that have finely dissected edges and are used in salads [French, short for *chicorée frisée* curly chicory]

Fri·sian \ˈfrizh-ən, ˈfrē-zhən\ *n* **1** : a member of a people that inhabit principally the Netherlands province of Friesland and the Frisian Islands in the North Sea **2** : the Germanic language of the Frisian people [Latin *Frisii* "Frisians"] — **Frisian** *adj*

frisk \ˈfrisk\ *vb* **1** : to leap, skip, or dance in a lively or playful way : GAMBOL **2** : to search (a person) rapidly especially for concealed weapons by running the hand over the clothing [obsolete *frisk* "lively"] — **frisk·er** *n*

frisky \ˈfris-kē\ *adj* **frisk·i·er; -est** : inclined to frisk : PLAYFUL ⟨*frisky* puppies⟩; *also* : LIVELY ⟨a *frisky* performance⟩ — **frisk·i·ly** \-kə-lē\ *adv* — **frisk·i·ness** \-kē-nəs\ *n*

frit·il·lar·ia \ˌfrit-l-ˈer-ē-ə, -ˈar-\ *n* : any of a genus of bulbous herbs related to the lilies and having mottled or checkered flowers [derived from Latin *fritillus* "dice cup"; from its spotted markings]

frit·il·lary \ˈfrit-l-ˌer-ē\ *n, pl* **-lar·ies** **1** : FRITILLARIA **2** : any of numerous butterflies that are usually orange with black spots

1**frit·ter** \ˈfrit-ər\ *n* : a small quantity of fried or sautéed batter often containing fruit, vegetables, or meat [Medieval French *friture,* derived from Latin *frigere* "to fry"]

2**fritter** *vb* **1** : to reduce or waste little by little ⟨*frittering* away their time⟩ **2** : to break into small fragments **3** : to dwindle away [*fritter,* n., "fragment"] — **frit·ter·er** \-ər-ər\ *n*

fri·vol·i·ty \friv-ˈäl-ət-ē\ *n, pl* **-ties** **1** : the quality or state of being frivolous **2** : a frivolous act or thing

friv·o·lous \ˈfriv-ləs, -ə-ləs\ *adj* **1** : of little importance : TRIVIAL **2** : not serious or practical ⟨a *frivolous* attitude⟩ [Latin *frivolus*] — **friv·o·lous·ly** *adv* — **friv·o·lous·ness** *n*

1**frizz** \ˈfriz\ *vb* : to curl in small tight curls [French *friser*]

2**frizz** *n* : a small tight curl or hair that is tightly curled — **frizzy** \ˈfriz-ē\ *adj*

1**friz·zle** \ˈfriz-əl\ *vb* **friz·zled; friz·zling** \ˈfriz-ling, -ə-ling\ : FRIZZ, CURL [probably related to Old English *frīs* "curly"] — **frizzle** *n* — **friz·zly** \ˈfriz-lē, -ə-lē\ *adj*

2**frizzle** *vb* **1** : to fry until crisp and curled **2** : to cook with a sizzling noise [*fry* + *sizzle*]

fro \ˈfrō\ *adv* : BACK 2a, AWAY — used in the phrase *to and fro* [Middle English *fra, fro* "from," from Old Norse *frā*]

frock \ˈfräk\ *n* **1** : a friar's habit **2** : an outer garment worn by men **3** : a woman's or child's dress [Medieval French *froc,* of Germanic origin]

frock coat *n* : a man's usually double-breasted knee-length coat

frog \ˈfrȯg, ˈfräg\ *n* **1 a** : any of various largely aquatic tailless leaping amphibians that have slender bodies with smooth moist skin and strong long hind legs with webbed feet — compare TOAD **b** : a condition in the throat that produces hoarseness ⟨a *frog* in one's throat⟩ **2** : the triangular elastic horny pad on the sole of the hoof of a horse **3** : an ornamental braiding for fastening the front of a garment by a loop through which a button passes **4** : a device permitting the wheels on one rail of a track to cross an intersecting rail **5** : a small holder with perforations or spikes for holding flowers in place in a bowl or vase [Old English *frogga*]

frog 3

frog kick *n* : a kick used in swimming in which the legs are moved up, out, and back in the manner of a frog

frog·man \-ˌman, -mən\ *n* : a swimmer having equipment (as face mask, flippers, and air supply) that permits an extended stay underwater usually for observation or demolition; *esp* : a member of a military unit so equipped

frog spit *n* : CUCKOO SPIT 1 — called also *frog spittle*

1**frol·ic** \ˈfräl-ik\ *vi* **frol·icked; frol·ick·ing** **1** : to make merry **2** : to play about happily : ROMP ⟨children *frolicking* on the beach⟩ [Dutch *vroolijk,* from earlier Dutch *vro* "happy"] — **frol·ick·er** *n*

2**frolic** *n* **1** : a playful mischievous action **2** : GAIETY 2, MERRIMENT

frol·ic·some \ˈfräl-ik-səm\ *adj* : full of gaiety : PLAYFUL

from \frəm, ˈfrəm, ˈfräm\ *prep* **1** — used as a function word to indicate a starting or focal point ⟨came here *from* the city⟩ ⟨cost *from* $5 to $10⟩ ⟨ran a business *from* home⟩ **2** — used as a function word to indicate separation: as (1) physical separation ⟨a child taken *from* its mother⟩ (2) an act or condition of removal, abstention, exclusion, release, subtraction, or differentiation ⟨refrain *from* interrupting⟩ ⟨protection *from* the sun⟩ ⟨subtract 3 *from* 9⟩ **3** — used as a function word to indicate the source, cause, agent, or basis ⟨reading aloud *from* a book⟩ ⟨suffering *from* a cold⟩ [Old English]

frond \ˈfränd\ *n* : a leaf or leaflike part: as **a** : a palm leaf **b** : a fern leaf **c** : a leaflike thallus or shoot (as of a lichen or seaweed) [Latin *frond-, frons* "foliage"] — **frond·ed** \ˈfrän-dəd\ *adj*

1**front** \ˈfrənt\ *n* **1 a** : FOREHEAD; *also* : the whole face **b** : DEMEANOR, BEARING **c** : external often feigned appearance ⟨put up a good *front*⟩ **2 a** : a region in which active warfare is taking place ⟨the western *front*⟩ **b** : a line of battle **c** : an area of activity or interest ⟨progress on the educational *front*⟩ **3** : the side of a building containing the principal entrance **4 a** : the forward part or surface ⟨the *front* of a shirt⟩ **b** : FRONTAGE 1 **c** : the boundary between two dissimilar air masses **5 a** : a position directly before or ahead of something else **b** : a position of leadership or superiority ⟨at the *front* of the profession⟩ **6** : a person, group, or thing used to mask the identity or true character or activity of the actual controlling agent ⟨the business was a *front* for organized crime⟩ **7** : a political coalition [Medieval French, from Latin *front-, frons*]

2**front** *vb* **1** : to have the front or face toward ⟨a cottage *fronting* on the lake⟩ ⟨the house *fronts* the street⟩ **2** : to serve as a front **3** : CONFRONT

3**front** *adj* **1** : of, relating to, or situated at the front **2** : pronounced with closure or narrowing at or toward the front of the oral passage ⟨the *front* vowels \i\ and \e\⟩ — **front** *adv*

front·age \ˈfrənt-ij\ *n* **1 a** : a piece of land that fronts something (as a river or road) **b** : the front side of a building **2** : the extent or measure of a frontage ⟨a cottage with 200 feet of lake *frontage*⟩

front·al \ˈfrənt-l\ *adj* **1** : of, relating to, or adjacent to the forehead or the frontal bone **2 a** : of, relating to, or situated at the front **b** : directed against the front or at the main point or issue ⟨a *frontal* assault⟩ — **fron·tal·ly** \-l-ē\ *adv*

frontal bone *n* : either of a pair of bones that unite to form the human forehead and the upper part of the cavities of the eye and nose

frontal lobe *n* : the front part of each cerebral hemisphere

front–end loader *n* : a vehicle with a hydraulic scoop in front for excavating and loading loose material

fron·tier \ˌfrən-ˈtiər, frän-\ *n* **1** : a border between two countries **2 a** : a region that forms the margin of settled territory in a country being populated **b** : the outer limits of knowledge or achievement ⟨the *frontiers* of science⟩ [Medieval French *frontere,* from *front* "front"] — **frontier** *adj*

fron·tiers·man \-ˈtiərz-mən\ *n* : a person living on a frontier

fron·tiers·wom·an \-ˌwu̇m-ən\ *n* : a woman living on a frontier

fron·tis·piece \ˈfrənt-ə-ˌspēs\ *n* : an illustration preceding and usually facing the title page of a book [Middle French *frontispice* "front of a building," from Late Latin *frontispicium,* from Latin *front-, frons* "front" + *specere* "to look at"]

Word History The process of folk etymology changes unfamiliar words to give them an apparent relationship to more familiar ones. This obscured the true origin of *frontispiece,* which has nothing to do with the word *piece* at all. The earliest known form of the word in English is *frontispice.* Latin *frons, frontis* originally meant "forehead" or "brow" and then came to mean "front" in general. This word combined with *specere,* "to look at," is the source of *frontispiece.* The earliest sense of *frontispice* was architectural: "the part of a building most easily seen, front." The word came to be used as well for the title page of a book, probably because of the once common practice of decorating title pages with columns and other architectural details. From this sense developed its current meaning.

front·let \ˈfrənt-lət\ *n* **1** : a band worn on the forehead **2** : the forehead especially of a bird when distinctively marked

front man *n* **1** : a person serving as a front or figurehead **2** : a lead performer in a musical group

front–runner \-ˈrən-ər\ *n* **1** : a competitor who is most effective when running in the lead **2** : the leader in a contest

[1]frost \ˈfro̊st\ *n* **1 a** : the process of freezing **b** : the temperature that causes freezing **c** : a covering of minute ice crystals on a cold surface **2** : coldness of manner or feeling : INDIFFERENCE [Old English]

[2]frost *vb* **1 a** : to cover with or as if with frost; *esp* : to put icing on (as cake) **b** : to produce a fine-grained slightly roughened surface on (as glass) **2** : to injure or kill by frost : FREEZE

[1]frost·bite \ˈfro̊st-ˌbīt, ˈfro̊s-\ *vt* : to blight or nip with frost

[2]frostbite *n* : the superficial or deep freezing of the tissues of some part of the body (as the feet or hands); *also* : damage to tissues caused by such freezing

frost heave *n* : an upthrust of ground or pavement caused by freezing of moist soil — called also *frost heaving*

frost·ing \ˈfro̊-sting\ *n* **1** : [1]ICING **2** : dull finish on metal or glass

frosty \ˈfro̊-stē\ *adj* **frost·i·er; -est** **1** : attended with or producing frost : FREEZING ⟨a *frosty* night⟩ **2** : covered or appearing as if covered with frost ⟨a *frosty* glass⟩ **3** : marked by coolness or extreme reserve in manner ⟨a *frosty* reception⟩ — **frost·i·ly** \-stə-lē\ *adv* — **frost·i·ness** \-stē-nəs\ *n*

[1]froth \ˈfro̊th\ *n, pl* **froths** \ˈfro̊ths, ˈfro̊t͟hz\ **1 a** : bubbles formed in or on a liquid by fermentation or agitation **b** : the foam produced by saliva that sometimes accompanies disease or exhaustion **2** : something light or frivolous and of little value [Old Norse *frotha*]

[2]froth \ˈfro̊th, ˈfro̊t͟h\ *vb* **1** : to cause to foam **2** : to cover with froth **3** : to produce or throw up froth

frothy \ˈfro̊-thē, -t͟hē\ *adj* **froth·i·er; -est** **1** : full of or consisting of froth **2** : gaily frivolous or light in content or treatment ⟨a *frothy* comedy⟩ — **froth·i·ly** \-thə-lē, -t͟hə-\ *adv* — **froth·i·ness** \-thē-nəs, -t͟hē-\ *n*

frou·frou \frü-ˌfrü\ *n* **1** : a rustling especially of a woman's skirts **2** : showy or frilly ornamentation especially in clothing [French]

fro·ward \ˈfrō-wərd, -ərd\ *adj* : inclined to disobey and oppose : CONTRARY [Middle English, "turned away, froward," from *fro* + *-ward*] — **fro·ward·ly** *adv* — **fro·ward·ness** *n*

frown \ˈfrau̇n\ *vb* **1** : to wrinkle the forehead in anger or concentration **2** : to show displeasure or disapproval by or as if by facial expression ⟨parents *frown* on rudeness⟩ **3** : to express with a frown ⟨*frown* one's disapproval⟩ [Medieval French *frogner* "to snort, frown"] — **frown** *n* — **frown·er** *n* — **frown·ing·ly** \ˈfrau̇-ning-lē\ *adv*

frow·sy *or* **frow·zy** \ˈfrau̇-zē\ *adj* **frow·si·er** *or* **frow·zi·er; -est** : having a slovenly or uncared-for appearance [origin unknown]

froze *past of* FREEZE

fro·zen \ˈfrōz-n\ *adj* **1 a** : treated, affected, or crusted over by freezing **b** : subject to long and severe cold ⟨the *frozen* north⟩ **2 a** : incapable of being changed, moved, or undone ⟨wages were *frozen*⟩ **b** : not available for present use ⟨*frozen* capital⟩ **c** : expressing or characterized by cold unfriendliness ⟨a *frozen* stare⟩ — **fro·zen·ly** *adv* — **fro·zen·ness** \-n-nəs, -əs\ *n*

fruc·ti·fy \ˈfrək-tə-ˌfī, ˈfru̇k-\ *vb* **-fied; -fy·ing** **1** : to bear fruit **2** : to make fruitful or productive [Medieval French *fructifier,* derived from Latin *fructus* "fruit"] — **fruc·ti·fi·ca·tion** \ˌfrək-tə-fə-ˈkā-shən, fru̇k-\ *n*

fruc·tose \ˈfrək-ˌtōs, ˈfru̇k-\ *n* : a very sweet sugar $C_6H_{12}O_6$ that dissolves easily and occurs especially in fruit juices and honey [Latin *fructus* "fruit"]

fru·gal \ˈfrü-gəl\ *adj* : characterized by or reflecting economy in the use of resources : THRIFTY [Latin *frugalis* "virtuous, frugal," from *frux* "fruit, value"] — **fru·gal·i·ty** \frü-ˈgal-ət-ē\ *n* — **fru·gal·ly** \ˈfrü-gə-lē\ *adv*

[1]fruit \ˈfrüt\ *n* **1** : a usually useful product of plant growth (as grain, vegetables, or cotton) ⟨*fruits* of the earth⟩ **2 a** : a product of fertilization in a plant with its envelopes or appendages; *esp* : the ripened ovary of a seed plant, its contents, and inseparably associated parts (as the pod of a pea) **b** : the ripened ovary of a seed plant (as an apple or raspberry) when sweet and pulpy **c** : a juicy plant part (as the stalk of a rhubarb) used chiefly as a dessert **3** : CONSEQUENCE, RESULT ⟨the *fruits* of their labors⟩ [Medieval French, from Latin *fructus* "fruit, use," from *frui* "to enjoy, have the use of"] — **fruit·ed** \-əd\ *adj*

[2]fruit *vb* : to bear or cause to bear fruit

fruit·age \ˈfrüt-ij\ *n* **1** : the condition or process of bearing fruit **2** : yield or amount of fruit

fruit bat *n* : any of numerous large Old World fruit-eating bats of warm regions — called also *flying fox*

fruit·cake \ˈfrüt-ˌkāk\ *n* : a rich cake containing nuts, dried or candied fruits, and spices

fruit·er·er \ˈfrüt-ər-ər\ *n, chiefly British* : a person who deals in fruit

fruit fly *n* : any of various small two-winged flies (as a drosophila) whose larvae feed on fruit or decaying vegetable matter

fruit·ful \ˈfrüt-fəl\ *adj* **1** : yielding or producing fruit **2** : abundantly productive : bringing results ⟨*fruitful* labor⟩ ***synonyms*** see FERTILE — **fruit·ful·ly** \-fə-lē\ *adv* — **fruit·ful·ness** *n*

fruiting body *n* : a plant organ specialized for producing spores

fru·i·tion \fru̇-ˈish-ən\ *n* **1** : the state of bearing fruit **2** : REALIZATION, ACCOMPLISHMENT ⟨brought the project to *fruition*⟩ [Late Latin *fruitio* "enjoyment," from Latin *frui* "to enjoy"]

fruit·less \ˈfrüt-ləs\ *adj* **1** : lacking or not bearing fruit **2** : producing no good effect : UNSUCCESSFUL ⟨a *fruitless* attempt⟩ — **fruit·less·ly** *adv* — **fruit·less·ness** *n*

fruit sugar *n* : FRUCTOSE

fruity \ˈfrüt-ē\ *adj* **fruit·i·er; -est** : relating to or suggesting fruit

frus·trate \ˈfrəs-ˌtrāt\ *vt* **1 a** : to prevent from carrying out a purpose ⟨*frustrate* a person⟩ **b** : to induce feelings of discouragement in **2** : to make ineffective ⟨*frustrate* a plan⟩ [Latin *frustrare,* from *frustra* "in vain"] — **frus·tra·tion** \ˌfrəs-ˈtrā-shən, frəs-\ *n*

synonyms FRUSTRATE, THWART, BAFFLE, FOIL mean to check or defeat another's plan or block achievement of a goal. FRUSTRATE implies making even the best or most persistent efforts vain and ineffectual ⟨*frustrated* attempts at educational reform⟩. THWART implies frustrating or checking especially by deliberately crossing or opposing ⟨*thwarted* by the enemy⟩. BAFFLE implies frustrating by confusing or puzzling ⟨*baffled* by the large number of rules⟩. FOIL implies checking or defeating so as to discourage further effort ⟨*foiled* by her parents, he stopped trying to see her⟩.

frus·tum \ˈfrəs-təm\ *n, pl* **frustums** *or* **frus·ta** \-tə\ : the part of a cone or pyramid that remains after cutting off the top with a plane parallel to the base [Latin, "piece, bit"]

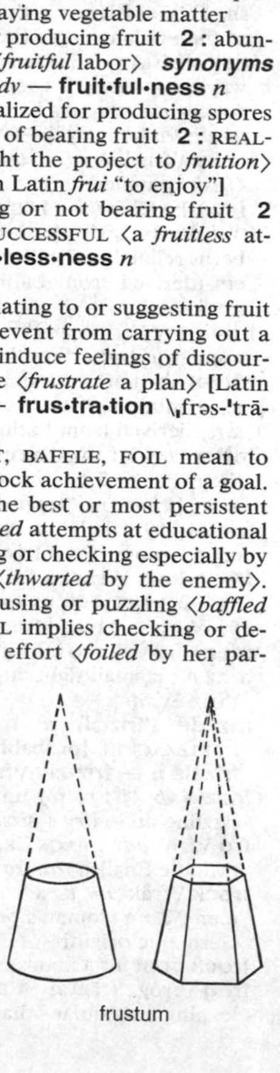
frustum

fru·ti·cose \ˈfrüt-i-ˌkōs\ *adj* : having a shrubby bushy thallus with flattened or cylindrical branches ⟨*fruticose* lichens⟩ — compare CRUSTOSE, FOLIOSE [Latin *fruticosus,* from *frutex* "shrub"]

[1]fry \ˈfrī\ *vb* **fried; fry·ing** **1** : to cook in a pan or on a griddle over heat especially in fat **2** *slang*

: ELECTROCUTE **3** : to get very hot or burn as if being fried ⟨bodies *frying* on the beach⟩ [Medieval French *frire,* from Latin *frigere*]

2fry *n, pl* **fries** **1 a** : a dish of something fried **b** : FRENCH FRY — usually used in plural ⟨a burger and *fries*⟩ **2** : a social gathering where fried food is eaten ⟨an annual fish *fry*⟩

3fry *n, pl* **fry** **1 a** : recently hatched or young fishes **b** : the young of animals other than fish **2** : very small adult fishes **3** : members of a group or class : PERSONS ⟨small *fry*⟩ [Medieval French *frie,* from *freier, frier* "to rub, spawn"]

fry bread *n* : quick bread cooked in deep fat

fry·er *also* **fri·er** \ˈfrī-ər, ˈfrīr\ *n* : something intended for or used in frying: as **a** : a young chicken **b** : a deep utensil for frying foods

frying pan *n* : a metal pan with a handle that is used for frying foods — called also *fry pan* — **out of the frying pan into the fire** : clear of one difficulty only to fall into a greater one

f–stop \ˈef-ˌstäp\ *n* : a camera lens aperture setting indicated by an f-number

FTP \ˌef-ˌtē-ˈpē\ *n* : a system for transferring computer files over the Internet [*f*ile *t*ransfer *p*rotocol]

fuch·sia \ˈfyü-shə\ *n* **1** : any of a genus of shrubs related to the evening primrose and having showy nodding flowers usually in deep pinks, reds, and purples **2** : a vivid reddish purple [Leonhard *Fuchs,* died 1566, German botanist]

fuchsia 1

fuch·sin *or* **fuch·sine** \ˈfyük-sən, -ˌsēn\ *n* : a synthetic dye that yields a brilliant bluish red [French *fuchsine,* probably from *fuchsia* "fuchsia"]

fu·co·xan·thin \ˌfyü-kō-ˈzan-thən\ *n* : a brown pigment occurring especially in the chloroplasts of brown algae [derived from Latin *fucus* "seaweed, a lichen yielding a violet dye" + Greek *xanthos* "yellow"]

fu·cus \ˈfyü-kəs\ *n* : ROCKWEED [Latin, "seaweed," from Greek *phykos*]

fud·dle \ˈfəd-l\ *vt* **fud·dled; fud·dling** \ˈfəd-ling, -l-ing\ : to make confused : MUDDLE [origin unknown]

fud·dy–dud·dy \ˈfəd-ē-ˌdəd-ē\ *n, pl* **-dies** : one that is old-fashioned, pompous, unimaginative, or concerned about trifles [origin unknown]

1fudge \ˈfəj\ *vb* **1 a** : to devise as a substitute : FAKE **b** : FALSIFY ⟨*fudged* the figures⟩ **2** : to exceed the proper bounds or limits of something ⟨*fudged* on the rules⟩; *also* : CHEAT 4 ⟨*fudged* on the exam⟩ **3** : to avoid commitment : HEDGE ⟨politicians *fudging* on the issues⟩ [origin unknown]

2fudge *n* **1** : foolish nonsense **2** : a soft creamy candy of sugar, milk, butter, and flavoring **3** : something that is fudged; *esp* : a bending of rules or a compromise

1fu·el \ˈfyü-əl\ *n* **1 a** : a material used to produce heat or power by burning **b** : a material from which atomic energy can be produced especially in a reactor **2** : a source of support : REINFORCEMENT [Medieval French *fuail, feuaile,* derived from Latin *focus* "hearth"]

2fuel *vb* **-eled** *or* **-elled; -el·ing** *or* **-el·ling** **1** : to provide with or take in fuel **2** : SUPPORT, STIMULATE ⟨*fuel* research with federal grants⟩

fuel cell *n* : a cell that continuously changes the chemical energy of a fuel (as hydrogen) and oxidant into electrical energy

fuel injection *n* : an electronically-controlled system for supplying a precise amount of fuel to an engine

fuel oil *n* : an oil that is used for fuel and that usually ignites at a higher temperature than kerosene

1fu·gi·tive \ˈfyü-jət-iv\ *adj* **1** : running away or trying to escape ⟨a *fugitive* slave⟩ **2** : moving from place to place **3** : likely to vanish suddenly : not fixed or lasting ⟨*fugitive* thoughts⟩ [Latin *fugitivus,* from *fugere* "to flee"] — **fu·gi·tive·ly** *adv* — **fu·gi·tive·ness** *n*

2fugitive *n* **1** : one that flees or tries to escape; *esp* : REFUGEE **2** : something elusive or hard to find

fu·gu \ˈfü-ˌgü, ˈfyü-\ *n* : any of various very poisonous puffer fishes that are used as food in Japan after the toxin-containing parts have been removed [Japanese]

fugue \ˈfyüg\ *n* **1** : a musical composition in which one or two themes are repeated or imitated by successively entering voices and developed in a continuous interweaving of the voice parts **2** : a disturbed state of mind in which a person does things of which he or she seems to be aware but does not remember upon recovery [probably from Italian *fuga* "flight, fugue," from Latin, "flight," from *fugere* "to flee"] — **fu·gal** \ˈfyü-gəl\ *adj*

füh·rer *or* **fueh·rer** \ˈfyu̇r-ər, ˈfir-\ *n* : LEADER 2c — used chiefly of the leader of the German Nazis [German]

1-ful \fəl\ *adj suffix, sometimes* **-ful·ler** *sometimes* **-ful·lest** **1** : full of ⟨event*ful*⟩ **2** : characterized by ⟨peace*ful*⟩ **3** : having the qualities of ⟨master*ful*⟩ **4** : tending, given, or liable to ⟨mourn*ful*⟩ ⟨help*ful*⟩

2-ful \ˌfu̇l\ *n suffix* : number or quantity that fills or would fill ⟨room*ful*⟩

ful·crum \ˈfu̇l-krəm, ˈfəl-\ *n, pl* **fulcrums** *or* **ful·cra** \-krə\ : the support about which a lever turns — see LEVER illustration [Latin, "bedpost," from *fulcire* "to prop"]

ful·fill *or* **ful·fil** \fu̇l-ˈfil\ *vt* **ful·filled; ful·fill·ing** **1** : to put into effect ⟨*fulfill* a promise⟩ **2** : to measure up to : SATISFY ⟨*fulfill* a need⟩ [Old English *fullfyllan,* from *full* + *fyllan* "to fill"] — **ful·fill·er** *n* — **ful·fill·ment** \-mənt\ *n*

1full \ˈfu̇l\ *adj* **1** : containing as much or as many as is possible or normal ⟨a bin *full* of corn⟩ **2 a** : complete as to number, amount, or duration ⟨a *full* share⟩ **b** : having all the distinguishing characteristics ⟨a *full* member⟩ **c** : being at the highest degree : MAXIMUM ⟨*full* strength⟩ **d** : lacking restraint or qualification ⟨my *full* support⟩ **e** : being fully illuminated ⟨the moon is *full* tonight⟩ **f** : completely occupied by runners ⟨come to bat with the bases *full*⟩ **g** : having three balls and two strikes ⟨a *full* count⟩ **3 a** : plump and rounded in outline ⟨a *full* figure⟩ **b** : having an abundance of material ⟨a *full* skirt⟩ **4 a** : possessing or containing a great number or amount ⟨a room *full* of pictures⟩ ⟨*full* of hope⟩ **b** : rich in detail ⟨a *full* report⟩ **5** : satisfied especially with food or drink **6** : having both parents in common ⟨*full* sisters⟩ **7** : having volume or depth of sound ⟨*full* tones⟩ **8** : completely occupied especially with a thought or plan ⟨*full* of one's own concerns⟩ [Old English] — **full·ness** *also* **ful·ness** *n* — **full of it** : not to be believed

2full *adv* **1 a** : VERY, EXTREMELY ⟨knew *full* well they were lying⟩ **b** : ENTIRELY ⟨fill a glass *full*⟩ **2** : EXACTLY, SQUARELY ⟨was hit *full* in the face⟩

3full *n* **1** : the highest or fullest state or degree ⟨the *full* of the moon⟩ **2** : the utmost extent ⟨enjoy life to the *full*⟩ — **in full** **1** : to the requisite or complete amount ⟨paid *in full*⟩ **2** : to the fullest extent : COMPLETELY ⟨read the book *in full*⟩

4full *vt* : to shrink and thicken (woolen cloth) by moistening, heating, and pressing [Medieval French *fuller, fouler* to full, trample, derived from Latin *fullo* "fuller"]

full·back \ˈfu̇l-ˌbak\ *n* **1** : an offensive football back who usually lines up between the halfbacks **2** : a primarily defensive player (as in soccer or field hockey) who usually plays near the goal to be defended

full–blood·ed \ˈfu̇l-ˈbləd-əd\ *adj* : of unmixed ancestry : PUREBRED — **full–blood·ed·ness** *n*

full–blown \-ˈblōn\ *adj* **1** : fully mature or developed ⟨a *full-blown* theory⟩ **2** : being at the height of bloom ⟨a *full-blown* rose⟩ **3** : possessing all necessary features

full–bod·ied \-ˈbäd-ēd\ *adj* : marked by richness and fullness

full–dress \-ˈdres\ *adj* : complete to the last detail ⟨a *full-dress* rehearsal⟩

full dress *n* : formal or ceremonial dress

full·er \ˈfu̇l-ər\ *n* : one that fulls cloth

full·er·ene \ˌfu̇l-ə-ˈrēn\ *n* : any of various hollow carbon molecules having especially a spherical shape [R. Buckminster *Fuller*; from the resemblance of the molecules to the geodesic domes designed by Fuller]

fuller's earth *n* : a clayish earthy substance used for filtering and as an absorbent

fuller's teasel *n* : TEASEL 1a

full–fledged \ˈfu̇l-ˈflejd\ *adj* **1** : fully developed : COMPLETE 4a **2** : having attained complete status ⟨a *full-fledged* lawyer⟩ **3** : FULL-BLOOM 3

full–grown \-ˈgrōn\ *adj* : having reached full growth or development : MATURE

\ə\ **a**but	\au̇\ **ou**t	\i\ **t**i**p**	\ȯ\ **saw**	\u̇\ **foot**
\ər\ **further**	\ch\ **ch**in	\ī\ **life**	\ȯi\ **coin**	\y\ **y**et
\a\ **mat**	\e\ **pet**	\j\ **j**ob	\th\ **th**in	\yü\ **few**
\ā\ **take**	\ē\ **easy**	\ng\ **sing**	\t͟h\ **th**is	\yu̇\ **cure**
\ä\ **cot, cart**	\g\ **go**	\ō\ **bone**	\ü\ **food**	\zh\ **vision**

full house *n* : a poker hand containing three cards of one rank plus a pair of cards of another rank
full–length \ˈfu̇l-ˌlength, -ˌlengkth, -ˌlenth\ *adj* **1** : showing or adapted to the entire length especially of the human figure ⟨a *full-length* dress⟩ **2** : having a length that is normal or standard for one of its kind ⟨a *full-length* play⟩
full moon *n* : the moon with its whole apparent disk illuminated
full–on \ˈfu̇l-ˌȯn, -ˌän\ *adj* : COMPLETE 4a, FULL-FLEDGED
full–scale \ˈfu̇l-ˈskāl\ *adj* **1** : identical to an original in proportion and size ⟨*full-scale* drawing⟩ **2** : involving full use of available resources ⟨a *full-scale* biography⟩
full–size \-ˌsīz\ *adj* **1** : having the usual or normal size for its kind **2** : having a size of 54 inches by 75 inches (about 1.4 meters by 1.9 meters) ⟨a *full-size* bed⟩
full tilt *adv* : at high speed
full time *n* : the standard working time for a given job or period — **full–time** *adj*
ful·ly \ˈfu̇l-lē, -ē\ *adv* **1** : in a full manner or degree : COMPLETELY **2** : at least ⟨*fully* nine tenths of us⟩
ful·mar \ˈfu̇l-mər, -ˌmär\ *n* : an Arctic seabird closely related to the petrels [of Scandinavian origin]
ful·mi·nant \ˈfu̇l-mə-nənt, ˈfəl-\ *adj* : coming on suddenly or with great severity ⟨a ~ disease⟩
ful·mi·nate \ˈfu̇l-mə-ˌnāt, ˈfəl-\ *vb* **1** : to utter or send out censure or condemnation **2** : to make a sudden loud noise : EXPLODE **3** : to come on suddenly or with great severity [Medieval Latin *fulminare,* from Latin, "to flash with lightning, strike with lightning," from *fulmen* "lightning"] — **ful·mi·na·tion** \ˌfu̇l-mə-ˈnā-shən, ˌfəl-\ *n* — **ful·mi·na·tor** \-ˌnāt-ər\ *n*
ful·some \ˈfu̇l-səm\ *adj* **1** : marked by abundance ⟨*fulsome* detail⟩ **2** : excessively complimentary or flattering ⟨*fulsome* praise⟩ [Middle English *fulsome* "copious, cloying," from *ful* "full" + *-som* "-some"] — **fulsome·ly** *adv* — **ful·some·ness** *n*
fu·ma·role \ˈfyü-mə-ˌrōl\ *n* : a hole in a volcanic region from which hot gases and vapors issue [Italian *fumarola,* derived from Latin *fumus* "fume"]
[1]**fum·ble** \ˈfəm-bəl\ *vb* **fum·bled; fum·bling** \-bə-ling, -bling\ **1** : to feel or grope about clumsily ⟨*fumbled* for the key⟩ **2** : to handle or manage something clumsily : fail to grasp firmly; *esp* : to fail to hold, catch, or handle the ball properly in a game (as baseball or football) [probably of Scandinavian origin] — **fum·bler** \-bə-lər, -blər\ *n* — **fum·bling·ly** *adv*
[2]**fumble** *n* **1** : an act or instance of fumbling **2** : a fumbled ball
[1]**fume** \ˈfyüm\ *n* **1** : a usually irritating or offensive smoke, vapor, or gas — usually used in plural ⟨exhaust *fumes*⟩ **2** : a state of excited irritation or anger [Medieval French *fum,* from Latin *fumus* "smoke, fume"] — **fumy** \ˈfyü-mē\ *adj*
[2]**fume** *vb* **1** : to expose to or treat with fumes **2** : to give off fumes **3 a** : to be in a fume **b** : to express irritable annoyance ⟨*fume* at the delay⟩
fu·mi·gant \ˈfyü-mi-gənt\ *n* : a substance used for fumigating
fu·mi·gate \ˈfyü-mə-ˌgāt\ *vt* : to apply smoke, vapor, or gas to especially for the purpose of disinfecting or of destroying pests [Latin *fumigare,* from *fumus* "smoke"] — **fu·mi·ga·tion** \ˌfyü-mə-ˈgā-shən\ *n* — **fu·mi·ga·tor** \ˈfyü-mə-ˌgāt-ər\ *n*
fu·mi·to·ry \ˈfyü-mə-ˌtōr-ē, -ˌtȯr-\ *n, pl* **-ries** : any of a genus of erect or climbing herbs with spikes of small flowers [Medieval French *fumeterre,* from Medieval Latin *fumus terrae,* literally, "smoke of the earth"]
[1]**fun** \ˈfən\ *n* **1** : something or someone that is amusing or enjoyable **2** : AMUSEMENT, ENJOYMENT ⟨sickness takes the *fun* out of life⟩ **3** : derisive jest : RIDICULE ⟨they made *fun* of me⟩ [English dialect *fun* "to hoax"]
[2]**fun** *vi* **funned; fun·ning** : to indulge in banter or play : JOKE
[3]**fun** *adj* **1** : providing entertainment, amusement, or enjoyment ⟨a *fun* party⟩ ⟨a *fun* person⟩ **2** : full of fun ⟨have a *fun* time⟩
[1]**func·tion** \ˈfəng-shən, ˈfəngk-\ *n* **1** : the job or duty of a person **2** : the special purpose for which a thing exists or is used **3** : a large ceremony or social event **4** : one of a group of related actions contributing to a larger action; *esp* : the normal and specific contribution of a bodily part to the operation of a living organism ⟨the *function* of the heart⟩ **5 a** : a mathematical relationship that assigns exactly one element of one set to each element of the same or another set **b** : something (as a quality or measurement) that depends on and varies with something else ⟨height is a *function* of age in children⟩ [Latin *functio* "performance," from *fungi* "to perform"] — **func·tion·less** \-ləs\ *adj*
[2]**function** *vi* **func·tioned; func·tion·ing** \-shə-ning, -shning\ **1** : to have a function : SERVE **2** : to be in action : OPERATE
func·tion·al \ˈfəng-shnəl, ˈfəngk-, -shən-l\ *adj* **1 a** : of, connected with, or being a function **b** : affecting functions but not structure ⟨*functional* heart disease⟩ — compare ORGANIC 1b **2** : serving in a larger whole; *also* : designed or developed chiefly from the point of view of use ⟨*functional* clothing⟩ **3** : performing or able to perform a regular function **4** : organized by functions — **func·tion·al·i·ty** \ˌfəng-shə-ˈnal-ət-ē, ˌfəngk-\ *n* — **func·tion·al·ly** \ˈfəng-shnəl-ē, ˈfəngk-, -shən-l-ē\ *adv*
functional illiterate *n* : a person having had some schooling but not meeting a minimum standard of literacy — **functional illiteracy** *n* — **functionally illiterate** *adj*
func·tion·ary \ˈfəng-shə-ˌner-ē, ˈfəngk-\ *n, pl* **-ar·ies** **1** : one who serves in a certain function **2** : one holding office in a government or political party
function word *n* : a word (as a preposition, helping verb, or conjunction) expressing primarily grammatical relationship
[1]**fund** \ˈfənd\ *n* **1** : an available quantity of material or intangible resources : SUPPLY **2 a** : a sum of money or other resources whose principal or interest is set apart for a specific objective **b** *pl* : available money **3** : an organization administering a special fund [Latin *fundus* "bottom, piece of landed property"]
[2]**fund** *vt* **1** : to provide funds for **2** : to convert (a short-term obligation) into a debt payable at a distant date or at no definite date and bearing a fixed interest ⟨*fund* a debt⟩ — **fund·er** *n*
fun·da·ment \ˈfən-də-mənt\ *n* **1** : FOUNDATION 2, BASE **2** : BUTTOCK 2a [Medieval French *foundement,* from Latin *fundamentum,* from *fundare* "to found," from *fundus* "bottom"]
[1]**fun·da·men·tal** \ˌfən-də-ˈment-l\ *adj* **1 a** : serving as an origin or source : PRIMARY **b** : serving as a basic support or essential structure or function : BASIC **2** : of or relating to essential structure or function : RADICAL ⟨a *fundamental* change⟩ **3** : of, relating to, or produced by the lowest part of a complex vibration **4** : of central importance ⟨the *fundamental* purpose⟩ ***synonyms*** see ESSENTIAL — **fun·da·men·tal·ly** \-l-ē\ *adv*
[2]**fundamental** *n* **1** : something fundamental; *esp* : one of the basic constituents essential to a thing or system ⟨*fundamentals* of arithmetic⟩ **2** : the part of a complex wave that has the lowest frequency and usually the greatest amplitude
fun·da·men·tal·ism \-l-ˌiz-əm\ *n* **1 a** *often cap* : a movement in 20th century Protestantism emphasizing the literally interpreted Bible as fundamental to Christian life and teaching **b** : the beliefs associated with fundamentalism **c** : adherence to such beliefs **2** : a movement or attitude stressing strict and literal adherence to a set of basic principles — **fun·da·men·tal·ist** \-l-əst\ *n* — **fundamentalist** *or* **fun·da·men·tal·is·tic** \-ˌment-l-ˈis-tik\ *adj*
fundamental particle *n* : ELEMENTARY PARTICLE
[1]**fu·ner·al** \ˈfyün-rəl, -ə-rəl\ *adj* **1** : of, relating to, or constituting a funeral **2** : FUNEREAL 2 [Late Latin *funeralis,* from Latin *funer-, funus,* n., "funeral"]
[2]**funeral** *n* **1** : a ceremony held for a dead person usually before burial or cremation **2** : a funeral procession
funeral director *n* : a person who manages funerals and is usually an embalmer
funeral home *n* : a set of rooms with facilities for the preparation of the dead for burial or cremation, for the viewing of the body, and for funerals — called also *funeral parlor*
fu·ne·re·al \fyu̇-ˈnir-ē-əl\ *adj* **1** : of or relating to a funeral **2** : suggesting a funeral ⟨*funereal* gloom⟩ [Latin *funereus,* from *funer-, funus* "funeral"] — **fu·ne·re·al·ly** \-ē-ə-lē\ *adv*
fun·gal \ˈfəng-gəl\ *adj* **1** : of, relating to, or resembling fungi **2** : caused by a fungus ⟨a *fungal* skin disease⟩
fungi- *combining form* : fungus ⟨*fungi*cide⟩
fun·gi·ble \ˈfən-jə-bəl\ *adj* **1** : having such a nature that one part or quantity may be replaced by another part or quantity in satisfaction of an obligation **2** : INTERCHANGEABLE **3** : FLEXIBLE 2 [Latin *fungi* "to perform" + *-ibilis* "-able"]
fun·gi·cide \ˈfən-jə-ˌsīd, ˌfəng-gə-\ *n* : a substance that destroys fungi or inhibits their growth — **fun·gi·cid·al** \ˌfən-jə-ˈsīd-l, fəng-gə-\ *adj* — **fun·gi·cid·al·ly** \-l-ē\ *adv*
fun·go \ˈfəng-gō\ *n, pl* **fungoes** : a fly ball hit by a player who tosses a ball in the air and hits it as it comes down [origin unknown]
fun·goid \ˈfəng-ˌgȯid\ *adj* : resembling, characteristic of, or being a fungus — **fungoid** *n*
fun·gous \ˈfəng-gəs\ *adj* : FUNGAL
fun·gus \ˈfəng-gəs\ *n, pl* **fun·gi** \ˈfən-ˌjī, ˈfəng-ˌgī\ *also* **fun·gus-**

es **1** : any of a kingdom (Fungi) of eukaryotic typically filamentous organisms (as molds, rusts, mildews, smuts, mushrooms, and yeasts) that lack chlorophyll, are saprophytic or parasitic, and were formerly classified as plants **2** : infection with a fungus [Latin] — **fungus** *adj*

fu•nic•u•lar \fyu̇-ˈnik-yə-lər, fə-\ *n* : a cable railway ascending a mountain; *esp* : one in which an ascending car counterbalances a descending car [derived from Latin *funiculus* "small rope"]

¹funk \ˈfəngk\ *n* : a strong offensive smell

²funk *vb* **1** : to become frightened and shrink back **2** : to be afraid of : DREAD

³funk *n* **1** : a state of paralyzing fear **2** : a depressed state of mind **3** : SLUMP ⟨the team went into a *funk*⟩ ⟨an economic *funk*⟩ [probably from obsolete Dutch dialect *fonck*]

⁴funk *n* **1** : music that combines forms of blues, gospel, or soul and is characterized by a strong backbeat **2** : the quality or state of being funky ⟨looking for clothes with *funk*⟩ [back-formation from *funky*]

funky \ˈfəng-kē\ *adj* **1** : having an offensive odor **2** : having an earthy style and feeling; *esp* : having the style and feeling of funk ⟨a *funky* beat⟩ **3 a** : odd or quaint in appearance or feeling **b** : lacking style or taste ⟨wearing some *funky* old hat⟩ **c** : unconventionally stylish : HIP [*funk* "offensive odor"] — **funk•i•ly** *adv* — **funk•i•ness** *n*

¹fun•nel \ˈfən-l\ *n* **1** : a utensil usually shaped like a hollow cone with a tube extending from the point to catch and direct a downward flow (as of liquid) **2** : a stack or flue (as of a ship) for the escape of smoke or for ventilation [Occitan *fonilh*, from Medieval Latin *fundibulum*, from Latin *infundibulum*, from *infundere* "to pour in," from *in-* + *fundere* "to pour"]

²funnel *vb* **-neled** *also* **-nelled; -nel•ing** *also* **-nel•ling** **1** : to form, take, or give the shape of a funnel ⟨*funneling* clouds⟩ **2** : to pass through or as if through a funnel ⟨funds were *funneled* into the project⟩

funnel cloud *n* : a funnel-shaped cloud that indicates the formation of a tornado; *also* : TORNADO

¹fun•ny \ˈfən-ē\ *adj* **fun•ni•er; -est** **1 a** : affording light mirth and laughter : AMUSING **b** : seeking or intended to amuse **2** : differing from the ordinary in a suspicious way : PECULIAR ⟨it's *funny* you should ask⟩ **3** : involving trickery or deception ⟨don't try anything *funny*⟩ — **fun•ni•ly** \ˈfən-l-ē\ *adv* — **fun•ni•ness** \ˈfən-ē-nəs\ *n* — **funny** *adv*

²funny *n, pl* **fun•nies** **1** : one that is funny; *esp* : JOKE 1 **2** *pl* : comic strips or the comic section of a newspaper — usually used with *the*

funny bone *n* **1** : a place at the back of the elbow where a blow may compress a nerve and cause a painful tingling sensation **2** : a sense of humor ⟨a joke that tickles my *funny bone*⟩

fun•plex \ˈfən-ˌpleks\ *n* : an entertainment complex that includes facilities for various sports and games and often restaurants

¹fur \ˈfər\ *vt* **furred; fur•ring** : to cover, line, trim, or clothe with fur [Medieval French *forrer, furrer* "to stuff, fill, line," from *fuerre* "sheath," of Germanic origin]

Word History The hairy coat of a mammal is called *fur*. But originally this coat could not be called *fur* until it had been removed from the animal and used to adorn a human being. The well-to-do of the late Middle Ages wore robes *furred* (lined and trimmed) with the pelts of animals. These trimmings and linings were called *furs*. The word was soon used for the soft hair of animals, even of living animals. But when robes were first *furred*, it was the act of lining rather than the material used that the verb *fur* suggested. Medieval French *forrer, furrer*, the source of English *fur*, originally meant "to line." *Forrer* was derived from the noun *fuerre*, a Germanic loanword in Medieval French which meant "sheath."

²fur *n* **1** : a piece of the dressed pelt of an animal used to make, trim, or line wearing apparel **2** : an article of clothing made of or with fur **3** : the hairy coat of a mammal especially when fine, soft, and thick **4** : a coating (as on the tongue) resembling fur — **fur•less** \ˈfər-ləs\ *adj* — **furred** \ˈfərd\ *adj*

fur•bear•er \ˈfər-ˌbar-ər, -ˌber-\ *n* : an animal that bears fur especially of a commerically desired quality

fur•be•low \ˈfər-bə-ˌlō\ *n* **1** : a pleated or gathered piece of material (as a ruffle or flounce) **2** : showy trimming [by folk etymology from French dialect *farbella*] — **furbelow** *vt*

fur•bish \ˈfər-bish\ *vt* **1** : to make lustrous : POLISH **2** : to give a new look to : RENOVATE [Medieval French *furbiss-*, stem of *furbir* "to furbish," of Germanic origin] — **fur•bish•er** *n*

fu•ri•ous \ˈfyu̇r-ē-əs\ *adj* **1** : being in a fury : FIERCE, ANGRY **2** : VIOLENT ⟨a *furious* wind⟩ — **fu•ri•ous•ly** *adv*

¹furl \ˈfərl\ *vt* : to wrap or roll (as a sail or a flag) close to or around something [Medieval French *ferlier* "to fasten," from *ferm, fer* "tight" (from Latin *firmus* "firm") + *lier* "to tie," from Latin *ligare*]

²furl *n* **1** : the act of furling **2** : something that is furled

fur•long \ˈfər-ˌlȯng\ *n* : a unit of distance equal to 220 yards (about 201 meters) [Old English *furlang*, from *furh* "furrow" + *lang* "long"]

¹fur•lough \ˈfər-lō\ *n* : a leave of absence from duty; *esp* : one granted to a soldier [Dutch *verlof*, literally, "permission"]

²furlough *vt* **1** : to grant a furlough to **2** : to lay off from work

fur•nace \ˈfər-nəs\ *n* : an enclosed structure in which heat is produced (as for heating a house or melting metals) [Medieval French *forneise*, from Latin *fornax*]

fur•nish \ˈfər-nish\ *vt* **1** : to provide with what is needed; *esp* : to equip with furniture **2** : SUPPLY, GIVE ⟨*furnished* them with food⟩ [Medieval French *furniss-*, stem of *furnir* "to complete, equip," of Germanic origin] — **fur•nish•er** *n*

fur•nish•ings \-nish-ingz\ *n pl* **1** : articles or accessories of dress **2** : objects that tend to increase comfort or utility; *esp* : articles of furniture for a room

fur•ni•ture \ˈfər-ni-chər\ *n* : equipment that is necessary, useful, or desirable; *esp* : movable articles (as chairs, tables, or beds) needed to fit a room for use [Medieval French *fourniture*, from *furnir* "to equip"]

fu•ror \ˈfyu̇r-ˌȯr, -ˌōr\ *n* **1** : a fit of anger : RAGE **2** : a fashionable craze : VOGUE **3** : an outburst of public excitement or indignation : UPROAR [Latin, from *furere* "to rage"]

fu•rore \-ˌōr, -ˌȯr\ *n* : FUROR 2, 3

fur•ri•er \ˈfər-ē-ər\ *n* : a person who prepares or deals in furs — **fur•ri•ery** \-ē-ə-rē\ *n*

fur•ring \ˈfər-ing\ *n* **1** : a fur trimming or lining **2** : the application of thin wood, brick, or metal to joists, studs, or walls to form a level surface or an air space; *also* : the material used in this process

¹fur•row \ˈfər-ō, ˈfə-rō\ *n* **1** : a trench in the earth made by or as if by a plow **2** : a narrow groove or wrinkle [Old English *furh*]

²furrow *vb* **1** : to make furrows in **2** : to form furrows

fur•ry \ˈfər-ē\ *adj* **fur•ri•er; -est** **1** : consisting of or resembling fur **2** : covered with fur

fur seal *n* : any of various eared seals with a dense soft undercoat

¹fur•ther \ˈfər-thər\ *adv* **1** : ¹FARTHER 1 **2** : in addition : MOREOVER **3** : to a greater degree or extent [Old English *furthor*, comparative of *forth*] ***usage*** see FARTHER

²further *vt* **fur•thered; fur•ther•ing** \ˈfərth-ring, -ə-ring\ : to help forward : PROMOTE ⟨*furthered* medical research⟩ — **fur•ther•er** \ˈfər-thər-ər\ *n*

³further *adj* **1** : ²FARTHER 1 **2** : going or extending beyond : ADDITIONAL ⟨*further* education⟩

fur•ther•ance \ˈfərth-rəns, -ə-rəns\ *n* : the act of furthering : ADVANCEMENT

fur•ther•more \ˈfər-thər-ˌmōr, -thə-, -ˌmȯr\ *adv* : in addition to what precedes : BESIDES

fur•ther•most \-ˌmōst\ *adj* : most distant : FARTHEST

fur•thest \ˈfər-thəst\ *adv or adj* : FARTHEST

fur•tive \ˈfərt-iv\ *adj* : done by stealth : SLY, SECRET ⟨a *furtive* look⟩ [Latin *furtivus*, from *furtum* "theft," from *fur* "thief"] — **fur•tive•ly** *adv* — **fur•tive•ness** *n*

fu•run•cle \ˈfyu̇r-ˌəng-kəl\ *n* : ¹BOIL [Latin *furunculus* "petty thief, boil," derived from *fur* "thief"]

fu•ry \ˈfyu̇r-ē\ *n, pl* **furies** **1** : an intense and often destructive rage ⟨threw the vase in a *fury*⟩ **2 a** *cap* : one of the avenging spirits in classical mythology **b** : a violent, angry, or spiteful person **3** : extreme fierceness or violence ⟨the *fury* of the storm⟩ [Latin *furia*, from *furere* "to rage"] ***synonyms*** see ANGER

furze \ˈfərz\ *n* : GORSE [Old English *fyrs*]

fu•sar•i•um \fyü-ˈzar-ē-əm, -ˈzer-\ *n* : any of a genus of fungi which includes forms that are causative agents of plant disease and others implicated in human and animal disease; *also* : a

\ə\ **abut**	\au̇\ **out**	\i\ **tip**	\ȯ\ **saw**	\u̇\ **foot**
\ər\ **further**	\ch\ **chin**	\ī\ **life**	\ȯi\ **coin**	\y\ **yet**
\a\ **mat**	\e\ **pet**	\j\ **job**	\th\ **thin**	\yü\ **few**
\ā\ **take**	\ē\ **easy**	\ng\ **sing**	\th\ **this**	\yu̇\ **cure**
\ä\ **cot, cart**	\g\ **go**	\ō\ **bone**	\ü\ **food**	\zh\ **vision**

plant disease caused by a fusarium [derived from Latin *fusus* "spindle"]

[1]**fuse** \ˈfyüz\ *vb* **1 :** to reduce to a liquid or plastic state by heat **2 :** to become fluid with heat **3 :** to unite by or as if by melting together **:** BLEND, INTEGRATE [Latin *fusus,* past participle of *fundere* "to pour, melt"]

[2]**fuse** *n* **:** an electrical safety device consisting of or including a wire or strip of fusible metal that melts and interrupts the circuit when the current becomes too strong

[3]**fuse** *n* **1 :** a continuous train (as of gunpowder) enclosed in a cord or cable for setting off an explosive charge by transmitting fire to it **2** *also* **fuze :** a mechanical or electrical detonating device for setting off the bursting charge of a projectile, bomb, or torpedo [Italian *fuso* "spindle," from Latin *fusus*]

[4]**fuse** *also* **fuze** *vt* **:** to equip with a fuse

fu·see \fyü-ˈzē\ *n* **:** a red signal flare used especially for protecting stalled trains and trucks

fu·se·lage \ˈfyü-sə-ˌläzh, ˈfyü-zə-\ *n* **:** the central body portion of an airplane which holds the crew, passengers, and cargo [French, from *fuselé* "spindle-shaped," derived from Latin *fusus* "spindle"]

fu·sel oil \ˈfyü-zəl-\ *n* **:** an acrid oily liquid occurring in insufficiently distilled alcoholic liquors and consisting chiefly of amyl alcohol [German *Fusel* "bad liquor"]

fus·ible \ˈfyü-zə-bəl\ *adj* **:** capable of being fused and especially liquefied by heat — **fus·ibil·i·ty** \ˌfyü-zə-ˈbil-ət-ē\ *n*

fu·si·form \ˈfyü-zə-ˌfȯrm\ *adj* **:** tapering toward each end ⟨*fusiform* swelling of the fingers⟩ [Latin *fusus* "spindle"]

fu·sil \ˈfyü-zəl\ *n* **:** a light musket equipped with a flintlock [French, "steel for striking fire, fusil," derived from Late Latin *focus* "fire," from Latin, "hearth"]

fu·sil·ier *or* **fu·sil·eer** \ˌfyü-zə-ˈliər\ *n* **1 :** a soldier armed with a fusil **2 :** a member of a British regiment formerly armed with fusils

fu·sil·lade \ˈfyü-sə-ˌläd, -zə-, -ˌläd\ *n* **1 :** a number of shots fired simultaneously or in rapid succession **2 :** a spirited outburst especially of criticism

fu·sion \ˈfyü-zhən\ *n* **1 :** the act or process of making fluid by heat **2 :** union by or as if by melting; *esp* **:** a merging of diverse elements into a unified whole **3 :** the union of atomic nuclei to form heavier nuclei resulting in the release of enormous quantities of energy when certain light elements unite

[1]**fuss** \ˈfəs\ *n* **1 a :** needless bustle or excitement **:** COMMOTION **b :** a show of flattering attention ⟨made a big *fuss* over their grandchildren⟩ **2 :** a state of agitation especially over a trivial matter [origin unknown]

[2]**fuss** *vi* **1 a :** to create or be in a state of restless activity; *esp* **:** to shower flattering attentions **b :** to pay undue attention to small details **2 :** to become upset **:** WORRY — **fuss·er** *n*

fuss·budg·et \ˈfəs-ˌbəj-ət\ *n* **:** one who fusses about trifles

fussy \ˈfəs-ē\ *adj* **fuss·i·er; -est 1 :** easily upset **:** IRRITABLE **2 a :** requiring or giving close attention to details ⟨a *fussy* job⟩ **b :** too particular **:** FINICKY ⟨*fussy* about food⟩ — **fuss·i·ly** \ˈfəs-ə-lē\ *adv* — **fuss·i·ness** \ˈfəs-ē-nəs\ *n*

fus·tian \ˈfəs-chən\ *n* **1 :** a strong cotton and linen fabric **2 :** pretentious writing or speech [Medieval French *fusteyne,* from Medieval Latin *fustaneum*] — **fustian** *adj*

fus·tic \ˈfəs-tik\ *n* **:** the wood of a tropical American tree related to the mulberries and yielding a yellow dye; *also* **:** a tree yielding fustic [Medieval French *fustoc,* from Arabic *fustuq,* from Greek *pistakē* "pistachio tree"]

fus·ty \ˈfəs-tē\ *adj* **fus·ti·er; -est 1 :** saturated with dust and stale odors **2 :** rigidly conservative **:** OLD-FASHIONED [Middle English, *foisted, foist* "musty," from *foist* "wine cask," from Medieval French *fust, fuist* "wood, tree trunk, cask," from Medieval Latin *fustis*] — **fus·ti·ly** \-tə-lē\ *adv* — **fus·ti·ness** \-tē-nəs\ *n*

fu·tile \ˈfyüt-l, ˈfyü-ˌtīl\ *adj* **1 :** having no result or effect **:** USELESS ⟨a *futile* struggle⟩ **2 :** UNIMPORTANT, TRIVIAL ⟨*futile* pleasures⟩ [Latin *futilis,* "brittle, pointless"] ***synonyms*** see VAIN — **fu·tile·ly** \-l-lē, -ˌtīl-lē\ *adv* — **fu·tile·ness** *n* — **fu·til·i·ty** \fyü-ˈtil-ət-ē\ *n*

fu·ton \ˈfü-ˌtän\ *n, pl* **futons** *also* **futon :** a usually cotton-filled mattress used on the floor or in a frame as a bed, couch, or chair [Japanese]

[1]**fu·ture** \ˈfyü-chər\ *adj* **1 a :** that is to be ⟨*future* events⟩ **b :** existing after death **2 :** of, relating to, or constituting a verb tense formed in English with *will* and *shall* and expressive of time yet to come **3 :** existing or occurring at a later time ⟨met his *future* wife⟩ [Latin *futurus* "about to be"]

[2]**future** *n* **1 a :** time that is to come ⟨sometime in the *future*⟩ **b :** what is going to happen ⟨predict the *future*⟩ **2 :** expectation of advancement or development ⟨a promising *future*⟩ **3 :** something (as a commodity) bought or sold for delivery at a future time — usually used in plural ⟨grain *futures*⟩ **4 a :** the future tense **b :** a verb form in the future tense

fu·ture·less \-ləs\ *adj* **:** having no prospect of future success or accomplishment ⟨a *futureless* acting career⟩ — **fu·ture·less·ness** *n*

future perfect *adj* **:** of, relating to, or constituting a verb tense formed in English with *will have* and *shall have* and expressing completion of an action by a specified time that is yet to come — **future perfect** *n*

fu·tur·ism \ˈfyü-chə-ˌriz-əm\ *n* **1 :** a movement in art, music, and literature begun in Italy about 1909 and marked especially by an effort to give formal expression to the dynamic energy and movement of mechanical processes **2 :** a point of view that finds meaning or fulfillment in the future rather than in the past or present

fu·tur·ist \ˈfyüch-rəst, -ə-rəst\ *n* **1 :** one who studies and predicts the future especially on the basis of current trends **2 :** one who advocates or practices futurism — **futurist** *adj*

fu·tur·is·tic \ˌfyü-chə-ˈris-tik\ *adj* **:** of or relating to the future or to futurism — **fu·tur·is·ti·cal·ly** \-ti-kə-lē, -klē\ *adv*

fu·tu·ri·ty \fyü-ˈtür-ət-ē, -ˈtyür-, -ˈchür-\ *n, pl* **-ties 1 :** FUTURE 1a **2 :** the quality or state of being future **3** *pl* **:** future events or prospects

fuze *variant of* FUSE

[1]**fuzz** \ˈfəz\ *n* **1 :** fine light particles or fibers (as of down or fluff) **2 :** a blurred effect [probably back-formation from *fuzzy*]

[2]**fuzz** *vb* **1 :** to fly off in or become covered with fluffy particles **2 :** to become or make fuzzy

fuzzy \ˈfəz-ē\ *adj* **fuzz·i·er; -est 1 :** covered with or resembling fuzz **2 :** not clear **:** INDISTINCT ⟨a *fuzzy* picture⟩ **3 :** being, relating to, or causing pleasant and usually sentimental emotions ⟨warm and *fuzzy* feelings⟩ [perhaps from Low German *fussig* "loose, spongy"] — **fuzz·i·ly** \ˈfəz-ə-lē\ *adv* — **fuzz·i·ness** \ˈfəz-ē-nəs\ *n*

-fy \ˌfī\ *vb suffix* **-fied; -fying 1 :** make ⟨beauti*fy*⟩ **:** form into ⟨dandi*fy*⟩ **2 :** invest with the attributes of **:** make similar to ⟨citi*fy*⟩ [Medieval French *-fier,* from Latin *-ficare,* from *-ficus* "-fic"]

fyn·bos \ˈfān-ˌbȯs\ *n* **:** an ecological community of coastal South Africa characterized by a diverse plant life and soil that is acidic and nutrient-poor; *also* **:** the type of plants characteristic of this community [Afrikaans, from *fyn* "fine, delicate" + *bos* "bush"]

G

g \'jē\ *n, pl* **g's** *or* **gs** \'jēz\ *often cap* **1 :** the 7th letter of the English alphabet **2 :** the musical tone G : the 5th note of a C-major scale **3 :** ACCELERATION OF GRAVITY; *also* : a unit of force equal to the force exerted by gravity on a body at rest and used to express the force to which a body is subjected when accelerated ⟨a force of three *G's*⟩ [sense 3 from *gravity*]

G *certification mark* — used to certify that a motion picture is of such a nature that persons of all ages may be allowed admission; compare NC-17, PG, PG-13, R

gab \'gab\ *vi* **gabbed; gab·bing :** to talk idly : CHATTER [probably short for *gabble*] — **gab** *n* — **gab·ber** *n*

gab·ar·dine \'gab-ər-ˌdēn\ *n* **1 :** GABERDINE 1 **2 a :** a firm durable twilled fabric having diagonal ribs **b :** a garment of gabardine [Middle French *gaverdine*]

gab·ble \'gab-əl\ *vb* **gab·bled; gab·bling** \'gab-ling, -ə-ling\ **1 :** to talk fast or foolishly : JABBER **2 :** to utter inarticulate sounds : BABBLE [probably imitative] — **gabble** *n* — **gab·bler** \'gab-lər, -ə-lər\ *n*

gab·bro \'gab-rō\ *n, pl* **gabbros :** a granular igneous rock containing much magnesium and little quartz [Italian] — **gab·bro·ic** \ga-'brō-ik\ *adj*

gab·by \'gab-ē\ *adj* **gab·bi·er; -est :** TALKATIVE, GARRULOUS

gab·er·dine \'gab-ər-ˌdēn\ *n* **1 a :** a long smock worn chiefly by Jews in medieval times **b :** an English laborer's smock **2 :** GABARDINE 2 [Middle French *gaverdine*]

gab·fest \'gab-ˌfest\ *n* **1 :** an informal gathering for general talk **2 :** a long conversation

ga·ble \'gā-bəl\ *n* **:** the triangular part of an outside wall of a building formed by the sides of the roof sloping down from the ridgepole to the eaves; *also* : a similar triangular structure [Medieval French, probably from Medieval Latin *gabulum* "gibbet," of Celtic origin] — **ga·bled** \-bəld\ *adj*

gable roof *n* **:** a roof having two sides sloping from a ridge and forming a gable at each end

1**gad** \'gad\ *vi* **gad·ded; gad·ding :** to be on the go without a specific purpose — usually used with *about* ⟨*gadding* about the city⟩ [Middle English *gadden*]

2**gad** *interj* — used as a mild oath [euphemism for *God*]

gad·about \'gad-ə-ˌbau̇t\ *n* **:** a person who flits about in social activity — **gadabout** *adj*

gad·fly \'gad-ˌflī\ *n* **1 :** any of various flies (as a horsefly or botfly) that bite or harass livestock **2 :** a person who annoys or provokes others especially by persistent criticism [Middle English *gad* "spike," from Old Norse *gaddr*]

gad·get \'gaj-ət\ *n* **:** an often new or unusual practical device ⟨a *gadget* for peeling potatoes⟩ [origin unknown] — **gad·ge·teer** \ˌgaj-ə-'tiər\ *n* — **gad·get·ry** \'gaj-ə-trē\ *n*

gad·o·lin·i·um \ˌgad-l-'in-ē-əm\ *n* **:** a magnetic metallic chemical element occurring in several minerals — see ELEMENT table [Johann *Gadolin*, died 1852, Finnish chemist]

gad·wall \'gad-ˌwȯl\ *n, pl* **gadwalls** *or* **gadwall :** a grayish brown medium-sized duck [origin unknown]

Gael \'gāl\ *n* **1 :** a Scottish Highlander **2 :** a Celtic especially Gaelic-speaking inhabitant of Ireland, Scotland, or the Isle of Man [Scottish Gaelic *Gàidheal* and Irish *Gaedheal*]

Gael·ic \'gā-lik\ *adj* **1 :** of or relating to the Gaels and especially the Celtic Highlanders of Scotland **2 :** of, relating to, or constituting the Goidelic speech of the Celts in Ireland, the Isle of Man, and the Scottish Highlands — **Gaelic** *n*

1**gaff** \'gaf\ *n* **1 a :** a spear or spearhead for taking fish or turtles **b :** a handled hook for holding or lifting heavy fish **c :** a metal spur for a gamecock **2 :** the spar upon which the head of a fore-and-aft sail is extended **3 :** ABUSE **4 :** GAFFE [French *gaffe*, from Occitan *gaf*]

2**gaff** *vt* **:** to strike, take, or handle with a gaff

gaffe \'gaf\ *n* **:** a noticeable blunder especially of manners [French, "gaff, gaffe"]

gaf·fer \'gaf-ər\ *n* **:** an old man [alteration of *godfather*]

1**gag** \'gag\ *vb* **gagged; gag·ging 1 a :** to prevent from speaking or crying out by stopping up the mouth **b :** to prevent from speaking freely **2 a :** to retch or cause to retch **b :** CHOKE 2 **3 :** to be unable to endure something : BALK **4 :** to tell jokes [Middle English *gaggen* "to strangle"]

2**gag** *n* **1 a :** something thrust into the mouth especially to prevent speech or outcry **b :** an official check or restraint on debate or free speech **2 :** JOKE 1a **3 :** PRANK, TRICK

ga·ga \'gä-ˌgä\ *adj* **1 :** CRAZY 2, FOOLISH **2 :** marked by wild enthusiasm : INFATUATED [French, from *gaga* "fool"]

1**gage** \'gāj\ *n* **1 :** a token of defiance; *esp* : a glove or cap cast on the ground as a pledge of combat **2 :** something given as a pledge of performance : SECURITY [Medieval French, of Germanic origin]

2**gage** *variant of* GAUGE

gag·gle \'ga-gəl\ *n* **1 :** FLOCK 1; *esp* : a flock of geese when not in flight **2 :** an unorganized group ⟨a *gaggle* of reporters⟩ [Middle English *gagyll*, from *gagelen* "to cackle"]

gag·man \'gag-ˌman\ *n* **1 :** a writer of jokes **2 :** COMEDIAN 2

gag order *n* **:** a court ruling prohibiting discussion (as by the press) of information relating to a case

gag rule *n* **:** a rule restricting freedom of debate or expression especially in a legislative body

gai·ety *also* **gay·ety** \'gā-ət-ē\ *n, pl* **-ties 1 :** MERRYMAKING 1 **2 :** high spirits **3 :** ELEGANCE, FINERY

gail·lar·dia \gə-'lärd-ē-ə, -'lärd-ə\ *n* **:** any of a genus of American herbs with showy flower heads that are related to the daisies [*Gaillard* de Marentonneau, 18th century French botanist]

gai·ly *also* **gay·ly** \'gā-lē\ *adv* **:** in a merry or lively manner

1**gain** \'gān\ *n* **1 :** resources or advantage acquired or increased : PROFIT ⟨financial *gains*⟩ **2 :** the obtaining of profit or possessions **3 :** an increase in amount, magnitude, or degree ⟨a *gain* in weight⟩ [Medieval French *gaigne, gain*, from *gaaignier* "to till, earn, gain," of Germanic origin]

2**gain** *vb* **1 a :** to get possession of often by effort ⟨*gain* an advantage⟩ **b :** to win in competition or conflict ⟨*gain* a victory⟩ **c :** to get by a natural development or process ⟨*gain* strength⟩ **d :** to arrive at ⟨*gained* the river that night⟩ **2 :** to win to one's side **3 :** to increase in ⟨*gain* momentum⟩ **4 :** to run fast ⟨my watch *gains* a minute a day⟩ **5 :** to get advantage : PROFIT ⟨*gained* from the deal⟩ **6 a :** INCREASE 1 **b :** to improve in health — **gain·er** *n* — **gain ground :** to make progress

gain·ful \'gān-fəl\ *adj* **:** producing gain : PROFITABLE ⟨*gainful* employment⟩ — **gain·ful·ly** \-fə-lē\ *adv* — **gain·ful·ness** *n*

gain·say \gān-'sā\ *vt* **gain·said** \-'sād, -'sed\; **gain·say·ing** \-'sā-ing\ **1 :** to declare untrue : DENY **2 :** to speak against : CONTRADICT [Middle English *gainsayen*, from *gain-* "against" + *sayen* "to say"] — **gain·say·er** *n*

gait \'gāt\ *n* **:** manner of moving on foot ⟨a slow unsteady *gait*⟩; *also* : a particular pattern or style of such movement ⟨the walk, trot, and canter are *gaits* of the horse⟩ [Medieval English *gait, gate* "gate, way"] — **gait·ed** \-əd\ *adj*

gai·ter \'gāt-ər\ *n* **1 :** a cloth or leather leg covering reaching from the instep to above the ankle or to mid-calf or knee **2 a :** an ankle-high shoe with elastic gores in the sides **b :** an overshoe with fabric upper [French *guêtre*]

ga·la \'gā-lə, 'gal-ə\ *n* **:** a festive celebration [Italian, from Middle French *gale* "festivity, pleasure"] — **gala** *adj*

ga·lac·tic \gə-'lak-tik\ *adj* **:** of or relating to a galaxy

ga·lac·tose \gə-'lak-ˌtōs\ *n* **:** a sugar $C_6H_{12}O_6$ less soluble and less sweet than glucose [French, from Greek *galakt-, gala* "milk"]

ga·la·go \gə-'lā-gō, -'läg-ō\ *n, pl* **-gos :** BUSH BABY [perhaps from Wolof (a language of western Africa) *golo* "monkey"]

Ga·la·tians \gə-'lā-shənz\ *n* **:** an argumentative letter of Saint Paul written to the Christians of Galatia and included as a book in the New Testament — see BIBLE table

galavant *variant of* GALLIVANT

ga·lax \'gā-ˌlaks\ *n* **:** an evergreen herb related to the heaths that has shiny leaves used in decorations [New Latin, probably from Greek *galaxias* "Milky Way, galaxy"]

gal·axy \'gal-ək-sē\ *n, pl* **-ax·ies** **1 a** *often cap* : MILKY WAY GALAXY **b** : one of the very large groups of stars and other matter that are found throughout the universe **2** : an assemblage of brilliant or notable persons or things [Late Latin *galaxias,* from Greek, from *galakt-, gala* "milk"]

Word History The system of stars that includes our sun looks, in the night sky, like a broad band of light. We call this band the *Milky Way*. The idea of the whiteness of the Milky Way being similar to that of milk is much older than the English language, however. *Galaxias,* the Greek word for the Milky Way, was derived from the Greek *gala,* "milk." English *galaxy,* derived from Greek *galaxias,* was not used until the 19th century as a term for other star systems as well as ours.

gale \'gāl\ *n* **1** : a strong current of air; *esp* : a wind of from 32 to 63 miles (about 51 to 101 kilometers) per hour **2** : an emotional outburst ⟨*gales* of laughter⟩ [origin unknown]

ga·le·na \gə-'lē-nə\ *n* : a bluish gray mineral PbS with metallic luster consisting of sulfide of lead and constituting the principal ore of lead [Latin, "lead ore"]

[1]**gall** \'gȯl\ *n* **1** : BILE 1 **2 a** : something hard to bear **b** : SPITE **3** : shameless boldness : NERVE [Old English *gealla*]

[2]**gall** *n* **1** : a skin sore (as on a horse's back) caused by chronic irritation **2** : a cause or state of exasperation [Old English *gealla,* from Latin *galla* "gall on a plant"]

[3]**gall** *vb* **1 a** : to fray and wear away by friction : CHAFE **b** : to become sore or worn by rubbing **2** : IRRITATE 1, VEX

[4]**gall** *n* : an abnormal growth of plant tissue usually caused by fungi or insect parasites [Medieval French *galle,* from Latin *galla*]

[1]**gal·lant** \gə-'lant, gə-'länt, 'gal-ənt\ *n* **1** : a fashionable young man **2 a** : LADIES' MAN **b** : SUITOR 3

[2]**gal·lant** \'gal-ənt (*usual in sense 2b*); gə-'lant, gə-'länt (*usual in sense 3*)\ *adj* **1** : showy in dress or bearing : SMART **2 a** : SPLENDID, STATELY ⟨a *gallant* ship⟩ **b** : SPIRITED, BRAVE **c** : CHIVALROUS 3a, NOBLE **3** : polite and attentive to women [Medieval French *galant,* from *galer* "to have a good time," from *gale* "pleasure," of Germanic origin] — **gal·lant·ly** *adv*

gal·lant·ry \'gal-ən-trē\ *n, pl* **-ries** **1** *archaic* : gallant appearance **2 a** : an act of marked courtesy **b** : courteous attention to a woman **3** : notable bravery

gall·blad·der \'gȯl-ˌblad-ər\ *n* : a membranous muscular sac in which bile from the liver is stored

gal·le·on \'gal-ē-ən\ *n* : a heavy square-rigged sailing ship of the 15th to early 18th centuries used for war or commerce especially by the Spanish [Spanish *galeón,* from Medieval French *galion,* from *galie* "galley"]

gal·lery \'gal-rē, -ə-rē\ *n, pl* **gal·ler·ies** **1 a** : a roofed walkway : COLONNADE **b** : an outdoor balcony **c** *South & Midland* : PORCH, VERANDA **d** : a structure projecting from one or more interior walls of an auditorium to seat additional people; *esp* : the highest such structure in a theater or the people who sit there **e** : a body of spectators at a sporting event (as a tennis or golf match) **2 a** : a long narrow room, hall, or passage; *esp* : one having windows along one side **b** : a subterranean passageway (as in a mine) **c** : a passage (as in earth or wood) made by an animal and especially an insect **3 a** : a room or building devoted to the exhibition of works of art **b** : an institution or business exhibiting or dealing in works of art **4** : a photographer's studio [Medieval Latin *galeria*] — **gal·ler·ied** \-rēd\ *adj*

gal·ley \'gal-ē\ *n, pl* **galleys** **1** : a large low ship propelled by oars and sails and used in ancient times and from the Middle Ages to the 19th century chiefly in the Mediterranean Sea **2** : the kitchen of a ship or airplane **3 a** : an oblong tray with upright sides to hold printer's type that has been set **b** : a proof from type in a galley [Medieval French *galie, galee,* derived from Middle Greek *galea*]

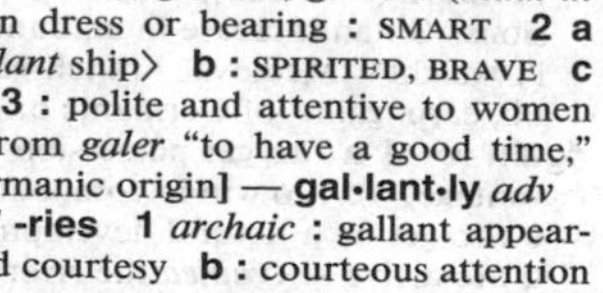

galley 1

gall·fly \'gȯl-ˌflī\ *n* : an insect (as a gall wasp) that deposits its eggs in plants and causes galls in which the larvae feed

Gal·lic \'gal-ik\ *adj* : of or relating to Gaul or France [Latin *Gallicus,* from *Gallia* "Gaul"]

gal·li·cism \'gal-ə-ˌsiz-əm\ *n, often cap* : a characteristic French idiom, expression, or trait

gal·li·gas·kins \ˌgal-i-'gas-kənz\ *n pl* : loose wide breeches worn in the 16th and 17th centuries [probably from Middle French *garguesques,* from Spanish *gregüescos,* from *griego* "Greek"]

gal·li·na·ceous \ˌgal-ə-'nā-shəs\ *adj* : of or relating to an order (Galliformes) of heavy-bodied largely land-dwelling birds including the pheasants, turkeys, grouse, and the common domestic chicken [Latin *gallinaceus* "of domestic fowl," from *gallina* "hen," from *gallus* "cock"]

gall·ing \'gȯ-ling\ *adj* : very irritating : VEXING

gal·li·nip·per \'gal-ə-ˌnip-ər\ *n* : any of several insects (as a large mosquito or crane fly) [origin unknown]

gal·li·nule \'gal-ə-ˌnül, -ˌnyül\ *n* : any of several aquatic birds related to the rails and having a platelike shield on the front of the head [Latin *gallinula* "pullet," from *gallina* "hen"]

gal·li·um \'gal-ē-əm\ *n* : a bluish white metallic element that is used especially in semiconductors — see ELEMENT table [Latin *gallus* "cock" (intended as translation of Paul *Lecoq* de Boisbaudran, died 1912, French chemist)]

gal·li·vant *also* **gal·a·vant** \'gal-ə-ˌvant\ *vi* : to travel or roam about for pleasure [perhaps derived from *gallant*]

gal·lon \'gal-ən\ *n* — see MEASURE table [Middle English *galon,* a liquid measure, from Medieval French *galun, jalun,* derived from Medieval Latin *galeta* "pail," a liquid measure]

gal·lon·age \'gal-ə-nij\ *n* : amount in gallons

[1]**gal·lop** \'gal-əp\ *n* **1** : a springing gait of a four-footed animal in which all four feet are off the ground at one time once in each stride; *esp* : a fast natural 3-beat or 4-beat gait of the horse — compare CANTER **2** : a ride or run at a gallop **3** : a rapid or hasty progression or pace [Middle French *galop*]

[2]**gallop** *vb* **1** : to move or ride at a gallop **2** : to run fast **3** : to cause to gallop — **gal·lop·er** *n*

gal·lows \'gal-ōz\ *n, pl* **gallows** *or* **gal·lows·es** **1** : a frame usually of two upright posts and a crosspiece from which criminals are hanged — called also *gallows tree* **2** : the punishment of hanging ⟨was sentenced to the *gallows*⟩ [Middle English *galwes,* pl. of *galwe,* from Old English *galga, gealga*]

gall·stone \'gȯl-ˌstōn\ *n* : a hard mass (as of cholesterol) formed in the gallbladder or bile passages

gall wasp *n* : a wasp that is a gallfly

ga·loot \gə-'lüt\ *n, slang* : FELLOW 4; *esp* : a person who is odd or foolish [origin unknown]

ga·lore \gə-'lōr, -'lȯr\ *adj* : ABUNDANT, PLENTIFUL — used after the word it modifies ⟨bargains *galore*⟩ [Irish Gaelic *go leor* "enough"]

ga·losh \gə-'läsh\ *n* : a high overshoe worn especially in snow and slush [Medieval French *galoche,* a kind of heavy-soled shoe]

ga·lumph \gə-'ləmf, -'ləmpf\ *vb* : to move in a loud and clumsy way [perhaps alteration of *gallop*]

gal·van·ic \gal-'van-ik\ *adj* **1** : of, relating to, or producing a direct current of electricity ⟨a *galvanic* cell⟩ **2** : having an electric effect : intensely exciting ⟨a *galvanic* personality⟩ [Luigi *Galvani,* died 1798, Italian physician and physicist] — **gal·van·i·cal·ly** \-i-kə-lē, -klē\ *adv*

gal·va·nize \'gal-və-ˌnīz\ *vt* **1 a** : to subject to the action of an electric current **b** : to stimulate or excite by or as if by an electric shock ⟨an issue that *galvanized* the public⟩ **2** : to coat (as iron) with zinc for protection — **gal·va·ni·za·tion** \ˌgal-və-nə-'zā-shən\ *n*

gal·va·nom·e·ter \ˌgal-və-'näm-ət-ər\ *n* : an instrument for detecting or measuring a small electric current by movements of a magnetic needle or of a coil in a magnetic field — **gal·va·no·met·ric** \ˌgal-və-nō-'me-trik\ *adj*

gal·vano·scope \gal-'van-ə-ˌskōp\ *n* : an instrument for detecting the presence and direction of an electric current by the deflection of a magnetic needle

gam·bit \'gam-bət\ *n* **1** : a chess opening in which a player risks one or more minor pieces to gain an advantage in position **2** : a carefully thought-out move : STRATAGEM [Italian *gambetto,* literally, "act of tripping someone," from *gamba* "leg," from Late Latin *gamba, camba,* from Greek *kampē* "bend"]

[1]**gam·ble** \'gam-bəl\ *vb* **gam·bled; gam·bling** \-bə-ling, -bling\ **1 a** : to play a game for money or property **b** : to bet on an uncertain outcome **2** : to bet something on the chance of gain : take a chance **3** : RISK 1, HAZARD [probably derived from obsolete English *gamen* "to play," from *game*] — **gam·bler** \-blər\ *n*

²gamble *n* **1 :** a risky undertaking **2 :** a betting on a game of chance

gam·boge \gam-ˈbōj, -ˈbüzh\ *n* **:** an orange to brown gum resin from southeast Asian trees that is used as a yellow pigment and purgative [derived from Portuguese *Camboja* "Cambodia"]

gam·bol \ˈgam-bəl\ *vi* **-boled** *or* **-bolled; -bol·ing** *or* **-bol·ling** \-bə-ling, -bling\ **:** to skip about in play **:** FROLIC [Middle French *gambade* "spring of a horse, gambol"] — **gambol** *n*

gam·brel roof \ˈgam-brəl-\ *n* **:** a roof with a lower steeper slope and an upper less steep one on each of its two sides [perhaps from Medieval French dialect *gamberel* "stick for suspending slaughtered animals," from *gambe* "leg," from Late Latin *gamba*]

gam·bu·sia \gam-ˈbyü-zhē-ə, -zhə\ *n* **:** any of several topminnows including some used to exterminate mosquito larvae in warm fresh waters [American Spanish *gambusino*]

¹game \ˈgām\ *n* **1 a :** activity engaged in for amusement **b :** FUN 1, SPORT ⟨made *game* of a nervous player⟩ **c :** the equipment for a game **2 a :** a strategy for gaining an end **b :** a line of work ⟨the newspaper *game*⟩ **3 a (1) :** a physical or mental contest following set rules **(2) :** a division of a larger contest **(3) :** the number of points necessary to win **(4) :** the manner of playing in a contest **b :** an activity that involves contest, rivalry, or struggle ⟨the dating *game*⟩ **c :** an activity of acting out a situation (as war) for training or testing **4 a (1) :** animals pursued or taken in hunting especially for sport or food **(2) :** the flesh of game animals **b :** an object of ridicule or attack — often used in the phrase *fair game* [Old English *gamen*]

²game *vb* **:** to play for a stake **:** GAMBLE

³game *adj* **1 a :** having a resolute unyielding spirit ⟨*game* to the end⟩ **b :** willing or ready to proceed ⟨were *game* for anything⟩ **2 :** of or relating to game ⟨*game* laws⟩ ⟨a *game* bird⟩ — **game·ly** *adv* — **game·ness** *n*

⁴game *adj* **:** LAME ⟨a *game* leg⟩

game·cock \ˈgām-ˌkäk\ *n* **:** a rooster trained for fighting

game fish *n* **1 :** a fish of the family that includes salmons, trouts, and chars **2 :** a fish regularly sought by anglers for sport

game fowl *n* **:** a domestic fowl of a strain developed for the production of fighting cocks

game·keep·er \ˈgām-ˌkē-pər\ *n* **:** a person in charge of the breeding and protection of game animals or birds on a private preserve

game of chance : a game (as a dice game) in which chance rather than skill determines the outcome

game plan *n* **:** GAME 2a

gam·er \ˈgā-mər\ *n* **1 :** a player who is determined and eager **2 :** a person who plays games (as computer or video games)

game show *n* **:** a television program on which contestants compete for prizes in a game (as a quiz)

game·ster \ˈgām-stər\ *n* **:** a person who plays games; *esp* **:** GAMBLER

gam·etan·gi·um \ˌgam-ə-ˈtan-jē-əm\ *n, pl* **-gia** \-jē-ə\ **:** a cell or organ (as of an alga, fern, or fungus) in which gametes are developed [*gamete* + Greek *angeion* "vessel"]

ga·mete \gə-ˈmēt, ˈgam-ˌēt\ *n* **:** a mature usually haploid germ cell capable of developing into a new individual upon uniting with another such cell of the opposite sex [Greek *gametēs* "husband," from *gamein* "to marry," from *gamos* "marriage"] — **ga·met·ic** \gə-ˈmet-ik\ *adj* — **ga·met·i·cal·ly** \-ˈmet-i-kə-lē, -klē\ *adv*

ga·me·to·cyte \gə-ˈmēt-ə-ˌsīt\ *n* **:** a cell that divides to produce gametes

ga·me·to·gen·e·sis \gə-ˌmēt-ə-ˈjen-ə-səs\ *n* **:** the production of gametes

ga·me·to·phyte \gə-ˈmēt-ə-ˌfīt\ *n* **:** the haploid individual or generation of a plant or fungus with alternating sexual and asexual generations that produces the gametes from which the asexual sporophyte develops — **ga·me·to·phyt·ic** \-ˌmēt-ə-ˈfit-ik\ *adj*

gam·in \ˈgam-ən\ *n* **1 :** a boy who hangs out on the streets **:** URCHIN **2 :** GAMINE 2 [French]

ga·mine \ga-ˈmēn\ *n* **1 :** a girl who hangs out on the streets **2 :** a small playfully mischievous girl [French, feminine of *gamin*]

gam·ing \ˈgā-ming\ *n* **1 :** the practice of gambling **2 :** the acting out of a situation (as war) for training or testing **3 :** the playing of video games

gam·ma \ˈgam-ə\ *n* **:** the 3rd letter of the Greek alphabet — Γ or γ

gamma globulin *n* **1 :** a protein part of blood plasma rich in antibodies **2 :** a solution of gamma globulin made from pooled human blood and given to provide immunity against some infectious disease (as measles and German measles)

gamma radiation *n* **:** radiation composed of gamma rays

gamma ray *n* **:** a photon similar to an X-ray but of shorter wavelength and higher energy that is emitted especially by various radioactive atomic nuclei

gam·mer \ˈgam-ər\ *n* **:** an old woman [alteration of *godmother*]

gam·ut \ˈgam-ət\ *n* **1 :** the whole series of recognized musical notes **2 :** an entire range or series ⟨ran the *gamut* from praise to criticism⟩ [Medieval Latin *gamma*, lowest note of a medieval musical scale (from Late Latin, 3rd letter of the Greek alphabet) + *ut*, lowest note of each group of six notes in the scale]

Word History In the 11th century, Guido d'Arezzo, a musician and former Benedictine monk, devised a system of musical notation that was later adopted throughout Europe. Guido's system consisted of groups of six notes, which he named *ut, re, mi, fa, sol,* and *la.* Guido called the first line of the bass staff *gamma,* and we can assume that *gamma ut* was the term his followers used for the note falling on this line, that is, the first note of the lowest group of six. This was later contracted to *gamut* and used for the whole scale as well as the lowest note. The term was further generalized to mean the whole range of a voice or instrument. Eventually *gamut* came to be used for an entire range of any sort.

gamy \ˈgā-mē\ *adj* **gam·i·er; -est 1 :** COURAGEOUS, PLUCKY **2 :** having the flavor of game especially when slightly spoiled ⟨*gamy* meat⟩ — **gam·i·ly** \ˈgā-mə-lē\ *adv* — **gam·i·ness** \ˈgā-mē-nəs\ *n*

-g·a·my \g-ə-mē\ *n combining form, pl* **-gamies 1 :** marriage ⟨exo*gamy*⟩ **2 :** union for propagation or reproduction ⟨syn*gamy*⟩ [Greek *-gamia,* from *gamos* "marriage"]

Gan·da \ˈgan-də\ *n, pl* **Ganda** *or* **Gandas 1 :** a member of a Bantu-speaking people of Uganda **2 :** the Bantu language of the Ganda people

¹gan·der \ˈgan-dər\ *n* **:** a male goose [Old English *gandra*]

²gander *n* **:** a usually appraising look ⟨take a *gander*⟩ [probably from ¹*gander*; from the outstretched neck of a person craning to look at something]

gan·dy dancer \ˈgan-dē-\ *n* **:** a laborer employed to maintain a section of railroad track [origin unknown]

¹gang \ˈgang\ *n* **1 :** a group of persons working or going about together ⟨a *gang* of laborers⟩ ⟨a *gang* of children playing⟩ **2 :** a group of persons working together for unlawful or antisocial purposes ⟨a *gang* of thieves⟩ **3 :** two or more similar implements or devices arranged to work together ⟨a *gang* of saws⟩ **4 :** a group of friends ⟨invited the *gang* over⟩ [Middle English, "journey, set of things or persons," from Old English, "act of going, journey," from *gangan* "to go"]

²gang *vi* **:** to form into or move or act as a gang

³gang *vi, Scottish* **:** GO, WALK [Old English *gangan*]

gang·bust·er \ˈgang-ˌbəs-tər\ *n* **:** one engaged in breaking up criminal gangs — **like gangbusters :** with great force, speed, or success ⟨came on *like gangbusters*⟩

gang·land \ˈgang-ˌland\ *n* **:** the world of organized crime

gan·gling \ˈgang-gling, -glən\ *adj* **:** LANKY, SPINDLY [perhaps from Scottish *gangrel* "vagrant, lanky person"]

gan·gli·on \ˈgang-glē-ən\ *n, pl* **-glia** \-glē-ə\ *also* **-gli·ons :** a mass of nerve tissue lying outside the brain or spinal cord and containing neurons; *also* **:** NUCLEUS c [Greek] — **gan·gli·on·at·ed** \ˈgang-glē-ə-ˌnāt-əd\ *adj* — **gan·gli·on·ic** \ˌgang-glē-ˈän-ik\ *adj*

gan·gly \ˈgang-glē\ *adj* **gan·gli·er; -est :** LANKY, GANGLING

gang·plank \ˈgang-ˌplangk\ *n* **:** a movable bridge used in boarding or leaving a ship at a pier [English dialect *gang* "passage, journey"]

gang·plow \-ˌplau̇\ *n* **:** a plow designed to turn two or more furrows at one time

¹gan·grene \ˈgang-ˌgrēn, gang-ˈ, ˈgan-ˌ, gan-ˈ\ *n* **:** local death of soft tissues due to loss of blood supply [Latin *gangraena,* from Greek *gangraina*] — **gan·gre·nous** \ˈgang-grə-nəs\ *adj*

²gangrene *vb* **:** to make or become gangrenous

gang·ster \ˈgang-stər\ *n* : a member of a gang of criminals — **gang·ster·ism** \-stə-ˌriz-əm\ *n*

gangue \ˈgang\ *n* : the rock or earth in which valuable metals or minerals occur [French, from German *gang* "vein of metal"]

gang up *vi* : to combine for a specific and often hostile purpose — often used with *on*

gang·way \ˈgang-ˌwā\ *n* **1 :** a passage into, through, or out of an enclosed place **2 :** GANGPLANK **3 :** a clear passage through a crowd — often used as an interjection ⟨*Gangway!* Coming through!⟩

gan·net \ˈgan-ət\ *n, pl* **gannets** *also* **gannet** : any of several large fish-eating seabirds that remain at sea for long periods and breed chiefly on offshore islands [Old English *ganot*]

gantlet *variant of* GAUNTLET

gan·try \ˈgan-trē\ *n, pl* **gantries 1 :** a platform made to carry a traveling crane and supported by towers or side frames running on parallel tracks; *also* **:** a movable structure with platforms at different levels used for erecting and servicing rockets before launching **2 :** a structure spanning several railroad tracks and displaying signals for each [from Medieval French dialect *gantier* "frame for supporting barrels," from Latin *cantherius* "trellis"]

gaol, gaol·er *chiefly British variant of* JAIL, JAILER

gap \ˈgap\ *n* **1 :** a break in a barrier **2 a :** a mountain pass **b :** RAVINE **3 :** a break in continuity : a blank space or separation ⟨a *gap* in her story⟩ ⟨a *gap* where the tooth had been⟩ **4 :** a wide difference (as in amount, character, or attitude) ⟨a wage *gap*⟩ [Old Norse, "chasm, hole"] — **gap** *vb*

[1]**gape** \ˈgāp\ *vi* **1 a :** to open the mouth wide **b :** to open or part widely **2 :** to stare openmouthed **3 :** YAWN 2 [Old Norse *gapa*] — **gap·er** *n* — **gap·ing·ly** *adv*

[2]**gape** *n* **1 :** an act of gaping **2 :** an unfilled space or extent **3 :** the line along which the mandibles of a bird close **4** *pl* **:** a disease of young birds in which nematode worms invade and irritate the trachea

gap junction *n* : a specialized area of contact between adjacent cells that allows for intercellular communication and transfer of substances

gar \ˈgär\ *n* : any of various fishes with a long body like that of a pike and long narrow jaws; *esp* : any of several predatory North American freshwater fishes with edible but tough flesh [short for *garfish*]

[1]**ga·rage** \gə-ˈräzh, -ˈräj\ *n* : a building where automobiles are housed or repaired [French] — **ga·rage·man** \-ˌman\ *n*

[2]**garage** *vt* : to keep or put in a garage

garage sale *n* : a sale of used household or personal articles held in the seller's own yard

[1]**garb** \ˈgärb\ *n* **1 :** a style of clothing **2 :** outward form : APPEARANCE [Middle French *garbe* "grace," from Italian *garbo*]

[2]**garb** *vt* : CLOTHE 1a, ARRAY

gar·bage \ˈgär-bij\ *n* **1 :** discarded or useless material **2 :** food waste [Middle English, "animal entrails"]

gar·bage·man \-ˌman\ *n* : a person who collects and hauls away garbage

gar·ban·zo \gär-ˈbän-zō\ *n, pl* **-zos :** CHICKPEA — called also *garbanzo bean*

gar·ble \ˈgär-bəl\ *vt* **gar·bled; gar·bling** \-bə-ling, -bling\ : to distort the meaning or sound of ⟨*garble* a story⟩ ⟨*garble* words⟩ [Middle English *garbelen* "to cull," from Italian *garbellare* "to sift," from Arabic *gharbala,* derived from Late Latin *cribellum* "sieve"] — **gar·bler** \-bə-lər, -blər\ *n*

gar·çon \gär-ˈsō^{n}\ *n, pl* **garçons** \-ˈsō^{n}, -ˈsō^{n}z\ : WAITER 1 [French, "boy, servant"]

[1]**gar·den** \ˈgärd-n\ *n* **1 :** a plot of ground where herbs, fruits, flowers, or vegetables are grown **2 a :** a public recreation area or park usually ornamented with plants and trees ⟨a botanical *garden*⟩ **b :** an open-air eating or drinking place [Medieval French *gardin, jardin,* of Germanic origin]

[2]**garden** *vb* **gar·dened; gar·den·ing** \ˈgärd-ning, -n-ing\ **1 :** to lay out or work in a garden **2 :** to make into a garden — **gar·den·er** \ˈgärd-nər, -n-ər\ *n*

[3]**garden** *adj* **1 :** of, relating to, used in, or frequenting gardens **2 :** of a kind grown under cultivation especially in the open ⟨*garden* plants⟩ **3 :** commonly found : GARDEN-VARIETY

garden heliotrope *n* : a tall Old World valerian widely grown for its fragrant tiny flowers and for its roots which yield the drug valerian

gar·de·nia \gär-ˈdē-nyə\ *n* : any of various Old World tropical trees and shrubs with leathery leaves and fragrant white or yellow flowers; *also* : one of the flowers [Alexander *Garden,* died 1791, Scottish naturalist]

garden–variety *adj* : not unusual : ORDINARY ⟨not the flu, just a *garden-variety* cold⟩

gar·fish \ˈgär-ˌfish\ *n* : GAR [Middle English *garfysshe*]

gar·gan·tu·an \gär-ˈganch-wən, -ə-wən\ *adj, often cap* : tremendous in size, degree, or volume : GIGANTIC [*Gargantua,* gigantic king in the novel *Gargantua* by Rabelais]

[1]**gar·gle** \ˈgär-gəl\ *vb* **gar·gled; gar·gling** \-gə-ling, -gling\ : to rinse the mouth or throat with a liquid kept in motion by air forced through it from the lungs especially for cleansing or disinfection [Middle French *gargouiller*]

[2]**gargle** *n* **1 :** a liquid used in gargling **2 :** a gargling sound

gar·goyle \ˈgär-ˌgȯil\ *n* : a spout in the form of a grotesque human or animal figure projecting from a roof gutter to throw rainwater away from a building [Medieval French *gargouille*] — **gar·goyled** \-ˌgȯild\ *adj*

gar·ish \ˈgaər-ish, ˈgeər-\ *adj* **1 a :** excessively vivid ⟨*garish* colors⟩ **b :** too bright ⟨*garish* lighting⟩ **2 :** tastelessly showy ⟨a *garish* display of wealth⟩ [origin unknown] ***synonyms*** see GAUDY — **gar·ish·ly** *adv* — **gar·ish·ness** *n*

[1]**gar·land** \ˈgär-lənd\ *n* : a wreath or rope of leaves or flowers or of other material [Medieval French *garlande*]

[2]**garland** *vt* : to form into or deck with a garland

gar·lic \ˈgär-lik\ *n* : a European bulbous herb related to the onion and widely grown for its pungent compound bulbs used in cooking; *also* : one of the bulbs [Old English *gārlēac,* from *gār* "spear" + *lēac* "leek"] — **gar·licky** \-li-kē\ *adj*

[1]**gar·ment** \ˈgär-mənt\ *n* : an article of clothing [Medieval French *garnement,* from *garnir* "to equip"]

[2]**garment** *vt* : to clothe with or as if with a garment

garment bag *n* : a bag used by travelers that folds in half and has a center handle for easy carrying

gar·ner \ˈgär-nər\ *vt* **1 :** to gather into storage **2 a :** to acquire by effort : EARN ⟨*garnered* financial support⟩ **b :** ACCUMULATE, COLLECT ⟨*garnered* many souvenirs on their travels⟩

gar·net \ˈgär-nət\ *n* **1 :** a brittle and more or less transparent usually red silicate mineral that occurs mainly in crystals and is used as a semiprecious stone and as an abrasive **2 :** a deep red color [Medieval French *gernete,* from *gernet* "dark red (like a pomegranate)," from *pomme grenate* "pomegranate"]

garnet paper *n* : a paper that has crushed garnet glued on one side and is used for smoothing and polishing

[1]**gar·nish** \ˈgär-nish\ *vt* **1 :** DECORATE 1, EMBELLISH **2 :** to add decorative or savory touches to (food) **3 :** to equip with accessories **4 :** GARNISHEE [Medieval French *garniss-,* stem of *garnir* "to warn, equip, garnish," of Germanic origin]

[2]**garnish** *n* **1 :** ORNAMENT 1a, EMBELLISHMENT **2 :** something (as parsley) used to garnish food or drink

gar·nish·ee \ˌgär-nə-ˈshē\ *vt* **-eed; -ee·ing :** to take (as a debtor's wages) by legal authority

gar·nish·ment \ˈgär-nish-mənt\ *n* **1 :** GARNISH **2 :** a legal warning to a party holding property of a debtor to give it to a creditor; *also* : the attachment of such property (as a bank account or pending wages) to satisfy a creditor

gar·ni·ture \ˈgär-ni-chər, -nə-ˌchür\ *n* : a decorative accessory : EMBELLISHMENT [Medieval French, "equipment," from *garnesture,* from *garnir* "to equip, garnish"]

gar·ret \ˈgar-ət\ *n* : a room or unfinished part of a house just under the roof [Medieval French *garite* "watchtower," from *garir* "to protect"]

[1]**gar·ri·son** \ˈgar-ə-sən\ *n* **1 :** a military post; *esp* : a permanent military installation **2 :** the troops stationed at a garrison [Medieval French *garisun* "protection," from *garir* "to protect," of Germanic origin]

[2]**garrison** *vt* **1 :** to station troops in ⟨*garrisoned* the town⟩ **2 :** to assign as a garrison

garrison house *n* **1 :** a house fortified against attack **2 :** a house having the second story overhanging the first in the front

[1]**gar·rote** *or* **ga·rotte** \gə-ˈrät, -ˈrōt; ˈgar-ət\ *n* **1 a :** a method of execution by strangling **b :** the apparatus used **2 :** an implement (as a wire with a handle at each end) for strangling [Spanish *garrote*]

[2]**garrote** *or* **garotte** *vt* : to strangle with or as if with a garrote — **gar·rot·er** *n*

gar·ru·lous \ˈgar-ə-ləs\ *adj* **1 :** pointlessly or annoyingly talkative **2 :** WORDY [Latin *garrulus,* from *garrire* "to chatter"] ***synonyms*** see TALKATIVE — **gar·ru·li·ty** \gə-ˈrü-lət-ē\ *n* — **gar·ru·lous·ly** \ˈgar-ə-ləs-lē\ *adv* — **gar·ru·lous·ness** *n*

¹gar·ter \ˈgärt-ər\ *n* **:** a band or strap worn to hold up a stocking or sock [Medieval French *gareter,* from *garet* "thigh, shank," of Celtic origin]

²garter *vt* **:** to support with or as if with a garter

garter snake *n* **:** any of numerous harmless viviparous American snakes with stripes along the back

¹gas \ˈgas\ *n, pl* **gas·es** *also* **gas·ses** **1 :** a fluid (as air) that has neither independent shape nor volume but tends to expand indefinitely **2 a :** a gas or gaseous mixture used for fuel; *esp* **:** NATURAL GAS **b :** a gaseous product of digestion **c :** a gas (as nitrous oxide) or gaseous mixture used to produce anesthesia **d :** a substance (as tear gas or mustard gas) that can be used to produce a poisonous, asphyxiating, or irritant atmosphere **3 :** empty talk **4 a :** GASOLINE **b :** the accelerator pedal of an automobile ‹take your foot off the *gas* and apply the brakes› [New Latin, alteration of Latin *chaos* "space, chaos"]

²gas *vb* **gassed; gas·sing** **1 a :** to treat chemically with gas **b :** to poison with gas **2 :** to supply with gas or especially gasoline ‹*gas* up the car› **3 :** to talk idly

gas chamber *n* **:** a room in which people are executed by poison gas

gas·con \ˈgas-kən\ *n* **1** *cap* **:** a native of Gascony **2 :** a boastful swaggering person — **Gascon** *adj*

gas·con·ade \ˌgas-kə-ˈnād\ *n* **:** arrogant boastful talk [French *gasconnade,* from *gasconner* "to boast," from *gascon* "gascon, boaster"] — **gasconade** *vi*

gas·eous \ˈgas-ē-əs, ˈgash-əs\ *adj* **1 :** having the form of or being gas; *also* **:** of or relating to gas **2 :** lacking substance or solidity

gas fitter *n* **:** a worker who installs or repairs gas pipes and appliances

gas gangrene *n* **:** progressive gangrene marked by gas in the dead and dying tissue and caused by toxin-producing bacteria

gas–guz·zler \ˈgas-ˈgəz-lər, -ˈgəz-ə-\ *n* **:** a usually large automobile that gets relatively poor mileage — **gas–guz·zling** \-liŋ\ *adj*

¹gash \ˈgash\ *n* **1 :** a deep long cut in flesh **2 :** a deep narrow depression or cut ‹a *gash* through the forest› ‹a *gash* in the hull of the ship›

²gash *vb* **:** to make a long deep gash in **:** CUT [Medieval French *garser* "to nip, scratch," derived from Greek *charassein* "to scratch, engrave"]

gas·ify \ˈgas-ə-ˌfī\ *vb* **-fied; -fy·ing** **1 :** to convert into gas **2 :** to become gaseous — **gas·ifi·ca·tion** \ˌgas-ə-fə-ˈkā-shən\ *n*

gas·ket \ˈgas-kət\ *n* **:** a material (as rubber) or a part used to make a joint leakproof [probably from French *garcette*]

gas·light \ˈgas-ˌlīt\ *n* **1 :** light made by burning a gas (as coal gas) **2 a :** a gas flame **b :** a gas lighting fixture — **gas·light·ing** \-iŋ\ *n* — **gas·lit** \-ˌlit\ *adj*

gas mask *n* **:** a mask connected to a chemical air filter and used to protect the face and lungs against harmful gases

gas·o·gene \ˈgas-ə-ˌjēn\ *or* **gaz·o·gene** \ˈgaz-\ *n* **1 :** a portable apparatus for carbonating liquids **2 :** an apparatus carried by a vehicle to produce gas for fuel by partial burning of charcoal or wood [French *gazogène,* from *gaz* "gas" + *-o-* + *-gène* "-gen"]

gas·o·hol \ˈgas-ə-ˌhȯl\ *n* **:** a fuel consisting of 10 percent ethanol and 90 percent gasoline [blend of *gasoline* and *alcohol*]

gas·o·line \ˈgas-ə-ˌlēn, ˌgas-ə-ˈ\ *n* **:** a flammable liquid that evaporates easily, consists of a mixture of hydrocarbons produced by blending products from natural gas and petroleum, and is used especially as a fuel for engines [*gas* + *-ol* + *-ine*]

gasp \ˈgasp\ *vb* **1 :** to draw in a breath sharply with shock or other emotion **2 :** to breathe laboriously **:** PANT **3 :** to utter in a gasping manner [Middle English *gaspen*] — **gasp** *n*

gas station *n* **:** a retail station for servicing motor vehicles especially with gasoline and oil

gas·sy \ˈgas-ē\ *adj* **gas·si·er; -est** **1 :** full of or containing gas **2 :** having the characteristics of gas **3 :** FLATULENT 1a — **gas·si·ness** *n*

gastr- *or* **gastro-** *also* **gastri-** *combining form* **1 :** belly **:** stomach ‹*gastr*itis› **2 :** gastric and ‹*gastro*intestinal› [Greek *gastr-, gastēr*]

gas·tric \ˈgas-trik\ *adj* **:** of, relating to, or located near the stomach ‹*gastric* ulcers›

gastric gland *n* **:** a gland secreting gastric juice

gastric juice *n* **:** a watery acid digestive fluid secreted by glands in the walls of the stomach

gas·trin \ˈgas-trən\ *n* **:** a hormone that induces secretion of gastric juice

gas·tri·tis \ga-ˈstrīt-əs\ *n* **:** inflammation of the stomach and especially of its mucous membrane

gas·troc·ne·mi·us \ˌgas-träk-ˈnē-mē-əs, -trək-\ *n* **:** the largest muscle of the calf of the leg that points the toe and flexes the leg below the knee [Greek *gastroknēmē* "calf of the leg," from *gastēr* "belly" + *knēmē* "shank"]

gas·tro·in·tes·ti·nal \ˌgas-trō-in-ˈtes-tən-l, -ˈtes-nəl\ *adj* **:** of, relating to, or including both stomach and intestine

gas·tron·o·my \ga-ˈsträn-ə-mē\ *n* **:** the art of appreciating fine food [French *gastronomie,* from Greek *gastronomia,* from *gastēr* "belly" + *nomos* "law"] — **gas·tro·nom·ic** \ˌgas-trə-ˈnäm-ik\ *adj* — **gas·tro·nom·i·cal** \-ˈnäm-i-kəl\ *adj*

gas·tro·pod \ˈgas-trə-ˌpäd\ *n* **:** any of a large class (Gastropoda) of mollusks (as snails) having a muscular ventral foot and usually a univalve shell and a distinct head bearing sensory organs — **gastropod** *adj*

gas·tro·trich \ˈgas-trə-ˌtrik\ *n* **:** any of a small group (Gastrotricha) of minute aquatic animals that glide by means of cilia on the lower surface of the body [derived from Greek *gastēr* "belly" + *trich-, thrix* "hair"]

gas·tro·vas·cu·lar \ˌgas-trō-ˈvas-kyə-lər\ *adj* **:** functioning in both digestion and circulation ‹the *gastrovascular* cavity of a starfish›

gas·tru·la \ˈgas-trə-lə\ *n, pl* **-las** *or* **-lae** \-ˌlē, -ˌlī\ **:** a cup-shaped 3-layered early embryo formed from the blastula by the movement of layers of cells to establish the ectoderm, mesoderm, and endoderm [New Latin, from *gastr-*] — **gas·tru·lar** \-lər\ *adj*

gas·tru·late \-ˌlāt\ *vi* **:** to become or form a gastrula — **gas·tru·la·tion** \ˌgas-trə-ˈlā-shən\ *n*

gas turbine *n* **:** an engine in which expanding gases from the combustion chamber drive the blades of a turbine

gas·works \ˈgas-ˌwərks\ *n pl* **:** a plant for manufacturing gas

¹gat \gat, ˈgat\ *archaic past of* GET

²gat \ˈgat\ *n, slang* **:** HANDGUN [short for *Gatling gun*]

gate \ˈgāt\ *n* **1 :** an opening in a wall or fence **2 :** a city or castle entrance often with towers or other defensive structures **3 :** the frame or door that closes a gate **4 :** a means of entrance or exit **5 :** a door, valve, or other device for controlling the passage especially of fluid **6 :** the total admission receipts or the number of spectators at a sports event **7** *slang* **:** DISMISSAL ‹got the *gate* for loafing› [Old English *geat*]

gate–crash·er \ˈgāt-ˌkrash-ər\ *n* **:** one who enters without paying admission or attends without invitation — **gate–crash** *vb*

gate·keep·er \-ˌkē-pər\ *n* **:** a person who tends or guards a gate

gate·leg table \ˈgāt-ˈleg-\ *n* **:** a table with drop leaves supported by movable paired legs

gate·post \ˈgāt-ˌpōst\ *n* **:** the post to which a gate is hung or the one against which it closes

gate·way \-ˌwā\ *n* **1 :** an opening for a gate in a wall or fence **2 :** a passage into or out of a place or state ‹Gibraltar is the *gateway* to the Mediterranean› ‹knowledge is the *gateway* to wisdom›

¹gath·er \ˈga*th*-ər, ˈge*th*-\ *vb* **gath·ered; gath·er·ing** \ˈga*th*-riŋ, ˈge*th*-, -ə-riŋ\ **1 :** to come together in a body **2 :** to bring together **:** COLLECT ‹*gather* a crowd› **3 a :** PICK 2b, HARVEST ‹*gather* flowers› **b :** to pick up little by little ‹*gather* ideas for the project› **4 a :** GROW, INCREASE ‹the storm *gathered* in intensity as it advanced› **b :** to swell and fill with pus **5 a :** to summon up ‹*gather* courage to dive› **b :** to prepare (as oneself) by mustering strength **c :** to gain by gradual increase ‹*gather* speed› **6 :** GUESS 1, INFER **7 a :** to draw about or close to something ‹*gather* a cloak about oneself› **b :** to pull (fabric) along a line of stitching into puckers [Old English *gaderian*] — **gath·er·er** *n*

synonyms GATHER, COLLECT, ASSEMBLE, CONGREGATE mean to come or bring together into a group, mass, or unit. GATHER is the general term for bringing or coming together from a spread-out or scattered state ‹a crowd *gathered* at the scene of the accident› ‹*gather* all the leaves into one pile›. COLLECT often implies careful selection or orderly arrange-

\ə\ **abut**	\au̇\ **out**	\i\ **tip**	\ȯ\ **saw**	\u̇\ **foot**
\ər\ **further**	\ch\ **chin**	\ī\ **life**	\ȯi\ **coin**	\y\ **yet**
\a\ **mat**	\e\ **pet**	\j\ **job**	\th\ **thin**	\yü\ **few**
\ā\ **take**	\ē\ **easy**	\ng\ **sing**	*th*\ **this**	\yu̇\ **cure**
\ä\ **cot, cart**	\g\ **go**	\ō\ **bone**	\ü\ **food**	\zh\ **vision**

ment ⟨*collect* rare coins⟩. ASSEMBLE implies an ordered gathering for a definite purpose often into a unified whole ⟨*assembled* a team of experts for an antarctic expedition⟩. CONGREGATE implies a spontaneous flocking together into a crowd or huddle ⟨people *congregating* on street corners⟩.

[2]**gather** *n* : a drawing together; *esp* : a puckering in cloth made by gathering

gath·er·ing *n* **1** : ASSEMBLY 1, MEETING **2** : a pus-filled swelling (as an abscess) **3** : the collecting of food and raw materials from the wild **4** : COLLECTION 3, COMPILATION **5** : a gather in cloth

Gat·ling gun \ˈgat-liŋ-\ *n* : a machine gun with a revolving cluster of barrels fired once each per revolution [Richard J. *Gatling,* died 1903, American inventor]

ga·tor \ˈgāt-ər\ *n* : ALLIGATOR

gauche \ˈgōsh\ *adj* : lacking social experience or grace : CRUDE [French, literally, "left"] ***synonyms*** see AWKWARD — **gauche·ness** *n*

gau·che·rie \ˌgōsh-ˈrē, -ə-ˈrē\ *n* : a tactless or awkward action

gau·cho \ˈgau̇-chō\ *n, pl* **gauchos** : a cowboy of the South American pampas [American Spanish]

gaud \ˈgȯd, ˈgäd\ *n* : a showy ornament or trinket [Middle English *gaude*]

gaudy \-ē\ *adj* **gaud·i·er; -est** : showily or tastelessly ornamented — **gaud·i·ly** \-l-ē\ *adv* — **gaud·i·ness** \-ē-nəs\ *n*

synonyms GAUDY, GARISH, FLASHY, TAWDRY mean overly or cheaply showy. GAUDY implies a tasteless use of overly bright colors or lavish decoration ⟨*gaudy* jewelry⟩. GARISH stresses a harsh brightness ⟨*garish* neon signs⟩. FLASHY applies to what appears dazzling but is quickly seen to be shallow and vulgar ⟨a *flashy* performance⟩. TAWDRY implies both gaudiness and cheapness of quality ⟨*tawdry* hotels⟩.

[1]**gauge** *also* **gage** \ˈgāj\ *n* **1 a** : measurement according to some standard or system: as (1) : the distance between the rails of a railroad (2) : the size of a shotgun expressed as the number of lead balls of the same size as the interior diameter of the barrel required to make a pound (3) : the thickness of sheet metal or the diameter of wire or a screw (4) : the fineness of a knitted fabric in loops per unit width **b** : SIZE 1, DIMENSIONS **2** : an instrument for measuring, testing, or registering ⟨a steam *gauge*⟩ [Medieval French] ***synonyms*** see STANDARD

[2]**gauge** *also* **gage** *vt* **gauged** *also* **gaged; gaug·ing** *also* **gag·ing** **1 a** : to measure exactly the size, dimensions, or other measurable quantity of **b** : to determine the capacity or contents of **2** : JUDGE 5, ESTIMATE ⟨*gauge* the response of the audience⟩ — **gaug·er** *n*

Gaul \ˈgȯl\ *n* **1** : a Celt of ancient Gaul **2** : FRENCHMAN

[1]**Gaul·ish** \ˈgȯ-lish\ *adj* : of or relating to the ancient Gauls or their language or land

[2]**Gaulish** *n* : the Celtic language of the ancient Gauls

gaunt \ˈgȯnt, ˈgänt\ *adj* **1** : excessively thin and angular often as a result of suffering or weariness **2** : grim and forbidding : DESOLATE [Middle English] ***synonyms*** see LANK — **gaunt·ly** *adv* — **gaunt·ness** *n*

[1]**gaunt·let** \ˈgȯnt-lət, ˈgänt-\ *n* **1** : a protective glove worn with medieval armor **2** : a protective glove used in industry **3** : a dress glove extending above the wrist [Medieval French *gantelet,* from *gant* "glove," of Germanic origin] — **gaunt·let·ed** \-lət-əd\ *adj*

[2]**gaunt·let** *also* **gant·let** \ˈgȯnt-lət, ˈgänt-\ *n* **1** : a double row of people armed with clubs who strike at a person forced to run between them **2** : CROSS FIRE 1; *also* : ORDEAL 2 [by folk etymology from earlier *gantelope,* from Swedish *gatlopp*]

gaur \ˈgau̇r\ *n* : a large wild ox of India and southeastern Asia [Hindi, from Sanskrit *gaura*]

gauss \ˈgau̇s\ *n, pl* **gauss** *also* **gauss·es** : a centimeter-gram-second unit of magnetic induction that is equal to 1×10^{-4} tesla [Karl F. *Gauss*]

gauze \ˈgȯz\ *n* **1** : a thin often transparent fabric **2** : a loosely woven cotton surgical dressing **3** : a woven fabric of metal or plastic filaments [Middle French *gaze*] — **gauzy** \ˈgȯ-zē\ *adj*

gave *past of* GIVE

gav·el \ˈgav-əl\ *n* : the mallet of a presiding officer or auctioneer [origin unknown]

ga·votte \gə-ˈvät\ *n* : a lively dance in 4/4 time of French peasant origin [French] — **gavotte** *vi*

[1]**gawk** \ˈgȯk\ *n* : a clumsy stupid person : LOUT [probably from English dialect *gawk* "left-handed"]

[2]**gawk** *vi* : to gape or stare stupidly [perhaps from obsolete *gaw* "to stare"]

gawky \ˈgȯ-kē\ *adj* **gawk·i·er; -est** : CLUMSY 1a, AWKWARD ⟨a tall *gawky* youth⟩ — **gawk·i·ly** \-kə-lē\ *adv* — **gawk·i·ness** \-kē-nəs\ *n*

gay \ˈgā\ *adj* **1** : happily excited : MERRY ⟨in a *gay* mood⟩ **2 a** : BRIGHT, LIVELY ⟨a *gay* sunny meadow⟩ **b** : brilliant in color **3** : given to social pleasures; *also* : tending to give in to sexual desires **4** : HOMOSEXUAL [Medieval French *gai*] — **gay** *adv* — **gay·ness** *n*

gayety *variant of* GAIETY

gayly *variant of* GAILY

gaze \ˈgāz\ *vi* : to fix the eyes in a steady intent look [Middle English *gazen*] — **gaze** *n* — **gaz·er** *n*

ga·ze·bo \gə-ˈzā-bō, -ˈzē-\ *n, pl* **-bos** : a freestanding roofed structure usually open on the sides [perhaps from *gaze* + Latin *-ebo* (as in *videbo* "I shall see")]

gaze·hound \ˈgāz-ˌhau̇nd\ *n* : SIGHT HOUND

ga·zelle \gə-ˈzel\ *n, pl* **gazelles** *also* **gazelle** : any of numerous small to medium graceful swift antelopes of Africa and Asia [French, from Arabic *ghazāl*]

[1]**ga·zette** \gə-ˈzet\ *n* **1** : NEWSPAPER **2** : an official journal [French, from Italian *gazetta*]

[2]**gazette** *vt, chiefly British* : to announce or publish in a gazette

gaz·et·teer \ˌgaz-ə-ˈtiər\ *n* : a geographical dictionary [from *The Gazetteer's: or, Newsman's Interpreter* (1693), a geographical index, from earlier *gazetteer* "journalist"]

ga·zil·lion \gə-ˈzil-yən\ *n* : ZILLION [alteration of *zillion*] — **gazillion** *adj* — **ga·zil·lionth** \-yənth, -yəntth\ *adj*

gazogene *variant of* GASOGENE

gaz·pa·cho \gəz-ˈpäch-ō, gəs-\ *n, pl* **-chos** : a spicy soup that is usually made from chopped vegetables (as tomato and cucumber) and is served cold

G clef *n* : TREBLE CLEF

[1]**gear** \ˈgiər\ *n* **1** : CLOTHING, GARMENTS **2** : EQUIPMENT, PARAPHERNALIA ⟨camping *gear*⟩ ⟨electronic *gear*⟩ **3** : the rigging of a ship or boat **4 a** (1) : a mechanism that performs a specific function in a complete machine ⟨steering *gear*⟩ (2) : a toothed wheel : COGWHEEL (3) : working order, relation, or adjustment ⟨got her career in *gear*⟩ **b** : one of two or more adjustments of a transmission (as of a bicycle or motor vehicle) that determine the direction of travel and the relative speed between the engine and the motion of the vehicle [probably from Old Norse *gervi*] — **gear·less** \-ləs\ *adj*

[2]**gear** *vb* **1 a** : to provide with gearing **b** : to connect by gearing **c** : to put into gear ⟨*gear* down⟩ **2 a** : to make ready for effective operation ⟨*gear* up for a new season⟩ **b** : to adjust or become adjusted so as to match or satisfy something ⟨*geared* to the needs of the blind⟩

gear·box \ˈgiər-ˌbäks\ *n* : TRANSMISSION 3

gear·ing *n* **1** : the act or process of providing or fitting with gears **2** : the parts by which motion is transmitted from one portion of machinery to another; *esp* : a train of gears

gear·shift \ˈgiər-ˌshift\ *n* : a mechanism by which the transmission gears in a power-transmission system are engaged and disengaged

gear·wheel \-ˌhwēl, -ˌwēl\ *n* : GEAR 2b

Geat \ˈgēt, ˈyaət\ *n* : a member of a Scandinavian people of southern Sweden to which the legendary hero Beowulf belonged [Old English *Gēat*] — **Geat·ish** \-ish\ *adj*

gecko \ˈgek-ō\ *n, pl* **geck·os** *or* **geck·oes** : any of numerous small harmless chiefly tropical and nocturnal insect-eating lizards [perhaps from Malay dialect *geʔkok*]

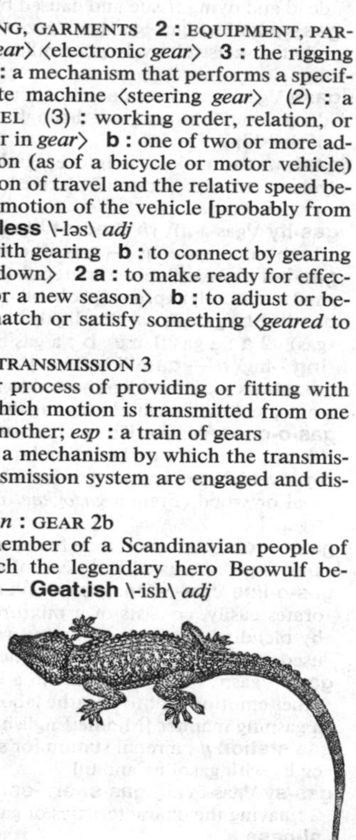

gecko

[1]**gee** \ˈjē\ *imperative verb* — used as a direction to turn to the right or move ahead; compare [4]HAW [origin unknown]

[2]**gee** *interj* — used to express surprise or enthusiasm [euphemism for *Jesus*]

geese *plural of* GOOSE

gee whiz \jē-ˈhwiz, ˈjē-, -ˈwiz\ *interj* : [2]GEE

gee·zer \ˈgē-zər\ *n* : an eccentric person; *esp* : an odd old man [probably from Scottish *guiser* "one in disguise"]

Ge·hen·na \gi-ˈhen-ə\ *n* **1 :** HELL 2 **2 :** a place or state of misery [Late Latin, from Greek *Geenna,* from Hebrew *Gē' Hinnōm,* literally, "valley of Hinnom"]

Gei·ger counter \ˈgī-gər-\ *n* **:** an electronic instrument for detecting the presence of cosmic rays or radioactive substances [Hans *Geiger,* died 1945, German physicist, and W. Müller, 20th century German physicist]

Geiger–Mül·ler counter \-ˈmyül-ər, -ˈmil-, -ˈməl-\ *n* **:** GEIGER COUNTER

gei·sha \ˈgā-shə, ˈgē-\ *n, pl* **geisha** *or* **geishas :** a Japanese girl or woman who is trained to provide entertaining company for men [Japanese, from *gei* "art" + *-sha* "person"]

[1]gel \ˈjel\ *n* **:** a solid jellylike colloid (as gelatin dessert) [*gelatin*]

[2]gel *vi* **gelled; gel·ling 1 :** to change into or take on the form of a gel **2 :** JELL 2 — **gel·able** \ˈjel-ə-bəl\ *adj*

gel·ate \ˈjel-ˌāt\ *vi* **:** GEL — **ge·la·tion** \ji-ˈlā-shən\ *n*

gel·a·tin *also* **gel·a·tine** \ˈjel-ət-n\ *n* **1 :** gummy or sticky material obtained from animal tissues by boiling; *esp* **:** a colloidal protein used as a food, in photography, and in medicine **2 a :** any of various substances resembling gelatin **b :** an edible jelly formed with gelatin **c :** a thin colored transparent sheet used to color a stage light [French *gélatine,* from Italian *gelatina,* derived from *gelare* "to freeze," from Latin]

ge·lat·i·nous \jə-ˈlat-nəs, -n-əs\ *adj* **1 :** resembling gelatin or jelly ⟨a *gelatinous* precipitate⟩ **2 :** of, relating to, or containing gelatin — **ge·lat·i·nous·ly** *adv* — **ge·lat·i·nous·ness** *n*

geld \ˈgeld\ *vt* **:** CASTRATE [Old Norse *gelda*]

geld·ing \ˈgel-ding\ *n* **:** a castrated animal; *esp* **:** a castrated male horse

gel electrophoresis *n* **:** electrophoresis in which molecules (as proteins and nucleic acids) migrate through a gel and separate into bands according to size

[1]gem \ˈjem\ *n* **1 a :** JEWEL **b :** a precious or sometimes semiprecious stone cut and polished for ornament **2 :** something prized for great beauty or perfection [Medieval French *gemme,* from Latin *gemma* "bud, gem"]

[2]gem *vt* **gemmed; gem·ming :** to adorn with or as if with gems

Ge·ma·ra \gə-ˈmär-ə, -ˈmȯr-\ *n* **:** a commentary on the Mishnah forming the second part of the Talmud [Aramaic *gĕmārā* "completion"]

gem·i·nate \ˈjem-ə-ˌnāt\ *vb* **:** DOUBLE 1a [Latin *geminare,* from *geminus* "twin"] — **gem·i·na·tion** \ˌjem-ə-ˈnā-shən\ *n*

Gem·i·ni \ˈjem-ə-nē, -ˌnī\ *n* **1 :** the 3rd zodiacal constellation pictorially represented as the twins Castor and Pollux sitting together and located between Taurus and Orion **2 :** the 3rd sign of the zodiac; *also* **:** one born under this sign [Latin, literally, "the twins" (Castor and Pollux)]

gem·ma \ˈjem-ə\ *n, pl* **gem·mae** \ˈjem-ˌē\ **:** BUD; *also* **:** an asexual reproductive body that becomes detached from a parent plant [Latin] — **gem·ma·tion** \je-ˈmā-shən\ *n*

gem·mule \ˈjem-yül\ *n* **:** a small bud; *esp* **:** an internal reproductive bud (as of a sponge) [French, from Latin *gemmula,* from *gemma* "bud"]

gem·ol·o·gy *or* **gem·mol·o·gy** \je-ˈmäl-ə-jē\ *n* **:** the science of gems — **gem·olog·i·cal** \ˌjem-ə-ˈläj-i-kəl\ *adj* — **gem·ol·o·gist** \je-ˈmäl-ə-jist\ *n*

gems·bok \ˈgemz-ˌbäk\ *n, pl* **gemsbok** *also* **gemsboks :** a large oryx formerly abundant in southern Africa [Afrikaans, from German *Gemsbock* "male chamois," from *Gems* "chamois" + *Bock* "male goat"]

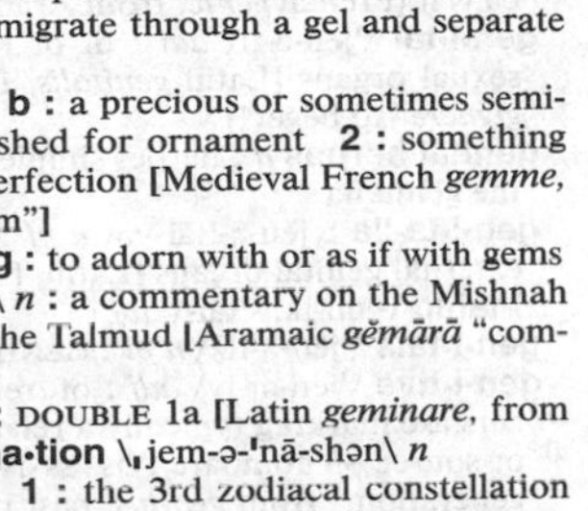

gemsbok

gem·stone \ˈjem-ˌstōn\ *n* **:** a mineral or petrified material that when cut and polished can be used in jewelry

[1]gen- *or* **geno-** *combining form* **1 :** race ⟨genocide⟩ **2 :** genus **:** kind ⟨genotype⟩ [Greek *genos* "birth, race, kind"]

[2]gen- *or* **geno-** *combining form* **:** gene ⟨genotype⟩

-gen \jən, ˌjen\ *also* **-gene** \ˌjēn\ *n combining form* **1 :** producer ⟨androgen⟩ **2 :** one that is (so) produced ⟨cultigen⟩ ⟨phosgene⟩ [Greek *-genēs* "born"]

gen·darme \ˈzhän-ˌdärm *also* ˈjän-\ *n* **:** a member of an armed national police force especially in France [French, derived from Middle French *gent d'armes,* literally, "armed people"]

gen·dar·mer·ie *or* **gen·dar·mery** \jän-ˈdärm-ə-rē, zhän-, -ˈdäm-\ *n, pl* **-mer·ies :** a body of gendarmes [French *gendarmerie,* from *gendarme*]

gen·der \ˈjen-dər\ *n* **1 a :** SEX 1 **b :** the behavioral, cultural, or psychological traits typically associated with one sex **2 :** any of two or more classes of words (as nouns or pronouns) or of forms of words (as adjectives) that are usually partly based on sex and that determine agreement with other words or grammatical forms ⟨in French the *gender* of "enfant" is masculine or feminine⟩ [Medieval French *genre, gendre,* from Latin *gener-, genus* "birth, race, kind, gender"]

gene \ˈjēn\ *n* **:** a specific sequence of nucleotides in DNA or sometimes RNA that is usually located on a chromosome and that is the functional unit of inheritance controlling the transmission and expression of one or more traits by specifying the structure of a particular protein (as an enzyme) or by controlling the function of other genetic material [German *Gen,* short for *Pangen,* from *Pan-* + *-gen*]

ge·ne·al·o·gy \ˌjē-nē-ˈäl-ə-jē, ˌjen-ē-, -ˈal-\ *n, pl* **-gies 1 :** an account of the descent of a person or family from an ancestor **2 :** the descent of a person or family from an ancestor **:** PEDIGREE, LINEAGE **3 :** the study of family pedigrees [Medieval French *genealogie,* from Late Latin *genealogia,* from Greek, from *genea* "race, family" + *-logia* "-logy"] — **ge·ne·a·log·i·cal** \ˌjē-nē-ə-ˈläj-i-kəl, ˌjen-ē-\ *adj* — **ge·ne·a·log·i·cal·ly** \-ˈläj-i-kə-lē, -klē\ *adv* — **ge·ne·al·o·gist** \-ˈäl-ə-jəst, -ˈal-\ *n*

gene pool *n* **:** the collection of genes in an interbreeding population

genera *plural of* GENUS

[1]gen·er·al \ˈjen-rəl, -ə-rəl\ *adj* **1 :** involving, applicable to, or affecting the whole **:** not local or partial ⟨a *general* election⟩ **2 :** relating to or covering all instances or individuals of a class or group ⟨a *general* conclusion⟩ **3 :** not limited in meaning **:** not specific or in detail ⟨a *general* outline⟩ **4 :** common to many ⟨a *general* custom⟩ **5 :** not special or specialized ⟨a test of *general* knowledge⟩ **6 :** not precise or definite ⟨*general* comments⟩ **7 :** superior in rank ⟨*general* manager⟩ ⟨inspector *general*⟩ [Medieval French, from Latin *generalis,* from *gener-, genus* "kind, class"] ***synonyms*** see UNIVERSAL

[2]general *n* **1 :** something that involves or is applicable to the whole **2 a :** GENERAL OFFICER **b :** an officer rank in the army, marine corps, and air force above lieutenant general — **in general :** for the most part **:** GENERALLY

general anesthesia *n* **:** anesthesia affecting the entire body and accompanied by loss of consciousness — **general anesthetic** *n*

general assembly *n* **1 :** a legislative assembly; *esp* **:** a U.S. state legislature **2** *cap G&A* **:** the supreme deliberative body of the United Nations

General Court *n* **:** the state legislature in Massachusetts and New Hampshire

general delivery *n* **:** a department of a post office that can be used by individuals as a mailing address

gen·er·a·lis·si·mo \ˌjen-rə-ˈlis-ə-ˌmō, -ə-rə-\ *n, pl* **-mos :** the chief commander of an army **:** COMMANDER IN CHIEF [Italian, from *generale* "general"]

gen·er·al·ist \ˈjen-rə-list, -ə-rə-\ *n* **:** a person whose skills or interests are varied or unspecialized

gen·er·al·i·ty \ˌjen-ə-ˈral-ət-ē\ *n, pl* **-ties 1 :** the quality or state of being general **2 a :** GENERALIZATION 2 **b :** a vague or inadequate statement **3 :** the greatest part **:** BULK

gen·er·al·i·za·tion \ˌjen-rə-lə-ˈzā-shən, -ə-rə-\ *n* **1 :** the act or process of generalizing **2 :** a general statement, law, principle, or proposition

gen·er·al·ize \ˈjen-rə-ˌlīz, -ə-rə-\ *vb* **1 :** to make general **:** give a general form to **2 a :** to draw general conclusions from ⟨*generalized* their experiences⟩ **b :** to reach a general conclusion especially from particular instances — **gen·er·al·iz·er** *n*

gen·er·al·ized *adj* **:** made general; *esp* **:** not highly specialized biologically nor strictly adapted (as to an environment)

gen·er·al·ly \ˈjen-rə-lē, -ə-rə-, ˈjen-ər-lē\ *adv* **:** in a general man-

\ə\ abut	\au̇\ out	\i\ tip	\ȯ\ saw	\u̇\ foot
\ər\ further	\ch\ chin	\ī\ life	\ȯi\ coin	\y\ yet
\a\ mat	\e\ pet	\j\ job	\th\ thin	\yü\ few
\ā\ take	\ē\ easy	\ng\ sing	\t͟h\ this	\yu̇\ cure
\ä\ cot, cart	\g\ go	\ō\ bone	\ü\ food	\zh\ vision

ner: as **a** : in disregard of specific instances and with regard to an overall picture ⟨*generally* speaking⟩ **b** : as a rule : USUALLY

general officer *n* : an officer ranking above a colonel in the army, marine corps, or air force

general of the air force : a commissioned officer of highest rank in the air force whose insignia is five stars

general of the army : a commissioned officer of highest rank in the army whose insignia is five stars

general paresis *n* : insanity caused by syphilis of the brain that leads to dementia and paralysis

general practitioner *n* : a physician or veterinarian who does not limit his or her practice to a specialty

general relativity *n* : RELATIVITY 2b

gen·er·al·ship \ˈjen-rəl-ˌship, -ə-rəl-\ *n* **1** : office or tenure of office of a general **2** : military skill in a high commander **3** : LEADERSHIP

general store *n* : a retail store that carries a wide variety of goods but is not divided into departments

general strike *n* : a strike by workers in all industries and enterprises of an area

gen·er·ate \ˈjen-ə-ˌrāt\ *vt* **1** : to bring into existence: as **a** : PROCREATE **b** : to originate especially by a vital or chemical process : PRODUCE ⟨*generate* an electric current⟩ **2** : to be the cause of (a situation, action, or state of mind) **3** : to trace out mathematically (a line, surface, or solid) by a moving point, line, or surface [Latin *generare,* from *gener-, genus* "descent, birth"] — **gen·er·a·tive** \-ə-ˌrāt-iv, -rət-\ *adj*

gen·er·a·tion \ˌjen-ə-ˈrā-shən\ *n* **1 a** : a group of living beings constituting a single step in the line of descent from an ancestor **b** : a group of individuals born and living at the same time **c** : a type or class of objects developed from an earlier type **2** : the average span of time between the birth of parents and that of their offspring **3** : the action or process of generating ⟨*generation* of income⟩ — **gen·er·a·tion·al** \-shnəl, -shən-l\ *adj*

generative nucleus *n* : the nucleus of a developing pollen grain that produces sperm nuclei — compare TUBE NUCLEUS

gen·er·a·tor \ˈjen-ə-ˌrāt-ər\ *n* : one that generates : as **a** : an apparatus in which vapor or gas is formed **b** : a machine by which mechanical energy is changed into electrical energy

gen·er·a·trix \ˌjen-ə-ˈrā-triks\ *n, pl* **-tri·ces** \-trə-ˌsēz\ : a point, line, or surface whose motion generates a line, surface, or solid

ge·ner·ic \jə-ˈner-ik\ *adj* **1 a** : of, relating to, or characteristic of a whole group or class : not specific : GENERAL **b** : not protected by a trademark registration ⟨*generic* drugs⟩ **2** : of, relating to, or having the rank of a biological genus — **ge·ner·i·cal·ly** \-ˈner-i-kə-lē, -klē\ *adv*

gen·er·os·i·ty \ˌjen-ə-ˈräs-ət-ē\ *n, pl* **-ties** **1 a** : liberality in spirit or act; *esp* : liberality in giving **b** : a generous act **2** : ABUNDANCE 1 ⟨*generosity* of spirit⟩

gen·er·ous \ˈjen-rəs, -ə-rəs\ *adj* **1** : free in giving or sharing : not mean or stingy ⟨a *generous* giver⟩ **2** : MAGNANIMOUS **3** : AMPLE, PLENTIFUL ⟨a *generous* supply⟩ [Latin *generosus* "highborn, magnanimous," from *gener-, genus* "birth, family, kind"] — **gen·er·ous·ly** *adv* — **gen·er·ous·ness** *n*

synonyms GENEROUS, BOUNTIFUL, MUNIFICENT mean giving freely and unstintingly. GENEROUS stresses unselfish warmheartedness in giving rather than the size or importance of the gift ⟨a *generous* offer of help⟩. BOUNTIFUL implies giving lavishly from ample means or an inexhaustible source of supply ⟨children spoiled by *bountiful* gifts⟩. MUNIFICENT suggests a scale of giving appropriate to lords and princes ⟨a *munificent* donation funded the program⟩.

gen·e·sis \ˈjen-ə-səs\ *n, pl* **-e·ses** \-ə-ˌsēz\ : the origin or coming into being of something [Latin, from Greek, from *gignesthai* "to be born"]

Genesis *n* : the mainly narrative first book of canonical Jewish and Christian Scriptures — see BIBLE table

gene–splic·ing \ˈjēn-ˌsplī-sing\ *n* : any of various techniques by which recombinant DNA is produced and introduced into an organism especially to change one or more of its characteristics

gen·et \ˈjen-ət\ *n* : an Old World flesh-eating mammal related to the civets [Medieval French *genete,* derived from Arabic *jarnayt*]

gene therapy *n* : the insertion of usually genetically altered genes into cells especially to replace defective genes in the treatment of genetic disorders

ge·net·ic \jə-ˈnet-ik\ *adj* **1** : of or relating to the origin, development, or causes of something **2 a** : of, relating to, or involving genetics **b** : of, relating to, caused by, or controlled by genes ⟨a *genetic* disease⟩ — **ge·net·i·cal** \-i-kəl\ *adj* — **ge·net·i·cal·ly** \-i-kə-lē, -klē\ *adv*

genetic code *n* **1** : the biochemical basis of heredity consisting of codons in DNA and RNA that determine the specific amino acid sequences in proteins or control a genetic process (as starting or stopping protein synthesis) **2** : the specific arrangement of the chemical groupings of the genetic code in the hereditary material of an organism

genetic drift *n* : random changes in gene frequency over time especially in small populations

genetic engineering *n* : the alteration of genetic material by intervention in genetic processes; *esp* : GENE-SPLICING — **genetically engineered** *adj* — **genetic engineer** *n*

ge·net·ics \jə-ˈnet-iks\ *n* **1** : a branch of biology that deals with heredity and variation of organisms **2** : the heredity and genetic processes of an organism, a group of organisms, or a condition (as a disease) — **ge·net·i·cist** \-ˈnet-ə-səst\ *n*

ge·nial \ˈjē-nyəl\ *adj* **1** : favorable to growth or comfort ⟨a *genial* climate⟩ **2** : being cheerful and cheering : FRIENDLY [Latin *genialis,* from *genius*] — **ge·nial·i·ty** \ˌjē-nē-ˈal-ət-ē, jēn-ˈyal-\ *n* — **ge·nial·ly** \ˈjē-nyə-lē\ *adv*

gen·ic \ˈjēn-ik, ˈjen-\ *adj* : GENETIC 2b — **gen·i·cal·ly** \-i-kə-lē, -klē\ *adv*

-gen·ic \ˈjen-ik *sometimes* ˈjē-nik\ *adj combining form* **1** : producing : forming ⟨carcino*genic*⟩ **2** : suitable for production or reproduction by (such) a medium ⟨tele*genic*⟩ [*-gen* and *-geny* + *-ic;* sense 2 from *photogenic*]

ge·nie \ˈjē-nē *also* ˈjen-ē\ *n, pl* **genies** **1** : JINNI **2** : a magic spirit believed to take human form and serve the person who calls it [French *génie,* from Arabic *jinnī*]

gen·i·tal \ˈjen-ə-tl\ *adj* : of or relating to reproduction or the sexual organs [Latin *genitalis,* from *genitus,* past participle of *gignere* "to beget"]

genital herpes *n* : herpes simplex of the type typically affecting the genitalia

gen·i·ta·lia \ˌjen-ə-ˈtāl-yə\ *n pl* : reproductive organs; *esp* : the external genital organs [Latin, from *genitalis* "genital"] — **gen·i·tal·ic** \-ˈtal-ik, -ˈtāl-\ *adj*

gen·i·tals \ˈjen-ə-tlz\ *n pl* : GENITALIA

gen·i·tive \ˈjen-ət-iv\ *adj* : of, relating to, or being a grammatical case marking typically a relationship especially of possessor or source — compare POSSESSIVE [Latin *genitivus,* literally, "of generation," from *genitus,* past participle of *gignere* "to beget"] — **gen·i·ti·val** \ˌjen-ə-ˈtī-vəl\ *adj* — **genitive** *n*

gen·i·to·uri·nary \ˌjen-ə-tō-ˈyu̇r-ə-ˌner-ē\ *adj* : of or relating to the genital and urinary organs or functions

ge·nius \ˈjē-nyəs, -nē-əs\ *n, pl* **ge·nius·es** *or* **ge·nii** \-nē-ˌī\ **1** *pl genii* : an attendant spirit of a person or place **2** : a strong leaning or inclination : PENCHANT **3 a** : a peculiar, distinctive, or identifying character or spirit **b** : the associations and traditions of a place **4** *pl genii* **a** : JINNI **b** : a person who influences another for good or bad ⟨my cousin was my evil *genius*⟩ **5** *pl geniuses* **a** : a single strongly marked capacity or aptitude **b** : extraordinary intellectual power especially as manifested in creative activity **c** : a person endowed with such power; *esp* : one with a very high IQ [Latin, "tutelary spirit, natural inclinations," from *gignere* "to beget"] ***synonyms*** see TALENT

Word History According to ancient mythology, there are supernatural beings whose nature is intermediate between that of a god and that of humans. It was believed that at birth each person is assigned one of these spirits to act as a guardian throughout life. The Latin name for such a spirit was *genius,* from *gignere* "to beget." *Genius,* in the sense of "attendant spirit," was borrowed from Latin into English in the early 15th century. Part of the role of such a *genius* was to guard a person's character, and in the 16th century *genius* came to be used for a person's character. Later this led to the sense of "a strongly marked aptitude," and eventually *genius* came to mean "an extraordinary native intellectual power."

geno- — see GEN-

geno·cide \ˈjen-ə-ˌsīd\ *n* : the deliberate and systematic destruction of a racial, political, or cultural group — **geno·cid·al** \ˌjen-ə-ˈsīd-l\ *adj*

ge·nome \ˈjē-ˌnōm\ *n* : one haploid set of chromosomes with the genes they contain; *also* : the genetic material of an organism [German *Genom,* from *Gen* "gene" + Chromos*om* "chromosome"] — **ge·no·mic** \ji-ˈnō-mik, -ˈnäm-ik\ *adj*

ge·no·mics \jē-ˈnō-miks\ *n* : a branch of science concerned especially with investigating the structure and function of all or part of an organism's genetic material

ge·no·type \ˈjē-nə-ˌtīp, ˈjen-ə-\ *n* **:** the genetic constitution of an individual or group — **ge·no·typ·ic** \ˌjē-nə-ˈtip-ik, ˌjen-ə-\ *adj* — **ge·no·typ·i·cal·ly** \-i-kə-lē, -klē\ *adv*

-g·e·nous \j-ə-nəs\ *adj combining form* **1 :** producing : yielding **2 :** having (such) an origin ⟨endo*genous*⟩ [*-gen* + *-ous*]

genre \ˈzhän-rə, ˈzhäⁿ-, ˈzhäng-; ˈzhäⁿr, ˈzhäⁿ-ər\ *n* **1 :** a distinctive type or category of literary, artistic, or musical composition **2 :** KIND 1b, SORT **3 :** painting that depicts scenes or events from everyday life usually realistically [French, from Middle French, "kind, gender"]

gens \ˈjenz, ˈgens\ *n, pl* **gen·tes** \ˈjen-ˌtēz, ˈgen-ˌtās\ **:** a Roman clan embracing the families of the same stock in the male line with the members worshipping a common ancestor [Latin]

gent \ˈjent\ *n* **:** FELLOW 4a [short for *gentleman*]

gen·teel \jen-ˈtēl\ *adj* **1 a :** having an aristocratic quality **:** STYLISH **b :** ELEGANT 1, GRACEFUL **c :** POLITE **2 a :** maintaining the appearance of superior or middle-class social status or respectability **b :** marked by false delicacy, prudery, or affectation [Middle French *gentil* "gentle"] — **gen·teel·ly** \-ˈtēl-lē\ *adv* — **gen·teel·ness** *n*

gen·tian \ˈjen-chən\ *n* **:** any of various herbs with opposite smooth leaves and showy usually blue flowers [Medieval French *genciane,* from Latin *gentiana*]

gentian violet *n, often cap G&V* **:** a violet dye in the form of a green powder produced chemically and used as a biological stain and as an antiseptic in bacterial and fungus infections

gen·tile \ˈjen-ˌtīl\ *n* **1** *often cap* **:** a person who is not Jewish **2 :** HEATHEN 1, PAGAN **3** *often cap* **:** a person who is not a Mormon [Late Latin *gentilis,* from Latin *gent-, gens* "clan, nation"] — **gentile** *adj, often cap*

gen·til·i·ty \jen-ˈtil-ət-ē\ *n, pl* **-ties** **1 :** good birth and family **2 a :** good manners **b :** falsely delicate or prudish attitude or behavior **3 :** maintenance of the appearance of superior or middle-class social status

[1]**gen·tle** \ˈjent-l\ *adj* **gen·tler** \ˈjent-lər, -l-ər\; **gen·tlest** \ˈjent-ləst, -l-əst\ **1 a :** belonging or suitable to a family of high social station **b :** NOBLE ⟨of *gentle* blood⟩ **c :** AMIABLE, KIND ⟨*gentle* reader⟩ **2 a :** easily handled ⟨a *gentle* horse⟩ **b :** not harsh **:** MILD ⟨*gentle* soap⟩ **c :** not stern or rough ⟨*gentle* words⟩ **3 :** SOFT, DELICATE ⟨a *gentle* touch⟩ **4 :** MODERATE ⟨a *gentle* slope⟩ [Medieval French *gentil,* from Latin *gentilis* "of a gens, of one's family," from *gent-, gens* "gens, nation"] — **gen·tle·ness** \ˈjent-l-nəs\ *n* — **gent·ly** \ˈjent-lē\ *adv*

[2]**gentle** *vt* **gen·tled; gen·tling** \ˈjent-ling, -l-ing\ **1 :** to make mild, docile, soft, or moderate **2 :** to soothe or calm down

gen·tle·folk \ˈjent-l-ˌfōk\ *also* **gen·tle·folks** \-ˌfōks\ *n pl* **:** persons of good family and breeding

gen·tle·man \ˈjent-l-mən\ *n* **1 :** a man of noble or gentle birth **2 a :** a well-bred man of good education and social position **b :** a thoughtful, polite, well-mannered male ⟨reminded her young son to be a *gentleman*⟩ **3 :** MAN — used in the plural as a form of address in speaking to a group of men

gen·tle·man·ly \-lē\ *adj* **:** characteristic of or having the character of a gentleman — **gen·tle·man·li·ness** *n*

gentleman's agreement *n* **:** an agreement based on trust rather than a legal document — called also *gentlemen's agreement*

gen·tle·wom·an \ˈjent-l-ˌwu̇m-ən\ *n* **1 :** a woman of good family or breeding **2 :** a woman attending a lady of rank **3 :** a woman with very good manners

gen·tri·fi·ca·tion \ˌjen-trə-fə-ˈkā-shən\ *n* **:** the process of renewal and rebuilding accompanied by a wave of middle- or upper-class people moving into the area and displacing poorer residents — **gen·tri·fy** \ˈjen-trə-ˌfī\ *vb*

gen·try \ˈjen-trē\ *n* **1 :** people of good birth, breeding, and education often of the ruling class **:** ARISTOCRACY **2 :** PEOPLE; *esp* **:** persons of a designated class ⟨the academic *gentry*⟩ [Medieval French *genterise,* alteration of *gentelise,* from *gentil* "gentle"]

gen·u·flect \ˈjen-yə-ˌflekt\ *vi* **:** to kneel on one knee and then rise again especially as an act of reverence [Late Latin *genuflectere,* from Latin *genu* "knee" + *flectere* "to bend"] — **gen·u·flec·tion** \ˌjen-yə-ˈflek-shən\ *n*

gen·u·ine \ˈjen-yə-wən\ *adj* **1 :** being actually what it seems to be **:** REAL ⟨*genuine* gold⟩ **2 :** SINCERE, HONEST ⟨a *genuine* interest⟩ [Latin *genuinus* "innate, genuine"] ***synonyms*** see AUTHENTIC — **gen·u·ine·ly** *adv* — **gen·u·ine·ness** *n*

ge·nus \ˈjē-nəs\ *n, pl* **gen·era** \ˈjen-ə-rə\ **1 :** a category of biological classification ranking between the family and the species, comprising structurally or genetically related species and being designated by a capitalized singular noun formed in Latin **2 :** a class of objects divided into several subordinate groups [Latin *gener-, genus* "birth, race, kind"]

-g·e·ny \j-ə-nē\ *n combining form, pl* **-genies** **:** generation : production ⟨phylo*geny*⟩ [Greek *-geneia* "act of being born," from *-genēs* "born"]

geo- *combining form* **:** earth : ground : soil ⟨*geo*logy⟩ [Greek *gē* "earth, land"]

geo·cach·ing \ˈjē-ō-ˌkash-ing\ *n* **:** a game in which players use a GPS device to search for a cache of items hidden at given geographical coordinates — **geo·cach·er** \-ˌkash-ər\ *n*

geo·cen·tric \ˌjē-ō-ˈsen-trik\ *adj* **1 :** relating to or measured from the earth's center **2 :** having or relating to the earth as a center — compare HELIOCENTRIC

geo·chem·is·try \-ˈkem-ə-strē\ *n* **:** a science that deals with the chemical composition of and chemical changes in the solid matter of the earth or another body (as the moon) — **geo·chem·i·cal** \-ˈkem-i-kəl\ *adj* — **geo·chem·i·cal·ly** \-i-kə-lē, -klē\ *adv* — **geo·chem·ist** \-ˈkem-ist\ *n*

geo·chro·nol·o·gy \ˌjē-ō-krə-ˈnäl-ə-jē\ *n* **:** the chronology of the past as indicated by geologic data — **geo·chro·no·log·i·cal** \-ˌkrän-l-ˈäj-i-kəl, -ˌkrōn-\ *adj*

ge·ode \ˈjē-ˌōd\ *n* **:** a nodule of stone having a cavity lined with crystals or mineral matter; *also* **:** the cavity in a geode [Latin *geodes,* a gem, from Greek *geōdēs* "earthlike," from *gē* "earth"]

[1]**ge·o·de·sic** \ˌjē-ə-ˈdes-ik, -ˈdēs-, -ˈdez-, -ˈdēz-\ *adj* **:** made of a framework of light straight-sided polygons in tension ⟨a *geodesic* dome⟩ [derived from Greek *geōdaisia* "measuring or surveying of land," from *geō-* "ge-" + *daiesthai* "to divide"]

[2]**geodesic** *n* **:** the shortest line between two points on a surface

geo·det·ic survey \ˌjē-ə-ˈdet-ik-\ *n* **:** a survey of a large land area in which corrections are made for the curvature of the earth's surface [*geodetic* derived from Greek *geōdaisia* "land measuring"] — **geodetic surveying** *n*

ge·og·ra·pher \jē-ˈäg-rə-fər\ *n* **:** a specialist in geography

ge·o·graph·ic \ˌjē-ə-ˈgraf-ik\ *or* **ge·o·graph·i·cal** \-i-kəl\ *adj* **1 :** of or relating to geography **2 :** belonging to or characteristic of a particular region ⟨*geographic* features of the plains⟩ — **ge·o·graph·i·cal·ly** \-i-kə-lē, -klē\ *adv*

ge·og·ra·phy \jē-ˈäg-rə-fē\ *n, pl* **-phies** **1 :** a science that deals with the distribution and interaction of the diverse physical and cultural features of the earth's surface **2 :** the natural features of an area

geologic time *n* **:** the long period of time marked by the sequence of events in the earth's geological history

☞ The Geologic Time Table is on the following page.

ge·ol·o·gy \jē-ˈäl-ə-jē\ *n, pl* **-gies** **1 a :** a science that deals with the history of the earth and its life especially as recorded in rocks **b :** a study of the features of a celestial body (as the moon) **2 :** the geologic features of an area — **geo·log·ic** \ˌjē-ə-ˈläj-ik\ *or* **geo·log·i·cal** \-i-kəl\ *adj* — **geo·log·i·cal·ly** \-i-kə-lē, -klē\ *adv* — **ge·ol·o·gist** \jē-ˈäl-ə-jəst\ *n*

geo·mag·net·ic \ˌjē-ō-mag-ˈnet-ik\ *adj* **:** of or relating to the earth's magnetism — **geo·mag·ne·tism** \-ˈmag-nə-ˌtiz-əm\ *n*

ge·om·e·ter \jē-ˈäm-ət-ər\ *n* **:** a specialist in geometry

geo·met·ric \ˌjē-ə-ˈme-trik\ *or* **geo·met·ri·cal** \-ˈme-tri-kəl\ *adj* **1 :** of, relating to, or based on the methods or principles of geometry **2 :** utilizing rectilinear or simple curvilinear motifs or outlines in design — **geo·met·ri·cal·ly** \-tri-kə-lē, -klē\ *adv*

geo·me·tri·cian \jē-ˌäm-ə-ˈtrish-ən, ˌjē-ə-mə-\ *n* **:** GEOMETER

geometric mean *n* **1 :** the square root of the product of two terms; *also* **:** the *n*th root of the product of *n* numbers **2 :** a term between any two terms of a geometric progression

geometric progression *n* **:** a sequence (as 1, ½, ¼) in which the ratio of a term to the term before it is always the same

geo·met·rid \jē-ˈäm-ə-trəd, ˌjē-ə-ˈme-trəd\ *n* **:** any of a family of medium-sized moths with large wings and larvae that are loopers — **geometrid** *adj*

ge·om·e·try \jē-ˈäm-ə-trē\ *n* **1 a :** a branch of mathematics that deals with the measurement, properties, and relationships of points, lines, angles, surfaces, and solids **b :** a particular

GEOLOGIC TIME

EONS	ERAS	PERIODS AND SYSTEMS	EPOCHS AND SERIES	APPROXIMATE BEGINNING OF INTERVAL (YEARS AGO)	BIOLOGICAL FORMS
Phanerozoic	Cenozoic	Quaternary	Holocene	10,000	
			Pleistocene	1,800,000	Earliest humans
		Tertiary	Pliocene	5,000,000	
			Miocene	24,000,000	Earliest hominids
			Oligocene	34,000,000	
			Eocene	55,000,000	Earliest grasses
			Paleocene	65,000,000	Earliest large mammals
		Cretaceous-Tertiary boundary (65 million years ago): extinction of dinosaurs			
	Mesozoic	Cretaceous	Upper	98,000,000	
			Lower	144,000,000	Earliest flowering plants; dinosaurs dominate the land
		Jurassic		208,000,000	Earliest birds
		Triassic		248,000,000	Earliest dinosaurs & mammals
	Paleozoic	Permian		286,000,000	
		Carboniferous			
		Pennsylvanian		320,000,000	Earliest reptiles
		Mississippian		360,000,000	Earliest winged insects
		Devonian		410,000,000	Earliest amphibians & bony fish
		Silurian		438,000,000	Earliest land plants & insects
		Ordovician		505,000,000	Earliest corals
		Cambrian		544,000,000	Earliest fish
Proterozoic	Precambrian			2,500,000,000	Earliest colonial algae & soft-bodied invertebrates
Archean				3,800,000,000	Earliest surviving fossils of primitive single-celled organisms
Hadean				4,600,000,000	No surviving fossils

type or system of geometry **2 a :** the arrangement of the parts of a device ⟨the *geometry* of an electron tube⟩ **b :** SHAPE ⟨the *geometry* of a crystal⟩ [Medieval French *geometrie,* from Latin *geometria,* from Greek *geōmetria,* from *geōmetrein* "to measure the earth," from *geō-* "ge-" + *metron* "measure"]

geo·mor·phol·o·gy \ˌjē-ə-mȯr-ˈfäl-ə-jē\ *n* **:** a science that deals with the relief features of the earth or of another body (as the moon) — **geo·mor·pho·log·i·cal** \-ˌmȯr-fə-ˈläj-i-kəl\ *adj*

geo·phys·ics \ˌjē-ə-ˈfiz-iks\ *n* **:** a science that deals with the various physical processes and phenomena occurring in or near the earth — **geo·phys·i·cal** \-ˈfiz-i-kəl\ *adj* — **geo·phys·i·cal·ly** \-kə-lē, -klē\ *adv* — **geo·phys·i·cist** \-ˈfiz-ə-səst\ *n*

geo·pol·i·tics \ˌjē-ō-ˈpäl-ə-ˌtiks\ *n* **:** a study of the influence of such factors as geography, economics, and population on the politics and especially the foreign policy of a state — **geo·po·lit·i·cal** \-pə-ˈlit-i-kəl\ *adj* — **geo·po·lit·i·cal·ly** \-kə-lē, -klē\ *adv*

geor·gette \jȯr-ˈjet\ *n* **:** a thin strong clothing crepe having a dull pebbly surface [from *Georgette,* a trademark]

¹Geor·gian \ˈjȯr-jən\ *adj* **1 :** of, relating to, or characteristic of the reigns of the first four Georges of Great Britain ⟨*Georgian* architecture⟩ **2 :** of, relating to, or characteristic of the reign of George V of Great Britain

²Georgian *n* **:** one belonging to either of the Georgian periods

geo·sci·ence \ˌjē-ō-ˈsī-əns\ *n* **:** the sciences (as geology, geophysics, and geochemistry) dealing with the earth

geo·sta·tion·ary \ˌjē-ō-ˈstā-shə-ˌner-ē\ *adj* **:** being or having an orbit such that a satellite remains in a fixed position above the earth's surface

geo·syn·chro·nous \ˌjē-ō-ˈsing-krə-nəs, -ˈsin-\ *adj* **:** GEOSTATIONARY

geo·syn·cline \-ˈsin-ˌklīn\ *n* **:** a great downward bend of the earth's crust

geo·tax·is \-ˈtak-səs\ *n* **:** a taxis in which the force of gravity is the controlling stimulus — **geo·tac·tic** \-ˈtak-tik\ *adj*

geo·ther·mal \-ˈthər-məl\ *or* **geo·ther·mic** \-mik\ *adj* **:** of, relating to, or using the heat of the earth's interior; *also* **:** produced by such heat ⟨*geothermal* steam⟩

ge·ot·ro·pism \jē-ˈä-trə-ˌpiz-əm\ *n* **:** a tropism involving turning or movement toward the earth — **geo·tro·pic** \ˌjē-ə-ˈtrō-pik, -ˈträp-ik\ *adj*

ge·ra·ni·um \jə-ˈrā-nē-əm\ *n* **1 :** any of a widely distributed genus of herbs with usually deeply cut leaves, and typically white, pink, or purple flowers in which glands alternate with the petals **2 :** any of a genus of herbs native to southern Africa with showy flowers of usually red, pink, or white flowers — called also *pelargonium* [Latin, from Greek *geranion,* from *geranos* "crane"]

ger·bil \ˈjər-bəl\ *n* **:** any of numerous Old World burrowing desert rodents with long hind legs adapted for leaping [French *gerbille*]

ger·i·at·ric \ˌjer-ē-ˈa-trik\ *adj* **:** of or relating to geriatrics, the aged, or the process of aging [Greek *gēras* "old age" + *iatros* "physician"]

ger·i·at·rics \ˌjer-ē-ˈa-triks\ *n* **:** a branch of medicine that deals with the problems and diseases of old age and aging people — **ger·i·a·tri·cian** \ˌjer-ē-ə-ˈtrish-ən\ *n*

germ \ˈjərm\ *n* **1 a :** a small mass of living substance capable of developing into an organism or one of its parts **b :** the embryo in the seed of a cereal (as wheat) together with its cotyledon that is usually separated from the starchy endosperm of the seed during milling **2 :** something that serves or may serve as an origin **:** RUDIMENT ⟨the *germ* of an idea⟩ **3 :** MICROORGANISM; *esp* **:** one causing disease [French *germe,* from Latin *germen,* from *gignere* "to beget"]

Ger·man \ˈjər-mən\ *n* **1 a :** a native or inhabitant of Germany **b :** a person of German descent **2 :** the Germanic language of Germany, Austria, and parts of Switzerland **3** *often not cap* **a :** a dance consisting of improvised intricate figures intermingled with waltzes **b** *chiefly Midland* **:** a dancing party [Latin *Germanus,* any member of the Germanic peoples] — **German** *adj*

German cockroach *n* **:** a winged cockroach that is probably of African origin and is a common household pest in the U.S.

ger·man·der \jər-ˈman-dər, ˌjər-\ *n* **:** a plant of the mint family with dense spikes of purple flowers [derived from Greek *chamaidrys,* from *chamai* "on the ground" + *drys* "tree"]

ger·mane \jər-ˈmān, ˌjər-\ *adj* **:** having a significant connection **:** PERTINENT [Middle English *germain,* literally, "having the same parents," derived from Latin *germanus,* from *germen* "bud, sprout, germ"] — **ger·mane·ly** *adv*

[1]**Ger·man·ic** \jər-ˈman-ik, ˌjər-\ *adj* **1 :** GERMAN **2 :** of, relating to, or characteristic of the Germanic-speaking peoples **3 :** of, relating to, or constituting Germanic

[2]**Germanic** *n* **:** a branch of the Indo-European language family containing English, German, Dutch, Afrikaans, Frisian, the Scandinavian languages, and Gothic

ger·ma·ni·um \jər-ˈmā-nē-əm, ˌjər-\ *n* **:** a grayish white hard brittle chemical element that resembles silicon and is used especially as a semiconductor — see ELEMENT table [New Latin, from Medieval Latin *Germania* "Germany"]

ger·man·ize \ˈjər-mə-ˌnīz\ *vt, often cap* **:** to cause to acquire German characteristics — **ger·man·i·za·tion** \ˌjər-mə-nə-ˈzā-shən\ *n, often cap*

German measles *n sing or pl* **:** an acute contagious virus disease that is usually milder than typical measles but is likely to cause damage to the fetus when occurring early in pregnancy — called also *rubella*

Ger·mano- \jər-ˈman-ō, ˌjər-\ *combining form* **:** German

German shepherd *n* **:** any of a breed of large erect-eared dogs of German origin that are often used in police work and as guide dogs for the blind

German silver *n* **:** NICKEL SILVER

germ cell *n* **:** an egg or sperm or one of the cells from which they arise

germ-free \ˈjərm-ˌfrē\ *adj* **:** free of germs

ger·mi·cid·al \ˌjər-mə-ˈsīd-l\ *adj* **:** of or relating to a germicide; *also* **:** destroying germs

ger·mi·cide \ˈjər-mə-ˌsīd\ *n* **:** an agent that destroys germs

ger·mi·nal \ˈjər-mən-l\ *adj* **1 a :** being in the earliest stage of development ⟨*germinal* ideas of philosophy⟩ **b :** CREATIVE ⟨a *germinal* mind⟩ **2 :** of or relating to a germ cell or early embryo — **ger·mi·nal·ly** \-l-ē\ *adv*

ger·mi·nate \ˈjər-mə-ˌnāt\ *vb* **1 :** to cause to sprout or develop **2 :** to begin to grow **:** SPROUT **3 :** to come into being **:** EVOLVE ⟨an idea that *germinated* slowly⟩ [Latin *germinare* "to sprout," from *germin-, germen* "bud, sprout, germ"] — **ger·mi·na·tion** \ˌjər-mə-ˈnā-shən\ *n*

germ layer *n* **:** any of the three primary layers of cells formed in most embryos during and immediately following gastrulation — compare ECTODERM, ENDODERM 1, MESODERM

germ plasm *n* **1 :** germ cells viewed as the bearers of hereditary material **2 :** GENES

germ theory *n* **:** a theory that infectious and contagious diseases result from the action of microorganisms

germ warfare *n* **:** the use of harmful microorganisms (as bacteria) as weapons in war

ger·on·tol·o·gy \ˌjer-ən-ˈtäl-ə-jē\ *n* **:** the comprehensive study of aging and the problems of the aged [Greek *geront-, gerōn* "old man"] — **ger·on·to·log·i·cal** \ˌjer-ˌänt-l-ˈäj-i-kəl\ *adj* — **ger·on·tol·o·gist** \ˌjer-ən-ˈtäl-ə-jəst\ *n*

[1]**ger·ry·man·der** \ˌjer-ē-ˈman-dər, ˈjer-ē-ˌ, *also* ˌger-, ˈger-\ *n* **1 :** the act or method of gerrymandering **2 :** a district or pattern of districts varying greatly in size or population as a result of gerrymandering [Elbridge *Gerry,* died 1814, American statesman + *-mander* (as in *salamander*); from the shape of an election district formed during Gerry's governorship of Massachusetts]

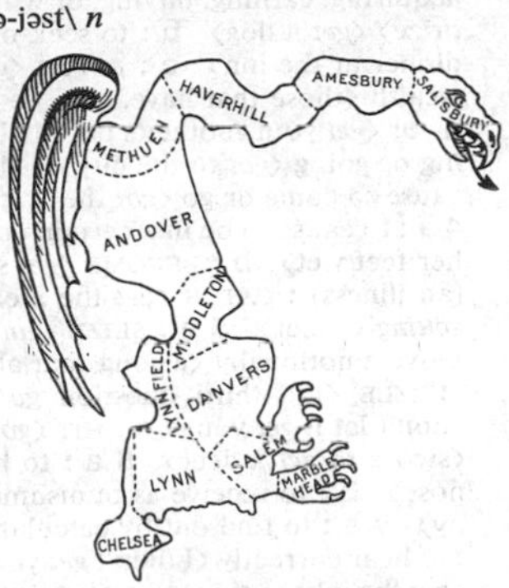

gerrymander 2

[2]**gerrymander** *vt* **-dered; -der·ing** \-də-ring, -dring\ **:** to divide (as a state or county) into election districts so as to give one political party an advantage over its opponents

ger·und \ˈjer-ənd\ *n* **1 :** a verbal noun in Latin that expresses generalized or uncompleted action **2 :** an English verbal noun in *-ing* used as a substantive and at the same time capable of taking adverbial modifiers and having an object [Late Latin *gerundium,* derived from Latin *gerere* "to bear, carry on"]

ge·run·dive \jə-ˈrən-div\ *n* **:** a Latin verbal adjective that expresses necessity or fitness of the action to be performed and has the same suffix as the gerund

ges·so \ˈjes-ō\ *n, pl* **ges·soes :** plaster of paris or gypsum mixed with a binder for use as a surface for painting or in making bas-reliefs [Italian, literally, "gypsum," from Latin *gypsum*]

gest *or* **geste** \ˈjest\ *n* **1 :** a remarkable deed **:** EXPLOIT **2 :** a tale of adventures; *esp* **:** a romance in verse [Medieval French *geste,* from Latin *gesta* "exploits," from *gerere* "to bear carry on, perform"]

ge·sta·po \gə-ˈstäp-ō\ *n, pl* **gestapos :** a secret-police organization employing underhanded and terrorist methods against persons suspected of disloyalty [German, from *Ge*heime *Sta*ats*po*lizei, literally, "secret state police"]

ges·tate \ˈjes-ˌtāt\ *vt* **1 :** to carry in the uterus during pregnancy **2 :** to conceive and gradually develop in the mind [back-formation from *gestation*]

ges·ta·tion \je-ˈstā-shən\ *n* **1 :** the carrying of young in the uterus **:** PREGNANCY **2 :** conception and development especially in the mind [Latin *gestatio,* from *gestare* "to bear," from

\ə\ **abut**	\au̇\ **out**	\i\ **tip**	\ȯ\ **saw**	\u̇\ **foot**
\ər\ **further**	\ch\ **chin**	\ī\ **life**	\ȯi\ **coin**	\y\ **yet**
\a\ **mat**	\e\ **pet**	\j\ **job**	\th\ **thin**	\yü\ **few**
\ā\ **take**	\ē\ **easy**	\ng\ **sing**	\t͟h\ **this**	\yu̇\ **cure**
\ä\ **cot, cart**	\g\ **go**	\ō\ **bone**	\ü\ **food**	\zh\ **vision**

gestus, past participle of *gerere* "to bear, carry"] — **ges·ta·tion·al** \-shnəl, -shən-l\ *adj*

ges·tic·u·late \je-ˈstik-yə-ˌlāt\ *vi* **:** to make gestures especially when speaking [Latin *gesticulari,* from *gestus,* past participle of *gerere* "to carry"] — **ges·tic·u·la·tor** \-ˌlāt-ər\ *n*

ges·tic·u·la·tion \je-ˌstik-yə-ˈlā-shən\ *n* **1 :** the action of making gestures **2 :** GESTURE; *esp* **:** an expressive gesture made in showing strong feeling or in enforcing an argument

ges·tic·u·la·tive \je-ˈstik-yə-ˌlāt-iv\ *adj* **:** inclined to or marked by gesticulation

[1]**ges·ture** \ˈjes-chər, ˈjesh-\ *n* **1 :** the use of motions of the limbs or body as a means of communication; *also* **:** an instance of such communication **2 :** something said or done by way of formality or courtesy, as a symbol or token, or for its effect on the attitudes of others ⟨a political *gesture*⟩ [Medieval Latin *gestura* "mode of action," from Latin *gestus,* past participle of *gerere* "to carry, carry on"]

[2]**gesture** *vb* **1 :** to make a gesture **2 :** to express or direct by a gesture

ge·sund·heit \gə-ˈzu̇nt-ˌhīt\ *interj* — used to wish good health especially to one who has just sneezed [German, literally, "health"]

[1]**get** \get, ˈget; *often* git, *without stress, when a heavily stressed syllable follows, as in "get up"*\ *vb* **got** \gät, ˈgät\; **got** *or* **got·ten** \ˈgät-n\; **get·ting** **1 a :** to gain possession of (as by receiving, acquiring, earning, buying, or winning) ⟨*get* a present⟩ ⟨*got* first prize⟩ ⟨*get* a dog⟩ **b :** to seek out and obtain ⟨planned to *get* dinner at the inn⟩ **c :** FETCH ⟨*get* me a pen⟩ **d :** to acquire wealth ⟨those that have, *get*⟩ **e :** to obtain by request or as a favor ⟨*get* your mother's permission⟩ **2 a :** to succeed in coming or going ⟨*got* to the city on time⟩ ⟨*got* home early⟩ **b :** to cause to come or go ⟨*got* the dog out in a hurry⟩ **3 :** BEGET 1 **4 a :** to cause to be in a certain condition ⟨*got* his hair cut⟩ ⟨*got* her feet wet⟩ **b :** BECOME ⟨*get* sick⟩ **c :** to come down with (an illness) **:** CATCH ⟨*get* the measles⟩ **d :** PREPARE ⟨started *getting* dinner⟩ **5 a :** SEIZE ⟨*got* the thief by the leg⟩ **b :** to move emotionally ⟨a song that always *got* them⟩ **c :** BAFFLE, PUZZLE ⟨the third question *got* everybody⟩ **d :** IRRITATE ⟨don't let it *get* you⟩ **e :** HIT ⟨*got* the dog in the leg⟩ **f :** KILL ⟨swore to *get* a deer⟩ **6 a :** to be subjected to ⟨*get* a broken nose⟩ **b :** to receive as punishment ⟨*got* six months for larceny⟩ **7 a :** to find out by calculation ⟨*got* the right answer⟩ **b :** to hear correctly ⟨I didn't *get* your name⟩ **c :** UNDERSTAND 1 ⟨*got* the joke⟩ **d :** MEMORIZE ⟨*got* the verse by heart⟩ **8 :** PERSUADE, INDUCE ⟨couldn't *get* them to agree⟩ **9 a :** HAVE — used in the present perfect form with present meaning ⟨I've *got* no money⟩ **b :** to be obliged — used in the present perfect form with present meaning ⟨we have *got* to leave⟩ **10 :** to establish communication with ⟨*got* me on the phone⟩ **11 :** to be able **:** MANAGE ⟨*got* to go to college⟩ **12 :** to leave at once **:** clear out ⟨told them to *get*⟩ **13 :** DELIVER 6 ⟨the car *gets* 30 miles to the gallon⟩ [Old Norse *geta* "to get, beget"] — **get ahead :** to achieve success — **get at 1 :** to reach effectively **2 :** to influence corruptly **3 :** to turn one's attention to **4 :** to try to prove or make clear ⟨what are you *getting* at⟩ — **get away with :** to perform without suffering unpleasant consequences — **get even :** to get revenge — **get even with :** to repay in kind — **get into :** to become strongly involved with or deeply interested in — **get it :** to receive a scolding or punishment — **get one's goat :** to make one angry or annoyed — **get over 1 :** OVERCOME ⟨*get over* difficulties⟩ **2 :** to recover from — **get through :** to reach the end of **:** COMPLETE — **get to 1 a :** BEGIN ⟨*gets to* worrying over nothing⟩ **b :** to be ready to deal with ⟨I'll *get to* my homework after dinner⟩ **2 :** to have an effect on **:** INFLUENCE; *esp* **:** BOTHER — **get together 1 :** to bring together **:** ACCUMULATE **2 :** to come together **:** ASSEMBLE **3 :** to reach agreement — **get wind of :** to become aware of — **get with it :** to become alert or aware

[2]**get** \ˈget\ *n* **1 :** something begotten **:** OFFSPRING, PROGENY **2 :** a return of a difficult shot in a game (as tennis)

get across *vb* **:** to become or make clear ⟨*got* the point *across*⟩

get along *vi* **1 a :** to proceed toward a destination **:** PROGRESS **b :** to approach old age **2 :** to meet one's needs **:** MANAGE **3 :** to be or remain on congenial terms

get around *vb* **1 :** EVADE **2 :** to get the better of **3 a :** to find or take the necessary time or effort **b :** to give attention or consideration ⟨will *get around* to it⟩ **4 :** to go from place to place **5 :** to become known ⟨word *got around*⟩

get·away \ˈget-ə-ˌwā\ *n* **1 :** the action or fact of getting away **:** ESCAPE **2 :** the action of starting (as in a race) **3 a :** a short vacation **b :** a place suitable for a short vacation

get back *vb* **1 :** to return to a person, place, or condition ⟨*getting back* to our earlier topic⟩ **2 :** to get revenge ⟨*got back* at him for the insult⟩ **3 :** to regain possession of

get by *vi* **1 :** to succeed with the least possible effort or accomplishment **2 :** to make ends meet **:** SURVIVE **3 :** to proceed without being discovered, criticized, or punished

Geth·sem·a·ne \geth-ˈsem-ə-nē\ *n* **:** a place or occasion of great suffering especially in mind or spirit [from *Gethsemane,* the garden outside Jerusalem mentioned in the New Testament as the scene of the agony and arrest of Jesus, from Greek *Gethsēmanē*]

get off *vb* **1 :** UTTER ⟨*get off* a joke⟩ **2 :** START 5a, LEAVE ⟨*got off* on the trip early⟩ **3 :** to escape or help to escape punishment or harm ⟨*got off* with just a warning⟩ **4 :** to leave work with permission or as scheduled

get on *vb* **1 :** GET ALONG ⟨they *get on* well⟩ **2 :** to start dealing with **3 :** to criticize (someone) repeatedly **4 :** to grow old

get out *vb* **1 :** to escape or cause to escape ⟨hoping to *get out* alive⟩ ⟨*get* oneself *out* of trouble⟩ **2 :** to become or cause to become known or public ⟨let a secret *get out*⟩; *esp* **:** PUBLISH

get·ter \ˈget-ər\ *n* **1 :** one that gets **2 :** a substance introduced into a vacuum tube or electric lamp to remove traces of gas

get–to·geth·er \ˈget-tə-ˌgeth-ər\ *n* **:** MEETING; *esp* **:** an informal social gathering

get·up \ˈget-ˌəp\ *n* **:** COSTUME 3, OUTFIT

get up \get-ˈəp, git-\ *vb* **1 a :** to arise from bed **b :** to rise to one's feet **2 :** to go ahead or faster — used as a command to a horse **3 :** to make preparations for **:** ORGANIZE **4 :** to produce in oneself by effort ⟨*got up* the courage⟩

gew·gaw \ˈgü-ˌgȯ, ˈgyü-\ *n* **:** a showy trifle **:** BAUBLE, TRINKET [origin unknown]

gey·ser \ˈgī-zər\ *n* **:** a spring that throws forth intermittent jets of heated water and steam [Icelandic *Geysir,* hot spring in Iceland, from *geysa* "to rush forth," from Old Norse]

gey·ser·ite \ˈgī-zə-ˌrīt\ *n* **:** a variety of opal that is deposited around some hot springs and geysers

g–force \ˈjē-ˌfȯrs\ *n* **:** the force of gravity or acceleration on a body ⟨pilots experiencing strong *g-forces* during takeoff⟩

[1]**ghast·ly** \ˈgast-lē\ *adj* **ghast·li·er; -est** **1 a :** very shocking or horrible ⟨a *ghastly* crime⟩ **b :** very unpleasant, disagreeable, or objectionable **2 :** resembling a ghost ⟨a *ghastly* face⟩ [Middle English *gastly,* from *gasten* "to terrify"] — **ghast·li·ness** *n*

synonyms GHASTLY, GRUESOME, GRIM, LURID mean horrifying and repellent in appearance or aspect. GHASTLY suggests the horrifying aspects of corpses and ghosts ⟨a *ghastly* ghost story⟩. GRUESOME suggests additionally the effects of cruelty or extreme violence ⟨a *gruesome* account of war⟩. GRIM implies a fierce and forbidding aspect ⟨a *grim* taskmaster⟩. LURID adds to GRUESOME the suggestion of fascination with violent death and especially murder ⟨*lurid* details of a crime⟩.

[2]**ghastly** *adv* **:** in a ghastly manner ⟨turned *ghastly* pale⟩

ghat \ˈgȯt, ˈgät\ *n* **:** a wide flight of stairs descending to a river in India [Hindi and Urdu *ghāṭ*]

gher·kin \ˈgər-kən\ *n* **1 :** a small prickly fruit related to the cucumber and used for pickling; *also* **:** the vine that bears gherkins **2 :** the immature fruit of the cucumber especially when used for pickling [Dutch *gurken,* plural of *gurk* "cucumber"]

ghet·to \ˈget-ō\ *n, pl* **ghettos** *also* **ghettoes** **1 :** a quarter of a city in which Jews were formerly required to live **2 :** a quarter of a city in which members of a minority group live because of social, legal, or economic pressure [Italian]

ghillie *variant of* GILLIE

[1]**ghost** \ˈgōst\ *n* **1 :** the seat of life **:** SOUL ⟨give up the *ghost*⟩ **2 :** a disembodied soul; *esp* **:** the soul of a dead person believed to be an inhabitant of the unseen world or to appear to the living in bodily likeness **3 :** SPIRIT 2b, DEMON **4 :** a faint shadowy trace or suggestion ⟨a *ghost* of a smile⟩ **5 :** a false image in a photographic negative or on a television screen caused especially by reflection **6 :** one who ghostwrites [Old English *gāst*] — **ghost·like** \-ˌlīk\ *adj* — **ghosty** \ˈgō-stē\ *adj*

[2]**ghost** *vb* **1 :** to haunt like a ghost **2 :** to move silently like a ghost **3 :** GHOSTWRITE

ghost·ly \ˈgōst-lē\ *adj* **ghost·li·er; -est** **1 :** of or relating to the soul **:** SPIRITUAL **2 :** of, relating to, or having the characteristics of a ghost **:** SPECTRAL — **ghost·li·ness** *n*

ghost town *n* **:** a once-flourishing town wholly or nearly deserted usually after exhaustion of some natural resource

ghost·write \ˈgōst-ˌrīt\ *vb* **-wrote** \-ˌrōt\; **-writ·ten** \-ˌrit-n\ **:** to write for and in the name of another [back-formation from *ghost-writer*] — **ghost–writ·er** *n*

ghoul \ˈgül\ *n* **1 :** a legendary evil being that robs graves and feeds on corpses **2 :** a person (as a grave robber) whose activities suggest those of a ghoul [Arabic *ghūl*] — **ghoul·ish** \ˈgü-lish\ *adj* — **ghoul·ish·ly** *adv* — **ghoul·ish·ness** *n*

[1]**GI** \jē-ˈī, ˈjē-\ *adj* **1 :** provided by an official U.S. military supply department ⟨*GI* shoes⟩ **2 :** of, relating to, or characteristic of U.S. military personnel **3 :** conforming to military regulations or customs ⟨a *GI* haircut⟩ [galvanized *i*ron; from abbreviation used in listing such articles as garbage cans, but taken as abbreviation for *government issue*]

[2]**GI** *n, pl* **GIs** *or* **GI's :** a member or former member of the U.S. armed forces; *esp* **:** an enlisted person

[1]**gi·ant** \ˈjī-ənt\ *n* **1 :** a legendary humanlike being of great stature and strength **2 a :** a living being of great size **b :** a person of extraordinary powers ⟨a literary *giant*⟩ **3 :** something unusually large or powerful [Medieval French *geant,* from Latin *gigant-, gigas,* from Greek]

[2]**giant** *adj* **:** having extremely large size, proportion, or power

giant anteater *n* **:** a large anteater of Central and South America that has shaggy gray fur and a bushy tail

giant cactus *n* **:** SAGUARO

gi·ant·ess \ˈjī-ənt-əs\ *n* **:** a female giant

gi·ant·ism \ˈjī-ənt-ˌiz-əm\ *n* **1 :** the quality or state of being a giant ⟨*giantism* in industry⟩ **2 :** GIGANTISM 2

giant panda *n* **:** PANDA 2

giant sequoia *n* **:** a California evergreen tree that is related to the bald cypresses and sometimes exceeds 270 feet (about 82 meters) in height — called also *big tree, sequoia*

giant squid *n* **:** any of a group of very large squids that may reach a length of 60 feet (18 meters)

giant star *n* **:** a star of great luminosity and of large mass

giant tortoise *n* **:** any of various large plant-eating tortoises of the Galápagos Islands and islands of the western Indian Ocean

giaour \ˈjaůr\ *n* **:** one outside the Islamic faith **:** INFIDEL [derived from Turkish *gâvur*]

gib \ˈgib\ *n* **:** a plate (as of metal) machined to hold other parts in place, to afford a bearing surface, or to take up wear [origin unknown]

gib·ber \ˈjib-ər\ *vi* **gib·bered; gib·ber·ing** \ˈjib-ring, -ə-ring\ **:** to speak rapidly and often foolishly [imitative] — **gibber** *n*

gib·ber·el·lic acid \ˌjib-ə-ˈrel-ik-\ *n* **:** a crystalline acid $C_{19}H_{22}O_6$ that is a gibberellin used especially in the malting of barley

gib·ber·el·lin \-ˈrel-ən\ *n* **:** any of several hormones that regulate plant growth [New Latin *Gibberella,* genus of fungi]

gib·ber·ish \ˈjib-rish, ˈgib-, -ə-rish\ *n* **:** obscure, confused, or meaningless speech or language [probably from *gibber*]

[1]**gib·bet** \ˈjib-ət\ *n* **1 :** GALLOWS 1 **2 :** an upright post with a projecting arm for hanging the bodies of executed criminals as a warning [Medieval French *gibet*]

[2]**gibbet** *vt* **1 a :** to hang on a gibbet **b :** to expose to public scorn **2 :** to execute by hanging

gib·bon \ˈgib-ən\ *n* **:** any of a genus of tailless apes of southeastern Asia that are the smallest and most arboreal anthropoid apes [French]

gibbon

gib·bos·i·ty \jib-ˈäs-ət-ē, gib-\ *n, pl* **-ties :** PROTUBERANCE, SWELLING

gib·bous \ˈjib-əs, ˈgib-\ *adj* **1 :** convexly rounded **2 :** seen with more than half but not all of the apparent disk illuminated ⟨*gibbous* moon⟩ [Late Latin *gibbosus* "humpbacked," from Latin *gibbus* "hump"]

[1]**gibe** *or* **jibe** \ˈjīb\ *vb* **:** to utter or reproach with taunting or sarcastic words [perhaps from Middle French *giber* "to shake, handle roughly"] — **gib·er** *n*

[2]**gibe** *or* **jibe** *n* **:** JEER, TAUNT

gib·lets \ˈjib-ləts\ *n pl* **:** the edible internal organs of a bird [Middle English *gibelet* "giblets piece, nonessential bit," from Medieval French *gibelot,* from "stew of wildfowl"] — **gib·let** \-lət\ *adj*

gid \ˈgid\ *n* **:** a disease usually of sheep caused by the larva of a tapeworm in the brain [back-formation from *giddy*]

gid·dy \ˈgid-ē\ *adj* **gid·di·er; -est 1 :** DIZZY ⟨*giddy* from the ride⟩ **2 :** causing dizziness ⟨a *giddy* height⟩ **3 :** lightheartedly silly **:** FRIVOLOUS [Old English *gydig* "possessed, mad"] — **gid·di·ly** \ˈgid-l-ē\ *adv* — **gid·di·ness** \ˈgid-ē-nəs\ *n*

gid·dy·ap \ˌgid-ē-ˈap\ *or* **gid·dy·up** \-ˈəp\ *imperative vb* — a command to a horse to go or go faster [alteration of *get up*]

gie \ˈgē\ *chiefly Scottish variant of* GIVE

GIF \ˈgif, ˈjif\ *n* **:** a computer file format for storing a video image; *also* **:** the image stored [*g*raphic *i*nterchange *f*ormat]

gift \ˈgift\ *n* **1 :** a special ability **:** TALENT ⟨a *gift* for music⟩ **2 :** something given voluntarily without compensation **:** PRESENT **3 :** the act or power of giving ⟨the appointment was not in my *gift*⟩ [Old Norse, "something given, talent"]

gift card *n* **:** a card that is worth a certain amount of money and that is given to someone to be used like money to pay for things (as goods or services from a business)

gift certificate *n* **:** a certificate that is worth a certain amount of money and that is given to someone to be used like money to pay for things (as goods and services from a business)

gift·ed \ˈgif-təd\ *adj* **:** having great natural ability ⟨a class for *gifted* children⟩

gift wrap *vt* **:** to wrap (merchandise intended as a gift) in specially attractive or fancy wrappings

[1]**gig** \ˈgig\ *n* **1 a :** a long light boat carried on a ship **b :** a rowboat designed for speed rather than for work **2 :** a light 2-wheeled one-horse carriage [Middle English *-gyge* (in *whyrlegyge* "whirligig"), of unknown origin]

[2]**gig** *n* **:** a pronged spear for catching fish [short for earlier *fizgig, fishgig,* of unknown origin]

[3]**gig** *vb* **gigged; gig·ging :** to spear or fish with a gig

[4]**gig** *n* **:** a military demerit [origin unknown]

[5]**gig** *vt* **gigged; gig·ging :** to give a military demerit to

[6]**gig** *n* **:** GIGABYTE

[7]**gig** *n* **:** an entertainer's job for a specified time [origin unknown]

giga- \ˈjig-ə, ˈgig-ə\ *combining form* **:** billion [Greek *gigas* "giant"]

giga·byte \-ˌbīt\ *n* **:** 1,073,741,824 bytes

giga·hertz \-ˌhərts, -ˌheərts\ *n* **:** a unit of frequency equal to one billion hertz

gi·gan·tesque \ˌjī-ˌgan-ˈtesk, -gən-\ *adj* **:** of huge proportions

gi·gan·tic \jī-ˈgant-ik\ *adj* **:** going beyond the ordinary or expected (as in size, weight, or strength) ⟨*gigantic* industry⟩ [Greek *gigantikos,* from *gigant , gigas* "giant"] **gi·gan·ti·cal·ly** \-ˈgant-i-kə-lē, -klē\ *adv*

gi·gan·tism \jī-ˈgan-ˌtiz-əm, jə-; ˈjī-gən-\ *n* **1 :** GIANTISM 1 **2 :** development to abnormally large size; *esp* **:** excessive bodily growth with delayed or inhibited reproduction

[1]**gig·gle** \ˈgig-əl\ *vi* **gig·gled; gig·gling** \ˈgig-ling, -ə-ling\ **:** to laugh in a silly way [imitative] — **gig·gler** \ˈgig-lər, -ə-lər\ *n*

[2]**giggle** *n* **:** the act of giggling **:** a light silly laugh

gig·gly \ˈgig-lē, -ə-lē\ *adj* **:** given to giggling

gig·o·lo \ˈjig-ə-ˌlō\ *n pl* **-los :** a man who is paid by a woman to be her lover and companion [French]

gi·got \ˈjig-ət, zhē-ˈgō\ *n, pl* **gigots** \-əts, -ˈgō, -ˈgōz\ **1 :** a leg (as of lamb) especially when cooked **2 :** a leg-of-mutton sleeve [Middle French, from *gigue* "fiddle"; from its shape]

Gi·la monster \ˈhē-lə-\ *n* **:** a large orange and black venomous lizard of the southwestern U.S.; *also* **:** a related Mexican lizard [*Gila* River, Arizona]

[1]**gild** \ˈgild\ *vt* **gild·ed** *or* **gilt** \ˈgilt\; **gild·ing 1 :** to cover with or as if with a thin coating of gold **2 :** to give a falsely attractive appearance to [Old English *gyldan*] — **gild·er** *n* — **gild the lily :** to add decoration to something that is already beautiful

[2]**gild** *variant of* GUILD

[1]**gill** \ˈjil\ *n* — see MEASURE table [Middle English *gille,* from Medieval Latin *gillus,* from Late Latin *gillo, gello* "water pot"]

[2]**gill** \ˈgil\ *n* **1 :** an organ (as of a fish) for obtaining oxygen from water **2** *pl* **:** the flesh under or about the chin or jaws **3 :** one of the radiating plates forming the undersurface of the cap of a mushroom [Middle English *gile,* of Scandinavian origin] — **gilled** \ˈgild\ *adj*

\ə\ **abut**	\aů\ **out**	\i\ **tip**	\ȯ\ **saw**	\ů\ **foot**
\ər\ **further**	\ch\ **chin**	\ī\ **life**	\ȯi\ **coin**	\y\ **yet**
\a\ **mat**	\e\ **pet**	\j\ **job**	\th\ **thin**	\yü\ **few**
\ā\ **take**	\ē\ **easy**	\ng\ **sing**	\t͟h\ **this**	\yů\ **cure**
\ä\ **cot, cart**	\g\ **go**	\ō\ **bone**	\ü\ **food**	\zh\ **vision**

gill arch *n* : one of the several curved bars of bone or cartilage that are paired on either side of the throat and support the gills of fishes and amphibians; *also* : any of the corresponding rudimentary ridges in the embryos of all higher vertebrates

gill filament *n* : one of the threadlike processes making up a gill

gil·lie *or* **ghil·lie** \ˈgil-ē\ *n, pl* **gillies** *or* **ghillies** **1** : a male attendant on a Scottish Highland chief **2** *chiefly Scottish & Irish* : a fishing and hunting guide **3** : a low-cut shoe with decorative lacing [Scottish Gaelic *gille* and Irish *giolla* "youth, gillie"]

gill net *n* : a net that allows the head of a fish to pass but entangles it as it seeks to withdraw — **gill–net** \ˈgil-ˌnet\ *vt*

gill raker *n* : one of the bony processes on each gill arch that divert debris away from the gills

gill slit *n* **1** : any of the openings in vertebrates with gills through which water taken in at the mouth moves to the outside bathing the gills **2** : a rudiment of a gill slit that occurs at some stage of development in the embryos of air-breathing vertebrates

gil·ly·flow·er \ˈjil-ē-ˌflau̇-ər, -ˌflau̇r\ *n* : CARNATION 2 [by folk etymology from Middle English *gilofre* "clove," from Medieval French *girofle,* from Latin *caryophyllum,* from Greek *karyophyllon,* from *karyon* "nut" + *phyllon* "leaf"]

[1]gilt \ˈgilt\ *adj* : of the color of gold [from past participle of [1]*gild*]

[2]gilt *n* **1** : gold or something that resembles gold laid on a surface **2** : superficial brilliance

[3]gilt *n* : a young female swine [Old Norse *gyltr*]

gilt–edged \ˈgilt-ˈejd\ *or* **gilt–edge** \-ˈej\ *adj* **1** : having a gilt edge **2** : of the best quality ⟨*gilt-edged* securities⟩

gim·bal \ˈgim-bəl, ˈjim-\ *n* : a device that permits a body to incline freely in any direction or suspends something (as a ship's compass) so that it will remain level when its support is tipped — usually used in plural; called also *gimbal ring* [from obsolete *gemel* "double ring," derived from Latin *geminus* "twin"]

gim·crack \ˈjim-ˌkrak\ *n* : a showy object of little use or value : GEWGAW [origin unknown] — **gimcrack** *adj* — **gim·crack·ery** \-ˌkrak-rē, -ə-rē\ *n*

gim·let \ˈgim-lət\ *n* : a small tool with a screw point, grooved shank, and cross handle for boring holes [Medieval French *guimbelet,* from Dutch *wimmelkijn,* from *wimmel* "wimble"]

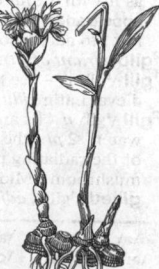

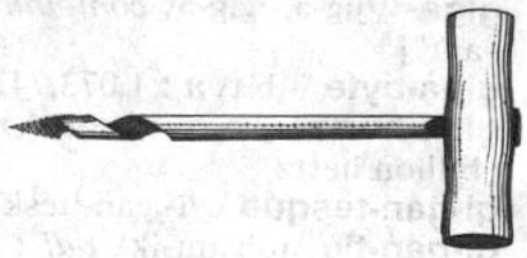
gimlet

gim·mick \ˈgim-ik\ *n* **1** : an ingenious or novel mechanical device : GADGET **2 a** : an important feature that is not immediately apparent : CATCH **b** : a new and ingenious scheme **c** : a trick or device used to attract business or attention ⟨a marketing *gimmick*⟩ [origin unknown] — **gim·micky** \-i-kē\ *adj*

[1]gimp \ˈgimp\ *n* : an ornamental flat braid or round cord used as a trimming [perhaps from Dutch]

[2]gimp *n* **1** : CRIPPLE 1a **2** : LIMP [origin unknown] — **gimpy** \ˈgim-pē\ *adj*

[1]gin \ˈjin\ *n* : a mechanical tool or device: as **a** : a snare or trap for game **b** : COTTON GIN [Medieval French *engin*]

[2]gin *vt* **ginned; gin·ning** **1** : SNARE 1 **2** : to separate (cotton fiber) from seeds and waste material — **gin·ner** *n*

[3]gin *n* **1** : a usually colorless alcoholic liquor flavored with juniper berries **2 a** : GIN RUMMY **b** : the act of laying down a full hand of matched cards in gin rummy [from earlier *geneva,* from obsolete Dutch *genever,* literally, "juniper," derived from Latin *juniperus*]

gin·ger \ˈjin-jər\ *n* **1** : any of a genus of tropical Old World herbs with pungent aromatic underground stems used especially as a spice; *also* : the underground stem of ginger or the spice prepared from it **2** : high spirit : PEP [Old English *gingifer,* from Medieval Latin *gingiber,* from Latin *zingiber,* from Greek *zingiberi*] — **gin·gery** \ˈjinj-rē, -ə-rē\ *adj*

ginger 1

ginger ale *n* : a carbonated nonalcoholic drink flavored with ginger extract

ginger beer *n* : a carbonated nonalcoholic drink heavily flavored with ginger or capsicum or both

gin·ger·bread \ˈjin-jər-ˌbred\ *n* **1** : a cake made with molasses and flavored with ginger **2** : lavish or superfluous ornament especially in architecture ⟨a Victorian house trimmed with *gingerbread*⟩ — **gingerbread** *adj* — **gin·ger·bready** \-ē\ *adj*

gin·ger·ly \ˈjin-jər-lē\ *adj* : very cautious or careful [perhaps from *ginger*] — **gin·ger·li·ness** *n* — **gingerly** *adv*

gin·ger·root \ˈjin-jər-ˌrüt, -ˌru̇t\ *n* : GINGER 1

gin·ger·snap \-ˌsnap\ *n* : a brittle cookie flavored with ginger

ging·ham \ˈging-əm\ *n* : a fabric usually of yarn-dyed cotton in plain weave [Malay *genggang* "striped cloth"]

gin·gi·vi·tis \ˌjin-jə-ˈvīt-əs\ *n* : inflammation of the gums [Latin *gingiva* "gum"]

gink·go \ˈging-kō\ *n, pl* **ginkgoes** *or* **ginkgos** : a large Chinese tree with fan-shaped leaves and foul-smelling fruit that is often grown as a shade tree — called also *maidenhair tree* [New Latin *Ginkgo,* from Japanese *ginkyō*]

gi·nor·mous \jī-ˈnȯr-məs\ *adj* : extremely large : HUGE [*gig*antic + *enormous*]

gin rummy *n* : a rummy game for two players in which each player is dealt 10 cards and a player may win by matching all cards in the hand in sets or may end play when unmatched cards count up to less than 10 [[3]*gin*]

gin·seng \ˈjin-ˌsang, -ˌseng\ *n* **1** : a perennial Chinese herb with small greenish flowers in a rounded cluster and scarlet berries; *also* : a closely related North American herb **2** : the forked aromatic root of the ginseng used as a medicine in China [Chinese (Beijing dialect) *rénshēn*]

Gipsy *chiefly British variant of* GYPSY

gi·raffe \jə-ˈraf\ *n, pl* **giraffes** *or* **giraffe** : a large swift African ruminant mammal that is the tallest living four-footed animal and that has a very long neck and a short coat with dark blotches separated by pale lines [Italian *giraffa,* from Arabic *zirāfa*]

gird \ˈgərd\ *vb* **gird·ed** *or* **girt** \ˈgərt\; **gird·ing** **1** : to encircle or fasten with or as if with a belt ⟨*gird* on a sword⟩ **2** : EQUIP, PROVIDE; *esp* : to invest especially with the sword of knighthood **3** : to get ready ⟨*girded* themselves for a fight⟩ [Old English *gyrdan*]

gird·er \ˈgərd-ər\ *n* : a horizontal main supporting beam

[1]gir·dle \ˈgərd-l\ *n* : something that encircles or confines: as **a** : a belt or sash encircling the waist **b** : a woman's supporting undergarment that extends from the waist to below the hips **c** : a bony arch for the support of a limb: (1) : SHOULDER GIRDLE (2) : PELVIC GIRDLE [Old English *gyrdel*]

[2]girdle *vt* **gir·dled; gir·dling** \ˈgərd-ling, -l-ing\ **1** : to encircle with or as if with a girdle **2** : to move around : CIRCLE ⟨*girdle* the earth⟩ **3** : to cut away the bark and cambium in a ring around (a plant)

girl \ˈgərl\ *n* **1 a** : a female child **b** : a young unmarried woman **c** *sometimes offensive* : a single or married woman of any age **2** *sometimes offensive* : a female servant or employee **3** : GIRLFRIEND 2 [Middle English *gurle, girle* "young person of either sex"] **girl·hood** \-ˌhu̇d\ *n*

girl·friend \ˈgərl-ˌfrend\ *n* **1** : a female friend **2** : a frequent or regular female companion in a romantic relationship

Girl Guide *n* : a member of a worldwide scouting movement for girls 7 to 18 years of age

girl·ish \ˈgər-lish\ *adj* : of, relating to, or having the characteristics of a female child — **girl·ish·ly** *adv* — **girl·ish·ness** *n*

Girl Scout *n* : a member of any of the scouting programs of the Girl Scouts of the United States of America for girls 6 through 17 years of age

Gi·rond·ist \jə-ˈrän-dəst\ *n* : a member of the moderate republican party in the French legislative assembly in 1791 [French *girondiste,* from *Gironde,* a political party, from *Gironde,* department of France]

girt \ˈgərt\ *vt* **1** : GIRD **2** : to fasten by means of a girth [Middle English *girten,* alteration of *girden*]

[1]girth \ˈgərth\ *n* **1** : a band or strap that encircles the body of an animal to fasten something (as a saddle) upon its back **2** : a measure around a body [Old Norse *gjǫrth*]

[2]girth *vt* **1** : ENCIRCLE 2 **2** : to bind or fasten with a girth

gist \ˈjist\ *n* : the main point of a matter : ESSENCE [Medieval French, "it lies," from *gisir* "to lie," derived from Latin *jacēre*]

[1]give \ˈgiv\ *vb* **gave** \ˈgāv\; **giv·en** \ˈgiv-ən\; **giv·ing** **1** : to make a present of **2 a** : GRANT, ACCORD ⟨*give* citizens the right to vote⟩ **b** : to offer or yield to another ⟨*gave* them my confidence⟩ **3 a** : to put into the possession or keeping of another **b** : to offer to another : PROFFER ⟨*give* one's hand to a visitor⟩ **4 a** : to present in public performance ⟨*give* a concert⟩ **b** : to present to view ⟨*gave* the signal⟩ **5** : to provide by way of entertainment ⟨*give* a party⟩ **6 :** to designate as a share or portion : ALLOT **7 :** ATTRIBUTE, ASCRIBE ⟨*gave* the credit to you⟩ **8 :** to grant as true : ASSUME **9 :** to yield as a product or result ⟨cows *give* milk⟩ **10 :** PAY ⟨*give* a fair price⟩ **11 a :** to deliver by bodily action ⟨*gave* it a push⟩ **b :** to carry out (a movement) : EXECUTE ⟨*gave* a sudden leap⟩ **c :** to award by formal verdict ⟨*give* judgment⟩ **12 :** to offer for consideration or acceptance ⟨*give* a reason⟩ **13 :** to apply fully : DEVOTE ⟨*give* oneself to a cause⟩ **14 :** to cause one to have or receive ⟨*gave* pleasure to the reader⟩ **15 :** to make gifts or donations ⟨better to *give* than to receive⟩ ⟨*give* blood⟩ **16 a :** to yield to physical force or strain **b :** to collapse from the application of force or pressure [Middle English *given,* of Scandinavian origin] — **giv·er** \ˈgiv-ər\ *n* — **give birth :** to have a baby — **give birth to :** to bring forth : BEAR — **give ground :** to withdraw before superior force : RETREAT — **give rise to :** to be the cause or source of : PRODUCE — **give the lie to :** to show to be false — **give way 1 a :** RETREAT **b :** to yield the right of way **2 :** to yield oneself without restraint or control **3 a :** COLLAPSE 3, FAIL **b :** CONCEDE 2

synonyms GIVE, PRESENT, DONATE, BESTOW, CONFER, AFFORD mean to hand over to someone without expecting something in return. GIVE is the general term applying to delivering, passing over, or transmitting in any manner ⟨*give* me those cups⟩ ⟨*give* a gift to a friend⟩. PRESENT implies more ceremony or formality and suggests a degree of complexity or value in what is given ⟨*presented* a trophy to the winner⟩. DONATE implies a free but usually publicized giving, as to charity ⟨*donated* new uniforms for the school band⟩. BESTOW implies the conveying of something as a gift and may suggest condescension on the part of the giver ⟨*bestow* unwanted advice⟩. CONFER implies a gracious giving (as of a favor or honor) ⟨*confer* an honorary degree⟩. AFFORD implies a giving or bestowing usually as a natural consequence of the character of the giver ⟨the trees *afford* shade⟩ ⟨a development that *affords* us some hope⟩.

[2]**give** *n* **1 :** capacity or tendency to yield to force or strain **2 :** the quality or state of being springy

give–and–take \ˌgiv-ən-ˈtāk\ *n* **1 :** the practice of making mutual concessions **2 :** a good-natured exchange of ideas

give·away \ˈgiv-ə-ˌwā\ *n* **1 :** an unintentional revelation or betrayal **2 :** something given away free; *esp* : PREMIUM 1c **3 :** a radio or television program on which prizes are given away

give away \ˌgiv-ə-ˈwā\ *vt* **1 :** to deliver (a bride) ceremonially to the bridegroom at a wedding **2 a :** to expose to detection or ridicule : BETRAY **b :** REVEAL 1, DISCLOSE

give back *vb* **1 :** RETREAT 1 **2 :** RETURN 5, RESTORE

give in *vi* : YIELD 5, SURRENDER

[1]**giv·en** \ˈgiv-ən\ *adj* **1 :** DISPOSED, INCLINED ⟨*given* to gossiping⟩ **2 :** FIXED 1c, SPECIFIED ⟨at a *given* time⟩ **3 :** granted as true : ASSUMED

[2]**given** *n* : something taken for granted : a basic assumption

given name *n* : a first name

give off *vt* : EMIT 1a ⟨*gave off* a sweet smell⟩

give out *vb* **1 :** EMIT 1 **2 :** ISSUE 2b ⟨*give out* new books⟩ **3 :** to become exhausted : COLLAPSE **4 :** to break down

give up *vb* **1 :** to yield control or possession of : SURRENDER **2 :** to abandon (oneself) to a feeling, influence, or activity **3 :** to withdraw from an activity or course of action

giz·mo *also* **gis·mo** \ˈgiz-mō\ *n, pl* **gizmos** *also* **gismos :** GADGET [origin unknown]

giz·zard \ˈgiz-ərd\ *n* : a muscular enlargement of the digestive passage (as of a bird or insect) that usually follows the crop and has a horny lining for grinding the food [Middle English *giser,* from Medieval French *gesir, giser,* from Latin *gigeria* "giblets"]

gla·brous \ˈglā-brəs\ *adj* : having a surface without hairs or projections : SMOOTH ⟨*glabrous* leaves⟩ [Latin *glaber* "smooth, bald"] — **gla·brous·ness** *n*

gla·cé \gla-ˈsā\ *adj* **1 :** made or finished so as to have a smooth glossy surface **2 :** coated with a glaze : CANDIED [French, from *glacer* "to freeze, ice, glaze," derived from Latin *glacies* "ice"]

gla·cial \ˈglā-shəl\ *adj* **1 a :** extremely cold : FRIGID **b :** lacking warmth and cordiality **2 a :** of, relating to, or produced by glaciers **b (1) :** of, relating to, or being any of those parts of geologic time when a large portion of the earth was covered by glaciers **(2)** *cap* : PLEISTOCENE — **gla·cial·ly** \-shə-lē\ *adv*

gla·ci·ate \ˈglā-shē-ˌāt\ *vt* **1 :** to cover with a glacier **2 :** to subject to glacial action; *also* : to produce glacial effects in or on — **gla·ci·a·tion** \ˌglā-shē-ˈā-shən, -sē-\ *n*

gla·cier \ˈglā-shər\ *n* : a large body of ice moving slowly down a slope or valley or spreading outward on a land surface [French, from Middle French dialect, from *glace* "ice," from Latin *glacies*]

gla·ci·ol·o·gy \ˌglā-shē-ˈäl-ə-jē, -sē-\ *n* : a branch of science dealing with snow or ice accumulation, glaciation, and glacial epochs — **gla·ci·ol·o·gist** \-jəst\ *n*

[1]**glad** \ˈglad\ *adj* **glad·der; glad·dest 1 a :** experiencing pleasure, joy, or delight : made happy **b :** made pleased, satisfied, or grateful ⟨was *glad* of their help⟩ **c :** very willing ⟨*glad* to do it⟩ **2 a :** marked by, expressive of, or caused by happiness ⟨a *glad* shout⟩ **b :** causing happiness and joy : PLEASANT ⟨*glad* tidings⟩ **3 :** full of brightness and cheerfulness [Old English *glæd* "shining, glad"] — **glad·ly** *adv* — **glad·ness** *n*

[2]**glad** *n* : GLADIOLUS

glad·den \ˈglad-n\ *vt* **glad·dened; glad·den·ing** \ˈglad-ning, -n-ing\ : to make glad

glade \ˈglād\ *n* : a grassy open space in a forest [perhaps from [1]*glad*]

glad·i·a·tor \ˈglad-ē-ˌāt-ər\ *n* **1 :** a person engaged in a fight to the death for public entertainment in ancient Rome **2 :** a person engaging in a fierce fight or controversy [Latin, from *gladius* "sword," of Celtic origin] — **glad·i·a·to·ri·al** \ˌglad-ē-ə-ˈtōr-ē-əl, -ˈtȯr-\ *adj*

glad·i·o·la \ˌglad-ē-ˈō-lə\ *n* : GLADIOLUS [back-formation from *gladiolus,* taken as a plural]

glad·i·o·lus \ˌglad-ē-ˈō-ləs\ *n, pl* **-o·li** \-lē, -ˌlē, -ˌlī\ *or* **-o·lus** *also* **-o·lus·es 1 :** any of a genus of chiefly African plants related to the irises with erect sword-shaped leaves and spikes of brilliantly colored flowers **2 :** the large middle portion of the sternum [Latin, from *gladius* "sword"]

gladiolus

glad·some \ˈglad-səm\ *adj* : giving or showing joy : CHEERFUL — **glad·some·ly** *adv* — **glad·some·ness** *n*

glad·stone \ˈglad-ˌstōn\ *n, often cap* : a traveling bag with flexible sides on a rigid frame that opens flat into two compartments [W. E. *Gladstone,* died 1898, British statesman]

glam·or·ize *also* **glam·our·ize** \ˈglam-ə-ˌrīz\ *vt* **1 :** to make glamorous **2 :** to look upon as glamorous — **glam·or·i·za·tion** \ˌglam-ə-rə-ˈzā-shən\ *n* — **glam·or·iz·er** *n*

glam·or·ous *also* **glam·our·ous** \ˈglam-rəs, -ə-rəs\ *adj* : excitingly attractive : full of glamour — **glam·or·ous·ly** *adv* — **glam·or·ous·ness** *n*

glam·our *also* **glam·or** \ˈglam-ər\ *n* : a romantic, exciting, and often illusory attractiveness; *esp* : alluring or fascinating personal attraction [Scottish *glamour* "magic spell," alteration of English *grammar*]

Word History In the Middle Ages the meaning of *grammar* was not restricted to the study of language but included learning in general. Since almost all learning was couched in language not spoken or understood by the unschooled populace, it was commonly believed that such subjects as magic and astrology were included in this broad sense of *grammar.* Scholars were often viewed with awe and more than a little suspicion by ordinary people. This connection between *grammar* and magic was evident in a number of languages, and in Scotland by the 18th century a form of *grammar,* altered to *glamer* or *glamour,* meant "a magic spell or enchantment." As *glamour* passed into more extended English usage, it came to mean "an elusive, mysteriously exciting attractiveness."

[1]**glance** \ˈglans\ *vi* **1 :** to strike something and fly off at an angle ⟨the bullet *glanced* off the wall⟩ **2 :** to flash or gleam with quick intermittent rays of light ⟨the pond *glanced* in the sunlight⟩ **3 a :** to take a quick or hasty look ⟨*glanced* up from the book⟩ **b :** to refer briefly to a subject [Middle English *glencen, glenchen*] ***synonyms*** see FLASH — **glanc·ing·ly** \-ing-lē\ *adv*

\ə\ **abut**	\au̇\ **out**	\i\ **tip**	\ȯ\ **saw**	\u̇\ **foot**
\ər\ **further**	\ch\ **chin**	\ī\ **life**	\ȯi\ **coin**	\y\ **yet**
\a\ **mat**	\e\ **pet**	\j\ **job**	\th\ **thin**	\yü\ **few**
\ā\ **take**	\ē\ **easy**	\ng\ **sing**	\t͟h\ **this**	\yu̇\ **cure**
\ä\ **cot, cart**	\g\ **go**	\ō\ **bone**	\ü\ **food**	\zh\ **vision**

[2]**glance** *n* **1** : a quick intermittent flash or gleam **2** : a deflected impact or blow **3 a** : a swift movement of the eyes **b** : a quick or cursory look — **at first glance** : on first consideration

gland \'gland\ *n* **1** : a cell or group of cells that prepares and secretes a product for further use in or for elimination from the plant or animal body **2** : LYMPH GLAND [French *glande,* derived from Latin *gland-, glans* "acorn"] — **gland** *adj*

glan·ders \'glan-dərz\ *n sing or pl* : an infectious often fatal bacterial disease especially of horses characterized by nodules that tend to ulcerate [Middle French *glandre* "glandular swelling on the neck," derived from Latin *glans* "acorn"] — **glan·dered** \-dərd\ *adj*

glan·du·lar \'glan-jə-lər\ *adj* **1** : of, relating to, or involving glands, gland cells, or their products **2** : having the characteristics or function of a gland — **glan·du·lar·ly** *adv*

glans \'glanz\ *n, pl* **glan·des** \'glan-ˌdēz\ : the conical vascular extremity of the penis or clitoris [Latin, literally, "acorn"]

glans penis *n* : the glans of the penis

[1]**glare** \'glaər, 'gleər\ *vb* **1 a** : to shine with a harsh uncomfortably brilliant light **b** : to stand out annoyingly or inappropriately **2 a** : to stare angrily or fiercely **b** : to express (as hostility) by staring angrily [Middle English *glaren*]

[2]**glare** *n* **1** : a harsh uncomfortably bright light; *esp* : painfully bright sunlight **2** : an angry or fierce stare **3** : a smooth slippery surface or sheet of ice

glar·ing *adj* **1** : having a fixed look of hostility, fierceness, or anger **2 a** : shining with or reflecting an uncomfortably bright light **b** : overly showy **3** : painfully obvious ⟨a *glaring* error⟩ ***synonyms*** see FLAGRANT — **glar·ing·ly** \-ing-lē\ *adv* — **glar·ing·ness** *n*

glary \'glaər-ē, 'gleər-\ *adj* **glar·i·er; -est** : having a dazzling brightness : GLARING

glas·nost \'glaz-nōst, 'glas-, 'gläz-, 'gläs-\ *n* : a policy in the former Soviet Union that permitted open discussion of political and social issues and freer spreading of news and information [Russian *glasnost',* literally, "publicity," from *glasnyĭ* "public," from *glas* "voice"]

[1]**glass** \'glas\ *n* **1 a** : a hard brittle usually transparent or translucent noncrystalline inorganic substance formed by melting a mixture (as of silica sand and metallic oxides) and cooling to a rigid condition **b** : a substance (as a rock formed by the rapid cooling of molten minerals) resembling glass **2 a** : something (as a water tumbler, lens, mirror, barometer, or telescope) that is made of glass or has a glass lens **b** *pl* : BINOCULARS **c** *pl* : a pair of glass or plastic lenses held in a frame and used to correct defects of vision or to protect the eyes — called also *eyeglasses, spectacles* **3** : the quantity held by a glass container [Old English *glæs*]

[2]**glass** *vt* : to fit or protect with glass

glass·blow·ing \-ˌblō-ing\ *n* : the art of shaping a mass of glass that has been softened by heat by blowing air into it through a tube — **glass·blow·er** \-ˌblō-ər, -ˌblōr\ *n*

glass ceiling *n* : an intangible barrier within the hierarchy of a company that prevents women or minorities from obtaining upper-level positions

glass·ful \'glas-ˌfu̇l\ *n* : the quantity held by a glass

glass·mak·ing \-ˌmā-king\ *n* : the art or process of manufacturing glass — **glass·mak·er** \-kər\ *n*

glass snake *n* : a limbless lizard of the southern U.S. resembling a snake and having a fragile tail that readily breaks off from the body often in pieces

glass sponge *n* : a sponge with a glassy skeleton of silica

glass·ware \'glas-ˌwaər, -ˌweər\ *n* : articles made of glass

glass wool *n* : glass fibers in a mass resembling wool used especially for thermal insulation and air filters

glassy \'glas-ē\ *adj* **glass·i·er; -est** **1** : resembling glass **2** : DULL, LIFELESS ⟨*glassy* eyes⟩ — **glass·i·ly** \'glas-ə-lē\ *adv* — **glass·i·ness** \'glas-ē-nəs\ *n*

Glau·ber's salt \'glau̇-bərz-\ *also* **Glau·ber salt** \'glau̇-bər-\ *n* : a colorless crystalline sulfate of sodium $Na_2SO_4{\cdot}10H_2O$ used especially as a cathartic [Johann R. *Glauber,* died 1668, German chemist]

glau·co·ma \glau̇-'kō-mə, glȯ-\ *n* : an abnormal condition of the eye marked by increased pressure within the eye that causes damage to the retina and gradual loss of vision [Latin, "cataract," from Greek *glaukōma,* derived from *glaukos* "gray"]

glau·cous \'glȯ-kəs\ *adj* **1 a** : of a pale yellowish green color **b** : of a light bluish gray or bluish white color **2** : having a powdery or waxy coating ⟨plums are *glaucous* fruits⟩ [Latin *glaucus,* from Greek *glaukos* "gleaming, gray"] — **glau·cous·ness** *n*

[1]**glaze** \'glāz\ *vb* **1** : to furnish or fit with glass **2 a** : to coat with or as if with glass **b** : to apply a glaze to **3** : to give a smooth glossy surface to **4** : to become glazed [Middle English *glasen,* from *glas* "glass"] — **glaz·er** *n*

[2]**glaze** *n* **1** : a smooth slippery coating of thin ice **2 a** : a transparent or translucent substance used as a coating (as on food or pottery) to produce a gloss **b** : a smooth glossy or lustrous surface or finish

gla·zier \'glā-zhər, -zē-ər\ *n* : a person who sets glass in window frames

glaz·ing \'glā-zing\ *n* : GLAZE

[1]**gleam** \'glēm\ *n* **1 a** : a transient subdued or partly obscured light **b** : a small bright light : GLINT **2** : a brief or faint appearance : TRACE ⟨a *gleam* of hope⟩ [Old English *glǣm*]

[2]**gleam** *vi* **1** : to shine with subdued light or moderate brightness **2** : to appear briefly or faintly

glean \'glēn\ *vb* **1** : to gather from a field or vineyard what has been left by harvesters **2** : to gather little by little ⟨*glean* knowledge from books⟩ [Medieval French *glener,* from Late Latin *glennare,* of Celtic origin] — **glean·er** *n*

glean·ings \'glē-ningz\ *n pl* : things gotten by gleaning

glee \'glē\ *n* **1** : exultant high-spirited joy : MERRIMENT **2** : an unaccompanied song for three or more voices [Old English *glēo* "entertainment, music"] ***synonyms*** see MIRTH

glee club *n* : a chorus organized for singing usually short choral pieces

glee·ful \'glē-fəl\ *adj* : full of glee : MERRY — **glee·ful·ly** \-fə-lē\ *adv* — **glee·ful·ness** *n*

gleet \'glēt\ *n* : chronic inflammation about a bodily opening accompanied by an abnormal discharge; *also* : this discharge [Middle English *glete* "mucous matter," from Medieval French *glette,* from Latin *glittus* "viscous"]

glen \'glen\ *n* : a small secluded narrow valley [Middle English (Scottish dialect), "valley," from Scottish Gaelic and Irish *gleann,* from Old Irish *glenn*]

glen·gar·ry \glen-'gar-ē\ *n, often cap* : a woolen cap of Scottish origin [*Glengarry,* valley in Scotland]

glia \'glē-ə, 'glī-\ *n* : cells of the brain, spinal cord, and ganglia that surround and support neurons [New Latin, from Greek, "glue"] — **gli·al** \-əl\ *adj*

glib \'glib\ *adj* **glib·ber; glib·best** : marked by careless ease and fluency and often insincerity in speaking or writing ⟨a *glib* talker⟩ ⟨a *glib* excuse⟩ [probably from Low German *glibberig* "slippery"] — **glib·ly** *adv* — **glib·ness** *n*

[1]**glide** \'glīd\ *vi* **1** : to move smoothly, continuously, and effortlessly **2** : to pass gradually and imperceptibly ⟨hours *gliding* by⟩ **3** : to descend gradually without engine power sufficient for level flight ⟨*glide* in an airplane⟩ [Old English *glīdan*]

[2]**glide** *n* **1** : the act or action of gliding **2 a** : PORTAMENTO **b** : a transitional sound produced by the passing of the vocal organs to or from the position for the articulation of a speech sound

glid·er \'glīd-ər\ *n* : one that glides: as **a** : an aircraft without an engine that glides on air currents **b** : a porch seat suspended from a frame

[1]**glim·mer** \'glim-ər\ *vi* **glim·mered; glim·mer·ing** \'glim-ring, -ə-ring\ : to shine faintly or unsteadily [Middle English *glimeren*]

[2]**glimmer** *n* **1 a** : a feeble or intermittent light **b** : a soft shimmer **2 a** : a faint idea : INKLING **b** : HINT, SPARK ⟨a *glimmer* of hope⟩

[1]**glimpse** \'glimps\ *vb* : to take a brief look : see momentarily or incompletely [Middle English *glimsen*] — **glimps·er** *n*

[2]**glimpse** *n* : a short hurried view ⟨catch a *glimpse* of someone rushing by⟩

[1]**glint** \'glint\ *vi* **1** *archaic* : GLANCE 1 **2 a** : to shine by reflection: **b** : to shine with small bright flashes **3** : to appear briefly or faintly ⟨fear *glinted* in their eyes⟩ [Middle English *glinten* "to dart obliquely, glint," of Scandinavian origin] ***synonyms*** see FLASH

[2]**glint** *n* **1** : a small bright flash of light : SPARKLE **2** : a brief or faint manifestation ⟨a *glint* of interest⟩

glis·san·do \gli-'sän-dō\ *n, pl* **-di** \-ˌdē\ *or* **-dos** : a rapid sliding up or down the musical scale [probably from French *glissade* "slide," from *glisser* "to slide"]

glis·ten \'glis-n\ *vi* **glis·tened; glis·ten·ing** \'glis-ning, -n-ing\

: to shine by reflection with a soft luster or sparkle [Old English *glisnian*] — **glisten** *n*

synonyms GLISTEN, GLITTER, SCINTILLATE mean to give out bright flashes of light. GLISTEN implies a subdued shining as from a wet or oily surface ⟨grass *glistening* with dew⟩. GLITTER implies a dancing brightness ⟨eyes *glittering* with greed⟩. SCINTILLATE suggests a series of quick flashes caused by or as if by the emission of sparks ⟨clear sky with *scintillating* stars⟩ ⟨*scintillating* conversation⟩.

glis·ter \ˈglis-tər\ *vi* **glis·tered; glis·ter·ing** \-tə-ring, -tring\ : GLISTEN [Middle English *glistren*] — **glister** *n*

glitch \ˈglich\ *n* **1 a** : a usually minor malfunction; *also* : BUG 2 **b** : a minor problem that causes a temporary setback : SNAG **2** : a false electronic signal [perhaps from Yiddish *glitsh* "slippery place"]

1glit·ter \ˈglit-ər\ *vi* **1 a** : to shine with brilliant or metallic luster ⟨*glittering* sequins⟩ **b** : to shine with strong emotion ⟨eyes *glittered* cruelly⟩ **2** : to be brilliantly attractive especially in a superficial way [perhaps from Old Norse *glitra*] ***synonyms*** see GLISTEN

2glitter *n* **1** : sparkling brilliancy, showiness, or attractiveness **2** : small glittering objects used for decoration — **glit·tery** \ˈglit-ə-rē\ *adj*

glitz \ˈglits\ *n* : extravagant showiness : GLITTER [perhaps from German *glitzern* "to glitter"] — **glitzy** \ˈglit-sē\ *adj*

gloam·ing \ˈglō-ming\ *n* : DUSK 1, TWILIGHT [Old English *glōming,* from *glōm* "twilight"]

gloat \ˈglōt\ *vi* : to think about something with great and often malicious delight [related to Middle English *glouten* "to scowl" and perhaps to Old Norse *glotta* "to grin scornfully"] — **gloat·er** *n* — **gloat·ing·ly** \-ing-lē\ *adv*

glob \ˈgläb\ *n* : a small drop : BLOB [perhaps blend of *globe* and *blob*]

glob·al \ˈglō-bəl\ *adj* **1** : SPHERICAL **2** : WORLDWIDE ⟨a *global* communications system⟩ **3** : of, relating to, or applying to the whole of something (as a computer program) ⟨a *global* search through the data⟩ — **glob·al·ly** \-bə-lē\ *adv*

glob·al·i·za·tion \ˌglō-bə-lə-ˈzā-shən\ *n* : the development of a worldwide economy marked especially by free trade, free flow of capital, and the tapping of cheaper foreign labor markets

Global Positioning System *n* : GPS

global warming *n* : a warming of the earth's atmosphere and oceans that is predicted to result from the enhancement of the greenhouse effect by air pollution

globe \ˈglōb\ *n* : something spherical or rounded: as **a** : a spherical representation of the earth or heavens **b** : EARTH 4 [Medieval French, from Latin *globus*]

globe·fish \-ˌfish\ *n* : PUFFER FISH

globe–trot·ter \-ˌträt-ər\ *n* : one that travels widely — **globe–trot·ting** \-ˌträt-ing\ *n or adj*

glob·u·lar \ˈgläb-yə-lər\ *adj* : having the shape of a globe

glob·ule \ˈgläb-yül\ *n* : a tiny globe or ball ⟨*globules* of fat⟩

glob·u·lin \ˈgläb-yə-lən\ *n* : any of a class of simple proteins insoluble in pure water but soluble in dilute salt solutions that occur widely in plant and animal tissues

glock·en·spiel \ˈgläk-ən-ˌshpēl, -ˌspēl\ *n* : a percussion instrument consisting of a series of graduated metal bars tuned to the chromatic scale and played with two hammers [German, from *Glocke* "bell" + *Spiel* "play"]

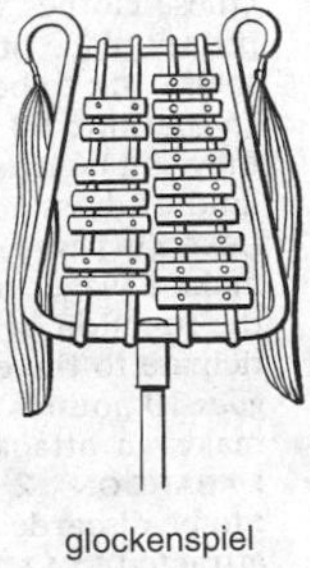

glockenspiel

glo·mer·u·lus \glä-ˈmer-ə-ləs, -yə-ləs\ *n, pl* **-li** \-lī, -lē\ : a clump of capillaries in a nephron of the kidney that passes fluid and dissolved substances to the surrounding Bowman's capsule [New Latin, from Latin *glomus* "ball"] — **glo·mer·u·lar** \-lər\ *adj*

1gloom \ˈglüm\ *vi* **1** : to look sullen or despondent **2** : to be or become overcast [Middle English *gloumen*]

2gloom *n* **1** : partial or total darkness **2 a** : lowness of spirits : DEJECTION **b** : an atmosphere of despondency

gloomy \ˈglü-mē\ *adj* **gloom·i·er; -est** **1** : dismally dark ⟨a *gloomy* cave⟩ **2** : low in spirits **3 a** : causing gloom ⟨*gloomy* weather⟩ ⟨*gloomy* news⟩ **b** : PESSIMISTIC 1 — **gloom·i·ly** \-mə-lē\ *adv* — **gloom·i·ness** \-mē-nəs\ *n*

Glo·ria \ˈglōr-ē-ə, ˈglȯr-\ *n* : either of two Christian doxologies: **a** *or* **Gloria in Ex·cel·sis** \-ˌin-eks-ˈchel-səs, -ek-ˈshel-\ : a hymn beginning "Glory be to God on high" **b** *or* **Gloria Pa·tri** \-ˈpä-trē\ : one beginning "Glory be to the Father" [Latin *gloria* "glory"]

glo·ri·fy \ˈglōr-ə-ˌfī, ˈglȯr-\ *vt* **-fied; -fy·ing** **1** : to make glorious by bestowing honor, praise, or admiration **2** : to present in a highly often overly favorable light ⟨*glorify* war⟩ **3** : to give glory to (as in worship) — **glo·ri·fi·ca·tion** \ˌglōr-ə-fə-ˈkā-shən, ˌglȯr-\ *n* — **glo·ri·fi·er** \ˈglōr-ə-ˌfī-ər, ˈglȯr-, -ˌfīr\ *n*

glo·ri·ous \ˈglōr-ē-əs, ˈglȯr-\ *adj* **1 a** : having or deserving glory **b** : entitling one to glory ⟨a *glorious* victory⟩ **2** : marked by great beauty, excellence, or splendor ⟨*glorious* weather⟩ **3** : extremely pleasant ⟨had a *glorious* time⟩ ***synonyms*** see SPLENDID — **glo·ri·ous·ly** *adv* — **glo·ri·ous·ness** *n*

1glo·ry \ˈglōr-ē, ˈglȯr-\ *n, pl* **glories** **1 a** : praise, honor, or distinction extended by common consent : RENOWN **b** : worshipful praise, honor, and thanksgiving ⟨giving *glory* to God⟩ **2 a** : something that brings praise or renown **b** : a brilliant asset ⟨was a *glory* to the profession⟩ **3 a** : RESPLENDENCE, MAGNIFICENCE ⟨the *glory* of ancient Greece⟩ **b** : the splendor and bliss of heaven **4** : a height of prosperity, achievement, or gratification ⟨in your *glory* when you're on stage⟩ [Latin *gloria*]

2glory *vi* : to rejoice proudly or intensely : EXULT ⟨he *gloried* in his fame⟩

1gloss \ˈgläs, ˈglȯs\ *n* **1** : brightness from a smooth surface : LUSTER, SHEEN **2** : a deceptively attractive appearance ⟨a *gloss* of good manners⟩ [related to Middle High German *glosen* "to glow, shine"]

2gloss *vt* **1 a** : to give a false appearance of acceptableness or adequacy to ⟨*gloss* over faults⟩ **b** : to deal with (a subject or problem) too lightly or not at all ⟨the controversy was *glossed* over by newspapers⟩ **2** : to make glossy

3gloss *n* **1** : a brief explanation (as in the margin of a text) of a hard or unusual word or expression **2 a** : GLOSSARY **b** : an interlinear translation **c** : a continuous commentary accompanying a text [Medieval French *glose,* from Medieval Latin *glosa, glossa,* from Greek *glōssa, glōtta,* literally, "tongue, language, obscure word"]

4gloss *vt* : to furnish glosses for : EXPLAIN

glos·sa·ry \ˈgläs-rē, ˈglȯs-, -ə-rē\ *n, pl* **-ries** **1** : a list in the back of a book of the hard or unusual words found in the text **2** : a dictionary of the special terms found in a particular field of study — **glos·sar·i·al** \gläs-ˈsar-ē-əl, -ˈser-\ *adj*

glos·so·pha·ryn·geal nerve \ˌgläs-ō-ˌfar-ən-ˈjē-əl-, ˌglȯs-; -fə-ˈrin-jē-əl-, -jəl-\ *n* : either of a pair of cranial nerves that supply chiefly the pharynx, posterior tongue, and parotid gland — called also *glossopharyngeal* [Greek *glōssa* "tongue"]

glossy \ˈgläs-ē, ˈglȯs-\ *adj* **gloss·i·er; -est** **1** : having surface luster ⟨*glossy* leather⟩ **2** : superficially sophisticated and attractive ⟨*glossy* advertisements⟩ — **gloss·i·ness** *n*

glot·tis \ˈglät-əs\ *n, pl* **glot·tis·es** *or* **glot·ti·des** \ˈglät-ə-ˌdēz\ : the elongated space in the larynx between the vocal cords; *also* : the structures that surround this space — compare EPIGLOTTIS [Greek *glōttis,* from *glōtta* "tongue"] — **glot·tal** \ˈglät-l\ *adj*

glove \ˈgləv\ *n* **1 a** : a covering for the hand having separate sections for each finger **b** : GAUNTLET 1 **2 a** : a padded leather covering for the hand used in baseball **b** : BOXING GLOVE [Old English *glōf*] — **gloved** \ˈgləvd\ *adj*

glove compartment *n* : a small storage cabinet in the dashboard of an automobile

1glow \ˈglō\ *vi* **1 a** : to shine with or as if with an intense heat **b** (1) : to have a rich warm usually ruddy color (2) : FLUSH, BLUSH **2 a** : to experience a sensation of heat **b** : to show exuberance or elation ⟨*glow* with pride⟩ [Old English *glōwan*]

2glow *n* **1** : brightness or warmth of color; *esp* : REDNESS **2 a** : warmth of feeling or emotion **b** : a sensation of warmth **3** : light that is emitted by something intensely hot but not flaming ⟨the *glow* of embers⟩

glow·er \ˈglau̇-ər, ˈglau̇r\ *vi* : to stare angrily [Middle English (Scottish dialect) *glowren*] — **glower** *n*

glow·worm \ˈglō-ˌwərm\ *n* : an insect or insect larva (as of a firefly) that gives off light

glox·in·ia \gläk-ˈsin-ē-ə\ *n* : any of a genus of tropical American tuberous herbs related to the African violets; *esp* : one from

\ə\ **abut**	\au̇\ **out**	\i\ **tip**	\ȯ\ **saw**	\u̇\ **foot**
\ər\ **further**	\ch\ **chin**	\ī\ **life**	\ȯi\ **coin**	\y\ **yet**
\a\ **mat**	\e\ **pet**	\j\ **job**	\th\ **thin**	\yü\ **few**
\ā\ **take**	\ē\ **easy**	\ng\ **sing**	\t͟h\ **this**	\yu̇\ **cure**
\ä\ **cot, cart**	\g\ **go**	\ō\ **bone**	\ü\ **food**	\zh\ **vision**

Brazil often grown for its showy bell-shaped or slipper-shaped flowers [B. P. *Gloxin,* 18th century German botanist]

gloze \'glōz\ *vt* : ²GLOSS 1 [Middle English *glosen* "to gloss, flatter," from *glose* "gloss"]

glu·ca·gon \'glü-kə-ˌgän\ *n* : a protein hormone secreted by the pancreas that increases the content of sugar in the blood [derived from *glucose*]

glu·cose \'glü-ˌkōs\ *n* : a sugar $C_6H_{12}O_6$; *esp* : a naturally occurring form that is found in plants, fruits, and blood and is a source of energy for living things [French, from Greek *gleukos* "must, sweet wine"]

glu·co·side \'glü-kə-ˌsīd\ *n* : GLYCOSIDE

¹glue \'glü\ *n* **1** : any of various strong adhesive substances; *esp* : a hard protein substance that absorbs water to form a viscous solution with strong adhesive properties **2** : a solution of glue used to stick things together [Medieval French *glu,* from Late Latin *glus*] — **glu·ey** \'glü-ē\ *adj* — **glu·i·ly** \'glü-ə-lē\ *adv*

²glue *vt* **glued; glu·ing** *also* **glue·ing** : to make fast with or as if with glue

glum \'gləm\ *adj* **glum·mer; glum·mest** **1** : SULLEN 1 **2** : DREARY, GLOOMY [related to Middle English *gloumen* "to gloom"] — **glum·ly** *adv* — **glum·ness** *n*

glume \'glüm\ *n* : either of two empty bracts at the base of the spikelet in a grass [Latin *gluma* "hull, husk"]

¹glut \'glət\ *vt* **glut·ted; glut·ting** **1** : to fill especially with food to excess : STUFF **2** : to flood with goods so that supply exceeds demand ⟨the market was *glutted* with fruit⟩ [probably from Medieval French *glutir* "to swallow," from Latin *gluttire*]

²glut *n* : an excessive quantity : OVERSUPPLY

glu·ta·mate \'glüt-ə-ˌmāt\ *n* : a salt or ester of glutamic acid

glu·tam·ic acid \glü-'tam-ik-\ *n* : an amino acid $C_5H_9NO_4$ widely distributed in plant and animal proteins and used in the form of a sodium salt as a seasoning [*gluten* + *amino* + *-ic*]

glu·ta·mine \'glüt-ə-ˌmēn\ *n* : an amino acid $C_5H_{10}N_2O_3$ that is found in plant and animal proteins and that yields glutamic acid and ammonia on hydrolysis

glu·ten \'glüt-n\ *n* : a tough elastic protein substance in flour especially from wheat that holds dough together and makes it sticky [Latin, "glue"] — **glu·ten·ous** \'glüt-nəs, -n-əs\ *adj*

glu·te·us \'glüt-ē-əs\ *n, pl* **-tei** \-ē-ˌī\ : any of the large muscles of the buttocks; *esp* : GLUTEUS MAXIMUS [New Latin, from Greek *gloutos* "buttock"] — **glu·te·al** \-ē-əl\ *adj*

gluteus max·i·mus \-'mak-sə-məs\ *n, pl* **glutei max·i·mi** \-'mak-sə-ˌmī\ : the largest and outermost of the three major muscles in each of the human buttocks [New Latin, literally, "largest gluteus"]

glu·ti·nous \'glüt-nəs, -n-əs\ *adj* : resembling glue : STICKY [Latin *glutinosus,* from *gluten* "glue"] — **glu·ti·nous·ly** *adv*

glut·ton \'glət-n\ *n* **1** : one that eats too much **2** : WOLVERINE [Medieval French *glutun, glotun,* from Latin *glutto*] — **glut·ton·ous** \'glət-nəs, -n-əs\ *adj* — **glut·ton·ous·ly** *adv*

glut·tony \'glət-nē, -n-ē\ *n, pl* **-ton·ies** : excess in eating or drinking

glyc·er·al·de·hyde \ˌglis-ə-'ral-də-ˌhīd\ *n* : a sweet crystalline compound $C_3H_6O_3$ that is formed as an intermediate in carbohydrate metabolism by the breakdown of sugars

gly·cer·ic acid \glis-'er-ik-\ *n* : a syrupy acid $C_3H_6O_4$ obtainable by oxidation of glycerol

glyc·er·ide \'glis-ə-ˌrīd\ *n* : an ester of glycerol especially with fatty acids — **glyc·er·id·ic** \ˌglis-ə-'rid-ik\ *adj*

glyc·er·in *or* **glyc·er·ine** \'glis-rən, -ə-rən\ *n* : GLYCEROL [French *glycérine,* from Greek *glykeros* "sweet"]

glyc·er·ol \'glis-ə-ˌrȯl, -ˌrōl\ *n* : a sweet colorless syrupy alcohol $C_3H_8O_3$ usually obtained by the hydrolysis of fats and oils

gly·cine \'glī-ˌsēn, 'glīs-n\ *n* : a sweet amino acid $C_2H_5NO_2$ formed especially by hydrolysis of proteins [Greek *glykys* "sweet"]

gly·co·gen \'glī-kə-jən\ *n* : a white tasteless substance that is the chief form in which glucose is stored in animal tissues [Greek *glykys* "sweet"]

gly·col·y·sis \glī-'käl-ə-səs\ *n* : energy-producing breakdown of carbohydrate (as glucose) by enzymes by way of phosphate derivatives — **gly·co·lyt·ic** \ˌglī-kə-'lit-ik\ *adj*

gly·co·side \'glī-kə-ˌsīd\ *n* : any of numerous derivatives of sugars that on hydrolysis yield a sugar (as glucose) — **gly·co·sid·ic** \ˌglī-kə-'sid-ik\ *adj*

gly·cos·uria \ˌglī-kō-'shu̇r-ē-ə, -kəs-'yu̇r-\ *n* : the presence of abnormal amounts of sugar in the urine [derived from Greek *glykys* "sweet" + *ouron* "urine"]

G–man \'jē-ˌman\ *n* : a special agent of the Federal Bureau of Investigation [probably from *g*overnment *man*]

gnarl \'närl\ *n* : a hard knob with twisted grain on a tree [probably from *knurl*] — **gnarled** \'närld\ *adj* — **gnarly** \'när-lē\ *adj*

gnash \'nash\ *vt* : to strike or grind (the teeth) together [alteration of Middle English *gnasten*]

gnat \'nat\ *n* : any of various small usually biting two-winged flies — compare ³FLY 2 [Old English *gnætt*]

gnaw \'nȯ\ *vb* **1 a** : to bite or chew with the teeth; *esp* : to wear away by persistent biting or nibbling ⟨a dog *gnawing* a bone⟩ **b** : to make by gnawing ⟨rats *gnawed* a hole⟩ **2 a** : to be a source of vexation to : PLAGUE **b** : to affect like gnawing ⟨*gnawing* hunger⟩ **3** : ERODE 1a, CORRODE [Old English *gnagan*] — **gnaw·er** \'nȯ-ər, 'nȯr\ *n*

gneiss \'nīs\ *n* : a metamorphic rock occurring in layers that is similar in composition to granite or feldspar [German *Gneis*]

gnome \'nōm\ *n* : a legendary dwarf living inside the earth and guarding precious ore or treasure [French] — **gnom·ish** \'nō-mish\ *adj*

gno·mon \'nō-ˌmän, -mən\ *n* : an object that by the position or length of its shadow serves as an indicator of the hour of the day; *esp* : the style of an ordinary sundial [Latin, from Greek *gnōmōn* "interpreter, pointer on a sundial," from *gignōskein* "to know"]

gnu \'nü, 'nyü\ *n, pl* **gnu** *or* **gnus** : WILDEBEEST [Khoikhoi (a southern African language) *t'gnu*]

¹go \'gō\ *vb* **went** \'went\; **gone** \'gȯn, 'gän\; **go·ing** \'gō-ing\; **goes** \'gōz\ **1** : to move on a course : PROCEED ⟨*go* slow⟩ **2** : to move away from one point to or toward another : LEAVE, DEPART **3 a** : to take a certain course or follow a certain procedure ⟨reports *go* through channels⟩ **b** : to pass by a process like journeying ⟨the message *went* by wire⟩ **c (1)** : EXTEND, RUN ⟨our land *goes* to the river⟩ **(2)** : to give access : LEAD ⟨that door *goes* to the cellar⟩ **4** : to be habitually in a certain state ⟨*goes* bareheaded⟩ **5 a** : to become lost, consumed, or spent ⟨where did the money *go*⟩ **b** : ELAPSE, PASS ⟨the evening *went* well⟩ **c** : to pass by sale ⟨*went* for a good price⟩ **d** : to become impaired or weakened ⟨my hearing started to *go*⟩ **e** : to give way under force or pressure : BREAK ⟨heavy rains made the dam *go*⟩ **6 a** : to be in general or on an average ⟨cheap, as yachts *go*⟩ **b** : to become especially as the result of a contest ⟨the decision *went* against them⟩ **7 a** : to apply oneself ⟨*went* to work on the problem⟩ **b** : to put or subject oneself ⟨*went* to great expense⟩ **8** : to make use of for decision, corroboration, or vindication : RESORT ⟨*go* to court to recover damages⟩ **9 a** : to begin or maintain an action or motion ⟨drums *going* strong⟩ **b** : to function properly ⟨get the motor to *go*⟩ **10** : to be known ⟨*goes* by a nickname⟩ **11 a** : to act in accordance ⟨a good rule to *go* by⟩ **b** : to come to be applied ⟨part of the budget *goes* for schools⟩ **c** : to pass by award, assignment, or lot ⟨the prize *went* to a sophomore⟩ **d** : to contribute to a result ⟨qualities that *go* to make a hero⟩ **12 a** : to be about, intending, or expecting something ⟨is *going* to leave town⟩ **b** : to come or arrive at a certain state or condition ⟨*go* to sleep⟩ **c** : to come to be ⟨the tire *went* flat⟩ **13 a** : FIT 2a ⟨these clothes will *go* in your suitcase⟩ **b** : to have a usual or proper place or position : BELONG ⟨these books *go* on the top shelf⟩ **c** : to be capable of being contained in another quantity ⟨5 *goes* into 60 12 times⟩ **14** : TEND, CONDUCE ⟨*goes* to show they can be trusted⟩ **15** : to be acceptable or satisfactory ⟨any kind of dress *goes*⟩ **16** : to proceed along or through : TRAVERSE ⟨if I was *going* your way⟩ ⟨*go* the whole route⟩ **17** : to make a wager or offer of ⟨willing to *go* $50⟩ **18 a** : to assume the function or obligation of ⟨*go* bail for a friend⟩ **b** : to participate to the extent of ⟨*go* halves⟩ **19** : WEIGH 1b ⟨this fish *goes* 10 pounds⟩ [Old English *gān*] — **go·er** *n* — **go at** **1** : to make an attack on **2** : UNDERTAKE 1 — **go back on** **1** : ABANDON **2** : BETRAY 2 **3** : FAIL 2a — **go by the board** : to be discarded — **go for** **1** : to pass for or serve as **2** : to be attracted to : LIKE **3** : ATTACK 1 — **go one better** : SURPASS 1, OUTDO — **go over** **1** : EXAMINE 1 **2 a** : REPEAT 1a **b** : to study or examine again — **go places** : to be on the way to success — **go steady** : to date one person exclusively — **go through** **1** : to subject to thorough examination, consideration, or study **2** : EXPERIENCE 2, UNDERGO **3** : to carry out : PERFORM ⟨*went through* the act perfectly⟩ — **go to bat for** : to give active support or help to — **go to one's head** : to cause one to become conceited or overconfident — **go to pieces** : to become shattered (as in nerves or health) — **go to**

town **1** : to act rapidly or efficiently **2** : to be very successful — **go with** : 3DATE 4a — **go without saying** : to be self-evident — **to go** **1** : remaining to pass or be done ⟨five minutes *to go*⟩ **2** : to be taken from a restaurant ⟨a sandwich *to go*⟩

2**go** *n, pl* **goes** **1** : the act or manner of going **2** : the height of fashion **3** : an often unexpected turn of affairs **4** : ENERGY 1, VIGOR ⟨full of *go*⟩ **5** : TRY ⟨give it a *go*⟩ **6 a** : a spell of activity **b** : SUCCESS 1c ⟨make a *go* of the business⟩ — **no go** : to no avail : USELESS — **on the go** : constantly or restlessly active

3**go** *adj* : ready to go ⟨declared all systems *go*⟩

4**go** *n* : a board game played between two players who alternately place black and white stones on a board checkered by 19 vertical and 19 horizontal lines in an attempt to enclose the opponent's stones [Japanese]

goad \'gōd\ *n* **1** : a pointed rod used to urge an animal on **2** : something that urges : SPUR [Old English *gād* "spear, goad"] — **goad** *vt*

go–ahead \'gō-ə-ˌhed\ *n* : a sign, signal, or authority to proceed : GREEN LIGHT

goal \'gōl\ *n* **1 a** : the terminal point of a race **b** : an area to be reached safely in children's games **2** : the end toward which effort is directed : AIM **3 a** : an area or object toward which players in various games attempt to advance a ball or puck to score points **b** : the score resulting from driving a ball or puck into a goal [Middle English *gol* "boundary, limit"]

goal·ie \'gō-lē\ *n* : GOALKEEPER

goal·keep·er \'gōl-ˌkē-pər\ *n* : a player who defends the goal in various games

goal line *n* : a line at or near either end of the playing area which marks the goal or on which the goal sits

goal·post \'gōl-ˌpōst\ *n* : one of two vertical posts that constitute the goal in various games

goal·ten·der \'gōl-ˌten-dər\ *n* : GOALKEEPER

goat \'gōt\ *n, pl* **goat** *or* **goats** **1** : any of various hollow-horned ruminant mammals related to the sheep but of lighter build and with backwardly arching horns, a short tail, and usually straight hair; *esp* : one long domesticated for its milk, wool, and flesh **2** : SCAPEGOAT 2 [Old English *gāt*] — **goat-like** \-ˌlīk\ *adj*

goat 1

goa·tee \gō-'tē\ *n* : a small pointed or tufted beard on a man's chin [from its resemblance to the beard of a he-goat]

goat·fish \'gōt-ˌfish\ *n* : any of a family of medium-sized often brightly colored fishes having two long barbels under the chin

goat·skin \-ˌskin\ *n* **1** : the skin of a goat **2** : leather made from goatskin

goat·suck·er \-ˌsək-ər\ *n* : NIGHTJAR [from the belief that it sucks milk from goats]

1**gob** \'gäb\ *n* **1** : LUMP 1, MASS **2** : a large amount — usually used in plural ⟨*gobs* of money⟩ [Middle English *gobbe,* probably back-formation from *gobet* "gobbet"]

2**gob** *n* : SAILOR 1a [origin unknown]

gob·bet \'gäb-ət\ *n* : LUMP 1, MASS [Middle French *gobet* "mouthful, piece"]

1**gob·ble** \'gäb-əl\ *vt* **gob·bled; gob·bling** \'gäb-ling, -ə-ling\ **1** : to swallow or eat greedily **2** : to take eagerly : GRAB — usually used with *up* [probably from 1*gob*]

2**gobble** *vi* : to utter the characteristic guttural cry of a male turkey [imitative] — **gobble** *n*

gob·ble·dy·gook *also* **gob·ble·de·gook** \'gäb-əl-dē-ˌgu̇k\ *n* : wordy and generally meaningless jargon [from *gobble,* n.]

gob·bler \'gäb-lər\ *n* : a male turkey

go–be·tween \'gō-bə-ˌtwēn\ *n* : a person who acts as a messenger or an intermediary between two parties

gob·let \'gäb-lət\ *n* : a drinking glass with a foot and stem — compare TUMBLER [Middle English *gobelet* "a bowl-shaped drinking vessel with handles," from Medieval French *goblet*]

goblet cell *n* : a mucus-secreting cell swollen at the free end by secretion [from its shape]

gob·lin \'gäb-lən\ *n* : an ugly grotesque sprite with evil or mischievous ways [Medieval French *gobelin,* from Medieval Latin *gobelinus,* derived from Greek *kobalos* "rogue"]

go·by \'gō-bē\ *n, pl* **gobies** *also* **goby** : any of numerous spiny-finned fishes with the pelvic fins often united to form a sucking disk [Latin *gobius,* a kind of fish, from Greek *kōbios*]

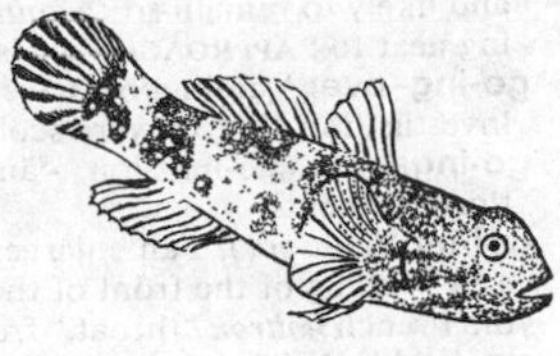
goby

go–cart \'gō-ˌkärt\ *n* **1** : STROLLER 2 **2** : a light open carriage

god \'gäd *also* 'gȯd\ *n* **1** *cap* : the supreme or ultimate reality; *esp* : the Being perfect in power, wisdom, and goodness whom humans worship as creator and ruler of the universe **2** : a being held to possess more than human powers ⟨ancient peoples worshipped many *gods*⟩ **3** : a natural or man-made physical object (as an image or idol) worshipped as divine **4** : something held to be the most important thing in existence ⟨make a *god* of money⟩ [Old English]

god·child \-ˌchīld\ *n* : a person for whom another person stands as sponsor at baptism

god·daugh·ter \-ˌdȯt-ər\ *n* : a female godchild

god·dess \'gäd-əs\ *n* **1** : a female god **2** : a woman whose great charm or beauty arouses adoration

god·fa·ther \'gäd-ˌfät͟h-ər *also* 'gȯd-\ *n* : a man who stands as sponsor for a child at its baptism

god·head \-ˌhed\ *n* **1** : divine nature or essence : DIVINITY **2** *cap* **a** : GOD 1 **b** : the nature of God especially as existing in three persons — used with *the* [Middle English *godhed,* from *god* + *-hed* "-hood"]

god·hood \-ˌhu̇d\ *n* : DIVINITY 1

god·less \'gäd-ləs *also* 'gȯd-\ *adj* : not acknowledging a deity or divine law — **god·less·ness** *n*

god·like \-ˌlīk\ *adj* : resembling or having the qualities of God or a god : DIVINE — **god·like·ness** *n*

god·ling \-ling\ *n* : an inferior or local god

god·ly \-lē\ *adj* **god·li·er; -est** : PIOUS, DEVOUT ⟨*godly* people⟩ — **god·li·ness** *n*

god·moth·er \-ˌmət͟h-ər\ *n* : a woman who stands as sponsor for a child at its baptism

god·par·ent \-ˌpar-ənt, -ˌper-\ *n* : a sponsor at baptism

God's acre *n* : CHURCHYARD; *esp* : a churchyard burial ground

god·send \'gäd-ˌsend *also* 'gȯd-\ *n* : a desirable or needed thing or event that comes unexpectedly [back-formation from *godsent*]

god·son \-ˌsən\ *n* : a male godchild

God·speed \-'spēd\ *n* : a prosperous journey : SUCCESS ⟨wished them *Godspeed*⟩ [Middle English *god speid,* from the phrase *God spede you* "God prosper you"]

god·wit \'gäd-ˌwit\ *n* : any of a genus of long-billed wading birds related to the sandpipers and curlews [origin unknown]

go–get·ter \'gō-ˌget-ər\ *n* : an aggressively enterprising person : HUSTLER — **go–get·ting** \-ˌget-ing\ *adj or n*

1**gog·gle** \'gäg-əl\ *vi* **gog·gled; gog·gling** \'gäg-ling, -ə-ling\ : to stare with wide or protuberant eyes [Middle English *gogelen* "to squint"] — **gog·gler** \gäg-lər, -ə-lər\ *n*

2**goggle** *adj* : PROTUBERANT, STARING ⟨*goggle* eyes⟩ — **gog·gly** \'gäg-lē, -ə-lē\ *adj*

gog·gle–eyed \ˌgäg-əl-'īd\ *adj* : having bulging or rolling eyes

gog·gles \'gäg-əlz\ *n pl* : protective eyeglasses set in a flexible frame that fits snugly against the face

Goi·del·ic \gȯi-'del-ik\ *n* : a branch of the Celtic languages that includes Irish Gaelic, Scottish Gaelic, and Manx [Irish *Gōidel* "Gael, Irishman"] — **Goidelic** *adj*

go in *vi* **1** : to make an approach (as in attacking) **2** : to take part in a game or contest **3** : to form a union or an alliance : JOIN ⟨asked us to *go in* with them⟩ — **go in for** **1** : to give support to **2** : to have or show an interest in or a liking for **3** : to take part in out of interest or liking ⟨*go in for* track⟩

1**go·ing** \'gō-ing\ *n* **1** : the act or instance of going **2** : the condition of the ground especially for walking or driving **3** : advance toward an objective : PROGRESS

\ə\ **abut**	\au̇\ **out**	\i\ **tip**	\ȯ\ **saw**	\u̇\ **foot**
\ər\ **further**	\ch\ **chin**	\ī\ **life**	\ȯi\ **coin**	\y\ **yet**
\a\ **mat**	\e\ **pet**	\j\ **job**	\th\ **thin**	\yü\ **few**
\ā\ **take**	\ē\ **easy**	\ng\ **sing**	\t͟h\ **this**	\yu̇\ **cure**
\ä\ **cot, cart**	\g\ **go**	\ō\ **bone**	\ü\ **food**	\zh\ **vision**

[2]**going** *adj* **1** : EXISTING, LIVING ⟨the best novelist *going*⟩ **2** : CURRENT, PREVAILING ⟨*going* prices⟩ **3** : being successful and likely to remain so ⟨a *going* concern⟩ — **going on** : drawing near to : APPROACHING ⟨is six years old *going on* seven⟩

go·ing–over \ˌgō-ing-ˈō-vər\ *n* **1** : a thorough examination or investigation **2** : a severe scolding or beating : DRUBBING

go·ings–on \ˌgō-ingz-ˈȯn, -ˈän\ *n pl* : usually undesirable actions or events

goi·ter \ˈgȯit-ər\ *n* : an enlargement of the thyroid gland visible as a swelling of the front of the neck [French *goitre,* from Middle French *goitron* "throat," from Latin *guttur*]

go–kart \ˈgō-ˌkärt\ *n* : a small motorized vehicle used especially for racing

gold \ˈgōld\ *n* **1** : a malleable ductile yellow metallic element that occurs chiefly free but also in a few minerals and is used especially in coins and jewelry — see ELEMENT table **2 a** : gold coins **b** : RICHES, MONEY **3** : a deep yellow **4** : a medal awarded as the first prize in a competition : a gold medal [Old English] — **gold** *adj*

gold digger *n* **1** : one who digs for gold **2** : a person who uses charm to get money or gifts from others

gold·en \ˈgōl-dən\ *adj* **1** : consisting of, relating to, or containing gold **2** : having the color of gold ⟨*golden* hair⟩ **3** : FLOURISHING, PROSPEROUS ⟨a *golden* age⟩ **4** : radiantly youthful and vigorous **5** : FAVORABLE 1, ADVANTAGEOUS ⟨a *golden* opportunity⟩ **6** : MELLOW, RESONANT ⟨a smooth *golden* tenor⟩ — **gold·en·ly** *adv* — **gold·en·ness** \-dən-nəs\ *n*

golden–brown alga *n* : any of a major group (Chrysophyta) of algae (as diatoms) with yellowish green to golden brown pigments usually hiding the chlorophyll — called also *golden alga*

golden eagle *n* : a dark brown eagle of northern regions with brownish yellow feathers on the head and neck

gold·en·eye \ˈgōl-də-ˌnī\ *n* **1** : a northern diving duck having the male strikingly marked in black and white **2** : LACEWING

golden glow *n* : a tall branching herb related to the daisies that has showy yellow flower heads

golden hamster *n* : a brownish yellow hamster native chiefly to Syria and often kept as a pet or used as a laboratory animal

golden mean *n* : the medium between extremes : MODERATION

golden retriever *n* : any of a breed of medium-sized retrievers with a moderately long golden coat

gold·en·rod \ˈgōl-dən-ˌräd\ *n* : any of numerous chiefly North American perennial herbs that are related to the daisies and that have heads of small late-blooming usually yellow flowers in loosely branched clusters

golden rule *n* : a rule that one should do to others as one would do to oneself

gol·den·seal \ˈgōl-dən-ˌsēl\ *n* : a perennial North American herb related to the buttercups with a thick knotted yellow rhizome and large rounded leaves

golden section *n* : division of a line segment such that the ratio of the smaller part to the larger is equal to the ratio of the larger to the whole segment

gold·field \ˈgōld-ˌfēld, ˈgōl-\ *n* : a gold-mining district

gold–filled \-ˈfild\ *adj* : covered with a layer of gold

gold·finch \-ˌfinch\ *n* **1** : a small largely red, black, and yellow European finch often kept as a cage bird **2** : any of several small American finches usually having the male in summer plumage yellow with black wings, tail, and crown

gold·fish \-ˌfish\ *n* : a small usually golden orange fish related to the carp and much used as an aquarium and pond fish

gold leaf *n* : a thin sheet of gold used especially for gilding

gold·smith \ˈgōld-ˌsmith, ˈgōl-\ *n* : a maker of or dealer in articles of gold

gold standard *n* : a monetary standard under which the basic unit of currency is defined by a stated quantity of gold

golf \ˈgälf, ˈgȯlf, ˈgäf, ˈgȯf\ *n* : a game in which a player using special clubs tries to sink a ball into each of 9 or 18 holes around a course using as few strokes as possible [Middle English (Scottish dialect)] — **golf** *vi* — **golf·er** *n*

Gol·gi apparatus \ˈgȯl-jē-\ *n* : a stack of flattened membranous sacs in the cytoplasm of a cell that is active in modifying and transporting cell products (as proteins) — called also *Golgi complex* [Camillo *Golgi,* died 1926, Italian physician]

Golgi body *n* : GOLGI APPARATUS; *also* : a single part of the Golgi apparatus

golly \ˈgäl-ē\ *interj* — used as a mild oath or to express surprise; usually used in the phrase *by golly* [euphemism for *God*]

gon- *or* **gono-** *combining form* : sexual : generative : semen : seed ⟨*gono*coccus⟩ [Greek *gonos* "procreation, seed," from *gignesthai* "to be born"]

-gon \ˌgän *also* gən\ *n combining form* : figure having (so many) angles ⟨nona*gon*⟩ [Greek *-gōnon,* from *gōnia* "angle"]

go·nad \ˈgō-ˌnad\ *n* : a sperm- or egg-producing gland (as a testis or ovary) [New Latin *gonad-, gonas,* from Greek *gonos*] — **go·nad·al** \gō-ˈnad-l\ *adj*

go·nad·o·trop·ic \gō-ˌnad-ə-ˈträp-ik\ *also* **go·nad·o·tro·phic** \-ˈtrō-fik\ *adj* : acting on or stimulating the gonads ⟨a *gonadotropic* hormone⟩

go·nad·o·tro·pin \-ˈtrō-pən\ *also* **go·nad·o·tro·phin** \-fən\ *n* : a gonadotropic hormone

gon·do·la \ˈgän-də-lə (*usual for sense 1*), gän-ˈdō-\ *n* **1** : a long narrow flat-bottomed boat with a high bow and stern used on the canals of Venice **2** : a railroad car with a flat bottom, fixed sides, and no top used chiefly for hauling heavy bulk commodities **3 a** : an elongated car attached to the underside of an airship **b** : an enclosure or metal-frame basket suspended from a balloon for carrying passengers or instruments **c** : an enclosed car suspended from a cable used especially as a ski lift [Italian dialect, probably from Greek *kontoura* "small vessel"]

gondola 1

gon·do·lier \ˌgän-də-ˈliər\ *n* : one who propels a gondola

gone \ˈgȯn, ˈgän\ *adj* **1** : PAST 2 ⟨thinking of *gone* summers⟩ **2 a** : ADVANCED, ABSORBED ⟨far *gone* in grief⟩ **b** : INFATUATED ⟨they're *gone* on each other⟩ **c** : PREGNANT 3 **3** : DEAD 1 [from past participle of *go*]

gon·er \ˈgȯn-ər, ˈgän-\ *n* : one whose case is hopeless

gon·fa·lon \ˈgän-fə-ˌlän\ *n* **1** : the ensign of certain princes or states (as the medieval republics of Italy) **2** : a flag that hangs from a crosspiece or frame [Italian *gonfalone*]

gong \ˈgäng, ˈgȯng\ *n* **1** : a metallic disk that produces a resounding tone when struck **2** : a flat saucer-shaped bell [Malay and Java, of imitative origin]

go·nid·i·um \gō-ˈnid-ē-əm\ *n, pl* **-ia** \-ē-ə\ : an asexual reproductive cell or group of cells especially in algae

gono·coc·cus \ˌgän-ə-ˈkäk-əs\ *n, pl* **-coc·ci** \-ˈkäk-ˌsī, -ˌī, -sē, -ē\ : the bacterium that causes gonorrhea [*gon-* + Greek *kokkos* "grain, seed, berry"] — **gono·coc·cal** \-ˈkäk-əl\ *or* **gono·coc·cic** \-ˈkäk-sik, -ik\ *adj*

gon·or·rhea \ˌgän-ə-ˈrē-ə\ *n* : a contagious inflammatory venereal disease of the genitourinary tract caused by the gonococcus — called also *clap* — **gon·or·rhe·al** \-ˈrē-əl\ *adj*

-g·o·ny \g-ə-nē\ *n combining form, pl* **-gonies** : reproduction [Greek *-gonia,* from *gonos* "procreation, seed"]

goo \ˈgü\ *n* : a viscid or sticky substance [perhaps short for *burgoo* "oatmeal gruel"]

goo·ber \ˈgü-bər, ˈgu̇b-ər\ *n, South & Midland* : PEANUT 1 [of Bantu origin; related to Kimbundu (Bantu language of northern Angola) *ŋguba* "peanut"]

[1]**good** \ˈgu̇d\ *adj* **bet·ter** \ˈbet-ər\; **best** \ˈbest\ **1 a** (1) : of a favorable character or tendency ⟨*good* news⟩ (2) : BOUNTIFUL, FERTILE ⟨*good* land⟩ (3) : COMELY, ATTRACTIVE ⟨*good* looks⟩ **b** (1) : SUITABLE, FIT ⟨*good* to eat⟩ (2) : SOUND 1b ⟨one *good* arm⟩ (3) : not depreciated ⟨bad money drives out *good*⟩ (4) : commercially reliable ⟨a *good* risk⟩ (5) : certain to last or live ⟨*good* for another year⟩ (6) : certain to pay or contribute ⟨*good* for a hundred dollars⟩ (7) : certain to elicit a specified result ⟨always *good* for a laugh⟩ **c** (1) : AGREEABLE, PLEASANT ⟨a *good* time⟩ (2) : SALUTARY, WHOLESOME ⟨*good* for a cold⟩ **d** (1) : CONSIDERABLE, AMPLE ⟨a *good* margin⟩ (2) : FULL ⟨waited a *good* four hours⟩ **e** (1) : WELL-FOUNDED, COGENT ⟨*good* reasons⟩ (2) : TRUE ⟨holds *good* for society at large⟩ (3) : deserving of respect : HONORABLE ⟨members in *good* standing⟩ (4) : legally valid ⟨a *good* title⟩ **f** (1) : ADEQUATE, SATISFACTORY ⟨*good* care⟩ (2) : conforming to a standard ⟨*good* English⟩ (3) : DISCRIMINATING, CHOICE ⟨*good* taste⟩ **2 a** (1) : COMMENDABLE, VIRTUOUS, JUST ⟨a *good* man⟩ (2) : RIGHT ⟨*good* conduct⟩ (3) : KIND, BENEVOLENT ⟨*good* intentions⟩ **b** : UPPER-CLASS ⟨a *good* family⟩ **c** : COMPETENT, SKILLFUL ⟨a *good* doctor⟩ **d** : LOYAL, FAITHFUL ⟨a *good* Catholic⟩ **3** : containing less fat and being less tender than higher grades — used of meat and especially beef [Old English *gōd*] — **as good as** : in effect : VIRTUALLY ⟨*as good as* dead⟩ — **good and** : VERY, ENTIRELY ⟨was *good and* mad⟩

[2]**good** *n* **1 a :** what is good or moral ⟨know *good* from evil⟩ **b :** praiseworthy character : GOODNESS **2 :** BENEFIT 1, WELFARE ⟨for the *good* of the community⟩ **3 a :** something that has economic utility or satisfies an economic need or desire **b** *pl* **:** PERSONAL PROPERTY **c** *pl* **:** CLOTH 1 **d** *pl* **:** WARES, COMMODITIES ⟨canned *goods*⟩ **4 :** good persons — used with *the* **5** *pl* **:** proof of wrongdoing ⟨got the *goods* on them⟩

[3]**good** *adv* **:** WELL

good book *n, often cap G&B* **:** BIBLE 1

good–bye *or* **good–by** \gu̇d-ˈbī, gəd-, gə-\ *n* **:** a concluding remark at parting ⟨said their *good-byes* and left⟩ — often used interjectionally as a farewell [alteration of *God be with you*]

good cholesterol *n* **:** HDL

good day *interj* — used as a greeting or farewell in the daytime

good evening *interj* — used as a greeting or farewell in the evening

good fellow *n* **:** an affable companionable person — **good–fel·low·ship** *n*

[1]**good–for–nothing** \ˈgu̇d-fər-ˌnəth-iŋ\ *adj* **:** of no use or value

[2]**good–for–nothing** *n* **:** a good-for-nothing person

Good Friday *n* **:** the Friday before Easter observed as the anniversary of the crucifixion of Christ [from its special sanctity]

good–heart·ed \ˈgu̇d-ˈhärt-əd\ *adj* **:** having a kindly generous disposition — **good–heart·ed·ly** *adv* — **good–heart·ed·ness** *n*

good–hu·mored \-ˈhyü-mərd, -ˈyü-\ *adj* **:** AMIABLE 2, CHEERFUL — **good–hu·mored·ly** *adv* — **good–hu·mored·ness** *n*

good·ish \ˈgu̇d-ish\ *adj* **:** fairly good

good–looking \ˈgu̇d-ˈlu̇k-iŋ\ *adj* **:** having a pleasing or attractive appearance — **good–looker** *n*

good·ly \ˈgu̇d-lē\ *adj* **good·li·er; -est 1 :** of pleasing appearance **2 :** LARGE, CONSIDERABLE ⟨a *goodly* number⟩

good·man \ˈgu̇d-mən\ *n* **1** *archaic* **:** the head of a household **2** *archaic* **:** MISTER 1

good morning *interj* — used as a greeting or farewell in the morning

good–na·tured \ˈgu̇d-ˈnā-chərd\ *adj* **:** of a pleasant and cooperative disposition — **good–na·tured·ly** *adv* — **good–na·tured·ness** *n*

good–neighbor policy *n* **:** a policy of friendship, cooperation, and noninterference in the affairs of another country

good·ness \ˈgu̇d-nəs\ *n* **1 :** the quality or state of being good; *esp* **:** excellence of character **2 :** the nutritious, flavorful, or beneficial portion or element

good–sized \ˈgu̇d-ˈsīzd\ *adj* **:** fairly large

good–tem·pered \-ˈtem-pərd\ *adj* **:** not easily angered or upset — **good–tem·pered·ly** *adv* — **good–tem·pered·ness** *n*

good·wife \ˈgu̇d-ˌwīf\ *n* **1** *archaic* **:** the mistress of a household **2** *archaic* **:** MRS. 1

good·will \ˈgu̇d-ˈwil\ *n* **1 :** a kindly feeling of approval or support **2 :** the favor or advantage that a business has built up over time **3 a :** cheerful consent **b :** willing effort

[1]**goody** \ˈgu̇d-ē\ *n, pl* **good·ies :** something that is particularly good to eat or otherwise attractive

[2]**goody** *interj* — used as an expression of delight especially by children

goody–goody \ˌgu̇d-ē-ˈgu̇d-ē\ *adj* **:** affectedly or self-righteously good or proper — **goody–goody** *n*

Goody Two–shoes \ˈgu̇d-ē-ˈtü-ˌshüz\ *n, often cap S* **:** a person who is goody-goody; *also* **:** a person who is uncommonly good

goo·ey \ˈgü-ē\ *adj* **goo·i·er; -est 1 :** STICKY 1 **2 :** very emotional or sentimental

[1]**goof** \ˈgüf\ *n* **1 :** a silly or stupid person **2 :** BLUNDER [probably from English dialect *goff* "simpleton"]

[2]**goof** *vb* **1 a :** to spend time idly or foolishly ⟨*goofing* off instead of working⟩ **b :** to engage in playful activity ⟨*goofing* around after school⟩ **2 :** BLUNDER 2 **3 :** to make a mess of **:** BUNGLE ⟨*goofed* up the assignment⟩

goof·ball \ˈgüf-ˌbȯl\ *n* **1** *slang* **:** a barbiturate sleeping pill **2 :** a goofy person

go off *vi* **1 :** EXPLODE 2 **2 :** to undergo decline or deterioration **3 :** to follow the expected or desired course **:** PROCEED

goofy \ˈgü-fē\ *adj* **goof·i·er; -est :** CRAZY 2b, SILLY — **goof·i·ly** \-fə-lē\ *adv* — **goof·i·ness** *n*

goo·gle \ˈgü-gəl\ *vt* **goo·gled; goo·gling** *often cap* **:** to use the Google search engine to obtain information about (as a person) on the Internet [*Google*, trademark for a search engine]

goo·gol \ˈgü-ˌgȯl\ *n* **:** a large number expressed as a one followed by one hundred zeros [coined by Milton Sirotta, nephew of Edward Kasner, died 1955, American mathematician]

goom·bah \ˈgüm-ˌbä\ *n* **1 :** a close friend or associate — used especially among Italian-American men **2 :** a member of a chiefly Italian-American mafia **:** MAFIOSO [Italian dialect *cumbà*, from *cumbare* "respected older man," literally, "godfather," from Medieval Latin *compater,* from *com-* "with" + *pater* "father"]

goon \ˈgün\ *n* **1 :** a stupid person **2 :** a man hired to terrorize or eliminate opponents [probably from English dialect *gooney* "simpleton"]

go on *vi* **1 a :** to continue on or as if on a journey ⟨life *goes on*⟩ **b :** keep on **:** CONTINUE ⟨*went on* talking⟩ **2 :** to take place **:** HAPPEN ⟨what's *going on*⟩ **3 :** to talk with enthusiasm

goo·ney \ˈgü-nē\ *n, pl* **gooneys :** an albatross of the Pacific that is chiefly blackish with a dusky bill and black feet and legs — called also *gooney bird* [probably from English dialect *gooney* "simpleton"]

goose \ˈgüs\ *n, pl* **geese** \ˈgēs\ **1 a :** any of numerous long-necked birds intermediate in size between the related swans and ducks **b :** a female goose as distinguished from a gander **2 :** SIMPLETON, DOLT **3** *pl* **goos·es :** a tailor's smoothing iron with a gooseneck handle [Old English *gōs*]

goose 1a

goose·ber·ry \ˈgüs-ˌber-ē, ˈgüz-\ *n* **:** the acid usually prickly fruit of any of several shrubs related to the currant

goose bumps *n pl* **:** a roughening of the skin caused especially by cold, fear, or a sudden feeling of excitement

goose egg *n* **:** ZERO, NOTHING

goose·flesh \ˈgüs-ˌflesh\ *n* **:** GOOSE BUMPS

goose·foot \-ˌfu̇t\ *n, pl* **goosefoots :** any of numerous mostly weedy smooth herbs with branched clusters of small petalless greenish or whitish flowers

goose·neck \-ˌnek\ *n* **:** something (as a flexible or jointed metal tube) curved like the neck of a goose or U-shaped — **goose-necked** \-ˌnekt\ *adj*

goose pimples *n pl* **:** GOOSE BUMPS

goose step *n* **:** a straight-legged stiff-kneed step used by troops of some armies when passing in review — **goose–step** \ˈgüs-ˌstep\ *vi*

go out *vi* **1 :** to go forth; *esp* **:** to leave one's house **2 :** to become extinguished ⟨the hall light *went out*⟩ **3 :** to go on strike **4 :** to become a candidate ⟨*went out* for the football team⟩

go over *vi* **1 :** to make one's way ⟨*going over* to the store⟩ **2 :** to win approval **:** SUCCEED ⟨the joke *went over* well⟩

go·pher \ˈgō-fər\ *n* **1 :** a burrowing land tortoise of the southern U.S. — called also *gopher tortoise* **2 a :** any of several burrowing American rodents with large cheek pouches — called also *pocket gopher* **b :** a small striped ground squirrel of the prairie region of the U.S. [origin unknown]

Gor·di·an knot \ˈgȯrd-ē-ən-\ *n* **:** a very intricate and difficult problem or task [*Gordius,* king of Phrygia, who tied a knot held to be capable of being untied only by the future ruler of Asia, and cut by Alexander the Great with his sword]

gor·di·ta \gȯr-ˈdēt-ə\ *n* **:** a deep-fried pocket of cornmeal dough filled with a seasoned mixture [Mexican Spanish, from *gorda* "thick tortilla," from Spanish, feminine of *gordo* "fat, thick," from Late Latin *gurdus* "dull, blunt"]

[1]**gore** \ˈgōr, ˈgȯr\ *n* **:** a tapering or triangular piece (as of cloth in a skirt) [Old English *gāra* "triangular piece of land"]

[2]**gore** *vt* **1 :** to cut into a tapering triangular form **2 :** to provide with a gore

[3]**gore** *vt* **:** to pierce or wound with a horn or tusk [Middle English *goren*]

[4]**gore** *n* **1 :** BLOOD; *esp* **:** clotted blood **2 :** very detailed gruesomeness [Old English *gor* "filth"]

\ə\ **abut**	\au̇\ **out**	\i\ **tip**	\ȯ\ **saw**	\u̇\ **foot**
\ər\ **further**	\ch\ **chin**	\ī\ **life**	\ȯi\ **coin**	\y\ **yet**
\a\ **mat**	\e\ **pet**	\j\ **job**	\th\ **thin**	\yü\ **few**
\ā\ **take**	\ē\ **easy**	\ŋ\ **sing**	\th\ **this**	\yu̇\ **cure**
\ä\ **cot, cart**	\g\ **go**	\ō\ **bone**	\ü\ **food**	\zh\ **vision**

[1]**gorge** \'gȯrj\ *n* **1** : THROAT 1 — often used with *rise* to indicate revulsion ⟨my *gorge* rises at the sight of blood⟩ **2** : a narrow passage, ravine, or steep-walled canyon [Middle French, from Late Latin *gurges,* from Latin, "whirlpool"]

Word History *Gurges,* the Latin word for "whirlpool," came in Late Latin to mean "throat" as well. The notions of downward passage and of voraciousness must have suggested to speakers of Late Latin that a word meaning "whirlpool" was an apt term for the throat. *Gurges* eventually became Middle French *gorge,* which was borrowed into English in the late 14th century, later developing such familiar meanings as "a ravine with steep, rocky walls," by metaphorical extension from the original "throat."

[2]**gorge** *vb* **1** : to eat greedily; *also* : to partake of something in large amounts ⟨*gorging* on books⟩ **2** : to stuff to capacity ⟨*gorged* themselves on pizza⟩ — **gorg•er** *n*

gor•geous \'gȯr-jəs\ *adj* : resplendently beautiful ⟨a *gorgeous* sunset⟩ [Middle French *gorgias* "elegant," from *gorgias* "wimple," from *gorge* "throat"] ***synonyms*** see SPLENDID — **gor•geous•ly** *adv* — **gor•geous•ness** *n*

Word History In the late Middle Ages, a standard article of feminine dress was the wimple, a cloth headdress that surrounded the neck and head, leaving only the face uncovered. Middle French *gorgias,* derived from *gorge,* "throat," was, strictly speaking, the name for the part of this garment that covered the throat and shoulders. But the word was also applied to the whole wimple. An elegant and elaborate wimple, or *gorgias,* was so much the mark of a well-to-do and fashionable lady that *gorgias* became an adjective meaning "elegant" or "fond of dress." In English it gradually came to emphasize "beauty" more than "elegance."

gor•get \'gȯr-jət\ *n* : a piece of armor protecting the throat and shoulders [Middle French, from *gorge* "throat"]

gor•gon \'gȯr-gən\ *n* **1** *cap* : any of three snaky-haired sisters in Greek mythology whose appearance turns the beholder to stone **2** : an ugly or repulsive woman [Greek *Gorgōn*]

Gor•gon•zo•la \ˌgȯr-gən-'zō-lə\ *n* : a blue cheese of Italian origin [Italian, from *Gorgonzola,* Italy]

go•ril•la \gə-'ril-ə\ *n* **1** : a typically black anthropoid ape of equatorial Africa that is much larger but less erect than the related chimpanzee **2** : THUG, GOON [Greek *Gorillai,* African creatures believed to be hairy women]

gor•man•dize \'gȯr-mən-ˌdīz\ *vb* : to eat greedily or ravenously [*gormand,* alteration of *gourmand*] — **gor•man•diz•er** *n*

gorp \'gȯrp\ *n* : a snack consisting of high-energy food (as raisins and nuts) [origin unknown]

gorse \'gȯrs\ *n* : an evergreen shrub of the legume family that has yellow flowers and leaves reduced to spines — called also *furze* [Old English *gorst*] — **gorsy** \'gȯr-sē\ *adj*

gory \'gȯr-ē, 'gȯr-\ *adj* **gor•i•er; -est** **1** : covered with blood **2** : involving much bloodshed **3** : BLOODCURDLING

gosh \'gäsh *also* 'gȯsh\ *interj* — used as a mild oath or to express surprise [euphemism for *God*]

gos•hawk \'gäs-ˌhȯk\ *n* : a long-tailed short-winged hawk of northern forests noted for its powerful flight and vigor [Old English *gōshafoc,* from *gōs* "goose" + *hafoc* "hawk"]

gos•ling \'gäz-ling, 'gȯz-, -lən\ *n* : a young goose [Middle English, from *gos* "goose"]

[1]**gos•pel** \'gäs-pəl\ *n* **1 a** *often cap* : the Christian message concerning Christ, the kingdom of God, and salvation **b** *cap* : any of the first four New Testament books that tell of the life, death, and resurrection of Jesus Christ; *also* : a similar apocryphal book **2** *cap* : a liturgical reading from one of the New Testament Gospels **3** : the message or teachings of a religious teacher **4** : something accepted or promoted as infallible truth or as a guiding principle **5** : gospel music [Old English *gōdspel,* from *gōd* "good" + *spell* "tale, news"]

[2]**gospel** *adj* **1** : relating to or in accordance with the gospel : EVANGELICAL **2** : of or relating to religious songs associated with evangelism and popular devotion ⟨a *gospel* singer⟩

gos•sa•mer \'gäs-ə-mər, 'gäz-\ *n* **1** : a film of cobwebs floating in air **2** : something light, delicate, or tenuous [Middle English *gossomer,* from *gos* "goose" + *somer* "summer"] — **gossamer** *adj* — **gos•sa•mery** \-mə-rē\ *adj*

[1]**gos•sip** \'gäs-əp\ *n* **1** : a person who habitually reveals personal or sensational facts **2 a** : rumor or report of an intimate nature **b** : chatty talk **c** : the subject matter of gossip [Middle English *gossib* "crony, godparent," from Old English *godsibb* "godparent," from *god* + *sibb* "kinsman"] — **gos•sipy** \-ə-pē\ *adj*

Word History Old English *sibb,* meaning "relative" or "kinsman," came from the adjective *sibb,* "related by blood" (the ancestor of modern English *sibling*). Old English *godsibb* was a person spiritually related to another, specifically by being a sponsor at baptism. Today we call such a person a *godparent.* Over the centuries *godsibb* changed both in form and in meaning. Middle English *gossib* came to be used for a close friend or crony as well as for a godparent. From there it was only a short step to the *gossip* of today, a person no longer necessarily friend, relative, or sponsor, but someone filled with irresistible tidbits of rumor.

[2]**gossip** *vi* : to relate gossip — **gos•sip•er** *n*

got *past of* GET

Goth \'gäth\ *n* : a member of a Germanic people that in the early centuries of the Christian era overran the Roman Empire [Late Latin *Gothi* "Goths"]

[1]**Goth•ic** \'gäth-ik\ *adj* **1** : of, relating to, or resembling the Goths, their civilization, or their language **2** : of or relating to a style of architecture prevalent in western Europe from the middle 12th to the early 16th century and characterized by weights and stresses converging at isolated points on slender vertical piers and counterbalancing buttresses and by pointed arches and vaulting **3** *often not cap* : of or relating to a literary style characterized by the use of desolate or remote settings and macabre, mysterious, or violent incidents — **goth•i•cal•ly** \-i-kə-lē, -klē\ *adv* — **Goth•ic•ness** *n*

[2]**Gothic** *n* **1** : the Germanic language of the Goths **2** : the Gothic architectural style or decoration **3** *often not cap* : a novel, film, or play in the gothic style

go–to \'gō-ˌtü\ *adj* : relied on for expert knowledge or skill ⟨the company's *go-to* guy⟩

gotten *past participle of* GET

gouache \'gwäsh\ *n* **1** : painting with watercolors that have been mixed with white pigment to produce an opaque effect **2** : a picture painted by gouache [French]

Gou•da \'gau̇d-ə, 'güd-\ *n* : a mild cheese of Dutch origin resembling Edam but containing more fat [*Gouda,* Netherlands]

[1]**gouge** \'gau̇j\ *n* **1** : a chisel with a curved blade for scooping or cutting holes **2** : a hole or groove made with or as if with a gouge [Middle French, from Late Latin *gulbia*]

[2]**gouge** *vt* **1** : to cut holes or grooves in with or as if with a gouge **2** : to force out (an eye) with the thumb **3** : to charge excessively : DEFRAUD, CHEAT — **goug•er** *n*

gou•lash \'gü-ˌläsh, -ˌlash\ *n* : a stew made with meat (as beef), vegetables, and paprika [Hungarian *gulyás,* short for *guyláshús,* literally, "herdsman's meat"]

gourd \'gōrd, 'gȯrd, 'gu̇rd\ *n* **1** : any of a family of chiefly herbaceous tendril-bearing vines including the cucumber, melon, squash, and pumpkin **2** : the fruit of a gourd; *esp* : any of various hard-shelled inedible fruits often used for ornament or for vessels and utensils [Medieval French *gurde, gourde,* from Latin *cucurbita*]

gourde \'gu̇rd\ *n* **1** : the basic monetary unit of Haiti **2** : a coin or note representing one gourde [American French]

gour•mand \'gu̇r-ˌmänd\ *n* **1** : one who is excessively fond of eating and drinking **2** : a person heartily interested in good food and drink [Medieval French *gourmant*] — **gour•mand•ism** \'gu̇r-ˌmän-ˌdiz-əm, -mən-\ *n*

gour•met \-ˌmā\ *n* : a connoisseur of food and drink [French, from Middle French *gromet* "groom, wine merchant's assistant," probably from Middle English *grom* "groom"]

gout \'gau̇t\ *n* **1** : a metabolic disease marked by a painful inflammation and swelling of the joints with deposits of salts of uric acid in and around the joints **2** : a fluid mass often gushing or bursting forth [Medieval French *gute* "drop, gout," from Latin *gutta* "drop"] — **gouty** \-ē\ *adj*

gov•ern \'gəv-ərn\ *vb* **1** : to exercise authority or authority over : RULE; *esp* : to control and direct the making and administration of policy in **2** : to control the speed of by automatic means **3 a** : to control, direct, or strongly influence the actions and conduct of ⟨*governed* by his emotions⟩ **b** : to hold in check : RESTRAIN ⟨our limited income *governs* our spending⟩ **4** : to require a word to be in a certain case or mood ⟨in English a transitive verb *governs* a pronoun in the objective case⟩ **5** : to constitute a rule or law for ⟨customs that *govern* human decisions⟩ [Middle French *governer,* from Latin *gubernare* "to steer, govern," from Greek *kybernan*] — **gov·ern·able** \-ər-nə-bəl\ *adj*

gov·ern·ance \'gəv-ər-nəns\ *n* : the exercise of control

gov·ern·ess \'gəv-ər-nəs\ *n* : a woman who teaches and trains a child especially in a private home

gov·ern·ment \'gəv-ər-mənt; 'gəb-m-ənt, 'gəv-; 'gəv-ərn-mənt\ *n* **1** : the act or process of governing; *esp* : authoritative direction or control **2 a** : the exercise of authority over a political unit : RULE **b** : the making of policy as distinguished from the administration of policy decisions **3 a** : the organization, machinery, or agency through which a political unit exercises authority and performs functions **b** : manner of governing : the institutions, laws, and customs through which a political unit is governed ⟨republican *government*⟩ **4** : the body of persons that constitutes the governing authority of a political unit: as **a** : the officials comprising the governing body of a political unit **b** *cap* : the executive branch of the U.S. federal government **5** : POLITICAL SCIENCE — **gov·ern·men·tal** \ˌgəv-ərn-'ment-l, -ər-\ *adj* — **gov·ern·men·tal·ly** \-l-ē\ *adv*

gov·er·nor \'gəv-ə-nər, -ər-\ *n* **1** : one that governs: as **a** : one that exercises authority especially over an area or group **b** : an official elected or appointed to act as ruler, chief executive, or nominal head of a political unit (as a colony, state, or province) **c** : COMMANDANT ⟨*governor* of a fortress⟩ **d** : the managing director and usually the principal officer of an institution or organization ⟨the *governor* of a bank⟩ **e** : a member of a group that directs or controls an institution or society **2** : TUTOR **3** : an attachment to a machine for automatic control of speed

gov·er·nor–gen·er·al \ˌgəv-ə-nər-'jen-rəl, -ər-nər, -ə-rəl\ *n, pl* **governors–general** *or* **governor–generals** : a governor of high rank; *esp* : one who governs a large territory or has deputy governors under him

governor's council *n* : an executive or legislative council chosen to advise or assist a governor

gov·er·nor·ship \'gəv-ə-nər-ˌship, -ər-nər-\ *n* **1** : the office or position of governor **2** : the term of office of a governor

gown \'gau̇n\ *n* **1 a** : a loose flowing outer garment formerly worn by men **b** : an official robe worn especially by a judge, clergyman, or teacher **c** : a woman's dress; *esp* : one suitable for afternoon or evening wear **d** : a loose robe (as a nightgown) **e** : a coverall worn in an operating room **2** : a body of students and faculty of a college or university [Middle French *gune, goune,* from Late Latin *gunna,* a fur or leather garment] — **gown** *vt* — **gowned** \'gau̇nd\ *adj*

GPS \ˌjē-ˌpē-'es\ *n* : a navigation system that uses satellite signals to determine the position of a radio receiver on or above the earth's surface; *also* : a radio receiver used in a GPS system [*G*lobal *P*ositioning *S*ystem]

graaf·ian follicle \'gräf-ē-ən-, 'graf-\ *n, often cap G* : a fluid-filled cavity in a mammal ovary enclosing a developing egg [Regnier de *Graaf,* died 1673, Dutch anatomist]

[1]**grab** \'grab\ *vb* **grabbed; grab·bing** : to take hastily : SNATCH [obsolete Dutch or Low German *grabben*] — **grab·ber** *n*

[2]**grab** *n* **1 a** : a sudden snatch **b** : an unlawful seizure ⟨a land *grab*⟩ **c** : something grabbed **2 a** : a device for clutching an object **b** : CLAMSHELL 2

[1]**grace** \'grās\ *n* **1 a** : help held to be given to humans by God especially in overcoming temptation or in leading a good life **b** : a state of freedom from sin and of love for God held to be enjoyed through divine grace **2** : a short prayer at a meal asking a blessing or giving thanks **3 a** : a disposition to kindness or mercy **b** : a temporary delay granted from the performance of an obligation (as the payment of a debt) **c** : APPROVAL, ACCEPTANCE ⟨stay in his good *graces*⟩ **4 a** : a charming trait or accomplishment **b** : a pleasing appearance or effect : charm **c** : ease of movement or bearing **5** : a musical trill, turn, or appoggiatura **6** *cap* — used as a form of address for a duke, a duchess, or an archbishop **7** *cap* : any of three sister goddesses who are the givers of charm and beauty in Greek mythology [Medieval French, from Latin *gratia* "favor, thanks," from *gratus* "pleasing, grateful"] — **grace·ful** \-fəl\ *adj* — **grace·ful·ly** \-fə-lē\ *adv* — **grace·ful·ness** *n*

[2]**grace** *vt* **1** : HONOR 1b **2** : ADORN, EMBELLISH

grace·less \'grās-ləs\ *adj* : lacking grace, charm, or elegance; *esp* : showing lack of feeling for what is fitting ⟨*graceless* behavior⟩ — **grace·less·ly** *adv* — **grace·less·ness** *n*

grace note *n* : a musical note added as an ornament; *esp* : APPOGGIATURA

gra·cious \'grā-shəs\ *adj* **1 a** : marked by kindness and courtesy ⟨a *gracious* host⟩ **b** : GRACEFUL **c** : characterized by charm, good taste, and urbanity ⟨*gracious* living⟩ **2** : MERCIFUL, COMPASSIONATE — used conventionally of royalty and high nobility — **gra·cious·ly** *adv* — **gra·cious·ness** *n*

grack·le \'grak-əl\ *n* **1** : any of several rather large American blackbirds with glossy iridescent black plumage **2** : any of various Asian starlings [derived from Latin *graculus* "jackdaw"]

grackle 2

grad \'grad\ *n or adj* : GRADUATE

gra·da·tion \grā-'dā-shən, grə-\ *n* **1 a** : a series forming successive stages **b** : a step, degree, or stage in a series **2** : an advance by regular degrees **3** : the act or process of arranging in grades — **gra·da·tion·al** \-shnəl, -shən-l\ *adj* — **gra·da·tion·al·ly** \-ē\ *adv*

[1]**grade** \'grād\ *n* **1** : position in a scale of rank, quality, or order ⟨the *grade* of sergeant⟩ ⟨leather of the highest *grade*⟩ **2** : a stage, step, or degree in a series, order, or ranking **3** : a class of things that are of the same rank, quality, or order **4 a** : a division of the school course representing a year's work ⟨finished the fourth *grade*⟩ **b** : the pupils in a school division **c** *pl* : the elementary school system ⟨teach in the *grades*⟩ **5** : a mark or rating especially of accomplishment in school ⟨a *grade* of 90 on a test⟩ **6** : a standard of quality ⟨government *grades* for meat⟩ **7 a** : the degree of slope (as of a road, railroad track, or embankment); *also* : a sloping road **b** : ground level **8** : a domestic animal with only one parent purebred [French, from Latin *gradus* "step, degree"]

[2]**grade** *vb* **1** : to arrange in grades : SORT ⟨*grade* apples⟩ **2** : to make level or evenly sloping ⟨*grade* a highway⟩ **3** : to give a grade to ⟨*grade* a pupil in arithmetic⟩ **4** : to assign to a grade or assign a grade to ⟨*grade* lumber⟩ **5** : to form a series having only slight differences ⟨colors that *grade* into one another⟩

grade crossing *n* : a crossing (as of highways, railroad tracks, or pedestrian walks) on the same level

grade point *n* : one of the points assigned to each course credit (as in a college) in accordance with the letter grade earned in the course — called also *quality point*

grade point average *n* : the average obtained by dividing the total number of grade points earned by the total number of credits taken — called also *quality point average*

grad·er \'grād-ər\ *n* **1** : one that grades **2** : a machine for leveling earth **3** : a pupil in a school grade ⟨a 5th *grader*⟩

grade school *n* : a public school including usually the first six or the first eight grades

gra·di·ent \'grād-ē-ənt\ *n* **1 a** : the rate of ascent or descent : INCLINATION ⟨the *gradient* of a rock layer⟩ **b** : a part (as of a road) sloping upward or downward : GRADE **2** : change in the value of a quantity per unit distance in a specified direction ⟨vertical temperature *gradient*⟩ [Latin *gradiens,* present participle of *gradi* "to step, go"]

[1]**grad·u·al** \'graj-ə-wəl, 'graj-əl\ *n, often cap* **1** : a book containing the choral parts of the Mass **2** : a response following the Epistle in the Mass [Medieval Latin *graduale,* from Latin *gradus* "step"; from its being sung on the steps of the altar]

[2]**gradual** *adj* **1** : proceeding by steps or degrees **2** : moving or changing by slight degrees [Medieval Latin *gradualis,* from Latin *gradus* "degree, step"] — **grad·u·al·ly** \'graj-ə-lē, -ə-wə-lē\ *adv* — **grad·u·al·ness** \'graj-ə-wəl-nəs, 'graj-əl-\ *n*

grad·u·al·ism \'graj-ə-wə-ˌliz-əm, -ə-ˌliz-\ *n* **1** : the policy of approaching a desired end by gradual stages **2** : the evolution of new species by gradual accumulation of small genetic changes over time — **grad·u·al·ist** \-ləst\ *n or adj* — **grad·u·al·is·tic** \ˌgraj-ə-wə-'lis-tik\ *adj*

[1]**grad·u·ate** \'graj-ə-wət, -ˌwāt\ *n* **1** : a holder of an academic degree or diploma **2** : a graduated cup, cylinder, or flask for measuring contents

[2]**graduate** *adj* **1** : holding an academic degree or diploma **2**

\ə\ **abut**	\au̇\ **out**	\i\ **tip**	\ȯ\ **saw**	\u̇\ **foot**
\ər\ **further**	\ch\ **chin**	\ī\ **life**	\ȯi\ **coin**	\y\ **yet**
\a\ **mat**	\e\ **pet**	\j\ **job**	\th\ **thin**	\yü\ **few**
\ā\ **take**	\ē\ **easy**	\ng\ **sing**	\t͟h\ **this**	\yu̇\ **cure**
\ä\ **cot, cart**	\g\ **go**	\ō\ **bone**	\ü\ **food**	\zh\ **vision**

: of, relating to, or engaged in studies beyond the bachelor's degree

[3]**grad·u·ate** \ˈgraj-ə-ˌwāt\ *vb* **1** : to grant or receive an academic degree or diploma **2** : to admit to a particular standing or grade **3 a** : to mark with degrees of measurement ⟨*graduate* a thermometer⟩ **b** : to divide into grades, classes, or intervals ⟨a *graduated* income tax⟩ **4** : to change gradually [Medieval Latin *graduare,* from Latin *gradus* "step, degree"] — **grad·u·a·tor** \-ˌwāt-ər\ *n*

grad·u·at·ed cylinder *n* : a tall narrow container with a volume scale used especially for measuring liquids

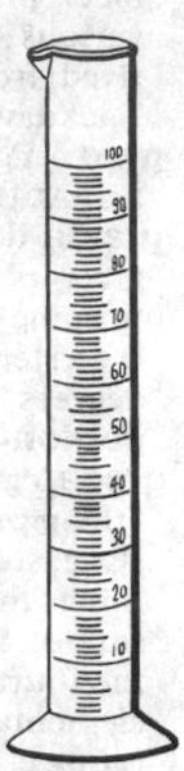

graduated cylinder

graduate school *n* : a division of a university or college devoted entirely to studies beyond the bachelor's degree and having authority to grant advanced degrees

grad·u·a·tion \ˌgraj-ə-ˈwā-shən\ *n* **1** : a mark or the marks on an instrument or vessel indicating degrees or quantity **2 a** : an act or process of graduating **b** : the ceremony or exercises marking the completion by a student of a course of study at a school or college : COMMENCEMENT **3** : arrangement in degrees or ranks

Graeco- — see GRECO-

graf·fi·ti \grə-ˈfēt-ē\ *n* : usually unauthorized writing or drawing on a public surface [Italian, plural of *graffito*] — **graffiti** *vt*

graf·fi·to \gra-ˈfēt-ō\ *n, pl* **-ti** \-ē\ : an inscription or drawing made on a public surface (as a rock or wall) [Italian]

[1]**graft** \ˈgraft\ *n* **1 a** : a grafted plant **b** : the point of insertion of a scion upon a stock **2 a** : the act of grafting **b** : something used in grafting: as (1) : SCION 1 (2) : living tissue used in surgical grafting **3** : the getting of money or advantage by dishonest means through misuse of an official position; *also* : the money or advantage gained [Medieval French *greffe, graife* "stylus, graph," from Medieval Latin *graphium,* from Latin, "stylus," derived from Greek *graphein* "to write"]

[2]**graft** *vb* **1 a** : to unite (plants or scion and stock) to form a graft; *also* : to insert a shoot from a plant into (a different plant) to grow **b** : to join as if by grafting **2** : to implant (living tissue) surgically ⟨*graft* skin over the burn⟩ **3** : to gain money or advantage by dishonest means — **graft·er** *n*

gra·ham cracker \ˈgrā-əm-, ˈgram-\ *n* : a slightly sweet cracker made chiefly of whole wheat flour

graham flour *n* : whole wheat flour [Sylvester *Graham,* died 1851, American dietary reformer]

grail \ˈgrāl\ *n* **1** *cap* : the cup or platter used according to medieval legend by Christ at the Last Supper and thereafter the object of knightly quests **2** : the object of a long or difficult quest [Medieval French *greal, graal* "bowl, grail," from Medieval Latin *gradalis*]

[1]**grain** \ˈgrān\ *n* **1 a** : a seed or fruit of a cereal grass **b** : the seeds or fruits of various food plants and especially the cereal grasses **c** : plants producing grain **2 a** : a small hard particle or crystal (as of sand) **b** : the least amount possible ⟨a *grain* of truth⟩ **3 a** : a granulated surface or appearance **b** : the outer or hair side of a skin or hide **4** : a unit of weight based on the weight of a grain of wheat — see MEASURE table **5 a** : the arrangement of fibers in wood **b** : appearance or texture due to constituent particles or fibers ⟨the *grain* of a stone⟩ **c** : the direction of threads in cloth **6** : natural disposition : TEMPER ⟨lying goes against my *grain*⟩ [Medieval French, from Latin *granum*] — **grained** \ˈgrānd\ *adj*

[2]**grain** *vt* **1** : to form into grains : GRANULATE **2** : to paint in imitation of the grain of wood or stone — **grain·er** *n*

grain alcohol *n* : ETHANOL

grain elevator *n* : ELEVATOR 1c

grain sorghum *n* : any of several sorghums cultivated primarily for grain — compare SORGO

grainy \ˈgrā-nē\ *adj* **grain·i·er; -est** **1** : consisting of or resembling grains : GRANULAR **2** : resembling the grain of wood — **grain·i·ness** *n*

gram \ˈgram\ *n* **1** : a metric unit of mass equal to 1/1000 kilogram and nearly equal to one cubic centimeter of water at its maximum density — see METRIC SYSTEM table **2** : the weight of a gram under the acceleration of gravity [French *gramme,* from Late Latin *gramma,* a small weight, from Greek *gramma* "letter, writing, a small weight"]

-gram \ˌgram\ *n combining form* : drawing : writing : record ⟨spectro*gram*⟩ ⟨tele*gram*⟩ [Greek *gramma* "letter, writing," from *graphein* "to write"]

grama \ˈgram-ə\ *n* : any of several pasture grasses of the western U.S. — called also *grama grass* [Spanish]

gram–atomic weight *n* : the quantity of an element that has a weight in grams numerically equal to the atomic weight — called also *gram-atom*

gra·mer·cy \grə-ˈmər-sē\ *interj, archaic* — used to express gratitude or astonishment [Medieval French *grand merci* "great thanks"]

gram·i·ci·din \ˌgram-ə-ˈsīd-n\ *n* : a toxic crystalline antibiotic produced by a soil bacterium and used against bacteria in local infections [*gram*-positive + *-i-* + *-cide* + *-in*]

gram·mar \ˈgram-ər\ *n* **1** : the study of the classes of words, their inflections, and their functions and relations in sentences **2** : the facts of language with which grammar deals **3 a** : a grammar textbook **b** : speech or writing evaluated according to its conformity to grammatical rules ⟨bad *grammar*⟩ [Medieval French *gramaire,* from Latin *grammatica,* from Greek *grammatikē,* derived from *gramma* "letter, writing," from *graphein* "to write"] — **gram·mar·i·an** \grə-ˈmer-ē-ən, -ˈmar-\ *n*

grammar school *n* **1 a** : a secondary school emphasizing Latin and Greek in preparation for college **b** : a British college preparatory school **2** : ELEMENTARY SCHOOL

gram·mat·i·cal \grə-ˈmat-i-kəl\ *adj* **1** : of or relating to grammar **2** : conforming to the rules of grammar ⟨a *grammatical* sentence⟩ — **gram·mat·i·cal·ly** \-kə-lē, -klē\ *adv*

gramme *chiefly British variant of* GRAM

gram molecular weight *n* : the quantity of a chemical compound that has a weight in grams numerically equal to the molecular weight — called also *gram-molecule*

gram–neg·a·tive \ˈgram-ˈneg-ət-iv\ *adj* : not holding the purple dye when stained by the Gram's stain

gram·o·phone \ˈgram-ə-ˌfōn\ *n* : PHONOGRAPH [from *Gramophone,* a trademark]

gram–pos·i·tive \ˈgram-ˈpäz-ət-iv, -ˈpäz-tiv\ *adj* : holding the purple dye when stained by the Gram's stain

gram·pus \ˈgram-pəs\ *n* **1** : a dolphin with teeth in the lower jaw only **2** : KILLER WHALE [Middle French *graspeis,* from *gras* "fat" + *peis* "fish"]

Gram's stain \ˈgramz-\ *or* **Gram stain** \ˈgram-\ *n* : a technique of staining bacteria with gentian violet such that some bacteria retain the stain and others do not — compare GRAM-NEGATIVE, GRAM-POSITIVE [Hans C. J. *Gram,* died 1938, Danish physician]

gran \ˈgran\ *n* : GRANDMOTHER 1

grana *plural of* GRANUM

gran·a·dil·la \ˌgran-ə-ˈdil-ə\ *n* : the edible usually egg-shaped fruit of a tropical American passionflower [Spanish, literally, "small pomegranate"]

gra·na·ry \ˈgrān-rē, ˈgran-, -ə-rē\ *n, pl* **-ries** **1** : a storehouse for threshed grain **2** : a region producing grain in abundance [Latin *granarium,* from *granum* "grain"]

[1]**grand** \ˈgrand\ *adj* **1** : higher in rank than others of the same class : FOREMOST, PRINCIPAL ⟨the *grand* prize⟩ **2** : INCLUSIVE, COMPLETE ⟨a *grand* total⟩ **3** : of great size, scope, or extent ⟨*grand* ideas⟩ **4 a** : LAVISH ⟨a *grand* celebration⟩ **b** : impressive especially because of size, bearing, dignity, or grandeur ⟨a *grand* palace⟩ **5** : very good : FINE ⟨have a *grand* old time⟩ [Middle French, "large, great, grand," from Latin *grandis*] — **grand·ly** \ˈgran-dlē, -lē\ *adv* — **grand·ness** \ˈgrand-nəs, ˈgran-\ *n*

synonyms GRAND, MAGNIFICENT, MAJESTIC, GRANDIOSE mean large and impressive. GRAND often adds to greatness of size implications of handsomeness and dignity ⟨the royal wedding was a *grand* affair⟩. MAGNIFICENT implies an impressive largeness achieved without sacrifice of dignity or taste ⟨*magnificent* paintings⟩. MAJESTIC adds to MAGNIFICENT connotations of awe-inspiring grandeur or loftiness ⟨a *majestic* waterfall⟩. GRANDIOSE commonly implies inflated pretension or pomposity ⟨*grandiose* schemes of world conquest⟩.

[2]**grand** *n* **1** : GRAND PIANO **2** *pl* **grand** *slang* : a thousand dollars

gran·dam \ˈgran-ˌdam, -dəm\ *or* **gran·dame** \-ˌdām, -dəm\ *n* **1** : GRANDMOTHER 1 **2** : an old woman [Medieval French *graund dame,* literally, "great lady"]

grand·aunt \ˈgran-ˈdant, -ˈdänt\ *n* : an aunt of one's father or mother

grand·child \'grand-ˌchīld, 'gran-\ *n* : a child of one's son or daughter

grand·dad·dy \'gran-ˌdad-ē\ *n* **1** : GRANDFATHER 1a **2** : one that is the first, earliest, or most venerable of its kind

grand·daugh·ter \'gran-ˌdȯt-ər\ *n* : a daughter of one's son or daughter

grand duchess *n* **1** : the wife or widow of a grand duke **2** : a woman who rules a grand duchy in her own right

grand duchy *n* : the territory or dominion of a grand duke or grand duchess

grand duke *n* **1** : the sovereign duke of any of various European states **2** : a son or male descendant of a Russian czar

grande dame \grän^nd-'dȧm, grän-\ *n, pl* **grandes dames** *also* **grande dames** *same or* -dȧmz\ **1** : a usually elderly woman of great prestige **2** : GRANDDADDY 2 [French, literally, "great lady"]

gran·dee \gran-'dē\ *n* : a man of high rank or station; *esp* : a high-ranking Spanish or Portuguese nobleman [Spanish *grande,* from *grande* "large, great," from Latin *grandis*]

gran·deur \'gran-jər\ *n* : the quality or state of being grand : awe-inspiring magnificence [Medieval French, from *grand*]

grand·fa·ther \'grand-ˌfäth-ər, 'gran-\ *n* **1 a** : the father of one's father or mother **b** : ANCESTOR 1 **2** : GRANDDADDY 2 — **grand·fa·ther·ly** \-lē\ *adj*

grandfather clause *n* : a clause creating an exemption based on circumstances previously existing

grandfather clock *n* : a tall pendulum clock standing on the floor — called also *grandfather's clock*

gran·dil·o·quence \gran-'dil-ə-kwəns\ *n* : lofty or pompous eloquence : BOMBAST [derived from Latin *grandiloquus* "using lofty language," from *grandis* "grand" + *loqui* "to speak"] — **gran·dil·o·quent** \-kwənt\ *adj* — **gran·dil·o·quent·ly** *adv*

gran·di·ose \'gran-dē-ˌōs\ *adj* **1** : impressive because of uncommon largeness, scope, effect, or grandeur **2** : characterized by deliberately assumed grandeur or splendor or by absurd exaggeration [French, from Italian *grandioso,* from *grande* "great," from Latin *grandis*] ***synonyms*** see GRAND — **gran·di·ose·ly** *adv* — **gran·di·os·i·ty** \ˌgran-dē-'äs-ət-ē\ *n*

grand jury *n* : a jury that chiefly examines accusations made against persons and if the evidence warrants makes formal charges on which the accused persons are tried

grand·ma \'grand-ˌmä, 'gran-, -ˌmȯ; 'gram-ˌä, -ˌȯ\ *n* : GRANDMOTHER 1

grand mal \'grand-'mäl, 'gran-\ *n* : severe epilepsy [French, literally, "great illness"]

grand march *n* : a march at the opening of a ball in which all the guests participate

grand·moth·er \'grand-ˌməth-ər, 'gran-\ *n* **1** : the mother of one's father or mother **2** : a female ancestor

grand·neph·ew \-'nef-yü\ *n* : a grandson of one's brother or sister

grand·niece \-'nēs\ *n* : a granddaughter of one's brother or sister

grand opera *n* : opera in which the plot is serious or tragic and the entire text is set to music

grand·pa \'grand-ˌpä, 'gran-, -ˌpȯ; 'gram-ˌpä, -ˌpȯ\ *n* : GRANDFATHER 1a

grand·par·ent \'grand-ˌpar-ənt, 'gran-, -ˌper-\ *n* : a parent of one's father or mother

grand piano *n* : a piano with horizontal frame and strings

grand·sire \'grand-ˌsīr, 'gran-\ *n* **1** *or* **grand·sir** \'gran-sər\ *dialect* : GRANDFATHER 1a **2** *archaic* : an aged man

grand slam *n* **1** : the winning of all the tricks of one hand in a card game (as bridge) **2** : a clean sweep or total success (as in winning all of a number of specified contests) **3** : a home run hit with the bases loaded — **grand–slam** *adj*

grand·son \'grand-ˌsən, 'gran-\ *n* : a son of one's son or daughter

grand·stand \-ˌstand\ *n* : a usually roofed stand for spectators at a racecourse or stadium

grand tour *n* **1** : an extended European tour once a part of the education of aristocratic British youth **2** : an extensive and usually educational tour

grand·un·cle \'gran-'dəng-kəl\ *n* : an uncle of one's father or mother

grand unified theory *n* : a theory that unites all the forces of nature (as gravity and electromagnetism) into a single framework

grange \'grānj\ *n* **1** : FARM; *esp* : a farmhouse with outbuildings **2** *cap* : one of the lodges of a national fraternal association of farmers; *also* : the association itself [Medieval French, "granary," from Medieval Latin *granica,* from Latin *granum* "grain"]

grang·er \'grān-jər\ *n* : a member of a Grange

gran·ite \'gran-ət\ *n* **1** : a very hard igneous rock formed essentially of quartz and orthoclase or microcline and used especially for building and for monuments **2** : unyielding firmness or endurance [Italian *granito,* from *granire* "to granulate," from *grano* "grain," from Latin *granum*] — **gra·nit·ic** \grə-'nit-ik\ *adj*

gran·ite·ware \'gran-ət-ˌwaər, -ˌweər\ *n* : enameled ironware

gran·ny *or* **gran·nie** \'gran-ē\ *n, pl* **grannies** : GRANDMOTHER 1 [by shortening and alteration]

granny knot *n* : an insecure knot often made instead of a square knot — see KNOT illustration

Granny Smith \-'smith\ *n* : a tart green apple of Australian origin [Maria Ann *Smith,* died 1870, who cultivated it]

gra·no·la \grə-'nō-lə\ *n* : a mixture typically of rolled oats and various added ingredients (as brown sugar, raisins, coconut, and nuts) that is eaten especially for breakfast or as a snack [from *Granola,* a trademark]

[1]**grant** \'grant\ *vt* **1 a** : to consent to : ALLOW ⟨*grant* your request⟩ **b** : to permit as a right, privilege, or favor ⟨*granted* them a day off to volunteer⟩ **2** : to give the possession or benefit of formally or legally ⟨*grant* a pardon⟩ **3 a** : to be willing to concede **b** : to assume to be true ⟨*granted* you are right, you may find it hard to prove your point⟩ [Medieval French *granter, graanter,* derived from Latin *credere* "to believe, trust"] — **grant·er** \-ər\ *n* — **grant·or** \'grant-ər, grant-'ȯr\ *n*

synonyms GRANT, CONCEDE mean to give as a favor or a right. GRANT implies giving something that could be withheld ⟨*granted* them a chance to rewrite the book report⟩. CONCEDE implies yielding with reluctance to a rightful or compelling claim ⟨forced to *concede* that they were right⟩.

[2]**grant** *n* **1** : the act of granting ⟨land ceded by *grant*⟩ **2** : something granted; *esp* : a gift (as of money or land) for a particular purpose ⟨a research *grant*⟩ **3 a** : a transfer of property by deed or writing **b** : the instrument by which such a transfer is made; *also* : the property so transferred

grant·ee \grant-'ē\ *n* : one to whom a grant is made

gran·tia \'grant-ē-ə\ *n* : a small cylindrical sponge with a skeleton containing calcium [Robert E. *Grant,* died 1874, Scottish anatomist]

grant–in–aid \ˌgrant-n-'ād\ *n, pl* **grants–in–aid** \ˌgrant-sə-'nād\ **1** : a grant from public funds paid to a local government in aid of a public undertaking **2** : a grant to a school or individual for an educational or artistic project

gran·u·lar \'gran-yə-lər\ *adj* : consisting of or appearing to consist of granules : having a grainy texture — **gran·u·lar·i·ty** \ˌgran-yə-'lar-ət-ē\ *n*

gran·u·late \'gran-yə-ˌlāt\ *vb* **1** : to form or crystallize into grains or granules **2** : to form granulations

gran·u·la·tion \ˌgran-yə-'lā-shən\ *n* **1** : the act or process of granulating or the condition of being granulated **2** : a product of granulating (as a tiny knot of vascular tissue in a healing wound)

granulation tissue *n* : tissue made up of granulations that temporarily replaces lost tissue in a wound

gran·ule \'gran-yül\ *n* **1** : a small grain or particle ⟨*granules* of sugar⟩ **2** : a small short-lived bright spot on the sun's photosphere [Late Latin *granulum,* from Latin *granum* "grain"]

gra·num \'grā-nəm\ *n, pl* **gra·na** \-nə\ : one of the stacks of chlorophyll-containing flattened membranous sacs in plant chloroplasts [Latin, "grain, seed"]

grape \'grāp\ *n* **1** : a smooth-skinned juicy light green or deep red to purplish black berry eaten dried or fresh as a fruit or used to make wine **2** : a climbing woody vine whose clustered fruits are grapes **3** : GRAPESHOT [Medieval French, of Germanic origin] — **grapy** \'grā-pē\ *adj*

grape·fruit \'grāp-ˌfrüt\ *n* **1** *pl* **grapefruit** *or* **grapefruits** : a large citrus fruit with a bitter yellow rind and a highly flavored somewhat acid juicy pulp **2 :** a tree that bears grapefruit [from its growing in clusters like grapes]

grape hyacinth *n* **:** any of several small bulbous spring-flowering herbs related to the lilies and bearing spikes of clustered usually blue flowers

grape hyacinth

grape•shot \ˈgrāp-ˌshät\ *n* **:** a cluster of small iron balls used as shot for a cannon

grape sugar *n* **:** DEXTROSE

grape•vine \ˈgrāp-ˌvīn\ *n* **1 :** GRAPE 2 **2 a :** an informal means of circulating information, rumor, or gossip **b :** a secret source of information

[1]**graph** \ˈgraf\ *n* **1 :** the collection of all the points whose coordinates satisfy a given function ⟨the *graph* of $y = x^2$⟩ **2 :** a diagram that represents the change in one variable in comparison with that of one or more other variables [short for *graphic* formula]

[2]**graph** *vt* **1 :** to represent by a graph **2 :** to plot on a graph

-graph \ˌgraf\ *n combining form* **1 :** something written or drawn ⟨mono*graph*⟩ **2 :** instrument for making or transmitting records or images ⟨chrono*graph*⟩ [Greek *graphein* "to write"]

-g•ra•pher \g-rə-fər\ *n combining form* **:** one that writes about (specified) material or in a (specified) way ⟨bio*grapher*⟩

[1]**graph•ic** \ˈgraf-ik\ *also* **graph•i•cal** \-i-kəl\ *adj* **1 :** of or relating to the graphic arts **2 :** being written, drawn, or engraved **3 a :** described or related with vivid clarity or striking imaginative power **b :** sharply outlined or detailed **4 :** of, relating to, or represented by a graph **5 :** of or relating to writing [Latin *graphicus,* from Greek *graphikos,* from *graphein* "to write"] — **graph•i•cal•ly** \-i-kə-lē, -klē\ *adv* — **graph•ic•ness** *n*

synonyms GRAPHIC, VIVID, PICTURESQUE mean giving a clear visual impression in words. GRAPHIC stresses the evoking of a lifelike picture ⟨a *graphic* account of combat⟩. VIVID suggests conveying a strong or lasting impression of reality ⟨a *vivid* story about heroes⟩. PICTURESQUE implies the presenting of a striking or effective picture composed of features notable for their distinctness and charm ⟨a *picturesque* account of their adventures⟩.

[2]**graphic** *n* **1 a :** a product of graphic art **b** *pl* **:** the graphic media **2 :** a picture, map, or graph used for illustration or demonstration **3** *pl* **:** a display (as of pictures or graphs) generated by a computer on a screen, printer, or plotter

graphical user interface *n* **:** software that enables a computer user to interact easily with a computer especially by using icons and menus

graphic arts *n pl* **:** the fine and applied arts of representation, decoration, and writing or printing on flat surfaces together with the techniques and crafts associated with each

graphic equalizer *n* **:** an electronic device for controlling the response of an audio system to a number of frequency bands

graphic novel *n* **:** a fictional story that is presented in comic-strip format and published as a book

graphics tablet *n* **:** a device by which pictures, graphs, or maps are put into a computer in a manner similar to drawing

graph•ite \ˈgraf-ˌīt\ *n* **1 :** a soft black carbon with a metallic luster that conducts electricity and is used especially in making lead pencils, as a dry lubricant, and for electrodes **2 :** a composite material containing carbon fibers for strength ⟨a *graphite* tennis racquet⟩ [German *Graphit,* from Greek *graphein* "to write"] — **gra•phit•ic** \gra-ˈfit-ik\ *adj*

graph•i•tize \ˈgraf-ə-ˌtīz\ *vt* **1 :** to convert into graphite **2 :** to impregnate or coat with graphite — **graph•it•iza•tion** \ˌgraf-ˌīt-ə-ˈzā-shən\ *n*

gra•phol•o•gy \gra-ˈfäl-ə-jē\ *n* **:** the study of handwriting especially to analyze character — **gra•phol•o•gist** \-jəst\ *n*

graph paper *n* **:** paper ruled (as into small squares) for drawing graphs or making diagrams

-g•ra•phy \g-rə-fē\ *n combining form, pl* **-graphies 1 :** writing or representation in a (specified) manner or by a (specified) means or of a (specified) object ⟨phono*graphy*⟩ ⟨photo*graphy*⟩ ⟨steno*graphy*⟩ **2 :** writing on a (specified) subject or in a (specified) field ⟨lexico*graphy*⟩

grap•nel \ˈgrap-nᵊl\ *n* **:** a small anchor with four or five flukes used especially to recover a sunken object or to anchor a small boat [Middle English *grapenel,* derived from Middle French *grape* "hook"]

[1]**grap•ple** \ˈgrap-əl\ *n* **:** the act of grappling or seizing [Middle English *grappel* "grappling hook," from Medieval French *grape* "hook"]

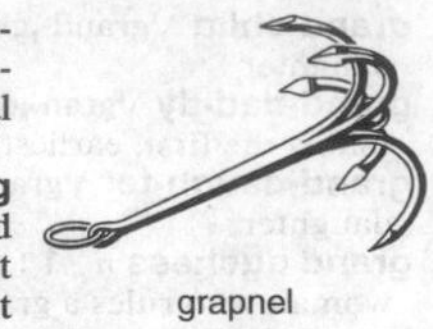
grapnel

[2]**grapple** *vb* **grap•pled; grap•pling** \ˈgrap-ling, -ə-ling\ **1 :** to seize or hold with or as if with a hooked implement **2 :** to struggle in or as if in a close fight **3 :** to attempt to deal **:** COPE ⟨*grapple* with a problem⟩ — **grap•pler** \ˈgrap-lər, -ə-lər\ *n*

grappling hook *n* **:** a metal hook attached to a rope and used for grabbing or grappling — called also *grappling iron*

grap•to•lite \ˈgrap-tə-ˌlīt\ *n* **:** any of numerous fossil colonial animals of the Paleozoic era having individual animals in cups arranged along a support of chitin [Greek *graptos* "painted," from *graphein* "to write, paint"]

[1]**grasp** \ˈgrasp\ *vb* **1 :** to make the effort of seizing with or as if with the hand **:** CLUTCH ⟨*grasping* at straws⟩ **2 :** to clasp or embrace with or as if with the fingers or arms ⟨*grasp* a bat⟩ **3 :** UNDERSTAND 1, COMPREHEND ⟨*grasp* a new idea⟩ [Middle English *graspen*] ***synonyms*** see TAKE — **grasp•able** \ˈgras-pə-bəl\ *adj* — **grasp•er** *n*

[2]**grasp** *n* **1 a :** HANDLE 1 **b :** EMBRACE **2 :** HOLD, CONTROL ⟨in the tyrant's *grasp*⟩ **3 a :** the reach of the arm **b :** the power of seizing and holding ⟨success within our *grasp*⟩ **4 :** UNDERSTANDING 2, COMPREHENSION

grasp•ing *adj* **:** desiring material possessions urgently and excessively and often to the point of ruthlessness ***synonyms*** see COVETOUS — **grasp•ing•ly** \ˈgras-ping-lē\ *adv*

[1]**grass** \ˈgras\ *n* **1 :** herbage suitable or used for grazing animals **2 :** any of a large family of mostly herbaceous plants with jointed stems, slender sheathing leaves, and fruits consisting of seedlike grains **3 a :** grass-covered land **b :** LAWN **4 :** MARIJUANA [Old English *græs*] — **grass•like** \-ˌlīk\ *adj*

[2]**grass** *vt* **1 :** to seed with grass **2 :** to provide (as cattle) with grass for food

grass•hop•per \ˈgras-ˌhäp-ər\ *n* **:** any of numerous plant-eating insects (order Orthoptera) with hind legs adapted for leaping

grass•land \-ˌland\ *n* **:** land covered naturally or under cultivation with grasses and other low-growing herbs

grass roots *n pl* **:** society at the local and popular level especially in rural areas away from political or cultural centers ⟨*grass roots* support⟩

grassy \ˈgras-ē\ *adj* **grass•i•er; -est 1 :** covered or abounding with grass **2 :** resembling grass ⟨a *grassy* odor⟩

[1]**grate** \ˈgrāt\ *n* **1 :** a frame containing parallel or crossed bars (as in a prison window) **2 :** a frame or basket of iron bars for holding burning fuel (as in a furnace or a fireplace) [Medieval Latin *crata, grata* "hurdle," from Latin *cratis*]

[2]**grate** *vt* **:** to furnish with a grate

[3]**grate** *vb* **1 :** to make into small particles by rubbing against something rough ⟨*grate* cheese⟩ **2 :** to grind or rub against something with a rasping noise ⟨a door that *grates* on its hinges⟩ **3 :** to have a harsh or rasping effect ⟨a noise that *grates* on one's nerves⟩ [Medieval French *grater* "to scratch," of Germanic origin] — **grat•er** *n*

grate•ful \ˈgrāt-fəl\ *adj* **1 a :** appreciative of benefits received **b :** expressing gratitude **2 :** affording pleasure or contentment; *esp* **:** pleasing by reason of comfort supplied or discomfort alleviated ⟨*grateful* warmth of a fire on a frosty day⟩ [obsolete *grate* "pleasing, thankful," from Latin *gratus*] — **grate•ful•ly** \-fə-lē\ *adv* — **grate•ful•ness** *n*

synonyms GRATEFUL, THANKFUL mean feeling or expressing gratitude. GRATEFUL applies to an appreciation for having received favors from other persons ⟨I was very *grateful* for your help⟩. THANKFUL suggests a more generalized acknowledgement of what is vaguely felt to be providential ⟨*thankful* for a good harvest⟩.

grat•i•fi•ca•tion \ˌgrat-ə-fə-ˈkā-shən\ *n* **1 :** the act of gratifying **:** the state of being gratified **2 :** a source of satisfaction or pleasure

grat•i•fy \ˈgrat-ə-ˌfī\ *vt* **-fied; -fy•ing 1 :** to give or be a source of pleasure or satisfaction to **2 :** to give in to **:** INDULGE ⟨*gratify* a whim⟩ [Middle French *gratifier* "to reward," from Latin *gratificari* "to show kindness to," from *gratus* "pleasing" + *-ificari,* passive of *-ificare* "-ify"]

grat•ing \ˈgrāt-ing\ *n* **1 :** a partition, covering, or frame of parallel bars or crossbars **:** GRATE **2 :** a system of close parallel lines on a polished surface used to produce spectra by diffraction

gra·tis \'grat-əs, 'grāt-\ *adv or adj* : without charge or recompense : FREE [Latin *gratiis, gratis,* from *gratia* "favor"]

grat·i·tude \'grat-ə-ˌtüd, -ˌtyüd\ *n* : the state of being grateful : THANKFULNESS [Medieval Latin *gratitudo,* from Latin *gratus* "grateful"]

gra·tu·i·tous \grə-'tü-ət-əs, -'tyü-\ *adj* **1** : done or provided without return or expectation of return or payment; *also* : acting without compensation **2** : not called for by the circumstances : UNWARRANTED ⟨a *gratuitous* insult⟩ [Latin *gratuitus,* from *gratus* "pleasing, grateful"] — **gra·tu·i·tous·ly** *adv* — **gra·tu·i·tous·ness** *n*

gra·tu·i·ty \grə-'tü-ət-ē, -'tyü-\ *n, pl* **-ties** : something given freely; *also* : something given in return for a favor or service : TIP

gra·va·men \grə-'vām-ən\ *n, pl* **-vamens** *or* **-va·mi·na** \-'vam-ə-nə\ : the significant part (as of a grievance or complaint) : BASIS [Late Latin, "burden," from Latin *gravare* "to burden," from *gravis* "heavy"]

[1]grave \'grāv\ *vt* **graved; grav·en** \'grā-vən\ *or* **graved; grav·ing** **1 a** : to carve or shape with a chisel : SCULPTURE **b** : to carve or cut (as letters or figures) into a hard surface : ENGRAVE **2** : to impress or fix (as a thought) deeply [Old English *grafan* "to dig, engrave"]

[2]grave *n* **1 a** : an excavation for burial of a body **b** : TOMB 2 **2** : DEATH 1 — used with *the* [Old English *græf*]

[3]grave \'grāv, *in sense 4 also* 'gräv\ *adj* **1 a** : meriting serious consideration : IMPORTANT ⟨a *grave* issue⟩ **b** : threatening great harm or danger : MORTAL ⟨*grave* risks⟩ **2** : dignified in appearance or demeanor : SERIOUS **3** : drab in color : SOMBER **4** : of, marked by, or being an accent mark having the form ` [Middle French, from Latin *gravis* "heavy, grave"] ***synonyms*** see SERIOUS — **grave·ly** *adv* — **grave·ness** *n*

[4]gra·ve \'grä-vā\ *adv or adj* : in a slow and solemn manner — used as a direction in music [Italian, from Latin *gravis* "grave"]

[1]grav·el \'grav-əl\ *n* **1** : loose rounded fragments of rock coarser than sand **2** : a deposit of small hard masses in the kidneys and urinary bladder [Medieval French *gravele,* from *grave, greve* "pebbly ground"]

[2]gravel *adj* : GRAVELLY 2

[3]gravel *vt* **grav·eled** *or* **grav·elled; grav·el·ing** *or* **grav·el·ling** \'grav-ling, -ə-ling\ : to cover or spread with gravel

grave·less \'grāv-ləs\ *adj* **1** : not buried ⟨*graveless* bones⟩ **2** : not requiring graves : DEATHLESS

grav·el·ly \'grav-lē, -ə-lē\ *adj* **1** : of, containing, or covered with gravel **2** : having a harsh grating sound ⟨a *gravelly* voice⟩

grav·er \'grā-vər\ *n* **1** : SCULPTOR, ENGRAVER **2** : any of various cutting or shaving tools

grave·stone \'grāv-ˌstōn\ *n* : a stone marking a grave

grave·yard \-ˌyärd\ *n* : CEMETERY

grav·id \'grav-əd\ *adj* **1** : PREGNANT 3 **2** : full of eggs ⟨a *gravid* fish⟩ [Latin *gravidus,* from *gravis* "heavy"]

gra·vi·me·ter \gra-'vim-ət-ər, 'grav-ə-ˌmēt-\ *n* : an instrument for measuring variations in the force of gravity (as on the earth or moon) [French *gravimètre,* from Latin *gravis* "weight" + *-meter*]

grav·i·tate \'grav-ə-ˌtāt\ *vi* **1** : to move or tend to move under the influence of gravitation **2** : to be attracted to or toward something

grav·i·ta·tion \ˌgrav-ə-'tā-shən\ *n* **1** : a force of attraction between two material particles or bodies : GRAVITY 3b **2** : the action or process of gravitating — **grav·i·ta·tion·al** \-shnəl, -shən-l\ *adj* — **grav·i·ta·tion·al·ly** \-ē\ *adv* — **grav·i·ta·tive** \'grav-ə-ˌtāt-iv\ *adj*

gravitational lens *n* : a massive celestial object (as a galaxy) that bends and focuses the light of another more distant object (as a quasar) by gravity

grav·i·ty \'grav-ət-ē\ *n, pl* **-ties** **1 a** : dignity or sobriety of bearing **b** : IMPORTANCE 1; *esp* : SERIOUSNESS ⟨the *gravity* of the crime⟩ **2** : WEIGHT **3 a** : the gravitational attraction of the earth's mass for bodies at or near its surface **b** : a force of attraction between two material particles or bodies that is proportional to the product of their masses and inversely proportional to the square of the distance between them **c** : ACCELERATION OF GRAVITY [Latin *gravitas,* from *gravis* "heavy, grave"] — **gravity** *adj*

gra·vure \grə-'vyůr, grā-\ *n* : PHOTOGRAVURE [French, from *graver* "to cut, engrave," of Germanic origin]

gra·vy \'grā-vē\ *n, pl* **gravies** **1** : a sauce made from the thickened and seasoned juices of cooked meat **2** : something additional or unexpected that is pleasing or valuable [Medieval French *gravé* "broth, stew"]

[1]gray *also* **grey** \'grā\ *adj* **1** : of the color gray; *also* : dull in color **2** : having gray hair **3** : dull or cheerless in mood or outlook : DISMAL ⟨a *gray* day⟩ [Old English *grǣg*] — **gray·ish** \'grā-ish\ *adj* — **gray·ness** *n*

[2]gray *also* **grey** *n* **1** : something of a gray color **2** : one of the series of shades formed by a blending of black and white

[3]gray *also* **grey** *vb* : to make or become gray

gray·beard \'grā-ˌbiərd\ *n* : an old man

gray·ling \'grā-ling\ *n, pl* **grayling** *also* **graylings** : any of several freshwater fishes related to the trouts and salmons and valued for food and sport

gray matter *n* **1** : nerve tissue especially of the brain and spinal cord that is composed mostly of the cell bodies of neurons and is brownish gray in color **2** : BRAINS, INTELLECT

gray scale *n* : a series of gray tones ranging from black to white — **gray-scale** \'grā-ˌskāl\ *adj*

gray squirrel *n* : a common light gray to black squirrel native to eastern North America and introduced into Great Britain

gray wolf *n* : a large usually gray-colored wolf of northern regions that has become rare in the more southern parts of its range — called also *timber wolf*

[1]graze \'grāz\ *vb* **1** : to feed on growing herbage or the herbage of ⟨cattle *grazing* on the hill⟩ **2** : to put cattle to feed on the herbage of ⟨the farmer *grazed* the field⟩ **3** : to put to graze ⟨*grazing* the cattle⟩ [Old English *grasian,* from *græs* "grass"]
synonyms GRAZE, BROWSE mean to feed on growing vegetation. GRAZE applies especially to animals wandering freely on open grassland ⟨*grazing* in the hay field⟩. BROWSE implies specifically feeding on leaves and shoots of trees or shrubs ⟨*browsing* on bamboo shoots⟩.

[2]graze *n* **1** : an act of grazing **2** : herbage for grazing

[3]graze *vt* **1** : to rub or touch lightly in passing : touch against and glance off **2** : to scratch or scrape by rubbing against something [perhaps from [1]*graze*]

[4]graze *n* : a scraping along a surface or an abrasion made by it; *esp* : a superficial skin abrasion

[1]grease \'grēs\ *n* **1** : rendered animal fat **2** : oily matter **3** : a thick lubricant [Medieval French *creisse, greisse, gresse,* from Latin *crassus,* adj., "fat"]

[2]grease \'grēs, 'grēz\ *vt* **1** : to smear or daub with grease **2** : to lubricate with grease — **greas·er** *n*

grease·paint \'grēs-ˌpānt\ *n* : theater makeup

grease pencil *n* : a pencil with a lead like a crayon for marking on hard surfaces (as glass)

grease·wood \-ˌwůd\ *n* : a low stiff shrub related to the goosefoots and common in alkaline soils in the western U.S.

greasy \'grē-sē, -zē\ *adj* **greas·i·er; -est** **1** : smeared with grease **2** : containing grease ⟨*greasy* food⟩ **3** : resembling grease or oil : SMOOTH, SLIPPERY — **greas·i·ly** \-sə-lē, -zə-\ *adv* — **greas·i·ness** \-sē-nəs, -zē-\ *n*

[1]great \'grāt, *in South also* 'greət, 'gret\ *adj* **1** : very large in size or extent ⟨a *great* expanse of land⟩ **2** : large in number ⟨4 is *greater* than 2⟩ **3** : being much beyond the average or ordinary ⟨in *great* pain⟩ **4** : EMINENT, DISTINGUISHED ⟨a *great* artist⟩ **5** : long continued ⟨a *great* while⟩ **6** : more distant in relationship by one generation ⟨*great*-grandchildren⟩ **7** : markedly superior in character or quality; *esp* : NOBLE ⟨*great* of heart⟩ **8 a** : remarkably skilled ⟨*great* at tennis⟩ **b** : marked by enthusiasm : KEEN ⟨*great* on science fiction⟩ **9** — used as a generalized term of approval ⟨had a *great* time⟩ [Old English *grēat*] ***synonyms*** see LARGE — **great·ly** *adv* — **great·ness** *n*

[2]great *adv* : in a great manner : SUCCESSFULLY, WELL ⟨things are going *great*⟩

[3]great *n, pl* **great** *or* **greats** : an outstandingly superior or skillful person ⟨the *greats* of baseball⟩

great ape *n* : any of a family of apes including the gorilla, orangutan, and chimpanzee

great auk *n* : an extinct large flightless auk formerly abundant along North Atlantic coasts

great–aunt *n* : GRANDAUNT
Great Bear *n* : URSA MAJOR
great blue heron *n* : a large grayish blue American heron with a crested head
great circle *n* : a circle on the surface of a sphere that has the same center as the sphere; *esp* : such a circle on the surface of the earth a portion of which is the shortest distance between any two points on the earth's surface
great·coat \'grāt-ˌkōt\ *n* : a heavy overcoat
Great Dane *n* : any of a breed of tall powerful smooth-coated dogs
great divide *n* **1** : a watershed between major drainage systems **2** : a significant point of division; *esp* : DEATH
greatest common divisor *n* : the largest whole number that is an exact divisor of each of two or more whole numbers — called also *greatest common factor*
great·heart·ed \'grāt-'härt-əd\ *adj* **1** : COURAGEOUS **2** : MAGNANIMOUS 2 — **great·heart·ed·ly** *adv* — **great·heart·ed·ness** *n*
great horned owl *n* : a large American owl with two tufts of long feathers resembling ears or horns at the top of the head
great–nephew *n* : GRANDNEPHEW
great–niece *n* : GRANDNIECE
great power *n* : one of the nations that figure most decisively in international affairs : SUPERPOWER
Great Russian *n* : a member of the dominant Slavic-speaking ethnic group of Russia
great–uncle *n* : GRANDUNCLE
great white shark *n* : a large shark of warm seas that is quick to attack humans and is bluish gray when young but becomes whitish when older
greave \'grēv\ *n* : armor for the leg below the knee [Medieval French *greve*]
grebe \'grēb\ *n* : any of a family of swimming and diving birds closely related to the loons [French *grèbe*]

grebe

Gre·cian \'grē-shən\ *adj* : GREEK 1 [derived from Latin *Graecia* "Greece"] — **Grecian** *n*
Greco- *or* **Graeco-** \'grek-ō, 'grē-kō\ *combining form* **1** : Greece : Greeks **2** : Greek and [Latin *Graecus*]
greed \'grēd\ *n* : a selfish and excessive desire for more of something (as money) than is needed [back-formation from *greedy*]
greedy \'grēd-ē\ *adj* **greed·i·er; -est** **1** : having a driving appetite for food or drink : very hungry **2** : having an eager and often selfish desire or longing ⟨*greedy* for praise⟩ **3** : wanting more than one needs or more than one's fair share (as of food or wealth) [Old English *grǣdig*] ***synonyms*** see COVETOUS — **greed·i·ly** \'grēd-l-ē\ *adv* — **greed·i·ness** \'grēd-ē-nəs\ *n*
1**Greek** \'grēk\ *n* **1 a** : a native or inhabitant of ancient or modern Greece **b** : a person of Greek descent **2 a** : the Indo-European language used by the Greeks from prehistoric times to the present **b** : ancient Greek as used from the time of the earliest records to the end of the 2nd century A.D. [Old English *Grēca,* from Latin *Graecus,* from Greek *Graikos*]
2**Greek** *adj* **1** : of, relating to, or characteristic of Greece, the Greeks, or Greek ⟨*Greek* architecture⟩ **2 a** : EASTERN ORTHODOX **b** : of or relating to the Orthodox church of Greece **3** : of or relating to the Eastern rite of the Roman Catholic Church
Greek cross *n* : an upright cross with all arms of equal length
Greek fire *n* : a composition of uncertain ingredients that burns even in water [from the Byzantine Greeks who used it in warfare]
Greek Orthodox *adj* : EASTERN ORTHODOX; *esp* : GREEK 2b
1**green** \'grēn\ *adj* **1** : of the color green **2 a** : covered by green foliage or herbage ⟨*green* hills⟩ **b** : consisting of green plants or of the leafy part of a plant ⟨a *green* salad⟩ **3** : YOUTHFUL, VIGOROUS **4** : not fully grown or ripe **5 a** : appearing sickly or pale **b** : ENVIOUS — used especially in the phrase *green with envy* **6** : not fully processed, treated, or seasoned ⟨*green* lumber⟩ **7 a** : lacking training, knowledge, or experience ⟨*green* troops⟩ **b** : GULLIBLE, NAIVE ⟨too *green* to suspect a trick⟩ **8 a** *often cap* : relating to or being an environmental political movement **b** : concerned with or supporting environmentalism **c** : tending to preserve environmental quality (as by being recyclable, biodegradable, or non-polluting) [Old English *grēne*] — **green·ish** \'grē-nish\ *adj* — **green·ly** *adv* — **green·ness** \'grēn-nəs\ *n*
2**green** *vb* : to make or become green
3**green** *n* **1** : a color whose hue is somewhat less yellow than that of growing fresh grass or of the emerald or is that of the part of the spectrum lying between blue and yellow **2** : something of a green color **3 a** : green vegetation **b** *pl* : leafy parts of plants used for some purpose (as ornament or food) ⟨turnip *greens*⟩ **4** : a grassy plain or plot; *esp* : PUTTING GREEN **5** : MONEY **6** *often cap* : ENVIRONMENTALIST; *esp* : a member of an activist political party focusing on environmental and social issues — **greeny** \'grē-nē\ *adj*
green alga *n* : any of a major group (Chlorophyta) of green-colored usually freshwater algae
green ano·le \-ə-'nō-lē\ *n* : a long-tailed arboreal lizard chiefly of the southeastern U.S. that can change from green to brown
green·back \'grēn-ˌbak\ *n* : a piece of paper currency issued by the U.S. government
Green·back·er \-ər\ *n* : a member of a post-Civil War American political party opposing reduction in the amount of paper money in circulation
green bean *n* : a kidney bean that is used as a snap bean while the pods are green
green·belt \'grēn-ˌbelt\ *n* : a belt of parkways, parks, or farmlands that encircles a community
green·bri·er \'grēn-ˌbrī-ər, -ˌbrīr\ *n* : any of a genus of vines related to the lilies; *esp* : a prickly vine of the eastern U.S. with clusters of small greenish flowers
green·ery \'grēn-rē, -ə-rē\ *n, pl* **-er·ies** : green foliage or plants : VERDURE
green gland *n* : a greenish excretory organ in the head of some crustaceans (as a lobster)
green·gro·cer \'grēn-ˌgrō-sər\ *n, chiefly British* : a retailer of fresh vegetables and fruit — **green·gro·cery** \-ˌgrōs-rē, -ə-rē\ *n*
green·horn \'grēn-ˌhȯrn\ *n* : an inexperienced person; *esp* : one easily tricked or cheated [obsolete *greenhorn* "animal with young horns"]
1**green·house** \-ˌhau̇s\ *n* : a structure enclosed (as by glass) and used for the cultivation or protection of plants
2**greenhouse** *adj* : relating to, causing, or caused by the greenhouse effect ⟨*greenhouse* warming⟩ ⟨a *greenhouse* gas⟩
greenhouse effect *n* : warming of the lower atmosphere as a result of the absorption (as by carbon dioxide and water vapor) of radiation received from the sun and reemitted by the earth
green light *n* : authority or permission to undertake a project [from the green traffic light which signals permission to proceed]
green·ling \'grēn-ling\ *n* : any of several food fishes of the rocky coasts of the northern Pacific
green manure *n* : an herbaceous crop (as clover) plowed under while green to enrich the soil
green mold *n* : a green or green-spored mold (as a penicillium)
green onion *n* : a young onion pulled before the bulb has enlarged and used especially in salads
green pepper *n* : a sweet pepper before it turns red at maturity
green revolution *n* : the great increase in the production of food grains resulting from improved plant varieties and farming methods
green·room \'grēn-ˌrüm, -ˌru̇m\ *n* : a room in a theater or concert hall where actors or musicians relax before, between, or after appearances
green snake *n* : either of two bright green harmless largely insect-eating North American snakes
green soap *n* : a soft soap made from vegetable oils and used especially to treat skin diseases
green·stick fracture \'grēn-'stik-\ *n* : a bone fracture in the young in which the bone is partly broken and partly bent
green·sward \'grēn-ˌswȯrd\ *n* : turf that is green with growing grass
green tea *n* : tea that is light in color from incomplete fermentation of the leaf before drying
green thumb *n* : an unusual ability to make plants grow — **green–thumbed** \'grēn-'thəmd\ *adj*
green turtle *n* : a large usually plant-eating sea turtle of warm waters with a smooth greenish shell

Green·wich mean time \'grin-ij-, 'gren-, -ich-\ *n* : the time of the meridian of Greenwich used as the basis of standard time throughout the world — called also *Greenwich time* [*Greenwich,* England]

green·wood \'grēn-ˌwu̇d\ *n* : a forest that is green with foliage

greet \'grēt\ *vt* **1** : to address with expressions of kind wishes upon meeting or arrival **2** : to meet or react to in a specified manner ⟨*greeted* the team with cheers⟩ **3** : to appear or present itself to ⟨offensive odors *greeted* the nose⟩ [Old English *grētan*] — **greet·er** *n*

greet·ing *n* **1** : a salutation at meeting **2** : an expression of good wishes : REGARDS — usually used in plural

greeting card *n* : a decorated card with a greeting or message of goodwill that is given usually on a special occasion

gre·gar·i·ous \gri-'gar-ē-əs, -'ger-\ *adj* **1** : tending to associate with others of one's kind : SOCIAL; *also* : tending to live in a flock, herd, or community rather than alone ⟨*gregarious* birds⟩ **2** : marked by a liking for companionship : SOCIABLE [Latin *gregarius* "of a flock or herd," from *greg-, grex* "flock, herd"] — **gre·gar·i·ous·ly** *adv* — **gre·gar·i·ous·ness** *n*

Gre·go·ri·an calendar \gri-'gōr-ē-ən-, -'gȯr-\ *n* : a calendar in general use introduced in 1582 by Pope Gregory XIII as a revision of the Julian calendar that was marked by the initial dropping of 10 days as well as the 366th day in any century year not divisible by 400 (as 1700, 1800, and 1900) and that was adopted by Great Britain and the American colonies in 1752

Gregorian chant *n* : a rhythmically free unaccompanied melody sung in unison in services of the Roman Catholic Church

grem·lin \'grem-lən\ *n* : a small sprite held to be responsible for malfunction of equipment especially in an airplane [origin unknown]

gre·nade \grə-'nād\ *n* **1** : a small bomb filled with a destructive agent (as gas, high explosive, or incendiary chemicals) and made to be hurled **2** : a device containing a gaseous or volatile substance (as tear gas) that when hurled releases its contents on impact [Middle French, literally, "pomegranate," from Late Latin *granata,* derived from Latin *granum* "grain"]

gren·a·dier \ˌgren-ə-'diər\ *n* : a soldier who carries and throws grenades

gren·a·dine \ˌgren-ə-'dēn, 'gren-ə-ˌ\ *n* : a syrup flavored with pomegranates and used in mixed drinks [French, from *grenade* "pomegranate"]

Gret·na Green \ˌgret-nə-'grēn\ *n* : a place where many eloping couples are married [*Gretna Green,* village in Scotland]

grew *past of* GROW

grey *variant of* GRAY

grey friar *n, often cap G&F* : a Franciscan friar

grey·hound \'grā-ˌhau̇nd\ *n* : any of a breed of tall slender graceful smooth-coated dogs noted for swiftness and keen sight and used for pursuing game and for racing [Old English *grīghund*]

greyhound

grey·lag \-ˌlag\ *n* : the common gray wild goose of Europe [probably from *gray* + *lag* "last," from *lag* "to fall behind"]

grid \'grid\ *n* **1** : GRATING 1 **2** : a perforated or ridged metal plate used as a conductor in a storage battery **3** : an electrode consisting of a mesh or a spiral of fine wire placed between two other elements of an electron tube **4 a** : a network of horizontal and perpendicular lines (as for locating points on a map) **b** : GRIDIRON 2 [back-formation from *gridiron*]

grid·dle \'grid-l\ *n* : a flat surface or pan on which food is cooked by dry heat [Medieval French *greil, gredile* "gridiron," from Latin *craticulum,* from *cratis* "wickerwork, hurdle"]

griddle cake *n* : PANCAKE

grid·iron \'grid-ˌī-ərn, -ˌīrn\ *n* **1** : a grate for broiling food **2** : something consisting of or covered with a network; *esp* : a football field [Middle English *gredire,* alteration of *gredile* "gridiron"]

grief \'grēf\ *n* **1** : deep sorrow : SADNESS, DISTRESS **2** : a cause of sorrow **3** : MISHAP, DISASTER ⟨the boat came to *grief* on the rocks⟩ **4** : TROUBLE 1b ⟨enough *grief* for one day⟩ [Medieval French *gref, grief* "injustice, calamity," from *gref,* adjective, "heavy, grave," from Latin *gravis*] ***synonyms*** see SORROW

griev·ance \'grē-vəns\ *n* **1** : a cause of distress (as an unsatisfactory working condition) affording reason for complaint or resistance **2** : the formal expression of a grievance

grieve \'grēv\ *vb* **1** : to cause to suffer : DISTRESS **2** : to feel or show grief : SORROW [Medieval French *grever,* from Latin *gravare* "to burden," from *gravis* "heavy, grave"] — **griev·er** *n*

griev·ous \'grē-vəs\ *adj* **1** : causing suffering or sorrow : DISTRESSING ⟨*grievous* poverty⟩ **2** : SERIOUS, GRAVE ⟨a *grievous* mistake⟩ — **griev·ous·ly** *adv* — **griev·ous·ness** *n*

grif·fin *or* **grif·fon** *also* **gryph·on** \'grif-ən\ *n* : a fabulous animal typically half eagle and half lion [Medieval French *grif, griffun,* from Latin *gryphus,* from Greek *gryps,* from *grypos* "curved"]

griffin

[1]grill \'gril\ *vt* **1** : to broil on a grill **2 a** : to torment as if by broiling **b** : to question intensely ⟨police *grilled* the suspect⟩ — **grill·er** *n*

[2]grill *n* **1** : a cooking utensil of parallel bars on which food is exposed to radiant heat (as from charcoal) **2** : food that is broiled usually on a grill **3** : a usually informal restaurant [French *gril,* from Latin *craticulum,* from *cratis* "wickerwork, hurdle"]

grille *or* **grill** \'gril\ *n* **1** : a grating forming a barrier or screen **2** : an opening covered with a grille [French *grille,* from Latin *craticula* "fine wickerwork, gridiron," from *cratis* "wickerwork, hurdle"]

grill·work \'gril-ˌwərk\ *n* : work constituting or resembling a grille

grilse \'grils\ *n, pl* **grilse** : a young salmon returning from the sea to spawn for the first time [Middle English *grills*]

grim \'grim\ *adj* **grim·mer; grim·mest** **1** : fierce in manner or action : SAVAGE 2 ⟨a *grim* battle⟩ **2 a** : stern and forbidding in appearance **b** : GLOOMY 3a ⟨*grim* news⟩ **3** : ghastly, repellent, or sinister in character ⟨a *grim* tale⟩ **4** : UNFLINCHING, UNYIELDING ⟨*grim* determination⟩ [Old English *grimm*] ***synonyms*** see GHASTLY — **grim·ly** *adv* — **grim·ness** *n*

grim·ace \'grim-əs, grim-'ās\ *n* : a twisting or distortion of the face or features expressive usually of disgust, disapproval, or pain [French, alteration of *grimache,* of Germanic origin] — **grimace** *vi*

gri·mal·kin \grim-'ȯl-kən, -'ȯ-kən, -'al-kən\ *n* : CAT 1a; *esp* : an old female cat [*gray* + English dialect *malkin* "cat"]

grime \'grīm\ *n* : soot, smut, or dirt adhering to or embedded in a surface; *also* : accumulated dirtiness and disorder [Dutch *grime* "soot, mask"] — **grime** *vt*

grimy \'grī-mē\ *adj* **grim·i·er; -est** : full of or covered with grime : DIRTY — **grim·i·ness** *n*

grin \'grin\ *vi* **grinned; grin·ning** : to draw back the lips so as to show the teeth especially in amusement or laughter [Old English *grennian*] — **grin** *n*

[1]grind \'grīnd\ *vb* **ground** \'grau̇nd\; **grind·ing** **1** : to reduce to powder or small fragments by crushing (as in a mill or with the teeth) **2** : to wear down, polish, or sharpen by friction **3** : to press with a grating noise : GRIT ⟨*grind* the teeth⟩ **4** : OPPRESS, HARASS **5** : to operate or produce by or as if by turning a crank **6** : to move with difficulty or friction especially so as to make a grating noise ⟨*grinding* the gears⟩ [Old English *grindan*]

[2]grind *n* **1** : an act of grinding **2 a** : monotonous or difficult labor, study, or routine **b** : one who works or studies excessively **3** : the result of grinding; *esp* : the size of particle obtained by grinding

grind·er \'grīn-dər\ *n* **1 a** : MOLAR **b** *pl* : TEETH **2** : one that grinds **3** : [2]SUBMARINE 2

grind out *vt* : to produce in a mechanical way ⟨*grind out* novels⟩

grind·stone \'grīn-ˌstōn\ *n* : a flat circular stone of natural sandstone that revolves on an axle and is used for grinding, shaping, or smoothing

griot \ˈgrē-ˌō\ *n* : any of a class of musician-entertainers of western Africa whose performances include tribal histories and genealogies [French]

[1]**grip** \ˈgrip\ *vt* **gripped; grip·ping** **1** : to seize firmly **2** : to hold strongly the interest of ⟨the story *grips* the reader⟩ [Old English *grippan*]

[2]**grip** *n* **1 a** : a strong or tight grasp **b** : strength in gripping **c** : manner or style of gripping; *esp* : a way of clasping the hand by which members of a secret order recognize or greet one another **2 a** : a firm hold giving control or mastery **b** : mental grasp : UNDERSTANDING **3** : a part or device for gripping **4** : a part by which something is grasped; *esp* : HANDLE **5** : SUITCASE

[1]**gripe** \ˈgrīp\ *vb* **1** *archaic* : CLUTCH 1 **2** : IRRITATE, VEX ⟨these rules *gripe* me⟩ **3** : to cause or experience spasms of pain in the intestines **4** : COMPLAIN 1 [Old English *grīpan*] — **grip·er** *n*

[2]**gripe** *n* **1** *archaic* **a** : GRIP 1a **b** : CONTROL 1, MASTERY **2** : COMPLAINT 1 **3** : a spasm of intestinal pain

grippe \ˈgrip\ *n* : an acute contagious virus disease; *esp* : INFLUENZA 1 [French, literally, "seizure"] — **grippy** \ˈgrip-ē\ *adj*

grip·sack \ˈgrip-ˌsak\ *n* : TRAVELING BAG

gris–gris \ˈgrē-ˌgrē\ *n, pl* **gris–gris** \-ˌgrēz\ : an amulet or incantation used chiefly by people of African ancestry [French]

gris·ly \ˈgriz-lē\ *adj* **gris·li·er; -est** : GHASTLY 1a, GRUESOME [Old English *grislic*] — **gris·li·ness** *n*

grist \ˈgrist\ *n* : grain to be ground or already ground [Old English *grīst*]

gris·tle \ˈgris-əl\ *n* : tough tissue usually of cartilage especially in table meats [Old English] — **gris·tli·ness** \ˈgris-lē-nəs, -ə-lē-\ *n* — **gris·tly** \ˈgris-lē, -ə-lē\ *adj*

grist·mill \ˈgrist-ˌmil\ *n* : a mill for grinding grain

[1]**grit** \ˈgrit\ *n* **1** : a hard sharp granule (as of sand); *also* : material (as an abrasive) composed of such granules **2** : firmness of mind or spirit [Old English *grēot*]

[2]**grit** *vb* **grit·ted; grit·ting** : to grind or cause to grind : GRATE

grits \ˈgrits\ *n pl* : coarsely ground hulled grain [Old English *grytt*]

grit·ty \ˈgrit-ē\ *adj* **grit·ti·er; -est** **1** : containing or resembling grit **2** : courageously persistent : PLUCKY — **grit·ti·ness** *n*

griz·zled \ˈgriz-əld\ *adj* : sprinkled, streaked, or mixed with gray [Medieval French *grisel* "gray," from *gris,* of Germanic origin]

[1]**griz·zly** \ˈgriz-lē\ *adj* **griz·zli·er; -est** : GRIZZLED

[2]**grizzly** *n, pl* **grizzlies** : GRIZZLY BEAR

grizzly bear *n* : a very large powerful brown bear found from the northwestern U.S. to Alaska

grizzly bear

groan \ˈgrōn\ *vi* **1** : to utter a deep moan of pain, grief, or annoyance **2** : to make a harsh sound under sudden or prolonged strain ⟨the floor *groaned* under the weight⟩ [Old English *grānian*] — **groan** *n* — **groan·er** *n*

[1]**groat** \ˈgrōt\ *n* **1** : hulled grain broken into fragments larger than grits — usually used in plural ⟨buckwheat *groats*⟩ **2** : a grain (as of oats) without the hull [Old English *grot*]

[2]**groat** *n* : a former British coin worth four pennies [Middle English *groot,* from Dutch]

gro·cer \ˈgrō-sər\ *n* : a dealer in staple foodstuffs and household supplies [Medieval French *groser* "wholesaler," from *gros,* adj., "coarse, wholesale"]

gro·cery \ˈgrōs-rē, -ə-rē\ *n, pl* **-cer·ies** **1** *pl* : commodities sold by a grocer ⟨buy the *groceries*⟩ **2** : a grocer's store

grog \ˈgräg\ *n* : alcoholic liquor; *esp* : liquor (as rum) cut with water [Old *Grog,* nickname of Edward Vernon, died 1757, English admiral who ordered the sailors' rum to be diluted] — **grog·shop** \-ˌshäp\ *n*

Word History The 18th century English admiral Edward Vernon is said to have been in the habit of wearing a cloak made of a kind of coarsely woven fabric called *grogram.* For this reason, the sailors under his command gave him the nickname "Old Grog." The Royal Navy in the West Indies had been given by custom a daily ration of rum, but in 1740 Vernon, alarmed at the damage to the physical and moral health of his men, ordered that the rum should be diluted with water. This mixture was christened *grog,* after its godfather. *Grog* is now sometimes used as a general term for any liquor, even undiluted.

grog·gy \ˈgräg-ē\ *adj* **grog·gi·er; -est** : weak and unsteady on the feet or in action [*grog*] — **grog·gi·ly** \ˈgräg-ə-lē\ *adv* — **grog·gi·ness** \ˈgräg-ē-nəs\ *n*

[1]**groin** \ˈgrȯin\ *n* **1** : the fold or depression marking the junction of the lower abdomen and the inner part of the thigh; *also* : the region of this junction **2** : the projecting curved line along which two intersecting structural vaults meet [Middle English *grynde,* from Old English, "abyss"]

[2]**groin** *vt* : to build or equip with groins

grom·met \ˈgräm-ət, ˈgrəm-\ *n* **1** : a ring of rope **2** : a small usually metal ring used to reinforce an eyelet or to protect something passed through it [obsolete French *gormette* "curb of a bridle"]

[1]**groom** \ˈgrüm, ˈgrům\ *n* **1 a** *archaic* : a male servant **b** : a person in charge of horses **2** : BRIDEGROOM [Middle English *grom* "man, servant"; sense 2 short for *bridegroom*]

[2]**groom** *vt* **1** : to clean and maintain the appearance of (as the coat of a horse or dog) **2** : to make neat, attractive, or acceptable

grooms·man \ˈgrümz-mən, ˈgrůmz-\ *n* : a male attendant of a bridegroom at his wedding

[1]**groove** \ˈgrüv\ *n* **1** : a long narrow channel or depression **2** : a fixed routine : RUT **3** : top form [Middle English *grove* "pit, cave," from Dutch *groeve*]

[2]**groove** *vb* **grooved; groov·ing** **1** : to form a groove in **2** : to become joined or fitted by a groove **3** : to enjoy oneself intensely

groovy \ˈgrü-vē\ *adj* **groov·i·er; -est** : MARVELOUS 3, WONDERFUL ⟨had a *groovy* time at the beach⟩

grope \ˈgrōp\ *vi* **1** : to feel about or cast about blindly or uncertainly in search ⟨*grope* for the right word⟩ **2** : to feel one's way by groping ⟨*grope* along a wall⟩ [Old English *grāpian*]

gros·beak \ˈgrōs-ˌbēk\ *n* : any of several finches of Europe and America having large stout conical bills [French *grosbec,* from *gros* "gross, thick" + *bec* "beak"]

grosbeak

gro·schen \ˈgrō-shən, ˈgrȯ-\ *n, pl* **groschen** : a former monetary unit equal to 1/100 schilling [German]

gros·grain \ˈgrō-ˌgrān\ *n* : a silk or rayon fabric with crosswise cotton ribs [French *gros grain* "coarse texture"]

[1]**gross** \ˈgrōs\ *adj* **1 a** : glaringly noticeable usually because of inexcusable badness ⟨a *gross* error⟩ **b** : OUT-AND-OUT, UTTER ⟨a *gross* fool⟩ **2 a** : BIG, BULKY; *esp* : excessively fat **b** : excessively luxuriant **3 a** : GENERAL 3, BROAD **b** : consisting of an overall total before any deductions ⟨*gross* earnings⟩ — compare NET **4** : EARTHY, CARNAL ⟨*gross* pleasures⟩ **5** : lacking knowledge or culture **6** : crudely vulgar ⟨*gross* humor⟩ **7** : inspiring disgust or distaste [Medieval French *gros* "thick, coarse," from Latin *grossus* "coarse"] ***synonyms*** see FLAGRANT — **gross·ly** *adv* — **gross·ness** *n*

[2]**gross** *n* : a whole amount before any deductions

[3]**gross** *vt* : to earn before deductions

[4]**gross** *n, pl* **gross** : a total of 12 dozen things ⟨a *gross* of pencils⟩ [probably from Medieval French *grosse* "sum, whole," from *gros* "thick, coarse"]

gross anatomy *n* : a branch of anatomy that deals with the structure of tissues and organs visible to the naked eye

gross national product *n* : the total value of the goods and services produced in a nation during a year

[1]**gro·tesque** \grō-ˈtesk\ *n* **1** : decorative art featuring fanciful human and animal forms often interwoven with foliage **2** : one that is grotesque [Middle French, from Italian *pittura grottesca,* literally, "cave painting," derived from *grotta* "cave"]

Word History During the Italian Renaissance the remaining buildings of the ancient city of Rome were heavily excavated, exposing chambers that became known, familiarly, as *grotte,* "caves" (the plural of *grotta*). The walls of many *grotte* were covered with exotic paintings. *Pittura grottesca,* or simply *grottesca,* the term for such a painting, became the name for a later but similar type of painting representing fantastic combinations of human and animal forms interwoven with strange fruits and flowers. The word was soon borrowed into English. The adjective *grotesque,* first applied only to decorative art of this kind, is now used to describe anything fanciful or bizarre.

[2]**grotesque** *adj* **:** of, relating to, or characteristic of the grotesque: as **a :** FANCIFUL 3, BIZARRE **b :** absurdly awkward or incongruous ***synonyms*** see FANTASTIC — **gro·tesque·ly** *adv* — **gro·tesque·ness** *n*

grot·to \ˈgrät-ō\ *n, pl* **grottoes** *also* **grottos** **1 :** CAVE **2 :** an artificial recess or structure made to resemble a natural cave [Italian *grotta, grotto,* from Latin *crypta* "cavern, crypt"]

grouch \ˈgraůch\ *n* **1 :** a fit of bad temper **2 :** an habitually irritable or complaining person [probably from English dialect *grutch* "grudge," derived from Middle English *grucchen* "to grumble"] — **grouch** *vi* — **grouch·i·ly** \ˈgraů-chə-lē\ *adv* — **grouch·i·ness** \-chē-nəs\ *n* — **grouchy** \-chē\ *adj*

[1]**ground** \ˈgraůnd\ *n* **1 a :** the bottom of a body of water ⟨the boat struck *ground*⟩ **b** *pl* **:** sediment at the bottom of a liquid **:** LEES **2 :** a basis for belief, action, or argument ⟨*grounds* for divorce⟩ **3 a :** a surrounding area **:** BACKGROUND ⟨a picture on a gray *ground*⟩ **b :** material that serves as a base **:** FOUNDATION **4 a :** the surface of the earth **b :** an area used for a particular purpose ⟨the parade *ground*⟩ **c** *pl* **:** the area around and belonging to a building ⟨the capitol *grounds*⟩ **5 :** SOIL 2, EARTH **6 a :** an object that makes an electrical connection with the earth **b :** a large conducting body (as the earth) used as a common return for an electric circuit [Old English *grund*]

[2]**ground** *vb* **1 :** to bring to or place on the ground ⟨*ground* a rifle⟩ **2 a :** to provide a reason or justification for **b :** to instruct in fundamentals ⟨well *grounded* in math⟩ **3 :** to connect electrically with a ground **4 a :** to restrict to the ground ⟨*ground* a pilot⟩ **b :** to prohibit from taking part in usual activities ⟨*grounded* her for a week⟩ **5 :** to run aground ⟨the ship *grounded* on a reef⟩ **6 :** to hit a ground ball

[3]**ground** *past of* GRIND

ground ball *n* **:** a baseball hit along the ground

ground·burst \ˈgraůnd-ˌbərst\ *n* **:** the detonation of a nuclear warhead at ground level

ground–cher·ry \ˈgraůnd-ˈcher-ē, ˈgraůn-\ *n* **:** a plant of the nightshade family that is sometimes grown for its edible yellow fruits enclosed in papery husks; *also* **:** its fruit

ground cover *n* **:** low-growing plants that cover the ground (as in a forest or in place of turf); *also* **:** a plant used as ground cover

ground crew *n* **:** the mechanics and technicians who maintain and service an airplane

ground·ed \ˈgraůn-dəd\ *adj* **:** mentally and emotionally stable **:** admirably sensible, realistic, and unpretentious ⟨remains *grounded* despite all the praise and attention⟩

ground·er \ˈgraůn-dər\ *n* **:** GROUND BALL

ground finch *n* **:** any of several dull-colored large-billed finches of the Galápagos Islands

ground floor *n* **:** the floor of a building most nearly on a level with the ground

ground glass *n* **:** glass with a roughened light-diffusing nontransparent surface

ground·hog \ˈgraůnd-ˌhȯg, -ˌhäg\ *n* **:** WOODCHUCK

Groundhog Day *n* **:** February 2 that traditionally indicates six more weeks of winter if sunny or an early spring if cloudy [from the legend that the groundhog comes out and is frightened back into hibernation if he sees his shadow]

ground·less \ˈgraůn-dləs\ *adj* **:** being without basis or reason ⟨*groundless* fears⟩ — **ground·less·ly** *adv* — **ground·less·ness** *n*

ground·ling \ˈgraůn-dling\ *n* **1 a :** a spectator who stood in the pit of an Elizabethan theater **b :** a person of vulgar or coarse tastes **:** PLEBEIAN **2 :** one that lives or works on or near the ground

ground loop *n* **:** a sharp uncontrollable turn made by an airplane in landing, taking off, or taxiing

ground·mass \ˈgraůnd-ˌmas, ˈgraůn-\ *n* **:** the fine-grained base of a rock in which larger crystals are embedded

ground·nut \-ˌnət\ *n* **1 :** a North American vine of the legume family with brownish purple fragrant flowers and an edible tuberous root; *also* **:** its root **2** *chiefly British* **:** PEANUT 1

ground pine *n* **:** any of several club mosses with long creeping stems and erect branches

ground plan *n* **1 :** a plan of a floor of a building **2 :** a basic plan

ground rule *n* **1 :** a sports rule adopted to modify play on a particular field, court, or course **2 :** a basic rule of procedure

ground·sel \ˈgraůnd-səl, ˈgraůn-\ *n* **:** any of a large genus of plants related to the daisies which have mostly yellow flower heads and some of which are poisonous [Old English *grundeswelge,* from *grund* "ground" + *swelgan* "to swallow"]

ground·sheet \-ˌshēt\ *n* **:** a waterproof sheet placed on the ground for protection from moisture

ground squirrel *n* **:** any of numerous burrowing rodents (as the gophers and chipmunks) differing from the related true squirrels in having cheek pouches and shorter fur

ground state *n* **:** the energy level of a system (as of an atom) having the least energy of all its possible states

ground swell *n* **1 :** a broad deep ocean swell caused by a distant storm or earthquake **2 :** a rapid spontaneous growth (as of political opinion)

ground·wa·ter \ˈgraůn-ˌdwȯt-ər, -ˌdwät-\ *n* **:** water within the earth that supplies wells and springs

ground wave *n* **:** a radio wave that is propagated along the surface of the earth

ground·work \ˈgraůn-ˌdwərk\ *n* **:** FOUNDATION 2, BASIS

ground zero *n* **1 :** the point directly above, below, or at which a nuclear explosion occurs **2 :** the center or origin of rapid, intense, or violent activity or change **3 :** the very beginning **:** SQUARE ONE

[1]**group** \ˈgrüp\ *n* **1 :** two or more figures forming a complete unit (as in a painting) **2 a :** a number of individuals assembled together or having common interests **b :** a number of objects regarded as a unit **3 a :** an assemblage of related organisms **b :** an assemblage of atoms forming part of a molecule ⟨a methyl *group* (CH_3)⟩ [French *groupe,* from Italian *gruppo,* of Germanic origin]

[2]**group** *vb* **1 :** to combine in a group **2 :** to assign to a group **:** CLASSIFY **3 :** to form a group

grou·per \ˈgrü-pər\ *n, pl* **groupers** *also* **grouper :** any of numerous mostly large solitary bottom-dwelling fishes of warm seas related to the sea basses [Portuguese *garoupa*]

group home *n* **:** a residence for persons needing care or supervision

group·ie \ˈgrü-pē\ *n* **:** a female fan of a rock group who usually follows it on tour

[1]**grouse** \ˈgraůs\ *n, pl* **grouse :** any of various chiefly ground-dwelling plump-bodied game birds that are usually reddish or grayish brown with feathered legs [origin unknown]

[2]**grouse** *vi* **:** COMPLAIN 1, GRUMBLE [origin unknown] — **grouser** *n*

grout \ˈgraůt\ *n* **1 :** thin mortar **2 :** PLASTER 2 [Old English *grūt* "coarse meal"] — **grout** *vt*

grove \ˈgrōv\ *n* **:** a small wood; *esp* **:** a group of trees without underbrush [Old English *grāf*]

grov·el \ˈgräv-əl, ˈgrəv-\ *vi* **grov·eled** *or* **grov·elled; grov·el·ing** *or* **grov·el·ling** \ˈgräv-ling, ˈgrəv-, -ə-ling\ **1 :** to lie or creep with the body prostrate especially as a sign of humbleness or abasement **2 :** to abase oneself **:** CRINGE [back-formation from *groveling* "prone," from Middle English *gruf* "on the face" + [2]*-ling*] — **grov·el·er** *or* **grov·el·ler** \-lər, -ə-lər\ *n*

grow \ˈgrō\ *vb* **grew** \ˈgrü\; **grown** \ˈgrōn\; **grow·ing** **1 a :** to spring up and develop to maturity **b :** to be able to grow in some place or situation ⟨rice *grows* in water⟩ **c :** to assume some relation through or as if through a process of natural growth ⟨a tree with limbs *grown* together⟩ **2 a :** to become larger and often more complex by addition of material either by assimilation into the living organism or by accretion in a natural inorganic process (as crystallization) **b :** INCREASE, EXPAND ⟨the city is *growing* rapidly⟩ ⟨*grow* in wisdom⟩ **3 :** ORIGINATE ⟨the project *grew* out of a mere suggestion⟩ **4 a :** to pass into a condition **:** BECOME ⟨*grew* pale⟩ **b :** to have an increasing influence ⟨habit *grows* on a person⟩ **5 :** to cause to grow **:** CULTIVATE, RAISE ⟨*grow* wheat⟩ [Old English *grōwan*] — **grow·er** \ˈgrō-ər, ˈgrōr\ *n*

growing pains *n pl* **1 :** pains in the legs of growing children having no demonstrable relation to growth **2 :** the stresses and strains attending a new project or development

\ə\ **abut**	\aů\ **out**	\i\ **tip**	\ȯ\ **saw**	\ů\ **foot**
\ər\ **further**	\ch\ **chin**	\ī\ **life**	\ȯi\ **coin**	\y\ **yet**
\a\ **mat**	\e\ **pet**	\j\ **job**	\th\ **thin**	\yü\ **few**
\ā\ **take**	\ē\ **easy**	\ng\ **sing**	\th\ **this**	\yů\ **cure**
\ä\ **cot, cart**	\g\ **go**	\ō\ **bone**	\ü\ **food**	\zh\ **vision**

growing point *n* **:** the tip of a plant shoot from which additional shoot tissues differentiate

growl \'grau̇l\ *vb* **1 a :** RUMBLE 1 **b :** to utter a deep guttural threatening sound ⟨the dog *growled*⟩ **2 :** to complain angrily [Middle English *groulen, grollen*] — **growl** *n* — **growl•er** *n*

grown \'grōn\ *adj* **:** ADULT 1, MATURE

grown–up \'grō-ˌnəp\ *adj* **:** ADULT ⟨*grown-up* behavior⟩ — **grown–up** *n*

growth \'grōth\ *n* **1 a :** stage or condition attained in growing **:** SIZE ⟨reach one's full *growth*⟩ **b :** a process of growing: as (1) **:** an increase in the size or amount of something (as an organism, a crystal, or wealth) (2) **:** progressive development ⟨the *growth* of civilization⟩ **2 :** a result or product of growing: as **a :** vegetation or a cover of vegetation ⟨a *growth* of new rye⟩ **b :** an abnormal mass of tissue (as a tumor) **3 :** a producing especially by growing ⟨fruits of one's own *growth*⟩

growth factor *n* **:** a substance (as a vitamin) that promotes the growth of an organism

growth hormone *n* **1 :** a hormone that is secreted by the pituitary gland and regulates growth **2 :** any of various plant substances (as gibberellin) that regulate growth

growth ring *n* **:** a layer of wood (as an annual ring) produced during a single period of growth

[1]**grub** \'grəb\ *vb* **grubbed; grub•bing 1 :** to clear or root out by digging ⟨*grub* land for planting⟩ **2 :** to work hard **:** DRUDGE **3 a :** to dig in the ground usually for a hidden object ⟨*grub* for potatoes⟩ **b :** to search about **:** RUMMAGE ⟨*grubbing* through the drawer⟩ [Middle English *grubben*] — **grub•ber** *n*

[2]**grub** *n* **1 :** a soft thick wormlike larva of an insect (as a beetle) **2 a :** DRUDGE **b :** a slovenly person **3 :** FOOD 2 [Middle English *grubbe,* from *grubben* "to grub"]

grub•by \'grəb-ē\ *adj* **grub•bi•er; -est 1 :** DIRTY 1, GRIMY **2 :** IGNOBLE 2 — **grub•bi•ly** \'grəb-ə-lē\ *adv* — **grub•bi•ness** \'grəb-ē-nəs\ *n*

grub•stake \'grəb-ˌstāk\ *n* **1 :** supplies or funds furnished a mining prospector on promise of a share in his finds **2 :** material assistance advanced for a project — **grubstake** *vt* — **grub•stak•er** *n*

[1]**grudge** \'grəj\ *vt* **:** BEGRUDGE 1 [Middle English *grucchen, grudgen* "to grumble, complain," from Medieval French *grucer, grucher,* of Germanic origin] — **grudg•er** *n* — **grudg•ing•ly** \'grəj-ing-lē\ *adv*

[2]**grudge** *n* **:** a feeling of deep-seated resentment or ill will

gru•el \'grü-əl\ *n* **:** a thin porridge [Medieval French, of Germanic origin]

gru•el•ing *or* **gru•el•ling** \'grü-ə-ling\ *adj* **:** taxing to the point of exhaustion **:** making severe demands **:** PUNISHING ⟨a *grueling* race⟩ [from obsolete *gruel* "to exhaust, punish," from *gruel,* n.]

grue•some \'grü-səm\ *adj* **:** inspiring horror or repulsion [alteration of earlier *growsome,* from English dialect *grow, grue* "to shiver," from Middle English *gruen* "to shiver," probably from Dutch *grūwen*] ***synonyms*** see GHASTLY — **grue•some•ly** *adv* — **grue•some•ness** *n*

gruff \'grəf\ *adj* **1 :** rough or stern in manner, speech, or look ⟨a *gruff* reply⟩ **2 :** being deep and harsh **:** HOARSE ⟨a *gruff* voice⟩ [Dutch *grof*] — **gruff•ly** *adv* — **gruff•ness** *n*

grum•ble \'grəm-bəl\ *vb* **grum•bled; grum•bling** \-bə-ling, -bling\ **1 :** to mutter in discontent **2 a :** to make low indistinct noises **b :** RUMBLE 1 [probably from Middle French *grommeler,* derived from Dutch *grommen*] — **grumble** *n* — **grum•bler** \-bə-lər, -blər\ *n* — **grum•bling•ly** *adv*

grump \'grəmp\ *n* **1 :** a fit of bad humor — usually used in plural **2 :** a person given to complaining [obsolete *grumps* "snubs, slights"] — **grump** *vi* — **grump•i•ly** \'grəm-pə-lē\ *adv* — **grump•i•ness** \-pē-nəs\ *n* — **grumpy** \-pē\ *adj*

grun•ion \'grən-yən\ *n* **:** a small fish of the California coast that regularly comes inshore to spawn at nearly full moon [probably from Spanish *gruñón* "grunter"]

[1]**grunt** \'grənt\ *vb* **1 :** to utter a grunt **2 :** to utter with a grunt [Old English *grunnettan,* from *grunian,* of imitative origin] — **grunt•er** *n*

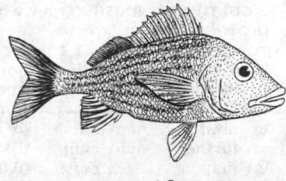

[2]**grunt** *n* **1 :** the characteristic deep short sound of a hog or a similar sound **2 :** any of numerous marine fishes related to the snappers **3 :** one who does routine unglamorous work ⟨*grunt* work⟩

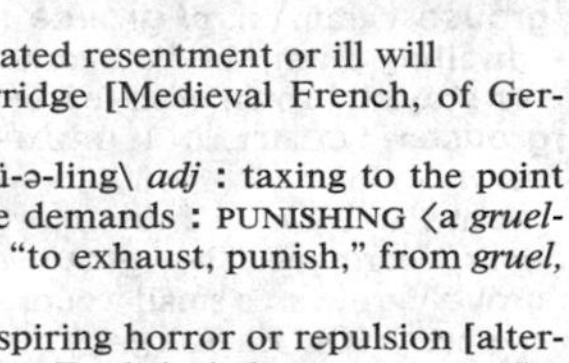
grunt 2

gryphon *variant of* GRIFFIN

G suit *n* **:** an aviator's or astronaut's suit designed to counteract the physiological effects of acceleration [gravity *suit*]

gua•ca•mo•le \ˌgwäk-ə-'mō-lē\ *n* **:** mashed avocado seasoned with condiments and often served as a spread or dip [Mexican Spanish, from Nahuatl *āhuacamōlli,* from *āhuacatl* "avocado" + *mōlli* "sauce"]

gua•na•co \gwə-'näk-ō\ *n, pl* **-cos** *also* **-co :** a South American mammal that has a soft thick fawn-colored coat and is related to the camel [Spanish, from Quechua *wanaku*]

gua•nine \'gwän-ˌēn\ *n* **:** a purine base $C_5H_5N_5O$ that codes genetic information in the polynucleotide chain of DNA and RNA — compare ADENINE, CYTOSINE, THYMINE, URACIL [*guano* + *-ine;* from its being found in guano]

gua•no \'gwän-ō\ *n, pl* **guanos :** a substance composed chiefly of the excrement of seabirds or bats and used as a fertilizer [Spanish, from Quechua *wanu* "fertilizer, dung"]

gua•ra•ni \ˌgwär-ə-'nē\ *n, pl* **-nis** *or* **-nies 1 :** the basic monetary unit of Paraguay **2 :** a coin representing one guarani [Spanish *guaraní*]

[1]**guar•an•tee** \ˌgar-ən-'tē, ˌgär-\ *n* **1 :** GUARANTOR **2 :** an agreement by which a person or firm guarantees something **3 :** something given as security **:** PLEDGE

[2]**guarantee** *vt* **-teed; -tee•ing 1 :** to undertake to answer to (a party) for the debt, failure to perform, or faulty performance of another **2 :** to undertake an obligation to establish, perform, or continue ⟨*guaranteed* annual wage⟩ **3 :** SECURE 1c

guar•an•tor \ˌgar-ən-'tȯr, 'gar-ən-tər, ˌgär-, 'gär-\ *n* **:** one that gives a guarantee

[1]**guar•an•ty** \'gar-ən-tē, 'gär-\ *n, pl* **-ties 1 :** GUARANTEE 2 **2 :** GUARANTEE 3 [Medieval French *garantie,* from *garantir* "to guarantee," from *garant* "warrant," of Germanic origin]

[2]**guaranty** *vt* **-tied; -ty•ing :** GUARANTEE

[1]**guard** \'gärd\ *n* **1 :** a defensive state or attitude ⟨asked dad for money when his *guard* was down⟩ **2 a :** the act or duty of defending **b :** PROTECTION 1 **3 a :** a person or a body of persons on sentinel duty **b** *pl* **:** troops attached to the person of the sovereign **4 a :** either of two football players who line up inside the tackles and next to the center **b :** either of two players stationed usually away from the basket in basketball **5 :** a protective or safety device (as on a machine) [Medieval French *garde,* from *garder* "to guard," of Germanic origin] — **off guard :** in an unprepared or unsuspecting state — **on guard :** defensively watchful **:** ALERT

[2]**guard** *vb* **1 :** to protect from danger **:** DEFEND **2 a :** to watch over so as to prevent escape, disclosure, or indiscretion ⟨*guard* a prisoner⟩ ⟨*guard* a secret⟩ **b :** to attempt to prevent (an opponent) from playing effectively or scoring **3 :** to be on guard **:** take precautions ⟨*guard* against infection⟩ ***synonyms*** see DEFEND

guard cell *n* **:** one of the two crescent-shaped epidermal cells that border and open and close a plant stoma

guard•ed \'gärd-əd\ *adj* **:** CAUTIOUS, CIRCUMSPECT ⟨a *guarded* answer⟩ — **guard•ed•ly** *adv*

guard hair *n* **:** one of the usually long coarse hairs forming a protective coating over the underfur of a mammal

guard•house \'gärd-ˌhau̇s\ *n* **1 :** a building occupied by a guard or used as a headquarters by soldiers on guard duty **2 :** a military jail

guard•i•an \'gärd-ē-ən\ *n* **1 :** one that guards **:** CUSTODIAN **2 :** one having the care of a person or the property of another — **guard•i•an•ship** \-ˌship\ *n*

guard of honor : HONOR GUARD

guard•rail \'gär-ˌdrāl\ *n* **:** a railing for guarding against danger or trespass; *esp* **:** a barrier placed at dangerous points along a highway

guard•room \'gär-ˌdrüm, -ˌdru̇m\ *n* **1 :** a room used by a military guard while on duty **2 :** a room where military prisoners are confined

guards•man \'gärdz-mən\ *n* **:** a member of a national guard, coast guard, or similar military body

gua•va \'gwäv-ə\ *n* **1 :** any of several tropical American shrubs or small trees of the myrtle family; *esp* **:** one widely grown for its yellow-skinned sweet-to-acid fruit **2 :** the fruit of a guava [Spanish *guaba, guayaba,* perhaps from Taino]

gua•yu•le \gwī-'ü-lē, wī-\ *n* **:** a low shrubby plant related to the daisies that is found in Mexico and the southwestern U.S. and has been grown as a source of rubber [American Spanish, from Nahuatl *cuauholli* or *huauholli*]

gu·ber·na·to·ri·al \ˌgü-bər-nə-ˈtōr-ē-əl, ˌgyü-, -bə-, -ˈtȯr-\ *adj* : of or relating to a governor [Latin *gubernator* "governor," from *gubernare* "to govern"]

Guern·sey \ˈgərn-zē\ *n, pl* **Guernseys** : any of a breed of reddish brown and white dairy cattle that are larger than Jerseys and produce rich yellowish milk [*Guernsey,* Channel Islands]

guer·ril·la *or* **gue·ril·la** \gə-ˈril-ə\ *n* : a person who engages in irregular warfare especially as a member of an independent unit carrying out harassment and sabotage [Spanish *guerrilla,* from *guerra* "war," of Germanic origin]

guess \ˈges\ *vb* **1** : to form an opinion from little or no evidence **2** : to arrive at a correct conclusion about by conjecture ⟨*guessed* the answer⟩ **3** : BELIEVE, SUPPOSE ⟨I *guess* you're right⟩ [Middle English *gessen,* perhaps of Scandinavian origin] ***synonyms*** see CONJECTURE — **guess** *n* — **guess·er** *n* — **guess·work** \ˈges-ˌwərk\ *n*

guest \ˈgest\ *n* **1 a** : a person entertained in one's house **b** : a person to whom hospitality is extended **c** : a patron of a commercial establishment (as a hotel or restaurant) **2** : an organism that lives in close association with another kind of organism [Old Norse *gestr*]

guf·faw \gə-ˈfȯ, ˌgə-\ *n* : a loud boisterous burst of laughter [imitative] — **guf·faw** *vi*

guid·ance \ˈgīd-ns\ *n* **1** : the act or process of guiding **2** : advice on vocational or educational problems given to students **3** : the process of controlling the course of a projectile by a built-in mechanism ⟨a missile *guidance* system⟩

[1]**guide** \ˈgīd\ *n* **1 a** : one that leads or directs another on a course **b** : a person who exhibits and explains points of interest **c** : something that provides guiding information ⟨a street *guide*⟩ **d** : a person who directs another's conduct or course of life **2 a** : a device for steadying or directing the motion of something **b** : a sheet or a card with a projecting tab for labeling that is inserted in a card index to facilitate reference [Medieval French, from Old Occitan *guida,* of Germanic origin]

[2]**guide** *vt* **1** : to act as a guide for : CONDUCT **2 a** : MANAGE, DIRECT ⟨*guide* a car through traffic⟩ **b** : to superintend the training of — **guid·able** \ˈgīd-ə-bəl\ *adj*

synonyms GUIDE, LEAD, STEER, PILOT mean to direct in a course or show the way to be followed. GUIDE implies intimate knowledge of the way and of all its difficulties and dangers ⟨*guided* the scouts through the cave⟩. LEAD implies showing the way and often keeping those that follow under control and in order ⟨*led* his team to victory⟩. STEER implies an ability to keep to a course and maneuver correctly ⟨*steering* the ship through a narrow channel⟩. PILOT suggests steering over a dangerous or complicated course or under difficult circumstances ⟨*piloted* the bill through the Senate⟩.

guide·book \ˈgīd-ˌbu̇k\ *n* : a book of information for travelers

guide dog *n* : a dog trained to lead the blind

guide·line \ˈgīd-ˌlīn\ *n* **1** : a line by which one is guided **2** : an indication or outline of policy or conduct

guided missile *n* : a missile whose course toward a target may be changed (as by radio signals or a built-in target-seeking device) during flight

guide word *n* : either of the terms at the head of a page of an alphabetical reference work (as a dictionary) indicating the alphabetically first and last words on the page

gui·don \ˈgīd-ˌän, -n\ *n* **1** : a small flag; *esp* : one carried by a military unit as a unit marker **2** : one who carries a guidon [Middle French]

guild *also* **gild** \ˈgild\ *n* : an association of people with similar interests or pursuits; *esp* : a medieval association of merchants or craftsmen [Old Norse *gildi* "payment, guild"] — **guild·ship** \-ˌship\ *n*

guil·der \ˈgil-dər\ *n* : GULDEN [Dutch *gulden*]

guild·hall \ˈgild-ˌhȯl\ *n* : a hall where a guild or corporation usually assembles

guile \ˈgīl\ *n* : deceitful cunning : DUPLICITY [Medieval French] — **guile·ful** \-fəl\ *adj* — **guile·ful·ly** \-fə-lē\ *adv* — **guile·ful·ness** *n*

guile·less \ˈgīl-ləs\ *adj* : free from deceit or cunning : NAIVE — **guile·less·ly** *adv* — **guile·less·ness** *n*

guil·le·mot \ˈgil-ə-ˌmät\ *n* : any of several narrow-billed auks of northern seas [French, from *Guillaume* "William"]

guil·lo·tine \ˈgil-ə-ˌtēn; ˌgē-ə-ˈ, ˈgē-ə-ˌ, -yə-\ *n* : a device for beheading by means of a heavy blade that slides down between vertical guides [French, from Joseph *Guillotin,* died 1814, French physician] — **guillotine** *vt*

guilt \ˈgilt\ *n* **1** : the fact of having committed an offense and especially one that is punishable by law **2** : the state of deserving blame **3** : a feeling of responsibility for offenses [Old English *gylt* "delinquency"] — **guilt·less** \-ləs\ *adj*

guilt–trip \ˈgilt-ˌtrip\ *vt* : to cause feelings of guilt in ⟨*guilt-tripped* them into helping⟩

guilty \ˈgil-tē\ *adj* **guilt·i·er; -est** **1** : having committed a breach of conduct or a crime **2 a** : suggesting or involving guilt ⟨a *guilty* look⟩ **b** : aware of or suffering from guilt ⟨a *guilty* conscience⟩ — **guilt·i·ly** \-tə-lē\ *adv* — **guilt·i·ness** \-tē-nəs\ *n*

guin·ea \ˈgin-ē\ *n* **1** : an English gold coin issued from 1663 to 1813 and fixed in 1717 at one pound and one shilling **2** : a former monetary unit equal to 21 shillings [*Guinea,* West Africa, supposed source of the gold from which it was made]

guinea fowl *n* : an African bird related to the pheasants, widely raised for food, and marked by a bare neck and head and white-speckled usually gray plumage

guinea hen *n* : GUINEA FOWL; *esp* : a female guinea fowl

guinea pig *n* **1** : a small stout-bodied short-eared nearly tailless rodent of South American origin often kept as a pet and widely used in biological research — called also *cavy* **2** : one that is the subject of a scientific experiment

guinea worm *n* : a slender nematode worm attaining a length of several feet and occurring as an adult under the skin of various mammals including humans

guise \ˈgīz\ *n* **1** : a form or style of dress : COSTUME ⟨appeared in the *guise* of a shepherd⟩ **2** : external appearance : SEMBLANCE ⟨swindled them under the *guise* of friendship⟩ [Medieval French, of Germanic origin]

gui·tar \gə-ˈtär, gi-\ *n* : a flat-bodied stringed instrument with a long fretted neck and usually six strings played with a pick or with the fingers [French *guitare,* from Spanish *guitarra,* from Arabic *qītār,* from Greek *kithara* "cithara"]

gu·lar \ˈgü-lər, ˈgyü-\ *adj* : of, relating to, or situated on the throat [Latin *gula* "throat"]

gulch \ˈgəlch\ *n* : RAVINE, COULEE [perhaps from English dialect *gulch* "to gulp"]

gul·den \ˈgül-dən, ˈgu̇l-\ *n, pl* **guldens** *or* **gulden** **1 a** : the basic monetary unit of the Netherlands until 2002 **b** : the basic monetary unit of Suriname **2** : a coin or note representing one gulden [Dutch *gulden florijn* "golden florin"]

gulf \ˈgəlf\ *n* **1** : a part of an ocean or sea extending into the land **2** : a deep hollow in the earth : CHASM, ABYSS **3** : WHIRLPOOL **4** : a wide gap ⟨the *gulf* between generations⟩ [Middle French *golfe,* from Italian *golfo,* from Late Latin *colpus,* from Greek *kolpos* "bosom, gulf"]

gulf·weed \ˈgəlf-ˌwēd\ *n* : any of several marine brown algae; *esp* : a branching olive-brown seaweed of tropical American seas with numerous air-filled sacs suggesting berries

[1]**gull** \ˈgəl\ *n* : any of numerous mostly white or gray long-winged web-footed aquatic birds [Middle English, of Celtic origin]

[1]gull

[2]**gull** *vt* : to take advantage of : DUPE [obsolete *gull* "gullet"]

[3]**gull** *n* : a person easily deceived or cheated : DECEIVE

gul·let \ˈgəl-ət\ *n* **1 a** : a tube that leads from the back of the mouth to the stomach : ESOPHAGUS **b** : THROAT 1 **2** : a tubular infolding of the protoplasm in various protozoans (as a paramecium) that functions especially in the intake of food **3** : the space between adjacent saw teeth [Medieval French *goulet* "narrow passage," from *gule* "throat," from Latin *gula*]

gull·ible \ˈgəl-ə-bəl\ *adj* : easily cheated or duped — **gull·ibil·i·ty** \ˌgəl-ə-ˈbil-ət-ē\ *n* — **gull·ibly** \ˈgəl-ə-blē\ *adv*

\ə\ abut	\au̇\ out	\i\ tip	\ȯ\ saw	\u̇\ foot
\ər\ further	\ch\ chin	\ī\ life	\ȯi\ coin	\y\ yet
\a\ mat	\e\ pet	\j\ job	\th\ thin	\yü\ few
\ā\ take	\ē\ easy	\ng\ sing	\t͟h\ this	\yu̇\ cure
\ä\ cot, cart	\g\ go	\ō\ bone	\ü\ food	\zh\ vision

gul·ly \ˈgəl-ē\ *n, pl* **gullies** : a trench worn in the earth by rainwater [obsolete *gully* "gullet," probably an alteration of Middle English *golet* "ravine, throat"] — **gully** *vb*
gully erosion *n* : soil erosion produced by running water
gulp \ˈgəlp\ *vb* **1** : to swallow hurriedly or greedily or in one swallow **2** : to keep back as if by swallowing ⟨*gulp* down a sob⟩ **3** : to catch the breath as if in taking a long drink [Middle English *gulpen*] — **gulp** *n* — **gulp·er** *n*
¹**gum** \ˈgəm\ *n* : the tissue along the jaws of animals that surrounds the necks of the teeth [Old English *gōma* "palate"]
²**gum** *vt* **gummed; gum·ming** **1** : to enlarge gullets of (a saw) **2** : to chew with the gums
³**gum** *n* **1** : any of numerous complex colloidal substances (as gum arabic) that are exuded by plants or are extracted from them by solvents, that are thick or sticky when moist but harden on drying and are either soluble in water or swell up in contact with water, and that are used in pharmacy (as for emulsifiers), for adhesives, as food thickeners, and in inks; *also* : any of various gummy plant exudates including natural resins, oleoresins, rubber, and rubberlike substances **2** : a substance or deposit resembling a plant gum (as in sticky quality) **3 a** : a tree (as a black gum) that yields gum **b** *Australian* : EUCALYPTUS **4** : the wood of a gum **5** : CHEWING GUM [Medieval French *gomme,* from Latin *cummi, gummi,* from Greek *kommi,* from Egyptian *gmyt*]
⁴**gum** *vt* **gummed; gum·ming** : to smear, seal, or clog with or as if with gum ⟨*gum* up the works⟩
gum arabic *n* : a water-soluble gum obtained from several acacias and used especially in adhesives, in confectionery, and in pharmacy
gum·bo \ˈgəm-ˌbō\ *n, pl* **gumbos** **1 a** : OKRA **b** : a soup thickened with okra pods **2** : any of various silty soils that when wet become very sticky [American French *gombo,* of Bantu origin]
gum·drop \-ˌdräp\ *n* : a sugar-coated candy made usually from corn syrup with gelatin or gum arabic
gum·ma \ˈgəm-ə\ *n, pl* **gummas** *also* **gum·ma·ta** \ˈgəm-ət-ə\ : a gummy or rubbery tumor associated especially with late stages of syphilis [Late Latin *gummat-, gumma* "gum," from Latin *gummi*] — **gum·ma·tous** \-ət-əs\ *adj*
gum·my \ˈgəm-ē\ *adj* **gum·mi·er; -est** **1** : consisting of, containing, or covered with gum **2** : VISCOUS 1, STICKY — **gum·mi·ness** *n*
gump·tion \ˈgəm-shən, ˈgəmp-\ *n* **1** : shrewd common sense **2** : courageous or ambitious initiative ⟨lacked the *gumption* to try⟩ [origin unknown]
gum resin *n* : a plant product consisting essentially of a mixture of gum and resin
gum·shoe \ˈgəm-ˌshü\ *n* : DETECTIVE — **gumshoe** *vi*
gum tragacanth *n* : TRAGACANTH
gum turpentine *n* : TURPENTINE 2a
gum·wood \ˈgəm-ˌwu̇d\ *n* : ³GUM 4
¹**gun** \ˈgən\ *n* **1 a** : a piece of artillery usually with high muzzle velocity and comparatively flat trajectory : CANNON **b** : a portable firearm (as a rifle or pistol) **c** : a device that throws a projectile **2 a** : a discharge of a gun especially as a salute or signal ⟨a 21-*gun* salute⟩ **b** : a signal marking a beginning or ending ⟨the opening *gun* of a campaign⟩ **3** : one who is skilled with a gun ⟨a hired *gun*⟩ **4** : something suggesting a gun in shape or function ⟨a grease *gun*⟩ **5** : THROTTLE 2 [Middle English *gunne*] — **gunned** \ˈgənd\ *adj*
²**gun** *vb* **gunned; gun·ning** **1** : to hunt or shoot with a gun **2** : to open up the throttle of quickly so as to increase speed ⟨*gun* the engine⟩
gun·boat \ˈgən-ˌbōt\ *n* : a small armed ship for patrolling coastal waters
gun·cot·ton \-ˌkät-n\ *n* : an explosive that consists of nitrocellulose and is used chiefly in smokeless powder
gun·fight \-ˌfīt\ *n* : a hostile encounter in which antagonists with guns shoot at each other — **gun·fight·er** *n*
gun·fire \-ˌfīr\ *n* : the firing of guns
gung ho \ˈgəng-ˈhō\ *adj* : very enthusiastic [*Gung ho!,* motto (supposed to mean "work together") of a U.S. Marine battalion in World War II, from Chinese (Beijing dialect) *gōnghé,* short for *Zhōngguó Gōngyè Hézuò Shè* "Chinese Industrial Cooperative Society"]
Word History The Chinese Industrial Cooperative Society was organized in 1938 to develop light industry in areas of China not overrun by the Japanese, and was supported by both Communists and Chiang Kai-shek's Nationalists. The Chinese name of the society, *Zhōngguó Gōngyè Hézuò Shè,* was conventionally shortened to *Gōnghé.* A U.S. Marine Corps officer, Evans Carlson, while an observer in China with the Communists' 8th Route Army in 1937–38, became an admirer of their spirit. When Carlson formed the Marines' 2nd Raider Battalion at Camp Elliot, California, in 1942, he tried to instill the Communists' unity of purpose in his men. He told them that "Gung ho" was the motto of the Chinese Industrial Cooperatives (which Carlson seems to have associated with the Communists) and meant "work together." In fact, though *gōng* may be translated "work" and *hé* "join," *Gōnghé* is the shortened form of a name and not the Chinese equivalent of "work together." Nonetheless, *gung ho* in the sense "zealous" spread to the entire Marine Corps and later from military to civilian use.
gun·man \-mən\ *n* : a man armed with a gun; *esp* : a professional killer
gun·ner \ˈgən-ər\ *n* **1** : a person (as a soldier) who operates a gun **2** : one who hunts with a gun
gun·nery \ˈgən-rē, -ə-rē\ *n* : the use of guns; *esp* : the science of the flight of projectiles and of the effective use of guns
gunnery sergeant *n* : an enlisted rank in the Marine Corps above staff sergeant and below master sergeant
gun·ny·sack \-ˌsak\ *n* : a sack made of a coarse heavy fabric (as burlap)
gun·point \ˈgən-ˌpȯint\ *n* : the muzzle of a gun — **at gunpoint** : under a threat of death by being shot
gun·pow·der \-ˌpau̇d-ər\ *n* : an explosive mixture of potassium nitrate, charcoal, and sulfur used in gunnery and blasting; *also* : any of various explosive powders used in guns
gun·shot \-ˌshät\ *n* **1** : shot or a projectile fired from a gun **2** : the range of a gun ⟨within *gunshot*⟩ **3** : the firing of a gun
gun–shy \-ˌshī\ *adj* **1** : afraid of loud noise (as that of a gun) **2** : markedly distrustful, afraid, or cautious
gun·smith \-ˌsmith\ *n* : one whose business is to design, make, or repair small firearms
gun·wale *also* **gun·nel** \ˈgən-l\ *n* : the upper edge of a ship's side [from its former use as a support for guns]
gup·py \ˈgəp-ē\ *n, pl* **guppies** : a small tropical topminnow frequently kept as an aquarium fish [R. J. L. *Guppy,* died 1916, Trinidadian naturalist]
gur·gle \ˈgər-gəl\ *vi* **gur·gled; gur·gling** \ˈgər-gə-ling, -gling\ **1** : to flow in a broken irregular current **2** : to make a sound like that of a gurgling liquid [probably imitative] — **gurgle** *n*
gur·nard \ˈgər-nərd\ *n, pl* **gurnard** *or* **gurnards** : SEA ROBIN [Medieval French *gurenard,* from *grognier* "to grunt," from Latin *grunnire,* of imitative origin]

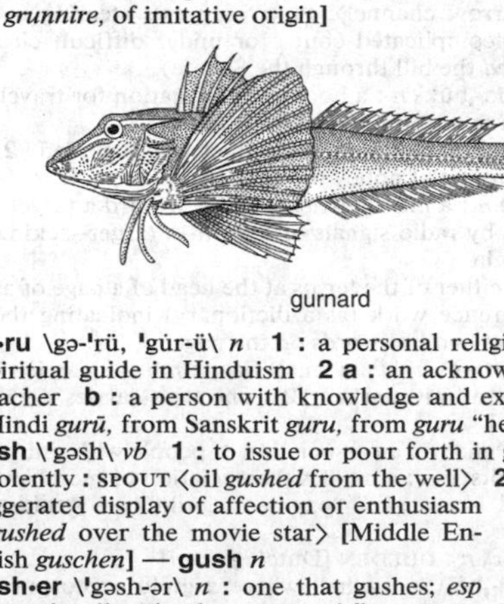
gurnard

gu·ru \gə-ˈrü, ˈgu̇r-ü\ *n* **1** : a personal religious teacher and spiritual guide in Hinduism **2 a** : an acknowledged leader or teacher **b** : a person with knowledge and expertise : EXPERT [Hindi *gurū,* from Sanskrit *guru,* from *guru* "heavy, venerable"]
gush \ˈgəsh\ *vb* **1** : to issue or pour forth in great quantity or violently : SPOUT ⟨oil *gushed* from the well⟩ **2** : to make an exaggerated display of affection or enthusiasm ⟨*gushed* over the movie star⟩ [Middle English *guschen*] — **gush** *n*
gush·er \ˈgəsh-ər\ *n* : one that gushes; *esp* : an oil well with a large natural flow
gushy \ˈgəsh-ē\ *adj* **gush·i·er; -est** : marked by exaggerated sentimentality — **gush·i·ly** \ˈgəsh-ə-lē\ *adv* — **gush·i·ness** \ˈgəsh-ē-nəs\ *n*
gus·set \ˈgəs-ət\ *n* : a usually triangular or diamond-shaped insert (as on a bridge) to give width or strength [Middle English, "piece of armor covering the joints in a suit of armor," from Medieval French *goussete*]

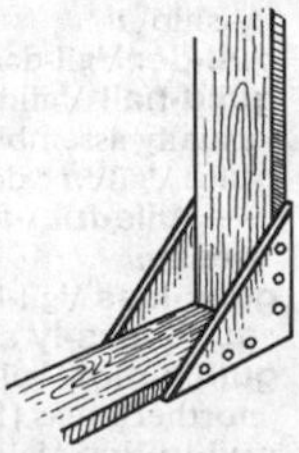
gusset

gust \ˈgəst\ *n* **1 :** a sudden brief rush of wind **2 :** a sudden outburst : SURGE ⟨a *gust* of rage⟩ [probably from Old Norse *gustr*] — **gust·i·ly** \ˈgəs-tə-lē\ *adv* — **gust·i·ness** \-tē-nəs\ *n* — **gusty** \-tē\ *adj*

gus·ta·tion \ˌgəs-ˈtā-shən\ *n* **:** the act or sensation of tasting [Latin *gustatio,* from *gustare* "to taste"]

gus·ta·to·ry \ˈgəs-tə-ˌtōr-ē, -ˌtȯr-\ *adj* **:** relating to, associated with, or being the sense or sensation of taste

gus·to \ˈgəs-ˌtō\ *n* **1 :** enthusiastic vigorous enjoyment or appreciation ⟨eat with *gusto*⟩ **2 :** very great vitality [Italian, from Latin *gustus* "taste"] ***synonyms*** see TASTE

[1]**gut** \ˈgət\ *n* **1 a :** VISCERA, ENTRAILS — usually used in plural **b :** the alimentary canal or part of it (as the intestine or stomach) **c :** ABDOMEN 1, BELLY **2** *pl* **:** the inner essential parts ⟨the *guts* of a car⟩ **3** *pl* **:** COURAGE [Old English *guttas,* pl.]

[2]**gut** *vt* **gut·ted; gut·ting 1 :** EVISCERATE 1 **2 :** to destroy the inside of ⟨fire *gutted* the building⟩

gut check *n* **:** a test of courage, character, or determination

gutsy \ˈgət-sē\ *adj* **guts·i·er; -est :** COURAGEOUS ⟨a *gutsy* hockey player⟩ ⟨a *gutsy* decision⟩ — **guts·i·ness** *n*

gut·ta–per·cha \ˌgət-ə-ˈpər-chə\ *n* **:** a tough plastic substance from the latex of several Malaysian trees that resembles but contains more resin than rubber and that is used especially as insulation and in dentistry [Malay *gĕtah-pĕrcha,* from *gĕtah* "sap, latex" + *pĕrcha* "scrap, rag"]

gut·ta·tion \ˌgə-ˈtā-shən\ *n* **:** oozing of drops of water from the surface of a leaf [Latin *gutta* "drop"]

[1]**gut·ter** \ˈgət-ər\ *n* **1 a :** a trough along the eaves to catch and carry off water from a roof **b :** a low area (as at a roadside) to carry off surface water **2 :** a narrow channel or groove [Medieval French *gutere, goter,* from *gute* "drop," from Latin *gutta*]

[2]**gutter** *vb* **1 :** to form gutters in **2 a :** to flow in small streams **b :** to melt away rapidly by becoming channeled down the sides ⟨a *guttering* candle⟩ **3 :** to flicker in a draft ⟨a flame *guttering* in the breeze⟩

gut·ter·snipe \-ˌsnīp\ *n* **:** a person of the lowest moral or economic station; *esp* **:** a street urchin

gut·tur·al \ˈgət-ə-rəl\ *adj* **1 :** of or relating to the throat **2 a :** formed or pronounced in the throat ⟨*guttural* sounds⟩ **b :** VELAR 1 **c :** being or marked by an utterance that is strange or disagreeable [Middle French, derived from Latin *guttur* "throat"] — **guttural** *n* — **gut·tur·al·ly** \-rə-lē\ *adv* — **gut·tur·al·ness** *n*

gut·ty \ˈgət-ē\ *adj* **gut·ti·er; -est 1 :** COURAGEOUS ⟨a *gutty* fighter⟩ **2 :** having a vigorous challenging quality ⟨*gutty* realism⟩

[1]**guy** \ˈgī\ *n* **:** a rope, chain, rod, or wire attached to something as a brace or guide [probably from Dutch *gei* "brail"]

[2]**guy** *vt* **guyed; guy·ing :** to steady or reinforce with a guy

[3]**guy** *n* **:** FELLOW 4a, b [Guy Fawkes, died 1606, English conspirator who plotted to blow up the Houses of Parliament]

Word History On November 4, 1605 in London, Guy Fawkes was arrested for having planted gunpowder in the cellars of the Houses of Parliament as his part in a conspiracy to blow up the Parliament buildings on the following day. He was later executed. The failure of the conspiracy is still celebrated in England on November 5, Guy Fawkes Day. On this day fireworks are displayed and effigies of Guy Fawkes are burned on bonfires. These effigies came to be called *guys.* The use of the word was extended to other similar effigies and then to people of grotesque appearance. In the U.S. the word was generalized to mean simply "man" or "fellow."

[4]**guy** *vt* **:** to make fun of : RIDICULE

guy·ot \ˈgē-ō\ *n* **:** a flat-topped seamount [Arnold H. *Guyot,* died 1884, American geographer and geologist]

guz·zle \ˈgəz-əl\ *vb* **guz·zled; guz·zling** \ˈgəz-ling, -ə-ling\ **1 :** to drink greedily ⟨*guzzled* soft drinks⟩ **2 :** to use up : CONSUME ⟨the automobile *guzzles* a lot of gasoline⟩ [origin unknown] — **guz·zler** \-lər, -ə-lər\ *n*

gybe *variant of* JIBE

gym \ˈjim\ *n* **:** GYMNASIUM 1

gym·kha·na \jim-ˈkän-ə, -ˈkan-\ *n* **:** a meet featuring sports contests (as horseback-riding events) [probably from Hindi *gẽdkhāna* and Urdu *gendkhāna,* literally, "ball court"]

gym·na·si·um *in sense 1* jim-ˈnā-zē-əm, *in sense 2* gim-ˈnä-zē-əm\ *n, pl* **-si·ums** *or* **-sia** \-zē-ə\ **1 :** a room or building for indoor sports activities **2 :** a German secondary school preparing students for the university [Latin, "exercise ground, school," from Greek *gymnasion,* from *gymnazein* "to exercise naked," from *gymnos* "naked"]

gym·nast \ˈjim-ˌnast, -nəst\ *n* **:** a person trained in gymnastics

gym·nas·tics \jim-ˈnas-tiks\ *n sing or pl* **:** physical exercises developing or exhibiting skill, strength, and control in the use of the body; *also* **:** a sport in which such exercises are performed — **gym·nas·tic** \-tik\ *adj* — **gym·nas·ti·cal·ly** \-ti-kə-lē, -klē\ *adv*

gym·no·sperm \ˈjim-nə-ˌspərm\ *n* **:** any of a group of woody vascular nonflowering plants (as pines, yews, and gingkos) that produce naked seeds not enclosed in an ovary or true fruit [derived from Greek *gymnos* "naked" + *sperma* "seed"] — **gym·no·sper·mous** \ˌjim-nə-ˈspər-məs\ *adj*

gy·ne·col·o·gy \ˌgī-ni-ˈkäl-ə-jē, ˌjin-\ *n* **:** a branch of medicine that deals with the diseases and routine medical care of the reproductive system of women [Greek *gynaik-, gynē* "woman"] — **gy·ne·co·log·ic** \-kə-ˈläj-ik\ *or* **gy·ne·co·log·i·cal** \-ˈläj-i-kəl\ *adj* — **gy·ne·col·o·gist** \-ˈkäl-ə-jəst\ *n*

gy·noe·ci·um \jin-ˈē-sē-əm, gīn-, -shē-\ *n, pl* **-cia** \-sēə, -shē-ə\ **:** the carpels in a flower [Latin *gynaeceum* "women's apartments," from Greek *gynaikeion,* from *gynaik-, gynē* "woman"]

-g·y·nous \j-ə-nəs\ *adj combining form* **1 :** of, relating to, or having (such or so many) wives or female mates ⟨poly*gynous*⟩ **2 :** situated (in a specified place) in relation to a female organ of a plant ⟨epi*gynous*⟩ [Greek *gynē* "woman"]

[1]**gyp** \ˈjip\ *n* **1 :** CHEAT 2, SWINDLER **2 :** FRAUD 1b, SWINDLE [probably short for *Gypsy*]

[2]**gyp** *vb* **gypped; gyp·ping :** CHEAT 1, SWINDLE

gyp·soph·i·la \jip-ˈsäf-ə-lə\ *n* **:** any of a large genus of Old World herbs related to the carnation and having loosely branched clusters of tiny flowers [Latin *gypsum* + *-phila* "-phil"]

gyp·sum \ˈjip-səm\ *n* **:** a colorless mineral $CaSO_4 \cdot 2H_2O$ that consists of hydrous sulfate of calcium occurring in crystals or masses and that is used especially as a soil improver and in making plaster of paris [Latin, from Greek *gypsos*]

Gyp·sy \ˈjip-sē\ *n, pl* **Gypsies 1 :** one of a people coming originally from India to Europe in the 14th or 15th century and living and maintaining a migratory way of life chiefly in south and southwest Asia, Europe, and North America **2 :** ROMANY 2 **3** *not cap* **:** one that resembles a Gypsy : WANDERER [alteration of *Egyptian*]

Word History In the early years of the 16th century there began to appear in Britain some members of a wandering race of people who were ultimately of Hindu origin and who called themselves and their language *Romany.* In Britain, however, it was popularly believed that they came from Egypt, so they were called *Egipcyans* or *Egyptians.* This was soon shortened to *Gipcyan,* and by 1600 the further altered form *Gipsy, Gypsey* began to appear in print.

gypsy moth *n* **:** an Old World tussock moth introduced about 1869 into the U.S. that has a hairy caterpillar which is a destructive defoliator of many trees

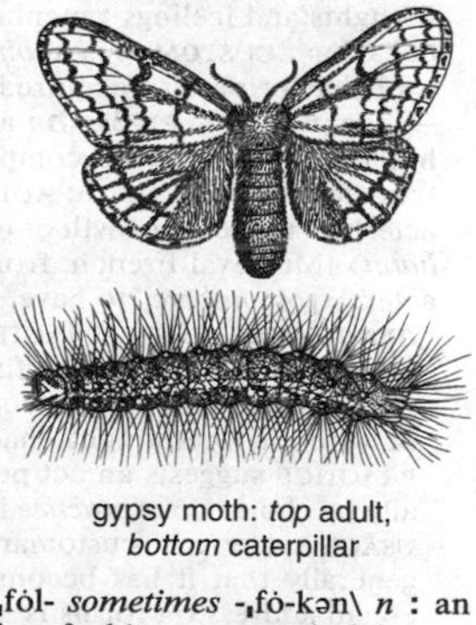
gypsy moth: *top* adult, *bottom* caterpillar

gyr- *or* **gyro-** *combining form* **1 :** ring : circle : spiral **2 :** gyroscope ⟨*gyro*compass⟩ [Greek *gyros* "rounded"]

gy·rate \ˈjī-ˌrāt\ *vi* **1 :** to revolve around a point or axis **2 :** to oscillate with or as if with a circular or spiral motion — **gy·ra·tion** \jī-ˈrā-shən\ *n* — **gy·ra·tion·al** \-shnəl, -shən-l\ *adj*

gyr·fal·con \ˈjər-ˌfal-kən *also* -ˌfȯl- *sometimes* -ˌfȯ-kən\ *n* **:** an arctic falcon that occurs in shades of white, gray, or dark brown and is the largest of all falcons [Medieval French *girfaucon,* probably from *gir* "vulture" + *faucon* "falcon"]

[1]**gy·ro** \ˈjī-rō\ *n, pl* **gyros 1 :** GYROCOMPASS **2 :** GYROSCOPE

[2]**gy·ro** \ˈyē-ˌrō, ˈzhir-ō\ *n, pl* **gyros :** a sandwich especially of lamb and beef, tomato, onion, and yogurt sauce on pita bread

\ə\ **abut**	\au̇\ **out**	\i\ **tip**	\ȯ\ **saw**	\u̇\ **foot**
\ər\ **further**	\ch\ **chin**	\ī\ **life**	\ȯi\ **coin**	\y\ **yet**
\a\ **mat**	\e\ **pet**	\j\ **job**	\th\ **thin**	\yü\ **few**
\ā\ **take**	\ē\ **easy**	\ng\ **sing**	\t͟h\ **this**	\yu̇\ **cure**
\ä\ **cot, cart**	\g\ **go**	\ō\ **bone**	\ü\ **food**	\zh\ **vision**

[New Greek *gyros* "turn"; from the rotation of the meat on a spit]

gy·ro·com·pass \ˈjī-rō-ˌkəm-pəs, -ˌkäm-\ *n* : a compass consisting of a constantly spinning gyroscope whose spin axis is always parallel to the earth's axis of rotation so that the compass always points to true north

gy·ro·scope \ˈjī-rə-ˌskōp\ *n* : a wheel or disk mounted to spin rapidly about an axis that is free to turn in various directions [from its original use to illustrate the rotation of the earth] — **gy·ro·scop·ic** \ˌjī-rə-ˈskäp-ik\ *adj*

gy·rus \ˈjī-rəs\ *n, pl* **gy·ri** \-ˌrī\ : a convoluted ridge between anatomical grooves; *esp* : CONVOLUTION 1 [Latin, "circle," from Greek *gyros*]

gyve \ˈjīv\ *n* : FETTER 1 [Middle English] — **gyve** *vt*

H

h \ˈāch\ *n, pl* **h's** *or* **hs** \ˈā-chəz\ *often cap* : the 8th letter of the English alphabet

ha *or* **hah** \ˈhä\ *interj* — used especially to express surprise, joy, or triumph [Middle English *ha*]

Hab·ak·kuk \ˈhab-ə-ˌkək, hə-ˈbak-ək\ *n* : a prophetic book of canonical Jewish and Christian Scriptures — see BIBLE table

ha·ba·ne·ra \ˌhäb-ə-ˈner-ə, ˌäb-\ *n* **1** : a Cuban dance in slow duple time **2** : the music for the habanera [Spanish *danza habanera,* literally, "Havanan dance"]

habdalah *variant of* HAVDALAH

ha·be·as cor·pus \ˌhā-bē-əs-ˈkȯr-pəs\ *n* **1** : any of several writs issued to bring a person before a court; *esp* : one ordering an inquiry to determine whether or not a person has been lawfully imprisoned **2** : the right of a citizen to obtain a writ of habeas corpus as a protection against illegal imprisonment [Medieval Latin, literally, "you should have the body" (the opening words of the writ)]

hab·er·dash·er \ˈhab-ər-ˌdash-ər, ˈhab-ə-ˌ\ *n* : a dealer in men's clothing and accessories [Medieval French *hapertas,* a kind of cloth]

hab·er·dash·ery \-ˌdash-rē, -ə-rē\ *n, pl* **-er·ies** **1** : goods sold by a haberdasher **2** : a haberdasher's shop

ha·bil·i·ment \hə-ˈbil-ə-mənt\ *n* **1** : the dress characteristic of an occupation or occasion — usually used in plural ⟨the *habiliments* of a priest⟩ **2** : CLOTHING — usually used in plural [Medieval French *abillement, habillemens,* from *abiller* "to prepare, equip," from *bille* "trimmed wood, log"]

¹hab·it \ˈhab-ət\ *n* **1** : a costume characteristic of a calling, rank, or function ⟨her riding *habit*⟩ ⟨a nun's *habit*⟩ **2** : bodily appearance or physical makeup : PHYSIQUE ⟨a man of fleshy *habit*⟩ **3** : the prevailing disposition or character of a person's thoughts and feelings : mental makeup **4** : a usual manner of behavior : CUSTOM ⟨his *habit* of taking a morning walk⟩ **5 a** : a behavior pattern acquired and fixed by frequent repetition — compare REFLEX 2a **b** : an acquired mode of behavior that has become nearly or completely involuntary ⟨got up early from force of *habit*⟩ **c** : ADDICTION ⟨a drug *habit*⟩ **6** : characteristic mode of growth or occurrence ⟨elms have a spreading *habit*⟩ [Medieval French, from Latin *habitus* "condition, character," from *habēre* "to have, hold"]

synonyms HABIT, PRACTICE, USAGE, CUSTOM mean a way of acting that has become fixed through repetition. HABIT implies doing something unconsciously and often involuntarily or without forethought ⟨had a *habit* of tapping his fingers⟩. PRACTICE suggests an act performed with regularity and usually by choice ⟨our *practice* is to honor all major credit cards⟩. USAGE suggests a customary action or practice followed so generally that it has become a social norm ⟨providing your e-mail address on forms is now common *usage*⟩. CUSTOM applies to practice or usage so long and continuously associated with an individual or group as to have the force of unwritten law ⟨the *custom* of wearing black at funerals⟩.

²habit *vt* : CLOTHE 1, DRESS

hab·it·able \ˈhab-ət-ə-bəl\ *adj* : suitable or fit to live in ⟨the *habitable* parts of the earth⟩ — **hab·it·abil·i·ty** \ˌhab-ət-ə-ˈbil-ət-ē\ *n* — **hab·it·able·ness** \ˈhab-ət-ə-bəl-nəs\ *n* — **hab·it·ably** \-blē\ *adv*

ha·bi·tant *n* **1** \ˈhab-ət-ənt\ : INHABITANT **2** \ˌhab-i-ˈtän, ˌab-\ : a French settler or a farmer of French origin in Canada

hab·i·tat \ˈhab-ə-ˌtat\ *n* **1** : the place or environment where a plant or animal naturally or normally lives or grows **2** : the place where something is commonly found [Latin, "it inhabits," from *habitare* "to inhabit"]

hab·i·ta·tion \ˌhab-ə-ˈtā-shən\ *n* **1** : the act of inhabiting : OCCUPANCY **2** : a dwelling place : RESIDENCE

hab·it–form·ing *adj* : causing addiction ⟨a *habit-forming* drug⟩

ha·bit·u·al \hə-ˈbich-ə-wəl, -ˈbich-wəl\ *adj* **1** : having the nature of a habit ⟨*habitual* tardiness⟩ **2** : doing or acting by force of habit ⟨*habitual* smokers⟩ **3** : done, followed, or used often or regularly ⟨took our *habitual* path⟩ ***synonyms*** see USUAL — **ha·bit·u·al·ly** \-ē\ *adv* — **ha·bit·u·al·ness** *n*

ha·bit·u·ate \hə-ˈbich-ə-ˌwāt, ha-\ *vt* : to make used to : ACCUSTOM

ha·bit·u·a·tion \-ˌbich-ə-ˈwā-shən\ *n* **1** : the act or process of habituating **2** : psychological dependence on a drug after a period of use — compare ADDICTION

hab·i·tude \ˈhab-ə-ˌtüd, -ˌtyüd\ *n* **1** : habitual disposition or mode of behavior or procedure **2** : CUSTOM 1b

ha·bi·tué \hə-ˈbich-ə-ˌwā, ha-\ *n* : a person who frequents a place or type of place ⟨café *habitués*⟩ [French, from *habituer* "to frequent," derived from Latin *habitus* "habit"]

hab·i·tus \ˈhab-ət-əs\ *n, pl* **habitus** \-ət-əs, -ə-ˌtüs\ : bodily habit; *also* : HABIT 6 [Latin]

Habsburg *variant of* HAPSBURG

ha·chure \ha-ˈshu̇r\ *n* : a short line used for shading and in representing surfaces in relief (as in map drawing) [French]

ha·ci·en·da \ˌhäs-ē-ˈen-də, ˌäs-\ *n* **1** : a large estate especially in a Spanish-speaking country : PLANTATION **2** : the main building of a farm or ranch [Spanish, derived from Latin *facienda,* literally, "things to be done," from *facere* "to do"]

¹hack \ˈhak\ *vb* **1 a** : to cut with repeated irregular or unskillful blows **b** : to sever with repeated blows : CHOP **2** : to cough in a short dry manner **3** : to manage successfully ⟨tried sales work but couldn't *hack* it⟩ **4 a** : to write computer programs for enjoyment **b** : to gain access to a computer illegally [Old English *-haccian*]

²hack *n* **1** : an implement for hacking **2** : NICK 1, NOTCH **3** : a short dry cough **4** : a hacking blow

³hack *n* **1 a** (1) : a horse let out for common hire (2) : a horse used in all kinds of work **b** : a horse worn out in service **c** : a light easy saddle horse; *esp* : a saddle horse trained to walk, trot, and canter **2 a** : HACKNEY 2 **b** (1) : TAXICAB (2) : CABDRIVER **3 a** : a person who works solely for mercenary reasons : HIRELING ⟨party *hacks*⟩ **b** : a writer who works mainly for hire **c** : HACKER 2 [short for *hackney*]

⁴hack *adj* **1** : working for hire especially with mediocre professional standards ⟨a *hack* journalist⟩ **2** : done by or characteristic of a hack ⟨*hack* writing⟩ **3** : HACKNEYED, TRITE

⁵hack *vi* **1** : to ride or drive at an ordinary pace or over the roads especially as distinguished from racing or hunting **2** : to operate a taxicab

hack·a·more \ˈhak-ə-ˌmōr, -ˌmȯr\ *n* : a bridle with a loop capable of being tightened about the nose in place of a bit or with a slip noose passed over the lower jaw [by folk etymology from Spanish *jáquima*]

hack·ber·ry \ˈhak-ˌber-ē\ *n* : any of a genus of trees and shrubs related to the elms and having small often edible berries; *also* : its wood [alteration of *hagberry,* a kind of cherry]

hack·er \ˈhak-ər\ *n* **1** : one that hacks **2** : a person who is unskilled at a particular activity **3** : an expert at programming and solving problems with a computer **4 :** a person who illegally gains access to information in a computer system

hack·ie \ˈhak-ē\ *n* **:** CABDRIVER

hack·le \ˈhak-əl\ *n* **1 :** one of the long narrow feathers on the neck or lower back of a bird **2 :** a comb for dressing fibers (as flax or hemp) **3** *pl* **a :** hairs that can be raised to an erect position along the neck and back especially of a dog **b :** TEMPER 4d, DANDER [Middle English *hakell*]

hack·man \ˈhak-mən\ *n* **:** CABDRIVER

hack·ma·tack \ˈhak-mə-ˌtak\ *n* **:** TAMARACK 1 [earlier *hakmantak,* probably from Western Abenaki (an Algonquian language of New Hampshire and Vermont)]

[1]**hack·ney** \ˈhak-nē\ *n, pl* **hack·neys** **1 a :** a horse suitable for ordinary riding or driving **b :** any of a breed of rather compact English horses with a flashy high-stepping action while trotting **2 :** a carriage or automobile kept for hire [Middle English *hakeney*]

[2]**hackney** *vt* **1 :** to make common or frequent use of **2 :** to make trite, vulgar, or commonplace

hack·neyed \ˈhak-nēd\ *adj* **:** lacking in freshness or originality ⟨a *hackneyed* expression⟩ ***synonyms*** see TRITE

hack·saw \ˈhak-ˌsȯ\ *n* **:** a fine-tooth saw with a blade under tension in a bow-shaped frame for cutting hard materials (as metal) — **hacksaw** *vb*

hack·work \-ˌwərk\ *n* **:** literary, artistic, or professional work done on order usually according to formula and in conformity with commercial standards

had *past of* HAVE

had·dock \ˈhad-ək\ *n, pl* **haddock** *also* **haddocks :** an important Atlantic food fish usually smaller than the related common cod [Middle English *haddok*]

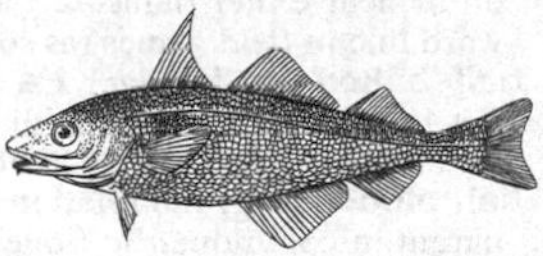

haddock

Ha·de·an \ˈhā-ˌdē-ən, hā-ˈdē-ən\ *adj* **:** of, relating to, or being the span of earth's history prior to the formation of the first rocks — see GEOLOGIC TIME table [*Hades*] — **Hadean** *n*

ha·des \ˈhād-ēz, -ˌēz\ *n, often cap* **:** HELL 1 [Greek *Haidēs,* god of the underworld, abode of the dead in Greek mythology]

hadj *variant of* HAJJ

Had·ley cell \ˈhad-lē-\ *n* **:** a pattern of atmospheric convection that tends to move heat from the equator toward higher latitudes [George Hadley, died 1768, English scientific writer]

hadn't \ˈhad-nt\ **:** had not

had·ron \ˈhad-ˌrän\ *n* **:** any of the subatomic particles (as protons and neutrons) that are made up of quarks and are subject to the strong force [Greek *hadros* "thick"]

hadst \hadst, ˈhadst, hədst, ədst\ *archaic past 2nd singular of* HAVE

hae \hā, ˈhā\ *chiefly Scottish variant of* HAVE

haem- *or* **haemo-** *chiefly British variant of* HEM-

haemat- *or* **haemato-** *chiefly British variant of* HEMAT-

haf·ni·um \ˈhaf-nē-əm\ *n* **:** a metallic chemical element that resembles zirconium chemically and that readily absorbs neutrons — see ELEMENT table [New Latin, from *Hafnia* (Copenhagen), Denmark]

[1]**haft** \ˈhaft\ *n* **:** the handle of a weapon or tool (as a sword or file) [Old English *hæft*]

[2]**haft** *vt* **:** to set in or furnish with a haft

haf·ta·rah *or* **haf·to·rah** \ˌhäf-tə-ˈrä, häf-ˈtō-rə\ *n* **:** one of the biblical selections from the Books of the Prophets read at the conclusion of the Jewish synagogue service [Hebrew *haphṭārāh* "conclusion"]

hag \ˈhag\ *n* **1 :** an ugly, untidy, or evil-looking old woman **2 :** WITCH 1 [Middle English *hagge* "demon, old woman"]

hag·fish \ˈhag-ˌfish\ *n* **:** an eellike fish related to the lampreys

Hag·ga·dah \hə-ˈgäd-ə, -ˈgȯd-\ *n, pl* **Hag·ga·doth** \-ˈgäd-ˌōt, -ˈgȯd-, -ˌōth\ **1 :** ancient Jewish lore forming especially the nonlegal part of the Talmud **2 :** the book of readings for the seder service [Hebrew *haggadhāh*] — **hag·gad·ic** \-ˈgad-ik, -ˈgäd-, -ˈgȯd-\ *adj, often cap*

Hag·gai \ˈhag-ē-ˌī, ˈhag-ˌī\ *n* **:** a prophetic book of canonical Jewish and Christian Scriptures — see BIBLE table

hag·gard \ˈhag-ərd\ *adj* **1 :** wild in appearance **2 :** having a worn or emaciated look **:** GAUNT [Middle French *hagard* "not tamed" (said of a hawk)]

hag·gis \ˈhag-əs\ *n* **:** a pudding popular especially in Scotland made of the heart, liver, and lungs of a sheep or a calf minced with suet, onions, oatmeal, and seasonings and boiled in the stomach of the animal [Middle English *hagese*]

[1]**hag·gle** \ˈhag-əl\ *vb* **hag·gled; hag·gling** \ˈhag-ling, -ə-ling\ **1 :** to cut roughly or clumsily **:** HACK **2 :** to argue especially over a price [derived from Middle English *haggen* "to hew"] — **haggler** \-lər, -ə-lər\ *n*

[2]**haggle** *n* **:** an act or instance of haggling

Hag·i·og·ra·pha \ˌhag-ē-ˈäg-rə-fə, ˌhā-jē-\ *n sing or pl* **:** the third part of the Jewish scriptures — compare LAW 3b, PROPHETS [Late Latin, from Late Greek, literally, "holy writings"]

hag·i·og·ra·phy \-fē\ *n* **1 :** biography of saints or venerated persons **2 :** idealizing or idolizing biography [Greek *hagios* "saint," from *hagios* "holy"] — **hag·i·og·ra·pher** \-fər\ *n*

hah *variant of* HA

ha–ha \hä-ˈhä, ˈhä-\ *interj* — used to express amusement or derision [Old English *ha ha*]

hai·ku \ˈhī-ˌkü\ *n, pl* **haiku :** an unrhymed verse form of Japanese origin having three lines containing 5, 7, and 5 syllables respectively; *also* **:** a poem written in this form [Japanese]

[1]**hail** \ˈhāl\ *n* **1 :** precipitation in the form of small balls or lumps usually consisting of concentric layers of clear ice and compact snow **2 :** something that gives the effect of falling hail ⟨a *hail* of bullets⟩ [Old English *hægl*]

[2]**hail** *vb* **1 :** to precipitate hail **2 :** to fall or strike like hail

[3]**hail** *interj* **1** — used to express acclamation **2** *archaic* — used as a greeting [Old Norse *heill,* from *heill* "healthy, hale"]

[4]**hail** *vb* **1 a :** SALUTE 1, GREET **b :** to greet with enthusiastic approval **:** ACCLAIM ⟨*hailed* the book as a masterpiece⟩ **2 :** to greet or summon by calling ⟨*hail* a taxi⟩ **3 :** to call out; *esp* **:** to call a greeting to a passing ship — **hail from :** to come from ⟨they *hail from* New York⟩

[5]**hail** *n* **1 :** an exclamation of greeting or acclamation **2 :** a calling to attract attention **3 :** hearing distance ⟨stayed within *hail*⟩

hail–fel·low \ˈhāl-ˌfel-ō\ *or* **hail–fellow–well–met** \-ˌwel-ˈmet\ *adj* **:** heartily friendly and informal [from the archaic salutation "Hail, fellow! Well met!"]

Hail Mary *n* **:** a Roman Catholic prayer to the Virgin Mary [translation of Medieval Latin *Ave, Maria,* from the opening words]

hail·stone \ˈhāl-ˌstōn\ *n* **:** a pellet of hail

hail·storm \-ˌstȯrm\ *n* **:** a storm accompanied by hail

hair \ˈhaər, ˈheər\ *n* **1 a :** a slender threadlike outgrowth of the epidermis of an animal; *esp* **:** one of the usually pigmented filaments that form the characteristic coat of a mammal **b :** the hairy covering of an animal or a body part **2 a :** a minute distance or amount ⟨won by a *hair*⟩ **b :** a precise degree ⟨aligned to a *hair*⟩ **3 :** a threadlike structure that resembles hair ⟨leaf *hairs*⟩ [Old English *hǣr*] — **haired** \ˈhaərd, ˈheərd\ *adj* — **hair·less** \ˈhaər-ləs, ˈheər-\ *adj* — **hair·like** \-ˌlīk\ *adj* — **in one's hair :** annoyingly always in one's presence ⟨can't work with you *in my hair* all day⟩ — **out of one's hair :** out of one's way ⟨stayed *out of his hair* while he prepared supper⟩

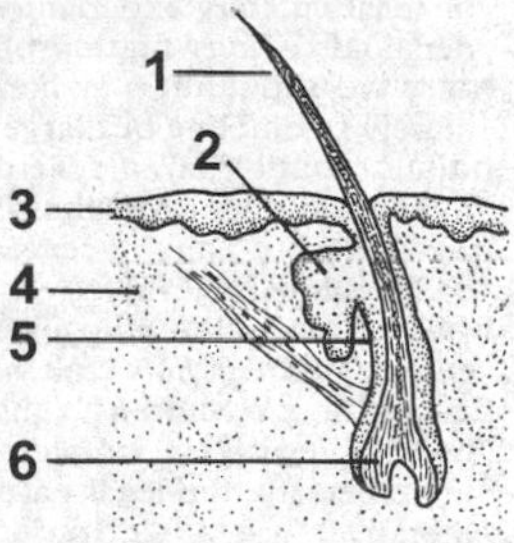

hair 1a: *1* shaft, *2* sebaceous gland, *3* epidermis, *4* dermis, *5* follicle, *6* root

[1]**hair·breadth** \ˈhaər-ˌbredth, ˈheər-\ *or* **hairs·breadth** \ˈhaərz-, ˈheərz-\ *n* **:** a very small distance or margin

[2]**hairbreadth** *adj* **:** very narrow **:** CLOSE ⟨a *hairbreadth* escape⟩

hair·brush \ˈhaər-ˌbrəsh, ˈheər-\ *n* **:** a brush for the hair

hair cell *n* **:** a sensory cell (as of the organ of Corti) bearing hairlike processes

hair·cloth \-ˌklȯth\ *n* **:** any of various stiff wiry fabrics (as of horsehair) used for upholstery or stiffening in garments

\ə\ **abut**	\au̇\ **out**	\i\ **tip**	\ȯ\ **saw**	\u̇\ **foot**
\ər\ **further**	\ch\ **chin**	\ī\ **life**	\ȯi\ **coin**	\y\ **yet**
\a\ **mat**	\e\ **pet**	\j\ **job**	\th\ **thin**	\yü\ **few**
\ā\ **take**	\ē\ **easy**	\ng\ **sing**	\th\ **this**	\yu̇\ **cure**
\ä\ **cot, cart**	\g\ **go**	\ō\ **bone**	\ü\ **food**	\zh\ **vision**

hair•cut \-ˌkət\ *n* **1 :** the act or process of cutting and shaping the hair **2 :** HAIRDO — **hair•cut•ter** \-ˌkət-ər\ *n* — **hair•cut•ting** \-ˌkət-iŋ\ *n*

hair•do \-ˌdü\ *n, pl* **hairdos :** a way of dressing a person's hair **:** COIFFURE

hair•dress•er \-ˌdres-ər\ *n* **:** a person who dresses or cuts hair — **hair•dress•ing** \-ˌdres-iŋ\ *n*

hair follicle *n* **:** the tubular sheath surrounding the lower part of a hair shaft

hair•line \-ˌlīn\ *n* **1 a :** a very slender line **b :** a very thin crack on a surface ⟨a *hairline* bone fracture⟩ **2 :** the line at which the hair meets the scalp ⟨a receding *hairline*⟩ — **hairline** *adj*

hair•net \-ˌnet\ *n* **:** a net worn over the hair to keep it in place

hair•pin \-ˌpin\ *n* **1 :** a U-shaped pin to hold the hair in place **2 :** something shaped like a hairpin; *esp* **:** a sharp turn in a road — **hairpin** *adj*

hair–rais•er \ˈhaər-ˌrā-zər, ˈheər-\ *n* **:** THRILLER

hair–rais•ing \-ˌrā-ziŋ\ *adj* **:** causing terror, excitement, or astonishment ⟨a *hair-raising* adventure⟩ — **hair–rais•ing•ly** \-ziŋ-lē\ *adv*

hair seal *n* **:** any of a family of seals with coarse hairy coats and no external ears — called also *earless seal*; compare EARED SEAL

hair shirt *n* **:** a shirt made of rough animal hair worn next to the skin as a penance

hair•split•ter \ˈhaər-ˌsplit-ər, ˈheər-\ *n* **:** one that makes excessively fine distinctions in reasoning — **hair•split•ting** \-ˌsplit-iŋ\ *adj or n*

hair spray *n* **:** a liquid sprayed on the hair to keep it in place

hair•spring \-ˌspriŋ\ *n* **:** a slender spiraled spring that regulates the motion of the balance wheel of a timepiece

hair•streak \-ˌstrēk\ *n* **:** any of various small usually dark butterflies with filaments projecting from the hind wings

hair•style \-ˌstīl\ *n* **:** HAIRDO

hair•styl•ist \-ˌstī-list\ *n* **:** HAIRDRESSER — **hair•styl•ing** \-liŋ\ *n*

hair–trig•ger \-ˈtrig-ər\ *adj* **1 :** immediately responsive to the slightest stimulus ⟨a *hair-trigger* temper⟩ **2 :** delicately adjusted or easily disrupted ⟨a *hair-trigger* balance⟩

hair•worm \ˈhaər-ˌwərm, ˈheər-\ *n* **:** any of various very slender worms (as a horsehair worm)

hairy \ˈhaər-ē, ˈheər-\ *adj* **hair•i•er; -est 1 :** bearing or covered with or as if with hair **2 :** made of or resembling hair **3 a :** tending to cause nervous tension (as from danger, difficulty, or fear) ⟨a *hairy* experience⟩ **b :** difficult to deal with or understand ⟨a *hairy* math problem⟩ — **hair•i•ness** *n*

hairy woodpecker *n* **:** a common North American woodpecker closely resembling but larger than the downy woodpecker

hajj *also* **hadj** \ˈhaj\ *n* **:** the pilgrimage to Mecca prescribed as a religious duty for Muslims [Arabic *ḥajj*]

hake \ˈhāk\ *n* **:** any of several marine food fishes related to the cod [Middle English]

hal- *or* **halo-** *combining form* **1 :** salt ⟨*halo*phyte⟩ **2 :** halogen ⟨*hal*ide⟩ [Greek *hals* "salt, sea"]

ha•la•cha *also* **ha•la•kha** \hä-ˈläk̲-ə, ˌhä-lə-ˈk̲ä\ *n, often cap* **:** the body of Jewish law supplementing the scriptural law and forming especially the legal part of the Talmud [Hebrew *halākhāh,* literally, "way"] — **ha•lach•ic** *also* **ha•lakh•ic** \hə-ˈlak-ik, -ˈläk-\ *adj, often cap*

ha•lal \hə-ˈläl\ *adj* **:** approved by Islamic law; *esp* **:** ritually fit for use ⟨*halal* foods⟩ [Arabic *ḥalāl* "permissible"]

ha•la•tion \hā-ˈlā-shən\ *n* **:** the spreading (as in a developed photographic image) of light beyond its proper boundaries [*halo* + *-ation*]

hal•berd \ˈhal-bərd, ˈhȯl-\ *also* **hal•bert** \-bərt\ *n* **:** a long-handled weapon used both as a spear and as a battle-ax especially in the 15th and 16th centuries [Medieval French *hallebarde*] — **hal•berd•ier** \ˌhal-bər-ˈdiər, ˌhȯl-\ *n*

halberd

[1]hal•cy•on \ˈhal-sē-ən\ *n* **1 :** a bird identified with the kingfisher and held in ancient legend to nest at sea about the time of the winter solstice and to calm the waves during incubation **2 :** KINGFISHER [Latin, from Greek *halkyōn*]

[2]halcyon *adj* **1 :** of or relating to the halcyon or its nesting period **2 a :** CALM 2, PEACEFUL **b :** HAPPY, GOLDEN ⟨the *halcyon* days of youth⟩

[1]hale \ˈhāl\ *adj* **:** free from defect, disease, or infirmity **:** SOUND, HEALTHY ⟨still *hale* at the age of 80⟩ [partly from Old English *hāl* "whole"; partly from Old Norse *heill*]

[2]hale *vt* **1 :** HAUL 1a, PULL **2 :** to compel to go ⟨*haled* them into court⟩ [Medieval French *haler*]

[1]half \ˈhaf, ˈháf\ *n, pl* **halves** \ˈhavz, ˈhávz\ **1 a :** one of two equal parts that make up something ⟨*half* of an apple⟩; *also* **:** a part approximately equal to one of these ⟨*half* the distance⟩ **b :** half an hour ⟨*half* past ten⟩ **2 :** one of a pair: as **a :** PARTNER **b :** SEMESTER, TERM **c :** one of the two equal periods that together make up the playing time of various games (as football) [Old English *healf*] — **by half :** by a great deal — **by halves :** in part **:** HALFHEARTEDLY — **in half :** into two equal or nearly equal parts

[2]half *adj* **1 :** being one of two equal parts ⟨a *half* sheet of paper⟩ **2 a :** amounting to nearly half ⟨a *half* mile⟩ **b :** falling short of the full or complete thing **:** PARTIAL ⟨a *half* smile⟩ — **half•ness** *n*

[3]half *adv* **1 a :** to the extent of half ⟨*half* full⟩ **b :** not completely **:** PARTIALLY ⟨*half* persuaded⟩ **2 :** by any means **:** AT ALL ⟨the song wasn't *half* bad⟩

half–and–half \ˌhaf-ən-ˈhaf, ˌháf-ən-ˈháf\ *n* **:** something that is half one thing and half another: as **a :** a mixture of two malt beverages **b :** a mixture of cream and whole milk — **half–and–half** *adj or adv*

half•back \ˈhaf-ˌbak, ˈháf-\ *n* **1 :** a football back who lines up on or near either flank **2 :** a player stationed behind the forward line in field games (as soccer or field hockey)

half–baked \-ˈbākt\ *adj* **1 a :** poorly developed or carried out **b :** lacking judgment, intelligence, or common sense ⟨a *half-baked* idea⟩ **2 :** imperfectly baked **:** UNDERDONE

half blood *n* **1 :** the relation between persons having only one parent in common; *also* **:** one so related to another **2** *often offensive* **:** HALF-BREED **3 :** GRADE 8 — **half–blood•ed** \-ˈbləd-əd\ *adj*

half boot *n* **:** a boot with a top reaching above the ankle and ending below the knees

half–breed \ˈhaf-ˌbrēd, ˈháf-\ *n, often disparaging* **:** the offspring of parents of different races; *esp* **:** the offspring of an American Indian and a white person — **half–breed** *adj, often disparaging*

half brother *n* **:** a brother related through one parent only

half–caste \ˈhaf-ˌkast, ˈháf-\ *n, often disparaging* **:** a person of mixed racial descent — **half–caste** *adj, often disparaging*

half–cocked \-ˌkäkt\ *adj* **:** lacking adequate preparation or forethought ⟨go off *half-cocked*⟩

half crown *n* **:** a formerly used British coin worth two shillings and sixpence

half–dol•lar \ˈhaf-ˈdäl-ər, ˈháf-\ *n* **1 :** a coin representing one half of a dollar **2 :** the sum of fifty cents

half eagle *n* **:** a 5-dollar gold piece issued by the U.S. from 1795–1916 and in 1929

half gainer *n* **:** a dive in which the diver executes a half-backward somersault and enters the water headfirst and facing the board

half–glas•ses \-ˈglas-əz\ *n pl* **:** eyeglasses that have half lenses and are used for reading only

half•heart•ed \ˈhaf-ˈhärt-əd, ˈháf-\ *adj* **:** lacking spirit or interest — **half•heart•ed•ly** *adv* — **half•heart•ed•ness** *n*

half hitch *n* **:** a simple knot so made as to be easily unfastened — see KNOT illustration

half hour *n* **1 :** thirty minutes **2 :** the middle point of an hour — **half–hour•ly** \ˈhaf-ˈau̇r-lē, ˈháf-\ *adv or adj*

half–knot \ˈhaf-ˌnät, ˈháf-\ *n* **:** a knot joining the ends of two cords and used in tying other knots

half–life \-ˌlīf\ *n* **1 :** the time required for half of the atoms of a radioactive substance to disintegrate **2 :** the time required for half the amount of a substance (as a drug in the body) to be eliminated or disintegrated by natural processes

half line *n* **:** a straight line extending from a point in one direction only

half–mast \ˈhaf-ˈmast, ˈháf-\ *n* **:** a point some distance but not necessarily halfway down below the top of a mast or staff or the peak of a gaff ⟨flags flying at *half-mast*⟩

half–moon \-ˌmün\ *n* **1 :** the moon when half its disk appears illuminated **2 :** something shaped like a crescent **3 :** the lunule of a fingernail

half note *n* : a musical note equal in value to one half of a whole note

half·pen·ny \ˈhāp-nē, -ə-nē, *US also* ˈhaf-ˌpen-ē, ˈhȧf-\ *n* **1** *pl* **half·pence** \ˈhā-pəns, *US also* ˈhaf-ˌpens, ˈhȧf-\ *or* **halfpennies** : a formerly used British coin worth one half of a penny **2** : the sum of half a penny **3** : a small amount — **halfpenny** *adj*

half plane *n* : the part of a plane on one side of an indefinitely extended straight line drawn in the plane

half rest *n* : a musical rest equal in time value to a half note

half sister *n* : a sister related through one parent only

half–slip \ˈhaf-ˌslip, ˈhȧf-\ *n* : an underskirt with an elasticized waistband

half–sole \ˈhaf-ˈsōl, ˈhȧf-\ *vt* : to put half soles on

half sole *n* : a shoe sole extending from the shank forward

half sovereign *n* : a formerly used British gold coin worth 10 shillings

half–staff \ˈhaf-ˈstaf, ˈhȧf-\ *n* : HALF-MAST

half step *n* : the pitch interval between any two adjacent tones on a keyboard instrument — called also *semitone*

half–tim·ber \ˈhaf-ˈtim-bər, ˈhȧf-\ *or* **half–tim·bered** \-bərd\ *adj* : constructed of wood framing with spaces filled with masonry ⟨a *half-timbered* house⟩

half·time \-ˌtīm\ *n* : an intermission marking the completion of half of a game (as in football)

half·tone \-ˌtōn\ *n* **1** : HALF STEP **2 a** : any of the shades of gray between the darkest and the lightest parts of a photographic image **b** : an image or print that reproduces the appearance of an original image using small dots of varying density

half–track \-ˌtrak\ *n* **1** : one of the endless-chain tracks used in place of rear wheels on a heavy-duty vehicle **2** : a motor vehicle propelled by half-tracks; *esp* : such a vehicle lightly armored for military use — **half–track** *or* **half–tracked** \-ˌtrakt\ *adj*

half–truth \-ˌtrüth\ *n* : a statement that is only partially true; *esp* : one that mingles truth and falsehood with deliberate intent to deceive

half·way \-ˈwā\ *adj* **1** : midway between two points ⟨a *halfway* mark⟩ **2** : PARTIAL 1 ⟨*halfway* measures⟩ — **halfway** *adv*

halfway house *n* : a residence for individuals after release from an institution (as a prison) that is designed to help them readjust to private life

half–wit \-ˌwit\ *n* : a foolish or imbecilic person — **half–wit·ted** \-ˈwit-əd\ *adj*

hal·i·but \ˈhal-ə-bət, ˈhäl-\ *n, pl* **halibut** *also* **halibuts** : either of two marine food fishes of the Atlantic or Pacific oceans that are the largest flatfishes reaching several hundred pounds [Middle English *halybutte,* from *haly* "holy" + *butte* "flatfish"; from its being eaten on holy days]

ha·lide \ˈhal-ˌīd, ˈhā-ˌlīd\ *n* : a compound of a halogen with another element or a radical

hal·i·dom \ˈhal-əd-əm\ *or* **hal·i·dome** \-ə-ˌdōm\ *n, archaic* : a holy place or relic [Old English *hāligdōm,* from *hālig* "holy"]

ha·lite \ˈhal-ˌīt, ˈhā-ˌlīt\ *n* : native salt : ROCK SALT

hal·i·to·sis \ˌhal-ə-ˈtō-səs\ *n* : a condition of having breath with an offensive odor [Latin *halitus* "breath," from *halare* "to breathe"]

hall \ˈhȯl\ *n* **1 a** : a large or imposing residence; *esp* : MANOR HOUSE **b** : a large building used for public purposes ⟨symphony *hall*⟩ **c** : one of the buildings of a college or university set apart for a special purpose ⟨residence *halls*⟩ **d** : a college or a division of a college at some universities ⟨Science *Hall*⟩ **e** : the common dining room of an English college **2** : the chief living room in a medieval castle **3 a** : the entrance room of a building : LOBBY **b** : a corridor or passage in a building **4** : a large room for assembly : AUDITORIUM **5** : a place used for public entertainment [Old English *heall*]

Hal·lel \hä-ˈlāl\ *n* : a selection comprising Psalms 113–118 chanted during a Jewish feast (as the Passover) [Hebrew *hallēl* "praise"]

[1]**hal·le·lu·jah** \ˌhal-ə-ˈlü-yə\ *interj* — used to express praise, joy, or thanks [Hebrew *hallĕlūyāh* "praise ye the Lord"]

[2]**hallelujah** *n* : a shout or song of praise or thanksgiving

[1]**hall·mark** \ˈhȯl-ˌmärk\ *n* **1 a** : an official mark stamped on gold and silver articles in England to attest their purity **b** : a mark placed on an article to indicate origin, purity, or genuineness **2** : a distinguishing characteristic or feature ⟨bears the *hallmarks* of genius⟩ [Goldsmiths' *Hall,* London, England, where gold and silver articles were assayed and stamped]

[2]**hallmark** *vt* : to stamp with a hallmark

hal·lo \hə-ˈlō, ha-\ *or* **hal·loo** \-ˈlü\ *variant of* HOLLO

Hall of Fame **1** : a structure housing memorials to famous individuals **2** : a group of individuals selected as particularly distinguished in a field or category (as a sport) — **Hall of Fam·er**

hal·low \ˈhal-ō\ *vt* **1** : to make holy or set apart for holy use **2** : to respect greatly [Old English *hālgian,* from *hālig* "holy"]

hal·lowed \ˈhal-ōd, -əd, in the Lord's Prayer also ˈhal-ə-wəd\ *adj* : SACRED ⟨*hallowed* traditions⟩

Hal·low·een \ˌhal-ə-ˈwēn, ˌhäl-\ *n* : October 31 observed especially by wearing costumes, trick-or-treating, and displaying jack-o'-lanterns [short for *All Hallow even,* the eve of All Saints' Day]

Hal·low·mas \ˈhal-ō-ˌmas, -məs\ *n* : ALL SAINTS' DAY

hal·lu·ci·nate \hə-ˈlüs-n-ˌāt\ *vb* : to have hallucinations or experience as a hallucination

hal·lu·ci·na·tion \hə-ˌlüs-n-ˈā-shən\ *n* : the perceiving of something (as a visual image or sound) that seems to be experienced through one of the senses but is not real and is usually the result of a mental disorder or as the effect of a drug; *also* : something so perceived or experienced [Latin *hallucinatio,* from *hallucinari* "to wander in mind"]

hal·lu·ci·na·to·ry \hə-ˈlüs-n-ə-ˌtōr-ē, -ˌtȯr-\ *adj* **1** : tending to produce hallucinations **2** : resembling, involving, or being a hallucination

hal·lu·ci·no·gen \hə-ˈlüs-n-ə-jən\ *n* : a substance (as LSD) that induces hallucinations — **hal·lu·ci·no·gen·ic** \-ˌlüs-n-ə-ˈjen-ik\ *adj*

hal·lux \ˈhal-əks\ *n, pl* **hal·lu·ces** \ˈhal-ə-ˌsēz, -yə-\ : BIG TOE [Latin]

hall·way \ˈhȯl-ˌwā\ *n* **1** : an entrance hall **2** : CORRIDOR 1

[1]**ha·lo** \ˈhā-lō\ *n, pl* **halos** *or* **haloes** **1** : a circle of light around the sun or moon caused by the presence of tiny ice crystals in the air **2** : something resembling a halo: as **a (1)** : NIMBUS 1 **(2)** : NIMBUS 2 **b** : a differentiated zone surrounding a central object **3** : the glory surrounding an idealized person or thing [Latin *halos,* from Greek *halōs* "threshing floor, disk, halo"]

[2]**halo** *vt* : to form into or surround with a halo

halo- — see HAL-

[1]**hal·o·gen** \ˈhal-ə-jən\ *n* : any of the five elements fluorine, chlorine, bromine, iodine, and astatine existing in the free state normally as diatomic molecules

[2]**halogen** *adj* : containing, using, or being a halogen ⟨a *halogen* lamp⟩

hal·o·ge·ton \ˌhal-ə-ˈjē-ˌtän\ *n* : a coarse annual Asian herb related to the goosefoots that is a noxious weed in western U.S. pastures [*hal-* + Greek *geitōn* "neighbor"]

hal·o·phyte \ˈhal-ə-ˌfīt\ *n* : a plant that thrives in salty soil — **hal·o·phyt·ic** \ˌhal-ə-ˈfit-ik\ *adj*

[1]**halt** \ˈhȯlt\ *adj* : LAME [Old English *healt*]

[2]**halt** *vi* **1** : to walk or proceed lamely : LIMP **2** : to stand in perplexity or doubt between alternate courses **3** : to display weakness or fault

[3]**halt** *n* : STOP ⟨call a *halt*⟩ [German, derived from Old High German *haltan* "to hold"]

[4]**halt** *vb* **1** : to cease marching or journeying **2** : to bring or come to a stop : END

[1]**hal·ter** \ˈhȯl-tər\ *n* **1 a** : a rope or strap for leading or tying an animal **b** : a headstall to which a lead may be attached **2** : a rope for hanging criminals : NOOSE **3** : a woman's blouse or top that is typically held in place by straps around the neck and across the back and leaves the back, arms, and midriff bare [Old English *hælftre*]

[2]**halter** *vt* **hal·tered; hal·ter·ing** \-tə-ring, -tring\ **1** : to catch with or as if with a halter; *also* : to put a halter on **2** : RESTRAIN 1, HAMPER

hal·tere \ˈhȯl-ˌtiər, ˈhal-\ *n, pl* **hal·teres** \-ˌtiərz; hȯl-ˈtir-ēz, hal-\ : one of a pair of club-shaped organs that are the modified second pair of wings of a two-winged fly and serve to maintain balance in flight [Latin *halter* "jumping weight," from Greek *haltēr,* from *hallesthai* "to jump"]

halt·ing \ˈhȯl-ting\ *adj* : marked by a lack of sureness or effectiveness ⟨the witness spoke in a *halting* manner⟩ — **halt·ing·ly** \-ting-lē\ *adv*

hal·vah *or* **hal·va** \häl-ˈvä, ˈhäl-ˌvä, -və\ *n* : a flaky candy made

\ə\ **abut**	\au̇\ **out**	\i\ **tip**	\ȯ\ **saw**	\u̇\ **foot**
\ər\ **further**	\ch\ **chin**	\ī\ **life**	\ȯi\ **coin**	\y\ **yet**
\a\ **mat**	\e\ **pet**	\j\ **job**	\th\ **thin**	\yü\ **few**
\ā\ **take**	\ē\ **easy**	\ng\ **sing**	\th\ **this**	\yu̇\ **cure**
\ä\ **cot, cart**	\g\ **go**	\ō\ **bone**	\ü\ **food**	\zh\ **vision**

of crushed sesame seeds in a base of syrup (as of honey) [Yiddish *halva,* derived from Arabic *ḥalwā* "sweetmeat"]

halve \ˈhav, ˈhȧv\ *vt* **1 a :** to divide into two equal parts **b :** to reduce to one half ⟨*halving* the cost⟩ **c :** to share equally **2 :** to play (a hole) in the same number of strokes as one's opponent at golf

halv•ers \ˈhav-ərz, ˈhȧv-\ *n pl* **:** half shares **:** HALVES

halves *plural of* HALF

hal•yard \ˈhal-yərd\ *n* **:** a rope or tackle for hoisting and lowering [Middle English *halier,* probably from Medieval French *haler* "to haul"]

[1]ham \ˈham\ *n* **1 :** a buttock with its associated thigh — usually used in plural **2 :** a cut of meat consisting of a thigh; *esp* **:** one from a hog **3 a :** an unskillful but showy performer **b :** an operator of an amateur radio station [Old English *hamm* "hollow of the knee"; sense 3 short for *hamfatter,* from "The Ham-Fat Man," minstrel song] — **ham** *adj*

[2]ham *vb* **hammed; ham•ming :** to execute with exaggerated speech or gestures **:** OVERACT ⟨*ham* it up for the camera⟩

hama•dry•ad \ˌham-ə-ˈdrī-əd, -ˌad\ *n* **:** WOOD NYMPH [Latin *hamadryas,* from Greek, from *hama* "together with" + *dryas* "dryad"]

ham•burg•er \ˈham-ˌbər-gər\ *or* **ham•burg** \-ˌbərg\ *n* **1 a :** ground beef **b :** a cooked patty of ground beef **2 :** a sandwich consisting of a patty of hamburger in a split round bun [German *Hamburger* "of Hamburg, Germany"]

hame \ˈhām\ *n* **:** one of two curved supports which are attached to the collar of a draft horse and to which the traces are fastened [Middle English]

ham•let \ˈham-lət\ *n* **:** a small group of houses in a rural area [Medieval French *hamelet,* from *ham* "village," of Germanic origin]

ham•man \hə-ˈmäm\ *n* **:** TURKISH BATH [Turkish *hamam* "bath," from Persian *hammām,* from Arabic *ḥammām*]

[1]ham•mer \ˈham-ər\ *n* **1 a :** a hand tool that consists of a solid head set crosswise on a handle and is used for pounding (as in driving nails) **b :** a power tool that substitutes a metal block or a drill for the hammerhead (as in driving posts or breaking rock) **2 :** something that resembles a hammer in shape or action: as **a :** an implement consisting of a handle or lever and a striking head used to sound a musical instrument (as a bell, the strings of a piano, or a xylophone) **b :** the part of a gun whose striking action causes explosion of the charge **3 :** MALLEUS **4 :** a metal sphere weighing about 16 pounds (7.3 kilograms) that is attached to a wire handle and is hurled in an athletic event [Old English *hamor*]

[2]hammer *vb* **ham•mered; ham•mer•ing** \ˈham-ring, -ə-ring\ **1 :** to strike blows especially repeatedly with or as if with a hammer **:** POUND **2 a :** to make repeated efforts ⟨*hammer* away at one's lessons⟩ **b :** to emphasize (as an opinion) by repetition ⟨*hammers* his point home⟩ **3 a :** to beat, drive, or shape with repeated blows of a hammer **b :** to fasten or build with a hammer **4 :** to strike or drive with a force suggesting a hammer blow or repeated blows ⟨*hammered* the ball over the fence⟩ **5 :** to criticize severely

hammer and sickle *n* **:** an emblem consisting of a crossed hammer and sickle used chiefly as a symbol of Soviet Communism

hammer and tongs *adv* **:** with great force and violence

ham•mered *adj* **:** having surface indentations produced or appearing to have been produced by hammering

ham•mer•head \ˈham-ər-ˌhed\ *n* **1 :** the striking part of a hammer **2 :** BLOCKHEAD **3 :** any of several sharks with the eyes on lateral extensions of the flat head

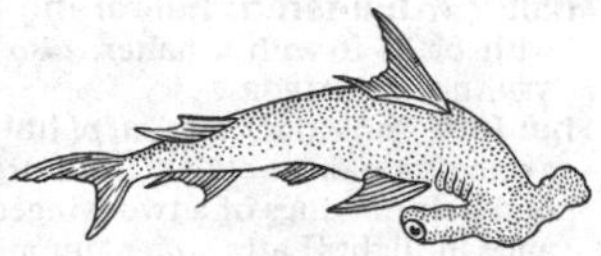

hammerhead 3

ham•mer•lock \-ˌläk\ *n* **:** a wrestling hold in which an opponent's arm is held bent behind the back

hammer out *vt* **:** to produce or bring about by persistent effort ⟨*hammered out* a policy⟩

ham•mer•stone \-ˌstōn\ *n* **:** a prehistoric hammering tool consisting of a rounded stone

ham•mer•toe \-ˌtō\ *n* **:** a toe and especially the second deformed by having the end part permanently bent

[1]ham•mock \ˈham-ək\ *n* **:** a swinging couch or bed usually made of netting or canvas and slung by cords from supports at each end [Spanish *hamaca,* from Taino, language of an aboriginal people of the Greater Antilles and the Bahamas]

[2]hammock *n* **1 :** HUMMOCK 1 **2 :** an area in the southeastern U.S. typically with rich soil and hardwood evergreen trees that is usually higher than its surroundings [earlier *hommoke, humock;* related to Middle Low German *hummel* "small height" and *hump* "bump"]

ham•my \ˈham-ē\ *adj* **ham•mi•er; -est :** marked by exaggerated speech or gestures — **ham•mi•ly** \-ə-lē\ *adv* — **ham•mi•ness** \-ē-nəs\ *n*

[1]ham•per \ˈham-pər\ *vt* **ham•pered; ham•per•ing** \-pə-ring, -pring\ **1 :** to restrict or interfere with the movement or operation of ⟨fog *hampered* the traffic⟩ **2 :** to interfere with **:** ENCUMBER [Middle English *hamperen*]

synonyms HAMPER, FETTER, SHACKLE, MANACLE mean to hinder or impede in moving, progressing, or acting. HAMPER may imply the effect of any hindering or restraining influence ⟨*hampered* the investigation by refusing to cooperate⟩. FETTER suggests a restraining so severe that freedom to move or progress is almost lost ⟨*fettered* by tradition⟩. SHACKLE and MANACLE are still stronger and suggest total loss of freedom to act or to move from one position ⟨a mind *shackled* by stubbornness⟩ ⟨a people *manacled* by tyranny⟩.

[2]hamper *n* **:** a large basket usually with a cover ⟨a clothes *hamper*⟩ [Medieval French *hanaper* "case to hold goblets," from *hanap* "goblet," of Germanic origin]

ham•ster \ˈham-stər, ˈhamp-\ *n* **:** any of various small short-tailed Old World rodents with large cheek pouches [German, of Slavic origin]

[1]ham•string \ˈham-ˌstring\ *n* **1 a :** either of two groups of tendons at the back of the human knee **b :** any of three muscles at the back of the thigh that function to extend the thigh, rotate the leg, and bend the knee **2 :** a large tendon above and behind the hock of a four-footed animal

[2]hamstring *vt* **-strung** \-ˌstrəng\; **-string•ing** \-ˌstring-ing\ **1 :** to cripple by cutting the leg tendons **2 :** to make ineffective or powerless **:** CRIPPLE

Han \ˈhän\ *n* **:** a Chinese dynasty dated 206 B.C.–A.D. 220 and marked by centralized bureaucratic control, a revival of learning, and the penetration of Buddhism

[1]hand \ˈhand\ *n* **1 a :** the free end part of the forelimb when modified (as in humans) for handling, grasping, and holding **b :** any of various anatomical parts (as the hind foot of an ape or the chela of a crab) that are like the hand in structure or function **2 :** something resembling a hand: as **a :** an indicator or pointer on a dial ⟨the *hands* of a clock⟩ **b :** a figure of a hand with index finger extended to point a direction or call attention to something **c :** a cluster of bananas developed from a single flower group **3 :** personal possession **:** CONTROL ⟨in the *hands* of the enemy⟩ **4 a :** SIDE, DIRECTION ⟨fighting on either *hand*⟩ **b :** a side or aspect of an issue or argument ⟨on the one *hand,* we can appeal for peace, and on the other *hand,* declare war⟩ **5 :** a pledge especially of marriage **6 a :** style of penmanship **:** HANDWRITING **b :** SIGNATURE ⟨some legal orders require a judge's *hand*⟩ **7 :** SKILL, ABILITY ⟨try one's *hand* at chess⟩ **8 a :** a part or share in doing something ⟨take a *hand* in the work⟩ **b :** ASSISTANCE, AID ⟨lend a *hand*⟩ **9 :** a unit of measure equal to 4 inches (about 10.2 centimeters) used especially for the height of horses **10 :** a round of applause **11 a** (1) **:** a player in a card game or board game (2) **:** the cards or pieces held by a player **b :** a single round in a game **12 a :** one who performs or executes a particular work ⟨two portraits by the same *hand*⟩ **b :** a hired worker **:** LABORER **c :** a member of a ship's crew ⟨all *hands* on deck⟩ **d :** one skilled in a particular activity or field **13 a :** HANDIWORK 1 **b :** style of execution **:** WORKMANSHIP ⟨the *hand* of a master⟩ **c :** the touch or feel of something [Old English] — **at hand 1 :** near in time or place **:** within reach ⟨use whatever ingredients are *at hand*⟩ **2 :** currently receiving or deserving attention ⟨the business *at hand*⟩ — **by hand :** with the hands — **in hand 1 :** in one's possession or control ⟨had matters well *in hand*⟩ **2 :** in preparation — **off one's hands :** out of one's care or charge — **on all hands** *or* **on every hand :** EVERYWHERE — **on hand 1 :** in present possession ⟨kept supplies *on hand*⟩ **2 :** about to appear ⟨trouble was *on hand*⟩ **3 :** in attendance **:** PRESENT — **on one's hands :** in one's possession or care ⟨too much time *on my hands*⟩ — **out of hand 1 :** without delay **:** FORTHWITH ⟨rejected her idea *out of hand*⟩ **2 :** done with

: FINISHED **3** : out of control **4** : with the hands ⟨fruit eaten *out of hand*⟩ — **to hand** **1** : into possession **2** : within reach

2**hand** *vt* **1** : to lead, guide, or assist with the hand : CONDUCT **2 a** : to give or pass with the hand ⟨*hand* a person a letter⟩ **b** : PRESENT, PROVIDE ⟨*handed* them a surprise⟩

hand and foot *adv* : TOTALLY, COMPLETELY ⟨waited on them *hand and foot*⟩

hand ax *n* : a prehistoric stone tool having one end pointed for cutting and the other end rounded for holding in the hand

hand•bag \ˈhand-ˌbag, ˈhan-\ *n* **1** : TRAVELING BAG **2** : a bag for carrying small personal articles and money

hand•ball \-ˌbȯl\ *n* : a game played in a walled court or against a single wall or board by two or four players who use their hands to strike a small rubber ball; *also* : the ball used in this game

hand•bar•row \-ˌbar-ō\ *n* : a flat rectangular frame with handles at both ends that is carried by two persons

hand•bill \-ˌbil\ *n* : a small printed sheet to be distributed by hand

hand•book \-ˌbu̇k\ *n* : a small book of facts or useful information usually about a particular subject : MANUAL

hand•breadth \-ˌbredth\ *or* **hands•breadth** \ˈhanz-\ *n* : any of various units of length based on the breadth of a hand varying from about 2½ to 4 inches (6 to 10 centimeters)

hand•car \ˈhand-ˌkär, ˈhan-\ *n* : a small four-wheeled railroad car propelled by a hand-operated mechanism or a small motor

hand•cart \-ˌkärt\ *n* : a cart drawn or pushed by hand

hand•clasp \-ˌklasp\ *n* : HANDSHAKE

1**hand•craft** \-ˌkraft\ *n* : HANDICRAFT

2**handcraft** *vt* : to fashion by handicraft

1**hand•cuff** \-ˌkəf\ *vt* : to apply handcuffs to : MANACLE

2**handcuff** *n* : a metal fastening that can be locked around a wrist and that is usually connected by a chain or bar with another handcuff

hand down *vt* **1** : to pass down in succession ⟨*handed down* from generation to generation⟩ **2** : to make official formulation of and express (the opinion of a court)

hand•ed \ˈhan-dəd\ *adj* : having or using such or so many hands ⟨a right-*handed* person⟩ — **hand•ed•ness** *n*

hand•ful \ˈhand-ˌfu̇l, ˈhan-\ *n, pl* **handfuls** \-ˌfu̇lz\ *or* **handsful** \ˈhanz-ˌfu̇l\ **1** : as much as or as many as the hand will grasp **2** : a small quantity or number ⟨a *handful* of people⟩ **3** : as much as one can control or manage ⟨the kids are quite a *handful*⟩

hand•glass *n* : a small mirror with a handle

hand•grip \ˈhand-ˌgrip, ˈhan-\ *n* **1** : a grasping with the hand **2** : HANDLE 1

hand•gun \ˈhand-ˌgən, ˈhan-\ *n* : a firearm held and fired with one hand

hand•held \-ˌheld\ *adj* : held in the hand; *esp* : designed to be operated while being held in the hand ⟨*handheld* computers⟩ — **handheld** *n*

hand•hold \ˈhand-ˌhōld\ *n* **1** : GRIP 1a **2** : HOLD 5

1**hand•i•cap** \ˈhan-di-ˌkap\ *n* **1 a** : a race or contest in which an artificial advantage is given to or disadvantage imposed on a contestant to equalize chances of winning **b** : the advantage given or disadvantage imposed **2 a** : a disadvantage that makes progress or success more difficult ⟨being lazy was a *handicap*⟩ **b** *sometimes offensive* : a physical disability [obsolete *handicap,* a game in which forfeits were held in a cap, from *hand in cap*]

Word History *Handicap,* from *hand in cap,* was an old form of barter. Two people who wished to make an exchange asked a third to act as umpire. All three put forfeit money in a cap, into which each of the two barterers put a hand. The umpire described the goods to be traded and set the additional amount the owner of the inferior article should pay the other in order that the exchange might be fair. The barterers withdrew their hands from the cap empty to signify refusal of the umpire's decision, or full to indicate acceptance. If both hands were full, the exchange was made and the umpire pocketed the forfeit money. If both were empty, the umpire took the money but there was no exchange. Otherwise, each barterer kept his own property, and the one who had accepted the umpire's decision took the forfeit money as well. Later, horse races arranged in accordance with the rules of *handicap* were called *handicap races.* The umpire decided how much extra weight the better horse should carry. The term was eventually extended to other contests, and the advantage or disadvantage imposed was called *handicap.*

2**handicap** *vt* **-capped; -cap•ping** **1 a** : to give a handicap to **b** : to assign handicaps to **2** : to put at a disadvantage

handicapped *adj, sometimes offensive* : having a physical or mental disability; *also* : of or reserved for individuals with a physical disability ⟨*handicapped* parking spaces⟩

hand•i•craft \ˈhan-di-ˌkraft\ *n* **1** : an occupation (as weaving or pottery making) requiring skill with the hands **2** : articles fashioned by those engaged in handicraft [alteration of *handcraft*] — **hand•i•craft•er** \-ˌkraf-tər\ *n* — **hand•i•crafts•man** \-ˌkrafs-mən\ *n*

hand•i•ly \ˈhan-də-lē\ *adv* **1** : in a skillful manner **2** : EASILY 1 ⟨won *handily*⟩ **3** : conveniently nearby

hand•i•ness \-dē-nəs\ *n* : the quality or state of being handy

hand in glove *or* **hand and glove** *adv* : in extremely close relationship or agreement

hand in hand *adv* **1** : with one's hand clasping another's hand **2** : in close association : TOGETHER ⟨hard work and success go *hand in hand*⟩

hand•i•work \ˈhan-di-ˌwərk\ *n* : work done by the hands or personally ⟨showed the *handiwork* of a master criminal⟩ [Old English *handgeweorc,* from *hand* + *geweorc* "work," from *ge-,* collective prefix + *weorc* "work"]

hand•ker•chief \ˈhang-kər-chəf, -ˌchif, -ˌchēf\ *n, pl* **-chiefs** *also* **-chieves** \-chəfs, -ˌchifs, -ˌchēvz *(used by many who have sing.* -chəf *or* -ˌchif), -ˌchēfs, -ˌchəvz, -ˌchivz\ **1** : a small piece of cloth used especially for wiping the face, nose, or eyes **2** : KERCHIEF 1

1**han•dle** \ˈhan-dl\ *n* **1** : a part that is designed especially to be grasped by the hand **2** : something that resembles a handle **3** : NAME 1, TITLE 6 [Old English] — **han•dled** \-dld\ *adj* — **off the handle** : into a state of sudden and violent anger

2**handle** *vb* **han•dled; han•dling** \-dling, -dl-ing\ **1 a** : to affect with the hand (as by touching or feeling) **b** : to manage with the hands ⟨*handle* a horse⟩ **2 a** : to deal with in writing or speaking or in the plastic arts ⟨learned how to *handle* color in using oil paints⟩ **b** : CONTROL, DIRECT ⟨a lawyer *handles* my affairs⟩ **c** : to train and act as second for (a boxer) **d** : to put up with : STAND ⟨can't *handle* the heat⟩ **3** : to deal with or act on ⟨*handle* a problem⟩ **4** : to deal or trade in ⟨a store that *handles* rugs⟩ **5** : to act, behave, or respond in a certain way when managed or directed ⟨a car that *handles* well⟩ [Old English *handlian*]

han•dle•able \ˈhan-dl-ə-bəl\ *adj* : capable of being handled

han•dle•bar \ˈhan-dl-ˌbär\ *n* : a straight or bent bar with a handle (as for steering a bicycle) at each end — usually used in plural

handlebar mustache *n* : a heavy mustache with long sections that curve upward at each end

hand lens *n* : a magnifying glass to be held in the hand

han•dler \ˈhan-dlər, -dl-ər\ *n* **1** : one that handles **2** : a person in immediate charge of an animal; *esp* : one who exhibits dogs at shows or field trials **3** : a person who trains or acts as a second for a boxer

hand•made \ˈhand-ˈmād, ˈhan-\ *adj* : made by hand and not by machine

hand•maid•en \-ˌmād-n\ *also* **hand•maid** \-ˌmād\ *n* : a female servant or attendant

hand–me–down \ˈhand-mē-ˌdau̇n, ˈhan-\ *adj* : put in use by one person or group after being used, discarded, or handed down by another — **hand–me–down** *n*

hand•off \ˈhan-ˌdȯf\ *n* : a football play in which the ball is handed by one player to another nearby

hand on *vt* : to pass along in succession : HAND DOWN

hand organ *n* : a barrel organ operated by a hand crank

hand•out \ˈhan-ˌdau̇t\ *n* **1** : a portion of food, clothing, or money given to or as if to a beggar **2** : an information sheet for free distribution **3** : a prepared statement released to the press

hand over *vt* : to give up possession or control of

hand•pick \ˈhand-ˈpik, ˈhan-\ *vt* : to select personally

hand•rail \ˈhan-ˌdrāl\ *n* : a narrow rail for grasping with the hand as a support (as on a staircase)

hand•saw \ˈhand-ˌsȯ, ˈhan-\ *n* : a saw used with one hand (as a woodworker's ripsaw or crosscut saw)

hands·breadth \'handz-ˌbredth\ *variant of* HANDBREADTH
hands down *adv* **1 :** without much effort **:** EASILY ⟨won the race *hands down*⟩ **2 :** without question ⟨is *hands down* the best pizza in town⟩
hand·sel \'han-səl\ *n* **1 :** a gift made as a token of good wishes or luck especially at the beginning of a new year **2 :** [3]EARNEST, FORETASTE [Middle English *hansell*]
hand·set \'hand-ˌset, han-\ *n* **:** a combined telephone transmitter and receiver mounted on a device that is held in the hand
hand·shake \-ˌshāk\ *n* **:** a clasping (as in greeting or farewell) of right hands by two people
hands–off \'han-'zȯf\ *adj* **:** marked by noninterference
hand·some \'han-səm\ *adj* **1 :** fairly large **:** SIZABLE ⟨a *handsome* fortune⟩ **2 :** marked by graciousness or generosity ⟨a *handsome* contribution⟩ **3 :** having a pleasing and often impressive or dignified appearance ⟨a *handsome* young lad⟩ ⟨a *handsome* building⟩ [Middle English *handsom* "easy to manipulate"] — **hand·some·ly** *adv* — **hand·some·ness** *n*
hand·spike \'han-ˌspīk\ *n* **:** a bar used as a lever (as in working a windlass on a boat) [by folk etymology from Dutch *handspaak,* from *hand* "hand" + *spaak* "pole"]
hand·spring \-ˌspring\ *n* **:** a tumbling feat in which the body turns forward or backward in a full circle from a standing position and lands first on the hands and then on the feet
hand·stand \-ˌstand\ *n* **:** an act of balancing the body on the hands with the trunk and legs in the air
hand–to–hand \'han-tə-ˌhand, -də-\ *adj* **:** involving physical contact — **hand to hand** \-'hand\ *adv*
hand–to–mouth \-tə-'mau̇th\ *adj* **:** having or providing nothing to spare ⟨a *hand-to-mouth* existence⟩ — **hand to mouth** *adv*
hand·wheel \'hand-ˌhwēl, 'han-, -ˌwēl\ *n* **:** a wheel worked by hand
hand·work \'han-ˌdwərk\ *n* **:** work done with the hands and not by machine
hand·wo·ven \'han-'dwō-vən\ *adj* **:** produced on a hand-operated loom
hand·writ·ing \'han-ˌdrīt-ing\ *n* **1 :** writing done by hand; *esp* **:** the form of writing peculiar to a particular person **2 :** something written by hand — **hand·writ·ten** \-ˌdrit-n\ *adj*
handy \'han-dē\ *adj* **hand·i·er; -est 1 a :** conveniently near **b :** convenient for use ⟨a *handy* reference book⟩ **c :** easily handled ⟨a *handy* sloop⟩ **2 :** clever in using the hands **:** DEXTEROUS ⟨*handy* with a needle⟩
handy·man \-dē-ˌman\ *n* **:** a person who does odd jobs
[1]**hang** \'hang\ *vb* **hung** \'həng\ *also* **hanged** \'hangd\; **hang·ing** \'hang-ing\ **1 a :** to fasten or be fastened to some elevated point without support from below **b :** to put to death or be put to death by hanging from a rope tied round the neck ⟨sentenced to be *hanged*⟩ **c :** to fasten so as to allow free motion upon a point of suspension ⟨*hang* a door⟩ **d :** to adjust the hem of (a skirt) so as to hang evenly and at a proper height when worn **2 :** to furnish with hanging decorations (as pictures or drapery) **3 :** to hold or bear in a suspended or inclined manner **:** DROOP ⟨*hang* your head in shame⟩ **4 :** to fasten to a wall ⟨*hang* wallpaper⟩ **5 :** to display (pictures) in a gallery **6 :** to remain poised or stationary in the air ⟨clouds *hanging* low overhead⟩ **7 :** to stay with persistence **8 :** to hover threateningly ⟨evils *hang* over the nation⟩ **9 :** DEPEND ⟨election *hangs* on one vote⟩ **10 a :** to take hold for support **:** CLING ⟨*hang* on my arm⟩ **b :** to be burdensome or oppressive ⟨time *hung* on our hands⟩ **11 :** to be in suspense **:** suffer delay ⟨the decision is still *hanging*⟩ **12 :** to lean, incline, or jut over or downward **13 :** to be in a state of close attention ⟨*hung* on their every word⟩ **14 :** to fit or fall from the figure in easy lines ⟨the coat *hangs* loosely⟩ **15 :** to pass time idly especially by relaxing or socializing — often used with *around* or *out* ⟨*hung* out with friends⟩ [Old English *hōn* (v.t.) and *hanglan* (v.i. and v.t.)] — **hang·able** \'hang-ə-bəl\ *adj* — **hang it up :** to stop an activity or effort — **hang loose :** to remain calm or relaxed — **hang tough :** to remain resolute in dealing with a challenge **:** HANG IN
[2]**hang** *n* **1 :** the manner in which a thing hangs ⟨the *hang* of a skirt⟩ **2 a :** peculiar and significant meaning ⟨the *hang* of an argument⟩ **b :** the special method of doing, using, or dealing with something **:** KNACK ⟨get the *hang* of driving a car⟩ — **give a hang** *or* **care a hang :** to be the least bit concerned or worried
[1]**hang·ar** \'hang-ər, 'hang-gər\ *n* **:** SHELTER, SHED; *esp* **:** a covered and usually enclosed area for housing and repairing aircraft [French]
[2]**hangar** *vt* **:** to place in a hangar
hang around *vb* **:** to pass time or stay aimlessly in or at ⟨*hung around* the house all day⟩
hang back *vi* **1 :** to lag behind others **2 :** to be reluctant **:** HESITATE
hang·dog \'hang-ˌdȯg\ *adj* **1 :** ASHAMED 1, GUILTY ⟨a *hangdog* look⟩ **2 :** ABJECT 3, COWED
hang·er \'hang-ər\ *n* **1 :** one that hangs or causes to be hung or hanged **2 :** a device by which or to which something is hung or hangs; *esp* **:** a device for hanging a garment from a hook or rod
hang·er–on \'hang-ər-ˌȯn, -ˌän\ *n, pl* **hangers–on :** one that hangs around a person, place, or institution in hope of personal gain
hang glider *n* **:** a small glider made usually in the form of a kite from which a person hangs in soaring — **hang glide** *vi* — **hang gliding** *n*

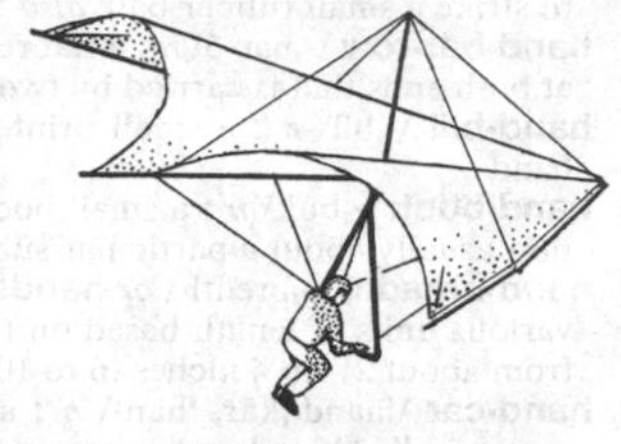
hang glider

hang in *vi* **:** to refuse to be discouraged or intimidated ⟨*hang in* there⟩
[1]**hang·ing** \'hang-ing\ *n* **1 :** an execution by strangling or breaking the neck by a suspended noose **2 :** something hung (as a curtain or tapestry) — usually used in plural **3 :** a downward slope
[2]**hanging** *adj* **1 :** situated or lying on steeply sloping ground ⟨*hanging* gardens⟩ **2 a :** jutting out or over **b :** supported only by the wall on one side ⟨a *hanging* staircase⟩ **3 :** adapted for sustaining a hanging object **4 :** punishable by death by hanging ⟨a *hanging* offense⟩
hang·man \'hang-mən\ *n* **1 :** a person who hangs condemned criminals **2 :** a game in which the object is for one player to guess the letters of an unknown word before the player who knows the word creates a stick figure of a hanged man by drawing one line for each incorrect guess
hang·nail \-ˌnāl\ *n* **:** a bit of skin hanging loose at the side or base of a fingernail [by folk etymology from earlier *agnail,* from Old English *angnægl* "corn on the foot or toe"]

Word History Old English *angnægl* meant "a corn on the foot." The second element of the word, *-nægl,* meant "nail," but it referred to an iron nail rather than to a toenail or fingernail. A hard corn was likened to the head of a nail. The first element, *ang-,* is related to Old English *ange,* "painful." Over the centuries *angnægl* became *agnail* and was used for a variety of ailments of the fingers or toes. This usage led to the belief that the *-nail* of *agnail* meant "toenail" or "fingernail." By then the adjective *ange* was obsolete, and the first element of *agnail* was not easy to interpret. So the compound was transformed to make sense to ordinary speakers of the language. The new form, *hangnail,* was used specifically for a bit of loose skin at the base of a fingernail.

hang on *vi* **1 :** to keep hold **:** hold onto something **2 :** to persist stubbornly ⟨a cold that *hung on* all spring⟩ — **hang on to :** to hold, grip, or keep persistently ⟨*hang on to* your money⟩
hang·out \'hang-ˌau̇t\ *n* **:** a favorite place for spending time
hang·over \'hang-ˌō-vər\ *n* **1 :** something (as a surviving custom) that remains from what is past **2 a :** disagreeable physical effects following heavy consumption of alcohol or the use of drugs **b :** a letdown following great excitement or excess
hang–up \'hang-ˌəp\ *n* **:** a source of mental or emotional difficulty
hang up \'hang-'əp, hang-\ *vb* **1 a :** to place on a hook or hanger ⟨*hang up* your coat⟩ **b :** to replace (a telephone receiver) on the cradle so that the connection is broken; *also* **:** to terminate a telephone conversation **2 :** to snag or cause to snag so as to be immovable ⟨the ship *hung up* on a sandbar⟩
hank \'hangk\ *n* **:** SKEIN [Middle English, of Scandinavian origin]
han·ker \'hang-kər\ *vi* **han·kered; han·ker·ing** \-kə-ring, -kring\ **:** to have an eager or persistent desire ⟨*hanker* after fame and fortune⟩ [probably from Flemish *hankeren,* from *hangen* "to hang"] ***synonyms*** see LONG — **han·ker·er** \-kər-ər\ *n*
han·ky–pan·ky \ˌhang-kē-'pang-kē\ *n* **:** questionable or underhanded activity [origin unknown]
Han·o·ver·i·an \ˌhan-ə-'vir-ē-ən, -'ver-\ *adj* **:** of, relating to, or

supporting the German ducal house of Hanover or the descendant British royal house that ruled from 1714 to 1901 [*Hanover,* Germany] — **Hanoverian** *n*

Han·sen's disease \'han-sənz-\ *n* : LEPROSY [Armauer *Hansen,* died 1912, Norwegian physician]

han·som \'han-səm\ *n* : a light 2-wheeled covered carriage with the driver's seat elevated behind — called also *hansom cab* [Joseph A. *Hansom,* died 1882, English architect]

Ha·nuk·kah *also* **Cha·nu·kah** *or* **Ha·nu·kah** \'kän-ə-kə, 'hän-\ *n* : an 8-day Jewish holiday celebrated in November or December in commemoration of the rededication of the Temple of Jerusalem after its defilement by Antiochus of Syria [Hebrew *ḥănukkāh* "dedication"]

¹hap \'hap\ *n* **1** : HAPPENING 1 **2** : CHANCE 1, FORTUNE [Old Norse *happ* "good luck"]

²hap *vb* **happed; hap·ping** **1** : HAPPEN 3 **2** : HAPPEN 4a

hap·haz·ard \hap-'haz-ərd, 'hap-\ *adj* : marked by lack of plan, order, or direction : AIMLESS ***synonyms*** see RANDOM — **haphazard** *adv* — **hap·haz·ard·ly** *adv* — **hap·haz·ard·ness** *n*

hap·ki·do \ˌhäp-'kēd-ō\ *n* : a Korean martial art based on kicking motions and using elements of aikido [Korean, from *hap-* "together, joined" + *ki* "breath, energy" + *to* "way, art"]

hap·less \'hap-ləs\ *adj* : having no luck : UNFORTUNATE ⟨a *hapless* child⟩ — **hap·less·ly** *adv* — **hap·less·ness** *n*

hap·loid \'hap-ˌlȯid\ *adj* : having the number of chromosomes characteristic of germ cells or half the number characteristic of body cells [Greek *haploeidēs* "single," from *haploos* "single"] — **haploid** *n* — **hap·loi·dy** \-ˌlȯid-ē\ *n*

hap·ly \'hap-lē\ *adv* : by chance, luck, or accident

hap·pen \'hap-ən, 'hap-m\ *vi* **hap·pened; hap·pen·ing** \'hap-ning, -ə-ning\ **1** : to occur by chance **2** : to take place **3** : to have occasion or opportunity without intention : CHANCE ⟨*happened* to overhear⟩ **4 a** : to find something by chance ⟨*happened* upon the right answer⟩ **b** : to appear casually or by chance **5** : to come especially by way of injury or harm ⟨I promise nothing will *happen* to you⟩ [Middle English *happenen,* from *hap*]

synonyms HAPPEN, CHANCE, OCCUR, TRANSPIRE mean to come about. HAPPEN applies to whatever comes about without cause or intention ⟨the incident *happened* last night⟩. CHANCE stresses lack of plan or apparent cause ⟨it *chanced* to rain that day⟩. OCCUR, often interchangeable with HAPPEN, stresses bringing to sight or to mind or attention ⟨theoretically possible, but not *occurring* in reality⟩ ⟨it never *occurred* to them that we would object⟩. TRANSPIRE can imply a coming out or becoming known ⟨what happened that day only *transpired* much later⟩ but is often equal to OCCUR.

¹hap·pen·ing *n* **1** : something that happens : OCCURRENCE **2 a** : an event or series of events designed to evoke a spontaneous reaction to sensory, emotional, or spiritual stimuli **b** : something (as an event) of special interest or importance

²happening *adj* **1** : very fashionable : IN ⟨a *happening* hairstyle⟩ **2** : offering much excitement or entertainment ⟨a *happening* dance club⟩

hap·pi·ly \'hap-ə-lē\ *adv* **1** : FORTUNATELY, LUCKILY ⟨*happily,* no one was injured⟩ **2** : in a happy manner or state ⟨lived *happily* ever after⟩ **3** : APTLY, SUCCESSFULLY ⟨the remarks were *happily* worded⟩

hap·pi·ness \'hap-i-nəs\ *n* **1 a** : a state of well-being and contentment : JOY **b** : a pleasurable satisfaction **2** : FELICITY 1, APTNESS

hap·py \'hap-ē\ *adj* **hap·pi·er; -est** **1** : favored by fortune : FORTUNATE **2** : notably well adapted or fitting ⟨a *happy* choice for governor⟩ **3 a** : enjoying well-being and contentment ⟨*happy* in their work⟩ **b** : expressing or suggestive of happiness : PLEASANT ⟨*happy* laughter⟩ **c** : feeling satisfaction ⟨*happy* to escape⟩ [Middle English, from *hap*] ***synonyms*** see LUCKY

happy camper *n* : one who is content

hap·py–go–lucky \ˌhap-ē-gō-'lək-ē\ *adj* : cheerfully unconcerned : CAREFREE

Haps·burg *or* **Habs·burg** \'haps-ˌbərg, 'häps-ˌbu̇rg\ *adj* : of or relating to the German royal house to which belong the rulers of Austria from 1278 to 1918 and of Spain from 1516 to 1700 and many of the Holy Roman emperors [*Habsburg,* Aargau canton, Switzerland] — **Hapsburg** *n*

hap·ten \'hap-ˌten\ *n* : a substance that stimulates antibody formation only when joined with a protein [German, from Greek *haptein* "to fasten"]

hara–kiri *also* **hari–kari** \ˌhar-i-'kir-ē, -'kar-ē\ *n* : suicide by disembowelment formerly practiced by the Japanese samurai [Japanese *harakiri,* from *hara* "belly" + *kiri* "cutting"]

ha·rangue \hə-'rang\ *n* **1** : a speech addressed to a public assembly **2** : a ranting speech or writing [Middle French *arengue,* from Italian *aringa*] — **harangue** *vb* — **ha·rangu·er** \-'rang-ər\ *n*

ha·rass \hə-'ras, 'har-əs\ *vt* **1 a** : to tire out by persistent efforts **b** (1) : to annoy persistently (2) : to create an unpleasant or hostile situation for by uninvited and unwelcome verbal or physical conduct **2** : to worry and impede with repeated attacks [French *harasser,* from Medieval French *harer* "to set a dog on," from *hare,* interj. used to incite dogs, of Germanic origin] — **ha·rass·er** *n* — **ha·rass·ment** \-mənt\ *n*

¹har·bin·ger \'här-bən-jər\ *n* : one that announces or shows what is coming : FORERUNNER ⟨robins are *harbingers* of spring⟩ [Middle English *herbergere* "host, one sent ahead to provide lodgings," from Medieval French, "host," from *herberge* "inn," of Germanic origin]

Word History The modern *harbinger* is simply a forerunner. But in late medieval and early modern times a *harbinger,* or *herbergere,* was the person sent before an army, a royal progress, or the like, to find lodgings for the whole company. Still earlier English *herbergeres* were hosts, the actual providers of lodgings. The Medieval French word from which the English was borrowed was itself derived from an early Germanic loanword. Medieval French *herberge* took from its Germanic ancestor both the literal meaning, "army encampment," and the figurative extension, "hostelry, inn." Modern English *harbor* is another descendant of the same old Germanic word.

²harbinger *vt* : to be a harbinger of : PRESAGE

¹har·bor \'här-bər\ *n* **1** : a place of security : REFUGE **2** : a protected part of a body of water deep enough to furnish anchorage; *esp* : one with port facilities [Middle English *herberge, herberwe,* from Old English *herebeorg* "military quarters," from *here* "army" + *beorg* "refuge" — see *Word History* at HARBINGER] — **har·bor·less** \-ləs\ *adj*

²harbor *vb* **har·bored; har·bor·ing** \-bə-ring, -bring\ **1 a** : to give shelter or refuge to **b** : to be the home or habitat of : CONTAIN **2** : to hold in the mind ⟨*harbored* a grudge⟩ **3** : to take shelter in or as if in a harbor — **har·bor·er** *n*

har·bor·age \'här-bə-rij\ *n* : SHELTER 1a, HARBOR

har·bour \'här-bər\ *chiefly British variant of* HARBOR

¹hard \'härd\ *adj* **1** : not easily penetrated, cut, or divided into parts : not soft **2 a** : high in alcoholic content ⟨*hard* liquor⟩ **b** : characterized by the presence of salts that prevent lathering with soap ⟨*hard* water⟩ **3 a** : having high penetrating power ⟨*hard* X-rays⟩ **b** : having or producing relatively great photographic contrast ⟨a *hard* negative⟩ **4 a** : metallic as distinct from paper ⟨*hard* money⟩ **b** : convertible into gold : stable in value ⟨*hard* currency⟩ **5 a** : physically fit ⟨in good *hard* condition⟩ **b** : resistant to stress or disease : free of weakness or defects **6 a** (1) : FIRM, DEFINITE ⟨a *hard* agreement⟩ (2) : FACTUAL, ACTUAL ⟨*hard* evidence⟩ **b** : CLOSE, SEARCHING ⟨a *hard* look⟩ **c** : free from sentimentality or illusion : REALISTIC ⟨good *hard* sense⟩ **d** : lacking sympathy or sentiment : UNFEELING ⟨a *hard* heart⟩ **7 a** : difficult to bear or endure : HARSH, SEVERE ⟨*hard* times⟩ **b** : RESENTFUL ⟨*hard* feelings⟩ **c** : making no concessions ⟨drive a *hard* bargain⟩ **d** : INCLEMENT ⟨a *hard* winter⟩ **e** (1) : intense in force, manner, or degree ⟨a *hard* blow⟩ (2) : demanding the exertion of energy : calling for stamina and endurance ⟨*hard* work⟩ **8** : DILIGENT, ENERGETIC ⟨a *hard* worker⟩ **9 a** : sharply or harshly defined or outlined : STARK ⟨*hard* shadows⟩ **b** : sounding as in *cow* and *geese* respectively — used of *c* and *g* **10 a** : difficult to accomplish or resolve : TROUBLESOME ⟨a *hard* problem⟩ **b** : difficult to comprehend or explain ⟨a *hard* concept⟩ **11** : being both addictive and harmful to health ⟨*hard* drugs⟩ **12** : persisting in the environment for a long time without breaking down ⟨*hard* insecticides⟩ [Old English *heard*]

²hard *adv* **1 a** : with great effort or energy : STRENUOUSLY ⟨worked *hard*⟩ ⟨try *hard*⟩ **b** : VIOLENTLY, FIERCELY ⟨the wind is blowing *hard*⟩ **c** : to the full extent — used in nautical directions **d** : in a searching, close, or concentrated manner ⟨stared *hard* at the sign⟩ **2 a** : HARSHLY, SEVERELY ⟨the recession hit them *hard*⟩ **b** : with rancor, bitterness, or grief ⟨took the defeat *hard*⟩ **3** : TIGHTLY, FIRMLY ⟨hold *hard* to something⟩ **4** : to the point of hardness ⟨dry *hard*⟩ **5** : close in time or space ⟨the school stood *hard* by a river⟩

hard–and–fast \ˌhärd-n-ˈfast\ *adj* : not to be modified or evaded : STRICT ⟨a *hard-and-fast* rule⟩

hard·back \ˈhärd-ˌbak\ *n* : a book bound in hard covers

hard·ball \-ˌbȯl\ *n* : BASEBALL

hard–bit·ten \-ˈbit-n\ *adj* : seasoned or strengthened by difficult experience : TOUGH ⟨*hard-bitten* campaigners⟩

hard·board \-ˌbōrd, -ˌbȯrd\ *n* : a very dense fiberboard usually smooth on one side

hard–boiled \-ˈbȯild\ *adj* **1** : boiled until both white and yolk become solid ⟨*hard-boiled* eggs⟩ **2 a** : lacking sentiment ⟨a *hard-boiled* drill sergeant⟩ **b** : HARDHEADED 2

hard candy *n* : a candy made of sugar and corn syrup boiled without crystallizing and often fruit-flavored

hard coal *n* : ANTHRACITE

hard copy *n* : a copy of information (as from computer storage) produced on paper in normal size ⟨print a *hard copy*⟩

hard–core \ˈhärd-ˌkōr, -ˌkȯr\ *adj* **1** : fanatically loyal, devoted, or committed ⟨*hard-core* supporters⟩ **2** : barely capable of being or willing to be reformed ⟨a *hard-core* criminal⟩ **3** : continuing for a long time ⟨*hard-core* unemployment⟩ — **hard core** *n*

hard disk *n* **1** : a small rigid metal disk with a magnetic coating on which computer data can be stored **2** : HARD DRIVE

hard drive *n* : a data-storage device consisting of a drive and one or more hard disks in a sealed case

hard–driv·ing \-ˌdrī-viŋ\ *adj* : intensely ambitious, energetic, or hardworking ⟨a *hard-driving* salesperson⟩

hard·en \ˈhärd-n\ *vb* **hard·ened; hard·en·ing** \ˈhärd-niŋ, -n-iŋ\ **1** : to make or become hard or harder **2** : to make unfeeling or unsympathetic ⟨*hardened* his heart⟩ **3** : to make or become hardy or strong ⟨muscles *hardened* by exercise⟩ **4** : to protect from blast, heat, or radiation ⟨*harden* a missile site⟩ **5 a** : to become firm, stable, or settled **b** : to express harshness or severity **6** : to make or become gradually adapted to unfavorable conditions — often used with *off* ⟨*harden* off seedlings before transplanting⟩ — **hard·en·er** \ˈhärd-nər, -n-ər\ *n*

hardening *n* : SCLEROSIS ⟨*hardening* of the arteries⟩

hard·hack \ˈhärd-ˌhak\ *n* : a North American spirea with dense terminal clusters of small usually pink flowers and leaves having a hairy rust-colored underside

hard·head·ed \-ˈhed-əd\ *adj* **1** : STUBBORN 1 **2** : marked by sound judgment : REALISTIC ⟨a *hardheaded* reappraisal⟩ — **hard·head·ed·ly** *adv* — **hard·head·ed·ness** *n*

hard·heart·ed \-ˈhärt-əd\ *adj* : lacking in sympathetic understanding — **hard·heart·ed·ly** *adv* — **hard·heart·ed·ness** *n*

har·di·hood \ˈhärd-ē-ˌhu̇d\ *n* **1** : unwavering courage and fortitude **2** : VIGOR 1, ROBUSTNESS

hard labor *n* : compulsory labor of imprisoned criminals that is a part of the prison discipline

hard–luck \ˈhärd-ˌlək\ *adj* : marked by, relating to, or experiencing bad luck ⟨*hard-luck* stories⟩

hard·ly \ˈhärd-lē\ *adv* **1** : in a severe manner : HARSHLY **2** : with difficulty : PAINFULLY **3** : almost not : BARELY ⟨it *hardly* ever rains⟩ **4** : certainly not ⟨it was *hardly* a surprise⟩

hard·ness *n* **1** : the quality or state of being hard **2** : the cohesion of the particles on the surface of a mineral as determined by its capacity to scratch another or be itself scratched

hard–of–hearing \ˌhärd-əv-ˈhiər-iŋ, -ə-ˈ\ *adj* : relating to or having a defective but functional sense of hearing

hard·pack \ˈhärd-ˌpak\ *n* : compacted snow

hard palate *n* : the bony front part of the roof of the mouth

hard·pan \ˈhärd-ˌpan\ *n* **1** : a cemented or compacted and often clayey layer in soil that roots cannot readily penetrate **2** : a fundamental part : BASIS

hard put *adj* : barely able ⟨*hard put* to find an explanation⟩

hard rubber *n* : a firm rubber or rubber product that is relatively incapable of being stretched

hard·scrab·ble \ˈhärd-ˌskrab-əl\ *adj* **1** : being or relating to a place with soil barely fit for growing crops ⟨a *hardscrabble* farm⟩ **2** : marked by poverty ⟨a *hardscrabble* life⟩

hard sell *n* : aggressive high-pressure salesmanship

hard·ship \ˈhärd-ˌship\ *n* **1** : PRIVATION 2, DISTRESS **2** : something that causes or involves distress or privation

hard·stand \-ˌstand\ *n* : a hard-surfaced area for parking an airplane

hard–sur·face \-ˈsər-fəs\ *vt* : to provide (as a road) with a paved surface

hard·tack \ˈhärd-ˌtak\ *n* : a hard biscuit or bread made of flour and water without salt

hard·top \-ˌtäp\ *n* : an automobile or a motorboat having a permanent rigid top; *also* : such an automobile styled to resemble a convertible

hard up *adj* **1** : short of money **2** : poorly provided ⟨*hard up* for friends⟩

hard·ware \ˈhär-ˌdwaər, -ˌdweər\ *n* **1** : articles (as fittings, cutlery, tools, utensils, or parts of machines) made of metal **2** : major items of equipment used for a particular purpose; *esp* : sophisticated electronic or military equipment

hardware cloth *n* : rugged galvanized screening

hard wheat *n* : a wheat with hard kernels high in gluten that yield a flour especially suitable for bread and macaroni

hard·wired \ˈhärd-ˌwīrd\ *adj* : implemented in the form of permanent electronic circuits; *also* : connected or united by or as if by permanent electrical connections ⟨a *hardwired* phone⟩ ⟨multiplication tables are *hardwired* into my brain⟩

[1]**hard·wood** \ˈhär-ˌdwu̇d\ *n* **1** : the wood of a tree that is a broad-leaved flowering plant as distinguished from that of a tree that is a conifer — compare SOFTWOOD 1 **2** : a tree that yields hardwood

[2]**hardwood** *adj* **1** : having or made of hardwood ⟨*hardwood* floors⟩ **2** : consisting of mature woody tissue ⟨a *hardwood* cutting⟩

hard–wood·ed \ˈhär-ˈdwu̇d-əd\ *adj* **1** : having wood that is hard ⟨a *hard-wooded* pine⟩ **2** : HARDWOOD 1

hard·work·ing \ˈhär-ˈdwər-kiŋ\ *adj* : INDUSTRIOUS, DILIGENT ⟨*hardworking* students⟩

har·dy \ˈhärd-ē\ *adj* **har·di·er; -est** **1** : BOLD 1, BRAVE **2** : full of confidence or brashness : BRAZEN **3 a** : used to fatigue or hardships : ROBUST **b** : able to withstand adverse conditions (as of weather) ⟨a *hardy* rose bush⟩ [Medieval French *hardi,* of Germanic origin] — **har·di·ly** \ˈhärd-l-ē\ *adv* — **har·di·ness** \ˈhärd-ē-nəs\ *n*

Har·dy–Wein·berg law \ˌhärd-ē-ˈwīn-ˌbərg-\ *n* : a fundamental principle of population genetics: population gene frequencies remain constant from generation to generation if mating is random and if mutation, selection, immigration, and emigration do not occur — called also *Hardy-Weinberg principle* [G. H. *Hardy,* died 1947, English mathematician and W. *Weinberg,* 20th century German physician]

hare \ˈhaər, ˈheər\ *n, pl* **hare** *or* **hares** : any of various swift mammals (order Lagomorpha) that differ from the closely related rabbits especially in having longer ears and hind legs and having the young open-eyed and furred at birth [Old English *hara*]

hare and hounds *n* : a game in which some of the players scatter bits of paper for a trail and others try to find and catch them

hare·bell \ˈhaər-ˌbel, ˈheər-\ *n* : a slender herb with bright blue bell-shaped flowers

harebell

hare·brained \-ˈbrānd\ *adj* : FLIGHTY, FOOLISH

hare·lip \-ˈlip\ *n, sometimes offensive* : CLEFT LIP

har·em \ˈhar-əm, ˈher-\ *n* **1 a** : the rooms assigned to the women in a Muslim household **b** : the women of a Muslim household **2** : a group of female animals (as horses) associated and usually mating with one male [Arabic *harīm*]

hari–kari *variant of* HARA-KIRI

hark \ˈhärk\ *vi* : to pay close attention : LISTEN [Middle English *herken*]

hark back *vi* : to turn back to an earlier topic or circumstance

har·le·quin \ˈhär-li-kən, -kwən\ *n* **1** : BUFFOON 1, CLOWN **2** : a variegated pattern (as of a textile) [Italian *arlecchino,* a character in comedy and pantomime with a shaved head, masked face, variegated tights, and wooden sword, from Middle French *Helquin,* a demon]

har·lot \ˈhär-lət\ *n* : PROSTITUTE [Medieval French *herlot* "rogue"]

har·lot·ry \-lə-trē\ *n, pl* **-ries** : PROSTITUTION

[1]**harm** \ˈhärm\ *n* **1** : physical or mental damage : INJURY **2**

: DAMAGE, HURT [Old English *hearm*] ***synonyms*** see INJURY

[2]**harm** *vt* : to cause harm to

harm•ful \ˈhärm-fəl\ *adj* : causing injury : DAMAGING — **harm•ful•ly** \-fə-lē\ *adv* — **harm•ful•ness** *n*

harm•less \ˈhärm-ləs\ *adj* **1** : free from harm, liability, or loss **2** : lacking capacity or intent to injure ⟨a *harmless* joke⟩ — **harm•less•ly** *adv* — **harm•less•ness** *n*

[1]**har•mon•ic** \här-ˈmän-ik\ *adj* **1** : of or relating to musical harmony as opposed to melody or rhythm **2** : HARMONIOUS 2 — **har•mon•i•cal•ly** \-ˈmän-i-kə-lē, -klē\ *adv*

[2]**harmonic** *n* **1 a** : OVERTONE 1; *esp* : one whose frequency is a multiple of the fundamental **b** : a flutelike tone produced (as on a violin) by lightly touching a vibrating string with a finger **2** : a component frequency of a harmonic motion (as of an electromagnetic wave) that is an integral multiple of the fundamental frequency

har•mon•i•ca \här-ˈmän-i-kə\ *n* : a small rectangular wind instrument with free metallic reeds sounded by exhaling and inhaling — called also *mouth organ*

harmonic motion *n* : a periodic motion that has a single frequency or amplitude (as of a sounding violin string or swinging pendulum) or is composed of two or more such simple periodic motions

har•mo•ni•ous \här-ˈmō-nē-əs\ *adj* **1** : musically concordant ⟨a *harmonious* song⟩ **2** : having the parts agreeably related : CONGRUOUS ⟨*harmonious* colors⟩ **3** : marked by accord in sentiment or action ⟨a *harmonious* family⟩ — **har•mo•ni•ous•ly** *adv* — **har•mo•ni•ous•ness** *n*

har•mo•ni•um \-nē-əm\ *n* : REED ORGAN

har•mo•nize \ˈhär-mə-ˌnīz\ *vb* **1** : to play or sing in harmony **2** : to be in harmony **3** : to bring into harmony or agreement **4** : to provide or accompany with harmony ⟨*harmonize* a melody⟩ — **har•mo•ni•za•tion** \ˌhär-mə-nə-ˈzā-shən\ *n* — **har•mo•niz•er** \ˈhär-mə-ˌnī-zər\ *n*

har•mo•ny \ˈhär-mə-nē\ *n, pl* **-nies** **1** *archaic* : tuneful sound **2 a** : the combination of simultaneous musical notes in a chord **b** : the structure of music with respect to the composition and progression of chords **c** : the science of the structure, relation, and progression of chords **3 a** : pleasing arrangement of parts ⟨a picture showing *harmony* of color and design⟩ **b** : ACCORD, AGREEMENT ⟨live in *harmony* with neighbors⟩ **c** : internal calm [Medieval French *armonie,* from Latin *harmonia,* from Greek, "joint, harmony," from *harmos* "joint"]

[1]**har•ness** \ˈhär-nəs\ *n* **1 a** : the gear of a draft animal other than a yoke **b** : TACKLE 1, EQUIPMENT; *esp* : military equipment for man or horse **c** : something that resembles a harness (as in holding or fastening something) ⟨a parachute *harness*⟩ **2 a** : occupational surroundings or routine ⟨back in *harness* after a vacation⟩ **b** : close association ⟨doesn't work well in *harness*⟩ [Medieval French *herneis* "baggage, gear"]

[2]**harness** *vt* **1 a** : to put a harness on **b** : to attach by means of a harness **2** : to join together : YOKE **3** : to put to work : UTILIZE ⟨*harness* the sun's energy to heat homes⟩

harness horse *n* : a horse for racing or working in harness

harness racing *n* : the sport of racing standardbred horses harnessed to 2-wheeled sulkies

[1]**harp** \ˈhärp\ *n* : an instrument having strings of graded length stretched across an open triangular frame and played by plucking with the fingers [Old English *hearpe*] — **harp•ist** \ˈhär-pəst\ *n*

harp

[2]**harp** *vi* **1** : to play on a harp **2** : to dwell on or come back to a subject tiresomely or monotonously ⟨always *harping* on my shortcomings⟩ — **harp•er** \ˈhär-pər\ *n*

har•poon \här-ˈpün\ *n* : a barbed spear used especially in hunting large fish or whales [probably from Dutch *harpoen,* from Medieval French *harpon* "brooch," from *harper* "to grapple"] — **harpoon** *vt* — **har•poon•er** *n*

harp•si•chord \ˈhärp-si-ˌkȯrd\ *n* : a keyboard instrument resembling the grand piano and producing tones by the plucking of wire strings [Italian *arpicordo,* from *arpa* "harp" + *corda* "string"]

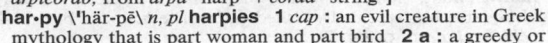

har•py \ˈhär-pē\ *n, pl* **harpies** **1** *cap* : an evil creature in Greek mythology that is part woman and part bird **2 a** : a greedy or grasping person : LEECH **b** : an angry and unpleasant woman [Latin *Harpyia,* from Greek]

har•que•bus \ˈhär-kwi-bəs, -ˌbəs\ *or* **ar•que•bus** \ˈär-\ *n* : a portable firearm of the 15th and 16th centuries later replaced by the musket [Middle French *harquebuse, arquebuse*]

har•ri•dan \ˈhar-əd-n\ *n* : a scolding old woman [perhaps from French *haridelle* "old horse, gaunt woman"]

[1]**har•ri•er** \ˈhar-ē-ər\ *n* **1** : any of a breed of hunting dogs resembling a small foxhound and originally bred for hunting rabbits **2** : a runner on a cross-country team [derived from *hare*]

[2]**harrier** *n* **1** : one that harries **2** : any of various slender long-legged hawks

[1]**har•row** \ˈhar-ō\ *n* : a cultivating implement set with spikes, spring teeth, or disks and used primarily for pulverizing and smoothing the soil [Middle English *harwe*]

[2]**harrow** *vt* **1** : to cultivate with a harrow **2** : TORMENT, VEX ⟨*harrowed* by grief⟩ — **har•row•er** \ˈhar-ə-wər\ *n*

har•ry \ˈhar-ē\ *vt* **har•ried; har•ry•ing** **1** : to make a raid on : PILLAGE **2** : to torment by or as if by constant attack ⟨*harried* by questions from the press⟩ [Old English *hergian*]

harsh \ˈhärsh\ *adj* **1** : having a coarse uneven surface unpleasant to the touch **2** : disagreeable to one of the senses ⟨a *harsh* light⟩; *also* : physically discomforting : PAINFUL ⟨a *harsh* wind⟩ **3** : unduly exacting : SEVERE ⟨*harsh* discipline⟩ **4** : lacking in aesthetic appeal or refinement : CRUDE ⟨*harsh* colors⟩ [Middle English *harsk,* of Scandinavian origin] ***synonyms*** see ROUGH — **harsh•en** \ˈhär-shən\ *vb* — **harsh•ly** *adv* — **harsh•ness** *n*

hart \ˈhärt\ *n, chiefly British* : a male red deer especially over five years old : STAG — compare HIND [Old English *heort*]

harte•beest \ˈhärt-ˌbēst, -ə-ˌbēst\ *n* : either of two large African antelopes with a long head and ringed horns [obsolete Afrikaans, from Dutch, from *hart* "deer" + *beest* "beast"]

har•um–scar•um \ˌhar-əm-ˈskar-əm, ˌher-əm-ˈsker-\ *adj* : casually or heedlessly careless [perhaps from archaic *hare* "to harass" + *scare*] — **harum–scarum** *n* — **harum–scarum** *adv*

ha•rus•pex \hə-ˈrəs-ˌpeks, ˈhar-əs-\ *n, pl* **ha•rus•pi•ces** \hə-ˈrəs-pə-ˌsēz\ : a diviner in ancient Rome basing predictions on inspection of the entrails of animals [Latin]

[1]**har•vest** \ˈhär-vəst\ *n* **1** : the season when crops are gathered **2** : the gathering of a crop **3** : a ripe crop; *also* : the quantity of a crop gathered in a single season **4** : an accumulated store or productive result ⟨a *harvest* of revenue⟩ [Old English *hærfest*]

[2]**harvest** *vb* **1 a** : to gather in a crop : REAP **b** : to gather as if by harvesting **2** : to win by achievement — **har•vest•able** \-və-stə-bəl\ *adj* — **har•vest•er** *n*

har•vest•man \ˈhär-vəst-mən, -vəs-\ *n* : DADDY LONGLEGS 2

harvest moon *n* : the full moon nearest the September equinox

has *present 3rd singular of* HAVE

has–been \ˈhaz-ˌbin\ *n* : one that has passed the peak of ability, power, effectiveness, or popularity

ha•sen•pfef•fer \ˈhäz-n-ˌpfef-ər, -ˌfef-\ *n* : a stew made of rabbit meat [German, from *Hase* "hare" + *Pfeffer* "pepper"]

[1]**hash** \ˈhash\ *vt* **1 a** : to chop into small pieces **b** : CONFUSE 1, MUDDLE **2** : to talk about : REVIEW ⟨*hash* over the evidence⟩ [French *hacher,* from *hache* "battle-ax," of Germanic origin]

[2]**hash** *n* **1** : chopped food; *esp* : chopped meat mixed with potatoes and browned **2** : a restatement of something that is already known **3** : JUMBLE, HODGEPODGE

[3]**hash** *n* : HASHISH

Hash•em•ite *or* **Hash•im•ite** \ˈhash-ə-ˌmīt\ *n* : a member of an Arab family having common ancestry with Muhammad and founding dynasties in countries of the eastern Mediterranean [*Hashim,* great-grandfather of Muhammad]

hash•ish \ˈhash-ˌēsh, ha-ˈshēsh\ *n* : the resin from the flowering tops of the female hemp plant that is smoked, chewed, or drunk for its intoxicating effect — called also *charas* [Arabic *ḥashīsh*]

hash•tag \ˈhash-ˌtag\ *n* : a word or phrase preceded by the symbol # that classifies or categorizes the accompanying text (such as a tweet) [from *hash sign* "the number sign #," perhaps altered from [5]*hatch*]

Ha•sid *also* **Has•sid** *or* **Cha•sid** *or* **Chas•sid** \ˈhas-əd, ˈkäs-\ *n, pl* **Ha•si•dim** *also* **Has•si•dim** *or* **Cha•si•dim** *or* **Chas•si•dim**

\ə\ **abut**	\au̇\ **out**	\i\ **tip**	\ȯ\ **saw**	\u̇\ **foot**
\ər\ **further**	\ch\ **chin**	\ī\ **life**	\ȯi\ **coin**	\y\ **yet**
\a\ **mat**	\e\ **pet**	\j\ **job**	\th\ **thin**	\yü\ **few**
\ā\ **take**	\ē\ **easy**	\ng\ **sing**	\t͟h\ **this**	\yu̇\ **cure**
\ä\ **cot, cart**	\g\ **go**	\ō\ **bone**	\ü\ **food**	\zh\ **vision**

\ˈhas-əd-əm, k̲ə-ˈsēd-\ : a member of an orthodox Jewish movement that was founded in Poland in the mid-18th century and that emphasizes joyous unrestrained religious worship and mystical devotion [Hebrew *ḥāsīdh* "pious"] — **Ha·sid·ic** *also* **Has·sid·ic** *or* **Cha·sid·ic** *or* **Chas·sid·ic** \hə-ˈsid-ik, ha-\ *adj* — Has·i·dism \ˈhas-ə-ˌdiz-əm\ *n*

Has·mo·nae·an *or* **Has·mo·ne·an** \ˌhaz-mə-ˈnē-ən\ *n* : a member of the Maccabees [*Hasmon,* ancestor of the Maccabees] — **Hasmonaean** *or* **Hasmonean** *adj*

hasn't \ˈhaz-nt\ : has not

hasp \ˈhasp\ *n* : any of several devices for fastening; *esp* : a fastener (as for a door or lid) consisting of a hinged metal strap that fits over a staple and is secured by a pin or padlock [alteration of Old English *hæpse*]

has·si·um \ˈhas-ē-əm\ *n* : a short-lived radioactive element produced artificially — see ELEMENT table [New Latin, from *Hassia* "Hesse (German state)," location of the laboratory that first produced the element]

[1]**has·sle** \ˈhas-əl\ *n* **1** : a heated argument : WRANGLE **2** : a violent skirmish : FIGHT **3 a** : a state of confusion : TURMOIL **b** : an annoying or troublesome concern [perhaps blend of *harass* and *hustle*]

[2]**hassle** *vb* **has·sled; has·sling** \ˈhas-ling, -ə-ling\ **1** : DISPUTE 1 ⟨*hassled* with the umpire⟩ **2** : to annoy persistently : HARASS

has·sock \ˈhas-ək\ *n* **1** : a tuft of bog grass or sedge **2 a** : a cushion to kneel on in prayer **b** : a cushion that serves as a seat or as a leg rest [Old English *hassuc* "coarse grass"]

hast \hast, ˈhast, əst, həst\ *archaic present 2nd singular of* HAVE

has·tate \ˈhas-ˌtāt\ *adj* : shaped like an arrow with flaring barbs ⟨a *hastate* leaf⟩ [Latin *hasta* "spear"]

[1]**haste** \ˈhāst\ *n* **1** : rapidity of motion or action : SWIFTNESS **2** : rash or headlong action **3** : undue eagerness to act : URGENCY [Medieval French, of Germanic origin]

synonyms HASTE, HURRY, SPEED mean quickness in movement or action. HASTE implies quickness impelled by urgency, eagerness, or rashness ⟨bought the car in *haste*⟩. HURRY suggests agitation, bustle, or confusion ⟨in the *hurry* of departure she forgot her toothbrush⟩. SPEED stresses swiftness without confusion and often with success ⟨increase your reading *speed*⟩.

[2]**haste** *vb* : to move or act swiftly : HASTEN, HURRY

has·ten \ˈhās-n\ *vb* **has·tened; has·ten·ing** \ˈhās-ning, -n-ing\ **1** : to urge on **2** : to speed up : ACCELERATE ⟨*hasten* one's steps⟩ **3** : to move or act quickly : HURRY ⟨*hasten* home⟩ — **has·ten·er** \-nər, -n-ər\ *n*

hasty \ˈhā-stē\ *adj* **hast·i·er; -est** **1 a** : done or made in a hurry ⟨made a *hasty* sketch of the scene⟩ **b** : fast and often superficial ⟨a *hasty* survey of the plan⟩ **2** : acting or done without forethought : RASH **3** : quick to anger : IRRITABLE ⟨a *hasty* temper⟩ — **hast·i·ly** \-stə-lē\ *adv* — **hast·i·ness** \-stē-nəs\ *n*

hasty pudding *n* **1** *British* : a porridge of oatmeal or flour boiled in water **2** *New England* **a** : cornmeal mush **b** : INDIAN PUDDING

hat \ˈhat\ *n* : a covering for the head usually having a shaped crown and brim [Old English *hæt*] — **under one's hat** : not disclosed : SECRET ⟨kept the news *under his hat*⟩

hat·box \ˈhat-ˌbäks\ *n* : a round piece of luggage especially for carrying hats

[1]**hatch** \ˈhach\ *n* **1** : an opening in the deck of a ship or in the floor or roof of a building; *also* : a small door or opening (as in an airplane) ⟨an escape *hatch*⟩ ⟨a cargo *hatch*⟩ **2** : the covering for a hatch [Old English *hæc*]

[2]**hatch** *vb* **1 a** : to produce (young) from the egg by applying heat ⟨the hen *hatched* chicks⟩ **b** : INCUBATE 1 ⟨the hen *hatched* the eggs⟩ **2 a** : to emerge from an egg, pupa, or chrysalis ⟨the chicks *hatched* today⟩ **b** : to give forth young ⟨the eggs *hatched* today⟩ **3** : to bring into being : ORIGINATE; *esp* : to concoct in secret ⟨*hatch* a plot⟩ [Middle English *hacchen*] — **hatch·abil·i·ty** \ˌhach-ə-ˈbil-ət-ē\ *n* — **hatch·able** \ˈhach-ə-bəl\ *adj*

[3]**hatch** *n* **1** : an act or instance of hatching **2** : a brood of hatched young

[4]**hatch** *vt* **1** : to inlay in fine lines **2** : to mark (as the shading in a picture) with fine closely spaced lines [Middle French *hacher* "to chop, slice up, hatch," from *hache* "battle-ax"]

[5]**hatch** *n* : a line used to give the effect of shading

hatch·ery \ˈhach-rē, -ə-rē\ *n, pl* **-er·ies** : a place for hatching eggs ⟨a fish *hatchery*⟩

hatch·et \ˈhach-ət\ *n* **1** : a short-handled ax for use with one hand **2** : TOMAHAWK [Medieval French *hachette,* from *hache* "battle-ax"]

hatchet face *n* : a thin sharp face — **hatch·et–faced** \ˌhach-ət-ˈfāst\ *adj*

hatchet man *n* : one hired for murder, coercion, or attack

hatch·ing \ˈhach-ing\ *n* : the engraving or drawing of fine lines close together to give the effect of shading; *also* : the pattern so made

hatch·ling \ˈhach-ling\ *n* : a recently hatched animal

hatch·ment \ˈhach-mənt\ *n* : a panel on which a coat of arms of a deceased person is temporarily displayed [perhaps alteration of *achievement*]

hatch·way \ˈhach-ˌwā\ *n* : a passage giving access to an enclosed space (as a cellar) and usually having a ladder or stairs

[1]**hate** \ˈhāt\ *n* **1 a** : intense hostility and aversion **b** : a very strong dislike : ANTIPATHY ⟨had a great *hate* of hard work⟩ **2** : an object of hatred [Old English *hete*]

[2]**hate** *vt* **1** : to feel extreme enmity toward ⟨*hate* one's enemies⟩ **2 a** : to have a strong aversion to : DETEST ⟨*hate* hypocrisy⟩ **b** : to find distasteful : DISLIKE ⟨*hates* cold weather⟩ — **hat·er** *n* — **hate one's guts** : to hate someone with great intensity

synonyms HATE, DETEST, ABHOR, LOATHE mean to feel strong aversion or intense dislike for. HATE implies strong dislike often coupled with malice ⟨*hated* the enemy with a passion⟩. DETEST suggests violent or intense dislike but may lack the hostility implied in HATE ⟨*detests* cowards⟩. ABHOR suggests a deep repugnance ⟨a crime *abhorred* by all⟩. LOATHE implies utter disgust and intolerance ⟨*loathed* the mere sight of them⟩.

hate·ful \ˈhāt-fəl\ *adj* **1** : full of hate : MALICIOUS ⟨*hateful* enemies⟩ **2** : exciting or deserving hate ⟨a *hateful* crime⟩ ***synonyms*** see REPUGNANT — **hate·ful·ly** \-fə-lē\ *adv* — **hate·ful·ness** *n*

hath \hath, ˈhath, əth, həth\ *archaic present 3rd singular of* HAVE

ha·tred \ˈhā-trəd\ *n* **1** : HATE 1 **2** : prejudiced hostility or animosity [Middle English, from *hate* + Old English *rǣden* "condition"]

hat·ter \ˈhat-ər\ *n* : one that makes, sells, or cleans and repairs hats

hat trick *n* : the scoring of three goals in one game by one player (as in hockey or soccer)

hau·berk \ˈhȯ-bərk\ *n* : a tunic of chain mail worn as armor from the 12th to the 14th century [Medieval French *hauberc,* of Germanic origin]

haugh·ty \ˈhȯt-ē, ˈhät-\ *adj* **haugh·ti·er; -est** : disdainfully proud [Medieval French *haut,* literally, "high," from Latin *altus*] ***synonyms*** see PROUD — **haugh·ti·ly** \-l-ē\ *adv* — **haugh·ti·ness** \-ē-nəs\ *n*

[1]**haul** \ˈhȯl\ *vb* **1 a** : to exert traction : DRAW, PULL ⟨the horse *hauled* a cart⟩ **b** : to obtain or move by or as if by hauling **c** : to transport in a vehicle **2** : SHIFT ⟨the wind *hauled* around to the south⟩ [Medieval French *haler,* of Germanic origin] — **haul·er** *n*

[2]**haul** *n* **1 a** : the act or process of hauling **b** : a device for hauling **2 a** : an amount collected : TAKE ⟨a burglar's *haul*⟩ **b** : the quantity of fish taken in a single draft of a net **3 a** : transportation by hauling **b** : the distance or route over which a load is transported ⟨a long *haul*⟩ **c** : a quantity transported : LOAD

haul·age \ˈhȯ-lij\ *n* **1** : the act or process of hauling **2** : a charge made for hauling

haulm \ˈhȯm\ *n* : the stems or tops of a crop plant (as peas or potatoes) especially after the crop has been gathered [Old English *healm*]

haunch \ˈhȯnch, ˈhänch\ *n* **1 a** : HIP 1 **b** : HINDQUARTER 2 — usually used in plural **2** : HINDQUARTER 1 [Medieval French *hanche,* of Germanic origin]

[1]**haunt** \ˈhȯnt, ˈhänt\ *vb* **1 a** : to visit often : FREQUENT **b** : to continually seek the company of **c** : to stay around or persist : LINGER **2 a** : to have a disturbing or harmful effect on ⟨problems we ignore now will come back to *haunt* us⟩ **b** : to recur constantly and spontaneously to ⟨the song *haunted* me all day⟩ **c** : to reappear continually in ⟨a sense of the supernatural that *haunts* his stories⟩ **3** : to visit or inhabit as a ghost [Medieval French *hanter*] — **haunt·er** *n* — **haunt·ing·ly** \-ing-lē\ *adv*

[2]**haunt** \ˈhȯnt, ˈhänt, *2 is usually* ˈhant\ *n* **1** : a place habitually frequented or repeatedly visited ⟨a favorite *haunt* of birds⟩ **2** *chiefly dialect* : GHOST 2

haus·to·ri·um \hȯ-ˈstōr-ē-əm, -ˈstȯr-\ *n, pl* **-ria** \-ē-ə\ : a food-absorbing outgrowth of a part (as a hypha) of a plant or plantlike organism [New Latin, from Latin *haurire* "to drink, drain"] — **haus·to·ri·al** \-ē-əl\ *adj*

haut·bois *or* **haut·boy** \ˈō-ˌbȯi, ˈhō-\ *n, pl* **hautbois** \-ˌbȯiz\ *or* **hautboys** : OBOE [Middle French *hautbois,* from *haut* "high" + *bois* "wood"]

haute cou·ture \ˌōt-kü-ˈtu̇r\ *n* : the establishments or designers that create high fashions for women; *also* : the fashions created [French, literally, "high sewing"]

hau·teur \hō-ˈtər\ *n* : ARROGANCE, HAUGHTINESS [French, from *haut* "high," from Latin *altus*]

hav·da·lah *also* **hab·da·lah** \ˌhäv-də-ˈlä, häv-ˈdō-lə\ *n, often cap* : a Jewish ceremony marking the close of a Sabbath or holy day [Hebrew *habhdālāh* "separation"]

[1]**have** \hav, ˈhav, həv, əv, v; *before "to" usually* ˈhaf\ *vb, past & past participle* **had** \had, ˈhad, həd, əd, d\; *present participle* **hav·ing** \ˈhav-ing\; *present 3rd sing* **has** \haz, ˈhaz, həz, əz, z, s; *before "to" usually* ˈhas\ **1 a** : to hold or maintain as a possession, privilege, or entitlement ⟨I *have* my rights⟩ ⟨they *have* a new car⟩ **b** : to hold in one's use, service, or affection or at one's disposal ⟨we don't *have* time to stay⟩ **c** : to consist of : CONTAIN ⟨April *has* 30 days⟩ **2** : to feel obligation or necessity in regard to ⟨*have* to go⟩ **3** : to stand in relationship to ⟨*have* enemies⟩ **4 a** : to get possession of : OBTAIN ⟨the best to be *had*⟩ **b** : RECEIVE ⟨*had* bad news⟩ **c** : ACCEPT; *esp* : to accept in marriage ⟨she wouldn't *have* him⟩ **5 a** : to be marked or characterized by ⟨*has* red hair⟩ **b** : SHOW ⟨*had* the courage to refuse⟩ **c** : USE 3, EXERCISE ⟨*have* mercy on us⟩ **6 a** : to experience especially by submitting to, undergoing, or suffering ⟨I *have* a cold⟩ **b** : to make the effort to perform (an action) or engage in (an activity) ⟨*have* a look at that mess⟩ ⟨*had* a fight⟩ **c** : to entertain in the mind ⟨*have* an opinion⟩ **7 a** : to cause to do or be done ⟨please *have* them stay⟩ **b** : to cause to be ⟨*have* the house painted⟩ **8** : PERMIT 1 ⟨we'll *have* no more of that⟩ **9** : to be competent in ⟨I *have* only a little French⟩ **10 a** : to hold an advantage over ⟨we *have* them now⟩ **b** : TRICK 1, FOOL ⟨was *had* by a partner⟩ **11** : BEAR 2a ⟨*have* a baby⟩ **12** : to partake of ⟨*have* dinner⟩ **13** : BRIBE ⟨can be *had* for a price⟩ **14** — used as an auxiliary verb with the past participle to form the present perfect, past perfect, or future perfect ⟨*has* gone home⟩ ⟨*had* already eaten⟩ ⟨will *have* finished⟩ [Old English *habban*] — **had better** *or* **had best** : would be wise to ⟨you *had better* start your work⟩ — **have at** : to go at or deal with : ATTACK — **have coming** : to deserve what one gets, benefits by, or suffers ⟨he *had* that punishment *coming*⟩ — **have done** : FINISH 1a, STOP — **have had it 1** : to have had or have done all one is going to be allowed to **2** : to have experienced, endured, or suffered all one can — **have it in for** : to intend to do harm to — **have it out** : to settle a matter of contention by discussion or fighting — **have one's eye on** : to watch constantly and attentively — **have to do with 1** : to deal with ⟨the program *has to do with* rare animals⟩ **2** : to have a specified relationship with or effect on ⟨brain size *has* nothing *to do with* intelligence⟩

[2]**have** \ˈhav\ *n* : one that has material wealth — compare HAVE-NOT

ha·ven \ˈhā-vən\ *n* **1** : HARBOR 2, PORT **2 a** : place of safety : ASYLUM [Old English *hæfen*]

have–not \ˈhav-ˌnät, -ˈnät\ *n* : one that is poor in material wealth — compare HAVE

haven't \ˈhav-ənt\ : have not

hav·er·sack \ˈhav-ər-ˌsak\ *n* : a bag similar to a knapsack but worn over one shoulder [French *havresac,* from German *habersack* "bag for oats," from *Haber* "oats" + *Sack* "bag"]

Ha·ver·sian canal \hə-ˈvər-zhən-\ *n* : any of the small canals by which blood vessels traverse bone [Clopton *Havers,* died 1702, English physician]

hav·oc \ˈhav-ək\ *n* **1** : wide and general destruction : DEVASTATION **2** : great confusion and disorder [Medieval French *havok,* from earlier *havot* "plunder"]

[1]**haw** \ˈhȯ\ *n* **1** : a hawthorn berry **2** : HAWTHORN [Old English *haga*]

[2]**haw** *vi* **1** : to utter the sound represented by *haw* ⟨hemmed and *hawed* before answering⟩ **2** : to hesitate in speaking : EQUIVOCATE [imitative]

[3]**haw** *n* : a vocalized pause in speaking or an instance of uttering this sound [imitative]

[4]**haw** *imperative verb* — used as a direction to turn to the left; compare GEE [origin unknown]

Ha·waii–Aleu·tian time \hə-ˈwä-ē-ə-ˈlü-shən-, -ˈwī-, -ˈwō-, -yē\ *n* : the time of the 10th time zone west of Greenwich that includes the Hawaiian Islands and the Aleutians west of the Fox group

Ha·wai·ian \hə-ˈwä-yən; -ˈwī-yən, -ən-; -ˈwō-yən\ *n* **1** : a native or resident of Hawaii; *esp* : one of Polynesian ancestry **2** : the Polynesian language of the Hawaiians — **Hawaiian** *adj*

Hawaiian guitar *n* : a usually electric stringed instrument consisting of a long neck and six to eight steel strings that are plucked while being pressed with a movable steel bar

[1]**hawk** \ˈhȯk\ *n* **1** : any of numerous birds of prey that are active mostly during the day, are smaller than the eagles, and include the accipiters and buteos **2** : a person who advocates immediate vigorous action in a dispute; *esp* : a supporter of a war or warlike policy — compare DOVE [Old English *hafoc*] — **hawk·ish** \ˈhȯ-kish\ *adj*

hawk 1

[2]**hawk** *vb* **1** : to hunt birds by means of a trained hawk **2** : to hunt on the wing like a hawk

[3]**hawk** *vt* : to offer for sale by calling out in the street ⟨*hawk* vegetables⟩ [back-formation from [2]*hawker*]

[4]**hawk** *vb* **1** : to utter a harsh guttural sound in or as if in clearing the throat **2** : to raise by hawking ⟨*hawk* up phlegm⟩ [imitative]

[1]**hawk·er** \ˈhȯ-kər\ *n* : FALCONER

[2]**hawker** *n* : one that hawks wares [Low German *höker,* from *höken* "to peddle"]

hawk moth *n* : any of numerous stout-bodied swift-flying moths with long strong narrow pointed forewings and small hind wings

hawks·bill \ˈhȯks-ˌbil\ *n* : a small sea turtle of tropical waters with a narrow pointed beak — compare TORTOISESHELL

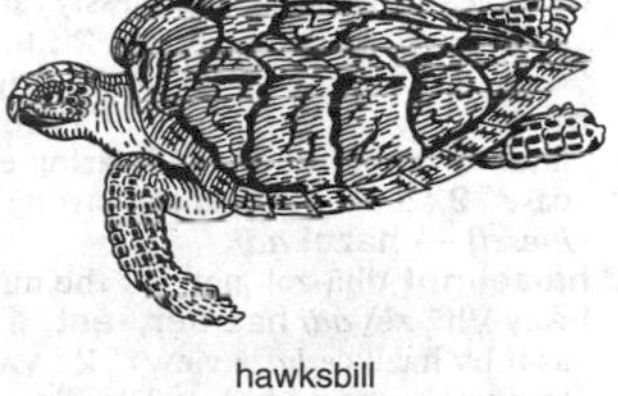

hawksbill

hawk·weed \ˈhȯ-ˌkwēd\ *n* : any of several plants related to the daisies and having usually yellow, red, or orange flowers — compare ORANGE HAWKWEED

hawse \ˈhȯz\ *n* **1 a** : HAWSEHOLE **b** : the part of a ship's bow that contains the hawseholes **2** : the distance between a ship's bow and its anchor [Old Norse *hals* "neck, hawse"]

hawse·hole \-ˌhōl\ *n* : a hole in the bow of a ship through which a cable passes

haw·ser \ˈhȯ-zər\ *n* : a large rope for towing, mooring, or securing a ship [Medieval French *haucer,* from *halcer, haucer* "to hoist," derived from Latin *altus* "high"]

haw·thorn \ˈhȯ-ˌthȯrn\ *n* : any of a genus of spring-flowering spiny shrubs or small trees related to the roses and having glossy and often lobed leaves, white or pink fragrant flowers, and small red fruits

[1]**hay** \ˈhā\ *n* : herbage (as grass) mowed and cured for fodder [Old English *hīeg*]

[2]**hay** *vb* **1** : to cut, cure, and store herbage for hay **2** : to feed with hay

hay·cock \ˈhā-ˌkäk\ *n* : a conical pile of hay

hay fever *n* : an acute allergic reaction to pollen that is usually seasonal and is marked by sneezing, nasal discharge and congestion, and itching and watering of the eyes

hay·loft \-ˌlȯft\ *n* : the upper part of a barn where hay is stored

hay·mak·er \-ˌmā-kər\ *n* : a powerful blow (as in boxing)

hay·mow \-ˌmau̇\ *n* : HAYLOFT

hay·rack \-ˌrak\ *n* **1 a** : a frame mounted on the running gear of a wagon and used especially in hauling hay or straw **b** : a

\ə\ **abut**	\au̇\ **out**	\i\ **tip**	\ȯ\ **saw**	\u̇\ **foot**
\ər\ **further**	\ch\ **chin**	\ī\ **life**	\ȯi\ **coin**	\y\ **yet**
\a\ **mat**	\e\ **pet**	\j\ **job**	\th\ **thin**	\yü\ **few**
\ā\ **take**	\ē\ **easy**	\ng\ **sing**	\t͟h\ **this**	\yu̇\ **cure**
\ä\ **cot, cart**	\g\ **go**	\ō\ **bone**	\ü\ **food**	\zh\ **vision**

wagon mounted with a hayrack **2 :** a feeding rack that holds hay for livestock

hay·rick \-ˌrik\ *n* **:** a large sometimes thatched outdoor stack of hay

hay·seed \-ˌsēd\ *n, pl* **hayseed** *or* **hayseeds** **1 a :** seed shattered from hay **b :** clinging bits of straw or chaff from hay **2** *pl* **hayseeds :** BUMPKIN, YOKEL

hay·stack \-ˌstak\ *n* **:** a stack of hay **:** HAYRICK

hay·wire \-ˌwīr\ *adv or adj* **1 :** being out of order ‹the radio is *haywire*› **2 :** emotionally or mentally upset **:** CRAZY ‹went *haywire* after the accident› [from the use of baling wire for makeshift repairs]

ha·zan \k̲ə-ˈzän, ˈk̲äz-ᵊn\ *n, pl* **ha·za·nim** \k̲ə-ˈzän-əm\ **:** CANTOR 2 [Hebrew *ḥazzān*]

[1]**haz·ard** \ˈhaz-ərd\ *n* **1 :** a game of chance played with two dice **2 :** a source of danger **3 :** ACCIDENT 1b, CHANCE **4 :** a golf-course obstacle [Medieval French *hasard,* from Arabic *al-zahr* "the die"] ***synonyms*** see DANGER

Word History *Hazard* was originally a game played with dice. The English word comes from Medieval French *hasard,* which was most likely borrowed from Arabic *az-zahr,* "the die" ("one of the dice"). *Hazard* was borrowed from the French by the medieval English, and within a few centuries what had been a venture on the outcome of a throw of the dice could be any venture or risk. Now "chance" or "venture" and "risk" or "peril" are the primary meanings of *hazard.* The game of *hazard* is only infrequently played, and the modern player probably assumes that the game is so called because of the chances taken in play.

[2]**hazard** *vt* **:** VENTURE, RISK ‹*hazard* a guess›

haz·ard·ous \ˈhaz-ərd-əs\ *adj* **:** DANGEROUS, RISKY — **haz·ard·ous·ly** *adv* — **haz·ard·ous·ness** *n*

[1]**haze** \ˈhāz\ *n* **1 :** fine dust, smoke, or light vapor causing lack of transparency in the air **2 :** a vague uncertain state of mind or mental perception

[2]**haze** *vb* **:** to make or become hazy or cloudy [probably back-formation from *hazy*]

[3]**haze** *vt* **1 :** to harass needlessly (as by exacting hard or disagreeable work or by mockery) **2 :** to play abusive and humiliating tricks on by way of initiation [origin unknown] — **haz·er** *n*

ha·zel \ˈhā-zəl\ *n* **1 :** any of a genus of shrubs or small trees related to the birches and bearing edible nuts enclosed in a leafy case **2 :** a light brown to a strong yellowish brown [Old English *hæsel*] — **hazel** *adj*

ha·zel·nut \ˈhā-zəl-ˌnət\ *n* **:** the nut of a hazel

hazy \ˈhā-zē\ *adj* **haz·i·er; -est** **1 :** obscured or darkened by or as if by haze ‹a *hazy* view› **2 :** VAGUE ‹a *hazy* idea› [origin unknown] — **haz·i·ly** \-zə-lē\ *adv* — **haz·i·ness** \-zē-nəs\ *n*

H–bomb \ˈāch-ˌbäm\ *n* **:** HYDROGEN BOMB

HDL \ˌāch-ˌdē-ˈel\ *n* **:** a lipoprotein of blood plasma that has little cholesterol and is associated with reduced risk of developing atherosclerosis — called also *good cholesterol, high-density lipoprotein*; compare LDL [*h*igh-*d*ensity *l*ipoprotein]

[1]**he** \hē, ˈhē, ē\ *pron* **1 :** that male one who is neither speaker nor hearer ‹*he* is my father› — compare HIM, HIS, IT, SHE, THEY **2** — used in a generic sense or when the sex of the person is not specified ‹*he* who hesitates is lost› ‹one should do the best *he* can› [Old English *hē*]

[2]**he** \ˈhē\ *n* **:** a male person or animal

[1]**head** \ˈhed\ *n* **1 :** the upper or front division of the body (as of a human or an insect) that contains the brain, the chief sense organs, and the mouth **2 a :** MIND, UNDERSTANDING ‹a good *head* for figures› **b :** mental or emotional control **:** POISE ‹a level *head*› **3 :** the side of a coin bearing a head or the major design **4 a :** PERSON, INDIVIDUAL ‹count *heads*› **b** *pl* **head** **:** one of a of number (as of livestock) ‹100 *head* of cattle› **5 a :** the end that is upper or higher or opposite the foot ‹the *head* of the bed› **b :** the source of a stream **c :** either end of something (as a drum) whose two ends need not be distinguished **6 a :** HEADMASTER **b :** a person responsible for directing the actions and duties of others **:** CHIEF, LEADER ‹the *head* of a company› **7 a :** an inflorescence (as of a sunflower or daisy) in the form of a rounded or flattened cluster of stemless flowers — called also *capitulum* **b :** a compact mass of plant parts (as leaves or flowers) ‹a *head* of cabbage› **8 a :** the leading element of a military column or a procession **b :** HEADWAY 1a **9 a :** the uppermost extremity or projecting part of an object **:** TOP **b :** the striking part of a weapon or tool **10 :** a body of water kept in reserve at a height **11 a :** the difference in elevation between two points in a body of fluid **b :** the resulting pressure of the fluid at the lower point expressible as this height; *also* **:** pressure of a fluid ‹a *head* of steam› **12 a :** the bow and adjacent parts of a ship **b :** a ship's toilet **13 :** the place of leadership or command ‹the one at the *head* of the group› **14 a** (1) **:** a word often in larger letters placed above a passage in order to introduce or categorize (2) **:** a separate part or topic **b :** a portion of a page or sheet that is above the first line of printing **15 :** the foam that rises on an effervescing liquid **16 a :** the part of a boil, pimple, or abscess at which it is likely to break **b :** CRISIS ‹events came to a *head*› **17 :** a part of a machine or machine tool containing a device (as a cutter or drill) ‹a machine with a grinding *head*›; *also* **:** the part of an apparatus that performs the chief function or a particular function ‹a shower *head*› [Old English *hēafod*] — **off one's head** **:** CRAZY, DISTRACTED — **out of one's head** **:** DELIRIOUS — **over one's head** **1 :** beyond one's comprehension **2 :** so as to pass over one's superior standing or authority

[2]**head** *adj* **1 :** of, relating to, or used for the head **2 :** PRINCIPAL, CHIEF ‹*head* cook› **3 :** situated at the head ‹the *head* table› **4 :** coming from in front ‹*head* sea›

[3]**head** *vb* **1 :** to cut back or off the upper or terminal growth of (a plant or plant part) **2 a :** to provide with or form a head ‹*head* an arrow› ‹this cabbage *heads* early› **b :** to form the head or top of ‹a tower *headed* by a spire› **3 :** to put oneself at the head of **:** act as leader to ‹*head* a revolt› **4 a :** to get in front of so as to hinder, stop, or turn back ‹*head* them off at the pass› **b :** to take a lead over (as in a race) **c :** to pass (a stream) by going round above the source **5 a :** to put something at the head of (as a list) **b :** to stand as the first or leading member of ‹*heads* the list› **6 :** to take or cause to take a specified course ‹*head* for home›

head·ache \ˈhed-ˌāk\ *n* **1 :** pain in the head **2 :** an annoying or baffling situation or problem — **head·achy** \-ˌā-kē\ *adj*

head·band \-ˌband\ *n* **:** a band worn on or around the head

head·board \-ˌbōrd, -ˌbȯrd\ *n* **:** a board forming the head (as of a bed)

head·cheese \-ˌchēz\ *n* **:** a jellied loaf or sausage made from the edible parts of the head, feet, and sometimes the tongue and heart especially of a pig

head cold *n* **:** a common cold centered in the nasal passages and adjacent mucous membranes

head·dress \ˈhed-ˌdres, ˈhe-\ *n* **:** a covering or ornament for the head

head·ed \ˈhed-əd\ *adj* **1 :** having a head or a heading ‹a *headed* bolt› **2 :** having such a head or so many heads ‹curly-*headed*› ‹three-*headed* monster›

head·er \ˈhed-ər\ *n* **1 :** one that removes heads; *esp* **:** a grain-harvesting machine that cuts off the grain heads and lifts them into a wagon **2 a :** a brick or stone laid in a wall with its end toward the face of the wall **b :** a beam fitted between trimmers and across the ends of tailpieces in a building frame **3 :** a fall or dive head foremost **4 :** a shot or pass made in soccer by hitting the ball with the head

head·first \ˈhed-ˈfərst\ *adv* **1 :** with the head foremost **2 :** HEADLONG, CARELESSLY ‹dove *headfirst* into uncharted territory› — **headfirst** *adj*

head gate *n* **:** a gate for controlling the water flowing into a channel (as an irrigation ditch)

head·gear \ˈhed-ˌgiər\ *n* **1 :** a covering or protective device for the head **2 :** a harness for a horse's head

head–hunt·ing \-ˌhənt-iŋ\ *n* **:** the practice of cutting off and preserving the heads of enemies as trophies — **head·hunt·er** *n*

head·ing \ˈhed-iŋ\ *n* **1 :** the compass direction in which the longitudinal axis of a ship or aircraft points **2 :** something that forms or serves as a head; *esp* **:** an inscription, headline, or title standing at the top or beginning (as of a letter or chapter)

head·land \ˈhed-lənd, -ˌland\ *n* **:** a point of usually high land jutting out into the sea **:** PROMONTORY

head·less \-ləs\ *adj* **1 :** having no head **2 :** having no leader **3 :** lacking good sense or prudence **:** FOOLISH — **head·less·ness** *n*

head·light \-ˌlīt\ *n* **:** a light on the front of a vehicle

[1]**head·line** \-ˌlīn\ *n* **1 :** the title over an item or article in a newspaper **2 :** a line at the top of a page (as in a book) giving a title or heading

[2]**headline** *vt* **1 :** to provide with a headline **2 :** to publicize highly **3 :** to be a leading performer or attraction in

head·lin·er \-ˌlī-nər\ *n* : the principal performer in a show : STAR
head·lock \ˈhed-ˌläk\ *n* : a wrestling hold in which one encircles the opponent's head with one arm
[1]**head·long** \-ˈlȯŋ\ *adv* **1** : HEADFIRST 1 **2** : without deliberation : RECKLESSLY ⟨dash *headlong* into traffic⟩ **3** : without pause or delay [Middle English *hedlong*, alteration of *hedling*, from *hed* "head" + *-ling*]
[2]**head·long** \-ˌlȯŋ\ *adj* **1** : lacking restraint : RASH ⟨*headlong* flight⟩ **2** : plunging headfirst ⟨a *headlong* dive into the pool⟩
head louse *n* : a sucking louse that lives on the human scalp
head·man \ˈhed-ˈman, -ˌman\ *n* : one who is a leader (as of a tribe, clan, or village) : CHIEF
head·mas·ter \ˈhed-ˌmas-tər\ *n* : a man heading the staff of a private school
head·mis·tress \-ˌmis-trəs\ *n* : a woman heading the staff of a private school
head·most \-ˌmōst\ *adj* : most advanced : LEADING
head–on \ˈhed-ˈȯn, -ˈän\ *adj* **1** : having the front facing in the direction of initial contact or line of sight **2** : in direct opposition or confontation : FRONTAL 2b ⟨a *head-on* attack⟩ — **head–on** *adv*
head over heels *adv* **1** : in or as if in a somersault ⟨fell *head over heels* down the hill⟩ **2** : very much ⟨*head over heels* in love⟩
head·phone \ˈhed-ˌfōn\ *n* : an earphone held over the ear by a band worn on the head — usually used in plural
head·piece \-ˌpēs\ *n* **1** : a protective or defensive covering for the head **2** : INTELLIGENCE 1a, BRAINS
head·pin \-ˌpin\ *n* : a pin that stands foremost in a triangular arrangement of bowling pins
head·quarter \ˈhed-ˌkwȯrt-ər, -ˌkwȯt-, hed-ˈ\ *vb* **1** : to make one's headquarters **2** : to place in headquarters
head·quar·ters \-ərz\ *n sing or pl* **1** : a place from which a commander exercises command **2** : the administrative center of an enterprise
head·rest \ˈhed-ˌrest\ *n* : a support for the head
head·sail \-ˌsāl, -səl\ *n* : a sail set forward of the mast
head·set \-ˌset\ *n* : a pair of headphones
head·ship \-ˌship\ *n* : the position, office, or dignity of a head
head·shrink·er \-ˌshriŋ-kər\ *n, slang* : PSYCHIATRIST
heads·man \ˈhedz-mən\ *n* : one that beheads : EXECUTIONER
head·stall \ˈhed-ˌstȯl\ *n* : a part of a bridle or halter that encircles the head
head·stand \-ˌstand\ *n* : the gymnastic feat of standing on one's head usually with support from the hands
head start *n* **1** : an advantage allowed at the start of a race **2** : a favorable or promising beginning
head·stock \ˈhed-ˌstäk\ *n* : a part of a lathe that holds the revolving spindle and its attachments
head·stone \-ˌstōn\ *n* : a memorial stone placed at the head of a grave
head·strong \-ˌstrȯŋ\ *adj* **1** : not easily restrained : WILLFUL ⟨a *headstrong* child⟩ **2** : directed by ungovernable will ⟨violent *headstrong* actions⟩
heads–up \ˈhedz-ˈəp\ *n* : a message that alerts or prepares : WARNING ⟨gave her the *heads-up* on the latest development⟩
head·wait·er \ˈhed-ˈwāt-ər\ *n* : the head of the dining-room staff of a restaurant or hotel
head·wa·ter \-ˌwȯt-ər, -ˌwät-\ *n* : the source and upper part of a stream — usually used in plural
head·way \-ˌwā\ *n* **1 a** : motion or rate of motion (as of a ship) in a forward direction **b** : ADVANCE, PROGRESS ⟨made *headway* in scientific research⟩ **2** : clear space (as under an arch) **3** : the time interval between two vehicles traveling in the same direction on the same route
headwind \-ˌwind\ *n* : a wind blowing in a direction opposite to a course of movement (as of a ship or aircraft)
head·word \ˈhed-ˌwərd\ *n* : a word or term placed at the beginning (as of a chapter or encyclopedia entry)
head·work \-ˌwərk\ *n* : mental work; *esp* : clever thinking
heady \ˈhed-ē\ *adj* **head·i·er; -est** **1** : WILLFUL, RASH ⟨*heady* opinions⟩ **2** : tending to make giddy ⟨*heady* wine⟩ — **head·i·ly** \ˈhed-l-ē\ *adv* — **head·i·ness** \ˈhed-ē-nəs\ *n*
heal \ˈhēl\ *vb* **1** : to make healthy or whole ⟨*heal* the sick⟩ **2** : to return to a sound or healthy condition ⟨the arm *healed*⟩ ⟨the wound *healed*⟩ [Old English *hǣlan*] ***synonyms*** see CURE
heal·er \ˈhē-lər\ *n* : one that heals
health \ˈhelth\ *n* **1 a** : the condition of being sound in body, mind, or spirit; *esp* : freedom from physical disease or pain **b** : the general condition of an individual ⟨in poor *health*⟩ ⟨enjoyed good *health*⟩ **2** : flourishing condition ⟨the economic *health* of a country⟩ **3** : a toast to someone's health or prosperity [Old English *hǣlth*, from *hāl* "whole, hale"]
health care *n* : efforts made to maintain or restore health especially by trained and licensed professionals
health food *n* : a food that is said to be especially good for one's health
health·ful \-fəl\ *adj* **1** : beneficial to health of body or mind ⟨*healthful* exercise⟩ **2** : HEALTHY 1 — **health·ful·ly** \-fə-lē\ *adv* — **health·ful·ness** *n*

synonyms HEALTHFUL, WHOLESOME, SALUBRIOUS, SALUTARY mean favorable to the health of mind or body. HEALTHFUL implies a positive contribution to a healthy condition ⟨a *healthful* diet⟩. WHOLESOME applies to what benefits, builds up, or sustains physically, mentally, or spiritually ⟨*wholesome* meals⟩ ⟨*wholesome* literature⟩. SALUBRIOUS applies chiefly to the helpful effects of climate or air ⟨cool and *salubrious* weather⟩. SALUTARY describes something corrective or beneficially effective, even though it may in itself be unpleasant ⟨the *salutary* influence of constructive criticism⟩.

health insurance *n* : insurance against loss through illness especially for medical expenses
health maintenance organization *n* : HMO
healthy \ˈhel-thē\ *adj* **health·i·er; -est** **1 a** : enjoying or typical of good health : WELL **b** : indicating good health ⟨a *healthy* complexion⟩ **2** : conducive to health **3 a** : PROSPEROUS, FLOURISHING ⟨a *healthy* economy⟩ **b** : not small or feeble : CONSIDERABLE ⟨a *healthy* serving⟩ — **health·i·ly** \-thə-lē\ *adv* — **health·i·ness** \-thē-nəs\ *n*

synonyms HEALTHY, WELL, SOUND mean enjoying or showing good health. HEALTHY implies full strength and vigor as well as freedom from disease ⟨a *healthy* family⟩. WELL implies merely freedom from disease or illness ⟨doesn't feel *well*⟩. SOUND stresses perfect health, absence of all defects, disease, or morbidity ⟨a *sound* mind in a *sound* body⟩.

[1]**heap** \ˈhēp\ *n* **1** : a collection of things thrown one on another : PILE ⟨a rubbish *heap*⟩ **2** : a great number or large quantity : LOT ⟨*heaps* of people⟩ ⟨a *heap* of fun⟩ [Old English *hēap*]
[2]**heap** *vt* **1** : to throw or lay in a heap : PILE ⟨*heap* up leaves⟩ **2** : to cast or bestow in large quantities ⟨*heaped* scorn on them⟩ **3** : to form a heap on : load heavily ⟨*heaped* food on their plates⟩
hear \ˈhiər\ *vb* **heard** \ˈhərd\; **hear·ing** \ˈhiər-iŋ\ **1** : to perceive or apprehend by the ear ⟨*hear* music⟩; *also* : to have the power of perceiving sound ⟨doesn't *hear* well⟩ **2** : to gain knowledge of by hearing : LEARN ⟨*heard* you're leaving⟩ **3** : to listen to : HEED ⟨*hear* me out⟩ **4 a** : to give a legal hearing to ⟨*hear* a case⟩ **b** : to take testimony from ⟨*hear* witnesses⟩ **5 a** : to get news ⟨*heard* from them yesterday⟩ **b** : to have knowledge ⟨had *heard* of them⟩ **6** : to entertain the idea ⟨wouldn't *hear* of it⟩ [Old English *hīeran*] — **hear·er** \ˈhir-ər\ *n*

synonyms HEAR, LISTEN mean to perceive through the ears. HEAR implies the actual sensation and response of the auditory nerves to a stimulus ⟨*heard* a sound⟩. LISTEN implies the conscious or voluntary effort to hear ⟨*listened* to the argument⟩.

hear·ing *n* **1 a** : the process, function, or power of perceiving sound; *esp* : the special sense by which noises and tones are received as stimuli **b** : EARSHOT ⟨stay within *hearing*⟩ **2 a** : a chance to present one's case **b** : a listening to arguments or testimony **c** : a session in which testimony is heard
hearing aid *n* : an electronic device for amplifying sound usually worn in or behind the ear of a person with poor hearing
hear·ken \ˈhär-kən\ *vi* **hear·kened; hear·ken·ing** \ˈhärk-niŋ, -ə-niŋ\ **1** : LISTEN 1 **2** : to give respectful attention [Old English *heorcnian*]
hear·say \ˈhiər-ˌsā\ *n* : something heard from another : RUMOR
hearsay evidence *n* : evidence based not on a witness's personal knowledge but on information given the witness by another
hearse \ˈhərs\ *n* : a vehicle for conveying the dead to the grave

\ə\ **abut**	\au̇\ **out**	\i\ **tip**	\ȯ\ **saw**	\u̇\ **foot**
\ər\ **further**	\ch\ **chin**	\ī\ **life**	\ȯi\ **coin**	\y\ **yet**
\a\ **mat**	\e\ **pet**	\j\ **job**	\th\ **thin**	\yü\ **few**
\ā\ **take**	\ē\ **easy**	\ŋ\ **sing**	\t͟h\ **this**	\yu̇\ **cure**
\ä\ **cot, cart**	\g\ **go**	\ō\ **bone**	\ü\ **food**	\zh\ **vision**

[Medieval French *herce* "harrow, frame for holding candles," from Latin *hirpex* "harrow"]

Word History In Medieval French the word *herce,* meaning "harrow," was applied to a triangular frame that was used for holding candles and was similar to the ancient form of a harrow. Both the literal and extended senses were used in English when the word was borrowed. It was a widespread practice to erect an elaborate framework over the coffin or tomb of a distinguished person. Because such frameworks were often decorated with lighted candles, the term *hearse* was applied to them. A series of extensions led to the use of *hearse* for a bier and then for a vehicle to carry the dead to the grave.

heart \ˈhärt\ *n* **1 a :** a hollow muscular organ of vertebrate animals that by its rhythmic contraction acts as a force pump maintaining the circulation of the blood **b :** a structure in an invertebrate animal similar in function to the vertebrate heart **2 :** something resembling a heart in shape **3 a :** a playing card marked with a red stylized heart; *also* **:** the suit made up of cards bearing hearts **b** *pl* **:** a card game in which the object is to avoid taking tricks containing hearts or win all of the hearts **4 a :** the whole personality including intellectual and emotional functions or traits **b :** PERSONALITY, DISPOSITION ⟨a cold *heart*⟩; *esp* **:** generous disposition **:** KINDNESS ⟨a person with a lot of *heart*⟩ **c :** COURAGE, SPIRIT ⟨take *heart*⟩ **5 a :** the central part ⟨the *heart* of the forest⟩ **b :** the most important part ⟨the *heart* of the issue⟩ [Old English *heorte*] — **by heart :** by rote — **to heart :** with deep concern

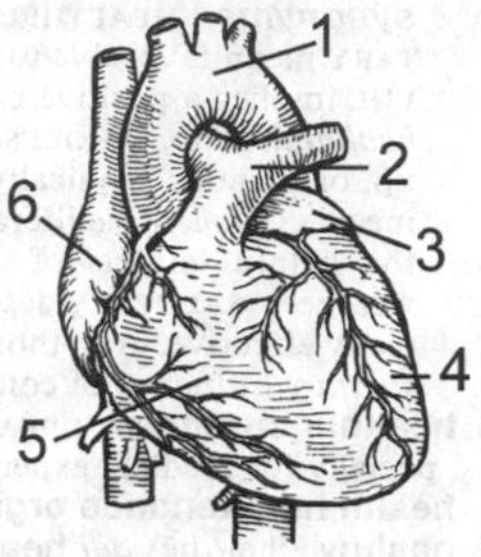

heart 1a: *1* aorta, *2* pulmonary artery, *3* left atrium, *4* left ventricle, *5* right ventricle, *6* right atrium

heart·ache \ˈhärt-ˌāk\ *n* **:** mental anguish **:** SORROW

heart attack *n* **:** an acute episode of death or damage of heart muscle due to insufficient blood flow to the heart usually as a result of the blocking of a coronary artery (as by a fatty deposit)

heart·beat \ˈhärt-ˌbēt\ *n* **1 :** one complete pulsation of the heart **2 :** a brief space of time ⟨would say yes in a *heartbeat*⟩

heart block *n* **:** lack of coordination of the heartbeat in which the atria and ventricles beat independently

heart·break \ˈhärt-ˌbrāk\ *n* **:** crushing grief or anguish

heart·break·ing \-ˌbrā-kiŋ\ *adj* **:** causing crushing grief — **heart·break·ing·ly** \-kiŋ-lē\ *adv*

heart·bro·ken \-ˌbrō-kən\ *adj* **:** overcome by grief

heart·burn \-ˌbərn\ *n* **:** a burning discomfort that seems to be localized about the heart and is usually due to spasms which pass acid from the stomach into the esophagus

heart·burn·ing \-ˌbər-niŋ\ *n* **:** intense or rancorous jealousy or resentment

heart disease *n* **:** an abnormal condition of the heart or of the heart and circulation

heart·ed \ˈhärt-əd\ *adj* **:** having a heart especially of a specified kind ⟨stout*hearted*⟩

heart·en \ˈhärt-ⁿn\ *vt* **heart·ened; heart·en·ing** \ˈhärt-niŋ, -ⁿn-iŋ\ **:** to cheer up **:** ENCOURAGE

heart·felt \ˈhärt-ˌfelt\ *adj* **:** deeply felt **:** EARNEST

hearth \ˈhärth\ *n* **1 a :** a brick, stone, or concrete area in front of a fireplace **b :** the floor of a fireplace **c :** the lowest section of a blast furnace **2 :** HOME 1a, FIRESIDE [Old English *heorth*]

hearth·stone \-ˌstōn\ *n* **1 :** stone forming a hearth **2 :** HOME 1a

heart·i·ly \ˈhärt-l-ē\ *adv* **1 :** with sincerity, goodwill, or enthusiasm ⟨set to work *heartily*⟩ ⟨eat *heartily*⟩ **2 :** CORDIALLY ⟨made them *heartily* welcome⟩ **3 :** COMPLETELY, THOROUGHLY

heart·land \ˈhärt-ˌland\ *n* **:** a central land area: as **a :** one thought of as economically and militarily important **b :** the central region of the U.S. in which mainstream or traditional values prevail

heart·less \-ləs\ *adj* **:** lacking feeling or compassion **:** CRUEL — **heart·less·ly** *adv* — **heart·less·ness** *n*

heart·rend·ing \-ˌren-diŋ\ *adj* **:** causing heartbreak

hearts·ease \ˈhärt-ˌsēz\ *n* **1 :** peace of mind **:** TRANQUILLITY **2 :** any of various violas; *esp* **:** WILD PANSY

heart·sick \ˈhärt-ˌsik\ *adj* **:** very despondent **:** DEPRESSED — **heart·sick·ness** *n*

heart·sore \-ˌsōr, -ˌsȯr\ *adj* **:** HEARTSICK

heart·string \-ˌstriŋ\ *n* **:** the deepest emotions or affections

heart·throb \-ˌthräb\ *n* **1 :** the throb of a heart **2 a :** sentimental emotion **:** PASSION **b :** SWEETHEART 2; *also* **:** a usually famous man (as an actor) known for his attractiveness

heart–to–heart \ˈhärt-tə-ˈhärt\ *adj* **:** SINCERE, FRANK ⟨a *heart-to-heart* talk⟩

heart·warm·ing \-ˌwȯrm-iŋ\ *adj* **:** making one feel good inside **:** cheering to one's emotions

heart·wood \ˈhärt-ˌwu̇d\ *n* **:** the older harder usually darker wood in the central part of a tree trunk — compare SAPWOOD

heart·worm \-ˌwərm\ *n* **:** a nematode worm that is a parasite especially in the heart of dogs and is transmitted by mosquitoes; *also* **:** infestation or disease caused by the heartworm

^{1}**hearty** \ˈhärt-ē\ *adj* **heart·i·er; -est 1 a :** giving unqualified support **:** THOROUGHGOING ⟨*hearty* agreement⟩ **b :** enthusiastically cordial ⟨a *hearty* welcome⟩ **c :** UNRESTRAINED ⟨*hearty* laughter⟩ **2 a :** exhibiting vigorous good health **b :** abundant and satisfying ⟨a *hearty* meal⟩ **c :** having a good appetite ⟨a *hearty* eater⟩ **3 :** ENERGETIC, STRONG ⟨gave a *hearty* pull⟩ — **heart·i·ness** *n*

^{2}**hearty** *n, pl* **heart·ies :** a hearty fellow; *also* **:** SAILOR

^{1}**heat** \ˈhēt\ *vb* **1 :** to make or become warm or hot **2 :** to make excited [Old English *hǣtan*]

^{2}**heat** *n* **1 a :** a condition of being hot **:** WARMTH **b :** a high degree of hotness **c :** a hot place or period **d :** a form of energy that causes substances to rise in temperature, fuse, evaporate, expand, or undergo any of various other changes and that flows to a body by contact with or radiation from bodies at higher temperatures **2 a :** intensity of feeling ⟨answered with some *heat*⟩ **b :** the height of an action or condition ⟨the *heat* of battle⟩ **c :** sexual receptiveness especially in a female mammal; *esp* **:** ESTRUS **3 :** pungency of flavor **4 :** a single continuous effort: as **a :** a single course in a race **b :** one of several preliminary races held to eliminate less competent contenders **5 a** *slang* **:** POLICE FORCE **b :** PRESSURE, COERCION ⟨the *heat* was on to get the job done⟩ — **heat·less** \ˈhēt-ləs\ *adj* — **heat-proof** \-ˈprüf\ *adj*

heat·ed \ˈhēt-əd\ *adj* **:** marked by anger ⟨*heated* words⟩ — **heat·ed·ly** *adv*

heat engine *n* **:** a mechanism for converting heat energy into mechanical energy

heat·er \ˈhēt-ər\ *n* **:** a device that imparts heat or holds something to be heated

heat exchanger *n* **:** a device (as an automobile radiator) for transferring heat from one fluid to another without allowing them to mix

heat exhaustion *n* **:** a condition marked by weakness, nausea, dizziness, and profuse sweating that results from physical exertion in a hot environment — called also *heat prostration*; compare HEATSTROKE

heath \ˈhēth\ *n* **1 :** any of a family of shrubby often evergreen plants that thrive on open barren usually acid and poorly drained soil; *esp* **:** a low evergreen shrub with whorls of needlelike leaves and clusters of small flowers **2 :** a tract of usually level and poorly drained uncultivated land commonly overgrown with low shrubs [Old English *hǣth*] — **heath·like** \-ˌlīk\ *adj* — **heathy** \ˈhē-thē\ *adj*

heath 1

^{1}**hea·then** \ˈhē-t͟hən\ *adj* **:** of or relating to heathens [Old English *hǣthen*]

^{2}**heathen** *n, pl* **heathens** *or* **heathen 1 :** an unconverted member of a people or nation that does not acknowledge the God of the Bible **2 :** an uncivilized or irreligious person — **hea·then·dom** \-dəm\ *n* — **hea·then·ism** \-t͟hə-ˌniz-əm\ *n*

hea·then·ish \ˈhē-t͟hə-nish\ *adj* **:** resembling or characteristic of heathens **:** BARBAROUS — **hea·then·ish·ly** *adv*

^{1}**heath·er** \ˈhet͟h-ər\ *n* **:** HEATH 1; *esp* **:** a common evergreen heath of northern and alpine regions with very small stemless leaves and tiny usually purplish pink flowers [Middle English *hather*] — **heath·ery** \ˈhet͟h-rē, -ə-rē\ *adj*

^{2}**heather** *adj* **1 :** of, relating to, or resembling heather **2 :** having flecks of various colors ⟨a soft *heather* tweed⟩

heath hen *n* **:** an extinct grouse of the northeastern U.S. related to the prairie chicken

heat lightning *n* : flashes of light without thunder caused by distant lightning reflected by high clouds
heat pump *n* : a device for heating or cooling a building by transferring heat contained in a fluid to or from the building
heat rash *n* : PRICKLY HEAT
heat shield *n* : a barrier of insulation to protect a space capsule from heat on its return to earth
heat sink *n* : a substance or device that absorbs or dissipates heat (as from an electronic device)
heat•stroke \ˈhēt-ˌstrōk\ *n* : a condition marked especially by cessation of sweating, high body temperature, and collapse that results from prolonged exposure to high temperature — compare HEAT EXHAUSTION
heat wave *n* : a period of unusually hot weather
[1]**heave** \ˈhēv\ *vb* **heaved** *or* **hove** \ˈhōv\; **heav•ing** **1** : to raise with an effort : LIFT ⟨*heave* a trunk onto a truck⟩ **2** : THROW, HURL ⟨*heave* a rock⟩ **3** : to utter with effort ⟨*heave* a sigh⟩ **4** : to rise and fall repeatedly ⟨the runner's chest was *heaving*⟩ **5** : to be thrown up or raised ⟨the ground *heaved* during the earthquake⟩ **6** : RETCH, VOMIT [Old English *hebban*] — **heav•er** *n* — **heave to** : to bring a ship to a stop
[2]**heave** *n* **1 a** : an effort to heave or raise **b** : a forceful throw : CAST **2** : an upward motion; *esp* : a rhythmical rising (as of the chest in breathing)
heav•en \ˈhev-ən\ *n* **1** : SKY 1 — usually used in plural **2 a** *often cap* : the dwelling place of God and the blessed dead **b** : a spiritual state of everlasting communion with God **3** *cap* : GOD 1 **4** : a place or condition of utmost happiness [Old English *heofon*]
heav•en•ly \ˈhev-ən-lē\ *adj* **1** : of or relating to heaven or the heavens **2** : suggesting the blessed state of heaven ⟨*heavenly* peace⟩ **3** : DELIGHTFUL ⟨a *heavenly* day⟩ — **heav•en•li•ness** *n*
heav•en•ward \ˈhev-ən-wərd\ *adv or adj* : toward heaven
heav•en•wards \-wərdz\ *adv* : HEAVENWARD
heavier–than–air *adj* : of greater weight than the air displaced
heav•i•ly \ˈhev-ə-lē\ *adv* **1** : in a heavy manner **2** : in a slow and laborious manner ⟨breathe *heavily*⟩ **3** : to a great degree : SEVERELY ⟨*heavily* punished⟩
[1]**heavy** \ˈhev-ē\ *adj* **heav•i•er; -est** **1 a** : having great weight **b** : weighty in proportion to bulk : having a high specific gravity ⟨*heavy* metals⟩ **c** : having or being atoms of greater than normal mass ⟨*heavy* isotopes⟩ **2** : hard to bear; *esp* : GRIEVOUS ⟨a *heavy* sorrow⟩ **3** : of great import : SERIOUS ⟨words *heavy* with meaning⟩ **4 a** : borne down by something oppressive : BURDENED **b** : PREGNANT 3; *esp* : approaching the time for giving birth **5 a** : slow or dull from loss of vitality or resiliency : SLUGGISH ⟨a tired *heavy* step⟩ **b** : lacking sparkle or vivacity ⟨a *heavy* writing style⟩ **c** : lacking mirth or gaiety **6** : dulled with weariness : DROWSY **7** : greater in volume, force, or power than the average ⟨*heavy* traffic⟩ ⟨*heavy* seas⟩ ⟨*heavy* infantry⟩ **8 a** : OVERCAST ⟨*heavy* skies⟩ **b** : full of clay and inclined to hold water ⟨*heavy* soils⟩ **c** : coming as if from a depth : LOUD ⟨*heavy* breathing⟩ **d** : OPPRESSIVE ⟨a *heavy* odor⟩ **e** : STEEP, ACUTE ⟨a *heavy* grade⟩ **f** : LABORIOUS, DIFFICULT ⟨a *heavy* task⟩ **g** : using or consuming much : IMMODERATE ⟨a *heavy* eater⟩ **9** : very rich and hard to digest ⟨a *heavy* dessert⟩ **10** : producing goods (as coal or steel) used in the production of other goods ⟨*heavy* industry⟩ **11** : having stress ⟨a *heavy* rhythm⟩ [Old English *hefig*] — **heav•i•ness** *n*
[2]**heavy** *adv* : in a heavy manner : HEAVILY ⟨walks *heavy*⟩
[3]**heavy** *n, pl* **heav•ies** **1** : HEAVYWEIGHT 2 **2 a** : a theatrical role or an actor representing a dignified or imposing person **b** : VILLAIN 4 **c** : VILLAIN 5
heavy chain *n* : either of the two larger of the four polypeptide chains comprising antibodies — compare LIGHT CHAIN
heavy–du•ty \ˌhev-ē-ˈdüt-ē, -ˈdyüt-\ *adj* : able or designed to withstand unusual strain ⟨*heavy-duty* garbage bags⟩
heavy–foot•ed \-ˈfu̇t-əd\ *adj* : heavy and slow in movement
heavy–hand•ed \-ˈhan-dəd\ *adj* **1** : CLUMSY 1 **2** : OPPRESSIVE, HARSH — **heavy–hand•ed•ly** *adv* — **heavy–hand•ed•ness** *n*
heavy•heart•ed \-ˈhärt-əd\ *adj* : SAD 1, MELANCHOLY — **heavy•heart•ed•ly** *adv* — **heavy•heart•ed•ness** *n*
heavy hydrogen *n* : DEUTERIUM
heavy•set \ˌhev-ē-ˈset\ *adj* : being stocky and compact and sometimes tending to stoutness in build
heavy water *n* : water enriched with deuterium
heavy•weight \ˈhev-ē-ˌwāt\ *n* **1** : one above average in weight **2** : one in the heaviest class of contestants; *esp* : a boxer in an unlimited weight division **3** : one with great power or stature
He•bra•ic \hi-ˈbrā-ik\ *adj* : of, relating to, or characteristic of the Hebrews or their language or culture
He•bra•ism \ˈhē-brā-ˌiz-əm\ *n* **1** : a characteristic feature of Hebrew occurring in another language **2** : the thought, spirit, or practice characteristic of the Hebrews
He•bra•ist \-ˌbrā-əst\ *n* : a specialist in Hebrew and Hebraic studies
He•brew \ˈhē-ˌbrü\ *n* **1** : a member of or descendant from one of a group of northern Semitic peoples including the Israelites; *esp* : ISRAELITE **2 a** : the Semitic language of the ancient Hebrews **b** : any of various later forms of this language [derived from Greek *Hebraios,* from Aramaic *ʽEbrai*] — **Hebrew** *adj*
He•brews \ˈhē-ˌbrüz\ *n* : a theological treatise addressed to early Christians and included as a book in the New Testament — see BIBLE table
hec•a•tomb \ˈhek-ə-ˌtōm\ *n* **1** : an ancient Greek and Roman sacrifice of 100 oxen or cattle **2** : a great slaughter or sacrifice of many victims [Latin *hecatombe,* from Greek *hekatombē,* from *hekaton* "hundred" + *bous* "cow"]
heck•le \ˈhek-əl\ *vt* **heck•led; heck•ling** \ˈhek-ling, -ə-ling\ : to interrupt with questions or comments usually in order to annoy or hinder : BADGER ⟨*heckled* the speaker⟩ [Middle English *hekelen* "to dress flax, scratch," from *heckele* "hackle"] — **heck•ler** \-lər, -ə-lər\ *n*
hect- *or* **hecto-** *combining form* : hundred [French, derived from Greek *hekaton*]
hect•are \ˈhek-ˌtaər, -ˌteər, -ˌtär\ *n* — see METRIC SYSTEM table
hec•tic \ˈhek-tik\ *adj* **1** : of, relating to, or being a fluctuating but persistent fever (as in tuberculosis) **2** : having a hectic fever **3** : RED, FLUSHED **4** : filled with excitement, activity, or confusion ⟨a *hectic* first day of school⟩ [derived from Late Latin *hecticus,* from Greek *hektikos* "habitual, consumptive," from *echein* "to have, hold"] — **hec•ti•cal•ly** \-ti-kə-lē, -klē\ *adv*
hec•to•gram \ˈhek-təˌgram\ *n* — see METRIC SYSTEM table
hec•to•graph \-ˌgraf\ *n* : a machine for making copies of a writing or drawing — **hectograph** *vt*
hec•to•li•ter \ˈhek-tə-ˌlēt-ər\ *n* — see METRIC SYSTEM table
hec•to•me•ter \ˈhek-tə-ˌmēt-ər\ *n* — see METRIC SYSTEM table
hec•tor \ˈhek-tər\ *vb* **hec•tored; hec•tor•ing** \-tə-ring, -tring\ **1** : to act like a bully : SWAGGER **2** : to intimidate by bluster or personal pressure [*Hector,* Trojan champion]
he'd \hēd, ˌhēd, ēd\ : he had : he would
hed•dle \ˈhed-l\ *n* : one of the sets of parallel cords or wires that with their mounting compose the harness used to guide warp threads in a loom [probably derived from Old English *hefeld*]
[1]**hedge** \ˈhej\ *n* **1 a** : a fence or boundary formed by a dense row of shrubs or low trees **b** : a fence or wall marking a boundary or forming a barrier **2** : a protection against financial loss **3** : a statement that intentionally avoids a direct answer or a promise [Old English *hecg*]
[2]**hedge** *vb* **1** : to enclose or protect with or as if with a hedge **2** : to obstruct with or as if with a barrier : HINDER ⟨*hedged* in by restrictions⟩ **3** : to protect oneself from losing by making a second balancing transaction ⟨*hedge* a bet⟩ **4** : to avoid giving a direct or definite answer or promise ⟨*hedged* when asked their opinion⟩ — **hedg•er** *n*
[3]**hedge** *adj* : of, relating to, or designed for a hedge
hedge•hog \ˈhej-ˌhȯg, -ˌhäg\ *n* **1** : any of several Eurasian and African insect-eating nocturnal mammals having sharp spines mixed with the hair on their back and able to roll themselves up into a spiny ball when threatened **2** : PORCUPINE

hedgehog 1

hedge•hop \-ˌhäp\ *vi* : to fly an airplane so low that it is sometimes necessary to climb to avoid obstacles (as trees) [back-formation from *hedgehopper*] — **hedge•hop•per** *n*

\ə\ **abut**	\au̇\ **out**	\i\ **tip**	\ȯ\ **saw**	\u̇\ **foot**
\ər\ **further**	\ch\ **chin**	\ī\ **life**	\ȯi\ **coin**	\y\ **yet**
\a\ **mat**	\e\ **pet**	\j\ **job**	\th\ **thin**	\yü\ **few**
\ā\ **take**	\ē\ **easy**	\ng\ **sing**	\t͟h\ **this**	\yu̇\ **cure**
\ä\ **cot, cart**	\g\ **go**	\ō\ **bone**	\ü\ **food**	\zh\ **vision**

hedge·row \-ˌrō\ *n* : a row of shrubs or trees enclosing or separating fields

he·do·nism \ˈhēd-n-ˌiz-əm\ *n* **1** : a doctrine that pleasure or happiness is the sole or chief good in life **2** : a way of life based on hedonism [Greek *hēdonē* "pleasure"] — **he·do·nist** \-n-əst\ *n* — **he·do·nis·tic** \ˌhēd-n-ˈis-tik\ *adj*

-he·dral \ˈhē-drəl\ *adj combining form* : having (such) a surface or (such or so many) surfaces ⟨di*hedral*⟩ [Greek *hedra* "seat"]

-he·dron \ˈhē-drən\ *n combining form, pl* **-hedrons** *or* **-he·dra** \-drə\ : crystal or geometric figure having a (specified) form or number of surfaces ⟨rhombo*hedron*⟩ [Greek *hedra* "seat"]

hee·bie–jee·bies \ˌhē-bē-ˈjē-bēz\ *n pl* : JITTERS, WILLIES [coined by Billy DeBeck, died 1942, American cartoonist]

¹heed \ˈhēd\ *vb* **1** : to pay attention **2** : to concern oneself with : MIND [Old English *hēdan*]

²heed *n* : ATTENTION 1, NOTICE ⟨pay *heed* to my words⟩

heed·ful \ˈhēd-fəl\ *adj* : taking heed : ATTENTIVE ⟨*heedful* of the rights of others⟩ — **heed·ful·ly** \-fə-lē\ *adv* — **heed·ful·ness** *n*

heed·less \-ləs\ *adj* : not taking heed : INATTENTIVE ⟨*heedless* of danger⟩ — **heed·less·ly** *adv* — **heed·less·ness** *n*

hee–haw \ˈhē-ˌhȯ\ *n* **1** : the bray of a donkey **2** : a loud rude laugh : GUFFAW [imitative] — **hee–haw** *vi*

¹heel \ˈhēl\ *n* **1 a** : the back part of the human foot behind the arch and below the ankle; *also* : the corresponding part of the hind limb of other vertebrates **b** : the part of the palm of the hand nearest the wrist **2 a** : a part (as of a shoe) that covers the human heel **b** : a solid attachment of a shoe or boot forming the back of the sole under the heel of the foot **3** : something resembling a heel in form, function, or position: as **a** : one of the crusty ends of a loaf of bread **b** (1) : the after end of a ship's keel (2) : the lower end of a mast **c** : the base of a tuber or cutting of a plant used for propagation **d** : the base of a ladder **4** : a contemptible person [Old English *hēla*] — **heel·less** \ˈhēl-ləs\ *adj* — **on the heels of** : immediately following — **to heel 1** : close behind **2** : into agreement or into line

²heel *vt* **1** : to furnish with a heel **2** : to supply especially with money ⟨a well-*heeled* customer⟩ **3** : to follow closely ⟨a dog *heeling* his master⟩ — **heel·er** *n*

³heel *vb* : to tilt or cause to tilt to one side : TIP ⟨a boat *heeling* badly⟩ [Old English *hieldan*]

⁴heel *n* : a tilt to one side

heel–and–toe \ˌhē-lən-ˈtō\ *adj* : marked by a stride in which the heel of one foot touches the ground before the toe of the other foot leaves it ⟨a *heel-and-toe* walking race⟩

¹heft \ˈheft\ *n* : physical or figurative weight [derived from *heave*]

²heft *vt* **1** : to heave up : HOIST **2** : to test the weight of by lifting

hefty \ˈhef-tē\ *adj* **heft·i·er; -est 1** : quite heavy **2 a** : marked by bigness, bulk, and usually strength **b** : POWERFUL, MIGHTY **c** : impressively large : SUBSTANTIAL — **heft·i·ly** \-tə-lē\ *adv* — **heft·i·ness** \-tē-nəs\ *n*

he·gem·o·ny \hi-ˈjem-ə-nē, ˈhej-ə-ˌmō-nē\ *n* : dominant influence or authority especially of one nation over others [Greek *hēgemonia,* from *hēgemōn* "leader," from *hēgeisthai* "to lead"]

he·gi·ra *also* **he·ji·ra** \hi-ˈjī-rə, ˈhej-ə-rə\ *n* : a journey especially when undertaken to seek refuge away from a dangerous or undesirable situation [the *Hegira,* flight of Muhammad from Mecca in A.D. 622, from Medieval Latin, from Arabic *hijrah,* literally, "departure"]

heif·er \ˈhef-ər\ *n* : a young cow; *esp* : one that has not had a calf [Old English *hēahfore*]

heigh–ho \ˈhī-ˈhō, ˈhā-\ *interj* — used typically to express boredom, weariness, or sadness or sometimes as a cry of encouragement

height \ˈhīt, ˈhītth\ *n* **1 a** : the highest part : SUMMIT **b** : the highest or most advanced point or level ⟨the *height* of stupidity⟩ **2 a** : the distance from the bottom to the top of something standing upright **b** : the extent of elevation above a level : ALTITUDE **3** : the condition of being tall or high **4 a** : an extent of land rising to a considerable degree above the surrounding country **b** : a high point or position [Old English *hīehthu*]

synonyms HEIGHT, ELEVATION, ALTITUDE mean distance upward. HEIGHT refers to something measured vertically whether high or low ⟨a wall 2 meters in *height*⟩ ⟨lettering not more than one centimeter in *height*⟩. ALTITUDE is preferable when referring to vertical distance above the surface of the earth or above sea level ⟨fly at an *altitude* of 5000 feet⟩. ELEVATION is used especially in reference to vertical height on land ⟨Mexico City has a high *elevation*⟩.

height·en \ˈhīt-n\ *vb* **height·ened; height·en·ing** \ˈhīt-ning, -n-ing\ **1 a** : to increase the amount or degree of : AUGMENT ⟨*heightened* the citizens' awareness⟩ **b** : to make or become brighter or more intense : DEEPEN ⟨excitement *heightened* the pinkness of their cheeks⟩ **c** : to bring out more strongly : point up ⟨*heighten* a contrast⟩ **2 a** : to raise high or higher : ELEVATE **b** : to raise above the ordinary or trite ***synonyms*** see INTENSIFY

Heim·lich maneuver \ˈhīm-lik-\ *n* : a technique for forcing an object out of the trachea of a choking person that involves standing behind the person with arms wrapped about the person's waist and applying sudden upward pressure with the fist to the abdomen above the navel [Henry J. Heimlich, born 1920, American surgeon]

hei·nous \ˈhā-nəs\ *adj* : hatefully or shockingly evil : ABOMINABLE [Medieval French *hainus, heinous,* from *haine* "hate," from *hair* "to hate," of Germanic origin] ***synonyms*** see OUTRAGEOUS — **hei·nous·ly** *adv* — **hei·nous·ness** *n*

heir \ˈaər, ˈeər\ *n* **1** : a person who inherits or is entitled to inherit property **2** : a person who has legal claim to a title, rank, or office when the person holding it dies ⟨*heir* to the throne⟩ [Medieval French, from Latin *heres*] — **heir·ship** \-ˌship\ *n*

heir apparent *n, pl* **heirs apparent** : an heir who cannot legally be deprived of the right to succeed (as to a throne or a title) if she or he outlives the present holder

heir·ess \ˈar-əs, ˈer-\ *n* : a woman who is an heir especially to great wealth

heir·loom \ˈaər-ˌlüm, ˈeər-\ *n* : a piece of personal property handed down by inheritance for several generations [Middle English *heirlome,* from *heir* + *lome* "implement"]

heir presumptive *n, pl* **heirs presumptive** : an heir whose present right to inherit could be lost through the birth of a nearer relative

¹heist \ˈhīst\ *vt* **1** *chiefly dialect* : HOIST **2 a** : to commit armed robbery on **b** : STEAL 2a [alteration of *hoist*]

²heist *n* : armed robbery : HOLDUP; *also* : THEFT

held *past of* HOLD

heli- *or* **helio-** *combining form* : sun ⟨*helio*centric⟩ [Greek *hēlios*]

helic- *or* **helico-** *combining form* : helix : spiral ⟨*helic*al⟩ [Greek *helik-, helix* "spiral"]

hel·i·cal \ˈhel-i-kəl, ˈhē-li-\ *adj* : of, relating to, or having the form of a helix; *also* : SPIRAL 1 — **hel·i·cal·ly** \-kə-lē, -klē\ *adv*

hel·i·con \ˈhel-ə-ˌkän, -i-kən\ *n* : a large circular bass tuba used in military bands [probably derived from Greek *helix* "spiral"]

¹he·li·cop·ter \ˈhel-ə-ˌkäp-tər, ˈhē-lə-\ *n* : an aircraft that is supported in the air by propellers revolving on a vertical axis [French *hélicoptère,* from Greek *helix* "helix" + *pteron* "wing"]

²helicopter *vb* : to travel or transport by helicopter

he·lio·cen·tric \ˌhē-lē-ō-ˈsen-trik\ *adj* **1** : referred to or measured from the sun's center or appearing as if seen from it ⟨a *heliocentric* position⟩ **2** : having or relating to the sun as a center ⟨a *heliocentric* theory of the solar system⟩ — compare GEOCENTRIC

he·lio·graph \ˈhē-lē-ə-ˌgraf\ *n* : an apparatus for signaling by means of the sun's rays reflected from a mirror — **heliograph** *vb*

he·li·o·sphere \ˈhē-lē-ə-ˌsfir, -ō-\ *n* : the region of space that is influenced by the sun or solar wind — **he·li·o·spher·ic** \ˌhē-lē-ə-ˈsfir-ik, -ō-\ *adj*

he·lio·trope \ˈhēl-yə-ˌtrōp\ *n* **1** : any of a genus of herbs or shrubs related to the forget-me-not — compare GARDEN HELIOTROPE **2** : BLOODSTONE **3** : a color varying from a moderate to reddish purple [Latin *heliotropium,* from Greek *hēliotropion,* from *hēlios* "sun" + *tropos* "turn"; from its flowers turning toward the sun]

he·li·ot·ro·pism \ˌhē-lē-ˈä-trə-ˌpiz-əm\ *n* : phototropism in which sunlight is the orienting stimulus — **he·lio·tro·pic** \ˌhē-lē-ə-ˈtrōp-ik, -ˈträp-\ *adj*

he·li·port \ˈhel-ə-ˌpōrt, ˈhē-lə-, -ˌpȯrt\ *n* : a landing and takeoff place for a helicopter

he·li·um \ˈhē-lē-əm\ *n* : a light colorless nonflammable gaseous element found in various natural gases and used especially for inflating airships and balloons — see ELEMENT table [New Latin, from Greek *hēlios* "sun"; from its first being observed in the sun's atmosphere]

he·lix \ˈhē-liks\ *n, pl* **he·li·ces** \ˈhel-ə-ˌsēz, ˈhē-lə-ˌsēz\ *also*

he·lix·es \ˈhē-lik-səz\ **1 :** something (as a wire coiled around a cylinder, a cone-shaped wire spring, or a corkscrew) spiral in form — compare DOUBLE HELIX **2 :** the incurved rim of the external ear **3 :** a curve formed by a point tracing a line around the surface of a cylinder or cone in such a way that the line always makes the same oblique angle with the cylinder or cone's cross sections; *also* **:** SPIRAL 1b [Latin, from Greek]

hell \ˈhel\ *n* **1 :** a nether world in which the dead are held to continue to exist **:** HADES **2 :** a place or state of punishment for the wicked after death **:** the home of evil spirits **3 :** a place or condition of misery or wickedness **4 :** a place or state of turmoil or destruction **5 :** something that causes torment; *esp* **:** a severe scolding [Old English]

he'll \hēl, ˌhel, hil, ēl, il\ **:** he shall **:** he will

hell·ben·der \ˈhel-ˌben-dər\ *n* **:** a large aquatic salamander of eastern and central U.S. streams

hell–bent \-ˌbent\ *adj* **:** stubbornly and often recklessly determined

hell·cat \-ˌkat\ *n* **:** a violently temperamental person; *esp* **:** SHREW 2

hel·le·bore \ˈhel-ə-ˌbōr, -ˌbȯr\ *n* **1 :** any of a genus of poisonous herbs related to the buttercups; *also* **:** its dried root formerly used in medicine **2 :** a poisonous herb related to the lilies; *also* **:** its dried root or a product of this containing alkaloids used in medicine and insecticides [Latin *helleborus,* from Greek *helleboros*]

hellebore 1

Hel·lene \ˈhel-ˌēn\ *n* **:** GREEK 1 [Greek *Hellēn*] — **Hel·len·ic** \he-ˈlen-ik, hə-\ *adj*

Hel·le·nism \ˈhel-ə-ˌniz-əm\ *n* **1 :** devotion to or imitation of especially ancient Greek thought, customs, or styles **2 :** Greek civilization **3 :** a body of humanistic and classical ideals associated with ancient Greece

Hel·le·nist \-nəst\ *n* **1 :** a person living in Hellenistic times who was Greek in language, outlook, and way of life but not in ancestry; *esp* **:** a hellenized Jew **2 :** a specialist in the language or culture of ancient Greece

Hel·le·nis·tic \ˌhel-ə-ˈnis-tik\ *adj* **1 :** of or relating to Greek history, culture, or art after the conquests of Alexander the Great **2 :** of or relating to the Hellenists — **Hel·le·nis·ti·cal·ly** \-ti-kə-lē, -klē\ *adv*

hel·le·nize \ˈhel-ə-ˌnīz\ *vb, often cap* **:** to make or become Greek or Hellenistic in form or culture — **hel·le·ni·za·tion** \ˌhel-ə-nə-ˈzā-shən\ *n, often cap*

hell·er \ˈhel-ər\ *n* **:** HELLION

hell·gram·mite \ˈhel-grə-ˌmīt\ *n* **:** the aquatic larva of a dobsonfly much used as fish bait [origin unknown]

hel·lion \ˈhel-yən\ *n* **:** a troublesome or mischievous person [probably from earlier *hallion* "scamp"]

hell·ish \ˈhel-ish\ *adj* **:** of, resembling, or befitting hell **:** DEVILISH — **hell·ish·ly** *adv* — **hell·ish·ness** *n*

hel·lo \hə-ˈlō, he-\ *n, pl* **hellos :** an expression or gesture of greeting — used interjectionally in greeting, in answering the telephone, or to express surprise [alteration of *hollo*]

[1]**helm** \ˈhelm\ *n* **:** HELMET 1 [Old English]

[2]**helm** *vt* **:** to cover or furnish with a helmet

[3]**helm** *n* **1 :** a lever or wheel controlling the rudder of a ship for steering; *also* **:** the entire apparatus for steering a ship **2 :** a position of control ⟨at the *helm* of the business⟩ [Old English *helma*]

hel·met \ˈhel-mət\ *n* **1 :** a covering or enclosing headpiece of ancient or medieval armor **2 :** any of various protective head coverings usually made of a hard material to resist impact **3 :** something resembling a helmet [Medieval French, from *helme* "helmet," of Germanic origin] — **helmet·like** \-ˌlīk\ *adj*

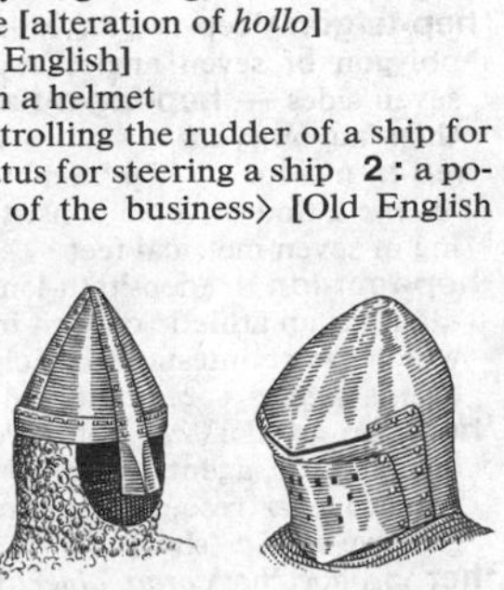
helmet 1

hel·minth \ˈhel-ˌminth, -ˌmintth\ *n* **:** a parasitic worm; *esp* **:** an intestinal worm (as a tapeworm) [Greek *helminth-, helmis*] — **hel·min·thic** \hel-ˈmin-thik, -ˈmint-\ *adj*

hel·min·thi·a·sis \ˌhel-ˌmin-ˈthī-ə-səs\ *n* **:** infestation with or disease caused by parasitic worms

hel·min·thol·o·gy \-ˈthäl-ə-jē\ *n* **:** a branch of zoology concerned with the study of parasitic worms

helms·man \ˈhelmz-mən\ *n* **:** the person at the helm **:** STEERSMAN

hel·ot \ˈhel-ət\ *n* **1** *cap* **:** a member of a class of serfs of ancient Sparta **2 :** SLAVE 1, SERF [Latin *Helotes,* pl., from Greek *Heilōtes*] — **hel·ot·ry** \-ə-trē\ *n*

[1]**help** \ˈhelp, *South also* ˈhep\ *vb* **1 :** to give aid or assistance ⟨*help* a child with a lesson⟩ **2 :** REMEDY, RELIEVE ⟨rest *helps* a cold⟩ **3 :** to further the advancement of **:** PROMOTE ⟨*helping* industrial development with loans⟩ **4 a :** to change for the better ⟨learn to live with what you can't *help*⟩ **b :** to refrain from ⟨couldn't *help* laughing⟩ **c :** to keep from occurring **:** PREVENT ⟨they couldn't *help* the accident⟩ **5 :** to serve with food or drink especially at a meal ⟨told guests to *help* themselves⟩ **6 :** to appropriate for the use of (oneself) ⟨*helped* herself to my bike⟩ [Old English *helpan*] — **so help me :** on my word **:** believe it or not

[2]**help** *n* **1 :** an act or instance of helping **:** AID, ASSISTANCE ⟨give *help*⟩ **2 :** the state of being helped **:** RELIEF ⟨a situation beyond *help*⟩ **3 :** a person or a thing that helps ⟨a *help* in time of trouble⟩ **4 :** a hired helper or a body of hired helpers ⟨hire additional *help* in a business⟩

help·er \ˈhel-pər\ *n* **:** one that helps; *esp* **:** a relatively unskilled worker who assists a skilled worker usually by manual labor

helper T cell *n* **:** a T cell that participates in an immune response by recognizing a foreign antigen and secreting substances which promote T cell and B cell proliferation and that is destroyed in large numbers by infection with HIV — called also *helper cell*

help·ful \ˈhelp-fəl\ *adj* **:** furnishing help ⟨a *helpful* friend⟩ ⟨a *helpful* book⟩ — **help·ful·ly** \-fə-lē\ *adv* — **help·ful·ness** *n*

help·ing \ˈhel-ping\ *n* **:** a portion of food **:** SERVING

helping verb *n* **:** a verb (as *have, be, may, do, shall, will, can, must*) that is used with another verb and expresses such things as person, number, mood, or tense — called also *auxiliary verb*

help·less \ˈhel-pləs\ *adj* **1 :** lacking protection or support **:** DEFENSELESS **2 :** lacking strength or effectiveness **:** POWERLESS ⟨was *helpless* to prevent them from going⟩ — **help·less·ly** *adv* — **help·less·ness** *n*

help·mate \ˈhelp-ˌmāt\ *n* **:** one that is a companion and helper; *esp* **:** WIFE [by folk etymology from *helpmeet*]

help·meet \-ˌmēt\ *n* **:** HELPMATE [[2]*help + meet,* adj.]

[1]**hel·ter–skel·ter** \ˌhel-tər-ˈskel-tər\ *adv* **1 :** in a confused and reckless manner **:** PELL-MELL **2 :** in no particular order **:** HAPHAZARDLY [perhaps from Middle English *skelten* "to come, go"]

[2]**helter–skelter** *n* **:** a disorderly confusion **:** TURMOIL

[3]**helter–skelter** *adj* **1 :** confusedly hurried **:** PRECIPITATE ⟨*helter-skelter* rush-hour traffic⟩ **2 :** HIT-OR-MISS, HAPHAZARD ⟨does things in a *helter-skelter* manner⟩

helve \ˈhelv\ *n* **:** a handle of a tool or weapon **:** HAFT [Old English *hielfe*]

Hel·ve·tian \hel-ˈvē-shən\ *adj* **:** of or relating to the Helvetii or Helvetia **:** SWISS — **Helvetian** *n*

Hel·ve·tii \-shē-ˌī\ *n pl* **:** an early Celtic people of western Switzerland in the time of Julius Caesar [Latin]

[1]**hem** \ˈhem\ *n* **:** a border of a garment or cloth made by folding back an edge and sewing it down [Old English]

[2]**hem** *vb* **hemmed; hem·ming 1 :** to finish with or make a hem in sewing **2 :** to surround in a restrictive manner **:** CONFINE ⟨*hemmed* in by the enemy⟩ — **hem·mer** *n*

[3]**hem** *vi* **hemmed; hem·ming 1 :** to utter the sound represented by *hem* **2 :** EQUIVOCATE ⟨*hemmed* and hawed and refused to act⟩

[4]**hem** *usually read as* ˈhem\ *interj* — often used to indicate a vocalized pause in speaking [imitative]

hem- *or* **hemo-** *combining form* **:** blood ⟨*hemo*cyanin⟩ [Greek *haima*]

he–man \ˈhē-ˈman\ *n* **:** a strong virile man

\ə\ **abut**	\au̇\ **out**	\i\ **tip**	\ȯ\ **saw**	\u̇\ **foot**
\ər\ **further**	\ch\ **chin**	\ī\ **life**	\ȯi\ **coin**	\y\ **yet**
\a\ **mat**	\e\ **pet**	\j\ **job**	\th\ **thin**	\yü\ **few**
\ā\ **take**	\ē\ **easy**	\ng\ **sing**	\t͟h\ **this**	\yu̇\ **cure**
\ä\ **cot, cart**	\g\ **go**	\ō\ **bone**	\ü\ **food**	\zh\ **vision**

hemat- *or* **hemato-** *combining form* : blood ⟨*hemato*logy⟩ [Greek *haimat-, haima*]

he·ma·tite \ˈhē-mə-ˌtīt\ *n* : a reddish brown or black mineral consisting of ferric oxide, constituting an important iron ore, and occurring in crystals or in a red earthy form

he·ma·tol·o·gy \ˌhē-mə-ˈtäl-ə-jē\ *n* : a branch of medicine that deals with the blood and blood-forming organs — **he·ma·to·log·ic** \ˈhē-mət-l-ˈäj-ik\ *adj* — **he·ma·tol·o·gist** \ˌhē-mə-ˈtäl-ə-jəst\ *n*

he·ma·to·ma \ˌhē-mə-ˈtō-mə\ *n, pl* **-mas** *also* **-ma·ta** \-mət-ə\ : a blood-containing tumor or swelling

he·ma·tox·y·lin \ˌhē-mə-ˈtäk-sə-lən\ *n* : a crystalline compound found in logwood and used chiefly as a biological stain [New Latin *Haematoxylon,* genus of plants that includes the logwood]

heme \ˈhēm\ *n* : a deep red iron-containing pigment obtained from hemoglobin [derived from Greek *haima* "blood"]

hem·ero·cal·lis \ˌhem-ə-rō-ˈkal-əs\ *n* : DAYLILY [Greek *hēmerokalles,* from *hēmera* "day" + *kallos* "beauty"]

hemi- *prefix* : half — compare SEMI [Greek *hēmi-*]

hemi·chor·date \ˌhem-i-ˈkȯrd-ət, -ˈkȯr-ˌdāt\ *n* : any of a small group (Hemichordata) of wormlike marine animals (as an acorn worm) having a proboscis that contains a structure superficially resembling the notochord of chordates

he·mip·ter·an \hi-ˈmip-tə-rən\ *n* : any of a large order (Hemiptera) of insects (as the true bugs) having flattened bodies, piercing and sucking mouth parts, and two pairs of wings with the forewings leathery at the base [Greek *pteron* "wing"] — **he·mip·ter·ous** \-tə-rəs\ *adj*

hemi·sphere \ˈhem-ə-ˌsfier\ *n* **1** : the northern or southern half of the earth as divided by the equator or the eastern or western half as divided by a meridian **2** : one of two halves of a sphere **3** : CEREBRAL HEMISPHERE — **hemi·spher·ic** \ˌhem-ə-ˈsfiər-ik, -ˈsfer-\ *or* **hemi·spher·i·cal** \-ˈsfir-i-kəl, -ˈsfer-\ *adj*

hemi·stich \ˈhem-i-ˌstik\ *n* : half a poetic line usually divided by a caesura [Latin *hemistichium,* from Greek *hēmistichion,* from *hēmi-* + *stichos* "line, verse"]

hem·line \ˈhem-ˌlīn\ *n* : the line formed by the lower edge of a dress, skirt, or coat

hem·lock \ˈhem-ˌläk\ *n* **1** : any of several poisonous herbs (as the poison hemlock or water hemlock) related to the carrot and having finely cut leaves and small white flowers **2** : any of a genus of evergreen trees related to the pines; *also* : the soft light splintery wood of a hemlock [Old English *hemlic*]

hemo- — see HEM-

he·mo·cy·a·nin \ˌhē-mō-ˈsī-ə-nən\ *n* : a copper-containing respiratory pigment in the blood of some mollusks and arthropods

he·mo·glo·bin \ˈhē-mə-ˌglō-bən\ *n* : an iron-containing protein that is the chief means of oxygen transport in the vertebrate body where it occurs in the red blood cells and is able to combine loosely with oxygen in regions (as the lungs) of high concentration and release it in regions (as the tissues of internal organs) of low concentration; *also* : any of various similar iron-containing compounds [derived from Greek *haima* "blood" + Latin *globus* "globe"]

hemoglobin S *n* : an abnormal hemoglobin that occurs in the red blood cells in sickle-cell anemia and sickle-cell trait

he·mo·phil·ia \ˌhē-mə-ˈfil-ē-ə\ *n* : an inherited blood defect that is sex-linked, is found almost always in males, and is marked by delayed clotting of blood and a resulting difficulty in stopping bleeding — **he·mo·phil·i·ac** \-ē-ˌak\ *adj or n*

hem·or·rhage \ˈhem-rij, -ə-rij\ *n* **1** : an abundant discharge of blood from the blood vessels **2** : a rapid and uncontrollable loss or outflow ⟨a financial *hemorrhage*⟩ [Latin *haemorrhagia,* from Greek *haimorrhagia,* from *haima* "blood" + *rhēgnynai* "to break"] — **hemorrhage** *vi* — **hem·or·rhag·ic** \ˌhem-ə-ˈraj-ik\ *adj*

hem·or·rhoid \ˈhem-ˌrȯid, -ə-ˌrȯid\ *n* : a swollen mass of dilated veins situated at or just within the anus — usually used in plural; called also *piles* [derived from Greek *haimorrhoides* "hemorrhoids," from *haima* "blood" + *rhein* "to flow"] — **hem·or·rhoid·al** \ˌhem-ə-ˈrȯid-l\ *adj*

hemp \ˈhemp\ *n* **1** : a tall Asian herb widely grown for its tough bast fiber that is used especially in cordage or for its flowers and leaves that yield drugs (as hashish and marijuana) that affect the mind or behavior **2** : the fiber of hemp [Old English *hænep*]

hemp·en \ˈhem-pən\ *adj* : made of hemp

[1]**hem·stitch** \ˈhem-ˌstich\ *vt* : to embroider (fabric) by drawing out parallel threads and stitching the exposed threads in groups to form various designs — **hem·stitch·er** *n*

[2]**hemstitch** *n* **1** : decorative needlework **2** : a stitch used in hemstitching

hen \ˈhen\ *n* **1** : a female chicken especially over a year old; *also* : a female bird **2** : the female of various mostly aquatic animals (as lobsters or fish) [Old English *henn*]

hen·bane \ˈhen-ˌbān\ *n* : a poisonous ill-smelling Eurasian herb of the nightshade family with sticky leaves

hence \ˈhens\ *adv* **1** : from this place : AWAY **2** : from this time ⟨a week *hence*⟩ **3** : CONSEQUENTLY, THEREFORE ⟨was a newcomer and *hence* had no close friends in the city⟩ [Middle English *hennes, henne,* from Old English *heonan*]

hence·forth \-ˌfōrth, -ˌfȯrth\ *adv* : from this point on

hence·for·ward \hens-ˈfȯr-wərd\ *adv* : HENCEFORTH

hench·man \ˈhench-mən\ *n* : a trusted follower or supporter ⟨a gangster's *henchman*⟩ [Middle English *henshman, hengestman* "groom," from *hengest* "stallion" + *man*]

hen·e·quen \ˈhen-i-kən, ˌhen-i-ˈken\ *n* : a strong hard cordage fiber from the leaves of a tropical American agave; *also* : the plant that yields henequen [Spanish *henequén*]

[1]**hen·na** \ˈhen-ə\ *n* **1** : an Old World tropical shrub with clusters of fragrant white flowers **2** : a reddish brown dye obtained from leaves of the henna and used especially on hair [Arabic *ḥinnā'*]

[2]**henna** *vb* **hen·naed** \ˈhen-əd\; **hen·na·ing** : to treat or dye with henna

hen·nery \ˈhen-ə-rē\ *n, pl* **-ner·ies** : a poultry farm; *also* : a poultry enclosure or house

hen party *n* : a party for women only

hen·peck \ˈhen-ˌpek\ *vt* : to subject (one's husband) to persistent nagging and domination

hen·ry \ˈhen-rē\ *n, pl* **henries** *also* **henrys** : a unit of inductance equal to the self-inductance of a circuit or the mutual inductance of two circuits in which the variation of one ampere per second results in an induced electromotive force of one volt [Joseph *Henry,* died 1878, American physicist]

hep *variant of* [3]HIP

hep·a·rin \ˈhep-ə-rən\ *n* : a compound found especially in the liver and lungs that slows the clotting of blood and is used medically [Greek *hēpar* "liver"]

he·pat·ic \hi-ˈpat-ik\ *adj* : of, relating to, affecting, or conveying to or away from the liver ⟨*hepatic* veins⟩ ⟨*hepatic* arteries⟩ [Latin *hepaticus,* from Greek *hēpatikos,* from *hēpar* "liver"]

he·pat·i·ca \hi-ˌpat-i-kə\ *n* : any of a genus of herbs related to the buttercups and having lobed leaves and delicate white, pink, or bluish flowers [Medieval Latin, from Latin *hepaticus* "hepatic"]

hep·a·ti·tis \ˌhep-ə-ˈtīt-əs\ *n, pl* **-tit·i·des** \-ˈtit-ə-ˌdēz\ *also* **-ti·tis·es** \-ˈtit-ə-səz\ : inflammation of the liver; *also* : any of several virus diseases marked especially by inflammation of the liver

hepped up \ˈhep-ˈtəp\ *adj* : ENTHUSIASTIC ⟨all *hepped up* about the new job⟩

Hep·ple·white \ˈhep-əl-ˌhwīt, -ˌwīt\ *adj* : of or relating to a style of furniture originating in late 18th century England [George *Hepplewhite,* died 1786, English cabinetmaker]

hepta- *or* **hept-** *combining form* : seven ⟨*hepta*meter⟩ [Greek *hepta*]

hep·ta·gon \ˈhep-tə-ˌgän\ *n* : a polygon of seven angles and seven sides — **hep·tag·o·nal** \hep-ˈtag-ən-l\ *adj*

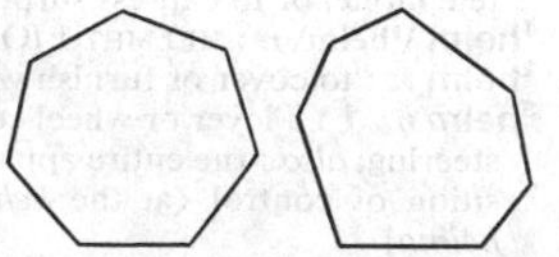

heptagon

hep·tam·e·ter \hep-ˈtam-ət-ər\ *n* : a line of verse consisting of seven metrical feet

hep·tath·lon \hep-ˈtath-lən, -ˌlän\ *n* : an athletic contest in which each contestant participates in 7 different track-and-field events [*hepta-* + *-athlon* (as in dec*athlon*)]

[1]**her** \hər, ər, ˌhər\ *adj* : of or relating to her or herself especially as possessor, agent, or object of an action ⟨*her* house⟩ ⟨*her* research⟩ ⟨*her* rescue⟩ — compare [1]SHE 1 [Old English *hiere,* genitive of *hēo* "she"]

[2]**her** \ər, hər, ˈhər\ *pron, objective case of* SHE

[1]**her·ald** \ˈher-əld\ *n* **1 a** : an official at a medieval tournament **b** : an officer acting as messenger between leaders of warring parties **c** : an officer responsible for granting and registering coats of arms **2** : an official crier or messenger **3** : one that

precedes or foreshadows : HARBINGER [Medieval French *heraud, herald,* of Germanic origin]

²**herald** *vt* **1** : to give notice of : ANNOUNCE **2** : to greet especially with enthusiasm : HAIL

he·ral·dic \he-ˈral-dik\ *adj* : of or relating to heralds or heraldry — **he·ral·di·cal·ly** \-di-kə-lē, -klē\ *adv*

her·ald·ry \ˈher-əl-drē\ *n, pl* **-ries** **1** : the practice of tracing a person's family history and determining its coat of arms **2** : COAT OF ARMS **3** : PAGEANTRY 2

herb \ˈərb, ˈhərb\ *n* **1** : an annual, biennial, or perennial seed-producing plant that does not develop persistent woody tissue but dies down at the end of a growing season **2** : a plant or plant part used in medicine or for seasoning [Medieval French *herbe,* from Latin *herba* "grass, herb"] — **herb·like** \ˈərb-ˌlīk, ˈhərb-\ *adj* — **herby** \ˈər-bē, ˈhər-\ *adj*

her·ba·ceous \ər-ˈbā-shəs, hər-\ *adj* **1** : of, relating to, or resembling an herb **2** : being a stem with little or no woody tissue and lasting usually only for a single growing season

herb·age \ˈər-bij, ˈhər-\ *n* **1** : herbaceous vegetation (as grass) especially when used for grazing **2** : the juicy parts of herbaceous plants

¹**herb·al** \ˈər-bəl, ˈhər-\ *n* : a book about plants and especially their medical properties

²**herbal** *adj* : of, relating to, utilizing, or made of herbs

herb·al·ist \ˈər-bə-ləst, ˈhər-\ *n* : a person who collects, grows, or deals in herbs

her·bar·i·um \ˌər-ˈbar-ē-əm, ˌhər-, -ˈber-\ *n, pl* **-ia** \-ē-ə\ **1** : a collection of dried plant specimens **2** : a place that houses an herbarium

her·bi·cide \ˈər-bə-ˌsīd, ˈhər-\ *n* : an agent used to destroy or inhibit plant growth — **her·bi·cid·al** \ˌər-bə-ˈsīd-l, ˌhər-\ *adj*

her·bi·vore \ˈər-bə-ˌvōr, ˈhər-, -ˌvȯr\ *n* : a plant-eating animal [derived from Latin *herba* "grass" + *vorare* "to devour"] — **her·biv·o·rous** \ˌər-ˈbiv-ə-rəs, ˌhər-\ *adj*

Her·cu·le·an \ˌhər-kyə-ˈlē-ən, ˌhər-ˈkyü-lē-\ *adj* **1** : of, relating to, or characteristic of Hercules **2** *often not cap* : of extraordinary power, size, or difficulty ⟨a *Herculean* task⟩ [*Hercules,* mythical hero]

Her·cu·les \ˈhər-kyə-ˌlēz\ *n* : a northern constellation between Corona Borealis and Lyra

Her·cu·les'–club \ˌhər-kyə-ˌlēz-ˈkləb\ *n* : a small prickly tree of the eastern U.S. that is related to the ginseng

¹**herd** \ˈhərd\ *n* **1** : a number of animals of one kind kept or living together **2** : the undistinguished masses : CROWD 2 [Old English *heord*]

²**herd** *vb* : to keep, assemble, or move in or as if in a herd — **herd·er** *n*

herds·man \ˈhərdz-mən\ *n* : a manager, breeder, or tender of livestock

¹**here** \ˈhiər\ *adv* **1 a** : in or at this place ⟨turn *here*⟩ **b** : NOW ⟨*here* it's morning already⟩ **2** : at or in this point or particular ⟨*here* we agree⟩ **3** : in the present life or state **4** : to this place ⟨come *here*⟩ **5** — used interjectionally in rebuke or encouragement ⟨*here,* that's enough⟩ [Old English *hēr*]

²**here** *n* : this place ⟨get away from *here*⟩

here·abouts \ˈhir-ə-ˌbau̇ts\ *or* **here·about** \-ˌbau̇t\ *adv* : in this vicinity

¹**here·af·ter** \hir-ˈaf-tər\ *adv* **1** : after this **2** : in some future time or state

²**hereafter** *n, often cap* **1** : FUTURE 1a **2** : an existence beyond earthly life ⟨belief in the *hereafter*⟩

here and there *adv* : in one place and another

here·by \hir-ˈbī\ *adv* : by this means

her·e·dit·a·ment \ˌher-ə-ˈdit-ə-mənt\ *n* : heritable property [Medieval Latin *hereditamentum,* from Late Latin *hereditare* "to inherit," from Latin *heres* "heir"]

he·red·i·tary \hə-ˈred-ə-ˌter-ē\ *adj* **1** : genetically transmitted or transmittable from parent to offspring ⟨*hereditary* traits⟩ **2 a** : received or passing by inheritance ⟨*hereditary* rank⟩ **b** : having title or possession through inheritance ⟨*hereditary* rulers⟩ **3** : of a kind established by tradition ⟨*hereditary* enemies⟩ **4** : of or relating to inheritance or heredity

he·red·i·ty \hə-ˈred-ət-ē\ *n, pl* **-ties** **1** : the genetic traits including both genes and their expressed characters derived from one's ancestors **2** : the transmission of qualities from ancestor to descendant through genes [Middle French *heredité* "inheritance," from Latin *hereditas,* from *hered-, heres* "heir"]

Her·e·ford \ˈhər-fərd *sometimes* ˈher-ə-\ *n* : any of an English breed of hardy red white-faced beef cattle widely raised in the western U.S. [*Hereford,* former county in England]

here·in \hir-ˈin\ *adv* : in this

here·of \hir-ˈəv, -ˈäv\ *adv* : of this

here·on \-ˈȯn, -ˈän\ *adv* : on this

her·e·sy \ˈher-ə-sē\ *n, pl* **-sies** **1** : religious opinion contrary to the doctrines of a church **2** : opinion or doctrine contrary to a dominant or generally accepted belief [Medieval French *heresie,* from Late Latin *haeresis,* from Greek *hairesis* "action of taking, choice, sect," from *hairein* "to take"]

her·e·tic \ˈher-ə-ˌtik\ *n* : a person who believes or teaches heretical doctrines

he·ret·i·cal \hə-ˈret-i-kəl\ *also* **her·e·tic** \ˈher-ə-ˌtik, hə-ˈret-ik\ *adj* : of, relating to, or characterized by heresy : UNORTHODOX — **he·ret·i·cal·ly** \hə-ˈret-i-kə-lē, -klē\ *adv*

here·to \hir-ˈtü\ *adv* : to this document

here·to·fore \ˈhirt-ə-ˌfōr, -ˌfȯr\ *adv* : up to this time : HITHERTO

here·un·der \hir-ˈən-dər\ *adv* : under or in accordance with this document or agreement

here·un·to \hir-ˈən-tü\ *adv* : to this ⟨we *hereunto* affix our signatures⟩

here·up·on \ˈhir-ə-ˌpȯn, -ˌpän\ *adv* : on this : immediately after this

here·with \hir-ˈwit͟h, -ˈwith\ *adv* : with this communication : enclosed in this

her·i·ot \ˈher-ē-ət\ *n* : a feudal duty or tribute due under English law to a lord on the death of a tenant [Old English *heregeatwe* "military equipment," from *here* "army" + *geatwe* "equipment"]

her·i·ta·ble \ˈher-ət-ə-bəl\ *adj* **1** : capable of being inherited **2 a** : HEREDITARY 1 **b** : HEREDITARY 2 — **her·i·ta·bil·i·ty** \ˌher-ət-ə-ˈbil-ət-ē\ *n*

her·i·tage \ˈher-ət-ij\ *n* **1** : property that descends to an heir **2** : something transmitted by or acquired from a predecessor : LEGACY **3** : TRADITION ⟨America's Puritan *heritage*⟩ [Medieval French, from *heriter* "to inherit," from Late Latin *hereditare,* from Latin *heres* "heir"]

synonyms HERITAGE, INHERITANCE mean something passed down. HERITAGE may imply anything passed on to heirs or succeeding generations, but applies usually to something other than actual property or material things ⟨our *heritage* of freedom⟩. INHERITANCE applies to anything acquired by an heir ⟨received a large *inheritance* from an aunt⟩ ⟨this optimistic nature was considered a maternal *inheritance*⟩.

her·maph·ro·dite \hər-ˈmaf-rə-ˌdīt\ *n* : a plant or animal having both male and female reproductive organs [Latin *hermaphroditus,* from Greek *hermaphroditos,* from *Hermaphroditos* "Hermaphroditus," legendary son of Hermes and Aphrodite who becomes joined in one body with a nymph while bathing] — **hermaph·ro·dit·ic** \hər-ˌmaf-rə-ˈdit-ik\ *adj*

her·met·ic \hər-ˈmet-ik\ *also* **her·met·i·cal** \-ˈmet-i-kəl\ *adj* **1** : AIRTIGHT 1 **2** : completely resistant to outside influence [Medieval Latin *hermeticus,* from *Hermes Trismegistus,* legendary inventor of a magic seal to keep vessels airtight] — **her·met·i·cal·ly** \-i-kə-lē, -klē\ *adv*

her·mit \ˈhər-mət\ *n* **1** : one that lives in solitude especially for religious reasons **2** : a spiced molasses cookie [Medieval French *eremite,* from Late Latin *eremita,* from Late Greek *erēmitēs,* from Greek *erēmia* "solitude, desert," from *erēmos* "desolate"]

her·mit·age \ˈhər-mət-ij\ *n* **1** : the habitation of a hermit **2** : a secluded residence : RETREAT

hermit crab *n* : any of various small marine crustaceans that occupy the empty shells of gastropods

her·nia \ˈhər-nē-ə\ *n, pl* **her·ni·as** *or* **her·ni·ae** \-nē-ˌē, -nē-ˌī\ : a protrusion of an organ or part (as the intestine) through connective tissue or through a wall of the cavity (as of the abdomen) in which it is normally enclosed — called also *rupture* [Latin]

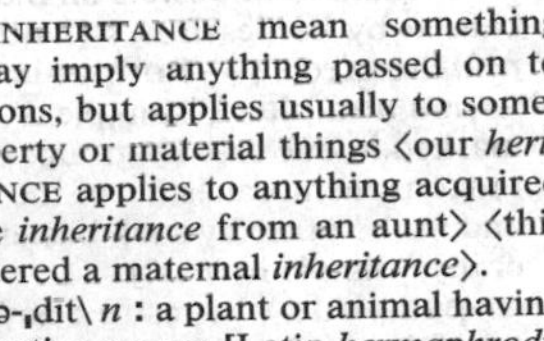

hermit crab

\ə\ **a**but	\au̇\ **ou**t	\i\ t**i**p	\ȯ\ s**aw**	\u̇\ f**oo**t
\ər\ f**ur**th**er**	\ch\ **ch**in	\ī\ l**i**fe	\ȯi\ c**oi**n	\y\ **y**et
\a\ m**a**t	\e\ p**e**t	\j\ **j**ob	\th\ **th**in	\yü\ f**ew**
\ā\ t**a**ke	\ē\ **ea**sy	\ng\ si**ng**	\t͟h\ **th**is	\yu̇\ c**u**re
\ä\ c**o**t, c**ar**t	\g\ **g**o	\ō\ b**o**ne	\ü\ f**oo**d	\zh\ vi**si**on

— **her·ni·al** \-nē-əl\ *adj* — **her·ni·ate** \-nē-ˌāt\ *vi*
he·ro \ˈhē-rō, ˈhiər-ō\ *n, pl* **heroes** **1 a :** a mythological or legendary figure often of divine descent endowed with great strength or ability **b :** an illustrious warrior **c :** a person admired for achievements and qualities **d :** one that shows great courage ⟨the *hero* of a rescue⟩ **2 :** the chief male figure in a literary work or in an event or period **3 :** SUBMARINE 2 [Latin *heros,* from Greek *hērōs*]
he·ro·ic \hi-ˈrō-ik\ *also* **he·ro·i·cal** \-ˈrō-i-kəl\ *adj* **1 :** of, relating to, or resembling heroes especially of antiquity ⟨the *heroic* age⟩ ⟨*heroic* legends⟩ **2 :** exhibiting or marked by courage, daring, or desperate enterprise ⟨a *heroic* rescue⟩ **3 :** large or impressive in size or range — **he·ro·i·cal·ly** \-i-kə-lē, -klē\ *adv*
heroic couplet *n* **:** a rhyming couplet in iambic pentameter
he·ro·ics \hi-ˈrō-iks\ *n pl* **1 :** heroic behavior **2 :** exaggerated display of heroic attitudes in action or expression
heroic verse *n* **:** the iambic pentameter used in English poetry (as epic) during the 17th and 18th centuries
her·o·in \ˈher-ə-wən\ *n* **:** a strongly addictive narcotic derived from the opium poppy and more potent than morphine [from *Heroin,* a former trademark] — **her·o·in·ism** \-wə-ˌniz-əm\ *n*
her·o·ine \ˈher-ə-wən\ *n* **1 :** a mythological or legendary woman of courage and daring **2 :** a woman admired for her achievements and qualities **3 :** the chief female figure in a literary work or in an event or period [Latin *heroina,* from Greek *hērōinē,* feminine of *hērōs* "hero"]
her·o·ism \ˈher-ə-ˌwiz-əm\ *n* **1 :** heroic conduct or qualities **2 :** great self-sacrificing courage ***synonyms*** see COURAGE
her·on \ˈher-ən\ *n, pl* **herons** *also* **heron :** any of various long-necked and long-legged wading birds with a long tapering bill and large wings [Medieval French *hairon,* of Germanic origin]
hero worship *n* **1 :** veneration of a hero **2 :** foolish or excessive praise for an individual
her·pes \ˈhər-pēz\ *n* **:** any of several virus diseases marked by the formation of blisters on the skin or mucous membranes and caused by herpesviruses [Latin, from Greek *herpēs,* from *herpein* "to creep"] — **her·pet·ic** \hər-ˈpet-ik\ *adj*
herpes sim·plex \-ˈsim-ˌpleks\ *n* **:** either of two kinds of herpes marked in one case by groups of watery blisters on the skin and mucous membranes (as of the mouth and lips) above the waist and in the other by such blisters on the genitals [New Latin, literally, "simple herpes"]
her·pes·virus \-ˈvī-rəs\ *n* **:** any of a group of viruses that contain DNA and include the causative agents of herpes
her·pe·tol·o·gy \ˌhər-pə-ˈtäl-ə-jē\ *n* **:** a branch of zoology dealing with reptiles and amphibians [Greek *herpeton* "reptile," from *herpein* "to creep"] — **her·pe·tol·o·gist** \ˌhər-pə-ˈtäl-ə-jəst\ *n*
Herr \heər, ˌheər\ *n, pl* **Her·ren** \ˌher-ən, heərn, ˌheərn\ — used by or to German-speaking people as a courtesy title equivalent to *Mr.* [German]
her·ring \ˈher-ing\ *n, pl* **herring** *or* **herrings :** a valuable soft-rayed food fish abundant in the temperate and colder parts of the north Atlantic; *also* **:** any of various similar and related fishes [Old English *hǣring*]
her·ring·bone \ˈher-ing-ˌbōn\ *n* **1 :** a pattern made up of rows of parallel lines with neighboring rows slanting in opposite directions **2 :** a twilled fabric with a herringbone pattern
herring gull *n* **:** a common large gull of the northern hemisphere that as an adult is largely white and gray with dark wing tips
hers \ˈhərz\ *pron, sing or pl in construction* **:** that which belongs to her **:** those which belong to her — used without a following noun as an equivalent in meaning to the adjective *her*
her·self \hər-ˈself, ər-\ *pron* **1 :** that identical female one — used reflexively or for emphasis ⟨she considers *herself* lucky⟩ ⟨she *herself* did it⟩; compare SHE 1 **2 :** her normal, healthy, or sane condition or self ⟨was *herself* again after a good night's sleep⟩
hertz \ˈhərts, ˈheərts\ *n* **:** a unit of frequency equal to one cycle per second — abbreviation *Hz* [Heinrich R. *Hertz,* died 1894, German physicist]
he's \hēz, ˌhēz, ēz\ **:** he is **:** he has
hes·i·tance \ˈhez-ə-təns\ *n* **:** HESITANCY
hes·i·tan·cy \-tən-sē\ *n, pl* **-cies** **1 :** the quality or state of being hesitant **2 :** an act or instance of hesitating
hes·i·tant \ˈhez-ə-tənt\ *adj* **:** tending to hesitate — **hes·i·tant·ly** *adv*
hes·i·tate \ˈhez-ə-ˌtāt\ *vi* **1 :** to stop or pause because of uncertainty or indecision ⟨*hesitate* before answering⟩ **2 :** to be reluctant ⟨never *hesitated* to ask a favor⟩ **3 :** to falter in speaking **:** STAMMER [Latin *haesitare* "to stick fast, hesitate," from *haesus,* past participle of *haerēre* "to stick"] — **hes·i·tat·er** *n* — **hes·i·tat·ing·ly** \-ˌtat-ing-lē\ *adv* — **hes·i·ta·tion** \ˌhez-ə-ˈtā-shən\ *n*

synonyms HESITATE, WAVER, VACILLATE, FALTER mean to show irresolution or uncertainty. HESITATE implies a pause before deciding, acting, or choosing ⟨*hesitated* before disagreeing⟩. WAVER implies hesitation after a decision and connotes weakness or a retreat ⟨*wavered* in her support of the bill⟩. VACILLATE implies prolonged hesitation from inability to reach a decision ⟨*vacillated* until events were out of control⟩. FALTER suggests a wavering or stumbling due to emotional stress, lack of courage, or fear ⟨never once *faltered* during his testimony⟩.

Hes·per·us \ˈhes-pə-rəs, -prəs\ *n* **:** Venus when appearing as an evening star [Latin, from Greek *Hesperos*]
Hes·sian \ˈhesh-ən\ *n* **1 :** a native or inhabitant of Hesse **2 :** a German mercenary serving in the British forces during the American Revolution
Hessian fly *n* **:** a small two-winged fly of European origin that is destructive in North America to wheat
heter- *or* **hetero-** *combining form* **:** other than usual **:** other **:** different ⟨*hetero*gamete⟩ [Greek *heteros* "other"]
het·ero·cyst \ˈhet-ə-rō-ˌsist\ *n* **:** a large transparent thick-walled cell that occurs in the filaments of some blue-green algae and is the site of nitrogen fixation
het·er·o·dox \ˈhet-ə-rə-ˌdäks\ *adj* **1 :** differing from or contrary to an acknowledged standard, a traditional form, or an established religion **:** UNORTHODOX **2 :** holding or expressing unorthodox beliefs or opinions [Late Latin *heterodoxus,* from Greek *heterodoxos,* from *heteros* "other" + *doxa* "opinion"]
het·er·o·doxy \-ˌdäk-sē\ *n, pl* **-dox·ies** **1 :** the quality or state of being heterodox **2 :** a heterodox opinion or doctrine
het·ero·dyne \ˈhet-ə-rə-ˌdīn\ *vt* **:** to combine (a radio frequency) with a different frequency so that a beat is produced — **heterodyne** *adj*
het·ero·ga·mete \ˌhet-ə-rō-gə-ˈmēt, -ˈgam-ˌēt\ *n* **:** either of a pair of gametes (as egg and sperm) that differ in form, size, or behavior — **het·ero·ga·met·ic** \-gə-ˈmet-ik\ *adj*
het·er·o·ge·ne·ity \ˌhet-ə-rō-jə-ˈnē-ət-ē\ *n* **:** the quality or state of being heterogeneous
het·er·o·ge·neous \ˌhet-ə-rə-ˈjē-nē-əs, -nyəs\ *adj* **:** differing in kind **:** consisting of dissimilar ingredients or constituents **:** MIXED ⟨a *heterogeneous* population⟩ [Medieval Latin *heterogeneus,* from Greek *heterogenēs,* from *heteros* "other" + *genos* "kind"] — **het·er·o·ge·neous·ly** *adv* — **het·er·o·ge·neous·ness** *n*
het·er·ol·o·gous \ˌhet-ə-ˈräl-ə-gəs\ *adj* **:** derived from a different species ⟨a *heterologous* organ transplant⟩ [*heter-* + *-logous* (as in *homologous*)]
het·ero·sex·u·al \ˌhet-ə-rō-ˈsek-shə-wəl, -shəl\ *adj* **:** of, relating to, or marked by a tendency to direct sexual desire toward members of the opposite sex — **heterosexual** *n* — **het·ero·sex·u·al·i·ty** \-ˌsek-shə-ˈwal-ət-ē\ *n*
het·er·o·sis \ˌhet-ə-ˈrō-səs\ *n* **:** the exceptional vigor or capacity for growth often exhibited by hybrid animals or plants — called also *hybrid vigor* — **het·er·ot·ic** \-ˈrät-ik\ *adj*
het·ero·troph \ˈhet-ə-rə-ˌtrōf, -ˌträf\ *n* **:** an organism that requires complex compounds of nitrogen and carbon (as that obtained from consuming plant or animal matter) for life and growth — **het·ero·tro·phic** \ˌhet-ə-rə-ˈtrō-fik\ *adj* — **het·ero·tro·phi·cal·ly** \-fi-kə-lē, -klē\ *adv*
het·ero·zy·gote \-ˈzī-ˌgōt\ *n* **:** a plant or animal with at least one gene pair containing different genes — **het·ero·zy·gos·i·ty** \-ˌzī-ˈgäs-ət-ē\ *n* — **het·ero·zy·gous** \ˌhet-ə-rō-ˈzī-gəs\ *adj*
het up \ˈhet-ˈəp\ *adj* **:** highly excited **:** UPSET
hew \ˈhyü\ *vb* **hewed; hewed** *or* **hewn** \ˈhyün\; **hew·ing** **1 :** to chop down **:** CHOP ⟨*hew* logs⟩ ⟨*hew* trees⟩ **2 :** to make or shape by or as if by cutting with an ax ⟨a cabin built of rough-hewn logs⟩ **3 :** to conform strictly **:** ADHERE ⟨*hew* to tradition⟩ [Old English *hēawan*] — **hew·er** *n*
[1]**hex** \ˈheks\ *vt* **1 :** to put a hex on **2 :** to affect as if by an evil spell **:** JINX [German *hexen,* from *Hexe* "witch"] — **hex·er** *n*
[2]**hex** *n* **1 :** [1]SPELL 1, JINX **2 :** a person who practices witchcraft
[3]**hex** *adj* **:** HEXAGONAL ⟨a bolt with a *hex* head⟩
[4]**hex** *n* **:** a hexadecimal number system

hexa- *or* **hex-** *combining form* : six ⟨*hexose*⟩ [Greek *hex*]

hexa·dec·i·mal \ˌhek-sə-ˈdes-ə-məl, -ˈdes-məl\ *adj* : of, relating to, or being a number system with a base of 16

hex·a·gon \ˈhek-sə-ˌgän\ *n* : a polygon of six angles and six sides

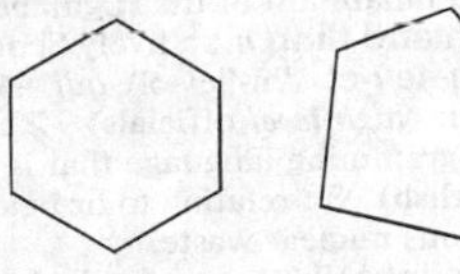

hexagon

hex·ag·o·nal \hek-ˈsag-ən-l\ *adj* **1** : having six angles and six sides **2** : having a hexagon as a section or base **3** : relating to or being a crystal system characterized by three equal lateral axes intersecting at angles of 60 degrees and a vertical axis of variable length at right angles ⟨quartz occurs in *hexagonal* crystals⟩ — **hex·ag·o·nal·ly** \-l-ē\ *adv*

hex·a·gram \ˈhek-sə-ˌgram\ *n* : a figure consisting of two equilateral triangles forming a 6-pointed star

hex·a·he·dron \ˌhek-sə-ˈhē-drən\ *n, pl* **-drons** *also* **-dra** \-drə\ : a polyhedron of six faces (as a cube)

hex·am·e·ter \hek-ˈsam-ət-ər\ *n* : a line of verse consisting of six metrical feet

hex·ane \ˈhek-ˌsān\ *n* : any of five isomeric volatile liquid hydrocarbons C_6H_{14} found in petroleum

[1]**hex·a·pod** \ˈhek-sə-ˌpäd\ *n* : INSECT 2

[2]**hexapod** *adj* **1** : having six feet **2** : of or relating to insects

hex·ose \ˈhek-ˌsōs\ *n* : a saccharide (as glucose) containing six carbon atoms in a molecule

hey \ˈhā\ *interj* — used especially to call attention or to express doubt, surprise, or joy [Middle English]

hey·day \ˈhā-ˌdā\ *n* : the time of greatest popularity, prosperity, or vigor

hi \ˈhī, ˈhī-ē\ *interj* — used especially as a greeting [Middle English *hy*]

hi·a·tus \hī-ˈāt-əs\ *n* **1** : a gap in or as if in a material object; *esp* : a break where a part is missing ⟨a *hiatus* in an old manuscript⟩ **2** : an interruption in time or continuity; *esp* : a period when something (as a program or activity) is suspended or interrupted **3** : the occurrence of two vowel sounds without pause or intervening consonantal sound [Latin, from *hiare* "to gape, yawn"]

hi·ba·chi \hi-ˈbäch-ē\ *n* : a charcoal grill [Japanese]

hi·ber·nate \ˈhī-bər-ˌnāt\ *vi* : to pass the winter in a torpid or resting state [Latin *hibernare* "to pass the winter," from *hibernus* "of winter"] — **hi·ber·na·tion** \ˌhī-bər-ˈnā-shən\ *n* — **hi·ber·na·tor** \ˈhī-bər-ˌnāt-ər\ *n*

hi·bis·cus \hī-ˈbis-kəs, hə-\ *n* : any of a large genus of herbs, shrubs, or small trees related to the mallows and having toothed leaves and large showy flowers [Latin, "marshmallow plant"]

[1]**hic·cup** *also* **hic·cough** \ˈhik-ˌəp, -əp\ *n* : a spasmodic drawing in of breath that is stopped by sudden closure of the glottis and is accompanied by a peculiar sound [imitative]

[2]**hiccup** *also* **hiccough** *vi* **hic·cuped** *also* **hic·cupped; hic·cup·ing** *also* **hic·cup·ping** : to make a hiccup or be affected with hiccups

hick \ˈhik\ *n* : an awkward unsophisticated person : BUMPKIN [*Hick*, nickname for Richard]

hick·o·ry \ˈhik-rē, -ə-rē\ *n, pl* **-ries** **1** : any of a genus of North American hardwood trees related to the walnuts that often produce hard-shelled sweet edible nuts **2** : the usually tough pale wood of a hickory [short for obsolete *pokahickory*, from Virginia Algonquian *pawcohiccora* "food prepared from pounded nuts"]

hi·dal·go \hid-ˈal-gō, ē-ˈthäl-\ *n, pl* **-gos** : a member of the lower nobility of Spain [Spanish]

[1]**hide** \ˈhīd\ *vb* **hid** \ˈhid\; **hid·den** \ˈhid-n\ *or* **hid; hid·ing** \ˈhīd-ing\ **1** : to put or get out of sight ⟨*hide* a treasure⟩ ⟨*hid* in a closet⟩ **2** : to keep secret ⟨*hid* their grief⟩ **3** : to screen from view ⟨a house *hidden* by trees⟩ **4** : to seek protection or evade responsibility ⟨*hides* behind dark glasses⟩ [Old English *hȳdan*] — **hid·er** \ˈhīd-ər\ *n*

synonyms HIDE, CONCEAL, SECRETE, BURY mean to withhold or withdraw from sight. HIDE may or may not suggest intent ⟨*hide* behind the couch⟩ ⟨a house *hidden* in the woods⟩. CONCEAL usually does imply intent and often specifically implies a refusal to divulge ⟨*concealed* the truth from their parents⟩. SECRETE suggests a depositing in a place unknown to others ⟨*secreted* the diary under the mattress⟩. BURY implies covering up so as to hide completely ⟨*buried* the treasure⟩.

[2]**hide** *n* : the skin of an animal whether raw or dressed [Old English *hȳd*]

[3]**hide** *vt* **hid·ed; hid·ing** : to give a beating to : FLOG

hide–and–seek \-n-ˈsēk\ *n* : a children's game in which one player gives the others time to hide and then tries to find them

hide·away \ˈhīd-ə-ˌwā\ *n* : RETREAT 2, HIDEOUT

hide·bound \ˈhīd-ˌbau̇nd\ *adj* **1** : having a dry skin lacking in pliancy and adhering closely to the underlying flesh ⟨a *hidebound* horse⟩ **2** : stubbornly conservative

hid·eous \ˈhid-ē-əs\ *adj* : horribly ugly or disgusting : FRIGHTFUL [Medieval French *hidus, hisdos* from *hisde, hide* "terror"] — **hid·eous·ly** *adv* — **hid·eous·ness** *n*

hide·out \ˈhīd-ˌau̇t\ *n* : a place of refuge or concealment

hie \ˈhī\ *vb* **hied; hy·ing** *or* **hie·ing** : HURRY 1, HASTEN [Old English *hīgian*]

hi·er·arch \ˈhī-ˌrärk, -ə-ˌrärk\ *n* **1** : a religious leader in a position of authority **2** : a person high in a hierarchy [Medieval Latin *hierarcha*, from Greek *hierarchēs*, from *hieros* "holy" + *archos* "ruler, leader"] — **hi·er·ar·chal** \ˌhī-ˈrär-kəl, -ə-ˈrär-\ *adj*

hi·er·ar·chy \ˈhī-ˌrär-kē, -ə-ˌrär-\ *n, pl* **-chies** **1** : a ruling body especially of clergy organized into ranks each subordinate to the one above it **2 a** : arrangement into a series according to rank **b** : persons or things arranged in ranks or classes — **hi·er·ar·chi·cal** \ˌhī-ˈrär-ki-kəl, -ə-ˈrär-\ *or* **hi·er·ar·chic** \-ˈrär-kik\ *adj* — **hi·er·ar·chi·cal·ly** \-ˈrär-ki-kə-lē, -klē\ *adv*

Word History The earliest examples of the use of *hierarchy* in English are found in works of the late 14th century and refer to the ranks or orders of angels. The first element of the word is from Greek *hieros*, "holy, sacred." The second element comes from Greek *archos*, "leader, ruler." A second sense of the word, appearing only slightly later than the first, is "a form of government administered by a priesthood." Later the term was extended from government to the classification of groups of people and then to the arrangement of objects, elements, or values in graduated series.

hi·er·o·glyph \ˈhī-rə-ˌglif, -ə-rə-\ *n* : a character used in a system of hieroglyphic writing [French *hiéroglyphe*, from Middle French *hieroglyphique*, adj., "hieroglyphic," from Late Latin *hieroglyphicus*, from Greek *hieroglyphikos*, from *hieros* "holy" + *glyphein* "to carve"]

hi·ero·glyph·ic \ˌhī-rə-ˈglif-ik, -ə-rə-\ *n* **1** : HIEROGLYPH **2** : a system of writing mainly in pictorial characters; *esp* : the picture script of the ancient Egyptian priesthood **3** : characters that resemble a hieroglyphic especially in being hard to decipher — **hieroglyphic** *adj*

hieroglyphic 2

hi–fi \ˈhī-ˈfī\ *n* **1** : HIGH FIDELITY **2** : equipment for reproduction of sound with high fidelity

hig·gle·dy–pig·gle·dy \ˌhig-əl-dē-ˈpig-əl-dē\ *adv* : in confusion : TOPSY-TURVY [origin unknown] — **higgledy–piggledy** *adj*

[1]**high** \ˈhī\ *adj* **1 a** : extending or raised up ⟨a *high* building⟩ **b** : having a specified elevation ⟨six meters *high*⟩ **2** : advanced toward fullness or culmination ⟨*high* summer⟩ **3** : elevated in pitch ⟨a *high* note⟩ **4** : relatively far from the equator ⟨*high* latitudes⟩ **5** : exalted in character : NOBLE ⟨a person of *high* purpose⟩ **6** : of greater degree, size, amount, or content than average or ordinary ⟨*high* pressure⟩ ⟨*high* prices⟩ **7** : of relatively great importance: as **a** : foremost in rank, dignity, or standing ⟨*high* society⟩ **b** : SERIOUS, GRAVE ⟨*high* crimes⟩ **8** : FORCIBLE, STRONG ⟨*high* winds⟩ **9 a** : showing elation or excitement ⟨*high* spirits⟩ **b** : intoxicated by or as if by drugs or alcohol **10** : advanced in complexity or development ⟨*higher* mathematics⟩ ⟨*higher* algae⟩ **11** : pronounced with some part of the tongue close to the palate ⟨\ē\ is a *high* vowel⟩ [Old English *hēah*]

[2]**high** *adv* **1** : at or to a high place, altitude, or degree ⟨hit the ball *high* into the bleachers⟩ **2** : RICHLY, LUXURIOUSLY ⟨lived *high* after winning the lottery⟩

[3]**high** *n* **1** : an elevated place or region: as **a** : HILL 1, KNOLL **b** : SKY 1, HEAVEN ⟨birds wheeling on *high*⟩ **c** : HEAVEN 2a ⟨a

judgment from on *high*〉 **2 :** a region of high barometric pressure **3 a :** a high point or level 〈prices reached a new *high*〉 **b :** the transmission gear of an automotive vehicle giving the highest ratio of propeller-shaft to engine-shaft speed and consequently the highest speed of travel **4 :** a state of elation, excitement, or intoxication produced by or as if by a drug

high·ball \'hī-,bȯl\ *n* **:** a drink of alcoholic liquor (as whiskey) with water or a carbonated beverage [earlier *highball* "fast train, signal for a train to proceed at full speed"]

high beam *n* **:** a vehicle headlight beam with a long-distance focus

high·bind·er \-,bīn-dər\ *n* **1 :** a professional killer operating in the Chinese quarter of an American city **2 :** a corrupt or scheming politician [the *Highbinders,* gang of vagabonds in New York City about 1806]

high blood pressure *n* **:** blood pressure that is abnormally high especially in the arteries or the bodily condition resulting from it — called also *hypertension*

high·born \'hī-'bȯrn\ *adj* **:** of noble birth

high·boy \'hī-,bȯi\ *n* **:** a tall chest of drawers mounted on a base with legs

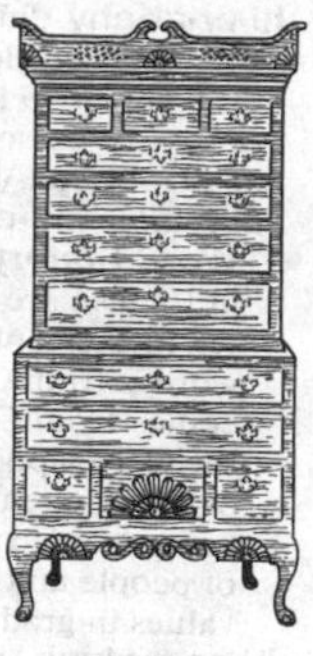
highboy

high·bred \-'bred\ *adj* **:** coming from superior stock

high·brow \-,brau̇\ *n* **:** a person who has or pretends to have superior learning or culture **:** INTELLECTUAL — **highbrow** *adj*

high·bush cranberry \-'bu̇sh-\ *n* **:** CRANBERRY BUSH

high chair *n* **:** a child's chair with long legs, a feeding tray, and a footrest

High Church *adj* **:** tending to stress the ceremonial, traditional, and priestly elements especially in Anglican worship — compare LOW CHURCH

high command *n* **1 :** the supreme headquarters of a military force **2 :** the highest leaders in an organization

high commissioner *n* **:** a principal or high-ranking commissioner; *esp* **:** an ambassadorial representative of the government of one country stationed in another

high–definition *adj* **:** relating to or being a television system that has higher resolution, a sharper image, and a wider screen than a conventional system

high–density lipoprotein *n* **:** HDL

higher education *n* **:** education provided by a college or university

high·er–up \,hī-ər-'əp\ *n* **:** a superior officer or official

high explosive *n* **:** an explosive (as TNT) that generates gas with extreme rapidity and has a shattering effect

high·fa·lu·tin \,hī-fə-'lüt-n\ *adj* **1 :** PRETENTIOUS 1 **2 :** POMPOUS 3, BOMBASTIC 〈*highfalutin* talk〉 [perhaps from *high* + *fluting,* present participle of *flute*]

high fidelity *n* **:** the reproduction of sound with a high degree of faithfulness to the original — **high–fidelity** *adj*

high five *n* **:** a slapping of upraised right hands by two people (as in celebration) — **high–five** \'hī-'fīv\ *vb*

high–flown \'hī-'flōn\ *adj* **:** FLOWERY 2, EXTRAVAGANT 〈*high-flown* language〉

high–fly·ing \-'flī-iŋ\ *adj* **1 :** rising to considerable height **2 :** marked by extravagance, pretension, or excessive ambition

high frequency *n* **:** a radio frequency in the range between 3 and 30 megahertz — abbreviation HF

High German *n* **:** German as natively used in southern and central Germany

high–grade \'hī-'grād\ *adj* **:** of superior grade or quality

high–hand·ed \-'han-dəd\ *adj* **:** DOMINEERING, OVERBEARING 〈*high-handed* actions〉 — **high–hand·ed·ly** *adv* — **high–hand·ed·ness** *n*

high–hat \'hī-'hat\ *adj* **:** snobbish and supercilious in attitude — **high–hat** *vt*

High Holiday *n* **:** either of two important Jewish holidays: **a :** ROSH HASHANAH **b :** YOM KIPPUR

high horse *n* **:** an arrogant mood or attitude 〈get off your *high horse* and start treating your classmates as equals〉

high jinks \'hī-,jiŋks\ *n pl* **:** wild or rowdy behavior [*jinks* "pranks, frolics"; origin unknown]

high jump *n* **:** a jump for height in a track-and-field contest — **high–jump** *vt* — **high jumper** *n*

[1]**high·land** \'hī-lənd\ *n* **:** elevated or mountainous land

[2]**highland** *adj* **1 :** of or relating to a highland **2** *cap* **:** of or relating to the Highlands of Scotland

high·land·er \-lən-dər\ *n* **1 :** an inhabitant of a highland **2** *cap* **:** an inhabitant of the Highlands of Scotland

Highland fling *n* **:** a lively Scottish folk dance

high–lev·el \'hī-'lev-əl\ *adj* **1 :** being of high importance or rank 〈*high-level* officials〉 **2 :** relating to or being a computer programming language that is similar to a natural language (as English) **3 :** relating to or being very radioactive and very hazardous nuclear waste

[1]**high·light** \'hī-,līt\ *n* **1 :** the brightest spot or area (as in a painting or drawing) **2 :** something (as an event or detail) that is of major interest 〈the *highlights* of a trip〉

[2]**highlight** *vt* **1 :** to throw a strong light on **2 a :** to center attention on **:** EMPHASIZE **b :** to be a highlight of 〈a bullfight *highlighted* their trip to Mexico〉 **3 a :** to mark (a text) with a highlighter **b :** to cause (as text) to stand out on a computer screen

high·light·er \-,līt-ər\ *n* **:** a pen with a broad felt tip and brightly colored transparent ink for marking selected passages in a text

high·ly \'hī-lē\ *adv* **1 :** to a high degree **:** EXTREMELY 〈*highly* pleased〉 **2 :** with much approval 〈speak *highly* of you〉

high mass *n, often cap H&M* **:** a mass that is sung in full ceremonial form — compare LOW MASS

high–mind·ed \'hī-'mīn-dəd\ *adj* **:** having or marked by elevated principles and feelings — **high–mind·ed·ly** *adv* — **high–mind·ed·ness** *n*

high–muck–a–muck \,hī-,mək-i-'mək\ *or* **high–muck·e·ty–muck** \,hī-mək-ət-ē-'mək\ *n* **:** an important and often arrogant person [by folk etymology from Chinook Jargon (a pidgin language used in northwestern America) *hayo makamak* "plenty to eat"]

high·ness \'hī-nəs\ *n* **1 :** the quality or state of being high **2** — used as a form of address for persons (as a prince, a princess, a duke, or a duchess) of exalted rank and usually of royal blood 〈Her *Highness* Princess Anne〉 〈His *Highness* the Duke of Edinburgh〉 〈Your *Highness*〉 〈Their *Highnesses*〉

high noon *n* **:** exactly noon

high–octane *adj* **:** having a high octane number and hence good antiknock properties 〈*high-octane* gasoline〉

high–pitched \'hī-'picht\ *adj* **:** having a high pitch 〈a *high-pitched* voice〉

[1]**high–pressure** *adj* **1 a :** having or involving a high or comparatively high pressure especially greatly exceeding that of the atmosphere **b :** having a high atmospheric pressure **2 a :** using or involving aggressive and insistent sales techniques **b :** imposing or involving severe strain or tension 〈a *high-pressure* job〉

[2]**high–pressure** *vt* **:** to sell or influence by high-pressure tactics

high relief *n* **:** sculptural relief in which at least half the thickness of the represented form is raised from the background — compare BAS-RELIEF

high–rise \'hī-'rīz\ *adj* **:** having many stories and being equipped with elevators 〈*high-rise* apartment buildings〉 — **high–rise** *n*

high·road \'hī-,rōd\ *n* **1 :** HIGHWAY **2 :** the easiest course

high school *n* **:** a school usually including grades 9–12 or 10–12 — **high schooler** *n*

high seas *n pl* **:** the open part of a sea or ocean especially outside territorial waters

high–sound·ing \'hī-'sau̇n-diŋ\ *adj* **:** PRETENTIOUS 1, IMPOSING

high–speed \'hī-'spēd\ *adj* **:** operated or adapted for operation at high speed

high–spir·it·ed \'hī-'spir-ət-əd\ *adj* **:** characterized by a bold or energetic spirit — **high–spir·it·ed·ly** *adv* — **high–spir·it·ed·ness** *n*

high–strung \-'strəŋ\ *adj* **:** having an extremely nervous or sensitive temperament

high·tail \'hī-,tāl\ *vi* **:** to retreat at full speed 〈*hightailed* it for home〉

high–tech \-'tek\ *adj* **:** of or relating to high technology

high technology *n* **:** technology involving advanced or sophisticated devices (as electronics or computers)

high–tension *adj* **:** having or using a high voltage

high–test *adj* **:** meeting a high standard; *also* **:** HIGH-OCTANE

high tide *n* **1 :** the tide when the water is at its greatest height **2 :** the culminating point **:** CLIMAX

high–toned \'hī-'tōnd\ *adj* **1 :** high in social, moral, or intellectual quality **2 :** PRETENTIOUS 1, POMPOUS

high–top \ˈhī-ˌtäp\ *adj* : extending up over the ankle ⟨*high-top* sneakers⟩ — **high–tops** \-ˌtäps\ *n pl*
high treason *n* : TREASON 2
high–water mark *n* : highest point : PEAK
high•way \ˈhī-ˌwā\ *n* : a public way; *esp* : a main direct road
high•way•man \-mən\ *n* : a person who robs travelers on a road
hi•jack *or* **high•jack** \ˈhī-ˌjak\ *vt* **1** : to steal by stopping a vehicle on the highway; *also* : to stop and steal from (a vehicle in transit) **2** : to commandeer a flying airplane (as by coercing the pilot at gunpoint) [origin unknown] — **hi•jack•er** *n*
[1]**hike** \ˈhīk\ *vb* **1 a** : to move or raise up often with a sudden motion **b** : to increase (as prices) usually sharply or suddenly **2** : to go on a hike [perhaps related to [1]*hitch*] — **hik•er** *n*
[2]**hike** *n* **1** : a long walk especially for pleasure or exercise **2** : an upward movement : RISE ⟨a price *hike*⟩
hi•lar•i•ous \hil-ˈar-ē-əs, -ˈer-; hī-ˈlar-, -ˈler-\ *adj* : marked by or causing hilarity : extremely funny [Latin *hilarus, hilaris* "cheerful," from Greek *hilaros*] — **hi•lar•i•ous•ly** *adv* — **hi•lar•i•ous•ness** *n*
hi•lar•i•ty \-ət-ē\ *n* : high-spirited and boisterous laughter or merriment ***synonyms*** see MIRTH
[1]**hill** \ˈhil\ *n* **1** : a usually rounded natural elevation of land lower than a mountain **2** : an artificial heap or mound (as of earth) **3** : several seeds or plants planted in a group rather than a row ⟨a *hill* of beans⟩ [Old English *hyll*]
[2]**hill** *vt* **1** : to form into a heap **2** : to draw earth around the roots or base of — **hill•er** *n*
hill•bil•ly \ˈhil-ˌbil-ē\ *n, pl* **-lies** : a person from a backwoods area [[1]*hill* + *Billy,* nickname for *William*]
hillbilly music *n* : COUNTRY MUSIC
hill•ock \ˈhil-ək\ *n* : a small hill — **hill•ocky** \-ə-kē\ *adj*
hill•side \ˈhil-ˌsīd\ *n* : the side of a hill
hill•top \ˈhil-ˌtäp\ *n* : the highest part of a hill
hilly \ˈhil-ē\ *adj* **hill•i•er; -est** : having many hills ⟨a *hilly* city⟩
hilt \ˈhilt\ *n* : a handle especially of a sword or dagger [Old English] — **to the hilt** : to the very limit : COMPLETELY
hi•lum \ˈhī-ləm\ *n, pl* **hi•la** \-lə\ **1** : a scar on a seed (as a bean) at the point of attachment of the ovule **2** : a notch in or opening from a bodily part suggesting the hilum of a bean [Latin, "trifle"] — **hi•lar** \-lər\ *adj*
him \im, him, ˈhim\ *pron, objective case of* HE
him•self \im-ˈself, him-\ *pron* **1 a** : that identical male one — used reflexively or for emphasis ⟨he considers *himself* lucky⟩ ⟨he *himself* did it⟩; compare [1]HE **b** — used reflexively when the sex of the antecedent is unspecified ⟨everyone must look out for *himself*⟩ **2** : his normal, healthy, or sane condition or self ⟨he's *himself* again⟩
[1]**hind** \ˈhīnd\ *n, pl* **hinds** *also* **hind** **1** *chiefly British* : a female red deer — compare HART **2** : any of various usually spotted groupers [Old English]
[2]**hind** *adj* : located behind : REAR ⟨*hind* legs⟩ [Middle English]
hind•brain \ˈhīnd-ˌbrān, ˈhīn-\ *n* : the posterior division of the embryonic vertebrate brain or the parts (as the cerebellum and medulla oblongata) developed from it
hin•der \ˈhin-dər\ *vb* **hin•dered; hin•der•ing** \-də-ring, -dring\ **1** : to make slow or difficult : HAMPER **2** : to hold back : CHECK [Old English *hindrian*]
synonyms HINDER, IMPEDE, OBSTRUCT, BLOCK mean to interfere with the activity or progress of. HINDER stresses causing harmful or annoying delay or interference with progress ⟨rain *hindered* the climb⟩. IMPEDE implies making forward progress difficult by clogging, hampering, or fettering ⟨tight clothing that *impedes* movement⟩. OBSTRUCT implies interfering with something by the sometimes intentional placing of obstacles in the way ⟨the view was *obstructed* by billboards⟩. BLOCK implies complete obstruction to passage or progress ⟨a landslide *blocked* the road⟩.
hind•gut \ˈhīnd-ˌgət, ˈhīn-\ *n* : the posterior part of the alimentary canal; *also* : INTESTINE
Hin•di \ˈhin-dē\ *n* **1** : a literary and official language of northern India **2** : a complex of Indic dialects of northern India for which Hindi is the usual literary language [Hindi & Urdu *hindī,* from *Hind* "India," from Persian] — **Hindi** *adj*
hind•most \ˈhīnd-ˌmōst, ˈhīn-\ *adj* : farthest to the rear
hind•quar•ter \-ˌkwȯrt-ər, -ˌkwȯt-\ *n* **1** : one side of the back half of the body or carcass of a four-footed animal ⟨a *hindquarter* of beef⟩ **2** *pl* : the part of a four-footed animal lying behind the attachment of the hind legs to the trunk
hin•drance \ˈhin-drəns\ *n* **1** : the state of being hindered **2** : the action of hindering **3** : something that hinders : IMPEDIMENT
hind•sight \ˈhīnd-ˌsīt, ˈhīn-\ *n* : the understanding of the nature of an event only after it has happened ⟨*hindsight* is easier than foresight⟩
[1]**Hin•du** *also* **Hin•doo** \ˈhin-ˌdü\ *n* **1** : an adherent of Hinduism **2** : a native or inhabitant of India [Persian *Hindū* "inhabitant of India," from *Hind* "India"]
[2]**Hindu** *also* **Hindoo** *adj* : of, relating to, or characteristic of the Hindus or Hinduism
Hindu–Arabic *adj* : relating to, being, or composed of Arabic numerals ⟨the *Hindu-Arabic* numeration system⟩
Hin•du•ism \-ˌiz-əm\ *n* : a body of social, cultural, and religious beliefs and practices native to the Indian subcontinent
Hin•du•stani \ˌhin-dü-ˈstan-ē, -ˈstän-ē\ *n* : a group of Indic dialects of northern India of which literary Hindi and Urdu are considered diverse written forms [Hindi & Urdu *Hindūstānī,* from Persian *Hindūstān* "India"] — **Hindustani** *adj*
hind wing *n* : either of the back wings of a four-winged insect situated behind the forewings
[1]**hinge** \ˈhinj\ *n* **1** : a jointed piece on which one surface (as a door, gate, or lid) turns or swings on another **2** : the joint between valves of a bivalve's shell — compare HINGE JOINT [Middle English *heng*]
[2]**hinge** *vb* **1** : to attach by or furnish with hinges **2** : to hang or turn as if on a hinge ⟨success *hinges* on the decision⟩
hinge joint *n* : a joint between bones (as at the elbow) that permits motion in but one plane
hin•ny \ˈhin-ē\ *n, pl* **hinnies** : a hybrid between a stallion and a female donkey — compare MULE [Latin *hinnus*]
[1]**hint** \ˈhint\ *n* **1 a** : a suggestion for action given briefly or in an indirect manner ⟨*hints* on lawn care⟩ **b** : a statement that communicates delicately and indirectly rather than directly **2 a** : a slight indication of the existence or nature of something : CLUE **b** : SMIDGEN, BIT [probably from *hent* "to seize," from Old English *hentan*]
[2]**hint** *vb* : to convey by or make a hint ***synonyms*** see SUGGEST — **hint•er** *n*
hin•ter•land \ˈhint-ər-ˌland\ *n* **1** : a region lying inland from a coast **2** : a region remote from urban areas or cultural centers [German, from *hinter* "hind" + *land* "land"]
[1]**hip** \ˈhip\ *n* : ROSE HIP [Old English *hēope*]
[2]**hip** *n* **1** : the part of the body that curves outward below the waist on either side and is formed by the side part of the pelvis and the upper part of the thigh **2** : HIP JOINT [Old English *hype*]
[3]**hip** *also* **hep** \ˈhep\ *adj* **hip•per; hip•pest** **1** : characterized by a keen informed awareness of or interest in the newest developments **2** : aware or appreciative of something ⟨got *hip* to their plan⟩ [origin unknown]
hip•bone \ˈhip-ˈbōn, -ˌbōn\ *n* : either of two large flaring bones that make up the lateral halves of the pelvis in mammals and are composed of the ilium, ischium, and pubis which are fused into one bone in the adult
hip girdle *n* : PELVIC GIRDLE
hip–hop \ˈhip-ˌhäp\ *n* **1** : a subculture especially of inner-city youths who are typically devotees of rap music **2** : the stylized rhythmic music that commonly accompanies rap; *also* : rap with this music [perhaps from [3]*hip* + [1]*hop*] — **hip–hop** *adj*
hip joint *n* : the articulation between the femur and the hipbone
hip•par•i•on \hip-ˈar-ē-ˌän, -ˈer-\ *n* : any of a genus of extinct Miocene and Pliocene 3-toed horses [Greek, "pony," from *hippos* "horse"]
[1]**hipped** \ˈhipt\ *adj* : having hips or such hips ⟨broad-*hipped*⟩
[2]**hipped** *adj* : DEPRESSED 1a [derived from *hypochondria*]
[3]**hipped** *adj* : extremely absorbed or interested ⟨*hipped* on astrology⟩ [*hip* "to make aware," from [3]*hip*]
hip•pie *or* **hip•py** \ˈhip-ē\ *n, pl* **hippies** : a usually young person who rejects the values and practices of established society (as by dressing unconventionally or favoring communal living); *also* : a long-haired unconventionally dressed young person [[3]*hip* + *-ie*]

\ə\ **abut**	\au̇\ **out**	\i\ **tip**	\ȯ\ **saw**	\u̇\ **foot**
\ər\ **further**	\ch\ **chin**	\ī\ **life**	\ȯi\ **coin**	\y\ **yet**
\a\ **mat**	\e\ **pet**	\j\ **job**	\th\ **thin**	\yü\ **few**
\ā\ **take**	\ē\ **easy**	\ng\ **sing**	\t͟h\ **this**	\yu̇\ **cure**
\ä\ **cot, cart**	\g\ **go**	\ō\ **bone**	\ü\ **food**	\zh\ **vision**

hip·po \ˈhip-ō\ *n, pl* **hippos** : HIPPOPOTAMUS

hip·po·cam·pus \ˌhip-ə-ˈkam-pəs\ *n* : a curved ridge at the base of the brain that is involved in forming, storing, and processing memory [Greek *hippokampos* "sea horse"; so called from its supposed resemblance to the fish]

Hip·po·crat·ic oath \ˌhip-ə-ˈkrat-ik-\ *n* : an oath embodying a code of medical ethics usually taken by those about to begin medical practice [*Hippocrates,* died about 377 B.C., Greek physician believed to have formulated it]

hip·po·drome \ˈhip-ə-ˌdrōm\ *n* **1** : an oval stadium for horse and chariot races in ancient Greece **2** : an arena for spectacles (as horse shows or circuses) [Middle French, from Latin *hippodromos,* from Greek, from *hippos* "horse" + *dromos* "racecourse"]

hip·po·pot·a·mus \ˌhip-ə-ˈpät-ə-məs\ *n, pl* **-mus·es** *or* **-mi** \-ˌmī, -mē\ : a very large plant-eating 4-toed chiefly aquatic mammal of sub-Saharan Africa related to the swine and characterized by an extremely large head and mouth, very thick hairless grayish skin, and short legs; *also* : a smaller closely related mammal of western Africa [Latin, from Greek *hippopotamos,* from *hippos* "horse" + *potamos* "river"]

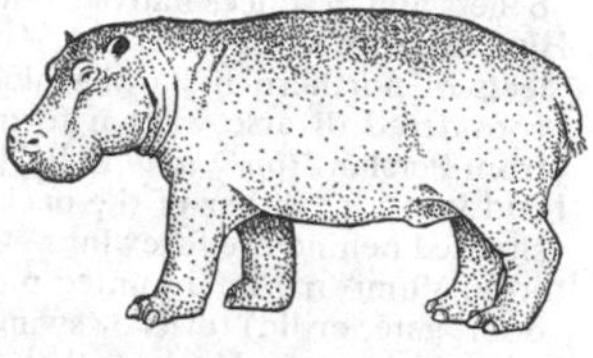
hippopotamus

Word History *Hippopotamos* was the name invented by the Greeks to describe the bulky, barrel-shaped animal that spends most of the day bathing in the rivers of Africa. The two elements of the word are *hippos,* "horse," and *potamos,* "river." In fact, however, the hippopotamus is more closely related to the hog than to the horse.

hip·py \ˈhip-ē\ *adj* **hip·pi·er; -est** : having large hips

hip roof *n* : a roof having sloping ends and sloping sides

hip·ster \ˈhip-stər\ *n* : a person who is hip

[1]**hire** \ˈhīr\ *n* **1 a** : payment for temporary use **b** : payment for services : WAGES **2 a** : the act of hiring **b** : the state of being hired : EMPLOYMENT [Old English *hȳr*] — **for hire** : available for use or service in return for payment

[2]**hire** *vb* **1 a** : to engage the personal services of for a set sum ⟨*hire* a new crew⟩ **b** : to engage the temporary use of for a fixed sum ⟨*hire* a hall⟩ **2** : to grant the personal services of for a fixed sum ⟨*hire* themselves out⟩ **3** : to take employment ⟨*hire* out as a cook⟩ — **hir·er** *n*

synonyms HIRE, LET, LEASE, RENT mean to engage or grant for use at a price. HIRE and LET, strictly speaking, are complementary terms, HIRE implying the act of engaging or taking for use and LET the granting of use ⟨we *hired* a car for the summer⟩ ⟨decided to *let* the cottage to a young couple⟩. LEASE strictly implies a letting under the terms of a contract but is often applied to hiring on a lease ⟨the diplomat *leased* an apartment for a year⟩ ⟨the landlord refused to *lease* to tenants with pets⟩. RENT stresses the payment of money for the full use of property and may imply either hiring or letting ⟨decided to *rent* instead of buy a house⟩.

hire·ling \ˈhīr-liŋ\ *n* : a person who serves for pay and usually for no other reason

hiring hall *n* : a union-operated placement office where registered applicants are referred in rotation to jobs

hir·sute \ˈhər-ˌsüt, ˈhiər-\ *adj* **1** : HAIRY 1 **2** : covered with coarse stiff hairs ⟨a *hirsute* leaf⟩ [Latin *hirsutus*] — **hir·sute·ness** *n*

[1]**his** \iz, hiz, ˌhiz\ *adj* : of or relating to him or himself especially as possessor, agent, or object of an action ⟨*his* house⟩ ⟨*his* writings⟩ ⟨*his* confirmation⟩ — compare [1]HE [Old English, genitive of *hē* "he"]

[2]**his** \ˈhiz\ *pron, sing or pl in constr* : that which belongs to him : those which belong to him — used without a following noun as an equivalent in meaning to the adjective *his*

[1]**His·pan·ic** \his-ˈpan-ik\ *adj* **1** : of or relating to the people, speech, or culture of Spain or of Spain and Portugal **2** : of, relating to, or being a person of Latin American descent living in the U.S.; *esp* : being one of Cuban, Mexican, or Puerto Rican origin [Latin *hispanicus* "derived from or relating to the people, speech, or culture of Spain or of Spain and Portugal," from *Hispania* "Iberian Peninsula, Spain"]

[2]**Hispanic** *n* : a Hispanic person

his·pid \ˈhis-pəd\ *adj* : rough or covered with bristles, stiff hairs, or minute spines ⟨*hispid* leaves⟩ [Latin *hispidus*] — **his·pid·i·ty** \his-ˈpid-ət-ē\ *n*

hiss \ˈhis\ *vb* **1** : to utter the characteristic prolonged sibilant sound of an alarmed animal (as a snake or cat) or a similar sound **2** : to express disapproval by hissing [Middle English *hissen,* of imitative origin] — **hiss** *n* — **hiss·er** *n*

hissy fit \ˈhis-ē-\ *n* : TANTRUM [from *hissy* "tantrum," perhaps alteration of *hysterical*]

hist \s *often prolonged and usually with* p *preceding and* t *following; often read as* ˈhist\ *interj* — used to attract attention

hist- *or* **histo-** *combining form* : tissue ⟨*hist*amine⟩ [Greek *histos* "mast, loom, beam, web," from *histanai* "to cause to stand"]

his·ta·mine \ˈhis-tə-ˌmēn, -mən\ *n* : a compound occurring in many animal tissues that plays an important part in allergic reactions (as hives, asthma, and hay fever)

his·ti·dine \ˈhis-tə-ˌdēn\ *n* : a crystalline amino acid $C_6H_9N_3O_2$ formed in the splitting of most proteins

his·to·gram \ˈhis-tə-ˌgram\ *n* : a bar graph of a frequency distribution that uses the widths of rectangles to represent the interval of a class of values and the heights to represent the number of items in each class [Greek *histos* "mast, pole, web"]

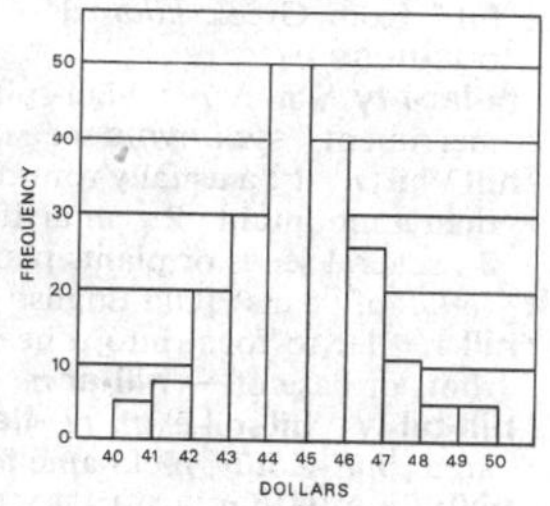

histogram

his·tol·o·gy \his-ˈtäl-ə-jē\ *n, pl* **-gies** **1** : a branch of anatomy that deals with the minute structure of animal and plant tissues as revealed by the microscope **2** : tissue structure or organization — **his·to·log·ical** \ˌhis-tə-ˈläj-i-kəl\ *adj* — **his·tol·o·gist** \his-ˈtäl-ə-jəst\ *n*

his·tone \ˈhis-ˌtōn\ *n* : a simple water-soluble protein that forms a compact structure with DNA in the nucleosomes of eukaryotic chromatin [German *Histon*]

his·to·plas·mo·sis \ˌhis-tə-plaz-ˈmō-səs\ *n* : a disease that is caused by a fungus infection especially of the lungs

his·to·ri·an \his-ˈtōr-ē-ən, -ˈtȯr-\ *n* **1** : a student or writer of history; *esp* : one that produces a scholarly historical study **2** : a writer of chronicles : CHRONICLER

his·tor·ic \his-ˈtȯr-ik, -ˈtär-\ *adj* : HISTORICAL; *esp* : famous in history ⟨*historic* events⟩

his·tor·i·cal \-i-kəl\ *adj* **1 a** : of, relating to, or having the character of history ⟨*historical* fact⟩ **b** : based on history ⟨*historical* novels⟩ **c** : used in the past and reproduced in historical presentations **2** : famous in history — **his·tor·i·cal·ly** \-i-kə-lē, -klē\ *adv* — **his·tor·i·cal·ness** \-kəl-nəs\ *n*

historical present *n* : the present tense used to relate past events

his·to·ric·i·ty \ˌhis-tə-ˈris-ət-ē\ *n* : historical actuality : FACT

his·to·ri·og·ra·pher \his-ˌtōr-ē-ˈäg-rə-fər, -ˌtȯr-\ *n* : HISTORIAN — **his·to·rio·graph·i·cal** \-ˈgraf-i-kəl\ *also* **his·to·rio·graph·ic** \-ē-ə-ˈgraf-ik\ *adj* — **his·to·rio·graph·i·cal·ly** \-i-kə-lē, -klē\ *adv* — **his·to·ri·og·ra·phy** \-ē-ˈäg-rə-fē\ *n*

his·to·ry \ˈhis-tə-rē, -trē\ *n, pl* **-ries** **1** : STORY 1a, TALE **2 a** : a chronological record of significant events usually with an explanation of their causes **b** : an account of a patient's medical background **3** : a branch of knowledge that records and explains past events **4 a** : events that form the subject matter of a history **b** : past events [Medieval French *estoire, histoire,* from Latin *historia,* from Greek, "inquiry, history," from *istōr, histōr* "knowing, learned"]

his·tri·on·ic \ˌhis-trē-ˈän-ik\ *adj* **1** : of or relating to actors, acting, or the theater **2** : deliberately affected : THEATRICAL [Late Latin *histrionicus,* from Latin *histrio* "actor"] ***synonyms*** see DRAMATIC — **his·tri·on·i·cal·ly** \-ˈän-i-kə-lē, -klē\ *adv*

his·tri·on·ics \-ˈän-iks\ *n sing or pl* **1** : theatrical performances **2** : deliberate display of emotion for effect

[1]**hit** \ˈhit\ *vb* **hit; hit·ting** **1 a** : to strike usually with force ⟨*hit* a ball⟩ ⟨the ball *hit* against the house⟩ **b** : to make usually forceful contact with something ⟨fell and *hit* the ground⟩ **2 a** : ATTACK ⟨tried to guess when and where the enemy would *hit*⟩ **b** : to affect unfavorably ⟨the loss of the contract *hit* the company hard⟩ **3** : to arrive with a forceful effect ⟨when the storm *hit*⟩ **4 a** : COME, STUMBLE ⟨*hit* upon the solution⟩ **b** : to experience or find especially by chance ⟨*hit* a run of bad luck⟩ **c** : to get to : REACH ⟨*hit* town that night⟩ ⟨prices *hit* a new high⟩ **d**

: to accord with accurately ⟨styles that *hit* modern taste⟩ **5 :** to fire the charge in the cylinders ⟨an automobile engine not *hitting*⟩ [Old English *hyttan,* probably from Old Norse *hitta* "to meet with, hit"] — **hit·ter** *n* — **hit it off :** to get along well — **hit the ground running :** to begin or proceed quickly, energetically, or effectively — **hit the spot :** to give complete or special satisfaction

[2]hit *n* **1 a :** a blow striking an object aimed at **b :** COLLISION **2 a :** a stroke of luck **b :** something that is conspicuously successful ⟨the show was a *hit*⟩ **3 :** a telling remark **4 :** BASE HIT **5 :** a single dose of a narcotic drug **6 :** an instance of a computer user connecting to a given Web site ⟨a million *hits* per day⟩ **7 :** a successful match in a computer search

hit–and–miss \ˌhit-n-ˈmis\ *adj* **:** sometimes successful and sometimes not **:** HAPHAZARD

hit–and–run \-ˈrən\ *adj* **1 :** being or relating to a baseball play in which a runner on first base starts for the next base as the pitcher starts to pitch and the batter attempts to hit the ball **2 :** being or involving a motor-vehicle driver who does not stop after being involved in an accident **3 :** involving or intended for quick action or results

[1]hitch \ˈhich\ *vb* **1 :** to move by jerks ⟨*hitch* a chair toward the table⟩ **2 a :** to catch or fasten by or as if by a hook or knot ⟨*hitch* a horse to a rail⟩ **b :** to connect to or with a hitch **3 :** HITCHHIKE [Middle English *hytchen*] — **hitch·er** *n*

[2]hitch *n* **1 :** a jerky movement or pull **2 :** a sudden stop **:** an unforeseen obstacle **:** HALT ⟨the plan went off without a *hitch*⟩ **3 :** the connection between something towed (as a plow or trailer) and its mover (as a tractor, automobile, or animal) **4 :** a knot used for a temporary fastening ⟨barrel *hitch*⟩ **5 :** a period of time especially of military service ⟨a *hitch* in the infantry⟩

hitch·hike \ˈhich-ˌhīk\ *vb* **:** to travel by securing free rides from passing vehicles — **hitch·hik·er** *n*

hitch up *vi* **:** to harness and hitch a draft animal or team to a vehicle

[1]hith·er \ˈhi*th*-ər\ *adv* **:** to this place ⟨come *hither*⟩ [Old English *hider*]

[2]hither *adj* **:** being on the near or adjacent side ⟨the *hither* side of the hill⟩

hith·er·most \-ˌmōst\ *adj* **:** nearest on this side

hith·er·to \-ˌtü\ *adv* **:** up to this time ⟨*hitherto* unknown facts⟩

hith·er·ward \ˈhi*th*-ər-wərd, -ə-\ *adv* **:** HITHER

hit–or–miss \ˌhit-ər-ˈmis\ *adj* **:** marked by a lack of care, forethought, system, or plan

hit or miss *adv* **:** in a hit-or-miss manner **:** HAPHAZARDLY

Hit·tite \ˈhi-ˌtīt\ *n* **1 :** a member of a conquering people in Asia Minor and Syria ruling an empire in the 2nd millennium B.C. **2 :** an Indo-European language of the Hittite people known from cuneiform texts [Hebrew *Ḥittī,* from Hittite *ḫatti*] — **Hittite** *adj*

HIV \ˌāch-ˌī-ˈvē\ *n* **:** any of a group of retroviruses that infect and destroy helper T cells of the immune system causing the marked reduction in their numbers that is diagnostic of AIDS — called also *AIDS virus, human immunodeficiency virus*

[1]hive \ˈhīv\ *n* **1 a :** a container for housing honeybees **b :** the usually aboveground nest of bees **c :** a colony of bees **2 :** a place swarming with busy occupants [Old English *hȳf*] — **hive·less** \-ləs\ *adj*

[2]hive *vb* **1 a :** to collect (as bees) into a hive **b :** to enter and take over a hive **2 :** to store up in or as if in a hive ⟨*hive* honey⟩ **3 :** to live in close association

hives *n sing or pl* **:** an allergic disorder in which the skin or mucous membrane is affected by itching swellings [origin unknown]

HMO \ˌāch-ˌem-ˈō\ *n* **:** an organization that provides comprehensive health care to voluntarily enrolled individuals and families by participating medical professionals and facilities which receive fixed periodic payments [*h*ealth *m*aintenance *o*rganization]

ho \ˈhō\ *interj* — used especially to attract attention ⟨land *ho*⟩ [Middle English]

hoa·gie \ˈhō-gē\ *n* **:** SUBMARINE 2 [origin unknown]

[1]hoar \ˈhōr, ˈhȯr\ *adj* **:** HOARY [Old English *hār*]

[2]hoar *n* **:** FROST 1c [Middle English *hor* "hoariness," from *hor,* adjective]

hoard \ˈhōrd, ˈhȯrd\ *n* **:** a supply or fund stored up usually in secret [Old English *hord*] — **hoard** *vt* — **hoard·er** *n*

hoar·frost \ˈhōr-ˌfrȯst, ˈhȯr-\ *n* **:** FROST 1c

hoarse \ˈhōrs, ˈhȯrs\ *adj* **1 :** harsh in sound ⟨a crow's *hoarse* caw⟩ **2 :** having a rough grating voice ⟨*hoarse* from a cold⟩ [Middle English *hos, hors,* probably from Old Norse] — **hoarse·ly** *adv* — **hoarse·ness** *n*

hoary \ˈhōr-ē, ˈhȯr-\ *adj* **hoar·i·er; -est 1 :** grayish or whitish especially from age ⟨an old dog's *hoary* muzzle⟩ **2 :** very old **:** ANCIENT ⟨*hoary* legends⟩ — **hoar·i·ness** *n*

[1]hoax \ˈhōks\ *vt* **:** to trick into believing or accepting as genuine something false and often preposterous [probably from *hocus*] — **hoax·er** *n*

[2]hoax *n* **1 :** an act intended to trick or fool **2 :** something false passed off or accepted as genuine

[1]hob \ˈhäb\ *n* **1** *English dialect* **:** HOBGOBLIN 1, ELF **2 :** MISCHIEF, TROUBLE ⟨raise *hob*⟩ [Middle English *hobbe,* from *Hobbe,* nickname for *Robert*]

[2]hob *n* **1 :** a projection at the back or side of a fireplace on which something may be kept warm **2 :** a cutting tool used for cutting the teeth of worm wheels or gears [origin unknown]

[3]hob *vt* **hobbed; hob·bing 1 :** to furnish with hobnails **2 :** to cut with a hob

[1]hob·ble \ˈhäb-əl\ *vb* **hob·bled; hob·bling** \ˈhäb-ling, -ə-ling\ **1 a :** to move along unsteadily or with difficulty; *esp* **:** to limp along ⟨*hobble* on crutches⟩ **b :** to cause to limp **:** make lame ⟨*hobbled* by an ankle injury⟩ **2 a :** to keep (as a horse) from straying by joining two legs with a short length (as of rope) **b :** to place under handicap **:** HAMPER, IMPEDE [Middle English *hoblen*] — **hob·bler** \ˈhäb-lər, -ə-lər\ *n*

[2]hobble *n* **1 :** a hobbling movement **2 :** something used to hobble an animal

hob·ble·de·hoy \ˈhäb-əl-di-ˌhȯi\ *n* **:** an awkward gawky youth [origin unknown]

hobble skirt *n* **:** a skirt very narrow at the ankles

hob·by \ˈhäb-ē\ *n, pl* **hobbies :** an interest or activity which is outside a person's regular occupation and is pursued for pleasure [short for *hobbyhorse*] — **hob·by·ist** \-ē-əst\ *n*

hob·by·horse \ˈhäb-ē-ˌhȯrs\ *n* **1 :** a stick with an imitation horse's head at one end which children pretend to ride **2 a :** a toy horse hung by springs from a frame **b :** ROCKING HORSE **3 :** a topic to which one constantly returns [Middle English *hoby, hobyn* "small light horse," perhaps from *Hobbin,* nickname for *Robert* or *Robyn*]

hob·gob·lin \ˈhäb-ˌgäb-lən\ *n* **1 :** a mischievous elf or goblin **2 :** BOGEY 2, BUGABOO

hob·nail \ˈhäb-ˌnāl\ *n* **:** a short large-headed nail used to stud the soles of heavy shoes as a protection against wear [[2]*hob*] — **hob·nailed** \-ˌnāld\ *adj*

hob·nob \-ˌnäb\ *vi* **hob·nobbed; hob·nob·bing :** to associate familiarly ⟨*hobnobbing* with royalty⟩ [from the obsolete phrase *drink hobnob* "to drink alternately to one another"] — **hob·nob·ber** *n*

ho·bo \ˈhō-bō\ *n, pl* **hoboes** *also* **hobos 1 :** a migratory worker **2 :** a homeless and usually penniless wanderer **:** TRAMP 1 [origin unknown] — **hobo** *vi*

Hob·son's choice \ˈhäb-sənz-\ *n* **:** apparently free choice with no real alternative [Thomas *Hobson,* died 1631, English liveryman, who required every customer to take the horse nearest the door]

[1]hock \ˈhäk\ *n* **1 :** the tarsal joint or region in the hind limb of a four-footed animal (as the horse) corresponding to the human ankle **2 :** a small cut of meat from either the front or hind leg just above the foot especially of a pig [Old English *hōh* "heel"]

[2]hock *n, often cap, chiefly British* **:** RHINE WINE [German *Hochheimer,* from *Hochheim,* Germany]

[3]hock *n* **:** [1]PAWN 2 ⟨got the watch out of *hock*⟩ [Dutch *hok* "pen, prison"]

[4]hock *vt* **:** PAWN ⟨*hocked* the silverware⟩

hock·ey \ˈhäk-ē\ *n* **1 :** FIELD HOCKEY **2 :** ICE HOCKEY [perhaps from Middle French *hoquet* "shepherd's crook," from *hoc* "hook," of Germanic origin]

ho·cus \ˈhō-kəs\ *vt* **ho·cussed** *or* **ho·cused; ho·cus·sing** *or* **ho·cus·ing 1 :** to play a trick on **:** DECEIVE **2 :** DRUG 1, DOPE [from *hocus-pocus*]

ho·cus–po·cus \ˌhō-kə-ˈspō-kəs\ *n* **1 :** a magic trick **2 :** nonsense that serves as a means of deception [probably from *hocus pocus,* imitation Latin phrase used by jugglers]

\ə\ **abut**	\au̇\ **out**	\i\ **tip**	\ȯ\ **saw**	\u̇\ **foot**
\ər\ **further**	\ch\ **chin**	\ī\ **life**	\ȯi\ **coin**	\y\ **yet**
\a\ **mat**	\e\ **pet**	\j\ **job**	\th\ **thin**	\yü\ **few**
\ā\ **take**	\ē\ **easy**	\ng\ **sing**	*th*\ **this**	\yu̇\ **cure**
\ä\ **cot, cart**	\g\ **go**	\ō\ **bone**	\ü\ **food**	\zh\ **vision**

hod \ˈhäd\ *n* **1 :** a long-handled wooden tray or trough used for carrying mortar or bricks on the shoulder **2 :** a bucket for holding or carrying coal [probably from Dutch *hodde*]

hod 1

hod carrier *n* **:** a laborer who carries supplies to bricklayers, stonemasons, cement finishers, or plasterers on the job

hodge•podge \ˈhäj-ˌpäj\ *n* **:** MISHMASH, JUMBLE [alteration of *hotchpotch*]

Word History An earlier form of *hodgepodge,* and still a form used commonly in Britain, is *hotchpotch.* This in turn is a rhyming alteration of Middle English *hochepot.* Medieval French *hochepot,* from which the English word is derived, is formed from *hochier,* "to shake," and *pot,* which has the same meaning as English *pot. Hochepot,* then, was a stew with many different ingredients all shaken (and presumably cooked) together in the same pot. This mixture of many ingredients in one pot prompted the extension of meaning to any heterogeneous mixture.

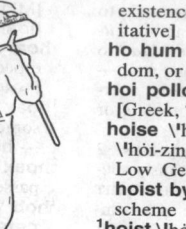

Hodg•kin's disease \ˈhäj-kənz-\ *n* **:** a disease characterized by progressive enlargement of the lymph glands, spleen, and liver and by progressive anemia [Thomas *Hodgkin,* died 1866, English physician]

hoe \ˈhō\ *n* **:** a farm or garden tool with a thin flat blade at nearly a right angle to a long handle that is used especially for weeding and loosening the earth [Medieval French *houe,* of Germanic origin] — **hoe** *vb* — **ho•er** \ˈhō-ər, ˈhȯr\ *n*

hoe•cake \ˈhō-ˌkāk\ *n* **:** a small cornmeal cake

hoe•down \-ˌdau̇n\ *n* **1 :** SQUARE DANCE **2 :** a gathering featuring square dances

[1]**hog** \ˈhȯg, ˈhäg\ *n, pl* **hogs** *also* **hog 1 a :** a domesticated swine especially when weighing more than 120 pounds (54 kilograms) — compare PIG 1a **b :** any of various animals related to the domesticated swine **2 a :** a selfish, gluttonous, or filthy person **b :** one that uses something to excess ⟨old cars that are gas *hogs*⟩ [Old English *hogg*]

[2]**hog** *vt* **hogged; hog•ging :** to take more than one's share of

ho•gan \ˈhō-ˌgän\ *n* **:** a Navajo Indian dwelling usually made of logs and mud with a door traditionally facing east [Navajo *hooghan*]

hogan

hog•back \ˈhȯg-ˌbak, ˈhäg-\ *n* **1 :** a ridge of land formed by the outcropping edges of tilted strata **2 :** a ridge with a sharp summit and steeply sloping sides

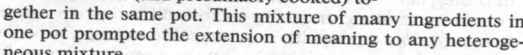

hog cholera *n* **:** a highly infectious often fatal virus disease of swine

hog•gish \ˈhȯg-ish, ˈhäg-\ *adj* **:** very selfish, gluttonous, or filthy — **hog•gish•ly** *adv* — **hog•gish•ness** *n*

hog heaven *n* **:** an extremely satisfying state or situation

hog•nose snake \ˈhȯg-ˌnōz-, ˈhäg-\ *or* **hog–nosed snake** \-ˌnōz-, -ˌnōzd-\ *n* **:** any of several rather small harmless stout-bodied North American snakes that have an upturned snout and that hiss or play dead when disturbed — called also *puff adder*

hogs•head \ˈhȯgz-ˌhed, ˈhägz-\ *n* **1 :** a large cask or barrel **2 :** any of various units of capacity; *esp* **:** a U.S. unit for liquids equal to 63 gallons (about 238 liters)

hog–tie \ˈhȯg-ˌtī, ˈhäg-\ *vt* **1 :** to tie together the feet of ⟨*hog-tie* a calf⟩ **2 :** to make helpless ⟨*hog-tied* by red tape⟩

hog•wash \-ˌwȯsh, -ˌwäsh\ *n* **1 :** SWILL 1, SLOP 4a **2 :** worthless or nonsensical language

hog wild *adj* **:** lacking in restraint **:** WILD ⟨fans going *hog wild* at the sight of the celebrity⟩

Ho•hen•stau•fen \ˈhō-ən-ˌshtau̇-fən, -ˌstau̇-\ *adj* **:** of or relating to the German royal family that reigned over the Holy Roman Empire from 1138 to 1254 and over Sicily from 1194 to 1266 — **Hohenstaufen** *n*

Ho•hen•zol•lern \ˈhō-ən-ˌzäl-ərn\ *adj* **:** of or relating to the German royal family that reigned in Prussia from 1701 to 1918 and in Germany from 1871 to 1918 — **Hohenzollern** *n*

ho–hum \ˈhō-ˈhəm\ *adj* **1 :** ROUTINE, ORDINARY ⟨a *ho-hum* existence⟩ **2 :** INDIFFERENT, BORED ⟨a *ho-hum* reaction⟩ [imitative]

ho hum \ˈhō-ˈhəm\ *interj* — used to express weariness, boredom, or disdain

hoi polloi \ˌhȯi-pə-ˈlȯi\ *n pl* **:** the common people **:** MASSES [Greek, "the many"]

hoise \ˈhȯiz\ *vt* **hoised** \ˈhȯizd\ *or* **hoist** \ˈhȯist\; **hois•ing** \ˈhȯi-zing\ **:** HOIST [alteration of *hysse* "to hoist," perhaps from Low German *hissen*] — **hoist with one's own petard** *or* **hoist by one's own petard :** affected or hurt by one's own scheme

[1]**hoist** \ˈhȯist\ *vb* **:** to raise or become raised into position by or as if by means of tackle [alteration of *hoise*] ***synonyms*** see LIFT — **hoist•er** *n*

[2]**hoist** *n* **1 :** an act of hoisting **:** LIFT **2 :** an apparatus for hoisting heavy loads

hoi•ty–toi•ty \ˌhȯit-ē-ˈtȯit-ē, ˌhīt-ē-ˈtīt-ē\ *adj* **1 :** GIDDY 3, FLIGHTY **2 :** HAUGHTY, PATRONIZING [derived from English dialect *hoit* "to play the fool"]

hok•ey \ˈhō-kē\ *adj* **hok•i•er; -est 1 :** CORNY **2 :** obviously contrived **:** PHONY ⟨believed his *hokey* story about how he could fly⟩ — **hok•ey•ness** *or* **hok•i•ness** \ˈhō-kē-nəs\ *n* — **hok•i•ly** \ˈhō-kə-lē\ *adv*

ho•key•po•key \ˌhō-kē-ˈpō-kē\ *n* **:** HOCUS-POCUS 2

ho•kum \ˈhō-kəm\ *n* **1 :** a device for evoking a desired response (as laughter or sentiment) from an audience **2 :** pretentious nonsense **:** BUNKUM [probably from *ho*cus-pocus + bun*kum*]

hol- *or* **holo-** *combining form* **:** complete **:** total **:** completely **:** totally ⟨*Holocene*⟩ [Greek *holos* "whole"]

[1]**hold** \ˈhōld\ *vb* **held** \ˈheld\; **hold•ing 1 a :** to maintain possession of **:** HAVE ⟨*hold* title to property⟩ **b :** to retain by force ⟨the soldiers *held* the bridge⟩ **2 a :** to restrain especially by keeping back ⟨*hold* your temper⟩ **b :** to keep from advancing or succeeding in attack **c :** to delay temporarily the handling of ⟨*hold* my calls⟩ ⟨*hold* that thought⟩ **d :** to bind legally or morally **:** CONSTRAIN ⟨I'll *hold* you to your word⟩ **3 a :** to have or keep in the grasp **b :** to cause to be or remain in a particular situation, position, or relation ⟨*hold* a ladder steady⟩ **c :** SUPPORT, SUSTAIN ⟨the floor will *hold* 10 metric tons⟩ **d :** to keep in custody **e :** to keep back from use ⟨will *hold* tickets for us⟩ **f :** to prevent from leaving or getting away ⟨*hold* the elevator⟩ **4 :** to bear or carry oneself ⟨*hold* oneself proudly⟩ ⟨*hold* still⟩ **5 a** (1) **:** to keep up without interruption or flagging ⟨*hold* silence⟩ (2) **:** to maintain or continue without change ⟨*hold* a course due east⟩ ⟨*hold* southwest for two miles⟩ **b :** to have strong appeal to ⟨the speaker *held* my attention⟩ **6 a :** to receive and retain **:** CONTAIN, ACCOMMODATE ⟨the can *holds* 20 liters⟩ **b :** to have in store ⟨what the future *holds*⟩ **7 a :** HARBOR, ENTERTAIN ⟨*hold* a theory⟩ **b :** CONSIDER, REGARD ⟨truths *held* to be self-evident⟩ **8 :** to schedule and carry out (as a social event or a conference) **9 a :** to have (as an office) by election or appointment ⟨*holds* a captaincy in the navy⟩ **b :** to have earned or been awarded ⟨*holds* a PhD⟩ **10 a :** to maintain position **:** not retreat **b :** to continue in the same way or state **:** LAST ⟨hope the weather *holds*⟩ ⟨their courage *held* against all odds⟩ **11 :** to maintain a grasp on something **:** remain fastened to something ⟨the anchor *held* in the rough sea⟩ **12 :** to be or remain valid **:** APPLY ⟨the rule *holds* in most cases⟩ **13 :** to hold oneself back from an intended or threatened action **:** HALT, PAUSE [Old English *healdan*] ***synonyms*** see CONTAIN — **hold a candle to :** to qualify for comparison with — **hold forth :** to talk or preach at length — **hold hands :** to join one's hand with another's especially as an expression of affection — **hold one's breath 1 :** to prevent oneself from breathing temporarily **2 :** to wait in anxious anticipation — **hold one's horses :** to slow down or stop for a moment ⟨*Hold your horses!* We'll go in a minute!⟩ — **hold one's own :** to prove equal to opposition — **hold one's tongue** *or* **hold one's peace :** to keep silent **:** keep one's thoughts to oneself — **hold sway :** to have a dominant influence **:** RULE — **hold the bag 1 :** to be left empty-handed **2 :** to bear alone a responsibility that should have been shared by others — **hold the fort 1 :** to maintain a firm position **2 :** to take care of usual affairs ⟨is *holding the fort* until the manager returns⟩ — **hold to :** to give firm assent to **:** adhere to strongly ⟨*held* to their beliefs⟩ — **hold water :** to stand up under criticism or analysis — **hold with :** to agree with or approve of

[2]**hold** *n* **1 :** STRONGHOLD 1 **2 a :** the act or manner of holding

: SEIZURE, GRASP ⟨took a firm *hold* on the rope⟩ **b :** a manner of grasping the opponent in wrestling **3 :** a bond by which someone or something is affected or controlled : POWER ⟨had a strong *hold* on public opinion⟩ **4 a :** full understanding ⟨finally got *hold* of the severity of the situation⟩ **b :** full or immediate control ⟨get a *hold* of yourself⟩ **c :** physical control or possession ⟨need to get *hold* of a road map⟩ **5 :** something that may be grasped or held **6 :** a prolonged note or rest in music; *also* : a sign 𝄐 denoting a hold **7 a :** an order or indication that something is to be reserved or delayed **b :** STOP, HALT ⟨put a *hold* on the launch⟩ — **on hold 1 :** in a state of interruption during a phone call when one party switches to another line without disconnecting the other party **2 :** in a state of indefinite suspension ⟨put our plans *on hold*⟩

[3]hold *n* **1 :** the interior of a ship below decks; *esp* : the cargo deck of a ship **2 :** the cargo compartment of an airplane [alteration of *hole*]

hold·all \ˈhōl-ˌdȯl\ *n, chiefly British* : an often cloth traveling case or bag

hold back *vb* **1 a :** to hinder the progress of **b :** to keep from advancing to the next stage, level, or grade **2 :** to refrain from revealing or giving up ⟨*held back* important information⟩

hold down *vt* : to assume or have responsibility for ⟨*holding down* two jobs⟩

hold·er \ˈhōl-dər\ *n* **1 :** a person that holds: **a (1) :** OWNER — often used in combination ⟨job*holder*⟩ (2) : TENANT 1 **b :** a person in possession of and legally entitled to receive payment of a bill, note, or check **2 :** a device that holds

hold·fast \ˈhōld-ˌfast, ˈhōl-\ *n* : a part by which a plant or animal clings (as to a flat surface or the body of a host)

hold·ing \ˈhōl-diŋ\ *n* **1 a :** land held (as for farming or residence) **b :** property (as bonds or stocks) owned — usually used in plural **2 :** a ruling of a court especially on an issue of law raised in a case

holding company *n* : a company that owns part or all of other companies for purposes of control

holding pattern *n* **1 :** the course flown (as over an airport) by an aircraft awaiting permission to land **2 :** a state of waiting or suspended activity or progress ⟨the project is in a *holding pattern*⟩

hold off *vb* **1 :** POSTPONE, DELAY ⟨*hold off* on making a decision⟩ ⟨will *hold off* production during the summer⟩ **2 :** to fight to a standoff : WITHSTAND ⟨*held* the enemy *off*⟩

hold on *vi* **1 :** to maintain a grasp on something ⟨*hold on* to the ledge⟩ **2 :** WAIT ⟨*hold on* and I'll see if she's available⟩ — **hold on to :** to maintain possession of or adherence to ⟨*hold on to* your dreams⟩

hold out \hōl-ˈdau̇t, ˈhōl-\ *vb* **1 :** PROFFER ⟨*held out* little chance of success⟩ **2 :** REPRESENT 4 ⟨*hold* oneself *out* to be a scholar⟩ **3 :** to remain unsubdued or operative; *also* : to continue to function or be available ⟨prayed the engine would *hold out*⟩ ⟨as long as our money *holds out*⟩ **4 :** to refuse to come to an agreement — **hold·out** \ˈhōl-ˌdau̇t\ *n* — **hold out on :** to withhold something (as information) from

hold over \hōl-ˈdō-vər, ˈhōl-\ *vb* **1 a :** to continue (as in office) beyond the normal term **b :** to retain from an earlier period ⟨that mistake is *held over* from a previous edition⟩ **2 :** to prolong the engagement or tenure of ⟨the film is *held over* for another week⟩ — **hold·over** \ˈhōl-ˌdō-vər\ *n*

hold up \hōl-ˈdəp, ˈhōl-\ *vt* **1 :** to rob at gunpoint **2 :** DELAY, IMPEDE ⟨only *holding* things *up*⟩ **3 :** to single out ⟨*held* his work *up* as perfect⟩ **4 :** to continue in the same condition without failing or losing effectiveness ⟨*holding up* well under the stress⟩ ⟨music that *holds up* twenty years later⟩

hold·up \ˈhōld-ˌəp\ *n* **1 :** DELAY **2 :** a robbery carried out at gunpoint

hole \ˈhōl\ *n* **1 :** an opening into or through a thing ⟨a *hole* in a wall⟩ **2 a :** a hollow place (as a pit or cave) **b :** a deep place in a body of water ⟨trout *holes*⟩ **3 :** an underground habitation : BURROW ⟨a fox in its *hole*⟩ **4 :** FLAW, FAULT ⟨a big *hole* in your argument⟩ **5 a :** a cavity in the putting green of a golf course into which the ball is played **b :** the play or the part of the course from the tee to the hole **6 a :** a mean or dingy place ⟨lives in a real *hole*⟩ **b :** a prison cell especially for solitary confinement **7 :** an awkward position : FIX [Old English *hol* and *holh*] — **hole** *vb* — **hol·ey** \ˈhō-lē\ *adj* — **in the hole 1 :** in debt **2 :** having a score below zero

hole in one *n* : ACE 4

hole–in–the–wall *n, pl* **holes–in–the–wall :** a small and often unpretentious out-of-the-way place (as a restaurant)

hole up *vb* : to take refuge or shelter in or as if in a hole or cave

hol·i·day \ˈhäl-ə-ˌdā\ *n* **1 :** HOLY DAY **2 :** a day of freedom from work; *esp* : a day of celebration or commemoration fixed by law **3** *chiefly Brit* : a period of relaxation : VACATION [Old English *hāligdæg,* from *hālig* "holy" + *dæg* "day"] — **holiday** *vi* — **hol·i·day·er** *n*

ho·li·ness \ˈhō-lē-nəs\ *n* **1 :** the quality or state of being holy **2** *cap* — used as a form of address for various high religious dignitaries ⟨His *Holiness* Pope John Paul II⟩ ⟨Your *Holiness*⟩

ho·lis·tic \hō-ˈlis-tik\ *adj* : relating to or concerned with wholes or with complete systems rather than with the analysis of, treatment of, or dissection into parts ⟨*holistic* medicine attempts to treat both the mind and the body⟩

hol·land \ˈhäl-ənd\ *n* : a cotton or linen fabric in plain weave usually heavily sized or glazed and used especially for window shades [Middle English *Holand,* county in the Netherlands, from Dutch *Holland*]

hol·lan·daise \ˌhäl-ən-ˈdāz-\ *n* : a sauce made basically of butter, yolks of eggs, and lemon juice or vinegar [French *sauce hollandaise,* literally, "Dutch sauce"]

hol·ler \ˈhäl-ər\ *vb* **hol·lered; hol·ler·ing** \ˈhäl-riŋ, -ə-riŋ\ **1 :** to cry or call out : SHOUT **2 :** COMPLAIN 1 [alteration of *hollo,* of unknown origin] — **holler** *n*

hol·lo \hä-ˈlō, hə-; ˈhäl-ō\ *or* **hal·lo** \hə-ˈlō, ha-\ *or* **hal·loo** \-ˈlü\ *interj* **1** — used to attract attention **2** — used as a call of encouragement or jubilation [origin unknown]

[1]hol·low \ˈhäl-ō\ *n* **1 :** an empty space within something : HOLE ⟨the *hollow* of a tree⟩ **2 :** a low spot in a surface; *esp* : VALLEY

[2]hollow *adj* **1 :** curved inward : SUNKEN ⟨*hollow* cheeks⟩ **2 :** having a hole inside : not solid throughout ⟨a *hollow* tree⟩ **3 :** apparently but not really valuable, sincere, or significant ⟨a *hollow* victory⟩ ⟨*hollow* promises⟩ **4 :** echoing like a sound made in a large empty enclosure or by beating on a hollow object [Middle English *holh, holw,* from Old English, "hole, hollow"] — **hol·low·ly** *adv* — **hol·low·ness** *n*

[3]hollow *vb* : to make or become hollow

hol·low·ware *or* **hol·lo·ware** \ˈhäl-ə-ˌwaər, -ˌweər\ *n* : vessels (as cups or vases) usually of pottery, metal, or glass that have significant depth and volume

hol·ly \ˈhäl-ē\ *n, pl* **hollies :** either of two trees or shrubs of U.S. or Eurasia with thick glossy spiny-margined evergreen leaves and usually bright red berries; *also* : the foliage or branches of a holly [Old English *holen*]

hol·ly·hock \ˈhäl-ē-ˌhäk, -ˌhȯk\ *n* : a tall widely grown perennial or biennial herb that is probably of Asian origin, is related to the mallows, and has large coarse rounded leaves and tall spikes of showy flowers [Middle English *holihoc,* from *holi* "holy" + *hoc* "mallow," from Old English]

hollyhock

Hol·ly·wood bed \ˈhäl-ē-ˌwu̇d-\ *n* : a mattress on a box spring supported by low legs and often having an upholstered headboard [*Hollywood,* district of Los Angeles, California]

hol·mi·um \ˈhōl-mē-əm, ˈhō-\ *n* : a rare metallic element that forms highly magnetic compounds — see ELEMENT table [New Latin, from *Holmia* (Stockholm), Sweden]

holo- — see HOL-

ho·lo·caust \ˈhäl-ə-ˌkȯst, ˈhō-lə- also ˈhȯ-lə-\ *n* **1 :** a sacrifice consumed by fire **2 :** a thorough destruction especially by fire **3 a** *often cap* : the mass slaughter of European civilians and especially Jews by the Nazis during World War II **b :** a mass slaughter of people; *esp* : GENOCIDE [Late Latin *holocaustum,* from Greek *holokauston,* from *holokaustos* "burnt whole," from *holos* "whole" + *kaustos* "burnt," from *kaiein* "to burn"]

Ho·lo·cene \ˈhō-lə-ˌsēn, ˈhäl-ə-\ *adj* : of, relating to, or being the present epoch of geological history which is dated from the close of the Pleistocene — see GEOLOGIC TIME table — **Holocene** *n*

\ə\ **abut**	\au̇\ **out**	\i\ **tip**	\ȯ\ **saw**	\u̇\ **foot**
\ər\ **further**	\ch\ **chin**	\ī\ **life**	\ȯi\ **coin**	\y\ **yet**
\a\ **mat**	\e\ **pet**	\j\ **job**	\th\ **thin**	\yü\ **few**
\ā\ **take**	\ē\ **easy**	\ng\ **sing**	\t͟h\ **this**	\yu̇\ **cure**
\ä\ **cot, cart**	\g\ **go**	\ō\ **bone**	\ü\ **food**	\zh\ **vision**

ho·lo·gram \'hō-lə-ˌgram, 'häl-ə-\ *n* : a three-dimensional image reproduced from a pattern of interference produced by a laser; *also* : the pattern of interference itself
ho·lo·graph \'hō-lə-ˌgraf, 'häl-ə-\ *n* : a document wholly in the handwriting of its author — **holograph** *adj* — **ho·lo·graph·ic** \ˌhō-lə-'graf-ik, ˌhäl-ə-\ *adj*
ho·log·ra·phy \hō-'läg-rə-fē\ *n* : the process of making or using a hologram — **ho·lo·graph** \'hō-lə-ˌgraf, 'häl-ə-\ *vt* — **ho·lo·graph·ic** \ˌhō-lə-'graf-ik, ˌhäl-ə-\ *adj* — **ho·lo·graph·i·cal·ly** \-i-kə-lē, -klē\ *adv*
ho·lo·thu·ri·an \ˌhō-lə-'thu̇r-ē-ən, ˌhäl-ə-, -'thyu̇r-\ *n* : SEA CUCUMBER [derived from Greek *holothourion,* "water polyp"] — **holothurian** *adj*
Hol·stein \'hōl-ˌstēn, -ˌstīn\ *n* : any of a breed of large usually black-and-white dairy cattle that produce large quantities of comparatively low-fat milk [short for *Holstein-Friesian*]
Hol·stein–Frie·sian \-'frē-zhən\ *n* : HOLSTEIN [*Holstein,* Germany + *Friesian,* variant of *Frisian*]
hol·ster \'hōl-stər, 'hōlt-\ *n* : a usually leather case for carrying a pistol [Dutch]
ho·ly \'hō-lē\ *adj* **ho·li·er; -est** **1** : exalted or worthy of complete devotion as one perfect in goodness **2** : DIVINE **3** : devoted to the deity or the work of the deity : SACRED ⟨a *holy* temple⟩ ⟨*holy* monks⟩ **4** : worshipped as or as if sacred ⟨*holy* scripture⟩ **5** — used as an intensive ⟨this is a *holy* mess⟩ or in combination as a mild oath ⟨*holy* cow⟩ [Old English *hālig*]
Holy Communion *n* : COMMUNION 1a
holy day *n* : a day set aside for special religious observance
holy day of obligation : a feast on which Roman Catholics are obliged to attend mass
Holy Father *n* : POPE
Holy Ghost *n* : HOLY SPIRIT
Holy Grail *n* : GRAIL
holy order *n, often cap H&O* **1 a** : MAJOR ORDER — usually used in plural **b** : one of the orders of the ministry in the Anglican or Episcopal church **2** : the rite or sacrament of ordination — usually used in plural
Holy Roman Empire *n* : an empire consisting mainly of a loose confederation of German and Italian territories under the rule of an emperor and that existed from the 9th or 10th century to 1806
Holy Saturday *n* : the Saturday before Easter
Holy See *n* : the see of the pope
Holy Spirit *n* : the third person of the Christian Trinity
ho·ly·stone \'hō-lē-ˌstōn\ *n* : a soft sandstone used to scrub a ship's wooden decks — **holystone** *vb*
Holy Synod *n* : the governing body of a national Eastern church
Holy Thursday *n* : MAUNDY THURSDAY
holy war *n* : a war or violent campaign waged often by religious extremists for what is considered to be a holy purpose
holy water *n* : water blessed by a priest and used as a purifying sacramental
Holy Week *n* : the week before Easter
Holy Writ *n* : BIBLE
hom- *or* **homo-** *combining form* : one and the same : similar : alike ⟨*homo*graph⟩ [Greek *homos* "same"]
hom·age \'äm-ij, 'häm-\ *n* **1** : a ceremony in which a person pledged allegiance to a lord and became his vassal **2** : something done or given as an acknowledgment of a vassal's duty to his lord **3 a** : respectful admiration : HONOR ⟨paid *homage* to his father at the banquet⟩ **b** : something that attests to the worth of another or shows respect : TRIBUTE ⟨review filled with *homages* to her talent⟩ [Medieval French *homage, omage,* from *home* "man, vassal," from Latin *homo* "human being"]
hom·bre \'äm-brē, -ˌbrā\ *n* : FELLOW 4a [Spanish, "man," from Latin *homo*]
hom·burg \'häm-ˌbərg\ *n* : a man's felt hat with a stiff curled brim and a high crown creased lengthwise [*Bad Homburg,* Germany]
[1]**home** \'hōm\ *n* **1 a** : the house in which one lives or in which one's family lives **b** : a dwelling house ⟨new *homes* for sale⟩ **2** : the social unit formed by a family living together in one dwelling ⟨a city of 20,000 *homes*⟩ **3** : the place where something is usually or naturally found : HABITAT ⟨the *home* of the elephant⟩ **4** : the country or place where one lives or where one's ancestors lived **5** : HEADQUARTERS 2 **6** : a place for the care of persons unable to care for themselves ⟨a *home* for old people⟩ **7** : the goal or point to be reached in some games; *esp* : HOME PLATE [Old English *hām* "village, home"] — **home·like** \-ˌlīk\ *adj* — **at home** **1** : relaxed and comfortable ⟨made herself right *at home* in the hotel room⟩ **2** : KNOWLEDGEABLE ⟨teachers *at home* in their subjects⟩
[2]**home** *adv* **1** : to or at home ⟨go *home*⟩ ⟨stay *home*⟩ **2** : to a final, closed, or standard position ⟨drive a nail *home*⟩ **3** : to a vital core ⟨the truth struck *home*⟩ — **home free** : out of jeopardy or difficulty
[3]**home** *adj* **1** : of, relating to, or being a home or place of origin ⟨*home* office⟩ **2** : prepared, done, or designed for use in a home ⟨*home* remedies⟩ ⟨a *home* computing system⟩ **3** : operating or happening in a home area ⟨the *home* team⟩
[4]**home** *vb* **1 a** : to go or return home **b** : to return home accurately from a distance ⟨a pigeon *homes* to its loft⟩ **c** : to proceed to or toward a source of radiated energy used as a guide ⟨missiles *home* in on radar⟩ **d** : to proceed or direct attention toward an objective ⟨we're *homing* in on a solution⟩ **2** : to send to or provide with a home
home·body \'hōm-ˌbäd-ē\ *n* : one whose life centers on home
[1]**home·bound** \'hōm-ˌbau̇nd\ *adj* : going homeward ⟨*homebound* travelers⟩
[2]**homebound** *adj* : confined to the home
home·boy \'hōm-ˌbȯi\ *n* **1** : a boy or man from one's neighborhood, hometown, or region **2** : a fellow member of a youth gang **3** : an inner-city youth
home·bred \-'bred\ *adj* : produced at home : INDIGENOUS
home brew *n* : an alcoholic beverage made at home
home·com·ing \'hōm-ˌkəm-ing\ *n* **1** : a return home **2 a** : the return of a group of people usually on a special occasion to a place formerly frequented **b** : an annual celebration for alumni at a school (as a college or university)
home computer *n* : a presonal computer used in the home
home economics *n* : the study of the care and management of a home — called also *home ec* \-'ek\ — **home economist** *n*
home front *n* : the sphere of civilian activity in war
home·girl \'hōm-ˌgərl\ *n* **1** : a girl or woman from one's neighborhood, hometown, or region **2** : a girl or woman who is a member of one's peer group
home·grown \'hōm-'grōn\ *adj* **1** : grown or produced at home or nearby **2** : native to or characteristic of a particular place ⟨the festival will feature *homegrown* artists⟩
home·land \'hōm-ˌland\ *n* : native land : FATHERLAND
home·less \'hōm-ləs\ *adj* : having no home or permanent place of residence — **home·less·ness** *n*
home·ly \'hōm-lē\ *adj* **home·li·er; -est** **1** : characteristic of a home or home life **2 a** : PLAIN, SIMPLE ⟨*homely* manners⟩ **b** : not elaborate or complex ⟨*homely* virtues⟩ **3** : plain or unattractive in appearance ⟨a *homely* person⟩ — **home·li·ness** *n*
home·made \'hōm-'mād, 'hō-\ *adj* : made in the home, on the premises, or by one's own efforts ⟨*homemade* bread⟩
home·mak·er \'hōm-ˌmā-kər\ *n* : a person who manages a household especially as a wife and mother — **home·mak·ing** \-king\ *n or adj*
homeo- *also* **homoio-** *combining form* : like : similar ⟨*homeo*stasis⟩ ⟨*homoio*thermic⟩ [Greek *homoios,* from *homos* "same"]
ho·me·op·a·thy \ˌhō-mē-'äp-ə-thē\ *n* : a system of medical practice that treats disease especially with minute doses of material that would in healthy persons produce symptoms similar to those of the disease treated — **ho·meo·path** \'hō-mē-ə-ˌpath\ *n* — **ho·meo·path·ic** \ˌhō-mē-ə-'path-ik\ *adj*
ho·meo·sta·sis \ˌhō-mē-ō-'stā-səs\ *n* : a tendency toward keeping a relatively stable internal environment in the body of an organism by means of complex physiological interactions — **ho·meo·stat·ic** \-mē-ō-'stat-ik\ *adj*
ho·meo·ther·mic \ˌhō-mē-ō-'thər-mik\ *adj* : WARM-BLOODED [Greek *homoios* "similar" + *thermē* "heat"] — **ho·meo·therm** \'hō-mē-ə-ˌthərm\ *n*
home page *n* : the page of a World Wide Web site typically encountered first that usually contains links to other pages of the site
home plate *n* : the base at which a batter stands when batting and which a base runner must touch in order to score
hom·er \'hō-mər\ *n* **1** : HOME RUN **2** : HOMING PIGEON
home range *n* : the area to which an animal confines its activities — compare TERRITORY
Ho·mer·ic \hō-'mer-ik\ *adj* : of, relating to, or characteristic of the Greek poet Homer, his age, or his writings — **Ho·mer·i·cal·ly** \-i-kə-lē, -klē\ *adv*

home·room \'hōm-ˌrüm, -ˌru̇m\ *n* : a classroom where students report usually at the beginning of each school day
home rule *n* : self-government in internal affairs by the citizens of a dependent political unit
home run *n* : a hit in baseball that enables the batter to round all the bases and score a run
home·school \'hōm-ˌsku̇l\ *vb* : to teach school subjects to one's children at home
home·school·er \-ˌskül-ər\ *n* **1** : a person who homeschools **2** : a child who is homeschooled
home·sick \'hōm-ˌsik\ *adj* : longing for home and family while absent from them — **home·sick·ness** *n*
[1]**home·spun** \-ˌspən\ *adj* **1 a** : spun or made at home **b** : made of homespun **2** : SIMPLE, HOMELY ⟨*homespun* humor⟩
[2]**homespun** *n* : a loosely woven usually woolen or linen fabric originally made from homespun yarn
[1]**home·stead** \'hōm-ˌsted\ *n* **1 a** : the home and adjoining land occupied by a family **b** : an ancestral home **2** : a tract of land acquired from U.S. public lands by filing a record and living on and cultivating it
[2]**homestead** *vb* : to acquire or settle on land for use as a homestead ⟨*homesteaded* in Alaska⟩ — **home·stead·er** *n*
home·stretch \'hōm-'strech\ *n* **1** : the part of a racecourse between the last curve and the winning post **2** : a final stage (as of a project)
home·town \-'tau̇n\ *n* : the city or town where one was born or grew up; *also* : the place of one's principal residence
home·ward \'hōm-wərd\ *or* **home·wards** \-wərdz\ *adv* : toward or in the direction of home — **homeward** *adj*
home·work \-ˌwərk\ *n* : work and especially school lessons to be done at home or outside regular class hours
hom·ey \'hō-mē\ *adj* **hom·i·er; -est** : characteristic or evocative of home — **hom·ey·ness** *or* **hom·i·ness** *n*
ho·mi·cid·al \ˌhäm-ə-'sīd-l, ˌhō-mə-\ *adj* : of, relating to, or having tendencies toward homicide — **ho·mi·cid·al·ly** \-l-ē\ *adv*
ho·mi·cide \'häm-ə-ˌsīd, 'hō-mə-\ *n* **1** : a person who kills another **2** : a killing of one human being by another [Medieval French, from Latin *homicida*, from *homo* "human being" + *-cida* "-cide"; in sense 2, from Medieval French, from Latin *homicidium*, from *homo* + *-cidium*, "-cide"]
hom·i·let·ic \ˌhäm-ə-'let-ik\ *adj* **1** : of the nature of a homily **2** : of or relating to homiletics — **hom·i·let·i·cal** \-i-kəl\ *adj* — **hom·i·let·i·cal·ly** \-i-kə-lē, -klē\ *adv*
hom·i·let·ics \-'let-iks\ *n* : the art of preaching
hom·i·ly \'häm-ə-lē\ *n, pl* **-lies** **1** : SERMON **2** : a moral lecture [Medieval French *omelie*, from Late Latin *homilia*, from Greek, "conversation, discourse," from *homilein* "to consort with, address," from *homilos* "crowd, assembly"]
homing pigeon *n* : a racing pigeon trained to return home
hom·i·nid \'häm-ə-nəd\ *n* : any of a family (Hominidae) of erect 2-footed primate mammals comprising recent human beings together with extinct ancestral and related forms [derived from Latin *homin-*, *homo* "human being"] — **hominid** *adj*
hom·i·noid \'häm-ə-ˌnȯid\ *n* : any of a group of primates that includes humans, gorillas, orangutans, chimpanzees, and gibbons together with their extinct ancestral and related forms — **hominoid** *adj*
hom·i·ny \'häm-ə-nē\ *n* : dried corn with the hull and germ removed [Virginia Algonquian *-homen*, literally, "that treated (in the way specified)"]
ho·mo \'hō-mō\ *n, pl* **homos** : any of a genus *Homo* of hominids that includes modern humans (*H. sapiens*) and several extinct related species (as *H. erectus*) [Latin, "human being"]
homo- — see HOM-
ho·mog·e·nate \hō-'mäj-ə-ˌnāt\ *n* : a product of homogenizing
ho·mo·ge·ne·i·ty \ˌhō-mə-jə-'nē-ət-ē, -'nā-ət-\ *n* : the quality or state of being homogeneous
ho·mo·ge·neous \-'jē-nē-əs, -nyəs\ *adj* **1** : of the same or a similar kind or nature **2** : of uniform structure or composition throughout [Medieval Latin *homogeneus*, from Greek *homogenēs*, from *homos* "same" + *genos* "kind"] — **ho·mo·ge·neous·ly** *adv* — **ho·mo·ge·neous·ness** *n*
ho·mog·e·nize \hə-'mäj-ə-ˌnīz, hō-\ *vt* **1** : to make homogeneous **2 a** : to reduce to small particles of uniform size and distribute evenly ⟨*homogenize* paint⟩ **b** : to break up the fat globules of (milk) into very fine particles — **ho·mog·e·ni·za·tion** \-ˌmäj-ə-nə-'zā-shən\ *n* — **ho·mog·e·niz·er** \-'mäj-ə-ˌnī-zər\ *n*
ho·mog·e·nous \-'mäj-ə-nəs\ *adj* : HOMOGENEOUS
ho·mo·graph \'häm-ə-ˌgraf, 'hō-mə-\ *n* : one of two or more words spelled alike but different in origin or meaning or pronunciation (as the *bow* of a ship, a *bow* and arrow) — **ho·mo·graph·ic** \ˌhäm-ə-'graf-ik, ˌhō-mə-\ *adj*
homoio- — see HOMEO-
ho·mol·o·gous \hō-'mäl-ə-gəs, hə-\ *adj* **1 a** : having the same relative position, value, or structure **b** (1) : exhibiting biological homology ⟨a *homologous* wing and arm⟩ (2) : having the same or allelic genes with corresponding genes arranged in the same order ⟨*homologous* chromosomes⟩ **2** : derived from or developed in response to organisms of the same species ⟨*homologous* tissue graft⟩ [Greek *homologos* "agreeing," from *homos* "same" + *legein* "to say"]
ho·mo·logue *or* **ho·mo·log** \'hō-mə-ˌlȯg, 'häm-ə-, -ˌläg\ *n* : something (as a chromosome) that is homologous
ho·mol·o·gy \hō-'mäl-ə-jē, hə-\ *n, pl* **-gies** **1** : a similarity often attributable to common origin **2 a** : structural likeness between corresponding parts (as the wing of a bat and the human arm) of different organisms due to evolution from a corresponding part in a common ancestor — compare ANALOGY **b** : structural likeness between a series of parts (as vertebrae) in the same individual
hom·onym \'häm-ə-ˌnim, 'hō-mə-\ *n* **1 a** : HOMOPHONE **b** : HOMOGRAPH **2** : one of two or more words spelled and pronounced alike but different in meaning ⟨*pool* of water and *pool* (the game) are *homonyms*⟩ [Latin *homonymum*, from Greek *homōnymon*, from *homōnymos* "having the same name," from *homos* "same" + *onyma, onoma* "name"] — **hom·onym·ic** \ˌhäm-ə-'nim-ik, ˌhō-mə-\ *adj*
ho·mo·pho·bia \ˌhō-mə-'fō-bē-ə\ *n* : irrational fear of, aversion to, or discrimination against homosexuality or homosexuals — **ho·mo·pho·bic** \-'fō-bik\ *adj*
ho·mo·phone \'häm-ə-ˌfōn, 'hō-mə-\ *n* : one of two or more words pronounced alike but different in meaning or derivation or spelling ⟨*to, too,* and *two* are *homophones*⟩ — **ho·mo·phon·ic** \ˌhäm-ə-'fän-ik, ˌhō-mə-\ *adj* — **ho·moph·o·nous** \hō-'mäf-ə-nəs\ *adj*
ho·mop·ter·ous \hō-'mäp-tə-rəs\ *adj* : of or relating to a group (Homoptera) of insects (as cicadas, aphids, or scale insects) having sucking mouthparts [derived from Greek *homos* "same" + *pteron* "wing"] — **ho·mop·ter·an** \-rən\ *adj or n*
Ho·mo sa·pi·ens \ˌhō-mō-'sap-ē-ənz, -'sā-pē-, -ˌenz\ *n* : HUMANKIND [New Latin, species name, from Latin *homo* "human being" + *sapiens* "wise, intelligent"]
ho·mo·sex·u·al \ˌhō-mə-'sek-shə-wəl, -shəl\ *adj* **1** : of, relating to, or exhibiting sexual desire toward a member of the same sex **2** : of, relating to, or involving sexual intercourse between persons of the same sex — **homosexual** *n* — **ho·mo·sex·u·al·i·ty** \-ˌsek-shə-'wal-ət-ē\ *n*
ho·mo·zy·gote \-'zī-ˌgōt\ *n* : a plant or animal with at least one gene pair that contains identical genes — **ho·mo·zy·gos·i·ty** \-zī-'gäs-ət-ē\ *n* — **ho·mo·zy·gous** \-'zī-gəs\ *adj*
hone \'hōn\ *vt* **1** : to sharpen or smooth with or as if with a fine abrasive stone **2** : to make more acute, intense, or effective ⟨top athletes *honing* their skills⟩ — **hon·er** *n*
hon·est \'än-əst\ *adj* **1 a** : free from fraud or deception : TRUTHFUL ⟨an *honest* plea⟩ **b** : GENUINE, REAL ⟨made an *honest* mistake⟩ **c** : not costly or fancy : PLAIN **2** : virtuous in the eyes of society : RESPECTABLE **3** : of a creditable nature : PRAISEWORTHY ⟨do an *honest* job⟩ **4 a** : marked by integrity **b** : marked by frankness or sincerity : STRAIGHTFORWARD **c** : INNOCENT 4, SIMPLE [Medieval French *honeste*, from Latin *honestus* "honorable," from *honos, honor* "honor"] — **hon·est·ly** *adv*
hon·es·ty \'än-ə-stē\ *n* **1** : fairness and straightforwardness of conduct : INTEGRITY **2** : TRUTHFULNESS, SINCERITY ⟨*honesty* is the best policy⟩
[1]**hon·ey** \'hən-ē\ *n, pl* **honeys** **1** : a thick sugary material prepared by bees from floral nectar and stored by them in a honeycomb for food **2 a** : SWEETHEART, DEAR — often used as a term of endearment **b** : a superlative example ⟨a *honey* of a play⟩ **3** : the quality or state of being sweet : SWEETNESS [Old English *hunig*] — **honey** *adj*

\ə\ **abut**	\au̇\ **out**	\i\ **tip**	\ȯ\ **saw**	\u̇\ **foot**
\ər\ **further**	\ch\ **chin**	\ī\ **life**	\ȯi\ **coin**	\y\ **yet**
\a\ **mat**	\e\ **pet**	\j\ **job**	\th\ **thin**	\yü\ **few**
\ā\ **take**	\ē\ **easy**	\ng\ **sing**	\th\ **this**	\yu̇\ **cure**
\ä\ **cot, cart**	\g\ **go**	\ō\ **bone**	\ü\ **food**	\zh\ **vision**

[2]**honey** *vb* **hon·eyed** *also* **hon·ied; hon·ey·ing 1** : to sweeten with or as if with honey **2** : FLATTER

hon·ey·bee \ˈhən-ē-ˌbē\ *n* : a social honey-producing bee; *esp* : a European bee widely kept in hives for the honey it produces

[1]**hon·ey·comb** \-ˌkōm\ *n* **1** : a mass of 6-sided wax cells built by honeybees in their nest to contain their young and store honey **2** : something that resembles a honeycomb in structure or appearance

[2]**honeycomb** *vb* : to make or become full of holes like a honeycomb

hon·ey·dew \ˈhən-ē-ˌdü, -ˌdyü\ *n* **1** : a sugary deposit secreted on the leaves of plants by aphids, scale insects, or sometimes by a fungus **2** : HONEYDEW MELON

honeydew melon *n* : a pale smooth-skinned winter melon with sweet greenish flesh

honeyed *adj* **1** : made with, resembling, or having honey ⟨*honeyed* candies⟩ **2** : pleasantly sweet ⟨a singer with a *honeyed* voice⟩

honey locust *n* : a tall usually spiny North American tree of the legume family with hard durable wood and long flat twisted pods

hon·ey·moon \ˈhən-ē-ˌmün\ *n* **1** : the time immediately after marriage **2** : a trip or vacation taken by a newly married couple [from the idea that the first month of marriage is the sweetest] — **honeymoon** *vi* — **hon·ey·moon·er** *n*

hon·ey·suck·le \-ˌsək-əl\ *n* : any of a genus of shrubs with fragrant tubular flowers rich in nectar; *also* : any of various plants (as a columbine or azalea) with tubular flowers rich in nectar [Old English *hunisūce,* from *hunig* "honey" + *sūcan* "to suck"]

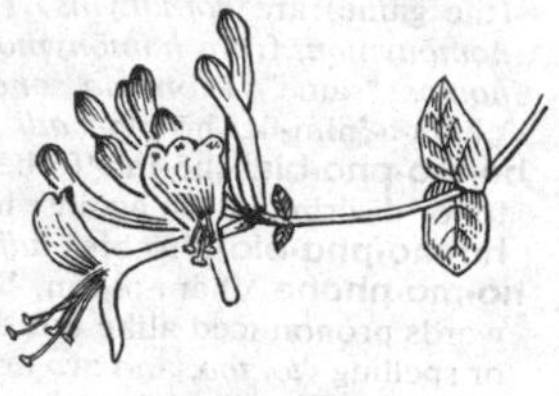

honeysuckle

honk \ˈhängk, ˈhȯngk\ *vb* : to utter the characteristic cry of a goose or a similar sound [imitative] — **honk** *n*

hon·ky–tonk \ˈhäng-kē-ˌtängk, ˈhȯng-kē-ˌtȯngk\ *n* : a cheap nightclub or dance hall [origin unknown]

[1]**hon·or** \ˈan-ər\ *n* **1 a** : good name or public esteem : REPUTATION **b** : a showing of usually merited respect : RECOGNITION ⟨a leader worthy of all possible *honor*⟩ **2** : PRIVILEGE ⟨whom have I the *honor* of addressing⟩ **3** *cap* — used especially as a title for a holder of high office ⟨if Your *Honor* please⟩ **4** : one whose worth brings respect or fame : CREDIT ⟨an *honor* to your profession⟩ **5** : an evidence or symbol of distinction: as **a** : an exalted title or rank **b** : BADGE 3, DECORATION **c** : a ceremonial rite or observance ⟨buried with full military *honors*⟩ **d** : an award in a contest or field of competition **e** *pl* (1) : an academic distinction conferred on a superior student (2) : a course of study for superior students that supplements or replaces a regular course ⟨took *honors* biology⟩ **6** : CHASTITY, PURITY **7 a** : a keen sense of ethical conduct : INTEGRITY ⟨refused as a matter of *honor*⟩ **b** : one's word given as a guarantee of performance ⟨on my *honor,* I will be there⟩ **8** *pl* : social courtesies or civilities extended by a host ⟨did the *honors* at the table⟩ [Medieval French *onur, honur,* from Latin *honos, honor*] ***synonyms*** see DEFERENCE

[2]**honor** *vt* **hon·ored; hon·or·ing** \ˈän-ring, -ə-ring\ **1 a** : to regard or treat with honor : RESPECT ⟨*honor* your parents⟩ **b** : to confer honor on **2** : to live up to or fulfill the terms of; *esp* : to accept and pay when due ⟨*honor* a check⟩ **3** : to salute with a bow in square dancing

hon·or·able \ˈän-rə-bəl, -ə-rə-; ˈän-ər-bəl\ *adj* **1** : deserving of honor and respect **2 a** : of great renown : ILLUSTRIOUS **b** *cap* — used as a title usually placed before the names of various high-ranking persons ⟨the *Honorable* John M. Doe⟩ **3** : performed or accompanied with marks of honor or respect ⟨an *honorable* burial⟩ **4 a** : doing credit to the possessor **b** : consistent with an untarnished reputation **5** : characterized by integrity : ETHICAL — **hon·or·ably** \-blē\ *adv*

hon·o·rar·i·um \ˌän-ə-ˈrer-ē-əm\ *n, pl* **-ia** \-ē-ə\ *also* **-i·ums** : a payment for a service on which custom forbids a price to be set [Latin, from *honorarius* "honorary"]

hon·or·ary \ˈän-ə-ˌrer-ē\ *adj* **1 a** : having or conferring distinction **b** : COMMEMORATIVE ⟨an *honorary* plaque⟩ **2** : conferred in recognition of achievement or service without the usual requirements or obligations ⟨an *honorary* degree⟩ **3** : UNPAID, VOLUNTARY ⟨*honorary* chairman⟩ [Latin *honorarius,* from *honor* "honor"] — **hon·or·ar·i·ly** \ˌän-ə-ˈrer-ə-lē\ *adv*

honor guard *n* : a guard assigned to a ceremonial duty

[1]**hon·or·if·ic** \ˌän-ə-ˈrif-ik\ *adj* **1** : conferring or conveying honor **2** : belonging to or constituting a class of grammatical forms used in speaking to or about a social superior

[2]**honorific** *n* : an honorific word, phrase, or form

honor roll *n* : a list of names of persons deserving honor; *esp* : a list of students achieving academic distinction

honor society *n* : a society for the recognition of scholarly achievement

honor system *n* : a system where persons are trusted to abide by the regulations without supervision or surveillance

hon·our \ˈän-ər\ *chiefly British variant of* HONOR

[1]**hood** \ˈhu̇d\ *n* **1 a** : a flexible covering for the head and neck **b** : a protective covering for the head and face **2 a** : an ornamental scarf worn over an academic gown **b** : a color marking, crest, or expandable fold on the head of an animal **3 a** : something that resembles a hood **b** : a cover for parts of mechanisms; *esp* : the movable metal covering over the engine of an automobile **c** : an enclosure provided with a draft for carrying off disagreeable or harmful fumes, sprays, or dust [Old English *hōd*] — **hood** *vt* — **hood·like** \-ˌlīk\ *adj*

[2]**hood** \ˈhu̇d, ˈhüd\ *n* : HOODLUM

-hood \ˌhu̇d\ *n suffix* **1** : state : condition : quality : character ⟨hardi*hood*⟩ **2** : time : period ⟨child*hood*⟩ **3** : instance of a (specified) state or quality ⟨false*hood*⟩ **4** : individuals sharing a (specified) state or character ⟨brother*hood*⟩ [Old English *-hād*]

hood·ed \ˈhu̇d-əd\ *adj* **1** : having or shaped like a hood **2** : being half-closed ⟨*hooded* eyes⟩ — **hood·ed·ness** *n*

hood·lum \ˈhüd-ləm\ *n* **1** : THUG, MOBSTER **2** : a young ruffian [perhaps from German dialect *hudelum* "disorderly"]

hoo·doo \ˈhüd-ü\ *n, pl* **hoodoos 1** : VOODOO 1 **2** : something that brings bad luck [perhaps alteration of *voodoo*] — **hoodoo** *vt* — **hoo·doo·ism** \-ˌiz-əm\ *n*

hood·wink \ˈhu̇d-ˌwingk\ *vt* **1** *archaic* : BLINDFOLD **2** : DECEIVE, CHEAT [[1]*hood* + *wink*]

hoo·ey \ˈhü-ē\ *n* : NONSENSE 1 [origin unknown]

[1]**hoof** \ˈhu̇f, ˈhüf\ *n, pl* **hooves** \ˈhu̇vz, ˈhüvz\ *or* **hoofs 1** : a curved covering of horn that protects the front of or encloses the ends of the toes of some mammals and that corresponds to a nail or claw **2** : a hoofed foot especially of a horse [Old English *hōf*] — **hoofed** \ˈhu̇ft, ˈhüft, ˈhu̇vd, ˈhüvd\ *adj* — **on the hoof** : before butchering : LIVING ⟨meat animals bought *on the hoof*⟩

[2]**hoof** *vb* **1** : to walk especially with haste ⟨*hoofed* it to class⟩ **2** : to dance especially as a performer ⟨watched the cast *hoofing* on stage⟩

hoof–and–mouth disease *n* : FOOT-AND-MOUTH DISEASE

hoof·beat \ˈhu̇f-ˌbēt, ˈhüf-\ *n* : the sound of a hoof striking a hard surface (as the ground)

[1]**hook** \ˈhu̇k\ *n* **1** : a curved or bent implement for catching, holding, or pulling **2** : something curved or bent like a hook **3** : a path of a ball that deviates from a straight course in a direction opposite to the dominant hand of the player propelling it **4** : a short blow delivered with a circular motion by a boxer while the elbow remains bent and rigid **5** : a selling point **6** : CRADLE 3a ⟨left the phone off the *hook*⟩ [Old English *hōc*] — **by hook or by crook** : by any means — **off the hook** : out of trouble — **on one's own hook** : by oneself : INDEPENDENTLY

[2]**hook** *vb* **1** : to form into a hook : CROOK, CURVE **2 a** : to seize, make fast, or connect by or as if by a hook **b** : to become secured or connected by or as if by a hook **3** : STEAL **4** : to make (as a rug) by drawing loops of thread, yarn, or cloth through a coarse fabric with a hook **5** : to hit or throw (a ball) so that a hook results

hoo·kah \ˈhu̇k-ə, ˈhü-kə\ *n* : WATER PIPE 2 [Arabic *ḥuqqa* "bottle of a water pipe"]

hook and eye *n* : a 2-part fastening device (as on a garment or a door) consisting of a metal hook that catches over a bar or into a loop

hooked \ˈhu̇kt\ *adj* **1** : shaped like or furnished with a hook **2** : made by hooking ⟨a *hooked* rug⟩ **3 a** : addicted to narcotics **b** : fascinated by or devoted to something ⟨*hooked* on skiing⟩

[1]**hook·er** \ˈhu̇k-ər\ *n* : one that hooks

[2]**hooker** *n* : a one-masted fishing boat; *also* : an outmoded or clumsy boat [Dutch *hoeker,* derived from *hoec* "fishhook"]

hook, line and sinker *adv* : without hesitation or reservation

: COMPLETELY ⟨fell for the story *hook, line and sinker*⟩ [from analogy with a well-hooked fish]

hook·up \ˈhu̇k-ˌəp\ *n* **1** : an assemblage (as of circuits) used for a specific purpose (as in radio); *also* : the plan of such an assemblage **2** : an arrangement of mechanical parts

hook up *vi* : to become associated especially in a working or social relationship

hook·worm \ˈhu̇k-ˌwərm\ *n* **1** : any of several parasitic nematode worms which have strong hooks or plates about the mouth and some of which are serious bloodsucking pests **2** : a diseased state marked by blood loss, paleness, and weakness due to hookworms in the intestine — called also *hookworm disease*

hooky *also* **hook·ey** \ˈhu̇k-ē\ *n, pl* **hook·ies** *also* **hookeys** : TRUANT — used chiefly in the phrase *play hooky* [probably from slang *hook, hook it* "to make off"]

hoo·li·gan \ˈhü-li-gən\ *n* : RUFFIAN, HOODLUM [perhaps from Patrick *Hooligan,* 19th century Irish hoodlum in London]

hoo·li·gan·ism \ˈhü-li-gə-ˌniz-əm\ *n* : rowdy, violent, or destructive behavior

¹**hoop** \ˈhüp, ˈhu̇p\ *n* **1** : a circular strip used especially for holding together the staves of containers or as a toy **2** : a circular figure or object : RING **3** : a circle or series of circles of flexible material used to expand a woman's skirt **4** : BASKETBALL — usually used in plural [Old English *hōp*]

²**hoop** *vt* : to bind or fasten with or as if with a hoop — **hoop·er** *n*

hoop·la \ˈhü-ˌplä\ *n* : great commotion and excitement : FUSS, BALLYHOO ⟨*hoopla* and fanfare of the bicentennial⟩ [French *houp-là,* interj.]

hoop·skirt \ˈhu̇p-ˈskərt, ˈhüp-\ *n* : a skirt stiffened with or as if with hoops

¹**hooray** *variant of* ¹HURRAH

²**hoo·ray** \hu̇-ˈrā\ *also* **hur·rah** \-ˈrȯ, -ˈrä\ *or* **hur·ray** \-ˈrā\ *interj* — used to express joy, approval, or encouragement

hoose·gow \ˈhüs-ˌgau̇\ *n* : JAIL [Spanish *juzgado* "panel of judges, courtroom," from *juzgar* "to judge," from Latin *judicare*]

¹**hoot** \ˈhüt\ *vb* **1** : to utter a loud shout usually in contempt **2** : to make the characteristic cry of an owl or a similar cry **3** : to assail or drive out by hooting ⟨*hooted* the speaker off the stage⟩ **4** : to express in or by hoots ⟨*hooted* disapproval⟩ [Middle English *houten,* of imitative origin] — **hoot·er** *n*

²**hoot** *n* **1** : the cry of an owl or a similar sound **2** : the least bit ⟨don't care a *hoot* about the book⟩ **3** : something or someone amusing ⟨this play is a *hoot*⟩

hoo·te·nan·ny \ˈhüt-n-ˌan-ē\ *n, pl* **-nies** : a gathering at which folksingers entertain often with the audience joining in [origin unknown]

¹**hop** \ˈhäp\ *vb* **hopped; hop·ping** **1** : to move by a quick springy leap or in a series of leaps; *esp* : to jump on one foot **2** : to jump over ⟨*hop* a puddle⟩ **3** : to move or get aboard by or as if by hopping ⟨*hop* a train⟩ ⟨*hop* in the car⟩ **4** : to make a quick trip especially by air **5** : to set about doing something ⟨*hop* to it⟩ [Old English *hoppian*]

²**hop** *n* **1 a** : a short brisk leap especially on one leg **b** : BOUNCE, REBOUND ⟨fielded the ball on the first *hop*⟩ **2** : DANCE, BALL ⟨the junior *hop*⟩ **3 a** : a flight in an airplane **b** : a short trip

³**hop** *n* **1** : a twining vine related to the mulberries and having lobed leaves and female flowers in cone-shaped catkins **2** *pl* : the ripe dried catkins of a hop used especially to impart a bitter flavor to malt liquors [Dutch *hoppe*]

⁴**hop** *vt* **hopped; hop·ping** : to flavor with hops

¹**hope** \ˈhōp\ *vb* **1** : to cherish a desire with anticipation ⟨*hope* to succeed⟩ ⟨*hope* for peace⟩ **2** : to long for with expectation of obtainment **3** : to expect with confidence : TRUST ⟨*hope* you'll accept the invitation⟩ [Old English *hopian*]

²**hope** *n* **1** *archaic* : TRUST, RELIANCE ⟨our *hope* is in the Lord⟩ **2 a** : desire accompanied by expectation of or belief in fulfillment ⟨in *hope* of an early recovery⟩ **b** : someone or something on which hopes are centered ⟨a fast halfback was the team's only *hope* for victory⟩ **c** : something hoped for

hope chest *n* : a young woman's accumulation of clothes and domestic furnishings (as silver or linen) kept in anticipation of her marriage; *also* : a chest for such an accumulation

¹**hope·ful** \ˈhōp-fəl\ *adj* **1** : having qualities which inspire hope ⟨a *hopeful* sign⟩ **2** : full of or inclined to hope — **hope·ful·ness** *n*

²**hopeful** *n* : a person who aspires to something or is considered promising ⟨a political *hopeful*⟩

hope·ful·ly \-fə-lē\ *adv* **1** : in a hopeful manner **2** : it is hoped : I hope : we hope ⟨*hopefully* the rain will end soon⟩

hope·less \ˈhō-pləs\ *adj* **1 a** : having no expectation of good or success **b** : not susceptible to remedy or cure : INCURABLE **2 a** : giving no ground for hope : DESPERATE ⟨a *hopeless* situation⟩ **b** : incapable of solution, management, or accomplishment : IMPOSSIBLE ⟨a *hopeless* task⟩ ***synonyms*** see DESPONDENT — **hope·less·ly** *adv* — **hope·less·ness** *n*

Ho·pi \ˈhō-pē\ *n, pl* **Hopi** *also* **Hopis** **1** : a member of an American Indian people of northeastern Arizona **2** : the Nahuatl-related language of the Hopi people [Hopi *hópi,* literally, "good, peaceful"]

hop·lite \ˈhäp-ˌlīt\ *n* : a heavily armed infantry soldier of ancient Greece [Greek *hoplitēs,* from *hoplon* "tool, weapon"]

hopped–up \ˈhäpt-ˈəp\ *adj* **1 a** : full of excitement or enthusiasm **b** : more interesting or attractive than normal **2** : SOUPED-UP ⟨put a *hopped-up* engine in the hot rod⟩

hop·per \ˈhäp-ər\ *n* **1 a** : one that hops or leaps **b** : a leaping insect; *esp* : an immature hopping form of an insect (as a grasshopper) **2 a** : a usually funnel-shaped receptacle for delivering material (as grain or coal) **b** : a freight car with a floor sloping to one or more hinged doors for discharging bulk materials — called also *hopper car* **c** : a tank holding liquid and having a device for releasing its contents through a pipe **3** : a box in which a bill to be considered by a legislative body is dropped [sense 2 from the shaking motion of hoppers used to feed grain into a mill]

¹**hopping** *adv* : to an extreme degree : EXTREMELY ⟨he was *hopping* mad⟩

²**hopping** *adj* **1** : intensely busy ⟨the restaurant was *hopping*⟩ **2** : extremely angry

hop·scotch \ˈhäp-ˌskäch\ *n* : a child's game in which a player tosses an object (as a stone) into areas of a figure outlined on the ground and hops through the figure and back to regain the object

ho·ra *also* **ho·rah** \ˈhōr-ə, ˈhȯr-ə\ *n* : a circle dance of Romania and Israel [Modern Hebrew *hōrāh,* from Romanian *horă*]

horde \ˈhōrd, ˈhȯrd\ *n* **1 a** : a political subdivision of central Asian nomads **b** : a nomadic people or tribe **2** : a great multitude : THRONG, SWARM ⟨*hordes* of tourists⟩ [Polish *horda,* from Ukrainian dialect *gorda,* alteration of *orda,* from Old Russian, from Turkic *orda, ordu* "Khan's residence"]

hore·hound \ˈhōr-ˌhau̇nd, ˈhȯr-\ *n* : an aromatic bitter mint with downy leaves; *also* : an extract or confection made from the dried leaves and flowering tops of this plant [Old English *hārhūne,* from *hār* "hoary" + *hūne* "horehound"]

ho·ri·zon \hə-ˈrīz-n\ *n* **1** : the apparent junction of earth and sky **2** : range of perception or experience ⟨reading broadens our *horizons*⟩ **3 a** : the geological deposit of a particular time **b** : a distinct layer of soil or its underlying material in a vertical section of land [Late Latin *horizont-, horizon,* from Greek *horizont-, horizōn,* from *horizein* "to bound," from *horos* "boundary"] — **ho·ri·zon·al** \-ˈrīz-nəl, -n-əl\ *adj*

hor·i·zon·tal \ˌhȯr-ə-ˈzänt-l, ˌhär-\ *adj* **1 a** : of, relating to, or situated near the horizon **b** : parallel to, in the plane of, or operating in a plane parallel to the horizon or to a baseline : LEVEL ⟨*horizontal* distance⟩ ⟨a *horizontal* engine⟩ **2** : relating to or consisting of individuals or groups of similar level in a hierarchy ⟨*horizontal* labor unions⟩ — **horizontal** *n* — **hor·i·zon·tal·ly** \-l-ē\ *adv*

horizontal bar *n* : a steel bar supported horizontally above the ground and used for swinging feats in gymnastics

hor·mone \ˈhȯr-ˌmōn\ *n* **1** : a product of living cells that circulates in body fluids (as blood) or sap and produces a specific and often stimulatory effect on cells usually at a distance from its point of origin; *also* : a synthetic substance that acts like a hormone **2** : SEX HORMONE [Greek *hormōn,* present participle of *horman* "to stir up, set in motion"] — **hor·mon·al** \hȯr-ˈmōn-l\ *adj* — **hor·mon·al·ly** \-l-ē\ *adv*

horn \ˈhȯrn\ *n* **1 a** : one of the hard growths of bone or keratin on the head of many hoofed animals: as (1) : one of the perma-

\ə\ **abut**	\au̇\ **out**	\i\ **tip**	\ȯ\ **saw**	\u̇\ **foot**
\ər\ **further**	\ch\ **chin**	\ī\ **life**	\ȯi\ **coin**	\y\ **yet**
\a\ **mat**	\e\ **pet**	\j\ **job**	\th\ **thin**	\yü\ **few**
\ā\ **take**	\ē\ **easy**	\ng\ **sing**	\t͟h\ **this**	\yu̇\ **cure**
\ä\ **cot, cart**	\g\ **go**	\ō\ **bone**	\ü\ **food**	\zh\ **vision**

nent paired hollow sheaths of keratin usually present in both sexes of cattle and their relatives that function chiefly for defense and arise from a bony core anchored to the skull (2) : ANTLER **b** : a tough fibrous material that consists chiefly of keratin and forms the sheath of a true horn and horny parts (as hooves or nails) **2** : a hollow animal's horn used to hold something (as gunpowder) **3** : something resembling or suggestive of a horn: as **a** : one of the curved ends of a crescent **b** : the knob on the pommel of a western-style saddle **4** : a manufactured product (as a plastic) resembling horn **5 a** : an animal's horn used as a musical instrument **b** : a brass wind instrument (as a trumpet or French horn) **c** : a usually electrical device that makes a noise like that of a horn ⟨an automobile *horn*⟩ [Old English] — **horned** \ˈhȯrnd\ *adj* — **horn·less** \ˈhȯrn-ləs\ *adj* — **horn·less·ness** *n* — **horn·like** \-ˌlīk\ *adj*

horn·beam \ˈhȯrn-ˌbēm\ *n* : any of a genus of trees related to the birches and having smooth gray bark and hard white wood

horn·bill \-ˌbil\ *n* : any of a family of large Old World birds with enormous bills

hornbill

horn·blende \-ˌblend\ *n* : a black, dark green, or brown mineral that is a variety of amphibole [German]

horn·book \-ˌbu̇k\ *n* **1** : an early primer for children consisting of a sheet of parchment or paper protected by a transparent sheet of horn **2** : a treatise of basic principles or skills

horned owl *n* : any of several owls with conspicuous tufts of feathers on the head; *esp* : GREAT HORNED OWL

horned pout *n* : a common bullhead of the eastern U.S.

horned toad *n* : any of several small harmless insect-eating lizards of the western U.S. and Mexico resembling toads and having hornlike spines

hor·net \ˈhȯr-nət\ *n* : any of the larger social wasps — compare YELLOW JACKET [Old English *hyrnet*]

hornet's nest *n* **1** : a troublesome or dangerous situation **2** : an angry reaction ⟨his rudeness stirred up a *hornet's nest*⟩

horn·felz \ˈhȯrn-ˌfelz\ *n* : a fine-grained rock produced by the action of heat especially on slate [German, from *Horn* "horn" + *Fels* "cliff, rock"]

horn in *vi* : to participate without invitation or consent : INTRUDE ⟨*horn in* on a conversation⟩

horn of plenty : CORNUCOPIA 1

horn·pipe \ˈhȯrn-ˌpīp\ *n* **1** : a single-reed wind instrument consisting of a wooden or bone pipe with finger holes and a bell and mouthpiece usually of horn **2** : a lively folk dance of the British Isles originally accompanied by hornpipe playing

horn·tail \-ˌtāl\ *n* : any of a various insects closely related to the sawflies but having the female with a stout hornlike ovipositor

horn·worm \-ˌwərm\ *n* : a hawk moth caterpillar having a hornlike tail process

horn·wort \-ˌwərt, -ˌwȯrt\ *n* : any of a genus of rootless mostly aquatic plants related to the liverworts

horny \ˈhȯr-nē\ *adj* **horn·i·er; -est** **1** : made of horn or of something resembling horn **2** : HARD, CALLOUS ⟨*horny* hands⟩

hor·o·scope \ˈhȯr-ə-ˌskōp, ˈhär-\ *n* **1** : a diagram of the relative positions of planets and signs of the zodiac at a specific time (as that of a person's birth) used by astrologers to infer character traits and foretell events **2** : an astrological forecast [Latin *horoscopus,* from Greek *hōroskopos,* from *hōra* "time, hour" + *skopos* "watcher"]

hor·ren·dous \hȯ-ˈren-dəs, hä-\ *adj* : DREADFUL, HORRIBLE [Latin *horrendus,* from *horrēre* "to shudder"] — **hor·ren·dous·ly** *adv*

hor·ri·ble \ˈhȯr-ə-bəl, ˈhär-\ *adj* **1** : marked by or arousing horror ⟨*horrible* scenes of death and destruction⟩ **2** : extremely unpleasant or bad ⟨had *horrible* weather in July⟩ — **hor·ri·bly** \-blē\ *adv*

hor·rid \ˈhȯr-əd, ˈhär-\ *adj* **1** : inspiring horror : SHOCKING ⟨the *horrid* rite of human sacrifice⟩ **2 a** : inspiring disgust or loathing ⟨a *horrid* man⟩ **b** : HORRIBLE 2 ⟨a *horrid* noise⟩ [Latin *horridus,* from *horrēre* "to shudder"] — **hor·rid·ly** *adv* — **hor·rid·ness** *n*

hor·rif·ic \hȯ-ˈrif-ik, hä-\ *adj* : causing horror

hor·ri·fy \ˈhȯr-ə-ˌfī, ˈhär-\ *vt* **-fied; -fy·ing** **1** : to cause to feel horror **2** : to fill with distaste : SHOCK

[1]**hor·ror** \ˈhȯr-ər, ˈhär-\ *n* **1 a** : painful and intense fear, dread, or dismay **b** : intense aversion or repugnance **2 a** : the quality of inspiring horror **b** : something that inspires horror ⟨the war was a *horror*⟩ **3** *pl* : a state of extreme depression or apprehension [Middle French, from Latin, "action of bristling," from *horrēre* "to bristle, shiver"]

[2]**horror** *adj* : causing feelings of horror : BLOODCURDLING ⟨a *horror* movie⟩

hors de combat \ˌȯrd-ə-kōⁿ-ˈbä\ *adv or adj* : out of combat : disabled especially from fighting [French]

hors d'oeuvre \ȯr-ˈdərv\ *n, pl* **hors d'oeuvres** *also* **hors d'oeuvre** \-ˈdərvz, -ˈdərv\ : any of various savory foods usually served as appetizers [French *hors-d'œuvre,* literally, "outside of the work"]

[1]**horse** \ˈhȯrs\ *n, pl* **hors·es** *also* **horse** **1 a** (1) : a large solid-hoofed plant- eating mammal domesticated since prehistoric times and used as a beast of burden, a draft animal, or for riding — compare PONY (2) : RACEHORSE ⟨play the *horses*⟩ **b** : a male horse : STALLION **2 a** : a frame that supports something (as wood while being cut or clothes while being dried) **b** (1) : POMMEL HORSE (2) : VAULTING HORSE **3** *slang* : HEROIN [Old English *hors*] — **from the horse's mouth** : from the original source

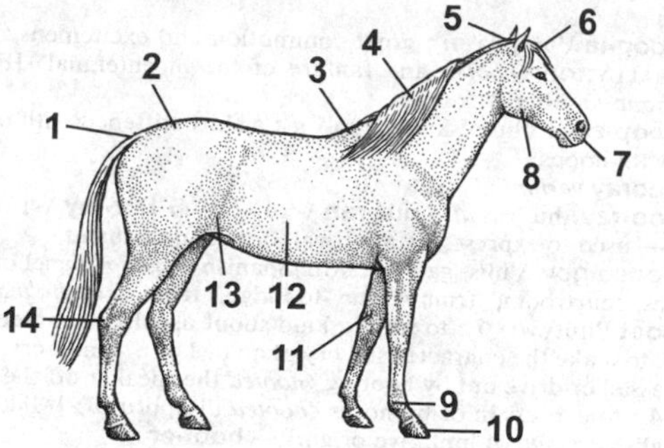

horse 1a: *1* dock, *2* croup, *3* withers, *4* mane, *5* poll, *6* forelock, *7* muzzle, *8* cheek, *9* fetlock, *10* hoof, *11* chestnut, *12* barrel, *13* flank, *14* hock

[2]**horse** *vt* **1** : to provide with a horse **2** : to lift, pull, or push by brute force

[3]**horse** *adj* **1 a** : of or relating to the horse **b** : hauled or powered by a horse ⟨a *horse* barge⟩ **2** : large or coarse of its kind ⟨*horse* corn⟩ **3** : mounted on horses ⟨*horse* guards⟩

horse around *vi* : to engage in horseplay

[1]**horse·back** \ˈhȯrs-ˌbak\ *n* : the back of a horse

[2]**horseback** *adv* : on horseback

horse·car \ˈhȯr-ˌskär\ *n* **1** : a streetcar drawn by horses **2** : a car for transporting horses

horse chestnut *n* : a large European tree that has palmate leaves and clusters of showy flowers and is widely grown as an ornamental and shade tree; *also* : its large glossy brown seed

horse·flesh \ˈhȯrs-ˌflesh\ *n* : horses for riding, driving, or racing

horse·fly \-ˌflī\ *n* : any of a family of swift usually large two-winged flies with bloodsucking females

horse·hair \-ˌhaər, -ˌheər\ *n* **1** : the hair of a horse especially from the mane or tail **2** : cloth made from horsehair

horsehair worm *n* : any of various long slender worms whose adults live in water and whose larvae are parasites of insects

horse·hide \ˈhȯrs-ˌhīd\ *n* : a horse's hide or leather made from it

horse latitudes *n pl* : either of two belts or regions in the neighborhood of 30° north and 30° south latitude characterized by high pressure, calms, and light changeable winds

horse·laugh \ˈhȯr-ˌslaf, -ˌsläf\ *n* : a loud boisterous laugh

horse·less carriage \ˈhȯr-sləs-\ *n* : AUTOMOBILE — used especially of early models

horse mackerel *n* : any of several large fishes (as a bluefin tuna)

horse·man \ˈhȯr-smən\ *n* **1 a** : a rider or driver of horses **b** : one skilled in managing horses **2** : a breeder or raiser of horses — **horse·man·ship** \-ˌship\ *n*

horse·mint \ˈhȯr-ˌsmint\ *n* : any of various coarse mints
horse nettle *n* : a coarse prickly weed of the nightshade family that has bright yellow fruit
horse opera *n* : WESTERN 2
horse·play \ˈhȯr-ˌsplā\ *n* : rough or boisterous play
horse·pow·er \ˈhȯr-ˌspau̇-ər, -ˌspau̇r\ *n* : a unit of power equal in the U.S. to 746 watts and nearly equal to the English unit of the same name that equals 550 foot-pounds of work per second
horse·rad·ish \ˈhȯrs-ˌrad-ish\ *n* **1** : a tall coarse white-flowered herb related to the mustards **2** : the pungent root of the horseradish; *also* : a seasoning prepared from the root
horse sense *n* : COMMON SENSE
horse·shoe \ˈhȯrs-ˌshü, ˈhȯrsh-\ *n* **1** : a usually U-shaped band of iron fitted and nailed to the rim of a horse's hoof to protect it **2** : something (as a valley) shaped like a horseshoe **3** *pl* : a game in which horseshoes or horseshoe-shaped pieces of metal are tossed at a stake in the ground in an attempt to encircle the stake or come closer than one's opponent — **horseshoe** *vt* — **horse·sho·er** \-ˌshü-ər\ *n*
horseshoe crab *n* : any of several closely related marine arthropods with a broad crescent-shaped cephalothorax and a spikelike tail — called also *king crab, limulus*
horse·tail \ˈhȯr-ˌstāl\ *n* : any of a genus of primitive perennial plants that reproduce by spores and have leaves reduced to tiny scales which encircle each node on the hollow jointed grooved stems — called also *equisetum, scouring rush*
horse trade *n* : negotiation accompanied by shrewd bargaining and concessions on both sides — **horse–trade** *vi* — **horse trader** *n*
horse·whip \ˈhȯr-ˌswip, ˈhȯrs-ˌhwip\ *vt* : to flog with or as if with a whip made to be used on a horse
horse·wom·an \ˈhȯr-ˌswu̇m-ən\ *n* **1** : a woman who is a rider or driver of horses **2** : a woman skilled in caring for or managing horses **3** : a woman who breeds or raises horses
hors·ey *also* **horsy** \ˈhȯr-sē\ *adj* **hors·i·er; -est 1** : of, relating to, or suggesting a horse **2 a** : having to do with horses or horse racing ⟨the *horsey* set⟩ **b** : characteristic of horsemen and horsewomen — **hors·i·ness** *n*
hor·ta·to·ry \ˈhȯrt-ə-ˌtōr-ē, -ˌtȯr-\ *adj* : given to or characterized by strong urging or encouragement [Late Latin *hortatorius,* from Latin *hortari* "to urge, exhort"]
hor·ti·cul·ture \ˈhȯrt-ə-ˌkəl-chər\ *n* : the science and art of growing fruits, vegetables, flowers, or ornamental plants [Latin *hortus* "garden"] — **hor·ti·cul·tur·al** \ˌhȯrt-ə-ˈkəlch-rəl, -ə-rəl\ *adj* — **hor·ti·cul·tur·al·ly** \-rə-lē\ *adv* — **hor·ti·cul·tur·ist** \-ˈkəlch-rəst, -ə-rəst\ *also* **hor·ti·cul·tur·al·ist** \-ˈkəl-chə-rə-list, -chrə-list\ *n*
ho·san·na \hō-ˈzan-ə\ *interj* — used as a cry of acclamation and adoration [Old English *osanna,* from Late Latin, from Greek *hōsanna,* from Hebrew *hōshīʿāh-nnā* "pray, save (us)!"]
[1]hose \ˈhōz\ *n, pl* **hose** *or* **hos·es 1** *pl* **hose a** (1) : a cloth leg covering that sometimes covers the foot (2) : STOCKING 1, SOCK **b** (1) : a close-fitting garment covering the legs and waist that is usually attached to a doublet by laces (2) : short breeches reaching to the knee **2** : a flexible tube for conveying a fluid (as from a faucet) [Old English *hosa* "stocking, husk"]
[2]hose *vt* : to spray, water, or wash with a hose
Ho·sea \hō-ˈzē-ə, -ˈzā-\ *n* : a prophetic book of canonical Jewish and Christian Scriptures — see BIBLE table
ho·siery \ˈhōzh-rē, ˈhōz-, -ə-rē\ *n* : HOSE 1a
hos·pice \ˈhäs-pəs\ *n* **1** : an inn for travelers; *esp* : one kept by a religious order **2** : a place or program designed to meet the physical and emotional needs of dying persons [French, from Latin *hospitium* "lodging," from *hospit-, hospes* "host"]
hos·pi·ta·ble \hä-ˈspit-ə-bəl, ˈhäs-pit-\ *adj* **1 a** : given to generous and cordial reception of guests ⟨our *hospitable* host⟩ **b** : promising or suggesting generous and cordial welcome **c** : offering a pleasant or sustaining environment ⟨a *hospitable* climate⟩ **2** : readily receptive : OPEN ⟨*hospitable* to new ideas⟩ — **hos·pi·ta·bly** \-blē\ *adv*
hos·pi·tal \ˈhäs-ˌpit-l\ *n* **1** : an institution where the sick or injured are given medical or surgical care **2** : a repair shop for specified small objects ⟨doll *hospital*⟩ [Medieval French, from Medieval Latin *hospitale* "hospice," from Latin *hospitalis* "of a guest," from *hospit-, hospes* "host, guest"]
hos·pi·tal·i·ty \ˌhäs-pə-ˈtal-ət-ē\ *n, pl* **-ties** : cordial reception and treatment (as of guests)
hos·pi·tal·ize \ˈhäs-ˌpit-l-ˌīz\ *vt* : to place in a hospital as a patient — **hos·pi·tal·iza·tion** \ˌhäs-ˌpit-l-ə-ˈzā-shən\ *n*
Hos·pi·tal·ler *or* **Hos·pi·tal·er** \-l-ər\ *n* : a member of a religious military order established in Jerusalem in the 12th century
[1]host \ˈhōst\ *n* **1** : ARMY 1a **2** : a very large number : MULTITUDE [Medieval French *ost,* from Late Latin *hostis,* from Latin, "stranger, enemy"]
[2]host *n* **1** : one who receives or entertains guests socially or as a business **2** : a living animal or plant on or in which a parasite lives **3** : MASTER OF CEREMONIES 3 **4** : a computer that controls network communications or that manages a database [Medieval French *hoste* "host, guest," from Latin *hospit-, hospes,* probably from *hostis* "stranger"]
[3]host *vb* **1** : to serve as host to, for, or at ⟨*host* a dinner⟩ ⟨*host* friends⟩ **2** : to serve as master of ceremonies for
[4]host *n, often cap* : the bread or wafer used in the Eucharist [Medieval French *oste, oiste,* from Latin *hostia* "sacrifice"]
hos·ta \ˈhōs-tə, ˈhäs-\ *n* : any of a genus of Asian plants that are related to the lilies and have leaves which grow from the base of the plant and stalks of white or violet flowers — called also *plantain lily* [New Latin, from Nicholas *Host,* died 1834, Austrian botanist]
hos·tage \ˈhäs tij\ *n* : a person held by one party in a conflict as a pledge that promises will be kept or terms met by the other party [Medieval French, from *hoste* "host, guest"]
host cell *n* : a living cell invaded by or capable of being invaded by an infectious agent (as a bacterium or virus)
hos·tel \ˈhäst-l\ *n* **1** : INN 1 **2** : a supervised lodging for usually young travelers — called also *youth hostel* [Medieval French, from Medieval Latin *hospitale* "hospice"]
hos·tel·er \ˈhäs-tə-lər\ *n* **1** : one that lodges guests or strangers **2** : a traveler who stops at hostels overnight
hos·tel·ry \ˈhäst-l-rē\ *n, pl* **-ries** : INN 1, HOTEL
host·ess \ˈhō-stəs\ *n* : a woman who acts as host; *esp* : one who greets and provides service for patrons — **hostess** *vb*
hos·tile \ˈhäst-l, ˈhäs-ˌtīl\ *adj* **1** : of or relating to an enemy ⟨*hostile* troops⟩ **2** : marked by open antagonism : UNFRIENDLY ⟨*hostile* to new ideas⟩ ⟨a *hostile* critic⟩ **3** : not hospitable ⟨a *hostile* environment⟩ [Latin *hostilis,* from *hostis* "enemy"] — **hos·tile·ly** \-l-lē, -ˌtīl-lē\ *adv*
hos·til·i·ty \hä-ˈstil-ət-ē\ *n, pl* **-ties 1 a** : deep-seated usually mutual ill will **b** (1) : hostile action (2) *pl* : overt acts of warfare **2** : conflict, opposition, or resistance in thought or principle ***synonyms*** see ENMITY
hos·tler \ˈäs-lər, ˈhäs-\ *also* **ost·ler** \ˈäs-\ *n* **1** : one who takes care of horses or mules **2** : one who moves or services locomotives [Medieval French *hosteler,* "innkeeper, hostler," from *hostel*]
[1]hot \ˈhät\ *adj* **hot·ter; hot·test 1 a** : having a relatively high temperature **b** : capable of burning, scalding, or searing **2** : having or showing intense feeling: as **a** : FIERY, VEHEMENT ⟨a *hot* temper⟩ **b** : VIOLENT 1 ⟨a *hot* battle⟩ **c** : LUSTFUL **d** : ZEALOUS ⟨*hot* for reform⟩ **3** : feeling or causing an uncomfortable degree of body heat ⟨it's *hot* in here⟩ **4 a** : newly made : FRESH ⟨*hot* off the press⟩ **b** : close to something sought or pursued ⟨guess again, you're getting *hotter*⟩ ⟨police were *hot* on their heels⟩ **5 a** : suggestive of heat or burning or glowing objects ⟨*hot* colors⟩ **b** : PUNGENT, SPICY ⟨*hot* sauces⟩ **6 a** : of intense and immediate interest ⟨a *hot* scandal⟩ **b** : temporarily capable of unusual performances ⟨felt *hot* with the dice⟩ **c** : currently popular ⟨cotton is the *hot* item for spring clothes⟩ **d** : very good ⟨a *hot* new lawyer⟩ **7 a** : electrically charged especially with high voltage **b** : RADIOACTIVE **8 a** : recently and illegally obtained ⟨the jewels are *hot*⟩ **b** : wanted by the police [Old English *hāt*] — **hot·ly** *adv* — **hot·ness** *n*
[2]hot *adv* : HOTLY
hot air *n* : empty talk ⟨his boasting was just *hot air*⟩
hot·bed \ˈhät-ˌbed\ *n* **1** : a bed of soil enclosed in glass, heated usually by fermenting manure, and used for forcing or for raising seedlings **2** : an environment set of circumstances that favors rapid growth or development ⟨a *hotbed* of activity⟩
hot–blood·ed \-ˈbləd-əd\ *adj* : easily roused or excited : PASSIONATE — **hot–blood·ed·ness** *n*

\ə\ **abut**	\au̇\ **out**	\i\ **tip**	\ȯ\ **saw**	\u̇\ **foot**
\ər\ **further**	\ch\ **chin**	\ī\ **life**	\ȯi\ **coin**	\y\ **yet**
\a\ **mat**	\e\ **pet**	\j\ **job**	\th\ **thin**	\yü\ **few**
\ā\ **take**	\ē\ **easy**	\ng\ **sing**	\t͟h\ **this**	\yu̇\ **cure**
\ä\ **cot, cart**	\g\ **go**	\ō\ **bone**	\ü\ **food**	\zh\ **vision**

hot•box \'hät-ˌbäks\ *n* **:** a bearing (as of a railroad car) overheated by friction
hot button *n* **:** an emotional and usually controversial issue that triggers immediate intense reaction
hot•cake \-ˌkāk\ *n* **:** PANCAKE — **like hotcakes :** at a rapid rate ⟨selling *like hotcakes*⟩
hotch•potch \'häch-ˌpäch\ *n* **:** HODGEPODGE [Medieval French *hochepot* "stew," from *hocher* "to shake" + *pot* "pot"]
hot cross bun *n* **:** a sweet bun that is marked with a cross on the top and often contains fruit (as raisins)
hot dog \'hät-ˌdȯg\ *n* **:** FRANKFURTER; *esp* **:** a cooked frankfurter usually served in a long split roll
ho•tel \hō-'tel\ *n* **:** an establishment that provides lodging and usually meals, entertainment, and various personal services for the public [French *hôtel,* from Medieval French *hostel* "hostel"]
[1]**hot•foot** \'hät-ˌfu̇t\ *adv* **:** in haste
[2]**hotfoot** *vi* **:** to go quickly **:** HURRY ⟨*hotfooted* it home⟩
[3]**hotfoot** *n, pl* **hotfoots :** a practical joke in which a match is secretly inserted into the side of a victim's shoe and lighted
hot•head \'hät-ˌhed\ *n* **:** a hotheaded person
hot•head•ed \-'hed-əd\ *adj* **1 :** easily angered **2 :** RASH 2, HEADSTRONG — **hot•head•ed•ly** *adv* — **hot•head•ed•ness** *n*
hot•house \'hät-ˌhau̇s\ *n* **:** a heated greenhouse — **hothouse** *adj*
hot•line \'hät-ˌlīn\ *n* **:** a direct telephone line for direct emergency use (as between heads of governments or to a counseling service)
hot link *n* **:** HYPERLINK
hot pepper *n* **1 :** a pungent often thin-walled and small pepper **2 :** a pepper plant of the nightshade family bearing hot peppers
hot plate *n* **:** a small portable appliance for heating or for cooking
hot rod *n* **:** an automobile rebuilt or modified for high speed and fast acceleration
hot–rod•der \'hät-ˌräd-ər\ *n* **:** a hot rod driver, builder, or enthusiast
hot seat *n* **:** a position of uneasiness, embarrassment, or anxiety
hot•shot \'hät-ˌshät\ *n* **:** a person who is talented or successful often in a showy or flashy way
hot spot *n* **1 :** a place of more than usual interest, activity, or popularity ⟨surfing *hot spots*⟩ **2 :** a place where hot magma from earth's interior rises through the mantle and crust to form a volcanic feature **3 :** an area of political, civil, or military unrest usually considered dangerous ⟨sent troops to a global *hot spot*⟩ **4 :** a place where a wireless Internet connection is available
hot spring *n* **:** a spring whose water emerges at a temperature higher than that of its surroundings
Hot•ten•tot \'hät-n-ˌtät\ *n* **:** KHOIKHOI [Afrikaans]
hot tub *n* **:** a large tub of hot water in which bathers soak; *also* **:** such a tub fitted with a device that creates forceful whirling currents of hot water
hot water *n* **:** a distressing or difficult situation **:** TROUBLE ⟨got in *hot water* at school⟩
hot–wire \'hät-ˌwīr\ *vt* **:** to start (as an automobile) by short-circuiting the ignition system
[1]**hound** \'hau̇nd\ *n* **1 a :** DOG 1a **b :** a dog of any of various hunting breeds typically having large drooping ears and a deep voice and following its prey by scent or sight **2 :** ENTHUSIAST; *esp* **:** one who eagerly seeks or collects something ⟨autograph *hounds*⟩ [Old English *hund*]
[2]**hound** *vt* **1 :** to pursue with or as if with hounds **2 :** HARASS 1
hour \'au̇r\ *n* **1 :** a time or office for daily devotion; *esp* **:** CANONICAL HOUR **2 :** one of the 24 divisions of a day **:** 60 minutes **3 a :** the time of day reckoned in two 12-hour periods ⟨the *hour* is now 10:00 a.m.⟩ **b** *pl* **:** the time reckoned in one 24-hour period ⟨in the military 4:00 p.m. is called 1600 *hours*⟩ **4 :** a customary or particular time ⟨the lunch *hour*⟩ ⟨in your *hour* of need⟩ **5 :** the work done or distance traveled at normal rate in an hour ⟨two *hours* away by car⟩ **6 :** a class session ⟨I have math this *hour*⟩ [Medieval French *ure, eure,* from Latin *hora* "hour of the day," from Greek *hōra*]
hour•glass \-ˌglas\ *n* **:** an instrument for measuring time in which usually sand runs from the upper to the lower part of a glass container in an hour — **hourglass** *adj*
hour hand *n* **:** the short hand that marks the hours on the face of a watch or clock
hou•ri \'hu̇r-ē, 'hü-rē\ *n* **:** one of the beautiful maidens that in Muslim belief live with the blessed in paradise [French, from Persian *hūri,* from Arabic *ḥūrīyah*]
hour•ly \'au̇r-lē\ *adj* **1 :** occurring hour by hour **2 :** computed in terms of one hour ⟨*hourly* wages⟩ **3 :** paid by the hour ⟨*hourly* workers⟩ — **hourly** *adv*
[1]**house** \'hau̇s\ *n, pl* **hous•es** \'hau̇-zəz\ **1 :** a building that serves as living quarters for one or more families **2 a :** an animal's shelter or habitation **b :** a building in which something is stored ⟨carriage *house*⟩ **3 a :** one of the 12 equal sectors in which the celestial sphere is divided in astrology **b :** a zodiacal sign that is the seat of a planet's greatest influence **4 a :** HOUSEHOLD **b :** FAMILY 2; *esp* **:** a royal or noble family ⟨the *house* of Windsor⟩ **5 a :** a residence for a religious community or for students **b :** the community or students in residence **6 a :** a legislative, deliberative, or consultative assembly; *esp* **:** one constituting a division of a bicameral body **b :** the place where an assembly meets **7 a :** a place of business or entertainment ⟨a movie *house*⟩ **b** (1) **:** a business organization ⟨a publishing *house*⟩ (2) **:** a gambling establishment ⟨a percentage of the bets always goes to the *house*⟩ **c :** the audience in a theater or concert hall ⟨played to a full *house*⟩ [Old English *hūs*] — **house•ful** \'hau̇s-ˌfu̇l\ *n* — **on the house :** without charge **:** FREE
[2]**house** \'hau̇z\ *vb* **1 a :** to provide with living quarters or shelter **b :** to store in a house **2 :** to encase, enclose, or shelter as if by putting in a house **3 :** to take shelter **:** LODGE
house•boat \'hau̇s-ˌbōt\ *n* **:** a usually flat-bottomed shallow-draft boat with a structure resembling a house built on deck for use as a dwelling on the water
house•bound \-ˌbau̇nd\ *adj* **:** confined to the house
house•boy \-ˌbȯi\ *n* **:** a boy or man hired to act as a general household servant
house•break \-ˌbrāk\ *vt* **:** to make housebroken
house•break•ing \-ˌbrā-king\ *n* **:** the act of breaking into and entering a person's dwelling house with the intent of committing a felony — **house•break•er** \-kər\ *n*
house•bro•ken \-ˌbrō-kən\ *adj* **:** trained to excretory habits acceptable in indoor living ⟨a *housebroken* dog⟩
house call *n* **:** a visit (as by a doctor) to a home to provide a requested service
house cat *n* **:** CAT 1a
house•clean \'hau̇-ˌsklēn\ *vb* **1 :** to clean a house and its furniture **2 :** to clean the surfaces and furnishings of (as a room) **3 :** to get rid of unwanted or undesirable items or people — **house•clean•ing** *n*
house•coat \'hau̇-ˌskōt\ *n* **:** a woman's often long-skirted informal garment for wear around the house
house•fly \'hau̇s-ˌflī\ *n* **:** a two-winged fly that is common about human habitations and can act as a carrier of disease
house•guest \-ˌgest\ *n* **:** GUEST 1a
[1]**house•hold** \'hau̇s-ˌhōld, 'hau̇-ˌsōld\ *n* **:** those who dwell under the same roof and compose a family; *also* **:** a social unit made up of those living together in the same dwelling
[2]**household** *adj* **1 :** of or relating to a household **:** DOMESTIC **2 :** FAMILIAR, COMMON ⟨a *household* name⟩
house•hold•er \'hau̇s-ˌhōl-dər, 'hau̇-ˌsōl-\ *n* **:** one who occupies a dwelling alone or as the head of a household
house•hus•band \-ˌhəz-bənd\ *n* **:** a husband who does housekeeping usually while his wife earns the family income
house•keep \'hau̇-ˌskēp\ *vi* **-kept** \-ˌskept\; **-keep•ing :** to care for and manage a house [back-formation from *housekeeper*]
house•keep•er \-ˌskē-pər\ *n* **:** a person employed to housekeep
house•keep•ing \-ping\ *n* **:** the care and management of a house and home affairs
house•lights \'hau̇-ˌslīts\ *n pl* **:** the lights that illuminate the parts of a theater occupied by the audience
house•maid \-ˌsmād\ *n* **:** a woman or girl employed to do housework
housemaid's knee *n* **:** bursitis of the knee
house•man \'hau̇-smən, -ˌsman\ *n* **:** a man who performs general work about a house **:** HOUSEBOY
house•mas•ter \-ˌsmas-tər\ *n* **:** a man in charge of a house in a boy's boarding school
house•mate \-ˌsmāt\ *n* **:** a person who lives with another in a house
house•moth•er \'hau̇-ˌsmət͟h-ər\ *n* **:** a woman acting as hostess, chaperone, and often housekeeper in a group residence
House of Burgesses : the representative assembly of colonial Virginia

house of cards : a structure, situation, or institution that is insubstantial, shaky, or in constant danger of collapse

House of Commons : the lower house of the British and Canadian parliaments

house of correction : an institution where persons are confined who have committed a minor offense and are considered capable of being reformed

House of Lords : the upper house of the British Parliament composed of the lords temporal and spiritual

house of representatives : the lower house of a legislative body (as the U.S. Congress)

house organ *n* **:** a periodical distributed by a business concern among its employees, sales personnel, and customers

house·par·ent \ˈhau̇-ˌsper-ənt\ *n* **:** an adult in charge of a dormitory, hall, hostel, or group residence

house party *n* **:** a party lasting over one or more nights at a residence (as a home or fraternity house)

house·plant \ˈhau̇-ˌsplant\ *n* **:** a plant grown or kept indoors

house–rais·ing \ˈhau̇s-ˌrā-ziŋ\ *n* **:** the putting up of a house or its framework by a gathering of neighbors

house rule *n* **:** a rule (as in a game) that applies only among a certain group or in a certain place

house seat *n* **:** a theater seat reserved by the management for a special guest

house sitter *n* **:** a person who occupies a dwelling to provide security and maintenance while the usual occupant is away — **house–sit** \ˈhau̇s-ˌsit\ *vi* — **house–sit·ting** \-ˌsit-iŋ\ *n*

house sparrow *n* **:** a sparrow native to Eurasia that is widely naturalized in the New World — called also *English sparrow*

house·top \ˈhau̇-ˌstäp\ *n* **:** ROOF 1

house·wares \-ˌswerz\ *n pl* **:** furnishings for a house; *esp* **:** small articles of household equipment (as cooking utensils)

house·warm·ing \-ˌswȯr-miŋ\ *n* **:** a party to celebrate moving into a new home

house·wife \ˈhau̇-ˌswīf, *2 is often* ˈhəz-əf, ˈhəs-əf\ *n* **1 :** a usually married woman in charge of a household **2 :** a small container for small articles (as thread) — **house·wife·li·ness** \ˈhau̇-ˌswī-flē-nəs\ *n* — **house·wife·ly** \-flē\ *adj* — **house·wif·ery** \-ˌswī-fə-rē, -frē\ *n*

house·work \ˈhau̇-ˌswərk\ *n* **:** the work of housekeeping

[1]**hous·ing** \ˈhau̇-ziŋ\ *n* **1 a :** the shelter of a temporary or permanent structure (as a tent or house) **:** LODGING **b :** dwellings provided for people ⟨*housing* for the elderly⟩ **2 a :** something that covers or protects **b :** a support (as a frame) for mechanical parts

[2]**housing** *n* **:** a usually ornamental covering for the back and sides of a horse [Medieval French *huce, houce,* of Germanic origin]

housing development *n* **:** a group of individual dwellings or apartment buildings typically of similar design that are usually built and sold or leased by one management

housing project *n* **:** a publicly supported and manged housing development planned usually for low-income families

hove *past of* HEAVE

hov·el \ˈhəv-əl, ˈhäv-\ *n* **1 :** an open shed or shelter **2 :** a small mean house **:** HUT [Middle English]

hov·er \ˈhəv-ər, ˈhäv-\ *vb* **hov·ered; hov·er·ing** \ˈhəv-riŋ, ˈhäv-, -ə-riŋ\ **1 a :** to hang fluttering in the air or on the wing ⟨hawks *hovering* over their prey⟩ **b :** to remain suspended over a place or object ⟨smoke *hovering* above the campfire⟩ **2 a :** to move to and fro near a place ⟨waiters *hovered* about⟩ **b :** to fluctuate around a certain point **c :** to be in a state of uncertainty, irresolution, or suspense ⟨*hovering* between life and death⟩ [Middle English *hoveren*] — **hover** *n* — **hov·er·er** \-ər-ər\ *n*

hov·er·craft \-ˌkraft\ *n* **:** a vehicle supported above the surface of land or water by a cushion of air produced by fans blowing downward

[1]**how** \hau̇, ˈhau̇\ *adv* **1 a :** in what manner or way ⟨learn *how* to study⟩ **b :** for what reason **:** WHY ⟨*how* can you do that⟩ **c :** with what meaning **:** to what effect ⟨*how* do you mean that⟩ **2 :** to what degree or extent ⟨*how* far will you travel⟩ **3 :** in what state or condition ⟨*how* are you⟩ **4 :** at what price ⟨*how* do you sell your eggs⟩ [Old English *hū*] — **how about :** what do you say to or think of ⟨*how about* another game⟩ — **how come :** how does it happen that **:** WHY ⟨*how come* you're so early⟩

[2]**how** *conj* **1 :** the way, manner, or condition in which ⟨remember *how* they fought⟩ ⟨asked *how* they were⟩ **2 :** HOWEVER ⟨do it *how* you like⟩

[3]**how** \ˈhau̇\ *n* **:** MANNER, METHOD ⟨the *hows* and whys⟩

[1]**how·be·it** \hau̇-ˈbē-ət\ *conj* **:** ALTHOUGH

[2]**howbeit** *adv* **:** NEVERTHELESS

how·dah \ˈhau̇d-ə\ *n* **:** a seat or covered pavilion on the back of an elephant or camel [Hindi & Urdu *hauda,* from Arabic *hawdaj*]

howdah

how·dy \ˈhau̇-dē\ *interj* — used to express a greeting [from *how do you do*]

[1]**how·ev·er** \hau̇-ˈev-ər\ *conj* **:** in whatever way or manner that ⟨go *however* you like⟩

[2]**however** *adv* **1 a :** in whatever manner or way ⟨I'll get there *however* I can⟩ **b :** to whatever degree or extent ⟨no prank, *however* innocent, was done⟩ **2 :** in spite of that **:** on the other hand ⟨still seems possible, *however,* that conditions will improve⟩ **3 :** how in the world ⟨*however* did you do it⟩

how·it·zer \ˈhau̇-ət-sər\ *n* **:** a short cannon used to fire projectiles in a high trajectory [Dutch *houwitser,* derived from Czech *houfnice,* a machine for hurling missiles]

howl \ˈhau̇l\ *vb* **1 :** to make a loud sustained doleful sound ⟨the wind *howled* all night⟩ **2 :** to cry out or declare without restraint under strong impulse (as pain, grief, or amusement) ⟨*howled* with laughter⟩ ⟨*howled* his protest⟩ **3 :** to affect, effect, or drive by adverse outcry ⟨*howl* down all opposition⟩ [Middle English *houlen*] — **howl** *n*

howl·er \ˈhau̇-lər\ *n* **1 a :** one that howls **b :** HOWLER MONKEY **2 :** a stupid and ridiculous blunder

howler monkey *n* **:** any of a genus of South and Central American monkeys that have a long grasping tail and are able to make loud howling noises

how·so·ev·er \ˌhau̇-sə-ˈwev-ər\ *adv* **1 :** in whatever manner **2 :** to whatever degree or extent

hoy·den \ˈhȯid-n\ *n* **:** a girl or woman of saucy, boisterous, or carefree behavior [perhaps from obsolete Dutch *heiden* "country lout," from Dutch, "heathen"] — **hoy·den·ish** \-ish\ *adj*

HTML \ˌāch-ˌtē-ˌem-ˈel\ *n* **:** a computer language used to create pages for the World Wide Web that can include text, pictures, sound, and hyperlinks [*h*yper*t*ext *m*arkup *l*anguage]

hua·ra·che \wə-ˈräch-ē, hə-\ *n* **:** a low-heeled sandal having an upper made of interwoven leather thongs [Mexican Spanish, from Tarascan (American Indian language of Mexico) *kʷaṛáči*]

hub \ˈhəb\ *n* **1 :** the central part of a circular object (as a wheel or propeller) **2 a :** a center of activity ⟨the *hub* of the universe⟩ **b :** a central device that connects computers to each other ⟨a network *hub*⟩ [probably alteration of [2]*hob*]

hub·bub \ˈhəb-ˌəb\ *n* **1 :** a noisy confusion of sound **:** UPROAR **2 :** TURMOIL [perhaps of Irish origin]

hu·bris \ˈhyü-brəs\ *n* **:** exaggerated pride or self-confidence [Greek *hybris*]

huck·le·ber·ry \ˈhək-əl-ˌber-ē\ *n* **1 :** an American shrub related to the blueberry; *also* **:** its edible dark blue to black usually acid berry **2 :** BLUEBERRY [perhaps alteration of *hurtleberry* "huckleberry"]

huck·ster \ˈhək-stər\ *n* **1 :** [2]HAWKER, PEDDLER **2 :** a writer of promotional material especially for radio or television [Dutch *hokester,* from *hoeken* "to peddle"]

[1]**hud·dle** \ˈhəd-l\ *vb* **hud·dled; hud·dling** \ˈhəd-liŋ, -l-iŋ\ **1** *British* **:** to throw together, arrange, or complete carelessly or hurriedly **2 :** to crowd, push, or pile together ⟨*huddled* in a doorway⟩ **3 a :** to gather in a group for conference **:** CONFER **b :** to gather in a huddle during a football game **4 :** to curl up **:** CROUCH ⟨a child *huddled* in its crib⟩ [probably from Middle English *hoderen*] — **hud·dler** \ˈhəd-lər, -l-ər\ *n*

[2]**huddle** *n* **1 :** a close-packed group **:** BUNCH **2 a :** CONFERENCE 1 **b :** a brief gathering of football players away from the line of scrimmage to receive instructions for the next down

hue \ˈhyü\ *n* **1 :** outward appearance **:** ASPECT **2 a :** COLOR 1

\ə\ **abut**	\au̇\ **out**	\i\ **tip**	\ȯ\ **saw**	\u̇\ **foot**
\ər\ **further**	\ch\ **chin**	\ī\ **life**	\ȯi\ **coin**	\y\ **yet**
\a\ **mat**	\e\ **pet**	\j\ **job**	\th\ **thin**	\yü\ **few**
\ā\ **take**	\ē\ **easy**	\ng\ **sing**	\t͟h\ **this**	\yu̇\ **cure**
\ä\ **cot, cart**	\g\ **go**	\ō\ **bone**	\ü\ **food**	\zh\ **vision**

gradation of color **c** : the attribute of colors that permits them to be classed as red, yellow, green, blue, or an intermediate between any neighboring pair of these colors [Old English *hīw*] ***synonyms*** see COLOR — **hued** \ˈhyüd\ *adj*

hue and cry *n* **1** : a loud outcry formerly used in the pursuit of one suspected of a crime **2** : a clamor of protest **3** : HUBBUB [earlier *hue* "outcry," from Medieval French *hue,* from *huer* "to shout, hoot"]

¹huff \ˈhəf\ *vi* **1** : PUFF 1a, b ⟨tourists *huffing* up the steps behind their guide⟩ **2 a** : BLUSTER 2, RANT ⟨*huffing* and puffing about taxes⟩ **b** : to react indignantly ⟨*huffed* off in a fit of anger⟩

²huff *n* : a fit of anger or pique ⟨all in a *huff* over nothing⟩

huffy \ˈhəf-ē\ *adj* **huff·i·er; -est** **1** : HAUGHTY **2 a** : aroused to indignation : OFFENDED **b** : easily offended : TOUCHY — **huff·i·ly** \ˈhəf-ə-lē\ *adv* — **huff·i·ness** *n*

hug \ˈhəg\ *vb* **hugged; hug·ging** **1** : to press tightly especially in the arms : EMBRACE **2** : to hold fast : CHERISH ⟨*hugged* their fancied grievances⟩ **3** : to stay close to ⟨drives along *hugging* the curb⟩ [perhaps of Scandinavian origin] — **hug** *n* — **hug·ga·ble** \ˈhəg-ə-bəl\ *adj* — **hug·ger** *n*

huge \ˈhyüj, ˈyüj\ *adj* : very large or extensive: as **a** : of great size or area **b** : great in scale or degree ⟨a *huge* success⟩ **c** : great in scope or character ⟨*huge* talent⟩ [Medieval French *ahuge*] ***synonyms*** see ENORMOUS — **huge·ly** *adv* — **huge·ness** *n*

hug·ger–mug·ger \ˈhəg-ər-ˌməg-ər\ *n* **1** : SECRECY 2 **2** : a disorderly jumble [origin unknown] — **hugger–mugger** *adj*

Hu·gue·not \ˈhyü-gə-ˌnät\ *n* : a French Protestant of the 16th and 17th centuries [Middle French, from Middle French dialect *eyguenot,* "adherent of a Swiss political movement," from German dialect *Eidgnosse* "confederate"]

huh *a snort or a strong* h-*sound followed with varying intonation by an* m-*sound or by* əⁿ; *often read as* ˈhə\ *interj* — used to express surprise, disbelief, confusion, or interrogation [imitative of a grunt]

hu·la \ˈhü-lə\ *also* **hu·la–hu·la** \ˌhü-lə-ˈhü-lə\ *n* : a Polynesian dance characterized by rhythmic movement of the hips and imitative hand gestures [Hawaiian]

Hu·la–Hoop \ˈhü-lə-ˌhüp, -ˌhu̇p\ *trademark* — used for a plastic hoop that is twirled around the body by hip movement

¹hulk \ˈhəlk\ *n* **1 a** : a heavy clumsy ship **b** : the body of an old ship unfit for service or of an abandoned wreck **2** : a bulky, unwieldy, or clumsy person or thing [Old English *hulc,* probably from Medieval Latin *holcas,* from Greek *holkas,* from *helkein* "to pull, drag"]

²hulk *vi* : to appear impressively large ⟨factories *hulked* along the river⟩

hulk·ing \ˈhəl-king\ *adj* : MASSIVE 2a, PONDEROUS

¹hull \ˈhəl\ *n* **1 a** : the outer covering of a fruit or seed **b** : the persistent calyx or involucre that clings to the base of some fruits (as a strawberry) **2** : the frame or body of a ship, flying boat, or airship **3** : COVERING, CASING [Old English *hulu*]

²hull *vt* : to remove the hulls of ⟨*hulled* strawberries⟩ — **hull·er** *n*

hul·la·ba·loo \ˈhəl-ə-bə-ˌlü\ *n, pl* **-loos** : a confused noise : UPROAR [perhaps from *hallo,* interjection used to attract attention + Scottish *balloo,* interjection used to hush children]

hum \ˈhəm\ *vb* **hummed; hum·ming** **1 a** : to utter a sound like that of the speech sound \m\ prolonged **b** : to make the characteristic buzzing sound of an insect in motion or a similar sound **c** : to give forth a low continuous blend of sound **2** : to sing with the lips closed and without articulation **3** : to be busily active [Middle English *hummen*] — **hum** *n* — **hum·mer** *n*

¹hu·man \ˈhyü-mən, ˈyü-\ *adj* **1** : of, relating to, or characteristic of humans ⟨the *human* body⟩ ⟨*human* history⟩ **2** : consisting of humans ⟨the *human* race⟩ **3 a** : having human form or attributes ⟨the dog's expression was almost *human*⟩ **b** : liable to or representative of the sympathies or frailties of human nature ⟨to err is *human*⟩ [Medieval French *humain,* from Latin *humanus*] — **hu·man·ness** \-mən-nəs\ *n*

synonyms HUMANE and HUMAN mean characteristic of or common to humanity. HUMAN applies to any feeling or quality shared by humanity in general ⟨*human* love⟩ ⟨*human* achievements⟩. HUMANE suggests the gentler side of human nature and implies compassion for people or animals in difficulty or need ⟨the growth of the *humane* treatment of prisoners⟩.

²human *n* : an individual of the species of primate mammal that walks on two feet, is related to the great apes, and is distinguished by a greatly developed brain with capacity for speech and abstract reasoning — **hu·man·like** \-ˌlīk\ *adj*

human being *n* : HUMAN

hu·mane \hyü-ˈmān, yü-\ *adj* **1** : marked by compassion, sympathy, or consideration for humans or animals **2** : characterized by broad humanistic culture ⟨*humane* studies⟩ [Middle English *humain*] ***synonyms*** see HUMAN — **hu·mane·ly** *adv* — **hu·mane·ness** \-ˈmān-nəs\ *n*

human immunodeficiency virus *n* : HIV

hu·man·ism \ˈhyü-mə-ˌniz-əm, ˈyü-\ *n* **1** : a revival of classical letters, an individualistic and inquiring spirit, and an emphasis on secular concerns characteristic of the Renaissance **2** : a doctrine, attitude, or way of life centered on human interests or values; *esp* : a philosophy that stresses the dignity and worth of human beings and their capacity for self-realization through reason and that often rejects supernaturalism — **hu·man·ist** \-nəst\ *n or adj* — **hu·man·is·tic** \ˌhyü-mə-ˈnis-tik, ˌyü-\ *adj*

hu·man·i·tar·i·an \ˌhyü-ˌman-ə-ˈter-ē-ən, ˌyü-\ *n* : a person promoting human welfare and social reform : PHILANTHROPIST — **humanitarian** *adj* — **hu·man·i·tar·i·an·ism** \-ē-ə-ˌniz-əm\ *n*

hu·man·i·ty \hyü-ˈman-ət-ē, yü-\ *n, pl* **-ties** **1** : the quality or state of being humane : COMPASSION **2** : the quality or state of being human ⟨the common *humanity* of all peoples⟩ **3** *pl* : the branches of learning having primarily a cultural character **4** : the totality of human beings both past and present

hu·man·ize \ˈhyü-mə-ˌnīz, ˈyü-\ *vb* **1 a** : to represent as human or with human attributes **b** : to adapt to human nature or use **2** : to make or become humane or more humane ⟨*humanize* industry⟩ — **hu·man·iza·tion** \ˌhyü-mə-nə-ˈzā-shən, ˌyü-\ *n*

hu·man·kind \ˈhyü-mən-ˌkīnd, ˈyü-\ *n* : the human race : HUMANITY 4

hu·man·ly \ˈhyü-mən-lē, ˈyü-\ *adv* **1** : with regard to human needs, emotions, or weakness ⟨*humanly* inaccurate⟩ ⟨need to provide *humanly* for the downtrodden⟩ **2 a** : from the viewpoint of human beings **b** : within the range of human capacity ⟨a task not *humanly* possible⟩

human nature *n* : the nature of humans; *esp* : the fundamental dispositions and traits of humans

hu·man·oid \-mə-ˌnȯid\ *adj* : having human form or characteristics — **humanoid** *n*

human resources *n pl* : a division of an organization concerned with personnel; *esp* : PERSONNEL 2

human rights *n pl* : rights (as freedom from unlawful imprisonment) regarded as belonging fundamentally to all persons

human trafficking *n* : organized criminal activity in which human beings are treated as possessions to be controlled and exploited (as by being forced into prostitution or involuntary labor)

¹hum·ble \ˈhəm-bəl, ˈəm-\ *adj* **hum·bler** \-bə-lər, -blər\; **hum·blest** \-bə-ləst, -bləst\ **1** : modest or meek in spirit or manner : not proud or assertive **2** : expressing a spirit of deference or submission ⟨a *humble* apology⟩ **3** : low in rank or status : UNPRETENTIOUS ⟨*humble* birth⟩ ⟨a *humble* position⟩ [Medieval French, from Latin *humilis* "low, humble," from *humus* "earth"] — **hum·bly** \-blē\ *adv*

²humble *vt* **hum·bled; hum·bling** \-bə-ling, -bling\ **1** : to make humble in spirit or manner **2** : to destroy the power, independence, or prestige of ⟨*humbled* their opponents with a crushing attack⟩ — **hum·bler** \-bə-lər, -blər\ *n*

hum·ble–bee \ˈhəm-bəl-ˌbē\ *n* : BUMBLEBEE [Middle English *humbylbee*]

humble pie *n* : a figurative serving of humiliation usually in the form of a forced submission, apology, or retraction ⟨made him eat *humble pie*⟩

hum·bug \ˈhəm-ˌbəg\ *n* **1 a** : something designed to deceive and mislead : FRAUD ⟨took their fervent denials as *humbug*⟩ **b** : CHARLATAN **2** : DRIVEL, NONSENSE ⟨the speech was full of *humbug*⟩ **3** *Brit* : a hard usually mint-flavored candy [origin unknown] — **humbug** *vb* — **hum·bug·gery** \-ˌbəg-rē, -ə-rē\ *n*

hum·ding·er \ˈhəm-ˈding-ər\ *n* : a striking or extraordinary person or thing [probably alteration of *hummer*]

hum·drum \ˈhəm-ˌdrəm\ *adj* : COMMONPLACE, ORDINARY [reduplication of *hum*]

hu·mec·tant \hyü-ˈmek-tənt\ *n* : a substance that promotes retention of moisture [Latin *humectare* "to moisten," from *humectus* "moist," from *humēre* "to be moist"]

hu·mer·al \ˈhyüm-rəl, -ə-rəl\ *adj* : of, relating to, or situated in the region of the humerus or shoulder or an analogous region — **humeral** *n*

humeral veil *n* : an oblong vestment worn around the shoulders and over the hands by a priest holding a sacred vessel (as a monstrance)

hu·mer·us \'hyü-mərs, -ə-rəs\ *n, pl* **hu·meri** \'hyü-mə-ˌrī, -ˌrē\ : the long bone of the upper arm or forelimb extending from the shoulder to the elbow [Latin, "upper arm, shoulder"]

hu·mic \'hyü-mik, 'yü-\ *adj* : of, relating to, or derived from humus ‹a *humic* acid›

hu·mid \'hyü-məd, 'yü-\ *adj* : containing or characterized by perceptible moisture ‹a *humid* day› ‹a *humid* climate› [Latin *humidus,* from *humēre* "to be moist"] — **hu·mid·ly** *adv*

hu·mid·i·fi·er \hyü-'mid-ə-ˌfī-ər, -ˌfīr\ *n* : a device for supplying or maintaining humidity

hu·mid·i·fy \hyü-'mid-ə-ˌfī, yü-\ *vt* **-fied; -fy·ing** : to make (as the air of a room) humid — **hu·mid·i·fi·ca·tion** \-ˌmid-ə-fə-'kā-shən\ *n*

hu·mid·i·ty \-'mid-ət-ē\ *n, pl* **-ties** : DAMPNESS, MOISTURE; *esp* : the amount of moisture in the air — compare RELATIVE HUMIDITY

hu·mi·dor \'hyü-mə-ˌdȯr, 'yü-\ *n* : a case (as for storing cigars) in which the air is kept properly humidified [*humid* + *-or* (as in *cuspidor*)]

hu·mil·i·ate \hyü-'mil-ē-ˌāt, yü-\ *vt* : to reduce to a lower position in one's own eyes or others' eyes : MORTIFY ‹the public reprimand *humiliated* the general› [Late Latin *humiliare,* from Latin *humilis* "low, humble"] — **hu·mil·i·a·tion** \-ˌmil-ē-'ā-shən\ *n*

hu·mil·i·ty \hyü-'mil-ət-ē, yü-\ *n* : the quality or state of being humble

hum·ming·bird \'həm-ing-ˌbərd\ *n* : any of numerous tiny brightly colored American birds related to the swifts and having narrow swiftly beating wings, a slender bill, and a long tongue for sipping nectar

hum·mock \'həm-ək\ *n* **1** : a rounded mound of earth : KNOLL **2** : a ridge or pile of ice [alteration of [2]*hammock*] — **hummocky** \-ə-kē\ *adj*

hu·mon·gous *also* **hu·mun·gous** \hyü-'məng-gəs\ *adj* : extremely large : HUGE ‹*humongous* amounts of money› [perhaps alteration of *huge* + *monstrous*]

[1]**hu·mor** \'hyü-mər, 'yü-\ *n* **1** : a normal functioning bodily semifluid or fluid (as the blood or lymph) — compare AQUEOUS HUMOR, VITREOUS HUMOR **2** : an often temporary state of mind induced especially by circumstances **3** : WHIM 1, FANCY **4** : the amusing quality of things ‹the *humor* of a situation› **5** : the power to see or tell about the amusing side of things : a keen perception of the comic or the ridiculous **6** : something comical or amusing [Medieval French *umor, umour* from Latin *humor* "moisture"] ***synonyms*** see MOOD, WIT — **hu·mor·less** \-ləs\ *adj* — **hu·mor·less·ness** *n* — **out of humor** : out of sorts

Word History In the Middle Ages it was believed that everything on Earth was made of different combinations of four elements: earth, air, fire, and water. These elements in turn were thought to be composed of combinations of what were known as the Four Contraries: hot, cold, moist, and dry. In people these same four contraries were thought to combine into the four humors: choler, blood, melancholy, and phlegm. The balance or imbalance of these humors determined a person's temperament. Coming from a Latin word meaning "moisture," *humor* originally reflected the combinations of heat and moisture that accounted for a person's disposition. *Humor* became a general term for "disposition" and soon came to mean "a mood or state of mind." From this developed the sense of "whim or fancy," from which are derived the senses of *humor* which refer to the comical or amusing.

[2]**humor** *vt* **hu·mored; hu·mor·ing** \'hyüm-ring, 'yüm-, -ə-ring\ : to comply with the wishes or mood of ‹*humor* a sick child›

hu·mor·al \'hyüm-rəl, 'yüm-, -ə-rəl\ *adj* : of, relating to, proceeding from, or involving a bodily humor and especially a hormone

hu·mor·esque \ˌhyü-mə-'resk, ˌyü-\ *n* : a typically whimsical or fanciful musical composition [German *Humoreske,* from *Humor* "humor," from Medieval Latin]

hu·mor·ist \'hyüm-rəst, 'yüm-, -ə-rəst\ *n* : a person specializing in or noted for humor

hu·mor·ous \'hyüm-rəs, 'yüm-, -ə-rəs\ *adj* : full of, characterized by, or expressive of humor : FUNNY ‹a *humorous* story› ***synonyms*** see WITTY — **hu·mor·ous·ly** *adv* — **hu·mor·ous·ness** *n*

hu·mour *chiefly British variant of* HUMOR

[1]**hump** \'həmp\ *n* **1** : a rounded bulge or lump (as on the back of a camel) **2** : KNOLL, HUMMOCK **3** : a difficult phase or obstacle ‹not finished, but finally over the *hump*› [related to Low German *hump* "bump"] — **humped** \'həmpt\ *adj*

[2]**hump** *vb* **1** : to exert oneself vigorously : HUSTLE **2** : to make hump-shaped : HUNCH

hump·back \'həmp-ˌbak\ *n* **1** : a humped or crooked back **2** : HUNCHBACK 1 **3** : HUMPBACK WHALE

hump·backed \-'bakt\ *or* **hump·back** \-ˌbak\ *adj* : having a humped back

humpback whale

humpback whale *n* : a large baleen whale that is black above and white below and has very long flippers

humpy \'həm-pē\ *adj* **hump·i·er; -est** : full of or covered with humps ‹*humpy* terrain›

hu·mus \'hyü-məs, 'yü-\ *n* : the brown or black organic portion of soil formed by partial decomposition of plant or animal matter [Latin, "earth"]

Hun \'hən\ *n* **1** : a member of a nomadic central Asian people gaining control of a large part of central and eastern Europe under Attila about A.D. 450 **2** *often not cap* : a person who is wantonly destructive [Old English *Hunas,* plural, from Late Latin *Hunni*]

[1]**hunch** \'hənch\ *vb* **1** : to thrust oneself forward ‹*hunch* nearer the fire› **2 a** : to assume a bent or crooked posture : curl up ‹sat *hunched* over the table› **b** : to bend over into a humped or crooked position ‹*hunch* one's shoulders› [origin unknown]

[2]**hunch** *n* **1** : HUMP 1 **2** : a strong intuitive feeling

hunch·back \'hənch-ˌbak\ *n* **1** : a person with a humpback **2** : HUMPBACK 1 — **hunch·backed** \-'bakt\ *adj*

hun·dred \'hən-drəd, -dərd\ *n, pl* **hundreds** *or* **hundred** **1** — see NUMBER table **2** : a great number ‹*hundreds* of times› **3** : a 100-dollar bill ‹gave me change for a *hundred*› [Old English] — **hundred** *adj*

hundreds digit *n* : the numeral (as 4 in 456) occupying the hundreds place in a number expressed in the Arabic system of writing numbers

hundreds place *n* : the place three to the left of the decimal point in a number expressed in the Arabic system of writing numbers

hun·dredth \'hən-drədth, -drətth\ *n* **1** : one of 100 equal parts of something **2** : one numbered 100 in a countable series — see NUMBER table — **hundredth** *adj*

hun·dredths place \'hən-drədths-, -drətths-\ *n* : the second place to the right of a decimal point in a number expressed in the Arabic system of writing numbers ‹4 is in the *hundredths place* in the number 1.246›

hun·dred·weight \'hən-drə-ˌdwāt, -dər-ˌdwāt\ *n, pl* **-weight** *or* **-weights** **1** : a unit of weight equal to 100 pounds (about 45.4 kilograms) — called also *short hundredweight*; see MEASURE table **2** *British* : a unit of weight equal to 112 pounds (about 50.8 kilograms) — called also *long hundredweight*

[1]**hung** *past and past participle of* HANG

[2]**hung** *adj* : unable to reach a decision or verdict ‹a *hung* jury›

Hun·gar·i·an \ˌhəng-'ger-ē-ən, -'gar-\ *n* **1 a** : a native or inhabitant of Hungary : MAGYAR **b** : a person of Hungarian descent **2** : the language of the Hungarians — **Hungarian** *adj*

[1]**hun·ger** \'həng-gər\ *n* **1 a** : a desire or a need for food **b** : an uneasy feeling or weakened condition resulting from lack of food **2** : a strong desire : CRAVING ‹a *hunger* for praise› [Old English *hungor*] — **hunger** *adj*

[2]**hunger** *vi* **hun·gered; hun·ger·ing** \-gə-ring, -gring\ **1** : to feel or suffer hunger **2** : to have an eager desire

hunger strike *n* : refusal (as by a prisoner) to eat enough to sustain life

hun·gry \'həng-grē\ *adj* **hun·gri·er; -est** **1** : feeling or showing hunger **2** : EAGER, AVID **3** : not rich or fertile : BARREN — **hun·gri·ly** \-grə-lē\ *adv* — **hun·gri·ness** \-grē-nəs\ *n*

hung up *adj* **1** : delayed for a time **2** : anxiously nervous **3**

\ə\ abut	\au̇\ out	\i\ tip	\ȯ\ saw	\u̇\ foot
\ər\ further	\ch\ chin	\ī\ life	\ȯi\ coin	\y\ yet
\a\ mat	\e\ pet	\j\ job	\th\ thin	\yü\ few
\ā\ take	\ē\ easy	\ng\ sing	\t͟h\ this	\yu̇\ cure
\ä\ cot, cart	\g\ go	\ō\ bone	\ü\ food	\zh\ vision

: having great or excessive interest in or preoccupation with someone or something ⟨still *hung up* on his old girlfriend⟩

hunk \ˈhəŋk\ *n* **1** : a large lump or piece **2** : a male who is physically very attractive [Dutch dialect *hunke*]

hun·ker \ˈhəŋ-kər\ *vi* **1** : CROUCH 1, SQUAT **2** : to settle in for a sustained period ⟨*hunkered* down for the long winter⟩ [probably related to Dutch *hucken, huken* "to squat"]

hun·kers \-kərz\ *n pl* : HINDQUARTER 2

hun·ky–do·ry \ˌhəŋ-kē-ˈdōr-ē, -ˈdȯr-\ *adj* : quite satisfactory : FINE [obsolete English dialect *hunk* "home base" + *-dory*, of unknown origin]

[1]hunt \ˈhənt\ *vb* **1 a** : to seek out and pursue (game) for food or sport ⟨*hunt* deer⟩ **b** : to use in hunting game ⟨*hunts* a pack of dogs⟩ **2** : to pursue with intent to capture **3 a** : to attempt to find something **b** : to search out : SEEK **4** : to drive or chase especially by harrying ⟨*hunt* a criminal out of town⟩ **5** : to search through in quest of prey ⟨*hunts* the woods⟩ **6** : to take part in a hunt [Old English *huntian*]

[2]hunt *n* **1** : the act, the practice, or an instance of hunting **2** : a group of hunters; *esp* : a group of hunters on horseback and their hunting dogs

hunt·er \ˈhənt-ər\ *n* **1 a** : a person who hunts game **b** : a dog or horse used or trained for hunting **2** : a person who searches for something

hunt·er–gath·er·er \ˈhənt-ər-ˈgath-ər-ər, -ˈgeth-\ *n* : a member of a culture in which food is obtained by hunting, fishing, and gathering rather than by agriculture or animal husbandry

hunt·ing *n* : the act of one that hunts; *esp* : the pursuit of game

Hun·ting·ton's disease \ˈhənt-iŋ-tənz-\ *n* : a hereditary nervous disorder that may develop in adult life and progress to dementia — called also *Huntington's chorea* [from George *Huntington*, died 1916, American physician]

hunt·ress \ˈhən-trəs\ *n* : a woman who is a hunter; *also* : a female animal that hunts prey

hunts·man \ˈhəns-mən\ *n* **1** : HUNTER 1a **2** : a person who manages a hunt and looks after the hounds

[1]hur·dle \ˈhərd-l\ *n* **1** : a movable panel used for enclosing land or livestock **2 a** : a barrier to be jumped in a race **b** *pl* : any of various track events in which a series of hurdles must be jumped **3** : OBSTACLE [Old English *hyrdel*]

[2]hurdle *vt* **hur·dled; hur·dling** \ˈhərd-liŋ, -l-iŋ\ **1** : to leap over while running **2** : OVERCOME 1, SURMOUNT — **hur·dler** \ˈhərd-lər, -l-ər\ *n*

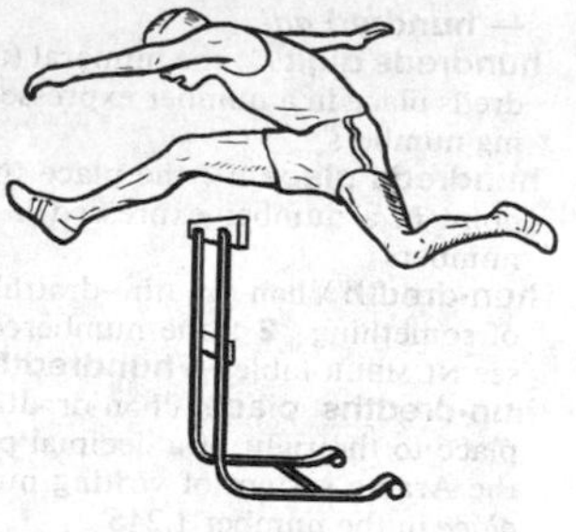

hurdle 2

hur·dy–gur·dy \ˌhərd-ē-ˈgərd-ē\ *n, pl* **-dies** : a musical instrument in which the sound is produced by turning a crank; *esp* : BARREL ORGAN [probably imitative]

hurl \ˈhərl\ *vb* **1 a** : to move forward or progress with haste : HURTLE **b** : to throw violently or powerfully ⟨*hurl* a spear⟩ **2** : PITCH 6 **3** : VOMIT **4** : to utter with vehemence ⟨*hurled* insults at him⟩ [Middle English *hurlen*] ***synonyms*** see THROW — **hurl·er** *n*

hurl·ing \ˈhər-liŋ\ *n* : an Irish game resembling field hockey played between two teams of 15 players each

hur·ly–bur·ly \ˌhər-lē-ˈbər-lē\ *n, pl* **-lies** : UPROAR, TUMULT [probably derived from *hurl*]

Hu·ron \ˈhyu̇r-ən, ˈhyu̇r-ˌän\ *n* : a member of a group of American Indian peoples originally of the St. Lawrence valley and what is now Ontario [French, literally, "boor"]

[1]hur·rah \hu̇-ˈrȯ, -ˈrä, ˈhü-ˌ\ *also* **hoo·ray** \-ˈrā\ *n* **1 a** : FANFARE 2, EXCITEMENT **b** : CHEER 5 **2** : FUSS 2, CONTROVERSY

[2]hur·rah *or* **hur·ray** *variant of* [2]HOORAY

hur·ri·cane \ˈhər-ə-ˌkān, -i-kən, ˈhə-rə-, ˈhə-ri-\ *n* : a tropical cyclone with winds of 74 miles (119 kilometers) or greater that is usually accompanied by rain, thunder, and lightning [Spanish *huracán*, from Taino (Arawakan language of the Greater Antilles) *hurakán*]

hurricane lamp *n* : a candlestick or lamp with a glass chimney

hur·ried \ˈhər-ēd, ˈhə-rēd\ *adj* **1** : going or working with speed ⟨the *hurried* life of the city⟩ **2** : done in a hurry : HASTY ⟨a *hurried* meal⟩ — **hur·ried·ly** *adv*

[1]hur·ry \ˈhər-ē, ˈhə-rē\ *vb* **hur·ried; hur·ry·ing** **1 a** : to carry or cause to go with haste ⟨*hurry* them to the airport⟩ **b** : to move or act with haste ⟨please *hurry* up⟩ **2 a** : to impel to greater speed : PROD **b** : to hasten the doing of ⟨*hurry* a repair job⟩ **c** : to perform with undue haste [perhaps from Middle English *horyen*] — **hur·ri·er** *n*

[2]hurry *n, pl* **hurries** **1** : disorderly activity : COMMOTION **2 a** : agitated and often bustling or disorderly haste **b** : a state of eagerness or urgency : RUSH ⟨in a *hurry* to get there⟩ ***synonyms*** see HASTE

[1]hurt \ˈhərt\ *vb* **hurt; hurt·ing** **1 a** : to inflict physical pain upon **b** : to do harm to : DAMAGE ⟨the storm didn't *hurt* the house⟩ **2 a** : to cause anguish to : OFFEND ⟨was *hurt* by their taunts⟩ **b** : HAMPER ⟨the scandal *hurt* their election chances⟩ **3 a** : to feel or be a source of pain ⟨I *hurt* all over⟩ ⟨my tooth *hurts*⟩ **b** : to be in need ⟨was *hurting* for money⟩ [Middle English *hurten*, probably from Medieval French *hurter* "to strike, prick, collide with," probably of Germanic origin] — **hurt·er** *n*

[2]hurt *n* **1** : a cause of injury or damage **2 a** : a bodily injury or wound **b** : mental distress : SUFFERING **3** : WRONG 1a, HARM

hurt·ful \ˈhərt-fəl\ *adj* : causing injury or suffering : DAMAGING — **hurt·ful·ly** \-fə-lē\ *adv* — **hurt·ful·ness** *n*

hur·tle \ˈhərt-l\ *vb* **hur·tled; hur·tling** \ˈhərt-liŋ, -l-iŋ\ **1** : to move with or as if with a rushing sound ⟨boulders *hurtled* down the hill⟩ **2** : HURL, FLING ⟨*hurtled* the stone through the air⟩ [Middle English *hurtlen* "to collide," from *hurten* "to cause to strike, hurt"]

[1]hus·band \ˈhəz-bənd\ *n* : a married man [Old English *hūsbonda* "master of a house," from Old Norse *hūsbōndi*, from *hūs* "house" + *bōndi* "householder"]

[2]husband *vt* **1 a** : to manage prudently and economically **b** : use carefully : CONSERVE ⟨*husbanded* their resources⟩ **2** *archaic* : to find a husband for : MATE — **hus·band·er** *n*

hus·band·man \ˈhəz-bənd-mən, -bən-\ *n* : FARMER; *also* : a specialist in farm husbandry

hus·band·ry \-bən-drē\ *n* **1** : the management or careful use of resources : ECONOMY **2** : FARMING, AGRICULTURE; *esp* : the technical and scientific aspects of farming and especially of the care, raising, or breeding of domestic animals — compare ANIMAL HUSBANDRY

[1]hush \ˈhəsh\ *vb* **1** : to make quiet, calm, or still : SOOTHE ⟨*hush* a baby⟩ **2** : to become quiet **3** : to keep from public knowledge : SUPPRESS ⟨*hush* up a scandal⟩ [back-formation from *husht* "hushed," from Middle English *huissht*, interjection used to enjoin silence]

[2]hush *n* : a silence or calm especially following noise : QUIET

hush–hush \ˈhəsh-ˌhəsh\ *adj* : hidden or kept from knowledge or view : CONFIDENTIAL

[1]husk \ˈhəsk\ *n* **1** : a usually thin dry outer covering of various seeds or fruits (as barley and corn) : HULL **2** : an outer layer : SHELL [Middle English]

[2]husk *vt* : to strip the husk from — **husk·er** *n*

husk·ing *n* : a gathering of farm families to husk corn — called also *husking bee*

[1]husky \ˈhəs-kē\ *adj* **husk·i·er; -est** : resembling, containing, or full of husks

[2]husky *adj* **husk·i·er; -est** : hoarse with or as if with emotion [probably from obsolete *husk* "to have a dry cough"] — **husk·i·ly** \ˈhəs-kə-lē\ *adv* — **husk·i·ness** \-kē-nəs\ *n*

[3]hus·ky \ˈhəs-kē\ *n, pl* **hus·kies** **1** : a heavy-coated working dog especially of the New World arctic region **2** : SIBERIAN HUSKY [probably alteration of *Huskemaw, Uskemaw* "Eskimo," from Cree *aškimeˀw*]

[4]husky *n, pl* **husk·ies** : one that is husky

[5]husky *adj* **husk·i·er; -est** : BURLY, ROBUST [probably from [1]*husk*]

hus·sar \hə-ˈzär, ˌhə-, -ˈsär\ *n* : a member of any of various European military units originally of light cavalry [Hungarian *huszár* "hussar (obsolete), highway robber," from Serbian & Croatian *husar* "pirate," from Medieval Latin *cursarius* "corsair"]

Huss·ite \ˈhəs-ˌīt, ˈhu̇s-\ *n* : a member of the Bohemian religious and nationalist movement originating with John Huss — **Hussite** *adj*

hus·sy \ˈhəz-ē, ˈhəs-\ *n, pl* **hus·sies** **1** : a lewd or brazen woman **2** : a pert or mischievous girl [alteration of *housewife*]

hus·tings \ˈhəs-tiŋz\ *n pl* : a place where political campaign speeches are made; *also* : the proceedings in an election campaign [Old English *hūsting* "local court," from Old Norse *hūsthing,* from *hūs* "house" + *thing* "assembly"]

hus·tle \ˈhəs-əl\ *vb* **hus·tled; hus·tling** \ˈhəs-ling, -ə-ling\ **1** : to push, crowd, or force forward roughly ‹*hustled* the prisoner to jail› **2 a** : to move or work with energetic activity **b** : to sell something to or obtain something from by energetic and especially underhanded activity **c** : to sell or promote aggressively ‹*hustling* new products› **d** : to lure less skillful players into competing against oneself at (a gambling game) ‹*hustle* pool› [Dutch *husselen* "to shake"] — **hustle** *n* — **hus·tler** \ˈhəs-lər, -ə-lər\ *n*

hut \ˈhət\ *n* : an often small and temporary dwelling or shelter : SHACK [Medieval French *hute,* of Germanic origin] — **hut** *vb*

hutch \ˈhəch\ *n* **1 a** : a chest or compartment for storage **b** : a low cupboard usually surmounted by open shelves **2** : a pen or coop for an animal **3** : SHANTY, SHACK [Medieval French *huche*]

hut·ment \ˈhət-mənt\ *n* **1** : a camp of huts **2** : HUT

Hu·tu \ˈhü-ˌtü\ *n, pl* **Hutu** *or* **Hutus** : a member of a Bantu-speaking people of Rwanda and Burundi [Kinyarwanda & Kirundi (Bantu languages of East Africa)]

hutzpah *or* **hutzpa** *variant of* CHUTZPAH

huz·zah *or* **huz·za** \hə-ˈzä, ˌhə-\ *interj* — used to express joy or approbation [origin unknown]

hy·a·cinth \ˈhī-ə-ˌsinth, -ˌsintth\ *n* **1** : a red or brownish gem zircon or garnet **2** : a bulbous Mediterranean herb related to the lilies and widely grown for its showy dense spikes of fragrant bell-shaped flowers — compare GRAPE HYACINTH, WATER HYACINTH **3** : a light violet to moderate purple [Latin *hyacinthus,* a precious stone,a flowering plant, from Greek *hyakinthos*] — **hy·a·cin·thine** \ˌhī-ə-ˈsin-thən, -ˈsint-\ *adj*

hyacinth 2

Hy·a·des \ˈhī-ə-ˌdēz\ *n pl* : a V-shaped cluster of stars in the head of the constellation Taurus held by the ancients to indicate rainy weather when they rise with the sun [Latin, from Greek]

hy·a·line \ˈhī-ə-lən, -ˌlīn\ *adj* : transparent or nearly so and usually homogeneous ‹a *hyaline* membrane› [derived from Greek *hyalos* "glass"]

hy·a·lite \ˈhī-ə-ˌlīt\ *n* : a colorless opal that is clear or translucent or whitish [German *Hyalit,* from Greek *hyalos* "glass"]

hy·brid \ˈhī-brəd\ *n* **1** : an offspring of genetically different parents especially of different races, breeds, varieties, species, or genera **2** : something of mixed origin or composition **3** : something (as a vehicle) that has two different types of components performing essentially the same function [Latin *hybrida*] — **hybrid** *adj* — **hy·brid·ism** \ˈhī-brə-ˌdiz-əm\ *n* — **hy·brid·i·ty** \hī-ˈbrid-ət-ē\ *n*

hy·brid·ize \ˈhī-brə-ˌdīz\ *vb* : to produce or cause to produce hybrids : INTERBREED — **hy·brid·iza·tion** \ˌhī-brəd-ə-ˈzā-shən\ *n* — **hy·brid·iz·er** \ˈhī-brə-ˌdī-zər\ *n*

hybrid vigor *n* : HETEROSIS

hy·da·tid \ˈhīd-ə-təd, -ˌtid\ *n* : the larval cyst of a tapeworm that occurs in the host's tissues as a fluid-filled sac containing smaller sacs of scolices [Greek *hydatid-, hydatis* "watery cyst," from *hydat-, hydōr* "water"]

hydr- *or* **hydro-** *combining form* **1** : water ‹*hydro*electric› ‹*hydrous*› **2** : hydrogen ‹*hydro*carbon› [Greek, from *hydōr*]

Hy·dra \ˈhī-drə\ *n* **1** : a many-headed serpent or monster in Greek mythology slain by Hercules **2** : a southern constellation of great length **3** *not cap* : any of numerous small tubular freshwater animals related to the jellyfishes and having a mouth surrounded by tentacles at one end [Latin, from Greek]

hy·dran·gea \hī-ˈdrān-jə\ *n* : any of a genus of shrubby plants, pink, or bluish with showy clusters of usually sterile white or tinted flowers [*hydr-* + Greek *angeion* "vessel"]

hy·drant \ˈhī-drənt\ *n* : a discharge pipe with a valve and spout at which water may be drawn from a water main

[1]**hy·drate** \ˈhī-ˌdrāt\ *n* : a compound formed by the union of water with some other substance ‹a *hydrate* of copper sulfate›

[2]**hydrate** *vt* **1** : to cause to take up or combine with water or the elements of water **2** : to supply with ample fluid or moisture — **hy·dra·tion** \hī-ˈdrā-shən\ *n*

hy·drau·lic \hī-ˈdrȯ-lik\ *adj* **1** : operated, moved, or effected by means of water **2** : of or relating to hydraulics ‹*hydraulic* engineer› **3** : operated by the resistance offered or the pressure transmitted when a quantity of liquid is forced through a comparatively small orifice or through a tube ‹*hydraulic* brakes› **4** : hardening or setting under water ‹*hydraulic* cement› [Latin *hydraulicus,* from Greek *hydraulikos,* from *hydraulis* "hydraulic organ," from *hydr-* + *aulos* "reed instrument"] — **hy·drau·li·cal·ly** \-li-kə-lē, -klē\ *adv*

hydraulic ram *n* : a pump that forces running water to a higher level by utilizing the kinetic energy of flow

hy·drau·lics \-liks\ *n* : science that deals with practical applications of liquid (as water) in motion

hy·dra·zine \ˈhī-drə-ˌzēn\ *n* : a colorless fuming corrosive liquid N_2H_4 used especially in fuels for rocket engines

hy·dride \ˈhī-ˌdrīd\ *n* : a compound of hydrogen usually with a more electropositive element or radical

hy·dro \ˈhī-drō\ *n* : hydroelectric power

hy·dro·bro·mic acid \ˌhī-drə-ˈbrō-mik-\ *n* : a strong acid that is a solution of the bromide of hydrogen in water

hy·dro·car·bon \ˌhī-drə-ˈkär-bən\ *n* : an organic compound (as acetylene) containing only carbon and hydrogen

hy·dro·ceph·a·lus \ˌhī-drō-ˈsef-ə-ləs\ *also* **hy·dro·ceph·a·ly** \-lē\ *n* : an abnormal condition in which an increased amount of cerebrospinal fluid results in expansion of the cerebral ventricles, enlargement of the skull, and wasting away of the brain [derived from Greek *hydr-* + *kephalē* "head"] — **hy·dro·ce·phal·ic** \-sə-ˈfal-ik\ *adj or n*

hy·dro·chlo·ric acid \ˌhī-drə-ˈklōr-ik-, -ˈklȯr-\ *n* : an aqueous solution of hydrogen chloride HCl that is a strong corrosive liquid acid, is normally present in dilute form in gastric juice, and is widely used in industry and in the laboratory

hy·dro·chlo·ride \-ˈklōr-ˌid, -ˈklȯr-\ *n* : a compound of hydrochloric acid

hy·dro·chlo·ro·fluo·ro·car·bon \-ˌklȯr-ō-ˌflȯr-ō-ˈkär-bən\ *n* : a compound containing carbon, chlorine, fluorine, and hydrogen

hy·dro·cor·ti·sone \-ˈkȯrt-ə-ˌsōn, -ˌzōn\ *n* : CORTISOL

hy·dro·cy·an·ic acid \ˌhī-drō-sī-ˈan-ik-\ *n* : an aqueous solution of hydrogen cyanide HCN that is a weak poisonous acid and is used in fumigating

hy·dro·dy·nam·ics \ˌhī-drō-dī-ˈnam-iks\ *n* : a branch of physics that deals with the motion of fluids and the forces acting on solid bodies immersed in fluids and in motion relative to them — **hy·dro·dy·nam·ic** \-ik\ *adj*

hy·dro·elec·tric \ˌhī-drō-i-ˈlek-trik\ *adj* : of or relating to production of electricity by waterpower — **hy·dro·elec·tric·i·ty** \-ˌlek-ˈtris-ət-ē, -ˈtris-tē\ *n*

hy·dro·flu·or·ic acid \ˌhī-drō-flü-ˈȯr-ik, -ˈär-\ *n* : an aqueous solution of hydrogen fluoride HF that is a weak poisonous acid and is used especially in finishing and etching glass

hy·dro·foil \ˈhī-drə-ˌfȯil\ *n* **1** : a body similar to an airfoil but designed for action in or on the water **2** : a motorboat that has metal fins attached by struts to the front and back of the ship for lifting the hull clear of the water as speed is reached

hy·dro·gen \ˈhī-drə-jən\ *n* : a univalent chemical element that is the simplest and lightest of the elements and occurs as a colorless odorless highly flammable diatomic gas — see ELEMENT table; compare DEUTERIUM, TRITIUM [French *hydrogène,* from *hydr-* "hydr-" + *-gène* "-gen"; from the fact that water is generated by its combustion] — **hy·drog·e·nous** \hī-ˈdräj-ə-nəs\ *adj*

hy·dro·ge·nate \ˈhī-drə-jə-ˌnāt, hī-ˈdräj-ə-\ *vt* : to combine or treat with hydrogen; *esp* : to add hydrogen to the molecule of ‹*hydrogenate* a vegetable oil to form a fat› — **hy·dro·ge·na·tion** \ˌhī-drə-jə-ˈnā-shən, hī-ˌdräj-ə-\ *n*

hydrogen bomb *n* : a bomb whose violent explosive power is due to the sudden release of atomic energy resulting from the union of light nuclei (as of hydrogen atoms)

hydrogen chloride *n* : a colorless pungent poisonous gas HCl that fumes in moist air and yields hydrochloric acid when dissolved in water

hydrogen fluoride *n* : a colorless corrosive fuming poisonous liquid or gas HF that yields hydrofluoric acid when dissolved in water

\ə\ **abut**	\au̇\ **out**	\i\ **tip**	\ȯ\ **saw**	\u̇\ **foot**
\ər\ **further**	\ch\ **chin**	\ī\ **life**	\ȯi\ **coin**	\y\ **yet**
\a\ **mat**	\e\ **pet**	\j\ **job**	\th\ **thin**	\yü\ **few**
\ā\ **take**	\ē\ **easy**	\ng\ **sing**	\th\ **this**	\yu̇\ **cure**
\ä\ **cot, cart**	\g\ **go**	\ō\ **bone**	\ü\ **food**	\zh\ **vision**

hydrogen ion *n* **1 :** the cation H^+ of acids consisting of a hydrogen atom whose electron has been transferred to the anion of the acid **2 :** HYDRONIUM

hydrogen peroxide *n* **:** an unstable liquid compound H_2O_2 used especially as an oxidizing and bleaching agent, an antiseptic, and a propellant

hydrogen sulfide *n* **:** a flammable poisonous gas H_2S of disagreeable odor found especially in many mineral waters and in decomposing matter

hy·drog·ra·phy \hī-ˈdräg-rə-fē\ *n* **1 :** the study of bodies of water (as seas, lakes, rivers) especially with reference to their use by man **2 :** the mapping of bodies of water — **hy·drog·ra·pher** \-fər\ *n* — **hy·dro·graph·ic** \ˌhī-drə-ˈgraf-ik\ *adj*

[1]**hy·droid** \ˈhī-ˌdrȯid\ *adj* **:** of or relating to the hydrozoans; *esp* **:** resembling a typical hydra

[2]**hydroid** *n* **:** HYDROZOAN; *esp* **:** a hydrozoan polyp as distinguished from a hydrozoan jellyfish

hydrologic cycle *n* **:** the series of conditions through which water naturally passes from vapor in the atmosphere, through precipitation upon land or water surfaces, and finally back into the atmosphere as a result of evaporation and transpiration

hy·drol·o·gy \hī-ˈdräl-ə-jē\ *n* **:** a science dealing with the properties, distribution, and circulation of water on and below the surface of the land and in the atmosphere — **hy·dro·log·ic** \ˌhī-drə-ˈläj-ik\ *or* **hy·dro·log·i·cal** \-ˈläj-i-kəl\ *adj* — **hy·drol·o·gist** \hī-ˈdräl-ə-jəst\ *n*

hy·drol·y·sis \hī-ˈdräl-ə-səs\ *n* **:** a chemical process of decomposition involving splitting of a bond and addition of the elements of water — **hy·dro·lyt·ic** \ˌhī-drə-ˈlit-ik\ *adj*

hy·dro·lyze \ˈhī-drə-ˌlīz\ *vb* **:** to subject to or undergo hydrolysis

hy·drom·e·ter \hī-ˈdräm-ət-ər\ *n* **:** an instrument for determining the specific gravity of a liquid and hence its strength (as of alcoholic liquor or battery acid) — **hy·dro·met·ric** \ˌhī-drə-ˈme-trik\ *adj*

hy·dro·ni·um \hī-ˈdrō-nē-əm\ *n* **:** a hydrated hydrogen ion H_3O^+ [*hydr-* + *-onium* (as in ammonium)]

hy·dro·phil·ic \ˌhī-drə-ˈfil-ik\ *adj* **:** of, relating to, or having a strong affinity for water

hy·dro·pho·bia \ˌhī-drə-ˈfō-bē-ə\ *n* **1 :** RABIES **2 :** a morbid dread of water

hy·dro·pho·bic \-ˈfō-bik, -ˈfäb-ik\ *adj* **1 :** of, relating to, or suffering from hydrophobia **2 :** lacking affinity for water ⟨*hydrophobic* molecules⟩ — **hy·dro·pho·bic·i·ty** \-fō-ˈbis-ət-ē\ *n*

hy·dro·phone \ˈhī-drə-ˌfōn\ *n* **:** an instrument for listening to sound transmitted through water

hy·dro·phyte \-ˌfīt\ *n* **:** a plant growing in water or in waterlogged soil — **hy·dro·phyt·ic** \ˌhī-drə-ˈfit-ik\ *adj*

[1]**hy·dro·plane** \ˈhī-drə-ˌplān\ *n* **1 :** a speedboat with fins or a bottom so designed that the hull is raised wholly or partly out of the water **2 :** SEAPLANE

[2]**hydroplane** *vi* **:** to skim over the water; *esp* **:** to skid on a wet surface (as pavement) ⟨the car *hydroplaned*⟩

hy·dro·pon·ics \ˌhī-drə-ˈpän-iks\ *n* **:** the growing of plants in nutrient solutions [*hydr-* + *-ponics* (as in *geoponics* "agriculture," from Greek *geōponein* "to plow," from *geō-* "ge-" + *ponein* "to toil")] — **hy·dro·pon·ic** \-ik\ *adj* — **hy·dro·pon·i·cal·ly** \-ˈpän-i-kə-lē, -klē\ *adv*

hy·dro·power \ˈhī-drə-ˌpau̇-ər, -ˌpau̇r\ *n* **:** hydroelectric power

hy·dro·qui·none \ˌhī-drō-kwin-ˈōn, -ˈkwin-ˌōn\ *n* **:** a white crystalline compound used as a photographic developer and as an antioxidant and stabilizer [derived from *hydr-* + *quinine*]

hy·dro·sphere \ˈhī-drə-ˌsfiər\ *n* **1 :** the water vapor that surrounds the earth as part of the atmosphere **2 :** the surface waters of the earth and the water vapor in the atmosphere

hy·dro·stat·ic \ˌhī-drə-ˈstat-ik\ *adj* **:** of or relating to liquids at rest or to the pressures they exert or transmit

hy·dro·stat·ics \-iks\ *n* **:** a branch of physics that deals with the characteristics of liquids at rest and especially with the pressure in a liquid or exerted by a liquid on an immersed body

hy·dro·ther·a·py \-ˈther-ə-pē\ *n* **:** the use of water in the treatment of disease

hy·dro·ther·mal vent \ˌhī-drə-ˈthər-məl-\ *n* **:** an opening in the ocean floor from which mineral-rich hot water emerges

hy·drot·ro·pism \hī-ˈdrä-trə-ˌpiz-əm\ *n* **:** a tropism (as in plant roots) in which water or water vapor is the orienting factor — **hy·dro·tro·pic** \ˌhī-drə-ˈtrō-pik, -ˈträp-ik\ *adj*

hy·drous \ˈhī-drəs\ *adj* **:** containing water usually chemically combined

hy·drox·ide \hī-ˈdräk-ˌsīd\ *n* **:** a negatively charged ion consisting of one atom of oxygen and one atom of hydrogen

hy·droxy·ap·a·tite \hī-ˌdräk-sē-ˈap-ə-ˌtīt\ *n* **:** a compound of phosphate and calcium that occurs as the chief structural component of vertebrate bone

hy·drox·yl \hī-ˈdräk-səl\ *n* **:** a chemical group that consists of one atom of oxygen and one atom of hydrogen

hy·dro·zo·an \ˌhī-drə-ˈzō-ən\ *n* **:** any of a class (Hydrozoa) of coelenterates including the jellyfishes and single or colonial polyps (as hydras or corals) — **hydrozoan** *adj*

hy·e·na \hī-ˈē-nə\ *n* **:** any of several large strong nocturnal flesh-eating Old World mammals [Latin *hyaena,* from Greek *hyaina,* from *hys* "hog"]

hy·giene \ˈhī-ˌjēn\ *n* **1 :** a science dealing with the establishment and maintenance of health **2 :** conditions or practices (as of cleanliness) tending to promote or aid health [French *hygiène,* from Greek *hygienos* "healthful," from *hygiēs* "healthy"]

hy·gien·ic \ˌhī-ˈjen-ik, -ˈjen-\ *adj* **1 :** of or relating to hygiene **2 :** having or showing good hygiene ⟨*hygienic* conditions⟩ — **hy·gien·i·cal·ly** \-i-kə-lē, -klē\ *adv*

hy·gien·ist \hī-ˈjēn-əst, -ˈjen-\ *n* **:** a person specializing in hygiene; *esp* **:** DENTAL HYGIENIST

hygr- *or* **hygro-** *combining form* **:** humidity **:** moisture ⟨*hygro*graph⟩ [Greek *hygros* "wet"]

hy·gro·graph \ˈhī-grə-ˌgraf\ *n* **:** an instrument for automatic recording of variations in atmospheric humidity

hy·grom·e·ter \hī-ˈgräm-ət-ər\ *n* **:** any of several instruments for measuring the humidity of the atmosphere — **hy·gro·met·ric** \ˌhī-grə-ˈme-trik\ *adj* — **hy·grom·e·try** \hī-ˈgräm-ə-trē\ *n*

hy·gro·scop·ic \ˌhī-grə-ˈskäp-ik\ *adj* **1 :** readily taking up and retaining moisture ⟨salt is somewhat *hygroscopic*⟩ **2 :** taken up and retained ⟨*hygroscopic* moisture⟩

hying *present participle of* HIE

Hyk·sos \ˈhik-ˌsōs\ *adj* **:** of or relating to a Semitic dynasty ruling Egypt from about 1750 to 1580 B.C. [Greek *Hyksōs,* perhaps from Egyptian *ḥqȝ* "ruler" + *ḫȝst* "foreign land"]

hy·men \ˈhī-mən\ *n* **:** a fold of mucous membrane partly closing the opening of the vagina — called also *maidenhead* [Late Latin, from Greek *hymēn* "membrane"] — **hy·men·al** \ˈhī-mən-l\ *adj*

hy·me·nop·tera \ˌhī-mə-ˈnäp-tə-rə\ *n pl* **:** insects that are hymenopterans

hy·me·nop·ter·an \-rən\ *n, pl* **-tera** \-rə\ **:** any of an order (Hymenoptera) of highly specialized and often colonial insects (as bees, wasps, and ants) that have usually four membranous wings and the abdomen on a slender stalk [derived from Greek *hymēn* "membrane" + *pteron* "wing"] — **hymenopteran** *adj* — **hy·me·nop·ter·ous** \-rəs\ *adj*

hymn \ˈhim\ *n* **1 :** a song of praise especially to God **2 :** a religous song [Old English *ymen,* from Latin *hymnus,* from Greek *hymnos*]

hym·nal \ˈhim-nəl\ *n* **:** a book of hymns

hymn·book \ˈhim-ˌbu̇k\ *n* **:** HYMNAL

hym·no·dy \ˈhim-nəd-ē\ *n* **1 :** hymn singing **2 :** hymn writing **3 :** the hymns of a time, place, or church [Late Latin *hymnodia,* from Greek *hymnōidia,* from *hymnos* "hymn" + *aeidein* "to sing"]

hy·oid bone \ˈhī-ˌȯid-\ *n* **:** a U-shaped bone or complex of bones supporting the tongue, larynx, and their muscles [Greek *hyoeidēs* "shaped like the letter upsilon (Υ)," from *hy* "upsilon"] — **hy·oid** \ˈhī-ˌȯid\ *adj or n*

hyp- — see HYPO-

[1]**hype** \ˈhīp\ *vt* **hyped; hyping 1 :** to give spirit or action to **:** EXCITE ⟨*hyped* herself up for the game⟩ **2 :** INCREASE 1 [*hype,* noun, "a narcotics addict," from *hypodermic*] — **hyped–up** \ˈhīp-ˈdəp\ *adj*

[2]**hype** *n* **1 :** an instance of tricking **:** DECEPTION **2 :** PUBLICITY; *esp* **:** extravagant or contrived promotional publicity ⟨all the *hype* before the boxing match⟩ — **hype** *vt*

hyper- *prefix* **1 :** above **:** beyond **:** SUPER- ⟨*hyper*sonic⟩ **2 a :** excessively ⟨*hyper*critical⟩ **b :** excessive ⟨*hyper*xemia⟩ **3 :** that is or exists in a space of more than three dimensions ⟨*hyper*space⟩ **4 :** bridging points within an entity (as a database or network) nonsequentially ⟨*hyper*text⟩ [Greek *hyper*]

hyperacuity
hyperacute
hyperaggressive
hyperaggressiveness
hyperalert
hyperaware
hyperawareness
hypercautious

hypercivilized
hypercompetitive
hyperconcentration
hyperconscious
hyperconsciousness
hyperefficient
hyperemotional
hyperenergetic
hyperexcitability
hyperexcitable
hyperexcited
hyperexcitement
hyperfastidious
hyperimmune
hyperimmunization
hyperimmunize
hyperintellectual
hyperintelligent
hyperintense
hypermasculine
hypermodern
hypermodernist
hypernationalistic
hyperpigmentation
hyperpigmented
hyperproducer
hyperproduction
hyperpure
hyperrational
hyperrationality
hyperreactive
hyperreactivity
hyperreactor
hyperresponsive
hyperromantic
hypersaline
hypersalinity
hyperstimulate
hyperstimulation
hypersusceptibility
hypersusceptible
hypertense
hypertypical
hypervigilance
hypervigilant
hypervirulent

hy·per·acid·i·ty \ˌhī-pə-rə-ˈsid-ət-ē\ *n* **:** the condition of containing more than the normal amount of acid — **hy·per·acid** \ˌ-pə-ˈras-əd\ *adj*

hy·per·ac·tive \-ˈrak-tiv\ *adj* **:** excessively or abnormally active — **hy·per·ac·tiv·i·ty** \-ˌrak-ˈtiv-ət-ē\ *n*

hy·per·bo·la \hī-ˈpər-bə-lə\ *n, pl* **-las** *or* **-lae** \-ˌlē\ **:** a curve formed in a geometric plane by a point moving in such a way that the difference of the distances between it and two fixed points is a constant [Greek *hyperbolē*]

hy·per·bo·le \hī-ˈpər-bə-lē\ *n* **:** extravagant exaggeration [Latin, from Greek *hyperbolē* "excess, hyperbole, hyperbola," from *hyperballein* "to exceed," from *hyper* "beyond" + *ballein* "to throw"]

hy·per·bol·ic \ˌhī-pər-ˈbäl-ik\ *adj* **1 :** of, characterized by, or given to hyperbole **2 :** of or relating to a hyperbola — **hy·per·bol·i·cal·ly** \-i-kə-lē, -klē\ *adv*

hy·per·bo·re·an \ˌhī-pər-ˈbōr-ē-ən, -ˈbȯr-; -bə-ˈrē-ən\ *n* **1** *often cap* **:** a member of a people held by the ancient Greeks to live beyond the north wind in a region of perpetual sunshine **2 :** an inhabitant of a cool northern climate [Latin *Hyperborei,* pl., from Greek *Hyperboreoi,* from *hyper* "beyond" + *Boreas* "north wind"]

hy·per·cor·rec·tion \ˌhī-pər-kə-ˈrek-shən\ *n* **:** a mistaken word or form (as *widely* used for *wide* in "open widely") used especially to avoid what one believes to be a grammatical error but is not — **hy·per·cor·rect** \-ˈrekt\ *adj* — **hy·per·cor·rect·ly** *adv* — **hy·per·cor·rect·ness** \-ˈrek-nəs, -ˈrekt-\ *n*

hy·per·crit·i·cal \ˌhī-pər-ˈkrit-i-kəl\ *adj* **:** excessively critical — **hy·per·crit·i·cal·ly** \-kə-lē, -klē\ *adv*

hy·per·emia \ˌhī-pə-ˈrē-mē-ə\ *n* **:** excess of blood in a body part **:** CONGESTION — **hy·per·emic** \-mik\ *adj*

hy·per·gly·ce·mia \ˌhī-pər-glī-ˈsē-mē-ə\ *n* **:** excess of sugar in the blood [Greek *glykys* "sweet"] — **hy·per·gly·ce·mic** \-mik\ *adj*

hy·per·in·fla·tion \ˌhī-pər-in-ˈflā-shən\ *n* **:** inflation growing at a very high rate in a very short time

hy·per·ki·net·ic \-kə-ˈnet-ik, -kī-\ *adj* **:** characterized by fast-paced or frenzied activity ⟨a *hyperkinetic* police drama⟩

hy·per·link \ˈhī-pər-ˌlingk\ *n* **:** a computerized connector that allows one to move quickly from one place in a document to another place in the same or a different document usually with a single mouse click

hy·per·opia \ˌhī-pə-ˈrō-pē-ə\ *n* **:** a condition in which visual images come to a focus behind the retina and vision is better for distant than for near objects

hy·per·pla·sia \ˌhī-pər-ˈplā-zhə, -zhē-ə\ *n* **:** an abnormal or unusual increase in the elements (as tissue cells) composing a bodily part — **hy·per·plas·tic** \-ˈplas-tik\ *adj*

hy·per·re·al·ism \ˌhī-pər-ˈri-ə-ˌliz-əm, -ˈrē\ *n* **:** realism in art showing real life in an unusual or striking way — **hy·per·re·al·ist** \-list\ *adj* — **hy·per·re·al·is·tic** \-ˌri-ə-ˈlis-tik, -ˌrē-\ *adj*

hy·per·sen·si·tive \-ˈsen-sət-iv, -ˈsen-stiv\ *adj* **1 :** excessively or abnormally sensitive **2 :** abnormally susceptible to a drug, antigen, or other agent — **hy·per·sen·si·tive·ness** *n* — **hy·per·sen·si·tiv·i·ty** \-ˌsen-sə-ˈtiv-ət-ē\ *n*

hy·per·sex·u·al \-ˈseksh-wəl, -ə-wəl; -ˈsek-shəl\ *adj* **:** showing excessive concern with or indulgence in sexual activity — **hy·per·sex·u·al·i·ty** \-ˌsek-shə-ˌwa-lə-tē\ *n*

hy·per·son·ic \-ˈsän-ik\ *adj* **1 :** of or relating to speed five or more times that of sound in air — compare SONIC **2 :** moving, capable of moving, or utilizing air currents that move at hypersonic speed ⟨a *hypersonic* wind tunnel⟩

hy·per·space \ˈhī-pər-ˌspās\ *n* **1 :** space of more than three dimensions **2 :** a fictional space held to support extraordinary events (as travel faster than the speed of light)

hy·per·ten·sion \ˌhī-pər-ˈten-chən\ *n* **:** HIGH BLOOD PRESSURE — **hy·per·ten·sive** \-ˈten-siv\ *adj or n*

hy·per·text \ˈhī-pər-ˌtekst\ *n* **:** a database format in which information related to that on a display can be accessed directly from the display (as by a mouse click); *also* **:** text or other material in this format

hypertext markup language *n* **:** HTML

hypertext transfer protocol *n* **:** a set of communications standards that controls the exchange of computer data especially on the World Wide Web

hy·per·thy·roid·ism \-ˈthī-ˌrȯid-ˌiz-əm, -rəd-\ *n* **:** excessive activity of the thyroid gland; *also* **:** the resulting abnormal state of health — **hy·per·thy·roid** \-ˌrȯid\ *adj*

hy·per·ton·ic \-ˈtän-ik\ *adj* **:** having a higher osmotic pressure than a surrounding medium or a fluid under comparison — **hy·per·to·nic·i·ty** \-tə-ˈnis-ət-ē\ *n*

hy·per·tro·phy \hī-ˈpər-trə-fē\ *n, pl* **-phies :** excessive development of a bodily part; *esp* **:** an increase in the size of a part (as by cellular enlargement) without an increase in the number of its constituent cells — **hy·per·tro·phic** \ˌhī-pər-ˈträf-ik, -ˈtrōf-\ *adj* — **hypertrophy** *vb*

hy·per·ven·ti·late \ˌhī-pər-ˈvent-l-ˌāt\ *vi* **:** to breathe rapidly and deeply **:** undergo hyperventilation

hy·per·ven·ti·la·tion \-ˌvent-l-ˈā-shən\ *n* **:** excessive rate and depth of respiration leading to abnormal loss of carbon dioxide from the blood

hy·pha \ˈhī-fə\ *n, pl* **hy·phae** \-fē\ **:** one of the threads that make up the mycelium of a fungus [Greek *hyphē* "web"] — **hy·phal** \-fəl\ *adj*

¹hy·phen \ˈhī-fən\ *n* **:** a punctuation mark - used to divide or to compound words or word elements [Greek, from *hyph' hen* "under one"]

²hyphen *vt* **:** HYPHENATE

hy·phen·ate \ˈhī-fə-ˌnāt\ *vt* **:** to connect or divide with a hyphen — **hy·phen·ation** \ˌhī-fə-ˈnā-shən\ *n*

hyp·no·sis \hip-ˈnō-səs\ *n, pl* **-no·ses** \-ˈnō-ˌsēz\ **:** a trancelike state resembling sleep that is induced in a person by another whose suggestions are readily accepted and acted upon by the person in this state [derived from Greek *hypnos* "sleep"]

hyp·no·ther·a·py \ˌhip-nō-ˈther-ə-pē\ *n* **:** the use of hypnotism in medical or psychiatric practice

¹hyp·not·ic \hip-ˈnät-ik\ *adj* **1 :** tending to produce sleep **:** SOPORIFIC **2 :** of or relating to hypnosis or hypnotism [Late Latin *hypnoticus,* from Greek *hypnotikos,* from *hypnoun* "to put to sleep," from *hypnos* "sleep"] — **hyp·not·i·cal·ly** \-i-kə-lē, -klē\ *adv*

²hypnotic *n* **:** a sleep-inducing agent **:** SOPORIFIC

hyp·no·tism \ˈhip-nə-ˌtiz-əm\ *n* **1 :** the study of or act of inducing hypnosis **2 :** HYPNOSIS — **hyp·no·tist** \-təst\ *n*

hyp·no·tize \-ˌtīz\ *vt* **1 :** to induce hypnosis in **2 :** to dazzle or overcome by or as if by suggestion — **hyp·no·tiz·able** \-ˌtī-zə-bəl\ *adj*

¹hy·po \ˈhī-pō\ *n* **:** SODIUM THIOSULFATE; *also* **:** a solution of sodium thiosulfate [short for *hyposulfite* "thiosulfate"]

²hypo *n, pl* **hypos :** a hypodermic syringe or injection

hypo- *or* **hyp-** *prefix* **1 :** under **:** beneath **:** down ⟨*hypo*dermic⟩ **2 :** less than normal or normally ⟨*hypo*tension⟩ **3 :** in a lower state of oxidation **:** in a low and usually the lowest position in a series of compounds ⟨*hypo*chlorous acid⟩ [Greek *hypo*]

hy·po·al·ler·gen·ic \ˌhī-pī-ˌal-ər-ˈjen-ik\ *adj* **:** having little likelihood of causing an allergic response ⟨*hypoallergenic* soap⟩

hy·po·chlo·rite \ˌhī-pə-ˈklōr-ˌīt, -ˈklȯr-\ *n* **:** a salt or ester of hypochlorous acid

hy·po·chlo·rous acid \ˌhī-pə-ˈklōr-əs-, -ˈklȯr-\ *n* **:** an unstable weak acid HClO used especially in the form of salts as an oxidizing agent, bleaching agent, and disinfectant

hy·po·chon·dria \ˌhī-pə-ˈkän-drē-ə\ *n* **:** abnormal concern about one's health especially when accompanied by anxiety, depression, and a false belief that one has a physical disease or ailment [Late Latin, pl., "upper abdomen" (formerly regarded as the seat of hypochondria), from Greek, literally, "the parts under the cartilage (of the breastbone)," from *hypo* "under" + *chondros* "cartilage"]

Word History Many ancient theories of disease have been discarded. That dire humor, black bile (or melancholy), was said to be a secretion of the spleen or kidneys and was believed to produce a morbid state of depression and with it an excessive concern with one's health. This disease was named for the region below the breastbone in which it had its origin, the *hypochondria.* This Late Latin word is a derivative of Greek *hypo,* "under," and *chondros,* "cartilage of the breastbone."

[1]**hy·po·chon·dri·ac** \-drē-ˌak\ *adj* **:** HYPOCHONDRIACAL [French *hypochondriaque,* from Greek *hypochon* + *driakos,* from *hypochondria*]

[2]**hypochondriac** *n* **:** a person affected by hypochondria

hy·po·chon·dri·a·cal \-kən-ˈdrī-ə-kəl, -ˌkän-\ *adj* **:** affected or produced by hypochondria — **hy·po·chon·dri·a·cal·ly** \-ˈdrī-ə-kə-lē, -klē\ *adv*

hy·po·cot·yl \ˈhī-pə-ˌkät-l\ *n* **:** the part of the main stem of a plant embryo or seedling below the cotyledons

hy·poc·ri·sy \hip-ˈäk-rə-sē\ *n, pl* **-sies :** a pretending to be what one is not or to believe what one does not; *esp* **:** a pretending to be more virtuous or religious than one really is

hyp·o·crite \ˈhip-ə-ˌkrit\ *n* **1 :** a person who puts on a false appearance of virtue or religion **2 :** a person who acts in contradiction to his or her stated beliefs or feelings [Medieval French *ypocrite,* from Late Latin *hypocrita,* from Greek *hypokritēs* "actor, hypocrite," from *hypokrinesthai* "to answer, act on the stage"]

hyp·o·crit·i·cal \ˌhip-ə-ˈkrit-i-kəl\ *adj* **:** characterized by hypocrisy; *also* **:** being a hypocrite — **hyp·o·crit·i·cal·ly** \-i-kə-lē, klē\ *adv*

[1]**hy·po·der·mic** \ˌhī-pə-ˈdər-mik\ *adj* **:** of, relating to, or injected into the parts beneath the skin — **hy·po·der·mi·cal·ly** \-mi-kə-lē, -klē\ *adv*

[2]**hypodermic** *n* **1 :** HYPODERMIC INJECTION **2 :** HYPODERMIC SYRINGE

hypodermic injection *n* **:** an injection made into the tissues beneath the skin

hypodermic needle *n* **1 :** NEEDLE 1c **2 :** a hypodermic syringe complete with needle

hypodermic syringe *n* **:** a small syringe used with a hollow needle for injection of material into or beneath the skin

hypodermic syringe

hy·po·der·mis \ˌhī-pə-ˈdər-məs\ *n* **:** a layer of tissue immediately beneath an outermost layer; *esp* **:** a layer just beneath the epidermis of a plant and often modified to serve as a supporting and protecting layer

hy·po·glos·sal nerve \ˌhī-pə-ˈgläs-əl-\ *n* **:** either of the 12th and final pair of cranial nerves that are motor nerves arising from the medulla oblongata and supply muscles of the tongue [Greek *glōssa* "tongue"]

hy·po·gly·ce·mia \ˌhī-pə-ˌglī-ˈsē-mē-ə\ *n* **:** abnormal decrease of sugar in the blood [Greek *glykys* "sweet"] — **hy·po·gly·ce·mic** \-mik\ *adj*

hy·poph·y·sis \hī-ˈpäf-ə-səs\ *n, pl* **-y·ses** \-ə-ˌsēz\ **:** PITUITARY GLAND [Greek, "attachment beneath," from *hypophyein* "to grow beneath," from *hypo* "under" + *phyein* "to grow"] — **hy·poph·y·se·al** \hī-ˌpäf-ə-ˈsē-əl\ *adj*

hy·po·style \ˈhī-pə-ˌstīl\ *adj* **:** having the roof resting on rows of columns [Greek *hypostylos,* from *hypo* "under" + *stylos* "pillar"]

hy·po·ten·sion \ˌhī-pō-ˈten-chən\ *n* **:** LOW BLOOD PRESSURE — **hy·po·ten·sive** \-ˈten-siv\ *adj or n*

hy·pot·e·nuse \hī-ˈpät-n-ˌüs, -ˌüz, -ˌyüs, -ˌyüz\ *n* **1 :** the side of a right triangle that is opposite the right angle **2 :** the length of a hypotenuse [Latin *hypotenusa,* from Greek *hypoteinousa,* from *hypoteinein* "to subtend," from *hypo* "under" + *teinein* "to stretch"]

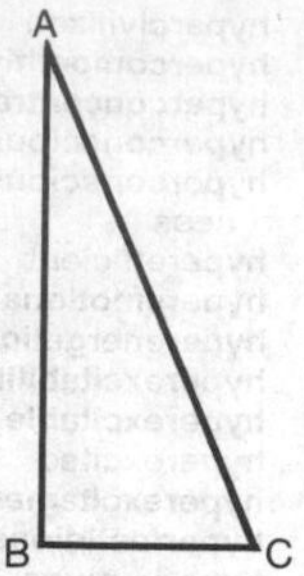

AC hypotenuse

hy·po·thal·a·mus \ˌhī-pō-ˈthal-ə-məs\ *n* **:** a part of the brain that lies beneath the thalamus, produces hormones which pass to the front part of the pituitary gland, and is important in the regulation of the activities of the autonomic nervous system — **hy·po·tha·lam·ic** \-thə-ˈlam-ik\ *adj*

hy·po·ther·mia \ˌhī-pō-ˈthər-mē-ə\ *n* **:** reduction of the body temperature to an abnormally low level — **hy·po·ther·mic** \-mik\ *adj*

hy·poth·e·sis \hī-ˈpäth-ə-səs\ *n, pl* **-e·ses** \-ə-ˌsēz\ **1 :** something not proved but assumed to be true for purposes of argument or further study or investigation **2 :** the conditional clause in a conditional statement [Greek, "supposition," from *hypotithenai* "to put under, suppose," from *hypo* "under," + *tithenai* "to put"]

synonyms HYPOTHESIS, THEORY, LAW mean a formula derived by inference from scientific data that explains a principle operating in nature. HYPOTHESIS implies insufficient evidence to provide more than a tentative explanation ⟨a *hypothesis* explaining the extinction of the dinosaurs⟩. THEORY implies a greater range of evidence and greater likelihood of truth ⟨the *theory* of evolution⟩. LAW implies a statement of order and relation in nature that has been found to be invariable under the same conditions ⟨the *law* of gravitation⟩.

hy·poth·e·size \hī-ˈpäth-ə-ˌsīz\ *vb* **1 :** to make a hypothesis **2 :** to adopt as a hypothesis

hy·po·thet·i·cal \ˌhī-pə-ˈthet-i-kəl\ *adj* **:** being or involving a hypothesis **:** CONJECTURAL ⟨a *hypothetical* situation⟩ — **hy·po·thet·i·cal·ly** \-i-kə-lē, -klē\ *adv*

hy·po·thy·roid·ism \ˌhī-pō-ˈthī-ˌrȯid-ˌiz-əm\ *n* **:** deficient activity of the thyroid gland; *also* **:** the resultant abnormal state of health — **hy·po·thy·roid** \-ˌrȯid\ *adj*

hy·po·ton·ic \ˌhī-pə-ˈtän-ik\ *adj* **:** having a lower osmotic pressure than a fluid under comparison — **hy·po·to·nic·i·ty** \-tə-ˈnis-ət-ē\ *n*

hyp·ox·ia \hip-ˈäk-sē-ə, hī-ˈpäk-\ *n* **:** a deficiency of oxygen reaching the tissues of the body — **hyp·ox·ic** \-sik\ *adj*

hyp·som·e·ter \hip-ˈsäm-ət-ər\ *n* **:** any of various instruments for determining the height of trees by triangulation [Greek *hypsos* "height"]

hy·rax \ˈhī-ˌraks\ *n, pl* **hy·rax·es** *also* **hy·ra·ces** \ˈhī-rə-ˌsēz\ **:** any of several small thickset mammals of Africa and the Middle East with short ears, legs, and tail and feet with soft pads and broad nails [Greek, "shrew"]

hys·sop \ˈhis-əp\ *n* **1 :** a plant used in purificatory sprinkling rites by the ancient Hebrews **2 :** a woody European mint with pungent aromatic leaves sometimes used in folk medicine for bruises [Old English *ysope,* from Latin *hyssopus,* from Greek *hyssōpos,* of Semitic origin]

hys·ter·ec·to·my \ˌhis-tə-ˈrek-tə-mē\ *n, pl* **-mies :** surgical removal of the uterus [Greek *hystera* "womb" + *extemnein* "to cut out"]

hys·te·ria \his-ˈter-ē-ə, -ˈtir-\ *n* **1 :** a neurosis marked by emotional excitability and a tendency to develop sensory and physical disturbances with no apparent organic basis **2 :** behavior exhibiting unmanageable fear or emotional excess [derived from Greek *hystera* "womb"; from the former notion that hysterical women were suffering from disturbances of the womb] — **hys·ter·ic** \-ˈter-ik\ *n* — **hys·ter·i·cal** \-ˈter-i-kəl\ *also* **hys·ter·ic** *adj* — **hys·ter·i·cal·ly** \-i-kə-lē, -klē\ *adv*

hys·ter·ics \his-ˈter-iks\ *n sing or pl* **:** a fit of uncontrollable laughter or crying

I

i \ˈī\ *n, pl* **i's** *or* **is** \ˈīz\ *often cap* **1 :** the 9th letter of the English alphabet **2 :** one in Roman numerals **3 :** a grade rating a student's work as incomplete

I \ī, ˈī, ə\ *pron* **:** the one who is speaking or writing ⟨*I* feel fine⟩ ⟨it wasn't *I*⟩ — compare MINE, MY, WE [Old English *ic*] ***usage*** see ME, MYSELF

-i- — used as a connective vowel to join word elements especially of Latin origin ⟨pest*i*cide⟩ [Latin, stem vowel of most nouns and adjectives in combination]

-ia *n suffix* **1 :** pathological condition ⟨hyster*ia*⟩ **2 :** genus of plants or animals ⟨Fuchs*ia*⟩ **3 :** territory **:** world **:** society ⟨suburb*ia*⟩ [New Latin, from Latin and Greek, suffix forming feminine nouns]

-ial *adj suffix* **:** [1]-AL ⟨manor*ial*⟩ [Latin *-ialis,* from *-i-* + *-alis* "-al"]

iamb \ˈī-ˌam, -ˌamb\ *or* **iam·bus** \ī-ˈam-bəs\ *n, pl* **iambs** \ˈī-ˌamz\ *or* **iam·bus·es :** a metrical foot consisting of one unaccented syllable followed by one accented syllable (as in *away*) [Latin *iambus* "metrical foot of one short syllable followed by one long syllable," from Greek *iambos*] — **iam·bic** \ī-ˈam-bik\ *adj or n*

-ian — see -AN

-iana — see -ANA

-i·a·sis \ˈī-ə-səs\ *n suffix, pl* **-i·a·ses** \-ˌsēz\ **:** disease having characteristics of or produced by (something specified) ⟨ameb*iasis*⟩ [New Latin, from Greek, suffix of action]

iat·ro·gen·ic \ī-ˌa-trə-ˈjen-ik\ *adj* **:** caused by a physician or surgeon or by medical treatment ⟨*iatrogenic* illness⟩ [Greek *iatros* "physician"]

-i·a·try \ˈī-ə-trē, *in a few words* ē-ˌa-trē\ *n combining form* **:** medical treatment **:** healing ⟨psych*iatry*⟩ [Greek *iatreia* "art of healing," from *iatros* "physician"]

Ibe·ri·an \ī-ˈbir-ē-ən\ *n* **:** a member of one or more peoples anciently inhabiting the peninsula comprising Spain and Portugal [*Iberia,* peninsula in Europe] — **Iberian** *adj*

ibex \ˈī-ˌbeks\ *n, pl* **ibex** *or* **ibex·es :** any of several wild goats living chiefly in high mountain areas of the Old World and having large recurved horns transversely ridged in front [Latin]

ibi·dem \ˈib-ə-ˌdem, ib-ˈīd-əm\ *adv* **:** in the same place [Latin]

-ibil·i·ty — see -ABILITY

ibis \ˈī-bəs\ *n, pl* **ibis** *or* **ibis·es :** any of several wading birds related to the herons but distinguished by a long slender downward curving bill [Latin, from Greek, from Egyptian *hbw*]

ibis

-ible — see -ABLE

IC \ī-ˈsē, ˈī-\ *n* **:** INTEGRATED CIRCUIT

[1]-ic \ik\ *adj suffix* **1 :** having the character or form of **:** being **:** consisting of ⟨panoram*ic*⟩ ⟨run*ic*⟩ **2 a :** of or relating to ⟨alderman*ic*⟩ **b :** related to, derived from, or containing ⟨alcohol*ic*⟩ ⟨ole*ic*⟩ **3 :** in the manner of **:** like that of **:** characteristic of ⟨Byron*ic*⟩ **4 :** associated or dealing with **:** utilizing ⟨electron*ic*⟩ **5 :** characterized by **:** exhibiting ⟨nostalg*ic*⟩**:** affected with ⟨parapleg*ic*⟩ **6 :** caused by ⟨amoeb*ic*⟩ **7 :** tending to produce ⟨analges*ic*⟩ **8 :** having a valence higher than in compounds or ions named with an adjective ending in *-ous* ⟨ferric iron⟩ [Latin *-icus*]

[2]-ic *n suffix* **:** one having the character or nature of **:** one belonging to or associated with **:** one exhibiting or affected by ⟨alcohol*ic*⟩**:** one that produces [Latin *-icus,* from *-icus,* adj. suffix]

-i·cal \i-kəl\ *adj suffix* **:** -IC ⟨geologi*cal*⟩ ⟨symmetri*cal*⟩ — sometimes differing from *-ic* in that adjectives formed with *-ical* have a wider range of meaning than corresponding adjectives in *-ic* [Late Latin *-icalis,* from nouns in *-icus* + Latin *-alis* "-al"]

ICBM \ˌī-ˌsē-ˌbē-ˈem\ *n* **:** an intercontinental ballistic missile

[1]ice \ˈīs\ *n* **1 a :** frozen water **b :** a sheet or stretch of frozen water **2 :** a state of coldness (as from formality or reserve) **3 :** a substance resembling ice **4 :** a frozen dessert; *esp* **:** one containing no milk or cream [Old English *īs*] — **on ice 1 :** with every likelihood of being won or accomplished **2 :** in reserve or safekeeping

[2]ice *vb* **1 a :** to coat or become coated with ice **:** change into ice **b :** to chill with ice **c :** to supply with ice **2 :** to cover with or as if with icing **3 :** SECURE 1b ⟨another goal to *ice* the win⟩ **4 :** to shoot (an ice hockey puck) the length of the rink and beyond the opponents' goal line

ice age *n* **1 :** a time of widespread glaciation **2** *cap I&A* **:** the Pleistocene glacial epoch

ice bag *n* **:** a waterproof bag to hold ice for local application of cold to the body

ice·berg \ˈīs-ˌbərg\ *n* **:** a large floating mass of ice detached from a glacier [probably from Danish or Norwegian *isberg,* from *is* "ice" + *berg* "mountain"]

iceberg lettuce *n* **:** a crisp light green lettuce that has the leaves arranged in a compact head

ice·boat \-ˌbōt\ *n* **:** a skeleton boat or frame on runners propelled on ice usually by sails

iceboat

ice·bound \-ˌbau̇nd\ *adj* **:** surrounded or obstructed by ice

ice·box \-ˌbäks\ *n* **:** REFRIGERATOR

ice·break·er \-ˌbrā-kər\ *n* **1 :** a ship equipped to make and maintain a channel through ice **2 :** something (as a funny comment or game) that makes one feel less reserved and more at ease (as at a social occasion)

ice cap *n* **:** a glacier forming on an extensive area of relatively level land and flowing outward from its center

ice–cold \ˈī-ˈskōld\ *adj* **:** extremely cold

ice cream \ˈī-ˈskrēm, ī-ˈ, ˈī-ˌ\ *n* **:** a flavored and sweetened frozen food containing cream or butterfat and usually eggs

ice–cream cone *n* **:** a thin crisp edible cone for holding ice cream; *also* **:** one filled with ice cream

ice dancing *n* **:** a sport in which ice-skating pairs perform to music routines similar to ballroom dances

ice field *n* **1 :** an extensive sheet of sea ice **2 :** ICE CAP

ice floe *n* **:** a flat free mass of floating sea ice

ice hockey *n* **:** a game played on an ice rink between two teams of six players on ice skates whose object is to drive a puck into the opponents' goal with a hockey stick

ice·house \ˈīs-ˌhau̇s\ *n* **:** a building for storing ice

[1]Ice·lan·dic \ī-ˈslan-dik\ *adj* **:** of, relating to, or characteristic of Iceland, the Icelanders, or Icelandic

[2]Icelandic *n* **:** the Germanic language of the Icelandic people

Ice·land moss \ˌī-slənd-, -slən-, -ˌsland-, -ˌslan-\ *n* **:** an arctic lichen sometimes used medicinally or as food

Iceland spar *n* **:** a pure transparent variety of calcite

ice·man \ˈī-ˌsman\ *n* **:** one who sells or delivers ice

ice pack *n* **1 :** an expanse of pack ice **2 :** ice placed in a container or folded in a towel and applied to the body

ice pick *n* **:** a hand tool ending in a spike for chipping ice

ice sheet *n* **:** ICE CAP

ice–skate \ˈīs-ˌskāt, ˈī-\ *vi* **:** to skate on ice — **ice–skater** *n*

ice skate *n* **:** a shoe with a metal runner attached to the bottom for skating on ice

ice storm *n* **:** a storm in which falling rain freezes as it lands

ice water *n* **:** chilled or iced water especially for drinking

ich·neu·mon \ik-ˈnü-mən, -ˈnyü-\ *n* **1 :** MONGOOSE **2 :** ICH-

NEUMON WASP [Latin, from Greek *ichneumōn,* literally, "tracker," from *ichneuein* "to track," from *ichnos* "footprint"]

Word History The ancient Egyptians thought very highly of the African mongoose (a close relative of the mongoose of India) because they believed that it sought out and devoured the eggs of crocodiles. The Greeks, hearing this story, named the beast *ichneumōn,* which means "tracker." In English we call any mongoose, including the Indian, *ichneumon.* The Greek word *ichneumōn* was also used for a certain kind of small wasp that hunts spiders. We use *ichneumon* today for an insect rather distantly related to the Greek *ichneumōn.*

ichneumon wasp *n* **:** any of numerous small insects which are related to the wasps and whose larvae are usually internal parasites of other insect larvae — called also *ichneumon fly*

ichor \ˈī-ˌkȯr, ˈī-kər, ˈik-\ *n* **:** an ethereal fluid taking the place of blood in the veins of the ancient Greek gods [Greek *ichōr*] — **ichor·ous** \-ə-rəs\ *adj*

ichthy- *or* **ichthyo-** *combining form* **:** fish ⟨*ichthyo*logy⟩ [Greek *ichthys*]

ich·thy·ol·o·gy \ˌik-thē-ˈäl-ə-jē\ *n* **:** a branch of zoology that deals with fishes — **ich·thy·o·log·i·cal** \ˌik-thē-ə-ˈläj-i-kəl\ *adj* — **ich·thy·ol·o·gist** \ˌik-thē-ˈäl-ə-jəst\ *n*

ich·thyo·saur \ˈik-thē-ə-ˌsȯr\ *n* **:** any of an order (Ichthyosauria) of extinct marine reptiles of the Mesozoic era with a fish-shaped body and long snout [Greek *sauros* "lizard"] — **ich·thyo·sau·ri·an** \ˌik-thē-ə-ˈsȯr-ē-ən\ *adj or n*

-i·cian \ˈish-ən\ *n suffix* **:** specialist **:** practitioner ⟨beaut*ician*⟩ [Medieval French *-icien,* from Latin *-ica* "-ic, -ics" + Medieval French *-ien* "-ian"]

ici·cle \ˈī-ˌsik-əl\ *n* **:** a hanging mass of ice formed by the freezing of dripping water [Middle English *isikel,* from *is* "ice" + *ikel* "icicle," from Old English *gicel*]

Word History Old English *gicel,* "icicle," became Middle English *ikyl* or *ikel* and later modern English *ickle,* which still survives as a dialect word in Yorkshire, England. The word for ice in Old English is *īs,* and in a manuscript of about the year 1000 we find Latin *stiria,* "icicle," glossed somewhat redundantly as *īses gicel,* that is, "an icicle of ice." Some three hundred years later in Middle English this became the compound we know today as *icicle,* which means precisely what it did a thousand years ago.

¹ic·ing \ˈī-sing\ *n* **1 :** a sweet and usually creamy mixture used to coat baked goods — called also *frosting* **2 :** something that adds to the interest, value, or appeal of an item or event — often used in the phrase *icing on the cake*

²icing *n* **:** an illegal act by an ice-hockey player of shooting a puck the length of the rink and beyond the oponents' goal line

icon *also* **ikon** \ˈī-ˌkän\ *n* **1 :** a usually pictorial representation **2 :** a conventional religious image typically painted on a small wooden panel and used in the devotions of Eastern Christians **3 :** an object of uncritical devotion **:** IDOL **4 :** EMBLEM 1, SYMBOL **5 :** a graphic symbol on a computer display screen that represents an object (as a file) or function (as the command to print out a document) [Latin, from Greek *eikōn,* from *eikenai* "to resemble"] — **icon·ic** \ī-ˈkän-ik\ *adj* — **icon·i·cal·ly** \-ˈkän-i-kə-lē, -klē\ *adv*

icon·o·clasm \ī-ˈkän-ə-ˌklaz-əm\ *n* **:** the doctrine, practice, or attitude of an iconoclast

icon·o·clast \-ˌklast\ *n* **1 :** a person who destroys religious images or opposes their veneration **2 :** a person who attacks established beliefs or institutions [Medieval Latin *iconoclastes,* from Middle Greek *eikonoklastēs,* literally, "image destroyer," from Greek *eikōn* "image" + *klan* "to break"] — **icon·o·clas·tic** \ī-ˌkän-ə-ˈklas-tik\ *adj* — **icon·o·clas·ti·cal·ly** \-ti-kə-lē, -klē\ *adv*

ico·sa·he·dron \ī-ˌkō-sə-ˈhē-drən, -ˌkäs-ə-\ *n, pl* **-drons** *or* **-dra** \-drə\ **:** a polyhedron having 20 faces [Greek *eikosaedron,* from *eikosi* "twenty" + *-edron* "-hedron"]

-ics \iks, ˌiks\ *n sing or pl suffix* **1 :** study **:** knowledge **:** skill **:** practice ⟨linguist*ics*⟩ **2 :** characteristic actions or activities ⟨acrobat*ics*⟩ **3 :** characteristic qualities, operations, or phenomena ⟨acoust*ics*⟩

ic·ter·us \ˈik-tə-rəs\ *n* **:** JAUNDICE 1 [Greek *ikteros*] — **ic·ter·ic** \ik-ˈter-ik\ *adj*

ic·tus \ˈik-təs\ *n* **:** the recurring stress or beat in a rhythmic or metrical series of sounds [Latin *ictus,* literally, "blow," from *icere* "to strike"]

icy \ˈī-sē\ *adj* **ic·i·er; -est** **1 a :** covered with, full of, or consisting of ice ⟨*icy* roads⟩ **b :** intensely cold ⟨*icy* weather⟩ **2 :** characterized by coldness **:** FRIGID ⟨an *icy* stare⟩ — **ic·i·ly** \-sə-lē\ *adv* — **ic·i·ness** \-sē-nəs\ *n*

id \ˈid\ *n* **:** the one of the three divisions of the mind in psychoanalytic theory that is completely unconscious and is the source of psychic energy derived from instinctual needs and drives — compare EGO, SUPEREGO [Latin, "it"]

I'd \īd, ˌīd\ **:** I had **:** I should **:** I would

-ide \ˌīd\ *also* **-id** \əd, id, ˌid\ *n suffix* **1 :** binary chemical compound ⟨hydrogen sulf*ide*⟩ ⟨cyan*ide*⟩ **2 :** chemical compound derived from or related to another (usually specified) compound ⟨anhydr*ide*⟩ ⟨gluco*side*⟩ [French *-ide* (as in *oxide*)]

idea \ī-ˈdē-ə, ˈīd-ē-ə, *especially Southern* ˈīd-ē\ *n* **1 :** a plan of action **:** INTENTION ⟨my *idea* is to study law⟩ **2 :** something imagined or pictured in the mind **:** NOTION ⟨form an *idea* of a foreign country from reading⟩ **3 :** a central meaning or purpose ⟨the *idea* of the game is to keep from getting caught⟩ [Latin, "form, notion," from Greek, from *idein* "to see"] — **idea·less** \ī-ˈdē-ə-ləs\ *adj*

synonyms IDEA, CONCEPT, CONCEPTION mean what exists in the mind as a representation (as of something comprehended) or as a formulation (as a plan). IDEA may apply to a mental image of something seen, known, or imagined or to an abstraction or to something assumed or vaguely sensed ⟨a new *idea* for redecorating a room⟩ ⟨*ideas* about the nature of democracy⟩ ⟨my *idea* of paradise⟩. CONCEPT may apply to the idea formed after knowing many instances of a type or to an idea of what a thing ought to be ⟨the *concepts* of modern architecture⟩ ⟨the *concept* of the role of a citizen in a democracy⟩. CONCEPTION is often interchangeable with CONCEPT, but it may stress the act of imagining or formulating rather than the result ⟨our changing *conception* of what constitutes art⟩.

¹ide·al \ī-ˈdē-əl, -ˈdēl\ *adj* **1 :** existing only in the mind **:** not real **2 :** embodying or symbolizing an ideal **:** PERFECT ⟨an *ideal* place for a picnic⟩ ⟨*ideal* weather⟩

²ideal *n* **1 :** a standard of perfection, beauty, or excellence **2 :** a perfect type **:** a model for imitation **3 :** an ultimate object or aim of endeavor **:** GOAL — **ide·al·less** \ī-ˈdē-əl-ləs, -ˈdēl-\ *adj*

ide·al·ism \ī-ˈdē-ə-ˌliz-əm, -ˈdē-ˌliz-\ *n* **1 a :** a theory that ultimate reality lies in a realm transcending phenomena **b :** a theory that reality lies essentially in consciousness or reason **2 a :** a theory that only the perceptible is real **b :** a theory that only mental states or entities are knowable **3 a :** the practice of forming ideals or living under their influence **b :** something that is idealized **4 :** literary or artistic theory or practice that affirms the value of imagination over the representation of objective reality — compare REALISM

ide·al·ist \ī-ˈdē-ə-ləst, -ˈdē-ləst\ *n* **1 a :** an adherent of a philosophical theory of idealism **b :** an artist or author who advocates or practices idealism in art or writing **2 :** one guided by ideals; *esp* **:** one that places ideals before practical considerations — **ide·al·is·tic** \-ˌdē-ə-ˈlis-tik, -ˌdē-ˈlis-\ *adj* — **ide·al·is·ti·cal·ly** \-ti-kə-lē, -klē\ *adv*

ide·al·ize \ī-ˈdē-ə-ˌlīz, -ˈdē-ˌlīz\ *vt* **:** to think of or represent as ideal ⟨*idealize* life on a farm⟩ — **ide·al·i·za·tion** \ī-ˌdē-ə-lə-ˈzā-shən, -ˌdē-lə-\ *n* — **ide·al·iz·er** *n*

ide·al·ly \ī-ˈdē-ə-lē, -ˈdē-lē\ *adv* **1 :** in idea or imagination **:** MENTALLY ⟨it's possible only *ideally,* not in fact⟩ **2 :** conformably to an ideal **:** PERFECTLY ⟨*ideally* suited to the position⟩

ide·ation \ˌīd-ē-ˈā-shən\ *n* **:** the capacity for or the act of forming or entertaining ideas — **ide·ate** \ˈīd-ē-ˌāt\ *vb* — **ide·ation·al** \ˌīd-ē-ˈā-shnəl, -shən-l\ *adj*

idem \ˈīd-ˌem, ˈēd-, ˈid-\ *pron* **:** the same as something previously mentioned — used chiefly in bibliographies [Latin, "same"]

iden·ti·cal \ī-ˈdent-i-kəl, ə-\ *adj* **1 :** being the same ⟨the *identical* place we stopped before⟩ **2 :** being essentially the same or exactly alike ⟨*identical* hats⟩ — **iden·ti·cal·ly** \-i-kə-lē, -klē\ *adv* — **iden·ti·cal·ness** \-kəl-nəs\ *n*

identical twin *n* **:** either member of a pair of twins that are produced from a single fertilized egg cell, carry the same genes, and are physically similar

iden·ti·fi·ca·tion \ī-ˌdent-ə-fə-ˈkā-shən, ə-\ *n* **1 :** an act of identifying **:** the state of being identified **2 :** evidence of identity ⟨carry *identification*⟩

iden·ti·fy \ī-ˈdent-ə-ˌfī, ə-\ *vt* **-fied; -fy·ing** **1 a :** to cause to be or become identical **b :** to think of as united (as in principle) ⟨groups that are *identified* with conservation⟩ **2 :** to establish the identity of ⟨*identified* the dog as my lost pet⟩ — **iden·ti·fi-**

able \-ˌfī-ə-bəl\ *adj* — **iden·ti·fi·ably** \-blē\ *adv* — **iden·ti·fi·er** \-ˌfī-ər, -ˌfīr\ *n*

iden·ti·ty \ī-ˈdent-ət-ē, ə-\ *n, pl* **-ties** **1 :** the fact or condition of being exactly alike **:** SAMENESS ⟨an *identity* of interests⟩ **2 :** distinguishing character or personality **:** INDIVIDUALITY **3 :** the fact of being the same as something described or known to exist ⟨establish the *identity* of stolen goods⟩ **4 a :** an equation that is true for all values substituted for the variables **b :** IDENTITY ELEMENT [Middle French *identité,* from Late Latin *identitas,* from Latin *idem* "same," from *is* "that"]

identity element *n* **:** an element of a set that leaves any other element of the set unchanged when combined with it using a given mathematical operation ⟨ø is the *identity element* of the set of whole numbers under addition⟩

identity theft *n* **:** the illegal use of someone else's personal information (as a Social Security number) in order to obtain money or credit

ideo·gram \ˈīd-ē-ə-ˌgram, ˈid-\ *n* **1 :** a picture or symbol used in a system of writing to represent a thing or an idea but not a particular word or phrase for it **2 :** a character or symbol used in a system of writing to represent an entire word

ideo·graph \-ˌgraf\ *n* **:** IDEOGRAM — **ideo·graph·ic** \ˌīd-ē-ə-ˈgraf-ik, ˌid-\ *adj* — **ideo·graph·i·cal·ly** \-ˈgraf-i-kə-lē, -klē\ *adv*

ide·ol·o·gy \ˌīd-ē-ˈäl-ə-jē, ˌid-\ *n, pl* **-gies** **1 :** a systematic body of concepts especially about human life or culture **2 :** a manner or the content of thinking characteristic of an individual, group, or culture **3 :** the integrated assertions, theories, and aims that constitute a political, social and economic program [French *idéologie,* from Greek *idea* "form, notion, idea"] — **ideo·log·i·cal** \-ē-ə-ˈläj-i-kəl\ *adj* — **ideo·log·i·cal·ly** \-i-kə-lē, -klē\ *adv* — **ide·ol·o·gist** \-ē-ˈäl-ə-jəst\ *n*

ides \ˈīdz\ *n pl* **:** the 15th day of March, May, July, or October or the 13th day of any other month in the ancient Roman calendar [Medieval French, from Latin *idus*]

idio- *combining form* **:** one's own **:** personal **:** separate **:** distinct ⟨*idio*lect⟩ [Greek *idios* "one's own, private"]

id·i·o·cy \ˈid-ē-ə-sē\ *n, pl* **-cies** **:** something notably stupid or foolish

id·io·lect \ˈid-ē-ə-ˌlekt\ *n* **:** the speech pattern of one individual [*idio-* + *-lect* (as in *dialect*)]

id·i·om \ˈid-ē-əm\ *n* **1 :** the language peculiar to a group ⟨doctors speaking in their professional *idiom*⟩ **2 :** the characteristic form of expression of a language ⟨know the vocabulary of a foreign language but not its *idiom*⟩ **3 :** an expression that cannot be understood from the meanings of its separate words but must be learned as a whole ⟨the expression *give way,* meaning "retreat," is an *idiom*⟩ [Late Latin *idioma* "individual peculiarity of language," from Greek *idiōmat-, idiōma,* from *idios* "one's own"] — **id·i·om·at·ic** \ˌid-ē-ə-ˈmat-ik\ *adj* — **id·i·om·at·i·cal·ly** \-ˈmat-i-kə-lē, -klē\ *adv* — **id·i·om·at·ic·ness** \-ˈmat-ik-nəs\ *n*

id·io·syn·cra·sy \ˌid-ē-ə-ˈsing-krə-sē\ *n, pl* **-sies** **1 :** a peculiarity of constitution or temperament **:** a characteristic or quality distinguishing an individual **2 :** characteristic peculiarity (as of temperament) [Greek *idiosynkrasia,* from *idios* "one's own" + *synkerannynai* "to blend," from *syn-* + *kerannynai* "to mix"] ***synonyms*** see ECCENTRICITY — **id·io·syn·crat·ic** \ˌid-ē-ō-sin-ˈkrat-ik\ *adj* — **id·io·syn·crat·i·cal·ly** \-ˈkrat-i-kə-lē, -klē\ *adv*

id·i·ot \ˈid-ē-ət\ *n* **:** a silly or foolish person [Latin *idiota* "ignorant person," from Greek *idiōtēs* "one in a private station, layman, ignorant person," from *idios* "one's own, private"] — **idiot** *adj*

Word History The Greek adjective *idios* means "one's own" or "private." The derivative noun *idiōtēs* means "private person." A Greek *idiōtēs* was a person who was not in the public eye, who held no public office. From this sense came the sense "common man," and later "ignorant person" — a natural extension, for the common people of ancient Greece were not, in general, particularly learned. English *idiot* originally meant "ignorant person," but the more usual reference now is to a person who lacks basic intelligence or common sense rather than education.

id·i·ot·ic \ˌid-ē-ˈät-ik\ *adj* **:** showing complete lack of thought **:** FOOLISH, SENSELESS — **id·i·ot·i·cal·ly** \-ˈät-i-kə-lē, -klē\ *adv*

id·i·ot·proof \ˈid-ē-ət-ˌprüf\ *adj* **:** extremely easy to operate or maintain ⟨an *idiotproof* VCR⟩

¹idle \ˈīd-l\ *adj* **idler** \ˈīd-lər, -l-ər\; **idlest** \ˈīd-ləst, -l-əst\ **1 :** lacking worth or basis ⟨*idle* rumor⟩ **2 a :** not employed or occupied ⟨*idle* workers⟩ **b :** not turned to normal or appropriate use ⟨*idle* farmland⟩ **3 :** disliking work **:** LAZY [Old English *īdel*] ***synonyms*** see INACTIVE — **idle·ness** \ˈīd-l-nəs\ *n* — **idly** \ˈīd-lē\ *adv*

²idle *vb* **idled; idling** \ˈīd-ling, -l-ing\ **1 a :** to spend time in idleness **b :** to move idly **2 :** to run disengaged so that power is not used for useful work ⟨the engine is *idling*⟩ **3 :** to pass in idleness **:** WASTE — **idler** \ˈīd-lər, -l-ər\ *n*

synonyms IDLE, LOAF, LOUNGE, LOLL, LAZE mean to spend time doing nothing. IDLE may be used in reference to persons that move lazily or without purpose ⟨*idled* the day away⟩. LOAF suggests either resting or wandering about as though there were nothing to do ⟨he makes the beds and then *loafs* the rest of the day⟩. LOUNGE, though occasionally used as equal to *idle* or *loaf,* typically conveys an additional implication of resting or reclining against a support or of physical comfort and ease in relaxation ⟨he *lounged* against the wall⟩. LOLL also carries an implication of a posture similar to that of *lounge,* but places greater stress upon an indolent or relaxed attitude ⟨*lolling* on the couch⟩. LAZE usually implies the relaxation of a busy person enjoying a vacation or moments of leisure ⟨*lazed* about between appointments⟩.

idol \ˈīd-l\ *n* **1 :** an image of a god made or used as an object of worship **2 :** one that is very greatly or excessively loved and admired [Medieval French *idle,* from Late Latin *idolum,* from Greek *eidōlon* "phantom, idol"]

idol·a·ter \ī-ˈdäl-ət-ər\ *n* **1 :** a worshipper of idols **2 :** a person that admires or loves intensely and often blindly [Medieval French *idolatre,* from Late Latin *idolatres,* from Greek *eidōlatrēs,* from *eidōlon* "idol" + *-latrēs* "worshipper"]

idol·a·tress \ī-ˈdäl-ə-trəs\ *n* **:** a female idolater

idol·a·trous \ī-ˈdäl-ə-trəs\ *adj* **1 :** of or relating to idolatry **2 :** having the character of idolatry **3 :** given to idolatry — **idol·a·trous·ly** *adv* — **idol·a·trous·ness** *n*

idol·a·try \-trē\ *n, pl* **-tries** **1 :** the worship of a physical object as a god **2 :** excessive attachment or devotion to something

idol·ize \ˈīd-l-ˌīz\ *vb* **1 :** to worship idolatrously **2 :** to love or admire to excess — **idol·i·za·tion** \ˌīd-l-ə-ˈzā-shən\ *n* — **idol·iz·er** \ˈīd-l-ˌī-zər\ *n*

idyll *also* **idyl** \ˈīd-l\ *n* **1 a :** a simple poetic or prose work descriptive of peaceful rustic life or pastoral scenes **b :** a narrative poem having an epic, romantic, or tragic theme **2 :** a fit subject for an idyll [Latin *idyllium,* from Greek *eidyllion,* from *eidos* "form"]

idyl·lic \ī-ˈdil-ik\ *adj* **1 :** pleasing in natural simplicity ⟨an *idyllic* landscape⟩ **2 :** of, relating to, or being an idyll ⟨*idyllic* works⟩ — **idyl·li·cal·ly** \-ˈdil-i-kə-le, -ik-lē\ *adv*

-ie *also* **-y** \ē\ *n suffix, pl* **-ies** **1 :** little one **:** dear little one ⟨bird*ie*⟩ ⟨sonn*y*⟩ **2 :** one belonging to **:** one having to do with ⟨cabb*ie*⟩ **3 :** one of (such) a kind or quality ⟨tough*ie*⟩ ⟨smart*y*⟩ [Middle English]

-ier — see -ER

¹if \if, əf, ˌif\ *conj* **1 :** in the event that ⟨come *if* you can⟩ **2 :** WHETHER ⟨asked *if* the mail had come⟩ **3** — used as a function word to introduce an exclamation expressing a wish ⟨*if* it would only rain⟩ **4 :** even though **:** although perhaps ⟨a fun *if* silly movie⟩ **5 :** and perhaps not even ⟨few *if* any changes are expected⟩ — often used with *not* ⟨difficult *if* not impossible⟩ [Old English *gif*] — **if anything :** on the contrary even **:** perhaps even ⟨*if anything* you should apologize⟩

²if \ˈif\ *n* **1 :** CONDITION 3, STIPULATION ⟨too many *ifs* make the contract confusing⟩ **2 :** SUPPOSITION ⟨a theory full of *ifs*⟩

-if·er·ous \ˈif-rəs, -ə-rəs\ *adj combining form* **:** -FEROUS

if·fy \ˈif-ē\ *adj* **1 :** having many uncertain or unknown qualities or conditions ⟨an *iffy* proposition⟩ **2 :** of inconsistent or unreliable quality — **if·fi·ness** *n*

-i·form \ə-ˌfȯrm\ *adj combining form* **:** -FORM

-i·fy \ə-ˌfī\ *vb suffix* **-i·fied; -i·fy·ing** **:** -FY

ig·loo \ˈig-lü\ *n, pl* **igloos** **1**

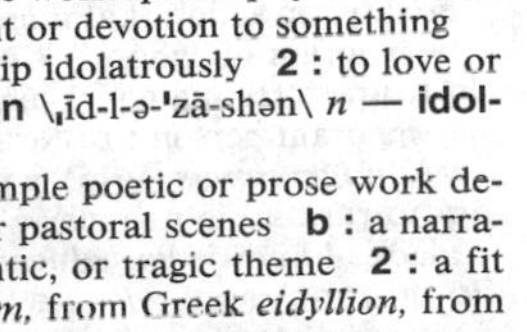

igloo 1

\ə\ **abut**	\au̇\ **out**	\i\ **tip**	\ȯ\ **saw**	\u̇\ **foot**
\ər\ **further**	\ch\ **chin**	\ī\ **life**	\ȯi\ **coin**	\y\ **yet**
\a\ **mat**	\e\ **pet**	\j\ **job**	\th\ **thin**	\yü\ **few**
\ā\ **take**	\ē\ **easy**	\ng\ **sing**	\t͟h\ **this**	\yu̇\ **cure**
\ä\ **cot, cart**	\g\ **go**	\ō\ **bone**	\ü\ **food**	\zh\ **vision**

: an Eskimo house usually made of sod, wood, or stone when permanent or of blocks of snow or ice in the shape of a dome when built for temporary purposes **2** : a structure shaped like a dome [Inuit *iglu* "house"]

ig•ne•ous \ˈig-nē-əs\ *adj* **1** : of, relating to, or resembling fire : FIERY **2** : formed by solidification of magma ⟨*igneous* rock⟩ [Latin *igneus,* from *ignis* "fire"]

ig•nis fatuus \ˌig-nəs-ˈfach-ə-wəs\ *n, pl* **ig•nes fat•ui** \-ˌnēz-ˈfach-ə-ˌwī\ **1** : a light that sometimes appears in the night over marshy ground and is often attributable to the combustion of gas from decomposed organic matter **2** : WILL-O'-THE-WISP 2 [Medieval Latin, literally, "foolish fire"]

ig•nite \ig-ˈnīt\ *vb* **1 a** : to set afire ⟨*ignite* a piece of paper⟩; *also* : KINDLE ⟨*ignite* a fire⟩ **b** : to cause (a fuel mixture) to burn **2** : to catch fire ⟨dry wood *ignites* quickly⟩ **3 a** : to heat up : EXCITE ⟨rumors *ignited* fears in the uninformed population⟩ **b** : to set in motion : SPARK ⟨*ignite* a debate⟩ [Latin *ignire,* from *ignis* "fire"] — **ig•nit•abil•i•ty** \-ˌnīt-ə-ˈbil-ət-ē\ *n* — **ig•nit•able** \-ˈnīt-ə-bəl\ *adj* — **ig•nit•er** *also* **ig•ni•tor** \-ˈnīt-ər\ *n*

ig•ni•tion \ig-ˈnish-ən\ *n* **1** : the act or action of igniting : KINDLING **2 a** : the process or means (as an electric spark) of igniting a fuel mixture **b** : a device that activates an ignition system (as in an automobile) ⟨put the key in the *ignition*⟩

ig•no•ble \ig-ˈnō-bəl\ *adj* **1** : of low birth : PLEBEIAN **2** : characterized by baseness or meanness ⟨*ignoble* conduct⟩ [Latin *ignobilis,* from *in-* + *gnobilis, nobilis* "noble"] — **ig•no•ble•ness** *n* — **ig•no•bly** \-blē\ *adv*

ig•no•min•i•ous \ˌig-nə-ˈmin-ē-əs\ *adj* **1** : marked by disgrace or shame : DISHONORABLE **2** : deserving of shame : DESPICABLE **3** : SHAMEFUL, DEGRADING ⟨an *ignominious* defeat⟩ — **ig•no•min•i•ous•ly** *adv* — **ig•no•min•i•ous•ness** *n*

ig•no•mi•ny \ˈig-nə-ˌmin-ē, ig-ˈnäm-ə-nē\ *n, pl* **-nies** **1** : deep personal humiliation and disgrace **2** : disgraceful conduct, quality, or action [Latin *ignominia,* from *ig-* (as in *ignorare* "to be ignorant of, ignore") + *nomen* "name, repute"]

ig•no•ra•mus \ˌig-nə-ˈrā-məs\ *n, pl* **-mus•es** *also* **-mi** : an utterly ignorant person : DUNCE [from *Ignoramus,* an ignorant lawyer in *Ignoramus* (1615), a play by George Ruggle]

ig•no•rance \ˈig-nə-rəns\ *n* : the state or fact of being ignorant : lack of knowledge, education, or awareness

ig•no•rant \-rənt\ *adj* **1 a** : lacking knowledge or education **b** : resulting from or showing lack of knowledge ⟨an *ignorant* mistake⟩ **2** : not knowing : UNAWARE ⟨*ignorant* of the true facts⟩ — **ig•no•rant•ly** *adv* — **ig•no•rant•ness** *n*

synonyms IGNORANT, ILLITERATE, UNLETTERED, UNTUTORED, UNLEARNED mean not having knowledge. IGNORANT indicates a lack of knowledge in general or of a particular thing ⟨*ignorant* about nuclear physics⟩. ILLITERATE applies to either an absolute or a relative inability to read or write ⟨determine which part of the population is still *illiterate*⟩. UNLETTERED implies ignorance of the knowledge gained by reading ⟨an allusion meaningless to the *unlettered*⟩. UNTUTORED suggests a lack of formal learning or training ⟨the two paintings look identical to the *untutored* eye⟩. UNLEARNED suggests ignorance of advanced subjects ⟨poetry written not for academics but for the *unlearned* audience⟩.

ig•nore \ig-ˈnōr, -ˈnȯr\ *vt* : to refuse to take notice of ⟨*ignore* an interruption⟩ ⟨*ignored* his pleas for help⟩ [French *ignorer* "to be ignorant of," from Latin *ignorare* "to be ignorant of, ignore," from *ignarus* "ignorant, unknown," from *in-* + *gnoscere, noscere* "to know"] ***synonyms*** see NEGLECT — **ig•nor•able** \-ˈnōr-ə-bəl\ *adj* — **ig•nor•er** *n*

igua•na \i-ˈgwän-ə\ *n* : any of various large chiefly plant-eating tropical American lizards with a serrated crest on the back and a large dewlap [Spanish, from Arawak & Carib *iwana*]

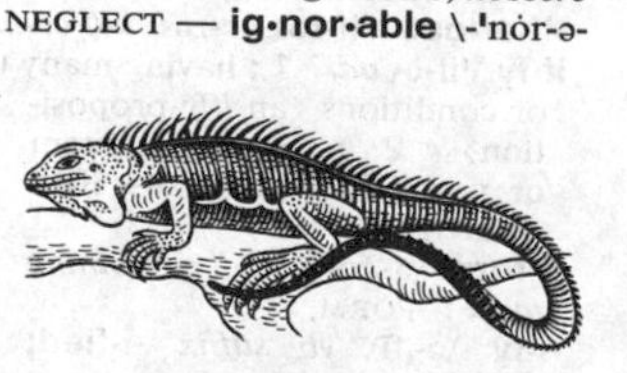
iguana

iguan•odon \i-ˈgwän-ə-ˌdän\ *n* : a large plant-eating dinosaur of the early Cretaceous period that usually walked on all four legs [New Latin *iguanadon,* from Spanish *iguana* + Greek *odōn* "tooth"]

IHS \ˌī-ˌā-ˈches\ — used as a Christian symbol and monogram for *Jesus* [Late Latin, part transliteration of Greek ΙΗΣ, abbreviation for ΙΗΣΟΨΣ *Iēsous* "Jesus"]

ike•ba•na \ˌik-ā-ˈbän-ə\ *n* : the Japanese art of flower arranging that emphasizes form and balance [Japanese, from *ikeru* "to keep alive, arrange" + *hana* "flower"]

ikon *variant of* ICON

il- — see IN-

-ile \əl, ᵊl, ˌīl, ˌil\ *adj suffix* : tending to or capable of ⟨*contractile*⟩ [Latin *-ilis*]

il•e•i•tis \ˌil-ē-ˈīt-əs\ *n* : inflammation of the ileum

il•e•um \ˈil-ē-əm\ *n, pl* **il•ea** \-ē-ə\ : the last part of the small intestine between the jejunum and the large intestine [Latin, "groin, viscera"] — **il•e•al** \-ē-əl\ *adj*

ilex \ˈī-ˌleks\ *n* : HOLLY [Latin, a kind of oak]

il•i•um \ˈil-ē-əm\ *n, pl* **il•ia** \-ē-ə\ : the broad upper and largest of the three bones composing either half of the pelvis [Latin *ilium, ileum* "groin"] — **il•i•ac** \-ē-ˌak\ *adj*

ilk \ˈilk\ *n* : SORT 1, KIND ⟨it's even worse than other films of that *ilk*⟩ [Old English *ilca* "same"]

¹ill \ˈil\ *adj* **worse** \ˈwərs\; **worst** \ˈwərst\ **1** : showing or implying evil intention ⟨*ill* deeds⟩ **2 a** : causing suffering or distress : DISAGREEABLE ⟨*ill* weather⟩ **b** : not normal or sound : FAILING ⟨*ill* health⟩ **c** : not in good health ⟨an *ill* person⟩ **d** : NAUSEATED ⟨felt *ill*⟩ **3** : UNFORTUNATE, UNLUCKY ⟨an *ill* omen⟩ **4** : UNKIND, UNFRIENDLY ⟨*ill* feelings⟩ **5** : not right or proper ⟨an *ill* use of power⟩ [Old Norse *illr* "evil"]

²ill *adv* **worse; worst** **1 a** : with displeasure ⟨the remark was *ill* received⟩ **b** : HARSHLY ⟨*ill* treated⟩ **2** : in a reprehensible manner ⟨an *ill*-spent youth⟩ **3** : SCARCELY ⟨can *ill* afford it⟩ **4** : BADLY, POORLY ⟨*ill* equipped⟩

³ill *n* **1** : EVIL, MISFORTUNE ⟨for good or *ill*⟩ **2** : SICKNESS ⟨childhood *ills*⟩ **3** : TROUBLE, AFFLICTION ⟨the *ills* of society⟩ **4** : something that reflects unfavorably ⟨spoke no *ill* of them⟩

I'll \īl, ˌīl\ : I shall : I will

ill–ad•vised \ˌil-əd-ˈvīzd\ *adj* : showing lack of wise and sufficient advice or consideration : UNWISE — **ill–ad•vis•ed•ly** \-ˈvī-zəd-lē\ *adv*

ill–bred \ˈil-ˈbred\ *adj* : badly brought up : IMPOLITE

il•le•gal \il-ˈlē-gəl, -ˈē-\ *adj* : not lawful — **il•le•gal•i•ty** \ˌil-ē-ˈgal-ət-ē\ *n* — **il•le•gal•ly** \il-ˈlē-gə-lē, -ˈē-\ *adv*

il•leg•ible \il-ˈlej-ə-bəl, -ˈej-\ *adj* : impossible or very hard to read ⟨*illegible* handwriting⟩ ***synonyms*** see UNREADABLE — **il•leg•ibil•i•ty** \il-ˌej-ə-ˈbil-ət-ē\ *n* — **il•leg•ibly** \il-ˈlej-ə-blē, -ˈej-\ *adv*

il•le•git•i•mate \ˌil-i-ˈjit-ə-mət\ *adj* **1** : born of a father and mother who are not married **2** : not correctly deduced or reasoned ⟨an *illegitimate* conclusion⟩ **3** : not lawful or proper — **il•le•git•i•ma•cy** \-ˈjit-ə-mə-sē\ *n* — **il•le•git•i•mate•ly** *adv*

ill–fat•ed \ˈil-ˈfāt-əd\ *adj* : doomed to failure or disaster ⟨an *ill-fated* expedition⟩

ill–fa•vored \-ˈfā-vərd\ *adj* : unattractive in physical appearance; *esp* : having an ugly face

ill–got•ten \-ˈgät-n\ *adj* : acquired by illicit or improper means ⟨*ill-gotten* gains⟩

ill–hu•mored \ˈil-ˈhyü-mərd, -ˈyü-\ *adj* : SURLY, IRRITABLE ⟨became *ill-humored* when tired⟩ — **ill–hu•mored•ly** *adv*

il•lib•er•al \il-ˈlib-rəl, -ˈib-, -ə-rəl\ *adj* **1** : not liberal **2** : not broad-minded : BIGOTED ⟨*illiberal* thinking⟩ **3** : opposed to liberalism ⟨*illiberal* tendencies⟩ — **il•lib•er•al•i•ty** \il-ˌib-ə-ˈral-ət-ē\ *n* — **il•lib•er•al•ly** \-ˈlib-rə-lē, -ˈib-, -ə-rə-\ *adv* — **il•lib•er•al•ness** *n*

il•lic•it \il-ˈlis-ət, -ˈis-\ *adj* : not permitted : UNLAWFUL — **il•lic•it•ly** *adv*

il•lim•it•able \il-ˈlim-ət-ə-bəl, -ˈim-\ *adj* : incapable of being limited : BOUNDLESS — **il•lim•it•abil•i•ty** \-ˌlim-ət-ə-ˈbil-ət-ē, -ˌim-\ *n* — **il•lim•it•able•ness** \-ˈlim-ət-ə-bəl-nəs, -ˈim-\ *n* — **il•lim•it•ably** \-blē\ *adv*

il•lit•er•a•cy \il-ˈlit-ə-rə-sē, -ˈit-; -ˈli-trə-sē, -ˈi-trə-\ *n, pl* **-cies** **1** : the quality or state of being illiterate; *esp* : inability to read or write **2** : a mistake or crudity typical of one who is illiterate

il•lit•er•ate \il-ˈlit-ə-rət, -ˈit-; -ˈli-trət, -ˈi-trət\ *adj* **1** : having little or no education; *esp* : unable to read or write **2 a** : showing or marked by a lack of familiarity with language and literature **b** : showing ignorance of the fundamentals of a particular field of knowledge ***synonyms*** see IGNORANT — **illiterate** *n* — **il•lit•er•ate•ly** *adv* — **il•lit•er•ate•ness** *n*

ill–man•nered \ˈil-ˈman-ərd\ *adj* : marked by bad manners : RUDE

ill–na•tured \-ˈnā-chərd\ *adj* : having a bad disposition — **ill–na•tured•ly** *adv*

ill·ness \'il-nəs\ *n* : an unhealthy condition of body or mind : SICKNESS
il·log·i·cal \il-'läj-i-kəl, -'äj-\ *adj* : not observing the principles of logic or good reasoning — **il·log·i·cal·ly** \-i-kə-lē, -klē\ *adv* — **il·log·i·cal·ness** \-kəl-nəs\ *n*
ill–starred \'il-'stärd\ *adj* : ILL-FATED ⟨*ill-starred* lovers⟩
ill–tem·pered \-'tem-pərd\ *adj* : ILL-NATURED, QUARRELSOME — **ill–tem·pered·ly** *adv*
ill–treat \-'trēt\ *vt* : to treat cruelly or improperly : MALTREAT — **ill–treat·ment** \-mənt\ *n*
il·lu·mi·nant \il-'ü-mə-nənt\ *n* : an illuminating device (as an electric lamp) or substance (as natural gas)
il·lu·mi·nate \-ˌnāt\ *vt* **1 a** : to supply or brighten with light : light up ⟨*illuminate* a building⟩ **b** : to enlighten spiritually or intellectually **2 a** : to make clear : EXPLAIN **b** : to bring to the fore : HIGHLIGHT ⟨a crisis can *illuminate* how interdependent we all are⟩ **3** : to decorate with designs or pictures in gold or colors ⟨*illuminate* a manuscript⟩ [Latin *illuminare,* from *in-* + *luminare* "to light up," from *lumen* "light"] — **il·lu·mi·na·tive** \-ˌnāt-iv\ *adj* — **il·lu·mi·na·tor** \-ˌnāt-ər\ *n*
il·lu·mi·na·tion \il-ˌü-mə-'nā-shən\ *n* **1** : the action of illuminating or state of being illuminated: as **a** : spiritual or intellectual enlightenment **b** : decorative lighting or lighting effects **c** : decoration by the art of illuminating **2** : the quantity of light or the luminous flux per unit area on an intercepting surface at any given point
il·lu·mine \il-'ü-mən\ *vt* : ILLUMINATE
ill–us·age \'il-'yü-sij, -'yü-zij\ *n* : harsh, unkind, or abusive treatment
ill–use \-'yüz\ *vt* : to use badly : MALTREAT, ABUSE
il·lu·sion \il-'ü-zhən\ *n* **1 a** : a misleading image presented to the vision **b** : perception of something actually existing so as to misinterpret its real nature **c** : a figure or pattern capable of being perceived in several ways — called also *optical illusion* **2** : the state or fact of being led to accept as true something unreal or imagined **3** : a misleading or inaccurate idea or impression of reality [Medieval French, from Latin *illusio* "action of mocking," from *illudere* "to mock at," from *in-* + *ludere* "to play, mock"] *synonyms* see DELUSION — **il·lu·sion·ary** \-zhə-ˌner-ē\ *adj*

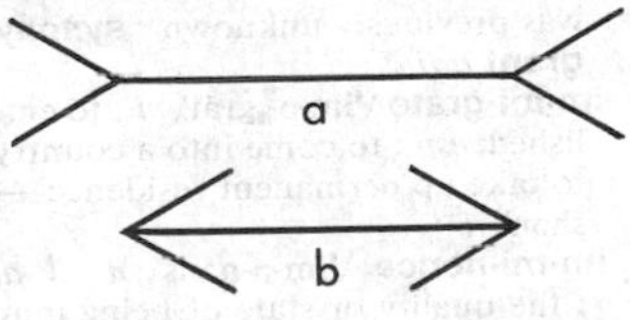

illusion 1c: *a* equals *b* in length

il·lu·sion·ist \il-'üzh-nəst, -ə-nəst\ *n* : a person who produces illusions; *esp* : a magician or performer of sleight of hand
il·lu·sive \il-'ü-siv, -'ü-ziv\ *adj* : ILLUSORY — **il·lu·sive·ly** *adv* — **il·lu·sive·ness** *n*
il·lu·so·ry \il-'üs-rē, -'üz-, -ə-rē\ *adj* : based on or producing illusion : DECEPTIVE ⟨an *illusory* hope⟩ — **il·lu·so·ri·ly** \-rə-lē\ *adv* — **il·lu·so·ri·ness** \-rē-nəs\ *n*
il·lus·trate \'il-ə-ˌstrāt\ *vt* **1** : to make clear especially by serving as or giving an example or instance ⟨*illustrate* an argument with documented evidence⟩ **2 a** : to provide with pictures or figures intended to explain or decorate ⟨*illustrate* a book⟩ **b** : to show clearly : DEMONSTRATE ⟨*illustrate* the operation of a computer⟩ [Latin *illustrare,* from *in-* + *lustrare* "to purify, make bright"] — **il·lus·tra·tor** \-ˌstrāt-ər\ *n*
il·lus·tra·tion \ˌil-ə-'strā-shən\ *n* **1** : the action of illustrating : the condition of being illustrated **2 a** : an example or instance intended to make something clear **b** : a picture or diagram intended to explain or decorate
il·lus·tra·tive \il-'əs-trət-iv\ *adj* : serving, tending, or designed to illustrate ⟨an *illustrative* diagram⟩ — **il·lus·tra·tive·ly** *adv*
il·lus·tri·ous \il-'əs-trē-əs\ *adj* : notably outstanding because of rank or achievement : EMINENT — **il·lus·tri·ous·ly** *adv* — **il·lus·tri·ous·ness** *n*
ill will *n* : unfriendly feeling : MALICE
ill–wish·er \'il-'wish-ər\ *n* : one that wishes ill to another
il·ly \'il-lē, 'il-ē\ *adv* : BADLY, ILL ⟨*illy* chosen⟩
il·men·ite \'il-mə-ˌnīt\ *n* : a metallic-black mineral that consists of an oxide of iron and titanium and that is a major ore of titanium [German *Ilmenit,* from *Ilmen* range, Ural Mountains, Russia]
IM \ˈī-'em\ *vb* **IM'd; IM'ing 1** : to send an instant message to ⟨*IM'd* my friends⟩ **2** : to communicate by instant message ⟨were *IM'ing* at lunch⟩ [*i*nstant *m*essage]
im- — see IN-
I'm \īm, ˌīm\ : I am
[1]**im·age** \'im-ij\ *n* **1** : a reproduction or imitation of the form of a person or thing; *esp* : STATUE **2 a** : a picture of an object produced by a lens, a mirror, or an electronic system **b** : a likeness of an object produced on a photographic material **c** : a picture produced on a display screen (as of a television or computer) **3** : a mental picture or impression of something ⟨a soldier haunted by *images* of battle⟩ **4** : a vivid or graphic representation or description **5** : FIGURE OF SPEECH **6** : a person strikingly like another person ⟨he's the *image* of his father⟩ **7** : a set of values given by a mathematical function from a set of values in its domain [Medieval French, from Latin *imago*]
[2]**image** *vt* **im·aged; im·ag·ing 1** : to call up a mental picture of : IMAGINE **2** : to describe or portray in language especially vividly **3** : to form an image of ⟨a probe *imaging* Jupiter's rings⟩ **4 a** : REFLECT, MIRROR ⟨a face *imaged* in a mirror⟩ **b** : to make appear : PROJECT ⟨a film *imaged* on a screen⟩
im·ag·ery \'im-ij-rē, -ə-rē\ *n, pl* **-er·ies 1** : the product of image makers : IMAGES; *also* : the art of making images **2** : figurative language ⟨*imagery* of a poem⟩ **3** : mental images; *esp* : the products of imagination
imag·in·able \im-'aj-nə-bəl, -ə-nə-\ *adj* : capable of being imagined : CONCEIVABLE ⟨any *imaginable* place⟩ — **imag·in·ably** \-blē\ *adv*
imag·i·nary \im-'aj-ə-ˌner-ē\ *adj* **1** : existing only in imagination : FANCIED ⟨an *imaginary* friend⟩ **2** : of, relating to, or being an imaginary number — **imag·i·nar·i·ly** \-ˌaj-ə-'ner-ə-lē\ *adv* — **imag·i·nar·i·ness** \-'aj-ə-ˌner-ē-nəs\ *n*
imaginary number *n* : a complex number in which the part (as $3\sqrt{-1}$ in $2 + 3\sqrt{-1}$) containing the positive square root of minus 1 is not equal to zero — called also *imaginary*
imag·i·na·tion \im-ˌaj-ə-'nā-shən\ *n* **1** : the act or power of forming a mental image of something not present to the senses or never before wholly perceived in reality **2 a** : creative ability **b** : ability to confront and deal with a problem : RESOURCEFULNESS ⟨use your *imagination* and get us out of here⟩ **3 a** : a creation of the mind; *esp* : an idealized or poetic creation **b** : fanciful or empty assumption
imag·i·na·tive \im-'aj-nət-iv, -ə-nət-, -'aj-ə-ˌnāt-\ *adj* **1** : of, relating to, or characterized by imagination **2** : given to imagining : having a lively imagination **3** : of or relating to images; *esp* : showing a command of imagery — **imag·i·na·tive·ly** *adv* — **imag·i·na·tive·ness** *n*
imag·ine \im-'aj-ən\ *vb* **imag·ined; imag·in·ing** \-'aj-ning, -ə-ning\ **1** : to form a mental image of something not present : use the imagination **2** : SUPPOSE, GUESS ⟨I *imagine* it will rain⟩ [Medieval French *imaginer,* from Latin *imaginari,* from *imagin-, imago* "image"]
imag·in·ings \-'aj-ningz, -ə-ningz\ *n pl* : products of the imagination : THOUGHTS, IMAGES
Im·ag·ism \'im-ij-ˌiz-əm\ *n, often cap* : a 20th century movement in poetry advocating free verse and the expression of ideas and emotions through clear precise images — **im·ag·ist** \-ij-əst\ *n or adj, often cap* — **im·ag·is·tic** \ˌim-ij-'is-tik\ *adj* — **im·ag·is·ti·cal·ly** \ˌim-ij-'is-ti-kə-lē, -klē\ *adv*
ima·go \im-'ā-gō, -'äg-ō\ *n, pl* **imagoes** *or* **ima·gi·nes** \-'ā-gə-ˌnēz, -'äg-ə-\ : an insect in its final adult, sexually mature, and usually winged state [Latin, "image"] — **ima·gi·nal** \-'ā-gən-l, -'äg-ən-\ *adj*
imam \i-'mäm, -'mam\ *n, often cap* **1** : the prayer leader of a mosque **2** : a Muslim leader held to be a divinely appointed, sinless, infallible successor of Muhammad **3** : any of various rulers that claim descent from Muhammad and exercise spiritual and temporal leadership over a Muslim region [Arabic *imām*]
imam·ate \-'mäm-ˌāt, -'mam-\ *n, often cap* **1** : the office of an imam **2** : the region or country ruled over by an imam
im·bal·ance \im-'bal-əns, 'im-\ *n* : lack of balance : the state of being out of equilibrium or out of proportion
im·be·cile \'im-bə-səl, -ˌsil\ *n* : FOOL 1, SIMPLETON [French *imbécile,* from *imbécile* "weak, weak-minded," from Latin *imbecillus*] — **imbecile** *or* **im·be·cil·ic** \ˌim-bə-'sil-ik\ *adj* — **im·be·cile·ly** \'im-bə-səl-lē, -sə-lē, -ˌsil-lē\ *adv*

\ə\ abut	\au̇\ out	\i\ tip	\ȯ\ saw	\u̇\ foot
\ər\ further	\ch\ chin	\ī\ life	\ȯi\ coin	\y\ yet
\a\ mat	\e\ pet	\j\ job	\th\ thin	\yü\ few
\ā\ take	\ē\ easy	\ng\ sing	\t͟h\ this	\yu̇\ cure
\ä\ cot, cart	\g\ go	\ō\ bone	\ü\ food	\zh\ vision

im·be·cil·i·ty \ˌim-bə-ˈsil-ət-ē\ *n, pl* **-ties** **1 :** utter foolishness; *also* **:** FUTILITY **2 :** something foolish or nonsensical

imbed *variant of* EMBED

im·bibe \im-ˈbīb\ *vb* **1 :** to receive into the mind and retain ⟨*imbibe* knowledge⟩ **2 a :** DRINK 1a **b :** to take in or up **:** ABSORB ⟨sponges *imbibe* moisture⟩ [Latin *imbibere* "to drink in," from *in-* + *bibere* "to drink"] — **im·bib·er** *n*

im·bri·cate \ˈim-brə-ˌkāt\ *vb* **:** OVERLAP ⟨*imbricated* shingles⟩ [Late Latin *imbricare* "to cover with tiles," from Latin *imbrex* "roofing tile," from *imber* "rain"] — **im·bri·ca·tion** \ˌim-brə-ˈkā-shən\ *n*

im·bro·glio \im-ˈbrōl-yō\ *n, pl* **-glios** **1 :** a confused mass ⟨an *imbroglio* of papers and books⟩ **2 a :** an intricate or complicated situation (as in a drama or novel) **b :** a painful or embarrassing misunderstanding **:** EMBROILMENT ⟨an *imbroglio* between foreign ministers⟩ **c :** SCANDAL 3a ⟨survived the political *imbroglio*⟩ [Italian, from *imbrogliare* "to embroil," from French *embrouiller*]

im·bue \im-ˈbyü\ *vt* **1 :** to permeate or influence as if by dyeing ⟨*imbued* with a deep sense of loyalty⟩ **2 :** to tinge or dye deeply **3 :** ENDOW 2 ⟨the brightly painted walls *imbue* the room with warmth⟩ [Latin *imbuere*] ***synonyms*** see INFUSE

im·i·ta·ble \ˈim-ət-ə-bəl\ *adj* **:** capable or worthy of being imitated or copied

im·i·tate \ˈim-ə-ˌtāt\ *vt* **1 :** to follow as a pattern, model, or example **2 :** to be or appear similar to **:** RESEMBLE **3 :** to copy exactly ⟨*imitated* a dog's bark⟩ [Latin *imitari*] — **im·i·ta·tor** \-ˌtāt-ər\ *n*

synonyms IMITATE, MIMIC, APE, MOCK mean to follow the example of another. IMITATE suggests following a model or a pattern but may allow for some variation ⟨*imitate* a poet's style⟩. MIMIC implies a close copying as of voice or mannerism often for fun, ridicule, or lifelike imitation ⟨*mimicked* the bird's notes⟩ ⟨children *mimicking* adults⟩. APE may suggest copying in a clumsy or inept manner ⟨young writers *aping* the style of best selling authors⟩. MOCK usually implies imitation with derision ⟨*mocked* the dictator's swaggering walk⟩.

[1]**im·i·ta·tion** \ˌim-ə-ˈtā-shən\ *n* **1 :** an act of imitating **2 :** something produced as a copy **3 :** the repetition in a voice part of the melodic theme, phrase, or motive previously found in another part

[2]**imitation** *adj* **:** resembling something else especially of greater worth **:** not real ⟨*imitation* leather⟩

im·i·ta·tive \ˈim-ə-ˌtāt-iv\ *adj* **1 a :** marked by imitation **b :** reproducing or representing a natural sound ⟨*hiss* is an *imitative* word⟩ **2 :** inclined to imitate **3 :** imitating something superior — **im·i·ta·tive·ly** *adv* — **im·i·ta·tive·ness** *n*

im·mac·u·late \im-ˈak-yə-lət\ *adj* **1 :** having no stain or blemish **:** PURE ⟨an *immaculate* heart⟩ **2 :** containing no flaw or error **3 :** spotlessly clean ⟨*immaculate* linen⟩ [Latin *immaculatus,* from *in-* + *maculare* "to stain," from *macula* "spot, stain"] — **im·mac·u·late·ly** *adv* — **im·mac·u·late·ness** *n*

im·ma·te·ri·al \ˌim-ə-ˈtir-ē-əl\ *adj* **1 :** not consisting of matter **2 :** of no consequence **:** UNIMPORTANT — **im·ma·te·ri·al·i·ty** \-ˌtir-ē-ˈal-ət-ē\ *n* — **im·ma·te·ri·al·ly** \-ˈtir-ē-ə-lē\ *adv* — **im·ma·te·ri·al·ness** *n*

im·ma·ture \ˌim-ə-ˈtůr, -ˈtyůr\ *adj* **1 :** not mature or fully developed **:** YOUNG, UNRIPE ⟨an *immature* bird⟩ ⟨*immature* fruit⟩ **2 :** showing less than an expected degree of maturity ⟨emotionally *immature* adults⟩ — **immature** *n* — **im·ma·ture·ly** *adv* — **im·ma·ture·ness** *n* — **im·ma·tu·ri·ty** \-ˈtůr-ət-ē, -ˈtyůr-\ *n*

im·mea·sur·able \im-ˈezh-rə-bəl, -ˈezh-ə-rə-, -ˈezh-ər-bəl, -ˈāzh-, ˈim-\ *adj* **:** incapable of being measured **:** indefinitely extensive ⟨the *immeasurable* sea⟩ — **im·mea·sur·able·ness** *n* — **im·mea·sur·ably** \-blē\ *adv*

im·me·di·a·cy \im-ˈēd-ē-ə-sē\ *n, pl* **-cies** **1 :** the quality or state of being immediate **2 :** something that is of immediate importance — usually used in plural

im·me·di·ate \im-ˈēd-ē-ət\ *adj* **1 :** next in line or relationship ⟨the monarch's *immediate* heir⟩ **2 :** closest in importance ⟨our *immediate* interest⟩ **3 :** acting directly and alone without anything intervening ⟨the *immediate* cause of disease⟩ **4 :** not distant or separated **:** NEXT ⟨their *immediate* neighbors⟩ **5 :** close in time ⟨the *immediate* past⟩ **6 :** made or done at once ⟨ask for an *immediate* reply⟩ [Late Latin *immediatus,* derived from Latin *in-* "[1]in-" + *medius* "middle"] — **im·me·di·ate·ness** *n*

im·me·di·ate·ly *adv* **1 :** with nothing between **:** DIRECTLY ⟨the house *immediately* beyond this one⟩ **2 :** without delay **:** STRAIGHTWAY ⟨do it *immediately*⟩

im·me·mo·ri·al \ˌim-ə-ˈmōr-ē-əl, -ˈmȯr-\ *adj* **:** extending beyond the reach of memory, record, or tradition ⟨since time *immemorial*⟩ — **im·me·mo·ri·al·ly** \-ē-ə-lē\ *adv*

im·mense \im-ˈens\ *adj* **1 :** very great in size or degree; *esp* **:** beyond ordinary means of measurement ⟨the *immense* and boundless universe⟩ **2 :** supremely good **:** EXCELLENT [Medieval French, from Latin *immensus* "immeasurable," from *in-* + *mensus,* past participle of *metiri* "to measure"] ***synonyms*** see ENORMOUS — **im·mense·ly** *adv* — **im·mense·ness** *n*

im·men·si·ty \im-ˈen-sət-ē\ *n, pl* **-ties** **1 :** the quality or state of being immense **2 :** something immense

im·merse \im-ˈərs\ *vt* **1 :** to plunge into something that surrounds or covers; *esp* **:** to plunge or dip into a fluid **2 :** to baptize by submerging in water **3 :** ENGROSS, ABSORB ⟨completely *immersed* in my work⟩ [Latin *immersus,* past participle of *immergere* "to immerse," from *in-* + *mergere* "to merge"]

im·mers·ible \i-ˈmər-sə-bəl\ *adj* **:** capable of being totally submerged in water without damage ⟨an *immersible* electric frying pan⟩

im·mer·sion \im-ˈər-zhən, -shən\ *n* **:** the act of immersing or the state of being immersed: as **a :** baptism by complete submersion of the person in water **b :** absorbing involvement ⟨*immersion* in politics⟩ **c :** instruction based on extensive exposure to surroundings or conditions that are native or related to the object of study; *esp* **:** foreign language instruction in which only the language being taught is used ⟨learned French through *immersion*⟩

im·mi·grant \ˈim-i-grənt\ *n* **:** one that immigrates: **a :** a person who comes to a country to become a permanent resident **b :** a plant or animal that becomes established in an area where it was previously unknown ***synonyms*** see EMIGRANT — **immigrant** *adj*

im·mi·grate \ˈim-ə-ˌgrāt\ *vi* **:** to enter and usually become established; *esp* **:** to come into a country of which one is not a native to take up permanent residence — **im·mi·gra·tion** \ˌim-ə-ˈgrā-shən\ *n*

im·mi·nence \ˈim-ə-nəns\ *n* **1** *also* **im·mi·nen·cy** \-nən-sē\ **:** the quality or state of being imminent **2 :** something imminent; *esp* **:** impending evil or danger

im·mi·nent \-nənt\ *adj* **:** ready to take place; *esp* **:** hanging threateningly over one's head [Latin *imminens,* present participle of *imminēre* "to project, threaten"] ***synonyms*** see IMPENDING — **im·mi·nent·ly** *adv* — **im·mi·nent·ness** *n*

im·mis·ci·ble \im-ˈis-ə-bəl, ˈim-\ *adj* **:** incapable of mixing ⟨ether and water are *immiscible*⟩ — **im·mis·ci·bil·i·ty** \im-ˌis-ə-ˈbil-ət-ē\ *n*

im·mis·er·a·tion \ˌim-iz-ə-ˈrā-shən\ *n* **:** the act of making miserable; *esp* **:** IMPOVERISHMENT [[2]*in-* + *miserable* + *-ation*]

im·mo·bile \im-ˈō-bəl, -ˌbēl, -ˌbīl, ˈim-\ *adj* **1 :** incapable of being moved **:** FIXED **2 :** not moving **:** MOTIONLESS ⟨kept the patient *immobile*⟩ — **im·mo·bil·i·ty** \ˌim-ō-ˈbil-ət-ē\ *n*

im·mo·bi·lize \im-ˈō-bə-ˌlīz\ *vt* **:** to make immobile; *esp* **:** to prevent freedom of movement or effective use of — **im·mo·bi·li·za·tion** \im-ˌō-bə-lə-ˈzā-shən\ *n* — **im·mo·bi·liz·er** \im-ˈō-bə-ˌlī-zər\ *n*

im·mod·er·ate \im-ˈäd-rət, ˈim-, -ə-rət\ *adj* **:** lacking in moderation **:** EXCESSIVE — **im·mod·er·a·cy** \-ˈäd-rə-sē, -ə-rə-\ *n* — **im·mod·er·ate·ly** *adv* — **im·mod·er·ate·ness** *n* — **im·mod·er·a·tion** \ˌim-ˌäd-ə-ˈrā-shən\ *n*

im·mod·est \im-ˈäd-əst, ˈim-\ *adj* **:** not modest; *esp* **:** INDECENT ⟨*immodest* clothing⟩ — **im·mod·est·ly** *adv* — **im·mod·es·ty** \-ə-stē\ *n*

im·mo·late \ˈim-ə-ˌlāt\ *vt* **1 :** to offer in sacrifice; *esp* **:** to kill as a sacrificial victim **2 :** KILL 1, DESTROY [Latin *immolare,* from *in-* + *mola* "meal"; from the custom of sprinkling victims with sacrificial meal] — **im·mo·la·tion** \ˌim-ə-ˈlā-shən\ *n* — **im·mo·la·tor** \ˈim-ə-ˌlāt-ər\ *n*

im·mor·al \im-ˈȯr-əl, ˈim-, -ˈär-\ *adj* **:** not moral — **im·mor·al·ly** \-ə-lē\ *adv*

im·mor·al·ist \-ə-ləst\ *n* **:** an advocate of immorality

im·mo·ral·i·ty \ˌim-ˌȯ-ˈral-ət-ē, ˌim-ə-ˈral-\ *n, pl* **-ties** **1 :** the quality or state of being immoral; *esp* **:** UNCHASTITY **2 :** an immoral act or practice

[1]**im·mor·tal** \im-ˈȯrt-l, ˈim-\ *adj* **1 :** not subject to death ⟨*immortal* gods⟩ **2 :** connected with or relating to immortality ⟨*immortal* longings⟩ **3 :** lasting forever ⟨*immortal* fame⟩ — **im·mor·tal·ly** \-l-ē\ *adv*

[2]**immortal** *n* **1 a :** one exempt from death **b** *pl, often cap* **:** the

gods of the Greek and Roman pantheon **2 :** a person whose fame is lasting ⟨one of the *immortals* of baseball⟩

im·mor·tal·i·ty \ˌim-ˌȯr-ˈtal-ət-ē\ *n* **:** the quality or state of being immortal: **a :** unending existence **b :** lasting fame

im·mor·tal·ize \im-ˈȯrt-l-ˌīz\ *vt* **:** to make immortal — **im·mor·tal·iza·tion** \-ˌȯrt-l-ə-ˈzā-shən\ *n* — **im·mor·tal·iz·er** \-ˈȯrt-l-ˌī-zər\ *n*

im·mor·telle \ˌim-ˌȯr-ˈtel\ *n* **:** EVERLASTING 3 [French, feminine of *immortel* "immortal"]

im·mov·able \im-ˈü-və-bəl, ˈim-\ *adj* **1 a :** incapable of being moved ⟨*immovable* mountains⟩ **b :** STATIONARY 1 **2 a :** STEADFAST, UNYIELDING ⟨an *immovable* purpose⟩ **b :** not capable of being moved emotionally — **im·mov·abil·i·ty** \ˌim-ˌü-və-ˈbil-ət-ē\ *n* — **im·mov·able·ness** \im-ˈü-və-bəl-nəs, ˈim-\ *n* — **im·mov·ably** \-blē\ *adv*

im·mune \im-ˈyün\ *adj* **1 a :** FREE, EXEMPT ⟨*immune* from punishment⟩ **b :** marked by protection ⟨some criminal leaders are *immune* from arrest⟩ **2 :** not susceptible or responsive ⟨*immune* to fatigue⟩ ⟨*immune* to persuasion⟩; *esp* **:** having a high degree of resistance to an illness or disease ⟨*immune* to the chicken pox⟩ **3 a :** containing or producing antibodies ⟨an *immune* serum⟩ **b :** produced by or concerned with immunity or an immune response [Latin *immunis,* from *in-* "[1]in-" + *munia* "services, obligations"] — **immune** *n*

immune response *n* **:** a bodily response to a foreign substance, cell, or tissue that involves the formation of antibodies and lymphocytes capable of reacting with it and rendering it harmless — called also *immune reaction*

immune system *n* **:** the bodily system that protects the body from foreign substances, cells, and tissues by producing the immune response and that includes especially the thymus, spleen, lymph nodes, macrophages, lymphocytes including the B cells and T cells, and antibodies

im·mu·ni·ty \im-ˈyü-nət-ē\ *n, pl* **-ties :** the quality or state of being immune; *esp* **:** bodily power to resist an infectious disease usually by preventing development of the causative microorganism or by neutralizing its poisons

im·mu·nize \ˈim-yə-ˌnīz\ *vt* **:** to make immune — **im·mu·ni·za·tion** \ˌim-yə-nə-ˈzā-shən\ *n*

immuno- *combining form* **:** physiological immunity ⟨*immuno*logy⟩

im·mu·no·de·fi·cien·cy \-di-ˈfish-ən-sē\ *n* **:** inability to produce a normal number of antibodies or T cells capable of acting in an immune response

im·mu·no·gen·ic \ˌim-yə-nō-ˈjen-ik\ *adj* **:** producing immunity or an immune response — **im·mu·no·gen·i·cal·ly** \-ˈjen-i-kə-lē, -klē\ *adv* — **im·mu·no·ge·nic·i·ty** \-jə-ˈnis-ət-ē\ *n*

im·mu·nol·o·gy \ˌim-yə-ˈnäl-ə-jē\ *n* **:** a science that deals with the immune system, immunity, and immune responses — **im·mu·no·log·ic** \-yən-l-ˈäj-ik\ *or* **im·mu·no·log·i·cal** \-i-kəl\ *adj* — **im·mu·no·log·i·cal·ly** \-i-kə-lē, -klē\ *adv* — **im·mu·nol·o·gist** \ˌim-yə-ˈnäl-ə-jəst\ *n*

im·mu·no·sup·pres·sion \ˌim-yə-nō-sə-ˈpresh-ən\ *n* **:** suppression (as by drugs) of natural immune responses — **im·mu·no·sup·press** \sə-ˈpres\ *vt* — **im·mu·no·sup·pres·sant** \-ˈpres-nt\ *n or adj* — **im·mu·no·sup·pres·sive** \-ˈpres-iv\ *adj*

im·mure \im-ˈyu̇r\ *vt* **1 a :** to enclose within or as if within walls **b :** to shut up **:** IMPRISON **2 :** to build into a wall; *esp* **:** to entomb in a wall [Medieval Latin *immurare,* from Latin *in-* + *murus* "wall"] — **im·mure·ment** \-mənt\ *n*

im·mu·ta·ble \im-ˈyüt-ə-bəl, ˈim-\ *adj* **:** not capable of change — **im·mu·ta·bil·i·ty** \im-ˌyüt-ə-ˈbil-ət-ē\ *n* — **im·mu·ta·ble·ness** \im-ˈyüt-ə-bəl-nəs, ˈim-\ *n* — **im·mu·ta·bly** \-blē\ *adv*

imp \ˈimp\ *n* **1 :** a small demon **2 :** a mischievous child [Old English *impa* "bud, shoot, scion"]

[1]im·pact \im-ˈpakt\ *vt* **1 a :** to fix firmly by or as if by packing or wedging **b :** to press together **2 a :** to have a direct effect or impact on **:** impinge on ⟨tourism was severely *impacted* by poor weather⟩ **b :** to strike forcefully; *also* **:** to cause to strike forcefully [Latin *impactus,* past participle of *impingere* "to push against, impinge"]

[2]im·pact \ˈim-ˌpakt\ *n* **1 a :** an impinging or striking (as of one body against another) **b :** a forceful contact or onset; *also* **:** the impetus communicated in or as if in such contact **2 :** the force of impression of one thing on another **:** EFFECT ⟨the *impact* of technology on society⟩

im·pact·ed \im-ˈpak-təd\ *adj* **1 :** packed or wedged in **2 :** wedged between the jawbone and another tooth ⟨an *impacted* molar⟩

im·pac·tion \im-ˈpak-shən\ *n* **:** the act of becoming or the state of being impacted; *esp* **:** accumulation and packing of something (as feces) in a body passage or cavity

impact printer *n* **:** a printing device in which a printing element directly strikes a surface (as in a typewriter)

im·pair \im-ˈpaər, -ˈpeər\ *vt* **:** to damage or make worse by or as if by diminishing in quantity, value, excellence, strength, or efficiency ⟨smoking can *impair* one's health⟩ [Medieval French *empeirer,* derived from Latin *in-* "[2]in-" + Late Latin *pejorare* "to make worse," from Latin *pejor* "worse"] — **im·pair·er** *n* — **im·pair·ment** \-mənt\ *n*

im·paired \-ˈpaərd, -ˈpeərd\ *adj* **1 a :** functioning in a defective or less than perfect way ⟨*impaired* heart action⟩ **b :** having a defective physical or mental function — often used in combination ⟨a hearing-*impaired* person⟩ **2 :** intoxicated by alcohol or drugs ⟨driving while *impaired*⟩

im·pa·la \im-ˈpal-ə, -ˈpäl-\ *n* **:** a large brownish African antelope that in the male has slender curving horns [Zulu]

impala

im·pale \im-ˈpāl\ *vt* **:** to pierce with or as if with something pointed; *esp* **:** to torture or kill by fixing on a sharp stake [Medieval Latin *impalare,* from Latin *in-* + *palus* "stake"] — **im·pale·ment** \-mənt\ *n* — **im·pal·er** \-ˈpā-lər\ *n*

im·pal·pa·ble \im-ˈpal-pə-bəl, ˈim-\ *adj* **1 :** incapable of being felt by the touch **:** INTANGIBLE ⟨the *impalpable* feeling of accomplishment⟩ **2 :** not readily discerned or understood ⟨*impalpable* evils⟩ — **im·pal·pa·bil·i·ty** \im-ˌpal-pə-ˈbil-ət-ē\ *n* — **im·pal·pa·bly** \im-ˈpal-pə-blē, ˈim-\ *adv*

im·pan·el *or* **em·pan·el** \im-ˈpan-l\ *vt* **-eled** *or* **-elled; -el·ing** *or* **-el·ling :** to enter in or on a panel or list **:** ENROLL ⟨*impanel* a jury⟩

im·par·a·dise \im-ˈpar-ə-ˌdīs, -ˌdīz\ *vt* **:** ENRAPTURE

im·par·i·ty \im-ˈpar-ət-ē, ˈim-\ *n, pl* **-ties :** INEQUALITY 1, DISPARITY

im·part \im-ˈpärt\ *vt* **1 :** to give from or as if from one's store or abundance ⟨the sun *imparts* warmth⟩ **2 :** to communicate the knowledge of **:** DISCLOSE ⟨*imparted* their plans⟩ [Latin *impartire,* from *in-* + *partire* "to divide, part"] — **im·part·able** \-ə-bəl\ *adj* — **im·par·ta·tion** \ˌim-ˌpär-ˈtā-shən\ *n* — **im·part·ment** \im-ˈpart-mənt\ *n*

im·par·tial \im-ˈpär-shəl, ˈim-\ *adj* **:** not partial **:** UNBIASED ***synonyms*** see FAIR — **im·par·ti·al·i·ty** \ˌim-ˌpär-shē-ˈal-ət-ē, -ˌpär-ˈshal-\ *n* — **im·par·tial·ly** \im-ˈpärsh-lē, ˈim-, -ə-lē\ *adv*

im·pass·able \im-ˈpas-ə-bəl, ˈim-\ *adj* **:** incapable of being passed, traveled, crossed, or climbed — **im·pass·abil·i·ty** \ˌim-ˌpas-ə-ˈbil-ət-ē\ *n* — **im·pass·able·ness** \im-ˈpas-ə-bəl-nəs, ˈim-\ *n* — **im·pass·ably** \-blē\ *adv*

im·passe \ˈim-ˌpas, im-ˈ\ *n* **1 :** an impassable road or way **2 a :** a predicament from which there is no obvious escape **b :** DEADLOCK [French, from *in-* "[1]in-" + *passer* "to pass"]

im·pas·si·ble \im-ˈpas-ə-bəl, ˈim-\ *adj* **1 a :** incapable of experiencing pain **b :** incapable of being harmed **2 :** incapable of feeling **:** IMPASSIVE [Late Latin *impassibilis,* derived from Latin *in-* + *passus,* past participle of *pati* "to suffer"] — **im·pas·si·bil·i·ty** \ˌim-ˌpas-ə-ˈbil-ət-ē\ *n* — **im·pas·si·bly** \im-ˈpas-ə-blē, ˈim-\ *adv*

im·pas·sioned \im-ˈpash-ənd\ *adj* **:** filled with passion or zeal **:** showing great warmth or intensity of feeling ⟨delivered an *impassioned* speech⟩

synonyms IMPASSIONED, PASSIONATE, ARDENT, FERVENT mean showing intense feeling. IMPASSIONED implies warmth and intensity without violence and suggests a fluent verbal expression ⟨an *impassioned* plea for justice⟩. PASSIONATE implies extreme emotion sometimes accompanied by anger or violence ⟨a *passionate* denunciation of the traitor⟩. ARDENT implies an intense degree of zeal, devotion, or enthusiasm ⟨an *ardent* supporter of human rights⟩. FERVENT stresses sincerity and steadiness of emotional warmth or zeal ⟨*fervent* good wishes⟩.

im·pas·sive \im-ˈpas-iv, ˈim-\ *adj* : not feeling or not showing any emotion ⟨an *impassive* stare⟩ — **im·pas·sive·ly** *adv* — **im·pas·sive·ness** *n* — **im·pas·siv·i·ty** \ˌim-ˌpas-ˈiv-ət-ē\ *n*

synonyms IMPASSIVE, STOIC, APATHETIC, STOLID, PHLEGMATIC mean unresponsive to something that might normally excite interest or emotion. IMPASSIVE stresses the absence of any external sign of emotion in action or facial expression ⟨met the good news with an *impassive* look⟩. STOIC implies an apparent indifference to pleasure or especially to pain often as a matter of principle or self-discipline ⟨was firmly *stoic* even in adversity⟩. APATHETIC may imply a puzzling or deplorable indifference or inertness ⟨the public was *apathetic* to the plight of the homeless⟩. STOLID implies an habitual absence of interest, responsiveness, or curiosity ⟨*stolid* workers wedded to routine⟩. PHLEGMATIC implies a temperament hard to arouse ⟨a *phlegmatic* man unmoved by tears⟩.

im·pas·to \im-ˈpas-tō, -ˈpäs-\ *n* : the thick application of a pigment to a canvas or panel in painting; *also* : the body of pigment so applied [Italian, derived from *in-* "in" + *pasta* "paste," from Late Latin]

im·pa·tience \im-ˈpā-shəns, ˈim-\ *n* : the quality or state of being impatient

im·pa·tiens \im-ˈpā-shənz, -shəns\ *n* : any of a large genus of annual herbs with often showy flowers [Latin, "impatient"]

im·pa·tient \im-ˈpā-shənt, ˈim-\ *adj* **1 a** : not patient : restless or short of temper especially under irritation, delay, or opposition ⟨an *impatient* disposition⟩ **b** : INTOLERANT ⟨*impatient* of delay⟩ **2** : prompted or marked by impatience ⟨an *impatient* answer⟩ **3** : eagerly desirous : ANXIOUS ⟨*impatient* to get home⟩ — **im·pa·tient·ly** *adv*

im·peach \im-ˈpēch\ *vt* **1 a** : to charge (a public official) formally with misconduct in office **b** : to remove from office especially for misconduct **2** : to cast doubt on; *esp* : to challenge the credibility or validity of ⟨*impeach* the testimony of a witness⟩ [Medieval French *empecher, enpechier* "to hinder," from Late Latin *impedicare* "to fetter," from Latin *in-* + *pedica* "fetter," from *ped-, pes* "foot"] — **im·peach·able** \-ˈpē-chə-bəl\ *adj* — **im·peach·ment** \-ˈpēch-mənt\ *n*

im·pearl \im-ˈpərl\ *vt* : to form into pearls; *also* : to form of or adorn with pearls

im·pec·ca·ble \im-ˈpek-ə-bəl, ˈim-\ *adj* **1** : not capable of sinning or liable to sin **2** : free from fault or blame : FLAWLESS ⟨a person of *impeccable* character⟩ [Latin *impeccabilis,* from *in-* + *peccare* "to sin"] — **im·pec·ca·bil·i·ty** \ˌim-ˌpek-ə-ˈbil-ət-ē\ *n* — **im·pec·ca·bly** \im-ˈpek-ə-blē, ˈim-\ *adv*

im·pe·cu·nious \ˌim-pi-ˈkyü-nyəs, -nē-əs\ *adj* : having very little or no money usually habitually : PENNILESS [derived from Latin *pecunia* "money"] — **im·pe·cu·ni·os·i·ty** \-ˌkyü-nē-ˈäs-ət-ē\ *n* — **im·pe·cu·ni·ous·ly** *adv* — **im·pe·cu·ni·ous·ness** *n*

im·ped·ance \im-ˈpēd-ns\ *n* : the apparent opposition in an electrical circuit to the flow of an alternating current as a result of a combination of resistance and reactance

im·pede \im-ˈpēd\ *vt* : to interfere with the progress of : BLOCK ⟨traffic *impeded* by heavy rain⟩ [Latin *impedire,* from *in-* "[2]in-" + *ped-, pes* "foot"] ***synonyms*** see HINDER — **im·ped·er** *n*

im·ped·i·ment \im-ˈped-ə-mənt\ *n* **1** : something that impedes **2** : a defect in speech

im·ped·i·men·ta \im-ˌped-ə-ˈment-ə\ *n pl* : things (as baggage or supplies) that impede progress or movement [Latin, "impediments"]

im·pel \im-ˈpel\ *vt* **im·pelled; im·pel·ling** **1** : to urge or drive forward or into action ⟨felt *impelled* to speak up in their defense⟩ **2** : to impart motion to : PROPEL ⟨*impel* water through a pipe⟩ [Latin *impellere,* from *in-* + *pellere* "to drive"] ***synonyms*** see MOVE — **im·pel·ler** *also* **im·pel·lor** \-ˈpel-ər\ *n*

im·pend \im-ˈpend\ *vi* : to hover threateningly : MENACE ⟨warning of a danger that *impends*⟩ **2** : to be about to occur [Latin *impendēre,* from *in-* + *pendēre* "to hang"]

im·pend·ing *adj* : threatening to occur soon : APPROACHING

synonyms IMPENDING, IMMINENT mean threatening to occur very soon. IMPENDING implies signs that keep one in suspense ⟨an *impending* thunderstorm kept us from going on a picnic⟩. IMMINENT emphasizes the shortness of time before happening ⟨his arrival was now *imminent*⟩.

im·pen·e·tra·bil·i·ty \im-ˌpen-ə-trə-ˈbil-ət-ē\ *n* : the quality or state of being impenetrable

im·pen·e·tra·ble \im-ˈpen-ə-trə-bəl, ˈim-\ *adj* **1 a** : incapable of being penetrated or pierced ⟨*impenetrable* rock⟩ ⟨*impenetrable* jungle⟩ **b** : inaccessible to knowledge, reason, or sympathy : IMPERVIOUS **2** : incapable of being comprehended : INSCRUTABLE ⟨an *impenetrable* mystery⟩ — **im·pen·e·tra·ble·ness** *n* — **im·pen·e·tra·bly** \-blē\ *adv*

im·pen·i·tence \im-ˈpen-ə-təns\ *n* : the quality or state of being impenitent

im·pen·i·tent \im-ˈpen-ə-tənt, ˈim-\ *adj* : not penitent : not sorry for having done wrong — **im·pen·i·tent·ly** *adv*

[1]im·per·a·tive \im-ˈper-ət-iv\ *adj* **1 a** : of, relating to, or constituting the grammatical mood that expresses a command, request, or strong encouragement **b** : expressive of a command, entreaty, or exhortation ⟨an *imperative* gesture⟩ **2** : not to be avoided or evaded : URGENT ⟨*imperative* business⟩ [Late Latin *imperativus,* from Latin *imperare* "to command"] — **im·per·a·tive·ly** *adv* — **im·per·a·tive·ness** *n*

[2]imperative *n* **1** : the imperative mood or a verb form expressing it **2** : something that is imperative: **a** : COMMAND 2, ORDER **b** : an obligatory act or duty

im·pe·ra·tor \ˌim-pə-ˈrät-ər, -ˈrä-ˌtȯr\ *n* : a supreme leader of the ancient Romans : EMPEROR [Latin] — **im·per·a·to·ri·al** \ˌim-per-ə-ˈtōr-ē-əl, -ˈtȯr-\ *adj*

im·per·cep·ti·ble \ˌim-pər-ˈsep-tə-bəl\ *adj* **1** : not perceptible by a sense or by the mind **2** : extremely slight, gradual, or subtle — **im·per·cep·ti·bil·i·ty** \-ˌsep-tə-ˈbil-ət-ē\ *n* — **im·per·cep·ti·bly** \-ˈsep-tə-blē\ *adv*

im·per·cep·tive \ˌim-pər-ˈsep-tiv\ *adj* : not perceptive ⟨an *imperceptive* reader⟩ — **im·per·cep·tive·ness** *n*

im·per·cip·i·ence \ˌīm-pər-ˈsip-ē-əns\ *n* : the quality or state of being imperceptive — **im·per·cip·i·ent** \-ənt\ *adj*

[1]im·per·fect \im-ˈpər-fikt, ˈim-\ *adj* **1** : not perfect: **a** : DEFECTIVE ⟨*imperfect* pearls⟩ **b** : having stamens or pistils but not being a flower with both **2** : of, relating to, or constituting a verb tense used to designate a continuing state or an incomplete action especially in the past — **im·per·fect·ly** \-fik-lē, -tlē\ *adv* — **im·per·fect·ness** \-fik-nəs, -fikt-\ *n*

[2]imperfect *n* : the imperfect tense of a verb; *also* : a verb in this tense

imperfect fungus *n* : any of various fungi of which only the asexual stage involving production of conidia is known

im·per·fec·tion \ˌim-pər-ˈfek-shən\ *n* : the quality or state of being imperfect; *also* : BLEMISH, FAULT

im·per·fo·rate \im-ˈpər-fə-rət, ˈim-, -frət, -fə-ˌrāt\ *adj* : lacking perforations or rouletting ⟨*imperforate* postage stamps⟩ — **imperforate** *n*

[1]im·pe·ri·al \im-ˈpir-ē-əl\ *adj* **1 a** : of, relating to, or befitting an empire or an emperor ⟨by *imperial* decree⟩ **b** : of or relating to the Commonwealth of Nations and British Empire **2 a** : SUPREME 2 **b** : REGAL 1, IMPERIOUS **3** : of superior or unusual size or excellence **4** : belonging to a British series of weights and measures ⟨an *imperial* gallon⟩ [Medieval French, from Late Latin *imperialis,* from Latin *imperium* "command, empire"] — **im·pe·ri·al·ly** \-ē-ə-lē\ *adv*

[2]imperial *n* : a pointed beard growing below the lower lip [from the beard worn by Napoléon III]

imperial

im·pe·ri·al·ism \im-ˈpir-ē-ə-ˌliz-əm\ *n* **1** : imperial government, authority, or system **2** : the policy or practice of extending the power and dominion of one nation by direct territorial acquisitions or by indirect control over the political or economic life of other areas — **im·pe·ri·al·ist** \-ləst\ *n* — **imperialist** *or* **im·pe·ri·al·is·tic** \im-ˌpir-ē-ə-ˈlis-tik\ *adj* — **im·pe·ri·al·is·ti·cal·ly** \-ti-kə-lē, -klē\ *adv*

im·per·il \im-ˈper-əl\ *vt* **-iled** *or* **-illed; -il·ing** *or* **-il·ling** : to bring into peril : ENDANGER — **im·per·il·ment** \-əl-mənt\ *n*

im·pe·ri·ous \im-ˈpir-ē-əs\ *adj* **1** : befitting or characteristic of one of eminent rank or attainments **2** : marked by arrogant assurance : DOMINEERING **3** : IMPERATIVE, URGENT ⟨*imperious* problems⟩ [Latin *imperiosus,* from *imperium* "command, empire"] ***synonyms*** see MASTERFUL — **im·pe·ri·ous·ly** *adv* — **im·pe·ri·ous·ness** *n*

im·per·ish·a·ble \im-ˈper-ish-ə-bəl, ˈim-\ *adj* : not perishable or subject to decay : INDESTRUCTIBLE ⟨*imperishable* fame⟩ — **im·per·ish·abil·i·ty** \ˌim-ˌper-ish-ə-ˈbil-ət-ē\ *n* — **im·per·ish·able·ness** \im-ˈper-ish-ə-bəl-nəs, ˈim-\ *n* — **im·per·ish·a·bly** \-blē\ *adv*

im·pe·ri·um \im-ˈpir-ē-əm\ *n* **1 a** : supreme power or dominion **b** : the right to supreme power : SOVEREIGNTY **2** : EMPIRE 1a(2) [Latin]

im·per·ma·nent \im-ˈpər-mə-nənt, ˈim-\ *adj* : not permanent : TRANSIENT — **im·per·ma·nence** \-nəns\ *n* — **im·per·ma·nent·ly** *adv*

im·per·me·able \im-ˈpər-mē-ə-bəl, ˈim-\ *adj* : not permitting passage (as of a fluid) through its substance : IMPERVIOUS — **im·per·me·abil·i·ty** \ˌim-ˌpər-mē-ə-ˈbil-ət-ē\ *n*

im·per·mis·si·ble \ˌim-pər-ˈmis-ə-bəl\ *adj* : not permissible — **im·per·mis·si·bil·i·ty** \-ˌmis-ə-ˈbil-ət-ē\ *n* — **im·per·mis·si·bly** \-ˈmis-ə-blē\ *adv*

im·per·son·al \im-ˈpərs-nəl, ˈim-, -n-əl\ *adj* **1** : of, relating to, or being a verb used with no expressed subject or with a merely formal subject ⟨*methinks* in "methinks you are wrong" and *rained* in "it rained" are *impersonal* verbs⟩ **2 a** : having no personal reference or connection ⟨*impersonal* criticism⟩ **b** : not engaging the human personality or emotions ⟨the *impersonal* attitude of a doctor⟩ **c** : not existing as a person ⟨an *impersonal* deity⟩ — **im·per·son·al·i·ty** \ˌim-ˌpərs-n-ˈal-ət-ē\ *n* — **im·per·son·al·ize** \im-ˈpərs-nə-ˌlīz, ˈim-, -n-ə-ˌlīz\ *vt* — **im·per·son·al·ly** \-nə-lē, -n-ə-lē\ *adv*

im·per·son·ate \im-ˈpərs-n-ˌāt\ *vt* : to act the part of or pretend to be (some other person) ⟨*impersonate* a police officer⟩ — **im·per·son·ation** \-ˌpərs-n-ˈā-shən\ *n* — **im·per·son·ator** \-ˈpərs-n-ˌāt-ər\ *n*

im·per·ti·nence \im-ˈpərt-n-əns, ˈim-\ *n* **1** : the quality or state of being impertinent **2** : a rude act or remark

im·per·ti·nen·cy \-ən-sē\ *n, pl* **-cies** : IMPERTINENCE

im·per·ti·nent \-ənt\ *adj* **1** : not pertinent : IRRELEVANT **2** : not restrained within due or proper bounds : RUDE, INSOLENT ⟨an *impertinent* answer⟩ — **im·per·ti·nent·ly** *adv*

im·per·turb·able \ˌim-pər-ˈtər-bə-bəl\ *adj* : marked by extreme calm, impassivity, and steadiness : SERENE — **im·per·turb·abil·i·ty** \-ˌtər-bə-ˈbil-ət-ē\ *n* — **im·per·turb·ably** \-ˈtər-bə-blē\ *adv*

im·per·vi·ous \im-ˈpər-vē-əs, ˈim-\ *adj* **1** : not allowing entrance or passage : IMPENETRABLE ⟨a coat *impervious* to rain⟩ **2** : not capable of being affected or disturbed ⟨*impervious* to criticism⟩ — **im·per·vi·ous·ly** *adv* — **im·per·vi·ous·ness** *n*

im·pe·ti·go \ˌim-pə-ˈtē-gō, -ˈtī-\ *n* : an acute contagious skin disease characterized by small pus-filled blisters and yellowish crusts [Latin, from *impetere* "to attack"] — **im·pe·tig·i·nous** \-ˈtij-ə-nəs\ *adj*

im·pet·u·os·i·ty \im-ˌpech-ə-ˈwäs-ət-ē\ *n, pl* **-ties** **1** : the quality or state of being impetuous **2** : an impetuous action or impulse

im·pet·u·ous \im-ˈpech-wəs, -ə-wəs\ *adj* **1** : marked by force and violence **2** : marked by impulsive vehemence [Medieval French from Late Latin *impetuosus,* from Latin *impetus*] — **im·pet·u·ous·ly** *adv* — **im·pet·u·ous·ness** *n*

im·pe·tus \ˈim-pət-əs\ *n* **1 a** : a driving force : IMPULSE **b** : INCENTIVE, STIMULUS **2** : MOMENTUM 1 ⟨the *impetus* of a bullet⟩ [Latin, "assault, impetus," from *impetere* "to attack," from *in-* + *petere* "to go to, seek"]

im·pi·e·ty \im-ˈpī-ət-ē, ˈim-\ *n, pl* **-ties** **1** : the quality or state of being impious : IRREVERENCE **2** : an impious act

im·pinge \im-ˈpinj\ *vi* **1** : to strike or dash especially with a sharp collision ⟨sound waves *impinge* upon the eardrums⟩ **2** : to come into close contact **3** : ENCROACH, INFRINGE ⟨*impinge* on another person's rights⟩ [Latin *impingere,* from *in-* + *pangere* "to fasten, drive in"] — **im·pinge·ment** \-mənt\ *n*

im·pi·ous \ˈim-pē-əs; im-ˈpī-, ˈim-\ *adj* : lacking in reverence or proper respect — **im·pi·ous·ly** *adv*

imp·ish \ˈim-pish\ *adj* : of, relating to, or befitting an imp; *esp* : MISCHIEVOUS — **imp·ish·ly** *adv* — **imp·ish·ness** *n*

im·pla·ca·ble \im-ˈplak-ə-bəl, ˈim-, -ˈplā-kə-\ *adj* : not placable : not capable of being appeased, pacified, or mitigated ⟨an *implacable* enemy⟩ — **im·pla·ca·bil·i·ty** \ˌim-ˌplak-ə-ˈbil-ət-ē, -ˌplā-kə-\ *n* — **im·pla·ca·bly** \-blē\ *adv*

im·plant \im-ˈplant\ *vt* **1 a** : to fix or set securely or deeply **b** : to set permanently in the consciousness or habit patterns ⟨*implant* patriotism in children⟩ **2** : to insert in living tissue (as for growth or absorption) ⟨cartilage *implanted* into the damaged knee joint⟩ — **implant** *n* — **im·plan·ta·tion** \ˌim-ˌplan-ˈtā-shən\ *n* — **im·plant·er** *n*

im·plau·si·ble \im-ˈplȯ-zə-bəl, ˈim-\ *adj* : not plausible — **im·plau·si·bil·i·ty** \ˌim-ˌplȯ-zə-ˈbil-ət-ē\ *n* — **im·plau·si·bly** \im-ˈplȯ-zə-blē, ˈim-\ *adv*

¹im·ple·ment \ˈim-plə-mənt\ *n* **1** : a piece of equipment : TOOL **2** : one that serves as an instrument or tool [Late Latin *implementum* "action of filling up," from Latin *implēre* "to fill up," from *in-* + *plēre* "to fill"]

synonyms IMPLEMENT, TOOL, UTENSIL, INSTRUMENT mean a device for performing work. IMPLEMENT may apply to anything necessary to perform a task ⟨farm *implements*⟩. TOOL suggests an implement adapted for a specific task and implies the need of skill in its use ⟨a carpenter's *tools*⟩. UTENSIL suggests a device useful for domestic tasks ⟨kitchen *utensils*⟩ or some routine unskilled activity ⟨writing *utensils*⟩. INSTRUMENT suggests a device capable of delicate or precise work ⟨a surgeon's *instruments*⟩.

²im·ple·ment \-ˌment\ *vt* **1** : CARRY OUT 1, FULFILL; *esp* : to give practical effect to by positive action ⟨*implement* the provisions of a treaty⟩ **2** : to provide implements for — **im·ple·men·ta·tion** \ˌim-plə-mən-ˈtā-shən, -ˌmen-\ *n*

im·pli·cate \ˈim-plə-ˌkāt\ *vt* : to bring into connection : INVOLVE ⟨the confession *implicated* several others in the crime⟩ [Latin *implicare,* literally, "to enfold, involve," from *in-* + *plicare* "to fold"]

im·pli·ca·tion \ˌim-plə-ˈkā-shən\ *n* **1 a** : the act of implicating : the state of being implicated **b** : an incriminating involvement **2 a** : the act of implying : the state of being implied **b** : something implied **3** : a sentence which is composed of two parts beginning with "if" and "then" and for which the "then" part is true whenever the "if" part is true ⟨"If P then Q" is an *implication*⟩ — **im·pli·ca·tive** \ˈim-plə-ˌkāt-iv\ *adj* — **im·pli·ca·tive·ly** *adv* — **im·pli·ca·tive·ness** *n*

im·plic·it \im-ˈplis-ət\ *adj* **1** : understood though not directly stated ⟨an *implicit* agreement⟩ **2** : being without reserve : COMPLETE, UNQUESTIONING ⟨*implicit* trust⟩ — compare EXPLICIT 1 [Latin *implicitus,* past participle of *implicare* "to enfold, implicate"] — **im·plic·it·ly** *adv* — **im·plic·it·ness** *n*

im·plode \im-ˈplōd\ *vi* **1** : to burst inward **2** : to break down or fall apart from within : SELF-DESTRUCT ⟨the firm *imploded* from the CEO's excessive greed⟩ [*in-* + *-plode* (as in *explode*)] — **im·plo·sion** \-ˈplō-zhən\ *n* — **im·plo·sive** \-ˈplō-siv, -ziv\ *adj*

im·plore \im-ˈplōr, -ˈplȯr\ *vt* **1** : to call upon in supplication : BESEECH **2** : to call or pray for earnestly [Latin *implorare,* from *in-* + *plorare* "to cry out"] ***synonyms*** see BEG

im·ply \im-ˈplī\ *vt* **im·plied; im·ply·ing** **1 a** : to include or involve as a natural or necessary though not definitely stated part or effect ⟨the rights of citizenship *imply* certain obligations⟩ **b** : to involve as a necessary consequence or condition ⟨"If A then B" means that A *implies* B⟩ **2** : to express indirectly : suggest rather than say plainly ⟨remarks that *implied* consent⟩ [Medieval French *emplier* "to enfold," from Latin *implicare* "to enfold, implicate"] ***usage*** see INFER

im·po·lite \ˌim-pə-ˈlīt\ *adj* : not polite : RUDE — **im·po·lite·ly** *adv* — **im·po·lite·ness** *n*

im·pol·i·tic \im-ˈpäl-ə-ˌtik\ *adj* : not politic : UNWISE ⟨*impolitic* remarks⟩ — **im·po·lit·i·cal** \-pə-ˈlit-i-kəl\ *adj* — **im·po·lit·i·cal·ly** \-kə-lē, -klē\ *adv* — **im·pol·i·tic·ly** *adv*

im·pon·der·able \im-ˈpän-də-rə-bəl, ˈim-, -drə-bəl\ *adj* : not ponderable : incapable of being weighed or evaluated with exactness ⟨an *imponderable* phenomenon⟩ — **im·pon·der·abil·i·ty** \im-ˌpän-də-rə-ˈbil-ət-ē, -drə-ˈbil-\ *n* — **imponderable** *n* — **im·pon·der·ably** \-blē\ *adv*

¹im·port \im-ˈpōrt, -ˈpȯrt, ˈim-ˌ\ *vb* **1 a** : MEAN ⟨their words *imported* a need for change⟩ **b** : to be of importance : MATTER **2** : to bring from a foreign or external source; *esp* : to bring (as goods) into a place or country from another country ⟨*import* coffee⟩ **3** : to transfer (as existing data) into a computer program from another file rather than typing it in manually [Latin *importare* "to bring in," from *in-* + *portare* "to carry"] — **im·port·able** \-ə-bəl\ *adj* — **im·port·er** *n*

[2]**im·port** \ˈim-ˌpōrt, -ˌpȯrt\ *n* **1** : MEANING **2** : IMPORTANCE **3 a** : something imported **b** : IMPORTATION 1

im·por·tance \im-ˈpȯrt-ns, -əns\ *n* **1** : the quality or state of being important **2** : an important aspect or bearing : SIGNIFICANCE

im·por·tant \im-ˈpȯrt-nt, -ənt\ *adj* **1** : having great meaning or influence ⟨an *important* change in printing methods⟩ **2** : having considerable power or authority ⟨an *important* official⟩ **3** : showing a feeling of personal importance — **im·por·tant·ly** *adv*

im·por·ta·tion \ˌim-ˌpōr-ˈtā-shən, -ˌpȯr-, -pər-\ *n* **1** : the act or practice of importing **2** : IMPORT 3a

imported fire ant *n* : either of two small South American fire ants that are pests in the southeastern U.S. especially in fields used to grow crops

im·por·tu·nate \im-ˈpȯrch-nət, -ə-nət\ *adj* **1** : overly persistent in request or demand **2** : BURDENSOME, TROUBLESOME — **im·por·tu·nate·ly** *adv* — **im·por·tu·nate·ness** *n*

[1]**im·por·tune** \ˌim-pər-ˈtün, -ˈtyün; im-ˈpȯr-chən\ *adj* : IMPORTUNATE [Latin *importunus,* from *in-* + *-portunus* (as in *opportunus* "opportune")] — **im·por·tune·ly** *adv*

[2]**importune** *vb* **1** : to press, beg, or urge with troublesome persistence **2** : ANNOY, TROUBLE — **im·por·tun·er** *n*

im·por·tu·ni·ty \ˌim-pər-ˈtü-nət-ē, -ˈtyü-\ *n, pl* **-ties** **1** : the quality or state of being importunate **2** *pl* : importunate requests or demands

im·pose \im-ˈpōz\ *vb* **1 a** : to establish or apply as a charge or penalty : LEVY ⟨*impose* a fine⟩ ⟨*impose* a tax⟩ **b** : to establish by force **2** : to use trickery or deception to get what one wants ⟨*impose* on an ignorant person⟩ **3** : to arrange (as type or printing plates) in proper order for printing **4** : to take unwarranted advantage of something ⟨*impose* upon a friend's good nature⟩ [Middle French *imposer,* from Latin *imponere,* literally, "to put upon," from *in-* + *ponere* "to put"] — **im·pos·er** *n*

im·pos·ing \im-ˈpō-ziŋ\ *adj* : impressive because of size, bearing, dignity, or grandeur ⟨an *imposing* building⟩ — **im·pos·ing·ly** \-ziŋ-lē\ *adv*

im·po·si·tion \ˌim-pə-ˈzish-ən\ *n* **1** : the act of imposing **2** : something imposed: as **a** : LEVY 1, TAX **b** : an overly burdensome requirement or demand **3** : TRICK 1a, DECEPTION

im·pos·si·bil·i·ty \im-ˌpäs-ə-ˈbil-ət-ē\ *n, pl* **-ties** **1** : the quality or state of being impossible **2** : something impossible

im·pos·si·ble \im-ˈpäs-ə-bəl, ˈim-\ *adj* **1 a** : not capable of being or of occurring **b** : very difficult to accomplish or deal with ⟨an *impossible* situation⟩ **2 a** : extremely undesirable : OBJECTIONABLE, UNACCEPTABLE ⟨living in *impossible* conditions⟩ — **im·pos·si·bly** \-blē\ *adv*

[1]**im·post** \ˈim-ˌpōst\ *n* : TAX; *esp* : a customs duty [Middle French, from Medieval Latin *impositum,* from Latin *imponere* "to impose"]

[2]**impost** *n* : a block, capital, or molding (as of a pillar or pier) from which an arch extends

1 [2]impost

im·pos·tor *or* **im·pos·ter** \im-ˈpäs-tər\ *n* : one that practices deceit; *esp* : a person who fraudulently pretends to be someone else [Late Latin, from Latin *imponere* "to impose"]

im·pos·ture \im-ˈpäs-chər\ *n* : the act or conduct of an impostor

im·po·tence \ˈim-pət-əns\ *n* : the quality or state of being impotent

im·po·tent \ˈim-pət-ənt\ *adj* **1** : not potent : lacking in power, strength, or vigor : HELPLESS **2** : unable to engage in sexual intercourse because of inability to have and maintain an erection; *also* : STERILE 1 — **impotent** *n* — **im·po·tent·ly** *adv*

im·pound \im-ˈpau̇nd\ *vt* **1** : to shut up in or as if in a pound : CONFINE **2** : to seize and hold in legal custody ⟨*impound* funds pending decision of a case⟩ **3** : to collect (water) in a reservoir

im·pound·ment \im-ˈpau̇nd-mənt, -ˈpau̇n-\ *n* **1** : the act of impounding : the state of being impounded **2** : a body of water formed by impounding

im·pov·er·ish \im-ˈpäv-rish, -ə-rish\ *vt* **1** : to make poor **2** : to use up the strength, richness, or fertility of ⟨*impoverished* soil⟩ [Medieval French *empoveriss-,* stem of *empoverir,* from *en-* + *povre* "poor," from Latin *pauper*] — **im·pov·er·ish·er** *n* — **im·pov·er·ish·ment** \-mənt\ *n*

im·prac·ti·ca·ble \im-ˈprak-ti-kə-bəl, ˈim-\ *adj* **1** : not practicable : not capable of being put into practice or use ⟨an *impracticable* plan⟩ **2** : IMPASSABLE ⟨an *impracticable* road⟩ — **im·prac·ti·ca·bil·i·ty** \im-ˌprak-ti-kə-ˈbil-ət-ē\ *n* — **im·prac·ti·ca·ble·ness** \im-ˈprak-ti-kə-bəl-nəs, ˈim-\ *n* — **im·prac·ti·ca·bly** \-blē\ *adv*

im·prac·ti·cal \im-ˈprak-ti-kəl, ˈim-\ *adj* : not practical: as **a** : not wise to put into or keep in practice or effect ⟨an *impractical* rule detested by many⟩ **b** : IDEALISTIC ⟨an *impractical* viewpoint⟩ **c** : not capable of dealing sensibly with practical matters **d** : IMPRACTICABLE 1 ⟨the new gadgets were complicated and *impractical*⟩ — **im·prac·ti·cal·i·ty** \im-ˌprak-ti-ˈkal-ət-ē\ *n* — **im·prac·ti·cal·ness** \im-ˈprak-ti-kəl-nəs, ˈim-\ *n*

im·pre·cate \ˈim-pri-ˌkāt\ *vb* : to invoke evil upon : CURSE [Latin *imprecari,* from *in-* "[2]in-" + *precari* "to pray"] — **im·pre·ca·tion** \ˌim-pri-ˈkā-shən\ *n* — **im·pre·ca·to·ry** \ˈim-pri-kə-ˌtōr-ē, im-ˈprek-ə-, -ˌtȯr-\ *adj*

im·pre·cise \ˌim-pri-ˈsīs\ *adj* : not precise ⟨an *imprecise* estimate⟩ — **im·pre·cise·ly** *adv* — **im·pre·cise·ness** *n* — **im·pre·ci·sion** \-ˈsizh-ən\ *n*

im·preg·na·ble \im-ˈpreg-nə-bəl\ *adj* : not capable of being taken by assault : UNCONQUERABLE ⟨an *impregnable* fortress⟩ [Middle French *imprenable,* from *in-* "not" + *prenable* "vulnerable to capture," from *prendre* "to take," from Latin *prehendere*] — **im·preg·na·bil·i·ty** \-ˌpreg-nə-ˈbil-ət-ē\ *n* — **im·preg·na·ble·ness** \-ˈpreg-nə-bəl-nəs\ *n* — **im·preg·na·bly** \-blē\ *adv*

im·preg·nate \im-ˈpreg-ˌnāt\ *vt* **1 a** : to make pregnant **b** : to introduce sperm cells into **2** : to cause (a material or substance) to be filled, permeated, or saturated ⟨*impregnate* wood with a preservative⟩ [Late Latin *impraegnare,* from Latin *in-* + *praegnas* "pregnant"] ***synonyms*** see SOAK — **im·preg·na·tion** \ˌim-ˌpreg-ˈnā-shən\ *n* — **im·preg·na·tor** \im-ˈpreg-ˌnāt-ər\ *n*

im·pre·sa·rio \ˌim-prə-ˈsär-ē-ˌō, -ˈsar-, -ˈser-\ *n, pl* **-rios** **1** : the manager or conductor of an opera or concert company **2** : one who puts on an entertainment **3** : PRODUCER 2, MANAGER [Italian, from *impresa* "undertaking"]

[1]**im·press** \im-ˈpres\ *vt* **1 a** : to apply with pressure so as to imprint **b** : to produce (as a mark) by pressure **c** : to mark by or as if by pressure or stamping **2 a** : to produce a vivid impression of ⟨*impress* an idea on the mind⟩ **b** : to affect especially forcibly or deeply ⟨*impressed* with your sincerity⟩; *also* : to gain the admiration or interest of ⟨always trying to *impress* people⟩ [Latin *impressus,* past participle of *imprimere* "to press into, imprint," from *in-* + *premere* "to press"] — **im·press·ibil·i·ty** \im-ˌpres-ə-ˈbil-ət-ē\ *n* — **im·press·ible** \-ˈpres-ə-bəl\ *adj*

[2]**im·press** \ˈim-ˌpres\ *n* **1** : the act of impressing **2 a** : a mark made by pressure **b** : an image of something formed by or as if by pressure; *esp* : SEAL **c** : a product of pressure or influence **3** : a characteristic or distinctive mark : STAMP **4** : EFFECT 4, IMPRESSION

[3]**im·press** \im-ˈpres\ *vt* **1** : to seize for public service; *esp* : to force into naval service **2** : to enlist the aid or services of by strong argument or appeal [*in-* + *press*]

[4]**im·press** \ˈim-ˌpres\ *n* : IMPRESSMENT

im·pres·sion \im-ˈpresh-ən\ *n* **1** : the act or process of impressing **2** : the effect produced by impressing: as **a** : a stamp, form, or figure resulting from physical contact **b** : an especially marked influence or effect on feeling, sense, or mind **3 a** : a characteristic trait or feature resulting from influence **b** : an effect of change or improvement **c** : a telling image impressed on the senses or the mind **4 a** : one instance of the meeting of a printing surface and the material being printed; *also* : a single print or copy so made **b** : all the copies of a publication (as a book) printed at one time **5** : a usually indistinct or imprecise notion or remembrance **6** : an imitation of outstanding features in an artistic or theatrical medium; *esp* : an imitation in caricature of a noted personality as a form of theatrical entertainment

im·pres·sion·able \im-ˈpresh-nə-bəl, -ə-nə-\ *adj* : capable of being easily impressed : easily molded or influenced : PLASTIC — **im·pres·sion·abil·i·ty** \-ˌpresh-nə-ˈbil-ət-ē, -ə-nə-\ *n* — **im·pres·sion·able·ness** \-ˈpresh-nə-bəl-nəs, -ə-nə-\ *n* — **im·pres·sion·ably** \-blē\ *adv*

im·pres·sion·ism \im-ˈpresh-ə-ˌniz-əm\ *n* **1** *often cap* : a theory or practice in painting especially among French painters of about 1870 of representing the natural appearances of objects by means of dabs or strokes of primary unmixed colors in order to give the effect of actual reflected light **2 a** : the depiction of scene, emotion, or character by details evoking impressions rather than by re-creating reality **b** : a style of musical composition designed to create moods through rich and varied harmonies

im·pres·sion·ist \im-ˈpresh-nəst, -ə-nəst\ *n* **1** *often cap* : one (as a painter) who practices or adheres to the theories of impressionism **2** : an entertainer who does impressions

im·pres·sion·is·tic \-ˌpresh-ə-ˈnis-tik\ *adj* **1** *or* **impressionist** *often cap* : of, relating to, or constituting impressionism ⟨an *impressionistic* style of painting⟩ **2** : based on or involving impression rather than knowledge or fact ⟨*impressionistic* descriptions⟩ — **im·pres·sion·is·ti·cal·ly** \-ti-kə-lē, -klē\ *adv*

im·pres·sive \im-ˈpres-iv\ *adj* : making or tending to make a marked impression : stirring deep feeling especially of awe or admiration ⟨an *impressive* speech⟩ — **im·pres·sive·ly** *adv* — **im·pres·sive·ness** *n*

im·press·ment \im-ˈpres-mənt\ *n* : the act of seizing for public use or of impressing into public service

im·pri·ma·tur \ˌim-prə-ˈmät-ər\ *n* **1 a** : a license to print or publish **b** : official approval of a publication by a censor **2** : APPROVAL 1 [New Latin, "let it be printed," from *imprimere* "to print," from Latin, "to impress, imprint"]

[1]**im·print** \im-ˈprint, ˈim-ˌ\ *vb* **1** : to mark by or as if by pressure : STAMP, IMPRESS **2** : to fix firmly (as in the memory) **3** : to go through the process of imprinting

[2]**im·print** \ˈim-ˌprint\ *n* : something imprinted or printed: as **a** : [2]IMPRESS 2 **b** : a publisher's name often with address and date of publication printed at the foot of a title page **c** : an indelible distinguishing effect or influence

im·print·ing \ˈim-ˌprint-ing, im-ˈ\ *n* : a rapid learning process that takes place early in the life of a social animal (as a goose) and results in the formation of a pattern of behavior (as recognizing and being attracted to one's own kind or a substitute)

im·pris·on \im-ˈpriz-n\ *vt* **-pris·oned; -pris·on·ing** \-ˈpriz-ning, -n-ing\ : to confine in or as if in prison — **im·pris·on·ment** \-ˈpriz-n-mənt\ *n*

im·prob·able \im-ˈpräb-ə-bəl, ˈim-\ *adj* : unlikely to be true or to occur — **im·prob·a·bil·i·ty** \im-ˌpräb-ə-ˈbil-ət-ē\ *n* — **im·prob·a·ble·ness** \im-ˈpräb-ə-bəl-nəs, ˈim-\ *n* — **im·prob·a·bly** \-ˈpräb-ə-blē\ *adv*

im·pro·bi·ty \im-ˈprō-bət-ē, ˈim-, -ˈpräb-ət-\ *n* : DISHONESTY

im·promp·tu \im-ˈpräm-tü, -ˈprämp-, -tyü\ *adj* **1** : made or done on or as if on the spur of the moment **2** : produced without previous study or preparation ⟨an *impromptu* speech⟩ [French, from *impromptu* "extemporaneously," from Latin *in promptu* "in readiness"] — **impromptu** *adv or n*

im·prop·er \im-ˈpräp-ər, ˈim-\ *adj* **1** : not proper, fit, or suitable ⟨*improper* dress for the occasion⟩ **2** : INCORRECT, INACCURATE ⟨an *improper* deduction⟩ **3** : not in accordance with good taste or good manners ⟨*improper* language⟩ ***synonyms*** see INDECOROUS — **im·prop·er·ly** *adv* — **im·prop·er·ness** *n*

improper fraction *n* : a fraction whose numerator is equal to or larger than the denominator

im·pro·pri·ety \ˌim-prə-ˈprī-ət-ē\ *n, pl* **-ties** **1** : the quality or state of being improper **2** : an improper act or remark; *esp* : an unacceptable use of a word or of language

im·prov \ˈim-ˌpräv\ *adj* : of, relating to, or being improvisation and especially an improvised comedy routine — **improv** *n*

im·prove \im-ˈprüv\ *vb* **1** : to make greater in amount or degree : INCREASE **2 a** : to increase in value or quality : make or grow better **b** : to increase the value of (land or property) by making it more useful for humans (as by cultivation or the erection of buildings) **c** : to grade and drain (a road) and apply surfacing material other than pavement **3** : to make good use of ⟨*improved* their time by studying⟩ **4** : to make improvements ⟨*improve* on the carburetor⟩ [Medieval French *emprouer* "to invest profitably," from *en-* + *pru, prou* "advantage," from Late Latin *prode,* from Latin *prodesse* "to be advantageous"] — **im·prov·able** \-ˈprü-və-bəl\ *adj* — **im·prov·er** *n*

im·prove·ment \im-ˈprüv-mənt\ *n* **1** : the act or process of improving **2 a** : the state of being improved; *esp* : increased value or excellence **b** : an instance or result of improvement **3** : something that increases value especially of real estate ⟨make *improvements* in an old house⟩

im·prov·i·dent \im-ˈpräv-əd-ənt, ˈim-, -ə-ˌdent\ *adj* : not providing for the future : THRIFTLESS — **im·prov·i·dence** \-əd-əns, -ə-ˌdens\ *n* — **im·prov·i·dent·ly** *adv*

im·prov·i·sa·tion \im-ˌpräv-ə-ˈzā-shən, ˌim-prə-və-\ *n* **1** : the act or art of improvising **2** : something that is improvised — **im·prov·i·sa·tion·al** \-shnəl, -shən-l\ *adj* — **im·prov·i·sa·tion·al·ly** *adv*

im·prov·i·sa·tor \im-ˈpräv-ə-ˌzāt-ər\ *n* : IMPROVISER — **im·prov·i·sa·to·ri·al** \-ˌpräv-ə-zə-ˈtōr-ē-əl, -ˈtȯr-\ *or* **im·prov·i·sa·to·ry** \-ˈpräv-ə-zə-ˌtōr-ē, -ˌtȯr-\ *adj*

im·pro·vise \ˈim-prə-ˌvīz\ *vb* **1** : to compose, recite, or sing on the spur of the moment **2** : to make, invent, or arrange without planning or preparation ⟨the quarterback *improvised* a play⟩ **3** : to make out of what is conveniently on hand ⟨*improvise* a bed using leaves and straw⟩ [French *improviser,* from Italian *improvvisare,* from Latin *improvisus* "sudden, unforeseen," from *in-* + *providēre* "to see ahead, provide"] — **im·pro·vis·er** *n*

im·pru·dent \im-ˈprüd-nt, ˈim-\ *adj* : not prudent : lacking discretion, wisdom, or good judgment ⟨an *imprudent* investor⟩ — **im·pru·dence** \-ns\ *n* — **im·pru·dent·ly** *adv*

im·pu·dent \ˈim-pyəd-ənt\ *adj* : showing contempt for or disregard of others : INSOLENT, DISRESPECTFUL [Latin *impudens* "shameless, impudent," from *in-* + *pudēre* "to feel shame"] — **im·pu·dence** \-əns\ *n* — **im·pu·dent·ly** *adv*

im·pugn \im-ˈpyün\ *vt* : to oppose or attack as false : cast doubt on [Medieval French *empugner,* from Latin *impugnare,* from *in-* + *pugnare* "to fight"] — **im·pugn·er** *n*

im·puis·sance \im-ˈpwis-ns, ˈim-, -ˈpyü-ə-səns\ *n* : WEAKNESS 1, POWERLESSNESS

im·pulse \ˈim-ˌpəls\ *n* **1 a** : a force that starts a body into motion : IMPULSION **b** : the motion produced by such an impulsion **2** : a sudden spontaneous arousing of the mind and spirit to do something : an inclination to act ⟨an *impulse* to run away⟩ ⟨acts on *impulse*⟩ **3** : NERVE IMPULSE **4** : the product of the average value of a force and the time during which it acts [Latin *impulsus,* from *impellere* "to impel"] ***synonyms*** see MOTIVE

im·pul·sion \im-ˈpəl-shən\ *n* **1 a** : the action of impelling : the state of being impelled **b** : an impelling force **c** : IMPETUS 1 **2** : IMPULSE 2 **3** : COMPULSION 2

im·pul·sive \im-ˈpəl-siv\ *adj* : acting or liable to act on impulse : moved or caused by an impulse ***synonyms*** see SPONTANEOUS — **im·pul·sive·ly** *adv* — **im·pul·sive·ness** *n*

im·pu·ni·ty \im-ˈpyü-nət-ē\ *n* : immunity or freedom from punishment, harm, or loss [Latin *impunitas,* from *impune* "without punishment," from *in-* + *poena* "pain, penalty"]

im·pure \im-ˈpyu̇r, ˈim-\ *adj* : not pure: as **a** : UNCHASTE, OBSCENE ⟨*impure* language⟩ **b** : containing something unclean : FOUL ⟨*impure* water⟩ **c** : ritually unclean **d** : mixed or impregnated with an extraneous and usually unwanted substance ⟨an *impure* chemical⟩ — **im·pure·ly** *adv* — **im·pure·ness** *n*

im·pu·ri·ty \im-ˈpyu̇r-ət-ē, ˈim-\ *n, pl* **-ties** **1** : the quality or state of being impure **2** : something that is impure or that makes something else impure ⟨*impurities* in water⟩

im·pu·ta·tion \ˌim-pyə-ˈtā-shən\ *n* **1** : the act of imputing : as **a** : ATTRIBUTION, ASCRIPTION **b** : ACCUSATION 2 **c** : INSINUATION 1 **2** : something imputed — **im·pu·ta·tive** \-ˈpyüt-ət-iv\ *adj* — **im·pu·ta·tive·ly** *adv*

im·pute \im-ˈpyüt\ *vt* **1** : to place the responsibility or blame for often falsely or unjustly : CHARGE **2** : to credit to a person or a cause : ATTRIBUTE [Latin *imputare,* from *in-* "[2]in-" + *putare* "to reckon"] ***synonyms*** see ASCRIBE — **im·put·abil·i·ty** \-ˌpyüt-ə-ˈbil-ət-ē\ *n*

[1]**in** \in, ˈin, ən, ᵊn\ *prep* **1 a** — used as a function word to indicate inclusion, location, or position within limits ⟨*in* the lake⟩ ⟨*in* the summer⟩ **b** : INTO 1 ⟨went *in* the house⟩ **2** : by means of : WITH ⟨written *in* pencil⟩ **3 a** — used as a function word to indicate manner, state, or situation ⟨alike *in* some respects⟩ ⟨left *in* a hurry⟩ **b** : INTO 2a ⟨broke *in* pieces⟩ **4** — used as a function word to indicate purpose ⟨said *in* reply⟩ [Old English]

[2]**in** \ˈin\ *adv* **1 a** : to or toward the inside ⟨went *in* and closed the door⟩ **b** : to or toward some particular place ⟨flew *in* on the

\ə\ abut	\au̇\ out	\i\ tip	\ȯ\ saw	\u̇\ foot
\ər\ further	\ch\ chin	\ī\ life	\ȯi\ coin	\y\ yet
\a\ mat	\e\ pet	\j\ job	\th\ thin	\yü\ few
\ā\ take	\ē\ easy	\ng\ sing	\t͟h\ this	\yu̇\ cure
\ä\ cot, cart	\g\ go	\ō\ bone	\ü\ food	\zh\ vision

first plane⟩ **c** : at close quarters : NEAR ⟨play close *in*⟩ **d** : into the midst of something ⟨mix *in* the flour⟩ **e** : to or at its proper place ⟨fit a piece *in*⟩ **f** : into line ⟨fell *in* with our plans⟩ **2 a** : within a particular place; *esp* : within the customary place of residence or business ⟨tell them I'm not *in*⟩ **b** : in the position of insider ⟨*in* on the scheme⟩ **c** : on good terms ⟨*in* with the right people⟩ **d** : in a position of assured success ⟨with those grades she was certainly *in*⟩ **e** : in style or season ⟨boots are *in* this year⟩ **f** : at hand or on hand ⟨the evidence is all *in*⟩ ⟨harvests are *in*⟩

[3]**in** \ˈin\ *adj* **1 a** : being inside or within ⟨the *in* part⟩ **b** : being in position, operation, or power ⟨the *in* party⟩ **2** : directed or bound inward : INCOMING ⟨the *in* train⟩ **3 a** : extremely fashionable ⟨the *in* thing to do⟩ **b** : keenly aware of and responsive to what is new and fashionable ⟨the *in* crowd⟩

[4]**in** \ˈin\ *n* **1** : one who is in office or power or on the inside **2** : INFLUENCE, PULL ⟨had an *in* with the boss⟩

[1]**in-** *or* **il-** *or* **im-** *or* **ir-** *prefix* : not : NON-: UN- — usually *il-* before *l* ⟨*il*logical⟩, *im-* before *b, m,* or *p* ⟨*im*balance⟩ ⟨*im*moral⟩ ⟨*im*practical⟩, *ir-* before *r* ⟨*ir*reducible⟩, and *in-* before other sounds ⟨*in*conclusive⟩ [Latin]

[2]**in-** *or* **il-** *or* **im-** *or* **ir-** *prefix* **1** : in : within : into : toward : on — usually *il-* before *l, im-* before *b, m,* or *p, ir-* before *r,* and *in-* before other sounds ⟨*in*filtrate⟩ **2** : [1]EN- ⟨*im*plant⟩ [Latin, from *in* "in, into"]

[1]**-in** \ən, [a]n, ˌin\ *n suffix* : chemical compound ⟨*in*sulin⟩ [French *-ine,* from Latin *-īna,* feminine of *-īnus* "[1]-ine"]

[2]**-in** \-ˌin\ *n combining form* : organized public protest by means of or in favor of : demonstration ⟨teach-*in*⟩ ⟨love-*in*⟩ [*in* (as in *sit-in*)]

in·abil·i·ty \ˌin-ə-ˈbil-ət-ē\ *n* : lack of sufficient power, resources, or capacity ⟨his *inability* to carry a tune⟩

in absentia \ˌin-ab-ˈsen-chə, -chē-ə\ *adv* : in one's absence : while absent ⟨was awarded the degree *in absentia*⟩ [Latin, "in absence"]

in·ac·ces·si·ble \ˌin-ak-ˈses-ə-bəl, -ik-\ *adj* : not accessible ⟨an *inaccessible* area⟩ — **in·ac·ces·si·bil·i·ty** \-ˌses-ə-ˈbil-ət-ē\ *n* — **in·ac·ces·si·bly** \-ˈses-ə-blē\ *adv*

in·ac·cu·ra·cy \in-ˈak-yə-rə-sē, ˈin-\ *n, pl* **-cies** **1** : the quality or state of being inaccurate **2** : MISTAKE, ERROR

in·ac·cu·rate \-rət\ *adj* : not accurate : FAULTY ⟨*inaccurate* information⟩ — **in·ac·cu·rate·ly** *adv*

in·ac·tion \in-ˈak-shən, ˈin-\ *n* : lack of action or activity : IDLENESS

in·ac·ti·vate \in-ˈak-tə-ˌvāt, ˈin-\ *vt* : to make inactive — **in·ac·ti·va·tion** \in-ˌak-tə-ˈvā-shən\ *n*

in·ac·tive \in-ˈak-tiv, ˈin-\ *adj* : not active: as **a** : INDOLENT 2, SLUGGISH **b** : being out of use or activity **c** : relating to members of the armed forces who are not performing or available for military duties **d** : chemically or biologically inert — **in·ac·tive·ly** *adv* — **in·ac·tiv·i·ty** \ˌin-ak-ˈtiv-ət-ē\ *n*

synonyms INACTIVE, INERT, IDLE mean not engaged in work or activity. INACTIVE applies to anyone or anything not in action or in operation or at work ⟨an *inactive* mine⟩ ⟨an *inactive* seasonal worker⟩. INERT as applied to a thing implies being powerless to move itself or to affect other things ⟨an *inert* gas⟩ ⟨*inert* drugs no longer effective⟩ and as applied to a person suggests an inherent or habitual indisposition to activity ⟨politically *inert* citizens⟩. IDLE applies to people who are not busy or occupied or to their powers or implements ⟨*idle* laborers hoping for work⟩.

in·ad·e·qua·cy \in-ˈad-i-kwə-sē, ˈin-\ *n, pl* **-cies** **1** : the quality or state of being inadequate **2 a** : an inadequate amount **b** : failure to meet expectations ⟨feelings of *inadequacy*⟩

in·ad·e·quate \-kwət\ *adj* : not adequate : not enough or not good enough ⟨*inadequate* food supplies⟩ ⟨*inadequate* equipment⟩ — **in·ad·e·quate·ly** *adv* — **in·ad·e·quate·ness** *n*

in·ad·mis·si·ble \ˌin-əd-ˈmis-ə-bəl\ *adj* : not admissible ⟨*inadmissible* evidence⟩ — **in·ad·mis·si·bil·i·ty** \-ˌmis-ə-ˈbil-ət-ē\ *n*

in·ad·ver·tence \ˌin-əd-ˈvərt-ns\ *n* **1** : the fact or action of being inattentive **2** : a result of inattention : OVERSIGHT [Medieval Latin *inadvertentia,* from Latin *in-* + *advertere* "to notice"] — **in·ad·ver·ten·cy** \-n-sē\ *n*

in·ad·ver·tent \-nt\ *adj* **1** : INATTENTIVE **2** : UNINTENTIONAL ⟨an *inadvertent* omission⟩ — **in·ad·ver·tent·ly** *adv*

in·ad·vis·able \ˌin-əd-ˈvī-zə-bəl\ *adj* : not wise to do : not advisable — **in·ad·vis·abil·i·ty** \-ˌvī-zə-ˈbil-ət-ē\ *n*

in·alien·able \in-ˈāl-yə-nə-bəl, ˈin-, -ˈā-lē-ə-nə-\ *adj* : not capable of being taken away, given up, or transferred ⟨*inalienable* rights⟩ — **in·alien·abil·i·ty** \in-ˌāl-yə-nə-ˈbil-ət-ē, -ˌā-lē-ə-nə-\ *n* — **in·alien·ably** \in-ˈāl-yə-nə-blē, ˈin-, -ˈā-lē-ə-nə-\ *adv*

in·al·ter·a·ble \in-ˈȯl-tə-rə-bəl, ˈin-, -trə-\ *adj* : not alterable : UNALTERABLE — **in·al·ter·abil·i·ty** \in-ˌȯl-tə-rə-ˈbil-ət-ē, -trə-\ *n* — **in·al·ter·able·ness** \in-ˈȯl-tə-rə-bəl-nəs, -trə-\ *n* — **in·al·ter·ably** \-blē\ *adv*

in·amo·ra·ta \in-ˌam-ə-ˈrät-ə\ *n* : a woman with whom one is in love [Italian *innamorata,* from *innamorare* "to inspire with love," from *in-* "[2]in-" + *amore* "love," from Latin *amor*]

inane \in-ˈān\ *adj* : lacking significance, meaning, or point : SILLY ⟨*inane* comments⟩ [Latin *inanis* "empty, insubstantial"] ***synonyms*** see INSIPID — **inane·ly** *adv* — **inane·ness** \-ˈān-nəs\ *n*

in·an·i·mate \in-ˈan-ə-mət, ˈin-\ *adj* **1** : not animate: **a** : not endowed with life or spirit ⟨an *inanimate* object⟩ **b** : lacking consciousness or power of motion ⟨an *inanimate* body⟩ **2** : not animated or lively : DULL — **in·an·i·mate·ly** *adv* — **in·an·i·mate·ness** *n*

in·a·ni·tion \ˌin-ə-ˈnish-ən\ *n* : a weakened condition resulting from or as if from lack of food and water [Medieval Latin *inanitio,* from Latin *inanire* "to empty," from *inanis* "empty, inane"]

inan·i·ty \in-ˈan-ət-ē\ *n, pl* **-ties** **1** : the quality or state of being inane; *esp* : foolish or trivial character **2** : something that is inane; *esp* : a senseless or foolish remark

in·ap·par·ent \ˌin-ə-ˈpar-ənt, -ˈper-\ *adj* : not apparent ⟨an *inapparent* infection⟩

in·ap·peas·able \ˌin-ə-ˈpē-zə-bəl\ *adj* : UNAPPEASABLE

in·ap·pe·tence \in-ˈap-ət-əns\ *n* : loss or lack of appetite

in·ap·pli·ca·ble \in-ˈap-li-kə-bəl, ˈin-; ˌin-ə-ˈplik-ə-\ *adj* : not applicable : UNSUITABLE, IRRELEVANT — **in·ap·pli·ca·bil·i·ty** \in-ˌap-li-kə-ˈbil-ət-ē, ˌin-ə-ˌplik-ə-\ *n* — **in·ap·pli·ca·bly** \in-ˈap-li-kə-blē, ˈin-; ˌin-ə-ˈplik-ə-\ *adv*

in·ap·po·site \(ˌ)i-na-pə-zət\ *adj* : not apposite : not apt or pertinent ⟨*inapposite* comments⟩ — **in·ap·po·site·ly** *adv*

in·ap·pre·cia·ble \ˌin-ə-ˈprē-shə-bəl\ *adj* : too small to be perceived : very slight ⟨an *inappreciable* amount⟩ — **in·ap·pre·cia·bly** \-blē\ *adv*

in·ap·pro·pri·ate \ˌin-ə-ˈprō-prē-ət\ *adj* : not appropriate : UNSUITABLE ⟨*inappropriate* behavior⟩ — **in·ap·pro·pri·ate·ly** *adv* — **in·ap·pro·pri·ate·ness** *n*

in·apt \in-ˈapt, ˈin-\ *adj* **1** : not suitable **2** : INEPT 1 — **in·apt·ly** *adv* — **in·apt·ness** \-ˈapt-nəs, -ˈap-\ *n*

in·ap·ti·tude \-ˈap-tə-ˌtüd, -ˌtyüd\ *n* : lack of aptitude

in·ar·gu·able \in-ˈär-gyə-wə-bəl\ *adj* : not arguable : not open to doubt or debate ⟨an *inarguable* fact⟩

in·ar·gu·ably \-blē\ *adv* : cannot be argued : UNQUESTIONABLY ⟨*inarguably,* December is the best month for retailers⟩

in·ar·tic·u·late \ˌin-är-ˈtik-yə-lət\ *adj* **1 a** : not understandable as spoken words ⟨*inarticulate* cries⟩ **b** : incapable of speech especially under emotional stress **c** : incapable of being expressed by speech ⟨*inarticulate* longings⟩ **d** : not voiced or expressed ⟨*inarticulate* rules of conduct⟩ **2** : incapable of giving coherent, clear, or effective expression to one's ideas or feelings ⟨an *inarticulate* speaker⟩ — **in·ar·tic·u·late·ly** *adv* — **in·ar·tic·u·late·ness** *n*

in·ar·tis·tic \ˌin-är-ˈtis-tik\ *adj* **1** : not conforming to the principles of art **2** : not appreciative of art — **in·ar·tis·ti·cal·ly** \-ˈtis-ti-kə-lē, -klē\ *adv*

in·as·much as \ˌin-əz-ˌməch-əz\ *conj* **1** : to the extent that **2** : in view of the fact that : SINCE

in·at·ten·tion \ˌin-ə-ˈten-chən\ *n* : failure to pay attention

in·at·ten·tive \-ˈtent-iv\ *adj* : not attentive : not paying attention ⟨the student was *inattentive* in class⟩ — **in·at·ten·tive·ly** *adv* — **in·at·ten·tive·ness** *n*

[1]**in·au·gu·ral** \in-ˈȯ-gyə-rəl, -gə-rəl, -grəl\ *adj* **1** : of or relating to an inauguration ⟨the *inaugural* address⟩ **2** : marking a beginning : first in a projected series ⟨the *inaugural* run of a new luxury liner⟩

[2]**inaugural** *n* **1** : an inaugural address **2** : INAUGURATION

in·au·gu·rate \in-ˈȯ-gyə-ˌrāt, -gə-\ *vt* **1** : to introduce into office with suitable ceremonies : INSTALL ⟨*inaugurate* a president⟩ **2** : to celebrate or mark the opening of ⟨*inaugurate* the new athletic field⟩ **3** : to commence or enter upon : BEGIN ⟨*inaugurate* a reform⟩ [Latin *inaugurare* "to practice augury, inaugurate," from *in-* + *augur* "augur"; from the consulting of omens at inaugurations] — **in·au·gu·ra·tor** \-ˌrāt-ər\ *n*

in·au·gu·ra·tion \in-ˌȯ-gyə-ˈrā-shən, -gə-\ *n* : an act of inaugurating; *esp* : a ceremonial introduction into office

in·aus·pi·cious \ˌin-ȯ-ˈspish-əs\ *adj* : not auspicious : UNPROMISING — **in·aus·pi·cious·ly** *adv* — **in·aus·pi·cious·ness** *n*

in·au·then·tic \ˌin-ˌȯ-ˈthen-tik\ *adj* : not authentic ⟨*inauthentic* costumes⟩ — **in·au·then·tic·i·ty** \-ˌthen-ˈtis-ət-ē\ *n*

1in–between \ˌin-bi-ˈtwēn\ *adj* : INTERMEDIATE

2in–be·tween *n* : INTERMEDIATE

1in between *adv* : BETWEEN ⟨were neither young nor old but fell somewhere *in between*⟩

2in between *prep* : BETWEEN ⟨a meadow lies *in between* the house and the woods⟩

in·board \ˈin-ˌbōrd, -ˌbȯrd\ *adv* **1** : inside the line of a ship's bulwarks or hull **2** : toward the center line of a vehicle or craft (as a ship or aircraft) — **inboard** *adj*

in·born \ˈin-ˈbȯrn\ *adj* **1** : born in or with one : not acquired by training or experience : NATURAL ⟨an *inborn* ability to sense danger⟩ **2** : HEREDITARY 1, INHERITED ⟨an *inborn* defect in metabolism⟩ ***synonyms*** see INNATE

in·bound \ˈin-ˈbau̇nd\ *adj* : inward bound ⟨*inbound* traffic⟩

in·breathe \ˈin-ˈbrē<u>th</u>\ *vt* : INHALE 2

in·bred \ˈin-ˈbred\ *adj* **1 a** : present from birth **b** : planted in by early teaching or training : INCULCATED **2** : subjected to or produced by inbreeding ***synonyms*** see INNATE

in·breed \ˈin-ˈbrēd\ *vb* **-bred** \-ˈbred\; **-breed·ing** : to produce by, subject to, or engage in inbreeding

in·breed·ing \ˈin-ˌbrēd-ing\ *n* **1** : the interbreeding of closely related individuals especially to preserve and fix desirable characters of and to eliminate unfavorable characters from a stock **2** : confinement to a narrow range or a local or limited field of choice

In·ca \ˈing-kə\ *n* **1** : a noble or a member of the Quechuan peoples of Peru maintaining an empire until the Spanish conquest **2** : a member of any people under Inca influence [Spanish, from Quechua *inka* "ruler of the Inca empire"] — **In·can** \-kən\ *adj*

in·cal·cu·la·ble \in-ˈkal-kyə-lə-bəl, ˈin-\ *adj* **1** : not capable of being calculated; *esp* : too large or numerous to be calculated **2** : not capable of being known in advance : UNCERTAIN — **in·cal·cu·la·bil·i·ty** \in-ˌkal-kyə-lə-ˈbil-ət-ē\ *n* — **in·cal·cu·la·bly** \-blē\ *adv*

in·can·des·cence \ˌin-kən-ˈdes-ns\ *n* : a glowing condition of a body due to its high temperature

1in·can·des·cent \-nt\ *adj* **1 a** : white or glowing with intense heat **b** : strikingly bright, radiant, or clear **c** : BRILLIANT ⟨*incandescent* wit⟩ **2 a** : of, relating to, or being light produced by incandescence **b** : producing light by incandescence [derived from Latin *incandescere* "to become hot," from *in-* + *candēre* "to glow"] — **in·can·des·cent·ly** *adv*

2incandescent *n* : LIGHTBULB a

incandescent lamp *n* : LIGHTBULB a

in·can·ta·tion \ˌin-ˌkan-ˈtā-shən\ *n* : a use of spells or charms spoken or sung as part of a ritual of magic; *also* : a formula of words so used [Middle French, from Late Latin *incantatio*, from Latin *incantare* "to enchant"] — **in·can·ta·tion·al** \-shnəl, -shən-l\ *adj* — **in·can·ta·to·ry** \in-ˈkant-ə-ˌtōr-ē, -ˌtȯr-\ *adj*

in·ca·pa·ble \in-ˈkā-pə-bəl, ˈin-\ *adj* : lacking capacity, ability, or qualification for the purpose or end in view: as **a** : not being in a state or of a kind to admit : INSUSCEPTIBLE ⟨*incapable* of precise measurement⟩ **b** : not able or fit for the doing or performance : UNQUALIFIED, INCOMPETENT ⟨*incapable* of understanding the matter⟩ — **in·ca·pa·bil·i·ty** \in-ˌkā-pə-ˈbil-ət-ē\ *n* — **in·ca·pa·ble·ness** \in-ˈkā-pə-bəl-nəs, ˈin-\ *n* — **in·ca·pa·bly** \-blē\ *adv*

in·ca·pac·i·tate \ˌin-kə-ˈpas-ə-ˌtāt\ *vt* **1** : to deprive of natural capacity or power : DISABLE **2** : to make legally incapable or ineligible — **in·ca·pac·i·ta·tion** \-ˌpas-ə-ˈtā-shən\ *n*

in·ca·pac·i·ty \ˌin-kə-ˈpas-ət-ē, -ˈpas-tē\ *n, pl* **-ties** : lack of ability or power ⟨a seeming *incapacity* for telling the truth⟩

in·car·cer·ate \in-ˈkär-sə-ˌrāt\ *vt* : IMPRISON, CONFINE [Latin *incarcerare*, from *in-* + *carcer* "prison" — see *Word History* at CANCEL] — **in·car·cer·a·tion** \in-ˌkär-sə-ˈrā-shən\ *n*

1in·car·na·dine \in-ˈkär-nə-ˌdīn, -ˌdēn\ *adj* : RED 1a; *esp* : BLOODRED [Middle French *incarnadin*, from Italian *incarnadino*, from *incarnato* "flesh-colored," from Late Latin *incarnare* "to incarnate"]

2incarnadine *vt* : to make incarnadine : REDDEN

1in·car·nate \in-ˈkär-nət, -ˌnāt\ *adj* **1** : invested with bodily and especially human nature and form **2** : EMBODIED, PERSONIFIED ⟨a fiend *incarnate*⟩ [Late Latin *incarnatus*, past participle of *incarnare* "to incarnate," from Latin *in-* + *carn-*, *caro* "flesh"]

2in·car·nate \-ˌnāt\ *vt* : to make incarnate : as **a** : to give bodily form and substance to ⟨*incarnates* the devil as a serpent⟩ **b** : to give a concrete or actual form to

in·car·na·tion \ˌin-ˌkär-ˈnā-shən\ *n* **1 a** (1) : the embodiment of a deity or spirit in an earthly form (2) *cap* : the union of divinity with humanity in Jesus Christ **b** : a concrete or actual form of a quality or concept; *esp* : a person showing a trait or typical character to a marked degree **2** : the act of incarnating : the state of being incarnate ⟨she is the *incarnation* of goodness⟩ — **in·car·na·tion·al** *adj*

in·cau·tious \in-ˈkȯ-shəs, ˈin-\ *adj* : lacking in caution : CARELESS — **in·cau·tious·ly** *adv* — **in·cau·tious·ness** *n*

1in·cen·di·ary \in-ˈsen-dē-ˌer-ē\ *n, pl* **-ar·ies 1 a** : a person who commits arson : ARSONIST **b** : an incendiary agent (as a bomb) **2** : a person who excites quarrels : AGITATOR [Latin *incendiarius*, from *incendium* "conflagration," from *incendere* "to set on fire"]

2incendiary *adj* **1** : of, relating to, or involving arson **2** : tending to excite or inflame quarrels : INFLAMMATORY ⟨*incendiary* speeches⟩ **3 a** : igniting combustible materials spontaneously **b** : of, relating to, or being a weapon (as a bomb) containing chemicals that ignite on bursting or on contact **4** : extremely hot ⟨*incendiary* chili peppers⟩

1in·cense \ˈin-ˌsens\ *n* **1** : material used to produce a fragrant odor when burned **2 a** : the perfume given off by some spices and gums when burned **b** : a pleasing scent [Medieval French *encens*, from Late Latin *incensum*, from Latin *incendere* "to set on fire"]

2in·cense \in-ˈsens\ *vt* : to inflame with anger or indignation ⟨*incensed* by their bad behavior⟩ [probably from Latin *incensus*, past participle of *incendere*, "to set on fire, provoke"]

in·cen·ter \ˈin-ˌsent-ər\ *n* : the point in a triangle where the three lines that bisect its angles intersect

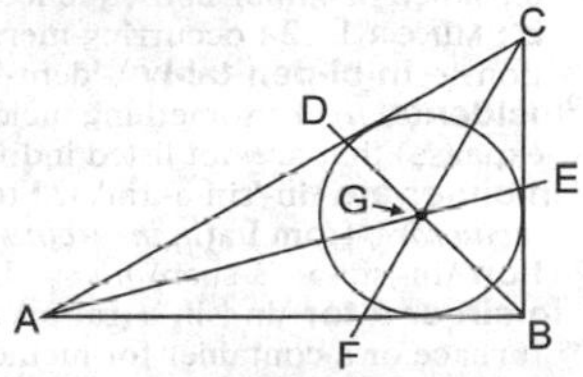

incenter: *ABC* triangle; *AE, BD, CF* bisectors; *G* incenter

in·cen·tive \in-ˈsent-iv\ *n* : something that arouses or spurs one on to action or effort : STIMULUS [Late Latin *incentivum*, from Latin *incentivus* "setting the tune," from *incinere* "to play (a tune)," from *in-* + *canere* "to sing"] — **incentive** *adj*

in·cep·tion \in-ˈsep-shən\ *n* : an act, process, or instance of beginning : COMMENCEMENT ⟨the program has been a success since its *inception*⟩ [Latin *inceptio*, from *incipere* "to begin," from *in-* + *capere* "to take"] ***synonyms*** see ORIGIN

in·cep·tive \in-ˈsep-tiv\ *adj* : of or relating to a beginning — **in·cep·tive·ly** *adv*

in·cer·ti·tude \in-ˈsərt-ə-ˌtüd, ˈin-, -ˌtyüd\ *n* : UNCERTAINTY: **a** : absence of assurance : DOUBT, INDECISION **b** : the quality or state of being unstable or insecure

in·ces·sant \in-ˈses-nt, ˈin-\ *adj* : continuing without interruption : UNCEASING ⟨*incessant* rains⟩ [Late Latin *incessans*, from Latin *in-* + *cessare* "to delay"] ***synonyms*** see CONTINUAL — **in·ces·sant·ly** *adv*

in·cest \ˈin-ˌsest\ *n* : sexual intercourse between persons so closely related that they are forbidden by law to marry; *also* : the statutory crime of such a relationship [Latin *incestum*, "sexual impurity," from *incestus* "impure," from *in-* + *castus* "pure"]

in·ces·tu·ous \in-ˈses-chə-wəs\ *adj* **1** : constituting or involving incest **2** : guilty of incest **3** : excessively or improperly intimate or exclusive ⟨magazines having an *incestuous* relationship with advertisers⟩ — **in·ces·tu·ous·ly** *adv* — **in·ces·tu·ous·ness** *n*

1inch \ˈinch\ *n* **1** : a unit of length equal to 1/36 yard (2.54 centimeters) — see MEASURE table **2** : a small amount, distance, or degree ⟨wouldn't move an *inch*⟩ **3** *pl* : STATURE 1, HEIGHT **4** : a small advantage especially from lenient or compassionate treatment — usually used in the phrase *give an inch* ⟨did not

\ə\ **abut**	\au̇\ **out**	\i\ **tip**	\ȯ\ **saw**	\u̇\ **foot**
\ər\ **further**	\ch\ **chin**	\ī\ **life**	\ȯi\ **coin**	\y\ **yet**
\a\ **mat**	\e\ **pet**	\j\ **job**	\th\ **thin**	\yü\ **few**
\ā\ **take**	\ē\ **easy**	\ng\ **sing**	\<u>th</u>\ **this**	\yu̇\ **cure**
\ä\ **cot, cart**	\g\ **go**	\ō\ **bone**	\ü\ **food**	\zh\ **vision**

give an inch during negotiations⟩ [Old English *ynce,* from Latin *uncia* "12th part, inch, ounce"] — **every inch** : to the utmost degree ⟨looks *every inch* a winner⟩ — **inch by inch** : very gradually or slowly — **within an inch of** : almost to the point of ⟨came *within an inch of* succeeding⟩

[2]**inch** *vb* : to move by small degrees

[3]**inch** *n, chiefly Scottish* : ISLAND 1 [Scottish Gaelic *innis*]

in·cho·ate \in-ˈkō-ət, ˈin-kə-ˌwāt\ *adj* : being recently begun or only partly in existence or operation; *esp* : imperfectly formed or formulated ⟨*inchoate* suspicions⟩ [Latin *inchoatus,* past participle of *inchoare* "to start work on," perhaps from *in-* + *cohum* "part of a yoke"] — **in·cho·ate·ly** *adv* — **in·cho·ate·ness** *n*

inch·worm \ˈinch-ˌwərm\ *n* : LOOPER 1

in·ci·dence \ˈin-səd-əns, -sə-ˌdens\ *n* **1 a** : ANGLE OF INCIDENCE **b** : the arrival of something (as a projectile or a ray of light) at a surface **2 a** : an act or the fact or manner of falling upon or affecting : OCCURRENCE **b** : rate of occurrence or influence ⟨a high *incidence* of crime⟩

[1]**in·ci·dent** \ˈin-səd-ənt, -sə-ˌdent\ *n* **1 a** : an occurrence that is a separate item of experience : HAPPENING **b** : an accompanying minor occurrence **2** : an action likely to lead to grave consequences especially in diplomatic matters **3** : something dependent on or subordinate to something else of greater importance [Medieval French, from Medieval Latin *incidens,* from Latin *incidere* "to fall into, occur," from *in-* + *cadere* "to fall"]
synonyms see OCCURRENCE

[2]**incident** *adj* **1** : occurring or likely to occur as a minor consequence or accompaniment ⟨a question *incident* to the main topic⟩ **2** : dependent on or relating to another thing **3** : falling or striking on something ⟨*incident* light rays⟩

[1]**in·ci·den·tal** \ˌin-sə-ˈdent-l\ *adj* **1 a** : being likely to happen as a chance or minor consequence ⟨*incidental* expenses of a trip⟩ **b** : MINOR 1 **2** : occurring merely by chance or without intention — **in·ci·den·tal·ly** \-ˈdent-lē, -l-ē\ *adv*

[2]**incidental** *n* **1** : something incidental **2** *pl* : minor items (as of expense) that are not listed individually

in·cin·er·ate \in-ˈsin-ə-ˌrāt\ *vt* : to burn to ashes [Medieval Latin *incinerare,* from Latin *in-* + *ciner-, cinis* "ashes"] — **in·cin·er·a·tion** \in-ˌsin-ə-ˈrā-shən\ *n*

in·cin·er·a·tor \in-ˈsin-ə-ˌrāt-ər\ *n* : one that incinerates; *esp* : a furnace or a container for incinerating waste materials

in·cip·i·ent \in-ˈsip-ē-ənt\ *adj* : beginning to come into existence or to become apparent ⟨an *incipient* solar system⟩ [Latin *incipiens,* present participle of *incipere* "to begin," from *in-* + *capere* "to take"] — **in·cip·i·en·cy** \-ən-sē\ *also* **in·cip·i·ence** \-əns\ *n* — **in·cip·i·ent·ly** *adv*

in·cise \in-ˈsīz\ *vt* **1** : to cut into **2** : ENGRAVE 1b [Latin *incisus,* past participle of *incidere* "to cut into," from *in-* + *caedere* "to cut"]

in·cised \-ˈsīzd\ *adj* : cut in; *esp* : decorated with incised figures

in·ci·sion \in-ˈsizh-ən\ *n* **1** : CUT, GASH; *esp* : a wound made in surgery by cutting the body **2** : an act of incising **3** : incisive quality

in·ci·sive \in-ˈsī-siv\ *adj* : impressively direct and decisive ⟨an *incisive* writing style⟩ ⟨an *incisive* and convincing argument⟩ — **in·ci·sive·ly** *adv* — **in·ci·sive·ness** *n*
synonyms INCISIVE, TRENCHANT, CUTTING, BITING mean having or manifesting a keen mind. INCISIVE implies a power to impress the mind by keen penetration, directness, and decisiveness ⟨no one could ignore that *incisive* command⟩. TRENCHANT implies an energetic cutting or deep probing so as to reveal distinctions or to get to the heart of the matter ⟨a *trenchant* critic of political pretensions⟩. CUTTING suggests sarcasm or penetrating accuracy that wounds the feelings ⟨hurt by his *cutting* remarks⟩ . BITING adds a greater implication of harsh vehemence or ironic force ⟨a *biting* commentary on the election⟩.

in·ci·sor \in-ˈsī-zər\ *n* : a front tooth adapted for cutting; *esp* : one of the cutting teeth located between the canines of a mammal — **incisor** *adj*

in·ci·ta·tion \ˌin-ˌsī-ˈtā-shən, ˌin-sə-\ *n* : INCITEMENT

in·cite \in-ˈsīt\ *vt* : to move to action : stir up : urge on [Medieval French *inciter,* from Latin *incitare* "to put in motion, rouse, cite"] — **in·cite·ment** \-ˈsīt-mənt\ *n* — **in·cit·er** *n*
synonyms INCITE, INSTIGATE, ABET, FOMENT mean to spur to action. INCITE stresses a stirring up and urging on and may or may not imply initiative ⟨propaganda *inciting* war⟩. INSTIGATE implies responsibility for initiating another's action and often connotes dubious or evil intention ⟨*instigated* a conspiracy⟩. ABET implies both assisting and encouraging ⟨traitors *abetting* the enemy⟩. FOMENT stresses persistence in goading ⟨*fomented* rebellion⟩.

in·ci·vil·i·ty \ˌin-sə-ˈvil-ət-ē\ *n, pl* **-ties** **1** : the quality or state of being uncivil **2** : a rude or discourteous act

in·clem·ent \in-ˈklem-ənt, ˈin-\ *adj* : physically severe : STORMY, ROUGH ⟨*inclement* weather⟩; *also* : marked by such weather ⟨an *inclement* day⟩ — **in·clem·en·cy** \-ən-sē\ *n* — **in·clem·ent·ly** *adv*

in·clin·able \in-ˈklī-nə-bəl\ *adj* **1** : having a tendency or inclination : DISPOSED ⟨*inclinable* to idleness⟩ **2** : disposed to favor or think well of ⟨*inclinable* to their request⟩ **3** : capable of being inclined ⟨an *inclinable* steering column⟩

in·cli·na·tion \ˌin-klə-ˈnā-shən, ˌing-\ *n* **1** : a particular disposition of mind or character; *esp* : LIKING ⟨had little *inclination* for housekeeping⟩ **2** : an act or the action of bending or inclining: as **a** : [2]BOW, NOD **b** : a tilting of something **3 a** : a departure from the true vertical or horizontal : SLANT ⟨the *inclination* of the earth's axis⟩; *also* : the degree of such departure **b** : an inclined surface : SLOPE **4** : a tendency to a particular state, character, or action ⟨the weather showed some *inclination* to snow⟩ — **in·cli·na·tion·al** \-shnəl, -shən-l\ *adj*

[1]**in·cline** \in-ˈklīn\ *vb* **1** : to bend the head or body forward : BOW **2** : to lean, tend, or become drawn toward an opinion or course of conduct ⟨*incline* toward the second of two proposals⟩ **3** : to deviate from a line, direction, or course : SLOPE, SLANT; *esp* : to deviate from the vertical or horizontal **4** : to cause to bend, bow, slope, or slant **5** : to have influence on : PERSUADE ⟨his love of books inclined him toward a literary career⟩ [Medieval French *incliner,* from Latin *inclinare,* from *in-* + *clinare* "to lean"] — **in·clin·er** *n*
synonyms INCLINE, BIAS, DISPOSE, PREDISPOSE mean to influence one to have or take an attitude toward something. INCLINE implies a tendency to favor one of two or more actions or conclusions ⟨I *incline* to agree⟩. BIAS suggests a settled and predictable leaning in one direction and implies unfair prejudice ⟨the experience *biased* him against imported goods⟩. DISPOSE suggests an affecting of one's mood or temper so as to incline one toward something ⟨her nature *disposes* her to trust others⟩. PREDISPOSE implies the operation of a disposing influence well in advance of the opportunity to manifest itself ⟨does fictional violence *predispose* them to accept real violence?⟩.

[2]**in·cline** \ˈin-ˌklīn\ *n* : an inclined plane : GRADE, SLOPE

in·clined \in-ˈklīnd, *2 also* ˈin-ˌ\ *adj* **1** : having an inclination, disposition, or tendency **2 a** : having a slant or slope **b** : making an angle with a line or plane

inclined plane *n* : a plane surface that makes an oblique angle with the plane of the horizon

inclose, inclosure *variant of* ENCLOSE, ENCLOSURE

in·clude \in-ˈklüd\ *vt* **1** : to shut up : ENCLOSE **2** : to take in or comprise as a part of a whole or group ⟨the recipe *included* many ingredients⟩ **3** : to contain between ⟨two sides and the *included* angle⟩ [Latin *includere,* from *in-* + *claudere* "to close"] — **in·clud·able** *or* **in·clud·ible** \-ˈklüd-ə-bəl\ *adj*
synonyms INCLUDE, COMPREHEND, INVOLVE mean to contain within as a part of the whole. INCLUDE suggests containing something as a constituent or subordinate part of a larger whole ⟨the price of dinner *includes* dessert⟩. COMPREHEND implies that something comes within the range or scope of a statement or definition ⟨his system *comprehends* all history⟩. INVOLVE suggests inclusion by virtue of the nature of the whole, whether by being its natural or inevitable consequence ⟨surrender *involves* submission⟩ ⟨the new job *involves* a lot of detail⟩. ***synonyms*** see in addition COMPRISE

in·clu·sion \in-ˈklü-zhən\ *n* **1** : the act of including : the state of being included **2** : something that is included; *esp* : a passive product of cell activity (as a starch grain) within the cytoplasm or nucleus [Latin *inclusio,* from *includere* "to include"]

in·clu·sive \in-ˈklü-siv, -ziv\ *adj* **1** : including the specified limits and everything in between ⟨March to June *inclusive*⟩ **2 a** : broad in orientation or scope ⟨an *inclusive* goal⟩ **b** : covering or intended to cover all items, costs, or services ⟨an *inclusive* insurance policy⟩ — **in·clu·sive·ly** *adv* — **in·clu·sive·ness** *n*

inclusive of *prep* : taking into account ⟨the cost of building *inclusive of* materials⟩

in·co·erc·ible \ˌin-kō-ˈər-sə-bəl\ *adj* : incapable of being controlled, checked, or confined

[1]**in·cog·ni·to** \ˌin-ˌkäg-ˈnēt-ō, in-ˈkäg-nə-ˌtō\ *adv or adj* : with

one's identity concealed [Italian, from Latin *incognitus* "unknown," from *in-* + *cognoscere* "to know"]

[2]incognito *n, pl* **-tos** **1** : one appearing or living incognito **2** : the state or disguise of an incognito

in·co·her·ence \ˌin-kō-ˈhir-əns, -ˈher-\ *n* **1** : the quality or state of being incoherent **2** : an incoherent utterance

in·co·her·ent \-ənt\ *adj* : not coherent: as **a** : not sticking closely or compactly together : LOOSE **b** : not clearly or logically connected ⟨an *incoherent* story⟩ **c** : not clear or intelligible in speech or thought ⟨*incoherent* with grief⟩ — **in·co·her·ent·ly** *adv*

in·com·bus·ti·ble \ˌin-kəm-ˈbəs-tə-bəl\ *adj* : not combustible : incapable of being burned

in·come \ˈin-ˌkəm\ *n* : a gain usually measured in money that comes from capital or labor; *also* : the amount of such gain received in a given period of time

in·com·er \ˈin-ˌkəm-ər\ *n, chiefly British* : one who comes in : IMMIGRANT, NEWCOMER

income tax \ˈin-kəm-\ *n* : a tax on the net income of an individual or business

[1]in·com·ing \ˈin-ˌkəm-ing\ *n* : the act of coming in : ARRIVAL

[2]incoming *adj* : coming in: as **a** : taking a place or position formerly held by another ⟨the *incoming* president⟩ **b** : arriving at a usual or designated destination ⟨*incoming* mail⟩ **c** : just starting or beginning ⟨the *incoming* year⟩

in·com·men·su·ra·ble \ˌin-kə-ˈmens-rə-bəl, -ˈmench-, -ə-rə-\ *adj* : not commensurable : lacking a basis of comparison in regard to a quality normally subject to comparison ⟨*incommensurable* theories⟩ — **in·com·men·su·ra·bly** \-blē\ *adv*

in·com·men·su·rate \ˌin-kə-ˈmens-rət, -ˈmench-rət, -ə-rət\ *adj* : not commensurate : as **a** : INADEQUATE ⟨funds *incommensurate* with need⟩ **b** : DISPROPORTIONATE ⟨a confidence *incommensurate* with his ability⟩

in·com·mode \ˌin-kə-ˈmōd\ *vt* : to give inconvenience or trouble to [Middle French *incommoder,* from Latin *incommodare,* from *incommodus* "inconvenient," from *in-* + *commodus* "convenient"]

in·com·mo·di·ous \ˌin-kə-ˈmōd-ē-əs\ *adj* : not commodious : INCONVENIENT ⟨could sleep in the most *incommodious* places⟩

in·com·mod·i·ty \-ˈmäd-ət-ē\ *n* : INCONVENIENCE 2, DISADVANTAGE

in·com·mu·ni·ca·ble \ˌin-kə-ˈmyü-ni-kə-bəl\ *adj* : not capable of being communicated or imparted — **in·com·mu·ni·ca·bil·i·ty** \-ˌmyü-ni-kə-ˈbil-ət-ē\ *n* — **in·com·mu·ni·ca·bly** \-ˈmyü-ni-kə-blē\ *adv*

in·com·mu·ni·ca·do \ˌin-kə-ˌmyü-nə-ˈkäd-ō\ *adv or adj* : without means of communication : in a situation or state not allowing communication ⟨a prisoner held *incommunicado*⟩ [Spanish *incomunicado,* from *incomunicar* "to deprive of communication"]

in·com·mu·ni·ca·tive \ˌin-kə-ˈmyü-nə-ˌkāt-iv, -ni-kət-\ *adj* : UNCOMMUNICATIVE

in·com·pa·ra·ble \in-ˈkäm-pə-rə-bəl, -prə-bəl\ *adj* **1** : having no equal (as in quality or worth) : MATCHLESS **2** : not suitable for comparison — **in·com·pa·ra·bil·i·ty** \in-ˌkäm-pə-rə-ˈbil-ət-ē, -prə-\ *n* — **in·com·pa·ra·bly** \in-ˈkäm-pə-rə-blē, -prə-\ *adv*

in·com·pat·i·bil·i·ty \ˌin-kəm-ˌpat-ə-ˈbil-ət-ē\ *n, pl* **-ties** **1** : the quality or state of being incompatible **2** *pl* : mutually antagonistic things or qualities

in·com·pat·i·ble \ˌin-kəm-ˈpat-ə-bəl\ *adj* : not compatible : as **a** : incapable of association or harmonious coexistence ⟨*incompatible* colors⟩ ⟨their personalities were *incompatible*⟩ **b** : unsuitable for use together because of undesirable chemical or bodily effects ⟨*incompatible* blood types⟩ **c** : infertile in a particular genetic cross ⟨*incompatible* plants⟩ — **in·com·pati·ble** *n* — **in·com·pat·i·bly** \-blē\ *adv*

in·com·pe·tence \in-ˈkäm-pət-əns, ˈin-\ *n* : the state or fact of being incompetent

in·com·pe·ten·cy \-ən-sē\ *n* : INCOMPETENCE

[1]in·com·pe·tent \in-ˈkäm-pət-ənt, ˈin-\ *adj* **1** : lacking the qualities (as knowledge, skill, or ability) necessary for effective independent action **2** : not legally qualified **3** : inadequate to or unsuitable for the purpose ⟨an *incompetent* heart valve⟩ ⟨an *incompetent* system of government⟩ — **in·com·pe·tent·ly** *adv*

[2]incompetent *n* : an incompetent person

in·com·plete \ˌin-kəm-ˈplēt\ *adj* : not complete : lacking some part : UNFINISHED, IMPERFECT — **in·com·plete·ly** *adv* — **in·com·plete·ness** *n*

incomplete metamorphosis *n* : insect metamorphosis (as of a grasshopper) in which there is no pupal stage between the immature stage and the adult and in which the young insect usually resembles the adult — compare COMPLETE METAMORPHOSIS

in·com·pre·hen·si·ble \in-ˌkäm-pri-ˈhen-sə-bəl\ *adj* : incapable of being understood — **in·com·pre·hen·si·bil·i·ty** \-ˌhen-sə-ˈbil-ət-ē\ *n* — **in·com·pre·hen·si·ble·ness** \-ˈhen-sə-bəl-nəs\ *n* — **in·com·pre·hen·si·bly** \-blē\ *adv*

in·com·pre·hen·sion \in-ˌkäm-pri-ˈhen-chən\ *n* : lack of understanding

in·com·press·ible \ˌin-kəm-ˈpres-ə-bəl\ *adj* : incapable of or resistant to compression — **in·com·press·ibil·i·ty** \-ˌpres-ə-ˈbil-ət-ē\ *n* — **in·com·press·ibly** \-ˈpres-ə-blē\ *adv*

in·com·put·able \ˌin-kəm-ˈpyüt-ə-bəl\ *adj* : greater than can be computed or counted — **in·com·put·ably** \-blē\ *adv*

in·con·ceiv·able \ˌin-kən-ˈsē-və-bəl\ *adj* : impossible to imagine or conceive — **in·con·ceiv·abil·i·ty** \-ˌsē-və-ˈbil-ət-ē\ *n* — **in·con·ceiv·able·ness** \-ˈsē-və-bəl-nəs\ *n* — **in·con·ceiv·ably** \-blē\ *adv*

in·con·clu·sive \ˌin-kən-ˈklü-siv, -ziv\ *adj* : leading to no conclusion or definite result ⟨*inconclusive* evidence⟩ — **in·con·clu·sive·ly** *adv* — **in·con·clu·sive·ness** *n*

in·con·for·mi·ty \ˌin-kən-ˈfȯr-mət-ē\ *n* : NONCONFORMITY 2

in·con·gru·ence \ˌin-kən-ˈgrü-əns; in-ˈkäng-grə-wəns, ˈin-\ *n* : INCONGRUITY

in·con·gru·ent \ˌin-kən-ˈgrü-ənt; in-ˈkäng-grə-wənt, ˈin-\ *adj* : marked by incongruity — **in·con·gru·ent·ly** *adv*

in·con·gru·i·ty \ˌin-kən-ˈgrü-ət-ē, -ˌkän-\ *n, pl* **-ties** **1** : the quality or state of being incongruous **2** : something that is incongruous

in·con·gru·ous \in-ˈkäng-grə-wəs, ˈin-\ *adj* : not consistent with or suitable to the surroundings or associations : not harmonious, appropriate, or proper ⟨*incongruous* colors⟩ ⟨an act *incongruous* with their duty⟩ — **in·con·gru·ous·ly** *adv* — **in·con·gru·ous·ness** *n*

in·con·se·quence \in-ˈkän-sə-ˌkwens, -si-kwəns, ˈin-\ *n* : the quality or state of being inconsequent

in·con·se·quent \-kwənt, -ˌkwent\ *adj* **1 a** : lacking reasonable sequence : ILLOGICAL **b** : not consecutive **2** : IRRELEVANT **3** : INCONSEQUENTIAL 2 — **in·con·se·quent·ly** \-ˌkwent-lē, -kwənt-\ *adv*

in·con·se·quen·tial \in-ˌkän-sə-ˈkwen-chəl\ *adj* **1 a** : ILLOGICAL **b** : IRRELEVANT **2** : of no significance : UNIMPORTANT — **in·con·se·quen·ti·al·i·ty** \-ˌkwen-chē-ˈal-ət-ē\ *n* — **in·con·se·quen·tial·ly** \-ˈkwench-lē, -ə-lē\ *adv*

in·con·sid·er·able \ˌin-kən-ˈsid-ər-bəl, -ˈsid-ər-ə-bəl, -ˈsid-rə-bəl\ *adj* : not worth considering : SLIGHT, TRIVIAL — **in·con·sid·er·able·ness** *n* — **in·con·sid·er·ably** \-blē\ *adv*

in·con·sid·er·ate \ˌin-kən-ˈsid-rət, -ə-rət\ *adj* **1** : acting or tending to act without due thought **2** : careless of the rights or feelings of others — **in·con·sid·er·ate·ly** *adv* — **in·con·sid·er·ate·ness** *n* — **in·con·sid·er·a·tion** *n*

in·con·sis·ten·cy \ˌin-kən-ˈsis-tən-sē\ *n, pl* **-cies** **1** : the quality or state of being inconsistent **2** : an instance of being inconsistent

in·con·sis·tent \ˌin-kən-ˈsis-tənt\ *adj* **1 a** : not being in agreement or harmony : INCOMPATIBLE ⟨an explanation *inconsistent* with the facts⟩ **b** : containing incompatible elements ⟨an *inconsistent* argument⟩ **2** : not logical in thought or actions : CHANGEABLE ⟨a very *inconsistent* person⟩ — **in·con·sis·tent·ly** *adv*

in·con·sol·able \ˌin-kən-ˈsō-lə-bəl\ *adj* : incapable of being consoled : DISCONSOLATE — **in·con·sol·able·ness** *n* — **in·con·sol·ably** \-blē\ *adv*

in·con·so·nance \in-ˈkän-sə-nəns, ˈin-, -snəns\ *n* : lack of consonance or harmony : DISAGREEMENT

in·con·so·nant \-sə-nənt, -snənt\ *adj* : DISCORDANT

in·con·spic·u·ous \ˌin-kən-ˈspik-yə-wəs\ *adj* : not readily noticeable — **in·con·spic·u·ous·ly** *adv* — **in·con·spic·u·ous·ness** *n*

\ə\ abut	\au̇\ out	\i\ tip	\ȯ\ saw	\u̇\ foot
\ər\ further	\ch\ chin	\ī\ life	\ȯi\ coin	\y\ yet
\a\ mat	\e\ pet	\j\ job	\th\ thin	\yü\ few
\ā\ take	\ē\ easy	\ng\ sing	\th\ this	\yu̇\ cure
\ä\ cot, cart	\g\ go	\ō\ bone	\ü\ food	\zh\ vision

in·con·stan·cy \in-ˈkän-stən-sē, ˈin-\ *n, pl* **-cies** : the quality or state of being inconstant
in·con·stant \-stənt\ *adj* : given to changing frequently without apparent reason : CHANGEABLE — **in·con·stant·ly** *adv*
in·con·test·able \ˌin-kən-ˈtes-tə-bəl\ *adj* : not open to doubt or contest : INDISPUTABLE, UNQUESTIONABLE ⟨an *incontestable* fact⟩ — **in·con·test·abil·i·ty** \-ˌtes-tə-ˈbil-ət-ē\ *n* — **in·con·test·ably** \-ˈtes-tə-blē\ *adv*
in·con·ti·nent \in-ˈkänt-n-ənt, ˈin-\ *adj* **1** : not continent : lacking in self-restraint **2** : unable to retain urine or feces in the body voluntarily — **in·con·ti·nence** \-əns\ *n* — **in·con·ti·nent·ly** *adv*
in·con·trol·la·ble \ˌin-kən-ˈtrō-lə-bəl\ *adj* : UNCONTROLLABLE
in·con·tro·vert·ible \in-ˌkän-trə-ˈvərt-ə-bəl\ *adj* : not open to question : INDISPUTABLE ⟨*incontrovertible* evidence⟩ — **in·con·tro·vert·ibly** \-blē\ *adv*
[1]**in·con·ve·nience** \ˌin-kən-ˈvē-nyəns\ *n* **1** : the quality or state of being inconvenient; *esp* : lack of suitability for personal ease or comfort **2** : something inconvenient
[2]**inconvenience** *vt* : to cause inconvenience to
in·con·ve·nient \-nyənt\ *adj* : not convenient : causing difficulty, discomfort, or annoyance — **in·con·ve·nient·ly** *adv*
in·con·vert·ible \ˌin-kən-ˈvərt-ə-bəl\ *adj* : not convertible into something else; *esp* : not exchangeable for a foreign currency or coin — **in·con·vert·ibil·i·ty** \-ˌvərt-ə-ˈbil-ət-ē\ *n* — **in·con·vert·ibly** \-ˈvərt-ə-blē\ *adv*
in·con·vinc·ible \ˌin-kən-ˈvin-sə-bəl\ *adj* : incapable of being convinced
in·co·or·di·na·tion \ˌin-kō-ˌȯrd-n-ˈā-shən\ *n* : lack of coordination especially of muscular movement
[1]**in·cor·po·rate** \in-ˈkȯr-pə-ˌrāt\ *vb* **1** : to unite with or work into something already existent **2** : to unite or combine to form a single body or a consistent whole **3** : to give material form to : EMBODY **4** : to form, form into, or become a corporation ⟨*incorporate* a firm⟩ ⟨an *incorporated* town⟩ [Late Latin *incorporare,* from Latin *in-* + *corpor-, corpus* "body"] — **in·cor·po·ra·tion** \in-ˌkȯr-pə-ˈrā-shən\ *n* — **in·cor·po·ra·tive** \in-ˈkȯr-pə-ˌrāt-iv, -pə-rət-, -prət-\ *adj* — **in·cor·po·ra·tor** \-pə-ˌrāt-ər\ *n*
[2]**in·cor·po·rate** \in-ˈkȯr-pə-rət, -prət\ *adj* : INCORPORATED
in·cor·po·rat·ed \-pə-ˌrāt-əd\ *adj* : united in one body; *esp* : formed into a legal corporation
in·cor·po·re·al \ˌin-kȯr-ˈpōr-ē-əl, -ˈpȯr-\ *adj* : having no material body or form : IMMATERIAL — **in·cor·po·re·al·ly** \-ə-lē\ *adv*
in·cor·po·re·i·ty \ˌin-ˌkȯr-pə-ˈrē-ət-ē\ *n* : the quality or state of being incorporeal : IMMATERIALITY
in·cor·rect \ˌin-kə-ˈrekt\ *adj* **1 a** : INACCURATE, FAULTY ⟨an *incorrect* copy⟩ **b** : not true : WRONG ⟨an *incorrect* answer⟩ **2** : UNBECOMING, IMPROPER ⟨*incorrect* behavior⟩ — **in·cor·rect·ly** *adv* — **in·cor·rect·ness** \-ˈrekt-nəs, -ˈrek-nəs\ *n*
[1]**in·cor·ri·gi·ble** \in-ˈkȯr-ə-jə-bəl, ˈin-, -ˈkär-\ *adj* : not to be corrected or improved: as **a** : incapable of being reformed ⟨an *incorrigible* gambler⟩ **b** : UNRULY, UNMANAGEABLE ⟨*incorrigible* hair⟩ — **in·cor·ri·gi·bil·i·ty** \in-ˌkȯr-ə-jə-ˈbil-ət-ē, -ˌkär-\ *n* — **in·cor·ri·gi·ble·ness** \in-ˈkȯr-ə-jə-bəl-nəs, ˈin-, -ˈkär-\ *n* — **in·cor·ri·gi·bly** \-blē\ *adv*
[2]**incorrigible** *n* : an incorrigible person
in·cor·rupt·ible \ˌin-kə-ˈrəp-tə-bəl\ *adj* : not to be corrupted: as **a** : not subject to decay **b** : incapable of being bribed or morally corrupted — **in·cor·rupt·ibil·i·ty** \-ˌrəp-tə-ˈbil-ət-ē\ *n* — **in·cor·rupt·ibly** \-ˈrəp-tə-blē\ *adv*
[1]**in·crease** \in-ˈkrēs, ˈin-ˌ\ *vb* **1** : to make or become greater (as in size, number, value, or power) ⟨*increase* speed⟩ ⟨skill *increases* with practice⟩ **2** : to multiply by the production of young [Medieval French *encreistre,* from Latin *increscere,* from *in-* + *crescere* "to grow"] — **in·creas·able** \-ˈkrē-sə-bəl, -ˌkrē-\ *adj* — **in·creas·er** *n*
[2]**in·crease** \ˈin-ˌkrēs, in-ˈ\ *n* **1** : the act of increasing : addition or enlargement in size, extent, or quantity **2** : something (as offspring, produce, or profit) added to an original stock or amount by enlargement or growth — **on the increase** : becoming greater in size, number or amount ⟨crime is *on the increase*⟩
in·creas·ing·ly \in-ˈkrē-sing-lē, ˈin-ˌkrē-\ *adv* : to an increasing degree : more and more ⟨an *increasingly* dangerous situation⟩
in·cred·i·ble \in-ˈkred-ə-bəl, ˈin-\ *adj* **1** : too extraordinary or improbable to be believed ⟨making *increible* claims⟩ **2** : AMAZING, EXTRAORDINARY ⟨*incredible* skill⟩ — **in·cred·i·bil·i·ty** \in-ˌkred-ə-ˈbil-ət-ē\ *n* — **in·cred·i·bly** \in-ˈkred-ə-blē, ˈin-\ *adv*
in·cre·du·li·ty \ˌin-kri-ˈdü-lət-ē, -ˈdyü-\ *n* : the quality or state of being incredulous : DISBELIEF ***synonyms*** see UNBELIEF
in·cred·u·lous \in-ˈkrej-ə-ləs, ˈin-\ *adj* **1** : tending to disbelieve : SKEPTICAL **2** : indicating or caused by disbelief ⟨an *incredulous* smile⟩ — **in·cred·u·lous·ly** *adv*
in·cre·ment \ˈing-krə-mənt, ˈin-\ *n* **1** : an increasing or growth especially in quantity or value : ENLARGEMENT, INCREASE; *also* : QUANTITY **2 a** : something gained or added **b** : one of a series of regular consecutive additions **c** : a minute increase in quantity [Latin *incrementum,* from *increscere* "to increase"]
in·cre·men·tal \ˌing-krə-ˈment-l, ˌin-\ *adj* : of, relating to, being, or occurring in especially small increments ⟨*incremental* change⟩ — **in·cre·men·tal·ly** \-l-ē\ *adv*
in·crim·i·nate \in-ˈkrim-ə-ˌnāt\ *vt* : to charge with or show evidence or proof of involvement in a crime or fault : ACCUSE [Late Latin *incriminare,* from Latin *in-* + *crimen* "crime, accusation"] — **in·crim·i·na·tion** \in-ˌkrim-ə-ˈnā-shən\ *n* — **in·crim·i·na·to·ry** \in-ˈkrim-nə-ˌtōr-ē, -ə-nə-, -ˌtȯr-\ *adj*
incrust *variant of* ENCRUST
in·crus·ta·tion \ˌin-ˌkrəs-ˈtā-shən\ *also* **en·crus·ta·tion** \ˌin-, ˌen-\ *n* **1** : the act of encrusting : the state of being encrusted **2** : a hard coating : CRUST **3 a** : OVERLAY **b** : INLAY 1
in·cu·bate \ˈing-kyə-ˌbāt, ˈin-\ *vb* **1** : to sit upon (eggs) to hatch by warmth **2** : to maintain (as bacteria or a chemically active system) under conditions favorable for development or reaction **3** : to undergo incubation [Latin *incubare,* from *in-* + *cubare* "to lie"]
in·cu·ba·tion \ˌing-kyə-ˈbā-shən, ˌin-\ *n* **1** : the act or process of incubating **2** : INCUBATION PERIOD
incubation period *n* : the period between infection by a pathogen and the manifestation of an illness or disease
in·cu·ba·tor \ˈing-kyə-ˌbāt-ər, ˈin-\ *n* : one that incubates; *esp* : an apparatus providing suitable conditions (as of warmth and moisture) for incubating something ⟨an *incubator* for premature babies⟩
in·cu·bus \ˈing-kyə-bəs, ˈin-\ *n, pl* **-bi** \-ˌbī, -ˌbē\ *also* **-bus·es** **1** : an evil spirit held to lie upon persons in their sleep **2** : NIGHTMARE 1 **3** : one that oppresses or burdens like a nightmare [Late Latin, from Latin *incubare* "to lie on, incubate"]
in·cul·cate \in-ˈkəl-ˌkāt, ˈin-ˌkəl-\ *vt* : to impress on the mind by frequent repetition ⟨*inculcated* a deep sense of responsibility in their children⟩ [Latin *inculcare,* literally, "to tread on," from *in-* + *calcare* "to trample," from *calx* "heel"] — **in·cul·ca·tion** \ˌin-ˌkəl-ˈkā-shən\ *n* — **in·cul·ca·tor** \in-ˈkəl-ˌkāt-ər, ˈin-ˌkəl-\ *n*
in·cul·pa·ble \in-ˈkəl-pə-bəl, ˈin-\ *adj* : free from guilt : BLAMELESS
in·cul·pate \in-ˈkəl-ˌpāt, ˈin-ˌkəl-\ *vt* : INCRIMINATE [derived from Latin *in-* "[2]in-" + *culpare* "to blame," from *culpa* "blame, fault"] — **in·cul·pa·tion** \ˌin-ˌkəl-ˈpā-shən\ *n*
in·cum·ben·cy \in-ˈkəm-bən-sē\ *n, pl* **-cies** **1** : the quality or state of being incumbent **2** : the office or period of office of an incumbent
[1]**in·cum·bent** \-bənt\ *n* : the holder of an office or position [Latin *incumbere* "to lie down on"]
[2]**incumbent** *adj* **1** : imposed as a duty : OBLIGATORY ⟨incumbent on us to take action⟩ **2** : being an incumbent; *esp* : occupying a specified office ⟨an *incumbent* president⟩ **3** : lying or resting on something else
in·cum·ber *archaic variant of* ENCUMBER
in·cu·nab·u·lum \ˌin-kyə-ˈnab-yə-ləm, ˌing-\ *n, pl* **-la** \-lə\ **1** : a book printed before 1501 **2** : a work of art or of industry of an early period [New Latin, from Latin *incunabula* "bands holding the baby in a cradle," from *in-* + *cunae* "cradle"]
in·cur \in-ˈkər\ *vt* **in·curred; in·cur·ring** : to become liable or subject to : bring down upon oneself ⟨*incur* punishment⟩ ⟨*incur* expenses⟩ [Latin *incurrere,* literally, "to run into," from *in-* + *currere* "to run"] — **in·cur·rence** \in-ˈkər-əns, -ˈkə-rəns\ *n*
[1]**in·cur·able** \in-ˈkyu̇r-ə-bəl, ˈin-\ *adj* : not capable of being cured — **in·cur·abil·i·ty** \in-ˌkyu̇r-ə-ˈbil-ət-ē\ *n* — **in·cur·ably** \-blē\ *adv*
[2]**incurable** *n* : a person suffering from a disease that is beyond cure
in·cu·ri·ous \in-ˈkyu̇r-ē-əs, ˈin-\ *adj* : showing no interest or concern : INDIFFERENT ⟨a blank *incurious* stare⟩ — **in·cu·ri·ous·ly** *adv* — **in·cu·ri·ous·ness** *n*
in·cur·rent \in-ˈkər-ənt, -ˈkə-rənt\ *adj* : characterized by a current that flows inward ⟨*incurrent* pores of a sponge⟩
in·cur·sion \in-ˈkər-zhən\ *n* : a sudden usually temporary invasion : RAID [Latin *incursio,* from *incurrere* "to run into"]

in·cur·vate \ˈin-ˌkər-ˌvāt, in-ˈ\ *vt* : to cause to curve inward : BEND — **in·cur·vate** \ˈin-ˌkər-ˌvāt, in-ˈkər-vət\ *adj* — **in·cur·va·tion** \ˌin-ˌkər-ˈvā-shən\ *n* — **in·cur·va·ture** \in-ˈkər-və-ˌchu̇r, ˈin-, -chər\ *n*

in·curve \in-ˈkərv, ˈin-\ *vb* : to bend so as to curve inward

in·cus \ˈing-kəs\ *n, pl* **in·cu·des** \ing-ˈkyüd-ēz, ˈing-kyə-ˌdēz\ : the middle of a chain of three small bones in the ear of a mammal — called also *anvil*; compare MALLEUS, STAPES [Latin, "anvil"]

in·debt·ed \in-ˈdet-əd\ *adj* : owing something (as money, gratitude, or recognition)

in·debt·ed·ness *n* **1** : the condition of being indebted **2** : something owed

in·de·cen·cy \in-ˈdēs-n-sē, ˈin-\ *n* **1** : lack of decency **2** : an indecent act or word

in·de·cent \-nt\ *adj* : not decent : as **a** : grossly improper or offensive ⟨*indecent* language⟩ **b** : UNSEEMLY, INAPPROPRIATE ⟨remarried in *indecent* haste⟩ — **in·de·cent·ly** *adv*

in·de·ci·pher·able \ˌin-dē-ˈsī-fə-rə-bəl, -frə-\ *adj* : incapable of being deciphered ⟨*indecipherable* instructions⟩

in·de·ci·sion \ˌin-di-ˈsizh-ən\ *n* : slowness or hesitation in making up one's mind

in·de·ci·sive \-ˈsī-siv\ *adj* **1** : not decisive : INCONCLUSIVE ⟨an *indecisive* battle⟩ **2** : characterized by indecision : UNCERTAIN ⟨an *indecisive* person⟩ — **in·de·ci·sive·ly** *adv* — **in·de·ci·sive·ness** *n*

in·de·clin·able \ˌin-di-ˈklī-nə-bəl\ *adj* : having no grammatical inflections

in·dec·o·rous \in-ˈdek-ə-rəs, ˈin-; ˌin-di-ˈkōr-əs, -ˈkȯr-\ *adj* : not decorous : conflicting with accepted standards of good conduct or good taste — **in·dec·o·rous·ly** *adv* — **in·dec·o·rous·ness** *n*

synonyms INDECOROUS, IMPROPER, UNSEEMLY, UNBECOMING mean not conforming to what is accepted as right, fitting, or in good taste. INDECOROUS suggests a violation of accepted standards of good manners ⟨talking in church is *indecorous*⟩. IMPROPER applies to a broader range of violation of rules not only of social behavior but also of ethical practice or logical procedure ⟨*improper* use of campaign donations⟩ ⟨telling *improper* jokes⟩. UNSEEMLY adds a suggestion of an offensiveness to good taste ⟨an *unseemly* display of poor manners⟩. UNBECOMING suggests behavior or language that does not suit one's character or status ⟨conduct *unbecoming* to an officer⟩.

in·de·co·rum \ˌin-di-ˈkōr-əm, -ˈkȯr-\ *n* : lack of decorum

in·deed \in-ˈdēd\ *adv* **1** : without any question : TRULY — often used interjectionally to express disbelief or surprise **2** : in reality **3** : as a matter of fact : all things considered

in·de·fat·i·ga·ble \ˌin-di-ˈfat-i-gə-bəl\ *adj* : capable of working a long time without tiring : TIRELESS ⟨an *indefatigable* writer⟩ [Middle French, from Latin *indefatigabilis,* from *in-* + *defatigare* "to fatigue," from *de-* + *fatigare* "to fatigue"] — **in·de·fat·i·ga·bil·i·ty** \-ˌfat-i-gə-ˈbil-ət-ē\ *n* — **in·de·fat·i·ga·ble·ness** \-ˈfat-i-gə-bəl-nəs\ *n* — **in·de·fat·i·ga·bly** \-blē\ *adv*

in·de·fea·si·ble \ˌin-di-ˈfē-zə-bəl\ *adj* : not capable of being abolished or annulled ⟨*indefeasible* rights⟩ [*in-* + earlier *defeasible* "capable of being annulled," from Medieval French *defaisible,* from *deffaire* "to undo, destroy," from Medieval Latin *disfacere,* from Latin *dis-* + *facere* "to do"] — **in·de·fea·si·bil·i·ty** \-ˌfē-zə-ˈbil-ət-ē\ *n* — **in·de·fea·si·bly** \-ˈfē-zə-blē\ *adv*

in·de·fec·ti·ble \ˌin-di-ˈfek-tə-bəl\ *adj* **1** : not subject to failure or decay : LASTING **2** : free of faults : FLAWLESS — **in·de·fec·ti·bil·i·ty** \-ˌfek-tə-ˈbil-ət-ē\ *n* — **in·de·fec·ti·bly** \-ˈfek-tə-blē\ *adv*

in·de·fen·si·ble \ˌin-di-ˈfen-sə-bəl\ *adj* : not capable of being defended or justified ⟨an *indefensible* position⟩ — **in·de·fen·si·bil·i·ty** \-ˌfen-sə-ˈbil-ət-ē\ *n* — **in·de·fen·si·bly** \-ˈfen-sə-blē\ *adv*

in·de·fin·able \ˌin-di-ˈfī-nə-bəl\ *adj* : incapable of being precisely described or analyzed — **in·de·fin·abil·i·ty** \-ˌfī-nə-ˈbil-ət-ē\ *n* — **in·de·fin·able·ness** \-ˈfī-nə-bəl-nəs\ *n* — **in·de·fin·ably** \-blē\ *adv*

in·def·i·nite \in-ˈdef-nət, ˈin-, -ə-nət\ *adj* **1** : typically designating an unidentified or not immediately identifiable person or thing ⟨the *indefinite* articles *a* and *an*⟩ **2** : not precise in meaning or details : VAGUE ⟨an *indefinite* answer⟩ **3** : not fixed or limited (as in amount or length) ⟨an *indefinite* period⟩ — **in·def·i·nite·ly** *adv* — **in·def·i·nite·ness** *n*

in·de·his·cent \ˌin-di-ˈhis-nt\ *adj* : remaining closed at maturity ⟨*indehiscent* fruits⟩ — **in·de·his·cence** \-ns\ *n*

in·del·i·ble \in-ˈdel-ə-bəl\ *adj* **1** : not capable of being erased, removed, or blotted out ⟨an *indelible* impression⟩ **2** : making marks not easily erased ⟨an *indelible* pencil⟩ [Latin *indelebilis,* from *in-* + *delēre* "to delete"] — **in·del·i·bil·i·ty** \in-ˌdel-ə-ˈbil-ət-ē\ *n* — **in·del·i·bly** \in-ˈdel-ə-blē\ *adv*

in·del·i·ca·cy \in-ˈdel-i-kə-sē, ˈin-\ *n* **1** : the quality or state of being indelicate **2** : something that is indelicate

in·del·i·cate \-kət\ *adj* : offensive to good manners or taste : IMMODEST, COARSE — **in·del·i·cate·ly** *adv* — **in·del·i·cate·ness** *n*

in·dem·ni·fy \in-ˈdem-nə-ˌfī\ *vt* **-fied; -fy·ing** **1** : to insure or protect against loss, damage, or injury **2** : to compensate for loss, damage, or injury ⟨*indemnify* victims of a disaster⟩ **3** : to make compensation for : make good ⟨have their losses *indemnified*⟩ [Latin *indemnis* "unharmed," from *in-* + *damnum* "damage"] — **in·dem·ni·fi·ca·tion** \-ˌdem-nə-fə-ˈkā-shən\ *n* — **in·dem·ni·fi·er** \-ˈdem-nə-ˌfī-ər, -ˌfīr\ *n*

in·dem·ni·ty \in-ˈdem-nət-ē\ *n, pl* **-ties** **1** : protection from loss, damage, or injury : INSURANCE **2** : freedom from penalty for past offenses **3** : compensation for loss, damage, or injury

¹in·dent \in-ˈdent\ *vt* **1 a** : to notch the edge of : make jagged **b** : to cut into for the purpose of mortising or dovetailing **2** : to set in from the margin ⟨*indent* the first line of a paragraph⟩ [Medieval French *endenter,* from *en-* + *dent* "tooth," from Latin *dent-, dens*] — **in·dent·er** *n*

²indent *vt* **1** : to force inward so as to form a depression **2** : to form a dent in — **in·dent·er** *n*

³indent *n* **1** : INDENTATION 1b **2** : DENT 1

in·den·ta·tion \ˌin-ˌden-ˈtā-shən\ *n* **1 a** : an angular cut in an edge **b** : a recess in a surface **2 a** : the action of indenting : the state of being indented **b** : INDENTION 2 **3** : DENT 1

in·den·tion \in-ˈden-chən\ *n* **1** : INDENTATION 2a **2** : the space left by indentation

¹in·den·ture \in-ˈden-chər\ *n* **1** : a written agreement : CONTRACT **2** : a contract that binds a person to serve another for a specified period — often used in plural [Medieval French *endenture* "document carrying two or more copies and divided by an irregular notched cut so that the sections might be proved to belong to the same document by matching the divided edges," from *endenter* "to indent, notch"]

²indenture *vt* : to bind (as an apprentice) by indentures

in·de·pen·dence \ˌin-də-ˈpen-dəns\ *n* : the quality or state of being independent : freedom from outside control

Independence Day *n* : a civil holiday for the celebration of the anniversary of the beginnings of national independence; *esp* : July 4 observed as a legal holiday in the U.S. in commemoration of the adoption of the Declaration of Independence in 1776

in·de·pen·den·cy \ˌin-də-ˈpen-dən-sē\ *n* : FREEDOM 1b, INDEPENDENCE

¹in·de·pen·dent \ˌin-də-ˈpen-dənt\ *adj* **1** : not subject to control or rule by another : SELF-GOVERNING, FREE ⟨an *independent* nation⟩ **2** : not having connections with another : SEPARATE ⟨*independent* conclusions⟩ **3** : not supported by or relying on another : having or providing enough money to live on ⟨a person of *independent* means⟩ **4** : not easily influenced : showing self-reliance ⟨an *independent* person⟩ **5** : having full meaning in itself and capable of standing alone as a simple sentence : MAIN ⟨an *independent* clause⟩ **6** : not committed to a political party **7 a** : not expressed in terms of or having a value determined by another ⟨an *independent* set of vectors⟩ **b** : having probabilities such that the occurrence or nonoccurrence of one event does not influence the outcome of another ⟨the outcomes of the tossing of two dice are *independent*⟩ ***synonyms*** see FREE — **in·de·pend·ent·ly** *adv*

²independent *n* : one that is independent; *esp, often cap* : one not committed to a political party

independent assortment *n* : formation of random combinations of chromosomes and genes in meiosis with one of each pair of homologous chromosomes passing into each gamete independently of each other pair

independent variable *n* : a mathematical variable that is independent of the other variables in an expression or function and

\ə\ **abut**	\au̇\ **out**	\i\ **tip**	\ȯ\ **saw**	\u̇\ **foot**
\ər\ **further**	\ch\ **chin**	\ī\ **life**	\ȯi\ **coin**	\y\ **yet**
\a\ **mat**	\e\ **pet**	\j\ **job**	\th\ **thin**	\yü\ **few**
\ā\ **take**	\ē\ **easy**	\ng\ **sing**	\th\ **this**	\yu̇\ **cure**
\ä\ **cot, cart**	\g\ **go**	\ō\ **bone**	\ü\ **food**	\zh\ **vision**

whose value determines one or more of the values of the other variables — compare DEPENDENT VARIABLE
in–depth \in-ˈdepth\ *adj* : THOROUGH 1, COMPREHENSIVE
in·de·scrib·able \ˌin-di-ˈskrī-bə-bəl\ *adj* : incapable of being described : being beyond description ⟨*indescribable* beauty⟩ — **in·de·scrib·able·ness** *n* — **in·de·scrib·ably** \-bə-blē\ *adv*
in·de·struc·ti·ble \ˌin-di-ˈstrək-tə-bəl\ *adj* : impossible to destroy — **in·de·struc·ti·bil·i·ty** \-ˌstrək-tə-bil-ət-ē\ *n* — **in·de·struc·ti·ble·ness** *n* — **in·de·struc·ti·bly** \-ˈstrək-tə-blē\ *adv*
in·de·ter·min·able \ˌin-di-ˈtərm-nə-bəl, -ə-nə-\ *adj* : incapable of being definitely decided or ascertained — **in·de·ter·min·able·ness** *n* — **in·de·ter·min·ably** \-blē\ *adv*
in·de·ter·mi·nate \ˌin-di-ˈtərm-nət, -ə-nət\ *adj* **1 a :** not definitely or precisely determined : VAGUE ⟨*indeterminate* plans⟩ **b :** not leading to a definite end or result **2 :** having the capacity for growing in length indefinitely; *esp* : having or being an inflorescence in which the main stem continues to grow without forming a terminal flower and the lower flowers on the stem bloom first — **in·de·ter·mi·na·cy** \-nə-sē\ *n* — **in·de·ter·mi·nate·ly** *adv* — **in·de·ter·mi·nate·ness** *n*
in·de·ter·mi·na·tion \-ˌtər-mə-ˈnā-shən\ *n* : a state of mental indecision
[1]**in·dex** \ˈin-ˌdeks\ *n, pl* **in·dex·es** *or* **in·di·ces** \-də-ˌsēz\ **1 a :** a device (as the pointer on a scale) that serves to indicate a value or quantity **b :** something (as a physical feature or mode of expression) that leads one to a particular fact or conclusion : INDICATION ⟨the price of goods is an *index* of business conditions⟩ **2 :** a guide (as a table or file) for facilitating reference; *esp* : an alphabetical list of items in a printed work that gives with each item the page number where it may be found **3** *pl usually indices* : a mathematical number, symbol, or expression associated with another to indicate a mathematical operation to be performed or to indicate use or position in an arrangement ⟨3 is the *index* in $\sqrt[3]{5}$ to specify a cube root of 5⟩ **4 :** a character ☞ used to direct attention — called also *fist* **5 :** a number (as a ratio) derived from a series of observations and used as an indicator or measure; *esp* : INDEX NUMBER [Latin *indic-, index,* from *indicare* "to indicate"] — **in·dex·i·cal** \in-ˈdek-si-kəl\ *adj*
[2]**index** *vt* **1 a :** to provide with an index **b :** to list in an index **2 :** to serve as an index of — **in·dex·er** *n*
index finger *n* : the finger next to the thumb
index fossil *n* : a fossil that is found over a relatively short span of geological time and can be used in dating formations in which it is found
index number *n* : a number used to indicate change in magnitude (as of cost or price) as compared with the magnitude at some other specified time
index of refraction : REFRACTIVE INDEX
in·dia ink \ˌin-dē-ə-\ *n, often cap 1st I* **1 :** a solid black pigment (as lampblack) used in drawing and lettering **2 :** a fluid consisting of a fine suspension of india ink in a liquid
In·dia·man \ˈin-dē-ə-mən\ *n* : a large sailing ship formerly used in trade with India
In·di·an \ˈin-dē-ən\ *n* **1 a :** a native or inhabitant of India or the East Indies **b :** a person of Indian descent **2 a :** AMERICAN INDIAN **b :** one of the native languages of American Indians [sense 2 from Columbus's belief that the lands he discovered were part of Asia] — **Indian** *adj*
Indian club *n* : a wooden club that resembles a tenpin and is swung for exercise
Indian corn *n* **1 :** [1]CORN 1 **2 :** [1]CORN 2 **3 :** [1]CORN 3 **4 :** corn that is of a variety having seeds of various colors (as reddish brown, dark purple, and yellow) and is typically used for ornamental purposes
Indian elephant *n* : ELEPHANT b
Indian giver *n, sometimes offensive* : a person who gives something to another and then takes it back or expects an equivalent in return — **Indian giving** *n*
Indian meal *n* : CORNMEAL
Indian paintbrush *n* **1 :** any of a large genus of chiefly American herbs related to the snapdragons and having spikes of flowers with brightly colored bracts **2 :** ORANGE HAWKWEED
Indian pipe *n* : a waxy white leafless saprophytic herb with a solitary nodding bell-shaped flower

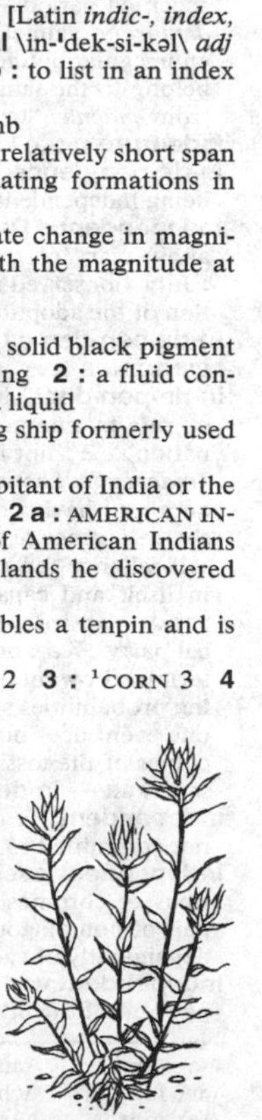
Indian paintbrush 1

Indian pudding *n* : a pudding made chiefly of cornmeal, milk, and molasses
Indian summer *n* : a period of mild weather in late autumn or early winter
Indian tobacco *n* : any of several plants resembling or used in place of tobacco; *esp* : a North American wild lobelia with small blue or white flowers
Indian wrestling *n* : any of various contests of strength or of strength and balance in which two individuals try to overcome each other using only one arm or one leg; *esp* : ARM WRESTLING
India paper *n* : a thin tough opaque printing paper
india rubber *n, often cap I* : RUBBER 2a
In·dic \ˈin-dik\ *adj* **1 :** of or relating to the subcontinent of India : INDIAN **2 :** of, relating to, or constituting the Indian branch of the Indo-European languages — **Indic** *n*
in·di·cate \ˈin-də-ˌkāt\ *vt* **1 a :** to point out or point to **b :** to be a sign, symptom, or index of **2 :** to state or express briefly : SUGGEST [Latin *indicare,* from *in-* + *dicare* "to proclaim"]
in·di·ca·tion \ˌin-də-ˈkā-shən\ *n* **1 :** the action of indicating **2 :** something that indicates : SIGN **3 :** the degree or amount indicated on a graduated instrument
[1]**in·dic·a·tive** \in-ˈdik-ət-iv\ *adj* **1 :** of, relating to, or constituting the grammatical mood that represents the denoted act or state as an objective fact ⟨in "I am here," the verb "am" is in the *indicative* mood⟩ **2 :** indicating something not visible or obvious : SUGGESTIVE ⟨remarks *indicative* of anger⟩ — **in·dic·a·tive·ly** *adv*
[2]**indicative** *n* : the indicative mood of a verb or a verb in this mood
in·di·ca·tor \ˈin-də-ˌkāt-ər\ *n* **1 :** one that indicates: as **a :** a pointer on an instrument (as a dial) **b :** a pressure gauge **2 :** a substance used to show visually (as by change of color) the condition of a solution with respect to the presence of free acid, alkali, or other substance — **in·dic·a·to·ry** \in-ˈdik-ə-ˌtōr-ē, -ˌtȯr-\ *adj*
indices *plural of* INDEX
in·di·cia \in-ˈdish-ə, -ˈdish-ē-ə\ *n pl* **1 :** distinctive marks : INDICATIONS **2 :** postal markings often imprinted on mail or on labels to be affixed to mail [Latin, pl. of *indicium* "sign," from *indicare* "to indicate"]
in·dict \in-ˈdīt\ *vt* **1 :** to charge with a fault or offense : ACCUSE **2 :** to charge with a crime by the finding of a grand jury [Medieval French *enditer* "to write down, indite"] — **in·dict·able** \-ə-bəl\ *adj* — **in·dict·er** *or* **in·dict·or** \-ˈdīt-ər\ *n*
in·dict·ment \in-ˈdīt-mənt\ *n* **1 :** the act or process of indicting **2 :** a formal statement charging a person with an offense that is drawn up by a prosecuting attorney and reported by a grand jury after an inquiry
in·dif·fer·ence \in-ˈdif-ərns, -ˈdif-rəns, -ˈdif-ə-rəns\ *n* **1 :** lack of feeling for or against something **2 :** lack of importance ⟨a matter of *indifference* to them⟩

synonyms INDIFFERENCE, UNCONCERN mean a lack of emotional responsiveness. INDIFFERENCE implies neutrality of feeling from lack of inclination, preference, or prejudice ⟨showed *indifference* toward the game's outcome⟩. UNCONCERN suggests a lack of sensitivity or regard for others' needs or troubles ⟨an *unconcern* for the poor and helpless⟩.

in·dif·fer·ent \in-ˈdif-ərnt, -ˈdif-rənt, -ˈdif-ə-rənt\ *adj* **1 :** having no preference : not interested or concerned ⟨*indifferent* to the troubles of others⟩ **2 :** showing neither liking nor dislike ⟨an *indifferent* audience⟩ **3 :** neither good nor bad : MEDIOCRE ⟨*indifferent* health⟩ **4 :** of no special influence or value : UNIMPORTANT **5 :** capable of development in more than one direction — **in·dif·fer·ent·ly** *adv*
in·di·gence \ˈin-di-jəns\ *n* : POVERTY 1, NEEDINESS
in·dig·e·nous \in-ˈdij-ə-nəs\ *adj* : originating in or produced, growing, or living naturally in a particular region or environment ⟨*indigenous* plants⟩ ⟨*indigenous* tribes⟩ [Late Latin *indigenus,* from Latin *indigena,* n., "native," derived from *indu, endo* "in, within" + *gignere* "to beget"] ***synonyms*** see NATIVE — **in·dig·e·nous·ly** *adv* — **in·dig·e·nous·ness** *n*
in·di·gent \ˈin-di-jənt\ *adj* : POOR 1, NEEDY [Medieval French, from Latin *indigēre* "to need"]
in·di·gest·ible \ˌin-dī-ˈjes-tə-bəl, -də-\ *adj* : not digestible : hard to digest — **in·di·gest·ibil·i·ty** \-ˌjes-tə-ˈbil-ət-ē\ *n*
in·di·ges·tion \-ˈjes-chən\ *n* **1 :** inability to digest or difficulty in digesting something **2 :** a case or attack of indigestion

marked especially by a burning sensation or discomfort in the upper stomach — **in·di·ges·tive** \-ˈjes-tiv\ *adj*

in·dig·nant \in-ˈdig-nənt\ *adj* **:** filled with or marked by indignation [Latin *indignari* "to be indignant," from *indignus* "unworthy," from *in-* + *dignus* "worthy"] — **in·dig·nant·ly** *adv*

in·dig·na·tion \ˌin-dig-ˈnā-shən\ *n* **:** anger aroused by something unjust, unworthy, or mean

in·dig·ni·ty \in-ˈdig-nət-ē\ *n, pl* **-ties** **1 :** an act that offends against a person's dignity or self-respect **:** INSULT **2 :** humiliating treatment ***synonyms*** see AFFRONT

in·di·go \ˈin-di-ˌgō\ *n, pl* **-gos** *or* **-goes** **1 :** a blue dye made artificially and formerly obtained from plants and especially indigo plants **2 :** a deep reddish blue [Italian dialect, from Latin *indicum,* from Greek *indikon,* from *indikos* "Indian," from *Indos* "India"]

indigo plant *n* **:** any of various plants especially of the legume family that yield indigo

indigo snake *n* **:** a very large harmless blue-black or brownish snake of the southern U.S. and Texas

in·di·rect \ˌin-də-ˈrekt, -dī-\ *adj* **1 :** not straight **:** not the shortest ⟨an *indirect* route⟩ **2 :** not straightforward **:** ROUNDABOUT ⟨*indirect* methods⟩ **3 :** not having a plainly seen connection ⟨an *indirect* cause⟩ **4 :** not going straight to the point ⟨an *indirect* accusation⟩ **5 :** stating what an original speaker said with changes in wording that adapt the statement grammatically to the rest of the sentence ⟨*they would come* in "they said that they would come" is in *indirect* discourse⟩ — **in·di·rect·ly** *adv* — **in·di·rect·ness** \-ˈrekt-nəs, -ˈrek-\ *n*

in·di·rec·tion \-ˈrek-shən\ *n* **1 :** lack of straightforwardness and openness **:** DECEITFULNESS **2 :** lack of direction **:** AIMLESSNESS

indirect lighting *n* **:** lighting in which the light emitted by a source is diffusely reflected (as by the ceiling)

indirect object *n* **:** a grammatical object representing the secondary goal of the action of its verb ⟨*me* in "gave me the book" is an *indirect object*⟩

in·dis·cern·ible \ˌin-dis-ˈər-nə-bəl, -diz-\ *adj* **:** incapable of being discerned

in·dis·creet \ˌin-dis-ˈkrēt\ *adj* **:** not discreet **:** IMPRUDENT — **in·dis·creet·ly** *adv* — **in·dis·creet·ness** *n*

in·dis·cre·tion \ˌin-dis-ˈkresh-ən\ *n* **1 :** lack of discretion **:** IMPRUDENCE **2 :** an indiscreet act or remark

in·dis·crim·i·nate \ˌin-dis-ˈkrim-nət, -ə-nət\ *adj* **:** showing lack of discrimination **:** not making careful distinctions ⟨an *indiscriminate* reader⟩ ⟨*indiscriminate* criticism⟩ — **in·dis·crim·i·nate·ly** *adv* — **in·dis·crim·i·nate·ness** *n*

in·dis·crim·i·na·tion \-ˌkrim-ə-ˈnā-shən\ *n* **:** lack of discrimination

in·dis·pens·able \ˌin-dis-ˈpen-sə-bəl\ *adj* **:** absolutely needed **:** ESSENTIAL ⟨an *indispensable* employee⟩ ***synonyms*** see NECESSARY — **in·dis·pens·abil·i·ty** \-ˌpen-sə-ˈbil-ət-ē\ *n* — **indispensable** *n* — **in·dis·pens·able·ness** \-ˈpen-sə-bəl-nəs\ *n* — **in·dis·pens·ably** \-blē\ *adv*

in·dis·pose \ˌin-dis-ˈpōz\ *vt* **1 :** to make unfit **:** DISQUALIFY **2 :** to make averse **:** DISINCLINE

in·dis·posed \-ˈpōzd\ *adj* **1 :** slightly ill **2 :** UNWILLING, AVERSE

in·dis·po·si·tion \ˌin-ˌdis-pə-ˈzish-ən\ *n* **1 :** a slight illness **2 :** AVERSION 1, RELUCTANCE

in·dis·put·able \ˌin-dis-ˈpyüt-ə-bəl; in-ˈdis-pyət-, ˈin-\ *adj* **:** not disputable **:** UNQUESTIONABLE ⟨*indisputable* proof⟩ — **in·dis·put·able·ness** *n* — **in·dis·put·ably** \-blē\ *adv*

in·dis·sol·u·ble \ˌin-dis-ˈäl-yə-bəl\ *adj* **:** not capable of being dissolved, undone, broken up, or decomposed ⟨an *indissoluble* contract⟩ — **in·dis·sol·u·bil·i·ty** \-ˌäl-yə-ˈbil-ət-ē\ *n* — **in·dis·sol·u·ble·ness** \-ˈäl-yə-bəl-nəs\ *n* — **in·dis·sol·u·bly** \-blē\ *adv*

in·dis·tinct \ˌin-dis-ˈtingt, -ˈtingkt\ *adj* **:** not distinct: as **a :** BLURRED ⟨*indistinct* figures in the fog⟩ **b :** FAINT 4a, DIM ⟨an *indistinct* light in the distance⟩ **c :** not clearly recognizable or understandable **:** UNCERTAIN — **in·dis·tinct·ly** *adv* — **in·dis·tinct·ness** *n*

in·dis·tinc·tive \-ˈting-tiv, -ˈtingk-\ *adj* **:** lacking distinctive qualities

in·dis·tin·guish·able \ˌin-dis-ˈting-gwish-ə-bəl\ *adj* **:** not capable of being clearly distinguished — **in·dis·tin·guish·able·ness** *n* — **in·dis·tin·guish·ably** \-blē\ *adv*

in·dite \in-ˈdīt\ *vt* **1 :** INVENT, COMPOSE ⟨*indite* a poem⟩ **2 :** to put down in writing ⟨*indite* a message⟩ [Medieval French *enditer* "to write down, proclaim," from Latin *indictus,* past participle of *indicere* "to proclaim," from *in-* + *dicere* "to say"] — **in·dit·er** *n*

in·di·um \ˈin-dē-əm\ *n* **:** a malleable fusible silvery metallic chemical element — see ELEMENT table [New Latin, from Latin *indicum* "indigo"; from the indigo lines in its spectrum]

[1]**in·di·vid·u·al** \ˌin-də-ˈvij-ə-wəl, -ˈvij-əl\ *adj* **1 a :** of or relating to an individual ⟨*individual* traits⟩ **b :** intended for one person ⟨*individual* servings⟩ **2 :** PARTICULAR, SEPARATE ⟨*individual* copies⟩ **3 :** having marked individuality ⟨an *individual* style⟩ [Medieval Latin *individualis* "inseparable, individual," from Latin *individuus* "indivisible," from *in-* + *dividere* "to divide"] ***synonyms*** see CHARACTERISTIC — **in·di·vid·u·al·ly** \-ē\ *adv*

[2]**individual** *n* **1 :** a particular being or thing as distinguished from a class, species, or collection **2 :** a particular person ⟨an odd *individual*⟩

in·di·vid·u·al·ism \-ˈvij-ə-wə-ˌliz-əm, -ˈvij-ə-ˌliz-\ *n* **1 :** a doctrine that the interests of the individual are of the greatest importance **2 :** a doctrine that the individual has certain political or economic rights with which the state must not interfere **3 a :** INDIVIDUALITY 1 **b :** an individual peculiarity **:** IDIOSYNCRASY

in·di·vid·u·al·ist \-ləst\ *n* **1 :** a person showing marked individuality or independence in thought or behavior **2 :** a supporter of individualism — **individualist** *or* **in·di·vid·u·al·is·tic** \-ˌvij-ə-wə-ˈlis-tik, -ˌvij-ə-ˈlis-\ *adj* — **in·di·vid·u·al·is·ti·cal·ly** \-ti-kə-lē, -klē\ *adv*

in·di·vid·u·al·i·ty \ˌin-də-ˌvij-ə-ˈwal-ət-ē\ *n, pl* **-ties** **1 :** the qualities that distinguish one person or thing from all others **2 :** the quality or state of existing as an individual **:** separate or distinct existence

in·di·vid·u·al·ize \-ˈvij-ə-wə-ˌlīz, -ˈvij-ə-ˌlīz\ *vt* **1 :** to make individual in character **2 :** to treat or notice individually **3 :** to adapt to the needs of an individual — **in·di·vid·u·al·iza·tion** \-ˌvij-ə-wə-lə-ˈzā-shən, -ˌvij-ə-lə-\ *n*

in·di·vis·i·ble \ˌin-də-ˈviz-ə-bəl\ *adj* **:** not capable of being divided or separated — **in·di·vis·i·bil·i·ty** \-ˌviz-ə-ˈbil-ət-ē\ *n* — **in·di·vis·i·ble·ness** \-ˈviz-ə-bəl-nəs\ *n* — **in·di·vis·i·bly** \-blē\ *adv*

Indo- *combining form* **1 :** India or the East Indies **2 :** Indo-European

In·do–Ar·y·an \ˌin-dō-ˈar-ē-ən, -ˈer-; -ˈär-yən\ *n* **1 :** a member of one of the peoples of the Indian subcontinent speaking an Indo-European language **2 :** one of the early Indo-European invaders of southern Asia **3 :** a branch of the Indo-European language family that includes Hindi, Bengali, Punjabi, and other languages spoken primarily in India, Pakistan, Bangladesh, and Sri Lanka — **Indo–Aryan** *adj*

in·doc·ile \in-ˈdäs-əl, ˈin-\ *adj* **:** unwilling to be taught or disciplined **:** INTRACTABLE — **in·do·cil·i·ty** \ˌin-dä-ˈsil-ət-ē, -dō-\ *n*

in·doc·tri·nate \in-ˈdäk-trə-ˌnāt\ *vt* **1 :** to instruct especially in fundamentals **2 :** to teach the beliefs or doctrines of a particular group — **in·doc·tri·na·tion** \in-ˌdäk-trə-ˈnā-shən\ *n* — **in·doc·tri·na·tor** \in-ˈdäk-trə-ˌnāt-ər\ *n*

[1]**In·do–Eu·ro·pe·an** \ˌin-dō-ˌyu̇r-ə-ˈpē-ən\ *adj* **:** of, relating to, or constituting a family of languages comprising those spoken in most of Europe and in the parts of the world colonized by Europeans since 1500 and also in Persia, the subcontinent of India, and some other parts of Asia

[2]**Indo–European** *n* **1 :** the Indo-European languages **2 :** a member of a people who originally spoke one of the Indo-European languages

in·dole·ace·tic acid \ˌin-ˌdōl-ə-ˌsēt-ik-\ *n* **:** a crystalline plant hormone that promotes growth and rooting of plants [*indole,* a crystalline compound, derived from Latin *indicum* "indigo"]

in·dole·bu·tyr·ic acid \-byü-ˌtir-ik-\ *n* **:** a crystalline acid similar to indoleacetic acid in its effects on plants

in·do·lent \ˈin-də-lənt\ *adj* **1 :** slow to develop or heal **2 :** averse to activity, effort, or movement **:** habitually lazy ⟨the heat made us *indolent*⟩ [Late Latin *indolens* "insensitive to pain," from Latin *in-* + *dolēre* "to feel pain"] — **in·do·lence** \-ləns\ *n* — **in·do·lent·ly** *adv*

in·dom·i·ta·ble \in-ˈdäm-ət-ə-bəl\ *adj* **:** incapable of being subdued : UNCONQUERABLE [Late Latin *indomitabilis,* from Latin *in-* + *domitare* "to tame, daunt"] — **in·dom·i·ta·bil·i·ty** \-ˌdäm-ət-ə-ˈbil-ət-ē\ *n* — **in·dom·i·ta·ble·ness** \-ˈdäm-ət-ə-bəl-nəs\ *n* — **in·dom·i·ta·bly** \-blē\ *adv*

synonyms INDOMITABLE, INVINCIBLE mean incapable of being conquered. INDOMITABLE stresses courage or determination that cannot be overcome or subdued ⟨an *indomitable* explorer⟩. INVINCIBLE more often applies to a person and implies having strength and ability superior to all others ⟨an *invincible* warrior⟩.

In·do·ne·sian \ˌin-də-ˈnē-zhən, -shən\ *n* **1 :** a native or inhabitant of the Malay archipelago **2 a :** a native or inhabitant of the Republic of Indonesia **b :** the language based on Malay that is the national language of the Republic of Indonesia — **Indonesian** *adj*

in·door \ˌin-ˌdōr, -ˌdȯr\ *adj* **1 :** of or relating to the interior of a building **2 :** done, living, used, or belonging within a building ⟨an *indoor* sport⟩

in·doors \in-ˈdōrz, ˈin-, -ˈdȯrz\ *adv* **:** in or into a building ⟨games to be played *indoors*⟩

indorse, indorsement *variant of* ENDORSE, ENDORSEMENT

in·du·bi·ta·ble \in-ˈdü-bət-ə-bəl, ˈin-, -ˈdyü-\ *adj* **:** too evident to be doubted **:** UNQUESTIONABLE — **in·du·bi·ta·ble·ness** *n* — **in·du·bi·ta·bly** \-blē\ *adv*

in·duce \in-ˈdüs, -ˈdyüs\ *vt* **1 :** to lead on to do something **:** PERSUADE **2 :** BRING ABOUT, CAUSE ⟨an illness *induced* by overwork⟩ **3 :** to conclude or infer by reasoning from particular instances **4 :** to produce (as an electric current) by induction [Latin *inducere,* from *in-* + *ducere* "to lead"] — **in·duc·er** *n* — **in·duc·ible** \-ˈdü-sə-bəl, -ˈdyü-\ *adj*

in·duce·ment \in-ˈdü-smənt, -ˈdyü-\ *n* **1 :** the act of inducing **2 :** something that induces ⟨advertising gimmicks that are mere *inducements* to buy⟩

in·duct \in-ˈdəkt\ *vt* **1 :** to place formally in office **:** INSTALL **2 :** to enroll into military service [Medieval Latin *inductus,* past participle of *inducere* "to induct," from Latin, "to lead in, induce"] — **in·duct·ee** \ˌin-ˌdək-ˈtē\ *n*

in·duc·tance \in-ˈdək-təns\ *n* **:** a property of an electric circuit by which an electromotive force is induced in it by a variation of current either in the circuit itself or in a neighboring circuit

in·duc·tion \in-ˈdək-shən\ *n* **1 a :** the act or process of inducting (as into office) **b :** an initial experience **:** INITIATION **c :** the procedure by which a civilian is inducted into military service **2 a :** reasoning from particular instances to a general conclusion; *also* **:** the conclusion so reached **b :** mathematical demonstration of the validity of a law concerning all positive whole numbers by proving that the law holds for the number 1 and that if it holds for any positive whole number k then it also holds for $k + 1$ **3 a :** the act of causing or bringing on or about **b :** the process by which an electrical conductor becomes electrified when near a charged body, by which a body becomes magnetized when in a magnetic field or in the flux set up by a magnetizing force, or by which an electromotive force is produced in a circuit by varying the magnetic field linked with the circuit **c :** the way in which one embryonic tissue or structure influences the development and differentiation of another

induction coil *n* **:** an apparatus for obtaining intermittent high voltage consisting of a primary coil through which the direct current flows, an interrupter, and a secondary coil of a larger number of turns in which the high voltage is induced

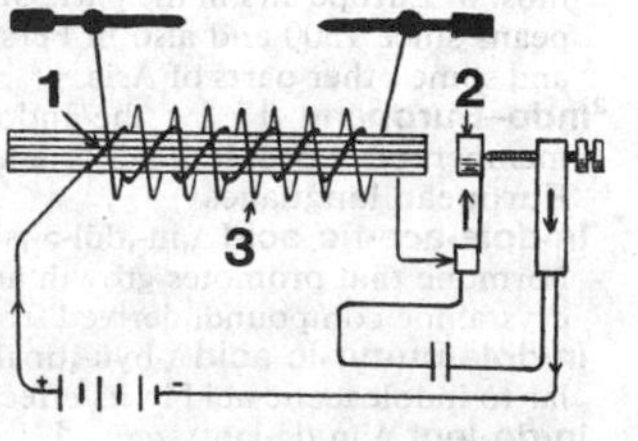

induction coil: *1* primary coil, *2* interrupter, *3* secondary coil

induction heating *n* **:** the heating of material by means of an electric current that is caused to flow through the material or its container by electromagnetic induction

in·duc·tive \in-ˈdək-tiv\ *adj* **:** relating to, employing, or based on induction — **in·duc·tive·ly** *adv*

in·duc·tor \in-ˈdək-tər\ *n* **1 :** one that inducts **2 :** a part of an electrical apparatus that acts upon another or is itself acted upon by induction **3 :** ORGANIZER 2

indue *variant of* ENDUE

in·dulge \in-ˈdəlj\ *vb* **1 :** to give in to one's own or another's desires **:** HUMOR ⟨*indulged* their grandchildren's whims⟩ **2 :** to allow oneself the pleasure of having or doing something ⟨decided to *indulge* in an ice cream sundae⟩ [Latin *indulgēre*] — **in·dulg·er** *n*

in·dul·gence \in-ˈdəl-jəns\ *n* **1 :** a release from punishment in this world or in purgatory gained by performing pious acts authorized by the Roman Catholic Church **2 a :** the act of indulging **:** the state of being indulgent **b :** an indulgent act **c :** something indulged in

in·dul·gent \-jənt\ *adj* **:** disinclined to be severe or rigorous **:** LENIENT ⟨an *indulgent* parent⟩ — **in·dul·gent·ly** *adv*

in·dult \ˈin-ˌdəlt, in-ˈ\ *n* **:** a special often temporary privilege granted in the Roman Catholic Church [Medieval Latin *indultum,* from Latin *indultus,* past participle of *indulgēre* "to indulge"]

[1]in·du·rate \ˈin-də-rət, -dyə-; in-ˈdu̇r-ət, -ˈdyu̇r-\ *adj* **:** physically or morally hardened

[2]in·du·rate \ˈin-də-ˌrāt, -dyə-\ *vb* **1 :** to make unfeeling, stubborn, or obdurate **2 :** to make hardy **:** INURE **3 :** to make firm or hard ⟨great heat *indurates* clay⟩ ⟨*indurated* tissue⟩ **4 :** to grow hard **:** HARDEN [Latin *indurare,* from *in-* + *durare* "to harden," from *durus* "hard"] — **in·du·ra·tion** \ˌin-də-ˈrā-shən, -dyə-\ *n* — **in·du·ra·tive** \ˈin-də-ˌrāt-iv, -dyə-; in-ˈdu̇r-ət-, -ˈdyu̇r-\ *adj*

in·du·rat·ed \-ˌrāt-əd\ *adj* **:** having become firm or hard ⟨*indurated* volcanic ash⟩

in·dus·tri·al \in-ˈdəs-trē-əl\ *adj* **1 :** of, relating to, or engaged in industry **2 :** characterized by highly developed industries ⟨an *industrial* nation⟩ **3 :** derived from human industry ⟨*industrial* wealth⟩ **4 :** used in industry ⟨*industrial* diamonds⟩ — **in·dus·tri·al·ly** \-trē-ə-lē\ *adv*

industrial arts *n sing or pl* **:** a subject taught in elementary and secondary schools that aims at developing manual skill and familiarity with tools and machines

in·dus·tri·al·ism \in-ˈdəs-trē-ə-ˌliz-əm\ *n* **:** social organization in which large-scale industries are dominant

in·dus·tri·al·ist \-ləst\ *n* **:** one owning or engaged in the management of an industry **:** MANUFACTURER

in·dus·tri·al·ize \in-ˈdəs-trē-ə-ˌlīz\ *vb* **:** to make or become industrial ⟨*industrialize* an agricultural region⟩ — **in·dus·tri·al·i·za·tion** \-ˌdəs-trē-ə-lə-ˈzā-shən\ *n*

industrial revolution *n* **:** a rapid major change in an economy (as in England in the late 18th century) marked by the general introduction of power-driven machinery or by an important change in the prevailing types and methods of use of such machines

industrial school *n* **:** a school specializing in the teaching of the industrial arts

industrial union *n* **:** a labor union open to workers in an industry irrespective of their occupation or craft — compare TRADE UNION

in·dus·tri·ous \in-ˈdəs-trē-əs\ *adj* **:** constantly, regularly, or habitually active or occupied **:** DILIGENT ⟨an *industrious* worker⟩ ***synonyms*** see BUSY — **in·dus·tri·ous·ly** *adv* — **in·dus·tri·ous·ness** *n*

in·dus·try \ˈin-dəs-trē, -ˌdəs-\ *n, pl* **-tries** **1 :** diligence in an employment or pursuit; *esp* **:** steady or habitual effort **2 a :** systematic labor especially for some useful purpose or the creation of something of value ⟨live by one's own *industry*⟩ **b :** a department or branch of a craft, art, business, or manufacture; *esp* **:** one that employs a large number of persons and considerable capital usually in manufacturing **c :** a distinct group of productive or profit-making enterprises ⟨the steel *industry*⟩ ⟨the tourist *industry*⟩ **d :** manufacturing activity as a whole ⟨commerce and *industry*⟩ [Medieval French *industrie* "diligence," from Latin *industria*] ***synonyms*** see BUSINESS

[1]-ine \ˌīn, ən, in, ˌin, ˌēn\ *adj suffix* **1 :** of or relating to ⟨alkal*ine*⟩ **2 :** made of **:** like ⟨opal*ine*⟩ [sense 1 from Latin *-īnus;* sense 2 from Latin *-īnus,* from Greek *-inos*]

[2]-ine \ˌēn, ˈēn, ən, in, ˌin\ *n suffix* **1 :** chemical substance: as **a :** halogen element ⟨chlor*ine*⟩ **b :** basic or base-containing carbon compound that contains nitrogen ⟨cyst*ine*⟩ **c :** mixture of compounds (as of hydrocarbons) ⟨gasol*ine*⟩ **d :** hydride ⟨ar*sine*⟩ **2 :** neutral chemical compound [Latin *-īna,* from *-īnus,* adj. suffix]

ine·bri·ate \in-ˈē-brē-ˌāt\ *vt* **:** to make drunk **:** INTOXICATE [Latin *inebriare,* from *in-* + *ebrius* "drunk"] — **ine·bri·ate** \-brē-ət\ *adj or n* — **ine·bri·a·tion** \in-ˌē-brē-ˈā-shən\ *n*

ine·bri·at·ed *adj* **:** affected by or as if by alcohol **:** INTOXICATED

in·e·bri·e·ty \ˌin-i-ˈbrī-ət-ē\ *n* : the state of being inebriated : DRUNKENNESS

in·ed·i·ble \in-ˈed-ə-bəl, ˈin-\ *adj* : not fit or safe for food ⟨*inedible* mushrooms⟩

in·ed·u·ca·ble \in-ˈej-ə-kə-bəl\ *adj* : incapable of being educated

in·ef·fa·ble \-ˈef-ə-bəl\ *adj* : INEXPRESSIBLE, UNUTTERABLE ⟨*ineffable* bliss⟩ [Medieval French, from Latin *ineffabilis,* from *in-* + *effari* "to utter," from *ex-* + *fari* "to speak"] — **in·ef·fa·bil·i·ty** \in-ˌef-ə-ˈbil-ət-ē\ *n* — **in·ef·fa·ble·ness** \in-ˈef-ə-bəl-nəs, ˈin-\ *n* — **in·ef·fa·bly** \-blē\ *adv*

in·ef·face·able \ˌin-ə-ˈfā-sə-bəl\ *adj* : not effaceable : INERADICABLE ⟨an *ineffaceable* memory⟩

in·ef·fec·tive \ˌin-ə-ˈfek-tiv\ *adj* **1** : not producing an intended effect : INEFFECTUAL ⟨an *ineffective* law⟩ **2** : not performing as well as expected or needed : INCAPABLE ⟨an *ineffective* leader⟩ — **in·ef·fec·tive·ly** *adv* — **in·ef·fec·tive·ness** *n*

in·ef·fec·tu·al \ˌin-ə-ˈfek-chə-wəl, -ˈfek-chəl, -ˈfeksh-wəl\ *adj* **1** : not producing the proper or usual effect : FUTILE ⟨an *ineffectual* attempt⟩ **2** : INEFFECTIVE 2 — **in·ef·fec·tu·al·ly** \-ē\ *adv* — **in·ef·fec·tu·al·ness** *n*

in·ef·fi·ca·cious \ˌin-ˌef-ə-ˈkā-shəs\ *adj* : lacking the power to produce a desired effect : INADEQUATE — **in·ef·fi·ca·cious·ly** *adv* — **in·ef·fi·ca·cious·ness** *n* — **in·ef·fi·ca·cy** \-ˈef-ə-kə-sē\ *n*

in·ef·fi·cien·cy \ˌin-ə-ˈfish-ən-sē\ *n, pl* **-cies** **1** : the quality or state of being inefficient **2** : something that is inefficient

in·ef·fi·cient \ˌin-ə-ˈfish-ənt\ *adj* : not efficient : as **a** : not producing the intended or desired effect ⟨*inefficient* regulations⟩ **b** : wasteful of time or energy ⟨*inefficient* operating procedures⟩; *esp* : accomplishing little relative to the time spent or effort expended ⟨an *inefficient* worker⟩ — **in·ef·fi·cient·ly** *adv*

in·elas·tic \ˌin-ə-ˈlas-tik\ *adj* **1** : not elastic **2** : slow to respond to changing conditions — **in·elas·tic·i·ty** \ˌin-i-ˌlas-ˈtis-ət-ē\ *n*

in·el·e·gance \in-ˈel-i-gəns, ˈin-\ *n* : lack of elegance

in·el·e·gant \in-ˈel-i-gənt, ˈin-\ *adj* : lacking in refinement, grace, or good taste — **in·el·e·gant·ly** *adv*

in·el·i·gi·ble \in-ˈel-ə-jə-bəl, ˈin-\ *adj* : not qualified or worthy to be chosen — **in·el·i·gi·bil·i·ty** \ˌin-ˌel-ə-jə-ˈbil-ət-ē\ *n* — **ineligible** *n*

in·eluc·ta·ble \ˌin-i-ˈlək-tə-bəl\ *adj* : not to be avoided, changed, or resisted : INEVITABLE ⟨an *ineluctable* fate⟩ [Latin *ineluctabilis,* from *in-* + *eluctari* "to struggle clear of," from *ex-* + *luctari* "to struggle"] — **in·eluc·ta·bil·i·ty** \-ˌlək-tə-ˈbil-ət-ē\ *n* — **in·eluc·ta·bly** \-ˈlək-tə-blē\ *adv*

in·ept \in-ˈept\ *adj* **1** : lacking in fitness or aptitude : UNFIT **2** : not suited to the occasion : INAPPROPRIATE **3** : lacking sense or reason : FOOLISH **4** : generally incompetent : BUNGLING [Middle French *inepte,* from Latin *ineptus,* from *in-* + *aptus* "apt"] ***synonyms*** see AWKWARD — **in·ep·ti·tude** \-ˈep-tə-ˌtüd, -ˌtyüd\ *n* — **in·ept·ly** *adv* — **in·ept·ness** \-ˈept-nəs, -ˈep-nəs\ *n*

in·equal·i·ty \ˌin-i-ˈkwäl-ət-ē\ *n* **1** : the quality of being unequal or uneven **2** : an instance of being unequal (as an irregularity in a surface) **3** : a formal logical or mathematical statement that two quantities usually separated by a special sign (as <, >, or ≠ respectively meaning "is less than," "is greater than," or "is not equal to") are not equal

in·eq·ui·ta·ble \in-ˈek-wət-ə-bəl, ˈin-\ *adj* : not equitable : UNFAIR, UNJUST — **in·eq·ui·ta·bly** \-blē\ *adv*

in·eq·ui·ty \-wət-ē\ *n* **1** : INJUSTICE 1, UNFAIRNESS **2** : an instance of injustice or unfairness

in·erad·i·ca·ble \ˌin-i-ˈrad-i-kə-bəl\ *adj* : incapable of being eradicated ⟨an *ineradicable* belief⟩

in·ert \in-ˈərt\ *adj* **1** : not having the power to move itself **2** : deficient in active properties; *esp* : lacking a usual or anticipated chemical or biological action **3** : very slow to move or act : SLUGGISH [Latin *inert-, iners* "unskilled, idle," from *in-* + *art-, ars* "skill, art"] ***synonyms*** see INACTIVE — **in·ert·ly** *adv* — **in·ert·ness** *n*

in·er·tia \in-ˈər-shə, -shē-ə\ *n* **1** : a property of matter by which it remains at rest or in uniform motion in the same straight line unless acted upon by some external force; *also* : an analogous property of other physical quantities (as electricity) **2** : a disposition not to move, change, or exert oneself : INERTNESS [Latin, "lack of skill," from *iners* "unskilled"] — **in·er·tial** \-shəl\ *adj*

inertial guidance *n* : guidance (as of a spacecraft) by means of self-contained automatically controlling devices that respond to changes in velocity or direction

in·es·cap·able \ˌin-ə-ˈskā-pə-bəl\ *adj* : incapable of being escaped : INEVITABLE — **in·es·cap·ably** \-blē\ *adv*

in·es·sen·tial \ˌin-ī-ˈsen-chəl\ *adj* **1** : having no essence or being **2** : not essential

in·es·ti·ma·ble \in-ˈes-tə-mə-bəl, ˈin-\ *adj* **1** : incapable of being estimated or computed ⟨the storm caused *inestimable* damage⟩ **2** : too valuable or excellent to be measured or appreciated — **in·es·ti·ma·bly** \-blē\ *adv*

in·ev·i·ta·ble \in-ˈev-ət-ə-bəl\ *adj* : bound to happen : CERTAIN [Latin *inevitabilis,* from *in-* + *evitare* "to avoid," from *ex-* + *vitare* "to shun"] — **in·ev·i·ta·bil·i·ty** \in-ˌev-ət-ə-ˈbil-ət-ē\ *n* — **in·ev·i·ta·ble·ness** \in-ˈev-ət-ə-bəl-nəs, ˈin-\ *n*

in·ev·i·ta·bly \-blē\ *adv* **1** : in an inevitable way ⟨they *inevitably* become good friends⟩ **2** : as is to be expected ⟨*inevitably,* it rained⟩

in·ex·act \ˌin-ig-ˈzakt\ *adj* : not precisely correct or true : INACCURATE ⟨*inexact* measurements⟩ — **in·ex·ac·ti·tude** \-ˈzak-tə-ˌtüd, -ˌtyüd\ *n* — **in·ex·act·ly** \-ˈzak-tlē, -lē\ *adv* — **in·ex·act·ness** \-ˈzakt-nəs, -ˈzak-\ *n*

in·ex·cus·able \ˌin-ik-ˈskyü-zə-bəl\ *adj* : impossible to excuse or justify ⟨*inexcusable* rudeness⟩ — **in·ex·cus·able·ness** *n* — **in·ex·cus·ably** \-blē\ *adv*

in·ex·haust·ible \ˌin-ig-ˈzȯ-stə-bəl\ *adj* **1** : plentiful enough not to give out or be used up : UNFAILING ⟨an *inexhaustible* supply⟩ **2** : not subject to fatigue or wear — **in·ex·haust·ibil·i·ty** \-ˌzȯ-stə-ˈbil-ət-ē\ *n* — **in·ex·haust·ibly** \-ˈzȯ-stə-blē\ *adv*

in·ex·o·ra·ble \in-ˈeks-rə-bəl, ˈin-, -ə-rə-\ *adj* : not to be persuaded or moved by entreaty : RELENTLESS [Latin *inexorabilis,* from *in-* + *exorabilis* "pliant," from *exorare* "to prevail upon," from *ex-* + *orare* "to speak"] — **in·ex·o·ra·bil·i·ty** \in-ˌeks-rə-ˈbil-ət-ē, -ə-rə-\ *n* — **in·ex·o·ra·ble·ness** \in-ˈeks-rə-bəl-nəs, -ə-rə-\ *n* — **in·ex·o·ra·bly** \-blē\ *adv*

in·ex·pe·di·ent \ˌin-ik-ˈspēd-ē-ənt\ *adj* : not suited to bring about a desired result : UNWISE — **in·ex·pe·di·en·cy** \-ən-sē\ *n* — **in·ex·pe·di·ent·ly** *adv*

in·ex·pen·sive \ˌin-ik-ˈspen-siv\ *adj* : reasonable in price : CHEAP — **in·ex·pen·sive·ly** *adv* — **in·ex·pen·sive·ness** *n*

in·ex·pe·ri·ence \ˌin-ik-ˈspir-ē-əns\ *n* **1** : lack of practical experience **2** : lack of knowledge of the ways of the world — **in·ex·pe·ri·enced** \-ənst\ *adj*

in·ex·pert \in-ˈek-ˌspərt, ˌin-ik-ˈ\ *adj* : not expert : UNSKILLED — **in·ex·pert·ly** *adv* — **in·ex·pert·ness** *n*

in·ex·plain·able \ˌin ik-ˈsplā-nə-bəl\ *adj* : INEXPLICABLE ⟨an *inexplainable* feeling⟩

in·ex·plic·able \ˌin-ik-ˈsplik-ə-bəl; in-ˈek-splik-, ˈin-\ *adj* : incapable of being explained, interpreted, or accounted for — **in·ex·plic·abil·i·ty** \ˌin-ik-ˌsplik-ə-ˈbil-ət-ē, in-ˌek-splik-ə-ˈbil-\ *n* — **in·ex·plic·able·ness** \ˌin-ik-ˈsplik-ə-bəl-nəs; in-ˈek-splik-, ˈin-\ *n* — **in·ex·plic·ably** \-blē\ *adv*

in·ex·plic·it \ˌin-ik-ˈsplis-ət\ *adj* : not explicit ⟨*inexplicit* directions⟩

in·ex·press·ible \ˌin-ik-ˈspres-ə-bəl\ *adj* : being beyond one's power to express : INDESCRIBABLE ⟨*inexpressible* joy⟩ — **in·ex·press·ibil·i·ty** \-ˌspres-ə-ˈbil-ət-ē\ *n* — **in·ex·press·ible·ness** \-ˈspres-ə-bəl-nəs\ *n* — **in·ex·press·ibly** \-blē\ *adv*

in·ex·pres·sive \-ˈspres-iv\ *adj* : lacking expression or meaning ⟨an *inexpressive* face⟩ — **in·ex·pres·sive·ly** *adv* — **in·ex·pres·sive·ness** *n*

in·ex·tin·guish·able \ˌin-ik-ˈsting-gwish-ə-bəl\ *adj* : impossible to extinguish ⟨an *inextinguishable* longing⟩

in ex·tre·mis \ˌin-ik-ˈstrā-məs, -ˌmēs\ *adv* : in extreme circumstances; *esp* : at the point of death [Latin]

in·ex·tric·able \ˌin-ik-ˈstrik-ə-bəl; in-ˈek-strik-, ˈin-\ *adj* **1** : forming a tangle from which one cannot free oneself **2** : not capable of being disentangled ⟨an *inextricable* knot⟩ — **in·ex·tric·ably** \-blē\ *adv*

in·fal·li·ble \in-ˈfal-ə-bəl, ˈin-\ *adj* **1** : not capable of being wrong ⟨an *infallible* memory⟩ **2** : not liable to fail, deceive, or disappoint : CERTAIN ⟨an *infallible* remedy⟩ — **in·fal·li·bil·i·ty** \in-ˌfal-ə-ˈbil-ət-ē\ *n* — **in·fal·li·bly** \in-ˈfal-ə-blē, ˈin-\ *adv*

in·fal·ling \ˈin-ˌfȯ-liŋ\ *adj* **:** moving under the influence of gravity toward a celestial object (as a star or black hole)

in·fa·mous \ˈin-fə-məs\ *adj* **1 :** having an evil reputation ⟨an *infamous* person⟩ **2 :** DETESTABLE, DISGRACEFUL ⟨an *infamous* crime⟩ [Latin *infamis,* from *in-* + *fama* "fame, reputation"] — **in·fa·mous·ly** *adv*

in·fa·my \-mē\ *n, pl* **-mies 1 :** evil reputation brought about by something grossly criminal, shocking, or brutal **2 a :** an infamous act **b :** the state of being infamous

in·fan·cy \ˈin-fən-sē\ *n, pl* **-cies 1 :** early childhood **2 :** a beginning or early period of existence **3 :** the legal status of a minor

[1]in·fant \ˈin-fənt\ *n* **1 :** a child in the first period of life **2 :** MINOR 1 [Medieval French *enfaunt,* from Latin *infans,* from *infans* "incapable of speech, young," from *in-* + *fari* "to speak"]

Word History Latin *infans* means literally "not speaking, incapable of speech." In classical Latin the noun *infans* designated a very young child who had not yet learned to talk. But later *infans* became the most common word for any child, however talkative. In the Romance languages, too, the descendants of Latin *infans* are words that mean "child." In English the word *infant,* which was borrowed from the French, was originally used for any child. But the word usually is used now in the earlier Latin sense "a very young child, a baby."

[2]infant *adj* **:** of, relating to, or being in infancy

in·fan·ti·cide \in-ˈfant-ə-ˌsīd\ *n* **1 :** the killing of an infant **2 :** one who deliberately kills an infant

in·fan·tile \ˈin-fən-ˌtīl, -təl, -ˌtēl\ *adj* **:** of, relating to, or resembling infants or infancy; *also* **:** CHILDISH — **in·fan·til·i·ty** \ˌin-fən-ˈtil-ət-ē\ *n*

infantile paralysis *n* **:** POLIOMYELITIS

in·fan·til·ism \ˈin-fən-ˌtīl-ˌiz-əm, -təl-, -ˌtēl-\ *n* **:** retention of childish physical or emotional qualities in adult life

in·fan·try \ˈin-fən-trē\ *n, pl* **-tries 1 :** soldiers trained, armed, and equipped to fight on foot **2 :** a branch of an army composed of infantry [Middle French *infanterie,* from Italian *infanteria,* from *infante* "boy, foot soldier," from Latin *infans* "infant"] — **in·fan·try·man** \-mən\ *n*

Word History In the Middle Ages in France, a young soldier of good family who had not yet been made a knight was called *enfant,* which means literally "child." Similarly, in Italy one of the soldiers who followed a mounted knight on foot was an *infante.* Soon foot soldiers collectively became *infanteria,* which was borrowed into French as *infanterie* and into English as *infantry.*

in·farct \ˈin-ˌfärkt\ *n* **:** an area of dead tissue (as of the heart wall) caused by blockage of local blood circulation [Latin *infarctus,* past participle of *infarcire* "to stuff in," from *in-* + *farcire* "to stuff"] — **in·farc·tion** \in-ˈfärk-shən\ *n*

in·fat·u·ate \in-ˈfach-ə-ˌwāt\ *vt* **:** to fill with a foolish or extravagant love or admiration [Latin *infatuare,* from *in-* + *fatuus* "fatuous"] — **in·fat·u·a·tion** \in-ˌfach-ə-ˈwā-shən\ *n*

in·fea·si·ble \(ˌ)in-ˈfē-zə-bəl\ *adj* **:** not feasible **:** IMPRACTICABLE ⟨an *infeasible* plan⟩ — **in·fea·si·bil·i·ty** \-ˌfē-zə-ˈbil-ət-ē\ *n*

in·fect \in-ˈfekt\ *vt* **1 :** to contaminate with a disease-producing substance or organism ⟨*infected* bedding⟩ **2 a :** to communicate a germ or disease to ⟨coughing people who *infect* others⟩ **b :** to enter and cause disease in ⟨bacteria that *infect* wounds⟩ **c :** to become copied to ⟨a virus has *infected* the computer⟩ **3 :** to cause to share one's feelings ⟨*infected* everyone with their enthusiasm⟩ [Latin *infectus,* past participle of *inficere* "to infect," from *in-* "[3]in" + *facere* "to make, do"] — **in·fec·tor** \-ˈfek-tər\ *n*

in·fec·tion \in-ˈfek-shən\ *n* **1 :** an act or process of infecting **2 a :** the state produced by the establishment of a germ in or on a suitable host **b :** a disease resulting from infection **3 :** an infective agent (as a bacterium or virus); *also* **:** material contaminated with an infective agent **4 :** the communication of emotions or qualities through example or contact

in·fec·tious \in-ˈfek-shəs\ *adj* **1 a :** capable of causing infection ⟨*infectious* viruses⟩ **b :** communicable by infection ⟨*infectious* diseases⟩ **2 :** spreading or capable of spreading rapidly to others ⟨their enthusiasm was *infectious*⟩ — **in·fec·tious·ly** *adv* — **in·fec·tious·ness** *n*

infectious mononucleosis *n* **:** an acute infectious disease characterized by fever, swelling of the lymph glands, and an abnormal increase in the number of lymphocytes in the blood

in·fec·tive \in-ˈfek-tiv\ *adj* **:** producing or able to produce infection — **in·fec·tiv·i·ty** \in-ˌfek-ˈtiv-ət-ē\ *n*

in·fe·lic·i·tous \ˌin-fi-ˈlis-ət-əs\ *adj* **:** not apt **:** not suitably chosen for the occasion ⟨an *infelicitous* remark⟩ — **in·fe·lic·i·tous·ly** *adv*

in·fe·lic·i·ty \-ət-ē\ *n, pl* **-ties 1 :** a lack of suitability or aptness **2 :** an unsuitable or inappropriate act or utterance

in·fer \in-ˈfər\ *vt* **in·ferred; in·fer·ring 1 :** to derive as a conclusion from facts or premises **2 :** GUESS 1, SURMISE **3 :** HINT, SUGGEST [Latin *inferre,* literally, "to carry into," from *in-* + *ferre* "to carry"] — **in·fer·able** \-ˈfər-ə-bəl\ *adj* — **in·fer·rer** \-ˈfər-ər\ *n*

usage *Infer* is mostly used to mean to arrive at a conclusion and is commonly followed by *from* ⟨I *infer* from your letter that everything was satisfactory⟩. *Imply* is used to mean to draw attention to a fact or relationship by suggestion or hint rather than by direct statement ⟨the letter *implies* that the service was not satisfactory⟩. The use of *infer* with a personal subject in the sense of imply (as in "Are you *inferring* that I made a mistake?") is widely criticized as a confusion, though in any given context, in fact, the meaning is never in doubt. Further, the use is mostly oral and has seldom been a problem in edited prose in recent years.

in·fer·ence \ˈin-fə-rəns, -frəns\ *n* **1 :** the act or process of inferring **2 :** something inferred; *esp* **:** a proposition arrived at by inference

in·fe·ri·or \in-ˈfir-ē-ər\ *adj* **1 a :** situated lower down **b :** situated below another usually similar part of the upright body ⟨*inferior* vena cava⟩ **2 :** of low or lower degree or rank **3 :** of little or less importance, value, or merit [Latin, comparative of *inferus* "low, situated beneath"] — **inferior** *n* — **in·fe·ri·or·i·ty** \in-ˌfir-ē-ˈȯr-ət-ē, -ˈär\ *n* — **in·fe·ri·or·ly** \in-ˈfir-ē-ər-lē\ *adv*

inferiority complex *n* **:** an acute sense of personal inferiority resulting either in timidity or in exaggerated aggressiveness

inferior planet *n* **:** a planet (as Venus) whose orbit lies closer to the sun than that of Earth

inferior vena cava *n* **:** a branch of the vena cava that returns blood to the heart from the lower parts of the body including the internal organs below the lungs and the lower limbs

in·fer·nal \in-ˈfərn-l\ *adj* **1 :** of or relating to a netherworld of the dead **2 a :** of or relating to hell **b :** suggestive of or appropriate to hell **:** FIENDISH **3 :** DAMNABLE 2 ⟨an *infernal* nuisance⟩ [Medieval French, from Late Latin *infernus* "hell," from Latin, "lower"] — **in·fer·nal·ly** \-l-ē\ *adv*

infernal machine *n* **:** an apparatus designed to explode and destroy life or property

in·fer·no \in-ˈfər-nō\ *n, pl* **-nos :** a place or a state that resembles or suggests hell especially in intense heat or raging fire [Italian, "hell," from Late Latin *infernus*]

in·fer·tile \in-ˈfərt-l, ˈin-\ *adj* **:** not fertile or productive **:** BARREN — **in·fer·til·i·ty** \ˌin-fər-ˈtil-ət-ē\ *n*

in·fest \in-ˈfest\ *vt* **1 :** to spread or swarm in or over in a troublesome manner ⟨a neighborhood *infested* with crime⟩ ⟨shark-*infested* waters⟩ **2 :** to live in or on as a parasite ⟨horses *infested* with worms⟩ [Middle French *infester,* from Latin *infestare,* from *infestus* "hostile"] — **in·fes·ta·tion** \ˌin-ˌfes-ˈtā-shən\ *n* — **in·fest·er** \in-ˈfes-tər\ *n*

in·fi·del \ˈin-fəd-l, -fə-ˌdel\ *n* **:** a person who does not believe in a particular religion [Medieval French *infidele,* from Latin *infidelis* "unfaithful," from *in-* + *fidelis* "faithful," from *fides* "faith"] — **infidel** *adj*

in·fi·del·i·ty \ˌin-fə-ˈdel-ət-ē, -fī-\ *n, pl* **-ties 1 :** lack of faith in a religion **2 :** unfaithfulness especially to one's spouse

in·field \ˈin-ˌfēld\ *n* **1 :** the area of a baseball field enclosed by the three bases and home plate **2 :** the area enclosed by a racetrack or running track — **in·field·er** \-ˌfēl-dər\ *n*

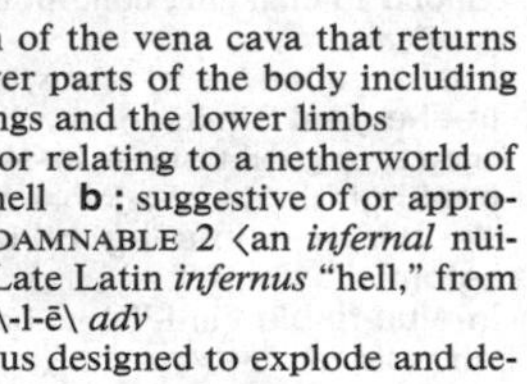

infield 1

in·fight·ing \ˈin-ˌfīt-iŋ\ *n* **1 :** fighting or boxing at close quarters **2 :** prolonged and often bitter disagreement among members of a group — **in·fight·er** *n*

in·fil·trate \in-ˈfil-ˌtrāt, ˈin-fil-\ *vb* **1 :** to pass into or through by filtering or permeating **2 :** to enter or become established gradually or inconspicuously — **in·fil·tra·tion** \ˌin-fil-ˈtrā-shən\ *n* — **in·fil·tra·tor** \ˈin-fil-ˌtrāt-ər, in-ˈfil-\ *n*

in·fi·nite \ˈin-fə-nət\ *adj* **1 :** being without limits of any kind

: ENDLESS ⟨*infinite* space⟩ **2 :** seeming to be without limits : VAST, INEXHAUSTIBLE ⟨*infinite* patience⟩ ⟨*infinite* wealth⟩ **3 a :** extending, lying, or being beyond any preassigned value however large ⟨the number of positive numbers is *infinite*⟩ **b :** having an infinite number of elements or terms ⟨an *infinite* set⟩ — **infinite** *n* — **in·fi·nite·ly** *adv* — **in·fi·nite·ness** *n*

in·fin·i·tes·i·mal \in-ˌfin-ə-ˈtes-ə-məl\ *adj* **:** immeasurably or incalculably small — **in·fin·i·tes·i·mal·ly** \-mə-lē\ *adv*

in·fin·i·tive \in-ˈfin-ət-iv\ *n* **:** an uninflected verb form serving as a noun or as a modifier and yet showing certain characteristics of a verb (as association with objects and adverbial modifiers) ⟨*have* in "let me have it" and *to run* in "able to run fast" are *infinitives*⟩ — **infinitive** *adj*

in·fin·i·tude \in-ˈfin-ə-ˌtüd, -ˌtyüd\ *n* **1 :** INFINITY 1a **2 :** something infinite especially in extent **3 :** an infinite number or quantity

in·fin·i·ty \in-ˈfin-ət-ē\ *n, pl* **-ties 1 a :** the quality of being infinite **b :** unlimited extent of time, space, or quantity **2 :** INFINITUDE 3 **3 :** a distance so great that the rays of light from a point source at that distance may be regarded as parallel ⟨a camera focused at *infinity*⟩

in·firm \in-ˈfərm\ *adj* **1 :** poor or weakened in vitality; *esp* **:** feeble from age **2 :** not solid or stable : INSECURE — **in·firm·ly** *adv*

in·fir·ma·ry \in-ˈfərm-rē, -ə-rē\ *n, pl* **-ries :** a place (as in a school or factory) where sick or injured people ar cared for; *also* : HOSPITAL

in·fir·mi·ty \in-ˈfər-mət-ē\ *n, pl* **-ties 1 :** the quality or state of being infirm : FEEBLENESS, FRAILTY **2 a :** DISEASE 1, AILMENT **b :** a personal failing : FOIBLE

in fla·gran·te de·lic·to \ˌin-flə-ˌgränt-ē-di-ˈlik-tō, -ˌgrant-\ *adv* **:** in the very act of committing a misdeed [Medieval Latin, "while the crime is blazing"]

in·flame \in-ˈflām\ *vb* **1 :** to set on fire : KINDLE **2 a :** to excite to excessive or uncontrollable action or feeling; *esp* **:** to make angry **b :** to make more heated or violent : INTENSIFY ⟨insults served only to *inflame* the feud⟩ **3 :** to cause to redden or grow hot from anger or excitement **4 :** to cause inflammation in (bodily tissue) **5 :** to become affected with inflammation — **in·flam·er** *n*

in·flam·ma·ble \in-ˈflam-ə-bəl\ *adj* **1 :** FLAMMABLE **2 :** easily inflamed : EXCITABLE — **in·flam·ma·bil·i·ty** \-ˌflam-ə-ˈbil-ət-ē\ *n* — **inflammable** *n* — **in·flam·ma·ble·ness** \-ˈflam-ə-bəl-nəs\ *n* — **in·flam·ma·bly** \-blē\ *adv*

in·flam·ma·tion \ˌin-flə-ˈmā-shən\ *n* **1 :** the act of inflaming : the state of being inflamed **2 :** a local bodily response to injury in which an affected area becomes red, hot, painful, and congested with blood

in·flam·ma·to·ry \in-ˈflam-ə-ˌtōr-ē, -ˌtȯr-\ *adj* **1 :** tending to excite anger, disorder, or tumult **2 :** causing or accompanied by inflammation ⟨*inflammatory* diseases⟩

in·flate \in-ˈflāt\ *vb* **1 :** to swell with air or gas ⟨*inflate* a balloon⟩ **2 :** to puff up : ELATE ⟨*inflated* with pride⟩ **3 :** to increase abnormally ⟨*inflated* prices⟩ ⟨*inflated* currency⟩ [Latin *inflare,* from *in-* + *flare* "to blow"] ***synonyms*** see EXPAND — **in·flat·able** \in-ˈflāt-ə-bəl\ *adj* — **in·fla·tor** \-ˈflāt-ər\ *n*

in·fla·tion \in-ˈflā-shən\ *n* **1 a :** an act of inflating : the state of being inflated **b :** a hypothetical period of very fast expansion of the universe immediately after the big bang **2 :** a continuing rise in the general price level usually attributed to an increase in the volume of money and credit relative to available goods and services

in·fla·tion·ary \-shə-ˌner-ē\ *adj* **:** of, relating to, or tending to cause inflation ⟨*inflationary* policies⟩

in·flect \in-ˈflekt\ *vb* **1 :** to turn from a direct line or course : CURVE **2 :** to vary a word by inflection **3 :** to vary the pitch of the voice [Latin *inflectere,* from *in-* + *flectere* "to bend"]

in·flec·tion \in-ˈflek-shən\ *n* **1 :** the act or result of curving or bending **2 :** a change in the pitch of a person's voice **3 :** the change in the form of a word showing its case, gender, number, person, tense, mood, voice, or comparison — **in·flec·tion·al** \-shnəl, -shən-l\ *adj* — **in·flec·tion·al·ly** \-ē\ *adv*

in·flex·ible \in-ˈflek-sə-bəl, ˈin-\ *adj* **1 :** not easily bent or twisted : RIGID, STIFF **2 :** not easily influenced or persuaded : FIRM ⟨an *inflexible* judge⟩ **3 :** incapable of change ⟨*inflexible* laws⟩ — **in·flex·ibil·i·ty** \in-ˌflek-sə-ˈbil-ət-ē\ *n* — **in·flex·ibly** \in-ˈflek-sə-blē, ˈin-\ *adv*

in·flict \in-ˈflikt\ *vt* **1 :** to give by or as if striking ⟨*inflict* a wound⟩ **2 :** to cause (something damaging or painful) to be endured : IMPOSE ⟨*inflict* punishment⟩ [Latin *inflictus,* past participle of *infligere* "to inflict," from *in-* + *fligere* "to strike"] — **in·flic·tion** \in-ˈflik-shən\ *n* — **in·flic·tive** \-ˈflik-tiv\ *adj*

in·flo·res·cence \ˌin-flə-ˈres-ns\ *n* **1 a :** the mode of development and arrangement of flowers on a stem **b :** a flowering stem with all its parts; *also* **:** a flower cluster or sometimes a solitary flower **2 :** the forming and unfolding of blossoms [Late Latin *inflorescere* "to begin to bloom," from Latin *in-* + *florescere* "to begin to bloom," from *florēre* "to blossom, flourish"] — **in·flo·res·cent** \-nt\ *adj*

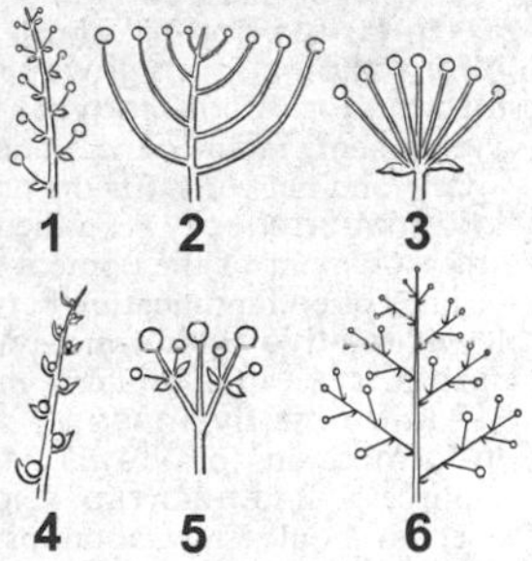

inflorescence 1a: *1* raceme, *2* corymb, *3* umbel, *4* spike, *5* cyme, *6* panicle

in·flow \ˈin-ˌflō\ *n* **1 :** the act of flowing in **2 :** something that flows in

[1]in·flu·ence \ˈin-ˌflü-əns\ *n* **1 :** the act or power of producing an effect without apparent exertion of force or direct exercise of command **2 :** corrupt interference with authority for personal gain **3 :** a person or thing that exerts influence [Medieval French, from Medieval Latin *influentia* "ethereal fluid thought to flow from the stars and affect people's actions," from Latin *influere* "to flow in," from *in-* + *fluere* "to flow"]

[2]influence *vt* **1 :** to affect or alter (as behavior) by indirect or intangible means **2 :** to have an effect on the condition or development of : MODIFY — **in·flu·enc·er** *n*

synonyms INFLUENCE, AFFECT, SWAY mean to produce or have an effect upon. INFLUENCE is used of a force that brings about a change or determines a course of action or behavior ⟨traditions that *influenced* resistance to change⟩. AFFECT implies a stimulus strong enough to bring about a reaction or modification without a total change ⟨rainfall *affects* the growth of plants⟩ ⟨the new law *affects* only some aspects of commerce⟩. SWAY suggests that the forces either are not resisted or are irresistible and bring about a change ⟨advertising that *sways* public taste⟩.

in·flu·en·tial \ˌin-flü-ˈen-chəl\ *adj* **:** having or exerting influence — **in·flu·en·tial·ly** \-ˈench-lē, -ə-lē\ *adv*

in·flu·en·za \ˌin-flü-ˈen-zə\ *n* **1 :** an acute and very contagious virus disease with sudden onset, fever, exhaustion, severe aches and pains, and inflammation of the respiratory tract **2 :** any of various usually virus diseases of humans or domestic animals that are typically marked by fever and respiratory symptoms and often affect the whole body [Italian, literally, "influence," from Medieval Latin *influentia*]

Word History Italian *influenza* has the same meaning as its English cognate *influence.* But in the 15th century sudden epidemics whose earthly causes were not apparent were blamed on the influence of the stars, so in Italy epidemic diseases were given the name *influenza.* The report of a Roman epidemic which spread through much of Europe in 1743 brought the word to England.

in·flux \ˈin-ˌfləks\ *n* **:** a flowing in : INFLOW [Medieval Latin *influxus,* from Latin *influere* "to flow in"]

in·fold *vb* **1** \in-ˈfōld\ **:** ENFOLD **2** \ˈin-ˌfōld\ **:** to fold inward or toward one another

in·form \in-ˈfȯrm\ *vb* **1 :** to let a person know something : TELL **2 :** to give information so as to accuse or cast suspicion ⟨*inform* against someone to the police⟩ [Medieval French *enformer* "to give form to, inform," from Latin *informare,* from *in-* + *forma* "form"]

in·for·mal \in-ˈfȯr-məl, ˈin-\ *adj* **1 :** conducted or carried out without formality or ceremony **2 :** appropriate for ordinary or casual use ⟨*informal* clothes⟩ — **in·for·mal·i·ty** \ˌin-fȯr-ˈmal-ət-ē, -fər-\ *n* — **in·for·mal·ly** \in-ˈfȯr-mə-lē, ˈin-\ *adv*

in·for·mant \in-ˈfȯr-mənt\ *n* **:** INFORMER

in·for·ma·tion \ˌin-fər-ˈmā-shən\ *n* **1 :** the communication or

reception of knowledge or intelligence **2 a :** knowledge obtained from investigation, study, or instruction **b :** knowledge of a particular event or situation : NEWS **c :** FACT 3, DATA **d :** a signal or mark put into or put out by a computing machine — **in·for·ma·tion·al** \-shnəl, -shən-ᵊl\ *adj*
information superhighway *n* : INTERNET
information technology *n* : the technology involving the development, maintenance, and use of computer systems, software, and networks for the processing and distribution of data
information theory *n* : a theory that deals statistically with the measurement of the content of information and with the efficiency of communication between humans and machines
in·for·ma·tive \in-ˈfȯr-mət-iv\ *adj* : imparting knowledge : INSTRUCTIVE ⟨an *informative* meeting⟩ — **in·for·ma·tive·ly** *adv* — **in·for·ma·tive·ness** *n*
in·formed \in-ˈfȯrmd\ *adj* **1 :** having information ⟨*informed* sources⟩ **2 :** EDUCATED, KNOWLEDGEABLE ⟨what an *informed* person should know about psychology⟩
in·form·er \in-ˈfȯr-mər\ *n* : one that informs; *esp* : a person who informs against someone else
infra- *prefix* **1 :** below ⟨*infra*human⟩ ⟨*infra*sonic⟩ **2 :** below in a scale or series ⟨*infra*red⟩ [Latin *infra*]
in·frac·tion \in-ˈfrak-shən\ *n* : the act of infringing : VIOLATION [Latin *infractio,* from *infractus,* past participle of *infringere* "to infringe"]
in·fra·hu·man \ˌin-frə-ˈhyü-mən, -ˈyü-\ *adj* : less or lower than human ⟨*infrahuman* primates⟩ — **infrahuman** *n*
in·fra·red \ˌin-frə-ˈred, -frä-\ *adj* **1 :** lying outside the visible spectrum at its red end — used of heat radiation of wavelengths longer than those of visible light **2 :** relating to, producing, or employing infrared radiation — **infrared** *n*
in·fra·son·ic \-ˈsän-ik\ *adj* **1 :** having a frequency below the audibility range of the human ear **2 :** utilizing or produced by infrasonic waves or vibrations
in·fra·struc·ture \ˈin-frə-ˌstrək-chər\ *n* **1 :** the underlying foundation or basic framework (as of a system or organization) **2 :** the system of public works of a country, state, or region; *also* : the resources (as personnel, buildings, or equipment) required for an activity
in·fre·quent \in-ˈfrē-kwənt, ˈin-\ *adj* **1 :** seldom happening or occurring : RARE ⟨*infrequent* disagreements⟩ **2 :** placed or occurring at considerable distances or intervals ⟨made *infrequent* stops⟩ — **in·fre·quen·cy** \-kwən-sē\ *n* — **in·fre·quent·ly** *adv*
synonyms INFREQUENT, UNCOMMON, SPORADIC mean not common or abundant. INFREQUENT implies occurrence at wide intervals in time or space ⟨*infrequent* family visits⟩ ⟨*infrequent* road signs⟩. UNCOMMON suggests a frequency below normal expectation ⟨litter is now *uncommon* along roadways⟩. SPORADIC implies occurrence in scattered instances or isolated outbursts ⟨*sporadic* cases of influenza⟩.
in·fringe \in-ˈfrinj\ *vb* **1 :** to fail to obey or act in agreement with : VIOLATE 1 ⟨*infringe* a treaty⟩ ⟨*infringe* a patent⟩ **2 :** ENCROACH 1 ⟨*infringe* upon a person's rights⟩ [Latin *infringere,* literally, "to break off," from *in-* "[2]in-" + *frangere* "to break"] — **infringement** *n* — **in·fring·er** *n*
in·fun·dib·u·lum \ˌin-fən-ˈdib-yə-ləm\ *n, pl* **-la** \-lə\ : any of various funnel-shaped organs or parts (as the stalk by which the pituitary gland is connected to the hypothalamus) [Latin, "funnel," from *infundere* "to pour in," from *in-* + *fundere* "to pour"] — **in·fun·dib·u·lar** \-lər\ *adj*
in·fu·ri·ate \in-ˈfyu̇r-ē-ˌāt\ *vt* : to make furious : ENRAGE — **in·fu·ri·at·ing·ly** \-ˌāt-ing-lē\ *adv* — **in·fu·ri·a·tion** \-ˌfyu̇r-ē-ˈā-shən\ *n*
in·fuse \in-ˈfyüz\ *vt* **1 :** to put in as if by pouring ⟨*infused* courage into their followers⟩ **2 :** to make full ⟨*infused* with a desire to help⟩ **3 :** to steep (as tea) without boiling [Latin *infusus,* past participle of *infundere* "to pour in," from *in-* + *fundere* "to pour"] — **in·fus·er** *n*
synonyms INFUSE, SUFFUSE, IMBUE mean to introduce one thing into another so as to affect it throughout. INFUSE implies a pouring in of something that gives new life or significance ⟨new members *infused* enthusiasm into the club⟩. SUFFUSE implies a spreading through of something that gives an unusual color or quality ⟨a room *suffused* with light⟩. IMBUE implies the introduction of a quality that fills and permeates the whole being ⟨*imbue* students with intellectual curiosity⟩.
in·fus·ible \in-ˈfyü-zə-bəl, ˈin-\ *adj* : difficult or impossible to fuse ⟨*infusible* clays⟩ — **in·fus·ibil·i·ty** \in-ˌfyü-zə-ˈbil-ət-ē\ *n* — **in·fus·ible·ness** \in-ˈfyü-zə-bəl-nəs, ˈin-\ *n*
in·fu·sion \in-ˈfyü-zhən\ *n* **1 :** the act or process of infusing ⟨an *infusion* of new ideas⟩ **2 :** a product extracted especially from a plant material by infusing **3 :** the continuous slow introduction of a solution (as of glucose) into a vein
in·fu·so·ri·an \ˌin-fyü-ˈzōr-ē-ən, -ˈzȯr-\ *n* : any of a heterogeneous group of minute organisms found especially in decomposing infusions of organic matter; *esp* : a ciliated protozoan — **in·fu·so·ri·al** \-ē-əl\ *or* **infusorian** *adj*
[1]-ing \ing; *in some dialects usually, in other dialects informally,* ən, in, *or* (*after certain consonants*) ᵊn, ᵊm, ᵊng\ *vb suffix or adj suffix* — used to form the present participle ⟨sail*ing*⟩ and sometimes to form an adjective resembling a present participle but not derived from a verb ⟨swashbuckl*ing*⟩ [Middle English, from Old English *-ung, -ing, ēn*]
[2]-ing *n suffix* : one of a (specified) kind ⟨sweet*ing*⟩ [Old English *-ing, -ung*]
[3]-ing *n suffix* **1 :** action or process ⟨runn*ing*⟩ ⟨sleep*ing*⟩: instance of an action or process ⟨a meet*ing*⟩ **2 a :** product or result of an action or process ⟨an engrav*ing*⟩ — often in plural ⟨earn*ings*⟩ **b :** something used in an action or process ⟨a bed cover*ing*⟩ **3 :** action or process connected with (a specified thing) ⟨boat*ing*⟩ **4 :** something connected with, consisting of, or used in making (a specified thing) ⟨roof*ing*⟩ **5 :** something related to (a specified concept) ⟨off*ing*⟩ [Old English, suffix forming nouns from verbs]
in·gath·er·ing \ˈin-ˌgath-ring, -ə-ring\ *n* **1 :** COLLECTION 1, HARVEST **2 :** ASSEMBLY 3
in·ge·nious \in-ˈjē-nyəs\ *adj* : having or showing ingenuity : very clever [Middle French *ingenieus,* from Latin *ingeniosus,* from *ingenium* "natural capacity," from *in-* + *gignere* "to beget"] — **in·ge·nious·ly** *adv* — **in·ge·nious·ness** *n*
in·ge·nue *or* **in·gé·nue** \ˈan-jə-ˌnü, ˈän-; ˈa^{n}-zhə-, ˈä^{n}-\ *n* : a naive girl or young woman; *also* : an actress representing such a person [French *ingénue,* from *ingénu* "ingenuous," from Latin *ingenuus*]
in·ge·nu·i·ty \ˌin-jə-ˈnü-ət-ē, -ˈnyü-\ *n, pl* **-ties** **1 a :** skill or cleverness in devising or combining : INVENTIVENESS **b :** cleverness or aptness of design or contrivance **2 :** an ingenious device or contrivance [obsolete *ingenuity* "ingenuousness"]
in·gen·u·ous \in-ˈjen-yə-wəs\ *adj* **1 :** FRANK 1 **2 :** showing innocent or childlike simplicity : NAIVE [Latin *ingenuus* "native, freeborn, ingenuous," from *in-* + *gignere* "to beget"] — **in·gen·u·ous·ly** *adv* — **in·gen·u·ous·ness** *n*
in·gest \in-ˈjest\ *vt* : to take in for or as if for digestion [Latin *ingestus,* past participle of *ingerere* "to carry in," from *in-* + *gerere* "to carry"] — **in·gest·ible** \-ˈjes-tə-bəl\ *adj* — **in·ges·tion** \-ˈjes-chən\ *n* — **in·ges·tive** \-ˈjes-tiv\ *adj*
in·ges·ta \in-ˈjes-tə\ *n pl* : material taken into the body by way of the mouth [New Latin]
in·gle \ˈing-gəl, -əl\ *n* **1 :** a fire in a fireplace **2 :** an indoor fireplace [Scottish Gaelic *aingeal*]
in·gle·nook \-ˌnu̇k\ *n* **1 :** a corner by the fire or chimney **2 :** a high-backed wooden bench placed close to a fireplace

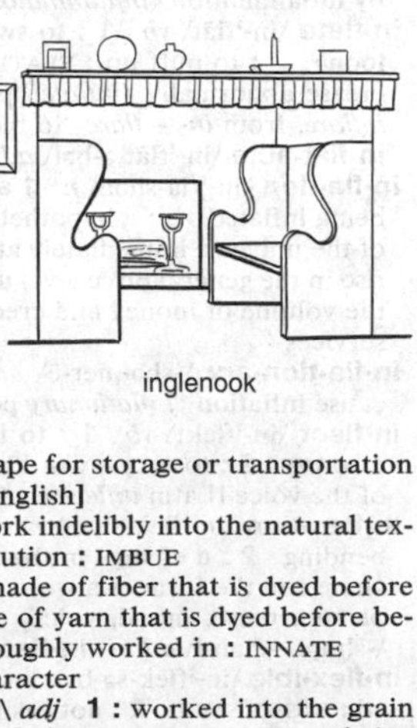
inglenook

in·glo·ri·ous \in-ˈglōr-ē-əs, ˈin-, -ˈglȯr-\ *adj* **1 :** not glorious : lacking fame or honor **2 :** bringing disgrace : SHAMEFUL ⟨*inglorious* defeat⟩ — **in·glo·ri·ous·ly** *adv* — **in·glo·ri·ous·ness** *n*
in·got \ˈing-gət\ *n* : a mass of metal cast into a convenient shape for storage or transportation to be later processed [Middle English]
[1]in·grain \in-ˈgrān, ˈin-\ *vt* : to work indelibly into the natural texture or mental or moral constitution : IMBUE
[2]in·grain \ˈin-ˌgrān\ *adj* **1 a :** made of fiber that is dyed before being spun into yarn **b :** made of yarn that is dyed before being woven or knitted **2 :** thoroughly worked in : INNATE
[3]ingrain *n* : innate quality or character
in·grained \ˈin-ˌgrānd, in-ˈ, ˈin-ˈ\ *adj* **1 :** worked into the grain or fiber **2 :** forming a part of the essence or inmost being : DEEP-SEATED ⟨*ingrained* prejudice⟩ — **in·grain·ed·ly** \-ˈgrā-nəd-lē, -ˈgrā-\ *adv*
in·grate \ˈin-ˌgrāt\ *n* : an ungrateful person [Latin *ingratus* "ungrateful," from *in-* + *gratus* "grateful"]

in·gra·ti·ate \in-ˈgrā-shē-ˌāt\ *vt* : to gain favor or favorable acceptance for by deliberate effort ⟨*ingratiate* oneself with a new boss⟩ [[2]*in-* + Latin *gratia* "grace"] — **in·gra·ti·a·tion** \-ˌgrā-shē-ˈā-shən\ *n* — **in·gra·tia·to·ry** \-ˈgrā-shə-ˌtōr-ē, -shē-ə-, -ˌtȯr-\ *adj*

in·gra·ti·at·ing *adj* **1** : capable of winning favor : PLEASING ⟨an *ingratiating* smile⟩ **2** : intended or adopted in order to gain favor ⟨*ingratiating* manners⟩ — **in·gra·ti·at·ing·ly** \-ˌāt-ing-lē\ *adv*

in·grat·i·tude \in-ˈgrat-ə-ˌtüd, ˈin-, -ˌtyüd\ *n* : forgetfulness of or poor return for kindness received : UNGRATEFULNESS

in·gre·di·ent \in-ˈgrēd-ē-ənt\ *n* : one of the substances that make up a mixture ⟨*ingredients* of a cake⟩ [Latin *ingrediens,* present participle of *ingredi* "to go into," from *in-* + *gradi* "to go"] ***synonyms*** see ELEMENT — **ingredient** *adj*

in·gress \ˈin-ˌgres\ *n* **1** : the act of entering : ENTRANCE **2** : the power or liberty of entrance or access ⟨free *ingress* to the circus grounds⟩ [Latin *ingressus,* from *ingredi* "to go into"]

in·ground \ˈin-ˌgraund\ *adj* : built into the ground ⟨an *inground* pool⟩

in·grow·ing \ˈin-ˌgrō-ing\ *adj* : growing or tending inward

in·grown \-ˌgrōn\ *adj* : grown in; *esp* : having the free tip or edge embedded in the flesh ⟨an *ingrown* toenail⟩ — **in·grown·ness** \-ˌgrōn-nəs\ *n*

in·growth \ˈin-ˌgrōth\ *n* **1** : a growing inward (as to fill a void) **2** : something that grows in or into a space

in·gui·nal \ˈing-gwən-l\ *adj* : of, relating to, or located in the region of the groin [Latin *inguinalis,* from *inguen* "groin"]

in·gur·gi·tate \in-ˈgər-jə-ˌtāt\ *vt* : to swallow greedily or in large quantity [Latin *ingurgitare,* from *in-* + *gurges* "whirlpool"] — **in·gur·gi·ta·tion** \-ˌgər-jə-ˈtā-shən\ *n*

in·hab·it \in-ˈhab-ət\ *vt* : to live or dwell in [Latin *inhabitare,* from *in-* + *habitare* "to dwell," from *habēre* "to have"] — **in·hab·it·able** \-ə-bəl\ *adj* — **in·hab·i·ta·tion** \-ˌhab-ə-ˈtā-shən\ *n* — **in·hab·it·er** \-ˈhab-ət-ər\ *n*

in·hab·it·an·cy \-ən-sē\ *n* : OCCUPANCY

in·hab·it·ant \in-ˈhab-ət-ənt\ *n* : one that lives permanently in a place

[1]**in·hal·ant** \in-ˈhā-lənt\ *n* : something (as an allergen or medicated spray) that is inhaled

[2]**inhalant** *adj* **1** : of or relating to an inhalant **2** : INCURRENT ⟨an *inhalant* siphon of a clam⟩

in·ha·la·tion \ˌin-hə-ˈlā-shən, ˌin-ə-ˈlā-, ˌin-l-ˈā-\ *n* : the act or an instance of inhaling — **in·ha·la·tion·al** \-shnəl, -shən-l\ *adj*

in·ha·la·tor \ˈin-hə-ˌlāt-ər, ˈin-ə-ˌlāt-, ˈin-l-ˌāt-\ *n* : a device used in inhaling something (as oxygen and carbon dioxide); *esp* : INHALER 1

in·hale \in-ˈhāl\ *vb* **1** : to draw in by breathing **2** : to breathe in [[2]*in-* + *-hale* (as in *exhale*)]

in·hal·er \in-ˈhā-lər\ *n* **1** : a device by means of which medicinal material is inhaled **2** : one that inhales

in·har·mon·ic \ˌin-här-ˈmän-ik\ *adj* : not harmonic

in·har·mo·ni·ous \-ˈmō-nē-əs\ *adj* : not harmonious : DISCORDANT ⟨*inharmonious* sounds⟩ ⟨*inharmonious* ideas⟩ — **in·har·mo·ni·ous·ly** *adv* — **in·har·mo·ni·ous·ness** *n*

in·here \in-ˈhiər\ *vi* : to be inherent : BELONG ⟨power to make laws *inheres* in the state⟩ [*inhaerēre,* from *in-* + *haerēre* "to stick, adhere"]

in·her·ent \in-ˈhir-ənt, -ˈher-\ *adj* : belonging to or being a part of the nature of a person or thing : INTRINSIC ⟨an *inherent* sense of fair play⟩ ⟨fluidity is an *inherent* quality of gas⟩ — **in·her·ence** \-əns\ *n* — **in·her·ent·ly** *adv*

in·her·it \in-ˈher-ət\ *vt* **1** : to come into possession of : RECEIVE **2** : to receive by legal right from a person at the person's death **3 a** : to receive by genetic transmission ⟨*inherit* blue eyes⟩ **b** : to have handed on to one by a predecessor ⟨the president *inherited* the problem of unemployment⟩ [Medieval French *enheriter* "to make heir," from Late Latin *inhereditare,* from Latin *in-* + *hereditas* "inheritance," from *hered-, heres* "heir"] — **in·her·i·tor** \-ət-ər\ *n* — **in·her·i·tress** \-ə-trəs\ *or* **in·her·i·trix** \-ə-ˌtriks\ *n*

in·her·it·able \in-ˈher-ət-ə-bəl\ *adj* : capable of being inherited — **in·her·it·able·ness** *n*

in·her·it·ance \in-ˈher-ət-əns\ *n* **1** : the act of inheriting **2** : something that is or may be inherited ***synonyms*** see HERITAGE

in·hib·it \in-ˈhib-ət\ *vt* **1** : to prevent or hold back from doing something : RESTRAIN, REPRESS ⟨fear can *inhibit* the natural expression of feelings⟩ **2** : to prevent or slow down the activity or occurrence of ⟨oil *inhibits* rust⟩ ⟨a drug which *inhibits* an infection⟩ [Latin *inhibitus,* past participle of *inhibēre* "to inhibit," from *in-* + *habēre* "to have, hold"] ***synonyms*** see FORBID — **in·hib·i·tive** \-ət-iv\ *adj* — **in·hib·i·to·ry** \-ə-ˌtōr-ē, -ˌtȯr-\ *adj*

in·hib·it·ed \-ət-əd\ *adj* : finding it difficult to show desires, feelings, and thoughts

in·hi·bi·tion \ˌin-ə-ˈbish-ən, ˌin-hə-\ *n* **1 a** : the act of inhibiting : the state of being inhibited **b** : something that forbids **2** : an inner force that interferes with free activity, expression, or functioning

in·hib·i·tor \in-ˈhib-ət-ər\ *n* : one that inhibits; *esp* : an agent that slows or interferes with a chemical action ⟨rust *inhibitor*⟩

in·hos·pi·ta·ble \ˌin-ˌhäs-ˈpit-ə-bəl; in-ˈhäs-pit-, ˈin-\ *adj* **1** : not showing hospitality **2** : providing no shelter or food : BARREN ⟨miles of *inhospitable* desert⟩ — **in·hos·pi·ta·ble·ness** *n* — **in·hos·pi·ta·bly** \-blē\ *adv*

in·hos·pi·tal·i·ty \in-ˌhäs-pə-ˈtal-ət-ē\ *n* : the quality or state of being inhospitable

in·hu·man \in-ˈhyü-mən, in-ˈyü-, ˈin-\ *adj* **1 a** : lacking pity or kindness : SAVAGE **b** : lacking human warmth : IMPERSONAL **c** : not fit, adequate, or worthy to meet human needs ⟨living in *inhuman* conditions⟩ **2** : of or suggesting a nonhuman class of beings — **in·hu·man·ly** *adv* — **in·hu·man·ness** \-əs\ *n*

in·hu·mane \ˌin-hyü-ˈmān, ˌin-yü-\ *adj* : not humane : INHUMAN 1 ⟨inhumane treatment of prisoners⟩ — **in·hu·mane·ly** *adv*

in·hu·man·i·ty \-ˈman-ət-ē\ *n, pl* **-ties** **1** : the quality or state of being cruel or barbarous **2** : a cruel or barbarous act

in·hume \in-ˈhyüm\ *vt* : BURY 1, INTER [derived from Medieval Latin *inhumare,* from Latin *in-* + *humus* "earth"]

in·im·i·cal \in-ˈim-i-kəl\ *adj* **1 a** : having the disposition of an enemy : HOSTILE **b** : reflecting or indicating hostility : UNFRIENDLY ⟨*inimical* stares⟩ **2** : HARMFUL, ADVERSE ⟨habits *inimical* to health⟩ [Late Latin *inimicalis,* from Latin *inimicus* "enemy"] — **in·im·i·cal·ly** \-ˈim-i-kə-lē, -klē\ *adv*

in·im·i·ta·ble \in-ˈim-ət-ə-bəl, ˈin-\ *adj* : not capable of being imitated : MATCHLESS ⟨her own *inimitable* style⟩ — **in·im·i·ta·bil·i·ty** \in-ˌim-ət-ə-ˈbil-ət-ē\ *n* — **in·im·i·ta·ble·ness** \in-ˈim-ət-ə-bəl-nəs, ˈin-\ *n* — **in·im·i·ta·bly** \-blē\ *adv*

in·iq·ui·tous \in-ˈik-wət-əs\ *adj* : characterized by iniquity : WICKED — **in·iq·ui·tous·ly** *adv* — **in·iq·ui·tous·ness** *n*

in·iq·ui·ty \in-ˈik-wət-ē\ *n, pl* **-ties** **1** : shameful injustice : WICKEDNESS **2** : an unjust or wicked act or thing [Medieval French *iniquité,* from Latin *iniquitas,* from *iniquus* "uneven, unfair," from *in-* + *aequus* "equal, fair"]

[1]**ini·tial** \in-ˈish-əl\ *adj* **1** : of, relating to, or existing at the beginning : INCIPIENT ⟨*initial* stages of a disease⟩ **2** : placed or standing at the beginning : FIRST ⟨the *initial* letter of a word⟩ [Latin *initialis,* from *initium* "beginning," from *inire* "to go in," from *in-* + *ire* "to go"] — **ini·tial·ly** \in-ˈish-lē, -ə-lē\ *adv*

[2]**initial** *n* **1** : the first letter of a name **2** : a large letter beginning a text or a division or paragraph

[3]**initial** *vt* **ini·tialed** *or* **ini·tialled; ini·tial·ing** *or* **ini·tial·ling** \-ˈish-ling, -ə-ling\ : to affix initials or an initial to : mark with an initial ⟨*initial* a memorandum⟩

initial side *n* : a straight line containing a point about which another line rotates to generate an angle — compare TERMINAL SIDE

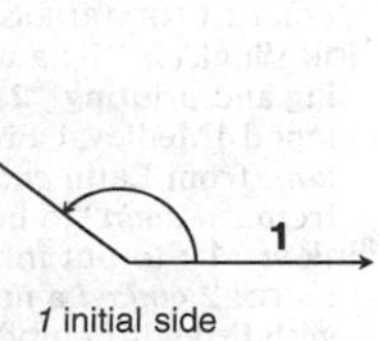

1 initial side

[1]**ini·ti·ate** \in-ˈish-ē-ˌāt\ *vt* **1** : to set going : BEGIN ⟨*initiate* a new policy⟩ **2** : to instruct in the basics or principles of something : INTRODUCE ⟨*initiate* tourists to the local customs⟩ **3** : to admit into membership by or as if by special ceremonies — **ini·ti·a·tor** \-ˌāt-ər\ *n*

[2]**ini·tiate** \in-ˈish-ət, -ē-ət\ *adj* : INITIATED

[3]**ini·tiate** \in-ˈish-ət, -ē-ət\ *n* **1** : a person who is undergoing or has passed an initiation **2** : an expert in a special field

ini·ti·a·tion \in-ˌish-ē-ˈā-shən\ *n* **1** : the act of initiating : the process of being initiated **2** : the ceremonies by which a person is made a member of a society or club

\ə\ **abut**	\au̇\ **out**	\i\ **tip**	\ȯ\ **saw**	\u̇\ **foot**
\ər\ **further**	\ch\ **chin**	\ī\ **life**	\ȯi\ **coin**	\y\ **yet**
\a\ **mat**	\e\ **pet**	\j\ **job**	\th\ **thin**	\yü\ **few**
\ā\ **take**	\ē\ **easy**	\ng\ **sing**	\t͟h\ **this**	\yu̇\ **cure**
\ä\ **cot, cart**	\g\ **go**	\ō\ **bone**	\ü\ **food**	\zh\ **vision**

ini·tia·tive \in-ˈish-ət-iv\ *n* **1 :** a first step or movement ⟨take the *initiative* in making friends⟩ **2 :** energy or ability displayed in initiating something : ENTERPRISE ⟨has the desire to win but lacks *initiative*⟩ **3 a :** the right to initiate legislative action **b :** a procedure enabling a specified number of voters to propose a law for approval of the electorate or the legislature — compare REFERENDUM

ini·tia·to·ry \in-ˈish-ə-ˌtōr-ē, -ˈish-ē-ə-, -ˌtȯr-\ *adj* **1 :** constituting a beginning : INTRODUCTORY ⟨*initiatory* remarks⟩ **2 :** serving to initiate ⟨*initiatory* ceremonies⟩

in·ject \in-ˈjekt\ *vt* **1 a :** to throw, drive, or force into something ⟨*inject* fuel into an engine⟩ **b :** to force a fluid into especially for medical purposes **2 :** to introduce as an additional element ⟨*injected* humor into the speech⟩ [Latin *injectus,* past participle of *inicere* "to inject," from *in-* + *jacere* "to throw"] — **in·ject·able** \-ˈjek-tə-bəl\ *adj* — **in·jec·tor** \-tər\ *n*

in·jec·tion \in-ˈjek-shən\ *n* **1 :** an act or instance of injecting (as by a syringe or pump) **2 :** something (as a medication) that is injected

injection molding *n* **:** a method of forming articles (as of plastic) by heating the molding material until it can flow and injecting it into a mold — **injection–molded** *adj*

in·ju·di·cious \ˌin-jü-ˈdish-əs\ *adj* **:** not judicious : INDISCREET, UNWISE ⟨an *injudicious* outburst⟩ — **in·ju·di·cious·ly** *adv* — **in·ju·di·cious·ness** *n*

in·junc·tion \in-ˈjəng-shən, -ˈjəngk-\ *n* **1 :** the act or an instance of enjoining : ORDER **2 :** a court order requiring a party to do or refrain from doing a specified act ⟨sought an *injunction* against the strike⟩ [Late Latin *injunctio,* from Latin *injungere* "to enjoin"] — **in·junc·tive** \-ˈjəng-tiv, -ˈjəngk-\ *adj*

in·jure \ˈin-jər\ *vt* **in·jured; in·jur·ing** \ˈinj-ring, -ə-ring\ **1 a :** to do an injustice to : WRONG **b :** to harm, impair, or tarnish the standing of ⟨*injured* his reputation⟩ **c :** to give pain to ⟨*injure* one's pride⟩ **2 a :** to inflict bodily hurt on ⟨injured by a *falling* brick⟩ **b :** to impair the soundness of ⟨*injured* her health⟩ **c :** to inflict material damage or loss on ⟨houses *injured* by the storm⟩ [Late Latin *injuriare,* from Latin *injuria* "injury"]

in·ju·ri·ous \in-ˈju̇r-ē-əs\ *adj* **:** causing injury : HARMFUL ⟨*injurious* to health⟩ — **in·ju·ri·ous·ly** *adv* — **in·ju·ri·ous·ness** *n*

in·ju·ry \ˈinj-rē, -ə-rē\ *n, pl* **-ries 1 :** an act that damages or hurts : WRONG **2 :** hurt, damage, or loss sustained [Latin *injuria,* from *in-* + *jur-, jus* "justice, right"]

synonyms INJURY, DAMAGE, HARM mean the act or result of inflicting something that causes loss or pain. INJURY implies an act or result detrimental to one's rights, well-being, freedom, property, or success ⟨the accident resulted in both physical and emotional *injuries*⟩. DAMAGE applies to injury involving loss ⟨the pest did considerable *damage* to the crop⟩ ⟨scandal that resulted in *damage* to the company's prestige⟩. HARM applies to any evil that injures and often suggests suffering, pain, or annoyance ⟨assured that there would be no bodily *harm*⟩.

in·jus·tice \in-ˈjəs-təs, ˈin-\ *n* **1 :** violation of the rights of another : UNFAIRNESS **2 :** an unjust act

[1]ink \ˈiŋk\ *n* **1 :** a usually liquid and colored material for writing and printing **2 :** the black protective secretion of a cephalopod [Medieval French *encre, enke,* from Late Latin *encaustum,* from Latin *encaustus* "burned in," from Greek *enkaustos,* from *enkaiein* "to burn in," from *en-* + *kaiein* "to burn"]

[2]ink *vt* **1 :** to put ink on; *also* **:** to draw or write on in ink **2 a :** SIGN 2 ⟨*inked* a new contract⟩ **b :** SIGN 4 ⟨*inked* the players with little difficulty⟩ — **ink·er** *n*

ink·ber·ry \ˈiŋk-ˌber-ē\ *n* **1 :** a black-berried North American holly **2 :** POKEWEED **3 :** the fruit of an inkberry

ink·blot test \ˈiŋk-ˌblät-\ *n* **:** any of several psychological tests based on the interpretation of irregular figures (as blots of ink)

[1]ink·horn \ˈiŋk-ˌhȯrn\ *n* **:** a small portable bottle (as of horn) for holding ink

[2]inkhorn *adj* **:** ostentatiously learned : PEDANTIC ⟨*inkhorn* terms⟩

ink–jet \ˈiŋk-ˈjet\ *adj* **:** of, relating to, or being a printer in which electrically charged droplets of ink are sprayed onto the paper

in·kling \ˈiŋ-kliŋ\ *n* **1 :** a slight suggestion : HINT **2 :** a slight knowledge or vague notion ⟨didn't have an *inkling* of what it all meant⟩ [Middle English *yngkiling* "whisper, mention," probably from *inclen* "to hint at"]

ink·stand \ˈiŋk-ˌstand\ *n* **:** INKWELL; *also* **:** a pen and inkwell

ink·well \ˈiŋ-ˌkwel\ *n* **:** a container for ink

inky \ˈiŋ-kē\ *adj* **ink·i·er; -est :** of, resembling, or covered with ink ⟨*inky* blackness of the sea⟩ ⟨*inky* hands⟩ — **ink·i·ness** *n*

inky cap *n* **:** a small mushroom whose cap dissolves into an inky fluid after the spores mature — called also *ink cap*

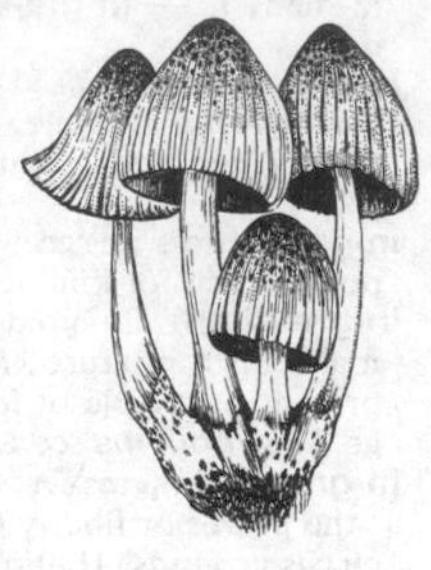

inky cap

in·laid \ˈin-ˈlād\ *adj* **1 a :** set into a surface in a decorative design ⟨tables with *inlaid* marble⟩ **b :** decorated with a design or material set into a surface ⟨a table with an *inlaid* top⟩ **2 :** having a design that goes all the way through to the backing ⟨*inlaid* linoleum⟩

in·land \ˈin-ˌland, -lənd\ *n* **:** the land away from the coast or boundaries : INTERIOR — **inland** *adj or adv* — **in·land·er** \ˈin-ˌlan-dər, -lən-\ *n*

in–law \ˈin-ˌlȯ\ *n* **:** a relative by marriage [back-formation from *mother-in-law,* etc.]

[1]in·lay \in-ˈlā, ˈin-\ *vt* **in·laid; in·lay·ing :** to set into a surface or ground material for decoration or reinforcement — **in·lay·er** *n*

[2]in·lay \ˈin-ˌlā\ *n* **1 :** inlaid work or material used in inlaying **2 :** a tooth filling shaped to fit a cavity and then cemented into place

in·let \ˈin-ˌlet, -lət\ *n* **1 :** a small or narrow indentation into the land formed by a body of water **2 :** an opening for intake

in–line \ˈin-ˈlīn, ˌin-\ *adj or adv* **:** having the parts or units arranged in a straight line; *also* **:** being so arranged

in–line skate *n* **:** a roller skate whose wheels are set in-line for greater speed and maneuverability — **in–line skater** *n* — **in–line skating** *n*

in·mate \ˈin-ˌmāt\ *n* **:** one of a group occupying a single residence; *esp* **:** a person confined to an institution (as a hospital or prison)

in me·di·as res \in-ˌmed-ē-əs-ˈrās, -ˌmēd-ē-əs-ˈrēz\ *adv* **:** in or into the middle of a narrative or plot [Latin, literally, "into the midst of things"]

in me·mo·ri·am \ˌin-mə-ˈmōr-ē-əm, -ˈmȯr-\ *prep* **:** in memory of — used especially in epitaphs [Latin]

in·most \ˈin-ˌmōst\ *adj* **:** INNERMOST [Old English *innemest,* superlative of *inne* "in, within," from *in*]

inn \ˈin\ *n* **1 :** a public house that provides lodging and food for travelers : HOTEL **2 :** TAVERN 1 [Old English]

in·nards \ˈin-ərdz\ *n pl* **1 :** the internal organs of a human being or animal; *esp* **:** VISCERA **2 :** the internal parts of a structure or mechanism [alteration of *inwards*]

in·nate \in-ˈāt, ˈin-ˌ\ *adj* **1 :** existing in or belonging to an individual from birth : NATIVE **2 :** belonging to the essential nature of something : INHERENT [Latin *innatus,* past participle of *innasci* "to be born in," from *in-* + *nasci* "to be born"] — **in·nate·ly** *adv* — **in·nate·ness** *n*

synonyms INNATE, INBORN, INBRED, CONGENITAL mean not acquired after birth. INNATE applies to qualities or characteristics that are part of the essential nature of a person or thing ⟨develop the *innate* talent of the young⟩ ⟨the *innate* defect of the scheme⟩. INBORN suggests a quality or tendency either present at birth or so deep-seated as to seem so ⟨an *inborn* ability to act⟩. INBRED suggests something deeply rooted and acquired from parents by heredity or early nurture ⟨an *inbred* hatred of injustice⟩. CONGENITAL applies to something acquired during fetal development ⟨*congenital* heart defects⟩.

in·ner \ˈin-ər\ *adj* **1 a :** situated farther in ⟨an *inner* room⟩ **b :** being near a center especially of influence ⟨the *inner* circle of party leaders⟩ **2 :** of or relating to the mind or spirit ⟨valued a rich *inner* life⟩ — **in·ner·ly** *adv*

inner city *n* **:** the usually older and more densely populated central section of a city — **inner–city** *adj*

inner ear *n* **:** the part of the ear that is most important for hearing and balance, is located in a cavity in the temporal bone, includes the vestibule, semicircular canals, and cochlea, and contains the endings of the auditory nerve

inner light *n, often cap I&L* **:** a divine presence held (as in Quaker doctrine) to enlighten and guide the soul

in·ner·most \ˈin-ər-ˌmōst\ *adj* **1 :** situated farthest inward **2 :** most intimate : DEEPEST ⟨one's *innermost* feelings⟩

in·ner·sole \ˌin-ər-ˈsōl\ *n* **:** INSOLE

inner tube *n* : an airtight inflatable ring-shaped rubber tube used inside a pneumatic tire to hold air under pressure

in·ner·vate \in-ˈər-ˌvāt, ˈin-ər-, ˈin-ˌər-\ *vt* : to supply with nerves — **in·ner·va·tion** \ˌin-ər-ˈvā-shən, ˌin-ˌər-\ *n*

in·ning \ˈin-ing\ *n* **1** : a division of a baseball game consisting of a turn at bat for each team; *also* : a baseball team's turn at bat ending with the 3rd out **2** : a chance or turn for action or accomplishment ⟨time for the opposition to have its *innings*⟩ [[2]*in*]

inn·keep·er \ˈin-ˌkē-pər\ *n* : the landlord of an inn

in·no·cence \ˈin-ə-səns\ *n* **1** : the quality or state of being innocent **2** : BLUET

in·no·cent \-sənt\ *adj* **1** : free from sin : PURE **2** : free from guilt or blame : GUILTLESS ⟨*innocent* of the crime⟩ **3** : free from evil influence or effect : HARMLESS ⟨*innocent* fun⟩ **4** : lacking or reflecting a lack of sophistication, guile, or self-consciousness [Medieval French, from Latin *innocens,* from *in-* + *nocens* "wicked," from *nocēre* "to harm"] — **innocent** *n* — **in·no·cent·ly** *adv*

in·noc·u·ous \in-ˈäk-yə-wəs\ *adj* **1** : causing no injury : HARMLESS ⟨an *innocuous* chemical⟩ **2 a** : not likely to give offense : INOFFENSIVE ⟨an *innocuous* joke⟩ **b** : not likely to arouse strong feelings : INSIPID ⟨*innocuous* poems⟩ [Latin *innocuus* from *in-* + *nocēre* "to harm"] — **in·noc·u·ous·ly** *adv* — **in·noc·u·ous·ness** *n*

in·nom·i·nate \in-ˈäm-ə-nət\ *adj* : having no name; *also* : ANONYMOUS [Late Latin *innominatus,* from Latin *in-* + *nominare* "to name, nominate"]

innominate artery *n* : a short artery arising from the arched first part of the aorta and dividing into the carotid and subclavian arteries of the right side

innominate bone *n* : HIPBONE

innominate vein *n* : either of two large veins that occur one on each side of the neck, that receive blood from the head and neck, and that unite to form the superior vena cava

in·no·vate \ˈin-ə-ˌvāt\ *vb* **1** : to introduce as or as if new **2** : to make changes [Latin *innovare,* from *in-* + *novus* "new"] — **in·no·va·tive** \-ˌvāt-iv\ *adj* — **in·no·va·tor** \-ˌvāt-ər\ *n*

in·no·va·tion \ˌin-ə-ˈvā-shən\ *n* **1** : the introduction of something new **2** : a new idea, method, or device

in·nu·en·do \ˌin-yə-ˈwen-dō\ *n, pl* **-dos** *or* **-does** : a subtle or indirect suggestion; *esp* : an unfavorable insinuation [Latin, "by nodding," from *innuere* "to nod to, to make a sign to," from *in-* + *nuere* "to nod"]

in·nu·mer·a·ble \in-ˈüm-rə-bəl, -ˈyüm-, -ə-rə-\ *adj* : too many to be numbered : COUNTLESS ⟨*innumerable* stars in the sky⟩; *also* : very many ⟨visited the museum *innumerable* times⟩ — **in·nu·mer·a·bly** \-blē\ *adv*

in·nu·mer·ous \in-ˈüm-rəs, -ˈyüm-, -ə-rəs\ *adj* : INNUMERABLE

in·ob·ser·vance \ˌin-əb-ˈzər-vəns\ *n* **1** : lack of attention : HEEDLESSNESS **2** : failure to fulfill : NONOBSERVANCE — **in·ob·ser·vant** \-vənt\ *adj*

in·oc·u·late \in-ˈäk-yə-ˌlāt\ *vt* **1 a** : to introduce a microorganism into ⟨beans *inoculated* with nitrogen-fixing bacteria⟩ **b** : to introduce (a microorganism) into a suitable situation for growth **c** : to introduce a material (as a vaccine) into the body especially by injection in order to treat or prevent a disease ⟨*inoculate* children against the measles⟩ **2** : to introduce something into the mind of ⟨*inoculate* them with a love of freedom⟩ **3** : to protect or be protected as if by inoculation ⟨*inoculated* themselves against verbal attacks⟩ [Latin *inoculare* "to insert a bud in a plant," from *in-* + *oculus* "eye, bud"] — **in·oc·u·la·tive** \-ˌlāt-iv\ *adj* — **in·oc·u·la·tor** \-ˌlāt-ər\ *n*

Word History We often give to inanimate objects the names of parts of the body. We speak, for example, of the foot of a mountain, the leg of a table, the lip of a pitcher. And an undeveloped bud on a potato is an eye. In Latin, any bud of a plant may be called *oculus* "eye." And the verb *inoculare* means "to insert or graft a bud from one plant into another." When *inoculate* was first borrowed into English it had the same meaning as the Latin verb. Later, by extension, *inoculate* came to mean "to introduce a microorganism or serum into."

in·oc·u·la·tion \in-ˌäk-yə-ˈlā-shən\ *n* **1** : the act or process or an instance of inoculating **2** : INOCULUM

in·oc·u·lum \in-ˈäk-yə-ləm\ *n, pl* **-la** \-lə\ : material used for inoculation [New Latin, from Latin *inoculare*]

in·of·fen·sive \ˌin-ə-ˈfen-siv\ *adj* : not offensive : HARMLESS — **in·of·fen·sive·ly** *adv* — **in·of·fen·sive·ness** *n*

in·op·er·a·ble \in-ˈäp-rə-bəl, ˈin-, -ə-rə-\ *adj* **1** : not treatable by surgery ⟨an *inoperable* tumor⟩ **2** : not being in working order : INOPERATIVE

in·op·er·a·tive \-ˈäp-rət-iv, -ə-rət-; -ˈäp-ə-ˌrāt-\ *adj* : not operative: as **a** : not functioning ⟨an *inoperative* clock⟩ **b** : having no effect or force ⟨an *inoperative* law⟩ — **in·op·er·a·tive·ness** *n*

in·oper·cu·late \ˌin-ō-ˈpər-kyə-lət\ *adj* : lacking an operculum ⟨*inoperculate* snails⟩

in·op·por·tune \in-ˌäp-ər-ˈtün, ˌin-, -ˈtyün\ *adj* : INCONVENIENT ⟨happened at an *inopportune* time⟩ — **in·op·por·tune·ly** *adv* — **in·op·por·tune·ness** \-ˈtün-nəs, -ˈtyün-\ *n*

in order that *conj* : THAT 2a

in·or·di·nate \in-ˈȯrd-n-ət, -ˈȯrd-nət\ *adj* : exceeding reasonable limits : IMMODERATE ⟨an *inordinate* curiosity⟩ [Latin *inordinatus* "disordered," from *in-* + *ordinare* "to arrange," from *ordin-, ordo* "order"] ***synonyms*** see EXCESSIVE — **in·or·di·nate·ly** *adv* — **in·or·di·nate·ness** *n*

in·or·gan·ic \ˌin-ȯr-ˈgan-ik\ *adj* **1** : being or composed of matter of other than plant or animal origin : MINERAL **2** : of or relating to a branch of chemistry concerned with substances not usually classed as organic — **in·or·gan·i·cal·ly** \-ˈgan-i-kə-lē, -klē\ *adv*

in·pa·tient \ˈin-ˌpā-shənt\ *n* : a hospital patient who receives lodging and food as well as treatment — compare OUTPATIENT

[1]**in·put** \ˈin-ˌpu̇t\ *n* **1** : something that is put in: as **a** : power or energy put into a machine or system **b** : information fed into a computer **2** : ADVICE, COMMENT **3** : a point at which an input (as power, an electronic signal, or data) is made **4** : the act or process of putting in

[2]**input** *vt* **in·put·ted** *or* **input; in·put·ting** : to enter (data) into a computer

in·quest \ˈin-ˌkwest\ *n* **1** : a judicial or official inquiry or investigation especially before a jury **2** : a body of persons assembled to conduct an inquest **3** : the finding of an inquest [Medieval French *enqueste,* derived from Latin *inquirere* "to inquire"]

in·qui·line \ˈin-kwə-ˌlīn, ˈing-, -lən\ *n* : an animal that habitually lives in the nest or den of another kind of animal [Latin *inquilinus* "tenant, lodger," from *in-* + *colere* "to cultivate, dwell"]

in·quire \in-ˈkwīr\ *vb* **1** : to ask about ⟨*inquired* the way to the library⟩ **2** : to make an investigation or inquiry : INVESTIGATE ⟨*inquired* into the accident⟩ **3** : to seek information by questioning ⟨*inquire* about her health⟩ [Medieval French *enquerre,* from Latin *inquirere,* from *in-* + *quaerere* "to seek"] — **in·quir·er** *n* — **in·quir·ing·ly** \-ing-lē\ *adv* — **inquire after** : to ask about the health of

in·qui·ry \ˈin-ˌkwī-rē, in-ˈ, ˈin-kwə-rē, ˈing-\ *n, pl* **-ries** **1 a** : the act of inquiring ⟨learn by *inquiry*⟩ **b** : a request for information **2** : a search for truth or knowledge **3** : a systematic examination : INVESTIGATION

in·qui·si·tion \ˌin-kwə-ˈzish-ən\ *n* **1** : the act of inquiring **2** : a judicial or official inquiry **3 a** *cap* : a former Roman Catholic tribunal for the discovery and punishment of heresy **b** : an investigation conducted with little regard for individual rights **c** : a severe questioning [Medieval French, from Latin *inquisitio,* from *inquirere* "to inquire"] — **in·qui·si·tion·al** \-ˈzish-nəl, -ən-l\ *adj*

in·quis·i·tive \in-ˈkwiz-ət-iv\ *adj* **1** : given to examination or investigation **2** : given to asking questions; *esp* : too curious about other people's affairs ***synonyms*** see CURIOUS — **in·quis·i·tive·ly** *adv* — **in·quis·i·tive·ness** *n*

in·quis·i·tor \in-ˈkwiz-ət-ər\ *n* : one that inquires; *esp* : one that conducts an inquisition — **in·quis·i·to·ri·al** \-ˌkwiz-ə-ˈtōr-ē-əl, -ˈtȯr-\ *adj* — **in·quis·i·to·ri·al·ly** \-ē-ə-lē\ *adv*

in re \in-ˈrē, -ˈrā\ *prep* : in the matter of : CONCERNING, RE [Latin]

in·road \ˈin-ˌrōd\ *n* **1** : a sudden hostile entry : RAID **2** : an advance or penetration often at the expense of someone or something ⟨*inroads* by the competition in the do-it-yourself market⟩

in·rush \ˈin-ˌrəsh\ *n* : a crowding or flooding in : INFLUX ⟨an *inrush* of air⟩ ⟨an *inrush* of tourists⟩

in·sa·lu·bri·ous \ˌin-sə-ˈlü-brē-əs\ *adj* : not conducive to health : UNWHOLESOME ⟨an *insalubrious* climate⟩ — **in·sa·lu·bri·ty** \-brət-ē\ *n*

\ə\ **abut**	\au̇\ **out**	\i\ **tip**	\ȯ\ **saw**	\u̇\ **foot**
\ər\ **further**	\ch\ **chin**	\ī\ **life**	\ȯi\ **coin**	\y\ **yet**
\a\ **mat**	\e\ **pet**	\j\ **job**	\th\ **thin**	\yü\ **few**
\ā\ **take**	\ē\ **easy**	\ng\ **sing**	\t͟h\ **this**	\yu̇\ **cure**
\ä\ **cot, cart**	\g\ **go**	\ō\ **bone**	\ü\ **food**	\zh\ **vision**

in·sane \in-ˈsān, ˈin-\ *adj* **1 :** not sane : unsound in mind **2 :** showing evidence of an unsound mind ⟨an *insane* look⟩ **3 :** used by or for insane persons ⟨an *insane* asylum⟩ **4 :** utterly foolish or unreasonable — **in·sane·ly** *adv* — **in·sane·ness** \-ˈsān-nəs\ *n*

synonyms INSANE, MAD, CRAZY mean not wholly sound in mind. INSANE technically means such unsoundness of mind that one is not responsible for one's actions; in general use it implies utter folly or irrationality ⟨an *insane* scheme⟩. MAD carries implications of wildness or rashness or lack of restraint ⟨*mad* pursuit of fortunes⟩. CRAZY suggests a distraught state of mind induced by intense emotion ⟨*crazy* with frustration⟩.

in·san·i·tary \in-ˈsan-ə-ˌter-ē, ˈin-\ *adj* : unclean enough to endanger health : CONTAMINATED

in·san·i·ty \in-ˈsan-ət-ē\ *n, pl* **-ties** **1 :** the condition of being insane : serious mental disorder **2 :** such unsoundness of mind as excuses one from criminal or civil responsibility **3 a :** extreme folly or unreasonableness **b :** something utterly foolish or unreasonable

in·sa·tia·ble \in-ˈsā-shə-bəl, ˈin-\ *adj* : incapable of being satisfied ⟨*insatiable* thirst⟩ ⟨an *insatiable* desire for knowledge⟩ — **in·sa·tia·bil·i·ty** \in-ˌsā-shə-ˈbil-ət-ē\ *n* — **in·sa·tia·ble·ness** \in-ˈsā-shə-bəl-nəs, ˈin-\ *n* — **in·sa·tia·bly** \-blē\ *adv*

in·sa·tiate \-ˈsā-shət, -shē-ət\ *adj* : not satiated or satisfied; *also* : INSATIABLE ⟨*insatiate* desires⟩ — **in·sa·tiate·ly** *adv* — **in·sa·tiate·ness** *n*

in·scribe \in-ˈskrīb\ *vt* **1 a :** to write, engrave, or print as a lasting record ⟨*inscribe* a name on a monument⟩ **b :** to enter on a list : ENROLL **2 a :** to write, engrave, or print characters on ⟨*inscribe* a locket⟩ **b :** to autograph or address as a gift ⟨*inscribe* a book⟩ **3 :** to dedicate (as a poem) to someone **4 :** to draw within a figure so as to touch in as many places as possible ⟨a hexagon *inscribed* in a circle⟩ [Latin *inscribere,* from *in-* + *scribere* "to write"] — **in·scrib·er** *n*

in·scrip·tion \in-ˈskrip-shən\ *n* **1 :** something that is inscribed **2 :** the wording on a coin, medal, or seal : LEGEND **3 :** the dedication of a book or work of art **4 :** the act of inscribing [Latin *inscriptio,* from *inscribere* "to inscribe"] — **in·scrip·tion·al** \-shnəl, -shən-l\ *adj*

in·scru·ta·ble \in-ˈskrüt-ə-bəl\ *adj* : not readily understood : ENIGMATIC ⟨*inscrutable* motives⟩ [Late Latin *inscrutabilis,* from Latin *in-* + *scrutari* "to search"] — **in·scru·ta·bil·i·ty** \-ˌskrüt-ə-ˈbil-ət-ē\ *n* — **in·scru·ta·ble·ness** \-ˈskrüt-ə-bəl-nəs\ *n* — **in·scru·ta·bly** \-blē\ *adv*

in·seam \ˈin-ˌsēm\ *n* : the seam on the inside of the leg of a pair of pants; *also* : the length of this seam

in·sect \ˈin-ˌsekt\ *n* **1 :** any of numerous small animals (as spiders or centipedes) that are usually more or less obviously segmented — not used technically **2 :** any of a class (Insecta) of arthropods (as bugs or bees) with well-defined head, thorax, and abdomen, three pairs of jointed legs, and typically one or two pairs of wings [Latin *insectum,* from *insecare* "to cut into," from *in-* + *secare* "to cut"]

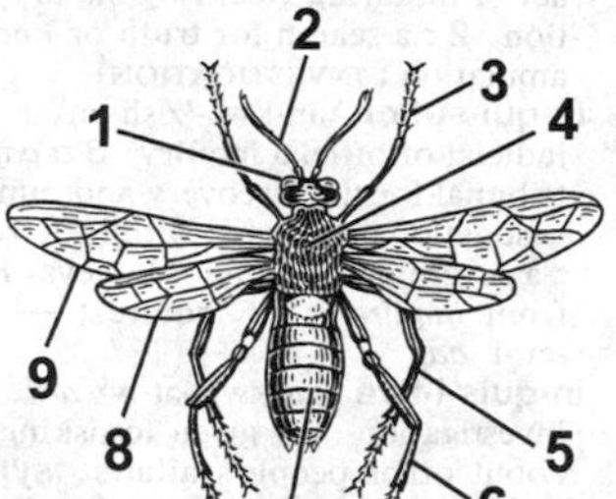

insect 2: *1* compound eye, *2* antenna, *3* front leg, *4* thorax, *5* middle leg, *6* back leg, *7* abdomen, *8* hind wing, *9* forewing

Word History The bodies of insects are segmented. This makes them look as if notches have been cut into them at intervals. For this reason the Greek philosopher Aristotle gave insects the name *entomon,* "a thing cut into," derived from the prefix *en-,* "in," and the verb *temnein,* "to cut." (From this Greek word we derive our name for the study of insects, *entomology.*) Later, when the Romans wanted a word for this kind of creature, they did not simply borrow the Greek word but translated it *insectum,* from the verb *insecare* "to cut into." The Latin word was borrowed into English.

in·sec·ta·ry \ˈin-ˌsek-tə-rē\ *also* **in·sec·tar·i·um** \ˌin-ˌsek-ˈter-ē-əm\ *n, pl* **-taries** \-tə-rēz\ *also* **-tar·ia** \-ˈter-ē-ə\ : a place for rearing or keeping live insects

in·sec·ti·cide \in-ˈsek-tə-ˌsīd\ *n* : an agent that destroys insects — **in·sec·ti·cid·al** \-ˌsek-tə-ˈsīd-l\ *adj*

in·sec·ti·vore \in-ˈsek-tə-ˌvōr, -ˌvȯr\ *n* **1 :** any of an order (Insectivora) of small usually nocturnal mammals (as the moles, shrews, and hedgehogs) that feed mainly on insects **2 :** an insectivorous plant or animal [derived from Latin *insectum* "insect" + *vorare* "to devour"]

in·sec·tiv·o·rous \ˌin-ˌsek-ˈtiv-rəs, -ə-rəs\ *adj* : feeding on insects as food

in·se·cure \ˌin-si-ˈkyu̇r\ *adj* **1 :** not confident or sure : UNCERTAIN ⟨felt *insecure* about their support⟩ **2 :** not well protected ⟨an *insecure* investment⟩ **3 :** not firmly fastened or fixed : SHAKY ⟨the hinge is loose and *insecure*⟩ **4 a :** not stable or well-adjusted **b :** lacking self-assurance ⟨*insecure* people⟩ — **in·se·cure·ly** *adv* — **in·se·cure·ness** *n* — **in·se·cu·ri·ty** \-ˈkyu̇r-ət-ē\ *n*

in·sem·i·nate \in-ˈsem-ə-ˌnāt\ *vt* : to introduce semen into the genital tract of (a female) — **in·sem·i·na·tion** \-ˌsem-ə-ˈnā-shən\ *n*

in·sen·sate \in-ˈsen-ˌsāt, ˈin-\ *adj* **1 :** lacking awareness or sensation : INANIMATE **2 :** lacking sense or understanding; *also* : FOOLISH **3 :** lacking humane feeling : BRUTAL ⟨*insensate* hatred⟩ — **in·sen·sate·ly** *adv*

in·sen·si·ble \in-ˈsen-sə-bəl, ˈin-\ *adj* **1 :** incapable or deprived of feeling or sensation: as **a :** not endowed with life or spirit : INSENTIENT ⟨*insensible* earth⟩ **b :** UNCONSCIOUS 2b ⟨knocked *insensible* by the accident⟩ **c :** lacking or deprived of sensory perception : INSENSITIVE ⟨*insensible* to pain⟩ **2 :** IMPERCEPTIBLE 1 ⟨*insensible* differences in weight⟩; *also* : SLIGHT, GRADUAL ⟨*insensible* motion⟩ **3 :** APATHETIC, INDIFFERENT ⟨*insensible* to fear⟩; *also* : UNAWARE ⟨*insensible* of their danger⟩ **4 :** not intelligible : MEANINGLESS **5 :** lacking delicacy or refinement — **in·sen·si·bil·i·ty** \in-ˌsen-sə-ˈbil-ət-ē\ *n* — **in·sen·si·ble·ness** \in-ˈsen-sə-bəl-nəs, ˈin-\ *n* — **in·sen·si·bly** \-blē\ *adv*

in·sen·si·tive \in-ˈsen-sət-iv, ˈin-, -ˈsen-stiv\ *adj* : not sensitive; *esp* : lacking feeling — **in·sen·si·tive·ly** *adv* — **in·sen·si·tive·ness** *n* — **in·sen·si·tiv·i·ty** \in-ˌsen-sə-ˈtiv-ət-ē\ *n*

in·sen·tient \in-ˈsen-chənt, ˈin-, -chē-ənt\ *adj* : lacking perception, consciousness, or animation — **in·sen·tience** \-chəns, -chē-əns\ *n*

in·sep·a·ra·ble \in-ˈsep-rə-bəl, ˈin-, -ə-rə-\ *adj* **1 :** incapable of being separated ⟨*inseparable* issues⟩ **2 :** seemingly always together ⟨*inseparable* friends⟩ — **in·sep·a·ra·bil·i·ty** \in-ˌsep-rə-ˈbil-ət-ē, -ə-rə-\ *n* — **in·sep·a·ra·ble·ness** \in-ˈsep-rə-bəl-nəs, ˈin-, -ə-rə-\ *n* — **in·sep·a·ra·bly** \-blē\ *adv*

¹in·sert \in-ˈsərt\ *vb* **1 :** to put or place in ⟨*inserted* the key in the lock⟩ **2 :** to introduce into the body of something : INTERPOLATE ⟨*insert* an explanation into a text⟩ **3 :** to set in and make fast ⟨*insert* strips of lace in the sleeves⟩ **4 :** to be in attachment to the part to be moved ⟨a muscle which *inserts* on the humerus⟩ [Latin *insertus,* past participle of *inserere* "to insert," from *in-* + *serere* "to join"] ***synonyms*** see INTRODUCE — **in·sert·er** *n*

²in·sert \ˈin-ˌsərt\ *n* : something that is inserted or is for insertion; *esp* : written or printed material inserted (as between the pages of a newspaper)

in·ser·tion \in-ˈsər-shən\ *n* **1 :** the act or process of inserting **2 :** something that is inserted: as **a :** the part of a muscle that inserts on a part to be moved **b :** embroidery or needlework inserted as ornament between two pieces of fabric **c :** a section of genetic material that is inserted into an existing gene sequence **3 :** the mode or place of attachment of an organ or part — **in·ser·tion·al** \-shnəl, -shən-l\ *adj*

¹in·set \ˈin-ˌset\ *n* : something that is inset: as **a :** a small graphic representation (as a map or picture) set within the compass of a larger one **b :** a piece of cloth set into a garment for decoration

²in·set \ˈin-ˌset, in-ˈ\ *vt* **inset** *or* **in·set·ted; in·set·ting** : to set in : insert as an inset

¹in·shore \ˈin-ˈshōr, -ˈshȯr\ *adj* **1 :** situated or carried on near shore ⟨*inshore* fishing⟩ **2 :** moving toward shore ⟨an *inshore* wind⟩

²inshore *adv* : to or toward shore ⟨debris drifting *inshore*⟩

¹in·side \in-ˈsīd, ˈin-ˌ\ *n* **1 :** an inner side or surface **2 a :** an interior or internal part **b :** inward nature, thoughts, or feeling **c :** VISCERA, ENTRAILS — usually used in plural

²inside *adv* **1 :** on the inside ⟨don't forget to clean the car *inside*⟩ **2 :** in or into the interior ⟨went *inside*⟩

³inside *adj* **1 :** of, relating to, or being on or near the inside ⟨an *inside* wall⟩ **2 :** relating or known to a special group of people ⟨*inside* information⟩

⁴inside *prep* **1 a :** in or into the interior of ⟨went *inside* the house⟩ **b :** on the inner side of ⟨put the dot *inside* the curve⟩ **2 :** before the end of : WITHIN ⟨*inside* an hour⟩

inside of *prep* : INSIDE

in·sid·er \in-ˈsīd-ər, ˈin-\ *n* **:** a person who has access to confidential information

inside track *n* **:** an advantageous competitive position [from the fact that the inner side of a curved racetrack is shorter than the outer]

in·sid·i·ous \in-ˈsid-ē-əs\ *adj* **1 a :** awaiting a chance to entrap : TREACHEROUS ⟨an *insidious* foe⟩ **b :** harmful but enticing ⟨*insidious* drugs⟩ **2 :** having a gradual and cumulative effect ⟨an *insidious* disease⟩ [Latin *insidiosus,* from *insidiae* "ambush," from *insidēre* "to sit in, sit on," from *in-* + *sedēre* "to sit"] — **in·sid·i·ous·ly** *adv* — **in·sid·i·ous·ness** *n*

in·sight \ˈin-ˌsīt\ *n* **1 :** the power or act of seeing into a situation **2 :** the act of understanding the inner nature of things or of seeing intuitively

in·sig·nia \in-ˈsig-nē-ə\ *also* **in·sig·ne** \-nē\ *n, pl* **-nia** *or* **-ni·as** **:** a distinguishing mark especially of authority, office, or honor : BADGE, EMBLEM [Latin *insignia,* pl. of *insigne* "mark, badge," from *in-* + *signum* "mark, sign"]

in·sig·nif·i·cant \ˌin-sig-ˈnif-i-kənt\ *adj* **:** not significant: as **a** : lacking meaning or importance : INCONSEQUENTIAL ⟨*insignificant* details⟩ **b :** lacking weight, position, or influence : CONTEMPTIBLE ⟨an *insignificant* hanger-on⟩ **c :** LITTLE, TRIVIAL ⟨an *insignificant* amount⟩ — **in·sig·nif·i·cance** \-kəns\ *n* — **in·sig·nif·i·cant·ly** *adv*

in·sin·cere \ˌin-sin-ˈsiər\ *adj* **:** lacking in sincerity — **in·sin·cere·ly** *adv* — **in·sin·cer·i·ty** \-ˈser-ət-ē, -ˈsir-\ *n*

in·sin·u·ate \in-ˈsin-yə-ˌwāt\ *vt* **1 :** to introduce gradually or in a subtle, indirect, or secretive way ⟨*insinuated* himself into a position of influence⟩ ⟨*insinuate* doubts into their minds⟩ **2** : to suggest in a subtle or indirect way : IMPLY ⟨*insinuated* that I had cheated⟩ [Latin *insinuare,* from *in-* + *sinuare* "to bend, curve," from *sinus* "curve"] — **in·sin·u·a·tor** \-ˌwāt-ər\ *n*

in·sin·u·at·ing *adj* **1 :** tending gradually to cause doubt, distrust, or change of outlook ⟨*insinuating* remarks⟩ **2 :** intended to win favor and confidence by subtle or artful means ⟨an *insinuating* manner⟩ — **in·sin·u·at·ing·ly** \-ˌwāt-ing-lē\ *adv*

in·sin·u·a·tion \in-ˌsin-yə-ˈwā-shən\ *n* **1 :** a subtle suggestion : INNUENDO **2 :** the artful pursuit of favor : INGRATIATION

in·sip·id \in-ˈsip-əd\ *adj* **1 :** lacking taste or savor : TASTELESS **2 :** lacking in interest, stimulation, or challenge : DULL, FLAT ⟨*insipid* fiction⟩ [Late Latin *insipidus,* from Latin *in-* + *sapidus* "savory," from *sapere* "to taste"] — **in·si·pid·i·ty** \ˌin-sə-ˈpid-ət-ē\ *n* — **in·sip·id·ly** \in-ˈsip-əd-lē\ *adv*

synonyms INSIPID, VAPID, BANAL, INANE mean devoid of qualities that make for spirit and character. INSIPID implies a lack of sufficient taste or savor to please or interest ⟨*insipid* art and dull prose⟩ ⟨a fruit with *insipid* flesh⟩. VAPID suggests lack of liveliness, force, or spirit ⟨*vapid* song lyrics⟩. BANAL stresses the complete absence of freshness, novelty, or immediacy ⟨a *banal* tale of unrequited love⟩. INANE implies lacking any significant or convincing quality ⟨a purposeless *inane* life⟩ ⟨*inane* criticism⟩.

in·sist \in-ˈsist\ *vb* **1 :** to place special emphasis or great importance ⟨*insists* on punctuality⟩ **2 :** to request urgently ⟨*insisted* that I come⟩ **3 :** to maintain in a persistent or positive manner ⟨*insisted* that their rights had been violated⟩ [Latin *insistere* "to stand upon, insist," from *in-* + *sistere* "to stand"]

in·sis·tence \in-ˈsis-təns\ *n* **1 :** the act of insisting **2 :** the quality or state of being insistent : URGENCY ⟨the *insistence* of a need⟩

in·sis·tent \-tənt\ *adj* **:** compelling attention : PERSISTENT ⟨*insistent* demands⟩ — **in·sist·ent·ly** *adv*

in situ \in-ˈsī-tü *also* -ˈsi-\ *adv or adj* **:** in the natural or original position ⟨the cancer cells remained *in situ*⟩ [Latin, "in position"]

in·so·far as \ˈin-sə-ˌfär-əz\ *conj* **:** to the extent or degree that

in·so·la·tion \ˌin-ˌsō-ˈlā-shən\ *n* **1 :** solar radiation that has been received **2 :** the rate of delivery of all direct solar energy per unit of horizontal surface [Latin *insolatio* "exposure to the sun," from *insolare* "to expose to the sun," from *in-* + *sol* "sun"]

in·sole \ˈin-ˌsōl\ *n* **1 :** an inside sole of a shoe **2 :** a loose thin strip placed inside a shoe for warmth and comfort

in·so·lent \ˈin-sə-lənt\ *adj* **1 :** arrogant or rude in speech or conduct ⟨an *insolent* child⟩ **2 :** exhibiting boldness or rudeness ⟨an *insolent* act⟩ [Latin *insolens* "unaccustomed, overbearing," from *in-* + *solens,* present participle of *solēre* "to be accustomed"] ***synonyms*** see PROUD — **in·so·lence** \-ləns\ *n* — **in·so·lent·ly** *adv*

in·sol·u·ble \in-ˈsäl-yə-bəl, ˈin-\ *adj* **:** not soluble: as **a :** incapable of being solved or explained **b :** incapable of being dissolved in a liquid and especially in water; *also* **:** soluble only with difficulty or to a slight degree — **in·sol·u·bil·i·ty** \in-ˌsäl-yə-ˈbil-ət-ē\ *n* — **insoluble** *n* — **in·sol·u·ble·ness** \in-ˈsäl-yə-bəl-nəs, ˈin-\ *n* — **in·sol·u·bly** \-blē\ *adv*

in·solv·able \in-ˈsäl-və-bəl, -ˈsȯl-\ *adj* **:** admitting no solution ⟨an apparently *insolvable* problem⟩ — **in·solv·ably** \-blē\ *adv*

in·sol·vent \in-ˈsäl-vənt, ˈin-\ *adj* **1 :** unable to pay debts **2** : insufficient to pay all debts ⟨an *insolvent* estate⟩ — **in·sol·ven·cy** \-vən-sē\ *n* — **insolvent** *n*

in·som·nia \in-ˈsäm-nē-ə\ *n* **:** prolonged and usually abnormal inability to get enough sleep [Latin, from *insomnis* "sleepless," from *in-* + *somnus* "sleep"] — **in·som·ni·ac** \-nē-ˌak\ *adj or n*

in·so·much as \ˌin-sə-ˌməch-əz\ *conj* **:** inasmuch as

insomuch that \-t͟hət\ *conj* **:** to such a degree that : so that

in·sou·ci·ance \in-ˈsü-sē-əns\ *n* **:** a lighthearted unconcern : NONCHALANCE [French] — **in·sou·ci·ant** \-ənt\ *adj* — **in·sou·ci·ant·ly** *adv*

in·spect \in-ˈspekt\ *vb* **1 :** to examine closely (as for judging quality or condition) ⟨*inspect* meat⟩ **2 :** to view and examine officially ⟨*inspect* the troops⟩ **3 :** to make an examination [Latin *inspectus,* past participle of *inspicere* "to inspect," from *in-* + *specere* "to look"] — **in·spec·tive** \-ˈspek-tiv\ *adj*

in·spec·tion \in-ˈspek-shən\ *n* **1 a :** the act of inspecting : EXAMINATION **b :** recognition of a familiar pattern leading to immediate solution of a mathematical problem ⟨solve an equation by *inspection*⟩ **2 :** a checking or testing of an individual against established standards

in·spec·tor \in-ˈspek-tər\ *n* **1 :** a person employed to make inspections ⟨meat *inspector*⟩ **2 :** a police officer ranking next below a superintendent or deputy superintendent — **in·spec·tor·ate** \-tə-rət, -trət\ *n* — **in·spec·tor·ship** \-tər-ˌship\ *n*

in·spi·ra·tion \ˌin-spə-ˈrā-shən\ *n* **1 :** a divine influence on a person **2 :** the drawing of air into the lungs in breathing : INHALATION **3 :** the act or power of stimulating the intellect or emotions ⟨the *inspiration* of music⟩ **4 a :** the quality or state of being inspired ⟨the artist's *inspiration* came from many sources⟩ **b :** something that is inspired ⟨a scheme that was an *inspiration*⟩ **5 :** one that inspires — **in·spi·ra·tion·al** \-shnəl, -shən-l\ *adj* — **in·spi·ra·tion·al·ly** \-ē\ *adv*

in·spire \in-ˈspīr\ *vb* **1 a :** to move or guide by divine or supernatural influence ⟨prophets *inspired* by God⟩ **b :** to exert an animating, enlivening, or exalting influence on ⟨*inspired* by their mother⟩ **c :** to spur on : IMPEL, MOTIVATE ⟨a childhood that *inspired* them to get an education⟩ **d :** to cause to have a particular thought or feeling : AFFECT ⟨the old house *inspired* her with a longing for the past⟩ **2 :** INHALE **3 a :** to communicate to an agent supernaturally ⟨words *inspired* by God⟩ **b** : to draw forth or bring out : AROUSE ⟨*inspire* trust in listeners⟩ **4 :** BRING ABOUT, OCCASION ⟨studies that *inspired* several inventions⟩ [Latin *inspirare,* literally, "to breathe into," from *in-* + *spirare* "to breathe"] — **in·spir·er** *n*

in·spir·it \in-ˈspir-ət\ *vt* **:** to fill with spirit, courage, or energy

in·sta·bil·i·ty \ˌin-stə-ˈbil-ət-ē\ *n* **:** the quality or state of being unstable

in·stall \in-ˈstȯl\ *vt* **1 :** to induct into an office, rank, or order ⟨*installed* the new president⟩ **2 :** to put in an indicated place, condition, or status ⟨*install* oneself in the best chair⟩ **3 :** to set up for use or service ⟨*install* a furnace⟩ ⟨*installed* the software⟩ [Medieval French *installer,* from Medieval Latin *installare,* from *in-* "in" + *stallum* "stall," from Old High German *stal*] — **in·stall·er** *n*

in·stal·la·tion \ˌin-stə-ˈlā-shən\ *n* **1 :** the act of installing : the state of being installed **2 :** something that is installed for use **3 :** a military camp, fort, or base **4 :** a work of art that usually consists of multiple components often in mixed media and that is exhibited in a usually large space in an arrangement specified by the artist

[1]**in·stall·ment** *also* **in·stal·ment** \in-ˈstȯl-mənt\ *n* : INSTALLATION 1

[2]**installment** *also* **instalment** *n* **1** : one of the parts into which a debt is divided when payment is made at intervals **2** : one of several parts (as of a publication) presented at intervals [earlier *estallment* "payment by parts," derived from Medieval French *estaler* "to place, fix," from *estal* "place," of Germanic origin] — **installment** *adj*

installment plan *n* : a system of paying for something in installments

[1]**in·stance** \ˈin-stəns\ *n* **1** : SUGGESTION, REQUEST ⟨entered a contest at the *instance* of his teacher⟩ **2** : an individual illustrative of a category ⟨an *instance* of rare courage⟩ **3** : a step, stage, or situation viewed as part of a process or series of events ⟨in the first *instance*⟩ — **for instance** \fər-ˈin-stəns, ˈfrin-stəns\ : as an example ⟨big dogs, like German shepherds, *for instance*⟩
synonyms INSTANCE, CASE, EXAMPLE mean something that exhibits distinguishing characteristics in its category. INSTANCE applies to any individual person, act, or thing that may be offered to illustrate or explain ⟨a good *instance* of the power of suggestion⟩. CASE is used to direct attention to a real or assumed occurrence or situation that is to be considered, studied, or dealt with ⟨a *case* of mistaken identity⟩. EXAMPLE applies to a typical or illustrative instance or case ⟨a fine *example* of Georgian architecture⟩.

[2]**instance** *vt* **1** : to illustrate or demonstrate by an instance **2** : to mention as a case or example : CITE

[1]**in·stant** \ˈin-stənt\ *n* : a very short period of time : MOMENT [Medieval Latin *instans,* from Latin, "instant," from *instare* "to stand upon, urge," from *in-* + *stare* "to stand"]

[2]**instant** *adj* **1** : PRESSING 1, URGENT ⟨in *instant* need⟩ **2** : IMMEDIATE, DIRECT ⟨an *instant* response⟩ **3 a** : partially prepared by the manufacturer to make final preparation easy ⟨*instant* mashed potatoes⟩ **b** : immediately soluble in water ⟨*instant* coffee⟩ [Latin *instans,* from *instare* "to stand upon, urge"]

in·stan·ta·neous \ˌin-stən-ˈtā-nē-əs, -nyəs\ *adj* **1** : done, occurring, or acting in an instant ⟨death was *instantaneous*⟩ **2** : done without delay **3** : occurring or present at a particular instant ⟨*instantaneous* velocity⟩ [Medieval Latin *instantaneus,* from *instans* "instant"] — **in·stan·ta·neous·ly** *adv* — **in·stan·ta·neous·ness** *n*

in·stan·ter \in-ˈstant-ər\ *adv* : at once : INSTANTLY [Medieval Latin, from *instans* "instant"]

in·stant·ly \ˈin-stənt-lē\ *adv* **1** : with urgency or great persistence : URGENTLY ⟨pleaded *instantly*⟩ **2** : without the least delay : IMMEDIATELY ⟨responded *instantly* to my request⟩

instant messaging *n* : a means or system for transmitting electronic messages instantly — **instant message** *n*

in·star \ˈin-ˌstär\ *n* : a stage in the life of an insect between two successive molts [Latin, "equivalent, figure"]

in·stead \in-ˈsted\ *adv* : as a substitute or alternative ⟨was going to write but called *instead*⟩

instead of \in-ˌsted-əv, -ˌsted-ə, -ˌstid-\ *prep* : as a substitute for or alternative to ⟨called *instead of* writing⟩

in·step \ˈin-ˌstep\ *n* **1** : the arched middle part of the human foot **2** : the part of a shoe or stocking that fits over the instep

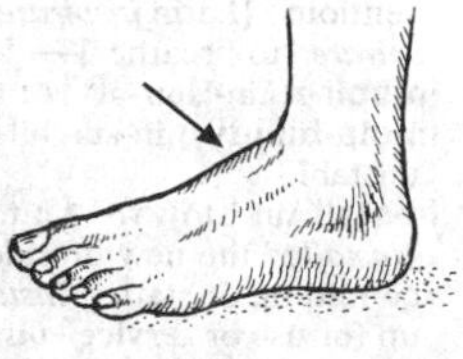
instep 1

in·sti·gate \ˈin-stə-ˌgāt\ *vt* : to goad or urge forward [Latin *instigare*] ***synonyms*** see INCITE — **in·sti·ga·tion** \ˌin-stə-ˈgā-shən\ *n* — **in·sti·ga·tive** \ˈin-stə-ˌgāt-iv\ *adj* — **in·sti·ga·tor** \-ˌgāt-ər\ *n*

in·still \in-ˈstil\ *vt* **1** : to cause to enter drop by drop **2** : to impart gradually ⟨*instill* a love of music⟩ [Latin *instillare,* from *in-* + *stillare* "to drip"] — **in·stil·la·tion** \ˌin-stə-ˈlā-shən\ *n* — **in·still·er** \in-ˈstil-ər\ *n* — **in·still·ment** \-ˈstil-mənt\ *n*

[1]**in·stinct** \ˈin-ˌstingt, -ˌstingkt\ *n* **1** : a natural aptitude, impulse, or capacity **2 a** : a complex pattern of response by an organism to environmental stimuli that is largely inborn and unalterable **b** : behavior based on reactions below the conscious level [Latin *instinctus* "impulse," from *instinguere* "to incite"]

[2]**in·stinct** \in-ˈstingt, -ˈstingkt, ˈin-ˌ\ *adj* : entirely filled ⟨a heart *instinct* with faith⟩

in·stinc·tive \in-ˈsting-tiv, -ˈstingk-\ *adj* : of, relating to, or prompted by instinct ***synonyms*** see SPONTANEOUS — **in·stinc·tive·ly** *adv*

in·stinc·tu·al \in-ˈsting-chə-wəl, -chəl\ *adj* : of, relating to, or based on instinct : INSTINCTIVE ⟨*instinctual* behavior⟩ — **in·stinc·tu·al·ly** *adv*

[1]**in·sti·tute** \ˈin-stə-ˌtüt, -ˌtyüt\ *vt* **1** : to set up : ESTABLISH ⟨*instituted* a new policy⟩ **2** : to set going : BEGIN ⟨*institute* an investigation⟩ [Latin *institutus,* past participle of *instituere* "to institute," from *in-* + *statuere* "to set up," from *status* "condition, state"] — **in·sti·tut·er** *or* **in·sti·tu·tor** \-ˌtüt-ər, -ˌtyüt-\ *n*

[2]**institute** *n* **1** : something that is instituted; *esp* : a basic principle recognized as authoritative **2 a** : an organization for the promotion of a cause : ASSOCIATION ⟨an *institute* for scientific research⟩ **b** : a place for study usually in a specialized field ⟨an art *institute*⟩ **3** : a brief course of instruction on selected topics relating to a particular field

in·sti·tu·tion \ˌin-stə-ˈtü-shən, -ˈtyü-\ *n* **1** : the act of instituting : ESTABLISHMENT **2 a** : an established custom, practice, or law in a society or culture ⟨the *institution* of marriage⟩ ⟨the turkey dinner is a Thanksgiving *institution*⟩ **b** : something or someone firmly associated with a place or thing ⟨she had become an *institution* in the theater⟩ **3 a** : an established organization or corporation and especially one of a public nature ⟨a financial *institution*⟩ ⟨educational *institutions*⟩ **b** : ASYLUM 4 — **in·sti·tu·tion·al** \-shnəl, -shən-l\ *adj* — **in·sti·tu·tion·al·ly** \-ē\ *adv*

in·sti·tu·tion·al·ize \-ˈtü-shnə-ˌlīz, -ˈtyü-, -shən-l-ˌīz\ *vt* **1** : to make into or treat like an institution **2** : to put in the care of an institution — **in·sti·tu·tion·al·i·za·tion** \-ˌtü-shnəl-ə-ˈzā-shən, -ˌtyü-, -shən-l-\ *n*

in·struct \in-ˈstrəkt\ *vt* **1** : to impart knowledge to : TEACH ⟨the tutor *instructs* him in math⟩ **2** : to give information to : INFORM ⟨*instructed* us that the cafeteria was downstairs⟩ **3** : to give directions or commands to ⟨*instructed* us to arrive promptly⟩ [Latin *instructus,* past participle of *instruere* "to construct, instruct," from *in-* + *struere* "to build"] ***synonyms*** see COMMAND, TEACH

in·struc·tion \in-ˈstrək-shən\ *n* **1 a** : PRECEPT ⟨*instructions* of ethical behavior⟩ **b** : COMMAND 2, ORDER ⟨had *instructions* to close the windows before we left⟩ **c** *pl* : an outline or manual of procedure to be followed : DIRECTIONS ⟨*instructions* for assembling a bookcase⟩ **d** : a code that tells a computer to perform a particular operation **2** : the action or practice of an instructor or teacher — **in·struc·tion·al** \-shnəl, -shən-l\ *adj*

in·struc·tive \in-ˈstrək-tiv\ *adj* : giving knowledge : serving to instruct or inform ⟨an *instructive* experience⟩ — **in·struc·tive·ly** *adv* — **in·struc·tive·ness** *n*

in·struc·tor \-tər\ *n* : one that instructs : TEACHER; *esp* : a college teacher below professorial rank — **in·struc·tor·ship** \-ˌship\ *n*

in·stru·ment \ˈin-strə-mənt\ *n* **1** : a means whereby something is achieved, performed, or furthered ⟨imagination is an *instrument* of innovation⟩ **2 a** : IMPLEMENT; *esp* : one designed for precision work ⟨a surgical *instrument*⟩ **b** : a device used to produce music **3** : a formal legal document (as a deed, bond, or agreement) **4 a** : a measuring device for determining the present value of a quantity under observation **b** : an electrical or mechanical device used in navigating an airplane; *esp* : such a device used as the sole means of navigating [Latin *instrumentum,* from *instruere* "to arrange, instruct"] ***synonyms*** see IMPLEMENT

in·stru·men·tal \ˌin-strə-ˈment-l\ *adj* **1 a** : acting as an instrument or means ⟨*instrumental* in sending a thief to jail⟩ **b** : of, relating to, or done with an instrument or tool ⟨*instrumental* analysis of the chemical compound⟩ **2** : relating to, composed for, or performed on a musical instrument ⟨an unusual *instrumental* arrangement⟩ — **in·stru·men·tal·ly** \-l-ē\ *adv*

in·stru·men·tal·ist \-l-əst\ *n* : a player of a musical instrument

in·stru·men·tal·i·ty \ˌin-strə-mən-ˈtal-ət-ē, -ˌmen-\ *n, pl* **-ties** **1** : the quality or state of being instrumental **2** : something by which an end is achieved : MEANS ⟨orderly conduct was restored through the *instrumentality* of strict rules⟩

in·stru·men·ta·tion \ˌin-strə-mən-ˈtā-shən, -ˌmen-\ *n* **1** : the use or application of instruments for observation, measurement, or control **2** : the arrangement or composition of music for instruments **3** : instruments for a particular purpose

instrument flying *n* : navigation of an airplane by instruments only

instrument landing *n* : a landing made with little or no external visibility by means of instruments within an airplane and by ground radio devices

instrument panel *n* : a panel on which instruments are mounted; *esp* : DASHBOARD 2

in·sub·or·di·nate \ˌin-sə-ˈbȯrd-n-ət, -ˈbȯrd-nət\ *adj* : unwilling to submit to authority : DISOBEDIENT — **in·sub·or·di·nate·ly** *adv* — **in·sub·or·di·na·tion** \ˌin-sə-ˌbȯrd-n-ˈā-shən\ *n*

in·sub·stan·tial \ˌin-səb-ˈstan-chəl\ *adj* : not substantial: as **a** : lacking substance or reality : IMAGINARY ⟨*insubstantial* dreams⟩ **b** : lacking firmness or solidity ⟨a flimsy, *insubstantial* shelf⟩ — **in·sub·stan·ti·al·i·ty** \-ˌstan-chē-ˈal-ət-ē\ *n*

in·suf·fer·able \in-ˈsəf-rə-bəl, ˈin-, -ə-rə-\ *adj* : incapable of being endured : INTOLERABLE ⟨an *insufferable* bore⟩ ⟨*insufferable* wrongs⟩ — **in·suf·fer·able·ness** *n* — **in·suf·fer·ably** \-blē\ *adv*

in·suf·fi·cien·cy \ˌin-sə-ˈfish-ən-sē\ *n, pl* **-cies** **1** : the quality or state of being insufficient: as **a** : lack of mental or moral fitness **b** : lack of adequate supply **c** : inability of an organ or body part to function normally ⟨cardiac *insufficiency*⟩ **2** : something insufficient ⟨aware of their own *insufficiencies*⟩

in·suf·fi·cient \-ˈfish-ənt\ *adj* : not sufficient : INADEQUATE; *also* : INCOMPETENT — **in·suf·fi·cient·ly** *adv*

in·su·lar \ˈins-ə-lər, -yə-; ˈin-shə-lər\ *adj* **1** : of, relating to, or forming an island **2** : characteristic of an isolated people; *esp* : having or reflecting a narrow viewpoint [Late Latin *insularis,* from Latin *insula* "island"] — **in·su·lar·ism** \-lə-ˌriz-əm\ *n* — **in·su·lar·i·ty** \ˌins-ə-ˈlar-ət-ē, -yə-; ˌin-shə-ˈlar-\ *n* — **in·su·lar·ly** *adv*

in·su·late \ˈin-sə-ˌlāt\ *vt* : to place in a detached situation : ISOLATE; *esp* : to separate from conducting bodies by means of nonconductors so as to prevent transfer of electricity, heat, or sound [Latin *insula* "island"]

in·su·la·tion \ˌin-sə-ˈlā-shən\ *n* **1** : the act of insulating : the state of being insulated **2** : material used in insulating

in·su·la·tor \ˈin-sə-ˌlāt-ər\ *n* : one that insulates; *esp* : a material that is a poor conductor of heat or electricity or a device made of such material

in·su·lin \ˈin-sə-lən, -slən\ *n* : a pancreatic hormone secreted by the islets of Langerhans and needed especially for the normal utilization of glucose by the body and when inadequately produced results in diabetes mellitus [New Latin *insula* "islet (of Langerhans)," from Latin, "island"]

insulin shock *n* : a condition of deficient blood sugar that is associated with excessive insulin in the system and that if left untreated may result in progressive development of coma

¹in·sult \in-ˈsəlt\ *vt* **1** : to treat with insolence, indignity, or contempt : AFFRONT **2** : to make little of : BELITTLE [Latin *insultare,* literally, "to spring upon," from *in-* + *saltare* "to leap"] ***synonyms*** see OFFEND — **in·sult·er** *n*

²in·sult \ˈin-ˌsəlt\ *n* **1** : an act or speech showing disrespect or contempt **2** : damage to the body or one of its parts; *also* : a cause of this ⟨thermal *insult*⟩ ***synonyms*** see AFFRONT

in·su·per·a·ble \in-ˈsü-pə-rə-bəl, ˈin-, -prə-bəl\ *adj* : incapable of being surmounted or overcome ⟨*insuperable* difficulties⟩ [Latin *insuperabilis,* from *in-* + *superare* "to surmount," from *super* "over"] — **in·su·per·a·bly** \-blē\ *adv*

in·sup·port·able \ˌin-sə-ˈpōrt-ə-bəl, -ˈpȯrt-\ *adj* : not supportable: **a** : UNENDURABLE ⟨an *insupportable* burden⟩ **b** : UNJUSTIFIABLE ⟨*insupportable* charges⟩ — **in·sup·port·ably** \-blē\ *adv*

in·sup·press·ible \ˌin-sə-ˈpres-ə-bəl\ *adj* : not suppressible — **in·sup·press·ibly** \-blē\ *adv*

in·sur·able \in-ˈshu̇r-ə-bəl\ *adj* : capable of being insured — **in·sur·abil·i·ty** \in-ˌshu̇r-ə-ˈbil-ət-ē\ *n*

in·sur·ance \in-ˈshu̇r-əns\ *n* **1 a** : the business of insuring persons or property **b** : coverage by contract whereby one party undertakes to guarantee another against loss by a specified event or peril (as theft or fire) **c** : the sum for which something is insured **2** : a means of guaranteeing protection or safety ⟨wears a helmet as *insurance* against head injury⟩

in·sure \in-ˈshu̇r\ *vt* **1** : to give or procure insurance on or for **2** : to make certain : ENSURE

in·sured *n* : a person whose life or property is insured

in·sur·er \in-ˈshu̇r-ər\ *n* : one that insures

in·sur·gence \in-ˈsər-jəns\ *n* : UPRISING

in·sur·gen·cy \-jən-sē\ *n, pl* **-cies** **1** : the quality or state of being insurgent; *esp* : a state of revolt against a government that is less than an organized revolution **2** : UPRISING

¹in·sur·gent \in-ˈsər-jənt\ *n* : a person who revolts; *esp* : a rebel not recognized as a belligerent [Latin *insurgere* "to rise up," from *in-* + *surgere* "to rise"]

²insurgent *adj* : rising in opposition to authority : REBELLIOUS — **in·sur·gent·ly** *adv*

in·sur·mount·able \ˌin-sər-ˈmau̇nt-ə-bəl\ *adj* : incapable of being surmounted

in·sur·rec·tion \ˌin-sə-ˈrek-shən\ *n* : an act or instance of revolting against civil authority or an established government [Medieval French, from Late Latin *insurrectio,* from Latin *insurgere* "to rise up"] — **in·sur·rec·tion·ary** \-shə-ˌner-ē\ *adj or n* — **in·sur·rec·tion·ist** \-shə-nəst\ *n*

in·sus·cep·ti·ble \ˌint-sə-ˈsep-tə-bəl\ *adj* : not susceptible ⟨*insusceptible* to flattery⟩ — **in·sus·cep·ti·bil·i·ty** \-ˌsep-tə-ˈbil-ət-ē\ *n*

in·tact \in-ˈtakt\ *adj* : untouched especially by anything that harms or diminishes : ENTIRE, UNINJURED [Latin *intactus,* from *in-* + *tangere* "to touch"] — **in·tact·ness** \-ˈtakt-nəs, -ˈtak-nəs\ *n*

in·ta·glio \in-ˈtal-yō, -ˈtag-lē-ˌō\ *n, pl* **-glios** **1 a** : an engraving or incised figure in a hard material (as stone) depressed below the surface of the material **b** : the process of making intaglios **c** : printing (as in photogravure) done from a plate in which the image is sunk below the surface **2** : something (as a gem) carved in intaglio [Italian, from *intagliare* "to engrave," from Medieval Latin *intaliare,* from Latin *in-* + Late Latin *taliare* "to cut"]

intaglio 1a

in·take \ˈin-ˌtāk\ *n* **1** : a place where liquid or air is taken into something (as a pump) **2** : the act of taking in ⟨a sharp *intake* of breath⟩ **3** : something taken in ⟨inadequate food *intake*⟩

¹in·tan·gi·ble \in-ˈtan-jə-bəl, ˈin-\ *adj* : not tangible: as **a** : incapable of being touched ⟨light is *intangible*⟩ **b** : incapable of being thought of as matter or substance : ABSTRACT ⟨goodwill is an *intangible* asset⟩ — **in·tan·gi·bil·i·ty** \in-ˌtan-jə-ˈbil-ət-ē\ *n* — **in·tan·gi·ble·ness** \in-ˈtan-jə-bəl-nəs, ˈin-\ *n* — **in·tan·gi·bly** \-blē\ *adv*

²intangible *n* : something intangible: as **a** : an asset (as goodwill) that is not corporeal **b** : an abstract quality or attribute (as loyalty or creativity)

in·te·ger \ˈint-i-jər\ *n* **1** : a number that is a natural number (as 1, 2, or 3), the negative of a natural number, or 0 — called also *whole number* **2** : a complete entity [Latin, "whole, entire"]

¹in·te·gral \ˈint-i-grəl (*usually so in mathematics*); in-ˈteg-rəl, -ˈtēg-\ *adj* **1 a** : essential to completeness : CONSTITUENT ⟨an *integral* part of the plan⟩ **b** : of, relating to, or being a mathematical integer ⟨9 is an *integral* factor of 72⟩ **c** : relaing to or concerned with mathematical integrals or integration **d** : formed as a unit with another part **2** : composed of integral parts : INTEGRATED ⟨an *integral* locking system⟩ **3** : lacking nothing essential : ENTIRE — **in·te·gral·i·ty** \ˌint-ə-ˈgral-ət-ē\ *n* — **in·te·gral·ly** \ˈint-i-grə-lē; in-ˈteg-rə-, -ˈtēg-\ *adv*

²integral *n* : the result of a mathematical integration

integral calculus *n* : a branch of mathematics concerned with the theory and applications of integrals and integration (as the determination of lengths, areas, and volumes) — compare DIFFERENTIAL CALCULUS

in·te·grate \ˈint-ə-ˌgrāt\ *vb* **1** : to form into a whole : UNITE ⟨*integrate* the countries' economies⟩ **2** : to find the integral of ⟨*integrate* the function⟩ **3 a** : to unite with something else ⟨free enterprise *integrated* with some government controls⟩ **b** : to incorporate into a larger unit ⟨*integrate* migrant workers into the organized labor movement⟩ **4 a** : to end the segregation of and bring into common and equal membership in society or an organization **b** : DESEGREGATE ⟨*integrate* school districts⟩ **5** : to become integrated [Latin *integrare,* from *integer* "whole, entire"]

\ə\ **abut**	\au̇\ **out**	\i\ **tip**	\ȯ\ **saw**	\u̇\ **foot**
\ər\ **further**	\ch\ **chin**	\ī\ **life**	\ȯi\ **coin**	\y\ **yet**
\a\ **mat**	\e\ **pet**	\j\ **job**	\th\ **thin**	\yü\ **few**
\ā\ **take**	\ē\ **easy**	\ng\ **sing**	\t͟h\ **this**	\yu̇\ **cure**
\ä\ **cot, cart**	\g\ **go**	\ō\ **bone**	\ü\ **food**	\zh\ **vision**

integrated circuit *n* : a tiny complex of electronic components and their connections that is produced in or on a small slice of material (as silicon) — **integrated circuitry** *n*

integrated pest management *n* : management of agricultural and horticultural pests that utilizes various methods (as biological control) which minimize the use of chemicals

in·te·gra·tion \ˌint-ə-ˈgrā-shən\ *n* **1** : the act, the process, or an instance of integrating; *esp* : incorporation as equals into society or an organization of persons from different groups (as races) **2 a** : the operation of finding a function that has a given differential **b** : the operation of solving a differential equation

in·te·gra·tion·ist \-shə-nəst, -shnəst\ *n* : a person who believes in, advocates, or practices social integration

in·teg·ri·ty \in-ˈteg-rət-ē\ *n* **1** : an unimpaired condition : SOUNDNESS **2** : adherence to a code of especially moral or artistic values **3** : the quality or state of being complete or undivided : COMPLETENESS

in·teg·u·ment \in-ˈteg-yə-mənt\ *n* : something that covers or encloses; *esp* : an enclosing layer (as a skin, membrane, or cuticle) of an organism or one of its parts [Latin *integumentum,* from *integere* "to cover," from *in-* + *tegere* "to cover"] — **in·teg·u·men·ta·ry** \-ˈment-ə-rē, -ˈmen-trē\ *adj*

in·tel·lect \ˈint-l-ˌekt\ *n* **1 a** : the power of knowing **b** : the capacity for thought especially when highly developed **2** : a person of superior intellect [Latin *intellectus,* from *intellegere* "to understand"]

in·tel·lec·tion \ˌint-l-ˈek-shən\ *n* **1** : exercise of the intellect : REASONING **2** : a specific act of the intellect : THOUGHT — **in·tel·lec·tive** \-ˈek-tiv\ *adj* — **in·tel·lec·tive·ly** *adv*

[1]**in·tel·lec·tu·al** \ˌint-l-ˈek-chə-wəl, -chəl\ *adj* **1 a** : having to do with the intellect or understanding **b** : originating in or chiefly guided by intellect rather than by emotion or experience **c** : performed by the intellect ⟨*intellectual* processes⟩ **2** : having intellect to a high degree : engaged in or given to learning and thinking ⟨an *intellectual* writer⟩ **3** : requiring study and thought ⟨*intellectual* games⟩ ***synonyms*** see MENTAL — **in·tel·lec·tu·al·i·ty** \-ˌek-chə-ˈwal-ət-ē\ *n* — **in·tel·lec·tu·al·ly** \-ˈek-chə-wə-lē, -chə-lē\ *adv* — **in·tel·lec·tu·al·ness** \-chə-wəl-nəs, -chəl-\ *n*

[2]**intellectual** *n* : an intellectual person

intellectual disability *n* : significant impairment in intellectual ability accompanied by deficits in skills necessary for independent daily functioning : MENTAL RETARDATION

in·tel·lec·tu·al·ism \ˌint-l-ˈek-chə-wə-ˌliz-əm, -chə-ˌliz-\ *n* : devotion to the exercise of intellect or to intellectual pursuits — **in·tel·lec·tu·al·ist** \-ləst\ *n* — **in·tel·lec·tu·al·is·tic** \-ˌek-chə-wə-ˈlis-tik, -chə-ˈlis-\ *adj*

in·tel·lec·tu·al·ize \ˌint-l-ˈek-chə-wə-ˌlīz, -chə-ˌlīz\ *vt* : to give rational form or content to

intellectual property *n* : property (as an idea, a method, or written work) that derives from the work of the mind

in·tel·li·gence \in-ˈtel-ə-jəns\ *n* **1 a** : the ability to learn and understand or to deal with new or challenging situations : REASON, INTELLECT **b** : mental acuteness : SHREWDNESS **2** : an intelligent being **3** : the act of understanding : COMPREHENSION **3 a** : information communicated : NEWS **b** : information concerning an enemy or possible enemy; *also* : a group or agency gathering such intelligence

intelligence quotient *n* : IQ

intelligence test *n* : a test designed to determine a person's intelligence compared to others

in·tel·li·gent \in-ˈtel-ə-jənt\ *adj* **1 a** : having or indicating a high or satisfactory degree of intelligence ⟨humans are *intelligent* beings⟩ **b** : revealing or reflecting good judgment or sound thought ⟨an *intelligent* decision⟩ **2** : controlled by a computer ⟨an *intelligent* terminal⟩ [Latin *intelligens,* from *intelligere, intellegere* "to understand," from *inter-* + *legere* "to select"] ***synonyms*** see CLEVER — **in·tel·li·gent·ly** *adv*

in·tel·li·gen·tsia \in-ˌtel-ə-ˈjen-sē-ə, -ˈgen-\ *n* : intellectuals as a group [Russian *intelligentsiya,* from Latin *intelligentia* "intelligence"]

in·tel·li·gi·ble \in-ˈtel-ə-jə-bəl\ *adj* : capable of being understood — **in·tel·li·gi·bil·i·ty** \-ˌtel-ə-jə-ˈbil-ət-ē\ *n* — **in·tel·li·gi·ble·ness** \-ˈtel-ə-jə-bəl-nəs\ *n* — **in·tel·li·gi·bly** \-blē\ *adv*

in·tem·per·ance \in-ˈtem-pə-rəns, ˈin-, -prəns\ *n* : lack of moderation; *esp* : habitual or excessive use of intoxicants

in·tem·per·ate \-pə-rət, -prət\ *adj* : not temperate: as **a** : not moderate or mild : EXTREME, SEVERE ⟨*intemperate* weather⟩ **b** : lacking or showing lack of restraint or self-control **c** : given to excessive use of intoxicants — **in·tem·per·ate·ly** *adv* — **in·tem·per·ate·ness** *n*

in·tend \in-ˈtend\ *vt* : to have in mind as a purpose or aim : PLAN ⟨*intended* no harm⟩ ⟨*intends* to write her memoirs⟩ [Medieval French *entendre,* from Latin *intendere* "to stretch out, direct, aim at," from *in-* + *tendere* "to stretch"]

in·ten·dant \in-ˈten-dənt\ *n* : an administrative official (as a governor) especially under the French, Spanish, or Portuguese monarchies [French, from Latin *intendere* "to intend, attend"]

[1]**in·tend·ed** \in-ˈten-dəd\ *adj* **1** : planned for the future ⟨one's *intended* career⟩ **2** : INTENTIONAL ⟨an *intended* insult⟩

[2]**intended** *n* : the person to whom another is engaged

in·tense \in-ˈtens\ *adj* **1 a** : existing in an extreme degree ⟨*intense* heat⟩ **b** : having or showing a characteristic in extreme degree ⟨*intense* colors⟩ **2** : marked by or expressive of great zeal, energy, determination or concentration ⟨*intense* effort⟩ **3 a** : exhibiting strong feeling or earnestness of purpose ⟨an *intense* actor⟩ **b** : deeply felt ⟨*intense* convictions⟩ [Medieval French, from Latin *intensus,* from *intendere* "to stretch out, intend"] — **in·tense·ly** *adv* — **in·tense·ness** *n*

in·ten·si·fy \in-ˈten-sə-ˌfī\ *vb* **-fied; -fy·ing** **1** : to make or become intense or more intensive : STRENGTHEN **2** : to make or become more acute : SHARPEN — **in·ten·si·fi·ca·tion** \-ˌten-sə-fə-ˈkā-shən\ *n* — **in·ten·si·fi·er** \-ˈten-sə-ˌfī-ər, -ˌfīr\ *n*

synonyms INTENSIFY, HEIGHTEN, AGGRAVATE, ENHANCE mean to increase markedly in measure or degree. INTENSIFY implies a deepening or strengthening of a thing or its characteristics ⟨*intensify* efforts for peace⟩ ⟨colors were *intensified* by the clear atmosphere⟩. HEIGHTEN suggests a lifting above the ordinary or accustomed ⟨tried to *heighten* awareness of possible danger⟩. AGGRAVATE stresses the worsening of something already bad ⟨inflation *aggravated* the economic depression⟩. ENHANCE suggests a raising above normal in desirability or attractiveness ⟨shrubbery *enhances* a lawn⟩.

in·ten·si·ty \in-ˈten-sət-ē\ *n, pl* **-ties** **1** : the quality or state of being intense; *esp* : extreme degree of strength, force, energy, or feeling **2** : the magnitude of force or energy per unit (as of surface, charge, or mass) ⟨the *intensity* of an electric or magnetic field⟩ **3** : SATURATION 2

[1]**in·ten·sive** \in-ˈten-siv\ *adj* **1** : involving or marked by special effort : THOROUGH, EXHAUSTIVE ⟨an *intensive* campaign⟩ ⟨*intensive* agriculture⟩ **2** : serving to give emphasis ⟨an *intensive* adverb, as "dreadfully" in "it was dreadfully cold"⟩ — **in·ten·sive·ly** *adv* — **in·ten·sive·ness** *n*

[2]**intensive** *n* : an intensive word

intensive care *n* : continuous monitoring and treatment of seriously ill patients using special medical equipment and services; *also* : a unit in a hospital providing intensive care

[1]**in·tent** \in-ˈtent\ *n* **1** : the act, fact, or state of mind of intending ⟨with *intent* to injure⟩ **2** : MEANING, SIGNIFICANCE ⟨understand the *intent* of the message⟩ [Medieval French *entente,* from Late Latin *intentus,* from Latin *intendere* "to intend"]

[2]**intent** *adj* **1** : directed with strained or eager attention ⟨an *intent* gaze⟩ **2 a** : closely occupied ⟨*intent* upon their plans⟩ **b** : set on some end or purpose ⟨*intent* on going⟩ — **in·tent·ly** *adv* — **in·tent·ness** *n*

in·ten·tion \in-ˈten-chən\ *n* **1** : a determination to act in a certain way ⟨done without *intention*⟩ **2** : an intended object : PURPOSE, END ⟨carry out one's *intention*⟩ **3** : IMPORT, SIGNIFICANCE ⟨grasp the *intention* of a speaker⟩

synonyms INTENTION, PURPOSE, DESIGN, AIM mean what one intends to accomplish or attain. INTENTION implies little more than what one has in mind to do or bring about ⟨announced his *intention* to learn to cook⟩. PURPOSE suggests a more settled determination ⟨being successful was her *purpose* in life⟩. DESIGN implies a carefully calculated plan ⟨the order of events came by accident, not *design*⟩. AIM adds implications of definite purpose and effort to attain or accomplish an end ⟨her *aim* was to reduce waste in manufacturing⟩.

in·ten·tion·al \in-ˈtench-nəl, -ˈten-chən-l\ *adj* : done by intention or design : DELIBERATE ⟨*intentional* damage⟩ ***synonyms*** see VOLUNTARY — **in·ten·tion·al·i·ty** \-ˌten-chə-ˈnal-ət-ē\ *n* — **in·ten·tion·al·ly** \in-ˈtench-nə-lē, -ˈten-chən-l-ē\ *adv*

in·ter \in-ˈtər\ *vt* **in·terred; in·ter·ring** : to deposit (a dead body) in the earth or in a tomb [Medieval French *enterrer,* from Latin *in-* + *terra* "earth"]

inter- *prefix* **1** : between : among : in the midst ⟨*inter*penetrate⟩ ⟨*inter*stellar⟩ **2** : reciprocal : reciprocally ⟨*inter*marry⟩

3 : located between ⟨*inter*face⟩ 4 : carried on between ⟨*inter*national⟩ 5 : occurring between : intervening ⟨*inter*glacial⟩ 6 : shared by or derived from two or more ⟨*inter*faith⟩ [Latin, from *inter*]

interagency	**interdependence**	**interoffice**
interatomic	**interdependency**	**interoperate**
interbank	**interdependent**	**interoperative**
interborough	**interdependently**	**interparish**
interbranch	**interdialectal**	**interparty**
intercampus	**interdistrict**	**interplanetary**
intercaste	**interdivisional**	**interpopulation**
intercell	**interelectronic**	**interprofessional**
intercellular	**interethnic**	**interprovincial**
interchannel	**interfaculty**	**interregional**
interchurch	**interfamily**	**interreligious**
intercity	**interfiber**	**interrow**
interclan	**interfraternity**	**interschool**
interclass	**intergang**	**intersectional**
interclub	**intergeneration**	**intersegment**
intercoastal	**intergenerational**	**intersegmental**
intercolonial	**intergeneric**	**intersocietal**
intercommunal	**intergroup**	**intersociety**
intercommunity	**interhemispheric**	**intersystem**
intercompany	**interindustry**	**interterminal**
intercorporate	**interinstitutional**	**interterritorial**
intercountry	**interisland**	**intertribal**
intercounty	**interlay**	**intertroop**
intercultural	**interlayer**	**interunion**
interculturally	**interleague**	**interunit**
interculture	**interlibrary**	**interuniversity**
interdenomina-tional	**intermolecular**	**interurban**
interdepartmental	**intermolecularly**	**intervalley**
interdepartmental-ly	**intermountain**	**intervillage**
interdepend	**internuclear**	**interwar**
	interocean	**interzonal**
	interoceanic	**interzone**

in·ter·act \ˌint-ə-ˈrakt\ *vi* : to act upon one another

in·ter·ac·tion \ˌint-ə-ˈrak-shən\ *n* : the action or influence of people, groups, or things on one another — **in·ter·ac·tion·al** \-shnəl, -shə-nəl\ *adj*

in·ter·ac·tive \-ˈrak-tiv\ *adj* 1 : active between people, groups, or things 2 : involving the actions or input of a user ⟨an *interactive* museum exhibit⟩; *esp* : of, relating to, or allowing two-way electronic communications (as between a person and a computer) — **in·ter·ac·tive·ly** *adv* — **in·ter·ac·tiv·i·ty** \-ˌrak-ˈtiv-ət-ē\ *n*

in·ter alia \ˌint-ə-ˈrā-lē-ə, -ˈrä-\ *adv* : among other things [Latin]

in·ter·breed \ˌint-ər-ˈbrēd\ *vb* **-bred** \-ˈbred\; **-breed·ing** : to breed or cause to breed together : as **a** : CROSSBREED **b** : to breed within a closed population

in·ter·ca·lary \in-ˈtər-kə-ˌler-ē, ˌint-ər-ˈkal-ə-rē\ *adj* : inserted between other things or parts

in·ter·ca·late \in-ˈtər-kə-ˌlāt\ *vt* 1 : to insert (as a day) in a calendar 2 : to insert between or among existing elements or layers [Latin *intercalare,* from *inter-* + *calare* "to call, proclaim"] — **in·ter·ca·la·tion** \-ˌtər-kə-ˈlā-shən\ *n*

in·ter·cede \ˌint-ər-ˈsēd\ *vi* 1 : to act as a go-between between unfriendly parties 2 : to beg or plead in behalf of another ⟨*intercede* for a friend⟩ [Latin *intercedere,* from *inter-* + *cedere* "to go"] ***synonyms*** see INTERPOSE

[1]**in·ter·cept** \ˌint-ər-ˈsept\ *vt* 1 : to stop or seize on the way to or before arrival at a destination ⟨*intercept* a letter⟩ ⟨*intercept* a pass in football⟩ 2 : to include part of (a curve, surface, or solid) between two points, curves, or surfaces ⟨a line *intercepted* between points A and B⟩ [Latin *interceptus,* past participle of *intercipere* "to prevent, hinder," from *inter-* + *capere* "to take, seize"]

[2]**in·ter·cept** \ˈint-ər-ˌsept\ *n* : the distance from the origin of a coordinate system to a point where a graph (as of a line) crosses a coordinate axis

in·ter·cep·tion \ˌint-ər-ˈsep-shən\ *n* : the act of intercepting : the state of being intercepted

in·ter·cep·tor *also* **in·ter·cep·ter** \ˌint-ər-ˈsep-tər\ *n* : one that intercepts; *esp* : a light high-speed fast-climbing fighter plane designed for defense against raiding bombers

in·ter·ces·sion \ˌint-ər-ˈsesh-ən\ *n* 1 : the act of interceding : MEDIATION 2 : prayer, petition, or entreaty in favor of another [Latin *intercessio,* from *intercedere* "to intercede"] — **in·ter·ces·sion·al** \-ˈsesh-nəl, -ən-l\ *adj* — **in·ter·ces·sor** \-ˈses-ər\ *n* — **in·ter·ces·so·ry** \-ˈses-rē, -ə-rē\ *adj*

[1]**in·ter·change** \ˌint-ər-ˈchānj\ *vb* 1 : to put each of (two things) in the place of the other ⟨*interchange* two tires⟩ 2 : EXCHANGE ⟨*interchange* ideas⟩ 3 : to change places mutually — **in·ter·chang·er** *n*

[2]**in·ter·change** \ˈint-ər-ˌchānj\ *n* 1 : the act, the process, or an instance of interchanging : EXCHANGE 2 : a joining of two or more highways by a system of separate levels that permit traffic to pass from one to another without the crossing of traffic streams

in·ter·change·able \ˌint-ər-ˈchān-jə-bəl\ *adj* : capable of being interchanged; *esp* : permitting mutual substitution ⟨*interchangeable* parts⟩ — **in·ter·change·abil·i·ty** \-ˌchān-jə-ˈbil-ət-ē\ *n* — **in·ter·change·able·ness** \-ˈchān-je-bəl-nəs\ *n* — **in·ter·change·ably** \-blē\ *adv*

in·ter·col·le·giate \ˌint-ər-kə-ˈlē-jət, -jē-ət\ *adj* : existing or carried on between colleges ⟨*intercollegiate* athletics⟩

in·ter·com \ˈint-ər-ˌkäm\ *n* : a two-way communication system with microphone and loudspeaker at each station for localized use

in·ter·com·mu·ni·cate \ˌint-ər-kə-ˈmyü-nə-ˌkāt\ *vi* 1 : to exchange communication with one another 2 : to afford passage from one to another ⟨the rooms *intercommunicate*⟩ — **in·ter·com·mu·ni·ca·tion** \-ˌmyü-nə-ˈkā-shən\ *n*

intercommunication system *n* : INTERCOM

in·ter·com·mu·nion \ˌint-ər-kə-ˈmyü-nyən\ *n* : interdenominational participation in communion

in·ter·con·nect \ˌint-ər-kə-ˈnekt\ *vb* : to connect with one another ⟨the rooms *interconnect*⟩ ⟨*interconnected* switches⟩ — **in·ter·con·nec·tion** \-ˈnek-shən\ *n*

in·ter·con·ti·nen·tal \ˌint-ər-ˌkänt-n-ˈent-l\ *adj* 1 : extending among or carried on between continents ⟨*intercontinental* trade⟩ 2 : capable of traveling between continents ⟨an *intercontinental* missile⟩

in·ter·con·ver·sion \ˌint-ər-kən-ˈvər-zhən, -shən\ *n* : mutual conversion ⟨*interconversion* of chemical compounds⟩ — **in·ter·con·vert** \-ˈvərt\ *vt* — **in·ter·con·vert·ible** \-ˈvərt-ə-bəl\ *adj*

in·ter·cool·er \ˌint-ər-ˈkü-lər\ *n* : a device for cooling a fluid between successive heat-generating processes

in·ter·cos·tal \ˌint-ər-ˈkäs-tl\ *adj* : situated or extending between the ribs ⟨*intercostal* spaces⟩ ⟨an *intercostal* muscle⟩ [Latin *costa* "rib"] — **intercostal** *n*

in·ter·course \ˈint-ər-ˌkōrs, -ˌkȯrs\ *n* 1 : connection or relations between persons or groups : COMMUNICATION ⟨social *intercourse*⟩ 2 : physical sexual contact between individuals that involves the genitalia of at least one person; *esp* : SEXUAL INTERCOURSE [derived from Latin *intercursus* "act of running between," from *intercurrere* "to run between," from *inter-* + *currere* "to run"]

in·ter·crop \ˌint-ər-ˈkräp\ *vb* : to grow two or more crops at one time (as in alternate rows) on the same piece of land

in·ter·cross \ˈint-ər-ˌkrȯs\ *n* : an instance or a product of crossbreeding — **in·ter·cross** \ˌint-ər-ˈkrȯs\ *vb*

[1]**in·ter·dict** \ˈint-ər-ˌdikt\ *n* 1 : a Roman Catholic ecclesiastical censure withdrawing most sacraments and Christian burial from a person or district 2 : PROHIBITION 2 [Medieval French *entredite,* from Latin *interdictum* "prohibition," from *interdicere* "to interpose, forbid," from *inter-* + *dicere* "to say"]

[2]**in·ter·dict** \ˌint-ər-ˈdikt\ *vt* : to prohibit or forbid especially by an interdict — **in·ter·dic·tion** \ˌint-ər-ˈdik-shən\ *n* — **in·ter·dic·tor** \-ˈdik-tər\ *n* — **in·ter·dic·to·ry** \-ˈdik-tə-rē, -trē\ *adj*

in·ter·dig·i·tate \-ˈdij-ə-ˌtāt\ *vi* : to interlock like the fingers of folded hands [Latin *digitus* "finger"] — **in·ter·dig·i·ta·tion** \-ˌdij-ə-ˈtā-shən\ *n*

in·ter·dis·ci·pli·nary \ˌint-ər-ˈdis-ə-plə-ˌner-ē\ *adj* : involving two or more academic disciplines

[1]**in·ter·est** \ˈin-trəst; ˈint-ə-ˌrest, -ə-rəst, -ərst; ˈin-ˌtrest\ *n* 1 : a right, title, or legal share in something 2 : BENEFIT 1a, WELFARE; *also* : SELF-INTEREST 3 **a** : a charge for borrowed money that is generally a percentage of the amount borrowed **b** : the profit in goods or money that is made on invested capital

\ə\ **abut**	\au̇\ **out**	\i\ **tip**	\ȯ\ **saw**	\u̇\ **foot**
\ər\ **further**	\ch\ **chin**	\ī\ **life**	\ȯi\ **coin**	\y\ **yet**
\a\ **mat**	\e\ **pet**	\j\ **job**	\th\ **thin**	\yü\ **few**
\ā\ **take**	\ē\ **easy**	\ng\ **sing**	\th\ **this**	\yu̇\ **cure**
\ä\ **cot, cart**	\g\ **go**	\ō\ **bone**	\ü\ **food**	\zh\ **vision**

4 : a group financially interested in an industry or enterprise ⟨mining *interests*⟩; *esp* : LOBBY 2 **5 a** : readiness to be concerned with or moved by something **b** : the quality in a thing that arouses interest ⟨your plans are of great *interest* to me⟩ [derived from Latin *interesse* "to be between, make a difference, concern," from *inter-* + *esse* "to be"]

²interest *vt* **1** : to persuade to participate or take part ⟨couldn't *interest* her in a game of chess⟩ **2** : to arouse the interest of ⟨the gossip does not *interest* me⟩

in•ter•est•ed *adj* **1** : having the attention occupied ⟨*interested* listeners⟩ **2** : being involved ⟨*interested* parties⟩ — **in•ter•est•ed•ly** *adv*

interest group *n* : a group of persons having a common interest that often provides a basis for action

in•ter•est•ing *adj* : holding the attention : arousing interest

in•ter•est•ing•ly *adv* **1** : in an interesting manner ⟨a story *interestingly* told⟩ **2** : as a matter of interest ⟨*interestingly,* there are two alike⟩

¹in•ter•face \ˈint-ər-ˌfās\ *n* **1** : a surface forming a common boundary of two bodies, spaces, or phases ⟨an *interface* between oil and water⟩ **2** : a place at which two independent systems meet and act on or communicate with each other; *also* : a means of communication at an interface — **in•ter•fa•cial** \ˌint-ər-ˈfā-shəl\ *adj*

²interface *vb* **1** : to connect or become connected through an interface **2** : to serve as an interface for

in•ter•fac•ing \-ˌfā-sing\ *n* : fabric attached especially between the facing and the outside of a garment (as in a collar or cuff) for stiffening or reinforcing

in•ter•faith \ˈint-ər-ˌfāth\ *adj* : involving persons of different religious faiths ⟨*interfaith* conference⟩

in•ter•fere \ˌint-ər-ˈfiər, ˌint-ə-ˈfiər\ *vi* **1** : to strike one foot against the opposite foot or ankle in walking or running — used especially of horses **2** : to come in collision or be in opposition : CLASH ⟨our neighbor's arrival *interfered* with our plan⟩ **3** : to meddle in the affairs of others ⟨don't *interfere* with my business⟩ **4** : to act so as to augment, diminish, or otherwise affect one another ⟨*interfering* light waves⟩ **5** : to hinder illegally an attempt of a player to receive a pass or to play a ball or puck [Medieval French *s'entreferir* "to strike one another," from *entre-* "inter-" + *ferir* "to strike," from Latin *ferire*] ***synonyms*** see INTERPOSE — **in•ter•fer•er** *n*

in•ter•fer•ence \ˌint-ər-ˈfir-əns, ˌint-ə-ˈfir-\ *n* **1 a** : the act or process of interfering **b** : something that interferes : OBSTRUCTION **2** : the mutual effect on meeting of two waves (as of light or sound) whereby the resulting neutralization at some points and reinforcement at others produces in the case of light waves alternate light and dark bands or colored bands **3 a** : the legal blocking of an opponent in football **b** : the illegal hindering of an opponent (as in baseball) **4 a** : confusion of received radio signals due to undesired signals or electrical effects **b** : an electrical effect that produces such confusion — **in•ter•fer•en•tial** \-fə-ˈren-chəl, -ˌfir-ˈen-\ *adj*

in•ter•fer•om•e•ter \ˌin-tər-fə-ˈräm-ət-ər\ *n* : an instrument that uses the interference of waves (as of light) for making precise measurements (as of distance or wavelength) — **in•ter•fer•o•met•ric** \-ˌfir-ə-ˈmet-rik\ *adj* — **in•ter•fer•om•e•try** \-fə-ˈräm-ə-trē\ *n*

in•ter•fer•on \ˌin-tər-ˈfir-ˌän\ *n* : any of a group of proteins that are produced by cells and that prevent viruses attacking the cells from replicating [*interfere* + *-on*]

in•ter•fer•tile \ˌint-ər-ˈfərt-l\ *adj* : capable of interbreeding — **in•ter•fer•til•i•ty** \-fər-ˈtil-ət-ē\ *n*

in•ter•fuse \ˌint-ər-ˈfyüz\ *vb* **1** : to combine by fusing : BLEND ⟨*interfuse* rock and country music⟩ **2** : to add as if by fusing : INFUSE ⟨a factual account *interfused* with wit⟩ — **in•ter•fu•sion** \-ˈfyü-zhən\ *n*

in•ter•ga•lac•tic \ˌint-ər-gə-ˈlak-tik\ *adj* : situated or occurring in the spaces between galaxies

¹in•ter•gla•cial \ˌint-ər-ˈglā-shəl\ *adj* : occurring or relating to the time between successive glaciations

²interglacial *n* : a period of warm climate between glaciations

in•ter•gov•ern•men•tal \-ˌgəv-ərn-ˈment-l, -ər-\ *adj* : existing or occurring between two or more governments or levels of government ⟨*intergovernmental* meetings⟩

in•ter•grade \ˌint-ər-ˈgrād\ *vi* : to merge gradually one with another through a continuous series of intermediates — **in•ter•gra•da•tion** \-grā-ˈdā-shən, -grə-\ *n* — **in•ter•gra•da•tion•al** \-shnəl, -shən-l\ *adj*

in•ter•im \ˈint-ə-rəm\ *n* : an intervening time : INTERVAL [Latin, adv., "meanwhile," from *inter* "between"] — **interim** *adj*

¹in•te•ri•or \in-ˈtir-ē-ər\ *adj* **1** : being or acting within a limiting boundary **2** : remote from the border or shore : INLAND [Latin] — **in•te•ri•or•ly** *adv*

²interior *n* **1** : the internal or inner part of something : INSIDE ⟨the brightly decorated *interior* of the bowl⟩ **2** : the inland part (as of a country or island) ⟨traveled to the *interior* of Australia⟩ **3** : inner nature : CHARACTER **4** : the internal affairs of a state or nation ⟨department of the *interior*⟩

interior angle *n* **1** : the inner of the two angles formed where two sides of a polygon come together **2** : any of the four angles formed in the area between a pair of parallel lines when a third line cuts them

interior decoration *n* : INTERIOR DESIGN

interior decorator *n* : INTERIOR DESIGNER

interior design *n* : the art of planning the layout and furnishings of the interior of a building

interior designer *n* : a person who specializes in interior design

in•te•ri•or•i•ty \in-ˌtir-ē-ˈór-ət-ē, -ˈär-\ *n* **1** : interior quality or character **2** : inner life or substance : psychological existence

in•ter•ject \ˌint-ər-ˈjekt\ *vt* : to throw in between or among other things : INSERT ⟨*interject* a remark⟩ [Latin *interjectus,* past participle of *intericere* "to interject," from *inter-* + *jacere* "to throw"] ***synonyms*** see INTRODUCE — **in•ter•jec•tor** \-ˈjek-tər\ *n* — **in•ter•jec•to•ry** \-tə-rē, -trē\ *adj*

in•ter•jec•tion \ˌint-ər-ˈjek-shən\ *n* **1** : an interjecting of something **2** : something interjected ⟨the speaker was interrupted by *interjections* from the audience⟩ **3** : a word or cry expressing sudden or strong feeling and usually lacking grammatical connection — **in•ter•jec•tion•al** \-shnəl, -shən-l\ *adj* — **in•ter•jec•tion•al•ly** \-ē\ *adv*

in•ter•lace \ˌint-ər-ˈlās\ *vb* **1** : to unite by or as if by lacing together ⟨*interlaced* fibers⟩ **2** : to vary by alternating : INTERSPERSE **3** : to cross one another as if woven together ⟨*interlacing* boughs⟩ — **in•ter•lace•ment** \-ˈlā-smənt\ *n*

in•ter•lard \ˌint-ər-ˈlärd\ *vt* : to insert or introduce at intervals : INTERSPERSE ⟨a speech *interlarded* with quotations⟩

in•ter•leave \ˌint-ər-ˈlēv\ *vt* **-leaved; -leav•ing** : to arrange in or as if in alternating layers

in•ter•leu•kin \ˌin-tər-ˈlü-kən\ *n* : any of various proteins that are produced by lymphocytes, macrophages, and monocytes and that function especially in regulation of the immune system [*inter-* + *leuk-* + ¹*-in*]

¹in•ter•line \ˌint-ər-ˈlīn\ *vt* : to insert between lines already written or printed — **in•ter•lin•ea•tion** \-ˌlin-ē-ˈā-shən\ *n*

²interline *vt* : to provide (a garment) with an interlining

in•ter•lin•ear \ˌint-ər-ˈlin-ē-ər\ *adj* **1** : inserted between lines already written or printed **2** : written or printed in different languages or texts in alternate lines — **in•ter•lin•ear•ly** *adv*

in•ter•lin•ing \ˈint-ər-ˌlī-ning\ *n* : a lining (as of a coat) between the ordinary lining and the outside fabric

in•ter•link \ˌint-ər-ˈlingk\ *vt* : to link together

in•ter•lock \ˌint-ər-ˈläk\ *vb* : to lock together : UNITE ⟨a series of rings *interlocking* to form a chain⟩ — **in•ter•lock** \ˈint-ər-ˌläk\ *n*

in•ter•loc•u•tor \ˌint-ər-ˈläk-yət-ər\ *n* **1** : one who takes part in dialogue or conversation **2** : a man in a minstrel show who questions the end men

in•ter•lop•er \ˌint-ər-ˈlō-pər, ˈint-ər-ˌ\ *n* : a person who intrudes or interferes wrongly : INTRUDER [probably related to Dutch *loper* "runner," from *lopen* "to run"]

in•ter•lude \ˈint-ər-ˌlüd\ *n* **1** : a performance or entertainment between the acts of a play **2** : an intervening period, space, or event : INTERVAL ⟨an *interlude* of peace between wars⟩ **3** : a musical composition inserted between the parts of a longer composition, a drama, or a religious service [Medieval Latin *interludium,* from Latin *inter-* + *ludus* "play"]

in•ter•mar•riage \ˌint-ər-ˈmar-ij\ *n* : marriage between members of different racial, social, or religious groups

in•ter•mar•ry \-ˈmar-ē\ *vi* **1** : to marry each other **2** : to become connected by intermarriage

in•ter•med•dle \ˌint-ər-ˈmed-l\ *vi* : to meddle impertinently and usually so as to interfere — **in•ter•med•dler** \-ˈmed-lər, -l-ər\ *n*

¹in•ter•me•di•ary \ˌint-ər-ˈmēd-ē-ˌer-ē\ *adj* **1** : INTERMEDIATE ⟨an *intermediary* stage⟩ **2** : acting as a mediator ⟨an *intermediary* agent⟩

²intermediary *n, pl* **-ar•ies** : MEDIATOR 1, GO-BETWEEN ⟨acting as *intermediary* between the warring factions⟩

¹in·ter·me·di·ate \ˌint-ər-ˈmed-e-ət\ *adj* **:** being or occurring at the middle place or degree or between extremes [Medieval Latin *intermediatus,* from Latin *intermedius,* from *inter-* + *medius* "middle"] — **in·ter·me·di·ate·ly** *adv* — **in·ter·me·di·ate·ness** *n*

²intermediate *n* **1 :** an intermediate term, thing, or class **2 :** MEDIATOR 1, GO-BETWEEN

in·ter·ment \in-ˈtər-mənt\ *n* **:** BURIAL

in·ter·mesh \ˌin-tər-ˈmesh\ *vb* **:** to mesh together **:** INTERLOCK

in·ter·mez·zo \ˌint-ər-ˈmet-sō, -ˈmed-zō\ *n, pl* **-zi** \-sē, -zē\ *or* **-zos 1 :** a short light piece between the acts of a serious drama or opera **2 a :** a movement coming between the major sections of an extended musical work (as a symphony) **b :** a short independent instrumental composition [Italian, derived from Latin *intermedius* "intermediate"]

in·ter·mi·na·ble \in-ˈtərm-nə-bəl, ˈin-, -ə-nə-\ *adj* **:** ENDLESS; *esp* **:** wearisomely dragged out ⟨an *interminable* speech⟩ — **in·ter·mi·na·ble·ness** *n* — **in·ter·mi·na·bly** \-blē\ *adv*

in·ter·min·gle \ˌint-ər-ˈming-gəl\ *vb* **:** INTERMIX

in·ter·mis·sion \ˌint-ər-ˈmish-ən\ *n* **1 :** INTERRUPTION ⟨worked without *intermission*⟩ **2 :** a pause or interval between the parts of an entertainment (as the acts of a play) [Latin *intermissio,* from *intermittere* "to intermit"]

in·ter·mit \-ˈmit\ *vb* **-mit·ted; -mit·ting :** to stop for a time or at intervals [Latin *intermittere,* from *inter-* + *mittere* "to send"] — **in·ter·mit·ter** *n*

in·ter·mit·tent \-ˈmit-nt\ *adj* **:** coming and going at intervals **:** not continuous ⟨*intermittent* rain⟩ — **in·ter·mit·tence** \-ˈmit-ns\ *n* — **in·ter·mit·tent·ly** *adv*

in·ter·mix \ˌint-ər-ˈmiks\ *vb* **:** to mix together — **in·ter·mix·ture** \-ˈmiks-chər\ *n*

¹in·tern \ˈin-ˌtərn, in-ˈ\ *vt* **:** to confine or impound especially during a war ⟨*intern* enemy aliens⟩ [French *interner,* from Latin *internus* "internal"]

²in·tern *also* **in·terne** \ˈin-ˌtərn\ *n* **:** an advanced student or graduate usually in a professional field (as medicine or teaching) gaining supervised practical experience (as in a hospital or classroom) [French *interne,* from *interne* "internal," from Latin *internus*]

³in·tern \ˈin-ˌtərn\ *vi* **:** to work as an intern

in·ter·nal \in-ˈtərn-l\ *adj* **1 a :** existing or situated within the limits or surface of something ⟨*internal* structure⟩ **b :** relating to or occurring or located in the interior of the body ⟨*internal* organs⟩ ⟨*internal* pain⟩ **2 :** relating or belonging to or existing within the mind **3 :** INTRINSIC, INHERENT ⟨test a theory for *internal* consistency⟩ **4 :** of or relating to the domestic affairs of a state ⟨*internal* revenue⟩ [Latin *internus*] — **in·ter·nal·i·ty** \ˌin-ˌtər-ˈnal-ət-ē\ *n* — **in·ter·nal·ly** \in-ˈtərn-l-ē\ *adv*

internal combustion engine *n* **:** an engine run by a fuel mixture ignited within the engine cylinder instead of in an external furnace

internal medicine *n* **:** a branch of medicine that deals with diseases not requiring surgery

internal respiration *n* **:** exchange of gases between the cells of the body and the blood — compare EXTERNAL RESPIRATION

internal rhyme *n* **:** rhyme between a word within a line and another at the end of the same line or within another line

internal secretion *n* **:** HORMONE 1

¹in·ter·na·tion·al \ˌint-ər-ˈnash-nəl, -ən-l\ *adj* **1 :** involving or affecting two or more nations ⟨*international* trade⟩ **2 :** of, relating to, or constituting a group having members in two or more nations ⟨an *international* union⟩ **3 :** active, known, or reaching beyond national boundaries ⟨an *international* reputation⟩ — **in·ter·na·tion·al·i·ty** \-ˌnash-ə-ˈnal-ət-ē\ *n* — **in·ter·na·tion·al·ly** \-ˈnash-nə-lē, -ən-l-ē\ *adv*

²international *n* **:** one that is international; *esp* **:** an organization of international scope

international date line *n* **:** an imaginary line along the 180th meridian named as the place where each calendar day begins

in·ter·na·tion·al·ism \ˌint-ər-ˈnash-nəl-ˌiz-əm, -ˈnash-ən-l-\ *n* **1 :** international character or outlook **2 a :** a policy of political and economic cooperation among nations **b :** an attitude favoring such a policy — **in·ter·na·tion·al·ist** \-əst\ *n or adj*

in·ter·na·tion·al·ize \-ˈnash-nəl-ˌīz, -ˈnash-ən-l-\ *vt* **:** to make international ⟨*internationalized* the company's business⟩; *also* **:** to place under international control ⟨*internationalize* the city⟩ — **in·ter·na·tion·al·i·za·tion** \-ˌnash-nəl-ə-ˈzā-shən, -ˌnash-ən-l-\ *n*

international law *n* **:** a body of rules that control or affect the rights of nations in their relations with each other

International System of Units *n* **:** a system of units based on the metric system and used by international agreement especially for scientific work

international unit *n* **:** a quantity (as of a vitamin) that produces a particular biological effect agreed upon as an international standard of activity

in·ter·nec·ine \ˌint-ər-ˈnes-ˌēn, -ˈnē-ˌsīn; in-ˈtər-nə-ˌsēn\ *adj* **1 :** marked by slaughter **:** DEADLY **2 :** of, relating to, or involving conflict within a group ⟨bitter *internecine* feuds⟩ [Latin *internecinus,* from *internecare* "to destroy, kill," from *inter-* + *necare* "to kill," from *nex* "violent death"]

in·tern·ee \ˌin-ˌtər-ˈnē\ *n* **:** an interned person

In·ter·net \ˈint-ər-ˌnet\ *n* **:** an electronic communications network that connects computer networks and organizational computer facilities around the world

in·ter·neu·ron \ˌint-ər-ˈnü-ˌrän, -ˈnyü-; -ˈnůr-ˌän, -ˈnyůr-\ *n* **:** a neuron that carries a nerve impulse from one neuron to another

in·ter·nist \in-ˈtər-nəst\ *n* **:** a specialist in internal medicine [*internal* medicine]

in·tern·ment \in-ˈtərn-mənt\ *n* **:** the act of interning **:** the state of being interned

in·ter·node \ˈint-ər-ˌnōd\ *n* **:** a space or part between two nodes (as of a stem) **:** SEGMENT

in·tern·ship \ˈin-tərn-ˌship\ *n* **1 :** the state or position of being an intern **2 :** a period of service as an intern

in·ter·nun·ci·al \ˌint-ər-ˈnən-sē-əl, -ˈnůn-\ *adj* **1 :** of or relating to an internuncio **2 :** of, relating to, or being an interneuron

in·ter·nun·cio \-sē-ˌō\ *n* **:** a papal legate of lower rank than a nuncio [Italian *internunzio,* literally, "messenger between two parties," from Latin *internuntius,* from *inter-* + *nuntius* "messenger"]

in·tero·cep·tive \ˌint-ə-rō-ˈsep-tiv\ *adj* **:** of, relating to, or being stimuli arising within the body and especially the internal organs [*inter-* (as in *interior*) + *-o-* + *-ceptive* (as in *receptive*)] — **in·tero·cep·tor** \-ˈsep-tər\ *n*

in·ter·pen·e·trate \ˌint-ər-ˈpen-ə-ˌtrāt\ *vb* **1 :** to penetrate between, within, or throughout **:** PERMEATE **2 :** to penetrate mutually — **in·ter·pen·e·tra·tion** \-ˌpen-ə-ˈtrā-shən\ *n*

in·ter·per·son·al \-ˈpərs-nəl, -n-əl\ *adj* **:** being, relating to, or involving relations between persons — **in·ter·per·son·al·ly** *adv*

in·ter·phase \ˈint-ər-ˌfāz\ *n* **:** the period between the end of one mitotic or meiotic division and the beginning of the next

in·ter·plant \ˌint-ər-ˈplant\ *vt* **:** to plant (a crop) between plants of another kind

in·ter·play \ˈint-ər-ˌplā\ *n* **:** mutual action or influence **:** INTERACTION — **in·ter·play** \ˌint-ər-ˈplā\ *vi*

in·ter·po·late \in-ˈtər-pə-ˌlāt\ *vb* **1 a :** to alter or corrupt (as a text) by inserting new matter **b :** to insert (words) into a text or into a conversation **2 :** to insert between other things or parts **3 :** to estimate values of (data or a function) between two known values **4 :** to make insertions [Latin *interpolare* "to refurbish," from *inter-* + *-polare,* from *polire* "to polish"] ***synonyms*** see INTRODUCE — **in·ter·po·la·tion** \-ˌtər-pə-ˈlā-shən\ *n* — **in·ter·po·la·tive** \-ˈtər-pə-ˌlāt-iv\ *adj* — **in·ter·po·la·tor** \-ˌlāt-ər\ *n*

in·ter·pose \ˌint-ər-ˈpōz\ *vb* **1 a :** to place in an intervening position **b :** to put (oneself) between **:** INTRUDE **2 :** to introduce or throw in between the parts of a conversation or argument **3 :** to be or come between; *esp* **:** to step in between opposing parties [Middle French *interposer,* from Latin *interponere,* from *inter-* + *ponere* "to put"] — **in·ter·pos·er** *n* — **in·ter·po·si·tion** \-pə-ˈzish-ən\ *n*

synonyms INTERPOSE, INTERFERE, INTERVENE, INTERCEDE mean to come or go between. INTERPOSE implies no more than this ⟨*interposed* in the argument⟩. INTERFERE implies a getting in the way or otherwise hindering ⟨strikes *interfere* with production plans⟩. INTERVENE may imply an occurring in space or time between two things or a stepping in to halt or settle a dispute ⟨years *intervening* between graduation and marriage⟩. INTERCEDE implies acting in behalf of an offender or between two parties needing reconciliation ⟨the United Nations *intercedes* in international disputes⟩.

in·ter·pret \in-ˈtər-prət\ *vb* **1 :** to explain the meaning of ⟨*interpret* a dream⟩ **2 :** to understand according to one's belief or judgment ⟨*interpret* an act as hostile⟩ **3 :** to bring out the meaning of by performing ⟨an actor *interprets* a role⟩ **4 :** to translate orally for others [Latin *interpretari,* from *interpres* "agent, interpreter"] ***synonyms*** see EXPLAIN — **in·ter·pret·able** \-prət-ə-bəl\ *adj*

in·ter·pre·ta·tion \in-ˌtər-prə-ˈtā-shən\ *n* **1 :** the act or the result of interpreting **:** EXPLANATION **2 :** an instance of artistic interpretation in performance — **in·ter·pre·ta·tion·al** \-shnəl, -shən-l\ *adj* — **in·ter·pre·ta·tive** \-ˈtər-prə-ˌtāt-iv\ *adj* — **in·ter·pre·ta·tive·ly** *adv*

in·ter·pret·er \in-ˈtər-prət-ər\ *n* **1 :** one that interprets; *esp* **:** a person who translates orally for people speaking different languages **2 :** a computer program that translates an instruction into machine language and executes it before going to the next instruction

in·ter·pre·tive \in-ˈtər-prət-iv\ *adj* **1 :** of, relating to, or based on interpretation ⟨*interpretive* errors⟩ **2 :** designed to interpret **:** EXPLANATORY ⟨*interpretive* exhibits⟩

in·ter·ra·cial \ˌint-ər-ˈrā-shəl, ˌint-ə-ˈrā-\ *adj* **:** of, involving, or designed for members of different races

in·ter·reg·num \ˌint-ə-ˈreg-nəm\ *n, pl* **-nums** *or* **-na** \-nə\ **1 :** a period between two successive reigns or regimes **2 :** a lapse or pause in a continuous series [Latin, from *inter-* + *regnum* "reign"]

in·ter·re·late \ˌint-ər-ri-ˈlāt, ˌint-ə-ri-\ *vb* **:** to bring into or have a mutual relationship — **in·ter·re·la·tion** \-ˈlā-shən\ *n* — **in·ter·re·la·tion·ship** \-ˌship\ *n*

in·ter·ro·gate \in-ˈter-ə-ˌgāt\ *vt* **:** to question usually formally and systematically ⟨*interrogate* a prisoner of war⟩ [Latin *interrogare,* from *inter-* + *rogare* "to ask"] — **in·ter·ro·ga·tion** \-ˌter-ə-ˈgā-shən\ *n* — **in·ter·ro·ga·tion·al** \-shnəl, -shən-l\ *adj* — **in·ter·ro·ga·tor** \-ˈter-ə-ˌgāt-ər\ *n*

interrogation point *n* **:** QUESTION MARK

[1]**in·ter·rog·a·tive** \ˌint-ə-ˈräg-ət-iv\ *adj* **1 :** having the form or force of a question **2 :** used in a question ⟨an *interrogative* pronoun⟩ — **in·ter·rog·a·tive·ly** *adv*

[2]**interrogative** *n* **:** a word (as *who, what, which*) used in asking questions

in·ter·rog·a·to·ry \-ˈräg-ə-ˌtōr-ē, -ˌtȯr-\ *adj* **:** containing, expressing, or implying a question

in·ter·rupt \ˌint-ə-ˈrəpt\ *vb* **1 :** to stop or hinder by breaking in ⟨*interrupt* a conversation⟩ **2 :** to break the uniformity or continuity of ⟨a loud crash *interrupted* the silence⟩ ⟨*interrupt* a sequence⟩ **3 :** to break in upon an action; *esp* **:** to break in with questions or remarks while another is speaking [Latin *interruptus,* past participle of *interrumpere* "to interrupt," from *inter-* + *rumpere* "to break"] — **in·ter·rupt·ible** \-ˈrəp-tə-bəl\ *adj* — **in·ter·rup·tion** \-ˈrəp-shən\ *n* — **in·ter·rup·tive** \-ˈrəp-tiv\ *adj*

in·ter·rupt·er \ˌint-ə-ˈrəp-tər\ *n* **:** one that interrupts; *esp* **:** a device for interrupting an electric current usually automatically

in·ter·scho·las·tic \ˌint-ər-skə-ˈlas-tik\ *adj* **:** existing or carried on between schools ⟨*interscholastic* athletics⟩

in·ter se \ˌint-ər-ˈsā, -ˈsē\ *adv or adj* **:** among or between themselves [Latin]

in·ter·sect \ˌint-ər-ˈsekt\ *vb* **1 :** to pierce or divide by passing through or across **:** CROSS ⟨the line *intersects* the plane⟩ **2 :** to meet and cross at a point ⟨the two streets *intersect*⟩ ⟨*intersecting* lines⟩ [Latin *intersectus,* past participle of *intersecare* "to intersect," from *inter-* + *secare* "to cut"]

in·ter·sec·tion \ˌint-ər-ˈsek-shən\ *n* **1 :** the act or process of intersecting **2 :** the place where two or more things (as streets) intersect ⟨a busy *intersection*⟩ **3 :** the set of elements shared by two or more sets; *esp* **:** the set of points shared by two geometric figures

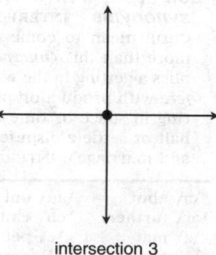

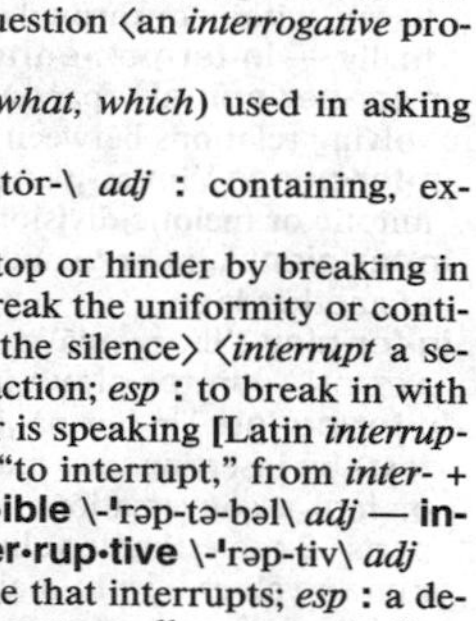
intersection 3

in·ter·sex \ˈint-ər-ˌseks\ *n* **:** an intersexual individual

in·ter·sex·u·al \ˌint-ər-ˈsek-shə-wəl, -shəl\ *adj* **1 :** existing between sexes ⟨*intersexual* hostility⟩ **2 :** intermediate in sexual characters between a typical male and a typical female — **in·ter·sex·u·al·i·ty** \-ˌsek-shə-ˈwal-ət-ē\ *n* — **in·ter·sex·u·al·ly** \-ˈseksh-wə-lē, -ə-wə-; -ˈseksh-lē, -ə-lē\ *adv*

[1]**in·ter·space** \ˈint-ər-ˌspās\ *n* **:** an intervening space **:** INTERVAL

[2]**in·ter·space** \ˌint-ər-ˈspās\ *vt* **:** to occupy or fill the space between

in·ter·spe·cif·ic \ˌint-ər-spi-ˈsif-ik\ *or* **in·ter·spe·cies** \-ˈspē-shēz, -sēz\ *adj* **:** existing or arising between species ⟨*interspecific* hybrids⟩

in·ter·sperse \ˌint-ər-ˈspərs\ *vt* **1 :** to place here and there among other things ⟨*interspersing* photos throughout the text⟩ **2 :** to vary with things inserted here and there ⟨a serious talk *interspersed* with jokes⟩ [Latin *interspersus* "interspersed," from *inter-* + *sparsus,* past participle of *spargere* "to scatter"] — **in·ter·sper·sion** \-ˈspər-zhən\ *n*

in·ter·state \ˌint-ər-ˈstāt\ *adj* **:** of, connecting, or existing between two or more states especially of the U.S. ⟨*interstate* highways⟩

in·ter·stel·lar \-ˈstel-ər\ *adj* **:** located or taking place among the stars ⟨*interstellar* space⟩

in·ter·stice \in-ˈtər-stəs\ *n, pl* **in·ter·stic·es** \-stə-ˌsēz, -stə-səz\ **:** a little space between two things **:** CHINK, CREVICE [Latin *interstitium,* from *inter-* + *-stit-, -stes* "standing" (as in *superstes* "standing over")]

in·ter·sti·tial \ˌint-ər-ˈstish-əl\ *adj* **1 :** relating to or situated in the interstices **2 :** situated within organs or tissues ⟨*interstitial* connective tissue⟩; *also* **:** affecting the interstitial tissues of a body part — **in·ter·sti·tial·ly** \-ˈstish-ə-lē\ *adv*

in·ter·tid·al \-ˈtīd-l\ *adj* **:** of, relating to, or being the area that is above low-tide mark but exposed to tidal flooding

in·ter·trop·i·cal \-ˈträp-i-kəl\ *adj* **:** relating to or being between or within the tropics

in·ter·twine \-ˈtwīn\ *vb* **:** to twine or cause to twine about one another **:** INTERLACE — **in·ter·twine·ment** \-mənt\ *n*

in·ter·twist \-ˈtwist\ *vb* **:** INTERTWINE — **intertwist** *n*

in·ter·val \ˈint-ər-vəl\ *n* **1 :** a space of time between events or states ⟨the *interval* between elections⟩ ⟨an *interval* of three months⟩ **2 a :** a space between things ⟨the *interval* between two desks⟩ **b :** difference in pitch between tones **3 :** a set of numbers between two numbers and either including or excluding one or both of them [Medieval French *entreval,* from Latin *intervallum* "space between ramparts, interval," from *inter-* + *vallum* "rampart"]

in·ter·vene \ˌint-ər-ˈvēn\ *vi* **1 :** to happen as an unrelated event ⟨rain *intervened* and we postponed the match⟩ **2 :** to come between events or points of time ⟨barely one minute *intervened* between the two phone calls⟩ **3 :** to interpose in order to stop, settle, or change something ⟨*intervene* in a quarrel⟩ **4 :** to be or lie between ⟨*intervening* hills⟩ [Latin *intervenire* "to come between," from *inter-* + *venire* "to come"] ***synonyms*** see INTERPOSE — **in·ter·ve·nor** \-ˈvē-nər, -ˌnȯr\ *or* **in·ter·ven·er** \-ˈvē-nər\ *n* — **in·ter·ven·tion** \-ˈven-chən\ *n* — **in·ter·ven·tion·al** \-ˈvench-nəl, -ˈven-chən-l\ *adj*

in·ter·ven·tion·ism \-ˈven-chə-ˌniz-əm\ *n* **:** the theory or practice of intervening; *esp* **:** interference by one country in the political affairs of another — **in·ter·ven·tion·ist** \-ˈvench-nəst, -ə-nəst\ *n or adj*

in·ter·ver·te·bral disk \-ˈvərt-ə-brəl-\ *n* **:** any of the tough disks situated between adjacent vertebrae and consisting of an outer fibrous ring enclosing an inner jellylike portion

in·ter·view \ˈint-ər-ˌvyü\ *n* **1 :** a formal consultation usually to evaluate qualifications (as of a prospective student or employee) **2 :** a meeting at which information is obtained (as by a journalist) from a person; *also* **:** an account of such a meeting — **interview** *vt* — **in·ter·view·er** *n*

in·ter·vo·cal·ic \ˌint-ər-vō-ˈkal-ik\ *adj* **:** immediately preceded and immediately followed by a vowel

in·ter·weave \ˌint-ər-ˈwēv\ *vb* **-wove** \-ˈwōv\ *also* **-weaved; -wo·ven** \-ˈwō-vən\ *also* **-weaved; -weav·ing** **1 :** to weave together **2 :** to blend or cause to blend together

[1]**in·tes·tate** \in-ˈtes-ˌtāt, -ˈtes-tət\ *adj* **1 :** not having made a will ⟨died *intestate*⟩ **2 :** not disposed of by will ⟨*intestate* personal property⟩ — **in·tes·ta·cy** \-ˈtes-tə-sē\ *n*

[2]**intestate** *n* **:** one who dies intestate

in·tes·ti·nal \in-ˈtes-tən-l\ *adj* **1 :** of or relating to the intestine **2 :** affecting or occurring in the intestine — **in·tes·ti·nal·ly** \-l-ē\ *adv*

intestinal fortitude *n* **:** COURAGE, GRIT [euphemism for *guts*]

in·tes·tine \in-ˈtes-tən\ *n* **:** the tubular part of the alimentary canal that extends from the stomach to the anus — compare

LARGE INTESTINE, SMALL INTESTINE [Medieval French *intestin,* from Latin *intestinus* "internal," from *intus* "within"]

in·ti·fa·da \ˌint-ə-ˈfäd-ə\ *n* : UPRISING, REBELLION; *esp* : an armed uprising of Palestinians against Israeli occupation of the West Bank and Gaza Strip [Arabic *intifāḍa,* literally, "the act of shaking up"]

in·ti·ma·cy \ˈint-ə-mə-sē\ *n* **1** : the state of being intimate **2** : something of a personal or private nature

[1]in·ti·mate \ˈint-ə-ˌmāt\ *vt* **1** : to announce formally : DECLARE **2** : to communicate indirectly : HINT [Late Latin *intimare* "to put in, announce," from Latin *intimus* "innermost"] ***synonyms*** see SUGGEST — **in·ti·mat·er** *n* — **in·ti·ma·tion** \ˌint-ə-ˈmā-shən\ *n*

[2]in·ti·mate \ˈint-ə-mət\ *adj* **1** : belonging to or characterizing one's deepest nature ⟨*intimate* reflections⟩ **2** : marked by very close association or contact ⟨*intimate* familiarity with the rules⟩ **3 a** : marked by a warm friendship developing through long association ⟨*intimate* friends⟩ **b** : suggesting informal warmth or privacy ⟨*intimate* clubs⟩ **4** : of a very personal or private nature ⟨*intimate* secrets⟩ [derived from Latin *intimus* "innermost"] — **in·ti·mate·ly** *adv* — **in·ti·mate·ness** *n*

[3]in·ti·mate \ˈint-ə-mət\ *n* : an intimate friend : CONFIDANT

in·tim·i·date \in-ˈtim-ə-ˌdāt\ *vt* : to make timid or fearful, *esp* : to compel or deter by or as if by threats — **in·tim·i·da·tion** \-ˌtim-ə-ˈdā-shən\ *n* — **in·tim·i·da·tor** \-ˈtim-ə-ˌdāt-ər\ *n*

in·to \ˈin-tə, -tü\ *prep* **1 a** — used as a function word to indicate entry, introduction, or inclusion ⟨enter *into* an alliance⟩ ⟨came *into* the room⟩ **2 a** : to the state, condition, or form of ⟨got *into* trouble⟩ **b** : to the occupation, action, or possession of ⟨go *into* farming⟩ **c** : involved with or interested in ⟨was never *into* drugs⟩ ⟨*into* Japanese art⟩ **3** : to a position of contact with : AGAINST ⟨ran *into* a wall⟩

in·tol·er·able \in-ˈtäl-rə-bəl, -ˈtäl-ə-rə-bəl, -ˈtäl-ər-bəl, ˈin-\ *adj* **1** : not tolerable : UNBEARABLE ⟨*intolerable* pain⟩ **2** : EXCESSIVE, EXTREME ⟨*intolerable* sentimentality⟩ — **in·tol·er·abil·i·ty** \in-ˌtäl-rə-ˈbil-ət-ē, -ə-rə-\ *n* — **in·tol·er·able·ness** *n* — **in·tol·er·ably** \-blē\ *adv*

in·tol·er·ance \in-ˈtäl-ə-rəns, ˈin-\ *n* **1** : the quality or state of being intolerant **2** : exceptional sensitivity (as to a drug or food); *esp* : inability of the body to properly digest, process, or absorb a substance (as glucose)

in·tol·er·ant \-rənt\ *adj* **1** : unable or unwilling to endure **2 a** : unwilling to grant equality or freedom especially in religious matters **b** : unwilling to grant or share social, political, or professional advantages **3** : exhibiting physiological intolerance ⟨lactose *intolerant*⟩ — **in·tol·er·ant·ly** *adv*

in·to·nate \ˈin-tə-ˌnāt\ *vt* : UTTER 1, INTONE

in·to·na·tion \ˌin-tə-ˈnā-shən\ *n* **1** : the act of intoning; *also* : something intoned **2** : the ability to sing or play music in tune **3** : the rise and fall in pitch of the voice in speech — **in·to·na·tion·al** \-shnəl, -shən-l\ *adj*

in·tone \in-ˈtōn\ *vb* : to utter in musical or prolonged tones : CHANT — **in·ton·er** *n*

in to·to \in-ˈtōt-ō\ *adv* : TOTALLY, ENTIRELY ⟨accepted the plan *in toto*⟩ [Latin, "on the whole"]

in·tox·i·cant \in-ˈtäk-si-kənt\ *n* : something that intoxicates; *esp* : an alcoholic drink — **intoxicant** *adj*

in·tox·i·cate \in-ˈtäk-sə-ˌkāt\ *vt* **1 a** : POISON 1a **b** : to affect by alcohol or a drug especially to the point where physical and mental control is greatly diminished **2** : to excite or elate to the point of enthusiasm or frenzy ⟨*intoxicated* with joy⟩

in·tox·i·ca·tion \in-ˌtäk-sə-ˈkā-shən\ *n* **1 a** : an abnormal state that is essentially a poisoning ⟨carbon monoxide *intoxication*⟩ **b** : the condition of being drunk : INEBRIATION **2** : a strong excitement or elation ⟨the *intoxication* of success⟩

in·tra- \ˌin-trə, -trä, -ˌträ\ *prefix* **1 a** : within ⟨*intra*cellular⟩ **b** : between layers of ⟨*intra*dermal⟩ **2** : INTRO- 1 ⟨*intra*venous⟩ [Latin *intra*]

in·tra·cel·lu·lar \ˌin-trə-ˈsel-yə-lər\ *adj* : being or occurring within a cell ⟨*intracellular* parasites⟩ — **in·tra·cel·lu·lar·ly** *adv*

in·tra·com·pa·ny \-ˈkəmp-nē, -ə-nē\ *adj* : occurring within or taking place between branches or employees of a company ⟨*intracompany* communications⟩

in·trac·ta·ble \in-ˈtrak-tə-bəl, ˈin-\ *adj* **1** : not easily managed or controlled ⟨an *intractable* child⟩ **2** : not easily relieved or cured ⟨*intractable* pain⟩ — **in·trac·ta·bil·i·ty** \in-ˌtrak-tə-ˈbil-ət-ē\ *n* — **in·trac·ta·bly** \-blē\ *adv*

in·tra·cu·ta·ne·ous \ˌin-trə-kyu̇-ˈtā-nē-əs\ *adj* : INTRADERMAL

in·tra·day \ˈin-trə-ˌdā\ *adj* : occurring in the course of a single day ⟨*intraday* stock trading⟩

in·tra·der·mal \-ˈdər-məl\ *adj* : situated or done within or between the layers of the skin — **in·tra·der·mal·ly** \-mə-lē\ *adv*

in·tra·dos \ˈin-trə-ˌdäs, -ˌdō; in-ˈtrā-ˌdäs\ *n, pl* **-dos** \-ˌdōz, -ˌdäs\ *or* **-dos·es** \-ˌdäs-əz\ : the interior curve of an arch [French, from Latin *intra* "within" + French *dos* "back," from Latin *dorsum*]

1 intrados

in·tra·mu·ral \ˌin-trə-ˈmyu̇r-əl\ *adj* : being, occurring, or undertaken within the limits usually of a school ⟨*intramural* sports⟩ — **in·tra·mu·ral·ly** \-ˈmyu̇r-ə-lē\ *adv*

in·tra·mus·cu·lar \-ˈməs-kyə-lər\ *adj* : located in, occurring in, or injected into a muscle — **in·tra·mus·cu·lar·ly** *adv*

in·tra·net \ˈin-trə-ˌnet\ *n* : a computer network that works like the World Wide Web but that limits access to it to certain users (as employees of a company)

in·tran·si·geance \in-ˈtrans-ə-jəns, -ˈtranz-\ *n* : INTRANSIGENCE — **in·tran·si·geant** \-jənt\ *adj or n* — **in·tran·si·geant·ly** *adv*

in·tran·si·gence \-jəns\ *n* : the quality or state of being intransigent

in·tran·si·gent \-jənt\ *adj* : refusing to compromise or to give up an extreme position or attitude : UNCOMPROMISING ⟨*intransigent* in their opposition⟩ [Spanish *intransigente,* from *in-* + *transigir* "to compromise," from Latin *transigere* "to transact"] — **intransigent** *n* — **in·tran·si·gent·ly** *adv*

in·tran·si·tive \in-ˈtrans-ət-iv, -ˈtranz-, ˈin-\ *adj* : not transitive; *esp* : characterized by not having or containing a direct object ⟨an *intransitive* verb⟩ — **in·tran·si·tive·ly** *adv* — **in·tran·si·tive·ness** *n*

in·tra·plate \ˈin-trə-ˌplāt\ *adj* : relating to or occurring within the interior of a tectonic plate ⟨an *intraplate* earthquake⟩

in·tra·spe·cif·ic \ˌin-trə-spi-ˈsif-ik\ *also* **in·tra·spe·cies** \-ˈspē-shēz, -sēz\ *adj* : occurring within a species or involving members of one species ⟨*intraspecific* variation⟩

in·tra·state \ˌin-trə-ˈstāt\ *adj* : existing or occurring within a state

in·tra·uter·ine \-ˈyüt-ə-rən, -ˌrīn\ *adj* : situated, used, or occurring within the uterus ⟨an *intrauterine* growth⟩

intrauterine device *n* : a small plastic or metal device inserted into the uterus and left there to prevent pregnancy — called also *IUD*

in·tra·ve·nous \ˌin-trə-ˈvē-nəs\ *adj* : being within or entering by way of the veins ⟨*intravenous* feeding⟩ — **in·tra·ve·nous·ly** *adv*

in·tra·vi·tal \-ˈvīt-l\ *adj* : done, acting on, or found in a living subject

in·tra·zon·al \ˌin-trə-ˈzōn-l\ *adj* : of, relating to, or being a soil or a major soil group having relatively well-developed characteristics — compare AZONAL, ZONAL

intrench *variant of* ENTRENCH

in·trep·id \in-ˈtrep-əd\ *adj* : resolutely firm and fearless [Latin *intrepidus,* from *in-* + *trepidus* "alarmed"] — **in·tre·pid·i·ty** \ˌin-trə-ˈpid-ət-ē\ *n* — **in·trep·id·ly** \in-ˈtrep-əd-lē\ *adv* — **in·trep·id·ness** *n*

in·tri·ca·cy \ˈin-tri-kə-sē\ *n, pl* **-cies** **1** : the quality or state of being intricate **2** : something intricate ⟨the *intricacies* of the plot⟩

in·tri·cate \ˈin-tri-kət\ *adj* : having many complexly interrelating parts, elements, or considerations : COMPLICATED ⟨an *intricate* design⟩ ⟨difficult to solve the *intricate* puzzle⟩ [Latin *intricatus,* past participle of *intricare* "to entangle," from *in-* + *tricae* "trifles, complications"] ***synonyms*** see COMPLEX — **in·tri·cate·ly** *adv* — **in·tri·cate·ness** *n*

[1]in·trigue \in-ˈtrēg\ *vb* **1** : to get or accomplish by intrigue ⟨*intrigued* their way into power⟩ **2** : PLOT 3, SCHEME **3** : to arouse the interest or curiosity of ⟨was *intrigued* by the tale⟩

\ə\ abut	\au̇\ **out**	\i\ **tip**	\ȯ\ **saw**	\u̇\ **foot**
\ər\ **further**	\ch\ **chin**	\ī\ **life**	\ȯi\ **coin**	\y\ **yet**
\a\ **mat**	\e\ **pet**	\j\ **job**	\th\ **thin**	\yü\ **few**
\ā\ **take**	\ē\ **easy**	\ng\ **sing**	\th\ **this**	\yu̇\ **cure**
\ä\ **cot, cart**	\g\ **go**	\ō\ **bone**	\ü\ **food**	\zh\ **vision**

[French *intriguer,* from Italian *intrigare* "to entangle," from Latin] — **in·trigu·er** *n*

2in·trigue \ˈin-ˌtrēg, in-ˈ\ *n* **1 :** a secret and involved scheme : PLOT **2 :** a secret love affair ***synonyms*** see PLOT

in·trin·sic \in-ˈtrin-zik, -ˈtrin-sik\ *adj* **:** belonging to the essential nature or makeup of a thing ⟨the *intrinsic* value of a gem⟩ [Middle French *intrinsèque* "internal," from Latin *intrinsĕcus* "inwardly"] — **in·trin·si·cal** \-zi-kəl, -si-\ *adj* — **in·trin·si·cal·ly** \-kə-lē, -klē\ *adv*

intro- *prefix* **1 :** in : into ⟨*intro*duce⟩ **2 :** inward ⟨*intro*vert⟩ [Latin, from *intro* "inside, to the inside"]

in·tro·duce \ˌin-trə-ˈdüs, -ˈdyüs\ *vt* **1 :** to lead or bring in especially for the first time ⟨*introduce* a nonnative species⟩ ⟨*introduce* a topic into the discussion⟩ **2 :** to bring into practice or use ⟨*introduce* a new fashion⟩ **3 a :** to cause to be acquainted ⟨*introduce* two strangers⟩ **b :** to present or announce formally or officially ⟨*introduce* a legislative bill⟩ **4 :** to make preliminary remarks about ⟨*introduced* the star of the show⟩ **5 :** to put in : INSERT ⟨*introduce* a probe into a cavity⟩ **6 :** to bring to a knowledge of something ⟨*introduced* them to new ideas⟩ [Latin *introducere,* from *intro-* + *ducere* "to lead"] — **in·tro·duc·er** *n*

synonyms INTRODUCE, INSERT, INTERPOLATE, INTERJECT mean to put among or between others. INTRODUCE is a general term for bringing or putting a thing or person into a body or thing already in existence ⟨*introduce* a new topic into the conversation⟩. INSERT implies putting into an open, fixed, or prepared space between or among things ⟨*inserted* the peg in the hole⟩. INTERPOLATE applies especially to the inserting of something extraneous or spurious ⟨*interpolated* her own comments into the report⟩. INTERJECT strongly implies an abrupt or forced introduction ⟨*interjected* a question⟩.

in·tro·duc·tion \ˌin-trə-ˈdək-shən\ *n* **1 a :** the action of introducing **b :** something introduced **2 :** the part of a book that leads up to and explains what will be found in the main part : PREFACE **3 :** a book for beginners in a subject ⟨an *introduction* to chemistry⟩

in·tro·duc·to·ry \ˌin-trə-ˈdək-tə-rē, -trē\ *adj* **:** serving to introduce : PRELIMINARY — **in·tro·duc·to·ri·ly** \-tə-rə-lē, -trə-\ *adv*

in·troit \ˈin-ˌtrō-ət, -ˌtrȯit, in-ˈ\ *n* **1** *often cap* **:** the first part of the proper of the Mass consisting of an antiphon, verse from a psalm, and the Gloria Patri **2 :** a piece of music sung or played at the beginning of a worship service [Medieval Latin *introitus,* from Latin, "entrance," from *introire* "to go in," from *intro-* + *ire* "to go"]

in·tron \ˈin-ˌträn\ *n* **:** a DNA sequence in a gene that does not code information for protein synthesis and is removed before translation of messenger RNA — compare EXON [*int*e*r*vening sequence + *-on*]

in·tro·spec·tion \ˌin-trə-ˈspek-shən\ *n* **:** a reflective examination of one's own thoughts or feelings [Latin *introspectus,* past participle of *introspicere* "to look into," from *intro-* + *specere* "to look"] — **in·tro·spect** \-ˈspekt\ *vb* — **in·tro·spec·tion·al** \-ˈspek-shnəl, -shən-l\ *adj* — **in·tro·spec·tive** \-ˈspek-tiv\ *adj* — **in·tro·spec·tive·ly** *adv*

in·tro·vert \ˈin-trə-ˌvərt\ *n* **1 :** a person whose attention and interests are directed wholly or predominantly toward what is within the self **2 :** a shy or reserved person [earlier *introvert* "to turn inward," from *intro-* + *-vert* (as in *divert*)] — **in·tro·ver·sion** \ˌin-trə-ˈvər-zhən, -shən\ *n* — **introvert** *adj* — **in·tro·vert·ed** \ˈin-trə-ˌvərt-əd\ *adj*

in·trude \in-ˈtrüd\ *vb* **1 :** to bring or force in unasked ⟨*intrude* one's views into a discussion⟩ **2 :** to come or go in without invitation : TRESPASS ⟨*intrude* on another's property⟩ **3 :** to enter or cause to enter as if by force [Latin *intrudere* "to thrust in," from *in-* + *trudere* "to thrust"] — **in·trud·er** *n*

synonyms INTRUDE, OBTRUDE mean to thrust oneself or something in without invitation or authorization. INTRUDE implies rudeness, officiousness, or encroachment ⟨no wish to *intrude* on your privacy⟩. OBTRUDE suggests more strongly the impropriety, boldness, futility, or disagreeableness of an intrusion ⟨*obtrude* personal matters in a serious discussion⟩.

in·tru·sion \in-ˈtrü-zhən\ *n* **1 :** the act of intruding : the state of being intruded **2 :** the forcible entry of magma into or between other rock formations; *also* **:** the intruded magma [Medieval French, from Medieval Latin *intrusio,* from Latin *intrudere* "to thrust in"]

in·tru·sive \in-ˈtrü-siv, -ziv\ *adj* **1 a :** characterized by intrusion ⟨*intrusive* behavior⟩ **b :** intruding where one is not welcome or invited ⟨*intrusive* neighbors⟩ **2 :** having been forced while in a molten state into cavities or between layers ⟨*intrusive* rock⟩ — **intrusive** *n* — **in·tru·sive·ly** *adv* — **in·tru·sive·ness** *n*

in·tu·it \in-ˈtü-ət, -ˈtyü-\ *vt* **:** to know, sense, or understand by intuition [back-formation fr. *intuition*] — **in·tu·it·able** \-ə-bəl\ *adj*

in·tu·i·tion \ˌin-tu̇-ˈish-ən, -tyu̇-\ *n* **1 :** the power of knowing immediately and without conscious reasoning **2 :** something known or understood at once and without an effort of the mind ⟨act upon an *intuition*⟩ [Late Latin *intuitio* "act of contemplating," from Latin *intuēri* "to contemplate," from *in-* + *tuēri* "to look at"] — **in·tu·i·tion·al** \-ˈish-nəl, -ən-l\ *adj*

in·tu·i·tive \in-ˈtü-ət-iv, -ˈtyü-\ *adj* **1 :** knowing or understanding by intuition ⟨an *intuitive* person⟩ **2 :** having or characterized by intuition ⟨an *intuitive* mind⟩ **3 :** known or understood by intuition ⟨*intuitive* knowledge⟩ — **in·tu·i·tive·ly** *adv* — **in·tu·i·tive·ness** *n*

In·u·it \ˈin-ü-wət, -yü-\ *n* **1** *pl* **Inuit** *or* **Inuits a** (1) **:** the Eskimo people of North America and Greenland (2) **:** the Eskimo people of Canada **b :** a member of such people **2 a :** ESKIMO 2 **b :** the group of Eskimo dialects spoken from northwestern Canada to Greenland [Inuit, plural of *inuk* "person"]

in·u·lin \ˈin-yə-lən\ *n* **:** a white polysaccharide that consists of fructose molecules and occurs as a storage carbohydrate especially in the roots or tubers of plants of the composite family [derived from Latin *inula,* a kind of composite plant]

in·un·date \ˈin-ən-ˌdāt\ *vt* **1 :** to cover with a flood : DELUGE 1 ⟨a tidal wave *inundates* the island⟩ **2 :** DELUGE 2, OVERWHELM ⟨*inundated* with work⟩ [Latin *inundare,* from *in-* + *unda* "wave"] — **in·un·da·tion** \ˌin-ən-ˈdā-shən\ *n* — **in·un·da·tor** \ˈin-ən-ˌdāt-ər\ *n* — **in·un·da·to·ry** \in-ˈən-də-ˌtōr-ē, -ˌtȯr-\ *adj*

Inu·pi·at \in-ˈü-pē-ˌät, in-ˈyü-\ *also* **Inu·pi·aq** \-ˌäk\ *n* **1** *pl* **Inupiat** *or* **Inupiats** *also* **Inupiaq** *or* **Inupiaqs :** a member of the Eskimo people of northern Alaska **2 :** the language of the Inupiat people [Inupiat *in^yupiaq,* plural of *in^yupiat,* literally, "real person"]

in·ure \in-ˈu̇r, -ˈyu̇r\ *vb* **1 :** to make less sensitive : HARDEN ⟨*inured* to cold⟩ **2 :** to become advantageous ⟨profits that *inure* from education⟩ [Middle English *enuren,* from *in ure* "customary," from *putten in ure* "to use, put into practice," partial translation of Medieval French *mettre en uevre,* from Middle French *uevre* "work," from Latin *opera*] — **in·ure·ment** \-mənt\ *n*

in utero \in-ˈyüt-ə-ˌrō\ *adv or adj* **:** in the uterus : before birth ⟨*in utero* development⟩ ⟨exposed to the disease *in utero*⟩ [Latin]

in vac·uo \in-ˈvak-yə-ˌwō\ *adv* **:** in a vacuum [New Latin]

in·vade \in-ˈvād\ *vt* **1 :** to enter for conquest or plunder ⟨*invade* a country⟩ **2 :** to encroach upon : INFRINGE ⟨*invaded* their privacy⟩ **3 :** to spread progressively over or into and usually affect injuriously ⟨bacteria *invading* tissue⟩ ⟨stores *invading* a residential section⟩ [Latin *invadere,* from *in-* + *vadere* "to go"] — **in·vad·er** *n*

in·vag·i·nate \in-ˈvaj-ə-ˌnāt\ *vb* **:** to fold or cause to fold in so that an outer becomes an inner surface [Medieval Latin *invaginare* "to enclose, sheathe," from Latin *in-* + *vagina* "sheath"] — **in·vag·i·na·tion** \-ˌvaj-ə-ˈna-shən\ *n*

1in·val·id \in-ˈval-əd, ˈin-\ *adj* **:** having no force or effect : not valid ⟨an *invalid* license⟩ ⟨an *invalid* assumption⟩ [Latin *invalidus* "weak," from *in-* + *validus* "strong"] — **in·va·lid·i·ty** \ˌin-və-ˈlid-ət-ē\ *n* — **in·val·id·ly** \in-ˈval-əd-lē, ˈin-\ *adv*

2in·va·lid \ˈin-və-ləd\ *adj* **1 :** suffering from disease or disability : SICKLY **2 :** of, relating to, or suited to one that is sick [French *invalide,* from Latin *invalidus* "weak"]

3invalid *like* 2\ *n* **:** one who is sickly or disabled — **in·va·lid·ism** \-ˌiz-əm\ *n*

4in·va·lid \ˈin-və-ləd, -ˌlid\ *vt* **1 :** to make an invalid of ⟨*invalided* by heart disease⟩ **2 :** to remove from active duty by reason of sickness or disability ⟨*invalided* home after the battle⟩

in·val·i·date \in-ˈval-ə-ˌdāt, ˈin-\ *vt* **:** to make invalid ⟨a petition *invalidated* by false signatures⟩; *esp* **:** to weaken or destroy the effect of ⟨evidence *invalidating* their claim⟩ ***synonyms*** see NULLIFY — **in·val·i·da·tion** \in-ˌval-ə-ˈdā-shən\ *n* — **in·val·i·da·tor** \in-ˈval-ə-ˌdāt-ər\ *n*

in·valu·able \in-ˈval-yə-wə-bəl, -yə-bəl\ *adj* **:** having value too great to be estimated : PRICELESS ⟨*invaluable* help⟩ — **in·valu·able·ness** *n* — **in·valu·ably** \-blē\ *adv*

in·vari·able \in-ˈver-ē-ə-bəl, -ˈvar-, ˈin-\ *adj* **:** not changing or capable of change : CONSTANT ⟨an *invariable* daily routine⟩ — **in-**

vari·abil·i·ty \in-ˌver-ē-ə-ˈbil-ət-ē, -ˌvar-\ *n* — **invariable** *n* — **in·vari·able·ness** *n*
in·vari·ably \in-ˈver-ē-ə-blē, -ˈvar-, ˈin-\ *adv* : on every occasion : ALWAYS ⟨*invariably* late⟩
in·vari·ant \in-ˈver-ē-ənt, -ˈvar-, ˈin-\ *adj* : CONSTANT, UNCHANGING ⟨an *invariant* factor⟩ — **in·vari·ance** \-əns\ *n* — **invariant** *n*
in·va·sion \in-ˈvā-zhən\ *n* **1** : an act of invading; *esp* : entrance of an army into a country for conquest **2** : the entry or spread of some usually harmful thing ⟨bacterial *invasion* of tissue⟩ [Medieval French, from Late Latin *invasio,* from Latin *invadere* "to invade"]
in·va·sive \-ˈvā-siv, -ziv\ *adj* : tending to spread; *esp* : tending to invade healthy tissue ⟨*invasive* cancer cells⟩ — **in·va·sive·ness** *n*
in·vec·tive \in-ˈvek-tiv\ *n* : condemnation expressed in a harsh or bitter tone ⟨let loose a stream of *invective* against his opponent⟩ [Medieval French *invectif* "condemnatory," from Latin *invectivus,* from *invehere* "to carry in"] ***synonyms*** see ABUSE
in·veigh \in-ˈvā\ *vi* : to protest or complain bitterly : RAIL ⟨*inveigh* against high taxes⟩ [Latin *invehi* "to attack, inveigh," from *invehere* "to carry in," from *in-* + *vehere* "to carry"] — **inveigh·er** *n*
in·vei·gle \in-ˈvā-gəl, -ˈvē-\ *vt* **in·vei·gled; in·vei·gling** \-gəling, -gling\ **1** : to win over by flattery : ENTICE ⟨was *inveigled* into helping out⟩ **2** : to acquire by ingenuity or flattery : WANGLE ⟨*inveigled* a promotion from his supervisor⟩ [Medieval French *enveegler, aveogler, avogler* "to blind, hoodwink," from *avogle, enveugle* "blind," from Medieval Latin *ab oculis,* literally, "lacking eyes"] — **in·vei·gle·ment** \-gəl-mənt\ *n* — **in·vei·gler** \-gə-lər, -glər\ *n*

Word History When we permit ourselves to be *inveigled* we are blinded, figuratively speaking, by flattery. The ancestor of our word *inveigle* is a Medieval Latin phrase meaning "blind." Literally, *ab oculis* is "lacking (or away from) eyes" — the Latin preposition *ab* expresses separation. From *ab oculis* are derived the French adjective *aveugle* "blind" and the verb *aveugler* "to blind." French *aveugler,* like its English equivalent, *blind,* is often used figuratively. When English borrowed the French verb in the late Middle Ages, only the figurative use was taken. English *inveigle* originally meant "to blind or delude in judgment." This sense is now obsolete, but the present meaning is not far removed.

in·vent \in-ˈvent\ *vt* **1** : to think up : make up ⟨*invented* the whole incident⟩ **2** : to create or produce for the first time ⟨*invent* a new form of transportation⟩ [Latin *inventus,* past participle of *invenire* "to come upon, find," from *in-* + *venire* "to come"] — **in·ven·tor** \-ˈvent-ər\ *n*
in·ven·tion \in-ˈven-chən\ *n* **1** : something invented: as **a** : an original device or process **b** : a product of the imagination; *esp* : FALSEHOOD **2** : the act, process, or power of inventing
in·ven·tive \in-ˈvent-iv\ *adj* : gifted with the skill and imagination to invent — **in·ven·tive·ly** *adv* — **in·ven·tive·ness** *n*
¹in·ven·to·ry \ˈin-vən-ˌtōr-ē, -ˌtȯr-\ *n, pl* **-ries** **1** : an itemized list of assets or goods on hand **2** : the stock of goods on hand **3** : the making of an inventory — **in·ven·to·ri·al** \ˌin-vən-ˈtōr-ē-əl, -ˈtȯr-\ *adj* — **in·ven·to·ri·al·ly** \-ē-ə-lē\ *adv*
²inventory *vt* **-ried; -ry·ing** : to make an inventory of
in·ver·ness \ˌin-vər-ˈnes\ *n* : a loose belted coat having a cape with a close-fitting round collar [*Inverness,* Scotland]
¹in·verse \in-ˈvərs, ˈin-, ˈin-ˌ\ *adj* **1** : opposite in order, nature, or effect ⟨an *inverse* relationship between interest rates and bond prices⟩ **2** : being an inverse function ⟨*inverse* sine⟩ [Latin *inversus,* from *invertere* "to invert"]
²in·verse \ˈin-ˌvərs, in-ˈvərs\ *n* **1** : something of a contrary nature or quality : OPPOSITE **2** : a statement in logic formed by contradicting both the hypothesis and the conclusion of a proposition ⟨the *inverse* of "if A then B" is "if not-A then not-B"⟩ **3** : INVERSE FUNCTION; *also* : an operation that undoes the effect of another operation ⟨subtraction is the *inverse* of addition⟩
inverse function *n* : a function that is derived from a given function by interchanging the two variables ⟨$y = x^3$ is the *inverse function* of $x = y^3$⟩
in·verse·ly *adv* **1** : in an inverse order or manner **2** : in the manner of inverse variation
inversely proportional *adj* : related by inverse variation — compare DIRECTLY PROPORTIONAL
inverse square law *n* : a statement in physics: a physical quantity (as illumination) varies with the distance from the source inversely as the square of the distance
inverse variation *n* **1** : mathematical relationship between two variables which can be expressed by an equation in which the product of the two variables is equal to a constant **2** : an equation or function expressing inverse variation — compare DIRECT VARIATION
in·ver·sion \in-ˈvər-zhən, -shən\ *n* **1** : the act or process of inverting **2** : a reversal of position, order, or relationship **3** : an increase in the temperature of the air with increasing altitude
in·ver·sive \in-ˈvər-siv, -ziv\ *adj* : marked by inversion
in·vert \in-ˈvərt\ *vt* **1** : to reverse the position, order, or relationship of **2 a** : to turn inside out or upside down **b** : to turn inward **3** : to find the mathematical reciprocal of ⟨to divide using fractions, *invert* the divisor and multiply⟩ [Latin *invertere,* from *in-* + *vertere* "to turn"] ***synonyms*** see REVERSE — **in·vert·ible** \-ə-bəl\ *adj*
in·ver·tase \in-ˈvərt-ˌās, -ˌāz; ˈin-vər-ˌtās, -ˌtāz\ *n* : an enzyme that splits sucrose into glucose and fructose
¹in·ver·te·brate \in-ˈvərt-ə-brət, -ˌbrāt, ˈin-\ *adj* : lacking a spinal column ⟨an *invertebrate* animal⟩; *also* : of or relating to invertebrate animals ⟨*invertebrate* zoology⟩
²invertebrate *n* : an animal (as a worm, clam, spider, or butterfly) that lacks a spinal column
in·vert·er \in-ˈvərt-ər\ *n* : a device for converting direct current into alternating current
in·vert sugar \ˌin-ˌvərt-\ *n* : a mixture of dextrose and levulose found in fruits or produced artificially from sucrose
¹in·vest \in-ˈvest\ *vt* **1 a** : INSTALL 1 **b** : to furnish with power or authority **2** : to cover completely : ENVELOP **3** : to surround with troops or ships : BESIEGE **4** : to endow with a quality or characteristic ⟨*invest* an incident with mystery⟩ [Latin *investire* "to clothe, surround," from *in-* + *vestis* "garment"]
²invest *vb* **1** : to lay out money in order to earn a financial return ⟨*invest* in bonds and real estate⟩ **2** : to expend for future benefits or advantages ⟨*invest* time and effort in a project⟩ **3** : to involve or engage especially emotionally ⟨were deeply *invested* in their children's lives⟩ [Italian *investire* "to clothe, invest money," from Latin, "to clothe"] — **in·vest·able** \-ˈves-tə-bəl\ *adj* — **in·ves·tor** \-tər\ *n*
in·ves·ti·gate \in-ˈves-tə-ˌgāt\ *vb* : to observe or study by close and systematic examination [Latin *investigare* "to track, investigate," from *in-* + *vestigium* "footprint"] — **in·ves·ti·ga·tion** \-ˌves-tə-ˈgā-shən\ *n* — **in·ves·ti·ga·tion·al** \-ˈgā-shnəl, -shə-nl\ *adj* — **in·ves·ti·ga·tive** \-ˈves-tə-ˌgāt-iv\ *adj* — **in·ves·ti·ga·tor** \-ˌgāt-ər\ *n* — **in·ves·ti·ga·to·ry** \-ˈves-ti-gə-ˌtōr-ē, -ˌtȯr-\ *adj*
in·ves·ti·ture \in-ˈves-tə-ˌchu̇r, -chər\ *n* : the act of installing a person in an office, rank or order ⟨an Honor Society *investiture*⟩ [Medieval Latin *investitura,* from Latin *investire* "to clothe"]
¹in·vest·ment \in-ˈvest-mənt, -ˈves-\ *n* **1** : an outer layer of any kind : ENVELOPE, COATING **2** : INVESTITURE **3** : SIEGE 1, BLOCKADE
²investment *n* : an outlay of money for income or profit; *also* : the sum invested or the property purchased
in·vet·er·ate \in-ˈvet-ə-rət, -ˈve-trət\ *adj* **1** : firmly established by age or by being long continued ⟨*inveterate* attitudes⟩ **2** : HABITUAL ⟨an *inveterate* collector⟩ [Latin *inveteratus,* from *inveterare* "to age," from *in-* + *veter-, vetus* "old"] — **in·vet·er·ate·ly** *adv*
in·vi·a·ble \in-ˈvī-ə-bəl, ˈin-\ *adj* : incapable of surviving — **in·vi·a·bil·i·ty** \in-ˌvī-ə-ˈbil-ət-ē\ *n*
in·vid·i·ous \in-ˈvid-ē-əs\ *adj* : tending to cause dislike, ill will, or envy ⟨*invidious* criticism⟩ [Latin *invidiosus* "envious, invidious," from *invidia* "envy"] — **in·vid·i·ous·ly** *adv* — **in·vid·i·ous·ness** *n*
in·vig·o·rate \in-ˈvig-ə-ˌrāt\ *vt* : to give life and energy to : ANIMATE — **in·vig·o·ra·tion** \-ˌvig-ə-ˈrā-shən\ *n* — **in·vig·o·ra·tor** \-ˈvig-ə-ˌrāt-ər\ *n*
in·vin·ci·ble \in-ˈvin-sə-bəl, ˈin-\ *adj* : incapable of being defeated, overcome, or subdued ⟨an *invincible* army⟩ [Middle French, from Late Latin *invincibilis,* from Latin *in-* + *vincere* "to con-

\ə\ **abut**	\au̇\ **out**	\i\ **tip**	\ȯ\ **saw**	\u̇\ **foot**
\ər\ **further**	\ch\ **chin**	\ī\ **life**	\ȯi\ **coin**	\y\ **yet**
\a\ **mat**	\e\ **pet**	\j\ **job**	\th\ **thin**	\yü\ **few**
\ā\ **take**	\ē\ **easy**	\ng\ **sing**	\t͟h\ **this**	\yu̇\ **cure**
\ä\ **cot, cart**	\g\ **go**	\ō\ **bone**	\ü\ **food**	\zh\ **vision**

quer"] ***synonyms*** see INDOMITABLE — **in·vin·ci·bil·i·ty** \ˌin-ˌvin-sə-ˈbil-ət-ē\ *n* — **in·vin·ci·ble·ness** *n* — **in·vin·ci·bly** \in-ˈvin-sə-blē, ˈin-\ *adv*

in·vi·o·la·ble \in-ˈvī-ə-lə-bəl, ˈin-\ *adj* **1** : too sacred to be violated ⟨an *inviolable* oath⟩ **2** : incapable of being assaulted or destroyed ⟨an *inviolable* fortress⟩ — **in·vi·o·la·bil·i·ty** \in-ˌvī-ə-lə-ˈbil-ət-ē\ *n* — **in·vi·o·la·bly** \in-ˈvī-ə-lə-blē, ˈin-\ *adv*

in·vi·o·late \in-ˈvī-ə-lət, ˈin-\ *adj* **1** : not violated or profaned; *esp* : PURE **2** : INVIOLABLE 2 — **in·vi·o·late·ly** *adv* — **in·vi·o·late·ness** *n*

in·vis·i·ble \in-ˈviz-ə-bəl\ *adj* **1 a** : incapable of being seen ⟨sound is *invisible*⟩ **b** : inaccessible to view : HIDDEN ⟨the sun is *invisible* on a cloudy day⟩ **2** : IMPERCEPTIBLE, INCONSPICUOUS ⟨an *invisible* hair net⟩ — **in·vis·i·bil·i·ty** \in-ˌviz-ə-ˈbil-ət-ē\ *n* — **invisible** *n* — **in·vis·i·ble·ness** *n* — **in·vis·i·bly** \in-ˈviz-ə-blē, ˈin-\ *adv*

in·vi·ta·tion \ˌin-və-ˈtā-shən\ *n* **1** : the act of inviting **2** : the written, printed, or spoken expression by which a person is invited — **in·vi·ta·tion·al** \-shnəl, -shən-l\ *adj*

[1]**in·vite** \in-ˈvīt\ *vt* **1** : to increase the likelihood of : INDUCE ⟨*invite* disaster by speeding⟩ **2 a** : to request the presence or participation of **b** : to request formally or politely : ENCOURAGE ⟨*invite* suggestions⟩ [Latin *invitare*] — **in·vit·er** *n*

[2]**in·vite** \ˈin-ˌvīt\ *n* : INVITATION

in·vit·ing \in-ˈvīt-ing\ *adj* : ATTRACTIVE, TEMPTING ⟨a very *inviting* dinner⟩ — **in·vit·ing·ly** \-ing-lē\ *adv*

in vi·tro \in-ˈvē-ˌtrō\ *adv or adj* : outside the living body and in an artificial environment ⟨an egg fertilized *in vitro*⟩ [New Latin, literally, "in glass"]

in vi·vo \in-ˈvē-vō\ *adv or adj* : inside the living body of a plant or animal ⟨*in vivo* activity⟩ [New Latin, literally, "in the living"]

in·vo·ca·tion \ˌin-və-ˈkā-shən\ *n* **1** : the act or process of invoking **2** : a prayer for blessing or guidance especially at the beginning of a religious service **3** : a formula for conjuring : INCANTATION **4** : an act of legal or moral enforcement ⟨*invocation* of the law⟩ — **in·vo·ca·tion·al** \-shnəl, -shən-l\ *adj*

[1]**in·voice** \ˈin-ˌvȯis\ *n* : an itemized statement given to a buyer by a seller and usually specifying the price of goods or services and the terms of sale; *also* : a shipment of goods sent with such a statement [Middle French *envois,* pl. of *envoi* "message," from *envoier* "to send on one's way," from Latin *in* "in, on" + *via* "way"]

[2]**invoice** *vt* : to submit an invoice for : BILL

in·voke \in-ˈvōk\ *vt* **1 a** : to call on for aid or protection (as in prayer) **b** : to appeal to as an authority or for support ⟨*invoke* a law⟩ **2** : to call forth by magic : CONJURE ⟨*invoke* spirits⟩ **3** : to put into effect or operation : IMPLEMENT ⟨*invoke* the harshest penalty⟩ **4** : BRING ABOUT, CAUSE ⟨the solution *invoked* new problems⟩ [Medieval French *invoquer,* from Latin *invocare,* from *in-* + *vocare* "to call"] — **in·vok·er** *n*

usage *Invoke* is usually used to mean to appeal to or cite ⟨*invoke* a constitutional principle⟩ or to implement ⟨*invoke* sanctions⟩. *Evoke* is usually used to mean to elicit ⟨his actions *evoked* disapproval⟩, to bring to mind ⟨a smell that *evokes* images of childhood⟩, or to re-create imaginatively ⟨her descriptions *evoke* the place perfectly⟩. *Evoke* is sometimes used in place of *invoke* in the sense to appeal to or cite ⟨*evoked* the authority of the constitution⟩ but it is preferable to use *invoke* in such cases.

in·vo·lu·cre \ˈin-və-ˌlü-kər\ *n* : one or more whorls of bracts situated immediately below a flower, flower cluster, or fruit [French, from New Latin *involucrum* "sheath," from Latin, "wrapper," from *involvere* "to wrap"] — **in·vo·lu·cral** \ˌin-və-ˈlü-krəl\ *adj*

in·vol·un·tary \in-ˈväl-ən-ˌter-ē, ˈin-\ *adj* **1** : not made or done willingly or from choice **2** : COMPULSORY ⟨*involuntary* servitude⟩ **3** : not subject to direct control by the will : REFLEX — **in·vol·un·tar·i·ly** \in-ˌväl-ən-ˈter-ə-lē\ *adv*

involuntary muscle *n* : SMOOTH MUSCLE

in·vo·lu·tion \ˌin-və-ˈlü-shən\ *n* **1 a** : the act or an instance of enfolding or entangling : INVOLVEMENT **b** : INTRICACY 1, COMPLEXITY **2** : EXPONENTIATION **3** : an inward curving or penetration **4 a** : a shrinking or return to a former size **b** : the regressive changes that accompany aging and are marked by a decrease of bodily vigor [Latin *involutio,* from *involvere* "to wrap, involve"] — **in·vo·lu·tion·al** \-shnəl, -shən-l\ *adj* — **in·vo·lu·tion·ary** \-shə-ˌner-ē\ *adj*

in·volve \in-ˈvälv, -ˈvȯlv\ *vt* **1 a** : to draw in as a participant : ENGAGE ⟨many workers are *involved* in the job⟩ **b** : to oblige to take part ⟨was *involved* in a lawsuit⟩ **c** : to occupy (as oneself) absorbingly ⟨was *involved* in the hero's fate⟩ **2 a** : to have within or as part of itself : INCLUDE ⟨one problem *involves* others⟩ **b** : to require as a necessary accompaniment : ENTAIL ⟨the road job *involved* building 10 bridges⟩ **c** : to have an effect on : AFFECT ⟨the renovations *involved* the whole school⟩ [Latin *involvere* "to roll up, wrap, involve," from *in-* + *volvere* "to roll"] ***synonyms*** see INCLUDE — **in·volve·ment** \-mənt\ *n* — **in·volv·er** *n*

in·volved \-ˈvälvd, -ˈvȯlvd\ *adj* **1** : INTRICATE 1 ⟨an *involved* plot⟩ **2** : difficult to deal with because of confusion or disorder : TANGLED ***synonyms*** see COMPLEX — **in·volv·ed·ly** \-ˈväl-vəd-lē, -ˈvȯl-\ *adv*

in·vul·ner·a·ble \in-ˈvəln-rə-bəl, -ə-rə-; -ˈvəl-nər-bəl\ *adj* **1** : incapable of being wounded, injured, or damaged **2** : immune to or secure against attack : IMPREGNABLE — **in·vul·ner·a·bil·i·ty** \in-ˌvəln-rə-ˈbil-ət-ē, -ə-rə-\ *n* — **in·vul·ner·a·ble·ness** \in-ˈvəln-rə-bəl-nəs, -ə-rə-; -ˈvəl-nər-bəl-\ *n* — **in·vul·ner·a·bly** \-blē\ *adv*

[1]**in·ward** \ˈin-wərd\ *adj* **1** : situated on the inside : INNER **2** : of or relating to the mind or spirit ⟨an *inward* peace⟩ **3** : directed toward the interior ⟨an *inward* flow⟩

[2]**inward** *or* **in·wards** \-wərdz\ *adv* **1** : toward the inside, center, or interior ⟨slope *inward*⟩ **2** : toward the inner being ⟨turned their thoughts *inward*⟩

[3]**inward** *n* : something that is inward

in·ward·ly \ˈin-wərd-lē\ *adv* **1** : in the mind or spirit **2 a** : on the inside ⟨bled *inwardly*⟩ **b** : to oneself : PRIVATELY ⟨chuckled *inwardly*⟩

in·ward·ness *n* **1** : fundamental nature : ESSENCE **2** : absorption in one's own mental or spiritual life

in·weave \in-ˈwēv, ˈin-\ *vt* **-wove** \-ˈwōv\ *also* **-weaved; -wo·ven** \-ˈwō-vən\ *also* **-weaved; -weav·ing** : to weave in or together : INTERLACE

in–wrought \in-ˈrȯt, ˈin-\ *adj* : having or being a decorative element worked or woven in

in–your–face \ˌin-yər-ˌfās\ *adj* : characterized by or expressive of bold and often defiant aggressiveness ⟨*in-your-face* basketball⟩; *also* : aggressively intrusive ⟨*in-your-face* advertising⟩

iod- *or* **iodo-** *combining form* : iodine ⟨*iod*ize⟩ ⟨*iodo*form⟩ [French *iode*]

io·dide \ˈī-ə-ˌdīd\ *n* : a compound of iodine with another element or radical

io·dine \ˈī-ə-ˌdīn, -əd-n, -ə-ˌdēn\ *n* **1** : a nonmetallic usually univalent chemical element that is obtained usually as heavy shining blackish gray crystals and is used especially in medicine, photography, and analysis — see ELEMENT table **2** : a solution of iodine in alcohol used as an antiseptic [French *iode,* from Greek *ioeidēs* "violet colored," from *ion* "violet"]

io·dize \ˈī-ə-ˌdīz\ *vt* : to treat with iodine or an iodide ⟨*iodized* salt⟩

io·do·form \ī-ˈōd-ə-ˌfȯrm, -ˈäd-\ *n* : a yellow crystalline volatile iodine compound that is used as an antiseptic dressing [*iod-* + *-form* (as in *chloroform*)]

io·dop·sin \ˌī-ə-ˈdäp-sən\ *n* : a violet light-sensitive pigment in the retinal cones that is formed from vitamin A and is important in daylight vision — compare RHODOPSIN [Greek *ioeidēs* "violet colored" + *opsis* "sight, vision"]

Io moth \ˌī-ō-\ *n* : a large North American moth with a large eyelike spot on each yellowish hind wing [Latin *Io,* a mythical maiden loved by Zeus, from Greek *Iō*]

Io moth

ion \ˈī-ən, ˈī-ˌän\ *n* : an atom or group of atoms that carries a positive or negative electric charge as a result of having lost or gained one or more electrons [Greek *iōn,* present participle of *ienai* "to go"]

-ion *n suffix* **1 a** : act or process ⟨validat*ion*⟩ **b** : result of an act or process ⟨regulat*ion*⟩ **2** : state or condition ⟨deflat*ion*⟩ [Latin *-ion-, -io*]

Io·ni·an \ī-ˈō-nē-ən\ *n* **1** : one of an ancient Greek people who settled on the islands of the Aegean Sea and on the western shore of Asia Minor **2 :** a native or inhabitant of Ionia — **Ioni·an** *adj*

ion·ic \ī-ˈän-ik\ *adj* **:** of, relating to, or existing in the form of ions

Ion·ic \ī-ˈän-ik\ *adj* **1 :** of or relating to Ionia or the Ionians **2 :** belonging to or resembling the Ionic order of architecture characterized especially by the spiral volutes of its capital

ionic bond *n* **:** a chemical bond formed between ions of opposite charge

io·ni·um \ī-ˈō-nē-əm\ *n* **:** a natural radioactive isotope of thorium having a mass number of 230 [*ion;* from its ionizing action]

ion·ize \ˈī-ə-ˌnīz\ *vb* **:** to convert or become converted wholly or partly into ions — **ion·i·za·tion** \ˌī-ə-nə-ˈzā-shən\ *n* — **ion·iz·er** \ˈī-ə-ˌnī-zər\ *n*

iono·sphere \ī-ˈän-ə-ˌsfiər\ *n* **:** the part of the earth's atmosphere beginning at an altitude of about 30 miles (50 kilometers) and extending outward that contains free electrically charged particles — **iono·spher·ic** \ī-ˌän-ə-ˈsfiər-ik, -ˈsfer-\ *adj*

io·ta \ī-ˈōt-ə\ *n* **1 :** the 9th letter of the Greek alphabet — Ι or ι **2 :** a tiny amount **:** JOT ⟨not one *iota* of truth⟩

IOU \ˌī-ō-ˈyü\ *n* **:** a paper that has on it the letters IOU, a stated sum, and a signature and that is given as an acknowledgment of debt [from the pronunciation of *I owe you*]

-ious *adj suffix* **:** OUS ⟨capac*ious*⟩ [partly from Latin *-iosus,* from *-i-* + *-osus* "-ous"; partly from Latin *-ius,* adj. suffix]

IPA \ˌī-ˌpē-ˈā\ *n* **:** an alphabet designed to represent each human speech sound with a different character [*I*nternational *P*honetic *A*lphabet]

IP address \ˈī-ˈpē-\ *n* **:** the address of a computer on the Internet that consists of a series of numbers [*I*nternet *p*rotocol]

ip·e·cac \ˈip-i-ˌkak\ *also* **ipe·ca·cu·an·ha** \ē-ˌpek-ə-kü-ˈan-yə\ *n* **1 :** either of two South American creeping plants **2 :** the dried rhizome and roots of an ipecac that are the source of a medicinal syrup used to cause vomiting in the treatment of accidental poisoning; *also* **:** the medicinal syrup [Portuguese *ipecacuanha,* from Tupi *ipekakwánʸa*]

ip·se dixit \ˌip-sē-ˈdik-sət\ *n* **:** an assertion made but not proved **:** DICTUM [Latin, "he himself said it"]

ip·so facto \ˌip-sō-ˈfak-tō\ *adv* **:** by the very nature of the case [New Latin, literally, "by the fact itself"]

IQ \ˈī-ˈkyü\ *n* **1 :** a number used to express the relative intelligence of a person and determined by dividing the mental age of the person (as reported on a standardized test) by their age in years and multiplying by 100 **2 :** proficiency in or knowledge of a specified subject ⟨loves football but has a low hockey *IQ*⟩ [*i*ntelligence *q*uotient]

ir- — see IN-

Ira·ni·an \ir-ˈā-nē-ən\ *n* **1 :** a native or inhabitant of Iran **2 :** a branch of the Indo-European family of languages that includes Persian — **Iranian** *adj*

iras·ci·ble \ir-ˈas-ə-bəl, ī-ˈras-\ *adj* **:** marked by hot temper and easily aroused anger [Middle French, from Late Latin *irascibilis,* from Latin *irasci* "to become angry," from *ira* "ire"] — **iras·ci·bil·i·ty** \ir-ˌas-ə-ˈbil-ət-ē, ī-ˌras-\ *n* — **iras·ci·ble·ness** \ir-ˈas-ə-bəl-nəs, ī-ˈras-\ *n* — **iras·ci·bly** \-blē\ *adv*

synonyms IRASCIBLE, CHOLERIC, TESTY, TOUCHY mean easily angered. IRASCIBLE implies a tendency to be fiery tempered ⟨an *irascible* actor who was hard to work with⟩. CHOLERIC may suggest impatient excitability and unreasonable irritability ⟨an impulsive, *choleric* ruler who lost many allies⟩. TESTY implies a quick temper irritated by trivial annoyances ⟨grew *testy* when tired⟩. TOUCHY suggests oversensitive readiness to take offense or flare up at slight or implied criticism ⟨was *touchy* about having her judgment questioned⟩.

irate \ī-ˈrāt\ *adj* **1 :** ANGRY 1a ⟨*irate* taxpayers⟩ **2 :** ANGRY 1b — **irate·ly** *adv* — **irate·ness** *n*

ire \ˈīr\ *n* **:** WRATH 1, ANGER [Medieval French, from Latin *ira*] — **ire** *vt* — **ire·ful** \-fəl\ *adj* — **ire·ful·ly** \-fə-lē\ *adv*

iren·ic \ī-ˈren-ik\ *adj* **:** favoring, conducive to, or operating toward peace, moderation, or goodwill ⟨*irenic* intentions⟩ [Greek *eirēnikos,* from *eirēnē* "peace"] — **iren·i·cal·ly** \-ˈren-i-kə-lē, -klē\ *adv*

ir·i·des·cence \ˌir-ə-ˈdes-ns\ *n* **:** a play of colors producing rainbow effects (as in a soap bubble) [derived from Latin *irid-, iris* "rainbow"]

ir·i·des·cent \-nt\ *adj* **:** having or showing iridescence — **ir·i·des·cent·ly** *adv*

irid·i·um \ir-ˈid-ē-əm\ *n* **:** a rare silver-white hard brittle very heavy metallic chemical element — see ELEMENT table [New Latin, from Latin *irid-, iris* "rainbow"; from the colors produced by its dissolving in hydrochloric acid]

iris \ˈī-rəs\ *n, pl* **iris·es** *or* **iri·des** \ˈī-rə-ˌdēz, ˈir-ə-\ **1 :** the colored part of the eye that surrounds the pupil and changes in size to control the amount of light entering the eye **2 :** any of a large genus of perennial herbaceous plants with sword-shaped basal leaves and large showy flowers **3 :** IRIS DIAPHRAGM [Latin, "rainbow, iris plant," from Greek, "rainbow, iris plant, iris of the eye"]

iris diaphragm *n* **:** an adjustable diaphragm of thin opaque plates used for changing the diameter of a central opening to control the amount of light passing (as into a microscope or camera)

iris diaphragm

Irish \ˈī-rish\ *n* **1** *pl in construction* **:** the natives or inhabitants of Ireland or their descendants **2 :** the Celtic language of Ireland — **Irish** *adj* — **Irish·man** \-mən\ *n* — **Irish·wom·an** \-ˌwu̇m-ən\ *n*

Irish Gaelic *n* **:** IRISH 2

Irish·ism \ˈī-rish-ˌiz-əm\ *n* **:** a word, phrase, or expression characteristic of the Irish

Irish moss *n* **:** either of two red algae; *also* **:** these algae when dried and bleached for use especially as thickeners, emulsifiers, or soothing agents (as in food or lotions)

Irish potato *n* **:** POTATO 2b

Irish setter *n* **:** any of a breed of bird dogs resembling English setters but with a mahogany-red coat

Irish terrier *n* **:** any of a breed of active medium-sized terriers having a dense usually reddish stiff coat

Irish wolfhound *n* **:** any of a breed of very tall heavily built hounds having a rough stiff relatively short coat

irk \ˈərk\ *vt* **:** to make weary, irritated, or bored [Middle English *irken*] ***synonyms*** see ANNOY

irk·some \ˈərk-səm\ *adj* **:** tending to irk **:** TEDIOUS — **irk·some·ly** *adv* — **irk·some·ness** *n*

¹iron \ˈī-ərn, ˈīrn\ *n* **1 :** a heavy malleable ductile magnetic silver-white metallic chemical element that readily rusts in moist air, occurs in meteorites and combined in rocks, is widely used, and is vital to biological processes — see ELEMENT table **2 a :** something (as handcuffs or chains) used to bind or restrain — usually used in plural **b :** a heated metal implement used for branding **c :** FLATIRON **d :** one of a set of golf clubs with flat metal heads **3 :** great strength or hardness [Old English *īsern, īren*]

²iron *adj* **1 :** of, relating to, or made of iron **2 :** resembling iron (as in hardness or strength) **3 a :** being strong and healthy **:** ROBUST ⟨an *iron* constitution⟩ **b :** INFLEXIBLE, UNRELENTING ⟨*iron* determination⟩

³iron *vb* **1 :** to furnish or cover with iron **2 :** to smooth or press with a heated flatiron ⟨*iron* a shirt⟩ **3 :** to iron clothes ⟨spent all day *ironing*⟩

Iron Age *n* **:** the period of human culture characterized by the first smelting and use of iron and beginning somewhat before 1000 B.C. in western Asia and Egypt

¹iron·clad \-ˈklad\ *adj* **1 :** sheathed in iron armor **2 :** RIGOROUS, EXACTING ⟨*ironclad* laws⟩

²iron·clad \-ˌklad\ *n* **:** an armored naval vessel

iron curtain *n* **:** a political, military, and ideological barrier that cuts off and isolates an area; *esp* **:** one between an area under Soviet control and other areas

iron hand *n* **:** stern or rigorous control ⟨rule with an *iron hand*⟩

iron horse *n* **:** LOCOMOTIVE

iron·ic \ī-ˈrän-ik\ *adj* **1 :** relating to, containing, or constituting irony ⟨an *ironic* turn of events⟩ **2 :** given to irony — **iron·i·cal** \-i-kəl\ *adj* — **iron·i·cal·ly** \-i-kə-lē, -klē\ *adv*

iron lung *n* **:** a device for artificial respiration in which rhythmic alternations in the air pressure in a chamber surrounding a patient's chest force air into and out of the lungs

\ə\ **abut**	\au̇\ **out**	\i\ **tip**	\ȯ\ **saw**	\u̇\ **foot**
\ər\ **further**	\ch\ **chin**	\ī\ **life**	\ȯi\ **coin**	\y\ **yet**
\a\ **mat**	\e\ **pet**	\j\ **job**	\th\ **thin**	\yü\ **few**
\ā\ **take**	\ē\ **easy**	\ng\ **sing**	\t͟h\ **this**	\yu̇\ **cure**
\ä\ **cot, cart**	\g\ **go**	\ō\ **bone**	\ü\ **food**	\zh\ **vision**

iron oxide *n* : an oxide of iron: as **a** : FERRIC OXIDE **b** : the oxide FeO that occurs as a black powder
iron pyrites *n* : PYRITE — called also *iron pyrite*
iron·stone \ˈī-ərn-ˌstōn, ˈīrn-\ *n* **1** : a hard sedimentary rock rich in iron **2** : a hard white pottery first made in England during the 18th century — called also *ironstone china*
iron sulfide *n* : a compound (as a pyrite) of iron and sulfur
iron·ware \-ˌwaər, -ˌweər\ *n* : articles made of iron
iron·weed \-ˌwēd\ *n* : any of several mostly weedy plants related to the daisies and bearing clusters of red, purple, or white flowers
iron·wood \-ˌwu̇d\ *n* **1** : any of numerous trees and shrubs with exceptionally tough or hard wood **2** : the wood of an ironwood
iron·work \-ˌwərk\ *n* **1** : work in iron **2** *pl* : a mill or building where iron or steel is smelted or heavy iron or steel products are made — **iron·work·er** \-ˌwər-kər\ *n*
iro·ny \ˈī-rə-nē\ *n, pl* **-nies** **1 a** : the humorous or sardonic use of words to express the opposite of what one really means (as when words of praise are given but blame is intended) **b** : an ironic expression or utterance **2 a** : inconsistency between an actual and an expected result **b** : a result marked by such inconsistency [Latin *ironia,* from Greek *eirōnia,* from *eirōn* "dissembler"]
Ir·o·quoi·an \ˌir-ə-ˈkwȯi-ən\ *n* **1** : an American Indian language family of eastern North America **2** : a member of the peoples speaking Iroquoian languages — **Iroquoian** *adj*
Ir·o·quois \ˈir-ə-ˌkwȯi\ *n, pl* **Iroquois** \-ˌkwȯi, -ˌkwȯiz\ : a member of an American Indian confederacy of New York consisting originally of the Cayugas, Mohawks, Oneidas, Onondagas, and Senecas and later including the Tuscaroras [French, probably of Algonquian origin]
ir·ra·di·ant \ir-ˈād-ē-ənt\ *adj* : emitting rays of light — **ir·ra·di·an·cy** \-ən-sē\ *n*
ir·ra·di·ate \ir-ˈād-ē-ˌāt\ *vt* **1 a** : to cast rays of light on : ILLUMINATE **b** : to affect or treat by exposure to radiations (as of ultraviolet light, X-rays, or gamma rays) **2** : to emit like rays of light : RADIATE — **ir·ra·di·a·tion** \-ˌād-ē-ˈā-shən\ *n* — **ir·ra·di·a·tive** \-ˈād-ē-ˌāt-iv\ *adj*
ir·ra·tio·nal \ir-ˈash-nəl, ˈir-, -ən-l\ *adj* **1 a** : incapable of reasoning ⟨*irrational* beasts⟩ **b** : not governed by or according to reason ⟨an *irrational* hatred of strangers⟩ **2** : being an irrational number ⟨an *irrational* root⟩ — **ir·ra·tio·nal·i·ty** \ir-ˌash-ə-ˈnal-ət-ē\ *n* — **ir·ra·tio·nal·ly** \ir-ˈash-nə-lē, ˈir-, -ˈash-ən-l-ē\ *adv* — **ir·ra·tio·nal·ness** \-nəl-nəs, -ən-l-nəs\ *n*
synonyms IRRATIONAL, UNREASONABLE mean not guided by reason. IRRATIONAL may imply mental derangement but oftener suggests lack of control or guidance by reason ⟨*irrational* fears⟩. UNREASONABLE suggests control by some force other than reason (as greed or rage) which makes for a deficiency in good sense ⟨*unreasonable* demands⟩.
irrational number *n* : a real number (as $\sqrt{2}$) that cannot be expressed as the quotient of two whole numbers
ir·re·claim·able \ˌir-i-ˈklā-mə-bəl\ *adj* : incapable of being reclaimed — **ir·re·claim·ably** \-blē\ *adv*
ir·rec·on·cil·able \ir-ˌek-ən-ˈsī-lə-bəl; ir-ˈek-ən-, ˈir-\ *adj* : impossible to reconcile, adjust, or harmonize ⟨*irreconcilable* enemies⟩ — **ir·rec·on·cil·abil·i·ty** \ir-ˌek-ən-ˌsī-lə-ˈbil-ət-ē\ *n* — **ir·rec·on·cil·ably** \ir-ˌek-ən-ˈsī-lə-blē; ir-ˈek-ən-ˌ, ˈir-\ *adv*
ir·re·cov·er·able \ˌir-i-ˈkəv-rə-bəl, -ə-rə-\ *adj* : not capable of being recovered ⟨an *irrecoverable* debt⟩ — **ir·re·cov·er·ably** \-blē\ *adv*
ir·re·deem·able \ˌir-i-ˈdē-mə-bəl\ *adj* **1** : not redeemable; *esp* : not convertible into gold or silver at the will of the holder **2** : being beyond remedy : HOPELESS ⟨*irredeemable* mistakes⟩ — **ir·re·deem·ably** \-blē\ *adv*
ir·re·duc·ible \ˌir-i-ˈdü-sə-bəl, -ˈdyü-\ *adj* : not reducible — **ir·re·duc·ibil·i·ty** \-ˌdü-sə-ˈbil-ət-ē, -ˌdyü-\ *n* — **ir·re·duc·ibly** \-ˈdü-sə-blē, -ˈdyü-\ *adv*
ir·re·fut·able \ˌir-i-ˈfyüt-ə-bəl; ir-ˈef-yət-, ˈir-\ *adj* : not capable of being proved wrong : INDISPUTABLE ⟨*irrefutable* proof⟩ — **ir·re·fut·abil·i·ty** \ˌir-i-ˌfyüt-ə-ˈbil-ət-ē, ir-ˌef-yət-ə-ˈbil-\ *n* — **ir·re·fut·ably** \ˌir-i-ˈfyüt-ə-blē; ir-ˈef-yət-, ˈir-\ *adv*
[1]**ir·reg·u·lar** \ir-ˈeg-yə-lər, ˈir-\ *adj* **1 a** : not conforming to established laws, customs, or moral principles **b** : not belonging to a recognized or organized body ⟨*irregular* troops⟩ ⟨*irregular* Democrats⟩ **2** : not conforming to the normal or usual manner of inflection ⟨the *irregular* verbs *sell* and *cast*⟩; *esp* : STRONG 13 ⟨the *irregular* verb *write*⟩ **3** : having one or more similar floral parts unequal in size, form, or arrangement; *esp* : ZYGOMORPHIC **4** : lacking continuity or regularity of occurrence ⟨*irregular* intervals⟩ ⟨*irregular* payments⟩ — **ir·reg·u·lar·ly** *adv*
[2]**irregular** *n* : a soldier (as a guerrilla) who is not a member of a regular military force
ir·reg·u·lar·i·ty \ir-ˌeg-yə-ˈlar-ət-ē\ *n, pl* **-ties** **1** : the quality or state of being irregular **2** : something (as dishonest conduct) that is irregular **3** : CONSTIPATION
ir·rel·e·vant \ir-ˈel-ə-vənt, ˈir-\ *adj* : not relevant : not applicable or pertinent — **ir·rel·e·vance** \-vəns\ *or* **ir·rel·e·van·cy** \-vən-sē\ *n* — **ir·rel·e·vant·ly** *adv*
ir·re·li·gious \-ˈlij-əs\ *adj* **1** : lacking religious emotions, doctrines, or practices **2** : indicating lack of religion ⟨*irreligious* talk⟩ — **ir·re·li·gious·ly** *adv*
ir·re·me·di·a·ble \ˌir-i-ˈmēd-ē-ə-bəl\ *adj* : not remediable; *also* : INCURABLE — **ir·re·me·di·a·ble·ness** *n* — **ir·re·me·di·a·bly** \-blē\ *adv*
ir·re·mov·able \ˌir-i-ˈmü-və-bəl\ *adj* : not removable — **ir·re·mov·abil·i·ty** \-ˌmü-və-ˈbil-ət-ē\ *n* — **ir·re·mov·ably** \-ˈmü-və-blē\ *adv*
ir·rep·a·ra·ble \ir-ˈep-rə-bəl, ˈir-, -ə-rə-\ *adj* : not capable of being repaired or made good ⟨an *irreparable* loss⟩ — **ir·rep·a·ra·ble·ness** *n* — **ir·rep·a·ra·bly** \-blē\ *adv*
ir·re·place·able \ˌir-i-ˈplā-sə-bəl\ *adj* : not replaceable
ir·re·press·ible \ˌir-i-ˈpres-ə-bəl\ *adj* : not capable of being checked or held back ⟨*irrepressible* laughter⟩ — **ir·re·press·ibil·i·ty** \-ˌpres-ə-ˈbil-ət-ē\ *n* — **ir·re·press·ibly** \-ˈpres-ə-blē\ *adv*
ir·re·proach·able \-ˈprō-chə-bəl\ *adj* : not reproachable : BLAMELESS — **ir·re·proach·able·ness** *n* — **ir·re·proach·ably** \-blē\ *adv*
ir·re·sist·ible \-ˈzis-tə-bəl\ *adj* : impossible to successfully resist or oppose ⟨an *irresistible* attraction⟩ — **ir·re·sist·ibil·i·ty** \-ˌzis-tə-ˈbil-ət-ē\ *adj* — **ir·re·sist·ible·ness** \-ˈzis-tə-bəl-nəs\ *n* — **ir·re·sist·ibly** \-blē\ *adv*
ir·res·o·lute \ir-ˈez-ə-ˌlüt, ˈir-, -lət\ *adj* : uncertain how to act or proceed : HESITANT — **ir·res·o·lute·ly** *adv* — **ir·res·o·lute·ness** *n* — **ir·res·o·lu·tion** \ir-ˌez-ə-ˈlü-shən\ *n*
irrespective of *prep* : without regard to : regardless of
ir·re·spon·si·ble \ˌir-i-ˈspän-sə-bəl\ *adj* : not responsible: as **a** : not answerable to higher authority **b** : said or done with no sense of responsibility ⟨*irresponsible* charges⟩ **c** : lacking a sense of responsibility **d** : unable especially mentally or financially to bear responsibility — **ir·re·spon·si·bil·i·ty** \-ˌspän-sə-ˈbil-ət-ē\ *n* — **ir·re·spon·si·bly** \-ˈspän-sə-blē\ *adv*
ir·re·triev·able \ˌir-i-ˈtrē-və-bəl\ *adj* : not capable of being regained or remedied ⟨an *irretrievable* mistake⟩ — **ir·re·triev·ably** \-blē\ *adv*
ir·rev·er·ence \ir-ˈev-rəns, ˈir-, -ˈev-ə-rəns, -ˈev-ərns\ *n* **1** : lack of reverence **2** : an irreverent act or utterance
ir·rev·er·ent \-ˈev-rənt, -ˈev-ə-rənt, -ˈev-ərnt\ *adj* : showing lack of reverence : DISRESPECTFUL — **ir·rev·er·ent·ly** *adv*
ir·re·vers·ible \ˌir-i-ˈvər-sə-bəl\ *adj* : incapable of being reversed — **ir·re·vers·ibil·i·ty** \-ˌvər-sə-ˈbil-ət-ē\ *n* — **ir·re·vers·ibly** \-ˈvər-sə-blē\ *adv*
ir·rev·o·ca·ble \ir-ˈev-ə-kə-bəl, ˈir-\ *adj* : not capable of being revoked ⟨an *irrevocable* decision⟩ — **ir·rev·o·ca·bil·i·ty** \ir-ˌev-ə-kə-ˈbil-ət-ē\ *n* — **ir·rev·o·ca·bly** \ir-ˈev-ə-kə-blē, ˈir-\ *adv*
ir·ri·gate \ˈir-ə-ˌgāt\ *vb* **1** : WET, MOISTEN: as **a** : to supply (as land or crops) with water by artificial means **b** : to flush with a liquid ⟨*irrigate* a wound⟩ **2** : to practice irrigation [Latin *irrigare,* from *in-* + *rigare* "to water"] — **ir·ri·ga·tion** \ˌir-ə-ˈgā-shən\ *n* — **ir·ri·ga·tor** \ˈir-ə-ˌgāt-ər\ *n*
ir·ri·ta·bil·i·ty \ˌir-ət-ə-ˈbil-ət-ē\ *n, pl* **-ties** : the quality or state of being irritable: as **a** : quick excitability to annoyance, impatience, or anger **b** : the property of living tissue and organisms that permits them to react to stimuli
ir·ri·ta·ble \ˈir-ət-ə-bəl\ *adj* **1** : capable of being irritated; *esp* : readily or easily irritated **2** : responsive to stimuli — **ir·ri·ta·ble·ness** *n* — **ir·ri·ta·bly** \-blē\ *adv*
ir·ri·tant \ˈir-ə-tənt\ *adj* : causing irritation; *esp* : tending to produce physical irritation — **irritant** *n*
ir·ri·tate \ˈir-ə-ˌtāt\ *vb* **1** : to excite impatience, anger, or displeasure in : ANNOY **2** : to make sore or inflamed [Latin *irritare*] — **ir·ri·ta·tive** \-ˌtāt-iv\ *adj*
synonyms IRRITATE, EXASPERATE, PROVOKE mean to excite a feeling of anger or annoyance. IRRITATE implies arousing feelings that may range from impatience to rage ⟨*irritated* me with constant nagging⟩. EXASPERATE suggests intense an-

noyance or extreme impatience ⟨an *exasperating* habit of putting off important decisions⟩. PROVOKE implies an often deliberate arousing of strong annoyance or vexation that may excite to action ⟨only says things like that to *provoke* me⟩.

ir·ri·ta·tion \ˌir-ə-ˈtā-shən\ *n* **1** : the act of irritating **2** : something that irritates **3** : the state of being irritated

ir·rupt \ir-ˈəpt, ˈir-\ *vi* **1** : to rush in forcibly or violently **2** : to increase suddenly in numbers ⟨rabbits *irrupt* in cycles⟩ [Latin *irruptus,* past participle of *irrumpere* "to break in, irrupt," from *in-* + *rumpere* "to break"] — **ir·rup·tion** \ir-ˈəp-shən, ˈir-\ *n* — **ir·rup·tive** \-ˈəp-tiv\ *adj* — **ir·rup·tive·ly** \-ˈəp-tiv-lē\ *adv*

is *present 3rd singular of* BE [Old English]

is- *or* **iso-** *combining form* **1** : equal : uniform ⟨*iso*bar⟩ **2** : isomeric ⟨*iso*leucine⟩ [Greek *isos*]

Isa·iah \ī-ˈzā-ə\ *n* : a prophetic book of canonical Jewish and Christian Scriptures — see BIBLE table

isch·emia \is-ˈkē-mē-ə\ *n* : deficient supply of blood to a body part that is due to obstruction of the inflow of arterial blood [Greek *ischaimos* "styptic," from *ischein* "to restrain" + *haima* "blood"] — **isch·emic** \-mik\ *adj*

is·chi·um \ˈis-kē-əm\ *n, pl* **-chia** \-kē-ə\ : the lower and posterior of the three main bones composing either half of the pelvis [Latin, "hip joint," from Greek *ischion*] — **is·chi·al** \-kē-əl\ *adj*

-ise \ˌīz\ *vb suffix, chiefly British* : -IZE

-ish \ish\ *adj suffix* **1** : of, relating to, or being ⟨Finn*ish*⟩ **2 a** : characteristic of ⟨girl*ish*⟩: having the undesirable qualities of ⟨mul*ish*⟩ **b** : inclined or liable to ⟨book*ish*⟩ ⟨qualm*ish*⟩ **c** (1) : somewhat ⟨small*ish*⟩ (2) : having the approximate age of ⟨forty*ish*⟩ (3) : being or occurring at the approximate time of ⟨eight*ish*⟩ [Old English *-isc*]

Ish·ma·el \ˈish-mā-əl, -mē-\ *n* : a social outcast [*Ishmael,* outcast son of Abraham and Hagar, from Hebrew *Yishmāʿēl*]

Ish·ma·el·ite \ˈish-mā-ə-ˌlīt, -mē-\ *n* : a member of an ancient Semitic people of the deserts of southwestern Asia held to be descended from Ishmael and sometimes held to be ancestral to the modern Arabs

isin·glass \ˈīz-n-ˌglas, ˈī-zing-\ *n* **1** : a very pure gelatin prepared from the air bladders of fishes (as sturgeons) **2** : mica in thin sheets [probably by folk etymology from Dutch *huizenblas,* from *huus* "sturgeon" + *blase* "bladder"]

Is·lam \is-ˈläm, iz-, -ˈlam, ˈis-ˌ, ˈiz-ˌ\ *n* **1** : a religion dominant in much of Asia and northern Africa since the 7th century A.D. that is marked by belief in Allah as the sole deity, in Muhammad as his prophet, and in the Koran **2 a** : the civilization erected upon Islamic faith **b** : the group of modern nations in which Islam is the dominant religion [Arabic *islām* "submission (to the will of God)"] — **Is·lam·ic** \is-ˈläm-ik, iz-, -ˈlam-\ *adj* — **Is·lam·ize** \ˈiz-lə-ˌmīz\ *vt*

is·land \ˈī-lənd\ *n* **1** : an area of land surrounded by water and smaller than a continent **2** : something suggestive of an island in its isolation [Middle English *iland,* from Old English *īgland*]

Word History The words *island* and *isle* are etymologically distinct. *Island* can be traced back to Old English *īgland,* composed of two elements *īg* and *land. Land,* as we might expect, means "land," but *īg* is also found in Old English as a word meaning "island." In a sense, then, *īgland* is "island-land." English *isle,* on the other hand, is derived through Medieval French from Latin *insula.* In the 16th century, under the influence of *isle,* the letter *s* was added to *iland,* the earlier form of *island.*

is·land·er \ˈī-lən-dər\ *n* : a native or inhabitant of an island

island universe *n* : a galaxy other than the Milky Way

isle \ˈīl\ *n* : ISLAND 1; *esp* : a small island [Medieval French, from Latin *insula* — see *Word History* at ISLAND]

is·let \ˈī-lət\ *n* **1** : a little island **2** : ISLET OF LANGERHANS

islet of Lang·er·hans \-ˈläng-ər-ˌhäns, -ˌhänz\ *n, pl* **islets of Langerhans** : one of the clusters of small slightly granular endocrine cells that form interlacing strands in the pancreas and secrete insulin and glucagon [Paul *Langerhans,* died 1888, German physician]

ism \ˈiz-əm\ *n* **1** : a distinctive doctrine, cause, or theory **2** : an oppressive and especially discriminatory attitude or belief [*-ism*]

-ism \ˌiz-əm\ *n suffix* **1 a** : act : practice : process ⟨plagiar*ism*⟩ **b** : manner of action or behavior characteristic of a (specified) person or thing ⟨animal*ism*⟩ **c** : prejudice or discrimination on the basis of a (specified) attribute ⟨rac*ism*⟩ ⟨sex*ism*⟩ **2 a** : state : condition : property ⟨barbarian*ism*⟩ **b** : abnormal state or condition resulting from excess of a (specified) thing ⟨alcohol*ism*⟩ **3 a** : doctrine : theory : cult ⟨Buddh*ism*⟩ **b** : adherence to a system or a class of principles ⟨stoic*ism*⟩ **4** : characteristic or peculiar feature or trait ⟨colloquial*ism*⟩ [Greek *-isma* and *-ismos,* from verbs in *-izein* "-ize"]

isn't \ˈiz-nt\ : is not

iso·bar \ˈī-sə-ˌbär\ *n* : a line drawn on a map connecting places having the same atmospheric pressure at a given time or for a given period [*is-* + Greek *baros* "weight"] — **iso·bar·ic** \ˌī-sə-ˈbär-ik, -ˈbar-\ *adj*

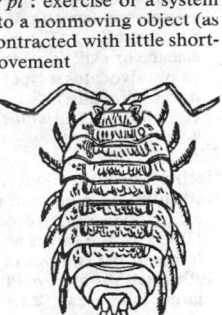

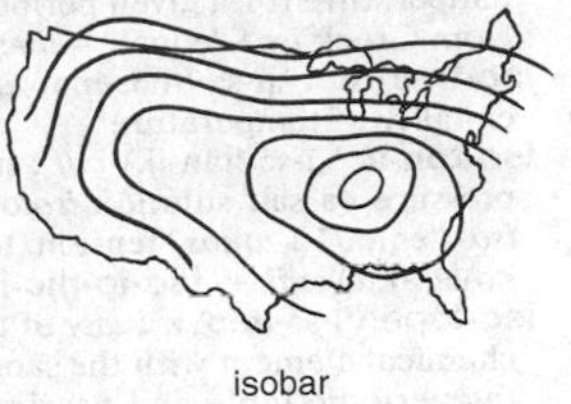

isobar

iso·ga·mete \ˌī-sō-gə-ˈmēt, -ˈgam-ˌēt\ *n* : a gamete indistinguishable from another gamete with which it can unite to form a zygote — **iso·ga·met·ic** \-gə-ˈmet-ik\ *adj*

iso·gon·ic line \ˌī-sə-ˌgän-ik-\ *n* : a line on a map joining points on the earth's surface at which the magnetic declination is the same [Greek *gōnia* "angle"]

iso·late \ˈī-sə-ˌlāt *also* ˈis-ə-\ *vb* **1** : to set apart from others; *also* : QUARANTINE **2** : to select from among others; *esp* : to separate from other substances so as to obtain pure or in a free state [back-formation from *isolated* "set apart," from French *isolé,* from Italian *isolato,* from *isola* "island," from Latin *insula*]

iso·la·tion \ˌī-sə-ˈlā-shən, ˌis-ə-\ *n* : the act of isolating : the condition of being isolated

iso·la·tion·ism \-shə-ˌniz-əm\ *n* : a national policy of avoiding international political and economic relations (as alliances) — **iso·la·tion·ist** \-shə-nəst, -shnəst\ *n or adj*

iso·leu·cine \ˌī-sō-ˈlü-ˌsēn\ *n* : a crystalline essential amino acid isomeric with leucine

iso·mer \ˈī-sə-mər\ *n* : one of two or more chemical compounds or groups that have the same numbers of atoms of the same elements but differ in structural arrangement [back-formation from *isomeric,* from Greek *isomerēs* "equally divided," from *isos* "equal" + *meros* "part"] — **iso·mer·ic** \ˌī-sə-ˈmer-ik\ *adj* — **isom·er·ism** \ī-ˈsäm-ə-ˌriz-əm\ *n*

iso·met·ric \ˌī-sə-ˈme-trik\ *adj* **1** : of, relating to, or characterized by equality of measure **2** : relating to or being a crystallographic system characterized by three equal axes at right angles **3** : of, relating to, or being muscular contraction of the type that occurs in doing isometrics — **iso·met·ri·cal·ly** \-tri-kə-lē, -klē\ *adv*

iso·met·rics \ˌī-sə-ˈme-triks\ *n sing or pl* : exercise or a system of exercises in which force is applied to a nonmoving object (as a wall) so that opposing muscles are contracted with little shortening of muscle fibers and no joint movement

iso·pod \ˈī-sə-ˌpäd\ *n* : any of a large order (Isopoda) of small sessile-eyed aquatic or terrestrial crustaceans (as a wood louse) with a body composed of seven free thoracic segments each bearing a pair of legs — **isopod** *adj*

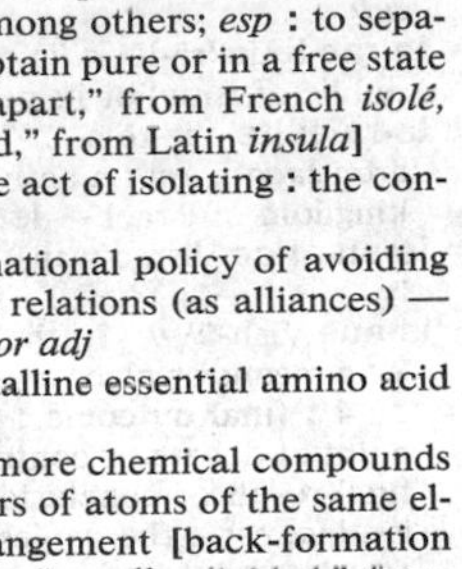

isopod

iso·prene \ˈī-sə-ˌprēn\ *n* : a compound C_5H_8 used especially in making synthetic rubber [probably from Greek *isos* "equal" + *propylene* "a gaseous hydrocarbon C_3H_6"]

iso·pro·pyl alcohol \ˌī-sə-ˈprō-pəl-\ *n* : a volatile flammable alcohol C_3H_8O used especially as a solvent and rubbing alcohol [*isopropyl* from *is-* + *prop-* (derived from *propionic acid*) + *-yl*]

isos·ce·les \ī-ˈsäs-ˌlēz, -ə-ˌlēz\ *adj* **1** : being a triangle with two equal sides **2** : being a trapezoid whose two nonparallel sides are equal [Late Latin, from Greek *isoskelēs,* from *isos* "equal" + *skelos* "leg"]

isos·ta·sy \ī-ˈsäs-tə-sē\ *n* : general equilibrium in vertical movement between segments of the earth's crust maintained by a yielding flow of rock material beneath the surface under the

\ə\ **abut**	\au̇\ **out**	\i\ **tip**	\ȯ\ **saw**	\u̇\ **foot**
\ər\ **further**	\ch\ **chin**	\ī\ **life**	\ȯi\ **coin**	\y\ **yet**
\a\ **mat**	\e\ **pet**	\j\ **job**	\th\ **thin**	\yü\ **few**
\ā\ **take**	\ē\ **easy**	\ng\ **sing**	\t͟h\ **this**	\yu̇\ **cure**
\ä\ **cot, cart**	\g\ **go**	\ō\ **bone**	\ü\ **food**	\zh\ **vision**

force of gravity [Greek *isos* "equal" + *-stasia* "condition of standing," from *histanai* "to cause to stand"] — **iso·stat·ic** \ˌī-sə-ˈstat-ik\ *adj*

iso·therm \ˈī-sə-ˌthərm\ *n* : a line on a map connecting points having the same temperature at a given time or the same mean temperature for a given period [French *isotherme* "isothermal," from Greek *isos* "equal" + *thermē* "heat"]

iso·ther·mal \ˌī-sə-ˈthər-məl\ *adj* : of, relating to, or marked by equality of temperature

iso·ton·ic \ˌī-sə-ˈtän-ik\ *adj* : having the same or equal osmotic pressure ⟨a salt solution *isotonic* with red blood cells⟩ [Greek *isos* "equal" + *tonos* "tension, tone"] — **iso·ton·i·cal·ly** \-ˈtän-i-kə-lē, -klē\ *adv* — **iso·to·nic·i·ty** \-tō-ˈnis-ət-ē\ *n*

iso·tope \ˈī-sə-ˌtōp\ *n* : any of two or more species of atoms of a chemical element with the same atomic number and position in the periodic table and nearly identical chemical behavior but with differing atomic mass or mass number and different physical properties [Greek *isos* "equal" + *topos* "place"] — **iso·top·ic** \ˌī-sə-ˈtäp-ik, -ˈtō-pik\ *adj* — **iso·top·i·cal·ly** \-ˈtäp-i-kə-lē, -ˈtō-pi-, -klē\ *adv*

Is·ra·el \ˈiz-rē-əl\ *n* **1** : the Jewish people **2** : a group of people held to be God's elect [derived from Hebrew *Yiśrāʼēl*] — **Israel** *adj*

Is·rae·li \iz-ˈrā-lē\ *adj* : of, relating to, or characteristic of the republic of Israel or its people — **Israeli** *n*

Is·ra·el·ite \ˈiz-rē-ə-ˌlīt\ *n* : a descendant of the Hebrew patriarch Jacob; *esp* : a native or inhabitant of the ancient northern kingdom of Israel — **Israelite** *or* **Is·ra·el·it·ish** \-ˌlīt-ish\ *adj*

is·su·ance \ˈish-ə-wəns\ *n* : the act of issuing especially officially

[1]is·sue \ˈish-ü\ *n* **1** : the action of going, coming, or flowing out **2** : a means or place of going out : EXIT, OUTLET **3** : PROGENY 2 **4** : final outcome : RESULT **5 a** : a matter in dispute : a point of debate or controversy **b** : CONCERN, PROBLEM **c** : a final result or conclusion : DECISION **6** : something issued or issuing; *esp* : the copies of a periodical published at one time ⟨the latest *issue* of a magazine⟩ [Medieval French, from *issir* "to come out, go out," from Latin *exire,* from *ex-* + *ire* "to go"]

[2]issue *vb* **1** : to go, come, or flow out : DISCHARGE ⟨water *issuing* from a pipe⟩ **2 a** : to cause to come forth : EMIT **b** : to distribute officially ⟨*issue* a new stamp⟩ **c** : to send out for sale or circulation : PUBLISH **3** : to come as an effect : RESULT — **is·su·er** *n*

[1]-ist \əst\ *n suffix* **1 a** : one that performs a (specified) action ⟨cycl*ist*⟩: one that makes or produces ⟨novel*ist*⟩ **b** : one that plays a (specified) musical instrument ⟨harp*ist*⟩ **c** : one that operates a (specified) mechanical instrument or contrivance ⟨automobil*ist*⟩ **2** : one that specializes in a (specified) art or science or skill ⟨geolog*ist*⟩ ⟨ventriloqu*ist*⟩ **3** : one that adheres to or advocates a (specified) doctrine or system or code of behavior ⟨royal*ist*⟩ ⟨social*ist*⟩ or that of a (specified) individual ⟨Calvin*ist*⟩ ⟨Darwin*ist*⟩ [Greek *-istēs,* from verbs in *-izein* "-ize"]

[2]-ist *adj suffix* : -ISTIC

[1]isth·mi·an \ˈis-mē-ən\ *n* : a native or inhabitant of an isthmus

[2]isthmian *adj* : of, relating to, or situated in or near an isthmus: as **a** *often cap* : of or relating to the Isthmus of Corinth in Greece or the games anciently held there **b** *often cap* : of or relating to the Isthmus of Panama

isth·mus \ˈis-məs\ *n* **1** : a narrow strip of land connecting two larger land areas **2** : a narrow anatomical part or passage connecting two larger structures or cavities [Latin, from Greek *isthmos*]

-is·tic \ˈis-tik\ *also* **-is·ti·cal** \ˈis-ti-kəl\ *adj suffix* : of, relating to, or characteristic of ⟨altru*istic*⟩ [Greek *-istikos,* from *-istēs* "-ist" + *-ikos* "-ic"]

is·tle \ˈist-lē\ *n* : a strong fiber (as for cordage or basketry) obtained from various tropical American plants (as an agave) [American Spanish *ixtle,* from Nahuatl *ichtli*]

[1]it \it, ˈit, ət\ *pron* **1** : that one — used usually in reference to a lifeless thing ⟨caught the ball and threw *it* back⟩, a plant, a person or animal whose sex is unknown or disregarded ⟨don't know who *it* is⟩, a group of individuals or things, or an abstract entity; compare HE, ITS, SHE, THEY **2** — used as subject of a verb that expresses a condition or action without reference to an agent ⟨*it* is raining⟩ **3 a** — used to mark the logical place of a noun, phrase, or clause that has been shifted to a later place in a sentence ⟨*it* is necessary to repeat the whole thing⟩; often used to shift emphasis to a part of a statement other than the subject ⟨*it* was in this city that the treaty was signed⟩ **b** — used with many verbs as a direct object with little or no meaning ⟨footed *it* back to camp⟩ **4** : the general state of affairs or circumstances ⟨how is *it* going⟩ [Old English *hit*]

[2]it \ˈit\ *n* : the player in a game who performs the principal action of the game (as trying to catch others in a game of tag)

Ital·ian \ə-ˈtal-yən, i-\ *n* **1 a** : a native or inhabitant of Italy **b** : a person of Italian descent **2** : the Romance language of the Italians — **Italian** *adj*

Italian sonnet *n* : a sonnet consisting of an octave rhyming *abba abba* and a sestet rhyming in any of several patterns (as *cde cde* or *cdc dcd*)

[1]ital·ic \ə-ˈtal-ik, i-, ī-\ *adj* **1** *cap* : of or relating to ancient Italy, its peoples, or their Indo-European languages **2** : of or relating to a type style with characters that slant upward to the right (as in *"these words are italic"*)

[2]italic *n* : an italic character or type

ital·i·cize \ə-ˈtal-ə-ˌsīz, i-, ī-\ *vt* **1** : to print in italics **2** : to underscore with a single line

[1]itch \ˈich\ *vb* **1** : to have or produce an itch **2** : to cause to itch **3** : to have a strong persistent desire ⟨*itching* to get a new car⟩ [Middle English *icchen,* from Old English *giccan*]

[2]itch *n* **1 a** : an uneasy irritating sensation in the skin usually held to result from mild stimulation of pain receptors **b** : a skin disorder accompanied by an itch; *esp* : SCABIES **2** : a constant restless desire ⟨an *itch* to travel⟩ — **itch·i·ness** \ˈich-ē-nəs\ *n* — **itchy** \-ē\ *adj*

it'd \ˌit-əd\ : it had : it would

[1]-ite \ˌīt\ *n suffix* **1 a** : native : resident ⟨Brooklyn*ite*⟩ **b** : descendant ⟨Ishmael*ite*⟩ **c** : adherent : follower ⟨Jacob*ite*⟩ **2** : product ⟨metabol*ite*⟩ **3** : fossil ⟨ammon*ite*⟩ **4** : mineral ⟨hal*ite*⟩: rock ⟨quartz*ite*⟩ **5** : segment or constituent part ⟨so*mite*⟩ [Greek *-itēs*]

[2]-ite *n suffix* : salt or ester of an acid with a name ending in *-ous* ⟨nitr*ite*⟩ [French, alteration of *-ate* "[1]-ate"]

item \ˈīt-əm\ *n* **1** : a separate thing in a list, account, group, or series : ARTICLE ⟨check each *item* before you pack it⟩ **2** : a separate piece of news or information : a short news paragraph ⟨column of local *items*⟩ [Latin *item* "also," from *ita* "thus"]

synonyms ITEM, DETAIL, PARTICULAR mean one of the distinct parts of a whole. ITEM applies to each separate thing specified in a list or in a group of things that might be listed or enumerated ⟨get every *item* on the list⟩. DETAIL applies to one of the small component parts of a larger whole such as a task, building, painting, narration, or process ⟨leave the *details* to me⟩. PARTICULAR stresses the smallness, singleness, and especially the concreteness of a detail or item ⟨a description that included few *particulars*⟩.

item·ize \ˈīt-ə-ˌmīz\ *vt* : to set down in detail : LIST ⟨*itemize* expenditures⟩ — **item·iza·tion** \ˌīt-ə-mə-ˈzā-shən\ *n*

it·er·ate \ˈit-ə-ˌrāt\ *vt* : REITERATE, REPEAT [Latin *iterare,* from *iterum* "again"] — **it·er·a·tive** \ˈit-ə-ˌrāt-iv, -rət-\ *adj*

it·er·a·tion \ˌit-ə-ˈrā-shən\ *n* : REPETITION; *esp* : a computational process in which a series of operations is repeated a number of times

itin·er·ant \ī-ˈtin-ə-rənt, ə-ˈtin-\ *adj* : traveling from place to place ⟨*itinerant* preachers⟩ [Late Latin *itinerari* "to journey," from Latin *itiner-, iter* "journey"] — **itinerant** *n* — **itin·er·ant·ly** *adv*

itin·er·ary \ī-ˈtin-ə-ˌrer-ē, ə-\ *n, pl* **-ar·ies** **1** : the route of a journey **2** : a travel diary **3** : a traveler's guidebook — **itinerary** *adj*

-i·tis \ˈīt-əs\ *n suffix, pl* **-i·tis·es** *also* **-it·i·des** \ˈit-ə-ˌdēz\ *or* **-i·tes** \ˈīt-ēz\ **1** : disease or inflammation ⟨bronch*itis*⟩ **2** : heated or excessive response to [Greek]

it'll \ˌit-l\ : it shall : it will

its \its, ˌits, əts\ *adj* : of or relating to it or itself especially as possessor, agent, or object of an action ⟨going to *its* kennel⟩ ⟨a child proud of *its* first drawings⟩ ⟨*its* final enactment into law⟩

it's \its, ˌits, əts\ : it is : it has

it·self \it-ˈself, ət-\ *pron* **1** : that identical one — used reflexively or for emphasis ⟨watched the cat giving *itself* a bath⟩ ⟨the letter *itself* was missing⟩; compare IT 1 **2** : its normal, healthy, or sane condition or self

-ity \ət-ē\ *n suffix, pl* **-ities** : quality : state : degree ⟨asinin*ity*⟩ [Medieval French or Latin; Medieval French *-ité,* from Latin *-itat-, -itas*]

IUD \ˌī-ˌyü-ˈdē\ *n* : INTRAUTERINE DEVICE

-ium *n suffix* **1 :** chemical element ⟨europ*ium*⟩ **2 :** chemical radical ⟨ammon*ium*⟩ [Latin, ending of some neuter nouns]

-ive \iv\ *adj suffix* **:** that performs or tends toward an (indicated) action ⟨regress*ive*⟩ [Latin *-ivus*]

I've \īv, ˌīv\ **:** I have

ivied \ˈī-vēd\ *adj* **:** overgrown with ivy

ivo·ry \ˈīv-rē, -ə-rē\ *n, pl* **-ries 1 :** the hard creamy-white modified dentine that composes the tusks of a tusked mammal (as an elephant or walrus) **2 :** a pale yellow **3 :** something (as piano keys) made of ivory or of a similar substance [Medieval French *ivoire,* from Latin *eboreus* "of ivory," from *ebur* "ivory," from Egyptian *ꜣb, ꜣbw* "elephant, ivory"]

ivo·ry–billed woodpecker \-ˈbild-\ *n* **:** a large black-and-white woodpecker of the southeastern U.S. that has a large whitish bill and in the male a red crest and that is presumed to be extinct

ivory black *n* **:** a fine black pigment made by calcining ivory

ivory tower *n* **1 :** a lack of concern with practical matters or urgent problems **2 :** a secluded place for meditation **:** RETREAT

ivy \ˈī-vē\ *n, pl* **ivies 1 :** a widely grown climbing woody vine with glossy evergreen leaves, small yellowish flowers, and black berries **2 :** any of several climbing plants (as Virginia creeper or poison ivy) resembling ivy [Old English *īfig*]

Ivy League *adj* **:** of, relating to, or characteristic of a group of long-established eastern United States colleges widely regarded as high in scholastic and social prestige [from the prevalence of ivy-covered buildings on the campuses of the older United States colleges]

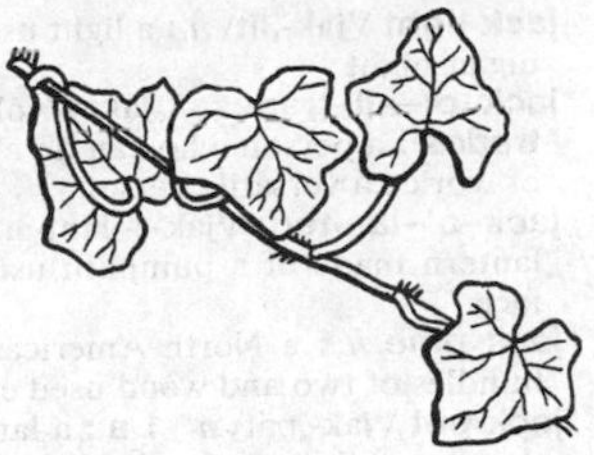

ivy 1

-i·za·tion \ə-ˈzā-shən *also especially when an unstressed syllable precedes* ī-ˈzā-\ *n suffix* **:** action, process, or result of making ⟨social*ization*⟩ ⟨union*ization*⟩ ⟨special*ization*⟩

-ize \ˌīz\ *vb suffix* **1 a** (1) **:** cause to be or conform to or resemble ⟨american*ize*⟩ **:** cause to be formed into ⟨union*ize*⟩ (2) **:** subject to a (specified) action ⟨satir*ize*⟩ (3) **:** impregnate or treat or combine with ⟨macadam*ize*⟩ **b :** treat like ⟨idol*ize*⟩ **2 a :** become **:** become like ⟨crystall*ize*⟩ **b :** be productive in or of ⟨hypothes*ize*⟩ **:** engage in a (specified) activity ⟨botan*ize*⟩ [Greek *-izein*]

J

j \ˈjā\ *n, pl* **j's** *or* **js** \ˈjāz\ *often cap* **:** the 10th letter of the English alphabet

jab \ˈjab\ *vb* **jabbed; jab·bing :** to thrust quickly or abruptly with or as if with something sharp **:** POKE [Middle English *jobben*] — **jab** *n*

jab·ber \ˈjab-ər\ *vb* **jab·bered; jab·ber·ing** \ˈjab-ring, -ə-ring\ **:** to utter or speak rapidly, indistinctly, or unintelligibly [Middle English *jaberen*] — **jabber** *n* — **jab·ber·er** \ˈjab-ər-ər\ *n*

jab·ber·wocky \ˈjab-ər-ˌwäk-ē\ *n* **:** meaningless speech or writing [*Jabberwocky,* nonsense poem by Lewis Carroll]

ja·bot \zha-ˈbō, ˈjab-ˌō\ *n* **:** a ruffle of cloth or lace that falls from the collar down the front of a dress or shirt [French]

jac·a·ran·da \ˌjak-ə-ˈran-də\ *n* **:** a tropical American tree often grown for its showy clusters of blue flowers [Portuguese]

ja·cinth \ˈjās-nth, ˈjas-; zhä-ˈsant\ *n* **:** HYACINTH 1 [Medieval French *jacinte,* from Latin *hyacinthus,* a flowering plant]

[1]**jack** \ˈjak\ *n* **1** *often cap* **:** SAILOR 1a **2 a :** a device for turning a spit (as in roasting meat) **b :** any of various portable mechanisms for exerting pressure or lifting a heavy body a short distance **3 :** any of various animals: as **a :** a male donkey **b :** JACKRABBIT **4 a :** a small target ball in lawn bowling **b :** a small national flag flown by a ship **c** (1) **:** a small 6-pointed metal object used in a game (2) *pl* **:** a game played with jacks **5 :** a playing card bearing the stylized figure of a man **6** *slang* **:** MONEY 1 **7 :** a socket in an electric circuit used with a plug to make a connection with another circuit [*Jack,* nickname for *John*]

[2]**jack** *vb* **1 :** to hunt or fish for game at night with a jacklight **2 :** to move or lift by or as if by a jack **3 :** to raise the level or quality of ⟨*jack* up prices⟩ — **jack·er** *n*

jack·al \ˈjak-əl, -ˌȯl\ *n* **1 :** any of several wild dogs of Africa and Asia similar to but smaller than the related wolves **2 :** a person who performs routine or menial tasks for another [Turkish *çakal,* from Persian *shagāl,* from Sanskrit *śṛgāla*]

jack·a·napes \ˈjak-ə-ˌnāps\ *n* **1 :** MONKEY 1, APE **2 :** an impudent or conceited person [Middle English *Jack Napis,* nickname for William de la Pole, died 1450, duke of Suffolk]

jack·ass \ˈjak-ˌas\ *n* **:** DONKEY; *esp* **:** a male donkey

jack·boot \ˈjak-ˌbüt\ *n* **1 :** a heavy military boot reaching above the knee and worn especially in the 17th and 18th centuries **2 :** a laceless military boot reaching to the calf

jack·daw \ˈjak-ˌdȯ\ *n* **:** a common black and gray Eurasian bird smaller than the related crows

jack·et \ˈjak-ət\ *n* **1 :** a short coat usually having a front opening, collar, and sleeves **2 :** an outer covering or casing: as **a :** a tough metal covering on a bullet or projectile **b :** a coating or covering of a nonconducting material used to prevent heat radiation **c :** a detachable outer paper wrapper on a bound book [Medieval French *jackés,* from *jaque* "short jacket," from *jacques* "peasant," from the name *Jaques* "James"] — **jack·et·ed** \-ət-əd\ *adj*

Jack Frost *n* **:** frost or frosty weather personified

jack·ham·mer \ˈjak-ˌham-ər\ *n* **:** a pneumatic percussive tool for drilling or breaking up hard substances (as rock or pavement)

jack–in–the–box \ˈjak-ən-t͟hə-ˌbäks\ *n, pl* **jack–in–the–boxes** *or* **jacks–in–the–box :** a small box out of which a figure (as of a clown's head) springs when the lid is raised

jack–in–the–pul·pit \ˌjak-ən-t͟hə-ˈpu̇l-ˌpit\ *n, pl* **jack–in–the–pulpits** *also* **jacks–in–the–pulpit :** a North American spring-flowering woodland herb with an upright club-shaped flower cluster arched over by a green and purple spathe

[1]**jack·knife** \ˈjak-ˌnīf\ *n* **1 :** a large strong pocketknife **2 :** a dive in which the diver bends from the waist and touches the ankles before straightening out

[2]**jackknife** *vi* **1 :** to double up like a jackknife **2 :** to turn or rise and form an angle of 90 degrees or less with each other — used especially of a pair of connected vehicles

jack-in-the-pulpit

jack·leg \ˈjak-ˌleg\ *adj* **1 :** lacking skill or training **:** AMATEUR ⟨a *jackleg* carpenter⟩ **2 :** designed as a temporary expedient **:** MAKESHIFT

\ə\ **abut**	\au̇\ **out**	\i\ **tip**	\ȯ\ **saw**	\u̇\ **foot**
\ər\ **further**	\ch\ **chin**	\ī\ **life**	\ȯi\ **coin**	\y\ **yet**
\a\ **mat**	\e\ **pet**	\j\ **job**	\th\ **thin**	\yü\ **few**
\ā\ **take**	\ē\ **easy**	\ng\ **sing**	\t͟h\ **this**	\yu̇\ **cure**
\ä\ **cot, cart**	\g\ **go**	\ō\ **bone**	\ü\ **food**	\zh\ **vision**

jack·light \ˈjak-ˌlīt\ *n* : a light used especially in hunting or fishing at night

jack–of–all–trades \ˌjak-ə-ˈvȯl-ˌtrādz\ *n, pl* **jacks–of–all–trades** : a person who can do a satisfactory job at varied kinds of work : a versatile person

jack–o'–lan·tern \ˈjak-ə-ˌlant-ərn\ *n* **1** : IGNIS FATUUS **2** : a lantern made of a pumpkin usually cut to look like a human face

jack pine *n* : a North American pine with twisted needles in bundles of two and wood used especially for pulpwood

jack·pot \ˈjak-ˌpät\ *n* **1 a** : a large pot (as in poker) formed by the accumulation of stakes from previous play **b** (1) : a combination on a slot machine that wins a top prize or all the coins in the machine (2) : the sum so won **2** : an impressive often unexpected success or reward

jack·rab·bit \-ˌrab-ət\ *n* : any of several large hares of western North America with long ears and long hind legs [*jack*ass + *rabbit;* from its long ears]

jackrabbit

jack·screw \-ˌskrü\ *n* : a screw-operated jack for lifting or for exerting pressure

Jack·so·ni·an \jak-ˈsō-nē-ən\ *adj* : of, relating to, or characteristic of Andrew Jackson or his political principles or policies — **Jacksonian** *n*

jack stand *n* : a stand of adjustable height that is used to support an automobile

jack·stone \ˈjak-ˌstōn\ *n* **1** : JACK 4c(1) **2** *pl* : JACK 4c(2)

jack·straw \-ˌstrȯ\ *n* **1** : one of the pieces used in the game jackstraws **2** *pl* : a game in which a set of straws or thin strips are dropped in a heap with each player in turn trying to remove one at a time without disturbing the rest

jack–tar \-ˈtär\ *n, often cap* : SAILOR 1a

Jac·o·be·an \ˌjak-ə-ˈbē-ən\ *adj* : of, relating to, or characteristic of James I of England or his age [New Latin *Jacobus* "James"] — **Jacobean** *n*

Jac·o·bin \ˈjak-ə-bən\ *n* : a member of a radical political group advocating egalitarian democracy and engaging in terrorist activities during the French Revolution of 1789 [French, from *Jacobin* "Dominican" (from Late Latin *Jacobus* "James"; from the location of the first Dominican convent in Paris in the street of Saint James—*Rue Saint Jacques*); from the group's having been founded in a former Dominican convent] — **Jac·o·bin·ism** \-bə-ˌniz-əm\ *n*

Jac·o·bite \ˈjak-ə-ˌbīt\ *n* : a partisan of James II of England or of the Stuarts after the revolution of 1688 — **Jac·o·bit·i·cal** \ˌjak-ə-ˈbit-i-kəl\ *adj* — **Jac·o·bit·ism** \ˈjak-ə-ˌbīt-ˌiz-əm\ *n*

Jacob's ladder *n* : a ship's ladder of rope or chain with wooden or iron steps [from the ladder seen in a dream by Jacob in Genesis 28:12]

Ja·cob·son's organ \ˈjā-kəb-sənz-\ *n* : VOMERONASAL ORGAN [Ludvig L. *Jacobson*, died 1843, Danish anatomist]

jac·quard \ˈjak-ˌärd\ *n, often cap* : a fabric of intricate variegated weave or pattern [Joseph *Jacquard*, died 1834, French inventor]

[1]**jade** \ˈjād\ *n* **1** : a broken-down, vicious, or worthless horse **2** : a disreputable woman [Middle English]

Word History The English word *jade* that is used for a horse or a woman is not related to the name of the green stone jade. The origin of the earlier *jade* is uncertain. It was first used in Middle English to mean "a broken-down horse." Later the word for a worthless horse was often applied to a woman (or, very rarely, to a man) considered worthless. Now a *jade* is more often a disreputable woman than a broken-down horse. *Jaded,* meaning "worn out," is also derived from the equine *jade.* Originally, to *jade* a horse was to make a *jade* of it, to wear it out or break it down by overwork or abuse. It was not long before people, too, could be called *jaded.*

[2]**jade** *vb* **1 a** : to wear out by overwork or abuse **b** : to tire by tedious tasks **2** : to become weary

[3]**jade** *n* : a tough dense usually green gemstone that takes a high polish [French, from obsolete Spanish (*piedra de la*) *ijada,* literally, "loin stone"]

Word History Gemstones were once believed to have magical and medicinal properties. Jade was supposed to be especially effective in combating kidney disorders. The 16th century Spanish, who brought jade home with them from the New World, named the powerful green stone *piedra de la ijada,* "loin stone." Not only in Spain but throughout western Europe jade became popular both as an ornament and as a cure or preventive for internal problems. In England jade was formerly called *spleen stone,* but this term has not survived. Our modern word *jade* was borrowed from the French, who had so transformed Spanish *ijada.*

jad·ed *adj* **1** : very fatigued **2** : dulled by overindulgence ⟨*jaded* viewers⟩ — **jad·ed·ly** *adv* — **jad·ed·ness** *n*

jade green *n* : a light bluish green

jae·ger \ˈyā-gər\ *n* : any of several large dark-colored birds of northern seas that harass weaker birds and steal their prey [German *jäger* "hunter"]

[1]**jag** \ˈjag\ *vb* **jagged** \ˈjagd\; **jag·ging** : to make ragged : NOTCH [Middle English *jaggen*]

[2]**jag** *n* : a sharp projecting part : BARB

[3]**jag** *n* **1** : a small load (as of hay) **2** : SPREE ⟨a crying *jag*⟩ ⟨drinking *jags*⟩ [origin unknown]

jag·ged \ˈjag-əd\ *adj* : sharply notched : ROUGH ⟨a *jagged* edge⟩ — **jag·ged·ly** *adv* — **jag·ged·ness** *n*

jag·uar \ˈjag-ˌwär, ˈjag-yə-ˌwär\ *n* : a large cat of tropical America that is larger and stockier than the leopard and is brownish yellow or buff with black spots [Portuguese, from Tupi *jawára* "large carnivore"]

jag·ua·run·di \ˌzhag-wə-ˈrən-dē\ *n* : a slender long-tailed short-legged grayish wildcat of Central and South America [American Spanish, from Old Guarani (native American language of Bolivia, Paraguay, and southern Brazil) *yaguarundi*]

jai alai \ˈhī-ˌlī, ˌhī-ə-ˈlī\ *n* : a court game played usually by two or four players in which the ball is caught and hurled against the front wall with a long curved wicker basket strapped to the hand [Spanish, from Basque, from *jai* "festival" + *alai* "merry"]

[1]**jail** \ˈjāl\ *n* : PRISON; *esp* : a building for the temporary custody of prisoners [Medieval French *gaiole, jaiole,* from Late Latin *caveola* "little cage," from Latin *cavea* "cage"]

Word History *Jail* and *cage,* similar in meaning but quite different in form, are actually etymologically related. Both are descendants of Latin *cavea,* which means "cavity" or "cage." In medieval France the direct descendant of Latin *cavea* appeared in a variety of forms. Among these variants were *gave, gage, cage,* and *jaie.* It was *cage* that survived into modern French, and it was *cage* that was borrowed into English. During the Late Latin period a diminutive of Latin *cavea* was formed. This diminutive, *caveola,* developed into Medieval French *jaole, jaiole,* and *geole.* This Medieval French word is the source of our British and American English variants *gaol* and *jail.*

[2]**jail** *vt* : to confine in or as if in a jail

jail·bird \ˈjāl-ˌbərd\ *n* : a person confined in jail; *esp* : an habitual criminal

jail·break \-ˌbrāk\ *n* : an escape from jail

jail·er *or* **jail·or** \ˈjā-lər\ *n* : the keeper of a jail

Jain \ˈjīn\ *or* **Jai·na** \ˈjī-nə\ *n* : an adherent of Jainism [Hindi &Urdu *Jain,* from Sanskrit *Jaina*]

Jain·ism \ˈjī-ˌniz-əm\ *n* : a religion of India originating in the 6th century B.C. and teaching liberation of the soul by right knowledge, right faith, and right conduct

jal·ap \ˈjal-əp, ˈjäl-\ *n* : the dried tuberous root especially of a Mexican plant related to the morning glories; *also* : a purgative drug prepared from this [French, from Spanish *jalapa,* from *Jalapa,* Mexico]

ja·lopy \jə-ˈläp-ē\ *n, pl* **-lop·ies** : a dilapidated old automobile or airplane [origin unknown]

jal·ou·sie \ˈjal-ə-sē\ *n* **1** : a blind with adjustable horizontal slats for admitting light and air while excluding sun and rain **2** : a window made of adjustable glass louvers that control ventilation [French, literally, "jealousy"]

[1]**jam** \ˈjam\ *vb* **jammed; jam·ming** **1 a** : to press into a close or tight position ⟨*jam* a hat on⟩ **b** : to cause to be wedged so as to be unworkable ⟨*jam* the typewriter keys⟩ **c** : to block passage of : OBSTRUCT **d** : to fill full or to excess : PACK **2** : to push forcibly; *esp* : to apply the brakes suddenly with full force **3** : to squeeze or crush painfully ⟨*jammed* a finger⟩ **4** : to make unintelligible by sending out interfering signals or messages

⟨*jam* a radio program⟩ **5 :** to become unworkable through the jamming of a movable part ⟨the gun *jammed*⟩ **6 :** to force one's way into a tight space [origin unknown] — **jam·mer** *n*

[2]jam *n* **1 a :** an act or instance of jamming **b :** a crowded mass that impedes or blocks ⟨a traffic *jam*⟩ **2 :** a difficult state of affairs

[3]jam *n* **:** a spread made by boiling fruit and sugar to a thick consistency [probably from [1]*jam*]

jamb \ˈjam\ *n* **:** an upright piece forming the side of an opening (as of a door) [Medieval French *jambe,* literally, "leg," from Late Latin *gamba*]

jam·ba·laya \ˌjəm-bə-ˈlī-ə\ *n* **:** rice cooked with ham, sausage, chicken, shrimp, or oysters and seasoned with herbs [Louisiana French, from Occitan *jambalaia* "stew of rice and fowl"]

jam·bo·ree \ˌjam-bə-ˈrē\ *n* **1 :** a large festive gathering **2 :** a national or international camping assembly of boy scouts [origin unknown]

James \ˈjāmz\ *n* **:** a moral lecture addressed to early Christians and included as a book in the New Testament — see BIBLE table

jam session *n* **:** an informal performance by jazz musicians characterized by group improvisation [[2]*jam*]

[1]jan·gle \ˈjang-gəl\ *vb* **jan·gled; jan·gling** \-gə-ling, -gling\ **1 :** to quarrel verbally **2 :** to make or cause to make a harsh or discordant sound [Medieval French *jangler,* of Germanic origin] — **jan·gler** \-gə-lər, -glər\ *n*

[2]jangle *n* **1 :** noisy quarreling **2 :** discordant sound

jan·is·sary *or* **jan·i·zary** \ˈjan-ə-ˌser-ē, -ˌzer-\ *n, pl* **-sar·ies** *or* **-zar·ies** *often cap* **:** a soldier of a select corps of Turkish troops organized in the 14th century and abolished in 1826 [Italian *gianizzero,* from Turkish *yeniçeri*]

jan·i·tor \ˈjan-ət-ər\ *n* **1 :** DOORKEEPER **2 :** a person who has the care of a building [Latin, from *janus* "arch, gate"] — **jan·i·to·ri·al** \ˌjan-ə-ˈtōr-ē-əl, -ˈtȯr-\ *adj*

Jan·u·ary \ˈjan-yə-ˌwer-ē\ *n* **:** the 1st month of the year according to the Gregorian calendar [Latin *Januarius,* from *Janus,* a Roman god]

[1]ja·pan \jə-ˈpan\ *n* **1 :** a varnish giving a hard brilliant surface coating **2 :** work varnished and figured in the Japanese manner

[2]japan *vt* **ja·panned; ja·pan·ning :** to cover with or as if with a coat of japan

Jap·a·nese \ˌjap-ə-ˈnēz, -ˈnēs\ *n, pl* **Japanese 1 a :** a native or inhabitant of Japan **b :** a person of Japanese descent **2 :** the language of the Japanese — **Japanese** *adj*

Japanese beetle *n* **:** a small metallic green and brown scarab beetle introduced into North America from Japan that as a grub feeds on roots and decaying vegetation and as an adult consumes foliage and fruits

Japanese maple *n* **:** a widely grown maple of Japan, China, and Korea with usually green, red, or purplish leaves

[1]jape \ˈjāp\ *vt* **:** to make mocking fun of [Middle English *japen*] — **jap·er** \ˈjā-pər\ *n* — **jap·ery** \ˈjā-pə-rē, -prē\ *n*

[2]jape *n* **:** JEST 2, GIBE

[1]jar \ˈjär\ *vb* **jarred; jar·ring 1 a :** to make a harsh or discordant sound **b :** to affect disagreeably **c :** to be out of harmony; *esp* **:** BICKER **d :** to have a harsh or disagreeable effect **2 :** to undergo severe vibration **3 :** to make unstable or loose **:** SHAKE [probably imitative]

[2]jar *n* **1 :** a harsh grating sound **2 :** CONFLICT 2, DISCORD **3 :** JOLT 1 **4 :** an unsettling shock

[3]jar *n* **1 :** a widemouthed container usually of earthenware or glass **2 :** the quantity that a jar will hold [Middle French *jarre,* from Old Occitan *jarra,* from Arabic *jarra* "earthen water vessel"] — **jar·ful** \-ˌfu̇l\ *n*

jar·di·niere \ˌjärd-n-ˈiər\ *n* **:** an ornamental stand or receptacle for potted plants or flowers [French *jardinière,* literally, "female gardener"]

jar·gon \ˈjär-gən, -ˌgän\ *n* **1 a :** confused unintelligible language **:** GIBBERISH **b :** a hybrid language or dialect used for communication between peoples of different speech **2 :** the technical or specialized vocabulary of a particular profession or group **3 :** obscure and often pretentiously wordy language [Medieval French *jargun, gargon*] ***synonyms*** see DIALECT

jas·mine \ˈjaz-mən\ *also* **jes·sa·mine** \ˈjes-mən, -ə-mən\ *n* **:** any of numerous often climbing shrubs related to the olive and having extremely fragrant flowers; *also* **:** any of various plants (as yellow jessamine) noted for sweet-scented flowers [Middle French *jasmin,* from Arabic *yāsamīn,* from Persian]

jas·per \ˈjas-pər\ *n* **:** an opaque fine-grained quartz occurring in several colors; *esp* **:** green chalcedony [Middle French *jaspre,* from Latin *jaspis,* from Greek *iaspis,* of Semitic origin] — **jas·pery** \-pə-rē\ *adj*

jasmine

jaun·dice \ˈjȯn-dəs, ˈjän-\ *n* **1 :** yellowish discoloration of the skin, tissues, and body fluids caused by the deposition of bile pigments; *also* **:** a disease or abnormal condition marked by jaundice **2 :** a state or attitude marked by satiety, distaste, or hostility [Medieval French *jaunice, galniz,* from *jaune, gaune* "yellow," derived from Latin *galbinus* "greenish yellow"]

jaun·diced \-dəst\ *adj* **1 :** affected with or as if with jaundice **2 :** showing or influenced by envy, distaste, or hostility

jaunt \ˈjȯnt, ˈjänt\ *n* **:** a short trip taken for pleasure [origin unknown] — **jaunt** *vi*

jaun·ty \ˈjȯnt-ē, ˈjänt-\ *adj* **jaun·ti·er; -est :** sprightly in manner or appearance **:** LIVELY [French *gentil* "genteel"] — **jaun·ti·ly** \ˈjȯnt-l-ē, ˈjänt-\ *adv* — **jaun·ti·ness** \ˈjȯnt-ē-nəs, ˈjänt-\ *n*

Ja·va man \ˌjäv-ə-, ˌjav-\ *n* **:** an extinct hominid of the Pleistocene that is known from fragments of skeletons found in Java and is classified with the direct ancestor of modern humans

Ja·va·nese \ˌjav-ə-ˈnēz, ˌjäv-, -ˈnēs\ *n* **1 :** a member of an Indonesian people inhabiting the island of Java **2 :** an Austronesian language of the Javanese people — **Javanese** *adj*

jav·e·lin \ˈjav-lən, -ə-lən\ *n* **1 :** a light spear **2 :** a slender usually metal shaft thrown for distance in an athletic field event [Medieval French *javeline,* of Celtic origin]

[1]jaw \ˈjȯ\ *n* **1 a :** either of two cartilaginous or bony structures in most vertebrates that support the soft parts enclosing the mouth and usually bear teeth on their oral margin — compare MANDIBLE 1a(1), MAXILLA 1 **b :** the structures including the jaws and soft parts that make up the walls of the mouth and that serve to open and close it — usually used in plural **c :** any of various organs of invertebrates that perform the function of the vertebrate jaws **2 :** something resembling the jaw of an animal in form or action ⟨the *jaws* of a mountain pass⟩; *esp* **:** one of a set of opposing parts that open and close for holding or crushing something between them ⟨the *jaws* of a vise⟩ [Middle English] — **jawed** \ˈjȯd\ *adj*

[2]jaw *vi* **1 :** to talk in a scolding or boring way **2 :** to speak forcefully or persuasively

jaw·bone \ˈjȯ-ˈbōn, -ˌbōn\ *n* **:** one of the bones of an animal's jaw; *esp* **:** MANDIBLE 1a(1)

jaw·break·er \-ˌbrā-kər\ *n* **1 :** a word that is difficult to pronounce **2 :** a round hard candy

jaw·less fish \ˌjȯ-ləs-\ *n* **:** any of a group (Agnatha) of primitive fishes that lack a jaw, have a skeleton of cartilage, and include living and extinct forms (as the cyclostomes and ostracoderms)

jaw·line \ˈjȯ-ˌlīn\ *n* **:** the outline of the lower jaw

jay \ˈjā\ *n* **:** any of several noisy crested birds of the crow family that are smaller and usually more brightly colored than a crow [Medieval French, from Late Latin *gaius*]

Jay·cee \ˈjā-ˈsē\ *n* **:** a member of a major national and international civic organization [from the initials of *J*unior *C*itizens, former name of the organization]

jay·vee \ˈjā-ˈvē\ *n* **1 :** JUNIOR VARSITY **2 :** a member of a junior varsity team [*j*unior *v*arsity]

jay·walk \ˈjā-ˌwȯk\ *vi* **:** to cross a street carelessly without heeding traffic regulations and signals — **jay·walk·er** *n*

[1]jazz \ˈjaz\ *vt* **1 :** ENLIVEN — usually used with *up* **2 :** to play in the manner of jazz [origin unknown]

[2]jazz *n* **1 :** music of American origin developed mainly from blues and ragtime and marked especially by solo instrumental improvisation **2 :** empty talk **:** HUMBUG **3 :** STUFF 5c

jazzy \ˈjaz-ē\ *adj* **jazz·i·er; -est 1 :** having the characteristics of jazz **2 :** marked by unrestraint, animation, or flashiness — **jazz·i·ly** \ˈjaz-ə-lē\ *adv* — **jazz·i·ness** \ˈjaz-ē-nəs\ *n*

jeal·ous \ˈjel-əs\ *adj* **1 a :** intolerant of rivalry or unfaithful-

\ə\ **a**but	\au̇\ **ou**t	\i\ t**i**p	\ȯ\ s**aw**	\u̇\ f**oo**t
\ər\ f**ur**ther	\ch\ **ch**in	\ī\ l**i**fe	\ȯi\ c**oi**n	\y\ **y**et
\a\ m**a**t	\e\ p**e**t	\j\ **j**ob	\th\ **th**in	\yü\ f**ew**
\ā\ t**a**ke	\ē\ **ea**sy	\ng\ si**ng**	\t͟h\ **th**is	\yu̇\ c**u**re
\ä\ c**o**t, c**a**rt	\g\ **g**o	\ō\ b**o**ne	\ü\ f**oo**d	\zh\ vi**si**on

ness **b** : suspicious that a person one loves is not faithful **2** : hostile toward a rival or one believed to enjoy an advantage : ENVIOUS **3** : careful in guarding a right or possession ⟨their *jealous* love of freedom⟩ [Medieval French *gelus,* from Late Latin *zelus* "zeal"] ***synonyms*** see ENVIOUS — **jeal•ous•ly** *adv*

jeal•ou•sy \ˈjel-ə-sē\ *n, pl* **-sies** **1** : a jealous disposition, attitude, or feeling **2** : zealous vigilance

jean \ˈjēn\ *n* **1** : a durable twilled cotton cloth used especially for sportswear and work clothes **2** *pl* : close-fitting pants made of jean, denim, or corduroy [short for *jean fustian,* from Middle English *Gene* "Genoa, Italy" + *fustian*]

jeep \ˈjēp\ *n* : a small general-purpose motor vehicle with ¼-ton capacity and four-wheel drive used by the United States Army in World War II [alteration of *gee pee,* from *g*eneral-*p*urpose, influenced by the name Eugene the *Jeep,* character in the comic strip *Thimble Theater* by Elzie C. Segar]

Word History In March 1936 in newspapers across the country, Popeye's girlfriend, Olive Oyl, was delivered a box labeled "Eugene the Jeep." The box contained a small, friendly animal that made the sound "jeep." Comic strip writer Elzie Segar continued this story through much of 1936. In 1937 work was begun by several American manufacturers to develop an all-purpose vehicle for military use. When the vehicle was ready, it was apparently designated *g.p.* for *general purpose.* Probably owing in part to the popularity of Eugene the Jeep, the pronunciation of the letters *g.p.* became shortened to one syllable and the spelling *jeep* was adopted. For a similar alteration, compare the spelling and pronunciation of *veep,* from *v.p.,* an abbreviation of *vice president.*

Jeep *trademark* — used for a civilian automotive vehicle

jee•pers \ˈjē-pərz\ *interj* — used as a mild oath or to express surprise [euphemism for *Jesus*]

[1]**jeer** \ˈjiər\ *vb* **1** : to speak or cry out in derision or mockery **2** : DERIDE, MOCK [origin unknown] ***synonyms*** see SCOFF — **jeer•er** \ˈjir-ər\ *n* — **jeer•ing•ly** \-ing-lē\ *adv*

[2]**jeer** *n* : a jeering remark or sound : TAUNT

Jef•fer•so•ni•an \ˌjef-ər-ˈsō-nē-ən\ *adj* : of, relating to, or characteristic of Thomas Jefferson or his political principles — **Jeffersonian** *n*

jehad *variant of* JIHAD

Je•ho•vah \ji-ˈhō-və\ *n* : GOD 1 [New Latin, from Hebrew *Yahweh*]

Jehovah's Witness *n* : a member of a group that by distributing literature and by personal evangelism witness to beliefs in the theocratic rule of God, the sinfulness of organized religions and governments, and an approaching millennium

je•june \ji-ˈjün\ *adj* **1** : lacking nutritive value ⟨*jejune* diets⟩ **2** : not interesting : DULL **3** : lacking maturity : CHILDISH ⟨*jejune* remarks⟩ [Latin *jejunus* "empty of food, hungry, meager"] — **je•june•ly** *adv* — **je•june•ness** \-ˈjün-nəs\ *n*

je•ju•num \ji-ˈjü-nəm\ *n* : the section of the small intestine between the duodenum and the ileum [Latin, from *jejunus* "empty of food, hungry, meager"] — **je•ju•nal** \-ˈjün-l\ *adj*

jell \ˈjel\ *vb* **1** : to make or become jelly **2** : to take shape ⟨an idea began to *jell* in my mind⟩ [back-formation from *jelly*]

Jell–O \ˈjel-ō\ *trademark* — used for a fruit-flavored gelatin dessert

[1]**jel•ly** \ˈjel-ē\ *n, pl* **jellies** **1** : a food with a soft elastic consistency due usually to gelatin or pectin; *esp* : a fruit product made by boiling sugar and the juice of fruit **2** : a substance resembling jelly in consistency [Medieval French *gelee,* from *geler* "to freeze, congeal," from Latin *gelare*] — **jel•ly•like** \-ē-ˌlīk\ *adj*

[2]**jelly** *vb* **jel•lied; jel•ly•ing** **1** : JELL 1 **2** : to set in jelly ⟨*jellied* salmon⟩

jelly bean *n* : a sugar-glazed bean-shaped candy

jel•ly•fish \ˈjel-ē-ˌfish\ *n* **1 a** : a free-swimming marine coelenterate animal that reproduces sexually and has a gelatinous, disk-shaped, and usually nearly transparent body and tentacles with nematocysts **b** : any of various sea animals (as a ctenophore) that resemble a jellyfish **2** : a weak spineless person

jellyfish 1a

jelly roll *n* : a thin sheet of sponge cake spread with jelly and rolled up

jen•net \ˈjen-ət\ *n* **1** : a small Spanish horse **2** : a female donkey [Medieval French *genet,* from Catalan]

jen•ny \ˈjen-ē\ *n, pl* **jennies** **1 a** : a female bird ⟨a *jenny* wren⟩ **b** : a female donkey **2** : SPINNING JENNY [from the name *Jenny*]

jeop•ar•dize \ˈjep-ər-ˌdīz\ *vt* : to expose to danger : IMPERIL

jeop•ar•dy \ˈjep-ərd-ē\ *n* **1** : exposure to death, loss, or injury : DANGER **2** : the danger of conviction and punishment that an accused person is subjected to when on trial for a criminal offense [Medieval French *juparti, jeuparti* "alternative," literally, "divided game"]

Word History In French *jeu parti* means literally "divided game." In Medieval French, the major criterion for a *jeuparti* was the involvement of alternative possibilities or opposed viewpoints. A *jeuparti* could be a poem in dialogue form representing the discussion of problems. Or it could be a situation in a game like chess in which the relative worth of alternative plays is uncertain. The word was borrowed into English in this sense. Any position that provides equal chances of success and of failure can be described in terms of a similar position in chess and called a *jeopardy.* But the word was early used in its present extended sense, "risk or danger, with a greater probability of losing than of winning."

jer•boa \jər-ˈbō-ə\ *n* : any of several social nocturnal jumping rodents of dry regions of Asia and northern Africa with long hind legs and a long tail [Arabic *yarbūʿ*]

jerboa

Jer•e•mi•ah \ˌjer-ə-ˈmī-ə\ *n* : a prophetic book of canonical Jewish and Christian Scriptures — see BIBLE table

[1]**jerk** \ˈjərk\ *vb* **1** : to give a sharp quick push, pull, or twist to **2 a** : to make or move in jerks : move with a jerk **3** : to mix and dispense (as sodas) [probably from Middle English *yerken* "to bind tightly"] — **jerk•er** *n*

[2]**jerk** *n* **1 a** : a single quick motion **b** : a jolting, bouncing, or thrusting motion **2 a** : an involuntary muscular movement or spasm due to reflex action **b** *pl* : involuntary twitchings due to nervous excitement **3** : an annoyingly stupid or foolish person

[3]**jerk** *vt* : to preserve (meat) in long strips dried in the sun [back-formation from [2]*jerky*]

jer•kin \ˈjər-kən\ *n* : a close-fitting hip-length sleeveless jacket [origin unknown]

jerk•wa•ter \ˈjər-ˌkwȯt-ər, -ˌkwät-\ *adj* : being small and remote ⟨*jerkwater* towns⟩ [earlier *jerkwater* "rural train"]

Word History In the early days of the steam locomotive many rural railroad lines were not so well-provided with water tanks as were the main lines. It was sometimes necessary for trains on the rural lines to stop at streams while the crew went to fetch (or *jerk*) water in buckets. For this reason rural trains were given the name *jerkwater.* Eventually the term came to be applied to anything small or insignificant.

[1]**jerky** \ˈjər-kē\ *adj* **jerk•i•er; -est** **1** : moving by sudden starts and stops **2** : FOOLISH ⟨a *jerky* idea⟩ — **jerk•i•ly** \-kə-lē\ *adv* — **jerk•i•ness** \-kē-nəs\ *n*

[2]**jerky** *n* : jerked meat [Spanish *charqui,* from Quechua *ch'arki*]

jer•ry–build \ˈjer-ē-ˌbild\ *vt* **-built** \-ˌbilt\; **-build•ing** : to build cheaply and flimsily [back-formation from *jerry-built* "flimsily built," of unknown origin] — **jer•ry–build•er** *n*

jer•ry–rigged \ˈjer-ē-ˌrigd\ *adj* : organized or constructed in a crude or improvised manner [probably a blend of *jerry-built* and *jury-rigged*]

jer•sey \ˈjər-zē\ *n, pl* **jerseys** **1** : a plain knitted fabric of wool, cotton, nylon, rayon, or silk **2** : any of various close-fitting knitted garments for the upper body **3** *cap* : any of a breed of small short-horned usually fawn-colored dairy cattle noted for their rich milk [*Jersey,* one of the Channel islands]

Je•ru•sa•lem artichoke \jə-ˌrü-sə-ləm-, -sləm-; -ˌrüz-ləm-, -ə-ləm-\ *n* : a perennial sunflower of the U.S. and Canada grown for its tubers that are eaten as a vegetable [*Jerusalem* by folk etymology from Italian *girasole* "sunflower"]

Jerusalem cherry *n* : either of two plants of the nightshade family grown as houseplants for their showy orange or red berries [*Jerusalem,* Palestine]

jess \ˈjes\ *n* : a strap placed on a leg of a hawk for attachment of a leash [Medieval French *gez, jettes,* derived from *geter, jeter* "to throw, release (a hawk)"]

jessamine *variant of* JASMINE

[1]**jest** \'jest\ *n* **1 a :** an act intended to cause laughter **:** PRANK **b :** a comic incident **2 :** a witty remark **3 a :** a frivolous mood or manner ⟨spoken in *jest*⟩ **b :** a state of gaiety and merriment **4 :** [3]BUTT 2, LAUGHINGSTOCK [Medieval French *geste* "deed, action, tale," from Latin *gesta* "deeds," from *gerere* "to carry, perform"]

synonyms JEST, JOKE, QUIP, WISECRACK mean something said to evoke laughter. JEST applies to an utterance not seriously intended whether sarcastic, ironic, witty, or merely playful ⟨the bantering *jests* about his clothes were all in good fun⟩. JOKE may apply to an act as well as an utterance and suggests no intent to hurt feelings ⟨hid our keys as a *joke*⟩. QUIP suggests a quick, witty, neatly phrased remark ⟨responded with timely *quips* at her opponent's expense⟩. WISECRACK stresses cleverness of phrasing and sarcasm especially in a retort ⟨spent most of the debate making *wisecracks* rather than discussing the issue seriously⟩.

[2]**jest** *vi* **1 :** to utter taunts **:** GIBE **2 :** to speak or act without seriousness **3 :** JOKE 1

jest·er \'jes-tər\ *n* **1 :** FOOL 2a ⟨court *jester*⟩ **2 :** one given to jests

Je·su·it \'jezh-wət, -ə-wət, 'jez-\ *n* **:** a member of the Roman Catholic Society of Jesus founded by Saint Ignatius of Loyola in 1534 and devoted to missionary and educational work — **je·su·it·ic** \ˌjezh-ə-'wit-ik, ˌjez-\ *adj, often cap* — **je·su·it·i·cal·ly** \-i-kə-lē, -klē\ *adv, often cap*

[1]**jet** \'jet\ *n* **1 :** a dense velvet-black coal that takes a good polish and is often used for jewelry **2 :** an intense black [Medieval French *jaiet,* from Latin *gagates,* from Greek *gagatēs,* from *Gagas,* town and river in Asia Minor]

[2]**jet** *vb* **jet·ted; jet·ting :** to spout or emit in a stream **:** SPURT [Middle French *jeter,* literally, "to throw," from Latin *jactare,* from *jacere* "to throw"]

[3]**jet** *n* **1 a :** a forceful rush of liquid, gas, or vapor especially through a narrow opening or a nozzle **b :** a nozzle for a jet of fluid (as gas or water) **2 a :** JET ENGINE **b :** JET AIRPLANE

[4]**jet** *vi* **jet·ted; jet·ting :** to travel by jet airplane

jet airplane *n* **:** an airplane powered by one or more jet engines — called also *jet plane*

jet engine *n* **:** an airplane engine that uses atmospheric oxygen to burn fuel and produces a rearward discharge of heated air and exhaust gases

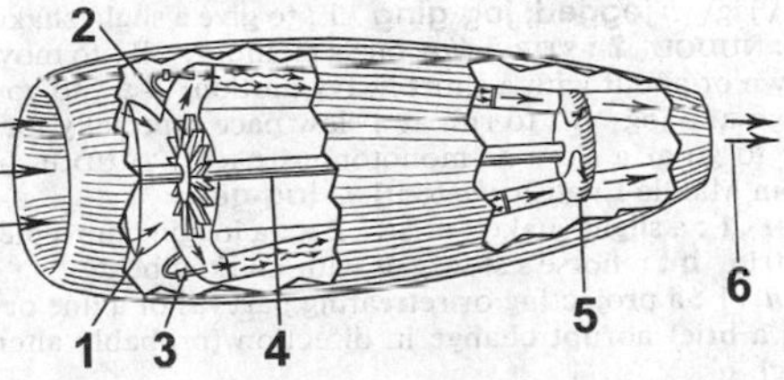

jet engine: *1* air intake, *2* compressor, *3* fuel injection, *4* drive shaft, *5* turbine, *6* exhaust

jet lag *n* **:** a condition that occurs following long flight through several time zones and is characterized by various physical and mental effects (as fatigue and irritability)

jet–pro·pelled \ˌjet-prə-'peld\ *adj* **1 :** propelled by a jet engine **2 :** suggestive of the speed and force of a jet airplane

jet propulsion *n* **:** propulsion of a body in a forward direction as a result of the rearward discharge of a jet of fluid; *esp* **:** propulsion of an airplane by jet engines

jet·sam \'jet-səm\ *n* **:** goods thrown overboard to lighten a ship in distress; *esp* **:** such goods when washed ashore [alteration of *jettison*]

jet set *n* **:** an international social group of wealthy people who frequent fashionable resorts — **jet–set·ter** \'jet-ˌset-ər\ *n*

jet stream *n* **:** a long narrow meandering current of high-speed winds blowing from a generally westerly direction several miles above the earth's surface

[1]**jet·ti·son** \'jet-ə-sən\ *n* **:** a voluntary sacrifice of cargo to lighten a ship's load in time of distress [Medieval French *geteson* "act of throwing," from Latin *jactatio,* from *jactare* "to throw"]

[2]**jettison** *vt* **1 a :** to throw (goods) overboard to lighten a ship in distress **b :** to drop from an aircraft or spacecraft in flight **2 :** to cast away or aside **:** DISCARD — **jet·ti·son·able** \-sə-nə-bəl\ *adj*

jet·ty \'jet-ē\ *n, pl* **jetties 1 :** a pier built out into the water to influence the current or to protect a harbor **2 :** a landing wharf [Medieval French *geté, jetee,* from *jeter* "to throw"]

Jew \'jü\ *n* **1 a :** a member of the tribe of Judah **b :** ISRAELITE **2 :** a member of a nation existing in Palestine from the 6th century B.C. to the 1st century A.D. **3 a :** a person of Jewish descent **b :** one whose religion is Judaism [Medieval French *ju, jeu,* from Latin *Judaeus,* from Greek *Ioudaios,* from Hebrew *Yĕhūdhī,* from *Yĕhūdhāh,* "Judah, Jewish kingdom"]

[1]**jew·el** \'jü-əl\ *n* **1 :** an ornament of precious metal set with stones or finished with enamel and worn as an accessory of dress **2 :** one that is highly esteemed **3 :** a precious stone **:** GEM **4 :** a bearing for a pivot in a watch made of a crystal, precious stone, or glass [Medieval French *juel,* from *ju, jeu* "game, play," from Latin *jocus* "joke, game"]

[2]**jewel** *vt* **-eled** *or* **-elled; -el·ing** *or* **-el·ling :** to adorn or equip with jewels

jewel box *n* **:** a thin plastic case for a CD or DVD

jew·el·er *or* **jew·el·ler** \'jü-ə-lər\ *n* **:** a maker or repairer of or dealer in jewelry

jew·el·ry \'jü-əl-rē\ *n* **:** JEWELS; *esp* **:** objects of precious metal set with gems and worn for personal adornment

jew·el·weed \'jü-əl-ˌwēd\ *n* **:** TOUCH-ME-NOT

jew·fish \'jü-ˌfish\ *n* **:** any of various large groupers that are usually dusky green, brown, or blackish, thickheaded, and rough-scaled; *also* **:** any of various other large fishes

Jew·ish \'jü-ish\ *adj* **:** of, relating to, or characteristic of the Jews — **Jew·ish·ly** *adv* — **Jew·ish·ness** *n*

Jewish calendar *n* **:** a calendar in use among Jewish peoples that is reckoned from the year 3761 B.C. and dates in its présent form from about A.D. 360

Jew·ry \'jür-ē, 'jü-rē\ *n* **1** *pl* **Jewries :** a community of Jews **2 :** the Jewish people

Jew's harp *or* **Jews' harp** \'jüz-ˌhärp\ *n* **:** a small lyre-shaped instrument that when placed between the teeth gives tones from a metal tongue struck by the finger

[1]**jib** \'jib\ *n* **:** a triangular sail set on a stay forward of the mast or foremast [origin unknown]

[2]**jib** *vb* **jibbed; jib·bing 1 :** to shift or swing from one side of a ship to the other **2 :** to cause (a sail) to jib

[3]**jib** *n* **1 :** the projecting arm of a crane **2 :** a derrick boom [probably from *gibbet*]

jib·boom \'jib-'büm, -'üm\ *n* **:** a spar that serves as an extension of the bowsprit

[1]**jibe** *or* **gybe** \'jīb\ *vb* **1 :** to shift suddenly from one side to the other **2 :** to change the course of a ship when sailing with the wind aft so that the sail jibes **3 :** to cause (a sail) to jibe [perhaps from Dutch *gijben*]

[2]**jibe** *variant of* GIBE

[3]**jibe** *vi* **:** to be in accord **:** AGREE [origin unknown]

ji·ca·ma \'hē-kə-mə\ *n* **:** a starchy root of a tropical American vine of the legume family that is eaten raw or cooked [Mexican Spanish *jícama,* from Nahuatl *xīcamatl*]

jif·fy \'jif-ē\ *n* **:** MOMENT 1, INSTANT ⟨in a *jiffy*⟩ [origin unknown]

[1]**jig** \'jig\ *n* **1 :** a lively springy dance in triple rhythm **2 :** TRICK, GAMBIT — used chiefly in the phrase *the jig is up* **3 a :** any of several fishing lures that are jerked up and down and drawn through the water **b :** a device used to maintain mechanically the correct position of a piece of work and a tool or of parts of work during assembly [perhaps from Middle French *giguer* "to frolic," from *gigue* "fiddle," of Germanic origin]

[2]**jig** *vb* **jigged; jig·ging 1 :** to dance a jig **2 :** to jerk up and down or to and fro **3 :** to fish or catch with a jig **4 :** to machine by means of a jig-controlled tool operation

[1]**jig·ger** \'jig-ər\ *n* **1 :** one that jigs or operates a jig **2 :** JIG 3a **3 :** the mast nearest the stern of a 4-masted ship **4 a :** a mechanical device; *esp* **:** one operating with a jerky reciprocating motion **b :** CONTRIVANCE 2, GADGET **5 :** a measure used in mixing drinks that usually holds 1 to 2 ounces (30 to 60 milliliters)

\ə\ **abut**	\au̇\ **out**	\i\ **tip**	\ȯ\ **saw**	\u̇\ **foot**
\ər\ **further**	\ch\ **chin**	\ī\ **life**	\ȯi\ **coin**	\y\ **yet**
\a\ **mat**	\e\ **pet**	\j\ **job**	\th\ **thin**	\yü\ **few**
\ā\ **take**	\ē\ **easy**	\ng\ **sing**	\t͟h\ **this**	\yu̇\ **cure**
\ä\ **cot, cart**	\g\ **go**	\ō\ **bone**	\ü\ **food**	\zh\ **vision**

^{2}**jigger** *n* : CHIGGER [perhaps from Wolof (a language of western Africa) *jiga* "insect"]

jig•gle \ˈjig-əl\ *vb* **jig•gled; jig•gling** \ˈjig-ling, -ə-ling\ : to move or cause to move with quick little jerks [derived from ^{2}*jig*] — **jiggle** *n*

jig•saw \ˈjig-ˌsȯ\ *n* **1 :** SCROLL SAW **2 :** a handheld electric saw with a narrow blade that moves up and down for cutting curved and irregular lines or open-worked patterns

jigsaw puzzle *n* : a puzzle consisting of small irregular pieces that are to be fitted together to form a picture

ji•had *also* **je•had** \ji-ˈhäd, -ˈhad\ *n* **1 :** a holy war waged on behalf of Islam as a religious duty **2 :** a crusade for a principle or belief [Arabic *jihād*]

^{1}**jilt** \ˈjilt\ *n* : a person who jilts a lover [from earlier *jillet* "flirtatious girl," from the name *Jill*]

^{2}**jilt** *vt* : to drop (one's lover) capriciously or unfeelingly

jim crow \ˈjim-ˈkrō\ *n, often cap J&C* : ethnic discrimination especially against blacks by legal enforcement or traditional sanctions [from *Jim Crow,* stereotype black man in a 19th century song-and-dance act] — **jim crow•ism** \-ˌiz-əm\ *n, often cap J&C*

jim–dan•dy \ˈjim-ˈdan-dē\ *n* : something excellent of its kind

^{1}**jim•my** \ˈjim-ē\ *n, pl* **jimmies :** a short crowbar [from *Jimmy,* nickname for *James*]

^{2}**jimmy** *vt* **jim•mied; jim•my•ing :** to force open with or as if with a jimmy ⟨*jimmy* a window⟩

jim•son•weed \ˈjim-sən-ˌwēd, ˈjimp-\ *n, often cap* : a poisonous tall annual weed of the nightshade family with rank-smelling foliage, large white or violet trumpet-shaped flowers, and a prickly fruit — called also *thorn apple* [alteration of *Jamestown weed,* from *Jamestown,* Virginia]

^{1}**jin•gle** \ˈjing-gəl\ *vb* **jin•gled; jin•gling** \-gə-ling, -gling\ **1 :** to make or cause to make a light clinking sound **2 :** to rhyme or sound in a catchy repetitious manner [Middle English *ginglen,* of imitative origin] — **jin•gler** \-gə-lər, -glər\ *n*

^{2}**jingle** *n* **1 :** a light clinking sound **2 a :** a catchy repetition of sounds in a poem **b :** a short verse or song with such repetition — **jin•gly** \-gə-lē, -glē\ *adj*

^{1}**jin•go** \ˈjing-gō\ *interj* — used as a mild oath usually in the phrase *by jingo* [probably euphemism for *Jesus*]

^{2}**jingo** *n, pl* **jingoes :** one characterized by jingoism [from the fact that the phrase *by jingo* appeared in the refrain of a chauvinistic song] — **jin•go•ish** \-ish\ *adj*

jin•go•ism \ˈjing-gō-ˌiz-əm\ *n* : extreme chauvinism or nationalism marked especially by a belligerent foreign policy — **jin•go•ist** \-əst\ *n* — **jin•go•is•tic** \ˌjing-gō-ˈis-tik\ *adj* — **jin•go•is•ti•cal•ly** \-ˈis-ti-kə-lē, -klē\ *adv*

jin•ni \jə-ˈnē, ˈjin-ē\ *or* **jinn** \ˈjin\ *n pl* **jinn** *or* **jinns :** one of a type of spirit in Muslim demonology held to exist on earth in various forms and have supernatural powers [Arabic *jinnī* "demon"]

jin•rick•sha \jin-ˈrik-ˌshȯ\ *n* : RICKSHAW [Japanese]

^{1}**jinx** \ˈjings, ˈjingks\ *n* **1 :** one that brings bad luck **2 :** the state or spell of bad luck brought on by a jinx [perhaps alteration of *jynx,* a kind of woodpecker; from the use of woodpeckers in witchcraft]

^{2}**jinx** *vt* : to bring bad luck to

jit•ney \ˈjit-nē\ *n, pl* **jitneys 1** *slang* **:** NICKEL 2a **2 :** BUS 1a [origin unknown; sense 2 from the original 5-cent fare]

jit•ter•bug \ˈjit-ər-ˌbəg\ *n* **1 :** a dance in which couples swing, balance, and twirl in standardized patterns often with vigorous acrobatics **2 :** one who dances the jitterbug [from earlier *jitter* "to be nervous," of unknown origin] — **jitterbug** *vi*

jit•ters \ˈjit-ərz\ *n pl* : extreme nervousness [origin unknown] — **jit•tery** \-ə-rē\ *adj*

jiujitsu *or* **jiujutsu** *variant of* JUJITSU

^{1}**jive** \ˈjīv\ *n* **1 :** swing music or dancing performed to it **2 a :** glib, deceptive, or silly talk **b :** the jargon of hipsters **c :** a special jargon of difficult or slang terms [origin unknown]

^{2}**jive** *vb* **1 :** KID 1 **2 :** to dance to or play jive

^{1}**job** \ˈjäb\ *n* **1 a :** a piece of work; *esp* : one undertaken at a stated rate **b :** something produced by or as if by work **2 a :** something done for private advantage **b :** a criminal act; *esp* : ROBBERY **3 a :** TASK, DUTY **b :** a regular position for pay ⟨lost their *jobs*⟩ **4 :** plastic surgery for cosmetic purposes ⟨a nose *job*⟩ [perhaps from obsolete *job* "lump"] ***synonyms*** see TASK — **job•less** \-ləs\ *adj* — **job•less•ness** *n*

^{2}**job** *vb* **jobbed; job•bing 1 :** to do occasional pieces of work for hire **2 :** to hire or let by the job

Job \ˈjōb\ *n* : a narrative and poetic book of canonical Jewish and Christian Scriptures — see BIBLE table

job action *n* : a temporary action (as a slowdown) by workers as a protest and means of enforcing demands

job•ber \ˈjäb-ər\ *n* **1 :** one that buys goods and sells them to other dealers (as retailers) : MIDDLEMAN **2 :** one that works by the job

job•hold•er \ˈjäb-ˌhōl-dər\ *n* : one having a regular job

job lot *n* **1 :** a miscellaneous collection of goods for sale as a lot usually to a retailer **2 :** a miscellaneous and often inferior collection or group

Job's tears \ˈjōbz-\ *n* : an Asian grass with large hard usually pearly white seeds often used as beads

Job's tears

^{1}**jock** \ˈjäk\ *n* **1 :** JOCKEY 1 **2 :** DISC JOCKEY

^{2}**jock** *n* **1 :** ATHLETIC SUPPORTER **2 :** ATHLETE [short for earlier *jock strap*]

^{1}**jock•ey** \ˈjäk-ē\ *n, pl* **jockeys 1 :** one who rides a horse especially as a professional in a race **2 :** OPERATOR 1a [*Jockey,* Scottish nickname for *John*]

^{2}**jockey** *vb* **jock•eyed; jock•ey•ing 1 :** to ride (a horse) as a jockey **2 :** to move or maneuver skillfully ⟨*jockey* a truck into a lot⟩ ⟨*jockey* for power⟩ **3 :** FINESSE 2a, OUTWIT

jock itch *n* : a skin infection of the groin and upper thigh that is caused by a fungus and is marked by itching, redness, and flaking [^{2}*jock*]

jock strap *n* : ATHLETIC SUPPORTER

jo•cose \jō-ˈkōs\ *adj* **1 :** given to joking : MERRY **2 :** characterized by joking : HUMOROUS [Latin *jocosus,* from *jocus* "joke"] — **jo•cose•ly** *adv*

joc•u•lar \ˈjäk-yə-lər\ *adj* **1 :** JOCOSE 1 **2 :** said or done in jest [Latin *jocularis,* from *joculus* "little jest," from *jocus* "joke"] — **joc•u•lar•i•ty** \ˌjäk-yə-ˈlar-ət-ē\ *n* — **joc•u•lar•ly** *adv*

joc•und \ˈjäk-ənd *also* ˈjōk-ənd\ *adj* : happily excited : MERRY [Late Latin *jocundus* "pleasant, agreeable," from Latin *jucundus,* from *juvare* "to help"] — **joc•und•ly** *adv*

jodh•pur \ˈjäd-pər\ *n* **1** *pl* **:** tight pants that are worn for horseback riding **2 :** an ankle-high boot fastened with a strap that is buckled at the side [*Jodhpur,* India]

Jo•el \ˈjō-əl\ *n* : a narrative book of canonical Jewish and Christian Scriptures — see BIBLE table

^{1}**jog** \ˈjäg\ *vb* **jogged; jog•ging 1 :** to give a slight shake or push to : NUDGE **2 :** STIR 5 ⟨*jog* one's memory⟩ **3 :** to move up and down or about with a short heavy motion **4 a :** to go or cause to go at a jog **b :** to run at a slow pace especially for exercise **c :** to go at a slow or monotonous pace : TRUDGE [probably from Middle English *shoggen*] — **jog•ger** *n*

^{2}**jog** *n* **1 :** a slight shake : PUSH **2 a :** a jogging movement, pace, or trip **b :** a horse's slow gait with marked beats

^{3}**jog** *n* **1 :** a projecting or retreating part (as of a line or surface) **2 :** a brief abrupt change in direction [probably alteration of ^{2}*jag*]

^{1}**jog•gle** \ˈjäg-əl\ *vb* **jog•gled; jog•gling** \ˈjäg-ling, -ə-ling\ **1 :** to shake slightly **2 :** to move shakily or jerkily [derived from ^{1}*jog*]

^{2}**joggle** *n* : ^{2}JOG 2a

John \ˈjän\ *n* **1 :** the fourth Gospel in the New Testament — see BIBLE table **2 :** any of three short didactic letters addressed to early Christians and included in the New Testament — see BIBLE table

john•boat \ˈjän-ˌbōt\ *n* : a narrow flat-bottomed square-ended boat propelled by a pole or paddle and used on inland waterways [from the name *John*]

John Bull \ˈjän-ˈbu̇l\ *n* **1 :** the English nation personified : the English people **2 :** a typical Englishman [*John Bull,* character typifying the English nation in *The History of John Bull* (1712) by John Arbuthnot, died 1735, Scottish physician and writer]

John Doe \-ˈdō\ *n* **1 :** a party to legal proceedings whose true name is unknown **2 :** MAN IN THE STREET

John Do•ry \-ˈdōr-ē, -ˈdȯr-\ *n, pl* **John Dories :** a yellow to olive marine food fish with a dark spot on each side [earlier *dory,* from Medieval French *doree,* literally, "gilded one"]

John Han•cock \-ˈhan-ˌkäk\ *n* : an autograph signature [from the prominence of John Hancock's signature on the Declaration of Independence]

john•ny \ˈjän-ē\ *n, pl* **johnnies :** a short gown opening in the back that is worn by persons (as hospital patients) undergoing medical examination or treatment [from *Johnny,* nickname for *John*]

john·ny·cake \ˈjän-ē-ˌkāk\ *n* **:** a bread made with cornmeal

John·ny–come–late·ly \ˌjän-ē-kəm-ˈlāt-lē\ *n, pl* **Johnny–come–latelies** *or* **Johnnies–come–lately** **1 :** a late or recent arrival **2 :** UPSTART

John·ny–jump–up \ˌjän-ē-ˈjəm-ˌpəp\ *n* **:** WILD PANSY; *also* **:** any of various other small-flowered pansies or violets

John·ny–on–the–spot \ˌjän-ē-ˌȯn-t͟hə-ˈspät, -ē-ˌän-\ *n* **:** one that is on hand and ready to act whenever needed

Johnny Reb \-ˈreb\ *n* **:** a Confederate soldier [*reb,* short for *rebel*]

John·so·ni·an \jän-ˈsō-nē-ən\ *adj* **:** of, relating to, or characteristic of Samuel Johnson or his writings

joie de vi·vre \ˌzhwäd-ə-ˈvēvr\ *n* **:** keen enjoyment of life [French, literally, "joy of living"]

[1]**join** \ˈjȯin\ *vb* **1 a :** to bring or fasten together in close physical contact ‹*join* hands› **b :** to connect (as points) by a line **2 :** to come or bring into close associaton ‹*join* a club› ‹*joined* them in marriage› **3 :** to come into the company of ‹*join* friends for lunch› **4 a :** to come together so as to be connected ‹nouns *join* to form compounds› **b :** ADJOIN ‹the two estates *join*› **5 :** to take part in a collective activity ‹*join* in singing› [Medieval French *joindre,* from Latin *jungere*] — **join·able** \-ə-bəl\ *adj*

synonyms JOIN, COMBINE, UNITE, CONNECT mean to bring or come together in some kind of union. JOIN suggests a physical contact or conjunction between two or more things ‹*join* the ends with glue› ‹*joined* forces to win›. COMBINE implies some merging or mingling with corresponding loss of identity of each unit ‹*combining* jazz and rock to create a new kind of music›. UNITE implies a greater loss of separate identity ‹the colonies *united* to form a republic›. CONNECT suggests a loose or external attachment with little or no loss of separate identity ‹the treaty *connects* the two nations›.

[2]**join** *n* **:** a point of joining **:** JOINT

join·er \ˈjȯi-nər\ *n* **:** one that joins: as **a :** a person whose craft is to construct articles by joining pieces of wood **b :** a gregarious person who joins many organizations

join·ery \ˈjȯin-rē, -ə-rē\ *n* **1 :** the craft or trade of a joiner **2 :** articles made by a joiner

[1]**joint** \ˈjȯint\ *n* **1 a** (1) **:** the point of contact between elements of an animal skeleton together with the parts that surround and support it (2) **:** NODE 4 **b :** a part or space included between two animal or plant joints **c :** a large piece of meat for roasting **2 a :** a place where two things or parts are joined ‹a *joint* in a pipe› **b :** a space between the adjacent surfaces of two bodies joined and held together by an adhesive material (as cement or mortar) ‹a thin *joint*› **c :** a fracture or crack in rock **3 a :** a shabby or disreputable place of entertainment **b :** PLACE 2b, ESTABLISHMENT **4 :** a marijuana cigarette [Medieval French *jointe,* from *joindre* "to join"] — **joint·ed** \-əd\ *adj*

[2]**joint** *adj* **1 :** UNITED 1 ‹the *joint* effect of study and play› **2 :** common to two or more: as **a :** done or shared by two or more ‹a *joint* report› ‹*joint* efforts› **b :** sharing in something (as a right or duty ‹*joint* owners›

[3]**joint** *vb* **1 a :** to unite by a joint **b :** to provide with a joint **2 :** to separate the joints of — **joint·er** *n*

joint·ly *adv* **:** TOGETHER ‹owned *jointly*›

joint–stock company *n* **:** a form of business organization intermediate in many respects between a partnership and a corporation

joist \ˈjȯist\ *n* **:** any of the small timbers or metal beams placed parallel from wall to wall in a building to support the floor or ceiling [Medieval French *giste,* derived from Latin *jacēre* "to lie"]

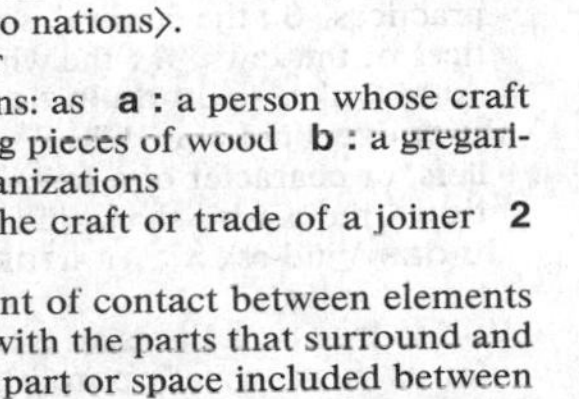

J joist

jo·jo·ba \hə-ˈō-bə\ *n* **:** a shrub or small tree of southwestern North America with edible seeds that yield a liquid wax used especially in cosmetics [Mexican Spanish, from Uto-Aztecan (a family of American Indian languages spoken in the western U.S. south to Central America)]

[1]**joke** \ˈjōk\ *n* **1 a :** something said or done to provoke laughter; *esp* **:** a brief oral narrative with a climactic humorous twist **b** (1) **:** the humorous or ridiculous element in something (2) **:** RAILLERY, KIDDING ‹can't take a *joke*› **c :** PRACTICAL JOKE **d :** LAUGHINGSTOCK **2 :** something not to be taken seriously [Latin *jocus*] ***synonyms*** see JEST

[2]**joke** *vb* **1 :** to make jokes **:** JEST **2 :** to make the object of a joke **:** KID — **jok·ing·ly** \ˈjō-king-lē\ *adv*

jok·er \ˈjō-kər\ *n* **1 :** a person who jokes **2 :** an extra card used in some card games **3 :** a part (as of an agreement) meaning something quite different from what it seems to mean and changing the apparent intention of the whole **4 :** HUMAN BEING, FELLOW; *esp* **:** an obnoxious or incompetent person

jol·li·fi·ca·tion \ˌjäl-i-fə-ˈkā-shən\ *n* **:** MERRYMAKING 1

jol·li·ty \ˈjäl-ət-ē\ *n, pl* **-ties :** the quality or state of being jolly ***synonyms*** see MIRTH

[1]**jol·ly** \ˈjäl-ē\ *adj* **jol·li·er; -est 1 a** (1) **:** full of high spirits **:** JOYOUS (2) **:** given to conviviality **:** JOVIAL **b :** CHEERFUL **2 :** extremely pleasant or agreeable **:** SPLENDID [Medieval French *jolif,* probably derived from Old Norse *jōl* "midwinter festival"] ***synonyms*** see MERRY

[2]**jolly** *adv* **:** VERY ‹had a *jolly* good time›

[3]**jolly** *vb* **jol·lied; jol·ly·ing 1 :** to engage in good-natured banter **2 :** to put in good humor especially in order to gain an end

jol·ly boat \ˈjäl-ē-\ *n* **:** a medium-sized ship's boat used for general rough or small work [origin unknown]

Jol·ly Rog·er \ˌjäl-ē-ˈräj-ər\ *n* **:** a black flag with a white skull and crossbones

[1]**jolt** \ˈjōlt\ *vb* **1 :** to move or cause to move with a sudden jerky motion **2 :** to give a knock or blow to **:** JAR **3 :** to disturb the composure of **:** SHOCK **4 :** to interfere with roughly, abruptly, and disconcertingly [probably blend of obsolete *joll* "to strike" and *jot* "to bump"] — **jolt·er** *n*

[2]**jolt** *n* **1 :** an abrupt sharp jerky blow or movement **2 :** a sudden shock, surprise, or disappointment

Jo·nah \ˈjō-nə\ *n* **1 :** a narrative book of canonical Jewish and Christian Scriptures — see BIBLE table **2 :** JINX 1 [sense 2 from the fact that by disobeying God's command Jonah caused a storm to endanger the ship he was traveling in]

jon·gleur \zhōⁿ-ˈglər\ *n* **:** a wandering medieval minstrel [French, from Medieval French *jogleour,* derived from Latin *jocus* "joke"]

jon·quil \ˈjän-kwəl, ˈjäng-\ *n* **:** a Mediterranean daffodil that is widely grown for its yellow or white fragrant short-tubed clustered flowers [French *jonquille,* from Spanish *junguillo,* from *junco* "reed," from Latin *juncus*]

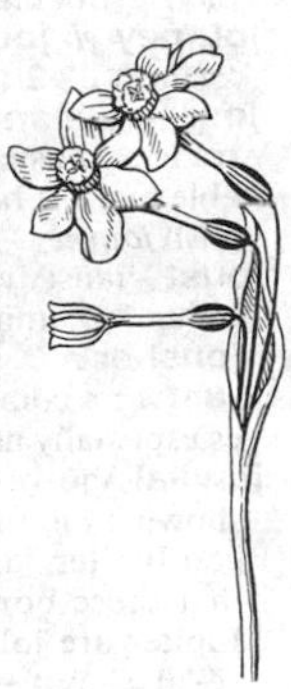
jonquil

Jor·dan almond \ˌjȯrd-n-\ *n* **:** a large Spanish almond especially when salted or coated with colored sugar [Middle English *jardin almande,* from Medieval French *jardin* "garden" + Middle English *almande* "almond"]

jo·seph \ˈjō-zəf\ *n* **:** a long cloak worn especially by women in the 18th century [probably from *Joseph,* Old Testament patriarch; from his coat of many colors (Genesis 37:3)]

josh \ˈjäsh\ *vb* **:** to tease good-naturedly [origin unknown] — **josh·er** *n*

Josh·ua \ˈjäsh-wə, -ə-wə\ *n* **:** a mainly narrative book of canonical Jewish and Christian Scriptures — see BIBLE table

Joshua tree *n* **:** a tall branched yucca of the southwestern U.S. with short leaves and clustered greenish white flowers

joss \ˈjäs, ˈjȯs\ *n* **:** a Chinese idol or cult image [Chinese Pidgin English, from Portuguese *deus* "god," from Latin]

joss house *n* **:** a Chinese temple or shrine

[1]**jos·tle** \ˈjäs-əl\ *vb* **jos·tled; jos·tling** \ˈjäs-ling, -ə-ling\ **1 :** to move against so as to jar **:** push roughly ‹*jostled* by a crowd› **2 :** to make one's way by pushing and shoving **:** ELBOW [earlier *justle,* derived from *joust*]

[2]**jostle** *n* **1 :** a jostling encounter or experience **2 :** the state of being jostled together

[1]**jot** \ˈjät\ *n* **:** the least bit **:** IOTA [Latin *iota, jota* "iota"]

Word History "Till heaven and earth pass, one jot or one tittle shall in no wise pass from the law, till all be fulfilled." This

\ə\ **abut**	\au̇\ **out**	\i\ **tip**	\ȯ\ **saw**	\u̇\ **foot**
\ər\ **further**	\ch\ **chin**	\ī\ **life**	\ȯi\ **coin**	\y\ **yet**
\a\ **mat**	\e\ **pet**	\j\ **job**	\th\ **thin**	\yü\ **few**
\ā\ **take**	\ē\ **easy**	\ng\ **sing**	\t͟h\ **this**	\yu̇\ **cure**
\ä\ **cot, cart**	\g\ **go**	\ō\ **bone**	\ü\ **food**	\zh\ **vision**

is Christ's assurance (Matthew 5:18) that He was not "come to destroy the law or the prophets." Not the smallest letter, not a single stroke of a letter, we are told, will be lost. *Jot* is an anglicized form of Latin *jota* (or *iota*), itself simply a transliteration of the Greek name of the ninth letter of the Greek alphabet. The original Aramaic version must have referred to *yōdh,* the smallest letter in the Hebrew alphabet. The transfer across language boundaries was easily made because the Greek equivalent *iōta* was also the smallest letter in its alphabet. A *jot* now simply means "a very small part."

[2]**jot** *vt* **jot·ted; jot·ting :** to write briefly or hurriedly : set down in the form of a note ⟨*jot* this down⟩

jot·ting \ˈjät-iŋ\ *n* : a brief note : MEMORANDUM

joule \ˈjül\ *n* : a unit of work or energy equal to the work done by a force of one newton acting through a distance of one meter [James P. *Joule,* died 1889, English physicist]

jounce \ˈjau̇ns\ *vb* : to move or cause to move in an up-and-down manner [Middle English *jouncen*] — **jounce** *n*

jour·nal \ˈjərn-ᵊl\ *n* **1 a :** a brief account of daily events **b :** a record of experiences, ideas, or reflections kept for private use **c :** a record of transactions kept by a deliberative or legislative body **2 a :** a daily newspaper **b :** a periodical that deals with current events [Medieval French, "service book containing the day hours," from *jurnal* "daily," from Latin *diurnalis,* from *diurnus* "of the day," from *dies* "day"]

jour·nal·ese \ˌjərn-ᵊl-ˈēz, -ˈēs\ *n* : a style of writing held to be characteristic of newspapers

jour·nal·ism \ˈjərn-ᵊl-ˌiz-əm\ *n* **1 :** the collection and editing of material of current interest for presentation through news media (as newspapers or television) **2 :** writing designed for or characteristic of newspapers or popular magazines

jour·nal·ist \-ᵊl-əst\ *n* : a person engaged in journalism

jour·nal·is·tic \ˌjərn-ᵊl-ˈis-tik\ *adj* : of, relating to, or characteristic of journalism or journalists — **jour·nal·is·ti·cal·ly** \-ti-kə-lē, -klē\ *adv*

jour·nal·ize \ˈjərn-ᵊl-ˌīz\ *vt* : to record in a journal

[1]**jour·ney** \ˈjər-nē\ *n, pl* **journeys :** travel or passage from one place to another [Medieval French *jurnee* "day's journey," from *jur* "day," from Late Latin *diurnum,* from Latin *diurnus* "of a day," from *dies* "day"]

[2]**journey** *vb* **jour·neyed; jour·ney·ing 1 :** to go on a journey : TRAVEL **2 :** to travel over or through — **jour·ney·er** *n*

jour·ney·man \ˈjər-nē-mən\ *n* **1 :** a worker who has learned a trade and usually works for wages **2 :** an experienced and reliable but not brilliant worker, athlete, or performer [Middle English *journey* "journey, day's labor"]

[1]**joust** \ˈjau̇st\ *vi* : to engage in a joust : TILT [Medieval French *juster* "to unite, joust," derived from Latin *juxta* "near"] — **joust·er** *n*

[2]**joust** *n* : a combat on horseback between two knights with lances especially as part of a tournament

jo·vi·al \ˈjō-vē-əl\ *adj* : markedly good-humored especially as shown by jollity and good-fellowship [Late Latin *jovialis* "of the god Jupiter," from Latin *Jov-, Juppiter* "Jupiter"; from the belief that those born under the astrological influence of the planet Jupiter are jolly] ***synonyms*** see MERRY — **jo·vi·al·i·ty** \ˌjō-vē-ˈal-ət-ē\ *n* — **jo·vi·al·ly** \ˈjō-vē-ə-lē\ *adv*

[1]**jowl** \ˈjau̇l\ *n* **1 :** JAW; *esp* **:** the lower jaw **2 :** CHEEK 1 [Old English *ceafl*]

[2]**jowl** *n* : loose flesh hanging from the cheeks, lower jaw, or throat [Middle English *cholle,* probably from Old English *ceole* "throat"] — **jowly** \-ē\ *adj*

[1]**joy** \ˈjȯi\ *n* **1 :** a feeling of great pleasure or happiness that comes from success, good fortune, or a sense of well-being : GLADNESS **2 :** something that gives great pleasure or happiness ⟨a *joy* to behold⟩ [Medieval French *joie,* from Latin *gaudium,* from *gaudēre* "to rejoice"]

[2]**joy** *vi* : to experience great pleasure or delight : REJOICE

joy·ful \ˈjȯi-fəl\ *adj* : experiencing, causing, or showing joy : HAPPY — **joy·ful·ly** \-fə-lē\ *adv* — **joy·ful·ness** *n*

joy·less \ˈjȯi-ləs\ *adj* : not feeling or causing joy : CHEERLESS — **joy·less·ly** *adv* — **joy·less·ness** *n*

joy·ous \ˈjȯi-əs\ *adj* : JOYFUL — **joy·ous·ly** *adv* — **joy·ous·ness** *n*

joy·ride \ˈjȯi-ˌrīd\ *n* : a ride taken for pleasure and often marked by reckless driving — **joy·rid·er** *n* — **joy·rid·ing** *n*

joy·stick \-ˌstik\ *n* : a control lever for a device (as a computer display or an airplane) that allows motion in two or more directions

JPEG \ˈjā-ˌpeg\ *n* : a type of computer file especially for storing photographic images [*J*oint *P*hotographic *E*xperts *G*roup]

ju·bi·lant \ˈjü-bə-lənt\ *adj* : feeling or expressing great joy : EXULTANT [Latin *jubilare* "to rejoice"] — **ju·bi·lant·ly** *adv*

ju·bi·la·tion \ˌjü-bə-ˈlā-shən\ *n* **1 :** an act of rejoicing : the state of being jubilant **2 :** an expression of great joy

ju·bi·lee \ˈjü-bə-ˌlē, ˌjü-bə-ˈlē\ *n* **1 a :** a special anniversary; *esp* : a 50th anniversary **b :** a celebration of such an anniversary **2 a :** a period of time proclaimed by the Roman Catholic pope ordinarily every 25 years as a time of special solemnity **b :** a special plenary indulgence granted during a year of jubilee to Roman Catholics who perform specified works of repentance and piety [Late Latin *jubilaeus* "year of emancipation and restoration provided by ancient Hebrew law," from Late Greek *iōbēlaios,* from Hebrew *yōbhēl,* literally, "ram's horn"]

Word History Ancient Hebrew law established every 50th year as a year of emancipation and restoration. All Hebrew slaves were freed; lands were restored to their former owners; fields were left uncultivated. This year took its name, *yōbhēl,* from the ram's horn trumpets used to proclaim its coming. When the Old Testament was translated into Greek and later into Latin, the translators borrowed the Hebrew name. The Greek form *iōbēlaios* was borrowed into Latin as *jubilaeus.* Since *jubilee* came into English with the translation of the Bible from Latin, it has acquired new meanings.

Ju·da·ic \jü-ˈdā-ik\ *adj* : of, relating to, or characteristic of Jews or Judaism [Latin *judaicus,* from Greek *ioudaikos,* from *Ioudaios* "Jew"] — **Ju·da·ical** \-ˈdā-ə-kəl\ *adj*

Ju·da·ism \ˈjüd-ə-ˌiz-əm, ˈjüd-ē-\ *n* **1 :** a religion developed among the ancient Hebrews and marked by belief in one God who is creator, ruler, and redeemer of the universe and by the moral and ceremonial laws of the Old Testament and the rabbinic tradition **2 :** conformity to Jewish rites, ceremonies, and practices **3 :** the cultural, social, and religious beliefs and practices of the Jews **4 :** the whole body of Jews — **Ju·da·ist** \-ə-əst, -ē-əst\ *n* — **Ju·da·is·tic** \ˌjüd-ə-ˈis-tik, ˌjüd-ē-\ *adj*

Ju·da·ize \ˈjüd-ə-ˌīz, ˈjüd-ē-\ *vb* **1 :** to adopt the customs, beliefs, or character of a Jew **2 :** to make Jewish — **Ju·da·i·za·tion** \ˌjüd-ə-ə-ˈzā-shən, ˌjüd-ē-ə-\ *n* — **Ju·da·iz·er** *n*

Ju·das \ˈjüd-əs\ *n* : TRAITOR [*Judas* Iscariot, apostle who betrayed Jesus]

Judas tree *n* : a Eurasian tree of the legume family often grown for its showy usually purplish pink flowers [from the belief that Judas Iscariot hanged himself from a tree of this kind]

Jude \ˈjüd\ *n* : a short epistle addressed to early Christians and included as a book in the New Testament — see BIBLE table

[1]**judge** \ˈjəj\ *vb* **1 :** to form an authoritative opinion **2 :** to decide as a judge : TRY **3 :** to determine or pronounce after inquiry and deliberation : CONSIDER **4 :** GOVERN, RULE — used of a Hebrew tribal leader **5 :** to form an estimate, conclusion, or evaluation about something : THINK [Medieval French *juger,* from Latin *judicare,* from *judic-, judex* "judge," from *jus* "right, law" + *dicere* "to say"] — **judg·er** *n*

[2]**judge** *n* **1 :** a public official authorized to decide questions brought before a court **2** *often cap* **:** a tribal hero exercising authority over the Hebrews after the death of Joshua **3 :** one who decides in a contest or competition : UMPIRE **4 :** one who gives an authoritative opinion : CRITIC — **judge·ship** \-ˌship\ *n*

Judg·es \ˈjəj-əz\ *n* : a narrative and historical book of Jewish and Christian Scriptures — see BIBLE table

judg·ment *or* **judge·ment** \ˈjəj-mənt\ *n* **1 a :** the act of judging **b :** a decision or opinion formed or given after judging **2 a :** a formal decision given by a court **b :** a court decree that a defendant has an obligation to the plaintiff for a specified amount **3** *cap* **:** the final judging of humankind by God **4 :** the process of forming an opinion by discerning and comparing **5 :** the capacity for judging — **judg·men·tal** \ˌjəj-ˈment-ᵊl\ *adj*

judgment call *n* : a subjective decision, ruling, or opinion

Judgment Day *n* : the day of the Last Judgment

ju·di·ca·ture \ˈjüd-i-kə-ˌchu̇r\ *n* **1 :** the administration of justice **2 :** JUDICIARY 1 [Middle French, from Medieval Latin *judicatura,* from Latin *judicare* "to judge"]

ju·di·cial \ju̇-ˈdish-əl\ *adj* **1 :** of or relating to a judgment, the function of judging, the administration of justice, or the judiciary **2 :** pronounced, ordered, or enforced by a court ⟨a *judicial* decision⟩ **3 :** of, characterized by, or expressing judgment : CRITICAL [Latin *judicialis,* from *judicium* "judgment," from *judex* "judge"] — **ju·di·cial·ly** \-ˈdish-lē, -ə-lē\ *adv*

ju·di·cia·ry \jü-ˈdish-ē-ˌer-ē, -ˈdish-ə-rē\ *n, pl* **-ries 1 a :** a system of courts of law **b :** the judges of these courts **2 :** a branch of government in which judicial power is vested — **judiciary** *adj*

ju·di·cious \jü-ˈdish-əs\ *adj* **:** having, exercising, or characterized by sound judgment **:** DISCREET ***synonyms*** see WISE — **ju·di·cious·ly** *adv* — **ju·di·cious·ness** *n*

Ju·dith \ˈjüd-əth\ *n* **:** a book of Scripture included in the Roman Catholic canon of the Old Testament and in the Protestant Apocrypha — see BIBLE table

ju·do \ˈjüd-ō\ *n, pl* **judos :** a form of wrestling developed in Japan from jujitsu [Japanese *jūdō,* from *jū* "weakness, gentleness" + *dō* "art"]

jug \ˈjəg\ *n* **1 a :** a large deep earthenware, glass, or plastic container with a narrow mouth and a handle **b :** JUGFUL **2 :** JAIL [perhaps from *jug,* nickname for *Joan*]

jug·ful \ˈjəg-ˌfu̇l\ *n, pl* **jugfuls** \-ˌfu̇lz\ *or* **jugs·ful** \ˈjəgz-ˌfu̇l\ **:** the quantity held by a jug

jug·ger·naut \ˈjəg-ər-ˌnȯt\ *n* **:** a massive inexorable force or object that crushes whatever is in its path [Hindi *Jagannāth,* title of Vishnu, literally, "lord of the world"]

Word History One of the titles of the Hindu god Vishnu is *Jagannāth,* which means "lord of the world." Every year the image of *Jagannāth* is taken from his temple at Puri, India, and drawn through the streets on an enormous chariot. In earlier times, some of the worshippers at the procession would allow themselves to be crushed beneath the wheels of the chariot in sacrifice to *Jagannāth*. The English form of the god's name, *Juggernaut,* came to be used in the sense of a massive inexorable force or object that crushes everything in its path.

[1]**jug·gle** \ˈjəg-əl\ *vb* **jug·gled; jug·gling** \ˈjəg-ling, -ə-ling\ **1 :** to keep several objects in motion in the air at the same time **2 :** to do several things at the same time ⟨*juggling* three jobs⟩ **3 :** to make changes to in order to achieve a desired result ⟨had to *juggle* my schedule⟩ [Medieval French *jugler* "to joke, sing," from Latin *joculari* "to joke," from *joculus* "little joke," from *jocus* "joke"] — **jug·gler** \ˈjəg-lər, -ə-lər\ *n*

[2]**juggle** *n* **:** an act or instance of juggling

jug·glery \ˈjəg-lə-rē\ *n, pl* **-gler·ies 1 :** the art or practice of a juggler **2 :** TRICKERY

[1]**jug·u·lar** \ˈjəg-yə-lər\ *adj* **1 :** of, relating to, or situated in or on the throat or neck **2 :** of or relating to the jugular vein [Late Latin *jugularis,* from Latin *jugulum* "collarbone, throat"]

[2]**jugular** *n* **:** JUGULAR VEIN

jugular vein *n* **:** any of several veins on each side of the neck that return blood from the head

juice \ˈjüs\ *n* **1 a :** the fluid contents that can be separated from plant cells or structures ⟨orange *juice*⟩ **b :** the fluid part of meat **2 a :** the natural fluids (as blood and lymph) of an animal body; *esp* **:** any of several chiefly digestive secretions **b :** the liquid or moisture contained in something **3 :** a medium (as electricity or gasoline) that supplies power [Medieval French *jus* "broth, juice," from Latin] — **juiced** \jüst\ *adj* — **juice·less** \ˈjüs-ləs\ *adj*

juic·er \ˈjü-sər\ *n* **:** an appliance for extracting juice from fruits or vegetables

juice up *vt* **:** to give life, energy, or spirit to

juicy \ˈjü-sē\ *adj* **juic·i·er; -est 1 :** having much juice **:** SUCCULENT **2 a :** rich in interest **:** COLORFUL **b :** agreeably interesting or titillating ⟨a *juicy* scandal⟩ — **juic·i·ly** \-sə-lē\ *adv* — **juic·i·ness** \-sē-nəs\ *n*

ju·jit·su *or* **ju·jut·su** *or* **jiu·jit·su** *or* **jiu·jut·su** \jü-ˈjit-sü\ *n* **:** the Japanese art of unarmed fighting employing holds, throws, and paralyzing blows [Japanese *jūjutsu,* from *jū* "weakness" + *jutsu* "art, skill"]

ju·jube \ˈjü-ˌjüb, *2 is often* ˈjü-jü-ˌbē\ *n* **1 :** the edible fruit of an Asian tree related to the buckthorns; *also* **:** this tree **2 :** a fruit-flavored gumdrop or lozenge [Medieval Latin *jujuba,* from Latin *zizyphum,* from Greek *zizyphon*]

juke·box \ˈjük-ˌbäks\ *n* **:** a machine that plays music when money is put into it [from dialect *jukehouse* "brothel," of Atlantic Creole origin]

juke joint *n* **:** a small inexpensive establishment for eating, drinking, or dancing to the music of a jukebox

ju·lep \ˈjü-ləp\ *n* **:** a drink of alcoholic liquor and sugar poured over crushed ice and garnished with mint — called also *mint julep* [Medieval French, a drink made from syrup, from Arabic *julāb,* from Persian *gulāb,* from *gul* "rose" + *āb* "water"]

Ju·lian calendar \ˌjül-yən-\ *n* **:** a calendar introduced in Rome in 46 B.C. establishing the 12-month year of 365 days with each 4th year having 366 days and the months each having 31 or 30 days except for February which has 28 or in leap years 29 days — compare GREGORIAN CALENDAR [Gaius *Julius* Caesar, who introduced it]

Ju·ly \jü-ˈlī\ *n* **:** the 7th month of the year according to the Gregorian calendar [Old English *Julius,* from Latin, from Gaius *Julius* Caesar]

[1]**jum·ble** \ˈjəm-bəl\ *vb* **jum·bled; jum·bling** \-bə-ling, -bling\ **:** to move or mix in a confused mass [perhaps imitative]

[2]**jumble** *n* **:** a disorderly mass or pile

jum·bo \ˈjəm-bō\ *n, pl* **jumbos :** a very large specimen of its kind [*Jumbo,* a huge elephant exhibited by P.T. Barnum] — **jumbo** *adj*

[1]**jump** \ˈjəmp\ *vb* **1 a :** to spring or cause to spring into the air **:** LEAP ⟨*jump* up⟩ ⟨*jumped* off the step⟩ ⟨*jump* a horse over a ditch⟩ **b :** to give a sudden movement **:** START **c :** to move over a position occupied by an opponent's piece in a board game **d :** to begin a forward movement — used with *off* **2 a :** to rise or cause to rise suddenly in rank or status **b :** to undergo or cause to undergo a sudden sharp increase ⟨prices *jumped*⟩ **3 :** to pounce suddenly or unexpectedly **:** ATTACK **4 :** to bustle with activity **5 a :** to leap over **b :** BYPASS ⟨*jump* electrical connections⟩ **c :** ANTICIPATE ⟨*jump* the starting gun⟩ **d :** to escape from usually in a hasty or furtive manner ⟨*jump* town⟩ **e :** to abscond while at liberty under (bail) **f :** to depart from (a normal course) ⟨*jump* the track⟩ **g :** to get aboard by jumping ⟨*jump* a train⟩ **h :** to occupy illegally ⟨*jump* a mining claim⟩ [probably related to Low German *gumpen* "to jump"]

[2]**jump** *n* **1 a (1) :** an act of jumping **:** LEAP **(2) :** a sports competition featuring a leap, spring, or bound **(3) :** a distance covered by a leap **b :** a sudden involuntary movement **c :** a move made in a board game by jumping **2 a :** a sharp sudden increase **b :** one in a series of moves **3 :** an advantage at the start

jump ball *n* **:** a method of putting a basketball into play in which the referee tosses the ball up between two opposing players who jump and try to tap it to a teammate

jump drive *n* **:** a small usually rectangular device used for storing and transferring computer data **:** FLASH DRIVE

[1]**jump·er** \ˈjəm-pər\ *n* **1 :** one that jumps **2 :** any of various devices operating with a jumping motion **3 :** a wire used to close a break or cut out part of a circuit

[2]**jumper** *n* **1 :** a loose blouse or jacket worn by workmen **2 :** a sleeveless one-piece dress worn usually with a blouse **3** *pl* **:** a child's coverall [probably from English dialect *jump* "jumper"]

jumper cables *n pl* **:** a pair of electrical cables with clips used to make a connection to jump-start a vehicle

jumping bean *n* **:** a seed of any of several Mexican shrubs of the spurge family that tumbles about because of the movements of the larva of a small moth inside it

jumping jack *n* **1 :** a toy figure of a man jointed and made to jump or dance by means of strings or a sliding stick **2 :** a conditioning exercise that involves jumping from a standing position to one with legs spread and arms raised and then back to the original standing position

jumping mouse *n* **:** any of several small hibernating North American rodents with long hind legs and tail and no cheek pouches

jump·ing–off place \ˌjəm-ping-ˈȯf-\ *n* **1 :** a remote or isolated place **2 :** a place from which an enterprise is launched

jump seat *n* **1 :** a movable carriage seat **2 :** a folding seat between the front and rear seats of a passenger automobile

jump shot *n* **:** a shot made by a basketball player at the peak of a jump

jump–start \ˈjəmp-ˈstärt\ *vt* **:** to start (a vehicle or its engine) by temporary connection to an external power source (as another vehicle's battery)

jumpy \ˈjəm-pē\ *adj* **jump·i·er; -est :** very nervous **:** JITTERY — **jump·i·ness** *n*

jun·co \ˈjəng-kō\ *n, pl* **juncos** *or* **juncoes :** any of a genus of small North American finches usually with a pink bill, ashy

\ə\ **abut**	\au̇\ **out**	\i\ **tip**	\ȯ\ **saw**	\u̇\ **foot**
\ər\ **further**	\ch\ **chin**	\ī\ **life**	\ȯi\ **coin**	\y\ **yet**
\a\ **mat**	\e\ **pet**	\j\ **job**	\th\ **thin**	\yü\ **few**
\ā\ **take**	\ē\ **easy**	\ng\ **sing**	\th\ **this**	\yu̇\ **cure**
\ä\ **cot, cart**	\g\ **go**	\ō\ **bone**	\ü\ **food**	\zh\ **vision**

gray head and back, and conspicuous white lateral tail feathers [Spanish, "reed," from Latin *juncus*]

junc·tion \ˈjəŋ-shən, ˈjəŋk-\ *n* **1 :** an act of joining **:** the state of being joined **2 :** a place or point of meeting ⟨a railroad *junction*⟩ **3 :** something that joins [Latin *junctio,* from *jungere* "to join"] — **junc·tion·al** \-shnəl, -shən-l\ *adj*

junc·ture \ˈjəŋ-chər, ˈjəŋk-\ *n* **1 :** an instance of joining **:** UNION **2 a :** JOINT 2a, CONNECTION **b :** the manner of transition between two consecutive sounds in speech **3 :** a point of time; *esp* **:** one made critical by a concurrence of circumstances — **junc·tur·al** \-chə-rəl, -shrəl\ *adj*

synonyms JUNCTURE, EMERGENCY, CRISIS mean a critical or crucial time or state of affairs. JUNCTURE stresses the significant convergence of events ⟨an important *juncture* in our country's history⟩. EMERGENCY emphasizes the sudden unforeseen nature of a situation and the need for quick action ⟨knows how to deal with *emergencies*⟩. CRISIS applies to a juncture whose outcome will make a decisive difference ⟨faces a serious financial *crisis*⟩.

June \ˈjün\ *n* **:** the 6th month of the year according to the Gregorian calendar [Latin *Junius*]

June·ber·ry \ˈjün-ˌber-ē\ *n* **:** SERVICEBERRY 2

june bug *n, often cap J* **:** any of various large leaf-eating beetles that fly chiefly in late spring and have as larvae white grubs that live in soil and feed on roots — called also *june beetle*

jun·gle \ˈjəŋ-gəl\ *n* **1 a :** a thick tangled mass of tropical vegetation **b :** a tract overgrown with jungle or other vegetation **2 :** a hobo camp **3 :** a place of ruthless struggle for survival [Hindi *jaṅgal* & Urdu *jangal* "forest," from Sanskrit *jaṅgala* "desert region"] — **jun·gly** \-gə-lē, -glē\ *adj*

jungle fowl *n* **:** any of several Asian wild birds related to the pheasants; *esp* **:** one from which domestic chickens are held to have descended

jungle gym *n* **:** a structure of vertical and horizontal bars for use of children at play

[1]**ju·nior** \ˈjün-yər\ *n* **1 :** a person who is younger or of lower rank than another **2 :** a student in the next-to-last year before graduating from an educational institution of secondary or higher level [Latin, from *junior,* comparative of *juvenis* "young"]

[2]**junior** *adj* **1 a :** YOUNGER — used chiefly to distinguish a son with the same given name or names as his father and usually placed in its abbreviated form after a surname ⟨John M. Doe, *Jr.*⟩ **b :** of more recent date **2 :** lower in standing or rank ⟨*junior* partner⟩ **3 :** of or relating to juniors in a school or college

ju·nior·ate \ˈjün-yə-ˌrāt, -rət\ *n* **1 :** a course of high school or college study for candidates for the priesthood, brotherhood, or sisterhood; *esp* **:** one preparatory to the course in philosophy **2 :** a seminary for the juniorate

junior college *n* **:** an educational institution that offers two years of studies corresponding to the first two years of a four-year college

junior high school *n* **:** a school usually including the 7th, 8th, and 9th grades

junior varsity *n* **:** a team composed of players lacking the experience or qualifications for the varsity

ju·ni·per \ˈjü-nə-pər\ *n* **1 a :** any of a genus of evergreen shrubs and trees related to the pines but producing female cones resembling berries **b :** the berrylike cone or fruit of a juniper **2 :** any of various coniferous trees resembling true junipers [Latin *juniperus*]

[1]**junk** \ˈjəŋk\ *n* **1 :** hard salted beef for use on shipboard **2 a (1) :** waste (as iron or glass) that may be used again in some form **(2) :** articles discarded as worthless **b :** a shoddy product **:** TRASH [Middle English *jonke* "pieces of old rope or cable"] — **junk·man** \-ˌman\ *n* — **junky** *adj*

[2]**junk** *vt* **:** to get rid of as worthless **:** SCRAP

[3]**junk** *n* **:** a flat-bottomed sailing vessel of Chinese waters having an overhanging bow, high stern, high masts with lugsails, and a deep rudder [Portuguese *junco,* from Javanese *joṅ*]

junk e-mail *n* **:** SPAM

Jun·ker \ˈyu̇ŋ-kər\ *n* **:** a member of the Prussian landed aristocracy [German, from Old High German *junchērro,* literally, "young lord"]

[1]**jun·ket** \ˈjəŋ-kət\ *n* **1 :** a dessert of sweetened flavored milk with a jellylike consistency **2 a :** a festive social affair **b :** JOURNEY, TRIP; *esp* **:** a trip made by an official at public expense [Middle English *joncate,* derived from Latin *juncus* "reed, rush"]

[3]junk

Word History Long ago a type of cream cheese was prepared in baskets made of reeds or rushes. In the Middle Ages this cream cheese was called *joncate,* a derivative of Latin *juncus,* which means "reed" or "rush." *Junket* was first used for cream cheese and later for a dessert made of sweetened curdled milk. In the early modern period, indeed, *junket* was a popular term for any sweet dish. From this sense of *junket* developed the extended sense "a feast or banquet." *Junket* came to be used for large picnics and later for any pleasure outing or trip.

[2]**junket** *vi* **1 :** BANQUET, FEAST **2 :** to go on a junket

junk food *n* **:** food that is high in calories but low in nutritional content

junk·ie *also* **junky** \ˈjəŋ-kē\ *n, pl* **junk·ies** **1 :** a person who sells or is addicted to narcotics **2 :** a person who gets an unusual amount of pleasure from or is dependent on something ⟨a sugar *junkie*⟩ [English slang *junk* "narcotics," from [1]*junk*]

jun·ta \ˈhu̇n-tə, ˈjənt-ə, ˈhən-tə\ *n* **1 :** a council or committee for political or governmental purposes; *esp* **:** a group of persons controlling a government after a revolutionary seizure of power **2 :** JUNTO [Spanish, from *junto* "joined," from Latin *jungere* "to join"]

jun·to \ˈjənt-ō\ *n, pl* **juntos :** a group of persons joined for a common purpose [probably alteration of *junta*]

Ju·pi·ter \ˈjü-pət-ər\ *n* **:** the largest of the planets and 5th in order of distance from the sun — see PLANET table [Latin *Jupiter,* chief Roman god]

Ju·ras·sic \ju̇-ˈras-ik\ *n* **:** the period of the Mesozoic era between the Triassic and Cretaceous marked by the presence of dinosaurs and the first appearance of birds; *also* **:** the corresponding system of rocks — see GEOLOGIC TIME table [French *jurassique,* from *Jura* mountain range] — **Jurassic** *adj*

ju·rid·i·cal \ju̇-ˈrid-i-kəl\ *adj* **1 :** of or relating to the administration of justice or the office of a judge **2 :** of or relating to law or jurisprudence **:** LEGAL [Latin *juridicus,* from *jur-, jus* "right, law" + *dicere* "to say"] — **ju·rid·i·cal·ly** \-kə-lē, -klē\ *adv*

ju·ris·dic·tion \ˌju̇r-əs-ˈdik-shən\ *n* **1 :** the power, right, or authority to interpret and apply the law **2 :** the authority of a sovereign power to govern or legislate **3 :** the limits or territory within which authority may be exercised [Latin *jurisdictio,* from *jur-, jus* "right, law" + *dictio* "act of saying," from *dicere* "to say"] — **ju·ris·dic·tion·al** \-shnəl, -shən-l\ *adj* — **ju·ris·dic·tion·al·ly** \-ē\ *adv*

ju·ris·pru·dence \ˌju̇r-ə-ˈsprüd-ns\ *n* **1 :** a system of laws **2 :** the science or philosophy of law **3 :** a department of law ⟨medical *jurisprudence*⟩ [Late Latin *jurisprudentia,* from *jur-, jus* "right, law" + *prudens* "skilled, prudent"] — **ju·ris·pru·den·tial** \-sprü-ˈden-chəl\ *adj* — **ju·ris·pru·den·tial·ly** \-ˈdench-lē, -ə-lē\ *adv*

ju·rist \ˈju̇r-əst\ *n* **:** one having a thorough knowledge of law [Middle French *juriste,* from Latin *jur-, jus* "law, right"]

ju·ris·tic \ju̇-ˈris-tik\ *adj* **1 :** of or relating to a jurist or jurisprudence **2 :** of, relating to, or recognized in law — **ju·ris·ti·cal·ly** \-ti-kə-lē, -klē\ *adv*

ju·ror \ˈju̇r-ər, ˈju̇r-ˌȯr\ *n* **:** a member of or a person summoned to serve on a jury

[1]**ju·ry** \ˈju̇r-ē\ *n, pl* **juries** **1 :** a body of persons sworn to hear evidence on a matter submitted to them and to give their verdict according to the evidence presented **2 :** a committee that judges and awards prizes at an exhibition or contest [Medieval French *juree,* from *jurer* "to swear," from Latin *jurare,* from *jur-, jus* "law"] — **ju·ry·man** \-mən\ *n* — **ju·ry·wom·an** \-ˌwu̇m-ən\ *n*

[2]**jury** *adj* **:** improvised for temporary use especially in an emergency **:** MAKESHIFT ⟨a *jury* mast⟩ [Middle English *jory* (as in *jory saile* "improvised sail")]

ju·ry-rig \ˈju̇r-ē-ˌrig\ *vt* **:** to build, construct, or arrange in a makeshift fashion

[1]**just** \ˈjəst\ *adj* **1 a :** having a basis in or conforming to fact or reason **:** REASONABLE ⟨a *just* comment⟩ **b** *archaic* **:** faithful to an original **c :** conforming to a standard of correctness **:** PROP-

ER ⟨*just* proportions⟩ **2 a** (1) : morally right or good : RIGHTEOUS ⟨a *just* war⟩ (2) : MERITED, DESERVED ⟨*just* punishment⟩ **b** : legally right ⟨a *just* title⟩ [Latin *justus,* from *jus* "right, law"] ***synonyms*** see FAIR — **just·ly** *adv* — **just·ness** \ˈjəst-nəs, ˈjəs-\ *n*

²**just** \jəst, ˌjəst, jist, ˌjist, jest, ˌjest\ *adv* **1 a** : EXACTLY, PRECISELY ⟨*just* right⟩ **b** : very recently ⟨the bell *just* rang⟩ **2 a** : by a very small margin : BARELY ⟨*just* over the line⟩ **b** : only a little ⟨*just* west of here⟩ **3 a** : no more than : MERELY ⟨*just* a note⟩ **b** : QUITE, VERY ⟨*just* wonderful⟩

jus·tice \ˈjəs-təs\ *n* **1 a** : the maintenance or administration of what is just **b** : JUDGE 1 **c** : the administration of law **2 a** : the quality of being just, impartial, or fair **b** : RIGHTEOUSNESS ⟨defend the *justice* of their cause⟩ **c** : the quality of conforming to law [Medieval French *justise,* from Latin *justitia,* from *justus* "just"] — **do justice 1 a** : to act justly **b** : to treat fairly or properly **c** : to consume in a manner showing due appreciation **2** : to conduct in a way worthy of one's capabilities

justice of the peace : a local magistrate empowered chiefly to try minor cases, to administer oaths, and to perform marriages

jus·ti·fi·able \ˈjəs-tə-ˌfī-ə-bəl\ *adj* : capable of being justified : EXCUSABLE — **jus·ti·fi·ably** \-blē\ *adv*

jus·ti·fi·ca·tion \ˌjəs-tə-fə-ˈkā-shən\ *n* **1** : the act, process, or state of being justified by God **2 a** : the act or an instance of justifying : VINDICATION **b** : something that justifies : DEFENSE

jus·ti·fy \ˈjəs-tə-ˌfī\ *vb* **-fied; -fy·ing 1 a** : to prove or show to be just, right, or reasonable : VINDICATE **b** : to show a sufficient lawful reason for an act done **2** : to release from the guilt of sin and accept as righteous **3** : to adjust or arrange exactly; *esp* : to cause (as lines of typewritten text) to come out even at the right margin ***synonyms*** see MAINTAIN — **jus·ti·fi·er** \-ˌfī-ər, -ˌfīr\ *n*

¹**jut** \ˈjət\ *vb* **jut·ted; jut·ting** : to shoot or cause to shoot out, up, or forward : PROJECT [perhaps short for *jutty* "to project beyond"]

²**jut** *n* : something that juts : PROJECTION

jute \ˈjüt\ *n* : a glossy fiber from either of two Asian plants that is used chiefly for making sacks, burlap, and twine; *also* : a plant producing jute [Bengali *jhuṭo*]

Jute \ˈjüt\ *n* : a member of a Germanic people invading England from Jutland and settling in Kent in the 5th century A.D. — compare ANGLO-SAXON [Medieval Latin *Jutae* "Jutes"] — **Jut·ish** \ˈjüt-ish\ *adj*

¹**ju·ve·nile** \ˈjü-və-ˌnīl, -vən-l\ *adj* **1 a** : showing incomplete development : IMMATURE **b** : CHILDISH 2 ⟨*juvenile* conduct⟩ **2** : derived from sources within the earth and coming to the surface for the first time ⟨*juvenile* water⟩ **3** : of, relating to, or characteristic of children or young people [Latin *juvenilis,* from *juvenis* "young person," from *juvenis* "young"] — **ju·ve·nil·i·ty** \ˌjü-və-ˈnil-ət-ē\ *n*

²**juvenile** *n* **1 a** : a young person **b** : a book for young people **2 a** : a fledged bird not yet in adult plumage **b** : a 2-year-old racehorse **3** : an actor or actress who plays youthful parts

juvenile delinquency *n* : violation of the law or antisocial behavior by a juvenile — **juvenile delinquent** *n*

juvenile diabetes *n* : TYPE 1 DIABETES

jux·ta·pose \ˈjək-stə-ˌpōz\ *vt* : to place side by side [probably back-formation from *juxtaposition*]

jux·ta·po·si·tion \ˌjək-stə-pə-ˈzish-ən\ *n* : a placing or being placed side by side [Latin *juxta* "near" + English *position*] — **jux·ta·po·si·tion·al** \-ˈzish-nəl, -ən-l\ *adj*

K

k \ˈkā\ *n, pl* **k's** *or* **ks** \ˈkāz\ *often cap* **1** : the 11th letter of the English alphabet **2** : THOUSAND **3** : a unit of computer memory equal to 1024 bytes

Kaa·ba \ˈkäb-ə\ *n* : a small stone building in the court of the Great Mosque at Mecca that contains a sacred black stone and is the point toward which Muslims turn in praying [Arabic *kaʿbah,* literally, "square building"]

kabbala *or* **kabbalah** *or* **kabala** *variant of* CABALA

ka·bob *or* **ke·bab** *also* **ke·bob** \ˈkā-ˌbäb, kə-ˈ\ *n* : cubes of meat cooked with vegetables usually on a skewer [derived from Arabic or Persian *kabāb,* from Turkish *kebap*]

Ka·bu·ki \kə-ˈbü-kē, ˈkäb-ů-ˌkē\ *n* : traditional Japanese popular drama with singing and dancing performed in a stylized manner [Japanese, literally, "art of singing and dancing"]

kad·dish \ˈkäd-ish\ *n, often cap* : a Jewish prayer recited in the daily ritual of the synagogue and by mourners at public services after the death of a close relative [Aramaic *qaddīsh* "holy"]

kaf·fee·klatsch \ˈkȯf-ē-ˌkläch, ˈkäf-, -ˌklach, -ˌkləch\ *n, often cap* : an informal social gathering for coffee and talk [German, from *Kaffee* "coffee" + *Klatsch* "gossip"]

Kaf·fir *or* **Kaf·ir** \ˈkaf-ər\ *n* : a member of a group of southern African Bantu-speaking peoples [Arabic *kāfir* "infidel"]

kaf·ir \ˈkaf-ər\ *n* : a grain sorghum with stout somewhat juicy stalks and erect heads

kaftan *variant of* CAFTAN

kai·ser \ˈkī-zər\ *n* : EMPEROR; *esp* : the ruler of Germany from 1871 to 1918 [Old Norse *keisari,* from Latin *Caesar,* cognomen of the Emperor Augustus] — **kai·ser·dom** \-zərd-əm\ *n* — **kai·ser·ism** \-zə-ˌriz-əm\ *n*

Word History Although Julius Caesar was never emperor, his name became synonymous with the office of emperor of the Roman empire. Caesar adopted his grandnephew Gaius Octavius, who, upon his adoption, took the name Gaius Julius Caesar Octavianus. This man, after the death of Julius Caesar, gained control in Italy and became the first Roman emperor, with the title *Augustus,* "exalted, august." Later Roman emperors adopted his name, Caesar, to indicate their right to the imperial title. Subsequently other European languages borrowed this name from Latin as a word for emperor.

ka·ka \ˈkäk-ə\ *n* : a brownish New Zealand parrot with gray and red markings that is a good mimic and talker [Maori]

kal·an·choe \ˌkal-ən-ˈkō-ē, kə-ˈlang-kə-wē\ *n* : any of a genus of chiefly African succulent tropical plants including several grown as ornamentals [New Latin]

kale \ˈkāl\ *n* : a hardy cabbage with curled often finely cut leaves that do not form a dense head [Scottish, from Old English *cāl*]

ka·lei·do·scope \kə-ˈlīd-ə-ˌskōp\ *n* **1** : an instrument containing loose bits of colored glass between two flat plates and two plane mirrors so placed that changes of position of the bits of glass are reflected in an endless variety of symmetrical patterns **2** : a changing pattern or scene **3** : a diverse collection ⟨a *kaleidoscope* of subjects⟩ [Greek *kalos* "beautiful" + *eidos* "shape, form" + English -scope] — **ka·lei·do·scop·ic** \-ˌlīd-ə-ˈskäp-ik\ *adj* — **ka·lei·do·scop·i·cal·ly** \-ˈskäp-i-kə-lē, -klē\ *adv*

kalends *variant of* CALENDS

Kal·muck *or* **Kal·muk** \ˈkal-ˌmək, kal-ˈ\ *n* **1** : a member of a Buddhist Mongol people originally of northern Sinkiang, China **2** : the language of the Kalmucks [Russian *Kalmyk*]

ka·ma·ai·na \ˌkäm-ə-ˈī-nə\ *n* : one who has lived in Hawaii for a long time [Hawaiian *kamaʻāina,* from *kama* "child" + *ʻāina* "land"]

kame \ˈkām\ *n* : a short ridge or mound of material deposited by

\ə\ **abut**	\aů\ **out**	\i\ **tip**	\ȯ\ **saw**	\ů\ **foot**
\ər\ **further**	\ch\ **chin**	\ī\ **life**	\ȯi\ **coin**	\y\ **yet**
\a\ **mat**	\e\ **pet**	\j\ **job**	\th\ **thin**	\yü\ **few**
\ā\ **take**	\ē\ **easy**	\ng\ **sing**	\t͟h\ **this**	\yů\ **cure**
\ä\ **cot, cart**	\g\ **go**	\ō\ **bone**	\ü\ **food**	\zh\ **vision**

water from a melting glacier [Scottish, literally, "comb," from Old English *camb*]

ka·mi·ka·ze \ˌkäm-i-ˈkäz-ē\ *n* : a member of a corps of Japanese pilots in World War II assigned to make a crash on a target; *also* : an airplane flown in such an attack [Japanese, literally, "divine wind"]

Word History In 1281 Kublai Khan sent an immense fleet against Japan. Although Japan was prepared, the Mongol horde was not easy to resist. But after some weeks of fighting, a great and sudden storm arose and destroyed the Mongol fleet. To the Japanese this salvation was *kamikaze,* "divine wind." In the Second World War Japan sent out pilots willing to give up their lives to help save their country by destroying American ships. These were the members of a special corps named *kamikaze* after the storm that had saved Japan seven centuries earlier.

kan·ga·roo \ˌkang-gə-ˈrü\ *n, pl* **-roos** : any of various plant-eating leaping marsupial mammals of Australia, New Guinea, and adjacent islands with a small head, long powerful hind legs, a long thick tail used as a support and in balancing, and short forelegs not used in locomotion [Guugu Yimidhirr (Australian aboriginal language of northern Queensland) *gaŋurru*]

kangaroo court *n* **1** : a court whose status or procedures are irresponsible or irregular **2** : judgment or punishment given outside of legal procedure

kangaroo rat *n* : a burrowing rodent of dry regions of western North America that travels by hopping on its long hind legs

kangaroo rat

Kant·ian \ˈkant-ē-ən, ˈkänt-\ *adj* : of, relating to, or characteristic of Kant or his philosophy

ka·o·lin \ˈkā-ə-lən\ *n* : a fine usually white clay that is used in ceramics and refractories and as an adsorbent [French *kaolin,* from *Gaoling,* hill in China]

ka·o·lin·ite \ˈkā-ə-lə-ˌnīt\ *n* : a white mineral consisting of a silicate of aluminum that is the principle mineral in kaolin

ka·pok \ˈkā-ˌpäk\ *n* : a mass of silky fibers that cover the seeds of the ceiba tree and are used as a filling for mattresses, life preservers, and sleeping bags and as insulation [Malay]

Ka·po·si's sarcoma \ˈkap-ə-sēz-, kə-ˈpō-, -shēz-\ *n* : a form of cancer typically affecting the skin and mucous membranes that is associated especially with AIDS and is characterized usually by the formation of colored blotches on the skin [Mortiz *Kaposi,* died 1902, Hungarian dermatologist]

kap·pa \ˈkap-ə\ *n* : the 10th letter of the Greek alphabet — Κ or κ

ka·put \kä-ˈpu̇t, kə-, -ˈpüt\ *adj* **1** : utterly defeated or destroyed **2** : made useless or unable to function **3** : hopelessly outmoded [German *kaputt,* from French *capot* "not having made a trick at piquet"]

Word History To win all the tricks in the card game piquet is *faire capot,* "to make *capot,*" in French, while *être capot,* "to be *capot,*" is to have lost all the tricks in a game. In German *capot* was transliterated as *kaput,* and from the sense of having lost a game German *kaput* developed the senses "broken," "finished," "utterly destroyed." *Kaput* was borrowed into English from German early in the 20th century.

kar·a·kul \ˈkar-ə-kəl\ *n* **1** *often cap* : any of a breed of hardy fat-tailed Asian sheep with coarse wiry fur **2** : the usually curly glossy black coat of a very young karakul lamb valued as fur [*Karakul,* village in Uzbekistan]

karakul 1

kar·a·o·ke \ˌkar-ē-ˈō-kē, kə-ˈrō-kē\ *n* : a device that plays music to which the user sings along and that records the user's singing with the music [Japanese, from *kara* "empty" + *ōke,* short for *ōkesutora* "orchestra"]

kar·at *or* **car·at** \ˈkar-ət\ *n* : a unit of fineness for gold equal to 1/24 part of pure gold in an alloy [probably from Medieval French *carat,* from Medieval Latin *carratus* "[2]carat"]

ka·ra·te \kə-ˈrät-ē\ *n* : a Japanese art of self-defense in which an attacker is disabled with kicks and punches [Japanese, literally, "empty hand"]

kar·ma \ˈkär-mə, ˈkər-\ *n, often cap* **1** : the force generated by one's actions that is held in Hinduism and Buddhism to sustain the cycle of deaths and rebirths and to determine destiny in one's next existence **2** : a distinctive spirit or atmosphere that can be sensed [Sanskrit *karma,* "fate, work"] — **kar·mic** \-mik\ *adj*

kar·roo *or* **ka·roo** \kə-ˈrü\ *n* : a dry tableland of southern Africa [Afrikaans *karo,* from Khoikhoi (a language of southern Africa) *karo, karro* "hard, dry"]

karst \ˈkärst\ *n* : an irregular limestone region with depressions, underground streams, and caverns [German]

kart \ˈkärt\ *n* : GO-KART — **kart·ing** *n*

kary- *or* **karyo-** *combining form* : nucleus of a cell ⟨*karyo*kinesis⟩ [Greek *karyon* "nut"]

karyo·ki·ne·sis \ˌkar-ē-ō-kə-ˈnē-səs, -kī-ˈnē-\ *n* : MITOSIS

[1]**karyo·type** \ˈkar-ē-ə-ˌtīp\ *n* : the set of characteristics that distinguish the chromosomes of a particular cell or group; *also* : the chromosomes themselves or a representation of them — **karyo·typ·ic** \ˌkar-ē-ə-ˈtip-ik\ *adj*

[2]**karyotype** *vt* : to determine or analyze the karyotype of

kash·ruth *or* **kash·rut** \kä-ˈshrüt, -ˈshrüth\ *n* **1** : the state of being kosher **2** : the Jewish dietary laws [Hebrew *kashrūth,* literally, "fitness"]

Kas·site \ˈkas-ˌīt\ *n* : a member of a people from the Iranian plateau ruling Babylon between 1600 and 1200 B.C.

ka·ty·did \ˈkāt-ē-ˌdid\ *n* : any of various large green American long-horned grasshoppers with stridulating organs on the forewings of the males that produce a loud shrill sound [imitative]

kau·ri \ˈkau̇r-ē\ *n* **1 a** : any of several trees resembling pines; *esp* : a tall New Zealand timber tree **b** : the tough white straight-grained wood of a kauri **2** : a recent or fossil resin from New Zealand kauris used especially in varnish and linoleum [Maori *kawri*]

kay·ak \ˈkī-ˌak\ *n* **1** : an Eskimo canoe made of a frame entirely covered with skins except for a small opening in the center where one or two paddlers sit **2** : a covered canoe resembling a kayak [Inuit *qajaq*]

ka·zoo \kə-ˈzü\ *n, pl* **kazoos** : a toy musical instrument containing a membrane which produces a buzzing tone when one hums or sings into the mouth hole [imitative]

kea \ˈkē-ə\ *n* : a large mosty dull green New Zealand parrot that is normally insectivorous but sometimes attacks and kills sheep for their flesh [Maori]

kebab *or* **kebob** *variant of* KABOB

[1]**kedge** \ˈkej\ *vt* : to move (a ship) by hauling on a line attached to a small anchor dropped at the distance and in the direction desired [Middle English *caggen*]

[2]**kedge** *n* : a small anchor used especially in kedging

[1]**keel** \ˈkēl\ *n* **1 a** : a timber or plate running lengthwise along the center of the bottom of a ship and usually projecting from the bottom **b** : SHIP **2 a** : something (as the breastbone of a bird) like a ship's keel in form or use; *esp* : a ridged part **b** : the lower two petals of a pea flower [Old Norse *kjǫlr*]

[2]**keel** *vb* **1 a** : to turn over **b** : to fall in or as if in a faint — usually used with *over* **2** : to provide with a keel

keel·boat \ˈkēl-ˌbōt\ *n* : a shallow covered riverboat with a keel that is usually rowed, poled, or towed and that is used for freight — **keel·boat·man** \-mən\ *n*

keel·haul \-ˌhȯl\ *vt* **1** : to haul under the keel of a ship as punishment or torture **2** : to rebuke severely [Dutch *kielhalen,* from *kiel* "keel" + *halen* "to haul"]

[1]**keen** \ˈkēn\ *adj* **1** : having a fine edge or point : SHARP ⟨a *keen* knife⟩ **2** : CUTTING 2, STINGING ⟨a *keen* wind⟩ **3** : EAGER, ENTHUSIASTIC ⟨*keen* about baseball⟩ **4 a** : very alert and perceptive ⟨a *keen* mind⟩ **b** : extremely sensitive (as in seeing or hearing) ⟨*keen* eyesight⟩ [Old English *cēne* "brave, fierce"] ***synonyms*** see SHARP — **keen·ly** *adv* — **keen·ness** \ˈkēn-nəs\ *n*

[2]**keen** *vb* : to lament with a keen [Irish Gaelic *caoinim* "I lament"] — **keen·er** *n*

³keen *n* : a loud wailing lament for the dead

¹keep \ˈkēp\ *vb* **kept** \ˈkept\; **keep·ing** **1 a** : to perform as a duty : FULFILL ⟨*keep* a promise⟩ **b** : to observe in a fitting or customary manner : not neglect ⟨*keep* a holiday⟩ **2 a** : GUARD ⟨*keep* us from harm⟩ **b** : to take care of ⟨*keep* a war orphan⟩ ⟨*keep* house⟩ **3** : to continue doing something : MAINTAIN ⟨*keep* silence⟩ ⟨*keep* on working⟩ **4** : HOLD, DETAIN ⟨*keep* a prisoner in jail⟩ **5 a** : to cause to remain in a given place, situation, or condition ⟨*keep* someone waiting⟩ **b** : to remain unspoiled ⟨milk may not *keep* in hot weather⟩ **6** : to hold back : WITHHOLD ⟨*keep* a secret⟩ **7** : to possess permanently ⟨*keep* what you have earned⟩ **8** : REFRAIN ⟨unable to *keep* from talking⟩ **9** : to have in one's service or at one's disposal ⟨*keep* servants⟩ ⟨*keep* a car⟩ **10** : to preserve a record in ⟨*keep* a diary⟩ **11** : STAY, REMAIN ⟨*keep* off the grass⟩ **12** : to have on hand regularly for sale ⟨*keep* neckties⟩ [Old English *cēpan*] — **keep one's end up** : to do one's share or duty

synonyms KEEP, OBSERVE, CELEBRATE, COMMEMORATE mean to notice or honor a day, occasion, or deed. KEEP stresses the idea of not neglecting or violating ⟨*keep* the Sabbath⟩. OBSERVE is likely to imply marking by ceremonious performance ⟨not all holidays are *observed* nationally⟩. CELEBRATE suggests acknowledging an occasion by festivity ⟨*celebrate* Thanksgiving with a huge dinner⟩. COMMEMORATE implies remembrance and suggests observances that tend to call to mind what the occasion stands for ⟨*commemorate* Memorial Day with the laying of wreaths⟩.

²keep *n* **1** : FORTRESS; *esp* : the strongest part of a medieval castle **2** : the means by which one is kept; *esp* : one's food and lodging ⟨earned their *keep*⟩ — **for keeps 1 a** : with the provision that one keep one's winnings ⟨play marbles *for keeps*⟩ **b** : with deadly seriousness **2** : PERMANENTLY ⟨came home *for keeps*⟩

keep·er \ˈkē-pər\ *n* : a person who watches, guards, maintains, or takes care of something ⟨the *keeper* of a store⟩

keep·ing \ˈkē-piŋ\ *n* **1** : OBSERVANCE ⟨the *keeping* of a holiday⟩ **2** : CUSTODY 1, CARE **3** : AGREEMENT, HARMONY ⟨in *keeping* with good taste⟩

keep·sake \ˈkēp-ˌsāk\ *n* : something kept or given to be kept as a memento [*keep* + *-sake* (as in *namesake*)]

keep up *vb* **1** : MAINTAIN, SUSTAIN ⟨*keep* standards *up*⟩ **2** : to keep informed ⟨*keep up* on politics⟩ **3** : to continue without interruption ⟨rain *kept up* all night⟩ **4** : to stay even with others (as in a race)

keg \ˈkeg, ˈkag, ˈkāg\ *n* **1** : a small cask or barrel holding 30 gallons (about 114 liters) or less **2** : the contents of a keg [Middle English *kag,* of Scandinavian origin]

kelp \ˈkelp\ *n* **1** : any of various large brown seaweeds; *also* : a mass of these **2** : the ashes of seaweed used as a fertilizer and a source of iodine [Middle English *culp*]

kel·pie \ˈkel-pē\ *n* : any of a breed of Australian sheepdogs developed in Australia from British sheepdogs [*Kelpie,* the name of an early dog of this breed]

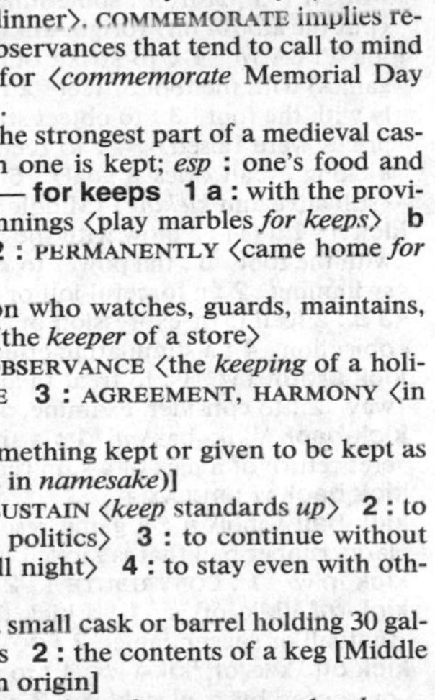

kelpie

kel·vin \ˈkel-vən\ *n* : a unit of temperature equal to $\frac{1}{273.16}$ of the Kelvin scale temperature of the triple point of water

Kel·vin \ˈkel-vən\ *adj* : relating to, conforming to, or having a temperature scale on which the unit of measurement is the same size as the Celsius degree and according to which absolute zero is 0 K which is the equivalent of −273.15°C — abbreviation *K* [William Thomson, Lord *Kelvin*]

Kemp's ridley \ˈkemps-\ *n* : a small gray sea turtle of the Atlantic coast of the U.S. and Gulf of Mexico [Richard M. *Kemp,* late 19th century amateur naturalist]

¹ken \ˈken\ *vb* **kenned; ken·ning** *chiefly Scottish* : KNOW [Old Norse *kenna* "to perceive"]

²ken *n* **1** : range of vision **2** : range of understanding

ke·naf \kə-ˈnaf\ *n* : an African hibiscus that yields a strong cordage fiber; *also* : its fiber [Persian]

ken·do \ˈken-dō\ *n* : a traditional Japanese sport of fencing with bamboo staves [Japanese *kendō,* from *ken* "sword" + *dō* "art"]

¹ken·nel \ˈken-l\ *n* **1** : a shelter for a dog **2** : an establishment for the breeding or boarding of dogs or cats [derived from Latin *canis* "dog"]

²kennel *vb* **-neled** *or* **-nelled; -nel·ing** *or* **-nel·ling** : to put, keep, or take shelter in or as if in a kennel

Ken·tucky bluegrass \kən-ˌtək-ē-\ *n* : a Eurasian grass that is naturalized in North America and is widely grown in pastures, meadows, and lawns

Kentucky coffee tree *n* : a tall North American tree of the legume family with large woody pods whose seeds have been used as a substitute for coffee

Kentucky rifle *n* : a muzzle-loading long-barreled flintlock rifle developed in the 18th century

ke·pi \ˈkā-pē, ˈkep-ē\ *n* : a military cap with a round flat top sloping toward the front and a visor [French *képi,* from German dialect *käppi* "cap"]

ker·a·tin \ˈker-ət-n\ *n* : any of various sulfur-containing fibrous proteins that form the chemical basis of hair and horny tissues (as nails) [Greek *kerat-, keras* "horn"] — **ke·ra·ti·nous** \kə-ˈrat-n-əs, ˌker-ə-ˈtī-nəs\ *adj*

kerb \ˈkərb\ *n, British* : CURB 4

ker·chief \ˈkər-chəf, -ˌchēf\ *n, pl* **kerchiefs** \-chəfs, -ˌchēfs\ *also* **kerchieves** \-ˌchēvz\ **1** : a square of cloth worn especially by women as a head covering or around the neck **2** : HANDKERCHIEF 1 [Medieval French *coverchef, cuerchief,* from *covrir* "to cover" + *chef* "head," from Latin *caput*]

kerf \ˈkərf\ *n* : a slit or notch made by a saw or cutting torch [Old English *cyrf* "action of cutting"]

ker·mes \ˈkər-mēz\ *n* : the dried bodies of the females of various scale insects used as a red dyestuff [French *kermès,* from Arabic *qirmiz*]

ker·mis *or* **ker·mess** \ˈkər-məs\ *n* : an outdoor festival of the Low Countries [Dutch *kermis*]

kern *or* **kerne** \ˈkərn, ˈkeərn\ *n* : a foot soldier of medieval Ireland or Scotland [Irish *cethern* "band of soldiers"]

ker·nel \ˈkərn-l\ *n* **1 a** : the inner softer part of a seed, fruit stone, or nut **b** : a whole seed of a cereal (as corn) **2** : a central or essential part : CORE [Old English *cyrnel,* from *corn* "grain"]

kern·ite \ˈkər-ˌnīt\ *n* : a mineral that consists of sodium, boron, and water [*Kern* county, California]

ker·o·sene *also* **ker·o·sine** \ˈker-ə-ˌsēn, ˌker-ə-ˈ, ˈkar-, ˌkar-\ *n* : a thin oil consisting of a mixture of hydrocarbons usually obtained by distillation of petroleum and used for a fuel and as a solvent [Greek *kēros* "wax"]

ker·ria \ˈker-ē-ə\ *n* : a yellow-flowered shrub of China and Japan that is related to the roses [William *Kerr,* died 1814, English gardener]

Ker·ry blue terrier \ˌker-ē-\ *n* : any of an Irish breed of medium-sized terriers with a long head, deep chest, and silky bluish coat [County *Kerry,* Ireland]

ker·sey \ˈkər-zē\ *n* : a coarse ribbed woolen cloth for hose and work clothes [*Kersey,* England]

kes·trel \ˈkes-trəl\ *n* : a small European falcon that hovers in the air against a wind [Medieval French *crecerelle*]

kestrel

ketch \ˈkech\ *n* : a 2-masted fore-and-aft-rigged sailing vessel similar to a yawl but with the mizzenmast farther forward [Middle English *cache*]

ketch·up *also* **catch·up** \ˈkech-əp, ˈkach-\ *or* **cat·sup** \ˈkech-əp, ˈkach-; ˈkat-səp\ *n* : a thick seasoned sauce usually made from tomatoes [Malay *kēchap* "fish sauce"]

ke·tone \ˈkē-ˌtōn\ *n* : any of various organic compounds with a carbonyl group attached to two carbon atoms [German *Keton*] — **ke·ton·ic** \kē-ˈtän-ik\ *adj*

ket·tle \ˈket-l\ *n* **1** : a metallic vessel for boiling liquids; *esp* : TEAKETTLE **2** : a steep-sided hollow without surface drainage

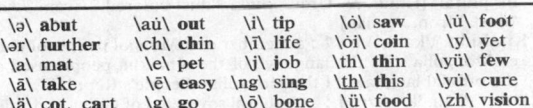

formed especially by the melting of a glacier [Old Norse *ketill,* derived from Latin *catillus* "small bowl," from *catinus* "bowl"]

ket•tle•drum \-ˌdrəm\ *n* : a kettle-shaped drum whose head can be tuned to different pitches by changing its tension

[1]**key** \ˈkē\ *n, pl* **keys** **1 a :** a usually metal instrument by which the bolt of a lock is turned **b :** a device having the form or function of a key ⟨a *key* for winding a clock⟩ **2 a :** a means of gaining or preventing entrance, possession, or control **b :** an instrumental or deciding factor **3 a :** something that gives an explanation or solution **b :** a list of words or phrases giving an explanation of symbols or abbreviations **c :** a series of phrases or statements that describe observable characteristics by which plants or animals of a particular group differ and are used to aid in identification **d :** a map legend **4 :** a small piece of wood or metal used as a wedge or for preventing motion between parts **5 :** one of the levers with a flat surface that is pressed by a finger in operating or playing an instrument (as a typewriter, piano, or clarinet) **6 :** SAMARA **7 :** a system of seven tones based on their relationship to a tonic; *esp* **:** the tonality of a scale **8 a :** characteristic style or tone **b :** the tone or pitch of a voice **9 :** a small switch for opening or closing an electric circuit [Old English *cǣg*]

[2]**key** *vb* **keyed** \ˈkēd\; **key•ing** **1 :** to lock or secure with a key **2 :** to regulate the musical pitch of **3 :** to make appropriate ⟨remarks *keyed* to an event⟩ **4 :** to make nervous or tense — usually used with *up* **5 :** to use a key **6 :** [2]KEYBOARD

[3]**key** *adj* **:** of basic importance **:** FUNDAMENTAL

[4]**key** *n* **:** a low island or reef; *esp* **:** one of the coral islets off the southern coast of Florida [Spanish *cayo,* from Taino]

[1]**key•board** \ˈkē-ˌbōrd, -ˌbȯrd\ *n* **1 :** a bank of keys on a musical instrument (as a piano) **2 :** an arrangement of keys by which a machine (as a typewriter or computer) is operated **3 :** a small usually portable musical instrument that is played by means of a keyboard like that on a piano and that produces a variety of sounds electronically

[2]**keyboard** *vb* **1 :** to operate a machine with a keyboard **2 :** to capture or set (as data or text) by means of a machine with a keyboard — **key•board•er** *n*

key•hole \ˈkē-ˌhōl\ *n* **:** a hole for receiving a key

keyhole saw *n* **:** a narrow pointed fine-toothed handsaw used especially for cutting tight curves

[1]**key•note** \-ˌnōt\ *n* **1 :** the first and fundamental tone of a scale **2 :** the fundamental or central fact, idea, or mood

[2]**keynote** *vt* **1 :** to set the keynote of **2 :** to deliver the keynote address at — **key•not•er** *n*

keynote address *n* **:** an address designed to present the issues of primary interest to a gathering and often to arouse unity and enthusiasm — called also *keynote speech*

key•pad \ˈkē-ˌpad\ *n* **:** a small keyboard (as on a calculator)

key•punch \ˈkē-ˌpənch\ *n* **:** a machine with a keyboard used to cut holes or notches in punch cards — **keypunch** *vt* — **key•punch•er** *n*

key signature *n* **:** the sharps or flats placed after a clef in music to indicate the key

key•stone \ˈkē-ˌstōn\ *n* **1 :** the wedge-shaped piece at the crown of an arch that locks the other pieces in place **2 :** something on which associated things depend for support **3 :** a species of plant or animal that is considered essential to maintaining the stability of an ecosystem

K keystone 1

key•stroke \-ˌstrōk\ *n* **:** the act or an instance of pushing down a key on a keyboard — **keystroke** *vb*

key•word \ˌwərd\ *n* **:** a word of interest or significance especially from a document ⟨a *keyword* search of the database⟩

kha•ki \ˈkak-ē, ˈkäk-, *Canadian often* ˈkärk-\ *n* **1 :** a light yellowish brown **2 a :** a khaki-colored cloth made usually of cotton or wool **b :** a military uniform of this cloth — usually used in plural [Hindi & Urdu *khākī* "dust-colored," from *khāk* "dust," from Persian]

Khal•kha \ˈkal-kə\ *n* **1 :** a member of a Mongol people of Outer Mongolia **2 :** the language of the Khalkha people used as the official language of the Mongolian People's Republic

[1]**khan** \ˈkän, ˈkan\ *n* **1 :** a medieval sovereign of China and ruler over the Turkish, Tatar, and Mongol tribes **2 :** a local chieftain or man of rank in some countries of central Asia [Medieval French *kan, kaan,* of Turkic origin] — **khan•ate** \-ˌāt\ *n*

[2]**khan** *n* **:** an inn or rest house in some Asian countries [Arabic *khān*]

khe•dive \kə-ˈdēv\ *n* **:** a Turkish governor of Egypt from 1867 to 1914 [French *khédive,* from Turkish *hidiv*]

Khmer \kə-ˈmeər\ *n* **1 :** a member of an aboriginal people of Cambodia **2 :** the official language of Cambodia — **Khmer•ian** \-ˈmer-ē-ən\ *adj*

Khoi•khoi \ˈkȯi-ˌkȯi\ *n, pl* **Khoikhoi** **1 :** a member of a group of pastoral peoples who lived in far southern Africa when first encountered by Europeans in the 17th century and who now live mainly in Namibia **2 :** the languages spoken by the Khoikhoi

kib•butz \kib-ˈu̇ts, -ˈüts\ *n, pl* **kib•but•zim** \-ˌu̇t-ˈsēm, -ˌüt-\ **:** a collective farm or settlement in Israel [Modern Hebrew *qibbūṣ*]

kibe \ˈkīb\ *n* **:** CHILBLAIN [Middle English]

ki•bitz *also* **kib•bitz** \ˈkib-əts\ *vb* **1 :** to act or observe as a kibitzer **2 :** to exchange comments **:** CHAT [Yiddish *kibetsn*]

kib•itz•er \ˈkib-ət-sər\ *n* **:** one who looks on and often offers unwanted advice or comment especially at a card game

ki•bosh \ˈkī-ˌbäsh\ *n* **:** something that serves as a check or stop ⟨put the *kibosh* on⟩ [origin unknown]

[1]**kick** \ˈkik\ *vb* **1 :** to strike out (as in defense or at a ball in games) with the foot or feet **2 :** to strike, thrust, or hit violently with the foot **3 :** to object strongly **:** PROTEST ⟨*kick* because prices were raised⟩ **4 :** to recoil when fired **5 :** to score by kicking a ball ⟨*kick* a goal⟩ **6 :** to be full of pep and energy ⟨still alive and *kicking*⟩ [Middle English *kiken*] — **kick•er** *n*

[2]**kick** *n* **1 a** (1) **:** a blow with the foot (2) **:** a propelling of a ball with the foot **b :** the power to kick **c :** a motion of the legs in swimming **2 :** a forceful jolt or thrust; *esp* **:** the recoil of a gun **3 a :** a feeling or expression of opposition **b :** the grounds for objection **4 :** a stimulating effect especially of pleasure

kick around *vt* **1 :** to treat in an inconsiderate or high-handed way **2 :** to consider, examine, or discuss from various angles

kick•back \ˈkik-ˌbak\ *n* **1 :** a sharp violent reaction **2 :** a secret return of a part of a sum received

kick back *vi* **:** RELAX 1

kick•ball \-ˌbȯl\ *n* **:** a game resembling baseball played with a large rubber ball that is kicked instead of hit with a bat

kick in *vb* **1 :** CONTRIBUTE 1 **2 :** START 2b

kick•off \ˈkik-ˌȯf\ *n* **1 :** a kick that puts the ball into play in a football or soccer game **2 :** COMMENCEMENT 1

kick off \kik-ˈȯf, ˈkik-\ *vb* **1 :** to start or resume play in football or soccer by a placekick **2 :** to begin or begin something **:** COMMENCE ⟨*kicked* the campaign *off* with a dinner⟩

kick out *vt* **:** to throw out ⟨*kicked* them *out* of the club⟩

kick•stand \-ˌstand\ *n* **:** a metal bar or rod attached to a 2-wheeled vehicle (as a bicycle) and used to prop up the vehicle when it is not in use

[1]**kid** \ˈkid\ *n* **1 :** the young of a goat or of a related animal **2 a :** the flesh, fur, or skin of a kid **b :** something (as leather) made of kid **3 :** CHILD 2a, YOUNGSTER [Middle English *kide,* of Scandinavian origin] — **kid•dish** \ˈkid-ish\ *adj*

[2]**kid** *vb* **kid•ded; kid•ding** **1 :** to deceive as a joke **:** FOOL **2 :** to make fun of **:** TEASE [probably from [1]*kid*] — **kid•der** *n* — **kid•ding•ly** \ˈkid-ing-lē\ *adv*

kid•do \ˈkid-ō\ *n* **:** CHILD 2a [[1]*kid*]

kid glove *n* **:** a dress glove made of kidskin — **kid–gloved** \ˈkid-ˈgləvd\ *adj* — **with kid gloves :** with special consideration

kid•nap \ˈkid-ˌnap\ *vb* **kid•napped** *also* **kid•naped** \-ˌnapt\; **kid•nap•ping** *also* **kid•nap•ing** \-ˌnap-ing\ **:** to carry away a person by unlawful force or by fraud and against his or her will [probably back-formation from *kidnapper,* from [1]*kid* + obsolete *napper* "thief"] — **kid•nap•per** *also* **kid•nap•er** \-ˌnap-ər\ *n*

kid•ney \ˈkid-nē\ *n, pl* **kidneys** **1 :** either of a pair of oval to bean-shaped organs situated in the body cavity near the spinal column that excrete waste in the form of urine **2 :** an excretory organ of an invertebrate animal [Middle English]

kidney bean *n* **:** an edible seed and especially a large dark red seed of any of several varieties of cultivated bean plants; *also* **:** a plant that produces kidney beans

kidney stone *n* **:** a calculus (as of calcium salts) in the kidney

kid•skin \ˈkid-ˌskin\ *n* **:** the skin of a young goat or leather made from or resembling this

kie·sel·guhr *or* **kie·sel·gur** \ˈkē-zəl-ˌgu̇r\ *n* : loose or porous diatomaceous earth [German *Kieselgur*]

[1]**kill** \ˈkil\ *vb* **1** : to deprive of life : put to death **2** : DESTROY, RUIN ⟨*kill* all chance of success⟩ **3** : to use up ⟨*kill* time⟩ **4** : DEFEAT ⟨*kill* a proposed law⟩ **5** : to mark for omission ⟨*kill* a news story⟩ **6** : to hit (a shot) so hard in various games that a return is impossible [Middle English *killen*]

synonyms KILL, SLAY, MURDER, ASSASSINATE mean to deprive of life. KILL simply states the fact of death by any agency in any manner ⟨was *killed* in an accident⟩. SLAY, chiefly literary, implies deliberateness and violence but not necessarily motive ⟨*slain* heroes of the revolution⟩. MURDER implies motive and premeditation and usually secrecy and stresses full moral responsibility ⟨convicted of *murdering* a rival⟩. ASSASSINATE applies to open or secret killing often for political motives ⟨terrorists *assassinated* the Senator⟩.

[2]**kill** *n* **1** : an act of killing **2 a** : an animal killed in a hunt, season, or particular period of time **b** : an enemy airplane, submarine, or ship destroyed by military action

kill·deer \ˈkil-ˌdiər\ *n, pl* **killdeers** *or* **killdeer** : a North American plover with a plaintive penetrating cry [imitative]

[1]**kill·er** \ˈkil-ər\ *n* **1** : one that kills **2** : KILLER WHALE

[2]**killer** *adj* **1** : strikingly impressive or effective ⟨a *killer* smile⟩ **2** : extremely difficult to deal with ⟨a *killer* exam⟩; *also* : causing death or devastation ⟨a *killer* tornado⟩

killer cell *n* : a lymphocyte (as a killer T cell) that is active in destroying other cells

killer T cell *n* : a T cell that functions in an immune response by destroying a cell (as one infected with a virus) having specific antigenic molecules on its surface — called also *cytotoxic T cell*

killer whale *n* : a gregarious largely black flesh-eating toothed whale 20 to 30 feet (about 6 to 9 meters) long

killer whale

kil·li·fish \ˈkil-ē-ˌfish\ *n* : any of numerous small fishes including some used as bait, in mosquito control, and as aquarium fishes [earlier *killie,* perhaps from Dutch *kil* "river, stream"]

kill·ing \ˈkil-iŋ\ *n* **1** : the act of one that kills **2** : a quick profit

kill·joy \ˈkil-ˌjȯl\ *n* : a person who spoils others' fun

kiln \ˈkiln, ˈkil\ *n* : an oven, furnace, or heated enclosure for processing a substance by burning, firing, or drying [Old English *cyln,* from Latin *culina* "kitchen"] — **kiln** *vt*

ki·lo \ˈkē-lō\ *n, pl* **kilos** : KILOGRAM

kilo- *combining form* : thousand [French, from Greek *chilioi*]

ki·lo·byte \ˈkē-lə-ˌbīt, ˈkil-ə-\ *n* : 1024 bytes

ki·lo·cal·o·rie \ˈkē-lə-ˌkal-rē, ˈkil-ə-, -ə-rē\ *n* : CALORIE 1b

kilo·cy·cle \ˈkil-ə-ˌsī-kəl\ *n* : 1000 cycles; *esp* : KILOHERTZ

ki·lo·gram \ˈkē-lə-ˌgram, ˈkil-ə-\ *n* **1** : the base unit of mass in the metric system that has been agreed upon by international convention and is nearly equal to the mass of 1000 cubic centimeters of water at its maximum density — see METRIC SYSTEM table **2** : the weight of a kilogram mass that is under a gravitational acceleration equal to that of the earth ⟨he weighs 80 *kilograms*⟩

ki·lo·hertz \ˈkil-ə-ˌhərts, ˈkē-lə-, -ˌheərts\ *n* : 1000 hertz

ki·lo·joule \ˈkil-ə-ˌjül\ *n* : 1000 joules

kilo·li·ter \ˈkil-ə-ˌlēt-ər\ *n* — see METRIC SYSTEM table

ki·lo·me·ter \kil-ˈäm-ət-ər, ˈkil-ə-ˌmēt-\ *n* — see METRIC SYSTEM table

ki·lo·pas·cal \ˌkil-ə-pas-ˈkal\ *n* : 1000 pascals

ki·lo·ton \ˈkil-ə-ˌtən, ˈkē-lə- *also* -ˌtän\ *n* **1** : 1000 tons **2** : an explosive force equivalent to that of 1000 tons of TNT

ki·lo·volt \-ˌvōlt\ *n* : 1000 volts

kilo·watt \ˈkil-ə-ˌwät\ *n* : 1000 watts

kilowatt–hour *n* : a unit of work or energy equal to that expended by one kilowatt in one hour or to 3.6 million joules

kilt \ˈkilt\ *n* **1** : a knee-length pleated skirt usually of tartan worn by men in Scotland **2** : a garment that resembles a Scottish kilt [Middle English *kilten* "to gather up (a skirt)," of Scandinavian origin] — **kilt·ed** \ˈkil-təd\ *adj*

kil·ter \ˈkil-tər\ *n* : proper condition : ORDER ⟨out of *kilter*⟩ [origin unknown]

kim·ber·lite \ˈkim-bər-ˌlīt\ *n* : a mineral especially of southern Africa that often contains diamonds [*Kimberley,* South Africa]

ki·mo·no \kə-ˈmō-nō, -nə\ *n, pl* **-nos** **1** : a loose robe with wide sleeves and a broad sash traditionally worn as an outer garment by the Japanese **2** : a loose dressing gown worn chiefly by women [Japanese, "clothes"]

kimono 1

[1]**kin** \ˈkin\ *n* **1** : a person's relatives : KINDRED **2** : KINSMAN [Old English *cynn*]

[2]**kin** *adj* : KINDRED, RELATED

-kin \kən\ *also* **-kins** \kənz\ *n suffix* : little ⟨nap*kin*⟩ [Dutch *-kin*]

[1]**kind** \ˈkīnd\ *n* **1 a** : a natural group : VARIETY ⟨different *kinds* of sharks⟩ **b** : a group united by common qualities, traits, or interests : CATEGORY **c** : a doubtful or barely admissible member of a category ⟨a *kind* of gray⟩ **2** : essential quality or character ⟨punishment different in *kind* rather than degree⟩ **3 a** : goods or commodities as distinguished from money **b** : the equivalent of what has been offered or received [Old English *cynd* "birth, nature"]

synonyms KIND, TYPE, SORT, NATURE mean a number of individuals thought of as a group because of common qualities. KIND may suggest natural grouping ⟨a zoo having animals of every *kind*⟩. TYPE may suggest strong and clearly marked similarity throughout the items included so that each is typical of the group ⟨one of three basic body *types*⟩. SORT often suggests some disparagement ⟨the *sort* of newspaper that prints sensational stories⟩. NATURE may imply inherent, essential resemblance rather than obvious or superficial likenesses ⟨two problems of a similar *nature*⟩.

[2]**kind** *adj* **1** : having the will to do good and to bring happiness to others **2** : showing or growing out of gentleness or goodness of heart ⟨a *kind* act⟩

kin·der·gar·ten \ˈkin-dər-ˌgärt-n, -də-, -ˌgärd-\ *n* : a school or class for children usually from four to six years old [German, from *Kinder* "children" + *Garten* "garden"]

kin·der·gart·ner \-ˌgärt-nər, -ˌgärd-\ *n* **1** : a kindergarten pupil **2** : a kindergarten teacher

kind·heart·ed \ˈkīnd-ˈhärt-əd\ *adj* : having or showing a kind and sympathetic nature — **kind·heart·ed·ly** *adv* — **kind·heart·ed·ness** *n*

kin·dle \ˈkin-dl\ *vb* **kin·dled; kin·dling** \-dliŋ, -dl-iŋ\ **1** : to set on fire or catch fire : start burning ⟨*kindle* a fire⟩ **2** : to stir up : AROUSE ⟨*kindle* anger⟩ **3** : to light up as if with flame : GLOW ⟨with *kindling* eyes⟩ [Old Norse *kynda*] — **kin·dler** \-dlər, -dl-ər\ *n*

kin·dling \ˈkin-dliŋ\ *n* : material that burns easily for starting a fire

[1]**kind·ly** \ˈkīn-dlē\ *adj* **kind·li·er; -est** **1** : of an agreeable or beneficial nature : PLEASANT ⟨*kindly* climate⟩ **2** : of a sympathetic or generous nature : FRIENDLY ⟨*kindly* people⟩ — **kind·li·ness** *n*

[2]**kindly** *adv* **1** : READILY ⟨does not take *kindly* to criticism⟩ **2 a** : in a kind manner **b** : as a gesture of goodwill **c** : in a gracious manner : COURTEOUSLY **d** : as a matter of courtesy : PLEASE ⟨would you *kindly* be seated⟩

kind·ness \ˈkīnd-nəs, ˈkīn-\ *n* **1** : a kind deed : FAVOR **2** : the quality or state of being kind

kind of \ˌkīn-dəv, -də\ *adv* : to a moderate degree : SOMEWHAT ⟨it's *kind of* cold in here⟩

[1]**kin·dred** \ˈkin-drəd\ *n* **1** : a group of related individuals **2** : a person's relatives [Middle English, from *kin* + Old English *rǣden* "condition," from *rǣdan* "to advise, read"]

[2]**kindred** *adj* : of like nature or character ⟨a *kindred* spirit⟩

kine \ˈkīn\ *archaic plural of* COW

ki·ne·sics \kə-ˈnē-siks, kī-, -ziks\ *n* : the study of body motions (as blushes, shrugs, or eye movement) that communicate [Greek *kinēsis* "motion" + English *-ics*]

ki·ne·si·ol·o·gy \kə-ˌnē-sē-ˈäl-ə-jē, kī-, -ˌnē-zē-\ *n* : the study of the mechanical and anatomical relations involved in human movement

-ki·ne·sis \kə-ˈnē-səs, kī-, ˌkī-\ *n combining form, pl* **-ki·ne·ses** \-ˌsēz\ : division ⟨karyo*kinesis*⟩ [Greek *kinēsis* "motion," from *kinein* "to move"]
kin·es·the·sia \ˌkin-əs-ˈthē-zhə, -zhē-ə\ *or* **kin·es·the·sis** \-ˈthē-səs\ *n, pl* **-the·sias** *or* **-the·ses** \-ˈthē-ˌsēz\ : the sensation of bodily position, movement, or effort arising from receptors in the joints, tendons, and muscles; *also* : the sense involved [Greek *kinein* "to move" + *aisthēsis* "perception"] — **kin·es·thet·ic** \-ˈthet-ik\ *adj* — **kin·es·thet·i·cal·ly** \-ˈthet-i-kə-lē, -klē\ *adv*
ki·net·ic \kə-ˈnet-ik, kī-\ *adj* : of or relating to the motion of material bodies and the forces and energy associated with them [Greek *kinētikos,* from *kinein* "to move"]
kinetic energy *n* : energy associated with motion
ki·net·ics \kə-ˈnet-iks, kī-\ *n sing or pl* **1** : a science that deals with the effects of forces upon the motions of material bodies or with changes in a physical or chemical system **2** : the means by which a physical or chemical change is effected
kinetic theory *n* : a theory that states that all matter is composed of particles in motion and that the rate of motion varies directly with the temperature
ki·net·o·chore \kə-ˈnet-ə-ˌkȯr\ *n* : a structure on the centromere to which the spindle fibers attach during mitosis and meiosis [Greek *kinētos* "moving" + *chōros* "place"]
kin·folk \ˈkin-ˌfōk\ *n* : a person's relatives
king \ˈking\ *n* **1** : a male ruler of a country; *esp* : one whose position is hereditary and who rules for life **2** *cap* **a** : GOD 1 **b** : CHRIST **3** : one that holds a dominant position; *esp* : a chief among competitors **4** : the principal piece in a set of chessmen that can move ordinarily one square in any direction and has the power to capture but may never enter or remain in check **5** : a playing card bearing the stylized figure of a king **6** : a checker that has been crowned [Old English *cyning*]
king·bird \-ˌbərd\ *n* : any of several American tyrant flycatchers
king crab *n* **1** : HORSESHOE CRAB **2** : any of several very large crabs; *esp* : one of the northern Pacific Ocean caught for food
king·dom \ˈking-dəm\ *n* **1** : a country whose ruler is a king or queen **2** : a sphere in which something or someone is dominant **3 a** : one of the three primary divisions into which natural objects are classified — compare ANIMAL KINGDOM, MINERAL KINGDOM, PLANT KINGDOM **b** : a major category (as Plantae) in biological taxonomy that ranks above the phylum and below the domain
kingdom come *n* : a destroyed state ⟨blew it to *kingdom come*⟩
king·fish \ˈking-ˌfish\ *n* : any of various sea fishes (as a king mackerel)
king·fish·er \-ˌfish-ər\ *n* : any of various usually crested and bright-colored birds with a short tail and a long stout sharp bill
King James Version \-ˈjāmz-\ *n* : AUTHORIZED VERSION
king·let \ˈking-lət\ *n* : any of several small insect-eating birds
king·ly \ˈking-lē\ *adj* **1** : having royal rank **2** : of, relating to, or befitting a king — **king·li·ness** *n* — **kingly** *adv*
king mackerel *n* : a mackerel of the warmer waters of the Atlantic Ocean that is a food and sport fish
king·pin \ˈking-ˌpin\ *n* **1** : the number 5 bowling pin **2** : the chief person in a group or undertaking
king post *n* : a vertical member connecting the apex of a triangular truss with the base
Kings \ˈkingz\ *n* : either of two narrative and historical books of canonical Jewish and Christian Scriptures — see BIBLE table
King's English *n* : standard or correct English speech or usage
king·ship \ˈking-ˌship\ *n* **1** : the position, office, or dignity of a king **2** : the quality of being a king **3** : government by a king
king–size \ˈking-ˌsīz\ *or* **king–sized** \-ˌsīzd\ *adj* : longer or larger than the usual or standard size
king snake *n* : any of numerous harmless brightly marked large snakes chiefly of the southern and central U.S.
king's ransom *n* : a very large sum of money
[1]**kink** \ˈkingk\ *n* **1** : a short tight twist or curl **2** : a mental or physical peculiarity : QUIRK **3** : a cramp or stiffness in some part of the body : CRICK **4** : an imperfection (as in design) likely to cause difficulties in operation [Dutch]
[2]**kink** *vb* : to form a kink : make a kink in
kin·ka·jou \ˈking-kə-ˌjü\ *n* : a slender long-tailed nocturnal mammal of Central and South America that is related to the raccoon, lives in trees, and has yellowish brown fur and a prehensile tail [French, alteration of *quincajou* "wolverine"]
kinky \ˈking-kē\ *adj* **kink·i·er; -est** **1** : tightly twisted or curled **2** : involving or liking unusual sexual behavior — **kink·i·ness** *n*
-kins — see -KIN
kins·folk \ˈkinz-ˌfōk\ *n pl* : a person's relatives
kin·ship \ˈkin-ˌship\ *n* : the quality or state of being kin
kins·man \ˈkinz-mən\ *n* : RELATIVE 3; *esp* : a male relative
kins·wom·an \ˈkinz-ˌwu̇m-ən\ *n* : a female relative
ki·osk \ˈkē-ˌäsk, kē-ˈ\ *n* **1** : an open summerhouse or pavilion **2** : a small light structure with one or more open sides used especially as a newsstand or a telephone booth **3** : a small structure that provides information and services on a computer screen [Turkish *köşk,* from Persian *kūshk* "portico"]

kinkajou

Ki·o·wa \ˈkī-ə-ˌwȯ, -ˌwä\ *n, pl* **Kiowa** *or* **Kiowas** **1** : a member of an American Indian people of what are now Colorado, Kansas, New Mexico, Oklahoma, and Texas **2** : the language of the Kiowa people
[1]**kip·per** \ˈkip-ər\ *n* : a kippered herring or salmon [Old English *cypera* "spawning salmon"]
[2]**kipper** *vt* **kip·pered; kip·per·ing** \ˈkip-ring, -ə-ring\ : to cure by salting and smoking
Kir·ghiz \kiər-ˈgēz\ *n, pl* **Kirghiz** *or* **Kir·ghiz·es** : a member of a Turkic people of Kyrgyzstan and adjacent areas of central Asia
kirk \ˈkiərk, ˈkərk\ *n* **1** *chiefly Scottish* : CHURCH 1 **2** *cap* : the national church of Scotland as distinguished from the Church of England or the Episcopal Church in Scotland [Old Norse *kirkja,* from Old English *cirice*]
kir·tle \ˈkərt-l\ *n* **1** : a tunic or coat worn by men especially in the Middle Ages **2** : a long gown or dress worn by a woman [Old English *cyrtel*]
[1]**kiss** \ˈkis\ *vb* **1** : to touch with the lips as a mark of affection or greeting **2** : to touch gently or lightly ⟨a soft wind *kissing* the trees⟩ [Old English *cyssan*] — **kiss·able** \-ə-bəl\ *adj*
[2]**kiss** *n* **1** : a caress with the lips **2** : a gentle touch or contact **3 a** : a small cookie made of meringue **b** : a bite-size candy
kiss·er \ˈkis-ər\ *n* **1** : one that kisses **2** *slang* : MOUTH 1; *also* : FACE 1
kissing bug *n* : any of various large bloodsucking bugs including some capable of inflicting painful bites
[1]**kit** \ˈkit\ *n* **1 a** : a collection of articles for personal use **b** : a set of tools or supplies **c** : a set of parts to be assembled ⟨model-airplane *kit*⟩ **d** : a packaged collection of related material ⟨convention *kit*⟩ **2** : a container (as a bag or case) for a kit **3** : a group of persons or things — used in the phrase *the whole kit and caboodle* [Middle English, "wooden tub"]
[2]**kit** *n* **1** : KITTEN **2** : a young or undersized fur-bearing animal; *also* : its pelt
[3]**kit** *n* : a small narrow violin [origin unknown]
kitch·en \ˈkich-ən\ *n* : a place (as a room) with cooking facilities [Old English *cycene,* from Late Latin *coquina,* from Latin *coquere* "to cook"]
kitchen cabinet *n* **1** : a cupboard with drawers and shelves for use in a kitchen **2** : an informal group of advisers to the head of a government
kitch·en·ette \ˌkich-ə-ˈnet\ *n* : a small kitchen or an alcove containing cooking facilities
kitchen garden *n* : a garden of vegetables for personal use
kitchen midden *n* : a refuse heap; *esp* : a mound (as of shells or bones) marking the site of a prehistoric human habitation
kitchen police *n* : KP
kitch·en·ware \ˈkich-ən-ˌwaər, -ˌweər\ *n* : utensils and appliances for use in a kitchen
kite \ˈkīt\ *n* **1** : any of various usually small hawks with long narrow wings and a deeply forked tail **2** : a light frame covered with paper, plastic, or cloth, often provided with a balancing tail, and designed to be flown in the air at the end of a long string [Old English *cȳta*]
kit fox *n* : SWIFT FOX; *also* : a fox of the southwestern U.S. and Mexico with very large ears and a black-tipped tail that is often considered to be a subspecies of the swift fox
kith \ˈkith\ *n* : familiar friends, neighbors, or relatives ⟨*kith* and kin⟩ [Old English *cȳthth,* from *cūth* "known"]

kitsch \ˈkich\ *n* : something that appeals to popular or lowbrow taste and is often of poor quality [German]

kit·ten \ˈkit-n\ *n* : a young cat; *also* : a young individual of various other small mammals [Middle English *kitoun,* derived from Late Latin *cattus* "cat"]

kit·ten·ish \ˈkit-nish, -n-ish\ *adj* : resembling a kitten; *esp* : PLAYFUL — **kit·ten·ish·ly** *adv* — **kit·ten·ish·ness** *n*

kit·ti·wake \ˈkit-ē-ˌwāk\ *n* : either of two cliff-nesting gulls that winter on the open ocean [imitative]

[1]**kit·ty** \ˈkit-ē\ *n, pl* **kitties** : CAT 1a; *esp* : KITTEN

[2]**kitty** *n, pl* **kitties** **1** : a fund in a poker game made up of contributions from each pot **2** : a sum of money or a collection of goods made up of small contributions : POOL [[1]*kit*]

kit·ty–cor·ner *also* **cat·ty–cor·ner** *or* **cat·er·cor·ner** \ˈkit-ē-ˌkȯr-nər, ˈkat-, ˈkat-ə-\ *or* **kit·ty–cor·nered** *or* **cat·ty–cor·nered** *or* **cat·er·cor·nered** \-nərd\ *adv or adj* : in a crosswire position : or a diagonal line ⟨the house stood *kitty-corner* across the square⟩ [*kitty-corner* alteration of *cater-corner,* from obsolete *cater* "four"]

ki·va \ˈkē-və\ *n* : a Pueblo Indian ceremonial structure that is usually round and partly underground [Hopi]

Ki·wa·ni·an \kə-ˈwän-ē-ən\ *n* : a member of one of the major national and international service clubs

ki·wi \ˈkē-ˌwē\ *n* **1** : a flightless New Zealand bird with rudimentary wings, stout legs, a long bill, and grayish brown hairlike plumage **2** : KIWIFRUIT [Maori]

kiwi 1

ki·wi·fruit \-ˌfrüt\ *n* : the edible fruit of a Chinese vine having a fuzzy brown skin and slightly tart green flesh

Klan \ˈklan\ *n* : an organization of Ku Kluxers; *also* : a subordinate unit of such an organization — **Klansman** \ˈklanz-mən\ *n*

Klee·nex \ˈklē-ˌneks\ *trademark* — used for a cleansing tissue

klep·to·ma·nia \ˌklep-tə-ˈmā-nē-ə, -nyə\ *n* : a persistent abnormal impulse to steal especially without economic motive [Greek *kleptein* "to steal"] — **klep·to·ma·ni·ac** \-nē-ˌak\ *adj or n*

klez·mer \ˈklez-mər\ *n, pl* **klez·mo·rim** \klez-ˈmȯr-əm\ **1** : a Jewish instrumentalist especially of traditional eastern European music **2** : the music played by klezmorim [Yiddish, from Hebrew *kĕlēy zemer* musical instruments]

klieg light *or* **kleig light** \ˈklēg-ˈlīt\ *n* : an arc lamp used in taking motion pictures [John H. *Kliegl,* died 1959, and Anton T. *Kliegl,* died 1927, German-born American lighting experts]

klutz \ˈkləts\ *n* : a clumsy person [Yiddish *klots,* literally, "wooden beam"] — **klutz·i·ness** \ˈklət-sē-nəs\ *n* — **klutzy** \ˈklət-sē\ *adj*

knack \ˈnak\ *n* **1** : a clever way of doing something : TRICK **2** : a natural ability [Middle English *knak*] ***synonyms*** see TALENT

knack·er \ˈnak-ər\ *n, British* : a buyer of worn-out animals or their carcasses especially for use as animal feed and fertilizer [probably from English dialect *knacker* "saddle maker"]

knap·sack \ˈnap-ˌsak\ *n* : a case strapped on the back to carry supplies or personal belongings [Low German *knappsack,* from *knappen* "to eat" + *sack* "bag"]

knap·weed \ˈnap-ˌwēd\ *n* : any of several weedy plants related to the cornflower [Middle English *knopwed,* from *knop* "knob" + *wed* "weed"]

knave \ˈnāv\ *n* **1** *archaic* **a** : a male servant **b** : a man of humble birth or position **2** : a tricky deceitful person : ROGUE **3** : JACK 5 [Old English *cnafa* "boy, servant"]

knav·ery \ˈnāv-rē, -ə-rē\ *n, pl* **-er·ies** **1** : the practices of a knave : RASCALITY **2** : a roguish or mischievous act

knav·ish \ˈnā-vish\ *adj* : of, relating to, or characteristic of a knave; *esp* : DISHONEST — **knav·ish·ly** *adv*

knead \ˈnēd\ *vt* **1** : to work and press into a mass with or as if with the hands **2** : to form or shape as if by kneading [Old English *cnedan*] — **knead·er** *n*

[1]**knee** \ˈnē\ *n* **1** : the joint or region in the middle part of the human leg in which the femur, tibia, and kneecap come together; *also* : a corresponding part of a four-footed animal **2** : something resembling the human knee; *esp* : a cone-shaped process rising from the roots of various swamp-growing trees (as a cypress of the southern U.S.) **3** : the part of a garment covering the knee [Old English *cnēow*] — **kneed** \ˈnēd\ *adj* — **to one's knees** : into a state of submission or defeat

[2]**knee** *vt* **kneed; knee·ing** : to strike with the knee

knee·cap \ˈnē-ˌkap\ *n* : a thick flat triangular bone that forms the front part of the knee and protects the front of the joint — called also *patella*

knee–deep \-ˈdēp\ *adj* : sunk to the knees ⟨*knee-deep* in mud⟩

knee–high \-ˈhī\ *adj* : rising or reaching upward to the knees

knee·hole \-ˌhōl\ *n* : a space (as under a desk) for the knees

knee–jerk \ˈnē-ˌjərk\ *adj* : readily predictable : AUTOMATIC ⟨*knee-jerk* reactions⟩; *also* : reacting in a predictable way ⟨*knee-jerk* political opponents⟩

knee jerk *n* : an involuntary forward kick produced by a light blow on the tendon below the kneecap

kneel \ˈnēl\ *vi* **knelt** \ˈnelt\ *or* **kneeled** \ˈnēld\; **kneel·ing** : to bend the knee : fall or rest on the knees [Old English *cnēowlian*] — **kneel·er** *n*

[1]**knell** \ˈnel\ *vb* **1** : to ring especially for a death, funeral, or disaster : TOLL **2** : to sound as a knell **3** : to summon or announce by or as if by a knell [Old English *cnyllan*]

[2]**knell** *n* **1** : a stroke or sound of a bell especially when rung slowly for a death, funeral, or disaster **2** : an indication of the end or failure of something ⟨sounded the death *knell* for our hopes⟩

knew *past of* KNOW

knick·er·bock·er \ˈnik-ər-ˌbäk-ər, ˈnik-ə-ˌ\ *n* **1** *cap* : a native or resident of the city or state of New York; *esp* : a descendant of the early Dutch settlers of New York **2** *pl* : KNICKERS [Diedrich *Knickerbocker,* fictitious author of *History of New York* (1809) by Washington Irving]

knick·ers \ˈnik-ərz\ *n pl* : loose-fitting short pants gathered just below the knee [short for *knickerbockers*]

knick·knack *also* **nick·nack** \ˈnik-ˌnak\ *n* : a small article intended for ornament [reduplication of *knack*]

[1]**knife** \ˈnīf\ *n, pl* **knives** \ˈnīvz\ **1 a** : a cutting instrument consisting of a sharp blade fastened to a handle **b** : a weapon resembling a knife **2** : a sharp cutting blade or tool in a machine [Old English *cnīf*]

[2]**knife** *vb* **1** : to stab, slash, or wound with a knife **2** : to move like a knife ⟨*knifed* through the water⟩

knife–edge \ˈnī-ˌfej\ *n* : a sharp wedge usually of steel used as a fulcrum for a lever beam in a precision instrument (as a balance)

[1]**knight** \ˈnīt\ *n* **1 a** : a mounted warrior of feudal times serving a superior (as a king); *esp* : one who after a period of early service has been awarded a special military rank and has sworn to obey certain rules of conduct **b** : a man honored by a sovereign for merit and in Great Britain ranking below a baronet **c** : a person of another age or area resembling a medieval knight in rank or way of life **d** : a member of any of various orders or societies **e** : a man devoted to the service of a lady as her attendant or champion **2** : a chess piece that has an L-shaped move of two squares in any row and one square in a perpendicular row over squares that may be occupied [Old English *cniht* "boy, warrior"]

[2]**knight** *vt* : to make a knight of

knight–er·rant \ˈnīt-ˈer-ənt\ *n, pl* **knights–errant** : a knight traveling in search of adventures in which to exhibit his military skill and generosity — **knight–er·rant·ry** \ˈnīt-ˈer-ən-trē\ *n*

knight·hood \ˈnīt-ˌhu̇d\ *n* **1** : the rank, dignity, or profession of a knight **2** : the qualities befitting a knight **3** : knights as a class or body

knight·ly \ˈnīt-lē\ *adj* **1** : of, relating to, or characteristic of a knight **2** : made up of knights — **knight·li·ness** *n* — **knight·ly** *adv*

Knight of Co·lum·bus \-kə-ˈləm-bəs\ *n, pl* **Knights of Columbus** : a member of a fraternal and benevolent society of Roman Catholic men [Christopher *Columbus*]

Knight Templar *n, pl* **Knights Templars** *or* **Knights Templar** **1** : TEMPLAR 1 **2** : a member of an order of Freemasonry

\ə\ abut	\au̇\ out	\i\ tip	\ȯ\ saw	\u̇\ foot
\ər\ further	\ch\ chin	\ī\ life	\ȯi\ coin	\y\ yet
\a\ mat	\e\ pet	\j\ job	\th\ thin	\yü\ few
\ā\ take	\ē\ easy	\ng\ sing	\t͟h\ this	\yu̇\ cure
\ä\ cot, cart	\g\ go	\ō\ bone	\ü\ food	\zh\ vision

knish \kə-ˈnish\ *n* : a small round or square piece of dough stuffed with a filling (as potato) and baked or fried [Yiddish, from Polish *knysz*]

[1]**knit** \ˈnit\ *vb* **knit** *or* **knit·ted; knit·ting** **1** : to form a fabric or garment by interlacing yarn or thread in connected loops with needles ⟨*knit* a sweater⟩ **2** : to draw or come together closely as if knitted : unite firmly ⟨wait for a broken bone to *knit*⟩ **3** : WRINKLE ⟨*knit* one's brows⟩ **4** : to bind by some tie ⟨*knit* by common interests⟩ [Old English *cnyttan*] — **knit·ter** *n*

[2]**knit** *n* **1** : KNIT STITCH **2 a** : a knit fabric **b** *pl* : KNITWEAR

knit stitch *n* : a basic knitting stitch usually made with the yarn at the back of the work by inserting the right needle into the front part of a loop on the left needle from the left side, catching the yarn with the point of the right needle, and bringing it through the first loop to form a new loop — compare PURL STITCH

knit·ting *n* **1** : the action or method of one that knits **2** : work done or being done by one that knits

knitting needle *n* : a slender rod (as of plastic or metal) with one or both ends pointed used for hand knitting

knit·wear \ˈnit-ˌwaər, -ˌweər\ *n* : knitted clothing

knob \ˈnäb\ *n* **1 a** : a rounded bulge : LUMP **b** : a small rounded ornament or handle **2** : a rounded usually isolated hill or mountain [Middle English *knobbe*] — **knobbed** \ˈnäbd\ *adj* — **knob·by** \ˈnäb-ē\ *adj*

[1]**knock** \ˈnäk\ *vb* **1 a** : to strike something with a sharp blow **b** : to drive, force, or make by so striking **2** : to collide with something **3 a** : BUSTLE ⟨*knocked* around in the kitchen most of the afternoon⟩ **b** : WANDER ⟨*knocked* about the world for years⟩ **4** : to make a pounding noise especially as a result of abnormal ignition ⟨an automobile engine that *knocks*⟩ **5** : to find fault with ⟨always *knocking* her teammates⟩ [Old English *cnocian*] — **knock cold** : KNOCK OUT 1 — **knock dead** : to move strongly especially to admiration or applause ⟨a performer who really *knocked* them *dead*⟩ — **knock for a loop** : to cause to be overwhelmed : SHOCK — **knock together** : to make or assemble especially hurriedly or in a makeshift way

[2]**knock** *n* **1 a** : a sharp blow **b** : a severe misfortune or hardship **2 a** : a pounding noise **b** : a sharp metallic noise in an automobile engine caused by abnormal ignition

[1]**knock·about** \ˈnäk-ə-ˌbau̇t\ *adj* **1** : suitable for rough use **2** : being noisy and rough ⟨*knockabout* games⟩

[2]**knockabout** *n* : a sloop with a simple rig and no bowsprit and topmast

[1]**knock·down** \ˈnäk-ˌdau̇n\ *n* **1** : a knocking down of something or someone (as a boxer) **2** : something that strikes down or overwhelms **3** : something easily assembled or disassembled

[2]**knockdown** *adj* **1** : having such force as to strike down or overwhelm **2** : that can easily be assembled or disassembled

knock down \näk-ˈdau̇n, ˈnäk-\ *vt* **1** : to strike to the ground with or as if with a sharp blow **2** : to dispose of to a bidder at an auction sale **3** : to take apart : DISASSEMBLE

knock·er \ˈnäk-ər\ *n* : one that knocks; *esp* : a device hinged to a door for use in knocking

knock–knee \ˈnäk-ˈnē, -ˌnē\ *n* : a condition in which the legs curve inward at the knees — **knock–kneed** \-ˈnēd\ *adj*

knock off *vb* : to discontinue doing something : STOP

knock·out \ˈnäk-ˌau̇t\ *n* **1 a** : the act of knocking out : the condition of being knocked out **b** : a blow that knocks out an opponent **2** : something or someone sensationally striking or attractive — **knockout** *adj*

knock out \näk-ˈau̇t, ˈnäk-\ *vt* **1** : to make unconscious **2** : to make inoperative or useless

knock over *vt* : STEAL: **a** : HIJACK 1 **b** : ROB 1

knock·wurst \ˈnäk-wərst, -ˌwu̇rst\ *n* : a short thick sausage [German *Knackwurst,* from *knacken* "to crackle (when being fried)" + *Wurst* "sausage"]

knoll \ˈnōl\ *n* : a small round hill : MOUND [Old English *cnoll*]

[1]**knot** \ˈnät\ *n* **1** : an interlacing (as of string or ribbon) that forms a lump or knob **2** : something hard to solve : PROBLEM **3** : a bond of union; *esp* : the marriage bond **4 a** : a projecting lump or swelling in tissue **b** : the base of a woody branch enclosed in the stem from which it arises; *also* : its section in lumber **5** : a cluster of persons or things : GROUP **6** : one nautical mile per hour [Old English *cnotta*]

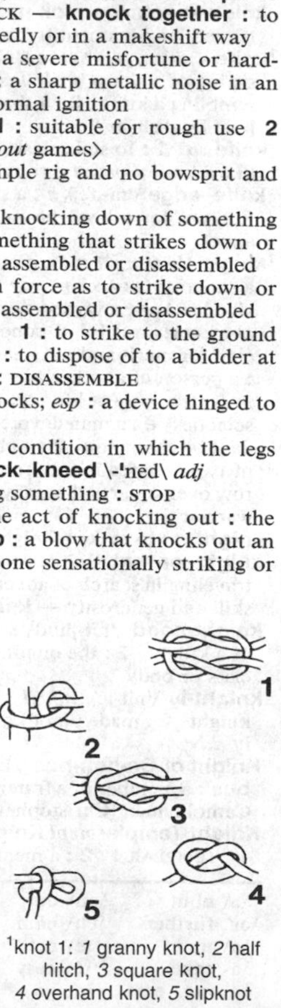
[1]knot 1: *1* granny knot, *2* half hitch, *3* square knot, *4* overhand knot, *5* slipknot

[2]**knot** *vb* **knot·ted; knot·ting** **1** : to tie in or with a knot : form knots in **2** : to unite closely or intricately : ENTANGLE

[3]**knot** *n* : either of two sandpipers that breed in the Arctic and winter in temperate or warm regions [Middle English *knott*]

knot·grass \ˈnät-ˌgras\ *n* : a weed related to buckwheat with jointed stems, bluish gray grassy leaves, and tiny flowers

knot·hole \-ˌhōl\ *n* : a hole in a board or tree trunk where a knot has come out

knot·ted *adj* **1** : tied in or with a knot **2** : full of knots : GNARLED **3** : KNOTTY 2 **4** : ornamented with knots or knobs

knot·ty \ˈnät-ē\ *adj* **knot·ti·er; -est** **1** : marked by or full of knots **2** : puzzling because of intricacy : COMPLEX

knout \ˈnau̇t, ˈnüt\ *n* : a whip for flogging criminals [Russian *knut,* of Scandinavian origin]

[1]**know** \ˈnō\ *vb* **knew** \ˈnü, ˈnyü\; **known** \ˈnōn\; **know·ing** **1 a** (1) : to perceive directly : have direct awareness of (2) : to have understanding of ⟨*know* yourself⟩ (3) : to recognize the nature of ⟨*knew* them to be honest⟩ **b** (1) : to perceive and remember the identity of : RECOGNIZE ⟨*knew* me by my walk⟩ (2) : to be acquainted or familiar with (3) : to have experience of **2 a** : to be able to declare truthfully ⟨*know* that the earth is round⟩ **b** : to have a practical understanding of ⟨*knows* how to write⟩ **3** : to have knowledge ⟨ask someone who *knows*⟩ **4** : to be or become aware ⟨*knew* about us⟩ [Old English *cnāwan*] — **know·able** \ˈnō-ə-bəl\ *adj* — **know·er** \ˈnō-ər, ˈnōr\ *n*

[2]**know** *n* : KNOWLEDGE — **in the know** : well-informed; *esp* : having confidential or exclusive information

know–how \ˈnō-ˌhau̇\ *n* : knowledge of how to do something smoothly and efficiently

[1]**know·ing** \ˈnō-ing\ *n* : ACQUAINTANCE 1, COGNIZANCE

[2]**knowing** *adj* **1** : having or reflecting knowledge, information, or intelligence ⟨a *knowing* glance⟩ **2** : shrewdly and keenly alert **3** : INTENTIONAL — **know·ing·ly** \-ing-lē\ *adv*

know–it–all \ˈnō-ət-ˌȯl\ *n* : a person who claims to know everything and needs no advice

knowl·edge \ˈnäl-ij\ *n* **1** : understanding gained by actual experience ⟨a *knowledge* of carpentry⟩ **2 a** : the state of being aware of something or of having information **b** : the range of one's information or awareness ⟨to the best of my *knowledge*⟩ **3** : the act of understanding : clear perception of truth **4** : the sum of what is known : the body of truth, information, and principles acquired by mankind [Middle English *knowlege* "acknowledgment, cognizance," from *knowlechen* "to acknowledge," from *knowen* "to know"]

knowl·edge·able \ˈnäl-i-jə-bəl\ *adj* : having or exhibiting knowledge or intelligence : WISE — **knowl·edge·able·ness** *n* — **knowl·edge·ably** \-blē\ *adv*

knowledge engineering *n* : a branch of artificial intelligence that emphasizes the development and use of expert systems — **knowledge engineer** *n*

known *adj* : generally recognized ⟨a *known* authority on art⟩

know–noth·ing \ˈnō-ˌnəth-ing\ *n* **1** : IGNORAMUS **2** *cap K&N* : a member of a 19th-century secret American political organization hostile to the political influence of recent immigrants and Roman Catholics

[1]**knuck·le** \ˈnək-əl\ *n* **1** : the rounded lump formed by the ends of two bones where they come together in a joint; *esp* : such a lump at a finger joint **2** : a cut of meat consisting of a tarsal or carpal joint with the adjoining flesh **3** *pl* : a set of joined metal finger rings worn over the front of the fist for use as a weapon — called also *brass knuckles* [Middle English *knokel*]

[2]**knuckle** *vi* **knuck·led; knuck·ling** \ˈnək-ling, -ə-ling\ : to place the knuckles on the ground in shooting a marble

knuck·le·ball \ˈnək-əl-ˌbȯl\ *n* : a slow baseball pitch that moves erratically and unpredictably and that is thrown with little spin by gripping the ball with the knuckles or the tips of the fingers pressed against the top

knuck·le·bone \ˈnək-əl-ˌbōn\ *n* : a bone of a knuckle joint

knuckle down *vi* : to apply oneself earnestly

knuckle under *vi* : to give in : SUBMIT

knurl \ˈnərl\ *n* **1** : a small protuberance or knob **2** : one of a series of small ridges or beads on a metal surface (as of a thumbscrew) to aid in gripping [probably blend of *knur* "gnarl" (from Middle English *knorre*) and *gnarl*] — **knurled** \ˈnərld\ *adj* — **knurly** \ˈnər-lē\ *adj*

[1]**KO** \kā-ˈō, ˈkā-ō\ *n, pl* **KO's** : a knockout in boxing [*k*nock *o*ut]

[2]**KO** *vt* **KO'd; KO'·ing** : to knock out in boxing

ko·ala \kō-ˈäl-ə, kə-ˈwäl-ə\ *n* : an Australian tree-dwelling marsupial that has large hairy ears, thick gray fur, sharp claws for climbing, and no tail and feeds on eucalyptus leaves — called also *koala bear* [from a word in Dharuk, an Australian aboriginal language formerly spoken around Port Jackson]

ko·bold \ˈkō-ˌbȯld\ *n* **1** : a gnome that in German folklore inhabits underground places **2** : an often mischievous spirit of German folklore [German]

Koch's postulates \ˈkȯks-\ *n pl* : a statement of the four steps required to identify a microorganism as the cause of a disease [Robert *Koch,* died 1910, German bacteriologist]

ko·di·ak bear \ˈkōd-ē-ˌak-\ *n* : a large brown bear of the southern coast of Alaska and nearby islands [*Kodiak* Island, Alaska]

kohl \ˈkōl\ *n* : a preparation used especially in Arabia and Egypt to darken the edges of the eyelids [Arabic *kuḥl*]

kohl·ra·bi \kōl-ˈräb-ē, -ˈrab-\ *n, pl* **-bies** : a cabbage that forms no head but has a swollen fleshy edible stem [German, from Italian *cavolo rapa,* from *cavolo* "cabbage" + *rapa* "turnip"]

kohlrabi

koi \ˈkȯi\ *n* : a carp bred for a variety of colors and often stocked in ornamental ponds [Japanese]

ko·la nut \ˈkō-lə-\ *n* : the bitter seed of an African tree containing much caffeine and used in beverages and medicine for its stimulant effect [of African origin]

ko·lin·sky \kə-ˈlin-skē\ *n, pl* **-skies** **1** : any of several Asian weasels **2** : the fur or pelt of a kolinsky [origin unknown]

kol·khoz \käl-ˈkȯz, -ˈkȯs\ *n, pl* **kol·kho·zy** \-ˈkȯ-zē\ *or* **kol·khoz·es** : a collective farm of the former Union of Soviet Socialist Republics — compare SOVKHOZ [Russian, from *kol*lektivnoe *khoz*yaĭstvo "collective farm"]

Kol Nidre \kōl-ˈnid-rā\ *n* : an Aramaic prayer chanted in the synagogue on the eve of Yom Kippur [Aramaic *kol nidhrē* "all the vows"; from its opening phrase]

Ko·mo·do dragon \kə-ˈmōd-ō-\ *n* : an Indonesian lizard that is the largest of all known lizards and may reach 10 feet (3 meters) in length [*Komodo* Island, Indonesia]

koodoo *variant of* KUDU

kook \ˈkük\ *n* : a person whose ideas or actions are eccentric or crazy [from *cuckoo*] — **kooky** \ˈkü-kē\ *adj*

kook·a·bur·ra \ˈku̇k-ə-ˌbər-ə, ˈku̇k-, -ˌbə-rə\ *n* : an Australian kingfisher that is about the size of a crow and has a call resembling loud laughter [Wiradhuri (Australian aboriginal language of central New South Wales) *gugubarra*]

ko·peck *or* **ko·pek** \ˈkō-ˌpek\ *n* **1** : a monetary unit equal to 1/100 ruble **2** : a coin representing one kopeck [Russian *kopeĭka*]

Ko·ran \kə-ˈran, -ˈrän; ˈkōr-ˌan, ˈkȯr-\ *n* : the book composed of sacred writings accepted by Muslims as revelations made to Muhammad by Allah [Arabic *qur'ān*] — **Ko·ran·ic** \kə-ˈran-ik\ *adj*

Ko·re·an \kə-ˈrē-ən\ *n* **1** : a native or inhabitant of Korea **2** : the language of the Korean people — **Korean** *adj*

ko·ru·na \ˈkȯr-ə-ˌnä, ˈkär-\ *n, pl* **ko·ru·ny** \-ə-nē\ *or* **korunas** *or* **ko·run** \-ən\ **1** : the basic monetary unit of the Czech republic and Slovakia **2** : a coin representing one koruna [Czech, literally, "crown," from Latin *corona*]

[1]**ko·sher** \ˈkō-shər\ *adj* **1 a** : accepted by Jewish law; *esp* : ritually fit for use **b** : selling or serving food ritually fit according to Jewish law **2** : PROPER 1 ⟨made sure the deal was *kosher*⟩ [Yiddish, from Hebrew *kāshēr* "fit, proper"]

[2]**kosher** *vt* **ko·shered; ko·sher·ing** \-shə-riŋ, -shriŋ\ : to make kosher

kou·miss *or* **ku·miss** \kü-ˈmis, ˈkü-məs\ *n* : a fermented milk beverage made originally by the nomadic peoples of central Asia from mare's milk [Russian *kumys*]

[1]**kow·tow** \kau̇-ˈtau̇, ˈkau̇-ˌ\ *n* : an act of kowtowing [Chinese (Beijing dialect) *kòutóu,* from *kòu* "to to knock" + *tóu* "head"]

[2]**kowtow** *vi* **1** : to kneel and touch the forehead to the ground to show honor, worship, or deep respect **2** : to show slavish respect

KP \ˈkā-ˈpē\ *n, pl* **KPs** **1** : the military duty of helping to prepare, serve, and clean up after meals **2** : a person assigned to KP [*k*itchen *p*olice]

[1]**kraal** \ˈkrȯl, ˈkräl\ *n* **1** : a village of southern African natives **2** : an enclosure for domestic animals especially in southern Africa [Afrikaans, from Portuguese *curral* "enclosure, corral"]

[2]**kraal** *vt* : to pen in a kraal

kraft \ˈkraft\ *n* : a strong paper or cardboard used especially for boxes and paper bags [German, literally, "strength"]

krait \ˈkrīt\ *n* : any of several brightly banded extremely venomous Asian snakes [Hindi & Urdu *karait*]

kra·ken \ˈkräk-ən\ *n* : a sea monster of Scandinavian legend [Norwegian]

K ration \ˈkā-\ *n* : a lightweight packaged ration of emergency foods developed for the U.S. armed forces in World War II [probably alteration of *C-ration* (a canned ration), but taken as initial of Ancel B. *K*eys, born 1904, American physiologist]

kraut \ˈkrau̇t\ *n* : SAUERKRAUT

Krebs cycle \ˈkrebz-\ *n* : a sequence of reactions in the living organism in which oxidation of acetyl groups of acetyl-CoA to carbon dioxide provides energy stored in ATP — called also *citric acid cycle* [H. A. *Krebs,* died 1900, German-born British biochemist]

krem·lin \ˈkrem-lən\ *n* **1** : the citadel of a Russian city **2** *cap* : the Russian government [derived from Russian *kreml';* sense 2 from the *Kremlin,* citadel of Moscow and governing center of the Soviet Union and post-Soviet Russia]

kreu·zer \ˈkrȯit-sər\ *n* : a small coin formerly used in Austria and Germany [German]

krill \ˈkril\ *n* : small planktonic crustaceans and their larvae that form a major food of baleen whales [Norwegian *kril* "recently hatched fishes"]

kris \ˈkrēs\ *n* : a Malay or Indonesian dagger with a ridged and twisting blade [Malay *kĕris*]

kris

[1]**kro·na** \ˈkrō-nə\ *n, pl* **kro·nur** \-nər\ **1** : the basic monetary unit of Iceland **2** : a coin representing one krona [Icelandic *krōna,* literally, "crown"]

[2]**kro·na** \ˈkrō-nə, ˈkrü-\ *n, pl* **kro·nor** \-ˌnȯr, -nər\ **1** : the basic monetary unit of Sweden **2** : a coin representing one krona [Swedish, literally, "crown"]

[1]**kro·ne** \ˈkrō-nə\ *n, pl* **kro·nen** \-nən\ **1** : the basic monetary unit of Austria from 1892 to 1925 **2** : a coin representing one krone [German, literally, "crown"]

[2]**kro·ne** \ˈkrō-nə\ *n, pl* **kro·ner** \-nər\ **1** : the basic monetary unit of Denmark and Norway **2** : a coin representing one krone [Danish, literally, "crown"]

kryp·ton \ˈkrip-ˌtän\ *n* : a colorless inert gaseous chemical element found in air and used especially in electric lamps — see ELEMENT table [Greek *kryptos* "hidden," from *kryptein* "to hide"]

K–T \ˈkā-ˈtē-\ *adj* : of, relating to, or occurring at the K-T boundary ⟨*K-T* extinctions⟩

K–T boundary *n* : the transition between the Cretaceous and Tertiary periods of geologic time marked by the extinction of many species including the dinosaurs; *also* : a geologic layer marking this boundary [*K* (alternative for *C* as abbreviation for *Cretaceous*) + Tertiary]

ku·do \ˈkyüd-ō, ˈküd-\ *n, pl* **kudos** : AWARD, HONOR [back-formation from *kudos* (taken as a plural)]

usage *Kudos* was introduced into English in the 19th century; it was used in contexts where a reader unfamiliar with Greek could not be sure whether it was singular or plural. By the 1920s it began to appear as a plural, and about 25 years later, *kudo* began to appear. Some commentators hold that since *kudos* is a singular word it cannot be used as a plural and that the word *kudo* is impossible. But *kudo* does exist; it is simply one of the most recent words created by back-formation from another word misunderstood as a plural, as *cherry* and *pea* were.

ku·dos \ˈkyü-ˌdäs, ˈkü-, -ˌdōs\ *n* : FAME, GLORY [Greek *kydos*]

\ə\ **about**	\au̇\ **out**	\i\ **tip**	\ȯ\ **saw**	\u̇\ **foot**
\ər\ **further**	\ch\ **chin**	\ī\ **life**	\ȯi\ **coin**	\y\ **yet**
\a\ **mat**	\e\ **pet**	\j\ **job**	\th\ **thin**	\yü\ **few**
\ā\ **take**	\ē\ **easy**	\ŋ\ **sing**	\t͟h\ **this**	\yu̇\ **cure**
\ä\ **cot, cart**	\g\ **go**	\ō\ **bone**	\ü\ **food**	\zh\ **vision**

ku·du *also* **koo·doo** \'küd-ü\ *n, pl* **kudu** *or* **kudus** *also* **koodoo** *or* **koodoos** : a large grayish brown African antelope with long ringed spirally twisted horns [Afrikaans *koedoe,* from Khoikhoi *kudu-b, kudu-s*]

kud·zu \'kud-zü\ *n* : a fast-growing trailing Asian vine of the legume family that is grown for forage and for erosion control and that is often a serious weed in the southeastern U.S. [Japanese *kuzu*]

Ku Klux·er \'kü-ˌklək-sər, 'kyü-\ *n* : a member of the Ku Klux Klan — **Ku Klux·ism** \-ˌklək-ˌsiz-əm\ *n*

Ku Klux Klan \ˌkü-ˌklǝks-'klan, ˌkyü-, *also* ˌklü-\ *n* **1** : a post-Civil War secret society favoring white supremacy **2** : a 20th-century secret fraternal group held to confine its membership to American-born Protestant whites

ku·lak \kü-'lak, kyü-\ *n* : a prosperous or wealthy peasant farmer in early 20th century Russia [Russian, literally, "fist"]

kul·tur \kul-'tur\ *n, often cap* : German culture held to be superior especially by militant Nazi and Hohenzollern expansionists [German, "culture," from Latin *cultura*]

kum·quat \'kəm-ˌkwät\ *n* **1** : a small yellowish orange fruit related to the citruses and having sweet spongy rind and somewhat tart pulp used especially for preserves **2** : a tree or shrub that bears kumquats [Chinese (dialect of Guangzhou & Hong Kong) *gām-gwat,* from *gām* "gold" + *gwāt* "citrus fruit"]

kung fu \ˌkəng-'fü, ˌkuŋ-\ *n* : a Chinese system of self-defense that resembles karate [Chinese (Beijing dialect) *gōngfu* "skill, art"]

Kurd \'kurd, 'kərd\ *n* : a member of a nomadic herding and agricultural people inhabiting a plateau region in bordering parts of Turkey, Iran, Iraq, Syria, and Armenia and Azerbaijan — **Kurd·ish** \-ish\ *adj*

Kurd·ish \'kurd-ish, 'kərd-\ *n* : the Iranian language of the Kurds

Kwan·zaa *also* **Kwan·za** \'kwän-zə\ *n* : an African-American cultural festival held from December 26 to January 1 [Swahili *kwanza* "first," in the phrase *matunda ya kwanza* "first fruits"]

kwash·i·or·kor \ˌkwäsh-ē-'ȯr-kər\ *n* : a disease of young children resulting from inadequate intake of protein [from a word in Ga (language of coastal Ghana) meaning "influence a child is said to be under when a second child comes"]

ky·pho·sis \kī-'fō-səs\ *n* : exaggerated outward curvature of the spine resulting in a rounded upper back — compare LORDOSIS, SCOLIOSIS [Greek *kyphōsis,* from *kyphos* "humpbacked"] — **ky·phot·ic** \-'fät-ik\ *adj*

ky·rie \'kir-ē-ˌā\ *n, often cap* : a short liturgical prayer that begins with or consists of the words "Lord have mercy" [Late Latin *kyrie eleison,* transliteration of Greek *kyrie eleēson* "Lord, have mercy"]

ky·rie elei·son \'kir-ē-ˌā-ə-'lā-ə-ˌsän, -ə-sən\ *n, often cap K&E* : KYRIE

L

l \'el\ *n, pl* **l's** *or* **ls** \'elz\ *often cap* **1** : the 12th letter of the English alphabet **2** : fifty in Roman numerals

la \'lä\ *n* : the 6th note of the diatonic scale [Medieval Latin]

lab \'lab\ *n* : LABORATORY

lab coat *n* : a loose-fitting usually white coat with deep pockets that is worn by personnel in a laboratory or medical facility

[1]**la·bel** \'lā-bəl\ *n* **1** : a slip (as of paper or cloth) with writing on it that is attached to something for identification or description **2** : a descriptive or identifying word or phrase : EPITHET **3** : a usually radioactive isotope used in labeling [Medieval French, *labelle* "strip of cloth, ribbon"]

[2]**label** *vt* **la·beled** *or* **la·belled; la·bel·ing** *or* **la·bel·ling** \'lā-bə-ling, -bling\ **1 a** : to affix a label to ⟨*label* a medicine bottle⟩ **b** : to describe as : CALL ⟨*labeled* their opponents cheats⟩ **2 a** : to make (an atom or chemical element) traceable (as through the steps of a biochemical process) by substitution of a detectable isotope **b** : to distinguish (as a compound or cell) by introducing a traceable constituent (as a dye or labeled atom) — **la·bel·er** \-bə-lər, -blər\ *n*

la·bel·lum \lə-'bel-əm\ *n, pl* **-bel·la** \-'bel-ə\ : the median and often spurred petal of the corolla of an orchid [Latin, "little lip," from *labrum* "lip"] — **la·bel·late** \lə-'bel-ət\ *adj*

[1]**la·bi·al** \'lā-bē-əl\ *adj* **1** : of, relating to, or situated near the lips or labia **2** : uttered with the participation of one or both lips ⟨the *labial* sounds \f\, \p\, and \ü\⟩ [Latin *labium* "lip"] — **la·bi·al·ly** \-ə-lē\ *adv*

[2]**labial** *n* : a labial consonant

[1]**la·bi·ate** \'lā-bē-ət, -bē-ˌāt\ *adj* **1** : LIPPED; *esp* : having a tubular corolla or calyx divided into two unequal parts projecting one over the other like lips **2** : of or relating to the mint family

[2]**labiate** *n* : a plant of the mint family

la·bile \'lā-ˌbīl, -bəl\ *adj* **1** : readily open to change : ADAPTABLE **2** : readily or continually undergoing chemical or physical change : UNSTABLE ⟨a *labile* mineral⟩ [French, from Late Latin *labilis* "slipping easily," from Latin *labi* "to slip"] — **la·bil·i·ty** \lā-'bil-ət-ē\ *n*

labio- *combining form* : labial and ⟨*labio*dental⟩

la·bio·den·tal \ˌlā-bē-ō-'dent-l\ *adj* : uttered with the participation of lip and teeth ⟨the *labiodental* sounds \f\ and \v\⟩ — **labiodental** *n*

la·bi·um \'lā-bē-əm\ *n, pl* **-bia** \-bē-ə\ **1** : any of the folds at the margin of the vulva **2** : the lower lip of a labiate corolla **3 a** : the lower mouthpart of an insect **b** : a liplike part of various invertebrates [Latin, "lip"]

[1]**la·bor** \'lā-bər\ *n* **1 a** : expenditure of physical or mental effort especially when difficult or compulsory **b (1)** : human activity that provides the goods or services in an economy **(2)** : the services performed by workers for wages as distinguished from those rendered by entrepreneurs for profits **c (1)** : the physical activities (as contraction of the uterus) involved in childbirth **(2)** : the period of such labor **2** : TASK **3** : a product of labor **4 a** : those who do manual labor or work for wages **b** : labor unions or their officials **5** *usually* **La·bour** \-bər\ : the Labour party of the United Kingdom or of another nation of the Commonwealth of Nations [Medieval French, from Latin]

[2]**labor** *vb* **la·bored; la·bor·ing** \-bə-ring, -bring\ **1** : to exert one's body or mind : WORK **2** : to move with great effort ⟨the truck *labored* up the hill⟩ **3** : to suffer from some disadvantage or distress ⟨*labor* under a delusion⟩ **4** : to pitch or roll heavily ⟨the ship *labored* in a rough sea⟩ **5** : to treat or work out in elaborate detail ⟨*labor* the obvious⟩

[3]**labor** *adj* **1** : of or relating to labor **2** *cap* : of, relating to, or constituting a political party held to represent the interests of workers or made up largely of organized labor groups

lab·o·ra·to·ry \'lab-rə-ˌtōr-ē, -ə-rə-, -ˌtȯr-\ *n, pl* **-ries** : a place equipped for experimental study in a science or for testing and analysis; *also* : a place providing opportunity for experimentation, observation, or practice in a field of study [Medieval Latin *laboratorium,* from Latin *laborare* "to labor," from *labor* "labor"]

labor camp *n* **1** : a penal colony where forced labor is performed **2** : a camp for migratory laborers

Labor Day *n* : the 1st Monday in September observed in the U.S. and Canada as a legal holiday in recognition of the worker

la·bored *adj* **1** : produced or performed with labor; *esp* : not freely or easily done ⟨*labored* breathing⟩ **2** : lacking ease of expression ⟨a *labored* speech⟩

la·bor·er \'lā-bər-ər\ *n* : one that works; *esp* : a person who does unskilled physical work for wages

la·bo·ri·ous \lə-'bōr-ē-əs, -'bȯr-\ *adj* **1** : INDUSTRIOUS **2** : requiring or characterized by hard or toilsome effort : LABORED — **la·bo·ri·ous·ly** *adv* — **la·bo·ri·ous·ness** *n*

La·bor·ite \'lā-bə-ˌrīt\ *n* **1** : a member of a political party devoted chiefly to the interests of labor **2** *usually* **La·bour·ite** \-bə-ˌrīt\ : a member of the British Labour party

la·bor·sav·ing \ˈlā-bər-ˌsā-viŋ\ *adj* : adapted to replace or decrease human labor and especially manual labor

labor union *n* : an organization of workers formed to advance its members' interests in respect to wages, benefits, and working conditions

la·bour \ˈlā-bər\ *chiefly British variant of* LABOR

lab·ra·dor·ite \ˈlab-rə-ˌdȯr-ˌīt\ *n* : an iridescent feldspar used especially in jewelry [*Labrador* peninsula, Canada]

Labrador retriever *n* : any of a breed of medium-sized retrievers developed from stock originating in Newfoundland and characterized by a short dense black, yellow, or chocolate coat, broad head and chest, and thick round tail [*Labrador,* Newfoundland]

Labrador retriever

la·brum \ˈlā-brəm\ *n* : the upper mouthpart of an arthropod in front of or above the mandibles [Latin, "lip"]

la·bur·num \lə-ˈbər-nəm\ *n* : any of several poisonous Eurasian shrubs and trees of the legume family with pendulous racemes of bright yellow flowers [Latin]

lab·y·rinth \ˈlab-ə-ˌrinth, -ˌrintth\ *n* **1** : a place constructed of or full of passageways and blind alleys : MAZE **2** : something extremely complex or tortuous **3** : a tortuous anatomical structure; *esp* : the internal ear or its bony or membranous part [Latin *labyrinthus,* from Greek *labyrinthos*] — **lab·y·rin·thine** \ˌlab-ə-ˈrin-thən, -ˈrint-\ *adj*

lac \ˈlak\ *n* : a resinous substance secreted by a scale insect and used in the manufacture of shellac, lacquers, and sealing wax [Persian *lak* and Hindi & Urdu *lākh,* from Sanskrit *lākṣā*]

[1]**lace** \ˈlās\ *n* **1** : a cord or string used for drawing together two edges (as of a garment or a shoe) **2** : an ornamental braid for trimming coats or uniforms **3** : a fine openwork usually figured fabric made of thread and used chiefly for household coverings or for ornament of dress [Medieval French *laz,* from Latin *laqueus* "noose, snare"] — **laced** \ˈlāst\ *adj* — **lace·less** \ˈlā-sləs\ *adj* — **lace·like** \ˈlā-ˌslīk\ *adj*

[2]**lace** *vb* **1** : to draw together the edges of with or as if with a lace passed through eyelets ⟨*laced* her shoes⟩ **2 a** : to adorn with or as if with lace **b** : INTERTWINE, THREAD ⟨*lace* the ribbon through the holes⟩ **3** : BEAT 1a, LASH **4 a** : to add a dash of an alcoholic liquor to **b** : to give savor or zest to — **lac·er** *n*

[1]**lac·er·ate** \ˈlas-ə-rət\ *adj* : having the edges deeply and irregularly cut ⟨a flower with *lacerate* petals⟩

[2]**lac·er·ate** \ˈlas-ə-ˌrāt\ *vt* **1** : to tear roughly : injure by tearing ⟨a *lacerated* knee⟩ **2** : to cause sharp mental or emotional pain to : DISTRESS [Latin *lacerare*] — **lac·er·a·tive** \-ˌrāt-iv\ *adj*

lac·er·a·tion \ˌlas-ə-ˈrā-shən\ *n* **1** : an act or instance of lacerating **2** : a torn and ragged wound

lace·wing \ˈlā-ˌswiŋ\ *n* : any of various insects with delicate lacelike wings, long antennae, and often brilliant eyes

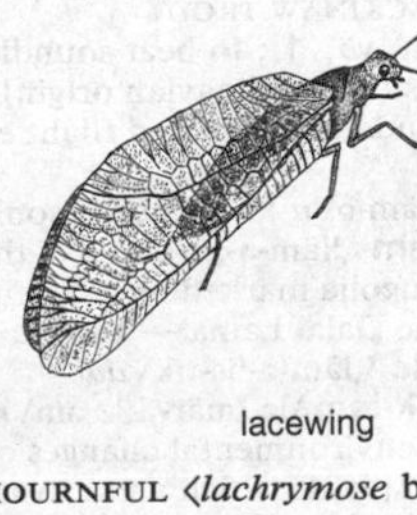
lacewing

lach·ry·mal *or* **lac·ri·mal** \ˈlak-rə-məl\ *adj* : of, relating to, or being the glands that produce tears [Latin *lacrima* "tear"]

lach·ry·mose \ˈlak-rə-ˌmōs\ *adj* **1** : given to tears or weeping : TEARFUL **2** : tending to cause tears : MOURNFUL ⟨*lachrymose* ballads⟩ — **lach·ry·mose·ly** *adv*

lac·ing \ˈlā-siŋ\ *n* **1** : the action of one that laces **2** : something that laces : LACE

la·cin·i·ate \lə-ˈsin-ē-ət, -ˌāt\ *adj* : bordered with a fringe; *esp* : cut into deep irregular usually pointed lobes ⟨*laciniate* leaves⟩ [Latin *lacinia* "flap"] — **la·cin·i·a·tion** \lə-ˌsin-ē-ˈā-shən\ *n*

[1]**lack** \ˈlak\ *vb* **1** : to be missing ⟨the will to win is *lacking*⟩ **2** : to need, want, or be deficient in ⟨*lack* financial support⟩

[2]**lack** *n* **1** : the fact or state of being in short supply ⟨a *lack* of good manners⟩ **2** : something that is lacking or is needed ⟨money is the club's biggest *lack*⟩ [Middle English *lak*]

lack·a·dai·si·cal \ˌlak-ə-ˈdā-zi-kəl\ *adj* : lacking life, spirit, or zest : LANGUID [derived from *lackaday,* interj. used to express regret, from *alack the day*] — **lack·a·dai·si·cal·ly** \-kə-lē, -klē\ *adv*

lack·ey \ˈlak-ē\ *n, pl* **lackeys** **1** : a liveried retainer : FOOTMAN **2** : a servile follower [Middle French *laquais*]

lack·lus·ter \ˈlak-ˌləs-tər\ *adj* : lacking in sheen, radiance, or vitality : DULL — **lackluster** *n*

la·con·ic \lə-ˈkän-ik\ *adj* : sparing of words : TERSE [Latin *laconicus* "Spartan," from Greek *lakōnikos;* from the Spartan reputation for terseness of speech] — **la·con·i·cal·ly** \-ˈkän-i-kə-lē, -klē\ *adv*

lac·quer \ˈlak-ər\ *n* **1** : any of various durable natural varnishes; *esp* : one from an Asian sumac **2** : any of various clear or colored synthetic organic coatings that typically dry to form a film by evaporation of the solvent; *esp* : a solution of a cellulose derivative (as nitrocellulose) [Portuguese *lacré* "sealing wax," from *laca* "lac," from Arabic *lakk,* from Persian *lak*] — **lacquer** *vt*

lac·ri·ma·tion \ˌlak-rə-ˈmā-shən\ *n* : the secretion of tears especially when abnormal or excessive [Latin *lacrimatio,* from *lacrimare* "to weep," from *lacrima* "tear"]

lac·ri·ma·tor *or* **lach·ry·ma·tor** \ˈlak-rə-ˌmāt-ər\ *n* : TEAR GAS

la·crosse \lə-ˈkrȯs\ *n* : a game played on a field in which the players use a long-handled stick with a triangular head with a mesh pouch to catch, carry, or throw the ball [Canadian French *la crosse,* literally, "the crooked stick"]

lact- *or* **lacti-** *or* **lacto-** *combining form* **1** : milk ⟨*lacto*genic⟩ **2 a** : lactic acid ⟨*lact*ate⟩ **b** : lactose ⟨*lact*ase⟩ [Latin *lact-, lac*]

lac·tase \ˈlak-ˌtās\ *n* : an enzyme that breaks down lactose and related compounds and occurs especially in the intestines of young mammals and in yeasts

[1]**lac·tate** \ˈlak-ˌtāt\ *n* : a salt or ester of lactic acid

[2]**lactate** *vi* : to secrete milk — **lac·ta·tion** \lak-ˈtā-shən\ *adj* — **lac·ta·tion·al** \-shnəl, -shən-l\ *adj*

[1]**lac·te·al** \ˈlak-tē-əl\ *adj* **1** : relating to, consisting of, producing, or resembling milk **2 a** : conveying or containing a milky fluid **b** : of or relating to the lacteals [Latin *lacteus* "of milk," from *lact-, lac* "milk"]

[2]**lacteal** *n* : one of the lymphatic vessels beginning in the villi of the small intestine and carrying chyle to the thoracic duct

lac·tic \ˈlak-tik\ *adj* : relating to or producing lactic acid ⟨*lactic* fermentation⟩

lactic acid *n* : an organic acid $C_3H_6O_3$ that is present normally especially in muscle tissue as a by-product of the breakdown of carbohydrates (as glycogen) in the absence of oxygen, is produced from carbohydrates usually by bacterial fermentation, and is used especially in food and medicine

lac·tif·er·ous \lak-ˈtif-rəs, -ə-rəs\ *adj* **1** : secreting or conveying milk ⟨*lactiferous* ducts⟩ **2** : yielding or containing a milky juice ⟨*lactiferous* plants⟩ — **lac·tif·er·ous·ness** *n*

lac·to·ba·cil·lus \ˌlak-tō-bə-ˈsil-əs\ *n* : any of a genus of bacteria that produce lactic acid

lac·to·gen·ic \ˌlak-tə-ˈjen-ik\ *adj* : inducing the secretion of milk

lac·tose \ˈlak-ˌtōs\ *n* : a sugar $C_{12}H_{22}O_{11}$ present in milk that breaks down into glucose and galactose and on fermentation yields especially lactic acid

la·cu·na \lə-ˈkü-nə, -ˈkyü-\ *n, pl* **-cu·nae** \-ˈkyü-nē, -ˈkü-ˌnī\ *also* **-cu·nas** \-ˈkü-nəz,-ˈkyü-\ **1** : a blank space or a missing part : GAP **2** : a small cavity or pit in an anatomical structure [Latin, "pool, pit, gap," from *lacus* "lake"] — **la·cu·nar** \-ˈkü-nər, -ˈkyü-\ *also* **la·cu·nate** \-nət\ *adj*

la·cus·trine \lə-ˈkəs-trən\ *adj* : of, relating to, or growing in lakes [derived from Latin *lacus* "lake"]

lacy \ˈlā-sē\ *adj* **lac·i·er; -est** : resembling or consisting of lace

lad \ˈlad\ *n* **1** : BOY 1, YOUTH **2** : FELLOW, CHAP [Middle English *ladde*]

lad·der \ˈlad-ər\ *n* **1** : a structure for climbing that consists of two long sidepieces joined at intervals by crosspieces on which one may step **2** : something that suggests a ladder in form or

\ə\ **abut**	\au̇\ **out**	\i\ **tip**	\ȯ\ **saw**	\u̇\ **foot**
\ər\ **further**	\ch\ **chin**	\ī\ **life**	\ȯi\ **coin**	\y\ **yet**
\a\ **mat**	\e\ **pet**	\j\ **job**	\th\ **thin**	\yü\ **few**
\ā\ **take**	\ē\ **easy**	\ŋ\ **sing**	\t͟h\ **this**	\yu̇\ **cure**
\ä\ **cot, cart**	\g\ **go**	\ō\ **bone**	\ü\ **food**	\zh\ **vision**

use **3 :** a series of usually ascending steps or stages **:** SCALE ⟨climbed the corporate *ladder*⟩ [Old English *hlǣder*]

lad·die \ˈlad-ē\ *n* **:** a young lad

lade \ˈlād\ *vb* **lad·ed; lad·ed** *or* **lad·en** \ˈlād-n\; **lad·ing** **1 a :** to put a load or burden on or in **:** LOAD ⟨*lade* a vessel⟩ **b :** SHIP 1a, STOW ⟨*lading* a rich cargo⟩ **2 :** to burden heavily **:** OPPRESS ⟨was *laden* with responsibilities⟩ **3 :** LADLE [Old English *hladan*]

la–di–da \ˌläd-ē-ˈdä\ *adj* **:** affectedly refined or polished [perhaps from earlier *lardy-dardy* "foppish"]

ladies' man *n* **:** a man who shows a marked liking for the company of women or is especially attentive to women

lad·ing \ˈlād-ing\ *n* **1 :** the act of one that lades **2 :** CARGO, FREIGHT

la·di·no clover \lə-ˈdī-nō-, -nə-\ *n* **:** a large rapidly growing white clover widely planted especially for forage [perhaps from *Lodi,* Italy]

[1]**la·dle** \ˈlād-l\ *n* **:** a deep-bowled long-handled spoon or dipper used especially for dipping up and moving liquids [Old English *hlædel,* from *hladan* "to lade"] — **la·dle·ful** \-ˌfu̇l\ *n*

[2]**ladle** *vt* **la·dled; la·dling** \ˈlād-ling, -l-ing\ **:** to take up and move in or as if in a ladle ⟨*ladle* soup⟩

la·dy \ˈlād-ē\ *n, pl* **ladies** **1 a :** a woman of property, rank, or authority; *esp* **:** one having a standing equivalent to that of a lord **b :** a woman receiving the homage or devotion of a knight or lover **2 a :** a woman of superior social position **b :** a woman of refinement and manners **c :** WOMAN — often used in a courteous reference ⟨show the *lady* to her seat⟩ **3 :** WIFE 2 **4 a** *cap* — used as a title of a woman of rank in Great Britain **b :** a woman who is a member of an order of knighthood — compare DAME 1c **5** *cap* **:** VIRGIN MARY — usually used with *Our* [Old English *hlǣfdīge,* from *hlāf* "loaf of bread" + *-dīge* "one that kneads"]

Word History Over the centuries the meaning of *lady* has become more and more generalized, and it is now widely used as a courteous term for a woman. *Lady* was formerly used to refer primarily to women of superior social standing. The Old English form, *hlǣfdīge,* was originally used to mean "female head of a household" or "mistress of servants." This sense reflects something of the ultimate etymology, for *hlǣfdīge* is composed of Old English *hlāf,* "loaf," and *-dīge,* "kneader of bread," which is related to our modern English *dough.*

lady beetle *n* **:** LADYBUG

la·dy·bird \-ˌbərd\ *n* **:** LADYBUG

la·dy·bug \-ˌbəg\ *n* **:** any of numerous small, nearly hemispherical, and often brightly colored and spotted beetles that mostly feed both as larvae and adults on other insects (as aphids) [Our *Lady,* the Virgin Mary]

lady chapel *n, often cap L&C* **:** a chapel dedicated to the Virgin Mary

Lady Day *n* **:** the feast of the Annunciation

la·dy·fin·ger \ˈlād-ē-ˌfing-gər\ *n* **:** a small finger-shaped sponge cake

la·dy·fish \-ˌfish\ *n* **:** a large silvery fish of the western Atlantic that is related to the tarpon and is often caught for sport — called also *bonefish, tenpounder*

la·dy–in–wait·ing \ˌlād-ē-in-ˈwāt-ing\ *n, pl* **ladies–in–waiting** **:** a lady appointed to attend a queen or princess

la·dy·like \ˈlād-ē-ˌlīk\ *adj* **1 :** resembling a lady in appearance or manners **2 :** suitable to a lady ⟨*ladylike* behavior⟩

la·dy·love \ˌlād-ē-ˌləv, ˌlād-ē-ˈ\ *n* **:** a beloved woman

la·dy·ship \ˈlād-ē-ˌship\ *n* **:** the condition of being a lady **:** the rank or dignity of a lady — used as a title for a woman having the rank of lady ⟨her *Ladyship*⟩ ⟨your *Ladyship*⟩ ⟨their *Ladyships*⟩

lady's slipper *or* **lady slipper** \ˈlād-ēz-ˌslip-ər, -ē-ˌslip-\ *n* **:** any of several North American temperate-zone orchids with flowers whose shape suggests a slipper

lady's slipper

[1]**lag** \ˈlag\ *vi* **lagged; lag·ging** **1 a :** to stay or fall behind **:** LINGER ⟨*lagged* behind the other hikers⟩ **b :** to move, function, or develop with comparative slowness ⟨*lagged* behind the production schedule⟩ **2 :** to slacken little by little **:** FLAG ⟨interest never *lagged* during the play⟩ **3 :** to pitch or shoot something (as a marble) at a mark [probably of Scandinavian origin] — **lag·ger** *n*

[2]**lag** *n* **1 a :** the action or condition of lagging ⟨a city experiencing a *lag* in economic development⟩ **b :** comparative slowness or retardation **2 a :** an amount of lagging or the time during which lagging continues **b :** INTERVAL 1

la·ger \ˈläg-ər\ *n* **:** a beer brewed by slow fermentation and stored in refrigerated cellars for maturing [German *Lagerbier,* from *Lager* "storehouse" + *Bier* "beer"]

lag·gard \ˈlag-ərd\ *adj* **:** lagging or tending to lag **:** DILATORY — **laggard** *n* — **lag·gard·ly** *adv or adj* — **lag·gard·ness** *n*

la·gniappe \ˈlan-ˌyap, lan-ˈ\ *n* **:** something given free or by way of good measure; *esp* **:** a small gift given to a customer by a merchant at the time of a purchase [American French, from American Spanish *la ñapa* "the lagniappe"]

lago·morph \ˈlag-ə-ˌmȯrf\ *n* **:** any of an order (Lagomorpha) of plant-eating gnawing mammals having two pairs of incisors in the upper jaw one behind the other and comprising the rabbits, hares, and pikas — compare RODENT [derived from Greek *lagōs* "hare" + *morphē* "form"]

la·goon \lə-ˈgün\ *n* **:** a shallow sound, channel, or pond near or connected with a larger body of water [French *lagune,* from Italian *laguna,* from Latin *lacuna* "pit, pool," from *lacus* "lake"]

la·ical \ˈlā-ə-kəl\ *or* **la·ic** \ˈlā-ik\ *adj* **:** of or relating to the laity **:** SECULAR — **laic** *n* — **la·ical·ly** \ˈlā-ə-kə-lē, -klē\ *adv*

la·icism \ˈlā-ə-ˌsiz-əm\ *n* **:** a political system characterized by the exclusion of church control and influence

la·icize \ˈlā-ə-ˌsīz\ *vt* **1 :** to reduce to lay status **2 :** to put under the direction of or open to the laity — **la·ici·za·tion** \ˌlā-ə-sə-ˈzā-shən\ *n*

laid *past and past participle of* LAY

laid–back \ˈlād-ˈbak\ *adj* **:** having a relaxed style or manner

lain *past participle of* LIE

lair \ˈlaər, ˈleər\ *n* **1 :** the resting or living place of a wild animal **:** DEN **2 :** REFUGE 1, HIDEAWAY [Old English *leger*]

laird \ˈlaərd, ˈleərd\ *n, chiefly Scottish* **:** a landed proprietor [Middle English (northern & Scots) *lard, lord,* "lord"]

lais·sez–faire \ˌle-ˌsā-ˈfaər, ˌlā-, -ˌzā-, -ˈfeər\ *n* **:** a doctrine opposing governmental interference in economic affairs beyond the minimum necessary for the maintenance of peace and property rights [French *laissez faire,* imperative of *laisser faire* "to let (people) do (as they choose)"] — **laissez–faire** *adj*

la·ity \ˈlā-ət-ē\ *n, pl* **-ities** **1 :** the people of a religious faith as distinguished from its clergy **2 :** the mass of the people as distinguished from those of a particular profession or skill [*[5]lay*]

[1]**lake** \ˈlāk\ *n* **:** a large inland body of standing water; *also* **:** a pool of liquid (as lava, oil, or pitch) [Old English *lacu* "stream, pool," from Latin *lacus* "lake, pool, pit"]

[2]**lake** *n* **1 :** any of numerous bright pigments composed of a soluble dye adsorbed on or combined with an inorganic substance **2 :** a vivid red [French *laque* "lac," from Old Occitan *laca,* from Arabic *lakk,* from Persian *lak*]

lake dwelling *n* **:** a dwelling built on piles in a lake; *esp* **:** one built in prehistoric times — **lake dweller** *n*

lake herring *n* **:** a cisco chiefly of the northern U.S. and Canada that is of commercial importance

lake trout *n* **:** any of various trout and salmon found in lakes; *esp* **:** MACKINAW TROUT

[1]**lam** \ˈlam\ *vb* **1 :** to beat soundly **:** THRASH **2 :** to flee hastily [perhaps of Scandinavian origin]

[2]**lam** *n* **:** sudden or hurried flight especially from the law ⟨on the *lam*⟩

la·ma \ˈläm-ə\ *n* **:** a Lamaist monk [Tibetan *blama*]

La·ma·ism \ˈläm-ə-ˌiz-əm\ *n* **:** the form of Buddhism of Tibet and Mongolia marked by a dominant hierarchy of monks headed by the Dalai Lama — **La·ma·ist** \ˈläm-ə-əst\ *n or adj* — **La·ma·is·tic** \ˌläm-ə-ˈis-tik\ *adj*

La·marck·ism \lə-ˈmär-ˌkiz-əm\ *n* **:** a theory of evolution asserting that environmental changes cause structural changes in animals and plants which are transmitted to offspring [J.B. de Monet *Lamarck*] — **La·marck·i·an** \-ˈmär-kē-ən\ *adj*

la·ma·sery \ˈläm-ə-ˌser-ē\ *n, pl* **-ser·ies** **:** a monastery of lamas [French *lamaserie,* from *lama* "lama"]

La·maze \lə-ˈmäz\ *adj* **:** relating to or being a method of childbirth involving psychological and physical techniques (as controlled deep breathing) designed to minimize pain [Fernand *Lamaze,* died 1957, French obstetrician]

[1]**lamb** \ˈlam\ *n* **1 a :** a young sheep; *esp* **:** one less than a year old or without permanent teeth **b :** the young of various animals

(as the smaller antelopes) **2 :** an innocent, weak, or gentle person **3 :** the flesh of a lamb used as food [Old English]

[2]**lamb** *vb* **1 :** to bring forth a lamb **2 :** to tend (ewes) at lambing time — **lamb·er** \ˈlam-ər\ *n*

lam·baste *or* **lam·bast** \lam-ˈbāst, -ˈbast\ *vt* **1 :** to assault violently : BEAT **2 :** to attack verbally [probably from [1]*lam* + *baste* "to thrash"]

lamb·da \ˈlam-də\ *n* **:** the 11th letter of the Greek alphabet — Λ or λ

lam·bent \ˈlam-bənt\ *adj* **1 :** playing lightly over a surface : FLICKERING ‹a *lambent* flame› **2 :** softly radiant ‹*lambent* eyes› **3 :** marked by lightness or brilliance especially of expression ‹*lambent* humor› [Latin *lambens,* present participle of *lambere* "to lick"] — **lam·ben·cy** \-bən-sē\ *n*

lamb·kin \ˈlam-kən\ *n* **:** a little lamb

lam·bre·quin \ˈlam-bər-kən, -bri-kən\ *n* **:** VALANCE [French]

lamb's ears *n sing or pl* **:** a widely grown southwest Asian herb of the mint family having leaves covered with fuzzy silver-white hairs

lamb·skin \ˈlam-ˌskin\ *n* **:** a lamb's skin or a small fine-grade sheepskin or the leather made from either

lamb's–quar·ter \ˈlamz-ˌkwȯrt-ər, -ˌkwȯt-\ *n* **:** a goosefoot with leaves that are sometimes used in salads or cooked as a vegetable — called also *lamb's-quarters*

[1]**lame** \ˈlām\ *adj* **1 a :** having a body part and especially a limb so disabled as to impair freedom of movement **b :** marked by stiffness and soreness ‹a *lame* shoulder› **2 :** lacking substance : WEAK ‹a *lame* excuse› [Old English *lama*] — **lame·ly** *adv* — **lame·ness** *n*

[2]**lame** *vt* **1 :** to make lame **2 :** to make weak or ineffective

la·mé \lä-ˈmā, la-\ *n* **:** a brocaded fabric woven with metallic filling threads often of gold or silver [French]

lame duck *n* **:** an elected official continuing to hold political office after being defeated and before a successor is inaugurated

la·mel·la \lə-ˈmel-ə\ *n, pl* **-mel·lae** \-ˈmel-ē, -ˌī\ *also* **-mellas :** a thin flat scale, layer, or membrane [Latin, "little plate," from *lamina* "thin plate"] — **la·mel·lar** \lə-ˈmel-ər\ *adj* — **la·mel·late** \-ˈmel-ət\ *adj*

[1]**la·ment** \lə-ˈment\ *vb* **1 :** to mourn aloud : WAIL **2 :** to feel or express sorrow for : BEWAIL [Latin *lamentari,* from *lamentum* "lament"] — **lam·en·ta·tion** \ˌlam-ən-ˈtā-shən\ *n*

[2]**lament** *n* **1 :** a crying out in grief : WAILING **2 :** a mournful song or poem

lam·en·ta·ble \ˈlam-ən-tə-bəl, lə-ˈment-ə-\ *adj* **1 :** deserving to be regretted : DEPLORABLE ‹a *lamentable* error› **2 :** expressing grief : MOURNFUL — **lam·en·ta·ble·ness** *n* — **lam·en·ta·bly** \-blē\ *adv*

Lam·en·ta·tions \ˌlam-ən-ˈtā-shənz\ *n* **:** a poetic book on the fall of Jerusalem in canonical Jewish and Christian Scriptures — see BIBLE table

la·mia \ˈlā-mē-ə\ *n* **:** a female demon; *esp* **:** a female vampire [Latin, from Greek]

lam·i·na \ˈlam-ə-nə\ *n, pl* **-nae** \-ˌnē, -ˌnī\ *or* **-nas 1 :** a thin plate or scale **2 :** BLADE 1b [Latin] — **lam·i·nar** \-nər\ *adj*

lam·i·nar·ia \ˌlam-ə-ˈner-ē-ə, -ˈnar-\ *n* **:** any of various large kelps with an unbranched cylindrical or flattened stalk and a smooth or wavy blade [derived from Latin *lamina* "lamina"] — **lam·i·nar·i·an** \-ē-ən\ *adj or n*

[1]**lam·i·nate** \ˈlam-ə-ˌnāt\ *vt* **1 :** to roll or compress into a thin plate **2 :** to make by uniting superposed layers of one or more materials — **lam·i·na·tor** \-ˌnāt-ər\ *n*

[2]**lam·i·nate** \-nət, -ˌnāt\ *adj* **1 :** consisting of laminae **2 :** bearing or covered with laminae

[3]**lam·i·nate** \-nət, -ˌnāt\ *n* **:** a product made by laminating

lam·i·nat·ed \-ˌnāt-əd\ *adj* **:** composed of layers of firmly united material; *esp* **:** made by bonding or impregnating superposed layers of paper, wood, or fabric with resin and compressing under heat

lam·i·na·tion \ˌlam-ə-ˈnā-shən\ *n* **1 :** the process of laminating **2 :** a laminate structure **3 :** LAMINA

Lam·mas \ˈlam-əs\ *n* **:** August 1 originally celebrated in England as a harvest festival [Old English *hlāfmæsse,* from *hlāf,* "loaf" + *mæsse* "mass"]

lam·mer·gei·er *or* **lam·mer·gey·er** \ˈlam-ər-ˌgī-ər, -ˌgīr\ *n* **:** the largest Eurasian and African bird of prey found chiefly in mountainous regions [German *Lämmergeier,* from *Lämmer* "lambs" + *Geier* "vulture"]

lamp \ˈlamp\ *n* **:** a device for producing light or heat: as **a :** a vessel with a wick for burning an inflammable liquid (as oil) **b :** a lightbulb that emits light produced by electricity **c :** a decorative appliance housing a lightbulb that is usually covered by a shade [Medieval French *lampe,* from Latin *lampas,* from Greek, from *lampein* "to shine"]

lamp·black \-ˌblak\ *n* **:** a finely powdered deep black soot made by incomplete burning of carbon-containing material and used chiefly as a pigment (as in paints and ink)

lamp·light \ˈlam-ˌplīt\ *n* **:** the light of a lamp

lamp·light·er \ˈlam-ˌplīt-ər\ *n* **:** one that lights a lamp; *esp* **:** a person employed to light gas street lights

[1]**lam·poon** \lam-ˈpün\ *n* **:** SATIRE 1; *esp* **:** a harsh satire usually aimed at an individual [French *lampon*]

[2]**lampoon** *vt* **:** to make the subject of a lampoon : RIDICULE — **lam·poon·er** *n* — **lam·poon·ery** \-ˈpün-rē, -ə-rē\ *n*

lamp·post \ˈlamp-ˌpōst\ *n* **:** a post supporting a usually outdoor lamp or lantern

lam·prey \ˈlam-prē\ *n, pl* **lampreys :** any of a family of eellike jawless fishes having a large sucking mouth with horny teeth — called also *lamprey eel* [Medieval French *lampreie,* from Medieval Latin *lampreda*]

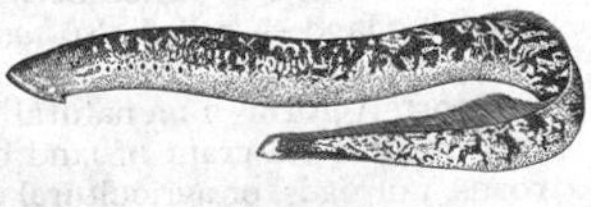
lamprey

lamp·shell \ˈlamp-ˌshel\ *n* **:** BRACHIOPOD

LAN \ˈlan, ˌel-ˌā-ˈen\ *n* **:** LOCAL AREA NETWORK

la·nai \lə-ˈnī, lä-\ *n* **:** a roofed patio used as a living room [Hawaiian]

la·nate \ˈlā-ˌnāt, ˈlan-ˌāt\ *adj* **:** covered with fine hair or filaments : WOOLLY ‹*lanate* leaves› [Latin *lanatus,* from *lana* "wool"]

Lan·cas·tri·an \lan-ˈkas-trē-ən, lang-\ *adj* **:** of or relating to the English royal house that ruled from 1399 to 1461 — compare YORKIST [John of Gaunt, duke of *Lancaster,* died 1399]

[1]**lance** \ˈlans\ *n* **1 :** a weapon consisting of a long shaft with a sharp head and carried by knights or light cavalry **2 :** a sharp object suggestive of a lance; *esp* **:** LANCET **3 :** LANCER 1b [Medieval French, from Latin *lancea*]

[2]**lance** *vt* **1 :** to pierce with or as if with a lance **2 :** to open with or as if with a lancet ‹*lance* a boil›

lance corporal *n* **:** an enlisted person with a rank in the marine corps above private first class and below corporal [*lance* (as in obsolete *lancepesade* "lance corporal," from Middle French *lancepessade*)]

lance·let \ˈlan-slət\ *n* **:** any of various small translucent marine animals that are related to the vertebrates, are fishlike in appearance, and usually live partly buried on the ocean floor — called also *amphioxus*

lan·ce·o·late \ˈlan-sē-ə-ˌlāt\ *adj* **:** shaped like a lance head; *esp* **:** being narrow and tapering to a point at the tip ‹*lanceolate* leaves› [Late Latin *lanceolatus,* from Latin *lanceola* "small lance," from *lancea* "lance"]

lanc·er \ˈlan-sər\ *n* **1 a :** one that carries a lance **b :** a light cavalryman armed with a lance **2** *pl but sing in construction* **a :** a set of five quadrilles each in a different meter **b :** the music for such dances

lan·cet \ˈlan-sət\ *n* **:** a sharp-pointed and usually 2-edged surgical instrument used to make small incisions

lancet arch *n* **:** an acutely pointed arch

[1]**land** \ˈland\ *n* **1 :** the solid part of the surface of the earth **2 :** a portion of the earth's solid surface distinguished by ownership boundaries: as **a :** COUNTRY 2 **b :** privately or publicly owned territory ‹buy some *land*› **3 :** REALM, DOMAIN ‹in the *land* of dreams› **4 :** the people of a country : NATION [Old English] — **land·less** \ˈlan-dləs\ *adj*

[2]**land** *vb* **1 a :** to set or go ashore from a ship : DISEMBARK ‹*land* troops› ‹troops *landed*› **b :** to stop at or near a place on shore ‹the boat *landed* at the dock› **2 :** to alight or cause to alight on a surface ‹the plane *landed*› ‹*landed* the plane in a cornfield› **3 :** to bring to or arrive at a specified destination, position, or condition ‹*landed* downtown› ‹never *landed* a punch› ‹carelessness *landed* them in trouble› **4 a :** to catch with a hook

and bring in ⟨*land* a fish⟩ **b** : GAIN, SECURE ⟨*land* a job⟩ — **land·er** *n*

lan·dau \ˈlan-ˌdau̇, -ˌdȯ\ *n* : a four-wheeled carriage with a top divided into two sections that can be lowered, thrown back, or removed [*Landau,* Bavaria, Germany]

landau

land·ed \ˈlan-dəd\ *adj* **1** : owning land ⟨*landed* proprietors⟩ **2** : consisting of real estate ⟨*landed* property⟩

land·fall \ˈland-ˌfȯl, ˈlan-\ *n* : a sighting or reaching of land after a voyage or flight; *also* : the land first sighted

land·fill \-ˌfil\ *n* **1** : a system of trash and garbage disposal in which the waste is buried between layers of earth to build up low-lying land — called also *sanitary landfill* **2** : an area built up by landfill

land·form \-ˌfȯrm\ *n* : a natural feature of a land surface

land grant *n* : a grant of land by a government especially for roads, railroads, or agricultural colleges

land·hold·er \ˈland-ˌhōl-dər\ *n* : one that holds or owns land — **land·hold·ing** \-diŋ\ *n*

land·ing \ˈlan-diŋ\ *n* **1** : the action of one that lands **2** : a place for discharging or taking on passengers and cargo **3** : a level part of a staircase (as at the end of a flight of stairs)

landing craft *n* : any of various naval craft designed for putting troops and equipment ashore

landing field *n* : a field where aircraft may land and take off

landing gear *n* : the part that supports the weight of an aircraft or spacecraft when on the ground

landing strip *n* : AIRSTRIP

land·la·dy \ˈland-ˌlād-ē, ˈlan-\ *n* : a woman who is a landlord

land·line \-ˌlīn\ *n* : a line of communication (as by telephone) consisting of a cable laid on land

land·locked \-ˌläkt\ *adj* **1** : enclosed or nearly enclosed by land ⟨a *landlocked* country⟩ **2** : confined to fresh water by some barrier ⟨*landlocked* salmon⟩

land·lord \-ˌlȯrd\ *n* **1** : the owner of real estate which is leased or rented to another **2** : a person who runs an inn or rooming house : INNKEEPER

land·lub·ber \ˈlan-ˌdləb-ər, -ləb-\ *n* : one whose life is spent on land; *esp* : one who is unacquainted with the sea or seamanship — **land·lub·ber·ly** *adj*

land·mark \ˈland-ˌmärk, ˈlan-\ *n* **1** : an object (as a stone or tree) that marks the boundary of land **2 a** : a conspicuous object on land that directs toward or identifies a place **b** : an anatomical structure used as a point of orientation in locating other structures **3** : an event or development that marks a turning point or a stage ⟨the album was a musical *landmark*⟩ **4** : a structure of unusual historic interest

land·mass \-ˌmas\ *n* : a large area of land

land mine *n* : a mine placed just below the surface of the ground and designed to be exploded by the weight of vehicles or troops passing over it

land–office business *n* : extensive and rapid business [from the fact that government land offices were swamped with would-be homesteaders when public lands were opened for homesteading]

land·own·er \ˈlan-ˌdō-nər\ *n* : an owner of land — **land·own·ing** \-niŋ\ *adj*

land–poor \ˈland-ˌpu̇r, ˈlan-\ *adj* : owning so much unprofitable or encumbered land as to lack funds to develop it or pay the charges due on it

land reform *n* : usually legislative measures intended to achieve a fairer distribution of agricultural land

[1]**land·scape** \ˈland-ˌskāp, ˈlan-\ *n* **1** : a picture of natural inland scenery **2** : a portion of land that the eye can see in one glance [Dutch *landschap,* from *land* + *-schap* "-ship"]

[2]**landscape** *vt* : to modify or improve (a tract of land) by grading, clearing, or gardening

landscape gardener *n* : a person skilled in the development and decorative planting of gardens and grounds

land·slide \ˈland-ˌslīd, ˈlan-\ *n* **1** : the slipping down of a mass of rocks or earth on a steep slope; *also* : the mass of material that slides **2** : an overwhelming victory especially in an election

lands·man \ˈlandz-mən, ˈlanz-\ *n* : LANDLUBBER

land·ward \ˈlan-dwərd\ *adv or adj* : to or toward the land

lane \ˈlān\ *n* **1** : a narrow way between fences, hedges, or buildings **2** : a relatively narrow way: as **a** : an ocean route for ships; *also* : AIR LANE **b** : a strip of roadway for a single line of vehicles **c** : a long hardwood surface with pins at one end for use in bowling [Old English *lanu*]

Lan·go·bard \ˈlaŋ-gə-ˌbärd\ *n* : LOMBARD 1 [Latin *Langobardus*]

lan·gos·ti·no \ˌlaŋ-gə-ˈstē-nō\ *n* : any of several edible crustaceans that are or resemble small lobsters or large shrimp; *esp* : LANGOUSTINE [Spanish, from *langosta* "spiny lobster, locust"]

lan·gouste \lä^{n}-ˈgüst\ *n* : SPINY LOBSTER [French]

lan·gous·tine \ˌlaŋ-gə-ˈstēn\ *n* : a small edible lobster of European seas having long slender claws [French, from *langouste* "grasshopper, lobster"]

lang syne \laŋ-ˈzīn\ *n, chiefly Scottish* : times past [Middle English (Scots), from *lang* "long" + *syne* "since"] — **lang syne** *adv, chiefly Scottish*

lan·guage \ˈlaŋ-gwij\ *n* **1 a** : the words, their pronunciation, and the methods of combining them used and understood by a large group of people **b** (1) : audible, articulate, and meaningful sound as produced by the action of the vocal organs (2) : a systematic means of communicating ideas by signs or marks with understood meanings ⟨sign *language*⟩ (3) : the means by which animals communicate ⟨*language* of the bees⟩ **2 a** : form or manner of verbal expression; *esp* : STYLE ⟨forceful *language*⟩ **b** : the words and expressions of a particular group or field ⟨the *language* of medicine⟩ **3** : the study of language especially as a school subject **4** : a system of signs and symbols and rules for using them that is used to carry information ⟨BASIC is a computer *language*⟩ [Medieval French *langage,* from *lange, langue* "tongue, language," from Latin *lingua*]

language arts *n pl* : the subjects (as reading, spelling, literature, and composition) that aim at developing the student's understanding and skills for using language

lan·guid \ˈlaŋ-gwəd\ *adj* **1** : drooping or flagging from or as if from exhaustion **2** : sluggish in character or disposition : LISTLESS **3** : lacking force or quickness of movement : LAZY [Middle French *languide,* from Latin *languidus,* from *languēre* "to languish"] — **lan·guid·ly** *adv* — **lan·guid·ness** *n*

lan·guish \ˈlaŋ-gwish\ *vi* **1 a** : to be or become languid **b** : to lose strength or force : DECLINE **2 a** : to become dispirited ⟨*languished* in prison⟩ **b** : to suffer neglect ⟨a bill *languishing* in the Senate⟩ **3** : to assume a weary or sad look appealing for sympathy [Medieval French *languiss-,* stem of *languir* "to languish," derived from Latin *languēre*] — **lan·guish·ment** \-gwish-mənt\ *n*

lan·guor \ˈlaŋ-gər, -ər\ *n* **1** : weakness or weariness of body or mind **2** : a state of dreamy inactivity [Medieval French *langur,* from Latin *languor,* from *languēre* "to languish"] ***synonyms*** see LETHARGY — **lan·guor·ous** \-gə-rəs, -ə-rəs\ *adj* — **lan·guor·ous·ly** *adv*

lan·gur \läŋ-ˈgu̇r\ *n* : any of several slender long-tailed Asian monkeys [Hindi *lãgūr*]

La Ni·ña \lä-ˈnē-nyə, -nyä\ *n* : an irregularly occurring movement of deep cold water to the ocean surface along the western coast of South America that often occurs after an El Niño and that disrupts weather patterns especially in a manner opposite that of an El Niño [Spanish, "the (female) child"]

lank \ˈlaŋk\ *adj* **1** : not well filled out : THIN ⟨*lank* cattle⟩ **2** : hanging straight and limp without spring or curl ⟨*lank* hair⟩ [Old English *hlanc*] — **lank·ly** *adv* — **lank·ness** *n*

synonyms LANK, LANKY, GAUNT, RAWBONED mean thin because of an absence of excess flesh. LANK implies tallness as well as leanness of figure ⟨the *lank* legs of the heron⟩. LANKY suggests awkwardness and loose-jointedness as well as thinness ⟨a *lanky* adolescent, all arms and legs⟩. GAUNT implies marked thinness as from overwork, suffering, or undernourishment ⟨the prisoner's *gaunt* face⟩. RAWBONED suggests a large ungainly build without implying undernourishment ⟨a *rawboned* farmer⟩.

lanky \ˈlaŋ-kē\ *adj* **lank·i·er; -est** : being tall, thin, and usually loose-jointed ***synonyms*** see LANK — **lank·i·ly** \-kə-lē\ *adv* — **lank·i·ness** \-kē-nəs\ *n*

lan·ner \ˈlan-ər\ *n* : a widely distributed Old World falcon; *esp* : a female lanner [Medieval French *laner*]

lan·o·lin \ˈlan-l-ən\ *n* : the fatty coating of sheep's wool especially when refined for use in ointments and cosmetics [derived from Latin *lana* "wool" + *oleum* "oil"]

lan·ta·na \lan-ˈtän-ə\ *n* **:** any of a genus of tropical shrubs and herbs that are related to vervains and have showy heads of small bright flowers [Italian dialect, "viburnum"]

lan·tern \ˈlant-ərn\ *n* **1 :** a usually portable light that has a protective transparent or translucent covering **2 a :** the chamber in a lighthouse containing the light **b :** a structure with glazed or open sides above an opening in a roof for light, ventilation, or decoration **3 :** PROJECTOR 2b [Medieval French *lanterne,* from Latin *lanterna,* from Greek *lamptēr,* from *lampein* "to shine"]

lantern 2b

lantern fish *n* **:** any of a family of small deep-sea fishes that have a large mouth and eyes and usually many spots on the body that emit light

lantern fly *n* **:** any of several large brightly marked insects that are related to the cicadas and aphids and have the front of the head lengthened into a hollow structure

lantern jaw *n* **:** a long thin jaw — **lan·tern–jawed** \ˌlant-ərn-ˈjȯd\ *adj*

lan·tha·nide \ˈlan-thə-ˌnīd-, ˈlant-\ *n* **:** any of the series of elements with atomic numbers from that of lanthanum to that of lutetium

lan·tha·num \ˈlan-thə-nəm, ˈlant-\ *n* **:** a white soft malleable metallic chemical element — see ELEMENT table [New Latin, from Greek *lanthanein* "to escape notice"]

la·nu·go \lə-ˈnü-gō, -ˈnyü-\ *n* **:** a dense cottony or downy growth of hair; *esp* **:** the soft fine hair that covers the fetus of some mammals including humans [Latin, "down," from *lana* "wool"]

lan·yard \ˈlan-yərd\ *n* **1 :** a piece of rope or line for fastening something in ships **2 a :** a cord worn around the neck to hold a knife or a whistle **b :** a cord worn on a uniform as a symbol of a military citation **3 :** a strong cord with a hook at one end used in firing cannon [Medieval French *lanier* "thong, lanyard"]

Lao \ˈlau̇\ *n, pl* **Lao** *or* **Laos 1 :** a member of a people living in Laos and northeastern Thailand **2 :** the Tai language of the Lao people — **Lao** *adj*

Lao·tian \lā-ˈō-shən, ˈlau̇-shən\ *n* **1 :** a native or inhabitant of Laos; *also* **:** LAO 1 **2 :** LAO 2 — **Laotian** *adj*

[1]**lap** \ˈlap\ *n* **1 :** a loose panel in a garment **:** FLAP **2 a :** the clothing that lies on the knees and thighs of a seated person **b :** the front part of the lower trunk and thighs of a seated person **3 :** responsible custody **:** CONTROL ⟨dropped the problem into my *lap*⟩ [Old Englsih *læppa*] — **lap·ful** \ˈlap-ˌfu̇l\ *n* — **the lap of luxury :** an environment of great comfort and wealth

[2]**lap** *vb* **lapped; lap·ping 1 :** [4]WIND 6b, WRAP ⟨*lap* a bandage around the wrist⟩ **2 :** ENVELOP, SWATHE ⟨*lap* the child in a blanket⟩ **3 a :** to place or lay so that one covers part of another ⟨*lap* shingles on a roof⟩ **b :** to project or spread beyond a certain point **4 :** to smooth or polish (as a metal surface) to a fine finish or accurate fit — **lap·per** *n*

[3]**lap** *n* **1 a :** the amount by which one object overlaps or projects beyond another **b :** the part of an object that overlaps another **2 :** a smoothing and polishing tool **3 a :** one circuit around a racecourse **b :** one segment of a journey **c :** one complete turn

[4]**lap** *vb* **lapped; lap·ping 1 a :** to take in food or drink with the tongue **b :** to take in or absorb eagerly or quickly **:** DEVOUR — used with *up* **2 :** to wash or splash gently [Old English *lapian*] — **lap·per** *n*

[5]**lap** *n* **1 a :** an act or instance of lapping **b :** the amount that can be carried to the mouth by one lick or scoop of the tongue **2 :** a gentle splashing sound

lap·a·ro·scope \ˈlap-ə-rə-ˌskōp\ *n* **:** a fiber-optic instrument inserted through an incision in the abdominal wall and used to visually examine the interior of the abdomen [Greek *lapara* "flank"]

lap·a·ros·co·py \ˌlap-ə-ˈräs-kə-pē\ *n* **1 :** visual examination of the interior of the abdomen by means of a laparoscope **2 :** an operation involving use of a laparoscope

lap·board \ˈlap-ˌbōrd, -ˌbȯrd\ *n* **:** a board used on the lap as a table or desk

lap·dog \-ˌdȯg\ *n* **:** a small dog that may be held in the lap

la·pel \lə-ˈpel\ *n* **:** the part of the front of a garment that is turned back and is usually a continuation of the collar [derived from [1]*lap*]

[1]**lap·i·dary** \ˈlap-ə-ˌder-ē\ *n, pl* **-dar·ies :** a person who cuts, polishes, and engraves precious stones [Latin *lapidarius,* from *lapid-, lapis* "stone"]

[2]**lapidary** *adj* **1 :** of or relating to precious stones or the art of cutting them **2 :** of, relating to, or suitable for engraved inscriptions

lap·in \ˈlap-ən\ *n* **:** rabbit fur usually sheared and dyed [French, "rabbit"]

la·pis la·zu·li \ˌlap-əs-ˈlazh-ə-lē, -ˈlaz-\ *n* **:** a deep blue semiprecious stone that is essentially a complex silicate often with spangles of pyrites [Medieval Latin, from Latin *lapis* "stone" + Medieval Latin *lazulum* "lapis lazuli," from Arabic *lāzaward*]

lap joint *n* **:** a joint made by overlapping two ends or edges and fastening them together — **lap–jointed** \ˈlap-ˈjȯint-əd\ *adj*

Lapp \ˈlap\ *n, sometimes offensive* **:** SAMI

lap·pet \ˈlap-ət\ *n* **1 :** a fold or flap on a garment or headdress **2 :** a flat overlapping or hanging piece

[1]**lapse** \ˈlaps\ *n* **1 a :** a slight error or slip ⟨a *lapse* in manners⟩ **b :** a temporary deviation or fall especially from a higher to a lower state ⟨a *lapse* from grace⟩ **2 :** a becoming less **:** DECLINE **3 a :** the ending of a right or privilege by neglect to exercise it or failure to meet requirements **b :** DISUSE, DISCONTINUANCE ⟨*lapse* of a custom⟩ **4 :** a passage of time; *also* **:** INTERVAL [Latin *lapsus,* from *labi* "to slip"]

[2]**lapse** *vi* **1 a :** to fall from a better or higher state into a poorer or lower one ⟨*lapsed* into carelessness⟩ **b :** to sink or slip gradually ⟨*lapse* into silence⟩ **2 :** to come to an end **:** CEASE **3 :** to let something (as insurance or a legacy) come to an end or to pass to another by omission or negligence — **laps·er** *n*

lapse rate *n* **:** the rate of decrease in temperature of an air mass with increase in altitude

[1]**lap·top** \ˈlap-ˌtäp\ *adj* **:** of a size and design that makes use on one's lap convenient

[2]**laptop** *n* **:** a portable computer that is small enough for laptop use, has its main parts (as keyboard and display screen) combined into a single unit, and can run on battery power

lap·wing \ˈlap-ˌwing\ *n* **:** a crested Old World plover with a slow irregular flapping flight and a shrill wailing cry [Old English *hlēapewince*]

lar·board \ˈlär-bərd\ *n* **:** [3]PORT [Middle English *ladeborde*] — **lar·board** *adj*

lar·ce·ny \ˈlärs-nē, -n-ē\ *n, pl* **-nies :** the unlawful taking and carrying away of personal property with intent to deprive the owner of it permanently **:** THEFT [Medieval French *larecin* "theft," from Latin *latrocinium* "robbery," from *latro* "mercenary soldier"] — **lar·ce·nous** \ˈlärs-nəs, -n-əs\ *adj*

larch \ˈlärch\ *n* **1 :** any of a genus of trees of the pine family with short deciduous needles **2 :** the wood of a larch [probably from German *Lärche,* from Latin *larix*]

[1]**lard** \ˈlärd\ *vt* **1 :** to insert strips of pork fat or bacon into (meat) before cooking **2 :** to smear with lard, fat, or grease **3 :** to enrich with something excessive or superfluous ⟨a book *larded* with illustrations⟩

[2]**lard** *n* **:** a soft white fat obtained from fatty tissue of the hog by heating [Medieval French, from Latin *lardum*] — **lardy** \ˈlärd-ē\ *adj*

lar·der \ˈlärd-ər\ *n* **:** a place where foods are kept [Medieval French, from *lard,* "lard"]

large \ˈlärj\ *adj* **:** exceeding most other things of like kind especially in quantity or size **:** BIG [Medieval French, "broad, wide, generous," from Latin *largus* "generous, plentiful"] — **large·ness** *n* — **larg·ish** \ˈlär-jish\ *adj* — **at large 1 :** at liberty **:** FREE ⟨an escaped prisoner still *at large*⟩ **2 :** as a whole **:** in general ⟨society *at large*⟩ **3 :** representing a whole area rather than one of its subdivisions — used in combination with a preceding noun ⟨a delegate-*at-large*⟩

synonyms LARGE, BIG, GREAT mean above average in magnitude. LARGE is likely to be chosen when the dimensions, extent, capacity, or quantity are being considered ⟨a *large* sum of money⟩. BIG suggests emphasis on bulk, weight, or volume ⟨*big* boxes⟩. GREAT may imply physical magnitude usually with connotations of wonder or awe but more often implies degree of intensity ⟨*great* kindness⟩ ⟨*great* fear⟩. LARGE figuratively implies breadth, comprehensiveness, or generosity. BIG suggests impressiveness often at the expense of solidity. GREAT implies eminence, distinction, or supremacy.

large calorie *n* : CALORIE 1b

large·heart·ed \ˈlärj-ˈhärt-əd\ *adj* : having a generous nature

large intestine *n* : the last part of the vertebrate intestine that is wider and shorter than the small intestine, consists of the cecum, colon, and rectum and functions especially in the removal of water from digestive residues to form feces

large·ly \ˈlärj-lē\ *adv* : in a large manner; *esp* : for the most part : CHIEFLY, MOSTLY

large–mind·ed \ˈlärj-ˈmīn-dəd\ *adj* : generous or comprehensive in outlook, range, or capacity — **large–mind·ed·ly** *adv* — **large–mind·ed·ness** *n*

large·mouth bass \ˌlärj-ˌmau̇th-\ *n* : a large North American bass of sluggish warm waters that is blackish green above and lighter below — called also *largemouth black bass*

large–scale \ˈlärj-ˈskāl\ *adj* : larger than others of its kind

large–scale integration *n* : the process of placing a large number of circuits on a small chip

lar·gesse *also* **lar·gess** \lär-ˈzhes, lär-ˈjes\ *n* **1** : liberal giving **2** : a generous gift [Medieval French *largesse,* from *large* "generous"]

[1]**lar·ghet·to** \lär-ˈget-ō\ *adv or adj* : slower than andante but not so slow as largo — used as a direction in music [Italian, "somewhat slow," from *largo* "slow"]

[2]**larghetto** *n, pl* **-tos** : a larghetto movement

[1]**lar·go** \ˈlär-gō\ *adv or adj* : in a very slow and broad manner — used as a direction in music [Italian, "slow, broad," from Latin *largus* "plentiful"]

[2]**largo** *n, pl* **largos** : a largo movement

lar·i·at \ˈlar-ē-ət, ˈler-\ *n* : a long light rope used to catch livestock or to tether grazing animals [American Spanish *la reata* "the lasso"]

[1]**lark** \ˈlärk\ *n* : any of a family of Old World ground-dwelling songbirds that are usually brownish in color; *esp* : SKYLARK — compare MEADOWLARK [Old English *lāwerce*]

[2]**lark** *n* : something done solely for fun or adventure [*lark* "to do something for fun," probably alteration of *lake* "to frolic"] — **lark** *vi*

lark·spur \ˈlärk-ˌspər\ *n* : DELPHINIUM; *esp* : a cultivated annual delphinium grown for its flowers

lar·rup \ˈlar-əp\ *vt* **1** *dialect* : WHIP 2a **2** *dialect* : to defeat decisively [perhaps imitative]

lar·va \ˈlär-və\ *n, pl* **lar·vae** \-ˌvē, -ˌvī\ *also* **larvas** **1** : the immature, wingless, and often wormlike form (as a caterpillar or grub) that hatches from the egg of many insects **2** : the early form of any animal that at birth or hatching is fundamentally unlike its parent ⟨the tadpole is the *larva* of the frog⟩ [Latin, "specter, mask"] — **lar·val** \-vel\ *adj*

Word History Many insects hatch from their eggs looking very different from their eventual adult forms. The caterpillar is a young butterfly but seems to have little in common with that winged creature. The immature insect appears to be in disguise, to be masked. Biologists in the 18th-century were struck by this and gave the immature insect form the name *larva,* from a Latin word that means "mask."

lar·vi·cide \ˈlär-və-ˌsīd\ *n* : an agent for killing larval pests — **lar·vi·cid·al** \ˌlär-və-ˈsīd-l\ *adj*

[1]**la·ryn·geal** \lə-ˈrin-jəl, -jē-əl, ˌlar-ən-ˈjē-əl\ *adj* : of, relating to, or used on the larynx [derived from Greek *laryng-, larynx* "larynx"]

[2]**laryngeal** *n* : an anatomical part associated with the larynx

lar·yn·gi·tis \ˌlar-ən-ˈjīt-əs\ *n* : inflammation of the larynx — **lar·yn·git·ic** \-ˈjit-ik\ *adj*

lar·ynx \ˈlar-ings, -ingks\ *n, pl* **la·ryn·ges** \lə-ˈrin-ˌjēz\ *or* **lar·ynx·es** : the modified upper part of the trachea that in humans and most mammals contains the vocal cords [Greek *laryng-, larynx*]

la·sa·gna \lə-ˈzän-yə\ *n* : broad flat noodles baked with a sauce usually of tomatoes, cheese, and meat or vegetables [Italian *lasagna,* derived from Latin *lasanum* "chamber pot," from Greek *lasanon*]

las·civ·i·ous \lə-ˈsiv-ē-əs\ *adj* : LEWD 1, LUSTFUL [Latin *lascivia* "wantonness," from *lascivus* "wanton"] — **las·civ·i·ous·ly** *adv* — **las·civ·i·ous·ness** *n*

[1]**la·ser** \ˈlā-zər\ *n* : a device that utilizes the natural oscillations of atoms or molecules between energy levels for generating a beam of electromagnetic waves with a narrow frequency range [*l*ight *a*mplification by *s*timulated *e*mission of *r*adiation]

[2]**laser** *vt* : to subject to the action of a laser : treat with a laser

laser printer *n* : a high-quality computer printer that uses a laser to form the image to be printed

[1]**lash** \ˈlash\ *vb* **1** : to move violently or suddenly ⟨a cat *lashing* its tail⟩ **2** : to strike with or as if with a whip ⟨rain *lashing* the window⟩ **3** : to attack or retort verbally — usually used with *out* [Middle English] — **lash·er** *n*

[2]**lash** *n* **1 a** (1) : a stroke with or as if with a whip (2) : the flexible part of a whip; *also* : WHIP **b** : a beating, whipping, or driving force **2** : a verbal attack **3** : EYELASH

[3]**lash** *vt* : to bind with a rope, cord, or chain [Medieval French *lacer* "to lace"] — **lash·er** *n*

lash·ing *n* : something used for binding, wrapping, or fastening

LA·SIK \ˈlā-sik\ *n* : a surgical operation to reshape the cornea for correction of nearsightedness, farsightedness, or astigmatism in which the surface layer of the cornea is separated to create a hinged flap providing access to the inner cornea where varying amounts of tissue are removed by a laser [*las*er-assisted *i*n situ *k*eratomileusis (plastic surgery on the cornea)]

lass \ˈlas\ *n* **1** : young woman : GIRL **2** : SWEETHEART 2 [Middle English *las*]

lass·ie \ˈlas-ē\ *n* : LASS 1, GIRL

las·si·tude \ˈlas-ə-ˌtüd, -ˌtyüd\ *n* **1** : FATIGUE 2a, WEARINESS **2** : LANGUOR 2, LISTLESSNESS [Latin *lassitudo,* from *lassus* "weary"]

las·so \ˈlas-ō, la-ˈsü\ *n, pl* **lassos** *or* **lassoes** : a rope or long thin strip of leather with a noose that is used especially for catching livestock [Spanish *lazo,* from Latin *laqueus* "noose, snare"] — **lasso** *vt*

[1]**last** \ˈlast\ *vb* **1** : to continue in being or operation : go on ⟨the meeting *lasted* three hours⟩ **2 a** : to remain valid or important : ENDURE ⟨a book that will *last*⟩ **b** : to manage to continue ⟨won't *last* on that job⟩ **3** : to be enough for the needs of ⟨supplies to *last* you for a week⟩ [Old English *lǣstan* "to last, follow"] — **last·er** *n*

Word History English *last* has several homonyms. The verb *last* means "to continue" or "to endure." In Old English, *lǣstan* was used like its modern decendant to mean "to continue," but it also meant "to follow." The original meaning was probably "to follow a track." Old English *lǣstan* is related to the Old English noun *lāst,* which means "footprint" or "track." This noun is the ancestor of the shoemaker's *last,* a form in the shape of a foot. The very common adjective and adverb *last,* which mean "after the others," are not related to this verb and noun. They come from Old English *latost,* superlative of *læt,* "late, slow."

[2]**last** *adj* **1 a** : following all the rest ⟨*last* on the list⟩ **b** : being the only remaining ⟨my *last* dollar⟩ **2** : belonging to the final stage (as of life) ⟨his *last* hours⟩ **3 a** : next before the present ⟨*last* week⟩ **b** : most up-to-date : LATEST **4** : least likely ⟨the *last* thing they'd want⟩ **5 a** : CONCLUSIVE, ULTIMATE ⟨no *last* answer to that problem⟩ **b** : highest in degree : SUPREME [Old English *latost,* superlative of *læt* "late"] — **last·ly** *adv*

synonyms LAST, FINAL, ULTIMATE mean following all others (as in time, order, or importance). LAST applies to something that comes at the end of a series but does not always imply that the series is completed or stopped ⟨the *last* stop on the bus line⟩ ⟨the *last* news bulletin I heard⟩. FINAL stresses a definite closing of a series, process, or stage of progress ⟨*final* exams⟩. ULTIMATE implies the last degree or stage of a long process beyond which further progress or change is impossible ⟨*ultimate* collapse of civilization⟩.

[3]**last** *adv* **1** : after all others : at the end ⟨ran *last* in the race⟩ **2** : most lately ⟨saw them *last* in New York⟩ **3** : in conclusion ⟨and *last,* I'd like to talk about money⟩

[4]**last** *n* : something that is last — **at last** *or* **at long last** : at the end of a period of time : FINALLY

[5]**last** *n* : a wooden or metal form which is shaped like the human foot and on which a shoe is shaped or repaired [Old English *lǣste,* from *lāst* "footprint"]

[6]**last** *vt* : to shape with a last — **last·er** *n*

last–ditch \ˈlast-ˌdich\ *adj* : made as a final effort especially to avert disaster ⟨a *last-ditch* effort to raise money⟩

last·ing *adj* : existing or continuing a long while : ENDURING — **last·ing·ly** \ˈlas-ting-lē\ *adv* — **last·ing·ness** *n*

synonyms LASTING, PERMANENT, DURABLE mean enduring for so long as to seem fixed or established. LASTING implies a capacity to continue indefinitely ‹*lasting* friendships›. PERMANENT may add the implication of being designed to stand or continue indefinitely ‹a *permanent* arrangement› ‹*permanent* buildings›. DURABLE implies power to resist destructive agencies ‹*durable* fabrics›.

Last Judgment *n* : JUDGMENT 3

last laugh *n* : the satisfaction of ultimate triumph or success especially after being scorned or regarded as a failure ‹she got the *last laugh* on her early critics›

last rites *n* : ANOINTING OF THE SICK

last straw *n* : the last of a series (as of events or indignities) that brings one beyond the point of endurance [from the fable of the last straw that broke the camel's back when added to his burden]

Last Supper *n* : the supper eaten by Jesus and his disciples on the night of his betrayal

last word *n* **1** : the final remark in a verbal exchange **2** : the power of final decision **3** : the most advanced, up-to-date, or fashionable one of its kind ‹the *last word* in cars›

lat \ˈlat\ *n* : LATISSIMUS DORSI — usually used in plural

[1]**latch** \ˈlach\ *vi* **1** : to catch or get hold ‹*latch* onto a pass› **2** : to attach oneself [Old English *læccan*]

[2]**latch** *n* : a device that holds something in place by entering a notch or cavity; *esp* : a catch that holds a door or gate closed and that sometimes is operated by a key on one side and a knob on the other

[3]**latch** *vt* : to make fast with or as if with a latch : SHUT 1

latch·key \ˈlach-ˌkē\ *n* : a key to an outside and especially a front door

latchkey child *n* : a school-aged child of working parents who must spend part of the day unsupervised (as at home) — called also *latchkey kid*

latch·string \-ˌstriŋ\ *n* : a string for raising a latch so as to release it

[1]**late** \ˈlāt\ *adj* **1 a** : coming or remaining after the due, usual, or proper time ‹a *late* spring› **b** : of or relating to an advanced stage in time or development ‹the *late* Middle Ages›; *esp* : far advanced toward the close of the day or night ‹*late* hours› **2 a** : living comparatively recently ‹the *late* president› **b** : being something or holding a position or relationship recently but not now ‹the *late* belligerents› **c** : made, appearing, or happening in times close to the present ‹a *late* discovery› [Old English *læt*] ***synonyms*** see RECENT — **late·ness** *n*

[2]**late** *adv* **1 a** : after the usual or proper time **b** : at or to an advanced point of time ‹stayed *late* at the party› **2** : not long ago : RECENTLY ‹a person *late* of Chicago› — **of late** : LATELY, RECENTLY

late·com·er \ˈlāt-ˌkəm-ər\ *n* : one that arrives late; *also* : a recent arrival

[1]**la·teen** \lə-ˈtēn\ *adj* : of, relating to, or being a sailing rig used especially along the north coast of Africa and characterized by a triangular sail extended by a long spar slung to a low mast [French *voile latine,* literally, "Latin (Mediterranean) sail"]

[2]**lateen** *n* **1** *also* **la·teen·er** \-ˈtē-nər\ : a lateen-rigged ship **2** : a lateen sail

lateen 1

Late Greek *n* : the Greek language used in the 3rd to 6th centuries

Late Latin *n* : the Latin language used by writers in the 3rd to 6th centuries

late·ly \ˈlāt-lē\ *adv* : in recent time ‹what have you done for me *lately*›

lat·en \ˈlāt-n\ *vb* : to grow or cause to grow late

la·ten·cy \ˈlāt-n-sē\ *n, pl* **-cies** : the quality or state of being latent : DORMANCY

la·tent \ˈlāt-nt\ *adj* : present but not visible, active, or symptomatic ‹the car's *latent* defects› ‹a *latent* infection› [Latin *latens,* from *latēre* "to lie hidden"] — **la·tent·ly** *adv*

synonyms LATENT, DORMANT, QUIESCENT mean not now showing signs of activity or existence. LATENT applies to a power or quality that has not yet come forth but may emerge and develop ‹talents which were *latent* in childhood›. DORMANT suggests inactivity as though sleeping ‹a *dormant* volcano›. QUIESCENT suggests a temporary cessation of activity ‹*quiescent* lung disease›.

latent heat *n* : heat energy absorbed or evolved in a process (as fusion or vaporization)

latent period *n* : the interval (as the incubation period of a disease) between the introduction of a cause and the occurrence of its effect

lat·er·ad \ˈlat-ə-ˌrad\ *adv* : toward the side [Latin *later-, latus* "side"]

[1]**lat·er·al** \ˈlat-ə-rəl, ˈla-trəl\ *adj* **1** : of or relating to the side : situated on, directed toward, or coming from the side ‹the *lateral* branches of a tree› **2** : being a part of the boundary of a geometric solid that is not a base or completely included in a base ‹a *lateral* edge of a prism› ‹a *lateral* face› [Latin *lateralis,* from *later-, latus* "side"] — **lat·er·al·ly** \-ē\ *adv*

[2]**lateral** *n* **1** : a lateral part or branch **2** : a pass in football thrown to the side or to the rear

lateral line *n* : a sense organ of the skin of most fishes that is sensitive to low vibrations and extends along each side of the body

lat·er·ite \ˈlat-ə-ˌrīt\ *n* : a residual product of rock decay that is red in color and rich in the oxides of iron and hydroxide of aluminum [Latin *later* "brick"] — **lat·er·it·ic** \ˌlat-ə-ˈrit-ik\ *adj*

lat·est \ˈlāt-əst\ *n* : the most recent style or development ‹have you heard the *latest?*›

late·wood \ˈlāt-ˌwu̇d\ *n* : SUMMERWOOD

la·tex \ˈlā-ˌteks\ *n, pl* **la·ti·ces** \ˈlāt-ə-ˌsēz, ˈlat-\ *or* **la·tex·es** **1** : a milky juice that is produced by the cells of various plants and is the source of rubber, gutta-percha, chicle, and balata **2** : a water emulsion of a synthetic rubber or plastic used especially in paints and adhesives [Latin, "fluid"] — **lat·i·cif·er·ous** \ˌlāt-ə-ˈsif-rəs, ˌlat-, -ə-rəs\ *adj*

lath \ˈlath *also* ˈlath\ *n, pl* **laths** *or* **lath** : a thin narrow strip of wood used especially as a base for plaster [Middle English] — **lath** *vt*

lathe \ˈlath\ *n* : a machine in which a piece of material is held and turned while being shaped by a tool [probably from Middle English *lath* "supporting stand"]

[1]**lath·er** \ˈlath-ər\ *n* **1 a** : a thick foam or froth formed when a detergent is agitated in water **b** : foam or froth from profuse sweating (as on a horse) **2** : an overwrought state : DITHER ‹worked myself into a *lather*› [Old English *lēathor*] — **lath·ery** \ˈlath-rē,-ə-rē\ *adj*

[2]**lather** *vb* **lath·ered; lath·er·ing** \ˈlath-riŋ, -ə-riŋ\ **1 a** : to spread lather over ‹to *lather* one's face for shaving› **b** : to form a lather or a froth like lather ‹this soap *lathers* well› **2** : to beat severely : FLOG — **lath·er·er** \ˈlath-ər-ər\ *n*

[1]**Lat·in** \ˈlat-n\ *adj* **1 a** : of, relating to, or composed in Latin ‹*Latin* grammar› **b** : ROMANCE ‹*Latin* languages› **2** : of or relating to the part of the Catholic Church that until recently used a Latin rite **3** : of or relating to the peoples or countries using Romance languages; *esp* : of or relating to the peoples or countries of Latin America [Old English, from Latin *Latinus,* from *Latium,* ancient country of Italy]

[2]**Latin** *n* **1** : the Italic language of ancient Rome and until modern times the dominant language of school, church, and state in western Europe **2** : a Catholic of the Latin rite **3** : a member of one of the peoples speaking Romance languages; *esp* : a native or inhabitant of Latin America

La·ti·na \lə-ˈtē-nə\ *n* **1** : a woman or girl who is a native or inhabitant of Latin America **2** : a woman or girl of Latin-American origin living in the U.S. — **Latina** *adj*

Latin alphabet *n* : an alphabet that was used for writing Latin and that has been modified for writing many modern languages (as English)

Lat·in·ate \ˈlat-n-ˌāt\ *adj* : of, relating to, resembling, or derived from Latin

Latin cross *n* : a cross having a long upright shaft and a shorter crossbar above the middle

Lat·in·ism \ˈlat-n-ˌiz-əm\ *n* **1 a** : a characteristic feature of

\ə\ **abut**	\au̇\ **out**	\i\ **tip**	\ȯ\ **saw**	\u̇\ **foot**
\ər\ **further**	\ch\ **chin**	\ī\ **life**	\ȯi\ **coin**	\y\ **yet**
\a\ **mat**	\e\ **pet**	\j\ **job**	\th\ **thin**	\yü\ **few**
\ā\ **take**	\ē\ **easy**	\ŋ\ **sing**	\th\ **this**	\yu̇\ **cure**
\ä\ **cot, cart**	\g\ **go**	\ō\ **bone**	\ü\ **food**	\zh\ **vision**

Latin occurring in another language **b :** a word or phrase derived from Latin **2 :** Latin quality or character

Lat·in·ist \-n-əst\ *n* **:** a specialist in the Latin language or Roman culture

la·tin·i·ty \lə-ˈtin-ət-ē, lə-\ *n, often cap* **1 :** a way of speaking or writing Latin **2 :** LATINISM 2

lat·in·ize \ˈlat-n-ˌīz\ *vt, often cap* **:** to give Latin characteristics or forms to — **lat·in·i·za·tion** \ˌlat-n-ə-ˈzā-shən\ *n, often cap*

La·ti·no \lə-ˈtē-nō\ *n* **1 :** a native or inhabitant of Latin America **2 :** a person of Latin-American origin living in the U.S. [American Spanish, probably short for *latinoamericano* Latin American] — **Latino** *adj*

lat·ish \ˈlāt-ish\ *adj* **:** somewhat late

la·tis·si·mus dor·si \lə-ˈtis-ə-məs-ˈdȯr-sī\ *n, pl* **la·tis·si·mi dorsi** \-ˌmī-\ **:** a broad flat superficial muscle chiefly of the middle and lower back [New Latin, "broadest (muscle) of the back"]

lat·i·tude \ˈlat-ə-ˌtüd, -ˌtyüd\ *n* **1 a :** angular distance north or south from the earth's equator measured in degrees **b :** angular distance of a celestial body from the ecliptic **c :** a region or locality as marked by its latitude **2 :** the range of exposures within which a film or plate will produce a negative or positive of satisfactory quality **3 :** freedom from narrow restrictions ⟨were allowed great *latitude* in their editorials⟩ [Latin *latitudin-, latitudo* "width," from *latus* "wide"] — **lat·i·tu·di·nal** \ˌlat-ə-ˈtüd-nəl, -ˈtyüd-, -n-əl\ *adj* — **lat·i·tu·di·nal·ly** \-ē\ *adv*

latitude 1a

lat·i·tu·di·nar·i·an \ˌlat-ə-ˌtüd-n-ˈer-ē-ən, -ˌtyüd-\ *adj* **:** not insisting on strict conformity to a particular doctrine or standard **:** TOLERANT; *esp* **:** tolerant of variations in religious opinion or doctrine — **latitudinarian** *n* — **lat·i·tu·di·nar·i·an·ism** \-ē-ə-ˌniz-əm\ *n*

la·trine \lə-ˈtrēn\ *n* **1 :** a receptacle (as a pit in the earth) for use as a toilet **2 :** BATHROOM [French, from Latin *latrina* "washing place, latrine," derived from *lavere* "to wash"]

lat·ter \ˈlat-ər\ *adj* **1 a :** more recent **:** LATER **b :** of or relating to the end **:** FINAL **2 :** of, relating to, or being the second of two things referred to [Old English *lætra,* comparative of *læt* "late"]

lat·ter–day \ˌlat-ər-ˌdā\ *adj* **1 :** of a later or subsequent time **2 :** of present or recent times

Latter–day Saint *n, often cap D* **:** a member of a religious body founded by Joseph Smith in 1830 and accepting the Book of Mormon as divine revelation **:** MORMON

lat·ter·ly \ˈlat-ər-lē\ *adv* **:** LATELY, RECENTLY

lat·tice \ˈlat-əs\ *n* **1 a :** a framework or structure of crossed wood or metal strips **b :** a window, door, or gate having a lattice **2 :** a regular geometrical arrangement of points or objects over an area or in space ⟨the *lattice* of atoms in a crystal⟩ [Medieval French *latiz*] — **lattice** *vt* — **lat·ticed** \-əst\ *adj*

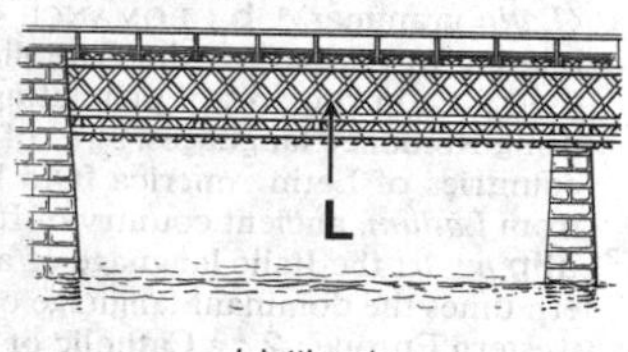

L lattice 1a

lat·tice·work \ˈlat-ə-ˌswərk\ *n* **:** a lattice or work made of lattices

¹Lat·vi·an \ˈlat-vē-ən\ *adj* **:** of, relating to, or characteristic of Latvia, the Latvians, or Latvian

²Latvian *n* **1 :** a native or inhabitant of Latvia **2 :** the Baltic language of the Latvian people

¹laud \ˈlȯd\ *n* **1** *pl, often cap* **:** an office of solemn praise to God forming with matins the first of the canonical hours **2 :** PRAISE 1, ACCLAIM [derived from Latin *laud-, laus* "praise"]

²laud *vt* **:** PRAISE 2, EXTOL

laud·able \ˈlȯd-ə-bəl\ *adj* **:** worthy of praise **:** COMMENDABLE — **laud·able·ness** \ˈlȯd-ə-bəl-nəs\ *n* — **laud·ably** \-blē\ *adv*

lau·da·num \ˈlȯd-nəm, -n-əm\ *n* **1 :** a formerly used preparation of opium **2 :** a tincture of opium [New Latin]

lau·da·tion \lȯ-ˈdā-shən\ *n* **:** the act of praising **:** EULOGY

lau·da·to·ry \ˈlȯd-ə-ˌtōr-ē, -ˌtȯr-\ *adj* **:** of, relating to, or expressing praise

¹laugh \ˈlaf, ˈlȧf\ *vb* **1 a :** to show emotion (as mirth, joy, or scorn) with a chuckle or explosive vocal sound **b :** to become amused or derisive ⟨*laughed* at their early efforts⟩ **2 :** to produce the sound or appearance of laughter **3 :** to utter with a laugh ⟨to *laugh* one's consent⟩ [Old English *hliehhan*] — **laugh·er** *n*

²laugh *n* **1 :** the act or sound of laughing **2 :** a cause for derision or merriment

laugh·able \ˈlaf-ə-bəl, ˈlȧf-\ *adj* **:** of a kind to provoke laughter or derision **:** RIDICULOUS — **laugh·able·ness** *n* — **laugh·ably** \-blē\ *adv*

synonyms LAUGHABLE, RISIBLE, LUDICROUS, RIDICULOUS mean provoking laughter or mirth. LAUGHABLE and RISIBLE may apply to anything that arouses laughter ⟨a *laughable* attempt at skating⟩ ⟨a *risible* movie⟩. LUDICROUS suggests obvious absurdity or preposterousness that excites both laughter and scorn or sometimes pity ⟨a thriller with a *ludicrous* plot⟩. RIDICULOUS implies extreme absurdity, foolishness, or ineptness ⟨a *ridiculous* display of anger⟩.

laughing gas *n* **:** NITROUS OXIDE

laughing jackass *n* **:** KOOKABURRA

laugh·ing·ly \ˈlaf-ing-lē, ˈlȧf-\ *adv* **:** with laughter

laughing matter *n* **:** something not to be taken seriously ⟨this is no *laughing matter*⟩

laugh·ing·stock \ˈlaf-ing-ˌstäk, ˈlȧf-\ *n* **:** an object of ridicule

laugh·ter \ˈlaf-tər, ˈlȧf-\ *n* **:** the action or sound of laughing [Old English *hleahtor*]

¹launch \ˈlȯnch, ˈlänch\ *vb* **1 a :** to throw or spring forward **:** HURL ⟨*launch* a spear⟩ **b :** to send off (a self-propelled object) ⟨*launch* a rocket⟩ **2 :** to set (a ship) afloat **3 a :** to put in operation **:** BEGIN ⟨*launch* an attack⟩ **b :** to give (a person) a start ⟨*launched* their children in the family business⟩ **4 a :** to make a start (as on a course of action) ⟨had *launched* on a difficult course of study⟩ **b :** to throw oneself energetically **:** PLUNGE ⟨*launched* into a dreary monologue⟩ [Medieval French *lancher, lancer,* from Late Latin *lanceare* "to wield a lance," from Latin *lancea* "lance"]

²launch *n* **:** an act of launching

³launch *n* **:** a small motorboat that is open or that has the front part of the hull covered [Portuguese *lancha*]

launch·er \ˈlȯn-chər, ˈlän-\ *n* **:** one that launches: as **a :** a device for firing a grenade from a rifle **b :** a device for launching a rocket or rocket shell

launch·pad *or* **launching pad** *n* **:** a nonflammable platform from which a rocket can be launched

laun·der \ˈlȯn-dər, ˈlän-\ *vb* **laun·dered; laun·der·ing** \-də-ring, -dring\ **1 :** to wash (as clothes) in water; *also* **:** to wash and iron ⟨a freshly *laundered* shirt⟩ **2 :** to wash or wash and iron clothing or household linens [Middle English *launder* "launderer," from Medieval French *lavandere,* from Medieval Latin *lavandarius,* from Latin *lavare* "to wash"] — **laun·der·er** \-dər-ər\ *n*

Laun·dro·mat \ˈlȯn-drə-ˌmat, ˈlän-\ *service mark* — used for a self-service laundry

laun·dry \ˈlȯn-drē, ˈlän-\ *n, pl* **-dries** **1 :** clothes or linens that have been or are to be laundered **2 :** a place where laundering is done

lau·re·ate \ˈlȯr-ē-ət, ˈlär-\ *n* **:** a recipient of honor for achievement in an art or science; *esp* **:** POET LAUREATE [Latin *laureatus* "crowned with laurel," from *laurea* "laurel wreath," from *laurus* "laurel"] — **laureate** *adj* — **lau·re·ate·ship** \-ˌship\ *n*

lau·rel \ˈlȯr-əl, ˈlär-\ *n* **1 :** an evergreen shrub or tree of southern Europe related to the sassafras and cinnamon with foliage used by the ancient Greeks to crown victors in various contests **2 :** a tree or shrub (as a mountain laurel) like the true laurel **3 a :** a crown of laurel awarded as an honor **b :** a recognition of achievement **:** HONOR — usually used in plural [derived from Latin *laurus*]

la·va \ˈläv-ə, ˈlav-\ *n* **:** molten rock coming from a volcano; *also* **:** such rock that has cooled and hardened [Italian, derived from Latin *labes* "fall"]

la·va·bo \lə-ˈväb-ō\ *n, pl* **-bos** *often cap* **:** a ceremony at Mass in which the celebrant after offering the oblations washes his hands and says Psalm 25:6–12 [Latin, "I shall wash," from *lavare* "to wash"]

la·vage \lə-ˈväzh\ *n* **:** a washing out (as of a wound or hollow organ) for medicinal reasons [French, from *laver* "to wash," from Latin *lavare*]

la·va·liere *also* **la·val·liere** \ˌläv-ə-ˈliər, ˌlav-\ *n* **:** a pendant on a fine chain that is worn as a necklace [French *lavallière* "necktie with a large knot"]

lav·a·to·ry \ˈlav-ə-ˌtōr-ē, -ˌtȯr-\ *n, pl* **-ries** **1 :** a vessel for washing; *esp* **:** a fixed bowl or basin with running water and drainpipe **2 :** a room with conveniences for washing and usually with one or more toilets **3 :** TOILET 2b [Medieval Latin *lavatorium,* from Latin *lavare* "to wash"]

lave \ˈlāv\ *vb* **1 a :** WASH 1 **b** *archaic* **:** to wash oneself **:** BATHE **2 :** to flow along or against ⟨water *laving* the shore⟩ [Old English *lafian,* from Latin *lavare*]

lav·en·der \ˈlav-ən-dər\ *n* **1 :** a Mediterranean mint widely cultivated for its narrow aromatic leaves and spikes of lilac-purple flowers which are dried and used in sachets and from which is extracted a fragrant oil used chiefly in perfumes; *also* **:** any of several related plants used similarly **2 :** a pale purple [Medieval French *lavendre,* from Medieval Latin *lavandula*]

¹la·ver \ˈlā-vər\ *n* **:** a large basin used for ceremonial ablutions in ancient Judaism [Medieval French *lavour,* derived from Latin *lavare* "to wash"]

²la·ver \ˈlā-vər, ˈlä-\ *n* **:** any of several mostly edible seaweeds [Latin, a water plant]

¹lav·ish \ˈlav-ish\ *adj* **1 :** spending or giving more than is necessary **:** EXTRAVAGANT ⟨*lavish* with money⟩ ⟨*lavish* of praise⟩ **2 :** produced or given freely or in abundance ⟨*lavish* hospitality⟩ [Middle English *laves, lavage,* probably from Medieval French *lavasse, lavache* "downpour of rain," from *laver* "to wash," from Latin *lavare*] — **lav·ish·ly** *adv* — **lav·ish·ness** *n*

²lavish *vt* **:** to spend or give freely ⟨*lavish* affection on them⟩

law \ˈlȯ\ *n* **1 a :** a rule of conduct or action established by custom or laid down by the supreme governing authority of a community, state, or nation **b :** a body of such rules and customs **2 a :** the state of order brought about by observance and enforcement of laws ⟨preserve *law* and order⟩ **b :** an agent or agency for enforcing laws ⟨an officer of the *law*⟩ **c :** the action of laws and especially court action as a means of achieving justice or redressing wrongs **3 a** *often cap* **:** the revelation of the divine will set forth in the Old Testament **b** *cap* **:** the first part of the Jewish scriptures — see BIBLE table; compare PROPHETS, WRITINGS **4 a :** the legal profession **b :** law as an area of knowledge ⟨study *law*⟩ **5 :** a rule of construction or procedure (as in an art, craft, or game) **6 :** something that has the force of authority and must be obeyed ⟨in the classroom the teacher's word is *law*⟩ **7 :** a rule or principle stating something that always works in the same way under the same conditions ⟨the *law* of gravity⟩ [Old English *lagu,* of Scandinavian origin]

synonyms LAW, REGULATION, STATUTE, ORDINANCE mean a principle that governs action or procedure. LAW implies imposition by a sovereign authority and obligation of obedience by all ⟨obey the *law*⟩. REGULATION carries an implication of authority exercised in order to control an organization or system ⟨*regulations* affecting nuclear power plants⟩. STATUTE implies a law enacted by a legislative body often as distinguished from the common or unwritten law ⟨a *statute* requiring the use of seatbelts⟩. ORDINANCE applies to an order governing some detail or procedure enforced by a limited authority such as a municipality ⟨city *ordinances* for traffic regulation⟩.

synonyms see in addition HYPOTHESIS

law–abid·ing \ˈlȯ-ə-ˌbīd-ing\ *adj* **:** obedient to the law

law·break·er \ˈlȯ-ˌbrā-kər\ *n* **:** a person who breaks the law — **law·break·ing** \-king\ *adj or n*

law·ful \ˈlȯ-fəl\ *adj* **1 :** permitted or not prohibited by law ⟨conduct a demonstration in a *lawful* manner⟩ **2 :** established or recognized by law **:** RIGHTFUL ⟨the *lawful* owner⟩ — **law·ful·ly** \-fə-lē, -flē\ *adv* — **law·ful·ness** \-fəl-nəs\ *n*

synonyms LAWFUL, LEGAL, LEGITIMATE, LICIT mean being in accordance with law. LAWFUL stresses conformity to law of any kind ⟨the *lawful* sovereign⟩. LEGAL applies to what is sanctioned by law or in conformity with law, especially as it is written or administered by the courts ⟨*legal* residents of the state⟩. LEGITIMATE implies a legal right or one supported by tradition, custom, or accepted standards ⟨the *legitimate* heir to the throne⟩ ⟨a *legitimate* question⟩. LICIT emphasizes strict conformity to law specifically regulating the way something is performed or carried on ⟨the *licit* use of drugs by hospitals⟩.

law·giv·er \ˈlȯ-ˌgiv-ər\ *n* **1 :** one who gives a code of laws to a people **2 :** LEGISLATOR

law·less \ˈlȯ-ləs\ *adj* **1 :** having no laws **:** not based on or regulated by law ⟨the *lawless* frontier⟩ **2 :** not controlled by law **:** UNRULY, DISORDERLY ⟨a *lawless* mob⟩ — **law·less·ly** *adv* — **law·less·ness** *n*

law·mak·er \ˈlȯ-ˌmā-kər\ *n* **:** a person who has a part in framing laws **:** LEGISLATOR — **law·mak·ing** *adj or n*

¹lawn \ˈlȯn, ˈlän\ *n* **:** a fine sheer linen or cotton fabric of plain weave that is thinner than cambric [probably from *Laon,* France] — **lawny** \-ē\ *adj*

²lawn *n* **:** ground (as around a house) covered with grass that is kept mowed [Middle English *launde* "glade, pasture," from Medieval French *land, launde* "wood, unwooded field," of Celtic origin]

lawn bowling *n* **:** a bowling game played on a green with wooden balls which are rolled at a jack

lawn mower *n* **:** a machine for cutting grass on lawns

lawn tennis *n* **:** TENNIS

law of cosines : a theorem in trigonometry: the square of a side of a plane triangle equals the sum of the squares of the remaining sides minus twice the product of those sides and the cosine of the angle included between them

law of definite proportions : a statement in chemistry: every definite compound always contains the same elements in the same proportions by mass

law of dominance : MENDEL'S LAW 3

law of independent assortment : MENDEL'S LAW 2

law of Mo·ses \-ˈmō-zəz, -zəs\ **:** PENTATEUCH

law of segregation : MENDEL'S LAW 1

law of sines : a theorem in trigonometry: the ratio of the length of each side of a plane triangle to the sine of the opposite angle is the same for all three sides and angles

law·ren·ci·um \lȯ-ˈren-sē-əm\ *n* **:** a short-lived radioactive element produced artificially — see ELEMENT table [New Latin, from Ernest O. *Lawrence,* died 1958, American physicist]

law·suit \ˈlȯ-ˌsüt\ *n* **:** a suit in law **:** a legal case

law·yer \ˈlȯ-yər, ˈlȯi-ər\ *n* **:** one whose profession is to conduct lawsuits and to advise clients on legal matters and represent them in court

lax \ˈlaks\ *adj* **1 :** lacking in restraint or the power to restrain ⟨*lax* bowels⟩ **2 :** not strict or stringent ⟨*lax* discipline⟩ **3 a :** not firm or rigid **b :** having an open or loose texture ⟨a *lax* flower cluster⟩ **4 :** produced with the speech muscles in a relatively relaxed state ⟨the *lax* vowels \i\ and \u̇\⟩ — compare TENSE [Latin *laxus* "loose"] — **lax·ly** \ˈlak-slē\ *adv* — **lax·ness** *n*

¹lax·a·tive \ˈlak-sət-iv\ *adj* **:** having a tendency to loosen or relax; *esp* **:** relieving constipation

²laxative *n* **:** a usually mild laxative drug — compare PURGATIVE

lax·i·ty \ˈlak-sət-ē\ *n* **:** the quality or state of being lax ⟨*laxity* in discipline⟩

¹lay \ˈlā\ *vb* **laid** \ˈlād\; **lay·ing** **1 :** to beat or strike down ⟨wheat *laid* flat by a hailstorm⟩ **2 a :** to put or set on or against something ⟨*lay* the book on the table⟩ ⟨*lay* a watch to one's ear⟩ **b :** to place or put down in order or position ⟨*lay* bricks⟩ ⟨*lay* the table⟩ **3 :** to place for rest or sleep; *esp* **:** BURY 1 **4 :** to produce and deposit eggs ⟨the hens won't *lay*⟩ **5 a :** to put forward for consideration **:** SUBMIT ⟨*laid* their case before the committee⟩ **b :** ASSERT, ALLEGE ⟨*lay* claim to the estate⟩ **c :** to place (as emphasis or importance) on something ⟨*lay* great stress on neatness⟩ **6 :** SET, IMPOSE ⟨*lay* a tax on liquor⟩ **7 a :** CONTRIVE, DEVISE ⟨*lay* plans⟩ **b :** to make ready or put in operation ⟨*laid* a trap⟩ **8 a :** BET 1 ⟨*lay* $10 on the race⟩ **b :** BET 2 ⟨*lay* you ten to one⟩ **9 :** to cause to settle or subside ⟨a shower *laid* the dust⟩; *also* **:** CALM, ALLAY ⟨*laid* their fears⟩ **10 :** to assign as a burden of reproach ⟨*laid* the blame on me⟩ **11 :** to bring to a specified condition ⟨*lay* waste the land⟩ **12** *nonstandard* **:** ¹LIE [Old English *lecgan*] — **lay eyes on :** to catch sight of **:** SEE — **lay into :** to attack especially verbally

usage LAY has been used as an intransitive verb (that is, a verb that does not have an indirect object) meaning "lie" for over 700 years (as in "tried to make the book *lay* flat," or "*lay* down on the job"). By the late 1700s, however, it was being labeled as a mistake. Since then grammarians have succeeded in eliminating the use from most literary and learned writing, but it persists in speech and informal writing. Part of the problem lies in the confusing similarity of the inflected forms of the two words (the past tense and past participle of *lay* are both *laid;* the past tense of *lie* is *lay* and the past participle of *lie* is *lain*). Remember that even though many people use *lay* for *lie,* you will likely be criticized if you do.

[2]lay *n* **1 :** the way in which a thing lies or is laid in relation to something else ⟨*lay* of the land⟩ **2 :** the state of one that lays eggs ⟨hens coming into *lay*⟩

[3]lay *past of* LIE

[4]lay *n* **1 :** a simple narrative poem **:** BALLAD **2 :** MELODY 2, SONG [Medieval French *lai*]

[5]lay *adj* **1 :** of or relating to the laity **:** not ecclesiastical **2 :** of or relating to members of a religious house occupied with domestic or manual work ⟨a *lay* brother⟩ **3 :** not of or from a particular profession ⟨the *lay* public⟩ [Medieval French *lai,* from Late Latin *laicus,* from Greek *laikos* "of the people," from *laos* "people"]

lay·away \ˈlā-ə-ˌwā\ *n* **:** a purchasing agreement by which a seller agrees to hold merchandise on which a deposit has been made until the price is paid in full by the buyer

lay away *vt* **:** to put aside for future use or delivery

lay by *vt* **:** to store for future use **:** SAVE

lay down *vt* **1 :** to give up **:** SURRENDER ⟨*lay down* your arms⟩ **2 a :** ESTABLISH, PRESCRIBE ⟨*lays down* standards⟩ **b :** to assert or command dogmatically ⟨*lay down* the law⟩

[1]lay·er \ˈlā-ər, ˈle-ər, ˈler\ *n* **1 :** one that lays ⟨the hens were poor *layers*⟩ **2 :** one thickness, course, or fold laid or lying over or under another ⟨a *layer* of rock⟩ **3 a :** a branch or shoot of a plant that roots while still attached to the parent plant **b :** a plant developed by layering — **lay·ered** \ˈlā-ərd, ˈle-ərd, ˈlerd\ *adj*

[2]layer *vt* **1 :** to propagate (a plant) by means of layers **2 :** to separate into layers **3 :** to form by adding layers

lay·er·age \ˈlā-ə-rij, ˈle-ə-\ *n* **:** the practice, art, or process of rooting plants by layering

lay·ette \lā-ˈet\ *n* **:** a complete outfit of clothing and equipment for a newborn infant [French, from Middle French, from *laye* "box," from Dutch *lade*]

lay figure \ˈlā-\ *n* **1 :** a jointed model of the human body used by artists to show the disposition of drapery **2 :** a person so compliant as to be a puppet [obsolete *layman* "lay figure," from Dutch *ledeman, leeman,* from *lid* "limb" + *man* "man"]

lay in *vt* **:** to store up **:** LAY BY ⟨*lay in* a supply of groceries⟩

lay·man \ˈlā-mən\ *n* **1 :** a person who is not a member of the clergy **2 :** a person who is not a member of a particular profession

lay·off \ˈlā-ˌȯf\ *n* **1 :** the act of laying off an employee or a workforce **2 :** a period of inactivity or idleness

lay off \lā-ˈȯf, ˈlā-\ *vb* **1 :** to mark or measure off **2 :** to cease to employ (a worker) often temporarily **3 a :** to leave undisturbed ⟨*lay off* me, will you⟩ **b :** AVOID, QUIT ⟨*lay off* smoking⟩ **4 :** to stop or rest from work

lay on *vi* **:** ATTACK, BEAT

lay·out \ˈlā-ˌau̇t\ *n* **1 :** ARRANGEMENT, PLAN ⟨the *layout* of a house⟩ **2 :** something that is laid out ⟨a model train *layout*⟩ **3 :** the way in which a piece of printed matter is arranged ⟨the *layout* of a page⟩; *also* **:** DUMMY 6 **4 :** a set or outfit especially of tools

lay out \lā-ˈau̇t, ˈlā-\ *vt* **1 :** to prepare (a corpse) for burial **2 :** to plan in detail ⟨*lay out* a campaign⟩ **3 :** ARRANGE 1, DESIGN **4 :** SPEND 1

lay·over \ˈlā-ˌō-vər\ *n* **:** STOPOVER 1

lay over \lā-ˈō-vər, ˈlā-\ *vi* **:** to make a temporary halt or stop ⟨*laid over* in New York for three days before flying back⟩

lay·peo·ple \ˈlā-ˌpē-pəl\ *n* **:** LAYPERSONS

lay·per·son \ˈlā-ˌpərs-n\ *n* **:** a member of the laity

lay reader *n* **:** a layperson authorized to conduct parts of the church service not requiring a priest or minister

lay to \lā-ˈtü, ˈlā-\ *vb* **:** to bring (a ship) into the wind and hold stationary **:** lie to

lay–up \ˈlā-ˌəp\ *n* **1 :** the action of laying up or the condition of being laid up **2 :** a jumping one-hand shot in basketball made from close under the basket by laying the ball over the rim or bouncing it off the backboard

lay up \lā-ˈəp, ˈlā-\ *vt* **1 :** to store up **:** lay by **2 :** to disable or confine with illness or injury ⟨a knee injury *laid* her *up* for a week⟩ **3 :** to take out of active service

lay·wom·an \-ˌwu̇m-ən\ *n* **:** a woman who is a member of the laity

la·zar \ˈlaz-ər, ˈlā-zər\ *n* **:** a person afflicted with a repulsive disease; *esp* **:** LEPER [Medieval Latin *lazarus,* from Late Latin *Lazarus,* beggar in parable in Luke 16:20–31]

laz·a·ret·to \ˌlaz-ə-ˈret-ō\ *or* **laz·a·ret** \-ˈret, -ˈrēt\ *n, pl* **-rettos** *or* **-rets** **1** *usually lazaretto* **:** a hospital for contagious diseases **2 :** a building or a ship used for detention in quarantine **3** *usually lazaret* **:** a space in a ship between decks used as a storeroom [Italian dialect *lazzaretto,* alteration of *Nazaretto,* from *Santa Maria di Nazareth,* church in Venice that maintained a hospital]

laze \ˈlāz\ *vb* **:** to pass time in idleness or relaxation **:** IDLE [back-formation from *lazy*] ***synonyms*** see IDLE

la·zy \ˈlā-zē\ *adj* **la·zi·er; -est** **1 :** not willing to act or work **:** IDLE, INDOLENT **2 :** SLOW, SLUGGISH ⟨a *lazy* stream⟩ [perhaps from Low German *lasich* "feeble"] — **la·zi·ly** \-zə-lē\ *adv* — **la·zi·ness** \-zē-nəs\ *n* — **la·zy·ish** \-zē-ish\ *adj*

la·zy·bones \ˈlā-zē-ˌbōnz\ *n sing or pl* **:** a lazy person

lazy eye *n* **:** AMBLYOPIA; *also* **:** an eye affected with amblyopia

lazy Su·san \ˌlā-zē-ˈsüz-n\ *n* **:** a revolving tray placed on a dining table for serving food, condiments, or relishes

LCD \ˌel-ˌsē-ˈdē\ *n* **:** an electronic display that consists of a liquid with properties like a crystal which can reflect light [*l*iquid *c*rystal *d*isplay]

LDL \ˌel-ˌdē-ˈel\ *n* **:** a lipoprotein of blood plasma that has a high proportion of cholesterol and is associated with increased probability of developing atherosclerosis — called also *bad cholesterol, low-density lipoprotein*; compare HDL [*l*ow-*d*ensity *l*ipoprotein]

lea *or* **ley** \ˈlē, ˈlā\ *n* **1 :** GRASSLAND, PASTURE **2** *usually ley* **:** arable land used temporarily for hay or grazing [Old English *lēah*]

leach \ˈlēch\ *vt* **:** to pass a liquid and especially water through to carry off the soluble components; *also* **:** to dissolve out by such means ⟨*leach* alkali from ashes⟩ [*leach* "vessel through which water is passed to extract lye"]

[1]lead \ˈlēd\ *vb* **led** \ˈled\; **lead·ing** \ˈlēd-ing\ **1 :** to force to go with one ⟨police *led* the prisoner to jail⟩ **2 a :** to guide on the way **:** show the way ⟨you *lead* and we will follow⟩ **b :** to serve as a route or passage ⟨this road *leads* straight into town⟩ **c :** to be an entrance or connection ⟨that door *leads* to the kitchen⟩ **3 :** to serve as a channel for ⟨a pipe *leads* water to the house⟩ **4 :** to pass one's days in **:** LIVE ⟨*lead* an active life⟩ **5 a :** to march or go at the head of ⟨*lead* a parade⟩ **b :** to have first place in ⟨*leads* the world in coffee exports⟩; *also* **:** to serve as an example — often used in the phrase *lead the way* ⟨*lead* the way on political reform⟩ **c :** to have a margin over ⟨*leading* by 20 points at halftime⟩ **d :** to direct the operations, activity, or performance of ⟨*lead* an orchestra⟩ ⟨*leads* a Bible-study group⟩ **e :** to serve as guide for by performing one's own part ⟨*led* the choir in singing⟩ **6 a :** to influence to come to a conclusion ⟨you *led* me to believe you loved me⟩ **b :** to tempt or talk into going ⟨*led* them all astray⟩ **7 a :** to play as the first card or suit in a round ⟨*lead* trumps⟩ **b :** to be the first player of a round at cards ⟨*led* with an ace⟩ **8 :** to begin a series of blows in boxing ⟨*leading* with a right⟩ **9 :** to have as a definite aim or result ⟨study that *leads* to a degree⟩ [Old English *lǣdan*] ***synonyms*** see GUIDE

[2]lead *n* **1 a** (1) **:** position at the front **:** VANGUARD (2) **:** INITIATIVE 1 (3) **:** the act or privilege of leading in cards; *also* **:** the card or suit led **b :** EXAMPLE, PRECEDENT ⟨follow their *lead*⟩ **c :** a margin or measure of advantage or superiority or position in advance ⟨has a 2-length *lead*⟩ **2 :** one that leads: as **a :** INDICATION 2, CLUE **b :** a principal role in a dramatic production; *also* **:** one who plays such a role **c :** LEASH 1 **d :** an introductory section of a news story; *also* **:** a news story of chief importance **e :** the first in a series or exchange of blows in boxing **3 :** an insulated electrical conductor **4 :** a position taken by a base runner off a base toward the next

[3]lead *adj* **:** acting or serving as a lead or leader ⟨the *lead* article in this month's issue⟩

[4]lead \ˈled\ *n* **1 :** a soft malleable bluish white heavy metallic chemical element that is found mostly in combination and is used especially in pipes, cable sheaths, solder, batteries, and shields against radioactivity — see ELEMENT table **2 a :** a mass of lead used on a line for finding the depth of water (as in the ocean) **b** *pl* **:** lead framing for panes in windows **c :** a thin strip of metal used to separate lines of type in printing **3 a :** a thin stick of marking substance (as graphite) in or for a pencil

b : WHITE LEAD **4** : bullets in quantity **5** : TETRAETHYL LEAD [Old English *lēad*] — **lead·less** \-ləs\ *adj*

[5]**lead** \ˈled\ *vt* **1** : to cover, line, or weight with lead **2** : to fix (glass) in position with lead **3** : to place lead or other spacing material between the lines of (type matter) **4** : to treat or mix with lead or a lead compound ⟨*leaded* gasoline⟩

lead acetate *n* : a poisonous soluble salt of lead $PbC_4H_6O_4 \cdot 3H_2O$ used in dyeing and printing

lead arsenate *n* : an acid salt of lead $PbHAsO_4$ used as an insecticide

lead dioxide *n* : a poisonous compound PbO_2 that is used as an oxidizing agent and as an electrode in batteries — called also *lead peroxide*

lead·en \ˈled-n\ *adj* **1 a** : made of lead **b** : of the color of lead : dull gray **2** : low in quality : POOR **3 a** : oppressively heavy **b** : SLUGGISH **c** : lacking spirit or animation : DULL ⟨*leaden* spirits⟩ — **lead·en·ly** *adv* — **lead·en·ness** \-n-nəs, -n-əs\ *n*

lead·er \ˈlēd-ər\ *n* **1** : one that leads: as **a** : one that goes along to guide and show the way **b** : one that directs or has authority over others: (1) : COMMANDER 1 (2) : FOREMAN, STRAW BOSS **c** : one that is foremost or that sets an example ⟨a *leader* in fashion⟩ **d** : CONDUCTOR b **e** : an animal placed at the head of a team **f** *pl* : dots or hyphens used (as in an index) to lead the eye horizontally across the page; *also* : ELLIPSIS 2 **g** : a pipe for conducting fluid **h** : an article offered at an attractive special low price to stimulate business **2 a** : a main shoot of a plant **b** : TENDON, SINEW **3** : a short length of material for attaching a lure or hook to the end of a fishing line — **lead·er·less** \-ləs\ *adj* — **lead·er·ship** \-ˌship\ *n*

lead–in \ˈlēd-ˌin\ *n* : something (as a television show or segment) that leads into something else — **lead–in** *adj*

lead·ing \ˈlēd-ing\ *adj* **1** : coming or ranking first or among the first : FOREMOST **2** : exercising leadership **3** : serving to guide or direct ⟨a *leading* question⟩ **4** : given most prominent display

leading lady *n* : an actress who plays the leading feminine role in a play or movie

leading light *n* : a prominent or influential member (as of a field of study, political movement, or artistic endeavor)

leading man *n* : an actor who plays the leading male role in a play or movie

leading tone *n* : the seventh musical degree of a major or minor scale — called also *subtonic* [from its leading harmonically to the tonic]

lead monoxide \ˈled-\ *n* : a yellow to brownish red poisonous compound PbO used in rubber manufacture and glassmaking

lead·off \ˈlēd-ˌȯf\ *n* **1** : a beginning or leading action **2** : one that leads off — **lead–off** *adj*

lead off \lēd-ˈȯf, ˈlēd-\ *vt* **1** : to make a start on : BEGIN **2** : to bat first for a baseball team in (an inning)

lead on *vt* : to entice or induce to adopt or continue in a course of action or belief especially when unwise or mistaken ⟨*led on* by the promise of wealth⟩

lead oxide *n* : an oxide of lead; *esp* : LEAD MONOXIDE

lead pencil \ˈled-\ *n* : a pencil using graphite as the marking material

lead poisoning *n* : a chronic abnormal condition that is produced by absorption of lead into the body and results in various bodily symptoms (as fatigue, nausea, appetite loss, anemia, and paralysis or weakness of muscles)

lead sulfide *n* : a black compound PbS that is used in light-sensitive electrical cells

lead up \lēd-ˈəp, ˈlēd-\ *vi* **1** : to prepare the way — used with *to* ⟨events *leading up* to the war⟩ **2** : to make a gradual or indirect approach to a topic — used with *to*

[1]**leaf** \ˈlēf\ *n, pl* **leaves** \ˈlēvz\ **1 a** : a usually green flat lateral outgrowth from a plant stem that functions primarily in food manufacture by photosynthesis **b** : FOLIAGE ⟨trees in full *leaf*⟩ **2** : something suggestive of a leaf: as **a** : a part of a book or folded sheet containing a page on each side

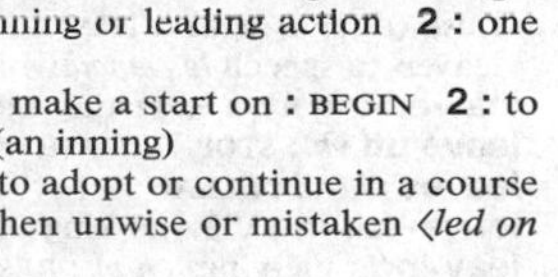

leaf 1a: *1* petiole, *2* rachis, *3* stipule, *4* leaflet

b : a part (as of window shutters, folding doors, or gates) that slides or is hinged **c** : a movable or removable part of a table top **d** : a thin sheet (as of metal) : LAMINA **e** : one of the plates of a leaf spring [Old English *lēaf*] — **leaf·less** \ˈlē-fləs\ *adj* — **leaf·like** \ˈlē-ˌflīk\ *adj*

[2]**leaf** *vi* **1** : to produce leaves **2** : to turn the pages of a book

leaf·age \ˈlē-fij\ *n* : FOLIAGE

leaf bud *n* : a bud that develops into a leafy shoot and does not produce flowers

leaf–cut·ter \ˈlēf-ˌkət-ər\ *n* : any of various chiefly tropical American ants that cut and carry off leaves of plants which they use in culturing fungi for food — called also *leaf-cutting ant*

leaf fat *n* : the fat that lines the abdominal cavity and encloses the kidneys; *esp* : such fat of a hog used in the manufacture of lard

leaf·hop·per \ˈlēf-ˌhäp-ər\ *n* : any of numerous small leaping insects that are related to the cicadas and aphids and suck the juices of plants

leaf lard *n* : high quality lard made from leaf fat

leaf·let \ˈlē-flət\ *n* **1 a** : one of the divisions of a compound leaf **b** : a small or young foliage leaf **2** : a leaflike organ or part (as one of the flaps of a heart valve) **3** : a usually folded printed sheet intended for free distribution

leaf miner *n* : any of various small insects (as moths or two-winged flies) that as larvae burrow in and eat the tissue of leaves

leaf mold *n* : a compost or layer composed chiefly of decayed leaves

leaf spring *n* : a usually crescent-shaped spring made of several strips of metal of unequal length stacked and fastened together and arranged in length from longest to shortest

leaf·stalk \ˈlēf-ˌstȯk\ *n* : PETIOLE 1

leafy \ˈlē-fē\ *adj* **leaf·i·er; -est** **1** : having or abounding in leaves ⟨*leafy* woodlands⟩ **2** : consisting mostly of leaves ⟨*leafy* vegetables⟩ **3** : resembling a leaf

[1]**league** \ˈlēg\ *n* : any of various units of distance from about 2.4 to 4.6 statute miles (3.9 to 7.4 kilometers) [Late Latin *leuga*]

[2]**league** *n* **1 a** : an association or alliance of nations for a common purpose **b** : an association of persons or groups united for common interests or goals; *esp* : an association of athletic teams **2** : CLASS, CATEGORY ⟨a bit out of your *league*⟩ [Middle French *ligue*, from Italian *liga*, from *ligare* "to bind," from Latin] — **league** *vb*

leagu·er \ˈlē-gər\ *n* : a member of a league

[1]**leak** \ˈlēk\ *vb* **1** : to enter or escape or permit to enter or escape through an opening usually by a fault or mistake ⟨fumes *leak* in⟩ **2** : to become known despite efforts at concealment ⟨the secret *leaked* out⟩ **3** : to give out (information) secretly ⟨*leaked* the story to the press⟩ [from or akin to Dutch *leken*]

[2]**leak** *n* **1 a** : a hole, crack, or flaw that lets something enter or escape **b** : a person who leaks information **2** : LEAKAGE 1a — **leak·proof** \-ˌprüf\ *adj*

leak·age \ˈlē-kij\ *n* **1 a** : the act, process, or an instance of leaking **b** : loss of electricity due especially to faulty insulation **2** : something or the amount that leaks in or out

leaky \ˈlē-kē\ *adj* **leak·i·er; -est** : permitting fluid to leak in or out — **leak·i·ness** *n*

[1]**lean** \ˈlēn\ *vb* **leaned** \ˈlēnd, *chiefly British* ˈlent\; **lean·ing** \ˈlē-ning\ **1 a** : to incline, deviate, or bend from a vertical position **b** : to shift one's weight to one side for support : rest against something ⟨*lean* on me⟩ **2** : to rely for support or inspiration ⟨children who *lean* on their parents⟩ **3** : to incline in opinion, taste, or desire ⟨*lean* toward simplicity⟩ [Old English *hleonian*]

[2]**lean** *n* : the act or an instance of leaning : INCLINATION

[3]**lean** *adj* **1 a** : lacking or deficient in flesh : THIN ⟨*lean* cattle⟩ **b** : containing little or no fat ⟨*lean* meat⟩ **2** : lacking richness, sufficiency, or productiveness **3** : characterized by economy of style or expression ⟨*lean,* compact writing⟩ [Old English *hlǣne*] — **lean·ness** \ˈlēn-nəs\ *n*

[4]**lean** *n* : the part of meat that consists principally of fat-free muscle

lean·ing \ˈlē-ning\ *n* : INCLINATION 2, TENDENCY

leant \ˈlent\ *chiefly British past of* LEAN

\ə\ **abut**	\au̇\ **out**	\i\ **tip**	\ȯ\ **saw**	\u̇\ **foot**
\ər\ **further**	\ch\ **chin**	\ī\ **life**	\ȯi\ **coin**	\y\ **yet**
\a\ **mat**	\e\ **pet**	\j\ **job**	\th\ **thin**	\yü\ **few**
\ā\ **take**	\ē\ **easy**	\ng\ **sing**	\t͟h\ **this**	\yu̇\ **cure**
\ä\ **cot, cart**	\g\ **go**	\ō\ **bone**	\ü\ **food**	\zh\ **vision**

[1]**lean–to** \ˈlēn-ˌtü\ *n, pl* **lean–tos** **1 :** a wing or extension of a building having a lean-to roof **2 :** a rough shed or shelter with a lean-to roof

[2]**lean–to** *adj* **:** having only one slope or pitch ⟨a *lean-to* roof⟩

[1]**leap** \ˈlēp\ *vb* **leaped** *or* **leapt** \ˈlēpt, ˈlept\; **leap•ing** \ˈlē-piŋ\ **1 :** to spring or cause to spring free from or as if from the ground **:** JUMP ⟨*leap* over a fence⟩ ⟨*leap* a horse over a ditch⟩ **2 a :** to pass abruptly from one state or topic to another **b :** to act precipitately ⟨*leaped* at the chance⟩ [Old English *hlēapan*] — **leap•er** \ˈlē-pər\ *n*

[2]**leap** *n* **1 a :** an act of leaping **:** SPRING, BOUND **b** (1) **:** a place leaped over or from (2) **:** the distance covered by a leap **2 :** a sudden transition — **by leaps and bounds :** very rapidly ⟨improved *by leaps and bounds*⟩

leap•frog \ˈlēp-ˌfrȯg, -ˌfräg\ *n* **:** a game in which one player vaults over another who has bent down

leap year *n* **:** a year in the Gregorian calendar containing 366 days with February 29 as the extra day

learn \ˈlərn\ *vb* **learned** \ˈlərnd, ˈlərnt\ *also* **learnt** \ˈlərnt\; **learn•ing** **1 a :** to gain knowledge or understanding of or skill in by study, instruction, or experience **b :** MEMORIZE ⟨*learn* the lines of a play⟩ **c :** to come to realize ⟨*learned* that honesty paid⟩ **2** *substandard* **:** to cause to learn **:** TEACH **3 :** to find out **:** ASCERTAIN **4 :** to acquire knowledge ⟨never too late to *learn*⟩ [Old English *leornian*] ***synonyms*** see DISCOVER — **learn•able** \ˈlər-nə-bəl\ *adj* — **learn•er** *n*

usage *Learn* implies acquiring knowledge, while *teach* implies imparting it. Though *learn* has been used to mean "teach," it is no longer an accepted usage. The use of *learn* in this way still persists in speech but its appearance in writing occurs mainly in the representation of such speech or its deliberate imitation for effect ⟨I'll *learn* him a thing or two⟩.

learned *adj* **1** \ˈlər-nəd\ **:** characterized by or associated with learning ⟨*learned* professors⟩ **2** \ˈlərnd, ˈlərnt\ **:** acquired by learning ⟨*learned* responses⟩ — **learn•ed•ly** \ˈlər-nəd-lē\ *adv* — **learn•ed•ness** \ˈlər-nəd-nəs\ *n*

learn•ing *n* **1 :** the act or experience of one that learns **2 :** knowledge or skill acquired by instruction or study

learning disability *n* **:** any of various conditions (as attention deficit disorder and dyslexia) that interfere with a person's ability to learn and result in impaired functioning in language, reasoning, or academic skills — **learning disabled** *adj*

[1]**lease** \ˈlēs\ *n* **1 :** a contract by which one party grants the use of property or facilities to another for a fixed or open period of time usually for a specified rent; *also* **:** the act of making such a grant or the term for which it is made **2 :** a piece of land or property that is leased [Medieval French *les,* from *lesser, laissier* "to leave, hand over, lease," from Latin *laxare* "to loosen," from *laxus* "loose"]

[2]**lease** *vt* **1 :** to grant by lease **:** LET **2 :** to hold or use under a lease ***synonyms*** see HIRE

lease•hold \ˈlēs-ˌhōld\ *n* **1 :** a tenure by lease **2 :** land held by lease — **lease•hold•er** \-ˌhōl-dər\ *n*

leash \ˈlēsh\ *n* **1 :** a line for leading or restraining an animal **2 :** a set of three animals (as dogs) [Medieval French *lesse,* probably from *lesser* "to leave, let go," from Latin *laxare* "to loosen," from *laxus* "loose"] — **leash** *vt*

[1]**least** \ˈlēst\ *adj* **1 :** lowest in importance or position **2 a :** smallest in size or degree **b :** smallest possible **:** SLIGHTEST [Old English *lǣst,* superlative of *lǣssa* "less"]

[2]**least** *n* **:** one that is least (as in value, importance, or scope) ⟨I don't care in the *least*⟩ ⟨the *least* that can be said⟩ — **at least** **1 :** at the minimum **2 :** in any case

[3]**least** *adv* **:** in the smallest or lowest degree

least common denominator *n* **:** the least common multiple of the denominators of two or more fractions — called also *lowest common denominator*

least common multiple *n* **:** the smallest number that is a multiple of each of two or more numbers — called also *lowest common multiple*

least•wise \ˈlēst-ˌwīz\ *adv* **:** at least ⟨*leastwise,* that's what I heard⟩

[1]**leath•er** \ˈleth-ər\ *n* **1 :** animal skin dressed for use **2 :** something wholly or partly made of leather [Old English *lether-*] — **leather** *adj*

[2]**leather** *vt* **leath•ered; leath•er•ing** \ˈleth-riŋ, -ə-riŋ\ **1 :** to cover with leather **2 :** to beat with a strap **:** THRASH

leath•er•back \ˈleth-ər-ˌbak\ *n* **:** the largest existing sea turtle with a shell composed of small bones embedded in a thick leathery skin

Leath•er•ette \ˌleth-ə-ˈret\ *trademark* — used for a product colored, finished, and embossed in imitation of leather grains

leath•ern \ˈleth-ərn\ *adj* **:** made of, consisting of, or resembling leather

leath•er•neck \ˈleth-ər-ˌnek\ *n* **:** a U.S. marine [from the leather collar formerly part of the uniform]

leath•ery \ˈleth-rē, -ə-rē\ *adj* **:** resembling leather in appearance or texture **:** TOUGH ⟨a *leathery* face⟩ ⟨*leathery* leaves⟩

[1]**leave** \ˈlēv\ *vb* **left** \ˈleft\; **leav•ing** **1 a** (1) **:** to give by will **:** BEQUEATH ⟨*left* a fortune to his daughter⟩ (2) **:** to have remaining after one's death ⟨*leaves* a widow and two children⟩ **b :** to cause to remain as a trace or aftereffect ⟨the wound *left* a scar⟩; *also* **:** to cause to remain behind ⟨*leave* your valuables at home⟩ **2 a :** to cause or allow to be or remain in a specified condition ⟨*leave* the door open⟩ **b :** to fail to include or take along ⟨*left* my books at home⟩ ⟨the movie *leaves* a lot out⟩ **c :** to have as a remainder ⟨taking 4 from 7 *leaves* 3⟩ **d :** to permit to be or remain subject to another's action or control ⟨just *leave* everything to me⟩ **e :** [3]LET 3 **f :** to cause or allow to be or remain available ⟨*leave* room for expansion⟩ **3 a :** to go away from **:** DEPART ⟨*leave* the house⟩ **b :** to terminate association with **:** withdraw from ⟨*left* school before graduation⟩ **4 :** to put, deposit, or deliver especially before or in the process of departing ⟨*left* a package on your porch⟩ [Old English *lǣfan*] — **leave alone :** to refrain from bothering, disturbing, or using ⟨*leave* them alone⟩

usage *Leave* in the sense of "let" followed by a pronoun and an infinitive but without *to* ⟨*leave* it be⟩ is a mostly spoken idiom used in writing especially for humorous effect. The use of *leave* in the sense of "let" is more commonly accepted in British English than American English.

[2]**leave** *n* **1 a :** PERMISSION 2 **b :** authorized absence from duty or employment **2 :** an act of leaving **:** DEPARTURE [Old English *lēaf*]

[3]**leave** *vi* **leaved; leav•ing :** LEAF 1

leaved \ˈlēvd\ *adj* **:** having such or so many leaves ⟨broad-leaved⟩

[1]**leav•en** \ˈlev-ən\ *n* **1 a :** a substance (as yeast) used to produce gaseous fermentation (as in dough) **b :** a material (as baking powder) used to produce a gas that lightens dough or batter **2 :** something that modifies or lightens a mass or whole ⟨a *leaven* of common sense⟩ [Medieval French *levein,* derived from Latin *levare* "to raise"]

[2]**leaven** *vt* **leav•ened; leav•en•ing** \ˈlev-niŋ, -ə-niŋ\ **1 :** to raise (dough) with a leaven **2 :** to lighten or improve with a leaven ⟨a speech *leavened* with wit⟩

leav•en•ing *n* **:** a leavening agent **:** LEAVEN

leave off *vb* **:** STOP 7, CEASE

leaves *plural of* LEAF

leave–tak•ing \ˈlēv-ˌtā-kiŋ\ *n* **:** DEPARTURE 1a, FAREWELL

leav•ings \ˈlē-viŋz\ *n pl* **:** RESIDUE; *esp* **:** food leftovers

lech•ery \ˈlech-rē, -ə-rē\ *n, pl* **-er•ies :** excessive concern with or indulgence in sexual activity [Medieval French *lecherie,* from *lecher* "to lick," of Germanic origin] — **lecher** *n* — **lech•er•ous** \-rəs\ *adj* — **lech•er•ous•ly** *adv* — **lech•er•ous•ness** *n*

lec•i•thin \ˈles-ə-thən\ *n* **:** any of several waxy phosphorus-containing substances that are common in animals and plants, form colloidal solutions in water, and have emulsifying, wetting, and antioxidant properties [Greek *lekithos* "egg yolk"]

lec•tern \ˈlek-tərn\ *n* **:** READING DESK; *esp* **:** one from which scripture lessons are read in a church service [Medieval French *leitrun,* from Medieval Latin *lectrinum,* from Late Latin *lectrum,* from Latin *legere* "to read"]

lec•tor \ˈlek-tər\ *n* **:** one whose chief duty is to read the lessons in a church service [Latin, "reader," from *legere* "to read"]

[1]**lec•ture** \ˈlek-chər, -shər\ *n* **1 :** a discourse given before an audience especially for instruction **2 :** a dressing down **:** REPRIMAND [Late Latin *lectura* "act of reading," from Latin *legere* "to gather, read"]

[2]**lecture** *vb* **lec•tured; lec•tur•ing** \ˈlek-chə-riŋ, ˈlek-shriŋ\ **1 :** to give a lecture or a course of lectures **2 :** to instruct by lectures **3 :** to dress down **:** REPRIMAND — **lec•tur•er** \-chər-ər, -shrər\ *n*

led *past of* LEAD

LED \ˌel-ˌē-ˈdē\ *n* **:** a semiconductor device that emits light when a voltage is applied to it [*l*ight-*e*mitting *d*iode]

le·der·ho·sen \ˈlād-ər-ˌhōz-n\ *n pl* : knee-length leather trousers worn especially in Bavaria [German, literally, "leather trousers"]

ledge \ˈlej\ *n* **1** : a projecting ridge or raised edge along a surface : SHELF **2** : an underwater ridge or reef especially near the shore **3** : a narrow flat surface or shelf; *esp* : one that projects (as from a wall of rock) **4** : LODE, VEIN [Middle English *legge* "bar of a gate"]

led·ger \ˈlej-ər\ *n* : a book containing accounts to which debits and credits are posted in final form [Middle English *lygger, leger* "large breviary, beam," probably from *leyen, leggen* "to lay"]

ledger line *n* : a short line added above or below a musical staff for notes that are too high or too low to be placed on the staff

1lee \ˈlē\ *n* **1** : protecting shelter **2** : the side (as of a ship) or area that is sheltered from the wind [Old English *hlēo*]

2lee *adj* : of, relating to, or being the side sheltered from the wind — compare WEATHER

1leech \ˈlēch\ *n* **1** *archaic* : PHYSICIAN, SURGEON **2** : any of numerous flesh-eating or bloodsucking usually flattened freshwater annelid worms (class Hirudinea) having a sucker at each end **3** : a hanger-on who seeks advantage or gain : PARASITE [Old English *lǣce;* sense 2 from the worm's former use by physicians for bleeding patients]

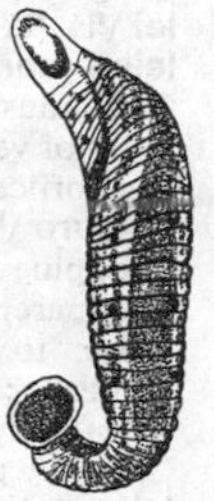

1leech 2

2leech *vb* **1** : to drain the substance of : EXHAUST **2** : to attach oneself to a person as a leech

3leech *n* **1** : either vertical edge of a square sail **2** : the after edge of a fore-and-aft sail [Middle English *leche*]

leek \ˈlēk\ *n* : a garden herb closely related to the onion and grown for its mildly pungent leaves and thick stalk [Old English *lēac*]

1leer \ˈliər\ *vi* : to cast a sidelong glance; *esp* : to give a knowing, malicious, or sexually suggestive look [probably from obsolete *leer* "cheek"]

2leer *n* : a knowing, malicious, or sexually suggestive look

leery \ˈliər-ē\ *adj* : SUSPICIOUS 2, WARY ⟨*leery* of strangers⟩

lees \ˈlēz\ *n pl* : the settlings of liquor during fermentation and aging : DREGS [Medieval French *lie,* from Medieval Latin *lia*]

lee shore *n* : a shore lying off a ship's leeward side and toward which a ship could be driven by storm winds

1lee·ward \ˈlē-wərd, *especially nautical* ˈlü-ərd\ *adj* : situated away from the wind : DOWNWIND — compare WINDWARD — **leeward** *adv*

2leeward *n* : the lee side

lee·way \ˈlē-ˌwā\ *n* **1** : off-course lateral movement of a ship to leeward when under way **2** : an allowable margin of freedom or variation : TOLERANCE ⟨enough *leeway* to arrive on time⟩

1left \ˈleft\ *adj* **1** : of, relating to, or being a bodily part on the side of the body in which the heart is mostly located **2** : located nearer to the left side of the body than to the right ⟨the *left* arm of my chair⟩; *also* : lying in the direction that an observer's left hand would naturally extend ⟨the *left* fork of the road⟩ **3** *often cap* : of, adhering to, or constituted by the political Left [Old English, "weak"; from the left hand's being the weaker in most people] — **left** *adv*

2left *n* **1 a** : the left hand **b** : the location or direction of or part on the left side **2** *often cap* **a** : the part of a legislative chamber located to the left of the presiding officer **b** : the members of a continental European legislative body occupying the left and holding more radical political views than other members **3** *cap* **a** : those professing views usually characterized by desire to reform or overthrow the established order especially in politics and usually advocating greater freedom or well-being of the common man **b** : a liberal as distinguished from a conservative position

3left *past of* LEAVE

left field *n* **1** : the part of the baseball outfield to the left looking out from the plate **2** : the position of the player defending left field — **left fielder** *n*

left–hand \ˌleft-ˌhand\ *adj* **1** : situated on the left **2** : LEFT-HANDED 1 **3** : LEFT-HANDED 2

left–hand·ed \ˈleft-ˈhan-dəd\ *adj* **1** : using the left hand regularly or more easily than the right **2** : relating to, designed for, or done with the left hand **3 a** : CLUMSY 1a, AWKWARD **b** : INSINCERE, DUBIOUS ⟨a *left-handed* compliment⟩ **4 a** : COUNTERCLOCKWISE **b** : having a structure involving a counterclockwise direction — **left–handed** *adv* — **left–hand·ed·ly** *adv* — **left–hand·ed·ness** *n* — **left–hand·er** \-ˈhan-dər\ *n*

left·ist \ˈlef-təst\ *n* : a liberal or radical in politics — **leftist** *adj*

left·over \ˈleft-ˌō-vər\ *n* : an unused or unconsumed residue; *esp* : food left over from one meal and served at another — **leftover** *adj*

left·ward \ˈleft-wərd\ *also* **left·wards** \-wərdz\ *adv* : toward or on the left — **leftward** *adj*

left wing *n* **1** : the leftist division of a group **2** : LEFT 3a — **left–wing** *adj* — **left–wing·er** \ˈleft-ˌwing-ər\ *n*

1leg \ˈleg\ *n* **1** : a limb of an animal used especially for supporting the body and for walking; *also* : the part of the vertebrate limb between the knee and foot **2** : something resembling an animal leg in shape or use ⟨the *legs* of a table⟩ **3** : the part of an article of clothing that covers the leg **4** : a side of a right triangle that is not the hypotenuse; *also* : a side of an isosceles triangle that is not the base **5 a** : the course and distance sailed by a boat on a single tack **b** : a portion of a trip : STAGE **c** : one section of a relay race **6** : a branch or part of an object or system ⟨the *legs* of a pair of compasses⟩ [Old Norse *leggr*]

2leg *vi* **legged; leg·ging** : to use the legs in walking or especially in running

leg·a·cy \ˈleg-ə-sē\ *n, pl* **-cies** **1** : something left to a person by will : INHERITANCE, BEQUEST **2** : something that has come from an ancestor or predecessor or the past ⟨a *legacy* of ill will⟩ [Medieval Latin *legatia* "office of a legate," from Latin *legatus* "legate"]

le·gal \ˈlē-gəl\ *adj* **1** : of or relating to law or lawyers **2 a** : deriving authority from or founded on law : DE JURE **b** : established by law; *esp* : STATUTORY **3** : conforming to or permitted by law or established rules **4** : recognized or made effective at law rather than in equity [Middle French, from Latin *legalis,* from *leg-, lex* "law"] ***synonyms*** see LAWFUL — **le·gal·ly** \-gə-lē\ *adv*

legal age *n* : the age at which a person enters into full adult legal rights and responsibilities (as of making contracts or wills)

legal holiday *n* : a holiday established by legal authority and characterized by legal restrictions on work and transaction of official business

le·gal·ism \ˈlē-gə-ˌliz-əm\ *n* : strict, literal, or excessive conformity to the law or to a religious or moral code — **le·gal·ist** \-gə-ləst\ *n* — **le·gal·is·tic** \ˌlē-gə-ˈlis-tik\ *adj* — **le·gal·is·ti·cal·ly** \-ti-kə-lē, -klē\ *adv*

le·gal·i·ty \li-ˈgal-ət-ē\ *n, pl* **-ties** : the quality or state of being legal

le·gal·ize \ˈlē-gə-ˌlīz\ *vt* : to make legal; *esp* : to give legal validity to — **le·gal·i·za·tion** \ˌlē-gə-lə-ˈzā-shən\ *n*

legal tender *n* : money that the law authorizes a debtor to pay with and requires a creditor to accept

leg·ate \ˈleg-ət\ *n* : an official representative (as an ambassador or envoy) [Latin *legatus* "deputy, emissary," from *legare* "to depute, send as emissary, bequeath," from *leg-, lex* "law"]

leg·a·tee \ˌleg-ə-ˈtē\ *n* : one to whom a legacy is bequeathed

le·ga·tion \li-ˈgā-shən\ *n* **1** : a diplomatic mission; *esp* : one headed by a minister **2** : the official residence and office of a diplomatic minister

le·ga·to \li-ˈgät-ō\ *adv or adj* : in a manner that is smooth and connected between successive tones — used as a direction in music [Italian, literally, "tied," from *legare* "to tie," from Latin *ligare*]

leg·end \ˈlej-ənd\ *n* **1 a** : a story coming down from the past whose truth is popularly accepted but cannot be checked **b** : a popular myth of recent origin **c** : a person or thing that inspires legends **2 a** : an inscription or title on an object (as a coin) **b** : CAPTION 2 **c** : an explanatory list of the symbols on a map or chart [Medieval Latin *legenda,* derived from Latin *legere* "to gather, read"] ***synonyms*** see MYTH

Word History The Latin verb *legere* originally meant "to gather." In the course of time the verb came to be used in a figurative sense, "to gather with the eye, see," which led to the sense "to read." In Medieval Latin the word *legenda,* meaning literally "a thing to be read," was used specifically to mean "the story of the life of a saint." Many saints' lives that were

\ə\ **abut**	\au̇\ **out**	\i\ **tip**	\ȯ\ **saw**	\u̇\ **foot**
\ər\ **further**	\ch\ **chin**	\ī\ **life**	\ȯi\ **coin**	\y\ **yet**
\a\ **mat**	\e\ **pet**	\j\ **job**	\th\ **thin**	\yü\ **few**
\ā\ **take**	\ē\ **easy**	\ng\ **sing**	\t͟h\ **this**	\yu̇\ **cure**
\ä\ **cot, cart**	\g\ **go**	\ō\ **bone**	\ü\ **food**	\zh\ **vision**

written in the Middle Ages incorporated a generous measure of fanciful material along with solid fact. This accounts for the use of English *legend* to mean "a traditional story popularly believed to be historical though not entirely verifiable." We owe other senses of *legend,* "inscription," "caption," "explanatory list," to the literal meaning of Latin *legenda,* "a thing to be read."

leg·end·ary \ˈlej-ən-ˌder-ē\ *adj* **1 :** of or resembling a legend ⟨*legendary* heroes⟩ **2 :** consisting of legends ⟨*legendary* writings⟩ ***synonyms*** see FABULOUS

leg·er·de·main \ˌlej-ərd-ə-ˈmān\ *n* **1 :** SLEIGHT OF HAND, MAGIC **2 :** a display of skill or adroitness [Medieval French *leger de main* "light of hand"]

legged \ˈleg-əd, ˈlegd\ *adj* **:** having legs especially of a specified kind or number ⟨four-*legged*⟩

leg·ging *or* **leg·gin** \ˈleg-ən, ˈleg-ing\ *n* **:** a covering for the leg

leg·gy \ˈleg-ē\ *adj* **leg·gi·er; -est 1 :** having disproportionately long legs **2 :** having long and attractive legs **3 :** SPINDLY ⟨a *leggy* plant⟩

leg·hold trap \ˈleg-ˌhōld-\ *n* **:** a jawed steel trap that is used to catch and hold an animal and operates by springing closed and clamping onto the leg of the animal that steps on it

leg·horn \ˈleg-ˌhȯrn, -ˌȯrn, ˈleg-ərn\ *n* **1 a :** a fine plaited straw made from an Italian wheat **b :** a hat of this straw **2 :** any of a Mediterranean breed of small hardy domestic chickens noted for their ability to produce many white eggs [*Leghorn,* Italy]

leg·i·ble \ˈlej-ə-bəl\ *adj* **:** capable of being read **:** PLAIN ⟨*legible* handwriting⟩ [Late Latin *legibilis,* from Latin *legere* "to read"] **— leg·i·bil·i·ty** \ˌlej-ə-ˈbil-ət-ē\ *n* **— leg·i·bly** \ˈlej-ə-blē\ *adv*

le·gion \ˈlē-jən\ *n* **1 :** the principal unit of the Roman army comprising 3000 to 6000 foot soldiers with cavalry **2 :** ARMY 1a **3 :** a very large number **:** MULTITUDE [Medieval French, from Latin *legio,* from *legere* "to gather, read"]

¹le·gion·ary \ˈlē-jə-ˌner-ē\ *adj* **:** of, relating to, or constituting a legion

²legionary *n, pl* **-ar·ies :** LEGIONNAIRE

le·gion·naire \ˌlē-jə-ˈnaər, -ˈneər\ *n* **:** a member of a legion [French *légionnaire*]

leg·is·late \ˈlej-ə-ˌslāt\ *vb* **1 :** to make or enact laws **2 :** to cause, establish, or regulate by legislation [back-formation from *legislator*]

leg·is·la·tion \ˌlej-ə-ˈslā-shən\ *n* **1 :** the action of making laws **2 :** the laws made by a legislator or legislative body

leg·is·la·tive \ˈlej-ə-ˌslāt-iv\ *adj* **1 :** having the power or performing the function of legislating **2 :** of or relating to a legislature or legislation **— leg·is·la·tive·ly** *adv*

legislative assembly *n, often cap L&A* **1 :** a bicameral legislature in an American state; *also* **:** its lower house **2 :** a unicameral legislature especially in a Canadian province

legislative council *n, often cap L&C* **:** a permanent committee from both houses of a state legislature that meets between sessions to study state problems and plan a legislative program

leg·is·la·tor \ˈlej-ə-ˌslāt-ər\ *n* **:** a person who makes laws for a state or community; *esp* **:** a member of a legislature [Latin *legis lator,* literally, "proposer of a law"]

leg·is·la·ture \ˈlej-ə-ˌslā-chər\ *n* **:** an organized body of persons with authority to make laws for a political unit

le·git \li-ˈjit\ *adj* **1** *slang* **:** LEGITIMATE 2 ⟨a *legit* business⟩ **2** *slang* **:** LEGITIMATE 3 ⟨his explanations were all *legit*⟩

le·git·i·ma·cy \lə-ˈjit-ə-mə-sē\ *n* **:** the quality or state of being legitimate

¹le·git·i·mate \li-ˈjit-ə-mət\ *adj* **1 :** born of parents who are married to each other ⟨*legitimate* children⟩ **2 :** being in accordance with law or established requirements **:** LAWFUL ⟨a *legitimate* claim⟩ **3 :** being in keeping with what is right or in accordance with accepted standards ⟨a *legitimate* excuse for absence⟩ **4 :** relating to acted plays not including burlesque, revues, or some forms of musical comedy ⟨*legitimate* theater⟩ ***synonyms*** see LAWFUL **— le·git·i·mate·ly** *adv*

²le·git·i·mate \-ˌmāt\ *vt* **:** to make lawful or legal [Medieval Latin *legitimare,* from Latin *legitimus* "lawful," from *leg-, lex* "law"] **— le·git·i·ma·tion** \li-ˌjit-ə-ˈmā-shən\ *n*

le·git·i·ma·tize \li-ˈjit-ə-mə-ˌtīz\ *vt* **:** LEGITIMATE

le·git·i·mize \li-ˈjit-ə-ˌmīz\ *vt* **:** LEGITIMATE

leg·less \ˈleg-ləs\ *adj* **:** having no legs ⟨a *legless* insect⟩

leg·man \ˈleg-ˌman\ *n* **1 :** a newspaper employee assigned usually to gather information **2 :** an assistant who gathers information and runs errands

leg–of–mut·ton \ˌleg-əv-ˈmət-n, -ə-\ *adj* **:** having the sharply tapering shape or outline of a leg of mutton ⟨*leg-of-mutton* sleeves⟩

leg·ume \ˈleg-ˌyüm, li-ˈgyüm\ *n* **1 a :** any of a large family of herbs, shrubs, and trees that have fruits which are dry single-celled pods that split into two valves when ripe, that bear nodules on the roots containing nitrogen-fixing bacteria, and that include important food and forage plants (as peas, beans, or clovers) **b :** the part (as seeds or pods) of a legume used as food; *also* **:** VEGETABLE 1b **2 :** the pod characteristic of a legume [French *légume,* from Latin *legumen,* from *legere* "to gather"] **— le·gu·mi·nous** \li-ˈgyü-mə-nəs, le-\ *adj*

leg up *n* **1 :** a helping hand **:** BOOST **2 a :** HEAD START 1 **b :** an advantageous beginning

leg·work \ˈleg-ˌwərk, ˈlāg-\ *n* **:** work (as gathering data) that involves physical activity and is the basis of more creative activity (as writing a book)

le·hua \lā-ˈhü-ə\ *n* **:** a showy tree of the myrtle family with bright red flowers and a hard wood; *also* **:** its flower [Hawaiian]

lei \ˈlā, ˈlā-ˌē\ *n* **:** a wreath usually of flowers [Hawaiian]

leish·man·i·a·sis \ˌlēsh-mə-ˈnī-ə-səs\ *n* **:** infection with or disease caused by flagellate protozoans that are parasitic in the tissues of vertebrates [Sir W. B. *Leishman,* died 1926, British medical officer]

lei·sure \ˈlēzh-ər, ˈlezh-, ˈlāzh-\ *n* **1 :** freedom provided by the stopping of activities; *esp* **:** time free from work or duties **2 :** apparent effortlessness **:** EASE [Medieval French *leisir,* from *leisir* "to be permitted," from Latin *licēre*] **— leisure** *adj* **— at leisure :** in one's leisure time **:** at one's convenience

lei·sure·ly \-lē\ *adj* **:** characterized by leisure **:** UNHURRIED ⟨a *leisurely* pace⟩ **— lei·sure·li·ness** *n* **— leisurely** *adv*

leit·mo·tiv *or* **leit·mo·tif** \ˈlīt-mō-ˌtēf\ *n* **:** a dominant recurring theme (as in a musical or literary work) [German *Leitmotiv,* from *leiten* "to lead" + *Motiv* "motive"]

lek \ˈlek\ *n* **:** an area where animals (as the prairie chicken) assemble and carry on display and courtship behavior; *also* **:** a group of animals assembled in such an area [Swedish, short for *lekställe* "mating ground," from *lek* "mating, sport" + *ställe* "place"]

lem·ma \ˈlem-ə\ *n* **:** the lower of the two bracts enclosing the flower in the spikelet of grasses [Greek, "husk," from *lepein* "to peel"]

lem·ming \ˈlem-ing\ *n* **:** any of several small short-tailed northern rodents with furry feet and small ears; *esp* **:** a European rodent that takes part in periodic mass migrations which often continue into the sea where large numbers are drowned [Norwegian]

¹lem·on \ˈlem-ən\ *n* **1 a :** a nearly oval many-seeded yellow fruit that is botanically a berry and has sour juice and a thick rind from which a fragrant oil is obtained **b :** a small thorny citrus tree that bears this fruit **2 :** DUD, FAILURE ⟨the new car proved to be a *lemon*⟩ [Medieval French *limon,* from Medieval Latin *limo,* from Arabic *laymūn, līmūn,* from Persian *līmū, līmun*]

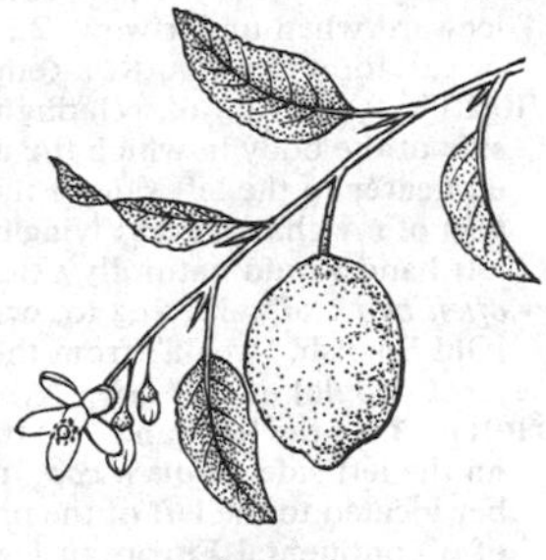

lemon 1

²lemon *adj* **1 a :** containing lemon **b :** having the flavor or scent of lemon **2 :** of the color lemon yellow

lem·on·ade \ˌlem-ə-ˈnād\ *n* **:** a drink made of lemon juice, sugar, and water

lemon balm *n* **:** a perennial European mint often grown for its fragrant lemon-scented leaves

lemon law *n* **:** a law offering car buyers relief (as by repair or refund) for defects detected during a specified period after purchase

lemon shark *n* **:** a medium-sized shark of warm waters that is yellowish brown to gray above with yellow or greenish sides and that has been known to attack people

lemon yellow *n* **:** a brilliant greenish yellow

lem·pi·ra \lem-ˈpir-ə\ *n* **1 :** the basic monetary unit of Honduras **2 :** a coin or note representing one lempira [American Spanish, from *Lempira,* 16th century Honduran Indian cacique]

le·mur \ˈlē-mər\ *n* **:** any of various arboreal and mostly nocturnal primates that usually have large eyes, very soft woolly fur, and a long furry tail and were formerly widespread but are now largely confined to Madagascar [Latin *lemures* "ghosts"]

Word History The ancient Romans believed that if the dead were not buried their spirits would return by night to haunt the living. In Latin such ghosts were called *lemures.* In none of the Latin writings that have survived does the singular of this word appear, but the normal singular form would be *lemur.* In the trees of Madagascar lives a kind of small nocturnal mammal. Its large-eyed face, glimpsed through the trees at night, must look quite ghostly. 18th century naturalists, struck by the nocturnal habits and strange appearance of the creature, named it *lemur,* after the ancient Roman ghosts.

lend \ˈlend\ *vb* **lent** \ˈlent\; **lend·ing** **1 :** to give or hand over as a loan ⟨*lend* a book⟩ ⟨*lend* money⟩ **2 :** to give temporarily ⟨*lend* assistance⟩ **3 :** to have the quality or nature that makes suitable ⟨a voice that *lends* itself to singing in opera⟩ [Old English *lǣnan,* from *lǣn* "loan"] ***usage*** see LOAN — **lend·er** *n*

lending library *n* **:** RENTAL LIBRARY

lend–lease \len-ˈdlēs\ *n* **:** the transfer of goods and services to an ally to aid in a common cause with payment being made by a return of the original items or their use in the common cause or by a similar transfer of other goods and services [U.S. *Lend-Lease* Act (1941)] — **lend–lease** *vt*

length \ˈlength, ˈlengkth, ˈlenth\ *n* **1 a :** the longer or longest dimension of an object **b :** a measured distance or dimension ⟨a 2-meter *length*⟩ — see MEASURE table, METRIC SYSTEM table **c :** the quality or state of being long ⟨criticized the *length* of the story⟩ **2 a :** duration or extent in time ⟨the *length* of an interview⟩ **b :** relative duration or stress of a sound **3 :** the length of something taken as a unit of measure ⟨that horse led by a *length*⟩ **4 :** a piece constituting or usable as part of a whole or of a connected series **:** SECTION ⟨a *length* of pipe⟩ **5 :** a vertical dimension of an article of clothing [Old English *lengthu,* from *lang* "long"] — **at length 1 :** in full **:** FULLY **2 :** at last **:** FINALLY

length·en \ˈleng-thən, ˈlengk-, ˈlen-\ *vb* **length·ened; length·en·ing** \ˈlength-ning, ˈlengkth-, ˈlenth-, -ə-ning\ **:** to make or become longer ***synonyms*** see EXTEND — **length·en·er** \-nər\ *n*

length·ways \ˈlength-ˌwāz, ˈlengkth-, ˈlenth-\ *adv* **:** LENGTHWISE

length·wise \-ˌwīz\ *adv* **:** in the direction of the length **:** LONGITUDINALLY — **lengthwise** *adj*

lengthy \ˈleng-thē, ˈlengk-, ˈlen-\ *adj* **length·i·er; -est 1 :** excessively drawn out **:** OVERLONG ⟨a *lengthy* speech⟩ **2 :** LONG 1 ⟨a *lengthy* journey⟩ — **length·i·ly** \-thə-lē\ *adv* — **length·i·ness** \-thē-nəs\ *n*

le·ni·en·cy \ˈlē-nē-ən-sē\ *or* **le·ni·ence** \-əns\ *n* **:** the quality or state of being lenient ***synonyms*** see MERCY

le·ni·ent \ˈlē-nē-ənt\ *adj* **:** of mild and tolerant disposition or effect; *esp* **:** INDULGENT ⟨was *lenient* with the naughty child⟩ [Latin *lenient-, leniens,* present participle of *lenire* "to soften, soothe," from *lenis* "soft, mild"] — **le·ni·ent·ly** *adv*

Len·in·ism \ˈlen-ə-ˌniz-əm\ *n* **:** the political, economic, and social principles and policies advocated by Lenin; *esp* **:** the theory and practice of communism developed by or associated with Lenin — **Len·in·ist** \-nəst\ *n or adj*

len·i·tive \ˈlen-ət-iv\ *adj* **:** easing pain or harshness **:** SOOTHING [Medieval French *lenitif,* from Medieval Latin *lenitivus,* from Latin *lenire* "to soothe," from *lenis* "mild"] — **lenitive** *n*

lens \ˈlenz\ *n* **1 a :** a piece of transparent substance (as glass) that has two opposite surfaces either both curved or one curved and the other plane and that is used either singly or combined in an optical instrument for forming an image by focusing rays of light **b :** a piece of glass or plastic used (as in protective goggles or sunglasses) to protect the eye **2 :** a device for directing or focusing radiation (as sound waves or electrons) other than light **3 :** something (as a geologic deposit) shaped like an optical lens **4 :** a transparent biconvex lens-shaped or nearly spherical body in the eye that focuses light rays (as upon the retina) [Latin, "lentil"; from its shape]

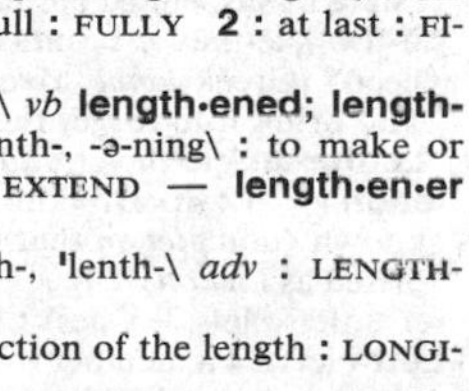

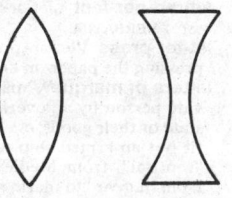

lens 1a: *left* convex, *right* concave

Lent \ˈlent\ *n* **:** a period of penitence and fasting observed on the 40 weekdays from Ash Wednesday to Easter by many churches [Old English *lengten* "springtime, Lent"]

Lent·en \ˈlent-n\ *adj* **:** of, relating to, or suitable to Lent; *esp* **:** MEAGER 2b ⟨*Lenten* fare⟩

len·ti·cel \ˈlent-ə-ˌsel\ *n* **:** a pore in a stem of a woody plant through which gases are exchanged between the atmosphere and the stem tissues [derived from Latin *lent-, lens* "lentil"]

len·tic·u·lar \len-ˈtik-yə-lər\ *adj* **:** shaped like a biconvex lens [Latin *lenticularis* "lentil-shaped," from *lenticula* "small lentil," from *lens* "lentil"]

len·til \ˈlent-l\ *n* **:** an annual Eurasian plant of the legume family widely grown for its flattened edible seeds and leafy stalks used as fodder; *also* **:** its seed [Medieval French *lentille,* from Latin *lenticula,* from *lent-, lens*]

len·to \ˈlen-ˌtō\ *adv or adj* **:** in a slow manner — used as a direction in music [Italian, from *lento,* adj., "slow," from Latin *lentus* "pliant, sluggish, slow"]

Leo \ˈlē-ō\ *n* **1 :** a zodiacal northern constellation east of Cancer **2 :** the 5th sign of the zodiac; *also* **:** one born under this sign [Latin, literally, "lion"]

le·o·nine \ˈlē-ə-ˌnīn\ *adj* **:** of, relating to, or resembling a lion [Latin *leoninus,* from *leo* "lion"]

leop·ard \ˈlep-ərd\ *n* **:** a large strong cat of southern Asia and Africa that is skilled at climbing and is usually tawny or buff with black spots arranged in broken rings or rosettes — called also *panther* [Medieval French *lepart, leupart,* from Late Latin *leopardus,* from Greek *leopardos,* from *leōn* "lion" + *pardos* "leopard"] — **leop·ard·ess** \-əs\ *n*

leopard frog *n* **:** a common spotted frog of northern North America; *also* **:** a related frog of the southeastern U.S.

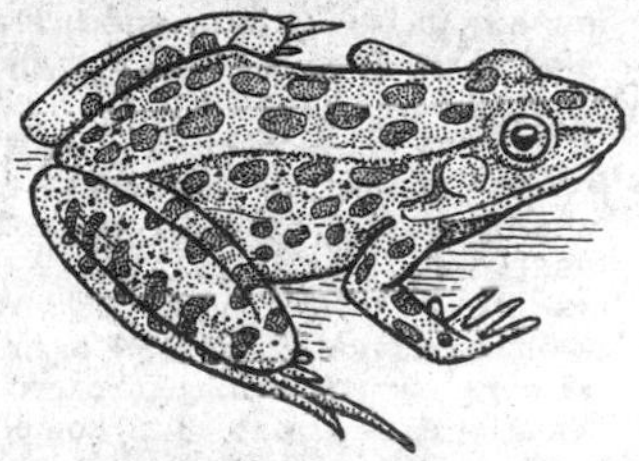

leopard frog

le·o·tard \ˈlē-ə-ˌtärd\ *n* **:** a stretchable close-fitting one-piece garment typically covering the torso that is worn for practice or performance by dancers, acrobats, and aerialists [Jules Léotard, 19th century French aerial gymnast]

lep·er \ˈlep-ər\ *n* **1 :** a person affected with leprosy **2 :** PARIAH 2, OUTCAST [Medieval French *lepre* "leprosy," from Late Latin *lepra,* from Greek, from *lepein* "to peel"]

lep·i·dop·tera \ˌlep-ə-ˈdäp-tə-rə\ *n pl* **:** insects that are lepidopterans [New Latin, from Greek *lepid-, lepis* "scale" + *pteron* "wing"]

lep·i·dop·ter·an \ˌlep-ə-ˈdäp-tə-rən\ *n* **:** any of a large order (Lepidoptera) of insects that comprise the butterflies, moths, and skippers, as adults have four wings usually covered with minute overlapping often brightly colored scales, and as larvae are caterpillars — **lepidopteran** *adj* — **lep·i·dop·ter·ous** \-tə-rəs\ *adj*

lep·re·chaun \ˈlep-rə-ˌkän, -ˌkȯn\ *n* **:** a mischievous elf of Irish folklore usually believed to reveal the hiding place of treasure if caught [Irish Gaelic *leipreachān*]

lep·ro·sy \ˈlep-rə-sē\ *n* **:** a chronic infectious bacterial disease marked by slow-growing spreading swellings accompanied by loss of sensation, wasting of muscles, and deformities — called also *Hansen's disease* [*leprous* + *-y*] — **lep·rot·ic** \le-ˈprät-ik\ *adj*

lep·rous \ˈlep-rəs\ *adj* **:** infected with, relating to, or resembling leprosy [Late Latin *leprosus,* from *lepra* "leprosy," from Greek, from *lepein* "to peel"] — **lep·rous·ly** *adv* — **lep·rous·ness** *n*

lep·to·ceph·a·lus \ˌlep-tə-ˈsef-ə-ləs\ *n, pl* **-li** \-ˌlī\ **:** the slender transparent first larva of various eels [New Latin, from Greek *leptos* "peeled, slender, small" + *kephalē* "head"]

les·bi·an \ˈlez-bē-ən\ *n* **:** a woman who is a homosexual [*Lesbos,* Greek island; from the reputed homosexual band associated with Sappho of Lesbos] — **lesbian** *adj* — **les·bi·an·ism** \-bē-ə-ˌniz-əm\ *n*

\ə\ **abut**	\au̇\ **out**	\i\ **tip**	\ȯ\ **saw**	\u̇\ **foot**
\ər\ **further**	\ch\ **chin**	\ī\ **life**	\ȯi\ **coin**	\y\ **yet**
\a\ **mat**	\e\ **pet**	\j\ **job**	\th\ **thin**	\yü\ **few**
\ā\ **take**	\ē\ **easy**	\ng\ **sing**	\t͟h\ **this**	\yu̇\ **cure**
\ä\ **cot, cart**	\g\ **go**	\ō\ **bone**	\ü\ **food**	\zh\ **vision**

lese maj·es·ty *or* **lèse ma·jes·té** \ˈlēz-ˈmaj-ə-stē\ *n* **1 a :** a crime committed against a sovereign power **b :** an offense violating the dignity of a ruler **2 :** a detraction from or affront to dignity or importance [Middle French *lese majesté,* from Latin *laesa majestas,* literally, "injured majesty"]

le·sion \ˈlē-zhən\ *n* **:** an abnormal structural change in an organ or part due to injury or disease; *esp* **:** one that is clearly marked off from healthy tissue around it [Middle French, "injury," from Latin *laesio,* from *laedere* "to injure"]

les·pe·de·za \ˌles-pə-ˈdē-zə\ *n* **:** any of a genus of herbaceous or shrubby plants of the legume family including some widely used for forage, soil improvement, and hay [derived from V. M. de *Zespedes,* 18th century Spanish governor of East Florida]

¹less \ˈles\ *adj* **1 :** of a smaller number **:** FEWER ⟨*less* than three⟩ **2 :** of lower rank, degree, or importance ⟨no *less* a person than the principal⟩ **3 a :** of reduced size or extent **b :** more limited in quantity ⟨in *less* time⟩ [Old English *lǣs,* adv. and n., and *lǣssa,* adj.] ***usage*** see FEWER

²less *adv* **:** to a lesser extent or degree ⟨*less* difficult⟩

³less *prep* **:** diminished by **:** MINUS ⟨full price *less* the discount⟩

⁴less *n, pl* **less 1 :** a smaller portion or quantity ⟨spent *less* than usual⟩ **2 :** something of less importance ⟨could have killed them for *less*⟩

-less \-ləs\ *adj suffix* **1 :** destitute of **:** not having ⟨wit*less*⟩ **2 :** unable to be acted on or to act (in a specified way) ⟨daunt*less*⟩ ⟨fade*less*⟩ [Old English *-lēas,* from *lēas* "devoid, false"]

les·see \le-ˈsē\ *n* **:** a tenant under a lease [Medieval French, from *lesser* "to lease"]

less·en \ˈles-n\ *vb* **less·ened; less·en·ing** \ˈles-ning, -n-ing\ **:** to make or become less ***synonyms*** see DECREASE

¹less·er \ˈles-ər\ *adj* **:** of less size, quality, or importance ⟨subtract the *lesser* number⟩ ⟨the *lesser* nobility⟩

²lesser *adv* **:** LESS ⟨*lesser*-known⟩

lesser celandine *n* **:** CELANDINE 2

lesser panda *n* **:** RED PANDA

¹les·son \ˈles-n\ *n* **1 :** a passage from sacred writings read in a worship service **2 :** a piece of instruction ⟨the story carries a *lesson*⟩; *esp* **:** a reading or exercise to be studied by a pupil ⟨master each *lesson*⟩ **3 a :** something learned by study or experience ⟨the *lessons* of life⟩ **b :** a rebuke or punishment meant to forestall the repetition of an offense ⟨gave the naughty child a *lesson*⟩ [Medieval French *leçon,* from Late Latin *lectio* "act of reading," from *legere* "to read"]

²lesson *vt* **les·soned; les·son·ing** \ˈles-ning, -n-ing\ **1 :** to give a lesson to **2 :** REBUKE

les·sor \ˈles-ˌȯr, le-ˈsȯr\ *n* **:** one that grants a lease [Medieval French *lessour,* from *lesser* "to lease"]

lest \lest, ˌlest\ *conj* **:** for fear that ⟨worried *lest* they be late⟩ [derived from Old English *lǣs* "less"]

¹let \ˈlet\ *vt* **let·ted; letted** *or* **let; let·ting** *archaic* **:** HINDER, PREVENT [Old English *lettan*]

²let \ˈlet\ *n* **1 :** something that impedes **:** OBSTRUCTION ⟨talk without *let* or hindrance⟩ **2 :** a shot or rally (as in tennis) that is not counted and that must be played over because of interference with the play

³let *vb* **let; let·ting 1 :** to cause to **:** MAKE ⟨*let* it be known⟩ **2 a** *chiefly British* **:** to offer or grant for rent or lease ⟨*let* rooms⟩ **b :** to assign or award especially after bids ⟨*let* a contract⟩ **3 a :** to allow to ⟨live and *let* live⟩ ⟨*let* me go⟩ **b :** to allow to go or pass ⟨*let* them through⟩ **4 —** used imperatively to introduce a request or proposal ⟨*let* us pray⟩ ⟨*let* x be any number⟩ **5 —** used as an auxiliary to express a warning ⟨*let* him try⟩ **6 :** to free from or as if from confinement ⟨*let* out a scream⟩ [Old English *lǣtan*] ***usage*** see ¹LEAVE **— let alone :** to leave undisturbed ⟨*let* the flowers *alone*⟩; *also* **:** to leave to oneself ⟨wanted to be *let alone*⟩ **— let go 1 :** to dismiss from employment ⟨the firm *let* him *go* at the end of the month⟩ **2 :** to relax or release one's hold — used with *of* ⟨*let go* of my arm⟩ **3 :** to fail to take care of **:** NEGLECT ⟨stopped exercising and *let* himself *go*⟩ **— let one's hair down :** to act without pretense or self-restraint **— let the cat out of the bag :** to give away a secret

synonyms LET, ALLOW, PERMIT mean not to forbid or prevent. LET may imply a positive giving of permission but more often implies failure to prevent either through inadvertence and negligence or through lack of power or effective authority ⟨*let* the cold in by forgetting to close the window⟩. ALLOW simply suggests a forbearing to prohibit ⟨the machinery was *allowed* to rust⟩. PERMIT implies willingness or acquiescence ⟨*permits* them to stay up late⟩. ***synonyms*** see in addition HIRE

-let \lət\ *n suffix* **1 :** small one ⟨book*let*⟩ **2 :** article worn on ⟨wrist*let*⟩ [Medieval French *-elet,* from *-el,* diminutive suffix (from Latin *-ellus*) + *-et*]

let alone *conj* **:** to say nothing of **:** not to mention ⟨lacked the courage, *let alone* the skill⟩

let·down \ˈlet-ˌdau̇n\ *n* **1 :** DISAPPOINTMENT 2 **2 :** a slackening of effort **:** RELAXATION

let down \let-ˈdau̇n, ˈlet-\ *vb* **1 :** to fail to support **:** DESERT ⟨*let down* a friend in a crisis⟩ **2 :** DISAPPOINT ⟨the end of the story *lets* the reader *down*⟩ **3 :** to slacken effort **:** RELAX

¹le·thal \ˈlē-thəl\ *adj* **1 :** of, relating to, or causing death **2 :** capable of causing death ⟨*lethal* chemicals⟩ [Latin *letalis, lethalis,* from *letum* "death"] ***synonyms*** see DEADLY **— le·thal·i·ty** \lē-ˈthal-ət-ē\ *n* **— le·thal·ly** \ˈlē-thə-lē\ *adv*

²lethal *n* **:** a lethal gene

lethal gene *n* **:** a gene that in some circumstances (as the homozygous condition) may prevent the development or cause the death of an organism or its germ cells

le·thar·gic \li-ˈthär-jik, le-\ *adj* **1 :** of, relating to, or characterized by lethargy **:** SLUGGISH **2 :** APATHETIC **— le·thar·gi·cal·ly** \-ji-kə-lē, -klē\ *adv*

leth·ar·gy \ˈleth-ər-jē\ *n* **1 :** abnormal drowsiness **2 :** the quality or state of being lazy or indifferent [Late Latin *lethargia,* from Greek *lēthargia,* from *lēthargos* "forgetful, lethargic," from *lēthē* "forgetfulness"]

synonyms LETHARGY, LANGUOR, STUPOR, TORPOR mean physical or mental inertness. LETHARGY implies drowsiness or apathy induced by disease, injury, or drugs. LANGUOR suggests inertia induced by enervating climate, illness, or amorous emotion. STUPOR implies a deadening of the mind and senses by shock, narcotics, or intoxicants. TORPOR implies a state of suspended animation or extreme sluggishness.

Le·the \ˈlē-thē\ *n* **:** OBLIVION, FORGETFULNESS ⟨the *Lethe* of sleep⟩ [Greek *Lēthē,* river of Hades whose water causes those who drink it to forget their past, from *lēthē* "forgetfulness"] **— Le·the·an** \ˈlē-thē-ən\ *adj*

let on *vb* **1 :** ADMIT ⟨know more than they *let on*⟩ **2 :** to make known ⟨don't *let on* that I told you⟩ **3 :** PRETEND ⟨not so surprised as I *let on*⟩

let's \lets, ˌlets, les, ˌles\ **:** let us

Lett \ˈlet\ *n* **:** a member of a people closely related to the Lithuanians and mainly inhabiting Latvia [German *Lette,* from Latvian *latvis*]

¹let·ter \ˈlet-ər\ *n* **1 :** a symbol in writing or print that stands for a speech sound and constitutes a unit of an alphabet **2 :** a written or printed message addressed to a person or organization **3** *pl* **a :** LITERATURE 2a **b :** LEARNING 2 **4 :** the strict meaning ⟨the *letter* of the law⟩ **5 a :** a single piece of type **b :** a style of type [Medieval French *lettre,* from Latin *littera* "letter of the alphabet" and *litterae,* pl., "epistle, literature"]

²letter *vt* **1 :** to set down in letters **:** PRINT **2 :** to mark with letters **— let·ter·er** \-ər-ər\ *n*

letter carrier *n* **:** a person who delivers mail

let·tered \ˈlet-ərd\ *adj* **1 a :** LEARNED, EDUCATED ⟨a *lettered* person⟩ **b :** of or relating to learning ⟨a *lettered* environment⟩ **2 :** marked with or as if with letters ⟨a *lettered* sign⟩

let·ter·head \ˈlet-ər-ˌhed\ *n* **:** stationery having a printed or engraved heading; *also* **:** the heading itself

let·ter·ing *n* **:** letters used in an inscription

let·ter–per·fect \ˌlet-ər-ˈpər-fikt\ *adj* **:** correct in every detail; *esp* **:** VERBATIM

let·ter·press \ˈlet-ər-ˌpres\ *n* **:** printing done directly by impressing the paper on an inked raised surface

letters of marque \-ˈmärk\ **:** written authority granted to a private person by a government to seize the subjects of a foreign state or their goods; *esp* **:** a license granted to a private person to fit out an armed ship to plunder the enemy [obsolete *marque* "reprisal," from Medieval French, from Old Occitan *marca,* from *marcar* "to mark, seize as pledge," of Germanic origin]

letters pat·ent \-ˈpat-nt\ *n pl* **:** a writing (as from a sovereign) that confers on a person a grant in a form open for public inspection

¹Lett·ish \ˈlet-ish\ *adj* **:** of or relating to the Letts or the Latvian language

²Lettish *n* **:** LATVIAN 2

let·tuce \ˈlet-əs\ *n* **:** a common garden vegetable related to the daisies and having crisp juicy leaves used especially in salads

[Medieval French *letuse,* probably from plural of *letue* "lettuce plant," from Latin *lactuca,* from *lac* "milk"]

Word History Many types of lettuce have a milky white juice, and it is this property that accounts for the name of the vegetable. The English singular form, *lettuce,* comes from Medieval French *letues,* the plural of *letue.* The Medieval French word is derived in turn from Latin *lactuca,* which is still used as the scientific name of the lettuce. The root of *lactuca* is Latin *lac,* which means "milk."

let·up \ˈlet-ˌəp\ *n* : a lessening of effort

let up \let-ˈəp, ˈlet-\ *vi* **1** : to lessen in force or intensity : ABATE **2** : STOP 7, CEASE **3** : to become less severe — used with *on* ⟨hope the principal *lets up* on me⟩

leu·cine \ˈlü-ˌsēn\ *n* : an essential amino acid obtained by the hydrolysis of most dietary proteins

leu·co·plast \ˈlü-kə-ˌplast\ *n* : a colorless plastid of a plant cell usually concerned with starch formation and storage [*leuk-* + *-plast* "granule," from Greek *plastos* "formed, molded"]

leuk- *or* **leuko-** *or* **leuc-** *or* **leuco-** *combining form* **1** : white : colorless : weakly colored ⟨*leuko*cyte⟩ **2** : leukocyte ⟨*leuke*mia⟩ [Greek *leukos*]

leu·ke·mia \lü-ˈkē-mē-ə\ *n* : a cancerous disease of warm-blooded animals including humans in which there is an abnormal increase in the number of white blood cells in the tissues and often in the blood — **leu·ke·mic** \-mik\ *adj*

leu·ko·cyte \ˈlü-kə-ˌsīt\ *n* : WHITE BLOOD CELL — **leu·ko·cyt·ic** \ˌlü-kə-ˈsit-ik\ *adj*

leu·ko·cy·to·sis \ˌlü-kə-ˌsī-ˈtō-səs\ *n, pl* **-to·ses** \-ˈtō-ˌsēz\ : an increase in the number of white blood cells in the circulating blood — **leu·ko·cy·tot·ic** \-ˈtät-ik\ *adj*

leu·ko·pe·nia \ˌlü-kə-ˈpē-nē-ə\ *n* : a condition in which the number of white blood cells circulating in the blood is abnormally low [Greek *penia* "poverty, lack"] — **leu·ko·pe·nic** \-nik\ *adj*

leu·ko·pla·kia \ˌlü-kō-ˈplā-kē-ə\ *n* : an abnormal condition in which thickened white patches occur on the mucous membranes (as of the mouth) [New Latin, from *leuk-* + Greek *plax* "flat surface"]

leu·ko·sis \lü-ˈkō-səs\ *n, pl* **-ko·ses** \-ˌsēz\ : LEUKEMIA

lev- *or* **levo-** *combining form* : turning the plane of polarization of light to the left ⟨*lev*ulose⟩ [Latin *laevus* "left"]

le·va·tor \li-ˈvāt-ər\ *n, pl* **lev·a·to·res** \ˌlev-ə-ˈtōr-ēz\ *or* **le·va·tors** \li-ˈvāt-ərz\ : a muscle that serves to raise a body part — compare DEPRESSOR [derived from Latin *levare* "to raise"]

¹lev·ee \ˈlev-ē; lə-ˈvē, -ˈvā\ *n* **1** : a reception held by a distinguished person originally on rising from bed **2** : a reception usually in honor of a particular person [French *lever,* from Medieval French, "act of arising," from *se lever* "to raise oneself, rise"]

²levee \ˈlev-ē\ *n* **1** : an embankment or dike to prevent flooding **2** : a river landing place : PIER [French *levée,* from Medieval French, "act of raising," from *lever* "to raise," from Latin *levare,* from *levis* "light in weight"]

¹lev·el \ˈlev-əl\ *n* **1** : a device for establishing a horizontal line or plane ⟨a carpenter's *level*⟩ ⟨a surveyor's *level*⟩ **2** : horizontal condition; *esp* : a condition of liquids marked by a horizontal surface of even altitude ⟨water seeks its own *level*⟩ **3** : a horizontal position, line, or surface often taken as an index of altitude ⟨placed at eye *level*⟩; *also* : a flat surface ⟨easier to walk on the *level*⟩ **4** : a position in a scale or rank (as of achievement, significance, importance, or value) ⟨students at the same learning *level*⟩ **5 a** : an amount of something especially in relation to typical or expected amounts ⟨production is at a low *level* this year⟩ ⟨a high *level* of hostility⟩ **b** : the concentration of a constituent especially of a body fluid (as blood) ⟨a high *level* of sugar in the blood⟩ [Medieval French *livel,* derived from Latin *libella,* from *libra* "pound, balance"] — **on the level** : BONA FIDE, HONEST ⟨the offer is *on the level*⟩

²level *vb* **lev·eled** *or* **lev·elled; lev·el·ing** *or* **lev·el·ling** \ˈlev-ling, -ə-ling\ **1** : to make (a line or surface) horizontal : make flat or level ⟨*leveled* the ground⟩ **2** : DIRECT 3 ⟨*leveled* a charge of fraud⟩ **3** : to bring to a common level or plane : EQUALIZE **4** : to lay level with the ground : RAZE ⟨the cyclone *leveled* the village⟩ **5** : to come to a level ⟨the jet *leveled* off at 10,000 feet⟩ — **lev·el·er** *or* **lev·el·ler** \ˈlev-lər, -ə-lər\ *n*

³level *adj* **1** : having no part higher than another **2** : being on a line with the horizon : HORIZONTAL **3 a** : of the same height or rank : being on a line : EVEN ⟨stood in water *level* with my shoulders⟩ **b** (1) : STEADY 1a ⟨a *level* stare⟩ (2) : CALM, UNEXCITED ⟨spoke in *level* tones⟩ — **lev·el·ly** \ˈlev-əl-lē, ˈlev-ə-le\ *adv* — **lev·el·ness** \-əl-nəs\ *n* — **level best** : very best

lev·el·head·ed \ˌlev-əl-ˈhed-əd\ *adj* : having or showing sound judgment : SENSIBLE — **lev·el·head·ed·ness** *n*

¹le·ver \ˈlev-ər, ˈlē-vər\ *n* **1 a** : a bar used for prying or dislodging something **b** : an instrument or means used to achieve a purpose : TOOL ⟨used food distribution as a *lever* to gain votes⟩ **2 a** : a rigid bar that pivots on a fulcrum and that is used to exert a pressure or sustain a weight at one point of its length by the application of a force at a second **b** : a projecting piece by which a mechanism is operated or adjusted [Medieval French *levier,* from *lever* "to raise," from Latin *levare,* from *levis* "light in weight"]

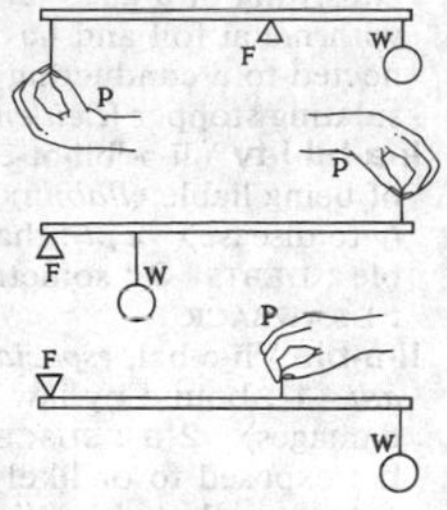

lever 2a: *P* pulling force, *F* fulcrum, *W* weight

²lever *vt* **le·vered; le·ver·ing** \ˈlev-ring, ˈlēv-, -ə-ring\ : to pry, raise, or move with or as if with a lever

le·ver·age \ˈlev-rij, ˈlēv-, -ə-rij\ *n* **1** : the action of a lever or the mechanical advantage gained by it **2** : power to influence or dominate ⟨the strike threat gave the union bargaining *leverage*⟩

lev·er·et \ˈlev-rət, -ə-rət\ *n* : a hare in its first year [Medieval French, "hare skin," from *levre* "hare," from Latin *lepor-, lepus*]

le·vi·a·than \li-ˈvī-ə-thən\ *n* **1 a** *often cap* : a sea monster often symbolizing evil in the Old Testament and Christian literature **b** : a large sea animal **2** : GIANT 3 [Late Latin, from Hebrew *liwyāthān*] — **leviathan** *adj*

Le·vi's \ˈlē-ˌvīz\ *trademark* — used for jeans

lev·i·tate \ˈlev-ə-ˌtāt\ *vb* : to rise or cause to rise in or as if in the air in seeming defiance of gravity [*levity*]

lev·i·ta·tion \ˌlev-ə-ˈtā-shən\ *n* : the act or process of levitating; *esp* : the rising or lifting of a person or thing by means held to be supernatural

Le·vite \ˈlē-ˌvīt\ *n* **1** : a member of the Hebrew tribe of Levi **2** : a descendant of Levi assigned to assist the priests in the care of the temple — **Le·vit·i·cal** \li-ˈvit-i-kəl\ *adj*

Le·vit·i·cus \li-ˈvit-i-kəs\ *n* : the third book of canonical Jewish and Christian Scriptures consisting mainly of priestly legislation — see BIBLE table

lev·i·ty \ˈlev-ət-ē\ *n, pl* **-ties** : an often inappropriate lack of seriousness : FRIVOLITY [Latin *levitas,* from *levis* "light in weight"]

lev·u·lose \ˈlev-yə-ˌlōs\ *n* : FRUCTOSE [derived from *lev-* + *-ose*]

¹levy \ˈlev-ē\ *n, pl* **lev·ies** **1 a** : the imposition or collection of an assessment **b** : an amount levied **2 a** : the raising of men for military service **b** : troops raised by levy [Medieval French *levé,* literally, "raising," from *lever* "to raise," from Latin *levare,* from *levis* "light in weight"]

²levy *vb* **lev·ied; lev·y·ing** **1 a** : to impose or collect by legal authority ⟨*levy* a tax⟩ **b** : to require (as a service) by authority **2** : to enlist or conscript for military service **3** : to carry on (war) : WAGE **4** : to seize property to satisfy a legal claim — **lev·i·er** *n*

lewd \ˈlüd\ *adj* **1** : lacking in sexual restraint : LICENTIOUS **2** : OBSCENE 2a, VULGAR [Middle English *lewed* "vulgar," from Old English *lǣwede* "laical, ignorant"] — **lewd·ly** *adv* — **lewd·ness** *n*

lex·i·cal \ˈlek-si-kəl\ *adj* **1** : of or relating to the vocabulary of a language **2** : of or relating to a lexicon or to lexicography — **lex·i·cal·ly** \-si-kə-lē, -klē\ *adv*

lex·i·cog·ra·pher \ˌlek-sə-ˈkäg-rə-fər\ *n* : a specialist in lexicography

lex·i·cog·ra·phy \-fē\ *n* **1** : the editing or making of a dictionary **2** : the principles and practices of dictionary making — **lex·i·co·graph·i·cal** \ˌlek-sə-kō-ˈgraf-i-kəl\ *or* **lex·i·co·graph·ic** \-ik\ *adj* — **lex·i·co·graph·i·cal·ly** \-i-kə-lē, -klē\ *adv*

lex·i·con \ˈlek-sə-ˌkän, -si-kən\ *n, pl* **lex·i·ca** \-si-kə\ *or* **lexi·cons** **1** : DICTIONARY 1 **2** : the vocabulary of a language, an individual speaker, or a subject [Late Greek *lexikon,* from *lexi-*

kos "of words," from Greek *lexis* "speech, word," from *legein* "to say"]

ley *variant of* LEA

Ley·den jar \ˌlīd-n-\ *n* **:** an electrical condenser consisting of a glass jar coated inside and outside with metal foil and having the inner coating connected to a conducting rod passed through an insulating stopper [*Leiden, Leyden,* Netherlands]

Leyden jar

li·a·bil·i·ty \ˌlī-ə-ˈbil-ət-ē\ *n, pl* **-ties** **1 :** the state of being liable ⟨*liability* for one's actions⟩ ⟨*liability* to disease⟩ **2** *pl* **:** that for which a person is liable **:** DEBTS **3 :** something that is a disadvantage **:** DRAWBACK

li·a·ble \ˈlī-ə-bəl, *especially in sense 2b also* ˈlī-bəl\ *adj* **1 :** bound by law **:** RESPONSIBLE ⟨*liable* for damages⟩ **2 a :** SUSCEPTIBLE ⟨*liable* to disease⟩ **b :** exposed to or likely to experience something usually undesirable ⟨*liable* to get hurt⟩ [Medieval French *lier* "to bind," from Latin *ligare*] ***usage*** see APT

li·aise \lē-ˈāz\ *vi* **1 :** to establish liaison **2 :** to act as a liaison officer [back-formation from *liaison*]

li·ai·son \ˈlē-ə-ˌzän, lē-ˈā-\ *n* **1 a :** a connecting link; *esp* **:** a linking or coordinating of activities **b :** AFFAIR 3a **2 :** the pronunciation of an otherwise absent consonant sound at the end of a word when immediately followed by a word beginning with a vowel sound **3 :** communication especially between parts of an armed force [French, from Medieval French *lier* "to bind," from Latin *ligare*]

li·a·na \lē-ˈän-ə, -ˈan-ə\ *n* **:** any of various usually woody vines especially of tropical rain forests that root in the ground [French *liane*]

li·ar \ˈlī-ər, ˈlīr\ *n* **:** a person who tells lies

li·ba·tion \lī-ˈbā-shən\ *n* **1 :** the act of pouring a liquid (as wine) in honor of a god; *also* **:** the liquid poured out **2 :** a drink usually of an alcoholic beverage [Latin *libatio,* from *libare* "to pour as an offering"] — **li·ba·tion·ary** \-shə-ˌner-ē\ *adj*

[1]**li·bel** \ˈlī-bəl\ *n* **1 :** a written or spoken statement or a representation that gives an unjustly unfavorable impression of a person or thing **2 :** the act or crime of injuring a person's reputation by way of something printed or written or by a visible representation (as a picture) — compare SLANDER [Medieval French, "written declaration," from Latin *libellus,* from *liber* "book"] — **li·bel·ous** \-bə-ləs\ *adj*

[2]**libel** *vt* **li·beled** *or* **li·belled; li·bel·ing** *or* **li·bel·ling** \-bə-ling, -bling\ **:** to make or publish a libel against — **li·bel·er** \-bə-lər\ *n* — **li·bel·ist** \-bə-list\ *n*

[1]**lib·er·al** \ˈlib-rəl, -ə-rəl\ *adj* **1 :** of, relating to, or based on the liberal arts ⟨a *liberal* education⟩ **2 a :** GENEROUS 1 ⟨a *liberal* giver⟩ **b :** AMPLE, BOUNTIFUL ⟨a *liberal* serving⟩ **3 :** not literal **:** LOOSE ⟨a *liberal* translation⟩ **4 :** BROAD-MINDED, TOLERANT; *esp* **:** not bound by orthodox or traditional forms or beliefs **5 a :** of, favoring, or based on the principles of liberalism **b** *cap* **:** of or making up a political party (as in the United Kingdom) advocating or associated with the principles of political liberalism [Medieval French, from Latin *liberalis* "suitable for a freeman, generous," from *liber* "free"] — **lib·er·al·ly** \-rə-lē\ *adv*

[2]**liberal** *n* **:** one who is liberal: as **a :** one who is open-minded or not strict in the observance of orthodox or traditional forms **b** *cap* **:** a member or supporter of a Liberal party **c :** an advocate of liberalism especially in individual rights

liberal arts *n pl* **:** the studies (as language, philosophy, history, literature, or abstract science) in a college or university intended to provide chiefly general knowledge and to develop the general intellectual capacities

lib·er·al·ism \ˈlib-rə-ˌliz-əm, -ə-rə-\ *n* **1 :** the quality or state of being liberal **2 a** *often cap* **:** a movement in modern Protestantism emphasizing intellectual liberty and the spiritual and ethical content of Christianity **b :** a theory in economics emphasizing individual freedom from restraint and usually based on free competition, the self-regulating market, and the gold standard **c :** a political philosophy based on belief in progress, the essential goodness of man, and the autonomy of the individual and standing for the protection of political and civil liberties **d** *cap* **:** the principles or policies of a Liberal party — **lib·er·al·ist** \-rə-ləst\ *n or adj* — **lib·er·al·is·tic** \ˌlib-rə-ˈlis-tik, -ə-rə-\ *adj*

lib·er·al·i·ty \ˌlib-ə-ˈral-ət-ē\ *n, pl* **-ties :** the quality or state of being liberal; *also* **:** an instance of being liberal

lib·er·al·ize \ˈlib-rə-ˌlīz, -ə-rə-\ *vb* **:** to make or become liberal — **lib·er·al·i·za·tion** \ˌlib-rə-lə-ˈzā-shən, -ə-rə-\ *n* — **lib·er·al·iz·er** \ˈlib-rə-ˌlī-zər, -ə-rə-\ *n*

lib·er·ate \ˈlib-ə-ˌrāt\ *vt* **1 :** to free from bondage or restraint **:** set at liberty **2 :** to free (as a gas) from combination [Latin *liberare,* from *liber* "free"] ***synonyms*** see FREE — **lib·er·a·tion** \ˌlib-ə-ˈrā-shən\ *n* — **lib·er·a·tor** \ˈlib-ə-ˌrāt-ər\ *n*

liberation theology *n* **:** a Christian movement especially in Latin America that combines political philosophy with a theology of salvation as liberation from injustice — **liberation theologian** *n*

lib·er·tar·i·an \ˌlib-ər-ˈter-ē-ən\ *n* **1 :** an advocate of the doctrine of free will **2 :** one who upholds liberty of thought and action — **libertarian** *adj* — **lib·er·tar·i·an·ism** \-ē-ə-ˌniz-əm\ *n*

lib·er·tine \ˈlib-ər-ˌtēn\ *n* **:** a person who is unrestrained by convention or morality; *esp* **:** one leading a dissolute life [Latin *libertinus* "freedman," derived from *liber* "free"] — **libertine** *adj* — **lib·er·tin·ism** \-ˌtē-ˌniz-əm\ *n*

lib·er·ty \ˈlib-ərt-ē\ *n, pl* **-ties** **1 :** the condition of being free and independent **:** FREEDOM **2 :** power to do what one pleases **:** freedom from restraint ⟨give the child some *liberty*⟩ **3 :** an action that goes beyond normal limits (as of proper behavior or common sense) ⟨took *liberties* with the truth⟩: as **a :** a breach of etiquette or propriety **:** FAMILIARITY **b :** RISK, CHANCE ⟨don't take foolish *liberties* with your health⟩ **4 :** a short authorized absence from naval duty [Medieval French *liberté,* from Latin *libertas,* from *liber* "free"] ***synonyms*** see FREEDOM — **at liberty** **1 :** not held back **:** FREE ⟨*at liberty* to go⟩ **2 :** at leisure **:** UNOCCUPIED ⟨is *at liberty* this afternoon⟩

liberty cap *n* **:** a close-fitting conical cap used as a symbol of liberty by the French revolutionists and in the U.S. especially before 1800

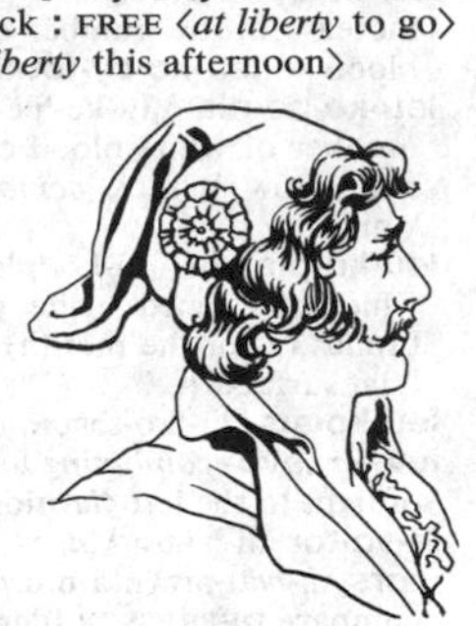
liberty cap

li·bid·i·nal \lə-ˈbid-ə-nəl\ *adj* **:** of or relating to the libido ⟨*libidinal* impulses⟩ — **li·bid·i·nal·ly** *adv*

li·bid·i·nous \lə-ˈbid-n-əs\ *adj* **1 :** having or marked by lustful desires **:** LEWD **2 :** LIBIDINAL — **li·bid·i·nous·ly** *adv* — **li·bid·i·nous·ness** *n*

li·bi·do \lə-ˈbēd-ō, -ˈbīd-\ *n, pl* **-dos** **1 :** instinctual psychic energy that in psychoanalytic theory is derived from primitive biological urges (as for self-preservation or sexual pleasure) **2 :** sexual drive [Latin *libidin-, libido* "desire, lust"]

Li·bra \ˈlī-brə, ˈlē-\ *n* **1 :** a southern zodiacal constellation between Virgo and Scorpio **2 :** the 7th sign of the zodiac; *also* **:** one born under this sign [Latin, literally, "scales, pound"]

li·brar·i·an \lī-ˈbrer-ē-ən\ *n* **:** a specialist in the care or management of a library — **li·brar·i·an·ship** \-ˌship\ *n*

li·brary \ˈlī-ˌbrer-ē\ *n, pl* **-brar·ies** **1 :** a place in which literary, reference, and artistic materials (as books, recordings, films) are kept for use but not for sale **2 :** a collection of literary or artistic materials (as books or prints) **3 :** a collection resembling or suggesting a library ⟨a *library* of cloned DNA fragments⟩ [Medieval Latin *librarium,* from Latin *liber* "book"]

library paste *n* **:** a thick white adhesive made from starch

li·bret·tist \lə-ˈbret-əst\ *n* **:** the writer of a libretto

li·bret·to \lə-ˈbret-ō\ *n, pl* **-tos** *or* **-ti** \-ē\ **:** the text of an opera or a musical; *also* **:** a book containing such a text [Italian, from *libro* "book," from Latin *liber*]

Lib·ri·um \ˈlib-rē-əm\ *trademark* — used for a tranquilizer containing chlordiazepoxide

lice *plural of* LOUSE

[1]**li·cense** *or* **li·cence** \ˈlīs-ns\ *n* **1 a :** permission to act **b :** freedom of action **2 a :** permission granted by competent authority to engage in a business, occupation, or activity otherwise unlawful **b :** a document, plate, or tag showing that a license has been granted **3 a :** freedom that is used irresponsibly **b :** licentious conduct **4 :** deviation from fact, form, or rule by an artist or writer for the sake of effect [Medieval French *licence,* from Latin *licentia,* from *licēre* "to be permitted"] ***synonyms*** see FREEDOM

[2]**license** *also* **licence** *vt* **1 :** to issue a license to **2 :** to permit or authorize especially by formal license — **li·cens·able** \-ə-bəl\ *adj*

licensed practical nurse *n* **:** a person who has undergone training and has obtained a license (as from a state) granting authorization to provide routine care for the sick
licensed vocational nurse *n* **:** a licensed practical nurse authorized by license to practice in the states of California or Texas
li·cens·ee \ˌlīs-ⁿn-ˈsē\ *n* **:** one that is licensed
license plate *n* **:** a plate or tag (as of metal) showing that a license has been secured and usually bearing a registration number
li·cen·tious \lī-ˈsen-chəs\ *adj* **:** loose and lawless in behavior; *esp* **:** LEWD — **li·cen·tious·ly** *adv* — **li·cen·tious·ness** *n*
lichee *variant of* LYCHEE
li·chen \ˈlī-kən\ *n* **:** any of numerous complex plantlike organisms made up of an alga and a fungus growing in symbiotic association on a solid surface (as a tree, a rock, or the ground) [Latin, from Greek *leichēn, lichēn,* from *leichein* "to lick"] — **li·chen·ous** \-kə-nəs\ *adj*
lich–gate *variant of* LYCH-GATE
lic·it \ˈlis-ət\ *adj* **:** conforming to the requirements of the law **:** PERMISSIBLE [Medieval French *licite,* from Latin *licitus,* from *licēre* "to be permitted"] ***synonyms*** see LAWFUL — **lic·it·ly** *adv*
[1]**lick** \ˈlik\ *vb* **1 a :** to draw the tongue over **b :** to dart or dart at or over like a tongue ⟨flames *licked* the ceiling⟩ **2 :** to lap up **3 a :** to strike repeatedly **:** THRASH **b :** DEFEAT 2 [Old English *liccian*] — **lick into shape :** to put into proper form or condition
[2]**lick** *n* **1 a :** an act or instance of licking **b :** a small amount **:** BIT ⟨not a *lick* of work⟩ **2 :** a sharp hit **:** BLOW **3 :** a place (as a spring) having a deposit of salt that animals regularly lick — **lick and a promise :** a careless performance of a task
lick·e·ty–split \ˌlik-ət-ē-ˈsplit\ *adv* **:** at great speed **:** very fast [probably derived from [1]*lick* + *split*]
lick·ing \ˈlik-ing\ *n* **1 :** a sound thrashing **2 :** a severe setback **:** DEFEAT
lick·spit·tle \ˈlik-ˌspit-l\ *n* **:** a fawning or abject subordinate **:** TOADY
lic·o·rice \ˈlik-rish, -ə-rish, -rəs\ *n* **1 :** a European plant of the legume family with spikes of blue flowers **2 :** the dried root of licorice; *also* **:** an extract from it used especially in liquors, confectionery, and medicine **3 :** a candy flavored with licorice or a substitute (as anise) [Medieval French *licoris,* from Late Latin *liquiritia,* from Latin *glycyrrhiza,* from Greek *glykyrrhiza,* from *glykys* "sweet" + *rhiza* "root"]
lic·tor \ˈlik-tər\ *n* **:** a Roman officer carrying the fasces as the insignia of his office with duties that included attending the chief magistrates in public appearances [Latin]
lid \ˈlid\ *n* **1 :** a movable cover ⟨the *lid* of a box⟩ **2 :** EYELID **3** *slang* **:** CAP 1, HAT **4 :** RESTRAINT 2a ⟨put a *lid* on all news coverage⟩ [Old English *hlid*] — **lid·ded** \ˈlid-əd\ *adj* — **lid·less** \ˈlid-ləs\ *adj*
li·do \ˈlēd-ō\ *n, pl* **lidos :** a fashionable beach resort [*Lido,* Italy]
[1]**lie** \ˈlī\ *vi* **lay** \ˈlā\; **lain** \ˈlān\; **ly·ing** \ˈlī-ing\ **1 a :** to be in, stay in, or take up a horizontal position ⟨decided to *lie* on the bed⟩ ⟨*lie* asleep⟩ **b** *archaic* **:** to have sexual intercourse — used with *with* **c :** to stay quietly (as in hiding) **2 :** to be in a helpless or defenseless state ⟨*lay* at the mercy of the invaders⟩ **3 :** to have direction **:** EXTEND ⟨the route *lay* to the west⟩ **4 a :** to occupy a specified relative place or position ⟨hills *lie* behind us⟩ **b :** to have an effect by mere presence, weight, or relative position ⟨guilt *lay* heavily on them⟩ **5 :** to have a place **:** EXIST ⟨the choice *lies* here⟩ **6 :** REMAIN ⟨machinery *lying* idle⟩ [Old English *licgan*] ***usage*** see LAY — **lie low 1 :** to stay in hiding **2 :** to bide one's time but remain ready for action
[2]**lie** *n* **1 :** the position in which something lies **2** *chiefly British* **:** [2]LAY 1 **3 :** the haunt of an animal **:** COVERT
[3]**lie** *vi* **lied; ly·ing** \ˈlī-ing\ **1 :** to make an untrue statement with intent to deceive ⟨*lie* about one's age⟩ **2 :** to create a false impression ⟨statistics sometimes *lie*⟩ [Old English *lēogan*]

synonyms LIE, PREVARICATE, EQUIVOCATE, FIB mean to tell an untruth. LIE is the blunt term, imputing dishonesty ⟨*lied* about where she had been⟩. PREVARICATE softens the bluntness of LIE by implying quibbling or confusing the issue ⟨during the hearings the witness did his best to *prevaricate*⟩. EQUIVOCATE implies using words having more than one sense so as to seem to say one thing but intend another ⟨*equivocated* endlessly in an attempt to mislead them⟩. FIB applies to a telling of a trivial untruth ⟨*fibbed* about the price of the necklace⟩.

[4]**lie** *n* **1 :** a deliberate telling of an untruth **2 :** something that misleads or deceives ⟨your show of innocence was a *lie*⟩
lie detector *n* **:** an instrument for detecting bodily changes (as an increase in heart rate) considered to accompany lying — compare POLYGRAPH
lie down *vi* **1 :** to submit meekly to defeat, disappointment, or insult ⟨refused to take the setback *lying down*⟩ **2 :** to fail to do one's part ⟨*lying down* on the job⟩
lief \ˈlēv, ˈlēf\ *adv* **:** SOON, GLADLY ⟨I'd as *lief* go as not⟩ [Old English *lēof* "dear, agreeable"]
[1]**liege** \ˈlēj\ *adj* **1 :** having the right to receive service and allegiance ⟨*liege* lord⟩ **2 :** owing or giving service to a lord ⟨a *liege* subject⟩ [Medieval French *lige,* from Late Latin *laeticus,* from *laetus* "serf," of Germanic origin]
[2]**liege** *n* **1 :** VASSAL 1 **2 :** a feudal superior
liege man *n* **1 :** VASSAL 1 **2 :** a devoted follower
lien \ˈlēn, ˈlē-ən\ *n* **:** a legal claim on the property of a person until he or she has met a certain obligation (as a debt) [Middle French *lien, loyen* "bond, restraint," from Latin *ligamen,* from *ligare* "to bind"]
lie to \lī ˈtü, ˈlī-\ *vi* **:** to stay stationary with head to windward
lieu \ˈlü\ *n, archaic* **:** PLACE, STEAD [Medieval French *liu, lieu,* from Latin *locus*] — **in lieu of :** in the place of **:** instead of
lieu·ten·an·cy \lü-ˈten-ən-sē\ *n, pl* **-cies :** the office, rank, or commission of a lieutenant
lieu·ten·ant \lü-ˈten-ənt\ *n* **1 a :** an officer empowered to act for a higher official **b :** a representative of another in the performance of duty **2 a** (1) **:** FIRST LIEUTENANT (2) **:** SECOND LIEUTENANT **b :** an officer rank in the Navy and Coast Guard above lieutenant junior grade and below lieutenant commander **c :** a fire or police department officer ranking below a captain [Medieval French, from *lieu* "place" + *tenant* "holding"]
lieutenant colonel *n* **:** an officer rank in the Army, Marine Corps, and Air Force above major and below colonel
lieutenant commander *n* **:** an officer rank in the Navy and Coast Guard above lieutenant and below commander
lieutenant general *n* **:** an officer rank in the Army, Marine Corps, and Air Force above major general and below general
lieutenant governor *n* **1 :** an elected official serving as deputy to the governor of an American state **2 :** the formal head of the government of a Canadian province appointed to represent the crown
lieutenant junior grade *n, pl* **lieutenants junior grade :** an officer rank in the Navy and Coast Guard above ensign and below lieutenant
[1]**life** \ˈlīf\ *n, pl* **lives** \ˈlīvz\ **1 a :** the quality that distinguishes a vital and functional being from a dead body or inanimate matter **b :** a state of an organism characterized especially by capacity for metabolism, growth, reaction to stimuli, and reproduction **2 :** the sequence of physical and mental experiences that make up the existence of an individual **3 :** BIOGRAPHY 1 **4 a :** the period during which an organism lives **b :** a specific phase or aspect of such a life ⟨adult *life*⟩ ⟨sex *life*⟩ **5 :** a way or manner of living **6 :** a vital or living being; *esp* **:** PERSON ⟨saving *lives*⟩ **7 :** ANIMATION, SPIRIT ⟨eyes full of *life*⟩ **8 :** the period of utility, duration, or existence of something ⟨*life* of a car⟩ **9 :** living beings ⟨forest *life*⟩ **10 a :** human activities **b :** animate activity and movement ⟨stirrings of *life*⟩ **11 :** one providing interest and vigor ⟨the *life* of the party⟩ [Old English *līf*]
[2]**life** *adj* **1 :** of or relating to animate being ⟨the *life* force⟩ **2 :** LIFELONG ⟨*life* tenure⟩ **3 :** using a living model ⟨a *life* class⟩
life–and–death *adj* **:** ending in life or death **:** deciding which will survive
life belt *n* **:** a life preserver in the form of a buoyant belt
life·blood \ˈlīf-ˈbləd\ *n* **:** something that gives strength and energy **:** the vital force or essence
life·boat \-ˌbōt\ *n* **:** a sturdy buoyant boat (as one carried by a ship) for use in an emergency and especially for saving lives at sea
life buoy *n* **:** a ring-shaped life preserver
life cycle *n* **1 :** the series of stages of form and activity through

\ə\ abut	\au̇\ **out**	\i\ **tip**	\ȯ\ **saw**	\u̇\ **foot**
\ər\ **further**	\ch\ **chin**	\ī\ **life**	\ȯi\ **coin**	\y\ **yet**
\a\ **mat**	\e\ **pet**	\j\ **job**	\th\ **thin**	\yü\ **few**
\ā\ **take**	\ē\ **easy**	\ng\ **sing**	\t͟h\ **this**	\yu̇\ **cure**
\ä\ **cot, cart**	\g\ **go**	\ō\ **bone**	\ü\ **food**	\zh\ **vision**

which an organism passes from a particular first stage (as the egg) in one individual to the same stage in its offspring **2 :** LIFE HISTORY 1a

life expectancy *n* **:** an expected number of years of life based on statistical probability

life•guard \ˈlīf-ˌgärd\ *n* **:** a usually expert swimmer employed to safeguard other swimmers

life history *n* **1 a :** a history of the changes through which an organism passes in its development from its first stage to its natural death **b :** LIFE CYCLE 1 **2 :** the history of an individual's development in a social environment

life insurance *n* **:** insurance providing for payment of a fixed sum to a specified individual upon death of the insured

life jacket *n* **:** a life preserver in the form of a sleeveless jacket or a collar which extends down the chest — called also *life vest*

life•less \ˈlīf-ləs\ *adj* **:** having no life: **a :** DEAD 1 **b :** INANIMATE ⟨*lifeless* as marble⟩ **c :** lacking qualities expressive of life and vigor **:** DULL ⟨*lifeless* voice⟩ **d :** destitute of living beings ⟨a *lifeless* desert⟩ — **life•less•ly** *adv* — **life•less•ness** *n*

life•like \ˈlīf-ˌlīk\ *adj* **:** accurately representing or imitating real life ⟨a *lifelike* portrait⟩ — **life•like•ness** *n*

life•line \ˈlīf-ˌlīn\ *n* **1 :** a line (as a rope) used for saving or protecting life: as **a :** a line along the outer edge of the deck of a boat or ship **b :** a line used to keep contact with a person (as a diver or astronaut) in a dangerous or potentially dangerous situation **2 :** something regarded as indispensable for the maintaining or protection of life

life•long \ˈlīf-ˌlȯng\ *adj* **:** continuing through life ⟨a *lifelong* friendship⟩

life preserver *n* **:** a device designed to save a person from drowning by buoying up the body while in the water

lif•er \ˈlī-fər\ *n* **:** a person sentenced to life imprisonment

life raft *n* **:** a raft usually made of wood or an inflatable material and designed for rescue use in an emergency at sea

life•sav•er \ˈlīf-ˌsā-vər\ *n* **1 :** one trained to save the lives of drowning persons **2 :** one that is at once timely and effective in times of distress or need

1**life•sav•ing** \ˈlīf-ˌsā-viŋ\ *adj* **:** designed for or used in saving lives ⟨*lifesaving* drugs⟩

2**lifesaving** *n* **:** the skill or practice of saving or protecting lives especially of drowning persons

life science *n* **:** a branch of science (as biology, medicine, and sometimes anthropology or sociology) that deals with living organisms and life processes — **life scientist** *n*

life–size \ˈlīf-ˈsīz\ *or* **life–sized** \-ˈsīzd\ *adj* **:** of natural size **:** of the size of the original ⟨a *life-size* statue⟩

life span *n* **1 :** the duration of existence of an individual **2 :** the average length of life of a kind of organism or of an object

life•style \ˈlīf-ˈstīl\ *n* **:** the usual way of life of a person, group, or society

life–support system *n* **:** a system that supplies some or all of the items (as oxygen, food, water, and proper air pressure) necessary for maintaining life or health

life•time \-ˌtīm\ *n* **:** the duration of an individual's existence

life vest *n* **:** LIFE JACKET

life•work \ˈlīf-ˈwərk\ *n* **:** the entire or principal work of one's lifetime; *also* **:** a work extending over a lifetime

1**lift** \ˈlift\ *vb* **1 :** to raise from a lower to a higher position, rate, or amount **:** ELEVATE **2 :** REVOKE, REPEAL ⟨*lift* an embargo⟩ **3 a :** STEAL ⟨had their wallets *lifted*⟩ **b :** PLAGIARIZE **4 :** to move from one place to another **:** TRANSPORT **5 :** RISE, ASCEND ⟨the jet *lifted* from the airport⟩ **6 :** to disperse upward ⟨until the fog *lifts*⟩ [Old Norse *lypta*] — **lift•er** *n*

synonyms LIFT, RAISE, HOIST, BOOST mean to move from a lower to a higher place or position. LIFT implies effort exerted to bring up from and especially clear of the ground and may apply to immaterial as well as material things. RAISE often suggests bringing something to a vertical or high position for which it is suited or intended. HOIST implies lifting something very heavy by mechanical means. BOOST suggests assisting to climb or advance by a push.

2**lift** *n* **1 :** the amount that may be lifted at one time **:** LOAD **2 :** the action or an instance of lifting **3 a :** ASSISTANCE, HELP **b :** a ride along one's way **4 :** the distance or extent to which something rises ⟨the *lift* of a canal lock⟩ **5 a** *chiefly British* **:** ELEVATOR 1b **b :** an apparatus for raising an automobile (as for repair) **c :** a conveyor for carrying people up or down a mountain slope **6 a :** an elevating influence **b :** an elevation of the spirits **7 :** the part of the total aerodynamic force acting on an airplane or airfoil that is upward and opposes the pull of gravity

lift•off \ˈlift-ˌȯf\ *n* **:** a vertical takeoff by an aircraft, rocket, or missile

lig•a•ment \ˈlig-ə-mənt\ *n* **:** a tough band of tissue that holds bones together or keeps an organ in place in the body [Latin *ligamentum* "band, tie," from *ligare* "to bind"] — **lig•a•men•tous** \ˌlig-ə-ˈment-əs\ *adj*

li•gate \ˈlī-ˌgāt, lī-ˈ\ *vt* **:** to tie with a ligature — **li•ga•tion** \lī-ˈgā-shən\ *n*

lig•a•ture \ˈlig-ə-ˌchu̇r, -chər\ *n* **1 :** a binding or tying of something **2 :** something that binds or connects **:** BOND **3 :** a thread or filament used in surgery especially for tying blood vessels **4 :** a printed or written character consisting of two or more letters or characters united ⟨the *ligature* æ⟩ [Late Latin *ligatura*, from Latin *ligare* "to bind"]

1**light** \ˈlīt\ *n* **1 a :** something that makes vision possible **b :** the sensation aroused by stimulation of the visual receptors **c :** electromagnetic radiation of any wavelength range (as infrared, visible, ultraviolet, and X-rays) and traveling in a vacuum with a speed of about 186,000 miles (300,000 kilometers) per second; *esp* **:** such radiation that is visible to the human eye **2 a :** DAYLIGHT 1 **b :** DAWN 1 **3 :** a source of light: as **a :** a celestial body **b :** CANDLE 1 **c :** an electric lamp ⟨turned on all the *lights*⟩ **4 a :** mental or spiritual insight **b :** TRUTH ⟨see the *light*⟩ **5 a :** public knowledge ⟨facts brought to *light*⟩ **b :** a particular aspect presented to view ⟨saw the matter in a false *light*⟩ **6 :** a particular illumination ⟨by the *light* of the moon⟩ **7 a :** WINDOW 1a **b :** SKYLIGHT **8** *pl* **:** way of thinking **:** BELIEFS ⟨worship according to one's *lights*⟩ **9 :** LEADING LIGHT, LUMINARY **10 :** a particular expression of the eye **11 a :** LIGHTHOUSE, BEACON **b :** TRAFFIC SIGNAL **12 :** a source of heat for lighting something [Old English *lēoht*] — **light•less** \-ləs\ *adj*

2**light** *adj* **1 :** having light **:** BRIGHT ⟨a *light* room⟩ **2 a :** not dark or swarthy in color ⟨a *light* skin⟩ **b :** medium in saturation and high in lightness ⟨*light* blue⟩

3**light** *vb* **light•ed** *or* **lit** \ˈlit\; **light•ing 1 :** to make or become light **:** BRIGHTEN **2 :** to burn or cause to burn **:** IGNITE **3 a :** to conduct with a light ⟨*light* them to their room⟩ **b :** ILLUMINATE ⟨rockets *lit* up the sky⟩

4**light** *adj* **1 a :** having little weight **:** not heavy ⟨*light* as a feather⟩ **b :** designed to carry a comparatively small load ⟨a *light* truck⟩ **c :** having relatively little weight in proportion to bulk ⟨aluminum is a *light* metal⟩ **2 a :** not important or serious **:** TRIVIAL **b :** not abundant **:** SCANTY ⟨*light* rain⟩ ⟨a *light* breakfast⟩ **3 a :** easily disturbed ⟨a *light* sleeper⟩ **b :** exerting little force or pressure **:** GENTLE ⟨a *light* touch⟩ **4 :** requiring little effort ⟨*light* exercise⟩ **5 :** capable of moving swiftly or nimbly ⟨the dancers were *light* on their feet⟩ **6 :** FRIVOLOUS ⟨*light* conduct⟩ **7 :** free from care **:** CHEERFUL **8 :** intended chiefly to entertain ⟨*light* reading⟩ **9 :** made with a lower calorie content or with less of some ingredient (as fat or alcohol) ⟨*light* salad dressing⟩ **10 :** well leavened **:** having a spongy or fluffy quality ⟨a *light* pastry⟩ **11 :** lightly armed or equipped ⟨*light* cavalry⟩ **12 :** being coarse and sandy **:** easily reduced to dust ⟨*light* soil⟩ **13 :** producing goods for direct consumption by the consumer ⟨*light* industry⟩ **14 :** UNACCENTED ⟨*light* syllables⟩ **15 :** having a clear soft quality ⟨a *light* voice⟩ [Old English *lēoht*]

5**light** *adv* **1 :** LIGHTLY **2 :** with little baggage ⟨travels *light*⟩

6**light** *vi* **light•ed** *or* **lit** \ˈlit\; **light•ing 1 :** SETTLE, ALIGHT ⟨birds *lit* on the lawn⟩ **2 a :** to strike or fall unexpectedly ⟨bad luck *lighted* on the party⟩ **b :** to arrive by chance **:** HAPPEN ⟨*lit* upon a solution⟩ [Old English *līhtan* "to dismount, alight"]

light adaptation *n* **:** the process by which the eye adapts to seeing in strong light — **light–adap•ted** \ˈlīt-ə-ˌdap-təd\ *adj*

light•bulb \ˈlīt-ˌbəlb\ *n* **:** an electric lamp: as **a :** one in which a filament gives off light when heated by an electric current — called also *incandescent lamp* **b :** FLUORESCENT LAMP

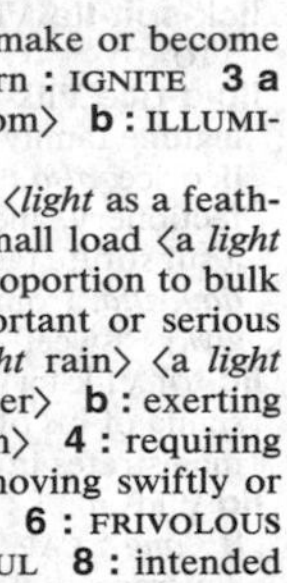

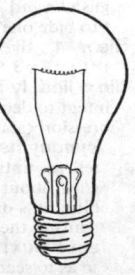

lightbulb

light chain *n* **:** either of the two smaller of the four polypeptide chains comprising antibodies — compare HEAVY CHAIN

light–emitting diode *n* **:** LED

1**light•en** \ˈlīt-n\ *vb* **light•ened; light•en•ing**

\ˈlīt-ning, -n-ing\ **1 :** to make or grow light or clear **:** BRIGHTEN **2 :** to make or become lighter — **light·en·er** \ˈlīt-nər, -n-ər\ *n*

[2]**lighten** *vb* **light·ened; light·en·ing** \ˈlīt-ning, -n-ing\ **1 :** to relieve of a burden in whole or in part ⟨*lighten* the plane⟩ ⟨*lighten* their duties⟩ **2 :** GLADDEN **3 :** to become lighter ***synonyms*** see RELIEVE — **light·en·er** \ˈlīt-nər, -n-ər\ *n*

[1]**ligh·ter** \ˈlīt-ər\ *n* **:** a large usually flat-bottomed barge used especially in unloading or loading ships [Dutch *lichten* "to unload"]

[2]**lighter** *vt* **:** to convey by a lighter

[3]**light·er** \ˈlīt-ər\ *n* **:** one that lights; *esp* **:** a device for lighting

lighter–than–air *adj* **:** of less weight than the air displaced

light·face \ˈlīt-ˌfās\ *n* **:** a typeface having thin light lines — **light·faced** \-ˈfāst\ *adj*

light·fast \ˈlīt-ˈfast\ *adj* **:** resistant to light and especially to sunlight; *esp* **:** colorfast to light — **light·fast·ness** \-ˌfast-nəs, -ˌfas-\ *n*

light–fin·gered \-ˈfing-gərd\ *adj* **1 :** adroit in stealing especially by picking pockets **2 :** having a light and dexterous touch **:** NIMBLE — **light–fin·gered·ness** *n*

light–foot·ed \-ˈfu̇t-əd\ *adj* **:** having a light and springy step or movement

light–head·ed \-ˈhed-əd\ *adj* **1 :** mentally disoriented **:** DIZZY **2 :** lacking in maturity or seriousness **:** FRIVOLOUS — **light–head·ed·ly** *adv* — **light–head·ed·ness** *n*

light·heart·ed \-ˈhärt-əd\ *adj* **:** free from care or anxiety **:** MERRY — **light·heart·ed·ly** *adv* — **light·heart·ed·ness** *n*

light heavyweight *n* **:** a boxer in a weight division having an upper limit of about 175 pounds

light·house \ˈlīt-ˌhau̇s\ *n* **:** a structure (as a tower) with a powerful light signal for guiding navigators at night

lighthouse

light·ing \ˈlīt-ing\ *n* **1 a :** ILLUMINATION 2 **b :** IGNITION 1 **2 :** an artificial supply of light or the apparatus providing it

light·ly \ˈlīt-lē\ *adv* **1 :** with little weight or force **:** GENTLY **2 :** in a small degree or amount ⟨sprinkle *lightly*⟩ **3 :** with little difficulty **:** EASILY ⟨was let off *lightly* with a warning⟩ **4 :** in an agile manner **:** NIMBLY **5 :** with indifference or carelessness ⟨took the rebuff *lightly*⟩

light meter *n* **1 :** a small portable device for measuring illumination **2 :** a device for indicating correct photographic exposure under varying conditions of illumination

light–mind·ed \ˈlīt-ˈmīn-dəd\ *adj* **:** lacking in seriousness **:** FRIVOLOUS — **light·mind·ed·ly** *adv*

[1]**light·ness** \ˈlīt-nəs\ *n* **1 :** the quality or state of being light or lighted **:** ILLUMINATION **2 :** the degree to which the achromatic element of a color is nearer white than black ⟨pink is high in *lightness*⟩

[2]**lightness** *n* **1 :** the quality or state of being light in weight **2 :** LEVITY **3 a :** physical agility **b :** cheery ease of style or manner **4 :** DELICACY ⟨*lightness* of touch⟩

[1]**light·ning** \ˈlīt-ning\ *n* **:** the flashing of light produced by a discharge of atmospheric electricity from one cloud to another or between a cloud and the earth; *also* **:** the discharge itself [Middle English, from *lightenen* "to lighten"]

[2]**lightning** *adj* **:** moving or accomplished with or as if with the speed of lightning ⟨a *lightning* attack⟩

lightning arrester *n* **:** a device for protecting an electrical apparatus from damage by lightning

lightning bug *n* **:** FIREFLY

lightning rod *n* **:** a metal rod set up on a building or a ship and connected with the earth or water below to decrease the chances of damage from lightning

light opera *n* **:** OPERETTA

light out *vi* **:** to leave in a hurry ⟨*lit out* for home⟩

light pen *n* **:** a pen-shaped device for immediate handling of information on the display screen of a computer

light·plane \ˈlīt-ˈplān\ *n* **:** a small and comparatively lightweight airplane; *esp* **:** a privately owned passenger airplane

light pollution *n* **:** artificial light (as from city lights) that interferes with astronomical observations

light·proof \ˈlīt-ˈprüf\ *adj* **:** impenetrable by light

light reaction *n* **:** the phase of photosynthesis that requires the presence of light and involves the synthesis of ATP from ADP and phosphate

lights \ˈlīts\ *n pl* **:** the lungs especially of a slaughtered animal [Middle English *lightes,* from [4]*light*]

light·ship \ˈlīt-ˌship\ *n* **:** a ship equipped with a powerful light signal and moored at a place dangerous to navigation

light·some \ˈlīt-səm\ *adj* **1 :** AIRY 3, NIMBLE **2 :** free from care **:** CHEERFUL — **light·some·ly** *adv* — **light·some·ness** *n*

light·tight \ˈlīt-ˌtīt\ *adj* **:** LIGHTPROOF

light trap *n* **:** a device for collecting or destroying insects by attracting them to a light and trapping or killing them

light water *n* **:** WATER 1a — compare HEAVY WATER

[1]**light·weight** \ˈlīt-ˌwāt\ *n* **1 :** one of less than average weight; *esp* **:** a boxer in a weight division having an upper limit of about 135 pounds **2 :** one of little consequence

[2]**lightweight** *adj* **1 :** of, relating to, or characteristic of a lightweight **2 :** having less than average weight **3 :** of no significance **:** UNIMPORTANT

light–year \ˈlīt-ˌyiər\ *n* **:** a unit of length in astronomy equal to the distance that light travels in one year or 5,880,000,000,000 miles (9,460,000,000,000 kilometers)

lign- *or* **ligni-** *or* **ligno-** *combining form* **:** wood ⟨*lignin*⟩ [Latin *lignum*]

lig·ne·ous \ˈlig-nē-əs\ *adj* **:** of or resembling wood **:** WOODY [Latin *ligneus,* from *lignum* "firewood, wood," from *legere* "to gather"]

lig·ni·fy \ˈlig-nə-ˌfī\ *vb* **-fied; -fy·ing :** to convert into or become wood or woody tissue — **lig·ni·fi·ca·tion** \ˌlig-nə-fə-ˈkā-shən\ *n*

lig·nin \ˈlig-nən\ *n* **:** a substance related to cellulose that provides rigidity and together with cellulose forms the woody cell walls of plants and the cementing material between them

lig·nite \ˈlig-ˌnīt\ *n* **:** a usually brownish black coal intermediate between peat and bituminous coal; *esp* **:** one in which the texture of the original wood is distinct

lig·num vi·tae \ˌlig-nəm-ˈvīt-ē\ *n, pl* **lignum vitaes :** any of several tropical American trees or their very hard heavy wood [New Latin, literally, "wood of life"]

lig·u·late \ˈlig-yə-lət, -ˌlāt\ *also* **lig·u·lat·ed** \-ˌlāt-əd\ *adj* **1 :** shaped like a strap ⟨*ligulate* ray flowers⟩ **2 :** having ligules

lig·ule \ˈlig-yül\ *n* **:** a scalelike projection especially on a plant: as **a :** an appendage of a leaf and especially of the sheath of a blade of grass **b :** the limb of a ray flower [Latin *ligula* "small tongue, strap"]

lik·able *or* **like·able** \ˈlī-kə-bəl\ *adj* **:** easily liked **:** PLEASANT, AGREEABLE — **lik·able·ness** *n*

[1]**like** \ˈlīk\ *vb* **1 :** to feel attraction toward or take pleasure in **:** ENJOY ⟨*likes* baseball⟩ **2 :** to feel toward **:** REGARD ⟨how do you *like* this plan⟩ **3 :** to wish to have **:** WANT ⟨would *like* a vacation⟩ **4 :** to feel inclined **:** CHOOSE ⟨allowed to do as they *liked*⟩ [Old English *lician* "to be suitable, be pleasing"]

[2]**like** *n* **:** LIKING, PREFERENCE ⟨*likes* and dislikes⟩

[3]**like** *adj* **1 :** the same or nearly the same (as in appearance, character, or quantity) ⟨suits of *like* design⟩ ⟨in *like* circumstances⟩ **2 :** LIKELY 1 [Old English *gelīc,* from *līc* "body"]

[4]**like** *prep* **1 a :** similar to ⟨their house is *like* a barn⟩ **b :** typical of ⟨was *like* them to do that⟩ **2 :** in the manner of **:** similarly to ⟨acts *like* a fool⟩ **3 :** as though there would be ⟨looks *like* rain⟩ **4 :** such as ⟨a subject *like* physics⟩

[5]**like** *n* **:** one that is like another **:** COUNTERPART, EQUAL ⟨may never see its *like* again⟩ — **the likes of :** such people as **:** such things as ⟨reads *the likes of* Shakespeare⟩

[6]**like** *adv* **1 :** LIKELY, PROBABLY ⟨*like* enough, you will⟩ **2 :** to some extent **:** SEEMINGLY ⟨came in nonchalantly *like*⟩ **3 :** close to ⟨the rate is more *like* 12 percent⟩

[7]**like** *conj* **1 :** AS IF ⟨acted *like* they were scared⟩ **2 :** in the same way that **:** AS ⟨did it *like* you told me⟩

-like *adj combining form* **:** resembling or characteristic of ⟨bell-*like*⟩ ⟨lady*like*⟩

like·li·hood \ˈlī-klē-ˌhu̇d\ *n* **:** PROBABILITY

[1]**like·ly** \ˈlī-klē\ *adj* **like·li·er; -est 1 :** being such as to make a certain happening or result probable ⟨the stronger team is *likely*

\ə\ **abut**	\au̇\ **out**	\i\ **tip**	\ȯ\ **saw**	\u̇\ **foot**
\ər\ **further**	\ch\ **chin**	\ī\ **life**	\ȯi\ **coin**	\y\ **yet**
\a\ **mat**	\e\ **pet**	\j\ **job**	\th\ **thin**	\yü\ **few**
\ā\ **take**	\ē\ **easy**	\ng\ **sing**	\t͟h\ **this**	\yu̇\ **cure**
\ä\ **cot, cart**	\g\ **go**	\ō\ **bone**	\ü\ **food**	\zh\ **vision**

to win⟩ **2 :** seeming like the truth : BELIEVABLE ⟨a *likely* story⟩ **3 :** PROMISING ⟨a *likely* place to fish⟩ [Old English *gelīclic* "fitting," from *gelīc* "like," and Old Norse *glīkligr,* from *glīkr* "like"] ***usage*** see APT

[2]likely *adv* : in all probability : PROBABLY

like–mind•ed \ˈlīk-ˈmīn-dəd\ *adj* : of the same mind or habit of thought — **like–mind•ed•ly** *adv* — **like–mind•ed•ness** *n*

lik•en \ˈlī-kən\ *vt* **lik•ened; lik•en•ing** \ˈlīk-ning, -ə-ning\ : to represent as like something : COMPARE

like•ness \ˈlīk-nəs\ *n* **1 :** the quality or state of being like : RESEMBLANCE **2 :** APPEARANCE 1a, SEMBLANCE ⟨in the *likeness* of a clown⟩ **3 :** COPY 1, PORTRAIT

synonyms LIKENESS, SIMILARITY, RESEMBLANCE mean agreement or correspondence in details. LIKENESS implies a closer correspondence than SIMILARITY which often implies that things are only somewhat alike ⟨a remarkable *likeness* to his father⟩ ⟨some *similarity* between the two⟩. RESEMBLANCE implies similarity chiefly in appearance or external qualities ⟨a statement that bears little *resemblance* to the truth⟩.

like•wise \ˈlīk-ˌwīz\ *adv* **1 :** in like manner : SIMILARLY ⟨go and do *likewise*⟩ **2 :** in addition : ALSO

lik•ing \ˈlī-king\ *n* : favorable regard : FONDNESS, TASTE

li•lac \ˈlī-lək, -ˌlak, -ˌläk\ *n* **1 :** any of a genus of shrubs and trees related to the olive; *esp* : a European shrub widely grown for its showy clusters of fragrant pink, purple, or white flowers **2 :** a moderate purple [obsolete French, from Arabic *līlak,* from Persian *nīlak* "bluish," from *nīl* "blue," from Sanskrit *nīla* "dark blue"]

lil•li•pu•tian \ˌlil-ə-ˈpyü-shən\ *adj, often cap* **1 :** extremely small : MINIATURE **2 :** SMALL-MINDED, PETTY [*Lilliput,* island in Swift's *Gulliver's Travels* (1726) inhabited by people six inches high]

[1]lilt \ˈlilt\ *vi* **1 :** to sing or speak rhythmically and with varying pitch **2 :** to move in a lively springy manner [Middle English *lulten* "to sound an alarm"] — **lilt•ing•ly** \ˈlil-ting-lē\ *adv*

[2]lilt *n* **1 :** a lively and usually happy song or tune **2 :** a rhythmical swing, flow, or cadence

[1]lily \ˈlil-ē\ *n, pl* **lil•ies** **1 :** any of a genus of erect perennial leafy-stemmed bulbous herbs widely grown for their showy funnel-shaped flowers; *also* : any of various related plants **2 :** any of various plants (as a water lily or a calla lily) with showy flowers [Old English *lilie,* from Latin *lilium*]

[2]lily *adj* : of, relating to, or resembling a lily

lily–liv•ered \ˌlil-ē-ˈliv-ərd\ *adj* : lacking courage : COWARDLY

Word History White, the lily's color, is a color associated with fear. A badly frightened person may turn pale—"white as a sheet." But the sudden fright that drains the blood from one's face is quite different from the habitual cowardice of one who is *lily-livered.* Although the liver does not turn pale with fear, it was once believed that a deficiency of choler or yellow bile—the humor that governed anger, spirit, and courage—would leave the liver colorless. A person deficient in choler, and so white-livered, or lily-livered, would be spiritless and a coward.

lily of the valley : a low perennial herb related to the lilies with usually two large oblong leaves and a stalk of fragrant nodding bell-shaped white flowers

lily pad *n* : a floating leaf of a water lily

lily–white \ˌlil-ē-ˈhwīt, -ˈwīt\ *adj* **1 :** white as a lily **2 :** FAULTLESS, PURE

li•ma bean \ˌlī-mə-\ *n* : a bushy or tall-growing tropical American bean plant widely grown for its flat edible usually pale green or whitish seeds; *also* : the seed of a lima bean [*Lima,* Peru]

[1]limb \ˈlim\ *n* **1 :** one of the projecting paired appendages (as wings) of an animal body used especially for movement and grasping; *esp* : a leg or arm of a human **2 :** a large primary branch of a tree [Old English *lim*] — **limbed** \ˈlimd\ *adj*

[2]limb *vt* : to cut off the limbs of (a felled tree)

[3]limb *n* **1 :** the outer edge of the apparent disk of a celestial body ⟨the eastern *limb* of the sun⟩ **2 :** the expanded portion of a bodily organ or structure; *esp* : the upper spreading portion of a corolla that is not made up of separate parts [Latin *limbus* "border"]

[1]lim•ber \ˈlim-bər\ *adj* : bending easily : SUPPLE ⟨a *limber* willow twig⟩ ⟨a *limber* gymnast⟩ [origin unknown] — **lim•ber•ly** *adv* — **lim•ber•ness** *n*

[2]limber *vb* **lim•bered; lim•ber•ing** \ˈlim-bə-ring, -bring\ : to become or cause to become limber ⟨*limbered* up with calisthenics⟩

limbic system \ˌlim-bik-\ *n* : a group of structures (as the hypothalamus and hippocampus) below the cortex of the brain that are concerned especially with emotion and motivation [Latin *limbus* "border"]

limb•less \ˈlim-ləs\ *adj* : having no limbs ⟨*limbless* amphibians⟩

[1]lim•bo \ˈlim-bō\ *n, pl* **limbos** **1** *often cap* : an abode of souls (as of unbaptized infants) barred from heaven through no fault of their own **2 a :** a place or state of restraint, confinement, or oblivion **b :** an intermediate or transitional place or state [Medieval Latin in *limbo* "on the border," from Latin *limbus* "border"]

[2]limbo *n, pl* **limbos :** a dance or contest that involves bending over backwards and passing under a horizontal pole lowered slightly for each successive pass [English of Trinidad and Barbados; related to Jamaican English *limba* "to bend," from English [1]*limber*]

Lim•burg•er \ˈlim-ˌbər-gər\ *n* : a creamy semisoft surface-ripened cheese with a pungent rind [*Limburg,* Belgium]

[1]lime \ˈlīm\ *n* **1 :** BIRDLIME **2 a :** a caustic highly infusible solid that consists of an oxide of calcium often together with magnesia, is obtained by calcining forms of calcium carbonate (as limestone or shells), and is used in mortar and plaster and in agriculture — called also *quicklime* **b :** a dry white powder consisting essentially of an hydroxide of calcium that is made by treating lime with water **c :** CALCIUM ⟨carbonate of *lime*⟩ [Old English *līm*]

[2]lime *vt* : to treat or cover with lime ⟨*lime* the lawn⟩

[3]lime *adj* : of, relating to, or containing lime or limestone

[4]lime *n* : a European linden tree [Old English *lind*]

[5]lime *n* : a fruit similar to the lemon but smaller and with yellowish green rind; *also* : the spiny tropical Asian citrus tree that bears limes [Medieval French, from Spanish *lima,* from Arabic *līma, līm*]

lime•ade \ˌlīm-ˈād, ˈlī-ˌmād\ *n* : a drink made of lime juice, sugar, and water

lime•kiln \ˈlīm-ˌkiln, -ˌkil\ *n* : a furnace for reducing limestone or shells to lime by burning

lime•light \-ˌlīt\ *n* **1 :** a stage light producing light by means of a flame directed on a cylinder of lime; *also* : the light produced by this device **2 :** the center of public attention

lim•er•ick \ˈlim-rik, -ə-rik\ *n* : a light or humorous verse form of 5 lines of which the 1st, 2nd, and 5th follow one rhyme and the 3rd and 4th follow another [*Limerick,* Ireland]

lime•stone \ˈlīm-ˌstōn\ *n* : a rock that is formed chiefly by accumulation of organic remains (as shells or coral), consists mainly of calcium carbonate, is extensively used in building, and yields lime when burned

lime•wa•ter \ˈlīm-ˌwȯt-ər, -ˌwät-\ *n* : an alkaline water solution of calcium hydroxide used as an antacid

limey *variant of* LIMY

[1]lim•it \ˈlim-ət\ *n* **1 a :** a geographic or political boundary **b** *pl* : [2]BOUND 3 **2 a :** something that bounds, restrains, or confines ⟨cooperate within *limits*⟩ **b :** the utmost extent ⟨reach the *limit* of one's tolerance⟩ **3 :** LIMITATION 2 **4 :** a prescribed maximum or minimum amount, quantity, or number **5 a :** a number that is related to a mathematical function in such a way that the difference between it and the value of the function becomes smaller and smaller as the function's independent variable approaches a given number ⟨the *limit* of $f(x) = (x^2 - 1) / (x - 1)$ as x approaches 1 is 2⟩ **b :** a number that is related to an infinite sequence of numbers in such a way that the difference between it and a term in the sequence becomes smaller and smaller the later the term happens in the sequence ⟨the *limit* of $\frac{1}{2}, \frac{2}{3}, \frac{3}{4}, \frac{4}{5}, \ldots$ is 1⟩ **6 :** something that is exasperating or intolerable [Medieval French *limite,* from Latin *limit-, limes* "boundary"]

[2]limit *vt* **1 :** to set limits to **2 :** to reduce in quantity or extent — **lim•it•able** \ˈlim-ət-ə-bəl\ *adj* — **lim•it•er** *n*

synonyms LIMIT, RESTRICT, CIRCUMSCRIBE, CONFINE mean to set boundaries for. LIMIT implies setting a point or line (as in time, space, or speed) beyond which something cannot or is not permitted to go ⟨visits are *limited* to 30 minutes⟩. RESTRICT suggests a narrowing or restraining within or as if within an encircling boundary ⟨laws intended to *restrict* the freedom of the press⟩. CIRCUMSCRIBE stresses a restriction on all sides and by clearly defined boundaries ⟨the authority of the investigating committee was carefully *circumscribed*⟩. CONFINE suggests severe restraint and a resulting cramping or hampering ⟨our options were *confined* by our modest income⟩.

lim·i·ta·tion \ˌlim-ə-ˈtā-shən\ *n* **1** : an act or instance of limiting **2** : the quality or state of being limited **3** : something that limits : RESTRAINT — **lim·i·ta·tion·al** \-shnəl, -shən-l\ *adj*

lim·it·ed *adj* **1 a** : confined within limits : RESTRICTED ⟨*limited* success⟩ **b** : having a limited number of passengers and offering superior and faster service and transportation ⟨a *limited* train⟩ **2** : relating to or being a government in which constitutional limitations are placed on the powers of one or more of its branches ⟨a *limited* monarchy⟩ — **lim·it·ed·ly** *adv* — **lim·it·ed·ness** *n*

limited war *n* : a war with an objective less than the total defeat of the enemy

lim·it·ing *adj* **1** : functioning as a limit : RESTRICTIVE ⟨*limiting* value⟩ **2** : serving to limit population size of organisms in an environment ⟨food is a *limiting* factor⟩

lim·it·less \ˈlim-ət-ləs\ *adj* : having no limits — **lim·it·less·ly** *adv* — **lim·it·less·ness** *n*

limn \ˈlim\ *vt* **limned; limn·ing** \ˈlim-ing, -ning\ **1** : to draw or paint on a surface **2 a** : to outline in clear sharp detail **b** : to describe or portray in symbols (as words or musical notes) [Middle English *limnen* "to illuminate (a manuscript)," derived from Latin *illuminare*] — **limn·er** \ˈlim-ər, -nər\ *n*

lim·nol·o·gy \lim-ˈnäl-ə-jē\ *n* : the scientific study of bodies of fresh water (as lakes) [Greek *limnē* "pool"] — **lim·no·log·i·cal** \ˌlim-nə-ˈläj-i-kəl\ *adj* — **lim·nol·o·gist** \lim-ˈnäl-ə-jəst\ *n*

li·mo·nite \ˈlī-mə-ˌnīt\ *n* : an ore of iron consisting of a hydrous ferric oxide or a mixture of oxides [German *Limonit,* from Greek *leimōn* "wet meadow"] — **li·mo·nit·ic** \ˌlī-mə-ˈnit-ik\ *adj*

lim·ou·sine \ˈlim-ə-ˌzēn, ˌlim-ə-ˈ\ *n* **1** : a large luxurious often chauffeur-driven sedan **2** : a small bus with doors along the sides ⟨an airport *limousine*⟩ [French, literally, "cloak," from *Limousin,* France]

[1]limp \ˈlimp\ *vi* **1** : to walk lamely **2** : to proceed slowly or with difficulty ⟨the ship *limped* into port⟩ [probably from Middle English *lympen* "to fall short"] — **limp·er** *n*

[2]limp *n* : a limping movement or gait ⟨walked with a *limp*⟩

[3]limp *adj* **1** : lacking firm texture, substance, or structure ⟨*limp* curtains⟩ ⟨a *limp* bookbinding⟩ **2 a** : WEARY 1, EXHAUSTED **b** : lacking strength or firmness : SPIRITLESS [related to [1]*limp*] — **limp·ly** *adv* — **limp·ness** *n*

synonyms LIMP, FLACCID, FLABBY mean lacking firmness in texture or substance. LIMP implies a lack or loss of stiffness and a tendency to droop ⟨arms *limp* from exhaustion⟩. FLACCID implies a loss of power to keep or return to shape ⟨*flaccid* muscles⟩. FLABBY implies hanging or sagging by its own weight as through loss of muscular tone ⟨*flabby* cheeks⟩.

lim·pa \ˈlim-pə\ *n* : rye bread made with molasses or brown sugar [Swedish]

lim·pet \ˈlim-pət\ *n* : any of numerous marine gastropod mollusks that have a low conical shell, browse over rocks or timbers, and cling very tightly when disturbed [Old English *lempedu,* from Medieval Latin *lampreda* "lamprey"]

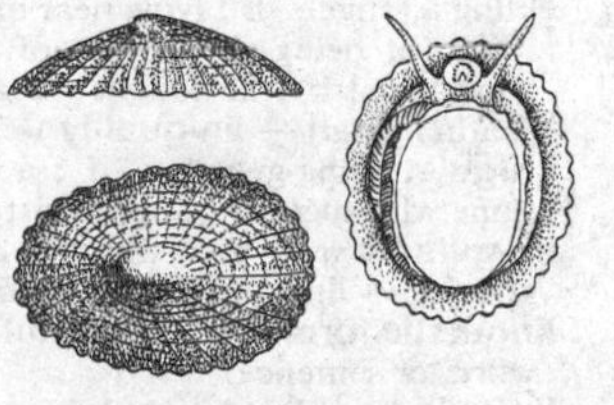

limpet

lim·pid \ˈlim-pəd\ *adj* **1** : marked by transparency ⟨a *limpid* pool of water⟩ **2** : clear and simple in style ⟨*limpid* prose⟩ [Latin *limpidus,* perhaps from *lympha* "water"] — **lim·pid·i·ty** \lim-ˈpid-ət-ē\ *n* — **lim·pid·ly** \ˈlim-pəd-lē\ *adv* — **lim·pid·ness** *n*

limp·kin \ˈlim-kən, ˈlimp-\ *n* : a large brown wading bird resembling a bittern but having a longer bill, neck, and legs and white stripes on head and neck [perhaps from [1]*limp*]

lim·u·lus \ˈlim-yə-ləs\ *n, pl* **-li** \-ˌlī, -ˌlē\ : HORSESHOE CRAB [derived from Latin *limus* "sidelong"]

limy *or* **lim·ey** \ˈlī-mē\ *adj* **lim·i·er; -est** : containing lime or limestone

lin·age \ˈlī-nij\ *n* **1** : the number of lines of printed or written matter **2** : payment for literary matter based on the number of lines

linch·pin \ˈlinch-ˌpin\ *n* : a locking pin inserted crosswise (as through the end of an axle or shaft) [Old English *lynis* "linch pin"]

lin·dane \ˈlin-ˌdān\ *n* : an insecticide consisting of not less than 99 percent of an isomer of a chloride of benzene [T. van der *Linden,* 20th-century Belgian chemist]

lin·den \ˈlin-dən\ *n* **1** : any of a genus of trees with large heart-shaped leaves and clustered yellowish flowers and that are often planted as ornamental or shade trees **2** : the light fine-grained white wood of a linden; *esp* : BASSWOOD [Old English, "made of linden wood," from *lind* "linden tree"]

[1]line \ˈlīn\ *n* **1** : a length of cord or cordlike material; *esp* : a comparatively strong slender cord ⟨a fishing *line*⟩ **2** : a cord, wire, or tape used in measuring and leveling **3 a** : piping for conveying a fluid (as steam or oil) **b** : wire connecting one telegraph or telephone station with another or a whole system of such wires **c** : the principal circuits of an electric power system ⟨a power *line*⟩ **4 a** : a row of words, letters, numbers, or symbols that are written, printed, or displayed (as on a page or TV screen); *also* : space for such a line **b** : a structural unit of something written (as a poem or computer program) **c** : a short letter : NOTE ⟨drop me a *line*⟩ **d** : the words making up a part in a drama — usually used in plural ⟨forgot my *lines*⟩ **5 a** : something (as a ridge, seam, or wrinkle) that is distinct, elongated, and narrow **b** : the course or direction of something in motion : ROUTE ⟨the *line* of flight of a bullet⟩ **c** : a boundary of an area ⟨the state *line*⟩ **d** : DISTINCTION 2 **e** : the track and roadbed of a railway **6** : a state of agreement ⟨bring ideas into *line*⟩ **7 a** : a course of conduct, action, or thought; *esp* : an official or public position ⟨the party *line*⟩ **b** : a field of activity or interest ⟨out of my *line*⟩ **c** : a glib persuasive way of talking **8 a** : LIMIT 2b, RESTRAINT ⟨overstep the *line* of good taste⟩ **b** *archaic* : position in life : LOT **9** : any of various things arranged in or as if in a row or sequence: as **a** : LINEAGE ⟨a noble *line*⟩ **b** : a strain produced and maintained by selective breeding or biological culture ⟨a high-fat *line* of cattle⟩ **c** (1) : the position of military forces in actual combat with the enemy at the front (2) : a military formation in which the different elements are abreast of each other (3) : naval ships arranged in a regular order (4) : fighting forces as distinguished from staff and supply personnel (5) : the force of a regular navy **d** : a set of objects of one general kind ⟨a *line* of merchandise⟩ **e** (1) : a group of public conveyances plying regularly under one management over a route (2) : a system of transportation; *also* : the company owning or operating it **f** : an arrangement of manufacturing processes in which each step is carried out separately and in proper order **g** : the football players who line up on or within one yard of the line of scrimmage **10** : a long narrow mark: as **a** : a circle of latitude or longitude on a map **b** : EQUATOR 2 **c** : any of the horizontal parallel strokes on a music staff **d** : LINE OF SCRIMMAGE **11** : a geometric element that is formed by a moving point and that has length but no width or thickness; *esp* : a straight line **12 a** : a defining outline : CONTOUR ⟨a ship's *lines*⟩ **b** : a general plan ⟨thinking along these *lines*⟩ **13** : a source of information : INSIGHT ⟨got a *line* on their plans⟩ **14** : a complete game of 10 frames in bowling — called also *string* [partly from Medieval French *ligne,* from Latin *linea,* derived from *linum* "flax"; partly from Old English *līne*] — **between the lines 1** : in an indirect way **2** : by way of inference ⟨read *between the lines*⟩ — **down the line 1** : all the way : FULLY **2** : in the future — **in line for** : due or in a position to receive — **on the line 1** : at great risk ⟨the champ's title is *on the line*⟩ **2** : on the border between two categories — **out of line** : beyond what is reasonable to put up with ⟨these prices are way *out of line*⟩ ⟨your behavior is getting *out of line*⟩

[2]line *vb* **1** : to mark or cover with a line **2** : to depict by lines : DRAW **3** : to place or form a line along

[3]line *vt* **1** : to cover the inner surface of ⟨*line* a box with paper⟩ **2** : to put something in the inside of : FILL **3** : to serve as the lining of ⟨tapestries *lined* the walls⟩ [Middle English *linen,* from *line* "flax, linen," from Old English *līn*]

lin·e·age \ˈlin-ē-ij\ *n* **1** : descent in a line from a common progenitor **2** : a group of individuals tracing descent from a common ancestor

lin·e·al \ˈlin-ē-əl\ *adj* **1** : LINEAR ⟨*lineal* measure⟩ **2 a** : con-

\ə\ **abut**	\au̇\ **out**	\i\ **tip**	\ȯ\ **saw**	\u̇\ **foot**
\ər\ **further**	\ch\ **chin**	\ī\ **life**	\ȯi\ **coin**	\y\ **yet**
\a\ **mat**	\e\ **pet**	\j\ **job**	\th\ **thin**	\yü\ **few**
\ā\ **take**	\ē\ **easy**	\ng\ **sing**	\t͟h\ **this**	\yu̇\ **cure**
\ä\ **cot, cart**	\g\ **go**	\ō\ **bone**	\ü\ **food**	\zh\ **vision**

sisting of or being in a direct line of ancestry or descent ⟨*lineal* descendants⟩ **b** : HEREDITARY 4 — **lin·e·al·ly** \-ē-ə-lē\ *adv*

lin·e·a·ment \ˈlin-ē-ə-mənt\ *n* : an outline, feature, or contour of a body or figure and especially of the face [Latin *lineamentum,* from *linea* "line"]

lin·ear \ˈlin-ē-ər\ *adj* **1 a** : relating to, consisting of, or resembling a line : STRAIGHT ⟨a direct *linear* approach⟩ **b** : involving a single dimension **c** : characterized by an emphasis on line ⟨*linear* art⟩ **d** (1) : containing variables and terms of the first degree only ⟨*linear* factors such as x – 1 and x – 2⟩ (2) : based on, involving, or expressed by linear functions or linear equations **2** : long and uniformly narrow ⟨the *linear* leaves of grasses⟩ — **lin·ear·i·ty** \ˌlin-ē-ˈar-ət-ē\ *n* — **lin·ear·ly** \ˈlin-ē-ər-lē\ *adv*

linear accelerator *n* : a device in which charged particles are accelerated in a straight line by successive impulses from a series of electric fields

linear combination *n* : a mathematical entity (as 4x + 5y + 6z) composed of sums and differences of elements (as variables or equations) each multiplied by a constant coefficient

linear equation *n* : an equation in which each term is a monomial of degree one or a constant

linear function *n* : a mathematical function in which the variables are raised only to the first power, are multiplied by constants, and are combined only by addition and subtraction

linear interpolation *n* : estimation of a function (as a logarithm) by assuming that it is a straight line between known values

linear measure *n* **1** : a measure of length **2** : a system of measures of length

linear programming *n* : a mathematical method of solving practical problems (as the distribution of resources) with linear functions whose variables are given specific limitations

line·back·er \ˈlīn-ˌbak-ər\ *n* : a defensive football player who lines up immediately behind the line of scrimmage

line·breed·ing \ˈlīn-ˈbrēd-ing\ *n* : the interbreeding of individuals within a particular line of descent usually to perpetuate desirable characters — **line·breed** *vb*

line drawing *n* : a drawing made in solid lines

line drive *n* : a batted baseball hit in a nearly straight line not far off the ground

line engraving *n* : an engraving cut by hand directly in the printing plate

line graph *n* : a graph in which line segments join points representing different values of a variable

line–item veto *n* : the power of a government executive to veto specific items in an appropriations bill without vetoing the entire bill

line·man \ˈlīn-mən\ *n* **1** : one who sets up or repairs electric wire communication or power lines — called also *linesman* **2** : a player in the forward line of a team; *esp* : a football player in the line

lin·en \ˈlin-ən\ *n* **1 a** : cloth made of flax and noted for its strength, coolness, and luster **b** : thread or yarn spun from flax **2** : clothing or household articles made of linen cloth or a similar fabric **3** : paper made from linen fibers or with a linen finish [Old English *līnen* "of flax," from *līn* "flax," from Latin *linum*] — **linen** *adj*

line of credit : the maximum credit allowed a buyer or borrower; *also* : an agreement providing credit up to a certain amount ⟨a home-equity *line of credit*⟩

line of duty : all that is authorized, required, or normally associated with some field of responsibility

line of force : an imaginary line serving as a convenience in indicating the direction in space in which a force (as from an electric, magnetic, or gravitational field) acts

line of scrimmage : an imaginary line in football parallel to the goal lines that marks the position of the ball at the start of each down

line of sight **1** : a line from an observer's eye to a distant point **2** : the line between two points; *esp* : the straight path between a radio transmitting antenna and receiving antenna when unobstructed by the horizon — **line–of–sight** *adj*

line out *vb* **1** : to indicate with or as if with lines : OUTLINE ⟨*line out* a route⟩ **2** : to arrange in an extended line **3** : to move rapidly ⟨*lined out* for home⟩

line printer *n* : a very fast printing device for a computer that prints a whole line at one time instead of one character at a time

¹lin·er \ˈlī-nər\ *n* **1** : one that makes, draws, or uses lines **2** : something with which lines are made **3 a** : a ship belonging to a regular line of ships **b** : an airplane belonging to an airline **4** : LINE DRIVE

²liner *n* : one that lines or is used to line or back something

line segment *n* : SEGMENT 2b

lines·man \ˈlīnz-mən\ *n* **1** : LINEMAN 1 **2** : an official who assists a referee by determining whether a puck or ball or a player is beyond a boundary line

line·up \ˈlī-ˌnəp\ *n* **1** : a line of persons arranged especially for inspection or for identification by police **2 a** : a list of players taking part in a game (as of baseball); *also* : the players on such a list **b** : an alignment of persons or things having a common purpose or interest

line up \lī-ˈnəp, ˈlī-\ *vb* **1 a** : to assume an orderly linear arrangement ⟨*line up* for inspection⟩ **b** : to take one's position in a formation **2** : to put into alignment **3** : to organize and make available ⟨*line up* supporters⟩

¹ling \ˈling\ *n* **1** : any of various fishes (as a hake or burbot) related to the cods **2** : LINGCOD [Middle English]

²ling *n* : a heath plant; *esp* : a common Old World heather [Old Norse *lyng*]

¹-ling \ling\ *n suffix* **1** : one connected with or having the quality of ⟨*hireling*⟩ **2** : young, small, or inferior one ⟨*duckling*⟩ [Old English]

²-ling \ling\ *or* **-lings** \lingz\ *adv suffix* : in (such) a direction or manner ⟨*sideling*⟩ [Middle English *-ling, -linges*]

ling·cod \ˈling-ˌkäd\ *n* : a large greenish-fleshed food fish of the Pacific coast of North America related to the greenlings

lin·ger \ˈling-gər\ *vi* **lin·gered; lin·ger·ing** \-gə-ring, -gring\ **1** : to be slow in leaving a place or activity ⟨*lingered* in bed⟩ **2** : to remain alive although close to dying **3** : to be slow to act [Middle English *lengeren* "to dwell," from Old English *lengan* "to prolong"] ***synonyms*** see STAY — **lin·ger·er** \-gər-ər\ *n* — **lin·ger·ing·ly** \-gə-ring-lē, -gring-\ *adv*

lin·ge·rie \ˌlän-jə-ˈrā, ˌlaⁿ-zhə-, -ˈrē\ *n* : women's intimate apparel [French, from Medieval French *linge* "linen," from Latin *lineus* "made of linen," from *linum* "flax, linen"]

lin·go \ˈling-gō\ *n, pl* **lingoes** **1** : strange or incomprehensible language or speech; *esp* : a foreign language **2** : JARGON 2 **3** : language characteristic of an individual [probably from Lingua Franca, "language," from Occitan, from Latin *lingua* "tongue"] ***synonyms*** see DIALECT

lin·gua fran·ca \ˌling-gwə-ˈfrang-kə\ *n, pl* **lingua francas** *or* **lin·guae fran·cae** \-ˌgwī-ˈfrang-ˌkī\ **1** *often cap* : a common language consisting of Italian mixed with French, Spanish, Greek, and Arabic that was formerly spoken in Mediterranean ports **2** : any of various languages used for mutual understanding by speakers of different languages [Italian, literally, "Frankish language"]

lin·gual \ˈling-gwəl, -gyə-wəl\ *adj* **1 a** : of, relating to, or resembling a tongue **b** : lying near or next to the tongue; *esp* : relating to or being the surface of a tooth next to the tongue **2** : produced by the tongue ⟨*lingual* sounds such as \t\ or \l\⟩ [Latin *lingua*] — **lin·gual·ly** \-ē\ *adv*

lin·guist \ˈling-gwəst\ *n* **1** : a person skilled in languages **2** : one who specializes in linguistics

lin·guis·tic \ling-ˈgwis-tik\ *adj* : of or relating to language or linguistics — **lin·guis·ti·cal·ly** \-ti-kə-lē, -klē\ *adv*

linguistic form *n* : a meaningful unit of speech (as a morpheme, word, or sentence)

lin·guis·tics \ling-ˈgwis-tiks\ *n* : the study of human speech including the units, nature, structure, and modification of language

lin·i·ment \ˈlin-ə-mənt\ *n* : a preparation that is thinner in consistency than an ointment and is used on the skin especially to relieve pain [Late Latin *linimentum,* from Latin *linere* "to smear"]

lin·ing \ˈlī-ning\ *n* : material that lines or that is used to line especially the inner surface of something (as a garment)

¹link \ˈlingk\ *n* **1** : a connecting structure: as **a** : a single ring or division of a chain **b** : a division of a surveyor's chain that is 7.92 inches (about 20.1 centimeters) long and is used as a measure of length **c** : CUFF LINK **d** : BOND 3b **e** : an intermediate rod or piece for transmitting force or motion **2** : something resembling a link of chain: as **a** : a segment of sausage in a chain **b** : a connecting element or factor ⟨a *link* with the past⟩ **c** : HYPERLINK [of Scandinavian origin]

²link *vb* : to join by or as if by a link : UNITE — **link·er** *n*

link·age \ˈling-kij\ *n* **1** : the manner or style of being united: as

a : the manner in which atoms or radicals are linked in a molecule **b** : BOND 3b **2** : the quality or state of being linked; *esp* : the occurrence of genes on the same chromosome so that they tend to be inherited and expressed together **3** : a system of links; *esp* : a system of links or bars jointed together by means of which lines or curves may be traced

linked \ˈlingt, ˈlingkt\ *adj* : marked by linkage and especially genetic linkage

linking verb *n* : a verb that connects the subject of a sentence with a word or phrase that tells how, what, or where the subject is 〈*feel* in "I feel bad," *seems* in "it seems a reasonable request," and *am* in "I am upstairs" are *linking verbs*〉 — compare ACTION VERB

links \ˈlings, ˈlingks\ *n pl* : a golf course [Old English *hlinc* "ridge, hill"]

link•up \ˈling-ˌkəp\ *n* **1** : establishment of contact : MEETING **2** : something that serves as a linking device or factor

Lin•nae•an *or* **Lin•ne•an** \lə-ˈnē-ən, -ˈnā-; ˈlin-ē-\ *adj* : of, relating to, or following the method of the Swedish botanist Linnaeus who established the system of binomial nomenclature [Carolus *Linnaeus* (Carl von Linné)]

lin•net \ˈlin-ət\ *n* : a common small Old World brownish finch of which the male has red on the breast and crown during breeding season [Middle French *linette,* from *lin* "flax," from Latin *linum*]

lin•ole•ic acid \ˌlin-ə-ˌlē-ik-, -ˌlā-\ *n* : a liquid unsaturated fatty acid found in various semidrying oils (as corn oil) and essential for the nutrition of some animals [Greek *linon* "flax" + English *oleic acid*]

lin•ole•nic acid \-ˌlē-nik-, -ˌlā-\ *n* : a liquid unsaturated fatty acid found especially in drying oils (as linseed oil) and essential for the nutrition of some animals [derived from *linoleic acid*]

li•no•leum \lə-ˈnō-lē-əm, -ˈnōl-yəm\ *n* : a floor covering with a canvas back and a surface of hardened linseed oil and a filler (as cork dust) [Latin *linum* "flax" + *oleum* "oil"]

Li•no•type \ˈlī-nə-ˌtīp\ *trademark* — used for a typesetting machine that produces each line of type in the form of a solid metal slug

lin•seed \ˈlin-ˌsēd\ *n* : FLAXSEED [Old English *līnsǣd,* from *līn* "flax" + *sǣd* "seed"]

linseed oil *n* : a yellowish drying oil obtained from flaxseed and used especially in paint, varnish, printing ink, and linoleum

lin•sey–wool•sey \ˌlin-zē-ˈwu̇l-zē\ *n* : a coarse sturdy fabric of wool and linen or cotton [Middle English *lynsy wolsye*]

lint \ˈlint\ *n* **1 a** : a soft fleecy material made from linen usually by scraping **b** : fuzz consisting of short fibers from yarn and fabric **2** : fibers forming a close thick coating about cotton seeds and constituting the staple of cotton [Middle English] — **linty** \-ē\ *adj*

lin•tel \ˈlint-l\ *n* : a horizontal piece across the top of an opening (as of a door) that carries the weight of the structure above it [alteration of Medieval French *linter* "threshhold," from Late Latin *limitaris,* from Latin *limit-, limes* "boundary"]

L lintel

lint•er \ˈlint-ər\ *n* **1** : a machine for removing linters **2** *pl* : the fuzz of short fibers that adheres to cottonseed after ginning

li•on \ˈlī-ən\ *n, pl* **lion** *or* **lions** **1 a** : a large tawny flesh-eating cat of open or rocky areas chiefly of sub-Saharan Africa though once widely distributed throughout Africa and southern Asia that has a tufted tail and a shaggy mane in the male **b** : any of several large wildcats; *esp* : COUGAR **2 a** : a person held to resemble a lion (as in courage or ferocity) **b** : a person of outstanding interest or importance 〈a literary *lion*〉 **3** *cap* : a member of one of the major service clubs [Medieval French, from Latin *leo,* from Greek *leōn*] — **li•on•ess** \ˈlī-ə-nəs\ *n* — **li•on•like** \ˈlī-ən-ˌlīk\ *adj*

li•on•ess \ˈlī-ə-nəs\ *n* : a female lion

li•on•heart•ed \ˌlī-ən-ˈhärt-əd\ *adj* : BOLD 1, COURAGEOUS

li•on•ize \ˈlī-ə-ˌnīz\ *vt* : to treat as an object of great interest or importance — **li•on•i•za•tion** \ˌlī-ə-nə-ˈzā-shən\ *n*

lion's den *n* : a place or state of extreme disadvantage, antagonism, or hostility

lion's share *n* : the largest portion

[1]**lip** \ˈlip\ *n* **1** : either of the two fleshy folds that surround the mouth **2** *slang* : BACK TALK **3 a** : a fleshy edge or margin 〈*lips* of a wound〉 **b** : an anatomical part or structure resembling a lip (as the protruding part of an orchid's corolla) **4 a** : the edge of a hollow vessel especially where it flares slightly **b** : a projecting edge 〈the *lip* of a cliff〉 **c** : a short open spout (as on a pitcher) **5** : EMBOUCHURE 1 [Old English *lippa*] — **lip•less** \-ləs\ *adj* — **lip•like** \-ˌlīk\ *adj*

[2]**lip** *adj* **1** : spoken with the lips only : INSINCERE 〈*lip* praise〉 **2** : produced with the lips : LABIAL 〈*lip* consonants〉

[3]**lip** *vt* **lipped; lip•ping** **1** : to touch with the lips; *esp* : KISS **2** : to speak usually softly

lip- *or* **lipo-** *combining form* : fat : fatty tissue : fatty 〈*lipoma*〉 [Greek *lipos*]

li•pase \ˈlī-ˌpās, -ˌpāz\ *n* : an enzyme that functions especially in the breakdown or digestion of fats

lip•id \ˈlip-əd\ *n* : any of various substances including fats, waxes, and phosphatides that with proteins and carbohydrates constitute the principal structural components of living cells

[1]**li•poid** \ˈlī-ˌpȯid, ˈlip-ˌȯid\ *or* **li•poi•dal** \lī-ˈpȯid-l, lip-ˈȯid-\ *adj* : resembling fat

[2]**lipoid** *n* : LIPID

li•po•ma \lī-ˈpō-mə, lip-ˈō-\ *n, pl* **-mas** *also* **-ma•ta** \-mət-ə\ : a tumor of fatty tissue — **li•po•ma•tous** \-mət-əs\ *adj*

li•po•pro•tein \ˌlī-pō-ˈprō-ˌtēn, ˌlip-ō-, -ˈprōt-ē-ən\ *n* : a protein containing a lipid group — compare HDL, LDL

li•po•suc•tion \ˈlip-ə-ˌsək-shən, ˈlī-pə-\ *n* : the surgical removal of fat from deposits beneath the skin (as of the thighs) especially for cosmetic purposes

lipped \ˈlipt\ *adj* : having a lip or lips especially of a certain kind or number 〈tight-*lipped*〉 〈a 2-*lipped* corolla〉

lip•py \ˈlip-ē\ *adj* **lip•pi•er; -est** : given to back talk

lip•read•ing \ˈlip-ˌrēd-ing\ *n* : the interpretation of speech by watching the speaker's lip and facial movements without hearing the voice — **lip–read** *vb* — **lip–read•er** *n*

lip service *n* : a declaration of advocacy, adherence, or allegiance expressed in words but not backed by deeds 〈pay *lip service* to the cause〉

lip•stick \ˈlip-ˌstik\ *n* : a waxy solid usually colored cosmetic in stick form for the lips; *also* : this cosmetic with its case

liq•ue•fac•tion \ˌlik-wə-ˈfak-shən\ *n* **1** : the process of making or becoming liquid **2** : the state of being liquid [Late Latin *liquefactio,* from Latin *liquefacere* "to liquefy"]

liquefied petroleum gas *n* : a compressed gas consisting of flammable light hydrocarbons and used especially as fuel or as raw material for chemical synthesis

liq•ue•fy *also* **liq•ui•fy** \ˈlik-wə-ˌfī\ *vb* **-fied; -fy•ing** : to make or become liquid [Medieval French *liquefier,* from Latin *liquefacere,* from *liquēre* "to be fluid" + *facere* "to make"] — **liq•ue•fi•able** \-ˌfī-ə-bəl\ *adj* — **liq•ue•fi•er** \-ˌfī-ər, -ˌfīr\ *n*

li•queur \li-ˈkər, -ˈkyu̇r, -ˈku̇r\ *n* : a usually sweetened alcoholic liquor flavored with fruit, spices, nuts, herbs, or seeds [French, literally, "liquor, liquid," from Latin *liquor*]

[1]**liq•uid** \ˈlik-wəd\ *adj* **1** : flowing freely like water **2** : neither solid nor gaseous : characterized by free movement of the constituent molecules among themselves but without the tendency to separate that characterizes gases 〈*liquid* mercury〉 **3 a** : shining and clear 〈large *liquid* eyes〉 **b** : being musical and free of harshness in sound **c** : smooth and unconstrained in movement **d** : pronounced without friction and capable of being prolonged like a vowel 〈the *liquid* consonant \l\〉 **4 a** : consisting of or capable of ready conversion into cash 〈*liquid* assets〉 **b** : capable of covering current liabilities quickly with current assests [Medieval French *liquide,* from Latin *liquidus,* from *liquēre* "to be fluid"] — **li•quid•i•ty** \lik-ˈwid-ət-ē\ *n* — **liq•uid•ly** \ˈlik-wəd-lē\ *adv* — **liq•uid•ness** *n*

[2]**liquid** *n* **1** : a liquid substance **2** : a liquid consonant

liquid air *n* : air in the liquid state prepared by subjecting it to great pressure and then cooling it by its own expansion and used chiefly as a refrigerant

liq•ui•date \ˈlik-wə-ˌdāt\ *vt* **1** : to pay off 〈*liquidate* a debt〉 **2** : to bring (as a business) to an end by selling off assets, paying debts, and dividing any remainder among the owners **3** : to do away with [Late Latin *liquidare* "to melt," from Latin *liquidus*

\ə\ **abut**	\au̇\ **out**	\i\ **tip**	\ȯ\ **saw**	\u̇\ **foot**
\ər\ **further**	\ch\ **chin**	\ī\ **life**	\ȯi\ **coin**	\y\ **yet**
\a\ **mat**	\e\ **pet**	\j\ **job**	\th\ **thin**	\yü\ **few**
\ā\ **take**	\ē\ **easy**	\ng\ **sing**	\t͟h\ **this**	\yu̇\ **cure**
\ä\ **cot, cart**	\g\ **go**	\ō\ **bone**	\ü\ **food**	\zh\ **vision**

"liquid"] — **liq·ui·da·tion** \ˌlik-wə-ˈdā-shən\ *n* — **liq·ui·da·tor** \ˈlik-wə-ˌdāt-ər\ *n*

liquid crystal display *n* : LCD

liquid measure *n* : a unit or series of units for measuring liquid capacity — see MEASURE table, METRIC SYSTEM table

1li·quor \ˈlik-ər\ *n* : a liquid substance; *esp* : a distilled alcoholic beverage [Medieval French *licour,* from Latin *liquor,* from *liquēre* "to be fluid"]

2liquor *vb* **li·quored; li·quor·ing** \ˈlik-ring, -ə-ring\ : to make or become drunk with alcoholic liquor — usually used with *up*

li·quo·rice *chiefly British variant of* LICORICE

li·ra \ˈlir-ə, ˈlē-rə\ *n* **1** *pl* **li·re** \ˈlē-rā\ *also* **liras** : the basic monetary unit of Italy until 2002 **2** *pl* **liras** : the basic monetary unit of Turkey **3** : a coin representing one lira [Italian, from Latin *libra,* a unit of weight]

lisle \ˈlīl\ *n* : a smooth tightly twisted thread usually made of long-staple cotton [*Lisle* "Lille, France"]

1lisp \ˈlisp\ *vb* **1** : to pronounce \s\ and \z\ imperfectly especially by giving them the sound of \th\ and \th\ **2** : to speak falteringly, childishly, or with a lisp [Old English *-wlyspian*] — **lisper** *n*

2lisp *n* **1** : a speech defect or mannerism marked by lisping **2** : a sound resembling a lisp

lis·some *also* **lis·som** \ˈlis-əm\ *adj* **1** : LITHE 1 **2** : NIMBLE 1 ⟨*lissome* grace⟩ [alteration of *lithesome*] — **lis·some·ly** *adv* — **lis·some·ness** *n*

1list \ˈlist\ *vb, archaic* : CHOOSE 3 [Old English *lystan* "to please, suit"]

2list *vb* **1** *archaic* : LISTEN **2** *archaic* : to listen to : HEAR [Old English *hlystan,* from *hlyst* "hearing"]

3list *n* **1** : a band or strip of material; *esp* : SELVAGE **2** *pl* **a** : an arena for jousting **b** : an arena for combat ⟨entered the *lists*⟩ **c** : a field of competition or controversy [Old English *līste*]

4list *n* : a deviation from the vertical : TILT [origin unknown]

5list *vb* : to lean or cause to lean to one side : TILT ⟨a ship *listing* to port⟩

6list *n* : a roll, record, or catalog of names or items ⟨guest *list*⟩ [French *liste,* from Italian *lista,* of Germanic origin]

7list *vb* **1 a** : to make a list of : ENUMERATE **b** : to include on a list : REGISTER ⟨securities *listed* on the exchange⟩ **2 a** : to place (oneself) in a specified category ⟨*lists* himself as a political liberal⟩ **b** : to have a list price ⟨a car that *lists* for $20,000⟩

lis·ten \ˈlis-n\ *vi* **lis·tened; lis·ten·ing** \ˈlis-ning, -n-ing\ **1** : to pay attention in order to hear ⟨*listen* for a signal⟩ ⟨*listen* to a new CD⟩ **2** : to give heed : follow advice ⟨*listen* to a warning⟩ [Old English *hlysnan* "to hear"] ***synonyms*** see HEAR — **lis·ten·er** \ˈlis-nər, -n-ər\ *n*

listen in *vi* **1** : to tune in to or monitor a broadcast **2** : to listen to a conversation without participating in it; *esp* : EAVESDROP — **lis·ten·er–in** \ˌlis-nər-ˈin, -n-ər-\ *n*

list·er \ˈlis-tər\ *n* : a double-moldboard plow that throws up ridges of earth on both sides of the furrow [derived from Old English *līste* "band or strip of material"]

list·ing \ˈlis-ting\ *n* **1** : an act or instance of making or including in a list **2** : something listed

list·less \ˈlist-ləs\ *adj* : marked by lack of energy or willingness to exert oneself : LANGUID [Middle English *list* "desire, inclination"] — **list·less·ly** *adv* — **list·less·ness** *n*

list price *n* : a price of an item as published in a catalog, price list, or advertisement before any discounts are taken

1lit *past of* LIGHT

2lit \ˈlit\ *n* : LITERATURE 2 — **lit** *adj*

lit·a·ny \ˈlit-n-ē\ *n, pl* **-nies** **1** : a prayer consisting of a series of supplications and responses said alternately by a leader and a group **2 a** : a resonant or repetitive chant ⟨a *litany* of cheers⟩ **b** : a long list ⟨a *litany* of complaints⟩ [Medieval French *letanie,* from Late Latin *litania,* from Greek *litaneia* "entreaty"]

litchi *variant of* LYCHEE

-lite \ˌlīt\ *n combining form* : mineral : rock : fossil ⟨cryo*lite*⟩ [French, from Greek *lithos* "stone"]

li·ter *or* **li·tre** \ˈlēt-ər\ *n* : a metric unit of capacity equal to one cubic decimeter — see METRIC SYSTEM table [French *litre,* from Medieval Latin *litra,* a measure, from Greek, a weight]

lit·er·a·cy \ˈlit-ə-rə-sē, ˈli-trə-sē\ *n* : the quality or state of being literate

lit·er·al \ˈlit-ə-rəl, ˈli-trəl\ *adj* **1 a** : according with the letter of the scriptures **b** : following the ordinary or usual meaning of a term or expression ⟨*literal* and figurative meanings⟩ **c** : free from exaggeration or embellishment ⟨the *literal* truth⟩ **d** : concerned mainly with facts : PROSAIC ⟨a very *literal* person⟩ **2** : of, relating to, or expressed in letters **3** : reproduced word for word ⟨a *literal* translation⟩ [Medieval French, from Latin *litteralis* "of a letter," from *littera* "letter"] — **lit·er·al·ness** *n*

lit·er·al·ism \ˈlit-ə-rə-ˌliz-əm, ˈli-trə-\ *n* **1** : adherence to the exact meaning of an idea or expression **2** : fidelity to fact : REALISM — **lit·er·al·ist** \-ləst\ *n* — **lit·er·al·is·tic** \ˌlit-ə-rə-ˈlis-tik, ˌli-trə-\ *adj*

lit·er·al·ly \ˈlit-ər-ə-lē, -ər-lē, ˈlit-rə-lē\ *adv* **1** : in a literal sense or manner : ACTUALLY ⟨the flying machine *literally* never got off the ground⟩ ⟨took the remark *literally*⟩ **2** : in effect : VIRTUALLY ⟨*literally* poured out new ideas⟩

usage Since some people take sense 2 to have the opposite meaning of sense 1, it has been frequently criticized as nonsense and a misuse. Instead, the use is not supposed to make sense, but rather merely to inject a bit of hyperbole (exaggeration) for emphasis. The usage often appears in contexts where no additional emphasis is necessary, though ⟨will *literally* scare you to death⟩.

lit·er·ary \ˈlit-ə-ˌrer-ē\ *adj* **1 a** : of, relating to, or having the characteristics of literature or humane learning **b** : BOOKISH 2 **2 a** : LITERATE 2a, WELL-READ **b** : of or relating to writers or writing as a profession — **lit·er·ar·i·ly** \ˌlit-ə-ˈrer-ə-lē\ *adv* — **lit·er·ar·i·ness** \ˈlit-ə-ˌrer-ē-nəs\ *n*

lit·er·ate \ˈlit-ə-rət, ˈli-trət\ *adj* **1 a** : characterized by education and culture **b** : able to read and write **2 a** : versed in literature or creative writing **b** : having knowledge or competence ⟨computer-*literate*⟩ — **literate** *n* — **lit·er·ate·ly** *adv* — **lit·er·ate·ness** *n*

li·te·ra·ti \ˌlit-ə-ˈrät-ē\ *n pl* **1** : INTELLIGENTSIA **2** : persons interested in literature or the arts [obsolete Italian *litterati,* from Latin *litteratus* "literate," from *littera* "letter"]

lit·er·a·tim \ˌlit-ə-ˈrāt-əm, -ˈrät-\ *adv or adj* : letter for letter [Medieval Latin, from Latin *littera* "letter"]

lit·er·a·ture \ˈlit-ə-rə-ˌchu̇r, ˈli-trə-, -chər\ *n* **1** : the writing of literary work especially as an occupation **2 a** : writings in prose or verse; *esp* : writings that are excellent in form or expression and that set forth ideas of permanent or universal interest **b** : the body of writings on a particular subject ⟨medical *literature*⟩ **c** : printed matter (as leaflets or circulars) **3** : a whole body of musical compositions

lith- *or* **litho-** *combining form* : stone ⟨*litho*logy⟩ [Greek *lithos*]

-lith \ˌlith\ *n combining form* **1** : structure or implement of stone ⟨mega*lith*⟩ **2** : calculus ⟨oto*lith*⟩ **3** : -LITE ⟨rego*lith*⟩ [Greek *lithos* "stone"]

li·tharge \ˈlith-ärj, lith-ˈ\ *n* : LEAD MONOXIDE [Medieval French *litarge,* from Latin *lithargyrus,* from Greek *lithargyros,* from *lithos* "stone" + *argyros* "silver"]

lithe \ˈlīth, ˈlīth\ *adj* **1** : easily bent : FLEXIBLE ⟨long *lithe* stems⟩ **2** : gracefully limber : SUPPLE ⟨*lithe* dancers⟩ [Old English *līthe* "gentle"] — **lithe·ly** *adv* — **lithe·ness** *n*

lithe·some \ˈlīth-səm, ˈlīth-\ *adj* : LITHE 2

lith·ia \ˈlith-ē-ə\ *n* : an oxide of lithium occurring as a white crystalline substance [New Latin, from Greek *lithos* "stone"]

lith·ic \ˈlith-ik\ *adj* **1** : of, relating to, or made of stone **2** : of or relating to lithium — **lith·i·cal·ly** \ˈlith-i-kə-lē, -klē\ *adv*

-lithic \ˈlith-ik\ *adj combining form* : relating to or characteristic of a (specified) stage in the use of stone as a cultural tool by humans ⟨Neo*lithic*⟩

lith·i·um \ˈlith-ē-əm\ *n* : a soft silver-white univalent chemical element that is the lightest metal known and is used especially in batteries and metallurgy — see ELEMENT table [New Latin, from *lithia* "oxide of lithium"]

1litho·graph \ˈlith-ə-ˌgraf\ *vt* : to produce, copy, or portray by lithography — **li·thog·ra·pher** \lith-ˈäg-rə-fər, ˈlith-ə-ˌgraf-ər\ *n*

2lithograph *n* : a print made by lithography — **litho·graph·ic** \ˌlith-ə-ˈgraf-ik\ *adj* — **litho·graph·i·cal·ly** \-ˈgraf-i-kə-lē, -klē\ *adv*

li·thog·ra·phy \lith-ˈäg-rə-fē\ *n* **1** : the process of printing from a flat surface (as a smooth stone or metal plate) on which the image to be printed is ink-receptive and the blank area ink-repellent **2** : PLANOGRAPHY

lith·o·pone \ˈlith-ə-ˌpōn\ *n* : a white pigment consisting essentially of zinc sulfide and barium sulfate [*lith-* + Greek *ponos* "work"]

litho·sphere \-ˌsfiər\ *n* : the outer part of the solid earth consisting of the crust and part of the mantle

Lith·u·a·ni·an \ˌlith-ə-ˈwā-nē-ən, -yə-ˈwā-, -nyən\ *n* **1** : a native or inhabitant of Lithuania **2 :** the Baltic language of the Lithuanian people — **Lithuanian** *adj*

lit·i·gant \ˈlit-i-gənt\ *n* **:** one engaged in a lawsuit — **litigant** *adj*

lit·i·gate \ˈlit-ə-ˌgāt\ *vb* **1 :** to carry on a legal contest by judicial process **2 :** to contest in law [Latin *litigare,* from *lit-, lis* "lawsuit" + *agere* "to drive, act, do"] — **lit·i·ga·tion** \ˌlit-ə-ˈgā-shən\ *n* — **lit·i·ga·tor** \ˈlit-ə-ˌgāt-ər\ *n*

li·ti·gious \lə-ˈtij-əs\ *adj* **1 a :** CONTROVERSIAL 2, ARGUMENTATIVE **b :** inclined to engage in lawsuits **2 :** of or relating to lawsuits — **li·ti·gious·ly** *adv* — **li·ti·gious·ness** *n*

lit·mus \ˈlit-məs\ *n* **:** a coloring matter from lichens that turns red in acid solutions and blue in alkaline solutions and is used as an acid-base indicator [of Scandinavian origin]

litmus paper *n* **:** paper impregnated with litmus and used as a pH indicator

li·to·tes \ˈlīt-ə-ˌtēz, lī-ˈtōt-ˌēz\ *n, pl* **litotes :** understatement in which an affirmative is expressed by the negative of the contrary (as in "not a bad singer") [Greek *litotēs,* from *litos* "simple"]

litre *variant of* LITER

¹lit·ter \ˈlit-ər\ *n* **1 a :** a covered and curtained couch having shafts that is used for carrying a single passenger **b :** a device (as a stretcher) for carrying a sick or injured person **2 a :** material spread in areas where farm animals (as cows or chickens) are kept especially to absorb their urine and feces **b :** the uppermost layer of organic debris on the forest floor **3 :** the offspring of an animal at one birth ⟨a *litter* of puppies⟩ **4 a :** trash, wastepaper, or garbage lying about ⟨roadside *litter*⟩ **b :** an untidy accumulation of objects [Medieval French *litiere,* from *lit* "bed," from Latin *lectus*]

Word History Latin *lectus,* "bed," is the ancestor of English *litter.* From *lectus* comes the French *lit,* "bed." *Litiere,* a Medieval French derivative of *lit,* was used not only for a bed but also for that type of vehicle we call a *litter.* English *litter,* borrowed from French, originally meant "bed" or "litter (vehicle)." The first sense, "bed," did not survive, but before it became obsolete it gave rise to other senses of *litter.* The straw, hay, or like material laid down or strewn about to serve as bedding was called *litter.* So were the offspring of an animal born, or "bedded," at one time. Once *litter* had been applied to straw laid down for bedding, it was not far-fetched to use the word for any odds and ends of rubbish lying scattered about.

²litter *vb* **1 :** to give birth to young **2 a :** to strew with litter **b :** to scatter about in disorder **c :** to lie about in disorder

lit·ter·a·teur \ˌlit-ə-rə-ˈtər, ˌli-trə-\ *n* **:** a literary person; *esp* **:** a professional writer [French *littérateur*]

lit·ter·bag \ˈlit-ər-ˌbag\ *n* **:** a bag used (as in an automobile) for temporary disposal of refuse

lit·ter·bug \ˈlit-ər-ˌbəg\ *n* **:** one who litters a public area

lit·ter·mate \-ˌmāt\ *n* **:** one of a litter of offspring considered in relation to the other members of the litter

¹lit·tle \ˈlit-l\ *adj* **lit·tler** \ˈlit-l-ər, ˈlit-lər\ *or* **less** \ˈles\ *or* **less·er** \ˈles-ər\; **lit·tlest** \ˈlit-l-əst, ˈlit-ləst\ *or* **least** \ˈlēst\ **1 a :** small in size or extent **:** TINY ⟨*little* feet⟩ **b :** YOUNG 1a ⟨was too *little* to remember⟩ **c :** small in comparison with related forms ⟨*little* blue heron⟩ **d :** having few members or inhabitants ⟨a *little* town⟩ **e :** small in condition, distinction, or scope ⟨big businesses taking over *little* ones⟩ **f :** NARROW 2, MEAN ⟨the pettiness of *little* minds⟩ **g :** pleasingly small ⟨a cute *little* thing⟩ **h :** being younger ⟨my *little* brother⟩ **2 a :** small in quantity or degree **:** not much ⟨have *little* money⟩ **b :** short in duration **:** BRIEF **3 :** small in importance or interest **:** TRIVIAL [Old English *lȳtel*] ***synonyms*** see SMALL — **lit·tle·ness** \ˈlit-l-nəs\ *n*

²little *adv* **less** \ˈles\; **least** \ˈlēst\ **1 a :** in only a small quantity or degree **:** SLIGHTLY ⟨*little* known facts⟩ **b :** not at all ⟨cared *little* for them⟩ **2 :** INFREQUENTLY, RARELY ⟨saw them very *little*⟩

³little *n* **1 :** a small amount or quantity **2 :** a short time or distance — **a little :** ²SOMEWHAT, RATHER ⟨found the play *a little* dull⟩ — **in little :** on a small scale; *esp* **:** in miniature

Little Bear *n* **:** URSA MINOR

Little Dipper *n* **:** DIPPER 3b

little finger *n* **:** the fourth and smallest finger of the hand counting the index finger as the first

Little Hours *n pl* **:** the offices of prime, terce, sext, and none forming part of the canonical hours

Little League *n* **:** a commercially sponsored baseball league for children from 8 to 12 years old — **Little Leaguer** *n*

little people *n pl* **1 :** tiny imaginary beings (as fairies, elves, and leprechauns) of folklore **2 :** CHILDREN **3 :** people of unusually small size **4 :** common people

little slam *n* **:** the winning of all tricks except one in bridge

little theater *n* **:** a small theater for low-cost dramatic productions designed for fairly limited audiences

little toe *n* **:** the outermost and smallest toe of the foot

¹lit·to·ral \ˈlit-ə-rəl; ˌlit-ə-ˈral, -ˈräl\ *adj* **:** of, relating to, or situated or growing on or near a shore especially of the sea [Latin *litoralis,* from *litor-, litus* "seashore"]

²littoral *n* **:** a coastal region

li·tur·gi·cal \lə-ˈtər-ji-kəl\ *adj* **1 :** of, relating to, or having the characteristics of liturgy **2 :** using or favoring the use of liturgy — **li·tur·gi·cal·ly** \-kə-lē, -klē\ *adv*

lit·ur·gist \ˈlit-ər-jəst\ *n* **:** one who adheres to, compiles, or leads a liturgy

lit·ur·gy \ˈlit-ər-jē\ *n, pl* **-gies 1** *often cap* **:** a communion rite **2 :** a rite or body of rites prescribed for public worship [Late Latin *liturgia,* from Greek *leitourgia* "public service, divine service"]

liv·abil·i·ty \ˌliv-ə-ˈbil-ət-ē\ *n* **1 :** survival expectancy **:** VIABILITY **2 :** suitability for human living

liv·able *also* **live·able** \ˈliv-ə-bəl\ *adj* **1 :** suitable for living in or with **2 :** capable of being endured **:** BEARABLE — **liv·able·ness** *n*

¹live \ˈliv\ *vb* **1 :** to be or continue alive **:** have life **2 :** to maintain oneself **:** SUBSIST ⟨*live* on fruits⟩ **3 :** to conduct or pass one's life ⟨*lived* up to their principles⟩ **4 :** to occupy a home **:** RESIDE ⟨*lives* next door⟩ **5 :** to attain eternal life **6 :** to remain in human memory or record **7 :** to have a life rich in experience **8 :** COHABIT **9 :** to pass through or spend the duration of ⟨*lived* their lives alone⟩ **10 :** to represent in action ⟨to *live* out their fantasies⟩ **11 :** to exhibit vigor, gusto, or enthusiasm in ⟨*lived* life to the fullest⟩ **12 :** to experience firsthand ⟨*living* a dream⟩ [Old English *libban*] — **live it up :** to live with gusto and often recklessness — **live up to :** to act or be in keeping with ⟨had no intention of *living up to* his promise⟩ — **live with :** to put up with **:** TOLERATE, ACCEPT ⟨had to *live with* their decision⟩

²live \ˈlīv\ *adj* **1 a :** having life **:** LIVING **b :** existing in fact or reality **:** ACTUAL ⟨spoke to a real *live* celebrity⟩ **2 :** abounding with life **:** VIVID **3 :** exerting force or containing energy: as **a :** AFIRE, GLOWING ⟨*live* coals⟩ **b :** carrying an electric current ⟨a *live* wire⟩ **c :** charged with explosives and containing shot or a bullet ⟨*live* ammunition⟩; *also* **:** UNEXPLODED ⟨a *live* bomb⟩ **d :** rotating or imparting motion ⟨a *live* spindle⟩ **e :** power-driven ⟨a *live* axle⟩ **4 :** of continuing or current interest **:** UNCLOSED ⟨*live* issues⟩ **5 :** being in the native uncut state ⟨*live* rock⟩ **6 :** of bright vivid color **7 :** being in play ⟨a *live* ball⟩ **8 a :** of or involving a presentation (as a play or concert) in which both the performers and an audience are physically present ⟨*live* entertainment⟩ **b :** broadcast directly at the time of production instead of from recorded or filmed material ⟨*live* television⟩ [short for *alive*]

live–ac·tion \ˈlīv-ˈak-shən\ *adj* **:** of, relating to, or featuring cinematography that is not produced by animation ⟨a *live-action* film⟩

live–bear·er \ˈlīv-ˌbar-ər, -ˌber-\ *n* **:** a fish that brings forth living young rather than eggs; *esp* **:** any of a family of numerous small surface-feeding fishes (as a molly or swordtail)

live–bear·ing \ˈlīv-ˈbaər-ing, -ˈbeər-\ *adj* **:** VIVIPAROUS

-lived \ˈlīvd, ˈlivd\ *adj combining form* **:** having a life of a specified kind or length ⟨long-*lived*⟩

live down *vt* **:** to live so as to wipe out the memory or effects of ⟨made a mistake and could not *live* it *down*⟩

live–for·ev·er \ˈliv-fə-ˌrev-ər\ *n* **:** SEDUM

live·li·hood \ˈlīv-lē-ˌhu̇d\ *n* **:** means of support or subsistence ⟨an honest *livelihood*⟩ [Old English *līflād* "course of life," from *līf* "life" + *lād* "course"]

live·long \ˌliv-ˌlȯng\ *adj* **:** WHOLE 3a, ENTIRE ⟨the *livelong* day⟩ [Middle English *lef long,* from *lef* "dear" + *long* "long"]

live·ly \ˈlīv-lē\ *adj* **live·li·er; -est 1 :** briskly alert and energetic **:** VIGOROUS, ANIMATED ⟨a *lively* discussion⟩ **2 :** ACTIVE 5a, INTENSE ⟨a *lively* interest in sports⟩ **3 :** SPIRITED, BRILLIANT ⟨a

\ə\ **abut**	\au̇\ **out**	\i\ **tip**	\ȯ\ **saw**	\u̇\ **foot**
\ər\ **further**	\ch\ **chin**	\ī\ **life**	\ȯi\ **coin**	\y\ **yet**
\a\ **mat**	\e\ **pet**	\j\ **job**	\th\ **thin**	\yü\ **few**
\ā\ **take**	\ē\ **easy**	\ng\ **sing**	\t͟h\ **this**	\yu̇\ **cure**
\ä\ **cot, cart**	\g\ **go**	\ō\ **bone**	\ü\ **food**	\zh\ **vision**

lively wit⟩ **4** : quick to rebound : RESILIENT **5** : full of life, movement, or incident ⟨a *lively* city⟩ — **live·li·ly** \ˈlīv-lə-lē\ *adv* — **live·li·ness** \ˈlīv-lē-nəs\ *n* — **lively** *adv*

synonyms LIVELY, ANIMATED, VIVACIOUS mean being keenly alive. LIVELY suggests briskness, alertness, or energy ⟨a *lively* debate⟩. ANIMATED applies to what is spirited, active, or vigorous ⟨an *animated* discussion of current events⟩. VIVACIOUS suggests attractive cheerfulness and a quick wit ⟨a *vivacious* party host⟩.

liv·en \ˈlī-vən\ *vb* **liv·ened; liv·en·ing** \ˈlīv-ning, -ə-ning\ : to make or become lively

live oak \ˈlīv-ˌōk\ *n* : any of several American evergreen oaks

[1]**liv·er** \ˈliv-ər\ *n* **1 a** : a large vascular glandular organ of vertebrates that secretes bile and regulates the concentration of various blood substances (as by converting sugars into glycogen) **b** : any of various large glands associated with the digestive tract of invertebrate animals **2** : the liver of an animal (as a calf or chicken) eaten as food [Old English *lifer*]

[2]**liv·er** \ˈliv-ər\ *n* : one that lives in a specified way ⟨a fast *liver*⟩

-liv·ered \ˈliv-ərd\ *adj combining form* : expressing courage or spirit that suggests a person having (such) a liver ⟨lily-*livered*⟩ ⟨chicken-*livered*⟩

liver fluke *n* : any of various trematodes that invade the liver of mammals

liv·er·ied \ˈliv-rēd, -ə-rēd\ *adj* : wearing a livery

liv·er·ish \ˈliv-rish, -ə-rish\ *adj* **1** : suffering from liver disorder : BILIOUS **2** : CROSS 3, MELANCHOLY — **liv·er·ish·ness** *n*

liver spots *n pl* : AGE SPOTS

liv·er·wort \ˈliv-ər-ˌwərt, -ˌwȯrt\ *n* : any of a class (Hepaticae) of bryophytes resembling the related mosses but differing especially in reproduction and development

liv·er·wurst \ˈliv-ər-ˌwərst, ˈliv-ə-, -ˌwu̇rst, -ˌwu̇st, -ˌwu̇sht\ *n* : sausage consisting chiefly of liver [German *Leberwurst,* from *Leber* "liver" + *Wurst* "sausage"]

liv·ery \ˈliv-rē, -ə-rē\ *n, pl* **-er·ies** **1** : a special uniform worn by the servants of a wealthy household ⟨a footman in *livery*⟩ **2** : distinctive dress ⟨the *livery* of a school⟩ **3 a** : the feeding, care, and stabling of horses for pay; *also* : the keeping of horses and vehicles for hire **b** : LIVERY STABLE [Medieval French *liveree, livree,* literally, "delivery," from *livrer* "to deliver," from Latin *liberare* "to liberate"]

liv·ery·man \-mən\ *n* : the keeper of a livery stable

livery stable *n* : a stable where horses and vehicles are kept for hire and where stabling is provided

lives *plural of* LIFE

live steam *n* : steam direct from a boiler and under full pressure

live·stock \ˈlīv-ˌstäk\ *n* : animals kept or raised for use or pleasure; *esp* : farm animals kept for use and profit

live wire *n* : an alert, active, or aggressive person — **live–wire** *adj*

liv·id \ˈliv-əd\ *adj* **1** : discolored by bruising : BLACK-AND-BLUE **2** : ASHEN, PALLID ⟨*livid* with fear⟩ **3** : very angry [French *livide,* from Latin *lividus,* from *livēre* "to be blue"] — **li·vid·i·ty** \liv-ˈid-ət-ē\ *n* — **liv·id·ly** \ˈliv-əd-lē\ *adv* — **liv·id·ness** *n*

[1]**liv·ing** \ˈliv-ing\ *adj* **1 a** : having life **b** : ACTIVE ⟨a *living* language⟩ **2** : exhibiting the life or motion of nature : NATURAL **3 a** : full of life or vigor ⟨made mathematics a *living* subject⟩ **b** : true to life : VIVID **c** : suited for living ⟨the *living* area⟩ **4** : VERY — used as an intensive

[2]**living** *n* **1** : the condition of being alive **2** : conduct or manner of life **3** : means of subsistence : LIVELIHOOD

living fossil *n* : an animal or plant (as the horseshoe crab or ginkgo tree) that has remained almost unchanged from earlier geologic times and whose close relatives are usually extinct

living room *n* : a room in a residence used for the common social activities of the occupants

living wage *n* : a wage sufficient to provide the necessities and comforts held to comprise an acceptable standard of living

living will *n* : a document in which the signer requests to be allowed to die rather than be kept alive by artificial means if no reasonable expectation of recovery exists — compare ADVANCE DIRECTIVE

liz·ard \ˈliz-ərd\ *n* : any of a group (Lacertilia) of reptiles distinguished from the related snakes by a fused inseparable lower jaw, external ears, eyes with movable lids, and usually two pairs of functional limbs [Medieval French *lesarde,* from Latin *lacerta*]

'll \l, əl, əl\ *vb* : WILL ⟨it'*ll* do for now⟩: SHALL ⟨I'*ll* be there⟩

lla·ma \ˈläm-ə\ *n* : any of several wild and domesticated South American cud-chewing mammals with long necks and hooves that are related to the camels but smaller and without a hump; *esp* : one domesticated in the Andes and used as a beast of burden and a source of wool [Spanish, from Quechua]

llama

lla·no \ˈlän-ō, ˈlan-\ *n, pl* **llanos** : an open grassy plain especially of Spanish America [Spanish, "plain," from Latin *planum*]

lo \ˈlō\ *interj* — used to call attention or to express wonder or surprise [Old English *lā*]

loach \ˈlōch\ *n* : any of a family of small Old World freshwater fishes related to the carps [Medieval French *loche*]

[1]**load** \ˈlōd\ *n* **1 a** : whatever is put on a person or pack animal to be carried : PACK **b** : whatever is put in a ship or vehicle or airplane for conveyance : CARGO; *esp* : a quantity of material assembled or packed as a shipping unit **c** : the quantity that can be carried at one time by a specified means — often used in combination ⟨a boat*load* of tourists⟩ **2** : a mass or weight supported by something ⟨branches bent low by their *load* of fruit⟩ **3 a** : something that weighs down the mind or spirits ⟨a *load* of care⟩ **b** : a burdensome or laborious responsibility ⟨always carried his share of the *load*⟩ **4** : a large quantity : LOT — usually used in plural **5 a** : a charge for a firearm **b** : the quantity of material loaded into a device at one time **6** : external resistance overcome by a machine **7 a** : power output (as of a power plant) **b** : a device to which power is delivered **8 a** : the amount of work that a person, department, or machine performs or is expected to perform **b** : the demand upon the operating resources of a system (as a telephone exchange or a refrigerating apparatus) **9** *slang* : EYEFUL ⟨get a *load* of that⟩ [Old English *lād* "support, carrying"]

[2]**load** *vb* **1 a** : to put a load in or on ⟨*load* a truck⟩; *also* : to receive a load **b** : to place in or on a means of conveyance ⟨*load* freight⟩ **c** : to copy or transfer (as data or a program) into a computer's memory **2 a** : to encumber or oppress with something heavy, laborious, or disheartening : BURDEN ⟨*loaded* down with debts⟩ **b** : to place as a burden or obligation ⟨*loaded* more work on us⟩ **3 a** : to increase the weight of by adding something heavy **b** : to weight or shape (dice) to fall unfairly **c** : to pack with one-sided or prejudicial influence : BIAS **d** : to charge with multiple meanings (as emotional associations or hidden implications) **e** : to weight (as a test) with factors influencing validity or outcome **4 a** : to supply in abundance or excess : HEAP **b** : to put runners on (first, second, and third base) in baseball **5 a** : to put a load or charge in (a device or piece of equipment) ⟨*load* a gun⟩ **b** : to place or insert especially as a load in a device or piece of equipment ⟨*load* film in a camera⟩ **6** : to alter by adding an adulterant or drug **7** : to go or go in as a load ⟨sightseers *loading* onto a bus⟩ — **load·er** *n* — **load up on 1** : to ingest in usually large amounts ⟨*loaded up on* his favorite food⟩ **2** : to acquire in usually large amounts ⟨*loaded up on* hot stocks⟩

load·ed *adj* **1** *slang* : DRUNK **2** : having a large amount of money **3 a** : equipped with an abundance of options ⟨bought a fully *loaded* car⟩ **b** : staffed with excellent players ⟨a *loaded* basketball team⟩

load line *n* : the line on a ship indicating the depth to which it sinks in the water when properly loaded

loadstar *variant of* LODESTAR

loadstone *variant of* LODESTONE

[1]**loaf** \ˈlōf\ *n, pl* **loaves** \ˈlōvz\ **1** : a shaped or molded mass of bread **2** : a dish (as of meat) baked in the form of a loaf [Old English *hlāf*]

[2]**loaf** *vb* **1** : to spend time in idleness : LOUNGE **2** : to pass idly ⟨*loaf* the time away⟩ [probably back-formation from *loafer*]

synonyms see IDLE

loaf·er \ˈlō-fər\ *n* **1** : one that loafs : IDLER **2** : a low step-in shoe [perhaps from German *Landläufer* "tramp," from *Land* "land" + *Läufer* "runner"]

loam \ˈlōm, ˈlüm\ *n* : SOIL; *esp* : a soil consisting of a crumbly mixture of varying proportions of clay, silt, and sand [Old English *lām* "clay, mud"] — **loamy** \ˈlō-mē, ˈlü-\ *adj*

[1]**loan** \ˈlōn\ *n* **1 a** : money let out at interest **b** : something

loaned for the borrower's temporary use **2 :** the grant of temporary use [Old Norse *lān*]

[2]**loan** *vt* **:** LEND

usage The verb *loan* came to America with early settlers and continued to be used even after it had dropped out of use in Great Britain. Various 19th-century commentators declared the use improper. Although a surprising number of critics still object to it, *loan* is entirely standard as a verb. You should note that it is used only literally ⟨*loaned* me a book⟩, while *lend* is the verb used for figurative expressions, such as *"lend* a hand" or *"lending* a touch of class."

loan shark *n* **:** a person who lends money at excessive rates of interest

loan•word \ˈlōn-ˌwərd\ *n* **:** a word taken from another language and at least partly naturalized

loath *also* **loth** \ˈlōth, ˈlōth\ *or* **loathe** *adj* **:** very unwilling or reluctant ⟨was *loath* to run for office again⟩ [Old English *lāth* "loathsome"]

loathe \ˈlōth\ *vt* **:** to dislike greatly and often with disgust or intolerance **:** DETEST ⟨*loathe* the smell of burning rubber⟩ [Old English *lāthian* "to dislike, be hateful," from *lāth* "hateful"] ***synonyms*** see HATE

loath•ing \ˈlō-thing\ *n* **:** extreme disgust **:** DETESTATION

[1]**loath•ly** \ˈlōth-lē, ˈlōth-\ *adj* **:** LOATHSOME, REPULSIVE

[2]**loath•ly** \ˈlōth-lē, ˈlōth-\ *adv* **:** not willingly **:** RELUCTANTLY

loath•some \ˈlōth-səm, ˈlōth-\ *adj* **:** utterly disgusting — **loath•some•ly** *adv* — **loath•some•ness** *n*

[1]**lob** \ˈläb\ *vb* **lobbed; lob•bing 1 :** to throw, hit, or propel easily or in a high arc **2 :** to direct (as a question or comment) so as to get a response **3 a :** to move slowly and heavily **b :** to move in an arc [*lob* "a loosely hanging object"]

[2]**lob** *n* **:** a ball that is lobbed

[1]**lob•by** \ˈläb-ē\ *n, pl* **lobbies 1 :** a corridor or hall connected with a larger room or series of rooms and used as a passageway or waiting room: as **a :** an anteroom of a legislative chamber **b :** a large hall serving as a foyer (as of a hotel or theater) **2 :** a group of persons engaged in lobbying especially as representatives of a particular interest group [Medieval Latin *lobium* "gallery," of Germanic origin]

[2]**lobby** *vb* **lob•bied; lob•by•ing 1 :** to try to influence public officials and especially members of a legislative body **2 :** to promote (as a project) or secure the passage of (as legislation) by influencing public officials — **lob•by•ist** \ˈläb-ē-əst\ *n*

lobe \ˈlōb\ *n* **:** a curved or rounded projection or division; *esp* **:** such a subdivision of a bodily organ or part [Middle French, from Late Latin *lobus,* from Greek *lobos*] — **lo•bar** \ˈlō-bər, -ˌbär\ *adj* — **lo•bate** \-ˌbāt\ *adj* — **lobed** \ˈlōbd\ *adj*

lobe–finned fish \ˈlōb-ˌfind-\ *n* **:** any of a group (Crossopterygii) of mostly extinct fishes (as a coelacanth) that have paired fins suggesting limbs and may be ancestral to the land-dwelling vertebrates — called also *lobe-fin, lobe-fin fish*

lo•be•lia \lō-ˈbēl-yə\ *n* **:** any of a genus of widely distributed herbs often grown for their terminal clusters of showy lipped flowers [Matthias de *Lobel,* died 1616, Flemish botanist]

lob•lol•ly pine \ˌläb-ˌläl-ē-\ *n* **:** a pine of the southeastern U.S. with thick flaky bark, long needles in groups of three, and spiny-tipped cones; *also* **:** its coarse-grained wood — called also *loblolly* [probably from English dialect *lob* "to boil" + obsolete English dialect *lolly* "broth"]

lo•bot•o•my \lō-ˈbät-ə-mē\ *n, pl* **-mies :** surgical cutting of nerve fibers connecting the frontal lobes of the brain to the thalamus performed especially formerly for the relief of some mental disorders

lob•ster \ˈläb-stər\ *n* **:** any of several large edible marine crustaceans with stalked eyes, a pair of large claws, and a long abdomen; *also* **:** SPINY LOBSTER [Old English *loppestre,* from *loppe* "spider"]

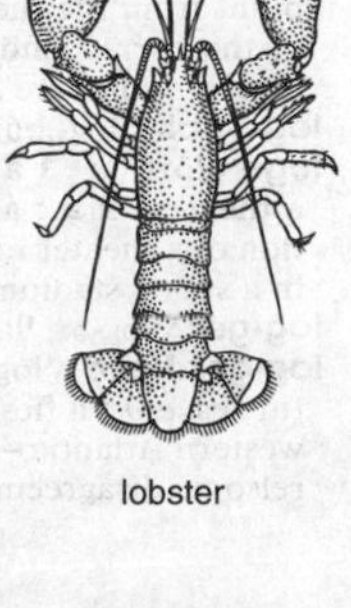
lobster

lobster pot *n* **:** a trap for catching lobsters

lob•ule \ˈläb-yül\ *n* **:** a small lobe; *also* **:** a subdivision of a lobe — **lob•u•lar** \ˈläb-yə-lər\ *adj* — **lob•u•lat•ed** \-ˌlāt-əd\ *also* **lob•u•late** \-ˌlāt\ *adj* — **lob•u•la•tion** \ˌläb-yə-ˈlā-shən\ *n*

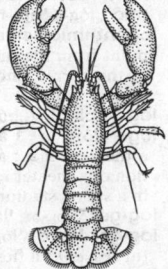

[1]**lo•cal** \ˈlō-kəl\ *adj* **1 :** characterized by or relating to position in space **2 :** characterized by, relating to, being from, or occupying a particular place ⟨*local* news⟩ **3 :** not broad or general; *esp* **:** involving or affecting only a small part of the body ⟨a *local* infection⟩ **4 a :** primarily serving the needs of a particular limited district ⟨*local* government⟩ **b :** making all the stops on a run ⟨a *local* train⟩ [Late Latin *localis,* from Latin *locus* "place"] — **lo•cal•ly** \-kə-lē\ *adv*

[2]**local** *n* **:** a local person or thing: as **a :** a local train or other public conveyance **b :** a local branch, lodge, or chapter (as of a labor union)

local area network *n* **:** a computer network that spans a small area (as an office building)

local color *n* **:** the presentation of the features and peculiarities of a particular locality and its inhabitants in writing

lo•cale \lō-ˈkal\ *n* **1 :** a place or locality that is the setting for a particular event or characteristic **2 :** SITE 2, SCENE ⟨the *locale* of a story⟩ [modification of French *local,* from *local,* adj., "local"]

lo•cal•ism \ˈlō-kə-ˌliz-əm\ *n* **1 :** often undue partiality for one's own locality **:** SECTIONALISM **2 :** a local idiom or peculiarity of speech

lo•cal•i•ty \lō-ˈkal-ət-ē\ *n, pl* **-ties :** a particular spot, situation, or location

lo•cal•ize \ˈlō-kə-ˌlīz\ *vb* **:** to make or become local **:** fix in or assign or confine to a definite place or locality ⟨pain *localized* in a joint⟩ — **lo•cal•i•za•tion** \ˌlō-kə-lə-ˈzā-shən\ *n*

local option *n* **:** the power granted by a legislature to a political subdivision to determine by popular vote whether a particular law is to apply locally

lo•cate \ˈlō-ˌkāt, lō-ˈ\ *vb* **1 :** to establish oneself or one's business **:** set or establish in a particular spot **2 a :** to seek out and find the location of **b :** to find the position of (a point) by means of coordinates **3 :** to find or fix the place of in a sequence [Latin *locare* "to place," from *locus* "place"]

lo•ca•tion \lō-ˈkā-shən\ *n* **1 :** a position or site occupied or available for occupancy or marked by some distinguishing feature **:** SITUATION **2 :** a tract of land (as a mining claim) whose boundaries and purpose have been designated **3 :** a place outside a studio where a motion picture is filmed ⟨on *location* in the desert⟩ **4 :** the act or process of locating — **lo•ca•tion•al** \-shnəl, -shən-l\ *adj* — **lo•ca•tion•al•ly** \-ē\ *adv*

loc•a•tive \ˈläk-ət-iv\ *adj* **:** of or being a grammatical case that denotes place — **locative** *n*

lo•ca•tor *also* **lo•cat•er** \ˈlō-ˌkāt-ər\ *n* **:** one that locates something (as a mining claim or the course of a road)

loch \ˈläk, ˈläk\ *n* **1** *Scottish* **:** LAKE **2** *Scottish* **:** a bay or arm of the sea especially when nearly landlocked [Scottish Gaelic]

loci *plural of* LOCUS

[1]**lock** \ˈläk\ *n* **1 a :** a tuft, tress, or ringlet of hair **b** *pl* **:** the hair of the head **2 :** a cohering bunch (as of wool, cotton, or flax) [Old English *locc*]

[2]**lock** *n* **1 a :** a fastening (as for a door) in which a bolt is operated (as by a key) **b :** the mechanism for exploding the charge or cartridge of a firearm **2 a :** an enclosure (as in a canal) with gates at each end used in raising or lowering boats as they pass from level to level **b :** AIR LOCK **3 :** a hold in wrestling that prevents movement of a part of the body ⟨a leg *lock*⟩ [Old English *loc*]

[3]**lock** *vb* **1 a :** to fasten the lock of **b :** to make or be made fast with or as if with a lock ⟨*lock* up the house⟩ **2 a :** to shut or keep or make secure or inaccessible by means of locks ⟨*locked* up my bike⟩ ⟨*locked* in jail⟩ **b :** to hold fast or inactive **:** FIX **3 a :** to make fast by the interlacing or interlocking of parts ⟨*lock* wheels⟩ **b :** to hold in a close embrace **c :** to grapple in conflict; *also* **:** to bind closely ⟨the company's owner and workers were *locked* in conflict⟩ **4 :** to move by raising or lowering in a lock **:** go or pass by means of a lock (as in a canal) — **lock•able** \ˈlä-kə-bəl\ *adj* — **lock horns :** to come into conflict

lock•er \ˈläk-ər\ *n* **1 a :** a drawer, cabinet, compartment, or chest usually with a lock **b :** a storage chest or compartment on shipboard **2 :** an insulated compartment for storing frozen food at a low temperature **3 :** one that locks

locker room *n* **:** a room for changing clothes and for storing clothing and equipment; *esp* **:** one for use by sports players

lock•et \ˈläk-ət\ *n* **:** a small case usually of precious metal that

\ə\ abut	\au̇\ out	\i\ tip	\ȯ\ saw	\u̇\ foot
\ər\ further	\ch\ chin	\ī\ life	\ȯi\ coin	\y\ yet
\a\ mat	\e\ pet	\j\ job	\th\ thin	\yü\ few
\ā\ take	\ē\ easy	\ng\ sing	\th\ this	\yu̇\ cure
\ä\ cot, cart	\g\ go	\ō\ bone	\ü\ food	\zh\ vision

has space for a memento and that is usually worn suspended from a chain or necklace [Middle French *loquet* "latch," from Dutch *loke*]

lock·jaw \ˈläk-ˌjȯ\ *n* : a symptom of tetanus characterized by spasm of the jaw muscles and inability to open the jaws; *also* : TETANUS 1

lock·nut \ˈläk-ˌnət\ *n* **1** : a nut screwed down tightly on another to prevent it from loosening **2** : a nut constructed to remain fast when tightly screwed down

lock·out \ˈläk-ˌau̇t\ *n* : the suspension of work or closing of a plant by an employer during a labor dispute in order to make the employees accept terms

lock out \läk-ˈau̇t, ˈläk-\ *vt* : to subject (a body of employees) to a lockout

lock·smith \ˈläk-ˌsmith\ *n* : a person who makes or repairs locks

lock·step \ˈläk-ˌstep\ *n* : a way of marching in step by a body of persons going one after another as closely as possible

lock·stitch \ˈläk-ˌstich\ *n* : a sewing machine stitch formed by the looping together of two threads one on each side of the material being sewn

lock, stock, and barrel *adv* : WHOLLY 1 ⟨sold out *lock, stock, and barrel*⟩ [from the principal parts of a flintlock]

lock·up \ˈläk-ˌəp\ *n* : JAIL; *esp* : one where persons are detained prior to court hearing

¹lo·co \ˈlō-kō\ *n, pl* **locos** *or* **locoes** **1** : LOCOWEED **2** : LOCOISM [Mexican Spanish, from Spanish, "crazy"]

²loco *adj, slang* : out of one's mind : CRAZY [Spanish]

lo·co·ism \ˈlō-kō-ˌiz-əm\ *n* : a nervous disease of horses, cattle, and sheep caused by chronic poisoning with locoweeds

lo·co·mo·tion \ˌlō-kə-ˈmō-shən\ *n* : the act or power of moving from place to place [Latin *locus* "place" + English *motion*]

¹lo·co·mo·tive \ˌlō-kə-ˈmōt-iv\ *adj* **1 a** : of, relating to, or functioning in locomotion **b** : having the ability to move independently from place to place **2** : of or relating to travel **3** : of, relating to, or being a machine that moves under its own power

²locomotive *n* : an engine that moves under its own power; *esp* : one that hauls cars on a railroad

lo·co·mo·tor \ˌlō-kə-ˈmōt-ər\ *adj* **1** : LOCOMOTIVE 1 **2** : affecting or involving the locomotive organs

locomotor ataxia *n* : a syphilitic disorder of the nervous system marked especially by disturbances of gait and difficulty in coordinating voluntary movements

lo·co·weed \ˈlō-kō-ˌwēd\ *n* : any of several plants of the legume family that are found in western North America and cause locoism in livestock

loc·ule \ˈläk-yül\ *n* : LOCULUS; *esp* : any of the cells of a compound ovary of a plant — **loc·uled** \-yüld\ *adj*

loc·u·lus \ˈläk-yə-ləs\ *n, pl* **-li** \-ˌlī, -ˌlē\ : a small chamber or cavity especially in a plant or animal body [Latin, "little place," from *locus* "place"]

lo·cum te·nens \ˌlō-kəm-ˈtē-ˌnenz\ *n, pl* **locum te·nen·tes** \-tə-ˈnen-ˌtēz\ : a person (as a doctor or clergyman) filling an office for a time or temporarily taking the place of another [Medieval Latin, literally, "one holding a place"]

lo·cus \ˈlō-kəs\ *n, pl* **lo·ci** \ˈlō-ˌsī, -ˌkī, -ˌkē\ **1** : PLACE 1b, LOCALITY **2** : the set of all points whose location is determined by stated conditions **3** : the position in a chromosome of a particular gene or allele [Latin]

lo·cus clas·si·cus \ˌlō-kəs-ˈklas-i-kəs\ *n, pl* **lo·ci clas·si·ci** \-ˌsī-ˈklas-ə-ˌsī, -ˌkī-ˈklas-ə-ˌkī, -ˌkē-ˈklas-ə-ˌkē\ : a standard passage important for the explanation of a word or subject [New Latin]

lo·cust \ˈlō-kəst\ *n* **1 a** : SHORT-HORNED GRASSHOPPER; *esp* : a migratory grasshopper often traveling in vast swarms and stripping the areas passed of vegetation **b** : CICADA — compare SEVENTEEN-YEAR LOCUST **2 a** : any of various hard-wooded trees (as a honey locust) of the legume family **b** : the wood of a locust [Latin *locusta*]

locust bean *n* : CAROB

lo·cu·tion \lō-ˈkyü-shən\ *n* **1** : a particular form of expression or phrasing ⟨complicated *locutions* in legal documents⟩ **2** : style of discourse : PHRASEOLOGY [Latin *locutio,* from *loqui* "to speak"]

lode \ˈlōd\ *n* : an ore deposit [Old English *lād* "way, course, support"]

lode·star *also* **load·star** \-ˌstär\ *n* **1** : a star that leads or guides; *esp* : NORTH STAR **2** : one that is a guide or a focus of attention

lode·stone *also* **load·stone** \-ˌstōn\ *n* **1** : magnetite having magnetic properties **2** : something that strongly attracts

¹lodge \ˈläj\ *vb* **1 a** : to provide temporary quarters for **b** : to establish or settle oneself in a place **c** : to rent lodgings to **2** : to serve as a receptacle for **3** : to bring or come to a rest and remain ⟨the bone *lodged* in the throat⟩ **4** : to lay (as a complaint) before a proper authority **5** : to fall or become beaten down ⟨the tall grass *lodged* in the storm⟩

²lodge *n* **1 a** : a house set apart for residence in a special season ⟨a hunting *lodge*⟩ **b** : a resort hotel ⟨a ski *lodge*⟩ **c** : a house for an employee on an estate ⟨a gamekeeper's *lodge*⟩ **2** : a den or lair especially of a group of gregarious animals (as beavers) **3** : the meeting place of a branch (as of a fraternal organization); *also* : the members of such a branch **4 a** : WIGWAM **b** : a family of North American Indians [Medieval French *loge* "hut, cabin," of Germanic origin]

lodge·pole pine \ˌläj-ˌpōl-\ *n* : any of several western North American pines with paired needles and short rough cones

lodg·er \ˈläj-ər\ *n* : one that lodges; *esp* : one that occupies a rented room in another's house

lodg·ing \ˈläj-ing\ *n* **1** : DWELLING; *esp* : a temporary dwelling or sleeping place **2** : a room in the house of another person used as a residence — usually used in plural

lodging house *n* : ROOMING HOUSE

loess \ˈles, ˈlu̇s, ˈlərs, ˈlō-əs\ *n* : a usually yellowish brown loamy deposit believed to be deposited chiefly by the wind [German *Löss*] — **loess·ial** \-ē-əl\ *adj*

¹loft \ˈlȯft\ *n* **1** : a room or floor above another : ATTIC **2 a** : a gallery in a church or hall ⟨an organ *loft*⟩ **b** : an upper floor of a warehouse or business building especially when not partitioned **c** : HAYLOFT **3 a** : the backward slant of the face of a golf-club head **b** : HEIGHT 2b ⟨the ball had too much *loft* to reach the green⟩ [Old Norse *lopt* "air, sky, loft"]

²loft *vb* **1** : to place, house, or store in a loft **2** : to strike or throw a ball high into the air ⟨*lofted* a high fly to center field⟩

lofty \ˈlȯf-tē\ *adj* **loft·i·er; -est** **1** : marked by a haughty overbearing manner ⟨a *lofty* air⟩ **2 a** : elevated in character and spirit ⟨*lofty* ideals⟩ **b** : elevated in position : SUPERIOR **3** : rising high in the air : TOWERING ⟨a *lofty* oak⟩ — **loft·i·ly** \-tə-lē\ *adv* — **loft·i·ness** \-tē-nəs\ *n*

¹log \ˈlȯg, ˈläg\ *n* **1** : a bulky piece of a cut or fallen tree; *esp* : a long piece of a tree trunk trimmed and ready for sawing **2** : an apparatus for measuring the rate of a ship's motion through the water that consists of a block fastened to a line and run out from a reel **3 a** : the daily record of a ship's speed and progress **b** : the full record of a ship's voyage or of an aircraft's flight **4** : a record of performance, events, or day-to-day activities ⟨a computer *log*⟩ [Middle English *logge*]

²log *vb* **logged; log·ging** **1** : to cut trees for lumber or clear (land) of trees in lumbering **2** : to make a note or record of : enter details of or about in a log **3 a** : to move (an indicated distance) or attain (an indicated speed) as noted in a log **b** (1) : to sail a ship or fly an airplane for (an indicated distance or an indicated period of time) (2) : to have (an indicated record) to one's credit

³log *n* : LOGARITHM

lo·gan·ber·ry \ˈlō-gən-ˌber-ē\ *n* : a red-fruited upright-growing dewberry; *also* : its berry [James H. *Logan,* died 1928, American lawyer]

log·a·rithm \ˈlȯg-ə-ˌrith-əm, ˈläg-\ *n* : the exponent that indicates the power to which a base number is raised to produce a given number ⟨the *logarithm* of 100 to the base 10 is 2⟩ [Greek *logos* "word, reckoning" + *arithmos* "number"] — **log·a·rith·mic** \ˌlȯg-ə-ˈrith-mik, ˌläg-\ *adj*

logarithmic scale *n* : a scale on which the actual distance of a point from the the scale's zero is proportional to the logarithm of the corresponding scale number rather than to the number itself — compare ARITHMETIC SCALE

log·book \ˈlȯg-ˌbu̇k, ˈläg-\ *n* **1** : LOG 3 **2** : LOG 4

loge \ˈlōzh\ *n* **1 a** : a small compartment : BOOTH **b** : a box in a theater **2 a** : a small partitioned area **b** : the forward section of a theater mezzanine **c** : a raised section or level of seats in a sports stadium [French, "hut, lodge, loge"]

log·ger \ˈlȯg-ər, ˈläg-\ *n* : one engaged in logging

log·ger·head \ˈlȯg-ər-ˌhed, ˈläg-\ *n* : any of several very large turtles; *esp* : a flesh-eating sea turtle of the warmer parts of the western Atlantic — **at loggerheads** : in or into a state of quarrelsome disagreement

log·gia \ˈläj-ē-ə, ˈlō-jä\ *n* : a roofed gallery open on at least one side [Italian, from Medieval French *loge* "lodge, hut"]

L loggia

log·ic \ˈläj-ik\ *n* **1** : a science that deals with the rules and tests of sound thinking and proof by reasoning **2** : REASONING 1; *esp* : sound reasoning ⟨no *logic* in that remark⟩ **3** : connection (as of facts or events) in a way that seems reasonable ⟨the *logic* of a situation⟩ **4** : the arrangement of circuit elements (as in a computer) needed for computation [Medieval French *logique*, from Latin *logica*, from Greek *logikē*, from *logos* "reason"] — **lo·gi·cian** \lō-ˈjish-ən\ *n*

log·i·cal \ˈläj-i-kəl\ *adj* **1** : of or relating to logic : used in logic **2** : conforming to or consistent with the rules of logic ⟨a *logical* argument⟩ **3** : skilled in logic ⟨a *logical* thinker⟩ **4** : being in agreement with what may be reasonably expected ⟨a *logical* result of an action⟩ — **log·i·cal·ly** \-kə-lē, -klē\ *adv* — **log·i·cal·ness** \-kəl-nəs\ *n*

log in *vi* : LOG ON — **log–in** \ˈlȯg-ˌin, ˈläg-\ *n*

lo·gis·tics \lō-ˈjis-tiks\ *n sing or pl* **1** : a branch of military science dealing with the procurement, maintenance, and transportation of military matériel, facilities, and personnel **2** : the handling of the details of an operation [French, literally, "art of calculating," from Greek *logistikē*, from *logizein* "to calculate," from *logos* "reason"] — **lo·gis·tic** \-tik\ *or* **lo·gis·ti·cal** \-ti-kəl\ *adj* — **lo·gis·ti·cal·ly** \-ti-kə-lē, -klē\ *adv*

log·jam \ˈlȯg-ˌjam, ˈläg-\ *n* **1** : a jumble of logs jammed together in a watercourse **2** : IMPASSE 2

Logo \ˈlō-gō\ *n* : a simplified language for programming and communicating with a computer that uses drawing on a display screen as a tool for teaching programming principles [probably derived from Greek *logos* "word, speech, reason"]

log on *vi* : to make a connection with a computer or network ⟨she *logged on* to the Internet⟩ — **log–on** \ˈlȯg-ˌȯn, ˈläg-ˌän\ *n*

Lo·gos \ˈlō-ˌgäs, -ˌgōs\ *n* : the divine wisdom manifest in the creation, government, and redemption of the world and often identified with the second person of the Trinity [Greek, "speech, word, reason"]

log·roll·ing \ˈlȯg-ˌrō-ling, ˈläg-\ *n* **1** : the trading of votes by legislators to secure favorable action on projects of interest to each one **2** : the rolling of logs in water by treading; *also* : a sport in which individuals treading logs try to dislodge one another — **log·roll·er** \-ˌrō-lər\ *n*

-logue *or* **-log** \ˌlȯg, ˌläg\ *n combining form* **1** : discourse : talk ⟨duo*logue*⟩ **2** : student : specialist [French *-logue*, derived from Greek *-logos*, from *legein* "to speak"]

log·wood \ˈlȯg-ˌwu̇d, ˈläg-\ *n* : a Central American and West Indian tree of the legume family; *also* : its hard brown or brownish red heartwood used in dyeing or an extract of this

lo·gy \ˈlō-gē\ *adj* **lo·gi·er; -est** : marked by sluggishness and lack of vitality [perhaps from Dutch *log* "heavy"]

-l·o·gy \l-ə-jē\ *n combining form* **1** : oral or written expression ⟨phraseo*logy*⟩ **2** : doctrine : theory : science ⟨ethno*logy*⟩ [Greek *-logia*, from *logos* "word, speech, reason"]

loin \ˈlȯin\ *n* **1 a** : the part of the body on each side of the spinal column and between the hip and the lower ribs **b** : a cut of meat comprising this part of one or both sides of a carcass with the adjoining half of the vertebrae included but without the flank **2** *pl* **a** : the pubic region **b** : the organs of reproduction [Middle French *loigne*, derived from Latin *lumbus*]

loin·cloth \-ˌklȯth\ *n* : a cloth worn about the loins often as the sole article of clothing in warm climates

loi·ter \ˈlȯit-ər\ *vi* **1** : to interrupt or delay an activity with aimless idle stops and pauses **2 a** : to hang around idly **b** : to lag behind [Middle English *loiteren*] — **loi·ter·er** \-ər-ər\ *n*

loll \ˈläl\ *vb* **1** : to hang or let hang loosely : DROOP **2** : to act or move in a lax, lazy, or indolent manner : LOUNGE ⟨*loll* around in the sun⟩ [Middle English *lollen*] ***synonyms*** see IDLE

lol·li·pop *or* **lol·ly·pop** \ˈläl-ē-ˌpäp\ *n* : a lump of hard candy on the end of a stick [perhaps from English dialect *lolly* "tongue" + [2]*pop*]

Lom·bard \ˈläm-ˌbärd, -bərd\ *n* **1** : a member of a Germanic people that invaded Italy in A.D. 568 and established a kingdom in the Po valley **2** : a native or inhabitant of Lombardy [Medieval French, from Italian *Lombardo*, from Latin *Langobardus*]

Lom·bar·dy poplar \ˌläm-ˌbärd-ē, -bərd-\ *n* : a tall slender poplar of European origin that tapers at the top and has strongly ascending upright branches [*Lombardy*, Italy]

lo·ment \ˈlō-ˌment, -mənt\ *n* : a dry fruit resembling a pod that has constrictions between the seeds and that breaks into one-seeded segments at maturity [Latin *lomentum* "wash made from bean meal," from *lavere* "to wash"]

lone \ˈlōn\ *adj* **1 a** : having no company : SOLITARY ⟨a *lone* traveler⟩ **b** : preferring solitude **2** : ONLY 2, SOLE ⟨the *lone* theater in town⟩ **3** : situated by itself : ISOLATED [Middle English, short for *alone*] — **lone·ness** \ˈlōn-nəs\ *n*

lone·ly \ˈlōn-lē\ *adj* **lone·li·er; -est** **1** : being without company : LONE ⟨a *lonely* hiker⟩ **2** : UNFREQUENTED, DESOLATE ⟨a *lonely* spot⟩ **3** : sad from being alone : LONESOME ***synonyms*** see ALONE — **lone·li·ness** *n*

lone·some \ˈlōn-səm\ *adj* **1** : sad from lack of companionship or separation from others **2 a** : not often visited or traveled over ⟨a *lonesome* stretch of highway⟩ **b** : lacking companionship : separated from others of its kind : LONE ***synonyms*** see ALONE — **lone·some·ly** *adv* — **lone·some·ness** *n*

lone wolf *n* : a person who prefers to work, act, or live alone

[1]long \ˈlȯng\ *adj* **long·er** \ˈlȯng-gər\; **long·est** \ˈlȯng-gəst\ **1** : of great or greater than usual extent from end to end ⟨a *long* corridor⟩ **2 a** : having a specified length ⟨six feet *long*⟩ **b** : forming the chief linear dimension ⟨the *long* side of the table⟩ **3 a** : lasting for a considerable or a specified time ⟨a *long* friendship⟩ ⟨two hours *long*⟩ **b** : prolonged beyond the usual time ⟨a *long* look⟩ **c** : lasting too long : TEDIOUS ⟨a *long* explanation⟩ **4 a** : containing many items in a series ⟨a *long* list⟩ **b** : having a specified number of units ⟨300 pages *long*⟩ **5 a** : being a syllable or speech sound of relatively great duration **b** : being the member of a pair of similarly spelled vowel or vowel-containing sounds that is descended from a vowel long in duration ⟨*long a* in *fate*⟩ ⟨*long i* in *sign*⟩ **6** : having the capacity to reach or extend a considerable distance ⟨a *long* left jab⟩ **7** : larger or longer than the standard **8 a** : extending far into the future ⟨take a *long* view of things⟩ **b** : extending beyond what is known ⟨a *long* guess⟩ **9** : strong in or well furnished with something ⟨*long* on common sense⟩ **10** : of an unusual degree of difference between the amounts wagered on each side ⟨*long* odds⟩ [Old English *long, lang*] — **at long last** : after a long wait : FINALLY

[2]long *adv* **1** : for or during a long time ⟨*long* a popular hangout⟩ **2** : for the duration of a specified period ⟨all summer *long*⟩ **3** : at a distant point of time ⟨*long* before we arrived⟩ — **so long** : GOOD-BYE

[3]long *vi* **longed; long·ing** \ˈlȯng-ing\ : to feel a strong desire or wish : YEARN ⟨*longing* to return home⟩ [Old English *langian*]

synonyms LONG, YEARN, HANKER, PINE mean to have a strong desire for something. LONG implies wishing with one's whole heart and often striving to attain ⟨*longed* for some rest⟩. YEARN suggests an eager, restless, or painful longing ⟨*yearned* to be understood⟩. HANKER suggests an uneasiness due to an unsatisfied and often unreasonable appetite or desire ⟨*hankered* for complete approval⟩. PINE implies a languishing or fruitless longing ⟨always *pining* for something better⟩.

long ball *n* : HOME RUN

long·boat \ˈlȯng-ˌbōt\ *n* : a large boat carried on a ship

long bone *n* : one of the bones supporting a vertebrate limb and consisting of a long nearly cylinder-shaped shaft that contains bone marrow and ends in enlarged heads that each form a joint with another bone

long·bow \ˈlȯng-ˌbō\ *n* : a wooden bow held vertically that is drawn by hand

long–day *adj* : flowering or developing to maturity only in response to alternating long light and short dark periods — compare DAY-NEUTRAL, SHORT-DAY

[1]long–dis·tance \-ˈdis-təns\ *adj* : of or relating to telephone communication with a distant point especially outside a specified area

[2]long–distance *adv* : by long-distance telephone

long distance *n* **1** : communication by long-distance telephone **2** : a telephone operator or exchange that gives long-distance connections

long division *n* : arithmetical division in which the several steps involved in the division are indicated in detail

lon·gev·i·ty \län-ˈjev-ət-ē, lòn-\ *n* **1** : a long duration of individual life **2** : length of life **3** : long continuance : PERMANENCE, DURABILITY [Late Latin *longaevitas,* from Latin *longaevus* "long-lived," from *longus* "long" + *aevum* "age"]

long·hair \ˈlòng-ˌhaər, -ˌheər\ *n* **1** : a person of artistic gifts or interests; *esp* : a lover of classical music **2** : an impractical intellectual **3** : a person with long hair; *esp* : HIPPIE **4** : a domestic cat having long outer fur

long–haired \-ˈhaərd, -ˈheərd\ *or* **longhair** *adj* : having long hair or fur ⟨a *long-haired* dog⟩

long·hand \ˈlòng-ˌhand\ *n* : HANDWRITING 1: as **a** : characters or words written out fully by hand **b** : cursive writing

long·head·ed \-ˈhed-əd\ *adj* **1** : having unusual foresight or wisdom **2** : having a head relatively long from front to back but narrow from side to side — **long·head·ed·ness** *n*

long·horn \ˈlòng-ˌhòrn\ *n* : any of the long-horned cattle of Spanish derivation formerly common in the southwestern U.S.

long–horned \-ˈhòrnd\ *adj* : having long horns or antennae ⟨*long-horned* beetles⟩

long·house \-ˌhau̇s\ *n* : a communal dwelling of some North American Indians (as the Iroquois)

longhouse

long hundredweight *n, British* : HUNDREDWEIGHT 2

lon·gi·corn \ˈlän-jə-ˌkòrn\ *adj* : of, relating to, or being beetles with long antennae [Latin *longus* "long" + *cornu* "horn"]

long·ing \ˈlòng-ing\ *n* : an eager desire often for the unattainable : CRAVING — **long·ing·ly** \-ing-lē\ *adv*

long·ish \ˈlòng-ish\ *adj* : somewhat long

lon·gi·tude \ˈlän-jə-ˌtüd, -ˌtyüd\ *n* : distance measured by degrees or time east or west from the prime meridian ⟨the *longitude* of New York is 74 degrees or about five hours west of Greenwich⟩ [Latin *longitudin-, longitudo* "length," from *longus* "long"]

longitude

lon·gi·tu·di·nal \ˌlän-jə-ˈtüd-nəl, -ˈtyüd-, -n-əl\ *adj* **1** : of or relating to length or the lengthwise dimension **2** : placed or running lengthwise — **lon·gi·tu·di·nal·ly** \-ē\ *adv*

long jump *n* : a jump for distance in track-and-field sports — **long jumper** *n*

long·leaf pine \ˌlòng-ˌlēf-\ *n* : a tall pine of the southeastern U.S. that has long needles in clusters of three and long cones and is a major timber tree; *also* : its tough coarse-grained durable reddish orange wood

long–leaved pine \ˌlòng-ˌlēvd-\ *n* : LONGLEAF PINE

long–lived \ˈlòng-ˈlīvd, -ˈlivd\ *adj* : living or lasting a long time — **long–lived·ness** \-ˈlīvd-nəs, -ˈlīv-, -ˈlivd-, -ˈliv-\ *n*

long·neck \-ˌnek\ *n* : beer served in a bottle that has a long neck

long–play·ing \ˈlòng-ˈplā-ing\ *adj* : of, relating to, or being a phonograph record designed to be played at 33⅓ revolutions per minute

long–range \-ˈrānj\ *adj* **1** : relating to or fit for long distances ⟨a *long-range* gun⟩ **2** : lasting over or taking into account a long period : LONG-TERM ⟨*long-range* planning⟩

long·ship \-ˌship\ *n* : a long sail and oar ship used by the Vikings

long·shore·man \ˈlòng-ˈshōr-mən, -ˈshòr-\ *n* : a laborer who loads and unloads ships at a seaport [*longshore* "existing along the seacoast," short for *alongshore*]

long shot \ˈlòng-ˌshät\ *n* **1** : an entry (as in a horse race) given little chance of winning **2** : a bet in which the chances of winning are slight but the possible winnings great **3** : a venture involving great risk but promising a great reward if successful — **by a long shot** : by a great deal

long–sight·ed \-ˈsīt-əd\ *adj, chiefly British* : FARSIGHTED — **long–sight·ed·ness** *n, chiefly British*

long–stand·ing \ˈlòng-ˈstan-ding\ *adj* : of long duration ⟨a *long-standing* dispute⟩

long–suf·fer·ing \-ˈsəf-ring, -ə-ring\ *adj* : patiently enduring lasting offense or hardship — **long–suffering** *n* — **long–suf·fer·ing·ly** \-ring-lē\ *adv*

long suit *n* **1** : a suit containing the most cards in a hand **2** : STRONG SUIT 2

long–tailed duck *n* : OLD-SQUAW

long–term \ˈlòng-ˈtərm\ *adj* **1** : extending over or involving a long period of time **2** : constituting a financial obligation based on a term usually of more than 10 years ⟨a *long-term* mortgage⟩

long–wind·ed \ˈlòng-ˈwin-dəd\ *adj* **1** : not easily subject to loss of breath **2** : tediously long in speaking or writing — **long–wind·ed·ly** *adv* — **long–wind·ed·ness** *n*

loo \ˈlü\ *n* **1** : an old card game **2** : money staked at loo [short for obsolete *lanterloo,* from French *lanturelu* "piffle"]

loo·fah *also* **luf·fa** \ˈlü-fə\ *n* : any of various Old World tropical plants of the gourd family with large fruits; *also* : a sponge consisting of the fibrous skeleton of its fruit

¹look \ˈlu̇k\ *vb* **1** : to exercise the power of vision upon : EXAMINE, SEE **2** : EXPECT 2 ⟨we *look* to see you soon⟩ **3** : to express by the eyes or facial expression **4** : to have an appearance that suits or agrees with ⟨*looks* my age⟩ **5** : to have the appearance of being : SEEM ⟨it *looks* unlikely⟩ **6** : to direct one's attention or eyes ⟨*look* in the mirror⟩ **7** : to have a specified outlook : POINT ⟨the house *looks* east⟩ **8** : to gaze in wonder or surprise : STARE [Old English *lōcian*] — **look after** : to take care of : attend to — **look at** **1** : CONSIDER 1 ⟨*looking at* the possibility of moving⟩ **2** : to confront or be confronted by ⟨*looking at* detention after school⟩ — **look for** **1** : to await with hope or anticipation : EXPECT **2** : to search for : SEEK — **look forward** : to anticipate with pleasure or satisfaction ⟨*looking forward* to your visit⟩ — **look into** : to examine carefully — **look on** *or* **look upon** **1** : CONSIDER 3, REGARD ⟨*looked upon* them as friends⟩ **2** : to observe as a spectator — **look the other way** : to direct one's attention away from something unpleasant or troublesome — **look to** **1** : to direct one's attention to ⟨*looking to* the future⟩ **2** : to rely upon ⟨*looks to* reading for relaxation⟩

²look *n* **1 a** : the act of looking **b** : GLANCE 3b **2 a** : the expression of the face **b** : physical appearance; *esp* : attractive physical appearance — usually used in plural **3** : the state or form in which something appears : ASPECT

look·er–on \ˌlu̇k-ər-ˈòn, -ˈän\ *n, pl* **lookers–on** : ONLOOKER, SPECTATOR

looking glass *n* : MIRROR 1

look·out \ˈlu̇k-ˌau̇t\ *n* **1** : a person engaged in watching; *esp* : one assigned to watch (as on a ship) **2** : an elevated place or structure offering a wide view for observation **3** : a careful looking or watching **4** : a probability for the future : OUTLOOK **5** : a matter of care or concern

¹loom \ˈlüm\ *n* : a frame or machine for weaving together threads or yarns into cloth [Old English *gelōma* "tool"]

loom

²loom *vi* **1** : to come into sight in an unnaturally large, indistinct, or distorted form ⟨*loomed* out of the fog⟩ **2** : to be about to happen ⟨trouble was *looming*⟩ [origin unknown]

loon \ˈlün\ *n* **1** : any of several large fish-eating diving birds with webbed feet, black head, and white-spotted black back **2** : a person of dull or disordered mind : LUNATIC [of Scandinavian origin; sense 2 from the popular phrase *crazy as a loon*]

loo·ny *also* **loo·ney** \ˈlü-nē\ *adj* **loo·ni·er; -est** : CRAZY 2, FOOLISH [derived from *lunatic*] — **loony** *n*

¹loop \ˈlüp\ *n* **1** : a fold or doubling of a line leaving an opening between the parts through which another line can be passed or into which a hook may be hooked **2** : a loop-shaped figure, bend, or course ⟨a *loop* in a river⟩ **3** : a circular airplane maneuver involving flying upside down **4 a** : the portion of a vibrating body between two nodes **b** : the middle point of such a portion **5** : a complete electric circuit **6** : a series of instructions for a computer that is repeated until a terminating condition is reached [Middle English *loupe*] — **for a loop :** into a state of amazement, confusion, or distress ⟨the news knocked us *for a loop*⟩

[2]**loop** *vb* **1 :** to make or form a loop **2 a :** to make a loop in, on, or about **b :** to fasten with a loop **3 :** to execute a loop in an airplane

loop·er \ˈlü-pər\ *n* **1 :** any of numerous small hairless moth larvae that move with a looping motion — called also *inchworm, measuring worm* **2 :** one that loops

loop·hole \ˈlüp-ˌhōl\ *n* **1 a :** a small opening in a wall through which small firearms may be discharged **b :** a similar opening to admit light and air or to permit observation **2 :** a means of escape; *esp* **:** an ambiguity or omission (as in the wording of a law or contract) that makes evasion of one's obligation possible

loop of Hen·le \-ˈhen-lē\ **:** a U-shaped part of the nephron of birds and mammals that lies in the midst of the convoluted portion and plays a part in resorption of water during urine formation [F. G. J. *Henle*, died 1885, German pathologist]

[1]**loose** \ˈlüs\ *adj* **1 a :** not rigidly fastened or securely attached **b :** having worked partly free from attachments ⟨a *loose* tooth⟩ **c :** not tight-fitting **2 a :** free from confinement, restraint, or obligation **b :** not brought together in a bundle, container, or binding **3 a :** not dense or compact in structure or arrangement ⟨*loose* soil⟩ **b :** not solid **:** WATERY ⟨*loose* stools⟩ **4 :** lacking in restraint or power of restraint ⟨*loose* conduct⟩ **5 a :** not tightly drawn or stretched **:** SLACK **b :** being flexible or relaxed ⟨stay *loose*⟩ **6 a :** lacking in precision, exactness, or care ⟨*loose* work⟩ **b :** permitting freedom of interpretation **7 :** not in the possession of either of two competing teams ⟨a *loose* ball⟩ [Old Norse *lauss*] — **loose·ly** *adv* — **loose·ness** *n*

[2]**loose** *vb* **1 a :** to let loose **:** RELEASE **b :** to free from restraint **2 :** to make loose **:** UNTIE ⟨*loose* a knot⟩ **3 :** to let fly **:** DISCHARGE **4 :** to make less rigid, tight, or strict **:** RELAX

loose end *n* **1 :** something left hanging loose **2 :** a fragment of unfinished business ⟨tying up *loose ends*⟩

loose–joint·ed \ˈlüs-ˈjȯint-əd\ *adj* **1 :** having flexible joints **2 :** moving with unusual freedom or ease — **loose–joint·ed·ness** *n*

loose–leaf \ˈlüs-ˈlēf\ *adj* **1 :** having leaves secured in book form in a cover whose spine contains a locking device that may be opened for adding, arranging, or removing leaves ⟨a *loose-leaf* notebook⟩ **2 :** of, relating to, or used with a loose-leaf binding ⟨*loose-leaf* paper⟩

loos·en \ˈlüs-ⁿn\ *vb* **loos·ened; loos·en·ing** \ˈlüs-niŋ, -ⁿn-iŋ\ **1 :** to release from restraint **2 :** to make or become loose or looser **3 :** to cause or permit to become less strict ⟨*loosened* the rules⟩

loose·strife \ˈlüs-ˌstrīf, ˈlü-\ *n* **1 :** any of a genus of herbs related to the primroses and having leafy stems and yellow or white flowers **2 :** any of a genus of herbs including some with showy spikes of purple flowers; *esp* **:** PURPLE LOOSESTRIFE [intended as translation of Greek *lysimacheios* "loosestrife" (as if from *lysis* "act of loosing" + *machesthai* "to fight"), from *Lysimachos,* 5th or 4th century B.C. Greek physician]

[1]**loot** \ˈlüt\ *n* **1 :** goods taken in war **:** SPOIL **2 :** something stolen or taken by force or violence **3 :** the action of looting [Hindi & Urdu *lūṭ*, from Sanskrit *luṇṭati* "he robs"]

[2]**loot** *vb* **1 :** to plunder or sack in war **2 :** to rob or steal especially on a large scale and by violence or corruption **3 :** to seize and carry away by force especially in war — **loot·er** *n*

lop \ˈläp\ *vt* **lopped; lop·ping 1 a :** to cut branches or twigs from **:** TRIM ⟨*lop* a tree⟩ **b :** to cut or shear from a woody plant ⟨*lop* dead branches⟩ **c :** to cut (as a portion or part) from something **2 :** to remove unnecessary or undesirable parts from — usually used with *off* [Middle English *loppe* "small branches and twigs cut from a tree"]

[1]**lope** \ˈlōp\ *n* **1 :** an easy natural gait of a horse resembling a canter **2 :** an easy bounding gait capable of being sustained for a long time [probably from Old Norse *hlaup* "leap"]

[2]**lope** *vi* **:** to go, move, or ride at a lope — **lop·er** *n*

lop–eared \ˈläp-ˈiərd\ *adj* **:** having ears that droop ⟨a *lop-eared* rabbit⟩ [earlier *lop* "to droop"]

loph·o·phore \ˈläf-ə-ˌfōr, -ˌfȯr\ *n* **:** a circular or horseshoe-shaped organ about the mouth of a brachiopod or bryozoan that bears tentacles and functions especially in food-getting [Greek *lophos* "crest"]

lop·per \ˈläp-ər\ *n* **:** shears with long handles used for pruning — usually used in plural

lop·sid·ed \ˈläp-ˈsīd-əd\ *adj* **1 :** leaning to one side **2 :** lacking in balance, symmetry, or proportion — **lop·sid·ed·ly** *adv* — **lop·sid·ed·ness** *n*

lo·qua·cious \lō-ˈkwā-shəs\ *adj* **:** given to too much talking [Latin *loquac-, loquax,* from *loqui* "to speak"] — **lo·qua·cious·ly** *adv* — **lo·qua·cious·ness** *n* — **lo·quac·i·ty** \-ˈkwas-ət-ē\ *n*

lo·quat \ˈlō-ˌkwät\ *n* **:** a small Asian evergreen tree related to the roses and bearing yellow plumlike fruits; *also* **:** its fruit used especially in preserves [Chinese (Guangdong dialect) *làuh-gwāt*]

loquat

[1]**lord** \ˈlȯrd\ *n* **1 :** one having power and authority over others: **a :** a ruler to whom service and obedience are due **b :** a person from whom a feudal fee or estate is held **c :** HUSBAND **2** *cap* **a :** GOD 1 **b :** Jesus as the lord of Christians **3 :** a man of rank or high position: as **a :** a feudal tenant whose right or title comes directly from the king **b** *often cap* **:** a British nobleman or a bishop in the Church of England entitled to sit in the House of Lords — used as a title **4** *pl, cap* **:** HOUSE OF LORDS [Old English *hlāford,* from *hlāf* "loaf" + *weard* "keeper, ward"]

Word History *Lord* is etymologically similar to *lady.* A lady is, etymologically, a kneader of bread and a lord a keeper of bread. Old English *hlāford* is formed from *hlāf,* "loaf, bread," and *weard,* "keeper, guard," the Old English form of modern *ward.* The earliest known instances of *hlāford* show the sense of "head of household." Apparently the *hlāf-* element was to be taken no more literally than is the first element of the modern term *breadwinner.*

[2]**lord** *vi* **:** to act in an arrogant or domineering manner — used with *it* ⟨*lords* it over his friends⟩

lord chancellor *n, pl* **lords chancellor :** a British officer of state who presides over the House of Lords, serves as the head of the British judiciary, and is usually a leading member of the cabinet

lord·ly \ˈlȯrd-lē\ *adj* **lord·li·er; -est 1 a :** of, relating to, or having the characteristics of a lord **b :** fit for a lord ⟨a *lordly* estate⟩ **2 :** haughtily proud or superior — **lord·li·ness** *n* — **lordly** *adv*

lor·do·sis \lȯr-ˈdō-səs\ *n* **:** abnormal inward curvature of the lower region of the spine — compare KYPHOSIS, SCOLIOSIS [Greek *lordōsis,* from *lordos* "curving forward"] — **lor·dot·ic** \-ˈdät-ik\ *adj*

Lord's day *n, often cap D* **:** SUNDAY

lord·ship \ˈlȯrd-ˌship\ *n* **1** *often cap* **:** the rank or dignity of a lord — used as a title ⟨his *Lordship* is not at home⟩ **2 :** the authority, power, or territory of a lord

Lord's Prayer *n* **:** the prayer with variant versions in Matthew and Luke that according to Luke Christ taught his disciples

Lord's Supper *n* **:** COMMUNION 1a

lore \ˈlōr, ˈlȯr\ *n* **:** KNOWLEDGE 4; *esp* **:** a particular body of knowledge or tradition ⟨forest *lore*⟩ [Old English *lār* "teaching"]

lor·gnette \lȯrn-ˈyet\ *n* **:** a pair of eyeglasses or opera glasses with a handle [French, from *lorgner* "to take a sidelong look at," from *lorgne* "squinting"]

lo·ri·ca \lə-ˈrī-kə\ *n, pl* **-cae** \-ˌkē, -ˌsē\ **1 :** a Roman cuirass of leather or metal **2 :** a hard protective case or shell (as of a rotifer) [Latin, from *lorum* "thong, rein"]

lor·i·keet \ˈlȯr-ə-ˌkēt, ˈlär-\ *n* **:** any of numerous small parrots of Australasia that feed chiefly on nectar [*lory,* a kind of parrot (from Malay *nuri, luri*) + *-keet* (as in *parakeet*)]

lo·ris \ˈlōr-əs, ˈlȯr-\ *n* **:** any of several small nocturnal slow-moving primates without a tail [French, probably from Dutch *loeris* "simpleton"]

lorn \ˈlȯrn\ *adj* **:** left alone **:** DESOLATE [Middle English, from *loren,* past participle of *lesen* "to lose," from Old English *lēosan*]

lor·ry \ˈlȯr-ē, ˈlär-\ *n, pl* **lorries** *chiefly British* **:** a motor truck especially if open [origin unknown]

lose \ˈlüz\ *vb* **lost** \ˈlȯst\; **los•ing** \ˈlü-ziŋ\ **1 :** to bring to destruction ⟨the ship was *lost* on the reef⟩ **2 :** to be unable to find or have at hand ⟨*lose* a billfold⟩ **3 :** to become deprived of especially accidentally or by death ⟨*lose* one's eyesight⟩ ⟨*lost* a child in the war⟩ **4 :** to fail to keep control of or allegiance of ⟨*lose* votes⟩ **5 a :** to fail to use : let slip by : WASTE ⟨no time to *lose*⟩ **b** (1) : to fail to win, gain, or obtain ⟨*lose* a contest⟩ (2) : to undergo defeat in ⟨*lost* every battle⟩ **c :** to fail to catch with the senses or the mind ⟨*lost* part of what they said⟩ **6 :** to cause the loss of ⟨one careless statement *lost* the election⟩ **7 :** to fail to keep, sustain, or maintain ⟨*lose* one's balance⟩ **8 a :** to cause to miss one's way or bearings ⟨*lost* myself in the maze of streets⟩ **b :** to make (oneself) withdrawn from immediate reality ⟨*lost* myself in daydreaming⟩ **9 a :** to wander or go astray from ⟨*lost* my way⟩ **b :** to go faster than : shake off ⟨*lost* their pursuers⟩ **10 :** to fail to keep in sight or in mind **11 :** to free oneself from : get rid of ⟨dieting to *lose* some weight⟩ **12** *slang* **:** REGURGITATE, VOMIT — often used in such phrases as *lose one's lunch* [Old English *losian* "to perish, lose," from *los* "destruction"] — **lose ground :** to suffer loss or disadvantage : fail to advance or improve — **lose it 1 :** to lose touch with reality; *also* : to go crazy **2 :** to become overwhelmed with strong emotions : lose one's composure ⟨so angry I almost *lost it*⟩ — **lose one's heart :** to fall in love

lose out *vi* : to fail to win in competition : fail to receive an expected reward or gain

los•er \ˈlü-zər\ *n* **1 :** a person or thing that loses **2 :** a person who is incompetent or unable to succeed; *also* : something doomed to fail or disappoint

losing *adj* **1 :** resulting in or likely to result in defeat ⟨a *losing* battle⟩ **2 :** marked by many losses or more losses than wins ⟨a *losing* record⟩

loss \ˈlȯs\ *n* **1 a :** the act of losing **b :** the harm or privation resulting from losing ⟨their death was a *loss* to the community⟩ **c :** an instance of losing **2 a :** a person or thing or an amount that is lost **b** *pl* : killed, wounded, or captured soldiers **3 a :** failure to gain, win, obtain, or utilize **b :** an amount by which the cost of something exceeds its selling price **4 :** decrease in amount, magnitude, or degree **5 :** DESTRUCTION 2, RUIN [Middle English *los,* probably a back-formation from *lost*] — **at a loss 1 :** uncertain as to how to proceed ⟨was *at a loss* to explain the problem⟩ **2 :** unable to produce what is needed ⟨was *at a loss* for a cure⟩ — **for a loss :** into a state of distress

loss leader *n* : an article sold at a loss in order to draw customers

lost \ˈlȯst\ *adj* **1 :** not made use of, won, or claimed **2 a :** unable to find the way **b :** no longer visible **c :** lacking assurance or self-confidence **3 :** ruined or destroyed physically or morally **4 a :** no longer possessed **b :** no longer known **5 a :** taken away or beyond reach or attainment ⟨regions *lost* to the faith⟩ **b :** made callous : INSENSIBLE ⟨*lost* to shame⟩ **6 :** wholly occupied or interested in a thought or activity : RAPT ⟨*lost* in reverie⟩ **7 :** hopelessly unattainable : FUTILE ⟨a *lost* cause⟩ [past participle of *lose*] — **lost•ness** \ˈlȯst-nəs, ˈlȯs-\ *n*

[1]lot \ˈlät\ *n* **1 :** an object used as a counter in determining a question by chance **2 :** the use of lots as a means of deciding something ⟨choose by *lot*⟩; *also* : the resulting choice **3 a :** something that comes to one by or as if by lot : SHARE **b :** one's way of life or worldly fate : FORTUNE **4 a :** a portion of land ⟨a building *lot*⟩ **b :** a motion-picture studio and its adjoining property **5 :** a number of units of an article or a parcel of articles offered as one item (as in an auction sale) **6 :** a number of associated persons : SET **7 :** a considerable quantity ⟨*lots* of money⟩ [Old English *hlot*] ***synonyms*** see FATE

[2]lot *vb* **lot•ted; lot•ting 1 :** to form or divide into lots **2 :** ALLOT

loth \ˈlōth, ˈlōth\ *variant of* LOATH

lo•thar•io \lō-ˈthar-ē-ˌō, -ˈther-, -ˈthär-\ *n, pl* **-ios** *often cap* : a man whose chief interest is seducing women [*Lothario,* seducer in the play *The Fair Penitent* (1703) by Nicholas Rowe]

lo•tion \ˈlō-shən\ *n* : a liquid preparation for cosmetic and medicinal use on the skin [Latin *lotio* "act of washing," from *lavere* "to wash"]

lots \ˈläts\ *adv* : MUCH 1a ⟨feeling *lots* better⟩ [pl. of [1]*lot*]

lot•tery \ˈlät-ə-rē, ˈlä-trē\ *n, pl* **-ter•ies 1 :** a drawing of lots in which prizes are given to the winners among persons buying a chance **2 :** a drawing of lots used to decide something

lot•to \ˈlät-ō\ *n* : a game of chance similar to bingo [Italian, "lottery, lotto," from French *lot* "lot," of Germanic origin]

lo•tus \ˈlōt-əs\ *n* **1** *also* **lo•tos** \ˈlōt-əs\ : a fruit held in Greek legend to cause indolence and forgetfulness; *also* : a tree bearing this fruit **2 :** any of various water lilies including several represented in ancient Egyptian and Hindu art and religious symbolism **3 :** any of various erect plants of the legume family including some used for hay and pasture [Latin, from Greek *lōtos*]

lotus–eater \ˈlōt-ə-ˌsēt-ər\ *n* **1 :** one of a people in classical mythology who subsist on the lotus and live in its induced dreamy indolence **2 :** DREAMER 2a, IDLER

loud \ˈlau̇d\ *adj* **1 a :** marked by intensity or volume of sound **b :** producing a loud sound **2 :** CLAMOROUS, NOISY **3 :** obtrusive or offensive in color or pattern ⟨a *loud* suit⟩ [Old English *hlūd*] — **loud** *adv* — **loud•ly** *adv* — **loud•ness** *n*

loud•en \ˈlau̇d-n\ *vb* **loud•ened; loud•en•ing** \ˈlau̇d-niŋ, -n-iŋ\ : to make or become loud or louder

loud•mouth \ˈlau̇d-ˌmau̇th\ *n* : a person given to loud offensive talk — **loud•mouthed** \-ˈmau̇thd, -ˌmau̇tht\ *adj*

loud•speak•er \ˈlau̇d-ˈspē-kər\ *n* : a device similar to a telephone receiver in operation but amplifying sound

Lou Geh•rig's disease \ˌlü-ˈger-igz-\ *n* : AMYOTROPHIC LATERAL SCLEROSIS [*Lou Gehrig,* died 1941, American baseball player who suffered from the disease]

lou•is d'or \ˌlü-ē-ˈdȯr\ *n, pl* **louis d'or 1 :** a French gold coin first struck in 1640 and issued up to the French Revolution **2 :** the French 20-franc gold piece issued after the French Revolution [French, from *Louis* XIII of France + *d'or* "of gold"]

Lou•is Qua•torze \ˌlü-ē-kə-ˈtȯrz\ *adj* : of, relating to, or characteristic of the architecture or furniture of the reign of Louis XIV of France [French, "Louis XIV"]

Louis Quinze \-ˈka^{n}z\ *adj* : of, relating to, or characteristic of the architecture or furniture of the reign of Louis XV of France [French, "Louis XV"]

Louis Seize \-ˈsāz, -ˈsez\ *adj* : of, relating to, or characteristic of the architecture or furniture of the reign of Louis XVI of France [French, "Louis XVI"]

Louis Treize \-ˈtrāz, -ˈtrez\ *adj* : of, relating to, or characteristic of the architecture or furniture of the reign of Louis XIII of France [French, "Louis XIII"]

[1]lounge \ˈlau̇nj\ *vb* **1 :** to move or act idly or lazily : LOAF **2 :** to stand, sit, or lie in a relaxed manner **3 :** to pass (time) idly ⟨*lounged* away the day⟩ [origin unknown] ***synonyms*** see IDLE — **loung•er** *n*

[2]lounge *n* **1 :** a place for lounging: as **a :** LIVING ROOM **b :** LOBBY **c :** a room in a public building or vehicle often combining lounging, smoking, and toilet facilities **2 :** a long couch

lounge car *n* : a railroad passenger car with seats for lounging and facilities for serving refreshments

loup–ga•rou \ˌlü-gə-ˈrü\ *n, pl* **loups–garous** \ˌlü-gə-ˈrü, -ˈrüz\ : WEREWOLF [Middle French, from Medieval French *leu garoul,* from *leu* "wolf" + *garoul* "werewolf"]

lour, louring, loury *variant of* LOWER, LOWERING, LOWERY

louse \ˈlau̇s\ *n* **1** *pl* **lice** \ˈlīs\ **a :** any of various small wingless usually flat insects (orders Anoplura and Mallophaga) parasitic on warm-blooded animals **b :** any of several other small arthropods (as a book louse or wood louse) that are not parasites **2** *pl* **lous•es** \ˈlau̇-səz\ : a contemptible person [Old English *lūs*]

louse up *vb* : to make a mess of something : BUNGLE

lousy \ˈlau̇-zē\ *adj* **lous•i•er; -est 1 :** infested with lice **2 a :** totally repulsive : CONTEMPTIBLE **b :** miserably poor or inferior ⟨got *lousy* grades⟩ **c :** somewhat ill ⟨felt *lousy* after dinner⟩ **d :** amply supplied ⟨*lousy* with money⟩ — **lous•i•ly** \-zə-lē\ *adv* — **lous•i•ness** \-zē-nəs\ *n*

lout \ˈlau̇t\ *n* : a clownish awkward fellow [perhaps from Old English *lūtan* "to bow in respect"] — **lout•ish** \-ish\ *adj* — **lout•ish•ly** *adv* — **lout•ish•ness** *n*

lou•ver *or* **lou•vre** \ˈlü-vər\ *n* **1 :** an opening provided with one or more slanted fixed or movable strips (as of metal or wood) to allow flow of air but to exclude rain or sun or to provide privacy; *also* : a similar device with movable strips for controlling the passage of air or light **2 :** one of the slanted strips of a louver [Medieval French *lover* "roof lantern or turret with slatted openings"] — **lou•vered** \-vərd\ *adj*

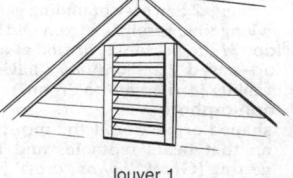

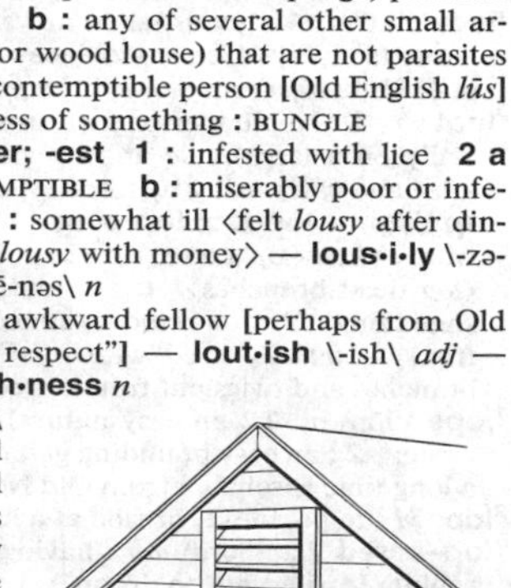

louver 1

lov·able *also* **love·able** \'ləv-ə-bəl\ *adj* : having qualities that attract affection — **lov·able·ness** *n* — **lov·ably** \-blē\ *adv*

lov·age \'ləv-ij\ *n* : any of several aromatic perennial herbs related to the carrot [Medieval French *luvasche, lovasche*]

[1]**love** \'ləv\ *n* **1 a** : strong affection for another based on kinship ties ⟨maternal *love* for a child⟩ **b** : attraction based on sexual desire **c** : affection based on admiration or benevolence **2** : warm attachment, enthusiasm, or devotion ⟨*love* of the sea⟩ **3 a** : the object of attachment or devotion **b** : a beloved person : DARLING **4 a** : unselfish loyal concern for the good of another: as (1) : the fatherly concern of God for humankind (2) : brotherly concern for others **b** : a person's adoration of God **5** : an amorous episode **6** : a score of zero in tennis [Old English *lufu*] — **in love** : feeling love for and devotion toward someone

[2]**love** *vb* **1** : to hold dear : CHERISH **2 a** : to feel a lover's passion, devotion, or tenderness for **b** : CARESS **3** : to like or desire actively : take pleasure in ⟨*loved* to play the violin⟩ **4** : to thrive in ⟨the rose *loves* sunlight⟩ **5** : to feel affection : experience desire

love apple *n* : TOMATO

love·bird \'ləv-ˌbərd\ *n* : any of various small usually gray or green parrots that are noted for the expression of caring behavior for their mates

love feast *n* **1** : a meal eaten in common by a Christian congregation in token of brotherly love **2** : a gathering held to reconcile differences or show someone honor

love·fest \'ləv-ˌfest\ *n* : LOVE FEAST 2; *also* : an expression or exchange of goodwill, praise, or affection

love handles *n pl* : fatty bulges along the sides of the body at the waist

love–in–a–mist \'ləv-ə-nə-ˌmist\ *n* : a European garden plant related to the buttercups that has usually blue or white flowers enveloped in finely dissected bracts

love knot *n* : a stylized knot sometimes used as an emblem of love

love·less \'ləv-ləs\ *adj* **1** : marked by the absence of love ⟨a *loveless* marriage⟩ **2** : not feeling or showing love **3** : not loved — **love·less·ly** *adv* — **love·less·ness** *n*

love·lorn \'ləv-ˌlȯrn\ *adj* : deprived of or deserted by one's lover — **love·lorn·ness** \-ˌlȯrn-nəs\ *n*

love·ly \'ləv-lē\ *adj* **love·li·er; -est** **1** : beautiful in moral or spiritual character : GRACIOUS **2** : delicately beautiful ⟨a *lovely* dress⟩ **3** : highly pleasing : FINE ⟨a *lovely* view⟩ ***synonyms*** see BEAUTIFUL — **love·li·ness** *n*

love·mak·ing \'ləv-ˌmā-king\ *n* **1** : COURTSHIP **2** : sexual activity — **love·mak·er** \-kər\ *n*

lov·er \'ləv-ər\ *n* **1 a** : a person in love; *esp* : a man in love **b** *pl* : two persons in love with each other **2** : DEVOTEE ⟨a *lover* of jazz⟩ **3 a** : PARAMOUR **b** : a person with whom one has sexual relations

lov·er·ly \-lē\ *adj* : befitting a lover

love seat *n* : a double chair, sofa, or settee for two persons

love·sick \'ləv-ˌsik\ *adj* **1** : languishing with love : YEARNING **2** : expressing a lover's longing ⟨*lovesick* poems⟩ — **love·sick·ness** *n*

love tap *n* : a gentle blow

lov·ing \'ləv-ing\ *adj* : feeling or showing love : AFFECTIONATE — **lov·ing·ly** \-ing-lē\ *adv*

loving cup *n* : a large ornamental drinking vessel with two or more handles; *esp* : one given as a prize or trophy

lov·ing–kind·ness \ˌləv-ing-'kīnd-nəs, -'kīn-\ *n* : tender and benevolent affection

[1]**low** \'lō\ *vi* : to utter a low or a similar sound [Old English *hlōwan*]

[2]**low** *n* : the characteristic deep sustained sound of a cow

[3]**low** \'lō\ *adj* **low·er** \'lō-ər, 'lōr\; **low·est** \'lō-əst\ **1 a** : not high or tall ⟨a *low* wall⟩ ⟨a *low* bridge⟩ **b** : having a low-cut neckline **2 a** : situated or passing below the normal level, surface, or base of measurement ⟨*low* ground⟩ **b** : marking a bottom ⟨the *low* point of a career⟩ **3** : PROSTRATE ⟨laid *low* by the flu⟩ **4** : not loud : SOFT; *also* : FLAT 10a **5 a** : being near the equator ⟨*low* latitudes⟩ **b** : being near the horizon ⟨the sun is *low*⟩ **6** : humble in status ⟨*low* birth⟩ **7 a** : lacking strength, health, or vitality **b** : lacking spirit or vivacity : DEPRESSED **8 a** : of lesser degree, size, or amount than average or ordinary ⟨*low* pressure⟩ **b** : less than usual in number, amount, or value ⟨a *low* price⟩ **9** : falling short of some standard: as **a** : lacking dignity or elevation ⟨a *low* style of writing⟩ **b** : morally reprehensible : BASE ⟨a *low* trick⟩ **c** : COARSE 3, VULGAR ⟨*low* language⟩ **10** : not advanced in complexity, development, or elaboration ⟨*low* organisms⟩ **11** : UNFAVORABLE a, DISPARAGING ⟨had a *low* opinion of it⟩ **12** : pronounced with a wide opening between the relatively flat tongue and the palate ⟨the *low* vowel \ä\⟩ [Old Norse *lāgr*] — **low** *adv* — **low·ness** *n*

[4]**low** *n* **1** : something that is low; *esp* : a region of low barometric pressure **2** : the arrangement of gears (as of an automobile) in a position to transmit the greatest power from the engine to the propeller shaft

low beam *n* : a vehicle headlight beam with a short-range focus for short distances

low blood pressure *n* : blood pressure that is abnormally low especially in the arteries — called also *hypotension*

low·born \'lō-'bȯrn\ *adj* : born in a low condition or rank

low·boy \'lō-ˌbȯi\ *n* : a chest of drawers about three feet (one meter) high with long legs

lowboy

low·bred \'lō-'bred\ *adj* : RUDE 2, VULGAR

low·brow \'lō-ˌbrau̇\ *adj* : of, relating to, or suitable for a person with little taste or intellectual interest — **lowbrow** *n*

Low Church *adj* : tending especially in Anglican worship to minimize the priesthood, sacraments, and formal rites and often to emphasize evangelical principles — compare HIGH CHURCH

low–density lipoprotein *n* : LDL

low·down \-ˌdau̇n\ *n* : information especially from a reliable or inside source

low–down \'lō-'dau̇n\ *adj* **1** : CONTEMPTIBLE, DESPICABLE **2** : deeply emotional ⟨*low-down* blues⟩

[1]**low·er** *also* **lour** \'lau̇-ər, 'lau̇r\ *vi* **1** : to look sullen : FROWN **2** : to become dark, gloomy, and threatening [Middle English *louren*]

[2]**lower** *also* **lour** *n* : a lowering look : FROWN

[3]**low·er** \'lō-ər, 'lōr\ *adj* **1** : relatively low in position, rank, or order ⟨a *lower* court⟩ **2** : less advanced in the scale of evolutionary development ⟨*lower* animals⟩ **3** : constituting the popular and more representative branch of a bicameral legislative body **4 a** : situated or held to be situated beneath the earth's surface **b** *cap* : of, relating to, or constituting an earlier geologic period or formation **5** : SOUTHERN 2 ⟨*lower* New York State⟩

[4]**low·er** \'lō-ər, 'lōr\ *vb* **1** : to move down : DROP; *also* : DIMINISH **2 a** : to let descend by its own weight **b** : to make the aim lower **c** : to reduce the height of **3 a** : to reduce in value or amount ⟨*lower* the price⟩ **b** (1) : to bring down : DEGRADE (2) : ABASE, HUMBLE **c** : to reduce the objective of — **lower the boom** : to deal a crushing blow or punishment

low·er·case \ˌlō-ər-'kās, ˌlōr-\ *adj* : being a letter that belongs to or conforms to the series a, b, c, etc. rather than A, B, C, etc. [from the printer's practice of keeping such letters in the lower of a pair of type cases] — **lowercase** *n*

lower class *n* : a social class occupying a position below the middle class and having the lowest status in a society

low·er·ing *also* **lour·ing** \'lau̇-ring, -ə-ring\ *adj* : dark and threatening : GLOOMY

low·er·most \'lō-ər-ˌmōst, 'lōr-\ *adj* : LOWEST

low·ery *also* **loury** \'lau̇-rē, -ə-rē\ *adj* : GLOOMY 1, LOWERING ⟨a *lowery* sky⟩

lowest common denominator *n* : LEAST COMMON DENOMINATOR

lowest common multiple *n* : LEAST COMMON MULTIPLE

lowest terms *n pl* : the form of a fraction in which the numerator and denominator have no factor in common except 1

low frequency *n* : a radio frequency in the range between 30 and 300 kilohertz — abbreviation *LF*

Low German *n* **1** : the German dialects of northern Germany

\ə\ abut	\au̇\ out	\i\ tip	\ȯ\ saw	\u̇\ foot
\ər\ further	\ch\ chin	\ī\ life	\ȯi\ coin	\y\ yet
\a\ mat	\e\ pet	\j\ job	\th\ thin	\yü\ few
\ā\ take	\ē\ easy	\ng\ sing	\th\ this	\yu̇\ cure
\ä\ cot, cart	\g\ go	\ō\ bone	\ü\ food	\zh\ vision

especially since the end of the medieval period **2 :** the West Germanic languages other than High German

low–grade \ˈlō-ˈgrād\ *adj* **1 :** of inferior grade or quality **2 :** being near that extreme of a specified range which is lowest, least intense, or least favorable ⟨a *low-grade* fever⟩

low–key \ˈlō-ˈkē\ *also* **low–keyed** \-ˈkēd\ *adj* **:** of low intensity **:** RESTRAINED

low·land \ˈlō-lənd, -ˌland\ *n* **:** low and usually level country — **lowland** *adj*

low·land·er \-lən-dər, -ˌlan-\ *n* **1** *cap* **:** an inhabitant of the Lowlands of Scotland **2 :** a native or inhabitant of a lowland region

low–lev·el \ˈlō-ˈlev-əl\ *adj* **1 :** occurring, done, or placed at a low level **2 :** being of low importance or rank ⟨a *low-level* job⟩ **3 :** being or relating to nuclear waste of relatively low radioactivity ⟨*low-level* waste⟩

[1]low·ly \ˈlō-lē\ *adv* **1 :** in a humble or meek manner **2 :** in a low position, manner, or degree **3 :** not loudly

[2]lowly *adj* **low·li·er; -est 1 :** HUMBLE 1, MEEK **2 :** of or relating to a low social or economic rank **3 :** LOW 10 ⟨*lowly* organisms like the amoeba⟩ **4 :** ranking low in some hierarchy — **low·li·ness** *n*

low–ly·ing \ˈlō-ˈlī-ŋ\ *adj* **:** having little upward extension or elevation ⟨*low-lying* clouds⟩

low mass *n, often cap L&M* **:** a mass that is said in the simplest ceremonial form — compare HIGH MASS

low–mind·ed \ˈlō-ˈmīn-dəd\ *adj* **:** inclined mentally to vulgar or unworthy things — **low–mind·ed·ly** *adv* — **low–mind·ed·ness** *n*

low–pres·sure \ˈlō-ˈpresh-ər\ *adj* **1 a :** having, exerting, or operating under a relatively small pressure **b :** having or resulting from a low atmospheric pressure **2 :** EASYGOING

low relief *n* **:** BAS-RELIEF

low–spir·it·ed \ˈlō-ˈspir-ət-əd\ *adj* **:** DEJECTED, DEPRESSED — **low–spir·it·ed·ly** *adv* — **low–spir·it·ed·ness** *n*

low tide *n* **:** the tide when the water is at its farthest ebb

[1]lox \ˈläks\ *n* **:** liquid oxygen [*l*iquid *ox*ygen]

[2]lox *n, pl* **lox** *or* **lox·es :** salmon that has been cured in brine and sometimes smoked [Yiddish *laks,* from Middle High German *lahs* "salmon"]

loy·al \ˈlȯi-əl, ˈlȯil\ *adj* **1 a :** faithful in allegiance to one's lawful government **b :** faithful to a private person to whom fidelity is due **2 :** faithful to a cause or ideal [Middle French, from Medieval French *leial,* from Latin *legalis* "legal"] ***synonyms*** see FAITHFUL — **loy·al·ly** \ˈlȯi-ə-lē\ *adv*

loy·al·ist \ˈlȯi-ə-ləst\ *n* **:** one who is loyal to a political cause, party, government, or sovereign; *esp* **:** TORY 2

loy·al·ty \ˈlȯi-əl-tē, ˈlȯil-\ *n, pl* **-ties :** the quality or state of being loyal ***synonyms*** see FIDELITY

loz·enge \ˈläz-nj\ *n* **1 a :** a diamond-shaped figure **b :** something shaped like a lozenge **2 :** a small often medicated candy [Medieval French]

LP \ˈel-ˈpē\ *n* **:** a phonograph record designed to be played at 33⅓ revolutions per minute [*l*ong-*p*laying]

LPN \ˌel-ˌpē-ˈen\ *n* **:** LICENSED PRACTICAL NURSE

LSD \ˌel-ˌes-ˈdē\ *n* **:** an illegal compound $C_{20}H_{25}N_3O$ derived from ergot that induces altered perceptions of reality (as of time or space), abnormal sensations, intense and changeable emotional states, and hallucinations, that may also produce delusions or paranoia, and that may sometimes cause panic in response to the effects experienced [German *Lysergsäure-Diäthylamid* "lysergic acid diethylamide"]

lu·au \ˈlü-ˌau̇\ *n* **:** a Hawaiian feast [Hawaiian *lu'au*]

lub·ber \ˈləb-ər\ *n* **1 :** a big clumsy fellow **2 :** an unskilled seaman [Middle English *lobre, lobur*] — **lub·ber·li·ness** \-lē-nəs\ *n* — **lub·ber·ly** \-lē\ *adj or adv*

lube \ˈlüb\ *n* **:** LUBRICANT

lu·bri·cant \ˈlü-bri-kənt\ *n* **:** something (as a grease or oil) capable of reducing friction when applied between moving parts — **lubricant** *adj*

lu·bri·cate \ˈlü-brə-ˌkāt\ *vb* **1 :** to make smooth or slippery **2 :** to apply a lubricant to ⟨*lubricate* a car⟩ **3 :** to act as a lubricant [Latin *lubricare,* from *lubricus* "slippery"] — **lu·bri·ca·tion** \ˌlü-brə-ˈkā-shən\ *n* — **lu·bri·ca·tive** \ˈlü-brə-ˌkāt-iv\ *adj* — **lu·bri·ca·tor** \-ˌkāt-ər\ *n*

lu·bri·cious \lü-ˈbrish-əs\ *or* **lu·bri·cous** \ˈlü-bri-kəs\ *adj* **1 :** LECHEROUS; *also* **:** SALACIOUS 1 **2 :** smooth or slippery in texture ⟨a *lubricious* skin⟩ [Latin *lubricus* "slippery, easily led astray"] — **lu·bri·cious·ly** *adv*

lu·bric·i·ty \lü-ˈbris-ət-ē\ *n, pl* **-ties :** the property or state of being lubricious; *also* **:** the capacity for reducing friction

lu·cent \ˈlüs-nt\ *adj* **1 :** glowing with light **:** LUMINOUS **2 :** marked by clearness or translucence [Latin *lucens,* present participle of *lucēre* "to shine"] — **lu·cent·ly** *adv*

lu·cerne *also* **lu·cern** \lü-ˈsərn\ *n, chiefly British* **:** ALFALFA [French *luzerne,* from Occitan *luserno*]

lu·cid \ˈlü-səd\ *adj* **1 a :** suffused with light **:** LUMINOUS **b :** penetrated with light **:** TRANSLUCENT ⟨snorkeling in the *lucid* sea⟩ **2 :** having full use of one's faculties **:** clear in mind **3 :** clear to the understanding **:** PLAIN ⟨*lucid* prose⟩ [Latin *lucidus*] — **lu·cid·i·ty** \lü-ˈsid-ət-ē\ *n* — **lu·cid·ly** *adv* — **lu·cid·ness** *n*

Lu·ci·fer \ˈlü-sə-fər\ *n* **:** DEVIL 1 [Old English, the morning star, a fallen angel, the Devil, from Latin, the morning star, from *lucifer* "light-bearing," from *luc-, lux* "light" + *-fer* "-ferous"]

Word History *Lucifer,* "bearer of light," is a strange name for the Devil. Latin *Lucifer* (from *lux,* "light," and *ferre,* "to carry") was the name of the chief morning star (the planet Venus), which heralds, if it does not exactly carry in, the dawn. In telling about the fall of Babylon, the Prophet Isaiah compares the king of Babylon to the morning star: "How art thou fallen from Heaven, O Lucifer, son of the morning!" (Isaiah 14:12). Later, Christians interpreted Isaiah's description of the downfall of Babylon as an allegory for the fall from heaven of the rebel archangel Satan. *Lucifer,* they concluded, must have been the Devil's original name.

lu·cif·er·ase \lü-ˈsif-ə-ˌrās\ *n* **:** an enzyme that catalyzes the oxidation of luciferin

lu·cif·er·in \lü-ˈsif-ə-rən\ *n* **:** a substance of luminescent organisms (as fireflies) that upon oxidation produces practically heatless light [Latin *lucifer* "light-bearing"]

Lu·cite \ˈlü-ˌsīt\ *trademark* — used for an acrylic resin or plastic consisting essentially of methacrylate

luck \ˈlək\ *n* **1 :** whatever happens to a person apparently by chance **:** FORTUNE ⟨we had a run of good *luck*⟩ **2 :** the accidental way events occur ⟨happening by pure *luck*⟩ **3 :** good fortune **:** SUCCESS ⟨out of *luck*⟩ [Dutch *luc*] — **luck·less** \ˈlək-ləs\ *adj*

lucky \ˈlək-ē\ *adj* **luck·i·er; -est 1 :** favored by luck **:** FORTUNATE **2 :** producing or resulting in good by chance ⟨a *lucky* hit⟩ **3 :** seeming to bring good luck ⟨a *lucky* coin⟩ — **luck·i·ly** \ˈlək-ə-lē\ *adv* — **luck·i·ness** \ˈlək-ē-nəs\ *n*

synonyms LUCKY, FORTUNATE, HAPPY mean meeting with unforeseen success. LUCKY stresses the operation of pure chance in producing a favorable result ⟨won because of a *lucky* bounce⟩. FORTUNATE suggests being rewarded beyond what one strictly deserves or succeeding beyond reasonable expectation ⟨*fortunate* in my investments⟩. HAPPY stresses good fortune and the resulting joy ⟨a series of *happy* accidents⟩.

lu·cra·tive \ˈlü-krət-iv\ *adj* **:** producing wealth **:** PROFITABLE ⟨invested in a *lucrative* business⟩ — **lu·cra·tive·ly** *adv* — **lu·cra·tive·ness** *n*

lu·cre \ˈlü-kər\ *n* **:** monetary gain **:** PROFIT; *also* **:** MONEY 1 [Latin *lucrum*]

lu·cu·bra·tion \ˌlü-kyə-ˈbrā-shən, -kə-\ *n* **1 :** laborious study **:** MEDITATION **2 :** studied or pretentious expression in speech or writing [Latin *lucubratio* "study by night," from *lucubrare* "to work by lamplight"]

lu·di·crous \ˈlüd-ə-krəs\ *adj* **1 :** amusing or laughable through obvious absurdity or incongruity **2 :** deserving scorn as absurdly inept, false, or foolish [Latin *ludicrus,* from *ludus* "play, sport"] ***synonyms*** see LAUGHABLE — **lu·di·crous·ly** *adv* — **lu·di·crous·ness** *n*

lu·es \ˈlü-ˌēz\ *n, pl* **lues :** SYPHILIS [Latin, "plague"] — **lu·et·ic** \lü-ˈet-ik\ *adj*

[1]luff \ˈləf\ *n* **1 :** the act of turning a sailing vessel's head into the wind **2 :** the forward edge of a fore-and-aft sail [Medieval French *lof* "weather side of a ship"]

[2]luff *vi* **:** to turn the head of a sailing vessel into the wind

luffa *variant of* LOOFAH

[1]lug \ˈləg\ *vb* **lugged; lug·ging 1 :** DRAG 1a, PULL **2 :** to carry laboriously **3 :** to introduce in a forced manner ⟨*lug* a story into the conversation⟩ [Middle English *luggen* "to pull by the hair or ear, drag"]

[2]lug *n* **1 :** a part (as a handle) that projects like an ear **2 :** a nut used to secure a wheel on an automotive vehicle **3 a :** a big clumsy fellow **b** : an ordinary commonplace person [Middle English *lugge*]

lug·gage \ˈlə-gij\ *n* : something that is lugged; *esp* : suitcases for a traveler's belongings : BAGGAGE

lug·ger \ˈlə-gər\ *n* : a boat that carries one or more lugsails

lugger

Lu·gol's solution \ˈlü-ˌgȯlz-, -ˌgälz-\ *n* : any of several deep brown solutions of iodine and potassium in water or alcohol that are used in medicine and as microscopic stains — called also *Lugol's iodine solution* [J.G.A. *Lugol,* died 1851, French physician]

lug·sail \ˈləg-ˌsāl, -səl\ *n* : a 4-sided sail fastened at the top to a yard that hangs at a slant and is hoisted and lowered with the sail [perhaps from [2]*lug*]

lu·gu·bri·ous \lu̇-ˈgü-brē-əs, -ˈgyü-\ *adj* : MOURNFUL; *esp* : overly or affectedly mournful [Latin *lugubris,* from *lugēre* "to mourn"] — **lu·gu·bri·ous·ly** *adv* — **lu·gu·bri·ous·ness** *n*

lug·worm \ˈləg-ˌwərm\ *n* : any of a genus of marine annelid worms that have a row of tufted gills along each side of the back and are used for bait [origin unknown]

Luke \ˈlük\ *n* : the third Gospel in the New Testament — see BIBLE table

luke·warm \ˈlü-ˈkwȯrm\ *adj* **1** : neither hot nor cold : TEPID ⟨a *lukewarm* bath⟩ **2** : not enthusiastic : HALFHEARTED ⟨received a *lukewarm* reception⟩ [Middle English, from *luke* "lukewarm" + *warm*] — **luke·warm·ly** *adv* — **luke·warm·ness** *n*

[1]lull \ˈləl\ *vt* **1** : to cause to sleep or rest : SOOTHE **2** : to cause to relax vigilance ⟨were *lulled* into a false sense of security⟩ [Middle English *lullen;* probably of imitative origin]

[2]lull *n* **1** : a temporary calm before or during a storm **2** : a temporary drop in activity

lul·la·by \ˈlə-lə-ˌbī\ *n, pl* **-bies** : a song to quiet children or lull them to sleep [Middle English *lulla,* interj. used to lull a child + *by,* interj. used to lull a child]

lum·ba·go \ˌləm-ˈbā-gō\ *n* : pain (as that caused by muscle strain) in the lower back [Latin, from *lumbus* "loin"]

lum·bar \ˈləm-bər, -ˌbär\ *adj* : of, relating to, or adjacent to the loins or the vertebrae between the thoracic vertebrae and sacrum ⟨*lumbar* region⟩ [Latin *lumbus* "loin"]

[1]lum·ber \ˈləm-bər\ *vi* **lum·bered; lum·ber·ing** \-bə-riŋ, -briŋ\ **1** : to move heavily or clumsily **2** : RUMBLE 1 [Middle English *lomeren*]

[2]lumber *n* **1** : surplus or disused articles (as furniture) that are stored away **2** : timber or logs especially when sawed up for use [perhaps from earlier *Lombard* "moneylender" (from the prominence of Lombards as moneylenders); from the use of pawnshops as storehouses of disused property] — **lumber** *adj*

[3]lumber *vb* **lum·bered; lum·ber·ing** \-bə-riŋ, -briŋ\ **1** : to clutter with or as if with lumber : ENCUMBER **2** : to heap together in disorder **3** : to cut timber or saw logs into lumber — **lum·ber·er** \-bər-ər\ *n*

lum·ber·jack \ˈləm-bər-ˌjak\ *n* : LOGGER

lum·ber·man \-mən\ *n* : a person who is engaged in or oversees the business of cutting, processing, and marketing lumber

lum·ber·yard \-ˌyärd\ *n* : a place where a stock of lumber is kept for sale

lu·men \ˈlü-mən\ *n, pl* **lumens** *also* **lu·mi·na** \-mə-nə\ **1** : the cavity or bore of a tube or tubular organ ⟨the *lumen* of a blood vessel⟩ ⟨the *lumen* of a catheter⟩ **2** : a unit of luminous flux equal to the light on a unit surface all points of which are at a unit distance from a uniform point source of one candle [Latin, "light, air shaft, opening"] — **lu·mi·nal** \ˈlü-mən-l\ *adj*

lumin- *or* **lumini-** *combining form* : light ⟨*lumini*ferous⟩ [Latin *lumin-, lumen*]

lu·mi·naire \ˌlü-mə-ˈnaər, -ˈneər\ *n* : a complete lighting unit (as for a streetlight) [French, "lamp, lighting"]

lu·mi·nance \ˈlü-mə-nəns\ *n* : luminous intensity (as of a surface)

lu·mi·nary \ˈlü-mə-ˌner-ē\ *n, pl* **-nar·ies** **1** : a source of light; *esp* : one of the celestial bodies **2** : a very famous and distinguished person — **luminary** *adj*

lu·mi·nes·cence \ˌlü-mə-ˈnes-ns\ *n* : emission of light at low temperatures as a by-product of a physiological, chemical, or electrical process; *also* : such light — **lu·mi·nesce** \-ˈnes\ *vi*

lu·mi·nes·cent \-ˈnes-nt\ *adj* : relating to, exhibiting, or adapted for the production of luminescence ⟨*luminescent* paint⟩

lu·mi·nif·er·ous \ˌlü-mə-ˈnif-rəs, -ə-rəs\ *adj* : transmitting, producing, or yielding light

lu·mi·nos·i·ty \ˌlü-mə-ˈnäs-ət-ē\ *n, pl* **-ties** **1** : the quality or state of being luminous : BRIGHTNESS **2** : something luminous

lu·mi·nous \ˈlü-mə-nəs\ *adj* **1** : emitting light : SHINING **2** : bathed in or exposed to steady light ⟨a plaza *luminous* with sunlight⟩ **3** : CLEAR 3c, INTELLIGIBLE ⟨a *luminous* poem⟩ — **lu·mi·nous·ly** *adv* — **lu·mi·nous·ness** *n*

luminous flux *n* : radiant flux in the visible-wavelength range

lum·mox \ˈləm-əks\ *n* : a clumsy person [origin unknown]

[1]lump \ˈləmp\ *n* **1** : a piece or mass of indefinite size or shape **2** : AGGREGATE, TOTALITY ⟨taken in the *lump*⟩ **3** : an abnormal swelling or growth **4** : a person who is heavy and awkward; *esp* : one who is stupid or dull **5** *pl* : DEFEAT 2b, LOSS [Middle English] — **lump in one's throat** : a constriction of the throat caused by emotion

[2]lump *vb* **1** : to group without discrimination **2** : to make into lumps **3** : to become formed into lumps

[3]lump *adj* : not divided into parts : ENTIRE ⟨a *lump* sum⟩

[4]lump *vt* : to put up with ⟨like it or *lump* it⟩ [origin unknown]

lump·ish \ˈləm-pish\ *adj* **1** : DULL 3, SLUGGISH **2** : CLUMSY 1a, UNGAINLY — **lump·ish·ly** *adv* — **lump·ish·ness** *n*

lumpy \ˈləm-pē\ *adj* **lump·i·er; -est** **1** : filled or covered with lumps **2** : having a heavy clumsy appearance — **lump·i·ly** \-pə-lē\ *adv* — **lump·i·ness** \-pē-nəs\ *n*

lu·na·cy \ˈlü-nə-sē\ *n, pl* **-cies** **1** : insanity especially interrupted by lucid intervals **2** : extreme foolishness [*lunatic*]

lu·na moth \ˌlü-nə-\ *n* : a large mostly pale green American moth with long tails on the hind wings [Latin *luna* "moon"]

lu·nar \ˈlü-nər\ *adj* **1** : of, relating to, or resembling the moon ⟨*lunar* craters⟩ ⟨a *lunar* landscape⟩ **2** : measured by the moon's revolution ⟨*lunar* month⟩ [Latin *lunaris,* from *luna* "moon"]

lunar caustic *n* : silver nitrate molded into sticks for use as a caustic

lunar eclipse *n* : an eclipse in which the moon passes partially or wholly through the umbra of the earth's shadow

lunar module *n* : a space vehicle module designed to carry astronauts from the command module to the surface of the moon and back — called also *lunar excursion module*

lu·nate \ˈlü-ˌnāt\ *adj* : shaped like a crescent

lu·na·tic \ˈlü-nə-ˌtik\ *adj* **1 a** : affected with lunacy : INSANE **b** : designed for insane persons ⟨*lunatic* asylum⟩ **2** : wildly foolish or reckless ⟨a *lunatic* idea⟩ [Late Latin *lunaticus,* from Latin *luna* "moon"; from the belief that lunacy fluctuated with the phases of the moon] — **lunatic** *n*

lunatic fringe *n* : the members of a political or social movement advocating extreme, eccentric, or fanatical views

lunch \ˈlənch\ *n* **1** : a light meal; *esp* : one eaten in the middle of the day **2** : the food prepared for a lunch [probably short for *luncheon*] — **lunch** *vb* — **lunch·er** *n* — **out to lunch** *slang* : out of touch with reality

lun·cheon \ˈlən-chən\ *n* : a light meal at midday; *esp* : a formal lunch [perhaps alteration of *nuncheon* "light snack," from Middle English *noneschench* "midday refreshment," literally, "noon drink," from *none* "noon" + *schench* "drink, cup"]

lun·cheon·ette \ˌlən-chə-ˈnet\ *n* : a place where light lunches are sold

lunch·room \ˈlənch-ˌrüm, -ˌru̇m\ *n* **1** : LUNCHEONETTE **2** : a room (as in a school) where lunches supplied on the premises or brought from home may be eaten

lune \ˈlün\ *n* : a crescent-shaped figure on a flat surface or a sphere formed by two intersecting arcs of circles [Latin *luna* "moon"]

lung \ˈləŋ\ *n* **1 a** : one of the usually paired thoracic organs that form the special breathing apparatus of air-breathing vertebrates **b** : any of various other respiratory organs of invertebrates **2 :** a device (as an iron lung) to promote and facilitate breathing [Old English *lungen*]

1lunge \ˈlənj\ *n* **1 :** a quick thrust or jab (as of a sword) usually made by leaning or striding forward **2 :** a sudden forward rush or reach ⟨made a *lunge* to catch the ball⟩ [modification of French *allonge* "extension, reach," from Medieval French *alongier* "to lengthen," derived from Latin *longus* "long"]

2lunge *vb* **1 :** to make or move with or as if with a lunge **2 :** to thrust or propel (as a blow) in a lunge

1lung·er \ˈlən-jər\ *n* **:** one that lunges

2lung·er \ˈləng-ər\ *n* **:** one suffering from a chronic disease of the lungs; *esp* **:** a tubercular person

lung·fish \ˈləng-ˌfish\ *n* **:** any of an order (Dipnoi) of fishes that breathe by a modified air bladder as well as gills

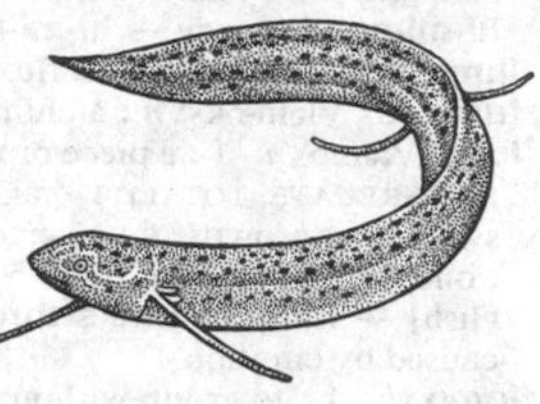

lungfish

lung·wort \ˈləng-ˌwərt, -ˌwȯrt\ *n* **:** a European herb that is related to the forget-me-not, has bristly leaves and bluish flowers, and was formerly used in the treatment of respiratory diseases

lunk·head \ˈləngk-ˌhed\ *n* **:** a dull-witted person **:** DOLT [*lunk,* probably alteration of *lump*] — **lunk·head·ed** \-ˈhed-əd\ *adj*

lu·nule \ˈlü-nyül\ *n* **:** a crescent-shaped body part or marking; *esp* **:** the whitish mark at the base of a fingernail [Latin *lunula* "crescent-shaped ornament," from *luna* "moon"]

Lu·per·ca·lia \ˌlü-pər-ˈkā-lē-ə\ *n* **:** an ancient Roman festival celebrated February 15 to ensure fertility for the people, fields, and flocks [Latin, from *Lupercus,* god of flocks] — **Lu·per·ca·li·an** \-lē-ən\ *adj*

1lu·pine *also* **lu·pin** \ˈlü-pən\ *n* **:** any of a genus of herbs of the legume family some of which are poisonous and others grown for their showy spikes of colorful flowers or for green manure, fodder, or their edible seeds [Latin *lupinus, lupinum,* from *lupinus* "of wolves," from *lupus* "wolf"]

2lu·pine \ˈlü-ˌpīn\ *adj* **:** of, relating to, or befitting or characteristic of wolves

lu·pus \ˈlü-pəs\ *n* **:** any of several diseases marked by skin lesions [Medieval Latin, from Latin, "wolf"]

1lurch \ˈlərch\ *n* **:** a decisive defeat (as in cribbage) in which an opponent wins a game by more than double the defeated player's score [Middle French *lourche* "defeated by a lurch, deceived"] — **in the lurch :** in a helpless or unsupported position ⟨left them *in the lurch*⟩

2lurch *n* **:** a sudden jerking, swaying, or tipping movement ⟨the car gave a *lurch*⟩; *also* **:** a staggering gait [origin unknown]

3lurch *vi* **1 :** to roll or tip abruptly **:** PITCH **2 :** to move with a lurch ⟨suddenly *lurched* forward⟩; *also* **:** STAGGER 1

lurch·er \ˈlər-chər\ *n, British* **:** a mongrel dog; *esp* **:** one used by poachers [Middle English *lorchen* "to prowl, steal," probably an alteration of *lurken* "to lurk"]

1lure \ˈlu̇r\ *n* **1 a :** an inducement to pleasure or gain **:** ENTICEMENT **b :** APPEAL 3, ATTRACTION **2 :** a decoy for attracting animals to capture; *esp* **:** an artificial bait used for catching fish [Medieval French *lure, leure,* a device used by a falconer to recall a hawk, of Germanic origin]

2lure *vt* **:** to tempt with a promise of pleasure or gain **:** ENTICE — **lur·er** *n*

synonyms LURE, ENTICE, DECOY, TEMPT, SEDUCE mean to lead astray from one's true or usual course. LURE implies an attraction that may be harmless ⟨the resort *lured* skiers from around the world⟩ or may suggest a drawing into danger, evil, or difficulty through deception ⟨*lured* naive investors with get-rich-quick schemes⟩. ENTICE suggests luring by artful or clever means ⟨advertising designed to *entice* new customers⟩. DECOY implies luring and trapping by trickery or false appearances ⟨attempting to *decoy* the enemy into an ambush⟩. TEMPT implies arousing a desire that may be contrary to one's conscience or better judgment ⟨*tempted* by the offer of more money⟩. SEDUCE implies leading astray especially from a proper or responsible course by persuasion or false promises ⟨was *seduced* into breaking the law⟩.

lu·rid \ˈlu̇r-əd\ *adj* **1 a :** causing horror or revulsion **:** GRUESOME ⟨*lurid* tales of murder⟩ **b :** SENSATIONAL 2 ⟨*lurid* magazine covers⟩ **2 :** ghastly pale **:** WAN, LIVID **3 :** shining with the red glow of fire seen through smoke [Latin *luridus* "pale yellow, sallow"] ***synonyms*** see GHASTLY — **lu·rid·ly** *adv* — **lu·rid·ness** *n*

lurk \ˈlərk\ *vi* **1 a :** to lie in ambush **b :** to move furtively or inconspicuously **:** SNEAK **c :** to persist in staying **2 :** to be present but unseen or unrecognized ⟨a *lurking* danger⟩ [Middle English *lurken*] — **lurk·er** *n*

lus·cious \ˈləsh-əs\ *adj* **1 :** having a delicious taste or smell ⟨*luscious* berries⟩ **2 :** having sensual appeal **:** SEDUCTIVE **3 :** richly luxurious or appealing to the senses; *also* **:** overly ornate [Middle English *lucius,* perhaps an alteration of *licius,* short for *delicious*] — **lus·cious·ly** *adv* — **lus·cious·ness** *n*

1lush \ˈləsh\ *adj* **1 :** producing or covered with luxuriant growth ⟨*lush* grass⟩ ⟨*lush* pastures⟩ **2 a :** doing well **:** VIGOROUS **b :** characterized by abundance **:** PLENTIFUL **3 a :** DELECTABLE 1, DELIGHTFUL **b :** SUMPTUOUS, OPULENT [Middle English *lusch* "soft, tender"] — **lush·ly** *adv* — **lush·ness** *n*

2lush *n* **1** *slang* **:** intoxicating liquor **:** DRINK **2 :** a habitual heavy drinker **:** DRUNKARD [origin unknown]

1lust \ˈləst\ *n* **1 :** usually intense sexual desire **2 :** an intense longing **:** CRAVING [Old English, "pleasure, delight, lust"]

2lust *vi* **:** to have an intense desire or need **:** CRAVE; *esp* **:** to have sexual desire

lus·ter *or* **lus·tre** \ˈləs-tər\ *n* **1 :** a shine or sheen especially from reflected light **:** GLOSS; *esp* **:** the appearance of the surface of a mineral with respect to its reflecting qualities ⟨a pearly *luster*⟩ **2 :** inner beauty **:** RADIANCE **3 :** GLORY 1a, SPLENDOR ⟨the *luster* of a famous name⟩ [Middle French *lustre,* from Italian *lustro,* from *lustrare* "to brighten," from Latin, "to purify ceremonially," from *lustrum* "a purification of the ancient Roman people made after the census every five years"] — **lus·ter·less** \-tər-ləs\ *adj*

lus·ter·ware \-ˌwaər, -ˌweər\ *n* **:** pottery decorated by applying to the glaze metallic compounds which become iridescent metallic films in the process of firing

lust·ful \ˈləst-fəl\ *adj* **:** excited by lust; *esp* **:** LECHEROUS — **lust·ful·ly** \-fə-lē\ *adv* — **lust·ful·ness** *n*

lus·trous \ˈləs-trəs\ *adj* **1 :** having a high gloss or shine **2 :** radiant in character or reputation **:** ILLUSTRIOUS — **lus·trous·ly** *adv* — **lus·trous·ness** *n*

lus·trum \ˈləs-trəm\ *n, pl* **lustrums** *or* **lus·tra** \-trə\ **1 a :** a purification of the ancient Roman people made after the census every five years **b :** the Roman census **2 :** a period of five years [Latin]

lusty \ˈləs-tē\ *adj* **lust·i·er; -est :** full of vitality **:** VIGOROUS — **lust·i·ly** \-tə-lē\ *adv* — **lust·i·ness** \-tē-nəs\ *n*

1lute \ˈlüt\ *n* **:** a stringed instrument with a large pear-shaped body, a neck with a fretted fingerboard, and a head with pegs for tuning [Medieval French *lut,* from Old Occitan *laut,* from Arabic *al-ʿūd,* literally, "the wood"]

2lute *n* **:** material (as cement or clay) for packing a joint or coating a porous surface to make it impervious to fluid [Latin *lutum* "mud"]

3lute *vt* **:** to seal or cover with lute ⟨*lute* a joint⟩

lu·te·al \ˈlüt-ē-əl\ *adj* **:** of, relating to, or involving the corpus luteum

lu·tein·iz·ing hormone \ˈlüt-ē-ə-ˌnīz-ing-, ˈlü-ˌtēn-ˌīz-\ *n* **:** a hormone secreted by the pituitary gland that in the female stimulates ovulation and the development of the corpora lutea and in the male stimulates production of testosterone by certain cells in the testis

lu·te·nist *or* **lu·ta·nist** \ˈlüt-n-əst, ˈlüt-nəst\ *n* **:** one who plays the lute [Medieval Latin *lutanista,* from *lutana* "lute," probably from Medieval French *lut*]

lu·teo·tro·pic hormone \ˌlüt-ē-ə-ˌtrō-pik-, -ˌträp-ik-\ *or* **lu·teo·tro·phic hormone** \-ˌtrō-fik-, -ˌträf-ik-\ *n* **:** PROLACTIN [*lute-* (as in *corpus luteum*) + Greek *trophē* "nourishment"]

lu·te·tium \lü-ˈtē-shē-əm, -shəm\ *n* **:** a soft metallic chemical element — see ELEMENT table [New Latin, from Latin *Lutetia,* ancient name of Paris]

1Lu·ther·an \ˈlü-thə-rən, -thrən\ *n* **:** a member of a Lutheran church

2Lutheran *adj* **1 :** of or relating to Martin Luther or his religious doctrines **2 :** of or relating to the Protestant churches adhering to Lutheran doctrines, liturgy, or polity — **Lu·ther·an·ism** \-ˌiz-əm\ *n*

lutz \ˈləts\ *n* **:** a backward figure-skating jump with a takeoff from the outside edge of one skate followed by a full turn in the air and a landing on the outside edge of the other skate [probably from Gustave *Lussi,* died 1993, Swiss-born American figure-skating coach]

lux \ˈləks\ *n, pl* **lux** *or* **lux·es** : a unit of illumination equal to one lumen per square meter [Latin, "light"]

lux·u·ri·ant \ləg-ˈzhu̇r-ē-ənt, ˌləg-; lək-ˈshu̇r-, ˌlək-\ *adj* **1 a** : yielding abundantly : PRODUCTIVE **b** : characterized by abundant growth : LUSH ⟨*luxuriant* vegetation⟩ **2 a** : exuberantly rich and varied : PROFUSE **b** : excessively elaborate : FLORID **3** : LUXURIOUS 3 ⟨*luxuriant* fabric⟩ — **lux·u·ri·ance** \-əns\ *n* — **lux·u·ri·ant·ly** *adv*

lux·u·ri·ate \-ē-ˌāt\ *vi* **1** : to grow profusely : PROLIFERATE **2** : to indulge oneself luxuriously : REVEL

lux·u·ri·ous \ləg-ˈzhu̇r-ē-əs, ˌləg-; lək-ˈshu̇r-, ˌlək-\ *adj* **1** : marked by or given to self-indulgence ⟨*luxurious* tastes⟩ **2** : of, relating to, or marked by luxury ⟨*luxurious* accommodations⟩ **3** : of the finest and richest kind ⟨*luxurious* silks⟩ — **lux·u·ri·ous·ly** *adv* — **lux·u·ri·ous·ness** *n*

lux·u·ry \ˈləksh-rē, ˈləgzh-, -ə-rē\ *n, pl* **-ries** **1** : a condition of abundance or great ease and comfort : sumptuous environment ⟨lived in *luxury*⟩ **2 a** : something adding to pleasure or comfort but not absolutely necessary ⟨one of life's *luxuries*⟩ **b** : an indulgence in something that provides pleasure, satisfaction, or ease [Medieval French *luxorie,* from Latin *luxuria* "rankness, luxury, excess"] — **luxury** *adj*

luxury box *n* : SKYBOX

¹-ly \lē\ *adj suffix* **1** : like in appearance, manner, or nature : having the characteristics of ⟨king*ly*⟩ ⟨sister*ly*⟩ **2** : characterized by regular recurrence in (specified) units of time : every ⟨year*ly*⟩ [Old English *-līc, -lic*]

²-ly *adv suffix* **1** : in a (specified) manner ⟨easi*ly*⟩ **2** : from a (specified) point of view ⟨theological*ly*⟩ **3** : with respect to ⟨part*ly*⟩ [Old English *-līce, -lice,* from *-līc,* adj. suffix]

ly·cée \lē-ˈsā\ *n* : a French public secondary school that prepares students for the university [French, from Middle French *lyceum,* from Latin *Lyceum*]

ly·ce·um \lī-ˈsē-əm, ˈlī-sē-\ *n* **1** : a hall for public lectures or discussions **2** : an association providing public lectures, concerts, and entertainments [Latin *Lyceum,* gymnasium near Athens where Aristotle taught, from Greek *Lykeion,* from *lykeios,* epithet of Apollo]

ly·chee *or* **li·tchi** *also* **li·chee** \ˈlē-chē, ˈlī-\ *n* **1** : the oval fruit of a Chinese tree related to the soapberries and having a hard scaly reddish outer covering and sweet whitish edible flesh surrounding a single large seed — called also *lychee nut* **2** : a tree bearing lychees [Chinese (Beijing dialect) *lìzhī*]

lych–gate *also* **lich–gate** \ˈlich-ˌgāt\ *n* : a roofed gate in a churchyard under which a bier rests during the first part of a burial service [Middle English *lich* "body, corpse," from Old English *līc*]

lych·nis \ˈlik-nəs\ *n* : any of a genus of often sticky-stemmed herbs related to the pinks and having clusters of usually red or white flowers [Latin, a kind of red flower, from Greek]

ly·co·pod \ˈlī-kə-ˌpäd\ *n* : CLUB MOSS; *esp* : LYCOPODIUM 1

ly·co·po·di·um \ˌlī-kə-ˈpōd-ē-əm\ *n* **1** : any of a large genus of erect or creeping club mosses with small or scalelike evergreen leaves **2** : a fine yellowish flammable powder of lycopodium spores used especially in pharmacy and in fireworks [Greek *lykos* "wolf" + *podion* "little foot," from *pod-, pous* "foot"]

Lyd·i·an \ˈlid-ē-ən\ *n* **1** : a native or inhabitant of Lydia **2** : an extinct Indo-European language of ancient Anatolia — **Lydian** *adj*

lye \ˈlī\ *n* **1** : a strong alkaline liquor rich in potassium carbonate leached from wood ashes and used especially in making soap and in washing **2** : any of various strong alkaline solutions; *also* : SODIUM HYDROXIDE **3** : a solid caustic [Old English *lēag*]

ly·gus bug \ˈlī-gəs-\ *n* : any of several small sucking bugs including some which are pests of crops [New Latin *Lygus,* genus name]

ly·ing \ˈlī-ing\ *adj* : FALSE 2a, UNTRUTHFUL ⟨a *lying* account of the accident⟩ [present participle of ³*lie*]

ly·ing–in \ˌlī-ing-ˈin\ *n, pl* **lyings–in** *or* **lying–ins** : the state during and immediately after childbirth — **lying–in** *adj*

Lyme disease \ˈlīm-\ *n* : an acute inflammatory disease that is caused by a spirochete transmitted by ticks, that is often characterized at first by a round spreading red patch on the skin at the place of infection and by fatigue, fever, and chills, and that may result in joint pain, arthritis, and disorders of the heart and nervous system if left untreated [*Lyme,* Connecticut, where it was first reported]

lymph \ˈlimf, ˈlimpf\ *n, pl* **lymphs** \ˈlimfs, ˈlimpfs, ˈlims, ˈlimps\ : a usually clear coagulable fluid that resembles blood plasma, contains white blood cells, circulates in lymphatic vessels, and bathes the cells of the body [Latin *lympha* "water goddess, water," perhaps from Greek *nymphē* "nymph"] — **lymph** *adj*

lymph·ad·e·ni·tis \ˌlim-ˌfad-n-ˈīt-əs\ *n* : inflammation of the lymph glands [Greek *adēn* "gland"]

¹lym·phat·ic \lim-ˈfat-ik\ *adj* **1 a** : of, relating to, or produced by lymph, lymphoid tissue, or lymphocytes **b** : conveying lymph **2** : lacking physical or mental energy — **lym·phat·i·cal·ly** \-ˈfat-i-kə-lē, -klē\ *adv*

²lymphatic *n* : a vessel that contains or conveys lymph — called also *lymph vessel*

lymphatic system *n* : the part of the circulatory system that consists of lymphocyte-containing tissue (as of the lymph nodes and tonsils), lymph, lymph-transporting vessels, and the thymus and spleen and is concerned especially with returning fluids and proteins back to the blood and with destroying foreign material (as bacteria or viruses) — called also *lymph system*

lymph node *n* : one of the rounded masses of tissue distributed along the lymphatic vessels and containing numerous lymphocytes which filter the flow of lymph — called also *lymph gland*

lym·pho·cyte \ˈlim-fə-ˌsīt, ˈlimp-\ *n* : any of the white blood cells arising in the bone marrow that are found especially in lymphoid tissue (as of the lymph nodes and spleen), blood, and lymph when mature and that play an important role in the immune response — compare B CELL, T CELL — **lym·pho·cyt·ic** \ˌlim-fə-ˈsit-ik, ˌlimp-\ *adj*

lym·phoid \ˈlim-ˌfȯid\ *adj* **1** : of, relating to, or resembling lymph **2** : of, relating to, or constituting the tissue characteristic of the lymph nodes

lym·pho·ma \lim-ˈfō-mə\ *n, pl* **-mas** *or* **-ma·ta** \-mət-ə\ : a usually malignant tumor of lymphoid tissue

lynch \ˈlinch\ *vt* : to put to death (as by hanging) by mob action without due process of law [*lynch law*] — **lynch·er** *n*

lynch law *n* : the punishment of presumed crimes or offenses usually by death without due process of law [William Lynch, died 1820, American vigilante]

lynx \ˈlings, ˈlingks\ *n, pl* **lynx** *or* **lynx·es** : any of several wildcats with relatively long legs, a short stubby tail, mottled coat, and often tufted ears: as **a** : the common large lynx of northern Europe and Asia **b** : BOBCAT **c** : a North American lynx distinguished from the bobcat by its larger size, longer tufted ears, large padded paws, and wholly black tail tip — called also *Canadian lynx* [Latin, from Greek]

lynx c

lynx–eyed \ˈlings-ˈīd, ˈlingks-\ *adj* : having keen sight

ly·on·naise \ˌlī-ə-ˈnāz\ *adj* : prepared with onions ⟨*lyonnaise* potatoes⟩ [French *à la lyonnaise* "in the manner of Lyons, France"]

Ly·ra \ˈlī-rə\ *n* : a northern constellation containing Vega [Latin, literally, "lyre"]

lyre \ˈlīr\ *n* : a stringed instrument of the harp class having a U-shaped frame and used by the ancient Greeks [Medieval French *lire,* from Latin *lyra,* from Greek]

lyre·bird \ˈlīr-ˌbərd\ *n* : either of two Australian birds of which the males have very long tail feathers that are arranged during courtship in a way resembling a lyre

¹lyr·ic \ˈlir-ik\ *adj* **1** : of or relating to a lyre **2 a** : resembling a song in form, feeling, or literary quality **b** : expressing a poet's own feeling **3** : having a light flexible voice ⟨a *lyric* soprano⟩

²lyric *n* **1** : a lyric poem or song **2** : the words of a song — often used in plural

lyr·i·cal \ˈlir-i-kəl\ *adj* **1** : resembling a song in mood or expres-

\ə\ **abut**	\au̇\ **out**	\i\ **tip**	\ȯ\ **saw**	\u̇\ **foot**
\ər\ **further**	\ch\ **chin**	\ī\ **life**	\ȯi\ **coin**	\y\ **yet**
\a\ **mat**	\e\ **pet**	\j\ **job**	\th\ **thin**	\yü\ **few**
\ā\ **take**	\ē\ **easy**	\ng\ **sing**	\th\ **this**	\yu̇\ **cure**
\ä\ **cot, cart**	\g\ **go**	\ō\ **bone**	\ü\ **food**	\zh\ **vision**

sion **2** : unrestrained in expressing enthusiasm, delight, or praise — **lyr·i·cal·ly** \-kə-lē, -klē\ *adj*

lyr·i·cism \ˈlir-ə-ˌsiz-əm\ *n* **1** : the quality or state of being lyric **2** : an intense personal style or quality in an art (as poetry)

lyr·i·cist \ˈlir-ə-səst\ *n* : a writer of lyrics

lyr·ist \ˈlīr-əst\ *n* : a lyre player

ly·ser·gic ac·id di·eth·yl·am·ide \lə-ˌsər-jik-ˈas-əd-ˌdī-ˌeth-ə-ˈlam-ˌīd, lī-\ *n* : LSD [*lysergic* from *lysis* + *ergot*]

ly·sin \ˈlīs-n\ *n* : a substance capable of causing lysis; *esp* : an antibody capable of causing disintegration of red blood cells or microorganisms

ly·sine \ˈlī-ˌsēn\ *n* : a crystalline essential amino acid obtained from the breakdown of various proteins

ly·sis \ˈlī-səs\ *n, pl* **ly·ses** \ˈlī-ˌsēz\ : a process of disintegration or dissolution (as of cells) [Greek, "act of loosening, breaking down," from *lyein* "to loosen"] — **lyt·ic** \ˈlit-ik\ *adj*

-ly·sis \l-ə-səs, ˈlī-səs\ *n combining form, pl* **-l·y·ses** \-l-ə-ˌsēz\ : decomposition ⟨electro*lysis*⟩

ly·so·some \ˈlī-sə-ˌsōm\ *n* : a saclike cellular organelle that contains hydrolytic enzymes

ly·so·zyme \ˈlī-sə-ˌzīm\ *n* : any of various enzymes that destroy the cell walls of certain bacteria and include some found in egg white, human tears, and saliva

-lyt·ic \ˈlit-ik\ *adj suffix* : of, relating to, or effecting (such) decomposition ⟨hydro*lytic*⟩ [Greek *lytikos* "able to loose," from *lyein* "to loosen"]

-lyze \ˌlīz\ *vb combining form* : produce or undergo lytic disintegration or dissolution ⟨electro*lyze*⟩ [probably derived from *-lysis*]

M

m \ˈem\ *n, pl* **m's** *or* **ms** \ˈemz\ **1** : the 13th letter of the English alphabet **2** : one thousand in Roman numerals

'm \m\ *vb* : AM ⟨I'*m* going⟩

ma \ˈmä, ˈmȯ\ *n, pl* **mas** : MOTHER [short for *mama*]

ma'am \ˈmam, *after "yes" often* əm\ *n* : MADAM

ma·ca·bre \mə-ˈkäb, -ˈkäb-rə, -ˈkäb-ər, -ˈkäbr\ *adj* **1** : having death as a subject : including a representation of death personified **2 a** : dwelling on the gruesome **b** : tending to produce horror in a beholder ⟨a *macabre* procession of starving peasants⟩ [French, from *danse macabre* "dance of death," from Medieval French *danse de Macabré*]

mac·ad·am \mə-ˈkad-əm\ *n* : macadamized roadway or pavement especially with a bituminous binder [John L. *McAdam,* died 1836, British engineer]

mac·a·da·mia nut \ˌmak-ə-ˈdā-mē-ə-\ *n* : a hard-shelled nut produced by an Australian evergreen tree and grown extensively in Hawaii — called also *macadamia* [John *Macadam,* died 1865, Australian chemist]

mac·ad·am·ize \mə-ˈkad-ə-ˌmīz\ *vt* : to construct or surface (as a road) by packing a layer of small broken stone on a well-drained earth roadbed and using a binder (as cement or asphalt) for the mass

ma·caque \mə-ˈkak, -ˈkäk\ *n* : any of various chiefly Asian monkeys including some with short or no tails; *esp* : RHESUS MONKEY [French, from Portuguese *macaco,* from *makaku,* plural of *kaku,* name for a monkey in one or more Bantu languages of Gabon and Congo]

macaque

mac·a·ro·ni \ˌmak-ə-ˈrō-nē\ *n, pl* **-nis** *or* **-nies** : a food made chiefly of semolina paste dried in the form of slender tubes [Italian *maccheroni,* pl. of *maccherone,* from Italian dialect *maccarone* "dumpling, macaroni"]

mac·a·roon \ˌmak-ə-ˈrün\ *n* : a cookie usually made of egg whites, sugar, and ground almonds or coconut [French *macaron,* from Italian dialect *maccarone* "dumpling, small cake, macaroni"]

ma·caw \mə-ˈkȯ\ *n* : any of numerous parrots of South and Central America including some of the largest and showiest of parrots [Portuguese *macao*]

Mac·ca·bees \ˈmak-ə-ˌbēz\ *n pl* **1** : a priestly family who led a Jewish revolt against Hellenism and Syrian rule and governed Palestine from 142 B.C. to 63 B.C. **2** : either of two narrative and historical books included in the Roman Catholic canon of the Old Testament and in the Protestant Apocrypha — see BIBLE table [Greek *Makkabaioi,* from plural of *Makkabaios,* surname of Judas Maccabeus 2nd century B.C. Jewish patriot] — **Mac·ca·be·an** \ˌmak-ə-ˈbē-ən\ *adj*

[1]**mace** \ˈmās\ *n* **1** : a heavy spiked club used as a weapon in the Middle Ages **2** : an ornamental staff borne as a symbol of authority [Medieval French]

[2]**mace** *n* : a spice consisting of the dried outer fibrous covering of the nutmeg [Medieval French *mascie, macis,* from Latin *macis*]

mac·er·ate \ˈmas-ə-ˌrāt\ *vb* **1** : to waste away or cause to waste away **2** : to cause to become soft or separated into constituent elements by or as if by steeping [Latin *macerare,* "to soften, steep"] — **mac·er·a·tion** \ˌmas-ə-ˈrā-shən\ *n*

Mac·Guf·fin *or* **Mc·Guf·fin** \mə-ˈgəf-ən\ *n* : an object, event, or character in a film or story that serves to set and keep the plot in motion despite usually lacking intrinsic importance

Mach \ˈmäk\ *n* : MACH NUMBER

Mach·a·bees \ˈmak-ə-ˌbēz\ *n pl* : MACCABEES

ma·chete \mə-ˈshet-ē, -ˈchet-ē; -ˈshet\ *n* : a large heavy knife used for cutting sugarcane and underbrush [Spanish]

Ma·chi·a·vel·lian \ˌmak-ē-ə-ˈvel-ē-ən, -ˈvel-yən\ *adj* **1** : of or relating to Niccolò Machiavelli or Machiavellianism **2** : characterized by cunning, deceitfulness, or bad faith — **Machiavellian** *n*

Ma·chi·a·vel·lian·ism \-ˌiz-əm\ *n* : the political theory of Machiavelli; *esp* : the view that any means however unscrupulous can justifiably be used in achieving political power

mach·i·nate \ˈmak-ə-ˌnāt, ˈmash-ə-\ *vb* : CONTRIVE, PLOT; *esp* : to plot or scheme to do harm [Latin *machinari,* from *machina* "machine, contrivance"] — **mach·i·na·tor** \-ˌnāt-ər\ *n*

mach·i·na·tion \ˌmak-ə-ˈnā-shən, ˌmash-ə-\ *n* : a crafty scheme or plot usually intended to accomplish some evil end — usually used in plural

[1]**ma·chine** \mə-ˈshēn\ *n* **1 a** : VEHICLE; *esp* : AUTOMOBILE **b** : a combination of parts that transmit forces, motion, and energy in a way that accomplishes some desired work **c** : an instrument (as a lever or pulley) designed to transmit or modify the application of power, force, or motion **2 a** : a person or organization that acts like a machine **b** : a combination of persons acting together for a common end together with the means they use; *esp* : a highly organized political group under the leadership of a boss or a small clique [Middle French, "structure, contrivance," from Latin *machina,* from Greek *mēchanē,* from *mēchos* "means, expedient"] — **ma·chine·like** \-ˌlīk\ *adj*

[2]**machine** *vt* : to shape or finish by machine-operated tools — **ma·chin·able** *also* **ma·chine·able** \-ˈshē-nə-bəl\ *adj*

machine gun *n* : an automatic gun capable of continuous firing — **ma·chine–gun** \mə-ˈshēn-ˌgən\ *vb* — **machine gunner** *n*

machine language *n* **1** : the set of symbolic instruction codes used to represent operations and data in a machine (as a computer) usually in binary form **2** : ASSEMBLY LANGUAGE

machine–readable *adj* : directly usable by a computer

ma·chin·ery \mə-ˈshēn-rē, -ə-rē\ *n* **1** : machines in general or as a working unit ⟨factory *machinery*⟩ **2** : the working parts of a machine or instrument having moving parts ⟨the *machinery* of a watch⟩ **3** : the organization or system by which something is done or carried on ⟨the *machinery* of government⟩

machine shop *n* : a workshop in which metal articles are machined and assembled

machine tool *n* : a machine (as a lathe or drill) that is operated by power and is designed for shaping solid work

ma·chin·ist \mə-ˈshē-nəst\ *n* : a person who makes or works on machines and engines

ma·chis·mo \mä-ˈchēz-mō, mə-, -ˈkēz-, -ˈkiz-, -ˈchiz-\ *n* : a strong sense of masculine pride : an exaggerated awareness and assertion of masculinity [Spanish, from *macho* "male"]

Mach number \ˈmäk-\ *n* : a number representing the ratio of the speed of a body to the speed of sound in the surrounding atmosphere ⟨a *Mach number* of 2 indicates a speed that is twice the speed of sound⟩ [Ernst *Mach,* died 1916, Austrian physicist]

[1]**ma·cho** \ˈmä-ˌchō\ *adj* : aggressively virile [Spanish, "male," from Latin *masculus*]

[2]**macho** *n, pl* **machos** **1** : MACHISMO **2** : one who exhibits machismo

mack·er·el \ˈmak-rəl, -ə-rəl\ *n, pl* **-el** *or* **-els** : a North Atlantic food fish that is green with blue bars above and silvery below; *also* : any of various usually small or medium-sized related fishes [Medieval French *makerel*]

mackerel sky *n* : a sky covered with rows of clouds resembling the patterns on a mackerel's back

mack·i·naw \ˈmak-ə-ˌnȯ\ *n* **1** : a flat-bottomed boat with pointed prow and square stern formerly much used on the upper Great Lakes **2** : a short heavy coat reaching to about mid-thigh [*Mackinaw* City, Michigan, formerly an Indian trading post]

mackinaw trout *n, often cap M* : a large dark North American char that is an important sport and food fish in northern lakes — called also *lake trout*

mack·in·tosh *also* **mac·in·tosh** \ˈmak-ən-ˌtäsh\ *n, chiefly British* : RAINCOAT [Charles *Macintosh,* died 1843, Scottish chemist and inventor]

Mac·Pher·son strut \mək-ˈfirs-n-, -ˈfərs-\ *n* : a component of an automobile suspension consisting of a shock absorber mounted within a coil spring [Earle S. *MacPherson,* died 1960, American engineer]

macr- *or* **macro-** *combining form* : large ⟨*macro*nucleus⟩ [Greek *makros* "long"]

mac·ro \ˈmak-rō\ *n, pl* **macros** : a single computer instruction that represents a series of operations [short for *macro instruction*]

mac·ro·bi·ot·ic \ˌmak-rō-bī-ˈät-ik\ *adj* : of, relating to, or being a diet consisting of cereals and whole grains supplemented especially with beans and vegetables — **mac·ro·bi·ot·ics** \-iks\ *n*

mac·ro·cosm \ˈmak-rə-ˌkäz-əm\ *n* : the great world : UNIVERSE [French *macrocosme,* from Medieval Latin *macrocosmos,* from Greek *makros* "long, large" + *kosmos* "order, universe"] — **mac·ro·cos·mic** \ˌmak-rə-ˈkäz-mik\ *adj* — **mac·ro·cos·mi·cal·ly** \-mi-kə-lē, -klē\ *adv*

mac·ro·eco·nom·ics \ˌmak-rō-ˌek-ə-ˈnäm-iks, -ˌē-kə-\ *n* : a study of economics in terms of whole systems especially with reference to general levels of output and income and to the interrelations among sectors of the economy — compare MICROECONOMICS — **mac·ro·eco·nom·ic** \-ik\ *adj*

mac·ro·ga·mete \ˌmak-rō-gə-ˈmēt, -ˈgam-ˌēt\ *n* : the larger and usually female gamete of an organism with two kinds of gametes — compare MICROGAMETE

mac·ro lens \ˈmak-ˌrō-\ *n* : a camera lens designed to focus at very short distances with up to life-size magnification of the image [*macr-,* from the fact that the focal length is greater than normal]

mac·ro·mol·e·cule \ˌmak-rō-ˈmäl-i-ˌkyül\ *n* : a large molecule built up from smaller chemical structures — **mac·ro·mo·lec·u·lar** \ˌmak-rō-mə-ˈlek-yə-lər\ *adj*

ma·cron \ˈmāk-ˌrän, ˈmak-, -rən\ *n* : a mark ¯ placed over a vowel (as in \māk\) to show that the vowel is long [Greek *makron,* from *makros* "long"]

mac·ro·nu·cle·us \ˌmak-rō-ˈnü-klē-əs, -ˈnyü-\ *n* : a large densely staining nucleus of most ciliated protozoans that controls various activities in the cell other than sexual reproduction

mac·ro·phage \ˈmak-rə-ˌfāj, -ˌfäzh\ *n* : a large phagocyte of the immune system — **mac·ro·phag·ic** \ˌmak-rə-ˈfaj-ik\ *adj*

mac·ro·scop·ic \ˌmak-rə-ˈskäp-ik\ *adj* **1** : large enough to be observed by the naked eye **2** : considered in terms of large units or elements [*macr-* + *-scopic* (as in *microscopic*)] — **mac·ro·scop·i·cal·ly** \-i-kə-lē, -klē\ *adv*

mac·u·la \ˈmak-yə-lə\ *n, pl* **-lae** \-ˌlē, -ˌlī\ *also* **-las** : an anatomical structure having the form of a spot differentiated from surrounding tissues; *esp* : MACULA LUTEA [Latin, "spot, stain"] — **mac·u·lar** \-lər\ *adj*

mac·u·la lu·tea \ˌmak-yə-lə-ˈlüt-ē-ə\ *n, pl* **mac·u·lae lu·te·ae** \-lē-ˈlüt-ē-ˌē, -lī-ˈlüt-ē-ˌī\ : a small yellowish area lying slightly lateral to the center of the retina that constitutes the region of most acute vision — called also *yellow spot* [New Latin, literally, "yellow spot"]

mac·u·la·tion \ˌmak-yə-ˈlā-shən\ *n* : the arrangement of spots and markings on an animal or plant

mac·ule \ˈmak-ˌyül\ *n* : a patch of skin altered in color but usually not elevated that is a characteristic feature of various diseases (as smallpox)

mad \ˈmad\ *adj* **mad·der; mad·dest** **1** : disordered in mind : INSANE **2** : being rash and foolish ⟨a *mad* promise⟩ **3** : FURIOUS, ENRAGED ⟨a *mad* bull⟩ **4 a** : FRANTIC 1 ⟨*mad* with pain⟩ **b** : marked by intense and often chaotic activity ⟨a *mad* scramble⟩ **5** : carried away by enthusiasm ⟨*mad* about dancing⟩ **6** : wildly merry ⟨a *mad* party⟩ **7** : affected with rabies : RABID ⟨a *mad* dog⟩ [Old English *gemǣd*] ***synonyms*** see INSANE — **mad·ly** *adv*

mad·am \ˈmad-əm\ *n, pl* **madams** **1** *pl* **mes·dames** \mə-ˈdäm, -ˈdam\ — used as a form of respectful address to a high-ranking woman **2** *cap* — used as a title before the surname of a high-ranking woman and especially before a designation of her rank or office ⟨*Madam* President⟩ **3** : a woman who runs a brothel [Medieval French *ma dame,* literally, "my lady"]

ma·dame \mə-ˈdam, ma-ˈ, *before a surname also,* ˌmad-əm\ *n, pl* **mes·dames** \mā-ˈdäm, -ˈdam\ — used as a courtesy title equivalent to Mrs. for a married woman not of English-speaking nationality [French, from Medieval French *ma dame* "my lady"]

mad·cap \ˈmad-ˌkap\ *adj* : being impulsive and rash ⟨a *madcap* scheme⟩ — **madcap** *n*

mad cow disease *n* : a fatal disease of cattle in which brain tissue degenerates in a manner resembling that of a porous sponge — called also *bovine spongiform encephalopathy*

mad·den \ˈmad-n\ *vt* : to make mad

mad·den·ing \ˈmad-ning, -n-ing\ *adj* : that irritates or infuriates ⟨a *maddening* habit⟩ — **mad·den·ing·ly** \-ning-lē, -n-ing-lē\ *adv*

mad·der \ˈmad-ər\ *n* **1** : a Eurasian herb with spear-shaped leaves, small yellowish flowers followed by dark berries, and red fleshy roots used to make a dye; *also* : any of several related plants **2** : madder root or a dye prepared from it [Old English *mædere*]

mad·ding \ˈmad-ing\ *adj* **1** : acting as if mad : FRENZIED ⟨the *madding* crowd⟩ **2** : MADDENING

made *past of* MAKE

Ma·dei·ra \mə-ˈdir-ə, -ˈder-\ *n* : an amber-colored dessert wine of the Madeira Islands; *also* : a similar wine made elsewhere

ma·de·moi·selle \ˌmad-mə-ˈzel, -ə-mə-, -mwə-ˈzel; mam-ˈzel\ *n, pl* **ma·de·moi·selles** \-ˈzelz\ *or* **mes·de·moi·selles** \ˌmād-mə-ˈzel, -ə-mə-, -mwə-ˈzel\ — used by or to French-speaking people as a courtesy title equivalent to Miss [Medieval French, from *ma damoisele* "my young lady"]

made–up \ˈmād-ˈəp\ *adj* **1** : marked by the use of make-up ⟨*made-up* eyelids⟩ **2** : fancifully conceived or falsely devised ⟨a *made-up* story⟩ **3** : fully manufactured

mad·house \ˈmad-ˌhau̇s\ *n* **1** : a place where insane persons are detained and treated **2** : a place of uproar or confusion

mad·man \ˈmad-ˌman, -mən\ *n* : a man who is or acts as if insane

mad·ness \ˈmad-nəs\ *n* **1** : the quality or state of being mad: as **a** : INSANITY **b** : extreme folly **c** : FURY 1, RAGE **2** : any of several disorders of animals marked by frenzied behavior; *esp* : RABIES

Ma·don·na lily \mə-ˌdän-ə-\ *n* : a white-flowered Eurasian lily often forced for spring bloom [*Madonna,* the Virgin Mary, from Italian *ma donna* "my lady"]

ma·dras \ˈmad-rəs; mə-ˈdras, -ˈdräs\ *n* : a fine usually corded or striped cotton fabric [*Madras,* India]

ma·dras·sa *or* **ma·dra·sa** *also* **ma·dras·sah** *or* **ma·dra·sah**

\mə-ˈdras-ə, -ˈdräs-\ *n* : a Muslim school, college, or university that is often part of a mosque [Arabic *madrasa*]

mad·ri·gal \ˈmad-ri-gəl\ *n* **1 a** : a short love poem suitable for a musical setting **b** : a musical setting for a madrigal **2** : a complex 16th century part-song [Italian *madrigale*] — **mad·ri·gal·ist** \-gə-ləst\ *n*

ma·dro·ne *or* **ma·dro·na** \mə-ˈdrō-nə\ *n* : an evergreen heath of western North America with shiny leaves and edible red berries [Spanish *madroño*]

mad·wom·an \ˈmad-ˌwu̇m-ən\ *n* : a woman who is or acts as if insane

Mae·ce·nas \mi-ˈsē-nəs\ *n* : a generous patron especially of literature or art [Latin, from Gaius *Maecenas,* died 8 B.C., Roman statesman and patron of literature]

mael·strom \ˈmāl-strəm\ *n* **1** : a whirlpool of great force and violence **2** : something resembling a whirlpool especially in whirling confusion ⟨a *maelstrom* of emotions⟩ [obsolete Dutch, from *malen* "to grind" + *strom* "stream"]

mae·nad \ˈmē-ˌnad\ *n* **1** : BACCHANTE **2** : an excessively excited or distraught woman [Latin *maenad-, maenas,* from Greek *mained-, mainas,* from *mainesthai* "to be mad"] — **mae·nad·ic** \mē-ˈnad-ik\ *adj*

mae·sto·so \mī-ˈstō-sō, -zō\ *adv or adj* : so as to be majestic and stately — used as a direction in music [Italian, from Latin *majestosus,* from *majestas* "majesty"]

mae·stro \ˈmī-strō\ *n, pl* **mae·stros** \-strōz\ *or* **mae·stri** \-ˌstrē\ : a master in an art; *esp* : an eminent composer, conductor, or teacher of music [Italian, literally, "master," from Latin *magister*]

Mae West \ˈmā-ˈwest\ *n* : an inflatable life jacket in the form of a collar extending down the chest that was worn by fliers in World War II [*Mae West,* died 1980, American actress noted for her full figure]

Ma·fia \ˈmäf-ē-ə, ˈmaf-\ *n* **1** : a secret terrorist society **2** : a secret criminal organization held to control illicit activities (as racketeering) throughout the world [Italian *Mafia, Maffia,* a Sicilian secret criminal society, from Italian dialect, probably from *mafiusu*]

ma·fi·o·so \ˌmäf-ē-ˈō-sō, ˌmaf-, -zō\ *n, pl* **-si** \-sē, -zē\ : a member of a Mafia [Italian, from Italian dialect *mafiusu* "gallant, swaggerer," perhaps alteration of *marfusu* "scoundrel"]

mag·a·zine \ˈmag-ə-ˌzēn, ˌmag-ə-ˈ\ *n* **1** : STOREHOUSE 1, WAREHOUSE **2** : a place for keeping explosives in a fort or ship **3** : a periodical containing miscellaneous stories, articles, or poems **4** : a supply chamber: as **a** : a chamber in a gun for holding cartridges **b** : a chamber for film on a camera or motion-picture projector [Middle French, from Old Occitan, from Arabic *makhāzin,* pl. of *makhzan* "storehouse"]

Ma·gen Da·vid *or* **Mo·gen David** \ˈmȯ-gən-ˈdȯ-vid, ˈmō-gən-ˈdā-vəd\ *n* : a hexagram used as a symbol of Judaism [Hebrew *māghēn Dāwīdh,* literally, "shield of David"]

ma·gen·ta \mə-ˈjent-ə\ *n* **1** : FUCHSIN **2** : a deep purplish red [*Magenta,* Italy]

mag·got \ˈmag-ət\ *n* **1** : a soft-bodied legless grub that is the larva of a two-winged fly (as the housefly) **2** : an odd or fantastic idea : WHIM [Middle English *magot,* probably alteration of *mathek, maddok;* sense 2 from the suggestion that a whim might be the result of a maggot in the brain] — **mag·goty** \-ət-ē\ *adj*

ma·gi \ˈmā-ˌjī\ *n pl, often cap* : the three wise men from the East who paid homage to the infant Jesus [Latin, plural of *magus* "Persian wise man, magician," from Greek *magos*]

[1]**mag·ic** \ˈmaj-ik\ *n* **1** : the art of persons who claim to be able to do things by the help of supernatural creatures or by their own knowledge of nature's secrets **2 a** : something that charms ⟨the *magic* of your smile⟩ **b** : seemingly hidden or secret power ⟨the *magic* of a great name⟩ **3** : SLEIGHT OF HAND 1 [Medieval French *magique,* from Latin *magice,* from Greek *magikos* "magical," from *magos* "Persian wise man, magician, sorcerer," of Iranian origin]

[2]**magic** *adj* **1** : of or relating to magic **2 a** : having seemingly supernatural qualities or powers **b** : ENCHANTING — **mag·i·cal** \ˈmaj-i-kəl\ *adj* — **mag·i·cal·ly** \-kə-lē, -klē\ *adv*

magic bullet *n* : a substance or therapy capable of destroying pathogenic agents (as cancer cells) or providing an effective remedy for a disease or condition without harmful side effects

ma·gi·cian \mə-ˈjish-ən\ *n* **1** : a person skilled in magic; *esp* : SORCERER **2** : a performer of sleight of hand

magic lantern *n* : an early type of slide projector

magic square *n* : a square containing rows of numbers arranged so that the sum of the numbers in each row, column, and diagonal is always the same

4	9	2
3	5	7
8	1	6

6	3	10	15
9	16	5	4
7	2	11	14
12	13	8	1

magic square

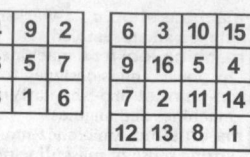

mag·is·te·ri·al \ˌmaj-ə-ˈstir-ē-əl\ *adj* **1** : of, relating to, or having the characteristics of a master or teacher **2** : of or relating to a magistrate or magistracy [Late Latin *magisterialis* "of authority," derived from Latin *magister* "master"] — **mag·is·te·ri·al·ly** \-ē-ə-lē\ *adv*

mag·is·tra·cy \ˈmaj-ə-strə-sē\ *n, pl* **-cies** **1** : the state of being a magistrate **2** : the office, power, or dignity of a magistrate **3** : a body of magistrates

ma·gis·tral \ˈmaj-ə-strəl, mə-ˈjis-trəl\ *adj* : MAGISTERIAL 1 — **ma·gis·tral·ly** \-ē\ *adv*

mag·is·trate \ˈmaj-ə-ˌstrāt, -strət\ *n* : an official entrusted with administration of the laws: as **a** : a principal official exercising executive powers over a major political unit **b** : a local official exercising administrative and often judicial functions **c** : a local judiciary official having jurisdiction in some criminal cases [Latin *magistratus* "magistracy, magistrate," from *magister* "master, political superior"]

mag·ma \ˈmag-mə\ *n* : molten rock material within the earth from which an igneous rock results by cooling [Latin *magmat-, magma* "dregs, sediment," from Greek, "pasty substance," from *massein* "to knead"] — **mag·mat·ic** \mag-ˈmat-ik\ *adj*

Mag·na Car·ta *also* **Mag·na Char·ta** \ˌmag-nə-ˈkärt-ə\ *n* **1** : a charter of civil liberties to which the English barons forced King John to give his assent in June 1215 at Runnymede **2** : a document constituting a fundamental guarantee of rights and privileges [Medieval Latin, literally, "great charter"]

mag·na cum lau·de \ˌmäg-nə-ˌku̇m-ˈlau̇d-ə, -ˈlau̇d-ē; ˌmag-nə-ˌkəm-ˈlȯd-ē\ *adv or adj* : with great academic distinction ⟨graduated *magna cum laude*⟩ [Latin, "with great praise"]

mag·na·nim·i·ty \ˌmag-nə-ˈnim-ət-ē\ *n, pl* **-ties** **1 a** : nobility of character : HIGH-MINDEDNESS **b** : GENEROSITY 1 **2** : a magnanimous act

mag·nan·i·mous \mag-ˈnan-ə-məs\ *adj* **1** : showing or suggesting a lofty and courageous spirit : NOBLE **2** : free of all meanness or pettiness [Latin *magnanimus,* from *magnus* "great" + *animus* "spirit"] — **mag·nan·i·mous·ly** *adv* — **mag·nan·i·mous·ness** *n*

mag·nate \ˈmag-ˌnāt, -nət\ *n* : a person of rank, power, influence, or distinction (as in an industry) [Late Latin *magnates,* pl., from Latin *magnus* "great"]

mag·ne·sia \mag-ˈnē-shə, -ˈnē-zhə\ *n* : MAGNESIUM OXIDE — compare MILK OF MAGNESIA [New Latin, from *magnes carneus,* a white earth, literally, "flesh magnet"] — **mag·ne·sian** \-shən, -zhən\ *adj*

mag·ne·sium \mag-ˈnē-zē-əm, -zhəm\ *n* : a silver-white metallic element that is light and easily worked, burns with a dazzling light, and is used in making lightweight alloys — see ELEMENT table [New Latin, from *magnesia*]

magnesium chloride *n* : a bitter salt $MgCl_2$ found in seawater and used in producing magnesium metal

magnesium hydroxide *n* : a weakly alkaline compound used especially as a laxative and an antacid

magnesium oxide *n* : a white highly infusible earthy solid MgO that consists of magnesium and oxygen and is used in refractories, fertilizers, and rubber and as an antacid and mild laxative

magnesium sulfate *n* : any of several sulfates of magnesium; *esp* : EPSOM SALT

mag·net \ˈmag-nət\ *n* **1** : a piece of some material (as the mineral iron oxide) that is able to attract iron; *esp* : a mass of iron or steel so treated that it has this property **2** : something that attracts ⟨the *magnet* of fame⟩ [Medieval French *magnete,* from Latin *magnes,* from Greek *magnēs lithos,* literally, "stone of Magnesia (ancient city in Asia Minor)"]

magnet- *or* **magneto-** *combining form* : magnetism : magnetic ⟨*magneto*electric⟩

mag·net·ic \mag-ˈnet-ik\ *adj* **1** : gifted with great power to attract ⟨a *magnetic* personality⟩ **2 a** : of or relating to a magnet or magnetism **b** : of or relating to the earth's magnetism ⟨the *magnetic* meridian⟩ **c** : capable of being magnetized **d** : working by magnetic attraction — **mag·net·i·cal·ly** \-ˈnet-i-kə-lē, -klē\ *adv*

magnetic bubble *n* : a tiny movable magnetized cylindrical volume in a thin magnetic material that along with other like volumes can be used to represent a bit of information (as in a computer)
magnetic disk *n* : [1]DISK 3c
magnetic field *n* : the portion of space near a magnetic body or a body carrying an electric current within which magnetic forces due to the body or current can be detected
magnetic north *n* : the northerly direction in the earth's magnetic field indicated by the north-seeking pole of a compass needle
magnetic pole *n* **1** : either of two small regions which are located respectively in the polar areas of the northern and southern hemispheres and toward which a compass needle points **2** : either of the poles of a magnet
magnetic resonance *n* : the excitation of particles (as electrons or atomic nuclei) in a magnetic field by exposure to electromagnetic radiation of a specific frequency
magnetic resonance imaging *n* : a diagnostic technique that produces computerized images of internal body tissues by using a powerful magnetic field and a series of radio wave pulses to cause hydrogen nuclei in the tissues to absorb and release energy in a characteristic manner — called also *MRI*
magnetic storm *n* : a marked temporary disturbance of the earth's magnetic field held to be related to sunspots
magnetic tape *n* : a thin ribbon (as of plastic) coated with a magnetic material on which information (as sound or television images) may be stored
mag•ne•tism \ˈmag-nə-ˌtiz-əm\ *n* **1 a** : the property of attracting certain metals or producing a magnetic field as shown by a magnet, a magnetized material, or a conductor carrying an electric current **b** : the science that deals with magnetic occurrences or conditions **2** : the power to attract or charm others
mag•ne•tite \ˈmag-nə-ˌtīt\ *n* : a black mineral Fe_3O_4 that is an oxide of iron, is strongly attracted by a magnet, and is an important iron ore
mag•ne•tize \ˈmag-nə-ˌtīz\ *vt* **1** : to attract like a magnet : CHARM **2** : to give magnetic properties to — **mag•ne•tiz•able** \-ˌtī-zə-bəl\ *adj* — **mag•ne•ti•za•tion** \ˌmag-nət-ə-ˈzā-shən\ *n* — **mag•ne•tiz•er** \ˈmag-nə-ˌtī-zər\ *n*
mag•ne•to \mag-ˈnēt-ō\ *n, pl* **-tos** : a small electric generator using permanent magnets; *esp* : one used to produce sparks in an internal-combustion engine [short for *magnetoelectric machine*]
mag•ne•to•elec•tric \mag-ˌnēt-ō-ə-ˈlek-trik\ *adj* : relating to electromotive forces developed by magnetic means ⟨*magnetoelectric* induction⟩
mag•ne•tom•e•ter \ˌmag-nə-ˈtäm-ət-ər\ *n* : an instrument for measuring magnetic intensity especially of the earth's magnetic field
mag•ne•to•sphere \mag-ˈnēt-ə-ˌsfiər, -ˈnet-\ *n* : a region of space surrounding an object (as a planet or star) that is dominated by the object's magnetic field
mag•ne•to•stric•tion \mag-ˌnēt-ō-ˈstrik-shən, -ˌnet-\ *n* : the change in the dimensions of various magnetic bodies caused by a change in their state of magnetization [*magnet-* + *-striction* (as in *constriction*)] — **mag•ne•to•stric•tive** \-ˈstrik-tiv\ *adj*
magnet school *n* : a school with superior facilities and staff designed to attract pupils throughout a city or school district
Mag•nif•i•cat \mag-ˈnif-i-ˌkat, -ˌkät; män-ˈyif-i-ˌkät\ *n* : the canticle of the Virgin Mary in Luke 1:46-55 [Latin, "magnifies," its first word]
mag•ni•fi•ca•tion \ˌmag-nə-fə-ˈkā-shən\ *n* **1** : the act of magnifying **2 a** : the state of being magnified **b** : the apparent enlargement of an object by an optical instrument — called also *power*
mag•nif•i•cence \mag-ˈnif-ə-səns\ *n* : the quality or state of being magnificent : SPLENDOR, GRANDEUR [Medieval French, from Latin *magnificentia,* from *magnificus* "noble, magnificent," from *magnus* "great" + *-ficus* "-fic"]
mag•nif•i•cent \-sənt\ *adj* **1** : having grandeur and beauty : SPLENDID ⟨*magnificent* palaces⟩ ⟨a *magnificent* view⟩ **2** : NOBLE 5 ***synonyms*** see GRAND — **mag•nif•i•cent•ly** *adv*
mag•nif•i•co \mag-ˈnif-i-ˌkō\ *n, pl* **-coes** *or* **-cos** **1** : a nobleman of Venice **2** : a person of high position [Italian, from *magnifico* "magnificent," from Latin *magnificus*]
mag•ni•fy \ˈmag-nə-ˌfī\ *vb* **-fied; -fy•ing** **1** : EXTOL, LAUD **2** : to exaggerate in importance ⟨*magnify* a fault⟩ **3** : to enlarge in fact or appearance ⟨a microscope *magnifies* an object seen through it⟩ [Medieval French *magnifier,* from Latin *magnificare,* from *magnificus* "great, magnificent"] — **mag•ni•fi•er** \-ˌfī-ər, -ˌfīr\ *n*
mag•ni•fy•ing glass *n* : a lens that magnifies an object seen through it
mag•ni•tude \ˈmag-nə-ˌtüd, -ˌtyüd\ *n* **1 a** : greatness especially in size or extent **b** : spatial quality : SIZE **2** : greatness in influence or effect **3** : degree of brightness; *esp* : a number representing the relative brightness of a star on a scale on which the lowest number represents the brightest star **4** : the intensity of an earthquake represented by a number on an arbitrary scale [Latin *magnitudo,* from *magnus* "large"]
mag•no•lia \mag-ˈnōl-yə\ *n* : any of a genus of North American and Asian shrubs and trees with usually showy white, yellow, rose, or purple flowers appearing in early spring [Pierre *Magnol,* died 1715, French botanist]
mag•num opus \ˌmag-nə-ˈmō-pəs\ *n* : a great work; *esp* : a literary or artistic masterpiece [Latin]
mag•pie \ˈmag-ˌpī\ *n* **1** : any of various noisy birds related to the jays but having a long tapered tail and black-and-white plumage **2** : a person who chatters constantly [*Mag* (nickname for *Margaret*) + [1]*pie*]
ma•guey \mə-ˈgā\ *n, pl* **magueys** **1** : any of various fleshy-leaved agaves (as the century plant) **2** : any of several hard fibers derived from magueys [Spanish, from Taino]
Mag•yar \ˈmag-ˌyär, ˈmäg-; ˈmäj-ˌär\ *n* **1** : a member of the dominant people of Hungary **2** : HUNGARIAN 2 [Hungarian] — **Magyar** *adj*
ma•ha•ra•ja *or* **ma•ha•ra•jah** \ˌmä-hə-ˈräj-ə, -ˈräzh-ə\ *n* : a Hindu prince ranking above a raja [derived from Sanskrit *mahārāja,* from *mahat* "great" + *rājan* "raja"]
ma•ha•ra•ni *or* **ma•ha•ra•nee** \-ˈrän-ē\ *n* **1** : the wife of a maharaja **2** : a Hindu princess ranking above a rani [Hindi & Urdu *mahārānī,* from *mahā* "great" (from Sanskrit *mahat*) + *rānī* "rani"]
ma•hat•ma \mə-ˈhät-mə, -ˈhat-\ *n* : a person revered for high-mindedness, wisdom, and selflessness — used as a title of honor especially by Hindus [Sanskrit *mahātman,* from *mahat* "great" + *ātman* "soul"]
Mah•di \ˈmäd-ē\ *n* **1** : the expected messiah of Muslim tradition **2** : a Muslim leader who assumes a messianic role [Arabic *mahdī,* literally, "one rightly guided"] — **Mah•dism** \ˈmä-ˌdiz-əm\ *n* — **Mah•dist** \ˈmäd-ist\ *n*
Ma•hi•can *or* **Mo•hi•can** \mə-ˈhē-kən\ *n, pl* **-can** *or* **-cans** **1** : a member of an American Indian people of the upper Hudson River valley **2** : the extinct Algonquian language of the Mahican people
ma•hi•ma•hi \ˌmä-hē-ˈmä-hē\ *n* : DOLPHIN 2; *also* : its flesh used for food
mah–jongg \mäzh-ˈäng, mäj-, -ˈȯng\ *n* : a game of Chinese origin for 4 players that is played with usually 144 tiles [from *Mah-Jongg,* a former trademark]
ma•hog•a•ny \mə-ˈhäg-ə-nē\ *n, pl* **-nies** **1** : the wood of any of various chiefly tropical trees: as **a** : the durable usually reddish brown and moderately hard and heavy wood of a West Indian tree that is widely used for cabinetwork **b** : any of several African woods that vary in color from pinkish to deep reddish brown **2** : any of various woods resembling or substituted for true mahogany **3** : a tree that yields mahogany **4** : a moderate reddish brown [origin unknown]
ma•ho•nia \mə-ˈhō-nē-ə\ *n* : any of a genus of shrubs (as the Oregon grape) related to the barberries [Bernard *McMahon,* died 1816, American botanist]
ma•hout \mə-ˈhau̇t\ *n* : a keeper and driver of an elephant [Hindi & Urdu *mahāwat, mahāut*]
maid \ˈmād\ *n* **1** : an unmarried girl or woman; *esp* : MAIDEN **2** : a female servant [Middle English *maide,* short for *maiden*]
[1]**maid•en** \ˈmād-n\ *n* : a young unmarried girl or woman [Old English *mægden, mǣden*] — **maid•en•hood** \-ˌhu̇d\ *n* — **maid•en•li•ness** \-lē-nəs\ *n* — **maid•en•ly** \-lē\ *adj*
[2]**maiden** *adj* **1 a** : not married ⟨my *maiden* aunt⟩ **b** : VIRGIN 1 **2** : of, relating to, or befitting a maiden **3** : FIRST, EARLIEST ⟨the ship's *maiden* voyage⟩ **4** : INTACT, FRESH

\ə\ **a**but	\au̇\ **ou**t	\i\ t**i**p	\ȯ\ s**aw**	\u̇\ f**oo**t
\ər\ f**ur**ther	\ch\ **ch**in	\ī\ l**i**fe	\ȯi\ c**oi**n	\y\ **y**et
\a\ m**a**t	\e\ p**e**t	\j\ **j**ob	\th\ **th**in	\yü\ f**ew**
\ā\ t**a**ke	\ē\ **ea**sy	\ng\ si**ng**	\t͟h\ **th**is	\yu̇\ c**u**re
\ä\ c**o**t, c**a**rt	\g\ **g**o	\ō\ b**o**ne	\ü\ f**oo**d	\zh\ vi**s**ion

maid·en·hair fern \ˈmād-n-ˌhaər-, -ˌheər-\ *n* : any of a genus of ferns with slender stems and delicate much-divided often feathery leaves — called also *maidenhair*

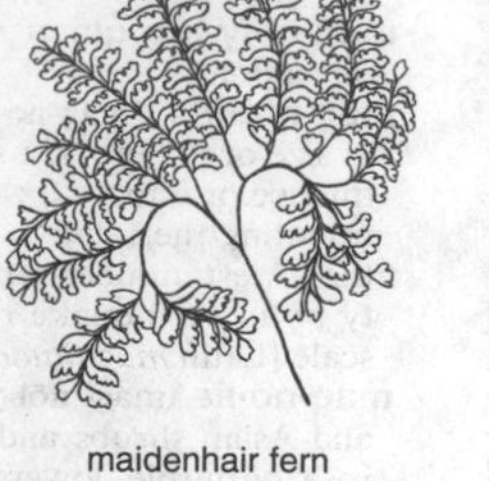
maidenhair fern

maidenhair tree *n* : GINKGO
maid·en·head \ˈmād-n-ˌhed\ *n* : HYMEN [Middle English *maidenhed* "maidenhood, virginity," from *maiden* + *-hed* "-hood"]
maiden name *n* : the surname of a woman before she is married
maid of honor **1** : an unmarried woman usually of noble birth who attends a queen or princess **2** : a bride's principal unmarried wedding attendant
maid·ser·vant \ˈmād-ˌsər-vənt\ *n* : a female servant
^{1}**mail** \ˈmāl\ *n* **1** : material (as letters or parcels) sent from one person to another especially through the post office **2** : the whole system used in the public sending and delivery of letters and parcels ⟨do business by *mail*⟩ **3** : something that comes in the mail; *esp* : the contents of a single delivery **4** : a conveyance that transports mail **5** : E-MAIL 2 [Middle English *male* "bag," from Medieval French, of Germanic origin]
^{2}**mail** *vt* : to send by mail : POST — **mail·able** \ˈmā-lə-bəl\ *adj* — **mail·er** *n*
^{3}**mail** *n* : a flexible network of small metal rings linked together for use as armor ⟨a coat of *mail*⟩ [Medieval French *maille,* from Latin *macula* "spot, mesh"] — **mailed** \ˈmāld\ *adj*
mail·box \ˈmāl-ˌbäks\ *n* **1** : a public box for the collection of mail **2** : a private box for the delivery of mail **3** : a computer file in which e-mail is collected
mail carrier *n* : LETTER CARRIER
mail·man \ˈmāl-ˌman\ *n* : LETTER CARRIER
mail order *n* : an order for goods that is received and filled by mail — **mail–order** \ˈmāl-ˌȯrd-ər\ *adj*
mail–order house *n* : a retail establishment whose business is conducted by mail
maim \ˈmām\ *vt* : to mutilate, disfigure, or wound seriously [Medieval French *maheimer, mahaigner,* probably of Germanic origin] — **maim·er** *n*
^{1}**main** \ˈmān\ *n* **1** : physical strength : FORCE — used in the phrase *with might and main* **2 a** : MAINLAND **b** : HIGH SEAS **3** : the chief part : essential point ⟨they are in the *main* well trained⟩ **4** : a principal pipe, duct, or circuit of a utility system ⟨gas *main*⟩ **5 a** : MAINMAST **b** : MAINSAIL [in sense 1, from Old English *mægen*; in other senses, from ^{2}*main* or by shortening]
^{2}**main** *adj* **1** : CHIEF 2, PRINCIPAL **2** : fully exerted : SHEER ⟨by *main* force⟩ **3** : connected with or located near the mainmast or mainsail **4** : being a clause that is capable of standing alone as a simple sentence but actually is part of a larger sentence that includes also a subordinate clause or another main clause
main·frame \ˈmān-ˌfrām\ *n* : a large fast computer that can do many jobs at once
main·land \ˈmān-ˌland, -lənd\ *n* : a continent or the main part of a continent as distinguished from an offshore island or sometimes from a cape or a peninsula — **main·land·er** \-ər\ *n*
main·line \ˈmān-ˈlīn\ *vb* **1** *slang* : to inject a narcotic drug (as heroin) into a principal vein **2** *slang* : to take by or as if by injecting into a principal vein
main·ly \ˈmān-lē\ *adv* : for the most part : CHIEFLY
main·mast \ˈmān-ˌmast, -məst\ *n* : the principal mast of a sailing ship
main·sail \ˈmān-ˌsāl, ˈmān-səl\ *n* : the principal sail on the mainmast
main sequence *n* : a group of stars that form a band on a graph of color versus brightness and that includes stars representing the stages a typical star passes through during most of its lifetime
main·spring \-ˌspriŋ\ *n* **1** : the principal spring in a mechanism especially of a watch or clock **2** : the chief motive, cause, or force underlying or causing an action
main·stay \-ˌstā\ *n* **1** : a forward stay which helps support the mainmast of a ship **2** : a chief support
main·stream \ˈmān-ˌstrēm\ *n* : a general movement or direction of activity or influence
main·tain \mān-ˈtān, mən-\ *vt* **1** : to keep in an existing state; *esp* : to keep in good condition ⟨*maintain* one's health⟩ ⟨*maintain* machinery⟩ **2** : to uphold and defend against opposition or danger ⟨*maintain* a position⟩ **3** : to continue in : keep up ⟨*maintain* one's balance⟩ ⟨*maintain* one's composure⟩ **4 a** : to provide for : SUPPORT ⟨*maintain* their family by working⟩ **b** : SUSTAIN ⟨enough food to *maintain* life⟩ **5** : to affirm in or as if in argument : ASSERT ⟨*maintained* that the earth is flat⟩ [Medieval French *maintenir, maynteiner,* from Latin *manu tenēre* "to hold in the hand"] — **main·tain·able** \-ˈtā-nə-bəl\ *adj* — **main·tain·er** *n*
synonyms MAINTAIN, ASSERT, VINDICATE, JUSTIFY mean to uphold as true, right, or just. MAINTAIN stresses firmness of conviction ⟨steadfastly *maintained* his innocence⟩. ASSERT suggests vigor of statement and determination to make others accept one's claim ⟨*asserted* her rights⟩. VINDICATE implies successfully defending what was under question or attack ⟨his success *vindicated* our faith in him⟩. JUSTIFY implies showing to be true or valid especially by appeal to a standard or to precedent ⟨an action used to *justify* military intervention⟩.
main·te·nance \ˈmānt-nəns, -n-əns\ *n* **1** : the act of maintaining : the state of being maintained **2** : something that maintains or supports; *esp* : a supply of necessities and conveniences **3** : the upkeep of property or machinery
maî·tre d'hô·tel \ˌmā-trə-dō-ˈtel\ *n, pl* **maîtres d'hôtel** *same*\ **1** : MAJORDOMO **2** : HEADWAITER [French, literally, "master of (the) house"]
maize \ˈmāz\ *n* **1** : ^{1}CORN 1 **2** : ^{1}CORN 2 **3** : ^{1}CORN 3 [Spanish *maíz,* from Taino *mahiz*]
ma·jes·tic \mə-ˈjes-tik\ *adj* : being stately and dignified : NOBLE ***synonyms*** see GRAND — **ma·jes·ti·cal·ly** \-ti-kə-lē, -klē\ *adv*
maj·es·ty \ˈmaj-ə-stē\ *n, pl* **-ties** **1 a** : sovereign power, authority, or dignity **b** *cap* — used as a form of address for reigning sovereigns and their consorts ⟨His *Majesty* King George⟩ ⟨Her *Majesty* Queen Elizabeth⟩ **2 a** : royal bearing or quality : GRANDEUR **b** : greatness of quality or character [Medieval French *majesté,* from Latin *majestas*]
^{1}**ma·jor** \ˈmā-jər\ *adj* **1 a** : greater in dignity, rank, or importance ⟨a *major* poet⟩ **b** : greater in number, quantity, or extent ⟨the *major* part of the blame⟩ **2** : having attained majority **3** : involving risk to life : SERIOUS ⟨a *major* illness⟩ **4 a** : notable or conspicuous in effect or scope ⟨a *major* improvement⟩ **b** : prominent or significant in size, amount, or degree ⟨earned some *major* cash⟩ **5** : of or relating to an academic major **6 a** : having half steps between the 3rd and 4th and the 7th and 8th degrees ⟨a *major* scale⟩ **b** : based on a major scale ⟨a *major* key⟩ [Latin, comparative of *magnus* "great, large"]
^{2}**major** *n* **1** : a major musical interval, scale, key, or mode **2** : an officer rank in the army, marine corps, and air force above captain and below lieutenant colonel **3** : an academic subject chosen by a student as a field of specialization
^{3}**major** *vi* **ma·jored; ma·jor·ing** \ˈmāj-riŋ, -ə-riŋ\ : to pursue an academic major
ma·jor·do·mo \ˌmā-jər-ˈdō-mō\ *n, pl* **-mos** : a man in charge of a great household and especially of a royal establishment [Spanish *mayordomo* or obsolete Italian *maiordomo,* from Medieval Latin *major domus,* literally, "chief of the house"]
ma·jor·ette \ˌmā-jə-ˈret\ *n* : DRUM MAJORETTE
major general *n* : an officer rank in the army, marine corps, and air force above brigadier general and below lieutenant general
major his·to·com·pat·i·bil·i·ty complex \-ˈhis-tō-kəm-ˌpat-ə-ˈbil-ət-ē-\ *n* : a group of genes in mammals that code for protein molecules which can display antigens on the surface of cells for recognition by T cells and that aid in the ability of the immune system to identify material that is foreign to the body
ma·jor·i·ty \mə-ˈjȯr-ət-ē, -ˈjär-\ *n, pl* **-ties** **1 a** : the age at which one is given full civil rights **b** : the status of one who has attained this age **2 a** : a number or percentage greater than half of a total **b** : the amount by which such a greater number exceeds the smaller number ⟨won by a *majority* of seven⟩ **c** : the greater part or share ⟨the *majority* of our fuel is imported⟩ **3** : the group or party that makes up the greater part of a whole body of persons **4** : the military office or rank of a major
synonyms MAJORITY, PLURALITY mean a margin of votes won. MAJORITY specifically refers to the number in excess of half of all the votes cast ⟨270 votes gave the winner a *majority* of 20 out of the total of 500 votes⟩. PLURALITY refers to the number that is in excess of those of the nearest rival but may not be more than half of the total votes cast ⟨won 35 percent, a *plurality* of the ballots cast⟩.

majority rule *n* : a political principle providing that a majority of an organized group shall have the power to make decisions binding upon the whole group
major league *n* : a league in the highest class of U.S. professional baseball; *also* : a league of major importance in another sport (as hockey)
major order *n* **1** : the order of priest or deacon in the Roman Catholic Church **2** : the order of bishop, priest, or deacon in the Eastern or Anglican Church
major penalty *n* : a 5-minute suspension of a player in ice hockey
major suit *n* : hearts or spades in bridge
[1]**make** \ˈmāk\ *vb* **made** \ˈmād\; **mak·ing** **1 a** : to begin or seem to begin an action ⟨*made* as if to go⟩ **b** : to act so as to appear ⟨*make* merry⟩ **2 a** : to cause to exist or occur : CREATE ⟨*make* a disturbance⟩ **b** : to cause to happen to or be experienced by someone ⟨*made* trouble for us⟩ **c** : to create for some purpose or goal ⟨they were *made* for each other⟩ **d** : to favor the growth or occurrence of ⟨haste *makes* waste⟩ **3 a** : to form or shape out of material or parts : FASHION, BUILD ⟨*make* a dress⟩ ⟨*make* a table⟩ **b** : to comprise or become combined into a whole : CONSTITUTE ⟨a house *made* of stone⟩ **4** : to frame or formulate in the mind ⟨*make* plans⟩ **5 a** : ESTIMATE 1, COMPUTE ⟨I *make* it an even $5⟩ **b** : to regard as being : CONSIDER ⟨he's not the fool you *make* him⟩ **c** : UNDERSTAND ⟨unable to *make* anything of the story⟩ **6 a** : to set in order ⟨*make* a bed⟩ **b** : PREPARE, FIX ⟨*make* lunch⟩ **7** : to cut and spread for drying ⟨*make* hay⟩ **8 a** : to cause to be or become ⟨*make* oneself useful⟩ **b** : APPOINT 2 ⟨*made* him CEO⟩ **c** : to develop into ⟨she will *make* a fine judge⟩ **9 a** : ENACT, ESTABLISH ⟨*make* laws⟩ **b** : to execute in an appropriate manner ⟨*make* a will⟩ **c** : SET, NAME ⟨*make* a price⟩ **10** : to complete an electric circuit **11 a** : to carry out a specific action ⟨*make* war⟩ ⟨*make* a speech⟩ **b** : to perform with a bodily movement ⟨*made* a bow⟩ **c** : FOLLOW, TRAVERSE ⟨*make* one's rounds⟩ **12** : to produce by action or effort spent on something ⟨*made* a mess of the job⟩ **13** : to cause to act in some manner : COMPEL ⟨*made* them return home⟩ **14** : to cause or assure the success of ⟨can either *make* you or break you⟩ **15 a** : to amount to in significance ⟨it *makes* a great difference⟩ **b** : to count as ⟨that *makes* your third turn⟩ **16** : REACH, ATTAIN ⟨the ship *makes* port tonight⟩ — often used with *it* ⟨you'll never *make* it that far⟩ **17 a** : to gain by or as if by working ⟨*makes* good money at the foundry⟩ **b** : to acquire by effort ⟨*makes* friends easily⟩ **c** : to gain a place on or in ⟨*made* the team⟩ ⟨the story *made* the papers⟩ **d** : to score in a game or sport ⟨*make* a point after a touchdown⟩ **18 a** : CATCH ⟨*make* the train⟩ **b** : to set out in pursuit ⟨*made* after the fox⟩ **19** : to provide the most satisfying experience of ⟨winning the prize *made* my day⟩ [Old English *macian* "to form, construct, do, act"] — **make a mountain out of a molehill** : to treat something unimportant as a matter of great importance — **make away with** : to carry off — **make believe** : FEIGN, PRETEND — **make do** : to get along with the means at hand — **make fun of** : to make an object of amusement or laughter — **make good 1** : to make complete : FULFILL ⟨*make good* a promise⟩ **2** : to make up for a deficiency ⟨*make good* the loss⟩ **3** : SUCCEED ⟨*made good* as a photographer⟩ — **make hay** : to make use of a situation or circumstance especially in order to gain an advantage — **make it 1** : to be successful ⟨trying to *make it* as an actor⟩ **2** : SURVIVE ⟨won't *make it* through the winter⟩ — **make time 1** : to travel fast **2** : to gain time — **make waves** : to create problems or a disturbance — **make way 1** : to give room for passing, entering, or occupying ⟨the crowd *made way* for the police⟩ **2** : to make progress
[2]**make** *n* **1** : the way in which a thing is made : manner of construction ⟨the *make* was so poor the chair fell apart⟩ **2** : the action of producing or manufacturing : the type or process of making or manufacturing ⟨the latest *make* of car⟩
[1]**make–be·lieve** \ˈmāk-bə-ˌlēv\ *n* : a pretending to believe (as in the play of children) : PRETENSE
[2]**make–believe** *adj* : PRETENDED, IMAGINARY ⟨a *make-believe* playmate⟩
make out *vb* **1** : to draw up in writing ⟨*make out* a shopping list⟩ **2** : to find or grasp the meaning of : UNDERSTAND ⟨couldn't *make out* what was going on⟩ **3** : to represent as being ⟨*made* them *out* to be heroes⟩ **4** : to see and identify with difficulty or effort ⟨*make out* a form in the fog⟩ **5** : SUCCEED, PROSPER ⟨*make out* well in business⟩ **6** : to engage in kissing and petting
make over *vt* **1** : to transfer the title of : CONVEY **2** : REMAKE, REMODEL **3** : REFORM 1
mak·er \ˈmā-kər\ *n* : one that makes: as **a** *cap* : GOD 1 **b** : a person who makes a promissory note **c** : MANUFACTURER
make·ready \ˈmā-ˌkred-ē\ *n* : final preparation (as of a form on a printing press) for running
make·shift \ˈmāk-ˌshift\ *n* : a temporary replacement : SUBSTITUTE — **makeshift** *adj*
make–up \ˈmā-ˌkəp\ *n* **1** : the way the parts or elements of something are put together : COMPOSITION ⟨last-minute changes in the *makeup* of the book⟩ **2** : materials (as wigs or cosmetics) used in making up ⟨put on *makeup* for a play⟩
make up \mā-ˈkəp, ˈmā-\ *vb* **1 a** : INVENT, CONCOCT ⟨*make up* a story⟩ **b** : to combine to produce a whole : COMPRISE ⟨nine players *make up* a team⟩ **2** : to form by fitting together or assembling **3** : to compensate for a deficiency or omission **4** : to become reconciled ⟨they quarreled and *made up*⟩ **5** : SETTLE, DECIDE ⟨*made up* their minds to leave⟩ **6 a** : to put on costumes or makeup (as for a play) **b** : to apply cosmetics
mak·ing \ˈmā-king\ *n* **1** : the action of one that makes **2** : a process or means of advancement or success ⟨misfortune is sometimes the *making* of a person⟩ **3** : material from which something can be developed ⟨there is the *making* of a racehorse in this colt⟩ **4** *pl* : the materials from which something can be made
ma·ko shark \ˈmā-kō-, ˈmä-\ *n* : either of two fast-swimming sharks that are often caught for sport [Maori *mako* "mako shark"]
mal- *combining form* **1** : bad : badly ⟨*mal*odorous⟩ ⟨*mal*practice⟩ **2** : abnormal : abnormally ⟨*mal*formation⟩ [Middle French, from *mal* "bad," from Latin *malus*]
mal·ab·sorp·tion \ˌmal-əb-ˈsȯrp-shən, -ˈzȯrp-\ *n* : faulty absorption especially of nutrient materials from the gastrointestinal tract
Mal·a·chi \ˈmal-ə-ˌkī\ *n* : a prophetic book of canonical Jewish and Christian Scriptures — see BIBLE table
mal·a·chite \ˈmal-ə-ˌkīt\ *n* : a green mineral that consists of a carbonate of copper and is used especially for ornamental objects [Latin *molochites*, from Greek *molochitēs*, from *molochē*, *malachē* "mallow"]
mal·a·col·o·gy \ˌmal-ə-ˈkäl-ə-jē\ *n* : a branch of zoology dealing with mollusks [French *malacologie*, derived from Greek *malakos* "soft"] — **mal·a·col·o·gist** \-jəst\ *n*
mal·ad·ap·ta·tion \ˌmal-ˌad-ˌap-ˈtā-shən\ *n* : poor or inadequate adaptation
mal·adapt·ed \ˌmal-ə-ˈdap-təd\ *adj* : unsuited or poorly suited (as to a particular use, purpose, or situation)
mal·adap·tive \ˌmal-ə-ˈdap-tiv\ *adj* **1** : marked by poor or inadequate adaptation **2** : not conducive to adaptation
mal·ad·just·ed \ˌmal-ə-ˈjəs-təd\ *adj* : poorly or inadequately adjusted; *esp* : lacking harmony with one's environment — **mal·ad·just·ment** \-ˈjəst-mənt, -ˈjəs-\ *n*
mal·ad·min·is·tra·tion \ˌmal-əd-ˌmin-ə-ˈstrā-shən\ *n* **1** : corrupt or incompetent administration (as of a public office) **2** : incorrect administration (as of a drug) — **mal·ad·min·is·ter** \-ˈmin-ə-stər\ *vt*
mal·adroit \ˌmal-ə-ˈdrȯit\ *adj* : not adroit : AWKWARD, CLUMSY — **mal·adroit·ly** *adv* — **mal·adroit·ness** *n*
mal·a·dy \ˈmal-əd-ē\ *n, pl* **-dies** : a disease or disorder of the body or mind : AILMENT [Medieval French *maladie*, from *malade* "sick," from Latin *male habitus* "in bad condition"]
Mal·a·gasy \ˌmal-ə-ˈgas-ē\ *n* **1** : a native or inhabitant of Madagascar or the Malagasy Republic **2** : the language of the Malagasy people — **Malagasy** *adj*
mal·aise \mə-ˈlāz, ma-; ma-ˈlez\ *n* : a vague feeling of bodily or mental disorder [French, from *mal-* + *aise* "ease, comfort"]
mal·a·mute *also* **mal·e·mute** \ˈmal-ə-ˌmyüt\ *n* : a sled dog of northern North America; *esp* : ALASKAN MALAMUTE [*Malemute*, an Inupiat of the Kotzebue Sound area, Alaska, from Inupiat *malimiut*]
mal·a·pert \ˌmal-ə-ˈpərt\ *adj* : impudently bold : SAUCY [Middle

English, from *mal-* + *apert* "open, frank," from Medieval French, "evident," from Latin *apertus* "open," from *aperire* "to open"] — **mal·a·pert·ly** *adv* — **mal·a·pert·ness** *n*

mal·ap·por·tioned \ˌmal-ə-ˈpōr-shənd\ *adj* **:** characterized by an unfair or unsuitable apportioning of representatives to a legislative body — **mal·ap·por·tion·ment** \-shən-mənt\ *n*

mal·a·prop·ism \ˈmal-ə-ˌpräp-ˌiz-əm\ *n* **1 :** a usually humorous misuse of a word especially for one of similar sound by someone unaware of the error **2 :** an example of malapropism [Mrs. *Malaprop,* character in Sheridan's *The Rivals* (1775) given to misusing words] — **mal·a·prop** \-ˌpräp\ *or* **mal·a·prop·ian** \ˌmal-ə-ˈpräp-ē-ən\ *adj*

mal·ap·ro·pos \ˌmal-ˌap-rə-ˈpō\ *adv* **:** in an inappropriate or inopportune way [French *mal à propos*] — **malapropos** *adj*

ma·lar \ˈmā-lər, -ˌlär\ *adj* **:** of or relating to the cheek or the side of the head [Latin *mala* "jawbone, cheek"]

ma·lar·ia \mə-ˈler-ē-ə\ *n* **:** a disease caused by protozoan parasites in the red blood cells, transmitted by the bite of mosquitoes, and characterized by periodic attacks of chills and fever [Italian, from *mala aria* "bad air"] — **ma·lar·i·al** \-ē-əl\ *adj* — **ma·lar·i·ous** \-ē-əs\ *adj*

ma·lar·key \mə-ˈlär-kē\ *n* **:** insincere or foolish talk [origin unknown]

mal·a·thi·on \ˌmal-ə-ˈthī-ən, -ˌän\ *n* **:** a pesticide $C_{10}H_{19}O_6PS_2$ that is less toxic to mammals than parathion and is used against insects and mites [from *Malathion,* a former trademark]

Ma·lay \mə-ˈlā, ˈmā-ˌlā\ *n* **1 :** a member of a people of the Malay Peninsula, eastern Sumatra, parts of Borneo, and adjacent islands **2 :** the language of the Malay people [obsolete Dutch *Malayo,* from Malay *Mĕlayu*] — **Malay** *adj* — **Ma·lay·an** \mə-ˈlā-ən, ˈmā-ˌlā-\ *adj or n*

mal·con·tent \ˌmal-kən-ˈtent\ *adj* **:** dissatisfied with the existing state of affairs — **malcontent** *n*

mal de mer \ˌmal-də-ˈmeər\ *n* **:** SEASICKNESS [French]

mal·dis·tri·bu·tion \ˌmal-ˌdis-trə-ˈbyü-shən\ *n* **:** bad or faulty distribution **:** undesirable inequality or unevenness of placement or apportionment (as of population, resources, or wealth) over an area or among members of a group

¹male \ˈmāl\ *adj* **1 a :** of, relating to, or being the sex that produces small usually motile gametes which fertilize the eggs of females **b :** STAMINATE; *esp* **:** having only staminate flowers and not producing fruit or seeds ⟨a *male* holly⟩ **2 a :** of, relating to, or characteristic of the male sex ⟨a deep *male* voice⟩ **b :** made up of males ⟨a *male* choir⟩ **3 :** designed for fitting into a corresponding hollow part [Medieval French *masle, male,* from Latin *masculus,* from *mas* "male"] — **male·ness** *n*

²male *n* **:** a male individual

mal·e·dic·tion \ˌmal-ə-ˈdik-shən\ *n* **:** a prayer for harm to befall someone **:** CURSE [Late Latin *maledictio,* from *maledicere* "to curse," from Latin, "to speak evil of," from *male* "badly" + *dicere* "to say"] — **mal·e·dic·to·ry** \-ˈdik-tə-rē, -trē\ *adj*

male·fac·tion \-ˈfak-shən\ *n* **:** an evil deed **:** CRIME

male·fac·tor \ˈmal-ə-ˌfak-tər\ *n* **1 :** one guilty of a crime or offense **2 :** EVILDOER [Latin, from *malefacere* "to do evil," from *male* "badly" + *facere* "to do"]

male fern *n* **:** a fern that yields a resinous substance used as a tapeworm remedy

ma·lef·i·cent \mə-ˈlef-ə-sənt\ *adj* **:** doing or producing harm or evil **:** HARMFUL [back-formation from *maleficence,* from Italian *maleficenza,* from Latin *maleficentia,* from *maleficus* "baleful, harmful," from *male* "badly" + *-ficus* "-fic"] — **ma·lef·i·cence** \-səns\ *n*

ma·lev·o·lent \mə-ˈlev-ə-lənt\ *adj* **:** having or showing intense often vicious ill will toward others [Latin *malevolens,* from *male* "badly" + *volens,* present participle of *velle* "to wish"] ***synonyms*** see MALICE — **ma·lev·o·lence** \-ˈlev-ə-ləns\ *n* — **ma·lev·o·lent·ly** *adv*

mal·fea·sance \mal-ˈfēz-ns, ˈmal-\ *n* **:** wrongful conduct especially by a public official [*mal-* + obsolete *feasance* "doing," from Middle French *faisance,* from *faire* "to make, do"]

mal·for·ma·tion \ˌmal-fȯr-ˈmā-shən, -fər-\ *n* **:** an irregular, abnormal, or defective formation or structure

mal·formed \mal-ˈfȯrmd, ˈmal-\ *adj* **:** marked by malformation

mal·func·tion \mal-ˈfəng-shən, ˈmal-, -ˈfəngk-\ *vi* **:** to fail to operate in the normal or usual manner — **malfunction** *n*

ma·lic acid \ˌmal-ik-, ˌmā-lik-\ *n* **:** an acid $C_4H_6O_5$ found especially in various fruits [French *acide malique,* from Latin *malum* "apple," from Greek *mēlon, malon*]

mal·ice \ˈmal-əs\ *n* **:** ILL WILL; *esp* **:** the deliberate intention of doing unjustified harm for the satisfaction of doing it [Medieval French, from Latin *malitia,* from *malus* "bad"]

synonyms MALICE, MALEVOLENCE, MALIGNITY mean the desire to see another experience pain, injury, or distress. MALICE may range from a passing mischievous impulse to a deep-seated unreasoning dislike and desire to cause harm and suffering ⟨felt no *malice* toward their former enemies⟩. MALEVOLENCE stresses evil intent or influence that is likely to lead to malicious action ⟨a look of dark *malevolence*⟩. MALIGNITY stresses the intensity and driving force of malevolence and suggests a quality that is part of one's nature ⟨a life consumed by *malignity* with no cause⟩.

ma·li·cious \mə-ˈlish-əs\ *adj* **1 :** feeling strong ill will **:** being mean and spiteful **2 :** done or carried on with malice or caused by malice ⟨*malicious* gossip⟩ — **ma·li·cious·ly** *adv* — **ma·li·cious·ness** *n*

¹ma·lign \mə-ˈlīn\ *adj* **1 :** operating so as to injure or hurt ⟨hindered by *malign* influences⟩ **2 :** moved by ill will toward others **:** MALEVOLENT [Medieval French *maligne,* from Latin *malignus,* from *male* "bad" + *gignere* "to beget"]

²malign *vt* **:** to utter injurious or false reports about **:** speak evil of **:** DEFAME ***synonyms*** see SLANDER

ma·lig·nan·cy \mə-ˈlig-nən-sē\ *n, pl* **-cies 1 :** the quality or state of being malignant **2 :** a malignant tumor

ma·lig·nant \-nənt\ *adj* **1 a :** evil in influence or effect **:** INJURIOUS **b :** passionately and relentlessly malevolent **2 :** tending or likely to produce death especially through being dispersed and growing throughout the body ⟨*malignant* tumors⟩ — **ma·lig·nant·ly** *adv*

ma·lig·ni·ty \mə-ˈlig-nət-ē\ *n, pl* **-ties 1 :** the quality or state of being malignant **:** MALIGNANCY **2 :** something (as an act or an event) that is malignant ***synonyms*** see MALICE

ma·li·hi·ni \ˌmäl-i-ˈhē-nē\ *n* **:** a newcomer to Hawaii [Hawaiian]

ma·lin·ger \mə-ˈling-gər\ *vi* **ma·lin·gered; ma·lin·ger·ing** \-gə-ring, -gring\ **:** to pretend or exaggerate incapacity or illness (as to avoid duty or work) [French *malingre* "sickly"] — **ma·lin·ger·er** \-gər-ər\ *n*

mall \ˈmȯl\ *n* **1 :** a shaded walk **:** PROMENADE **2 :** a grassy strip between two roadways **3 a :** an urban shopping area featuring stores and often restaurants surrounding a pedestrian walkway **b :** a usually large suburban building or group of buildings containing a variety of stores and often restaurants with associated passageways [The *Mall,* promenade in London, England]

mal·lard \ˈmal-ərd\ *n, pl* **mallard** *or* **mallards :** a common and widely distributed wild duck of the northern hemisphere the males of which have a green head and white-ringed neck and that is the source of the domestic ducks [Medieval French *mallart*]

mal·lea·ble \ˈmal-ē-ə-bəl, ˈmal-yə-bəl, ˈmal-ə-bəl\ *adj* **1 :** capable of being beaten out, extended, or shaped by hammer blows or by the pressure of rollers ⟨a *malleable* metal⟩ **2 :** ADAPTABLE, PLIABLE [Medieval Latin *malleabilis,* from *malleare* "to hammer," from Latin *malleus* "hammer"] — **mal·le·abil·i·ty** \ˌmal-ē-ə-ˈbil-ət-ē, ˌmal-yə-ˈbil-, ˌmal-ə-ˈ\ *n*

mal·lee \ˈmal-ē\ *n* **:** a dense growth of shrubby eucalypts; *also* **:** Australian land covered with mallee [probably from Wemba-Wemba (Australian aboriginal language of western Victoria) *mali*]

mal·let \ˈmal-ət\ *n* **:** a hammer usually having a barrel-shaped head: as **a :** a tool with a large head used for driving another tool (as a chisel) or for striking a surface without damaging it **b :** a long-handled club with a cylindrical head used for striking a ball (as in polo or croquet) **c :** a light hammer with a small rounded head used in playing certain musical instruments (as a vibraphone) [Medieval French *maillet,* from *mail* "hammer," from Latin *malleus*]

mal·le·us \ˈmal-ē-əs\ *n, pl* **mal·lei** \-ē-ˌī, -ē-ˌē\ **:** the outermost of the three small bones of the mammalian middle ear — compare INCUS, STAPES [Latin, "hammer"]

mal·low \ˈmal-ō\ *n* **:** any of a genus of herbs with lobed or dissected leaves, usually showy flowers, and a disk-shaped fruit [Old English *mealwe,* from Latin *malva*]

malm·sey \ˈmäm-zē, ˈmälm-\ *n, pl* **malmseys** *often cap* **:** a sweet aromatic wine originally produced in Greece [Medieval Latin *Malmasia* "Monemvasia," village in Greece]

mal·nour·ished \mal-ˈnər-isht, ˈmal-, -ˈnə-risht\ *adj* **:** marked by or affected with malnutrition **:** UNDERNOURISHED

mal·nu·tri·tion \ˌmal-nu̇-ˈtrish-ən, -nyu̇-\ *n* **:** faulty nutrition especially due to inadequate or unbalanced intake of nutrients — **mal·nu·tri·tion·al** \-ˈtrish-nəl, -ən-l\ *adj*

mal·oc·clu·sion \ˌmal-ə-ˈklü-zhən\ *n* **:** abnormality in the coming together of teeth in the upper and lower jaws when biting

mal·odor·ous \mal-ˈōd-ə-rəs, ˈmal-\ *adj* **:** having a bad smell — **mal·odor·ous·ly** *adv* — **mal·odor·ous·ness** *n*

Mal·pigh·i·an corpuscle \mal-ˌpig-ē-ən-, -ˌpē-gē-\ *n* **:** the part of a nephron that consists of a glomerulus and Bowman's capsule — called also *Malpighian body* [Marcello *Malpighi,* died 1694, Italian anatomist]

Malpighian tubule *n* **:** any of a group of long blind vessels opening into the intestine in various arthropods (as insects) and functioning in excretion

mal·po·si·tion \ˌmal-pə-ˈzish-ən\ *n* **:** wrong or faulty position

mal·prac·tice \mal-ˈprak-təs, ˈmal-\ *n* **1 :** violation of professional standards especially by negligence or improper conduct **2 :** an injurious, negligent, or improper practice — **mal·prac·ti·tion·er** \ˌmal-ˌprak-ˈtish-(ə-)nər\ *n*

¹malt \ˈmȯlt\ *n* **1 :** grain and especially barley softened by steeping in water, allowed to germinate, and used chiefly in brewing and distilling **2 :** MALTED MILK 2 [Old English *mealt*] — **malt** *adj* — **malty** \ˈmȯl-tē\ *adj*

²malt *vb* **1 :** to convert into malt **2 :** to make or treat with malt or malt extract **3 :** to become malt

malt·ase \ˈmȯl-ˌtās\ *n* **:** an enzyme that accelerates the hydrolysis of maltose to glucose

malted milk *n* **1 :** a soluble powder prepared from dried milk and malted cereals **2 :** a beverage made by dissolving malted milk in a liquid (as milk)

Mal·tese \mȯl-ˈtēz\ *n, pl* **Maltese 1 :** a native or inhabitant of Malta **2 :** the Semitic language of the Maltese people **3 :** any of a breed of toy dogs with a long silky white coat, a black nose, and dark eyes — **Maltese** *adj*

Maltese cross *n* **:** a cross with four arms of equal size that increase in width toward the outward ends

Mal·thu·sian \mal-ˈthü-zhən, mȯl-, -ˈthyü-\ *adj* **:** of or relating to Malthus or to his theory that population unless checked (as by war or disease) tends to increase at a faster rate than its means of subsistence — **Malthusian** *n* — **Mal·thu·sian·ism** \-zhə-ˌniz-əm\ *n*

malt·ose \ˈmȯl-ˌtōs\ *n* **:** a sugar formed especially from starch by the action of amylase and used in brewing and distilling — called also *malt sugar*

mal·treat \mal-ˈtrēt, ˈmal-\ *vt* **:** to treat unkindly or roughly **:** ABUSE ⟨*maltreat* animals⟩ — **mal·treat·ment** \-mənt\ *n*

ma·ma *also* **mam·ma** *or* **mom·ma** \ˈmäm-ə\ *n* **:** MOTHER [baby talk]

mam·ba \ˈmäm-bə, ˈmam-\ *n* **:** any of several African venomous snakes related to the cobras but lacking a hood [Zulu *im-amba*]

mam·bo \ˈmäm-bō\ *n, pl* **mambos :** a dance of Haitian origin related to the rumba [American Spanish] — **mambo** *vi*

mam·ma \ˈmam-ə\ *n, pl* **mam·mae** \ˈmam-ˌē, -ˌī\ **:** a mammary gland and its accessory parts [Latin, "mother, breast," of baby talk origin] — **mam·mate** \ˈmam-ˌāt\ *adj*

mam·mal \ˈmam-əl\ *n* **:** any of a class (Mammalia) of warm-blooded higher vertebrates comprising humans and all other animals that nourish their young with milk secreted by mammary glands and have the skin usually more or less covered with hair — **mam·ma·li·an** \mə-ˈmā-lē-ən, ma-ˈmā-\ *adj or n*

mam·mal·o·gy \mə-ˈmal-ə-jē, ma-ˈmal-\ *n* **:** a branch of zoology dealing with mammals — **mam·mal·o·gist** \-jəst\ *n*

mam·ma·ry \ˈmam-ə-rē\ *adj* **:** of, relating to, lying near, or affecting the mammae

mammary gland *n* **:** one of the large compound sebaceous glands that in female mammals are modified to secrete milk and in males are usually rudimentary, are situated in pairs on the abdominal side of the organism, and usually end in a nipple

mam·mil·la·ry \ˈmam-ə-ˌler-ē, ma-ˈmil-ə-rē\ *adj* **1 :** of, relating to, or resembling a breast **2 :** studded with breast-shaped protuberances [Latin *mammilla* "breast, nipple," from *mamma* "mother, breast"]

mam·mil·lat·ed \ˈmam-ə-ˌlāt-əd\ *adj* **:** having or being small bluntly rounded protuberances

mam·mo·gram \ˈmam-ə-ˌgram\ *n* **:** a photograph of the breasts made by X-rays; *also* **:** the procedure for producing a mammogram [Latin *mamma* "breast" + *-gram*]

mam·mog·ra·phy \mə-ˈmäg-rə-fē\ *n* **:** X-ray examination of the breasts (as for early detection of cancer) — **mam·mo·graph·ic** \ˌmam-ə-ˈgraf-ik\ *adj*

mam·mon \ˈmam-ən\ *n, often cap* **:** an often personified devotion to material possessions; *also* **:** WEALTH [Late Latin *mammona,* from Greek *mamōna,* from Aramaic *māmōnā* "riches"]

¹mam·moth \ˈmam-əth\ *n* **1 :** any of various large hairy extinct Pleistocene mammals of the elephant family with very long upward-curving tusks **2 :** something immense of its kind **:** GIANT [Russian *mamont, mamot*]

²mammoth *adj* **:** of very great size **:** GIGANTIC

mam·my \ˈmam-ē\ *n, pl* **mammies 1 :** MAMA **2 :** a black woman serving as a nurse to white children especially formerly in the southern U.S.

¹man \ˈman\ *n, pl* **men** \ˈmen\ **1 a :** HUMAN; *esp* **:** an adult male human **b :** the human race **:** HUMANKIND **c :** a bipedal primate mammal that is the sole living representative of the hominid family and is distinguished especially by notable development of the brain with a resultant capacity for speech and abstract reasoning; *also* **:** any living or extinct hominid **d :** one possessing in high degree the qualities considered distinctive of manhood **2 a :** VASSAL 1 **b :** an adult male servant **c** *pl* **:** the working force as distinguished from the employer **3 :** any person ⟨a *man* could easily be killed there⟩ **4 :** one of the pieces with which various games (as chess) are played [Old English]

²man *vt* **manned; man·ning 1 :** to supply with personnel (as for management or operation) ⟨*man* a business⟩ **2 :** to station members of a ship's crew at ⟨*man* the pumps⟩

man–about–town \ˌman-ə-ˌbau̇t-ˈtau̇n\ *n, pl* **men–about–town :** a worldly and socially active man

¹man·a·cle \ˈman-i-kəl\ *n* **1 :** a shackle for the hand or wrist **:** HANDCUFF **2 :** something that restrains or restricts [Medieval French *manicle,* from Latin *manicula* "handle," from *manicae* "shackles," from *manus* "hand"]

²manacle *vt* **-cled; -cling** \-kə-ling, -kling\ **1 :** to put manacles on **2 :** SHACKLE 2 ***synonyms*** see HAMPER

man·age \ˈman-ij\ *vb* **1 :** to oversee and make decisions about **:** DIRECT ⟨*manage* a factory⟩ **2 :** to make and keep compliant ⟨skill in *managing* problem children⟩ **3 :** to treat with care **:** use to best advantage ⟨there's enough food if it's *managed* well⟩ **4 :** to succeed in one's purpose ⟨*managed* to escape⟩ [Italian *maneggiare* "to handle," from *mano* "hand," from Latin *manus*] ***synonyms*** see CONDUCT

man·age·able \ˈman-ij-ə-bəl\ *adj* **:** capable of being managed — **man·age·abil·i·ty** \ˌman-ij-ə-ˈbil-ət-ē\ *n* — **man·age·able·ness** \ˈman-ij-ə-bəl-nəs\ *n* — **man·age·ably** \-blē\ *adv*

man·age·ment \ˈman-ij-mənt\ *n* **1 :** the act or art of managing **:** CONTROL, DIRECTION **2 :** skillfulness in managing **3 :** those who manage an enterprise

man·ag·er \ˈman-ij-ər\ *n* **:** one that manages: as **a :** a person who conducts business or household affairs **b :** a person whose work or profession is management **c :** a person who directs a team or an athlete — **man·a·ge·ri·al** \ˌman-ə-ˈjir-ē-əl\ *adj* — **man·a·ge·ri·al·ly** \-ē-ə-lē\ *adv* — **man·ag·er·ship** \ˈman-ij-ər-ˌship\ *n*

ma·ña·na \mən-ˈyän-ə\ *n* **:** an indefinite time in the future [Spanish, literally, "tomorrow"] — **mañana** *adv*

man–at–arms \ˌman-ət-ˈärmz\ *n, pl* **men–at–arms :** SOLDIER; *esp* **:** a heavily armed mounted soldier

man·a·tee \ˈman-ə-ˌtē\ *n* **:** any of several chiefly tropical plant-eating aquatic mammals that differ from the related dugong especially in having the tail broad and rounded — compare SIRENIAN [Spanish *manatí,* probably of Carib origin]

man·chi·neel \ˌman-chə-ˈnēl\ *n* **:** a tropical American tree with a blistering milky juice and poisonous apple-shaped fruits [French *mancenille,* from Spanish *manzanilla,* from *manzana* "apple"]

Man·chu \ˈman-chü, man-ˈ\ *n* **1 :** a member of the people of Manchuria who conquered China and established a dynasty there in 1644 **2 :** the language of the Manchu people [from Manchu *manju*] — **Manchu** *adj*

man·ci·ple \ˈman-sə-pəl\ *n* **:** a person responsible for procuring and distributing food especially for a college or monastery [Me-

\ə\ abut	\au̇\ out	\i\ tip	\ȯ\ saw	\u̇\ foot
\ər\ further	\ch\ chin	\ī\ life	\ȯi\ coin	\y\ yet
\a\ mat	\e\ pet	\j\ job	\th\ thin	\yü\ few
\ā\ take	\ē\ easy	\ng\ sing	\th\ this	\yu̇\ cure
\ä\ cot, cart	\g\ go	\ō\ bone	\ü\ food	\zh\ vision

dieval Latin *mancipium* "office of steward," from Latin *manceps* "purchaser," from *manus* "hand" + *capere* "to take"]

-man•cy \ˌman-sē\ *n combining form, pl* **-mancies** : divination ⟨necro*mancy*⟩ [Greek *manteia,* from *mantis* "diviner, prophet"]

man•da•mus \man-ˈdā-məs\ *n* : a writ issued by a superior court commanding that a specified official act or duty be performed [Latin, "we enjoin," its first word]

[1]man•da•rin \ˈman-də-rən, -drən\ *n* **1** : a public official under the Chinese Empire of any of nine superior grades **2** *cap* **a** : the primarily northern dialect of China used by the court and the official classes under the Empire **b** : the chief dialect of China that is spoken in about four fifths of the country and has a standard variety centering about Beijing **3** : a small spiny Chinese orange tree with yellow to reddish orange loose-rinded fruits; *also* : its fruit — compare TANGERINE [Portuguese *mandarim,* from Malay *mĕntĕri,* from Sanskrit *mantrin* "counselor," from *mantra* "counsel"] — **man•da•rin•ate** \-ˌāt\ *n*

[2]mandarin *adj* : of, relating to, or typical of a mandarin

mandarin orange *n* : MANDARIN 3

man•da•tary \ˈman-də-ˌter-ē\ *n, pl* **-tar•ies** : MANDATORY

man•date \ˈman-ˌdāt\ *n* **1** : a formal order from a superior court or official to an inferior one **2 a** : an authoritative command, instruction, or direction **b** : authorization or approval given to a representative **3 a** : a commission granted by the former League of Nations to a member nation to administer a conquered territory as guardian on behalf of the League **b** : a mandated territory [Latin *mandatum* "command," from *mandare* "to entrust, enjoin"] — **mandate** *vt*

[1]man•da•to•ry \ˈman-də-ˌtōr-ē, -ˌtȯr-\ *adj* **1** : containing or constituting a command ⟨*mandatory* tasks⟩ **2** : of, relating to, or holding a League of Nations mandate ⟨a *mandatory* power⟩

[2]mandatory *n, pl* **-ries** : one given a mandate

man•di•ble \ˈman-də-bəl\ *n* **1 a** (1) : a single bone or completely fused bones forming the lower jaw (2) : the lower jaw with its surrounding soft parts **b** : either the upper or lower segment of the bill of a bird **2** : an invertebrate mouthpart that holds or bites food; *esp* : either of the front pair of mouth appendages of an arthropod often forming strong biting jaws [Middle French, from Late Latin *mandibula,* from Latin *mandere* "to chew"] — **man•dib•u•lar** \man-ˈdib-yə-lər\ *adj*

man•do•lin \ˌman-də-ˈlin, ˈman-dl-ən\ *also* **man•do•line** \ˌman-də-ˈlēn, ˈman-dl-ən\ *n* : a musical instrument of the lute family that has a pear-shaped body and fretted neck and four to six pairs of strings [Italian *mandolino*] — **man•do•lin•ist** \ˌman-də-ˈlin-əst\ *n*

mandolin

man•drag•o•ra \man-ˈdrag-ə-rə\ *n* : MANDRAKE 1

man•drake \ˈman-ˌdrāk\ *n* **1** : a Mediterranean herb of the nightshade family with a large forked root resembling a human in form and formerly credited with magical properties; *also* : the root itself **2** : MAYAPPLE [probably alteration of Old English *mandragora,* from Latin *mandragoras,* from Greek]

man•drel \ˈman-drəl\ *n* **1** : an axle or spindle inserted into a hole in a piece of work to support it during machining **2** : a metal bar used as a core around which material may be cast, shaped, or molded [Medieval Latin *mandrellus,* probably derived from Old Occitan *mandre* "kingpin"]

man•drill \ˈman-drəl\ *n* : a large gregarious baboon of western Africa with a red rump and in the male with blue ridges on each side of the red-bridged nose [probably from [1]*man* + [3]*drill*]

mane \ˈmān\ *n* **1** : long heavy hair growing about the neck and head of some mammals (as horses and lions) **2** : long heavy hair on a person's head [Old English *manu*] — **maned** \ˈmānd\ *adj*

man–eat•er \ˈman-ˌēt-ər\ *n* : one (as a cannibal, shark, or tiger) that has or is thought to have an appetite for human flesh — **man–eat•ing** \-ˌēt-ing\ *adj*

ma•nège *also* **ma•nege** \ma-ˈnezh\ *n* **1** : a school for teaching horsemanship **2** : the art of horsemanship or of training horses [French *manège,* from Italian *maneggio* "training of a horse," from *maneggiare* "to handle, manage"]

ma•nes \ˈmän-ˌās, ˈmā-ˌnēz\ *n pl, often cap* : the deified spirits of the ancient Roman dead [Latin]

[1]ma•neu•ver \mə-ˈnü-vər, -ˈnyü-\ *n* **1 a** : a planned movement of military forces **b** : an armed forces training exercise; *esp* : an extensive exercise involving large-scale deployment of military forces **2 a** : a physical movement or procedure ⟨avoided a collision by a quick *maneuver*⟩ **b** : a variation from the straight and level flight path of an airplane **3** : a clever often evasive move or action : a shift of position to gain a tactical end ⟨tried by various *maneuvers* to win support from both sides⟩ [French *manœuvre,* from Medieval Latin *manuopera* "work done by hand," from Latin *manu operare* "to work by hand"]

Word History We owe both *manure* and *maneuver* to the same source, Latin *manu operare* "to do work by hand." This Latin phrase is the ancestor of the Medieval French verb *manouvrer.* The French verb originally meant "to work by hand" but later developed the more specific sense "to cultivate (land)." In the late Middle Ages the English borrowed the word as *manouren,* "to cultivate." From this verb we get the noun *manure* for the dung used to fertilize the land. Latin *manu operare* is also the source of French *manœuvre,* "maneuver." The original meaning of the French noun was "work done by hand," but the older sense gave way to a more general sense, "work." Still later the noun developed a new specific meaning, "military operation."

[2]maneuver *vb* **1** : to move (as troops or ships) in a maneuver **2** : to perform a maneuver **3** : to guide with adroitness and design : HANDLE, MANIPULATE **4** : to use stratagems : SCHEME — **ma•neu•ver•abil•i•ty** \-ˌnüv-rə-ˈbil-ət-ē, -ˌnyüv-, -ə-rə-\ *n* — **ma•neu•ver•able** \-ˈnüv-rə-bəl, -ˈnyüv-, -ə-rə-\ *adj*

man Fri•day \ˈman-ˈfrīd-ē\ *n* : a valued efficient helper or employee [*Friday,* native servant in *Robinson Crusoe* (1719), novel by Daniel Defoe]

man•ful \ˈman-fəl\ *adj* : showing courage and resolution — **man•ful•ly** \-fə-lē\ *adv* — **man•ful•ness** *n*

man•ga \ˈmäŋ-gə\ *n* : a Japanese comic book or graphic novel [Japanese]

man•ga•nese \ˈmang-gə-ˌnēz, -ˌnēs\ *n* : a grayish white usually hard and brittle metallic element that resembles iron but is not magnetic — see ELEMENT table [French *manganèse,* from Italian *manganese* "manganese dioxide"]

manganese dioxide *n* : a dark insoluble compound MnO_2 that consists of manganese and oxygen and is used as an oxidizing agent, in making glass, and in ceramics

mange \ˈmānj\ *n* : any of several persistent contagious skin diseases marked especially by itching and loss of hair in domestic animals and sometimes humans and caused by tiny parasitic mites [Medieval French *manjue,* from *manger* "to eat"]

man•ger \ˈmān-jər\ *n* : a trough or open box for livestock feed or fodder [Medieval French *maingure,* from *manger* "to eat," from Latin *manducare* "to chew, devour," from *manducus* "glutton," from *mandere* "to chew"]

[1]man•gle \ˈmang-gəl\ *vt* **man•gled; man•gling** \-gə-ling, -gling\ **1** : to cut, bruise, or hack with repeated blows or strokes **2** : to spoil or injure in making or performing : BOTCH ⟨a singer *mangling* the national anthem⟩ [Medieval French *mangler, mahangler,* perhaps from *mahaigner* "to maim"] — **man•gler** \-gə-lər, -glər\ *n*

[2]mangle *n* : a machine for ironing laundry by passing it between heated rollers [Dutch *mangel*]

[3]mangle *vt* **man•gled; man•gling** \-gə-ling, -gling\ : to press or smooth with a mangle — **man•gler** \-gə-lər, -glər\ *n*

man•go \ˈmang-gō\ *n, pl* **mangoes** *also* **mangos** : a yellowish red tropical fruit with a firm skin, hard central stone, and juicy aromatic mildly tart pulp; *also* : the evergreen tree related to the cashew that bears this fruit [Portuguese *manga,* probably from Malayalam (Dravidian language of southern India) *māṅṅa*]

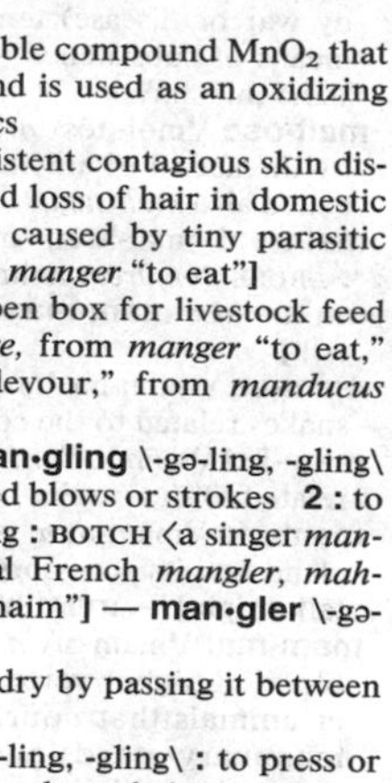
mango

man•go•steen \ˈmang-gə-ˌstēn\ *n* : a dark reddish purple fruit with thick rind and juicy flesh having a flavor suggestive of both peach and pineapple; *also* : a southeast Asian tree that bears this fruit [modification of Malay *manggisutan*]

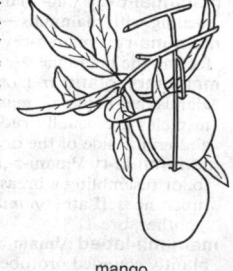

man•grove \ˈman-ˌgrōv, ˈmang-\ *n* : any of various tropical trees or shrubs that send out many prop roots and form dense masses in brackish marshes or shallow salt water [probably from Portuguese *mangue,* from Spanish *mangle,* probably from Taino]

mangy \ˈmān-jē\ *adj* **mang·i·er; -est** **1 :** affected with or resulting from mange **2 :** SHABBY 2, SEEDY ⟨a *mangy* rug⟩ — **mang·i·ness** \ˈmān-jē-nəs\ *n*

man·han·dle \ˈman-ˌhan-dl\ *vt* **1 :** to move or manage by human force **2 :** to handle roughly

man·hat·tan \man-ˈhat-n, mən-\ *n, often cap* **:** a cocktail consisting of vermouth and whiskey [*Manhattan,* borough of New York City]

man·hole \ˈman-ˌhōl\ *n* **:** a hole through which a person may go especially to gain access to an underground or enclosed structure

man·hood \ˈman-ˌhu̇d\ *n* **1 :** qualities generally associated with a man **2 :** the condition of being an adult male **3 :** adult males **:** MEN ⟨the nation's *manhood*⟩

man–hour \ˈman-ˈau̇-ər, -ˈau̇r\ *n* **:** a unit of one hour's work by one person used especially as a basis for wages and in accounting

man·hunt \ˈman-ˌhənt\ *n* **:** an organized hunt for a person and especially for one charged with a crime

ma·nia \ˈmā-nē-ə, -nyə\ *n* **1 :** excitement manifested especially by physical and mental hyperactivity and elevated mood **2 :** excessive or unreasonable enthusiasm **:** CRAZE [Late Latin, from Greek, from *mainesthai* "to be mad"]

1**ma·ni·ac** \ˈmā-nē-ˌak\ *adj* **:** affected with or suggestive of madness — **ma·ni·a·cal** \mə-ˈnī-ə-kəl\ *adj* — **ma·ni·a·cal·ly** \-kə-lē, -klē\ *adv*

2**maniac** *n* **1 :** MADMAN, LUNATIC **2 :** a person wildly enthusiastic about something **:** FAN

man·ic \ˈman-ik\ *adj* **:** affected with, relating to, characterized by, or resulting from mania — **manic** *n*

man·ic–de·pres·sive \ˌman-ik-di-ˈpres-iv\ *adj* **:** characterized by or affected with either mania, depression, or alternating mania and depression — **manic–depressive** *n*

1**man·i·cure** \ˈman-ə-ˌkyu̇r\ *n* **1 :** MANICURIST **2 :** a treatment for the care of the hands and nails [French, from Latin *manus* "hand" + French *-icure* (as in *pédicure* "pedicure")]

2**manicure** *vt* **1 :** to give a manicure to **2 :** to trim closely and evenly ⟨*manicure* the lawn⟩

man·i·cur·ist \-ˌkyu̇r-əst\ *n* **:** a person who gives manicures

1**man·i·fest** \ˈman-ə-ˌfest\ *adj* **:** clear to the senses or mind **:** OBVIOUS ⟨heard the verdict with *manifest* relief⟩ [Latin *manifestus,* "caught in the act, flagrant, obvious," perhaps from *manus* "hand" + *-festus,* related to Latin *infestus* "hostile"] — **man·i·fest·ly** *adv*

2**manifest** *vt* **:** to show plainly **:** make evident **:** DISPLAY

3**manifest** *n* **:** a list (as of cargo or passengers) especially for a ship or plane

man·i·fes·ta·tion \ˌman-ə-fə-ˈstā-shən, -ˌfes-ˈtā-\ *n* **1 a :** the act, process, or an instance of manifesting **b :** an outward or visible expression **2 :** a public demonstration of power and purpose ⟨rallies, parades, and other *manifestations*⟩

manifest destiny *n, often cap M&D* **:** a future event accepted as inevitable ⟨in the 19th century expansion to the Pacific was regarded as the *manifest destiny* of the United States⟩

man·i·fes·to \ˌman-ə-ˈfes-tō\ *n, pl* **-tos** *or* **-toes :** a public declaration of policy, purpose, or views [Italian, "denunciation, manifest," derived from Latin *manifestus* "manifest"]

1**man·i·fold** \ˈman-ə-ˌfōld\ *adj* **1 :** of many and various kinds ⟨*manifold* excuses⟩ **2 :** including or uniting various features ⟨a *manifold* personality⟩ [Old English *manigfeald,* from *manig* "many" + *-feald* "-fold"] — **man·i·fold·ly** *adv* — **man·i·fold·ness** \-ˌfōld-nəs, -ˌfōl-\ *n*

2**manifold** *n* **:** something that is manifold: as **a :** a whole consisting of many different elements **b :** a pipe fitting having several outlets for connecting one pipe with others **c :** a fitting on an internal-combustion engine that either receives exhaust gases or directs a fuel charge

3**manifold** *vb* **1 :** to make many or several copies ⟨*manifold* a manuscript⟩ **2 :** to make manifold

man·i·kin *also* **man·ni·kin** \ˈman-i-kən\ *n* **1 :** MANNEQUIN **2 :** a little man **:** DWARF, PYGMY

ma·nila *also* **ma·nil·la** \mə-ˈnil-ə\ *adj* **:** made of manila paper or from abaca

Manila hemp *n* **:** ABACA [*Manila,* Philippine Islands]

manila paper *n, often cap M* **:** a tough brownish paper made originally from abaca and used especially for wrapping

man in the street : a typical or ordinary person

man·i·oc \ˈman-ē-ˌäk\ *also* **man·di·o·ca** \ˌman-dē-ˈō-kə\ *n* **:** CASSAVA [French *manioc* and Spanish and Portuguese *mandioca,* from Tupi *maniˀóka, mandiˀóka*]

man·i·ple \ˈman-ə-pəl\ *n* **1 :** a long narrow band formerly worn at mass over the left arm by clerics of or above the order of subdeacon **2 :** a subdivision of a Roman legion consisting of either 120 or 60 men [Latin *manipulus* "handful," from *manus* "hand"]

ma·nip·u·late \mə-ˈnip-yə-ˌlāt\ *vt* **1 :** to treat or operate with or as if with the hands or by mechanical means especially with skill ⟨*manipulate* the trackball⟩ **2 a :** to manage or utilize skillfully ⟨*manipulate* masses of statistics⟩ **b :** to manage artfully, unfairly, or fraudulently ⟨*manipulate* accounts⟩ ⟨*manipulate* public opinion⟩ **c :** to influence (as prices) by artificial means [back-formation from *manipulation,* from French, derived from Latin *manipulus* "handful"] — **ma·nip·u·la·tion** \-ˌnip-yə-ˈlā-shən\ *n* — **ma·nip·u·la·tor** \-ˈnip-yə-ˌlāt-ər\ *n*

man·i·tou *or* **man·i·tu** \ˈman-ə-ˌtü\ *also* **man·i·to** \-ˌtō\ *n* **:** one of the Algonquian deities or spirits dominating the forces of nature [Ojibwa *manito·*]

man·kind *n sing or pl* **1** \ˈman-ˈkīnd, -ˌkīnd\ **:** the human race **:** the totality of human beings **2** \-ˌkīnd\ **:** men especially as distinguished from women

man·like \ˈman-ˌlīk\ *adj* **1 :** resembling human beings ⟨*manlike* apes⟩ **2 :** befitting or belonging to a man **:** MANLY

man·ly \ˈman-lē\ *adj* **man·li·er; -est** **1 :** having desirable qualities held to be appropriate to a man **:** STRONG, VIRILE **2 :** befitting a man ⟨*manly* sports⟩ — **man·li·ness** *n*

man–made \ˈman-ˈmād\ *adj* **:** made by humans rather than nature ⟨*man-made* systems⟩; *also* **:** SYNTHETIC ⟨*man-made* fibers⟩

man·na \ˈman-ə\ *n* **1 a :** food miraculously supplied to the Israelites in the wilderness **b :** divinely supplied spiritual nourishment **2 :** a usually sudden and unexpected source of gratification, pleasure, or gain [Old English, from Late Latin, from Greek, from Hebrew *mān*]

manned \ˈmand\ *adj* **:** carrying or performed by a person ⟨*manned* spaceflight⟩

man·ne·quin \ˈman-i-kən\ *n* **1 a :** an artist's, tailor's, or dressmaker's jointed figure of the human body **b :** a form representing the human figure used especially for displaying clothes **2 :** a woman who models clothing **:** MODEL [French, from Dutch *mannekijn* "little man," from *man* "man"]

man·ner \ˈman-ər\ *n* **1 a :** KIND ⟨what *manner* of person are you⟩ **b :** SORTS ⟨all *manner* of information⟩ **2 a :** a way of acting or proceeding ⟨worked in a brisk *manner*⟩ **b :** HABIT, CUSTOM ⟨spoke bluntly as is my *manner*⟩ **c :** STYLE ⟨painted in the artist's early *manner*⟩ **3** *pl* **a :** social conduct or rules of conduct as shown in prevalent customs **b :** characteristic or habitual deportment **:** BEHAVIOR ⟨mind your *manners*⟩ **c :** pleasing or socially acceptable deportment ⟨teach children *manners*⟩ [Medieval French *manere,* from Latin *manuarius* "of the hand," from *manus* "hand"]

man·nered \ˈman-ərd\ *adj* **1 :** having manners of a specified kind ⟨well-*mannered*⟩ **2 :** having an artificial character ⟨a highly *mannered* style⟩

man·ner·ism \ˈman-ə-ˌriz-əm\ *n* **:** an often affected peculiarity of action, bearing, or treatment ⟨the *mannerism* of constantly smoothing one's hair⟩ ***synonyms*** see AFFECTATION

man·ner·ly \ˈman-ər-lē\ *adj* **:** showing good manners **:** POLITE — **man·ner·li·ness** \-lē-nəs\ *n* — **mannerly** *adv*

man·nish \ˈman-ish\ *adj* **:** resembling or suggesting, suitable to, or characteristic of a man rather than a woman ⟨a *mannish* voice⟩ ⟨often wore *mannish* clothes⟩ — **man·nish·ly** *adv* — **man·nish·ness** *n*

man·ni·tol \ˈman-ə-ˌtȯl, -ˌtōl\ *n* **:** a slightly sweet crystalline alcohol $C_6H_{12}O_6$

ma·noeu·vre *chiefly British variant of* MANEUVER

man–of–war \ˌman-əv-ˈwȯr, -ə-\ *n, pl* **men–of–war** \ˌmen-\ **:** WARSHIP

ma·nom·e·ter \mə-ˈnäm-ət-ər\ *n* **:** an instrument for measuring pressure (as of gases and vapors) [derived from Greek *manos* "sparse, loose, rare"]

man·or \ˈman-ər\ *n* **:** a usually large landed estate; *esp* **:** one

\ə\ **abut**	\au̇\ **out**	\i\ **tip**	\ȯ\ **saw**	\u̇\ **foot**
\ər\ **further**	\ch\ **chin**	\ī\ **life**	\ȯi\ **coin**	\y\ **yet**
\a\ **mat**	\e\ **pet**	\j\ **job**	\th\ **thin**	\yü\ **few**
\ā\ **take**	\ē\ **easy**	\ng\ **sing**	\t͟h\ **this**	\yu̇\ **cure**
\ä\ **cot, cart**	\g\ **go**	\ō\ **bone**	\ü\ **food**	\zh\ **vision**

granted by a sovereign to a feudal lord [Medieval French *manoir* "residence," from *manoir* "to dwell," from Latin *manēre* "to stay"] — **ma·no·ri·al** \mə-ˈnōr-ē-əl, -ˈnȯr-\ *adj* — **ma·no·ri·al·ism** \-ē-ə-ˌliz-əm\ *n*

manor house *n* : the house of the lord of a manor

man–o'–war bird \ˌman-ə-ˈwȯr-ˌbərd\ *n* : FRIGATE BIRD

man power *n* **1** : power available from or supplied by the physical effort of humans **2** *usually* **man·pow·er** \ˈman-ˌpau̇-ər, -ˌpau̇r\ : the total supply of persons available and fitted for service (as in the armed forces or industry)

man·qué \mä^n-ˈkā\ *adj* : UNSUCCESSFUL — used after the word modified ⟨a poet *manqué*⟩ [French, from *manquer* "to lack, fall short"]

man·sard \ˈman-ˌsärd, -sərd\ *n* : a roof having two slopes on all sides with the lower slope much steeper than the upper [French *mansarde,* from François *Mansart,* died 1666, French architect]

manse \ˈmans\ *n* : the residence of a member of the clergy; *esp* : the house of a Presbyterian minister [Medieval Latin *mansa* "residence," from Latin *manēre* "to stay, dwell"]

man·ser·vant \ˈman-ˌsər-vənt\ *n, pl* **men·ser·vants** \ˈmen-ˌsər-vəns\ : a male servant

man·sion \ˈman-chən\ *n* : a large imposing residence [Medieval French, literally, "act of staying, lodging," from Latin *mansio,* from *manēre* "to stay"]

man–size \ˈman-ˌsīz\ *or* **man–sized** \-ˌsīzd\ *adj* **1** : suitable for or felt to require a man ⟨a *man-size* job⟩ **2** : larger than others of its kind ⟨a *man-size* model⟩

man·slaugh·ter \ˈman-ˌslȯt-ər\ *n* : the unlawful killing of a person without intent to do so

man·slay·er \-ˌslā-ər\ *n* : one that slays a person

man·sue·tude \ˈman-swi-ˌtüd, man-ˈsü-ə-ˌtüd, -ˌtyüd\ *n* : the quality or state of being gentle : MEEKNESS, TAMENESS [Latin *mansuetudo,* from *mansuescere* "to tame," from *manus* "hand" + *suescere* "to accustom"]

man·ta \ˈmant-ə\ *n* **1** : a square piece of cloth or blanket used in southwestern U.S. and Latin America as a cloak or shawl **2** : MANTA RAY [Spanish; sense 2 American Spanish, from Spanish; from its shape]

manta ray *n* : any of several extremely large rays that are widely distributed in warm seas and have enlarged pectoral fins resembling wings — called also *devilfish, manta*

man·teau \man-ˈtō\ *n* : a loose cloak, coat, or robe [French, from Medieval French *mantel*]

man·tel \ˈmant-l\ *n* **1** : the beam, stone, arch, or shelf above a fireplace **2** : the finish covering the chimney around a fireplace [Medieval French, "mantle"]

man·telet \ˈmant-lət\ *n* : a very short cape or cloak

man·tel·piece \ˈmant-l-ˌpēs\ *n* **1** : a mantel with its side elements **2** : the shelf of a mantel

man·ti·core \ˈmant-i-ˌkōr, -ˌkȯr\ *n* : a legendary animal with the head of a man, the body of a lion, and the tail of a dragon or scorpion [Latin *mantichora,* from Greek *mantichōras*]

man·tid \ˈman-təd\ *n* : MANTIS [*Mantis,* genus name]

man·til·la \man-ˈtē-ə, -ˈtē-yə, -ˈtil-ə\ *n* **1** : a light scarf worn over the head and shoulders especially by Spanish and Latin American women **2** : a short light cape or cloak [Spanish, from *manta* "manta"]

man·tis \ˈmant-əs\ *n, pl* **man·tis·es** *also* **man·tes** \ˈman-ˌtēz\ : any of various large usually green insects related to the grasshoppers and cockroaches that feed upon other insects and hold their prey in forelimbs raised as if in prayer [Greek, literally, "diviner, prophet"]

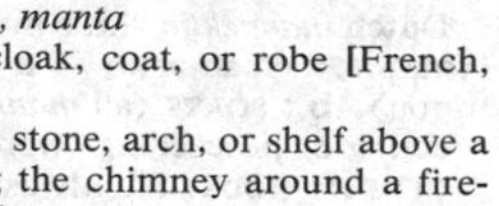
mantis

man·tis·sa \man-ˈtis-ə\ *n* : the decimal part of a logarithm [Latin *mantisa, mantissa* "something used to make up weight," from Etruscan]

[1]man·tle \ˈmant-l\ *n* **1** : a loose sleeveless outer garment : CLOAK **2 a** : something that covers or envelops **b** : a fold or lobe or pair of lobes of the body wall of a mollusk or brachiopod lining and secreting the shell in shell-bearing forms **3** : a lacy sheath that gives light by incandescence when placed over a flame **4** : the portion of the earth that lies between the crust and the core [Medieval French *mantel,* from Latin *mantellum*]

[2]mantle *vt* **man·tled; man·tling** \ˈmant-ling, -l-ing\ : to cover or envelop with or as if with a mantle

man·tle·rock \ˈmant-l-ˌräk\ *n* : unconsolidated material that overlies the earth's solid rock

man·trap \ˈman-ˌtrap\ *n* : a trap for catching men : SNARE

man·tua \ˈmanch-wə, -ə-wə\ *n* : a usually loose-fitting gown worn especially in the 17th and 18th centuries [French *manteau*]

[1]man·u·al \ˈman-yə-wəl, -yəl\ *adj* **1 a** : of, relating to, or involving the hands ⟨*manual* dexterity⟩ **b** : worked or done by hand and not a machine ⟨a *manual* transmission⟩ **2** : requiring or using physical skill and energy ⟨*manual* labor⟩ ⟨*manual* workers⟩ [Medieval French *manuel,* from Latin *manualis,* from *manus* "hand"] — **man·u·al·ly** \-ē\ *adv*

[2]manual *n* **1** : a small book; *esp* : HANDBOOK **2** : the set movements in the handling of a weapon during a military drill or ceremony

manual alphabet *n* : an alphabet for the deaf in which the letters are represented by finger positions

manual training *n* : a course of training to develop skill in using the hands (as in woodworking)

ma·nu·bri·um \mə-ˈnü-brē-əm, -ˈnyü-\ *n, pl* **-bria** \-brē-ə\ *also* **-briums** : an anatomical part suggesting a handle; *esp* : the uppermost segment of the sternum of humans and many other mammals [Latin, "handle," from *manus* "hand"]

man·u·fac·to·ry \ˌman-yə-ˈfak-tə-rē, ˌman-ə-, -trē\ *n, pl* **-ries** : FACTORY

[1]man·u·fac·ture \ˌman-yə-ˈfak-chər, ˌman-ə-\ *n* **1** : something made from raw materials **2** : the process of making wares by hand or by machinery especially when carried on systematically with division of labor **3** : the act or process of producing something ⟨the *manufacture* of blood by the body⟩ [Middle French, from Latin *manu factus* "made by hand"]

[2]manufacture *vt* **-fac·tured; -fac·tur·ing** \-ˈfak-chə-ring, -ˈfak-shring\ **1** : to make into a product suitable for use **2** : to make from raw materials by hand or by machinery especially systematically and with division of labor **3** : FABRICATE 2, INVENT — **man·u·fac·tur·ing** *n*

man·u·fac·tur·er \-ˈfak-chər-ər, -ˈfak-shrər\ *n* : one that manufactures; *esp* : an employer of workers in manufacturing

man·u·mis·sion \ˌman-yə-ˈmish-ən\ *n* : emancipation from slavery [Medieval French, from Latin *manumissio,* from *manumittere* "to manumit"]

man·u·mit \ˌman-yə-ˈmit\ *vt* **-mit·ted; -mit·ting** : to set free; *esp* : to release from slavery [Medieval French *manumettre,* from Latin *manumittere,* from *manus* "hand" + *mittere* "to let go, send"]

[1]ma·nure \mə-ˈnu̇r, -ˈnyu̇r\ *vt* : to enrich (land) by the application of manure [Middle English *manouren* "to cultivate," from Medieval French *mainouverer, meinourer* "to till (land), construct, create," from Medieval Latin *manu operare* "to perform manual labor," from Latin *manu* "by hand" + *operari* "to work" — see *Word History* at MANEUVER]

[2]manure *n* : material that fertilizes land; *esp* : refuse of stables and barnyards consisting of bodily waste of livestock with or without litter — **ma·nu·ri·al** \mə-ˈnu̇r-ē-əl, -ˈnyu̇r-\ *adj*

[1]man·u·script \ˈman-yə-ˌskript\ *adj* : written by hand or typed [Latin *manu scriptus* "written by hand"]

[2]manuscript *n* **1** : a written or typewritten composition or document **2** : writing as opposed to print

Manx \ˈmangs, ˈmangks\ *n, pl* **Manx** **1** *pl* : the people of the Isle of Man **2** : the Celtic language of the Manx people **3** : MANX CAT — **Manx** *adj*

Manx cat *n* : any of a breed of tailless domestic cats with short or long hair

[1]many \ˈmen-ē\ *adj* **more** \ˈmōr, ˈmȯr\; **most** \ˈmōst\ **1** : consisting of or amounting to a large but indefinite number ⟨worked for *many* years⟩ **2** : being one of a large but indefinite number ⟨*many* a person⟩ [Old English *manig*] — **as many** : the same in number ⟨saw three plays in *as many* days⟩

synonyms MANY, NUMEROUS, COUNTLESS mean consisting of a large number. MANY implies a relatively large number usually of like things in contrast with a few or several or with an exact number ⟨attracts *many* visitors each year⟩. NUMEROUS implies very many and often suggests crowding, thronging, or clustering ⟨ignored the *numerous* questions shouted by reporters⟩. COUNTLESS may imply a number too great to count or apparently without limit ⟨spent *countless* hours perfecting the invention⟩.

[2]**many** *pron, pl in construction* : a large number of persons or things ⟨*many* of them are already here⟩

[3]**many** *n, pl in construction* : a large but indefinite number ⟨a good *many* went⟩

many·fold \ˌmen-ē-ˈfōld\ *adv* : by many times

many–sid·ed \ˌmen-ē-ˈsīd-əd\ *adj* **1** : having many sides or aspects **2** : having many interests or aptitudes : VERSATILE — **many·sid·ed·ness** *n*

man·za·ni·ta \ˌman-zə-ˈnēt-ə\ *n* : any of various western North American evergreen shrubs of the heath family [American Spanish, from Spanish *manzana* "apple"]

Mao·ism \ˈmau̇-ˌiz-əm\ *n* : the theory and practice of Marxism-Leninism developed in China chiefly by Mao Zedong — **Mao·ist** \ˈmau̇-əst\ *n or adj*

Mao·ri \ˈmau̇-rē\ *n, pl* **Maori** *or* **Maoris** **1** : a member of a Polynesian people native to New Zealand **2** : the language of the Maori people — **Maori** *adj*

[1]**map** \ˈmap\ *n* **1 a** : a drawing or picture showing features of an area (as the surface of the earth) **b** : a drawing or picture of the sky showing the position of stars and planets **2** : the arrangement of genes on a chromosome as deduced from genetic experiments [Medieval Latin *mappa,* from Latin, "napkin, towel"]

[2]**map** *vt* **mapped; map·ping** **1 a** : to make a map of ⟨*map* the surface of the moon⟩ **b** : to assign (a set or element) in mathematical correspondence ⟨*map* the set of integers onto itself⟩ **2** : to plan in detail ⟨*map* out a campaign⟩ — **map·per** *n*

ma·ple \ˈmā-pəl\ *n* : any of a genus of trees or shrubs with opposite leaves and a 2-winged dry fruit; *also* : the hard light-colored close-grained wood of a maple [Old English *mapul-*]

maple sugar *n* : a sugar made by boiling maple syrup

maple syrup *n* : syrup made by concentrating the sap of maples and especially the sugar maple

map·ping \ˈmap-iŋ\ *n* **1** : the act or process of making a map **2** : FUNCTION 5a ⟨a one-to-one *mapping* of the positive integers onto their squares⟩

ma·quette \ma-ˈket\ *n* : a usually small preliminary model (as of a sculpture) [French]

ma·quis \ma-ˈkē, mä-\ *n, pl* **ma·quis** \-ˈkē, -ˈkēz\ **1** : thick scrubby evergreen underbrush of Mediterranean shores; *also* : an area of such underbrush **2** *often cap* : a guerrilla fighter in the French underground during World War II [French, from Italian *macchie,* plural of *macchia* "thicket, sketch, spot"]

mar \ˈmär\ *vt* **marred; mar·ring** **1** : to make a blemish on : DAMAGE, SPOIL **2** *archaic* **a** : [1]MANGLE 1, MUTILATE **b** : DESTROY 1 [Old English *mierran* "to waste"]

mar·a·bou *also* **mar·a·bout** \ˈmar-ə-ˌbü\ *n* **1 a** : a large dark gray African stork **b** : the long soft feathers from under the tail and wings of this bird used especially formerly in millinery **2 a** : a thrown raw silk **b** : a fabric (as a feathery trimming material) made of this silk [French *marabout,* literally, "marabout"]

marabou 1a

mar·a·bout \ˈmar-ə-ˌbü, -ˌbüt\ *n, often cap* : a dervish in Muslim Africa held to have supernatural power [French, from Portuguese *marabuto,* from Arabic *murābiṭ*]

ma·ra·ca \mə-ˈräk-ə, -ˈrak-\ *n* : a dried gourd or a rattle like a gourd that contains dried seeds or pebbles and is used as a percussion instrument [Portuguese *maracá,* from Tupi *maraká*]

mar·a·schi·no \ˌmar-ə-ˈskē-nō, -ˈshē-\ *n, often cap* **1** : a sweet liqueur distilled from the fermented juice of a bitter wild cherry **2** : a usually large cherry preserved in true or imitation maraschino [Italian, from *marasca* "bitter wild cherry"]

ma·ras·mus \mə-ˈraz-məs\ *n* : a condition of serious malnutrition occurring especially in children by a diet deficient in calories and protein [Late Latin, from Greek *marasmos,* from *marainein* "to waste away"]

Ma·ra·thi \mə-ˈrät-ē\ *n* : the chief Indo-Aryan language of the state of Maharashtra in India [Marathi *marāṭhī*]

mar·a·thon \ˈmar-ə-ˌthän\ *n* **1** : a long-distance race; *esp* : a footrace run on an open course of 26 miles 385 yards (42.2 kilometers) **2** : an unusually long and exhausting contest or activity [*Marathon,* Greece, site of a victory of Greeks over Persians in 490 B.C., the news of which was carried to Athens by a long-distance runner] — **marathon** *adj*

ma·raud \mə-ˈrȯd\ *vb* : to roam about and raid in search of plunder [French *marauder*] — **ma·raud·er** *n*

[1]**mar·ble** \ˈmär-bəl\ *n* **1 a** : a usually crystalline metamorphosed limestone that is capable of taking a high polish and is used in architecture and sculpture **b** : something made from marble; *esp* : a piece of sculpture **2 a** : a little ball (as of glass) used in various games **b** *pl* : a children's game played with these little balls [Medieval French *marbre,* from Latin *marmor,* from Greek *marmaros*]

[2]**marble** *vt* **mar·bled; mar·bling** \ˈmar-bə-liŋ, -bliŋ\ : to give a mottled appearance to ⟨*marble* the edges of a book⟩

[3]**marble** *adj* : made of, resembling, or suggestive of marble

mar·ble·ize \ˈmär-bə-ˌlīz\ *vt* : MARBLE

mar·bling \ˈmär-bə-liŋ, -bliŋ\ *n* **1** : coloration or markings resembling or suggestive of marble **2** : an intermixture of fat through the lean of a cut of meat

mar·bly \ˈmär-bə-lē, -blē\ *adj* : MARBLE

mar·ca·site \ˈmär-kə-ˌsīt, -ˌzīt, ˌmär-kə-ˈzēt\ *n* : a pale yellow to white mineral consisting of iron and sulfur [Medieval Latin *marcasita*]

[1]**mar·cel** \mär-ˈsel\ *n* : a deep soft wave made in the hair by the use of a heated curling iron [*Marcel* Grateau, died 1936, French hairdresser]

[2]**marcel** *vt* **mar·celled; mar·cel·ling** : to make a marcel in

[1]**march** \ˈmärch\ *n* : a border region : FRONTIER; *esp* : a district originally set up to defend a boundary ⟨the Welsh *marches*⟩ [Medieval French *marche,* of Germanic origin]

[2]**march** *vi* : to have common borders or frontiers

[3]**march** \ˈmärch, *imperatively often* härch *in the military*\ *vb* **1** : to move along usually with a steady regular stride in step with others **2 a** : to move in a direct purposeful manner : PROCEED **b** : to make steady progress : ADVANCE [Medieval French *marchier* "to trample," probably of Germanic origin] — **march·er** *n*

[4]**march** \ˈmärch\ *n* **1 a** : the action of marching **b** : the distance covered within a specific period of time by marching **c** : a regular even step used in marching **2** : forward movement **3** : a musical composition in duple rhythm (as $\frac{4}{4}$ time) with a strongly accentuated beat suitable to accompany marching

March \ˈmärch\ *n* : the 3rd month of the year according to the Gregorian calendar [Medieval French, from Latin *Martius,* from *Mart-, Mars,* the god Mars]

mär·chen \ˈmeər-k̲ən\ *n, pl* **marchen** : TALE 1; *esp* : FOLKTALE [German]

mar·chio·ness \ˈmär-shə-nəs, -shnəs\ *n* **1** : the wife or widow of a marquess **2** : a woman who holds the rank of marquess in her own right [Medieval Latin *marchionissa,* from *marchio* "marquess," from *marca* "border region," of Germanic origin]

march·pane \ˈmärch-ˌpān\ *n* : MARZIPAN [Italian *marzapane*]

march–past \ˈmärch-ˌpast\ *n* : a marching by especially of troops in review

Mar·di Gras \ˌmärd-ē-ˈgrä\ *n* **1** : Shrove Tuesday often observed with parades and festivities **2** : a carnival period climaxing on Shrove Tuesday [French, literally, "fat Tuesday"]

[1]**mare** \ˈmaər, ˈmeər\ *n* : an adult female of the horse or related animal (as a zebra) [Old English *mere*]

[2]**ma·re** \ˈmär-ˌā\ *n, pl* **ma·ria** \ˈmär-ē-ə\ : one of several large dark areas on the surface of the moon or Mars [Latin, "sea"]

ma·re clau·sum \ˌmär-ˌā-ˈklau̇-səm, -ˈklȯ-\ *n* : a navigable body of water (as a sea) under the jurisdiction of one nation and closed to other nations [New Latin, literally, "closed sea"]

mare's nest *n, pl* **mare's nests** *or* **mares' nests** **1** : a false discovery or a deliberate hoax **2** : a situation or condition of great confusion

mare's tail *n* : a cirrus cloud that has a long slender flowing appearance

mar·ga·rine \ˈmärj-rən, -ə-rən, -ə-ˌrēn\ *n* : a food product made

\ə\ **abut**	\au̇\ **out**	\i\ **tip**	\ȯ\ **saw**	\u̇\ **foot**
\ər\ **further**	\ch\ **chin**	\ī\ **life**	\ȯi\ **coin**	\y\ **yet**
\a\ **mat**	\e\ **pet**	\j\ **job**	\th\ **thin**	\yü\ **few**
\ā\ **take**	\ē\ **easy**	\ŋ\ **sing**	\t̲h̲\ **this**	\yu̇\ **cure**
\ä\ **cot, cart**	\g\ **go**	\ō\ **bone**	\ü\ **food**	\zh\ **vision**

usually from vegetable oils and skim milk often with vitamins A and D added and used as a spread and a cooking fat [French, derived from Greek *margaron* "pearl," probably back-formation from *margaritēs*]

mar·gay \ˈmär-ˌgā\ *n* **:** a small spotted wildcat resembling the ocelot and found from Mexico to Argentina [French, from Tupi *maracaja*]

marge \ˈmärj\ *n, archaic* **:** MARGIN 2

[1]**mar·gin** \ˈmär-jən\ *n* **1 :** the part of a page outside the main body of printed or written matter **2 :** the outside limit and adjoining area of something **3 a :** an allowance (as of time or money) to meet unexpected demands **b :** the point (as of rising costs or shortage of raw material) at which an economic activity becomes impracticable **4 a :** the difference between cost and selling price **b :** cash or collateral deposited to secure a broker from loss on a contract **c :** an allowance above or below a certain figure within which a purchase or sale is to be made **5 :** measure or degree of difference ⟨won by a single vote *margin*⟩ [Latin *margin-, margo* "border"] ***synonyms*** see BORDER — **mar·gined** \-jənd\ *adj*

[2]**margin** *vt* **1 :** to provide with an edging or border **2 :** BORDER 2

mar·gin·al \ˈmärj-nəl, -ən-l\ *adj* **1 :** written or printed in the margin of a page or sheet ⟨*marginal* notes⟩ **2 :** of, relating to, or situated at a margin or border **3 a :** close to the lower limit of qualification or acceptability ⟨*marginal* students⟩ **b :** yielding a supply of goods which when marketed at existing price levels will barely cover the cost of production ⟨*marginal* land⟩; *also* **:** relating to or derived from goods produced and marketed and with such result ⟨*marginal* profits⟩ — **mar·gin·al·i·ty** \ˌmär-jə-ˈnal-ət-ē\ *n* — **mar·gin·al·ly** \ˈmärj-nə-lē, -ən-l-ē\ *adv*

mar·gi·na·lia \ˌmär-jə-ˈnā-lē-ə\ *n pl* **:** marginal notes

mar·gin·al·ize \ˈmärj-nəl-ˌīz, -ən-l-\ *vt* **-ized; -iz·ing :** to relegate to an unimportant or powerless position within a society or group — **mar·gin·al·i·za·tion** \ˌmärj-nəl-ə-ˈzā-shən, -ən-l-\ *n*

marginal utility *n* **:** the amount of additional utility to a consumer provided by an additional unit of an economic good or service

mar·grave \ˈmär-ˌgrāv\ *n* **1 :** the military governor especially of a medieval German border province **2 :** a member of the German nobility corresponding in rank to a British marquess [Dutch *markgraaf*] — **mar·gra·vate** \-grə-ˌvāt\ *or* **mar·gra·vi·ate** \mär-ˈgrā-vē-ət\ *n* — **mar·gra·vi·al** \-vē-əl\ *adj*

mar·gra·vine \ˈmär-grə-ˌvēn, ˌmär-grə-ˈ\ *n* **:** the wife of a margrave

mar·gue·rite \ˌmär-gyə-ˈrēt, -gə-\ *n* **1 :** DAISY 1a **2 :** any of various single-flowered chrysanthemums [French, derived from Greek *margaritēs* "pearl"]

maria *plural of* [2]MARE

Mar·i·an \ˈmer-ē-ən, ˈmar-ē-, ˈmā-rē-\ *adj* **1 :** of or relating to Mary Tudor or her reign (1553-58) **2 :** of or relating to the Virgin Mary

Mar·i·an·ist \-ē-ə-nəst\ *n* **:** a member of the Roman Catholic Society of Mary of Paris devoted especially to education

mari·gold \ˈmar-ə-ˌgōld, ˈmer-\ *n* **1 :** POT MARIGOLD **2 :** any of a genus of tropical American herbs related to the daisies that are grown for their showy variously colored yellow, orange, or maroon flower heads [Middle English, from *Mary,* mother of Jesus + *gold*]

mar·i·jua·na *also* **mar·i·hua·na** \ˌmar-ə-ˈwän-ə *also* -ˈhwän-\ *n* **1 :** HEMP **2 :** the dried leaves and flowering tops of the female hemp plant that are sometimes smoked for their intoxicating effect [Mexican Spanish *mariguana, marihuana*]

ma·rim·ba \mə-ˈrim-bə\ *n* **:** a primitive xylophone with resonators beneath each bar; *also* **:** a modern form of this instrument [of Bantu origin]

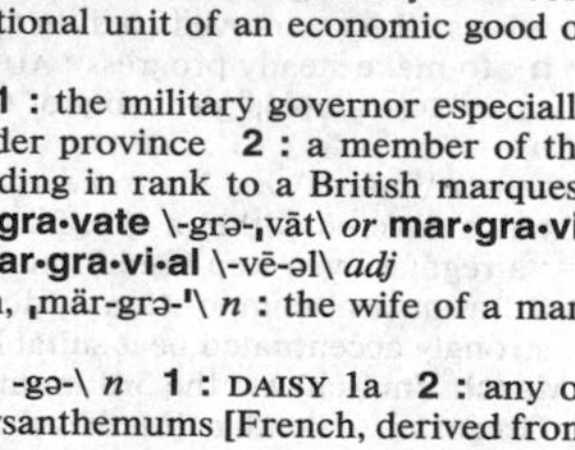

marimba

ma·ri·na \mə-ˈrē-nə\ *n* **:** a dock or basin providing secure moorings for boats and yachts [Italian and Spanish, "seashore," from *marino,* adj., "marine," from Latin *marinus*]

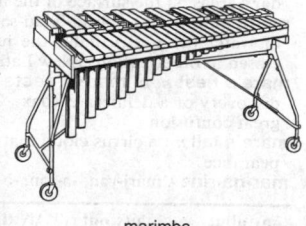

[1]**mar·i·nade** \ˌmar-ə-ˈnād\ *vt* **:** MARINATE

[2]**marinade** *n* **:** a savory usually acid sauce in which food (as meat) is soaked to enrich its flavor

mar·i·nate \ˈmar-ə-ˌnāt\ *vt* **:** to soak in a marinade [probably from Italian *marinare,* from *marino* "marine"]

[1]**ma·rine** \mə-ˈrēn\ *adj* **1 a :** of or relating to the sea ⟨*marine* life⟩ **b :** of or relating to the navigation of the sea **:** NAUTICAL ⟨a *marine* chart⟩ **c :** of or relating to the commerce of the sea ⟨*marine* insurance⟩ **2 :** of or relating to marines ⟨*marine* barracks⟩ [Latin *marinus,* from *mare* "sea"]

[2]**marine** *n* **1 :** the mercantile and naval shipping of a country **2 :** one of a class of soldiers serving on shipboard or in close association with a naval force; *esp* **:** a member of the United States Marine Corps

mar·i·ner \ˈmar-ə-nər\ *n* **:** one who navigates or assists in navigating a ship **:** SAILOR

Mar·i·ol·a·try \ˌmer-ē-ˈäl-ə-trē, ˌmar-\ *n* **:** excessive veneration of the Virgin Mary [*Mary* + Greek *latreia* "worship"]

mar·i·o·nette \ˌmar-ē-ə-ˈnet, ˌmer-\ *n* **:** a small usually wooden figure with jointed limbs moved by strings or wires [French *marionnette,* from the name *Marion*]

Mar·i·po·sa lily \ˌmar-ə-ˌpō-zə-, -sə-\ *n* **:** any of a genus of western North American plants related to the lilies and having showily blotched flowers [probably from American Spanish *mariposa,* from Spanish, "butterfly"]

Mar·ist \ˈmar-əst, ˈmer-\ *n* **:** a member of the Roman Catholic Society of Mary devoted to education

mar·i·tal \ˈmar-ət-l\ *adj* **1 :** of or relating to marriage **2 :** of or relating to a husband [Latin *maritalis,* from *maritus* "married"] ***synonyms*** see MATRIMONIAL — **mar·i·tal·ly** \-l-ē\ *adv*

mar·i·time \ˈmar-ə-ˌtīm\ *adj* **1 :** of or relating to navigation or commerce on the sea ⟨*maritime* law⟩ **2 :** of, relating to, or bordering on the sea ⟨a *maritime* province⟩ **3 :** having characteristics controlled primarily by oceanic winds and air masses ⟨a *maritime* climate⟩ [Latin *maritimus,* from *mare* "sea"]

mar·jo·ram \ˈmärj-rəm, -ə-rəm\ *n* **:** any of various usually fragrant and aromatic Old World mints often used as seasoning [Middle French *marjorane, marjolaine,* from Medieval Latin *marjorana*]

[1]**mark** \ˈmärk\ *n* **1 :** [1]MARCH **2 a** (1) **:** a conspicuous object serving as a guide for travelers (2) **:** something (as a line, notch, or fixed object) designed to record position ⟨high-water *mark*⟩ **b :** something aimed at **:** TARGET **c :** the starting line or position **d** (1) **:** an object of ridicule or abuse **:** BUTT; *also* **:** the victim or prospective victim of a swindle (2) **:** the point under discussion ⟨a comment beside the *mark*⟩ **e :** a standard of performance, quality, or condition **:** NORM **3 a** (1) **:** SIGN, INDICATION ⟨gave the necklace as a *mark* of esteem⟩ (2) **:** an impression (as a scratch, scar, or stain) made on something (3) **:** a distinguishing trait or quality **:** CHARACTERISTIC ⟨the *marks* of an educated person⟩ **b :** a symbol used for identification or indication of ownership **c :** a cross made in place of a signature **d :** a written or printed symbol (as a comma or colon) **e :** a symbol (as a number or letter) representing an estimation of the quality of work or conduct; *esp* **:** GRADE 5 **4 a :** ATTENTION, NOTICE ⟨nothing worthy of *mark*⟩ **b :** IMPORTANCE, DISTINCTION ⟨a person of *mark*⟩ **c :** a lasting or strong impression ⟨make one's *mark* in the world⟩ [Old English *mearc* "boundary, march, sign"] ***synonyms*** see SIGN

[2]**mark** *vt* **1 a** (1) **:** to fix or trace out the bounds of (2) **:** to plot the course of **:** CHART **b :** to set apart by a line or boundary ⟨*mark* off a mining claim⟩ **2 a :** to designate as if by a mark ⟨*marked* for greatness⟩ **b :** to make a mark on **c :** to furnish with natural marks ⟨wings *marked* with white⟩ **d :** to label so as to indicate price or quality **e :** to make note of in writing **:** JOT **f :** to indicate by a mark or symbol; *also* **:** RECORD **g :** to determine the quality or value of by means of marks or symbols **:** GRADE **h :** CHARACTERIZE, DISTINGUISH ⟨the flamboyance that *marks* her style⟩ **3 :** to take notice of **:** OBSERVE ⟨*mark* my words⟩ — **mark time 1 :** to keep the time of a marching step by moving the feet alternately without advancing **2 :** to function or operate without making progress

[3]**mark** *n* **1 :** the basic monetary unit of East Germany before reunification **2 :** DEUTSCHE MARK [German]

Mark \ˈmärk\ *n* **:** the second Gospel in the New Testament — see BIBLE table

mark·down \ˈmärk-ˌdau̇n\ *n* **1 :** a lowering of price **2 :** the amount by which an original selling price is reduced

mark down \märk-ˈdau̇n, ˈmärk-\ *vt* **:** to put a lower price on

marked \ˈmärkt\ *adj* **1 :** having marks ⟨a *marked* card⟩ **2 :** having a distinctive character **:** NOTICEABLE **3 a :** having fame or notoriety **b** : being an object of attack, suspicion, or vengeance ‹a *marked* man› — **mark·ed·ly** \ˈmär-kəd-lē\ *adv*

mark·er \ˈmär-kər\ *n* **1** : one that marks **2** : something used for marking

[1]**mar·ket** \ˈmär-kət\ *n* **1 a** : a meeting together of people to buy and sell; *also* : the people at such a meeting **b** : a public place where a market is held; *esp* : a place where provisions are sold at wholesale **c** : a retail establishment usually of a specified kind ‹a meat *market*› **2 a** : a geographical area of demand for commodities ‹our foreign *markets*› **b** : a specified category of potential buyers ‹the youth *market*› **c** : the course of commercial activity by which the exchange of commodities is effected ‹the *market* is dull› **d** : an opportunity for selling ‹a good *market* for used cars› **3** : the area of economic activity in which buyers and sellers come together and the forces of supply and demand affect prices [Middle English, derived from Latin *mercatus* "trade, marketplace," from *mercari* "to trade," from *merx* "merchandise"] — **in the market** : interested in buying ‹*in the market* for a house› — **on the market** : available for purchase; *also* : up for sale ‹put their house *on the market*›

[2]**market** *vb* **1** : to deal in a market **2** : to offer for sale in a market : SELL — **mar·ke·teer** \ˌmär-kə-ˈtiər\ *or* **mar·ket·er** \ˈmär-kət-ər\ *n* — **mar·ket·ing** \ˈmär-kət-iŋ\ *n*

mar·ket·able \ˈmär-kət-ə-bəl\ *adj* **1** : fit for sale **2** : wanted by purchasers : SALABLE — **mar·ket·abil·i·ty** \ˌmär-kət-ə-ˈbil-ət-ē\ *n*

market garden *n, British* : a plot in which vegetables are raised for market — **market gardener** *n, British* — **market gardening** *n, British*

mar·ket·place \ˈmär-kət-ˌplās\ *n* **1** : an open square or place in a town where markets or public sales are held **2** : the world of trade or economic activity

market price *n* : a price actually given in current market dealings

market research *n* : the gathering of factual information as to consumer preferences for goods and services

market value *n* : a price at which both buyers and sellers are willing to do business

mark·ing \ˈmär-kiŋ\ *n* **1** : the act, process, or an instance of making or giving a mark **2 a** : a mark made **b** : arrangement, pattern, or disposition of marks (as on the coat of a mammal)

mark·ka \ˈmär-ˌkä\ *n, pl* **mark·kaa** \ˈmär-ˌkä\ *or* **mark·kas** \-ˌkäz\ : the basic monetary unit of Finland until 2002 [Finnish, from Swedish *mark,* a unit of value]

marks·man \ˈmärk-smən\ *n* : a person skilled in shooting at a mark or target — **marks·man·ship** \-ˌship\ *n*

mark·up \ˈmär-ˌkəp\ *n* : an amount added to the cost price of an article to determine the selling price

mark up \mär-ˈkəp, ˈmär-\ *vt* : to put a higher price on

markup language *n* : a system (as HTML) for marking or tagging a document that indicates its logical structure (as paragraphs) and gives instructions for its layout on the page especially for electronic transmission and display

[1]**marl** \ˈmärl\ *n* : a loose or crumbling earthy deposit (as of sand or clay) that contains a substantial amount of calcium carbonate [Medieval French *marle,* from Medieval Latin *margila,* from Latin *marga,* from Gaulish] — **marly** \ˈmär-lē\ *adj*

[2]**marl** *vt* : to dress (land) with marl

mar·lin \ˈmär-lən\ *n* : any of several large saltwater sport fishes related to sailfishes [short for *marlinespike;* from the appearance of its beak]

mar·line \ˈmär-lən\ *also* **mar·lin** *n* : a small loosely twisted line of two strands used for seizing and as a covering for wire rope [Middle English *merlyn*]

mar·line·spike *also* **mar·lin·spike** \ˈmär-lən-ˌspīk\ *n* : a pointed iron tool used to separate strands of rope or wire (as in splicing)

mar·ma·lade \ˈmär-mə-ˌlād\ *n* : a clear jelly in which pieces of fruit and fruit rind are suspended [Portuguese *marmelada* "quince conserve," from *marmelo* "quince," from Latin *melimelum,* a kind of sweet apple, from Greek *melimēlon,* from *meli* "honey" + *mēlon* "apple"]

mar·mo·re·al \mär-ˈmōr-ē-əl, mär-ˈmȯr-\ *also* **mar·mo·re·an** \-ē-ən\ *adj* : of, relating to, or resembling marble or a marble statue [Latin *marmoreus,* from *marmor* "marble"] — **mar·mo·re·al·ly** \-ē-ə-lē\ *adv*

mar·mo·set \ˈmär-mə-ˌset, -mə-ˌzet\ *n* : any of numerous soft-furred bushy-tailed South and Central American monkeys with claws instead of nails except on the big toe [Middle French, "grotesque figure," from *marmouser* "to mumble"]

marmoset

mar·mot \ˈmär-mət\ *n* : any of a genus of stout-bodied short-legged burrowing rodents with coarse fur, a short bushy tail, and very small ears — compare WOODCHUCK [French *marmotte*]

[1]**ma·roon** \mə-ˈrün\ *vt* **1** : to put ashore and abandon on a desolate island or coast **2** : to leave isolated and helpless [probably from French *maron, marron,* "feral, fugitive," from American Spanish *cimarrón* "wild, savage"]

[2]**maroon** *n* : a dark red [French *marron* "Spanish chestnut"]

mar·quee \mär-ˈkē\ *n* **1** : a large tent set up for an outdoor party, reception, or exhibition **2** : a canopy usually of metal and glass projecting over an entrance ‹a theater *marquee*› [French *marquise,* literally, "marchioness"]

mar·quess \ˈmär-kwəs\ *or* **mar·quis** \ˈmär-kwəs, mär-ˈkē\ *n, pl* **mar·quess·es** *or* **mar·quis·es** \-kwə-səz\ *or* **mar·quis** \-ˈkē, -ˈkēz\ **1** : a nobleman of hereditary rank in Europe and Japan **2** : a member of the British peerage ranking below a duke and above an earl [Middle French *marquis,* alteration of *marchis,* from *marche* "border region, march"] — **mar·quess·ate** \ˈmär-kwə-sət\ *or* **mar·quis·ate** \ˈmär-kwə-zət, -sət\ *n*

mar·que·try \ˈmär-kə-trē\ *n, pl* **-tries** : decoration in which elaborate patterns are formed by the insertion of pieces of wood, shell, or ivory into a wood veneer that is then applied to a piece of furniture [Middle French *marqueterie,* from *marqueter* "to checker, inlay," from *marque* "mark"]

mar·quise \mär-ˈkēz\ *n, pl* **mar·quises** \-ˈkēz, -ˈkēz-əz\ : MARCHIONESS [French, from *marquis* "marquess"]

mar·qui·sette \ˌmär-kwə-ˈzet, -kə-\ *n* : a sheer meshed fabric used for clothing, curtains, and mosquito nets

mar·riage \ˈmar-ij\ *n* **1 a** (1) : the state of being united to a person of the opposite sex as husband or wife in a consensual and contractual relationship recognized by law (2) : the state of being united to a person of the same sex in a relationship like that of a traditional marriage ‹same-sex ~› **b** : the mutual relation of married persons : WEDLOCK **c** : the institution whereby individuals are joined in a marriage **2** : an act of marrying or the rite by which the married status is effected; *esp* : the wedding ceremony and attendant festivities or formalities **3** : an intimate or close union ‹the ~ of music and verse›

mar·riage·able \-ə-bəl\ *adj* : fit for or capable of marriage ‹of *marriageable* age›

marriage of convenience : a marriage contracted for social, political, or economic advantage

[1]**mar·ried** \ˈmar-ēd\ *adj* **1** : united in marriage : WEDDED ‹a *married* couple› **2** : of or relating to marriage

[2]**married** *n, pl* **marrieds** *or* **married** : a married person

married name *n* : a last name acquired by a woman through marriage

mar·ron \ma-ˈrō^{n}\ *n* **1** : a Mediterranean chestnut or its large sweet nut **2** *pl* : chestnuts preserved in vanilla-flavored syrup [French]

mar·row \ˈmar-ō\ *n* **1 a** : BONE MARROW **b** : the substance of the spinal cord **2** : HEART 5b, CORE [Old English *mearg*] — **mar·row·less** \-ō-ləs\ *adj* — **mar·rowy** \ˈmar-ə-wē\ *adj*

mar·row·bone \ˈmar-ə-ˌbōn\ *n* **1** : a bone (as a shinbone) rich in bone marrow **2** *pl* : a person's knees

mar·row·fat \ˈmar-ō-ˌfat\ *n* : any of several wrinkled-seeded garden peas

[1]**mar·ry** \ˈmar-ē\ *vb* **mar·ried; mar·ry·ing 1 a** : to join in marriage according to law or custom ‹were *married* yesterday› **b** : to give in marriage ‹*married* their daughter to the king› **c** : to take as husband or wife ‹*married* my neighbor› **d** : to take a spouse : WED **2** : to unite in a close and usually permanent relation [Medieval French *marier,* from Latin *maritare,* from *maritus* "married"]

\ə\ **abut**	\au̇\ **out**	\i\ **tip**	\ȯ\ **saw**	\u̇\ **foot**
\ər\ **further**	\ch\ **chin**	\ī\ **life**	\ȯi\ **coin**	\y\ **yet**
\a\ **mat**	\e\ **pet**	\j\ **job**	\th\ **thin**	\yü\ **few**
\ā\ **take**	\ē\ **easy**	\ŋ\ **sing**	\t͟h\ **this**	\yu̇\ **cure**
\ä\ **cot, cart**	\g\ **go**	\ō\ **bone**	\ü\ **food**	\zh\ **vision**

[2]**marry** *interj, archaic* — used to express amused or surprised agreement [Middle English *marie,* from *Marie,* the virgin Mary]

Mars \ˈmärz\ *n* : the planet 4th in order from the sun conspicuous for its red color — see PLANET table [Latin, from *Mars,* god of war]

marsh \ˈmärsh\ *n* : an area of soft wet land usually overgrown by grasses and sedges — compare SWAMP [Old English *mersc*]

[1]**mar·shal** \ˈmär-shəl\ *n* **1 a** : a high official in a medieval royal household **b** : a person who arranges and directs ceremonies **2** : an officer of the highest rank in some military forces **3** : a federal official having duties similar to those of a sheriff; *also* : a city official having similar duties [Medieval French *mareschal,* of Germanic origin] — **mar·shal·cy** \-sē\ *n* — **mar·shal·ship** \-ˌship\ *n*

Word History The Medieval French word *mareschal* was borrowed from a Germanic language. A *mareschal* is, etymologically, a "horse-servant"; the compound is related to Old English *mere* (modern English *mare*) and *scealc,* "servant." In addition to its original sense of "a groom or keeper of horses," Medieval French *mareschal* became the title of a high official in a royal court. In the Middle English period, the English borrowed *mareschal* in the sense "high official." The earlier sense, "keeper of horses," was borrowed a little later but is now obsolete.

[2]**marshal** *vt* **mar·shaled** *or* **mar·shalled; mar·shal·ing** *or* **mar·shal·ling** \ˈmärsh-ling, -ə-ling\ **1** : to arrange in proper position or order **2** : to lead ceremoniously or solicitously : USHER

marsh gas *n* : METHANE

marsh hawk *n* : NORTHERN HARRIER

marsh·land \ˈmärsh-ˌland\ *n* : a marshy area : MARSH

marsh·mal·low \ˈmärsh-ˌmel-ō, -ˌmal-\ *n* **1** : a pink-flowered European perennial herb related to the mallows that has a root sometimes used in confectionery and in medicine **2** : a white confection formerly made from the root of the marshmallow but now usually prepared from corn syrup, sugar, egg white, and gelatin

marshmallow 1

marsh marigold *n* : a swamp herb having bright yellow flowers resembling those of the related buttercups — called also *cowslip*

marshy \ˈmär-shē\ *adj* **marsh·i·er; -est** **1** : resembling or constituting a marsh **2** : of or relating to marshes — **marsh·i·ness** \-shē-nəs\ *n*

[1]**mar·su·pi·al** \mär-ˈsü-pē-əl\ *adj* : of, relating to, or being a marsupial

[2]**marsupial** *n* : any of an order (Marsupialia) of mammals (as a kangaroo or opossum) that have a pouch on the abdomen of the female containing the teats and serving to carry the young

mar·su·pi·um \-pē-əm\ *n, pl* **-pia** \-pē-ə\ **1** : the pouch of a female marsupial **2** : a structure analogous to the marsupium in which an invertebrate animal (as a mollusk) carries eggs or young [Latin, "purse, pouch," from Greek *marsypion*]

mart \ˈmärt\ *n* : MARKET 1b [Dutch *marct, mart,* derived from Latin *mercatus*]

mar·ten \ˈmärt-n\ *n, pl* **marten** *or* **martens** : a slender flesh-eating mammal larger than the related weasels; *also* : its soft gray or brown fur [Medieval French *martrine* "marten fur," from *martre* "marten," of Germanic origin]

mar·tial \ˈmär-shəl\ *adj* **1** : of, relating to, or suited for war or a warrior ⟨a *martial* stride⟩ **2** : of or relating to an army or to military life [Latin *martialis* "of Mars," from *Mart-, Mars* "Mars"] — **mar·tial·ly** \-shə-lē\ *adv*

synonyms MARTIAL, WARLIKE, MILITARY mean relating to or characteristic of war. MARTIAL suggests especially the pomp and ceremony of war and preparation for war ⟨*martial* music⟩. WARLIKE implies the feeling or temper that leads to or accompanies war ⟨*warlike* mountain tribes⟩. MILITARY applies to anything pertaining to the art or conduct of organized warfare especially on land ⟨*military* campaigns⟩.

martial art *n* : any of several arts of combat and self-defense (as karate) that are widely practiced as sport — **martial artist** *n*

martial law *n* : the law applied (as by military or police forces) in occupied territory or in an emergency

Mar·tian \ˈmär-shən\ *adj* : of or relating to the planet Mars or its hypothetical inhabitants — **Martian** *n*

mar·tin \ˈmärt-n\ *n* : a small Eurasian swallow with a forked tail, bluish black head and back, and white rump and underparts; *also* : any of various related birds [probably from Saint *Martin*]

mar·ti·net \ˌmärt-n-ˈet\ *n* : a strict disciplinarian [Jean *Martinet,* 17th century French army officer]

mar·tin·gale \ˈmärt-n-ˌgāl\ *n* : a strap connecting a horse's girth to the bit or reins so as to hold down its head [Middle French]

mar·ti·ni \mär-ˈtē-nē\ *n* : a cocktail consisting of gin or vodka and dry vermouth [probably alteration of *Martinez (cocktail),* from the name *Martinez*]

Mar·tin·mas \ˈmärt-n-məs, -ˌmas\ *n* : November 11 celebrated as the feast of Saint Martin [Middle English *martinmasse,* from Saint *Martin* + *masse* "mass"]

[1]**mar·tyr** \ˈmärt-ər\ *n* **1** : a person who suffers death rather than give up his or her religion **2** : one who sacrifices his or her life or something of great value for a principle or a cause **3** : a great or constant sufferer [Old English, from Late Latin, from Greek *martys* "witness"] — **mar·tyr·i·za·tion** \ˌmärt-ə-rə-ˈzā-shən\ *n* — **mar·tyr·ize** \ˈmärt-ə-ˌrīz\ *vb*

[2]**martyr** *vt* **1** : to put to death for adhering to a belief **2** : to inflict great pain on : TORTURE

mar·tyr·dom \ˈmärt-ər-dəm\ *n* **1** : the sufferings and death of a martyr **2** : TORMENT 1, 2, TORTURE

[1]**mar·vel** \ˈmär-vəl\ *n* : one that causes wonder or astonishment [Medieval French *merveille,* from Late Latin *mirabilia* "marvels," from Latin *mirabilis* "wonderful," from *mirari* "to wonder"]

[2]**marvel** *vb* **mar·veled** *or* **mar·velled; mar·vel·ing** *or* **mar·vel·ling** \ˈmarv-ling, -ə-ling\ : to become filled with surprise or astonishment ⟨*marveled* at the acrobat's feats⟩

mar·vel·ous *or* **mar·vel·lous** \ˈmärv-ləs, -ə-ləs\ *adj* **1** : causing wonder : ASTONISHING **2** : MIRACULOUS 1 **3** : of the highest quality : SPLENDID ⟨a *marvelous* party⟩ — **mar·vel·ous·ly** *adv* — **mar·vel·ous·ness** *n*

Marx·ian \ˈmärk-sē-ən, ˈmärk-shən\ *adj* : of, developed by, or influenced by the doctrines of Karl Marx ⟨*Marxian* socialism⟩

Marx·ism \ˈmärk-ˌsiz-əm\ *n* : the political, economic, and social doctrines developed by Karl Marx that provide the basis for Marxian socialism and much of modern Communism — **Marx·ist** \ˈmärk-səst\ *n or adj*

Marx·ism–Len·in·ism \-ˈlen-ə-ˌniz-əm\ *n* : a theory and practice of Communism developed by Lenin from Marxism primarily to fit Russian conditions — **Marx·ist–Len·in·ist** \-ˈlen-ə-nəst\ *n or adj*

Mary Jane \ˈmeər-ē-ˌjān, ˈmaər-ē-, ˈmā-rē-\ *n, slang* : MARIJUANA [by folk etymology]

Mary·knoll·er \-ˌnō-lər\ *n* : a member of the Catholic Foreign Mission Society of America founded at Maryknoll, N. Y., in 1911

mar·zi·pan \ˈmärt-sə-ˌpän, -ˌpan; ˈmär-zə-ˌpan\ *n* : a confection of almond paste, sugar, and egg white that is often shaped into forms [German, from Italian *marzapane*]

ma·sa \ˈmä-sə\ *n* : a dough used in Mexican cuisine (as for tortillas and tamales) that is made from ground corn soaked in a lime and water solution; *also* : MASA HARINA [Spanish, mash, dough]

masa ha·ri·na \-ä-ˈrē-nä\ *n* : a flour made from dried masa [Mexican Spanish, literally, masa flour]

mas·cara \ma-ˈskar-ə\ *n* : a cosmetic for coloring the eyelashes and eyebrows [probably from Italian *maschera* "mask"]

mas·con \ˈmas-ˌkän\ *n* : any of the large dense concentrations of mass under the surface of the maria of the moon [[2]*mass* + *con*centration]

mas·cot \ˈmas-ˌkät *also* -kət\ *n* : a person, animal, or object adopted by a group as a symbol and supposed to bring good luck [French *mascotte,* from Occitan *mascoto,* from *masco* "witch," from Medieval Latin *masca*]

Word History The Medieval Latin word *masca,* meaning "witch," was borrowed as *masco* into the Occitan language of southern France. *Mascoto,* a diminutive form of *masco,* was used to mean "witch." This word was borrowed into French as *mascotte* and was popularized by the operetta *La Mascotte,* composed by Edmond Audran in 1880. In this operetta *"la mascotte"* is the beautiful maiden Bettina, whose influence brings victories to the army of the prince of Pisa. *Mascot* appeared in English soon afterward, used to mean "a person or thing held to bring good luck."

[1]**mas·cu·line** \ˈmas-kyə-lən\ *adj* **1** : of the male sex **2** : characteristic of or belonging to men : MANLY **3** : of, relating to, or

constituting the class of words that ordinarily includes most of those referring to males ⟨a *masculine* noun⟩ ⟨*masculine* gender⟩ **4 :** having or occurring in a stressed final syllable ⟨*masculine* rhyme⟩ [Middle English *masculin,* from Latin *masculinus,* from *masculus,* noun, "male," from *mas* "male"] — **mas·cu·line·ly** *adv* — **mas·cu·lin·i·ty** \ˌmas-kyə-ˈlin-ət-ē\ *n*

[2]**masculine** *n* **1 :** a word or form of the masculine gender **2 :** the masculine gender

ma·ser \ˈmā-zər\ *n* **:** a device that utilizes the natural oscillations of atoms or molecules between energy levels for generating monochromatic microwave radiation [*m*icrowave *a*mplification by *s*timulated *e*mission of *r*adiation]

[1]**mash** \ˈmash\ *vt* **1 :** to reduce to a soft pulpy state by beating or pressure **2 :** to subject (as crushed malt) to the action of water with heating and stirring in preparing wort — **mash·er** *n*

[2]**mash** *n* **1 :** crushed malt or grain meal steeped and stirred in hot water to produce wort **2 :** a mixture of ground feeds for livestock **3 :** a soft pulpy mass [Old English *māx-*]

mash–up \ˈmash-ˌəp\ *n* **:** something created by combining elements from two or more sources: as **a :** a piece of music created by digitally overlaying an instrumental track with a vocal track from a different recording **b :** a movie or video having characters or situations from other sources **c :** a Web service or application that integrates data and functionalities from various online sources

[1]**mask** \ˈmask\ *n* **1 :** a cover for the face used for disguise or protection ⟨a Halloween *mask*⟩ ⟨a baseball catcher's *mask*⟩ **2 a :** GAS MASK **b :** a device usually covering the mouth and nose to aid inhalation ⟨an oxygen *mask*⟩ **3 :** a covering (as of gauze) for the mouth and nose to prevent infective droplets from being exhaled into the air **4 :** something that disguises or conceals **:** PRETENSE **5 :** one that wears a mask **6 :** a sculptured face made by a mold in plaster or wax **7 :** the face of a mammal (as a fox or dog) **8 :** MASQUE 2 [Middle French *masque,* from Italian *maschera*] ***synonyms*** see DISGUISE

[2]**mask** *vb* **1 :** to take part in a masquerade **2 :** to wear a mask **3 a :** CONCEAL, DISGUISE ⟨*masked* his real purpose⟩ **b :** to keep from being known or noticed ⟨*mask* odors⟩ **4 :** COVER 3

masked \ˈmaskt\ *adj* **:** marked by the wearing of masks or a mask

mask·er \ˈmas-kər\ *n* **:** one that wears a mask; *esp* **:** a participant in a masquerade

masking tape *n* **:** a tape with adhesive on one side that has many uses (as to cover a surface when painting near it)

mas·och·ism \ˈmas-ə-ˌkiz-əm, ˈmaz-\ *n* **:** enjoyment of one's own pain or suffering; *esp* **:** sexual pleasure from being hurt or punished [Leopold von Sacher-*Masoch,* died 1895, German novelist] — **mas·och·ist** \-kist\ *n* — **mas·och·is·tic** \ˌmas-ə-ˈkis-tik, ˌmaz-\ *adj* **mas·och·is·ti·cal·ly** \ ti kə lē, -klē\ *adv*

ma·son \ˈmās-n\ *n* **1 :** a skilled worker who builds with stone, brick, or cement **2** *cap* **:** FREEMASON [Medieval French, of Germanic origin]

Ma·son·ic \mə-ˈsän-ik\ *adj* **:** of, relating to, or characteristic of Freemasons or Freemasonry

Ma·son·ite \ˈmās-n-ˌīt\ *trademark* — used for a fiberboard made from steam-treated wood fiber

ma·son jar \ˌmās-n-\ *n* **:** a widemouthed jar used for home canning [John L. *Mason,* died 1902, American metalsmith]

mason jar

ma·son·ry \ˈmās-n-rē\ *n, pl* **-ries 1 a :** something built of materials used by masons **b :** the art, trade, or occupation of a mason **c :** work done by a mason **2** *cap* **:** FREEMASONRY 1

mason wasp *n* **:** a solitary wasp that constructs nests of hardened mud

masque \ˈmask\ *n* **1 :** MASQUERADE 1 **2 :** a short allegorical dramatic entertainment of the 16th and 17th centuries performed by masked actors [Middle French]

masqu·er \ˈmas-kər\ *n* **:** MASKER

[1]**mas·quer·ade** \ˌmas-kə-ˈrād\ *n* **1 a :** a social gathering of persons wearing masks and often costumes **b :** a costume for wear at such a gathering **2 :** a way of appearing or behaving that is not true or real [Middle French, from Italian dialect *mascarada,* from Italian *maschera* "mask"]

[2]**masquerade** *vi* **1 a :** to disguise oneself or go about disguised **b :** to take part in a masquerade **2 :** to assume the appearance of something one is not **:** POSE — **mas·quer·ad·er** *n*

[1]**mass** \ˈmas\ *n* **1** *cap* **:** a sequence of prayers and ceremonies forming the eucharistic service especially of the Roman Catholic Church **2** *often cap* **:** a celebration of the Eucharist **3 :** a musical setting for parts of the Mass [Old English *mæsse,* from Late Latin *missa* "dismissal after a religious service," from Latin *mittere* "to send, let go"]

[2]**mass** *n* **1 a :** a quantity of matter or the form of matter that holds or clings together in one body ⟨a *mass* of metal⟩ **b :** greatness of size **:** BULK **c :** the principal part **:** main body **2 :** the property of a body that is a measure of its inertia and is commonly taken as a measure of the quantity of matter it contains and that causes it to have weight in a gravitational field **3 :** a large quantity, amount, or number **4 a :** a large body of persons in a compact group **b** *pl* **:** the body of common people as contrasted with the elite [Medieval French *masse,* from Latin *massa,* from Greek *maza*] ***synonyms*** see BULK

[3]**mass** *vb* **:** to form or collect into a mass

[4]**mass** *adj* **1 a :** of, relating to, or designed for the mass of the people ⟨a *mass* market⟩ ⟨*mass* education⟩ **b :** participated in by or affecting a large number of individuals ⟨*mass* demonstrations⟩ **c :** occurring on a large scale ⟨*mass* production⟩ **2 :** viewed as a whole **:** TOTAL ⟨the *mass* effect of a design⟩

Mas·sa·chu·sett *or* **Mas·sa·chu·set** \ˌmas-ə-ˈchü-sət, -zət\ *n, pl* **Massachusetts** *or* **Massachusett** *or* **Massachusets** *or* **Massachuset 1 :** a member of an American Indian people of Massachusetts **2 :** the Algonquian language of the Massachusett people [Massachusett, a locality, literally, "at the big hill"]

[1]**mas·sa·cre** \ˈmas-i-kər\ *n* **1 :** the violent killing of many people **2 :** a slaughter of animals in large numbers [Middle French]

[2]**mas·sa·cre** *vt* **-cred; -cring** \-kə-ring, -kring\ **:** to kill by massacre **:** SLAUGHTER — **mas·sa·crer** \-kər-ər, -i-krər\ *n*

[1]**mas·sage** \mə-ˈsäzh, -ˈsäj\ *n* **:** manipulation of bodily tissues (as by rubbing, stroking, kneading, or tapping) especially with the hand or an instrument for relaxation or pain relief [French, from *masser* "to massage," from Arabic *massa* "to stroke"]

[2]**massage** *vt* **:** to subject to massage — **mas·sag·er** *n*

mas·sa·sau·ga \ˌmas-ə-ˈsȯ-gə\ *n* **:** a small North American rattlesnake [*Missisauga* river, Ontario, Canada]

mass driver *n* **:** a large electromagnetic catapult designed to hurl material (as from an asteroid) into space

mas·se·ter \mə-ˈsēt-ər, ma-\ *n* **:** a large muscle that raises the lower jaw and assists in chewing [Greek *masētēr,* from *masasthai* "to chew"] — **mas·se·ter·ic** \ˌmas-ə-ˈter-ik\ *adj*

mas·seur \ma-ˈsər, mə-\ *n* **:** a man whose job is to give massages [French, from *masser* "to massage"]

mas·seuse \-ˈsu̇z, -ˈsərz, -ˈsüz\ *n* **:** a woman whose job is to give massages [French, feminine of *masseur*]

mas·sif \ma-ˈsēf\ *n* **:** a principal mountain mass [French, from *massif* "massive"]

mas·sive \ˈmas-iv\ *adj* **1 :** forming or consisting of a large mass: **a :** WEIGHTY, HEAVY ⟨*massive* walls⟩ **b :** exceedingly large **:** GIGANTIC **c :** having no regular form but not necessarily lacking crystalline structure ⟨*massive* sandstone⟩ **2 a :** large, solid, or heavy in structure ⟨*massive* jaws⟩ **b :** large in scope or degree ⟨a *massive* effort⟩ **3 :** having mass ⟨a *massive* boson⟩ — **mas·sive·ly** *adv* — **mas·sive·ness** *n*

mass medium *n, pl* **mass media :** a communications medium (as newspapers, radio, or television) that is designed to reach mass audiences — usually used in plural

mass number *n* **:** an integer that approximates the mass of an isotope and designates the number of nucleons in the nucleus

mass–pro·duce \ˌmas-prə-ˈdüs, -ˈdyüs\ *vt* **:** to produce in quantity usually by machinery — **mass production** *n*

mass spectrograph *n* **:** an apparatus that separates a stream of charged particles into a spectrum according to their masses

mass spectrometry *n* **:** a method for identifying the structure of a chemical compound using an instrument that separates ions derived from the compound based on mass and charge — **mass spectrometer** *n* — **mass spectrometric** *adj*

mass spectrum *n* **:** the spectrum produced in mass spectrometry

massy \ˈmas-ē\ *adj* **mass·i·er; -est :** MASSIVE 1a, b

[1]**mast** \ˈmast\ *n* **1 :** a long pole or spar that rises from the keel or deck of a ship or boat and supports the sails and rigging **2 :** a

vertical or nearly vertical tall pole (as a post on a lifting crane) [Old English *mæst*] — **mast·ed** \ˈmas-təd\ *adj* — **before the mast :** as a common sailor

[2]mast *vt* **:** to furnish with a mast

[3]mast *n* **:** nuts (as acorns) accumulated on the forest floor and often serving as food for animals [Old English *mæst*]

mast cell *n* **:** a white blood cell that occurs especially in connective tissue and contains substances (as histamine) which play a role in allergic reactions [part translation of German *Mastzelle,* from *Mast* "food, meat" + *Zelle* "cell"]

mas·tec·to·my \ma-ˈstek-tə-mē\ *n, pl* **-mies :** surgical removal of all or part of a breast [Greek *mastos* "breast"]

[1]mas·ter \ˈmas-tər\ *n* **1 a :** a male teacher **b :** a person holding an academic degree higher than a bachelor's but lower than a doctor's **c** *often cap* **:** a revered religious leader **d :** an independent worker qualified to teach apprentices **e :** an artist or performer of great skill **2 a :** one having authority **:** RULER **b :** one that conquers or masters **:** SUPERIOR **c :** a person licensed to command a merchant ship **d :** an owner especially of a slave or animal **e :** the male head of a household **3 a** *archaic* **:** MISTER **b :** a youth or boy too young to be called *mister* — used as a title **4 :** a presiding officer in an institution or society **5 :** a master mechanism or device **6 :** an original from which copies can be made [Old English *magister* and Medieval French *meistre,* both from Latin *magister*]

[2]master *vt* **mas·tered; mas·ter·ing** \ˈmas-tə-ring, -tring\ **1 :** to get the better of **:** OVERCOME **2 :** to become skilled or proficient in or in the use of ⟨*master* arithmetic⟩

[3]master *adj* **1 :** being a master ⟨a *master* carpenter⟩ **2 :** being the chief or guiding one ⟨a *master* plan⟩ **3 :** being one that controls the operation of other mechanisms or that establishes a standard (as of dimension or weight) ⟨a *master* cylinder⟩ ⟨a *master* gauge⟩

mas·ter–at–arms \ˌmas-tər-ət-ˈärmz\ *n, pl* **masters–at–arms :** a petty officer charged with maintaining discipline aboard ship

master chief petty officer *n* **:** an enlisted man in the navy and coast guard ranking above a senior chief petty officer

master chief petty officer of the coast guard *n* **:** the ranking petty officer in the coast guard serving as adviser to the commandant

master chief petty officer of the navy *n* **:** the ranking petty officer in the navy serving as adviser to the chief of naval operations

mas·ter·ful \ˈmas-tər-fəl\ *adj* **1 :** inclined to take control or dominate **2 :** having or showing the power and skill of a master — **mas·ter·ful·ly** \-fə-lē\ *adv* — **mas·ter·ful·ness** *n*

synonyms MASTERFUL, DOMINEERING, IMPERIOUS mean tending to impose one's will on others. MASTERFUL implies a strong forceful personality and the ability to deal authoritatively with people and affairs ⟨her *masterful* personality soon dominated the movement⟩. DOMINEERING suggests an overbearing or tyrannical manner and an obstinate attempt to enforce one's will ⟨children controlled by *domineering* parents⟩. IMPERIOUS implies a commanding nature and often suggests arrogant assurance ⟨an *imperious* executive used to getting his own way⟩.

master gunnery sergeant *n* **:** a noncommissioned officer in the marine corps ranking above a master sergeant

master key *n* **:** a key designed to open several different locks

mas·ter·ly \ˈmas-tər-lē\ *adj* **1 :** suitable to or resembling that of a master; *esp* **:** showing superior knowledge or skill **2 :** having the power or skill of a master — **mas·ter·li·ness** *n* — **masterly** *adv*

mas·ter·mind \-ˌmīnd\ *n* **:** a person who invents or directs a project — **mastermind** *vt*

master of ceremonies 1 : a person who determines the forms to be observed on a public occasion **2 :** a person who acts as host at a formal event **3 :** a person who acts as host for an entertainment program (as on television)

mas·ter·piece \ˈmas-tər-ˌpēs\ *n* **1 :** a piece of work presented to a medieval guild as evidence of qualification for the rank of master **2 :** a work done with great skill; *esp* **:** a supreme intellectual or artistic achievement

master race *n* **:** a people held to be racially preeminent and hence fitted to rule or enslave other peoples

master sergeant *n* **:** an enlisted rank in the army above sergeant first class and below staff sergeant major, in the marine corps above gunnery sergeant and below sergeant major, and in the air force above technical sergeant and below senior master sergeant

mas·ter·ship \ˈmas-tər-ˌship\ *n* **1 :** the authority or control of a master **2 :** the office or position of a master **3 :** the skill or ability of a master

mas·ter·stroke \-ˌstrōk\ *n* **:** a masterly performance or move

mas·ter·work \-ˌwərk\ *n* **:** MASTERPIECE 2

mas·tery \ˈmas-tə-rē, -trē\ *n, pl* **-ter·ies 1 :** the position or authority of a master **2 :** the upper hand in a contest or competition **3 :** skill or knowledge that makes one master of something **:** COMMAND ⟨a *mastery* of French⟩

mast·head \ˈmast-ˌhed\ *n* **1 :** the top of a mast **2 a :** the printed matter in a newspaper or periodical that gives the title and pertinent details of ownership, advertising rates, and subscription rates **b :** the name of a newspaper displayed on the top of the first page

mas·tic \ˈmas-tik\ *n* **1 :** a yellowish to greenish resin of a small southern European tree used in varnish **2 :** a pasty material used as a protective coating or cement [Latin *mastiche,* from Greek *mastichē*]

mas·ti·cate \ˈmas-tə-ˌkāt\ *vb* **1 :** to grind or crush with or as if with the teeth in preparation for swallowing **:** CHEW **2 :** to soften or reduce to pulp by crushing or kneading [Late Latin *masticare,* from Greek *mastichan* "to gnash the teeth"] — **mas·ti·ca·tion** \mas-tə-ˈkā-shən\ *n* — **mas·ti·ca·tor** \ˈmas-tə-ˌkāt-ər\ *n*

[1]mas·ti·ca·to·ry \ˈmas-ti-kə-ˌtōr-ē, -ˌtȯr-\ *n, pl* **-ries :** a substance chewed to increase saliva

[2]masticatory *adj* **1 :** used for or adapted to chewing **2 :** of, relating to, or involving the organs involved in mastication ⟨*masticatory* paralysis⟩

mas·tiff \ˈmas-təf\ *n* **:** any of a breed of large powerful smooth-coated dogs often used as watchdogs and guard dogs [Medieval Latin *mastivus,* derived from Latin *mansuetus* "tame"]

mastiff

mas·ti·tis \mas-ˈtīt-əs\ *n, pl* **-tit·i·des** \-ˈtit-ə-ˌdēz\ **:** inflammation of the breast or udder usually caused by infection [Greek *mastos* "breast"]

mas·to·don \ˈmas-tə-ˌdän, -dən\ *also* **mas·to·dont** \ˈmas-tə-ˌdänt\ *n* **:** any of various huge extinct mammals existing from the Miocene through the Pleistocene and related to the mammoths and modern elephants [Greek *mastos* "breast" + *odōn, odous* "tooth"] — **mas·to·don·ic** \ˌmas-tə-ˈdän-ik\ *adj*

[1]mas·toid \ˈmas-ˌtȯid\ *adj* **:** of, relating to, or being the mastoid process; *also* **:** occurring in the region of the mastoid process [Greek *mastoeidēs,* literally, "breast-shaped," from *mastos* "breast"]

[2]mastoid *n* **:** a mastoid bone or process

mas·toid·itis \ˌmas-ˌtȯid-ˈīt-əs\ *n* **:** inflammation of the mastoid process

mastoid process *n* **:** a conical process of the temporal bone behind the ear

mas·tur·ba·tion \ˌmas-tər-ˈbā-shən\ *n* **:** sexual stimulation especially of one's own of the genital organs by bodily contact apart from sexual intercourse and usually by use of the hand [Latin *masturbatus,* past participle of *masturbari* "to masturbate"] — **mas·tur·bate** \ˈmas-tər-ˌbāt\ *vb*

[1]mat \ˈmat\ *n* **1 a :** a piece of coarse fabric made of rushes, straw, or wool **b :** a piece of material in front of a door to wipe the shoes on **c :** a piece of material used under a dish or vase or as an ornament **d :** a pad or cushion for gymnastics or wrestling **2 :** something made up of many intertwined or tangled strands or filaments ⟨a thick *mat* of vegetation⟩ [Old English *meatte,* from Late Latin *matta,* of Semitic origin]

[2]mat *vb* **mat·ted; mat·ting 1 :** to provide with a mat or matting **2 :** to become or cause to become a tangled mass

[3]mat \ˈmat\ *vt* **mat·ted; mat·ting 1** *also* **matte** *or* **matt :** to give a dull effect to **2 :** to provide (a picture) with a mat

[4]mat *variant of* [2]MATTE

[5]mat *n* **1 :** a border going around a picture between picture and frame or serving as the frame **2 :** a dull finish or a roughened surface (as of gilt or paint) [French *mat* "dull color," from *mat* "mat, lacking luster"]

mat·a·dor \ˈmat-ə-ˌdȯr\ *n* **:** a bullfighter who has the principal role in the bullfight [Spanish, literally, "killer," from *matar* "to kill"]

¹match \'mach\ *n* **1 a :** a person or thing equal or similar to another **b :** one able to cope with another ⟨a *match* for the enemy⟩ **c :** an exact counterpart **2 :** a pair that go well together ⟨curtains and carpet are a *match*⟩ **3 :** a contest between two or more parties ⟨a tennis *match*⟩ **4 a :** a marriage union **b :** a prospective marriage partner [Old English *gemæcca* "mate, equal"]

²match *vb* **1 :** to meet successfully as a competitor **2 a :** to place in competition with or opposition to : PIT **b :** to provide with a worthy competitor **3 :** to join or give in marriage **4 a :** to make or find the equal or the like of **b :** to cause to correspond **c :** to be the same as or suitable to one another ⟨these colors *match*⟩ **5 a :** to flip or toss (coins) and compare exposed faces **b :** to toss coins with — **match·er** *n*

³match *n* **1 :** an evenly burning wick or cord formerly used for igniting a charge of powder **2 :** a short slender piece of material (as wood) tipped with a mixture that ignites when subjected to friction [Medieval French *meche*]

match·board \'mach-ˌbōrd, -ˌbȯrd\ *n* **:** a board with a groove cut along one edge and a tongue along the other so as to fit snugly with the edges of similarly cut boards

match·book \'mach-ˌbu̇k\ *n* **:** a small folder containing rows of paper matches

match·less \'mach-ləs\ *adj* **:** having no equal : PEERLESS — **match·less·ly** *adv*

match·lock \'mach-ˌläk\ *n* **:** a slow-burning match cord lowered over a hole in the breech of a musket to light the charge; *also* **:** a musket equipped with such a lock

match·mak·er \-ˌmā-kər\ *n* **:** one that arranges a match and especially a marriage — **match·mak·ing** \-king\ *n*

match point *n* **:** the last point needed to win a match

match·wood \'mach-ˌwu̇d\ *n* **:** small bits of wood

¹mate \'māt\ *vt* **:** CHECKMATE 2

²mate *n* **:** CHECKMATE 1

³mate *n* **1 a :** ASSOCIATE 1, COLLEAGUE **b :** an assistant to a more skilled worker : HELPER ⟨plumber's *mate*⟩ **2 :** a deck officer on a merchant ship ranking below the captain **3 :** one of a pair: as **a :** either member of a married couple **b :** either member of a breeding pair of animals ⟨a dove and its *mate*⟩ **c :** either of two matched objects ⟨a *mate* to a glove⟩ [Middle English]

⁴mate *vb* **1 :** to join or fit together **2 a :** to bring together as mates **b :** to provide a mate for **3 :** COPULATE

ma·té *or* **ma·te** \'mä-ˌtā\ *n* **:** an aromatic beverage made from the leaves and shoots of a South American holly; *also* **:** this holly or its leaves and shoots [French and American Spanish; French *maté,* from American Spanish *mate* "maté, vessel for drinking maté," from Quechua *mati* "vessel"]

¹ma·te·ri·al \mə-'tir-ē-əl\ *adj* **1 :** relating to, derived from, or consisting of matter; *esp* **:** PHYSICAL ⟨the *material* world⟩ ⟨*material* comforts⟩ **2 :** having importance, relevance, or consequence ⟨facts *material* to the study⟩ **3 :** relating to or concerned with physical rather than spiritual or intellectual things ⟨*material* progress⟩ **4 :** of or relating to the production and distribution of economic goods and the social relationships of owners and laborers [Late Latin *materialis,* from Latin *materia* "matter"] — **ma·te·ri·al·i·ty** \-ˌtir-ē-'al-ət-ē\ *n* — **ma·te·ri·al·ly** \-'tir-ē-ə-lē\ *adv* — **ma·te·ri·al·ness** *n*

synonyms MATERIAL, PHYSICAL, CORPOREAL mean of or belonging to actuality. MATERIAL implies formation out of tangible matter; used in contrast with *spiritual* or *ideal* it suggests what is mundane, ignoble, or grasping ⟨a shallow person with only *material* values⟩. PHYSICAL applies to whatever is perceived by the senses and may contrast with *mental, spiritual,* or *imaginary* ⟨the *physical* benefits of exercise⟩. CORPOREAL stresses having such tangible qualities of a body as fixed shape and size and resistance to force ⟨artists have portrayed angels as *corporeal* beings⟩.

²material *n* **1 :** the elements, constituents, or substance of which something is composed or can be made ⟨building *materials*⟩ **2 a :** apparatus needed for doing or making something ⟨writing *materials*⟩ **b :** MATÉRIEL

ma·te·ri·al·ism \mə-'tir-ē-ə-ˌliz-əm\ *n* **1 a :** a theory that everything can be explained as being or coming from matter **b :** a doctrine that the only or the highest values lie in material well-being and material progress **c :** a doctrine that economic or social change is caused by material factors **2 :** a preoccupation with material rather than intellectual or spiritual things — **ma·te·ri·al·ist** \-ē-ə-ləst\ *n or adj* — **ma·te·ri·al·is·tic** \-ˌtir-ē-ə-'lis-tik\ *adj* — **ma·te·ri·al·is·ti·cal·ly** \-'lis-ti-kə-lē, -klē\ *adv*

ma·te·ri·al·ize \mə-'tir-ē-ə-ˌlīz\ *vb* **1 a :** to give form and substance to ⟨*materialize* an idea in words⟩ **b :** to appear or cause to appear in bodily form ⟨*materialize* a spirit⟩ **2 a :** to come into existence **b :** to put in an appearance; *esp* **:** to appear suddenly — **ma·te·ri·al·i·za·tion** \-ˌtir-ē-ə-lə-'zā-shən\ *n* — **ma·te·ri·al·iz·er** \-'tir-ē-ə-ˌlī-zər\ *n*

materials science *n* **:** the scientific study of materials used in construction or manufacturing — **materials scientist** *n*

ma·te·ria med·i·ca \mə-ˌtir-ē-ə-'med-i-kə\ *n* **1 :** material or substances used in medical remedies **2 :** a branch of medical science that deals with the sources, nature, properties, and preparation of drugs [New Latin, literally, "medical matter"]

ma·té·ri·el *or* **ma·te·ri·el** \mə-ˌtir-ē-'el\ *n* **:** equipment, apparatus, and supplies used by an organization or institution [French *matériel* "material"]

ma·ter·nal \mə-'tərn-l\ *adj* **1 :** of, relating to, or characteristic of a mother : MOTHERLY **2 a :** related through a mother ⟨*maternal* grandparents⟩ **b :** inherited or derived from the female parent ⟨*maternal* genes⟩ [Middle French *maternel,* from Latin *maternus,* from *mater* "mother"] — **ma·ter·nal·ly** \-l-ē\ *adv*

¹ma·ter·ni·ty \mə-'tər-nət-ē\ *n, pl* **-ties 1 :** the state of being a mother : MOTHERHOOD **2 :** the qualities of a mother : MOTHERLINESS

²maternity *adj* **1 :** designed for wear during pregnancy ⟨*maternity* clothes⟩ **2 :** effective for the time around childbirth ⟨*maternity* leave⟩

math \'math\ *n* **:** MATHEMATICS

math·e·mat·i·cal \ˌmath-ə-'mat-i-kəl, math-'mat-\ *adj* **1 :** of, relating to, or according with mathematics **2 :** very exact : PRECISE ⟨*mathematical* accuracy⟩ **3 :** possible but highly unlikely ⟨only a *mathematical* chance⟩ [Latin *mathematicus,* from Greek *mathēmatikos,* from *mathēma* "mathematics," from *manthanein* "to learn"] — **math·e·mat·i·cal·ly** \-i-kə-le, -klē\ *adv*

mathematical induction *n* **:** INDUCTION 2b

math·e·ma·ti·cian \ˌmath-mə-'tish-ən, -ə-mə-\ *n* **:** a specialist or expert in mathematics

math·e·mat·ics \ˌmath-ə-'mat-iks, math-'mat-\ *n* **:** the science of numbers and their properties, relations, combinations, and operations, and with shapes in space and their structure, measurement, and transformations

mat·i·nee *or* **mat·i·née** \ˌmat-n-'ā\ *n* **:** a musical or dramatic performance held in the daytime and especially in the afternoon [French *matinée,* literally, "morning," from *matin* "morning," from Latin *matutinum,* from *matutinus* "of the morning," from *Matuta,* goddess of morning]

mat·ins \'mat-nz\ *n pl, often cap* **1 :** the night office of prayer forming with lauds the first of the canonical hours **2 :** MORNING PRAYER [Medieval French *matines,* from Late Latin *matutinae,* from Latin *matutinus* "of the morning"]

matr- *or* **matri-** *or* **matro-** *combining form* **:** mother ⟨*matri*lineal⟩ [Latin *matr-, mater*]

ma·tri·arch \'mā-trē-ˌärk\ *n* **:** a woman who rules or dominates a family, group, or state; *esp* **:** a mother who is the head and ruler of her family and descendants [*matr-* + Greek *archein* "to rule"] — **ma·tri·ar·chal** \ˌmā-trē-'är-kəl\ *adj*

ma·tri·ar·chate \'mā-trē-ˌär-kət, -ˌkāt\ *n* **:** MATRIARCHY 1

ma·tri·ar·chy \'mā-trē-ˌär-kē\ *n, pl* **-chies 1 :** a family, group, or state governed or headed by a matriarch **2 :** a system of social organization in which descent and inheritance are traced through the female line

ma·tri·cide \'ma-trə-ˌsīd, 'mā-\ *n* **1 :** murder of a mother by her child **2 :** one who murders his or her own mother — **ma·tri·cid·al** \ˌma-trə-'sīd-l, ˌmā-\ *adj*

ma·tric·u·late \mə-'trik-yə-ˌlāt\ *vb* **:** to enroll as a member of a body and especially of a college or university [Medieval Latin *matriculare,* from Late Latin *matricula* "public roll," from *matrix* "list," from Latin, "female kept for breeding"] — **ma·tric·u·la·tion** \-ˌtrik-yə-'lā-shən\ *n*

ma·tri·lin·eal \ˌma-trə-'lin-ē-əl, ˌmā-\ *adj* **:** relating to, based on, or tracing descent through the maternal line ⟨a *matrilineal* society⟩ — **ma·tri·lin·eal·ly** \-ē-ə-lē\ *adv*

mat·ri·mo·ni·al \ˌma-trə-ˈmō-nē-əl, -nyəl\ *adj* **:** of or relating to matrimony — **mat·ri·mo·ni·al·ly** \-ē\ *adv*

mat·ri·mo·ny \ˈma-trə-ˌmō-nē\ *n, pl* **-nies :** the union of man and woman as husband and wife **:** MARRIAGE [Medieval French *matrimoignie,* from Latin *matrimonium,* from *mater* "mother, married woman"]

matrimony vine *n* **:** a shrub or vine of the nightshade family with often showy flowers and usually red berries

ma·trix \ˈmā-triks\ *n, pl* **ma·tri·ces** \ˈmā-trə-ˌsēz, ˈma-\ *or* **ma·trix·es** \ˈmā-trik-səz\ **1 :** a place or a surrounding or enclosing substance (as a rock) within which something (as a mineral) originates or develops **2 :** something (as a mold) that gives form, foundation, or origin to something else (as molten metal) enclosed in it **3 a :** the extracellular substance in which tissue cells (as of connective tissue) are embedded **b :** the thickened tissue at the base of a fingernail or toenail from which the nail grows **4 :** a group of mathematical elements arranged in rows and columns to form a rectangle that is subject to a special form of addition and multiplication [Latin, "female used for breeding, parent plant," from *mater* "mother"]

ma·tron \ˈmā-trən\ *n* **1 :** a usually mature and dignified or socially distinguished married woman **2 a :** a woman in charge of the household affairs of an institution **b :** a woman who supervises children or women (as in a school or a police station) [Medieval French *matrone,* from Latin *matrona,* from *mater* "mother, married woman"]

ma·tron·ly \-lē\ *adj* **:** of, resembling, or suitable for a matron

matron of honor : a bride's principal married wedding attendant — compare MAID OF HONOR

[1]**matte** *or* **matt** *variant of* [3]MAT 1

[2]**matte** *also* **mat** *or* **matt** \ˈmat\ *adj* **:** lacking luster or gloss [French *mat,* from Medieval French, "faded, defeated"]

[1]**mat·ter** \ˈmat-ər\ *n* **1 a :** a subject of interest or concern ⟨a *matter* of dispute⟩ **b :** something to be dealt with **:** AFFAIR, CONCERN ⟨a few personal *matters* to take care of⟩ **2 :** the subject or substance of a discourse or writing **3 a :** the substance of which a physical object is composed; *esp* **:** the material substance that occupies space and has mass and that makes up the observable universe **b :** material substance of a particular kind or function ⟨coloring *matter*⟩⟨the gray *matter* of the brain⟩ **c :** PUS **4 :** a more or less definite amount or quantity ⟨a *matter* of 10 years or so⟩ **5 :** something written or printed **6 :** MAIL ⟨first-class *matter*⟩ [Medieval French *matere,* from Latin *materia* "physical substance, matter," from *mater* "mother"] — **as a matter of fact :** in fact **:** ACTUALLY — **for that matter :** so far as that is concerned — **no matter :** without regard to ⟨fails *no matter* how he tries⟩ — **no matter what :** regardless of the costs, consequences, or results ⟨wants to win, *no matter what*⟩ — **the matter :** WRONG 4 ⟨nothing's *the matter* with me⟩

[2]**matter** *vi* **1 :** to be of importance **:** SIGNIFY **2 :** to form or discharge pus **:** SUPPURATE ⟨a *mattering* wound⟩

matter of course : something that is to be expected as a natural or logical result of something else

mat·ter–of–fact \ˌmat-ər-ə-ˈfakt\ *adj* **:** sticking to or concerned with facts ⟨a *matter-of-fact* account of the movie⟩; *also* **:** being plain, straightforward, or unemotional ⟨described the accident in a *matter-of-fact* manner⟩ — **mat·ter–of–fact·ly** *adv* — **mat·ter–of–fact·ness** \-ˈfakt-nəs, -ˈfak-\ *n*

mat·tery \ˈmat-ə-rē\ *adj* **:** producing or containing pus or material resembling pus

Mat·thew \ˈmath-yü\ *n* **:** the first Gospel in the New Testament — see BIBLE table

mat·ting \ˈmat-ing\ *n* **:** material for mats; *also* **:** mats or a supply of mats

mat·tock \ˈmat-ək\ *n* **:** an implement for digging consisting of a long wooden handle and a steel head one end of which comes to a blade and the other end to either a point or a cutting edge [Old English *mattuc*]

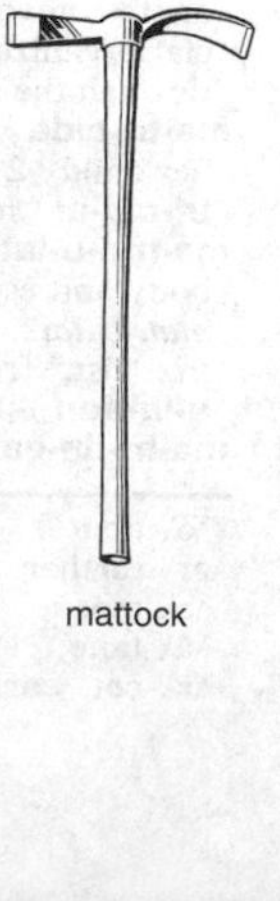
mattock

mat·tress \ˈma-trəs\ *n* **1 :** a fabric case filled with springy material used either as a bed or on a bedstead **2 :** an inflatable sack for use as a mattress — called also *air mattress* [Medieval French *materas,* from Medieval Latin *materacium,* from Arabic *maṭraḥ* "place where something is thrown"]

mat·u·ra·tion \ˌmach-ə-ˈrā-shən\ *n* **1 :** the process of becoming mature **2 :** the process by which diploid gamete-producing cells are transformed into haploid gametes — **mat·u·ra·tion·al** \-shnəl, -shən-l\ *adj*

[1]**ma·ture** \mə-ˈtu̇r, -ˈtyu̇r\ *adj* **1 :** based on slow careful consideration ⟨a *mature* judgment⟩ **2 a :** fully grown and developed **:** ADULT, RIPE ⟨*mature* fruit⟩ ⟨a youth physically but not yet emotionally *mature*⟩ **b :** having attained a final or desired state ⟨*mature* wine⟩ **c :** of, relating to, or being an older adult **:** ELDERLY ⟨airline discounts for *mature* travelers⟩ **3 :** characteristic of or suitable to a mature individual ⟨a *mature* outlook⟩ **4 :** due for payment ⟨the note becomes *mature* in 90 days⟩ [Latin *maturus* "ripe"] — **ma·ture·ly** *adv* — **ma·ture·ness** *n*

[2]**mature** *vb* **1 :** to bring to maturity or completion **2 :** to become fully developed or ripe **3 :** to become due ⟨when a bond *matures*⟩

ma·tu·ri·ty \mə-ˈtu̇r-ət-ē, -ˈtyu̇r-\ *n* **1 :** the quality or state of being mature; *esp* **:** full development **2 :** the date when an obligation (as a bond or note) becomes due

mat·zo *or* **mat·zoh** \ˈmät-sə, ˌ-sō\ *n, pl* **mat·zoth** \-ˌsōth, -ˌsōt, -sōs\ *or* **mat·zos** *or* **mat·zohs** \-səz, -səs, -ˌsōz\ **1 :** unleavened bread eaten at the Passover **2 :** a wafer of matzo [Yiddish *matse,* from Hebrew *maṣṣāh*]

maud·lin \ˈmȯd-lən\ *adj* **1 :** weakly and excessively sentimental **2 :** drunk enough to be emotionally silly [Middle English *Maudeleyn* "Mary Magdalene," from Medieval French *Madelaine,* from Late Latin *Magdalene,* from Greek *Magdalēnē* "(Mary) of Magdala (town on the Sea of Galilee)"; from the practice of depicting her as a weeping, penitent sinner]

Word History *Maudlin* is a doublet of *Magdalene,* the appellation of Mary, the woman mentioned in the Gospel of Luke (8:2): ". . . Mary, called Magdalene, out of whom went seven devils." Medieval representations of Mary Magdalene customarily showed her weeping, and by the 17th century *maudlin* had come to mean "tearful, weeping." Soon *maudlin* began to be used more generally to mean "tearfully or weakly emotional" and was used especially of anyone drunk enough to be emotionally silly, fuddled, or sentimental.

[1]**maul** \ˈmȯl\ *n* **:** a heavy hammer often with a wooden head used especially for driving wedges or posts [Medieval French *mail,* from Latin *malleus*]

[2]**maul** *vt* **1 a :** to beat severely **b :** to injure by beating **:** MANGLE **2 :** to handle roughly — **maul·er** *n*

maun·der \ˈmȯn-dər, ˈmän-\ *vi* **maun·dered; maun·der·ing** \-də-ring, -dring\ **1 :** WANDER 1 **2 :** to speak in an incoherent rambling way [British dialect *maunder* "to grumble"] — **maun·der·er** \-dər-ər\ *n*

Maun·dy Thursday \ˌmȯn-dē-, ˌmän-\ *n* **:** the Thursday before Easter [Medieval French *mandé,* ceremony of washing the feet of the poor on Maundy Thursday, from Medieval French *mandet,* Latin *mandatum* "command"; from Jesus' words in John 13:34]

mau·so·le·um \ˌmȯ-sə-ˈlē-əm, ˌmȯ-zə-\ *n, pl* **-le·ums** *or* **-lea** \-ˈlē-ə\ **:** a large tomb; *esp* **:** a usually stone building for entombing the dead above ground [Latin, from Greek *Mausōleion,* tomb of Mausolus, died 353 B.C., ruler of Caria]

mauve \ˈmōv, ˈmȯv\ *n* **:** a moderate purple, violet, or lilac color [French, "mallow," from Latin *malva*]

mav·er·ick \ˈmav-rik, -ə-rik\ *n* **1 :** an unbranded range animal; *esp* **:** a motherless calf **2 :** an independent individual who refuses to conform with the group [Samuel A. *Maverick,* died 1870, American pioneer]

Word History Samuel Augustus Maverick (1803-70) was a South Carolina-born lawyer who emigrated to Texas in 1835 and was a prominent figure in the early years of the state's history. Maverick's passion was not law or politics, however, but the acquisition of land; at his death he owned over 300,000 acres spread over 32 Texas counties. He was not a rancher and resided much of his life in San Antonio, but a minor episode in his career made his name part of every cowboy's vocabulary and a fixture of American English. In 1847 he bought a farm on the Gulf Coast with about 450 cattle that were left in charge of a single slave with no experience as a cowboy. Most of the calves were never penned and branded, and loss of animals led Maverick to eventually sell all of them in 1856. Presumably in the 1850's cowboys finding unbranded yearlings on land adjoining Maverick's began to call the animals *mavericks.* The vast extent of his land holdings and later legends about Maverick as a great cattle baron may have fostered the spread of this word throughout Texas and the West.

ma·vis \ˈmā-vəs\ *n* : SONG THRUSH [Medieval French *mauviz*]

maw \ˈmȯ\ *n* **1** : a receptacle (as a stomach or crop) into which food is taken by swallowing **2** : the throat, gullet, or jaws especially of a carnivore [Old English *maga*]

mawk·ish \ˈmȯ-kish\ *adj* **1** : having a bland or unpleasant taste **2** : sickly sentimental [Middle English *mawke* "maggot," probably from Old Norse *mathkr*] — **mawk·ish·ly** *adv* — **mawk·ish·ness** *n*

max \ˈmaks\ *n* **1** : MAXIMUM 1 **2** : MAXIMUM 2 — **max** *adj* — **to the max** : to the greatest extent possible

maxi \ˈmak-sē\ *n, pl* **maxis** : a long skirt, dress, or coat

maxi- *combining form* **1** : extra long ⟨*maxi*-yacht⟩ **2** : extra large ⟨*maxi*-problems⟩ [*maximum*]

max·il·la \mak-ˈsil-ə\ *n, pl* **max·il·lae** \-ˈsil-ˌē, -ˈsil-ˌī\ *or* **max·il·las** **1 a** : an upper jaw especially of a mammal in which the bony elements are closely fused **b** : either of two bones of the upper jaw that bear the upper teeth **2** : one of the first or second pair of mouth parts posterior to the mandibles in many arthropods (as insects or crustaceans) [Latin] — **max·il·lary** \ˈmak-sə-ˌler-ē\ *adj or n*

max·il·li·ped \mak-ˈsil-ə-ˌped\ *n* : any of three pairs of appendages situated next behind the maxillae in a crustacean

max·im \ˈmak-səm\ *n* **1** : a general truth, fundamental principle, or rule of conduct **2** : a proverbial saying [Medieval French *maxime,* from Medieval Latin *maxima,* from Latin *maximus,* superlative of *magnus* "great"]

max·i·mal \ˈmak-sə-məl, -sməl\ *adj* **1** : being an upper limit : HIGHEST ⟨a *maximal* dose⟩ **2** : most comprehensive : COMPLETE ⟨*maximal* recovery⟩ — **max·i·mal·ly** \-ē\ *adv*

max·i·mize \ˈmak-sə-ˌmīz\ *vb* **1** : to increase to a maximum ⟨*maximize* profits⟩ **2** : to make the most of ⟨*maximize* your opportunities⟩ **3** : to find a maximum value of **4** : to increase the size of (a program's window) to fill an entire computer screen — **max·i·mi·za·tion** \ˌmak-sə-mə-ˈzā-shən\ *n* — **max·i·miz·er** *n*

max·i·mum \ˈmak-sə-məm, -sməm\ *n, pl* **max·i·ma** \-sə-mə\ *or* **max·i·mums** **1 a** : the greatest quantity or value attainable or attained **b** : the period of highest, greatest, or utmost development **2** : an upper limit allowed (as by law) [Latin, neuter of *maximus,* superlative of *magnus* "large"] — **maximum** *adj*

max out *vb* **1** : to reach or cause to reach an upper limit or a peak **2** : to use up all available credit on ⟨*maxed out* the credit cards⟩

may \mā, ˈmā\ *auxiliary verb, past* **might** \mīt, ˈmīt\; *present sing & pl* **may** **1 a** : have permission to ⟨you *may* go⟩ **b** : be in some degree likely to ⟨you *may* be right⟩ **2** — used to express a wish or desire ⟨*may* the best man win⟩ **3** — used to express purpose ⟨I laughed that I *might* not weep⟩, contingency ⟨I'll stay come what *may*⟩, or concession ⟨he *may* be slow but he's thorough⟩ [Old English *mæg* "can, may"] ***usage*** see CAN

May \ˈmā\ *n* : the 5th month of the year according to the Gregorian calendar [Latin *Maius,* from *Maia,* a Roman goddess]

Ma·ya \ˈmī-ə\ *n, pl* **Maya** *or* **Mayas** : a member of a group of American Indian peoples of the Yucatán Peninsula and adjacent areas [Spanish] — **Ma·yan** \ˈmī-ən\ *adj*

Ma·yan \ˈmī-ən\ *n* **1** : a family of American Indian languages spoken in Central America and Mexico **2** : a member of any of the peoples speaking Mayan languages

may·ap·ple \ˈmā-ˌap-əl\ *n* : a North American woodland herb related to the barberries and having a poisonous rootstock, large leaves, and a single large waxy white flower followed by a yellow egg-shaped edible fruit; *also* : its fruit

may·be \ˈmā-bē, ˈmeb-ē\ *adv* : PERHAPS

May·day \mā-ˈdā, ˈmā-ˌ\ — an international radio-telephone signal word used as a distress call [French *m'aider* "help me"]

May Day \ˈmā-ˌdā\ *n* : May 1 celebrated as a springtime festival and in some countries as Labor Day

may·est *or* **mayst** \ˈmā-əst, māst, ˈmāst\ *archaic present 2nd singular of* MAY

may·flow·er \ˈmā-ˌflau̇-ər, -ˌflau̇r\ *n* : any of various spring-blooming plants; *esp* : ARBUTUS 2

may·fly \-ˌflī\ *n* : any of an order (Ephemeroptera) of insects with an aquatic nymph and a short-lived fragile adult having membranous wings

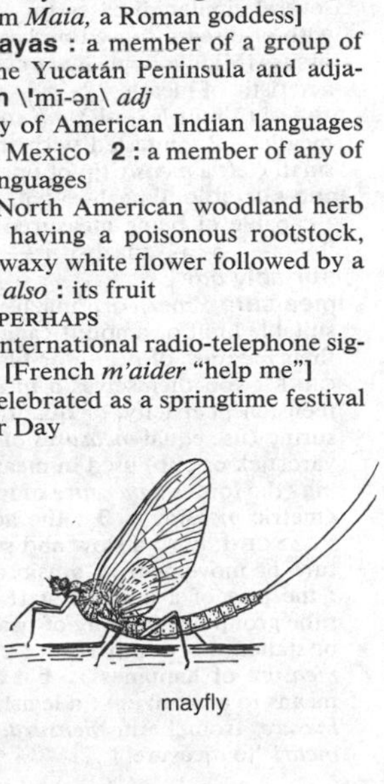

mayfly

may·hap \ˈmā-ˌhap, mā-ˈ\ *adv* : PERHAPS

may·hem \ˈmā-ˌhem, ˈmā-əm\ *n* **1** : willful and permanent crippling, mutilation, or disfigurement of any part of the body **2** : needless or willful damage or violence [Medieval French *mahaim,* from *maheimer* "to maim"]

may·ing \ˈmā-ing\ *n, often cap* : the celebrating of May Day

mayn't \ˈmā-ənt, mānt, ˈmānt\ : may not

may·on·naise \ˈmā-ə-ˌnāz, ˌmā-ə-ˈ\ *n* : a sauce made chiefly of egg yolk, vegetable oil, and vinegar or lemon juice [French]

may·or \ˈmā-ər, ˈme-ər, ˈmeər\ *n* : an official elected to act as chief executive or nominal head of a city or borough [Medieval French *maire,* from Latin *major,* comparative of *magnus* "large"] — **may·or·al** \ˈmā-ə-rəl, ˈme-ə-\ *adj*

may·or·al·ty \ˈmā-ə-rəl-tē, ˈme-; ˈmer-əl-\ *n, pl* **-ties** : the office or the term of office of a mayor

may·pole \ˈmā-ˌpōl\ *n, often cap* : a tall flower-wreathed pole forming a center for May Day sports and dances

may·pop \ˈmā-ˌpäp\ *n* : a climbing perennial passionflower of the southern U.S.; *also* : its large ovoid yellow edible tasteless fruit [alteration of *maracock,* perhaps from an Algonquian language of Virginia]

maze \ˈmāz\ *n* **1 a** : a confusingly intricate network of passages **b** : something often confusingly elaborate or complicated ⟨a *maze* of regulations⟩ **2** *chiefly dialect* : a state of confusion [Middle English, from *mazen* "to confuse"]

ma·zur·ka \mə-ˈzər-kə, -ˈzu̇r-\ *n* **1** : a Polish dance in moderate triple measure **2** : music for the mazurka usually in moderate ¾ or ⅜ time [Polish *mazurek*]

mazy \ˈmā-zē\ *adj* : resembling a maze

maz·zard \ˈmaz-ərd\ *n* : SWEET CHERRY; *esp* : wild or seedling sweet cherry used as a rootstock for grafting [origin unknown]

MC \em-ˈsē, ˈem-ˈsē\ *n* : MASTER OF CEREMONIES

Mc·Coy \mə-ˈkȯi\ *n* : something genuine ⟨the real *McCoy*⟩ [alteration of *Mackay* (in the phrase *the real Mackay,* of unknown origin]

McGuffin variant of MACGUFFIN

Mc·In·tosh \ˈmak-ən-ˌtäsh\ *n* : a juicy bright red eating apple with a thin skin, white flesh, and slightly tart flavor [John *McIntosh,* flourished 1796, Canadian settler]

Mc·Man·sion \mək-ˈman-chən\ *n* : a very large house usually built in a suburban neighborhood or development; *esp* : one regarded critically as oversized or ostentatious [*Mc-*, prefix denoting uniformity and mass appeal, after *McDonald's,* chain of fast-food restaurants]

me \mē, ˈmē\ *pron, objective case of* I [Old English *mē*]

usage *Me* is used in many constructions where strict grammarians prescribe *I*. This use of *me* in place of *I* is not so much ungrammatical as a matter of historical development. *I* is now chiefly used as the subject of an immediately following verb ⟨*I* went to the store⟩. *Me* occurs in every other position: absolutely ⟨who, *me?*⟩, emphatically ⟨*me* too⟩, and after prepositions, conjunctions, and verbs, including "be" ⟨come with *me*⟩ ⟨you're as big as *me*⟩ ⟨it's *me*⟩. The legitimacy of the use of *me* in these positions, especially in speech, is recognized in almost all usage books. *I* is sometimes recommended in formal and especially written contexts after forms of "be" ⟨it was *I* who discovered the mistake⟩ and after "as" and "than" when the first term of the comparison is the subject of a verb ⟨he is more knowledgeable than *I* on that subject⟩ ⟨she is just as responsible as *I*⟩. ***usage*** see in addition MYSELF

mea cul·pa \ˌmā-ə-ˈku̇l-pə\ *n* : a formal acknowledgment of personal fault or error [Latin, through my fault]

mead \ˈmēd\ *n* : an alcoholic fermented drink made of water, honey, malt, and yeast [Old English *medu*]

mead·ow \ˈmed-ō\ *n* : a usually flat area of land that is covered with tall grass [Middle English *medwe,* from Old English *mǣd*]

meadow beauty *n* : any of a genus of perennial North American herbs with showy flowers

meadow fescue *n* : a tall vigorous European fescue with broad flat leaves cultivated for pasture and hay

mead·ow·land \ˈmed-ō-ˌland\ *n* : land that is or is used for meadow

\ə\ **abut**	\au̇\ **out**	\i\ **tip**	\ȯ\ **saw**	\u̇\ **foot**
\ər\ **further**	\ch\ **chin**	\ī\ **life**	\ȯi\ **coin**	\y\ **yet**
\a\ **mat**	\e\ **pet**	\j\ **job**	\th\ **thin**	\yü\ **few**
\ā\ **take**	\ē\ **easy**	\ng\ **sing**	\t͟h\ **this**	\yu̇\ **cure**
\ä\ **cot, cart**	\g\ **go**	\ō\ **bone**	\ü\ **food**	\zh\ **vision**

mead·ow·lark \'med-ō-ˌlärk\ *n* : any of several North American songbirds that are largely brown and buff above with a yellow breast bearing a black crescent

meadowlark

meadow mushroom *n* : a common edible fungus that is often cultivated

meadow saffron *n* : AUTUMN CROCUS

mead·ow·sweet \'med-ō-ˌswēt\ *n* : any of several North American native or naturalized spireas with pink or white fragrant flowers

mea·ger *or* **mea·gre** \'mē-gər\ *adj* **1** : having little flesh : THIN **2 a** : lacking desirable qualities (as richness or strength) ⟨a *meager* life⟩ **b** : deficient in quality or quantity ⟨a *meager* serving⟩ [Medieval French *meigre,* from Latin *macer*] — **mea·ger·ly** *adv* — **mea·ger·ness** *n*

synonyms MEAGER, SCANTY, SPARSE mean falling short of what is normal, necessary, or desirable. MEAGER implies lack of fullness, richness, or plenty ⟨*meager* diets⟩. SCANTY stresses insufficiency in quantity, degree, or extent ⟨a *scanty* supply of fuel⟩. SPARSE implies a thin scattering of units ⟨a *sparse* population⟩.

1**meal** \'mēl\ *n* **1** : the food eaten or prepared for eating at one time **2** : the act or time of eating a meal [Old English *mǣl* "appointed time, meal"]

2**meal** *n* **1** : usually coarsely ground seeds of a cereal grass or pulse; *esp* : CORNMEAL **2** : something like meal especially in texture [Old English *melu*] ***synonyms*** see FLOUR

meal·time \'mēl-ˌtīm\ *n* : the usual time at which a meal is served

meal·worm \-ˌwərm\ *n* : a small brownish worm that is the larva of various beetles and that lives in grain products and is often raised as food for insect-eating animals or as bait

mealy \'mē-lē\ *adj* **meal·i·er; -est** **1** : containing meal **2** : being soft, dry, and crumbly **3** : covered with fine granules or with flecks (as of color) **4** : MEALYMOUTHED

mealy·bug \'mē-lē-ˌbəg\ *n* : any of numerous scale insects that have a white cottony or waxy covering and are destructive pests especially of fruit trees

mealy·mouthed \ˌmē-lē-'mau̇thd, -'mau̇tht\ *adj* : not willing to tell the truth in plain and simple language

1**mean** \'mēn\ *adj* **1** : lacking distinction or prominence : HUMBLE **2** : worthy of little regard : INFERIOR — often used in negative constructions as a term of praise ⟨a person of no *mean* ability⟩ **3** : of poor, shabby, or inferior quality or status ⟨*mean* city streets⟩ **4** : not honorable or worthy : UNKIND ⟨it is *mean* to take advantage of another's misfortunes⟩ **5** : STINGY 1, MISERLY **6** : SPITEFUL, MALICIOUS ⟨a *mean* remark⟩ **7** : causing trouble or bother ⟨a *mean* horse⟩ **8** : EXCELLENT, EFFECTIVE ⟨plays a *mean* guitar⟩ ⟨a lean, *mean* athlete⟩ [Middle English *imene, mene* "held in common, inferior," from Old English *gemǣne* "held in common"] — **mean·ness** *n*

2**mean** \'mēn\ *vb* **meant** \'ment\; **mean·ing** \'mē-ning\ **1 a** : to have as a purpose : INTEND ⟨I *mean* to go⟩ **b** : to intend for a particular purpose, use, or destination ⟨a book *meant* for children⟩ **2** : to serve to convey, show, or indicate ⟨what do these words *mean*⟩ ⟨those clouds *mean* rain⟩ **3** : to be of a specified degree of importance ⟨health *means* a lot to me⟩ [Old English *mǣnan*] — **mean business** : to be in earnest

3**mean** *n* **1** : a middle point between extremes **2 a** : a value that lies within a range of values and is computed according to a prescribed rule; *esp* : ARITHMETIC MEAN **b** : either of the middle two terms of a proportion **3** *pl* : something by the use or help of which a desired end is accomplished or furthered ⟨*means* of production⟩ ⟨ready to use any *means* at their disposal⟩ **4** *pl* : resources available for disposal; *esp* : WEALTH ⟨a person of *means*⟩ [Medieval French *meen,* from *mene, meen,* adj., "middle, medium"] ***synonyms*** see AVERAGE — **by all means** : without fail : CERTAINLY — **by means of** : through the use of — **by no means** : not at all : certainly not

4**mean** *adj* **1** : holding a middle position : INTERMEDIATE **2 a** : occupying a position about midway between extremes **b** : being the mean of a set of values : AVERAGE ⟨*mean* temperature⟩ [Medieval French *mene, meen* "middle, medium," from Latin *medianus* "median"]

1**me·an·der** \mē-'an-dər\ *n* **1** : a turn or winding of a stream **2** : a winding path or course [Latin *maeander,* from Greek *maiandros,* from *Maiandros* (now *Menderes*), river in Asia Minor]

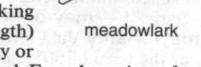

2**meander** *vi* **-dered; -der·ing** \-dəring, -dring\ **1** : to follow a winding or intricate course **2** : to wander aimlessly : RAMBLE ***synonyms*** see WANDER

1**mean·ing** \'mē-ning\ *n* **1 a** : the sense one intends to convey especially by language : PURPORT ⟨do not mistake my *meaning*⟩ **b** : the sense that is conveyed ⟨the *meaning* of the poem is clear⟩ **2** : INTENT 1, PURPOSE **3** : intent to convey information : SIGNIFICANCE 1 ⟨a glance full of *meaning*⟩

synonyms MEANING, SENSE, SIGNIFICATION, SIGNIFICANCE denote the idea conveyed to the mind by a word, sign, or symbol. MEANING is the general term used of anything (as a word, poem, action) requiring or allowing interpretation ⟨what is its *meaning* to you?⟩. SENSE applies especially to words or utterances and may denote one out of several meanings of any one word ⟨the word "charge" has many distinct *senses*⟩. SIGNIFICATION denotes the established meaning of a word, symbol, or written character ⟨use the word in its ordinary *signification*⟩. SIGNIFICANCE applies specifically to an underlying as distinguished from a surface meaning ⟨did not realize the *significance* of her remark⟩.

2**meaning** *adj* : conveying or intending to convey meaning : SIGNIFICANT ⟨a *meaning* look⟩ — **mean·ing·ly** \-ning-lē\ *adv*

mean·ing·ful \-fəl\ *adj* **1** : having a meaning or purpose ⟨*meaningful* work⟩ **2** : full of meaning : SIGNIFICANT ⟨a *meaningful* experience⟩ — **mean·ing·ful·ly** \-fə-lē\ *adv* — **mean·ing·ful·ness** *n*

mean·ing·less \'mē-ning-ləs\ *adj* **1** : lacking meaning or significance **2** : lacking motive ⟨a *meaningless* murder⟩ — **mean·ing·less·ly** *adv* — **mean·ing·less·ness** *n*

mean·ly \'mēn-lē\ *adv* **1** : in a poor, humble, or shabby manner ⟨*meanly* dressed⟩ **2** : in an ungenerous or ignoble manner

mean proportional *n* : GEOMETRIC MEAN 1; *esp* : the square root (as *x*) of the product of two numbers (as *a* and *b*) when expressed as the means of a proportion (as $a/x = x/b$)

mean solar day *n* : the average time interval between consecutive passes of the sun over a given meridian

mean–spir·it·ed \'mēn-'spir-ət-əd, ˌmēn-\ *adj* : feeling or showing a cruel desire to cause pain or harm ⟨a *mean-spirited* person⟩ ⟨a *mean-spirited* remark⟩

means test \'mēnz-\ *n* : an examination of a person's financial state to determine his or her eligibility for public assistance

meant *past of* MEAN

1**mean·time** \'mēn-ˌtīm\ *n* : the time between two events

2**meantime** *adv* : MEANWHILE

1**mean·while** \'mēn-ˌhwīl, -ˌwīl\ *n* : MEANTIME

2**meanwhile** *adv* **1** : during the meantime **2** : at the same time

mea·sle \'mē-zəl\ *n* : a tapeworm larva in the muscles of a domesticated mammal [singular of *measles*]

mea·sles \'mē-zəlz\ *n sing or pl* **1** : an acute contagious virus disease marked by fever and red spots on the skin; *also* : any of several similar diseases (as German measles) **2** : infestation with or disease caused by larval tapeworms in the muscles and tissues [Middle English *meseles,* pl. of *mesel* "measles, spot characteristic of measles"]

mea·sly \'mēz-lē, -ə-lē\ *adj* **mea·sli·er; -est** **1** : infected with measles **2** : infested with trichina worms **3** : contemptibly small ⟨left a *measly* tip of one quarter⟩

mea·sur·able \'mezh-rə-bəl, -ə-rə-; 'mezh-ər-bəl; 'māzh-\ *adj* : capable of being measured — **mea·sur·abil·i·ty** \ˌmezh-rə-'bil-ət-ē, -ə-rə-, ˌmāzh-\ *n* — **mea·sur·able·ness** *n* — **mea·sur·ably** *adv*

1**mea·sure** \'mezh-ər, 'māzh-\ *n* **1 a** : an adequate, fixed, or suitable limit or amount ⟨angry beyond *measure*⟩ ⟨all received their *measure* of praise or blame⟩ **b** : AMOUNT, EXTENT, DEGREE ⟨won themselves a *measure* of freedom⟩ **2 a** : the dimensions, capacity, or quantity of something as fixed by measuring ⟨use equal *measures* of ingredients⟩ **b** : something (as a yardstick or cup) used in measuring **c** : a unit used in measuring ⟨the foot is a *measure* of length⟩ **d** : a system of measuring ⟨metric *measure*⟩ **3** : the act or process of measuring **4 a** : DANCE 1; *esp* : a slow and stately dance **b** : rhythmic structure or movement in music or poetry : METER, CADENCE **c** : the part of a musical staff between two adjacent bars; *also* : the group or grouping of beats between these bars **5** : a basis or standard of comparison : CRITERION ⟨wealth is not always a *measure* of happiness⟩ **6** : an action planned or taken as a means to an end; *esp* : a legislative bill or act [Medieval French *mesure,* from Latin *mensura,* from *mensus,* past participle of *metiri* "to measure"]

MEASURES AND WEIGHTS[1]

UNIT	ABBREVIATION OR SYMBOL	EQUIVALENTS IN OTHER UNITS OF SAME SYSTEM	METRIC EQUIVALENT
		WEIGHT	
		Avoirdupois[2]	
ton			
short ton		2000 pounds, 20 short hundredweight	0.907 metric ton
long ton		2240 pounds, 20 long hundredweight	1.016 metric tons
hundredweight	cwt		
short hundredweight		100 pounds, 0.05 short ton	45.359 kilograms
long hundredweight		112 pounds, 0.05 long ton	50.802 kilograms
pound	lb *or* lb avdp *also* #	16 ounces, 7000 grains	0.454 kilogram
ounce	oz *or* oz avdp	16 drams, 437.5 grains, 0.0625 pound	28.350 grams
dram	dr *or* dr avdp	27.344 grains, 0.0625 ounce	1.772 grams
grain	gr	0.037 dram, 0.002286 ounce	0.0648 gram
		Troy	
pound	lb t	12 ounces, 240 pennyweight, 5760 grains	0.373 kilogram
ounce	oz t	20 pennyweight, 480 grains, 0.083 pound	31.103 grams
pennyweight	dwt *also* pwt	24 grains, 0.05 ounce	1.555 grams
grain	gr	0.042 pennyweight, 0.002083 ounce	0.0648 gram
		Apothecaries'	
pound	lb ap	12 ounces, 5760 grains	0.373 kilogram
ounce	oz ap *or* ℥	8 drams, 480 grains, 0.083 pound	31.103 grams
dram	dr ap *or* ʒ	3 scruples, 60 grains	3.888 grams
scruple	s ap *or* ℈	20 grains, 0.333 dram	1.296 grams
grain	gr	0.05 scruple, 0.002083 ounce, 0.0166 dram	0.0648 gram
		CAPACITY	
		U.S. liquid measure	
gallon	gal	4 quarts (231 cubic inches)	3.785 liters
quart	qt	2 pints (57.75 cubic inches)	0.946 liter
pint	pt	4 gills (28.875 cubic inches)	0.473 liter
gill	gi	4 fluid ounces (7.219 cubic inches)	118.294 milliliters
fluid ounce	fl oz *or f* ℥	8 fluid drams (1.805 cubic inches)	29.573 milliliters
fluid dram	fl dr *or f* ʒ	60 minims (0.226 cubic inch)	3.697 milliliters
minim	min *or* ♏	1/60 fluid dram (0.003760 cubic inch)	0.061610 milliliter
		U.S. dry measure	
bushel	bu	4 pecks (2150.42 cubic inches)	35.239 liters
peck	pk	8 quarts (537.605 cubic inches)	8.810 liters
quart	qt	2 pints (67.201 cubic inches)	1.101 liters
pint	pt	½ quart (33.600 cubic inches)	0.551 liter
		LENGTH	
mile	mi	5280 feet, 1760 yards, 320 rods	1.609 kilometers
rod	rd	5.50 yards, 16.5 feet	5.029 meters
yard	yd	3 feet, 36 inches	0.9144 meter
foot	ft *or* ′	12 inches, 0.333 yard	30.48 centimeters
inch	in *or* ″	0.083 foot, 0.028 yard	2.54 centimeters
		AREA	
square mile	sq mi *or* mi^2	640 acres, 102,400 square rods	2.590 square kilometers
acre	ac	4840 square yards, 43,560 square feet	0.405 hectare
square rod	sq rd *or* rd^2	30.25 square yards, 0.00625 acre	25.293 square meters
square yard	sq yd *or* yd^2	9 square feet, 1296 square inches	0.836 square meter
square foot	sq ft *or* ft^2	144 square inches, 0.111 square yard	0.093 square meter
square inch	sq in *or* in^2	0.0069 square foot, 0.00077 square yard	6.452 square centimeters
		VOLUME	
cubic yard	cu yd *or* yd^3	27 cubic feet, 46,656 cubic inches	0.765 cubic meter
cubic foot	cu ft *or* ft^3	1728 cubic inches, 0.0370 cubic yard	0.028 cubic meter
cubic inch	cu in *or* in^3	0.00058 cubic foot, 0.000021 cubic yard	16.387 cubic centimeters

[1]For U.S. equivalents of the metric units see Metric System table.
[2]The U.S. uses the avoirdupois units as the common system of measuring weight.

[2]**measure** *vb* **mea·sured; mea·sur·ing** \ˈmezh-ring, ˈmāzh-, -ə-ring\ **1** : to select or regulate with caution : GOVERN ⟨*measure* one's acts⟩ **2 a** : to mark or fix in multiples of a specific unit ⟨*measure* off three centimeters⟩ **b** : to allot or apportion in measured amounts ⟨*measure* out two cups⟩ **3** : to determine the dimensions, extent, or amount of ⟨*measure* the length of the table⟩ **4 a** : ESTIMATE ⟨*measure* the distance by eye⟩ **b** : to bring into comparison ⟨*measure* one's skill against a rival⟩ **5** : to serve as a measure of ⟨a thermometer *measures* temperature⟩ **6** : to have a certain measurement (as in length or breadth) ⟨the room *measures* 12 by 12 feet⟩ — **mea·sur·er** \-ər-ər\ *n*

mea·sured \-ərd\ *adj* **1 a** : marked by due proportion **b** : being slow and steady : EVEN ⟨a *measured* gait⟩ **2** : DELIBERATE, CALCULATED ⟨a *measured* response⟩ **3** : METRICAL 1, RHYTHMICAL

mea·sure·less \-ər-ləs\ *adj* : being without measure : IMMEASURABLE ⟨the *measureless* universe⟩

mea·sure·ment \ˈmezh-ər-mənt, ˈmāzh-\ *n* **1** : the act or pro-

\ə\ **abut**	\au̇\ **out**	\i\ **tip**	\ȯ\ **saw**	\u̇\ **foot**
\ər\ **further**	\ch\ **chin**	\ī\ **life**	\ȯi\ **coin**	\y\ **yet**
\a\ **mat**	\e\ **pet**	\j\ **job**	\th\ **thin**	\yü\ **few**
\ā\ **take**	\ē\ **easy**	\ng\ **sing**	\t͟h\ **this**	\yu̇\ **cure**
\ä\ **cot, cart**	\g\ **go**	\ō\ **bone**	\ü\ **food**	\zh\ **vision**

cess of measuring **2** : a figure, extent, or amount obtained by measuring : DIMENSION **3** : a system of measures

measure up *vi* **1** : to have necessary or fitting qualifications **2** : to be the equal (as in ability) — used with *to*

measuring worm *n* : LOOPER 1

meat \'mēt\ *n* **1 a** : something eaten for nourishment; *esp* : solid food as distinguished from drink **b** : the edible part of something as distinguished from the covering (as a shell or husk) ⟨walnut *meat*⟩ **2** : animal and especially mammal flesh used as food [Old English *mete*]

meat·ball \-ˌbȯl\ *n* : a small ball of chopped or ground meat

meat loaf *n* : a dish of ground meat seasoned and baked in the form of a loaf

me·a·tus \mē-'āt-əs\ *n, pl* **me·a·tus·es** *or* **me·a·tus** \-'āt-əs, -'āˌtüs\ : a natural body passage [Late Latin, from Latin, "going, passage," *meare* "to go, pass"]

meaty \'mēt-ē\ *adj* **meat·i·er; -est** **1** : full of meat : FLESHY **2** : rich in matter for thought : SUBSTANTIAL ⟨a *meaty* book⟩ — **meat·i·ness** \'mēt-ē-nəs\ *n*

mec·ca \'mek-ə\ *n, often cap* : a place regarded as a center for a specified group, activity, or interest ⟨the university is a *mecca* for chemistry students⟩ [*Mecca,* Saudi Arabia, a destination of pilgrims in the Islamic world]

[1]**me·chan·ic** \mi-'kan-ik\ *adj* : of or relating to manual work or skill ⟨*mechanic* arts⟩ [derived from Greek *mēchanikos,* from *mēchanē* "machine"]

[2]**mechanic** *n* **1** : a manual worker : ARTISAN **2** : a repairer of machines

me·chan·i·cal \mi-'kan-i-kəl\ *adj* **1 a** : of or relating to machinery ⟨*mechanical* skill⟩ **b** : made or operated by a machine or tool ⟨a *mechanical* concrete mixer⟩ ⟨a *mechanical* toy⟩ **2** : of or relating to mechanics or artisans **3** : done as if by machine : IMPERSONAL ⟨gave a *mechanical* reply⟩ **4** : relating to or in accordance with the principles of mechanics **5** : relating to a process that involves a purely physical change — **me·chan·i·cal·ly** \-i-kə-lē, -klē\ *adv*

mechanical advantage *n* : the ratio of the force that performs the useful work of a machine to the force that is applied to the machine

mechanical drawing *n* : a method of drawing that makes use of such instruments as compasses, squares, and triangles in order to insure mathematical precision; *also* : a drawing made by this method

mechanical engineering *n* : engineering that deals with the application of mechanics in industry and with the production of tools and machinery and their products — **mechanical engineer** *n*

me·chan·ics \mi-'kan-iks\ *n sing or pl* **1** : a branch of physical science that deals with energy and forces and their effect on bodies **2** : the practical application of mechanics to the making or operation of machines **3** : mechanical or functional details or procedure ⟨the *mechanics* of running⟩ ⟨the *mechanics* of writing plays⟩

mech·a·nism \'mek-ə-ˌniz-əm\ *n* **1** : a machine or mechanical device **2 a** : the parts by which a machine operates as a mechanical unit ⟨the *mechanism* of a watch⟩ **b** : the process, technique, or system for achieving a goal ⟨the *mechanism* of democratic government⟩ **3** : the doctrine that natural processes (as of life) are orderly and wholly subject to natural law — compare VITALISM **4** : the fundamental physical or chemical processes involved in or responsible for a natural phenomenon (as an action or reaction) — **mech·a·nist** \-nəst\ *n*

mech·a·nis·tic \'mek-ə-'nis-tik\ *adj* **1** : mechanically determined ⟨the *mechanistic* universe⟩ **2** : of or relating to a mechanism or the doctrine of mechanism — **mech·a·nis·ti·cal·ly** \-ti-kə-lē, -klē\ *adv*

mech·a·nize \'mek-ə-ˌnīz\ *vt* **1** : to make mechanical; *esp* : to make automatic **2 a** : to equip with machinery especially to replace human or animal labor **b** : to equip (a military force) with armed and armored motor-driven vehicles — **mech·a·ni·za·tion** \ˌmek-ə-nə-'zā-shən\ *n* — **mech·a·niz·er** \'mek-ə-ˌnī-zər\ *n*

me·co·ni·um \mi-'kō-nē-əm\ *n* : dark greenish matter in the bowel at birth [Latin, literally, "poppy juice," from Greek *mēkōnion,* from *mēkōn* "poppy"]

[1]**med·al** \'med-l\ *n* **1** : a metal disk bearing a religious emblem or picture **2** : a piece of metal often in the form of a coin issued to commemorate a person or event or as an award [Middle French *medaille,* from Italian *medaglia* "coin worth half a denarius, medal," derived from Late Latin *medialis* "medial"]

[2]**medal** *vi* **med·aled** *also* **med·alled; med·al·ing** *also* **med·al·ling** : to win a medal ⟨*medaled* in figure skating⟩

med·al·ist *or* **med·al·list** \-l-əst\ *n* **1** : a designer or maker of medals **2** : a recipient of a medal

me·dal·lion \mə-'dal-yən\ *n* **1** : a large medal **2** : something resembling a large medal; *esp* : a tablet or panel in a wall or window bearing a figure in relief, a portrait, or an ornament [French *médaillon,* from Italian *medaglione,* from *medaglia* "medal"]

med·dle \'med-l\ *vi* **med·dled** \-ld\; **med·dling** \'med-ling, -l-ing\ : to interest oneself in what is not one's concern ⟨*meddle* in another's business⟩ [Medieval French *mesler, medler* "to mix, meddle," derived from Latin *miscēre* "to mix"] — **med·dler** \'med-lər, -l-ər\ *n*

med·dle·some \'med-l-səm\ *adj* : given to meddling : INTRUSIVE — **med·dle·some·ness** *n*

Mede \'mēd\ *n* : a native or inhabitant of ancient Media in Persia

med·fly \'med-ˌflī\ *n, often cap* : MEDITERRANEAN FRUIT FLY

[1]**media** *plural of* MEDIUM

[2]**media** *n, pl* **medias** **1** : a medium of cultivation, conveyance, or expression; *esp* : MEDIUM 3 **2 a** *sing or pl* : forms or systems of communication designed to reach a large number of people : MASS MEDIA **b** *pl* : members of the mass media

usage The singular *media* and its plural *medias* seem to have originated in the field of advertising over 70 years ago. They are apparently still so used without stigma in that specialized field. In most other applications *media* is used as a plural of *medium.* The great popularity of *media* in references to the agencies of mass communication is leading to the formation of a mass noun, construed as a singular ⟨the news *media* is searching for breaking stories⟩. This use is not yet sufficiently well established to avoid criticism and is likely to be considered wrong especially when used in writing.

mediaeval *variant of* MEDIEVAL

me·di·al \'mēd-ē-əl\ *adj* **1 a** : MEDIAN 1 **b** : extending toward the middle **2** : situated between the beginning and the end of a word **3** : ORDINARY 2a, AVERAGE [Late Latin *medialis,* from Latin *medius* "middle"] — **medial** *n* — **me·di·al·ly** \-ə-lē\ *adv*

[1]**me·di·an** \'mēd-ē-ən\ *n* **1** : a median part **2** : a value in an ordered set of values below and above which there are an equal number of values or which is the average of the two middle values if there is no one middle number ⟨the *median* of the set 1, 3, 7, 12, 19 is 7 and the *median* of the set 2, 5, 7, 15 is 6⟩ **3 a** : a line from a vertex of a triangle to the midpoint of the opposite side **b** : a line joining the midpoints of the nonparallel sides of a trapezoid **4** : MEDIAN STRIP [Late Latin *mediana* (*vena*) "median (vein)," from Latin *medianus* "in the middle," from *medius* "middle"] ***synonyms*** see AVERAGE

[2]**median** *adj* **1** : being in the middle or in an intermediate position **2** : relating to or constituting a median

median strip *n* : a paved or planted strip separating the opposing lanes of a highway

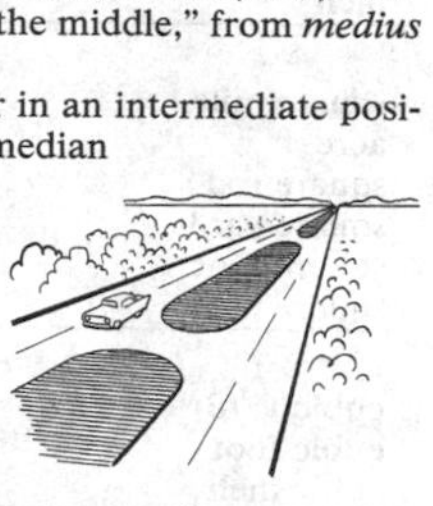

median strip

me·di·ant \'mēd-ē-ənt\ *n* : the third tone above the tonic [Italian *mediante,* from Late Latin *mediare* "to be in the middle"]

me·di·as·ti·num \ˌmēd-ē-ə-'stī-nəm\ *n, pl* **-na** \-nə\ : the space in the chest between the pleural sacs of the lungs that contains tissue and organs of the chest except the lungs and pleurae; *also* : this space with its contents [New Latin, from Medieval Latin *mediastinus* "medial," from Latin *medius* "middle"] — **me·di·as·ti·nal** \-'stīn-l\ *adj*

[1]**me·di·ate** \'mēd-ē-ət\ *adj* : acting through an intermediate agent or agency : not direct or immediate [Late Latin *mediatus* "intermediate," from *mediare* "to be in the middle," from Latin *medius* "middle"] — **me·di·ate·ly** *adv*

[2]**me·di·ate** \'mēd-ē-ˌāt\ *vb* **1** : to intervene between conflicting parties or viewpoints to promote reconciliation, settlement, or compromise **2 a** : to bring about by mediation ⟨*mediate* a settlement⟩ **b** : to bring accord out of by mediation ⟨*mediate* a dispute⟩ **3** : to transmit or act as an intermediate mechanism

me·di·a·tion \ˌmēd-ē-'ā-shən\ *n* : the act or process of mediating; *esp* : intervention by a third party in a dispute to promote reconciliation, settlement, or compromise between the conflicting parties

me·di·a·tor \ˈmē-dē-ˌāt-ər\ *n* **1 :** one that mediates; *esp* **:** an impartial third party (as a person, group, or country) that acts as a go-between in a dispute in order to arrange a peaceful settlement **2 :** a mediating agent in a chemical or biological process — **me·di·a·to·ry** \ˈmē-dē-ə-ˌtōr-ē, -ˌtȯr-\ *adj*

¹med·ic \ˈmed-ik\ *n* **:** any of a genus of herbs of the legume family resembling clovers and including some (as alfalfa) grown for hay and forage [Latin *medica,* from Greek *mēdikē,* from *mēdikos* "of Media"]

²medic *n* **:** a person engaged in medical work or study; *esp* **:** CORPSMAN [Latin *medicus* "physician"]

med·i·ca·ble \ˈmed-i-kə-bəl\ *adj* **:** CURABLE, REMEDIABLE — **med·i·ca·bly** \-blē\ *adv*

Med·ic·aid \ˈmed-i-ˌkād\ *n* **:** a program of medical aid designed for those unable to afford regular medical service and financed jointly by the state and federal governments

med·i·cal \ˈmed-i-kəl\ *adj* **1 :** of, relating to, or concerned with the science or practice of medicine ⟨a *medical* education⟩ **2 :** requiring, providing, or used in medical treatment ⟨*medical* emergencies⟩ ⟨a *medical* device⟩ [Late Latin *medicalis,* from Latin *medicus* "physician," from *mederi* "to heal"] — **med·i·cal·ly** \-k(ə-)lē, -klē\ *adv*

medical examiner *n* **:** an appointed public official with duties similar to a coroner but who is required to have specific medical training and is qualified to conduct medical examinations and autopsies

me·dic·a·ment \mi-ˈdik-ə-mənt\ *n* **:** a medicine or healing application

Medi·care \ˈmed-i-ˌkeər, -ˌkaər\ *n* **:** a government program of medical care especially for the aged

med·i·cate \ˈmed-ə-ˌkāt\ *vt* **1 :** to treat with medicine **2 :** to add a medicinal substance to ⟨*medicate* a soap⟩

med·i·ca·tion \ˌmed-ə-ˈkā-shən\ *n* **1 :** the act or process of medicating **2 :** a medicinal substance **:** MEDICAMENT

me·dic·i·nal \mə-ˈdis-nəl, -n-əl\ *adj* **:** tending or used to cure disease or relieve pain — **me·dic·i·nal·ly** \-ē\ *adv*

medicinal leech *n* **:** a large European freshwater leech that is sometimes used to drain blood (as from newly grafted tissue) and was formerly used to bleed patients thought to have excess blood

med·i·cine \ˈmed-ə-sən\ *n* **1 :** a substance or preparation used in treating disease **2 a :** the science and art dealing with the maintenance of health and the prevention, easing, or cure of disease **b :** the branch of medicine concerned with the nonsurgical treatment of disease **3 :** an object held to give control over natural or magical forces; *also* **:** a magical power or rite [Medieval French, from Latin *medicina,* from *medicus* "physician," from *mederi* "to heal"]

medicine ball *n* **:** a heavy usually large ball used especially for strengthening exercises

medicine dropper *n* **:** DROPPER 2

medicine man *n* **:** a person especially among the American Indians that is believed to communicate with the spirits and possess supernatural powers that can heal and keep away evil **:** SHAMAN

medicine show *n* **:** a traveling show using entertainers to attract a crowd that may buy remedies or nostrums

med·i·co \ˈmed-i-ˌkō\ *n, pl* **-cos :** a medical practitioner **:** PHYSICIAN; *also* **:** a medical student [Italian *medico* or Spanish *médico,* both from Latin *medicus*]

me·di·eval *also* **me·di·ae·val** \ˌmēd-ē-ˈē-vəl, ˌmed-, ˌmid-; mē-ˈdē-vəl, med-ˈē-, mid-ˈē-\ *adj* **:** of, relating to, or characteristic of the Middle Ages [New Latin *Medium Aevum* "Middle Ages"] — **me·di·eval·ly** \-və-lē\ *adv*

Medieval French *n* **:** the French language of the Middle Ages; *esp* **:** the French language from about 1000 to 1500

me·di·eval·ism \-və-ˌliz-əm\ *n* **1 :** medieval quality, character, or state **2 :** devotion to the institutions, arts, and practices of the Middle Ages — **me·di·eval·ist** \-ləst\ *n*

Medieval Latin *n* **:** the Latin used especially for liturgical and literary purposes from the 7th to the 15th centuries inclusive

me·di·o·cre \ˌmēd-ē-ˈō-kər\ *adj* **:** of moderate or low quality **:** ORDINARY ⟨a *mediocre* novel⟩ [Middle French, from Latin *mediocris,* from *medius* "middle" + *ocris* "stony mountain"]

me·di·oc·ri·ty \ˌmēd-ē-ˈäk-rət-ē\ *n, pl* **-ties 1 :** the quality or state of being mediocre **2 :** a mediocre person

med·i·tate \ˈmed-ə-ˌtāt\ *vb* **1 a :** to reflect on or muse over **:** CONTEMPLATE **b :** to engage in contemplation or reflection **2 :** to plan or project in the mind **:** INTEND, PURPOSE [Latin *meditari*] ***synonyms*** see PONDER — **med·i·ta·tor** \-ˌtāt-ər\ *n*

med·i·ta·tion \ˌmed-ə-ˈtā-shən\ *n* **:** the act or process of meditating **:** serious contemplation or reflection

med·i·ta·tive \ˈmed-ə-ˌtāt-iv\ *adj* **:** given to meditation — **med·i·ta·tive·ly** *adv* — **med·i·ta·tive·ness** *n*

Med·i·ter·ra·nean \ˌmed-ə-tə-ˈrā-nē-ən, -ˈrā-nyən\ *adj* **:** of or relating to the Mediterranean Sea or to the lands or peoples around it

Mediterranean fruit fly *n* **:** a small widely distributed yellowish brown two-winged fly whose larva lives and feeds in ripening fruit — called also *medfly*

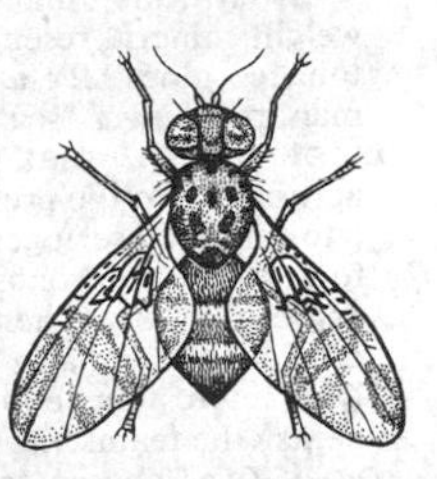
Mediterranean fruit fly

¹me·di·um \ˈmēd-ē-əm\ *n, pl* **me·di·ums** *or* **me·dia** \ˈmēd-ē-ə\ **1 :** something that is between or in the middle; *also* **:** a middle condition or degree **2 :** a means of effecting or conveying something; *esp* **:** a substance through which a force acts or through which something is transmitted ⟨air is the common *medium* of sound⟩ **3** *pl usually* **media a :** a form or system of communication, information, or entertainment — compare MASS MEDIUM **b :** something (as a magnetic disk) on which information may be stored **4 a :** GO-BETWEEN, INTERMEDIARY **b** *pl* **mediums :** a person through whom others seek to communicate with the spirits of the dead **5 :** material or technical means of artistic expression ⟨film was her *medium*⟩ **6 a :** a surrounding substance or condition **:** ENVIRONMENT ⟨marine fish live in a *medium* of salt water⟩ **b :** a condition in which something may function or flourish ⟨solitude is an effective *medium* for reflection⟩ **7** *pl* **media a :** a nutrient system for the artificial cultivation of organisms (as bacteria) or cells **b :** a fluid or solid in which parts from living things are placed (as for preservation or mounting) [Latin, from *medius* "middle"]

²medium *adj* **:** intermediate in amount, quality, position, or degree

medium frequency *n* **:** a radio frequency in the range between 300 and 3000 kilohertz — abbreviation *MF*

medium of exchange : something commonly accepted in exchange for goods and services and recognized as representing a standard of value

med·lar \ˈmed-lər\ *n* **:** a small hairy-leaved Eurasian tree related to the roses; *also* **:** its fruit that resembles a crab apple and is used especially in preserves [Medieval French *medlier,* from *medle* "medlar fruit," from Latin *mespilum,* from Greek *mespilon*]

med·ley \ˈmed-lē\ *n, pl* **medleys 1 :** MIXTURE 2; *esp* **:** a confused mixture **2 :** a musical composition made up of a series of songs or short musical pieces [Medieval French *medlee,* from *mesler, medler* "to mix, meddle"]

me·dul·la \mə-ˈdəl-ə\ *n, pl* **-dul·las** *or* **-dul·lae** \-ˌdəl-ē, -ˌī\ **1 a :** BONE MARROW **b :** MEDULLA OBLONGATA **2 :** the inner or deep part of an animal or plant structure (as the adrenal gland or the kidney) [Latin] — **med·ul·lary** \ˈmed-l-ˌer-ē, ˈmej-ə-ˌler-\ *adj*

medulla ob·lon·ga·ta \-ˌäb-ˌlȯng-ˈgät-ə\ *n* **:** the somewhat pyramid-shaped hind part of the vertebrate brain that is continuous with the spinal cord and contains the centers controlling involuntary vital functions [New Latin, literally, "oblong medulla"]

medullary sheath *n* **:** MYELIN SHEATH

med·ul·lat·ed \ˈmed-l-ˌāt-əd, ˈmej-ə-ˌlāt-\ *adj* **:** MYELINATED ⟨*medullated* nerve fibers⟩

me·du·sa \mi-ˈdü-sə, -ˈdyü-, -zə\ *n, pl* **-sae** \-ˌsē, -ˌzē\ *also* **-sas :** JELLYFISH 1a [*Medusa,* one of the three Gorgons] — **me·du·san** \-ˈdüs-n, -ˈdüz-, -ˈdyüs-, -ˈdyüz-\ *adj or n* — **me·du·soid** \-ˌȯid\ *adj or n*

meed \ˈmēd\ *n* **:** something deserved or earned **:** REWARD ⟨receive one's *meed* of praise⟩ [Old English *mēd*]

meek \ˈmēk\ *adj* **1 :** enduring injury with patience and without resentment **2 :** lacking self-assurance **:** HUMBLE ⟨they became *meek* when confronted with the evidence against them⟩ [of Scandinavian origin] — **meek·ly** *adv* — **meek·ness** *n*
meer·kat \ˈmir-ˌkat\ *n* **:** a burrowing mammal of southern Africa that feeds chiefly on insects, is grayish with faint black markings, and lives in usually large colonies [Afrikaans, from Dutch, "a kind of monkey," from earlier Dutch *meercatte,* probably from *meer* "sea" + *catte* "cat"]
meer·schaum \ˈmiər-shəm, -ˌshȯm\ *n* **1 :** a soft white lightweight mineral resembling a very fine clay used especially for tobacco pipes **2 :** a tobacco pipe made of meerschaum [German, from *Meer* "sea" + *Schaum* "foam"]
1meet \ˈmēt\ *vb* **met** \ˈmet\; **meet·ing** **1 :** to come upon or across or into the presence of ⟨*met* an old friend by chance⟩ **2 :** to come close together or into contact and join or cross ⟨a fork where two roads *meet*⟩ **3 a :** to get together with **:** JOIN ⟨agreed to *meet* them at school⟩ **b :** to become acquainted ⟨the couple *met* at a dance⟩ **c :** to make the acquaintance of ⟨*met* interesting people there⟩ **4 a :** to come together as opponents ⟨the teams *met* in the finals⟩ **b :** to struggle against **:** OPPOSE ⟨was chosen to *meet* the champion⟩ **c :** to cope with **:** MATCH ⟨tries to *meet* the competitor's price⟩ **d :** ENDURE 2b, BEAR ⟨learned to *meet* defeat bravely⟩ **5 :** to come together for a common purpose **:** ASSEMBLE ⟨*meet* weekly for discussion⟩ **6 :** to become noticed by ⟨sounds of revelry *meet* the ear⟩ **7 a :** to conform to or comply with **:** SATISFY ⟨*meets* all requirements⟩ **b :** to pay fully ⟨*meet* a financial obligation⟩ [Old English *mētan*] — **meet·er** *n* — **meet halfway :** to compromise with — **meet with :** to be subjected to **:** ENCOUNTER ⟨the proposal *met with* opposition⟩
2meet *n* **:** an assembly or meeting especially to engage in a competitive sport ⟨a track *meet*⟩
3meet *adj* **:** SUITABLE 2, PROPER [Old English *gemǣte*] — **meet·ly** *adv*
meet·ing \ˈmēt-ing\ *n* **1 :** the act of persons or things that meet ⟨a chance *meeting* with a friend⟩ **2 :** a coming together of a number of persons usually at a stated time and place and for a known purpose **:** ASSEMBLY, GATHERING ⟨the monthly club *meeting*⟩ **3 :** an assembly for religious worship ⟨a Quaker *meeting*⟩ **4 :** the place where two things come together **:** JUNCTION
meet·ing·house \-ˌhau̇s\ *n* **:** a building used for public assembly and especially for Protestant worship
meg \ˈmeg\ *n* **:** MEGABYTE
mega \ˈmeg-ə\ *adj* **1 :** VAST ⟨a *mega* electronics store⟩ **2 :** of the highest level of rank, excellence, or importance ⟨a *mega* movie star⟩
mega- *or* **meg-** *combining form* **1 :** great **:** large ⟨*mega*spore⟩ **2 :** million **:** multiplied by one million ⟨*mega*cycle⟩ ⟨*meg*ohm⟩ **3 :** to a superlative degree ⟨*mega*-successful⟩ [Greek *megas* "large"]
mega·bit \ˈmeg-ə-ˌbit\ *n* **:** one million bits
mega·byte \-ˌbīt\ *n* **:** 1,048,576 bytes; *also* **:** one million bytes
mega·cycle \-ˌsī-kəl\ *n* **:** one million cycles; *esp* **:** MEGAHERTZ
mega·dose \-ˌdōs\ *n* **:** a large dose (as of a vitamin)
mega·fau·na \-ˌfȯn-ə, -ˌfän-\ *n* **:** animals (as bears, bison, or mammoths) of particularly large size
mega·hertz \-ˌhərts, -ˌheərts\ *n* **:** one million hertz
mega·hit \-ˌhit\ *n* **:** something (as a motion picture) that is extremely successful
mega·lith \ˈmeg-ə-ˌlith\ *n* **:** one of the huge stones used in various prehistoric monuments — **mega·lith·ic** \ˌmeg-ə-ˈlith-ik\ *adj*

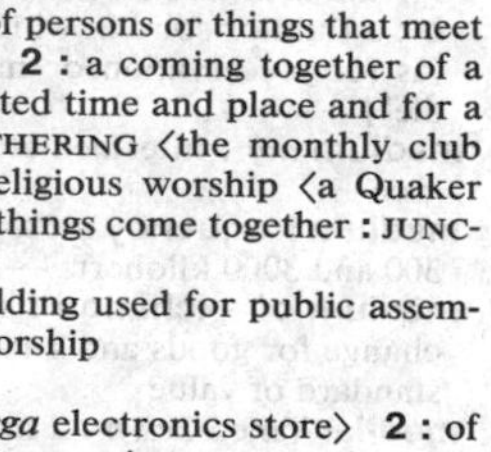
megaliths

meg·a·lo·ma·nia \ˌmeg-ə-lō-ˈmā-nē-ə, -nyə\ *n* **:** a disorder of mind marked by feelings of great personal power and importance [Greek *megal-, megas* "large"] — **meg·a·lo·ma·ni·ac** \-ˈmā-nē-ˌak\ *adj or n* — **meg·a·lo·ma·ni·a·cal** \-mə-ˈnī-ə-kəl\ *adj*
meg·a·lop·o·lis \ˌmeg-ə-ˈläp-ə-ləs\ *n* **1 :** a very large city **2 :** a thickly populated region centering in a metropolis or embracing several metropolises [Greek *megal-, megas* "large" + *polis* "city"] — **meg·a·lo·pol·i·tan** \ˌmeg-ə-lō-ˈpäl-ət-n\ *n or adj* — **meg·a·lo·pol·i·tan·ism** \-n-ˌiz-əm\ *n*
mega·phone \ˈmeg-ə-ˌfōn\ *n* **:** a cone-shaped device used to intensify or direct the voice — **mega·phon·ic** \ˌmeg-ə-ˈfän-ik\ *adj*
mega·pix·el \-ˌpik-səl\ *n* **:** one million pixels ⟨a two-*megapixel* digital camera⟩
mega·plex \-ˌpleks\ *n* **:** a large multiplex typically housing 16 or more movie theaters
mega·spore \ˈmeg-ə-ˌspōr, -ˌspȯr\ *n* **:** a plant spore that produces a female gametophyte
mega·ton \ˈmeg-ə-ˌtən\ *n* **:** an explosive force equal to that of one million tons of TNT
mega·watt \-ˌwät\ *n* **:** one million watts
me·gil·lah \mə-ˈgil-ə\ *n, slang* **:** a long involved story or account ⟨the whole *megillah*⟩ [Yiddish *megile,* from Hebrew *mĕgillāh* scroll, volume]
meg·ohm \ˈmeg-ˌōm\ *n* **:** one million ohms
me·grim \ˈmē-grəm\ *n* **1 :** a dizzy disordered state; *esp* **:** MIGRAINE **2 a :** WHIM, FANCY **b** *pl* **:** low spirits **:** mental depression [Medieval French *migraine*]
mei·o·sis \mī-ˈō-səs\ *n, pl* **-o·ses** \-ˈō-ˌsēz\ **:** the cellular process that results in the number of chromosomes in gamete-producing cells being reduced to one half and that involves a reduction division in which one of each pair of homologous chromosomes passes to each daughter cell followed by a mitotic division — compare MITOSIS 1 [Greek *meiōsis* "diminution," from *meioun* "to diminish," from *meiōn* "less"] — **mei·ot·ic** \mī-ˈät-ik\ *adj* — **mei·ot·i·cal·ly** \-ˈät-i-kə-lē, -klē\ *adv*
Mei·ster·sing·er \ˈmī-stər-ˌsing-ər, -stər-ˌzing-\ *n, pl* **-singer** *or* **-sing·ers :** a member of any of various German guilds formed chiefly in the 15th and 16th centuries for the cultivation of poetry and music [German, literally, "master singer"]
meit·ner·i·um \mīt-ˈnir-ē-əm, -ˈner-\ *n* **:** a short-lived radioactive element produced artificially — see ELEMENT table [New Latin, from Lise *Meitner,* died 1968, German physicist]
mel·a·mine \ˈmel-ə-ˌmēn\ *n* **:** a synthetic resin composed of carbon, hydrogen, and nitrogen and used in molded products, adhesives, and coatings [German *Melamin*]
mel·an·cho·lia \ˌmel-ən-ˈkō-lē-ə\ *n* **:** a mental condition characterized especially by extreme depression [Late Latin, "melancholy"] — **mel·an·cho·li·ac** \-lē-ˌak\ *n*
mel·an·chol·ic \ˌmel-ən-ˈkäl-ik\ *adj* **1 :** inclined to or affected with melancholy **:** DEPRESSED **2 :** affected with or relating to melancholia **3 :** tending to depress the spirits
1mel·an·choly \ˈmel-ən-ˌkäl-ē\ *n, pl* **-chol·ies :** depression of spirits **:** DEJECTION, SADNESS [Medieval French *malancolie,* from Late Latin *melancholia,* from Greek, from *melan-, melas* "black" + *cholē* "bile"; from the former belief that the condition was caused by an excess of black bile, a fluid once believed to be secreted by the spleen or kidneys]

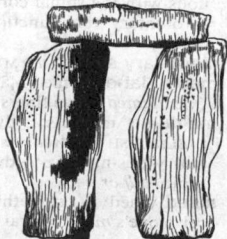

synonyms MELANCHOLY, SADNESS, DEPRESSION, DEJECTION mean a quality, state, or an instance of being sad. MELANCHOLY suggests a sad and serious pensiveness often without evident cause ⟨couldn't understand why he was troubled with *melancholy*⟩. SADNESS usually suggests a mood of regret, longing, or disappointment without bitterness or anger ⟨felt nothing but *sadness* when their friendship ended⟩. DEPRESSION suggests a condition in which one feels let down, disheartened, or enervated ⟨was in a deep *depression* and did not want to celebrate⟩. DEJECTION implies a usually passing mood of discouragement or hopelessness ⟨*dejection* is to be expected after losing a ball game⟩.

2melancholy *adj* **1 a :** depressed in spirits **:** DEJECTED, SAD **b :** PENSIVE 2 **2 a :** suggestive or expressive of melancholy ⟨sang in a *melancholy* voice⟩ **b :** causing sadness **:** DISMAL ⟨the *melancholy* conclusion that we were neither needed nor wanted⟩
Mel·a·ne·sian \ˌmel-ə-ˈnē-zhən, -shən\ *n* **:** a member of the dominant native group of Melanesia — **Melanesian** *adj*
mé·lange \mā-ˈläⁿzh, -ˈlänj\ *n* **:** a mixture often of incongruous elements ⟨a *mélange* of styles from all over the world⟩ [French, from Middle French, from *mesler, meler* "to mix"]
mel·a·nin \ˈmel-ə-nən\ *n* **:** a dark brown or black animal or plant pigment that in humans makes some skins darker than others [Greek *melan-, melas* "black"]
mel·a·nism \ˈmel-ə-ˌniz-əm\ *n* **:** an exceptionally dark pigmentation (as of skin, feathers, or hair) of an individual or kind of organism — **mel·a·nis·tic** \ˌmel-ə-ˈnis-tik\ *adj*
me·la·no·cyte \mə-ˈlan-ə-ˌsīt, ˈmel-ə-nō-\ *n* **:** a cell (as in the skin) that produces or contains melanin

mel·a·no·ma \ˌmel-ə-ˈnō-mə\ *n, pl* **-no·mas** *also* **-no·ma·ta** \-ˈnō-mət-ə\ : a usually malignant tumor containing dark pigment

mel·a·not·ic \-ˈnät-ik\ *adj* : having or characterized by black pigmentation ⟨*melanotic* tumors⟩

mel·a·to·nin \ˌmel-ə-ˈtō-nən\ *n* : a vertebrate hormone that is derived from serotonin, is secreted by the pineal gland especially in response to darkness, and has been linked to the regulation of bodily functions or activities (as sleep) that occur in approximately 24 hour cycles [Greek *melan-, melas* "black" + *-tonin* (as in *serotonin*)]

mel·ba toast \ˌmel-bə-\ *n* : very thin bread toasted till crisp [Nellie *Melba*, died 1931, Australian soprano]

Mel·chiz·e·dek \mel-ˈkiz-ə-ˌdek\ *adj* : of or relating to the higher order of the Mormon priesthood [*Melchizedek*, biblical priest-king]

¹meld \ˈmeld\ *vb* : to show or lay down a combination of cards in a card game [German *melden* "to announce"]

²meld *n* : a card or combination of cards that is or can be melded

³meld *vb* : MERGE 1, BLEND ⟨the vocals *meld* perfectly with the instrumental accompaniment⟩ [blend of *melt* and *weld*]

⁴meld *n* : BLEND 1, MIXTURE ⟨a *meld* of new and old ideas⟩

me·lee \ˈmā-ˌlā, mā-ˈlā\ *n* : a confused fight or struggle especially among several people [French *mêlée*, from Medieval French *meslee*, from *mesler* "to mix"]

me·lio·rate \ˈmēl-yə-ˌrāt, ˈmē-lē-ə-\ *vb* : to make or become better : IMPROVE [Late Latin *meliorare*, from Latin *melior* "better"] — **me·lio·ra·tion** \ˌmēl-yə-ˈrā-shən, ˌmē-lē-ə-\ *n* — **me·lio·ra·tive** \ˈmēl-yə-ˌrāt-iv, ˈmē-lē-ə-\ *adj* — **me·lio·ra·tor** \-ˌrāt-ər\ *n*

mel·lif·lu·ous \me-ˈlif-lə-wəs, mə-\ *adj* : smoothly or sweetly flowing ⟨*mellifluous* speech⟩ [Late Latin *mellifluus*, from Latin *mel* "honey" + *fluere* "to flow"] — **mel·lif·lu·ous·ly** *adv* — **mel·lif·lu·ous·ness** *n*

mel·lo·phone \ˈmel-ə-ˌfōn\ *n* : an althorn in circular form sometimes used as a substitute for the French horn [*mellow* + *-phone*]

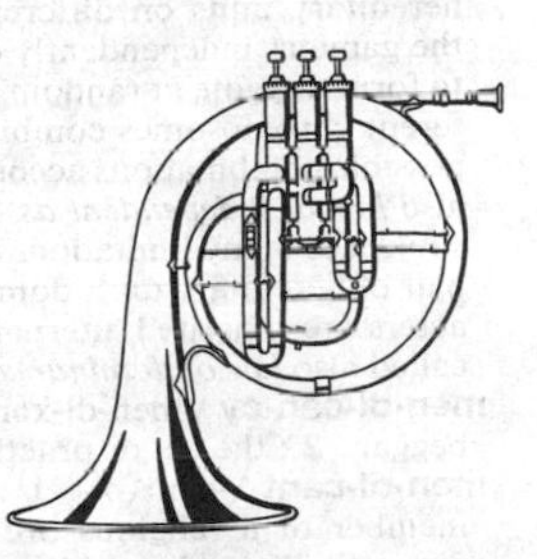

mellophone

¹mel·low \ˈmel-ō\ *adj* **1 a** : tender and sweet because of ripeness ⟨*mellow* peaches⟩ **b** : well aged and pleasingly mild ⟨a *mellow* wine⟩ **2 a** : made gentle by age or experience ⟨developed a *mellow* disposition from caring for his grandchildren⟩ **b** : PLEASANT 1, AGREEABLE ⟨*mellow* sounds⟩ **c** : LAID-BACK ⟨a *mellow* personality⟩ **3** : of soft and loamy consistency ⟨*mellow* soil⟩ **4** : being clear, full, and pure ⟨spoke in *mellow* tones⟩ [Middle English *melowe*] — **mel·low·ly** *adv* — **mel·low·ness** *n*

²mellow *vb* : to make or become mellow

me·lo·de·on \mə-ˈlōd-ē-ən\ *n* : a small reed organ in which a suction bellows draws air inward through the reeds [German *Melodion*, from *Melodie* "melody," derived from Late Latin *melodia* "melody"]

me·lod·ic \mə-ˈläd-ik\ *adj* : of or relating to melody : MELODIOUS — **me·lod·i·cal·ly** \-ˈläd-i-kə-lē, -klē\ *adv*

me·lo·di·ous \mə-ˈlōd-ē-əs\ *adj* **1** : having a pleasing melody **2** : of, relating to, or producing melody ⟨*melodious* birds⟩ — **me·lo·di·ous·ly** *adv* — **me·lo·di·ous·ness** *n*

mel·o·dist \ˈmel-əd-əst\ *n* : a composer or singer of melodies

melo·dra·ma \ˈmel-ə-ˌdräm-ə, -ˌdram-\ *n* **1 a** : a work (as a movie or play) characterized by extravagant theatricality and by the predominance of plot and physical action over characterization **b** : a dramatic category constituted by such works **2** : melodramatic events or behavior [French *mélodrame*, from Greek *melos* "song" + *drama* "drama"] — **melo·dram·a·tist** \ˈdram-ət-əst, -ˈdräm-\ *n*

melo·dra·mat·ic \-drə-ˈmat-ik\ *adj* **1** : of or relating to melodrama ⟨*melodramatic* elements of suspense and surprise⟩ **2** : resembling or suitable for melodrama : SENSATIONAL ⟨made a *melodramatic* announcement of the discovery⟩ ***synonyms*** see DRAMATIC — **melo·dra·mat·i·cal·ly** \-i-kə-lē, -klē\ *adv*

melo·dra·mat·ics \-ˈmat-iks\ *n sing or pl* : melodramatic conduct

mel·o·dy \ˈmel-əd-ē\ *n, pl* **-dies** **1** : pleasing succession of sounds : TUNEFULNESS **2** : a rhythmical series of musical tones of a given key so arranged as to make a pleasing effect **3** : the leading part in a harmonic composition [Medieval French *melodie*, from Late Latin *melodia*, from Greek *melōidia* "chanting, music," from *melos* "limb, musical phrase, song" + *aeidein* "to sing"]

mel·on \ˈmel-ən\ *n* : any of various fruits (as a cantaloupe, honeydew melon, or watermelon) of the gourd family that have juicy and typically sweet flesh usually eaten raw and a firm rind [Medieval French, from Late Latin *melo*, short for Latin *melopepo*, from Greek *mēlopepōn*, from *mēlon* "apple" + *pepōn*, a kind of gourd]

¹melt \ˈmelt\ *vb* **1** : to change from a solid to a liquid state usually through the application of heat ⟨snow *melts*⟩ **2** : DISSOLVE ⟨the sugar *melted* in the coffee⟩ **3** : to grow less : disappear as if by dissolving ⟨their fears *melted*⟩ **4** : to make or become gentle : SOFTEN ⟨a warm smile *melts* the heart⟩ **5** : to lose distinct outline or shape : BLEND, MERGE ⟨sky *melting* into sea⟩ [Old English *meltan*] — **melt·abil·i·ty** \ˌmel-tə-ˈbil-ət-ē\ *n* — **melt·able** \ˈmel-tə-bəl\ *adj* — **melt·er** *n*

²melt *n* : a melted substance

³melt *n* : SPLEEN 1 [Old English *milte*]

melt·down \ˈmelt-ˌdau̇n\ *n* **1** : the accidental melting of the core of a nuclear reactor **2** : a rapid or disastrous decline or collapse ⟨a financial *meltdown*⟩ **3** : a breakdown of self-control (as from fatigue or overstimulation)

melt down *vi* : to suffer a meltdown : COLLAPSE ⟨the economy *melted down*⟩

melting point *n* : the temperature at which a solid melts

melting pot *n* **1** : a container for melting something : CRUCIBLE **2 a** : a place (as a city or country) in which various nationalities or races live together and gradually blend into one community **b** : the population of such a place

mel·ton \ˈmelt-n\ *n* : a smooth heavy woolen cloth with a short nap used for overcoats [*Melton* Mowbray, England]

melt·wa·ter \ˈmelt-ˌwȯt-ər, -ˌwät-\ *n* : water derived from the melting of ice and snow

mem·ber \ˈmem-bər\ *n* **1** : a part (as an arm, leg, leaf, or branch) of the body of an animal or plant **2** : one of the individuals or units belonging to or forming part of a group or organization ⟨a club *member*⟩ ⟨*members* of the United Nations⟩ **3** : a part of a whole: as **a** : a part of a structure (as a building) ⟨a horizontal *member* in a bridge⟩ **b** : an element of a mathematical set **c** : the whole expression on one side or the other of a mathematical equation or inequality [Medieval French *membre*, from Latin *membrum*]

mem·ber·ship \-ˌship\ *n* **1** : the state or status of being a member **2** : all the members of an organization

mem·brane \ˈmem-ˌbrān\ *n* : a thin soft pliable sheet or layer especially of a plant or animal part (as a cell or organ) [Latin *membrana* "skin, parchment," from *membrum* "member"] — **mem·bra·nous** \ˈmem-brə-nəs\ *adj*

me·men·to \mi-ˈment-ō\ *n, pl* **-tos** *or* **-toes** : something that serves to warn or remind; *also* : SOUVENIR ⟨*mementos* of a trip⟩ [Latin, "remember," from *meminisse* "to remember"]

me·men·to mo·ri \mi-ˌment-ō-ˈmōr-ē, -ˈmȯr-ē\ *n, pl* **memento mori** : a reminder (as a death's-head) of mortality [Latin, "remember that you must die"]

memo \ˈmem-ō\ *n, pl* **mem·os** : MEMORANDUM

mem·oir \ˈmem-ˌwär, -ˌwȯr\ *n* **1 a** : a story of a personal experience **b** : AUTOBIOGRAPHY — usually used in plural **c** : BIOGRAPHY 1 **2 a** : REPORT 2 **b** *pl* : the proceedings of a learned society [French *mémoire*, literally, "memory," from Latin *memoria*]

mem·o·ra·bil·ia \ˌmem-ə-rə-ˈbil-ē-ə, -ˈbil-yə\ *n pl* **1** : things worthy of remembrance **2** : things valued or collected for their association with a particular field or interest ⟨baseball *memorabilia*⟩ [Latin, from *memorabilis* "memorable"]

mem·o·ra·ble \ˈmem-rə-bəl, -ə-rə-\ *adj* : worth remembering : NOTABLE [Latin *memorabilis*, from *memorare* "to remind, mention," from *memor* "mindful"] — **mem·o·ra·ble·ness** *n* — **mem·o·ra·bly** \-blē\ *adv*

mem·o·ran·dum \ˌmem-ə-ˈran-dəm\ *n, pl* **-dums** *or* **-da** \-də\

\ə\ **abut**	\au̇\ **out**	\i\ **tip**	\ȯ\ **saw**	\u̇\ **foot**
\ər\ **further**	\ch\ **chin**	\ī\ **life**	\ȯi\ **coin**	\y\ **yet**
\a\ **mat**	\e\ **pet**	\j\ **job**	\th\ **thin**	\yü\ **few**
\ā\ **take**	\ē\ **easy**	\ng\ **sing**	\t͟h\ **this**	\yu̇\ **cure**
\ä\ **cot, cart**	\g\ **go**	\ō\ **bone**	\ü\ **food**	\zh\ **vision**

1 a : an informal record or communication **b** : a written reminder **2** : an informal written note of a transaction or proposed legal instrument [Latin, neuter of *memorandus* "to be remembered," from *memorare* "to remind"]

[1]**me·mo·ri·al** \mə-ˈmōr-ē-əl, -ˈmȯr-\ *adj* : serving to preserve the memory of a person or an event ⟨a *memorial* service⟩ — **me·mo·ri·al·ly** \-ē-ə-lē\ *adv*

[2]**memorial** *n* **1** : something that keeps alive the memory of a person or event; *esp* : MONUMENT **2 a** : RECORD 2 **b** : a statement of facts accompanying a petition to a government official

Memorial Day *n* **1** : May 30 formerly observed as a legal holiday in most states of the U.S. in remembrance of war dead **2** : the last Monday in May observed as a legal holiday in most states of the U.S.

me·mo·ri·al·ize \mə-ˈmōr-ē-ə-ˌlīz, -ˈmȯr-\ *vt* **1** : to address or petition (as a government official) by a memorial **2** : COMMEMORATE 1 — **me·mo·ri·al·i·za·tion** \-ˌmōr-ē-ə-lə-ˈzā-shən, -ˌmȯr-\ *n*

mem·o·rize \ˈmem-ə-ˌrīz\ *vt* : to commit to memory : learn by heart — **mem·o·ri·za·tion** \ˌmem-rə-ˈzā-shən, -ə-rə-\ *n* — **mem·o·riz·er** \ˈmem-ə-ˌrī-zər\ *n*

mem·o·ry \ˈmem-rē, -ə-rē\ *n, pl* **-ries** **1 a** : the power or process of recalling what has been learned and retained **b** : the store of things learned and retained ⟨recite from *memory*⟩ **2** : commemorative remembrance ⟨a monument in *memory* of war dead⟩ **3 a** : something remembered ⟨has pleasant *memories* of the trip⟩ **b** : the time within which past events can be or are remembered ⟨within the *memory* of people living today⟩ **4 a** : a device (as in a computer) in which information can be inserted and stored and from which it can be extracted when wanted **b** : capacity for storing information ⟨a computer with 512 megabytes of *memory*⟩ [Medieval French *memoire, memorie,* from Latin *memoria,* from *memor* "mindful"]

synonyms MEMORY, REMEMBRANCE, RECOLLECTION, REMINISCENCE mean the capacity for or the act of remembering or the thing remembered. MEMORY applies both to the ability to recall mentally and to what is recalled ⟨gifted with a remarkable *memory*⟩ ⟨that day was now just a distant *memory*⟩. REMEMBRANCE stresses the act of remembering or the state of being remembered ⟨any *remembrance* of his deceased wife was painful⟩. RECOLLECTION adds an implication of deliberately recalling often with some effort ⟨after a moment's *recollection* he produced the name⟩. REMINISCENCE suggests the recalling of usually pleasant incidents, experiences, or feelings from one's remote past ⟨my grandmother's *reminiscences* of her Iowa girlhood⟩.

memory cell *n* : a long-lived lymphocyte that is capable of mounting a rapid effective immune response upon exposure to a previously encountered antigen

memory lane *n* : an imaginary path through the nostalgically remembered past — usually used in such phrases as *a walk down memory lane*

mem·sa·hib \ˈmem-ˌsä-ˌhib, -ˌib, -ˌsäb\ *n* : a white foreign woman of high social status living in India; *esp* : the wife of a British official — compare SAHIB [Hindi, from English *ma'am* + Hindi & Urdu *sahib* "sahib"]

men *plural of* MAN

[1]**men·ace** \ˈmen-əs\ *n* **1** : a show of intention to inflict harm : THREAT **2 a** : someone or something that represents a threat : DANGER **b** : an annoying person : NUISANCE [Medieval French, from Latin *minacia,* from *minax* "threatening," from *minari* "to threaten"]

[2]**menace** *vb* **1** : to make a show of intention to harm ⟨*menaced* them with upraised arms⟩ **2** : to appear likely to cause harm : ENDANGER ***synonyms*** see THREATEN — **men·ac·ing·ly** \ˈmen-ə-sing-lē\ *adv*

mé·nage \mā-ˈnäzh\ *n* : HOUSEHOLD [French, from Medieval French *mesnage* "dwelling," derived from Latin *mansio,* from *manēre* "to stay"]

me·nag·er·ie \mə-ˈnaj-ə-rē\ *n* **1** : a place where animals are kept and trained especially for exhibition **2** : a collection of wild or foreign animals kept especially for exhibition [French *ménagerie,* from *ménage* "household"]

men·ar·che \ˈme-ˌnär-kē\ *n* : the first menstrual period of an individual [Greek *mēn* "month" + *archē* "beginning"]

[1]**mend** \ˈmend\ *vb* **1 a** : to improve in manners or morals : REFORM **b** : to put into good shape or working order again : REPAIR **2** : to become corrected or improved **3** : to improve in health; *also* : HEAL [Middle English *menden,* short for *amenden* "to amend"] — **mend·able** \ˈmen-də-bəl\ *adj* — **mend·er** *n*

synonyms MEND, REPAIR, PATCH, FIX mean to put into good order something that has been injured or damaged or become defective. MEND implies making whole or sound something broken, torn, or injured ⟨*mended* the torn dress⟩. REPAIR applies to the fixing of more extensive damage or dilapidation ⟨*repaired* the back steps⟩. PATCH implies an often temporary fixing of a hole or break with new material ⟨*patched* the hole with concrete⟩. FIX tends to stress the arranging, straightening out, or adjusting of parts ⟨*fix* a clock⟩ ⟨get one's teeth *fixed*⟩.

[2]**mend** *n* **1** : an act of mending : REPAIR **2** : a mended place — **on the mend** : getting better (as in health)

men·da·cious \men-ˈdā-shəs\ *adj* : given to or characterized by deception or falsehood [Latin *mendac-, mendax*] — **men·da·cious·ly** *adv* — **men·da·cious·ness** *n*

men·dac·i·ty \men-ˈdas-ət-ē\ *n, pl* **-ties** : the quality or state of being mendacious; *also* : [4]LIE 1

men·de·le·vi·um \ˌmen-də-ˈlē-vē-əm\ *n* : a radioactive element produced artificially — see ELEMENT table [New Latin, from Dmitri *Mendelyev*]

Men·de·lian \men-ˈdē-lē-ən, -ˈdēl-yən\ *adj* : of, relating to, or according with Mendel's laws or Mendelism — **Mendelian** *n*

Mendelian inheritance *n* : inheritance of characters specifically transmitted by genes in accord with Mendel's laws

Men·del·ism \ˈmen-dl-ˌiz-əm\ *n* : the principles or the operations of Mendel's laws

Men·del's law \ˌmen-dlz-\ *n* **1** : a principle in genetics: hereditary units occur in pairs that separate during gamete formation so that every gamete receives but one member of a pair — called also *law of segregation* **2** : a principle in genetics subject to exceptions by the subsequent discovery of linkage: pairs of hereditary units on different chromosomes are distributed to the gametes independently of each other, the gametes combine to form a zygote at random, and pairs of hereditary units on different chromosomes combine in the zygote in all their various possible combinations according to the laws of chance — called also *law of independent assortment* **3** : a principle of genetics subject to many limitations and exceptions: because one of each pair of hereditary units dominates the other in expression, characters are inherited alternatively on an all or nothing basis — called also *law of dominance* [Gregor *Mendel*]

men·di·can·cy \ˈmen-di-kən-sē\ *n* **1** : the condition of being a beggar **2** : the act or practice of begging

men·di·cant \-kənt\ *n* **1** : one who lives by begging **2** : a member of a religious order (as the Franciscans) combining monastic life and outside religious activity and originally owning neither personal nor community property : FRIAR [Latin *mendicare* "to beg," from *mendicus* "beggar"] — **mendicant** *adj*

men·dic·i·ty \men-ˈdis-ət-ē\ *n* : MENDICANCY

men·folk \ˈmen-ˌfōk\ *or* **men·folks** \-ˌfōks\ *n pl* **1** : men in general **2** : the men of a family or community

men·ha·den \men-ˈhād-n, mən-\ *n, pl* **-den** *also* **-dens** : a fish related to the herring that is found along the Atlantic coast of the U.S. and is used for bait or converted into oil and fertilizer [of Algonquian origin]

men·hir \ˈmen-ˌhiər\ *n* : an upright monolith usually of prehistoric origin [French, from Breton, from *men* "stone" + *hir* "long"]

[1]**me·nial** \ˈmē-nē-əl, -nyəl\ *adj* **1** : of, relating to, or suitable for servants **2 a** : HUMBLE 2 ⟨answered in *menial* tones⟩ **b** : lacking interest or dignity ⟨a *menial* task⟩ [Medieval French *meignal,* from *mesnee, mayné* household, retinue, derived from Latin *mansio* "dwelling"] — **me·nial·ly** \-ē\ *adv*

[2]**menial** *n* : DOMESTIC

men·in·geal \ˌmen-ən-ˈjē-əl\ *adj* : of, relating to, or affecting the meninges

meninges *plural of* MENINX

men·in·gi·tis \ˌmen-ən-ˈjīt-əs\ *n, pl* **-git·i·des** \-ˈjit-ə-ˌdēz\ : inflammation of the meninges; *also* : a disease that is marked by such inflammation and may be either a relatively mild illness caused by a virus or a more severe life-threatening illness caused by a bacterium — **men·in·git·ic** \-ˈjit-ik\ *adj*

me·ninx \ˈmē-nings, -ningks; ˈmen-ings, -ingks\ *n, pl* **me·nin·ges** \mə-ˈnin-ˌjēz\ : any of the three membranes that envelop the brain and spinal cord [Greek *mēninx* "membrane"]

me·nis·cus \mə-ˈnis-kəs\ *n, pl* **me·nis·ci** \-ˈnis-ˌkī, -ˌī, -ˌkē\ *also*

me·nis·cus·es **1** : a crescent-shaped body : CRESCENT **2** : a lens that is convex on one side and concave on the other **3** : the curved upper surface of a liquid column that is concave when the containing walls are wetted by the liquid and convex when not [Greek *mēniskos,* from *mēnē* "moon, crescent"]

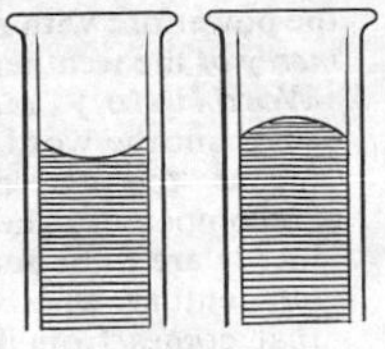
meniscus 3

Men·no·nite \ˈmen-ə-ˌnīt\ *n* : a member of one of the Protestant groups derived from the Anabaptist movement in Holland and noted for simplicity of life and rejection of oaths, public office, and military service [German *Mennonit,* from *Menno* Simons, died 1561, Frisian religious reformer]

me·no mos·so \ˌmā-nō-ˈmò-sō, -ˈmòs-\ *adv* : less rapidly — used as a direction in music [Italian]

meno·pause \ˈmen-ə-ˌpòz\ *n* : the period when menstruation naturally stops permanently usually between the ages of 45 and 55 [French *ménopause,* from *méno-* "menstruation" (from Greek *mēn* "month") + *pause* "pause"] — **meno·paus·al** \ˌmen-ə-ˈpò-zel\ *adj*

me·no·rah \mə-ˈnōr-ə, -ˈnòr-\ *n* : a candelabrum used in Jewish worship [Hebrew *mĕnōrāh* "candlestick"]

menservants *plural of* MANSERVANT

men·ses \ˈmen-ˌsēz\ *n sing or pl* : the menstrual flow [Latin, from pl. of *mensis* "month"]

Men·she·vik \ˈmen-chə-ˌvik, -ˌvēk\ *n, pl* **Men·she·viks** *or* **Men·she·vi·ki** \ˌmen-chə-ˈvik-ē, -ˈvē-kē\ : a member of a wing of the Russian Social Democratic party before and during the Russian Revolution believing in the gradual achievement of socialism by parliamentary methods in opposition to the Bolsheviks [Russian *men'shevik,* from *men'she* "less"; from their forming the minority group of the party] — **Men·she·vism** \ˈmen-chə-ˌviz-əm\ *n* — **Men·she·vist** \-vest\ *n or adj*

men·stru·al \ˈmen-strə-wəl, -stral\ *adj* : of or relating to menstruation

menstrual cycle *n* : the complete cycle of physiological changes from the beginning of one menstrual period to the beginning of the next

men·stru·ate \ˈmen-strə-ˌwāt, ˈmen-ˌstrāt\ *vi* : to undergo menstruation [Late Latin *menstruari,* from Latin *menstrua* "menses," from *menstruus* "monthly," from *mensis* "month"]

men·stru·a·tion \ˌmen-strə-ˈwā-shən, men-ˈstrā-shən\ *n* : a discharging of blood, secretions, and tissue debris from the uterus that recurs at approximately monthly intervals in breeding-age primate females that are not pregnant; *also* : PERIOD 5c

men·stru·um \ˈmen-strə-wəm\ *n, pl* **men·stru·ums** *or* **men·strua** \-strə-wə\ : a substance that dissolves a solid or holds it in suspension : SOLVENT [Medieval Latin, literally, "menses," from Latin *menstrua*]

men·su·ra·ble \ˈmen-sə-rə-bəl, ˈmen-chə-\ *adj* : capable of being measured : MEASURABLE [Late Latin *mensurabilis,* from *mensurare* "to measure," from Latin *mensura* "measure"] — **men·su·ra·bil·i·ty** \ˌmen-sə-rə-ˈbil-ət-ē, ˌmen-chə-\ *n*

men·su·ra·tion \ˌmen-sə-ˈrā-shən, ˌmen-chə-\ *n* **1** : the act of measuring : MEASUREMENT **2** : the branch of mathematics that deals with the measurement of lengths, areas, and volumes

mens·wear \ˈmenz-ˌwaər, -ˌweər\ *n* : clothing for men

-ment \mənt; *homographic verbs are* ˌment *also* mənt\ *n suffix* **1** : result, object, or means of a (specified) action ⟨embank*ment*⟩ ⟨entertain*ment*⟩ **2 a** : action : process ⟨develop*ment*⟩ **b** : place of a (specified) action ⟨encamp*ment*⟩ **3** : state : condition ⟨amaze*ment*⟩ [Latin *-mentum*]

men·tal \ˈment-l\ *adj* **1 a** : of or relating to the mind ⟨*mental* powers⟩; *esp* : of or relating to the total emotional and intellectual response of an individual to external reality **b** : carried on or experienced in the mind ⟨*mental* arithmetic⟩ **c** : relating to spirit or idea as opposed to matter **2 a** : of, relating to, or affected by a disorder of the mind ⟨a *mental* illness⟩ **b** : intended for the care or treatment of persons affected by mental disorders [Late Latin *mentalis,* from Latin *ment-, mens* "mind"] — **men·tal·ly** \-l-ē\ *adv*

synonyms MENTAL, INTELLECTUAL mean of or relating to the mind. MENTAL implies a contrast with what is physically or materially caused, expressed, or performed ⟨make a *mental* note⟩ ⟨form a *mental* picture⟩. INTELLECTUAL applies to the higher mental powers (as of generalizing or discriminating abstractions) and often implies a contrast with *moral, emotional,* or *practical* ⟨*intellectual* appreciation of music⟩ ⟨the *intellectual* value of scientific study⟩.

mental age *n* : a measure used in psychological testing that expresses an individual's mental attainment in terms of the number of years it takes an average child to reach the same level

men·tal·i·ty \men-ˈtal-ət-ē\ *n, pl* **-ties** **1** : mental power or capacity : INTELLIGENCE **2** : way of thinking

mental retardation *n* : a developmental disability present from birth or infancy that is marked by intellectual ability that is below average and is accompanied by significant limitations in abilities (as in communication or care of oneself) necessary for independent daily functioning

men·tee \men-ˈtē\ *n* : one who is being mentored : PROTÉGÉ, PUPIL

men·thol \ˈmen-ˌthòl, -ˌthōl\ *n* : a white crystalline alcohol $C_{10}H_{20}O$ that occurs especially in mint oils and has the odor and cooling properties of peppermint [German, derived from Latin *mentha* "mint"]

men·tho·lat·ed \ˈmen-thə-ˌlāt-əd\ *adj* : treated with or containing menthol

[1]**men·tion** \ˈmen-chən\ *n* : a brief reference to something : a passing remark [Medieval French *mencion,* from Latin *mentio*]

[2]**mention** *vt* **men·tioned; men·tion·ing** \ˈmench-ning, -ə-ning\ : to discuss or speak about briefly — **men·tion·able** \ˈmench-nə-bəl, -ə-nə-\ *adj* — **men·tion·er** \ˈmench-nər, -ə-nər\ *n* — **not to mention** : not even yet counting or considering : and notably in addition ⟨a plan that's risky, *not to mention* expensive⟩

[1]**men·tor** \ˈmen-ˌtòr, ˈment-ər\ *n* : a wise and faithful adviser or teacher [*Mentor,* adviser of Telemachus in Homer's *Odyssey*]

[2]**mentor** *vt* : to serve as a mentor : TUTOR

menu \ˈmen-yü, ˈmān-\ *n* **1** : a list of dishes served at a meal or available to order (as in a restaurant) **2** : the dishes making up a meal **3** : a list of computer operations shown on the display screen for a user to select from ⟨a *menu* of printing options⟩ [French, from *menu* "small, detailed," from Medieval French, from Latin *minutus* "minute" (adj.)]

Word History The French word *menu,* which means "a list of foods," comes from the adjective *menu,* which means "small," "slender," or "detailed." Presumably the last sense is the one that gave us the noun, since a *menu* is a detailed list. The French adjective *menu* is descended from Latin *minutus,* "small," which is also the source of the English adjective *minute.*

menu–driv·en \-ˌdriv-ən\ *adj* : relating to or being computer software in which options are offered to the user via menus

[1]**me·ow** \mē-ˈau̇\ *n* : the characteristic cry of a cat [imitative]

[2]**meow** *vi* : to utter a meow or similar sound

me·phit·ic \mə-ˈfit-ik\ *adj* : foul-smelling ⟨*mephitic* vapors⟩ [Latin *mephitis* "foul odor"]

mep·ro·bam·ate \ˌmep-rō-ˈbam-ˌāt\ *n* : a bitter drug $C_9H_{18}N_2O_4$ used as a tranquilizer

mer·can·tile \ˈmər-kən-ˌtēl, -ˌtīl\ *adj* **1** : of or relating to merchants or trade **2** : of, relating to, or having the characteristics of mercantilism ⟨a *mercantile* system⟩ [French, from Italian, from *mercante* "merchant," from Latin *mercans,* from *mercari* "to trade," from *merc-, merx* "merchandise"]

mer·can·til·ism \-ˌtēl-ˌiz-əm, -ˌtīl-\ *n* : an economic system developing during the 17th and 18th centuries to unify and increase the power and wealth of a nation by strict governmental regulation of the economy usually through policies designed to secure an accumulation of bullion, a favorable balance of trade, the development of agriculture and manufactures, and the establishment of foreign trading monopolies — **mer·can·til·ist** \-əst\ *n or adj* — **mer·can·til·is·tic** \ˌmər-kən-ˌtē-ˈlis-tik, -ˌtī-\ *adj*

Mer·ca·tor projection \mər-ˌkāt-ər-\ *n* : a map projection in which the meridians and

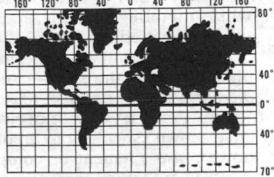

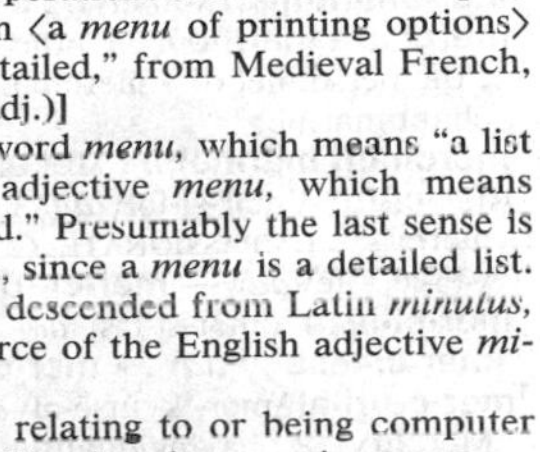

Mercator projection

\ə\ **abut**	\au̇\ **out**	\i\ **tip**	\ȯ\ **saw**	\u̇\ **foot**
\ər\ **further**	\ch\ **chin**	\ī\ **life**	\ȯi\ **coin**	\y\ **yet**
\a\ **mat**	\e\ **pet**	\j\ **job**	\th\ **thin**	\yü\ **few**
\ā\ **take**	\ē\ **easy**	\ng\ **sing**	\t͟h\ **this**	\yu̇\ **cure**
\ä\ **cot, cart**	\g\ **go**	\ō\ **bone**	\ü\ **food**	\zh\ **vision**

parallels cross each other at right angles as they do on the globe and provide accurate directional relations but cause increasing distortion of shape and size with increasing distance from the equator [Gerhardus *Mercator*]

1mer·ce·nary \ˈmərs-n-ˌer-ē\ *n, pl* **-nar·ies** : one that serves merely for wages; *esp* : a soldier hired by a foreign country to fight in its army [Latin *mercenarius,* from *merces* "wages," from *merc-, merx* "merchandise"]

2mercenary *adj* **1** : serving only for pay or reward **2** : greedy for money — **mer·ce·nari·ly** \ˌmərs-n-ˈer-ə-lē\ *adv* — **mer·ce·nari·ness** \ˈmərs-n-ˌer-ē-nəs\ *n*

mer·cer \ˈmər-sər\ *n, British* : a dealer in textile fabrics [Medieval French, from *merz* "merchandise," from Latin *merx*]

mer·cer·ize \ˈmər-sə-ˌrīz\ *vt* : to treat (cotton yarn or fabric) with a chemical so that the fibers are strengthened, take dyes better, and often acquire a sheen [John *Mercer,* died 1866, English calico printer]

merch \ˈmərch\ *n* : MERCHANDISE

1mer·chan·dise \ˈmər-chən-ˌdīz, -ˌdīs\ *n* : the goods that are bought and sold in trade [Medieval French *marchandise,* from *marcheant* "merchant"]

2merchandise \-ˌdīz\ *vb* : to buy and sell : TRADE; *esp* : to try to further the sale of goods or use of services by attractive presentation and publicity — **mer·chan·dis·er** *n*

1mer·chant \ˈmər-chənt\ *n* **1** : a buyer and seller of goods for profit; *esp* : one who carries on trade on a large scale or with foreign countries **2** : the operator of a retail business : STOREKEEPER [Medieval French *marchant,* derived from Latin *mercari* "to trade," from *merc-, merx* "merchandise"]

2merchant *adj* **1** : of, relating to, or used in trade ⟨a *merchant* ship⟩ **2** : of or relating to a merchant marine

mer·chant·able \-ə-bəl\ *adj* : of commercial quality : SALABLE ⟨*merchantable* goods⟩

mer·chant·man \-mən\ *n* : a ship used in commerce

merchant marine *n* **1** : the commercial ships of a nation **2 a** : the personnel of a merchant marine **b** : a member of a merchant marine

merchant mariner *n* : MERCHANT MARINE 2b

mer·ci·ful \ˈmər-si-fəl\ *adj* : having, showing, or disposed to mercy : COMPASSIONATE ⟨a *merciful* ruler⟩ — **mer·ci·ful·ly** \-fə-lē, -flē\ *adv* — **mer·ci·ful·ness** \-fəl-nəs\ *n*

mer·ci·less \ˈmər-si-ləs\ *adj* : having no mercy : PITILESS — **mer·ci·less·ly** *adv* — **mer·ci·less·ness** *n*

1mer·cu·ri·al \mər-ˈkyu̇r-ē-əl\ *adj* **1** : of or relating to the planet Mercury **2** : having qualities of eloquence, ingenuity, or thievishness **3** : marked by rapid and unpredictable change of mood ⟨a *mercurial* temperament⟩ **4** : of, relating to, or containing the element mercury ⟨*mercurial* medical preparations⟩ ⟨a *mercurial* thermometer⟩ — **mer·cu·ri·al·ly** \-ē-ə-lē\ *adv* — **mer·cu·ri·al·ness** *n*

2mercurial *n* : a drug or chemical containing mercury

mer·cu·ric \mər-ˈkyu̇r-ik\ *adj* : of, relating to, or containing mercury; *esp* : containing mercury that has a valence of two

mercuric chloride *n* : a heavy poisonous substance $HgCl_2$ used as a disinfectant and fungicide and in photography

Mer·cu·ro·chrome \mər-ˈkyu̇r-ə-ˌkrōm\ *trademark* — used for a germicidal and antiseptic red solution

mer·cu·rous \mər-ˈkyu̇r-əs, ˈmər-kyə-rəs\ *adj* : of, relating to, or containing mercury; *esp* : containing mercury that has a valence of one

mercurous chloride *n* : CALOMEL

mer·cu·ry \ˈmər-kyə-rē, -kə-rē, -krē\ *n* **1 a** : a heavy silver-white metallic element that is liquid at ordinary temperatures — called also *quicksilver*; see ELEMENT table **b** : the column of mercury in a thermometer or barometer **2** *cap* : the planet nearest the sun — see PLANET table [Medieval Latin *mercurius,* from Latin *Mercurius* "Mercury (Roman god)"]

mer·cy \ˈmər-sē\ *n, pl* **mercies** **1 a** : compassion or forbearance shown especially to an offender or to one subject to one's power; *also* : lenient or compassionate treatment ⟨begged for *mercy*⟩ **b** : imprisonment rather than death imposed as penalty for first-degree murder **2 a** : a blessing that is an act of divine favor or compassion **b** : a fortunate circumstance ⟨it was a *mercy* they found her before she froze⟩ **3** : compassionate treatment of those in distress ⟨works of *mercy* among the poor⟩ [Medieval French *merci,* from Medieval Latin *merces* "favor, mercy," from Latin, "price paid, wages," from *merc-, merx* "merchandise"] — **mercy** *adj* — **at the mercy of** : wholly in the power of : with no way to protect oneself against ⟨was *at the mercy of* the weather⟩

Word History *Mercy* is not something that can be bought or sold, but the word *mercy* is derived from Latin *merces,* which means "the price paid for something," "wages," "reward," or "recompense." The roots of what is now the primary sense of mercy are to be found in the Latin of Christian writers of the 6th century, who began to use *merces* for the spiritual reward that comes from kindness to those who do not necessarily have a claim to such mercy and from whom no recompense is to be expected.

synonyms MERCY, CLEMENCY, LENIENCY mean the disposition not to be harsh in one's dealings with others. MERCY implies kindness and compassion that withholds punishment even when justice demands it ⟨pleaded guilty and asked for *mercy* from the court⟩. CLEMENCY implies a mild or merciful disposition in one having the power or duty of punishing ⟨the ruler displayed *clemency* in dealing with the rebels⟩. LENIENCY implies a lack of severity in punishing ⟨criticized the courts for excessive *leniency*⟩.

mercy killing *n* : EUTHANASIA

1mere \ˈmiər\ *n* : a sheet of standing water : POOL [Old English]

2mere *adj, superlative* **mer·est** : being only this and nothing else : nothing more than ⟨a *mere* whisper⟩ ⟨a *mere* child⟩ [Latin *merus* "pure, unmixed"] — **mere·ly** *adv*

-mere \ˌmiər\ *n combining form* : part : segment ⟨meta*mere*⟩ [Greek *meros*]

me·ren·gue \mə-ˈreŋ-gā\ *n* : a ballroom dance of Haitian and Dominican origin in 2/4 time in which one foot is dragged on every step; *also* : the music for a merengue [American Spanish]

mer·e·tri·cious \ˌmer-ə-ˈtrish-əs\ *adj* : falsely attractive [Latin *meretricius* "of a prostitute," from *meretrix* "prostitute," from *merēre* "to earn"] — **mer·e·tri·cious·ly** *adv* — **mer·e·tri·cious·ness** *n*

mer·gan·ser \mər-ˈgan-sər\ *n, pl* **-sers** *or* **-ser** : any of various fish-eating diving ducks with a slender bill hooked at the end and a usually crested head [Latin *mergus,* a kind of waterfowl + *anser* "goose"]

merge \ˈmərj\ *vb* **1** : to be or cause to be swallowed up or absorbed in or within something else : MINGLE, BLEND ⟨*merging* traffic⟩ **2** : COMBINE 3, UNITE; *esp* : to undergo or cause to undergo a business merger [Latin *mergere* "to plunge"]

merg·er \ˈmər-jər\ *n* : the action or result of merging; *esp* : the combination of two or more business firms into one

me·rid·i·an \mə-ˈrid-ē-ən\ *n* **1** : the highest point attained **2 a** : an imaginary great circle on the earth's surface passing through the north and south poles and any given place between **b** : the half of such a circle included between the poles **c** : a representation of such a circle or half circle numbered for longitude on a globe or map [Medieval French *meridien* "noon," derived from Latin *meridianus* "of noon," from *meridies* "noon, south," from *medius* "mid" + *dies* "day"] — **meridian** *adj*

me·rid·i·o·nal \mə-ˈrid-ē-ən-l\ *adj* **1** : of, relating to, or situated in the south : SOUTHERN **2** : of, relating to, or characteristic of people living in the south especially of France **3** : of or relating to a meridian [Middle French *meridionel,* derived from Latin *meridies* "noon, south"] — **me·rid·i·o·nal·ly** \-l-ē\ *adv*

me·ringue \mə-ˈrang\ *n* **1** : a mixture of beaten egg white and sugar put on pies or cakes and browned **2** : a shell of baked meringue filled with fruit or ice cream [French]

me·ri·no \mə-ˈrē-nō\ *n, pl* **-nos** **1** : any of a breed of fine-wooled white sheep producing a heavy fleece of exceptional quality **2** : a soft wool or wool and cotton fabric resembling cashmere **3** : a fine wool and cotton yarn [Spanish] — **merino** *adj*

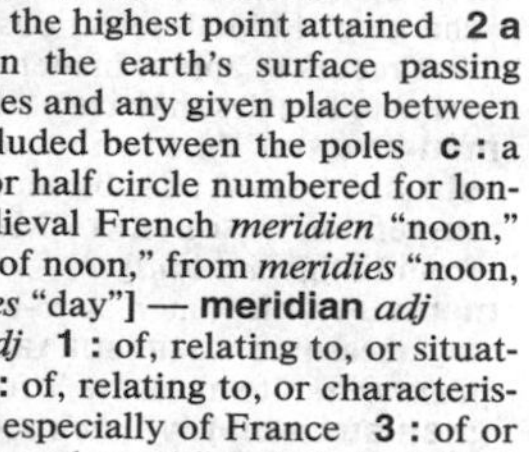
merino 1

mer·i·stem \ˈmer-ə-ˌstem\ *n* : a plant tissue made up of unspecialized cells capable of dividing indefinitely and of producing cells that differentiate into tissues and organs [Greek *meristos* "divided" + English *-em* (as in *system*)] — **mer·i·ste·mat·ic** \ˌmer-ə-stə-ˈmat-ik\ *adj*

1mer·it \ˈmer-ət\ *n* **1** : the qualities or actions that determine one's worthiness of reward or punishment ⟨opinions of his *merit* vary⟩ **2** : a praiseworthy quality : VIRTUE ⟨an answer having the *merit* of honesty⟩ **3 :** character or conduct deserving reward, honor, or esteem ⟨an idea of great *merit*⟩; *also* **:** ACHIEVEMENT 1 **4 :** individual significance or justification ⟨the accusation is without *merit*⟩ [Medieval French *merite,* from Latin *meritum,* from *merēre* "to deserve, earn"] — **mer·it·less** *adj*

[2]**merit** *vb* **:** to earn by service or performance **:** DESERVE

mer·i·to·ri·ous \ˌmer-ə-'tōr-ē-əs, -'tȯr-\ *adj* **:** deserving reward or honor **:** PRAISEWORTHY — **mer·i·to·ri·ous·ly** *adv* — **mer·i·to·ri·ous·ness** *n*

merit system *n* **:** a system by which appointments and promotions in the civil service are based on competence rather than political favoritism

mer·lin \'mər-lən\ *n* **:** a small falcon of northern regions [Medieval French *merilun*]

mer·maid \'mər-ˌmād\ *n* **:** an imaginary sea creature usually represented with a woman's body and a fish's tail [Old English *mere* "sea, mere"]

mer·man \-ˌman, -mən\ *n, pl* **mer·men** \-ˌmen, -mən\ **:** an imaginary sea creature usually represented with a man's body and a fish's tail

-m·er·ous \m-ə-rəs\ *adj combining form* **:** having (such or so many) parts ⟨penta*merous*⟩ [Greek *meros* "part"]

mer·ri·ment \'mer-i-mənt\ *n* **:** merry activity **:** FUN

mer·ry \'mer-ē\ *adj* **mer·ri·er; -est 1 :** full of good humor and good spirits **:** MIRTHFUL **2 :** marked by gaiety or festivity ⟨a *merry* Christmas⟩ [Old English *myrge, merge*] — **mer·ri·ly** \'mer-ə-lē\ *adv* — **mer·ri·ness** \'mer-ē-nəs\ *n*

synonyms MERRY, BLITHE, JOVIAL, JOLLY mean showing high spirits or lightheartedness. MERRY suggests high spirits and unrestrained enjoyment of frolic or festivity ⟨*merry* revelers⟩. BLITHE implies lightheartedness and carefree gaiety ⟨arrived late in his usual *blithe* way⟩. JOVIAL suggests behavior that stimulates conviviality and good-fellowship ⟨dinner put them in a *jovial* mood⟩. JOLLY suggests often habitual good spirits expressed in laughing, bantering, and jesting ⟨our *jolly* host enlivened the party⟩.

mer·ry–an·drew \ˌmer-ē-'an-ˌdrü\ *n, often cap M&A* **:** a person who clowns publicly [from the name *Andrew*]

mer·ry–go–round \'mer-ē-gō-ˌrau̇nd, -gə-\ *n* **1 :** a circular revolving platform fitted with seats and figures of animals on which people sit for a ride **2 :** a rapid round of activities **:** WHIRL ⟨*a merry-go-round* of parties⟩

mer·ry·mak·ing \-ˌmā-king\ *n* **1 :** merry activity **2 :** a merry occasion or party — **mer·ry·mak·er** \-kər\ *n*

mes- *or* **meso-** *combining form* **1 :** mid **:** in the middle ⟨*meso*carp⟩ **2 :** intermediate (as in size or type) ⟨*meson*⟩ [Greek, from *mesos*]

me·sa \'mā-sə\ *n* **:** a flat-topped hill or small plateau with steep sides [Spanish, literally, "table," from Latin *mensa*]

més·al·liance \ˌmā-ˌzal-'yä^{n}s, ˌmā-zə-'lī-əns\ *n, pl* **-liances** \-'yä^{n}s, -'yä^{n}s-əz; -'lī-ən-səz\ **:** a marriage with a person of inferior social position [French, from *més-* "mis-" + *alliance* "alliance"]

mes·cal \me-'skal, mə-\ *n* **1 :** PEYOTE 2 **2 a :** a usually colorless Mexican liquor distilled especially from the central leaves on maguey plants **b :** a plant from which mescal is produced [Spanish, from Nahuatl *mexcalli* "liquor made from the maguey plant"]

mescal button *n* **:** PEYOTE BUTTON

mes·ca·line \'mes-kə-lən, -ˌlēn\ *n* **:** a hallucination-inducing alkaloid $C_{11}H_{17}NO_3$ found in peyote buttons

mes·clun \'mes-klən\ *n* **:** a mixture of young tender greens (as lettuces and chicory); *also* **:** a salad made with mesclun [French, from Occitan, literally, "mixture"]

mesdames *plural of* MADAM *or of* MADAME *or of* MRS.

mesdemoiselles *plural of* MADEMOISELLE

me·seems \mi-'sēmz\ *vb impersonal, past* **me·seemed** \-'sēmd\ *archaic* **:** it seems to me

mes·en·ceph·a·lon \ˌmez-ˌen-'sef-ə-ˌlän, ˌmez-n-, ˌmēz-\ *n* **:** the middle division of the brain **:** MIDBRAIN — **mes·en·ce·phal·ic** \-ˌen-sə-'fal-ik, -n-sə-\ *adj*

mes·en·chyme \'mez-n-ˌkīm, 'mēz-\ *n* **:** a loosely organized mesodermal tissue that produces connective tissues, blood, lymphatics, bone, and cartilage [derived from *mes-* + *-enchyma* (as in *parenchyma*)] — **mes·en·chy·mal** \mə-'zeng-kə-məl, -'seng-; ˌmez-n-'kī-məl, ˌmēz-\ *adj*

mes·en·tery \'mez-n-ˌter-ē, 'mes-\ *n, pl* **-ter·ies :** a membranous tissue or one of the membranes that envelop and support internal organs (as the intestines) [Greek *mesenterion,* from *mes-* + *enteron* "intestine"] — **mes·en·ter·ic** \ˌmez-n-'ter-ik, ˌmes-\ *adj*

[1]**mesh** \'mesh\ *n* **1 :** one of the open spaces formed by the threads of a net or the wires of a sieve or screen **2 a :** a fabric of open texture with evenly spaced small holes **b :** NET 1a, NETWORK **3 :** SNARE 2 — usually used in plural ⟨caught in their own *meshes*⟩ **4 :** the coming or fitting together of the teeth of two gears [probably from early Dutch *maesche*] — **meshed** \'mesht\ *adj*

[2]**mesh** *vb* **1 :** to catch in or as if in a mesh **2 :** to fit together **:** INTERLOCK ⟨gears that *mesh*⟩

mesh·work \'mesh-ˌwərk\ *n* **:** NETWORK 2

me·si·al \'mē-zē-əl, -sē-\ *adj* **:** of, relating to, or being the surface of a tooth that is next to the tooth in front of it or that is closest to the middle of the front of the jaw — **me·si·al·ly** \-ə-lē\ *adv*

me·sic \'mez-ik, 'mes-\ *adj* **:** characterized by, relating to, or requiring a moderate amount of moisture ⟨*mesic* forests⟩

mes·mer·ism \'mez-mə-ˌriz-əm\ *n* **:** HYPNOTISM [F. A. *Mesmer,* died 1815, Austrian physician] — **mes·mer·ic** \mez-'mer-ik\ *adj* — **mes·mer·ist** \'mez-mə-rəst\ *n*

mes·mer·ize \'mez-mə-ˌrīz\ *vt* **1 :** HYPNOTIZE **2 :** FASCINATE 1, SPELLBIND — **mes·mer·iz·er** *n*

me·so·carp \'mez-ə-ˌkärp, 'mēz-, 'mēs-, 'mes-\ *n* **:** the often fleshy middle layer of the pericarp of a fruit — compare ENDOCARP, EXOCARP

me·so·derm \-ˌdərm\ *n* **:** the middle of the three primary germ layers of an embryo from which most of the muscular, skeletal, and connective tissues develop; *also* **:** tissue derived from this layer — **me·so·der·mal** \ˌmez-ə-'dər-məl, mēz-, ˌmēs-, ˌmes-\ *adj*

me·so·glea *also* **me·so·gloea** \ˌmez-ə-'glē-ə, ˌmēz-, ˌmēs-, ˌmes-\ *n* **:** a jellylike substance between the endoderm and ectoderm of sponges and coelenterates [*mes-* + Late Greek *gloia, glia* "glue"]

Me·so·lith·ic \ˌmez-ə-'lith-ik, ˌmēz-, ˌmes-, ˌmēs-\ *adj* **:** of or relating to a period of the Stone Age that is transitional between the Paleolithic and the Neolithic

me·so·mor·phic \ˌmez-ə-'mȯr-fik, ˌmēz-, ˌmēs-, ˌmes-\ *adj* **:** of a muscular or athletic type of body-build — **me·so·morph** \'mez-ə-ˌmorf, 'mēz-, 'mēs-, 'mes-\ *n*

me·son \'mez-ˌän, 'mes-; 'mā-ˌzän, 'mē-, -ˌsän\ *n* **:** any of a group of elementary particles that are subject to the strong force and are produced in nuclear collisions [*mes-* + *-on*]

me·so·pause \'mez-ə-ˌpȯz, 'mēz-, 'mēs-, 'mes-\ *n* **:** the upper boundary of the mesosphere where the temperature of the atmosphere reaches its lowest point

me·so·phyll \-ˌfil\ *n* **:** the parenchyma tissue of a foliage leaf consisting of photosynthetic and storage cells that lie between the surface layers

me·so·phyte \-ˌfīt\ *n* **:** a plant that grows under medium conditions of moisture — **me·so·phyt·ic** \ˌmez-ə-'fit-ik, ˌmēz-, ˌmēs-, ˌmes-\ *adj*

me·so·sphere \'mez-ə-ˌsfiər, 'mēz-, 'mēs-, 'mes-\ *n* **:** a layer of the atmosphere between the stratosphere and the thermosphere in which temperature decreases with increased altitude

me·so·the·li·um \ˌmez-ə-'thē-lē-əm, ˌmēz-, ˌmēs-, ˌmes-\ *n, pl* **-lia** \-lē-ə\ **:** epithelium derived from mesoderm — **me·so·the·li·al** \-lē-əl\ *adj*

me·so·tho·rax \-'thōr-ˌaks, -'thȯr-\ *n* **:** the middle of the three segments of the thorax of an insect

Me·so·zo·ic \-'zō-ik\ *n* **1 :** the 3rd of the four eras of geological history marked by the presence of dinosaurs, marine and flying reptiles, and evergreen trees — called also *Age of Reptiles*; see GEOLOGIC TIME table **2 :** the system of rocks corresponding to the Mesozoic — **Mesozoic** *adj*

mes·quite \mə-'skēt, me-\ *n* **:** a spiny deep-

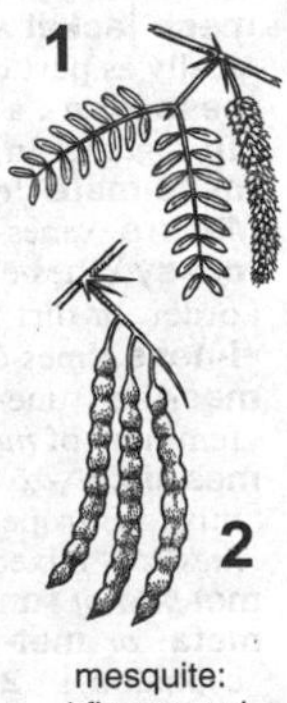

mesquite: *1* flower and leaves, *2* pods

\ə\ **abut**	\au̇\ **out**	\i\ **tip**	\ȯ\ **saw**	\u̇\ **foot**
\ər\ **further**	\ch\ **chin**	\ī\ **life**	\ȯi\ **coin**	\y\ **yet**
\a\ **mat**	\e\ **pet**	\j\ **job**	\th\ **thin**	\yü\ **few**
\ā\ **take**	\ē\ **easy**	\ng\ **sing**	\th\ **this**	\yu̇\ **cure**
\ä\ **cot, cart**	\g\ **go**	\ō\ **bone**	\ü\ **food**	\zh\ **vision**

rooted tree or shrub of the pea family that grows in the southwestern U.S. and in Mexico and bears pods rich in sugar and important as a livestock feed; *also* : the wood of the mesquite used especially in grilling food [Spanish, from Nahuatl *mizquitl*]

[1]**mess** \'mes\ *n* **1 a :** a quantity of food **b :** a dish of soft food ⟨a *mess* of porridge⟩ **2 a :** a group of people who regularly eat together; *also* : the meal they eat **b :** a place where meals are regularly served to a group : MESS HALL **3 :** a disordered, untidy, offensive, or unpleasant state or condition ⟨your room is in a *mess*⟩; *also* : one that is in such a state or condition ⟨his life was a *mess*⟩ **4 :** a large quantity or number ⟨a *mess* of problems⟩ [Medieval French *mes,* from Late Latin *missus* "course at a meal," from *mittere* "to put," from Latin, "to send"]

[2]**mess** *vb* **1 a :** to supply with meals **b :** to take meals with a mess **2 a :** to make dirty or untidy : DISARRANGE ⟨don't *mess* up your room⟩ **b :** to do incorrectly ⟨*messed* up the job⟩ **c :** to make an error ⟨tried again and still *messed* up⟩ **3 :** to interfere with ⟨the storm *messed* up our plans⟩ **4 a :** to work without a serious goal : PUTTER ⟨likes to *mess* around with paints⟩ **b :** to handle or play with something especially carelessly **c :** INTERFERE 3, MEDDLE ⟨don't *mess* with me⟩ **5 :** to rough up : MANHANDLE

mes•sage \'mes-ij\ *n* **1 :** a communication in writing, in speech, or by signals **2 :** a messenger's errand or function **3 :** an underlying theme or idea [Medieval French, from Medieval Latin *missaticum,* from Latin *missus,* past participle of *mittere* "to send"]

message board *n* : BULLETIN BOARD 2

messeigneurs *plural of* MONSEIGNEUR

mes•sen•ger \'mes-n-jər\ *n* **:** one that bears a message or does an errand [Medieval French *messager,* from *message* "message"]

messenger RNA *n* **:** an RNA produced by transcription that carries the code for a particular protein from the nuclear DNA to a ribosome and acts as a template for the formation of that protein — compare TRANSFER RNA

mess hall *n* **:** a hall or building (as on an army post) in which mess is served

mes•si•ah \mə-'sī-ə\ *n* **1** *cap* **a :** the expected king and deliverer of the Jews **b :** Jesus Christ regarded as the savior of the world by Christians **2 :** a professed or accepted leader of some hope or cause [Hebrew *māshīaḥ* and Aramaic *mĕshīḥā,* literally, "anointed"] — **mes•si•ah•ship** \-ˌship\ *n*

mes•si•an•ic \ˌmes-ē-'an-ik\ *adj* **1 :** of or relating to a messiah **2 :** marked by idealism and an aggressive crusading spirit ⟨*messianic* zeal⟩

mes•si•a•nism \'mes-ē-ə-ˌniz-əm, mə-'sī-ə-\ *n* **1 :** belief in a messiah as the savior of humankind **2 :** religious devotion to an ideal or cause

Mes•si•as \mə-'sī-əs\ *n* : MESSIAH 1 [Late Latin, from Greek, from Aramaic *mĕshīḥā*]

messieurs *plural of* MONSIEUR

mess jacket *n* **:** a fitted waist-length man's jacket worn especially as part of a dress uniform

mess kit *n* **:** a kit consisting of cooking and eating utensils that fit together in a compact unit

mess•mate \'mes-ˌmāt\ *n* **:** a member of a mess (as on a ship)

Messrs. \ˌmes-ərz\ *plural of* MR.

messy \'mes-ē\ *adj* **mess•i•er; -est :** marked by confusion, disorder, or dirt : UNTIDY — **mess•i•ly** \'mes-ə-lē\ *adv* — **mess•i•ness** \'mes-ē-nəs\ *n*

mes•ti•za \me-'stē-zə\ *n* **:** a woman who is a mestizo [Spanish, feminine of *mestizo*]

mes•ti•zo \-zō\ *n, pl* **-zos :** a person of mixed blood; *esp* **:** one of mixed European and American Indian ancestry [Spanish, from *mestizo* "mixed," derived from Latin *miscēre* "to mix"]

met *past of* MEET

meta- *or* **met-** *prefix* **1 :** situated behind or beyond ⟨*met*encephalon⟩ **2 :** change : transformation ⟨*meta*morphosis⟩ [Greek, from *meta* "among, with, after"]

met•a•bol•ic \ˌmet-ə-'bäl-ik\ *adj* **:** of, relating to, or based on metabolism ⟨*metabolic* activity⟩ ⟨a *metabolic* disorder⟩ — **met•a•bol•i•cal•ly** \-i-kə-lē, -klē\ *adv*

me•tab•o•lism \mə-'tab-ə-ˌliz-əm\ *n* **1 a :** the sum of the processes in the building up and destruction of the complex chemically reactive substances in the cells of living things; *esp* **:** the chemical changes in living cells by which energy is provided for vital processes and activities and new material is assimilated **b :** the sum of the processes by which a particular substance is handled in the living body **2 :** METAMORPHOSIS 3 [Greek *metabolē* "change," from *metaballein* "to change," from *meta-* + *ballein* "to throw"]

me•tab•o•lite \-ˌlīt\ *n* **1 :** a product of metabolism **2 :** a substance essential to a metabolic process

me•tab•o•lize \mə-'tab-ə-ˌlīz\ *vb* **:** to subject to or perform metabolism ⟨protein is *metabolized* in the body⟩

[1]**meta•car•pal** \ˌmet-ə-'kär-pəl\ *adj* **:** of, relating to, or being the metacarpus or a bone of the metacarpus

[2]**metacarpal** *n* **:** a bone of the metacarpus

meta•car•pus \-pəs\ *n* **:** the part of the hand or forefoot between the carpus and fingers or toes that typically contains five elongated bones

meta•cog•ni•tion \ˌmet-ə-käg-'nish-ən\ *n* **:** awareness or analysis of one's own learning or thinking processes

meta•gal•axy \ˌmet-ə-'gal-ək-sē\ *n* **:** the entire system of galaxies : UNIVERSE — **meta•ga•lac•tic** \-gə-'lak-tik\ *adj*

[1]**met•al** \'met-l\ *n* **1 :** any of various substances (as gold, tin, copper, or bronze) that have a more or less shiny appearance, are good conductors of electricity and heat, are opaque, can be melted, and are usually capable of being drawn into a wire or hammered into a thin sheet **2 :** any of the chemical elements that exhibit the properties of a metal, typically are crystalline solids, and have atoms that readily lose electrons **3 a :** METTLE 2a **b :** the substance out of which a person or thing is made [Medieval French, from Latin *metallum* "mine, metal," from Greek *metallon*] — **metal** *adj*

[2]**metal** *vt* **-aled** *or* **-alled; -al•ing** *or* **-al•ling :** to cover or furnish with metal

me•tal•lic \mə-'tal-ik\ *adj* **1 :** of, relating to, or being a metal **2 :** containing or made of metal **3 :** having iridescent and reflective properties **4 :** STRIDENT, HARSH ⟨a *metallic* voice⟩ — **me•tal•li•cal•ly** \-'tal-i-kə-lē, -klē\ *adv*

met•al•lif•er•ous \ˌmet-l-'if-rəs, -ə-rəs\ *adj* **:** yielding or containing metal

met•al•lize \'met-l-ˌīz\ *vt* **:** to treat or combine with a metal — **met•al•li•za•tion** \ˌmet-l-ə-'zā-shən\ *n*

met•al•log•ra•phy \ˌmet-l-'äg-rə-fē\ *n* **:** a study of the structure of metals especially with the microscope — **met•al•log•ra•pher** \-fər\ *n* — **me•tal•lo•graph•ic** \mə-ˌtal-ə-'graf-ik\ *adj*

met•al•loid \'met-l-ˌȯid\ *n* **:** a chemical element intermediate in properties between the typical metals and nonmetals

met•al•lur•gy \'met-l-ˌər-jē\ *n* **:** the science and technology of metals [derived from Greek *metallon* "metal" + *-ourgos* "working," from *ergon* "work"] — **met•al•lur•gi•cal** \ˌmet-l-'ər-ji-kəl\ *adj* — **met•al•lur•gist** \'met-l-ˌər-jəst\ *n*

met•al•ware \'met-l-ˌwaər, -ˌweər\ *n* **:** metal utensils for household use

met•al•work \'met-l-ˌwərk\ *n* **:** the product of metalworking; *esp* **:** a metal object of artistic merit — **met•al•work•er** \-ˌwər-kər\ *n*

met•al•work•ing \-ˌwər-king\ *n* **:** the act or process of shaping things out of metal

meta•mere \'met-ə-ˌmiər\ *n* **:** any of the series of segments into which the body of a higher invertebrate or vertebrate is divisible — **me•tam•er•ism** \mə-'tam-ə-ˌriz-əm\ *n* — **meta•mer•ic** \ˌmet-ə-'mer-ik, -'mir-\ *adj*

meta•mor•phic \ˌmet-ə-'mȯr-fik\ *adj* **1 :** of or relating to metamorphosis ⟨*metamorphic* changes⟩ **2 :** of, relating to, or produced by metamorphism ⟨a *metamorphic* rock⟩

meta•mor•phism \-'mȯr-ˌfiz-əm\ *n* **:** a change in rock that results in a more compact form by the action of pressure, heat, and water

meta•mor•phose \-ˌfōz, -ˌfōs\ *vb* **1 :** to change or cause to change in form : undergo metamorphosis **2 :** to cause (a rock) to undergo metamorphism ***synonyms*** see TRANSFORM

meta•mor•pho•sis \ˌmet-ə-'mȯr-fə-səs\ *n, pl* **-pho•ses** \-fə-ˌsēz\ **1 a :** a change of form, structure, or substance especially by witchcraft or magic **b :** a striking alteration in appearance, character, or circumstances **2 :** a fundamental and usually rather abrupt change in the form and often the habits of some animals from an immature stage (as a tadpole or caterpillar) to an adult stage (as a frog or butterfly) — compare COMPLETE METAMORPHOSIS, INCOMPLETE METAMORPHOSIS [Latin, from Greek *metamorphōsis,* from *metamorphoun* "to transform," from *meta-* + *morphē* "form"]

meta·phase \ˈmet-ə-ˌfāz\ *n* : the stage of mitosis and meiosis during which the chromosomes become arranged in the plane of the equator of the spindle

metaphase plate *n* : the plane at the equator of the spindle of a dividing cell in metaphase with the chromosomes arranged upon it — called also *equatorial plate*

met·a·phor \ˈmet-ə-ˌfȯr *also* -fər\ *n* : a figure of speech in which a word or phrase denoting one kind of object or idea is used in place of another to suggest a similarity between them (as in *the ship plows the sea*) — compare SIMILE [derived from Latin *metaphora,* from Greek, from *metapherein* "to transfer," from *meta-* + *pherein* "to carry"] — **met·a·phor·ic** \ˌmet-ə-ˈfȯr-ik, -ˈfär-\ *or* **met·a·phor·i·cal** \-i-kəl\ *adj* — **met·a·phor·i·cal·ly** \-i-kə-lē, -klē\ *adv*

meta·phys·i·cal \ˌmet-ə-ˈfiz-i-kəl\ *adj* **1** : of or relating to metaphysics **2** : SUPERNATURAL 1 **3** : highly abstract or difficult to understand **4** *often cap* : of or relating to poetry especially of the early 17th century that is highly intellectual and philosophical and marked by subtle and elaborate metaphors — **meta·phys·i·cal·ly** \-ˈfiz-i-kə-lē, -klē\ *adv*

meta·phy·si·cian \ˌmet-ə-fə-ˈzish-ən\ *n* : a student of or specialist in metaphysics

meta·phys·ics \ˌmet-ə-ˈfiz-iks\ *n* : the part of philosophy concerned with the ultimate causes and the underlying nature of things [Medieval Latin *Metaphysica,* title of Aristotle's treatise on the subject, from Greek *(ta) meta (ta) physika* "the (works) after the physical (works)"; from its position in his collected works]

meta·se·quoia \ˌmet-ə-si-ˈkwȯi-ə\ *n* : any of a genus of cone-bearing trees related to the bald cypresses and having needlelike leaves and consisting of one living and various extinct forms

meta·sta·ble \ˌmet-ə-ˈstā-bəl\ *adj* : marked by only a slight margin of stability ⟨a *metastable* chemical⟩

me·tas·ta·sis \mə-ˈtas-tə-səs\ *n, pl* **-ta·ses** \-ˌsēz\ **1** : the spread of a disease-producing agency (as cancer cells) from its original site to another part of the body; *also* : the process by which such spreading occurs **2** : a secondary growth of a malignant tumor resulting from metastasis [Late Latin, "transition," from Greek, from *methistanai* "to change," from *meta-* + *histanai* "to set, stand"] — **met·a·stat·ic** \ˌmet-ə-ˈstat-ik\ *adj* — **met·a·stat·i·cal·ly** \-ˈstat-i-kə-lē, -klē\ *adv*

me·tas·ta·size \mə-ˈtas-tə-ˌsīz\ *vi* : to spread or grow by or as if by metastasis

[1]**meta·tar·sal** \ˌmet-ə-ˈtär-səl\ *adj* : of, relating to, or being the metatarsus or a bone of the metatarsus

[2]**metatarsal** *n* : a bone of the metatarsus

meta·tar·sus \-səs\ *n* : the part of the foot in a human or of the hind foot in a four-footed animal between the toes and the tarsus that in humans comprises five elongated bones which form the front of the instep and ball of the foot

me·tath·e·sis \mə-ˈtath-ə-səs\ *n, pl* **-e·ses** \-ˌsēz\ : a change of place or condition; *esp* : transposition of two sounds or letters in a word (as in Modern English *bird* from Old English *bridd*) [Greek, from *metatithenai* "to transpose," from *meta-* + *tithenai* "to place"]

meta·tho·rax \ˌmet-ə-ˈthōr-ˌaks, -ˈthȯr-\ *n* : the hindmost of the three segments of the thorax of an insect

meta·zoa \ˌmet-ə-ˈzō-ə\ *n pl* : animals that are metazoans

meta·zo·an \-ˈzō-ən\ *n* : any of a group (Metazoa) including all animals with a body composed of cells differentiated into tissues and organs [derived from Greek *meta-* "after" and *zōion* "animal"] — **metazoan** *adj*

mete \ˈmēt\ *vt* : to distribute in a fair or proper manner ⟨*mete* out punishment⟩ [Old English *metan* "to measure"]

me·tem·psy·cho·sis \mə-ˌtem-si-ˈkō-səs, -ˌtemp-; ˌmet-əm-ˌsī-\ *n* : the passing of the soul at death into another body either human or animal [Greek *metempsychōsis,* derived from *meta-* + *en-* + *psychē* "soul"]

met·en·ceph·a·lon \ˌmet-ˌen-ˈsef-ə-ˌlän\ *n* : the anterior segment of the vertebrate hindbrain

me·te·or \ˈmēt-ē-ər, -ē-ˌȯr\ *n* : one of the small bodies of matter in the solar system observable when it falls into the earth's atmosphere where the heat of friction may cause it to glow brightly for a short time; *also* : the streak of light produced by the passage of a meteor [Medieval French *meteore,* from Medieval Latin *meteorum,* derived from Greek *meteōros* "high in the air"]

me·te·or·ic \ˌmēt-ē-ˈȯr-ik, -ˈär-\ *adj* **1** : of or relating to a meteor ⟨a *meteoric* shower⟩ **2** : resembling a meteor in speed or in sudden and temporary brilliance ⟨a *meteoric* rise to fame⟩ — **me·te·or·i·cal·ly** \-i-kə-lē, -klē\ *adv*

me·te·or·ite \ˈmēt-ē-ə-ˌrīt\ *n* : a meteor that reaches the surface of the earth

me·te·or·oid \-ˌrȯid\ *n* : a meteor in interplanetary space

me·te·o·rol·o·gy \ˌmēt-ē-ə-ˈräl-ə-jē\ *n* : a science that deals with the atmosphere and its phenomena and especially with weather and weather forecasting — **me·te·o·ro·log·ic** \-rə-ˈläj-ik\ *or* **me·te·o·ro·log·i·cal** \-i-kəl\ *adj* — **me·te·o·rol·o·gist** \-ˈräl-ə-jəst\ *n*

[1]**me·ter** \ˈmēt-ər\ *n* **1** : a systematic rhythm in verse that is usually repeated **2** : the repeated pattern of musical beats in a measure [Old English *mēter,* from Latin *metrum,* from Greek *metron* "measure, meter"]

[2]**meter** *n* : the basic metric unit of length equal to the distance traveled by light in a vacuum in $1/299{,}792{,}458$ second or to about 39.37 inches — see METRIC SYSTEM table [French *mètre,* from Greek *metron* "measure"]

[3]**meter** *n* : an instrument for measuring and sometimes recording the amount of something ⟨a gas *meter*⟩

[4]**meter** *vt* **1** : to measure by means of a meter **2** : to supply in a measured or regulated amount

-me·ter \m-ət-ər, *in some words,* ˌmēt-ər\ *n combining form* : instrument or means for measuring ⟨baro*meter*⟩

meter–kilogram–second *adj* : of, relating to, or being a system of units based on the meter as the unit of length, the kilogram as the unit of mass, and the second as the unit of time — abbreviation *mks*

me·ter·stick \ˈmēt-ər-ˌstik\ *n* : a measuring stick one meter long that is marked off in centimeters and usually millimeters

meth·ac·ry·late \meth-ˈak-rə-ˌlāt\ *n* : a light strong acrylic resin used as a substitute for glass [*meth*yl + *acryl*ic + [1]*-ate*]

meth·a·done \ˈmeth-ə-ˌdōn\ *also* **meth·a·don** \-ˌdän\ *n* : a synthetic addictive narcotic drug used especially to replace heroin in the treatment of heroin addiction

meth·am·phet·amine \ˌmeth-am-ˈfet-ə-ˌmēn, -əm-, -mən\ *n* : a derivative of amphetamine $C_{10}H_{15}N$ used especially in the treatment of obesity and often illegally as a stimulant of the central nervous system [*meth*yl + *amphetamine*]

meth·ane \ˈmeth-ˌān\ *n* : an odorless flammable gas CH_4 consisting of carbon and hydrogen and produced by decomposition of organic matter [*meth*yl + *-ane*]

meth·a·nol \ˈmeth-ə-ˌnȯl, -ˌnōl\ *n* : a volatile flammable poisonous liquid CH_3OH that consists of carbon, hydrogen, and oxygen and is used especially as a solvent and antifreeze

me·thinks \mi-ˈthiŋks, -ˈthiŋgks\ *vb impersonal, past* **me·thought** \-ˈthȯt\ *archaic* : it seems to me

me·thi·o·nine \mə-ˈthī-ə-ˌnēn\ *n* : a crystalline sulfur-containing essential amino acid $C_5H_{11}NO_2S$ that occurs in many proteins [*me*thyl + *thion-* (from Greek *theion* "sulfur") + [2]*-ine*]

meth·od \ˈmeth-əd\ *n* **1** : a way, technique, or process of or for doing something **2 a** : orderly arrangement, development, or classification : PLAN **b** : habitual regularity and orderliness [Latin *methodus,* from Greek *methodos,* from *meta-* + *hodos* "way"]

me·thod·i·cal \mə-ˈthäd-i-kəl\ *adj* **1** : arranged, characterized by, or performed with method or order **2** : habitually following a method : SYSTEMATIC — **me·thod·i·cal·ly** \-i-kə-lē, -klē\ *adv* — **me·thod·i·cal·ness** \-kəl-nəs\ *n*

Meth·od·ist \ˈmeth-əd-əst\ *n* : a member of one of the denominations deriving from the Wesleyan revival, accepting the possibility of salvation for all, having in the U.S. a modified episcopal government, and stressing personal and social morality — **Meth·od·ism** \-ə-ˌdiz-əm\ *n* — **Methodist** *adj*

meth·od·ize \ˈmeth-ə-ˌdīz\ *vt* : to reduce to method : SYSTEMATIZE

meth·od·ol·o·gy \ˌmeth-ə-ˈdäl-ə-jē\ *n, pl* **-gies** **1** : a body of methods and rules followed in a science or discipline **2** : the study of the principles or procedures of inquiry in a particular field — **meth·od·olog·i·cal** \ˌmeth-əd-l-ˈäj-i-kəl\ *adj* — **meth·od·ol·o·gist** \ˌmeth-ə-ˈdäl-ə-jəst\ *n*

meth·yl \ˈmeth-əl\ *n* **:** a chemical radical CH_3 consisting of carbon and hydrogen [back-formation from *methylene* "the radical CH_2," from French *méthylène,* from Greek *methy* "wine" + *hylē* "wood"]

methyl alcohol *n* **:** METHANOL

meth·y·lene blue \ˌmeth-ə-ˌlēn\ *n* **:** a basic dye used as a biological stain and as an antidote in cyanide poisoning

methyl orange *n* **:** a basic dye used as a chemical indicator

me·tic·u·lous \mə-ˈtik-yə-ləs\ *adj* **:** marked by extreme or excessive care in the consideration or treatment of details ⟨a *meticulous* researcher⟩ [Latin *meticulosus* "timid," from *metus* "fear"] ***synonyms*** see CAREFUL — **me·tic·u·lous·ly** *adv* — **me·tic·u·lous·ness** *n*

mé·tier *also* **me·tier** \mā-ˈtyā\ *n* **1 :** TRADE 2a **2 :** an area of activity in which one is an expert or successful **:** FORTE [French, derived from Latin *ministerium* "work, service," from *minister* "servant"]

mé·tis \mā-ˈtē, -ˈtēs\ *n, pl* **métis** \-ˈtē, -ˈtēs, -ˈtēz\ **:** a person of mixed blood; *esp, often cap* **:** the offspring of an American Indian and a person of European ancestry [French, derived from Latin *miscēre* "to mix"]

me·ton·y·my \mə-ˈtän-ə-mē\ *n, pl* **-mies :** a figure of speech in which the name of one thing is used for the name of another associated with or related to it (as "crown" in "lands belonging to the crown") [Latin *metonymia,* from Greek *metōnymia,* from *meta-* + *onyma* "name"] — **met·onym** \ˈmet-ə-ˌnim\ *n* — **met·onym·ic** \ˌmet-ə-ˈnim-ik\ *adj*

me–too \ˈmē-ˈtü\ *adj* **:** similar to or accepting successful or persuasive policies or practices used or promoted by someone else ⟨a *me-too* policy⟩ — **me–too·ism** \-ˌiz-əm\ *n*

me·tre *chiefly British variant of* METER

met·ric \ˈme-trik\ *adj* **1 :** of, relating to, or based on the metric system **2 :** METRICAL 1

-met·ric \ˈme-trik\ *or* **-met·ri·cal** \-tri-kəl\ *adj combining form* **1 :** of, employing, or obtained by (such) a meter ⟨baro*metric*⟩ **2 :** of or relating to (such) an art, process, or science of measuring ⟨titri*metric*⟩ ⟨geo*metrical*⟩

met·ri·cal \ˈme-tri-kəl\ *adj* **1 a :** of or relating to meter (as in poetry or music) **b :** arranged in meter ⟨*metrical* verse⟩ **2 :** of or relating to measurement — **met·ri·cal·ly** \-kə-lē, -klē\ *adv*

met·rics \ˈme-triks\ *n pl* **:** a part of prosody that deals with metrical structure

metric system *n* **:** a decimal system of weights and measures based on the meter as the unit of length and the kilogram as the unit of weight

metric ton *n* — see METRIC SYSTEM table

met·ro \ˈme-tro\ *n, pl* **metros :** SUBWAY 2 [French *métro,* short for *chemin de fer métropolitain* "metropolitan railroad"]

me·trol·o·gy \me-ˈträl-ə-jē\ *n* **:** the science of weights and measures or of measurements — **met·ro·log·i·cal** \ˌme-trə-ˈläj-i-kəl\ *adj*

met·ro·nome \ˈme-trə-ˌnōm\ *n* **:** an instrument designed to mark exact musical time by a regularly repeated tick [Greek *metron* "meter" + *-nomos* "controlling," from *nomos* "law"] — **met·ro·nom·ic** \ˌme-trə-ˈnäm-ik\ *adj* — **met·ro·nom·i·cal·ly** \-ˈnäm-i-kə-lē, -klē\ *adv*

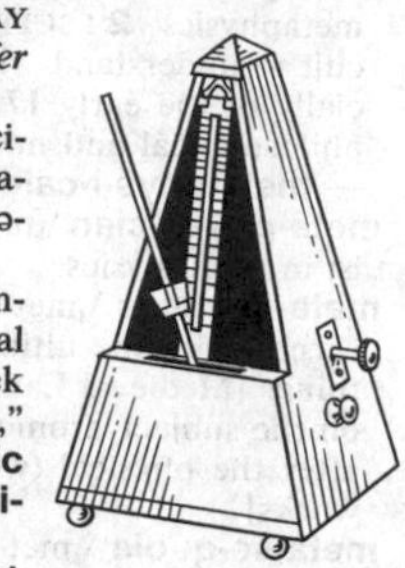
metronome

me·trop·o·lis \mə-ˈträp-ləs, -ə-ləs\ *n* **1 :** the city or state of origin of a colony (as

METRIC SYSTEM[1]

UNIT	ABBREVIATION	EQUIVALENT IN BASE UNIT	APPROXIMATE U.S. EQUIVALENT
		LENGTH	
kilometer	km	1,000 meters	0.62 mile
hectometer	hm	100 meters	328.08 feet
dekameter	dam	10 meters	32.81 feet
meter	m		39.37 inches
decimeter	dm	0.1 meter	3.94 inches
centimeter	cm	0.01 meter	0.39 inch
millimeter	mm	0.001 meter	0.039 inch
micrometer	μm	0.000001 meter	0.000039 inch
		AREA	
square kilometer	sq km *or* km^2	1,000,000 square meters	0.39 square mile
hectare	ha	10,000 square meters	2.47 acres
are	a	100 square meters	119.60 square yards
square centimeter	sq cm *or* cm^2	0.0001 square meter	0.16 square inch
		VOLUME	
cubic meter	m^3		1.31 cubic yards
cubic decimeter	dm^3	0.001 cubic meter	61.02 cubic inches
cubic centimeter	cu cm *or* cm^3 *also* cc	0.000001 cubic meter	0.061 cubic inch

CAPACITY

UNIT	ABBREVIATION	EQUIVALENT IN BASE UNIT	*cubic*	*dry*	*liquid*
kiloliter	kl	1,000 liters	1.31 cubic yards	28.38 bushels	264.17 gallons
hectoliter	hl	100 liters	3.53 cubic feet	2.84 bushels	26.42 gallons
dekaliter	dal	10 liters	0.35 cubic foot	1.14 pecks	2.64 gallons
liter	l		61.02 cubic inches	0.91 quart	1.06 quarts
cubic decimeter	dm^3	1 liter	61.02 cubic inches	0.91 quart	1.06 quarts
deciliter	dl	0.1 liter	6.10 cubic inches	0.18 pint	0.21 pint
centiliter	cl	0.01 liter	0.61 cubic inch		0.34 fluid ounce
milliliter	ml	0.001 liter	0.061 cubic inch		0.27 fluid dram

MASS AND WEIGHT

UNIT	ABBREVIATION	EQUIVALENT IN BASE UNIT	APPROXIMATE U.S. EQUIVALENT
metric ton	t	1,000,000 grams	1.10 short tons
kilogram	kg	1,000 grams	2.20 pounds
hectogram	hg	100 grams	3.53 ounces
dekagram	dag	10 grams	0.35 ounce
gram	g		0.035 ounce
decigram	dg	0.1 gram	1.54 grains
centigram	cg	0.01 gram	0.15 grain
milligram	mg	0.001 gram	0.015 grain

[1]For metric equivalents of U.S. units, see Measures and Weights table.

of ancient Greece) **2 :** the chief or capital city of a country, state, or region **3 a :** a city regarded as a center of a specified activity **b :** a large important city [Late Latin, from Greek *mētropolis,* from *mētēr* "mother" + *polis* "city"]

[1]**met·ro·pol·i·tan** \ˌme-trə-ˈpäl-ət-n\ *n* **1 :** the head of an ecclesiastical see **2 :** one who lives in a metropolis or who displays metropolitan manners or customs

[2]**metropolitan** *adj* **1 :** of or constituting a metropolitan or his see **2 :** of, relating to, or characteristic of a metropolis

-m·e·try \m-ə-trē\ *n combining form, pl* **-metries :** art, process, or science of measuring (something specified) ⟨photo*metry*⟩

met·tle \ˈmet-l\ *n* **1 :** quality of temperament or disposition **2 a :** vigor and strength of spirit : ARDOR **b :** staying quality : STAMINA [alteration of *metal*] — **on one's mettle :** eager and ready to do one's best

met·tle·some \-l-səm\ *adj* **:** full of mettle : SPIRITED

[1]**mew** \ˈmyü\ *n* **:** GULL; *esp* **:** a small gull of Eurasia and western North America [Old English *mǣw*]

[2]**mew** *n* **:** MEOW [Middle English *mewen*] — **mew** *vb*

[3]**mew** *n* **1 :** a cage for hawks **2** *pl, chiefly British* **a :** stables usually with living quarters built around a court **b :** a back street : ALLEY [Medieval French *mue,* from *muer* "to molt," from Latin *mutare* "to change"]

[4]**mew** *vt* **:** to shut up : CONFINE — often used with *up*

mewl \ˈmyül\ *vi* **:** to cry weakly : WHIMPER [imitative]

Mex·i·can \ˈmek-si-kən\ *n* **1 :** a native or inhabitant of Mexico **2 :** a person of Mexican descent — **Mexican** *adj*

Mexican bean beetle *n* **:** a spotted ladybug that is a garden pest which feeds on bean plants

Mexican jumping bean *n* **:** JUMPING BEAN

me·zu·zah *or* **me·zu·za** \mə-ˈzu̇z-ə\ *n, pl* **-zahs** *or* **-zas** *or* **-zot** \-ˌōt\ **:** a small parchment scroll inscribed with Deuteronomy 6:4–9 and 11:13–21 and the name Shaddai (the Almighty) and placed in a case fixed to the doorjamb by some Jewish families as a sign and reminder of their faith; *also* **:** such a scroll and its case [Hebrew *mĕzūzāh* "doorpost"]

mez·za·nine \ˈmez-n-ˌēn, ˌmez-n-ˈ\ *n* **1 :** a low story between two main stories of a building often projecting as a balcony **2 :** the lowest balcony in a theater or its first few rows [French, from Italian *mezzanino,* from *mezzano* "middle," from Latin *medianus* "middle, median"]

mez·zo for·te \ˌmet-sō-ˈfȯr-ˌtā, ˌmed-zō-, -ˈfȯrt-ē\ *adj or adv* **:** moderately loud — used as a direction in music [Italian, from *mezzo* "half, medium, middle"]

mez·zo pia·no \-pē-ˈän-ō\ *adj or adv* **:** moderately soft — used as a direction in music [Italian]

mez·zo–so·pra·no \-sə-ˈpran-ō, -ˈprän-\ *n* **:** a woman's voice with a range between that of the soprano and contralto; *also* **:** a singer having such a voice

mez·zo·tint \ˈmet-sō-ˌtint, ˈmed-zō-\ *n* **:** a process of engraving on copper or steel by scraping or burnishing a roughened surface to produce light and shade; *also* **:** an engraving produced by this process [Italian *mezzatinta,* from *mezza* (feminine of *mezzo* "medium") + *tinta* "tint"]

mho \ˈmō\ *n, pl* **mhos :** the unit of conductance equal to the reciprocal of the ohm [backward spelling of *ohm*]

mi \ˈmē\ *n* **:** the 3rd note of the diatonic scale [Medieval Latin]

mi·as·ma \mī-ˈaz-mə, mē-\ *n, pl* **-mas** *or* **-ma·ta** \-mət-ə\ **1 :** a vapor (as from a swamp) formerly believed to cause disease **2 :** an unhealthy or harmful influence or atmosphere ⟨the *miasma* of poverty⟩ [Greek, "defilement," from *miainein* "to pollute"] — **mi·as·mal** \-məl\ *adj* — **mi·as·mat·ic** \ˌmī-əz-ˈmat-ik\ *or* **mi·as·mic** \mī-ˈaz-mik, mē-\ *adj*

mic \ˈmīk\ *n* **:** MICROPHONE

mi·ca \ˈmī-kə\ *n* **:** any of various silicon-containing minerals that may be separated easily into thin transparent sheets [Latin, "grain, crumb"] — **mi·ca·ceous** \mī-ˈkā-shəs\ *adj*

Mi·cah \ˈmī-kə\ *n* **:** a prophetic book of canonical Jewish and Christian Scriptures — see BIBLE table

mice *plural of* MOUSE

mi·celle \mī-ˈsel\ *n* **1 :** an ordered region or structural unit in a fiber (as of cellulose) **2 :** a molecular aggregate that constitutes a colloidal particle [New Latin *micella,* from Latin *mica* "crumb"] — **mi·cel·lar** \-ˈsel-ər\ *adj*

Mich·ael·mas \ˈmik-əl-məs\ *n* **:** September 29 celebrated as the feast of St. Michael the Archangel [Old English *Michaeles mæsse* "Michael's mass"]

Michaelmas daisy *n* **:** a wild aster; *esp* **:** one blooming about Michaelmas

Mick·ey Finn \ˌmik-ē-ˈfin\ *n* **:** a drink of liquor doctored with a drug [probably from *Mickey* (Michael) *Finn,* flourished 1903, American saloon keeper who allegedly drugged his customers]

Mickey Mouse \-ˈmau̇s\ *adj* **1 :** not to be taken seriously ⟨a *Mickey Mouse* class⟩; *also* **:** WORTHLESS ⟨a *Mickey Mouse* lock⟩ **2 :** of little importance ⟨*Mickey Mouse* losses⟩ [*Mickey Mouse,* cartoon character created by Walt Disney]

Mic·mac \ˈmik-ˌmak\ *n, pl* **Micmac** *or* **Micmacs 1 :** a member of an American Indian people of eastern Canada **2 :** the Algonquian language of the Micmac people

micr- *or* **micro-** *combining form* **1 a :** small : minute ⟨*micro*film⟩ **b :** used for or involving minute quantities or variations ⟨*micro*scope⟩ **2 :** millionth ⟨*micro*second⟩ **3 :** using or used in microscopy ⟨*micro*projector⟩ [Greek *mikros*]

mi·cro \ˈmī-krō\ *adj* **:** MICROSCOPIC 3

mi·cro·am·pere \ˌmī-krō-ˈam-ˌpiər\ *n* **:** one millionth of an ampere

mi·crobe \ˈmī-ˌkrōb\ *n* **:** MICROORGANISM, GERM [*micr-* + Greek *bios* "life"] — **mi·cro·bi·al** \mī-ˈkrō-bē-əl\ *adj*

mi·cro·bi·ol·o·gy \ˌmī-krō-bī-ˈäl-ə-jē\ *n* **:** a branch of biology dealing especially with microscopic forms of life — **mi·cro·bi·o·log·i·cal** \-ˌbī-ə-ˈläj-i-kəl\ *also* **mi·cro·bi·o·log·ic** \-ˈläj-ik\ *adj* — **mi·cro·bi·o·log·i·cal·ly** \-i-kə-lē, -klē\ *adv* — **mi·cro·bi·ol·o·gist** \-bī-ˈäl-ə-jəst\ *n*

mi·cro·blog·ging \ˈmī-krō-ˌblȯ-ging, -ˌblä-\ *n* **:** blogging done with severe space or size constraints typically by posting frequent brief messages about personal activities

mi·cro·brew \ˈmī-krō-ˌbrü\ *n* **:** a beer produced by a microbrewery — **mi·cro·brewed** \-ˌbrüd\ *adj* — **mi·cro·brew·ing** \-ˌbrü-ing\ *n*

mi·cro·brew·ery \ˌmī-krō-ˈbrü-ə-rē, -ˈbru̇r-ē\ *n* **:** a small brewery making specialty beer in limited quantities — **mi·cro·brew·er** \ˈmī-krō-ˌbrü-ər, -ˌbru̇r\ *n*

mi·cro·burst \ˈmī-krō-ˌbərst\ *n* **:** a violent short-lived downdraft that creates wind shears at low altitudes

mi·cro·cap·sule \ˈmī-krō-ˌkap-səl, -sül\ *n* **:** a tiny capsule containing material (as a medicine) that is released when the capsule is broken, melted, or dissolved

mi·cro·chip \ˈmī-krō-ˌchip\ *n* **:** INTEGRATED CIRCUIT

mi·cro·cline \ˈmī-kro-ˌklīn\ *n* **:** a white to pale yellow, red, or green mineral $KAlSi_3O_8$ [German *Mikroklin,* from *mikr-* "micr-" + Greek *klinein* "to lean"]

mi·cro·coc·cus \ˌmī-krō-ˈkäk-əs\ *n, pl* **-coc·ci** \-ˈkäk-ˌsī, -ˌī\ **:** a small spherical bacterium

mi·cro·com·put·er \ˈmī-krō-kəm-ˌpyüt-ər\ *n* **1 :** PERSONAL COMPUTER **2 :** MICROPROCESSOR

mi·cro·cosm \ˈmī-krə-ˌkäz-əm\ *n* **:** a little world; *esp* **:** an individual or a community that is a miniature universe or a world in itself [Medieval Latin *microcosmus,* from Greek *mikros kosmos*] — **mi·cro·cos·mic** \ˌmī-krə-ˈkäz-mik\ *adj*

mi·cro·eco·nom·ics \ˌmī-krō-ˌek-ə-ˈnäm-iks, -ˌē-kə-\ *n* **:** study of economics in terms of individual areas of activity (as a firm, household, or prices) — compare MACROECONOMICS — **mi·cro·eco·nom·ic** \-ik\ *adj* — **mi·cro·econ·o·mist** \-i-ˈkän-ə-mist\ *n*

mi·cro·el·e·ment \ˌmī-krō-ˈel-ə-mənt\ *n* **:** TRACE ELEMENT

mi·cro·en·cap·su·lat·ed \-in-ˈkap-sə-ˌlāt-əd\ *adj* **:** enclosed in a microcapsule ⟨*microencapsulated* aspirin⟩ — **mi·cro·en·cap·su·la·tion** \-in-ˌkap-sə-ˈlā-shən\ *n*

mi·cro·en·ter·prise \-ˈen-tər-ˌprīz\ *n* **:** a very small business

mi·cro·far·ad \ˌmī-krō-ˈfar-ˌad, -ˈfar-əd\ *n* **:** one millionth of a farad

mi·cro·fi·ber \ˈmī-krō-ˌfī-bər\ *n* **:** a fine soft polyester fiber

mi·cro·fiche \ˈmī-krō-ˌfēsh, -ˌfish\ *n, pl* **-fiche** *or* **-fiches** \-ˌfēsh, -ˌfēsh-əz, -ˌfish, -ˌfish-əz\ **:** a sheet of microfilm containing rows of images usually of printed pages [French, from *micr-* "micr-" + *fiche* "peg, marker in a game, index card," from *ficher* "to stick in"]

mi·cro·fil·a·ment \ˌmī-krō-ˈfil-ə-mənt\ *n* **:** any of the very small actin-containing protein filaments in the cytoplasm of eukaryotic cells that function in maintaining cell structure and in movement within the cell

mi·cro·film \ˈmī-krə-ˌfilm\ *n* **:** a film bearing a photographic record on a greatly reduced scale of graphic matter (as printing) — **microfilm** *vb*

mi·cro·ga·mete \ˌmī-krō-gə-ˈmēt, -ˈgam-ˌēt\ *n* **:** the smaller and usually male gamete of an organism with two kinds of gametes — compare MACROGAMETE

mi·cro·gram \ˈmī-krə-ˌgram\ *n* **:** one millionth of a gram

mi·cro·graph \-ˌgraf\ *n* **:** a reproduction of the image of an object formed by a microscope

mi·cro·grav·i·ty \ˌmī-krə-ˈgrav-ət-ē\ *n* **:** a condition of weightlessness or of the near absence of gravity

mi·cro·groove \ˈmī-krō-ˈgrüv\ *n* **:** a minute closely spaced V-shaped groove used on long-playing phonograph records

mi·cro·me·te·or·ite \ˌmī-krō-ˈmē-tē-ə-ˌrīt\ *n* **:** a very small particle in space

[1]**mi·crom·e·ter** \mī-ˈkräm-ət-ər\ *n* **1 :** an instrument used with a telescope or microscope for measuring very small distances **2 :** MICROMETER CALIPER — **mi·crom·e·try** \-ə-trē\ *n*

[2]**mi·cro·me·ter** \ˈmī-krō-ˌmēt-ər\ *n* **:** a unit of length equal to one millionth of a meter — see METRIC SYSTEM table

mi·crom·e·ter caliper \mī-ˌkräm-ət-ər-\ *n* **:** a caliper having a spindle moved by a finely threaded screw for making precise measurements

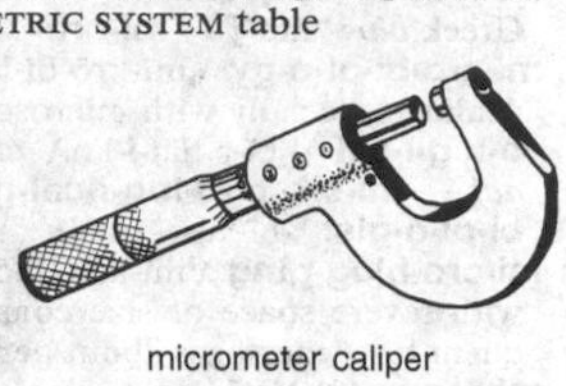

micrometer caliper

mi·cron \ˈmī-ˌkrän\ *n* **:** [2]MICROMETER [Greek *mikron,* neuter of *mikros* "small"]

Mi·cro·ne·sian \ˌmī-krə-ˈnē-zhən, -shən\ *n* **1 :** a native or inhabitant of Micronesia **2 :** a group of Austronesian languages spoken in the Micronesian islands — **Micronesian** *adj*

mi·cro·nu·cle·us \ˌmī-krō-ˈnü-klē-əs, -ˈnyü-\ *n* **:** a minute nucleus; *esp* **:** one concerned with reproductive and genetic functions in most ciliated protozoans

mi·cro·nu·tri·ent \-ˈnü-trē-ənt, -ˈnyü-\ *n* **1 :** TRACE ELEMENT **2 :** an organic compound (as a vitamin) essential in minute amounts to the growth and health of an animal

mi·cro·or·gan·ism \-ˈȯr-gə-ˌniz-əm\ *n* **:** an organism (as a bacterium) of microscopic or less than microscopic size

mi·cro·phone \ˈmī-krə-ˌfōn\ *n* **:** an instrument used to amplify, record, or transmit sounds

mi·cro·pho·to·graph \ˌmī-krə-ˈfōt-ə-ˌgraf\ *n* **1 :** a small photograph that is normally magnified for viewing **2 :** PHOTOMICROGRAPH

mi·cro·print \ˈmī-krə-ˌprint\ *n* **:** a photographic copy of printed or drawn matter in reduced size — **microprint** *vb*

mi·cro·pro·ces·sor \ˈmī-krō-ˌpräs-ˌes-ər, -ˌprōs-\ *n* **:** a cpu contained on an integrated-circuit chip

mi·cro·pro·jec·tor \ˌmī-krō-prə-ˈjek-tər\ *n* **:** a projector using a compound microscope to throw a greatly enlarged image of a microscopic object on a screen

mi·cro·pyle \ˈmī-krə-ˌpīl\ *n* **:** a tiny opening in an ovule of a seed plant through which the pollen tube penetrates to the embryo sac [*micr-* + Greek *pylē* "gate"] — **mi·cro·py·lar** \ˌmī-krə-ˈpī-lər\ *adj*

mi·cro·scope \ˈmī-krə-ˌskōp\ *n* **1 :** an optical instrument consisting of a lens or a combination of lenses for making enlarged images of minute objects **2 :** an instrument using radiations other than light for making enlarged images of minute objects

mi·cro·scop·ic \ˌmī-krə-ˈskäp-ik\ *also* **mi·cro·scop·i·cal** \-i-kəl\ *adj* **1 :** of, relating to, or conducted with the microscope or microscopy ⟨a *microscopic* examination⟩ **2 :** resembling a microscope especially in being able to see very tiny objects ⟨some insects have *microscopic* vision⟩ **3 :** able to be seen only through a microscope **:** very small ⟨a *microscopic* plant⟩ — **mi·cro·scop·i·cal·ly** \-ˈskäp-i-kə-lē, -klē\ *adv*

mi·cros·co·py \mī-ˈkräs-kə-pē\ *n* **:** the use of the microscope **:** investigation with the microscope — **mi·cros·co·pist** \-pəst\ *n*

mi·cro·sec·ond \ˌmī-krō-ˈsek-ənd, -ənt\ *n* **:** one millionth of a second

mi·cro·some \ˈmī-krə-ˌsōm\ *n* **:** a cellular particle that is obtained by centrifuging broken cells and that consists of various amounts of ribosomes, fragmented endoplasmic reticulum, and parts of mitochondria — **mi·cro·som·al** \ˌmī-krə-ˈsō-məl\ *adj*

mi·cro·sphere \ˈmī-krə-ˌsfiər\ *n* **:** a minute sphere ⟨a glass *microsphere* 30 micrometers in diameter⟩

mi·cro·spore \-ˌspōr, -ˌspȯr\ *n* **:** a plant spore that produces a male gametophyte

mi·cro·struc·ture \ˈmī-krō-ˌstrək-chər\ *n* **:** the microscopic structure of a material (as a mineral or body part)

mi·cro·sur·gery \ˌmī-krō-ˈsərj-rē, -ə-rē\ *n* **:** minute dissection or manipulation of living structures (as cells) for surgical or experimental purposes

mi·cro·tome \ˈmī-krə-ˌtōm\ *n* **:** an instrument for cutting sections (as of plant or animal tissues) for microscopic examination [*micr-* + Greek *tomos* "section," from *temnein* "to cut"]

mi·cro·tu·bule \ˌmī-krō-ˈtü-byül, -ˈtyü-\ *n* **:** any of the minute tubes in the cytoplasm of eukaryotic cells that are composed of protein and form an important part of cell structure, the mitotic spindle, cilia, and flagella

[1]**mi·cro·wave** \-ˌwāv\ *n* **1 :** a radio wave between one millimeter and one meter in wavelength **2 :** MICROWAVE OVEN

[2]**microwave** *vt* **:** to cook or heat in a microwave oven — **mi·cro·wav·able** *or* **mi·cro·wave·able** \ˌmī-krə-ˈwā-və-bəl\ *adj*

microwave oven *n* **:** an oven in which food is cooked by the heat produced as a result of penetration of the food by microwaves

mic·tu·rate \ˈmik-chə-ˌrāt, ˈmik-tə-\ *vi* **:** URINATE [Latin *micturire*] — **mic·tu·ri·tion** \ˌmik-chə-ˈrish-ən, ˌmik-tə-\ *n*

[1]**mid** \ˈmid\ *adj* **1 :** being the part in the middle or midst ⟨in *mid* ocean⟩ ⟨*mid*-August⟩ **2 :** occupying a middle position ⟨the *mid* finger⟩ **3 :** uttered with the tongue midway between its highest and its lowest elevation ⟨the *mid* vowel \e\ in pet⟩ [Old English *midde*]

[2]**mid** \mid, ˌmid\ *prep* **:** AMID

mid·brain \ˈmid-ˌbrān\ *n* **:** the middle division of the embryonic vertebrate brain or the corresponding part of the adult brain that contains the optic lobes and is situated between the forebrain and hindbrain

mid·course \-ˈkōrs, -ˈkȯrs\ *adj* **:** being or occurring in the middle part of a course (as of a spacecraft) ⟨a *midcourse* correction⟩

mid·day \ˈmid-ˌdā, -ˈdā\ *n* **:** the middle of the day — **midday** *adj*

mid·den \ˈmid-n\ *n* **:** a refuse heap; *esp* **:** KITCHEN MIDDEN [of Scandinavian origin]

[1]**mid·dle** \ˈmid-l\ *adj* **1 :** equally distant from the extremes **:** CENTRAL ⟨the *middle* house in the row⟩ **2 :** being at neither extreme **:** INTERMEDIATE ⟨of *middle* size⟩ **3** *cap* **:** constituting an intermediate division or period ⟨*Middle* Paleozoic⟩ ⟨*Middle* Dutch⟩ [Old English *middel*]

[2]**middle** *n* **1 :** a middle part, point, or position **2 :** WAIST 1a **3 :** the position of being among or in the midst of something ⟨in the *middle* of the crowd⟩ — **middle of nowhere :** an extremely remote and isolated place ⟨ran out of gas in the *middle of nowhere*⟩

middle age *n* **:** the period of life from about 45 to about 64 — **mid·dle–aged** \ˌmid-l-ˈājd\ *adj*

Middle Ages *n pl* **:** the period of European history from about A.D. 500 to about 1500

mid·dle·brow \ˈmid-l-ˌbrau̇\ *n* **:** a person who is moderately but not highly educated and refined — **middlebrow** *adj*

middle C *n* **:** the note designated by the first ledger line below the treble staff and the first above the bass staff

middle–class *adj* **:** of or relating to the middle class; *esp* **:** characterized by a fairly high material standard of living, sexual morality, and respect for property

middle class *n* **:** a social class occupying a position between the upper class and the lower class; *esp* **:** a fluid socioeconomic grouping composed principally of business and professional people, bureaucrats, and some farmers and skilled workers sharing common social characteristics and values

middle distance *n* **:** a part of a picture or scene between the foreground and the background

middle ear *n* **:** a small membrane-lined cavity that is separated from the outer ear by the eardrum and that transmits sound waves from the eardrum to the inner ear through a chain of tiny bones

Middle English *n* **:** the English language of the 12th to 15th centuries

middle finger *n* **:** the third digit of the hand if the thumb is counted as the first

Middle French *n* **:** the French language of the 14th to 16th centuries

Middle Greek *n* **:** the Greek language used in the 7th to 15th centuries

middle ground *n* **1 :** a standpoint or area midway between extreme or opposing positions, options, or objectives **2 :** MIDDLE DISTANCE

Middle High German *n* **:** the High German in use from about 1100 to 1500

middle lamella *n* **:** a layer of sticky material between the walls of adjacent plant cells that helps to hold them together

mid·dle·man \ˈmid-l-ˌman\ *n* **:** an agent between two parties; *esp* **:** a dealer, agent, or company intermediate between the producer of goods and the retailer or the consumer

middle name *n* **1 :** a name between one's first name and last name **2 :** a term that denotes a notable quality of a person ⟨patience is her *middle name*⟩

mid·dle–of–the–road \ˌmid-l-əv-t͟hə-ˈrōd, -ə-t͟hə-\ *adj* **:** standing for or following a course of action midway between extremes; *esp* **:** being neither liberal nor conservative in politics — **mid·dle–of–the–road·er** \-ˈrōd-ər\ *n*

Middle Passage *n* **:** the forced voyage of enslaved Africans across the Atlantic Ocean to the Americas

middle school *n* **:** a school usually including grades 5–8 or 6–8

mid·dle·weight \ˈmid-l-ˌwāt\ *n* **:** one of average weight; *esp* **:** a boxer in a weight division having an upper limit of about 160 pounds

[1]**mid·dling** \ˈmid-ling, -lən\ *adj* **1 :** of middle, medium, or moderate size, degree, or quality **2 :** MEDIOCRE **3 :** of, relating to, or being a middle class — **middling** *adv* — **mid·dling·ly** *adv*

[2]**middling** *n* **1 :** any of various commodities of medium quality or size **2** *pl* **:** a granular product of grain milling; *esp* **:** a wheat milling by-product used in animal feeds

mid·dy \ˈmid-ē\ *n, pl* **mid·dies 1 :** MIDSHIPMAN **2 :** a loosely fitting blouse with a collar that is wide and square at the back

mid·field \ˈmid-ˌfēld\ *n* **1 :** the middle portion of a field **2 :** the players on a team (as in lacrosse or soccer) that normally play in the midfield

mid·field·er \-ˌfēl-dər\ *n* **:** a member of a midfield

midge \ˈmij\ *n* **:** a very small fly **:** GNAT [Old English *mycg*]

midg·et \ˈmij-ət\ *n* **1 :** something (as an animal) much smaller than usual **2** *sometimes offensive* **:** a very small person [*midge*] — **midget** *adj*

mid·gut \ˈmid-ˌgət\ *n* **:** the middle part of an alimentary canal

mid·land \ˈmid-lənd, -ˌland\ *n* **1 :** the interior or central region of a country **2** *cap* **:** the dialect of English spoken in southern New Jersey; northern Delaware and Maryland; central and southern Pennsylvania, Ohio, Indiana, and Illinois; the Appalachian Mountain regions of Virginia, North Carolina, South Carolina, and Georgia; and Tennessee, Kentucky, and West Virginia — **midland** *adj, often cap*

mid·life \-ˈlīf\ *n* **:** MIDDLE AGE — **midlife** *adj*

mid·line \-ˌlīn\ *n* **:** a median line or plane; *esp* **:** one through a body or one of its parts that lies in a plane dividing it into halves that are mirror images of each other

mid·most \ˈmid-ˌmōst\ *adj* **1 :** being in or near the exact middle **2 :** most intimate **:** INNERMOST — **midmost** *adv or n*

mid·night \-ˌnīt\ *n* **:** the middle of the night; *esp* **:** 12 o'clock at night — **midnight** *adj* — **mid·night·ly** \-lē\ *adv or adj*

midnight sun *n* **:** the sun above the horizon at midnight in the arctic or antarctic summer

mid–ocean ridge \ˈmid-ˈō-shən-\ *n* **:** a raised area with a central valley on an ocean floor occurring at a boundary between two diverging tectonic plates where new crust is formed from magma rising from earth's interior

mid·point \ˈmid-ˌpȯint\ *n* **:** a point at or near the center or middle

mid·rib \-ˌrib\ *n* **:** the central vein of a leaf

mid·riff \-ˌrif\ *n* **1 :** DIAPHRAGM 1 **2 :** the middle region of the human torso [Old English *midhrif,* from *midde* "mid" + *hrif* "belly"]

mid·ship·man \ˈmid-ˌship-mən, mid-ˈship-\ *n* **:** one in training for a naval commission **:** a student naval officer

mid·ships \ˈmid-ˌships\ *adv* **:** AMIDSHIPS

mid·size \ˈmid-ˌsīz\ *adj* **:** of intermediate size ⟨a *midsize* car⟩

[1]**midst** \ˈmidst\ *n* **1 :** the interior or central part or point **:** MIDDLE ⟨in the *midst* of the forest⟩ **2 :** a position among the members of a group ⟨a visitor in our *midst*⟩ **3 :** the condition of being surrounded or beset ⟨in the *midst* of troubles⟩ [Middle English *middest,* alteration of *middes,* from *amiddes* "amid"]

[2]**midst** \midst, ˌmidst\ *prep* **:** AMID

mid·stream \ˈmid-ˈstrēm\ *n* **:** the middle of a stream

mid·sum·mer \ˈmid-ˈsəm-ər\ *n* **1 :** the middle of summer **2 :** the summer solstice

[1]**mid·way** \ˈmid-ˌwā, -ˈwā\ *adv or adj* **:** in the middle of the way or distance **:** HALFWAY

[2]**mid·way** \-ˌwā\ *n* **:** an avenue at a fair, carnival, or amusement park for concessions and light amusements [*Midway (Plaisance),* Chicago, site of the amusement section of the Columbian Exposition of 1893]

mid·week \ˈmid-ˌwēk\ *n* **:** the middle of the week — **midweek** *adj* — **mid·week·ly** \-lē\ *adj or adv*

mid·wife \ˈmid-ˌwīf\ *n* **:** a woman who helps other women in childbirth [Middle English *midwif,* from *mid* "with" (from Old English) + *wif* "woman"]

mid·wife·ry \mid-ˈwif-rē, -ə-rē; ˈmid-ˌwīf-\ *n* **:** the art or act of assisting at childbirth; *also* **:** OBSTETRICS

mid·win·ter \ˈmid-ˈwint-ər\ *n* **1 :** the middle of winter **2 :** the winter solstice

mid·year \-ˌyiər\ *n* **1 :** the middle of an academic or a calendar year **2 :** a midyear examination — **midyear** *adj*

mien \ˈmēn\ *n* **:** look, appearance, or bearing especially as showing mood or personality ⟨a kindly *mien*⟩ [derived from [1]*demean*]

[1]**miff** \ˈmif\ *n* **1 :** a fit of ill humor **2 :** a trivial quarrel [origin unknown]

[2]**miff** *vt* **:** to put into an ill humor **:** OFFEND ⟨was *miffed* by their behavior⟩

[1]**might** \mīt, ˈmīt\ *past of* MAY — used as an auxiliary verb to express permission ⟨asked if they *might* leave⟩, probability ⟨I *might* go, if urged⟩, possibility in the past ⟨thought you *might* try⟩, or a present condition contrary to fact ⟨if you were older, you *might* understand⟩ [Old English *meahte, mihte*]

[2]**might** \ˈmīt\ *n* **:** power to do something **:** FORCE ⟨the nation's *might*⟩ [Old English *miht*]

might·i·ly \ˈmīt-l-ē\ *adv* **1 :** in a mighty manner **:** VIGOROUSLY **2 :** very much

mightn't \ˈmīt-nt\ **:** might not

[1]**mighty** \ˈmīt-ē\ *adj* **might·i·er; -est 1 :** having might **:** POWERFUL, STRONG ⟨a *mighty* army⟩ **2 :** done by might **:** showing great power ⟨*mighty* deeds⟩ **3 :** great or imposing in size or extent ⟨a *mighty* famine⟩ — **might·i·ness** *n*

[2]**mighty** *adv* **:** VERY, EXTREMELY ⟨a *mighty* strong smell⟩

mi·gnon·ette \ˌmin-yə-ˈnet\ *n* **:** a garden plant with long spikes of small fragrant greenish white flowers [French *mignonnette*]

mi·graine \ˈmī-ˌgrān\ *n* **:** a condition marked by recurrent severe headache often restricted to one side of the head and accompanied by nausea and vomiting; *also* **:** an episode or attack of migraine [French, from Late Latin *hemicrania* "pain on one side of the head," from Greek *hēmikrania,* from *hēmi-* "hemi-" + *kranion* "cranium"] — **mi·grain·ous** \-ˌgrā-nəs\ *adj*

mi·grant \ˈmī-grənt\ *n* **:** a person, animal, or plant that migrates — **migrant** *adj*

mi·grate \ˈmī-ˌgrāt\ *vi* **1 :** to move from one country, place, or locality to another **2 :** to pass usually periodically from one region or climate to another for feeding or breeding **3 :** to change position or location in an organism or substance ⟨parasitic worms *migrating* from the lungs to the liver⟩ [Latin *migrare*] — **mi·gra·tion** \mī-ˈgrā-shən\ *n* — **mi·gra·tion·al** \-shnəl, -shən-l\ *adj*

mi·gra·to·ry \ˈmī-grə-ˌtōr-ē, -ˌtȯr-\ *adj* **:** of, relating to, or characterized by migration ⟨*migratory* birds⟩

mi·ka·do \mə-ˈkäd-ō\ *n, pl* **-dos :** an emperor of Japan [Japanese]

mike \ˈmīk\ *n* **:** MICROPHONE [by shortening and alteration]

mil \ˈmil\ *n* **:** a unit of length equal to 1/1000 inch (about .025 millimeter) used especially in measuring thickness [Latin *mille* "thousand"]

mi·lady \mil-ˈād-ē, in the United States also mī-ˈlād-\ *n* **1 :** an Englishwoman of noble or gentle birth **2 :** a woman of fashion [French, from English *my lady*]

milch \ˈmilk, ˈmilch, ˈmilks\ *adj* **:** MILK ⟨a *milch* cow⟩ [Old English *-milce*]

mild \ˈmīld\ *adj* **1 :** gentle in nature or behavior ⟨a *mild* disposition⟩ **2 a :** moderate in action or effect **:** not strong ⟨a *mild* drug⟩ **b :** not sharp, spicy, or bitter ⟨a *mild* cheese⟩ **3 :** not severe : TEMPERATE ⟨*mild* weather⟩ [Old English *milde*] — **mild·ly** \ˈmīld-lē, ˈmīl-\ *adv* — **mild·ness** \ˈmīld-nəs, ˈmīl-\ *n*

[1]**mil·dew** \ˈmil-ˌdü, -ˌdyü\ *n* : a superficial usually whitish growth produced on organic matter or living plants by fungi; *also* : a fungus producing mildew [Old English *meledēaw* "honeydew"] — **mil·dewy** \-ē\ *adj*

[2]**mildew** *vb* : to affect with or become affected with mildew

mile \ˈmīl\ *n* **1** : a unit of measure equal to 5280 feet (about 1609 meters) — called also *statute mile*; see MEASURE table **2** : NAUTICAL MILE [Old English *mīl,* from Latin *milia* "miles," from *milia passuum,* literally, "thousands of paces"]

mile·age \ˈmī-lij\ *n* **1** : an allowance for traveling expenses at a set rate per mile **2** : distance or length in miles **3 a** : the number of miles that something (as a car or tire) will travel before wearing out **b** : the average number of miles a vehicle will travel on a gallon of gasoline **4** : USEFULNESS, PROFIT ⟨gets a lot of *mileage* out of that old joke⟩

mile·post \ˈmīl-ˌpōst\ *n* : a post indicating the distance in miles from or to a stated place

mil·er \ˈmī-lər\ *n* : a person or a horse that competes in mile races

mile·stone \ˈmīl-ˌstōn\ *n* **1** : a stone serving as a milepost **2** : an important point in progress or development

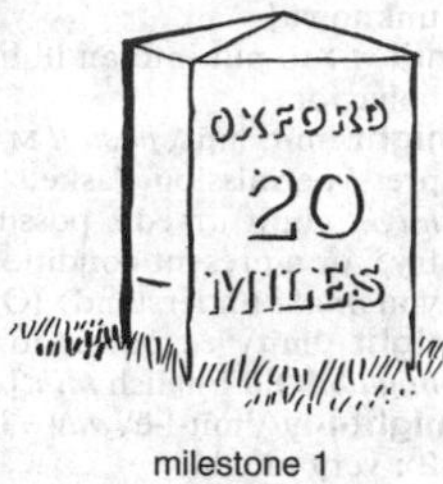

milestone 1

mil·foil \ˈmil-ˌfȯil\ *n* **1** : YARROW **2** : WATER MILFOIL [Medieval French, from Latin *millefolium,* from *mille* "thousand" + *folium* "leaf"]

mi·lieu \mēl-ˈyər, ˈmēl-ˌyü; mē-ˈlyœ\ *n, pl* **milieus** *or* **mi·lieux** *same or* -ˈyərz, -ˌyüz, -ˈlyœz\ : ENVIRONMENT 1 [French]

mil·i·tant \ˈmil-ə-tənt\ *adj* **1** : engaged in warfare **2** : aggressively active especially in a cause ⟨a *militant* conservationist⟩ — **mil·i·tan·cy** \-tən-sē\ *n* — **militant** *n* — **mil·i·tant·ly** *adv* — **mil·i·tant·ness** *n*

mil·i·ta·rism \ˈmil-ə-tə-ˌriz-əm\ *n* **1 a** : control or domination by a military class **b** : glorification of military virtues and ideals **2** : a policy of aggressive military preparedness — **mil·i·ta·rist** \-rəst\ *n* — **mil·i·ta·ris·tic** \ˌmil-ə-tə-ˈris-tik\ *adj* — **mil·i·ta·ris·ti·cal·ly** \-ˈris-ti-kə-lē,-klē\ *adv*

mil·i·ta·rize \ˈmil-ə-tə-ˌrīz\ *vt* **1** : to equip with military forces and defenses **2** : to give a military character to — **mil·i·ta·ri·za·tion** \ˌmil-ə-tə-rə-ˈzā-shən, -trə-ˈzā-\ *n*

[1]**mil·i·tary** \ˈmil-ə-ˌter-ē\ *adj* **1** : of, relating to, or characteristic of soldiers, arms, or war ⟨*military* drill⟩ **2** : carried on or supported by armed force ⟨*military* dictatorship⟩ **3** : of or relating to the army ⟨*military* and naval affairs⟩ [Latin *militaris,* from *milit-, miles* "soldier"] ***synonyms*** see MARTIAL — **mil·i·tar·i·ly** \ˌmil-ə-ˈter-ə-lē\ *adv*

[2]**military** *n, pl* **military** **1** : ARMED FORCES **2** : military persons; *esp* : army officers

military police *n* : a branch of an army that performs guard and police functions

mil·i·tate \ˈmil-ə-ˌtāt\ *vi* : to have an influence or effect ⟨factors *militating* against the success of an enterprise⟩ [Latin *militare* "to engage in warfare," from *milit-, miles* "soldier"]

mi·li·tia \mə-ˈlish-ə\ *n* : a body of citizens with military training who are called to active duty only in an emergency [Latin, "military service," from *milit-, miles* "soldier"] — **mi·li·tia·man** \-mən\ *n*

[1]**milk** \ˈmilk\ *n* **1** : a fluid secreted by the mammary glands of females for the nourishment of their young; *esp* : cow's milk used as food by humans **2** : a liquid (as the juice of a coconut) resembling milk [Old English *meolc, milc*]

[2]**milk** *vb* **1** : to draw milk from the breasts or udder of **2** : to draw or yield milk ⟨return in time for *milking*⟩ **3** : to draw something from as if by milking ⟨*milk* snakes for their venom⟩; *esp* : to draw unreasonable or excessive profit or advantage from ⟨*milk* a business⟩ — **milk·er** *n*

[3]**milk** *adj* : giving milk; *esp* : bred or suitable for milk production ⟨*milk* cows⟩

milk chocolate *n* : chocolate containing ground cacao beans, cocoa butter, and milk from which no solids (as of sugar or fat) have been removed

milk–liv·ered \ˈmil-ˈkliv-ərd\ *adj, archaic* : COWARDLY 1

milk·maid \ˈmilk-ˌmād\ *n* : DAIRYMAID

milk·man \-ˌman, -mən\ *n* : a person who sells or delivers milk

milk of magnesia : a milky white liquid preparation of magnesium hydroxide in water used as a laxative and antacid

milk shake *n* : a drink made of milk, a flavoring syrup, and often ice cream shaken or mixed thoroughly

milk snake *n* : a common harmless gray or tan snake with black-bordered brown blotches and an arrow-shaped spot on the head; *also* : KING SNAKE

milk·sop \ˈmilk-ˌsäp\ *n* : a timid unmanly man or boy

milk sugar *n* : LACTOSE

milk tooth *n* : one of the first temporary teeth of a young mammal that in humans number 20 — called also *baby tooth, deciduous tooth*

milk·weed \ˈmil-ˌkwēd\ *n* : any of various herbs with milky juice and flowers usually in dense clusters

milkweed

milky \ˈmil-kē\ *adj* **milk·i·er; -est** **1** : resembling milk in color or consistency **2** : TAME 3, TIMID **3** : consisting of, containing, or full of milk — **milk·i·ness** *n*

milky disease *n* : a destructive bacterial disease of some beetle grubs used especially in the control of Japanese beetles — called also *milky spore disease*

Milky Way *n* **1** : a broad luminous irregular band of light that stretches across the sky and is caused by the light of a vast multitude of faint stars **2** : MILKY WAY GALAXY

Milky Way galaxy *n* : the galaxy of which the sun and the solar system are a part and which contains the many stars that create the light of the Milky Way

[1]**mill** \ˈmil\ *n* **1** : a building with machinery for grinding grain into flour **2** : a machine used in treating (as by grinding, crushing, stamping, cutting, or finishing) raw material **3** : a building or group of buildings with machinery for manufacturing [Old English *mylen,* from Late Latin *molina,* derived from Latin *mola* "millstone, mill"] — **through the mill** : through a difficult experience

[2]**mill** *vb* **1** : to subject to an operation or process in a mill: as **a** : to grind into flour, meal, or powder **b** : to shape or dress by means of a rotary cutter **c** : to mix and condition (as rubber) by passing between rotating rolls **2** : to give a raised rim or a corrugated edge to (a coin) **3** : to hit out hard with the fists **4** : to move about in a disorderly mass ⟨guests *milling* about the hotel lobby⟩ **5** : to undergo milling

[3]**mill** *n* : one tenth of a cent [Latin *mille* "thousand"]

mill·dam \ˈmil-ˌdam\ *n* : a dam to make a millpond; *also* : MILLPOND

mil·le·nar·i·an \ˌmil-ə-ˈner-ē-ən\ *adj* **1** : of or relating to 1000 years **2** : of or relating to belief in the millennium — **millenarian** *n* — **mil·le·nar·i·an·ism** \-ē-ə-ˌniz-əm\ *n*

mil·le·nary \ˈmil-ə-ˌner-ē, mə-ˈlen-ə-rē\ *n, pl* **-nar·ies** **1** : a thousand units or things **2** : 1000 years : MILLENNIUM [Late Latin *millenarium,* derived from Latin *mille* "thousand"] — **millenary** *adj*

mil·len·ni·um \mə-ˈlen-ē-əm\ *n, pl* **-nia** \-ē-ə\ *or* **-ni·ums** **1 a** : a period of 1000 years **b** : a 1000th anniversary or its celebration **2** : a period of great happiness or of perfection in human existence [Latin *mille* "thousand" + *-ennium* (as in *biennium*)] — **mil·len·ni·al** \-ē-əl\ *adj*

mill·er \ˈmil-ər\ *n* **1** : one that operates a mill; *esp* : one that grinds grain into flour **2** : any of various moths whose wings are covered with powdery dust

mil·let \ˈmil-ət\ *n* **1** : any of several small-seeded annual cereal and forage grasses; *esp* : one with small shiny whitish seeds **2** : the seed of a millet [Medieval French *milet,* from *mil,* from Latin *milium*]

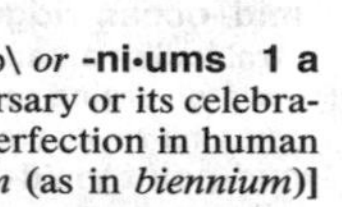
millet 1

milli- *combining form* : thousandth ⟨*milli*ampere⟩ [Latin *mille* "thousand"]

mil·li·amp \ˈmil-ē-ˌamp\ *n* : MILLIAMPERE

mil·li·am·pere \ˌmil-ē-ˈam-ˌpiər\ *n* : one thousandth of an ampere

mil·liard \ˈmil-ˌyärd, ˈmil-ē-ˌärd\ *n, British* : a thousand millions — see NUMBER table [French, derived from Latin *mille* "thousand"]

mil·li·bar \ˈmil-ə-ˌbär\ *n* : a unit used in measuring atmospheric pressure equal to $\frac{1}{1000}$ bar or 100 pascals [*bar,* unit of pressure equal to one million dynes per square centimeter, derived from Greek *baros* "weight"]

mil·li·gram \ˈmil-ə-ˌgram\ *n* — see METRIC SYSTEM table

mil·li·li·ter \ˈmil-ə-ˌlēt-ər\ *n* — see METRIC SYSTEM table

mil·li·me·ter \ˈmil-ə-ˌmēt-ər\ *n* — see METRIC SYSTEM table

mil·li·mi·cron \ˌmil-ə-ˈmī-ˌkrän\ *n* : NANOMETER

mil·li·ner \ˈmil-ə-nər\ *n* : a person who makes or sells women's hats [derived from *Milan,* Italy; from the importation of women's finery into England from Italy in the 16th century]

mil·li·nery \ˈmil-ə-ˌner-ē\ *n* **1** : women's hats **2** : the business or work of a milliner

mill·ing \ˈmil-ing\ *n* : a corrugated edge on a coin

milling machine *n* : a machine tool on which work usually of metal is secured to a carriage and shaped by being fed against rotating cutters

mil·lion \ˈmil-yən, ˈmi-yən\ *n, pl* **millions** *or* **million** **1** : one thousand times one thousand; *also* : a symbol representing this — see NUMBER table **2** : a very large or indefinitely great number ⟨*millions* of mosquitoes⟩ [Medieval French *milion,* from Italian *milione,* from *mille* "thousand," from Latin] — **million** *adj* — **mil·lionth** \-yənth, -yəntth\ *adj or n*

mil·lion·aire \ˌmil-yə-ˈnaər, -ˈneər, ˈmil-yə-ˌ, ˌmi-yə-ˈ, ˈmi-yə-ˌ\ *n* : one whose wealth is estimated at a million or more (as of dollars) [French *millionnaire,* from *million* "million," from Medieval French *milion*]

mil·li·pede *or* **mil·le·pede** \ˈmil-ə-ˌpēd\ *n* : any of a class (Diplopoda) of arthropods having a long usually cylindrical segmented body with a hard covering, two pairs of legs on most apparent segments, and unlike the related centipedes no poison fangs [Latin *millipeda,* "a small crawling animal," from *mille* "thousand" + *ped-, pes* "foot"]

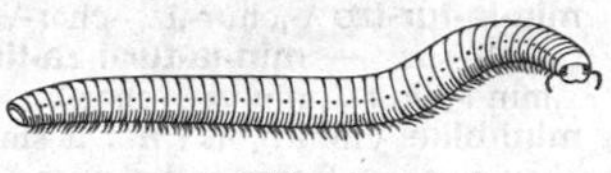

millipede

mil·li·sec·ond \ˈmil-ə-ˌsek-ənd\ *n* : one thousandth of a second

mil·li·volt \-ˌvōlt\ *n* : one thousandth of a volt

mill·pond \ˈmil-ˌpänd\ *n* : a pond produced by damming a stream to produce a head of water for operating a mill

mill·race \-ˌrās\ *n* : a canal in which water flows to and from a mill wheel; *also* : the current that drives the wheel

mill·stone \-ˌstōn\ *n* **1** : either of two circular stones used for grinding a substance (as grain) **2 a** : something that grinds or crushes **b** : a heavy burden

mill·stream \-ˌstrēm\ *n* **1** : a stream whose flow is utilized to run a mill **2** : the stream in a millrace

mill wheel *n* : a waterwheel that drives a mill

mill·wright \ˈmil-ˌrīt\ *n* : one whose occupation is planning and building mills or setting up their machinery

mi·lo \ˈmī-lō\ *n, pl* **milos** : a small usually early and drought-resistant grain sorghum [of Bantu origin]

mi·lord \mil-ˈȯr, -ˈȯrd\ *n* : an Englishman of noble or gentle birth [French, from English *my lord*]

milt \ˈmilt\ *n* : the sperm-containing fluid of fishes [probably from Dutch *milte*]

Mil·ton·ic \mil-ˈtän-ik\ *or* **Mil·to·ni·an** \mil-ˈtō-nē-ən\ *adj* : of, relating to, or characteristic of John Milton or his work

¹mime \ˈmīm *also* ˈmēm\ *n* **1 a** : an actor of mime **b** : MIMIC 2 **2** : an ancient play or skit representing scenes from life usually in a ridiculous manner **3** : the art of portraying a character or of narration by body movement : PANTOMIME [Latin *mimus,* from Greek *mimos*]

²mime *vb* **1** : to act as a mime : play a part with gesture and action usually without words **2** : to imitate closely : MIMIC **3** : to act out in the manner of a mime

mim·eo·graph \ˈmim-ē-ə-ˌgraf\ *n* : a machine for making copies of typewritten or written matter by means of a stencil [from *Mimeograph,* a former trademark] — **mimeograph** *vb*

mi·me·sis \mə-ˈmē-səs, mī-\ *n* : IMITATION 1, MIMICRY [Late Latin, from Greek *mimēsis,* from *mimeisthai* "to imitate"]

mi·met·ic \-ˈmet-ik\ *adj* **1** : IMITATIVE 2 **2** : relating to, characterized by, or exhibiting mimicry ⟨*mimetic* coloring of a butterfly⟩ [Late Latin *mimeticus,* from Greek *mimētikos,* from *mimeisthai* "to imitate"] — **mi·met·i·cal·ly** \-ˈmet-i-kə-lē, -klē\ *adv*

¹mim·ic \ˈmim-ik\ *n* **1** : MIME 1a **2** : one that mimics

²mimic *adj* **1 a** : IMITATIVE 2 **b** : IMITATION, MOCK ⟨*mimic* battle⟩ **2** : of or relating to mime or mimicry [Latin *mimicus,* from Greek *mimikos,* from *mimos* "mime"]

³mimic *vt* **mim·icked** \ˈmim-ikt\; **mim·ick·ing** **1** : to imitate closely : APE **2** : to ridicule by imitation **3** : SIMULATE **4** : to resemble by biological mimicry ***synonyms*** see IMITATE

mim·ic·ry \ˈmim-i-krē\ *n, pl* **-ries** **1** : the action, art, or an instance of mimicking **2** : a superficial resemblance of one organism to another or to natural objects among which it lives that secures it a selective advantage (as concealment or protection from predators)

mi·mo·sa \mə-ˈmō-sə, mī-, -zə\ *n* : any of a genus of trees, shrubs, and herbs of the legume family that are found in warm regions and produce small white or pink flowers in ball-shaped heads [derived from Latin *mimus* "mime"]

mi·na \ˈmī-nə\ *n* : an ancient unit of weight and value equal to $\frac{1}{60}$ talent [Latin, from Greek *mna,* of Semitic origin]

min·a·ret \ˌmin-ə-ˈret, ˈmin-ə-ˌ\ *n* : a tall slender tower of a mosque from a balcony of which the people are called to prayer [French, from Turkish *minare,* from Arabic *manārah* "lighthouse"]

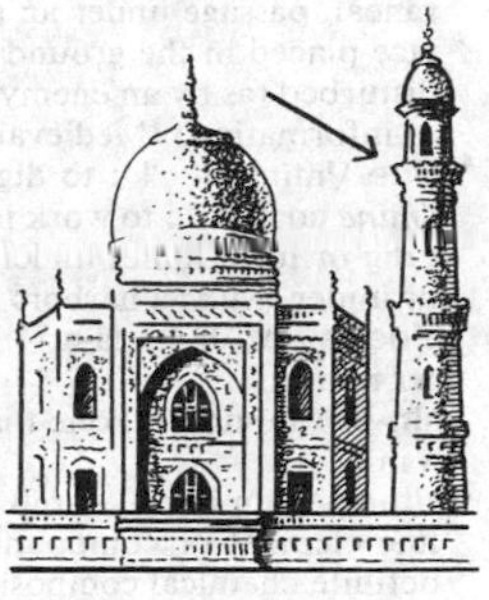

minaret

mi·na·to·ry \ˈmin-ə-ˌtōr-ē, ˈmī-nə-, -ˌtȯr-\ *adj* : having a menacing quality : THREATENING [Late Latin *minatorius,* from Latin *minari* "to threaten"]

¹mince \ˈmins\ *vb* **1** : to cut into very small pieces **2** : to utter with affectation **3** : to avoid being plainspoken in the use of (words) ⟨don't *mince* words with me⟩ **4** : to walk with short steps in a prim affected manner [Medieval French *mincer,* from Latin *minutia* "smallness," from *minutus* "minute"] — **minc·er** *n*

²mince *n* : small bits into which something is chopped; *esp* : MINCEMEAT

mince·meat \ˈmin-ˌsmēt\ *n* **1** : minced meat **2** : a finely chopped mixture of ingredients (as raisins, apples, or spices) with or without meat

minc·ing \ˈmin-sing\ *adj* : affectedly dainty or delicate — **minc·ing·ly** \-sing-lē\ *adv*

¹mind \ˈmīnd\ *n* **1** : MEMORY, RECOLLECTION ⟨keep it in *mind*⟩ **2 a** : the element or complex of elements in an individual that feels, perceives, thinks, wills, and especially reasons **b** : mental ability ⟨has the *mind* of a 5-year-old⟩ **3 a** : INTENTION 1, DESIRE ⟨that is not what I had in *mind*⟩ ⟨make up your *mind*⟩ **b** : one's view or opinion about something ⟨speak your *mind*⟩ **c** : CHOICE, LIKING ⟨to my *mind* it is satisfactory⟩ **d** : ATTENTION ⟨keep your *mind* on your work⟩ **4** : the normal or healthy condition of the mental faculties ⟨lose one's *mind*⟩ **5** : way of thinking or feeling : MOOD, DISPOSITION ⟨keep an open *mind* on the issue⟩ **6** : a person embodying mental qualities especially of a specified kind ⟨one of the greatest *minds* of the century⟩ **7** : IMAGINATION ⟨it's all in your *mind*⟩ **8** *dialect* : ATTENTION, HEED ⟨don't pay them any *mind*⟩ [Old English *gemynd*]

²mind *vb* **1** *chiefly dialect* : REMIND **2** *chiefly dialect* : REMEMBER 1 **3** : to attend to ⟨*mind* your own business⟩ **4** : to take notice of **5** : to give heed to ⟨*mind* your manners⟩; *also* : OBEY ⟨*mind* your parents⟩ **6 a** : to be concerned or troubled over ⟨never *mind* your mistake⟩ **b** : to have an objection : object to ⟨I don't *mind* if you go⟩ **7 a** : to be careful : make sure ⟨*mind* you finish it⟩ **b** : to be cautious of : watch out for ⟨*mind* the broken glass⟩ **8** : to have charge of : TEND ⟨*mind* the store⟩

mind·ed \ˈmīn-dəd\ *adj* **1** : having a specified kind of mind — usually used in combination ⟨narrow-*minded*⟩ **2** : INCLINED 1, DISPOSED ⟨was *minded* to help⟩

mind–ex·pand·ing \ˈmīn-dik-ˌspan-ding\ *adj* : PSYCHEDELIC 1a

mind·ful \ˈmīnd-fəl, ˈmīn-\ *adj* : bearing in mind : AWARE ⟨*mindful* of the needs of others⟩ — **mind·ful·ly** \-fə-lē\ *adv* — **mind·ful·ness** *n*

mind·less \ˈmīn-dləs, -ləs\ *adj* **1 a** : lacking the ability to think, feel, or respond ⟨a *mindless* killer⟩ **b :** showing no use of intelligence or thought **2 :** not mindful **:** HEEDLESS ⟨*mindless* of danger⟩ — **mind·less·ly** *adv* — **mind·less·ness** *n*

mind reader *n* **:** one who professes or is held to be able to perceive another's thought by telepathy — **mind reading** *n*

mind's eye *n* **:** the mental faculty of creating images or of recalling scenes previously seen

[1]**mine** \mīn, ˈmīn\ *adj, archaic* **:** MY — used before a word beginning with a vowel or *h* ⟨*mine* eyes⟩ ⟨*mine* host⟩ or sometimes as a modifier of a preceding noun ⟨mother *mine*⟩ [Old English *mīn*]

[2]**mine** \ˈmīn\ *pron, sing or pl in construction* **:** that which belongs to me **:** those which belong to me — used without a following noun as an equivalent in meaning to the adjective *my*

[3]**mine** \ˈmīn\ *n* **1 :** a pit or tunnel from which mineral substances (as coal or gold) are taken **2 :** a deposit of ore **3 :** a subterranean passage under an enemy position **4 :** an explosive device placed in the ground or in water and set to explode when disturbed (as by an enemy) **5 :** a rich source of supply ⟨a *mine* of information⟩ [Medieval French]

[4]**mine** \ˈmīn\ *vb* **1 :** to dig a mine **2 :** to obtain from a mine ⟨*mine* coal⟩ **3 :** to work in a mine **4 a :** to burrow in the earth **:** dig or form mines under a place **b :** to lay military mines in or under ⟨*mine* a harbor⟩

mine·lay·er \ˈmīn-ˌlā-ər\ *n* **:** a naval vessel for placing underwater mines

min·er \ˈmī-nər\ *n* **:** one that mines; *esp* **:** a person who works in a mine

[1]**min·er·al** \ˈmin-rəl, -ə-rəl\ *n* **1 :** a naturally occurring crystalline element or compound (as diamond or quartz) that has a definite chemical composition and results from processes other than those of plants and animals ⟨most rocks are composed of more than one *mineral*⟩ **2 :** any of various naturally occurring substances (as ore, coal, salt, sand, stone, petroleum, natural gas, or water) obtained for human use usually from the ground **3 a :** a natural substance that is neither plant nor animal **b :** an inorganic substance [Medieval Latin *minerale,* from *mineralis,* "of a mine," from *minera* "mine, ore," from Medieval French *miniere,* from *mine* "mine"]

[2]**mineral** *adj* **1 :** of, relating to, or having the characteristics of a mineral **:** INORGANIC **2 :** containing mineral salts or gases

min·er·al·ize \ˈmin-rə-ˌlīz, -ə-rə-\ *vb* **1 :** to transform a metal into an ore **2 :** PETRIFY ⟨*mineralized* bones⟩ **3 a :** to impregnate or supply with minerals **b :** to change into mineral form — **min·er·al·i·za·tion** \ˌmin-rə-lə-ˈzā-shən, -ə-rə-\ *n*

mineral kingdom *n* **:** a basic group of natural objects that includes inorganic objects — compare ANIMAL KINGDOM, PLANT KINGDOM

min·er·al·o·gy \ˌmin-ə-ˈräl-ə-jē, -ˈral-\ *n* **:** a science dealing with the properties and classification of minerals — **min·er·al·og·i·cal** \ˌmin-rə-ˈläj-i-kəl, -ə-rə-\ *adj* — **min·er·al·og·i·cal·ly** \-kə-lē, -klē\ *adv* — **min·er·al·o·gist** \ˌmin-ə-ˈräl-ə-jəst, -ˈral-\ *n*

mineral oil *n* **1 :** an oil (as petroleum) of mineral origin **2 :** a refined petroleum oil having no color, odor, or taste that is used especially as a laxative

mineral water *n* **:** water naturally or artificially impregnated with mineral salts (as of calcium and magnesium) or gases (as carbon dioxide)

mineral wool *n* **:** any of various lightweight materials that resemble wool in texture, are made from slag, rock, or glass, and are used especially in heat and sound insulation

min·e·stro·ne \ˌmin-ə-ˈstrō-nē, -ˈstrōn\ *n* **:** a rich thick vegetable soup usually made with dried beans and pasta (as macaroni) [Italian, from *minestrare* "to serve," from Latin *ministrare,* from *minister* "servant"]

mine·sweep·er \ˈmīn-ˌswē-pər\ *n* **:** a warship for removing or neutralizing mines

Ming \ˈming\ *n* **:** a Chinese dynasty dated 1368–1644 and noted for restoration of earlier traditions and in the arts for perfection of established techniques [Chinese (Beijing dialect) *míng* "luminous"]

min·gle \ˈming-gəl\ *vb* **min·gled; min·gling** \-gə-ling, -gling\ **1 a :** to bring or mix together or with something else usually without fundamental loss of identity **b :** to become mingled **2 :** to come in contact **:** ASSOCIATE ⟨*mingles* with all sorts of people⟩ **3 :** to move about (as at a party) to talk with different people [Middle English *menglen,* from *mengen* "to mix," from Old English *mengan*] ***synonyms*** see MIX

ming tree \ˈming-\ *n* **:** a dwarfed evergreen tree grown as bonsai; *also* **:** an artificial plant resembling this [perhaps from *Ming*]

mini \ˈmin-ē\ *n* **:** something small of its kind: as **a :** MINISKIRT **b :** MINICOMPUTER [*mini-*]

mini- *combining form* **:** miniature **:** of small dimensions ⟨*minibike*⟩ [*miniature*]

[1]**min·ia·ture** \ˈmin-ē-ə-ˌchu̇r, ˈmin-i-ˌchu̇r, ˈmin-yə-, -chər\ *n* **1 :** something much smaller than the usual size; *esp* **:** a copy on a much reduced scale **2 :** a painting in an illuminated book or manuscript **3 :** the art of painting miniatures **4 :** a very small portrait or painting (as on ivory or metal) [Italian *miniatura* "art of illuminating a manuscript," from Medieval Latin, from Latin *miniare* "to color with red lead," from *minium* "red lead"] — **min·ia·tur·ist** \-ˌchu̇r-əst, -chər-\ *n*

Word History Before printing was introduced in Europe, books were written by hand, and titles and initials were often written in red to contrast with the black ink of the text. The red coloring often used for this purpose and for decorative drawings was called, in Latin, *minium.* The Italian word *miniatura,* derived from Latin *minium,* was used for the art of illuminating a manuscript and for a picture in a manuscript. Because manuscript illustrations are relatively small, the word *miniature,* borrowed into English from Italian, came to be used for anything very small.

[2]**miniature** *adj* **:** very small **:** represented on a small scale

miniature golf *n* **:** a novelty golf game played on a miniature course having such obstacles as bridges, tunnels, and windmills

min·ia·tur·ize \-ˌchu̇r-ˌīz, -chər-\ *vt* **:** to design or construct in small size — **min·ia·tur·i·za·tion** \ˌmin-ē-ə-ˌchu̇r-ə-ˈzā-shən, ˌmin-i-ˌchu̇r-, ˌmin-yə-, -chər-\ *n*

mini·bike \ˈmin-i-ˌbīk\ *n* **:** a small one-passenger motorcycle having a low frame and elevated handlebars — **mini·bik·er** *n*

mini·bus \-ˌbəs\ *n* **:** a small bus or van

mini·car \-ˌkär\ *n* **:** a very small automobile

mini·com·put·er \ˈmin-i-kəm-ˌpyüt-ər\ *n* **:** a small computer that is between a mainframe and a personal computer in size, speed, and capacity

mini·course \-ˌkōrs, -ˌkȯrs\ *n* **:** a brief course of study

mini·disc \-ˌdisk\ *n* **:** a miniature optical disk

mini·dress \-ˌdres\ *n* **:** a short close-fitting dress

min·i·fy \ˈmin-ə-ˌfī\ *vt* **-fied; -fy·ing :** to make small or smaller **:** LESSEN [Latin *minimus* "smallest" + English *-fy*]

min·im \ˈmin-əm\ *n* **1 :** something very tiny **2** — see MEASURE table [Latin *minimus* "least, smallest"]

min·i·mal \ˈmin-ə-məl\ *adj* **:** relating to or being a minimum **:** LEAST — **min·i·mal·ly** \-mə-lē\ *adv*

mini–mart \ˈmin-ē-ˌmärt\ *n* **:** CONVENIENCE STORE

min·i·mize \ˈmin-ə-ˌmīz\ *vt* **1 :** to make as small as possible **:** reduce to a minimum ⟨*minimize* the chance of error⟩ **2 a :** to place a low estimate on ⟨*minimized* their losses⟩ **b :** to make (something) seem little or unimportant **:** BELITTLE ⟨*minimized* the danger⟩

min·i·mum \ˈmin-ə-məm\ *n, pl* **-i·ma** \-ə-mə\ *or* **-i·mums 1 a :** the least quantity or value possible or permissible **b :** the least of a set of numbers; *esp* **:** the smallest value of a function over a certain interval **2 :** the lowest degree or amount reached or recorded [Latin, neuter of *minimus* "smallest"] — **minimum** *adj*

minimum wage *n* **:** a wage fixed by legal authority or by contract as the least that may be paid either to employed persons generally or to a specific group of workers

min·ing \ˈmī-ning\ *n* **:** the process or business of working mines

min·ion \ˈmin-yən\ *n* **1 :** a servile dependent **2 :** FAVORITE 1, IDOL **3 :** a subordinate official [Middle French *mignon* "darling"]

mini·park \ˈmin-ē-ˌpärk\ *n* **:** a small city park

mini·school \ˈmin-i-ˌsku̇l\ *n* **:** an experimental school offering specialized or individualized instruction

min·is·cule \ˈmin-əs-ˌkyül\ *variant of* MINUSCULE

usage The adjective *minuscule* is derived from the Latin *minus* (meaning "less") but associations with *mini-* have produced the spelling variant *miniscule.* This variant dates to the end of the 19th century. It now occurs commonly in published writing, but continues to be widely regarded as an error.

mini·se·ries \ˈmin-ē-ˌsiər-ēz, -ˌēz\ *n* **:** a television production of a story presented in sequential episodes

mini·skirt \ˈmin-i-ˌskərt\ *n* **:** a woman's very short skirt — **mini·skirt·ed** \-əd\ *adj*

mini·state \-ˌstāt\ *n* **:** a small independent nation

[1]**min·is·ter** \ˈmin-ə-stər\ *n* **1 :** AGENT 3 **2 a :** one officiating or assisting at the administration of a sacrament **b :** a Protestant clergyman **c :** a person exercising the functions of a clergyman **3 :** a high government official entrusted with the management of a division of governmental activities **4 a :** a diplomatic representative (as an ambassador) sent to the seat of government of a foreign state **b :** a diplomatic representative ranking below an ambassador and usually sent to states of less importance [Medieval French *ministre,* from Latin *minister* "servant"]

[2]**minister** *vi* **min·is·tered; min·is·ter·ing** \-stə-ring, -string\ **:** to give aid or service ⟨*minister* to the sick⟩

min·is·te·ri·al \ˌmin-ə-ˈstir-ē-əl\ *adj* **1 :** of or relating to a minister or ministry **2 a :** prescribed by law as part of the duties of an administrative office **b :** done in obedience to a legal order without exercise of personal judgment or discretion — **min·is·te·ri·al·ly** \-ē-ə-lē\ *adv*

min·is·tra·tion \ˌmin-ə-ˈstrā-shən\ *n* **:** the act or process of ministering

min·is·try \ˈmin-ə-strē\ *n, pl* **-tries** **1 :** MINISTRATION **2 :** the office, duties, or functions of a minister ⟨study for the *ministry*⟩ **3 :** the body of ministers of religion **:** CLERGY **4 :** AGENCY 3, INSTRUMENTALITY **5 :** the period of service or office of a minister or ministry **6** *often cap* **a :** the body of ministers governing a nation or state from which a smaller cabinet is sometimes selected **b :** the group of ministers constituting a cabinet **7 a :** a government department presided over by a minister ⟨*ministry* of foreign affairs⟩ **b :** the building in which the business of a ministry is transacted

mini·van \ˈmin-i-ˌvan\ *n* **:** a small passenger van

min·i·ver \ˈmin-ə-vər\ *n* **:** a white fur worn by medieval nobles [Medieval French *menever,* from *menu vair* "small fur"]

mink \ˈmingk\ *n, pl* **mink** *or* **minks** \ˈmings, ˈmingks\ **:** either of two slender-bodied flesh-eating mammals resembling the related weasels, having partially webbed feet and a somewhat bushy tail, and living near water; *also* **:** the soft typically dark brown fur of a mink [Middle English]

mink

min·ne·sing·er \ˈmin-i-ˌsing-ər, ˈmin-ə-ˌzing-\ *n* **:** one of a class of German lyric poets and musicians of the 12th to the 14th centuries [German, from *minne* "love" + *singer* "singer"]

min·now \ˈmin-ō\ *n, pl* **minnows** *also* **minnow** **:** any of various small freshwater bottom-feeding fish (as the dace or shiner) related to the carps; *also* **:** any of various similar small fishes [Middle English *menawe*]

[1]**Mi·no·an** \mə-ˈnō-ən, mī-\ *adj* **:** of or relating to a Bronze Age culture centered in Crete (3000 B.C.–1100 B.C.) [Latin *minous* "of Minos (a legendary king of Crete)," from Greek *minōios,* from *Minōs* "Minos"]

[2]**Minoan** *n* **:** a native or inhabitant of ancient Crete

[1]**mi·nor** \ˈmī-nər\ *adj* **1 a :** inferior in dignity, rank, or importance ⟨a *minor* poet⟩ **b :** relatively small in number, quantity, or extent ⟨received a *minor* share of the blame⟩ **2 :** not having attained legal age **3 a :** having the 3rd, 6th, and sometimes the 7th degrees lowered a half step ⟨a *minor* scale⟩ **b :** based on a minor scale ⟨*minor* keys⟩ **c :** less by a half step than the corresponding major interval ⟨*minor* third⟩ **4 :** not involving risk to life **:** not serious ⟨*minor* illness⟩ **5 :** of or relating to an academic minor [Latin, "smaller, inferior"]

[2]**minor** *n* **1 :** a person who has not attained legal age **2 :** a minor musical interval, scale, key, or mode **3 :** an academic subject chosen by a student as a secondary field of specialization

[3]**minor** *vi* **:** to pursue an academic minor

mi·nor·i·ty \mə-ˈnȯr-ət-ē, mī-, -ˈnär-\ *n, pl* **-ties** **1 a :** the period before attainment of legal age **b :** the state of being a legal minor **2 :** the smaller in number of two groups constituting a whole; *esp* **:** a group (as in a legislature) having less than the number of votes necessary for control **3 :** a part of a population differing from others (as in race) and often treated differently

minority leader *n* **:** the leader of the minority party in a legislative body

minor league *n* **:** a league of professional clubs in a sport (as baseball) other than the recognized major leagues

minor order *n* **:** one of the Roman Catholic or Eastern clerical orders that are lower in rank than major orders and involve minor liturgical duties — normally used in plural

minor party *n* **:** a political party whose strength in elections is so small as to prevent its gaining control of a government except in rare and exceptional circumstances

minor penalty *n* **:** a two-minute suspension of a player in ice hockey

minor seminary *n* **:** a Roman Catholic seminary giving all or part of high school and junior college training

minor suit *n* **:** clubs or diamonds in bridge

min·ster \ˈmin-stər\ *n* **1 :** a church attached or once attached to a monastery **2 :** a large or important church [Old English *mynster* "monastery, minster," from Late Latin *monasterium* "monastery"]

min·strel \ˈmin-strəl\ *n* **1 :** a medieval musical entertainer; *esp* **:** a singer of verses to the accompaniment of a harp **2 a :** MUSICIAN **b :** POET 1 **3 a :** one of a troupe of performers typically giving a program of black American melodies and jokes and usually wearing blackface **b :** a performance by a troupe of minstrels [Medieval French *menestrel* "servant, minstrel," derived from Latin *minister* "servant"]

min·strel·sy \-sē\ *n, pl* **-sies** **1 :** the singing and playing of a minstrel **2 :** a body of minstrels **3 :** a group of songs or verse [Medieval French *menestralsie,* from *menestrel* "minstrel"]

[1]**mint** \ˈmint\ *n* **1 :** a place where coins, medals, or tokens are made **2 :** a huge amount ⟨worth a *mint*⟩ [Old English *mynet* "coin, money," from Latin *moneta* "mint, coin," from *Moneta,* epithet of the goddess Juno; from the fact that the Romans coined money in the temple of Juno Moneta]

[2]**mint** *vt* **1 :** to make (as coins) out of metal **2 :** CREATE 1, COIN — **mint·er** *n*

[3]**mint** *adj* **:** unmarred as if fresh from a mint ⟨*mint* coins⟩

[4]**mint** *n* **1 :** any of a family of herbs and shrubs (as basil and catnip) with square stems, opposite aromatic leaves, and commonly 2-lipped flowers; *esp* **:** any of a genus of mints (as peppermint or spearmint) that are fragrant and include some used in flavoring and cookery **2 :** a piece of candy flavored with mint [Old English *minte,* from Latin *mentha*]

mint·age \ˈmint-ij\ *n* **1 :** the action or process of minting coins **2 :** coins produced by minting

mint julep *n* **:** JULEP

min·u·end \ˈmin-yə-ˌwend\ *n* **:** a number from which another number is to be subtracted — compare SUBTRAHEND [Latin *minuendus* "to be lessened," from *minuere* "to lessen"]

min·u·et \ˌmin-yə-ˈwet\ *n* **1 :** a slow graceful dance consisting of forward balancing, bowing, and toe pointing **2 :** music for or in the rhythm of a minuet [French *menuet,* from Medieval French *menu* "small," from Latin *minutus*]

[1]**mi·nus** \ˈmī-nəs\ *prep* **1 :** with the subtraction of **:** LESS ⟨seven *minus* four is three⟩ **2 :** deprived of **:** WITHOUT ⟨*minus* his hat⟩ [Latin, "less," from *minor* "smaller"]

[2]**minus** *n* **1 :** a negative quantity **2 :** a negative quality; *esp* **:** DRAWBACK

[3]**minus** *adj* **1 :** mathematically negative ⟨*minus* 3⟩ **2 :** falling low in a specified range ⟨a grade of C *minus*⟩ **3 :** relating to or being a particular one of the two mating types that are required for successful fertilization in sexual reproduction in some lower plants (as a fungus)

mi·nus·cule \ˈmin-əs-ˌkyül, min-ˈəs-, ˈmin-yəs-, mī-ˈnəs-\ *adj* **:** very small ⟨*minuscule* amounts⟩ [French *minuscule* "lowercase letter," from Latin *minusculus* "rather small," from *minor* "smaller"]

minus sign *n* **:** a sign – used to show subtraction (as in $8 - 6 = 2$) or a quantity less than zero (as in $-10°$)

[1]**min·ute** \ˈmin-ət\ *n* **1 a :** the 60th part of an hour of time **b :** the 60th part of a degree of angular measure **2 :** the distance one can cover comfortably in a minute ⟨10 *minutes* from home to office⟩ **3 :** MOMENT 1 **4 a :** a brief note of instructions or recommendations written on a document **b :** an official memorandum authorizing or recommending some action **5** *pl* **:** a series of brief notes taken to provide a record of the proceedings of a meeting [Medieval French, from Late Latin *minuta,* from Latin *minutus* "small, minute"]

\ə\ **abut**	\au̇\ **out**	\i\ **tip**	\ȯ\ **saw**	\u̇\ **foot**
\ər\ **further**	\ch\ **chin**	\ī\ **life**	\ȯi\ **coin**	\y\ **yet**
\a\ **mat**	\e\ **pet**	\j\ **job**	\th\ **thin**	\yü\ **few**
\ā\ **take**	\ē\ **easy**	\ng\ **sing**	\t͟h\ **this**	\yu̇\ **cure**
\ä\ **cot, cart**	\g\ **go**	\ō\ **bone**	\ü\ **food**	\zh\ **vision**

[2]**minute** *vt* **min·ut·ed; min·ut·ing** : to make notes or a brief summary of ⟨*minute* a meeting⟩

[3]**mi·nute** \mī-ˈnüt, mə-, -ˈnyüt\ *adj* **1** : very small : INFINITESIMAL **2** : of small importance : TRIFLING **3** : marked by close attention to details ⟨*minute* description⟩ [Latin *minutus*] ***synonyms*** see CIRCUMSTANTIAL — **mi·nute·ness** *n*

minute hand *n* : the long hand that marks the minutes on the face of a watch or clock

mi·nute·ly \-lē\ *adv* **1** : into very small pieces **2** : in a minute manner or degree

min·ute·man \ˈmin-ət-ˌman\ *n* : a member of a militia ready to take up arms at a minute's notice during and immediately before the American Revolution

mi·nu·tia \mə-ˈnü-shē-ə, mī-, -ˈnyü-, -shə\ *n, pl* **-ti·ae** \-shē-ˌē, -shē-ˌī\ : a minute or minor detail — usually used in plural [Latin, from *minutus* "small, minute"]

minx \ˈmiŋs, ˈmiŋks\ *n* **1** : a pert girl **2** *obsolete* : a wanton woman [origin unknown]

Mio·cene \ˈmī-ə-ˌsēn\ *n* : the epoch of the Tertiary between the Oligocene and Pliocene; *also* : the corresponding series of rocks [Greek *meiōn* "less"] — **Miocene** *adj*

mir \ˈmiər\ *n* : a village community common in czarist Russia in which the land was owned jointly by the peasants and cultivable land was redistributed among the individual families at regular intervals [Russian]

mi·ra·cid·i·um \ˌmir-ə-ˈsid-ē-əm, ˌmī-rə-\ *n, pl* **-cid·ia** \-ē-ə\ : the free-swimming ciliated first larva that is characteristic of a group (Digenea) of trematode worms and that seeks out and penetrates a suitable snail intermediate host in which it develops into a sporocyst [New Latin, from Greek *meirax* "youth, stripling"]

mir·a·cle \ˈmir-i-kəl\ *n* **1** : an extraordinary event believed to manifest a supernatural work of God **2** : an extremely outstanding or unusual event, thing, or accomplishment [Medieval French, from Latin *miraculum* "a wonder, marvel," from *mirari* "to wonder at"]

miracle drug *n* : WONDER DRUG

miracle play *n* **1** : MYSTERY PLAY **2** : a medieval play based on the life of a saint or martyr

mi·rac·u·lous \mə-ˈrak-yə-ləs\ *adj* **1** : of the nature of a miracle : SUPERNATURAL **2** : resembling a miracle : MARVELOUS **3** : working or able to work miracles — **mi·rac·u·lous·ly** *adv* — **mi·rac·u·lous·ness** *n*

mi·rage \mə-ˈräzh\ *n* **1** : an optical effect that is sometimes seen at sea, in the desert, or over a hot pavement, that may have the appearance of a pool of water or a mirror in which distant objects are seen inverted, and that is caused by the bending or reflection of rays of light by a layer of heated air of varying density **2** : something only seemingly real [French, from *mirer* "to look at," from Latin *mirari* "to wonder at"]

Mi·ran·da \mə-ˈran-də\ *adj* : of, relating to, or being the legal rights of an arrested person to have an attorney and to remain silent so as to avoid self-incrimination ⟨a *Miranda* warning⟩ [from *Miranda v. Arizona,* the United States Supreme Court ruling establishing such rights]

[1]**mire** \ˈmīr\ *n* **1** : wet spongy earth (as of a bog or marsh) **2** : heavy often deep mud, slush, or dirt [Old Norse *mȳrr*]

[2]**mire** *vb* **1 a** : to sink or stick fast in mire **b** : ENTANGLE, INVOLVE ⟨*mired* in detail⟩ **2** : to soil with mud, slush, or dirt

[1]**mir·ror** \ˈmir-ər\ *n* **1** : a glass backed with a reflecting substance (as silver) **2** : a smooth or polished surface that reflects an image **3** : something that reflects a true likeness or gives a true description [Medieval French *mirur,* from *mirer* "to look at," from Latin *mirari* "to wonder at"]

[2]**mirror** *vt* **1** : to reflect in or as if in a mirror **2** : RESEMBLE ⟨his strategy *mirrored* that of his competitors⟩

mirror image *n* : something that has its parts arranged in reverse in comparison with another similar thing or that is reversed with reference to an axis or plane between the two things

mirth \ˈmərth\ *n* : gladness or gaiety as shown by or accompanied with laughter [Old English *myrgth,* from *myrge* "merry"]

synonyms MIRTH, GLEE, JOLLITY, HILARITY mean the quality or state of being glad or joyful. MIRTH implies generally lightness of heart and love of gaiety and specifically denotes laughter ⟨tried to suppress their *mirth*⟩. GLEE suggests an exulting sometimes malicious delight expressed in laughter or cries of joy ⟨shouted with *glee*⟩. JOLLITY suggests exuberance or lack of restraint in mirth or glee ⟨nothing could dampen her *jollity*⟩. HILARITY implies loud or irrepressible laughter or boisterousness ⟨shrieks of *hilarity*⟩.

mirth·ful \-fəl\ *adj* : full of, expressing, or producing mirth — **mirth·ful·ly** \-fə-lē\ *adv* — **mirth·ful·ness** *n*

miry \ˈmīr-ē\ *adj* **mir·i·er; -est** **1** : MARSHY 1 **2** : very muddy or slushy

mis- *prefix* **1 a** : badly : wrongly ⟨*mis*judge⟩ **b** : unfavorably **c** : in a suspicious manner ⟨*mis*doubt⟩ **2** : bad : wrong ⟨*mis*deed⟩ **3** : opposite or lack of ⟨*mis*trust⟩ **4** : not ⟨*mis*fire⟩ [Old English]

misaddress
misadjust
misadministration
misadvise
misaim
misalign
misalignment
misallocate
misallocation
misanalysis
misapplication
misapply
misarticulate
misassemble
misassumption
misattribute
misattribution
miscaption
miscatalog
mischannel
mischaracterization
mischaracterize
mischarge
mischoice
miscitation
misclassification
misclassify
miscomprehension
miscomputation
miscompute
misconnect
misconnection
miscopy
miscorrelation
miscount
miscut
misdate
misdefine
misdescribe
misdescription
misdevelop
misdiagnose
misdiagnosis
misdial
miseducate
miseducation
misemphasis
misemphasize
misemploy
misemployment
misestimate
misestimation
misevaluate
misevaluation
misfeed
misfield
misfocus
misfunction
misgauge
misgovern
misgovernment
misgrade
misidentification
misidentify
miskick
mislabel
mislearn
mislocate
mislocation
mismark
mismatch
mismate
mismeasure
mismeasurement
misperceive
misperception
misplan
misposition
misquotation
misquote
misregister
misregistration
misremember
misreport
misroute
misset
missort
misthrow
mistime
mistitle
mistranslate
mistranslation
mistruth
mistune
mistype
misutilization
miswrite

mis·ad·ven·ture \ˌmis-əd-ˈven-chər\ *n* : an unlucky adventure : MISHAP

mis·al·li·ance \ˌmis-ə-ˈlī-əns\ *n* : an improper or unsuitable alliance especially in marriage

mis·an·thrope \ˈmis-n-ˌthrōp\ *n* : a person who dislikes and distrusts other people [Greek *misanthrōpos* "hating humankind," from *misein* "to hate" + *anthrōpos* "human"]

mis·an·thro·py \mis-ˈan-thrə-pē, -ˈant-\ *n* : a dislike or hatred of other people — **mis·an·throp·ic** \ˌmis-n-ˈthräp-ik\ *adj* — **mis·an·throp·i·cal·ly** \-ˈthräp-i-kə-lē, -klē\ *adv*

mis·ap·pre·hend \ˌmis-ˌap-ri-ˈhend\ *vt* : MISUNDERSTAND — **mis·ap·pre·hen·sion** \-ˈhen-chən\ *n*

mis·ap·pro·pri·ate \ˌmis-ə-ˈprō-prē-ˌāt\ *vt* : to appropriate wrongly; *esp* : to take dishonestly for one's own use — **mis·ap·pro·pri·a·tion** \-ˌprō-prē-ˈā-shən\ *n*

mis·be·come \ˌmis-bi-ˈkəm\ *vt* : to be inappropriate or unbecoming to

mis·be·got·ten \ˌmis-bi-ˈgät-n\ *adj* **1** : ILLEGITIMATE 1 **2** : having or suggesting a disreputable or improper origin ⟨a *misbegotten* scheme⟩

mis·be·have \ˌmis-bi-ˈhāv\ *vi* : to behave in a wrong or improper manner — **mis·be·hav·ior** \-ˈhā-vyər\ *n*

mis·be·lief \ˌmis-bə-ˈlēf\ *n* : a mistaken or false belief

mis·be·liev·er \-ˈlē-vər\ *n* : one who is held to have false beliefs especially in religion

mis·brand \mis-ˈbrand, ˈmis-\ *vt* : to brand falsely or in a misleading way

mis·cal·cu·late \-ˈkal-kyə-ˌlāt\ *vb* : to calculate wrongly : make a mistake in calculation — **mis·cal·cu·la·tion** \ˌmis-ˌkal-kyə-ˈlā-shən\ *n*

mis·call \mis-ˈkȯl, ˈmis-\ *vt* : to call by a wrong name

mis·car·riage \mis-ˈkar-ij\ *n* **1** : a going astray: as **a** : a failure or blunder resulting usually from mismanagement ⟨a *miscarriage* of justice⟩ **b** : a failure (as of a letter) to arrive **c** : a failure of a purpose or plan **2** : the accidental separation and loss of a fetus from the body of its mother before it is capable of living independently

mis·car·ry \mis-ˈkar-ē\ *vi* **1** : to have a miscarriage : give birth prematurely **2** : to fail of the intended purpose : go wrong ⟨the plan *miscarried*⟩

mis·cast \mis-ˈkast, ˈmis-\ *vt* : to cast in an unsuitable role

mis·ceg·e·na·tion \mis-ˌej-ə-ˈnā-shən, ˌmis-i-jə-ˈnā-\ *n* : a mixture of races; *esp* : marriage, sexual intercourse, or cohabitation between a white person and a member of another race [Latin *miscēre* "to mix" + *genus* "kind, race"]

mis·cel·la·ne·ous \ˌmis-ə-ˈlā-nē-əs\ *adj* **1** : consisting of numerous things of different sorts **2 a** : marked by an interest in unrelated topics or subjects **b** : having the characteristics of a patchwork [Latin *miscellaneus,* from *miscellus* "mixed"] — **mis·cel·la·ne·ous·ly** *adv* — **mis·cel·la·ne·ous·ness** *n*

mis·cel·la·nist \ˈmis-ə-ˌlā-nəst\ *n* : a writer of miscellanies

mis·cel·la·ny \-nē\ *n, pl* **-nies** **1** : a mixture of various things **2** *pl* : a collection of writings : ANTHOLOGY

mis·chance \mis-ˈchans, ˈmis-\ *n* **1** : bad luck **2** : a piece of bad luck ***synonyms*** see MISFORTUNE

mis·chief \ˈmis-chəf, ˈmish-\ *n* **1** : injury or damage caused by a human agency **2** : a source of mischief; *esp* : a person who causes mischief **3 a** : action that annoys ⟨that child always gets into *mischief*⟩ **b** : mischievous quality [Medieval French *meschief* "calamity," from *mes-* "mis-" (of Germanic origin) + *chief* "head, end," from Latin *caput*]

mis·chie·vous \ˈmis-chə-vəs, ˈmish-\ *adj* **1** : causing mischief : intended to do harm ⟨*mischievous* gossip⟩ **2 a** : causing or tending to cause petty injury or annoyance **b** : irresponsibly playful **3** : showing a spirit of mischief — **mis·chie·vous·ly** *adv* — **mis·chie·vous·ness** *n*

usage A pronunciation \mis-ˈchē-vē-əs\ (rhyming with *devious*) and a consequent spelling *mischievious* are of long standing. While the evidence goes back to the 16th century, both the pronunciation and the spelling are still considered nonstandard.

mis·ci·ble \ˈmis-ə-bəl\ *adj* : capable of being mixed; *esp* : soluble in each other ⟨alcohol and water are *miscible*⟩ [Medieval Latin *miscibilis,* from Latin *miscēre* "to mix"] — **mis·ci·bil·i·ty** \ˌmis-ə-ˈbil-ət-ē\ *n*

mis·con·ceive \ˌmis-kən-ˈsēv\ *vt* : to interpret incorrectly : MISJUDGE — **mis·con·ceiv·er** *n* — **mis·con·cep·tion** \-ˈsep-shən\ *n*

[1]**mis·con·duct** \mis-ˈkän-dəkt, ˈmis-, -ˌdəkt\ *n* **1** : bad management **2** : improper or unlawful behavior

[2]**mis·con·duct** \ˌmis-kən-ˈdəkt\ *vt* **1** : MISMANAGE **2** : to behave (oneself) badly

mis·con·struc·tion \ˌmis-kən-ˈstrək-shən\ *n* : the act, the process, or an instance of misconstruing

mis·con·strue \ˌmis-kən-ˈstrü\ *vt* : to construe wrongly : MISINTERPRET

mis·cre·ant \ˈmis-krē-ənt\ *n* : one that behaves badly : RASCAL [Middle English *miscreaunt* "infidel," from Medieval French *mescreant,* present participle of *mescreire* "to disbelieve," from *mes-* "mis-" (of Germanic origin) + *creire* "to believe," from Latin *credere*] — **miscreant** *adj*

[1]**mis·cue** \mis-ˈkyü, ˈmis-\ *n* **1** : a faulty stroke (as in billiards) **2** : MISTAKE 2, SLIP

[2]**miscue** *vi* **1** : to make a miscue **2 a** : to miss a stage cue **b** : to answer a wrong cue

mis·deal \mis-ˈdēl, ˈmis-\ *vb* **-dealt** \-ˈdelt\; **-deal·ing** \-ˈdē-ling\ : to deal wrongly ⟨*misdeal* cards⟩ — **misdeal** *n*

mis·deed \mis-ˈdēd, ˈmis-\ *n* : a wrong deed; *esp* : an immoral or criminal action

mis·de·mean·or \ˌmis-di-ˈmē-nər\ *n* **1** : a crime less serious than a felony **2** : MISDEED

mis·di·rect \ˌmis-də-ˈrekt, -dī-\ *vt* : to direct incorrectly — **mis·di·rec·tion** \-ˈrek-shən\ *n*

mis·do \mis-ˈdü, ˈmis-\ *vt* **-did** \-ˈdid\; **-done** \-ˈdən\; **-do·ing** \-ˈdü-ing\; **-does** \-ˈdəz\ : to do wrongly or improperly — **mis·do·er** \-ˈdü-ər\ *n*

mis·do·ing \mis-ˈdü-ing, ˈmis-\ *n* **1** : wrong or improper behavior or action **2** : MISDEED

mis·doubt \mis-ˈdau̇t, ˈmis-\ *vt* **1** : to doubt the reality or truth of **2** : SUSPECT 1, FEAR — **misdoubt** *n*

mise–en–scène \ˌmē-ˌzäⁿ-ˈsen\ *n, pl* **mise–en–scènes** \-ˈsen, -ˈsenz\ **1** : the setting of a play **2** : physical setting : ENVIRONMENT [French *mise en scène* "putting onto the stage"]

mi·ser \ˈmī-zər\ *n* : a mean grasping person; *esp* : one who lives miserably in order to hoard wealth [Latin, "wretched, miserable"]

mis·er·a·ble \ˈmiz-ər-bəl, ˈmiz-rə-bəl, -ə-rə-\ *adj* **1 a** : wholly inadequate or scanty ⟨a *miserable* shanty⟩ **b** : causing great discomfort or unhappiness ⟨a *miserable* cold⟩ **2** : extremely poor or unhappy **3** : arousing pity **4** : SHAMEFUL ⟨played a *miserable* trick⟩ [Medieval French, from Latin *miserabilis* "pitiable, wretched," from *miserari* "to pity," from *miser* "wretched"] — **miserable** *n* — **mis·er·a·ble·ness** *n* — **mis·er·a·bly** \-blē\ *adv*

Mi·se·re·re \ˌmiz-ə-ˈriər-ē, -ˈreər-, ˌmē-zə-ˈrā-rā\ *n* : the 50th Psalm in the Vulgate [Latin, "be merciful" (the first word of the Psalm), from *misereri* "to be merciful," from *miser* "wretched"]

mi·ser·ly \ˈmī-zər-lē\ *adj* : of, relating to, or characteristic of a miser ***synonyms*** see STINGY — **mi·ser·li·ness** *n*

mis·ery \ˈmiz-rē, -ə-rē\ *n, pl* **-er·ies** **1** : a state of great suffering and want due to poverty or distress **2** : a source of suffering or discomfort ⟨the *miseries* of life in prison⟩ **3** : a state of great unhappiness and emotional distress ***synonyms*** see DISTRESS

mis·fea·sance \mis-ˈfēz-ns\ *n* : the performance of a lawful action in an illegal or improper manner [Middle French *mesfaisance,* from *mesfaire* "to do wrong," from *mes-* "mis-" (of Germanic origin) + *faire* "to do," from Latin *facere*]

mis·file \mis-ˈfīl, ˈmis-\ *vt* : to file in an inappropriate place

mis·fire \mis-ˈfīr, ˈmis-\ *vi* **1** : to have the explosive or propulsive charge fail to ignite at the proper time ⟨the engine *misfired*⟩ **2** : to fail to fire ⟨the gun *misfired*⟩ **3** : to miss an intended effect — **misfire** *n*

mis·fit \ˈmis-ˌfit, mis-ˈfit\ *n* **1** : something that fits badly **2** : a person poorly adjusted to his or her environment

mis·for·tune \mis-ˈfȯr-chən\ *n* **1** : bad fortune : ill luck **2** : an unfortunate condition or event : DISASTER

synonyms MISFORTUNE, MISCHANCE, MISHAP mean adverse fortune or an instance of this. MISFORTUNE is a general term for bad luck; applied to a single instance it implies resulting distress usually of some considerable duration. MISCHANCE emphasizes the immediate practical inconvenience or disruption of plans resulting from a chance happening or fall of circumstances. MISHAP implies a trivial instance of bad luck.

mis·give \mis-ˈgiv, ˈmis-\ *vb* **-gave** \-ˈgāv\; **-giv·en** \-ˈgiv-ən\; **-giv·ing** **1** : to suggest doubt or fear to **2** : to be fearful

mis·giv·ing \-ˈgiv-ing\ *n* : a feeling of doubt or suspicion especially concerning a future event

mis·guide \mis-ˈgīd, ˈmis-\ *vt* : to lead astray : MISDIRECT ⟨we have been *misguided* in our planning⟩ — **mis·guid·ance** \-ˈgīd-ns\ *n* — **mis·guid·er** *n*

mis·guid·ed \-ˈgīd-əd\ *adj* : marked or directed by mistaken ideas, principles, or motives ⟨*misguided* philanthropists⟩ — **mis·guid·ed·ly** *adv* — **mis·guid·ed·ness** *n*

mis·han·dle \mis-ˈhan-dl, ˈmis-\ *vt* **1** : to treat roughly : MALTREAT **2** : to manage wrongly

mis·hap \ˈmis-ˌhap, mis-ˈ\ *n* **1** *archaic* : bad luck : MISFORTUNE **2** : an unfortunate accident ***synonyms*** see MISFORTUNE

mis·hear \mis-ˈhiər, ˈmis-\ *vb* **1** : to hear wrongly **2** : to misunderstand what is heard

mis·hit \ˌmis-ˈhit\ *vt* : to hit in a faulty manner

mish·mash \ˈmish-ˌmash, -ˌmäsh\ *n* : a disorderly mixture : JUMBLE [Middle English and Yiddish; Middle English *mysse masche,* perhaps reduplication of *mash* "mash"; Yiddish *mish=mash,* perhaps reduplication of *mishn* "to mix"]

Mish·nah *or* **Mish·na** \ˈmish-nə\ *n* : the collection of Jewish halachic traditions compiled about A.D. 200 and made the basic half of the Talmud [Hebrew *mishnāh* "instruction"]

mis·im·pres·sion \ˌmis-im-ˈpresh-ən\ *n* : a mistaken impression

mis·in·form \ˌmis-n-ˈfȯrm\ *vt* : to give false or misleading information to — **mis·in·for·ma·tion** \ˌmis-ˌin-fər-ˈmā-shən\ *n*

mis·in·ter·pret \ˌmis-n-ˈtər-prət, *rapid* -pət\ *vt* : to understand

or explain wrongly — **mis·in·ter·pre·ta·tion** \-ˌtər-prə-ˈtā-shən, *rapid* -pə-ˈtā-\ *n*
mis·judge \mis-ˈjəj, ˈmis-\ *vb* : to judge wrongly or unjustly — **mis·judg·ment** \-ˈjəj-mənt\ *n*
mis·lay \mis-ˈlā, ˈmis-\ *vt* **-laid** \-ˈlād\; **-lay·ing** : to put in a place later forgotten : LOSE ⟨*mislaid* the car keys⟩
mis·lead \-ˈlēd\ *vt* **-led** \-ˈled\; **-lead·ing** : to lead in a wrong direction or into a mistaken action or belief ***synonyms*** see DECEIVE — **misleading** *adj*
mis·like \-ˈlīk\ *vt* : DISLIKE — **mislike** *n*
mis·man·age \mis-ˈman-ij, ˈmis-\ *vt* : to manage badly or improperly — **mis·man·age·ment** \-mənt\ *n*
mis·name \-ˈnām\ *vt* : to name incorrectly : MISCALL
mis·no·mer \mis-ˈnō-mər, ˈmis-\ *n* : a wrong or unsuitable name [Medieval French *mesnomer* "to misname," from *mes-* "mis-" (of Germanic origin) + *nomer* "to name," from Latin *nominare*]
mi·so \ˈmē-sō\ *n* : a high-protein fermented food paste consisting chiefly of soybeans, salt, and usually grain (as barley or rice) and ranging in taste from salty to sweet [Japanese]
mi·sog·a·mist \mə-ˈsäg-ə-məst\ *n* : one who hates marriage [derived from Greek *misein* "to hate" + *gamos* "marriage"] — **mi·sog·a·my** \-ˈsäg-ə-mē\ *n*
mi·sog·y·nist \mə-ˈsäj-ə-nəst\ *n* : one who hates or distrusts women [from *mysogyny,* from Greek *misogynia,* from *misein* "to hate" and *gynē* "woman"] — **mis·o·gyn·ic** \ˌmis-ə-ˈjin-ik, -ə-ˈgī-nik\ *adj* — **mi·sog·y·ny** \mə-ˈsäj-ə-nē\ *n*
mis·place \mis-ˈplās, ˈmis-\ *vt* **1** : to put in a wrong place **2** : MISLAY — **mis·place·ment** \-mənt\ *n*
mis·play \mis-ˈplā\ *n* : a wrong or unskillful play (as in a game or sport) — **mis·play** \mis-ˈplā, ˈmis-ˌplā\ *vt*
mis·print \mis-ˈprint, ˈmis-\ *vt* : to print incorrectly — **misprint** \ˈmis-ˌprint, mis-ˈ, ˈmis-ˈ\ *n*
mis·prize \mis-ˈprīz, ˈmis-\ *vt* **1** : SCORN 1 **2** : UNDERVALUE 1
mis·pro·nounce \ˌmis-prə-ˈnau̇ns\ *vt* : to pronounce incorrectly or in a way regarded as incorrect — **mis·pro·nun·ci·a·tion** \-ˌnən-sē-ˈā-shən\ *n*
mis·read \mis-ˈrēd, ˈmis-\ *vt* **-read** \-ˈred\; **-read·ing** \-ˈrēd-ing\ **1** : to read incorrectly **2** : to misinterpret in reading
mis·reck·on \mis-ˈrek-ən\ *vb* : MISCALCULATE
mis·rep·re·sent \ˌmis-ˌrep-ri-ˈzent\ *vt* : to give a false or misleading representation of — **mis·rep·re·sen·ta·tion** \mis-ˌrep-ri-ˌzen-ˈtā-shən\ *n*
[1]**mis·rule** \mis-ˈrül, ˈmis-\ *vt* : to rule or govern badly
[2]**misrule** *n* **1** : the action of misruling : the state of being misruled **2** : public disorder : ANARCHY
[1]**miss** \ˈmis\ *vb* **1** : to fail to hit, catch, reach, or get ⟨*miss* a target⟩ **2** : ESCAPE, AVOID ⟨just *missed* being hurt⟩ **3** : to leave out : OMIT **4** : to discover or feel the absence of ⟨*miss* an absent friend⟩ **5** : to fail to understand, sense, or experience ⟨*missed* the point⟩ **6** : MISFIRE ⟨the engine *missed*⟩ [Old English *missan*] — **miss out on** : to lose a good opportunity for — **miss the boat** : to fail to take advantage of an opportunity
[2]**miss** *n* **1** : a failure to reach a desired goal or result **2** : an instance of misfiring
[3]**miss** *n* **1** *cap* **a** — used as a courtesy title before the name of an unmarried woman **b** — used before the name of a place, an activity, an epithet, or a quality to form a title for a woman representing the thing indicated ⟨*Miss* America⟩ ⟨*Miss* Punctuality⟩ **2** : a woman whose marital status is unknown — used without a name as a conventional term of address [short for *mistress*]
mis·sal \ˈmis-əl\ *n* : a book containing the prayers to be said or sung in the Mass during the year [Medieval French *missal,* from Medieval Latin *missale,* from Late Latin *missa* "mass"]
mis·send \mis-ˈsend, ˈmis-\ *vt* **-sent** \-ˈsent\; **-send·ing** : to send (as mail) to a wrong address
mis·shape \mis-ˈshāp, mish-, ˈmis-, ˈmish-\ *vt* : to shape badly : DEFORM — **mis·shap·en** \-ˈshā-pən\ *adj*
mis·sile \ˈmis-əl\ *n* : an object (as a stone, arrow, artillery shell, bullet, or rocket) that is thrown or projected usually so as to strike something at a distance; *esp* : GUIDED MISSILE [Latin, from *missilis* "capable of being thrown," from *mittere* "to let go, send"]
mis·sile·man \-mən\ *n* : one who helps to design, build, or operate guided missiles
mis·sile·ry \-rē\ *n* **1** : MISSILES; *esp* : GUIDED MISSILES **2** : the science dealing with the design, manufacture, and use of guided missiles
miss·ing \ˈmis-ing\ *adj* : ABSENT; *also* : LOST ⟨*missing* in action⟩
missing link *n* **1** : an absent member needed to complete a series **2** : a hypothetical intermediate evolutionary form between one animal species or group and its presumed ancestors but that has not been found as a fossil ⟨find the *missing link* between humans and apes⟩
mis·sion \ˈmish-ən\ *n* **1 a** : a ministry commissioned by a religious organization to spread its faith or carry on humanitarian work **b** : assignment to or work in missionary enterprise **c** (1) : a mission establishment (2) : a local church or parish dependent on a larger religious organization for direction or financial support **d** *pl* : organized missionary work **e** : a course of sermons and services given to convert to or quicken Christian faith **2** : a group of persons sent to perform a service or carry on an activity: as **a** : a group sent to a foreign country to conduct negotiations **b** : a permanent embassy or legation **c** : a team of military or technical specialists or cultural leaders sent to a foreign country **3** : a task or function assigned or undertaken; *esp* : an official assignment ⟨my *mission* is to recover the stolen plans⟩ [Latin *missio* "act of sending," from *mittere* "to send"] — **mission** *adj*
[1]**mis·sion·ary** \ˈmish-ə-ˌner-ē\ *adj* **1** : relating to, engaged in, or devoted to missions **2** : characteristic of a missionary
[2]**missionary** *n, pl* **-ar·ies** : one sent to spread a religious faith among unbelievers
mis·sion·er \ˈmish-ə-nər\ *n* : MISSIONARY
Mis·sis·sip·pi·an \ˌmis-ə-ˈsip-ē-ən\ *adj* **1** : of or relating to Mississippi, its people, or the Mississippi River **2** : of, relating to, or being the period of the Paleozoic era between the Devonian and Pennsylvanian or the corresponding system of rocks — see GEOLOGIC TIME table — **Mississippian** *n*
mis·sive \ˈmis-iv\ *n* : a written communication : LETTER [Middle French *lettre missive,* literally, "letter intended to be sent"]
mis·spell \mis-ˈspel, ˈmis-\ *vt* : to spell incorrectly
mis·spell·ing \-ˈspel-ing\ *n* : an incorrect spelling
mis·spend \mis-ˈspend, ˈmis-\ *vt* **-spent** \-ˈspent\; **-spend·ing** : to spend unwisely ⟨a *misspent* youth⟩
mis·state \mis-ˈstāt, ˈmis-\ *vt* : to give a false or inaccurate account of — **mis·state·ment** \-mənt\ *n*
mis·step \-ˈstep\ *n* **1** : a wrong step **2** : a mistake in judgment or action : BLUNDER
missy \ˈmis-ē\ *n* : a young girl
[1]**mist** \ˈmist\ *n* **1** : water in the form of particles floating in the air or falling as fine rain **2** : something (as a haze or film) that blurs or hinders vision **3** : a cloud of small particles or objects resembling a mist [Old English] — **mist·like** \-ˌlīk\ *adj*
[2]**mist** *vb* **1** : to be or become misty **2** : to become dim or blurred **3** : to cover with mist
mis·tak·able \mə-ˈstā-kə-bəl\ *adj* : capable of being misunderstood or mistaken
[1]**mis·take** \mə-ˈstāk\ *vb* **mis·took** \-ˈstu̇k\; **mis·tak·en** \-ˈstā-kən\; **mis·tak·ing** **1** : to choose wrongly **2 a** : to understand wrongly : MISINTERPRET **b** : to estimate incorrectly ⟨*mistook* the strength of the enemy⟩ **3** : to identify wrongly — **mis·tak·en·ly** *adv* — **mis·tak·er** *n*
[2]**mistake** *n* **1** : a wrong judgment : MISUNDERSTANDING **2** : a wrong action or statement : BLUNDER ***synonyms*** see ERROR
[1]**mis·ter** \ˈmis-tər, *for sense 1* ˌmis-tər\ *n* **1** *cap* **a** — used sometimes in writing instead of the usual Mr. before the name of a man **b** — used before the name of a place, an activity, an epithet, or a quality to form a title for a man representing the thing indicated ⟨*Mister* Universe⟩ ⟨*Mister* Perfection⟩ **2** : SIR — used without a name as a term of direct address of a man who is a stranger ⟨hey, *mister,* do you want to buy a paper?⟩ [alteration of *master*]
[2]**mist·er** \ˈmis-tər\ *n* : a device for spraying a mist [[2]*mist* + [2]*-er*]
mis·tle·toe \ˈmis-əl-ˌtō\ *n* : a European plant with yellowish flowers and waxy white berries that grows on the branches and trunks of trees; *also* : any of various plants resembling and related to the mistletoe [Old English *misteltān,* from *mistel* "mistletoe" + *tān* "twig"]
mist net *n* : a large finely woven mesh net erected to entangle and capture birds or bats in flight
mis·tral \ˈmis-trəl, mi-ˈsträl\ *n* : a strong cold dry northerly wind of the north-

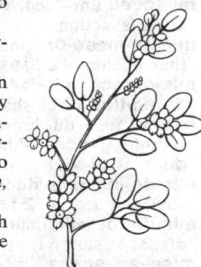

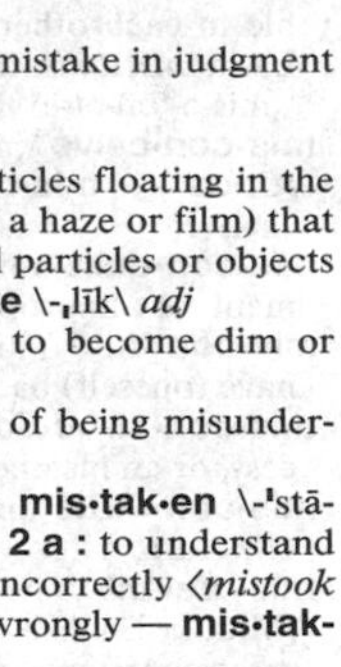

mistletoe

west Mediterranean [French, from Occitan, from *mistral* "masterful," from Late Latin *magistralis* "of a teacher," from *magister* "master"]

mis·treat \mis-ˈtrēt, ˈmis-\ *vt* **:** to treat badly **:** ABUSE — **mis·treat·ment** \-mənt\ *n*

mis·tress \ˈmis-trəs\ *n* **1 :** a woman (as the head of a household or school) who has power, authority, or ownership **2 :** something personified as female that rules or directs **3 a :** a woman other than his wife with whom a married man has a continuing sexual relationship **b** *archaic* **:** SWEETHEART **4** *cap* — used formerly as a courtesy title before the name of a woman [Medieval French *mestresse,* feminine of *mestre* "master," from Latin *magister*]

mis·tri·al \ˈmis-ˌtrī-əl, -ˌtrīl\ *n* **:** a trial that is legally void because of some error in the proceedings

1**mis·trust** \mis-ˈtrəst, ˈmis-\ *n* **:** a lack of confidence **:** DISTRUST — **mis·trust·ful** \-fəl\ *adj* — **mis·trust·ful·ly** \-fə-lē\ *adv* — **mis·trust·ful·ness** *n*

2**mistrust** *vt* **1 :** SUSPECT ⟨I *mistrust* their motives⟩ **2 :** to lack confidence in ⟨*mistrust* one's own ability⟩

misty \ˈmis-tē\ *adj* **mist·i·er; -est 1 :** full of mist ⟨a *misty* valley⟩ **2 :** blurred by or as if by mist ⟨*misty* eyes⟩ **3 :** VAGUE, INDISTINCT ⟨a *misty* memory⟩ — **mist·i·ly** \-tə-lē\ *adv* — **mist·i·ness** \-tē-nəs\ *n*

mis·un·der·stand \mis-ˌən-dər-ˈstand, ˌmis-\ *vb* **-stood** \-ˈstu̇d\; **-stand·ing 1 :** to fail to understand **2 :** to interpret incorrectly

mis·un·der·stand·ing \-ˈstan-diŋ\ *n* **1 :** a failure to understand **2 :** QUARREL 2

mis·us·age \mish-ˈü-sij, mish-ˈyü-, mis-ˈyü-, -zij\ *n* **1 :** bad treatment **:** ABUSE **2 :** wrong or improper use

1**mis·use** \mish-ˈüz, mish-ˈyüz, mis-ˈyüz\ *vt* **1 :** to use incorrectly **:** MISAPPLY ⟨*misuse* words⟩ **2 :** ABUSE 2a, MISTREAT

2**mis·use** \mish-ˈüs, mish-ˈyüs, mis-ˈyüz\ *n* **:** incorrect or improper use **:** MISAPPLICATION ⟨*misuse* of public funds⟩

mite \ˈmīt\ *n* **1 :** any of various tiny arachnids that together with the ticks make up an order (Acari) that often live on plants, animals, and stored foods, and that include important carriers of disease **2 :** a very small coin or sum of money **3 :** a very small object or creature [Old English *mīte*]

1**mi·ter** *or* **mi·tre** \ˈmīt-ər\ *n* **1 :** a high pointed headdress worn by a bishop or abbot in church ceremonies **2 a :** the beveled surface of a piece where a miter joint is made **b :** MITER JOINT [Medieval French *mitre,* from Latin *mitra* "headband, turban," from Greek]

2**miter** *or* **mitre** *vt* **mi·tered** *or* **mi·tred; mi·ter·ing** *or* **mi·tring** \ˈmīt-ə-riŋ\ **1 :** to match or fit together in a miter joint **2 :** to bevel the ends of for making a miter joint

miter box *n* **:** a device for guiding a handsaw at the proper angle in cutting wood for a miter joint

miter joint *n* **:** the joint or corner made by cutting the square edges of two boards at an angle and fitting them together

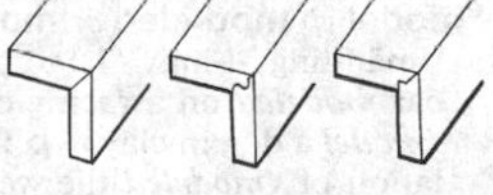
miter joint

mit·i·gate \ˈmit-ə-ˌgāt\ *vt* **:** to make less severe ⟨*mitigate* a punishment⟩ ⟨*mitigate* pain⟩ [Latin *mitigare* "to soften," from *mitis* "soft"] — **mit·i·ga·tion** \ˌmit-ə-ˈgā-shən\ *n* — **mit·i·ga·tive** \ˈmit-ə-ˌgāt-iv\ *adj* — **mit·i·ga·tor** \-ˌgāt-ər\ *n* — **mit·i·ga·to·ry** \ˈmit-i-gə-ˌtōr-ē, -ˌtȯr-\ *adj*

mi·to·chon·dri·on \ˌmīt-ə-ˈkän-drē-ən\ *n, pl* **-dria** \-drē-ə\ **:** any of various round or long cellular organelles that are located in the cytoplasm outside the nucleus, produce energy for the cell through metabolic processes utilizing oxygen, and are rich in fats, proteins, and enzymes [Greek *mitos* "thread" + *chondrion* "granule," from *chondros* "grain"] — **mi·to·chon·dri·al** \-drē-əl\ *adj*

mi·to·sis \mī-ˈtō-səs\ *n, pl* **-to·ses** \-ˌsēz\ **1 :** a process that takes place in the nucleus of a dividing cell, involves typically a series of steps consisting of prophase, metaphase, anaphase, and telophase, and results in the formation of two new nuclei each having the same number of chromosomes as the parent nucleus — compare MEIOSIS **2 :** a cell division in which mitosis occurs [New Latin, from Greek *mitos* "thread"] — **mi·tot·ic** \-ˈtät-ik\ *adj* — **mi·tot·i·cal·ly** \-ˈtät-i-kə-lē, -klē\ *adv*

mi·tral valve \ˌmī-trəl-\ *n* **:** a valve of the heart consisting of two triangular flaps which allow blood to flow only in one direction from the left atrium to the left ventricle — called also *bicuspid valve* [from its resemblance in shape to a miter]

mitt \ˈmit\ *n* **1 a :** a woman's glove that leaves the fingers uncovered **b :** MITTEN **c :** a baseball catcher's or first baseman's glove in the style of a mitten **2** *slang* **:** HAND 1a [short for *mitten*]

mit·ten \ˈmit-n\ *n* **:** a covering for the hand and wrist having a separate section for the thumb only [Medieval French *mitaine*]

mitz·vah \ˈmits-və\ *n, pl* **mitz·voth** \-ˌvōth, -ˌvōt, -ˌvōs\ *or* **mitz·vahs 1 :** a commandment of the Jewish law **2 :** a praiseworthy act [Hebrew *miṣwāh*]

1**mix** \ˈmiks\ *vb* **1 :** to combine or blend into one mass **2 :** to make by blending different things ⟨*mix* a salad dressing⟩ **3 :** to become one mass through blending ⟨oil will not *mix* with water⟩ **4 :** to associate with others on friendly terms ⟨*mixes* well in any company⟩ **5 :** CONFUSE ⟨*mix* up facts⟩ [Middle English *mixen,* back-formation from *mixte* "mixed," from Medieval French, from Latin *mixtus,* past participle of *miscēre* "to mix"]

synonyms MIX, MINGLE, BLEND, COALESCE mean to put or come together into a more or less uniform whole. MIX may or may not imply loss of each element's separate identity. MINGLE suggests that the elements are still somewhat distinguishable or separately active. BLEND implies that the elements lose some or all of their individuality. COALESCE stresses the action or process of like things growing into an organic unity.

2**mix** *n* **:** MIXTURE; *esp* **:** a commercially prepared mixture of food ingredients

mixed \ˈmikst\ *adj* **1 :** combining features of more than one kind; *esp* **:** combining features of different systems ⟨a *mixed* economy⟩ **2 :** involving individuals or items of more than one kind: as **a :** involving persons differing in race, national origin, or religion ⟨a *mixed* marriage⟩ **b :** involving individuals of both sexes ⟨*mixed* company⟩ **c :** containing two or more kinds of organisms in abundance ⟨a *mixed* forest⟩ **3 :** including or accompanied by inconsistent, incompatible, or contrary elements ⟨*mixed* emotions⟩ **4 :** deriving from two or more races or breeds ⟨a stallion of *mixed* blood⟩

mixed bud *n* **:** a bud that produces a branch and leaves as well as flowers

mixed media *n* **:** MULTIMEDIA ⟨a *mixed media* collage⟩

mixed nerve *n* **:** a nerve containing both sensory and motor fibers

mixed number *n* **:** a number (as 5⅔) composed of a whole number and a fraction

mix·er \ˈmik-sər\ *n* **1 :** one that mixes: as **a :** something used in mixing **b :** a party to give members of a group an opportunity to get acquainted **2 a :** a sociable person **b :** a nonalcoholic beverage used in preparing an alcoholic drink

mix·ture \ˈmiks-chər\ *n* **1 :** the act, the process, or an instance of mixing **2 a :** something mixed or being mixed ⟨add eggs to the *mixture*⟩ **b :** cloth made of thread of different colors **c :** a preparation consisting of two or more ingredients or kinds ⟨a smoking *mixture*⟩ **3 :** the relative proportion of the elements in a mixture ⟨the choke controls the *mixture* of fuel and air in the carburetor⟩ **4 :** two or more substances mixed together but not chemically united and not necessarily present in definite proportions ⟨sand mixed with sugar forms a *mixture*⟩ [Medieval French, from Latin *mixtura,* from *miscēre* "to mix"]

mix–up \ˈmik-ˌsəp\ *n* **1 :** a state or an instance of confusion ⟨a *mix-up* in plans⟩ **2 :** FIGHT 1a, MELEE

1**miz·zen** *also* **miz·en** \ˈmiz-n\ *n* **1 :** a fore-and-aft sail set on the mizzenmast **2 :** MIZZENMAST [Middle English *meson,* probably from Spanish *mesana* "sail set amidships"]

2**mizzen** *also* **mizen** *adj* **:** of or relating to the mizzenmast ⟨*mizzen* shrouds⟩

miz·zen·mast \-ˌmast, -məst\ *n* **:** the mast just behind the mainmast in a ship

mne·mon·ic \ni-ˈmän-ik\ *adj* **1 :** assisting or intended to assist memory ⟨*mnemonic* devices⟩ **2 :** of or relating to memory [Greek *mnēmonikos,* from *mnēmōn* "mindful," from *mimnēskesthai* "to remember"] — **mne·mon·i·cal·ly** \-ˈmän-i-kə-lē, -klē\ *adv*

MO \ˈem-ˈō\ *n, often not cap* **:** MODUS OPERANDI

\ə\ **abut**	\au̇\ **out**	\i\ **tip**	\ȯ\ **saw**	\u̇\ **foot**
\ər\ **further**	\ch\ **chin**	\ī\ **life**	\ȯi\ **coin**	\y\ **yet**
\a\ **mat**	\e\ **pet**	\j\ **job**	\th\ **thin**	\yü\ **few**
\ā\ **take**	\ē\ **easy**	\ng\ **sing**	\t͟h\ **this**	\yu̇\ **cure**
\ä\ **cot, cart**	\g\ **go**	\ō\ **bone**	\ü\ **food**	\zh\ **vision**

moa \ˈmō-ə\ *n* : any of various usually very large extinct flightless birds of New Zealand [Maori]

moa

Mo•ab•ite \ˈmō-ə-ˌbīt\ *n* : a member of an ancient Semitic people related to the Hebrews [*Moab,* ancient kingdom in Syria] — **Moabite** *or* **Mo•ab•it•ish** \-ˌbīt-ish\ *adj*

[1]moan \ˈmōn\ *n* **1** : COMPLAINT 1, LAMENTATION **2** : a low drawn-out sound usually indicative of pain or grief [Middle English *mone*]

[2]moan *vb* **1** : LAMENT 1 **2** : to utter with a moan or moans **3** : COMPLAIN 1

moat \ˈmōt\ *n* : a deep wide trench around the walls of a castle or fortress usually filled with water [Middle English *mote*]

[1]mob \ˈmäb\ *n* **1** : the lower classes of a community : RABBLE **2** : a large disorderly crowd often tending to violent or destructive actions **3** : an organized criminal group : GANG [Latin *mobile vulgus* "vacillating crowd"] ***synonyms*** see MULTITUDE

[2]mob *vt* **mobbed; mob•bing 1** : to crowd about and attack or annoy **2** : to crowd to capacity ⟨customers *mobbed* the store⟩

[1]mo•bile \ˈmō-bəl, -ˌbēl, -ˌbīl\ *adj* **1** : capable of moving or being moved : MOVABLE **2** : changing quickly in expression ⟨a *mobile* face⟩ **3** : tending to travel or migrate from place to place : MIGRATORY ⟨*mobile* workers⟩ **4** : readily moved by vehicles ⟨*mobile* troops⟩ **5** : characterized by movement from one class or group to another ⟨a *mobile* society⟩ **6** : CELLULAR 3 [Medieval French, from Latin *mobilis,* from *movēre* "to move"] — **mo•bil•i•ty** \mō-ˈbil-ət-ē\ *n*

[2]mo•bile \ˈmō-ˌbēl\ *n* : an artistic structure (as of sheet metal) with parts that can be moved by air currents especially when suspended

-mobile *n combining form* **1** : motorized vehicle ⟨snow*mobile*⟩ **2** : automotive vehicle bringing services to the public ⟨blood*mobile*⟩ ⟨book*mobile*⟩ [*automobile*]

mobile home *n* : a trailer that is used as a dwelling at a permanent site

mobile phone *n* : CELL PHONE

mo•bi•lize \ˈmō-bə-ˌlīz\ *vb* **1** : to put into movement or circulation **2** : to assemble and make ready for action ⟨*mobilize* army reserves⟩ — **mo•bi•li•za•tion** \ˌmō-bə-lə-ˈzā-shən, -blə-ˈzā-\ *n*

Mö•bi•us strip \ˌmœb-ē-əs, ˌmərb-, ˌmōb-\ *n* : a one-sided surface made by holding one end of a rectangle in place, twisting the rectangle to turn over the other end, and joining the two ends together [August F. *Möbius,* died 1868, German mathematician]

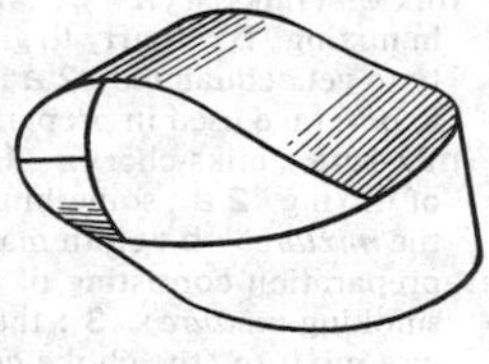
Möbius strip

mob•oc•ra•cy \mä-ˈbäk-rə-sē\ *n* **1** : mob rule **2** : the mob as a ruling class — **mob•o•crat•ic** \ˌmäb-ə-ˈkrat-ik\ *adj*

mob•ster \ˈmäb-stər\ *n* : a member of a criminal gang

moc•ca•sin \ˈmäk-ə-sən\ *n* **1** : a soft leather shoe without a heel and with the sole and sides made of one piece joined on top by a seam to a U-shaped piece across the front; *also* : a shoe resembling a true moccasin **2** : WATER MOCCASIN [Virginia Algonquian *mockasin*]

moccasin flower *n* : any of several lady's slippers; *esp* : a woodland orchid of eastern North America with usually pink or white flowers

mo•cha \ˈmō-kə\ *n* **1 a** : coffee of high quality grown in Arabia **b** : a flavoring made by mixing chocolate and coffee **2** : a pliable suede-finished glove leather from African sheepskins [*Mocha,* Yemen]

[1]mock \ˈmäk, ˈmȯk\ *vt* **1** : to laugh at scornfully : RIDICULE ⟨*mocked* his ideas⟩ **2** : DEFY 2 ⟨don't *mock* the rules⟩ **3** : to mimic in sport or derision ⟨*mocked* the statue's pose⟩ [Medieval French *moker*] ***synonyms*** see IMITATE, RIDICULE — **mock•er** *n* — **mock•ing•ly** \-ing-lē\ *adv*

[2]mock *n* **1** : an act of mocking : JEER **2** : an object of ridicule

[3]mock *adj* : not real : IMITATION ⟨*mock* grief⟩ ⟨a *mock* diamond⟩

[4]mock *adv* : in an insincere or sham manner — usually used in combination ⟨*mock*-serious⟩

mock•ery \ˈmäk-rē, ˈmȯk-, -ə-rē\ *n, pl* **-er•ies 1** : insulting or contemptuous action or speech **2** : one that is laughed at **3** : an insincere or a poor imitation ⟨the trial was a *mockery* of justice⟩ **4** : something ridiculously unsuitable

mock–he•ro•ic \ˌmäk-hi-ˈrō-ik, ˌmȯk-\ *adj* : ridiculing or burlesquing heroic style, character, or action

mock•ing•bird \ˈmäk-ing-ˌbərd, ˈmȯk-\ *n* : a common grayish North American songbird that is related to the catbirds and thrashers and is noted for the sweetness of its song and for its imitations of the notes of other birds

mock orange *n* : any of several shrubs widely grown for their showy white flowers

mock turtle soup *n* : a soup made with meat (as calf's head or veal) in imitation of green turtle soup

mock–up \ˈmäk-ˌəp, ˈmȯk-\ *n* : a full-sized structural model built accurately to scale chiefly for study, testing, or display

mod \ˈmäd\ *adj* : MODERN; *esp* : bold and free in style, behavior, or dress

mod•acryl•ic fiber \ˌmäd-ə-ˌkril-ik-\ *n* : a synthetic fiber used for clothing that dries quickly and resists burning [*modified acrylic*]

mod•al \ˈmōd-l\ *adj* **1** : of or relating to a mode or to form as opposed to substance **2** : relating to or being a modal auxiliary — **mo•dal•i•ty** \mō-ˈdal-ət-ē\ *n* — **mo•dal•ly** \ˈmōd-l-ē\ *adv*

modal auxiliary *n* : a verb (as *can, must, might, should*) that is typically used with another verb to indicate that the state or action expressed is something other than a simple fact (as a possibility or a necessity) ⟨in "we may go tomorrow" *may* is a *modal auxiliary*⟩

[1]mode \ˈmōd\ *n* **1** : an arrangement of the eight tones of an octave according to one of several fixed schemes of their intervals **2** : [2]MOOD **3 a** : a particular form or variety of something **b** : a form or manner of expression : STYLE **c** : a manner of doing something ⟨*mode* of travel⟩ **4** : the most frequent value of a set of data [Latin *modus* "measure, manner, musical mode"]

[2]mode *n* : a prevailing fashion or style (as of dress or behavior) [French, from Latin *modus*] ***synonyms*** see FASHION

[1]mod•el \ˈmäd-l\ *n* **1 a** : a small but exact copy of something ⟨a ship *model*⟩ **b** : a pattern or figure of something to be made ⟨clay *models* for a statue⟩ **2** : a person who sets a good example ⟨a *model* of politeness⟩ **3 a** : a person or thing that serves as an artist's pattern; *esp* : a person who poses for an artist **b** : a person employed to display garments or other merchandise; *esp* : MANNEQUIN **4** : a type of design of product (as a car or airplane) **5 a** : a description or analogy used to help visualize something (as an atom) that cannot be directly observed ⟨a *model* of a DNA molecule⟩ **b** : a system of assumptions, data, and inferences used to describe mathematically an object or state of affairs **c** : a computer simulation especially of a natural system ⟨climate *models*⟩ **6** : a theoretical projection of a possible or imaginary system [Middle French *modelle,* from Italian *modello,* from Latin *modulus* "small measure," from *modus* "measure, mode"]

[2]model *vb* **mod•eled** *or* **mod•elled; mod•el•ing** *or* **mod•el•ling** \ˈmäd-ling, -l-ing\ **1** : to plan or shape after a pattern ⟨a sports car *modeled* on a racing car⟩ **2 a** : to make a model : MOLD ⟨*model* a dog in clay⟩ **b** : to produce a representation or simulation of ⟨*modeled* the weather on a computer⟩ **3** : to act or serve as a model ⟨*model* for an artist⟩ — **mod•el•er** *or* **mod•el•ler** \ˈmäd-lər, -l-ər\ *n*

[3]model *adj* **1** : serving as or worthy of being a pattern ⟨a *model* student⟩ **2** : being a miniature representation of something ⟨a *model* airplane⟩

mo•dem \ˈmō-ˌdem\ *n* : a device that changes signals from one form to another that can be used by a different kind of equipment ⟨a *modem* for sending computer data over telephone lines⟩ [*mod*ulator + *dem*odulator]

[1]mod•er•ate \ˈmäd-rət, -ə-rət\ *adj* **1 a** : avoiding or lacking extremes (as of behavior or temperature) ⟨a *moderate* eater⟩ ⟨*moderate* climates⟩ **b** : CALM 2, REASONABLE ⟨were *moderate* in your protests⟩ **2 a** : tending toward the average ⟨a *moderate* rain⟩ **b** : neither very good nor very bad : MEDIOCRE ⟨*moderate* success⟩ **3** : avoiding extreme political or social measures ⟨a *moderate* candidate⟩ **4** : reasonable in price ⟨*moderate* rates⟩ **5** : of medium lightness and medium chroma ⟨a *moderate* blue⟩ [Latin *moderatus,* from *moderare* "to moderate"] — **mod•er•ate•ly** *adv* — **mod•er•ate•ness** *n*

synonyms MODERATE, TEMPERATE mean being neither very much nor very little. MODERATE implies absence or avoidance of excess ⟨*moderate* prices⟩ ⟨a *moderate* appetite⟩.

TEMPERATE suggests the exercise of restraint ⟨*temperate* use of alcohol⟩.

²**mod·er·ate** \ˈmäd-ə-ˌrāt\ *vb* **1 :** to make or become less violent, severe, or intense **2 :** to preside over a meeting

³**mod·er·ate** \ˈmäd-rət, -ə-rət\ *n* **:** one holding moderate views or belonging to a moderate group (as in politics)

mod·er·a·tion \ˌmäd-ə-ˈrā-shən\ *n* **1 :** the action of moderating **2 :** the quality or state of being moderate **:** an avoidance of extremes ⟨do everything in *moderation*⟩

mo·der·a·to \ˌmäd-ə-ˈrät-ō\ *adv or adj* **:** MODERATE 1a — used as a direction in music to indicate tempo [Italian, from Latin *moderatus*]

mod·er·a·tor \ˈmäd-ə-ˌrāt-ər\ *n* **1 :** one that moderates **2 :** a presiding officer (as of a town meeting or a discussion group) **3 :** a substance (as graphite) used for slowing down neutrons in a nuclear reactor — **mod·er·a·tor·ship** \-ˌship\ *n*

¹**mod·ern** \ˈmäd-ərn\ *adj* **1 :** of or relating to the period from about 1500 to the present ⟨*modern* history⟩ **2 :** of, relating to, or characteristic of the present or the immediate past **:** CONTEMPORARY **3 :** involving recent techniques, methods, and ideas **:** UP-TO-DATE [Late Latin *modernus,* from Latin *modo* "just now," from *modus* "measure, mode"] ***synonyms*** see RECENT — **mo·der·ni·ty** \mə-ˈdər-nət-ē, mä-\ *n* — **mod·ern·ly** \ˈmäd-ərn-lē\ *adv* — **mod·ern·ness** \-ərn-nəs\ *n*

²**modern** *n* **:** a modern person

Modern Greek *n* **:** Greek as used by the Greeks since the end of the Medieval period

Modern Hebrew *n* **:** Hebrew as used in present-day Israel

mod·ern·ism \ˈmäd-ər-ˌniz-əm\ *n* **1 :** a practice, usage, or expression peculiar to modern times **2** *often cap* **:** a movement to adapt religion to modern thought and especially to lessen traditional supernatural elements **3 :** the theory and practices of modern art; *esp* **:** an intentional break with the past and a search for new forms of expression — **mod·ern·ist** \-nəst\ *n or adj* — **mod·ern·is·tic** \ˌmäd-ər-ˈnis-tik\ *adj*

mod·ern·ize \ˈmäd-ər-ˌnīz\ *vb* **:** to make or become modern; *esp* **:** to adapt to present usage, style, or taste ⟨*modernize* an old house⟩ — **mod·ern·i·za·tion** \ˌmäd-ər-nə-ˈzā-shən\ *n* — **mod·ern·iz·er** \ˈmäd-ər-ˌnī-zər\ *n*

mod·est \ˈmäd-əst\ *adj* **1 :** having a moderate opinion of one's own good qualities and abilities **:** not boastful **2 :** showing moderation **:** not excessive ⟨a *modest* request⟩ **3 :** pure in thought, conduct, and dress **:** DECENT [Latin *modestus* "moderate"] ***synonyms*** see CHASTE, SHY — **mod·est·ly** *adv*

mod·es·ty \ˈmäd-ə-stē\ *n* **:** the quality of being modest; *esp* **:** freedom from conceit or impropriety

mo·di·cum \ˈmäd-i-kəm, ˈmōd-\ *n* **:** a limited quantity **:** a small amount ⟨a *modicum* of intelligence⟩ [Latin, neuter of *modicus* "moderate," from *modus* "measure, mode"]

mod·i·fi·ca·tion \ˌmäd-ə-fə-ˈkā-shən\ *n* **1 :** a limiting of the meaning or application (as of a statement) **2 :** partial alteration

mod·i·fi·er \ˈmäd-ə-ˌfī-ər, -ˌfīr\ *n* **:** a word (as an adjective or adverb) or group of words (as a phrase or clause) used with another word or group of words to limit or qualify its meaning

mod·i·fy \ˈmäd-ə-ˌfī\ *vb* **-fied; -fy·ing 1 a :** to make changes in **:** ALTER ⟨*modify* a plan⟩ **b :** to become modified **2 :** to lower or reduce in extent or degree **:** MODERATE ⟨*modify* a punishment⟩ **3 :** to limit in meaning **:** QUALIFY ⟨in the phrase "green gloves" "green" *modifies* "gloves"⟩ [Medieval French *modifier,* from Latin *modificare* "to measure, moderate," from *modus* "measure"] ***synonyms*** see CHANGE — **mod·i·fi·able** \-ˌfī-ə-bəl\ *adj* — **mod·i·fi·able·ness** *n*

mod·ish \ˈmōd-ish\ *adj* **:** FASHIONABLE 1, STYLISH ⟨was a *modish* dresser⟩ — **mod·ish·ly** *adv* — **mod·ish·ness** *n*

mod·u·lar \ˈmäj-ə-lər\ *adj* **1 :** of, relating to, or based on a module or a modulus **2 :** made in similar sizes or with similar units for flexibility and variety in use

modular arithmetic *n* **:** arithmetic that deals with whole numbers in such a way that all numbers are replaced by their remainders after division by a modulus ⟨5 hours after 10 o'clock is 3 o'clock because clocks follow a *modular arithmetic* with modulus 12⟩

mod·u·late \ˈmäj-ə-ˌlāt\ *vb* **1 :** to tune to a key or pitch **2 :** to adjust or regulate to a certain proportion ⟨*modulated* the voice⟩ **3 :** to vary the frequency, amplitude, or phase of (a carrier wave or signal) in order to transmit information (as by radio, television, telephony, or telegraphy) **4 :** to pass from one musical key to another usually in a gradual movement [Latin *modulari* "to play, sing," from *modulus* "small measure, rhythm," from *modus* "measure, mode"] — **mod·u·la·tor** \-ˌlāt-ər\ *n* — **mod·u·la·to·ry** \-lə-ˌtōr-ē, -ˌtȯr-\ *adj*

mod·u·la·tion \ˌmäj-ə-ˈlā-shən\ *n* **1 :** an action of modulating **2 :** the extent or degree by which something is modulated **3 :** variation of some quality (as the frequency or amplitude) of the carrier wave in radio, television, telephony, or telegraphy in accordance with the signal that is to be transmitted

mod·ule \ˈmäj-ül\ *n* **1 :** a standard or unit of measurement **2 a :** any of a series of units intended for use together **b :** a usually packaged functional subassembly of parts (as for an electronic device) **3 :** an independent unit that is a part of the total structure of a space vehicle [Latin *modulus* "small measure," from *modus* "measure, mode"]

mod·u·lo \ˈmäj-ə-ˌlō\ *prep* **:** with respect to a modulus of [New Latin, from *modulus* "small measure," from *modus* "measure, mode"]

mod·u·lus \ˈmäj-ə-ləs\ *n, pl* **-li** \-ˌlī, -ˌlē\ **1 :** a number that expresses the degree in which a property (as elasticity) is possessed by a substance or body **2 a :** ABSOLUTE VALUE 2 **b :** a fixed whole number by which all the numbers in a system of modular arithmetic are divided ⟨using *modulus* 5, the product of 3 times 4 equals 2 because 12 divided by 5 has remainder 2⟩ [New Latin, from Latin, "small measure," from *modus* "measure, mode"]

mo·dus ope·ran·di \ˌmōd-ə-ˌsäp-ə-ˈran-dē, -ˌdī\ *n, pl* **mo·di operandi** \ˌmō-ˌdē-ˌäp-, ˈmō-ˌdī-\ **:** a method of procedure [New Latin]

mo·dus vi·ven·di \ˌmō-dəs-vi-ˈven-dē, -ˌdī\ *n, pl* **mo·di vivendi** \ˈmō-ˌdē-vi-, ˈmō-ˌdī-\ **1 :** a feasible arrangement or practical compromise **2 :** a way of life [New Latin, "manner of living"]

Mogen David *variant of* MAGEN DAVID

¹**mo·gul** \ˈmō-gəl, ˈmō-ˌgəl, mō-ˈgəl\ *n* **1** *or* **mo·ghul** *often cap* **:** an Indian Muslim of or descended from one of several conquering groups of Mongol, Turkish, and Persian origin **2 :** a great personage **:** MAGNATE [Persian *Mughul,* from Mongolian *Mongγol* "Mongol"] — **mogul** *adj, often cap*

²**mogul** \ˈmō-gəl\ *n* **:** a bump on a ski slope [German dialect, related to *mugl* "small hill"]

mo·hair \ˈmō-ˌhaər, -ˌheər\ *n* **:** a fabric or yarn made of or with the long silky hair of the Angora goat; *also* **:** hair of this goat [obsolete Italian *mocaiarro,* from Arabic *mukhayyar,* literally, "choice"]

Mo·ham·med·an *also* **Mu·ham·mad·an** \mō-ˈham-əd-ən, mü-\ *adj* **:** of or relating to Muhammad or Islam — **Mohammedan** *n* — **Mo·ham·med·an·ism** \-ə-ˌniz-əm\ *n*

Mo·hawk \ˈmō-ˌhȯk\ *n, pl* **Mohawk** *or* **Mohawks :** a member of an Iroquoian people of northeastern and east central New York [of Algonquian origin]

Mo·he·gan \mō-ˈhē-gən, mə-\ *or* **Mo·hi·can** \-kən\ *n, pl* **Mohegan** *or* **Mohegans** *or* **Mohican** *or* **Mohicans :** a member of an American Indian people of southeastern Connecticut

Mohican *variant of* MAHICAN, MOHEGAN

Mo·ho \ˈmō-ˌhō\ *n* **:** the transition zone between the earth's crust and mantle [short for *Mohorovicic discontinuity,* from Andrija *Mohorovičić,* died 1936, Yugoslavian geologist]

Mo·ho·ro·vi·cic discontinuity \ˌmō-hə-ˈrō-və-ˌchich-\ *n* **:** MOHO

Mohs' scale \ˈmōz-, ˈmōs-, ˌmō-səz-\ *n* **:** a scale of hardness for minerals ranging from 1 for the softest to 10 for the hardest in which 1 represents the hardness of talc; 2, gypsum; 3, calcite; 4, fluorite; 5, apatite; 6, orthoclase; 7, quartz; 8, topaz; 9, corundum; and 10, diamond [Friedrich *Mohs,* died 1839, German mineralogist]

moi·ety \ˈmȯi-ət-ē\ *n, pl* **-ties :** one of two equal or approximately equal parts **:** HALF [Medieval French *meité, moité,* from Late Latin *medietas,* from Latin *medius* "middle"]

¹**moil** \ˈmȯil\ *vi* **:** to work hard **:** DRUDGE [Middle English *moillen* "to wet, dirty," from Medieval French *moiller* "to wet," derived from Latin *mollis* "soft"] — **moil·er** *n*

²**moil** *n* **1 :** hard work **:** DRUDGERY **2 :** CONFUSION 1

moi·ré \mȯ-ˈrā, mwä-\ *or* **moire** *same, or* ˈmȯir, ˈmȯr, ˈmwär\ *n* **:** a fabric with a shimmering watery look; *also* **:** an appearance suggesting this [French *moiré,* from *moire* "watered mohair," from English *mohair*] — **moiré** *adj*

moist \ˈmȯist\ *adj* **:** slightly wet **:** not completely dry **:** DAMP ⟨*moist* earth⟩ [Medieval French *moiste,* derived from Latin *mucidus* "slimy," from *mucus* "mucus"] — **moist·ly** *adv* — **moist·ness** \ˈmȯist-nəs, ˈmȯis-\ *n*

moist·en \ˈmȯis-ᵊn\ *vb* **moist·ened; moist·en·ing** \-n-ing, ˈmȯis-ning\ **:** to make or become moist — **moist·en·er** \ˈmȯis-ᵊn-ər, ˈmȯis-nər\ *n*

mois·ture \ˈmȯis-chər\ *n* **:** the small amount of liquid that causes moistness **:** DAMPNESS

mois·tur·ize \-chə-ˌrīz\ *vt* **:** to add moisture to

mo·jo \ˈmō-jō\ *n, pl* **mojoes** *or* **mojos :** a magic spell, hex, or charm; *also* **:** magical power [probably of African origin]

mol·al \ˈmō-ləl\ *adj* **:** of, relating to, or containing one mole of solute per 1000 grams of solvent — **mo·lal·i·ty** \mō-ˈlal-ət-ē\ *n*

[1]**mo·lar** \ˈmō-lər\ *n* **:** a tooth with a rounded or flattened surface adapted for grinding; *esp* **:** a grinding tooth of a mammal that is situated behind the premolars [Latin *molaris,* from *mola* "millstone"]

[2]**molar** *adj* **1 :** able or fitted to grind **2 :** of or relating to a molar

[3]**molar** *adj* **1 :** of or relating to a molecule or mole **2 :** containing one mole of solute per liter of solution — **mo·lar·i·ty** \mō-ˈlar-ət-ē\ *n*

mo·las·ses \mə-ˈlas-əz\ *n* **:** a thick brown syrup that is separated from raw sugar in sugar manufacture [Portuguese *melaço,* from Late Latin *mellaceum* "grape juice," from Latin *mel* "honey"]

[1]**mold** \ˈmōld\ *n* **:** light rich crumbly earth containing decayed organic matter [Old English *molde*]

[2]**mold** *n* **1 :** distinctive nature or character **:** TYPE ⟨a person of austere *mold*⟩ **2 :** the frame on or around which an object is constructed **3 a :** a cavity in which something is shaped ⟨a *mold* for metal type⟩ **b :** something shaped in a mold ⟨a *mold* of ice cream⟩ [Medieval French *molde, modle,* from Latin *modulus* "small measure," from *modus* "measure, mode"]

[3]**mold** *vb* **1 :** to knead into shape ⟨*mold* loaves of bread⟩ **2 :** to form or become formed in or as if in a mold ⟨*mold* butter⟩ — **mold·able** \ˈmōl-də-bəl\ *adj* — **mold·er** *n*

[4]**mold** *n* **:** an often woolly surface growth of fungus especially on damp or decaying organic matter; *also* **:** a fungus that produces mold [Middle English *mowlde*]

[5]**mold** *vi* **:** to become moldy

mold·board \ˈmōld-ˌbōrd, ˈmōl-, -ˌbȯrd\ *n* **:** a curved iron plate attached above the plowshare of a plow to lift and turn the soil

mol·der \ˈmōl-dər\ *vi* **mol·dered; mol·der·ing** \-də-ring, -dring\ **:** to crumble into particles [derived from [5]*mold*]

mold·ing \ˈmōl-ding\ *n* **1 :** the act or work of a person who molds **2 :** an object produced by molding **3 :** a strip of material having a shaped surface and used (as on a wall or the edge of a table) as a decoration or finish

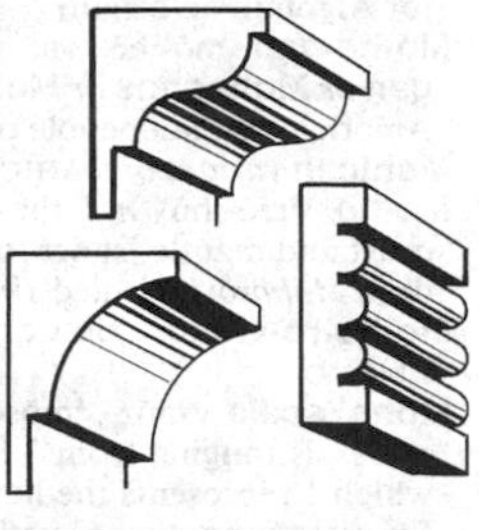
molding 3

moldy \ˈmōl-dē\ *adj* **mold·i·er; -est 1 :** of, resembling, or covered with a mold **2 a :** being old and moldering **b :** OUTMODED — **mold·i·ness** *n*

[1]**mole** \ˈmōl\ *n* **:** a small usually brown and sometimes protruding permanent spot on the skin [Old English *māl*]

[2]**mole** *n* **:** any of numerous burrowing insectivores with tiny eyes, concealed ears, and soft fur [Middle English]

[3]**mole** *n* **1 :** a heavy masonry structure built in the sea as a breakwater or pier **2 :** the harbor formed by a mole [Middle French, from Italian *molo,* from Late Greek *mōlos,* from Latin *moles,* literally, "mass"]

[4]**mole** *also* **mol** \ˈmōl\ *n* **:** a unit of amount of a pure substance that has a weight in mass units (as grams) numerically equal to its molecular weight [German *Mol,* short for *Molekulargewicht* "molecular weight"]

mo·lec·u·lar \mə-ˈlek-yə-lər\ *adj* **:** of, relating to, or produced by molecules

molecular biology *n* **:** a branch of biology that investigates the structure and function of usually large biological molecules (as DNA and proteins) in order to understand their role in biological processes and phenomena (as inheritance and cell function) — **molecular biologist** *n*

molecular formula *n* **:** a chemical formula that gives the total number of atoms of each element present in each molecule of a substance

molecular mass *n* **:** the mass of a molecule equal to the sum of the masses of all the atoms contained in it

molecular weight *n* **:** the weight of a molecule equal to the sum of the weights of the atoms contained in it

mol·e·cule \ˈmäl-i-ˌkyül\ *n* **1 :** the smallest portion of a substance that retains all the properties of the substance and is composed of one or more atoms **2 :** a very small bit **:** PARTICLE [French *molécule,* derived from Latin *moles* "mass"]

mole·hill \ˈmōl-ˌhil\ *n* **1 :** a ridge of earth pushed up by a mole **2 :** an unimportant obstacle or difficulty ⟨made a mountain out of a *molehill*⟩

mole·skin \-ˌskin\ *n* **1 :** the skin of the mole used as fur **2 a :** a heavy cotton fabric with a velvety nap on one side **b** *pl* **:** trousers of this fabric **c :** padding (as for blisters) made of moleskin with an adhesive backing

mo·lest \mə-ˈləst\ *vt* **1 :** to annoy, disturb, or persecute especially with hostile or injurious effect **2 :** to make unwanted sexual advances to; *esp* **:** to force physical sexual contact on [Medieval French *molester,* from Latin *molestare,* from *molestus* "burdensome," from *moles* "mass, burden"] — **mo·les·ta·tion** \ˌmō-ˌles-ˈtā-shən, ˌmōl-əs-, mäl-\ *n* — **mo·lest·er** \mə-ˈles-tər\ *n*

moll \ˈmäl\ *n* **:** a gangster's girl friend [probably from *Moll,* nickname for *Mary*]

mol·li·fy \ˈmäl-ə-ˌfī\ *vt* **-fied; -fy·ing 1 :** CALM 2, QUIET **2 :** to soothe in temper or disposition [Medieval French *mollifier,* from Late Latin *mollificare,* from Latin *mollis* "soft"] ***synonyms*** see PACIFY — **mol·li·fi·ca·tion** \ˌmäl-ə-fə-ˈkā-shən\ *n*

mol·lusk *or* **mol·lusc** \ˈmäl-əsk\ *n* **:** any of a large phylum (Mollusca) of invertebrate animals (as snails or clams) with a soft body lacking segments and usually enclosed in a calcareous shell [French *mollusque,* derived from Latin *molluscus* "thin-shelled (of a nut)," from *mollis* "soft"] — **mol·lus·can** \mə-ˈləs-kən, mä-\ *adj*

mol·ly *also* **mol·lie** \ˈmäl-ē\ *n, pl* **mollies :** any of several often colorful topminnows often kept in a tropical aquarium [François N. *Mollien,* died 1850, French statesman]

[1]**mol·ly·cod·dle** \ˈmäl-ē-ˌkäd-l\ *n* **:** a person who is used to being coddled or petted; *esp* **:** a pampered man or boy [from *Molly,* nickname for *Mary*]

[2]**mollycoddle** *vt* **-cod·dled; -cod·dling** \-ˌkäd-ling, -l-ing\ **:** CODDLE 2, PAMPER — **mol·ly·cod·dler** \-ˌkäd-lər, -l-ər\ *n*

Mo·lo·tov cocktail \ˌmäl-ə-ˌtȯf-, ˌmȯl-, ˌmōl-, -ˌtȯv-\ *n* **:** a crude incendiary device made of a bottle filled with a flammable liquid (as gasoline) and fitted with a wick or saturated rag that is ignited at the moment of hurling [Vyacheslav M. *Molotov*]

[1]**molt** \ˈmōlt\ *vb* **:** to shed hair, feathers, outer skin, shell, or horns periodically with the cast-off parts being replaced by a new growth [Middle English *mouten,* derived from Latin *mutare* "to change"] — **molt·er** *n*

[2]**molt** *n* **:** the act or process of molting

mol·ten \ˈmōlt-ᵊn\ *adj* **1** *obs* **:** made by melting and casting **2 :** melted especially by intense heat ⟨*molten* rock⟩ [Middle English, from past participle of *melten* "to melt"]

mol·to \ˈmōl-tō, ˈmȯl-\ *adv* **:** MUCH, VERY — used in music directions ⟨*molto* adagio⟩ [Italian, from Latin *multum,* from *multus,* adj., "much"]

mo·ly \ˈmō-lē\ *n* **:** a mythical herb with black root, white flowers, and magical powers [Latin, from Greek *mōly*]

mo·lyb·de·nite \mə-ˈlib-də-ˌnīt\ *n* **:** a metallic gray mineral consisting of molybdenum and sulfur and constituting a source of molybdenum

mo·lyb·de·num \-də-nəm\ *n* **:** a gray metallic element used in steel alloys to give greater strength and hardness — see ELEMENT table [New Latin, from Latin *molybdaena* "galena," from Greek *molybdaina,* from *molybdos* "lead"]

mom \ˈmäm, ˈməm\ *n* **:** MOTHER 1a [short for *momma*]

mo·ment \ˈmō-mənt\ *n* **1 :** a minute portion or point of time **:** INSTANT **2 a :** present time **b :** a time of importance or conspicuousness ⟨we have our *moments*⟩ **3 :** IMPORTANCE, CONSEQUENCE ⟨a matter of great *moment*⟩ [Medieval French, from Latin *momentum* "movement, particle sufficient to turn the scales, moment," from *movēre* "to move"]

mo•men•tar•i•ly \ˌmō-mən-ˈter-ə-lē\ *adv* **1** : for a moment ⟨the pain eased *momentarily*⟩ **2** *archaic* : INSTANTLY **3** : at any moment ⟨we expect them *momentarily*⟩

mo•men•tary \ˈmō-mən-ˌter-ē\ *adj* : lasting only a moment : SHORT-LIVED, TRANSITORY — **mo•men•tar•i•ness** *n*

mo•ment•ly \ˈmō-mənt-lē\ *adv* **1** : from moment to moment **2** : MOMENTARILY 1, 3

mo•men•tous \mō-ˈment-əs\ *adj* : very important : CONSEQUENTIAL ⟨a *momentous* decision⟩ — **mo•men•tous•ly** *adv* — **mo•men•tous•ness** *n*

mo•men•tum \mō-ˈment-əm\ *n, pl* **-men•ta** \-ˈment-ə\ *or* **-mentums 1** : property of a moving body that determines the length of time required to bring it to rest when under the action of a constant force or moment : the product of the mass of a body and its velocity **2** : IMPETUS 1 [Latin, "movement"]

momma *variant of* MAMA

mon- *or* **mono-** *combining form* **1** : one : single : alone ⟨*mono*mania⟩ ⟨*mono*plane⟩ **2** : containing one (usually specified) atom or group ⟨*mono*xide⟩ [Greek, from *monos* "alone, single"]

mo•nad•nock \mə-ˈnad-ˌnäk\ *n* : a hill or mountain of resistant rock surmounting a peneplain [Mount *Monadnock,* New Hampshire]

mon•arch \ˈmän-ərk, -ˌärk\ *n* **1** : a person who reigns over a kingdom or empire: **a** : a sovereign ruler ⟨an absolute *monarch*⟩ **b** : one acting primarily as chief of state and exercising only limited powers ⟨a constitutional *monarch*⟩ — compare CZAR, EMPEROR, KAISER, KING, QUEEN **2** : one holding preeminent position or power **3** : MONARCH BUTTERFLY [Late Latin *monarcha,* from Greek *monarchos,* from *mon-* + *archein* "to rule"] — **mo•nar•chal** \mə-ˈnär-kəl, mä-\ *or* **mo•nar•chi•al** \-kē-əl\ *adj*

monarch butterfly *n* : a large orange and black migratory American butterfly whose larva feeds on milkweed

monarch butterfly

mo•nar•chi•cal \mə-ˈnär-ki-kəl, mä-\ *or* **mo•nar•chic** \-ˈnär-kik\ *adj* : of, relating to, or characteristic of a monarch or monarchy — **mo•nar•chi•cal•ly** \-ki-kə-lē, -klē\ *adv*

mon•ar•chism \ˈmän-ər-ˌkiz-əm\ *n* : monarchical government or principles — **mon•ar•chist** \-kəst\ *n*

mon•ar•chy \ˈmän-ər-kē\ *n, pl* **-chies 1** : undivided or absolute rule by one person **2** : a nation or country having a monarch as chief of state **3** : a government having a hereditary chief of state with life tenure and powers varying from nominal to absolute

mo•nar•da \mə-ˈnärd-ə\ *n* : any of a genus of North American mints with showy flowers [Nicolás *Monardes,* died 1588, Spanish botanist]

mon•as•tery \ˈmän-ə-ˌster-ē\ *n, pl* **-ter•ies** : an establishment in which members of a religious community (as of monks) live and carry on their work [Late Latin *monasterium,* from Late Greek *monastērion,* from Greek, "hermit's cell," from *monazein* "to live alone," from *monos* "alone"]

mo•nas•tic \mə-ˈnas-tik\ *adj* **1** : of or relating to monks or monasteries **2** : separated from worldly affairs ⟨a *monastic* life⟩ — **monastic** *n* — **mo•nas•ti•cal•ly** \-ti-kə-lē, -klē\ *adv* — **mo•nas•ti•cism** \-tə-ˌsiz-əm\ *n*

mon•atom•ic \ˌmän-ə-ˈtäm-ik\ *adj* : consisting of one atom; *esp* : having one atom in the molecule

mon•au•ral \mä-ˈnȯr-əl, ˈmä-\ *adj* : MONOPHONIC 2 — **mon•au•ral•ly** \-rə-lē\ *adv*

Mon•day \ˈmən-dē\ *n* : the 2nd day of the week [Old English *mōnandæg,* derived from a translation of Latin *dies Lunae* "day of the moon"]

mo•ner•an \mō-ˈnir-ən\ *n* : PROKARYOTE [New Latin *Monera,* kingdom comprising prokaryotes, derived from Greek *monērēs* "single," from *monos*] — **moneran** *adj*

mon•e•tary \ˈmän-ə-ˌter-ē, ˈmən-\ *adj* : of or relating to money [Late Latin *monetarius,* from Latin *moneta* "mint, money"] ***synonyms*** see FINANCIAL

monetary unit *n* : the standard unit of value of a currency

mon•e•tize \ˈmän-ə-ˌtīz, ˈmən-\ *vt* : to coin into money; *also* : to establish as legal tender — **mon•e•ti•za•tion** \ˌmän-ət-ə-ˈzā-shən, ˌmən-\ *n*

mon•ey \ˈmən-ē\ *n, pl* **mon•eys** *or* **mon•ies** \-ēz\ **1** : something generally accepted as a medium of exchange, a measure of value, or a means of payment: as **a** : officially coined or stamped metal currency **b** : PAPER MONEY **c** : an amount or a sum of money **2** : wealth reckoned in terms of money **3** : a form or denomination of coin or paper money **4** : the 1st, 2nd, and 3rd place in a horse or dog race ⟨finished in the *money*⟩ **5** : persons or interests possessing or controlling great wealth [Medieval French *moneie,* from Latin *moneta* "mint, money"]

money changer *n* : one whose business is the exchanging of kinds or denominations of currency

mon•eyed *or* **mon•ied** \ˈmən-ēd\ *adj* **1** : having money : WEALTHY **2** : consisting of or derived from money

mon•ey•lend•er \ˈmən-ē-ˌlen-dər\ *n* : one whose business is lending money

mon•ey–mak•er \ˈmən-ē-ˌmā-kər\ *n* **1** : one who accumulates wealth **2** : a plan or product that produces profit — **mon•ey–mak•ing** \-kiŋ\ *adj or n*

money order *n* : an order for the payment of a specified amount of money to a named payee that can be purchased and cashed at issuing offices (as post offices or banks)

money plant *n* : a European herb related to the mustards and grown especially for its ornamental seed pods that are silvery white when dried

mon•ger \ˈməŋ-gər, ˈmäŋ-\ *n* **1** : a dealer in some commodity — usually used in combination ⟨fish*monger*⟩ **2** : one dealing in or promoting something petty or discreditable — usually used in combination ⟨hate*monger*⟩ [Old English *mangere,* from Latin *mango,* of Greek origin]

Mon•gol \ˈmäŋ-gəl, ˈmän-ˌgōl\ *n* **1** : a member of any of a group of traditionally pastoral peoples of Mongolia **2** : MONGOLIAN 2a [Mongolian *Moṅgyol*]

Mon•go•lian \män-ˈgōl-yən, mäŋ-\ *n* **1** : a native or inhabitant of Mongolia **2 a** : the language of the Mongol people **b** : a family of Altaic languages that includes the languages of the Mongols and the Kalmucks **3** : MONGOL 1 — **Mongolian** *adj*

Mon•gol•oid \ˈmäŋ-gə-ˌlȯid\ *adj* : of or relating to a race of humankind native to Asia — **Mongoloid** *n*

mon•goose \ˈmän-ˌgüs, ˈmäŋ\ *n, pl* **mon•goos•es** : any of various agile mammals with a long slender body and long tail that are about the size of a ferret and feed chiefly on small animals and fruit [Hindi & Marathi *māgūs*]

mon•grel \ˈməŋ-grəl, ˈmäŋ-\ *n* **1** : the offspring of parents of different breeds (as of dogs); *esp* : one of uncertain ancestry **2** : a person or thing of mixed origin [probably from Middle English *mong* "mixture," short for *ymong,* from Old English *gemong* "crowd"] — **mongrel** *adj* — **mon•grel•i•za•tion** \ˌməŋ-grə-lə-ˈzā-shən, ˌmäŋ-\ *n* — **mon•grel•ize** \ˈməŋ-grə-ˌlīz, ˈmäŋ-\ *vt*

mon•i•ker *also* **mon•ick•er** \ˈmän-i-kər\ *n, slang* : NAME 1, NICKNAME [probably from Shelta (language of Irish itinerants) *mŭnnik,* modification of Irish *ainm*]

mo•nism \ˈmō-ˌniz-əm, ˈmän-ˌiz-\ *n* : a view that a complex entity (as the universe) is basically one — **mo•nist** \ˈmō-nəst, ˈmän-əst\ *n* — **mo•nis•tic** \mō-ˈnis-tik, mä-\ *adj*

[1]**mon•i•tor** \ˈmän-ət-ər\ *n* **1 a** : a student appointed to assist a teacher **b** : one that warns or instructs **c** : one that monitors or is used in monitoring; *esp* : a screen used for display (as of television pictures or computer information) **2** : MONITOR LIZARD **3 a** : a heavily armored warship having low sides and revolving guns that was formerly used against shipping in harbors and in river patrol **b** : a gunboat used to bombard coastal areas and riverbanks [Latin, "one that warns, overseer," from *monēre* "to warn"] — **mon•i•to•ri•al** \ˌmän-ə-ˈtōr-ē-əl, -ˈtȯr-\ *adj* — **mon•i•tor•ship** \ˈmän-ət-ər-ˌship\ *n*

[2]**monitor** *vt* **mon•i•tored; mon•i•tor•ing** \ˈmän-ət-ə-riŋ, ˈmän-ə-triŋ\ : to watch, observe, or check especially for a special purpose ⟨*monitor* enemy communications⟩

monitor lizard *n* : any of various large flesh-eating lizards of tropical Africa, Australia, and Asia

mon•i•to•ry \ˈmän-ə-ˌtōr-ē, -ˌtȯr-\ *adj* : giving admonition : WARNING

monk \ˈməŋk\ *n* : a member of a religious community of men;

\ə\ **abut**	\au̇\ **out**	\i\ **tip**	\ȯ\ **saw**	\u̇\ **foot**
\ər\ **further**	\ch\ **chin**	\ī\ **life**	\ȯi\ **coin**	\y\ **yet**
\a\ **mat**	\e\ **pet**	\j\ **job**	\th\ **thin**	\yü\ **few**
\ā\ **take**	\ē\ **easy**	\ng\ **sing**	\t͟h\ **this**	\yu̇\ **cure**
\ä\ **cot, cart**	\g\ **go**	\ō\ **bone**	\ü\ **food**	\zh\ **vision**

esp : one of a religious order of men taking vows of poverty, chastity, and obedience and living in community under a rule [Old English *munuc,* from Late Latin *monachus,* from Late Greek *monachos,* from Greek *monos* "alone"] — **monk·hood** \-ˌhu̇d\ *n*

[1]**mon·key** \ˈməng-kē\ *n, pl* **monkeys** **1** : a primate mammal other than humans or usually the lemurs and tarsiers; *esp* : any of the smaller longer-tailed primates as contrasted with the apes **2** : a ludicrous figure : DUPE [probably of Low German origin] — **mon·key·ish** \-kē-ish\ *adj*

[2]**monkey** *vi* **mon·keyed; mon·key·ing** **1** : to act in a grotesque or mischievous manner **2 a** : FOOL 1b, TRIFLE **b** : MEDDLE, TAMPER

monkey business *n* : mischievous activity or behavior

mon·key·shine \ˈməng-kē-ˌshīn\ *n* : a mischievous trick : PRANK — usually used in plural

monkey wrench *n* **1** : a wrench having one fixed and one adjustable jaw at right angles to a straight handle **2** : something that disrupts ⟨the storm threw a *monkey wrench* into our plans⟩

monk·ish \ˈməng-kish\ *adj* **1** : of or relating to monks **2** : resembling that of a monk ⟨lived in *monkish* retirement⟩

monks·hood \ˈməngs-ˌhu̇d, ˈməngks-\ *n* : any of a genus of poisonous herbs related to the buttercups; *esp* : a poisonous Eurasian herb often cultivated for its showy hood-shaped white or purplish flowers

mono \ˈmä-nō\ *n* : INFECTIOUS MONONUCLEOSIS

mono- — see MON-

mono·ba·sic \ˌmän-ə-ˈbā-sik\ *adj* : having only one hydrogen atom replaceable by an atom or radical ⟨*monobasic* acid⟩

mono·chro·mat·ic \ˌmän-ə-krō-ˈmat-ik\ *adj* **1** : having or consisting of one color **2** : consisting of radiation (as light) of a single wavelength

mono·chrome \ˈmän-ə-ˌkrōm\ *n* : a painting, drawing, or photograph in a single hue — **monochrome** *adj*

mon·o·cle \ˈmän-i-kəl\ *n* : an eyeglass for one eye [French, from Late Latin *monoculus* "one-eyed," from Latin *mon-* "mon-" + *oculus* "eye"] — **mon·o·cled** \-kəld\ *adj*

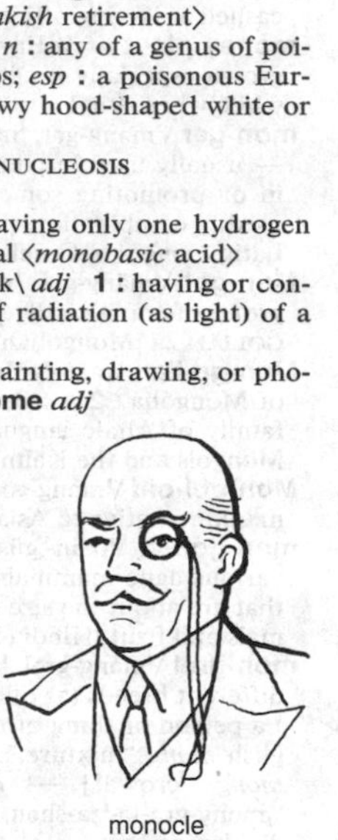

monocle

mono·clin·ic \ˌmän-ə-ˈklin-ik\ *adj* : being a crystal in which the three axes are of unequal length with two of them at right angles to each other and the third perpendicular to only one of the other two

mono·clo·nal \ˌmän-ə-ˈklō-nl\ *adj* : produced by, being, or composed of cells derived from a single cell ⟨*monoclonal* antibodies⟩ — **monoclonal** *n*

mon·o·cot \ˈmän-ə-ˌkät\ *n* : MONOCOTYLEDON — **monocot** *adj*

mono·cot·y·le·don \ˌmän-ə-ˌkät-l-ˈēd-n\ *n* : any of a group (Monocotyledoneae) of chiefly herbaceous flowering plants (as the palms and grasses) having an embryo with a single cotyledon and usually parallel-veined leaves and flower parts in groups of three — compare DICOTYLEDON — **mono·cot·y·le·don·ous** \-n-əs\ *adj*

mon·oc·u·lar \mä-ˈnäk-yə-lər, mə-\ *adj* : of, relating to, or suitable for use with only one eye

mono·cul·ture \ˈmän-ə-ˌkəl-chər\ *n* : the cultivation of a single crop to the exclusion of other uses of land

mono·cyte \ˈmän-ə-ˌsīt\ *n* : a large white blood cell that is formed in the bone marrow and migrates to the connective tissues via the bloodstream where it develops into a macrophage — **mono·cyt·ic** \ˌmän-ə-ˈsit-ik\ *adj*

mon·o·dy \ˈmän-əd-ē\ *n, pl* **-dies** **1** : ELEGY **2** : a style of musical composition in which one voice part carries the melody; *also* : a composition in this style [Medieval Latin *monodia* "lyric sung by one voice," from Greek *monōidia,* from *mon-* + *aidein* "to sing"] — **mo·nod·ic** \mə-ˈnäd-ik\ *or* **mo·nod·i·cal** \-i-kəl\ *adj* — **mon·o·dist** \ˈmän-əd-əst\ *n*

mon·oe·cious \mə-ˈnē-shəs, män-ˈē-\ *adj* : having pistils and stamens in different flowers on the same plant [derived from Greek *mon-* + *oikos* "house"] — **mon·oe·cism** \mə-ˈnē-ˌsiz-əm, män-ˈē-\ *n*

mo·nog·a·mous \mə-ˈnäg-ə-məs\ *adj* : of, relating to, or practicing monogamy — **mo·nog·a·mous·ly** *adv*

mo·nog·a·my \mə-ˈnäg-ə-mē\ *n* : marriage with only one person at a time — **mo·nog·a·mist** \-ˈnäg-ə-məst\ *n*

mono·gram \ˈmän-ə-ˌgram\ *n* : an identifying symbol or character usually made up of a person's initials — **monogram** *vt* — **mono·grammed** \-ˌgramd\ *adj*

mono·graph \ˈmän-ə-ˌgraf\ *n* : a learned treatise on a particular subject; *esp* : a written account of a single thing

mono·hy·brid \ˌmän-ə-ˈhī-brəd\ *n* : an individual or strain heterozygous for one single gene pair — **monohybrid** *adj*

mono·lay·er \ˈmän-ə-ˌlā-ər, -ˌle-ər, -ˌler\ *n* : a layer or film one cell, molecule, or atom in thickness

mono·lin·gual \ˌmän-ə-ˈling-gwəl\ *adj* : expressed in or knowing or using only one language

mon·o·lith \ˈmän-l-ˌith\ *n* **1** : a single great stone often in the form of a monument or column **2** : something (as a political organization) held to be a single massive whole exhibiting solid uniformity — **mon·o·lith·ic** \ˌmän-l-ˈith-ik\ *adj*

mon·o·logue *also* **mon·o·log** \ˈmän-l-ˌȯg, -ˌäg\ *n* **1** : a dramatic scene in which one person speaks alone **2** : a drama performed by one actor **3** : a literary composition (as a poem) in the form of a soliloquy **4** : a long speech monopolizing a conversation [Middle French *monologue,* from *mon-* "mon-" + *-logue*] — **mon·o·logu·ist** \ˈmän-l-ˌȯg-əst, -ˌäg-\ *or* **mo·no·lo·gist** *same or* mə-ˈnäl-ə-jest\ *n*

mono·ma·nia \ˌmän-ə-ˈmā-nē-ə, -ˈmā-nyə\ *n* : excessive concentration on a single object or idea — **mono·ma·ni·ac** \-ˈmā-nē-ˌak\ *n or adj*

mon·o·mer \ˈmän-ə-mər\ *n* : one of the molecular units of a polymer [*mon-* + *-mer* (as in *polymer*)] — **mon·o·mer·ic** \ˌmän-ə-ˈmer-ik\ *adj*

mo·nom·e·ter \mə-ˈnäm-ət-ər, mä-\ *n* : a line of verse consisting of one metrical foot

mo·no·mi·al \mä-ˈnō-mē-əl, mə-ˈnō-\ *n* : a mathematical expression that is a product of a constant and one or more variables raised to a power ⟨$6y$ and x^2y are *monomials*⟩ — comapre POLYNOMIAL [blend of *mon-* and *-nomial* (as in *binomial*)] — **monomial** *adj*

mono·mo·lec·u·lar \ˌmän-ō-mə-ˈlek-yə-lər\ *adj* : being only one molecule thick ⟨a *monomolecular* film⟩ — **mono·mo·lec·u·lar·ly** *adv*

mono·nu·cle·ar phagocyte system \ˌmän-ə-ˈnü-klē-ər-, -ˈnyü-\ *n* : RETICULOENDOTHELIAL SYSTEM

mono·nu·cle·o·sis \ˌmän-ə-ˌnü-klē-ˈō-səs, -ˌnyü-\ *n* : an abnormal increase in the blood of white blood cells having only one nucleus; *esp* : INFECTIOUS MONONUCLEOSIS

mono·phon·ic \ˌmän-ə-ˈfän-ik\ *adj* **1** : having a single melodic line with no accompaniment **2** : of or relating to sound transmission, recording, or reproduction involving a single transmission path — compare STEREOPHONIC

mon·oph·thong \ˈmän-əf-ˌthȯng, ˈmän-ə-ˌ\ *n* : a vowel sound that throughout its duration has a single constant articulatory position [Late Greek *monophthongos* "single vowel," from Greek *mon-* + *phthongos* "sound"] — **mon·oph·thon·gal** \ˌmän-əf-ˈthong-əl, män-ə-ˈ, -gəl\ *adj*

mono·plane \ˈmän-ə-ˌplān\ *n* : an airplane with only one pair of wings

mono·ploid \ˈmän-ə-ˌplȯid\ *adj* : having or being a single complete set of chromosomes [*mon-* + *-ploid* (as in *diploid*)] — **monoploid** *n*

mo·nop·o·list \mə-ˈnäp-ə-ləst\ *n* : one who has a monopoly or favors monopoly — **mo·nop·o·lis·tic** \mə-ˌnäp-ə-ˈlis-tik\ *adj* — **mo·nop·o·lis·ti·cal·ly** \-ˈlis-ti-kə-lē, -klē\ *adv*

mo·nop·o·lize \mə-ˈnäp-ə-ˌlīz\ *vt* : to get or have a monopoly of — **mo·nop·o·li·za·tion** \-ˌnäp-ə-lə-ˈzā-shən\ *n* — **mo·nop·o·liz·er** \-ˈnäp-ə-ˌlī-zər\ *n*

mo·nop·o·ly \mə-ˈnäp-lē, -ə-lē\ *n, pl* **-lies** **1** : exclusive ownership or control through legal privilege, command of supply, or group action **2** : exclusive possession **3** : a commodity controlled by one party **4** : a person or group having a monopoly [Latin *monopolium,* from Greek *monopōlion,* from *mon-* + *pōlein* "to sell"]

mono·rail \ˈmän-ə-ˌrāl\ *n* : a single rail serving as a track for cars that are balanced upon it

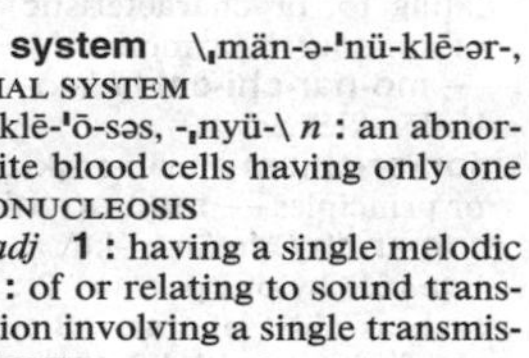

monorail

or suspended from it; *also* : a vehicle or system using such a track

mono·sac·cha·ride \ˌmän-ə-ˈsak-ə-ˌrīd\ *n* : a sugar (as glucose) that is not decomposable into simpler sugars by hydrolysis and that contains one or more hydroxyl groups — called also *simple sugar*

mono·so·di·um glutamate \ˌmän-ə-ˌsōd-ē-əm-\ *n* : a sodium salt $C_5H_8NO_4Na$ used for seasoning foods

mono·so·mic \ˌmän-ə-ˈsō-mik\ *adj* : having one less than the diploid number of chromosomes — **monosomic** *n* — **mono·so·my** \ˈmän-ə-ˌsō-mē\ *n*

mono·syl·la·ble \ˈmän-ə-ˌsil-ə-bəl, ˌmän-ə-ˈ\ *n* : a word of one syllable — **mono·syl·lab·ic** \ˌmän-ə-sə-ˈlab-ik\ *adj* — **mono·syl·lab·i·cal·ly** \-ˈlab-i-kə-lē, -klē\ *adv*

mono·the·ism \ˈmän-ə-ˌthē-ˌiz-əm\ *n* : a doctrine or belief that there is only one deity — **mono·the·ist** \-ˌthē-əst\ *n* — **mono·the·is·tic** \-thē-ˈis-tik\ *adj*

mono·tone \ˈmän-ə-ˌtōn\ *n* **1** : a succession of syllables, words, or sentences in one unvaried key or pitch ⟨speak in a *monotone*⟩ **2** : a single unvaried musical tone **3** : tedious sameness or repetition ⟨a *monotone* of yellow fields⟩ **4** : a person unable to produce or distinguish between musical intervals — **monotone** *adj* — **mono·ton·ic** \ˌmän-ə-ˈtän-ik\ *adj* — **mono·ton·i·cal·ly** \-ˈtän-i-kə-lē, -klē\ *adv*

mo·not·o·nous \mə-ˈnät-n-əs, -ˈnät-nəs\ *adj* **1** : uttered or sounded in one unvarying tone **2** : tediously uniform or unvarying ⟨*monotonous* scenery⟩ — **mo·not·o·nous·ly** *adv* — **mo·not·o·nous·ness** *n*

mo·not·o·ny \mə-ˈnät-n-ē, -ˈnät-nē\ *n, pl* **-nies** **1** : sameness of tone or sound **2** : lack of variety; *esp* : tiresome sameness ⟨the *monotony* of the empty landscape⟩

mono·treme \ˈmän-ə-ˌtrēm\ *n* : any of an order (Monotremata) of egg-laying mammals comprising the platypuses and echidnas [derived from Greek *mon-* + *trēma* "hole"]

mono·un·sat·u·rat·ed \ˌmän-ō-ˌən-ˈsach-ə-ˌrāt-əd\ *adj* : containing one double or triple bond per molecute — used especially of an oil, fat, or fatty acid

mono·va·lent \ˌmän-ə-ˈvā-lənt\ *adj* : UNIVALENT

mon·ovu·lar \män-ˈō-vyə-lər, ˈmän-\ *adj* : MONOZYGOTIC

mon·ox·ide \mə-ˈnäk-ˌsīd\ *n* : an oxide containing only one oxygen atom in the molecule

mono·zy·got·ic \ˌmän-ə-zī-ˈgät-ik\ *adj* : derived from a single egg ⟨*monozygotic* twins⟩

Mon·roe Doctrine \mən-ˌrō-\ *n* : a statement of U.S. foreign policy proclaimed in 1823 by President James Monroe expressing opposition to extension of European control or influence in the western hemisphere

mon·sei·gneur \ˌmōⁿ-ˌsān-ˈyər\ *n, pl* **mes·sei·gneurs** \ˌmā-ˌsān-ˈyər, -ˈyərz\ : a French dignitary — used as a title before another title of office or rank ⟨*Monseigneur* the Archbishop⟩ [French, literally, "my lord"]

mon·sieur \məs-ˈyə, məsh-; mə-ˈsiər\ *n, pl* **mes·sieurs** \məs-ˈyə, -ˈyəz, məsh-, mās-; mə-ˈsiər, -ˈsiərz\ — used by or to French-speaking people as a courtesy title equivalent to *Mr.* [Middle French, literally, "my lord"]

mon·si·gnor \män-ˈsē-nyər, mən-\ *n, pl* **mon·si·gnors** *or* **mon·si·gno·ri** \ˌmän-ˌsēn-ˈyōr-ē, -ˈyȯr-\ : a Roman Catholic prelate — used as a title before the surname or before the given name and the surname ⟨*Monsignor* Smith⟩ ⟨*Monsignor* John Smith⟩ [Italian *monsignore,* from French *monseigneur*] — **mon·si·gno·ri·al** \ˌmän-ˌsēn-ˈyōr-ē-əl, -ˈyȯr-\ *adj*

mon·soon \män-ˈsün\ *n* **1** : a periodic wind in the Indian Ocean and southern Asia **2** : the rainy season that accompanies the southwest monsoon in India and adjacent areas **3** : rainfall that is associated with the monsoon season [obsolete Dutch *monssoen,* from Portuguese *monção,* from Arabic *mawsim* "time, season"]

¹mon·ster \ˈmän-stər\ *n* **1** : an animal or plant of abnormal form or structure **2** : a creature of strange or horrible form **3** : one unusually large for its kind **4** : an extremely wicked or cruel person [Medieval French *monstre,* from Latin *monstrum* "omen, monster," from *monēre* "to warn"]

²monster *adj* : very large : ENORMOUS

mon·strance \ˈmän-strəns\ *n* : a vessel used for showing the Blessed Sacrament [Middle English *mustraunce, monstrans* "demonstration, monstrance," from Medieval French *mustrance* "show, sign," from Medieval Latin *monstrantia,* from Latin *monstrare* "to show"]

mon·stros·i·ty \män-ˈsträs-ət-ē\ *n, pl* **-ties** **1** : the condition of being monstrous **2** : something monstrous : MONSTER

mon·strous \ˈmän-strəs\ *adj* **1** : being great or overwhelming in size : GIGANTIC **2** : having the qualities or appearance of a monster **3 a** : very ugly or vicious : HORRIBLE **b** : shockingly wrong or ridiculous **4** : very different from the usual, natural, or expected — **mon·strous·ly** *adv* — **mon·strous·ness** *n*

synonyms MONSTROUS, PRODIGIOUS, TREMENDOUS, STUPENDOUS mean extremely impressive especially in size. MONSTROUS further implies ugliness or abnormality ⟨the *monstrous* waste of the project⟩. PRODIGIOUS suggests a marvelousness that strains belief ⟨made a *prodigious* effort to roll the stone aside⟩. TREMENDOUS implies an awe-inspiring or terrifying effect ⟨the *tremendous* size of the blue whale⟩. STUPENDOUS suggests a power to stun or astound ⟨a *stupendous* wedding cake⟩.

mon·tage \män-ˈtäzh, mōⁿ-, -ˈtȧzh\ *n* **1** : an artistic composition made up of several different kinds of items (as strips of newspaper or bits of wood) arranged together **2** : the production of a rapid succession of images in a motion picture to illustrate an association of ideas [French, from *monter* "to mount"]

mon·tane \män-ˈtān, ˈmän-ˌ\ *adj* : of, relating to, growing in, or being the relatively moist cool upland slopes below timberline characterized by large evergreen trees as the dominant form of life [Latin *montanus* "of a mountain," from *mont-, mons* "mountain"]

Mon·te·zu·ma's revenge \ˌmän-tə-ˈzü-məz-\ *n* : diarrhea contracted in Mexico especially by tourists [*Montezuma* II, died 1520, last Aztec emperor of Mexico]

month \ˈmənth, ˈməntth\ *n, pl* **months** \ˈməns, ˈmənths, ˈməntths\ : one of the 12 portions into which the year is divided [Old English *mōnath*]

¹month·ly \ˈmənth-lē, ˈməntth-\ *adj* **1** : occurring, done, produced, or issued every month **2** : computed in terms of one month **3** : lasting a month — **monthly** *adv*

²monthly *n, pl* **monthlies** **1** : a monthly periodical **2** *pl* : a menstrual period

mon·u·ment \ˈmän-yə-mənt\ *n* **1** : something that serves as a memorial; *esp* : a building, pillar, stone, or statue erected in memory of a person or event **2** : a work, saying, or deed that lasts or that is worth preserving **3** : a boundary marker (as a stone) **4** : a natural feature or historic site set aside and maintained by the government as public property [Latin *monumentum,* from *monēre* "to remind"]

mon·u·men·tal \ˌmän-yə-ˈment-l\ *adj* **1** : of, relating to, or suitable for a monument **2** : serving as or resembling a monument : MASSIVE; *also* : highly significant : OUTSTANDING ⟨a *monumental* achievement⟩ **3** : very great ⟨a *monumental* misunderstanding⟩ — **mon·u·men·tal·ly** \-l-ē\ *adv*

moo \ˈmü\ *vi* : to make the natural throat noise of a cow : LOW [imitative] — **moo** *n*

mooch \ˈmüch\ *vb* **1** : to wander about **2** : BEG, SPONGE [probably from French dialect *muchier* "to hide, lurk"] — **mooch·er** *n*

¹mood \ˈmüd\ *n* **1** : an emotional state or frame of mind : HUMOR ⟨in a good *mood*⟩; *also* : the expression of feeling in a work of art or literature **2 a** : a dominant attitude or spirit **b** : a distinctive atmosphere or context ⟨the dark *mood* of the movie⟩ [Old English *mōd* "mind, mood"]

synonyms MOOD, HUMOR, TEMPER mean a state of mind in which one emotion or desire temporarily has control. MOOD implies a pervasiveness and compelling quality of the emotion ⟨you can really write when you are in the *mood*⟩. HUMOR implies a mood resulting from one's special temperament or present physical condition ⟨a good dinner put us in a better *humor*⟩. TEMPER suggests the domination of a single strong emotion such as anger ⟨was in a foul *temper* that night⟩.

²mood *n* : a set of inflectional forms of a verb that show whether the action or state expressed is to be thought of as a fact, a command, or a wish or possibility — compare IMPERATIVE, INDICATIVE, SUBJUNCTIVE [alteration of ¹*mode*]

moody \ˈmüd-ē\ *adj* **mood·i·er; -est** **1** : frequently influenced by moods; *esp* : subject to fits of depression or temper **2**

: showing a moody state of mind ⟨a *moody* face⟩ — **mood·i·ly** \ˈmüd-ᵊl-ē\ *adv* — **mood·i·ness** \ˈmüd-ē-nəs\ *n*

[1]**moon** \ˈmün\ *n* **1 a :** the earth's natural satellite shining by the sun's reflected light, revolving about the earth from west to east in about 29½ days, having a diameter of about 2160 miles (3475 kilometers), a mean distance from the earth of about 238,900 miles (384,400 kilometers), and contributing the largest component to the raising of tides on earth **b :** SATELLITE 2 **2 :** an indefinite usually extended period of time ⟨took many *moons* to complete⟩ **3 :** MOONLIGHT [Old English *mōna*] — **moon·less** \-ləs\ *adj* — **moon·like** \-ˌlīk\ *adj*

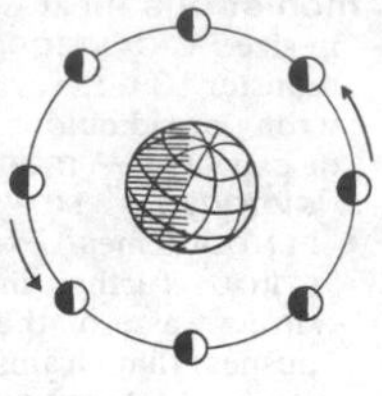

moon 1a

[2]**moon** *vb* **:** to spend time in idle thought **:** DREAM

moon·beam \ˈmün-ˌbēm\ *n* **:** a ray of light from the moon

moon blindness *n* **:** a recurrent eye disorder of the horse

moon·calf \-ˌkaf, -ˌkȧf\ *n* **:** a foolish or absentminded person **:** SIMPLETON

moon·fish \-ˌfish\ *n* **:** any of various often short deep-bodied silvery or yellowish marine fishes (as a platy) with a body that is flattened from side to side

moon·flow·er \-ˌflau̇-ər, -ˌflau̇r\ *n* **:** a tropical American morning glory with fragrant night-blooming flowers; *also* **:** any of several related plants

moon·let \ˈmün-lət\ *n* **:** a small natural or artificial satellite

[1]**moon·light** \-ˌlīt\ *n* **:** the light of the moon

[2]**moonlight** *vi* **-light·ed; -light·ing :** to hold a second usually nighttime job in addition to a regular one — **moon·light·er** *n*

moon·lit \ˈmün-ˌlit\ *adj* **:** lighted by the moon ⟨a *moonlit* night⟩

moon·roof \-ˌrüf, -ˌru̇f\ *n* **:** a glass sunroof

moon·scape \-ˌskāp\ *n* **:** the surface of the moon as seen or as pictured

moon·shine \-ˌshīn\ *n* **1 :** MOONLIGHT **2 :** empty talk **:** NONSENSE **3 :** intoxicating liquor; *esp* **:** illegally distilled corn whiskey — **moon·shin·er** \-ˌshī-nər\ *n*

moon·stone \-ˌstōn\ *n* **:** a transparent or translucent mineral with a pearly greenish or bluish luster that is a variety of feldspar and is used in jewelry

moon·struck \-ˌstrək\ *adj* **1 :** mentally unbalanced **2 :** romantically sentimental **3 :** lost in daydreams or fantasy

moony \ˈmü-nē\ *adj* **:** DREAMY 2, MOONSTRUCK

[1]**moor** \ˈmu̇r\ *n* **1** *chiefly British* **:** an expanse of open rolling infertile land **2 :** a boggy peaty area dominated by grasses and sedges [Old English *mōr*]

[2]**moor** *vb* **:** to secure (as a boat) with cables, lines, or anchors [Middle English *moren*] — **moor·age** \-ij\ *n*

Moor \ˈmu̇r\ *n* **:** one of a North African people of mixed Arab and Berber ancestry conquering Spain in the 8th century and ruling until 1492 [Medieval French *More,* from Latin *Maurus* "inhabitant of Mauretania"] — **Moor·ish** \-ish\ *adj*

Moore's law \ˈmōrz-, ˈmu̇rz-\ *n, often cap L* **:** an axiom of microprocessor development that usually holds that processing power doubles every 18 months relative to size or cost [Gordon E. *Moore,* born 1929, American computer industry executive]

moor·hen \ˈmu̇r-ˌhen\ *n* **:** the common gallinule of the New World, Eurasia, and Africa

moor·ing \ˈmu̇r-ing\ *n* **1 a :** a place where or an object to which a craft can be made fast **b :** a device (as a chain or line) by which an object is moored **2 :** moral or spiritual resources — usually used in plural

moor·land \ˈmu̇r-lənd, -ˌland\ *n* **:** land consisting of moors

moose \ˈmüs\ *n, pl* **moose :** a large ruminant mammal with humped shoulders and broad flattened antlers that is the largest existing member of the deer family and inhabits forested areas of Canada, the northern U.S., Europe, and Asia [of Algonquian origin]

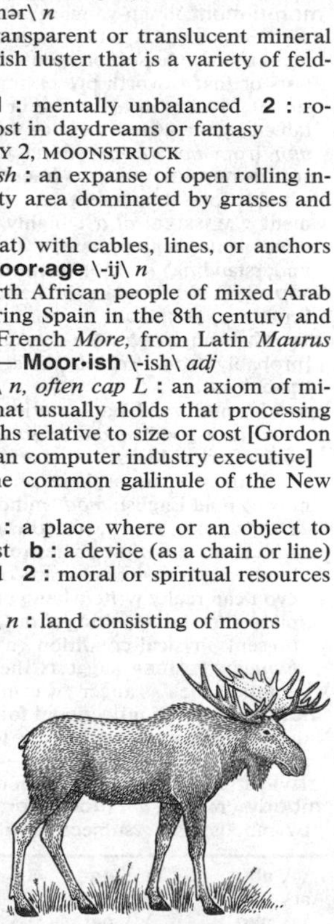

moose

[1]**moot** \ˈmüt\ *vt* **1 :** to bring up for discussion **2 :** DEBATE 1 [obsolete *moot* "discussion," from Old English *mōt* "assembly"]

[2]**moot** *adj* **1 :** subject to argument or discussion **:** DEBATABLE ⟨a *moot* question⟩ **2 :** ACADEMIC 4

moot court *n* **:** a mock court in which students of law argue hypothetical cases for practice

[1]**mop** \ˈmäp\ *n* **1 :** an implement for cleaning made of absorbent material fastened to a handle **2 :** something resembling a mop ⟨a *mop* of hair⟩ [Middle English *mappe*]

[2]**mop** *vb* **mopped; mop·ping :** to wipe or clean with or as if with a mop ⟨*mop* one's brow⟩ — **mop·per** *n*

[1]**mope** \ˈmōp\ *vi* **1 :** to be in a dull and dispirited state **2 :** to move slowly or aimlessly **:** DAWDLE [probably from obsolete *mop, mope* "fool"] — **mop·er** *n*

[2]**mope** *n* **1 :** a dull listless person **2** *pl* **:** low spirits **:** BLUES ⟨a fit of the *mopes*⟩

mo·ped \ˈmō-ˌped\ *n* **:** a lightweight low-powered motorbike that can be pedaled [Swedish, from *motor* "motor" + *pedal* "pedal"]

mop·pet \ˈmäp-ət\ *n* **:** a young child [obsolete *mop* "fool, child"]

mop–up \ˈmäp-ˌəp\ *n* **:** a concluding action or phase

mop up \mäp-ˈəp, ˈmäp-\ *vb* **1 :** to gather by or as if by mopping ⟨*mop up* spilt milk⟩ **2 :** to eliminate remaining resistance ⟨*mop up* enemy forces⟩ **3 :** to finish a task

mo·raine \mə-ˈrān\ *n* **:** an accumulation of earth and stones deposited by a glacier [French] — **mo·rain·al** \-ˈrān-ᵊl\ *adj* — **mo·rain·ic** \-ˈrā-nik\ *adj*

[1]**mor·al** \ˈmȯr-əl, ˈmär-\ *adj* **1 a :** of or relating to principles of right and wrong in behavior **:** ETHICAL **b :** expressing or teaching a conception of right behavior ⟨a *moral* poem⟩ **c :** conforming to a standard of right behavior **:** VIRTUOUS, GOOD ⟨a *moral* life⟩ **d :** capable of right and wrong action **2 :** probable but not proved **:** VIRTUAL ⟨a *moral* certainty⟩ [Medieval French, from Latin *moralis,* from *mor-, mos* "custom"] — **mor·al·ly** \-ə-lē\ *adv*

synonyms MORAL, ETHICAL, RIGHTEOUS, NOBLE mean conforming to a standard of what is right and good. MORAL and ETHICAL are both concerned with rightness or wrongness of actions and conduct, but MORAL is more often applied to the practice or acts of individuals ⟨the *moral* values of a community⟩. ETHICAL is applied more often to theoretical or general questions of rightness, fairness, or equity ⟨committed to the highest *ethical* principles⟩. RIGHTEOUS stresses guiltlessness or blamelessness and often suggests the sanctimonious ⟨wished to be *righteous* before the world⟩. NOBLE implies freedom from anything petty, mean, or dubious in conduct and character ⟨had the *noblest* of reasons for seeking office⟩.

[2]**moral** *n* **1 :** the moral significance or practical lesson (as of a story) **2** *pl* **:** moral conduct **3** *pl* **:** moral teachings or principles

mo·rale \mə-ˈral\ *n* **:** the mental and emotional condition (as of enthusiasm, spirit, loyalty) of an individual or a group with regard to the function or tasks at hand [French *moral,* from *moral,* adj., "moral"]

mor·al·ist \ˈmȯr-ə-ləst, ˈmär-\ *n* **1 :** one who leads a moral life **2 :** one who moralizes; *esp* **:** a person who teaches, studies, or points out morals **3 :** a person who is concerned with regulating the morals of others

mor·al·is·tic \ˌmȯr-ə-ˈlis-tik, ˌmär-\ *adj* **1 :** teaching or pointing out morals ⟨a *moralistic* story⟩ **2 :** narrowly conventional in morals ⟨*moralistic* attitudes⟩ — **mor·al·is·ti·cal·ly** \-ˈlis-ti-kə-lē, -klē\ *adv*

mo·ral·i·ty \mə-ˈral-ət-ē\ *n, pl* **-ties 1 :** moral quality or character ⟨judge the *morality* of an action⟩ **2 :** moral conduct **:** VIRTUE ⟨standards of *morality*⟩ **3 :** a system of morals **:** principles of conduct

morality play *n* **:** an allegorical play especially of the 15th and 16th centuries in which the characters personify moral qualities or abstractions (as beauty or death)

mor·al·ize \ˈmȯr-ə-ˌlīz, ˈmär-\ *vb* **1 :** to explain in moral terms **2 :** to make moral or morally better **3 :** to talk or write in a moralistic way — **mor·al·i·za·tion** \ˌmȯr-ə-lə-ˈzā-shən, ˌmär-\ *n* — **mor·al·iz·er** \ˈmȯr-ə-ˌlī-zər, ˈmär-\ *n*

mo·rass \mə-ˈras\ *n* **1 :** MARSH, SWAMP **2 :** a situation that traps, confuses, or hinders [Dutch *moeras*]

mor·a·to·ri·um \ˌmȯr-ə-ˈtōr-ē-əm, ˌmär-, -ˈtȯr-\ *n, pl* **-ri·ums** *or* **-ria** \-ē-ə\ **1 :** a legally authorized period of delay in the performance of an obligation (as the payment of a debt) ⟨a *moratorium* on war debt payments⟩ **2 :** a temporary ban or suspension ⟨a *moratorium* on atomic testing⟩ [New Latin, derived from Latin *morari* "to delay," from *mora* "delay"]

Mo·ra·vi·an \mə-ˈrā-vē-ən\ *n* **1 :** a member of a Christian denomination that traces its history back through the 15th century evangelical reform movement in Moravia and Bohemia **2 a :** a native or inhabitant of Moravia **b :** the group of Czech dialects spoken by the Moravian people — **Moravian** *adj*

mo·ray eel \mə-ˈrā-, ˈmȯr-ˌā-\ *n* **:** any of numerous often brightly colored eels of warm seas that have sharp teeth capable of inflicting severe bites and that include a Mediterranean eel sometimes used for food — called also *moray* [Portuguese *moréia,* from Latin *muraena,* from Greek *myraina*]

mor·bid \ˈmȯr-bəd\ *adj* **1 a :** of, relating to, or characteristic of disease ⟨*morbid* anatomy⟩ **b :** not healthful **:** DISEASED ⟨*morbid* conditions⟩ **2 :** characterized by gloomy or unwholesome ideas or feelings ⟨takes a *morbid* interest in funerals⟩ [Latin *morbidus* "diseased," from *morbus* "disease"] — **mor·bid·ly** *adv* — **mor·bid·ness** *n*

mor·bid·i·ty \mȯr-ˈbid-ət-ē\ *n, pl* **-ties 1 :** the quality or state of being morbid **2 :** the relative incidence of disease

[1]**mor·dant** \ˈmȯrd-nt\ *adj* **:** biting and caustic in thought, manner, or style **:** INCISIVE ⟨*mordant* criticism⟩ [Medieval French, present participle of *mordre* "to bite," from Latin *mordēre*] — **mor·dan·cy** \-n-sē\ *n* — **mor·dant·ly** *adv*

[2]**mordant** *n* **1 :** a chemical that fixes a dye in or on a substance by combining with the dye to form an insoluble compound **2 :** a corroding substance used in etching

[3]**mordant** *vt* **:** to treat with a mordant

mor·dent \ˈmȯrd-nt, mȯr-ˈdent\ *n* **:** a musical ornament made by a quick alternation of a principal tone with the tone below [Italian *mordente,* from Latin *mordēre* "to bite"]

[1]**more** \ˈmōr, ˈmȯr\ *adj* **1 :** greater in amount or degree ⟨felt *more* pain⟩ **2 :** ADDITIONAL, FURTHER ⟨bought *more* apples⟩ [Old English *māra*]

[2]**more** *adv* **1 a :** in addition ⟨a couple times *more*⟩ **b :** MOREOVER **2 :** to a greater or higher degree — often used with an adjective or adverb to form the comparative ⟨*more* active⟩ ⟨*more* actively⟩

[3]**more** *n* **1 :** a greater amount or number ⟨got *more* than we expected⟩ ⟨the *more* I thought about it⟩ **2 :** an additional amount or number ⟨the *more* the merrier⟩

mo·rel \mə-ˈrel, mȯ-\ *n* **:** any of several large edible fungi with a conical cap having a highly pitted surface — called also *morel mushroom* [French *morille,* probably derived from Latin *Maurus* "inhabitant of Mauretania"]

mo·rel·lo \mə-ˈrel-ō\ *n* **:** a cultivated sour cherry with dark red fruit [probably from Dutch dialect *amarelle, marelle,* from Medieval Latin *amarellum* "sour cherry," from Latin *amarus* "bitter, sour"]

more or less *adv* **1 :** to a varying or undetermined extent or degree **:** SOMEWHAT ⟨is *more or less* willing to help⟩ **2 :** with small variations **:** APPROXIMATELY ⟨is 16 acres *more or less*⟩

more·over \mōr-ˈō-vər, mȯr-\ *adv* **:** in addition to what has been said **:** BESIDES

mo·res \ˈmȯr-ˌāz, ˈmōr-, -ˌēz\ *n pl* **1 :** the fixed morally binding customs of a particular group **2 :** habitual behavior [Latin, pl. of *mor-, mos* "custom"]

Mor·gan \ˈmȯr-gən\ *n* **:** any of an American breed of light horses originated in Vermont and noted for stamina, docility, beauty, courage, and especially longevity [Justin *Morgan,* died 1798, American teacher]

mor·ga·nat·ic \ˌmȯr-gə-ˈnat-ik\ *adj* **:** of, relating to, or being a marriage between a person of royal or noble rank and a commoner who does not assume the superior partner's rank and whose children do not succeed to the title or inheritance of the parent of superior rank [New Latin *matrimonium ad morganaticum,* literally, "marriage with morning gift (given by the husband to the wife on the morning after consummation of the marriage)"] — **mor·ga·nat·i·cal·ly** \-i-kə-lē, -klē\ *adv*

morgue \ˈmȯrg\ *n* **1 :** a place where the bodies of dead persons are temporarily kept pending identification or release for burial or autopsy **2 :** a department of a newspaper where reference material is filed [French]

mor·i·bund \ˈmȯr-ə-ˌbənd, ˈmär-, -bənd\ *adj* **:** being in a dying state [Latin *moribundus,* from *mori* "to die"] — **mor·i·bun·di·ty** \ˌmȯr-ə-ˈbən-dət-ē, ˌmär-\ *n*

Mor·mon \ˈmȯr-mən\ *n* **:** LATTER-DAY SAINT; *esp* **:** a member of the Church of Jesus Christ of Latter-Day Saints [*Mormon,* ancient compiler of the Book of Mormon presented as divine revelation by Joseph Smith] — **Mor·mon·ism** \ˈmȯr-mə-ˌniz-əm\ *n*

morn \ˈmȯrn\ *n* **:** MORNING [Old English *morgen*]

morn·ing \ˈmȯr-ning\ *n* **1 a :** DAWN 1 **b :** the time from sunrise to noon **c :** the time from midnight to noon **2 :** the first or early part ⟨the *morning* of life⟩ [Middle English, from *morn* + *-ing* (as in *evening*)]

morning glory *n* **:** any of various usually twining plants with showy trumpet-shaped flowers that usually close by noon; *also* **:** any of various related herbs, vines, shrubs, or trees

Morning Prayer *n* **:** a morning service of the Anglican communion

morn·ings \ˈmȯr-ningz\ *adv* **:** in the morning repeatedly ⟨we work *mornings*⟩

morning sickness *n* **:** nausea and vomiting that occur typically in the morning especially during the early months of pregnancy

morning star *n* **:** a bright planet (as Venus) seen in the eastern sky before or at sunrise

mo·roc·co \mə-ˈräk-ō\ *n* **:** a fine leather made of goat skins tanned with sumac [*Morocco,* Africa]

mo·ron \ˈmōr-ˌän, ˈmȯr-\ *n* **:** a very stupid person [Greek *mōros* "foolish, stupid"] — **mo·ron·ic** \mə-ˈrän-ik, mȯ-\ *adj* — **mo·ron·i·cal·ly** \-ˈrän-i-kə-lē, -klē\ *adv*

mo·rose \mə-ˈrōs, mȯ-\ *adj* **1 :** having a sullen and gloomy disposition **2 :** marked by or expressive of gloom [Latin *morosus,* literally, "capricious," from *mor-, mos* "custom, will"] — **mo·rose·ly** *adv* — **mo·rose·ness** *n*

morph \ˈmȯrf\ *vb* **:** to change in form or character [short for *metamorphose*]

mor·pheme \ˈmȯr-ˌfēm\ *n* **:** a word or part of a word (as an affix or a base) that contains no smaller meaningful parts [French *morphème,* from Greek *morphē* "form"] — **mor·phe·mic** \mȯr-ˈfē-mik\ *adj*

mor·phia \ˈmȯr-fē-ə\ *n* **:** MORPHINE

-mor·phic \ˈmȯr-fik\ *adj combining form* **:** having (such) a form ⟨endo*morphic*⟩ [Greek *morphē* "form"]

mor·phine \ˈmȯr-ˌfēn\ *n* **:** a bitter white crystalline habit-forming narcotic drug $C_{17}H_{19}NO_3$ made from opium and used especially to deaden pain [French, from *Morpheus,* Greek god of dreams]

mor·phol·o·gy \mȯr-ˈfäl-ə-jē\ *n* **1 a :** a branch of biology that deals with the form and structure of animals and plants **b :** the form and structure of an organism or any of its parts **2 :** the part of grammar dealing with word formation and including inflection, derivation, and the formation of compounds **3 :** STRUCTURE, FORM ⟨the *morphology* of rocks⟩ [German *Morphologie,* derived from Greek *morphē* "form"] — **mor·pho·log·i·cal** \ˌmȯr-fə-ˈläj-i-kəl\ *adj* — **mor·pho·log·i·cal·ly** \-i-kə-lē, -klē\ *adv* — **mor·phol·o·gist** \mȯr-ˈfäl-ə-jəst\ *n*

-mor·phous \ˈmȯr-fəs\ *adj combining form* **:** having (such) a form [Greek *-morphos,* from *morphē* "form"]

mor·ris \ˈmȯr-əs, ˈmär-\ *n* **:** a vigorous English dance traditionally performed by men wearing costumes and bells [Middle English *moreys* "Moorish"]

mor·ris chair \ˈmȯr-əs-, ˈmär-\ *n* **:** an easy chair with an adjustable back and removable cushions [William *Morris,* died 1896, English poet and artist]

mor·row \ˈmär-ō, ˈmȯr-\ *n* **1** *archaic* **:** MORNING **2 :** the next day [Middle English *morn, morwen*]

Morse code \ˈmȯrs-\ *n* **:** either of two codes consisting of dots and dashes or long and short sounds used for transmitting messages by audible or visual signals [Samuel F. B. *Morse,* died 1872, American artist and inventor]

☞ The Morse Code Table is on the following page.

mor·sel \ˈmȯr-səl\ *n* **1 :** a small piece of food **:** BITE **2 :** a small quantity or piece [Medieval French, from *mors* "bite," from Latin *morsus,* from *mordēre* "to bite"]

[1]**mor·tal** \ˈmȯrt-l\ *adj* **1 :** capable of causing death **:** FATAL ⟨a *mortal* wound⟩ **2 :** subject to death ⟨*mortal* man⟩ **3 :** extremely hostile ⟨a *mortal* enemy⟩ **4 :** very great, intense, or severe ⟨in *mortal* fear⟩ **5 :** HUMAN ⟨*mortal* limitations⟩ **6 :** of, relating to, or connected with death ⟨*mortal* agony⟩ [Medieval French, from Latin *mortalis,* from *mort-, mors* "death"] ***synonyms*** see DEADLY — **mor·tal·ly** \-l-ē\ *adv*

\ə\ **abut**	\au̇\ **out**	\i\ **tip**	\ȯ\ **saw**	\u̇\ **foot**
\ər\ **further**	\ch\ **chin**	\ī\ **life**	\ȯi\ **coin**	\y\ **yet**
\a\ **mat**	\e\ **pet**	\j\ **job**	\th\ **thin**	\yü\ **few**
\ā\ **take**	\ē\ **easy**	\ng\ **sing**	\th̲\ **this**	\yu̇\ **cure**
\ä\ **cot, cart**	\g\ **go**	\ō\ **bone**	\ü\ **food**	\zh\ **vision**

INTERNATIONAL MORSE CODE

a ·–	n –·	á ·––·–	8 –––··
b –···	o –––	ä ·–·–	9 ––––·
c –·–·	p ·––·	é ··–··	0 –––––
d –··	q ––·–	ñ ––·––	, ––··–– (comma)
e ·	r ·–·	ö –––·	. ·–·–·– (period)
f ··–·	s ···	ü ··––	? ··––·· (question mark)
g ––·	t –	1 ·––––	" ·–··–· (quotation marks)
h ····	u ··–	2 ··–––	: –––··· (colon)
i ··	v ···–	3 ···––	' ·––––· (apostrophe)
j ·–––	w ·––	4 ····–	- –····– (hyphen)
k –·–	x –··–	5 ·····	/ –··–· (slash)
l ·–··	y –·––	6 –····	(–·––· (left parenthesis)
m ––	z ––··	7 ––···	) –·––·– (right parenthesis)

[2]**mortal** *n* **:** a human being

mor·tal·i·ty \mȯr-ˈtal-ət-ē\ *n, pl* **-ties** **1 :** the quality or state of being mortal **2 :** the death of large numbers **3 :** the human race **:** HUMANKIND **4 a :** the number of deaths in a given time or place **b :** the ratio of deaths to total population

mortality table *n* **:** a table of mortality statistics over a number of years used chiefly by insurance companies in computing premiums

mortal sin *n* **:** a sin (as murder) that is too serious or wicked to leave room for forgiveness

[1]**mor·tar** \ˈmȯrt-ər\ *n* **1 :** a strong bowl-shaped container in which substances are pounded or rubbed with a pestle **2 :** a muzzle-loading cannon that has a tube short in relation to its caliber and is used to throw projectiles at high angles [Old English *mortere* and Medieval French *mortier,* from Latin *mortarium*]

[1]mortar 1

[2]**mortar** *n* **:** a building material (as one made of lime and cement mixed with sand and water) that hardens and is spread between bricks or stones to hold them together — **mortar** *vt*

mor·tar·board \ˈmȯrt-ər-ˌbōrd, -ˌbȯrd\ *n* **1 :** a board for holding mortar while it is being applied **2 :** an academic cap with a broad projecting square top

[1]**mort·gage** \ˈmȯr-gij\ *n* **1 :** a transfer of rights to a piece of property usually as security for the payment of a loan or debt that becomes void when the debt is paid **2 :** the formal document recording such a transfer [Medieval French, from *mort* "dead" + *gage* "pledge, gage"]

[2]**mortgage** *vt* **1 :** to transfer rights to a piece of property by a mortgage **2 :** to subject to a claim or obligation

mort·gag·ee \ˌmȯr-gi-ˈjē\ *n* **:** a person to whom property is mortgaged

mort·ga·gor \ˌmȯr-gi-ˈjȯr\ *also* **mort·gag·er** \ˈmȯr-gi-jər\ *n* **:** a person who mortgages property

mor·ti·cian \mȯr-ˈtish-ən\ *n* **:** UNDERTAKER [Latin *mort-, mors* "death"]

mor·ti·fy \ˈmȯrt-ə-ˌfī\ *vb* **-fied; -fy·ing** **1 :** to subdue bodily appetites through penance and self-denial **2 :** to subject to humiliation or shame **3 :** to become necrotic or gangrenous [Medieval French *mortifier* "to destroy the vitality of, to deaden," from Late Latin *mortificare,* from Latin *mort-, mors* "death"] — **mor·ti·fi·ca·tion** \ˌmȯrt-ə-fə-ˈkā-shən\ *n*

[1]**mor·tise** *also* **mor·tice** \ˈmȯrt-əs\ *n* **:** a hole cut in a piece of wood or other material into which a projecting part of another piece fits so as to form a joint [Medieval French *mortais*]

[2]**mortise** *also* **mortice** *vt* **1 :** to join or fasten securely especially by a tenon and mortise **2 :** to cut a mortise in — **mor·tised** \-əst\ *adj*

[1]**mor·tu·ary** \ˈmȯr-chə-ˌwer-ē\ *adj* **:** of or relating to death or the burial of the dead [Latin *mortuarius* "of the dead," from *mortuus* "dead"]

[2]**mortuary** *n, pl* **-ar·ies** **:** a place in which dead bodies are kept until burial; *esp* **:** FUNERAL HOME

mor·u·la \ˈmȯr-ə-lə, ˈmär-, -yə-lə\ *n, pl* **-lae** \-ˌlē, -ˌlī\ *also* **-las** **:** an early embryo that is a solid mass of blastomeres that is formed by cleavage of a zygote and that typically precedes the blastula [New Latin, from Latin *morum* "mulberry," from Greek *moron*]

mo·sa·ic \mō-ˈzā-ik\ *n* **1 :** a surface decoration made by inlaying small pieces of variously colored material to form pictures or patterns; *also* **:** the process of making it **2 :** a picture or design made in mosaic **3 :** something resembling a mosaic; *esp* **:** a virus disease of plants characterized by mottling of the foliage **4 :** the part of a television camera tube consisting of many minute particles that convert light to an electric charge [Medieval Latin *musaicum,* derived from Latin *Musa* "Muse"] — **mosaic** *adj* — **mo·sa·i·cal·ly** \-ˈzā-i-kə-lē, -klē\ *adv*

mo·sa·saur \ˈmō-zə-ˌsȯr\ *n* **:** any of various very large extinct marine fish-eating lizards of the Cretaceous period with limbs resembling paddles [Latin *Mosa* "the river Meuse" + Greek *sauros* "lizard"]

mo·sey \ˈmō-zē\ *vi* **mo·seyed; mo·sey·ing** **:** to move in a leisurely or aimless manner **:** SAUNTER [origin unknown]

Mos·lem \ˈmäz-ləm *also* ˈmäs-\ *variant of* MUSLIM

mosque \ˈmäsk\ *n* **:** a Muslim place of worship [Middle French *mosquee,* from Italian *moschea,* from Spanish *mezquita,* from Arabic *masjid,* from *sajada* "to prostrate oneself, worship"]

mos·qui·to \mə-ˈskēt-ō\ *n, pl* **-toes** *also* **-tos** **:** any of numerous two-winged flies having females with a needlelike proboscis adapted to puncture the skin of animals and suck their blood [Spanish, from *mosca* "fly," from Latin *musca*] — **mos·qui·to·ey** \-ˈskēt-ə-wē\ *adj*

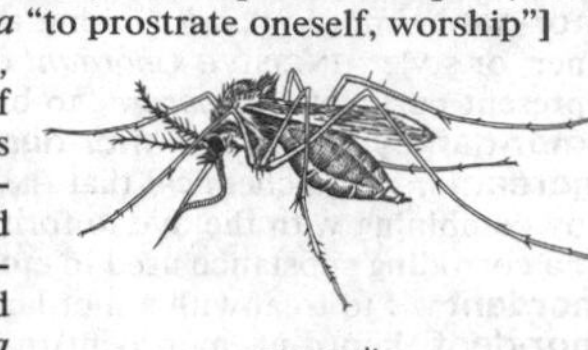
mosquito

mosquito net *n* **:** a net for keeping out mosquitoes

moss \ˈmȯs\ *n* **1 :** any of a class (Musci) of plants without flowers but with small leafy often tufted stems growing in patches and bearing sex organs at the tip **2 :** any of various plants (as lichens) resembling mosses — compare REINDEER MOSS [Old English *mos* "bog, swamp"] — **moss·like** \-ˌlīk\ *adj*

moss animal *n* **:** BRYOZOAN

moss pink *n* **:** a low-growing perennial phlox widely cultivated for its abundant usually pink or white flowers

mossy \ˈmȯ-sē\ *adj* **moss·i·er; -est** **1 :** covered with moss or something like moss ⟨a *mossy* grave⟩ **2 :** resembling moss

mossy zinc *n* **:** a granulated form of zinc made by pouring melted zinc into water

[1]**most** \ˈmōst\ *adj* **1 :** the majority of ⟨*most* people⟩ **2 :** greatest in quanitity, extent, or degree ⟨the *most* ability⟩ [Old English *mǣst*]

[2]**most** *adv* **1 :** to the greatest or highest degree — often used with an adjective or adverb to form the superlative **2 :** to a very great degree ⟨a *most* careful driver⟩

[3]**most** *n* **:** the greatest amount, number, or part — **at most** *or* **at the most :** as an extreme limit ⟨takes an hour at *most*⟩

[4]**most** *adv* **:** ALMOST

-most \ˌmōst\ *adj suffix* **:** most ⟨inner*most*⟩: most toward ⟨head*most*⟩ [Middle English, alteration of *-mest* (as in *formest* "foremost")]

most·ly \ˈmōst-lē\ *adv* **:** for the greatest part **:** MAINLY

Most Reverend — used as a title for an archbishop or a Roman Catholic bishop

mot \ˈmō\ *n, pl* **mots** \ˈmō, ˈmōz\ **:** a pithy or witty saying [French, "word, saying," derived from Late Latin *muttum* "grunt," from *muttire* "to mutter"]

mote \ˈmōt\ *n* **:** a small particle **:** SPECK [Old English *mot*]

mo·tel \mō-ˈtel\ *n* **:** a building or group of buildings used as a hotel in which the rooms are directly accessible from an outdoor parking area for automobiles [blend of *motor* and *hotel*]

mo·tet \mō-ˈtet\ *n* **:** a polyphonic choral composition on a sacred text usually without accompaniment [Medieval French, from *mot* "word"]

moth \ˈmȯth\ *n, pl* **moths** \ˈmȯt͟hz, ˈmȯths\ **:** any of various usually night-flying insects that are lepidopterans often with a stouter body, duller coloring, and proportionately smaller wings than the related butterflies and antennae which are often feathery [Old English *moththe*]

[1]**moth·ball** \ˈmȯth-ˌbȯl\ *n* **1 :** a ball (as of naphthalene) used to keep moths out of clothing **2** *pl* **:** protective storage ⟨put the ships in *mothballs* after the war⟩

[2]**mothball** *vt* **1 :** to deactivate (as a ship) and prevent deterioration chiefly by the removal of moisture **2 :** to withdraw from use or service and keep in reserve **:** put aside

moth–eat·en \ˈmȯth-ˌēt-n\ *adj* **1 :** eaten into by moth larvae

⟨*moth-eaten* clothes⟩ **2 a :** RUN-DOWN 1 **b :** OLD-FASHIONED 1

¹moth·er \ˈmə*th*-ər\ *n* **1 a :** a female parent **b :** a woman in authority; *esp* : the superior of a religious order **2 :** an old or elderly woman **3 :** SOURCE, ORIGIN ⟨necessity is the *mother* of invention⟩ [Old English *mōdor*] — **moth·er·hood** \-ˌhu̇d\ *n* — **moth·er·less** \-ləs\ *adj* — **moth·er·less·ness** *n*

²mother *adj* **1 a :** of, relating to, or being a mother **b :** being in the relation of a mother to others ⟨a *mother* church⟩ ⟨a *mother* country⟩ **2 :** derived from or as if from one's mother

³mother *vt* **moth·ered; moth·er·ing** \ˈmə*th*-ring, -ə-ring\ **:** to be or act as mother to

⁴mother *n* **:** a slimy mass of yeast cells and bacteria that forms on the surface of fermenting alcoholic liquids and is added to wine or cider to produce vinegar — called also *mother of vinegar* [archaic *mother* "dregs, lees"]

moth·er·board \ˈmə*th*-ər-ˌbōrd, -ˌbȯrd\ *n* **:** the main circuit board especially of a personal computer

Mother Car·ey's chicken \ˌmə*th*-ər-ˌkar-ēz-, -ˌker-\ *n* **:** STORM PETREL [origin unknown]

mother cell *n* **:** a cell that gives rise to other cells usually of a different sort

moth·er·house \ˈmə*th*-ər-ˌhau̇s\ *n* **1 :** the convent in which the superior of a religious community resides **2 :** the original convent of a religious community

Mother Hubbard \ˌmə*th*-ər-ˈhəb-ərd\ *n* **:** a loose usually shapeless dress [probably from *Mother Hubbard,* character in a nursery rhyme]

moth·er–in–law \ˈmə*th*-ər-ən-ˌlȯ, ˈmə*th*-ərn-ˌlȯ\ *n, pl* **mothers–in–law** \-ər-zən-ˌlȯ\ **:** the mother of one's husband or wife

moth·er·land \ˈmə*th*-ər-ˌland\ *n* **1 :** the land of origin of something **2 :** FATHERLAND

mother lode *n* **:** the main vein or deposit of an ore (as gold) in a region

moth·er·ly \ˈmə*th*-ər-lē\ *adj* **1 :** of, relating to, or characteristic of a mother ⟨*motherly* affection⟩ **2 :** resembling a mother **:** MATERNAL — **moth·er·li·ness** \-lē-nəs\ *n*

Mother Nature *n* **:** nature personified as a woman considered the source and guiding force of creation

moth·er–of–pearl \ˌmə*th*-ər-əv-ˈpərl, -ər-ə-ˈpərl\ *n* **:** the hard pearly iridescent substance forming the inner layer of a mollusk shell

mother of vinegar *n* **:** ⁴MOTHER

Mother's Day *n* **:** the 2nd Sunday in May appointed for the honoring of mothers

mother tongue *n* **1 :** one's native language **2 :** a language from which another language derives

mo·tif \mō-ˈtēf\ *n* **1 :** a recurring idea or theme (as in the arts) **2 :** a feature in a decoration or design ⟨a flower *motif* in wallpaper⟩ [French, "motive, motif"]

mo·tile \ˈmōt-l, ˈmō-ˌtīl\ *adj* **:** exhibiting or being capable of movement [Latin *motus,* past participle of *movēre* "to move"] — **mo·til·i·ty** \mō-ˈtil-ət-ē\ *n*

¹mo·tion \ˈmō-shən\ *n* **1 :** a formal proposal for action made in a deliberative assembly ⟨a *motion* to adjourn⟩ **2 a :** an act, process, or instance of changing place **:** MOVEMENT **b :** an act or instance of moving the body or its parts **:** GESTURE [Medieval French, from Latin *motio*"movement," from *movēre* "to move"] — **mo·tion·less** \-ləs\ *adj* — **mo·tion·less·ly** *adv* — **mo·tion·less·ness** *n*

²motion *vb* **mo·tioned; mo·tion·ing** \ˈmō-shə-ning, ˈmōsh-ning\ **:** to direct or signal by a movement or gesture

motion picture *n* **1 :** a series of pictures projected on a screen in rapid succession so as to produce the optical effect of a continuous picture in which the objects move **2 :** MOVIE 2

motion sickness *n* **:** sickness induced by motion (as in travel by air, car, or ship) and characterized especially by nausea

mo·ti·vate \ˈmōt-ə-ˌvāt\ *vt* **:** to provide with a motive **:** INDUCE — **mo·ti·va·tion** \ˌmōt-ə-ˈvā-shən\ *n* — **mo·ti·va·tion·al** \-shnəl, -shən-l\ *adv* — **mo·ti·va·tive** \ˈmōt-ə-ˌvāt-iv\ *adj*

¹mo·tive \ˈmōt-iv, 2 is *also* mō-ˈtēv\ *n* **1 :** something (as a need or desire) that causes a person to act ⟨their *motive* in running away was to avoid trouble⟩ **2 :** MOTIF 1 [Medieval French *motif, motive,* from *motif,* adj., "moving," derived from Latin *movēre* "to move"] — **mo·tive·less** \-ləs\ *adj*

synonyms MOTIVE, IMPULSE mean a stimulus to action. MOTIVE implies a desire or emotion causing the will to act ⟨a *motive* for the crime⟩. IMPULSE suggests a driving power arising from personal temperament often without explainable cause ⟨buying on *impulse*⟩.

²motive *adj* **:** of or relating to motion or the causing of motion ⟨*motive* power⟩

¹mot·ley \ˈmät-lē\ *adj* **1 :** having various colors **2 :** of various mixed kinds or parts ⟨a *motley* crowd⟩ [Middle English, perhaps from *mot* "mote, speck"]

²motley *n* **1 :** an old English woolen fabric of mixed colors **2 a :** a garment of motley constituting the characteristic dress of a court jester **b :** FOOL 2a, JESTER **3 :** a mixture of diverse elements

mo·to·cross \ˈmōt-ō-ˌkrȯs\ *n* **:** a motorcycle race on a course laid out over natural or simulated terrain; *also* **:** the sport of engaging in motocross races

mo·to·neu·ron \ˌmōt-ə-ˈnü-ˌrän, -ˈnyü-; -ˈnu̇r-ˌän, -ˈnyu̇r-\ *n* **:** MOTOR NEURON

¹mo·tor \ˈmōt-ər\ *n* **1 :** a small compact engine **2 :** INTERNAL-COMBUSTION ENGINE; *esp* **:** a gasoline engine **3 :** MOTOR VEHICLE; *esp* **:** AUTOMOBILE **4 :** a rotating machine that transforms electrical energy into mechanical energy [Latin, "one that moves," from *movēre* "to move"] — **mo·tor·less** *adj*

²motor *adj* **1 :** causing or imparting motion ⟨*motor* power⟩ **2 a :** of, relating to, or being a motor neuron or a nerve containing motor neurons **b :** concerned with or involving muscular movement ⟨*motor* areas of the brain⟩ ⟨a *motor* reaction⟩ **3 a :** equipped with or driven by a motor **b :** of or relating to an automobile **c :** designed for motor vehicles or motorists

³motor *vi* **:** to travel by automobile

mo·tor·bike \ˈmōt-ər-ˌbīk\ *n* **:** a small usually lightweight motorcycle

mo·tor·boat \ˈmōt-ər-ˌbōt\ *n* **:** a boat propelled by a motor

motor bus *n* **:** BUS 1a — called also *motor coach*

mo·tor·cade \ˈmōt-ər-ˌkād\ *n* **:** a procession of motor vehicles [*motor* + *-cade* (as in *cavalcade*)]

mo·tor·car \-ˌkär\ *n* **:** AUTOMOBILE

motor court *n* **:** MOTEL

mo·tor·cy·cle \ˈmōt-ər-ˌsī-kəl\ *n* **:** a 2-wheeled motor vehicle for one or two people — **motorcycle** *vi* — **mo·tor·cy·clist** \-ˌsī-kə-ləst, -kləst\ *n*

motor home *n* **:** a large automotive vehicle equipped as a self-contained traveling home

motor inn *n* **:** MOTEL; *esp* **:** a large multistory motel — called also *motor hotel*

mo·tor·ist \ˈmōt-ə-rəst\ *n* **:** a person who travels by automobile

mo·tor·ize \ˈmōt-ə-ˌrīz\ *vt* **1 :** to equip with a motor **2 :** to equip with motor-driven vehicles for transportation ⟨*motorized* troops⟩ — **mo·tor·i·za·tion** \ˌmōt-ə-rə-ˈzā-shən\ *n*

mo·tor·man \ˈmōt-ər-mən\ *n* **:** an operator of a motor-driven vehicle (as a streetcar or a subway train)

motor neuron *n* **:** a neuron that passes from the central nervous system or a ganglion toward or to a muscle and carries a nerve impluse that causes movement — compare SENSORY NEURON

motor pool *n* **:** a group of motor vehicles centrally controlled (as by a government agency) and dispatched for use as needed

motor scooter *n* **:** a low 2- or 3-wheeled automotive vehicle resembling a child's scooter but having a seat so that the rider does not straddle the engine

motor torpedo boat *n* **:** PT BOAT

mo·tor·truck \ˈmōt-ər-ˌtrək\ *n* **:** an automotive truck for transporting freight

motor vehicle *n* **:** an automotive vehicle not operated on rails; *esp* **:** one for use on highways

mot·tle \ˈmät-l\ *n* **1 :** a colored spot **2 :** a pattern of colored spots or blotches [probably back-formation from ¹*motley*] — **mottle** *vt* — **mot·tled** \-ld\ *adj* — **mot·tler** \ˈmät-lər, -l-ər\ *n*

mottled enamel *n* **:** spotted tooth enamel caused by drinking water containing excessive fluorides during the time calcium salts are being deposited in the teeth

mot·to \ˈmät-ō\ *n, pl* **mottoes** *also* **mottos** **1 :** a sentence, phrase, or word inscribed on something as suitable to its character or use ⟨a *motto* on a sundial⟩ **2 :** a short expression of a guiding principle [Italian, from Latin *muttum* "grunt," from *muttire* "to mutter"]

\ə\ **abut**	\au̇\ **out**	\i\ **tip**	\ȯ\ **saw**	\u̇\ **foot**
\ər\ **further**	\ch\ **chin**	\ī\ **life**	\ȯi\ **coin**	\y\ **yet**
\a\ **mat**	\e\ **pet**	\j\ **job**	\th\ **thin**	\yü\ **few**
\ā\ **take**	\ē\ **easy**	\ng\ **sing**	\t͟h\ **this**	\yu̇\ **cure**
\ä\ **cot, cart**	\g\ **go**	\ō\ **bone**	\ü\ **food**	\zh\ **vision**

moue \ˈmü\ *n* : [2]POUT 1 [French, of Germanic origin]
mou·flon *also* **mouf·flon** \mü-ˈflō^{n}\ *n* : a wild sheep of the mountains of Sardinia, Corsica, and western Asia with large curling horns in the male [French *mouflon,* from Italian dialect *muvrone,* from Late Latin *mufro*]
moujik *variant of* MUZHIK
mould *chiefly British variant of* MOLD
[1]**mound** \ˈmau̇nd\ *vt* : to form into a mound [origin unknown]
[2]**mound** *n* **1** : a small hill or heap of dirt (as one to mark a burial site) **2** : the slightly elevated ground on which a baseball pitcher stands [origin unknown]
Mound Builder *n* : a member of a prehistoric American Indian people whose extensive earthworks are found from the Great Lakes down the Mississippi River valley to the Gulf of Mexico
[1]**mount** \ˈmau̇nt\ *n* : a high hill : MOUNTAIN — used especially before a proper name ⟨*Mount* Everest⟩ [Old English *munt* and Medieval French *munt, mont*; both from Latin *mont-, mons*]
[2]**mount** *vb* **1 a** : RISE 7a, ASCEND **b** : to go up : CLIMB ⟨*mount* a ladder⟩ **2 a** : to get up onto ⟨*mount* a platform⟩ **b** : to get astride a horse **3** : to furnish with riding animals or vehicles ⟨*mounted* police⟩ **4** : to increase rapidly in amount ⟨debts *mounting*⟩ **5 a** : to prepare for use or display by fastening in proper position on a support ⟨*mount* a picture on cardboard⟩ **b** : to prepare (a specimen) for examination or display **6** : to furnish with scenery, properties, and costumes ⟨*mount* a play⟩ **7** : to post as a means of defense or observation ⟨*mount* guards⟩ **8** : to place (as artillery) in position ***synonyms*** see ASCEND — **mount·able** \ˈmau̇nt-ə-bəl\ *adj* — **mount·er** *n*
[3]**mount** *n* **1** : something on which a thing is mounted: as **a** : a jewelry setting **b** : a microscope slide with its accessories (as a cover glass) on which objects are placed for examination **2** : a means of conveyance; *esp* : SADDLE HORSE
moun·tain \ˈmau̇nt-n\ *n* **1** : a land mass that is higher than a hill **2** : a great quantity or amount ⟨a *mountain* of mail⟩ [Medieval French *muntaine,* derived from Latin *mont-, mons*]
mountain ash *n* : any of various trees related to the roses and having red or orange-red fruits and pinnate leaves
mountain bike *n* : a bicycle with wide knobby tires and many gears for use on all kinds of terrain — **mountain bike** *vi*
moun·tain·eer \ˌmau̇nt-n-ˈiər\ *n* **1** : a person who lives in the mountains **2** : a mountain climber
moun·tain·eer·ing \-ˈiər-ing\ *n* : the sport or technique of scaling mountains
mountain goat *n* : a ruminant mammal of the mountains of western North America that has a thick yellowish white hairy coat and slightly curved black horns and closely resembles a goat
mountain laurel *n* : a North American evergreen shrub of the heath family with glossy leaves and pink or white cup-shaped flowers
mountain lion *n* : COUGAR
moun·tain·ous \ˈmau̇nt-n-əs, ˈmau̇nt-nəs\ *adj* **1** : having many mountains ⟨*mountainous* country⟩ **2** : resembling a mountain especially in size : HUGE ⟨*mountainous* waves⟩ — **moun·tain·ous·ly** *adv*

mountain goat

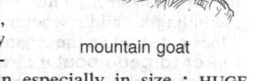

mountain sheep *n* : any of various wild sheep (as a bighorn sheep) inhabiting high mountains
moun·tain·side \ˈmau̇nt-n-ˌsīd\ *n* : the side of a mountain
mountain time *n, often cap M* : the time of the seventh time zone west of Greenwich that includes the Rocky Mountain states of the U.S.
moun·tain·top \ˈmau̇nt-n-ˌtäp\ *n* : the summit of a mountain
moun·te·bank \ˈmau̇nt-i-ˌbangk\ *n* **1** : a person who sells quack medicines : QUACK **2** : an unscrupulous impostor : SWINDLER [Italian *montimbanco,* from *montare* "to mount" + *in* "in, on" + *banco, banca,* "bench"]
Mount·ie \ˈmau̇nt-ē\ *n* : a member of the Royal Canadian Mounted Police
mount·ing \ˈmau̇nt-ing\ *n* : [3]MOUNT 1
mourn \ˈmōrn, ˈmȯrn\ *vb* **1** : to feel or show grief or sorrow; *esp* : to grieve over someone's death **2** : to display the customary signs of grief for a death especially by wearing clothes (as a black suit or dress) suitable for mourning [Old English *murnan*] — **mourn·er** *n* — **mourn·ing·ly** \-ing-lē\ *adv*
mourn·ful \ˈmōrn-fəl, ˈmȯrn-\ *adj* **1** : full of sorrow : SAD ⟨a *mournful* face⟩ **2** : causing sorrow : SADDENING ⟨*mournful* news⟩ **3** : of a melancholy nature ⟨took a *mournful* view of the future⟩ — **mourn·ful·ly** \-fə-lē\ *adv* — **mourn·ful·ness** *n*
mourn·ing \ˈmōr-ning, ˈmȯr-\ *n* **1** : an act of grieving **2** : an outward sign (as black clothes or a veil) of grief for a person's death ⟨wear *mourning*⟩ **3** : a period of time during which signs of grief are shown
mourning cloak *n* : a blackish brown butterfly of North America, Europe, and parts of Asia having a broad yellow border on the wings
mourning dove *n* : a dove of North America with a mournful cry
[1]**mouse** \ˈmau̇s\ *n, pl* **mice** \ˈmīs\ **1** : any of numerous small rodents with a pointed snout, rather small ears, an elongated body, and a slender usually nearly hairless tail **2** : a timid or spiritless person **3** : a dark-colored swelling caused by a blow; *esp* : BLACK EYE **4** : a small mobile manual device that controls movement of the cursor and selection of functions on a computer display [Old English *mūs*]
[2]**mouse** \ˈmau̇z, ˈmau̇s\ *vb* **1** : to hunt for mice **2** : to search or move stealthily or slowly **3** : to discover by careful searching ⟨*mouse* out a scandal⟩
mouse pad *n* : a thin flat pad (as of rubber) on which a computer mouse is used
mous·er \ˈmau̇-zər, -sər\ *n* : a catcher of mice and rats; *esp* : a cat proficient at mousing
mouse·trap \ˈmau̇-ˌstrap\ *n* : a trap for mice
mous·sa·ka \mü-ˈsäk-ə, ˌmü-sä-ˈkä\ *n* : a Middle Eastern dish of ground meat (as lamb or beef) and sliced eggplant often topped with a seasoned sauce [modern Greek *mousakas,* from Turkish *musakka,* from Arabic dialect *musaggaʿa,* literally, "chilled"]
[1]**mousse** \ˈmüs\ *n* **1** : a light spongy food; *esp* : a molded chilled dessert of sweetened and flavored whipped cream or egg whites and gelatin **2** : a foamy preparation used in styling hair [French, *literally,* "froth," of Germanic origin]
[2]**mousse** *vt* **moussed; mouss·ing** : to style (hair) with mousse
moustache *variant of* MUSTACHE
moustachio *variant of* MUSTACHIO
mousy *or* **mous·ey** \ˈmau̇-sē, -zē\ *adj* **mous·i·er; -est** : of, relating to, or resembling a mouse: as **a** : TIMID **b** : making no noise **c** : grayish brown : DRAB 1
[1]**mouth** \ˈmau̇th\ *n, pl* **mouths** \ˈmau̇thz, ˈmau̇ths\ **1** : the opening through which food passes into the body of an animal and which in vertebrates is typically surrounded externally by the lips and encloses the tongue, gums, and teeth **2** : GRIMACE ⟨make a *mouth*⟩ **3** : something that resembles a mouth especially in affording entrance or exit ⟨the *mouth* of a cave⟩ **4** : the place where a stream enters a larger body of water [Old English *mūth*] — **mouthed** \ˈmau̇thd, ˈmau̇tht\ *adj* — **mouth·like** \ˈmau̇th-ˌlīk\ *adj* — **down in the mouth** : DEPRESSED 1
[2]**mouth** \ˈmau̇th\ *vb* **1 a** : UTTER 2, PRONOUNCE **b** : to utter loudly or pompously **c** : to repeat without understanding or sincerity ⟨*mouth* platitudes⟩ **2 a** : to form with the lips without speaking ⟨she *mouthed* "quiet"⟩ **b** : MUMBLE 1 **3** : to take into the mouth; *esp* : EAT — **mouth·er** \ˈmau̇-thər\ *n*
mouth·breed·er \ˈmau̇th-ˌbrēd-ər\ *n* : a fish that carries its eggs and young in its mouth
mouth·ful \ˈmau̇th-ˌfu̇l\ *n* **1** : as much as the mouth will hold; *also* : the amount put into the mouth at one time **2 a** : a word or phrase that is very long or difficult to say **b** : a comment or remark that is rich in meaning ⟨you said a *mouthful*⟩ **3** : a small quantity
mouth hook *n* : one of a pair of hooked mouthparts of some fly larvae that function as jaws
mouth organ *n* : HARMONICA
mouth·part \ˈmau̇th-ˌpärt\ *n* : a structure or appendage near the mouth (as of an insect) especially when adapted for in gathering or eating food
mouth·piece \-ˌpēs\ *n* **1** : something placed at or forming a mouth **2** : a part (as of an instrument) to which the mouth is held ⟨a telephone *mouthpiece*⟩ **3 a** : one that expresses another's views : SPOKESPERSON **b** *slang* : a criminal lawyer
mouth–to–mouth *adj* : of, relating to, or being a method of artificial respiration in which the rescuer's mouth is placed tightly over the victim's mouth in order to force air into the lungs by blowing forcefully enough every few seconds to inflate them

mouth·wash \-ˌwȯsh, -ˌwäsh\ *n* **:** a usually antiseptic liquid preparation for cleaning the mouth and teeth or freshening the breath

mouthy \ˈmau̇-t͟hē, -thē\ *adj* **mouth·i·er; -est** **1 :** excessively talkative **2 :** given to or marked by pompous talk

mou·ton \ˈmü-ˌtän\ *n* **:** processed sheepskin that has been sheared and dyed to resemble beaver or seal [French, "sheep, mutton"]

[1]**mov·able** *or* **move·able** \ˈmü-və-bəl\ *adj* **1 :** capable of being moved ‹*movable* property› **2 :** changing date from year to year ‹Labor Day is a *movable* holiday› — **mov·abil·i·ty** \ˌmü-və-ˈbil-ət-ē\ *n* — **mov·able·ness** *n* — **mov·ably** \ˈmü-və-blē\ *adv*

[2]**movable** *or* **moveable** *n* **:** a piece of property (as an article of furniture) that can be moved

[1]**move** \ˈmüv\ *vb* **1 :** to change the place or position of **:** SHIFT ‹*move* the chair closer› **2 :** to go from one place to another ‹*move* into the shade› **3 :** to proceed in a given direction or toward a given condition ‹*moved* ahead in business› **4 :** to set in motion ‹*moved* their feet› **5 a :** to cause a person to act or decide **:** PERSUADE ‹*moved* me to change my mind› **b :** to take action **:** ACT **6 :** to affect the feelings of ‹the sad story *moved* them to tears› **7 a :** to propose something formally in a deliberative assembly ‹*move* that the meeting adjourn› **b :** to present a motion or make an appeal **8 :** to change hands or cause to change hands through sale or rental ‹the store's stock must be *moved*› **9 a :** to change residence ‹*move* to Iowa› **b :** to change position or posture **:** STIR ‹don't *move*› **10 :** to cause to operate or function **:** ACTUATE ‹this button *moves* the whole machine› **11 :** to live one's life in a specified environment ‹*moves* in the best circles› **12 :** to go away **:** DEPART ‹made the crowd *move* on› **13 :** to transfer a piece in a game (as chess or checkers) from one place to another **14 :** to evacuate or cause to evacuate ‹the medicine *moves* the bowels› [Medieval French *mover, moveir,* from Latin *movēre*]

synonyms MOVE, ACTUATE, DRIVE, IMPEL mean to set or keep in motion. MOVE is very general and implies no more than the fact of changing position ‹*moved* the furniture›. ACTUATE stresses the transmission of power so as to work or set in motion ‹turbines *actuated* by waterpower›. DRIVE implies imparting continuous forward motion and often stresses the effect rather than the impetus ‹a ship *driven* aground by winds›. IMPEL implies a greater impetus producing more headlong action ‹a candidate *impelled* by ambition›.

[2]**move** *n* **1 a :** the act of moving a piece in a game **b :** the turn of a player to move **2 a :** a step taken to gain an objective **:** MANEUVER **b :** the action of moving **:** MOVEMENT **c :** a change of residence or location — **on the move** **1 :** in a state of moving from one place to another **2 :** in a state of making progress

move·less \ˈmüv-ləs\ *adj* **:** not moving — **move·less·ness** *n*

move·ment \ˈmüv-mənt\ *n* **1 a :** the act or process of moving; *esp* **:** change of place, position, or posture **b :** an instance or manner of moving ‹observe the *movement* of a star› **c :** ACTION, ACTIVITY ‹a lot of *movements* of the crowd› **2 :** TENDENCY, TREND ‹a *movement* toward fairer pricing› **3 a :** a series of actions taken by a group to achieve an objective ‹a *movement* for reform› **b :** the group taking part in such a series ‹joined the *movement*› **4 :** a mechanical arrangement (as of wheels) for causing a particular motion (as in a clock or watch) **5 a :** RHYTHM 2 **b :** CADENCE 1a, TEMPO **c :** a section of a longer piece of music ‹a *movement* in a symphony› **6 :** BOWEL MOVEMENT

mov·er \ˈmü-vər\ *n* **:** one that moves or sets in motion; *esp* **:** a person or company that moves the belongings of others from one home or place of business to another

mov·ie \ˈmü-vē\ *n* **1 :** MOTION PICTURE 1 **2 a :** a representation of a story or other subject matter by means of motion pictures **b** *pl* **:** a showing of a movie ‹went to the *movies* yesterday› **3** *pl* **:** the business of making movies **:** the motion-picture industry [*moving picture*]

mov·ie·go·er \-ˌgō-ər\ *n* **:** a person who frequently attends the movies

mov·ing \ˈmü-viŋ\ *adj* **1 a :** marked by or capable of moving **b :** of or relating to a change of residence ‹*moving* expenses› **c :** used for moving belongings from one residence to another ‹a *moving* van› **2 :** causing motion or action **3 :** having the power to affect feelings or sympathies ‹a *moving* story about a lasting friendship› — **mov·ing·ly** \-viŋ-lē\ *adv*

moving picture *n* **:** MOTION PICTURE

[1]**mow** \ˈmau̇\ *n* **1 :** a stack of hay or straw especially in a barn **2 :** the part of a barn where hay or straw is stored [Old English *mūga* "heap, stack"]

[2]**mow** \ˈmō\ *vb* **mowed; mowed** *or* **mown** \ˈmōn\; **mow·ing** **1 :** to cut down with a scythe or machine ‹*mow* hay› **2 :** to cut the standing leafy plant cover from ‹*mow* a lawn› **3 :** to kill or destroy in great numbers ‹machine guns *mowed* down the attackers› **4 :** to overcome decisively ‹*mowed* down the opposing team› [Old English *māwan*] — **mow·er** \ˈmō-ər, ˈmōr\ *n*

mox·ie \ˈmäk-sē\ *n* **1 :** ENERGY 1, PEP **2 :** BRAVERY 1, COURAGE [from *Moxie,* a trademark for a soft drink]

moz·za·rel·la \ˌmät-sə-ˈrel-ə\ *n* **:** a moist white cheese with a mild flavor and smooth texture [Italian, from *mozza,* a kind of cheese, from *mozzare* "to cut off," derived from Latin *mutilus* "cut off"]

MP \ˈem-ˈpē\ *n* **1 :** a member of the military police **2 :** an elected member of a parliament [*m*ilitary *p*olice]

MPEG \ˈem-ˌpeg\ *n* **1 :** any of a group of computer file formats for the compression and storage of digital video and audio data **2 :** a computer file (as of a movie) in an MPEG format [*M*oving *P*icture *E*xperts *G*roup]

MP3 \ˌem-ˌpē-ˈthrē\ *n* **1 :** a computer file format for the compression and storage of digital audio data **2 :** a computer file (as a song) in MP3 format [from the file extension *.mp3*, short for *MPEG Audio Layer 3*]

Mr. \ˌmis-tər\ *n, pl* **Messrs.** \ˌmes-ərz\ **1 —** used as a courtesy title before the name of a man **2 —** used as a form of respectful address to a high-ranking man and followed by a designation of his rank or office ‹*Mr.* President› **3 —** used before the name of a place, an activity, or an epithet (as *clever*) to form a title for a man representing the thing indicated ‹*Mr.* Baseball› [*Mr.* from Middle English, abbreviation of *maister* "master"; *Messrs.* abbreviation of *Messieurs,* from French, pl. of *Monsieur*]

MRI \ˌem-ˌär-ˈī\ *n* **:** MAGNETIC RESONANCE IMAGING

Mrs. \ˌmis-əz, -əs; *especially South* ˌmiz-əz, -əs, *(for sense 1)* miz, ˌmis, *before given names* mis, ˌmis\ *n, pl* **Mes·dames** \mā-ˈdäm, -ˈdam\ **1 —** used as a courtesy title before the name of a married woman **2 —** used before the name of a place, an activity, or an epithet (as *clever*) to form a title for a married woman representing the thing indicated ‹*Mrs.* Golf› [*Mrs.* abbreviation of *mistress*; *Mesdames* from French, pl. of *Madame*]

MRSA \ˈmər-sə, ˌem-ˌär-ˌes-ˈā\ *n* **:** any of several strains of a staphylococcus that may cause usually mild infections of the skin or sometimes more severe infections (as of the blood) [*m*ethicillin-*r*esistant *S*taphylococcus *a*ureus]

Ms. \miz, ˈmiz\ *n, pl* **Mss.** *or* **Mses.** \ˈmiz-əz\ **—** used instead of *Miss* or *Mrs.* as a courtesy title (as when the marital status of a woman is unknown or irrelevant) ‹*Ms.* Mary Smith› [probably blend of *Miss* and *Mrs.*]

mu \ˈmyü, ˈmü\ *n* **:** the 12th letter of the Greek alphabet — M or μ

[1]**much** \ˈməch\ *adj* **more** \ˈmōr, ˈmȯr\; **most** \ˈmōst\ **1 :** great in quantity, amount, extent, or degree ‹has *much* money› ‹takes too *much* time› **2 :** great in importance or significance ‹nothing *much* happened› **3 :** more than enough ‹the large pizza is a bit *much* for one person› [Middle English *muche* "large, much," from *michel, muchel,* from Old English *micel, mycel*]

[2]**much** *adv* **more; most** **1 a :** to a great degree or extent **:** CONSIDERABLY ‹*much* happier› **b :** VERY ‹*much* obliged› **c** (1) **:** many times **:** OFTEN ‹*much* away from home› (2) **:** by or for a long time ‹didn't get to work *much* before noon› **d :** by far ‹was *much* the best student› **2 :** just about **:** NEARLY ‹*much* the same› — **as much** **1 :** the same in quantity ‹*as much* money› **2 :** to the same degree ‹likes it just *as much*›

[3]**much** *n* **1 :** a great quantity, amount, extent, or degree ‹*much* that was said is false› **2 :** something considerable or impressive ‹not *much* to look at›

mu·ci·lage \ˈmyü-sə-lij, -slij\ *n* **1 :** a gelatinous substance of various plants (as seaweeds or cacti) that contains protein and carbohydrates and is similar to plant gums **2 :** an aqueous solution of a gum or similar substance used especially as an adhesive [Late Latin *mucilago* "musty juice, mucus," from Latin *mucus*]

mu·ci·lag·i·nous \ˌmyü-sə-ˈlaj-ə-nəs\ *adj* **1 :** STICKY 1a, VISCID **2 :** producing or full of mucilage — **mu·ci·lag·i·nous·ly** *adv*

mu·cin \ˈmyüs-n\ *n* **:** any of various complex proteins found as viscid solutions in animal secretions and tissues [*mucus*] — **mu·cin·ous** \-əs\ *adj*

muck \ˈmək\ *n* **1 :** soft moist barnyard manure **2 :** DIRT 1a, FILTH **3 a :** dark highly organic soil **b :** MIRE 2, MUD [Middle English *muk*] — **mucky** \ˈmək-ē\ *adj*

muck·rake \ˈmək-ˌrāk\ *vi* **:** to search out and expose publicly real or seeming misconduct of a prominent person or business [obsolete *muckrake,* n., "rake for dung"] — **muck·rak·er** *n*

mu·co·sa \myü-ˈkō-zə\ *n, pl* **-sae** \-ˌzē, -ˌzī\ *or* **-sas :** MUCOUS MEMBRANE [New Latin, from Latin *mucosus* "mucous"] — **mu·co·sal** \-zəl\ *adj*

mu·cous \ˈmyü-kəs\ *adj* **1 :** of, relating to, or resembling mucus ⟨*mucous* discharges⟩ **2 :** secreting or containing mucus ⟨a *mucous* gland⟩ [Latin *mucosus,* from *mucus* "mucus"]

mucous membrane *n* **:** a membrane rich in mucous glands; *esp* **:** one that lines body passages and cavities (as of the nose or lungs) which communicate directly or indirectly with the exterior

mu·cro \ˈmyü-ˌkrō\ *n, pl* **mu·cro·nes** \myü-ˈkrō-ˌnēz\ **:** an abrupt sharp terminal point (as of a leaf) [Latin *mucron-, mucro* "point, edge"] — **mu·cro·nate** \ˈmyü-krə-ˌnāt\ *adj*

mu·cus \ˈmyü-kəs\ *n* **:** a slippery sticky secretion produced especially by mucous membranes which it moistens and protects [Latin, "nasal mucus"] — **mu·coid** \-ˌkȯid\ *adj*

mud \ˈməd\ *n* **:** soft wet earth [Middle English *mudde,* probably from Low German]

mud dauber *n* **:** any of various wasps that construct mud cells in which the female places an egg with spiders or insects paralyzed by a sting to serve as food for the larva

[1]**mud·dle** \ˈməd-l\ *vb* **mud·dled; mud·dling** \ˈməd-ling, -l-ing\ **1 :** CONFUSE 1b, BEFUDDLE ⟨*muddled* by too much advice⟩ **2 :** to throw into disorder ⟨*muddle* the household accounts⟩ **3 :** to think or act in a confused aimless way ⟨*muddle* through a task⟩ [probably from obsolete Dutch *moddelen,* from *modde* "mud"] — **mud·dler** \ˈməd-lər, -l-ər\ *n*

[2]**muddle** *n* **1 :** a state of confusion **2 :** a confused mess

mud·dle·head·ed \ˌməd-l-ˈhed-əd\ *adj* **1 :** mentally confused **2 :** INEPT 4, BUNGLING — **mud·dle·head·ed·ness** *n*

[1]**mud·dy** \ˈməd-ē\ *adj* **mud·di·er; -est 1 :** filled or covered with mud **2 :** resembling or suggesting mud ⟨a *muddy* color⟩ ⟨a *muddy* flavor⟩ **3 :** not clear or bright **:** DULL, CLOUDY ⟨a *muddy* complexion⟩ **4 :** CONFUSED, MUDDLED ⟨*muddy* thinking⟩ — **mud·di·ly** \ˈməd-l-ē\ *adv* — **mud·di·ness** \ˈməd-ē-nəs\ *n*

[2]**muddy** *vt* **mud·died; mud·dy·ing 1 :** to soil or stain with or as if with mud **2 :** to make turbid **3 :** to make cloudy or dull **4 :** CONFUSE 2

mud·flat \ˈməd-ˌflat\ *n* **:** a level area of land that lies just below the surface of water or that is repeatedly covered and left bare by the tide

mud·flow \ˈməd-ˌflō\ *n* **:** a moving mass of mud composed of soil and rainwater or melted snow

mud·guard \ˈməd-ˌgärd\ *n* **1 :** FENDER d **2 :** SPLASH GUARD

mud puppy *n* **:** a large North American salamander that has external gills and is gray to rusty brown usually with bluish black spots

mud·sling·er \ˈməd-ˌsling-ər\ *n* **:** one that uses abusive tactics (as invective or slander) especially against a political opponent — **mud·sling·ing** \-ˌsling-ing\ *n*

mud·stone \ˈməd-ˌstōn\ *n* **:** a hardened shale produced by the consolidation of mud

mud turtle *n* **:** any of various bottom-dwelling freshwater turtles related to the musk turtles

Muen·ster \ˈmən-stər, ˈmün-, ˈmyün-, ˈmu̇n-\ *n* **:** a semisoft cheese whose flavor may be bland or sharp [*Münster, Munster,* France]

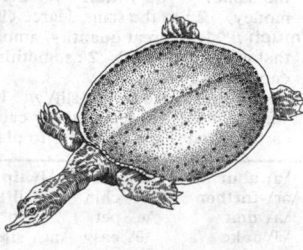

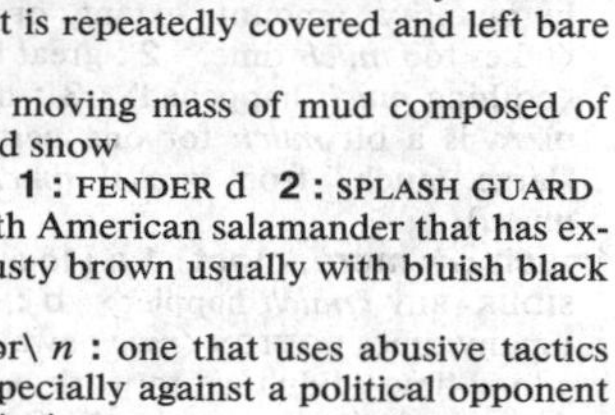

mud turtle

mu·ez·zin \mü-ˈez-n, myü-\ *n* **:** a Muslim crier who calls the hours of daily prayers [Arabic *mu'adhdhin*]

[1]**muff** \ˈməf\ *n* **:** a warm tube-shaped cover for the hands [Dutch *mof,* from Middle French *moufle* "mitten," from Medieval Latin *muffula*]

[2]**muff** *n* **:** a bungling performance; *esp* **:** a failure to hold a ball in attempting a catch [probably from [1]*muff*] — **muff** *vb*

muf·fin \ˈməf-ən\ *n* **:** a bread made of egg batter and baked in individual servings [probably from Low German *muffen,* pl. of *muffe* "cake"]

muf·fle \ˈməf-əl\ *vt* **muf·fled; muf·fling** \ˈməf-ling, -ə-ling\ **1 :** to wrap up so as to conceal or protect **2 :** to deaden the sound of **3 :** to keep down **:** SUPPRESS ⟨*muffled* the opposition⟩ [Middle English *muflen*]

muf·fler \ˈməf-lər\ *n* **1 :** a scarf for the neck **2 :** a device that deadens noises; *esp* **:** one forming part of the exhaust system of an automotive vehicle

[1]**muf·ti** \ˈməf-tē\ *n* **:** a professional jurist who interprets Muslim law [Arabic *muftī*]

[2]**mufti** *n* **:** civilian clothes especially when worn by a person in the armed forces

[1]**mug** \ˈməg\ *n* **1 :** a cylindrical drinking cup **2 :** the face or mouth of a person **3 :** [1]PUNK 2, THUG [origin unknown]

[2]**mug** *vb* **mugged; mug·ging 1 :** to pose or make faces especially to attract attention or for a camera **2 :** PHOTOGRAPH

[3]**mug** *vt* **mugged; mug·ging :** to assault with intent to rob [probably from earlier *mug* "to strike in the face," perhaps from [1]*mug*]

[1]**mug·ger** \ˈməg-ər\ *n* **:** a usually harmless freshwater crocodile of southeastern Asia with a broad heavy snout [Hindi & Urdu *magar,* from Sanskrit *makara* "water monster"]

[2]**mugger** *n* **:** one that attacks with intent to rob [[3]*mug*]

mug·gy \ˈməg-ē\ *adj* **mug·gi·er; -est :** being warm, damp, and stifling ⟨*muggy* weather preceded the thunderstorm⟩ [English dialect *mug* "drizzle"] — **mug·gi·ness** \ˈməg-ē-nəs\ *n*

mu·gho pine \ˌmü-gō-, ˌmyü-\ *n* **:** a shrubby spreading European pine widely grown as an ornamental [probably from French *mugho* "mugho pine," from Italian *mugo*]

mug shot *n* **:** a photograph of a person's face; *esp* **:** a police photograph of a suspect's face or profile

mug·wump \ˈməg-ˌwəmp\ *n* **1 :** a bolter from the Republican party in 1884 **2 :** a person who is independent (as in politics) or who remains undecided or neutral [obsolete slang, "chief, kingpin," from Massachusett (an American Indian language of Massachusetts) *mugquomp, muggumquomp* "war leader"]

Word History When James G. Blaine received the Republican Party's nomination for the presidency in 1884, some prominent Republicans refused to support his candidacy, supporting instead the Democratic candidate, Grover Cleveland. Republicans who remained loyal to their party called the bolters *mugwumps,* meaning men who thought themselves important. The word came originally from *mugquomp,* a word meaning "war leader" in the Algonquian language Massachusett.

Muhammadan *variant of* MOHAMMEDAN

mu·ja·hid·een *or* **mu·ja·hed·in** *also* **mu·ja·hed·een** \mü-ˌja-hid-ˈēn, mu̇-, -ˌjä-\ *n pl* **:** Islamic guerrilla fighters especially in the Middle East [Arabic *mujahidīn,* plural of *mujāhid,* literally, person who wages religious war]

mujik *variant of* MUZHIK

muk·luk \ˈmək-ˌlək\ *n* **1 :** an Eskimo boot of sealskin or reindeer skin **2 :** a boot with a soft leather sole often worn over several pairs of socks [Eskimo *maklak* "bearded seal"]

mu·lat·to \mu̇-ˈlat-ō, myu̇-\ *n, pl* **-toes** *or* **-tos 1 :** a person with one black and one white parent **2 :** a person of mixed white and black descent [Spanish *mulato,* from *mulo* "mule," from Latin *mulus*]

mul·ber·ry \ˈməl-ˌber-ē\ *n* **1 :** any of a genus of trees with edible usually purple fruits; *also* **:** this fruit **2 :** a dark purple or purplish black [Middle English *murberie, mulberie,* from Medieval French *mure, moure* "mulberry," from Latin *morum,* from Greek *moron*]

mulch \ˈməlch\ *n* **:** a protective covering (as of straw, compost, or paper) spread on the ground especially to reduce evaporation, prevent erosion, control weeds, or enrich the soil [perhaps from English dialect *melch* "soft, mild"] — **mulch** *vt*

[1]**mulct** \ˈməlkt\ *n* **:** [1]FINE, PENALTY [Latin *multa, mulcta*]

[2]**mulct** *vt* **1 :** to punish by a fine **2 a :** to defraud especially of money **:** SWINDLE **b :** to obtain by fraud, duress, or theft

[1]**mule** \ˈmyül\ *n* **1 a :** a hybrid between a horse and a donkey;

esp : the offspring of a male donkey and a female horse **b** : a usually sterile hybrid plant or animal **2** : a very stubborn person **3** : a machine for drawing and twisting fiber into yarn or thread and winding it onto spindles [Medieval French *mul,* from Latin *mulus*]

1mule 1a

2mule *n* : a shoe or slipper whose upper does not extend around the heel of the foot [Middle French, a kind of slipper, from Latin *mulleus* "shoe worn by magistrates"]

mule deer *n* : a long-eared deer of western North America that is larger and more heavily built than the white-tailed deer

mule skinner *n* : a driver of mules

mu·le·teer \ˌmyü-lə-ˈtiər\ *n* : a driver of mules [Middle French *muletier,* from *mulet* "mule," from Medieval French *mul*]

mu·ley \ˈmyü-lē, ˈmu̇l-ē\ *adj* : having no horns; *esp* : naturally hornless ⟨a *muley* cow⟩ [of Celtic origin]

mul·ish \ˈmyü-lish\ *adj* : STUBBORN 1a, OBSTINATE — **mul·ish·ly** *adv* — **mul·ish·ness** *n*

1mull \ˈməl\ *vb* : to consider at length : PONDER ⟨*mull* over an idea⟩ [Middle English *mullen* "to grind, pulverize," from *mul, mol,* "dust"]

2mull *vt* : to sweeten, spice, and heat ⟨*mulled* wine⟩ [origin unknown]

3mull *n* : granular forest humus with a layer of mixed organic matter and mineral soil merging gradually into the mineral soil beneath [Danish *muld,* from Old Norse *mold* "dust, soil"]

mul·lah \ˈməl-ə, ˈmu̇l-ə\ *n* : a Muslim trained in traditional religious law and doctrine and usually holding an official post [Turkish *molla* and Persian & Urdu *mulla,* from Arabic *mawlā*]

mul·lein *also* **mul·len** \ˈməl-ən\ *n* : a tall Erasian herb naturalized in North America that is related to the snapdragons and has coarse woolly leaves and spikes of usually yellow flowers [Medieval French *moleine*]

mul·let \ˈməl-ət\ *n, pl* **mullet** *or* **mullets** : any of a family of chiefly marine largely gray food fishes — compare RED MULLET [Medieval French *mulet,* from Latin *mullus* "red mullet," from Greek *myllos*]

mul·li·gan stew \ˈməl-i-gən-\ *n* : a stew made from whatever ingredients are available [probably from the name *Mulligan*]

mul·li·ga·taw·ny \ˌməl-i-gə-ˈtȯ-nē, -ˈtän-ē\ *n* : a soup usually of chicken stock seasoned with curry [Tamil *miḷakutaṇṇi,* from *miḷaku* "pepper" + *taṇṇi* "water"]

mul·lion \ˈməl-yən\ *n* : a slender vertical bar between units of windows, doors, or screens [probably from earlier *monial* "mullion"] — **mullion** *vt*

multi- *combining form* **1 a** : many : multiple : much ⟨*multi*valent⟩ **b** : more than two ⟨*multi*lateral⟩ **c** : more than one ⟨*multi*stage⟩ **2** : many times over ⟨*multi*millionaire⟩ [Latin, from *multus* "much, many"]

multiage
multiagency
multiarmed
multiauthor
multiauthored
multiaxial
mutlibarrel
multibarreled
multibillion
multibillionaire
multibladed
multibranched
multibuilding
multicampus
multicar
multicausal
multicell
multicelled
multicellular
multicellularity
multicenter
multichambered
multichannel
multicharacter
multicity
multicoated
multicolor
multicolored
multicolumn
multicomponent
multicounty
multicurrency
multiday
multidialectal
multidimensional
multidirectional
multidisc
multidisciplinary
multidiscipline
multidivisional
multidrug
multielement
multiengine
multifamily
multifilament
multifocal
multifunction
multifunctional
multigenerational
multigenic
multigrade
multigrain
multihandicapped
multiheaded
multihospital
multihued
multi–industry
multi–institutional
multilane
multilevel
multileveled
multilobed
multilocation
multimember
multimetallic
multimillennial
multimillion
multimillionaire
multimolecular
multination
multinucleate
multinucleated
mulitpage
multiparameter
multipart
multiparty
multiphase
multiphasic
multipiece
multiplant
multiplayer
multipole
multipower
multiproblem
multiproduct
multipurpose
multiroom
multiservice
multisided
multisite
multisize
multiskilled
multisource
multispecies
multispeed
multisport
multistemmed
multistep
multistoried
multistory
multisyllabic
multisystem
multitalented
multitiered
multiton
multitone
multitowered
multitrack
multitrillion
multiunion
multiunit
multiuse
multivalve
multivolume
multiwarhead
multiyear

mul·ti·cul·tur·al \ˌməl-ti-ˈkəlch-rəl, -ə-rəl\ *adj* : of, relating to, reflecting, or adapted to diverse cultures ⟨a *multicultural* society⟩ — **mul·ti·cul·tur·al·ism** \-rə-ˌliz-əm\ *n* — **mul·ti·cul·tur·al·ist** \-rə-list\ *n or adj*

mul·ti·eth·nic \-ˈeth-nik\ *adj* : made up of people of various ethnicities ⟨a *multiethnic* country⟩; *also* : of, relating to, reflecting, or adapted to diverse ethnicities ⟨*multiethnic* literature⟩ — **mul·ti·eth·nic·i·ty** \-ˌeth-ˈnis-ət-ē\ *n*

mul·ti·fac·et·ed \-ˈfas-ət-əd\ *adj* : having many facets or aspects ⟨a *multifaceted* approach to teaching⟩

mul·ti·far·i·ous \ˌməl-tə-ˈfar-ē-əs, -ˈfer-\ *adj* : of various kinds : being many and varied ⟨the *multifarious* complexities of language⟩ [Late Latin *multifarius,* from Latin *multifariam* "in many places"] — **mul·ti·far·i·ous·ness** *n*

mul·ti·flo·ra rose \ˌməl-tə-ˌflōr-ə-, -ˌflȯr-\ *n* : a vigorous thorny rose with clusters of small flowers

mul·ti·fold \ˈməl-ti-ˌfōld\ *adj* : MANY, NUMEROUS

mul·ti·form \ˈməl-ti-ˌfȯrm\ *adj* : having many forms, shapes, or appearances

mul·ti·lat·er·al \ˌməl-ti-ˈlat-ə-rəl, -ˌtī-, -ˈla-trəl\ *adj* **1** : having many sides **2** : involving more than two nations or parties ⟨a *multilateral* treaty⟩ — **mul·ti·lat·er·al·ism** \-ˌiz-əm\ *n* — **mul·ti·lat·er·al·ly** \-ē\ *adv*

mul·ti·lay·ered \-ˈlā-ərd, -ˈlerd\ *or* **mul·ti·lay·er** \-ˈlā-ər, -ˈler\ *adj* : having or involving several distinct layers, strata, or levels

1mul·ti·me·dia \-ˈmēd-ē-ə\ *adj* : using, involving, or composed of two or more communications media ⟨*multimedia* software that combines sound, video, and text⟩

2multimedia *n* : a technique (as the combining of sound, video, and text) for expressing ideas (as in communication, entertainment, or art) in which several media are employed; *also* : something (as software) using such a technique

mul·ti·modal \-ˈmōd-l\ *adj* : having or involving several modes, modalities, or maxima ⟨*multimodal* distributions⟩ ⟨*multimodal* therapy⟩

1mul·ti·na·tion·al \-ˈnash-nəl, -ən-l\ *adj* **1** : of or relating to more than two nationalities ⟨a *multinational* society⟩ **2 a** : of, relating to, or involving more than two nations ⟨a *multinational* alliance⟩ **b** : having divisions in more than two countries ⟨a *multinational* corporation⟩

2multinational *n* : a multinational corporation

mul·ti·par·tite \ˌməl-ti-ˈpär-ˌtīt\ *adj* : having numerous members or signatories ⟨a *multipartite* treaty⟩

mul·ti·plat·i·num \-ˈplat-nəm, -n-əm\ *adj* : having sold two million or more copies of an album

1mul·ti·ple \ˈməl-tə-pəl\ *adj* **1** : containing, involving, or consisting of more than one ⟨*multiple* copies⟩ **2** : MANY 1 ⟨*multiple* achievements⟩ [French, from Latin *multiplex,* from *multi-* + *-plex* "-fold"]

2multiple *n* : the product of a quantity and a whole number ⟨35 is a *multiple* of 7⟩

multiple allele *n* : an allele of a group of more than two different alleles any two of which can make up a particular gene pair on homologous chromosomes

multiple–choice *adj* **1** : having several answers given from which the correct one is to be chosen ⟨a *multiple-choice* ques-

\ə\ **abut**	\au̇\ **out**	\i\ **tip**	\ȯ\ **saw**	\u̇\ **foot**
\ər\ **further**	\ch\ **chin**	\ī\ **life**	\ȯi\ **coin**	\y\ **yet**
\a\ **mat**	\e\ **pet**	\j\ **job**	\th\ **thin**	\yü\ **few**
\ā\ **take**	\ē\ **easy**	\ng\ **sing**	\t͟h\ **this**	\yu̇\ **cure**
\ä\ **cot, cart**	\g\ **go**	\ō\ **bone**	\ü\ **food**	\zh\ **vision**

tion⟩ **2 :** made up of multiple-choice questions ⟨a *multiple-choice* test⟩

multiple fruit *n* **:** a fruit (as a mulberry) formed from a cluster of flowers

multiple sclerosis *n* **:** a disease caused by damage and loss of myelin surrounding nerve fibers resulting in patches of hardened tissue in the brain or spinal cord and in symptoms (as weakness or paralysis of the arms or legs or loss of balance and muscle coordination) that typically worsen and then subside partly or fully for a period before worsening again

[1]**mul·ti·plex** \ˈməl-tə-ˌpleks\ *adj* **1 :** MULTIPLE 1, MANY **2 :** being or relating to a system of transmitting several messages simultaneously on the same circuit or channel [Latin]

[2]**mutiplex** *n* **:** a complex that houses several movie theaters

mul·ti·pli·cand \ˌməl-tə-pli-ˈkand\ *n* **:** the number that is to be multiplied by another [Latin *multiplicandus* "to be multiplied," from *multiplicare* "to multiply"]

mul·ti·pli·ca·tion \ˌməl-tə-plə-ˈkā-shən\ *n* **1 :** the act or process of multiplying **2 a :** a mathematical operation that takes two numbers and gives an answer equal to the sum of a column containing one of the numbers repeated the number of times of the other number ⟨the *multiplication* of 8 and 3 is the same as the sum of 8 + 8 + 8⟩ **b :** a similar mathematical operation defined for sets of mathematical elements (as matrices or complex numbers) other than the real numbers

multiplication sign *n* **:** a symbol used to show multiplication: **a :** TIMES SIGN **b :** DOT 2c

mul·ti·pli·ca·tive \ˌməl-tə-ˈplik-ət-iv, ˈməl-tə-plə-ˌkāt-\ *adj* **:** of, relating to, or associated with a mathematical operation of multiplication — **mul·ti·pli·ca·tive·ly** *adv*

multiplicative identity *n* **:** an element of a set that when multiplied by any other element of the set leaves that element unchanged ⟨the number 1 is the *multiplicative identity* element in the set of all real numbers⟩

multiplicative inverse *n* **:** an element of a mathematical set that when multiplied by a given element gives the identity element — called also *reciprocal*

mul·ti·plic·i·ty \ˌməl-tə-ˈplis-ət-ē\ *n, pl* **-ties 1 :** the quality or state of being multiple or various **2 :** a great number ⟨a *multiplicity* of ideas⟩

mul·ti·pli·er \ˈməl-tə-ˌplī-ər, -ˌplīr\ *n* **:** one that multiplies: as **a :** a number by which another is multiplied **b :** a device for multiplying or for intensifying some effect

mul·ti·ply \ˈməl-tə-ˌplī\ *vb* **-plied; -ply·ing 1 a :** to increase in number **:** make or become more numerous **b :** to produce offspring **:** BREED, PROPAGATE **2 a :** to find the product of by multiplication ⟨*multiply* 7 and 8⟩ **b :** to perform the operation of multiplication ⟨first divide and then *multiply*⟩ [Medieval French *multiplier,* from Latin *multiplicare,* from *multiplex* "multiple"]

mul·ti·po·lar \ˌməl-ti-ˈpō-lər\ *adj* **1 :** having several poles ⟨*multipolar* mitoses⟩ **2 :** having several dendrites ⟨*multipolar* neurons⟩ **3 :** characterized by more than two centers of power or interest ⟨a *multipolar world*⟩ — **mul·ti·po·lar·i·ty** \-pō-ˈlar-ət-ē\ *n*

mul·ti·po·ten·tial \ˌməl-ti-pə-ˈten-chəl\ *adj* **:** having the potential of becoming any of several mature cell types ⟨a *multipotential* stem cell⟩

mul·ti·pronged \ˌməl-ti-ˈprȯngd, -ˈprängd\ *adj* **1 :** having several prongs ⟨*multipronged* fishing spears⟩ **2 :** having several distinct aspects or elements ⟨a *multipronged* attack on the problem⟩

mul·ti·ra·cial \ˌməl-ti-ˈrā-shəl, -ˌtī-\ *adj* **:** composed of, relating to, or representing various races

mul·ti·sen·so·ry \-ˈsens-rē, -ə-rē\ *adj* **:** relating to or involving several physiological senses ⟨a *multisensory* experience of sights, sounds, and aromas⟩

mul·ti·stage \-ˌstāj\ *adj* **:** operating in or involving two or more steps or stages ⟨a *multistage* rocket⟩

mul·ti·task·ing \ˈməl-ti-ˌtas-king\ *n* **:** the performance of multiple tasks at one time especially by a computer — **mul·ti·task** \-ˌtask\ *vi* — **mul·ti·task·er** \-ˌtas-kər\ *n*

mul·ti·tude \ˈməl-tə-ˌtüd, -ˌtyüd\ *n* **:** a very great number of things or people **:** HOST [Latin *multitudin-, multitudo,* from *multus* "much"]

synonyms MULTITUDE, CROWD, THRONG, MOB mean a large number of individuals. MULTITUDE implies great numbers ⟨a *multitude* of stars⟩. CROWD stresses packing together and loss of individuality ⟨a *crowd* of onlookers⟩. THRONG suggests a crowd in motion ⟨people came to the fair in *throngs*⟩. MOB implies disorganization and agitation and in specific use the intent of violence ⟨police dispersed the *mob*⟩.

mul·ti·tu·di·nous \ˌməl-tə-ˈtüd-nəs, -ˈtyüd-, -n-əs\ *adj* **:** consisting of a multitude ⟨a *multitudinous* gathering⟩ — **mul·ti·tu·di·nous·ly** *adv* — **mul·ti·tu·di·nous·ness** *n*

mul·ti·va·lent \ˌməl-ti-ˈvā-lənt, -ˌtī-\ *adj* **:** POLYVALENT

mul·ti·vi·ta·min \-ˈvīt-ə-mən\ *adj* **:** containing several vitamins and especially all known to be essential to health ⟨a *multivitamin* pill⟩ — **multivitamin** *n*

[1]**mum** \ˈməm\ *adj* **:** SILENT ⟨keep *mum*⟩ [probably imitative of a sound made with closed lips]

[2]**mum** *n* **:** CHRYSANTHEMUM

[3]**mum** *chiefly British variant of* MOM

mum·ble \ˈməm-bəl\ *vb* **mum·bled; mum·bling** \-bə-ling, -bling\ **1 :** to speak indistinctly usually with lips partly closed ⟨*mumble* one's words⟩ **2 :** to chew or bite with or as if with toothless gums ⟨a baby *mumbling* its food⟩ [Middle English *momelen,* of imitative origin] — **mumble** *n* — **mum·bler** \-bə-lər, -blər\ *n* — **mum·bly** \-bə-lē, -blē\ *adv*

mum·ble·ty–peg \ˈməm-bəl-tē-ˌpeg, -bəl-ˌpeg\ *n* **:** a game in which the players try to flip a knife from various positions so that the blade will stick into the ground [from the phrase *mumble the peg*; from the loser's originally having to pull out with his teeth a peg driven into the ground]

mum·bo jum·bo \ˌməm-bō-ˈjəm-bō\ *n* **1 :** an object of superstitious homage and fear **2 a :** a complicated ritual with elaborate trappings **b :** complicated activity or language that obscures and confuses [*Mumbo Jumbo,* a masked figure among Mandingos, a western African people]

mum·mer \ˈməm-ər\ *n* **1 :** ACTOR; *esp* **:** an actor in a pantomime **2 :** one who goes merrymaking in disguise during festivals [Middle French *momeur,* from *momer* "to go masked"]

mum·mery \ˈməm-ə-rē\ *n, pl* **-mer·ies 1 :** a performance by mummers **2 :** a ridiculous or pompous ceremony

mum·mi·fy \ˈməm-i-ˌfī\ *vb* **-fied; -fy·ing 1 :** to embalm and dry as or as if as a mummy **2 :** to dry up like the skin of a mummy **:** SHRIVEL — **mum·mi·fi·ca·tion** \ˌməm-i-fə-ˈkā-shən\ *n*

mum·my \ˈməm-ē\ *n, pl* **mummies 1 :** a body embalmed or treated for burial in the manner of the ancient Egyptians **2 :** an unusually well-preserved body [Medieval French *mumie* "powdered parts of a mummy used as a drug," from Medieval Latin *mumia* "mummy, powdered mummy," from Arabic *mūmiyah* "bitumen, mummy," from Persian *mūm* "wax"]

mumps \ˈməmps\ *n sing or pl* **:** an acute contagious virus disease marked by fever and by swelling especially of salivary glands [obsolete *mump* "grimace"]

munch \ˈmənch\ *vb* **:** to eat with a chewing action ⟨*munch* on celery⟩; *also* **:** to snack on ⟨watched TV and *munched* popcorn⟩ [Middle English *monchen,* probably of imitative origin] — **munch·er** *n*

munch·ies \ˈmən-chēz\ *n pl* **1 :** hunger pangs ⟨had the *munchies* after swimming⟩ **2 :** light snack foods

mun·dane \ˌmən-ˈdān, ˈmən-ˌ\ *adj* **1 :** of or relating to the world **:** WORLDLY **2 :** concerned with the practical, immediate, and ordinary ⟨*mundane* problems of everyday life⟩ [Medieval French *mundain,* from Late Latin *mundanus,* from Latin *mundus* "world"] ***synonyms*** see EARTHLY — **mun·dane·ly** *adv*

mung bean \ˈməng-\ *n* **:** a bushy bean plant that is widely grown in warm regions for its edible usually green or yellow seeds, for forage, and as the chief source of bean sprouts; *also* **:** its seed [Hindi & Urdu *mūg,* from Sanskrit *mudgah*]

mu·nic·i·pal \myu̇-ˈnis-ə-pəl\ *adj* **1 :** of or relating to the internal affairs of a nation **2 :** of or relating to a municipality ⟨*municipal* government⟩ [Latin *municipalis* "of a municipality," from *municeps* "inhabitant of a municipality," from *munus* "duty" + *capere* "to take"] — **mu·nic·i·pal·ly** \-pə-lē, -plē\ *adv*

mu·nic·i·pal·i·ty \myu̇-ˌnis-ə-ˈpal-ət-ē\ *n, pl* **-ties :** a primarily urban political unit (as a city or town) having corporate status and usually powers of self-government

mu·nif·i·cent \myu̇-ˈnif-ə-sənt\ *adj* **1 :** extremely liberal in giving **:** very generous **2 :** given generously or in plenty ⟨a *munificent* gift⟩ [derived from Latin *munificus* "generous," from *munus* "service, gift" + *-ficus* "-fic"] ***synonyms*** see GENEROUS — **mu·nif·i·cence** \-səns\ *n* — **mu·nif·i·cent·ly** *adv*

mu·ni·tion \myu̇-ˈnish-ən\ *n* **:** ARMAMENT 2, AMMUNITION [Middle French *munition* "rampart, defense," from Latin *muni-*

tio, from *munire* "to fortify," from *moenia* "walls"] — **mu·ni·tion** \-ˈnish-ən\ *vt*

mun·tin \ˈmənt-ᵊn\ *n* **:** a strip separating panes of glass in a sash [French *montant* "vertical dividing bar," from *monter* "to rise," derived from Latin *mont-, mons* "mount"]

1**mu·ral** \ˈmyu̇r-əl\ *adj* **1 :** of or relating to a wall **2 :** applied to and made a part of a wall surface ⟨a *mural* painting⟩ [Latin *muralis,* from *murus* "wall"]

2**mural** *n* **:** a mural painting — **mu·ral·ist** \-ə-ləst\ *n*

1**mur·der** \ˈmərd-ər\ *n* **1 :** the crime of unlawfully killing a person especially with deliberate intent or design **2 a :** something very difficult or dangerous ⟨the traffic was *murder*⟩ **b :** something outrageous or blameworthy ⟨got away with *murder*⟩ [partly from Old English *morthor;* partly from Medieval French *murdre,* of Germanic origin]

2**murder** *vb* **mur·dered; mur·der·ing** \ˈmərd-ring, -ə-ring\ **1 :** to kill a human being unlawfully and especially with deliberate intent or design **:** commit murder **2 :** to spoil by performing in a wretched manner ***synonyms*** see KILL — **mur·der·er** \ˈmərd-ər-ər\ *n* — **mur·der·ess** \ˈmərd-ə-rəs\ *n*

mur·der·ous \ˈmərd-rəs, -ə-rəs\ *adj* **1 a :** characterized by or causing murder or bloodshed ⟨*murderous* machine-gun fire⟩ ⟨a *murderous* act⟩ **b :** having the purpose or capability of murder ⟨with *murderous* intent⟩ ⟨a *murderous* glance⟩ **2 :** having the ability or power to overwhelm **:** DEVASTATING ⟨*murderous* heat⟩ — **mur·der·ous·ly** *adv* — **mur·der·ous·ness** *n*

mu·rex \ˈmyu̇r-ˌeks\ *n, pl* **mu·ri·ces** \ˈmyu̇r-ə-ˌsēz\ *or* **mu·rex·es :** any of a genus of sea snails that yield a purple dye [Latin, a kind of mollusk]

mu·ri·ate \ˈmyu̇r-ē-ˌāt\ *n* **:** CHLORIDE [French, back-formation from *(acide) muriatique* "muriatic acid"]

mu·ri·at·ic acid \ˌmyu̇r-ē-ˌat-ik-\ *n* **:** HYDROCHLORIC ACID [French *muriatique,* derived from Latin *muria* "brine"]

mu·rine \ˈmyu̇r-ˌīn\ *adj* **:** of or relating to the common house mouse or closely related rodents ⟨*murine* typhus⟩ [derived from Latin *mur-, mus* "mouse"]

murine typhus *n* **:** a mild disease that is marked especially by fever, headache, and red rash and is caused by a bacterium widespread in rodents and transmitted to humans by the bite of a flea

murk \ˈmərk\ *n* **:** intense darkness or gloom; *also* **:** FOG [Middle English *mirke*]

murky \ˈmər-kē\ *adj* **murk·i·er; -est 1 :** very dark or gloomy **2 :** FOGGY 1a, MISTY **3 :** difficult to understand ⟨a *murky* reply designed to confuse⟩ — **murk·i·ly** \-kə-lē\ *adv* — **murk·i·ness** \-kē-nəs\ *n*

mur·mur \ˈmər-mər\ *n* **1 :** a muttered complaint **:** GRUMBLE **2 :** a low indistinct sound ⟨the *murmur* of the wind⟩ **3 :** an irregular heart sound typically indicating an abnormality in the heart's function or structure [Medieval French *murmure* "disturbance," from Latin *murmur* "murmur, roar," of imitative origin] — **murmur** *vb* — **mur·mur·er** \ˈmər-mər-ər\ *n*

mur·mur·ous \ˈmərm-rəs, -ə-rəs\ *adj* **:** filled with or characterized by murmurs — **mur·mur·ous·ly** *adv*

Mur·phy's Law \ˈmər-fēz-\ *n* **:** an observation: anything that can go wrong will go wrong [probably from Edward A. Murphy, died 1990, American engineer]

mur·rain \ˈmər-ən, ˈmə-rən\ *n* **:** a pestilence or plague especially of domestic animals [Medieval French *morine,* from *morir* "to die," from Latin *mori*]

murre \ˈmər\ *n* **:** a common black-and-white web-footed bird of northern seas; *also* **:** any of several related seabirds [origin unknown]

mus·ca·dine \ˈməs-kə-ˌdīn\ *n* **:** a grape of the southern U.S. with musky fruits in small clusters; *also* **:** the fruit [probably alteration of *muscatel*]

mus·cat \ˈməs-ˌkat, -kət\ *n* **:** any of several cultivated grapes used in making wine and raisins [Middle French, from Occitan, from *muscat* "musky," from *musc* "musk," from Late Latin *muscus*]

mus·ca·tel \ˌməs-kə-ˈtel\ *n* **:** a sweet wine made from muscat grapes [Middle English *muskadell,* from Medieval Latin *muscadellum,* from Occitan *muscadel,* from *muscadel* "resembling musk," from *muscat* "muscat"]

1**mus·cle** \ˈməs-əl\ *n* **1 a :** a body tissue consisting of long cells that contract when stimulated and produce motion **b :** an organ that is essentially a mass of muscle tissue attached at either end to a fixed point (as to bone) and that by contracting moves or checks the movement of a body part **2 a :** muscular strength **:** BRAWN **b :** effective strength **:** POWER [Latin *musculus,* literally, "little mouse," from *mus* "mouse"]

Word History Diminutives like Latin *musculus,* "little mouse," are used not only to name small things but often to express such diverse feelings as endearment and ridicule as well. Some muscles, especially the major muscles of the arm and leg, look a little like stylized mice, their tendons playing the part of a mouse's tail. This fancied resemblance, which ignores the fact that muscles are often much larger than mice, accounts for the Latin word *musculus,* the ultimate source of English *muscle.*

2**muscle** *vb* **mus·cled; mus·cling** \ˈməs-ling, -ə-ling\ **1 :** to move or force by or as if by muscular effort ⟨*muscled* her out of office⟩ **2 :** to force one's way ⟨*muscle* in on a business⟩

mus·cle–bound \ˈməs-əl-ˌbau̇nd\ *adj* **:** having some of the muscles abnormally enlarged and lacking in elasticity

muscled *adj* **:** having muscles especially of a specified kind — often used in combination ⟨hard-*muscled* arms⟩

muscle spindle *n* **:** a structure at the ending of a group of nerve fibers in a muscle that is sensitive to stretching of the muscle, consists of small striated muscle fibers richly supplied with nerve fibers, and is enclosed in a sheath of connective tissue — called also *stretch receptor*

mus·co·vite \ˈməs-kə-ˌvīt\ *n* **1** *cap* **a :** a native or resident of the ancient principality of Moscow or of the city of Moscow **b :** RUSSIAN 1 **2 :** a mineral that consists of a colorless to pale brown potassium-containing mica [Medieval Latin or New Latin *Muscovia* "Moscow"] — **Muscovite** *adj*

Mus·co·vy duck \ˌməs-ˌkō-vē-\ *n* **:** a large tropical American duck widely kept in domestication [*Muscovy,* principality of Moscow, Russia]

mus·cu·lar \ˈməs-kyə-lər\ *adj* **1 a :** of, relating to, or constituting muscle **b :** performed by the muscles **2 a :** having well-developed muscles **b :** of or relating to physical strength **:** STRONG — **mus·cu·lar·i·ty** \ˌməs-kyə-ˈlar-ət-ē\ *n* — **mus·cu·lar·ly** \ˈməs-kyə-lər-lē\ *adv*

muscular dystrophy *n* **:** an inherited disease characterized by progressive wasting of muscles

mus·cu·la·ture \ˈməs-kyə-lə-ˌchu̇r\ *n* **:** the muscles of the body or of one of its parts

1**muse** \ˈmyüz\ *vb* **:** to consider carefully **:** PONDER, MEDITATE [Medieval French *muser* "to gape, muse," derived from Medieval Latin *musus* "mouth of an animal"] — **mus·er** *n*

2**muse** *n* **1** *cap* **:** any of nine sister goddesses in Greek mythology presiding over song and poetry and the arts and sciences **2 :** a source of inspiration [Medieval French, from Latin *Musa,* from Greek *Mousa*]

mu·sette \myü-ˈzet\ *n* **:** a small knapsack sometimes with one shoulder strap used especially by soldiers — called also *musette bag* [Medieval French, literally, "small bagpipe," from *muser* "to muse, play the bagpipe"]

mu·se·um \myu̇-ˈzē-əm\ *n* **:** a building or part of a building in which are displayed objects of permanent interest in one or more of the arts or sciences [Latin, "place for learned occupation," from Greek *Mouseion,* derived from *Mousa* "Muse"]

1**mush** \ˈməsh\ *n* **1 :** cornmeal boiled in water or milk **2 :** something soft and spongy or shapeless **3 :** sickeningly sweet sentimentality or courting [probably alteration of *mash*]

2**mush** *vi* **:** to travel over snow with a sled drawn by dogs — often used as a command to a dog team [probably from French *marchons,* "let's move," from *marcher* "to move, march," probably of Germanic origin] — **mush·er** *n*

3**mush** *n* **:** a trip across snow with a dog team

1**mush·room** \ˈməsh-ˌrüm,

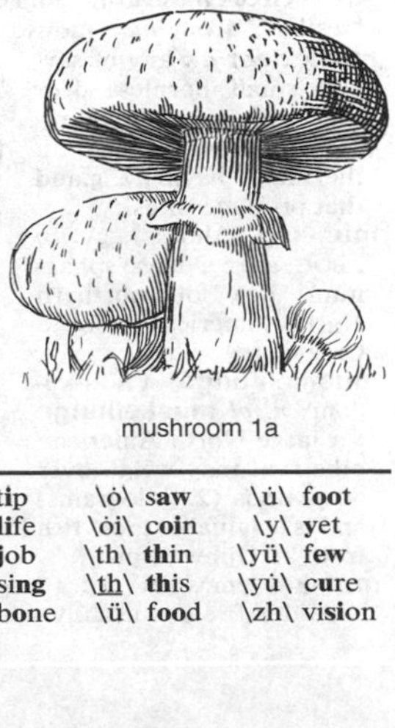

mushroom 1a

\ə\ **abut**	\au̇\ **out**	\i\ **tip**	\ȯ\ **saw**	\u̇\ **foot**
\ər\ **further**	\ch\ **chin**	\ī\ **life**	\ȯi\ **coin**	\y\ **yet**
\a\ **mat**	\e\ **pet**	\j\ **job**	\th\ **thin**	\yü\ **few**
\ā\ **take**	\ē\ **easy**	\ng\ **sing**	\t͟h\ **this**	\yu̇\ **cure**
\ä\ **cot, cart**	\g\ **go**	\ō\ **bone**	\ü\ **food**	\zh\ **vision**

-ˌrüm\ *n* **1 a :** a fleshy aboveground fruiting body of a fungus that consists typically of a stem bearing a flattened cap; *esp* **:** one that is edible **b :** FUNGUS 1 **2 :** one that springs up suddenly or multiplies rapidly **3 :** something resembling a mushroom [Medieval French *musherum, musseron,* from Late Latin *mussirio*]

²**mushroom** *vi* **1 :** to collect wild mushrooms **2 :** to spring up suddenly or multiply rapidly

mushroom cloud *n* **:** a mushroom-shaped cloud; *esp* **:** one caused by the explosion of a nuclear weapon

mushy \ˈməsh-ē\ *adj* **mush·i·er; -est 1 :** soft like mush **2 :** weakly sentimental — **mush·i·ly** \ˈməsh-ə-lē\ *adv* — **mush·i·ness** \ˈməsh-ē-nəs\ *n*

mu·sic \ˈmyü-zik\ *n* **1 a :** the art of combining tones or sounds in succession, in combination, or in temporal relationships so that they are pleasing, expressive, or intelligible **b :** vocal, instrumental, or mechanical sounds having rhythm, melody, or harmony **c :** the score of music compositions set down on paper ⟨did you bring your *music* with you⟩ **2 a :** an agreeable sound ⟨the *music* of a brook⟩ **b :** musical quality ⟨the *music* of verse⟩ **3 :** musical accompaniment ⟨a play set to *music*⟩ [Medieval French *musike,* from Latin *musica,* from Greek *mousikē* "art presided over by the Muses," from *Mousa* "Muse"]

¹**mu·si·cal** \ˈmyü-zi-kəl\ *adj* **1 a :** of or relating to music ⟨*musical* instruments⟩ **b :** having the pleasing harmonious qualities of music **:** MELODIOUS ⟨a *musical* voice⟩ **2 :** having an interest in or talent for music ⟨a *musical* family⟩ **3 :** set to or accompanied by music **4 :** of or relating to musicians or music lovers — **mu·si·cal·i·ty** \ˌmyü-zi-ˈkal-ət-ē\ *n* — **mu·si·cal·ly** \ˈmyü-zi-kə-lē, -klē\ *adv*

²**musical** *n* **:** a film or theatrical production consisting of musical numbers and dialogue that develop a plot — called also *musical comedy*; compare REVUE

musical chairs *n pl* **:** a children's game in which players march to music around a group of chairs numbering one less than the number of players and scramble for a seat when the music stops

mu·si·cale \ˌmyü-zi-ˈkal\ *n* **:** a usually private social gathering featuring a concert of music [French *soirée musicale,* literally, "musical evening"]

music box *n* **:** a box or case enclosing an apparatus that reproduces music mechanically when activated by clockwork

music hall *n* **:** a vaudeville theater

mu·si·cian \myu̇-ˈzish-ən\ *n* **:** one skilled in music; *esp* **:** a composer or professional performer of music — **mu·si·cian·ly** \-lē\ *adj* — **mu·si·cian·ship** \-ˌship\ *n*

mu·si·col·o·gy \ˌmyü-zi-ˈkäl-ə-jē\ *n* **:** a study of music as a branch of knowledge or field of research — **mu·si·co·log·i·cal** \-zi-kə-ˈläj-i-kəl\ *adj* — **mu·si·col·o·gist** \-zi-ˈkäl-ə-jəst\ *n*

mus·ing \ˈmyü-zing\ *n* **:** MEDITATION ⟨considered it in their *musings*⟩ — **musing** *adj* — **mus·ing·ly** \-zing-lē\ *adv*

musk \ˈməsk\ *n* **1 a :** a substance of penetrating persistent odor obtained usually from the male musk deer and used in perfume **b :** a comparable substance from another animal (as a skunk) or a synthetic substitute **2 a :** the odor of musk **b :** an odor resembling that of musk especially in heaviness or persistence [Medieval French *musc,* from Late Latin *muscus,* from Greek *moschos,* from Persian *mushk,* from Sanskrit *muṣka* "testicle," from *mūṣ* "mouse"]

musk deer *n* **:** any of several small hornless deer that live in the high regions of central Asia with the males having a gland that produces musk

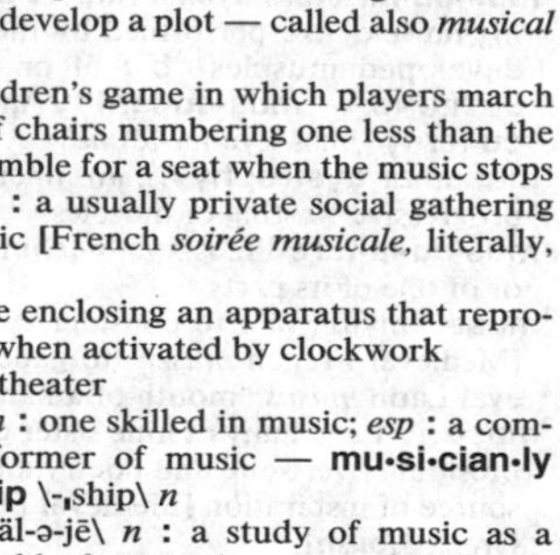

musk deer

mus·keg \ˈməs-ˌkeg\ *n* **:** BOG; *esp* **:** a dense sphagnum bog of northern North America [from a Cree word]

mus·kel·lunge \ˈməs-kə-ˌlənj\ *n, pl* **muskellunge :** a large North American pike that may weigh over 60 pounds (27 kilograms) and is a valuable sport fish [from Canadian French *maskinongé,* from an Ojibwa word]

mus·ket \ˈməs-kət\ *n* **:** a large-caliber muzzle-loading military shoulder firearm usually with a smooth bore [Middle French *mousquet,* from Italian *moschetto* "small artillery piece, sparrow hawk," from *mosca* "fly," from Latin *musca*]

Word History In the early history of firearms, cannons of lesser size sometimes took their names from birds of prey. Following this pattern, Italians applied *moschetto* or *moschetta,* "sparrow hawk" (a diminutive of *mosca,* "fly") to a small-caliber piece of ordnance in the 16th century. Spaniards borrowed this word as *mosquete* and the French as *mosquet* (later *mousquet*), but applied it to a heavy shoulder firearm rather than a cannon. The word *musket* was retained for the weapon after its original matchlock firing mechanism was replaced, eventually by the flintlock. As the practice of rifling firearms—incising the barrel with spiral grooves to improve the bullet's accuracy—became more common, *musket* gradually gave way to the newer word *rifle* in the 18th and 19th centuries.

mus·ke·teer \ˌməs-kə-ˈtiər\ *n* **:** a soldier armed with a musket

mus·ket·ry \ˈməs-kə-trē\ *n, pl* **-ries :** small-arms fire

mus·kie *or* **mus·ky** \ˈməs-kē\ *n, pl* **muskies :** MUSKELLUNGE

musk·mel·on \ˈməsk-ˌmel-ən\ *n* **:** any of various round to oval melons (as the cantaloupes or winter melons) of an Asian vine of the gourd family that have smooth or ridged skin and edible usually sweet flesh

Mus·ko·gee \məs-ˈkō-gē, ˌməs-\ *n, pl* **Muskogee** *or* **Muskogees :** a member of an American Indian people of what is now Georgia and eastern Alabama

musk ox *n* **:** a heavy-set shaggy-coated wild ox of tundra regions of Greenland, Canada, and Alaska with the males producing a strong musky odor from glands beneath the eyes

musk ox

musk·rat \ˈməs-ˌkrat\ *n, pl* **muskrat** *or* **muskrats :** a North American aquatic rodent with a long scaly tail, webbed hind feet, and dark glossy brown fur; *also* **:** its fur or pelt [probably by folk etymology from a word of Algonquian origin akin to Massachusett *musquash* "muskrat"]

musk turtle *n* **:** any of several small American freshwater turtles with a strong musky or foul-smelling odor

musky \ˈməs-kē\ *adj* **musk·i·er; -est :** having an odor of or resembling musk — **musk·i·ness** *n*

Mus·lim \ˈməz-ləm, ˈmu̇s-, ˈmu̇z-\ *n* **:** an adherent of Islam [Arabic *muslim,* literally, "one who surrenders (to God)"] — **Muslim** *adj*

mus·lin \ˈməz-lən\ *n* **:** a cotton fabric of plain weave [French *mousseline,* from Italian *mussolina,* from Arabic *mawṣilīy* "of Mosul," from *al-Mawṣil* "Mosul, Iraq"]

mus·quash \ˈməs-ˌkwäsh, -ˌkwȯsh\ *n* **:** MUSKRAT [Massachusett]

¹**muss** \ˈməs\ *n* **:** a state of disorder **:** MESS [origin unknown]

²**muss** *vt* **:** to make untidy **:** RUMPLE ⟨*mussed* my hair⟩

mus·sel \ˈməs-əl\ *n* **1 :** any of various edible saltwater bivalve mollusks with a long dark shell **2 :** any of various bivalve freshwater mollusks especially of rivers of the central U.S. having shells lined with mother-of-pearl [Old English *muscelle,* derived from Latin *musculus* "muscle, mussel"]

mussy \ˈməs-ē\ *adj* **muss·i·er; -est :** MESSY, UNTIDY — **muss·i·ly** \ˈməs-ə-lē\ *adv* — **muss·i·ness** \ˈməs-ē-nəs\ *n*

¹**must** \məst, məs, ˈməst\ *auxiliary verb, present & past all persons* **must 1 a :** be commanded or requested to ⟨you *must* stop that nonsense⟩ **b :** be urged to ⟨you *must* read that book⟩ **2 a :** be compelled, required, or obliged to (as by physical necessity, law, or social custom) ⟨one *must* eat to live⟩ ⟨we *must* be quiet⟩ **b :** be determined to ⟨if you *must* go⟩ **c :** be unreasonably compelled to ⟨why *must* you argue?⟩ **3 :** be logically inferred or supposed to ⟨it *must* be time⟩ **4 :** be reasonably certain to ⟨I *must* have lost it⟩ [Old English *mōste* "was allowed to, had to," past of *mōtan* "to be allowed to, have to"]

²**must** \ˈməst\ *n* **:** something necessary, required, or indispensable ⟨new shoes are a *must*⟩

³**must** *n* **:** the juice of fruit (as grapes) before and during fermentation [Old English, from Latin *mustum*]

mus·tache *also* **mous·tache** \ˈməs-ˌtash, məs-ˈ\ *n* **1 :** the hair growing on the human upper lip **2 :** hair or bristles about the mouth of a mammal (as walrus) [Middle French *moustache,* from Italian *mustaccio,* derived from Greek *mystax* "upper lip, mustache"]

mus·ta·chio *also* **mous·ta·chio** \məs-ˈtash-ō, -ˈtäsh-, -ē-ˌō\ *n, pl* **-chios :** MUSTACHE; *esp* **:** a large mustache [Italian *mustaccio*] — **mus·ta·chioed** *also* **mous·ta·chioed** \-ōd, -ē-ˌōd\ *adj*

mus·tang \ˈməs-ˌtang\ *n* **:** a small hardy wild horse of the western plains of the U.S. directly descended from horses brought in by the Spaniards; *also* **:** BRONCO [American Spanish *mestengo,* from Spanish, "stray," from *mesta* "annual roundup of stray cattle," from Medieval Latin *(animalia) mixta* "mixed animals"]

mus·tard \ˈməs-tərd\ *n* **1 :** any of several yellow-flowered herbs related to the turnips and cabbages **2 :** a pungent yellow powder of the small round seeds of a common mustard used as a seasoning or in medicine [Medieval French *mostarde,* from *moust* "must," from Latin *mustum*]

mustard gas *n* **:** a poisonous oily liquid $C_4H_8Cl_2S$ having severely irritating and especially blistering effects

mustard plaster *n* **:** a medicinal plaster containing powdered mustard that is applied to the skin (as of the back or chest) to cause redness and irritation in the surface layers of the skin and reduce inflammation deeper down

[1]**mus·ter** \ˈməs-tər\ *vb* **mus·tered; mus·ter·ing** \-tə-ring, -tring\ **1 :** to enlist or enroll a person in military service **2 a :** to assemble (as troops or a ship's company) for roll call or inspection **b :** CONGREGATE, ASSEMBLE **3 :** to call forth **:** ROUSE ⟨all the strength I could *muster*⟩ [Medieval French *monstrer, mustrer* "to show, muster," from Latin *monstrare,* from *monstrum* "sign, portent, monster"]

[2]**muster** *n* **1 a :** an act of assembling; *esp* **:** a formal military inspection **b :** critical examination ⟨slipshod work that would never pass *muster*⟩ **2 :** an assembled group

muster out *vt* **:** to discharge from service

mustn't \ˈməs-nt\ **:** must not

musty \ˈməs-tē\ *adj* **must·i·er; -est 1 a :** impaired by damp or mildew **:** MOLDY **b :** tasting or smelling of damp and decay **2 a :** TRITE, STALE ⟨a *musty* proverb⟩ **b :** OUTMODED 2, ANTIQUATED ⟨*musty* customs⟩ [earlier *must* "musk, mold," from Middle French, "musk," from *musc*] — **must·i·ly** \-tə-lē\ *adv* — **must·i·ness** \-tē-nəs\ *n*

mu·ta·ble \ˈmyüt-ə-bəl\ *adj* **1 :** prone to change **:** INCONSTANT **2 a :** capable of change in form or nature **b :** capable of or liable to mutation ⟨a *mutable* bacterium⟩ [Latin *mutabilis,* from *mutare* "to change"] — **mu·ta·bil·i·ty** \ˌmyüt-ə-ˈbil-ət-ē\ *n*

mu·ta·gen \ˈmyüt-ə-jən, -ˌjen\ *n* **:** an agent (as a chemical or radiation) inducing mutation — **mu·ta·gen·ic** \ˌmyüt-ə-ˈjen-ik\ *adj* — **mu·ta·ge·nic·i·ty** \-jə-ˈnis-ət-ē\ *n*

mu·tant \ˈmyüt-nt\ *adj* **:** of, relating to, or produced by mutation — **mutant** *n*

mu·tate \ˈmyü-ˌtāt\ *vb* **:** to undergo or cause to undergo mutation [Latin *mutare* "to change"] — **mu·ta·tive** \ˈmyü-ˌtāt-iv, ˈmyüt-ət-iv\ *adj*

mu·ta·tion \myü-ˈtā-shən\ *n* **1 :** a basic alteration **:** CHANGE **2 a :** a relatively permanent change in hereditary material involving either a change in the position of the genes on the chromosomes or a fundamental change in the chemical structure of the genes themselves **b :** an individual, strain, or trait resulting from mutation — **mu·ta·tion·al** \-shnəl, -shən-l\ *adj*

mu·ta·tis mu·tan·dis \mü-ˌtät-ə-smü-ˈtän-dəs\ *adv* **:** with the necessary changes having been made [Medieval Latin]

[1]**mute** \ˈmyüt\ *adj* **1 :** unable to speak **:** lacking the power of speech **2 :** marked by absence of speech ⟨a *mute* appeal for help⟩ **3 :** not pronounced **:** SILENT ⟨the *mute* "b" in "thumb"⟩ [Medieval French *muet,* from Latin *mutus*] — **mute·ly** *adv* — **mute·ness** *n* — **mut·ism** \ˈmyüt-ˌiz-əm\ *n*

[2]**mute** *n* **1 :** a person who cannot or does not speak **2 :** a device attached to or inserted into a musical instrument to deaden, soften, or muffle its tone **3 :** STOP 8

[3]**mute** *vt* **1 :** to muffle or reduce the sound of **2 :** to tone down ⟨*muted* their criticism⟩ ⟨*muted* the colors⟩

mu·ti·late \ˈmyüt-l-ˌāt\ *vt* **1 :** to cut off or permanently destroy a limb or essential part of **2 :** to make imperfect by cutting or alteration ⟨*mutilate* a document⟩ [Latin *mutilare*] — **mu·ti·la·tion** \ˌmyüt-l-ˈā-shən\ *n* — **mu·ti·la·tor** \ˈmyüt-l-ˌāt-ər\ *n*

mu·ti·neer \ˌmyüt-n-ˈiər\ *n* **:** one that mutinies

mu·ti·nous \ˈmyüt-n-əs, ˈmyüt-nəs\ *adj* **1 :** disposed to or engaged in mutiny **:** REBELLIOUS ⟨a *mutinous* crew⟩ **2 :** of, relating to, or constituting mutiny ⟨*mutinous* threats⟩ — **mu·ti·nous·ly** *adv* — **mu·ti·nous·ness** *n*

mu·ti·ny \ˈmyüt-n-ē, ˈmyüt-nē\ *n, pl* **-nies :** willful refusal to obey lawful authority; *esp* **:** revolt by a military group against a superior officer [obsolete *mutine* "to rebel," from Middle French *se mutiner,* from *mutin* "mutinous," from *meute* "revolt," derived from Latin *movēre* "to move"] — **mutiny** *vi*

mutt \ˈmət\ *n* **:** a mongrel dog **:** CUR [earlier *mutt* "fool," short for *muttonhead*]

mut·ter \ˈmət-ər\ *vb* **1 :** MUMBLE 1 **2 :** to murmur complainingly or angrily **:** GRUMBLE [Middle English *muteren*] — **mutter** *n* — **mut·ter·er** \ˈmət-ər-ər\ *n*

mut·ton \ˈmət-n\ *n* **:** the flesh of a mature sheep used for food [Medieval French *moton* "ram, sheep, mutton," of Celtic origin] — **mut·tony** \-ē\ *adj*

mut·ton·chops \-ˌchäps\ *n pl* **:** side-whiskers that are narrow at the temple and broad and round by the lower jaws — called also *muttonchop whiskers*

mu·tu·al \ˈmyüch-wəl, -ə-wəl, ˈmyü-chəl\ *adj* **1 a :** given and received in equal amount ⟨*mutual* favors⟩ **b :** having the same feelings one for the other ⟨*mutual* enemies⟩ **2 :** participated in, shared, or enjoyed by two or more at the same time **:** JOINT ⟨our *mutual* friend⟩ ⟨*mutual* defense⟩ **3 :** organized so that the members share in the profits, benefits, expenses, and liabilities ⟨*mutual* savings bank⟩ ⟨*mutual* life insurance company⟩ [Middle French *mutuel,* from Latin *mutuus* "lent, borrowed, mutual," from *mutare* "to change"] ***synonyms*** see RECIPROCAL — **mu·tu·al·i·ty** \ˌmyü-chə-ˈwal-ət-ē\ *n* — **mu·tu·al·ly** \ˈmyü-chə-wə-lē, -chə-lē\ *adv*

mutual fund *n* **:** an investment company that invests money of its shareholders in a group of securities usually of different types

mu·tu·al·ism \ˈmyüch-wə-ˌliz-əm, -ə-wə-, ˈmyü-chə-ˌliz-\ *n* **:** mutually beneficial association between different kinds of organisms — **mu·tu·al·is·tic** \ˌmyü-chə-wə-ˈlis-tik, -chə-ˈlis-\ *adj*

muu·muu \ˈmü-mü\ *n* **:** a loose often long dress having bright colors and patterns and originally worn in Hawaii [Hawaiian *mu'umu'u*]

mu·zhik *also* **mou·jik** *or* **mu·jik** \mü-ˈzhēk, -ˈzhik\ *n* **:** a Russian peasant [Russian]

[1]**muz·zle** \ˈməz-əl\ *n* **1 :** the projecting jaws and nose of an animal **:** SNOUT **2 :** a fastening or covering for the mouth of an animal used to prevent eating or biting **3 :** the open end of a weapon from which the missile is discharged [Medieval French *musel*]

muzzle 1

[2]**muzzle** *vt* **muz·zled; muz·zling** \ˈməz-ling, -ə-ling\ **1 :** to fit with a muzzle **2 :** to prevent free or normal expression by **:** GAG ⟨*muzzle* the press⟩ — **muz·zler** \ˈməz-lər, -ə-lər\ *n*

muz·zle–load·er \ˌməz-əl-ˈlōd-ər, -ə-ˈ\ *n* **:** a gun that is loaded through the muzzle — **muz·zle–load·ing** \-ˈlōd-ing\ *adj*

muz·zy \ˈməz-ē\ *adj* **muz·zi·er; -est 1 :** muddled or confused in mind **2 a :** not clear ⟨a *muzzy* photograph⟩ ⟨*muzzy* ideas⟩ **b :** DULL, GLOOMY ⟨a *muzzy* day⟩ [perhaps blend of *muddled* and *fuzzy*] — **muz·zi·ly** \ˈməz-ə-lē\ *adv* — **muz·zi·ness** \ˈməz-ē-nəs\ *n*

my \mī, ˈmī, mə\ *adj* **1 :** of or relating to me or myself especially as possessor, agent, or object of an action ⟨*my* car⟩ ⟨*my* promise⟩ ⟨*my* injuries⟩ **2 —** used interjectionally to express surprise ⟨oh *my*⟩ [Old English *mīn*]

my- *or* **myo-** *combining form* **:** muscle ⟨*myo*fibril⟩: muscle and ⟨*myo*neural⟩ [Greek *mys* "mouse, muscle"]

my·al·gia \mī-ˈal-jē-ə\ *n* **:** pain in one or more muscles — **my·al·gic** \-jik\ *adj*

my·as·the·nia gra·vis \ˌmī-əs-ˌthē-nē-ə-ˈgrav-əs, -ˈgräv-\ *n* **:** a disease characterized especially by progressive weakness of voluntary muscles without wasting [New Latin *myasthenia* "muscular debility" (from *my-* + Greek *asthenia* "asthenia") + Latin *gravis* "grave"]

\ə\ **abut**	\au̇\ **out**	\i\ **tip**	\ȯ\ **saw**	\u̇\ **foot**
\ər\ **further**	\ch\ **chin**	\ī\ **life**	\ȯi\ **coin**	\y\ **yet**
\a\ **mat**	\e\ **pet**	\j\ **job**	\th\ **thin**	\yü\ **few**
\ā\ **take**	\ē\ **easy**	\ng\ **sing**	\th\ **this**	\yu̇\ **cure**
\ä\ **cot, cart**	\g\ **go**	\ō\ **bone**	\ü\ **food**	\zh\ **vision**

myc- *or* **myco-** *combining form* : fungus ⟨*mycology*⟩ [Greek *mykēs*]

my·ce·li·um \mī-ˈsē-lē-əm\ *n, pl* **-lia** \-lē-ə\ : the vegetative part of the body of a fungus typically consisting of a mass of interwoven hyphae and often being submerged in another body (as of soil, organic matter, or the tissues of a plant or animal host) [derived from Greek *mykēs* "fungus" + *hēlos* "nail, wart, callus"] — **my·ce·li·al** \-lē-əl\ *adj*

My·ce·nae·an \ˌmī-sə-ˈnē-ən\ *also* **My·ce·ni·an** \mī-ˈsē-nē-ən\ *adj* : of or relating to the Bronze Age culture of the eastern Mediterranean area centering in Mycenae

my·co·bac·te·ri·um \ˌmī-kō-bak-ˈtir-ē-əm\ *n* : any of a genus of bacteria that includes the causative agents of tuberculosis and of leprosy as well as harmless saprophytes

my·col·o·gy \mī-ˈkäl-ə-jē\ *n* **1** : a branch of biology dealing with fungi **2** : fungal life — **my·co·log·i·cal** \ˌmī-kə-ˈläj-i-kəl\ *adj* — **my·col·o·gist** \mī-ˈkäl-ə-jəst\ *n*

my·co·plas·ma \ˌmī-kō-ˈplaz-mə\ *n, pl* **-mas** *also* **-ma·ta** \-mət-ə\ : any of a genus of bacteria without cell walls that are parasitic usually in mammals

my·cor·rhi·za \ˌmī-kə-ˈrī-zə\ *n, pl* **-zae** \-ˌzē\ *also* **-zas** : a symbiotic association of the mycelium of a fungus with the roots of a seed plant in which the fungus grows around or penetrates the root providing nutrients and water to it and receiving food from it [derived from Greek *myko-* "myc-" + *rhiza* "root"] — **my·cor·rhi·zal** \-zəl\ *adj*

my·co·sis \mī-ˈkō-səs\ *n, pl* **-co·ses** \-ˌsēz\ : infection with or disease caused by a fungus — **my·cot·ic** \-ˈkät-ik\ *adj*

my·e·lin \ˈmī-ə-lən\ *n* : a soft white somewhat fatty material that forms a thick layer around the axons of some neurons [derived from Greek *myelos* "marrow"]

my·e·lin·at·ed \ˈmī-ə-lə-ˌnāt-əd\ *adj* : having a myelin sheath ⟨*myelinated* nerve fibers⟩

myelin sheath *n* : a layer of myelin surrounding the axons of some neurons

my·i·a·sis \mī-ˈī-ə-səs, mē-\ *n, pl* **-a·ses** \-ə-ˌsēz\ : infestation (as of tissue) with fly maggots [Greek *myia* "fly"]

my·nah *or* **my·na** \ˈmī-nə\ *n* : any of various Asian starlings; *esp* : a dark brown bird of southeastern Asia with a white tail tip and wing markings and bright yellow bill and feet that is often tamed and trained to mimic words [Hindi & Urdu *mainā*, from Sanskrit *madana*]

mynah

myn·heer \mə-ˈner\ *n* : a man from the Netherlands — used as a title equivalent to *Mr.* [Dutch *mijnheer*, from *mijn* "my" + *heer* "master, sir"]

myo- — see MY-

myo·car·di·um \ˌmī-ə-ˈkärd-ē-əm\ *n* : the middle muscular layer of the heart wall [New Latin, from *my-* + Greek *kardia* "heart"] — **myo·car·di·al** \-ē-əl\ *adj*

myocardial infarction *n* : HEART ATTACK

myo·fi·bril \ˌmī-ō-ˈfīb-rəl, -ˈfib-\ *n* : any of the long thin parallel contractile subunits of a muscle cell that are composed of actin and myosin filaments

myo·glo·bin \ˌmī-ə-ˈglō-bən, ˈmī-ə-ˌ\ *n* : a red iron-containing protein pigment in muscles that is similar to hemoglobin

myo·neu·ral junction \ˌmī-ə-ˌnu̇r-əl-, -ˌnyu̇r-\ *n* : the region of contact between a motor neuron and a muscle fiber

my·o·pia \mī-ˈō-pē-ə\ *n* **1** : the condition of being nearsighted **2** : a lack of foresight or discernment : a narrow view of something [Greek *myōpia*, from *myōps* "nearsighted," *myein* "to be closed" + *ōps* "eye, face"] — **my·o·pic** \-ˈōp-ik, -ˈäp-\ *adj* — **my·o·pi·cal·ly** \-i-kə-lē, -klē\ *adv*

my·o·sin \ˈmī-ə-sən\ *n* : a protein of muscle that with actin is active in muscular contraction [derived from Greek *mys* "mouse, muscle"]

[1]**myr·i·ad** \ˈmir-ē-əd\ *n* **1** : ten thousand **2** : an indefinitely large number ⟨*myriads* of stars⟩ [Greek *myriad-*, *myrias*, from *myrioi* "countless, ten thousand"]

usage Recent criticism of the use of *myriad* as a noun, both in the plural form *myriads* and in the phrase *a myriad of*, seems to reflect a mistaken belief that the word was originally and is still properly only an adjective. The noun is in fact the older form, dating to the 16th century. The noun *myriad* has appeared in the works of such writers as Milton (plural *myriads*) and Thoreau (*a myriad of*), and it continues to occur frequently in reputable English. There is no reason to avoid it.

[2]**myriad** *adj* : consisting of a very great but indefinite number ⟨the *myriad* grains of sand on a beach⟩

myr·ia·pod *also* **myri·io·pod** \ˈmir-ē-ə-ˌpäd\ *n* : any of a group (Myriopoda) of arthropods including the millipedes and centipedes [derived from Greek *myrioi* "countless, ten thousand" + *pod-*, *pous* "foot"] — **myriapod** *also* **myriopod** *adj*

myr·mi·don \ˈmər-mə-ˌdän, ˈmər-məd-ən\ *n* **1** *cap* : any of a legendary Thessalian people following Achilles to the Trojan war **2** : a loyal follower; *esp* : a subordinate who executes orders without question or scruple [Greek *Myrmidōn*]

myrrh \ˈmər\ *n* : a brown slightly bitter aromatic gum resin obtained from African and Arabian trees and used especially in perfumes or formerly in incense [Old English *myrre*, from Latin *myrrha*, from Greek, of Semitic origin]

myr·tle \ˈmərt-l\ *n* **1** : a common evergreen bushy shrub of southern Europe with oval to lance-shaped shiny leaves, fragrant white or rosy flowers, and black berries **2 a** : any of the family of chiefly tropical shrubs or trees to which the common myrtle of Europe belongs **b** : [1]PERIWINKLE [French *mirtille*, from Medieval Latin *myrtillus*, from Latin *myrtos*, from Greek *myrtos*]

my·self \mī-ˈself, mə-\ *pron* **1** : that identical one that is I — used reflexively or for emphasis ⟨I'm going to get *myself* a new suit⟩ ⟨I *myself* will go⟩ **2** : my normal, healthy, or sane condition or self ⟨didn't feel *myself* yesterday⟩

usage *Myself* is often used where *I* or *me* might be expected: as subject ⟨others and *myself* continued to press for the legislation⟩, after *as*, *than*, or *like* ⟨paying such people as *myself* to tutor⟩ ⟨no one knows more about it than *myself*⟩ ⟨old-timers like *myself*⟩, and as object ⟨now here you see *myself* with the tour guide⟩ ⟨for my friends and *myself* it was a happy time⟩. Such uses almost always occur when the speaker or writer is referring to himself or herself as an object of discussion. The other reflexive personal pronouns (*herself*, *himself*, *themselves*) are similarly but less frequently used in the same circumstances. Critics have frowned on these uses since about the start of the 20th century, but they serve a definite purpose and are standard.

mys·te·ri·ous \mis-ˈtir-ē-əs\ *adj* : containing, suggesting, or implying a mystery ⟨*mysterious* noises⟩; *also* : difficult or impossible to understand ⟨the *mysterious* ways of nature⟩ — **mys·te·ri·ous·ly** *adv* — **mys·te·ri·ous·ness** *n*

mys·tery \ˈmis-tə-rē, -trē\ *n, pl* **-ter·ies** **1 a** : a religious truth that man can know by revelation alone and cannot fully understand **b** : any of the 15 events (as the Nativity, the Crucifixion, or the Assumption) serving as a subject for meditation during the saying of the rosary **2 a** : something that has not been or cannot be explained ⟨where they went is a *mystery*⟩ **b** : a deep secret ⟨kept our plans a *mystery*⟩ **3** : a piece of fiction dealing with a mysterious crime **4** : mysterious quality or character ⟨the *mystery* of that smile⟩ [Latin *mysterium*, from Greek *mystērion*, from *mystēs* "initiate"]

synonyms MYSTERY, ENIGMA, RIDDLE, PUZZLE mean something which baffles or perplexes. MYSTERY applies to what is not or cannot be fully understood or explained ⟨the disappearance of the money remained a *mystery*⟩. ENIGMA applies to words or actions very difficult to interpret correctly ⟨her remarks remain an *enigma*⟩. RIDDLE suggests especially a problem or enigma involving paradox or apparent contradiction ⟨the *riddle* of the reclusive movie star⟩. PUZZLE applies to an enigma or problem that challenges ingenuity for its solution ⟨his motives were a *puzzle*⟩.

mystery play *n* : a medieval play based on scriptural incidents (as the life, death, and resurrection of Christ)

[1]**mys·tic** \ˈmis-tik\ *adj* **1** : MYSTICAL 1 **2** : of or relating to mysteries or magical rites : OCCULT **3** : of or relating to mysticism or mystics **4 a** : MYSTERIOUS **b** : AWESOME 2 **c** : MAGICAL [Latin *mysticus* "of mysteries," from Greek *mystikos*, from *mystēs* "initiate"]

[2]**mystic** *n* : a person who seeks direct knowledge of God through contemplation and prayer

mys·ti·cal \ˈmis-ti-kəl\ *adj* **1** : having a spiritual meaning or reality that is neither apparent to the senses nor obvious to the intelligence **2** : of, relating to, or resulting from direct communion with God or ultimate reality **3 :** MYSTIC 2 — **mys·ti·cal·ly** \-ti-kə-lē, -klē\ *adv*

mys·ti·cism \ˈmis-tə-ˌsiz-əm\ *n* **1 :** the experience of mystical union or direct communion with ultimate reality **2 :** the belief that direct knowledge of God or of spiritual truth can be achieved by personal insight and inspiration **3 :** vague guessing or speculation

mys·ti·fy \ˈmis-tə-ˌfī\ *vb* **-fied; -fy·ing** **1 :** to make obscure or difficult to understand **2 :** to baffle and disturb the mind of **:** PERPLEX ⟨strange actions that *mystified* everyone⟩ ***synonyms*** see PUZZLE — **mys·ti·fi·ca·tion** \ˌmis-tə-fə-ˈkā-shən\ *n*

mys·tique \mi-ˈstēk\ *n* **:** an air or attitude of mystery and reverence developing around something or someone ⟨the *mystique* of mountain climbing⟩ [French, from *mystique* "mystic," from Latin *mysticus*]

myth \ˈmith\ *n* **1 :** a story often describing the adventures of superhuman beings that presents part of the beliefs of a people or explains a practice, belief, or natural phenomenon **2 :** PARABLE, ALLEGORY **3 a :** a person or thing having only an imaginary existence ⟨the dragon is a *myth*⟩ **b :** a false or unsupported belief **4 :** the whole body of myths [Greek *mythos*]

synonyms MYTH, LEGEND, FABLE mean a story often of supernatural or marvelous happenings. MYTH is a story dealing with gods or imaginary beings representing natural phenomena ⟨the Greek *myth* of Helios⟩. A LEGEND may include supernatural incidents but deals with human beings or particular places ⟨*legends* of Roman warriors⟩. A FABLE is an invented story in which talking animals or things illustrate human follies and weaknesses ⟨the *fable* of the fox in the barnyard⟩.

myth·i·cal \ˈmith-i-kəl\ *or* **myth·ic** \-ik\ *adj* **1 :** based on, described in, or being a myth ⟨Hercules is a *mythical* hero⟩ **2 :** IMAGINARY, INVENTED ⟨the novelist created a *mythical* town⟩ ***synonyms*** see FABULOUS — **myth·i·cal·ly** \-i-kə-lē, -klē\ *adv*

my·thol·o·gy \mith-ˈäl-ə-jē\ *n, pl* **-gies** **1 :** a body of myths; *esp* **:** the myths dealing with the gods and heroes of a people ⟨Greek *mythology*⟩ **2 :** a branch of knowledge that deals with myth — **myth·o·log·i·cal** \ˌmith-ə-ˈläj-i-kəl\ *adj* — **myth·o·log·i·cal·ly** \-kə-lē, -klē\ *adv* — **my·thol·o·gist** \mith-ˈäl-ə-jəst\ *n*

myth·os \ˈmith-ˌōs, -ˌäs\ *n, pl* **myth·oi** \-ˌȯi\ **:** a pattern of beliefs expressing often symbolically the characteristic or prevalent attitudes in a group or culture [Greek, "myth"]

myx·ede·ma \ˌmik-sə-ˈdē-mə\ *n* **:** a disorder caused by deficient thyroid secretion and marked by puffy swelling, dry skin and hair, and slowness in mental and physical functioning [Greek *myxa* "lamp wick, nasal mucus" + New Latin *edema* "edema"] — **myx·ede·ma·tous** \-ˈdem-ət-əs, -ˈdē-mət-\ *adj*

myxo·my·cete \ˌmik-sō-ˈmī-ˌsēt, -mī-ˈsēt\ *n* **:** SLIME MOLD [derived from Greek *myxa* "mucus" + *mykēt-, mykēs* "fungus"]

N

n \ˈen\ *n, pl* **n's** *or* **ns** \ˈenz\ *often cap* **1 :** the 14th letter of the English alphabet **2 :** an unspecified quantity ⟨sum of the numbers from one to *n*⟩ **3 :** the haploid number of chromosomes

-n — see -EN

nab \ˈnab\ *vt* **nabbed; nab·bing** **1 :** to seize and take into custody **:** ARREST **2 :** to seize suddenly [perhaps from English dialect *nap* "to grab, nab"]

na·bob \ˈnā-ˌbäb\ *n* **1 :** a governor of a province of the Mogul empire in India **2 :** a person of great wealth or prominence [Hindi *navāb* and Urdu *nawāb,* from Arabic *nuwwāb,* pl. of *nā'ib* "governor"]

na·celle \nə-ˈsel\ *n* **:** an enclosed shelter on an aircraft for an engine or sometimes for crew [French, literally, "small boat," from Late Latin *navicella,* from Latin *navis* "ship"]

na·cho \ˈnä-ˌchō\ *n, pl* **na·chos** **:** a tortilla chip topped with melted cheese and often additional toppings (as hot peppers or refried beans)

na·cre \ˈnā-kər\ *n* **:** MOTHER-OF-PEARL [French, from Italian *naccara* "drum, nacre," from Arabic *naqqāra* "drum"] — **na·cre·ous** \-krē-əs, -kə-rəs, -krəs\ *adj*

NAD \ˌen-ˌā-ˈdē\ *n* **:** a coenzyme $C_{21}H_{27}N_7O_{14}P_2$ of numerous dehydrogenases that occurs in most cells and plays an important role in respiration and photosynthesis as an oxidizing agent or when in the reduced form as a reducing agent — called also *nicotinamide adenine dinucleotide*

na·dir \ˈnā-ˌdiər, ˈnād-ər\ *n* **1 :** the point of the celestial sphere that is directly opposite the zenith and vertically downward from the observer **2 :** the lowest point ⟨our hopes had reached their *nadir*⟩ [Medieval French, from Arabic *naḍhīr* "opposite"]

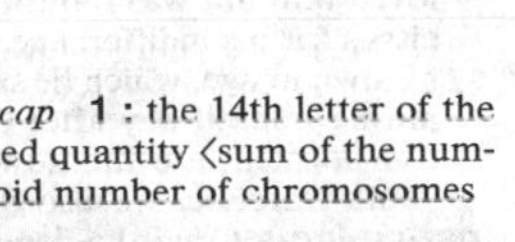

nadir 1: *1* nadir, *2* observer, *3* zenith

NADP \en-ˌā-ˌdē-ˈpē\ *n* **:** a coenzyme $C_{21}H_{28}N_7O_{17}P_3$ of numerous dehydrogenases that plays a role in respiration and photosynthesis similar to NAD — called also *nicotinamide adenine diphosphate*

¹nag \ˈnag\ *n* **:** HORSE 1a(1); *esp* **:** a horse that is old or in poor condition [Middle English *nagge*]

²nag *vb* **nagged; nag·ging** **1 :** to annoy by persistent faultfinding, scolding, or urging ⟨kept *nagging* me to let her come⟩ **2 :** to be a continuing source of annoyance ⟨a *nagging* toothache⟩ [probably of Scandinavian origin] — **nag·ger** *n*

³nag *n* **:** a person who nags on a regular basis

Na·huatl \ˈnä-ˌwät-l\ *n* **:** a group of closely related languages spoken by American Indian peoples (as the Aztecs) of Mexico and Central America [Spanish *náhuatl,* from Nahuatl *Nāhuatl*] — **Na·huat·lan** \-ˌwät-lən\ *adj or n*

Na·hum \ˈnā-əm, -həm\ *n* **:** a prophetic book of canonical Jewish and Christian Scriptures — see BIBLE table

na·iad \ˈnā-əd, ˈnī-, -ˌad\ *n, pl* **na·iads** *or* **na·ia·des** \-ə-ˌdēz\ **1 :** one of the nymphs in classical mythology living in and giving life to lakes, rivers, springs, and fountains **2 :** an aquatic insect nymph (as of a mayfly, dragonfly, damselfly, or stone fly) [Latin *naiad-, naias,* from Greek, from *nan* "to flow"]

¹nail \ˈnāl\ *n* **1 a :** a horny sheath protecting the end of each finger and toe in humans and most other primates **b :** a corresponding structure (as a claw) terminating a digit in other vertebrates **2 :** a slender pointed piece of metal driven into or through something for fastening [Old English *nægl*]

²nail *vt* **1 :** to fasten with or as if with a nail **2 :** CATCH, TRAP ⟨*nail* a thief⟩ **3 :** to hit or strike in a forceful or accurate manner ⟨*nailed* the ball⟩ **4 :** to perform or complete perfectly or impressively ⟨*nailed* a jump shot⟩ **5 :** to settle, establish or represent clearly and unmistakably — often used with *down* ⟨*nail down* all the details⟩ — **nail·er** *n*

nail·brush \ˈnāl-ˌbrəsh\ *n* **:** a small firm-bristled brush for cleaning the hands and fingernails

na·ive *or* **na·ïve** \nä-ˈēv\ *adj* **1 :** marked by unaffected simplicity **2 :** showing lack of informed judgment [French *naïve,* feminine of *naïf,* from Medieval French, "inborn, natural," from Latin *nativus* "native"] — **na·ive·ly** *adv* — **na·ive·ness** *n*

na·ïve·té *also* **na·ive·te** *or* **na·ive·té** \nä-ˌē-və-ˈtā, nä-ˈē-və-ˌ\ *n*

\ə\ **abut**	\au̇\ **out**	\i\ **tip**	\ȯ\ **saw**	\u̇\ **foot**
\ər\ **further**	\ch\ **chin**	\ī\ **life**	\ȯi\ **coin**	\y\ **yet**
\a\ **mat**	\e\ **pet**	\j\ **job**	\th\ **thin**	\yü\ **few**
\ā\ **take**	\ē\ **easy**	\ng\ **sing**	\th\ **this**	\yu̇\ **cure**
\ä\ **cot, cart**	\g\ **go**	\ō\ **bone**	\ü\ **food**	\zh\ **vision**

1 : the quality or state of being naive 2 : a naive remark or action [French *naïveté,* from *naïf* "naive"]

na·ive·ty *also* **na·ïve·ty** \nä-ˈē-vət-ē, -ˈēv-tē\ *n, pl* **-ties** *chiefly British* : NAÏVETÉ

na·ked \ˈnā-kəd, *especially South* ˈnek-əd\ *adj* **1** : having no clothes on : NUDE **2 a** : lacking a usual or natural covering (as of foliage or feathers) **b** : not sheathed ‹a *naked* sword› **c** : lacking protective enveloping parts (as membranes, scales, or shells) **3** : lacking embellishment : PLAIN ‹the *naked* truth› **4** : not aided by artificial means ‹seen by the *naked* eye› [Old English *nacod*] — **na·ked·ly** *adv* — **na·ked·ness** *n*

naked mole rat *n* : a burrowing rodent of Ethiopia, Somalia, and Kenya that resembles a mole, has nearly hairless wrinkled skin, is practically blind, and lives in underground colonies

nam·by–pam·by \ˌnam-bē-ˈpam-bē\ *adj* **1** : lacking in character or substance : INSIPID **2** : WEAK 1c, INDECISIVE [*Namby Pamby,* nickname given to Ambrose Phillips, died 1749, English poet, to ridicule his poetic style] — **namby–pamby** *n*

[1]**name** \ˈnām\ *n* **1** : a word or combination of words by which a person or thing is regularly known **2** : a descriptive often disparaging term ‹call someone *names*› **3** : REPUTATION; *esp* : a distinguished reputation ‹make a *name* for oneself› **4** : FAMILY, CLAN ‹was a disgrace to the *name*› **5** : appearance as opposed to fact ‹a friend in *name* only› [Old English *nama*]

[2]**name** *vt* **1** : to give a name to : CALL **2 a** : to mention or identify by name **b** : to accuse by name ‹*name* the culprit› **3** : to nominate for office : APPOINT ‹*named* the diplomat Secretary of State› **4** : to decide on : CHOOSE ‹*name* the date for a wedding› **5** : to mention explicitly : SPECIFY ‹*name* a price› — **name·able** \ˈnā-mə-bəl\ *adj* — **nam·er** *n*

[3]**name** *adj* **1** : of, relating to, or bearing a name ‹a *name* tag› **2** : having an established reputation ‹*name* brands›

name·less \ˈnām-ləs\ *adj* **1** : having no name **2** : not marked with a name ‹a *nameless* grave› **3** : not known by name : ANONYMOUS ‹a *nameless* author› **4** : not to be described ‹*nameless* fears› — **name·less·ly** *adv* — **name·less·ness** *n*

name·ly \ˈnām-lē\ *adv* : that is to say ‹the cat family, *namely,* lions, tigers, and related animals›

name·plate \-ˌplāt\ *n* : a plate or plaque bearing a name (as of a manufacturer)

name·sake \ˈnām-ˌsāk\ *n* : one that has the same name as another; *esp* : one named after another

nan·keen \nan-ˈkēn, ˈnan-\ *also* **nan·kin** \-ˈkēn, -ˈkin\ *n* : a durable brownish yellow cotton fabric originally woven by hand in China [*Nanking* (Nanjing), China]

nan·ny *also* **nan·nie** \ˈnan-ē\ *n, pl* **nan·nies** : a child's nurse or caregiver [probably of baby-talk origin]

nanny goat *n* : a female domestic goat [*Nanny,* nickname for *Anne*]

nano- \ˈnan-ō, -ə\ *combining form* **1** : billionth ‹*nano*second› **2** : nanoscale ‹*nano*particle› **3** : extremely small ‹*nano*technology› [Greek *nanos* "dwarf"]

nano·gram \ˈnan-ə-ˌgram\ *n* : one billionth of a gram

nano·me·ter \ˈnan-ə-ˌmēt-ər\ *n* : one billionth of a meter

nano·par·ti·cle \ˈnan-ə-ˌpärt-i-kəl\ *n* : a microscopic particle of a size usually measured in nanometers

nano·scale \ˈnan-ə-ˌskāl\ *adj* : having dimensions usually measured in nanometers

nano·sec·ond \ˈnan-ə-ˌsek-ənd, -ənt\ *n* : one billionth of a second

nano·tech \ˈnan-ō-ˌtek\ *n* : NANOTECHNOLOGY

nano·tech·nol·o·gy \ˌnan-ō-tek-ˈnäl-ə-jē\ *n* : the art of using and controlling materials on an atomic or molecular scale especially in order to create microscopic devices

nano·tube \ˈnan-ō-ˌtüb\ *n* : a microscopic tube ‹carbon *nanotubes*›

[1]**nap** \ˈnap\ *vi* **napped; nap·ping** **1** : to sleep briefly especially during the day : DOZE **2** : to be off guard ‹was caught *napping*› [Old English *hnappian*]

[2]**nap** *n* : a short sleep especially during the day : SNOOZE

[3]**nap** *n* : a hairy or downy surface (as on cloth) [Dutch *noppe* "tuft of wool, nap"] — **nap·less** \ˈnap-ləs\ *adj* — **napped** \ˈnapt\ *adj*

[4]**nap** *vt* **napped; nap·ping** : to raise a nap on (as cloth)

na·palm \ˈnā-ˌpäm, -ˌpälm\ *n* **1** : a thickener used in jelling gasoline (as for incendiary bombs) **2** : fuel jelled with napalm [derived from *naphtha* + *palmitic acid*]

nape \ˈnāp, ˈnap\ *n* : the back of the neck [Middle English]

naph·tha \ˈnaf-thə, ˈnap-\ *n* **1** : any of various volatile often flammable liquid hydrocarbon mixtures used chiefly as solvents and diluting agents **2** : PETROLEUM [Latin, from Greek, of Iranian origin]

naph·tha·lene \-ˌlēn\ *n* : a crystalline hydrocarbon $C_{10}H_8$ usually obtained by distillation of coal tar and used in chemical manufacture and as a moth repellent [derived from *naphtha*] — **naph·tha·le·nic** \ˌnaf-thə-ˈlēn-ik, ˌnap-, -ˈlen-\ *adj*

naph·thol \ˈnaf-ˌthȯl, ˈnap-, -ˌthōl\ *n* : either of two derivatives of napththalene found in coal tar or made synthetically and used as antiseptics and in the manufacture of dyes

Na·pier·ian logarithm \nə-ˌpir-ē-ən-, nā-\ *n* : NATURAL LOGARITHM [John *Napier,* died 1617, Scottish mathematician]

nap·kin \ˈnap-kən\ *n* **1** : a piece of material (as cloth or paper) used during a meal to wipe the lips or fingers and protect the clothes **2** : a small cloth or towel [Middle English *nappekin,* from *nape* "tablecloth," from Medieval French, from Latin *mappa* "napkin"]

na·po·leon \nə-ˈpōl-yən, -ˈpō-lē-ən\ *n* **1** : a former French 20-franc gold coin **2** : an oblong pastry consisting of layers of puff paste with a filling of cream, custard, or jelly [French *napoléon,* from *Napoléon* "Napoléon I"]

narc *also* **nark** \ˈnärk\ *n, slang* : a person (as a government agent) who investigates narcotics violations

nar·cis·sism \ˈnär-sə-ˌsiz-əm\ *n* : undue dwelling on one's own self or attainments : SELF-LOVE [German *Narzissismus,* from *Narziss* "Narcissus (mythological character)" — see *Word History* at NARCISSUS] — **nar·cis·sist** \ˈnär-sə-səst\ *n or adj* — **nar·cis·sis·tic** \ˌnär-sə-ˈsis-tik\ *adj*

nar·cis·sus \när-ˈsis-əs\ *n, pl* **nar·cis·si** \-ˈsis-ˌī, -ˌē\ *or* **nar·cis·sus·es** *or* **narcissus** : DAFFODIL; *esp* : one whose flowers have a short corona and are usually borne separately [*Narcissus,* Greek mythological character, from Latin, from Greek *Narkissos*]

Word History Narcissus, according to Greek mythology, was an unusually beautiful young man. The nymph Echo loved him but was rebuffed and wasted away. To punish Narcissus for his indifference, the gods made him fall in love with his own image, which he saw reflected in a fountain. He sat admiring himself day after day and finally pined away and was transformed into the flower that we call *narcissus.* From the youth Narcissus we also get a word for self-love, *narcissism.*

nar·co·lep·sy \ˈnär-kə-ˌlep-sē\ *n* : a condition characterized by brief attacks of deep sleep [derived from Greek *narkē* "deep sleep" + *lēpsis* "taking, seizure"]

nar·co·lep·tic \ˌnär-kə-ˈlep-tik\ *adj* : of, relating to, or affected with narcolepsy — **narcoleptic** *n*

nar·co·sis \när-ˈkō-səs\ *n, pl* **-co·ses** \-ˈkō-ˌsēz\ : a state of stupor, unconsciousness, or arrested activity produced by the influence of chemicals (as narcotics)

[1]**nar·cot·ic** \när-ˈkät-ik\ *n* **1 a** : a drug (as opium or morphine) that in moderate doses dulls the senses, relieves pain, and induces sleep but in excessive doses causes stupor, coma, or convulsions **b** : a drug (as marijuana or LSD) subject to restriction similar to that of addictive narcotics whether in fact physiologically addictive and narcotic or not **2** : something that soothes, relieves, or lulls [Medieval French *narcotique,* from *narcotique,* adj., from Medieval Latin *narcoticus,* from Greek *narkōtikos,* from *narkoun* "to benumb," from *narkē* "numbness"]

[2]**narcotic** *adj* **1** : having the properties of or yielding a narcotic **2** : of or relating to narcotics, to their use, or to addicts ‹*narcotic* laws› — **nar·cot·i·cal·ly** \-ˈkät-i-kə-lē, -klē\ *adv*

nar·co·tize \ˈnär-kə-ˌtīz\ *vt* **1 a** : to treat with or subject to a narcotic **b** : to put into a state of narcosis **2** : to soothe to unconsciousness or unawareness

nard \ˈnärd\ *n* : SPIKENARD 1b [Latin *nardus,* from Greek *nardos,* of Semitic origin]

na·res \ˈnaər-ˌēz, ˈneər-\ *n pl* : the pair of openings of the nose or nasal cavity of a vertebrate [Latin]

Nar·ra·gan·sett \ˌnar-ə-ˈgan-sət\ *n, pl* **Narragansett** *or* **Narragansetts** **1** : a member of an American Indian people of Rhode Island **2** : the Algonquian language of the Narragansett people [Narragansett *Nahicans, Nayohygunsic,* locale on Narragansett Bay]

nar·rate \ˈnar-ˌāt, na-ˈrāt\ *vt* : to recite the details of (as a story) : RELATE, TELL [Latin *narrare,* from *gnarus* "knowing"] — **nar·ra·tor** \ˈnar-ˌāt-ər; na-ˈrāt-, nə-; ˈnar-ət-\ *n*

nar·ra·tion \na-ˈrā-shən, nə-\ *n* **1** : the act or process or an instance of narrating **2** : NARRATIVE 1, STORY — **nar·ra·tion·al** \-shnəl, -shən-l\ *adj*

nar·ra·tive \ˈnar-ət-iv\ *n* **1 :** something (as a story) that is narrated **2 :** the art or practice of narration — **narrative** *adj* — **nar·ra·tive·ly** *adv*

1nar·row \ˈnar-ō\ *adj* **1 a :** of slender width ⟨a *narrow* space⟩ **b :** of less than standard or usual width ⟨*narrow* roads⟩ **2 :** limited in size or scope : RESTRICTED ⟨a *narrow* choice⟩ ⟨a *narrow* interpretation⟩ **3 :** not liberal in views : PREJUDICED ⟨*narrow* thinking⟩ **4 a :** barely sufficient : CLOSE ⟨won by a *narrow* margin⟩ **b :** barely successful ⟨a *narrow* escape⟩ **5 :** extremely close and careful ⟨a *narrow* inspection⟩ [Old English *nearu*] — **nar·row·ly** *adv* — **nar·row·ness** *n*

2narrow *n* **:** a narrow part or passage; *esp* **:** a strait connecting two bodies of water — usually used in plural

3narrow *vb* **:** to lessen in width or extent : CONTRACT

nar·row·band \-ˌband\ *adj* **:** involving a narrow range of frequencies ⟨*narrowband* communication⟩

nar·row–mind·ed \ˌnar-ō-ˈmīn-dəd\ *adj* **:** lacking in tolerance or breadth of vision — **nar·row–mind·ed·ly** *adv* — **nar·row–mind·ed·ness** *n*

nar·thex \ˈnär-ˌtheks\ *n* **1 :** the portico of an ancient church **2 :** a vestibule leading to the nave of a church [Late Greek *narthēx,* from Greek, "giant fennel, cane, casket"]

nar·whal \ˈnär-ˌhwäl, -ˌwäl, -ˌhwȯl, -ˌhwōl, -ˌwȯl, -ˌhwal, -ˌwal, -wəl\ *n* **:** an arctic sea animal about 20 feet (6 meters) long that is related to the dolphins and whales and in the male has a long twisted ivory tusk [Norwegian & Danish *narhval* and Swedish *narval,* derived from Old Norse *nāhvalr,* from *nār* "corpse" + *hvalr* "whale"]

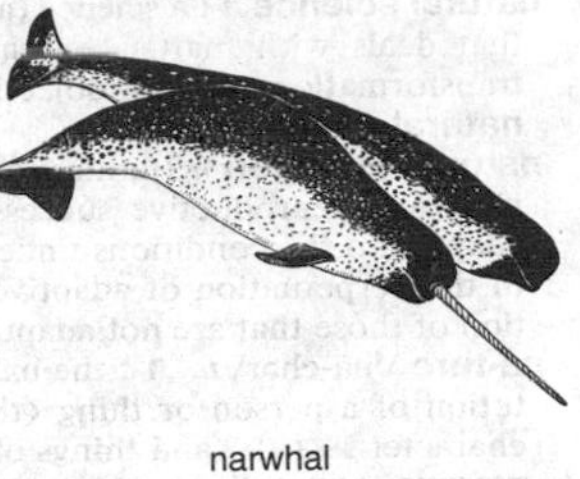

narwhal

nary \ˈnaər-ē, ˈneər-\ *adj, dialect* **:** not one [alteration of *ne'er a*]

1na·sal \ˈnā-zəl\ *n* **1 :** a nasal part **2 :** a nasal consonant [derived from Latin *nasus* "nose"]

2nasal *adj* **1 :** of or relating to the nose **2 :** uttered with passage of air through the nose ⟨the *nasal* consonants \m\, \n\, and \ng\⟩ ⟨the *nasal* vowels in French⟩ **3 :** characterized by resonance produced through the nose ⟨speaking in a *nasal* tone⟩ — **na·sal·i·ty** \nā-ˈzal-ət-ē\ *n* — **na·sal·ly** \ˈnā-zə-lē\ *adv*

nasal cavity *n* **:** an incompletely divided chamber that lies between the floor of the skull and the roof of the mouth and functions in the warming and filtering of inhaled air and in the sensing of odors

nas·cent \ˈnas-nt, ˈnās-\ *adj* **:** coming into existence : beginning to develop ⟨her *nascent* singing career⟩ [Latin *nascens,* from *nasci* "to be born"] — **nas·cence** \-ns\ *n* — **na·scen·cy** \-n-sē\ *n*

na·so·phar·ynx \ˌnā-zō-ˈfar-ings, -ingks\ *n* **:** the upper part of the pharynx continuous with the nasal passages — **na·so·pha·ryn·geal** \ˌnā-zō-fə-ˈrin-jəl, -ˌfar-ən-ˈjē-əl\ *adj*

nas·tic \ˈnas-tik\ *adj* **:** of, relating to, or being a movement of a plant part caused by disproportionate growth or increase of turgor in one surface [Greek *nastos* "close-pressed," from *nassein* "to press"]

nas·tur·tium \nə-ˈstər-shəm, na-\ *n* **:** any of a genus of Central and South American herbs with showy flowers and edible pungent seeds and leaves [Latin, a kind of cress]

nas·ty \ˈnas-tē\ *adj* **nas·ti·er; -est 1 :** very dirty or foul : FILTHY **2 :** morally offensive : VILE **3 :** DISAGREEABLE ⟨*nasty* weather⟩ **4 :** MEAN, ILL-NATURED ⟨a *nasty* temper⟩ **5 :** DISHONORABLE ⟨a *nasty* trick⟩ **6 :** HARMFUL, DANGEROUS ⟨a *nasty* fall on the ice⟩ [Middle English] ***synonyms*** see DIRTY — **nas·ti·ly** \-tə-lē\ *adv* — **nas·ti·ness** \-tē-nəs\ *n*

na·tal \ˈnāt-l\ *adj* **1 :** NATIVE **2 :** of, relating to, or present at birth [Latin *natalis,* from *natus,* past participle of *nasci* "to be born"]

na·tal·i·ty \nā-ˈtal-ət-ē, nə-\ *n, pl* **-ties :** BIRTHRATE

na·ta·tion \nā-ˈtā-shən, na-\ *n* **:** the action or art of swimming [Latin *natatio,* from *natare* "to swim"]

na·ta·to·ri·al \ˌnāt-ə-ˈtōr-ē-əl, ˌnat-, -ˈtȯr-\ *or* **na·ta·to·ry** \ˈnāt-ə-ˌtōr-ē, ˈnat-, -ˌtȯr-\ *adj* **:** of or relating to swimming

na·ta·to·ri·um \ˌnāt-ə-ˈtōr-ē-əm, ˌnat-, -ˈtȯr-\ *n* **:** an indoor swimming pool [Late Latin, from Latin *natare* "to swim"]

Natch·ez \ˈnach-əz\ *n, pl* **Natchez :** a member of an American Indian people of southwestern Mississippi [French, plural of *Nacha, Naché,* name of a Natchez town]

na·tion \ˈnā-shən\ *n* **1 a :** NATIONALITY 3a **b :** a community of people composed of one or more nationalities with its own territory and government **c :** the territory of a nation **2 :** a tribe or federation of tribes (as of American Indians) [Medieval French, from Latin *natio* "birth, race, nation," from *nasci* "to be born"]

1na·tion·al \ˈnash-nəl, -ən-l\ *adj* **1 :** of or relating to a nation ⟨*national* elections⟩ **2 :** comprising or characteristic of a nationality **3 :** belonging to or maintained by the federal government ⟨*national* cemeteries⟩ — **na·tion·al·ly** \-ē\ *adv*

2national *n* **1 :** a person who owes allegiance to or is under the protection of a nation without regard to the more formal status of citizen or subject **2 :** a competition that is national in scope — usually used in plural ⟨qualified for the figure skating *nationals*⟩ ***synonyms*** see CITIZEN

national anthem *n* **:** a song or hymn officially adopted and played or sung on formal occasions as a mark of loyalty to the nation

national bank *n* **:** a commercial bank organized under laws passed by Congress and chartered and supervised by the federal government

national guard *n* **1 :** a military force serving as a national police and defense force **2** *cap* **:** a militia force recruited by each state, equipped by the federal government, and subject to the call of either — **national guardsman** *n, often cap*

national income *n* **:** the total earnings from a nation's current production including wages of employees, interest, rental income, and business profits after taxes

na·tion·al·ism \ˈnash-nəl-iz-əm, -ən-l-\ *n* **:** loyalty and devotion to a nation especially as expressed by praise of one nation above all others and intense concern with promotion of its culture and interests

na·tion·al·ist \-nəl-əst, -ən-l-əst\ *n* **1 :** an advocate of nationalism **2 :** a member of a political party or group advocating national independence or strong national government — **nationalist** *adj* — **na·tion·al·is·tic** \ˌnash-nəl-ˈis-tik, -ən-l-ˈis-\ *adj*

na·tion·al·i·ty \ˌnash-ˈnal-ət-ē, -ə-ˈnal-\ *n, pl* **-ties 1 :** the fact or state of belonging to a nation ⟨a person of French *nationality*⟩ **2 :** political independence or existence as a separate nation **3 a :** a people having a common origin, tradition, and language and capable of forming or actually constituting a state **b :** an ethnic group within a larger unit (as a nation)

na·tion·al·ize \ˈnash-nəl-ˌīz, -ən-l-\ *vt* **1 :** to make national : make a nation of **2 :** to remove from private ownership and place under government control ⟨*nationalize* railroads⟩ — **na·tion·al·i·za·tion** \ˌnash-nəl-ə-ˈzā-shən, ˌnash-ən-l-\ *n* — **na·tion·al·iz·er** *n*

national monument *n* **:** a place of historic, scenic, or scientific interest set aside for preservation usually by presidential proclamation

national park *n* **:** an area of special scenic, historical, or scientific importance set aside and maintained by a national government and in the U.S. by an act of Congress

national socialism *n, often cap N&S* **:** NAZISM — **national socialist** *adj, often cap N&S*

na·tion·hood \ˈnā-shən-ˌhu̇d\ *n* **:** the quality or state of being a nation

na·tion·wide \ˌnā-shən-ˈwīd\ *adj* **:** extending throughout a nation ⟨a *nationwide* chain of stores⟩

1na·tive \ˈnāt-iv\ *adj* **1 :** INBORN, NATURAL ⟨*native* shrewdness⟩ **2 :** born in a particular place or country ⟨*native* Vermonters⟩ **3 :** belonging to a person because of the place or circumstances of birth ⟨one's *native* language⟩ **4 a :** grown, produced, or having its origin in a particular region ⟨*native* tomatoes⟩ ⟨*native* stone⟩ **b :** living or growing naturally in a particular region ⟨*native* plants⟩ **5 :** occurring in nature : not artificially prepared ⟨*native* salt⟩ **6** *cap* **:** of, relating to, or being a member of an indigenous people of North or South America : NATIVE AMERICAN [Medieval French *natif,* from Latin *nativus,* from *natus,* past participle of *nasci* "to be born"] — **na·tive·ly** *adv* — **na·tive·ness** *n*

\ə\ **abut**	\au̇\ **out**	\i\ **tip**	\ȯ\ **saw**	\u̇\ **foot**
\ər\ **further**	\ch\ **chin**	\ī\ **life**	\ȯi\ **coin**	\y\ **yet**
\a\ **mat**	\e\ **pet**	\j\ **job**	\th\ **thin**	\yü\ **few**
\ā\ **take**	\ē\ **easy**	\ng\ **sing**	\t͟h\ **this**	\yu̇\ **cure**
\ä\ **cot, cart**	\g\ **go**	\ō\ **bone**	\ü\ **food**	\zh\ **vision**

synonyms NATIVE, INDIGENOUS, ENDEMIC, ABORIGINAL mean belonging to a locality. NATIVE implies birth or origin in a place or region and may suggest special compatibility with it ⟨*native* tribal customs⟩. INDIGENOUS adds an implication of not having been introduced from elsewhere ⟨*indigenous* plants⟩. ENDEMIC stresses the notion that something is peculiar to a region ⟨the koala is *endemic* to Australia⟩. ABORIGINAL implies having no known predecessor in occupying a region ⟨the *aboriginal* peoples of Australia⟩.

[2]**native** *n* **1 :** one born or reared in a particular place **2 a :** an original inhabitant **b :** something (as an animal or plant) native to a particular locality **3 :** a local or lifelong resident

Native American *n* **:** a member of any of the indigenous peoples of the western hemisphere; *esp* **:** a Native American of North America and especially the U.S. — compare AMERICAN INDIAN — **Native American** *adj*

na·tiv·i·ty \nə-ˈtiv-ət-ē, nā-\ *n, pl* **-ties 1** *cap* **:** the birth of Christ **2 :** the process or circumstances of being born **:** BIRTH

nat·ty \ˈnat-ē\ *adj* **nat·ti·er; -est :** trimly neat and tidy **:** SMART ⟨a *natty* suit⟩ [perhaps from obsolete *net* "neat, clean"] — **nat·ti·ly** \ˈnat-l-ē\ *adv* — **nat·ti·ness** \ˈnat-ē-nəs\ *n*

[1]**nat·u·ral** \ˈnach-rəl, -ə-rəl\ *adj* **1 :** born in or with one **:** INNATE ⟨*natural* ability⟩ **2 :** being such by nature **:** BORN ⟨a *natural* athlete⟩ **3 :** BIOLOGICAL 2 ⟨one's *natural* parents⟩ **4 a :** growing without human care; *also* **:** not cultivated ⟨*natural* prairie⟩ **b :** existing in or produced by nature **:** not artificial ⟨*natural* scenery⟩ **c :** relating to or being natural food **5 :** having or showing qualities held to be part of human nature ⟨it is *natural* to love your children⟩ **6 a :** of or relating to nature as an object of study and research **b :** conforming to the laws of nature or of the physical world ⟨*natural* causes⟩ ⟨*natural* history⟩ **7 :** not made or altered by humans ⟨a *natural* complexion⟩ **8 :** marked by simplicity and sincerity ⟨*natural* manners⟩ **9 :** closely resembling the object imitated **:** LIFELIKE ⟨the people in the picture look *natural*⟩ **10 :** having neither sharps nor flats in the key signature or having a sharp or a flat changed in pitch by a natural sign — **nat·u·ral·ness** *n*

[2]**natural** *n* **1 :** a person born without the usual powers of reason and understanding **2 a :** a sign ♮ placed on a line or space of the musical staff to nullify the effect of a preceding sharp or flat **b :** a note or tone affected by the natural sign **3 a :** one having natural skills, talents, or abilities ⟨when it comes to debating, she's a *natural*⟩ **b :** one obviously suitable for a specific purpose **4 :** AFRO

natural childbirth *n* **:** a system of managing childbirth in which the mother receives preparatory education in order to remain conscious during and assist in delivery with minimal or no use of drugs or anesthetics

natural food *n* **:** food that has undergone minimal processing and contains no preservatives or artificial additives

natural gas *n* **:** gas issuing from the earth's crust through natural openings or bored wells; *esp* **:** a combustible mixture of methane and other hydrocarbons used chiefly as a fuel and raw material

natural history *n* **:** the study of natural objects and especially plants and animals as they live in nature from an amateur or popular point of view

natural immunity *n* **:** immunity typically present at birth as distinguished from that acquired by vaccination or exposure to a disease

nat·u·ral·ism \ˈnach-rə-ˌliz-əm, -ə-rə-\ *n* **1 :** a theory denying a supernatural explanation of the origin and development of the universe and holding that scientific laws account for everything in nature **2 :** realism in art or literature; *esp* **:** a theory in literature emphasizing realistic observation of life without idealization or the avoidance of the ugly

nat·u·ral·ist \-ləst\ *n* **1 :** one that advocates or practices naturalism **2 :** a person who specializes in natural history — **naturalist** *adj*

nat·u·ral·is·tic \ˌnach-rə-ˈlis-tik, -ə-rə-\ *adj* **:** of, characterized by, or according with naturalism — **nat·u·ral·is·ti·cal·ly** \-ti-kə-lē, -klē\ *adv*

nat·u·ral·ize \ˈnach-rə-ˌlīz, -ə-rə-\ *vb* **1 :** to introduce into common use ⟨*naturalize* a foreign word⟩ **2 :** to become or cause to become established as if native ⟨*naturalized* weeds⟩ **3 :** to make less artificial or conventional **4 :** to confer the rights and privileges of citizenship on (an alien) — **nat·u·ral·i·za·tion** \ˌnach-rə-lə-ˈzā-shən, -ə-rə-\ *n*

natural killer cell *n* **:** a large lymphocyte capable especially of destroying a tumor or virally infected cell without prior exposure to it

natural law *n* **:** a body of law or a specific principle held to be derived from nature and binding on human society in the absence of or in addition to law established or recognized by governmental authority

natural logarithm *n* **:** a logarithm whose base is the number *e*

nat·u·ral·ly \ˈnach-rə-lē, -ə-rə-; ˈnach-ər-lē\ *adv* **1 :** by natural character or ability ⟨*naturally* timid⟩ **2 :** according to the usual course of things ⟨we *naturally* dislike being hurt⟩ **3 a :** without artificial aid ⟨hair that curls *naturally*⟩ **b :** without affectation ⟨speak *naturally*⟩ **4 :** in a lifelike manner ⟨paints flowers *naturally*⟩

natural number *n* **:** the number 1 or any number (as 3, 12, or 432) obtained by repeatedly adding 1 to it **:** a positive whole number

natural philosophy *n* **:** NATURAL SCIENCE; *esp* **:** PHYSICAL SCIENCE

natural resource *n* **:** something (as a mineral, waterpower source, forest, or kind of animal) that occurs in nature and is valuable to humans (as in providing a source of energy, recreation, or scenic beauty)

natural science *n* **:** a science (as physics, chemistry, or biology) that deals with matter, energy, and their interrelations and transformations or with objectively measurable phenomena — **natural scientist** *n*

natural selection *n* **:** a natural process that results in the survival and reproductive success of individuals or groups best adapted to the conditions under which they live and that leads to the perpetuation of adaptive genetic traits and the elimination of those that are not adaptive

na·ture \ˈnā-chər\ *n* **1 :** the basic quality, character, or constitution of a person or thing ⟨the *nature* of steel⟩ **2 :** general character **:** KIND ⟨and things of that *nature*⟩ **3 :** DISPOSITION, TEMPERAMENT ⟨behavior contrary to one's *nature*⟩ **4 :** a power or set of forces thought of as controlling the universe **5 :** natural feeling especially as shown in one's attitude toward others **6 :** humanity's native state **:** primitive life ⟨return to *nature*⟩ **7 :** the whole physical universe ⟨the study of *nature*⟩ **8 :** the physical workings or drives of an organism ⟨sex is a part of *nature*⟩; *esp* **:** an excretory function — used in phrases like *the call of nature* **9 :** the genetically controlled qualities of an organism **10 :** natural scenery ⟨the beauties of *nature*⟩ [Medieval French, from Latin *natura,* from *natus,* past participle of *nasci* "to be born"] ***synonyms*** see KIND

[1]**naught** *also* **nought** \ˈnȯt, ˈnät\ *pron* **:** NOTHING ⟨their efforts came to *naught*⟩ [Old English *nāwiht,* from *nā* "no" + *wiht* "creature, thing"]

[2]**naught** *also* **nought** *n* **1 :** the quality or state of being nothing **:** NONEXISTENCE **2 :** ZERO 1 — see NUMBER table

naugh·ty \ˈnȯt-ē, ˈnät-\ *adj* **naugh·ti·er; -est 1 :** guilty of disobedience or misbehavior **2 :** not moral or proper [[2]*naught*] — **naugh·ti·ly** \ˈnȯt-l-ē, ˈnät-\ *adv* — **naugh·ti·ness** \ˈnȯt-ē-nəs, ˈnät-\ *n*

nau·pli·us \ˈnȯ-plē-əs\ *n, pl* **-plii** \-plē-ˌī, -ˌē\ **:** an early crustacean larva with three pairs of appendages and a median eye [Latin, a kind of shellfish, from Greek *nauplios*]

nau·sea \ˈnȯ-zē-ə, -sē-ə; ˈnȯ-zhə, -shə\ *n* **1 :** a stomach distress with distaste for food and an urge to vomit **2 :** extreme disgust [Latin, "seasickness, nausea," from Greek *nautia, nausia,* from *nautēs* "sailor," from *naus* "ship"]

Word History Nausea, stomach distress accompanied by an urge to vomit, is one of the most unpleasant symptoms of seasickness. Latin *nausea* and its Greek source *nausia* or *nautia* have the same meaning as English *nausea.* But these Greek and Latin words also have the specific sense of "seasickness." The Greek name for the illness is derived from the word *naus,* which means "ship."

nau·se·ate \ˈnȯ-zē-ˌāt, -sē-, -zhē-, -shē-\ *vb* **:** to affect or become affected with nausea or disgust

nau·se·at·ing \-ˌāt-ing\ *adj* **:** causing nausea and especially disgust ⟨*nauseating* sounds⟩ — **nau·se·at·ing·ly** *adv*

nau·seous \ˈnȯ-shəs, ˈnȯ-zē-əs\ *adj* **1 :** causing nausea or disgust ⟨*nauseous* odors⟩ **2 :** affected with nausea or disgust ⟨feel *nauseous*⟩ — **nau·seous·ly** *adv* — **nau·seous·ness** *n*

nau·ti·cal \ˈnȯt-i-kəl\ *adj* **:** of or relating to seamen, ships, or navigation on water [Latin *nauticus,* from Greek *nautikos,* from *nautēs* "sailor," from *naus* "ship"] — **nau·ti·cal·ly** \-kə-lē, -klē\ *adv*

nautical mile *n* : any of various units of distance used for sea and air navigation; *esp* : one equal to about 6076 feet (1852 meters)

nau·ti·loid \ˈnȯt-l-ˌȯid\ *n* : any of an ancient group (Nautiloidea) of cephalopods represented in the recent fauna only by the nautiluses — **nautiloid** *adj*

nau·ti·lus \ˈnȯt-l-əs\ *n, pl* **-lus·es** *or* **-li** \-l-ˌī, -ˌē\ **1** : any of a genus of cephalopod mollusks of the South Pacific and Indian oceans having a spiral chambered shell that is pearly on the inside — called also *chambered nautilus* **2** : PAPER NAUTILUS [Latin, "paper nautilus," from Greek *nautilos,* literally, "sailor," from *naus* "ship"]

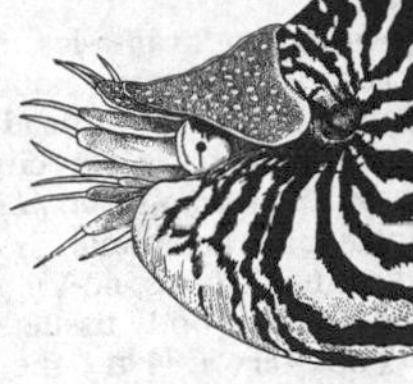
nautilus 1

Na·va·jo *also* **Na·va·ho** \ˈnav-ə-ˌhō, ˈnäv-\ *n, pl* **Navajo** *or* **Navajos** *also* **Navaho** *or* **Navahos** **1** : a member of an American Indian people of what is now northwestern New Mexico and the adjacent part of Arizona **2** : the language of the Navajo people [Spanish *Apache de Navajó,* literally, "Apache of Navajó," from *Navajó,* area occupied by Navajos]

na·val \ˈnā-vəl\ *adj* **1** : of or relating to a navy or warships ⟨*naval* shipyards⟩ **2** : possessing a navy ⟨a *naval* power⟩

naval stores *n pl* : products (as pitch, turpentine, or rosin) obtained from resinous conifers (as pines) [from their former use in the construction and maintenance of wooden sailing vessels]

[1]**nave** \ˈnāv\ *n* : the hub of a wheel [Old English *nafu* — see *Word History* at AUGER]

[2]**nave** *n* : the main body of a church interior; *esp* : the long central hall in a cruciform church that rises higher than the aisles flanking it [Medieval Latin *navis,* from Latin, "ship"]

na·vel \ˈnā-vəl\ *n* **1** : a depression in the middle of the abdomen marking the point of attachment of the umbilical cord or yolk stalk **2** : the central point : MIDDLE [Old English *nafela* — see *Word History* at AUGER]

navel orange *n* : a usually seedless orange having a pit at the apex where the fruit encloses a small secondary fruit

nav·i·ga·ble \ˈnav-i-gə-bəl\ *adj* **1 a** : deep enough and wide enough to afford passage to ships ⟨*navigable* waterways⟩ **b** : capable of being navigated ⟨*navigable* terrain⟩ **2** : capable of being steered ⟨a *navigable* balloon⟩ — **nav·i·ga·bil·i·ty** \ˌnav-i-gə-ˈbil-ət-ē\ *n* — **nav·i·ga·bly** \-blē\ *adv*

nav·i·gate \ˈnav-ə-ˌgāt\ *vb* **1 a** : to travel by water **b** : to sail over, on, or through ⟨*navigate* the Atlantic Ocean⟩ **2 a** : to direct one's course in a ship or aircraft **b** : to steer, direct, or control the course of (as a boat or aircraft) **3 a** : to get about : MOVE ⟨*navigates* quite well on crutches⟩ **b** : to make one's way about, over, or through ⟨*navigate* a Web site⟩ [Latin *navigare,* derived from *navis* "ship"]

nav·i·ga·tion \ˌnav-ə-ˈgā-shən\ *n* **1** : the act or practice of navigating **2** : the science of getting ships, aircraft, or spacecraft from place to place; *esp* : the method of determining position, course, and distance traveled **3** : ship traffic or commerce — **nav·i·ga·tion·al** \-shnəl, -shən-l\ *adj* — **nav·i·ga·tion·al·ly** \-ē\ *adv*

nav·i·ga·tor \ˈnav-ə-ˌgāt-ər\ *n* : a person who navigates or is qualified to navigate: as **a** : an officer on a ship or aircraft responsible for its navigation **b** : a person who explores by ship

nav·vy \ˈnav-ē\ *n, pl* **navvies** *chiefly British* : an unskilled laborer [from *navigator* "construction worker on a canal"]

na·vy \ˈnā-vē\ *n, pl* **navies** **1** : a group of ships : FLEET **2** : a nation's warships **3** *often cap* : a nation's complete naval establishment including yards, stations, ships, and personnel **4** : a dark blue [Medieval French *navie,* from Latin *navigia* "ships," from *navigare* "to navigate"]

navy bean *n* : a kidney bean grown especially for its small white nutritious seeds; *also* : its seed

navy yard *n* : a yard where naval vessels are built or repaired

na·wab \nə-ˈwäb\ *n* : NABOB [Urdu *nawāb*]

[1]**nay** \ˈnā\ *adv* **1** : NO 3 **2** : not merely this but also : not only so but ⟨the letter made me happy, *nay,* ecstatic⟩ [Old Norse *nei,* from *ne* "not" + *ei* "ever"]

[2]**nay** *n* **1** : REFUSAL 1, DENIAL **2 a** : a negative reply or vote **b** : one who votes no

Naz·a·rene \ˌnaz-ə-ˈrēn\ *n* **1** : a native or resident of Nazareth **2 a** : CHRISTIAN 1 **b** : a member of the Church of the Nazarene which follows Methodist policy — **Nazarene** *adj*

Na·zi \ˈnät-sē, ˈnat-\ *n* **1** : a member of a German fascist party controlling Germany from 1933 to 1945 under Adolf Hitler **2** *often not cap* : one held to resemble a German Nazi [German, from *Nationalsozialist* "national socialist"] — **nazi** *adj, often cap* — **na·zi·fi·ca·tion** \ˌnät-si-fə-ˈkā-shən, ˌnat-\ *n, often cap* — **na·zi·fy** \ˈnät-si-ˌfī, ˈnat-\ *vt, often cap*

Na·zism \ˈnät-ˌsiz-əm, ˈnat-\ *also* **Na·zi·ism** \-sē-ˌiz-əm\ *n* : the body of doctrines held and put into effect by the Nazis under Adolf Hitler including the totalitarian principle of government and predominance of especially Germanic groups assumed to be racially superior

NCO \ˌen-ˌsē-ˈō\ *n* : NONCOMMISSIONED OFFICER

NC–17 \ˈen-ˈsē-ˌsev-ən-ˈtēn, -ˈsev-ən-\ *certification mark* — used to certify that a motion picture is of such as nature that no one under the age of 17 can be admitted; compare G, PG, PG-13, R

-nd *symbol* — used after the figure 2 to indicate the ordinal number second ⟨2*nd*⟩ ⟨32*nd*⟩

ne- *or* **neo-** *combining form* : new and different period or form of ⟨*neo*-impressionism⟩ [Greek, from *neos* "new"]

Ne·an·der·thal \nē-ˈan-dər-ˌthȯl, -ˌtȯl; nā-ˈän-dər-ˌtäl\ *n* **1** *or* **Ne·an·der·tal** \-ˌtȯl, -ˌtäl\ : a hominid that lived from about 30,000 to 200,000 years ago with a stocky muscular build, prominent browridge, large nose, and a skull that was longer and wider than that of modern humans and that is known from skeletal remains in Europe, northern Africa, and western Asia — called also *Neanderthal man* **2** : one who suggests a caveman in appearance, behavior, or intelligence [*Neanderthal,* valley in western Germany] — **Neanderthal** *adj* — **Ne·an·der·thal·oid** \-ˌȯid\ *adj or n*

neap \ˈnēp\ *adj* : of, relating to, or constituting a neap tide [Old English *nēp* "being at the stage of neap tide"]

Ne·a·pol·i·tan ice cream \ˌnē-ə-ˌpäl-ət-n-\ *n* : a brick of from two to four layers of ice cream of different flavors [*Neapolitan* "of Naples, Italy," derived from Greek *Neapolis* "Naples"]

neap tide *n* : a tide of minimum range occurring at the first and the third quarters of the moon

[1]**near** \ˈniər\ *adv* **1** : at, within, or to a short distance or time ⟨winter is drawing *near*⟩ **2** : ALMOST, NEARLY ⟨*near* dead⟩ **3** : NEARLY 1 ⟨*near* related⟩ [partly from Old English *nēar* "nearer," comparative of *nēah* "nigh"; partly from Old Norse *nær* "nearer, near," from comparative of *nā-* "nigh"]

[2]**near** *prep* : close to ⟨standing *near* the door⟩

[3]**near** *adj* **1** : closely related or associated ⟨his *nearest* and dearest friend⟩ **2 a** : being little apart in time, place, value, or degree ⟨the *near* future⟩ **b** : barely avoided ⟨a *near* disaster⟩ **c** : almost not happening ⟨a *near* victory⟩ **3 a** : being the closer of two ⟨the *near* side⟩ **b** : being the left-hand one of a pair ⟨the *near* wheel of a cart⟩ **4** : DIRECT, SHORT ⟨the *nearest* route⟩ **5** : STINGY 1 **6 a** : closely resembling the standard or typical ⟨a *near* desert⟩ **b** : approximating the genuine ⟨*near* silk⟩ — **near·ness** *n*

[4]**near** *vb* : to draw near : APPROACH ⟨the ship was *nearing* the dock⟩

near·by \niər-ˈbī, ˈniər-ˌ\ *adv or adj* : close at hand

near–in·fra·red \ˌniər-ˌin-frə-ˈred, -frä-\ *adj* : relating to the shorter wavelengths of radiation in the infrared spectrum

near·ly \ˈniər-lē\ *adv* **1** : in a close manner or relationship ⟨*nearly* related⟩ **2** : almost but not quite ⟨*nearly* identical⟩ ⟨we *nearly* got hit⟩ **3** : to the least extent ⟨not *nearly* enough⟩

near miss *n* **1** : something that falls just short of success ⟨the new movie is a *near miss*⟩ **2 a** : a near collision **b** : CLOSE CALL ⟨the endless *near misses* on the hero's part⟩

near·sight·ed \ˈniər-ˈsīt-əd\ *adj* : able to see near things more clearly than distant ones : MYOPIC — **near·sight·ed·ly** *adv* — **near·sight·ed·ness** *n*

[1]**neat** \ˈnēt\ *n, pl* **neat** : the common domestic bovine (as a cow, bull, or ox) [Old English *nēat*]

[2]**neat** *adj* **1** : being orderly and clean : TIDY ⟨a *neat* closet⟩ ⟨a *neat* roommate⟩ **2** : not mixed or diluted : STRAIGHT ⟨*neat* cement⟩ **3** : marked by tasteful simplicity ⟨a *neat* outfit⟩ **4 a** : PRECISE, SYSTEMATIC ⟨*neat* plans⟩ **b** : marked by skill or in-

\ə\ **abut**	\au̇\ **out**	\i\ **tip**	\ȯ\ **saw**	\u̇\ **foot**
\ər\ **further**	\ch\ **chin**	\ī\ **life**	\ȯi\ **coin**	\y\ **yet**
\a\ **mat**	\e\ **pet**	\j\ **job**	\th\ **thin**	\yü\ **few**
\ā\ **take**	\ē\ **easy**	\ng\ **sing**	\t͟h\ **this**	\yu̇\ **cure**
\ä\ **cot, cart**	\g\ **go**	\ō\ **bone**	\ü\ **food**	\zh\ **vision**

genuity : ADROIT **5** : NET 1 ⟨a *neat* profit⟩ **6** : FINE, ADMIRABLE ⟨had a *neat* time⟩ ⟨a *neat* idea⟩ [Middle French *net,* from Latin *nitidus* "bright, neat," from *nitēre* "to shine"] — **neat·ly** *adv* — **neat·ness** *n*

neat·en \ˈnēt-n\ *vt* **neat·ened; neat·en·ing** \ˈnēt-ning, ˈnēt-n-ing\ : to set in order : make neat ⟨*neatened* papers on her desk⟩

neat's–foot oil \ˈnēts-ˌfu̇t-\ *n* : a pale yellow fatty oil made especially from the bones of cattle and used chiefly to condition leather

neb \ˈneb\ *n* **1 a** : the beak of a bird or tortoise : BILL **b** : NOSE 1, 3, 4; *also* : SNOUT **2** : NIB 2b, 3 [Old English]

neb·u·la \ˈneb-yə-lə\ *n, pl* **-las** *or* **-lae** \-ˌlē, -ˌlī\ **1** : any of many clouds of gas or dust in interstellar space **2** : GALAXY 1b [Latin, "mist, cloud"] — **neb·u·lar** \-lər\ *adj*

nebular hypothesis *n* : a hypothesis in astronomy: the solar system has evolved from a hot gaseous nebula

neb·u·lize \ˈneb-yə-ˌlīz\ *vt* : to reduce to a fine spray — **neb·u·li·za·tion** \ˌneb-yə-lə-ˈzā-shən\ *n* — **neb·u·liz·er** \ˈneb-yə-ˌlī-zər\ *n*

neb·u·los·i·ty \ˌneb-yə-ˈläs-ət-ē\ *n, pl* **-ties** **1** : the quality or state of being nebulous **2** : nebulous matter : NEBULA

neb·u·lous \ˈneb-yə-ləs\ *adj* **1** : VAGUE ⟨*nebulous* concepts⟩ **2** : of, relating to, or resembling a nebula : NEBULAR — **neb·u·lous·ly** *adv* — **neb·u·lous·ness** *n*

[1]**nec·es·sary** \ˈnes-ə-ˌser-ē\ *n, pl* **-sar·ies** : an indispensable item : ESSENTIAL ⟨*necessaries* of life⟩

[2]**necessary** *adj* **1 a** : of an inevitable nature : INESCAPABLE ⟨tests are a *necessary* part of school⟩ **b (1)** : being the only logically possible result ⟨a *necessary* conclusion⟩ **(2)** : logically required for a particular result ⟨a *necessary* truth⟩ **c** : being compulsory or required : MANDATORY ⟨it's *necessary* to attend all practices⟩ **2** : absolutely needed : ESSENTIAL ⟨secrecy was *necessary* to ensure her safety⟩ [Latin *necessarius,* from *necesse* "necessary," from *ne-* "not" + *cedere* "to withdraw"] — **nec·es·sar·i·ly** \ˌnes-ə-ˈser-ə-lē\ *adv*

synonyms NECESSARY, REQUISITE, INDISPENSABLE, ESSENTIAL mean needed or required, often urgently. NECESSARY applies to what cannot be done without or avoided and may stress lack of choice or uselessness of wishing or resisting ⟨make the *necessary* repairs⟩. REQUISITE implies being needful especially for fulfillment or attainment of a set purpose or standard ⟨has the *requisite* courses to meet graduation requirements⟩. INDISPENSABLE applies to something that cannot be done without if the end is to be attained ⟨a knife is an *indispensable* utensil for cutting food into slices⟩. ESSENTIAL implies being absolutely or urgently necessary ⟨food is *essential* to life⟩.

ne·ces·si·tate \ni-ˈses-ə-ˌtāt\ *vt* : to make necessary or unavoidable : REQUIRE, COMPEL ⟨the broken pipes *necessitated* calling a plumber⟩ — **ne·ces·si·ta·tion** \-ˌses-ə-ˈtā-shən\ *n*

ne·ces·si·tous \ni-ˈses-ət-əs\ *adj* **1** : hard up : NEEDY **2** : forced by necessity : NECESSARY ⟨*necessitous* bargaining⟩ — **ne·ces·si·tous·ly** *adv* — **ne·ces·si·tous·ness** *n*

ne·ces·si·ty \ni-ˈses-ət-ē, -ˈses-tē\ *n, pl* **-ties** **1** : conditions that cannot be changed ⟨compelled by *necessity*⟩ **2** : the quality or state of being in need; *esp* : POVERTY **3 a** : something that is necessary : REQUIREMENT ⟨*necessities* for daily living⟩ **b** : an urgent need or desire ⟨call in case of *necessity*⟩ ***synonyms*** see NEED

[1]**neck** \ˈnek\ *n* **1** : the part of the body connecting the head and the trunk **2** : the part of a garment covering or nearest to the neck **3 a** : something like a neck in shape or position ⟨the *neck* of a bottle⟩ ⟨a *neck* of land⟩ **b** : the part of a tooth between the crown and the root **4** : a narrow margin ⟨won by a *neck*⟩ [Old English *hnecca*] — **necked** \ˈnekt\ *adj*

[2]**neck** *vb* : to kiss and caress amorously

neck and neck *adv or adj* : very close (as in a race)

neck·er·chief \ˈnek-ər-chəf, -ˌchif, -ˌchēf\ *n, pl* **-chiefs** *also* **-chieves** *see* HANDKERCHIEF *pl*\ : a kerchief for the neck

neck·lace \ˈnek-ləs\ *n* : an ornament for the neck

neck·line \-ˌlīn\ *n* : the line formed by the neck opening of a garment

neck of the woods : NEIGHBORHOOD, REGION ⟨haven't been in that *neck of the woods* for a long time⟩

neck·tie \-ˌtī\ *n* : a band or strip of material worn about the neck and tied in front; *esp* : FOUR-IN-HAND

necr- *or* **necro-** *combining form* **1** : those that are dead ⟨*necrol*ogy⟩ **2** : dead body ⟨*necropsy*⟩ [Greek *nekros* "dead body"]

ne·crol·o·gy \nə-ˈkräl-ə-jē, ne-\ *n, pl* **-gies** **1** : a list of the recently dead **2** : OBITUARY — **nec·ro·log·i·cal** \ˌnek-rə-ˈläj-i-kəl\ *adj* — **ne·crol·o·gist** \nə-ˈkräl-ə-jəst, ne-\ *n*

nec·ro·man·cy \ˈnek-rə-ˌman-sē\ *n* **1** : the practice of conjuring up the spirits of the dead for purposes of magically revealing the future or influencing the course of events **2** : MAGIC 1, SORCERY — **nec·ro·man·cer** \-sər\ *n* — **nec·ro·man·tic** \ˌnek-rə-ˈmant-ik\ *adj* — **nec·ro·man·ti·cal·ly** \-ˈmant-i-kə-lē, -klē\ *adv*

ne·crop·o·lis \nə-ˈkräp-ə-ləs, ne-\ *n, pl* **-lis·es** *or* **-les** \-ˌlēz\ : CEMETERY; *esp* : a large elaborate cemetery of an ancient city [Late Latin, "city of the dead," from Greek *nekropolis,* from *nekros* "dead body" + *polis* "city"]

nec·rop·sy \ˈnek-ˌräp-sē\ *n, pl* **-sies** : AUTOPSY; *esp* : an autopsy performed on an animal

ne·cro·sis \nə-ˈkrō-səs, ne-\ *n, pl* **-cro·ses** \-ˈkrō-ˌsēz\ : usually localized death of body tissue — **ne·crot·ic** \-ˈkrät-ik\ *adj*

nec·tar \ˈnek-tər\ *n* **1 a** : the drink of the Greek and Roman gods **b** : a delicious drink **2** : a sweet liquid secreted by plants and especially by the flowers that is the chief raw material of honey [Latin, from Greek *nektar*]

nec·tar·ine \ˌnek-tə-ˈrēn\ *n* : a smooth-skinned peach; *also* : a tree producing this fruit

nec·tary \ˈnek-tə-rē, -trē\ *n, pl* **-tar·ies** : a plant gland that secretes nectar

née *or* **nee** \ˈnā\ *adj* : born with a given surname — used to identify a woman by her maiden family name ⟨Mrs. Jane Doe, *née* Smith⟩ [French *née,* feminine of *né* "born," from *naître* "to be born," from Latin *nasci*]

[1]**need** \ˈnēd\ *n* **1** : necessary duty ⟨no *need* to go⟩ **2 a** : a lack of something necessary, desirable, or useful ⟨a *need* for better health care⟩ **b** : REQUIREMENT 1 ⟨my *needs* are few and simple⟩; *also* : a physiological or psychological requirement for keeping a living thing in normal condition **3** : a condition requiring supply or relief ⟨call whenever the *need* arises⟩ **4** : POVERTY 1, DESTITUTION ⟨provide for those in *need*⟩ [Old English *nīed, nēd*]

synonyms NEED, NECESSITY, EXIGENCY mean a pressing lack of something essential. NEED implies urgency and may suggest distress ⟨a critical *need* for medical supplies⟩. NECESSITY stresses imperative demand or compelling cause ⟨the great *necessity* for a new investigation⟩. EXIGENCY implies unusual or special difficulty ⟨the *exigencies* of war⟩.

[2]**need** *vb* **1** : to be in want **2** : to have cause or occasion for ⟨they *need* advice⟩ **3** : to be obligated to — used as an auxiliary verb ⟨you *need* not answer⟩

need·ful \ˈnēd-fəl\ *adj* : NECESSARY 2, REQUISITE — **need·ful·ly** \-fə-lē\ *adv* — **need·ful·ness** *n*

[1]**nee·dle** \ˈnēd-l\ *n* **1 a** : a small slender usually steel instrument that has an eye for thread or surgical sutures at one end and is used for sewing **b** : any of various devices for carrying thread and making stitches (as in crocheting or knitting) **c** : a slender hollow usually stainless steel instrument for introducing material into or removing material from the body (as by insertion under the skin) **d** : an extremely thin solid usually stainless steel instrument used in acupuncture and inserted through the skin **2 a** : a thin bar of magnetized steel that is free to turn (as in a compass) to show the direction of a magnetic field **b** : a slender usually sharp-pointed indicator on a dial **3 a** : a slender pointed object resembling a needle (as a pointed crystal) **b** : OBELISK **c** : a needle-shaped leaf (as of a pine) **d** : a slender piece of jewel, steel, wood, or fiber used in a phonograph to transmit vibrations from the record **e** : a slender pointed rod controlling a fine inlet or outlet (as in a valve) [Old English *nǣdl*] — **nee·dle·like** \ˈnēd-l-ˌīk, -ˌīk\ *adj*

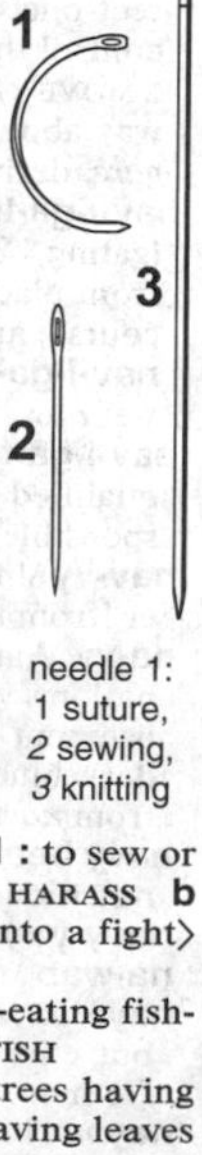

needle 1: *1* suture, *2* sewing, *3* knitting

[2]**needle** *vb* **nee·dled; nee·dling** \ˈnēd-ling, -l-ing\ **1** : to sew or pierce with or as if with a needle **2 a** : TEASE 2a, HARASS **b** : to incite to action by repeated gibes ⟨*needled* us into a fight⟩ — **nee·dler** \ˈnēd-lər, -l-ər\ *n*

nee·dle·fish \-ˌfish\ *n* **1** : any of various long flesh-eating fishes with long slender jaws and sharp teeth **2** : PIPEFISH

nee·dle·leaf \ˈnēd-l-ˌlēf, -ˌēf\ *adj* : populated with trees having leaves that are needles ⟨*needleleaf* forests⟩; *also* : having leaves that are needles ⟨*needleleaf* trees⟩

nee·dle·point \ˈnēd-l-ˌpȯint\ *n* **1** : lace worked with a needle in buttonhole stitch over a paper pattern **2 :** embroidery done on canvas usually in simple even stitches across counted threads — **needlepoint** *adj*

need·less \ˈnēd-ləs\ *adj* **:** UNNECESSARY ⟨*needless* expenses⟩ — **need·less·ly** *adv* — **need·less·ness** *n*

nee·dle·wom·an \ˈnēd-l-ˌwu̇m-ən\ *n* **:** a woman who does needlework; *esp* **:** SEAMSTRESS

nee·dle·work \-ˌwərk\ *n* **:** work done with a needle; *esp* **:** work (as embroidery) other than plain sewing — **nee·dle·work·er** *n*

needn't \ˈnēd-nt\ **:** need not

needs \ˈnēdz\ *adv* **:** of necessity **:** NECESSARILY ⟨must *needs* be recognized⟩ [Old English *nēdes,* from genitive of *nēd* "need"]

needy \ˈnēd-ē\ *adj* **need·i·er; -est 1 :** being in want **:** very poor ⟨*needy* families⟩ **2 :** needing a lot of affection, attention, or emotional support — **need·i·ness** *n*

ne'er \neər, ˈneər, naər, ˈnaər\ *adv* **:** NEVER

ne'er–do–well \ˈneər-du̇-ˌwel, ˈnaər-\ *n* **:** an idle worthless person — **ne'er–do–well** *adj*

ne·far·i·ous \ni-ˈfar-ē-əs, -ˈfer-\ *adj* **:** flagrantly wicked **:** EVIL [Latin *nefarius,* from *nefas* "crime," from *ne-* "not" + *fas* "right, divine law"] — **ne·far·i·ous·ly** *adv* — **ne·far·i·ous·ness** *n*

ne·gate \ni-ˈgāt\ *vt* **1 :** to deny the existence or truth of **2 :** to cause to be ineffective or invalid ⟨the discovery *negates* all previous theories⟩ [Latin *negare* "to say no, deny"] ***synonyms*** see NULLIFY — **ne·ga·tor** \-ˈgāt-ər\ *n*

ne·ga·tion \ni-ˈgā-shən\ *n* **1 a :** the action of negating **:** DENIAL **b :** a negative statement; *esp* **:** NEGATIVE 1a **2 :** something considered the opposite of something positive — **ne·ga·tion·al** \-shnəl, -shən-l\ *adj*

[1]**neg·a·tive** \ˈneg-ət-iv\ *adj* **1 :** marked by denial, prohibition, or refusal ⟨a *negative* reply⟩ **2 :** not positive or constructive ⟨a *negative* attitude⟩ **3 a :** less than zero and opposite in sign to a positive number ⟨–2 is a *negative* number⟩ **b :** taken in a direction opposite to one chosen as positive ⟨a *negative* angle⟩ **4 a :** of, being, or relating to electricity of a kind of which the electron is the elementary unit ⟨a *negative* charge⟩ **b :** being the part toward which the electric current flows from the external circuit ⟨the *negative* pole of a discharging storage battery⟩ **c :** electron-emitting — used of an electrode in an electron tube **5 a :** not affirming the presence of what is sought or suspected ⟨a *negative* TB test⟩ **b :** directed or moving away from a source of stimulation ⟨a *negative* tropism⟩ **6 :** having the light and dark parts in approximately inverse order to those of the original photographic subject ⟨a *negative* photographic image⟩ — **neg·a·tive·ly** *adv* — **neg·a·tive·ness** *n* — **neg·a·tiv·i·ty** \ˌneg-ə-ˈtiv-ət-ē\ *n*

[2]**negative** *n* **1 a :** a proposition by which something is denied or contradicted **b :** a reply that indicates the withholding of assent **:** REFUSAL **2 :** NEGATION 2 **3 a :** an expression (as the word *no*) of negation or denial **b :** a negative number **4 :** the side that argues or votes against something in a debate **5 :** a negative photographic image on transparent material used for printing positive pictures; *also* **:** the material that carries such an image **6 :** a negative result (as of a test) ⟨a high rate of false *negatives*⟩; *also* **:** a test yielding such a result

[3]**negative** *vt* **1 :** to refuse to accept or approve **:** VETO **2 :** DENY 4 **3 :** NEGATE 2

negative sign *n* **:** MINUS SIGN

neg·a·tiv·ism \ˈneg-ət-iv-ˌiz-əm\ *n* **:** an attitude of skepticism about nearly everything affirmed or suggested by others — **neg·a·tiv·ist** \-iv-əst\ *n* — **neg·a·tiv·is·tic** \ˌneg-ət-iv-ˈis-tik\ *adj*

[1]**ne·glect** \ni-ˈglekt\ *vt* **1 :** to give little attention, respect, or care to ⟨*neglected* their garden⟩ **2 :** to leave undone or unattended to especially through carelessness ⟨*neglect* one's duty⟩ ⟨*neglected* to mention a previous encounter⟩ [Latin *neglectus,* past participle of *neglegere, neclegere* "to neglect," from *nec-* "not" + *legere* "to gather"] — **ne·glect·er** *n*

synonyms NEGLECT, DISREGARD, IGNORE, OVERLOOK, SLIGHT, FORGET mean to pass over without giving due attention. NEGLECT implies giving insufficient attention to something that merits one's attention ⟨often *neglected* his studies⟩. DISREGARD suggests voluntary inattention ⟨don't *disregard* the wishes of your family⟩. IGNORE implies a failure to regard something obvious ⟨*ignored* the cruel remark⟩. OVERLOOK suggests disregarding or ignoring through haste or lack of care ⟨worked too fast and *overlooked* a possible solution⟩. SLIGHT implies contemptuous or disdainful disregarding or omitting ⟨felt as if he had been *slighted* by a close friend⟩. FORGET may suggest either a willful ignoring or a failure to impress something on one's mind ⟨*forget* what others say⟩.

[2]**neglect** *n* **1 :** an act or instance of neglecting ⟨his *neglect* of important responsibilities⟩ **2 :** the condition of being neglected ⟨the stone wall collapsed from years of *neglect*⟩

ne·glect·ful \ni-ˈglekt-fəl, -ˈglek-\ *adj* **:** given to neglecting **:** CARELESS ***synonyms*** see NEGLIGENT — **ne·glect·ful·ly** \-fə-lē\ *adv* — **ne·glect·ful·ness** *n*

neg·li·gee *also* **neg·li·gé** \ˌneg-lə-ˈzhā\ *n* **1 :** a woman's long flowing dressing gown **2 :** carelessly informal or incomplete attire [French *négligé,* from *négliger* "to neglect," from Latin *neglegere*]

neg·li·gence \ˈneg-li-jəns\ *n* **1 a :** the quality or state of being negligent **b :** failure to use the care that a reasonably prudent person would exercise in like circumstances **2 :** an act or instance of being negligent

neg·li·gent \-jənt\ *adj* **1 a :** marked by or given to neglect **b :** failing to use the care of a reasonably prudent person in like circumstances **2 :** marked by a carelessly easy manner [Latin *neglegens,* present participle of *neglegere* "to neglect"] — **neg·li·gent·ly** *adv*

synonyms NEGLIGENT, NEGLECTFUL, REMISS mean careless in a manner or to a degree deserving blame or condemnation. NEGLIGENT implies inattention to one's duty or business ⟨*negligent* about walking the dog⟩. NEGLECTFUL adds a stronger implication of laziness or deliberate inattention ⟨callously *neglectful* of the child's needs⟩. REMISS implies blameworthy carelessness or forgetfulness in performance of duty ⟨*remiss* in thanking them for the gifts⟩.

neg·li·gi·ble \ˈneg-li-jə-bəl\ *adj* **:** deserving neglect **:** TRIVIAL ⟨a *negligible* error⟩ — **neg·li·gi·bil·i·ty** \ˌneg-li-jə-ˈbil-ət-ē\ *n* — **neg·li·gi·bly** \ˈneg-li-jə-blē\ *adv*

ne·go·tia·ble \ni-ˈgō-shə-bəl, -shē-ə-bəl\ *adj* **:** capable of being negotiated: as **a :** transferable from one person to another by being delivered with or without endorsement so that the title passes to the recipient ⟨*negotiable* bonds⟩ **b :** capable of being traversed, dealt with, or accomplished ⟨a *negotiable* road⟩ ⟨*negotiable* demands⟩ **c :** open to discussion or change ⟨*negotiable* prices⟩ — **ne·go·tia·bil·i·ty** \-ˌgō-shə-ˈbil-ət-ē, -shē-ə-\ *n*

ne·go·tiant \ni-ˈgo-she-ənt, -shənt\ *n* **:** one that negotiates

ne·go·ti·ate \ni-ˈgō-shē-ˌāt\ *vb* **1 :** to confer with another so as to arrive at a settlement or agreement; *also* **:** to arrange for or bring about by such conference ⟨*negotiate* a treaty⟩ **2 :** to convert into cash or the equivalent value ⟨*negotiate* a check⟩ **3 :** to get through, around, or over successfully ⟨*negotiate* a turn⟩ [Latin *negotiari* "to carry on business," from *negotium* "business," from *neg-* "not" + *otium* "leisure"] — **ne·go·ti·a·tion** \-ˌgō-shē-ˈā-shən, -sē-ˈā-\ *n* — **ne·go·ti·a·tor** \-ˈgō-shē-ˌāt-ər\ *n* — **ne·go·tia·to·ry** \-shə-ˌtōr-ē, -shē-ə-, -ˌtȯr-\ *adj*

Ne·gri·to \nə-ˈgrēt-ō\ *n, pl* **-tos** *or* **-toes :** a member of a people (as the Andamanese) belonging to a group of dark-skinned peoples of small stature that live in Oceania and southeastern Asia [Spanish, from *negro* "Negro"]

ne·gri·tude \ˈneg-rə-ˌtüd, ˈnē-grə-, -ˌtyüd\ *n* **:** a consciousness of and pride in African culture and history [French *négritude,* from *nègre* "Negro"]

Ne·gro \ˈnē-grō\ *n, pl* **Negroes** *sometimes offensive* **:** a member of a race of humankind native to Africa and classified according to physical features (as dark skin pigmentation) [Spanish or Portuguese, from *negro,* adj., "black," from Latin *niger*] — **Negro** *adj, sometimes offensive* — **ne·groid** \ˈnē-ˌgrȯid\ *n or adj, often cap, sometimes offensive*

Ne·he·mi·ah \ˌnē-ə-ˈmī-ə, ˌnē-hə-\ *n* **:** a narrative and historical book of canonical Jewish and Christian Scriptures — see BIBLE table

neigh \ˈnā\ *vi* **:** to utter the characteristic loud prolonged cry of a horse or a similar sound [Old English *hnǣgan*] — **neigh** *n*

[1]**neigh·bor** \ˈnā-bər\ *n* **1 :** one living or located near another **2 :** a fellow being [Old English *nēahgebūr,* from *nēah* "near" + *gebūr* "dweller"]

[2]**neighbor** *vt* **neigh·bored; neigh·bor·ing** \-bə-ring, -bring\ **:** to be next to or near to

neigh·bor·hood \ˈnā-bər-ˌhu̇d\ *n* **1 :** the quality or state of being neighbors : NEARNESS **2 a :** a place or region near : VICINITY **b :** an approximate amount, extent, or degree ⟨cost in the *neighborhood* of $10⟩ **3 a :** the people living near one another **b :** a section lived in by neighbors and usually having distinguishing characteristics ⟨an older *neighborhood*⟩

neigh·bor·ly \ˈnā-bər-lē\ *adj* **:** of, relating to, or characteristic of congenial neighbors; *esp* **:** FRIENDLY ⟨a *neighborly* welcome⟩ — **neigh·bor·li·ness** *n*

[1]**nei·ther** \ˈnē-t͟hər *also* ˈnī-\ *pron* **:** not the one and not the other ⟨*neither* of the two⟩ [Middle English, alteration of *nauther,* from Old English *nāhwæther,* from *nā* "not" + *hwæther* "which of two, whether"]

[2]**neither** *conj* **1 :** not either ⟨*neither* black nor white⟩ **2 :** also not ⟨*neither* did I⟩

usage Although use with *or* is neither archaic nor wrong, *neither* is usually followed by *nor*. Some think that *neither* must be limited in reference to two, but reference to more than two has been quite common since the 17th century ⟨*neither* the post office, the bank, nor the library is open today⟩.

[3]**neither** *adj* **:** not either ⟨*neither* hand⟩

nek·ton \ˈnek-tən, -ˌtän\ *n* **:** free-swimming aquatic animals (as whales, sharks, or squid) whose distribution is essentially independent of wave and current action — compare PLANKTON [German, from Greek *nēktos* "swimming," from *nēchein* "to swim"] — **nek·ton·ic** \nek-ˈtän-ik\ *adj*

nel·son \ˈnel-sən\ *n* **:** a wrestling hold in which leverage is exerted against an opponent's arm, neck, and head [probably from the name *Nelson*]

ne·ma·to·cide \ˈnem-ət-ə-ˌsīd, ni-ˈmat-ə-\ *n* **:** a substance or preparation used to destroy nematodes

ne·ma·to·cyst \ˈnem-ət-ə-ˌsist, nə-ˈmat-ə-\ *n* **:** one of the minute stinging organs of various coelenterates (as jellyfishes and corals) used in catching prey [Greek *nēmat-, nēma* "thread"]

nem·a·tode \ˈnem-ə-ˌtōd\ *n* **:** any of a phylum (Nematoda) of elongated cylindrical worms parasitic in animals or plants or free-living in soil or water — called also *roundworm* [derived from Greek *nēmat-, nēma* "thread"]

Nem·bu·tal \ˈnem-byə-ˌtȯl\ *trademark* — used for the sodium salt of pentobarbital

ne·mer·te·an \ni-ˈmərt-ē-ən\ *n* **:** any of a phylum (Nemertea) of often vividly colored usually long flattened marine worms that typically burrow in the mud or sand along seacoasts — called also *ribbon worm* [derived from Greek *Nēmertēs,* Nemertes (a sea nymph)] — **nemertean** *adj* — **nem·er·tine** \ˈnem-ər-ˌtīn\ *adj or n*

nem·e·sis \ˈnem-ə-səs\ *n, pl* **-e·ses** \-ə-ˌsēz\ **1 a :** one that inflicts retribution or vengeance **b :** a formidable and usually victorious rival or opponent **2 a :** an act or instance of just punishment **b :** BANE 2 [*Nemesis,* Greek goddess of fate and punisher of pride]

ne·moph·i·la \ni-ˈmäf-ə-lə\ *n* **:** any of a genus of herbs chiefly of western North America that are widely grown for their showy blue or white sometimes spotted flowers [derived from Greek *nemos* "wooded pasture" + *philos* "loving"]

neo- — see NE-

neo·clas·sic \ˌnē-ō-ˈklas-ik\ *adj* **:** of or relating to a revival or adaptation of the classical style especially in literature, art, architecture, or music — **neo·clas·si·cal** \-ˈklas-i-kəl\ *adj* — **neo·clas·si·cism** \-ˈklas-ə-ˌsiz-əm\ *n*

neo–Dar·win·ism \-ˈdär-wə-ˌniz-əm\ *n* **:** a theory that explains evolution in terms of natural selection and the genetics of populations and specifically denies the possibility of inheriting acquired characters — **neo–Dar·win·i·an** \-där-ˈwin-ē-ən\ *adj or n* — **neo–Dar·win·ist** \-ˈdär-wə-nəst\ *n*

neo·dym·i·um \ˌnē-ō-ˈdim-ē-əm\ *n* **:** a silver-white to yellow metallic chemical element — see ELEMENT table [*ne-* + *-dymium* (from *didymium,* a mixture of rare-earth elements, from Greek *didymos* "double," from *dyo* "two")]

neo–im·pres·sion·ism \-im-ˈpresh-ə-ˌniz-əm\ *n, often cap N&I* **:** a late 19th century French art theory and practice marked by an attempt to make impressionism more precise in form and the use of a pointillistic painting technique — **neo–im·pres·sion·ist** \-ˈpresh-nəst, -ə-nəst\ *adj or n, often cap N&I*

Ne·o·lith·ic \ˌnē-ə-ˈlith-ik\ *adj* **:** of or relating to the latest period of the Stone Age characterized by polished stone implements — compare PALEOLITHIC

ne·ol·o·gism \nē-ˈäl-ə-ˌjiz-əm\ *n* **:** a new word, usage, or expression — **ne·ol·o·gist** \-jəst\ *n* — **ne·ol·o·gis·tic** \-ˌäl-ə-ˈjis-tik\ *adj*

neo·my·cin \ˌnē-ə-ˈmīs-n\ *n* **:** a broad-spectrum antibiotic or mixture of antibiotics produced by a soil streptomyces

[1]**ne·on** \ˈnē-ˌän\ *n* **1 :** a colorless odorless inert gaseous chemical element found in minute amounts in air and used in electric lamps — see ELEMENT table **2 a :** a discharge lamp in which the gas contains a large amount of neon **b :** a sign composed of such lamps [Greek, neuter of *neos* "new"]

[2]**neon** *adj* **1 :** of, relating to, or using neon ⟨*neon* lights⟩ **2 :** extremely bright **:** FLUORESCENT ⟨*neon* yellow⟩

neo·na·tal \ˌnē-ō-ˈnāt-l\ *adj* **:** of, relating to, or affecting the newborn — **neo·na·tal·ly** \-l-ē\ *adv*

neo·nate \ˈnē-ə-ˌnāt\ *n* **:** a newborn child

neo·or·tho·dox \ˌnē-ō-ˈȯr-thə-ˌdäks\ *adj* **:** of or relating to a 20th century Protestant theological movement characterized by a reaction against liberalism and emphasis on Reformation doctrines — **neo·or·tho·doxy** \-ˌdäk-sē\ *n*

neo–pa·gan \ˌnē-ō-ˈpā-gən\ *n* **:** a person who practices a contemporary form of paganism (as Wicca) — **neo–pagan** *adj* — **neo–pa·gan·ism** \-ˈpā-gə-ˌniz-əm\ *n*

neo·phyte \ˈnē-ə-ˌfīt\ *n* **1 :** a new convert **2 :** NOVICE 2 [Late Latin *neophytus,* from Greek *neophytos,* from *neophytos* "newly planted," from *neos* "new" + *phyein* "to bring forth"]

neo·plasm \ˈnē-ə-ˌplaz-əm\ *n* **:** TUMOR — **neo·plas·tic** \ˌnē-ə-ˈplas-tik\ *adj*

neo·prene \ˈnē-ə-ˌprēn\ *n* **:** a synthetic rubber that is used especially for special-purpose clothing (as wet suits) [*ne-* + *-prene* (as in *isoprene,* a flammable liquid used in synthetic rubber, probably from *is-* + *propyl* + *-ene*)]

ne·o·te·ny \nē-ˈät-n-ē\ *n* **:** attainment of sexual maturity during the larval stage; *also* **:** retention of immature characters in adulthood [derived from *ne-* + Greek *teinein* "to stretch"] — **ne·o·ten·ic** \ˌnē-ə-ˈten-ik\ *adj*

ne·pen·the \nə-ˈpen-thē, -ˈpent-\ *n* **1 :** a potion used by the ancients to dull pain and sorrow **2 :** something capable of making one forget grief or suffering [Latin *nepenthes,* from Greek *nēpenthēs* "banishing pain and sorrow," from *nē-* "not" + *penthos* "sorrow"] — **ne·pen·the·an** \-thē-ən\ *adj*

neph·e·line \ˈnef-ə-ˌlēn\ *also* **neph·e·lite** \-ˌlīt\ *n* **:** a usually glassy silicate mineral common in igneous rocks [French *néphéline,* from Greek *nephelē* "cloud"]

neph·ew \ˈnef-yü\ *n* **:** a son of one's brother, sister, brother-in-law, or sister-in-law [Medieval French *neveu,* from Latin *nepos* "grandson, nephew"]

neph·ric \ˈnef-rik\ *adj* **:** RENAL

ne·phrid·i·um \ni-ˈfrid-ē-əm\ *n, pl* **-ia** \-ē-ə\ **:** a tubular excretory organ of various invertebrates (as an earthworm) [New Latin, from Greek *nephros* "kidney"] — **ne·phrid·i·al** \-ē-əl\ *adj*

ne·phri·tis \ni-ˈfrīt-əs\ *n, pl* **ne·phrit·i·des** \-ˈfrit-ə-ˌdēz\ **:** inflammation of the kidneys — **ne·phrit·ic** \-ˈfrit-ik\ *adj*

neph·ron \ˈnef-ˌrän\ *n* **:** any of the functional units of the vertebrate kidney that filter blood and form urine [German, from Greek *nephros* "kidney"]

ne plus ul·tra \ˌnā-ˌpləs-ˈəl-trə, ˌnē-\ *n* **:** the highest point capable of being attained **:** ACME ⟨that hotel is the *ne plus ultra* of elegance⟩ [New Latin, "no more beyond"]

nep·o·tism \ˈnep-ə-ˌtiz-əm\ *n* **:** favoritism (as in appointment to a job) based on kinship [French *népotisme,* from Italian *nepotismo,* from *nepote* "nephew," from Latin *nepot-, nepos* "grandson, nephew"]

Nep·tune \ˈnep-ˌtün, -ˌtyün\ *n* **:** the planet 8th in order from the sun — see PLANET table [Latin *Neptunus,* Roman god of the sea] — **Nep·tu·ni·an** \nep-ˈtü-nē-ən, -ˈtyü-\ *adj*

nep·tu·ni·um \nep-ˈtü-nē-əm, -ˈtyü-\ *n* **:** a radioactive metallic chemical element that is similar to uranium and is obtained in nuclear reactors as a by-product in the production of plutonium — see ELEMENT table [New Latin, from *Neptunus,* the planet Neptune]

nerd \ˈnərd\ *n* **1 :** an unstylish, unattractive, or socially inept person **2 :** a person slavishly devoted to intellectual or academic pursuits [perhaps from *nerd,* a creature in the children's book *If I Ran the Zoo* by Dr. Seuss (Theodor Geisel)] — **nerd·ish** \ˈnərd-ish\ *adj* — **nerdy** \-ē\ *adj*

ne·re·id \ˈnir-ē-əd\ *n* **:** any of a genus of usually large greenish marine annelid worms [derived from Latin *Nereis*]

Ne·re·id \ˈnir-ē-əd\ *n* **:** any of the sea nymphs held in Greek mythology to be the daughters of the sea god Nereus [Latin *Nereid-, Nereis,* from Greek *Nēreid-, Nēreis,* from *Nēreus,* a sea god of Greek myth]

ne·rit·ic \nə-ˈrit-ik\ *adj* **:** of, relating to, or being the shallow water adjoining the seacoast [perhaps from New Latin *Nerita,* a genus of marine snails]

[1]**nerve** \ˈnərv\ *n* **1** : SINEW 1, TENDON ⟨strain every *nerve*⟩ **2** : any of the filamentous bands of nervous tissue connecting parts of the nervous system with the other organs and conducting nerve impulses **3 a** : power of endurance or control : FORTITUDE ⟨a test of mind and *nerve*⟩ **b** (1) : fearless boldness ⟨had the *nerve* to confront them⟩ (2) : rude, disrespectful, or contemptuous boldness : GALL ⟨what *nerve* of her to say that⟩ **4 a** : a sore or sensitive point ⟨that remark hit a *nerve*⟩ **b** *pl* : nervous agitation or irritability : NERVOUSNESS ⟨a case of the *nerves*⟩ **5** : VEIN 2b **6** : the sensitive pulp of a tooth [Latin *nervus* "sinew, nerve"] — **nerve** *adj* — **nerved** \ˈnərvd\ *adj*

[2]**nerve** *vt* : to give strength or courage to

nerve cell *n* : NEURON; *also* : CELL BODY

nerve center *n* **1** : CENTER 2b **2** : a source of leadership, control, or energy

nerve cord *n* **1** : the pair of closely united ventral longitudinal nerves with their segmental ganglia that is characteristic of many elongate invertebrates (as an earthworm) **2** : the dorsal tubular cord of nervous tissue above the notochord of a chordate that comprises or develops into the central nervous system

nerve ending *n* : a structure forming an end of a nerve axon that is distant from the cell body

nerve fiber *n* : any of the processes (as axons or dendrites) of a neuron

nerve gas *n* : a war gas damaging especially to the nervous and respiratory systems

nerve impulse *n* : the progressive alteration in electrical charge along a nerve fiber that follows stimulation and serves to transmit a record of sensation from a receptor to the spinal cord or brain, relay a signal to another neuron, or carry an instruction to act to a muscle or gland — called also *nervous impulse*

nerve·less \ˈnərv-ləs\ *adj* **1** : lacking strength or courage : FEEBLE **2** : showing control or balance : POISED, COOL — **nerve·less·ly** *adv* — **nerve·less·ness** *n*

nerve net *n* : a network of neurons apparently continuous one with another and conducting impulses in all directions; *also* : a nervous system (as in a jellyfish) consisting of such a network

nerve–rack·ing *or* **nerve–wrack·ing** \ˈnərv-ˌrak-ing\ *adj* : extremely trying on the nerves

nerv·ous \ˈnər-vəs\ *adj* **1** : marked by vigor of thought, feeling, or style : SPIRITED **2 a** : of, relating to, or composed of neurons ⟨*nervous* tissue⟩ **b** : of or relating to the nerves; *also* : originating in or affected by the nerves ⟨*nervous* energy⟩ **3 a** : easily excited or irritated : JUMPY ⟨a *nervous* person⟩ **b** : TIMID, APPREHENSIVE ⟨a *nervous* smile⟩ **4** : tending to cause nervousness or agitation : TRYING ⟨a *nervous* situation⟩ — **nerv·ous·ly** *adv* — **nerv·ous·ness** *n*

nervous breakdown *n* : an attack of mental or emotional disorder especially when severe enough to require hospital care

nervous system *n* : the bodily system that receives and interprets stimuli and transmits nerve impulses to the effector organs and that in vertebrates is made up of brain and spinal cord, nerves, ganglia, and parts of the receptor organs

nervy \ˈnər-vē\ *adj* **nerv·i·er; -est** **1 a** : showing calm courage : BOLD **b** : marked by impudence or presumption : BRASH ⟨a *nervy* salesperson⟩ **2** : NERVOUS 3a — **nerv·i·ness** *n*

ne·science \ˈnesh-əns, ˈnēsh-, -ē-əns\ *n* : lack of knowledge or awareness : IGNORANCE [Late Latin *nescientia,* from Latin *nescire* "not to know," from *ne-* "not" + *scire* "to know"] — **ne·scient** \-ənt\ *adj*

ness \ˈnes\ *n* : [1]CAPE, PROMONTORY [Old English *næss*]

-ness \nəs\ *n suffix* : state : condition : quality : degree ⟨hard*ness*⟩ [Old English]

Nes·sel·rode \ˈnes-əl-ˌrōd\ *n* : a mixture of candied fruits, nuts, and maraschino used in puddings, pies, and ice cream [Count Karl R. *Nesselrode,* died 1862, Russian statesman]

[1]**nest** \ˈnest\ *n* **1 a** : a place or structure where eggs are laid and hatched or young are raised ⟨the *nest* of a bird⟩ ⟨a mouse's *nest*⟩ **b** : the home or shelter of an animal (as a squirrel or chimpanzee) **2 a** : HOME 1 ⟨grown children who have left the *nest*⟩ **b** : DEN 2a, HANGOUT ⟨the thieves' *nest*⟩ **3** : the occupants or frequenters of a nest ⟨a *nest* of baby birds⟩ **4 a** : a group of similar things : AGGREGATION ⟨a *nest* of rusted wire⟩ **b** : HOTBED 2 ⟨a *nest* of rebellion⟩ **5** : a group of objects made to fit close together or one within another ⟨a *nest* of tables⟩ [Old English]

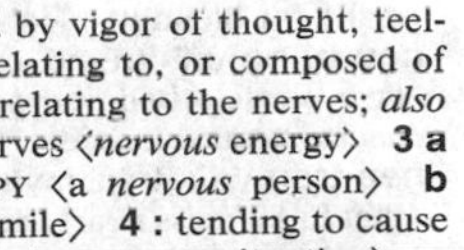

nest 5

[2]**nest** *vb* **1** : to build or occupy a nest ⟨robins *nested* in the underbrush⟩ **2** : to fit compactly together or within one another

nest egg *n* **1** : a natural or artificial egg left in a nest to induce a fowl to continue to lay there **2** : a fund of money set aside as a reserve

nest·er \ˈnes-tər\ *n* **1** : one that nests **2** *West* : a homesteader or squatter who takes up open range for a farm

nes·tle \ˈnes-əl\ *vb* **nes·tled; nes·tling** \ˈnes-ling, -ə-ling\ **1** : to settle snugly or comfortably **2 a** : to settle, shelter, or house as if in a nest **b** : to press closely and affectionately : CUDDLE [Old English *nestlian* "to make a nest," from *nest*] — **nes·tler** \-lər\ *n*

nest·ling \ˈnest-ling\ *n* : a young bird not yet able to leave the nest

[1]**net** \ˈnet\ *n* **1 a** : a meshed fabric twisted, knotted, or woven together at regular intervals **b** : something made of net: as (1) : a device for catching fish, birds, or insects (2) : a fabric barricade which divides a court in half (as in tennis or volleyball) and over which a ball or shuttlecock must be hit in play (3) : the fabric that encloses the sides and back of the goal in various games (as soccer or hockey) **2** : an entrapping device or situation ⟨caught in a *net* of suspicion⟩ **3** : a network of lines, fibers, or figures **4** *often cap* : INTERNET [Old English *nett*] — **net·like** \-ˌlīk\ *adj* — **net·ty** \ˈnet-ē\ *adj*

[2]**net** *vt* **net·ted; net·ting** **1** : to cover with or as if with a net **2** : to catch in or as if in a net — **net·ter** *n*

[3]**net** *adj* **1** : free from all charges or deductions ⟨a *net* profit⟩ ⟨*net* weight⟩ — compare GROSS 3b **2** : FINAL ⟨the *net* result⟩ [Medieval French, "clean, neat"]

[4]**net** *vt* **net·ted; net·ting** : to gain or produce as profit : CLEAR

[5]**net** *n* : a net amount, profit, or price

net·book \ˈnet-ˌbu̇k\ *n* : a small portable computer designed primarily for wireless Internet access

neth·er \ˈneth-ər\ *adj* **1** : situated down or below : LOWER **2** : situated beneath the earth's surface ⟨the *nether* regions⟩ [Old English *nithera,* from *nither* "down"]

neth·er·most \-ˌmōst\ *adj* : farthest down : LOWEST

neth·er·world \-ˌwərld\ *n* **1** : the world of the dead **2** : UNDERWORLD 3

net·i·quette \ˈnet-ɪ-kət, -ˌket\ *n* : etiquette governing communication on the Internet [blend of *net* and *etiquette*]

net·i·zen \ˈnet-ə-zən\ *n* : a user of the Internet [blend of *net* and *citizen*]

net·ting \ˈnet-ing\ *n* **1** : NETWORK 1 **2** : the act or process of making a net or network

[1]**net·tle** \ˈnet-l\ *n* : any of various tall herbs with stinging hairs on the leaves and stems [Old English *netel*]

[2]**nettle** *vt* **net·tled; net·tling** \ˈnet-ling, -l-ing\ **1** : to sting with or as if with nettles **2** : ANNOY, PROVOKE

net·tle·some \ˈnet-l-səm\ *adj* : causing annoyance

net–veined \ˈnet-ˈvānd\ *adj* : having veins that branch and interlace to form a network ⟨dicotyledons have *net-veined* leaves⟩ — compare PARALLEL-VEINED

[1]**net·work** \ˈnet-ˌwərk\ *n* **1** : a fabric or structure of cords or wires that cross at regular intervals and are knotted or secured at the crossings **2** : a system of lines or channels resembling a network **3 a** : an interconnected or interrelated chain, group, or system ⟨a *network* of hotels⟩ **b** : a system of computers connected by communications lines **4 a** : a group of radio or television stations linked by wire or radio relay **b** : a television or radio company that broadcasts over such a network

[2]**network** *vb* **1** : to cover with or as if with a network **2** : to join together in a network ⟨*networked* the classroom's computers⟩ **3** : to engage in networking — **net·work·er** \-ˌwər-kər\ *n*

net·work·ing *n* **1** : the exchange of information or services among individuals, groups, or institutions; *esp* : the cultivation of productive relationships for employment or business **2** : the establishment or use of a computer network

neur- *or* **neuro-** *combining form* : nerve ⟨*neur*al⟩ ⟨*neuro*logy⟩ [Greek *neuron* "sinew, nerve"]

neu·ral \ˈnu̇r-əl, ˈnyu̇r-\ *adj* **1** : of, relating to, or affecting a

\ə\ **abut**	\au̇\ **out**	\i\ **tip**	\ȯ\ **saw**	\u̇\ **foot**
\ər\ **further**	\ch\ **chin**	\ī\ **life**	\ȯi\ **coin**	\y\ **yet**
\a\ **mat**	\e\ **pet**	\j\ **job**	\th\ **thin**	\yü\ **few**
\ā\ **take**	\ē\ **easy**	\ng\ **sing**	\t͟h\ **this**	\yu̇\ **cure**
\ä\ **cot, cart**	\g\ **go**	\ō\ **bone**	\ü\ **food**	\zh\ **vision**

nerve or the nervous system **2 :** situated in the region of or on the same side of the body as the brain and spinal cord — **neu·ral·ly** \-ə-lē\ *adv*

neu·ral·gia \nu̇-ˈral-jə, nyu̇-\ *n* **:** acute pain that follows the course of a nerve; *also* **:** a condition marked by such pain — **neu·ral·gic** \-jik\ *adj*

neural network *n* **:** a computer design in which a number of processors are interconnected in a manner suggestive of the connections between neurons in a human brain and which is able to learn by a process of trial and error — called also *neural net*

neural tube *n* **:** a hollow longitudinal tube produced from dorsal ectodermal folds in the vertebrate embryo and giving rise to the brain and spinal cord

neu·ri·lem·ma \ˌnu̇r-ə-ˈlem-ə, ˌnyu̇r-\ *n* **:** the outer membranous sheath of a Schwann cell [derived from *neur-* + Greek *eilēma* "covering, coil," from *eilein* "to wind"] — **neu·ri·lem·mal** \-ˈlem-əl\ *adj*

neu·ri·tis \nu̇-ˈrīt-əs, nyu̇-\ *n, pl* **-rit·i·des** \-ˈrit-ə-ˌdēz\ *or* **-ri·tis·es :** inflammation of a nerve — **neu·rit·ic** \-ˈrit-ik\ *adj or n*

neu·ro·de·gen·er·a·tive \ˌnu̇r-ō-di-ˈjen-ə-rət-iv, ˌnyu̇r-\ *adj* **:** relating to or marked by deterioration of tissue of the nervous system ⟨*neurodegenerative* diseases⟩

neu·rog·lia \nu̇-ˈräg-lē-ə, nyu̇-; ˌnu̇r-ə-ˈglē-ə, ˌnyu̇r-, -ˈglī-\ *n* **:** GLIA [derived from *neur-* + Middle Greek *glia* "glue"] — **neu·rog·li·al** \-əl\ *adj*

neu·ro·hor·mone \ˌnu̇r-ō-ˈhȯr-ˌmōn, ˌnyu̇r-\ *n* **:** a hormone produced by or acting on nervous tissue

neu·rol·o·gist \nu̇-ˈräl-ə-jəst, nyu̇-\ *n* **:** a specialist in neurology; *esp* **:** a physician who specializes in identifying and treating diseases of the nervous system

neu·rol·o·gy \nu̇-ˈräl-ə-jē, nyu̇-\ *n* **:** the scientific study of the structure, functions, and disorders of the nervous system — **neu·ro·log·i·cal** \ˌnu̇r-ə-ˈläj-i-kəl, ˌnyu̇r-\ *or* **neu·ro·log·ic** \-ˈläj-ik\ *adj* — **neu·ro·log·i·cal·ly** \-i-kə-lē, -klē\ *adv*

neu·ro·mus·cu·lar \ˌnu̇r-ō-ˈməs-kyə-lər, ˌnyu̇r-\ *adj* **:** of or relating to nerves and muscles; *esp* **:** jointly involving or affecting nervous and muscular elements ⟨a *neuromuscular* disease⟩

neu·ron \ˈnü-ˌrän, ˈnyü-; ˈnu̇r-ˌän, ˈnyu̇r-\ *n* **:** a grayish or reddish cell with specialized processes that is the fundamental functional unit of nervous tissue [Greek *neuron* "nerve, sinew"] — **neu·ro·nal** \ˈnu̇r-ən-l, ˈnyu̇r-, nu̇-ˈrōn-l, nyu̇-\ *adj*

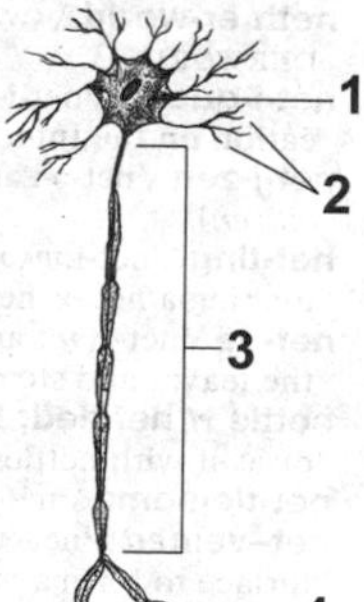

neuron: *1* cell body, *2* dendrite, *3* axon, *4* nerve ending

neu·rop·a·thy \nu̇r-ˈäp-ə-thē, nyu̇r-\ *n, pl* **-thies :** an abnormal and usually degenerative state of the nervous system or nerves; *also* **:** a condition resulting from a neuropathy

neu·ro·pep·tide \ˌnu̇r-ə-ˈpep-ˌtīd, ˌnyu̇r-\ *n* **:** a peptide produced within the body that influences the activity or functioning of the nervous system

neu·ro·sis \nu̇-ˈrō-səs, nyu̇-\ *n, pl* **-ro·ses** \-ˈrō-ˌsēz\ **:** any of various mental and emotional disorders that affect only part of a person's personality, are less serious than a psychosis, and involve extreme or atypical reactions (as abnormal fears, depression, or anxiety) to stress and conflict

neu·ros·po·ra \nu̇-ˈräs-pə-rə, nyu̇-\ *n* **:** any of a genus of often pink-spored ascomycetous fungi that are destructive in bakeries but important objects of genetic research [New Latin, from *neur-* + *spora* "spore"]

neu·ro·sur·geon \-ˈsər-jən\ *n* **:** a surgeon who specializes in performing surgery on the brain, spinal cord, or nerves — **neu·ro·sur·gery** \-ˈsərj-rē, -ə-rē\ *n*

1**neu·rot·ic** \nu̇-ˈrät-ik, nyu̇-\ *adj* **:** of, relating to, constituting, or affected with neurosis — **neu·rot·i·cal·ly** \-ˈrät-i-kə-lē, -klē\ *adv*

2**neurotic** *n* **1 :** a person affected with a neurosis **2 :** an emotionally unstable person

neu·ro·tox·ic \ˌnu̇r-ə-ˈtäk-sik, ˌnyu̇r-\ *adj* **:** poisonous to nervous tissue

neu·ro·tox·in \-ˈtäk-sən\ *n* **:** a poisonous protein that acts on the nervous system

neu·ro·trans·mit·ter \-trans-ˈmit-ər, -tranz-\ *n* **:** a substance (as norepinephrine or acetylcholine) that transmits nerve impulse across a synapse from one neuron to another

1**neu·ter** \ˈnüt-ər, ˈnyüt-\ *adj* **1 :** of, relating to, or constituting the class of words that ordinarily includes most of those referring to things that are neither male nor female ⟨a *neuter* noun⟩ ⟨the *neuter* gender⟩ **2 :** lacking sex organs; *also* **:** having imperfectly developed sex organs [Latin, literally, "neither," from *ne-* "not" + *uter* "which of two"]

2**neuter** *n* **1 a :** a word or form of the neuter gender **b :** the neuter gender **2 :** one that is neutral **3 a :** WORKER 2 **b :** a spayed or castrated animal

3**neuter** *vt* **:** ALTER 2, CASTRATE

1**neu·tral** \ˈnü-trəl, ˈnyü-\ *adj* **1 :** not favoring either side in a quarrel, contest, or war **2 :** of or relating to a neutral state or power ⟨*neutral* territory⟩ **3 a** (1) **:** having no distinctive characteristics ⟨a *neutral* personality⟩ (2) **:** not feeling strongly one way or the other **:** INDIFFERENT **b** (1) **:** ACHROMATIC (2) **:** having no color that stands out **c :** neither acid nor basic **d :** not electrically charged **4 :** produced with the tongue in the position it has when at rest ⟨the *neutral* vowels of \ə-ˈbəv\ *above*⟩ [derived from Medieval Latin *neutralitas* "middle ground," from Latin *neutralis* "of neuter gender," from *neuter* "neuter, neither"] — **neu·tral·ly** \-trə-lē\ *adv* — **neu·tral·ness** *n*

2**neutral** *n* **1 :** one that is neutral **2 :** a neutral color **3 :** a position of disengagement (as of gears)

neu·tral·ism \ˈnü-trə-ˌliz-əm, ˈnyü-\ *n* **:** a policy or the advocacy of neutrality especially in international affairs — **neu·tral·ist** \-ləst\ *n* — **neu·tral·is·tic** \ˌnü-trə-ˈlis-tik, ˌnyü-\ *adj*

neu·tral·i·ty \nü-ˈtral-ət-ē, nyü-\ *n* **:** the quality or state of being neutral; *esp* **:** the refusal to take part in a war between other powers

neu·tral·ize \ˈnü-trə-ˌlīz, ˈnyü-\ *vt* **1 :** to make chemically neutral ⟨*neutralize* the acid with a base⟩ **2 :** to destroy the effectiveness of **:** NULLIFY ⟨*neutralize* an opponent's move⟩ **3 :** to make electrically inert by combining equal positive and negative quantities **4 :** to provide for the neutrality of under international law ⟨*neutralize* a country⟩ — **neu·tral·i·za·tion** \ˌnü-trə-lə-ˈzā-shən, ˌnyü-\ *n* — **neu·tral·iz·er** \ˈnü-trə-ˌlī-zər, ˈnyü-\ *n*

neutral spirits *n pl* **:** ethanol of 190 or higher proof used especially for blending alcoholic liquors

neu·tri·no \nü-ˈtrē-nō, nyü-\ *n, pl* **-nos :** an uncharged elementary particle believed to have little or no mass [Italian, from *neutro* "neutral, neuter"]

neu·tron \ˈnü-ˌträn, ˈnyü-\ *n* **:** an uncharged elementary particle that has a mass nearly equal to that of the proton and is present in all known atomic nuclei except the hydrogen nucleus [*neutral* + *-on*]

neutron star *n* **:** a dense celestial object that consists of closely packed neutrons and results from the collapse of a much larger star

neu·tro·phil \ˈnü-trə-ˌfil, ˈnyü-\ *n* **:** a cell that has fine granules in the cytoplasm and is the chief phagocytic white blood cell [Latin *neuter* "neither"; from its staining to the same degree with acid or basic dyes]

né·vé \nā-ˈvā\ *n* **:** the partially compacted granular snow that forms the surface part of the upper end of a glacier; *also* **:** a field of granular snow [French (Swiss dialect), from Latin *niv-, nix* "snow"]

nev·er \ˈnev-ər\ *adv* **1 :** not ever **:** at no time ⟨I *never* saw them before⟩ **2 :** not in any degree, way, or condition ⟨*never* fear, we'll win⟩ [Old English *nǣfre,* from *ne* "not" + *ǣfre* "ever"]

nev·er·more \ˌnev-ər-ˈmōr, -ˈmȯr\ *adv* **:** never again

nev·er–nev·er land \ˌnev-ər-ˈnev-ər-\ *n* **:** an ideal or imaginary place

nev·er·the·less \ˌnev-ər-t͟hə-ˈles\ *adv* **:** in spite of that **:** HOWEVER ⟨an exhausting but *nevertheless* enjoyable day⟩

ne·vus \ˈnē-vəs\ *n, pl* **ne·vi** \-ˌvī\ **:** a pigmented area on the skin that is either flat or raised **:** 1MOLE [Latin *naevus*]

1**new** \ˈnü, ˈnyü\ *adj* **1 :** not old **:** RECENT, MODERN ⟨a *new* way of thinking⟩ **2 :** not the same as the former **:** taking the place of one that came before ⟨a *new* teacher⟩ **3 :** recently discovered, recognized, or learned about ⟨*new* lands⟩ **4 :** not formerly known or experienced ⟨*new* feelings⟩ **5 :** having been in a relationship or position but a short time ⟨*new* to her work⟩ ⟨a *new* member⟩ **6 :** beginning as a repetition of some previous act or thing ⟨a *new* year⟩ ⟨make a *new* start⟩ **7 :** renewed in strength and vigor ⟨felt like a *new* person after my vacation⟩ **8** *cap* : having been in use after medieval times : MODERN ⟨*New* Latin⟩ [Old English *nīwe*] — **new·ness** *n*

synonyms NEW, NOVEL, FRESH mean having recently come into existence or use. NEW may apply to what is freshly made and unused ⟨*new* bricks⟩ or has not been known before ⟨a *new* design⟩ or not experienced before ⟨start on a *new* job⟩. NOVEL applies to what is not only new but strange and unprecedented ⟨*novel* hair styles⟩. FRESH applies to what has not yet had time to grow dim, soiled, or stale ⟨put on a *fresh* shirt⟩ ⟨offering *fresh* ideas⟩.

²new *adv* : NEWLY, RECENTLY ⟨*new*-mown hay⟩

New Age *n* **1** : a group of cultural attitudes arising in late 20th century Western society that are adapted from a variety of ancient and modern cultures, that emphasize beliefs (as reincarnation) outside the mainstream, and that advance alternate approaches to spirituality, right living, and health **2** : a soothing form of instrumental music often used to promote relaxation — **new age** *adj, often cap N&A* — **New Ag·er** \-ˈā-jər\ *n*

new·bie \ˈnü-bē, ˈnyü-\ *n* : a newcomer especially to cyberspace

new·born \ˈnü-ˈbȯrn, ˈnyü-\ *adj* **1** : recently born **2** : born again — **newborn** *n*

new·com·er \ˈnü-ˌkəm-ər, ˈnyü-\ *n* **1** : one recently arrived **2** : NOVICE 2, BEGINNER

New Deal *n* **1** : the legislative and administrative program of President Franklin D. Roosevelt designed to promote economic recovery and social reform during the 1930s **2** : the period of the New Deal — **New Deal·er** \-ˈdē-lər\ *n*

new·el \ˈnü-əl, ˈnyü-\ *n* **1** : an upright post about which the steps of a circular staircase wind **2** : a post at the foot of a straight stairway or one at a landing [Medieval French *nuel, noel* "stone of a fruit, stone cut to form a newel," from Late Latin *nucalis* "like a nut," from Latin *nuc-, nux* "nut"]

new·fan·gled \ˈnü-ˈfang-gəld, ˈnyü-\ *adj* : of the newest style : NOVEL ⟨*newfangled* ideas⟩ [Middle English, from *newefangel,* from *new* + Old English *fangen,* past participle of *fōn* "to take, seize"]

new–fash·ioned \-ˈfash-ənd\ *adj* **1** : made in a new fashion or form **2** : UP-TO-DATE 2

new·found \-ˈfau̇nd\ *adj* : newly found ⟨a *newfound* friend⟩

New·found·land \ˈnü-fən-dlənd, ˈnyü-, -lənd, -ˌdland, -ˌland; nü-ˈfau̇n-dlənd, nyü-, -lənd\ *n* : any of a breed of very large thick-coated dogs probably developed in Newfoundland

new·ish \ˈnü-ish, ˈnyü-\ *adj* : rather new

New Latin *n* : Latin as used since the end of the medieval period especially in scientific description and classification

new·ly \ˈnü-lē, ˈnyü-\ *adv* **1** : LATELY, RECENTLY ⟨*newly* married⟩ **2** : ANEW, AFRESH ⟨a *newly* furnished house⟩

new·ly·wed \-ˌwed\ *n* : a person recently married

new math *n* : mathematics that is based on set theory especially as taught in elementary and secondary school — called also *new mathematics*

new moon *n* **1** : the moon's phase when it is in conjunction with the sun so that its dark side is toward the earth; *also* : the thin crescent moon seen shortly after sunset a few days after the actual occurrence of the new moon phase **2** : the 1st day of the Jewish month

news \ˈnüz, ˈnyüz\ *n* **1 a** : a report of recent events ⟨brought us the office *news*⟩ **b** : previously unknown information ⟨that's *news* to me⟩ **c** : something having a specified influence or effect ⟨snow was good *news* for the ski resorts⟩ **2 a** : material reported in a newspaper or news periodical or on a newscast **b** : matter that is newsworthy **c** : NEWSCAST ⟨watched the *news* on television⟩

news agency *n* : an organization that supplies news to subscribing newspapers, periodicals, and newscasters

news·boy \ˈnüz-ˌbȯi, ˈnyüz-\ *n* : a person who delivers or sells newspapers

news·cast \-ˌkast\ *n* : a radio or television news broadcast [*news* + broad*cast*] — **news·cast·er** \-ˌkas-tər\ *n*

news conference *n* : PRESS CONFERENCE

news·girl \ˈnüz-ˌgərl, ˈnyüz-\ *n* : a girl or woman who delivers or sells newspapers

news·group \-ˌgrüp\ *n* : an electronic bulletin board on the Internet that is devoted to a particular topic

news·let·ter \ˈnüz-ˌlet-ər, ˈnyüz-\ *n* : a newspaper containing news or information of interest chiefly to a special group

news·man \-mən, -ˌman\ *n* : one (as a reporter or correspondent) who gathers, reports, or comments on the news

news·mon·ger \-ˌməng-gər, -ˌmäng-\ *n* : GOSSIP 1

news·pa·per \ˈnüz-ˌpā-pər, ˈnyüz-, ˈnüs-, ˈnyüs-\ *n* **1** : a paper that is printed and distributed usually daily or weekly and contains news, articles of opinion, features, and advertising **2** : an organization publishing a newspaper **3** : the paper making up a newspaper

news·pa·per·man \-ˌman\ *n* : one who owns or is employed by a newspaper; *esp* : one who writes or edits copy for a newspaper

news·print \ˈnüz-ˌprint, ˈnyüz-\ *n* : a relatively cheap paper made from wood pulp and used mostly for newspapers

news·reel \-ˌrēl\ *n* : a short motion picture dealing with current events

news·stand \ˈnüz-ˌstand, ˈnyüz-\ *n* : a place where newspapers and periodicals are sold

New Style *adj* : using or according to the Gregorian calendar

news·wom·an \ˈnüz-ˌwu̇m-ən, ˈnyüz-\ *n* : a woman who gathers, reports, or comments on the news

news·wor·thy \ˈnüz-ˌwər-t͟hē, ˈnyüz-\ *adj* : sufficiently interesting to the general public to warrant reporting

newsy \ˈnü-zē, ˈnyü-\ *adj* **news·i·er; -est** : filled with news; *esp* : CHATTY ⟨a *newsy* letter⟩

newt \ˈnüt, ˈnyüt\ *n* : any of various small salamanders that live mostly in water [Middle English *newte,* the phrase *an ewte* (from Old English *efete* "eft") being understood as a *newte*]

newt

New Testament *n* : the second of the two chief divisions of the Christian Bible consisting of the books dealing with Christ's life and death and the work done by his apostles after his death — see BIBLE table

new·ton \ˈnüt-n, ˈnyüt-n\ *n* : a unit of force equal to the force required to give an acceleration of one meter per second per second to a mass of one kilogram [Sir Isaac *Newton*]

New·to·ni·an \nü-ˈtō-nē-ən, nyü-\ *adj* : of, relating to, or characteristic of Sir Isaac Newton, his discoveries, or his doctrines

New World *n* : the western hemisphere; *esp* : the continental landmass of North and South America

New Year \ˈnü-ˌyiər, ˈnyü-\ *n* **1** : NEW YEAR'S DAY, *also* : the first days of the year **2** : ROSH HASHANAH

New Year's Day *n* : January 1 observed as a legal holiday

¹next \ˈnekst\ *adj* : immediately preceding or following : NEAREST ⟨the *next* page⟩ ⟨the *next* house was empty⟩ [Old English *nīehst,* superlative of *nēah* "nigh"]

²next *adv* **1** : in the time, place, or order nearest or immediately succeeding ⟨open this package *next*⟩ **2** : on the first occasion to come ⟨when *next* we meet⟩

³next *prep* : next to

next of kin : a person's nearest relation or relations

¹next to *prep* : immediately following : adjacent to ⟨*next to* the head of the class⟩

²next to *adv* : very nearly : ALMOST ⟨*next to* impossible⟩

nex·us \ˈnek-səs\ *n, pl* **nex·us·es** \-sə-səz\ *or* **nex·us** \-səs, -ˌsüs\ : CONNECTION 2, LINK [Latin, from *nectere* "to bind"]

Nez Percé *or* **Nez Perce** \ˈnez-ˈpərs, ˈnes-ˈpeərs, *French* nā-per-sā\ *n, pl* **Nez Percé** *or* **Nez Percés** *same or* -ˈpər-səz, -ˈpeər-\ *or* **Nez Perce** *or* **Nez Perces** *same or* -ˈpər-səz, -ˈpeər-\ : a member of an American Indian people of what is now central Idaho and adjacent parts of Washington and Oregon [French, literally, "pierced nose"]

ni·a·cin \ˈnī-ə-sən\ *n* : an acid $C_6H_5NO_2$ of the vitamin B complex that is found widely in plants and animals and is used especially against pellagra — called also *nicotinic acid* [*ni*cotinic *acid* + *-in*]

ni·a·cin·amide \ˌnī-ə-ˈsin-ə-ˌmīd\ *n* : a compound $C_6H_6N_2O$ of the vitamin B complex found especially as a constituent of coenzymes and used similarly to niacin

Ni·ag·a·ra \nī-ˈag-rə, -ə-rə\ *n* : an overwhelming flood : TORRENT ⟨a *Niagara* of protests⟩ [*Niagara* Falls, waterfall of the Niagara river]

nib \ˈnib\ *n* **1** : BEAK 1, BILL **2 a** : the sharpened point of a quill pen **b** : a pen point **3** : a small pointed or projecting part [probably alteration of *neb*]

¹nib·ble \ˈnib-əl\ *vb* **nib·bled; nib·bling** \ˈnib-ling, -ə-ling\ **1 a**

\ə\ **abut**	\au̇\ **out**	\i\ **tip**	\ȯ\ **saw**	\u̇\ **foot**
\ər\ **further**	\ch\ **chin**	\ī\ **life**	\ȯi\ **coin**	\y\ **yet**
\a\ mat	\e\ pet	\j\ **job**	\th\ **thin**	\yü\ **few**
\ā\ take	\ē\ **easy**	\ng\ **sing**	\t͟h\ **this**	\yu̇\ **cure**
\ä\ cot, cart	\g\ go	\ō\ bone	\ü\ **food**	\zh\ **vision**

: to bite or chew gently or bit by bit **b** : to take away gradually ⟨*nibbling* our freedom⟩ **2** : to deal with something cautiously [origin unknown] — **nib·bler** \'nib-lər, -ə-lər\ *n*

²nibble *n* **1** : an act of nibbling; *esp* : a small bite or cautious approach **2 a** : a very small quantity **b** : a dainty morsel

Ni·be·lung \'nē-bə-ˌlu̇ŋ\ *n* **1** : a member of a race of dwarfs in Germanic legend from whom a hoard and ring were taken by Siegfried **2** : any of the followers of Siegfried **3** : any of the Burgundian kings in the medieval German epic *Nibelungenlied* [German]

nibs \'nibz\ *n* : an important or self-important person — used chiefly in the phrase *his* (or *her*) *nibs* [origin unknown]

ni·cad \'nī-ˌkad\ *n* : a rechargeable battery made with nickel and cadmium electrodes [¹*nickel* + *cad*mium]

nice \'nīs\ *adj* **1** : showing fastidious or finicky tastes **2** : marked by or demanding delicate discrimination or treatment ⟨a *nice* distinction⟩ **3 a** : PLEASING, AGREEABLE ⟨a *nice* time⟩ ⟨a *nice* person⟩ **b** : well-executed : GOOD ⟨a *nice* shot⟩ **4 a** : socially acceptable : WELL-BRED ⟨offensive to *nice* people⟩ **b** : VIRTUOUS, RESPECTABLE [Middle English, "foolish, wanton," from Medieval French, "silly, simple," from Latin *nescius* "ignorant," from *nescire* "not to know," from *ne-* "not" + *scire* "to know"] — **nice·ly** *adv* — **nice·ness** *n*

Word History While it is difficult to trace the precise development of the many senses of this word in English, a brief look at its history reveals that *nice* has come to have a number of meanings that are almost opposite to its earliest senses. *Nice* is derived from Latin *nescius,* "ignorant." It was earliest used in English, in the 13th and 14th centuries, to mean "foolish" or "stupid." Also in its early history in English *nice* had the sense of "wanton" or "dissolute." From these senses *nice* began in the 16th century to develop the meaning "coy" or "reserved," and then "fastidious" or "finicky." Not until the 18th century did *nice* come to be used in the variety of senses generally meaning "pleasurable" or "agreeable."

Ni·cene Creed \ˌnī-ˌsēn-\ *n* : a Christian creed issued by the first Council of Nicaea in A.D. 325 and later expanded that begins "I believe in one God" [Late Latin *nicaenus* "of Nicaea"]

nice–nel·ly \'nīs-'nel-ē\ *adj, often cap 2nd N* **1** : PRUDISH **2** : EUPHEMISTIC [from the name *Nelly*] — **nice nelly** *n, often cap 2nd N* — **nice–nel·ly·ism** \-ˌiz-əm\ *n, often cap 2nd N*

ni·ce·ty \'nī-sət-ē, -stē\ *n, pl* **-ties** **1** : a dainty, delicate, or elegant thing ⟨the *niceties* of life⟩ **2** : a small point : a fine detail ⟨the *niceties* of manners⟩ **3** : careful attention to details ⟨the greatest *nicety* is needed in making watches⟩ **4** : the point at which a thing is at its best ⟨roasted to a *nicety*⟩

¹niche \'nich\ *n* **1 a** : a recess in a wall especially for a statue **b** : something that resembles a niche **2** : a place, use, or work for which a person is best fitted **3 a** : a habitat supplying the factors necessary for the existence of an organism or species **b** : the ecological role of an organism in a community especially in regard to food consumption [French, from Middle French *nicher* "to nest," from Latin *nidus* "nest"]

²niche *vt* : to place in a niche

¹nick \'nik\ *n* **1** : a small groove, notch, or cut **2** : CHIP ⟨a *nick* in a cup⟩ **3** : the final critical moment ⟨in the *nick* of time⟩ [Middle English *nyke*]

²nick *vb* **1 a** : to make a nick in : NOTCH, CHIP **b** : to wound or cut slightly ⟨*nicked* himself shaving⟩ **2** : to make petty attacks : SNIPE

¹nick·el \'nik-əl\ *n* **1** : a silver-white hard malleable ductile metallic chemical element that is capable of a high polish, resistant to corrosion, and used chiefly in alloys and as a catalyst — see ELEMENT table **2 a** *also* **nick·le** : the United States 5-cent piece made of nickel and copper **b** : five cents [derived from German *Kupfernickel* "a compound of nickel and arsenic," probably from *Kupfer* "copper" + *Nickel* "goblin"; from the deceptive copper color of the ore]

²nick·el *vb* **-eled** *or* **-elled; -el·ing** *or* **-el·ling** \'nik-ling, -ə-ling\ : to plate with nickel

nic·kel·ic \nik-'el-ik\ *adj* : of, relating to, or containing nickel especially with a higher valence than two

nick·el·if·er·ous \ˌnik-ə-'lif-rəs, -ə-rəs\ *adj* : containing nickel

nick·el·ode·on \ˌnik-ə-'lōd-ē-ən\ *n* **1** : a theater presenting entertainment for an admission price of five cents **2** : JUKEBOX [probably from *nickel* + *-odeon* (as in archaic *melodeon* "music hall")]

nick·el·ous \'nik-ə-ləs\ *adj* : of, relating to, or containing nickel especially with a valence of two

nickel silver *n* : a silver-white alloy of copper, zinc, and nickel

nick·er \'nik-ər\ *vi* **nick·ered; nick·er·ing** \'nik-ring, -ə-ring\ : to neigh gently : WHINNY [perhaps alteration of *neigh*] — **nicker** *n*

nick·nack *variant of* KNICKKNACK

¹nick·name \'nik-ˌnām\ *n* **1** : a usually descriptive name given instead of or in addition to the one belonging to an individual **2** : a familiar form of a proper name [Middle English *nekename* "additional name," the phrase an *ekename* (from *eke* "also" + *name*) being understood as a *nekename*]

Word History *Nickname* was earliest used for a descriptive name given to a person, or even a place, in addition to the proper name. Today it can also mean "a shortened or familiar form of a proper name." In Middle English the word expressed the first of these senses very explicitly. The noun *eke,* meaning "an addition or extension," was combined with *name,* and an *ekename* was an additional name. By the 15th century an *ekename* began to be a *nekename,* in modern spelling a *nickname.* The Middle English noun *eke* is related to the verb *eke,* as in "eke out a living."

²nickname *vt* **1** : MISCALL **2** : to give a nickname to — **nick·nam·er** *n*

ni·co·ti·ana \nik-ˌō-shē-'an-ə, -'än-ə, -'ā-nə\ *n* : any of several tobaccos grown for their showy flowers [Jean *Nicot,* died 1600, French diplomat and scholar who introduced tobacco into France]

nic·o·tin·amide ad·e·nine di·nu·cle·o·tide \ˌnik-ə-'tē-nə-ˌmīd-ˌad-n-ˌēn-dī-'nü-klē-ə-ˌtīd, -'nyü-\ *n* : NAD

nicotinamide adenine dinucleotide phos·phate \-'fäs-ˌfāt\ *n* : NADP

nic·o·tine \'nik-ə-ˌtēn\ *n* : a poisonous alkaloid $C_{10}H_{14}N_2$ that is the chief active principle of tobacco and is used as an insecticide

nic·o·tin·ic \ˌnik-ə-'tē-nik, -'tin-ik\ *adj* : of or relating to nicotine

nicotinic acid *n* : NIACIN

nic·ti·tat·ing membrane \ˌnik-tə-ˌtāt-ing-\ *n* : a thin membrane found in many vertebrates at the inner angle or beneath the lower lid of the eye and capable of extending across the eyeball [derived from Latin *nictare* "to wink"]

niece \'nēs\ *n* : a daughter of one's brother, sister, brother-in-law, or sister-in-law [Medieval French, "granddaughter, niece," from Late Latin *neptia,* from Latin *neptis*]

nif·ty \'nif-tē\ *adj* **nif·ti·er; -est** : FINE, SWELL ⟨*nifty* new clothes⟩ [origin unknown] — **nifty** *n*

nig·gard \'nig-ərd\ *n* : a meanly covetous and stingy person [of Scandinavian origin] — **niggard** *adj*

nig·gard·ly \-lē\ *adj* **1** : grudgingly reluctant to spend or grant : STINGY **2** : provided in meanly limited supply : SCANTY — **nig·gard·li·ness** *n* — **niggardly** *adv*

nig·gling \'nig-ling, -ə-ling\ *adj* **1** : PETTY 2 **2** : demanding meticulous care [from earlier *niggle* "to carp," of unknown origin] — **niggling** *n* — **nig·gling·ly** \-lē\ *adv*

¹nigh \'nī\ *adv* **1** : near in place, time, or relationship **2** : NEARLY 1, ALMOST [Old English *nēah*]

²nigh *adj* **1** : not far : NEAR **2** : being on the left side ⟨the *nigh* horse⟩

³nigh *prep* : NEAR

⁴nigh *vb* : to draw near : APPROACH

night \'nīt\ *n* **1** : the time between dusk and dawn when there is no sunlight **2** : the beginning of darkness : NIGHTFALL **3** : the darkness of night [Old English *niht*]

night blindness *n* : subnormal vision in faint light (as at night) — **night–blind** \'nīt-ˌblīnd\ *adj*

night–blooming cereus *n* : any of several night-blooming cacti; *esp* : a slender sprawling or climbing cactus often grown for its large showy fragrant white flowers

night·cap \'nīt-ˌkap\ *n* **1** : a cloth cap worn with nightclothes **2** : a usually alcoholic drink taken at bedtime **3** : the final race or contest of a day's sports; *esp* : the final game of a baseball doubleheader

night·clothes \-ˌklōz, -ˌklōthz\ *n pl* : clothing worn in bed

night·club \-ˌkləb\ *n* : a place of entertainment open at night that usually serves food and liquor, has a floor show, and provides music and space for dancing

night crawler *n* : EARTHWORM; *esp* : a large earthworm found on the soil surface at night and often used as fish bait

night·dress \'nīt-ˌdres\ *n* **1** : NIGHTGOWN **2** : NIGHTCLOTHES

night·fall \-ˌfȯl\ *n* : the coming of night

night·gown \-ˌgau̇n\ *n* : a loose garment worn in bed

night·hawk \-ˌhȯk\ *n* **1** : any of several nightjars that resemble the related whip-poor-will **2** : NIGHT OWL

night·ie \ˈnīt-ē\ *n* : a nightgown for a woman or a child [*night*gown + *-ie*]

night·in·gale \ˈnīt-n-ˌgāl\ *n* **1** : an Old World thrush noted for the sweet usually nocturnal song of the male **2** : any of several other birds noted for their sweet song or for singing at night [Old English *nihtegale,* from *niht* "night" + *galan* "to sing"]

nightingale 1

night·jar \ˈnīt-ˌjär\ *n* : any of various related birds (as the whip-poor-wills and nighthawks) that are active at twilight or at night and catch insects in flight — called also *goatsucker* [from its harsh sound]

night latch *n* : a door lock having a spring bolt operated from the outside by a key and from the inside by a knob

night letter *n* : a telegram sent at night at a reduced rate for delivery the following morning — compare DAY LETTER

1**night·long** \ˈnīt-ˌlȯŋ\ *adj* : lasting the whole night

2**night·long** \-ˈlȯŋ\ *adv* : through the whole night

night·ly \ˈnīt-lē\ *adj* **1** : of or relating to the night or every night **2** : happening, done, or produced by night or every night — **nightly** *adv*

night·mare \-ˌmaər, -ˌmeər\ *n* **1** : a frightening dream **2** : an experience, situation, or object having the monstrous character of a nightmare or producing a feeling of anxiety or terror [Middle English "evil spirit thought to oppress people during sleep," from *night* + *mare* "incubus," from Old English] — **night·mar·ish** \-ish\ *adj*

night owl *n* : a person who habitually stays up late

night rider *n* : a member of a secret band who ride masked at night doing acts of violence for the purpose of punishing or terrorizing

night–robe \ˈnīt-ˌrōb\ *n* : NIGHTGOWN

nights \ˈnīts\ *adv* : in the nighttime repeatedly ⟨getting a degree by going to school *nights*⟩

night·shade \ˈnīt-ˌshād\ *n* **1** : any of a family of herbs, shrubs, and trees having clusters of usually white, yellow, or purple flowers, and fruits that are berries and including many poisonous forms (as belladonna) and important food plants (as the potato, tomato, and eggplant) **2** : BELLADONNA 1

night·shirt \-ˌshərt\ *n* : a nightgown resembling a shirt

night·stick \-ˌstik\ *n* : BILLY CLUB

night·tide \ˈnīt-ˌtīd\ *n* : NIGHTTIME

night·time \ˈnīt-ˌtīm\ *n* : the time from dusk to dawn

night·walk·er \-ˌwȯ-kər\ *n* : a person who roves about at night especially with criminal or immoral intent

ni·gri·tude \ˈnī-grə-ˌtüd, ˈnig-rə-, -ˌtyüd\ *n* : intense darkness : BLACKNESS [Latin *nigritudo,* from *niger* "black"]

ni·hil·ism \ˈnī-ə-ˌliz-əm, ˈnē-\ *n* : a doctrine or belief that conditions in the social organization are so bad as to make destruction desirable for its own sake independent of any constructive program [German *Nihilismus,* from Latin *nihil* "nothing"] — **ni·hil·ist** \-ə-ləst\ *n* — **nihilist** *or* **ni·hil·is·tic** \ˌnī-ə-ˈlis-tik, ˌnē-\ *adj*

ni·hil·i·ty \nī-ˈhil-ət-ē, nē-\ *n* : NOTHINGNESS

ni·hil ob·stat \ˌnī-ˌhil-ˈäb-ˌstät, ˌnē-ˌhil-, ˌnik-ˌil-, -ˌstat\ *n* : authoritative or official approval (as of a censor) [Latin, "nothing hinders"]

-nik \nik\ *n suffix* : one connected with or characterized by being ⟨beat*nik*⟩ [Yiddish, from Polish and Ukrainian]

nil \ˈnil\ *n* : nothing at all : ZERO [Latin, "nothing," contraction of *nihil*] — **nil** *adj*

Ni·lot·ic \nī-ˈlät-ik\ *adj* : of or relating to the Nile or the peoples of the Nile basin

nim·ble \ˈnim-bəl\ *adj* **nim·bler** \-bə-lər, -blər\; **-blest** \-bə-ləst, -bləst\ **1** : quick and light in motion : AGILE ⟨a *nimble* dancer⟩ **2** : quick in understanding and learning : CLEVER ⟨a *nimble* mind⟩ [Old English *numol* "holding much," from *niman* "to take"] — **nim·ble·ness** \-bəl-nəs\ *n* — **nim·bly** \-blē\ *adv*

nim·bo·stra·tus \ˌnim-bō-ˈstrāt-əs, -ˈstrat-\ *n* : a low dark gray cloud layer that usually produces precipitation

nim·bus \ˈnim-bəs\ *n, pl* **nim·bi** \-ˌbī, -ˌbē\ *or* **nim·bus·es** **1** : a luminous vapor, cloud, or atmosphere about a god or goddess when on earth **2** : an indication (as a circle) of radiant light or glory about the head of a drawn or sculptured divinity, saint, or sovereign **3** : a rain cloud [Latin, "rainstorm, cloud"]

nimbus 2

nim·rod \ˈnim-ˌräd\ *n* **1** : HUNTER 1a **2** *slang* : IDIOT, JERK [*Nimrod,* grandson of Noah]

nin·com·poop \ˈnin-kəm-ˌpüp, ˈniŋ-\ *n* : SIMPLETON, BOOBY [origin unknown]

nine \ˈnīn\ *n* **1** — see NUMBER table **2** : the ninth in a set or series **3** : something having nine units or members [Old English *nigon*] — **nine** *adj or pron*

nine days' wonder *n* : something that creates a short-lived sensation

nine·pin \ˈnīn-ˌpin\ *n* **1** : a pin used in ninepins **2** *pl* : a bowling game resembling tenpins played with nine pins in a diamond arrangement

nine·teen \nīn-ˈtēn, nīnt-, ˈnīn-, ˈnīnt-\ *n* — see NUMBER table [Old English *nigontēne*] — **nineteen** *adj or pron* — **nine·teenth** \-ˈtēnth, -ˈtēntth\ *adj or n*

nine·ty \ˈnīnt-ē\ *n, pl* **nineties** — see NUMBER table [Old English *nigontig*] — **ninety** *adj or pron* — **nine·ti·eth** \-ē-əth\ *adj or n*

nin·ja \ˈnin-jə, -ˌjä\ *n, pl* **ninja** *also* **ninjas** : a person trained in ancient Japanese martial arts and employed especially for espionage and assassinations [Japanese]

nin·ny \ˈnin-ē\ *n, pl* **ninnies** : FOOL 1, SIMPLETON [perhaps from *an innocent*]

nin·ny·ham·mer \ˈnin-ē-ˌham-ər\ *n* : NINNY

ninth \ˈnīnth, ˈnīntth\ *n, pl* **ninths** \ˈnīns, ˈnīnts, ˈnīnths, ˈnīntths\ **1** — see NUMBER table **2 a** : a musical interval embracing an octave and a second **b** : a chord containing a ninth — **ninth** *adj or adv*

ni·o·bi·um \nī-ˈō-bē-əm\ *n* : a lustrous platinum-gray ductile metallic chemical element that is used in alloys — see ELEMENT table [New Latin, from *Niobe,* a daughter of Tantalus; from its occurrence in ores with tantalum]

1**nip** \ˈnip\ *vb* **nipped; nip·ping** **1** : to catch hold of and squeeze tightly between two surfaces, edges, or points ⟨the dog *nipped* my ankle⟩ **2 a** : to sever by or as if by pinching sharply **b** : to destroy the growth, progress, maturing, or fulfillment of ⟨*nipped* the rumor in the bud⟩ **3** : to injure or make numb with cold : CHILL **4** : STEAL ⟨*nipped* the dessert⟩ **5** *chiefly British* : to move briskly, nimbly, or quickly [Middle English *nippen*]

2**nip** *n* **1** : something that nips: as **a** : a sharp stinging cold ⟨a *nip* in the air⟩ **b** : a biting or pungent flavor : TANG ⟨cheese with a *nip*⟩ **2** : the act of nipping : PINCH, BITE **3** : a small portion : BIT

3**nip** *n* : a small quantity of liquor ⟨takes a *nip* now and then⟩ [probably from *nipperkin,* a liquor container, of unknown origin]

4**nip** *vi* **nipped; nip·ping** : to take liquor in nips : TIPPLE

ni·pa \ˈnē-pə\ *n* : thatch made of leaves of a palm of southeastern Asia [probably from Italian, from Malay *nipah* "nipa palm"]

nip and tuck \ˌnip-ən-ˈtək\ *adj or adv* : so close that the lead or advantage shifts rapidly from one contestant to another ⟨a *nip and tuck* race⟩

nip·per \ˈnip-ər\ *n* **1** : a device (as pincers) for nipping — usually used in plural **2** : CHELA **3** *chiefly British* : CHILD; *esp* : a small boy

nip·ple \ˈnip-əl\ *n* **1** : the protuberance of a mammary gland upon which in the female the ducts open and from which milk is drawn **2** : something resembling a nipple; *esp* : the mouthpiece of a bottle from which an infant feeds [earlier *neble, nible,* probably from *neb, nib*]

Nip·pon·ese \ˌnip-ə-ˈnēz, -ˈnēs\ *adj* : JAPANESE 1 [*Nippon* "Japan"] — **Nipponese** *n*

\ə\ **abut**	\au̇\ **out**	\i\ **tip**	\ȯ\ **saw**	\u̇\ **foot**
\ər\ **further**	\ch\ **chin**	\ī\ **life**	\ȯi\ **coin**	\y\ **yet**
\a\ **mat**	\e\ **pet**	\j\ **job**	\th\ **thin**	\yü\ **few**
\ā\ **take**	\ē\ **easy**	\ŋ\ **sing**	\t͟h\ **this**	\yu̇\ **cure**
\ä\ **cot, cart**	\g\ **go**	\ō\ **bone**	\ü\ **food**	\zh\ **vision**

nip·py \ˈnip-ē\ *adj* **nip·pi·er; -est** **1** : brisk, quick, or nimble in movement **2** : CHILLY, CHILLING ⟨a *nippy* day⟩

nir·va·na \niər-ˈvän-ə, nər-\ *n, often cap* **1** : the final beatitude that transcends suffering, karma, and samsara and is sought in Hinduism and Buddhism through the extinction of desire and individual consciousness **2** : a place or state of oblivion to care, pain, or external reality [Sanskrit *nirvāna,* literally, "act of extinguishing"]

ni·sei \nē-ˈsā, ˈnē-\ *n, pl* **nisei** *also* **niseis** : a son or daughter of immigrant Japanese parents who is born and educated in America [Japanese, literally, "second generation"]

Nis·sen hut \ˌnis-n-\ *n* : a prefabricated shelter built of a semicircular arching roof of corrugated iron and a cement floor [Peter N. *Nissen,* died 1930, British mining engineer]

nit \ˈnit\ *n* **1** : the egg of a louse or other parasitic insect; *also* : the insect itself when young **2** : a minor shortcoming [Old English *hnitu*]

ni·ter *also* **ni·tre** \ˈnīt-ər\ *n* **1** : POTASSIUM NITRATE **2** : SODIUM NITRATE [Middle French *nitre* "sodium carbonate," from Latin *nitrum,* from Greek *nitron,* from Egyptian *ntry*]

nit·pick \ˈnit-ˌpik\ *vi* : to engage in nit-picking — **nit·pick·er** *n*

nit–pick·ing \ˈnit-ˌpik-ing\ *n* : minute and usually unjustified criticism

nitr- *or* **nitro-** *combining form* **1** : niter : nitrate **2 a** : nitrogen ⟨*nitr*ide⟩ **b** *usually* *nitro-* : containing the univalent group $-NO_2$ composed of one nitrogen and two oxygen atoms ⟨*nitro*benzene⟩

¹ni·trate \ˈnī-ˌtrāt, -trət\ *n* **1** : a salt or ester of nitric acid **2** : sodium nitrate or potassium nitrate used as a fertilizer

²ni·trate \-ˌtrāt\ *vt* : to treat or combine with nitric acid or a nitrate — **ni·tra·tion** \nī-ˈtrā-shən\ *n* — **ni·tra·tor** \ˈnī-ˌtrāt-ər\ *n*

ni·tric \ˈnī-trik\ *adj* : of, relating to, or containing nitrogen especially with a higher valence than in corresponding nitrous compounds

nitric acid *n* : a corrosive liquid acid HNO_3 used especially as an oxidizing agent, in nitrations, and in making fertilizers, explosives, and dyes

nitric oxide *n* : a colorless poisonous gas NO obtained by oxidation of nitrogen or ammonia

ni·tride \ˈnī-ˌtrīd\ *n* : a compound of nitrogen with a more electropositive element

ni·tri·fi·ca·tion \ˌnī-trə-fə-ˈkā-shən\ *n* : the process of combining or impregnating with nitrogen or a nitrogen compound; *esp* : the oxidation (as by bacteria) of ammonium salts to nitrites and the further oxidation of nitrites to nitrates

ni·tri·fi·er \ˈnī-trə-ˌfī-ər, -ˌfīr\ *n* : any of the nitrifying bacteria

ni·tri·fy·ing \-ˌfī-ing\ *adj* : active in nitrification

nitrifying bacteria *n pl* : bacteria of a family commonly found in the soil and obtaining energy through the process of nitrification

ni·trite \ˈnī-ˌtrīt\ *n* : a salt or ester of nitrous acid

ni·tro \ˈnī-trō\ *n* : any of various nitrated products; *esp* : NITROGLYCERIN

ni·tro·ben·zene \ˌnī-trō-ˈben-ˌzēn, -ˌben-ˈ\ *n* : a poisonous oily liquid compound made by nitration of benzene and used especially in chemical synthesis

ni·tro·cel·lu·lose \-ˈsel-yə-ˌlōs\ *n* : any of several compounds formed by the action of nitric acid on cellulose and used especially for making explosives, plastics, and varnishes

ni·tro·gen \ˈnī-trə-jən\ *n* : a colorless tasteless odorless chemical element that in the form of a diatomic gas constitutes 78 percent of the atmosphere and that is a constituent of all living tissues — see ELEMENT table [French *nitrogène,* from *nitre* "niter" + *-gène* "-gen"] — **ni·trog·e·nous** \nī-ˈträj-ə-nəs\ *adj*

nitrogen balance *n* : the ratio between nitrogen intake and nitrogen loss of the body or the soil

nitrogen cycle *n* : a continuous series of natural processes by which nitrogen passes successively from air to soil to organisms and back involving principally nitrogen fixation, nitrification, decay, and denitrification

nitrogen dioxide *n* : a toxic reddish brown gas NO_2 that is produced by combustion (as of gasoline) and is a component of smog

nitrogen fixation *n* : the conversion of atmospheric nitrogen into a combined form (as ammonia) chiefly by bacteria in soil and root nodules and its subsequent release in a form fit for plant use

nitrogen–fixing *adj* : capable of nitrogen fixation ⟨*nitrogen-fixing* bacteria⟩ — **nitrogen–fixer** *n*

nitrogen mustard *n* : any of various toxic blistering compounds that are analogous to mustard gas but with nitrogen replacing sulfur

nitrogen oxide *n* : any of various oxides of nitrogen: as **a** : NITRIC OXIDE **b** : NITROGEN DIOXIDE **c** : NITROUS OXIDE

ni·tro·glyc·er·in *or* **ni·tro·glyc·er·ine** \ˌnī-trō-ˈglis-rən, -ə-rən\ *n* : an oily explosive poisonous liquid obtained by nitrating glycerol and used chiefly in making dynamite and in medicine to expand blood vessels

ni·trous \ˈnī-trəs\ *adj* **1** : of, relating to, or containing niter **2** : of, relating to, or containing nitrogen especially with a lower valence than in corresponding nitric compounds

nitrous acid *n* : an unstable acid HNO_2 known only in solution or in the form of its salts

nitrous oxide *n* : a colorless gas N_2O that when inhaled produces loss of sensibility to pain preceded by exhilaration and sometimes laughter and is often used as an anesthetic in dentistry — called also *laughing gas*

nit·ty–grit·ty \ˈnit-ē-ˌgrit-ē, ˌnit-ē-ˈgrit-ē\ *n* : what is essential and basic : specific practical details [origin unknown] — **nitty–gritty** *adj*

nit·wit \ˈnit-ˌwit\ *n* : a scatterbrained or stupid person [probably from German dialect *nit* "not" + English *wit*]

¹nix \ˈniks\ *n* : a water sprite of Germanic folklore [German]

²nix *adv* : NO — used to express disagreement or the withholding of permission [German *nichts* "nothing"]

³nix *vt* : VETO, FORBID ⟨the court *nixed* the merger⟩

nix·ie \ˈnik-sē\ *n* : NIX [German *Nixe* "female nix"]

ni·zam \ni-ˈzäm, ˈnī-ˌzam, nī-ˈ\ *n* : one of a line of sovereigns of Hyderabad from 1713 to 1950 [Hindi & Urdu *nizām* "order, governor," derived from Arabic *niḍhām*] — **ni·zam·ate** \-ˌāt\ *n*

¹no \nō, ˈnō\ *adv* **1 a** : chiefly Scottish : NOT **b** — used to express the negative of an alternative choice or possibility ⟨shall we continue or *no*⟩ **2** : in no respect or degree — used in comparisons ⟨they are *no* better than they should be⟩ **3** : not so — used to express negation, dissent, denial, or refusal ⟨*no,* I'm not hungry⟩ **4** — used with a following adjective to imply a meaning expressed by the opposite positive statement ⟨*no* uncertain terms⟩ **5** — used to introduce a word that is stronger or more emphatic than the preceding one ⟨has the right, *no,* the duty to continue⟩ **6** — used as an interjection to express surprise, doubt, or incredulity ⟨*no* — you don't say⟩ [Old English *nā,* from *ne* "not" + *ā* "always"]

²no *adj* **1 a** : not any ⟨I've *no* money⟩ **b** : hardly any : very little ⟨finished in *no* time⟩ **2** : not a ⟨I'm *no* expert⟩

³no \ˈnō\ *n, pl* **noes** *or* **nos** \ˈnōz\ **1** : an act or instance of refusing or denying by the use of the word no **2 a** : a negative vote or decision **b** *pl* : persons voting in the negative

nob \ˈnäb\ *n, chiefly British* : one in a superior position in life [perhaps from earlier *nob* "head," probably from *knob*]

nob·by \ˈnäb-ē\ *adj* **nob·bi·er; -est** : CHIC, SMART

no·bel·i·um \nō-ˈbel-ē-əm\ *n* : a radioactive metallic element produced artificially — see ELEMENT table [Alfred B. *Nobel*]

No·bel Prize \nō-ˌbel-\ *n* : any of various annual prizes (as in peace, literature, medicine) established by the will of Alfred Nobel for the encouragement of persons who work for the interests of humanity

no·bil·i·ty \nō-ˈbil-ət-ē\ *n, pl* **-ties** **1** : the quality or state of being noble ⟨*nobility* of character⟩ **2** : noble rank ⟨confer *nobility* on a person⟩ **3** : a class or group of nobles ⟨the British *nobility*⟩ [Medieval French *nobilité,* from Latin *nobilitas,* from *nobilis* "noble"]

¹no·ble \ˈnō-bəl\ *adj* **no·bler** \-bə-lər, -blər\; **no·blest** \-bə-ləst, -bləst\ **1 a** : having outstanding qualities : ILLUSTRIOUS ⟨a *noble* warrior⟩ **b** : FAMOUS, NOTABLE ⟨*noble* deeds⟩ **2** : of high birth or exalted rank : ARISTOCRATIC **3** : having fine qualities ⟨a *noble* hawk⟩ **4** : grand or impressive especially in appearance : IMPOSING ⟨a *noble* edifice⟩ **5** : having or characterized by superiority of mind or character : LOFTY ⟨*noble* aims⟩ **6** : chemically inert or inactive especially toward oxygen ⟨a *noble* metal⟩ [Medieval French, from Latin *nobilis* "knowable, well known, noble," from *noscere* "to come to know"] ***synonyms*** see MORAL — **no·ble·ness** \-bəl-nəs\ *n* — **no·bly** \-blē\ *adv*

²noble *n* : a person of noble rank or birth

no·ble·man \ˈnō-bəl-mən\ *n* : a man of the nobility

no·blesse oblige \nō-ˌbles-ə-ˈblēzh\ *n* : the obligation to behave honorably that is associated with high rank or birth [French, literally, "nobility obligates"]

no·ble·wom·an \ˈnō-bəl-ˌwu̇m-ən\ *n* : a woman of the nobility

¹no·body \ˈnō-ˌbäd-ē, -bəd-ē\ *pron* : no person : not anybody

²nobody *n, pl* **no·bod·ies** : a person of no influence or importance

¹nock \ˈnäk\ *n* : a notch on the end of a bow or in an arrow in which the bowstring fits [Middle English *nocke* "notch on the end of a bow"]

²nock *vt* **1** : to make a nock in (a bow or an arrow) **2** : to fit (an arrow) against the bowstring for shooting

noc·tur·nal \näk-ˈtərn-l\ *adj* **1** : of, relating to, or occurring in the night ⟨a *nocturnal* journey⟩ **2** : active at night ⟨*nocturnal* insects⟩ [Late Latin *nocturnalis,* from Latin *nocturnus,* from *noct-, nox* "night"] — **noc·tur·nal·ly** \-l-ē\ *adv*

noc·turne \ˈnäk-ˌtərn\ *n* : a work of art dealing with night; *esp* : a dreamy pensive composition for the piano [French, "nocturnal," from Latin *nocturnus*]

noc·u·ous \ˈnäk-yə-wəs\ *adj* : likely to cause injury : HARMFUL [Latin *nocuus,* from *nocēre* "to harm"] — **noc·u·ous·ly** *adv*

¹nod \ˈnäd\ *vb* **nod·ded; nod·ding** **1** : to make a quick downward motion of the head (as in answering "yes" or in going to sleep); *also* : to cause (the head) to move in this way **2** : to move up and down ⟨the tulips *nodded* in the breeze⟩ **3** : to show by a nod of the head ⟨*nod* agreement⟩ **4** : to make a slip or an error in a moment of inattention [Middle English *nodden*] — **nod·der** *n*

²nod *n* : the action of nodding

nod·al \ˈnōd-l\ *adj* : relating to, being, or located at or near a node

nod·dle \ˈnäd-l\ *n* : HEAD 1 [Middle English *nodle* "back of the head or neck"]

nod·dy \ˈnäd-ē\ *n, pl* **noddies** **1** : a stupid person **2** : any of several stout-bodied terns of warm seas [probably from obsolete *noddypoll*]

node \ˈnōd\ *n* **1** : an entangling complication (as in a drama) **2 a** : a thickened or swollen enlargement (as of a rheumatic joint) **b** : a discrete mass of one kind of tissue enclosed in tissue of a different kind **3** : either of the two points where the orbit of a planet or comet intersects the ecliptic **4** : a point on a stem at which a leaf is attached **5** : a part of a vibrating body marked by absolute or relative freedom from vibratory motion [Latin *nodus* "knot, node"]

node of Ran·vier \-ˈrän-vē-ˌā\ : a small gap in the myelin sheath of a myelinated nerve fiber [Louis A. *Ranvier,* died 1922, French histologist]

nod·ule \ˈnäj-ül\ *n* : a small mass of rounded or irregular shape: as **a** : a small rounded lump of a mineral or mineral aggregate **b** : a swelling on the root of a plant of the legume family that contains nitrogen-fixing bacteria **c** : a small abnormal knobby bodily protuberance — **nod·u·lar** \ˈnäj-ə-lər\ *adj*

no·el \nō-ˈel\ *n* **1** : a Christmas carol **2** *cap* : the Christmas season [French *noël* "Christmas, carol," derived from Latin *natalis* "birthday," from *natalis* "natal"]

noes *plural of* NO

nog \ˈnäg\ *n* **1** : a strong ale formerly brewed in Norfolk, England **2** : EGGNOG [origin unknown]

nog·gin \ˈnäg-ən\ *n* **1** : a small mug or cup **2** : a small quantity (as a gill) of drink **3** : HEAD 1 [origin unknown]

¹no–good \ˌnō-ˌgu̇d\ *adj* : having no worth, use, or chance of success

²no–good \ˈnō-ˌgu̇d\ *n* : a no-good person or thing

no·how \ˈnō-ˌhau̇\ *adv* : in no manner or way ⟨*nohow* up to the job⟩

¹noise \ˈnȯiz\ *n* **1** : loud, confused, or senseless shouting or outcry **2 a** : SOUND; *esp* : one that lacks agreeable musical quality or is noticeably unpleasant **b** : an unwanted signal in an electronic communication system [Medieval French, "disturbance, noise," from Latin *nausea* "seasickness, nausea"] — **noise·less** \-ləs\ *adj* — **noise·less·ly** *adv* — **noise·less·ness** *n*

Word History The commotion and complaints so often associated with sufferers of seasickness have given us the word *noise,* a derivative of Latin *nausea,* which means "seasickness" or "nausea." The form *noise* developed in Medieval French, with the meanings "noisy strife," "quarrel," and "noise." Today in English *noise* may be used of sound in general, but it most often denotes disagreeable or undesirable sound.

²noise *vt* : to spread by rumor or report

noise·mak·er \-ˌmā-kər\ *n* : one that makes noise; *esp* : a device used to make noise at parties

noise pollution *n* : annoying or harmful noise (as of jet planes or automobiles) in an environment — called also *sound pollution*

noi·some \ˈnȯi-səm\ *adj* **1** : UNHEALTHY 1, NOXIOUS **2** : offensive especially to the sense of smell [Middle English *noysome,* from *noy* "annoyance," from Medieval French *anui,* from *anuier* "to annoy"] — **noi·some·ly** *adv* — **noi·some·ness** *n*

noisy \ˈnȯi-zē\ *adj* **nois·i·er; -est** **1** : making noise **2** : full of or characterized by noise — **nois·i·ly** \-zə-lē\ *adv* — **nois·i·ness** \-zē-nəs\ *n*

nol·le pro·se·qui \ˌnäl-ē-ˈpräs-ə-ˌkwī\ *n* : an entry on the record of a legal action that the prosecutor or plaintiff will proceed no further in an action or suit [Latin, "to be unwilling to pursue"]

no·lo con·ten·de·re \ˌnō-lō-kən-ˈten-də-rē\ *n* : a plea by the defendant in a criminal prosecution that without admitting guilt subjects him or her to conviction but does not preclude denial of the charges in another proceeding [Latin, "I do not wish to contend"]

nol–pros \ˈnäl-ˈpräs\ *vt* **nol–prossed; nol–pros·sing** : to discontinue by entering a nolle prosequi

no·mad \ˈnō-ˌmad\ *n* **1** : a member of a people that have no fixed residence but wander from place to place **2** : an individual who roams about aimlessly [Latin *nomad-, nomas* "member of a wandering pastoral people," from Greek, from *nemein* "to pasture"] — **no·mad·ic** \nō-ˈmad-ik\ *adj* — **no·mad·ism** \ˈnō-ˌmad-ˌiz-əm\ *n*

no–man's–land \ˈnō-ˌmanz-ˌland\ *n* **1** : an area of unowned, unclaimed, or uninhabited land **2** : an unoccupied area between opposing troops **3** : an area of indefinite or uncertain character

nom de guerre \ˌnäm-di-ˈgeər\ *n, pl* **noms de guerre** \ˌnäm-di-, ˌnämz-di-\ : PSEUDONYM [French, literally, "war name"]

nom de plume \ˌnäm-di-ˈplüm\ *n, pl* **noms de plume** \ˌnäm-di-, ˌnämz-di-\ : PEN NAME [French *nom* "name" + *de* "of" + *plume* "pen"]

no·men \ˈnō-mən\ *n, pl* **no·mi·na** \ˈnäm-ə-nə, ˈnō-mə-\ : the second of the usual three names of an ancient Roman [Latin, literally, "name"]

no·men·cla·ture \ˈnō-mən-ˌklā-chər\ *n* **1** : NAME 1, DESIGNATION **2** : a system of terms used in a particular science, discipline, or art; *esp* : the standardized New Latin names used in biology for kinds and groups of kinds of plants and animals — compare BINOMIAL NOMENCLATURE [Latin *nomenclatura* "assigning of names, list of names," from *nomen* "name" + *calare* "to call"] — **no·men·cla·tur·al** \ˌnō-mən-ˈklāch-rəl, -ə-rəl\ *adj*

¹nom·i·nal \ˈnäm-ən-l, ˈnäm-nəl\ *adj* **1** : of, relating to, or being a noun or a word or expression taking a noun construction **2** : of, relating to, or being a name **3 a** : existing or being something in name or form only ⟨the *nominal* head of the party⟩ **b** : very small : TRIFLING ⟨a *nominal* price⟩ [Latin *nominalis* "of a name," from Latin *nomen* "name"] — **nom·i·nal·ly** \-ē\ *adv*

²nominal *n* : a word or word group functioning as a noun

nom·i·nate \ˈnäm-ə-ˌnāt\ *vt* : to choose as a candidate for election, appointment, or honor; *esp* : to propose for office ⟨was *nominated* for president⟩ [Latin *nominare* "to name," from *nomen* "name"] — **nom·i·na·tor** \-ˌnāt-ər\ *n*

nom·i·na·tion \ˌnäm-ə-ˈnā-shən\ *n* **1** : the act, process, or an instance of nominating **2** : the state of being nominated ⟨three names have been placed in *nomination*⟩

nom·i·na·tive \ˈnäm-nət-iv, -ə-nət-\ *adj* : relating to or being a grammatical case marking typically the subject of a verb — **nominative** *n*

nom·i·nee \ˌnäm-ə-ˈnē\ *n* : a person who has been nominated

non- *before syllables with primary stress* nän, ˈnän *also* ˌnən, ˈnən; *before syllables with secondary or weak stress* ˌnän *also* ˌnən\ *prefix* : not : reverse of : absence of ⟨noncalcareous⟩ [Medieval French, from Latin *non* "not"]

nonabrasive	**nonacceptance**	**nonacting**
nonabsorbable	**nonaccountable**	**nonaction**
nonabsorbent	**nonaccredited**	**nonactivated**
nonabsorptive	**nonacid**	**nonadaptive**
nonabstract	**nonacidic**	**nonaddict**
nonacademic	**nonacquisitive**	**nonaddictive**

\ə\ **abut**	\au̇\ **out**	\i\ **tip**	\ȯ\ **saw**	\u̇\ **foot**
\ər\ **further**	\ch\ **chin**	\ī\ **life**	\ȯi\ **coin**	\y\ **yet**
\a\ **mat**	\e\ **pet**	\j\ **job**	\th\ **thin**	\yü\ **few**
\ā\ **take**	\ē\ **easy**	\ng\ **sing**	\t͟h\ **this**	\yu̇\ **cure**
\ä\ **cot, cart**	\g\ **go**	\ō\ **bone**	\ü\ **food**	\zh\ **vision**

nonadhesive
nonadjacent
nonadmission
nonaffiliated
nonaffluent
nonaggression
nonaggressive
nonagreement
nonagricultural
nonalcoholic
nonallergenic
nonallergic
nonalphabetic
nonanalytic
nonanthropological
nonantigenic
nonappearance
nonaquatic
nonaqueous
nonarbitrariness
nonarbitrary
nonaromatic
nonascetic
nonaspirin
nonassertive
nonassociated
nonathlete
nonathletic
nonattendance
nonauditory
nonauthoritarian
nonautomated
nonautomatic
nonautomotive
nonbacterial
nonbasic
nonbearing
nonbeing
nonbeliever
nonbelligerency
nonbelligerent
nonbetting
nonbinding
nonbiodegradable
nonbiological
nonbiologist
nonbiting
nonbonded
nonbreakable
nonbreeding
nonburnable
noncaking
noncancerous
noncanonical
noncarrier
noncash
non–Catholic
noncellular
noncertified
nonchauvinist
non–Christian
nonchurchgoer
noncitizen
nonclassical
nonclassified
nonclerical
nonclinical
noncoercive
noncognitive
noncoherent
noncollinear
noncombat
noncombative
noncombustible
noncommercial
noncommitment
noncommitted
noncommunicating
noncommunication
noncommunicative
noncommunist
noncommutative
noncommutativity
noncomparable
noncompatible
noncompetition
noncompetitive
noncompetitor
noncomplementary
noncompliance
noncompliant
noncomplying
noncompound
noncomprehension
noncompressible
nonconclusion
nonconcurrent
noncondensable
nonconditioned
nonconducting
nonconduction
nonconductive
nonconference
nonconfidential
nonconflicting
nonconfrontation
nonconfrontational
noncongruent
nonconjugated
nonconscious
nonconsecutive
nonconservation
nonconservative
nonconsolidated
nonconstitutional
nonconstruction
nonconstructive
nonconsumer
nonconsuming
noncontact
noncontagious
noncontemporary
noncontiguous
noncontinuous
noncontradiction
noncontradictory
noncontributory
noncontrollable
noncontrolled
noncontrolling
noncontroversial
nonconventional
nonconvertible
noncoplanar
noncorporate
noncorrodible
noncorroding
noncorrosive
noncoverage
noncreative
noncreativity
noncriminal
noncrisis
noncritical
noncrystalline
noncultivated
noncultivation
noncumulative
noncurrent
noncyclic
noncyclical
nondeceptive
nondecreasing
nondeferrable
nondegenerate
nondegradable
nondelinquent
nondelivery
nondemocratic
nondenominational
nondepartmental
nondependent
nonderivative
nondescriptive
nondetachable
nondevelopment
nondiabetic
nondirected
nondirectional
nondisclosure
nondiscrimination
nondiscriminatory
nondiscursive
nondisruptive
nondiversified
nondoctrinaire
nondocumentary
nondogmatic
nondollar
nondomestic
nondominant
nondramatic
nondurable
nonecclesiastical
nonedible
noneducational
noneffective
nonelastic
nonelected
nonelection
nonelective
nonelectric
nonelectrical
nonelectronic
nonelite
nonemergency
nonemotional
nonempirical
nonempty
nonencapsulated
nonending
nonenforcement
nonentanglement
nonequilibrium
nonequivalence
nonequivalent
nonessential
nonesterified
nonethical
nonethnic
nonexclusive
nonexempt
nonexpendable
nonexperimental
nonexpert
nonexplosive
nonexposed
nonextant
nonfact
nonfactor
nonfactual
nonfaculty
nonfading
nonfamily
nonfan
nonfarm
nonfarmer
nonfatal
nonfattening
nonfatty
nonfederal
nonfederated
nonfilamentous
nonfilterable
nonfinancial
nonfissionable
nonfluorescent
nonflying
nonfood
nonforfeiture
nonfossil
nonfraternization
nonfreezing
nonfrozen
nonfulfillment
nonfunctional
nonfunctioning
nongaseous
nongenetic
nonghetto
nonglamorous
nonglare
nongovernment
nongovernmental
nongraded
nongraduate
nongrammatical
nongranular
nongreasy
nongregarious
nongrowing
nongrowth
nonhandicapped
nonhardy
nonharmonic
nonhazardous
nonhereditary
nonhistorical
nonhomogeneous
nonhormonal
nonhostile
nonhuman
nonideal
nonidentical
nonidentity
nonideological
nonimmigrant
nonimmune
nonincreasing
nonindustrial
nonindustrialized
nonindustry
noninfected
noninfectious
noninfective
noninfested
noninflammable
noninflammatory
noninflationary
noninflectional
noninfluence
noninformation
noninjury
noninsecticidal
noninstitutional
noninstitutionalized
noninstructional
nonintegral
nonintegrated
nonintellectual
noninterchangeable
noninterference
nonintersecting
nonintoxicant
nonintoxicating
nonirradiated
nonirrigated
nonirritant
nonirritating
non–Jew
non–Jewish
nonleaded
nonlegal
nonlegume
nonleguminous
nonlethal
nonlexical
nonlife
nonlinguistic
nonliquid
nonliteral
nonliterary
nonliving
nonlocal
nonlogical
nonluminous
nonmagnetic
nonmalignant
nonmalleable
nonmammalian
nonmanagement
nonmanagerial
nonmanual
nonmanufacturing
nonmarital
nonmarket
nonmaterial
nonmaterialistic
nonmathematical
nonmathematician
nonmeaningful
nonmeasurable
nonmeat
nonmechanical
nonmechanistic
nonmedical
nonmember
nonmembership
nonmetaphorical
nonmetric
nonmetrical
nonmetropolitan
nonmicrobial
nonmigrant
nonmigratory
nonmilitant
nonmilitary
nonmimetic
nonmolecular
nonmoney
nonmotile
nonmotorized
nonmoving
nonmusical
nonmutant
nonnational
nonnative
nonnatural
nonnecessity
nonnegotiable
nonnitrogenous
nonnormative
nonnumerical
nonnutritious
nonnutritive
nonobscene
nonobservance
nonobservant
nonobvious
nonoccurrence
nonofficial
nonoily
nonoperating
nonoperational
nonoperative
nonorganic
nonorthodox
nonoverlapping
nonpaid
nonparallel
nonparasitic
nonparticipant
nonparticipating
nonparticipation
nonparticipatory
nonparty
nonpaying
nonpayment
nonperformance
nonperformer
nonperishable
nonpermissive
nonpersonal
nonphonemic
nonphonetic
nonphosphate
nonphysical
nonplastic
nonplay
nonplaying
nonpoisonous
nonpolarizable
nonpolitical
nonpolitically
nonpolluting
nonpoor
nonporous
nonpossession
nonpractical
nonpracticing
nonpregnant
nonprint
nonproducing
nonprofessional
nonprofessionally
nonprogressive
nonproprietary
nonpublic
nonpunitive
nonracial
nonracially
nonradioactive
nonrandom
nonrandomness
nonrated
nonrational
nonreactive
nonreactor
nonrealistic
nonreciprocal
nonrecognition
nonrecurrent
nonrecurring
nonrecyclable
nonreducing
nonredundant
nonrefillable
nonreflecting
nonregulated
nonregulation
nonrelative
nonrelevant
nonreligious
nonrenewal
nonrepayable
nonrepresentative
nonreproductive
nonresidential
nonresonant
nonrespondent
nonresponse
nonresponsive
nonrestricted
nonretractile
nonretroactive
nonreusable
nonreversible
nonrioter
nonrioting
nonrotating
nonroutine
nonruling
nonruminant
nonsalable

nonsaline
nonscientific
nonscientist
nonseasonal
nonsecretory
nonsecure
nonsegregated
nonsegregation
nonselected
nonselective
non–self–governing
nonsensitive
nonsensuous
nonsequential
nonsequentially
nonserious
nonsexist
nonsexual
nonshrink
nonshrinkable
nonsignificance
nonsignificant
nonsinkable
nonskater
nonskier
nonsmoker
nonsmoking
nonsolar
nonspatial
nonspeaker
nonspeaking
nonspecialist
nonspecific
nonspecifically
nonspectacular
nonspeculative
nonspherical
nonstationary
nonstatistical
nonsteady
nonstrategic
nonstructural
nonstructured
nonstudent
nonsubjective
nonsubsidized
nonsuccess
nonsugar
nonsurgical
nonswimmer
nonsymbolic
nonsymmetric
nonsymmetrical
nonsynchronous
nonsystematic
nonsystemic
nontaxable
nontechnical
nontemporal
nontenured
nontheatrical
nontheist
nontheistic
nontheoretical
nontherapeutic
nontidal
nontobacco
nontotalitarian
nontoxic
nontraditional
nontransferable
nontreatment
nontrivial
nontropical
nonturbulent
nontypical
nonunanimous
nonuniform
nonuniformity
nonunionized
nonurban
nonurgent
nonutilitarian
nonvalid
nonvalidity
nonvegetarian
nonvenomous
nonviable
nonviewer
nonviral
nonviscous
nonvisual
nonvocal
nonvocational
nonvoluntary
nonvoter
nonvoting
nonwinning
nonwoody
nonwork
nonworker
nonworking
nonyellowing

non·ad·di·tive \ˈnän-ˈad-ət-iv\ *adj* : not having a numerical value equal to the sum of values for the component parts

non·age \ˈnän-ij, ˈnō-nij\ *n* **1** : MINORITY 1 **2 a** : a period of youth **b** : lack of maturity [Medieval French, from *non-* + *age* "age"]

no·na·ge·nar·i·an \ˌnō-nə-jə-ˈner-ē-ən, ˌnän-ə-\ *n* : a person who is 90 or more but less than 100 years old [Latin *nonagenarius* "containing ninety," derived from *nonaginta* "ninety"] — **nonagenarian** *adj*

no·na·gon \ˈnō-nə-ˌgän\ *n* : a polygon of nine angles and nine sides [Latin *nonus* "ninth" + English *-gon*]

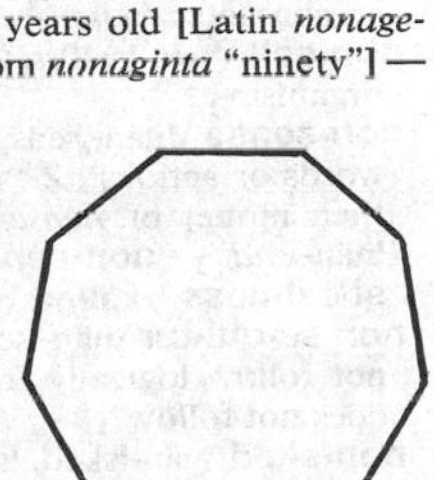
nonagon

non·aligned \ˌnän-l-ˈīnd\ *adj* : not allied with other nations

non·al·le·lic \ˌnän-ə-ˈlē-lik, -ˈlel-ik\ *adj* : not behaving as alleles toward one another ⟨*nonallelic* genes⟩

non·bond·ing \-ˈbän-ding\ *adj* : neither promoting nor inhibiting bonding between atoms ⟨a *nonbonding* electron⟩

non·cal·car·e·ous \ˌnän-kal-ˈkar-ē-əs, -ˈker-\ *adj* : lacking or deficient in lime ⟨*noncalcareous* soils⟩

non·ca·lor·ic \ˌnän-kə-ˈlȯr-ik, -ˈlōr-\ *adj* : free from or very low in calories ⟨a *noncaloric* sweetener⟩

[1]**nonce** \ˈnäns\ *n* : the one, particular, or present occasion, purpose, or use ⟨for the *nonce*⟩ [Middle English *nanes,* from incorrect division of *then anes* in such phrases as *to then anes* "for the one purpose"]

[2]**nonce** *adj* : occurring, used, or made only once or for a special occasion ⟨a *nonce* word⟩

non·cha·lant \ˌnän-shə-ˈlänt, ˈnän-shə-ˌ\ *adj* : giving an effect of easy unconcern or indifference ⟨face a crowd with *nonchalant* ease⟩ [French, from Medieval French *nonchaloir* "to disregard," from *non-* + *chaloir* "to concern," from Latin *calēre* "to be warm"] — **non·cha·lance** \-ˈläns, -ˌläns\ *n* — **non·cha·lant·ly** *adv*

non·cod·ing \ˈnän-ˈkōd-ing\ *adj* : not specifying the genetic code ⟨a *noncoding* DNA sequence⟩

non·com \ˈnän-ˌkäm\ *n* : NONCOMMISSIONED OFFICER

non·com·bat·ant \ˌnän-kəm-ˈbat-nt; nän-ˈkäm-bət-ənt, ˈnän-\ *n* : a member (as a chaplain) of the armed forces whose duties exclude fighting; *also* : CIVILIAN — **noncombatant** *adj*

non·com·e·do·gen·ic \-ˌkäm-əd-ō-ˈjen-ik\ *adj* : not tending to clog pores ⟨a *noncomedogenic* moisturizing lotion⟩

non·com·mis·sioned officer \ˌnän-kə-ˌmish-ənd-\ *n* : a subordinate officer (as a sergeant) in the armed forces appointed from enlisted personnel

non·com·mit·tal \ˌnän-kə-ˈmit-l\ *adj* : not telling or showing one's thoughts or decisions ⟨a *noncommittal* answer⟩ — **non·com·mit·tal·ly** \-l-ē\ *adv*

non com·pos men·tis \ˌnän-ˌkäm-pə-ˈsment-əs, ˌnōn-\ *adj* : not of sound mind [Latin, literally, "not having control of one's mind"]

non·con·duc·tor \ˌnän-kən-ˈdək-tər\ *n* : a substance that conducts heat, electricity, or sound only in very small degree

non·con·fi·dence \nän-ˈkän-fəd-əns, -fə-ˌdens\ *n* : lack of confidence especially of a parliamentary body in a government ⟨a vote of *nonconfidence*⟩

non·con·form·ist \ˌnän-kən-ˈfȯr-məst\ *n* **1** *often cap* : a person who does not conform to an established church and especially the Church of England **2** : a person who does not conform to a generally accepted pattern of thought or action — **nonconformist** *adj, often cap*

non·con·for·mi·ty \-ˈfȯr-mət-ē\ *n* **1 a** : failure or refusal to conform to an established church **b** *often cap* : the movement or principles of English Protestant dissent **c** *often cap* : the body of English Nonconformists **2** : refusal to conform to conventional rules or customs

non·co·op·er·a·tion \ˌnän-kō-ˌäp-ə-ˈrā-shən\ *n* : failure or refusal to cooperate especially with the government of a country — **non·co·op·er·a·tive** \-ˈäp-rət-iv, -ə-rət-, -ə-ˌrāt-\ *adj*

non·cus·to·di·al \-ˌkə-ˈstōd-ē-əl\ *adj* : relating to or being a parent who does not have sole custody of a child or who has custody a smaller portion of the time

non·dairy \ˈnän-ˈder-ē\ *adj* : containing no milk or milk products ⟨*nondairy* whipped topping⟩

non·de·script \ˌnän-di-ˈskript\ *adj* : belonging or seeming to belong to no particular class or kind [*non-* + Latin *descriptus,* past participle of *describere* "to describe"] — **nondescript** *n*

non·de·struc·tive \-di-ˈstrək-tiv\ *adj* : not destructive; *esp* : not causing destruction of material being investigated or treated ⟨*nondestructive* testing of metal⟩ — **non·de·struc·tive·ly** *adv* — **non·de·struc·tive·ness** *n*

non·dis·junc·tion \ˌnän-dis-ˈjəng-shən, -ˈjəngk-\ *n* : the failure of two homologous chromosomes to separate during meiosis so that one daughter cell has both and the other neither of the chromosomes — **non·dis·junc·tion·al** \-shnəl, -shən-l\ *adj*

non·di·vid·ing \-də-ˈvīd-ing\ *adj* : not undergoing cell division

[1]**none** \ˈnən\ *pron, sing or pl in construction* **1** : not any ⟨*none* of them went⟩ ⟨*none* of it is needed⟩ **2** : not one ⟨*none* of the family⟩ **3** : not any such thing or person ⟨half a loaf is better than *none*⟩ [Old English *nān,* from *ne* "not" + *ān* "one"]

[2]**none** *adj, archaic* : not any : NO

[3]**none** *adv* **1** : by no means : not at all ⟨*none* too soon⟩ **2** : in no way : to no extent ⟨*none* the worse for wear⟩

[4]**none** \ˈnōn\ *n, often cap* : the fifth of the canonical hours [Late Latin *nona,* from Latin, "9th hour of the day (from sunrise)," from *nonus* "ninth"]

non·elec·tro·lyte \ˌnän-ə-ˈlek-trə-ˌlīt\ *n* : a substance (as sugar) that does not ionize in water and is therefore a poor conductor of electricity

non·en·ti·ty \nä-ˈnent-ət-ē, -ˈnen-ət-\ *n* **1** : something that does not exist or exists only in the imagination **2** : one of no consequence or significance

nones \ˈnōnz\ *n pl* : the 9th day before the ides according to ancient Roman reckoning [Latin *nonae,* from *nonus* "ninth"]

none·such \ˈnən-ˌsəch\ *or* **non·such** \ˈnən-ˌsəch *also* ˈnän-\ *n* : a person or thing without an equal — **nonesuch** *adj*

none·the·less \ˌnən-t͟hə-ˈles\ *adv* : HOWEVER 2, NEVERTHELESS

non–Eu·clid·e·an \ˌnän-yu̇-ˈklid-ē-ən\ *adj* : not assuming or in accordance with all the postulates of Euclid's *Elements* ⟨*non-Euclidean* geometry⟩

non·ex·is·tence \-ig-ˈzis-təns\ *n* : absence of existence — **non·ex·is·tent** \-tənt\ *adj*
non·fat \ˈnän-ˈfat\ *adj* : lacking fat or solids of fat : having much or all of the fat removed ⟨*nonfat* milk⟩
non·fea·sance \nän-ˈfēz-ns, ˈnän-\ *n* : omission to do especially what ought to be done [*non-* + obsolete *feasance* "performance, doing," from Middle French *faisance* "act," from *faire* "to do," from Latin *facere*]
non·fer·rous \-ˈfer-əs\ *adj* **1** : not containing, including, or relating to iron **2** : of or relating to metals other than iron
non·fic·tion \ˈnän-ˈfik-shən\ *n* : literature or cinema that is not fictional — **non·fic·tion·al** \nän-ˈfik-shnəl, ˈnän-, -shən-l\ *adj*
non·flam·ma·ble \-ˈflam-ə-bəl\ *adj* : not flammable; *esp* : not easily ignited and not burning rapidly if ignited — **non·flam·ma·bil·i·ty** \-ˌflam-ə-ˈbil-ət-ē\ *n*
non·flow·er·ing \nän-ˈflau̇-ring, ˈnän-, -ə-ring\ *adj* : producing no flowers; *esp* : lacking a flowering stage in the life cycle
non·green \ˈnän-ˈgrēn\ *adj* : lacking chlorophyll ⟨*nongreen* plants⟩
non·ho·mol·o·gous \ˌnän-hō-ˈmäl-ə-gəs, -hə-\ *adj* : having different genes and not pairing during meiosis ⟨*nonhomologous* chromosomes⟩
no·nil·lion \nō-ˈnil-yən\ *n* — see NUMBER table [French, from Latin *nonus* "ninth" + French *-illion* (as in *million*)]
non·in·ter·ven·tion \ˌnän-ˌint-ər-ˈven-chən\ *n* : the state or habit of not intervening — **non·in·ter·ven·tion·ist** \-ˈvench-nəst, -ə-nəst\ *n or adj*
non·in·va·sive \-in-ˈvā-siv, -ziv\ *adj* : not tending to spread; *esp* : not tending to infiltrate and destroy healthy tissue ⟨*noninvasive* cancer of the bladder⟩ — **non·in·va·sive·ly** *adv*
non·in·volve·ment \-in-ˈvälv-mənt, -ˈvȯlv-\ *n* : absence of involvement or emotional attachment — **non·in·volved** \-ˈvälvd, -ˈvȯlvd\ *adj*
non·ju·ror \nän-ˈju̇r-ər, ˈnän-\ *n* : a person refusing to take an oath (as of allegiance) — **non·jur·ing** \-ˈju̇r-ing\ *adj*
non·lin·e·ar \nän-ˈlin-ē-ər, ˈnän-\ *adj* : not linear; *esp* : not representing or being a curve that can be graphed as a straight line ⟨*nonlinear* equations⟩
non·met·al \-ˈmet-l\ *n* : a chemical element (as carbon or nitrogen) that lacks metallic properties
non·me·tal·lic \ˌnän-mə-ˈtal-ik\ *adj* **1** : not metallic **2** : of, relating to, or being a nonmetal
non·neg·a·tive \nän-ˈneg-ət-iv, ˈnän-\ *adj* : being either positive or zero ⟨*nonnegative* numbers⟩
non·nu·cle·ar \ˈnän-ˈnü-klē-ər, -ˈnyü-\ *adj* **1** : not nuclear ⟨*nonnuclear* weapons⟩ **2** : not having nuclear weapons ⟨*nonnuclear* countries⟩
no–no \ˈnō-ˌnō\ *n, pl* **no–no's** *or* **no–nos** : something unacceptable or forbidden
non·ob·jec·tive \ˌnän-əb-ˈjek-tiv\ *adj* : representing or intended to represent no natural or actual object, figure, or scene ⟨*nonobjective* art⟩
no–nonsense *adj* : putting up with or including no nonsense : SERIOUS ⟨a *no-nonsense* manager⟩
[1]**non·pa·reil** \ˌnän-pə-ˈrel\ *adj* : having no equal [Medieval French *nompareil,* from *non-* + *pareil* "equal," from Latin *par*]
[2]**nonpareil** *n* **1** : one of unequaled excellence : PARAGON **2 a** : a small flat chocolate disk covered with white sugar pellets **b** : small sugar pellets of various colors
non·par·ti·san \nän-ˈpärt-ə-zən, ˈnän-\ *adj* : not partisan; *esp* : free from party affiliation, bias, or designation ⟨*nonpartisan* ballot⟩ ⟨a *nonpartisan* board⟩ — **non·par·ti·san·ship** \-ˌship\ *n*
non·pas·ser·ine \nän-ˈpas-ə-ˌrīn, ˈnän-\ *adj* : not passerine; *esp* : of, relating to, or being any of various birds (as pigeons, woodpeckers, kingfishers, and hummingbirds) that inhabit or frequent trees but are not passerines
non·patho·gen·ic \-ˌpath-ə-ˈjen-ik\ *adj* : not capable of inducing disease
non·per·sis·tent \ˌnän-pər-ˈsis-tənt, -ˈzis-\ *adj* : not persistent; *esp* : decomposed rapidly by environmental action ⟨*nonpersistent* insecticides⟩
[1]**non·plus** \nän-ˈpləs, ˈnän-\ *n* : a state of bafflement or perplexity : QUANDARY [Latin *non plus* "no more"]
[2]**nonplus** *vt* **non·plussed** *also* **non·plused; non·plus·sing** *also* **non·plus·ing** : to cause to be at a loss as to what to say, think, or do : PERPLEX
nonpoint \ˈnän-ˈpȯint\ *adj* : being a source of pollution (as runoff from farmland) that does not originate from a single point (as a pipe); *also* : being pollution or a pollutant that does not arise from a single identifiable source
non·po·lar \nän-ˈpō-lər, ˈnän-\ *adj* **1** : lacking electrical poles ⟨a *nonpolar* molecule⟩ **2** : of or characterized by covalence ⟨a *nonpolar* liquid⟩
non·pre·scrip·tion \-pri-ˈskrip-shən\ *adj* : capable of being bought without a doctor's prescription ⟨a *nonprescription* pain reliever⟩
non·pro·duc·tive \ˌnän-prə-ˈdək-tiv\ *adj* **1** : failing to produce or yield : UNPRODUCTIVE ⟨*nonproductive* land⟩ **2** : not directly concerned with production ⟨*nonproductive* labor⟩ — **non·pro·duc·tive·ness** *n*
non·prof·it \nän-ˈpräf-ət, ˈnän-\ *adj* : not conducted or maintained for the purpose of profit ⟨a *nonprofit* organization⟩
non·pro·tein \-ˈprō-ˌtēn, -ˈprōt-ē-ən\ *adj* : not being or derived from protein ⟨the *nonprotein* part of an enzyme⟩ ⟨*nonprotein* nitrogen⟩
non·re·new·able \-ri-ˈnü-ə-bəl, -ˈnyü-\ *adj* : not renewable; *esp* : not restored or replaced by natural processes ⟨*nonrenewable* resources such as fossil fuels and mineral ores⟩
non·rep·re·sen·ta·tion·al \ˌnän-ˌrep-ri-ˌzən-ˈtā-shnəl, -shən-l\ *adj* : NONOBJECTIVE
non·res·i·dent \nän-ˈrez-əd-ənt, ˈnän-, -ˈrez-dənt, -ˈrez-ə-ˌdent\ *adj* : not living in a specified or implied place — **non·res·i·dence** \-ˈrez-əd-əns, -ˈrez-dəns, -ˈrez-ə-ˌdens\ *n* — **nonresident** *n*
non·re·sis·tance \ˌnän-ri-ˈzis-təns\ *n* : the principles or practice of passive submission to authority even when unjust or oppressive; *also* : the principle or practice of not resisting violence by force
non·re·sis·tant \-tənt\ *adj* : not resistant; *esp* : susceptible to the effects of a harmful agent (as an antibiotic or insecticide) ⟨*nonresistant* bacteria⟩
non·re·stric·tive \ˌnän-ri-ˈstrik-tiv\ *adj* **1** : not restrictive **2** : not limiting the reference of a modified word or phrase ⟨a *nonrestrictive* clause⟩
non·rig·id \nän-ˈrij-əd, ˈnän-\ *adj* : maintaining form by pressure of contained gas : not rigid ⟨a *nonrigid* airship⟩
non·sched·uled \-ˈskej-üld, -əld\ *adj* : licensed to carry passengers or freight by air without a regular schedule ⟨*nonscheduled* airline⟩
non·sec·tar·i·an \ˌnän-sek-ˈter-ē-ən\ *adj* : not having a sectarian character ⟨a *nonsectarian* school⟩
non·self \ˈnän-ˈself\ *n* : material that is foreign to the body of an organism
non·sense \ˈnän-ˌsens, ˈnän-səns\ *n* **1** : foolish or meaningless words or actions **2** : things of no importance or value ⟨spent their money on *nonsense*⟩ — **non·sen·si·cal** \nän-ˈsen-si-kəl, ˈnän-\ *adj* — **non·sen·si·cal·ly** \-kə-lē, -klē\ *adv* — **non·sen·si·cal·ness** \-kəl-nəs\ *n*
non se·qui·tur \nän-ˈsek-wət-ər, ˈnän-\ *n* : a statement that does not follow logically from anything previously said [Latin, "it does not follow"]
non·sked \nän-ˈsked, ˈnän-\ *n* : a nonscheduled airline or transport plane
non·skid \nän-ˈskid, ˈnän-\ *adj* : designed or equipped to prevent skidding
non·sport·ing \-ˈspōrt-ing, -ˈspȯrt-\ *adj* : lacking the qualities characteristic of a hunting dog
non·stan·dard \-ˈstan-dərd\ *adj* **1** : not standard **2** : not conforming in pronunciation, grammatical construction, idiom, or word choice to the usage generally characteristic of educated native speakers of the language
non·stick \nän-ˈstik, ˈnän-\ *adj* : allowing easy removal of cooked food particles ⟨a *nonstick* coating on a pan⟩
non·stop \-ˈstäp\ *adj* : done or made without a stop ⟨a *nonstop* flight⟩ — **nonstop** *adv*
non·stri·at·ed muscle \nän-ˌstrī-ˌāt-əd-\ *n* : SMOOTH MUSCLE
nonsuch *variant of* NONESUCH
non·suit \nän-ˈsüt, ˈnän-\ *n* : a judgment against a plaintiff for failure to prosecute the case or inability to establish a prima facie case [Medieval French *nounsuyte,* from *noun-* "non-" + *siute* "following, pursuit"] — **nonsuit** *vt*
non·sup·port \ˌnän-sə-ˈpōrt, -ˈpȯrt\ *n* : failure to support; *esp* : failure (as of a parent) to honor an obligation to provide financial support to a dependent
non·syl·lab·ic \ˌnän-sə-ˈlab-ik\ *adj* : not constituting a syllable or the nucleus of a syllable
non·tar·get \-ˈtär-gət\ *adj* : not being the intended object of ac-

tion by a particular agent ⟨effect of insecticides on *nontarget* organisms⟩

non·tast·er \nän-ˈtā-stər, ˈnän-\ *n* : a person unable to taste the chemical phenylthiocarbamide

non·ther·mal \-ˈthər-məl\ *adj* : not produced by heat

non·threat·en·ing \-ˈthret-ning, -n-ing\ *adj* **1** : not constituting a threat ⟨a *nonthreatening* illness⟩ **2** : not likely to cause anxiety ⟨a *nonthreatening* environment⟩; *also* : INNOCUOUS 2

non trop·po \nän-ˈtrò-pō, ˈnän-, ˈnōn-\ *adv or adj* : not too much so : without excess — used as a direction in music [Italian, literally, "not too much"]

non·union \nän-ˈyün-yən, ˈnän-\ *adj* **1** : not belonging to a trade union ⟨*nonunion* carpenters⟩ **2** : not recognizing or favoring trade unions or their members

non·use \ˈnän-ˈyüs\ *n* **1** : failure to use ⟨*nonuse* of available material⟩ **2** : the fact or condition of not being used

non·us·er \ˈnän-ˈyü-zər\ *n* : one who does not make use of something (as an available public facility or a harmful drug)

non·vas·cu·lar plant \ˌnän-ˌvas-kyə-lər-\ *n* : a plant (as an alga or a moss) that has no vascular tissue for conveying fluids

non·ver·bal \nän-ˈvər-bəl, ˈnän-\ *adj* **1** : being other than verbal ⟨*nonverbal* symbols⟩ **2** : involving little use of language ⟨*nonverbal* tests⟩ — **non·ver·bal·ly** \-bə-lē\ *adv*

non·vin·tage \-ˈvin-tij\ *adj* : undated and usually blended to approximate a standard ⟨a *nonvintage* wine⟩

non·vi·o·lence \-ˈvī-ə-ləns\ *n* **1** : abstention on principle from violence; *also* : the principle of such abstention **2** : nonviolent demonstrations to secure political ends — **non·vi·o·lent** \-lənt\ *adj*

non·vol·a·tile \nän-ˈväl-ət-l\ *adj* : not volatile : not volatilizing readily

non·wo·ven \-ˈwō-vən\ *adj* **1** : made of fibers held together by interlocking or bonding (as by chemical means) but not woven ⟨*nonwoven* fabric⟩ **2** : made of nonwoven fabric ⟨a *nonwoven* dress⟩ — **nonwoven** *n*

non·ze·ro \nän-ˈzē-rō, -ˈziər-ō\ *adj* : either positive or negative but not zero

¹noo·dle \ˈnüd-l\ *n* **1** : a stupid person : SIMPLETON **2** : HEAD 1 [perhaps alteration of *noddle*]

²noodle *n* : a food paste made with egg and shaped into long flat strips [German *Nudel*]

nook \ˈnůk\ *n* **1** : an interior angle formed by two meeting walls : RECESS ⟨a chimney *nook*⟩ **2** : a secluded or sheltered place ⟨a shady *nook*⟩ [Middle English *noke, nok*]

noon \ˈnün\ *n* : the middle of the day : 12 o'clock in the daytime [Old English *nōn* "9th hour from sunrise," from Latin *nona*, from *nonus* "ninth"] — **noon** *adj*

Word History *Noon* has not always indicated that time of day at which the sun is most nearly overhead. According to the Roman method of reckoning time, the hours of the day were counted from sunrise to sunset. English *noon* is derived from Latin *nona*, from *nonus*, which means "ninth." *Noon*, then, was the ninth hour of the day, or about three p.m. A church service which was held daily at this time is called *none*, and perhaps in anticipation of this service or possibly of a mealtime, the time denoted by *none* or *noon* shifted to the hour of midday.

noon·day \-ˌdā\ *n* : MIDDAY

no one *pron* : NOBODY

noon·ing \ˈnü-ning, -nən\ *n, chiefly dialect* : a midday meal; *also* : a period at noon for eating or resting

noon·tide \ˈnün-ˌtīd\ *n* **1** : NOONTIME **2** : the highest or culminating point

noon·time \-ˌtīm\ *n* : the time of noon : MIDDAY

¹noose \ˈnüs\ *n* : a loop with a running knot that becomes tighter the more it is drawn [Middle English *nose*]

²noose *vt* : to catch or fasten with or as if with a noose

no–par *adj* : having no face value ⟨*no-par* stock⟩

nor \nər, nȯr, ˈnȯr\ *conj* : and not ⟨the book is too long; *nor* is the style easy⟩ ⟨not for you *nor* for me⟩ — used especially to introduce and negate the second member and each later member of a series of items of which the first is preceded by neither ⟨neither here *nor* there⟩ [Middle English, contraction of *nother* "neither, nor"] ***usage*** see NEITHER

nor·adren·a·line \ˌnȯr-ə-ˈdren-l-ən\ *n* : NOREPINEPHRINE [*normal* + *adrenaline*]

¹Nor·dic \ˈnȯrd-ik\ *adj* **1** : of or relating to the Germanic peoples of northern Europe and especially of Scandinavia **2** : of or relating to a physical type characterized by tall stature, long head, light skin and hair, and blue eyes [French *nordique*, from *nord* "north," from Old English *north*]

²Nordic *n* **1** : a native of northern Europe **2** : a person of Nordic physical type **3** : a member of a Scandinavian people

nor'easter *variant of* NORTHEASTER 2

nor·epi·neph·rine \ˈnȯr-ˌep-ə-ˈnef-rən\ *n* : a hormone $C_8H_{11}NO_3$ that causes blood vessels to contract and acts as a neurotransmitter in the sympathetic nervous system and some parts of the central nervous system [*normal* + *epinephrine*]

norm \ˈnȯrm\ *n* **1** : an authoritative standard : MODEL **2** : AVERAGE; *esp* : a set standard of development or achievement usually derived from the average or median achievement of a large group **3** : a common or typical practice or custom [Latin *norma*, literally, "carpenter's square"]

¹nor·mal \ˈnȯr-məl\ *adj* **1** : forming a right angle; *esp* : perpendicular to a tangent at a point of tangency **2** : according with or constituting a norm, rule, or principle **3 a** : of, relating to, or characterized by average intelligence or development **b** : free from disorder of body or mind : SOUND **4 a** : having a concentration of one gram equivalent of solute per liter ⟨a *normal* solution⟩ **b** : containing neither basic hydroxyl nor acid hydrogen ⟨a *normal* salt⟩ **c** : having a straight-chain structure ⟨a *normal* alcohol⟩ [Latin *normalis*, from *norma* "carpenter's square"] ***synonyms*** see REGULAR — **nor·mal·i·ty** \nȯr-ˈmal-ət-ē\ *n* — **nor·mal·ly** \ˈnȯr-mə-lē\ *adv*

Word History Latin *norma* means "rule" or "pattern" as well as "carpenter's square," for a square provides a standard or rule which ensures that a carpenter can make corners and edges that are straight and that form right angles. The Latin adjective *normalis*, formed from *norma*, originally meant "forming a right angle" or "according to a square," and it is from this Latin sense that we get the earliest sense of *normal* in English, "perpendicular." Latin *normalis* was also used in more extended senses, however, and by the Late Latin period its usual meaning was "according to rule." Most of the senses of our word *normal* are derived from this Late Latin usage.

²normal *n* **1** : one (as a line or person) that is normal **2** : a form or state regarded as the norm : STANDARD

normal curve *n* : a symmetrical bell-shaped curve that is generally used as an approximation to the graph of scores or measurements consisting of many bunched values near the average in the middle and a few large and a few small values arranged toward the opposite ends

nor·mal·cy \ˈnȯr-məl-sē\ *n* : the state or fact of being normal

nor·mal·ize \ˈnȯr-mə-ˌlīz\ *vt* : to bring or restore to a normal state

normal school *n* : a usually two-year school for training chiefly elementary teachers [translation of French *école normale*; from the fact that the first French school so named was intended to serve as a model]

Nor·man \ˈnȯr-mən\ *n* **1** : any of the Scandinavians who conquered Normandy in the 10th century **2** : any of the people of mixed Norman and French blood who conquered England in 1066 **3** : a native or inhabitant of the province of Normandy [Medieval French *Normant*, from Old Norse *Northmathr* "Norseman," from *northr* "north" + *mathr* "man"] — **Norman** *adj*

Norman–French *n* : the French language of the Normans

nor·ma·tive \ˈnȯr-mət-iv\ *adj* : of, conforming to, or prescribing norms — **nor·ma·tive·ly** *adv* — **nor·ma·tive·ness** *n*

Norse \ˈnȯrs\ *n, pl* **Norse** **1** *pl* **a** : the Scandinavian people **b** : the Norwegian people **2 a** : NORWEGIAN 2 **b** : any of the western Scandinavian dialects or languages **c** : the Scandinavian group of Germanic languages [probably from obsolete Dutch *noorsch*, adj., "Norwegian, Scandinavian," from *noordsch* "northern," from *noord* "north"] — **Norse** *adj*

Norse·man \ˈnȯr-smən\ *n* : any of the ancient Scandinavians

¹north \ˈnȯrth\ *adv* : to, toward, or in the north [Old English]

²north *adj* **1** : situated toward or at the north **2** : coming from the north

³north *n* **1 a** : the direction to the left of one facing east **b** : the compass point directly opposite to south **2** *cap* : regions or countries north of a specified or implied point

north·bound \ˈnȯrth-ˌbau̇nd\ *adj* : headed north

[1]**north·east** \nȯr-ˈthēst, *nautical* nȯ-ˈrēst\ *adv* : to, toward, or in the northeast

[2]**northeast** *n* **1 a** : the general direction between north and east **b** : the compass point midway between north and east : N 45° E **2** *cap* : regions or countries northeast of a specified or implied point

[3]**northeast** *adj* **1** : coming from the northeast **2** : situated toward or at the northeast

north·east·er \nȯr-ˈthē-stər, nȯ-ˈrē-\ *n* **1** : a strong northeast wind **2** *or* **nor'·east·er** \nȯ-ˈrē-\ : a storm with northeast winds

north·east·er·ly \nȯr-ˈthē-stər-lē\ *adv or adj* **1** : from the northeast **2** : toward the northeast

north·east·ern \-stərn\ *adj* **1** *often cap* : of, relating to, or characteristic of a region conventionally designated Northeast **2** : lying toward or coming from the northeast — **north·east·ern·most** \-stərn-ˌmōst\ *adj*

North·east·ern·er \-stər-nər, -stə-nər\ *n* : a native or inhabitant of a northeastern region (as of the U.S.)

[1]**north·east·ward** \nȯr-ˈthēs-twərd\ *adv or adj* : toward the northeast — **north·east·wards** \-twərdz\ *adj*

[2]**northeastward** *n* : NORTHEAST

north·er \ˈnȯr-t͟hər\ *n* **1** : a strong north wind **2** : a storm with north winds

[1]**north·er·ly** \-lē\ *adv or adj* **1** : from the north **2** : toward the north

[2]**northerly** *n, pl* **-lies** : a wind from the north

north·ern \ˈnȯr-t͟hərn, -t͟hən\ *adj* **1** *often cap* : of, relating to, or characteristic of a region conventionally designated North **2** : lying toward or coming from the north [Old English *northerne*] — **north·ern·most** \-ˌmōst\ *adj*

Northern *n* : the dialect of English spoken in the part of the U.S. north of a line running northwest through central New Jersey, below the northern tier of counties in Pennsylvania, through northern Ohio, Indiana, and Illinois, across central Iowa, and through the northwest corner of South Dakota

Northern Cross *n* : a cross formed by six stars in Cygnus

Northern Crown *n* : CORONA BOREALIS

North·ern·er \ˈnȯr-t͟hər-nər, -t͟hə-nər\ *n* : a native or inhabitant of the North (as of the U.S.)

northern harrier *n* : an American and Eurasian hawk that inhabits open and marshy regions and is brown or grayish with a white patch on the rump

northern hemisphere *n* : the half of the earth that lies north of the equator

northern lights *n pl* : AURORA BOREALIS

north·ing \ˈnȯr-thing, -t͟hing\ *n* **1** : difference in latitude to the north from the last preceding point of reckoning **2** : northerly progress

north·land \ˈnȯrth-ˌland, -lənd\ *n, often cap* : land in the north : the north of a country or region

North·man \-mən\ *n* : NORSEMAN

north–north·east \ˈnȯrth-ˌnȯr-ˈthēst, *nautical* -ˌnȯ-ˈrēst\ *n* : two points east of north : N 22° 30′ E

north–north·west \ˈnȯrth-ˌnȯrth-ˈwest, *nautical* -ˌnȯr-ˈwest\ *n* : two points west of north : N 22° 30′ W

north pole *n* **1 a** *often cap N&P* : the northernmost point of the earth **b** : the point in the sky directly overhead at the earth's north pole **2** : the pole of a magnet that points toward the north

north–seeking pole *n* : NORTH POLE 2

North Star *n* : the star toward which the northern end of the earth's axis very nearly points — called also *polestar*

[1]**north·ward** \ˈnȯrth-wərd\ *adv or adj* : toward the north — **north·wards** \-wərdz\ *adv*

[2]**northward** *n* : northward direction or part

[1]**north·west** \nȯrth-ˈwest, *nautical* nȯr-ˈwest\ *adv* : to, toward, or in the northwest

[2]**northwest** *n* **1 a** : the general direction between north and west **b** : the compass point midway between north and west : N 45° W **2** *cap* : regions or countries northwest of a specified or implied point

[3]**northwest** *adj* **1** : coming from the northwest **2** : situated toward or at the northwest

north·west·er \nȯrth-ˈwes-tər, nȯr-ˈwes-\ *n* **1** : a strong northwest wind **2** : a storm with northwest winds

north·west·er·ly \nȯrth-ˈwes-tər-lē\ *adv or adj* **1** : from the northwest **2** : toward the northwest

north·west·ern \nȯrth-ˈwes-tərn\ *adj* **1** *often cap* : of, relating to, or characteristic of a region conventionally designated Northwest **2** : lying toward or coming from the northwest — **north·west·ern·most** \-tərn-ˌmōst\ *adj*

North·west·ern·er \-tər-nər, -tə-nər\ *n* : a native or inhabitant of a northwestern region (as of the U.S.)

[1]**north·west·ward** \nȯrth-ˈwes-twərd\ *adv or adj* : toward the northwest — **north·west·wards** \-twərdz\ *adv*

[2]**northwestward** *n* : NORTHWEST

Nor·way maple \ˌnȯr-ˌwā-\ *n* : a Eurasian maple with dark green or often reddish or red-veined leaves that is often planted in the U.S. as a shade tree

Norway rat *n* : BROWN RAT

Norway spruce *n* : a widely grown spruce native to northern Europe with dark green needles and long cones

Nor·we·gian \nȯr-ˈwē-jən\ *n* **1 a** : a native or inhabitant of Norway **b** : a person of Norwegian descent **2** : the Germanic language of the Norwegian people [Medieval Latin *Norwegia* "Norway"] — **Norwegian** *adj*

nos *plural of* NO

[1]**nose** \ˈnōz\ *n* **1 a** : the part of the face or head that bears the nostrils and covers the front or outer part of the nasal cavity; *also* : this part together with the nasal cavity **b** : the front part of the head above or projecting beyond the jaws ⟨the length of a whale from the tip of the *nose* to the notch between the flukes⟩ **2** : the sense of smell : OLFACTION **3** : the vertebrate organ of smell **4** : something (as a point, edge, or projecting front part) that resembles a nose ⟨the *nose* of a plane⟩ **5 a** : the nose as a symbol of prying curiosity **b** : a knack for discovery or understanding ⟨a good *nose* for news⟩ [Old English *nosu*] — **nosed** \ˈnōzd\ *adj*

nose 4

[2]**nose** *vb* **1** : to detect by or as if by smell : SCENT **2 a** : to push or move with the nose **b** : to touch or rub with the nose **3** : to search impertinently : PRY **4** : to move ahead slowly or cautiously ⟨the car *nosed* out into traffic⟩

nose·band \ˈnōz-ˌband\ *n* : the part of a bridle or halter that passes over a horse's nose

nose·bleed \-ˌblēd\ *n* : a bleeding from the nose

nose cone *n* : a protective cone constituting the forward end of a rocket or missile

nose dive *n* **1** : the downward nose-first plunge of a flying object (as an airplane) **2** : a sudden extreme drop — **nose–dive** \ˈnōz-ˌdīv\ *vi*

no–see–um \nō-ˈsē-əm\ *n* : any of various tiny biting two-winged flies [from the words (as supposedly spoken by American Indians) *no see um* "you don't see them"]

nose·gay \ˈnōz-ˌgā\ *n* : a small bunch of flowers : POSY [*nose* + English dialect *gay* "ornament"]

nose·piece \-ˌpēs\ *n* **1** : a piece of armor for protecting the nose **2** : a fitting at the lower end of a microscope tube to which the objectives are attached

nose·wheel \-ˈhwēl, -ˈwēl\ *n* : a landing-gear wheel under the nose of an aircraft

no–show \nō-ˈshō\ *n* : a person who reserves space especially on an airplane but neither uses nor cancels the reservation

nos·tal·gia \nä-ˈstal-jə, nə-\ *n* : a wistful sentimental yearning for something past or irrecoverable [New Latin, from Greek *nostos* "return home" + New Latin *-algia* "-algia"] — **nos·tal·gic** \-jik\ *adj* — **nos·tal·gi·cal·ly** \-ji-kə-lē, -klē\ *adv*

nos·toc \ˈnäs-ˌtäk\ *n* : any of a genus of filamentous blue-green algae able to fix nitrogen [New Latin, genus name]

nos·tril \ˈnäs-trəl\ *n* : either of the outer openings of the nose with its adjoining passage; *also* : either fleshy lateral wall of the nose [Old English *nosthyrl,* from *nosu* "nose" + *thyrel* "hole"]

nos·trum \ˈnäs-trəm\ *n* **1** : a medicine of secret composition recommended especially by its preparer **2** : a questionable remedy or scheme : PANACEA [Latin, neuter of *noster* "our, ours," from *nos* "we"]

nosy *or* **nos·ey** \ˈnō-zē\ *adj* **nos·i·er; -est** : of a prying or inquisitive disposition or quality : INTRUSIVE, SNOOPY — **nos·i·ly** \-zə-lē\ *adv* — **nos·i·ness** \-zē-nəs\ *n*

not \nät, ˈnät\ *adv* **1** — used to make negative a group of words or a word ⟨the books are *not* here⟩ **2** — used to stand for the negative of a preceding group of words ⟨is sometimes hard to see and sometimes *not*⟩ [Middle English, alteration of *nought* "naught"]

no·ta·bil·i·ty \ˌnōt-ə-ˈbil-ət-ē\ *n, pl* **-ties** **1 :** the quality or state of being notable **2 :** NOTABLE

[1]**no·ta·ble** \ˈnōt-ə-bəl\ *adj* **1 :** worthy of note : REMARKABLE **2 :** DISTINGUISHED 1, PROMINENT — **no·ta·bly** \-blē\ *adv*

[2]**notable** *n* **:** a person of note or of great reputation

no·ta·rize \ˈnōt-ə-ˌrīz\ *vt* **:** to make legally authentic through the use of the powers granted to a notary public — **no·ta·ri·za·tion** \ˌnōt-ə-rə-ˈzā-shən\ *n*

no·ta·ry public \ˌnōt-ə-rē-\ *n, pl* **notaries public** *or* **notary publics :** a public officer who attests or certifies writings (as deeds) as authentic and takes affidavits, depositions, and protests of negotiable paper — called also *notary* [Latin *notarius* "clerk, secretary," derived from *nota* "note"]

no·tate \ˈnō-ˌtāt\ *vt* **:** to put into notation

no·ta·tion \nō-ˈtā-shən\ *n* **1 :** ANNOTATION, NOTE ⟨make *notations* for corrections on the margin⟩ **2 :** the act, process, or method of representing data symbolically by marks, signs, figures, or characters; *also* **:** a system of symbols (as letters, numerals, or musical notes) used in such notation — **no·ta·tion·al** \-shnəl, -shən-l\ *adj*

[1]**notch** \ˈnäch\ *n* **1 :** a V-shaped or rounded indentation **2 :** a narrow pass between mountains : GAP **3 :** DEGREE, STEP ⟨the team moved up a *notch* in the standings⟩ [perhaps derived from Middle French *oche* "notch"] — **notched** \ˈnächt\ *adj*

[2]**notch** *vt* **1 :** to cut or make notches in **2 a :** to mark or record with a notch **b :** ACHIEVE 2, SCORE ⟨*notched* another victory⟩

[1]**note** \ˈnōt\ *vt* **1 a :** to notice or observe with care **b :** to record in writing **2 :** to make special mention of : REMARK [Medieval French *noter,* from Latin *notare* "to mark, note," from *nota* "note"] — **not·er** *n*

[2]**note** *n* **1 a :** a musical sound **b :** an animal's cry, call, or sound ⟨a bird's *note*⟩ **c :** a special tone of voice ⟨a *note* of fear⟩ **2 a :** MEMORANDUM 1b **b :** a brief and informal record **c :** a written or printed comment or explanation ⟨*notes* in the back of the book⟩ **d :** a short informal letter **e :** a formal diplomatic or official communication **3 a :** a written promise to pay — called also *promissory note* **b :** a piece of paper money **4 :** a character in music that by its shape shows the length of time a tone is to be held and by its place on the staff shows the pitch of a tone **5 :** MOOD, QUALITY ⟨a *note* of optimism⟩ **6 a :** REPUTATION, DISTINCTION ⟨a person of *note*⟩ **b :** NOTICE, HEED ⟨take *note* of the exact time⟩ [Latin *nota* "mark, character, written note"] ***synonyms*** see SIGN

note·book \ˈnōt-ˌbu̇k\ *n* **1 :** a book for notes or memoranda **2 :** a portable computer that is similar to but usually smaller than a laptop

note·case \-ˌkās\ *n, British* **:** BILLFOLD, WALLET

not·ed \ˈnōt-əd\ *adj* **:** widely and favorably known ⟨a *noted* author⟩ ***synonyms*** see FAMOUS

note·wor·thy \ˈnōt-ˌwər-t͟hē\ *adj* **:** worthy of note : REMARKABLE — **note·wor·thi·ly** \-t͟hə-lē\ *adv* — **note·wor·thi·ness** \-t͟hē-nəs\ *n*

[1]**noth·ing** \ˈnəth-ing\ *pron* **1 :** not anything ⟨there's *nothing* in the box⟩ **2 :** one of no interest, value, or consequence [Old English *nān thing, nāthing,* from *nān* "no, none" + *thing*] — **nothing doing :** by no means : definitely no

[2]**nothing** *adv* **:** not at all : in no degree

[3]**nothing** *n* **1 a :** something that does not exist **b :** the absence of all magnitude or quantity : ZERO **2 :** something of little or no worth or importance — **noth·ing·ness** *n*

[1]**no·tice** \ˈnōt-əs\ *n* **1 a :** warning or indication of something : ANNOUNCEMENT **b :** notification of the ending of an agreement at a specified time **2 :** ATTENTION, HEED ⟨sit up and take *notice*⟩ **3 :** a written or printed announcement **4 :** a short critical account [Medieval French, "knowledge, notification," from Latin *notitia* "acquaintance, awareness," from *notus* "known," from *noscere* "to come to know"]

[2]**notice** *vt* **1 :** to make mention of : remark on **2 :** to take notice of : OBSERVE ⟨*notice* even the smallest details⟩

no·tice·able \ˈnōt-ə-sə-bəl\ *adj* **1 :** worthy of notice ⟨*noticeable* for its fine quality⟩ **2 :** capable of being or likely to be noticed ⟨a *noticeable* improvement⟩ — **no·tice·ably** \-blē\ *adv*

synonyms NOTICEABLE, REMARKABLE, PROMINENT, OUTSTANDING, CONSPICUOUS, STRIKING mean attracting notice or attention. NOTICEABLE applies to something unlikely to escape observation ⟨a piano recital with no *noticeable* errors⟩. REMARKABLE applies to something so extraordinary or exceptional as to invite comment ⟨a film of *remarkable* intelligence and wit⟩. PROMINENT applies to something commanding notice by standing out from its surroundings or background ⟨one of the most *prominent* families in the city⟩. OUTSTANDING applies to something that rises above and excels others of the same kind ⟨had made several *outstanding* contributions to science⟩. CONSPICUOUS applies to something that is obvious and certain to attract attention ⟨his loud voice made him *conspicuous* at the party⟩. STRIKING applies to something that impresses itself powerfully and deeply upon the observer's mind or vision ⟨the region's *striking* poverty⟩.

no·ti·fi·ca·tion \ˌnōt-ə-fə-ˈkā-shən\ *n* **1 :** the act or an instance of notifying **2 :** written or printed matter that gives notice

no·ti·fy \ˈnōt-ə-ˌfī\ *vt* **-fied; -fy·ing 1 :** to give notice of or report the occurrence of **2 :** to give notice to [Medieval French *notifier* "to make known," from Late Latin *notificare,* from Latin *notus* "known"] — **no·ti·fi·er** \-ˌfī-ər, -ˌfīr\ *n*

no·tion \ˈnō-shən\ *n* **1 a :** IDEA, CONCEPTION ⟨have a *notion* of a poem's meaning⟩ **b :** a belief held : OPINION **c :** WHIM, FANCY ⟨a sudden *notion* to go home⟩ **2** *pl* **:** small useful articles : SUNDRIES [Latin *notio,* from *noscere* "to come to know"]

no·tion·al \ˈnō-shnəl, -shən-l\ *adj* **1 :** existing in idea only **2 :** inclined to foolish or visionary fancies or moods

no·to·chord \ˈnōt-ə-ˌkȯrd\ *n* **:** a longitudinal flexible supporting rod of cells that exists in the embryos of all chordates, remains in the adults of some primitive forms (as lancelets and lampreys), and is replaced by the spinal column in most vertebrates [Greek *nōton* "back" + Latin *chorda* "cord"] — **no·to·chord·al** \ˌnōt-ə-ˈkȯrd-l\ *adj*

no·to·ri·e·ty \ˌnōt-ə-ˈrī-ət-ē\ *n, pl* **-ties :** the quality or state of being notorious

no·to·ri·ous \nō-ˈtōr-ē-əs, -ˈtȯr-\ *adj* **:** generally known and talked of; *esp* **:** widely and unfavorably known [Medieval Latin *notorius,* derived from Latin *noscere* "to come to know"] ***synonyms*** see FAMOUS — **no·to·ri·ous·ly** *adv* — **no·to·ri·ous·ness** *n*

no–trump \ˈnō-ˈtrəmp\ *adj* **:** being a bid, contract, or hand suitable to play (as in bridge) without any suit being trumps — **no–trump** *n*

[1]**not·with·stand·ing** \ˌnät-with-ˈstan-ding, -wit͟h-\ *prep* **:** in spite of ⟨they succeeded *notwithstanding* many obstacles⟩

[2]**notwithstanding** *adv* **:** NEVERTHELESS, HOWEVER

[3]**notwithstanding** *conj* **:** ALTHOUGH

nou·gat \ˈnü-gət\ *n* **:** a candy of nuts or fruit pieces in a sugar paste [French, from Occitan, from *noga* "nut," from Latin *nuc-, nux*]

nought \ˈnȯt, ˈnät\ *variant of* NAUGHT

noun \ˈnau̇n\ *n* **:** a word that is the name of something (as a person, animal, plant, place, thing, substance, quality, idea, action, or state) and that is typically used in a sentence as subject or object of a verb or as object of a preposition [Medieval French, "name, noun," from Latin *nomen*]

nour·ish \ˈnər-ish, ˈnə-rish\ *vt* **1 :** to promote the growth and development of **2 :** to provide with food : FEED ⟨plants *nourished* by rain and soil⟩ **3 :** SUPPORT, MAINTAIN ⟨a friendship *nourished* by trust⟩ [Medieval French *nuriss-,* stem of *nurrir, norrir* "to nourish," from Latin *nutrire*]

nour·ish·ing *adj* **:** giving nourishment ⟨*nourishing* food⟩

nour·ish·ment \ˈnər-ish-mənt, ˈnə-rish-\ *n* **1 :** something that nourishes : FOOD, NUTRIMENT **2 :** the act of nourishing : the state of being nourished

nou·veau riche \ˌnü-ˌvō-ˈrēsh\ *n, pl* **nou·veaux riches** *same*\ **:** a person newly rich [French, literally, "new rich"]

no·va \ˈnō-və\ *n, pl* **novas** *or* **no·vae** \-ˌvē, -ˌvī\ **:** a star that suddenly increases greatly in brightness and then within a few months or years grows dim again [New Latin, from Latin *novus* "new"]

[1]**nov·el** \ˈnäv-əl\ *adj* **:** new or striking in conception, kind, or style : having no precedent [Medieval French, "new," from Latin *novellus,* from *novus* "new"] ***synonyms*** see NEW

[2]**novel** *n* **:** a prose narrative longer than a short story that usually portrays imaginary characters and events [Italian *novella*] — **nov·el·is·tic** \ˌnäv-ə-ˈlis-tik\ *adj*

\ə\ **abut**	\au̇\ **out**	\i\ **tip**	\ȯ\ **saw**	\u̇\ **foot**
\ər\ **further**	\ch\ **chin**	\ī\ **life**	\ȯi\ **coin**	\y\ **yet**
\a\ **mat**	\e\ **pet**	\j\ **job**	\th\ **thin**	\yü\ **few**
\ā\ **take**	\ē\ **easy**	\ng\ **sing**	\t͟h\ **this**	\yu̇\ **cure**
\ä\ **cot, cart**	\g\ **go**	\ō\ **bone**	\ü\ **food**	\zh\ **vision**

nov·el·ette \ˌnäv-ə-ˈlet\ *n* : NOVELLA 2

nov·el·ist \ˈnäv-ləst, -ə-ləst\ *n* : a writer of novels

nov·el·ize \ˈnäv-ə-ˌlīz\ *vt* : to convert into the form of a novel — **nov·el·i·za·tion** \ˌnäv-ə-lə-ˈzā-shən\ *n*

no·vel·la \nō-ˈvel-ə\ *n, pl* **no·vel·le** \-ˈvel-ē\ **1** : a story with a compact and pointed plot **2** : a work of fiction intermediate in length and complexity between a short story and a novel [Italian, from *novello* "new," from Latin *novellus*]

nov·el·ty \ˈnäv-əl-tē\ *n, pl* **-ties** **1** : something new or unusual **2** : the quality or state of being novel **3** : a small manufactured article intended to amuse or for use as a plaything or an adornment — usually used in plural

No·vem·ber \nō-ˈvem-bər\ *n* : the 11th month of the year according to the Gregorian calendar [Medieval French *Novembre,* from Latin *November,* from *novem* "nine," from its having been originally the 9th month of the Roman calendar]

no·ve·na \nō-ˈvē-nə\ *n, pl* **-nas** *or* **-nae** \-ˌnē\ : a Roman Catholic devotion in which prayers are said for the same purpose on nine successive days [Medieval Latin, from Latin *novenus* "nine each," from *novem* "nine"]

nov·ice \ˈnäv-əs\ *n* **1** : a new member of a religious order who is preparing to take the vows of religion **2** : one who has no previous training or experience in a specific field or activity : BEGINNER [Medieval French, from Medieval Latin *novicius,* from Latin, "newly imported," from *novus* "new"]

no·vi·tiate \nō-ˈvish-ət\ *n* **1** : the period or state of being a novice **2** : NOVICE 1 **3** : a house where novices are trained [French *noviciat,* from Medieval Latin *noviciatus,* from *novicius* "novice"]

No·vo·cain \ˈnō-və-ˌkān\ *trademark* — used for the hydrochloride of procaine

no·vo·caine \ˈnō-və-ˌkān\ *n* : procaine in the form of its hydrochloride; *also* : an anesthetic that is applied to and acts on only a small part of the body [Latin *novus* "new" + *cocaine*]

^{1}**now** \naů, ˈnaů\ *adv* **1 a** : at the present time or moment ⟨I am busy *now*⟩ **b** : in the time immediately before the present ⟨they left just *now*⟩ **c** : in the time immediately to follow ⟨we will leave *now*⟩ **2** — used with the sense of present time weakened or lost to express command, request, or reproach ⟨*now* hear this⟩ **3** : SOMETIMES ⟨*now* one and *now* another⟩ **4** : under the present circumstances ⟨*now* what can we do⟩ **5** : at the time referred to ⟨*now* the trouble began⟩ **6** : by this time [Old English *nū*] — **now and then** : OCCASIONALLY

^{2}**now** *conj* : in view of the fact that : SINCE — often followed by *that* ⟨*now* that we are here⟩

^{3}**now** \ˈnaů\ *n* : the present time or moment ⟨up to *now*⟩

^{4}**now** \ˈnaů\ *adj* : of or relating to the present time : CURRENT ⟨the *now* president⟩

now·a·days \ˈnaů-ə-ˌdāz, ˈnaů-ˌdāz\ *adv* : at the present time [Middle English *now a dayes,* from *now* + *a dayes* "during the day"]

no·way \ˈnō-ˌwā\ *or* **no·ways** \-ˌwāz\ *adv* : NOWISE

no·where \ˈnō-ˌhweər, -ˌweər, -ˌhwaər, -ˌwaər, -hwər, -wər\ *adv* **1** : not in or at any place **2** : to no place **3** : not at all : not to the least extent — usually used with *near* ⟨*nowhere* near enough⟩ — **nowhere** *n*

no·wise \ˈnō-ˌwīz\ *adv* : in no way : not at all

nox·ious \ˈnäk-shəs\ *adj* : harmful or injurious especially to health or morals ⟨*noxious* fumes⟩ [Latin *noxius,* from *noxa* "harm"] — **nox·ious·ly** *adv* — **nox·ious·ness** *n*

noz·zle \ˈnäz-əl\ *n* : a projecting part with an opening that usually serves as an outlet ⟨the *nozzle* of a bellows⟩; *esp* : a short tube with a taper or constriction often used (as on a hose or pipe) to direct or speed up a flow of fluid [derived from *nose*]

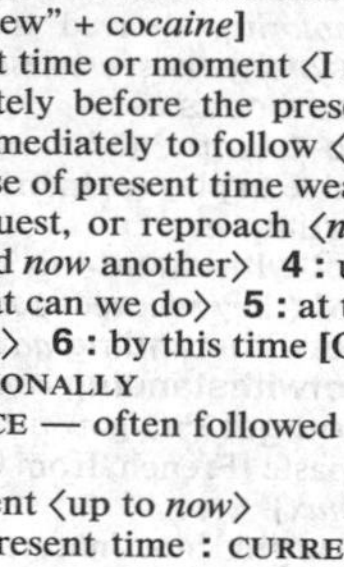

N nozzle

n't \$^{ə}$nt, nt, ənt\ *adv* : not — used in combination ⟨is*n't*⟩ ⟨does*n't*⟩

nth \ˈenth, ˈentth\ *adj* **1** : numbered with an indefinitely large or an unspecified ordinal number ⟨for the *nth* time⟩ **2** : EXTREME, UTMOST ⟨to the *nth* degree⟩

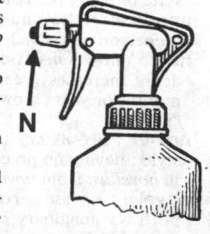

nu \ˈnü, ˈnyü\ *n* : the 13th letter of the Greek alphabet — Ν or ν

nu·ance \ˈnü-ˌäns, ˈnyü-, -ˌä^{n}s, nü-ˈ, nyü-ˈ\ *n* : a slight shade or degree of difference : a delicate gradation or variation (as in color, tone, or meaning) [French, from *nuer* "to make shades of color," from *nue* "cloud," from Latin *nubes*]

nub \ˈnəb\ *n* **1** : KNOB 1a, LUMP **2** : GIST, POINT ⟨the *nub* of the story⟩ [English dialect *knub*]

nub·bin \ˈnəb-ən\ *n* **1** : a small or imperfect ear of corn; *also* : any small shriveled or undeveloped fruit **2** : a small projecting part [perhaps from *nub*]

nub·ble \ˈnəb-əl\ *n* : a small knob or lump [derived from *nub*] — **nub·bly** \ˈnəb-lē, -ə-lē\ *adj*

nu·bile \ˈnü-bəl, ˈnyü-, -ˌbīl\ *adj* : of marriageable condition or age [French, from Latin *nubilis,* from *nubere* "to marry"]

nu·cel·lus \nü-ˈsel-əs, nyü-\ *n, pl* **-cel·li** \-ˈsel-ˌī\ : the central and chief part of a plant ovule containing the embryo sac [New Latin, from Latin *nucella* "small nut," from *nuc-, nux* "nut"] — **nu·cel·lar** \-ˈsel-ər\ *adj*

nu·chal \ˈnü-kəl, ˈnyü-\ *adj* : of, relating to, or lying in the region of the nape [Medieval Latin *nucha* "nape," from Arabic *nukhāʿ* "spinal marrow"] — **nuchal** *n*

nucle- *or* **nucleo-** *combining form* **1** : nucleus ⟨*nucleon*⟩ **2** : nucleic acid ⟨*nucleo*protein⟩

nu·cle·ar \ˈnü-klē-ər, ˈnyü-\ *adj* **1** : of, relating to, or being a nucleus (as of a cell) **2** : of or relating to the atomic nucleus ⟨*nuclear* reactions⟩ ⟨*nuclear* physics⟩ **3** : involving or produced by a nuclear reaction ⟨*nuclear* fuel⟩ ⟨*nuclear* energy⟩ **4** : being or involving a weapon whose destructive power results from an uncontrolled nuclear reaction ⟨*nuclear* war⟩ ⟨a *nuclear* state⟩ **5** : relating to or powered by nuclear energy ⟨a *nuclear* power plant⟩ ⟨the *nuclear* debate⟩

nuclear family *n* : a family group that consists only of father, mother, and children

nuclear medicine *n* : a branch of medicine involving the use of radioactive materials in the diagnosis and treatment of disease

nuclear membrane *n* : a double membrane enclosing a cell nucleus and having its outer part continuous with the endoplasmic reticulum — called also *nuclear envelope*

nuclear sap *n* : the part of a cell nucleus that is relatively fluid and does not include the chromatin and nucleoli

nu·cle·ase \ˈnü-klē-ˌās, ˈnyü-\ *n* : an enzyme that promotes hydrolysis of nucleic acids

nu·cle·ate \ˈnü-klē-ˌāt, ˈnyü-\ *vb* **1** : to gather about or into a center; *also* : to act as a nucleus for or provide with a nucleus **2** : to form, act as, or have a nucleus — **nu·cle·ation** \ˌnü-klē-ˈā-shən, ˌnyü-\ *n*

nu·cle·at·ed \ˈnü-klē-ˌāt-əd, ˈnyü-\ *or* **nu·cle·ate** \-klē-ət\ *adj* : having a nucleus or nuclei ⟨*nucleated* cells⟩

nu·cle·ic acid \nü-ˌklē-ik-, nyü-, -ˌklā-\ *n* : any of various acids (as a DNA or an RNA) that are composed of a chain of nucleotides and are found especially in cell nuclei

nu·cle·o·lus \nü-ˈklē-ə-ləs, nyü-\ *n, pl* **-li** \-ˌlī\ : a spherical body in a cell nucleus that is associated with a specific part of a chromosome and contains much ribosomal RNA [New Latin, from Latin *nucleus* "kernel"] — **nu·cle·o·lar** \-lər\ *adj*

nu·cle·on \ˈnü-klē-ˌän, ˈnyü-\ *n* : a proton or a neutron especially in the atomic nucleus

nu·cle·on·ics \ˌnü-klē-ˈän-iks, ˌnyü-\ *n* : a branch of physical science that deals with nucleons or with all phenomena of the atomic nucleus

nu·cleo·plasm \ˈnü-klē-ə-ˌplaz-əm, ˈnyü-\ *n* : the fluidlike substance in the nucleus of a cell

nu·cleo·pro·tein \ˌnü-klē-ō-ˈprō-ˌtēn, ˌnyü-, -ˈprōt-ē-ən\ *n* : any of the proteins joined to nucleic acid that occur especially in the nuclei of living cells and are an essential constituent of genes

nu·cle·o·side \ˈnü-klē-ə-ˌsīd, ˈnyü-\ *n* : a compound (as adenosine) that consists of a purine or pyrimidine base combined with deoxyribose or ribose and is found especially in DNA or RNA [*nucle-* + *-ose* + *-ide*]

nu·cle·o·some \ˈ-ˌsōm\ *n* : a compact structure that makes up the repeating subunit of chromatin and is composed of DNA tightly coiled around a core of histone proteins [*nucle-* + ^{3}*-some*]

nu·cle·o·tide \-ˌtīd\ *n* : any of several compounds that consist of a ribose or deoxyribose sugar joined to a purine or pyrimidine base and to a phosphate group and that are the basic structural units of RNA and DNA [derived from *nucle-* + *-ide*]

nu·cle·us \ˈnü-klē-əs, ˈnyü-\ *n, pl* **-clei** \-klē-ˌī\ *also* **-cle·us·es** : a central point, group, or mass of something: as **a** : the small, brighter, and denser part of a galaxy or of the head of a comet **b** : a part of the cell of eukaryotes that controls many cell functions (as reproduction and protein synthesis), contains the chromosomes, and is bounded by a nuclear membrane **c** : a mass of gray matter or group of cell bodies of neurons in the central nervous system **d :** a characteristic and stable complex of atoms or groups in a molecule **e :** the positively charged central part of an atom that comprises nearly all of the atomic mass and that consists of protons and usually neutrons [Latin, "kernel," from *nuc-, nux* "nut"]

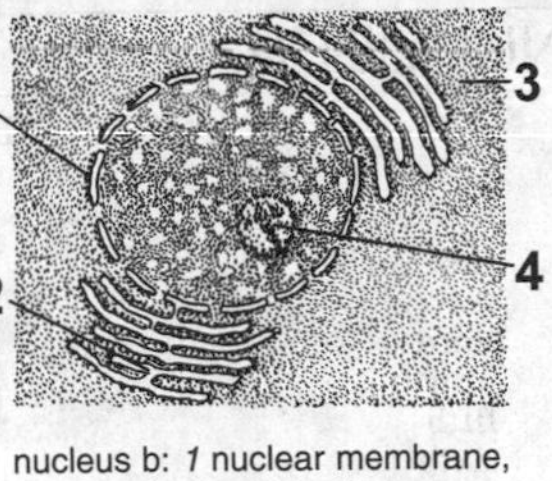

nucleus b: *1* nuclear membrane, *2* endoplasmic reticulum, *3* cytoplasm, *4* nucleolus

nu·clide \ˈnü-ˌklīd, ˈnyü-\ *n* **:** a species of atom characterized by the number of protons and neutrons and by the amount of energy contained in its nucleus [*nucleus* + Greek *eidos* "form, species"] — **nu·clid·ic** \nü-ˈklid-ik, nyü-\ *adj*

¹nude \ˈnüd, ˈnyüd\ *adj* **:** NAKED, BARE; *esp* **:** having no clothes on [Latin *nudus*] — **nude·ly** *adv* — **nude·ness** *n* — **nu·di·ty** \ˈnüd-ət-ē, ˈnyüd-\ *n*

²nude *n* **1 :** a nude human figure especially as depicted in art **2 :** the condition of being nude ⟨in the *nude*⟩

nudge \ˈnəj\ *vt* **:** to touch or push gently; *esp* **:** to seek the attention of by a push with the elbow [origin unknown] — **nudge** *n* — **nudg·er** *n*

nu·di·branch \ˈnüd-ə-ˌbrangk, ˈnyüd-\ *n, pl* **-branchs :** any of a group (Nudibranchia) of marine mollusks without a shell as adults and without true gills [derived from Latin *nudus* "nude" + Greek *branchia* "gill"] — **nudibranch** *adj*

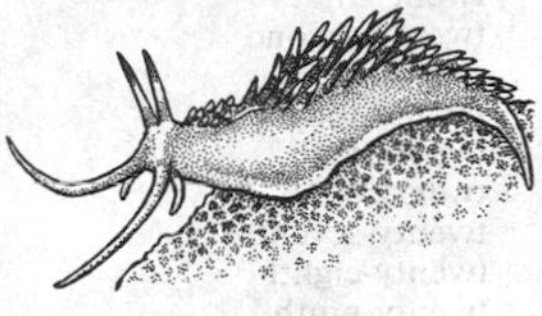
nudibranch

nud·ism \ˈnü-ˌdiz-əm, ˈnyü-\ *n* **:** the practice of going nude especially in groups and during periods of time spent in secluded places — **nud·ist** \ˈnüd-əst, ˈnyüd-\ *n*

nug·get \ˈnəg-ət\ *n* **:** a solid lump usually of precious metal [origin unknown]

nui·sance \ˈnüs-ns, ˈnyüs-\ *n* **:** one that is annoying, unpleasant, or obnoxious [Medieval French *nusaunce, noisance* "harm, injury," from *nuisir, nuire* "to harm," from Latin *nocēre*]

¹null \ˈnəl\ *adj* **1 :** having no legal or binding force **:** INVALID **2 :** amounting to nothing **:** NIL **3 :** having no value **4 :** having no elements ⟨the *null* set⟩ [Medieval French *nul,* literally, "not any," from Latin *nullus,* from *ne-* "not" + *ullus* "any"]

²null *n* **:** ZERO 2a

null and void *adj* **:** having no force, binding power, or validity

nul·li·fi·ca·tion \ˌnəl-ə-fə-ˈkā-shən\ *n* **1 :** the act of nullifying **:** the state of being nullified **2 :** the action of a state obstructing or attempting to prevent the operation and enforcement within its territory of a law of the United States — **nul·li·fi·ca·tion·ist** \-shə-nəst, -shnəst\ *n*

nul·li·fy \ˈnəl-ə-ˌfī\ *vt* **-fied; -fy·ing 1 :** to make null **:** VOID **2 :** to make of no value or consequence

synonyms NULLIFY, NEGATE, ANNUL, INVALIDATE mean to deprive of effective or continued existence. NULLIFY implies counteracting completely the force, effectiveness, or value of something ⟨all our work *nullified* by one act of carelessness⟩. NEGATE implies the destruction or canceling out of each of two things by the other ⟨the opposing arguments *negate* each other⟩. ANNUL suggests making ineffective by legal or official action ⟨the treaty *annuls* all previous agreements⟩. INVALIDATE implies a legal or moral flaw that makes something not acceptable or not valid ⟨the absence of a signature *invalidated* the will⟩.

numb \ˈnəm\ *adj* **1 :** lacking in sensation especially as a result of cold or the administration of an anesthetic **2 :** lacking in emotion **:** INDIFFERENT [Middle English *nomen,* from *nimen* "to take, seize," from Old English *niman*] — **numb** *vt* — **numb·ly** *adv* — **numb·ness** *n*

¹num·ber \ˈnəm-bər\ *n* **1 a :** the total of individual items taken together ⟨the *number* of people in the room⟩ **b :** an indefinite usually large total ⟨a *number* of accidents occur on wet roads⟩ **2 a :** the possibility of being counted ⟨mosquitoes in swarms beyond *number*⟩ **b :** the property involved in seeing things as units subject to separating ⟨observing the difference between few and many and calling it *number*⟩ **3 a :** a unit belonging to a mathematical system and subject to its laws ⟨a *number* divisible by 2⟩ **b** *pl* **:** ARITHMETIC 1 **4 :** a distinction of word form to denote reference to one or more than one ⟨a verb agrees in *number* with its subject⟩; *also* **:** a form or group of forms so distinguished — compare PLURAL, SINGULAR **5 a :** a symbol, letter, or word used to represent a mathematical number **b :** a number used to identify or designate ⟨*number* one on the list⟩ ⟨a phone *number*⟩ **6** *pl* **:** regular count especially of syllables in poetry **:** METER; *also* **:** metrical verse **7 :** a member of a sequence or series ⟨the best *number* on the program⟩ ⟨lost the last *number* of the magazine⟩ **8** *pl* **:** a form of lottery in which bets are placed on numbers regularly published [Medieval French *nombre,* from Latin *numerus*] — **by the numbers 1 :** in unison to a specific count or cadence **2 :** in a systematic, routine, or mechanical manner

☞The Table of Numbers is on the following page.

²number *vb* **num·bered; num·ber·ing** \-bə-ring, -bring\ **1 :** COUNT 1 **2 :** to claim as part of a total **:** INCLUDE **3 :** to restrict to a definite number ⟨your days are *numbered*⟩ **4 :** to assign a number to ⟨*number* the pages⟩ **5 :** to amount to in number ⟨the crew *numbers* 100⟩ **6 :** to reach a total number ⟨their fans *number* in the millions⟩ — **num·ber·able** \ˈnəm-bə-rə-bəl, -brə-bəl\ *adj* — **num·ber·er** \-bər-ər\ *n*

number crunch·er \-ˌkrən-chər\ *n* **1 :** a computer that performs fast numerical calculations especially on large amounts of data **2 :** a person concerned with complex numerical data — **number crunching** *n*

num·ber·less \ˈnəm-bər-ləs\ *adj* **:** too many to count

number line *n* **:** an infinite line whose points correspond to the real numbers according to their distance in a positive or negative direction from a point arbitrarily labeled zero

Num·bers \ˈnəm-bərz\ *n* **:** the mainly narrative fourth book of canonical Jewish and Christian Scriptures — see BIBLE table

number theory *n* **:** the study of the properties of whole numbers

numb·ing \ˈnəm-ing\ *adj* **:** causing numbness — **numb·ing·ly** \-ing-lē\ *adv*

numbskull *variant of* NUMSKULL

nu·mer·a·ble \ˈnüm-rə-bəl, ˈnyüm-, -ə-rə-\ *adj* **:** that can be counted

nu·mer·al \ˈnüm-rəl, ˈnyüm-, -ə-rəl\ *n* **1 :** a symbol representing a number **2** *pl* **:** numbers designating by year a school or college class that are awarded for distinction especially in sports [Late Latin *numeralis* "of numbers," from Latin *numerus* "number"]

nu·mer·ate \ˈnü-mə-ˌrāt, ˈnyü-\ *vt* **:** ENUMERATE [Latin *numerare* "to count," from *numerus* "number"]

nu·mer·a·tion \ˌnü-mə-ˈrā-shən, ˌnyü-\ *n* **1 :** the act or process or a system or instance of counting or naming one by one ⟨a base 10 system of *numeration*⟩ **2 :** the act of reading in words numbers expressed by numerals

nu·mer·a·tor \ˈnü-mə-ˌrāt-ər, ˈnyü-\ *n* **1 :** the part of a fraction that is above the line and signifies the number to be divided by the denominator **2 :** one that counts

nu·mer·ic \nu̇-ˈmer-ik, nyu̇-\ *adj* **:** NUMERICAL; *esp* **:** indicating a number or a system of numbers ⟨a *numeric* code⟩

nu·mer·i·cal \nu̇-ˈmer-i-kəl, nyu̇-\ *adj* **1 :** of or relating to numbers **2 :** shown in or involving numbers or a number system — **nu·mer·i·cal·ly** \-kə-lē, -klē\ *adv*

nu·mer·ol·o·gy \ˌnü-mə-ˈräl-ə-jē, ˌnyü-\ *n* **:** the study of the occult significance of numbers — **nu·mer·ol·o·gist** \-jəst\ *n*

nu·mer·ous \ˈnüm-rəs, ˈnyüm-, -ə-rəs\ *adj* **:** consisting of great numbers of units or individuals ⟨*numerous* occasions⟩ ***synonyms*** see MANY — **nu·mer·ous·ly** *adv* — **nu·mer·ous·ness** *n*

nu·mis·mat·ic \ˌnü-məz-ˈmat-ik, ˌnyü-, -məs-\ *adj* **1 :** of or relating to numismatics **2 :** of or relating to coins [French *numismatique,* from Latin *nomisma* "coin," from Greek, "current coin," from *nomizein* "to use," from *nomos* "custom, law"] — **nu·mis·mat·i·cal·ly** \-ˈmat-i-kə-lē, -klē\ *adv*

nu·mis·mat·ics \-iks\ *n* **:** the study or collection of coins, to-

\ə\ abut	\au̇\ out	\i\ tip	\ȯ\ saw	\u̇\ foot
\ər\ further	\ch\ chin	\ī\ life	\ȯi\ coin	\y\ yet
\a\ mat	\e\ pet	\j\ job	\th\ thin	\yü\ few
\ā\ take	\ē\ easy	\ng\ sing	\th\ this	\yu̇\ cure
\ä\ cot, cart	\g\ go	\ō\ bone	\ü\ food	\zh\ vision

TABLE OF NUMBERS

CARDINAL NUMBERS[1]

NAME[2]	SYMBOL Arabic	SYMBOL Roman[3]
zero *or* naught *or* cipher	0	
one	1	I
two	2	II
three	3	III
four	4	IV
five	5	V
six	6	VI
seven	7	VII
eight	8	VIII
nine	9	IX
ten	10	X
eleven	11	XI
twelve	12	XII
thirteen	13	XIII
fourteen	14	XIV
fifteen	15	XV
sixteen	16	XVI
seventeen	17	XVII
eighteen	18	XVIII
nineteen	19	XIX
twenty	20	XX
twenty-one	21	XXI
twenty-two	22	XXII
twenty-three	23	XXIII
twenty-four	24	XXIV
twenty-five	25	XXV
twenty-six	26	XXVI
twenty-seven	27	XXVII
twenty-eight	28	XXVIII
twenty-nine	29	XXIX
thirty	30	XXX
thirty-one *etc*	31	XXXI
forty	40	XL
fifty	50	L
sixty	60	LX
seventy	70	LXX
eighty	80	LXXX
ninety	90	XC
one hundred	100	C
one hundred and one *or* one hundred one *etc*	101	CI
two hundred	200	CC
three hundred	300	CCC
four hundred	400	CD
five hundred	500	D
six hundred	600	DC
seven hundred	700	DCC
eight hundred	800	DCCC
nine hundred	900	CM
one thousand *or* ten hundred *etc*	1,000	M
two thousand *etc*	2,000	MM
five thousand	5,000	$\overline{V}$
ten thousand	10,000	$\overline{X}$
one hundred thousand	100,000	$\overline{C}$
one million	1,000,000	$\overline{M}$

ORDINAL NUMBERS[4]

NAME[5]	SYMBOL[6]
first	1st
second	2d *or* 2nd
third	3d *or* 3rd
fourth	4th
fifth	5th
sixth	6th
seventh	7th
eighth	8th
ninth	9th
tenth	10th
eleventh	11th
twelfth	12th
thirteenth	13th
fourteenth	14th
fifteenth	15th
sixteenth	16th
seventeenth	17th
eighteenth	18th
nineteenth	19th
twentieth	20th
twenty-first	21st
twenty-second	22d *or* 22nd
twenty-third	23d *or* 23rd
twenty-fourth	24th
twenty-fifth	25th
twenty-sixth	26th
twenty-seventh	27th
twenty-eighth	28th
twenty-ninth	29th
thirtieth	30th
thirty-first *etc*	31st
fortieth	40th
fiftieth	50th
sixtieth	60th
seventieth	70th
eightieth	80th
ninetieth	90th
hundredth *or* one hundredth	100th
hundred and first *or* one hundred and first *etc*	101st
two hundredth	200th
three hundredth	300th
four hundredth	400th
five hundredth	500th
six hundredth	600th
seven hundredth	700th
eight hundredth	800th
nine hundredth	900th
thousandth *or* one thousandth	1,000th
two thousandth *etc*	2,000th
ten thousandth	10,000th
hundred thousandth *or* one hundred thousandth	100,000th
millionth *or* one millionth	1,000,000th

[1] The cardinal numbers are used in simple counting or in answer to "how many?" The words for these numbers may be used as nouns (he counted to *twelve*), as pronouns (*twelve* were found), or as adjectives (*twelve* girls).

[2] In formal writing the numbers one to one hundred and in less formal writing the numbers one to nine are commonly written out in words, while larger numbers are given in numerals. A number occurring at the beginning of a sentence is usually written out. Except in very formal writing numerals are used for dates. Arabic numbers from 1,000 to 9,999 are often written without commas (1000 to 9999). Year numbers are always written without commas (1783).

[3] The Roman numerals are written either in capitals or in lowercase letters.

[4] The ordinal numbers are used to show the order in which such items as names, objects, and periods of time are considered (the *twelfth* month; the *fourth* row of seats; the *18th* century).

[5] Each of the terms for the ordinal numbers except *first* and *second* is used for one of a number of parts into which a whole may be divided (a *fourth*; a *sixth*; a *tenth*) and as the denominator in fractions (*one fourth*; *three fifths*). When used as nouns the fractions are usually written as two words, although they are usually hyphenated as adjectives (a *two-thirds* majority). When fractions are written in numerals, the cardinal symbols are used (¼, ⅗, ⅚).

[6] The Arabic symbols for the cardinal numbers may sometimes be read as ordinals (January 1 = January first; 2 Samuel = Second Samuel). The Roman numerals are sometimes read as ordinals (Henry IV = Henry the Fourth); sometimes they are written with the ordinal suffixes (XIXth Dynasty).

DENOMINATIONS ABOVE ONE MILLION

American system[1]

NAME	VALUE IN POWERS OF TEN	NUMBER OF ZEROS[2]	NUMBER OF GROUPS OF THREE 0'S AFTER 1,000
billion	10^{9}	9	2
trillion	10^{12}	12	3
quadrillion	10^{15}	15	4
quintillion	10^{18}	18	5
sextillion	10^{21}	21	6
septillion	10^{24}	24	7
octillion	10^{27}	27	8
nonillion	10^{30}	30	9
decillion	10^{33}	33	10

British system[1]

NAME	VALUE IN POWERS OF TEN	NUMBER OF ZEROS[2]	POWERS OF 1,000,000
milliard	10^{9}	9	—
billion	10^{12}	12	2
trillion	10^{18}	18	3
quadrillion	10^{24}	24	4
quintillion	10^{30}	30	5
sextillion	10^{36}	36	6
septillion	10^{42}	42	7
octillion	10^{48}	48	8
nonillion	10^{54}	54	9
decillion	10^{60}	60	10

[1] The American system for numbers above one million was modeled on the French system but more recently the French system has been changed to correspond to the German and British systems. In the American system each of the denominations above 1,000 millions (the American *billion*) is 1,000 times greater than the one before (one trillion = 1,000 billions; one quadrillion = 1,000 trillions). In the British system the first denomination above 1,000 millions (the British *milliard*) is 1,000 times the preceding one, but each of the denominations above 1,000 milliards (the British *billion*) is 1,000,000 times the preceding one (one trillion = 1,000,000 billions; one quadrillion = 1,000,000 trillions). In recent years, however, British usage reflects increasing use of the American system in place of the British system.

[2] For ease in reading large numerals, the thousands, millions, and larger denominations are usually separated by commas (21,530; 1,155,465) or especially in technical writing by spaces (1 155 465). Serial numbers (as social security numbers) are often written with hyphens (042-24-4705).

kens, medals, or paper money — **nu·mis·ma·tist** \nü-ˈmiz-mət-əst, nyü-\ *n*

num·skull *or* **numb·skull** \ˈnəm-ˌskəl\ *n* : a stupid person

nun \ˈnən\ *n* : a woman belonging to a religious order; *esp* : one under solemn vows of poverty, chastity, and obedience [Old English *nunne,* from Late Latin *nonna*]

Nunc Di·mit·tis \ˌnəngk-də-ˈmit-əs\ *n* : the prayer of Simeon in Luke 2:29–32 used as a canticle [Latin, "now lettest thou depart"; from the first words of the canticle]

nun·ci·a·ture \ˈnən-sē-ə-ˌchu̇r, ˈnu̇n-, -chər\ *n* **1** : the office or period of office of a nuncio **2** : a papal delegation headed by a nuncio [Italian *nunciatura,* from *nuncio* "nuncio"]

nun·cio \ˈnən-sē-ˌō, ˈnu̇n-\ *n, pl* **-ci·os** : a papal representative of the highest rank permanently accredited to a civil government [Italian, from Latin *nuntius* "messenger, message"]

nun·cu·pa·tive \ˈnən-kyu̇-ˌpāt-iv, ˌnən-ˈkyü-pət-\ *adj* : not written : ORAL <a *nuncupative* will> [Medieval Latin *nuncupativus,* from Late Latin, "so-called," from Latin *nuncupare* "to name, call," probably derived from *nomen* "name" + *capere* "to take"]

nun·nery \ˈnən-rē, -ə-rē\ *n, pl* **-ner·ies** : a convent of nuns

¹nup·tial \ˈnəp-shəl, -chəl\ *adj* **1** : of or relating to marriage or the marriage ceremony **2** : characteristic of mating or the breeding season [Latin *nuptialis,* from *nuptiae* "wedding," from *nubere* "to marry"]

²nuptial *n* : WEDDING 1 — usually used in plural

¹nurse \ˈnərs\ *n* **1** : a woman who has the care of a young child **2** : a person who cares for the sick or infirm; *esp* : one who is specially licensed and practices independently or is supervised by a physician, surgeon, or dentist and who is skilled in promoting and maintaining health **3** : a worker of a social insect (as an ant or bee) that cares for the young [Medieval French *nurice,* from Late Latin *nutricia,* from Latin *nutricius* "nourishing, nutritious"]

²nurse *vb* **1** : to feed at the breast : SUCKLE **2** : REAR 3b, EDUCATE **3** : to manage with care or economy <*nurse* one's funds> **4** : to care for as a nurse <*nursed* them back to health> **5** : to hold in one's memory or consideration <*nurse* a grudge> **6** : to treat with special care <*nurse* a car over a rough road> **7** : to act or serve as a nurse [Middle English *nurshen* "to nourish," from *nurishen*] — **nurs·er** *n*

nurse·maid \ˈnər-ˌsmād\ *n* : a girl or woman employed to look after children

nurse–mid·wife \-ˈmid-ˌwīf\ *n* : a registered nurse with additional training as a midwife

nurse–prac·ti·tion·er \-prak-ˈtish-nər, -ə-nər\ *n* : a registered nurse who is qualified through advanced training to assume some of the duties and responsibilities formerly assumed only by a physician

nurs·ery \ˈnərs-rē, -ə-rē\ *n, pl* **-er·ies** **1 a** : a room or suite set apart in a house for the children **b** : a place where children are temporarily cared for in their parents' absence **c** : DAY NURSERY **2** : a place where plants (as trees or shrubs) are grown for transplanting, for use as stocks in grafting, or for sale

nurs·ery·maid \-ˌmād\ *n* : NURSEMAID

nurs·ery·man \-mən\ *n* : a person whose occupation is the growing of plants (as trees and shrubs) especially for sale

nursery rhyme *n* : a short rhyme for children that often tells a story

nursery school *n* : a school for children usually under five years of age

nurse's aid *n* : a worker who assists trained nurses in a hospital by performing unspecialized services (as giving baths)

nurse shark *n* : a nocturnal shark of warm waters [alteration of *nusse*]

nursing bottle *n* : BOTTLE 3a

nursing home *n* : a privately operated establishment where personal or nursing care is provided for persons (as the aged) who are unable to care for themselves properly

nurs·ling \ˈnərs-liŋ\ *n* **1** : one tended with special care **2** : a nursing child

¹nur·ture \ˈnər-chər\ *n* **1** : TRAINING 1, UPBRINGING **2** : something that nourishes : FOOD **3** : the sum of the environmental factors influencing the behavior and traits expressed by an organism [Medieval French *nureture,* from Late Latin *nutritura* "act of nursing," from Latin *nutrire* "to nourish, nurse"]

²nurture *vt* **nur·tured; nur·tur·ing** \ˈnərch-riŋ, -ə-riŋ\ **1** : to supply with nourishment **2** : EDUCATE 2 **3** : to further the development of : FOSTER — **nur·tur·er** \ˈnər-chər-ər\ *n*

¹nut \ˈnət\ *n* **1 a** : a hard-shelled dry fruit (as a peanut in the shell) or seed (as a Brazil nut) with a separable rind or shell and an inner kernel; *also* : this kernel **b** : a dry one-seeded fruit (as an acorn or chestnut) that has a woody outer layer and that does not split open when ripe **2** : a small block usually of metal with a hole in it that has an internal screw thread and is used on a bolt or screw for tightening or holding something **3** : the ridge in a stringed musical instrument over which the strings pass on the upper end of the fingerboard **4 a** : a foolish, eccentric, or crazy person **b** : ENTHUSIAST, FAN [Old English *hnutu*] — **nut·like** \-ˌlīk\ *adj*

²nut *vi* **nut·ted; nut·ting** : to gather or seek nuts

nut·crack·er \ˈnət-ˌkrak-ər\ *n* **1** : an instrument for cracking the shells of nuts **2** : a bird related to the crows that lives largely on seeds from the cones of the pine tree

\ə\ **abut**	\au̇\ **out**	\i\ **tip**	\ȯ\ **saw**	\u̇\ **foot**
\ər\ **further**	\ch\ **chin**	\ī\ **life**	\ȯi\ **coin**	\y\ **yet**
\a\ **mat**	\e\ **pet**	\j\ **job**	\th\ **thin**	\yü\ **few**
\ā\ **take**	\ē\ **easy**	\ng\ **sing**	\t͟h\ **this**	\yu̇\ **cure**
\ä\ **cot, cart**	\g\ **go**	\ō\ **bone**	\ü\ **food**	\zh\ **vision**

nut·hatch \ˈnət-ˌhach\ *n* **:** any of various small tree-climbing birds that feed on insects, have a narrow bill and short tail, and are noted for their habit of going down tree trunks headfirst [Middle English *notehache,* from *note* "nut" + *hache* "ax," from Medieval French, "battle-ax"]

nuthatch

nut·let \ˈnət-lət\ *n* **:** a small nut; *also* **:** a small fruit similar to a nut

nut·meg \ˈnət-ˌmeg\ *n* **1 :** the aromatic seed of an evergreen tree grown chiefly in Indonesia; *also* **:** this tree **2 :** a spice consisting of ground nutmeg seeds — compare MACE [Middle English *notemuge,* derived from Old Occitan *noz muscada,* from *noz* "nut" (from Latin *nux*) + *muscada,* feminine of *muscat* "musky"]

nut·pick \-ˌpik\ *n* **:** a small sharp-pointed table implement for extracting the kernels from nuts

nu·tria \ˈnü-trē-ə, ˈnyü-\ *n* **1 :** a South American rodent that lives in or near the water, has webbed feet and a nearly hairless tail, and has been introduced into the U.S. along the Gulf Coast and in the Pacific Northwest **2 :** the durable usually light brown fur of the nutria [Spanish, "otter," from Latin *lutra*]

[1]**nu·tri·ent** \ˈnü-trē-ənt, ˈnyü-\ *adj* **:** furnishing nourishment [Latin *nutriens,* present participle of *nutrire* "to nourish"]

[2]**nutrient** *n* **:** a nutritive substance or ingredient

nu·tri·ment \ˈnü-trə-mənt, ˈnyü-\ *n* **:** something that nourishes

nu·tri·tion \nu̇-ˈtrish-ən, nyu̇-\ *n* **1 :** the act or process of nourishing or being nourished; *esp* **:** the processes by which living things take in and utilize food substances **2 :** NOURISHMENT 1 [Late Latin *nutritio,* from Latin *nutrire* "to nourish"] — **nu·tri·tion·al** \-ˈtrish-nəl, -ən-l\ *adj* — **nu·tri·tion·al·ly** *adv*

nu·tri·tion·ist \-ˈtrish-nəst, -ə-nəst\ *n* **:** a specialist in the study of nutrition

nu·tri·tious \nu̇-ˈtrish-əs, nyu̇-\ *adj* **:** providing nutrients **:** NOURISHING [Latin *nutricius,* from *nutrix* "nurse"] — **nu·tri·tious·ly** *adv* — **nu·tri·tious·ness** *n*

nu·tri·tive \ˈnü-trət-iv, ˈnyü-\ *adj* **1 :** of or relating to nutrition **2 :** NUTRITIOUS — **nu·tri·tive·ly** *adv*

nuts \ˈnəts\ *adj* **1 :** ENTHUSIASTIC, KEEN **2 :** CRAZY 2a

nut·shell \ˈnət-ˌshel\ *n* **:** the shell of a nut — **in a nutshell :** in a small space **:** in brief

nut·ty \ˈnət-ē\ *adj* **nut·tier; -est 1 :** containing or suggesting nuts (as in flavor) **2 :** ECCENTRIC 2 ⟨a *nutty* idea⟩; *also* **:** mentally unbalanced — **nut·ti·ness** *n*

nux vom·i·ca \ˈnəks-ˈväm-i-kə\ *n, pl* **nux vomica :** the poisonous seed of a southeast Asian tree that contains strychnine; *also* **:** this tree [New Latin, literally, "emetic nut"]

nuz·zle \ˈnəz-əl\ *vb* **nuz·zled; nuz·zling** \ˈnəz-ling, -ə-ling\ **1 :** to push or rub with the nose **2 :** to lie close [Middle English *noselen* "to bring the nose toward the ground," from *nose*]

ny·lon \ˈnī-ˌlän\ *n* **1 :** any of numerous strong tough elastic synthetic materials used especially in textiles and plastics **2** *pl* **:** stockings made of nylon [coined word] — **nylon** *adj*

nymph \ˈnimf, ˈnimpf\ *n* **1 :** one of the minor divinities of nature in classical mythology represented as beautiful maidens dwelling in the mountains, forests, meadows, and waters **2 :** any of various immature insects; *esp* **:** an immature insect (as a dragonfly or grasshopper) that differs from the adult especially in size and in its incompletely developed wings and sex organs [Medieval French *nimphe,* from Latin *nympha* "bride, nymph," from Greek *nymphē*] — **nymph·al** \ˈnim-fəl, ˈnimp-\ *adj*

nys·tag·mus \nis-ˈtag-məs\ *n* **:** a rapid involuntary oscillation of the eyeballs [Greek *nystagmos* "drowsiness," from *nystazein* "to doze"]

O

o \ˈō\ *n, pl* **o's** *or* **os** \ˈōz\ *often cap* **1 :** the 15th letter of the English alphabet **2 :** ZERO

O *variant of* OH

o- *or* **oo-** *combining form* **:** egg **:** ovum ⟨oocyte⟩ [Greek *ōion* "egg"]

-o- — used as a connective vowel originally to join word elements of Greek origin and now also to join word elements of Latin or other origin ⟨speedometer⟩ [Greek, stem vowel of many nouns and adjectives in combination]

o' *also* **o** \ə\ *prep* **1** *chiefly dialect* **:** ON **2 :** OF ⟨one *o'*clock⟩

oaf \ˈōf\ *n* **:** a stupid or awkward person [alteration of *auf, alfe* "goblin's child," probably from Middle English *alven, elven* "elf, fairy," from Old English *elfen* "nymphs"] — **oaf·ish** \ˈō-fish\ *adj* — **oaf·ish·ly** *adv* — **oaf·ish·ness** *n*

oak \ˈōk\ *n, pl* **oaks** *or* **oak 1 :** any of various trees or shrubs closely related to the beeches and chestnuts and producing acorns **2 :** the usually tough hard durable wood of the oak much used for furniture and flooring [Old English *āc*] — **oak** *adj* — **oak·en** \ˈō-kən\ *adj*

oak 1

oak apple *n* **:** a large round gall produced on oak leaves by a gall wasp

oa·kum \ˈō-kəm\ *n* **:** hemp or jute fiber impregnated with tar or a tar derivative and used in caulking seams and packing joints [Old English *ācumba* "tow"]

oar \ˈōr, ˈȯr\ *n* **1 :** a long pole with a broad blade at one end used for propelling or steering a boat **2 :** OARSMAN [Old English *ār*] — **oared** \ˈōrd, ˈȯrd\ *adj*

oar·lock \ˈōr-ˌläk, ˈȯr-\ *n* **:** a usually U-shaped device for holding an oar in place

oars·man \ˈōrz-mən, ˈȯrz-\ *n* **:** a person who rows especially in a racing crew

oa·sis \ō-ˈā-səs\ *n, pl* **oa·ses** \-ˈā-ˌsēz\ **1 :** a fertile or green area in an arid region (as a desert) **2 :** something providing relief, refuge, or pleasant contrast [Late Latin, from Greek]

oat \ˈōt\ *n* **1 :** a cereal grass with long spikelets in loose clusters that is widely grown for its seed which is used for human food and livestock feed **2** *pl* **:** a crop or plot of the oat; *also* **:** oat seeds [Old English *āte*]

oat·en \ˈōt-n\ *adj* **:** of or relating to oats, oat straw, or oatmeal

oath \ˈōth\ *n, pl* **oaths** \ˈōt͟hz, ˈōths\ **1 a :** a solemn appeal to God or to some revered person or thing to bear witness to the truth of one's word or the sincerity of a promise or intention **b :** something (as a promise) made more certain by an oath **2 :** a careless or profane use of a sacred name; *also* **:** SWEARWORD [Old English *āth*]

oat·meal \ˈōt-ˌmēl, ōt-ˈ\ *n* **1 :** oats husked and crushed into coarse meal or flattened into flakes **2 :** porridge made from such meal or flakes

ob- *prefix* **:** inversely ⟨obovate⟩ [Latin, "in the way, against, toward," from *ob* "in the way of, on account of"]

Oba·di·ah \ˌō-bə-ˈdī-ə\ *n* **:** a prophetic book of canonical Jewish and Christian Scriptures — see BIBLE table

[1]**ob·bli·ga·to** \ˌäb-lə-ˈgät-ō\ *adj* **:** not to be omitted — used as a direction in music [Italian, "obligatory," from *obbligare* "to oblige," from Latin *obligare*]

[2]**obbligato** *n, pl* **-gatos** *also* **-ga·ti** \-ˈgät-ē\ **1 :** an elaborate and prominent accompanying part usually played by a solo instrument **2 :** an accompanying situation or occurrence

ob·du·ra·cy \ˈäb-də-rə-sē, -dyə-; äb-ˈdu̇r-ə-, -ˈdyu̇r-\ *n, pl* **-cies :** the quality or state of being obdurate

ob·du·rate \ˈäb-də-rət, -dyə-; äb-ˈdu̇r-ət, -ˈdyu̇r-\ *adj* **1 a**

: hardened in feelings **b** : stubbornly persistent in wrongdoing **2** : resisting change : UNYIELDING [Latin *obduratus,* past participle of *obdurare* "to harden," from *ob-* "against" + *durus* "hard"] — **ob·du·rate·ly** *adv* — **ob·du·rate·ness** *n*

obe·di·ence \ō-ˈbēd-ē-əns, ə-\ *n* **1** : an act or instance of obeying **2** : the quality or state of being obedient

obe·di·ent \-ənt\ *adj* : willing or inclined to obey [Medieval French, from Latin *oboediens,* from *oboedire* "to obey"] — **obe·di·ent·ly** *adv*

obei·sance \ō-ˈbās-ns, -ˈbēs-\ *n* **1** : a movement of the body made as a sign of respect : BOW **2** : DEFERENCE, HOMAGE [Medieval French *obeisance,* from *obeir* "to obey"] — **obei·sant** \-nt\ *adj*

obe·lia \ō-ˈbēl-yə\ *n* : any of a genus of small marine hydroids that form colonies branched like trees [New Latin, genus name]

ob·e·lisk \ˈäb-ə-ˌlisk\ *n* : a 4-sided pillar that tapers toward the top and ends in a pyramid [Middle French *obelisque,* from Latin *obeliscus,* from Greek *obeliskos,* from *obelos* "spit, pointed pillar"]

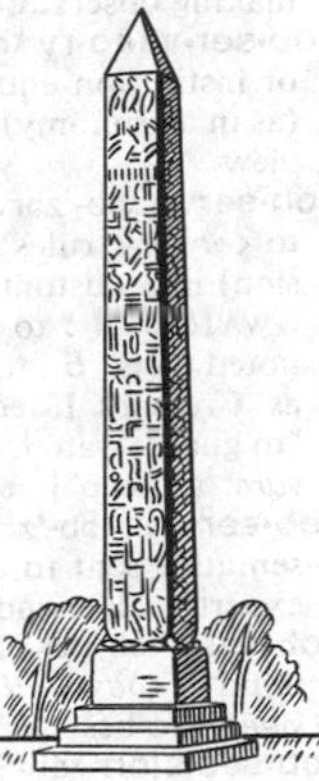
obelisk

obese \ō-ˈbēs\ *adj* : excessively fat [Latin *obesus,* from *obedere* "to eat up," from *ob-* "against" + *edere* "to eat"] — **obe·si·ty** \ō-ˈbē-sət-ē\ *n*

obey \ō-ˈbā, ə-\ *vb* **obeyed; obey·ing** **1** : to follow the commands or guidance of **2** : to comply with : EXECUTE ⟨*obey* an order⟩ **3** : to behave obediently [Medieval French *obeir,* from Latin *oboedire*] — **obey·er** *n*

ob·fus·cate \ˈäb-fə-ˌskāt, äb-ˈfəs-ˌkāt\ *vt* **1 a** : DARKEN **b** : to make obscure ⟨he is *obfuscating* the issue⟩ **2** : CONFUSE 2 [Late Latin *obfuscare,* from Latin *ob-* "in the way" + *fuscus* "dark brown"] — **ob·fus·ca·tion** \ˌäb-fəs-ˈkā-shən\ *n* — **ob·fus·ca·to·ry** \äb-ˈfəs-kə-ˌtōr-ē, -ˌtȯr-\ *adj*

ob–gyn \ˌō-ˌbē-ˈjin, -ˌjē-ˌwī-ˈen\ *n, pl* **ob–gyns** : a physician who specializes in obstetrics and gynecology [*ob*stetrician *gyn*ecologist]

obi \ˈō-bē\ *n* : a broad sash worn especially with a Japanese kimono [Japanese]

obit \ō-ˈbit, ˈō-bət\ *n* : OBITUARY

obit·u·ary \ə-ˈbich-ə-ˌwer-ē\ *n, pl* **-ar·ies** : a notice of a person's death usually with a short biographical account [Medieval Latin *obituarium,* from Latin *obitus* "death," from *obire* "to go to meet, die," from *ob-* "toward, against" + *ire* "to go"] — **obitu·ary** *adj*

[1]**ob·ject** \ˈäb-jikt\ *n* **1**: something that may be perceived by the senses ⟨I see an *object* in the distance⟩ **2 a** : something toward which thought, feeling, or action is directed ⟨the *object* of my affections⟩ **b** : a cause for attention or concern ⟨money is no *object*⟩ **3** : the goal or end of an effort or activity : PURPOSE ⟨the *object* is to raise money⟩ **4** : a noun or noun equivalent (as a pronoun, gerund, or phrase) that receives the action of a verb or completes the meaning of a preposition **5** : something (as an icon or window) in computer graphics that can be moved or used independently of other such things [Medieval Latin *objectum,* from Latin *obicere* "to throw in the way, present, hinder, object," from *ob-* "in the way" + *jacere* "to throw"] — **object·less** \ˈäb-jik-tləs\ *adj*

[2]**ob·ject** \əb-ˈjekt\ *vb* **1** : to offer or cite in opposition or as an objection ⟨*objected* that the price was too high⟩ **2** : to oppose something firmly usually with words ⟨the prosecution loudly *objected* to the question asked by the defense⟩ **3** : to feel distaste for something ⟨I *object* to racism⟩ [Latin *objectus,* past participle of *obicere* "to throw in the way, object"] — **ob·jector** \-ˈjek-tər\ *n*

object ball \ˈäb-jikt-, -jik-\ *n* : the ball first struck by the cue ball in billiards and pool

ob·jec·ti·fy \əb-ˈjek-tə-ˌfī\ *vt* **-fied; -fy·ing** **1** : to treat (as a person) as an object **2** : to make objective — **ob·jec·ti·fi·cation** \-ˌjek-tə-fə-ˈkā-shən\ *n*

ob·jec·tion \əb-ˈjek-shən\ *n* **1 a** : an act of objecting **b** : a reason or argument given in opposition ⟨my *objection* is this⟩ **2** : an expression or feeling of disapproval

ob·jec·tion·able \-shə-nə-bəl, -shnə-bəl\ *adj* : arousing disapproval : OFFENSIVE ⟨was written in *objectionable* language⟩ — **ob·jec·tion·able·ness** *n* — **ob·jec·tion·ably** \-blē\ *adv*

[1]**ob·jec·tive** \əb-ˈjek-tiv\ *adj* **1** : existing outside and independent of the mind ⟨*objective* reality⟩ — compare SUBJECTIVE 2 **2** : relating to, characteristic of, or constituting the case of words that follow transitive verbs or prepositions — compare ACCUSATIVE **3** : expressing or dealing with facts or conditions as perceived without distortion by personal feelings, prejudices, or interpretations ⟨an *objective* history of the war⟩ — **ob·jective·ly** *adv* — **ob·jec·tive·ness** *n* — **ob·jec·tiv·i·ty** \ˌäb-ˌjek-ˈtiv-ət-ē, əb-\ *n*

[2]**objective** *n* **1** : a lens or system of lenses (as in a microscope) that forms an image of an object **2** : something toward which effort is directed : an aim, goal, or end of action

objective complement *n* : a noun, adjective, or pronoun used in the predicate as complement to a verb and as qualifier of its direct object ⟨green in "paint the wall green" is an *objective complement*⟩

object lesson \ˈäb-jikt-\ *n* : something that serves as a practical example of a principle or abstract idea

ob·ject–ori·ent·ed programming \-ˌōr-ē-ˌent-əd-\ *n* : a type of computer programming that uses basic building blocks (as of data and variables) to construct a program

ob·jet d'art \ˌȯb-ˌzhā-ˈdär\ *n, pl* **ob·jets d'art** \same\ : an article of artistic value [French, literally, "art object"]

[1]**ob·late** \äb-ˈlāt, ˈäb-ˌ\ *adj* : flattened or depressed at the poles ⟨the *oblate* shape of the earth⟩ [probably from New Latin *oblatus,* from *ob-* "ob-" + *-latus* (as in *prolatus* "elongated in the direction of the poles," from Latin, past participle of *proferre* "to extend," from *pro-* + *ferre* "to carry")]

[2]**ob·late** \ˈäb-ˌlāt\ *n* **1** : a layman living in a monastery under a modified rule and without vows **2** : a member of one of several Roman Catholic communities of men or women [Medieval Latin *oblatus,* literally, "one offered up," from Latin, past participle of *offerre* "to offer"]

ob·la·tion \ə-ˈblā-shən, ō-\ *n* : something offered in worship or devotion [Medieval French, from Late Latin *oblatio,* from Latin *offerre* "to offer"]

[1]**ob·li·gate** \ˈäb-lə-ˌgāt\ *vt* : to bring under obligation : bind legally or morally ⟨*obligated* to repay the debt⟩ [Latin *obligare,* from *ob-* "toward" + *ligare* "to bind"]

[2]**ob·li·gate** \ˈäb-li-gət, -lə-ˌgāt\ *adj* : restricted to one particular mode of life ⟨an *obligate* parasite⟩ — **ob·li·gate·ly** *adv*

ob·li·ga·tion \ˌäb-lə-ˈgā-shən\ *n* **1** : an act of making oneself responsible for a course of action **2** : something (as a promise or contract) that requires one to do something **3** : a condition or feeling of being bound to a course of action **4** : something one must do : DUTY

oblig·a·to·ry \ə-ˈblig-ə-ˌtōr-ē, ä-, -ˌtȯr-\ *adj* **1** : legally or morally binding **2** : REQUIRED ⟨attendance was *obligatory*⟩

oblige \ə-ˈblīj\ *vb* **1** : to compel by physical, moral, or legal pressure : FORCE ⟨laws *oblige* citizens to pay taxes⟩ **2 a** : to put in one's debt by a favor ⟨*oblige* an acquaintance with a loan⟩ **b** : to do something as or as if a favor ⟨a person always willing to *oblige*⟩ [Medieval French *obliger,* from Latin *obligare* "to obligate"] — **oblig·er** *n*

oblig·ing \ə-ˈblī-jing\ *adj* : willing to do favors : HELPFUL — **oblig·ing·ly** \-jing-lē\ *adv* — **oblig·ing·ness** *n*

[1]**oblique** \ō-ˈblēk, ə-, -ˈblīk\ *adj* **1 a** : neither perpendicular nor parallel : INCLINED **b** : having the axis not perpendicular to the base ⟨an *oblique* cone⟩ **c** : having no right angle ⟨an *oblique* triangle⟩ **2** : not straightforward : INDIRECT ⟨*oblique* accusations⟩ [Latin *obliquus*] — **oblique·ly** *adv* — **oblique·ness** *n* — **obliq·ui·ty** \ō-ˈblik-wət-ē, ə-\ *n*

[2]**oblique** *n* **1** : something that is oblique **2** : any of several obliquely placed muscles; *esp* : one of the thin flat diagonal muscles of the abdominal wall

oblique angle *n* : an acute or obtuse angle

oblit·er·ate \ə-ˈblit-ə-ˌrāt, ō-\ *vt* : to remove or destroy completely : WIPE OUT ⟨wind *obliterated* the tracks⟩ [Latin *obliterare,* from *ob* "in the way of" + *littera* "letter"] ***synonyms*** see erase — **oblit·er·a·tion** \-ˌblit-ə-ˈrā-shən\ *n* — **oblit·er·a·tor** \-ˈblit-ə-ˌrāt-ər\ *n*

oblit·er·a·tive \ə-ˈblit-ə-ˌrāt-iv\ *adj* **1** : causing or characterized by obliteration **2** : tending to make inconspicuous ⟨*obliterative* behavior⟩

obliv·i·on \ə-ˈbliv-ē-ən, ō-, ä-\ *n* **1** : the state of forgetting or having forgotten; *esp* : the condition of being oblivious **2** : the condition or state of being forgotten [Medieval French, from Latin *oblivio,* from *oblivisci* "to forget"]

obliv·i·ous \-ē-əs\ *adj* **1** : lacking memory or mindful attention : FORGETFUL **2** : lacking active conscious knowledge : UNAWARE ⟨*oblivious* to the risk of swimming alone⟩ — **obliv·i·ous·ly** *adv* — **obliv·i·ous·ness** *n*

ob·long \ˈäb-ˌlȯŋ\ *adj* : longer in one direction than in the other ⟨an *oblong* shoebox⟩ ⟨an *oblong* watermelon⟩ [Latin *oblongus,* from *ob-* "toward" + *longus* "long"] — **oblong** *n*

ob·lo·quy \ˈäb-lə-kwē\ *n, pl* **-quies** **1** : a strongly condemning utterance : abusive language **2** : bad repute : DISCREDIT [Late Latin *obloquium,* from *obloqui* "to speak against," from *ob-* "against" + *loqui* "to speak"]

ob·nox·ious \äb-ˈnäk-shəs, əb-\ *adj* : extremely disagreeable or offensive [Latin *obnoxius,* from *ob* "in the way of, exposed to" + *noxa* "harm"] — **ob·nox·ious·ly** *adv* — **ob·nox·ious·ness** *n*

oboe \ˈō-bō\ *n* : a double-reed woodwind instrument having a conical tube and a bright penetrating tone [Italian, from French *hautbois,* from *haut* "high" + *bois* "wood"] — **obo·ist** \ˈō-ˌbō-əst\ *n*

oboe

obol \ˈäb-əl, ˈō-bəl\ *n* : an ancient Greek coin or weight equal to ⅙ drachma [Latin *obolus,* from Greek *obolos*]

ob·ovate \äb-ˈō-ˌvāt, ˈäb-\ *adj* : ovate with the base narrower ⟨an *obovate* leaf⟩

ob·scene \äb-ˈsēn, əb-\ *adj* **1** : disgusting to the senses : REPULSIVE **2** **a** : deeply offensive to morality or decency ⟨an *obscene* misuse of power⟩; *esp* : designed to incite to lust or depravity **b** : containing or being language not acceptable in polite usage ⟨*obscene* lyrics⟩ **c** : so excessive as to be offensive ⟨an *obscene* amount of money⟩ [Middle French, from Latin *obscenus*] ***synonyms*** see COARSE — **ob·scene·ly** *adv*

ob·scen·i·ty \-ˈsen-ət-ē\ *n, pl* **-ties** **1** : the quality or state of being obscene **2** : something that is obscene

[1]**ob·scure** \äb-ˈskyu̇r, əb-\ *adj* **1** : lacking or inadequately supplied with light : DIM **2** : not easily seen or distinguished : FAINT ⟨*obscure* markings⟩ **3** : not readily understood or clearly expressed **4** : relatively unknown: as **a** : SECLUDED ⟨an *obscure* village⟩ **b** : not famous or prominent ⟨an *obscure* poet⟩ **5** : constituting the unstressed vowel \ə\ or having unstressed \ə\ as its value [Medieval French *obscur,* from Latin *obscurus*] — **ob·scure·ly** *adv* — **ob·scure·ness** *n*

synonyms OBSCURE, DARK, VAGUE, CRYPTIC mean not clearly understandable. OBSCURE implies a veiling of meaning through defective expression or a withholding of full knowledge ⟨an *obscure* reference to ancient Roman law⟩. DARK implies an imperfect revelation often with ominous or sinister suggestion ⟨muttered *dark* hints of revenge⟩. VAGUE implies lacking clarity because imperfectly conceived, grasped, or thought out ⟨a *vague* sense of duty⟩. CRYPTIC implies a purposely concealed meaning ⟨made *cryptic* remarks about future plans⟩.

[2]**obscure** *vt* **1** : to make dark, dim, or indistinct **2** : to conceal or hide by or as if by covering **3** : to use the unstressed vowel \ə\ as the sound of

ob·scu·ri·ty \äb-ˈskyu̇r-ət-ē, əb-\ *n, pl* **-ties** **1** : one that is obscure **2** : the quality or state of being obscure

ob·se·qui·ous \əb-ˈsē-kwē-əs, äb-\ *adj* : humbly or excessively attentive (as to a person in authority) : FAWNING, SERVILE [Latin *obsequiosus* "compliant," from *obsequi* "to comply," from *ob-* "toward" + *sequi* "to follow"] — **ob·se·qui·ous·ly** *adv* — **ob·se·qui·ous·ness** *n*

ob·se·quy \ˈäb-sə-kwē\ *n, pl* **-quies** : a funeral or burial rite — usually used in plural [Medieval French *obsequie,* from Medieval Latin *obsequiae,* plural, alteration of Latin *exsequiae,* from *exsequi* "to follow out, execute," from *ex-* + *sequi* "to follow"]

ob·serv·able \əb-ˈzər-və-bəl\ *adj* **1** : NOTEWORTHY **2** : capable of being observed — **ob·serv·ably** \-blē\ *adv*

ob·serv·ance \əb-ˈzər-vəns\ *n* **1** : a customary practice or ceremony **2** : an act or instance of following a custom, rule, or law **3** : an act or instance of watching

ob·serv·ant \-vənt\ *adj* **1** : paying strict attention : WATCHFUL **2** : quick to observe : KEEN **3** : careful in observing : MINDFUL ⟨an *observant* and religious person⟩ — **ob·serv·ant·ly** *adv*

[1]**ob·ser·va·tion** \ˌäb-sər-ˈvā-shən, -zər-\ *n* **1 a** : an act or instance of observing a custom, rule, or law **b** : an act or the power of observing **2** : an act of usually measuring, noting, and recording facts or occurrences ⟨weather *observations*⟩ **3 a** : a conclusion drawn from observing **b** : an expression of opinion or judgment : COMMENT **4** : the state of being observed ⟨is under *observation* at the hospital⟩ — **ob·ser·va·tion·al** \-shnəl, -shən-l\ *adj*

[2]**observation** *adj* : designed for use in viewing something or in making observations ⟨an *observation* tower⟩

ob·ser·va·to·ry \əb-ˈzər-və-ˌtōr-ē, -ˌtȯr-\ *n, pl* **-ries** **1** : a place or institution equipped for observation of natural phenomena (as in astronomy) **2** : a place or structure commanding a wide view

ob·serve \əb-ˈzərv\ *vb* **1** : to conform one's action or practice to ⟨*observe* rules⟩ **2** : to celebrate or solemnize (as an occasion) in a customary or accepted way **3** : to pay attention to : WATCH **4** : to discover especially through consideration of noted facts **5** : to make a scientific observation of **6** : to utter as a remark [Medieval French *observer,* from Latin *observare* "to guard, watch, observe," from *ob-* "in the way, toward" + *servare* "to keep"] ***synonyms*** see KEEP

ob·serv·er \əb-ˈzər-vər\ *n* : one that observes: as **a** : a representative sent to observe but not participate officially **b** : an expert analyst and commentator in a field ⟨political *observers*⟩

ob·sess \əb-ˈses, äb-\ *vt* : to haunt or excessively preoccupy the mind of ⟨*obsessed* by fear⟩ [Latin *obsessus,* past participle of *obsidēre* "to besiege," from *ob-* "against" + *sedēre* "to sit"]

ob·ses·sion \äb-ˈsesh-ən, əb-\ *n* **1** : a prolonged disturbing preoccupation with an often unreasonable idea or feeling ⟨an *obsession* with money⟩ **2** : something that causes an obsession

ob·ses·sive \äb-ˈses-iv, əb-\ *adj* **1 a** : tending to cause obsession **b** : excessive often to an unreasonable degree ⟨an *obsessive* need for answers⟩ **2** : of, relating to, or characterized by obsession — **ob·ses·sive·ly** \-lē\ *adv*

ob·sid·i·an \əb-ˈsid-ē-ən\ *n* : a dark natural glass formed by the cooling of molten lava [Latin *obsidianus lapis,* mistaken manuscript reading for *obsianus lapis,* literally, "stone of Obsius (its supposed discoverer)"]

ob·so·les·cence \ˌäb-sə-ˈles-ns\ *n* : the process of becoming obsolete or the state of nearly being obsolete

ob·so·les·cent \ˌäb-sə-ˈles-nt\ *adj* : going out of use : becoming obsolete ⟨gradually replacing *obsolescent* equipment⟩ [Latin *obsolescens,* present participle of *obsolescere* "to grow old, become disused"] — **ob·so·lesce** \-ˈles\ *vi* — **ob·so·les·cent·ly** *adv*

ob·so·lete \ˌäb-sə-ˈlēt, ˈäb-sə-ˌ\ *adj* **1** : no longer in use ⟨an *obsolete* word⟩ **2** : of a kind or style that is no longer current : OUTMODED ⟨*obsolete* machinery⟩ [Latin *obsoletus,* from past participle of *obsolescere* "to grow old, become disused"] — **ob·so·lete·ly** *adv* — **ob·so·lete·ness** *n*

ob·sta·cle \ˈäb-sti-kəl\ *n* : something that stands in the way of progress or achievement ⟨drove around *obstacles* in the road⟩ ⟨lack of height proved no *obstacle* to his basketball career⟩ [Medieval French, from Latin *obstaculum,* from *obstare* "to stand in front of," from *ob-* "in the way" + *stare* "to stand"]

ob·stet·ric \əb-ˈste-trik, äb-\ *or* **ob·stet·ri·cal** \-tri-kəl\ *adj* : of or relating to childbirth or obstetrics [derived from Latin *obstetric-, obstetrix* "midwife," from *obstare* "to stand in front of"] — **ob·stet·ri·cal·ly** \-tri-kə-lē, -klē\ *adv*

ob·ste·tri·cian \ˌäb-stə-ˈtrish-ən\ *n* : a physician specializing in obstetrics

ob·stet·rics \əb-ˈste-triks, äb-\ *n* : a branch of medical science that deals with childbirth and with the care of women before, during, and after childbirth

ob·sti·na·cy \ˈäb-stə-nə-sē\ *n, pl* **-cies** **1** : the quality or state of being obstinate **2** : an instance of being obstinate

ob·sti·nate \ˈäb-stə-nət\ *adj* **1** : stubbornly sticking to an opinion, purpose, or course in spite of reason, arguments, or persuasion **2** : not easily subdued, remedied, or removed ⟨an *obstinate* fever⟩ [Latin *obstinatus,* past participle of *obstinare* "to be firm"] — **ob·sti·nate·ly** *adv* — **ob·sti·nate·ness** *n*

synonyms OBSTINATE, DOGGED, STUBBORN, PERTINACIOUS mean fixed and unyielding in course or purpose. OBSTI-

NATE implies usually an unreasonable persistence ⟨too *obstinate* to take advice⟩. DOGGED suggests a tenacious and unwavering persistence ⟨shoveled with a *dogged* regularity⟩. STUBBORN implies sturdiness in resisting change which may or may not be admirable ⟨met persuasion with *stubborn* resistance⟩. PERTINACIOUS suggests an annoying persistence ⟨a *pertinacious* salesperson who refused to take no for an answer⟩.

ob·strep·er·ous \əb-ˈstrep-rəs, äb-, -ə-rəs\ *adj* **1 :** uncontrollably or aggressively noisy **2 :** stubbornly resistant to control **:** UNRULY [Latin *obstreperus,* from *obstrepere* "to clamor against," from *ob-* "against" + *strepere* "to make a noise"] — **ob·strep·er·ous·ly** *adv* — **ob·strep·er·ous·ness** *n*

ob·struct \əb-ˈstrəkt, äb-\ *vt* **1 :** to block or close up by an obstacle **2 :** to hinder from passage, action, or operation **:** IMPEDE ⟨untruthful witnesses *obstructing* justice⟩ **3 :** to cut off from sight ⟨a wall *obstructing* the view⟩ [Latin *obstructus,* past participle of *obstruere* "to obstruct," from *ob-* "in the way" + *struere* "to build"] ***synonyms*** see HINDER — **ob·struc·tive** \-ˈstrək-tiv\ *adj or n* — **ob·struc·tor** \-tər\ *n*

ob·struc·tion \əb-ˈstrək-shən, äb-\ *n* **1 :** an act of obstructing **:** the state of being obstructed **2 :** something that obstructs

ob·struc·tion·ism \-shə-ˌniz-əm\ *n* **:** deliberate interference with the progress or business especially of a legislative body — **ob·struc·tion·ist** \-shə-nəst, -shnəst\ *n or adj* — **ob·struc·tion·is·tic** \-ˌstrək-shə-ˈnis-tik\ *adj*

ob·tain \əb-ˈtān, äb-\ *vb* **1 :** to gain or attain usually by planned action or effort **2 :** to be generally recognized or established **:** PREVAIL ⟨good manners *obtained*⟩ [Medieval French *obtenir,* from *obtinēre* "to hold on to, possess, obtain," from *ob-* "in the way" + *tenēre* "to hold"] — **ob·tain·able** \-ˈtā-nə-bəl\ *adj* — **ob·tain·er** *n* — **ob·tain·ment** \-ˈtān-mənt\ *n*

ob·trude \əb-ˈtrüd, äb-\ *vb* **1 :** to thrust out ⟨rocks *obtruding* from the cliff wall⟩ **2 :** to become too prominent or interfering ⟨that enormous sculpture *obtrudes* in such a small room⟩ **3 :** to force (as oneself or one's ideas) without basis or request ⟨was careful not to *obtrude* details of his personal life onto his coworkers⟩ [Latin *obtrudere* "to thrust at," from *ob-* "in the way" + *trudere* "to thrust"] ***synonyms*** see INTRUDE — **ob·trud·er** *n* — **ob·tru·sion** \-ˈtrü-zhən\ *n*

ob·tru·sive \əb-ˈtrü-siv, äb-, -ziv\ *adj* **1 a :** forward in manner or conduct ⟨*obtrusive* behavior⟩ **b :** too prominent ⟨an *obtrusive* painting⟩ **2 :** thrust out **:** PROTRUDING ⟨a sharp *obtrusive* edge⟩ [Latin *obtrusus,* past participle of *obtrudere* "to thrust at"] — **ob·tru·sive·ly** *adv* — **ob·tru·sive·ness** *n*

ob·tuse \äb-ˈtüs, -ˈtyüs\ *adj* **1 :** not pointed or acute **:** BLUNT ⟨an *obtuse* leaf⟩ **2 a :** being between 90° and 180° ⟨*obtuse* angle⟩ **b :** having an obtuse angle ⟨an *obtuse* triangle⟩ **3 a :** lacking sharpness or quickness of wit **:** STUPID, INSENSITIVE **b :** difficult to understand **:** not clear in thought or expression [Latin *obtusus* "blunt, dull," from *obtundere* "to beat against, blunt," from *ob-* "against" + *tundere* "to beat"] ***synonyms*** see BLUNT — **ob·tuse·ly** *adv* — **ob·tuse·ness** *n*

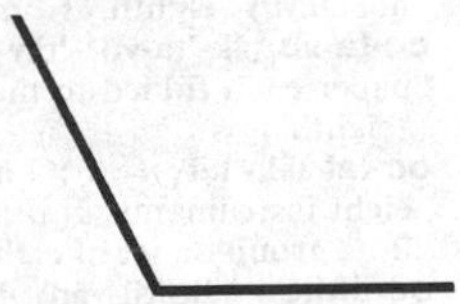
obtuse 2a: an obtuse angle

[1]**ob·verse** \äb-ˈvərs, ˈäb-ˌ\ *adj* **1 :** facing the observer or opponent **2 :** being a counterpart or complement **:** OPPOSITE [Latin *obversus,* from *obvertere* "to turn toward," from *ob-* "toward" + *vertere* "to turn"] — **ob·verse·ly** *adv*

[2]**ob·verse** \ˈäb-ˌvərs, äb-ˈ\ *n* **1 :** the side of something (as a coin or medal) bearing the principal design or lettering **2 :** a front or principal surface **3 :** COUNTERPART 2

ob·vi·ate \ˈäb-vē-ˌāt\ *vt* **:** to anticipate and prevent or make unnecessary ⟨*obviate* an objection⟩ [Late Latin *obviare* "to meet, withstand," from Latin *obviam* "in the way"] — **ob·vi·a·tion** \ˌäb-vē-ˈā-shən\ *n*

ob·vi·ous \ˈäb-vē-əs\ *adj* **:** easily discovered, seen, or understood **:** PLAIN ⟨an *obvious* mistake⟩ [Latin *obvius* "being in the way," from *obviam* "in the way," from *ob* "in the way of" + *via* "way"] — **ob·vi·ous·ness** *n*

ob·vi·ous·ly \-lē\ *adv* **1 :** in an obvious manner ⟨showed his anger *obviously*⟩ **2 :** as is plainly evident ⟨*obviously,* something is wrong⟩

oc·a·ri·na \ˌäk-ə-ˈrē-nə\ *n* **:** a wind instrument usually having an oval body with finger holes and producing soft flutelike tones [Italian, from *oca* "goose," from Late Latin *auca,* derived from Latin *avis* "bird"]

Oc·cam's razor \ˈäk-əmz-\ *n* **:** a scientific and philosophical rule that requires the simplest of competing explanations or theories be preferred to the more complex [William of *Occam,* died circa 1349, English philosopher]

[1]**oc·ca·sion** \ə-ˈkā-zhən\ *n* **1 :** a favorable opportunity or circumstance ⟨didn't have the *occasion* to talk to them⟩ **2 a :** a state of affairs that provides a ground or reason ⟨their mutual dislike was the *occasion* of the discord⟩ **b :** an occurrence or condition that brings something about; *esp* **:** the immediate inciting circumstance as distinguished from fundamental cause ⟨his comment was the *occasion* for their long-expected breakup⟩ **3 :** a time at which something happens **4 :** a need arising from a particular circumstance ⟨there was no *occasion* for his long-winded speech⟩ **5** *pl* **:** AFFAIR 1a, BUSINESS **6 :** a special event or ceremony **:** CELEBRATION [Latin *occasio,* from *occidere* "to fall, fall down," from *ob-* "toward" + *cadere* "to fall"] ***synonyms*** see CAUSE — **on occasion :** from time to time

[2]**occasion** *vt* **oc·ca·sioned; oc·ca·sion·ing** \-ˈkāzh-ning, -ə-ning\ **:** to give occasion to **:** CAUSE

oc·ca·sion·al \ə-ˈkāzh-nəl, -ən-l\ *adj* **1 :** of, relating to, or used or meant for a particular occasion ⟨*occasional* verse⟩ **2 a :** happening or met with now and then ⟨made *occasional* references to the war⟩ **b :** acting in a specified capacity from time to time ⟨an *occasional* lecturer⟩

oc·ca·sion·al·ly \-ē\ *adv* **:** from time to time ⟨goes out to eat *occasionally*⟩

Oc·ci·dent \ˈäk-səd-ənt, -sə-ˌdent\ *n* **:** WEST 2a [Medieval French, from Latin *occidens,* from *occidere* "to fall, set (of the sun)"]

oc·ci·den·tal \ˌäk-sə-ˈdent-l\ *adj, often cap* **1 :** of, relating to, or situated in the Occident **:** WESTERN **2 :** of or relating to Occidentals — **oc·ci·den·tal·ly** \-l-ē\ *adv*

Occidental *n* **:** a member of one of the occidental peoples; *esp* **:** a person of European ancestry

[1]**oc·cip·i·tal** \äk-ˈsip-ət-l\ *adj* **:** of or relating to the occiput or the occipital bone — **oc·cip·i·tal·ly** \-l-ē\ *adv*

[2]**occipital** *n* **:** OCCIPITAL BONE

occipital bone *n* **:** a compound bone that forms the back part of the skull and articulates with the atlas

occipital lobe *n* **:** the back part of the cerebral hemisphere that contains the visual areas of the brain

oc·ci·put \ˈäk-sə-pət, -ˌpət\ *n, pl* **occiputs** *or* **oc·cip·i·ta** \äk-ˈsip-ət-ə\ **:** the back part of the head or skull [Latin *occipit-, occiput,* from *ob-* "against" + *capit-, caput* "head"]

Oc·ci·tan \ˈäk-sə-ˌtan\ *n* **:** a Romance language spoken in southern France [French, from Medieval Latin *occitanus,* from Old Occitan *oc* "yes" (contrasted with Medieval French *oïl* "yes")]

oc·clude \ə-ˈklüd, ä-\ *vb* **1 :** to close up or block off or become closed up or blocked off **2 :** to take up and hold by absorption or adsorption **3 :** to come together with opposing surfaces in contact ⟨the teeth do not *occlude* properly⟩ [Latin *occludere,* from *ob-* "in the way" + *claudere* "to shut, close"] — **oc·clu·sive** \-ˈklü-siv, -ziv\ *adj*

occluded front *n* **:** OCCLUSION 3

oc·clu·sal \ə-ˈklü-səl, ä-, -zəl\ *adj* **:** of, relating to, or being the biting or grinding surface of a molar or premolar tooth; *also* **:** of or relating to occlusion of the teeth [Latin *occlusus,* past participle of *occludere* "to occlude"] — **oc·clu·sal·ly** \-ē\ *adv*

oc·clu·sion \ə-ˈklü-zhən\ *n* **1 :** the act of occluding **:** the state of being occluded **2 :** the coming together of the opposing surfaces of the upper and lower teeth; *also* **:** the relation between the surfaces when in contact **3 :** the front formed by a cold front overtaking a warm front and lifting the warm air over the cold air

[1]**oc·cult** \ə-ˈkəlt, ä-\ *vb* **:** to shut off from view **:** COVER, ECLIPSE

[2]**occult** *adj* **1 :** not revealed **:** SECRET **2 :** not easily understood **:** MYSTERIOUS **3 :** of or relating to the occult [Latin *occultus,* from *occulere* "to cover up, hide"] — **oc·cult·ly** *adv*

[3]**occult** *n* **:** matters thought to involve the action or influence of supernatural powers or some secret knowledge of them ⟨a student of the occult⟩

oc·cul·ta·tion \ˌäk-əl-ˈtā-shən, ˌäk-ˌəl-\ *n* **1 :** the state of being

\ə\ **abut**	\au̇\ **out**	\i\ **tip**	\ȯ\ **saw**	\u̇\ **foot**
\ər\ **further**	\ch\ **chin**	\ī\ **life**	\ȯi\ **coin**	\y\ **yet**
\a\ **mat**	\e\ **pet**	\j\ **job**	\th\ **thin**	\yü\ **few**
\ā\ **take**	\ē\ **easy**	\ng\ **sing**	\t͟h\ **this**	\yu̇\ **cure**
\ä\ **cot, cart**	\g\ **go**	\ō\ **bone**	\ü\ **food**	\zh\ **vision**

hidden from view or lost to notice **2** : the shutting out of the light of one celestial body by the intervention of another; *esp* : an eclipse of a star or planet by the moon

oc·cult·ism \ə-ˈkəl-ˌtiz-əm, ä-\ *n* : a belief in or study of supernatural powers — **oc·cult·ist** \-təst\ *n*

oc·cu·pan·cy \ˈäk-yə-pən-sē\ *n, pl* **-cies** **1** : the act or condition of occupying ⟨will take *occupancy* this week⟩ **2** : the fact or condition of being occupied ⟨*occupancy* by more than 400 persons is unlawful⟩

oc·cu·pant \ˈäk-yə-pənt\ *n* : one that occupies something or takes or has possession of it

oc·cu·pa·tion \ˌäk-yə-ˈpā-shən\ *n* **1** : an activity in which one engages; *esp* : one's business or vocation **2 a** : the taking possession of property : OCCUPANCY **b** : the taking possession or holding and controlling of an area by a foreign military force; *also* : such a military force — **oc·cu·pa·tion·al** \-shnəl, -shən-l\ *adj* — **oc·cu·pa·tion·al·ly** \-ē\ *adv*

occupational therapy *n* : therapy based on involvement in activities (as grooming oneself, learning, or working) typical of daily life especially to enable participation in such activities despite limits or impairments to mental or physical functioning — **occupational therapist** *n*

oc·cu·py \ˈäk-yə-ˌpī\ *vt* **-pied; -py·ing** **1 a** : to engage the attention or energies of ⟨*occupy* oneself with reading⟩ **b** : to fill up (an extent in space or time) ⟨sports *occupied* their spare time⟩ ⟨a liter of water *occupies* 1000 cubic centimeters of space⟩ **2** : to take or hold possession of ⟨*occupying* enemy territory⟩ **3** : to reside in as an owner or tenant [Medieval French *occuper* "to take possession of," from Latin *occupare*] — **oc·cu·pi·er** \-ˌpī-ər, -ˌpīr\ *n*

oc·cur \ə-ˈkər\ *vi* **oc·curred; oc·cur·ring** \-ˈkər-ing\ **1** : to be found or met with : APPEAR **2** : to take place **3** : to come to mind ⟨an idea that has *occurred* to me⟩ [Latin *occurrere,* from *ob-* "in the way" + *currere* "to run"] ***synonyms*** see HAPPEN

oc·cur·rence \ə-ˈkər-əns, -ˈkə-rəns\ *n* **1** : something that takes place; *esp* : something that happens unexpectedly ⟨a startling *occurrence*⟩ **2** : the action or process of taking place

synonyms OCCURRENCE, EVENT, INCIDENT, EPISODE mean something that happens or takes place. OCCURRENCE suggests a happening without plan, intent, or volition ⟨an encounter that was a chance *occurrence*⟩. EVENT usually implies a significant occurrence and frequently one resulting from or giving rise to another ⟨Columbus' voyage was one of the significant *events* of history⟩. INCIDENT suggests an occurrence of brief duration or secondary importance ⟨the plot of the play is strung with amusing *incidents*⟩. EPISODE stresses the distinctiveness or apartness of an incident ⟨their trip to Africa was a memorable *episode* in their lives⟩.

ocean \ˈō-shən\ *n* **1** : the whole body of salt water that covers nearly three fourths of the surface of the earth **2** : one of the large bodies of water into which the great ocean is divided **3** : an immense space or quantity [Latin *oceanus,* from Greek *ōkeanos*] — **oce·an·ic** \ˌō-shē-ˈan-ik\ *adj*

ocean·ar·i·um \ˌō-shə-ˈnar-ē-əm, -ˈner-\ *n, pl* **-i·ums** *also* **-ia** \-ē-ə\ : a large marine aquarium

ocean·front \ˈō-shən-ˌfrənt\ *n* : a shore area on the ocean

ocean·go·ing \ˈō-shən-ˌgō-ing\ *adj* : of, relating to, or designed for travel on the ocean

Oce·anid \ō-ˈsē-ə-nəd\ *n* : any of the ocean nymphs in Greek mythology

ocean·og·ra·phy \ˌō-shə-ˈnäg-rə-fē\ *n* : a science that deals with the ocean and its phenomena — **ocean·og·ra·pher** \-fər\ *n* — **ocean·o·graph·ic** \ˌō-shə-nə-ˈgraf-ik\ *also* **ocean·o·graph·i·cal** \-i-kəl\ *adj* — **ocean·o·graph·i·cal·ly** \-ˈgraf-i-kə-lē, -klē\ *adv*

ocel·lus \ō-ˈsel-əs\ *n, pl* **ocel·li** \-ˈsel-ˌī, -ˌē\ **1** : a tiny simple eye or eyespot of an invertebrate **2** : an eyelike colored spot (as on a peacock feather or the wings of some butterflies) [Latin, "little eye," from *oculus* "eye"] — **ocel·lat·ed** \ˈō-sə-ˌlāt-əd\ *adj*

oc·e·lot \ˈäs-ə-ˌlät, ˈō-sə-\ *n* : a medium-sized American wildcat ranging from Texas to northern Argentina and having a tawny yellow or grayish coat marked with black [French, from Nahuatl *ōcēlōtl* "jaguar"]

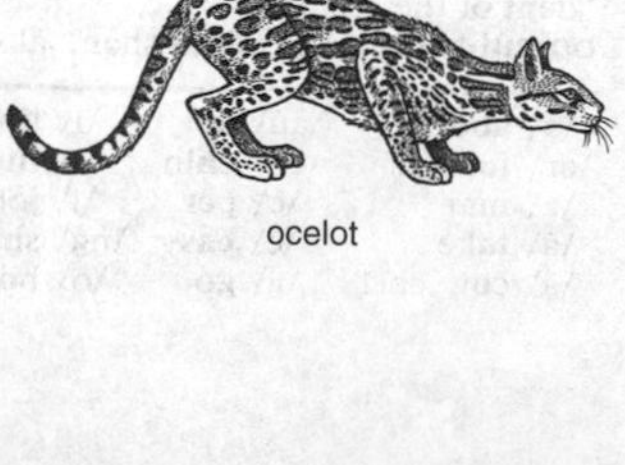
ocelot

ocher *or* **ochre** \ˈō-kər\ *n* **1** : an earthy usually red or yellow and often impure iron ore used as a pigment **2** : the color of yellow ocher [Medieval French *ocre,* from Latin *ochra,* from Greek *ōchra,* from *ōchros* "yellow"] — **ocher·ous** \ˈō-kə-rəs, -krəs\ *or* **ochre·ous** \ˈō-kə-rəs, -krəs, -krē-əs\ *adj*

-ock \ək, ik, ˌäk\ *n suffix* : small one ⟨hill*ock*⟩ [Old English *-oc*]

o'·clock \ə-ˈkläk\ *adv* **1** : according to the clock ⟨the time is three *o'clock*⟩ **2** — used for indicating position or direction as if on a clock dial ⟨an airplane approaching at eleven *o'clock*⟩ [contraction of *of the clock*]

oco·ti·llo \ˌō-kə-ˈtē-yō, -ˈtē-ō\ *n, pl* **-llos** : a thorny scarlet-flowered shrub of the southwestern U.S. and Mexico [Mexican Spanish]

ocotillo

octa- *or* **octo-** *also* **oct-** *combining form* : eight [Greek *oktō* and Latin *octo*]

oc·ta·gon \ˈäk-tə-ˌgän\ *n* : a polygon of eight angles and eight sides — **oc·tag·o·nal** \äk-ˈtag-ən-l\ *adj* — **oc·tag·o·nal·ly** \-l-ē\ *adv*

oc·ta·he·dron \ˌäk-tə-ˈhē-drən\ *n, pl* **-drons** *or* **-dra** \-drə\ : a polyhedron having eight faces — **oc·ta·he·dral** \-drəl\ *adj*

oc·tal \ˈäk-tl\ *adj* : of, relating to, or being a number system with a base of 8

oc·tam·e·ter \äk-ˈtam-ət-ər\ *n* : a line of verse consisting of eight metrical feet [Late Latin, "having eight feet," derived from Greek *oktō* "eight" + *metron* "measure"]

oc·tane \ˈäk-ˌtān\ *n* **1** : any of several isomeric liquid hydrocarbons C_8H_{18} **2** : OCTANE NUMBER

octane number *n* : a number that is used to measure or indicate the antiknock properties of a liquid motor fuel with a higher number indicating a smaller likelihood of knocking — called also *octane rating*

oc·tant \ˈäk-tənt\ *n* **1** : an instrument for observing altitudes of a celestial body from a moving ship or aircraft **2** : any of the eight parts into which a space is divided by three coordinate planes [Latin *octans* "eighth of a circle," from *octo* "eight"]

oc·tave \ˈäk-tiv, -təv, -ˌtāv\ *n* **1** : an 8-day period of observances beginning with a festival day **2** : a stanza or poem of eight lines; *esp* : the first eight lines of an Italian sonnet **3 a** : a musical interval embracing eight degrees **b** : a tone or note at this interval **c** : the whole series of notes, tones, or keys within this interval **4** : a group of eight [Medieval Latin *octava,* from Latin *octavus* "eighth," from *octo* "eight"]

oc·ta·vo \äk-ˈtā-vō, -ˈtäv-ō\ *n, pl* **-vos** : a book made of sheets of paper each folded to make 8 leaves [Latin, ablative of *octavus* "eighth"]

oc·tet \äk-ˈtet\ *n* **1** : a musical composition for eight voices or eight instruments; *also* : the performers of such a composition **2** : a group or set of eight

oc·til·lion \äk-ˈtil-yən\ *n* — see NUMBER table [French, from *oct-* "octa-" + *-illion* (as in *million*)]

Oc·to·ber \äk-ˈtō-bər\ *n* : the 10th month of the year according to the Gregorian calendar [Medieval French *Octobre,* from Latin *October,* from *octo* "eight"; from its having been originally the 8th month of the Roman calendar]

oc·to·ge·nar·i·an \ˌäk-tə-jə-ˈner-ē-ən\ *n* : a person whose age is between 80 and 89 [Latin *octogenarius* "containing 80," from *octogeni* "80 each," from *octoginta* "eighty," from *octo* "eight"]

oc·to·pus \ˈäk-tə-pəs\ *n, pl* **-pus·es** *or* **-pi** \-ˌpī, -ˌpē\ **1** : any of various cephalopod sea mollusks having eight muscular arms with two rows of suckers **2** : something suggestive of an octopus especially in having many centrally directed branches [Greek *oktōpous* "having 8 feet," from *oktō* "eight" + *pous* "foot"]

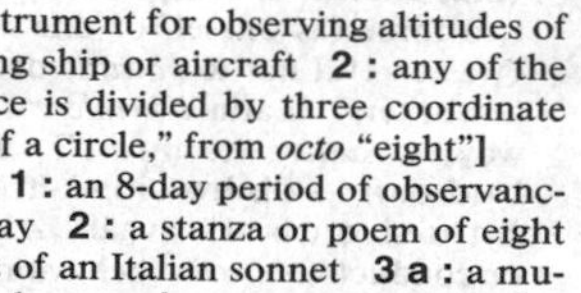
octopus 1

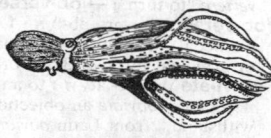

oc·to·roon \ˌäk-tə-ˈrün\ *n* : a person of one-eighth black ancestry [*octa-* + *-roon* (as in *quadroon*)]

oc·to·syl·lab·ic \ˌäk-tə-sə-ˈlab-ik\ *adj* **1** : having eight syllables **2** : composed of verses of eight syllables — **octosyllabic** *n*

¹oc·u·lar \ˈäk-yə-lər\ *adj* **1 a** : done or perceived by the eye ⟨*ocular* inspection⟩ **b** : based on what one has seen ⟨*ocular* testimony⟩ **2 :** of or relating to the eye ⟨*ocular* muscles⟩ [Late Latin *ocularis* "of eyes," from Latin *oculus* "eye"]

[2]ocular *n* **:** EYEPIECE

oc·u·list \ˈäk-yə-ləst\ *n* **1 :** OPHTHALMOLOGIST **2 :** OPTOMETRIST

oc·u·lo·mo·tor \ˌäk-yə-lə-ˈmōt-ər\ *adj* **1 :** moving or acting to move the eyeball **2 :** of or relating to the oculomotor nerve

oculomotor nerve *n* **:** either of the 3rd pair of cranial nerves that arise from the midbrain and supply most muscles of the eye — called also *oculomotor*

[1]OD \ˌō-ˈdē\ *n* **:** an overdose of a drug and especially a narcotic [*overdose*]

[2]OD *vi* **OD'd** *or* **ODed; OD'·ing; OD's :** to become ill or die from an OD

odd \ˈäd\ *adj* **1 :** being only one of a pair or set ⟨an *odd* shoe⟩ ⟨an *odd* chair⟩ **2 :** somewhat more than the number mentioned ⟨fifty-*odd* years ago⟩ **3 a :** being any number (as –3, –1, +1, and +3) that is not evenly divisible by 2 **b :** marked by an odd number ⟨an *odd* year⟩ **4 :** additional to or apart from what is usual, expected, or planned ⟨*odd* jobs⟩ ⟨done at *odd* moments⟩ ⟨*odd* bits of material⟩ **5 :** not usual or conventional **:** STRANGE ⟨an *odd* way of behaving⟩ ⟨what an *odd* place to keep cereal⟩ [Old Norse *oddi* "point of land, triangle, odd number"] ***synonyms*** see STRANGE — **odd·ness** *n*

Word History Although a triangle is a 3-angled figure, it is possible, by concentrating attention on the apex, to look at it as a point. An arrowhead, after all, is basically a triangle, and likewise a point of land reaching out into a body of water is roughly triangular in shape. The Old Norse word *oddi* was used both for a point of land and for a triangle. *Oddi* also developed the meaning "odd number," since the apex of a triangle is the unpaired angle and an odd number is a sum of pairs and one unpaired unit. English never called a triangle *odd,* but it did borrow the *odd* number from Old Norse *oddi.* Later anything singular or different came to be called *odd.*

odd·ball \ˈäd-ˌbȯl\ *n* **:** one that is eccentric

Odd Fellow *n* **:** a member of a major benevolent and fraternal order [Independent Order of *Odd Fellows*]

odd·i·ty \ˈäd-ət-ē\ *n, pl* **-ties 1 :** an odd person, thing, event, or trait **2 :** the quality or state of being odd ⟨the *oddity* of your behavior⟩

odd·ly \ˈäd-lē\ *adv* **1 :** in an odd manner **2 :** as is odd ⟨liked the work, *oddly* enough⟩

odd·ment \ˈäd-mənt\ *n* **1 :** something left over **:** REMNANT **2 :** something odd

odds \ˈädz\ *n pl* **1** *archaic* **:** unequal things or conditions **2 a :** DIFFERENCE ⟨won by considerable *odds*⟩ **b :** a difference by which one thing is favored over another ⟨the *odds* are in favor of our side⟩ **c :** the probability that one thing will happen rather than another ⟨the *odds* are against it⟩ **3 :** DISAGREEMENT — used with *at* ⟨the staff was at *odds* on everything⟩ **4 a :** an advantage granted by one making a bet to one accepting a bet and designed to equalize the chances of winning ⟨gave him *odds* of 3 to 1 but he still refused the bet⟩ **b :** the ratio between the amount to be won and the amount wagered on a bet ⟨the horse won at 6 to 1 *odds*⟩

odds and ends *n pl* **:** miscellaneous things or matters

odds–on \ˈäd-ˈzȯn, -ˈzän\ *adj* **1 :** having or viewed as having a better than even chance to win **2 :** not involving much risk ⟨an *odds-on* bet⟩

ode \ˈōd\ *n* **:** a lyric poem characterized usually by elevated feeling and style, varied length of line, and complex stanza forms [Late Latin, from Greek *ōidē,* literally, "song," from *aidein* "to sing"]

-ode \ˌōd\ *n combining form* **1 :** way **:** path ⟨electr*ode*⟩ **2 :** electrode ⟨di*ode*⟩ [Greek *hodos*]

odif·er·ous \ō-ˈdif-rəs, -ə-rəs\ *adj* **:** ODOROUS [contraction of *odoriferous*]

odi·ous \ˈōd-ē-əs\ *adj* **:** causing or deserving hatred or repugnance — **odi·ous·ly** *adv* — **odi·ous·ness** *n*

odi·um \ˈōd-ē-əm\ *n* **1 :** the state or fact of being generally hated and condemned usually for shameful conduct **2 :** the disgrace or shame attached to something considered hateful or low [Latin, "hatred," from *odisse* "to hate"]

odom·e·ter \ō-ˈdäm-ət-ər\ *n* **:** an instrument for measuring the distance traveled (as by a vehicle) [French *odomètre,* from Greek *hodometron,* from *hodos* "way, road" + *metron* "measure"]

odon·tol·o·gy \ˌō-ˌdän-ˈtäl-ə-jē\ *n* **:** a branch of forensic medicine that deals with teeth and marks left by teeth (as in identifying criminal suspects or the remains of a dead person) [French *odontologie,* from Greek *odont-, odous* "tooth"] — **odon·tol·o·gist** \-jəst\ *n*

odor \ˈōd-ər\ *n* **1 :** the quality of something that stimulates the sense of smell **:** SCENT; *also* **:** a sensation resulting from such stimulation **2 a :** a predominant quality **:** FLAVOR ⟨*odor* of sanctity⟩ **b :** a place in public esteem **:** ESTIMATION ⟨in bad *odor*⟩ [Medieval French *odour,* from Latin *odor*] ***synonyms*** see SMELL — **odored** \-ərd\ *adj* — **odor·less** \-ər-ləs\ *adj*

odor·ant \ˈōd-ə-rənt\ *n* **:** an odorous substance

odor·if·er·ous \ˌōd-ə-ˈrif-rəs, -ə-rəs\ *adj* **1 :** ODOROUS **2 :** morally offensive ⟨*odoriferous* legislation⟩ — **odor·if·er·ous·ly** *adv* — **odor·if·er·ous·ness** *n*

odor·ous \ˈōd-ə-rəs\ *adj* **:** having an odor — **odor·ous·ly** *adv* — **odor·ous·ness** *n*

odour \ˈōd-ər\ *chiefly British variant of* ODOR

od·ys·sey \ˈäd-ə-sē\ *n, pl* **-seys :** a long wandering usually marked by many changes of fortune [the *Odyssey,* epic poem attributed to Homer recounting the long wanderings of Odysseus]

Oe·di·pus complex \ˈed-ə-pəs, ˈēd-\ *n* **:** strong attraction of a child toward the parent of the opposite sex and hostile or jealous feelings toward the parent of the same sex that in Freudian theory may be a source of adult personality disorder if left unresolved [*Oedipus,* hero of ancient Greek legend who killed his father and married his mother] — **oe·di·pal** \ˈed-ə-pəl, ˈēd-\ *adj*

[1]o'er \ˈōr, ˈȯr\ *adv* **:** OVER

[2]o'er \ōr, ȯr, ˈōr, ˈȯr\ *prep* **:** OVER

oer·sted \ˈər-stəd\ *n* **:** a unit of magnetic intensity equal to the intensity of a magnetic field in a vacuum in which a unit magnetic pole experiences a mechanical force of one dyne in the direction of the field [Hans Christian *Oersted,* died 1851, Danish physicist]

oe·soph·a·gus *chiefly British variant of* ESOPHAGUS

oestr- *or* **oestro-** *chiefly British variant of* ESTR-

of \əv, ˈəv, ˈäv\ *prep* **1 :** from as a point of reckoning ⟨north *of* the lake⟩ **2 a :** from by origin or derivation ⟨a person *of* noble birth⟩ **b :** from as a consequence ⟨died *of* flu⟩ **c :** [1]BY 4 ⟨plays *of* Shakespeare⟩ **d :** on the part of ⟨love *of* parents for their children⟩ **e :** occurring in ⟨a fish *of* the western Atlantic⟩ **3 :** having as its material, parts, or contents ⟨a throne *of* gold⟩ ⟨cups *of* water⟩ **4 —** used as a function word to indicate the whole that includes the part denoted by the preceding word ⟨most *of* the army⟩ **5 a :** relating to **:** ABOUT ⟨stories *of* their travels⟩ **b :** in respect to ⟨slow *of* speech⟩ **6 a —** used as a function word indicating belonging or a possessive relationship ⟨queen *of* England⟩ ⟨courage *of* the pioneers⟩ **b —** used to indicate relationship between a result and something upon which an operation or procedure is performed to produce it ⟨the product *of* two numbers⟩ **7 —** used as a function word to indicate something that is removed ⟨cured *of* a cold⟩ ⟨eased *of* pain⟩ **8 —** used as a function word to indicate a particular example belonging to the class denoted by the preceding noun ⟨month *of* August⟩ ⟨the city *of* Rome⟩ **9 :** having as its object ⟨love *of* nature⟩ **10 :** having as a distinctive quality or possession ⟨a person *of* courage⟩ **11 :** [2]BEFORE 2 ⟨a quarter *of* ten⟩ [Old English, "off, of"]

[1]off \ˈȯf\ *adv* **1 a** (1) **:** from a place or position ⟨march *off*⟩; *esp* **:** away from land ⟨the ship stood *off* to sea⟩ (2) **:** at a distance in time or space ⟨a long way *off*⟩ **b** (1) **:** from a course **:** ASIDE ⟨turned *off* into a bypath⟩ (2) **:** away from the wind **2 :** into an unconscious state ⟨dozed *off*⟩ **3 a :** so as not to be supported ⟨rolled to the edge of the table and *off*⟩ or covering or enclosing ⟨blew the lid *off*⟩ or attached ⟨the handle came *off*⟩ **b :** so as to be divided ⟨surface marked *off* into squares⟩ **4 :** to a state of discontinuance or completion ⟨shut *off* an engine⟩ ⟨drink *off* a glass⟩ ⟨paint to finish it *off*⟩ **5 :** in absence from or suspension of regular work or service ⟨take time *off* for lunch⟩ [Old English *of*]

[2]off \ȯf, ˈȯf\ *prep* **1 a —** used as a function word to indicate physical separation from a position of rest, union, or attachment ⟨bounced *off* the wall⟩ ⟨take it *off* the table⟩ ⟨a path *off* the main walk⟩ **b** : to seaward of ⟨two miles *off* the coast⟩ **2** : from the possession of ⟨had his wallet stolen *off* him⟩ **3** — used as a function word to indicate the object of an action ⟨borrowed a dollar *off* him⟩ ⟨dined *off* oysters⟩ **4 a** : not now engaged in ⟨*off* duty⟩ **b** : below the usual standard or level of ⟨*off* my game⟩ ⟨a dollar *off* the list price⟩

[3]off \ˈȯf, ˈȯf\ *adj* **1 a** : SEAWARD **b** : RIGHT ⟨*off* horse in a team⟩ **c** : more removed or distant ⟨the *off* side of the building⟩ **2 a** : started on the way ⟨*off* on a spree⟩ **b** : CANCELED ⟨the picnic's *off*⟩ **c** : not operating ⟨current is *off*⟩ **d** : not placed so as to permit operation ⟨the switch is *off*⟩ **3 a** : not corresponding to fact : INCORRECT ⟨*off* in their reckoning⟩ **b** : not being at one's best : SUBNORMAL **c** : not entirely sane : ECCENTRIC **d** : REMOTE, SLIGHT ⟨an *off* chance⟩ **4 a** : spent off duty ⟨reading on our *off* days⟩ **b** : marked by a periodic decline in activity or business ⟨*off* season⟩ **5 a** : OFF-COLOR **b** : INFERIOR ⟨*off* grade of oil⟩ **c** : DOWN 1c ⟨stocks were *off*⟩ **6** : CIRCUMSTANCED ⟨comfortably *off*⟩

of•fal \ˈȯ-fəl, ˈäf-əl\ *n* **1** : the waste or by-product of a process: as **a** : trimmings of a hide **b** : the by-products of milling used especially for stock feeds **c** : the internal organs and trimmings of a butchered animal removed in dressing **2** : RUBBISH [Middle English, from *of* "off" + *fall*]

off and on *adv* : with periodic cessation ⟨rained *off and on* all day⟩

[1]off•beat \ˈȯf-ˌbēt\ *n* : the unaccented beat or part of a beat in a musical measure

[2]offbeat *adj* : ECCENTRIC, UNCONVENTIONAL ⟨an *offbeat* style⟩

off–col•or \ˈȯf-ˈkəl-ər\ *or* **off–col•ored** \-ərd\ *adj* **1** : not having the right or standard color **2** : verging on the indecent ⟨*off-color* remarks⟩

of•fend \ə-ˈfend\ *vb* **1 a** : to transgress the moral or divine law : SIN **b** : to break a law or rule : do wrong **2 a** : to cause difficulty, discomfort, or injury ⟨took off my shoe and removed the *offending* pebble⟩ **b** : to cause dislike, anger, or vexation **3** : to cause pain to **4** : to cause to feel vexed or resentful usually by violating what is proper ⟨that comment *offends* me⟩ [Medieval French *offendre,* from Latin *offendere* "to strike against, offend"] — **of•fend•er** *n*

synonyms OFFEND, OUTRAGE, INSULT, AFFRONT mean to cause hurt feelings or deep resentment. OFFEND may suggest a violating of ideas of what is right or proper without implying intent ⟨such blunt remarks *offended* the diplomats⟩. OUTRAGE implies offending beyond endurance and calling forth extreme feelings ⟨*outraged* by the vandalism⟩. INSULT suggests deliberately and insolently causing humiliation, hurt pride, or shame ⟨*insulted* every guest at the party⟩. AFFRONT implies treating with deliberate rudeness or contempt ⟨*affronted* by such arrogant neglect⟩.

of•fense *or* **of•fence** \ə-ˈfens; *especially for 2* ˈäf-ˌens, ˈȯf-\ *n* **1** : something that outrages the moral or physical senses **2 a** : the act of attacking : ASSAULT **b** : the side that is attacking in a contest or battle **3 a** : the act of displeasing or affronting **b** : the state of being insulted or morally outraged **4 a** : a breach of moral or social code : SIN **b** : an infraction of law : CRIME [Medieval French, from Latin *offensa,* from *offendere* "to offend"] — **offense•less** \-ləs\ *adj*

[1]of•fen•sive \ə-ˈfen-siv\ *adj* **1 a** : of, relating to, or designed for attack ⟨*offensive* weapons⟩ **b** (1) : of or relating to an attempt to score in a game or contest (2) : being on the offense ⟨the *offensive* team⟩ **2** : giving unpleasant sensations ⟨*offensive* smells⟩ **3** : causing displeasure or resentment : INSULTING ⟨an *offensive* word⟩ — **of•fen•sive•ly** *adv* — **of•fen•sive•ness** *n*

[2]offensive *n* **1** : the state or attitude of one making an attack ⟨on the *offensive*⟩ **2** : ATTACK ⟨launch an *offensive*⟩

[1]of•fer \ˈȯf-ər, ˈäf-\ *vb* **of•fered; of•fer•ing** \ˈȯf-ring, ˈäf-, -ə-ring\ **1** : to present as an act of worship : SACRIFICE **2** : to present for acceptance or rejection ⟨was *offered* a job⟩ **3 a** : to present for consideration or discussion : SUGGEST ⟨*offer* a solution to the problem⟩ **b** : to declare one's readiness or willingness ⟨*offered* to help me⟩ **4 a** : to put up ⟨*offered* stubborn resistance⟩ **b** : THREATEN ⟨*offered* to strike me with a cane⟩ **5** : to place (merchandise) on sale **6** : to present in performance or exhibition **7** : to propose as payment ⟨I'll *offer* you $700⟩ [derived from Latin *offerre* "to present, offer," from *ob-* "toward" + *ferre* "to carry"]

[2]offer *n* **1 a** : a presenting of something for acceptance ⟨an *offer* of marriage⟩ **b** : an agreement to do or give something on condition that the party to whom the proposal is made do or give something specified in return **2** : a price named by one proposing to buy **3** : an action or movement indicating a purpose or intention

of•fer•ing *n* **1 a** : the act of one who offers **b** : something offered; *esp* : a sacrifice ceremonially offered as a part of worship **c** : a contribution to the support of a church **2** : something offered for sale ⟨the novelist's latest *offering*⟩

of•fer•to•ry \ˈȯf-ər-ˌtōr-ē, ˈȯf-ə-ˌ, ˈäf-, -ˌtȯr-\ *n, pl* **-ries** **1** *often cap* **a** : the offering of the sacramental bread and wine to God before they are consecrated at Communion **b** : a verse from a psalm said or sung at the beginning of the offertory **2 a** : the period of collection and presentation of the offerings of the congregation at public worship **b** : the music played or sung during an offertory [Medieval Latin *offertorium,* derived from Latin *offerre* "to offer"]

[1]off•hand \ˈȯf-ˈhand\ *adv* : without previous thought or preparation ⟨couldn't give the figures *offhand*⟩

[2]offhand *adj* **1** : CASUAL ⟨a relaxed, *offhand* manner⟩ **2** : done or made offhand ⟨*offhand* excuses⟩

off•hand•ed \-ˈhan-dəd\ *adj* : OFFHAND — **off•hand•ed•ly** *adv* — **off•hand•ed•ness** *n*

of•fice \ˈȯf-əs, ˈäf-\ *n* **1 a** : a special duty, charge, or position; *esp* : a position of authority in government ⟨hold public *office*⟩ **b** : a position of responsibility or some degree of executive authority ⟨the *office* of president⟩ **2** : a prescribed form or service of worship; *esp, cap* : DIVINE OFFICE **3** : a religious or social ceremonial observance : RITE **4 a** : an assigned or assumed duty, task, or role **b** : FUNCTION 2 **c** : something done for another : SERVICE **5** : a place where a business is transacted or a service is supplied ⟨ticket *office*⟩: as **a** : a place in which functions of a public officer are performed **b** : the directing headquarters of an enterprise or organization **c** : the place in which a professional person (as a physician) conducts business **6 a** : a major administrative unit in some governments ⟨British Foreign *Office*⟩ **b** : a subdivision of some government departments ⟨Patent *Office*⟩ [Medieval French, from Latin *officium* "service, duty, office," from *opus* "work" + *facere* "to do"]

office boy *n* : a boy or man employed for odd jobs in a business office

of•fice•hold•er \-ˌhōl-dər\ *n* : one holding a public office

[1]of•fi•cer \ˈȯf-ə-sər, ˈäf-\ *n* **1** : POLICE OFFICER **2** : one who holds an office of trust, authority, or command ⟨bank *officers*⟩ **3 a** : one who holds a position of authority or command in the armed forces **b** : the master or any of the mates of a merchant or passenger ship

[2]officer *vt* **1** : to furnish with officers **2** : to command or direct as an officer

[1]of•fi•cial \ə-ˈfish-əl\ *n* **1** : one who holds an office : OFFICER **2** : one who enforces the rules of a game or sport especially as a referee or umpire

[2]official *adj* **1** : of or relating to an office, position, or trust ⟨*official* duties⟩ **2** : holding an office ⟨an *official* referee⟩ **3 a** : AUTHORITATIVE 1 ⟨*official* statement⟩ **b** : prescribed or recognized as authorized ⟨an *official* language⟩ **4** : befitting or characteristic of a person in office : FORMAL ⟨an *official* greeting⟩ — **of•fi•cial•ly** \-ˈfish-lē, -ə-lē\ *adv*

of•fi•cial•dom \ə-ˈfish-əl-dəm\ *n* : officials as a class

of•fi•cial•ism \-ˈfish-ə-ˌliz-əm\ *n* : lack of flexibility and initiative combined with excessive adherence to regulations (as in the behavior of government officials)

of•fi•ci•ant \ə-ˈfish-ē-ənt\ *n* : one (as a priest) that officiates at a religious rite

of•fi•ci•ate \ə-ˈfish-ē-ˌāt\ *vi* **1** : to perform a ceremony, function, or duty **2** : to act in an official capacity; *esp* : to serve as an officer or official **3** : to enforce the rules of (a game or sport) ⟨was asked to *officiate* the soccer match⟩ — **of•fi•ci•a•tion** \-ˌfish-ē-ˈā-shən\ *n*

of•fi•cious \ə-ˈfish-əs\ *adj* : offering one's services where they are neither asked nor needed : MEDDLESOME [Latin *officiosus* "obliging, helpful," from *officium* "service, office"] — **of•fi•cious•ly** *adv* — **of•fi•cious•ness** *n*

off•ing \ˈȯf-ing, ˈäf-\ *n* **1** : the part of the deep sea seen from the shore **2** : the near or foreseeable future ⟨sees trouble in the *offing*⟩

off•ish \ˈȯf-ish\ *adj* : inclined to be aloof — **off•ish•ness** *n*

off–key \ˈȯf-ˈkē\ *adj or adv* : varying in pitch from the proper tone of a melody ⟨sang *off-key*⟩

off–kil•ter \ˈȯf-ˈkil-tər\ *adj* **1** : not in perfect balance : ASKEW

⟨that homemade vase is *off-kilter*⟩ **2 :** being out of the ordinary or unconventional : ECCENTRIC ⟨an *off-kilter* character⟩ ⟨an *off-kilter* approach⟩

off–limits \ˈȯf-ˈlim-əts\ *adj* **1 :** not to be entered or visited by a designated class (as military personnel) ⟨officer's quarters are *off-limits* to civilians⟩ **2 :** not to be interfered with, considered, or spoken of ⟨questions about my salary are *off-limits*⟩

off–line \-ˈlīn\ *adj* **:** not connected to or served by a system and especially a computer or telecommunications system; *also* **:** done independently of a system ⟨*off-line* computer storage⟩ — **off–line** *adv*

off of *prep* **:** OFF

usage The *of* is often said to be unnecessary, but *off of* is an idiom. The objection to the inclusion of *of* is therefore irrelevant. *Off of* is much more common in speech than in writing.

off–peak \ˈȯf-ˈpēk\ *adj* **:** not being in the period of maximum use or business ⟨telephone during *off-peak* hours⟩

off·print \ˈȯf-ˌprint\ *n* **:** a separately printed excerpt (as from a magazine)

off–ramp \-ˌramp\ *n* **:** a ramp by which one leaves a limited-access highway

off–road \ˈȯf-ˈrōd\ *adj* **:** of, relating to, done with, or being a vehicle designed especially to operate away from public roads

off–road·er \-ˈrōd-ər\ *n* **1 :** a driver of an off-road vehicle **2 :** an off-road vehicle

off·screen \ˈȯf-ˈskrēn\ *adv or adj* **1 :** out of sight of the movie or television viewer **2 :** in private life ⟨costars romancing *offscreen*⟩

off–sea·son \ˈȯf-ˌsē-zn\ *n* **:** a time of suspended or reduced activity; *esp* **:** the time during which an athlete is not training or competing

1off·set \ˈȯf-ˌset\ *n* **1 a :** a short prostrate shoot arising from the base of a plant **b :** OFFSHOOT 1a **2 :** a horizontal ledge on the face of a wall formed by a decrease in its thickness above **3 :** an abrupt bend in an object by which one part is turned aside out of line **4 :** something that serves to counterbalance or to compensate for something else **5 a :** unintentional transfer of ink (as on a freshly printed sheet) **b :** a printing process in which an inked impression is first made on a rubber-blanketed cylinder and then transferred to the paper being printed

2off·set \ˈȯf-ˌset, *1 is also* ȯf-ˈ\ *vb* **-set; -set·ting 1 a :** BALANCE ⟨credits *offset* debits⟩ **b :** to compensate for **2 :** to form an offset in ⟨*offset* a wall⟩ ***synonyms*** see COMPENSATE

off·shoot \ˈȯf-ˌshüt\ *n* **1 a :** a collateral branch, descendant, or member **b :** a lateral branch (as of a mountain range) **2 :** a branch of a main stem especially of a plant

1off·shore \ˈȯf-ˈshōr, -ˈshȯr\ *adv* **1 :** from the shore **:** at a distance from the shore **2 :** out of the country **:** ABROAD ⟨lived *offshore* half the year⟩

2off·shore \ˈȯf-ˌ\ *adj* **1 :** coming or moving away from the shore ⟨an *offshore* breeze⟩ **2 a :** situated off the shore but within waters under a country's control ⟨*offshore* fisheries⟩ **b :** distant from the shore **3 :** situated or operating in a foreign country ⟨an *offshore* bank account⟩

off·side \ˈȯf-ˈsīd\ *adv or adj* **:** illegally in advance of the ball or puck

off–site \-ˈsīt\ *adj or adv* **:** not located or occurring at the site of a particular activity ⟨an *off-site* employee⟩ ⟨*off-site* computer work⟩

off·spring \ˈȯf-ˌspring\ *n, pl* **offspring** *also* **offsprings 1 :** the product of the reproductive processes of an animal or plant **:** YOUNG **2 :** RESULT ⟨books were the *offspring* of his impressive imagination⟩ [Old English *ofspring,* from *of* "off" + *springan* "to spring"]

off·stage \ˈȯf-ˈstāj, -ˌstāj\ *adv or adj* **1 :** on a part of a stage not visible to the audience **2 :** in private life ⟨known *offstage* as a kind person⟩ **3 :** out of public view ⟨much of the important work for the conference was done *offstage*⟩

off–the–cuff *adj or adv* **:** not prepared in advance **:** SPONTANEOUS ⟨*off-the-cuff* remarks⟩

off–the–record *adj* **:** given or made in confidence and not for publication ⟨made an *off-the-record* statement⟩

off–the–wall *adj* **:** highly unusual **:** BIZARRE ⟨an *off-the-wall* sense of humor⟩

off–white \ˈȯf-ˈhwīt, -ˈwīt\ *n* **:** a yellowish or grayish white

off year *n* **1 :** a year in which no major election is held **2 :** a year of diminished activity or production ⟨an *off year* for auto sales⟩

oft \ˈȯft\ *adv* **:** OFTEN ⟨an *oft* neglected factor⟩ [Old English]

of·ten \ˈȯ-fən, ˈȯf-tən\ *adv* **:** many times **:** FREQUENTLY [Middle English, from *oft,* from Old English]

of·ten·times \-ˌtīmz\ *or* **oft·times** \ˈȯf-ˌtīmz, ˈȯft-\ *adv* **:** OFTEN

ogee *also* **OG** \ˈō-ˌjē\ *n* **1 :** a molding with an S-shaped profile **2 :** a pointed arch having on each side a reversed curve near the apex [obsolete *ogee,* a kind of arch, from French *ogive*]

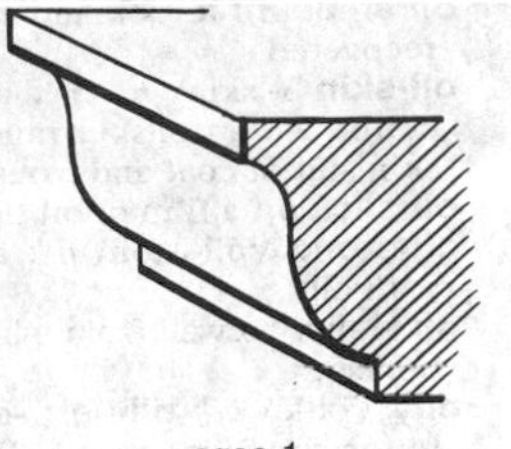

ogee 1

1ogle \ˈō-gəl\ *vb* **ogled; ogling** \-gə-ling, -gling\ **1 :** to glance in a flirtatious way **:** eye amorously **2 :** to look at especially with greedy or interested attention ⟨*ogling* the new sports car⟩ [probably from Low German *oegeln,* from *oog* "eye"] — **ogler** \-gə-lər, -glər\ *n*

2ogle *n* **:** a flirtatious glance

ogre \ˈō-gər\ *n* **1 :** a hideous man-eating giant of fairy tales and folklore **2 :** a dreaded person or object [French] — **ogre·ish** \ˈō-gə-rish, -grish\ *adj*

ogress \ˈō-grəs\ *n* **:** a female ogre

1oh *or* **O** \ō, ˈō\ *interj* **1 —** used to express an emotion (as astonishment, pain, or desire) **2 —** used in direct address ⟨*oh* sir, you forgot your change⟩ **3 —** used to express acknowledgment or understanding of a statement ⟨*oh,* that's how you do it⟩ **4 —** used to introduce an example or approximation ⟨there are probably, *oh,* three dozen sheep in the pasture⟩ [Middle English *o*]

2oh \ˈō\ *n* **:** ZERO [*o;* from the similarity of the symbol for zero (0) to the letter *O*]

ohm \ˈōm\ *n* **:** a unit of electric resistance equal to the resistance of a circuit in which a potential difference of one volt produces a current of one ampere [Georg Simon *Ohm,* died 1854, German physicist] — **ohm·ic** \ˈō-mik\ *adj*

ohm·me·ter \ˈōm-ˌmēt-ər, ˈō-\ *n* **:** an instrument for indicating resistance in ohms directly

Ohm's law *n* **:** a law in electricity that states that the current in a circuit is equal to the potential difference divided by the resistance of the circuit

-oholic *variant of* -AHOLIC

1-oid \ˌȯid\ *n suffix* **:** something resembling a (specified) object or having a (specified) quality ⟨planet*oid*⟩ [Latin *-oïdes,* from *-oïdes,* adj. suffix]

2-oid *adj suffix* **:** resembling **:** having the form or appearance of [Latin *-oïdes,* from Greek *-oeidēs,* from *-o-* + *eidos* "appearance, form"]

1oil \ˈȯil\ *n* **1 a :** any of numerous greasy combustible and usually liquid substances from plant, animal, or mineral sources that are soluble in ether but not in water **b :** PETROLEUM **2 :** a substance (as a cosmetic) of oily consistency ⟨bath *oil*⟩ **3 a :** an oil color used by an artist **b :** a painting done in oil colors [Medieval French *oile,* from Latin *oleum* "olive oil," from Greek *elaion,* from *elaia* "olive"]

2oil *vt* **:** to treat, furnish, or lubricate with oil

oil·can \-ˌkan\ *n* **:** a can for oil; *esp* **:** a spouted can designed to release oil drop by drop

oil·cloth \ˈȯil-ˌklȯth\ *n* **:** cloth treated with oil or paint and used for table and shelf coverings

oil color *n* **:** a pigment used for oil paint

oil·er \ˈȯi-lər\ *n* **1 :** a person who oils **2 :** a receptacle or device for applying oil

oil field *n* **:** a region rich in petroleum deposits

oil gland *n* **:** a gland (as of the skin) that produces an oily secretion

oil–im·mer·sion \ˌȯil-im-ˌər-zhən, -shən\ *adj* **:** being an objective lens of short focal distance designed to work with a drop of oil connecting the lens and the cover glass of the slide

oil of vitriol : concentrated sulfuric acid

oil of wintergreen : the methyl ester of salicylic acid used as a flavoring and in liniments

oil paint *n* **:** paint in which a drying oil is the vehicle

\ə\ **abut**	\au̇\ **out**	\i\ **tip**	\ȯ\ **saw**	\u̇\ **foot**
\ər\ **further**	\ch\ **chin**	\ī\ **life**	\ȯi\ **coin**	\y\ **yet**
\a\ **mat**	\e\ **pet**	\j\ **job**	\th\ **thin**	\yü\ **few**
\ā\ **take**	\ē\ **easy**	\ng\ **sing**	\t͟h\ **this**	\yu̇\ **cure**
\ä\ **cot, cart**	\g\ **go**	\ō\ **bone**	\ü\ **food**	\zh\ **vision**

oil painting *n* **1** : the act or art of painting in oil colors **2** : a picture painted in oils

oil·seed \ˈȯil-ˌsēd\ *n* : a seed or crop (as flaxseed) grown largely for oil

oil shale *n* : a rock and especially shale from which oil can be recovered

oil·skin \-ˌskin\ *n* **1** : an oiled waterproof cloth **2** : an oilskin raincoat **3** *pl* : an oilskin suit of coat and trousers

oilskin 3

oil slick *n* : a film of oil floating on water

oil·stone \ˈȯil-ˌstōn\ *n* : a whetstone for use with oil

oil well *n* : a well from which petroleum is obtained

oily \ˈȯi-lē\ *adj* **oil·i·er; -est** **1** : of, relating to, or consisting of oil **2 a** : covered or impregnated with oil : GREASY **b** : relatively high in naturally secreted oils ⟨*oily* skin⟩ **3** : excessively smooth or suave in manner : UNCTUOUS ⟨an *oily* game show host⟩ — **oil·i·ness** *n*

oint·ment \ˈȯint-mənt\ *n* : a semisolid usually greasy and medicated preparation for application to the skin [Medieval French *uignement, oignement,* derived from Latin *unguentum,* from *unguere* "to anoint"]

Ojib·wa *or* **Ojib·way** *or* **Ojib·we** \ō-ˈjib-wā\ *n, pl* **Ojibwa** *or* **Ojibwas** *or* **Ojibway** *or* **Ojibways** *or* **Ojibwe** *or* **Ojibwes** **1** : a member of an American Indian people of the region around Lake Superior and westward **2** : an Algonquian language of the Ojibwa people [Ojibwa *očipwe·*, an Ojibwa band]

[1]**OK** *or* **okay** \ō-ˈkā\ *adv or adj* : ALL RIGHT [abbreviation of *oll korrect,* alteration of *all correct*]

Word History In the late 1830s Boston newspapers were full of abbreviations. Apparently there was simply a fashion for abbreviation, and any expression might be abbreviated. The craze went so far as to produce abbreviations of intentional misspellings. Such popular expressions as *N.G.* (no go) and *A.R.* (all right) gave way to *K.G.* (know go) and *O.W.* (oll wright). *O.K.* (oll korrect) followed quite naturally. Several of these abbreviated misspellings gained some currency, but *OK* alone became widespread and survived.

[2]**OK** *or* **okay** *n* : APPROVAL 1 ⟨was given the *OK* to start work⟩

[3]**OK** *or* **okay** *vt* **OK'd** *or* **okayed; OK'·ing** *or* **okay·ing** : to give official sanction to : APPROVE

oka·pi \ō-ˈkäp-ē\ *n* : an African mammal closely related to the giraffe but lacking the long neck [native name in Africa]

okapi

okra \ˈō-krə\ *n* : a tall annual herb related to the hollyhocks and grown for its edible green pods which are used especially in soups and stews; *also* : these pods [of African origin]

-ol \ˌȯl, ˌōl\ *n suffix* : chemical compound (as an alcohol or phenol) containing hydroxyl ⟨glycer*ol*⟩ [*alcohol*]

[1]**old** \ˈōld\ *adj* **1 a** : dating from the remote past : ANCIENT ⟨*old* traditions⟩ **b** : persisting from an earlier time : of long standing ⟨an *old* friend⟩ **2** *cap* : belonging to an early period in the development of a language or literature ⟨*Old* Irish⟩ **3** : having existed for a specified period of time ⟨a child three years *old*⟩ **4** : of, relating to, or originating in a past era ⟨*old* chronicles record the event⟩ **5 a** : advanced in years or age ⟨an *old* person⟩ **b** : showing the characteristics of age ⟨looked *old* at 20⟩ **6** : FORMER ⟨my *old* students⟩ **7 a** : showing the effects of time or use ⟨*old* shoes⟩ **b** : no longer in use ⟨throw out those *old* rags⟩ **c** : TIRESOME ⟨gets *old* fast⟩ **8** : long familiar ⟨the same *old* story⟩ [Old English *eald*]

synonyms OLD, ANCIENT, ANTIQUE, ARCHAIC mean having come into existence or use in the distant past. OLD may imply actual or relative length of existence ⟨*old* castles⟩ ⟨*old* dogs⟩. ANCIENT implies occurrence, existence, or use in the distant past ⟨*ancient* history⟩. ANTIQUE applies to what has come down from a former or ancient time ⟨a collector of *antique* clocks⟩. ARCHAIC implies having the characteristics of a much earlier period ⟨an *archaic* chivalry⟩ ⟨"methinks" is an *archaic* construction⟩.

[2]**old** *n* **1** : of a specified age — usually used in combination ⟨a 7-year-*old*⟩ **2** : old or earlier time ⟨days of *old*⟩

Old Church Slavic *n* : the Slavic language used in the Bible translation of Cyril and Methodius as attested in manuscripts of the 10th and 11th centuries — called also *Old Church Slavonic*

old country *n* : an emigrant's country of origin

old·en \ˈōl-dən\ *adj* : of or relating to a bygone era

Old English *n* **1** : the language of the English people from the time of the earliest documents in the 7th century to about 1100 **2** : English of any period before Modern English

old–fan·gled \ˈōld-ˈfang-gəld\ *adj* : OLD-FASHIONED

old–fash·ioned \ˈōld-ˈfash-ənd, ˈōl-\ *adj* **1** : of, relating to, or characteristic of a past era **2** : adhering to customs of a past era **3** : OUTMODED

Old French *n* : the French language from the 9th to the 16th century; *esp* : French from the 9th to the 13th century

Old Glory *n* : the flag of the U.S.

old–growth \ˈōld-ˈgrōth\ *adj* : of, relating to, or being a forest characterized by the presence of large old trees, dead standing trees, and fallen rotting trees and that is usually in a late stage of ecological succession

old guard *n, often cap O&G* : the conservative and especially older members of an organization (as a political party)

old hand *n* : VETERAN 1

old hat *adj* **1** : OLD-FASHIONED **2** : lacking newness or freshness : TRITE

Old High German *n* : High German exemplified in documents prior to about 1150

Old Irish *n* : the Irish language in use from the 7th century to about 950

old·ish \ˈōl-dish\ *adj* : somewhat old or elderly

old lady *n* **1** : WIFE **2** : MOTHER 1a **3** : GIRLFRIEND; *esp* : a woman with whom a man lives

old–line \ˈōl-ˈdlīn, -ˈlīn\ *adj* **1** : having an established reputation ⟨planned to go to work right out of college with an *old line* company⟩ **2** : adhering to traditional policies or practices ⟨*old line* politicians⟩

old maid *n* **1** : SPINSTER 2 **2** : a prim fussy person **3** : a simple card game in which all but one of the cards are matched in pairs and the player holding the unmatched card at the end loses — **old–maid·ish** \ˈōld-ˈmād-ish, ˈōl-\ *adj*

old man *n* **1 a** : HUSBAND **b** : FATHER 1a **2** *cap* : one in authority; *esp* : COMMANDING OFFICER **3** : BOYFRIEND; *esp* : a man with whom a woman lives

old master *n* : a work of art by an established master and especially by any of the distinguished painters of the 16th, 17th, or 18th centuries; *also* : such an artist

Old Nick \ˈōld-ˈnik, ˈōl-\ *n* : DEVIL 1

Old Norse *n* : the Germanic language of the Scandinavian peoples prior to about 1350

Old Occitan *n* : the Occitan language as attested in documents from about 1100 to 1500

Old Prus·sian \-ˈprəsh-ən\ *n* : a Baltic language used in East Prussia until the 17th century

old–school *adj* **1** : adhering to traditional policies or practices ⟨an *old-school* coach⟩ **2** : characteristic of an earlier or original style, manner, or form ⟨*old-school* music⟩

old school *n* : adherents to traditional policies and practices

old–squaw \ˈōld-ˈskwȯ, ˈōl-\ *n* : a common sea duck of the more northern parts of the northern hemisphere — called also *long-tailed duck*

old·ster \ˈōld-stər, ˈōl-\ *n* : an old or elderly person

Old Style *n* : a style of reckoning time used before the adoption of the Gregorian calendar

Old Testament *n* : the first of the two chief divisions of the Christian Bible containing the books of the Jewish canon of the Scripture — see BIBLE table

old–time \ˈōld-ˌtīm, ˈōl-\ *adj* **1** : of, relating to, or characteristic of an earlier period **2** : of long standing ⟨*old-time* residents⟩

old–tim·er \-ˈtī-mər\ *n* **1 a** : VETERAN 1 **b** : OLDSTER **2** : something that is old-fashioned : ANTIQUE

old wives' tale *n* : an often traditional belief that is not based on fact : SUPERSTITION

old–world \ˈōl-ˈdwərld, -ˈwərld\ *adj* : of, relating to, or having the qualities of the Old World; *esp* : PICTURESQUE ⟨driving on narrow *old-world* streets⟩

Old World *n* : EASTERN HEMISPHERE; *esp* : the continent of Europe

ole·ag·i·nous \ˌō-lē-ˈaj-ə-nəs\ *adj* **1** : resembling or having the properties of oil; *also* : containing or producing oil **2** : UNCTUOUS 2 [Middle French *oleagineux,* from Latin *oleagineus* "of an olive tree," from *olea* "olive tree," from Greek *elaia*] — **ole·ag·i·nous·ly** *adv* — **ole·ag·i·nous·ness** *n*

ole·an·der \ˈō-lē-ˌan-dər\ *n* : a poisonous evergreen shrub related to the dogbanes and often grown for its showy clusters of fragrant usually white, pink, or purple flowers [Medieval Latin]

ole·as·ter \-ˌas-tər\ *n* : any of several trees and shrubs with usually silvery foliage and fruits suggesting small olives; *esp* : RUSSIAN OLIVE [Latin, from *olea* "olive tree"]

ole·cra·non \ˌō-lə-ˈkrā-ˌnän\ *n* : a process of the ulna that projects behind the elbow joint [Greek *ōlekranon,* from *ōlenē* "elbow" + *kranion* "skull"]

ole·fin \ˈō-lə-fən\ *n* : a chemical compound made up of carbon and hydrogen atoms that contains at least one double bond; *esp* : any of various long-chain synthetic polymers (as of ethylene) used especially as textile fibers [French *(gaz) oléfiant* "ethylene," from Latin *oleum* "oil"]

ole·ic \ō-ˈlē-ik\ *adj* **1** : relating to, derived from, or contained in oil **2** : of or relating to oleic acid [Latin *oleum* "oil"]

oleic acid *n* : an unsaturated fatty acid $C_{18}H_{34}O_2$ obtained from natural fats and oils

oleo \ˈō-lē-ˌō\ *n, pl* **ole·os** : MARGARINE

oleo·mar·ga·rine \ˌō-lē-ō-ˈmärj-rən, -ˈmärj-ə-rən, -ˈmärj-ə-ˌrēn\ *n* : MARGARINE [French *oléomargarine,* from Latin *oleum* "oil" + French *margarine*]

oleo·res·in \-ˈrez-n\ *n* : a plant product (as a turpentine) containing chiefly essential oil and resin — **oleo·res·in·ous** \-ˈrez-n-əs, -ˈrez-nəs\ *adj*

ole·um \ˈō-lē-əm\ *n, pl* **oleums** : a heavy oily fuming strongly corrosive solution of sulfur trioxide in anhydrous sulfuric acid [Latin, "olive oil"]

O level *n* **1** : the lowest of three levels of standardized British exams in a secondary school subject — called also *Ordinary level*; compare A LEVEL, S LEVEL **2 a** : the level of education required to pass an O-level exam **b** : a course leading to an O-level exam

ol·fac·tion \äl-ˈfak-shən, ōl-\ *n* : the sense of smell; *also* : the act or process of smelling

ol·fac·to·ry \äl-ˈfak-tə-rē, ōl-, -trē\ *adj* : of, relating to, or concerned with the sense of smell [Latin *olfactorius,* from *olfacere* "to smell," from *olēre* "to smell" + *facere* "to make, do"]

olfactory bulb *n* : either of two small round structures projecting from the lower surface of the brain above the nasal cavity that transmit stimuli from the olfactory nerves to other areas of the brain for processing

olfactory nerve *n* : either of the 1st pair of cranial nerves that arise in the sensory membranes of the nose and conduct smell stimuli to the brain by way of the olfactory bulb

ol·i·garch \ˈäl-ə-ˌgärk, ˈō-lə-\ *n* : a member or supporter of an oligarchy [Greek *oligarchēs,* from *oligos* "few" + *archein* "to rule"]

ol·i·gar·chy \-ˌgär-kē\ *n, pl* **-chies** **1** : government by a few persons **2** : a government in which a small group exercises control usually for corrupt or selfish purposes; *also* : the group of persons having such power **3** : an organization controlled by an oligarchy — **ol·i·gar·chic** \ˌäl-ə-ˈgär-kik\ *or* **ol·i·gar·chi·cal** \-ki-kəl\ *adj*

Oli·go·cene \ˈäl-i-gō-ˌsēn, ˈō-li-, ə-ˈlig-ə-\ *n* : the epoch of the Tertiary between the Eocene and Miocene; *also* : the corresponding series of rocks [Greek *oligos* "few, little"] — **Oligocene** *adj*

oli·go·chaete \-ˌkēt\ *n* : any of a class or order (Oligochaeta) of annelid worms lacking a specialized head and including the earthworms [derived from Greek *oligos* "few, little" + *chaitē* "long hair"] — **oligochaete** *adj*

olio \ˈō-lē-ˌō\ *n, pl* **oli·os** : JUMBLE, MEDLEY [Spanish *olla,* a kind of stew, literally, "pot," from Latin]

[1]**ol·ive** \ˈäl-iv, -əv\ *n* **1 a** : a Mediterranean evergreen tree grown for its fruit that is an important food and source of oil; *also* : this fruit **b** : any of various shrubs and trees resembling the olive **2** : a yellow to yellowish green color [Medieval French, from Latin *oliva,* from Greek *elaia*]

[2]**olive** *adj* **1** : of the color olive or olive green **2** : approaching olive in color or complexion

olive 1a

olive branch *n* **1** : a branch of the olive tree especially when used as a symbol of peace **2** : an offer or gesture of conciliation or goodwill ⟨make a call to his former friend as an *olive branch*⟩

olive drab *n* **1** : a grayish olive color **2 a** : a wool or cotton fabric of an olive drab color **b** : a uniform of this fabric

olive green *n* : a greenish olive color

olive oil *n* : a pale yellow to yellowish green oil obtained from the pulp of olives and used especially as a salad oil, in cooking, and in soaps

olive ridley *n* : a relatively small olive-colored turtle of the tropical regions of the Pacific, Indian, and Atlantic oceans — called also *olive ridley turtle*

ol·iv·ine \ˈäl-i-ˌvēn\ *n* : a usually green mineral that is a complex silicate of magnesium and iron [German *Olivin,* from Latin *oliva* "olive"]

ol·la po·dri·da \ˌäl-ə-pə-ˈdrēd-ə\ *n, pl* **olla podridas** \-ˈdrēd-əz\ *also* **ollas podridas** \ˌäl-əz-pə-drēd-əz, ˌäl-ə-pə-\ : JUMBLE, HODGEPODGE [Spanish, a kind of stew, literally, "rotten pot"]

Ol·mec \ˈäl-ˌmek, ˈōl-\ *n* : an ancient people of the southern east coast of Mexico who lived about 1200 to 400 B.C. [Nahuatl *Ōlmēcah,* a coastal people in Aztec history, from *Ōlmān,* their homeland]

olym·pi·ad \ə-ˈlim-pē-ˌad, ō-\ *n, often cap* **1** : one of the 4-year intervals between Olympic Games by which time was reckoned in ancient Greece **2** : a celebration of the modern Olympic Games; *also* : a competition resembling an olympiad ⟨the school's math *olympiad*⟩ [Latin *Olympiad-, Olympias,* from Greek, from *Olympia,* site of ancient Olympic Games]

[1]**Olym·pi·an** \-pē-ən\ *adj* **1** : of or relating to Olympus in Thessaly **2** : befitting or characteristic of the gods of Olympus : LOFTY

[2]**Olympian** *adj* **1** : of or relating to the ancient Greek region of Olympia **2** : of, relating to, or constituting the Olympic Games

[3]**Olympian** *n* : a participant in Olympic Games

[4]**Olympian** *n* **1** : one of the ancient Greek gods dwelling on Olympus **2** : a being of lofty detachment or superior attainments

Olym·pic \ə-ˈlim-pik, ō-\ *adj* **1** : [1]OLYMPIAN **2** : of or relating to the Olympic Games

Olympic Games *n pl* **1** : an ancient Panhellenic festival held every 4th year and made up of contests in sports, music, and literature with the victor's prize being a crown of wild olive **2** : a modern revival of the ancient Olympic Games made up of international athletic contests that are held at separate winter and summer gatherings every four years — called also *Olympics*

-o·ma \ˈō-mə\ *n suffix, pl* **-o·mas** \-məz\ *also* **-o·ma·ta** \-mət-ə\ : tumor ⟨lip*oma*⟩ [Greek *-ōmat-, -ōma,* ending of nouns denoting result formed from verbs in *-oun*]

Oma·ha \ˈō-mə-ˌhò, -ˌhä\ *n* **1** : a member of an American Indian people of what is now northeastern Nebraska **2** : the Siouan language of the Omaha [Omaha *umą́hą,* a self-designation]

oma·sum \ō-ˈmā-səm\ *n, pl* **-sa** \-sə\ : the third chamber of the stomach of a ruminant that is situated between the reticulum and the abomasum [Latin, "tripe of a bullock"]

om·buds·man \ˈäm-ˌbu̇dz-mən, ˈòm-, -bədz-; äm-ˈbu̇dz-, òm-\ *n* **1** : a government official who receives and investigates complaints made by individuals against public officials **2** : one that investigates, reports on, and helps settle complaints [Swedish, literally, "representative," from Old Norse *umbothsmathr,* from *umboth* "commission" + *mathr* "man"]

ome·ga \ō-ˈmeg-ə, -ˈmē-gə, -ˈmā-gə\ *n* **1** : the 24th and last letter of the Greek alphabet — Ω or ω **2 :** the extreme or final part **:** END

om·elet *or* **om·elette** \'äm-lət, -ə-lət\ *n* **:** beaten eggs cooked without stirring until set and served folded in half [French *omelette,* from Middle French *alemette,* alteration of *alemelle* "thin plate," from Latin *lamella* "small metal plate," from *lamina* "thin plate"]

Word History The word *omelet* bears little resemblance to the Latin word *lamina,* but the shape of an omelet is rather like a thin plate, which is what *lamina,* the ancestor of *omelet,* means. The Romans used *lamella,* a diminutive of *lamina,* to mean "a small metal plate." This became Middle French *alemelle.* The word acquired the additional meaning "eggs beaten and cooked without stirring," because such a dish resembled a thin plate. *Alemelle,* under the influence of the common suffix *-ette,* was altered to *alemette,* which became *omelette* in modern French.

omen \'ō-mən\ *n* **:** an event or phenomenon believed to be a sign of some future occurrence **:** PORTENT [Latin *omin-, omen*]

omen·tum \ō-'ment-əm\ *n, pl* **-ta** \-ə\ *or* **-tums :** a free fold of peritoneum or one connecting or supporting abdominal structures (as the stomach) [Latin] — **omen·tal** \-'ment-l\ *adj*

omer \'ō-mər\ *n* **1 :** an ancient Hebrew unit of dry capacity equal to 1/10 ephah **2** *often cap* **:** a 7-week period of anticipation for Shabuoth beginning with the second day of Passover [Hebrew *'ōmer*]

omi·cron \'äm-ə-,krän, 'ōm-\ *n* **:** the 15th letter of the Greek alphabet — O or *o*

om·i·nous \'äm-ə-nəs\ *adj* **:** being or showing an omen; *esp* **:** foretelling evil ⟨*ominous* events leading to war⟩ — **om·i·nous·ly** *adv* — **om·i·nous·ness** *n*

omis·si·ble \ō-'mis-ə-bəl, ə-\ *adj* **:** that may be omitted

omis·sion \ō-'mish-ən, ə-\ *n* **1 :** something neglected or left undone **2 :** the act of omitting **:** the state of being omitted [Medieval French, from Late Latin *omissio,* from Latin *omittere* "to omit"]

omit \ō-'mit, ə-\ *vt* **omit·ted; omit·ting 1 :** to leave out or leave unmentioned ⟨*omits* one important detail⟩ **2 :** to leave undone **:** NEGLECT ⟨had *omitted* to take out the trash⟩ [Latin *omittere,* from *ob-* "toward" + *mittere* "to let go, send"]

om·ma·tid·i·um \,äm-ə-'tid-ē-əm\ *n, pl* **-ia** \-ē-ə\ **:** one of the elements corresponding to a small simple eye that make up the compound eye of an arthropod [New Latin, from Greek *omma* "eye"] — **om·ma·tid·i·al** \-ē-əl\ *adj*

omni- *combining form* **:** all **:** universally ⟨*omni*directional⟩ [Latin, from *omnis*]

[1]**om·ni·bus** \'äm-ni-,bəs, -bəs\ *n* **1 :** a usually automotive public vehicle designed to carry a large number of passengers **:** BUS **2 :** a book containing reprints of a number of works [French, from Latin, "for all," from *omnis* "all"]

[2]**omnibus** *adj* **1 :** of, relating to, or providing for many things at once **2 :** containing or including many items ⟨an *omnibus* legislative bill⟩

om·ni·di·rec·tion·al \,äm-ni-də-'rek-shnəl, -dī-, -shən-l\ *adj* **:** being in or involving all directions; *esp* **:** receiving or sending radio waves equally well in all directions ⟨an *omnidirectional* antenna⟩

om·ni·far·i·ous \,äm-nə-'far-ē-əs, -'fer-\ *adj* **:** of all varieties, forms, or kinds [Late Latin *omnifarius,* from Latin *omni-* + *-farius* (as in *multifarius* "diverse")]

om·nip·o·tence \äm-'nip-ət-əns\ *n* **1 :** the quality or state of being omnipotent **2 :** something of unlimited power

[1]**om·nip·o·tent** \-ət-ənt\ *adj* **1** *often cap* **:** ALMIGHTY 1 **2 :** having virtually unlimited authority or influence ⟨an *omnipotent* ruler⟩ [Medieval French, from Latin *omnipotens,* from *omni-* + *potens* "powerful, potent"] — **om·nip·o·tent·ly** *adv*

[2]**omnipotent** *n* **1 :** one who is omnipotent **2** *cap* **:** GOD 1

om·ni·pres·ent \,äm-ni-'prez-nt\ *adj* **:** present in all places at all times — **om·ni·pres·ence** \-ns\ *n*

om·ni·range \'äm-ni-,rānj\ *n* **:** a system of radio navigation in which any bearing relative to a special radio transmitter on the ground may be chosen and flown by an airplane pilot

om·ni·science \-əns\ *n* **:** the quality or state of being omniscient

om·ni·scient \äm-'nish-ənt\ *adj* **1 :** having infinite awareness, understanding, and insight **2 :** possessed of universal or complete knowledge [derived from Medieval Latin *omniscientia* "omniscience," from Latin *omni-* + *scientia* "knowledge, science"] — **om·ni·scient·ly** *adv*

om·ni·um–gath·er·um \,äm-nē-əm-'gath-ə-rəm\ *n* **:** a miscellaneous collection (as of things or persons) [Latin *omnium* "of all" (from *omnis* "all") + English *gather* + Latin *-um,* n. ending]

om·ni·vore \'äm-ni-,vōr, -,vȯr\ *n* **:** one that is omnivorous

om·niv·o·rous \äm-'niv-rəs, -ə-rəs\ *adj* **1 :** feeding on both animal and vegetable substances **2 :** avidly taking in everything as if devouring or consuming ⟨an *omnivorous* reader⟩ [Latin *omnivorus,* from *omni-* + *vorare* "to devour"] — **om·niv·o·rous·ly** *adv*

[1]**on** \ȯn, 'ȯn, än, 'än\ *prep* **1 a —** used as a function word to indicate contact with and support by the top surface of ⟨the book is lying *on* the table⟩ **b —** used as a function word to indicate contact with an outer surface ⟨the fly landed *on* the ceiling⟩ ⟨I have a cut *on* my finger⟩ **c —** used as a function word to indicate position in close proximity with ⟨a village *on* the sea⟩ ⟨stay *on* your opponent⟩ **d —** used as a function word to indicate the location of something ⟨*on* your left⟩ ⟨*on* the south side of the house⟩ ⟨*on* the farm⟩ **2 a —** used as a function word to indicate a source of attachment or support ⟨*on* a string⟩ ⟨stand *on* one foot⟩ **b —** used as a function word to indicate a source of dependence ⟨you can rely *on* me⟩ ⟨feeds *on* insects⟩ **c —** used as a function word to indicate means of conveyance ⟨*on* the bus⟩ **d —** used as a function word to indicate presence in the possession of ⟨had some money *on* him⟩ **3 —** used as a function word to indicate a time frame during which something takes place ⟨a parade *on* Sunday⟩ or an instant, action, or occurrence when something begins or is done ⟨*on* cue⟩ ⟨*on* arriving home, I found your letter⟩ ⟨news *on* the hour⟩ **4 a —** used as a function word to indicate manner of doing something ⟨*on* the sly⟩ **b —** used as a function word to indicate means ⟨cut myself *on* a knife⟩ ⟨talk *on* the telephone⟩ **c —** used as a function word to indicate a medium of expression ⟨*on* stage⟩ ⟨best show *on* television⟩ **5 a** (1) **—** used as a function word to indicate active involvement in a condition or status ⟨*on* the increase⟩ ⟨*on* the lookout⟩ (2) **:** regularly using or showing the effects of using ⟨*on* drugs⟩ **b —** used as a function word to indicate involvement or participation ⟨*on* the team⟩ ⟨*on* duty⟩ **c —** used as a function word to indicate inclusion ⟨put it *on* the agenda⟩ **d —** used as a function word to indicate position or status with regard to a standard or objective ⟨*on* schedule⟩ **6 a —** used as a function word to indicate reason, ground, or basis (as for an action, opinion, or computation) ⟨I have it *on* good authority⟩ ⟨*on* one condition⟩ ⟨the interest will be 10 cents *on* the dollar⟩ **b —** used as a function word to indicate the cause or source ⟨profited *on* the sale of stock⟩ **c —** used as a function word to indicate the focus of obligation or responsibility ⟨put the blame *on* me⟩ **7 a —** used as a function word to indicate the object of collision, opposition, or hostile action ⟨bumped my head *on* a limb⟩ ⟨an attack *on* her beliefs⟩ **b —** used as a function word to indicate the object with respect to some disadvantage ⟨a 3-game lead *on* the opposing team⟩ ⟨the joke's *on* me⟩ **8 a —** used as a function word to indicate destination or the focus of some action, movement, or directed effort ⟨crept up *on* him⟩ ⟨working *on* my skiing⟩ ⟨made a payment *on* the loan⟩ **b —** used as a function word to indicate the focus of feelings, determination, or will ⟨have pity *on* me⟩ ⟨keen *on* sports⟩ **c —** used as a function word to indicate the object with respect to some misfortune ⟨the crops died *on* them⟩ **d —** used as a function word to indicate the subject of study, discussion, or consideration ⟨a book *on* insects⟩ ⟨reflect *on* that a moment⟩ ⟨agree *on* price⟩ **e :** with respect to ⟨go light *on* the salt⟩ ⟨short *on* cash⟩ **9 —** used as a function word to indicate succession in a series ⟨loss *on* loss⟩ [Old English *an, on*]

[2]**on** \'ȯn, 'än\ *adv* **1 a :** in or into contact with a supporting surface and especially positioned for use or operation ⟨put the plates *on*⟩ **b :** in or into a position of being attached to or covering a surface; *esp* **:** in or into the condition of being worn ⟨has new shoes *on*⟩ **2 a :** forward in space, time, or action ⟨later *on*⟩ ⟨went *on* home⟩ **b :** in continuance or succession ⟨and so *on*⟩ ⟨rambled *on*⟩ **3 :** into operation or a position permitting operation ⟨turn the light *on*⟩

[3]**on** \'ȯn, 'än\ *adj* **1 :** engaged in an activity or function (as a dramatic role) **2 a :** being in operation ⟨the radio is *on*⟩ **b :** placed so as to permit operation ⟨the switch is *on*⟩ **3 :** aware of something — usually used with *to* ⟨he was *on* to me⟩ **4 a :** taking place or being broadcast ⟨the game is *on*⟩ **b :** having been planned ⟨has nothing *on* for the weekend⟩

-on \,än\ *n suffix* **1 :** elementary particle ⟨nucle*on*⟩ **2 a :** unit

: quantum ⟨phot*on*⟩ **b** : basic hereditary component ⟨oper*on*⟩ [*ion*]

on–again, off–again *adj* : existing briefly and in an intermittent unpredictable way ⟨*on-again, off-again* fads⟩

on and off *adv* : OFF AND ON

on·a·ger \ˈän-i-jər\ *n* **1** : an Asian wild ass **2** : a heavy catapult used in ancient and medieval times [Latin, "wild ass," from Greek *onagros,* from *onos* "ass" + *agros* "field"]

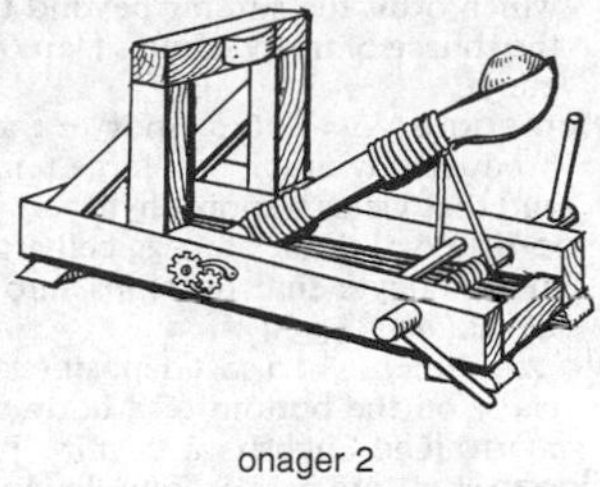

onager 2

on·board \ˈȯn-ˈbōrd, -ˈbȯrd, ˈän-\ *adj* : carried within or occurring aboard a vehicle (as a satellite or automobile) ⟨an *onboard* computer⟩

1**once** \ˈwəns\ *adv* **1** : one time and no more ⟨will repeat the question *once*⟩ **2** : at any one time : under any circumstances : EVER ⟨didn't *once* thank me⟩ **3** : at some indefinite time in the past : FORMERLY ⟨*once* lived in luxury⟩ **4** : by one degree of relationship ⟨a cousin *once* removed⟩ [Middle English *ones,* from genitive of *on* "one"] — **once and for all 1** : with finality ⟨let's settle this *once and for all*⟩ **2** : for the last time ⟨I'm asking you *once and for all*⟩ — **once in a while** : from time to time

2**once** *n* : one single time : one time at least ⟨just this *once*⟩ — **at once 1** : at the same time : SIMULTANEOUSLY **2** : IMMEDIATELY **3** : BOTH ⟨*at once* funny and sad⟩

3**once** *conj* : at the moment when : AS SOON AS ⟨*once* that's done, we can leave⟩

once–over \ˈwəns-ˌō-vər\ *n* : a swift examination or survey; *esp* : a swift comprehensive appraising glance ⟨gave me the *once-over*⟩

on·cho·cer·ci·a·sis \ˌäng-kō-ˌsər-ˈkī-ə-səs\ *n, pl* **-a·ses** \-ˌsēz\ : RIVER BLINDNESS [New Latin, from *Onchocerca,* genus of worms]

on·co·gene \ˈäng-kō-ˌjēn\ *n* : a gene having the potential to cause a normal cell to become cancerous [Greek *onkos* "mass"]

on·col·o·gy \än-ˈkäl-ə-jē, äng-\ *n* : a branch of medicine concerned with the study and treatment of tumors — **on·co·log·ic** \ˌäŋ-kə-ˈläj-ik\ *or* **on·co·log·i·cal** \-i-kəl\ *adj* — **on·col·o·gist** \än-ˈkäl-ə-jist, äŋ-\ *n*

on·com·ing \ˈȯn-ˌkəm-ing, ˈän-\ *adj* **1** : coming nearer in time or space ⟨*oncoming* traffic⟩ ⟨my *oncoming* vacation⟩ **2** : newly formed or prominent : RISING ⟨the *oncoming* generation⟩

1**one** \ˈwən, ˌwən\ *adj* **1** : being a single unit or thing ⟨*one* person left⟩ **2 a** : being one in particular ⟨early *one* morning⟩ **b** : being notably what is indicated ⟨*one* fine person⟩ **3 a** : being the same in kind or quality ⟨both of *one* species⟩ **b** : not divided : UNITED ⟨am *one* with you on this⟩ **4** : SOME 1 ⟨will see you again *one* day⟩ **5** : ONLY 2a ⟨the *one* person they wanted to see⟩ [Middle English *on,* from Old English *ān*]

2**one** \ˈwən\ *n* **1** — see NUMBER table **2** : the number denoting unity **3 a** : the first in a set or series ⟨day *one*⟩ **b** : an article of clothing of a size designated *one* ⟨wears a *one*⟩ **4** : a single person or thing ⟨I've got *one*, but I need the other⟩ **5** : a one-dollar bill — **for one** : as one example ⟨I *for one* disagree⟩

3**one** *pron* **1 a** : a single member or specimen of a usually specified class or group ⟨saw *one* of my friends⟩ **b** : a person in general : SOMEBODY ⟨*one* never knows⟩ **2** — used for *I* or *we* ⟨*one* hopes to see you there⟩

one another *pron* : EACH OTHER

one–dimensional *adj* **1** : having one dimension **2** : lacking depth : SUPERFICIAL ⟨*one-dimensional* characters⟩

one–horse *adj* **1** : drawn or operated by one horse **2** : small in scope or importance ⟨a *one-horse* town⟩

Onei·da \ō-ˈnīd-ə\ *n* : a member of an Iroquoian people originally of what is now central New York [Oneida *oneˀyóteˀ,* literally, "standing rock"]

onei·ric \ō-ˈnīr-ik\ *adj* : of or relating to dreams : DREAMY [Greek *oneiros* "dream"]

one–man *adj* : of or relating to just one individual: as **a** : consisting of just one individual ⟨a *one-man* committee⟩ **b** : done, presented, or made by only one individual ⟨a *one-man* play⟩ **c** : designed for or limited to one individual ⟨a *one-man* raft⟩

one·ness \ˈwən-nəs\ *n* : the quality, state, or fact of being one: as **a** : the state or fact of being one individual person or thing **b** : the quality, state, or fact of being complete : WHOLENESS **c** : pleasing or congruent arrangement of parts **d** : IDENTITY 1 **e** : a condition of being in agreement : UNITY

one–on–one \ˌwən-ȯn-ˈwən, -än-\ *adj or adv* **1** : playing directly against a single opposing player **2** : involving a direct encounter between one person and another ⟨enjoyed some *one-on-one* time with her daughter⟩

one–piece *adj* : consisting of or made in a single undivided piece ⟨a *one-piece* swimsuit⟩ — **one–piece** *n*

oner·ous \ˈän-ə-rəs, ˈō-nə-\ *adj* : being difficult or burdensome [Medieval French *honereus,* from Latin *onerosus,* from *oner-, onus* "burden"] — **oner·ous·ly** *adv* — **oner·ous·ness** *n*

one·self \wən-ˈself, ˌwən-\ *also* **one's self** \wən-, ˌwən-, ˌwənz-\ *pron* **1** : a person's self : one's own self — used reflexively as object of a preposition or verb or for emphasis in various constructions **2** : one's normal, healthy, or sane condition or self — **be oneself** : to conduct oneself in a usual or fitting manner

one–sid·ed \ˈwən-ˈsīd-əd\ *adj* **1 a** : having one side prominent : LOPSIDED 2 **b** : having or occurring on one side only ⟨a *one-sided* discussion⟩ **2** : limited to one side : BIASED ⟨take a *one-sided* view of a problem⟩ **3** : UNILATERAL ⟨a *one-sided* decision⟩

ones place *n* : UNITS PLACE

one–step \ˈwən-ˌstep\ *n* **1** : a ballroom dance in 2/4 time marked by quick walking steps backward and forward **2** : music used for the one-step — **one–step** *vi*

one·time \ˈwən-ˌtīm\ *adj* **1** : FORMER ⟨a *onetime* teacher⟩ **2** : occurring only once ⟨a *onetime* event⟩

one–to–one \ˌwən-tə-ˈwən, -də-\ *adj* : pairing each element of a set with one and only one element of another set

one–track *adj* : marked by narrowly restricted attention to or absorption in just one thing ⟨a *one-track* mind⟩

one–way *adj* **1** : that moves in, allows movement in, or functions in only one direction ⟨*one-way* traffic⟩ ⟨a *one-way* ticket⟩ **2** : ONE-SIDED 1b ⟨a *one-way* conversation⟩

on·go·ing \ˈȯn-ˌgō-ing, ˈän-\ *adj* **1 a** : being in process ⟨an investigation is now *ongoing*⟩ **b** : continuing without reaching a resolution or end ⟨an *ongoing* problem⟩ **2** : continuously moving forward : PROGRESSING ⟨contract negotiations are *ongoing*⟩

on·ion \ˈən-yən\ *n* : a widely grown Asian herb related to the lilies and having pungent edible bulbs used as a vegetable and to season foods; *also* : its bulb [Medieval French *oignon,* from Latin *unio*]

on·ion·skin \-ˌskin\ *n* : a thin strong translucent paper of very light weight

online *adj or adv* : connected to, served by, or available through a system and especially a computer or telecommunications system (as the Internet) ⟨an *online* database⟩; *also* : done while connected to a system ⟨*online* shopping⟩

on·look·er \ˈȯn-ˌlu̇k-ər, ˈän-\ *n* : SPECTATOR — **on·look·ing** \-ˌlu̇k-ing\ *adj*

1**on·ly** \ˈōn-lē\ *adj* **1** : unquestionably best : PEERLESS ⟨the *only* dog for me⟩ **2 a** : alone in a class or category : SOLE ⟨the *only* survivor⟩ **b** : having no brother or sister ⟨an *only* child⟩ **3** : FEW 1 ⟨one of the *only* areas not yet explored⟩ [Old English *ānlīc,* from *ān* "one" + *-līc* "-ly"]

2**only** *adv* **1 a** : as a single fact or instance and nothing more or different : MERELY ⟨*only* lost one game all season⟩ **b** : EXCLUSIVELY, SOLELY ⟨known *only* to me⟩ **2** : at the very least ⟨it was *only* too true⟩ **3 a** : in the final outcome ⟨will *only* make you sick⟩ **b** : with nevertheless the final result being ⟨won the battles, *only* to lose the war⟩ **4 a** : as recently as : not before ⟨*only* last week⟩ **b** : in the immediate past ⟨*only* just talked to them⟩

3**only** *conj* **1 a** : with this sole restriction that ⟨you may go, *only* come back early⟩ **b** : and yet : HOWEVER ⟨they look nice, *only* we can't use them⟩ **2** : were it not that : EXCEPT ⟨I'd go, *only* I'm too tired⟩

on·o·mas·tics \ˌän-ə-ˈmas-tiks\ *n sing or pl* : the study of the proper names of people and places [derived from Greek *onoma* "name"]

on·o·mat·o·poe·ia \ˌän-ə-ˌmat-ə-ˈpē-ə, -ˈpē-yə\ *n* **1** : the naming of a thing or action by a vocal imitation of the sound associated with it (as *buzz* or *hiss*) **2 :** the use of words whose sound suggests the sense (as for poetic effect) [Late Latin, from Greek *onomatopoiia,* from *onoma* "name" + *poiein* "to make"] — **on·o·mat·o·poe·ic** \-ˈpē-ik\ *or* **on·o·mat·o·po·et·ic** \-pō-ˈet-ik\ *adj* — **on·o·mat·o·poe·i·cal·ly** \-ˈpē-ə-kə-lē, -klē\ *or* **on·o·mat·o·po·et·i·cal·ly** \-pō-ˈet-i-kə-lē, -klē\ *adv*

On·on·da·ga \ˌän-ən-ˈdȯ-gə, ˌän-ə-ˈdȯ-\ *n, pl* **Onondaga** *or* **Onondagas** **1 :** a member of an American Indian people of New York and Canada **2 :** the Iroquoian language of the Onondaga people [Onondaga *onǫ́ˀtàˀke,* the chief Onondaga town]

on–ramp \ˈȯn-ˌramp, ˈän-\ *n* **:** a ramp by which one enters a limited-access highway

on·rush \ˈȯn-ˌrəsh, ˈän-\ *n* **1 :** a rushing forward or onward **2 :** ONSET ⟨the first *onrush* of grief⟩

on–screen \ˈȯn-ˌskrēn, ˈän-\ *adv or adj* **1 :** in a motion picture or television program ⟨briefly appears *on-screen*⟩ ⟨the *on-screen* action⟩ **2 :** on a computer or television screen ⟨the *on-screen* cursor⟩

on·set \-ˌset\ *n* **1 :** ATTACK 1 **2 :** BEGINNING 4a

on·shore \ˈȯn-ˌshōr, ˈän-, -ˌshȯr\ *adj* **1 :** moving toward the shore ⟨*onshore* winds⟩ **2 :** situated on land ⟨*onshore* oil refineries⟩ **3 :** DOMESTIC ⟨*onshore* financial markets⟩ — **on·shore** \ˈȯn-ˈ, ˈän-ˈ\ *adv*

onside \-ˈsīd\ *adv or adj* **:** in a position legally to play the ball or puck

on–site \-ˈsīt\ *adv or adj* **:** of a particular place especially of business ⟨printed *on-site*⟩ ⟨*on-site* day care⟩

on·slaught \ˈän-ˌslȯt, ˈȯn-\ *n* **:** an especially fierce attack [Dutch *aanslag* "act of striking"]

onstage \-ˈstāj\ *adv or adj* **:** on or onto a stage **:** on a part of the stage visible to the audience

on–the–job *adj* **:** of, relating to, or being something learned, gained, or done while working at a job ⟨*on-the-job* training⟩

on·to \ˌȯn-tə, ˌän-; ˈȯn-tü, ˈän-\ *prep* **1 :** to a position on ⟨climbed *onto* the roof⟩ **2 :** in or into a state of awareness about ⟨police were *onto* the plot⟩

on·tog·e·ny \än-ˈtäj-ə-nē\ *n, pl* **-nies :** the development or course of development especially of an individual organism [Greek *ont-, ōn,* present participle of *einai* "to be"] — **on·to·ge·net·ic** \ˌän-tə-jə-ˈnet-ik\ *adj* — **on·to·ge·net·i·cal·ly** \-ˈnet-i-kə-lē, -klē\ *adv*

onus \ˈō-nəs\ *n* **1 a :** something (as a duty) that is burdensome or trying **b :** an obligation (as to do something) that is disagreeable **2 :** BLAME 2 [Latin]

¹on·ward \ˈȯn-wərd, ˈän-\ *also* **on·wards** \-wərdz\ *adv* **:** toward or at a point lying ahead in space or time **:** FORWARD ⟨kept moving *onward*⟩

²onward *adj* **:** directed or moving onward **:** FORWARD ⟨the *onward* march of time⟩

on·y·choph·o·ran \ˌän-i-ˈkäf-ə-rən\ *n* **:** PERIPATUS [derived from Greek *onych-, onyx* "claw" + *-phoros* "-phore"] — **onychophoran** *adj*

on·yx \ˈän-iks\ *n* **:** chalcedony in parallel layers of different colors [Latin *onych-, onyx,* from Greek, literally, "claw, nail"]

oo- — see O-

oo·cyte \ˈō-ə-ˌsīt\ *n* **:** an egg before maturation

oo·dles \ˈüd-lz\ *n pl* **:** a great quantity [origin unknown]

oog·a·mous \ō-ˈäg-ə-məs\ *adj* **:** reproducing by egg and sperm **:** HETEROGAMETIC — **oog·a·my** \-mē\ *n*

oo·gen·e·sis \ˌō-ə-ˈjen-ə-səs\ *n, pl* **-gen·e·ses** \-ə-ˌsēz\ **:** the process of female gamete formation including formation of an oocyte from an oogonium followed by meiosis and maturation of the egg — **oo·ge·net·ic** \-jə-ˈnet-ik\ *adj*

oo·go·ni·um \ˌō-ə-ˈgō-nē-əm\ *n, pl* **-nia** \-nē-ə\ **1 :** a female sexual organ in various algae and fungi **2 :** a cell that gives rise to oocytes [derived from Greek *ōion* "egg" + *gonos* "procreation, seed"] — **oo·go·ni·al** \-nē-əl\ *adj*

¹ooh \ˈü\ *interj* — used to express amazement, joy, or surprise

²ooh *vi* **:** to exclaim in amazement, joy, or surprise ⟨*oohing* and aahing over her gifts⟩ — **ooh** *n*

oo·lite \ˈō-ə-ˌlīt\ *n* **:** a rock consisting of small round grains usually of calcium carbonate cemented together — **oo·lit·ic** \ˌō-ə-ˈlit-ik\ *adj*

oo·long \ˈü-ˌlȯŋ\ *n* **:** tea made from leaves that have been partially fermented before drying [Chinese *oōlióng(dé),* literally, black dragon (tea)]

oomph \ˈu̇mf, ˈu̇mpf\ *n* **1 :** personal charm or magnetism **:** GLAMOUR **2 :** SEX APPEAL **3 :** lively and animated character **:** ENTHUSIASM [imitation of a sound made under exertion]

oops *or* **whoops** *also* **woops** \ˈu̇ps, ˈwu̇ps\ *interj* — used to express mild apology, surprise, or dismay

Oort cloud \ˈōrt-, ˈȯrt-\ *n* **:** a spherical shell of small bodies which orbit the sun far beyond the orbit of Pluto that may be the source of many comets [Jan *Oort,* died 1992, Dutch astronomer]

oo·spore \ˈō-ə-ˌspōr, -ˌspȯr\ *n* **:** a spore (as of a fungus) that is produced by union of a large female cell with a small male cell and that yields a sporophyte

oo·tid \ˈō-ə-ˌtid\ *n* **:** an egg cell after the second meiotic division of an oocyte that develops into a mature egg [derived from Greek *ōion* "egg"]

¹ooze \ˈüz\ *n* **1 :** a soft deposit (as of mud, slime, or shells) especially on the bottom of a body of water **2 :** soft wet ground **:** MUD [Old English *wāse* "mire"]

²ooze *vb* **1 :** to pass or flow slowly through or as if through small openings ⟨sap *oozed* from the tree⟩ **2 :** to move slowly or imperceptibly **3 :** EXUDE 2, GIVE OFF ⟨*oozing* glamour⟩

³ooze *n* **1 :** the action of oozing **2 :** something that oozes [Middle English *wose* "sap, juice," from Old English *wōs*]

oozy \ˈü-zē\ *adj* **ooz·ier; -est 1 :** containing or composed of ooze **2 :** exuding moisture **:** SLIMY

opac·i·ty \ō-ˈpas-ət-ē\ *n, pl* **-ties 1 :** obscurity of meaning **2 :** mental dullness **3 :** the quality or state of being opaque to radiant energy (as light) **4 :** an opaque spot on an otherwise or normally transparent structure (as the lens of the eye) [French *opacité* "shadiness," from Latin *opacitas,* from *opacus* "shaded, dark"]

opal \ˈō-pəl\ *n* **:** a usually amorphous mineral that is a hydrated silica softer and less dense than quartz and typically with an iridescent play of colors and that is used as a gem [Latin *opalus,* derived from Sanskrit *upala* "stone, jewel"]

opal·es·cent \ˌō-pə-ˈles-nt\ *adj* **:** reflecting an iridescent light — **opal·esce** \-ˈles\ *vi* — **opal·es·cence** \-ˈles-ns\ *n*

opal·ine \ˈō-pə-ˌlīn, -ˌlēn\ *adj* **:** resembling opal

opaque \ō-ˈpāk\ *adj* **1 :** exhibiting opacity **:** not transmitting radiant energy (as light) **2 a :** not easily understood **:** OBSCURE **b :** DULL 1, STUPID [Latin *opacus*] — **opaque** *n* — **opaque·ly** *adv* — **opaque·ness** *n*

ope \ˈōp\ *vb, archaic* **:** OPEN

op–ed \ˈäp-ˈed\ *n, often cap O&E* **:** a page of special features usually opposite the editorial page of a newspaper [short for *opposite editorial*]

¹open \ˈō-pən, ˈōp-m\ *adj* **1 :** having no enclosing or confining barrier ⟨cattle grazing on an *open* range⟩ **2 :** being in a position or adjustment to permit passage **:** not shut or locked ⟨an *open* door⟩ ⟨the car is *open*⟩ **3 a :** completely free from concealment **:** exposed to general view or knowledge ⟨their hostilities eventually erupted with *open* war⟩ **b :** exposed or vulnerable to attack or question ⟨*open* to doubt⟩ **4 a :** not covered ⟨an *open* car⟩ ⟨her eyes were *open*⟩ **b :** having no protective cover ⟨an *open* wound⟩ **5 :** not restricted to a particular group or category of people ⟨*open* to the public⟩ ⟨an *open* tournament⟩ **6 :** fit to be traveled over **:** presenting no obstacle to passage or view ⟨the *open* road⟩ ⟨*open* country⟩ **7 a :** having the parts or surfaces laid out in an expanded position ⟨an *open* book⟩ **b :** having the lips parted ⟨stood there with his mouth wide *open*⟩ **c :** not buttoned or zipped ⟨an *open* shirt⟩ **8 a :** available to follow or make use of ⟨the only course of action *open* to us⟩ **b :** not taken up with duties or engagements ⟨keep an hour *open* on Friday⟩ **c :** not finally decided ⟨the salary is *open*⟩ ⟨an *open* question⟩ **d :** available for a qualified applicant **:** VACANT ⟨the job is still *open*⟩ **e :** remaining available for use or filling until canceled ⟨an *open* order for more items⟩ **f :** available for future purchase ⟨these items are in *open* stock⟩ **9 a :** characterized by ready accessibility and a usually generous attitude ⟨*open* to suggestions⟩ **b :** free from reserve or pretense **:** FRANK **c :** accessible to the influx of new factors (as foreign goods) ⟨an *open* market⟩ **10 a** (1) **:** having openings, interruptions, or spaces ⟨*open* mesh⟩ (2) **:** sparsely distributed **:** SCATTERED ⟨*open* population⟩ **b :** not made up of a continuous closed circuit of channels ⟨the insect circulatory system is *open*⟩ **11 :** being in operation ⟨an *open* microphone⟩; *esp* **:** ready for business, patronage, or use ⟨the store is *open* from 9 to 5⟩ ⟨the new highway will be *open* next week⟩ **12 a :** free from checking or hampering restraints ⟨an *open* economy⟩ **b :** relatively unguarded by opponents ⟨passed to an *open* teammate⟩ **13 :** containing none of its endpoints ⟨an *open* interval⟩ **14 a :** being an incomplete electrical circuit **b :** not allowing the flow of electricity ⟨an *open* switch⟩ [Old English] ***synonyms*** see FRANK — **open·ly** \ˈō-pən-lē\ *adv* — **open·ness** \ˈō-pən-nəs\ *n*

²open *vb* **opened** \ˈō-pənd, ˈōp-md\; **open·ing** \ˈōp-ning, -ə-ning\ **1 a :** to change or move from a shut or closed condition ⟨*open* a switch⟩ ⟨the door *opened* slowly⟩ **b :** to make or become available for passage by or as if by clearing away obstacles ⟨*open* a road blocked with snow⟩ ⟨the clouds *opened*⟩ **c :** to make more perceptive or responsive ⟨*open* your mind to new ways of thinking⟩ **2 a :** to make or become functional ⟨*open* a new store⟩ ⟨the office *opens* early⟩ **b :** to access for use ⟨*open* the computer file⟩ **3 :** to give access or make accessible ⟨*open* the way for changes⟩ ⟨the rooms *open* onto a hall⟩ **4 :** to make an opening or openings in ⟨*open* a boil⟩ **5 :** to spread out : UNFOLD ⟨an *opening* flower⟩ ⟨*open* a book⟩ **6 :** to enter upon : BEGIN, START ⟨*open* fire⟩ ⟨*open* talks⟩ **7 :** to speak out **8 :** to provide the opening performance of a show before the main event — **open·able** \ˈōp-nə-bəl, -ə-nə-\ *adj*

³open *n* **1 a :** open and unobstructed space or water **b :** OUTDOORS **2 :** an open contest, competition, or tournament **3 :** a public or unconcealed state or position ⟨now that the secret is out in the *open*⟩

open adoption *n* **:** an adoption that involves contact between biological and adoptive parents and sometimes between biological parents and the adopted child

open–air *adj* **:** OUTDOOR ⟨*open-air* theaters⟩

open air *n* **:** space where air is unconfined; *esp* **:** OUTDOORS

open–and–shut \ˌōp-nən-ˈshət, -ə-nən-\ *adj* **1 :** perfectly simple : OBVIOUS **2 :** easily settled ⟨an *open-and-shut* case⟩

open arms *n pl* **:** an eager or warm welcome ⟨greeted them with *open arms*⟩

open dating *n* **:** the marking of perishable food products with a clearly readable date indicating when the food was packaged or the last date on which it should be sold or used

open door *n* **1 :** a recognized right of admittance : freedom of access; *also* **:** a policy providing such freedom ⟨the company has an *open door* for its employees⟩ **2 :** a policy giving opportunity for commercial relations with a country to all nations on equal terms — **open–door** *adj*

open–end *adj* **:** organized or formulated to allow for contingencies ⟨an *open-end* mortgage⟩

open–end·ed \ˌō-pən-ˈend-əd\ *adj* **:** not fixed: as **a :** adaptable to the needs of a situation ⟨an *open-ended* budget⟩ **b :** allowing or designed to allow spontaneous and unguided responses ⟨ask an *open-ended* question⟩

open·er \ˈōp-nər, -ə-nər\ *n* **:** something used for opening ⟨a bottle *opener*⟩ ⟨a conversation *opener*⟩ — **for openers :** to begin with

open–eyed \ˌō-pə-ˈnīd\ *adj* **1 :** having the eyes open **2 :** carefully watchful : DISCERNING

open·hand·ed \ˌō-pən-ˈhan-dəd\ *adj* **:** generous in giving — **open·hand·ed·ly** *adv* — **open·hand·ed·ness** *n*

open–heart *adj* **:** of, relating to, or performed on a heart temporarily stopped and surgically opened for repair of defects or damage ⟨*open-heart* surgery⟩

open·heart·ed \-ˈhärt-əd\ *adj* **1 :** FRANK 1 **2 :** responsive to emotional appeal — **open·heart·ed·ly** *adv* — **open·heart·ed·ness** *n*

open–hearth *adj* **:** being or relating to a process of making steel from pig iron in a furnace that reflects heat from the roof onto the material

open house *n* **1 a :** ready and usually informal hospitality or entertainment for all comers **b :** an event during which a school is open to the public and which usually provides an opportunity for parents and guardians to speak with faculty and tour school facilities **2 :** a house or apartment open for inspection especially by prospective buyers or tenants

open·ing \ˈōp-ning, -ə-ning\ *n* **1 a :** an act or instance of making or becoming open **b :** an act or instance of beginning ⟨the *opening* of school⟩; *esp* **:** a formal and usually public event by which something new is put into operation ⟨store's grand *opening*⟩ **2 :** something that is open: as **a :** HOLE **b :** SPAN 2b **3 :** something that constitutes a beginning: as **a :** a usually planned series of moves made at the start of a game of chess or checkers **b :** a first performance **4 a :** OCCASION 1, CHANCE ⟨waited for an *opening* to pitch the idea⟩ **b :** an opportunity for employment

open letter *n* **:** a published letter of protest or appeal intended for the general public

open–mind·ed \ˌō-pən-ˈmīn-dəd\ *adj* **:** willing to listen to arguments or ideas : not prejudiced — **open–mind·ed·ly** *adv* — **open–mind·ed·ness** *n*

open·mouthed \ˌō-pən-ˈmau̇t͟hd, -ˈmau̇tht\ *adj* **1 :** having the mouth wide open **2 :** struck with amazement or wonder — **open·mouthed·ly** \-ˈmau̇-t͟həd-lē, -ˈmau̇th-tlē\ *adv* — **open·mouthed·ness** \-ˈmau̇-t͟həd-nəs, -ˈmau̇tht-nəs, -ˈmau̇th-nəs\ *n*

open–pol·li·nat·ed \ˌō-pən-ˈpäl-ə-ˌnāt-əd\ *adj* **:** pollinated by natural agencies (as wind or insects) without human interference

open season *n* **1 :** a period when it is legal to kill or catch game or fish protected at other times by law **2 :** a time during which someone or something is the object of sustained attack or criticism ⟨*open season* on politicians⟩

open secret *n* **:** something supposedly secret but in fact generally known

open sentence *n* **:** a statement (as in mathematics) that contains at least one blank or unknown and that becomes true or false when the blank is filled or a quantity is substituted for the unknown

open sesame \ˌō-pən-ˈses-ə-mē\ *n* **:** something that unfailingly brings about a desired end [from *open sesame,* the magical command used by Ali Baba to open the door of the robbers' den in the story *Ali Baba and the Forty Thieves* in the *Arabian Nights' Entertainments*]

open shop *n* **:** an establishment that employs both members and nonmembers of a labor union

open up *vb* **1 :** to make available ⟨*opened up* the records to the public⟩ **2 a :** to make visible **b :** to come into view ⟨the road *opens up* ahead⟩ **3 :** to open by cutting into **4 :** to begin firing **5 :** to become communicative ⟨tried to get him to *open up*⟩

open·work \ˈō-pən-ˌwərk\ *n* **:** work constructed so as to show openings through its substance — **open–worked** \ˌō-pən-ˈwərkt\ *adj*

¹opera *plural of* OPUS

²op·era \ˈäp-rə, -ə-rə\ *n* **1 :** a drama set to music and made up of vocal pieces with orchestral accompaniment and orchestral overtures and interludes **2 :** a performance of an opera; *also* **:** a building where operas are performed [Italian, "work, opera," from Latin "work, pains"]

op·er·a·ble \ˈäp-rə-bəl, -ə-rə-\ *adj* **1 :** fit, possible, or desirable to use **2 :** likely to result in a favorable outcome upon surgical treatment ⟨an *operable* cancer⟩

opé·ra bouffe \ˌäp-rə-ˈbüf, -ə-rə-\ *n* **:** satirical comic opera [French, from Italian *opera buffa*]

opé·ra co·mique \ˌäp-rə-käm-ˈēk, -ə-rə-, -kō-ˈmēk\ *n* **:** COMIC OPERA [French]

opera glasses *n pl* **:** small low-power binoculars or field glasses for use in a theater

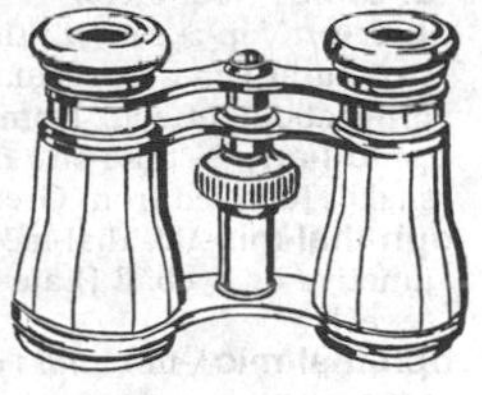

opera glasses

opera hat *n* **:** a man's collapsible top hat

op·er·ant \ˈäp-ə-rənt\ *adj* **:** of, relating to, or being operant conditioning or a behavior reinforced by operant conditioning

operant conditioning *n* **:** conditioning in which the desired behavior (as bar-pressing by a rat) or increasingly closer approximations to it are followed by a reinforcement (as delivery of food) that is needed, pleasant, or desired

op·er·ate \ˈäp-ə-ˌrāt, -ə-ˌrāt\ *vb* **1 :** to perform or cause to perform an appointed function ⟨learn to *operate* a car safely⟩ **2 :** to produce an effect ⟨a drug that *operates* quickly⟩ **3 :** to carry on the activities of ⟨*operate* a farm⟩; *esp* **:** MANAGE ⟨*operate* a business⟩ **4 :** to perform surgery ⟨*operate* on a patient⟩ ⟨*operated* on a defective heart valve⟩ [Latin *operari* "to work," from *oper-, opus* "work"]

op·er·at·ic \ˌäp-ə-ˈrat-ik\ *adj* **1 :** of or relating to opera **2**

: grand, dramatic, or romantic in style or effect — **op·er·at·i·cal·ly** \-i-kə-lē, -klē\ *adv*

op·er·at·ing \'äp-ˌrāt-ing, -ə-ˌrāt-\ *adj* : of, relating to, or used for or in operations ⟨*operating* expenses⟩ ⟨a hospital *operating* room⟩

operating system *n* : software that controls the operation of a computer and directs the processing of the user's programs (as by controlling input and output functions)

op·er·a·tion \ˌäp-ə-'rā-shən\ *n* **1 :** performance of a practical work **2 :** the quality or state of being functional or operative ⟨the factory is now in *operation*⟩ **3 :** a procedure performed on a living body usually with medical instruments especially to restore health or repair damage or defect **4 :** a process (as addition or multiplication) of deriving one mathematical expression from others according to a rule **5 a :** a usually military action, mission, or maneuver including its planning and execution **b** *pl* **:** the office of an airfield which controls flying from the field **c** *pl* **:** the agency of an organization that carries on the principal planning and operating functions of a headquarters and subordinate offices **6 :** a single step in a computer program **7 :** a usually small business or establishment ⟨ran a small *operation*⟩ — **op·er·a·tion·al** \-shnəl, -shən-l\ *adj* — **op·er·a·tion·al·ly** \-ē\ *adv*

[1]**op·er·a·tive** \'äp-rət-iv, -ə-rət-; 'äp-ə-ˌrāt-\ *adj* **1 a :** producing an appropriate or intended effect **b :** most significant or essential ⟨the *operative* word in a phrase⟩ **2 :** exerting force or influence **:** OPERATING ⟨an *operative* motive⟩ **3 a :** having to do with physical operations ⟨*operative* costs⟩ **b :** engaged in work ⟨an *operative* craftsman⟩ **4 :** based on or consisting of an operation ⟨*operative* dentistry⟩ — **op·er·a·tive·ly** *adv* — **op·er·a·tive·ness** *n*

[2]**operative** *n* **:** OPERATOR: as **a :** ARTISAN, MECHANIC **b :** a secret agent **c :** DETECTIVE

op·er·a·tor \'äp-ˌrāt-ər, -ə-ˌrāt-\ *n* **1 :** one that operates: as **a :** one that operates a machine or device ⟨telephone *operator*⟩ **b :** one that operates a business **c :** one that deals in stocks or commodities **2 :** a shrewd person who knows how to get around restrictions or difficulties **3 :** a binding site in a DNA chain at which a genetic repressor binds to inhibit the initiation of transcription of messenger RNA by one or more nearby structural genes — called also *operator gene*; compare OPERON

oper·cu·lum \ō-'pər-kyə-ləm\ *n, pl* **-la** \-lə\ *also* **-lums** **1 :** a body part that suggests a lid: as **a :** a plate on the foot of a gastropod mollusk that closes the shell **b :** the covering of the gills of a fish **2 :** a lid or covering flap (as of a moss capsule) [Latin, "cover," from *operire* "to shut, cover"] — **oper·cu·lar** \-lər\ *adj* — **oper·cu·late** \-lət\ *adj*

op·er·et·ta \ˌäp-ə-'ret-ə\ *n* **:** a usually romantic comic opera that includes songs and dancing [Italian, from *opera* "opera"] — **op·er·et·tist** \-'ret-əst\ *n*

op·er·on \'äp-ə-ˌrän\ *n* **:** the combination of an operator and the structural genes it regulates [French *opéron,* from *opérer* "to bring about, effect," from Latin *operari* "to work"]

ophid·i·an \ō-'fid-ē-ən\ *adj* **:** of, relating to, or resembling snakes [derived from Greek *ophis* "snake"] — **ophidian** *n*

oph·thal·mia \äf-'thal-mē-ə, äp-\ *n* **:** inflammation of the conjunctiva or eyeball [Late Latin, from Greek, from *ophthalmos* "eye"]

oph·thal·mic \-mik\ *adj* **:** of, relating to, or situated near the eye **:** OCULAR

oph·thal·mol·o·gist \ˌäf-thə-'mäl-ə-jəst, ˌäp-, -thəl-, -ˌthal-\ *n* **:** a physician specializing in ophthalmology — compare OPTICIAN, OPTOMETRIST

oph·thal·mol·o·gy \-jē\ *n* **:** a branch of medical science dealing with the structure, functions, and diseases of the eye — **oph·thal·mo·log·ic** \-mə-'läj-ik\ *or* **oph·thal·mo·log·i·cal** \-i-kəl\ *adj* — **oph·thal·mo·log·i·cal·ly** \ˌäf-thə-mə-'läj-i-kə-lē, ˌäp-, -thəl-, -ˌthal-, -klē\ *adv*

oph·thal·mo·scope \äf-'thal-mə-ˌskōp, äp-\ *n* **:** an instrument for use in viewing the interior of the eye and especially the retina

-opia \'ō-pē-ə\ *n combining form* **:** condition of having (such) vision ⟨hyper*opia*⟩ [Greek *ōps* "eye"]

[1]**opi·ate** \'ō-pē-ət, -ˌāt\ *n* **1 :** a drug (as morphine or codeine) containing or derived from opium and tending to induce sleep and relieve pain; *also* **:** NARCOTIC 1 **2 :** something that induces rest or inaction or quiets uneasiness

[2]**opiate** *adj* **1 a :** containing or mixed with opium **b :** of, relating to, binding, or being an opiate **2 a :** inducing sleep **:** NARCOTIC **b :** causing dullness or inaction

opine \ō-'pīn\ *vb* **1 :** to state as an opinion **2 :** to express opinions [Middle French *opiner,* from Latin *opinari* "to have an opinion"]

opin·ion \ə-'pin-yən\ *n* **1 a :** a view, judgement, or appraisal formed in the mind about a particular matter ⟨his *opinion* on the death penalty⟩ **b :** REGARD 2a ⟨has a high *opinion* of him⟩ **2 a :** belief stronger than an impression but not positive knowledge **b :** a generally held view **3 a :** a formal statement by an expert after careful study **b :** the formal expression (as by a judge or court) of the reasons and principles upon which a legal decision is based [Medieval French, from Latin *opinio*]

synonyms OPINION, BELIEF, CONVICTION mean a judgment one holds as true. OPINION implies a conclusion still open to dispute ⟨differing *opinions* on the safety of nuclear power⟩. BELIEF implies deliberate acceptance and intellectual assent ⟨a basic *belief* in a supreme being⟩. CONVICTION applies to a firm, unshakable belief ⟨a *conviction* that all life is sacred⟩.

opin·ion·at·ed \-yə-ˌnāt-əd\ *adj* **:** adhering unduly to one's own opinions or preconceived notions — **opin·ion·at·ed·ly** *adv* — **opin·ion·at·ed·ness** *n*

opin·ion·ative \-ˌnāt-iv\ *adj* **1 :** of, relating to, or consisting of opinion **2 :** OPINIONATED

opi·um \'ō-pē-əm\ *n* **1 :** a bitter brownish addictive narcotic drug consisting of the dried juice from the unripe seed capsules of the opium poppy **2 :** something having an effect like that of opium [Latin, from Greek *opion,* from *opos* "sap"]

opium poppy *n* **:** an annual Eurasian poppy grown since ancient times for opium, for its edible oily seeds, and for its showy flowers

opos·sum \ə-'päs-əm, 'päs-əm\ *n, pl* **opossums** *also* **opossum :** any of various American marsupials that usually have a pointed snout and prehensile tail; *esp* **:** a common largely nocturnal mammal of North America that eats both animal and vegetable matter and is an expert climber [of Algonquian origin]

[1]**op·po·nent** \ə-'pō-nənt\ *n* **1 :** a person or thing that opposes another person or thing **2 :** a muscle that counteracts and resists the action of another [Latin *opponens,* present participle of *opponere* "to oppose"]

synonyms OPPONENT, ANTAGONIST, ADVERSARY mean one who is opposed to another. OPPONENT implies a position on the other side as in a debate, election, or conflict ⟨a lively debate between political *opponents*⟩. ANTAGONIST implies sharper opposition in a struggle for supremacy ⟨the press is the *antagonist* of reclusive celebrities⟩. ADVERSARY suggests active hostility ⟨declared war on their *adversaries*⟩.

[2]**opponent** *adj* **1 :** ANTAGONISTIC **2 :** situated in front

op·por·tune \ˌäp-ər-'tün, -'tyün\ *adj* **1 :** suitable or convenient for a particular occurrence ⟨found an *opportune* moment to ask⟩ **2 :** occurring at an appropriate time ⟨an *opportune* offer of help⟩ [Middle French *opportun,* from Latin *opportunus,* from *ob* "toward" + *portus* "port, harbor"] — **op·por·tune·ly** *adv* — **op·por·tune·ness** \-'tün-nəs, -'tyün-\ *n*

op·por·tun·ism \-'tü-ˌniz-əm, -'tyü-\ *n* **:** the art, policy, or practice of taking advantage of opportunities or circumstances especially with little regard for principles or ultimate consequences

op·por·tun·ist \ˌäp-ər-'tü-ˌnəst, -'tyü-\ *n* **:** one that is opportunistic or that practices opportunism — **opportunist** *adj*

op·por·tu·nis·tic \-tü-'nis-tik, -tyü-\ *adj* **:** taking advantage of opportunities as they arise: as **a :** exploiting opportunities with little regard to principle or consequences ⟨a politician considered *opportunistic*⟩ **b :** feeding on whatever food is available ⟨*opportunistic* feeders⟩ **c :** being or caused by a usually harmless microorganism that can become pathogenic under some circumstances (as when a person is already weakened by illness) ⟨*opportunistic* infections⟩ — **op·por·tu·nis·ti·cal·ly** \-ti-k(ə-)lē\ *adv*

op·por·tu·ni·ty \ˌäp-ər-'tü-nət-ē, -'tyü-\ *n, pl* **-ties** **1 :** a favorable juncture of circumstances, time, and place **2 :** a good chance for advancement or progress

op·pos·able \ə-'pō-zə-bəl\ *adj* **1 :** capable of being opposed or resisted **2 :** capable of being placed against one or more of the remaining digits of a hand or foot ⟨the *opposable* human thumb⟩ — **op·pos·abil·i·ty** \ə-ˌpō-zə-'bil-ət-ē\ *n*

op·pose \ə-'pōz\ *vt* **1 :** to place over against something for resistance, counterbalance, or contrast **2 :** to offer resistance to

[French *opposer,* from Latin *opponere,* from *ob-* "against" + *ponere* "to put, place"] — **op·pos·er** *n*

synonyms OPPOSE, RESIST, WITHSTAND mean to set oneself against someone or something. OPPOSE may apply to any conflict ranging from mild objection to bitter hostility or warfare ⟨*opposed* the plan⟩. RESIST implies a recognition of a hostile or threatening force and a positive effort to counteract it ⟨*resist* temptation⟩. WITHSTAND usually suggests a more passive resistance ⟨trying to *withstand* peer pressure⟩.

[1]**op·po·site** \'äp-ə-zət, 'äp-sət\ *adj* **1 a :** being at the other end, side, or corner ⟨*opposite* sides of a rectangle⟩ **b :** being one of two angles of a four-sided figure (as a square) that are not next to each other **c :** attached to a stem or axis in pairs whose members are exactly across from each other ⟨*opposite* leaves⟩ — compare ALTERNATE **2 a :** occupying an opposing and often hostile position ⟨*opposite* sides of the question⟩ **b :** as different as possible **:** CONTRADICTORY ⟨*opposite* meanings⟩ **3 :** contrarily turned or moving ⟨go in *opposite* directions⟩ **4 :** being the other of a matching or contrasting pair ⟨a member of the *opposite* sex⟩ [Medieval French, from Latin *oppositus,* past participle of *opponere* "to oppose"] ***synonyms*** see CONTRARY — **op·po·site·ly** *adv* — **op·po·site·ness** *n*

[2]**opposite** *n* **1 :** something that is opposed or contrary **2 :** ANTONYM **3 :** ADDITIVE INVERSE; *esp* **:** the additive inverse of a real number ⟨+3 and –3 are *opposites*⟩

[3]**opposite** *adv* **:** on or to an opposite side

[4]**opposite** *prep* **:** across from and usually facing

op·po·si·tion \ˌäp-ə-'zish-ən\ *n* **1 :** a setting opposite or being set opposite; *also* **:** a configuration in which the difference in celestial longitude of two heavenly bodies is 180° **2 :** an act of setting opposite or the condition of being set opposite ⟨put them in *opposition* to each other⟩ **3 :** resistant or contrary action or condition ⟨offer *opposition* to a plan⟩ ⟨the *opposition* of two forces⟩ **4 a :** something that opposes; *esp* **:** a body of persons opposing something **b** *often cap* **:** a political party opposing and prepared to replace the party in power — **op·po·si·tion·al** \-'zish-nəl, -ən-l\ *adj*

op·press \ə-'pres\ *vt* **1 :** to crush or burden by harsh rule ⟨a country *oppressed* by a dictator's rule⟩ **2 :** to burden in spirit as if with weight ⟨*oppressed* by debts⟩ [Medieval French *oppresser,* from Latin *oppressus,* past participle of *opprimere* "to oppress," from *ob-* "against" + *premere* "to press"] ***synonyms*** see DEPRESS — **op·pres·sor** \-'pres-ər\ *n*

op·pres·sion \ə-'presh-ən\ *n* **1 a :** unjust or cruel exercise of authority or power **b :** something that oppresses cruelly or unjustly **2 :** a sense of being weighed down in body or mind **:** DEPRESSION

op·pres·sive \ə-'pres-iv\ *adj* **1 :** unreasonably burdensome or severe ⟨*oppressive* laws⟩ **2 :** TYRANNICAL ⟨*oppressive* rulers⟩ **3 :** overpowering or depressing to the spirit or senses ⟨*oppressive* heat⟩ — **op·pres·sive·ly** *adv* — **op·pres·sive·ness** *n*

op·pro·bri·ous \ə-'prō-brē-əs\ *adj* **1 :** expressing contemptuous distaste and usually reproach ⟨*opprobrious* language⟩ **2 :** deserving of strong disapproval and contempt ⟨an *opprobrious* person⟩ — **op·pro·bri·ous·ly** *adv* — **op·pro·bri·ous·ness** *n*

op·pro·bri·um \-brē-əm\ *n* **1 :** public disgrace or bad reputation that follows from conduct considered grossly wrong or vicious **2 :** very strong disapproval or reproach ⟨a term of *opprobrium*⟩ [Latin, from *opprobrare* "to reproach," from *ob* "in the way of" + *probrum* "reproach"]

op·so·nin \'äp-sə-nən\ *n* **:** a constituent of blood serum that makes foreign cells more susceptible to the action of the phagocytes [Latin *opsonare* "to buy provisions, cater," from Greek *opsōnein*] — **op·son·ic** \äp-'sän-ik\ *adj*

-op·sy \ˌäp-sē, əp-\ *n combining form, pl* **-opsies :** examination ⟨necr*opsy*⟩ [Greek *opsis* "appearance"]

opt \'äpt\ *vi* **:** to make a choice; *esp* **:** to decide in favor of something ⟨*opted* to go⟩ [French *opter,* from Latin *optare*]

op·tic \'äp-tik\ *adj* **:** of or relating to vision or the eye [Medieval Latin *opticus,* from Greek *optikos,* from *opsesthai* "to be going to see"]

op·ti·cal \'äp-ti-kəl\ *adj* **1 :** relating to optics **2 :** of or relating to vision **:** VISUAL **3 a :** of, relating to, or using light ⟨an *optical* telescope⟩ **b :** involving the use of a light-sensitive device to acquire information for a computer ⟨*optical* character recognition⟩ ⟨an *optical* scanner⟩ — **op·ti·cal·ly** \-kə-lē, -klē\ *adv*

optical disk *n* **:** a disk with a plastic coating on which information (as music or visual images) is recorded digitally (as in the form of tiny pits) and which is read by using a laser

optical fiber *n* **:** a single fiber-optic strand

optical illusion *n* **:** ILLUSION 1c

optically active *adj* **:** capable of rotating the plane of polarized light to the right or left ⟨an *optically active* sugar⟩

op·ti·cian \äp-'tish-ən\ *n* **1 :** a maker of or dealer in optical items and instruments **2 :** a person who reads prescriptions for correction of vision, orders, prepares, and sometimes grinds lenses for eyeglasses, sells eyeglasses and contact lenses, and fits and adjusts eyeglasses — compare OPHTHALMOLOGIST, OPTOMETRIST

optic lobe *n* **:** either of two prominences of the midbrain concerned with vision

optic nerve *n* **:** either of the 2nd pair of cranial nerves that conduct visual nerve impulses from the retina to the brain

op·tics \'äp-tiks\ *n* **:** a science that deals with the nature and properties of light and the effects that it undergoes and produces

op·ti·mal \'äp-tə-məl\ *adj* **:** most desirable or satisfactory **:** OPTIMUM — **op·ti·mal·ly** \-mə-lē\ *adv*

op·ti·mism \'äp-tə-ˌmiz-əm\ *n* **1 :** a doctrine that this world is the best possible world **2 :** an inclination to put the most favorable construction upon actions and events or to anticipate the best possible outcome [French *optimisme,* from Latin *optimus* "best"] — **op·ti·mist** \-məst\ *n or adj* — **op·ti·mis·tic** \ˌäp-tə-'mis-tik\ *adj* — **op·ti·mis·ti·cal·ly** \-ti-kə-lē, -klē\ *adv*

op·ti·mize \'äp-tə-ˌmiz\ *vt* **-mized; -miz·ing :** to make as perfect, effective, or functional as possible

op·ti·mum \'äp-tə-məm\ *n, pl* **-ma** \-mə\ *also* **-mums 1 :** the amount or degree of something that is most favorable to some end **2 :** greatest degree attained under implied or specified conditions [Latin, from *optimus* "best"] — **optimum** *adj*

op·tion \'äp-shən\ *n* **1 a :** the power or right to choose **b :** a contract conveying the right to buy or sell something at a specified price during a specified period **c :** a right of an insured person to choose the form in which payments due him or her are to be made **2 :** something that may be chosen **3 :** an offensive football play in which a back may choose whether to pass or run with the ball — called also *option play* [French, from Latin *optio*] ***synonyms*** see CHOICE

op·tion·al \'äp-shnəl, -shən-l\ *adj* **:** permitting a choice **:** not compulsory — **op·tion·al·ly** \-ē\ *adv*

op·tom·e·trist \äp-'täm-ə-trəst\ *n* **:** a specialist licensed to practice optometry — compare OPTICIAN, OPHTHALMOLOGIST

op·tom·e·try \-trē\ *n* **:** the profession concerned especially with examining the eye for defects of vision and prescribing correctional lenses or eye exercises and with diagnosing and sometimes treating diseases of the eye [derived from Greek *opsesthai* "to be going to see"] — **op·to·met·ric** \ˌäp-tə-'me-trik\ *adj*

opt out *vi* **:** to choose not to participate in something ⟨*opted out* of the project⟩

op·u·lence \'äp-yə-ləns\ *n* **1 :** WEALTH 1, RICHES **2 :** ABUNDANCE, PROFUSION

op·u·lent \-lənt\ *adj* **:** marked by opulence: as **a :** WEALTHY 1 **b :** amply provided or fashioned often to the point of excess ⟨living in *opulent* comfort⟩ [Latin *opulentus,* from *ops* "power, wealth, help"] — **op·u·lent·ly** *adv*

opun·tia \ō-'pən-chə, -chē-ə\ *n* **:** any of a genus of American cacti with usually yellow flowers and flat or cylindrical jointed stem segments having spines or prickly hairs — compare PRICKLY PEAR [Latin, a kind of plant, derived from *Opus,* ancient city in Greece]

opus \'ō-pəs\ *n, pl* **opera** \'ō-pə-rə, 'äp-ə-\ *also* **opus·es** \'ō-pə-səz\ **:** WORK 7; *esp* **:** a musical composition or set of compositions [Latin, "work"]

[1]**or** \ər, ȯr, ˌȯr\ *conj* — used as a function word to indicate an alternative ⟨coffee *or* tea⟩ ⟨sink *or* swim⟩ [Middle English *other, or,* from Old English *oththe*]

[2]**or** *prep, archaic* **:** BEFORE [Old Norse *ār,* adv., "early, before"]

[3]**or** *conj, archaic* **:** BEFORE

[4]**or** \'ȯr\ *n* **:** the heraldic color gold or yellow [Medieval French, "gold," from Latin *aurum*]

[1]**-or** \ər, ˌȯr, 'ȯr\ *n suffix* **:** one that does a (specified) thing ⟨elevat*or*⟩ [Latin]

\ə\ **abut**	\au̇\ **out**	\i\ **tip**	\ȯ\ **saw**	\u̇\ **foot**
\ər\ **further**	\ch\ **chin**	\ī\ **life**	\ȯi\ **coin**	\y\ **yet**
\a\ **mat**	\e\ **pet**	\j\ **job**	\th\ **thin**	\yü\ **few**
\ā\ **take**	\ē\ **easy**	\ng\ **sing**	\t͟h\ **this**	\yu̇\ **cure**
\ä\ **cot, cart**	\g\ **go**	\ō\ **bone**	\ü\ **food**	\zh\ **vision**

[2]**-or** *n suffix* : condition : activity ⟨demeanor⟩ [Latin]

or·a·cle \ˈȯr-ə-kəl, ˈär-\ *n* **1 a** : a person (as a priestess of ancient Greece) through whom a deity is held to speak **b** : a shrine in which a deity so reveals hidden knowledge or the divine purpose **c** : an answer or revelation given by an oracle **2 a** : a person giving wise or authoritative decisions or opinions **b** : an authoritative or wise expression or answer [Medieval French, from Latin *oraculum,* from *orare* "to speak"]

orac·u·lar \ȯ-ˈrak-yə-lər, ə-\ *adj* **1** : resembling an oracle in wisdom, solemnity, or obscurity **2** : of, relating to, or being an oracle — **orac·u·lar·i·ty** \-ˌrak-yə-ˈlar-ət-ē\ *n* — **orac·u·lar·ly** \-ˈrak-yə-lər-lē\ *adv*

[1]**oral** \ˈōr-əl, ˈȯr-, ˈär-\ *adj* **1 a** : uttered by the mouth or in words : SPOKEN ⟨an *oral* agreement⟩ **b** : using speech or the lips ⟨*oral* reading⟩ **2** : of, relating to, given through, or situated near the mouth ⟨*oral* hygiene⟩ ⟨the *oral* surface of a starfish⟩ [Latin *or-, os* "mouth"] — **oral·ly** \-ə-lē\ *adv*

[2]**oral** *n* : an oral examination — usually used in plural

oral contraceptive *n* : BIRTH CONTROL PILL

or·ange \ˈȯr-inj, ˈär-, -ənj\ *n* **1 a** : a roundish fruit that is a berry with a yellowish to reddish orange rind and a sweet edible juicy pulp **b** : any of various small evergreen citrus trees that have glossy leaves, fragrant white flowers, and bear oranges **2** : a color between red and yellow [Medieval French *orrange, araunge,* from Old Occitan *auranja,* from Arabic *nāranj,* from Persian *nārang,* from Sanskrit *nāraṅga* "orange tree"] — **orange** *adj*

or·ange·ade \ˌȯr-in-ˈjād, ˌär-, -ən-\ *n* : a drink made of orange juice, sugar, and water

orange hawkweed *n* : a European hawkweed that has bright orange-red flower heads and is a weed in northeastern North America — called also *Indian paintbrush*

Or·ange·man \ˈȯr-inj-mən, ˈär-\ *n* **1** : a member of a secret society organized in the north of Ireland in 1795 to defend the British sovereign and to support the Protestant religion **2** : a Protestant Irishman especially of Ulster [William III of England, prince of *Orange*]

orange pe·koe \-ˈpē-ˌkō\ *n* : tea made from the smallest and youngest leaves of the shoot

or·ange·ry \ˈȯr-inj-rē, ˈär-, -ənj-, -ə-rē\ *n, pl* **-ries** : a protected place (as a greenhouse) for growing oranges in cool climates

or·ange·wood \-ˌwu̇d\ *n* : the wood of the orange tree used especially in turnery and carving

or·ang·ey *or* **or·angy** \ˈȯr-in-jē, ˈär-\ *adj* : resembling or suggestive of an orange (as in color or flavor)

orang·u·tan *or* **orang·ou·tan** \ə-ˈrang-ə-ˌtang, -ˌtan\ *n* : a largely plant-eating and tree-dwelling anthropoid ape of Borneo and Sumatra that is about two thirds as large as the gorilla and has long thin reddish brown hair, a nearly hairless face, and very long arms [Bazaar Malay (Malay-based pidgin), from Malay *orang* "man" + *hutan* "forest"]

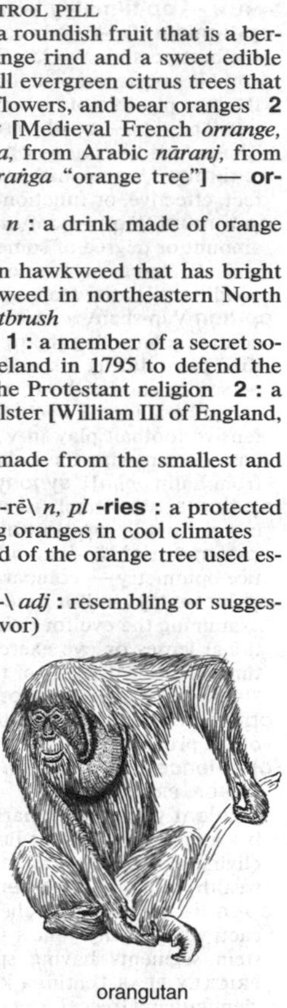

orangutan

orate \ȯ-ˈrāt\ *vi* : to speak in an elevated and often pompous manner [back-formation from *oration*]

ora·tion \ə-ˈrā-shən, ȯ-\ *n* : an elaborate discourse delivered in a formal and dignified manner [Latin *oratio,* from *orare* "to speak, pray"]

or·a·tor \ˈȯr-ət-ər, ˈär-\ *n* **1** : one that delivers an oration **2** : one noted for skill and power in public speaking

Or·a·to·ri·an \ˌȯr-ə-ˈtōr-ē-ən, ˌär-, -ˈtȯr-\ *n* : a member of the Congregation of the Oratory of St. Philip Neri founded in Rome in 1575 and comprising independent communities of secular priests under obedience but without vows — **Oratorian** *adj*

or·a·tor·i·cal \ˌȯr-ə-ˈtȯr-i-kəl, ˌär-ə-ˈtär-\ *adj* : of, relating to, or characteristic of an orator or oratory — **or·a·tor·i·cal·ly** \-kə-lē, -klē\ *adv*

or·a·to·rio \ˌȯr-ə-ˈtōr-ē-ˌō, ˌär-, -ˈtȯr-\ *n, pl* **-ri·os** : a lengthy choral work usually of a religious nature consisting chiefly of recitatives, arias, and choruses without action or scenery [Italian, from the *Oratorio* di San Filippo Neri (Oratory of Saint Philip Neri) in Rome]

[1]**or·a·to·ry** \ˈȯr-ə-ˌtōr-ē, ˈär-, -ˌtȯr-\ *n, pl* **-ries** **1** : a place of prayer; *esp* : a private or institutional chapel **2** *cap* : an Oratorian congregation or church [Late Latin *oratorium,* from Latin *orare* "to speak, pray"]

[2]**oratory** *n* **1** : the art of speaking in public effectively **2** : public speaking that uses oratory [Latin *oratoria,* from *oratorius* "oratorical," from *orare* "to speak, pray"]

[1]**orb** \ˈȯrb\ *n* : a spherical body: as **a** : a heavenly body (as a planet) **b** : EYE 1a **c** : a sphere surmounted by a cross symbolizing kingly power and justice [Medieval French *orbe,* from Latin *orbis* "circle, disk, orb"]

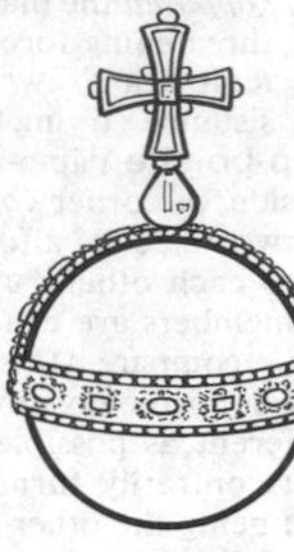

orb c

[2]**orb** *vt* **1** : to form into a disk or circle **2** *archaic* : ENCIRCLE 1, ENCLOSE

or·bic·u·lar \ȯr-ˈbik-yə-lər\ *adj* : SPHERICAL, CIRCULAR [Late Latin *orbicularis,* derived from Latin *orbis* "circle, disk"] — **or·bic·u·lar·i·ty** \-ˌbik-yə-ˈlar-ət-ē\ *n* — **or·bic·u·lar·ly** \-ˈbik-yə-lər-lē\ *adv*

[1]**or·bit** \ˈȯr-bət\ *n* : the bony socket of the eye — called also *eye socket*

[2]**orbit** *n* **1 a** : a path described by one body in its revolution about another ⟨the earth's *orbit* about the sun⟩; *also* : one complete revolution of a body in its orbit **b** : a circular path **2** : a range or sphere of activity or influence [Latin *orbita* "wheel track, orbit"] — **or·bit·al** \-l\ *adj*

[3]**orbit** *vb* **1** : to revolve in an orbit around : CIRCLE **2** : to send up and make revolve in an orbit ⟨*orbit* a satellite⟩ **3** : to travel in circles

orbital *n* : a region around a nucleus in an atom or molecule that may contain zero, one, or two electrons [*orbital,* adj.]

or·bit·er \ˈȯr-bət-ər\ *n* **1** : one that orbits **2** : SPACE SHUTTLE

orb weaver *n* : any of a group of spiders that spin a large elaborate wheel-shaped flat web

or·chard \ˈȯr-chərd\ *n* : a planting especially of fruit trees or nut trees; *also* : the trees of such a planting [Old English *ortgeard,* from Latin *hortus* "garden" + Old English *geard* "yard"] — **or·chard·ist** \-əst\ *n* — **or·chard·man** \-mən, -ˌman\ *n*

or·ches·tra \ˈȯr-kə-strə, -ˌkes-trə\ *n* **1 a** : the space in front of the stage in a modern theater that is used by an orchestra **b** : the forward section of seats on the main floor of a theater **2** : a group of instrumentalists including especially string players organized to perform ensemble music [Latin, "space occupied by the chorus in a Greek theater," from Greek *orchēstra,* from *orcheisthai* "to dance"]

or·ches·tral \ȯr-ˈkes-trəl\ *adj* **1** : of, relating to, or composed for an orchestra **2** : suggestive of an orchestra or its musical qualities — **or·ches·tral·ly** \-trə-lē\ *adv*

or·ches·trate \ˈȯr-kə-ˌstrāt\ *vt* **1 a** : to compose or arrange (music) for an orchestra **b** : to provide (as a ballet) with composed or arranged music **2** : to organize and manage skillfully ⟨*orchestrate* a political campaign⟩ — **or·ches·tra·tor** *also* **or·ches·trat·er** \ˈȯr-kə-ˌstrāt-ər\ *n*

or·ches·tra·tion \ˌȯr-kə-ˈstrā-shən\ *n* **1** : the arrangement of a musical composition for performance by an orchestra **2** : harmonious organization ⟨the seamless *orchestration* of events⟩

or·chid \ˈȯr-kəd\ *n* **1** : any of a large family of perennial plants that have usually showy 3-petaled flowers with the middle petal enlarged into a lip and differing from the others in shape and color; *also* : this flower **2** : a light purple [derived from Latin *orchis*]

or·chis \ˈȯr-kəs\ *n* : ORCHID; *esp* : a woodland plant having fleshy roots and flowers with the lip spurred [Latin,"orchid," from Greek, "testicle, orchid"]

or·dain \ȯr-ˈdān\ *vb* **1** : to endow officially with ministerial or priestly authority **2 a** : to establish or order by appointment, decree, or law **b** : to determine beforehand : PREDESTINE [Medieval French *ordener,* from Latin *ordinare* "to put in order, appoint," from *ordin-, ordo* "order"] — **or·dain·er** *n* — **or·dain·ment** \-ˈdān-mənt\ *n*

or·deal \ȯr-ˈdēl\ *n* **1** : a primitive method of deciding guilt or innocence by submitting the accused to dangerous or painful tests believed to be under supernatural control ⟨*ordeal* by fire⟩ **2** : a severe trial or experience [Old English *ordāl*]

[1]**or·der** \ˈȯrd-ər\ *vb* **1** : to put in or bring about order ⟨*ordered* the books alphabetically⟩ **2 a** : to direct or command with an order ⟨*order* them to stop⟩ **b** : to give an order for ⟨*order* breakfast⟩ **c** : to command to go or come to a certain place ⟨*ordered* back to the base⟩ **3** : to place an order ⟨have you *ordered* already?⟩ — **orderable** *adj* — **or·der·er** *n*

²order *n* **1 a :** a group of people formally united in some way: as (1) **:** a fraternal society ⟨the Masonic *Order*⟩ (2) **:** a community under religious rule; *esp* **:** one requiring members to take solemn vows **b :** a badge or medal of such an order; *also* **:** a military decoration **2 a :** any of the several grades of the Christian ministry **b** *pl* **:** Christian ordination ⟨decided to take *orders*⟩ **3 a :** a rank, class, or special group in a community or society **b :** a class grouped according to quality, value, or natural characteristics; *esp* **:** a category of taxonomic classification ranking above the family and below the class **4 a :** relative standing or position **:** RANK ⟨an artist of the first *order*⟩ ⟨emergencies of this *order*⟩ **b :** the arrangement or sequence of objects in position or of events in time ⟨list the items in *order* of importance⟩ **c :** DEGREE 7 **d :** the number of columns or rows or the number of columns and rows in a magic square, determinant, or matrix ⟨the *order* of a matrix with 2 rows and 3 columns is 2 by 3⟩ **e :** the established mode or arrangement ⟨the old *order*⟩ **f :** regular or harmonious arrangement ⟨the *order* of nature⟩; *also* **:** a condition characterized by such an arrangement ⟨kept my room in *order*⟩ **5 a :** RITE 1 ⟨the *order* of worship⟩ **b :** the customary mode of procedure especially in debate ⟨point of *order*⟩ **6 a :** the state of peace and respect for law or proper authority ⟨restored *order* in the capital⟩ **b :** a specific rule, regulation, or authoritative direction **7 a :** a style of building **b :** an architectural column with its related structures forming the unit of a style **8 :** proper condition ⟨out of *order*⟩ **9 a :** a written direction to pay money to someone **b :** a commission to purchase, sell, or supply goods or to perform work **c :** goods or items bought or sold **d :** an assigned or requested undertaking ⟨landing men on the moon was a tall *order*⟩ [Medieval French *ordre,* from Latin *ordo* "arrangement, group, class, order"] — **or·der·less** *adj* — **in order : APPROPRIATE** ⟨an apology is *in order*⟩ — **in order to :** for the purpose of — **on the order of 1 :** after the manner of **:** LIKE ⟨a composer *on the order of* Mozart⟩ **2 :** ABOUT, APPROXIMATELY ⟨spent *on the order of* $2000⟩ — **to order :** according to the specifications of an order ⟨shoes made *to order*⟩

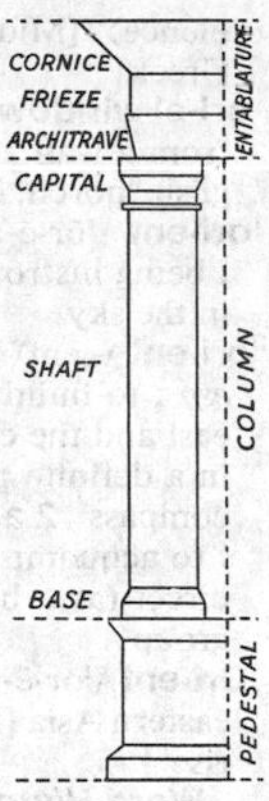

order 7b

or·dered \'ȯrd-ərd\ *adj* **:** characterized by order: as **a :** marked by discipline or regularity ⟨led an *ordered* life⟩ **b :** marked by regular or harmonious arrangement ⟨an *ordered* landscape⟩ **c :** having elements arranged or identified according to a rule; *esp* **:** having the property that for any two different elements *a* and *b* either *a* is greater than *b* or *a* is less than *b* ⟨the set of positive numbers is *ordered*⟩ **d :** having elements labeled by ordinal numbers ⟨an *ordered* pair has a first and a second element⟩

¹or·der·ly \'ȯrd-ər-lē\ *adj* **1 a :** arranged or disposed according to some order or pattern **:** REGULAR ⟨an *orderly* row of houses⟩ **b :** marked by order **:** TIDY **c :** METHODICAL ⟨an *orderly* mind⟩ **d :** governed by law or system ⟨an *orderly* universe⟩ **2 :** well behaved **:** PEACEFUL ⟨an *orderly* crowd⟩ — **or·der·li·ness** *n* — **orderly** *adv*

²orderly *n, pl* **-lies 1 :** a soldier assigned to perform various tasks for a superior officer **2 :** a hospital attendant who does routine or heavy work

¹or·di·nal \'ȯrd-nəl, -n-əl\ *n* **1** *cap* **:** a book of rites for ordination **2 :** ORDINAL NUMBER [derived from Latin *ordin-, ordo* "order"]

²ordinal *adj* **:** of a specified order or rank (as sixth) in a series

ordinal number *n* **:** a number designating the place (as first, second, third) occupied by an item in an ordered sequence — see NUMBER table; compare CARDINAL NUMBER

or·di·nance \'ȯrd-nəns, 'ȯrd-n-əns\ *n* **1 :** an authoritative decree or direction **:** ORDER **2 :** a law enacted by governmental authority; *esp* **:** a municipal regulation **3 :** a prescribed usage, practice, or ceremony [Medieval French *ordenance,* "order, disposition," from Medieval Latin *ordinantia,* from Latin *ordinare* "to put in order"] ***synonyms*** see LAW

or·di·nand \ˌȯrd-n-'and\ *n* **:** a candidate for ordination [derived from Late Latin *ordinare* "to ordain," from Latin, "to put in order"]

¹or·di·nary \'ȯrd-n-ˌer-ē\ *n, pl* **-nar·ies 1 a :** a prelate (as the bishop of a diocese) exercising jurisdiction over a territory or group **b :** a judge of probate in some states of the U.S. **2** *often cap* **:** the parts of the Mass that do not vary from day to day **3 :** regular or customary condition or course of things ⟨nothing out of the *ordinary*⟩ **4 a** *British* **:** a meal served at a fixed price **b** *chiefly British* **:** a restaurant serving regular meals [Medieval Latin *ordinarius,* from Latin *ordinarius,* adj., "ordinary"]

²ordinary *adj* **1 :** of a kind to be expected in the normal order of events **:** ROUTINE, NORMAL **2 a :** of common quality, rank, or ability ⟨*ordinary* people⟩ **b :** deficient in quality **:** INFERIOR [Latin *ordinarius,* from *ordin-, ordo* "order"] — **or·di·nari·ly** \ˌȯrd-n-'er-ə-lē\ *adv* — **or·di·nar·i·ness** \'ȯrd-n-ˌer-ē-nəs\ *n*

Ordinary level *n* **:** O LEVEL

ordinary seaman *n* **:** a seaman with less experience than an able seaman

or·di·nate \'ȯrd-nət, -n-ət, -n-ˌāt\ *n* **:** the vertical coordinate of a point in a plane Cartesian coordinate system obtained by measuring parallel to the y-axis — called also *y-coordinate*; compare ABSCISSA [New Latin *linea ordinate applicata,* literally, "line applied in an orderly manner"]

or·di·na·tion \ˌȯrd-n-'ā-shən\ *n* **:** the act of ordaining **:** the state of being ordained

ord·nance \'ȯrd-nəns\ *n* **1 a :** military supplies including weapons, ammunition, vehicles, and equipment **b :** a service of the army in charge of ordnance **2 :** ARTILLERY 1, CANNON [Medieval French *ordenance* "disposition, preparation, military provisions"]

Or·do·vi·cian \ˌȯrd-ə-'vish-ən\ *n* **:** the period of the Paleozoic era between the Cambrian and Silurian; *also* **:** the corresponding system of rocks — see GEOLOGIC TIME table [Latin *Ordovices,* ancient people in northern Wales] — **Ordovician** *adj*

or·dure \'ȯr-jər\ *n* **1 :** EXCREMENT **2 :** something morally degrading or depraving [Medieval French, from *ord* "filthy," from Latin *horridus* "horrid"]

ore \'ōr, 'ȯr\ *n* **:** a mineral containing a constituent for which it is mined and worked ⟨get iron from its *ore*⟩ [Old English *ōra* "ore" and *ār* "brass"]

øre \'ər-ə\ *n, pl* **øre 1 a :** a monetary unit equal to ¹⁄₁₀₀ of a Swedish krona **b :** a monetary unit equal to ¹⁄₁₀₀ krone **2 :** a coin representing one ore [Swedish *öre* and Danish and Norwegian *øre*]

ore·ad \'ōr-ē-ˌad, 'ȯr-, -ē-əd\ *n* **:** any of the nymphs of mountains and hills in Greek mythology [Latin *oread-, oreas,* from Greek *oreiad-, oreias,* derived from *oros* "mountain"]

oreg·a·no \ə-'reg-ə-ˌnō\ *n, pl* **-nos :** a bushy perennial mint with leaves used as a seasoning and a source of aromatic oil — called also *wild marjoram* [American Spanish *orégano,* from Spanish, "wild marjoram," from Latin *origanum*]

Or·e·gon grape \ˌȯr-i-gən-, ˌär-, -ˌgän-\ *n* **:** a yellow-flowered shrub related to the barberries that is native to western North America and bears edible bluish black berries [*Oregon,* United States]

Oregon grape

or·gan \'ȯr-gən\ *n* **1 a :** a keyboard instrument in which sets of pipes are sounded by compressed air and produce a variety of timbres — called also *pipe organ* **b :** REED ORGAN **c :** an electronic keyboard instrument that approximates the sounds of the pipe organ **d :** any of various similar cruder instruments **2 :** a differentiated animal or plant structure (as a kidney or leaf) consisting of cells and tissues and performing some specific function — compare SYSTEM 1b(1) **3 :** a means of performing some function or accomplishing some end ⟨the courts and other *organs* of government⟩ **4 :** a publication (as a newspaper) expressing the opinions or serving the interests of a special group [Old English *organa* and Medieval French *organe,* both from Latin *organum* "a musical instrument"]

organ- *or* **organo-** *combining form* **1 :** organ **2 :** organic ⟨*organo*phosphate⟩

or·gan·dy *also* **or·gan·die** \'ȯr-gən-dē\ *n, pl* **-dies :** a very fine transparent muslin with a stiff finish [French *organdi*]

\ə\ **abut**	\au̇\ **out**	\i\ **tip**	\ȯ\ **saw**	\u̇\ **foot**
\ər\ **further**	\ch\ **chin**	\ī\ **life**	\ȯi\ **coin**	\y\ **yet**
\a\ **mat**	\e\ **pet**	\j\ **job**	\th\ **thin**	\yü\ **few**
\ā\ **take**	\ē\ **easy**	\ng\ **sing**	\t͟h\ **this**	\yu̇\ **cure**
\ä\ **cot, cart**	\g\ **go**	\ō\ **bone**	\ü\ **food**	\zh\ **vision**

or·gan·elle \ˌȯr-gə-ˈnel\ *n* : a structure (as a mitochondrion or ribosome) that performs a specialized function in a cell [New Latin *organella,* from Latin *organum*]

organ–grind·er \ˈȯr-gən-ˌgrīn-dər\ *n* : one that cranks a hand organ; *esp* : a street musician who operates a barrel organ

or·gan·ic \ȯr-ˈgan-ik\ *adj* **1 a** : of, relating to, or arising in a bodily organ **b** : affecting the structure of the organism — compare FUNCTIONAL 1b **2 a** (1) : of, relating to, or derived from living organisms ⟨*organic* matter⟩ (2) : relating to, yielding, dealing in, or involving foods produced with the use of feed or fertilizer of plant or animal origin and without chemically formulated fertilizers, growth substances, antibiotics, or pesticides ⟨*organic* foods⟩ ⟨*organic* farming⟩ **b** (1) : of, relating to, or containing carbon compounds (2) : of, relating to, or dealt with by a branch of chemistry concerned with carbon compounds **3 a** : forming an integral element of a whole **b** : having systematic coordination of parts : ORGANIZED ⟨an *organic* whole⟩ **c** : developing in the manner of a living plant or animal ⟨society is *organic*⟩ — **or·gan·i·cal·ly** \-i-kə-lē, -klē\ *adv*

or·gan·ism \ˈȯr-gə-ˌniz-əm\ *n* **1** : a complex structure of interdependent and subordinate elements whose relations and properties are largely determined by their function in the whole **2** : an individual constituted to carry on the activities of life by means of organs separate in function but mutually dependent : a living person, plant, or animal — **or·gan·is·mic** \ˌȯr-gə-ˈniz-mik\ *also* **or·gan·is·mal** \-məl\ *adj* — **or·gan·is·mi·cal·ly** \-mi-kə-lē, -klē\ *adv*

or·gan·ist \ˈȯr-gə-nəst\ *n* : one who plays an organ

or·ga·ni·za·tion \ˌȯrg-nə-ˈzā-shən, -ə-nə-\ *n* **1** : the act or process of organizing or of being organized **2** : the condition or manner of being organized **3 a** : ASSOCIATION 2 **b** : an administrative body or its personnel **c** : an administrative and functional unit (as a business or a political party) — **or·ga·ni·za·tion·al** \-shnəl, -shən-l\ *adj* — **or·ga·ni·za·tion·al·ly** \-ē\ *adv*

or·ga·nize \ˈȯr-gə-ˌnīz\ *vb* **1** : to develop an organic structure : undergo or cause to undergo organization **2** : to arrange or form into a complete and functioning whole **3 a** : to set up an administrative structure for ⟨*organize* a business⟩ **b** : to enroll or associate in an organization (as a union) **4** : to arrange by systematic planning and united effort ⟨*organize* a prom⟩

or·ga·nized \-ˌnīzd\ *adj* **1** : having a formal organization to plan and carry out activities ⟨*organized* baseball⟩ ⟨*organized* crime⟩ **2** : affiliated by membership in an organization (as a union) ⟨*organized* steelworkers⟩

or·ga·niz·er \-ˌnī-zər\ *n* **1** : one that organizes **2** : a region of a developing embryo that is able to cause a specific type of development in undifferentiated tissue — called also *inductor*

or·gano·chlo·rine \ȯr-ˌgan-ə-ˈklōr-ˌēn, -ˈklȯr-, -ən\ *adj* : of, relating to, or being a chlorinated hydrocarbon used especially as a pesticide (as DDT) — **organochlorine** *n*

organ of Cor·ti \-ˈkȯr-tē\ : a complex structure in the cochlea that contains thousands of hair cells and is the chief part of the ear by which sound waves are perceived and converted into nerve impulses to be transmitted to the brain [Alfonso *Corti,* died 1876, Italian anatomist]

or·gano·phos·phate \-ˈfäs-ˌfāt\ *n* : an organophosphorus pesticide — **organophosphate** *adj*

or·gano·phos·pho·rus \-ˈfäs-fə-rəs, -frəs\ *adj* : of, relating to, or being a phosphorus-containing organic compound and especially a pesticide (as malathion) — **organophosphorus** *n*

organ pipe cactus *n* : any of several tall cacti of the southwestern U.S. and Mexico that usually branch at the base to form several upright stems

or·gan·za \ȯr-ˈgan-zə\ *n* : a sheer dress fabric resembling organdy and usually made of silk, rayon, or nylon [probably from *Lorganza,* a trademark]

or·gasm \ˈȯr-ˌgaz-əm\ *n* : the climax of sexual excitement [Greek *orgasmos,* from *organ* "to grow ripe, be lustful"] — **or·gas·mic** \ȯr-ˈgaz-mik\ *or* **or·gas·tic** \-ˈgas-tik\ *adj*

or·gi·as·tic \ˌȯr-jē-ˈas-tik\ *adj* : of, relating to, or marked by orgies [Greek *orgiastikos,* from *orgiazein* "to celebrate orgies," from *orgia* "orgy"] — **or·gi·as·ti·cal·ly** \-ti-kə-lē, -klē\ *adv*

or·gu·lous \ˈȯr-gyə-ləs\ *adj* : PROUD 1a, HAUGHTY [Medieval French *orguillus,* from *orguil* "pride," of Germanic origin]

or·gy \ˈȯr-jē\ *n, pl* **orgies** **1** : secret ceremonial rites held in honor of an ancient Greek or Roman deity and usually characterized by ecstatic singing and dancing **2** : drunken revelry **3** : any excessive indulgence ⟨the riot was an *orgy* of senseless violence⟩ [Middle French *orgie,* from Latin *orgia,* pl., from Greek]

ori·el window \ˈōr-ē-əl-, ˈȯr-\ *n* : a large bay window projecting from a wall and supported by a corbel or bracket [Middle English "porch, oriel," from Medieval French *oriol* "porch"]

[1]**ori·ent** \ˈōr-ē-ənt, ˈȯr-, -ē-ˌent\ *adj* **1** *archaic* : ORIENTAL **2** : being lustrous and sparkling ⟨*orient* gems⟩ **3** *archaic* : rising in the sky

[2]**ori·ent** \-ˌent\ *vt* **1 a** : to cause to face or point toward the east; *esp* : to build (as a church) with the longitudinal axis pointing east and the chief altar at the eastern end **b** : to set or arrange in a definite position especially in relation to the points of the compass **2 a** : to set right by adjusting to facts or principles **b** : to acquaint with an existing situation or environment **3** : to direct (as a book or film) toward the interests of a particular group

Ori·ent \ˈōr-ē-ənt, ˈȯr-, -ē-ˌent\ *n* : EAST 2; *esp* : the countries of eastern Asia [Medieval French, from Latin *oriens,* from *oriri* "to rise"]

Word History The noun *orient* is derived from the Latin adjective *oriens,* which comes from the present participle of the verb *oriri,* "to rise or come forth." The earliest English sense of *orient* is "the place on the horizon where the sun rises when it is near one of the equinoxes," that is, the east. *Orient* has come to be used today to refer to the Asian countries to the east of Europe. With the spread of Christianity into Europe it became customary to build churches with their longitudinal axes pointing eastward toward Jerusalem. This practice gave rise to the use of *orient* as a verb meaning "to cause to face or point to the east." This sense became generalized to yield the sense "to set or arrange in any determinate position, especially in relation to the points of the compass."

ori·en·tal \ˌōr-ē-ˈent-l, ˌȯr-\ *adj, often cap* : of, relating to, or situated in Asia — **ori·en·tal·ly** \-lē\ *adv*

Oriental *n* **1** *sometimes offensive* : one who is a native of east Asia or is of east Asian descent **2** : ORIENTAL RUG

ori·en·tal·ism \-l-ˌiz-əm\ *n, often cap* **1** : something (as a style or manner) associated with or characteristic of Asia or Asians **2** : learning in Asian subjects or languages — **ori·en·tal·ist** \-l-əst\ *n or adj, often cap*

ori·en·tal·ize \-l-ˌīz\ *vb, often cap* **1** : to make Asian : give Asian qualities to **2** : to adopt Asian characteristics — **ori·en·tal·i·za·tion** \-ˌent-ə-lə-ˈzā-shən\ *n, often cap*

Oriental poppy *n* : an Asian perennial poppy commonly grown for its very large showy flowers

Oriental rug *n* : a handwoven or hand-knotted rug or carpet made in a country of central or southern Asia

ori·en·tate \ˈōr-ē-ən-ˌtāt, ˈȯr-, -ˌen-\ *vb* **1** : to face or turn to the east **2** : ORIENT 1b

ori·en·ta·tion \ˌōr-ē-ən-ˈtā-shən, ˌȯr-, -ˌen-\ *n* **1 a** : the act or process of orienting **b** : the state of being oriented **2** : change of position by a cell or organism or by one of their parts in response to external stimulus — **ori·en·ta·tion·al** \-shnəl, -shən-l\ *adj*

ori·en·teer \ˌōr-ē-ən-ˈtiər, ˌȯr-, ˌen-\ *n* : a person who engages in orienteering

ori·en·teer·ing \ˌōr-ē-ən-ˈtiər-ing, ˌȯr-, -ˌen-\ *n* : a competitive or noncompetitive recreational activity in which participants find their way over an unfamiliar course (as in the woods) using a map and compass [Swedish *orientering,* from *orientera* "to orient"]

or·i·fice \ˈȯr-ə-fəs, ˈär-\ *n* : an opening (as a vent, mouth, hole, or aperture) through which something may pass [Medieval French, from Late Latin *orificium,* from Latin *or-, os* "mouth"] — **or·i·fi·cial** \ˌȯr-ə-ˈfish-əl, ˌär-\ *adj*

ori·flamme \ˈȯr-ə-ˌflam, ˈär-\ *n* : a banner, symbol, or ideal inspiring devotion or courage [Middle English *oriflamble* "the banner of St. Denis," from Medieval French *oriflambe* "small flag"]

ori·ga·mi \ˌȯr-ə-ˈgäm-ē\ *n* : the Japanese art or process of folding squares of paper into representational shapes [Japanese]

orig·a·num \ə-ˈrig-ə-nəm\ *n* : any of several mints with fragrant aromatic leaves used as seasonings; *esp* : OREGANO [Latin, "wild marjoram," from Greek *origanon*]

or·i·gin \ˈȯr-ə-jən, ˈär-\ *n* **1** : ANCESTRY 1, PARENTAGE **2 a** : rise, beginning, or derivation from a source **b** : primary source or cause **3** : the more fixed, more central, or larger attachment of a muscle **4** : the intersection of the axes in a coordinate system [derived from Latin *origin-, origo,* from *oriri* "to rise"]

synonyms ORIGIN, SOURCE, INCEPTION, ROOT mean the point at which something begins its course or existence. ORIGIN applies to the things or persons from which something is ultimately derived and often to the causes operating before the thing itself comes into being ⟨a study on the *origin* of baseball⟩. SOURCE stresses the point from which something springs into being ⟨an insect bite was the *source* of the infection⟩. INCEPTION stresses the beginning point without implying causes ⟨a member from the *inception* of the club⟩. ROOT suggests a first, ultimate, or fundamental source not always discernible ⟨their quarrel had *roots* deep in the past⟩.

[1]**orig·i·nal** \ə-ˈrij-ən-l, -ˈrij-nəl\ *n* **1** *archaic* **:** the source or cause from which something arises **2 a :** that from which a copy, reproduction, or translation is made **b :** a work composed firsthand **3 a :** a person who is original in thought or action **b :** a unique or eccentric person

[2]**original** *adj* **1 :** of or relating to a beginning **:** existing from the start **:** FIRST ⟨the *original* part of an old house⟩ ⟨*original* owners⟩ **2 a :** not copied, reproduced, or translated ⟨*original* paintings⟩ ⟨an *original* idea⟩ **b :** being the one from which a copy, reproduction, or translation is made **3 :** independent and creative in thought or action **:** INVENTIVE ⟨an *original* artist⟩ — **orig·i·nal·ly** \-ē\ *adv*

orig·i·nal·i·ty \ə-ˌrij-ə-ˈnal-ət-ē\ *n* **1 :** the quality or state of being original **:** FRESHNESS, NOVELTY **2 :** the power or ability to think, act, or do something in ways that are new ⟨an artist of great *originality*⟩

original sin *n* **1 :** the state of sin that according to Christian theology humans are born in as a result of the sin of Adam and Eve **2 :** a wrong of great magnitude ⟨the *original sin* of slavery⟩

orig·i·nate \ə-ˈrij-ə-ˌnāt\ *vb* **1 :** to bring into existence **:** give rise to ⟨*originate* a plan⟩ **2 :** to take or have origin **:** come into existence — **orig·i·na·tion** \ə-ˌrij-ə-ˈnā-shən\ *n* — **orig·i·na·tor** \ə-ˈrij-ə-ˌnāt-ər\ *n*

orig·i·na·tive \ə-ˈrij-ə-ˌnāt-iv\ *adj* **:** having ability to originate **:** CREATIVE — **orig·i·na·tive·ly** *adv*

ori·ole \ˈōr-ē-ˌōl, ˈȯr-, -ē-əl\ *n* **1 :** any of various usually brightly colored Old World birds related to the crows **2 :** any of various New World birds that build hanging nests woven from various materials (as grass and leaf fibers) and the males of which are usually black and yellow or orange and the females chiefly greenish or yellowish [French *oriol,* from Latin *aureolus* "golden," from *aureus,* from *aurum* "gold"]

oriole 2

Ori·on \ə-ˈrī-ən, ō-\ *n* **:** a constellation on the equator east of Taurus represented on charts by the figure of a hunter with belt and sword [Latin, a hunter of Greek mythology, a constellation, from Greek *Ōriōn*]

or·i·son \ˈȯr-ə-sən, ˈär-, -zən\ *n* **:** PRAYER [Medieval French, *ureison, oreison,* from Late Latin *oratio,* from Latin *orare* "to speak, pray"]

Or·lean·ist \ˈȯr-lē-ə-nəst; ȯr-ˈlē-nəst, -ə-nəst\ *n* **:** a supporter of the Orleans family in its claim to the throne of France by descent from a younger brother of Louis XIV

Or·lon \ˈȯr-ˌlän\ *trademark* — used for acrylic fiber

or·mo·lu \ˈȯr-mə-ˌlü\ *n* **:** a brass made to imitate gold and used for decorative purposes [French *or moulu,* literally, "ground gold"]

[1]**or·na·ment** \ˈȯr-nə-mənt\ *n* **1 a :** something that adorns or adds beauty **:** DECORATION, EMBELLISHMENT **b :** a manner or quality that adorns **2 :** the act of adorning or being adorned **3 :** an embellishing note in music that does not belong to the essential harmony or melody [Medieval French *ornement,* from Latin *ornamentum,* from *ornare* "to adorn"]

[2]**or·na·ment** \-ˌment\ *vt* **:** to provide with ornament **:** EMBELLISH

[1]**or·na·men·tal** \ˌȯr-nə-ˈment-l\ *adj* **:** of, relating to, or serving as ornament — **or·na·men·tal·ly** \-l-ē\ *adv*

[2]**ornamental** *n* **:** a decorative object; *esp* **:** a plant cultivated for its beauty rather than for use

or·na·men·ta·tion \ˌȯr-nə-mən-ˈtā-shən, -ˌmen-\ *n* **1 :** the act or process of ornamenting **:** the state of being ornamented **2 a :** a decorative device **b :** the ornaments of something

or·nate \ȯr-ˈnāt\ *adj* **1 :** marked by elaborate rhetoric or florid style **2 :** elaborately or excessively decorated [Latin *ornatus,* past participle of *ornare* "to furnish, adorn"] — **or·nate·ly** *adv* — **or·nate·ness** *n*

or·nery \ˈȯrn-rē, ˈärn-, -ə-rē\ *adj* **or·ner·i·er; -est :** having a touchy and self-willed disposition [alteration of *ordinary*] — **or·ner·i·ness** *n*

ornith- *or* **ornitho-** *combining form* **:** bird ⟨*ornitho*logy⟩ [Greek *ornith-, ornis*]

or·ni·thine \ˈȯr-nə-ˌthēn\ *n* **:** a crystalline amino acid $C_5H_{12}N_2O_2$ that functions in the body especially in urea production [*ornith*uric acid (an acid of which it is a component, found in the urine of birds) + *-ine*]

or·nith·is·chi·an \ˌȯr-nə-ˈthis-kē-ən\ *n* **:** any of an order (Ornithischia) of herbivorous dinosaurs (as a stegosaurus) that have the pubis of the pelvis rotated backward to a position parallel and close to the ischium — compare SAURISCHIAN [New Latin *Ornithischia,* from Greek *ornis* "bird" + *ischion* "hip joint"] — **ornithischian** *adj*

or·ni·thol·o·gy \ˌȯr-nə-ˈthäl-ə-jē\ *n* **:** a branch of zoology dealing with birds — **or·ni·tho·log·i·cal** \ˌȯr-ˌnith-ə-ˈläj-i-kəl\ *adj* — **or·ni·tho·log·i·cal·ly** \-i-kə-lē, -klē\ *adv* — **or·ni·thol·o·gist** \ˌȯr-nə-ˈthäl-ə-jəst\ *n*

orog·e·ny \ȯ-ˈräj-ə-nē\ *n, pl* **-nies :** the process of mountain formation [Greek *oros* "mountain"] — **oro·gen·ic** \ˌōr-ə-ˈjen-ik, ˌȯr-\ *adj*

[1]**or·phan** \ˈȯr-fən\ *n* **1 :** a child whose parents are dead **2 :** a young animal that has lost its mother **3 :** one deprived of some protection or advantage ⟨*orphans* of the storm⟩ [Late Latin *orphanus,* from Greek *orphanos*] — **or·phan·hood** \-ˌhu̇d\ *n*

[2]**orphan** *vt* **or·phaned; or·phan·ing** \ˈȯrf-ning, -ə-ning\ **:** to cause to become an orphan

or·phan·age \ˈȯrf-nij, -ə-nij\ *n* **:** an institution for the care of orphans

or·pi·ment \ˈȯr-pə-mənt\ *n* **:** a rare yellow to orange mineral that is a sulfide of arsenic used as a pigment [Medieval French, from Latin *auripigmentum,* from *aurum* "gold" + *pigmentum* "pigment"]

or·pine \ˈȯr-pən\ *n* **:** a pink- or purple-flowered sedum formerly used in folk medicine [Medieval French *orpin,* from *orpiment* "orpiment"]

or·ris \ˈȯr-əs, ˈär-\ *n* **:** ORRISROOT [probably derived from Latin *iris* "iris"]

or·ris·root \-ˌrüt, -ˌru̇t\ *n* **:** the fragrant rootstock of any of three European irises used especially in perfumery

orth- *or* **ortho-** *combining form* **1 :** straight **:** upright **:** vertical **2 :** perpendicular ⟨*ortho*rhombic⟩ **3 :** correct **:** corrective ⟨*ortho*dontics⟩ [Greek *orthos* "straight, right"]

or·tho·cen·ter \ˈȯr-thə-ˌsent-ər\ *n* **:** the point where the three altitudes of a triangle or their extensions intersect

or·tho·chro·mat·ic \ˌȯr-thə-krō-ˈmat-ik\ *adj* **:** sensitive to all colors except red ⟨an *orthochromatic* film⟩

or·tho·clase \ˈȯr-thə-ˌklās\ *n* **:** a mineral consisting especially of potassium feldspar [German *Orthoklas,* from *orth-* "orth-" + Greek *klasis* "breaking," from *klan* "to break"]

orth·odon·tia \ˌȯr-thə-ˈdän-chē-ə, -chə\ *n* **:** ORTHODONTICS

orth·odon·tics \-ˈdänt-iks\ *n* **:** a branch of dentistry dealing with irregularities in the arrangement and placing of the teeth and with their correction (as by means of braces) [*orth-* + Greek *odont-, odous* "tooth"] — **orth·odon·tic** \-ˈdänt-ik\ *adj*

orth·odon·tist \-ˈdänt-əst\ *n* **:** a dentist who specializes in orthodontics

or·tho·dox \ˈȯr-thə-ˌdäks\ *adj* **1 :** holding established beliefs especially in religion ⟨an *orthodox* Christian⟩ **2 :** approved as measuring up to some standard **:** CONVENTIONAL ⟨*orthodox* dress for a church wedding⟩ **3** *cap* **a :** EASTERN ORTHODOX **b :** of or relating to Orthodox Judaism [Late Latin *orthodoxus,* from Late Greek *orthodoxos,* from Greek *orthos* "right" + *doxa* "opinion"] — **or·tho·dox·ly** *adv*

Orthodox Judaism *n* **:** Judaism that adheres to the Torah and

Talmud as interpreted in the authoritative rabbinic law code and applies their principles and regulations to modern living

or·tho·doxy \'ȯr-thə-ˌdäk-sē\ *n, pl* **-dox·ies** **1 :** the quality or state of being orthodox **2 :** an orthodox belief or practice

or·thog·o·nal \ȯr-'thäg-ən-l\ *adj* **1 :** intersecting or lying at right angles ⟨*orthogonal* coordinate axes⟩ **2 :** having perpendicular slopes or tangents at the point of intersection ⟨*orthogonal* curves⟩ [Middle French, from Latin *orthogonius,* from Greek *orthogōnios,* from *orthos* "straight, upright" + *gōnia* "angle"] — **or·thog·o·nal·ly** \ȯr-'thäg-nə-lē, -ən-l-ē\ *adv*

or·thog·ra·phy \ȯr-'thäg-rə-fē\ *n, pl* **-phies** **1 a :** the writing of words with the proper letters according to standard usage **b :** a manner of representing the sounds of a language by written or printed symbols ⟨17th century *orthography*⟩ **2 :** a part of language study that deals with letters and spelling — **or·tho·graph·ic** \ˌȯr-thə-'graf-ik\ *adj* — **or·tho·graph·i·cal·ly** \-'graf-ik-ə-lē, -ik-lē\ *adv*

or·tho·pe·dic \ˌȯr-thə-'pēd-ik\ *adj* **1 :** of, relating to, or used in orthopedics **2 :** marked by or affected with a skeletal deformity, disorder, or injury [French *orthopédique,* from *orthopédie* "orthopedics," from *orth-* "orth-" + Greek *paid-, pais* "child"] — **or·tho·pe·di·cal·ly** \-'pēd-i-kə-lē, -klē\ *adv*

or·tho·pe·dics \-'pēd-iks\ *n sing or pl* **:** a medical specialty concerned with the correction or prevention of deformities, disorders or injuries of the skeletal system and associated structures (as tendons, muscles, and ligaments)

or·tho·pe·dist \ˌȯr-thə-'pēd-əst\ *n* **:** a physician who specializes in orthopedics

or·thop·ter·an \ȯr-'thäp-tə-rən\ *n* **:** any of an order (Orthoptera) of insects (as crickets and grasshoppers) with biting mouthparts, two pairs of wings or none, enlarged hind femurs and an incomplete metamorphosis [New Latin *Orthoptera* from *orth-* + Greek *pteron* "wing"] — **orthopteran** *adj*

or·tho·rhom·bic \ˌȯr-thə-'räm-bik\ *adj* **:** of, relating to, or constituting a system of crystallization characterized by three unequal axes at right angles to each other

or·thot·ic \ȯr-'thät-ik\ *n* **:** a device (as a brace or splint) for supporting, immobilizing, or treating muscles, joints, or skeletal parts which are weak, ineffective, deformed, or injured [Greek *orthōsis* "straightening," from *orthoun* "to straighten," from *orthos* "straight"]

or·thot·ics \ȯr-'thät-iks\ *n* **:** a branch of medical science that deals with the design and fitting of orthotics

¹-o·ry \ˌōr-ē, ˌȯr-ē, ə-rē, rē\ *n suffix, pl* **-ories** **1 :** place of or for ⟨observat*ory*⟩ **2 :** something that serves for ⟨cremat*ory*⟩ [Latin *-orium,* from neuter of *-orius,* adj. suffix]

²-ory *adj suffix* **1 :** of, relating to, or characterized by ⟨gustat*ory*⟩ **2 :** serving for, producing, or maintaining ⟨classificat*ory*⟩ [Latin *-orius*]

oryx \'ōr-iks, 'ȯr-, 'är-\ *n, pl* **oryx** *or* **oryx·es** **:** any of a genus of large heavily built African and Arabian antelopes that have horns that are straight or that curve backward [Latin, a kind of gazelle, from Greek "pickax, antelope," from *oryssein* "to dig"]

os \'äs\ *n, pl* **os·sa** \'äs-ə\ **:** BONE [Latin]

Osage \ō-'sāj, 'ō-ˌ\ *n, pl* **Osag·es** *or* **Osage** **:** a member of an American Indian people originally of Missouri [derived from Osage *wažáže,* a self-designation]

Osage orange *n* **:** an ornamental usually thorny tree of the U.S. related to the mulberries and having shiny ovate leaves and hard bright orange wood; *also* **:** its yellowish green round fruit

Os·car \'äs-kər\ *trademark* — used especially for any of a number of golden statuettes awarded annually by a professional organization for notable achievement in motion pictures

os·cil·late \'äs-ə-ˌlāt\ *vi* **1 a :** to swing backward and forward like a pendulum **:** VIBRATE **b :** to move or travel back and forth between two points **2 :** to vary between opposing beliefs, feelings, or theories **3 :** to vary above and below a mean value [Latin *oscillare* "to swing," from *oscillum* "swing"] ***synonyms*** see SWAY — **os·cil·la·to·ry** \ä-'sil-ə-ˌtōr-ē, -ˌtȯr-\ *adj*

os·cil·la·tion \ˌäs-ə-'lā-shən\ *n* **1 :** the act or fact of oscillating **:** VIBRATION **2 :** VARIATION 1, FLUCTUATION **3 :** a flow of electricity changing periodically from a maximum to a minimum; *esp* **:** a flow periodically changing direction **4 :** a single swing or change (as of an oscillating body) from one extreme limit to the other — **os·cil·la·tion·al** \-shnəl, -shən-l\ *adj*

os·cil·la·tor \'äs-ə-ˌlāt-ər\ *n* **1 :** one that oscillates **2 :** a device for producing alternating current; *esp* **:** a radio-frequency or audio-frequency generator

os·cil·lo·scope \ä-'sil-ə-ˌskōp, ə-\ *n* **:** an instrument in which the variations in a fluctuating electrical quantity appear temporarily as a visible wave form on the fluorescent screen of a cathode-ray tube

os·cu·lum \'äs-kyə-ləm\ *n, pl* **-la** \-lə\ **:** an opening of a sponge for the outflow of water [Latin, "little mouth, kiss," from *os* "mouth"]

¹-ose \ˌōs, 'ōs *sometimes* ˌōz, 'ōz\ *adj suffix* **:** full of **:** having **:** possessing the qualities of ⟨cym*ose*⟩ [Latin *-osus*]

²-ose \ˌōs, ˌōz\ *n suffix* **1 :** carbohydrate; *esp* **:** sugar ⟨pent*ose*⟩ **2 :** primary hydrolysis product ⟨prote*ose*⟩ [French, from *glucose*]

Osee \'ō-ˌzē, ō-'zā-ə\ *n* **:** HOSEA

osier \'ō-zhər\ *n* **1 :** any of various willows with pliable twigs used for furniture and basketry **2 :** a willow rod used in making baskets **3 :** any of several American dogwoods [Medieval French, from Medieval Latin *auseria* "osier bed"]

-o·sis \'ō-səs\ *n suffix, pl* **-o·ses** \-ˌsēz\ *or* **-o·sis·es** **1 :** action **:** process **:** condition ⟨hypn*osis*⟩ **2 :** abnormal or diseased condition ⟨leuk*osis*⟩ [Greek *-ōsis*]

os·mi·um \'äz-mē-əm\ *n* **:** a hard brittle blue-gray or blue-black metallic element with a high melting point that is the heaviest metal known and that is used especially as a catalyst and in hard alloys — see ELEMENT table [New Latin, from Greek *osmē* "odor"]

os·mom·e·ter \äz-'mäm-ət-ər, äs-\ *n* **:** an apparatus for measuring the pressure produced by osmosis

os·mose \'äz-ˌmōs, 'äs-\ *vi* **:** to diffuse by osmosis [back-formation from *osmosis*]

os·mo·sis \äz-'mō-səs, äs-\ *n* **1 :** a diffusion through a semipermeable membrane typically separating a solvent and a solution that tends to equalize their concentrations; *esp* **:** the passage of solvent in distinction from the passage of solute **2 :** a taking in (as of knowledge) as if by the process of osmosis [derived from Greek *ōsmos* "act of pushing," from *ōthein* "to push"] — **os·mot·ic** \-'mät-ik\ *adj* — **os·mot·i·cal·ly** \-'mät-i-kə-lē, -klē\ *adv*

osmotic shock *n* **:** a rapid change in the pressure produced by osmosis (as by transfer to a medium of different concentration) affecting a living system

os·prey \'äs-prē, -ˌprā\ *n, pl* **ospreys** **:** a large fish-eating hawk with long wings that is dark brown above and mostly white below [derived from Latin *ossifraga* "sea eagle," literally, "bone breaker"]

osprey

ossa *plural of* OS

os·se·ous \'äs-ē-əs\ *adj* **:** BONY 1 [Latin *osseus,* from *os* "bone"]

os·si·cle \'äs-i-kəl\ *n* **:** a small bone or bony structure (as the malleus, incus, or stapes) [Latin *ossiculum* "small bone," from *os* "bone"]

os·si·fi·ca·tion \ˌäs-ə-fə-'kā-shən\ *n* **1 :** formation of or conversion into bone or a bony substance **2 :** an area of ossified tissue

os·si·fy \'äs-ə-ˌfī\ *vb* **-fied; -fy·ing** **1 :** to become or change into bone or bony tissue **2 :** to become or make callous or set in one's ways

oste- *or* **osteo-** *combining form* **:** bone ⟨*osteo*pathy⟩ [Greek *osteon*]

os·ten·si·ble \ä-'sten-sə-bəl\ *adj* **:** shown outwardly **:** PROFESSED ⟨her *ostensible* motive⟩ [French, from Latin *ostendere* "to show," from *obs-* "in front of" + *tendere* "to stretch"]

os·ten·si·bly \ä-'sten-sə-blē\ *adv* **:** to all outward appearances ⟨was *ostensibly* frank, but deceitful in actuality⟩

os·ten·ta·tion \ˌäs-tən-'tā-shən\ *n* **:** showy or excessive display [Medieval French, from Latin *ostentatio,* from *ostentare* "to display," from *ostendere* "to show"]

os·ten·ta·tious \-shəs\ *adj* **:** marked by or fond of conspicuous and sometimes pretentious display — **os·ten·ta·tious·ly** *adv* — **os·ten·ta·tious·ness** *n*

os·teo·ar·thri·tis \ˌäs-tē-ō-ˌär-'thrīt-əs\ *n* **:** arthritis marked by degeneration of the cartilage and bone of joints

os·te·o·blast \'äs-tē-ə-ˌblast\ *n* **:** a cell that forms bone [derived from Greek *osteon* "bone" + *blastos* "bud, embryo"]

os·te·o·clast \'äs-tē-ə-ˌklast\ *n* **:** a large cell that dissolves bone [derived from Greek *osteon* "bone" + *klastos* "broken"]

os·te·o·cyte \ˈäs-tē-ə-ˌsīt\ *n* **:** a mature bone cell that develops from an osteoblast trapped in one of the tiny spaces in bone

os·te·ol·o·gy \ˌäs-tē-ˈäl-ə-jē\ *n* **1 :** a branch of anatomy dealing with the bones **2 :** the bony structure of an organism [New Latin *osteologia* from Greek, "description of bones," from *osteon* "bone" + *logos* "word"] — **os·te·o·log·i·cal** \-tē-ə-ˈläj-ikəl\ *adj*

os·teo·my·eli·tis \ˌäs-tē-ō-ˌmī-ə-ˈlīt-əs\ *n* **:** an infectious usually painful inflammatory disease of bone that may result in the death of bone tissue [*oste-* + Greek *myelos* "marrow" + English *-itis*]

os·teo·path \ˈäs-tē-ə-ˌpath\ *n* **:** a practitioner of osteopathy

os·te·op·a·thy \ˌäs-tē-ˈäp-ə-thē\ *n* **:** a system of treating diseases that places emphasis on manipulation especially of bones but does not exclude other treatment (as the use of drugs and surgery) — **os·teo·path·ic** \ˌäs-tē-ə-ˈpath-ik\ *adj* — **os·teo·path·i·cal·ly** \-ˈpath-i-kə-lē, -klē\ *adv*

os·te·o·po·ro·sis \ˌäs-tē-ō-pə-ˈrō-səs\ *n* **:** a condition affecting especially older women that is characterized by a decrease in the density of bone and an enlargement of the spaces within bone resulting in fragile bones susceptible to breakage [New Latin, from *oste-* "bone" (from Greek *osteon*) + *porosis* "the process of becoming thin or porous"]

os·ti·ole \ˈäs-tē-ˌōl\ *n* **:** a small opening [Latin *ostiolum* "little door," from *ostium* "door"]

os·ti·um \ˈäs-tē-əm\ *n, pl* **os·tia** \-tē-ə\ **:** a mouthlike opening in a bodily part (as a blood vessel) [Latin, "door, mouth of a river"]

ostler *variant of* HOSTLER

os·tra·cism \ˈäs-trə-ˌsiz-əm\ *n* **1 :** a method of temporary banishment by popular vote without trial or special accusation practiced in ancient Greece **2 :** exclusion by general consent from common privileges or social acceptance

os·tra·cize \ˈäs-trə-ˌsīz\ *vt* **1 :** to exile by ostracism **2 :** to exclude from a group by common consent [Greek *ostrakizein* "to banish by voting with potsherds," from *ostrakon* "shell, potsherd"]

Word History Greek *ostrakon* is a word for a shell or for an earthen vessel or a broken fragment of such a vessel. Such potsherds served ancient Athens as ballots in a particular kind of popular vote. Once a year the citizens would gather in the agora or marketplace of Athens to decide who, if anyone, should be banished temporarily for the good of the city. Each voter wrote a name on his *ostrakon.* If at least 6000 votes were cast and if a majority of them named one man, then that man was banished, or ostracized.

os·tra·cod \ˈäs-trə-ˌkäd\ *also* **os·tra·code** \-ˌkōd\ *n* **:** any of a group (Ostracoda) of very small marine and freshwater crustaceans [derived from Greek *ostrakon* "shell"]

os·tra·co·derm \ˈäs-trə-kō-ˌdərm, äs-ˈtrak-ə-\ *n* **:** any of the extinct primitive jawless fishes usually having a bony covering of plates or scales [derived from Greek *ostrakon* "shell" + *derma* "skin"]

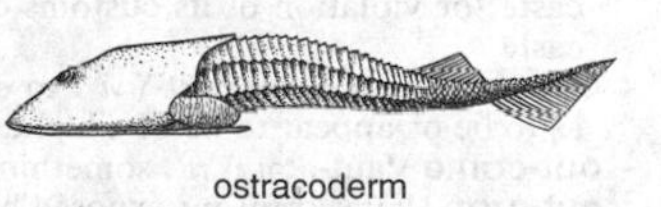
ostracoderm

os·trich \ˈäs-trich, ˈös-\ *n* **1 :** a 2-toed flightless bird of Africa that is the largest of existing birds often weighing 300 pounds (140 kilograms), is able to run quickly, and has large wing and tail feathers used especially formerly in dusters and fans and to adorn hats and clothing **2 :** one that attempts to avoid danger by refusing to face it [Medieval French *ostriz, ostrige,* derived from Latin *avis* "bird" + Late Latin *struthio* "ostrich," from Greek *strouthos* "sparrow, ostrich"]

Os·tro·goth \ˈäs-trə-ˌgäth\ *n* **:** a member of the eastern division of the Goths — compare VISIGOTH [Late Latin *Ostrogothi* "Ostrogoths"]

Os·we·go tea \ä-ˌswē-gō-\ *n* **:** a North American mint with showy scarlet flowers [*Oswego* river, New York]

ot- *or* **oto-** *combining form* **:** ear ⟨*ot*itis⟩ [Greek *ōt-, ous*]

1**oth·er** \ˈəth-ər\ *adj* **1 a :** being the one (as of two or more) left ⟨held my *other* arm straight⟩ **b :** being the ones distinct from those first mentioned ⟨thought the *other* members dull⟩ **c :** SECOND ⟨every *other* day⟩ **2 :** not the same **:** DIFFERENT ⟨*other* times and customs⟩ **3 :** ADDITIONAL ⟨some *other* guests are coming⟩ **4 :** recently past ⟨the *other* evening⟩ [Old English *ōther*]

2**other** *n* **1 a :** one that remains of two or more ⟨lift one foot and then the *other*⟩ **b :** a thing opposite to or excluded by something else ⟨from one side to the *other*⟩ **2 :** a different or additional one ⟨the *others* came later⟩

3**other** *pron, sometimes pl in constr* **:** a different or additional one ⟨something or *other* happened⟩

4**other** *adv* **:** OTHERWISE

1**other than** *prep* **:** EXCEPT FOR, BESIDES ⟨*other than* that, nothing happened⟩

2**other than** *conj* **:** EXCEPT, BUT ⟨cannot enter *other than* by special permission⟩

oth·er·wise \ˈəth-ər-ˌwīz\ *adv* **1 :** in a different way **:** DIFFERENTLY ⟨could not do *otherwise*⟩ **2 :** in different circumstances ⟨*otherwise* we might have won⟩ **3 :** in other respects ⟨the *otherwise* busy street⟩ [Old English *on ōthre wīsan* "in another manner"] — **otherwise** *adj*

oth·er·world \ˈəth-ər-ˌwərld\ *n* **:** a world beyond death or beyond present reality — **oth·er·world·li·ness** \-ˌwərl-dlē-nəs, -lē-\ *n* — **oth·er·world·ly** \-ˌwərl-dlē, -lē\ *adj*

otic \ˈōt-ik\ *adj* **:** of, relating to, or located near the ear

-ot·ic \ˈät-ik\ *adj suffix* **1 :** of, relating to, or characterized by a (specified) action, process, or condition ⟨symbi*otic*⟩ **2 :** having an abnormal or diseased condition of a (specified) kind ⟨leuk*otic*⟩ [Greek *-ōtikos*]

oti·tis \ō-ˈtīt-əs\ *n* **:** inflammation of the ear

oto·lar·yn·gol·o·gy \ˈōt-ō-ˌlar-ən-ˈgäl-ə-jē\ *n* **:** a medical specialty dealing with the ear, nose, and throat

oto·lith \ˈōt-l-ˌith\ *n* **:** a calcium-containing stony mass in the inner ear — **oto·lith·ic** \ˌōt-l-ˈith-ik\ *adj*

Ot·ta·wa \ˈät-ə-wə, -ˌwä, -ˌwȯ\ *n* **:** a member of an American Indian people of Michigan and southern Ontario

ot·ter \ˈät-ər\ *n, pl* **otters** *also* **otter 1 :** any of several aquatic mammals that are related to the weasels and minks, have webbed and clawed feet and dark brown fur, and feed on other animals (as fish, clams, and crabs) that live in or near the water — compare SEA OTTER **2 :** the fur or pelt of an otter [Old English *otor*]

ot·to·man \ˈät-ə-mən\ *n, pl* **-mans 1** *cap* **:** a citizen or political official of the Ottoman Empire **2 a :** an upholstered often overstuffed seat or couch usually without a back **b :** an overstuffed footstool [French, derived from Arabic *ʿothmānī,* from *ʿOthmān* "Othman (founder of the Ottoman Empire)"]

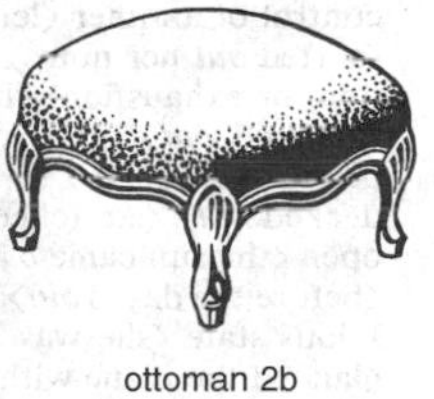
ottoman 2b

Ott·o·man \ˈät-ə-mən\ *adj* **:** of or relating to the Ottoman Empire, its rulers, or its citizens or political officials [derived from Arabic *ʿothmānī* from *ʿothmān* Osman I, founder of the Ottoman Empire]

ouch \ˈau̇ch\ *interj* — used to express sudden pain [probably imitative]

ought \ˈȯt\ *auxiliary verb* — used to express obligation ⟨*ought* to pay our debts⟩, advisability ⟨*ought* to take care of yourself⟩, natural expectation ⟨*ought* to be here by now⟩, or logical consequence ⟨the result *ought* to be infinity⟩ [Middle English *oughte,* past of *owen* "to owe"]

oughtn't \ˈȯt-nt\ **:** ought not

1**ounce** \ˈau̇ns\ *n* **1 a :** a unit of weight equal to 1/12 troy pound (about 31 grams) — see MEASURE table **b :** a unit of weight equal to 1/16 avoirdupois pound (about 28 grams) **c :** a small amount ⟨an *ounce* of sense⟩ **2 :** FLUID OUNCE [Medieval French *unce,* from Latin *uncia* "twelfth part, ounce," from *unus* "one"]

Word History The ancient Romans used a system of weights and measures based on units that were divided into 12 parts. The Latin *uncia,* meaning "a 12th part," was used for the 12th part of a *pes* or "foot." From this is derived Old English *ince* or *ynce,* which became modern English *inch.* The Roman pound, called *libra* in Latin, was also divided into 12 parts similarly designated by the word *uncia.* In this sense *uncia* followed a different path. It became Medieval French *unce,* which was borrowed into Middle English as *unce* or *ounce.*

[2]**ounce** *n* : SNOW LEOPARD [Medieval French *unce* "lynx," from *lonce* (understood as *l'once* "the ounce"), from Latin *lynx*]

our \är, aůr, 'aůr\ *adj* : of or relating to us or ourselves or ourself especially as possessors or possessor, agents or agent, or objects or object of an action ⟨*our* throne⟩ ⟨*our* actions⟩ ⟨*our* being chosen⟩ [Old English *ūre*]

Our Father *n* : LORD'S PRAYER

ours \aůrz, 'aůrz, ärz\ *pron, sing or pl in constr* : that which belongs to us — used without a following noun as a pronoun equivalent in meaning to the adjective *our* ⟨your yard is big and *ours* is small⟩

our·self \är-'self, aůr-\ *pron* : MYSELF — used (as by a sovereign or writer) to refer to the single-person subject when *we* is used instead of *I*

our·selves \-'selvz\ *pron pl* **1** : those identical ones that are we — used reflexively or for emphasis ⟨we're doing it solely for *ourselves*⟩ ⟨we *ourselves* will never go⟩; compare WE 1 **2** : our normal, healthy, or sane condition or selves ⟨we weren't feeling *ourselves* that day⟩

-ous \əs\ *adj suffix* **1** : full of : having : possessing the qualities of ⟨clamor*ous*⟩ ⟨poison*ous*⟩ **2** : having a valence lower than in compounds or ions named with an adjective ending in *-ic* ⟨mercur*ous*⟩ [Medieval French *-ous, -us,* from Latin *-osus*]

oust \'aůst\ *vt* : to force or drive out (as from office or from possession of something) : EXPEL ⟨*oust* a corrupt official⟩ [Medieval French *oster, ouster* "to take off," from Latin *obstare* "to stand in the way," from *ob-* "in the way" + *stare* "to stand"]
synonyms see EJECT

oust·er \'aůs-tər\ *n* : the act or an instance of ousting or being ousted : EXPULSION [Middle French *oster, ouster* "to oust"]

[1]**out** \'aůt\ *adv* **1 a** : in a direction away from the inside or the center ⟨look *out* of a window⟩ **b** : OUTSIDE 1 ⟨it's raining *out*⟩ **c** : OUT-OF-BOUNDS **2** : from among others ⟨picked *out* a hat⟩ **3** : away from home, business, or the usual or proper place ⟨*out* to lunch⟩ ⟨left a word *out*⟩ **4** : into a state of loss or deprivation ⟨vote the party *out* of office⟩ **5** : into the possession or control of another ⟨lent *out* money⟩ **6** : into groups or shares ⟨sorted *out* her notes⟩ **7 a** : to the point of depletion, extinction, or exhaustion ⟨the food ran *out*⟩ ⟨turn the light *out*⟩ ⟨all tuckered *out*⟩ **b** : to completion or satisfaction ⟨work the problem *out*⟩ **c** : to the full or a great extent or degree ⟨all decked *out*⟩ ⟨stretched *out* on the floor⟩ **8 a** : in or into the open ⟨the sun came *out*⟩ **b** : ALOUD ⟨cried *out*⟩ **9** : at an end ⟨before the day is *out*⟩ **10 a** : in or into an insensible or unconscious state ⟨she was *out* cold⟩ **b** : in or into a useless state ⟨landed the plane with one engine *out*⟩ **11 a** : so as to put out a batter or base runner ⟨the catcher threw *out* the runner trying to steal second base⟩ **b** : so as to be put out ⟨grounded *out* to the shortstop⟩ [Old English *ūt*]

[2]**out** *vi* : to become known ⟨the truth will *out*⟩

[3]**out** *adj* **1 a** : situated outside : EXTERNAL ⟨the *out* edge⟩ **b** : OUT-OF-BOUNDS **2** : situated at a distance : OUTLYING ⟨the *out* islands⟩ **3** : not being in power ⟨the *out* party⟩ **4** : ABSENT ⟨a basket with its bottom *out*⟩ **5** : removed by the defense from play as a batter or base runner in a baseball inning ⟨the batter was *out*⟩ **6** : directed outward or serving to direct something outward : OUTGOING ⟨put the letter in the *out* basket⟩ **7** : no longer in fashion ⟨that style of pants is definitely *out*⟩ **8** : not to be considered : out of the question ⟨that choice was *out* as far as we were concerned⟩ **9** : DETERMINED 1 ⟨was *out* to get revenge⟩ **10** : engaged in or attempting a particular activity ⟨won on his first time *out*⟩

[4]**out** \aůt, 'aůt\ *prep* — used as a function word to indicate an outward movement ⟨run *out* the door⟩ ⟨looked *out* the window⟩

[5]**out** \'aůt\ *n* **1** : one who is out of power **2 a** : the putting out of a batter or base runner in baseball **b** : a player who has been put out **3** : a way of escaping from an embarrassing situation or a difficulty — **on the outs** : on unfriendly terms

out- *prefix* : in a manner that goes beyond, surpasses, or excels ⟨*out*maneuver⟩ [[1]*out*]

outachieve
outact
outbluff
outbox
outbrawl
outbuy
outcatch
outclimb
outcoach
outcompete
outdance
outdazzle
outdebate
outdesign
outdress
outdrink
outdrive
outearn
outeat
outfight
outfish
outfly
outfumble
outglitter
outgross
outhit
outhunt
outhustle
outjump
outkick
outleap
outlearn
outman
outmarch
outmuscle
outperform
outplay
outpoll
outpopulate
outpower
outpray
outprice
outproduce
outpunch
outrow
outsail
outscheme
outscore
outshout
outsing
outsit
outskate
outsparkle
outspeed
outsprint
outstride
outswear
outswim
outtalk
outthink
outthrow
outtrade
outvote
outwait
outwalk
outwrestle
outwrite

out–and–out \ˌaůt-n-'aůt, -'daůt\ *adj* : being wholly what is stated ⟨an *out-and-out* crook⟩

out·bal·ance \aůt-'bal-əns, 'aůt-\ *vt* : OUTWEIGH

out·bid \-'bid\ *vt* **-bid; -bid·ding** : to make a higher bid than

[1]**out·board** \'aůt-ˌbōrd, -ˌbȯrd\ *adj* **1** : situated outboard **2** : having or using an outboard motor

[2]**outboard** *adv* **1** : outside the line of a ship's bulwarks or hull : away from the center line of a ship **2** : in a position closer or closest to either of the wing tips of an airplane or of the sides of an automobile

outboard motor *n* : a small internal-combustion engine with propeller attached for mounting at the stern of a small boat

out·bound \'aůt-ˌbaůnd\ *adj* : outward bound ⟨*outbound* traffic⟩

out·brave \aůt-'brāv, 'aůt-\ *vt* **1** : to face or resist defiantly **2** : to exceed in courage

out·break \'aůt-ˌbrāk\ *n* **1** : a sudden or violent increase in activity, use, or acceptance ⟨the *outbreak* of war⟩ **2** : something that breaks out: as **a** : EPIDEMIC ⟨an *outbreak* of measles⟩ **b** : INSURRECTION, REVOLT

out·breed *vt* **-bred** \-ˌbred, -'bred\; **-breed·ing** **1** \'aůt-ˌbrēd\ : to subject to outbreeding **2** \aůt-', 'aůt-'\ : to breed faster than

out·breed·ing \'aůt-ˌbrēd-ing\ *n* : the interbreeding of relatively unrelated individuals

out·build·ing \'aůt-ˌbil-ding\ *n* : a building separate from and smaller than the main one

out·burst \-ˌbərst\ *n* **1** : a violent expression of feeling **2** : a surge of activity or growth ⟨a new *outburst* of creative power⟩

out·cast \-ˌkast\ *n* : a person cast out by society : PARIAH — **outcast** *adj*

out·caste \-ˌkast\ *n* **1** : one who has been ejected from a Hindu caste for violation of its customs or rules **2** : one who has no caste

out·class \aůt-'klas, 'aůt-\ *vt* : to excel or surpass so decisively as to be or appear to be of a higher class

out·come \'aůt-ˌkəm\ *n* : something that follows as a result

[1]**out·crop** \'aůt-ˌkräp\ *n* : exposed bedrock or an unconsolidated deposit at the surface of the ground

[2]**out·crop** \'aůt-'kräp\ *vi* : to come to the surface : APPEAR

out·crop·ping \-'kräp-ing\ *n* : [1]OUTCROP

out·cross \'aůt-ˌkrȯs\ *n* : a cross between relatively unrelated individuals or strains; *also* : the offspring of such a cross — **outcross** *vt*

out·cry \'aůt-ˌkrī\ *n* **1** : a loud cry : CLAMOR **2** : a strong protest

out·dat·ed \aůt-'dāt-əd, 'aůt-\ *adj* : OUTMODED

out·dis·tance \aůt-'dis-təns, 'aůt-\ *vt* : to go far ahead of (as in a race) : OUTSTRIP

out·do \aůt-'dü, 'aůt-\ *vt* **-did** \-'did\; **-done** \-'dən\; **-do·ing** \-'dü-ing\ : to go beyond in action or performance : SURPASS

out·door \ˌaůt-ˌdōr, -ˌdȯr\ *also* **out·doors** \-ˌdōrz, -ˌdȯrz\ *adj* **1** : of or relating to the outdoors ⟨an *outdoor* setting⟩ **2** : done outdoors ⟨*outdoor* games⟩ **3** : not roofed or enclosed ⟨an *outdoor* theater⟩ [*out (of) door, out (of) doors*]

[1]**out·doors** \aůt-'dōrz, 'aůt-, -'dȯrz\ *adv* : outside a building : in or into the open air

[2]**outdoors** *n* **1** : the open air **2** : the world away from human dwellings

out·draw \aůt-'drȯ, 'aůt-\ *vt* **-drew** \-'drü\; **-drawn** \-'drȯn\; **-draw·ing** **1** : to attract a larger audience or following than **2** : to draw a handgun more quickly than

out·er \'au̇t-ər\ *adj* **1 :** EXTERNAL 1 ⟨*outer* appearance⟩ **2 a :** situated farther out ⟨the *outer* wall⟩ **b :** being away from a center ⟨the *outer* planets of the solar system⟩

outer ear *n* **:** the outer visible portion of the ear that collects and directs sound waves toward the eardrum by way of a canal which extends inward through the temporal bone

out·er·most \'au̇t-ər-ˌmōst\ *adj* **:** farthest out

outer space *n* **:** SPACE 5; *esp* **:** the region beyond the solar system

out·er·wear \'au̇t-ər-ˌwaər, -ˌweər\ *n* **1 :** clothing for outdoor wear **2 :** outer clothing as opposed to underwear

out·face \au̇t-'fās, 'au̇t-\ *vt* **1 :** STARE DOWN **2 :** to confront without fear or weakening **:** DEFY

out·fall \'au̇t-ˌfȯl\ *n* **:** the outlet of a river, stream, lake, drain, or sewer

out·field \-ˌfēld\ *n* **:** the part of a baseball field beyond the infield and between the foul lines — **out·field·er** \-ˌfēl-dər\ *n*

[1]**out·fit** \'au̇t-ˌfit\ *n* **1 :** the equipment or clothing especially for some special purpose or occasion ⟨a camping *outfit*⟩ ⟨a sports *outfit*⟩ **2 :** a group of persons working together or associated in the same undertaking ⟨soldiers belonging to the same *outfit*⟩

[2]**outfit** *vt* **1 :** to furnish with an outfit **:** EQUIP ⟨*outfit* an expedition⟩ **2 :** SUPPLY 3 — **out·fit·ter** *n*

out·flank \au̇t-'flaŋk, 'au̇t-\ *vt* **:** to get around the flank of (an opposing force)

out·flow \'au̇t-ˌflō\ *n* **1 :** a flowing out **2 :** something that flows out

out·foot \au̇t-'fu̇t, 'au̇t-\ *vt* **:** to outdo in speed **:** OUTSTRIP

out·fox \-'fäks\ *vt* **:** OUTSMART

out·gen·er·al \-'jen-rəl, -ə-rəl\ *vt* **:** to surpass in generalship **:** OUTMANEUVER

out·go \'au̇t-ˌgō\ *n, pl* **outgoes :** something (as goods or money) that is paid out **:** EXPENDITURE

out·go·ing \'au̇t-ˌgō-iŋ\ *adj* **1 a :** going out ⟨the *outgoing* tide⟩ **b :** retiring from a place or position ⟨the *outgoing* governor⟩ **2 :** FRIENDLY, RESPONSIVE ⟨an *outgoing* person⟩

out·grow \au̇t-'grō, 'au̇t-\ *vt* **-grew** \-'grü\; **-grown** \-'grōn\; **-grow·ing 1 :** to grow faster than **2 :** to grow too large or too mature for ⟨*outgrow* one's clothes⟩ ⟨*outgrew* childish fancies⟩

out·growth \'au̇t-ˌgrōth\ *n* **1 :** a product of growing out ⟨an *outgrowth* of hair⟩ **2 :** CONSEQUENCE, BY-PRODUCT ⟨crime is often an *outgrowth* of poverty⟩

out·guess \au̇t-'ges, 'au̇t-\ *vt* **:** to anticipate the intentions, plans, or actions of

out·house \'au̇t-ˌhau̇s\ *n* **:** OUTBUILDING; *esp* **:** PRIVY

out·ing \'au̇t-iŋ\ *n* **:** a brief usually outdoor pleasure trip

out·land·er \'au̇t-ˌlan-dər\ *n* **:** a person belonging to another culture or region

out·land·ish \au̇t-'lan-dish, 'au̇t-\ *adj* **1 :** of or relating to another country **2 a :** strikingly out of the ordinary **:** BIZARRE ⟨an *outlandish* costume⟩ **b :** beyond proper or reasonable limits or standards ⟨*outlandish* behavior⟩ **3 :** remote from civilization ⟨lived in *outlandish* places⟩ ***synonyms*** see STRANGE — **out·land·ish·ly** *adv* — **out·land·ish·ness** *n*

out·last \au̇t-'last, 'au̇t-\ *vt* **:** to last longer than

[1]**out·law** \'au̇t-ˌlȯ\ *n* **1 :** a person excluded from the benefit or protection of the law **2 a :** a lawless person or a fugitive from the law **b :** one (as a person or organization) under a ban or restriction [Old English *ūtlaga,* from Old Norse *ūtlagi,* from *ūt* "out" + *lag-, lǫg* "law"] — **outlaw** *adj*

[2]**outlaw** *vt* **1 a :** to deprive of the benefit and protection of law **b :** to make illegal **2 :** to place under a ban or restriction — **out·law·ry** \'au̇t-ˌlȯ-rē\ *n*

out·lay \'au̇t-ˌlā\ *n* **1 :** the act of expending **2 :** EXPENDITURE 2

out·let \'au̇t-ˌlet, -lət\ *n* **1 :** a place or opening through which something is let out **2 :** a means of release or satisfaction for an emotion or impulse **3 :** a place (as in a wall) at which an electrical device can be plugged into the wiring system **4 a :** a market for a commodity **b :** a retail store or distributor

[1]**out·line** \'au̇t-ˌlīn\ *n* **1 :** a line that traces or forms the outer limits of an object or figure and shows its shape **2 a :** a drawing or picture giving only the outlines of something **b :** this method of drawing **3 a :** a brief summary often in numbered divisions **b :** a preliminary account of a project **:** PLAN **4 :** a brief treatment of a subject ⟨an *outline* of world history⟩

[2]**outline** *vt* **1 :** to draw the outline of **2 :** to indicate the main features or parts of

out·live \au̇t-'liv, 'au̇t-\ *vt* **:** to live longer than **:** OUTLAST

out·look \'au̇t-ˌlu̇k\ *n* **1 a :** a place offering a view **b :** a view from a particular place **2 :** POINT OF VIEW **3 :** the prospect for the future

out·ly·ing \'au̇t-ˌlī-iŋ\ *adj* **:** far from a center or main body ⟨an *outlying* suburb⟩

out·ma·neu·ver \ˌau̇t-mə-'nü-vər, -'nyü-\ *vt* **1 :** to get the better of by more skillful maneuvering **2 :** to be more maneuverable than

out·match \ˌau̇t-'mach\ *vt* **:** to prove superior to **:** OUTDO

out·mod·ed \au̇t-'mōd-əd, 'au̇t-\ *adj* **1 :** no longer in style ⟨an *outmoded* dress⟩ **2 :** no longer acceptable or usable ⟨*outmoded* beliefs⟩ ⟨*outmoded* equipment⟩

out·most \'au̇t-ˌmōst\ *adj* **:** farthest out **:** OUTERMOST

out·num·ber \au̇t-'nəm-bər, 'au̇t-\ *vt* **:** to be greater in number than ⟨girls *outnumber* boys in the class⟩

out of *prep* **1 a :** from within to the outside of ⟨walked *out of* the room⟩ **b** — used as a function word to indicate a change in quality, state, or form ⟨woke up *out of* a deep sleep⟩ **c :** beyond the range or limits of ⟨*out of* sight⟩ **2 :** BECAUSE OF, FROM ⟨fled *out of* fear⟩ **3** — used as a function word to indicate the constituent material, basis, or source ⟨built *out of* old lumber⟩ **4** — used as a function word to indicate the state or condition of being without something especially that was there before ⟨all *out of* milk⟩ ⟨*out of* a job⟩ **5 :** from among ⟨one *out of* four survived⟩ **6** — used as a function word to indicate the center of an enterprise or activity ⟨runs her business *out of* her home⟩

out–of–bounds \ˌau̇t-əv-'bau̇nz, -ə-\ *adv or adj* **:** outside the prescribed area of play

out–of–date \ˌau̇t-əv-'dāt, -ə-\ *adj* **:** OUTMODED ⟨*out-of-date* ideas⟩

out–of–door \ˌau̇t-əv-'dōr, -ə-, -'dȯr\ *or* **out–of–doors** \-'dōrz, -'dȯrz\ *adj* **:** OUTDOOR

out–of–doors *n* **:** OUTDOORS

out of doors *adv* **:** OUTDOORS

out–of–the–way \ˌau̇t-əv-t͟hə-'wā, -ə-\ *adj* **1 :** not centrally or conveniently located ⟨an *out-of-the-way* restaurant⟩ **2 :** not commonly found or met **:** UNUSUAL

out·pace \ˌau̇t-'pās\ *vt* **1 :** to surpass in speed **2 :** OUTDO 1

out·pa·tient \'au̇t-ˌpa-shənt\ *n* **:** a patient who visits a hospital or other medical facility for diagnosis or treatment without staying overnight — compare INPATIENT

out·post \'au̇t-ˌpōst\ *n* **1 a :** a guard stationed at a distance from a military post **b :** the position occupied by an outpost **2 a :** an outlying settlement **b :** an outer limit **:** FRONTIER

out·pour \au̇t-'pōr, -'pȯr\ *vt* **:** to pour out — **out·pour** \'au̇t-ˌ\ *n*

out·pour·ing \'au̇t-ˌpōr-iŋ, -ˌpȯr-\ *n* **1 :** the act of pouring out **2 a :** something that pours out or is poured out **:** OUTFLOW **b :** an outburst of emotion

[1]**out·put** \-ˌpu̇t\ *n* **1 :** something produced: as **a :** agricultural or industrial production ⟨steel *output*⟩ **b :** mental or artistic production ⟨literary *output*⟩ **c :** the amount produced by a person in a given time **d :** power or energy delivered by a machine or system ⟨generator *output*⟩ ⟨solar *output*⟩ **e :** the information produced by a computer **2 :** a point at which something (as power, an electronic signal, or data) comes out

[2]**output** *vt* **out·put·ted** *or* **output; out·put·ting :** to produce as output

out·race \ˌau̇t-'rās\ *vt* **:** OUTPACE 1

[1]**out·rage** \'au̇t-ˌrāj\ *n* **1 :** a violent or brutal act **2 a :** INJURY 1, INSULT **b :** an act that violates accepted standards of behavior or taste ⟨an *outrage* against respectability⟩ **3 :** the anger or resentment aroused by injury or insult [Medieval French *utrage, outrage* "excess, insult," from *outre, utre* "beyond, in excess" (from Latin *ultra*) + *-age*]

Word History The English word *outrage* is related neither to *out* nor to *rage.* It is ultimately derived from Latin *ultra,* "beyond." Latin *ultra* became *outre* in Medieval French. *Outre* was combined with the common suffix *-age* to produce the word *outrage,* which meant "excess, insult," and the Medieval French word was borrowed into English in the Middle English period. Medieval French *outre* is also the ancestor of French *outré,* which was borrowed into English in modern times.

\ə\ **abut**	\au̇\ **out**	\i\ **tip**	\ȯ\ **saw**	\u̇\ **foot**
\ər\ **further**	\ch\ **chin**	\ī\ **life**	\ȯi\ **coin**	\y\ **yet**
\a\ **mat**	\e\ **pet**	\j\ **job**	\th\ **thin**	\yü\ **few**
\ā\ **take**	\ē\ **easy**	\ŋ\ **sing**	\t͟h\ **this**	\yu̇\ **cure**
\ä\ **cot, cart**	\g\ **go**	\ō\ **bone**	\ü\ **food**	\zh\ **vision**

[2]outrage *vt* **1 a** : RAPE 2 **b** : to subject to violent injury or abuse **2** : to arouse anger or great resentment in ***synonyms*** see OFFEND

out·ra·geous \au̇t-ˈrā-jəs\ *adj* : being beyond all bounds of decency or justice : extremely offensive, insulting, or shameful : SHOCKING — **out·ra·geous·ly** *adv* — **out·ra·geous·ness** *n*

synonyms OUTRAGEOUS, ATROCIOUS, HEINOUS mean exceedingly bad or horrible. OUTRAGEOUS implies exceeding the limits of what is tolerable or decent ⟨*outrageous* manners⟩. ATROCIOUS implies merciless cruelty, savagery, or contempt of ordinary values ⟨*atrocious* working conditions⟩. HEINOUS implies being so flagrantly evil as to induce hatred or horror ⟨a *heinous* crime⟩.

out·rank \au̇t-ˈraŋk, ˈau̇t-\ *vt* : to rank higher than : be more important than

ou·tré \ü-ˈtrā\ *adj* : going beyond what is usual or proper : BIZARRE [French, from *outrer* "to carry to excess," from Medieval French *outre* "beyond" — see *Word History* at OUTRAGE]

out·reach \au̇t-ˈrēch, ˈau̇t-\ *vb* **1 a** : to be greater in reach than **b** : to go beyond : EXCEED ⟨the demand *outreaches* the supply⟩ **2** : to get the better of by trickery : OVERREACH **3** : to go too far

out·ride \ˌau̇t-ˈrīd\ *vt* **-rode** \-ˈrōd\; **-rid·den** \-ˈrid-n\; **-rid·ing** \-ˈrīd-iŋ\ **1** : to ride better, faster, or farther than : OUTSTRIP **2** : to ride out (a storm)

out·rid·er \ˈau̇t-ˌrīd-ər\ *n* **1** : a mounted attendant **2** : FORERUNNER 1, HARBINGER

out·rig·ger \ˈau̇t-ˌrig-ər\ *n* **1 a** : a projecting frame on a float or shaped log attached to the side of a boat to prevent upsetting **b** : a projecting beam run out from a ship's side to help secure the masts or from a mast to extend a rope or sail **c** : a boat fitted with an outrigger **2** : a projecting frame to support the elevator or tailplanes of an airplane or the rotor of a helicopter

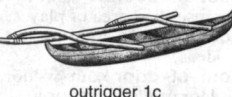

outrigger 1c

[1]out·right \au̇t-ˈrīt, ˈau̇t-ˌ\ *adv* **1 a** : with nothing kept back : COMPLETELY ⟨repeal a law *outright*⟩ **b** : without restraint ⟨laughed *outright*⟩ **2** : at once : INSTANTANEOUSLY ⟨killed *outright*⟩

[2]out·right \ˈau̇t-ˌrīt\ *adj* **1** : being exactly what is stated ⟨an *outright* lie⟩ **2** : given without reservation ⟨an *outright* gift⟩

out·run \au̇t-ˈrən, ˈau̇t-\ *vt* **-ran** \-ˈran\; **-run; -run·ning** : to run faster than; *also* : EXCEED ⟨their needs *outran* their funds⟩

out·sell \-ˈsel\ *vt* **-sold** \-ˈsōld\; **-sell·ing** **1** : to exceed in sales ⟨cigarettes far *outsold* cigars⟩ **2** : to surpass in selling

out·set \ˈau̇t-ˌset\ *n* : BEGINNING 1, START

out·shine \au̇t-ˈshīn, ˈau̇t-\ *vt* **-shone** \-ˈshōn\; **-shin·ing** **1 a** : to shine brighter than **b** : to exceed in splendor or showiness **2** : SURPASS ⟨*outshone* most of the competitors⟩

out·shoot \-ˈshüt\ *vt* **-shot** \-ˈshät\; **-shoot·ing** **1** : to surpass in shooting or making shots **2** : to go beyond

[1]out·side \au̇t-ˈsīd, ˈau̇t-ˌ\ *n* **1** : a place or region beyond an enclosure or boundary **2** : an outer side or surface **3** : the utmost limit or extent ⟨would sell 500 copies at the *outside*⟩

[2]outside *adj* **1** : of, relating to, or being on or toward the outside ⟨the *outside* edge⟩ **2 a** : situated or performed outside a particular place ⟨*outside* noises⟩ **b** : giving access to the outside ⟨the *outside* door⟩ **3** : MAXIMUM ⟨cost more than our *outside* estimate⟩ **4 a** : not included or originating in a particular group or organization ⟨*outside* influences⟩ **b** : not part of one's regular routine or duties ⟨*outside* activities⟩ ⟨*outside* reading⟩ **5** : barely possible : REMOTE ⟨an *outside* chance⟩

[3]outside *adv* : on or to the outside : OUTDOORS

[4]outside *prep* **1** — used as a function word to indicate movement to or position on the outer side of ⟨*outside* the house⟩ **2** : beyond the limits of ⟨*outside* the law⟩ **3** : EXCEPT ⟨nobody *outside* a few close friends⟩

outside of *prep* **1** : OUTSIDE 2 **2** : EXCEPT FOR ⟨*outside* of her brother she is alone in the house⟩

out·sid·er \au̇t-ˈsīd-ər, ˈau̇t-\ *n* **1** : a person who does not belong to a particular group **2** : a contender not expected to win

[1]out·size \ˈau̇t-ˌsīz\ *n* : an unusual size; *esp* : a size larger than the standard

[2]outsize *also* **out·sized** \-ˌsīzd\ *adj* : unusually large or heavy

out·skirts \ˈau̇t-ˌskərts\ *n pl* : the outlying parts of a place or town

out·smart \au̇t-ˈsmärt, ˈau̇t-\ *vt* : to get the better of; *esp* : OUTWIT

out·soar \-ˈsōr, -ˈsȯr\ *vt* : to soar beyond or above

out·sole \ˈau̇t-ˌsōl\ *n* : the outside sole of a boot or shoe

out·source \ˈau̇t-ˌsȯrs\ *vt* : to obtain (as some goods or services needed by a business or organization) under contract with an outside supplier

out·spend \au̇t-ˈspend\ *vt* **1** : to exceed the limits of in spending ⟨*outspends* his income⟩ **2** : to spend more than ⟨*outspent* the other candidate⟩

out·spo·ken \au̇t-ˈspō-kən\ *adj* : direct and open in speech or expression : FRANK ⟨an *outspoken* person⟩ ⟨*outspoken* criticism⟩ — **out·spo·ken·ness** \-kən-nəs\ *n*

out·spread \au̇t-ˈspred\ *vt* **-spread; -spread·ing** : to spread out : EXTEND — **out·spread** \ˈau̇t-ˌspred\ *adj*

out·stand·ing \au̇t-ˈstan-diŋ\ *adj* **1** : standing out or projecting **2 a** : not paid ⟨*outstanding* bills⟩ **b** : remaining in existence ⟨among problems still *outstanding*⟩ **c** : publicly issued and sold ⟨20,000 shares *outstanding*⟩ **3 a** : standing out from a group : CONSPICUOUS ⟨*outstanding* talent⟩ **b** : DISTINGUISHED 1, EMINENT ⟨*outstanding* scholars⟩ ***synonyms*** see NOTICEABLE — **out·stand·ing·ly** \au̇t-ˈstan-diŋ-lē\ *adv*

out·stay \au̇t-ˈstā, ˈau̇t-\ *vt* **1** : to stay beyond or longer than ⟨*outstay* one's welcome⟩ **2** : to surpass in staying power ⟨*outstayed* the early leaders to win at the finish⟩

out·stretch \au̇t-ˈstrech\ *vt* : to stretch out or beyond

out·strip \au̇t-ˈstrip\ *vt* **1** : to go faster or farther than ⟨*outstripped* the other runners⟩ **2 a** : EXCEL ⟨*outstripped* all rivals⟩ **b** : EXCEED ⟨demand *outstrips* supply⟩ [*out-* + obsolete *strip* "to move fast"]

out–there \ˈau̇t-t͟haər, -ˈt͟heər\ *adj* : UNCONVENTIONAL ⟨*out-there* styles⟩

[1]out·ward \ˈau̇t-wərd\ *adj* **1** : moving or directed toward the outside or away from a center ⟨an *outward* flow⟩ **2** : exposed to view or notice : not private or inward ⟨*outward* optimism⟩

[2]outward *or* **out·wards** \-wərdz\ *adv* **1** : toward the outside ⟨the city stretches *outward* for miles⟩ ⟨fold it *outward*⟩ **2** *obs* : EXTERNALLY

out·ward·ly \ˈau̇t-wərd-lē\ *adv* : on the outside : in outward appearance ⟨*outwardly* calm⟩

out·wear \au̇t-ˈwaər, ˈau̇t-, -ˈweər\ *vt* **-wore** \-ˈwōr, -ˈwȯr\; **-worn** \-ˈwōrn, -ˈwȯrn\; **-wear·ing** : to wear or last longer than ⟨a fabric that *outwears* most others⟩

out·weigh \-ˈwā\ *vt* : to exceed in weight, value, or importance

out·wit \au̇t-ˈwit\ *vt* : to get the better of by superior cleverness : OUTSMART

[1]out·work \au̇t-ˈwərk, ˈau̇t-\ *vt* : to outdo in working

[2]outwork \ˈau̇t-ˌwərk\ *n* : a minor defensive position constructed outside a fortified area

out·worn \au̇t-ˈwōrn, ˈau̇t-, -ˈwȯrn\ *adj* : no longer useful or accepted : OUT-OF-DATE ⟨an *outworn* system⟩

ou·zel \ˈü-zəl\ *n* **1** : a European blackbird or a related bird **2** : DIPPER 2 [Old English *ōsle*]

ov- *or* **ovi-** *or* **ovo-** *combining form* : egg ⟨*ovicidal*⟩ [Latin *ovum*]

ova *plural of* OVUM

[1]oval \ˈō-vəl\ *adj* : having the shape of an egg; *also* : broadly elliptical

[2]oval *n* : an oval figure or object

oval window *n* : an oval opening between the middle ear and inner ear having the base of the stapes attached to its membrane

ovar·i·an \ō-ˈvar-ē-ən, -ˈver-\ *adj* : of, relating to, or produced by an ovary ⟨*ovarian* hormones⟩

ova·ry \ˈōv-rē, -ə-rē\ *n, pl* **-ries** **1** : one of the typically paired female reproductive organs that produce eggs and in vertebrates female sex hormones **2** : the enlarged rounded part at the base of the pistil of a flowering plant in which seeds are produced [New Latin *ovarium,* from Latin *ovum* "egg"]

ovate \ˈō-ˌvāt\ *adj* : shaped like an egg especially with the basal end broader ⟨*ovate* leaves⟩

ova·tion \ō-ˈvā-shən\ *n* **1** : a ceremony honoring a Roman general who had won a victory less important than one for which a triumph was granted **2** : a public expression of praise : enthusiastic applause ⟨a standing *ovation*⟩ [Latin *ovatio,* from *ovare* "to exult"]

ov·en \ˈəv-ən\ *n* : a chamber used for baking, heating, or drying [Old English *ofen*]

ov·en·bird \-ˌbərd\ *n* : an American warbler that builds a dome-shaped nest on the ground [from the shape of its nest]

[1]over \ˈō-vər\ *adv* **1 a** : across a barrier or intervening space ⟨fly *over* to London⟩ **b** : forward beyond an edge or brink and often down ⟨went too near the edge and fell *over*⟩ **c** : across the brim ⟨the soup boiled *over*⟩ **d** : so as to bring the underside up ⟨turned the cards *over*⟩ **e** : from a vertical to a prone or inclined position ⟨tripped and fell *over*⟩ ⟨knocked the lamp *over*⟩ **f** : from one person or side to another ⟨hand it *over*⟩ **g** : ACROSS 3 ⟨got their point *over*⟩ **h** : to one's home ⟨invite some friends *over*⟩ **i** : at a distance from a certain point ⟨two streets *over*⟩ **j** : to agreement or concord ⟨won them *over*⟩ **2 a** : beyond a quantity, limit, or norm often by a specified amount or to a specified degree ⟨the show ran a minute *over*⟩; *also* : in or to excess **b** : till a later time (as the next day) : OVERNIGHT ⟨stay *over*⟩ ⟨sleep *over*⟩ **3** : so as to cover the whole surface ⟨windows boarded *over*⟩ **4** — used on a two-way radio transmission to indicate that a message is complete and a reply is expected **5 a** : THROUGH 2a ⟨read it *over*⟩ **b** : once more : AGAIN ⟨do it *over*⟩ [Old English *ofer*]

[2]**over** *prep* **1** : higher than : ABOVE ⟨flew *over* the city⟩ ⟨towered *over* his mother⟩ **2 a** : having authority, power, or jurisdiction in regard to ⟨respected those *over* me⟩ **b** : having superiority, advantage, or preference in comparison to ⟨a big lead *over* the others⟩ **3 a** : more than ⟨costs *over* $5⟩ **b** : ABOVE 4 **4 a** : on or down on especially so as to cover ⟨laid a blanket *over* the child⟩ **b** : all through or throughout ⟨went *over* my notes⟩ ⟨showed me *over* the house⟩ **c** : by or through the medium of ⟨heard it *over* the radio⟩ **5 a** : moving above and across ⟨jump *over* a stream⟩ **b** : down from : OFF ⟨fell *over* the edge⟩ ⟨lives *over* the way⟩ **6** : THROUGHOUT 2, DURING ⟨*over* the past 25 years⟩ **7** — used as a function word to indicate an object of interest or consideration ⟨laughed *over* my misadventures⟩, an activity ⟨spent an hour *over* cards⟩, or concern ⟨trouble *over* money⟩ **8** : for values of the unknown from ⟨find the solution set of the equation *over* the real numbers⟩

[3]**over** *adj* **1** : being outside or above **2 a** : EXCESSIVE ⟨*over* imagination⟩ **b** : having or showing an excess or surplus ⟨the balance is $3 *over* in your books⟩ **3** : being at an end ⟨the day is *over*⟩ — **over easy** : fried on one side then turned and fried lightly on the other side ⟨eggs *over easy*⟩

over- *prefix* **1** : so as to exceed or surpass **2** : excessive **3** : excessively

overabstract
overabundance
overabundant
overaccentuate
overadvertise
overaggressive
overambitious
overanalysis
overanalytical
overanalyze
overanxiety
overanxious
overapplication
overarousal
overarticulate
overassert
overassertion
overassertive
overassessment
overattention
overbake
overbill
overbleach
overboil
overbold
overbright
overbroad
overbrowse
overbusy
overcareful
overcaution
overcautious
overcentralization
overcentralize
overcivilized
overclean
overcommerciali-zation
overcommercialize
overcommunicate
overcommunica-tion
overcomplex
overcomplicate
overcomplicated
overcompress
overconcentration
overconcern
overconcerned
overconfidence
overconfident
overconfidently
overconscientious
overconscious
overconservative
overconsume
overconsumption
overcontrol
overcook
overcorrect
overcount
overcritical
overdecorate
overdependence
overdependent
overdramatic
overdramatize
overdrink
overeager
overeagerness
overearnest
overedit
overeducate
overeducated
overeducation
overelaborate
overelaboration
overemotional
overemphasis
overemphasize
overemphatic
overenergetic
overenrolled
overenthusiasm
overenthusiastic
overequipped
overexaggerate
overexaggeration
overexcite
overexcited
overexercise
overexert
overexertion
overexpand
overexpansion
overexpectation
overexplain
overexploit
overexploitation
overextravagant
overexuberant
overfamiliar
overfamiliarity
overfastidious
overfat
overfertilization
overfertilize
overfond
overfussy
overgeneralization
overgeneralize
overgenerosity
overgenerous
overgenerously
overglamorize
overharvest
overhasty
overhunt
overhype
overidealize
overimaginative
overimpress
overindebtedness
overindulge
overindulgence
overindulgent
overindustrialize
overinflate
overinflated
overinflation
overinform
overinformed
overingenious
overingenuity
overinsistent
overintellectualize
overintense
overintensity
overinvestment
overlabor
overlabored
overladen
overlarge
overlavish
overliteral
overload
overlong
overloud
overlush
overmature
overmaturity
overmedicate
overmedication
overmodest
overmodestly
overmuscled
overnice
overnourish
overobvious
overopinionated
overoptimism
overoptimist
overoptimistic
overoptimistically
overorganize
overorganized
overornament
overparticular
overpay
overpayment
overplan
overpraise
overprecise
overprescribe
overprescription
overprivileged
overproduce
overproduction
overpromise
overpromote
overprotect
overprotection
overprotective
overprotectiveness
overpump
overreact
overreaction
overrefined
overrefinement
overregulate
overregulation
overreliance
overreport
overrespond
overrich
oversalt
oversanguine
oversaturate
oversaturation
overscrupulous
oversensitive
oversensitiveness
oversensitivity
overserious
overseriously
oversimplistic
oversolicitous
oversophisticated
overspecialization
overspecialize
overspeculate
overspeculation
overstaff
overstimulate
overstimulation
overstrain
overstress
overstretch
oversubtle
oversuspicious
overtalk
overtalkative
overtax
overtaxation
overthin
overthink
overtighten
overtip
overtired
overtrain
overtreat
overtreatment
overutilization
overutilize
overviolent
overvivid
overwater
overwind
overwithhold
overzealous
overzealousness

over·achiev·er \ˌō-və-rə-ˈchē-vər\ *n* : one who achieves success over and above the standard or expected level especially at an early age — **overachieve** *vi* — **over·achieve·ment** \-ˈchēv-mənt\ *n*

over·act \ˌō-və-ˈrakt\ *vb* **1** : to act more than is necessary **2** : to overact a part **3** : to exaggerate in acting — **over·ac·tion** \-ˈrak-shən\ *n*

over·ac·tive \-ˈrak-tiv\ *adj* : excessively or abnormally active ⟨an *overactive* thyroid⟩ — **over·ac·tiv·i·ty** \-rak-ˈtiv-ət-ē\ *n*

over against *prep* : as opposed to : in contrast with

[1]**over·age** \ˌō-və-ˈrāj\ *adj* : older than is normal for one's position, function, or grade ⟨*overage* students⟩ [[2]*over* + *age*]

[2]**over·age** \ˈōv-rij, -ə-rij\ *n* : EXCESS 1, SURPLUS [[3]*over* + *-age*]

overalls

[1]**over·all** \ˌō-və-ˈrȯl\ *adv* : as a whole : GENERALLY ⟨we find your work satisfactory, *overall*⟩

[2]**over·all** \ˌō-və-ˈrȯl, ˈō-və-ˌ\ *adj* **1** : including everything ⟨*overall* expenses⟩ **2** : viewed as a whole : GENERAL

over·alls \ˈō-və-ˌrȯlz\ *n pl* : trousers of strong material usually with a bib and shoulder straps

over and above *prep* : [1]BESIDES

over and over *adv* : many times : OFTEN

over·arm \ˈō-və-ˌrärm\ *adj* : done with the arm raised above the shoulder ⟨swim with an *overarm* stroke⟩

over·awe \ˌō-və-ˈrȯ\ *vt* : to restrain or subdue by awe

over·bal·ance \ˌō-vər-ˈbal-əns\ *vb* **1 :** to have greater weight or importance than ⟨their good qualities more than *overbalanced* their shortcomings⟩ **2 :** to lose or cause to lose balance ⟨a boat *overbalanced* by shifting cargo⟩

over·bear \ˌō-vər-ˈbaər, -ˈbeər\ *vt* **-bore** \-ˈbōr, -ˈbȯr\; **-borne** \-ˈbōrn, -ˈbȯrn\ *also* **-born** \-ˈbȯrn\; **-bear·ing 1 :** to bring down by a stronger weight or force : OVERPOWER **2 a :** to domineer over **b :** to surpass in importance or forcefulness : OUTWEIGH

over·bear·ing \-ˈbaər-ing, -ˈbeər-\ *adj* **:** blatantly arrogant : DOMINEERING — **over·bear·ing·ly** \-ing-lē\ *adv*

over·bid \ˌō-vər-ˈbid\ *vb* **-bid; -bid·ding :** to bid too high; *esp* **:** to bid more than the value of (as one's hand at cards) — **over·bid** \ˈō-vər-ˌbid\ *n*

over·bite \ˈō-vər-ˌbīt\ *n* **:** the projection of the the upper front teeth over the lower front teeth when the biting surfaces of the teeth in the upper and lower jaws are in contact

[1]**over·blown** \ˌō-vər-ˈblōn\ *adj* **:** past the prime of bloom ⟨*overblown* roses⟩ [[3]*blow*]

[2]**overblown** *adj* **1 :** excessively large in girth : FAT **2 :** PRETENTIOUS ⟨*overblown* oratory⟩ [[1]*blow*]

over·board \ˈō-vər-ˌbōrd, -ˌbȯrd\ *adv* **1 :** over the side of a ship into the water **2 :** to extremes of enthusiasm ⟨go *overboard* for a new fad⟩ **3 :** into discard : ASIDE ⟨threw the rules *overboard*⟩

over·breed \ˌō-vər-ˈbrēd\ *vt* **:** to breed (a plant or animal) to excess especially without regard to the quality of the breeding stock ⟨*overbred* dogs⟩

over·build \ˌō-vər-ˈbild\ *vb* **-built** \-ˈbilt\; **-build·ing :** to build beyond need or demand

[1]**over·bur·den** \ˌō-vər-ˈbərd-n\ *vt* **:** to burden too heavily

[2]**over·bur·den** \ˈō-vər-ˌbərd-n\ *n* **:** material overlying a deposit of useful geological materials or bedrock

over·buy \ˌō-vər-ˈbī\ *vb* **-bought** \-ˈbȯt\; **-buy·ing :** to buy beyond need or ability to pay

over·call \ˌō-vər-ˈkȯl\ *vb* **1 :** to make a higher bridge bid than (the previous bid or player) **2 :** to bid over an opponent's bid in bridge when one's partner has not bid or doubled — **over·call** \ˈō-vər-ˌkȯl\ *n*

over·cap·i·tal·ize \ˌō-vər-ˈkap-ət-l-ˌīz\ *vt* **:** to assign a value to (the capital of a business) greater than justified by assets or prospects — **over·cap·i·tal·i·za·tion** \-ˌkap-ət-l-ə-ˈzā-shən\ *n*

[1]**over·cast** *vt* **-cast; -cast·ing 1** \ˌō-vər-ˈkast, ˈō-vər-ˌ\ **:** DARKEN 1, OVERSHADOW **2** \ˈō-vər-ˌ\ **:** to sew (raw edges of a seam) with long slanting widely spaced stitches to prevent raveling

[2]**over·cast** \ˈō-vər-ˌkast, ˌō-vər-ˈ\ *adj* **:** clouded over : GLOOMY ⟨an *overcast* night⟩

[3]**over·cast** \ˈō-vər-ˌkast\ *n* **:** COVERING; *esp* **:** a covering of clouds over the sky

over·charge \ˌō-vər-ˈchärj\ *vb* **1 :** to charge too much **2 :** to load too full ⟨*overcharge* an old cannon⟩ **3 :** EXAGGERATE 1 — **over·charge** \ˈō-vər-ˌchärj\ *n*

over·class \ˈō-vər-ˌklas\ *n* **:** the highest social class **:** the segment of a society usually having the most wealth, influence, education, and prestige

over·cloud \ˌō-vər-ˈklau̇d\ *vt* **:** to overspread with clouds

over·coat \ˈō-vər-ˌkōt\ *n* **:** a warm coat worn over indoor clothing

over·come \ˌō-vər-ˈkəm\ *vb* **-came** \-ˈkām\; **-come; -com·ing 1 :** to get the better of : SURMOUNT ⟨*overcome* an enemy⟩ ⟨*overcome* temptation⟩ **2 :** to make helpless or exhausted ⟨*overcome* by gas⟩ **3 :** to gain superiority : WIN ⟨we shall *overcome*⟩

over·com·pen·sa·tion \-ˌkäm-pən-ˈsā-shən, -ˌpen-\ *n* **:** excessive compensation; *esp* **:** excessive reaction to a feeling of inferiority, guilt, or inadequacy — **over·com·pen·sate** \-ˈkäm-pən-ˌsāt\ *vb* — **over·com·pen·sa·to·ry** \-kəm-ˈpen-sə-ˌtōr-ē, -ˌtȯr-\ *adj*

over·crowd \ˌō-vər-ˈkrau̇d\ *vb* **1 :** to cause to be too crowded **2 :** to crowd together too much

over·de·vel·op \ˌō-vər-di-ˈvel-əp\ *vt* **:** to develop excessively; *esp* **:** to subject (an exposed photographic plate or film) too long to the developing process — **over·de·vel·op·ment** \-mənt\ *n*

over·do \ˌō-vər-ˈdü\ *vb* **-did** \-ˈdid\; **-done** \-ˈdən\; **-do·ing** \-ˈdü-ing\ **1 :** to do too much **2 :** EXAGGERATE 1 **3 :** to cook too long **4 :** to tire oneself

[1]**over·dose** \ˈō-vər-ˌdōs\ *n* **:** too great a dose; *also* **:** a lethal or toxic amount — **over·dos·age** \ˌō-vər-ˈdō-sij\ *n*

[2]**over·dose** \ˌō-vər-ˈdōs\ *vb* **1 :** to give an overdose or too many doses to **2 :** to take or experience an overdose ⟨*overdosed* on heroin⟩

over·draft \ˈō-vər-ˌdraft, -ˌdráft\ *n* **:** an overdrawing of a bank account; *also* **:** the amount overdrawn

over·draw \ˌō-vər-ˈdrȯ\ *vb* **-drew** \-ˈdrü\; **-drawn** \-ˈdrȯn\; **-draw·ing 1 a :** to draw checks on (a bank account) for more than the balance **b :** to make an overdraft **2 :** EXAGGERATE 1, OVERSTATE ⟨*overdrew* the dangers in the task⟩

[1]**over·dress** \ˌō-vər-ˈdres\ *vb* **:** to dress too formally for an occasion

[2]**over·dress** \ˈō-vər-ˌdres\ *n* **:** a dress worn over another

over·drive \ˈō-vər-ˌdrīv\ *n* **:** an automotive gear mechanism so arranged as to provide a higher car speed for a specific engine speed than that provided by ordinary high gear

over·due \ˌō-vər-ˈdü, -ˈdyü\ *adj* **1 a :** unpaid when due ⟨*overdue* bills⟩ **b :** delayed beyond an appointed time ⟨an *overdue* train⟩ ⟨the flight is two hours *overdue*⟩ **2 :** more than ready ⟨a country *overdue* for reform⟩

over·eat \ˌō-vər-ˈēt\ *vt* **over·ate** \-ˈāt\; **over·eat·en** \-ˈēt-n\; **over·eat·ing :** to eat to excess — **over·eat·er** \-ˈēt-ər\ *n*

over·es·ti·mate \ˌō-və-ˈres-tə-ˌmāt\ *vt* **1 :** to estimate as being more than the actual size, quantity, or number **2 :** to place too high a value on : OVERRATE — **over·es·ti·mate** \-mət\ *n* — **over·es·ti·ma·tion** \-ˌres-tə-ˈmā-shən\ *n*

over·ex·pose \ˌō-və-rik-ˈspōz\ *vt* **:** to expose excessively; *esp* **:** to expose (photographic material) for a longer time than is needed — **over·ex·po·sure** \-ˈspō-zhər\ *n*

over·ex·tend \-ˈstend\ *vt* **:** to extend or expand beyond a safe or reasonable point ⟨*overextend* credit⟩; *esp* **:** to commit (oneself) financially beyond what can be paid — **over·ex·ten·sion** \-ˈsten-chən\ *n*

over·feed \ˌō-vər-ˈfēd\ *vb* **over·fed** \-ˈfed\ **-feed·ing 1 :** to feed to excess **2 :** to eat to excess

over·fill \ˌō-vər-ˈfil\ *vb* **:** to fill to overflowing

over·fish \-ˈfish\ *vt* **:** to fish to the depletion of (a kind of fish) or to the detriment of (a fishing ground)

over·flight \ˈō-vər-ˌflīt\ *n* **:** a passage over an area in an aircraft

[1]**over·flow** \ˌō-vər-ˈflō\ *vb* **1 :** to cover with or as if with water : INUNDATE **2 :** to flow over the top or edge of ⟨the stream *overflowed* its banks⟩ **3 :** to flow over bounds ⟨the stream *overflows* every spring⟩ **4 :** to fill a space to capacity and spread beyond its limits ⟨the crowd *overflowed* into the street⟩

[2]**over·flow** \ˈō-vər-ˌflō\ *n* **1 :** a flowing over : FLOOD **2 :** SURPLUS 1, EXCESS **3 :** an outlet or receptacle for surplus liquid

over·fly \ˌō-vər-ˈflī\ *vt* **-flew** \-flü\; **-flown** \-flōn\; **-fly·ing :** to fly over especially in an aircraft or spacecraft

over·gar·ment \ˈō-vər-ˌgär-mənt\ *n* **:** an outer garment

over·glaze \-ˌglāz\ *adj* **:** applied or suitable for use over a fired glaze ⟨*overglaze* decoration on china⟩ — **overglaze** *n*

over·graze \ˌō-vər-ˈgrāz\ *vt* **:** to allow animals to graze (as a pasture) to the point of damaging the vegetation

over·grow \ˌō-vər-ˈgrō\ *vb* **-grew** \-ˈgrü\; **-grown** \-ˈgrōn\; **-grow·ing 1 :** to grow over so as to cover **2 :** to grow beyond or rise above : OUTGROW **3 :** to grow excessively **4 :** to become grown over — **over·growth** \ˈō-vər-ˌgrōth\ *n*

over·grown \ˌō-vər-ˈgrōn\ *adj* **:** grown unusually or too big ⟨*overgrown* boys⟩ ⟨*overgrown* cities⟩

[1]**over·hand** \ˈō-vər-ˌhand\ *adj* **:** made with the hand brought down from above ⟨an *overhand* tennis stroke⟩ — **overhand** *adv* — **over·hand·ed** \ˌō-vər-ˈhan-dəd\ *adv*

[2]**overhand** *n* **:** an overhand stroke (as in tennis)

overhand knot \ˌō-vər-ˌhand-, -ˌhan-\ *n* **:** a small knot often used to prevent the end of a cord from fraying — see KNOT illustration

[1]**over·hang** \ˈō-vər-ˌhang, ˌō-vər-ˈ\ *vb* **-hung** \-ˌhəng, -ˈhəng\; **-hang·ing** \-ˌhang-ing, -ˈhang-\ **1 :** to jut, project, or be suspended over **2 :** to loom over threateningly

[2]**over·hang** \ˈō-vər-ˌhang\ *n* **:** a part that overhangs ⟨the *overhang* of a roof⟩

over·haul \ˌō-vər-ˈhȯl\ *vt* **1 :** to make a thorough examination of and the necessary repairs and adjustments on ⟨*overhaul* an engine⟩ **2 :** OVERTAKE 1 — **over·haul** \ˈō-vər-ˌhȯl\ *n*

[1]**over·head** \ˌō-vər-ˈhed\ *adv* **:** above one's head : ALOFT

[2]**over·head** \ˈō-vər-ˌhed\ *adj* **1 :** operating or

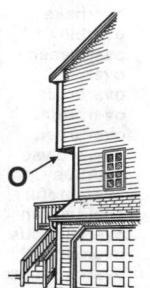

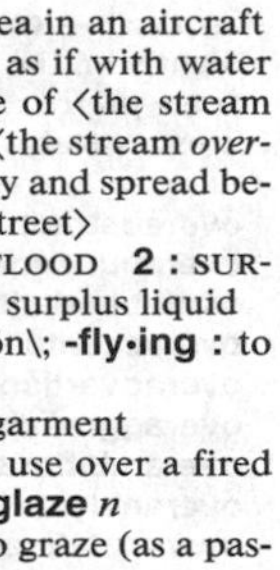

O overhang

lying above ⟨an *overhead* door⟩ **2 :** of or relating to business overhead

3**over·head** \ˈō-vər-ˌhed\ *n* **1 :** general business expenses (as rent, insurance or heating) **2 :** a stroke (as in tennis) made above head height : SMASH

over·hear \ˌō-vər-ˈhiər\ *vb* **-heard** \-ˈhərd\; **-hear·ing** \-ˈhiər-iŋ\ : to hear without the speaker's knowledge or intention

over·heat \ˌō-vər-ˈhēt\ *vb* : to heat too much : become too hot

over·joy \ˌō-vər-ˈjȯi\ *vt* : to fill with great joy

1**over·kill** \ˌō-vər-ˈkil\ *vt* : to obliterate (a target) with more nuclear force than required

2**over·kill** \ˈō-vər-ˌkil\ *n* **1 :** the capability of destroying a target with more nuclear force than required **2 :** EXCESS 1 ⟨advertising *overkill*⟩

over·land \ˈō-vər-ˌland, -lənd\ *adv or adj* : by, on, or across land

over·lap \ˌō-vər-ˈlap\ *vb* **1 :** to extend over or past and cover a part of ⟨that piece *overlaps* the edge⟩ **2 :** to have something in common or in common with ⟨political and social interests that often *overlap*⟩ **3 :** to occupy the same area in part ⟨the photos *overlap*⟩ — **over·lap** \ˈō-vər-ˌlap\ *n*

1**over·lay** \ˌō-vər-ˈlā\ *vt* **-laid** \-ˈlād\; **-lay·ing** **1 :** to lay or spread over or across : SUPERIMPOSE ⟨*overlay* silver on gold⟩ **2 :** OVERLIE 1 ⟨silver *overlaying* gold⟩

2**over·lay** \ˈō-vər-ˌlā\ *n* : something (as a veneer on wood) that is overlaid

over·leap \ˌō-vər-ˈlēp\ *vt* **1 :** to leap over or across ⟨*overleap* a ditch⟩ **2 :** to defeat (oneself) by going too far

over·lie \ˌō-vər-ˈlī\ *vt* **-lay** \-ˈlā\; **-lain** \-ˈlān\; **-ly·ing** \-ˈlī-iŋ\ **1 :** to lie over or on **2 :** to kill by lying on

over·look \ˌō-vər-ˈlu̇k\ *vt* **1 :** to look over : INSPECT **2 a :** to look down on from above **b :** to provide a view of from above ⟨the hill *overlooks* a lake⟩ **3 a :** to fail to see : MISS **b :** to pass over : IGNORE **c :** EXCUSE ⟨*overlook* a beginner's mistakes⟩ **4 :** to watch over : SUPERVISE ***synonyms*** see NEGLECT

over·lord \ˈō-vər-ˌlȯrd\ *n* **1 :** a lord who has supremacy over other lords **2 :** an absolute ruler — **over·lord·ship** \-ˌship\ *n*

over·ly \ˈō-vər-lē\ *adv* : to an excessive degree : TOO

over·man \ˌō-vər-ˈman\ *vt* : to have or get too many workers for the needs of ⟨*overman* a ship⟩

over·mas·ter \ˌō-vər-ˈmas-tər\ *vt* : SUBDUE 1

over·match \ˌō-vər-ˈmach\ *vt* **1 :** to be more than a match for : DEFEAT **2 :** to match with a superior opponent ⟨a boxer who was badly *overmatched*⟩

1**over·much** \ˌō-vər-ˈməch\ *adj or adv* : too much

2**over·much** \ˈō-vər-ˌməch, ˌō-vər-ˈ\ *n* : too great an amount

1**over·night** \ˌō-vər-ˈnīt\ *adv* **1 :** on or during the evening or night ⟨stayed away *overnight*⟩ **2 :** SUDDENLY ⟨became famous *overnight*⟩

2**overnight** *adj* **1 :** of, lasting, or staying the night ⟨an *overnight* trip⟩ ⟨*overnight* guests⟩ **2 :** SUDDEN 1a ⟨an *overnight* success⟩ **3 :** traveling during the night ⟨an *overnight* train⟩ **4 :** delivered within one day's time ⟨*overnight* mail⟩

3**over·night** \ˈō-vər-ˌnīt, ˌō-vər-ˈ\ *vb* **1 :** to stay overnight **2 :** to send (as a package or letter) by a mail service for delivery within one day's time

4**over·night** \ˈō-vər-ˌnīt\ *n* : an overnight stay

overnight bag *n* : a suitcase of a size to carry clothing and personal articles for an overnight trip — called also *overnight case*

over·night·er \ˌō-vər-ˈnī-tər\ *n* **1 :** OVERNIGHT BAG **2 :** an overnight trip **3 :** a person who stays overnight

1**over·pass** \ˌō-vər-ˈpas\ *vt* **1 :** SURPASS 1 **2 :** to pass across, over, or beyond : CROSS ⟨*overpass* the bounds of politeness⟩ **3 :** OVERLOOK 3b

2**over·pass** \ˈō-vər-ˌpas\ *n* : a crossing (as by means of a bridge) of two highways or of a highway and pedestrian path or railroad at different levels; *also* : the upper level of an overpass

over·per·suade \ˌō-vər-pər-ˈswād\ *vt* : to persuade to act contrary to conviction or preference — **over·per·sua·sion** \-ˈswā-zhən\ *n*

over·play \ˌō-vər-ˈplā\ *vt* **1 a :** to present (as a dramatic role) extravagantly **b :** to give undue emphasis **2 :** to rely too much on the strength of ⟨*overplayed* your hand⟩

over·plus \ˈō-vər-ˌpləs\ *n* : EXCESS 1, SURPLUS

over·pop·u·late \ˌō-vər-ˈpäp-yə-ˌlāt\ *vt* : to populate too densely : cause to have too great a population ⟨the city was *overpopulated* and polluted⟩

over·pop·u·la·tion \ˌō-vər-ˌpäp-yə-ˈlā-shən\ *n* : the condition of having a population so dense as to cause environmental deterioration, a reduced quality of life, or a population crash

over·pow·er \ˌō-vər-ˈpau̇-ər, -ˈpau̇r\ *vt* **1 :** to overcome by superior force : DEFEAT **2 :** OVERWHELM ⟨*overpowered* by hunger⟩

over·pow·er·ing \ˌō-vər-ˈpau̇r-iŋ\ *adj* : having great power or influence ⟨*overpowering* beauty⟩ — **over·pow·er·ing·ly** *adv*

over·pre·dict \ˌō-vər-pri-ˈdikt\ *vt* : to predict by an amount that exceeds the actual value ⟨*overpredict* inflation⟩ — **over·pre·dic·tion** \-ˈdik-shən\ *n*

over·pres·sure \ˈō-vər-ˌpresh-ər\ *n* : pressure significantly above what is usual or normal

over·price \ˌō-vər-ˈprīs\ *vb* : to price too high

1**over·print** \ˌō-vər-ˈprint\ *vt* : to print over with something additional

2**over·print** \ˈō-vər-ˌprint\ *n* : something added by overprinting; *esp* : a printed marking added to a postage or revenue stamp (as to commemorate a special event)

over·pro·por·tion \ˌō-vər-prə-ˈpōr-shən, -ˈpȯr-\ *vt* : to make disproportionately large — **overproportion** *n* — **over·pro·por·tion·ate** \-shə-nət, -shnət\ *adj* — **over·pro·por·tion·ate·ly** *adv*

over·qual·i·fied \-ˈkwäl-ə-ˌfīd\ *adj* : having more education, training, or experience than a job calls for

over·rate \ˌō-vər-ˈrāt, -və-\ *vt* : to rate, value, or estimate too highly ⟨*overrates* his importance to the team⟩

over·reach \-ˈrēch\ *vb* **1 :** to reach above or beyond **2 :** to defeat (oneself) by seeking to do or gain too much **3 :** to get the better of : OUTWIT **4 :** to go to excess — **over·reach·er** *n*

over·rep·re·sent·ed \-ˌrep-ri-ˈzent-əd\ *adj* : represented excessively; *esp* : having a number of representatives that is higher than the average — **over·rep·re·sen·ta·tion** \-ˌzen-ˈtā-shən\ *n*

over·ride \-ˈrīd\ *vt* **-rode** \-ˈrōd\; **-rid·den** \-ˈrid-n\; **-rid·ing** \-ˈrīd-iŋ\ **1 :** to ride over or across : TRAMPLE **2 :** to ride (as a horse) too much or too hard **3 a :** to prevail over : DOMINATE **b :** to set aside : ANNUL ⟨the congress *overrode* the president's veto⟩ **4 :** to extend or pass over; *esp* : OVERLAP

overriding *adj* : most important : CHIEF ⟨an *overriding* concern⟩

over·ripe \-ˈrīp\ *adj* : passed beyond maturity or ripeness toward decay ⟨an *overripe* pear⟩

over·rule \-ˈrül\ *vt* **1 :** to rule against ⟨the judge *overruled* the objection⟩ **2 :** to set aside : REVERSE ⟨a higher court *overruled* the judge's action⟩

1**over·run** \-ˈrən\ *vt* **-ran** \-ˈran\; **-run; -run·ning** **1 a** (1) **:** to defeat and occupy the positions of ⟨the enemy *overran* the outpost⟩ (2) **:** to invade and occupy or ravage **b :** to spread, swarm, or grow over : INFEST ⟨a ship *overrun* with rats⟩ ⟨weeds *overran* the garden⟩ **2 a :** to run or go beyond ⟨the plane *overran* the runway⟩ **b :** EXCEED ⟨*overran* my allotted time⟩ **3 :** to flow over ⟨the river *overran* its banks⟩

2**over·run** \ˈō-vər-ˌrən, -və-\ *n* : an act or instance of overrunning ⟨a cost *overrun*⟩; *also* : the amount by which something overruns

over·sea \ˌō-vər-ˈsē, ˈō-vər-ˌ\ *adj or adv* : OVERSEAS

over·seas \-ˈsēz, -ˌsēz\ *adv or adj* : beyond or across the sea

over·see \ˌō-vər-ˈsē\ *vt* **-saw** \-ˈsȯ\; **-seen** \-ˈsēn\; **-see·ing** **1 :** to look down upon **2 a :** to look over : EXAMINE **b :** SUPERINTEND ⟨*oversee* a road crew⟩

over·seer \ˈō-vər-ˌsiər, -ˌsē-ər, ˌō-vər-ˈ, -və-\ *n* : one that oversees : SUPERINTENDENT

over·sell \ˌō-vər-ˈsel\ *vt* **-sold** \-ˈsōld\; **-sell·ing** **1 a :** to sell too much to **b :** to sell too much of **2 :** to make excessive claims or claims for

over·set \ˌō-vər-ˈset\ *vt* **-set; -set·ting** : to turn or tip over : OVERTURN — **over·set** \ˈō-vər-ˌset\ *n*

over·sexed \ˌō-vər-ˈsekst\ *adj* : exhibiting an excessive sexual drive or interest

over·shad·ow \ˌō-vər-ˈshad-ō\ *vt* **1 :** to cast a shadow over : DARKEN **2 :** to exceed in importance : OUTWEIGH

over·shoe \ˈō-vər-ˌshü\ *n* : an outer shoe; *esp* : GALOSH

over·shoot \ˌō-vər-ˈshüt\ *vt* **-shot** \-ˈshät\; **-shoot·ing** **1 :** to pass swiftly beyond ⟨the train *overshot* the platform⟩ **2 :** to shoot or pass over or beyond so as to miss ⟨*overshot* the target⟩ ⟨the plane *overshot* the runway⟩

over·shot \ˈō-vər-ˌshät\ *adj* **1 :** having the upper jaw extending

\ə\ **abut**	\au̇\ **out**	\i\ **tip**	\ȯ\ **saw**	\u̇\ **foot**
\ər\ **further**	\ch\ **chin**	\ī\ **life**	\ȯi\ **coin**	\y\ **yet**
\a\ **mat**	\e\ **pet**	\j\ **job**	\th\ **thin**	\yü\ **few**
\ā\ **take**	\ē\ **easy**	\ŋ\ **sing**	\t͟h\ **this**	\yu̇\ **cure**
\ä\ **cot, cart**	\g\ **go**	\ō\ **bone**	\ü\ **food**	\zh\ **vision**

beyond the lower **2 :** moved by water passing over and flowing from above ⟨an *overshot* waterwheel⟩
over·sight \'ō-vər-ˌsīt\ *n* **1 :** the act or duty of overseeing : SUPERVISION **2 :** an unintentional omission or error
over·sim·pli·fy \ˌō-vər-'sim-plə-ˌfī\ *vb* : to simplify to such an extent as to bring about distortion, misunderstanding or error — **over·sim·pli·fi·ca·tion** \-ˌsim-plə-fə-'kā-shən\ *n*
over·size \ˌō-vər-'sīz\ *or* **over·sized** \-'sīzd\ *adj* : being of more than standard or ordinary size ⟨*oversize* pillows⟩ ⟨an *oversize* shirt⟩
over·skirt \'ō-vər-ˌskərt\ *n* : a skirt worn over another skirt
over·sleep \ˌō-vər-'slēp\ *vi* **-slept** \-'slept\; **-sleep·ing :** to sleep beyond the time for waking
over·spend \-'spend\ *vb* **-spent** \-'spent\; **-spend·ing 1 :** to spend more than **2 :** to spend beyond one's means or to excess
over·spread \ˌō-vər-'spred\ *vt* **-spread; -spread·ing :** to spread over or above ⟨branches *overspreading* a garden path⟩ — **over·spread** \'ō-vər-ˌspred\ *n*
over·state \ˌō-vər-'stāt\ *vt* : to state in too strong terms : EXAGGERATE — **over·state·ment** \-mənt\ *n*
over·stay \ˌō-vər-'stā\ *vt* : to stay beyond the time or the limits of ⟨*overstay* one's welcome⟩
over·step \-'step\ *vt* : to step over or go beyond : EXCEED ⟨*overstepped* their authority⟩
over·stock \ˌō-vər-'stäk\ *vb* : to stock beyond requirements or facilities — **over·stock** \'ō-vər-ˌstäk\ *n*
over·strew \ˌō-vər-'strü\ *vt* **-strewed; -strewed** *or* **-strewn** \-'strün\; **-strew·ing 1 :** to scatter about **2 :** to cover here and there
over·strung \ˌō-vər-'strəng\ *adj* : too highly strung : too sensitive
over·stuffed \ˌō-vər-'stəft\ *adj* **1 :** stuffed too full **2 :** covered completely and deeply with upholstery ⟨an *overstuffed* chair⟩
over·sub·scribe \ˌō-vər-səb-'skrīb\ *vt* : to subscribe for more of than is available, asked for, or offered for sale — **over·sub·scrip·tion** \-'skrip-shən\ *n*
over·sup·ply \ˌō-vər-sə-'plī\ *n* : SURPLUS — **oversupply** *vt*
overt \ō-'vərt, 'ō-ˌvərt, 'ō-vərt\ *adj* : open to view : MANIFEST ⟨*overt* hostility⟩ [Medieval French from *ovrir* "to open," derived from Latin *aperire*] — **overt·ly** *adv* — **overt·ness** *n*
over·take \ˌō-vər-'tāk\ *vt* **-took** \-'tu̇k\; **-tak·en** \-'tā-kən\; **-tak·ing 1 a :** to catch up with **b :** to catch up with and pass by **2 :** to come upon suddenly ⟨a blizzard *overtook* the hunting party⟩
over–the–count·er *adj* **1 :** not traded on an organized securities exchange **2 :** sold lawfully without prescription ⟨an *over-the-counter* pain reliever⟩
over·throw \ˌō-vər-'thrō\ *vt* **-threw** \-'thrü\; **-thrown** \-'thrōn\; **-throw·ing 1 :** OVERTURN 1, UPSET **2 :** to bring down : DEFEAT ⟨a government *overthrown* by rebels⟩ **3 :** to throw a ball over or past ⟨*overthrew* second base⟩ — **over·throw** \'ō-vər-ˌthrō\ *n*
over·time \'ō-vər-ˌtīm\ *n* **1 :** time exceeding a set limit; *esp* : working time exceeding a standard day or week **2 :** the wage paid for overtime work — **overtime** *adv or adj*
over·tone \'ō-vər-ˌtōn\ *n* **1 :** one of the higher tones that with the fundamental comprise a musical tone : HARMONIC 1a **2 :** a secondary effect, quality, or meaning : SUGGESTION ⟨the words carried an unfriendly *overtone*⟩
over·top \ˌō-vər-'täp\ *vt* **1 :** to rise above the top of : surpass in height ⟨*overtopped* my cousin by 3 inches⟩ **2 :** to be superior to **3 :** SURPASS
over·trick \'ō-vər-ˌtrik\ *n* : a card trick won in excess of the number bid
over·trump \ˌō-vər-'trəmp\ *vb* : to trump with a higher trump card than the highest previously played to the same trick
over·ture \'ō-vər-ˌchu̇r, -və-, -chər\ *n* **1 :** an opening offer : a first proposal ⟨made *overtures* for peace⟩ **2 a :** an orchestral introduction to a musical dramatic work **b :** an orchestral concert piece written especially as a single movement in sonata form [Middle English, literally, "opening," from Medieval French, derived from Latin *apertura* "aperture"]
over·turn \ˌō-vər-'tərn\ *vb* **1 :** to turn over : UPSET ⟨waves *overturned* the boat⟩ **2 a :** INVALIDATE, DESTROY ⟨*overturned* the group's unity⟩ **b :** REVERSE 2a ⟨*overturn* a supreme court ruling⟩ — **over·turn** \'ō-vər-ˌtərn\ *n*
over·use \ˌō-vər-'yüs\ *n* : excessive use — **over·use** \-'yüz\ *vt*
over·val·ue \ˌō-vər-'val-yü\ *vt* **1 :** to assign an excessive value to ⟨*overvalue* a stock⟩ **2 :** to value too highly : place too much importance on ⟨*overvalued* his contribution to the group's efforts⟩ — **over·val·u·a·tion** \-ˌval-yə-'wā-shən\ *n*
over·view \'ō-vər-ˌvyü\ *n* : a general survey : SUMMARY
over·watch \ˌō-vər-'wäch\ *vt* : to watch over
over·ween·ing \ˌō-vər-'wē-ning\ *adj* **1 :** unduly confident : PRESUMPTUOUS **2 :** EXCESSIVE, IMMODERATE ⟨*overweening* greed⟩ [Middle English *overwening,* present participle of *overwenen* "to be arrogant," from *over* + *wenen* "to believe"] — **over·ween·ing·ly** \-ning-lē\ *adv*
over·weigh \ˌō-vər-'wā\ *vt* **1 :** to exceed in weight : OVERBALANCE ⟨it *overweighed* other considerations⟩ **2 :** OPPRESS 2
[1]**over·weight** \'ō-vər-ˌwāt, *2 is usually* ˌō-vər-'\ *n* **1 :** weight above what is required or allowed **2 :** excessive or burdensome weight
[2]**over·weight** \ˌō-vər-'wāt\ *vt* **1 :** to give too much weight or consideration to ⟨you *overweight* their opinion⟩ **2 :** to weight excessively ⟨*overweighted* prose⟩ **3 :** OUTWEIGH
[3]**over·weight** \ˌō-vər-'wāt\ *adj* : exceeding expected, normal, or proper weight; *esp* : exceeding the bodily weight normal for one's age, height, and build
over·whelm \-'hwelm, -'welm\ *vt* **1 :** to defeat utterly **2 a :** to cover completely : SUBMERGE ⟨a wave *overwhelmed* the boat⟩ **b :** to overcome by superior force of numbers **3 :** to overpower in thought or feeling : PROSTRATE ⟨*overwhelmed* by grief⟩ [Middle English *overwhelmen,* "to upset, overthrow," from *over* + *whelmen* "to turn over, cover up"]
over·whelm·ing \-'hwel-ming, -'wel-\ *adj* : tending or serving to overwhelm ⟨*overwhelming* force⟩; *also* : EXTREME 1c, GREAT ⟨an *overwhelming* majority⟩ — **over·whelm·ing·ly** *adv*
over·win·ter \ˌō-vər-'wint-ər\ *vi* : to spend or survive the winter ⟨the butterfly *overwinters* in Mexico⟩
over·work \ˌō-vər-'wərk\ *vb* **1 :** to work or cause to work too hard, too long, or to exhaustion **2 :** to decorate all over ⟨a tombstone *overworked* with designs⟩ **3 a :** to work too much on : OVERDO **b :** to make excessive use of ⟨*overworked* phrases⟩ — **overwork** *n*
over·write \ˌō-vər-'rīt, -və-\ *vb* **-wrote** \-'rōt\; **-writ·ten** \-'rit-n\; **-writ·ing** \-'rīt-ing\ **1 :** to write over the surface of **2 :** to write in a too elaborate or pretentious style ⟨*overwritten* accounts of simple events⟩ **3 :** to write too much
over·wrought \ˌō-vər-'rȯt, -və-\ *adj* **1 :** extremely excited **2 :** decorated to excess [past participle of *overwork*]
ovi- *or* **ovo-** — see OV-
ovi·cid·al \ˌō-və-'sīd-l\ *adj* : capable of killing eggs ⟨an *ovicidal* insecticide⟩ — **ovi·cide** \'ō-və-ˌsīd\ *n*
ovi·duct \'ō-və-ˌdəkt\ *n* : a tube for the passage of eggs from the ovary of an animal
ovine \'ō-ˌvīn\ *adj* : of or relating to sheep [Late Latin *ovinus,* from Latin *ovis* "sheep"] — **ovine** *n*
ovip·a·rous \ō-'vip-rəs, -ə-rəs\ *adj* : producing eggs that develop and hatch outside the maternal body [Latin *oviparus,* from *ovum* "egg" + *parere* "to produce"]
ovi·pos·it \'ō-və-ˌpäz-ət\ *vi* : to lay eggs — used especially of insects [probably back-formation from *ovipositor*] — **ovi·po·si·tion** \ˌō-və-pə-'zish-ən\ *n*
ovi·pos·i·tor \'ō-və-ˌpäz-ət-ər\ *n* : a specialized organ (as of an insect) for depositing eggs [Latin *ovum* "egg" + *positor* "one that places," from *ponere* "to place"]
ovi·rap·tor \'ō-və-ˌrap-tər\ *n* : any of a genus of bipedal dinosaurs of the late Cretaceous period that had a toothless jaw and a crested skull and are thought to have incubated their eggs in a nest [New Latin, from Latin *ovum* "egg" + *raptor* "plunderer"]
ovoid \'ō-ˌvȯid\ *also* **ovoi·dal** \ō-'vȯid-l\ *adj* : shaped like an egg : OVATE — **ovoid** *n*
ovo·vi·vip·a·rous \ˌō-vō-ˌvī-'vip-rəs, -ə-rəs\ *adj* : producing eggs that develop within the maternal body and hatch within or immediately after release from the parent
ovu·late \'äv-yə-ˌlāt, 'ōv-\ *vi* : to produce eggs or discharge them from an ovary — **ovu·la·tion** \ˌäv-yə-'lā-shən, ˌōv-\ *n*
ovule \'äv-ˌyül, 'ōv-\ *n* **1 :** an outgrowth of the ovary of a seed plant that after fertilization develops into a seed **2 :** a small egg; *esp* : one in an early stage of growth [New Latin *ovulum,* from Latin *ovum* "egg"] — **ovu·lar** \-yə-lər\ *adj*
ovum \'ō-vəm\ *n, pl* **ova** \-və\ : a female gamete : MACROGAMETE — called also *egg, egg cell* [Latin, "egg"]
ow \'au̇, 'ü\ *interj* — used to express sudden pain
owe \'ō\ *vb* **1 :** to have (an emotion or attitude) to someone or something ⟨*owes* the boss a grudge⟩ **2 a (1) :** to be under obligation to pay or repay ⟨*owes* me $5⟩ **(2) :** to be obligated to

render (as duty or a service) **b** : to be indebted to ⟨*owes* the grocer for supplies⟩ **c** : to be in debt ⟨*owes* for the house⟩ [Old English *āgan* "to possess, own, owe"] — **owe it** : to have a responsibility to do something ⟨*owes it* to voters to explain his reasons⟩

ow·ing \ˈō-iŋ\ *adj* : due to be paid

owing to *prep* : BECAUSE OF ⟨delayed *owing to* traffic⟩

owl \ˈau̇l\ *n* : any of an order (Strigiformes) of birds of prey that are active chiefly at night and have a large head and eyes, short hooked bill, and strong talons [Old English *ūle*]

owl

owl·et \ˈau̇-lət\ *n* : a young or small owl

owl·ish \ˈau̇-lish\ *adj* : resembling or suggesting an owl — **owl·ish·ly** *adv* — **owl·ish·ness** *n*

[1]**own** \ˈōn\ *adj* : belonging to oneself or itself — usually used following a possessive case or possessive adjective ⟨wanted my *own* room⟩ [Old English *āgen*]

[2]**own** *vb* **1 a** : to have or hold as property : POSSESS **b** : to have power or control over ⟨wanted to *own* her own life⟩ **2** : ACKNOWLEDGE, ADMIT ⟨*own* a debt⟩ **3** : CONFESS — used with *to* or *up* ⟨*owned* to being scared⟩ ⟨if you broke the window, *own up*⟩ — **own·er** \ˈō-nər\ *n* — **own·er·ship** \-ˌship\ *n*

[3]**own** *pron, sing or pl in constr* : one or ones belonging to oneself — used after a possessive and without a following noun ⟨want rooms of their *own*⟩ — **on one's own** **1** : for or by oneself : without help or control ⟨made the decision *on his own*⟩ **2** : left to rely entirely on one's own resources ⟨if you mess up, you're *on your own*⟩

ox \ˈäks\ *n, pl* **ox·en** \ˈäk-sən\ *also* **ox** **1** : a common large domestic bovine mammal kept for milk, draft, and meat and of which the female is a cow and the male a bull; *esp* : an adult castrated male **2** : any of various related bovine mammals (as the buffalo) [Old English *oxa*]

ox- *or* **oxo-** *combining form* : oxygen [French, from *oxygène*]

ox·a·late \ˈäk-sə-ˌlāt\ *n* : a salt or ester of oxalic acid

ox·al·ic acid \äk-ˌsal-ik-\ *n* : a poisonous strong acid $C_2H_2O_4$ that occurs in various plants (as spinach) as oxalates and is used especially as a bleaching or cleaning agent and in making dyes [French *acide oxalique,* from Latin *oxalis* "wood sorrel"]

ox·al·is \äk-ˈsal-əs\ *n* : WOOD SORREL [Latin, from Greek, from *oxys* "sharp"]

ox·blood \ˈäks-ˌbləd\ *n* : a moderate reddish brown

ox·bow \ˈäks-ˌbō\ *n* **1** : a U-shaped collar worn by a draft ox **2 a** : a U-shaped bend in a river **b** : a U-shaped lake formed when such a bend becomes isolated when bypassed by the river channel — called also *oxbow lake* — **oxbow** *adj*

ox·cart \-ˌkärt\ *n* : a cart drawn by oxen

ox·eye \ˈäk-ˌsī\ *n* : any of several plants related to the daisies and having heads with both disk and ray flowers; *esp* : DAISY 1b

oxeye daisy *n* : DAISY 1b

ox·ford \ˈäks-fərd\ *n* **1** : a low shoe laced or tied over the instep **2** : a soft durable cotton or synthetic fabric made in plain or basket weaves — called also *oxford cloth* [*Oxford,* England]

ox·heart \ˈäks-ˌhärt\ *n* : any of various large sweet cherries

ox·i·dant \ˈäk-səd-ənt\ *n* : OXIDIZING AGENT

ox·i·dase \ˈäk-sə-ˌdās, -ˌdāz\ *n* : any of various enzymes that catalyze oxidations

ox·i·da·tion \ˌäk-sə-ˈdā-shən\ *n* **1** : the process of oxidizing **2** : the state or result of being oxidized — **ox·i·da·tive** \ˈäk-sə-ˌdāt-iv\ *adj*

oxidation–reduction *n* : a chemical reaction in which one or more electrons are transferred from one atom or molecule to another

oxidation state *n* : a positive or negative number that represents the effective charge of an atom or element and indicates the extent of or possibility of its oxidation ⟨the usual *oxidation state* of sodium is +1 and of oxygen −2⟩ — called also *oxidation number*

ox·ide \ˈäk-ˌsīd\ *n* : a compound of oxygen with another element or a chemical group [French, from *ox-* (from *oxygène* "oxygen" + *-ide* (from *acide* "acid")]

ox·i·dize \ˈäk-sə-ˌdīz\ *vb* **1** : to combine with oxygen **2** : to dehydrogenate especially by the action of oxygen **3** : to remove one or more electrons from (an atom, ion, or molecule) **4** : to become oxidized — **ox·i·diz·er** *n*

oxidizing agent *n* : a substance (as oxygen or nitric acid) that oxidizes by taking up electrons

Ox·o·ni·an \äk-ˈsō-nē-ən\ *n* : a student or graduate of Oxford University [Medieval Latin *Oxonia* "Oxford"] — **Oxonian** *adj*

ox·tail \ˈäk-ˌstāl\ *n* : the tail of cattle; *esp* : the skinned tail for use as food (as in soup)

oxy \ˈäk-sē\ *adj* : OXYGENIC; *esp* : containing oxygen or additional oxygen — often used in combination ⟨*oxy*hemoglobin⟩ ⟨*oxy*hydrogen⟩ [French, from *oxygène* "oxygen"]

oxy·acet·y·lene \ˌäk-sē-ə-ˈset-l-ən, -l-ˌēn\ *adj* : of, relating to, or utilizing a mixture of oxygen and acetylene ⟨*oxyacetylene* torch⟩

ox·y·gen \ˈäk-si-jən\ *n* : a reactive element that is found in water, rocks and minerals, many organic compounds, and free as a colorless tasteless odorless gas in the atmosphere of which it forms about 21 percent, that is capable of combining with all elements except the inert gases, that is active in physiological processes, and that is involved in combustion processes — see ELEMENT table [French *oxygène,* from Greek *oxys* "sharp, acidic" + French *-gène* "-gen"]

ox·y·gen·ate \ˈäk-si-jə-ˌnāt, äk-ˈsij-ə-\ *vt* : to impregnate, combine, or supply (as blood) with oxygen — **ox·y·gen·ation** \ˌäk-si-jə-ˈnā-shən, äk-ˌsij-ə-\ *n*

oxygen debt *n* : a cumulative deficit of oxygen that develops during periods of intense bodily activity and must be made good when the body returns to rest

ox·y·gen·ic \ˌäk-si-ˈjen-ik\ *adj* **1** : of or relating to oxygen **2** : generating or producing oxygen ⟨*oxygenic* photosynthesis⟩

oxygen mask *n* : a device worn over the nose and mouth through which oxygen is supplied from a storage tank

oxygen tent *n* : a canopy which can be placed over a bedridden person and within which a flow of oxygen can be maintained

oxy·he·mo·glo·bin \ˌäk-si-ˈhē-mə-ˌglō-bən\ *n* : a compound of hemoglobin with oxygen that is the chief means of transportation of oxygen from the air (as in the lungs) by way of the blood to the tissues

oxy·hy·dro·gen \ˌäk-si-ˈhī-drə-jən\ *adj* : of, relating to, or utilizing a mixture of oxygen and hydrogen ⟨an *oxyhydrogen* torch⟩

ox·y·mo·ron \ˌäk-si-ˈmōr-ˌän, -ˈmȯr-\ *n, pl* **oxymorons** *also* **ox·y·mo·ra** \-ˈmōr-ə, -ˈmȯr-ə\ : a combination of contradictory or incongruous words (as *cruel kindness*) [Late Greek *oxymōron,* from *oxymōros* "pointedly foolish," from Greek *oxys* "sharp, keen" + *mōros* "foolish"] — **ox·y·mo·ron·ic** \-mə-ˈrän-ik\ *adj* — **ox·y·mo·ron·i·cal·ly** \-i-klē, -kə-lē\ *adv*

oxy·to·cin \ˌäk-si-ˈtōs-n\ *n* : a pituitary hormone that stimulates the contraction of smooth muscle in the uterus and the secretion of milk [derived from Greek *oxys* "sharp, quick" + *tokos* "childbirth," from *tiktein* "to bear"]

oy \ˈȯi\ *interj* — used especially to express annoyance or dismay ⟨*oy,* what a mess⟩ [Yiddish]

oyez \ō-ˈyā, -ˈyes\ *imperative verb* — used by a court or public crier to gain attention before a proclamation [Medieval French, "hear ye," from *oir* "to hear," from Latin *audire*]

oys·ter \ˈȯi-stər\ *n* : any of various marine bivalve mollusks having a rough irregular shell and including important edible shellfish [Medieval French *oistre,* from Latin *ostrea,* from Greek *ostreon*]

oyster bed *n* : a place where oysters grow or are cultivated

oyster catcher *n* : any of a genus of wading birds with stout legs, a heavy wedge-shaped bill, and often black and white plumage

oyster cracker *n* : a small salted usually round cracker

oys·ter·man \ˈȯi-stər-mən\ *n* : a gatherer, opener, breeder, or seller of oysters

oyster plant *n* : SALSIFY

Oz \ˈäz\ *n* : an ideal or fantastical place [from *Oz,* mythical land in a series of books by L. Frank Baum]

ozone \ˈō-ˌzōn\ *n* **1** : a form O_3 of oxygen that has three atoms in the molecule, is a faintly blue irritating gas with a pungent odor, and is used especially in disinfection and deodorization and in oxidation and bleaching **2** : pure and refreshing air

\ə\ **a**but	\au̇\ **ou**t	\i\ t**i**p	\ȯ\ s**aw**	\u̇\ f**oo**t
\ər\ f**ur**ther	\ch\ **ch**in	\ī\ l**i**fe	\ȯi\ c**oi**n	\y\ **y**et
\a\ m**a**t	\e\ p**e**t	\j\ **j**ob	\th\ **th**in	\yü\ f**ew**
\ā\ t**a**ke	\ē\ **ea**sy	\ŋ\ si**ng**	\t͟h\ **th**is	\yu̇\ c**u**re
\ä\ c**o**t, c**a**rt	\g\ **g**o	\ō\ b**o**ne	\ü\ f**oo**d	\zh\ vi**si**on

[German *Ozon,* from Greek *ozōn,* present participle of *ozein* "to smell"] — **ozo·nic** \ō-ˈzō-nik\ *adj* — **ozo·nif·er·ous** \ˌō-ˌzō-ˈnif-rəs, -ə-rəs\ *adj*

ozone hole *n* **:** an area of the ozone layer (as near the south pole) that is seasonally depleted of ozone

ozone layer *n* **:** an atmospheric layer at heights of about 20 to 30 miles (32 to 48 kilometers) that is normally characterized by high ozone content which blocks most solar ultraviolet radiation from entry into the lower atmosphere

ozo·no·sphere \ō-ˈzō-nə-ˌsfiər\ *n* **:** OZONE LAYER

P

p \ˈpē\ *n, pl* **p's** *or* **ps** \ˈpēz\ *often cap* **:** the 16th letter of the English alphabet

pa \ˈpä, ˈpȯ\ *n* **:** FATHER 1a [short for *papa*]

PABA \ˈpab-ə, ˌpē-ˌā-ˈbē-ˌā\ *n* **:** PARA-AMINOBENZOIC ACID [*para-aminobenzoic acid*]

pab·u·lum \ˈpab-yə-ləm\ *n* **:** FOOD; *esp* **:** a suspension or solution of nutrients suitable for absorption [Latin, "food, fodder"]

pa·ca \ˈpäk-ə, ˈpak-\ *n* **:** either of two large South and Central American rodents usually with a white-spotted brownish coat [Portuguese from Tupi *páka*]

[1]pace \ˈpās\ *n* **1 a :** rate of movement; *esp* **:** an established rate of moving from place to place **b :** rate of progress ⟨the *pace* of the story was slow⟩ **2 a :** a manner of walking **:** TREAD **b :** GAIT; *esp* **:** a fast 2-beat gait of a horse in which the legs on the same side move in pairs and support the animal alternately on the right and left **3 :** a single step or a measure based on the length of a human step [Medieval French *pas* "step," from Latin *passus,* from *pandere* "to spread"]

[2]pace *vb* **1 a :** to walk with slow measured steps ⟨*paced* to and fro⟩ **b :** to move along **:** PROCEED **2 :** to go or cover at a pace — used of a horse **3 a :** to measure by paces — often used with *off* **b :** to cover at a walk ⟨could hear him *pacing* the floor⟩ ⟨*pace* off twenty feet⟩ **4 a :** to set or regulate the pace of **b :** PRECEDE 2, LEAD **c :** to keep pace with — **pac·er** *n*

pace·mak·er \ˈpā-ˌsmā-kər\ *n* **1 :** one that sets the pace for another **2 a :** a group of cells or a bodily part (as of the heart) that serves to establish and maintain a rhythmic activity **b :** an electrical device for steadying or establishing the heartbeat

pa·chi·si \pə-ˈchē-zē\ *n* **:** an ancient board game played with dice and counters [Hindi and Urdu *pacīsī* from *pacīs* "twenty-five"]

pachy·derm \ˈpak-i-ˌdərm\ *n* **:** any of various usually thick-skinned mammals (as an elephant or a rhinoceros) that have hooves or nails resembling hooves; *esp* **:** ELEPHANT [French *pachyderme,* from Greek *pachydermos* "thick-skinned," from *pachys* "thick" + *derma* "skin"] — **pachy·der·ma·tous** \ˌpak-i-ˈdər-mət-əs\ *adj*

pach·ys·an·dra \ˌpak-ə-ˈsan-drə\ *n* **:** any of a genus of evergreen perennial trailing plants often used as a ground cover [derived from Greek *pachys* "thick" + *andr-, anēr* "man"]

pa·cif·ic \pə-ˈsif-ik\ *adj* **1 a :** tending to lessen conflict **b :** rejecting the use of force as an instrument of policy **2 a :** having a soothing appearance or effect ⟨mild *pacific* breezes⟩ **b :** having a mild and calm nature **:** PEACEABLE ⟨a quiet *pacific* people⟩ [Latin *pacificus,* from *pac-, pax* "peace"] — **pa·cif·i·cal·ly** \-ˈsif-i-kə-lē, -klē\ *adv*

pac·i·fi·ca·tion \ˌpas-ə-fə-ˈkā-shən\ *n* **:** the act or process of pacifying **:** the state of being pacified

Pacific salmon *n* **:** SALMON 1b

Pacific time *n* **:** the time of the 8th time zone west of Greenwich that includes the Pacific coastal region of the U.S.

pac·i·fi·er \ˈpas-ə-ˌfī-ər, -ˌfīr\ *n* **1 :** one that pacifies **2 :** a usually nipple-shaped device for babies to suck on

pac·i·fism \ˈpas-ə-ˌfiz-əm\ *n* **:** opposition to war or violence as a means of settling disputes; *esp* **:** refusal to bear arms on moral or religious grounds — **pac·i·fist** \-fəst\ *n* — **pacifist** *or* **pac·i·fis·tic** \ˌpas-ə-ˈfis-tik\ *adj*

pac·i·fy \ˈpas-ə-ˌfī\ *vt* **-fied; -fy·ing 1 :** to ease the anger or agitation of **:** SOOTHE ⟨*pacify* a crying child⟩ **2 :** to restore to a peaceful state **:** SUBDUE ⟨*pacify* a country⟩ [Latin *pacificare,* from *pac-, pax* "peace"] — **pac·i·fi·able** \-ˌfī-ə-bəl\ *adj*

synonyms PACIFY, APPEASE, PLACATE, MOLLIFY mean to calm the feelings of. PACIFY suggests a soothing or calming ⟨*pacified* by a sincere apology⟩. APPEASE implies quieting insistent demands by making concessions ⟨some were willing to *appease* the dictator in order to keep peace⟩. PLACATE suggests changing resentment or bitterness to goodwill ⟨the builders *placated* the people of the neighborhood by including a playground in their plans⟩. MOLLIFY implies soothing hurt feelings or rising anger ⟨a speech that *mollified* the demonstrators⟩.

[1]pack \ˈpak\ *n* **1 a :** a bundle arranged for carrying especially on the back **b :** a group or pile of related objects ⟨a *pack* of cards⟩ **2 :** a large amount or number **:** HEAP ⟨a *pack* of lies⟩ **3 :** an act, instance, or method of packing; *also* **:** arrangement in a pack **4 a :** a group of often predatory animals of the same kind ⟨a wolf *pack*⟩ **b :** a group of persons with a common interest ⟨a *pack* of thieves⟩ **c :** an organized troop (as of Cub Scouts) **5 :** a concentrated or compacted mass (as of snow or ice) **6 :** absorbent material (as gauze pads) used to apply medicine or moisture or to press upon a bodily part or plug body openings in order to stop bleeding — compare ICE PACK 2 **7 a :** a cosmetic paste for the face **b :** an application or treatment of oils or creams for conditioning the scalp and hair [Middle English, of Low German or Dutch origin]

[2]pack *vb* **1 a :** to make into a compact bundle ⟨*pack* papers into an envelope⟩ **b :** to stow one's personal belongings in luggage ⟨I'll go home and *pack*⟩ **c :** to fill completely ⟨the stadium was *packed*⟩ **d :** to arrange closely and securely in a protective container ⟨glasses *packed* for shipment⟩ **2 a :** to crowd together so as to fill full **:** CRAM ⟨the crowd was *packed* into the hall⟩ **b :** to increase the density of **:** COMPRESS **3 :** to fill or cover so as to prevent passage (as of air or steam) ⟨*pack* a joint in a pipe⟩ **4 a :** to send or go away without ceremony ⟨*pack* the children off to school⟩ **b :** to bring to an end **:** GIVE UP — used with *up* or *in* ⟨might *pack* up the assignment⟩ — used especially in the phrase *pack it in* **5 a :** to transport on foot or on the back of an animal ⟨*pack* water from a spring⟩ **b :** to wear or carry as equipment ⟨*pack* a gun⟩ **c :** to be supplied or equipped with **:** POSSESS ⟨a storm *packing* hurricane winds⟩ **6 :** to assemble in a group **:** CONGREGATE — **pack·abil·i·ty** \ˌpak-ə-ˈbil-ət-ē\ *n* — **pack·able** \ˌpak-ə-bəl\ *adj*

[3]pack *vt* **:** to influence the makeup of so as to bring about a desired result ⟨*pack* a jury⟩ [obsolete *pack* "to make a secret agreement"]

[1]pack·age \ˈpak-ij\ *n* **1 a :** a small or moderate-sized pack **:** PARCEL **b :** a unit of a product uniformly wrapped or sealed **2 :** a covering wrapper or container **3 :** something that suggests a package: as **a :** PACKAGE DEAL **b :** a collection of related items to be considered together ⟨presented his tax *package* to the nation⟩

[2]package *vt* **:** to make into or enclose in a package — **pack·ag·er** *n*

package deal *n* **:** an offer or agreement involving a number of related items or one making acceptance of one item dependent on the acceptance of another

package store *n* **:** a store that sells alcoholic beverages only in containers that may not lawfully be opened on the premises

pack animal *n* **:** an animal (as a horse or donkey) used for carrying packs

packed \ˈpakt\ *adj* **1 a :** COMPRESSED ⟨*packed* snow⟩ **b :** that is crowded or stuffed — often used in combination ⟨an action-

packed story⟩ **2 :** filled to capacity ⟨played to a *packed* house⟩

pack·er \ˈpak-ər\ *n* **:** one that packs: as **a :** a dealer who prepares and packs foods for the market ⟨a meat *packer*⟩ **b :** [2]PORTER 1 **c :** one that conveys goods on pack animals

pack·et \ˈpak-ət\ *n* **1 :** a small bundle or parcel **2 :** a passenger boat carrying mail and cargo on a regular schedule [Medieval French *pacquet,* of Germanic origin]

pack·horse \ˈpak-ˌhȯrs\ *n* **:** a horse used as a pack animal

pack ice *n* **:** sea ice formed into a mass by the crushing together of chunks and sheets of ice

pack·ing \ˈpak-ing\ *n* **:** material used to pack or caulk something

pack·ing·house \ˈpak-ing-ˌhau̇s\ *n* **:** an establishment for processing and packing foodstuffs and especially meat and its by-products — called also *packing plant*

pack rat *n* **1 :** WOOD RAT; *esp* **:** a bushy-tailed rodent of western North America that hoards food and miscellaneous objects **2 :** a person who collects or hoards especially unneeded items

pack·sack \ˈpak-ˌsak\ *n* **:** a case used to carry gear on the back when traveling on foot **:** BACKPACK

pack·sad·dle \ˈpak-ˌsad-l\ *n* **:** a saddle that supports the load on the back of a pack animal

pack·thread \-ˌthred\ *n* **:** strong thread or small twine used for sewing or tying packs or parcels

pact \ˈpakt\ *n* **:** [4]COMPACT; *esp* **:** an international treaty [Medieval French, from Latin *pactum,* from *pacisci* "to agree, contract"]

[1]**pad** \ˈpad\ *vb* **pad·ded; pad·ding 1 :** to go on foot **2 :** to move along with a muffled step [perhaps from Dutch *paden* "to follow a path," from *pad* "path"]

[2]**pad** *n* **1 a :** a thin flat mat or cushion **b :** padding used to shape an article of clothing **c :** a guard worn to shield body parts against impact **d :** a piece of usually folded absorbent material (as gauze) **e :** a piece of material that holds ink for inking the surface of a rubber stamp **2 a :** the foot of some mammals (as foxes) **b :** the cushioned bottom of the foot or toes of some mammals (as dogs) **3 :** a floating leaf of a water plant **4 :** a collection of sheets of paper glued together at one end **5 :** LAUNCHPAD **6 a :** BED 1a **b :** living quarters [origin unknown]

[3]**pad** *vt* **pad·ded; pad·ding 1 :** to furnish with a pad or padding **2 :** to expand or increase especially with needless misleading or fraudulent matter ⟨*pad* the sales figures⟩

[4]**pad** *n* **:** a soft muffled or slapping sound [imitative]

pad·ding \ˈpad-ing\ *n* **:** material used to pad something

[1]**pad·dle** \ˈpad-l\ *vi* **pad·dled; pad·dling** \ˈpad-ling, -l-ing\ **1 :** to move the hands or feet about in shallow water **2 :** TODDLE ⟨the small child *paddled* over to them⟩ [origin unknown]

[2]**paddle** *n* **1 a :** an implement with a flat blade to propel and steer a small craft (as a canoe) **b :** an implement used for stirring, mixing, or hitting **c :** a short bat with a broad flat blade used to hit the ball in various games (as table tennis) **d :** a small usually numbered sign that is raised by a bidder at an auction to signal a bid **2 :** one of the broad boards at the circumference of a paddle wheel or waterwheel **3 :** a small hand-held device with a dial used to control movement of an object along a line on a computer display screen [Middle English *padell* "spade-shaped tool for cleaning a plow"]

[3]**paddle** *vb* **pad·dled; pad·dling** \ˈpad-ling, -l-ing\ **1 :** to go, propel, or carry by or as if by means of a paddle or paddle wheel **2 a :** to beat or stir with or as if with a paddle **b :** to punish with or as if with a paddle — **pad·dler** \ˈpad-lər, -l-ər\ *n*

pad·dle·fish \ˈpad-l-ˌfish\ *n* **:** a large food fish of the Mississippi River valley with a paddle-shaped snout and with roe used in caviar

paddle wheel *n* **:** a wheel with paddles around its circumference used to propel a boat

pad·dock \ˈpad-ək, -ik\ *n* **:** a usually enclosed area used especially for pasturing or exercising animals; *esp* **:** an enclosure where racehorses are saddled and paraded before a race [alteration of Middle English *parrok,* from Old English *pearroc* from Medieval Latin *parricus*]

pad·dy \ˈpad-ē\ *n, pl* **paddies 1 :** RICE; *esp* **:** threshed unmilled rice **2 :** wet land in which rice is grown [Malay *padi*]

pad·dy wagon \ˈpad-ē-\ *n* **:** PATROL WAGON [probably from English slang *Paddy* "Irishman, policeman," from *Paddy,* nickname for *Patrick*]

pad·lock \ˈpad-ˌläk\ *n* **:** a removable lock with a hinged bow-shaped piece attached at one end so that the other end can be passed through a staple (as on a hasp) and then snapped into a catch in the lock [Middle English *padlok* from *pad-* (of unknown origin + *lok* "lock"] — **padlock** *vt*

pa·dre \ˈpäd-rā, -rē\ *n* **1 :** a Christian clergyman; *esp* **:** PRIEST **2 :** a military chaplain [Spanish or Italian or Portuguese, literally, "father," from Latin *pater*]

pae·an \ˈpē-ən\ *n* **:** a joyous song of praise, tribute, thanksgiving, or triumph [Latin, "hymn of thanksgiving especially to Apollo," from Greek *paian,* from *Paian,* epithet of Apollo]

paed- *or* **paedo-** — see PED-

pa·el·la \pä-ˈel-ə, -ˈā-yə\ *n* **:** a saffron-flavored dish containing rice, meat, seafood, and vegetables [Catalan, literally, "pot, pan," from Middle French *paelle,* from Latin *patella* "small pan"]

pa·gan \ˈpā-gən\ *n* **1 :** HEATHEN 1 **2 :** an irreligious person **3 :** NEO-PAGAN [Late Latin *paganus,* from Latin, "country dweller," from *pagus* "country district"] — **pagan** *adj* — **pa·gan·ish** \-gə-nish\ *adj* — **pa·gan·ism** \-gə-ˌniz-əm\ *n* — **pa·gan·ize** \-gə-ˌnīz\ *vt*

[1]**page** \ˈpāj\ *n* **1 :** a medieval youth being trained for knighthood in the service of a knight; *also* **:** a youth attending a person of rank **2 :** one employed to deliver messages, assist patrons, or serve as a guide [Medieval French]

[2]**page** *vt* **1 :** to serve in the capacity of a page **2 :** to summon by calling out the name of **3 :** to contact via a pager

[3]**page** *n* **1 a :** one side of a printed or written leaf; *also* **:** the entire leaf **b :** the matter printed or written on a page ⟨set several *pages* of type⟩ **2 a :** a written record ⟨the *pages* of history⟩ **b :** an event or circumstance worth recording ⟨an exciting *page* in one's life⟩ **3 a :** a large section of computer memory **b :** the information found at a single World Wide Web address ⟨a Web *page*⟩ [Middle French, from Latin *pagina*]

[4]**page** *vt* **1 :** to number or mark the pages of **2 :** to turn the pages (as of a book) especially in a quick steady manner

pag·eant \ˈpaj-ənt\ *n* **1 a :** a mere show **:** PRETENSE **b :** a showy display **2 :** a usually elaborate entertainment consisting of scenes based on history or legend ⟨a Christmas *pageant*⟩ [Middle English *padgeant,* literally, "scene of a play," from Medieval French *pagine, pagent,* from Medieval Latin *pagina,* perhaps from Latin, "page"]

pag·eant·ry \ˈpaj-ən-trē\ *n, pl* **-ries 1 :** pageants and the presentation of pageants **2 :** colorful, rich, or splendid display

page boy *n* **1 :** a boy serving as a page **2** *usually* **page·boy** \ˈpāj-ˌbȯi\ **:** a woman's often shoulder-length haircut with the ends turned under in a smooth roll

pag·er \ˈpā-jər\ *n* **:** one that pages; *esp* **:** a small electronic device that beeps, vibrates, or flashes when it receives a special radio signal in order to alert the person carrying it to an incoming message

pag·i·nate \ˈpaj-ə-ˌnāt\ *vt* **:** [4]PAGE 1

pag·i·na·tion \ˌpaj-ə-ˈnā-shən\ *n* **1 :** the paging of written or printed matter **2 :** the number and arrangement of pages (as of a book) or an indication of these

pa·go·da \pə-ˈgōd-ə\ *n* **:** an east Asian temple or memorial in the form of a tower usually with roofs curving upward at the division of each of several stories [Portuguese *pagode* "statue of a deity, Hindu or Buddhist temple"]

paid *past of* PAY

pail \ˈpāl\ *n* **:** a usually cylindrical vessel that is open at the top and has a handle **:** BUCKET [Middle English *payle, paille*] — **pail·ful** \-ˌfu̇l\ *n*

[1]**pain** \ˈpān\ *n* **1** *pl* **:** PUNISHMENT ⟨prescribed *pains* and penalties⟩ **2 a** (1) **:** physical suffering associated with disease, injury, or other bodily disorder ⟨a *pain* in the back⟩ ⟨in constant *pain*⟩ (2) **:** a basic bodily sensation induced by a harmful stimulus, characterized by physical discomfort (as pricking, throbbing, or aching), and typically leading to attempts to escape its cause **b :** acute mental or emotional distress **:** GRIEF **3** *pl* **:** the suffering experienced during childbirth **4** *pl* **:** care or effort taken in accomplishing something ⟨took *pains* with their work⟩ **5 :** someone or something that annoys or is trouble-

some ⟨studying can be a real *pain*⟩ [Medieval French *peine,* from Latin *poena,* from Greek *poinē* "payment, penalty"] *synonyms* see EFFORT — **pain** *adj* — **pain·less** \-ləs\ *adj* — **pain·less·ly** *adv* — **pain·less·ness** *n* — **on pain of** *or* **under pain of** : subject to penalty or punishment by — **pain in the neck** : a source of annoyance : NUISANCE

[2]**pain** *vb* **1** : to cause pain in or to : HURT **2** : to give or experience pain

pain·ful \ˈpān-fəl\ *adj* **1 a** : feeling or giving pain **b** : that troubles or distresses ⟨a *painful* interview⟩ **2** : requiring effort or care — **pain·ful·ly** \-fə-lē\ *adv* — **pain·ful·ness** *n*

pagoda

pain·kill·er \ˈpān-ˌkil-ər\ *n* : something (as a drug) that relieves pain — **pain·kill·ing** \-ing\ *adj*

pains·tak·ing \ˈpān-ˌstā-king\ *adj* : marked by diligent care and effort — **pains·tak·ing·ly** \-king-lē\ *adv*

[1]**paint** \ˈpānt\ *vb* **1** : to apply paint or a comparable covering or coloring substance to ⟨*paint* a wall⟩ **2 a** : to represent in lines and colors on a surface by applying pigments ⟨*paint* a picture⟩ **b** : to produce or evoke as if by painting ⟨*paints* glowing pictures of their vacation⟩ **3** : to practice the art of painting **4** : to use cosmetics [Medieval French *peint* "painted," from *peindre* "to paint," from Latin *pingere* "to tattoo, embroider, paint"]

[2]**paint** *n* **1** : MAKEUP; *esp* : a cosmetic to add color **2 a** : a mixture of a pigment and a suitable liquid to form a closely adherent coating when spread on a surface in a thin coat **b** : an applied coating of paint ⟨scrape old *paint* from woodwork⟩

paint·brush \ˈpānt-ˌbrəsh\ *n* **1** : a brush for applying paint **2 a** : INDIAN PAINTBRUSH 1 **b** : ORANGE HAWKWEED

painted bunting *n* : a brightly colored bunting found from the southern U.S. to Panama

painted lady *n* : a migratory butterfly with wings mottled in brown, orange, black, and white

painted turtle *n* : a common freshwater turtle of North America with a greenish black upper shell with yellow bands and red markings and a yellow lower shell

[1]**paint·er** \ˈpānt-ər\ *n* : one that paints: as **a** : an artist who paints **b** : a worker who applies paint as an occupation — **paint·er·ly** \-lē\ *adj*

[2]**pain·ter** \ˈpānt-ər\ *n* : a line used for securing or towing a boat [Middle English *paynter,* probably from Middle French (dialect of Normandy) *pentoir, penteur* "clothesline," from *pendre* "to hang"]

[3]**pain·ter** *n* : COUGAR [alteration of *panther*]

paint·ing \ˈpānt-ing\ *n* **1** : a product of painting; *esp* : a painted work of art **2** : the art or occupation of painting

[1]**pair** \ˈpaər, ˈpeər\ *n, pl* **pairs** *also* **pair 1** : two corresponding things either naturally matched or intended to be used together ⟨a *pair* of gloves⟩ **2** : a single unit made up of two corresponding pieces ⟨a *pair* of scissors⟩ **3** : a set of two: as **a** : two mated animals **b** : a couple in love, engaged, or married **c** : two members of a deliberative body who hold opposing views and agree not to vote on a specific issue **4** *chiefly dialect* : a set or series of small objects (as beads) [Medieval French *paire,* from Latin *paria* "equal things," from *par* "equal"]

[2]**pair** *vb* : to join in a pair or in pairs ⟨*paired* the guests⟩

pair of compasses : COMPASS 2c

pai·sa \pī-ˈsä\ *n* **1** *pl* **paisa** : a monetary unit of Nepal and Pakistan equal to 1/100 rupee **2** *pl* **pai·se** \-ˈsā\ : a monetary unit equal to 1/100 Indian rupee **3** : a coin representing one paisa [Hindi & Urdu *paisā,* originally a quarter-anna coin]

pais·ley \ˈpāz-lē\ *adj, often cap* **1** : made typically of soft wool with colorful curved abstract figures **2** : having a pattern like that of a paisley fabric [*Paisley,* Scotland] — **paisley** *n*

Pai·ute \ˈpī-ˌüt, -ˌyüt\ *n* **1** : a member of an American Indian people originally of Utah, Arizona, Nevada, and California **2** : the languages of the Paiute people

pa·ja·mas \pə-ˈjäm-əz, -ˈjam-\ *n pl* : a loose usually 2-piece lightweight suit designed especially for sleeping [Hindi & Urdu *pājāma* "lightweight trousers," from Persian *pā* "leg" + *jāma* "garment"]

[1]**pal** \ˈpal\ *n* : a close friend [Romany *phral, phal* "brother, friend," from Sanskrit *bhrātr̥* "brother"]

[2]**pal** *vi* **palled; pal·ling** : to be or associate as pals

pal·ace \ˈpal-əs\ *n* **1 a** : the official residence of a sovereign **b** *chiefly British* : the official residence of an archbishop or bishop **2 a** : a large stately house **b** : a large public building **c** : a gaudy place for public amusement or refreshment ⟨a movie *palace*⟩ [Medieval French *palais,* from Latin *palatium,* from *Palatium,* hill in Rome where the emperors' residences were built]

pal·a·din \ˈpal-əd-ən\ *n* **1** : a knightly hero or champion **2** : a strong supporter of a cause [Middle French, from Italian *paladino,* from Medieval Latin *palatinus* "courtier," from Late Latin, "imperial official," from Latin, "palatine"]

pa·laes·tra \pə-ˈles-trə\ *n, pl* **-trae** \-ˌtrē\ **1** : a school in ancient Greece or Rome for sports (as wrestling) **2** : GYMNASIUM 1 [Latin, from Greek *palaistra,* from *palaiein* "to wrestle"]

pal·at·able \ˈpal-ət-ə-bəl\ *adj* **1** : agreeable to the taste : SAVORY **2** : agreeable to the mind : ACCEPTABLE — **pal·at·abil·i·ty** \ˌpal-ət-ə-ˈbil-ət-ē\ *n* — **pal·at·ably** \-blē\ *adv*

pal·a·tal \ˈpal-ət-l\ *adj* **1** : of or relating to the palate **2** : pronounced with the front or blade of the tongue near or touching the hard palate ⟨the \y\ in "yeast" and the \sh\ in "she" are *palatal* sounds⟩ — **palatal** *n* — **pal·a·tal·ly** \-l-ē\ *adv*

pal·a·tal·ize \ˈpal-ət-l-ˌīz\ *vt* : to pronounce as or change into a palatal sound — **pal·a·tal·i·za·tion** \ˌpal-ət-l-ə-ˈzā-shən\ *n*

pal·ate \ˈpal-ət\ *n* **1** : the roof of the mouth that separates the mouth from the nasal cavity and is made up of a bony front part and a soft flexible back part **2 a** : intellectual relish or taste **b** : the sense of taste [Latin *palatum*]

pa·la·tial \pə-ˈlā-shəl\ *adj* **1** : of, relating to, or being a palace **2** : suitable to a palace : MAGNIFICENT — **pa·la·tial·ly** \-shə-lē\ *adv* — **pa·la·tial·ness** *n*

pa·lat·i·nate \pə-ˈlat-n-ət\ *n* : the territory of a palatine

[1]**pal·a·tine** \ˈpal-ə-ˌtīn\ *adj* **1 a** : of or relating to a palace especially of a Roman or Holy Roman emperor **b** : PALATIAL **2 a** : possessing royal privileges **b** : of or relating to a palatine or a palatinate [Latin *palatinus,* from *palatium* "palace"]

[2]**palatine** *n* **1 a** : a high officer of an imperial palace **b** : a feudal lord having sovereign power within his domains **2** *cap* : a native or inhabitant of the Palatinate

[3]**palatine** *adj* : of, relating to, or lying near the palate

[4]**palatine** *n* : a palatine bone

[1]**pa·lav·er** \pə-ˈlav-ər, -ˈläv-\ *n* **1** : a long parley usually between persons of different cultures or levels of sophistication **2 a** : idle talk **b** : misleading or beguiling speech [Portuguese *palavra* "word, speech," from Late Latin *parabola* "parable, speech"]

[2]**palaver** *vi* : to talk at length or idly

[1]**pale** \ˈpāl\ *adj* **1 a** : lacking color or intensity of color **b** : not vivid in hue or luster; *esp* : low in saturation and high in lightness ⟨a *pale* pink⟩ **c** : not having the warm skin color of a person in good health : PALLID **2** : not bright or brilliant : DIM [Medieval French, from Latin *pallidus* "pallid"] — **pale·ly** \ˈpāl-lē\ *adv* — **pale·ness** \ˈpāl-nəs\ *n* — **pal·ish** \ˈpā-lish\ *adj*

[2]**pale** *vb* : to make or become pale

[3]**pale** *vt* : to enclose with pales : FENCE

[4]**pale** *n* **1** : a stake or picket of a fence or palisade **2 a** : an enclosed place **b** : a territory within specified bounds or under a particular jurisdiction **3** : limits within which one is protected or privileged ⟨conduct beyond the *pale* of decency⟩ [Medieval French *pel, pal* "stake," from Latin *palus*]

pale- *or* **paleo-** *or* **palae-** *or* **palaeo-** *combining form* **1** : involving or dealing with ancient forms or conditions ⟨*paleo*botany⟩ **2** : early : primitive : archaic ⟨*Paleo*lithic⟩ [Greek *palaios* "ancient," from *palai* "long ago"]

pa·lea \ˈpā-lē-ə\ *n, pl* **-le·as** *or* **-le·ae** \-lē-ˌē\ : the upper bract of the flower of a grass [Latin, "chaff"]

pale·face \ˈpāl-ˌfās\ *n* : a white person

pa·leo·bot·a·ny \ˌpā-lē-ō-ˈbät-n-ē, -ˈbät-nē\ *n* : a branch of botany dealing with fossil plants — **pa·leo·bot·a·nist** \-ˈbät-n-əst, -ˈbät-nəst\ *n*

Pa·leo·cene \ˈpā-lē-ə-ˌsēn\ *n* : the earliest epoch of the Tertiary; *also* : its series of rocks — **Paleocene** *adj*

pa·le·og·ra·phy \ˌpā-lē-ˈäg-rə-fē\ *n* **1 a** : an ancient manner of writing **b** : ancient writings **2** : the study of ancient writings and inscriptions — **pa·le·og·ra·pher** \-fər\ *n* — **pa·leo·graph·ic** \ˌpā-lē-ə-ˈgraf-ik\ *adj* — **pa·leo·graph·i·cal·ly** \-ˈgraf-i-kə-lē, -klē\ *adv*

Pa·leo·lith·ic \ˌpā-lē-ə-ˈlith-ik\ *adj* : of, relating to, or being the earliest period of the Stone Age which is characterized by rough or crudely chipped stone implements — compare NEOLITHIC

pa·le·on·tol·o·gy \ˌpā-lē-ˌän-ˈtäl-ə-jē\ *n* **:** a science dealing with the life of past geological periods as known especially from fossil remains [French *paléontologie,* from Greek *palaios* "ancient" + *onta* "existing things," from *ont-, ōn,* present participle of *einai* "to be" + French *-logie* "-logy"] — **pa·le·on·to·log·i·cal** \-ˌänt-l-ˈäj-i-kəl\ *also* **pa·le·on·to·log·ic** \-ˈäj-ik\ *adj* — **pa·le·on·tol·o·gist** \-än-ˈtäl-ə-jəst\ *n*

Pa·le·o·zo·ic \ˌpā-lē-ə-ˈzō-ik\ *n* **:** the second earliest era of geological history that extends from the beginning of the Cambrian to the close of the Permian and is marked by the greatest development of nearly all classes of invertebrates except the insects and in the later epochs by the appearance of amphibians, reptiles, and land plants; *also* **:** the corresponding system of rocks — see GEOLOGIC TIME table — **Paleozoic** *adj*

pal·ette \ˈpal-ət\ *n* **1 :** a thin board or tablet on which a painter mixes pigments **2 a :** the set of colors put on the palette **b :** a particular range, quality, or use of color [French, from Middle French *pale* "spade, shovel," from Latin *pala*]

palette knife *n* **:** a knife with a flexible steel blade and no cutting edge used to mix or to apply colors

pal·frey \ˈpȯl-frē\ *n, pl* **palfreys** *archaic* **:** a saddle horse other than a warhorse; *esp* **:** one suitable for a woman [Medieval French *palefrei,* from Medieval Latin *palafredus,* from Late Latin *paraveredus* "post-horse for secondary roads," from Greek *para-* "beside, subsidiary" + Late Latin *veredus* "post-horse," of Gaulish origin]

pal·imp·sest \ˈpal-əm-ˌsest, -əmp-\ *n* **:** writing material (as a parchment) used again after earlier writing has been erased [Latin *palimpsestus,* from Greek *palimpsēstos* "scraped again," from *palin* "back, again" + *psēn* "to scrape"]

pal·in·drome \ˈpal-ən-ˌdrōm\ *n* **:** a word, verse, or sentence (as "Able was I ere I saw Elba") or a number (as 1881) that reads the same backward or forward [Greek *palindromos* "running back again," from *palin* "back, again" + *dramein* "to run"]

pal·ing \ˈpā-ling\ *n* **1 :** [4]PALE 1, PICKET **2 a :** material for pales **b :** a fence of pales

pal·in·ode \ˈpal-ə-ˌnōd\ *n* **1 :** an ode or song recanting or retracting something in an earlier poem **2 :** a formal retraction [Greek *palinōidia,* from *palin* "back" + *aeidein* "to sing"]

[1]**pal·i·sade** \ˌpal-ə-ˈsād\ *n* **1 a :** a fence of stakes especially for defense **b :** a long strong stake pointed at the top and set close with others as a defense **2 :** a line of steep cliffs [French *palissade,* derived from Latin *palus* "stake"]

[2]**palisade** *vt* **:** to surround or fortify with palisades

palisade cell *n* **:** a cell of the palisade layer

palisade layer *n* **:** a layer of columnar or cylindrical cells rich in chloroplasts and found just under the upper epidermis of a leaf — called also *palisade parenchyma;* compare SPONGY LAYER

[1]**pall** \ˈpȯl\ *n* **1 :** a chalice cover made of a square piece of stiffened linen **2 :** a heavy cloth draped over a coffin **3 a :** something that covers, darkens, or produces a gloomy effect ⟨a *pall* of black smoke⟩ **b :** a feeling of gloom ⟨his bad mood cast a *pall* over the celebration⟩ [Old English *pæll* "cloak, mantle," from Latin *pallium*]

[2]**pall** *vi* **:** to become dull or uninteresting **:** lose the ability to give pleasure [Middle English *pallen,* from *appallen* "to become pale, make pale"]

[1]**pal·la·di·um** \pə-ˈlād-ē-əm\ *n, pl* **-dia** \-ē-ə\ **:** something that protects or defends **:** SAFEGUARD [Latin, a statue of Pallas Athene which was held to ensure the safety of Troy, from Greek *palladion,* from *Pallad-, Pallas* "Pallas"]

[2]**palladium** *n* **:** a silver-white ductile malleable metallic chemical element that is used especially as a catalyst and in alloys — see ELEMENT table [New Latin, from *Pallad-, Pallas,* an asteroid, from Latin, "Pallas, goddess of wisdom," from Greek]

pall·bear·er \ˈpȯl-ˌbar-ər, -ˌber-\ *n* **:** a person who carries or escorts the coffin at a funeral

[1]**pal·let** \ˈpal-ət\ *n* **1 :** a straw-filled tick or mattress **2 :** a small, hard, or temporary bed [Middle English *pailet,* from Medieval French *paillete* "bundle of straw," from *paille* "straw," from Latin *palea* "chaff, straw"]

[2]**pallet** *n* **1 :** a flat-bladed tool for forming, beating, or rounding clay or glass **2 :** PALETTE 1 **3 :** a lever or surface in a timepiece that receives an impulse from the escapement wheel and imparts motion to a balance or pendulum [Middle French *palette* "small shovel," from *pale* "spade, shovel," from Latin *pala*]

pal·li·ate \ˈpal-ē-ˌāt\ *vt* **1 :** to make (as a disease) less intense or severe **2 :** to cover by excuses and apologies [Late Latin *palliare* "to cloak, conceal," from Latin *pallium* "cloak"] — **pal·li·a·tion** \ˌpal-ē-ˈā-shən\ *n* — **pal·li·a·tor** \ˈpal-ē-ˌāt-ər\ *n*

pal·li·a·tive \ˈpal-ē-ˌāt-iv, ˈpal-yət-\ *adj* **:** serving to palliate — **palliative** *n* — **pal·li·a·tive·ly** *adv*

pal·lid \ˈpal-əd\ *adj* **:** lacking color **:** WAN [Latin *pallidus,* from *pallēre* "to be pale"] — **pal·lid·i·ty** \pa-ˈlid-ət-ē\ *n* — **pal·lid·ly** \ˈpal-əd-lē\ *adv* — **pal·lid·ness** *n*

pal·li·um \ˈpal-ē-əm\ *n, pl* **-lia** \-ē-ə\ *or* **-li·ums 1 :** a draped rectangular cloak worn by men of ancient Greece and Rome **2 :** a white woolen band with pendants in front and back worn over the chasuble by a pope or archbishop [Latin]

pal·lor \ˈpal-ər\ *n* **:** lack of color especially of the face **:** PALENESS [Latin, from *pallēre* "to be pale"]

pal·ly \ˈpal-ē\ *adj* **:** sharing the relationship of pals **:** INTIMATE

[1]**palm** \ˈpäm, ˈpälm\ *n* **1 :** any of a family of mostly tropical or subtropical trees, shrubs, or vines that are monocotyledons usually with a simple but often tall stem topped by a crown of very large feathery or fan-shaped leaves **2 a :** a palm leaf especially when carried as a symbol of victory or rejoicing **b :** a symbol of success; *also* **:** VICTORY, TRIUMPH [Old English, from Latin *palma,* literally, "palm of the hand"; from the resemblance of the tree's leaves to an outstretched hand] — **palm·like** \-ˌlīk\ *adj*

[2]**palm** *n* **1 :** the under part of the hand between the fingers and the wrist **2 :** a unit of length based on the width or length of the hand [Medieval French *paume,* from Latin *palma*]

[3]**palm** *vt* **1 :** to conceal in or pick up stealthily with the hand ⟨*palm* a card⟩ **2 :** to pass off by fraud ⟨shoddy goods fit only to be *palmed* on the unwary⟩ **3 :** to allow (a basketball) to come to rest momentarily in the hand while dribbling thus committing a violation

pal·mar \ˈpal-mər, ˈpäm-ər, ˈpäl-mər\ *adj* **:** of, relating to, situated in, or involving the palm of the hand

pal·mate \ˈpal-ˌmāt, ˈpäm-ˌāt, ˈpäl-ˌmāt\ *adj* **:** resembling a hand with the fingers spread: as **a :** having lobes or veins radiating from a common point ⟨a *palmate* leaf⟩ **b :** having the distal portion broad, flat, and lobed ⟨a *palmate* antler⟩ — **pal·mate·ly** *adv*

palm·er \ˈpäm-ər, ˈpäl-mər\ *n* **:** a person wearing two crossed palm leaves as a sign of a pilgrimage to the Holy Land

pal·met·to \pal-ˈmet-ō\ *n, pl* **-tos** *or* **-toes :** any of several usually low-growing palms with fan-shaped leaves; *esp* **:** one native to the coastal southeastern U.S. and the Bahamas [Spanish *palmito,* from *palma* "palm," from Latin]

palmetto

palm·ist·ry \ˈpäm-ə-strē, ˈpäl-mə-\ *n* **:** the art or practice of reading a person's character or future from markings on the palms [Middle English *pawmestry,* probably from *paume* "palm" + *maistrie* "mastery"] — **palm·ist** \ˈpäm-əst, ˈpäl-məst\ *n*

pal·mit·ic acid \pal-ˈmit-ik-, pä-, päl-\ *n* **:** a waxy fatty acid occurring free or especially in the form of glycerides in most fats and fatty oils

pal·mi·tin \ˈpal-mət-ən, ˈpäm-ət-, ˈpäl-mət-\ *n* **:** an ester of glycerol and palmitic acid [French *palmitine,* derived from Latin *palma* "palm"]

palm off *vt* **:** to get rid of or pass on (as something fake, useless, or of poor quality) usually in a dishonest way ⟨*palmed off* phony antiques on unsuspecting customers⟩

palm oil *n* **:** an edible fat obtained from the fruit of several palms and used especially in soap, candles, and lubricating greases

Palm Sunday *n* **:** the Sunday before Easter celebrated in commemoration of Christ's triumphal entry into Jerusalem [from the palm branches strewn in Christ's way]

palm·top \ˈpäm-ˌtäp, ˈpälm-\ *n* **:** a small portable computer that fits in the palm of the hand

palmy \ˈpäm-ē, ˈpäl-mē\ *adj* **palm·i·er; -est 1 :** abounding in or bearing palms **2 :** marked by prosperity **:** FLOURISHING

pal·o·mi·no \ˌpal-ə-ˈmē-nō\ *n, pl* **-nos** : a horse of a light tan or cream color with lighter mane and tail [American Spanish, from Spanish, "like a dove," from Latin *palumbinus,* from *palumbes,* a kind of pigeon]

palp \ˈpalp\ *n* : PALPUS

pal·pa·ble \ˈpal-pə-bəl\ *adj* **1** : that can be touched or felt : TANGIBLE **2** : easily perceptible : NOTICEABLE **3** : easily understood : MANIFEST [Late Latin *palpabilis,* from Latin *palpare* "to stroke"] — **pal·pa·bil·i·ty** \ˌpal-pə-ˈbil-ət-ē\ *n* — **pal·pa·bly** \ˈpal-pə-blē\ *adv*

pal·pate \ˈpal-ˌpāt\ *vt* : to examine by touch especially medically [derived from Latin *palpare* "to stroke"] — **pal·pa·tion** \pal-ˈpā-shən\ *n*

pal·pi·tate \ˈpal-pə-ˌtāt\ *vi* : to beat rapidly and strongly : THROB, QUIVER ⟨*palpitating* with excitement⟩ [Latin *palpitare,* from *palpare* "to stroke"] — **pal·pi·tant** \ˈpal-pət-ənt\ *adj*

pal·pi·ta·tion \ˌpal-pə-ˈtā-shən\ *n* : an act or instance of palpitating; *esp* : an abnormally rapid beating of the heart

pal·pus \ˈpal-pəs\ *n, pl* **pal·pi** \-ˌpī, -pē\ : a segmented sense organ on an arthropod mouthpart [Latin, "caress, soft palm of the hand"] — **pal·pate** \ˈpal-ˌpāt\ *adj*

pal·sied \ˈpȯl-zēd\ *adj* : affected with or as if with palsy

pal·sy \ˈpȯl-zē\ *n, pl* **palsies** **1** : PARALYSIS 1 **2** : a condition marked by uncontrollable tremor of the body or a part [Middle English *palesie, parlesey,* from Medieval French *paralisie,* from Latin *paralysis*] — **palsy** *vt*

pal·ter \ˈpȯl-tər\ *vi* **pal·tered; pal·ter·ing** \-tə-ring, -tring\ **1** : EQUIVOCATE **2** : HAGGLE 2, BARGAIN [origin unknown]

pal·try \ˈpȯl-trē\ *adj* **pal·tri·er; -est** **1** : CHEAP 2, SHODDY **2** : contemptibly limited : MEAN, LITTLE ⟨*paltry* minds⟩ **3** : PETTY 2, TRIVIAL [obsolete *paltry* "trash"] — **pal·tri·ness** *n*

pal·y·nol·o·gy \ˌpal-ə-ˈnäl-ə-jē\ *n* : a branch of science dealing with pollen and spores [Greek *palynein* "to sprinkle," from *palē* "fine meal"] — **pal·y·no·log·i·cal** \-nə-ˈläj-i-kəl\ *adj* — **pal·y·nol·o·gist** \-ˈnäl-ə-jəst\ *n*

pam·pa \ˈpam-pə, ˈpäm-\ *n, pl* **pampas** \-pəz, -pəs\ : an extensive generally grass-covered plain of South America east of the Andes [American Spanish, from Quechua] — **pam·pe·an** \ˈpam-pē-ən, ˈpäm-, pam-ˈ, päm-ˈ\ *adj*

pam·per \ˈpam-pər\ *vt* **pam·pered; pam·per·ing** \ˈpam-pə-ring, -pring\ : to treat with extreme or excessive care and attention [Middle English *pamperen,* probably of Dutch origin] — **pam·per·er** \-pər-ər\ *n*

pam·phlet \ˈpam-flət, ˈpamp-\ *n* : an unbound printed publication with no cover or a paper cover [Middle English *pamflet* "unbound booklet," from Medieval Latin *pamfletus,* from *Pamphilus, seu De Amore* "Pamphilus, or About Love," popular Latin poem of the 12th century]

Word History *Pamphilus, seu De Amore* ("Pamphilus, or About Love"), written in the late 12th century by an author now unknown, is a poem detailing a series of amusing amorous adventures. This poem was very popular in its day. In the late Middle Ages the names of short literary works were often given diminutive forms. *Pamphilus* became *Pamphilet* (at least in French—the name, although probably used, is not attested in English). And Middle English *pamflet* was soon the word for any written work too short to be called a book.

¹**pam·phle·teer** \ˌpam-flə-ˈtiər, ˌpamp-\ *n* : a writer of pamphlets attacking something or urging a cause

²**pamphleteer** *vi* : to write and publish pamphlets

¹**pan** \ˈpan\ *n* **1 a** : a usually broad, shallow, and open container for household use **b** : a broad shallow open vessel: as (1) : either of the receptacles of a pair of scales (2) : a round shallow metal container used to wash waste from metal (as gold) **2** : a basin or depression in the earth ⟨a salt *pan*⟩ **3** : HARDPAN 1 [Old English *panne,* derived from Latin *patina,* from Greek *patanē*]

²**pan** *vb* **panned; pan·ning** **1** : to wash earthy material in a pan to concentrate bits of native metal; *also* : to separate (metal) from debris by panning **2** : to yield precious metal in panning **3** : to criticize severely

pan- *combining form* **1** : all : completely ⟨*pan*chromatic⟩ **2** : involving all of a (specified) group ⟨*Pan*-American⟩ **3** : total : general ⟨*pan*leucopenia⟩ [Greek, from *pan,* neuter of *pas* "all, every"]

pan·a·cea \ˌpan-ə-ˈsē-ə\ *n* : a remedy for all ills or difficulties : CURE-ALL [Latin, from Greek *panakeia,* from *panakēs* "all-healing," from *pan-* + *akos* "remedy"]

pa·nache \pə-ˈnash, -ˈnäsh\ *n* **1** : an ornamental tuft (as of feathers) especially on a helmet **2** : dash or colorfulness in style and action : VERVE [Middle French *pennache,* from Italian *pennacchio,* from Late Latin *pinnaculum* "small wing, gable," from Latin *pinna* "wing, battlement"]

pan·a·ma \ˈpan-ə-ˌmä, -ˌmȯ\ *n, often cap* : a lightweight hat made of narrow strips from the young leaves of a tropical American tree [American Spanish *panamá,* from *Panama,* Central America]

Pan–Amer·i·can \ˌpan-ə-ˈmer-ə-kən\ *adj* : of, relating to, or involving the independent republics of North America and South America

Pan–Amer·i·can·ism \-kə-ˌniz-əm\ *n* : a movement for greater cooperation among the Pan-American nations

¹**pan·cake** \ˈpan-ˌkāk\ *n* : a flat cake usually made of thin batter and cooked on both sides (as on a griddle)

²**pancake** *vb* : to make or cause to make a pancake landing

pancake landing *n* : a landing in which an airplane is leveled off higher than for a normal landing causing it to stall and drop in an approximately horizontal position with little forward motion

pan·chro·mat·ic \ˌpan-krō-ˈmat-ik\ *adj* : sensitive to light of all colors in the visible spectrum ⟨*panchromatic* film⟩

pan·cre·as \ˈpang-krē-əs, ˈpan-\ *n* : a large gland of vertebrates that lies near the stomach and secretes digestive enzymes and the hormone insulin [Greek *pankreat-, pankreas,* "sweetbread," from *pan-* + *kreas* "flesh, meat"] — **pan·cre·at·ic** \ˌpang-krē-ˈat-ik, ˌpan-\ *adj*

pancreatic duct *n* : the duct leading from the pancreas and opening into the duodenum

pancreatic juice *n* : a clear alkaline secretion of pancreatic enzymes that flows into the duodenum and acts on food already partly digested by the gastric juice and saliva

pan·da \ˈpan-də\ *n* **1** : RED PANDA **2** : a large black and white mammal of chiefly central China that feeds primarily on bamboo shoots and is now usually considered to be closely related to the bears — called also *giant panda* [French, perhaps from a language of the southeast Himalayas]

panda 2

pan·da·nus \pan-ˈdā-nəs, -ˈdan-əs\ *n* : SCREW PINE; *also* : a fiber made from the leaves of the screw pine and used in woven products (as mats) [Malay *pandan*]

pan·dem·ic \pan-ˈdem-ik\ *n* : an outbreak of disease occurring over a wide area and affecting many people ⟨an influenza *pandemic*⟩ [derived from Greek *pan-* + *dēmos* "people"] — **pandemic** *adj*

pan·de·mo·ni·um \ˌpan-də-ˈmō-nē-əm\ *n* : a wild uproar : TUMULT [*Pandemonium,* capital of Hell in Milton's *Paradise Lost,* from Greek *pan-* + *daimōn* "evil spirit, demon"]

¹**pan·der** \ˈpan-dər\ *n* **1 a** : a go-between in love intrigues **b** : one who solicits clients for a prostitute **2** : one who caters to or exploits the weaknesses of others [*Pandarus*]

²**pander** *vi* **pan·dered; pan·der·ing** \-də-ring, -dring\ : to act as a pander — **pan·der·er** \-dər-ər\ *n*

Pan·do·ra's box \pan-ˌdōr-əz-, -ˌdȯr-\ *n* : a source of many usually unforeseen troubles [from the box containing all the ills of humankind opened by the mythical Pandora against the command of Zeus]

pan·dow·dy \pan-ˈdau̇d-ē\ *n, pl* **-dies** : a deep-dish apple dessert covered with a rich crust [origin unknown]

pane \ˈpān\ *n* **1** : a piece, section, or side of something **2 a** : a framed sheet of glass in a window or door **b** : one of the sections into which a sheet of postage stamps is cut for distribution [Medieval French *pan* "strip of cloth, pane," from Latin *pannus* "cloth, rag"]

pan·e·gy·ric \ˌpan-ə-ˈjir-ik, -ˈjī-rik\ *n* : a formal speech or writing eulogizing someone or something; *also* : formal or elaborate praise [Latin *panegyricus,* from Greek *panēgyrikos,* from *panēgyrikos* "for a festival," from *panēgyris* "festival assembly," from *pan-* + *agyris* "assembly"] — **pan·e·gy·ri·cal** \-ˈjir-i-kəl, -ˈjī-ri-\ *adj* — **pan·e·gy·rist** \ˌpan-ə-ˈjir-əst, -ˈjī-rəst\ *n*

¹**pan·el** \ˈpan-l\ *n* **1 a** : a schedule containing names of persons summoned as jurors; *also* : JURY 1 **b** : a group of persons who

discuss a topic before an audience **c :** a group of entertainers or guests engaged as players in a quiz or guessing game on a radio or television program **2 :** a separate or distinct part of a surface: as **a :** a usually rectangular and sunken or raised section of a surface (as of a door, wall, or ceiling) set off by a margin **b :** a unit of construction material (as plywood) made to form part of a surface (as of a wall) **c :** a vertical section (as a gore) of cloth **d :** a section of a switchboard; *also* **:** a mount for controls (as of an electrical device) **3 :** a thin flat piece of wood on which a picture is painted; *also* **:** a painting on such a surface [Middle English, "piece of cloth, jury list on a piece of parchment," from Medieval French, "piece of cloth," derived from Latin *pannus* "cloth"]

[2]**panel** *vt* **-eled** *or* **-elled; -el·ing** *or* **-el·ling :** to furnish or decorate with panels

pan·el·ing \'pan-l-ing\ *n* **:** panels joined in a continuous surface; *esp* **:** decorative wood panels so combined

pan·el·ist \'pan-l-əst\ *n* **:** a member of a panel for discussion or entertainment

panel truck *n* **:** a small light motortruck with a fully enclosed body

pan·fish \'pan-ˌfish\ *n* **:** a small food fish (as a sunfish) usually caught with hook and line and not sold commercially

pang \'pang\ *n* **:** a sudden sharp attack or spasm (as of pain or emotional distress) ‹hunger *pangs*› [origin unknown]

pan·go·lin \'pang-gə-lən; pan-'gō-lən, pang-\ *n* **:** any of several Asian and African toothless mammals having the body covered with large overlapping horny scales [Malay dialect *pĕngguling*]

[1]**pan·han·dle** \'pan-ˌhan-dl\ *n* **:** a narrow projection of a larger territory (as a state)

[2]**panhandle** *vb* **-dled; -dling** \-dling, -dl-ing\ **:** to beg for money or food on the street — **pan·han·dler** \-dlər\ *n*

Pan·hel·len·ic \ˌpan-hə-'len-ik\ *adj* **1 :** of or relating to all Greece or all the Greeks **2 :** of or relating to the Greek-letter sororities or fraternities in American colleges and universities or to an association representing them

[1]**pan·ic** \'pan-ik\ *n* **1 a :** a sudden overpowering fright; *also* **:** acute extreme anxiety **b :** a sudden unreasoning terror often causing mass flight **2 :** a sudden widespread fright concerning financial affairs that causes hurried selling and a sharp fall in prices **3** *slang* **:** one that is very funny [Greek *panikon* "fear caused by Pan, panic," from *panikos,* literally, "of Pan," from *Pan* "Pan"] ***synonyms*** see FEAR — **panic** *adj* — **pan·icky** \'pan-i-kē\ *adj*

Word History The Greek god Pan is often represented playing the panpipes, which he was believed to have invented. According to the story, Pan was once chasing a nymph named Syrinx. Unable to escape across a river, Syrinx asked the river nymphs for help, and they changed her into a bed of reeds. Pan cut pieces of those reeds and made a panpipe. Pan was also believed to have given a great shout which instilled fear into the giants in their battle against the gods. And in Athens Pan was worshipped because the citizens believed that it was he who had caused the Persians to flee in fear from the battle of Marathon. From this more awesome aspect of Pan's nature comes the word *panic.*

[2]**panic** *vb* **pan·icked** \-ikt\; **pan·ick·ing 1 :** to affect or be affected with panic **2 :** to cause to laugh loudly ‹*panic* an audience with a gag›

panic attack *n* **:** a sudden episode of intense fear

pan·i·cle \'pan-i-kəl\ *n* **:** a branched flower cluster (as of a lilac or some grasses) in which each branch from the main axis bears more than one flower [Latin *panicula,* from *panus* "stalk of a panicle"] — **pan·i·cled** \-kəld\ *adj* — **pa·nic·u·late** \pə-'nik-yə-lət\ *adj*

pan·ic–strick·en \'pan-ik-ˌstrik-ən\ *adj* **:** overcome with panic

pa·ni·no \pə-'nē-nō\ *n, pl* **pa·ni·ni** \pə-'nē-nē\ **:** a usually grilled sandwich made with Italian bread [Italian, diminutive of *pane* "bread," from Latin *panis*]

Pan·ja·bi \ˌpən-'jäb-ē, -'jab-\ *n* **:** PUNJABI

pan·jan·drum \pan-'jan-drəm\ *n* **:** a powerful personage or pretentious official [Grand *Panjandrum,* title of an imaginary personage in nonsense lines by Samuel Foote, died 1777, English playwright]

pan·leu·ko·pe·nia \ˌpan-ˌlü-kə-'pē-nē-ə\ *n* **:** an acute usually fatal viral disease of cats characterized by fever, diarrhea and dehydration, and destruction of white blood cells

pan·nier \'pan-yər, 'pan-ē-ər\ *n* **1 :** a large basket; *esp* **:** one of wicker carried on the back of an animal or the shoulder of a person **2 a :** either of a pair of hoops formerly used by women to expand their skirts at the hips **b :** an overskirt draped and puffed out at the sides [Medieval French *paner, panier,* from Latin *panarium,* from *panis* "bread"]

pannier 2b

pan·ni·kin \'pan-i-kən\ *n, chiefly British* **:** a small pan or cup

pan·o·ply \'pan-ə-plē\ *n, pl* **-plies 1 a :** a full suit of armor **b :** ceremonial attire **2 :** something that covers or hides protectively **3 :** a magnificently impressive array or display [Greek *panoplia,* from *pan-* + *hopla* "arms, armor"] — **pan·o·plied** \-plēd\ *adj*

pan·ora·ma \ˌpan-ə-'ram-ə, -'räm-\ *n* **1 a :** CYCLORAMA **b :** a picture exhibited a part at a time by being unrolled before the spectator **2 a :** a full and unobstructed view in every direction **b :** a comprehensive presentation of a subject **3 :** a mental picture of a series of images or events [*pan-* + Greek *horama* "sight," from *horan* "to see"] — **pan·oram·ic** \-'ram-ik\ *adj*

pan out *vi* **:** to turn out; *esp* **:** SUCCEED ‹plans that *panned out* as he had hoped they would› [[2]*pan*]

pan·pipe \'pan-ˌpīp\ *n* **:** a primitive wind instrument consisting of a graduated series of short vertical pipes bound together with the mouthpieces in an even row — often used in plural [*Pan,* its traditional inventor — see *Word History* at PANIC]

pan·sy \'pan-zē\ *n, pl* **pansies :** a garden plant originated by hybridization of various violets and violas; *also* **:** its showy velvety 5-petaled flower [Medieval French *pensee,* from *pensee* "thought," from *penser* "to think," from Latin *pensare* "to ponder"]

[1]**pant** \'pant\ *vb* **1 a :** to take short rapid breaths **b :** to make a puffing sound **c :** to progress with panting ‹the car *panted* up the hill› **2 :** to long eagerly **:** YEARN **3 :** to utter with panting ‹ran up and *panted* out the message› [Middle English, from Medieval French *panteiser,* derived from Greek *phantasioun* "to have hallucinations," from *phantasia* "imagination"]

[2]**pant** *n* **1 :** a panting breath **2 :** a puffing sound

pan·ta·lets *or* **pan·ta·lettes** \ˌpant-l-'ets\ *n pl* **:** long drawers with a ruffle at the bottom of each leg

pan·ta·loon \ˌpant-l-'ün\ *n* **1** *pl* **:** close-fitting trousers usually with straps passing under the insteps **2 :** loose-fitting usually shorter than ankle-length trousers [Italian *Pantaleone, Pantalone,* character in 16th-century Italian improvised comedies]

pan·the·ism \'pan-thē-ˌiz-əm, 'pant-\ *n* **:** a doctrine that equates God with the forces and laws of the universe — **pan·the·ist** \-thē-əst\ *n* — **pan·the·is·tic** \ˌpan-thē-'is-tik, ˌpant-\ *adj*

pan·the·on \'pan-thē-ˌän, 'pant-\ *n* **1 :** a temple dedicated to all the gods **2 :** a building serving as the burial place of or containing memorials to famous dead **3 :** the gods of a people; *esp* **:** the gods officially recognized [Latin, from Greek *pantheion,* from *pan-* + *theos* "god"]

pan·ther \'pan-thər, 'pant-\ *n, pl* **panthers** *also* **panther 1 :** LEOPARD; *esp* **:** one that is black **2 :** COUGAR **3 :** JAGUAR [Medieval French *pantere,* from Latin *panthera,* from Greek *panthēr*]

pant·ies \'pant-ēz\ *n pl* **:** a woman's or child's undergarment covering the lower trunk

pan·to·graph \'pant-ə-ˌgraf\ *n* **:** an instrument for manually copying a figure (as a map or plan) to scale [French *pantographe,* from Greek *pant-, pas* "all" + French *-graphe* "-graph"] — **pan·to·graph·ic** \ˌpant-ə-'graf-ik\ *adj*

pan·to·mime \'pant-ə-ˌmīm\ *n* **1 :** PANTOMIMIST **2 :** a dramatic or dancing performance in which a story is told primarily by expressive bodily or facial movements of the performers **3 :** conveyance of information by bodily or facial movements [Latin *pantomimus,* from Greek *pant-, pas* "all" + Latin *mimus* "mime"] — **pantomime** *vb* — **pan·to·mim·ic** \ˌpant-ə-'mim-ik\ *adj*

pan·to·mim·ist \'pant-ə-ˌmim-əst, -ˌmīm-\ *n* **:** an actor or dancer in or a composer of pantomimes

\ə\ **abut**	\au̇\ **out**	\i\ **tip**	\ȯ\ **saw**	\u̇\ **foot**
\ər\ **further**	\ch\ **chin**	\ī\ **life**	\ȯi\ **coin**	\y\ **yet**
\a\ **mat**	\e\ **pet**	\j\ **job**	\th\ **thin**	\yü\ **few**
\ā\ **take**	\ē\ **easy**	\ng\ **sing**	\t͟h\ **this**	\yu̇\ **cure**
\ä\ **cot, cart**	\g\ **go**	\ō\ **bone**	\ü\ **food**	\zh\ **vision**

pan·to·then·ic acid \ˌpant-ə-ˌthen-ik-\ *n* : a viscous oily acid of the vitamin B complex found in all living tissues and necessary for growth [Greek *pantothen* "from all sides," from *pant-, pas* "all"]

pan·trop·i·cal \ˌpan-ˈträp-ikəl\ *also* **pan·trop·ic** \-ik\ *adj* : occurring or growing throughout the tropics

pan·try \ˈpan-trē\ *n, pl* **pantries** : a small room in which food and dishes are kept or from which food is brought to the table [Medieval French *paneterie,* from *paneter* "servant in charge of the pantry," from *pain* "bread," from Latin *panis*]

pants \ˈpans\ *n pl* **1** : an outer garment extending from the waist to the ankle and covering each leg separately **2** : UNDERPANTS; *esp* : PANTIES [short for *pantaloons*]

panty hose *n pl* : a one-piece undergarment for women that consists of hosiery combined with panties

panty·waist \ˈpant-ē-ˌwāst\ *n* **1** : a child's garment consisting of short pants buttoned to a waist **2** : SISSY

pan·zer \ˈpan-zər, ˈpänt-sər\ *adj* : of or relating to a panzer division or similar armored unit [German *Panzer* "tank, armor, coat of mail," from Middle High German *panzier* "armor for the torso," from Medieval French *pancier,* from *pance* "belly," from Latin *pantex*]

panzer division *n* : a German armored division

[1]**pap** \ˈpap\ *n* **1** *chiefly dialect* : NIPPLE 1, TEAT **2** : something shaped like a nipple [Middle English *pappe*]

[2]**pap** *n* : soft or bland food for infants or invalids [Middle English]

pa·pa *also* **pop·pa** \ˈpäp-ə\ *n* : FATHER 1a [French (baby talk)]

pa·pa·cy \ˈpā-pə-sē\ *n, pl* **-cies** **1** : the office of pope **2** : a line of popes **3** : the term of a pope's reign **4** *cap* : the government of the Roman Catholic Church [Medieval Latin *papatia,* from Late Latin *papa* "pope"]

pa·pa·in \pə-ˈpā-ən, -ˈpī-ən\ *n* : a protease in papaya juice used especially as a meat tenderizer and in medicine

pa·pal \ˈpā-pəl\ *adj* : of or relating to the pope or the papacy [Medieval French, from Medieval Latin *papalis,* from Late Latin *papa* "pope"] — **pa·pal·ly** \-pə-lē\ *adv*

papaw *variant of* PAWPAW

pa·pa·ya \pə-ˈpī-ə\ *n* : a tropical American tree with large lobed leaves and oblong yellow edible fruit with many black seeds in a central cavity; *also* : its fruit [Spanish, of American Indian origin]

[1]**pa·per** \ˈpā-pər\ *n* **1 a** : a felted sheet of usually vegetable fibers laid down on a fine screen from a water suspension **b** : a sheet or piece of paper **2 a** : a piece of paper containing a written or printed statement; *esp* : a document of identification or authorization **b** : a written composition (as a piece of schoolwork) **3** : a paper container or wrapper **4** : NEWSPAPER **5** : WALLPAPER [Medieval French *paper,* from Latin *papyrus* "papyrus, paper"]

[2]**paper** *vb* **pa·pered; pa·per·ing** \ˈpā-pə-ring, -pring\ **1** : to cover or line with paper; *esp* : to apply wallpaper to **2** : to hang wallpaper — **pa·per·er** \-pər-ər\ *n*

[3]**paper** *adj* **1 a** : of, relating to, or made of paper or a related composition **b** : resembling paper : PAPERY **2** : NOMINAL 3a ⟨a *paper* blockade⟩

pa·per·back \ˈpā-pər-ˌbak\ *n* : a book with a flexible paper binding — **paperback** *adj*

paper birch *n* : a North American birch with white bark that peels off the tree easily

pa·per·board \-ˌbōrd, -ˌbȯrd\ *n* : CARDBOARD

paper boy *n* : NEWSBOY

paper chromatography *n* : chromatography that uses paper as the adsorbent material through which a solution flows

paper cutter *n* : a machine or device for cutting or trimming sheets of paper

pa·per·hang·er \-ˌhang-ər\ *n* : one that applies wallpaper — **pa·per·hang·ing** \-ˌhang-ing\ *n*

paper money *n* : money consisting of government notes and bank notes

paper mulberry *n* : an Asian tree related to the mulberries and widely grown as a shade tree

paper nautilus *n* : an 8-armed cephalopod mollusk related to the octopus that in the female has a thin fragile shell — called also *argonaut*

paper profit *n* : a profit that can be realized only by selling something that has gone up in value

paper trail *n* : documents (as financial records or published materials) from which a person's actions may be traced or opinions learned

paper wasp *n* : a wasp that builds a nest out of papery material

pa·per·weight \ˈpā-pər-ˌwāt\ *n* : an object used to hold down loose papers by its weight

pa·per·white \-ˌhwīt, -ˌwīt\ *n* : a narcissus bearing clusters of small very fragrant pure white flowers

paper work *n* : routine clerical or record-keeping work often incidental to a more important task

pa·pery \ˈpā-pə-rē, -prē\ *adj* : resembling paper in thinness or consistency — **pa·per·i·ness** *n*

pa·pier–mâ·ché \ˌpā-pər-mə-ˈshā, ˌpap-ˌyā-mə-, -ma-\ *n* : a light strong molding material of wastepaper pulped with glue and other additives [French, literally, "chewed paper"] — **papier–mâché** *adj*

pa·pil·la \pə-ˈpil-ə\ *n, pl* **-pil·lae** \-ˈpil-ē, -ˌī\ : a small projecting bodily structure (as one on the surface of the tongue that often contains taste buds) that suggests a nipple [Latin, "nipple"] — **pap·il·la·ry** \ˈpap-ə-ˌler-ē, pə-ˈpil-ə-rē\ *adj* — **pap·il·late** \ˈpap-ə-ˌlāt, pə-ˈpil-ət\ *adj*

pap·il·lo·ma \ˌpap-ə-ˈlō-mə\ *n, pl* **-mas** *also* **-ma·ta** \-mət-ə\ : a usually benign epithelial tumor

pa·pist \ˈpā-pəst\ *n, often cap, usu disparaging* : ROMAN CATHOLIC [Middle French *papiste,* from *pape* "pope," from Late Latin *papa*] — **papist** *adj* — **pa·pist·ry** \-pə-strē\ *n*

pa·poose \pa-ˈpüs, pə-\ *n* : a North American Indian infant [Narragansett *papoòs*]

pap·pus \ˈpap-əs\ *n, pl* **pap·pi** \ˈpap-ˌī, -ē\ : a downy or bristly appendage or tuft of appendages crowning the seed or fruit of some seed plants and functioning in its dispersal [Latin, from Greek *pappos*]

pa·pri·ka \pə-ˈprē-kə, pa-\ *n* : a mild red seasoning consisting of the dried finely ground pods of various cultivated sweet peppers; *also* : a sweet pepper used for making paprika [Hungarian, from Serbian & Croatian, from *papar* "ground pepper," derived from Latin *piper*]

Pap smear \ˈpap-\ *n* : a method for the early detection of cancer especially of the uterine cervix using a special cell-staining technique to identify diseased tissue — called also *Pap test* [George N. *Papanicolaou,* died 1962, American medical scientist]

pa·py·rus \pə-ˈpī-rəs\ *n, pl* **pa·py·ri** \-rē, -ˌrī\ *also* **pa·py·rus·es** **1** : a tall sedge of the Nile valley **2** : the pith of the papyrus plant especially when made into strips and pressed to make a material to write on **3** : a writing on or written scroll of papyrus [Latin, from Greek *papyros*]

papyrus 1

par \ˈpär\ *n* **1 a** : the established value of the monetary unit of one country expressed in terms of the monetary unit of another country using the same metal as the standard of value **b** : the face value of a security ⟨stocks that sell near *par*⟩ **2** : common level : EQUALITY ⟨their abilities are about on a *par*⟩ **3** : an accepted standard (as of health) ⟨not feeling up to *par*⟩ **4** : the score standard set for each hole of a golf course [Latin, "one that is equal," from *par* "equal"] — **par** *adj*

[1]**para-** \ˌpar-ə, ˈpar-ə\ *or* **par-** *prefix* **1 a** : beside : alongside ⟨*para*thyroid⟩ **b** : beyond : outside of **2 a** : closely related to or resembling ⟨*para*typhoid⟩ **b** : associated in a subsidiary or accessory capacity ⟨*para*professional⟩ **3** : faulty : abnormal [Greek, from *para*]

[2]**para-** \ˈpar-ə\ *combining form* : parachute ⟨*para*troops⟩ [*parachute*]

para–ami·no·ben·zo·ic acid \ˈpar-ə-ə-ˌmē-ˌnō-ˌben-ˌzō-ik-, ˈpar-ə-ˌam-ə-ˌnō-\ *n* : a colorless organic acid that is a derivative of benzoic acid and is a growth factor of the vitamin B complex often used as a sunscreen

par·a·ble \ˈpar-ə-bəl\ *n* : a short simple story illustrating a moral or spiritual truth [Medieval French, from Late Latin *parabola,* from Greek *parabolē* "comparison," from *paraballein* "to compare," from *para-* + *ballein* "to throw"]

pa·rab·o·la \pə-ˈrab-ə-lə\ *n* **1** : the curve formed by the intersection of a cone with a plane parallel to a straight line in its surface : a curve generated by a point moving so that its distance from a fixed point is equal to its distance from a fixed line **2** : something bowl-shaped [Greek *parabolē* "comparison, parable, parabola"] — **par·a·bol·ic** \ˌpar-ə-ˈbäl-ik\ *adj* — **par·a·bol·i·cal·ly** \-ˈbäl-i-kə-lē, -klē\ *adv*

[1]**para·chute** \ˈpar-ə-ˌshüt\ *n* **1 :** a folding umbrella-shaped device of light fabric used especially for making a safe descent after jumping from an airplane **2 :** something (as the tuft of hairs on a dandelion seed) suggestive of a parachute in form, use, or operation [French, from *para-* (as in *parasol*) + *chute* "fall"]

[2]**parachute** *vb* **:** to convey or descend by means of a parachute

para·chut·ist \ˈpar-ə-ˌshüt-əst\ *n* **:** one that descends by parachute

Par·a·clete \ˈpar-ə-ˌklēt\ *n* **:** HOLY SPIRIT [Late Latin *Paracletus, Paraclitus,* from Greek *Paraklētos,* literally, "advocate, intercessor," from *parakalein* "to invoke," from *para-* + *kalein* "to call"]

[1]**pa·rade** \pə-ˈrād\ *n* **1 :** pompous show or display **2 :** a ceremonial formation of a body of troops before a superior officer **3 :** a public procession (as of military units and bands) **4 :** a place of promenade; *also* **:** those who promenade [French, from Medieval French, from *parer* "to prepare," from Latin *parare*]

[2]**parade** *vb* **1 a :** to cause to maneuver or march **b :** to march in a procession **2 :** PROMENADE **3 :** to exhibit ostentatiously **:** show off — **pa·rad·er** *n*

para·di·chlo·ro·ben·zene \ˌpar-ə-ˌdī-ˌklōr-ə-ˈben-ˌzēn, -ˌklȯr-, -ˌben-ˈ\ *n* **:** a white crystalline chlorinated benzene used chiefly in mothballs and as a deodorizer

par·a·digm \ˈpar-ə-ˌdīm, -ˌdim\ *n* **1 :** MODEL, PATTERN ⟨an essay that is a *paradigm* of clear writing⟩ **2 :** an example of a conjugation or declension showing a word in all its inflectional forms [Late Latin *paradigma,* from Greek *paradeigma,* from *paradeiknynai* "to show side by side," from *para-* + *deiknynai* "to show"] — **par·a·dig·mat·ic** \ˌpar-ə-dig-ˈmat-ik\ *adj*

par·a·dise \ˈpar-ə-ˌdīs, -ˌdīz\ *n* **1 :** the garden of Eden **2 :** HEAVEN 2a **3 :** a place or state of bliss [Medieval French *paradis,* from Late Latin *paradisus,* from Greek *paradeisos,* literally, "enclosed park," of Iranian origin]

par·a·di·si·a·cal \ˌpar-ə-də-ˈsī-ə-kəl, -ˌdī-, -ˈzī-\ *or* **par·a·dis·i·ac** \-ˈdiz-ē-ˌak\ *adj* **:** of, relating to, or resembling paradise [Late Latin *paradisiacus,* from *paradisus* "paradise"] — **par·a·di·si·a·cal·ly** \-də-ˈsī-ə-kə-lē, -klē\ *adv*

par·a·dox \ˈpar-ə-ˌdäks\ *n* **1 a :** a statement that seems to contradict common sense and yet is perhaps true **b :** a self-contradictory statement that at first seems true **2 :** something (as a person, condition, or act) with seemingly contradictory qualities or phases [Latin *paradoxum,* from Greek *paradoxon,* from *paradoxos* "contrary to expectation," from *para-* + *dokein* "to think, seem"] — **par·a·dox·i·cal** \ˌpar-ə-ˈdäk-si-kəl\ *adj* — **par·a·dox·i·cal·ly** \-kə-lē, -klē\ *adv* — **par·a·dox·i·cal·ness** \-kəl-nəs\ *n*

[1]**par·af·fin** \ˈpar-ə-fən\ *n* **1 :** a flammable waxy crystalline mixture of hydrocarbons obtained especially from distillates of wood, coal, or petroleum and used chiefly in coating and sealing, in candles, and in drugs and cosmetics **2 :** a hydrocarbon of the methane series **3** *chiefly British* **:** KEROSENE [German, from Latin *parum* "too little" + *affinis* "bordering on, associated with"; from the small affinity it has for other bodies] — **par·af·fin·ic** \ˌpar-ə-ˈfin-ik\ *adj*

[2]**paraffin** *vt* **:** to coat or saturate with paraffin

par·a·gon \ˈpar-ə-ˌgän, -gən\ *n* **:** a model of excellence or perfection [Middle French, from Italian *paragone,* literally, "touchstone," from *paragonare* "to test on a touchstone," from Greek *parakonan* "to sharpen," from *para-* + *akonē* "whetstone," from *akē* "point"]

[1]**para·graph** \ˈpar-ə-ˌgraf\ *n* **1 a :** a subdivision of a piece of writing or a speech that consists of one or more sentences and develops in an organized manner one point of a subject or gives the words of one speaker **b :** a short written article (as in a newspaper) that is complete in one undivided section **2 :** a character ¶ used as a reference mark or to indicate the beginning of a paragraph [Medieval Latin *paragraphus* "sign marking a paragraph," from Greek *paragraphos* "marginal sign used to mark change of speakers in a dialogue," from *paragraphein* "to write alongside," from *para-* + *graphein* "to write"] — **para·graph·ic** \ˌpar-ə-ˈgraf-ik\ *adj*

[2]**paragraph** *vb* **1 :** to divide into paragraphs **2 :** to write paragraphs

par·a·keet \ˈpar-ə-ˌkēt\ *n* **:** any of numerous usually small slender parrots with a long pointed tail [Spanish *periquito,* from Middle French *perroquet* "parrot"]

par·al·de·hyde \pa-ˈral-də-ˌhīd, pə-\ *n* **:** a liquid derivative of acetaldehyde used especially to calm nervousness or induce sleep

Par·a·li·pom·e·non \ˌpar-ə-lə-ˈpäm-ə-ˌnän, -lī-\ *n* **:** CHRONICLES [Late Latin, from Greek *Paraleipomenōn,* genitive of *Paraleipomena,* literally, "things left out," from *paraleipein* "to leave out," from *para-* + *leipein* "to leave"; from its forming a supplement to Samuel and Kings]

par·al·lax \ˈpar-ə-ˌlaks\ *n* **:** the apparent displacement or the difference in apparent direction of an object as seen from two different points not on a straight line with the object; *esp* **:** the difference in direction of a celestial body as measured from two points on the earth's orbit [Middle French *parallaxe,* from Greek *parallaxis,* from *parallassein* "to change," from *para-* + *allassein* "to change," from *allos* "other"] — **par·al·lac·tic** \ˌpar-ə-ˈlak-tik\ *adj*

[1]**par·al·lel** \ˈpar-ə-ˌlel\ *adj* **1 a :** lying or moving in the same direction but always the same distance apart ⟨*parallel* lines⟩ **b :** everywhere equally distant ⟨concentric spheres are *parallel*⟩ **2 a :** relating to or being an electrical circuit having a number of conductors in parallel **b :** relating to or being a connection in a computer system in which the bits of a byte are transmitted over separate wires at the same time **3 a :** marked by likeness or correspondence **:** SIMILAR, ANALOGOUS ⟨*parallel* situations⟩ **b :** having corresponding syntactical elements ⟨*parallel* clauses⟩ [Latin *parallelus* from Greek *parallēlos,* from *para* "beside" + *allēlōn* "of one another," from *allos* "other"] ***synonyms*** see SIMILAR

[2]**parallel** *n* **1 a :** a parallel line, curve, or surface **b** (1) **:** one of the imaginary circles on the surface of the earth paralleling the equator and marking the latitude (2) **:** the corresponding line on a globe or map **c :** a character ll used as a reference mark **2 a :** something equal or similar in all essential particulars **:** COUNTERPART **b :** SIMILARITY 2, ANALOGUE **3 :** a tracing of similarity ⟨draw a *parallel* between two eras⟩ **4 a :** the state of being physically parallel **:** PARALLELISM **b :** an arrangement of electrical devices in a circuit in which the same potential difference is applied to two or more resistances with each resistance on a parallel branch of the circuit

[3]**parallel** *vt* **1 :** to indicate similarity or analogy of **:** COMPARE **2 a :** to show something equal to **:** MATCH **b :** to correspond to **3 :** to place so as to be parallel in direction with something **4 :** to extend, run, or move in a direction parallel to

[4]**parallel** *adv* **:** in a parallel manner

parallel bars *n pl* **:** a pair of bars that are parallel to each other on an adjustable support and are used for swinging and balancing exercises in gymnastics

par·al·lel·epi·ped \ˌpar-ə-ˌlel-ə-ˈpī-pəd, -ˈpip-əd\ *n* **:** a 6-faced polyhedron all of whose faces are parallelograms lying in pairs of parallel planes [Greek *parallēlepipedon,* from *parallēlos* "parallel" + *epipedon* "plane surface," from *epipedos* "flat," from *epi-* + *pedon* "ground"]

parallel evolution *n* **:** evolution characterized by parallelism

par·al·lel·ism \ˈpar-ə-ˌlel-ˌiz-əm\ *n* **1 :** the quality or state of being parallel **2 :** RESEMBLANCE 1, CORRESPONDENCE **3 :** similarity of syntactical construction of adjacent word groups especially for rhetorical effect or rhythm **4 :** the independent development of a similar trait in related species following divergence from a common ancestor

par·al·lel·o·gram \ˌpar-ə-ˈlel-ə-ˌgram\ *n* **:** a four-sided figure whose opposite sides are parallel and of equal length [Greek *parallēlogrammon,* derived from *parallēlos* "parallel" + *grammē* "line," from *graphein* "to write"]

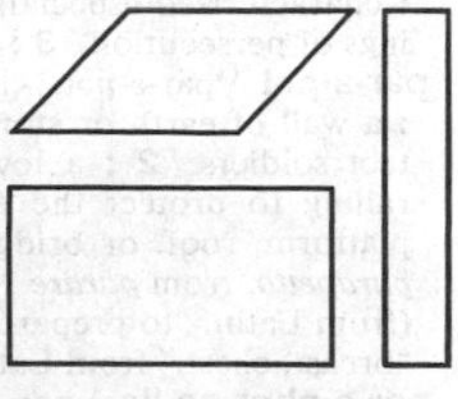

parallelogram

par·al·lel–veined \ˌpar-ə-ˌlel-ˈvānd, -ləl-\ *adj* **:** having veins that are arranged nearly parallel to one another and do not branch and interlace ⟨monocotyledons have *parallel-veined* leaves⟩ — compare NET-VEINED

pa·ral·y·sis \pə-ˈral-ə-səs\ *n, pl* **-y·ses** \-ə-ˌsēz\ **1 :** complete or partial loss of function especially when involving motion or sensation in a part of the body **2 :** loss of the ability to move or act

\ə\ **abut**	\au̇\ **out**	\i\ **tip**	\ȯ\ **saw**	\u̇\ **foot**
\ər\ **further**	\ch\ **chin**	\ī\ **life**	\ȯi\ **coin**	\y\ **yet**
\a\ **mat**	\e\ **pet**	\j\ **job**	\th\ **thin**	\yü\ **few**
\ā\ **take**	\ē\ **easy**	\ng\ **sing**	\t͟h\ **this**	\yu̇\ **cure**
\ä\ **cot, cart**	\g\ **go**	\ō\ **bone**	\ü\ **food**	\zh\ **vision**

⟨*paralysis* of highway traffic⟩ [Latin, from Greek, from *paralyein* "to loosen, disable," from *para-* + *lyein* "to loosen"]

¹**par·a·lyt·ic** \ˌpar-ə-ˈlit-ik\ *adj* **1** : affected with, characterized by, or causing paralysis **2** : of, relating to, or resembling paralysis

²**paralytic** *n* : one affected with paralysis

par·a·lyze \ˈpar-ə-ˌlīz\ *vt* **1** : to affect with paralysis **2** : to make powerless, ineffective, or unable to act or function ⟨a labor dispute that *paralyzed* the industry⟩ [French *paralyser,* back-formation from *paralysie* "paralysis," from Latin *paralysis*] — **par·a·ly·za·tion** \ˌpar-ə-lə-ˈzā-shən\ *n*

para·mag·net·ic \ˌpar-ə-mag-ˈnet-ik\ *adj* : being or relating to a slightly magnetizable substance (as aluminum) — **para·mag·ne·tism** \-ˈmag-nə-ˌtiz-əm\ *n*

par·a·me·cium \ˌpar-ə-ˈmē-sē-əm, -shē-əm, -shəm\ *n, pl* **-cia** \-sē-ə, -shē-ə, -shə\ *also* **-ciums** : any of a genus of somewhat slipper-shaped chiefly freshwater protozoans that move by cilia [New Latin, from Greek *paramēkēs* "oblong," from *para-* + *mēkos* "length"]

para·med·ic \ˌpar-ə-ˈmed-ik\ *n* **1** : one who assists a physician (as by giving injections and taking X-rays) **2** : a specially trained medical technician licensed to provide a wide range of emergency services (as intravenous administration of drugs) before or during transport to a hospital

para·med·i·cal \-ˈmed-i-kəl\ *adj* : concerned with helping with the work of highly trained medical professionals ⟨a *paramedical* aide⟩

pa·ram·e·ter \pə-ˈram-ət-ər\ *n* **1 a** : a mathematical constant that has a value which can be chosen in such a way that each different possible value causes a different member of a system (as a group of functions) to be described ⟨one of the *parameters* in the $y = mx + b$ equation of a line is the slope m⟩ **b** : a quantity (as a mean) that describes a statistical population **c** : an independent variable used to express the coordinates of a point ⟨if the coordinates (x, y) of a point are given by the functions $x = f(t)$ and $y = g(t)$ then the *parameter* is the variable t⟩ **2** : any set of physical properties whose values determine the characteristics or behavior of something ⟨*parameters* of the atmosphere such as temperature, pressure, and density⟩ **3** : a characteristic element : CHARACTERISTIC, FACTOR ⟨political dissent as a *parameter* of modern life⟩ [*para-* + Greek *metron* "measure"] — **para·met·ric** \ˌpar-ə-ˈme-trik\ *adj*

par·a·mount \ˈpar-ə-ˌmau̇nt\ *adj* : superior to all others : SUPREME [Medieval French *paramont,* from *par* "by" (from Latin *per*) + *amont* "above," from *a* "to" (from Latin *ad*) + *mont* "mountain"]

par·amour \ˈpar-ə-ˌmu̇r\ *n* : a partner in a sexual relationship other than that of husband and wife [Medieval French *par amour* "by way of love"]

par·a·noia \ˌpar-ə-ˈnȯi-ə\ *n* **1** : a serious mental disorder marked by feelings of persecution or an exaggerated sense of one's own importance usually without hallucinations **2** : a tendency toward excessive or unreasonable feelings of suspicion or distrust of others [Greek, "madness," from *paranous* "demented," from *para-* + *nous* "mind"] — **par·a·noi·ac** \-ˈnȯi-ˌak, -ˈnȯi-ik\ *adj or n*

par·a·noid \ˈpar-ə-ˌnȯid\ *adj* **1** : resembling paranoia **2** : characterized especially by suspiciousness, distrust, and feelings of persecution **3** : extremely fearful — **paranoid** *n*

par·a·pet \ˈpar-ə-pət, -ˌpet\ *n* **1** : a wall of earth or stone to protect soldiers **2** : a low wall or railing to protect the edge of a platform, roof, or bridge [Italian *parapetto,* from *parare* "to shield" (from Latin, "to prepare") + *petto* "breast, chest," from Latin *pectus*]

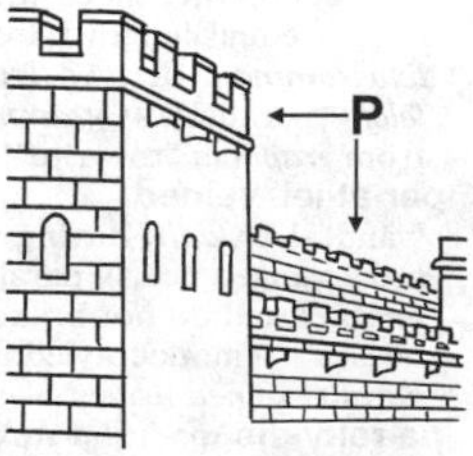

P parapet 1

par·a·pher·na·lia \ˌpar-ə-fər-ˈnāl-yə, -fə-ˈnāl-\ *n sing or pl* **1** : personal belongings **2** : articles of equipment [Medieval Latin, derived from Greek *parapherna* "goods a bride brings over and above the dowry," from *para-* + *phernē* "dowry," from *pherein* "to bear"]

¹**para·phrase** \ˈpar-ə-ˌfrāz\ *n* : a restatement of a text, passage, or work giving the meaning in another form

²**paraphrase** *vb* : to make a paraphrase of : give the meaning of something in different words — **para·phras·er** *n*

para·ple·gia \ˌpar-ə-ˈplē-jə, -jē-ə\ *n* : paralysis of the lower half of the body including of both legs [Greek *paraplēgiē* "paralysis of one side of the body," from *para-* + *-plēgia* "paralysis," from *plēssein* "to strike"] — **para·ple·gic** \-jik\ *adj or n*

para·po·di·um \ˌpar-ə-ˈpōd-ē-əm\ *n, pl* **-dia** \-ē-ə\ : either of a pair of fleshy lateral processes borne by most segments of a polychaete worm [derived from Greek *para-* + *podion* "small foot," from *pod-, pous* "foot"]

para·pro·fes·sion·al \-prə-ˈfesh-nəl, -ən-l\ *n* : a trained aide who assists a professional person

para·psy·chol·o·gy \ˌpar-ə-sī-ˈkäl-ə-jē\ *n* : a branch of study involving the investigation of telepathy, clairvoyance, and related psychological phenomena

para·sail·ing \ˈpar-ə-ˌsā-ling\ *n* : the recreational sport of soaring in a parachute while being towed usually by a motorboat

par·a·site \ˈpar-ə-ˌsīt\ *n* **1** : a person who lives at the expense of another **2** : an organism living in or on another organism in parasitism **3** : something that resembles a biological parasite in dependence on something else for existence or support without making a useful or adequate return [Middle French, "one habitually dining at the tables of others, sycophant," from Latin *parasitus,* from Greek *parasitos,* from *para-* + *sitos* "grain, food"] — **par·a·sit·ic** \ˌpar-ə-ˈsit-ik\ *also* **par·a·sit·i·cal** \-ˈsit-i-kəl\ *adj* — **par·a·sit·i·cal·ly** \-i-kə-lē, -klē\ *adv*

par·a·sit·ism \ˈpar-ə-ˌsīt-ˌiz-əm\ *n* : an intimate association between organisms of two or more kinds in which a parasite obtains benefits from a host which it usually injures

par·a·sit·ize \ˈpar-ə-sə-ˌtīz, -ˌsīt-ˌīz\ *vt* : to infest or live on or with as a parasite

par·a·si·tol·o·gy \ˌpar-ə-sə-ˈtäl-ə-jē, -ˌsīt-ˈäl-\ *n* : a branch of biology dealing with parasites and parasitism especially among animals — **par·a·si·tol·o·gist** \-jəst\ *n*

para·sol \ˈpar-ə-ˌsȯl\ *n* : a lightweight umbrella used as a sunshade [French, from Italian *parasole,* from *parare* "to shield" (from Latin, "to prepare") + *sole* "sun," from Latin *sol*]

para·sym·pa·thet·ic \ˌpar-ə-ˌsim-pə-ˈthet-ik\ *adj* : of, relating to, being, or acting on the parasympathetic nervous system

parasympathetic nervous system *n* : the part of the autonomic nervous system that is concerned especially with controlling the body during normal routine situations and that tends to induce secretion of the digestive and salivary glands, slow the heart rate, and increase the tone of smooth muscles (as of the intestine) and that acts on bodily organs by releasing acetylcholine at the ends of nerve fibers supplying them — compare SYMPATHETIC NERVOUS SYSTEM

para·thi·on \ˌpar-ə-ˈthī-ən, -ˌän\ *n* : an extremely toxic insecticide that is a derivative of a sulfur-containing phosphoric acid [derived from *para-* + *thi-*]

par·a·thor·mone \ˌpar-ə-ˈthȯr-ˌmōn\ *n* : PARATHYROID HORMONE

¹**para·thy·roid** \-ˈthī-ˌrȯid\ *n* : PARATHYROID GLAND

²**parathyroid** *adj* : of, relating to, or produced by the parathyroid glands

parathyroid gland *n* : any of usually four small endocrine glands adjacent to or embedded in the thyroid gland that produce parathyroid hormone

parathyroid hormone *n* : a hormone that is produced by the parathyroid glands and regulates the amount of calcium and phosphorus in the blood

para·troops \ˈpar-ə-ˌtrüps\ *n pl* : troops trained and equipped to parachute from an airplane — **para·troop** \-ˌtrüp\ *adj* — **para·troop·er** \-ˌtrü-pər\ *n*

¹**para·ty·phoid** \ˌpar-ə-ˈtī-ˌfȯid, -tī-ˈ\ *adj* **1** : resembling typhoid fever **2** : of or relating to paratyphoid or its causative organisms ⟨*paratyphoid* infection⟩

²**paratyphoid** *n* : a disease caused by bacteria that resembles typhoid fever and usually occurs from eating contaminated food

par·boil \ˈpär-ˌbȯil\ *vt* : to boil briefly usually before cooking in another manner [Middle French *parbouillir* "to boil thoroughly," from Late Latin *perbullire,* from Latin *per-* + *bullire* "to boil"]

¹**par·cel** \ˈpär-səl\ *n* **1** : a part of a whole : PORTION **2** : a plot of land **3** : a group or collection of persons or things ⟨told a *parcel* of lies⟩ **4** : a wrapped bundle : PACKAGE [Medieval French, derived from Latin *particula* "small part, particle"]

²**parcel** *vt* **par·celed** *or* **par·celled; par·cel·ing** *or* **par·cel·ling** \ˈpär-sə-ling, -sling\ **1** : to divide into parts : DISTRIBUTE **2** : to make up into a parcel

parcel post *n* **1** : a mail service handling parcels **2** : packages handled by parcel post

parch \'pärch\ *vb* **1** : to toast under dry heat **2** : to dry up : shrivel with heat [Middle English]

parched \'pärcht\ *adj* : deprived of natural moisture ‹*parched* hillsides› ‹a *parched* throat›; *also* : THIRSTY ‹*parched* hikers›

parch·ment \'pärch-mənt\ *n* **1** : the skin of a sheep or goat prepared for use as a writing material **2** : a paper made to resemble parchment **3** : something (as a diploma) written on parchment [Medieval French *parchemin,* from Latin *pergamena,* from Greek *pergamēnē,* from *Pergamēnos* "of Pergamum," from *Pergamon* "Pergamum"]

[1]**pard** \'pärd\ *n* : LEOPARD [Medieval French *parde,* from Latin *pardus,* from Greek *pardos*]

[2]**pard** *n, chiefly dialect* : CHUM [short for *pardner,* alteration of *partner*]

[1]**par·don** \'pärd-n\ *n* **1 a** : the excusing of an offense without a penalty **b** : a release from the legal penalties of an offense **2** : excuse for a fault or discourtesy [Medieval French *pardun,* from *parduner* "to pardon," from Late Latin *perdonare* "to grant freely," from Latin *per-* + *donare* "to give"] — **par·don·able** \'pärd-nə-bəl, -n-ə-bəl\ *adj* — **par·don·ably** \-blē\ *adv*

[2]**pardon** *vt* **par·doned; par·don·ing** \'pärd-ning, -n-ing\ **1** : to free from penalty **2** : to allow (an offense) to pass without punishment : FORGIVE ***synonyms*** see EXCUSE

pare \'paər, 'peər\ *vt* **1** : to cut or shave off the outside or the ends of ‹*pare* an apple› **2** : to reduce as if by paring ‹*pare* expenses› [Medieval French *parer* "make, prepare, pare," from Latin *parare* "to prepare, acquire"]

par·e·gor·ic \ˌpar-ə-'gȯr-ik, -'gōr-, -'gär-\ *n* : a solution of opium and camphor in alcohol used especially to relieve pain [French *parégorique* "alleviating pain," from Latin *paregoricus,* from Greek *parēgorikos,* from *parēgorein* "to talk over, soothe," from *para-* + *agora* "assembly"]

pa·ren·chy·ma \pə-'reng-kə-mə\ *n* **1** : the distinctive functional tissue of an animal organ (as a gland) as distinguished from its supporting tissue or framework **2** : a tissue of higher plants consisting of thin-walled living cells that remain capable of cell division even when mature, are agents of photosynthesis and storage, and make up much of the substance of leaves and roots and the pulp of fruits as well as parts of stems and supporting structures [New Latin, from Greek, "tissue of the viscera," from *parenchein* "to pour in beside," from *para-* + *en-* + *chein* "to pour"] — **par·en·chy·mal** \pə-'reng-kə-məl\ *also* **pa·ren·chy·ma·tous** \ˌpar-ən-'kim-ət-əs, -'kīm-\ *adj*

par·ent \'par-ənt, 'per-\ *n* **1 a** : a person who is a father or mother **b** : an animal or plant that produces offspring **2** : the source or originator of something [Medieval French, from Latin *parens,* from *parere* "to give birth to"] — **parent** *adj*

par·ent·age \-ənt-ij\ *n* : descent from parents or ancestors : LINEAGE ‹a person of noble *parentage*›

pa·ren·tal \pə-'rent-l\ *adj* : of, typical of, or being parents ‹*parental* affection› — **pa·ren·tal·ly** \-l-ē\ *adv*

pa·ren·the·sis \pə-'ren-thə-səs\ *n, pl* **-the·ses** \-thə-ˌsēz\ **1 a** : a word, phrase, or sentence inserted in a passage to explain or comment on it **b** : DIGRESSION **2** : one of a pair of marks ( ) used to enclose a parenthesis or to group a symbolic unit in a mathematical expression [Late Latin, from Greek, literally, "act of inserting," from *parentithenai* "to insert," from *para-* + *en-* + *tithenai* "to place"] — **par·en·thet·ic** \ˌpar-ən-'thet-ik\ *or* **par·en·thet·i·cal** \-'thet-i-kəl\ *adj* — **par·en·thet·i·cal·ly** \-i-kə-lē, -klē\ *adv*

pa·ren·the·size \pə-'ren-thə-ˌsīz, -'rent-\ *vt* : to make a parenthesis of

par·ent·hood \'par-ənt-ˌhu̇d, 'per-\ *n* : the position, function, or standing of a parent

pa·re·sis \pə-'rē-səs, 'par-ə-\ *n, pl* **-re·ses** \-ˌsēz\ **1** : slight or partial paralysis **2** : GENERAL PARESIS [Greek, "paralysis, neglect," from *parienai* "to let fall," from *para-* + *hienai* "to let go, send"] — **pa·ret·ic** \pə-'ret-ik\ *adj or n*

par excellence \ˌpär-ˌek-sə-'läⁿs\ *adv or adj* : in the highest degree [French, literally, "by excellence"]

par·fait \pär-'fā\ *n* **1** : a flavored custard containing whipped cream and syrup frozen without stirring **2** : a cold dessert made of layers of fruit, syrup, ice cream, and whipped cream [French, from *parfait* "perfect," from Latin *perfectus*]

par·he·lion \pär-'hēl-yən\ *n, pl* **-lia** \-yə\ : any one of several bright spots often tinged with color that often appear on both sides of the sun and at the same altitude as the sun [Latin *parelion,* from Greek *parēlion,* from *para-* + *hēlios* "sun"]

pa·ri·ah \pə-'rī-ə\ *n* **1** : a member of a low caste of southern India **2** : a person despised or rejected by society : OUTCAST [Tamil *paraiyan,* literally, "drummer"]

pa·ri·e·tal \pə-'rī-ət-l\ *adj* : of, relating to, or forming the walls of a part or cavity and especially the upper back wall of the head [Medieval Latin *parietalis,* from *pariet-, paries* "wall of a cavity or hollow organ," from Latin, "wall"]

parietal bone *n* : either of a pair of bones of the roof of the skull between the frontal bones and the occipital bones

pari–mu·tu·el \ˌpar-i-'myü-chə-wəl, -chəl\ *n* : a system of betting (as on a race) in which those who bet on the competitors finishing in the first three places share the total amount bet minus a percentage for the management [French *pari mutuel,* literally, "mutual stake"]

par·ing \'paər-ing, 'peər-\ *n* **1** : the act of cutting away an edge or surface **2** : something pared off ‹apple *parings*›

par·ish \'par-ish\ *n* **1 a** : a section of a diocese in the charge of a priest or minister **b** : the persons who live in and attend the church of such a section **2** : the members of any church **3** : a civil division of the state of Louisiana corresponding to a county in other states [Medieval French *paroche, parosse,* from Late Latin *parochia,* from Late Greek *paroikia,* from *paroikos* "Christian," from Greek, "stranger," from *para-* + *oikos* "house"]

pa·rish·io·ner \pə-'rish-nər, -ə-nər\ *n* : a member or resident of a parish

par·i·ty \'par-ət-ē\ *n, pl* **-ties** : the quality or state of being equal or equivalent [Latin *paritas,* from *par* "equal"]

[1]**park** \'pärk\ *n* **1** : a tract of land attached to a country house and used for recreation **2 a** : a piece of ground in or near a city or town kept as a place of beauty and recreation **b** : an area maintained in its natural state as a public property **3 a** : a space occupied by military animals, vehicles, or materials **b** : PARKING LOT **4** : an enclosed arena or stadium used especially for ball games [Medieval French *parc* "enclosure," from Medieval Latin *parricus*]

[2]**park** *vb* **1 a** : to leave a vehicle temporarily on a public way or in a parking lot or garage **b** : to land or leave an airplane **2** : to set and leave temporarily

par·ka \'pär-kə\ *n* : a winter jacket with a hood [Aleut, "skin, outer garment," from Russian dialect, of Uralic origin]

parking lot *n* : an outdoor area for the parking of motor vehicles

Par·kin·son's disease \'pär-kən-sənz-\ *n* : a neurological disease chiefly of later life that tends to get steadily worse, is linked to decreased dopamine production by the brain, and is marked especially by stiff and trembling muscles, slowness of movement, and a shuffling walk

park·way \'pär-ˌkwā\ *n* : a broad landscaped thoroughfare

par·lance \'pär-ləns\ *n* : choice of words : IDIOM [Middle French, from *parler* "to speak"]

[1]**par·lay** \'pär-ˌlā, -lē\ *vt* **1** : to bet in a parlay **2 a** : to exploit successfully ‹*parlay* a good idea into a fortune› **b** : to increase or transform into something of much greater value ‹*parlayed* a drawback into an asset›

[2]**parlay** *n* : a series of bets in which the original stake plus its winnings are risked on the successive wagers [French *paroli,* from Italian dialect, perhaps from *paro* "equal," from Latin *par*]

par·ley \'pär-lē\ *vi* **par·leyed; par·ley·ing** : to speak with another : CONFER; *esp* : to discuss terms with an enemy [Medieval French *parlee* "speech," from *parler* "to speak," from Medieval Latin *parabolare,* from Late Latin *parabola* "speech, parable"] — **parley** *n*

par·lia·ment \'pär-lə-mənt *also* 'pärl-yə-\ *n* **1** : a formal conference on public affairs; *esp* : a council of state in early medieval England **2 a** : an assemblage of the nobility, clergy, and commons called together by the British sovereign as the supreme legislative body in the United Kingdom **b** : a similar assemblage in another nation or state **3 a** : the supreme legislative body of a political unit comprising a series of successive parliaments **b** : the British House of Commons [Medieval French *parlement,* from *parler* "to speak"]

par·lia·men·tar·i·an \ˌpär-lə-ˌmen-ˈter-ē-ən, -mən- *also* ˌpärl-yə-\ *n* : an expert in parliamentary procedure

par·lia·men·ta·ry \-ˈment-ə-rē, -ˈmen-trē\ *adj* **1** : of, relating to, or enacted by a parliament **2** : of or relating to government by a cabinet whose members belong to and are responsible to the legislature **3** : being in accordance with the rules and customs of a parliament or other deliberative body

par·lor \ˈpär-lər\ *n* **1** : a room in a home, hotel, or club used for conversation or the reception of guests **2** : any of various business places ⟨funeral *parlor*⟩ ⟨beauty *parlor*⟩ [Medieval French *parlour,* from *parler* "to speak"]

parlor car *n* : an extra-fare railroad passenger car equipped with individual chairs and formerly used for day travel

par·lous \ˈpär-ləs\ *adj* : full of uncertainty or risk ⟨*parlous* times⟩ [Middle English, alteration of *perilous*] — **par·lous·ly** *adv*

pa·ro·chi·al \pə-ˈrō-kē-əl\ *adj* **1** : of or relating to a parish **2** : limited in range or scope : NARROW, PROVINCIAL ⟨a *parochial* attitude⟩ [Medieval French, from Late Latin *parochialis,* from *parochia* "parish"] — **pa·ro·chi·al·ism** \-kē-ə-ˌliz-əm\ *n* — **pa·ro·chi·al·ly** \-kē-ə-lē\ *adv*

parochial school *n* : a school maintained by a religious body

par·o·dy \ˈpar-əd-ē\ *n, pl* **-dies** **1** : a literary or musical work in which the style of an author or work is closely imitated for comic effect or in ridicule **2** : a feeble or ridiculous imitation [Latin *parodia,* from Greek *parōidia,* from *para-* + *aidein* "to sing"] ***synonyms*** see CARICATURE — **par·o·dist** \-əd-əst\ *n* — **parody** *vt*

[1]**pa·role** \pə-ˈrōl\ *n* **1** : a promise confirmed by a pledge; *esp* : the promise of a prisoner of war to fulfill stated conditions in return for release **2** : a conditional release of a prisoner before the sentence has expired [French, "speech, parole," from Medieval French, from Late Latin *parabola* "speech, parable"]

[2]**parole** *vt* : to release (a prisoner) on parole — **pa·rol·ee** \pə-ˌrō-ˈlē, ˌpar-ə-ˈlē\ *n*

pa·rot·id \pə-ˈrät-əd\ *adj* : of or relating to the parotid gland [New Latin *parotis* "parotid gland," from Latin, "tumor near the ear," from Greek *parōtis,* from *para-* + *ōt-, ous* "ear"]

parotid gland *n* : either of a pair of large salivary glands situated below and in front of the ear

par·ox·ysm \ˈpar-ək-ˌsiz-əm\ *n* **1** : a fit, attack, or sudden increase of symptoms (as of a disease) that occurs at intervals ⟨a *paroxysm* of coughing⟩ **2** : a sudden violent emotion or action ⟨*paroxysms* of rage⟩ [Medieval Latin *paroxysmus,* from Greek *paroxysmos,* from *paroxynein* "to stimulate," from *para-* + *oxynein* "to provoke," from *oxys* "sharp"] — **par·ox·ys·mal** \ˌpar-ək-ˈsiz-məl\ *adj*

par·quet \ˈpär-ˌkā, pär-ˈ\ *n* **1** : a flooring of parquetry **2** : the lower floor of a theater especially in front of the balcony [French, from Medieval French, "small enclosure," from *parc* "park"]

par·que·try \ˈpär-kə-trē\ *n, pl* **-tries** : a patterned wood inlay used especially for floors

parr \ˈpär\ *n, pl* **parr** *also* **parrs** : a young salmon actively feeding in fresh water [origin unknown]

par·ri·cide \ˈpar-ə-ˌsīd\ *n* **1** : one who murders one's father or mother or a close relative **2** : the act of a parricide [Latin *parricida* "killer of a close relative"] — **par·ri·cid·al** \ˌpar-ə-ˈsīd-l\ *adj*

[1]**par·rot** \ˈpar-ət\ *n* **1** : any of numerous usually brightly colored tropical birds characterized by a strong hooked bill, by toes arranged in pairs with two in front and two behind, and often by the ability to mimic speech **2** : a person who repeats words mechanically and without understanding [probably from Middle French *perroquet*]

[2]**parrot** *vt* : to repeat mechanically ⟨the child *parroted* his mother's words⟩

parrot fever *n* : PSITTACOSIS

parrot fish *n* : any of various chiefly tropical marine fishes related to the perches that have the teeth fused into a cutting plate resembling a beak

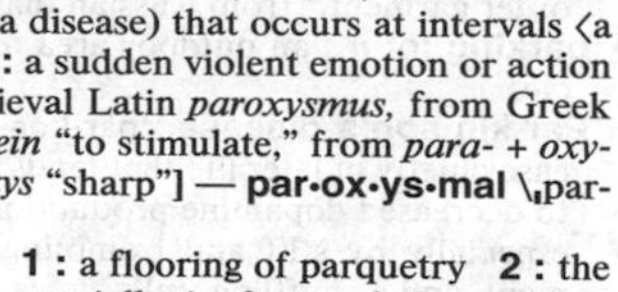

parrot fish

par·ry \ˈpar-ē\ *vb* **par·ried; par·ry·ing** **1** : to ward off a weapon or blow : turn aside skillfully **2** : to evade especially by a clever answer ⟨*parry* an embarrassing question⟩ [probably from French *parez,* imperative of *parer,* from Old Occitan *parar,* from Latin *parare* "to prepare"] — **parry** *n*

parse \ˈpärs, ˈpärz\ *vb* **1** : to analyze a sentence by naming its parts and their relations to each other **2** : to give the part of speech of a word and explain its relation to other words in a sentence [Latin *pars orationis* "part of speech"]

par·sec \ˈpär-ˌsek\ *n* : a unit of measure for interstellar space equal to 3.26 light-years [*par*allax + *sec*ond]

Par·si *also* **Par·see** \ˈpär-ˌsē\ *n* : a Zoroastrian descended from Persian refugees settled principally at Bombay [Persian *pārsī,* from *Pārs* "Persia"]

par·si·mo·ny \ˈpär-sə-ˌmō-nē\ *n* : extreme frugality : STINGINESS [Latin *parsimonia,* from *parsus,* past participle of *parcere* "to spare"] — **par·si·mo·ni·ous** \ˌpär-sə-ˈmō-nē-əs\ *adj* — **par·si·mo·ni·ous·ly** *adv*

pars·ley \ˈpär-slē\ *n, pl* **parsleys** : a European biennial herb related to the carrot and widely grown for its finely divided leaves which are used as a flavoring or garnish; *also* : the leaves [Old English *petersilie,* from Latin *petroselinum,* from Greek *petroselinon,* from *petros* "stone" + *selinon* "celery"]

pars·nip \ˈpär-snəp\ *n* : a Eurasian biennial herb related to the carrot and grown for its long white root which is cooked as a vegetable; *also* : this root [Middle English *pasnepe,* from Medieval French *pasnaie,* from Latin *pastinaca*]

par·son \ˈpärs-n\ *n* **1** : RECTOR 1 **2** : CLERGYMAN; *esp* : a Protestant pastor [Medieval French *persone,* from Medieval Latin *persona,* literally, "person," from Latin]

par·son·age \ˈpär-snij, ˈpärs-n-ij\ *n* : the house provided by a church for its pastor

[1]**part** \ˈpärt\ *n* **1 a** : one of the portions into which something is divisible and which together constitute the whole **b** : one of several or many equal units of which something is composed ⟨a fifth *part* for each⟩ **c** : a portion of a plant or animal body : MEMBER, ORGAN ⟨wash the injured *part*⟩ **d** : a vocal or instrumental line or melody in music written in harmony; *also* : the score for it **e** : a constituent member of a machine or apparatus; *also* : a spare piece or member **2** : something falling to one in a division or apportionment : SHARE **3** : one's shared or allotted task ⟨one must do one's *part*⟩ **4** : one of the sides in a conflict ⟨take someone's *part* in a quarrel⟩ **5** : a portion of an unspecified territorial area — usually used in plural ⟨took off for *parts* unknown⟩ **6** : a function or course of action performed **7 a** : an actor's lines in a play **b** : the role of a character in a play **8** : a constituent of character or capacity : TALENT ⟨a person of many *parts*⟩ **9** : the line where the hair is divided in combing [Medieval French and Old English, both from Latin *part-, pars*] — **for the most part** : in general ⟨*for the most part* the class was well behaved⟩ — **in part** : in some degree : PARTIALLY ⟨the program was sponsored *in part* by public donations⟩ — **on the part of** : with regard to the one specified ⟨an enthusiastic response *on the part of* students⟩

synonyms PART, PORTION, PIECE, SEGMENT mean something less than the whole. PART is the general term and is interchangeable with any of the others. PORTION suggests an assigned or allotted part ⟨a minor *portion* of the voting population⟩ ⟨each child received a *portion* of the cake⟩. PIECE applies to a separate or detached part ⟨a *piece* of pie⟩. SEGMENT applies to a part separated or marked out by natural lines of cleavage ⟨*segments* of an orange⟩.

[2]**part** *vb* **1 a** : to leave someone — used with *from* or *with* **b** : to take leave of one another ⟨the friends had to *part*⟩ **2** : to become separated into parts **3** : to go away : DEPART **4** : to give up possession or control ⟨wouldn't *part* with the old car⟩ **5 a** : to divide into parts **b** : to separate by combing on each side of a line **6 a** : to keep separate ⟨the channel that *parts* England and France⟩ **b** : to hold (as fighters) apart [Medieval French *partir,* from Latin *partire* "to divide," from *part-, pars* "part"]

[3]**part** *adv* : in a measure : PARTLY ⟨was only *part* right⟩

par·take \pär-ˈtāk, pər-\ *vi* **par·took** \-ˈtu̇k\; **par·tak·en** \-ˈtā-kən\; **par·tak·ing** **1 a** : to take a share ⟨*partake* of a meal⟩ **b** : PARTICIPATE ⟨all may *partake* in the ceremony⟩ **2** : to have some of the qualities or attributes of something ⟨their actions *partook* of rebellion⟩ [back-formation from *partaker,* from *part taker*] — **par·tak·er** *n*

part·ed \ˈpärt-əd\ *adj* : divided into parts

par·terre \pär-ˈteər\ *n* **1** : an ornamental garden with paths between the beds **2 :** the part of the floor of a theater behind the orchestra [French, from *par terre* "on the ground"]

par·the·no·car·py \ˈpär-thə-nō-ˌkär-pē\ *n* **:** the production of fruits without fertilization [Greek *parthenos* "virgin" + *karpos* "fruit"] — **par·the·no·car·pic** \ˌpär-thə-nō-ˈkär-pik\ *adj*

par·the·no·gen·e·sis \ˌpär-thə-nō-ˈjen-ə-səs\ *n, pl* **-gen·e·ses** \-ə-ˌsēz\ **:** reproduction especially among lower plants and invertebrate animals in which an unfertilized gamete develops into a new individual [Greek *parthenos* "virgin"] — **par·the·no·ge·net·ic** \-jə-ˈnet-ik\ *also* **par·the·no·gen·ic** \-jen-ik\ *adj* — **par·the·no·ge·net·i·cal·ly** \-ˈnet-i-kə-lē, -klē\ *adv*

par·tial \ˈpär-shəl\ *adj* **1 :** of, relating to, or being a part rather than the whole ⟨a *partial* eclipse⟩ **2 :** markedly or overly fond of someone or something ⟨*partial* to milk shakes⟩ **3 :** inclined to favor one side or party over another ⟨the judge was *partial*⟩ [Late Latin *partialis,* from Latin *part-, pars* "part"] — **par·tial·ly** \ˈpärsh-lē, -ə-lē\ *adv*

partial denture *n* **:** an often removable artificial replacement for one or more teeth

par·ti·al·i·ty \ˌpär-shē-ˈal-ət-ē, pär-ˈshal-\ *n, pl* **-ties** **1 :** the quality or state of being partial **:** BIAS **2 :** a special taste or liking

partial product *n* **:** a product of the multiplicand and one digit of a two or more digit multiplier

par·ti·ble \ˈpärt-ə-bəl\ *adj* **:** DIVISIBLE

par·tic·i·pant \pər-ˈtis-ə-pənt, pär-\ *n* **:** one that participates

par·tic·i·pate \pər-ˈtis-ə-ˌpāt, pär-\ *vi* **:** to engage or have a share in something in common with others [Latin *participare,* from *particeps* "participant," from part-, *pars* "part" + *capere* "to take"] — **par·tic·i·pa·tion** \-ˌtis-ə-ˈpā-shən\ *n* — **par·tic·i·pa·tor** \-ˈtis-ə-ˌpāt-ər\ *n* — **par·tic·i·pa·to·ry** \-ˈtis-ə-pə-ˌtōr-ē, -ˌtȯr-\ *adj*

par·ti·cip·i·al \ˌpärt-ə-ˈsip-ē-əl\ *adj* **:** of, relating to, or formed with or from a participle ⟨*participial* phrase⟩ — **par·ti·cip·i·al·ly** \-ē-ə-lē\ *adv*

par·ti·ci·ple \ˈpärt-ə-ˌsip-əl\ *n* **:** a verb form that sometimes can also be used like an adjective ⟨"burning" and "collapsed" are *participles* in "the burning building had collapsed"⟩ [Medieval French, from Latin *participium,* from *particeps* "participant"]

par·ti·cle \ˈpärt-i-kəl\ *n* **1 :** one of the minute subdivisions of matter (as a molecule, atom, electron); *also* **:** ELEMENTARY PARTICLE **2 a :** a tiny amount or fragment **b :** the smallest possible part **3 :** a word (as an article, preposition, or conjunction) expressing a general meaning or a connective or limiting relation [Latin *particula,* from *part-, pars* "part"]

par·ti·cle·board \-ˌbōrd, -ˌbȯrd\ *n* **:** a board made of very small pieces of wood stuck together

par·ti–col·or \ˈpärt-ē-ˌkəl-ər\ *or* **par·ti–col·ored** \-ərd\ *adj* **:** showing different colors or tints; *esp* **:** having a predominant color broken by patches of one or more other colors ⟨a *particolor* cat⟩ [obsolete English *party* "parti-colored," from Middle English *parti,* from Medieval French, "of two colors," from *partir* "to divide, part"]

[1]**par·tic·u·lar** \pər-ˈtik-yə-lər, pə-, -ˈtik-ə-lər, -ˈtik-lər\ *adj* **1 :** of or relating to a single person or thing **2 :** of or relating to details **:** MINUTE **3 :** distinctive among others **:** SPECIAL **4 a :** attentive to details **:** EXACT **b :** hard to please **:** EXACTING [Medieval French *particuler,* from Late Latin *particularis,* from Latin *particula* "small part, particle"] ***synonyms*** see CIRCUMSTANTIAL

[2]**particular** *n* **:** an individual fact, detail, or item ***synonyms*** see ITEM — **in particular :** in distinction from others **:** SPECIFICALLY

par·tic·u·lar·i·ty \-ˌtik-yə-ˈlar-ət-ē\ *n, pl* **-ties** **1 a :** a minute detail **b :** an individual characteristic **:** PECULIARITY **2 :** attentiveness to detail **:** EXACTNESS, CARE

par·tic·u·lar·ize \-ˈtik-yə-lə-ˌrīz, -ˈtik-lə-\ *vb* **:** to go into details **:** state in detail **:** SPECIFY — **par·tic·u·lar·i·za·tion** \-ˌtik-yə-lə-rə-ˈzā-shən, -ˌtik-lə-\ *n*

par·tic·u·lar·ly \pər-ˈtik-yə-lē, pə-, -yə-lər-lē, -ˈtik-lē, -ˈtik-ə-lē\ *adv* **1 :** in detail **2 :** to an unusual degree

par·tic·u·late \pər-ˈtik-yə-lət, pär-, -ˌlāt\ *adj* **:** relating to or existing as minute separate particles — **particulate** *n*

particulate inheritance *n* **:** MENDELIAN INHERITANCE

[1]**part·ing** \ˈpärt-ing\ *n* **1 :** FAREWELL 2 **2 :** a place or point where a division or separation occurs — **parting of the ways** **1 :** PARTING 2 **2 :** a place or time at which a choice must be made

[2]**parting** *adj* **:** involving, given, taken, or performed at parting ⟨a *parting* kiss⟩

par·ti·san \ˈpärt-ə-zən\ *n* **1 :** a person who supports the position of another; *esp* **:** a devoted adherent to the cause of another **2 :** an irregular soldier who operates behind enemy lines [Middle French, from north Italian dialect *partiźan,* from *part* "part, party," from Latin *part-, pars*] — **partisan** *adj* — **par·ti·san·ship** \-ˌship\ *n*

par·tite \ˈpär-ˌtīt\ *adj* **:** divided into a usually specified number of parts [Latin *partitus,* from *partire* "to divide," from *part-, pars* "part"]

par·ti·tion \pər-ˈtish-ən, pär-\ *n* **1 a :** the action of parting **:** DIVISION **b :** separation of a class or whole into components; *esp* **:** the division of a united territory among two or more governments **2 :** an interior dividing wall **3 :** PART 1a, SECTION — **partition** *vt* — **par·ti·tion·er** \-ˈtish-nər, -ə-nər\ *n*

par·ti·tive \ˈpärt-ət-iv\ *adj* **1 :** of, relating to, or denoting a part ⟨a *partitive* construction⟩ **2 :** serving to indicate the whole of which a part is specified ⟨*partitive* genitive⟩ — **partitive** *n* — **par·ti·tive·ly** *adv*

part·ly \ˈpärt-lē\ *adv* **:** in some measure or degree

[1]**part·ner** \ˈpärt-nər\ *n* **1 a :** one associated in action with another **:** COLLEAGUE **b :** either of a couple who dance together **c :** one of usually two persons who play together in a game against an opposing side **d :** a person with whom one shares an intimate relationship **:** one member of a couple **2 :** a member of a partnership [Middle English *partener* "sharer," alteration of *parcener,* from Medieval French, "partner, joint heir," from *parcion* "division, share," from Latin *partitio,* from *partire* "to divide"]

[2]**partner** *vb* **:** to join as a partner **:** be or act as a partner

part·ner·ship \ˈpärt-nər-ˌship\ *n* **1 :** the state of being a partner **2 :** a business organization owned by two or more persons who agree to share the profits and usually are liable individually for losses

part of speech : a traditional class of words distinguished according to the kind of idea denoted and the function performed in a sentence — compare ADJECTIVE, ADVERB, CONJUNCTION, INTERJECTION, NOUN, PREPOSITION, PRONOUN, VERB

partook *past of* PARTAKE

par·tridge \ˈpär-trij\ *n, pl* **partridge** *or* **par·tridg·es** **:** any of several stout-bodied Old World birds that are related to the common domestic chicken and are often hunted as game; *also* **:** any of various similar and related North American birds (as a bobwhite or ruffed grouse) [Medieval French *perdriz,* from Latin *perdix,* from Greek]

partridge

par·tridge·ber·ry \-ˌber-ē\ *n* **:** a trailing evergreen plant of the eastern U.S. and Canada with small somewhat round leaves and edible slightly tart scarlet berries; *also* **:** its berry

part–song \ˈpärt-ˌsȯng\ *n* **:** a usually unaccompanied song of two or more voice parts with one part carrying the melody

part–time \ˈpärt-ˈtīm\ *adj* **:** involving or working less than customary or standard hours — **part–time** *adv*

par·tu·ri·ent \pär-ˈtu̇r-ē-ənt, -ˈtyu̇r-\ *adj* **:** bringing forth or about to bring forth young; *also* **:** of or relating to parturition [Latin *parturiens,* present participle of *parturire* "to be in labor," from *parere* "to bring forth"]

par·tu·ri·tion \ˌpärt-ə-ˈrish-ən, ˌpar-chə-\ *n* **:** CHILDBIRTH [Late Latin *parturitio,* from Latin *parturire* "to be in labor"]

[1]**par·ty** \ˈpärt-ē\ *n, pl* **parties** **1 :** a side in a dispute or contest ⟨the *parties* to a lawsuit⟩ **2 :** a group of persons organized for the purpose of directing the policies of a government **3 :** a person or group participating in an activity or affair ⟨a *party* to the transaction⟩ ⟨a mountain-climbing *party*⟩ **4 :** a particular individual **:** PERSON ⟨get the right *party* on the telephone⟩ **5 :** a detail of soldiers **6 :** a social gathering; *also* **:** the entertainment

\ə\ **abut**	\au̇\ **out**	\i\ **tip**	\ȯ\ **saw**	\u̇\ **foot**
\ər\ **further**	\ch\ **chin**	\ī\ **life**	\ȯi\ **coin**	\y\ **yet**
\a\ **mat**	\e\ **pet**	\j\ **job**	\th\ **thin**	\yü\ **few**
\ā\ **take**	\ē\ **easy**	\ng\ **sing**	\t͟h\ **this**	\yu̇\ **cure**
\ä\ **cot, cart**	\g\ **go**	\ō\ **bone**	\ü\ **food**	\zh\ **vision**

provided for it [Medieval French *partie* "part, party," from *partir* "to divide, part"] — **party** *adj*

[2]**party** *vi* **par·tied; par·ty·ing** : to give or attend parties

party line *n* **1** : a single telephone circuit connecting two or more subscribers with the exchange **2** : the principles or policies of an individual or organization; *esp* : the official policies of a Communist party — **par·ty–lin·er** \ˌpärt-ē-ˈlī-nər\ *n*

par·ve·nu \ˈpär-və-ˌnü, -ˌnyü\ *n* : one who has recently or suddenly risen to wealth or power and has not yet secured the social position appropriate to it : UPSTART [French, from *parvenir* "to arrive," from Latin *pervenire,* from *per-* "through" + *venire* "to come"] — **parvenu** *adj*

par·vo·vi·rus \ˈpär-vō-ˌvī-rəs\ *n* : a contagious disease of dogs that is caused by a virus and is marked by loss of appetite, drowsiness, diarrhea, vomiting, and sometimes death [New Latin *Parvovirus,* a genus of small viruses, from Latin *parvus* "small"]

pas·cal \pas-ˈkal\ *n* **1** : a unit of pressure in the metric system equal to one newton per square meter **2** *cap P or all cap* : a computer programming language developed from ALGOL [Blaise *Pascal*]

Pas·cal's triangle \pas-ˈkalz-\ *n* : a system of numbers arranged in rows resembling a triangle with each row consisting of the coefficients in the expansion $(a + b)^n$ for $n = 1, 2, 3, \ldots$ [Blaise *Pascal*]

Pasch \ˈpask\ *n* **1** : PASSOVER **2** : EASTER [Medieval French *pasche,* from Late Latin *pascha,* from Greek, from Hebrew *pesaḥ*] — **pas·chal** \ˈpas-kəl\ *adj*

Paschal Lamb *n* : AGNUS DEI 2

pas de deux \ˌpäd-ə-ˈdər, -ˈdü, -ˈdœ\ *n, pl* **pas de deux** \-ˈdər, -ˈdərz, -ˈdü, -ˈdüz, -ˈdœ, -ˈdœz\ : a dance or figure for two performers [French, literally, "step for two"]

pas de trois \-ˈtrwä, -trə-ˈwä\ *n, pl* **pas de trois** \-ˈtrwä, -ˈtrwäz, -trə-ˈwä, -trə-ˈwäz\ : a dance or figure for three performers [French, literally, "step for three"]

pa·sha \ˈpäsh-ə, ˈpash-ə, pə-ˈshä\ *n* : a high-ranking official (as in Turkey or northern Africa) [Turkish *paşa*]

Pash·to \ˈpəsh-tō\ *also* **Push·tu** \-tü\ *n* : the Iranian language of the Pashtuns [Persian *pashtu,* from Pashto]

Pash·tun *also* **Push·tun** \ˌpəsh-ˈtün\ *n, pl* **Pashtuns** *also* **Pushtuns** *or* **Pashtun** *also* **Pushtun** : a member of a people of eastern and southern Afghanistan and adjacent parts of Pakistan [Pashto *paštun, paxtun*]

pasque·flow·er \ˈpask-ˌflau̇-ər, -ˌflau̇r\ *n* : any of several anemones with compound leaves arranged like a hand with fingers spread and large usually white or purple flowers in early spring [Middle French *passefleur,* from *passer* "to pass" + *fleur* "flower," from Latin *flor-, flos*]

[1]**pass** \ˈpas\ *vb* **1** : GO 1, PROCEED **2 a** : to go away : DEPART **b** : DIE 1 — often used with *on* or *away* **3** : to go by : move past **4 a** : to go or cause or let go across, over, or through **b** : to go unchallenged ⟨let that remark *pass*⟩ **5 a** : to change or transfer ownership **b** : to go from the control or possession of one person or group to that of another ⟨the throne *passed* to the heir⟩ **6 a** : HAPPEN 2, OCCUR **b** : to take place as a mutual exchange or transaction ⟨words *passed*⟩ **7 a** : to become approved by a legislative body **b** : to go through or let go through an inspection, test, or course of study successfully **8 a** : to serve as a medium of exchange **b** : to be held or regarded ⟨*passed* for an honest person⟩ **9** : to execute a pass in a game **10** : to decline to bid, bet, or draw an additional card in a card game **11** : to go beyond; *esp* : SURPASS ⟨*passes* all expectations⟩ **12** : to leave out in an account or narration **13 a** : to live through : UNDERGO **b** : to cause or permit to elapse : SPEND ⟨*pass* time⟩ **14** : to secure the approval of ⟨the bill *passed* the Senate⟩ **15 a** : to give official sanction or approval to ⟨*pass* a law⟩ **b** : OVERLOOK 3b **16 a** : to put in circulation ⟨*pass* bad checks⟩ **b** : to transfer from one person to another ⟨*pass* the salt⟩ **c** : to take a turn with (as a rope) around something **d** : to transfer (as a ball) to another player on the same team **e** : to go from one state or form to another ⟨*passes* from a liquid to a gaseous state⟩ **17 a** : to pronounce judicially ⟨*pass* sentence⟩ **b** : UTTER 2 **18** : to cause to march or go by in order ⟨*pass* the troops in review⟩ **19** : to emit or discharge from the bowels [Medieval French *passer,* derived from Latin *passus* "step, pace"] — **pass·er** *n* — **pass muster** : to gain approval or acceptance — **pass the buck** : to shift a responsibility to someone else — **pass the hat** : to take up a collection of money

[2]**pass** *n* **1** : an opening or way for passing along or through **2** : a gap in a mountain range

[3]**pass** *n* **1** : the act or an instance of passing : PASSAGE **2** : REALIZATION ⟨brought their dreams to *pass*⟩ **3** : a usually difficult or disturbing state of affairs **4 a** : a written permission to enter or leave or to move about freely ⟨a soldier's 3-day *pass*⟩ **b** : a ticket allowing one free transportation or free admission **5 a** : a transference of objects by sleight of hand **b** : a moving of the hands over or along something **6** : a transfer of a ball or a puck from one player to another on the same team **7** : a refusal to bid, bet, or draw an additional card in a card game **8** : EFFORT, TRY; *esp* : a sexually inviting approach

pass·able \ˈpas-ə-bəl\ *adj* **1** : capable of being passed, crossed, or traveled on ⟨*passable* roads⟩ **2** : barely good enough ⟨a *passable* meal⟩ — **pass·ably** \-blē\ *adv*

pas·sage \ˈpas-ij\ *n* **1** : the action or process of passing from one place or condition to another **2 a** : a road, path, channel, or course by which something can pass ⟨nasal *passages*⟩ ⟨a river *passage*⟩ **b** : a corridor or lobby giving access to the different rooms or parts of a building or apartment **3 a** : a specific act of traveling especially by sea or air **b** : the right to travel as a passenger ⟨take *passage* on a freighter⟩ **4** : the passing of a legislative measure : ENACTMENT **5 a** : INCIDENT 1a **b** : something that takes place between two persons mutually ⟨a *passage* of wit⟩ **6 a** : a usually brief portion of a written work or speech that concerns a point under discussion or is noteworthy for content or style **b** : a phrase or short section of a musical composition

pas·sage·way \-ˌwā\ *n* : a way that allows passage

pass·book \ˈpas-ˌbu̇k\ *n* : BANKBOOK

pas·sé \pa-ˈsā\ *adj* **1** : no longer active or in use : OBSOLETE **2** : OLD-FASHIONED 1 [French, from *passer* "to pass"]

passed ball *n* : a pitched ball that passes the catcher when he should have stopped it and that allows a base runner to advance

pas·sel \ˈpas-əl\ *n* : a large number [alteration of *parcel*]

pas·sen·ger \ˈpas-n-jər\ *n* **1** : WAYFARER **2** : a traveler in a public or private conveyance [Medieval French *passager,* from *passage* "act of passing," from *passer* "to pass"]

passenger pigeon *n* : an extinct but formerly abundant North American migratory pigeon

passenger pigeon

passe–par·tout \ˌpas-pər-ˈtü\ *n* **1** : something that passes or enables one to pass everywhere **2** : strong paper gummed on one side and used especially for mounting pictures [French, from *passe partout* "pass everywhere"]

pass·er·by \ˌpas-ər-ˈbī\ *n, pl* **pass·ers·by** \-ərz-\ : one that passes by

pas·ser·ine \ˈpas-ə-ˌrīn\ *adj* : of or relating to the largest order (Passeriformes) of birds including more than half of all living birds and consisting chiefly of songbirds of perching habits [Latin *passerinus* "of sparrows," from *passer* "sparrow"] — **passerine** *n*

pas seul \pä-ˈsərl, -ˈsəl, -ˈsœl\ *n* : a solo dance or dance figure [French, literally, "solo step"]

pas·sim \ˈpas-əm, -ˌim\ *adv* : here and there — used to indicate that something (as a phrase) is to be found at many places in the same book or work [Latin, from *passus* "scattered," from *pandere* "to spread"]

[1]**pass·ing** \ˈpas-ing\ *n* : the act of one that passes or causes to pass; *esp* : DEATH — **in passing** : by the way : INCIDENTALLY

[2]**passing** *adj* **1** : going by or past ⟨the *passing* crowd⟩ **2** : having a brief duration ⟨a *passing* whim⟩ **3** : marked by haste or inattention : SUPERFICIAL ⟨a *passing* glance⟩ **4** : given on satisfactory completion of an examination or course of study ⟨a *passing* grade⟩

[3]**passing** *adv* : to a surpassing degee : EXCEEDINGLY ⟨*passing* fair⟩

pas·sion \ˈpash-ən\ *n* **1** *often cap* : the sufferings of Christ between the night of the Last Supper and his death **2 a** *pl* : the emotions as distinguished from reason **b** : violent, intense, or overmastering feeling **c** : an outbreak of anger **3 a** : ardent affection : LOVE **b** : a strong liking ⟨a *passion* for cars⟩ **c** : sexual desire **d** : an object of desire or deep interest ⟨bowling is their *passion*> [Medieval French, from Late Latin *passio* "suffering," from Latin *pati* "to suffer"] — **pas·sion·al** \-ən-l\ *adj* — **pas·sion·less** \-ən-ləs\ *adj*

synonyms PASSION, FERVOR, ARDOR mean intense emotion. PASSION implies an emotion that is deeply stirring or ungovernable ⟨was a slave to his *passions*⟩. FERVOR implies a strong, steadily glowing emotion ⟨sang their hymns with deep *fervor*⟩. ARDOR suggests a warm excited feeling likely to be fitful or short-lived ⟨the cost dampened their *ardor* for travel⟩. ***synonyms*** see in addition FEELING

pas·sion·ate \ˈpash-nət, -ə-nət\ *adj* **1 a :** easily aroused to anger **b :** filled with anger **:** ANGRY **2 :** capable of, affected by, or expressing intense feeling **3 :** strongly affected with sexual desire ***synonyms*** see IMPASSIONED — **pas·sion·ate·ly** *adv* — **pas·sion·ate·ness** *n*

pas·sion·flow·er \ˈpash-ən-ˌflau̇-ər, -ˌflau̇r\ *n* **:** any of a genus of chiefly tropical climbing vines or erect herbs having showy flowers and pulpy often edible fruits [from the fancied resemblance of parts of the flower to the cross, nails, and crown of thorns used in Christ's crucifixion]

passionflower

passion fruit *n* **:** the edible fruit of a passionflower; *esp* **:** the small roundish purple or yellow fruit of a passionflower native to Brazil

Pas·sion·ist \ˈpash-nəst, -ə-nəst\ *n* **:** a member of a Roman Catholic monastic order devoted chiefly to missionary work and retreats

passion play *n, often cap 1st P* **:** a play representing scenes connected with Christ's suffering and crucifixion

Passion Sunday *n* **:** the 5th Sunday in Lent

Pas·sion·tide \ˈpash-ən-ˌtīd\ *n* **:** the last two weeks of Lent

Passion Week *n* **1 :** HOLY WEEK **2 :** the 2nd week before Easter

[1]**pas·sive** \ˈpas-iv\ *adj* **1 a :** not active but acted on **:** receptive to or affected by outside force, agency, or influence ⟨*passive* spectators⟩ **b :** of, relating to, or being a verb form or voice indicating that the person or thing represented by the subject is subjected to the action represented by the verb ⟨"was bitten" in "I was bitten by a dog" is *passive*⟩ **2 :** receiving or enduring without resistance **:** SUBMISSIVE ⟨*passive* surrender to fate⟩ [Latin *passivus,* from *passus,* past participle of *pati* "to be acted upon, suffer"] — **pas·sive·ly** *adv* — **pas·sive·ness** *n* — **pas·siv·i·ty** \pa-ˈsiv-ət-ē\ *n*

[2]**passive** *n* **1 :** a passive verb form **2 :** the passive voice of a language

passive–aggressive *adj* **:** being, marked by, or displaying behavior characterized by the expression of negative feelings, resentment, and aggression in an unassertive way (as through procrastination and stubbornness — **passive–aggressive** *n*

passive immunity *n* **:** temporary immunity acquired by transfer of antibodies (as by injection of serum from an individual with active immunity)

passive resistance *n* **:** resistance especially to a government or an occupying power characterized mainly by noncooperation

passive smoking *n* **:** the involuntary inhalation of tobacco smoke (as from another's cigarette) especially by a nonsmoker

passive transport *n* **:** the movement (as by diffusion or osmosis) of substances across a cell membrane from regions of lower concentration to those of higher concentration without the expenditure of energy

pass·key \ˈpas-ˌkē\ *n* **1 :** MASTER KEY **2 :** SKELETON KEY

pass off *vt* **1 :** to make public or offer for sale with intent to deceive **2 :** to give a false identity or character to

pass out *vi* **1 :** to lose consciousness **2 :** DIE 1

Pass·over \ˈpas-ˌō-vər\ *n* **:** a Jewish holiday celebrated in March or April in commemoration of the liberation of the Hebrews from slavery in Egypt [from the exemption of the Israelites from the slaughter of the firstborn of Egypt (Exodus 12:23-27)]

pass·port \ˈpas-ˌpōrt, -ˌpȯrt\ *n* **1 a :** an official document issued to a person that is usually necessary for exit from and reentry into the country, that allows the person to travel in foreign countries, and that requests protection for the person in foreign countries **b :** an identification document required by law to be carried by persons living or traveling in a country **2 :** something that secures admission or acceptance ⟨education as a *passport* to success⟩ [Medieval French *passeport,* from *passer* "to pass" + *port* "port"]

pass up *vt* **:** DECLINE 4b, c, REJECT

pass·word \ˈpas-ˌwərd\ *n* **1 :** a word or phrase that a person must utter before being allowed to pass a guard **2 :** a sequence of characters required for access to a computer system **3 :** WATCHWORD 1

[1]**past** \ˈpast\ *adj* **1 a :** AGO ⟨10 years *past*⟩ **b :** just gone by ⟨for the *past* few days⟩ **2 :** having existed or taken place in a period before the present **:** BYGONE **3 :** of, relating to, or being a verb tense that in English is usually formed by internal vowel change (as in *sang*) or by the addition of a suffix (as in *laughed*) and that expresses elapsed time **4 :** no longer serving ⟨*past* president⟩ [Middle English, from past participle of *passen* "to pass"]

[2]**past** *prep* **1 a :** beyond the age for or of ⟨*past* playing with toys⟩ **b :** AFTER ⟨half *past* two⟩ **2 a :** at the farther side of **:** BEYOND **b :** in a course or direction going close to and then beyond ⟨drove *past* the house⟩ **3 :** beyond the range, scope, or sphere of ⟨a situation *past* belief⟩

[3]**past** *n* **1 a :** time gone by **b :** something that happened or was done in the past **2 a :** PAST TENSE **b :** a verb form in the past tense **3 :** a past life, history, or course of action; *esp* **:** a past life that is secret

[4]**past** *adv* **:** so as to reach and go beyond a point near at hand

pas·ta \ˈpäs-tə\ *n* **1 :** a wheaten paste in processed form (as spaghetti) or in the form of fresh dough (as ravioli) **2 :** pasta prepared for eating [Italian, from Late Latin "paste, dough"]

[1]**paste** \ˈpāst\ *n* **1 a :** a dough rich in fat used for pastry **b :** a candy made by evaporating fruit with sugar or by flavoring a gelatin, starch, or gum arabic preparation **c :** a smooth food product made by evaporation or grinding ⟨almond *paste*⟩ **d :** a shaped dough (as spaghetti or ravioli) prepared from wheat products (as semolina, farina, or flour) **2 :** a soft plastic mixture or composition: as **a :** a preparation of flour and water or starch and water used for sticking things together **b :** a clay mixture prepared for shaping into pottery or porcelain **3 :** a very brilliant glass used for the manufacture of artificial gems [Medieval French, from Late Latin *pasta* "dough, paste"]

[2]**paste** *vt* **1 :** to cause to adhere by paste **:** STICK **2 :** to cover with or as if with something pasted on ⟨*paste* a wall with notes⟩

[3]**paste** *vt* **:** to hit hard [alteration of *baste*]

paste·board \ˈpāst-ˌbōrd, ˈpās-, -ˌbȯrd\ *n* **:** cardboard with paper pasted to the outside to provide a smooth surface; *also* **:** CARDBOARD

[1]**pas·tel** \pas-ˈtel\ *n* **1 a :** a paste made of ground color and used for making crayons **b :** a crayon made of such paste **2 :** a drawing in pastel **3 :** any of various pale or light colors [French, from Italian *pastello,* from Late Latin *pastellus* "woad," from *pasta* "paste"]

[2]**pastel** *adj* **1 a :** of or relating to a pastel **b :** made with pastels **2 :** pale and light in color

pas·tern \ˈpas-tərn\ *n* **:** the part of the foot of a horse between the fetlock and the top of the hoof; *also* **:** the corresponding part of some other animals [Middle French *pasturon,* from *pasture* "pastern, tether attached to the foot of a horse"]

pas·teur·i·za·tion \ˌpas-chə-rə-ˈzā-shən, ˌpas-tə-\ *n* **:** partial sterilization of a substance and especially a liquid (as milk) at a temperature and period of exposure that destroys objectionable organisms without major chemical alteration of the substance [Louis *Pasteur*] — **pas·teur·ize** \ˈpas-chə-ˌrīz, ˈpas-tə-\ *vt* — **pas·teur·iz·er** \-ˌrī-zər\ *n*

pas·tiche \pas-ˈtēsh, päs-\ *n* **:** a composition (as in literature or music) made up of selections from different works **:** POTPOURRI [French, from Italian *pasticcio,* literally, "pasty," derived from Late Latin *pasta* "paste"]

pas·tille \pas-ˈtēl\ *n* **1 :** a small mass of aromatic paste for fumigating or scenting the air of a room **2 :** LOZENGE 2 [French *pastille,* from Latin *pastillus* "small loaf, lozenge"]

pas·time \ˈpas-ˌtīm\ *n* **:** something that helps to make time pass agreeably **:** DIVERSION

past master *n* **1 :** one who has held the office of master (as in a guild, club, or lodge) **2 :** one who is expert

pas·tor \ˈpas-tər\ *n* **:** a member of the clergy who is in charge of a church or parish [Medieval French *pastour,* from Latin *pastor* "herdsman," from *pascere* "to feed"] — **pas·tor·ship** \-ˌship\ *n*

[1]**pas·to·ral** \ˈpas-tə-rəl, -trəl\ *adj* **1 a :** of or relating to shepherds or rural life **b :** devoted to or based on livestock raising **c :** RURAL **d :** depicting rural life and people especially in an idealistic way ‹*pastoral* poetry› **2 :** of or relating to the pastor of a church — **pas·to·ral·ly** \-tə-rə-lē, -trə-lē\ *adv* — **pas·to·ral·ness** *n*

[2]**pas·to·ral** \ˈpas-tə-rəl, -trəl; *sense 2 is often* ˌpas-tə-ˈräl, -ˈral\ *n* **1 :** a letter of a spiritual overseer; *esp* **:** one written by a bishop to his diocese **2 a :** a literary work dealing with shepherds or rural life in a usually artificial manner **b :** pastoral poetry or drama **c :** a rural picture or scene **d :** PASTORALE

pas·to·rale \ˌpas-tə-ˈräl, -ˈral\ *n* **:** an instrumental or vocal composition having a pastoral theme [Italian, from *pastorale* "pastoral"]

pas·tor·ate \ˈpas-tə-rət, -trət\ *n* **1 :** the office, duties, or term of service of a pastor **2 :** a body of pastors

past participle *n* **:** a participle that expresses completed action, that is traditionally one of the principal parts of the verb, and that is used in English in the formation of perfect tenses in the active voice and of all tenses in the passive voice ‹"raised" in "Many hands were raised" and "thrown" in "The ball has been thrown" are *past participles*›

past perfect *adj* **:** of, relating to, or being a verb tense formed in English with *had* and expressing an action or state completed at or before a past time spoken of — **past perfect** *n*

pas·tra·mi *also* **pas·tromi** \pə-ˈsträm-ē\ *n* **:** a highly seasoned smoked beef prepared especially from shoulder cuts [Yiddish *pastrame,* from Romanian *pastramă*]

past·ry \ˈpā-strē\ *n, pl* **pastries 1 :** sweet baked goods made of dough or having a crust made of enriched dough **2 :** a piece of pastry [[1]*paste*]

past tense *n* **:** a verb tense expressing action or state in the past

pas·tur·age \ˈpas-chə-rij\ *n* **:** PASTURE

[1]**pas·ture** \ˈpas-chər\ *n* **1 :** plants (as grass) for the feeding especially of grazing animals **2 :** land or a plot of land used for grazing [Medieval French, from Late Latin *pastura,* from Latin *pastus,* past participle of *pascere* "to feed"]

[2]**pasture** *vb* **1 :** to feed on or put (as cattle) to feed on pasture **:** GRAZE **2 :** to use as pasture

pas·ture·land \ˈpas-chər-ˌland\ *n* **:** PASTURE 2

[1]**pas·ty** \ˈpas-tē\ *n, pl* **pasties :** [2]PIE; *esp* **:** a meat pie [Middle French *pasté,* from *paste* "dough, paste"]

[2]**pasty** \ˈpā-stē\ *adj* **past·i·er; -est :** resembling paste; *esp* **:** pallid and unhealthy in appearance — **past·i·ness** *n*

PA system \pē-ˈā-\ *n* **:** PUBLIC-ADDRESS SYSTEM

[1]**pat** \ˈpat\ *n* **1 :** a light blow especially with the hand or a flat instrument **2 :** a light tapping sound **3 :** something (as butter) provided in a small flat portion [Middle English *patte*]

[2]**pat** *adv* **:** in a pat manner **:** APTLY, PERFECTLY

[3]**pat** *vb* **pat·ted; pat·ting 1 :** to strike lightly with the hand or a flat instrument **2 :** to flatten, smooth, or shape with light blows ‹*pat* one's hair into place› **3 :** to soothe or show approval by striking gently ‹*pat* someone's hand›

[4]**pat** *adj* **1 a :** exactly suited to the purpose or occasion **:** APT ‹a *pat* answer› **b :** suspiciously suitable ‹*pat* excuses› **2 :** learned, mastered, or memorized exactly ‹have a lesson down *pat*›

[1]**patch** \ˈpach\ *n* **1 :** a piece of material used to mend or cover a hole, a torn place, or a weak spot **2 :** a tiny piece of black silk or court plaster formerly worn on the face especially by women to cover a defect or to heighten beauty **3 :** a shield worn over the socket of an injured or missing eye **4 :** a small piece **:** SCRAP **5 a :** a small area or plot distinguished from its surroundings ‹a *patch* of oats› ‹a *patch* of blistered skin› **b :** a spot of color **:** BLOTCH ‹a *patch* of white on a dog's head› **6 :** a piece of cloth attached to a garment as an ornament or insignia [Middle English *pacche*]

[2]**patch** *vt* **1 :** to repair, cover, or fill up a hole or weak spot in **2 :** to provide with a patch **3 a :** to make out of patches **b :** to repair or put together especially hastily or clumsily **c :** to deal with successfully **:** SETTLE — usually used with *up* ‹*patched* up their differences› ***synonyms*** see MEND

pa·tchou·li *also* **pa·tchou·ly** \ˈpach-ə-lē, pə-ˈchü-lē\ *n, pl* **-lis** *or* **-lies 1 :** a mint of southeastern Asia that yields a fragrant essential oil; *also* **:** a heavy perfume made from the oil of patchouli [Tamil *paccuḷi*]

patch pocket *n* **:** a flat pocket applied to the outside of a garment

patch test *n* **:** a test for determining sensitivity to an allergy-producing substance made by applying to the unbroken skin small pads soaked with the allergen to be tested

patch·work \ˈpach-ˌwərk\ *n* **1 :** something made up of various different parts **:** HODGEPODGE **2 :** pieces of cloth of various colors and shapes sewed together usually in a pattern — **patchwork** *adj*

patchwork 2

patchy \ˈpach-ē\ *adj* **patch·i·er; -est :** consisting of or marked by patches; *also* **:** SPOTTY 2

pate \ˈpāt\ *n* **:** HEAD; *esp* **:** the crown of the head [Middle English] — **pat·ed** \ˈpāt-əd\ *adj*

pâ·té \pä-ˈtā, pa-\ *n* **1 :** a meat or fish pie or patty **2 :** a spread of finely mashed seasoned and spiced meat [French, from Medieval French *pasté,* from *paste* "dough, paste"]

pâ·té de foie gras \pä-ˌtād-ə-ˌfwä-ˈgrä, pa-\ *n, pl* **pâtés de foie gras** \-ˌtād-ə-, -ˌtāz-də-\ **:** a rich pâté of fat goose liver and truffles [French, literally, "pâté of fat liver"]

pa·tel·la \pə-ˈtel-ə\ *n, pl* **-tel·lae** \-ˈtel-ē, -ˌī\ *or* **-tellas :** KNEECAP [Latin, from *patina* "shallow dish, pan"] — **pa·tel·lar** \-ˈtel-ər\ *adj*

pat·en \ˈpat-n\ *n* **1 :** a plate of precious metal for holding the eucharistic bread **2 :** a shallow dish or plate **3 :** a thin metal disk [Medieval French *patene,* from Latin *patina* "shallow dish, pan"]

[1]**pa·tent** *1-4 are* ˈpat-nt, *5 is* ˈpāt-, *6 is* ˈpāt-, ˈpat-\ *adj* **1 :** open to public inspection — used chiefly in the phrase *letters patent* **2 :** protected by a patent ‹*patent* locks› **3 :** marketed as a proprietary commodity ‹*patent* drugs› **4 :** of, relating to, or concerned with the granting of patents especially for inventions ‹a *patent* lawyer› **5 :** offering free passage **:** UNOBSTRUCTED ‹a *patent* opening› **6 :** EVIDENT, OBVIOUS ‹a *patent* lie› [Medieval French, from Latin *patens,* from *patēre* "to be open"] — **pa·ten·cy** \ˈpāt-n-sē\ *n* — **pa·tent·ly** \ˈpāt-n-tlē, ˈpat-, -lē\ *adv*

[2]**pat·ent** \ˈpat-nt\ *n* **1 :** an official document conferring a right or privilege **2 :** a writing securing to an inventor for a term of years the exclusive right to make, use, or sell his or her invention; *also* **:** the right so granted **3 :** something (as a privilege) resembling a patent

[3]**patent** *vt* **1 :** to grant a privilege, right, or license to by patent **2 :** to obtain or secure by patent; *esp* **:** to secure by letters patent exclusive right to make, use, or sell **3 :** to obtain or grant a patent right to — **pat·ent·able** \ˈpat-n-tə-bəl\ *adj*

pat·en·tee \ˌpat-n-ˈtē\ *n* **:** one to whom a grant is made or a privilege secured by patent

pat·ent leather \ˌpat-n-, ˌpat-nt-\ *n* **:** a leather with a hard smooth glossy surface

patent medicine *n* **:** a packaged medicinal preparation (as cough syrup) available for sale to the public without a doctor's prescription that is typically protected by a trademark, has contents which may not be fully disclosed, and especially in the past was often of unproven effectiveness

patent office *n* **:** a government office for examining claims to patents and granting patents

pat·en·tor \ˈpat-n-tər, ˌpat-n-ˈtȯr\ *n* **:** one that grants a patent

patent right *n* **:** a right granted by letters patent; *esp* **:** the exclusive right to an invention

pa·ter *n* **1** *often cap* \ˈpä-ˌteər\ **:** PATERNOSTER 1 **2** \ˈpāt-ər\ *chiefly British* **:** FATHER 1a [sense 2 from Latin *pater* "father"]

pa·ter·fa·mil·i·as \ˌpāt-ər-fə-ˈmil-ē-əs\ *n* **1 :** the male head of a household **2 :** the father of a family [Latin, from *pater* "father" + *familia* "family"]

pa·ter·nal \pə-ˈtərn-l\ *adj* **1 :** of or relating to a father **:** FATHERLY **2 :** received or inherited from one's father **3 :** related through the father ‹a *paternal* grandfather› [Late Latin *paternalis,* from Latin *paternus,* from *pater* "father"] — **pa·ter·nal·ly** \-l-ē\ *adv*

pa·ter·nal·ism \-l-ˌiz-əm\ *n* **:** the principle or practice of governing or of exercising authority (as over employees) in a way suggesting that of a father over his children — **pa·ter·nal·ist** \-l-əst\ *adj or n* — **pa·ter·nal·is·tic** \-ˌtərn-l-ˈis-tik\ *adj*

pa·ter·ni·ty \pə-ˈtər-nət-ē\ *n* **1** : the quality or state of being a father **2** : origin or descent from a father

pat·er·nos·ter \ˌpät-ər-ˈnäs-tər, ˈpat-ər-ˌ, ˈpä-ˌteər-ˈ, -ˈnäs-ˌteər\ *n* **1** *often cap* : LORD'S PRAYER **2** : a word formula repeated as a prayer or magical charm [Latin *pater noster* "our father"]

path \ˈpath, ˈpàth\ *n, pl* **paths** \ˈpathz, ˈpaths, ˈpàthz, ˈpàths\ **1** : a course or way formed by or as if by repeated footsteps **2** : a track constructed for a particular use (as horseback riding) **3 a** : the way traversed by something : COURSE, ROUTE **b** : a way of life, conduct, or thought [Old English *pæth*] — **path·less** *adj*

path- *or* **patho-** *combining form* : pathological state : disease ⟨*path*ogen⟩ [Greek *pathos,* literally, "suffering"]

-path \ˌpath\ *n combining form* **1** : practitioner of a (specified) system of medicine that emphasizes one aspect of disease or its treatment ⟨osteo*path*⟩ **2** : one suffering from (such) an ailment ⟨psycho*path*⟩

Pa·than \pə-ˈtän\ *n* : PASHTUN [Hindi & Urdu *Paṭhān,* from Pashto (eastern dialect) *Paxtana,* plural of *Paxtun*]

pa·thet·ic \pə-ˈthet-ik\ *adj* **1** : arousing tenderness, pity, or sorrow : PITIABLE **2** : marked by sorrow or melancholy : SAD ⟨a *pathetic* story⟩ [Late Latin *patheticus,* from Greek *pathētikos* "capable of feeling, pathetic," from *paschein* "to experience, suffer"] — **pa·thet·i·cal·ly** \-ˈthet-i-kə-lē, -klē\ *adv*

path·find·er \ˈpath-ˌfīn-dər, ˈpàth-\ *n* : one that discovers a way and especially a new route in unexplored regions

patho·gen \ˈpath-ə-jən\ *n* : a specific cause (as a bacterium or virus) of disease

patho·gen·ic \ˌpath-ə-ˈjen-ik\ *adj* : causing or capable of causing disease — **patho·ge·nic·i·ty** \-jə-ˈnis-ət-ē\ *n*

patho·log·i·cal \ˌpath-ə-ˈläj-i-kəl\ *also* **patho·log·ic** \-ik\ *adj* **1** : of or relating to pathology **2** : altered or caused by disease; *also* : indicative of disease **3** : being such to a degree that is extreme, excessive, or markedly abnormal ⟨a *pathological* liar⟩ ⟨*pathological* fear⟩ — **patho·log·i·cal·ly** \-i-kə-lē, -klē\ *adv*

pa·thol·o·gy \pə-ˈthäl-ə-jē, pa-\ *n, pl* **-gies** **1** : the study of diseases and especially of the bodily changes produced by them **2** : something abnormal; *esp* : the disorders in structure and function that constitute disease or characterize a particular disease — **pa·thol·o·gist** \pə-ˈthäl-ə-jəst, pa-\ *n*

pa·thos \ˈpā-ˌthäs, -ˌthòs\ *n* **1** : an element in experience or in artistic representation arousing pity or compassion **2** : an emotion of sympathetic pity [Greek, "suffering, experience, emotion," from *paschein* "to experience, suffer"]

path·way \ˈpath-ˌwā, ˈpàth-\ *n* **1** : PATH **2** : a network of interconnecting neurons along which a nerve impulse travels **3** : the sequence of chemical reactions by which one substance is converted into another

-p·a·thy \p-ə-thē\ *n combining form, pl* **-pathies** **1** : feeling : suffering ⟨em*pathy*⟩ : being acted upon ⟨tele*pathy*⟩ **2** : disease of (such) a part or kind **3** : system of medicine based on (such) a factor ⟨osteo*pathy*⟩ [Greek *-patheia,* from *pathēs* "suffering," from *pathos*]

pa·tience \ˈpā-shəns\ *n* : the capacity, habit, or fact of being patient

[1]**pa·tient** \ˈpā-shənt\ *adj* **1** : bearing pains or trials calmly or without complaint **2** : being kindly and tolerant **3** : not hasty or impetuous **4** : steadfast despite opposition, difficulty, or adversity ⟨years of *patient* labor⟩ [Middle French *pacient,* from Latin *patiens,* from *pati* "to suffer"] — **pa·tient·ly** *adv*

[2]**patient** *n* : an individual awaiting or under medical care and treatment

pat·i·na \ˈpat-ə-nə, pə-ˈtē-nə\ *n, pl* **patinas** *or* **pat·i·nae** \ˈpat-ə-ˌnē, -ˌnī\ **1** : a usually green film formed on copper and bronze by long exposure or by chemicals and often valued aesthetically **2** : a surface appearance (as a coloring or mellowing) of something grown beautiful especially with age or use [Italian, from Latin, "shallow dish, pan"]

pa·tio \ˈpat-ē-ˌō *also* ˈpät-\ *n, pl* **pa·ti·os** **1** : COURTYARD; *esp* : an inner court open to the sky **2** : an often paved recreation area that adjoins a dwelling [Spanish]

pa·tois \ˈpa-ˌtwä, ˈpä-\ *n, pl* **patois** \-ˌtwäz\ **1 a** : a dialect other than the standard or literary dialect **b** : illiterate or provincial speech **2** : JARGON 2 [French]

patr- *or* **patri-** *or* **patro-** *combining form* : father ⟨*patr*istic⟩ [Latin *pater* and Greek *patēr*]

pa·tri·arch \ˈpā-trē-ˌärk\ *n* **1 a** : one of the Old Testament fathers of the human race or of the Hebrew people **b** : a man who is father or founder **c** (1) : the oldest male member or representative of a group (2) : a venerable old man **2 a** : a bishop of the leading ancient sees of Constantinople, Alexandria, Antioch, Jerusalem, and Rome **b** : the head of any of various Eastern churches **c** : a Roman Catholic bishop next in rank to the pope [Medieval French *patriarche,* from Late Latin *patriarcha,* from Greek *patriarchēs,* from *patria* "lineage" (from *patēr* "father") + *-archēs* "-arch"] — **pa·tri·ar·chal** \ˌpā-trē-ˈär-kəl\ *adj*

pa·tri·arch·ate \ˈpā-trē-ˌär-kət, -ˌkāt\ *n* **1 a** : the office, jurisdiction, or time in office of a patriarch **b** : the residence or headquarters of a patriarch **2** : PATRIARCHY 2

pa·tri·ar·chy \-ˌär-kē\ *n, pl* **-chies** **1** : social organization marked by the supremacy of the father in the clan or family and the reckoning of descent and inheritance in the male line **2** : a society organized according to the principles of patriarchy

pa·tri·cian \pə-ˈtrish-ən\ *n* **1** : a member of one of the original citizen families of ancient Rome **2** : a person of high birth and cultivation : ARISTOCRAT [Medieval French, from Latin *patricius,* from *patres* "senators," from pl. of *pater* "father"] — **patrician** *adj* — **pa·tri·ci·ate** \-ˈtrish-ē-ət, -ē-ˌāt\ *n*

pat·ri·cide \ˈpa-trə-ˌsīd\ *n* **1** : one who murders his or her own father **2** : the murder of one's own father — **pat·ri·cid·al** \ˌpa-trə-ˈsīd-l\ *adj*

pat·ri·mo·ny \ˈpa-trə-ˌmō-nē\ *n, pl* **-nies** **1 a** : an estate inherited from one's father or ancestors **b** : something derived from one's father or ancestors : HERITAGE **2** : an estate or endowment belonging by ancient right to a church [Medieval French *patrimoine,* from Latin *patrimonium,* from *pater* "father"] — **pat·ri·mo·ni·al** \ˌpa-trə-ˈmō-nē-əl\ *adj*

pa·tri·ot \ˈpā-trē-ət, -trē-ˌät\ *n* : a person who loves his or her country and zealously supports it [Middle French *patriote* "compatriot," from Late Latin *patriota,* from Greek *patriōtēs,* from *patria* "lineage," from *patēr* "father"]

pa·tri·ot·ic \ˌpā-trē-ˈät-ik\ *adj* **1** : inspired by patriotism **2** : suitable to or characteristic of a patriot — **pa·tri·ot·i·cal·ly** \-ˈät-i-kə-lē, -klē\ *adv*

pa·tri·o·tism \ˈpā-trē-ə-ˌtiz-əm\ *n* : love for or devotion to one's country

pa·tris·tic \pə-ˈtris-tik\ *adj* : of or relating to the church fathers or their writings — **pa·tris·ti·cal** \-ti-kəl\ *adj*

[1]**pa·trol** \pə-ˈtrōl\ *n* **1 a** : the action or duty of going the rounds of an area for observation or guarding **b** : the person or group performing such an action **2** : a detachment of persons employed for reconnaissance, security, or combat **3** : a subdivision of a Boy Scout or Girl Scout troop [French *patrouille,* from *partouiller* "to patrol," from Middle French, "to tramp around in the mud," derived from Medieval French *patte* "paw"]

[2]**patrol** *vb* **pa·trolled; pa·trol·ling** : to be on patrol : carry out a patrol of — **pa·trol·ler** *n*

pa·trol·man \pə-ˈtrōl-mən\ *n* : one who patrols; *esp* : a police officer assigned to a beat

patrol wagon *n* : an enclosed motor vehicle used by police to carry prisoners

pa·tron \ˈpā-trən\ *n* **1** : a person chosen as a special guardian or supporter ⟨a *patron* of poets⟩ **2** : one who gives generous support or approval ⟨a *patron* of the arts⟩ **3** : a regular client or customer [Medieval French, from Medieval Latin *patronus* "patron saint, patron of a benefice, pattern," from Latin, "defender," from *pater* "father" — see *Word History* at PATTERN]

pat·ron·age \ˈpa-trə-nij, ˈpā-\ *n* **1** : the support or influence of a patron **2** : business or trade provided by customers **3 a** : the power to distribute government jobs on a basis other than merit alone **b** : the distribution of jobs on this basis **c** : the jobs so distributed

pa·tron·ess \ˈpā-trə-nəs\ *n* : a woman who is a patron

pa·tron·ize \ˈpā-trə-ˌnīz, ˈpa-\ *vt* **1** : to act as a patron to or of ⟨*patronize* the arts⟩ **2** : to treat with a superior air : be condescending toward **3** : to do business with ⟨*patronize* a neighborhood store⟩ — **pa·tron·iz·ing·ly** \-ˌnī-zing-lē\ *adv*

patron saint *n* : a saint to whose protection and intercession a person, a society, a church, or a place is dedicated

pat·ro·nym·ic \ˌpa-trə-ˈnim-ik\ *n* : a name derived from that of the father or a paternal ancestor [Late Latin *patronymicum,* de-

\ə\ **abut**	\au̇\ **out**	\i\ **tip**	\ȯ\ **saw**	\u̇\ **foot**
\ər\ **further**	\ch\ **chin**	\ī\ **life**	\ȯi\ **coin**	\y\ **yet**
\a\ **mat**	\e\ **pet**	\j\ **job**	\th\ **thin**	\yü\ **few**
\ā\ **take**	\ē\ **easy**	\ng\ **sing**	\th\ **this**	\yu̇\ **cure**
\ä\ **cot, cart**	\g\ **go**	\ō\ **bone**	\ü\ **food**	\zh\ **vision**

rived from Greek *patronymia,* from *patēr* "father" + *onyma* "name"] — **patronymic** *adj*

pa·troon \pə-ˈtrün\ *n* **:** the proprietor of a manorial estate granted by the Dutch especially in New York or New Jersey [Dutch, literally, "boss, superior," from French *patron* "patron"]

pat·sy \ˈpat-sē\ *n, pl* **patsies :** one who is duped or victimized **:** SUCKER [perhaps from Italian *pazzo* "fool"]

[1]**pat·ter** \ˈpat-ər\ *vb* **1 :** to say or speak in a rapid or mechanical manner **2 :** to talk glibly and volubly [Middle English *patren,* from *paternoster*] — **pat·ter·er** *n*

[2]**patter** *n* **1 :** a specialized lingo **:** CANT; *esp* **:** the jargon of criminals (as thieves) **2 :** the spiel of a street hawker or of a circus barker **3 :** empty chatter **4 a :** the rapid-fire talk of a comedian **b :** the talk with which an entertainer accompanies a routine

[3]**patter** *vi* **1 :** to strike or pat rapidly and repeatedly ⟨rain *pattering* on a roof⟩ **2 :** to run with quick light-sounding steps [from [3]*pat*]

[4]**patter** *n* **:** a quick succession of light sounds or pats ⟨the *patter* of little feet⟩

[1]**pat·tern** \ˈpat-ərn\ *n* **1 :** a form or model proposed for imitation **:** EXEMPLAR **2 :** something designed or used as a model for making things ⟨a dress *pattern*⟩ **3 a :** an artistic or mechanical design ⟨cloth with a small *pattern*⟩ **b :** form or style in literary or musical composition **4 :** a natural or chance configuration ⟨frost *patterns*⟩ **5 :** a complex of individual or group characteristics (as traits or behavior) ⟨behavior *patterns*⟩ ⟨the *pattern* of American industry⟩ **6 :** frequent or widespread incidence ⟨a *pattern* of dissent⟩ ⟨a *pattern* of violence⟩ [Middle English *patron,* from Medieval French, from Medieval Latin *patronus* "pattern, patron," from Latin, "defender," from *patr-, pater* "father"]

Word History Latin *patronus* is derived from *pater,* "father," and the duties of a Roman *patronus* were comparable to those of a father. He was a protector of his city or province; a defender in a court of law was his client's *patronus;* the man who freed his slave became that slave's *patronus.* The use of *patronus* in Medieval Latin shifted to suit the new requirements of the Christian era. Such a father figure as a patron saint or the patron of a benefice was called a *patronus,* as was anyone who served like a father as a model or pattern to be emulated. Middle English *patron* (borrowed from Medieval French) had a range of meaning similar to that of its Medieval Latin ancestor. During the 16th century another pronunciation of *patron* appeared, represented by such spellings as *pattern.* By the beginning of the 18th century the two forms, *patron* and *pattern,* were identified with separate senses and became two distinct words.

[2]**pattern** *vt* **:** to make or fashion according to a pattern

pat·ty *also* **pat·tie** \ˈpat-ē\ *n, pl* **patties 1 :** a little pie **2 a :** a small flat cake of chopped food ⟨a hamburger *patty*⟩ **b :** a small flat candy ⟨mint *patties*⟩ [French *pâté*]

pau·ci·ty \ˈpȯ-sət-ē\ *n* **:** smallness of number or quantity ⟨a *paucity* of tenor voices⟩ ⟨*paucity* of experience⟩ [Latin *paucitas,* from *paucus* "little"]

Paul·ist \ˈpȯ-ləst\ *n* **:** a member of the Roman Catholic Congregation of the Missionary Priests of St. Paul the Apostle founded in the United States in 1858

pau·low·nia \pȯ-ˈlō-nē-ə\ *n* **:** a Chinese tree widely grown in warm regions for its showy clusters of fragrant violet flowers [Anna *Pavlovna,* died 1865, Russian princess]

paunch \ˈpȯnch, ˈpänch\ *n* **1 a :** the belly together with its contents **b :** POTBELLY 1 **2 :** RUMEN [Medieval French *pance,* from Latin *pantex*]

paunchy \ˈpȯn-chē, ˈpän-\ *adj* **:** having a potbelly — **paunch·i·ness** *n*

pau·per \ˈpȯ-pər\ *n* **:** a very poor person; *esp* **:** one supported by charity [Latin, "poor"] — **pau·per·ism** \-pə-ˌriz-əm\ *n* — **pau·per·ize** \-ˌrīz\ *vt*

[1]**pause** \ˈpȯz\ *n* **1 :** a temporary stop **2 a :** a break in a verse **b :** a brief suspension of the voice to indicate the limits and relations of sentences and their parts **3 :** temporary inaction often because of doubt or uncertainty **4 :** the sign denoting a musical hold **5 :** a reason or cause for pausing ⟨it was a thought to give one *pause*⟩ [Latin *pausa,* from Greek *pausis,* from *pauein* "to stop"]

[2]**pause** *vi* **1 :** to stop temporarily **2 :** to linger for a time ⟨*pause* on a high note⟩

pa·vane \pə-ˈvän, -ˈvan\ *also* **pa·van** *same or* ˈpav-ən\ *n* **1 :** a stately court dance by couples that was introduced from southern Europe into England in the 16th century **2 :** music for the pavane [Middle French *pavane,* from Italian dialect *pavana,* feminine of *pavano* "of Padua," from *Pava* "Padua"]

pave \ˈpāv\ *vt* **1 :** to lay or cover with material (as stone or concrete) that makes a firm level surface for travel **2 :** to cover firmly and solidly as if with paving material [Medieval French *paver,* from Latin *pavire* "to strike, pound"] — **pave the way :** to prepare a smooth easy way ⟨*pave the way* for those who come after⟩

pave·ment \ˈpāv-mənt\ *n* **1 :** a paved surface **2 :** the material with which something is paved

pa·vil·ion \pə-ˈvil-yən\ *n* **1 :** a usually large luxurious tent **2 :** a lightly constructed often ornamental building serving as a shelter in a park, garden, or athletic field **3 :** a part of a building projecting from the main body of the structure **4 :** a building either partly or completely detached from the main building or main group of buildings [Medieval French *pavilloun, pavilioun,* from Latin *papilio* "butterfly"]

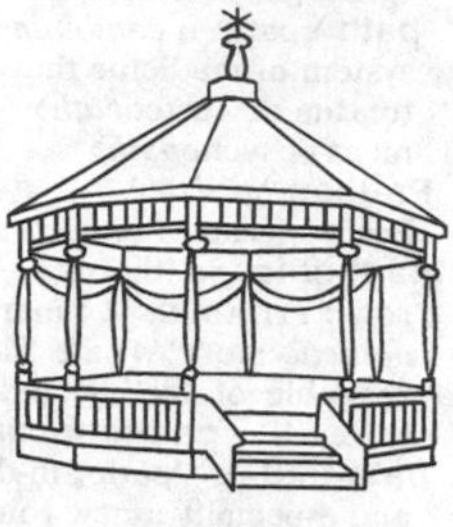
pavilion 2

pav·ing \ˈpā-ving\ *n* **:** PAVEMENT

[1]**paw** \ˈpȯ\ *n* **1 :** the foot of a four-footed animal (as a lion or dog) that has claws; *also* **:** the foot of an animal **2 :** a human hand especially when large or clumsy [Medieval French *powe, poe*]

[2]**paw** *vb* **1 :** to touch, strike, or scrape with a paw or hoof **2 :** to feel or touch clumsily or rudely ⟨merchandise *pawed* by customers⟩ **3 :** to flail at or grab wildly ⟨hands *pawing* the air⟩ **4 :** to search especially carelessly or roughly ⟨*pawed* through the box of letters⟩

pawl \ˈpȯl\ *n* **:** a pivoted tongue or sliding bolt on one part of a machine that is adapted to fall into notches on another part (as a ratchet wheel) so as to permit motion in only one direction [perhaps from Dutch *pal*]

[1]**pawn** \ˈpȯn, ˈpän\ *n* **1 :** something deposited with another as security for a loan **:** PLEDGE **2 :** the state of being pledged ⟨the watch was in *pawn*⟩ [Medieval French *pan*]

[2]**pawn** *vt* **:** to give temporarily as security ⟨*pawned* the silverware⟩ — **pawn·er** \ˈpȯ-nər, ˈpän-ər\ *n*

[3]**pawn** *n* **1 :** a piece in chess of least value that can move only one square forward at a time after its first move and can capture only diagonally forward **2 :** one used or exploited to further the purposes of another [Medieval French *peoun, paun,* from Medieval Latin *pedon-, pedo* "foot soldier," from Latin *ped-, pes* "foot"]

pawn·bro·ker \ˈpȯn-ˌbrō-kər, ˈpän-\ *n* **:** one who lends money to customers who have pledged personal property as security — **pawn·bro·king** \-king\ *n*

Paw·nee \pȯ-ˈnē, pä-\ *n* **:** a member of an American Indian people of what is now Nebraska and Kansas

pawn·shop \ˈpȯn-ˌshäp, ˈpän-\ *n* **:** a pawnbroker's shop

paw·paw *also* **pa·paw** *n* **1** \pə-ˈpȯ\ **:** PAPAYA **2** \ˈpäp-ȯ, ˈpȯp-\ **:** a North American tree related to the custard apples and having purple flowers and an edible green-skinned fruit; *also* **:** its fruit [probably from Spanish *papaya*]

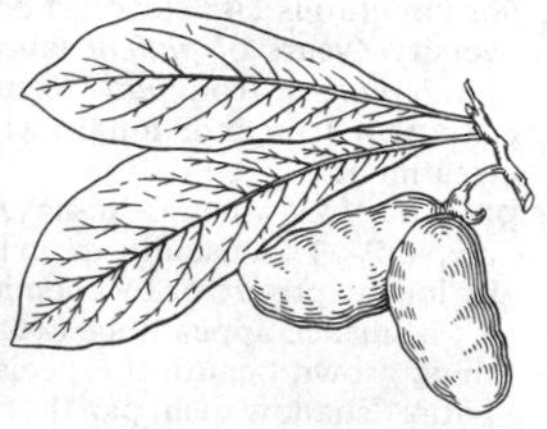
pawpaw 2

[1]**pay** \ˈpā\ *vb* **paid** \ˈpād\ *also in sense 7* **payed; pay·ing 1 :** to give money especially in return for services received or for something bought ⟨*pay* the taxi driver⟩ ⟨*pay* for a ticket⟩ **2 :** to pay what is indicated or required by ⟨*pay* a bill⟩ ⟨*pay* a tax⟩ **3 :** to get even with ⟨*pay* someone back for an injury⟩ **4 :** to give or offer freely ⟨*pay* a compliment⟩ ⟨*pay* attention⟩ **5 :** to return as profit ⟨an investment *paying* 5 percent⟩ **6 :** to make or secure suitable return for expense or trouble **:** be worth the effort or pains required ⟨it *pays* to drive carefully⟩ **7 :** to make (as a rope) slack and allow to run out — usually used with *out* [Medieval French *paier,* from Latin *pacare* "to pacify," from *pac-, pax* "peace"]

Word History Etymologically, to *pay* is "to pacify." The Latin verb *pacare,* "to pacify," is derived from *pax,* "peace." In the Middle Ages, *pacare* was used specifically to mean "to pacify a creditor by paying a debt" and eventually, more generally, "to pay." Medieval French *paier* had both the original sense "to pacify or appease" and the later, "to pay." Middle English *payen,* too, borrowed from the French in the late 12th or early 13th century, was used in both senses. But the original sense of *pay* is now long obsolete.

synonyms PAY, COMPENSATE, REMUNERATE mean to give money or its equivalent in return for something. PAY implies the discharge of an obligation incurred ⟨*pay* the worker's wages⟩. COMPENSATE implies making up for services rendered or help given or loss suffered ⟨gave $10 more to *compensate* us for our trouble⟩. REMUNERATE suggests paying for services rendered rather than for material goods.

[2]**pay** *n* **1 a :** the act or fact of paying or being paid **:** PAYMENT **b :** the status of being paid by an employer **:** EMPLOY **2 :** something paid; *esp* **:** WAGES, SALARY

[3]**pay** *adj* **1 :** containing or leading to something precious or valuable (as gold or oil) ⟨*pay* rock⟩ **2 :** equipped with a coin slot for receiving a fee for use ⟨a *pay* phone⟩ **3 :** requiring payment ⟨*pay* TV⟩

pay·able \ˈpā-ə-bəl\ *adj* **:** that may, can, or must be paid; *esp* **:** DUE ⟨accounts *payable*⟩

pay·check \ˈpā-ˌchek\ *n* **1 :** a check in payment of wages or salary **2 :** WAGES, SALARY

pay dirt *n* **1 :** earth or ore that yields a profit to a miner **2 :** a useful or remunerative discovery or object ⟨really hit *pay dirt* with that invention⟩

pay·ee \pā-ˈē\ *n* **:** one to whom money is or is to be paid

pay·er \ˈpā-ər\ *also* **pay·or** \ˈpā-ər, pā-ˈȯr\ *n* **:** one that pays

pay·load \ˈpā-ˌlōd\ *n* **:** something (as cargo, passengers, instruments, or explosives) carried by a vehicle, missile, rocket, or spacecraft in addition to what is necessary for its operation

pay·mas·ter \-ˌmas-tər\ *n* **:** an officer or agent of an employer whose duty it is to pay salaries or wages

pay·ment \ˈpā-mənt\ *n* **1 :** the act of paying **2 :** money given to pay for something ⟨*payments* on a car⟩ ⟨*payment* for a day's work⟩

pay·off \ˈpā-ˌȯf\ *n* **1 :** payment at the outcome of an enterprise ⟨a big *payoff* from an investment⟩ **2 :** the climax of an incident or enterprise ⟨the *payoff* of a story⟩

pay off \pā-ˈȯf, ˈpā-\ *vt* **1 :** to pay in full often through small payments made at intervals ⟨*pay off* a mortgage⟩ **2 :** to take revenge on ⟨*pay off* an enemy⟩

pay·ola \pā-ˈō-lə\ *n* **:** secret or indirect payment for a commercial favor [[1]*pay* + *-ola* (as in *Pianola,* a trademark for a player piano)]

pay–per–view *n* **:** a cable television service by which customers can order access to a particular broadcast for a fee

pay·roll \ˈpā-ˌrōl\ *n* **:** a list of persons entitled to receive pay with the amounts due to each; *also* **:** the amount of money necessary to pay those on such a list

pay station *n* **:** a pay telephone or a booth containing a pay telephone

pay up *vb* **:** to pay (as an overdue debt) in full

PC \ˌpē-ˈsē\ *n, pl* **PCs** *or* **PC's :** PERSONAL COMPUTER

PCB \ˌpē-ˌsē-ˈbē\ *n* **:** POLYCHLORINATED BIPHENYL

PDA \ˌpē-ˌdē-ˈā\ *n* **:** a small handheld electronic device used especially to store and organize personal information (as addresses, schedules, and notes) [*p*ersonal *d*igital *a*ssistant]

PDQ \ˌpē-ˌdē-ˈkyü\ *adv, often not cap* **:** IMMEDIATELY 2 [abbreviation of *pretty damned quick*]

pea \ˈpē\ *n, pl* **peas** *also* **pease** \ˈpēz\ **1 a :** an annual Eurasian vine of the legume family grown for its rounded smooth or wrinkled edible protein-rich seeds **b :** the seed of the pea **c** *pl* **:** the immature pods of the pea with their included seeds **2 :** any of various plants related to the pea [back-formation from Middle English *pease* (taken as a pl.), from Old English *pise,* from Latin *pisa,* pl. of *pisum,* from Greek *pison*]

peace \ˈpēs\ *n* **1 :** a state of tranquillity or quiet: as **a :** freedom from civil disturbance or foreign war **b :** a state of security or order within a community protected by law or custom ⟨breach of the *peace*⟩ **2 :** freedom from disquieting or oppressive thoughts or emotions **3 :** harmony in personal relations **4 a :** a state or period of agreement between governments **b :** a pact or agreement between combatants to end hostilities [Medieval French *pes, pees,* from Latin *pax*]

peace·able \ˈpē-sə-bəl\ *adj* **1 :** inclined toward peace **:** not quarrelsome **2 :** free from strife or disorder — **peace·ably** \-blē\ *adv*

peace·ful \ˈpēs-fəl\ *adj* **1 :** PEACEABLE 1 ⟨a *peaceful* person⟩ **2 :** untroubled by conflict, agitation, or commotion **:** QUIET, TRANQUIL ⟨a *peaceful* countryside⟩ **3 :** free from violence or force ⟨settled the conflict by *peaceful* means⟩ — **peace·ful·ly** \-fə-lē\ *adv* — **peace·ful·ness** *n*

peace·mak·er \ˈpē-ˌsmā-kər\ *n* **:** a person who arranges a peace **:** one who settles an argument or stops a fight — **peace·mak·ing** \-king\ *n or adj*

peace offering *n* **:** a gift or service to procure peace or reconciliation

peace officer *n* **:** a civil officer (as a police officer or sheriff) whose duty it is to preserve the public peace

peace pipe *n* **:** an ornamented ceremonial pipe of the American Indians — compare CALUMET

peace·time \ˈpē-ˌstīm\ *n* **:** a time when a nation is not at war

[1]**peach** \ˈpēch\ *n* **1 :** a low spreading Chinese tree related to the plums and cherries that is grown in most temperate areas for its sweet juicy fruit with pulpy white or yellow flesh, thin fuzzy skin, and single seed enclosed in a rough stony covering; *also* **:** its fruit **2 :** a moderate yellowish pink **3 :** one likened to a peach (as in beauty, or excellence) [Medieval French *pesche, peche* "peach fruit," from Late Latin *persica,* from Latin *(malum) persicum,* literally, "Persian fruit"]

[2]**peach** *vi* **:** to turn informer **:** BLAB [Middle English *pechen,* short for *apechen* "to accuse, impeach," derived from Late Latin *impedicare* "to entangle"]

peachy \ˈpē-chē\ *adj* **peach·i·er; -est** **1 :** resembling a peach **2 :** unusually fine **:** DANDY

[1]**pea·cock** \ˈpē-ˌkäk\ *n* **1 :** a male peafowl distinguished by a small crest of upright feathers on the head and by greatly elongated feathers in the tail mostly tipped with eyelike spots and erected and spread at will in a fan shimmering with iridescent color; *also* **:** PEAFOWL **2 :** one showing off personal attributes or possessions (as clothing) [Middle English *pecok,* from *pe-* (from Old English *pēa* "peafowl," from Latin *pavo* "peacock") + *cok* "cock"]

peacock 1

[2]**peacock** *vi* **:** to make a proud self-important display

peacock blue *n* **:** a moderate greenish blue

pea·fowl \ˈpē-ˌfau̇l\ *n* **:** a very large pheasant of southeastern Asia and India that is often kept in captivity for its beauty [*pea-* (as in *peacock*) + *fowl*]

pea green *n* **:** a moderate yellow-green

pea·hen \ˈpē-ˌhen, -ˈhen\ *n* **:** a female peafowl

pea jacket \ˈpē-\ *n* **:** a heavy woolen double-breasted jacket worn chiefly by sailors [by folk etymology from Dutch *pijjekker,* from *pij,* a kind of cloth + *jekker* "jacket"]

[1]**peak** \ˈpēk\ *n* **1 :** a pointed or projecting part; *esp* **:** the visor of a cap or hat **2 :** PROMONTORY **3 :** a sharp or pointed ridge or end ⟨the *peak* of a roof⟩ **4 a :** the top of a hill or mountain ending in a point **b :** a whole hill or mountain especially when isolated **5 :** the narrow part of a ship's bow or stern **6 :** the highest level or value or greatest degree of development ⟨the *peak* of perfection⟩ [perhaps alteration of *pike*] ***synonyms*** see SUMMIT

[2]**peak** *vb* **:** to come or cause to come to a peak, point, or maximum

[3]**peak** *adj* **:** being at or reaching the maximum ⟨an athlete in *peak* condition⟩ ⟨a *peak* year for sales⟩

[1]**peaked** \ˈpēkt, ˈpē-kəd\ *adj* **:** having a peak **:** POINTED — **peaked·ness** \ˈpēkt-nəs, ˈpēk-nəs, ˈpē-kəd-nəs\ *n*

[2]**peak·ed** \ˈpē-kəd\ *adj* **:** being pale and wan **:** SICKLY [from *peak* "to become sickly," of unknown origin]

[1]**peal** \ˈpēl\ *n* **1 :** a loud ringing of bells **2 :** a loud sound or suc-

\ə\ abut	\au̇\ **out**	\i\ **tip**	\ȯ\ **saw**	\u̇\ **foot**
\ər\ **further**	\ch\ **chin**	\ī\ **life**	\ȯi\ **coin**	\y\ **yet**
\a\ **mat**	\e\ **pet**	\j\ **job**	\th\ **thin**	\yü\ **few**
\ā\ **take**	\ē\ **easy**	\ng\ **sing**	\t͟h\ **this**	\yu̇\ **cure**
\ä\ **cot, cart**	\g\ **go**	\ō\ **bone**	\ü\ **food**	\zh\ **vision**

cession of sounds ⟨a *peal* of laughter⟩ ⟨a *peal* of thunder⟩ [Middle English, "appeal, summons to church," short for *appel* "appeal," from *appelen* "to appeal"]

[2]**peal** *vb* **:** to sound in peals ⟨bells *pealing* in the distance⟩

pea·like \ˈpē-ˌlīk\ *adj* **1 :** resembling a pea (as in firmness or shape) **2 :** being showy and resembling a butterfly in shape ⟨*pealike* flowers⟩

pea·nut \ˈpē-nət, -ˌnət\ *n* **1 :** a low-branching widely cultivated annual herb of the legume family with showy yellow flowers and pods that ripen underground; *also* **:** this pod or one of the oily edible seeds it contains **2 :** an insignificant or tiny person **3** *pl* **:** a trifling amount

peanut butter *n* **:** a paste made by grinding roasted skinned peanuts

peanut oil *n* **:** a colorless to yellow fatty oil from peanuts that is used chiefly as a salad oil, in margarine, in soap, and as an inert medium in medicinal preparations and cosmetics

pear \ˈpaər, ˈpeər\ *n* **:** a pome fruit that is usually narrower toward the stem end and typically has a pale green or brownish skin and firm juicy flesh; *also* **:** a tree that bears pears and is related to the apple [Old English *peru,* from Latin *pirum*]

[1]**pearl** \ˈpərl\ *n* **1 a :** a dense usually lustrous body formed of layers of nacre as an abnormal growth within the shell of some mollusks and used as a gem **b :** MOTHER-OF-PEARL **2 :** something resembling a pearl (as in shape, color, or value) **3 :** a slightly bluish medium gray [Medieval French *perle,* probably derived from Latin *perna* "mussel"]

[2]**pearl** *vb* **1 :** to set or adorn with pearls **2 :** to sprinkle or bead with pearly drops **3 :** to form into drops or beads like pearls or into small round grains **4 :** to give a pearly color or luster to **5 :** to fish or search for pearls — **pearl·er** *n*

[3]**pearl** *adj* **1 a :** of, relating to, or resembling pearl **b :** made of or adorned with pearls **2 :** having grains of medium size ⟨*pearl* barley⟩

pearl gray *n* **1 :** a yellowish to light gray **2 :** a pale blue

pearl onion *n* **:** a very small usually pickled onion used especially in appetizers and as a garnish

pearly \ˈpər-lē\ *adj* **pearl·i·er; -est :** resembling, containing, or adorned with pearls or mother-of-pearl

peart \ˈpiərt\ *adj, chiefly South & Midland* **:** in good spirits **:** LIVELY [alteration of *pert*]

peas·ant \ˈpez-nt\ *n* **1 :** a European small farmer or farm laborer; *also* **:** one of similar agricultural status elsewhere **2 :** an uncouth person or one of low social status [Medieval French *paisant,* from *païs* "country," from Late Latin *pagensis* "inhabitant of a district," from Latin *pagus* "district"]

peas·ant·ry \ˈpez-n-trē\ *n* **:** peasants as a group ⟨a nation's *peasantry*⟩ ⟨the local *peasantry*⟩

pease *plural of* PEA

pea·shoot·er \ˈpē-ˈshüt-ər\ *n* **:** a toy blowgun for shooting peas

pea soup *n* **1 :** a thick soup made of dried peas **2 :** a heavy fog

peat \ˈpēt\ *n* **1 :** TURF 2b **2 :** a dark brown or black vegetable matter that is formed when some plants (as sphagnum moss) partly decay underwater and is sometimes dug up and dried for use as fuel [Medieval Latin *peta* "piece of peat"] — **peaty** \ˈpēt-ē\ *adj*

peat moss *n* **:** SPHAGNUM

pea·vey *or* **pea·vy** \ˈpē-vē\ *n, pl* **peaveys** *or* **peavies :** a lever like a cant hook but with the end armed with a strong sharp spike used in handling logs [Joseph *Peavey,* died 1873, American blacksmith]

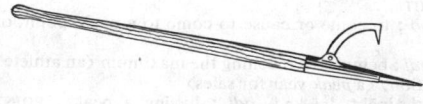

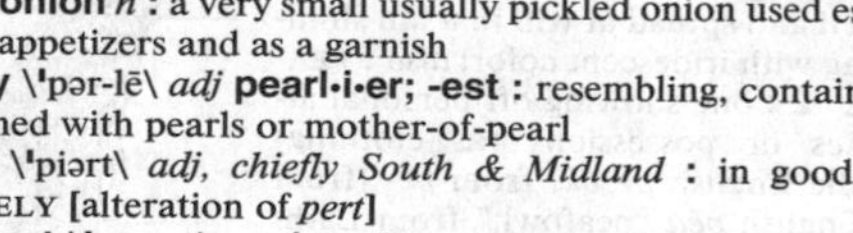

peavey

[1]**peb·ble** \ˈpeb-əl\ *n* **1 :** a small usually round stone especially when worn by the action of water **2 :** an irregular, crinkled, or grainy surface [Middle English *pobble,* from Old English *papolstān*] — **peb·bly** \ˈpeb-lē, -ə-lē\ *adj*

[2]**pebble** *vt* **peb·bled; peb·bling** \ˈpeb-ling, -ə-ling\ **:** to treat (as leather) so as to produce a rough and irregularly indented surface

pe·can \pi-ˈkän, -ˈkan\ *n* **:** a large hickory of the south central U.S. grown for its edible nut; *also* **:** its thin-shelled oblong nut [American French *pacane,* from Illinois (an Algonquian language) *pakani*]

pec·ca·dil·lo \ˌpek-ə-ˈdil-ō\ *n, pl* **-loes** *or* **-los :** a slight offense or fault [Spanish *pecadillo,* from *pecado* "sin," from Latin *peccatum,* from *peccare* "to sin"]

pec·ca·ry \ˈpek-ə-rē\ *n, pl* **-ries :** either of two American chiefly tropical mammals that are active chiefly at night and resemble but are smaller than the related pigs [of Carib origin]

peccary

[1]**peck** \ˈpek\ *n* **1 —** see MEASURE table **2 :** a large quantity **:** great deal ⟨a *peck* of trouble⟩ [Medieval French *pek*]

[2]**peck** *vb* **1 a** (1) **:** to strike, pick up, or move with a pointed bill or tool ⟨chickens *pecking* corn⟩ (2) **:** to make by pecking ⟨*peck* a hole⟩ **b :** to strike at or pick up something with or as if with a bill **2 :** to eat daintily **:** NIBBLE, PICK [Middle English *pecken*] — **peck·er** *n*

[3]**peck** *n* **1 :** an impression or hole made by pecking **2 :** a quick sharp stroke

pecking order *also* **peck order** *n* **1 :** a basic pattern of social organization within a flock of poultry in which each bird pecks another lower in the scale without being pecked in return and submits to pecking by one of higher rank **2 :** a social order with ranks or classes

pec·ten \ˈpek-tən\ *n* **:** SCALLOP 1a [Latin, "comb, scallop"]

pec·tin \ˈpek-tən\ *n* **:** any of various water-soluble substances in plant tissues that yield a gel which is the basis of fruit jellies; *also* **:** a commercial product rich in pectins [French *pectine,* derived from Greek *pēktikos* "coagulating," from *pēgnynai* "to fix, coagulate"]

pec·ti·nate \ˈpek-tə-ˌnāt\ *adj* **:** having narrow parallel projections or divisions resembling the teeth of a comb [Latin *pectinatus,* from *pecten* "comb"] — **pec·ti·na·tion** \ˌpek-tə-ˈnā-shən\ *n*

[1]**pec·to·ral** \ˈpek-tə-rəl, -trəl\ *adj* **1 :** of, relating to, or situated in, near, or on the chest **2 :** coming from the breast or heart as the seat of emotion **:** SUBJECTIVE [Latin *pectoralis,* from *pector-, pectus* "breast"]

[2]**pectoral** *n* **1 :** PECTORAL FIN **2 :** PECTORAL MUSCLE

pectoral cross *n* **:** a cross worn on the breast especially by a prelate

pectoral fin *n* **:** either of a pair of fins of a fish that correspond to the forelimbs of a four-footed animal — compare PELVIC FIN

pectoral girdle *n* **:** SHOULDER GIRDLE

pectoral muscle *n* **:** any of the muscles which connect the front walls of the chest with the bones of the upper arm and shoulder and of which there are two on each side in humans

pec·u·late \ˈpek-yə-ˌlāt\ *vt* **:** EMBEZZLE [Latin *peculari,* from *peculium* "private property"] — **pec·u·la·tion** \ˌpek-yə-ˈlā-shən\ *n* — **pec·u·la·tor** \ˈpek-yə-ˌlāt-ər\ *n*

pe·cu·liar \pi-ˈkyül-yər\ *adj* **1 :** characteristic of only one person, group, or thing **:** DISTINCTIVE **2 :** different from the usual or normal: **a :** SPECIAL 1a, PARTICULAR **b :** distinctly odd or eccentric [Latin *peculiaris* "of private property, special," from *peculium* "private property," from *pecu* "cattle"] ***synonyms*** see STRANGE, CHARACTERISTIC — **pe·cu·liar·ly** *adv*

pe·cu·liar·i·ty \pi-ˌkyül-ˈyar-ət-ē, -ˌkyü-lē-ˈar-\ *n, pl* **-ties 1 :** the quality or state of being peculiar **2 :** a distinguishing characteristic **3 :** an odd trait or habit **:** QUIRK

pe·cu·ni·ary \pi-ˈkyü-nē-ˌer-ē\ *adj* **:** of, relating to, or consisting of money ⟨*pecuniary* aid⟩ ⟨*pecuniary* policies⟩ [Latin *pecuniarius,* from *pecunia* "money"] ***synonyms*** see FINANCIAL

ped- *or* **pedo-** *or* **paed-** *or* **paedo-** *combining form* **:** child ⟨*ped*iatrics⟩ [Greek *paid-, paido-,* from *paid-, pais* "child, boy"]

-ped \ˌped *also* pəd\ *or* **-pede** \ˌpēd\ *n combining form* **:** foot ⟨maxilli*ped*⟩ [Latin *ped-, pes*]

ped·a·gog·ics \ˌped-ə-ˈgäj-iks, -ˈgōj-\ *n* **:** PEDAGOGY

ped·a·gogue *also* **ped·a·gog** \ˈped-ə-ˌgäg\ *n* **:** TEACHER, SCHOOLMASTER; *esp* **:** a dull, formal, and pedantic teacher [Latin *paedagogus,* from Greek *paidagōgos,* slave who escorted children to school, from *paid-* "paed-" + *agōgos* "leader," from *agein* "to lead"]

ped·a·go·gy \ˈped-ə-ˌgō-jē *also* -ˌgäj-ē\ *n* **:** the art, science, or profession of teaching; *esp* **:** EDUCATION 2 — **ped·a·gog·ic**

\ˌped-ə-ˈgäj-ik\ *or* **ped·a·gog·i·cal** \-ˈgäj-i-kəl\ *adj* — **ped·a·gog·i·cal·ly** \-i-kə-lē, -klē\ *adv*

[1]**ped·al** \ˈped-l\ *n* **1 :** a lever acted on by the foot in the playing of musical instruments **2 :** a foot lever or treadle by which a part is activated in a mechanism [Middle French *pedale,* from Italian, derived from Latin *ped-, pes* "foot"]

[2]**pedal** *adj* **:** of or relating to the foot

[3]**pedal** *vb* **ped·aled** *also* **ped·alled; ped·al·ing** *also* **ped·al·ling** \ˈped-l-ing, ˈped-ling\ **1 a :** to use or work the pedals of something **b :** to work the pedals of ⟨*pedal* a bike⟩ **2 :** to ride a bicycle ⟨*pedal* down the street⟩

pedal point *n* **:** a single tone that is normally sustained in the bass and sounds against changing harmonies in the other parts

pedal pushers *n pl* **:** women's and girls' calf-length pants

ped·ant \ˈped-nt\ *n* **1 :** a person who shows off his or her learning **2 :** a dull formal teacher who emphasizes petty details [Middle French, from Italian *pedante*] — **pe·dan·tic** \pə-ˈdant-ik\ *adj* — **pe·dan·ti·cal·ly** \-ˈdant-i-kə-lē, -klē\ *adv*

ped·ant·ry \ˈped-n-trē\ *n, pl* **-ries 1 :** pedantic presentation or application of knowledge or learning **2 :** an instance of pedantry

ped·dle \ˈped-l\ *vb* **ped·dled; ped·dling** \ˈped-ling, -l-ing\ **1 :** to travel about especially from house to house with wares for sale **2 :** to sell or offer for sale from place to place usually in small quantities **:** HAWK **3 :** to offer or promote as valuable ⟨*peddled* the theory in her book⟩ [back-formation from *peddler,* from Middle English *pedlere*] — **ped·dler** *or* **ped·lar** \ˈped-lər\ *n*

ped·es·tal \ˈped-əst-l\ *n* **1 :** the support or foot of a column; *also* **:** the base of any upright structure (as a vase, lamp, or statue) **2 :** a position of high regard or esteem ⟨placed on a *pedestal* by one's children⟩ [Middle French *piedestal,* from Italian *piedestallo,* from *pie di stallo* "foot of a stall"]

[1]**pe·des·tri·an** \pə-ˈdes-trē-ən\ *adj* **1 :** lacking imagination or originality **:** COMMONPLACE ⟨*pedestrian* writing⟩ **2 a :** going or performed on foot **b :** of or relating to walking **3 :** of or designed for pedestrians [Latin *pedester,* literally, "going on foot," derived from *ped-, pes* "foot"]

[2]**pedestrian** *n* **:** a person going on foot

pe·des·tri·an·ism \-ˌiz-əm\ *n* **1 a :** the practice of walking **b :** fondness for walking **2 :** the quality or state of being unimaginative or commonplace

pe·di·a·tri·cian \ˌpēd-ē-ə-ˈtrish-ən\ *n* **:** a specialist in pediatrics

pe·di·at·rics \ˌpēd-ē-ˈa-triks\ *n* **:** a branch of medicine dealing with the development, care, and diseases of children and infants [*ped-* + Greek *iatros* "physician"] — **pe·di·at·ric** \-trik\ *adj*

pedi·cab \ˈped-i-ˌkab\ *n* **:** a small 3-wheeled hooded passenger vehicle that is pedaled [Latin *ped-, pes* "foot" + English *cab*]

ped·i·cel \ˈped-ə-ˌsel\ *n* **:** a slender basal part of an organism or one of its parts; *esp* **:** a stalk that supports a single flower [New Latin *pedicellus,* from Latin *pediculus* "little foot, pedicel," from *ped-, pes* "foot"]

pe·dic·u·lo·sis \pi-ˌdik-yə-ˈlō-səs\ *n* **:** infestation with lice [Latin *pediculus* "louse," from *pedis* "louse"] — **pe·dic·u·lous** \-ˈdik-yə-ləs\ *adj*

ped·i·cure \ˈped-i-ˌkyu̇r\ *n* **1 :** a person who provides care for the feet, toes, and toenails **2 a :** care of the feet, toes, and toenails **b :** a single treatment of these parts [French *pédicure,* from Latin *ped-, pes* "foot" + *curare* "to take care," from *cura* "care"] — **ped·i·cur·ist** \-ˌkyu̇r-əst\ *n*

ped·i·gree \ˈped-ə-ˌgrē\ *n* **1 :** a table or list showing the line of ancestors of an animal or person **2 a :** an ancestral line **:** LINEAGE **b :** the origin and history of something (as a document or a collector's coin or stamp) **3 a :** distinguished ancestry **b :** purity of a breed of an individual or strain recorded by a pedigree [Middle English *pedegru,* from Middle French *pie de grue* "crane's foot"; from the shape made by the lines of a genealogical chart] — **ped·i·greed** \-ˌgrēd\ *adj*

ped·i·ment \ˈped-ə-mənt\ *n* **:** a triangular space forming the gable of a 2-pitched roof in classic architecture; *also* **:** a similar form used as a decoration (as over a door or a window) [obsolete *periment,* probably alteration of *pyramid*] — **ped·i·men·tal** \ˌped-ə-ˈment-l\ *adj*

pedi·palp \ˈped-ə-ˌpalp\ *n* **:** either of the second pair of head appendages of an arachnid (as a spider) borne near the mouth and often modified for a special function (as grasping prey) [New Latin *pedipalpus,* from *ped-, pes* "foot" + *palpus* "palpus"]

pedo- — see PED-

pe·dom·e·ter \pi-ˈdäm-ət-ər\ *n* **:** an instrument that measures the distance a walker covers by responding to body motion at each step [French *pédomètre,* from Latin *ped-, pes* "foot" + French *-mètre* "-meter"]

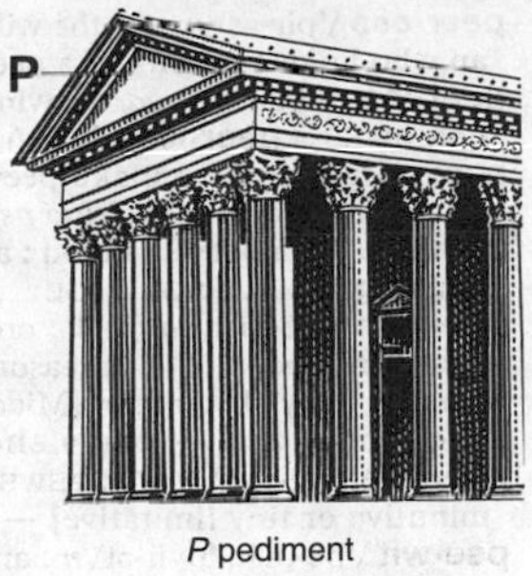

P pediment

pe·dun·cle \ˈpē-ˌdəng-kəl, pi-ˈ\ *n* **1 :** a stalk bearing a flower or flower cluster **2 :** a narrow part by which some larger part or the body of an organism is attached [New Latin *pedunculus,* from Latin *ped-, pes* "foot"] — **pe·dun·cu·lat·ed** \pi-ˈdəng-kyə-ˌlāt-əd\ *or* **pe·dun·cu·late** \-lət\ *adj*

[1]**peek** \ˈpēk\ *vi* **1 a :** to look slyly or stealthily **b :** to peer through a crack or hole or from a place of concealment **2 :** to take a brief look **:** GLANCE [Middle English *piken*]

[2]**peek** *n* **:** a brief or stealthy look

[1]**peel** \ˈpēl\ *vb* **1 :** to strip off an outer layer of ⟨*peel* an apple⟩ **2 :** to remove by or as if by stripping or tearing ⟨*peel* the label off the can⟩ ⟨*peeled* off my coat⟩ **3 a :** to come off in strips or patches ⟨the paint is *peeling*⟩ **b :** to lose an outer layer (as of skin) ⟨your face is *peeling*⟩ [Medieval French *peler,* from Latin *pilare* "to remove the hair from," from *pilus* "hair"] — **peel·er** *n*

[2]**peel** *n* **:** an outer covering and especially the skin or rind of a fruit

[3]**peel** *n* **:** a usually long-handled spade-shaped utensil used chiefly by bakers for getting something into or out of an oven [Medieval French *pele,* from Latin *pala*]

peel·ing \ˈpē-ling\ *n* **:** a peeled-off piece or strip (as of rind)

peel off *vi* **:** to veer away from an airplane formation especially for diving or landing

peen \ˈpēn\ *n* **:** the usually hemispherical or wedge-shaped end of the head of some hammers opposite the face that is used for cutting and shaping [probably of Scandinavian origin]

[1]**peep** \ˈpēp\ *vi* **1 :** to utter the characteristic feeble shrill cry of a newly hatched bird or a similar sound **2 :** to utter the slightest sound [Middle English *pepen,* of imitative origin]

[2]**peep** *n* **1 :** a feeble shrill sound **2 :** a slight utterance especially of complaint or protest ⟨not another *peep* out of you⟩

[3]**peep** *vb* **1 a :** to peer through a crevice **b :** to look cautiously or slyly **2 :** to begin to emerge from concealment **:** show slightly **3 :** to cause (as the head of one peeping) to protrude slightly [Middle English *pepen,* perhaps alteration of *piken* "to peek"]

[4]**peep** *n* **1 :** the first glimpse or faint appearance ⟨at the *peep* of dawn⟩ **2 :** a brief or furtive look

[1]**peep·er** \ˈpē-pər\ *n* **:** any of various tree frogs that peep shrilly; *esp* **:** SPRING PEEPER

[2]**peeper** *n* **1 :** one that peeps; *esp* **:** PEEPING TOM **2 :** EYE 1a

peep·hole \ˈpēp-ˌhōl\ *n* **:** a hole or crevice to peep through

peeping tom \-ˈtäm\ *n, often cap* **:** a person who spies into the windows of private dwellings **:** one who furtively watches others [*Peeping Tom,* legendary 11th century tailor of Coventry supposed to have been struck blind for peeping at Lady Godiva]

peep show *n* **:** a display of objects or pictures viewed through a small hole usually fitted with a lens

peep sight *n* **:** a rear sight for a gun having an adjustable metal piece pierced with a small hole to look through in aiming

[1]**peer** \ˈpiər\ *n* **1 :** one that is of equal standing with another **:** EQUAL **2** *archaic* **:** COMPANION, FELLOW **3 a :** a member (as a duke, marquess, earl, viscount, or baron) of one of the five ranks of the British peerage **b :** NOBLE [Medieval French *per,* from *per,* adj., "equal," from Latin *par*]

[2]**peer** *vi* **1 :** to look narrowly or curiously; *esp* **:** to look searchingly at something difficult to discern **2 :** to come slightly into view [perhaps from *appear*]

peer·age \ˈpiər-ij\ *n* **1 :** the body of peers **2 :** the rank or dignity of a peer **3 :** a book containing a list of peers

peer·ess \ˈpir-əs\ *n* **1 :** the wife or widow of a peer **2 :** a woman who holds the rank of a peer in her own right

peer·less \ˈpiər-ləs\ *adj* **:** having no equal **:** MATCHLESS, INCOMPARABLE — **peer·less·ly** *adv* — **peer·less·ness** *n*

[1]**peeve** \ˈpēv\ *vt* **:** to make peevish or resentful **:** ANNOY, IRRITATE [back-formation from *peevish*]

[2]**peeve** *n* **1 :** a peevish mood **:** a feeling of resentment **2 :** a particular grievance **:** GRUDGE

pee·vish \ˈpē-vish\ *adj* **1 :** cross and complaining in temperament or mood **2 :** unreasonably stubborn **:** OBSTINATE **3 :** marked by ill temper [Middle English *pevish* "spiteful"] — **pee·vish·ly** *adv* — **pee·vish·ness** *n*

pee·wee \ˈpē-ˌwē\ *n* **1 :** PEWEE **2 :** something or someone diminutive or tiny [imitative] — **peewee** *adj*

pee·wit \ˈpē-ˌwit, ˈpyü-ət\ *n* **:** any of several birds; *esp* **:** LAPWING [imitative]

[1]**peg** \ˈpeg\ *n* **1 :** a small usually cylindrical pointed or tapered piece (as of wood) used especially to pin down or fasten things or to fit into or close holes ⟨a tent *peg*⟩ **2 :** a projecting piece used as a support or boundary marker **3 a :** any of the pins of a stringed musical instrument that are turned to regulate the pitch of the strings **b :** a step or degree especially in estimation ⟨took you down a *peg*⟩ **4 :** a pointed prong or claw for catching or tearing **5** *British* **:** a small drink (as of whiskey) **6 :** a hard throw in baseball ⟨a quick *peg* to first base⟩ [Middle English *pegge*]

[2]**peg** *vb* **pegged; peg·ging 1 a :** to fasten or mark with pegs **b :** to pin down **:** RESTRICT **c :** to fix or hold (as prices) at a planned level **d :** to place in a definite category **2 :** THROW 2 **3 :** to work steadily and diligently **4 :** to move along vigorously or hastily **:** HUSTLE

Peg·a·sus \ˈpeg-ə-səs\ *n* **:** a northern constellation near the vernal equinoctial point [*Pegasus,* winged horse in Greek mythology]

Peg–Board \ˈpeg-ˌbōrd, -ˌbȯrd\ *trademark* — used for material (as fiberboard) with evenly spaced holes into which hooks may be inserted for the storage and display of articles

peg leg *n* **:** an artificial leg; *esp* **:** one fitted at the knee

peg·ma·tite \ˈpeg-mə-ˌtīt\ *n* **:** a coarse variety of granite occurring in dikes or veins [French, from Greek *pēgma* "something fastened together," from *pēgnynai* "to fasten together"]

peg–top \ˈpeg-ˈtäp\ *or* **peg–topped** \-ˈtäpt\ *adj* **:** wide at the top and narrow at the bottom ⟨*peg-top* trousers⟩

peg top *n* **1 :** a pear-shaped top with a sharp metal peg spun by a string as it is thrown from the hand **2** *pl* **:** peg-top trousers

pei·gnoir \pān-ˈwär, pen-\ *n* **:** a woman's loose negligee or dressing gown [French, literally, "garment worn while combing the hair," from *peigner* "to comb the hair," from Latin *pectinare,* from *pecten* "comb"]

pe·jor·a·tive \pi-ˈjȯr-ət-iv, -ˈjär-; ˈpej-rət-, -ə-rət-\ *adj* **:** tending to disparage or belittle **:** DEPRECIATORY ⟨*pejorative* language⟩ [Late Latin *pejoratus,* past participle of *pejorare* "to make or become worse," from Latin *pejor* "worse"] — **pe·jor·a·tive·ly** *adv*

Pe·kin \pi-ˈkin, ˈpē-ˌ\ *n* **:** any of a breed of large white ducks of Chinese origin used for meat production [*Pekin, Peking* (Beijing), China]

Pe·king·ese *or* **Pe·kin·ese** \ˌpē-kən-ˈēz, -king-, -ˈēs\ *n, pl* **Pekingese** *or* **Pekinese 1 a :** a native or resident of Peking **b :** the Chinese dialect of Peking **2 :** any of a Chinese breed of small short-legged dogs with a broad flat face and a profuse long soft coat

Pe·king man \ˌpē-ˌking-\ *n* **:** an extinct Pleistocene hominid known from skeletal and cultural remains found in cave deposits in northeastern China and now classified with the direct ancestor of modern humans

pel·age \ˈpel-ij\ *n* **:** the hairy covering of a mammal [French, from *poil* "hair," from Latin *pilus*]

pe·lag·ic \pə-ˈlaj-ik\ *adj* **:** of, relating to, living, or occurring in the open sea **:** OCEANIC ⟨*pelagic* birds⟩ [Latin *pelagicus,* from Greek *pelagikos,* from *pelagos* "sea"]

pel·ar·go·ni·um \ˌpel-är-ˈgō-nē-əm, ˌpel-ər-\ *n* **:** GERANIUM 2 [derived from Greek *pelargos* "stork"]

Pe·las·gian \pə-ˈlaz-jē-ən, -jən; -ˈlaz-gē-ən\ *n* **:** any of an ancient people mentioned by classical writers as early inhabitants of Greece and the eastern islands of the Mediterranean [Greek *Pelasgoi* "Pelasgians"] — **Pelasgian** *adj*

pe·lecy·pod \pə-ˈles-ə-ˌpäd\ *adj or n* **:** BIVALVE [derived from Greek *pelekys* "ax" + *pod-, pous* "foot"]

pelf \ˈpelf\ *n* **:** MONEY 2, RICHES [Medieval French *pelfre* "booty"]

pel·i·can \ˈpel-i-kən\ *n* **:** any of a genus of large web-footed birds with a very large pouched bill in which fish are caught [Old English *pellican,* from Late Latin *pelecanus,* from Greek *pelekan*]

pelican

pel·la·gra \pə-ˈlag-rə, -ˈlāg-, -ˈläg-\ *n* **:** a disease associated with a diet deficient in niacin and protein and marked by skin rash, digestive disorders, and mental symptoms (as irritability and confusion) [Italian, derived from Latin *pellis* "skin" + Greek *agra* "hunt, catch"] — **pel·la·grous** \-rəs\ *adj*

[1]**pel·let** \ˈpel-ət\ *n* **1 a :** a usually small round or cylindrical body (as of food or medicine) **b :** a wad of indigestible material (as of bones and fur) regurgitated by a bird of prey (as an owl) **2 a :** a usually stone ball used as a missile in medieval times **b :** BULLET 1 **c :** a piece of small shot [Medieval French *pelote,* derived from Latin *pila* "ball"]

[2]**pellet** *vt* **1 :** to form into pellets **2 :** to strike with pellets

pel·let·ize \ˈpel-ət-ˌīz\ *vt* **-ized; iz·ing :** to make or compact into pellets ⟨*pelletize* ore⟩ — **pel·let·i·za·tion** \ˌpel-ət-ə-ˈzā-shən\ *n* — **pel·let·iz·er** \ˈpel-ət-ˌī-zər\ *n*

pel·li·cle \ˈpel-i-kəl\ *n* **:** a thin skin, film, or membrane (as of a paramecium) [Middle French *pellicule,* from Medieval Latin *pellicula,* from Latin *pellis* "skin"] — **pel·lic·u·lar** \pə-ˈlik-yə-lər\ *adj*

pell–mell \ˈpel-ˈmel\ *adv* **1 :** in confusion or disorder **2 :** in confused or headlong haste [Middle French *pelemele*] — **pell–mell** *adj or n*

pel·lu·cid \pə-ˈlü-səd\ *adj* **1 :** extremely clear or transparent **2 :** reflecting light evenly from all surfaces **3 :** very easy to understand [Latin *pellucidus,* from *per* "through" + *lucidus* "lucid"] — **pel·lu·cid·i·ty** \ˌpel-yü-ˈsid-ət-ē\ *n* — **pel·lu·cid·ly** \pə-ˈlü-səd-lē\ *adv* — **pel·lu·cid·ness** *n*

pe·lo·rus \pə-ˈlōr-əs, -ˈlȯr-\ *n* **:** a navigational instrument having a disk marked in degrees and two sights by which bearings are taken [origin unknown]

[1]**pelt** \ˈpelt\ *n* **:** a usually undressed skin with its hair, wool, or fur [Middle English]

[2]**pelt** *vb* **1 a :** to strike with or deliver a succession of blows or missiles ⟨*pelted* them with snowballs⟩ **b :** BOMBARD 2 ⟨was *pelted* with questions by the reporters⟩ **2 :** HURL, THROW **3 :** to beat or dash repeatedly ⟨hail *pelting* the roof⟩ **4 :** to move rapidly and vigorously or with pounding blows or thuds ⟨turned and *pelted* for home⟩ [Middle English *pelten*] — **pelt·er** *n*

[3]**pelt** *n* **:** BLOW, WHACK

pelt·ry \ˈpel-trē\ *n, pl* **peltries :** animal pelts; *esp* **:** raw undressed skins

pel·vic \ˈpel-vik\ *adj* **:** of, relating to, or located in or near the pelvis ⟨*pelvic* bones⟩ — **pelvic** *n*

pelvic fin *n* **:** either of a pair of fins of a fish that correspond to the hind limbs of a four-footed animal — compare PECTORAL FIN

pelvic girdle *n* **:** an arch of bone or cartilage that supports the hind limbs of a vertebrate

pel·vis \ˈpel-vəs\ *n, pl* **pel·vis·es** *or* **pel·ves** \ˈpel-ˌvēz\ **1 :** a basin-shaped structure in the skeleton of many vertebrates formed by the pelvic girdle and adjoining bones of the spine; *also* **:** its cavity **2 :** the funnel-shaped cavity of the kidney into which urine is discharged [Latin, "basin"]

pel·y·co·saur \ˈpel-i-kə-ˌsȯər\ *n* **:** any of an order (Pelycosauria) of primitive Permian reptiles that resembled mammals and often had the back processes on the vertebrae greatly developed [derived from Greek *pelyx* "bowl" + *sauros* "lizard"]

Pem·broke Welsh corgi \ˈpem-ˌbrōk-, -ˌbrůk-\ *n* **:** any of a breed of Welsh corgis with pointed ears, straight legs, and short tail — called also *Pembroke* [*Pembroke,* Wales]

pem·mi·can \ˈpem-i-kən\ *n* **:** dried lean meat pounded fine and mixed with melted fat and used for food especially by North American Indians [Cree *pimikha'n*]

[1]**pen** \'pen\ *n* **1 :** a small enclosure for animals; *also* **:** the animals in a pen ⟨a *pen* of sheep⟩ **2 :** a small place of confinement or storage [Middle English]

[2]**pen** *vt* **penned; pen·ning :** to shut in a pen

[3]**pen** *n* **1 :** an implement for writing or drawing with ink or a similar fluid: as **a :** QUILL **b :** a small thin convex metal device tapering to a split point and fitting into a holder **c :** a penholder containing a pen **d :** FOUNTAIN PEN **e :** BALLPOINT **2 a :** a writing instrument regarded as a means of expression **b :** WRITER **3 :** the internal horny feather-shaped shell of a squid [Medieval French *penne* "feather, pen," from Latin *penna, pinna* "feather"]

[4]**pen** *vt* **penned; pen·ning :** to write especially with a pen

[5]**pen** *n* **:** a female swan [origin unknown]

[6]**pen** *n, slang* **:** PENITENTIARY

pe·nal \'pē-nl\ *adj* **:** of, relating to, or involving punishment, penalties, or punitive institutions ⟨*penal* laws⟩ ⟨a *penal* colony⟩ [Medieval French, from Latin *poenalis,* from *poena* "punishment"] — **pe·nal·ly** \-l-ē\ *adv*

penal code *n* **:** a code of laws concerning crimes and offenses and their punishment

pe·nal·ize \'pēn-l-,īz, 'pen-\ *vt* **1 :** to subject to a penalty ⟨*penalize* an athlete for a foul⟩ **2 :** to place at a disadvantage **:** HANDICAP ⟨the system *penalized* slow learners⟩ — **pe·nal·i·za·tion** \,pēn-l-ə-'zā-shən, ,pen-\ *n*

pen·al·ty \'pen-l-tē\ *n, pl* **-ties 1 :** punishment for a crime or offense **2 :** something forfeited when a person fails to do what he agreed to do **3 :** disadvantage, loss, or hardship due to some action or condition **4 :** a punishment or handicap imposed for breaking a rule in a sport or game

pen·ance \'pen-əns\ *n* **1 :** an act of self-abasement, mortification, or devotion performed to show sorrow or repentance for sin **2 :** a sacrament in the Roman Catholic and Eastern churches consisting in sorrow for sin, confession to a priest, a penance imposed by the confessor, and absolution [Medieval French, from Medieval Latin *poenitentia* "penitence"]

pence \'pens\ *plural of* PENNY

pen·chant \'pen-chənt\ *n* **:** a strong leaning **:** LIKING [French, from *pencher* "to lean, incline," derived from Latin *pendere* "to weigh"]

synonyms PENCHANT, FLAIR mean a strong instinct or liking for something. PENCHANT may imply a decided taste and strong inclination for ⟨a *penchant* for gardening⟩. FLAIR implies instinctive ability or perception and acumen ⟨a real *flair* for cooking⟩.

[1]**pen·cil** \'pen-səl\ *n* **1 a :** an implement for writing, drawing, or marking consisting of or containing a slender cylinder or strip of a solid marking substance **b :** a small medicated or cosmetic roll or stick **2 :** an aggregate of rays of light especially when diverging from or converging to a point **3 :** something long and thin like a pencil [Medieval French *pincel* "artist's brush," from Latin *penicillus,* literally, "little brush," from *penis* "tail, penis"]

[2]**pencil** *vt* **-ciled** *or* **-cilled; -cil·ing** *or* **-cil·ling** \-sə-ling, -sling\ **:** to mark, draw, or write with or as if with a pencil — **pen·cil·er** \-sə-lər, -slər\ *n*

pen·dant *also* **pen·dent** \'pen-dənt\ *n* **:** something that hangs down especially as an ornament [Medieval French *pendant,* from *pendre* "to hang," from Latin *pendēre*]

pen·den·cy \'pen-dən-sē\ *n* **:** the state of being pending

pen·dent *or* **pen·dant** \'pen-dənt\ *adj* **1 :** supported from above **:** SUSPENDED **2 :** jutting or leaning over **:** OVERHANGING **3 :** remaining undetermined **:** PENDING — **pen·dent·ly** *adv*

[1]**pend·ing** \'pen-ding\ *prep* **1 :** DURING **2 :** while awaiting ⟨*pending* a reply⟩ [French *pendant,* from *pendre* "to hang"]

[2]**pending** *adj* **:** not yet decided ⟨court cases *pending*⟩

pen·du·lar \'pen-jə-lər, -dyə-lər, -dl-ər\ *adj* **:** being or resembling the movement of a pendulum

pen·du·lous \'pen-jə-ləs\ *adj* **1 :** suspended so as to swing freely ⟨*pendulous* vines⟩ **2 :** inclined or hanging downward ⟨flabby *pendulous* jowls⟩ [Latin *pendulus,* from *pendēre* "to hang"] — **pen·du·lous·ly** *adv*

pen·du·lum \'pen-jə-ləm, -dyə-ləm, -dl-əm\ *n* **:** a body suspended from a fixed point so as to swing freely to and fro under the action of gravity ⟨the *pendulum* of a clock⟩ [Latin, neuter of *pendulus* "pendulous"]

pe·ne·plain *also* **pe·ne·plane** \'pē-ni-,plān, 'pen-\ *n* **:** a land surface of considerable area and slight relief shaped by erosion [Latin *paene, pene* "almost" + English *plain* or *plane*]

pen·e·tra·ble \'pen-ə-trə-bəl\ *adj* **:** capable of being penetrated — **pen·e·tra·bil·i·ty** \,pen-ə-trə-'bil-ət-ē\ *n* — **pen·e·tra·ble·ness** \'pen-ə-trə-bəl-nəs\ *n* — **pen·e·tra·bly** \-blē\ *adv*

pen·e·trate \'pen-ə-,trāt\ *vb* **1 a :** to pass into or through **b :** to enter by overcoming resistance **:** PIERCE **2 :** to come to understand **3 :** to move deeply **4 :** to seep through **:** PERMEATE [Latin *penetrare*] ***synonyms*** see ENTER

pen·e·trat·ing *adj* **1 :** having the power of entering or piercing **:** SHARP, BITING ⟨*penetrating* cold⟩ ⟨a *penetrating* shriek⟩ **2 :** ACUTE, DISCERNING ⟨a *penetrating* mind⟩ — **pen·e·trat·ing·ly** \-,trāt-ing-lē\ *adv*

pen·e·tra·tion \,pen-ə-'trā-shən\ *n* **1 :** the act or process of penetrating **2 a :** the depth to which something penetrates **b :** the power to penetrate; *esp* **:** the ability to discern deeply and acutely

pen·e·tra·tive \'pen-ə-,trāt-iv\ *adj* **:** tending or able to penetrate — **pen·e·tra·tive·ly** *adv* — **pen·e·tra·tive·ness** *n*

pen·guin \'pen-gwən, 'peng-\ *n* **:** any of various erect short-legged flightless aquatic birds of the southern hemisphere with the wings modified as flippers and used in swimming [obsolete English *penguin* "great auk," perhaps from Welsh *pen gwyn* "white head" (applied to the bird in winter plumage)]

penguin

pen·hold·er \'pen-,hōl-dər\ *n* **:** a holder or handle for a pen

pen·i·cil·lin \,pen-ə-'sil-ən\ *n* **:** any of several antibiotics or a mixture of these produced by penicillia or synthetically and used especially against cocci

pen·i·cil·lin·ase \-'sil-ə-,nās, -,nāz\ *n* **:** BETA-LACTAMASE

pen·i·cil·li·um \-'sil-ē-əm\ *n, pl* **-lia** \-ē-ə\ **:** any of a genus of fungi comprising mostly blue molds found chiefly on moist nonliving organic matter (as decaying fruit) [New Latin, from Latin *penicillus* "brush, little tail"]

pen·in·su·la \pə-'nin-sə-lə, -'nin-slə, -'nin-chə-lə\ *n* **:** a portion of land nearly surrounded by water; *also* **:** a piece of land jutting out into the water [Latin *paeninsula,* from *paene* "almost" + *insula* "island"] — **pen·in·su·lar** \-lər\ *adj*

pe·nis \'pē-nəs\ *n, pl* **pe·nis·es** *also* **pe·nes** \'pē-,nēz\ **:** a male organ of copulation containing a channel through which sperm is discharged from the body that in mammals including humans also serves to discharge urine from the body [Latin, "penis, tail"] — **pe·nile** \-,nīl\ *adj*

pen·i·tence \'pen-ə-təns\ *n* **:** sorrow for one's sins or faults **:** REPENTANCE

synonyms PENITENCE, REPENTANCE, CONTRITION mean regret for sin or wrongdoing. PENITENCE implies humble realization of and regret for one's faults. REPENTANCE emphasizes the change of mind of one who not only regrets errors but abandons them for a new standard. CONTRITION suggests penitence shown by signs of grief or pain.

[1]**pen·i·tent** \-tənt\ *adj* **:** feeling or expressing pain or sorrow for sins or offenses **:** REPENTANT [Medieval French, from Latin *paenitens,* from *paenitēre* "to be sorry"] — **pen·i·tent·ly** *adv*

[2]**penitent** *n* **1 :** a person who repents of sin **2 :** a person under church censure but admitted to penance especially under the direction of a confessor

pen·i·ten·tial \,pen-ə-'ten-chəl\ *adj* **:** of or relating to penitence or penance — **pen·i·ten·tial·ly** \-'tench-lē, -ə-lē\ *adv*

[1]**pen·i·ten·tia·ry** \,pen-ə-'tench-rē, -ə-rē\ *n, pl* **-ries :** a public institution in which criminals are confined; *esp* **:** a state or federal prison in the United States

[2]**penitentiary** *adj* **:** of, relating to, or incurring confinement in a penitentiary

pen·knife \'pen-,nīf\ *n* **:** a small pocketknife [from its original use for mending quill pens]

pen·man \'pen-mən\ *n* **1 a :** COPYIST 1, SCRIBE **b :** one who is expert in penmanship **2 :** AUTHOR 1

\ə\ **abut**	\au̇\ **out**	\i\ **tip**	\ȯ\ **saw**	\u̇\ **foot**
\ər\ **further**	\ch\ **chin**	\ī\ **life**	\ȯi\ **coin**	\y\ **yet**
\a\ **mat**	\e\ **pet**	\j\ **job**	\th\ **thin**	\yü\ **few**
\ā\ **take**	\ē\ **easy**	\ng\ **sing**	\th\ **this**	\yu̇\ **cure**
\ä\ **cot, cart**	\g\ **go**	\ō\ **bone**	\ü\ **food**	\zh\ **vision**

pen·man·ship \ˈpen-mən-ˌship\ *n* **1** : the art or practice of writing with the pen **2** : quality or style of handwriting
pen name *n* : an author's pseudonym
pen·nant \ˈpen-ənt\ *n* **1 a** : a nautical flag tapering to a point or swallowtail and used for identification or signaling **b** : a long narrow flag or banner that tapers to a point **2** : a flag emblematic of championship [alteration of *pendant*]
pen·ni·less \ˈpen-i-ləs, ˈpen-l-əs\ *adj* : having no money at all : very poor
pen·non \ˈpen-ən\ *n* **1** : a long usually triangular or swallow-tailed streamer typically attached to the head of a lance as an ensign **2** : PENNANT 1a [Medieval French *penun,* from *penne* "feather, pen"]
Penn·syl·va·nia Dutch \ˌpen-səl-ˌvā-nyə-\ *n* **1** : a people living mostly in eastern Pennsylvania whose characteristic cultural traditions go back to the German migrations of the 18th century **2** : a German dialect spoken by the Pennsylvania Dutch — **Pennsylvania Dutchman** *n*
Penn·syl·va·nian \-ˈvā-nyən\ *adj* **1** : of or relating to Pennsylvania or its people **2** : of, relating to, or being the period of the Paleozoic era between the Mississippian and Permian or the corresponding system of rocks — see GEOLOGIC TIME table — **Pennsylvanian** *n*
pen·ny \ˈpen-ē\ *n, pl* **pen·nies** \-ēz\ *or* **pence** \ˈpens\ **1 a** : a monetary unit of the United Kingdom formerly equal to 1/240 pound but now equal to 1/100 pound **b** : a similar monetary unit of any of various other countries in or formerly in the Commonwealth of Nations **c** : a coin representing this unit **2** : DENARIUS **3** *pl pennies* : a cent of the United States or Canada **4** : a sum of money ⟨earn an honest *penny*⟩ [Old English *penning*]
penny ante *n* : poker played for very low stakes
penny arcade *n* : an amusement center where each device for entertainment may be operated for a small sum and originally for a penny
penny dreadful *n* : a novel of violent adventure or crime originally costing one penny
pen·ny pinch·er \ˈpen-ē-ˌpin-chər\ *n* : a stingy person — **penny–pinch·ing** \-ching\ *adj or n*
pen·ny·roy·al \ˌpen-ē-ˈrȯi-əl, -ˈrȯil; ˈpen-i-ˌrīl\ *n* : a European perennial mint with small aromatic leaves; *also* : a North American mint that yields an oil used in folk medicine and as a mosquito repellent [probably alteration of Middle French *puliol real,* from *puliol* "pennyroyal" (derived from Latin *puleium* + *real* "royal"]
pen·ny·weight \ˈpen-ē-ˌwāt\ *n* — see MEASURE table
pen·ny–wise \-ˌwīz\ *adj* : wise or prudent only in small matters
pen·ny·worth \ˈpen-ē-ˌwərth\ *n, pl* **-worth** *or* **-worths** : a penny's worth : as much as a penny will buy
Pe·nob·scot \pə-ˈnäb-skət, -ˌskät\ *n, pl* **Penobscot** *or* **Penobscots** : a member of an Algonquian people of the Penobscot river valley and the Penobscot Bay region
pe·nol·o·gy \pi-ˈnäl-ə-jē\ *n* : a branch of criminology dealing with prison management and the treatment of offenders [Greek *poinē* "penalty"] — **pe·no·log·i·cal** \ˌpēn-l-ˈäj-i-kəl\ *adj* — **pe·nol·o·gist** \pi-ˈnäl-ə-jəst\ *n*
pen pal *n* : a friend made and kept through correspondence often without any face-to-face acquaintance
pen·sile \ˈpen-ˌsīl\ *adj* : suspended from above [Latin *pensilis,* from *pensus,* past participle of *pendēre* "to hang"]
[1]**pen·sion** *n* **1** \ˈpen-chən\ : a fixed sum paid regularly to a person; *esp* : one paid to a person following retirement or to surviving dependents **2** \pä^{n}s-yō^{n}\ : a boardinghouse especially in continental Europe [Medieval French, from Latin *pensio,* from *pendere* "to weigh, pay"] — **pen·sion·less** \ˈpen-chən-ləs\ *adj*
[2]**pension** \ˈpen-chən\ *vt* **pen·sioned; pen·sion·ing** \ˈpench-ning, -ə-ning\ : to grant or pay a pension to
pen·sion·er \ˈpench-nər, -ə-nər\ *n* **1** : a person who receives or lives on a pension **2** : a mercenary dependent : HIRELING
pen·sive \ˈpen-siv\ *adj* **1** : musingly or dreamily thoughtful **2** : suggestive of sad thoughtfulness : MELANCHOLY [Medieval French *pensif,* from *penser* "to think," from Latin *pensare* "to ponder," from *pendere* "to weigh"] — **pen·sive·ly** *adv* — **pen·sive·ness** *n*
pen·ste·mon *also* **pent·ste·mon** \pen-ˈstē-mən, ˈpen-stə-\ *n* : any of a genus of chiefly American herbs of the snapdragon family with showy blue, purple, red, yellow, or white flowers [derived from Greek *penta-* + *stēmōn* "thread"]
pen·stock \ˈpen-ˌstäk\ *n* **1** : a sluice or gate for regulating a flow (as of water) **2** : a conduit or pipe for conducting water

pent \ˈpent\ *adj* : shut up : held back ⟨*pent*-up feelings⟩ [probably from past participle of obsolete *pend* "to confine"]
penta- *or* **pent-** *combining form* : five ⟨*pentode*⟩ [Greek, from *pente*]
pen·ta·gon \ˈpent-i-ˌgän\ *n* : a polygon of five angles and five sides

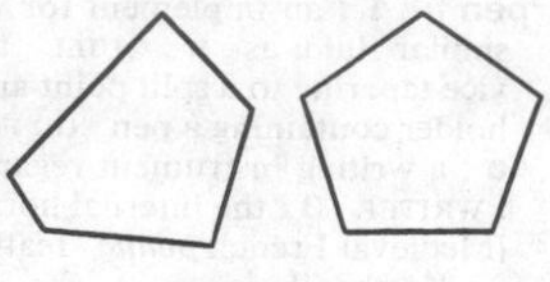
pentagon

Pentagon *n* : the American military establishment [the *Pentagon* building, headquarters of the United States Department of Defense]
pen·tag·o·nal \pen-ˈtag-ən-l\ *adj* **1** : having five sides and five angles **2** : having a pentagon as a cross section or as a base ⟨a *pentagonal* pyramid⟩
pen·tam·e·ter \pen-ˈtam-ət-ər\ *n* : a line consisting of five metrical feet [Latin, derived from Greek *penta-* "five" + *metron* "measure"]
pen·tane \ˈpen-ˌtān\ *n* : any of three isomeric hydrocarbons C_5H_{12} occurring in petroleum and natural gas
Pen·ta·teuch \ˈpent-ə-ˌtük, -ˌtyük\ *n* : the first five books of the Old Testament [Late Latin *Pentateuchus,* from Greek *Pentateuchos,* from *penta-* "five" + *teuchos* "tool, vessel, book"]
pen·tath·lon \pen-ˈtath-lən, -ˌlän\ *n* : an athletic contest in which each contestant participates in five different events [Greek, from *penta-* "five" + *athlon* "contest"]
Pen·te·cost \ˈpent-i-ˌkȯst, -ˌkäst\ *n* **1** : SHABUOTH **2** : the 7th Sunday after Easter observed as a church festival in commemoration of the descent of the Holy Spirit on the apostles [Old English *pentecosten,* from Late Latin *pentecoste,* from Greek *pentēkostē,* literally, "50th (day)," from *pentēkonta* "fifty"]
Pen·te·cos·tal \ˌpent-i-ˈkäs-tl, -ˈkȯs-\ *adj* **1** : of, relating to, or suggesting Pentecost **2** : of, relating to, or constituting any of various usually fundamentalist sects that stress religious revivals — **Pentecostal** *n* — **Pen·te·cos·tal·ism** \-tə-ˌliz-əm\ *n*
pent·house \ˈpent-ˌhau̇s\ *n* **1** : a roof or a shed attached to and sloping from a wall or building **2** : a structure (as an apartment) built on the roof of a building [Middle English *pentis,* from Medieval French *apentiz,* from *appendre* "to attach, hang against," probably from Latin *appendere* "to hang, weigh out"]
Word History In Middle English *pentis* meant primarily "a shed or roof attached to a wall or building." *Pentis,* borrowed from Medieval French *apentiz,* is derived from Latin *appendere,* which means "to hang." A *pentis,* then, was a smaller building or structure attached to a larger one. It was widely though mistakenly believed that *pentis* was related to Middle French *pente* "slope," and this belief was likely encouraged by the fact that many such structures did have sloping roofs. The second syllable of the word was altered by folk etymology to *-house.*
pent·land·ite \ˈpent-lən-ˌdīt\ *n* : a bronzy yellow mineral $(Fe,Ni)_9S_8$ that is a nickel iron sulfide and the principal ore of nickel [Joseph *Pentland,* died 1873, Irish scientist]
pen·to·bar·bi·tal \ˌpent-ə-ˈbär-bə-ˌtȯl\ *n* : a barbiturate used especially in the form of its sodium or calcium salt chiefly as a sedative and to induce sleep [*penta-* + *-o-* + *barbital*]
pen·tom·ic \pen-ˈtäm-ik\ *adj* **1** : made up of five battle groups ⟨a *pentomic* division⟩ **2** : organized into pentomic divisions ⟨*pentomic* armies⟩ [blend of *penta-* and *atomic*]
pen·tose \ˈpen-ˌtōs\ *n* : any of various sugars $C_5H_{10}O_5$ (as ribose) containing five carbon atoms in the molecule
Pen·to·thal \ˈpent-ə-ˌthȯl\ *trademark* — used for a substance that is used as an intravenous anesthetic of short duration and as a hypnotic
pent·ox·ide \pent-ˈäk-ˌsīd\ *n* : an oxide containing five atoms of oxygen in the molecule
pentstemon *variant of* PENSTEMON
pe·nu·che \pə-ˈnü-chē\ *n* : fudge made usually of brown sugar, butter, cream or milk, and nuts [Mexican Spanish *panocha* "raw sugar," from Spanish, "ear of maize," derived from Latin *panicula* "panicle," from *panus* "swelling"]
pe·nult \ˈpē-ˌnəlt, pi-ˈ\ *n* : the next to the last syllable of a word [Latin *paenultima,* from *paenultimus* "almost last," from *paene* "almost" + *ultimus* "last"]
pen·ul·ti·mate \pi-ˈnəl-tə-mət\ *adj* **1** : next to the last **2** : of or relating to a penult — **penultimate** *n* — **pen·ul·ti·mate·ly** *adv*
pen·um·bra \pə-ˈnəm-brə\ *n, pl* **-brae** \-ˌbrē, -ˌbrī\ *or* **-bras** **1** : the partial shadow surrounding a perfect shadow (as in an

eclipse) **2 :** the shaded region around the dark central portion of a sunspot [Latin *paene* "almost" + *umbra* "shadow"] — **pen·um·bral** \-brəl\ *adj*

pe·nu·ri·ous \pə-ˈnu̇r-ē-əs, -ˈnyu̇r-\ *adj* **1 :** marked by or suffering from penury **2 :** given to or marked by extreme frugality *synonyms* see STINGY — **pe·nu·ri·ous·ly** *adv* — **pe·nu·ri·ous·ness** *n*

pen·u·ry \ˈpen-yə-rē\ *n* **1 :** extreme poverty **:** PRIVATION **2 :** absence of resources **:** SCANTINESS [Latin *penuria* "want"]

pe·on \ˈpē-ˌän, -ən\ *n* **1 :** a member of the landless laboring class in Spanish America **2 :** a person held in compulsory servitude to work out an indebtedness **3 :** DRUDGE, MENIAL [Portuguese *peão* and French *pion,* both from Medieval Latin *pedo* "foot soldier," from Latin *ped-, pes* "foot"]

pe·on·age \ˈpē-ə-nij\ *n* **1 :** the condition of a peon **2 :** the use of laborers bound in servitude because of debt

pe·o·ny \ˈpē-ə-nē\ *n, pl* **-nies :** any of a genus of perennial chiefly Eurasian plants widely grown for their large usually double flowers of red, pink, or white [Medieval French *peonie, pioiné,* from Latin *paeonia,* from Greek *paiōnia,* from *Paiōn* "Paeon (physician of the gods)"]

[1]**peo·ple** \ˈpē-pəl\ *n, pl* **people 1** *pl* **:** HUMANS, PERSONS — often used in compounds instead of persons ⟨sales*people*⟩ **2** *pl* **:** the members of a family **:** KINDRED; *also* **:** ANCESTORS **3** *pl* **:** the mass of a community as distinguished from a special class **4** *pl* **peoples :** a body of persons united by a common culture, tradition, or sense of kinship, typically having common language, institutions, and beliefs, and often politically organized ⟨English-speaking *peoples*⟩ **5 :** a body of enfranchised citizens **:** ELECTORATE [Medieval French *pople, peple, peuple,* from Latin *populus*]

[2]**people** *vt* **peo·pled; peo·pling** \ˈpē-pə-ling, -pling\ **1 :** to supply or fill with people **2 :** to dwell in **:** INHABIT

[1]**pep** \ˈpep\ *n* **:** brisk energy or initiative and high spirits **:** LIVELINESS [short for *pepper*]

[2]**pep** *vt* **pepped; pep·ping :** to inject pep into **:** STIMULATE ⟨*pep* them up⟩

pep·lum \ˈpep-ləm\ *n* **:** a short section attached to the waistline of a blouse, jacket, or dress [Latin, from Greek *peplon* "a garment worn like a shawl by women of ancient Greece"]

pe·po \ˈpē-pō\ *n* **:** a fleshy many-seeded fruit (as a pumpkin, squash, melon, or cucumber) of the gourd family that has a hard rind and is technically classed as a berry [Latin, a kind of melon]

[1]**pep·per** \ˈpep-ər\ *n* **1 a :** either of two pungent products from the fruit of an Indian plant used chiefly as seasoning: (1) **:** BLACK PEPPER (2) **:** WHITE PEPPER **b :** a woody vine with rounded leaves and flowers arranged in a spike that is widely cultivated in the tropics for its red berries from which pepper is prepared **c :** any of several somewhat similar products obtained from other plants **2 a :** CAPSICUM; *esp* **:** one whose fruits are hot peppers or sweet peppers **b :** the hollow fruit of a pepper that is usually green when unripe and yellow or red when ripe [Old English *pipor,* from Latin *piper,* from Greek *peperi*] — **pepper** *adj*

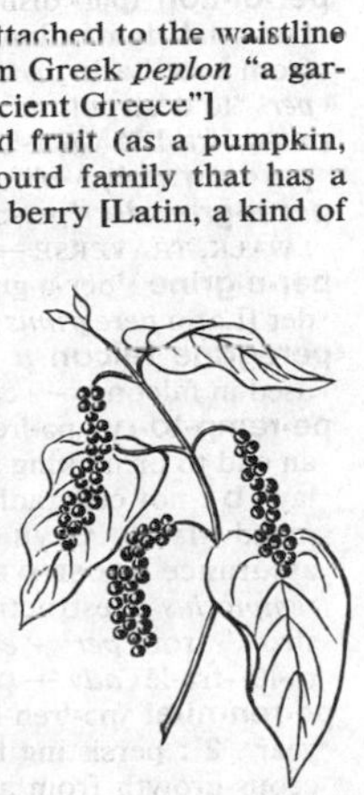

pepper 1b

[2]**pepper** *vt* **pep·pered; pep·per·ing** \ˈpep-ring, -ə-ring\ **1 a :** to sprinkle or season with pepper **b :** to shower with missiles (as shot) **2 :** to hit with rapid repeated blows **3 :** to sprinkle or cover as if with pepper

pep·per–and–salt \ˌpep-ər-ən-ˈsȯlt, ˌpep-ərn-ˈsȯlt\ *adj* **:** SALT-AND-PEPPER

pep·per·corn \ˈpep-ər-ˌkȯrn\ *n* **:** a dried berry of the black pepper

peppered moth *n* **:** a European moth that typically has white wings with small black specks but often has black wings in areas with heavy air pollution

pep·per·grass \ˈpep-ər-ˌgras\ *n* **:** any of a genus of cresses having a rounded fruit with a notch or depression at the top

pepper mill *n* **:** a hand mill for grinding peppercorns

pep·per·mint \-ˌmint, -mənt\ *n* **1 :** a pungent and aromatic mint that has dark green leaves and whorls of small usually pink flowers in spikes and is the source of an oil used especially to flavor candies **2 :** candy flavored with peppermint

pep·per·o·ni \ˌpep-ə-ˈrō-nē\ *n* **:** a highly seasoned beef and pork sausage [Italian *peperoni* "cayenne peppers," pl. of *peperone,* from *pepe* "pepper," from Latin *piper,* from Greek *peperi*]

pep·per·pot \ˈpep-ər-ˌpät\ *n* **1 :** PEPPER SHAKER **2 :** a thick highly seasoned soup of tripe, meat, dumplings, and vegetables

pepper shaker *n* **:** a container with a perforated top for sprinkling pepper on food

pep·pery \ˈpep-rē, -ə-rē\ *adj* **1 :** of, relating to, or having the qualities of pepper **:** HOT, PUNGENT **2 :** having a hot temper **:** TOUCHY **3 :** FIERY, STINGING ⟨*peppery* words⟩

pep pill *n* **:** any of various stimulant drugs (as an amphetamine) in pill or tablet form

pep·py \ˈpep-ē\ *adj* **pep·pi·er; -est :** full of pep — **pep·pi·ness** *n*

pep·sin \ˈpep-sən\ *n* **1 :** a protease secreted by glands in the wall of the stomach that begins the digestion of most proteins **2 :** a preparation of pepsin obtained especially from the stomach of the hog and used medicinally [German, from Greek *pepsis* "digestion," from *pessein* "to cook, digest"]

pep·sin·o·gen \pep-ˈsin-ə-jən\ *n* **:** a product of the gastric glands that is converted into pepsin in the acid medium of the stomach

pep talk *n* **:** a usually brief, high-pressure, and emotional utterance designed to influence or encourage an audience

pep·tic \ˈpep-tik\ *adj* **1 :** relating to or promoting digestion **2 :** of, relating to, producing, or caused by pepsin ⟨*peptic* digestion⟩ **3 :** resulting from the action of digestive juices ⟨*peptic* ulcers of the stomach and duodenum⟩ [Latin *pepticus,* from Greek *peptikos,* from *peptos* "cooked," from *peptein, pessein* "to cook, digest"]

pep·ti·dase \ˈpep-tə-ˌdās, -ˌdāz\ *n* **:** an enzyme that hydrolyzes simple peptides or their derivatives

pep·tide \ˈpep-ˌtīd\ *n* **:** any of various amides derived from two or more amino acids by combination of the amino group of one acid with the carboxyl group of another and usually obtained by partial hydrolysis of proteins [*pep*tone + *-ide*]

peptide bond *n* **:** the chemical bond between carbon and nitrogen in the CO-NH group that unites the amino acids in a peptide

pep·tone \ˈpep-ˌtōn\ *n* **:** any of various water-soluble products of partial hydrolysis of proteins [German *pepton,* from Greek *peptos* "cooked," from *pessein* "to cook, digest"]

Pe·quot \ˈpē-ˌkwät\ *n* **:** a member of an Algonquian people of what is now southeastern Connecticut [Narragansett *Pequttôog*]

per \pər, ˈpər\ *prep* **1 :** by the means or agency of ⟨*per* bearer⟩ **2 :** to or for each ⟨$10 *per* day⟩ **3 :** as indicated by **:** according to ⟨*per* list price⟩ [Latin, "through, by"]

per- *prefix* **1 :** throughout **:** thoroughly **2 a :** containing the largest possible or a relatively large proportion of a (specified) chemical element ⟨*per*oxide⟩ **b :** containing an element in its highest or a high oxidation state ⟨*per*chloric acid⟩ [Latin, "through, throughout, thoroughly, to destruction," from *per*]

[1]**per·ad·ven·ture** \ˈpər-əd-ˌven-chər, ˈper-; ˌpər-əd-ˈ, ˌper-\ *adv, archaic* **:** PERHAPS, POSSIBLY [Medieval French *par aventure* "by chance"]

[2]**peradventure** *n* **:** a possibility of error or uncertainty

per·am·bu·late \pə-ˈram-byə-ˌlāt\ *vb* **1 :** to travel over or through especially on foot **:** TRAVERSE **2 :** STROLL, RAMBLE [Latin *perambulare,* from *per-* + *ambulare* "to walk"] — **per·am·bu·la·tion** \-ˌram-byə-ˈlā-shən\ *n*

per·am·bu·la·tor \pə-ˈram-byə-ˌlāt-ər\ *n* **1 :** one that perambulates **2** *chiefly British* **:** a baby carriage — **per·am·bu·la·to·ry** \-lə-ˌtōr-ē, -ˌtȯr-\ *adj*

per an·num \ˌpər-ˈan-əm\ *adv* **:** in or for each year **:** ANNUALLY [Medieval Latin]

per·cale \pər-ˈkāl, ˌpər-, -ˈkal\ *n* **:** a fine closely woven cotton cloth [Persian *pargālah*]

per cap·i·ta \ˌpər-ˈkap-ət-ə\ *adv or adj* **:** per unit of population **:** by or for each person ⟨*per capita* income⟩ [Medieval Latin, "by heads"]

per·ceiv·able \pər-ˈsē-və-bəl\ *adj* **:** that can be perceived — **per·ceiv·ably** \-blē\ *adv*

per·ceive \pər-ˈsēv\ *vt* **1 :** to attain awareness or understanding

\ə\ **abut**	\au̇\ **out**	\i\ **tip**	\ȯ\ **saw**	\u̇\ **foot**
\ər\ **further**	\ch\ **chin**	\ī\ **life**	\ȯi\ **coin**	\y\ **yet**
\a\ **mat**	\e\ **pet**	\j\ **job**	\th\ **thin**	\yü\ **few**
\ā\ **take**	\ē\ **easy**	\ng\ **sing**	\t͟h\ **this**	\yu̇\ **cure**
\ä\ **cot, cart**	\g\ **go**	\ō\ **bone**	\ü\ **food**	\zh\ **vision**

of **2 :** to become aware of through the senses and especially through sight [Medieval French *perceivre,* from Latin *percipere,* from *per-* "thoroughly" + *capere* "to take"] — **per·ceiv·er** *n*

[1]**per·cent** \pər-ˈsent\ *adv* **:** in the hundred **:** of each hundred [*per* + Latin *centum* "hundred"]

[2]**percent** *n, pl* **percent** **1 :** one part in a hundred **:** HUNDREDTH ⟨40 *percent* of the budget⟩ **2 :** PERCENTAGE ⟨a large *percent* of her allowance⟩

[3]**percent** *adj* **1 :** measured or counted on the basis of a whole divided into one hundred parts ⟨a five *percent* increase⟩ **2 :** paying interest at a specified percent ⟨a 7 *percent* bond⟩

per·cent·age \pər-ˈsent-ij\ *n* **1 a :** a part of a whole expressed in hundredths ⟨a high *percentage* of students attended⟩ **b :** the result obtained by multiplying a number by a percent ⟨the *percentage* equals the rate times the base⟩ **2 a :** a share of winnings or profits ⟨my agent collects a *percentage*⟩ **b :** ADVANTAGE, PROFIT ⟨no *percentage* in going it alone⟩ **3 :** an indeterminate part **:** PROPORTION **4 a :** PROBABILITY 3 ⟨a gambler who plays the *percentages*⟩ **b :** favorable odds

per·cen·tile \pər-ˈsen-ˌtīl\ *n* **:** a measure widely used in educational testing that expresses the standing of a score or grade in terms of the percentage of scores or grades falling with or below it ⟨a person in the 75th *percentile* has done as well as or better than 75 percent of the people with whom he or she is being compared⟩

per cen·tum \pər-ˈsent-əm\ *n* **:** PERCENT

per·cep·ti·ble \pər-ˈsep-tə-bəl\ *adj* **:** capable of being perceived especially by the senses ⟨a *perceptible* change in the tone of her voice⟩ — **per·cep·ti·bil·i·ty** \-ˌsep-tə-ˈbil-ət-ē\ *n* — **per·cep·ti·bly** \-ˈsep-tə-blē\ *adv*

per·cep·tion \pər-ˈsep-shən\ *n* **1 a :** a result of perceiving **:** OBSERVATION, DISCERNMENT **b :** a mental image **:** CONCEPT **2 :** awareness of surrounding objects, conditions, or forces through physical sensation ⟨color *perception*⟩ **3 a :** INSIGHT 2 **b :** a capacity for comprehension [Latin *perceptio* "act of perceiving," from *percipere* "to perceive"] — **per·cep·tion·al** \-shnəl, -shən-l\ *adj*

per·cep·tive \pər-ˈsep-tiv\ *adj* **1 :** responsive to sensory stimulus **:** DISCERNING **2 a :** capable of or exhibiting keen perception **:** OBSERVANT **b :** characterized by sympathetic understanding or insight — **per·cep·tive·ly** *adv* — **per·cep·tive·ness** *n* — **per·cep·tiv·i·ty** \pər-ˌsep-ˈtiv-ət-ē\ *n*

per·cep·tu·al \pər-ˈsep-chə-wəl\ *adj* **:** of, relating to, or involving stimulation of the senses as opposed to abstract concept — **per·cep·tu·al·ly** \-wə-lē\ *adv*

[1]**perch** \ˈpərch\ *n* **1 :** a bar or peg on which something is hung **2 a :** a roost for a bird **b :** a resting place or vantage point **:** SEAT **c :** a prominent position **3** *chiefly British* **:** ROD 2 [Medieval French *perche,* from Latin *pertica* "pole"]

[2]**perch** *vb* **1 :** to place on a perch, a height, or precarious spot ⟨*perched* itself on the table⟩ **2 :** to alight, settle, or rest on or as if on a perch

[3]**perch** *n, pl* **perch** *or* **perch·es** **1 :** a small largely olive-green and yellow European freshwater fish; *also* **:** YELLOW PERCH **2 :** any of numerous fishes related to or resembling the true perches [Medieval French *perche,* from Latin *perca,* from Greek *perkē*]

per·chance \pər-ˈchans\ *adv* **:** PERHAPS, POSSIBLY [Medieval French *par chance* "by chance"]

Per·che·ron \ˈpər-chə-ˌrän, -shə-\ *n* **:** any of a breed of powerful rugged draft horses that originated in France [French, from *Perche,* region in northern France]

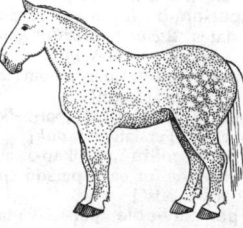

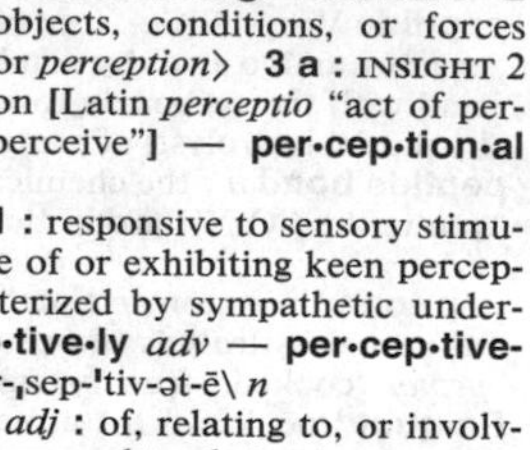
Percheron

per·chlo·rate \pər-ˈklōr-ˌāt, ˌpər-, -ˈklȯr-\ *n* **:** a salt or ester of perchloric acid

per·chlo·ric acid \pər-ˌklōr-ik-, ˌpər-, -ˌklȯr-\ *n* **:** a fuming corrosive strong acid $HClO_4$ that is a powerful oxidizing agent when heated

per·cip·i·ent \pər-ˈsip-ē-ənt\ *adj* **:** capable of or characterized by perception **:** DISCERNING ⟨a *percipient* critic⟩ [Latin *percipiens,* present participle of *percipere* "to perceive"] — **per·cip·i·ence** \-ē-əns\ *n* — **percipient** *n*

per·co·late \ˈpər-kə-ˌlāt\ *vb* **1 a :** to cause (a liquid) to pass through a permeable substance especially for extracting a constituent **b :** to ooze or trickle through a permeable substance **:** SEEP ⟨water *percolating* through sand⟩ **c :** to prepare (coffee) in a percolator **2 :** to be or become diffused through **:** PENETRATE **3 a :** to become percolated **b :** to become lively or effervescent [Latin *percolare,* from *per-* "through" + *colare* "to sieve"] — **per·co·la·tion** \ˌpər-kə-ˈlā-shən\ *n*

per·co·la·tor \ˈpər-kə-ˌlāt-ər\ *n* **:** one that percolates; *esp* **:** a coffeepot in which boiling water rising through a tube is repeatedly deflected downward through a perforated basket containing the ground coffee beans

per·cuss \pər-ˈkəs\ *vt* **:** to tap sharply; *esp* **:** to practice percussion on

per·cus·sion \pər-ˈkəsh-ən\ *n* **1 :** the act of tapping sharply: as **a :** the striking of a percussion cap so as to set off the charge in a firearm **b :** the beating or striking of a musical instrument **c :** the act or technique of tapping the surface of a body part to learn the condition of the parts beneath by the resultant sound **2 :** the striking of sound sharply on the ear **3 :** percussion instruments especially as forming a section of a band or orchestra [Medieval French *percussioun,* from Latin *percussio,* from *percutere* "to beat," from *per-* "thoroughly" + *quatere* "to shake"] — **percussion** *adj*

percussion cap *n* **:** CAP 4

percussion instrument *n* **:** a musical instrument (as a drum) sounded by striking

per·cus·sion·ist \pər-ˈkəsh-nəst, -ə-nəst\ *n* **:** one skilled in the playing of percussion instruments

per·cus·sive \pər-ˈkəs-iv\ *adj* **:** of or relating to percussion; *esp* **:** operative or operated by striking — **per·cus·sive·ly** *adv* — **per·cus·sive·ness** *n*

per·cu·ta·ne·ous \ˌpər-kyü-ˈtā-nē-əs\ *adj* **:** effected, occurring, or performed through the skin — **per·cu·ta·ne·ous·ly** *adv*

[1]**per di·em** \ˌpər-ˈdē-əm, -ˈdī-\ *adv* **:** by the day **:** for each day [Medieval Latin] — **per diem** *adj*

[2]**per diem** *n* **1 :** a daily allowance (as for traveling expenses) **2 :** a daily fee

per·di·tion \pər-ˈdish-ən\ *n* **1** *archaic* **:** utter destruction **2 a :** eternal damnation **b :** HELL [Medieval French *perdiciun,* from Late Latin *perditio,* from Latin *perdere* "to destroy," from *per-* "to destruction" + *dare* "to give"]

per·du·ra·ble \pər-ˈdu̇r-ə-bəl, -ˈdyu̇r-\ *adj* **:** very durable — **per·du·ra·bly** \-blē\ *adv*

per·e·gri·nate \ˈper-ə-grə-ˌnāt\ *vb* **:** to travel especially on foot **:** WALK, TRAVERSE — **per·e·gri·na·tion** \ˌper-ə-grə-ˈnā-shən\ *n*

per·e·grine \ˈper-ə-grən, -ˌgrēn\ *adj* **:** having a tendency to wander [Latin *peregrinus* "foreign"]

peregrine falcon *n* **:** a swift widely distributed falcon often used in falconry — called also *peregrine*

pe·remp·to·ry \pə-ˈrem-tə-rē, -ˈremp-, -trē\ *adj* **1 a :** putting an end to or making impossible a right of action, debate, or delay **b :** not contradictable **2 :** expressive of urgency or command **:** IMPERATIVE ⟨*peremptory* tone⟩ **3 a :** marked by self-assurance **:** POSITIVE **b :** HAUGHTY, DICTATORIAL [Latin *peremptorius* "destructive," from *perimere* "to take entirely, destroy," from *per-* + *emere* "to take"] — **pe·remp·to·ri·ly** \-tə-rə-lē, -trə-lē\ *adv* — **pe·remp·to·ri·ness** \-tə-rē-nəs, -trē-nəs\ *n*

pe·ren·ni·al \pə-ˈren-ē-əl\ *adj* **1 :** present at all seasons of the year **2 :** persisting for several years usually with new herbaceous growth from a part (as an underground stem) that survives from one growing season to the next ⟨*perennial* daisies⟩ **3 a :** lasting indefinitely **b :** continuing without interruption **:** CONSTANT **c :** regularly repeated **:** RECURRENT [Latin *perennis,* from *per-* "throughout" + *annus* "year"] — **perennial** *n* — **pe·ren·ni·al·ly** \-ē-ə-lē\ *adv*

[1]**per·fect** \ˈpər-fikt\ *adj* **1 a :** being entirely without fault or defect **b :** satisfying all requirements **c :** corresponding to an ideal standard **2 :** faithfully reproducing the original **3 a :** being exactly as stated ⟨*perfect* stillness⟩ **b :** lacking in no essential detail **:** COMPLETE **c :** of an extreme kind ⟨a *perfect* fool⟩ **4 :** of, relating to, or constituting a verb form or verbal that expresses an action or state completed at the time of speaking or at a time spoken of **5 :** belonging to the musical consonances unison, fourth, fifth, and octave **6 :** having both stamens and pistils in the same flower [Medieval French *parfit,* from Latin *perfectus,* from *perficere* "to carry out, perfect," from *per-* "thoroughly" + *facere* "to make, do"] ***synonyms*** see WHOLE — **per·fect·ness** \-fikt-nəs, -fik-nəs\ *n*

[2]**per·fect** \pər-ˈfekt, *also* ˈpər-fikt\ *vt* **1 :** to make perfect **:** IMPROVE, REFINE **2 :** to bring to final form — **per·fect·er** *n*

[3]**per·fect** \ˈpər-fikt\ *n* **:** the perfect tense of a language; *also* **:** a verb form in the perfect tense

per·fect·ible \pər-ˈfek-tə-bəl, *also* ˈpər-fik-\ *adj* **:** capable of improvement or perfection (as in moral state) — **per·fect·ibil·i·ty** \pər-ˌfek-tə-ˈbil-ət-ē *also* ˌpər-fik-\ *n*

per·fec·tion \pər-ˈfek-shən\ *n* **1 :** the quality or state of being perfect: as **a :** freedom from fault or defect **:** FLAWLESSNESS **b :** MATURITY 1 **c :** saintly quality or state **2 a :** an exemplification of supreme excellence **b :** an unsurpassable degree of accuracy or excellence **3 :** the act or process of perfecting

per·fec·tion·ist \pər-ˈfek-shə-nəst, -shnəst\ *n* **:** a person who will not accept or be content with anything less than perfection — **perfectionist** *adj*

per·fect·ly \ˈpər-fik-tlē, -fik-lē\ *adv* **1 :** in a perfect manner ⟨understand *perfectly*⟩ **2 :** to an adequate extent **:** QUITE ⟨*perfectly* willing to go⟩

perfect number *n* **:** a whole number that is equal to the sum of all its divisors except itself ⟨28 is a *perfect number* because it is the sum of 1 + 2 + 4 + 7 + 14⟩

perfect participle *n* **:** PAST PARTICIPLE

perfect pitch *n* **:** ABSOLUTE PITCH

perfect square *n* **:** a whole number whose square root is a whole number ⟨9 is a *perfect square*⟩

perfect tense *n* **:** a verb tense that expresses an action or state completed at the time of speaking or a time spoken of

per·fer·vid \ˌpər-ˈfər-vəd\ *adj* **:** extremely fervent

per·fid·i·ous \pər-ˈfid-ē-əs\ *adj* **:** of, relating to, or characterized by perfidy ***synonyms*** see FAITHLESS — **per·fid·i·ous·ly** *adv* — **per·fid·i·ous·ness** *n*

per·fi·dy \ˈpər-fəd-ē\ *n* **:** the quality or state of being faithless or disloyal [Latin *perfidia,* from *perfidus* "faithless," from *per-* "detrimental to" + *fides* "faith"]

per·fo·rate \ˈpər-fə-ˌrāt\ *vb* **1 :** to make a hole through or through something; *esp* **:** to make perforations in (as sheets of postage stamps) **2 :** to pass through or into by or as if by making a hole [Latin *perforare* "to bore through," from *per-* "through" + *forare* "to bore"] — **per·fo·rate** \ˈpər-fə-rət, -frət, -fə-ˌrāt\ *adj* — **per·fo·ra·tor** \-fə-ˌrāt-ər\ *n*

per·fo·ra·tion \ˌpər-fə-ˈrā-shən\ *n* **1 :** the act or process of perforating **2 a :** a hole or pattern made by or as if by piercing or boring **b :** any of the series of holes made between rows of postage stamps in a sheet

per·force \pər-ˈfōrs, -ˈfȯrs\ *adv* **:** by force of circumstances ⟨we went *perforce*⟩ [Medieval French *par force* "by force"]

per·form \pər-ˈfȯrm\ *vb* **1 :** to stick to the terms of **:** FULFILL ⟨*perform* a contract⟩ **2 a :** to carry out **:** DO ⟨*perform* miracles⟩ **b :** ACT, FUNCTION ⟨the car *performed* well⟩ **3 a :** to do in a formal manner or according to prescribed ritual **b :** to give a performance of **:** PRESENT ⟨the first time they had *performed* Hamlet⟩ [Medieval French *parfurmer,* from earlier *parfurnir,* from *per-* "thoroughly" + *furnir* "to complete"] — **per·form·able** \-ˈfȯr-mə-bəl\ *adj* — **per·form·er** *n*

per·for·mance \pər-ˈfȯr-məns\ *n* **1 a :** the execution of an action **b :** something accomplished **:** DEED, FEAT **2 :** the fulfillment of a claim, promise, or request **3 a :** the action of representing a character in a play **b :** a public presentation or exhibition ⟨a benefit *performance*⟩ **4 a :** the ability to perform **:** EFFICIENCY **b :** the manner in which a mechanism performs — **per·for·ma·to·ry** \-mə-ˌtōr-ē, -ˌtȯr-\ *adj*

per·form·ing *adj* **:** of, relating to, or constituting an art (as drama) that involves public performance

[1]**per·fume** \ˈpər-ˌfyüm, pər-ˈ, ˌpər-ˈ\ *n* **1 :** the scent of something sweet-smelling **2 :** a substance that emits a pleasant odor; *esp* **:** a fluid preparation of natural essences (as from plants or animals) or synthetics and a fixative used for scenting [Middle French *perfum*]

[2]**per·fume** \pər-ˈfyüm, ˌpər-ˈ, ˈpər-ˌ\ *vt* **:** to fill with an odor (as of something pleasant) ⟨a kitchen *perfumed* with spices⟩

per·fum·er \pər-ˈfyü-mər, pə-ˈfyü-\ *n* **:** one that makes or sells perfumes

per·fum·ery \pər-ˈfyüm-rē, pə-ˈfyüm-, -ə-rē\ *n, pl* **-er·ies 1 :** the art or process of making perfume **2 :** the products made by a perfumer

per·func·to·ry \pər-ˈfəng-tə-rē, -ˈfəngk-, -trē\ *adj* **1 :** characterized by routine or superficiality **:** MECHANICAL **2 :** lacking in interest or enthusiasm **:** INDIFFERENT [Late Latin *perfunctorius,* from Latin *perfungi* "to accomplish, get through with," from *per-* "through" + *fungi* "to perform"] — **per·func·to·ri·ly** \-tə-rə-lē, -trə-lē\ *adv* — **per·func·to·ri·ness** \-tə-rē-nəs, -trē-nəs\ *n*

per·fuse \pər-ˈfyüz\ *vt* **1 :** SUFFUSE **2 a :** to cause to flow or spread **:** DIFFUSE **b :** to force a fluid through (an organ or tissue) especially by way of the blood vessels [Latin *perfusus,* past participle of *perfundere* "to pour over," from *per-* "through" + *fundere* "to pour"] — **per·fu·sion** \-ˈfyü-zhən\ *n*

per·go·la \ˈpər-gə-lə, pər-ˈgō-\ *n* **:** a structure consisting of posts supporting an open roof in the form of a trellis [Italian, from Latin *pergula*]

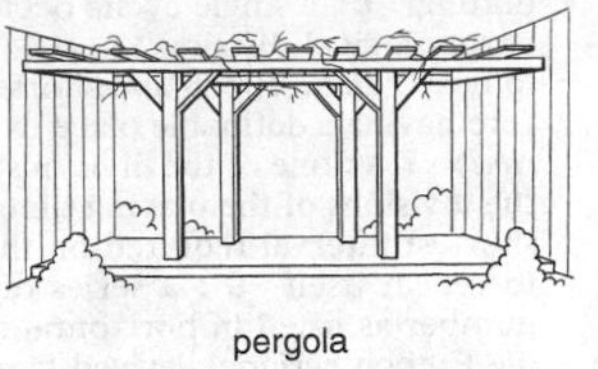

pergola

per·haps \pər-ˈhaps, pər-ˈaps, ˈpraps\ *adv* **:** possibly but not certainly **:** MAYBE [*per* + *hap*]

pe·ri \ˈpiər-ē\ *n, pl* **peris :** a supernatural being in Persian folklore descended from fallen angels and excluded from paradise until penance is accomplished [Persian *perī* "fairy, genius," from earlier *parīk*]

peri- *prefix* **1 :** all around **:** about ⟨*peri*scope⟩ **2 :** near ⟨*peri*helion⟩ **3 :** enclosing **:** surrounding ⟨*peri*odontal⟩ [Greek, "around, in excess," from *peri* "around"]

peri·anth \ˈper-ē-ˌanth, -ˌantth\ *n* **:** the outer part of a flower comprised of the calyx and corolla especially when the two whorls are fused into one [*peri-* + Greek *anthos* "flower"]

peri·car·di·um \ˌper-ə-ˈkärd-ē-əm\ *n, pl* **-dia** \-ē-ə\ **:** the cone-shaped sac of membrane that encloses the heart and the roots of the great blood vessels of vertebrates [New Latin, from Greek *perikardios* "around the heart," from *peri-* + *kardia* "heart"] — **peri·car·di·al** \-ē-əl\ *adj*

peri·carp \ˈper-ə-ˌkärp\ *n* **:** the ripened and variously modified walls of a plant ovary that form the substance of a fruit and enclose the seeds — compare ENDOCARP, EXOCARP, MESOCARP

peri·cy·cle \ˈper-ə-ˌsī-kəl\ *n* **:** a thin layer of cells that surrounds the stele in most vascular plants [French *péricycle,* from Greek *perikyklos* "spherical," from *peri-* + *kyklos* "circle"]

peri·derm \ˈper-ə-ˌdərm\ *n* **:** an outer layer of tissue; *esp* **:** a cortical protective layer of many roots and stems — **peri·der·mal** \ˌper-ə-ˈdər-məl\ *adj*

peri·gee \ˈper-ə-ˌjē\ *n* **:** the point nearest the center of a planet or satellite (as the earth or moon) reached by an object orbiting it — compare APOGEE [Greek *perigeios* "near the earth," from *peri-* "near" + *gē* "earth"]

pe·rig·y·nous \pə-ˈrij-ə-nəs\ *adj* **1 :** growing from a ring or cup of the receptacle surrounding a pistil ⟨*perigynous* petals⟩ **2 :** having perigynous flower parts — **pe·rig·y·ny** \-nē\ *n*

per·i·he·lion \ˌper-ə-ˈhēl-yən\ *n, pl* **-he·lia** \-ˈhēl-yə\ **:** the point in the path of a celestial body (as a planet) that is nearest to the sun — compare APHELION [New Latin, from *peri-* + Greek *hēlios* "sun"]

[1]**per·il** \ˈper-əl\ *n* **1 :** exposure to the risk of being injured, destroyed, or lost ⟨fire put the city in *peril*⟩ **2 :** something that imperils **:** RISK ⟨*perils* of the highway⟩ [Medieval French, from Latin *periculum* "danger"] ***synonyms*** see DANGER

[2]**peril** *vt* **-iled** *also* **-illed; -il·ing** *also* **-il·ling :** to expose to danger **:** HAZARD, RISK

per·il·ous \ˈper-ə-ləs\ *adj* **:** full of or involving peril **:** HAZARDOUS — **per·il·ous·ly** *adv* — **per·il·ous·ness** *n*

pe·rim·e·ter \pə-ˈrim-ət-ər\ *n* **1 :** the boundary of a figure or area; *also* **:** the length of this boundary **2 :** a line or strip bounding or protecting an area **3 :** outer limits [French *périmètre,* from Latin *perimetros,* from Greek, from *peri-* + *metron* "measure"]

per·i·ne·um \ˌper-ə-ˈnē-əm\ *n, pl* **-nea** \-ˈnē-ə\ **:** an area between the thighs which marks the approximate lower boundary of the pelvis and through which the urinary and genital ducts and rectum pass; *also* **:** the area between the anus and the posterior part of the external genitalia [Late Latin *perinaion,* from Greek, from *peri-* + *inan* "to empty out"] — **per·i·ne·al** \-ˈnē-əl\ *adj*

[1]**pe·ri·od** \ˈpir-ē-əd\ *n* **1 a :** an utterance from one full stop to another **:** SENTENCE **b :** PERIODIC SENTENCE **2 a :** the full pause with which a sentence closes **b :** END 2a, STOP **3 :** a punctuation mark . used chiefly to mark the end of a declara-

\ə\ **abut**	\au̇\ **out**	\i\ **tip**	\ȯ\ **saw**	\u̇\ **foot**
\ər\ **further**	\ch\ **chin**	\ī\ **life**	\ȯi\ **coin**	\y\ **yet**
\a\ **mat**	\e\ **pet**	\j\ **job**	\th\ **thin**	\yü\ **few**
\ā\ **take**	\ē\ **easy**	\ng\ **sing**	\t͟h\ **this**	\yu̇\ **cure**
\ä\ **cot, cart**	\g\ **go**	\ō\ **bone**	\ü\ **food**	\zh\ **vision**

tive sentence or an abbreviation **4 :** the completion of a cycle, a series of events, or a single action : CONCLUSION **5 a :** a portion of time determined by some recurring phenomenon **b :** the interval of time required for a motion or phenomenon to complete a cycle and begin to repeat itself ⟨the *period* of a pendulum⟩ **c :** a single cyclic occurrence of menstruation **6 a :** a chronological division : STAGE **b :** a division of geologic time longer than an epoch and shorter than an era **c :** a stage of culture having a definable place in time and space ⟨the colonial *period*⟩ **7 a :** one of the divisions of the academic day **b :** one of the divisions of the playing time of a game **8 :** the length of the shortest interval required on the x-axis for a periodic function to repeat itself **9 :** a series of elements of increasing atomic number as listed in horizontal rows in the periodic table [Middle French *periode,* derived from Greek *periodos* "circuit, period of time, rhetorical period," from *peri-* + *hodos* "way"]

synonyms PERIOD, EPOCH, ERA, AGE mean a division of time. PERIOD may designate any extent of time. EPOCH applies to a period begun by some striking or significant event ⟨the steam engine marked a new *epoch* in industry⟩. ERA suggests a period in history marked by a new or distinct order ⟨the *era* of exploration⟩. AGE is applied to a fairly definite period strongly dominated by a central figure ⟨the *age* of Jackson⟩ or by a prominent feature ⟨the nuclear *age*⟩.

²**period** *adj* **:** of, relating to, or representing a particular historical period ⟨*period* furniture⟩

pe·ri·od·ic \ˌpir-ē-ˈäd-ik\ *adj* **1 :** occurring or recurring at regular intervals **2 :** consisting of or containing stages or values repeated at equal intervals : CYCLIC ⟨*periodic* vibrations⟩ ⟨*periodic* decimals⟩ **3 :** of or relating to a period — **pe·ri·od·ic·i·ty** \ˌpir-ē-ə-ˈdis-ət-ē\ *n*

¹**pe·ri·od·i·cal** \ˌpir-ē-ˈäd-i-kəl\ *adj* **1 :** PERIODIC 1 **2 a :** published with a fixed interval between the issues or numbers **b :** published in, characteristic of, or connected with a periodical — **pe·ri·od·i·cal·ly** \-kə-lē, -klē\ *adv*

²**periodical** *n* **:** a periodical publication

periodic law *n* **:** a law in chemistry : the elements when arranged in the order of their atomic numbers show a periodic variation in most of their properties

periodic sentence *n* **:** a usually complex sentence that has no subordinate or trailing elements following its principal clause (as in "yesterday, while I was walking down the street, I saw them")

periodic table *n* **:** an arrangement of chemical elements based on the periodic law

peri·odon·tal \ˌper-ē-ō-ˈdänt-l\ *adj* **1 :** surrounding or occurring about the teeth ⟨*periodontal* tissue⟩ **2 :** affecting periodontal tissues ⟨*periodontal* disease⟩

periodontal membrane *n* **:** the fibrous layer of connective tissue covering the cementum of a tooth and holding it in place in the jawbone

peri·odon·tics \-ˈdänt-iks\ *n* **:** a branch of dentistry that deals with diseases of the structures (as the gums) that support and surround the teeth [*peri-* + Greek *odont-, odous* "tooth"] — **peri·odon·tist** \-ist\ *n*

peri·os·te·um \ˌper-ē-ˈäs-tē-əm\ *n, pl* **-tea** \-tē-ə\ **:** the membrane of connective tissue that covers all bones except at the surfaces in a joint [Late Latin *periosteon,* from Greek *periosteos* "around the bone," from *peri-* + *osteon* "bone"] — **peri·os·te·al** \-tē-əl\ *adj*

peri·pa·tet·ic \ˌper-ə-pə-ˈtet-ik\ *adj* **:** moving about from place to place : ITINERANT ⟨a *peripatetic* preacher⟩ [Latin *peripateticus,* from Greek *peripatētikos,* from *peripatein* "to walk about," from *peri-* + *patein* "to walk"] — **peri·pa·tet·i·cal·ly** \-ˈtet-i-kə-lē, -klē\ *adv*

pe·rip·a·tus \pə-ˈrip-ət-əs\ *n* **:** any of a class (Onychophora) of primitive tropical wormlike invertebrates that appear intermediate between annelid worms and arthropods [Greek *peripatos* "act of walking about," from *peri-* + *patein* "to walk"]

¹**pe·riph·er·al** \pə-ˈrif-rəl, -ə-rəl\ *adj* **1 :** of, relating to, located in, or forming a periphery ⟨*peripheral* vision⟩ **2 :** of, relating to, or being part of the peripheral nervous system **3 :** having an auxiliary function — **pe·riph·er·al·ly** \-ē\ *adv*

²**peripheral** *n* **:** a device connected to a computer to provide communication (as input and output) or extra storage capacity

peripheral nervous system *n* **:** the part of the nervous system that is outside the central nervous system and consists of the autonomic nervous system, the spinal nerves, and the cranial nerves except the optic nerve

pe·riph·ery \pə-ˈrif-rē, -ə-rē\ *n, pl* **-er·ies** **1 :** the perimeter of a circle or other closed curve; *also* **:** the perimeter of a polygon **2 :** the external boundary or surface of a body **3 a :** the outward bounds of something as distinguished from its more internal regions or center **b :** an area lying beyond the strict limits of a thing [Medieval French *peripherie,* from Late Latin *peripheria,* from Greek *periphereia,* from *peripherein* "to carry around," from *peri-* + *pherein* "to carry"]

pe·riph·ra·sis \pə-ˈrif-rə-səs\ *n, pl* **-ra·ses** \-rə-ˌsēz\ **:** use of a longer phrasing in place of a possible shorter and usually plainer form of expression : CIRCUMLOCUTION [Latin, from Greek, from *periphrazein* "to express periphrastically," from *peri-* + *phrazein* "to point out"]

per·i·phras·tic \ˌper-ə-ˈfras-tik\ *adj* **1 :** of, relating to, or characterized by periphrasis **2 :** formed by the use of function words or auxiliaries instead of by inflection ⟨*more fair* is a *periphrastic* comparative⟩ — **per·i·phras·ti·cal·ly** \-ti-kə-lē, -klē\ *adv*

peri·scope \ˈper-ə-ˌskōp\ *n* **:** a tubular optical instrument containing lenses and mirrors by which an observer (as on a submerged submarine) obtains an otherwise obstructed field of view — **peri·scop·ic** \ˌper-ə-ˈskäp-ik\ *adj*

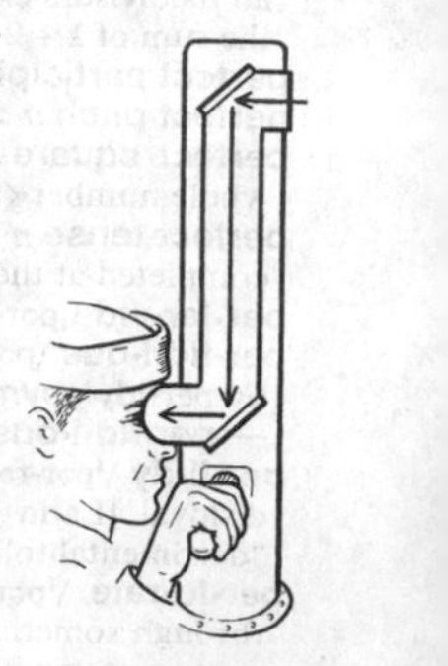

periscope

per·ish \ˈper-ish\ *vi* **:** to pass away completely **:** become destroyed or ruined : DIE [Medieval French *periss-,* stem of *perir* "to perish," from Latin *perire,* from *per-* "to destruction" + *ire* "to go"]

per·ish·able \ˈper-ish-ə-bəl\ *adj* **:** liable to spoil or decay ⟨*perishable* products such as fruit⟩ — **per·ish·abil·i·ty** \ˌper-ish-ə-ˈbil-ət-ē\ *n* — **perishable** *n*

pe·ris·so·dac·tyl \pə-ˌris-ə-ˈdak-tl\ *n* **:** any of an order (Perissodactyla) of hoofed mammals (as the horse or rhinoceros) with an odd number of functional toes on each foot [Greek *perissos* "excessive, odd in number" + *daktylos* "finger, toe"] — **perissodactyl** *adj*

peri·stal·sis \ˌper-ə-ˈstȯl-səs, -ˈstäl-, -ˈstal-\ *n, pl* **-stal·ses** \-ˌsēz\ **:** successive waves of involuntary contraction passing along the walls of a hollow muscular structure (as the intestine) and forcing the contents (as food or waste) onward [derived from Greek *peristellein* "to wrap around," from *peri-* + *stellein* "to place"] — **peri·stal·tic** \-ˈstȯl-tik, -ˈstal-\ *adj*

peri·style \ˈper-ə-ˌstīl\ *n* **1 :** a colonnade surrounding a building or court **2 :** an open space enclosed by a row of columns [French *péristyle,* from Latin *peristylum,* from Greek *peristylon,* derived from *peri-* + *stylos* "pillar"]

peri·to·ne·um \ˌper-ət-n-ˈē-əm\ *n, pl* **-ne·ums** *or* **-nea** \-ˈē-ə\ **:** the smooth transparent membrane that lines the cavity of the abdomen and encloses the abdominal and pelvic organs [Late Latin, from Greek *peritonaios* "stretched around," from *peri-* + *teinein* "to stretch"] — **peri·to·ne·al** \-ˈē-əl\ *adj*

peri·to·ni·tis \ˌper-ət-n-ˈīt-əs\ *n* **:** inflammation of the peritoneum

peri·wig \ˈper-i-ˌwig\ *n* **:** WIG [French *perruque*]

¹**per·i·win·kle** \ˈper-i-ˌwing-kəl\ *n* **:** a European evergreen herb that spreads along the ground and is widely grown as a ground cover and for its blue or white flowers [Old English *perwince,* from Latin *pervinca*]

²**periwinkle** *n* **:** any of various small edible marine snails of coastal regions; *also* **:** the shell of a periwinkle [Old English *pīnewincle*]

per·jure \ˈpər-jər\ *vt* **per·jured; per·jur·ing** \ˈpərj-ring, -ə-ring\ **:** to make (oneself) guilty of perjury [Middle French *perjurer,* from Latin *perjurare,* from *per-* "to destruction, to the bad" + *jurare* "to swear"]

per·jur·er \ˈpər-jər-ər\ *n* **:** a person guilty of perjury

per·ju·ri·ous \pər-ˈju̇r-ē-əs\ *adj* **:** marked by perjury — **per·ju·ri·ous·ly** *adv*

per·ju·ry \ˈpərj-rē, -ə-rē\ *n, pl* **-ries** **:** violation of an oath by knowingly swearing to what is untrue : false swearing

perk \ˈpərk\ *vb* **1 :** to stick up or out jauntily ⟨a dog *perking* its ears⟩ **2 :** to regain vigor or cheerfulness ⟨*perked* up as the cold got better⟩ **3 :** to smarten the appearance of ⟨*perked* the room up with new curtains⟩ [Middle English *perken*]

perky \ˈpər-kē\ *adj* **perk·i·er; -est :** JAUNTY, LIVELY — **perk·i·ly** \-kə-lē\ *adv* — **perk·i·ness** \-kē-nəs\ *n*

per·lite \ˈpər-ˌlīt\ *n* : a porous volcanic glassy mineral that when expanded by heat forms a lightweight material capable of absorbing liquids (as water) [French, from *perle* "pearl"]

[1]**perm** \ˈpərm\ *n* : PERMANENT

[2]**perm** *vt* : to give (hair) a permanent

per·ma·frost \ˈpər-mə-ˌfrȯst\ *n* : a permanently frozen layer at variable depth below the earth's surface in frigid regions [*permanent frost*]

per·ma·nence \ˈpər-mə-nəns\ *n* : the quality or state of being permanent

per·ma·nen·cy \-nən-sē\ *n, pl* **-cies** : PERMANENCE

[1]**per·ma·nent** \ˈpər-mə-nənt\ *adj* : lasting or intended to last for a very long time without fundamental or marked change [Medieval French *parmanant,* from Latin *permanēre* "to endure," from *per-* "throughout" + *manēre* "to remain"] ***synonyms*** see LASTING — **per·ma·nent·ly** *adv* — **per·ma·nent·ness** *n*

[2]**permanent** *n* : a long-lasting hair wave produced by mechanical and chemical means

permanent magnet *n* : a magnet that retains its magnetism after removal of the magnetizing force

permanent press *adj* : of, relating to, or made from a fabric chemically treated to resist wrinkling

permanent tooth *n* : one of the second set of teeth of a mammal that follow the milk teeth, typically persist into old age, and in humans are 32 in number

per·man·ga·nate \pər-ˈmang-gə-ˌnāt\ *n* : POTASSIUM PERMANGANATE

per·me·abil·i·ty \ˌpər-mē-ə-ˈbil-ət-ē\ *n, pl* **-ties** **1** : the quality or state of being permeable **2** : the property of a substance that determines the degree to which it is magnetizable

per·me·able \ˈpər-mē-ə-bəl\ *adj* : having pores or openings that permit liquids or gases to pass through ⟨a *permeable* membrane⟩ ⟨*permeable* limestone⟩ — **per·me·able·ness** *n* — **per·me·ably** \-blē\ *adv*

per·me·ate \ˈpər-mē-ˌāt\ *vb* **1** : to pass through the pores or small openings of ⟨water *permeates* sand⟩ **2** : to spread throughout : PERVADE ⟨a room *permeated* with the odor of tobacco⟩ [Latin *permeare,* from *per-* "through" + *meare* "to go, pass"] — **per·me·a·tion** \ˌpər-mē-ˈā-shən\ *n* — **per·me·a·tive** \ˈpər-mē-ˌāt-iv\ *adj*

Perm·ian \ˈpər-mē-ən\ *n* : the most recent period of the Paleozoic era; *also* : the corresponding system of rocks — see GEOLOGIC TIME table [*Perm,* region in eastern Russia] — **Permian** *adj*

per·mis·si·ble \pər-ˈmis-ə-bəl\ *adj* : that may be permitted : ALLOWABLE — **per·mis·si·bil·i·ty** \-ˌmis-ə-ˈbil-ət-ē\ *n* — **per·mis·si·ble·ness** \-ˈmis-ə-bəl-nəs\ *n* — **per·mis·si·bly** \-blē\ *adv*

per·mis·sion \pər-ˈmish-ən\ *n* **1** : the act of permitting **2** : the consent of a person in authority : AUTHORIZATION [Medieval French, from Latin *permissio,* from *permittere* "to permit"]

per·mis·sive \pər-ˈmis-iv\ *adj* **1 a** : granting or tending to grant permission **b** : allowing freedom (as of choice or behavior) ⟨*permissive* parents⟩ **2** : not forbidden : ALLOWABLE — **per·mis·sive·ly** *adv* — **per·mis·sive·ness** *n*

[1]**per·mit** \pər-ˈmit\ *vb* **per·mit·ted; per·mit·ting** **1** : to consent to expressly or formally : give permission **2** : to make possible : give an opportunity : ALLOW ⟨if time *permits*⟩ [Latin *permittere* "to let through, permit," from *per-* "through" + *mittere* "to let go, send"] ***synonyms*** see LET — **per·mit·ter** *n*

[2]**per·mit** \ˈpər-ˌmit, pər-ˈ\ *n* : a written statement of permission given by one having authority ⟨a *permit* to learn to drive⟩

per·mu·ta·tion \ˌpər-myu̇-ˈtā-shən\ *n* **1** : a thorough change in character or condition : TRANSFORMATION **2 a** : the act or process of changing the order of a set of objects **b** : an ordered arrangement of a set of objects — **per·mu·ta·tion·al** \-shnəl, -shən-l\ *adj*

per·mute \pər-ˈmyüt\ *vt* : to change the order or arrangement of; *esp* : to arrange in all possible ways [Medieval French *permuter,* from Latin *permutare,* from *per-* "thoroughly" + *mutare* "to change"]

per·ni·cious \pər-ˈnish-əs\ *adj* : very destructive or injurious ⟨a *pernicious* disease⟩ ⟨a *pernicious* habit⟩ [Medieval French, from Latin *perniciosus,* from *pernicies* "destruction," from *per-* + *nec-, nex* "violent death"] — **per·ni·cious·ly** *adv* — **per·ni·cious·ness** *n*

pernicious anemia *n* : a severe anemia in which the red blood cells progressively decrease in number and increase in size and which is caused by reduced ability to absorb vitamin B_{12}

per·nick·e·ty \pər-ˈnik-ət-ē\ *adj* : PERSNICKETY [perhaps alteration of *particular*]

per·ora·tion \ˌper-ər-ˈā-shən, ˈpər-\ *n* **1** : the concluding part of a speech and especially an oration **2** : a very rhetorical speech — **per·orate** \ˈper-ər-ˌāt\ *vi* — **per·ora·tion·al** \ˌper-ər-ˈā-shnəl, ˌpər-, -shən-l\ *adj*

[1]**per·ox·ide** \pə-ˈräk-ˌsīd\ *n* **1** : an oxide containing a high proportion of oxygen; *esp* : a compound (as hydrogen peroxide) in which oxygen is joined to oxygen **2** : HYDROGEN PEROXIDE

[2]**peroxide** *vt* : to bleach (hair) with hydrogen peroxide

[1]**per·pen·dic·u·lar** \ˌpər-pən-ˈdik-yə-lər\ *adj* **1 a** : exactly vertical or upright **b** : being at right angles to a given line or plane **2** : extremely steep : PRECIPITOUS [Medieval French *perpendiculer,* from Latin *perpendicularis,* from *perpendiculum* "plumb line," from *per-* + *pendēre* "to hang"] ***synonyms*** see VERTICAL — **per·pen·dic·u·lar·i·ty** \-ˌdik-yə-ˈlar-ət-ē\ *n* — **per·pen·dic·u·lar·ly** \-ˈdik-yə-lər-lē\ *adv*

[2]**perpendicular** *n* : a line at right angles to another line or surface

per·pe·trate \ˈpər-pə-ˌtrāt\ *vt* : to be guilty of doing or performing : COMMIT ⟨*perpetrate* a crime⟩ [Latin *perpetrare,* from *per-* + *patrare* "to accomplish"] — **per·pe·tra·tion** \ˌpər-pə-ˈtrā-shən\ *n* — **per·pe·tra·tor** \ˈpər-pə-ˌtrāt-ər\ *n*

per·pet·u·al \pər-ˈpech-ə-wəl, -ˈpech-əl\ *adj* **1 a** : continuing forever : EVERLASTING **b** (1) : valid for all time ⟨a *perpetual* right-of-way⟩ (2) : holding (as an office) for life or for an unlimited time **2** : going on and on without interruption : CONSTANT **3** : blooming continuously throughout the season [Medieval French, from Latin *perpetuus* "uninterrupted," from *per-* "through" + *petere* "to go to"] — **per·pet·u·al·ly** \-ē\ *adv*

perpetual calendar *n* : a table for finding the day of the week for any one of a wide range of dates

per·pet·u·ate \pər-ˈpech-ə-ˌwāt\ *vt* : to make perpetual or cause to last indefinitely ⟨*perpetuate* a tradition⟩ — **per·pet·u·a·tion** \-ˌpech-ə-ˈwā-shən\ *n* — **per·pet·u·a·tor** \-ˈpech-ə-ˌwāt-ər\ *n*

per·pe·tu·i·ty \ˌpər-pə-ˈtü-ət-ē, -ˈtyü-\ *n, pl* **-ties** **1** : perpetual existence or duration ⟨the *perpetuity* of their fame⟩ **2** : endless time : ETERNITY

per·plex \pər-ˈpleks\ *vt* **1** : to make mentally uncertain : BEWILDER, NONPLUS **2** : to make intricate or involved : COMPLICATE [Latin *perplexus* "involved, perplexed," from *per-* "thoroughly" + *plexus* "involved," from *plectere* "to braid, twine"] ***synonyms*** see PUZZLE

per·plexed \-ˈplekst\ *adj* **1** : filled with uncertainty **2** : full of difficulty : COMPLICATED — **per·plexed·ly** \-ˈplek-səd-lē, -ˈpleks-tlē\ *adv*

per·plex·i·ty \pər-ˈplek-sət-ē\ *n, pl* **-ties** **1** : the state of being perplexed : BEWILDERMENT **2** : something that perplexes

per·qui·site \ˈpər-kwə-zət\ *n* **1** : a profit made from one's employment in addition to one's regular pay; *esp* : such a profit when expected or promised **2** : TIP [Medieval French *perquisit* "property acquired by other means than inheritance," from Medieval Latin *perquisitum,* from *perquirere* "to purchase, acquire," from Latin, "to search for thoroughly," from *per-* "thoroughly" + *quaerere* "to seek"]

per·ry \ˈper-ē\ *n* : pear cider [Medieval French *peré,* from Latin *pirum* "pear"]

per se \ˌpər-ˈsā\ *adv* : by, of, or in itself or oneself or themselves : as such : INTRINSICALLY [Latin]

per second per second *adv* : per second every second — used of acceleration

per·se·cute \ˈpər-si-ˌkyüt\ *vt* **1** : to harass in a manner to injure, grieve, or afflict; *esp* : to cause to suffer because of belief **2** : to annoy with persistent or urgent approaches : PESTER [Medieval French *persecuter,* derived from Late Latin *persequi,* from Latin, "to pursue," from *per-* "through" + *sequi* "to follow"] — **per·se·cu·tor** \-ˌkyüt-ər\ *n* — **per·se·cu·to·ry** \-kyu̇-ˌtōr-ē, -ˌtȯr-\ *adj*

per·se·cu·tion \ˌpər-si-ˈkyü-shən\ *n* **1** : the act or practice of persecuting especially those who differ in origin, religion, or social outlook **2** : the condition of being persecuted, harassed, or annoyed

\ə\ **abut**	\au̇\ **out**	\i\ **tip**	\ȯ\ **saw**	\u̇\ **foot**
\ər\ **further**	\ch\ **chin**	\ī\ **life**	\ȯi\ **coin**	\y\ **yet**
\a\ **mat**	\e\ **pet**	\j\ **job**	\th\ **thin**	\yü\ **few**
\ā\ **take**	\ē\ **easy**	\ng\ **sing**	\th\ **this**	\yu̇\ **cure**
\ä\ **cot, cart**	\g\ **go**	\ō\ **bone**	\ü\ **food**	\zh\ **vision**

Per·seus \ˈpər-ˌsüs, -sē-əs\ *n* : a northern constellation between Taurus and Cassiopeia [Latin *Perseus,* son of Zeus, from Greek]

per·se·ver·ance \ˌpər-sə-ˈvir-əns\ *n* : the action, condition, or an instance of persevering : STEADFASTNESS

per·se·vere \ˌpər-sə-ˈviər\ *vi* : to keep at something in spite of difficulties, opposition, or discouragement [Medieval French *parseverer,* from Latin *perseverare,* from *per-* "through" + *severus* "severe"]

per·se·ver·ing \-ˈviər-ing\ *adj* : showing perseverance : PERSISTENT — **per·se·ver·ing·ly** \-ing-lē\ *adv*

Per·sian \ˈpər-zhən\ *n* **1** : one of the people of Persia: as **a** : one of the ancient Iranians who under Cyrus and his successors dominated western Asia **b** : a member of one of the peoples forming the modern Iranian nation **2 a** : any of several Iranian languages dominant in Persia at different periods **b** : the modern language of Iran and western Afghanistan **3** : a thin soft silk formerly used especially for linings — **Persian** *adj*

Persian cat *n* : any of a breed of stocky round-headed domestic cats with long silky fur

Persian cat

Persian lamb *n* : a pelt obtained from karakul lambs slightly older than those yielding broadtail and characterized by very silky tightly curled glossy fur

per·si·flage \ˈpər-sə-ˌfläzh, ˈper-\ *n* : frivolous or lightly jesting talk : BANTER [French, from *persifler* "to banter," from *per-* "thoroughly" + *siffler* "to whistle, hiss, boo," derived from Latin *sibilare*]

per·sim·mon \pər-ˈsim-ən\ *n* **1** : any of a genus of trees with hard fine wood, oblong leaves, and small bell-shaped white flowers; *esp* : one of the eastern U.S. or Japan **2** : the usually orange several-seeded fruit of a persimmon that resembles a plum, is technically a berry, and is edible when fully ripe but usually very bitter when unripe [Virginia Algonquian *pessemmin*]

per·sist \pər-ˈsist, -ˈzist\ *vi* **1** : to go on resolutely in spite of opposition, warnings, or pleas : PERSEVERE **2** : to last on and on : continue to exist ⟨rain *persisting* for days⟩ [Medieval French *persister,* from Latin *persistere,* from *per-* + *sistere* "to take a stand, stand firm"] — **per·sist·er** *n*

per·sis·tence \pər-ˈsis-təns, -ˈzis-\ *n* **1** : the act or fact of persisting **2** : the quality or state of being persistent; *esp* : PERSEVERANCE

per·sis·ten·cy \-tən-sē\ *n* : PERSISTENCE 2

per·sis·tent \-tənt\ *adj* **1** : continuing, existing, or acting for a long or longer than usual time ⟨a *persistent* cough⟩ ⟨*persistent* gills⟩ **2** : DOGGED, TENACIOUS ⟨a *persistent* salesman⟩ [Latin *persistens,* present participle of *persistere* "to persist"] — **per·sis·tent·ly** *adv*

per·snick·e·ty \pər-ˈsnik-ət-ē\ *adj* : fussy about small details : FASTIDIOUS [alteration of *pernickety*]

per·son \ˈpərs-n\ *n* **1** : HUMAN, INDIVIDUAL — used in combination especially by those who prefer to avoid *man* in compounds applicable to both sexes ⟨chair*person*⟩ **2** : a character or part in or as if in a play : GUISE **3 a** : bodily appearance **b** : the body of a human being **4 a** : the individual personality of a human being : SELF **b** : bodily presence ⟨appear in *person*⟩ **5** : an entity (as a human being or corporation) recognized by law as having rights and duties **6** : reference to the speaker, to one spoken to, or to one spoken of as indicated especially by means of certain pronouns [Medieval French *persone,* from Latin *persona* "actor's mask, character in a play, person," derived from Greek *prosōpon* "face, mask"]

per·son·able \ˈpərs-nə-bəl, -n-ə-bəl\ *adj* : attractive in looks and manner : PLEASING — **per·son·able·ness** *n*

per·son·age \ˈpərs-nij, -n-ij\ *n* **1** : a person of rank or distinction **2** : a character in a book or play

[1]**per·son·al** \ˈpərs-nəl, -n-əl\ *adj* **1** : of, relating to, or belonging to a person : PRIVATE **2 a** : done in person or proceeding from a single person **b** : carried on between individuals directly **3** : relating to the person or body ⟨*personal* hygiene⟩ **4** : closely related to an individual : INTIMATE **5** : denoting grammatical person

[2]**personal** *n* : a short newspaper paragraph relating to a person or group or to personal matters

personal computer *n* : a small general-purpose computer with a microprocessor

personal digital assistant *n* : PDA

personal effects *n pl* : personal property (as clothing and toilet articles) normally worn or carried on the person

personal equation *n* : variation (as in scientific observation) due to the personal peculiarities of an individual; *also* : a correction or allowance made for such variation

personal foul *n* : a foul (as in basketball or lacrosse) which involves unnecessary roughness or illegal obstruction of an opponent

per·son·al·i·ty \ˌpərs-n-ˈal-ət-ē, ˌpər-ˈsnal-\ *n, pl* **-ties** **1** : the state of being a person **2** : the emotional and behavioral characteristics of a person : INDIVIDUALITY **3** : pleasing qualities of character ⟨lack *personality*⟩ **4** : a person who has strongly marked qualities ⟨a great stage *personality*⟩ **5** : a personal remark : a slighting reference to a person ⟨use *personalities* in an argument⟩

per·son·al·ize \ˈpərs-nə-ˌlīz, -n-ə-\ *vt* **1** : PERSONIFY 1 **2** : to make personal or individual; *esp* : to mark as belonging to a particular person ⟨*personalized* stationery⟩

per·son·al·ly \ˈpərs-nə-lē, -n-ə-\ *adv* **1** : in person ⟨attend to the matter *personally*⟩ **2** : as a person : in personality ⟨*personally* attractive but not very trustworthy⟩ **3** : for oneself : as far as oneself is concerned ⟨*personally,* I am against it⟩

personal pronoun *n* : a pronoun (as *I, you,* or *they*) expressing a distinction of person

personal property *n* : movable property (as money, clothing, or furnishings) : CHATTELS

per·son·al·ty \ˈpərs-nəl-tē, -n-əl-\ *n, pl* **-ties** : PERSONAL PROPERTY

per·so·na non gra·ta \pər-ˌsō-nə-ˌnän-ˈgrat-ə, -ˈgrät-\ *adj* : personally unacceptable or unwelcome [New Latin, "unacceptable person"]

per·son·ate \ˈpərs-n-ˌāt\ *vt* **1** : IMPERSONATE, REPRESENT **2** : to invest with personality or personal characteristics — **per·son·ation** \ˌpərs-n-ˈā-shən\ *n* — **per·son·ative** \ˈpərs-n-ˌāt-iv\ *adj* — **per·son·ator** \-ˌāt-ər\ *n*

per·son·i·fi·ca·tion \pər-ˌsän-ə-fə-ˈkā-shən\ *n* **1** : the act of personifying **2** : an imaginary being thought of as representing a thing or an idea **3** : EMBODIMENT 1, INCARNATION ⟨you are the *personification* of generosity⟩ **4** : a figure of speech in which a lifeless object or abstract quality is spoken of as if alive

per·son·i·fy \pər-ˈsän-ə-ˌfī\ *vt* **-fied; -fy·ing** **1** : to think of or represent as a person ⟨*personify* the forces of nature⟩ **2** : to represent in a physical form ⟨the law was *personified* in the sheriff⟩ **3** : to serve as the perfect type or example of — **per·son·i·fi·er** \-ˌfī-ər, -ˌfīr\ *n*

per·son·nel \ˌpərs-n-ˈel\ *n* **1 a** : a group of persons employed (as in a factory, office, or organization) **b personnel** *pl* : employed persons of a particular group ⟨50,000 military *personnel*⟩ ⟨the changing *personnel* of the theater⟩ **2** : a division of an organization concerned with personnel [French, from German *Personale, Personal,* from Medieval Latin *personale,* from *personalis* "personal"]

[1]**per·spec·tive** \pər-ˈspek-tiv\ *n* **1** : the art or technique of painting or drawing a scene so that objects in it have apparent depth and distance **2** : the power to see or think of things in their true relationship to each other ⟨lose one's *perspective*⟩ **3** : the true relationship of objects or events to one another ⟨view events in proper *perspective*⟩ **4 a** : a visible scene; *esp* : one giving a definite impression of distance **b** : a mental view or prospect **5** : the appearance to the eye of objects in respect to their relative distance and positions [Middle French, probably from Italian *prospettiva,* from *prospetto* "view, prospect," from Latin *prospectus*]

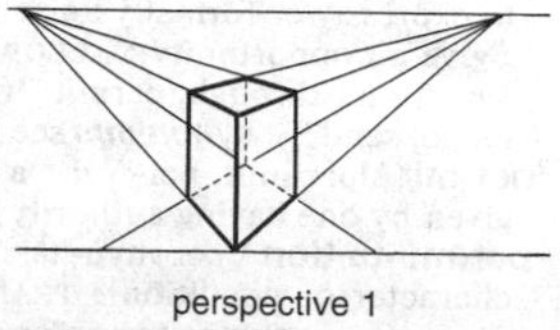
perspective 1

[2]**perspective** *adj* : of, relating to, or seen in perspective — **per·spec·tive·ly** *adv*

per·spi·ca·cious \ˌpər-spə-ˈkā-shəs\ *adj* : having or showing keen understanding or discernment [Latin *perspicax,* from *perspicere* "to look through, see clearly," from *per-* "through" + *specere* "to look"] — **per·spi·ca·cious·ly** *adv* — **per·spi·ca·cious·ness** *n*

per·spi·cac·i·ty \ˌpər-spə-ˈkas-ət-ē\ *n* : the quality or state of being perspicacious

per·spic·u·ous \pər-ˈspik-yə-wəs\ *adj* : plain to the understanding : CLEAR [Latin *perspicuus* "transparent, perspicuous," from *perspicere* "to look through"] — **per·spi·cu·i·ty** \ˌpər-spə-ˈkyü-ət-ē\ *n* — **per·spic·u·ous·ly** \pər-ˈspik-yə-wə-slē\ *adv* — **per·spic·u·ous·ness** *n*

per·spi·ra·tion \ˌpər-spə-ˈrā-shən\ *n* **1** : the act or process of perspiring **2** : a saline fluid secreted by the sweat glands : SWEAT

per·spire \pər-ˈspīr\ *vi* : to secrete and emit perspiration : SWEAT [French *perspirer,* from Latin *per-* "through" + *spirare* "to blow, breathe"]

per·suad·able \pər-ˈswād-ə-bəl\ *adj* : capable of being persuaded

per·suade \pər-ˈswād\ *vt* : to win over to a belief or to a course of action by argument or earnest request : induce to do or believe something [Latin *persuadēre,* from *per-* "thoroughly" + *suadēre* "to advise, urge"] — **per·suad·er** *n*

per·sua·si·ble \pər-ˈswā-zə-bəl, -ˈswā-sə-\ *adj* : PERSUADABLE

per·sua·sion \pər-ˈswā-zhən\ *n* **1** : the act of persuading **2** : the power or ability to persuade : persuasive quality **3** : the state of being persuaded **4** : a way of believing : BELIEF; *esp* : a system of religious beliefs **5** : a group having the same religious beliefs [Latin *persuasio,* from *persuadēre* "to persuade"]

per·sua·sive \pər-ˈswā-siv, -ziv\ *adj* : tending to persuade : having the power or effect of persuading ⟨a *persuasive* speech⟩ — **per·sua·sive·ly** *adv* — **per·sua·sive·ness** *n*

pert \ˈpərt\ *adj* **1 a** : saucily free and forward : IMPUDENT **b** : being trim and chic : JAUNTY **c** : piquantly stimulating **2** : VIVACIOUS, LIVELY [Middle English, "open, bold, pert," short for *apert* "evident," from Medieval French, from Latin *apertus* "open," from *aperire* "to open"] — **pert·ly** *adv* — **pert·ness** *n*

per·tain \pər-ˈtān\ *vi* **1** : to belong as a part, quality, or function ⟨duties that *pertain* to an office⟩ **2** : to have reference ⟨books *pertaining* to birds⟩ [Medieval French *partenir,* from Latin *pertinēre* "to reach to, belong," from *per-* "through" + *tenēre* "to hold"]

per·ti·na·cious \ˌpərt-n-ˈā-shəs\ *adj* **1** : holding strongly to an opinion, purpose, or course of action **2** : stubbornly or annoyingly persistent [Latin *pertinax,* from *per-* "thoroughly" + *tenax* "tenacious," from *tenēre* "to hold"] ***synonyms*** see OBSTINATE — **per·ti·na·cious·ly** *adv* — **per·ti·na·cious·ness** *n* — **per·ti·nac·i·ty** \ˌpərt-n-ˈas-ət-ē\ *n*

per·ti·nent \ˈpərt-n-ənt\ *adj* : having to do with the subject or matter that is being considered : being to the point ⟨a *pertinent* suggestion⟩ [Medieval French, from Latin *pertinēre* "to pertain"] — **per·ti·nence** \-n-əns\ *or* **per·ti·nen·cy** \-n-ən-sē\ *n* — **per·ti·nent·ly** *adv*

per·turb \pər-ˈtərb\ *vt* **1** : to disturb greatly in mind : DISQUIET **2** : to throw into confusion : AGITATE [Medieval French *perturber,* from Latin *perturbare* "to throw into confusion," from *per-* "thoroughly" + *turbare* "to disturb"] ***synonyms*** see DISTURB — **per·turb·able** \-ˈtər-bə-bəl\ *adj*

per·tur·ba·tion \ˌpərt-ər-ˈbā-shən, ˌpər-ˌtər-\ *n* **1** : the action of perturbing : the state of being perturbed **2** : a disturbance of the regular motion of a celestial body produced by some force additional to that which causes its regular motion — **per·tur·ba·tion·al** \-shnəl, -shən-l\ *adj*

per·tus·sis \pər-ˈtəs-əs\ *n* : WHOOPING COUGH [Latin *per-* "thoroughly" + *tussis* "cough"]

pe·ruke \pə-ˈrük\ *n* : WIG [Middle French *perruque,* from Italian *parrucca*]

pe·ruse \pə-ˈrüz\ *vt* **1 a** : to examine or study attentively and in detail **b** : to look over or through in a casual or hasty manner **2** : READ 1a (1); *esp* : to read over in an attentive or leisurely manner [Middle English *perusen* "to use up, deal with in sequence," from Latin *per-* "thoroughly" + Middle English *usen* "to use"] — **pe·rus·al** \-ˈrü-zəl\ *n* — **pe·rus·er** *n*

per·vade \pər-ˈvād\ *vt* : to spread or become diffused throughout every part of [Latin *pervadere* (past participle *pervasus*) "to go through, pervade," from *per-* "through" + *vadere* "to go"] — **per·va·sion** \-ˈvā-zhən\ *n* — **per·va·sive** \-ˈvā-siv, -ziv\ *adj* — **per·va·sive·ly** *adv* — **per·va·sive·ness** *n*

per·verse \pər-ˈvərs, ˈpər-ˌ\ *adj* **1** : turned away from what is right or good : CORRUPT **2 a** : obstinate in opposing what is right, reasonable, or accepted : WRONGHEADED **b** : arising from or showing stubbornness or obstinacy **3** : marked by peevishness or petulance : CRANKY **4** : marked by perversion : PERVERTED [Medieval French *purvers,* from Latin *perversus,* from *pervertere* "to pervert"] — **per·verse·ly** *adv* — **per·verse·ness** *n* — **per·ver·si·ty** \pər-ˈvər-sət-ē, -stē\ *n*

per·ver·sion \pər-ˈvər-zhən\ *n* **1** : the action of perverting : the condition of being perverted **2** : a perverted form of something; *esp* : atypical sexual behavior or interest

[1]**per·vert** \pər-ˈvərt\ *vt* **1 a** : to cause to turn aside or away from what is good or true or morally right : CORRUPT **b** : to cause to turn aside or away from what is generally done or accepted : MISDIRECT **2 a** : to divert to a wrong end or purpose : MISUSE **b** : to twist the meaning or sense of : MISINTERPRET [Medieval French *pervertir,* from Latin *pervertere* "to overturn, corrupt, pervert," from *per-* + *vertere* "to turn"] ***synonyms*** see DEBASE — **per·ver·sive** \-ˈvər-siv, -ziv\ *adj* — **per·vert·er** *n*

[2]**per·vert** \ˈpər-ˌvərt\ *n* : one that is perverted; *esp* : one given to some form of sexual perversion

per·vert·ed \pər-ˈvərt-əd\ *adj* **1** : CORRUPT 1, TWISTED **2** : marked by perversion — **per·vert·ed·ly** *adv* — **per·vert·ed·ness** *n*

per·vi·ous \ˈpər-vē-əs\ *adj* : allowing entrance or passage : PERMEABLE ⟨*pervious* rock⟩ [Latin *pervius,* from *per-* "through" + *via* "way"] — **per·vi·ous·ness** *n*

Pe·sach \ˈpā-ˌsäk\ *n* : PASSOVER [Hebrew *pesaḥ*]

pe·se·ta \pə-ˈsāt-ə\ *n* : the basic monetary unit of Spain until 2002 [Spanish, from *peso* "peso"]

pes·ky \ˈpes-kē\ *adj* **pes·ki·er; -est** : TROUBLESOME 1, VEXATIOUS [probably derived from *pest*] — **pes·ki·ly** \-kə-lē\ *adv* — **pes·ki·ness** \-kē-nəs\ *n*

pe·so \ˈpā-sō\ *n, pl* **pesos** **1** : an old silver coin of Spain and Spanish America equal to eight reals **2 a** : the basic monetary unit of any of several countries (as Argentina, Chile, Colombia, Cuba, Dominican Republic, Mexico, Philippines, and Uruguay) **b** : a coin or note representing one peso [Spanish, literally, "weight," from Latin *pensum,* from *pendere* "to weigh"]

pes·si·mism \ˈpes-ə-ˌmiz-əm\ *n* **1** : an inclination to emphasize bad, disagreeable, or unpleasant aspects, conditions, and possibilities or to expect the worst **2** : a belief that evil is more common or powerful than good [French *pessimisme,* from Latin *pessimus* "worst"] — **pes·si·mist** \-məst\ *n*

pes·si·mis·tic \ˌpes-ə-ˈmis-tik\ *adj* : marked by, given to, or exhibiting pessimism ⟨a *pessimistic* report on the economy⟩ ⟨*pessimistic* about our chances of winning⟩ — **pes·si·mis·ti·cal·ly** \-ti-kə-lē, -klē\ *adv*

pest \ˈpest\ *n* **1** : an epidemic disease with a high mortality; *esp* : PLAGUE **2** : something resembling a pest in destructiveness; *esp* : a plant or animal harmful to humans or human concerns (as agriculture) **3** : one that pesters or annoys : NUISANCE [Middle French *peste,* from Latin *pestis*]

pes·ter \ˈpes-tər\ *vt* **pes·tered; pes·ter·ing** \-tə-ring, -tring\ : ANNOY, BOTHER [Middle French *empestrer* "to hobble (a horse), embarrass," derived from Late Latin *pastoria* "tether"]

pest·hole \ˈpest-ˌhōl\ *n* : a place in which epidemic diseases are common

pest·house \-ˌhau̇s\ *n* : a shelter or hospital for those infected with a contagious or epidemic disease

pes·ti·cide \ˈpes-tə-ˌsīd\ *n* : an agent used to destroy pests — **pes·ti·cid·al** \ˌpes-tə-ˈsīd-l\ *adj*

pes·tif·er·ous \pe-ˈstif-rəs, -ə-rəs\ *adj* **1** : dangerous to society : PERNICIOUS **2** : carrying or causing infection **3** : causing annoyance : TROUBLESOME — **pes·tif·er·ous·ly** *adv* — **pes·tif·er·ous·ness** *n*

pes·ti·lence \ˈpes-tə-ləns\ *n* : a contagious or infectious epidemic disease that spreads quickly and has devastating effects; *esp* : BUBONIC PLAGUE

pes·ti·lent \-lənt\ *adj* **1** : dangerous or destructive to life : DEADLY ⟨a *pestilent* drug⟩ **2** : harmful or dangerous to society : PERNICIOUS ⟨the *pestilent* influence of the slums⟩ **3** : causing displeasure or annoyance ⟨a *pestilent* child⟩ **4** : INFECTIOUS, CONTAGIOUS ⟨a *pestilent* disease⟩ [Latin *pestilens* "pestilential," from *pestis* "plague"] — **pes·ti·lent·ly** *adv*

pes·ti·len·tial \ˌpes-tə-ˈlen-chəl\ *adj* : causing or likely to cause pestilence : PESTILENT — **pes·ti·len·tial·ly** \-lench-lē, -ə-lē\ *adv*

\ə\ **abut**	\au̇\ **out**	\i\ **tip**	\ȯ\ **saw**	\u̇\ **foot**
\ər\ **further**	\ch\ **chin**	\ī\ **life**	\ȯi\ **coin**	\y\ **yet**
\a\ **mat**	\e\ **pet**	\j\ **job**	\th\ **thin**	\yü\ **few**
\ā\ **take**	\ē\ **easy**	\ng\ **sing**	\th\ **this**	\yu̇\ **cure**
\ä\ **cot, cart**	\g\ **go**	\ō\ **bone**	\ü\ **food**	\zh\ **vision**

pes·tle \ˈpes-əl, ˈpes-tl\ *n* : a usually club-shaped implement for pounding or grinding substances in a mortar [Medieval French *pestel,* from Latin *pistillum*] — **pestle** *vb*

pes·to \ˈpes-tō\ *n* : a sauce made especially of fresh basil, garlic, oil, pine nuts, and grated cheese [Italian, from *pesto* "pounded" (adjective), from *pestare* "to pound," from Late Latin *pistare,* from Latin *pinsere* "to pound, grind"]

[1]**pet** \ˈpet\ *n* **1 a** : a pampered and usually spoiled child **b** : a person who is treated with unusual kindness or consideration : DARLING **2** : a domesticated animal kept for pleasure rather than utility [perhaps from Middle English *pety* "small"]

[2]**pet** *adj* **1** : kept or treated as a pet ⟨a *pet* rabbit⟩ **2** : expressing fondness or endearment ⟨a *pet* name⟩ **3** : FAVORITE ⟨a *pet* project⟩

[3]**pet** *vb* **pet·ted; pet·ting 1** : to stroke in a gentle or loving manner **2** : to treat with unusual kindness and consideration : PAMPER **3** : to engage in amorous embracing, caressing, and kissing — **pet·ter** *n*

[4]**pet** *n* : a fit of peevishness, sulkiness, or anger [origin unknown]

pet·al \ˈpet-l\ *n* : one of the often brightly colored modified leaves making up the corolla of a flower [Greek *petalon*] — **pet·aled** *or* **pet·alled** \-ld\ *adj* — **pet·al·like** \-l-ˌlīk, -l-ˌīk\ *adj*

pe·tard \pə-ˈtärd, -ˈtär\ *n* : a case containing an explosive to break down a door or gate or breach a wall [Middle French, from *peter* "to break wind," from *pet* "expulsion of intestinal gas," from Latin *peditum,* from *pedere* "to break wind"]

pet·cock \ˈpet-ˌkäk\ *n* : a small cock, faucet, or valve for letting out air, releasing compression, or draining [*pet-* (perhaps from *petty*) + *cock*]

pe·ter \ˈpēt-ər\ *vi* : to diminish gradually and come to an end : GIVE OUT 3 ⟨the stream *peters* out⟩ [origin unknown]

Pe·ter \ˈpēt-ər\ *n* : either of two letters written to early Christians and included as books of the New Testament — see BIBLE table

Pe·ter's pence *n* **1** : an annual tribute of a penny formerly paid by each householder in England to the papal see **2** : a voluntary annual contribution made by Roman Catholics to the pope [from the tradition that Saint Peter founded the papal see]

pet·i·ole \ˈpet-ē-ˌōl\ *n* **1** : the slender stem of a leaf **2** : STALK; *esp* : a narrow segment joining the abdomen and thorax in some insects (as wasps) [Latin *petiolus* "small foot, fruit stalk," probably derived from *pes* "foot"] — **pet·i·o·late** \ˈpet-ē-ə-ˌlāt, ˌpet-ē-ˈō-lət\ *adj* — **pet·i·oled** \ˈpet-ē-ˌōld\ *adj*

pet·it \ˈpet-ē, ˈpet-ət\ *adj* : PETTY 1 — used chiefly in legal compounds [Medieval French, "small"]

pe·tite \pə-ˈtēt\ *adj* : having a small trim figure — usually used of a woman [French, feminine of *petit* "small"] — **pe·tite·ness** *n*

pe·tit four \ˌpet-ē-ˈfōr, -ˈfȯr\ *n, pl* **petits fours** *or* **petit fours** \-ē-ˈfōrz, -ˈfȯrz\ : a small frosted and ornamented cake cut from pound or sponge cake [French, literally, "small oven"]

[1]**pe·ti·tion** \pə-ˈtish-ən\ *n* **1** : an earnest request : ENTREATY **2** : a formal written request made to a superior or authority **3** : something asked or requested [Medieval French, from Latin *petitio,* from *petere* "to seek, request"] — **pe·ti·tion·ary** \-ˈtish-ə-ˌner-ē\ *adj*

[2]**petition** *vb* **pe·ti·tioned; pe·ti·tion·ing** \-ˈtish-ning, -ə-ning\ : to make a request to or for : SOLICIT; *esp* : to make a formal written request — **pe·ti·tion·er** \-ˈtish-nər, -ə-nər\ *n*

pet·it jury \ˈpet-ē-\ *n* : a jury of 12 persons who listen to the testimony in a trial and try to determine which side is in the right

pe·tit mal \pə-ˌtē-ˈmal, -ˈmäl\ *n* : epilepsy characterized by mild seizures but no loss of consciousness [French, literally, "small illness"]

pet·it point \ˈpet-ē-ˌpȯint\ *n* : TENT STITCH; *also* : embroidery made with this stitch [French, literally, "small point"]

pet peeve *n* : a frequent subject of complaint

petr- *or* **petri-** *or* **petro-** *combining form* **1** : stone : rock ⟨*pe*trology⟩ **2** : petroleum ⟨*petro*chemical⟩ [Greek *petros* "stone" and *petra* "rock"]

pe·trel \ˈpe-trəl, ˈpē-\ *n* : any of various small long-winged seabirds (as the storm petrel) that fly far from land [alteration of earlier *pitteral*]

Pe·tri dish \ˌpē-trē-\ *n* : a small shallow dish of thin glass or plastic with a loose cover used especially for cultures in bacteriology [Julius R. *Petri,* died 1921, German bacteriologist]

pet·ri·fac·tion \ˌpe-trə-ˈfak-shən\ *n* **1** : the process of petrifying or state of being petrified **2** : something that is petrified

pet·ri·fi·ca·tion \ˌpe-trə-fə-ˈkā-shən\ *n* : PETRIFACTION

pet·ri·fy \ˈpe-trə-ˌfī\ *vb* **-fied; -fy·ing 1** : to convert (an organic object) into stone or stony material by the infiltration of water and the deposition of dissolved minerals ⟨*petrified* wood⟩ **2** : to make or become rigid or inert like stone: **a** : to make lifeless or inactive : DEADEN **b** : to paralyze with fear, amazement, or awe : STUN [Middle French *petrifier,* from *petr-* "petr-" + *-ifier* "-fy"]

petrel

Pe·trine \ˈpē-ˌtrīn\ *adj* : of, relating to, or characteristic of the apostle Peter or the doctrines associated with his name [Late Latin *Petrus* "Peter"]

pet·ro·chem·i·cal \ˌpe-trō-ˈkem-i-kəl\ *n* : a chemical isolated or derived from petroleum or natural gas

pe·trog·ra·phy \pə-ˈträg-rə-fē\ *n* : the description and systematic classification of rocks — compare PETROLOGY — **pe·trog·ra·pher** \-fər\ *n* — **pet·ro·graph·ic** \ˌpe-trə-ˈgraf-ik\ *or* **pet·ro·graph·i·cal** \-ˈgraf-i-kəl\ *adj*

pet·rol \ˈpe-trəl, -ˌträl\ *n, chiefly British* : GASOLINE [French *essence de pétrole,* literally, "essence of petroleum"]

pet·ro·la·tum \ˌpe-trə-ˈlāt-əm\ *n* : PETROLEUM JELLY [New Latin, from Medieval Latin *petroleum*]

pe·tro·leum \pə-ˈtrō-lē-əm, -ˈtrōl-yəm\ *n* : an oily flammable liquid widely distributed in the upper strata of the earth that is a complex mixture mostly of hydrocarbons and is the source of gasoline and lubricants and a major industrial raw material [Medieval Latin, from Latin *petr-* "petr-" + *oleum* "oil"]

petroleum jelly *n* : a tasteless odorless oily substance from petroleum that is used especially in ointments and dressings

pe·trol·o·gy \pə-ˈträl-ə-jē\ *n* : a science that deals with the origin, history, occurrence, structure, chemical composition, and classification of rocks — compare PETROGRAPHY — **pet·ro·log·ic** \ˌpe-trə-ˈläj-ik\ *or* **pet·ro·log·i·cal** \-ˈläj-i-kəl\ *adj* — **pet·ro·log·i·cal·ly** \-i-kə-lē, -klē\ *adv* — **pe·trol·o·gist** \pə-ˈträl-ə-jəst\ *n*

[1]**pet·ti·coat** \ˈpet-ē-ˌkōt\ *n* **1 a** : an outer skirt formerly worn by women and small children **b** : a skirt worn under a dress or outer skirt **2** : something (as a valance) resembling a petticoat [Middle English *petycote* "short tunic, petticoat," from *pety* "small" + *cote* "coat"]

[2]**petticoat** *adj* : FEMALE 2 ⟨*petticoat* rule⟩

pet·ti·fog \ˈpet-ē-ˌfȯg, -ˌfäg\ *vi* **-fogged; -fog·ging 1** : to engage in legal trickery **2** : to quibble over insignificant details : CAVIL [back-formation from *pettifogger,* probably from *petty* + obsolete *fogger* "pettifogger"] — **pet·ti·fog·ger** *n* — **pet·ti·fog·gery** \-ˌfȯg-rē, -ˌfäg-, -ə-rē\ *n*

petting zoo *n* : a collection of farm animals or gentle exotic animals for children to pet and feed

pet·tish \ˈpet-ish\ *adj* : FRETFUL 1, PEEVISH — **pet·tish·ly** *adv* — **pet·tish·ness** *n*

pet·ty \ˈpet-ē\ *adj* **pet·ti·er; -est 1** : having secondary rank or importance : MINOR, SUBORDINATE ⟨a *petty* prince⟩ **2** : having little or no importance or significance ⟨*petty* details⟩ **3** : marked by or reflective of narrow interests and sympathies [Middle English *pety* "small, minor," from Middle French *petit* "small"] — **pet·ti·ly** \ˈpet-l-ē\ *adv* — **pet·ti·ness** \ˈpet-ē-nəs\ *n*

petty cash *n* : cash kept on hand for payment of minor items

petty officer *n* : an officer in the navy or coast guard appointed from among the enlisted ranks that is comparable to a noncommissioned officer in the army

petty officer first class *n* : an enlisted rank in the navy and coast guard above petty officer second class and below chief petty officer

petty officer second class *n* : an enlisted rank in the navy and coast guard above petty officer third class and below petty officer first class

petty officer third class *n* : an enlisted rank in the navy and coast guard above seaman and below petty officer second class

pet·u·lant \ˈpech-ə-lənt\ *adj* : characterized by temporary or capricious ill humor : PEEVISH [Latin *petulans*] — **pet·u·lance** \-ləns\ *n* — **pet·u·lant·ly** *adv*

pe·tu·nia \pə-ˈtü-nyə, -ˈtyü-\ *n* : any of a genus of tropical South American herbs of the nightshade family widely grown for their showy funnel-shaped flowers [New Latin, from obsolete French *petun* "tobacco," from Tupi *petíma*]

pew \ˈpyü\ *n* **1 :** a compartment in the auditorium of a church providing seats for several persons **2 :** one of the benches with backs and sometimes doors fixed in rows in a church [Medieval French *puie* "balustrade," derived from Latin *podium* "parapet, podium"]

pe·wee \ˈpē-wē, -ˌwē\ *n* **:** any of various small largely gray or olive-colored American flycatchers [imitative]

pew·ter \ˈpyüt-ər\ *n* **1 :** any of various tin-based alloys; *esp* **:** a dull alloy with lead formerly used for domestic utensils **2 :** wares (as table utensils) of pewter [Medieval French *peutre*] — **pewter** *adj*

pew·ter·er \ˈpyüt-ər-ər\ *n* **:** one that makes pewter wares

pey·o·te \pā-ˈōt-ē\ *also* **pey·otl** \-ˈōt-l\ *n* **1 :** a drug containing mescaline that causes hallucinations and is obtained from the dried and flattened tops of a small spineless cactus of the southwestern U.S. and Mexico **2 :** the cactus from which peyote is obtained — called also *mescal* [Mexican Spanish *peyote,* from Nahuatl *peyotl*]

peyote button *n* **:** one of the dried round and flattened tops of the peyote cactus — called also *mescal button*

pfen·nig \ˈfen-ig, -ik\ *n, pl* **pfennigs** *or* **pfen·ni·ge** \ˈfen-i-gə\ **:** a former monetary unit equal to 1⁄100 deutsche mark [German]

PG \ˈpē-ˈjē\ *certification mark* — used to certify that a motion picture is of such a nature that all ages may be allowed admission but parental guidance is suggested

PG–13 \-ˌthər-ˈtēn, -ˌthərt-\ *certification mark* — used to certify that a motion picture is of such a nature that persons of all ages may be admitted but parental guidance is suggested especially for children under 13

pH \pē-ˈāch, ˈpē-\ *n* **:** a number used in expressing acidity or alkalinity that is the negative logarithm of the effective hydrogen-ion concentration on a scale whose values run from 0 to 14 with 7 representing neutrality, numbers less than 7 increasing acidity, and numbers greater than 7 increasing alkalinity; *also* **:** the condition with respect to acidity or alkalinity

Word History In 1909 the Danish chemist Søren Peter Lauritz Sørensen developed the concept of pH. He suggested that the concentration of hydrogen ions in a solution should be expressed in terms of the negative logarithm (the power to which 10 is raised). Sørensen's *p* stood for *Potenz,* the German word for "(mathematical) power," and *H* represents the hydrogen ion.

phage \ˈfāj *also* ˈfäzh\ *n* **:** BACTERIOPHAGE

-phage \ˌfāj *also* ˌfäzh\ *n combining form* **:** one that eats ⟨bacteriophage⟩ [Greek *phagein* "to eat"]

phago·cyte \ˈfag-ə-ˌsīt\ *n* **:** a cell (as a white blood cell) that engulfs and breaks down foreign material (as bacteria) and waste [Greek *phagein* "to eat"] — **phago·cyt·ic** \ˌfag-ə-ˈsit-ik\ *adj*

phago·cy·to·sis \ˌfag-ə-sī-ˈtō-səs\ *n* **:** the engulfing and usually the destruction of particulate matter by phagocytes — **phago·cy·tot·ic** \-ˈtät-ik\ *adj*

-ph·a·gous \f-ə-gəs\ *adj combining form* **:** eating [Greek *-phagos,* from *phagein* "to eat"]

pha·lan·ger \fə-ˈlan-jər\ *n* **:** any of various marsupial mammals of the Australian region ranging in size from a mouse to a large cat that typically dwell in trees, are active at night, and have dense fur [derived from Greek *phalanx* "log, line of battle, bone of the finger or toe"]

pha·lanx \ˈfā-ˌlangs, -ˌlangks\ *n, pl* **pha·lanx·es** *or* **pha·lan·ges** \fə-ˈlan-ˌjēz, fā-\ **1 :** a body of heavily armed infantry in ancient Greece formed in close deep ranks and files; *also* **:** a body of troops in close array **2** *pl* ***phalanges* :** one of the bones of a finger or toe of a vertebrate **3** *pl usually* ***phalanxes*** **a :** a massed arrangement of persons, animals, or things ⟨a *phalanx* of armed guards⟩ **b :** an organized body of persons ⟨a *phalanx* of lawyers⟩ [Latin, from Greek, literally, "log"] — **pha·lan·geal** \fə-ˈlan-jē-əl, -jəl\ *adj*

phal·a·rope \ˈfal-ə-ˌrōp\ *n* **:** any of various small shorebirds that resemble sandpipers but have lobed toes and are good swimmers [French, derived from Greek *phalaris* "coot" + *pod-, pous* "foot"]

phal·lus \ˈfal-əs\ *n, pl* **phal·li** \ˈfal-ˌī, -ˌē\ *or* **phal·lus·es** **1 :** a symbol or representation of the human penis **2 :** PENIS [Latin, from Greek *phallos*] — **phal·lic** \ˈfal-ik\ *adj*

Phan·er·o·zo·ic \ˌfan-ə-rə-ˈzō-ik\ *adj* **:** of, relating to, or being an eon of geologic history that comprises the Paleozoic, Mesozoic, and Cenozoic eras or the corresponding systems of rocks — see GEOLOGIC TIME table [Greek *phaneros* visible] — **Phanerozoic** *n*

phan·tasm \ˈfan-ˌtaz-əm\ *n* **1 :** a product of fantasy: as **a :** delusive appearance **:** ILLUSION **b :** GHOST 2, SPECTER **c :** a figment of the imagination **:** FANTASY **2 :** a deceptive or illusory appearance of a thing [Medieval French *fantasme,* from Latin *phantasma,* from Greek, from *phantazein* "to present to the mind," from *phainein* "to show"] — **phan·tas·mal** \fan-ˈtaz-məl\ *adj* — **phan·tas·mic** \-ˈtaz-mik\ *adj*

phan·tas·ma·go·ria \fan-ˌtaz-mə-ˈgōr-ē-ə, -ˈgȯr-\ *n* **1 :** an exhibition or display of optical effects and illusions **2 a :** a constantly shifting complex succession of things seen or imagined **b :** a scene that constantly changes **3 :** a bizarre or fantastic combination, collection, or assemblage [French *phantasmagorie,* derived from *phantasme* "phantasm," from Medieval French *fantasme*] — **phan·tas·ma·go·ric** \-ˈgōr-ik, -ˈgȯr-, -ˈgär-\ *or* **phan·tas·ma·gor·i·cal** \-i-kəl\ *adj*

phantasy *variant of* FANTASY

[1]**phan·tom** \ˈfant-əm\ *n* **1 a :** something (as a specter) apparent to sense but with no substantial existence **b :** something elusive or visionary **:** WILL-O'-THE-WISP **c :** an object of continual dread or abhorrence **:** BUGBEAR **2 :** something existing in appearance only **3 :** a representation of something abstract, ideal, or incorporeal [Medieval French *fantosme,* from Latin *phantasma* "phantasm"]

[2]**phantom** *adj* **1 :** of the nature of, suggesting, or being a phantom **2 :** FICTITIOUS, DUMMY ⟨*phantom* voters⟩

phar·aoh \ˈfeər-ō, ˈfaər-ō, ˈfā-rō\ *n, often cap* **:** a ruler of ancient Egypt [Late Latin *pharaon-, pharao,* from Greek *pharaō,* from Hebrew *parʿōh,* from Egyptian *pr-ʿ3*] — **phar·a·on·ic** \ˌfer-ā-ˈän-ik, ˌfar-\ *adj, often cap*

phar·i·sa·ic \ˌfar-ə-ˈsā-ik\ *adj* **1 :** PHARISAICAL **2** *cap* **:** of or relating to the Pharisees

phar·i·sa·i·cal \-ˈsā-ə-kəl\ *adj* **:** marked by hypocritical censorious self-righteousness — **phar·i·sa·i·cal·ly** \-kə-lē, -klē\ *adv* — **phar·i·sa·i·cal·ness** \-kəl-nəs\ *n*

phar·i·sa·ism \ˈfar-ə-sā-ˌiz-əm, -ˌsā-\ *n* **1** *cap* **:** the doctrines or practices of the Pharisees **2** *often cap* **:** pharisaical character, spirit, or attitude

phar·i·see \ˈfar-ə-ˌsē\ *n* **1** *cap* **:** a member of a Jewish sect of New Testament times noted for strict observance of rites and ceremonies of the written law and for insistence on the validity of their own oral traditions concerning the law **2 :** a pharisaical person [Old English *farise,* from Late Latin *pharisaeus,* from Greek *pharisaios,* from Aramaic *pĕrīshayyā,* pl. of *pĕrīshā,* literally, "separated"]

[1]**phar·ma·ceu·ti·cal** \ˌfär-mə-ˈsüt-i-kəl\ *adj* **:** of, relating to, or engaged in pharmacy or the manufacture and sale of pharmaceuticals ⟨a *pharmaceutical* company⟩ [Late Latin *pharmaceuticus,* from Greek *pharmakeutikos,* from *pharmakeuein* "to administer drugs"] — **phar·ma·ceu·ti·cal·ly** \-i-kə-lē, -klē\ *adv*

[2]**pharmaceutical** *n* **:** a medicinal drug or preparation

phar·ma·cist \ˈfär-mə-səst\ *n* **:** a specialist in pharmacy

pharmaco- *combining form* **:** medicine **:** drug ⟨*pharmacology*⟩ [Greek *pharmakon*]

phar·ma·col·o·gy \ˌfär-mə-ˈkäl-ə-jē\ *n* **1 :** the science of drugs, their composition, effects, and use in medicine **2 :** the properties and reactions of drugs especially with relation to their medicinal value — **phar·ma·co·log·i·cal** \-kə-ˈläj-i-kəl\ *also* **phar·ma·co·log·ic** \-ˈläj-ik\ *adj* — **phar·ma·co·log·i·cal·ly** \-i-kə-lē, -klē\ *adv* — **phar·ma·col·o·gist** \-ˈkäl-ə-jəst\ *n*

phar·ma·co·poe·ia *also* **phar·ma·co·pe·ia** \ˌfär-mə-kə-ˈpē-ə\ *n* **1 :** a book describing drugs, chemicals, and medicinal preparations **2 :** a collection or stock of drugs [Late Greek *pharmakopoiia* "preparation of drugs," from Greek *pharmakon* "drug" + *poiein* "to make"] — **phar·ma·co·poe·ial** \-əl\ *adj*

phar·ma·cy \ˈfär-mə-sē\ *n, pl* **-cies** **1 :** the art, practice, or profession of preparing, preserving, compounding, and dispensing drugs; *esp* **:** the profession of mixing drugs according to a doctor's prescription **2 a :** a place where medicines are compounded or dispensed **b :** DRUGSTORE **3 :** PHARMACOPOEIA 2 [Late Latin *pharmacia* "administration of drugs," from Greek *pharmakeia,* from *pharmakeuein* "to administer drugs," from *pharmakon* "magic charm, poison, drug"]

\ə\ **abut**	\au̇\ **out**	\i\ **tip**	\ȯ\ **saw**	\u̇\ **foot**
\ər\ **further**	\ch\ **chin**	\ī\ **life**	\ȯi\ **coin**	\y\ **yet**
\a\ **mat**	\e\ **pet**	\j\ **job**	\th\ **thin**	\yü\ **few**
\ā\ **take**	\ē\ **easy**	\ng\ **sing**	\t͟h\ **this**	\yu̇\ **cure**
\ä\ **cot, cart**	\g\ **go**	\ō\ **bone**	\ü\ **food**	\zh\ **vision**

pha·ryn·geal \fə-ˈrin-jē-əl, -jəl; ˌfar-ən-ˈjē-əl\ *adj* **:** relating to or located or produced in the region of the pharynx

phar·yn·gi·tis \ˌfar-ən-ˈjīt-əs\ *n* **:** inflammation of the pharynx

phar·ynx \ˈfar-ings, -ingks\ *n, pl* **pha·ryn·ges** \fə-ˈrin-ˌjēz\ *also* **phar·ynx·es :** the muscular tubular passage of the vertebrate digestive and respiratory tracts that extends from the back of the nasal cavity and mouth to the esophagus and through which air passes to the larynx and food to the esophagus; *also* **:** a corresponding part of an invertebrate [Greek, "throat, pharynx"]

[1]**phase** \ˈfāz\ *n* **1 :** the apparent shape of the moon or a planet at any time in its series of changes with respect to illumination ⟨the new moon and the full moon are *phases* of the moon⟩ **2 a :** a stage or interval in a development or cycle **b :** an aspect or part under consideration **3 :** the stage of progress in a regularly recurring motion or a cyclic process (as a wave or vibration) in relation to a reference point **4 a :** a homogeneous physically distinct portion of matter present in a nonhomogeneous system **b :** one of the fundamental states of matter usually considered to include the solid, liquid, and gaseous forms [Greek *phasis* "appearance of a star, phase of the moon," from *phainein* "to show"] — **pha·sic** \ˈfā-zik\ *adj*

[2]**phase** *vb* **phased; phas·ing 1 :** to carry out by planned phases **2 :** to introduce in stages — usually used with *in*

phase–contrast microscope *n* **:** a microscope that translates differences in phase of the light transmitted through or reflected by the object into differences of intensity in the image — called also *phase microscope*

pheas·ant \ˈfez-nt\ *n, pl* **pheasant** *or* **pheasants :** any of numerous large long-tailed brightly colored Old World birds related to the domestic chicken including many of which are reared as ornamental or game birds [Medieval French *fesant, faisan,* from Latin *phasianus,* from Greek *phasianos,* from *Phasis,* river in Colchis]

pheasant

phel·lem \ˈfel-ˌem\ *n* **:** CORK 1b [Greek *phellos* "cork" + English *-em* (as in *phloem*)]

phel·lo·gen \ˈfel-ə-jən\ *n* **:** an outer layer of meristem that produces cells inwardly and outwardly in many roots and stems [Greek *phellos* "cork"]

phen- *or* **pheno-** *combining form* **:** related to or derived from benzene ⟨*phen*ol⟩ **:** containing phenyl ⟨*pheno*barbital⟩ [French *phène* "benzene," from Greek *phainein* "to show"; from its occurrence in gas used for illumination]

phe·no·bar·bi·tal \ˌfē-nō-ˈbär-bə-ˌtȯl\ *n* **:** a crystalline barbiturate drug used as a sedative and to induce sleep

phe·nol \ˈfē-ˌnōl, -ˌnȯl, fi-ˈ\ *n* **1 :** a caustic poisonous crystalline acidic compound C_6H_5OH present in the tars of coal and wood that in dilute solution is used as a disinfectant **2 :** any of various acidic compounds analogous to phenol and regarded as hydroxyl derivatives of aromatic hydrocarbons — **phe·no·lic** \fi-ˈnō-lik, -ˈnäl-ik\ *adj*

phe·no·lic \fi-ˈnō-lik, -ˈnäl-ik\ *n* **:** a resin or plastic made by condensation of a phenol with an aldehyde and used especially for molding and insulating and in coatings and adhesives

phe·nol·phtha·lein \ˌfē-ˌnōl-ˈthal-ē-ən, -ˈthal-ˌēn, -ˈthāl-\ *n* **:** a white or yellowish white crystalline compound used as a laxative and as an acid-base indicator because its solution is red in alkalies and is decolorized by acids [*phenol* + *phthalein,* a kind of dye, from *phthalic acid,* an acid, short for obsolete *naphthalic acid,* from *naphthalene*]

phe·nom·e·nal \fi-ˈnäm-ən-l\ *adj* **1 :** of, relating to, or being a phenomenon **2 :** EXTRAORDINARY 1, REMARKABLE ⟨a *phenomenal* memory⟩ — **phe·nom·e·nal·ly** \-l-ē\ *adv*

phe·nom·e·non \fi-ˈnäm-ə-ˌnän, -nən\ *n, pl* **-na** \-nə, -ˌnä\ *or* **-nons 1 :** an observable fact or event **2 :** a fact or event that can be scientifically described and explained **3 a :** a rare or significant fact or event **b** *pl* *phenomenons* **:** an exceptional person, thing, or event [Late Latin *phaenomenon,* from Greek *phainomenon,* from *phainesthai* "to appear," from *phainein* "to show"]

phe·no·thi·azine \ˌfē-nō-ˈthī-ə-ˌzēn\ *n* **:** any of various tranquilizing drugs (as chlorpromazine) used especially in the treatment of schizophrenia [*phen-* + *thi-* + *azine,* a type of nitrogen compound, derived from French *azote* "nitrogen," derived from Greek *a-* + *zōē* "life"]

phe·no·type \ˈfē-nə-ˌtīp\ *n* **:** the observable characters of an organism resulting from the interaction of genotype and environment [German *Phänotypus,* from Greek *phainein* "to show" + *typos* "type"] — **phe·no·typ·ic** \ˌfē-nə-ˈtip-ik\ *adj* — **phe·no·typ·i·cal·ly** \-i-kə-lē, -klē\ *adv*

phe·nyl \ˈfen-l, ˈfēn-\ *n* **:** a univalent radical C_6H_5– derived from benzene by removal of one hydrogen atom — **phe·nyl·ic** \fi-ˈnil-ik\ *adj*

phe·nyl·al·a·nine \ˌfen-l-ˈal-ə-ˌnēn, ˌfēn-\ *n* **:** an essential amino acid $C_9H_{11}NO_2$ obtained by the hydrolysis of proteins and converted in the body to tyrosine

phe·nyl·ke·ton·uria \-ˌkēt-n-ˈůr-ē-ə, -ˈyůr-\ *n* **:** an inherited disorder marked by the inability to break down and process phenylalanine and typically resulting in mental retardation unless phenylalanine is restricted from the diet from birth [*phenyl* + *ketone* + *-uria* (from Greek *ouron* "urine")]

phen·yl·thio·car·ba·mide \ˌfen-l-ˌthī-ō-ˈkär-bə-ˌmīd\ *n* **:** a crystalline compound $C_7H_8N_2S$ that is extremely bitter or tasteless depending on the presence or absence of a single dominant gene in the taster — called also *PTC*

phe·re·sis \fə-ˈrē-səs\ *n* **:** APHERESIS

pher·o·mone \ˈfer-ə-ˌmōn\ *n* **:** a chemical substance (as a scent) that is produced by an animal and serves as a signal to stimulate behavior (as mating) of other individuals of the same species [*phero-* (from Greek *pherein* "to carry") + *-mone* (as in *hormone*)] — **pher·o·mon·al** \ˌfer-ə-ˈmōn-l\ *adj*

phi \ˈfī\ *n* **:** the 21st letter of the Greek alphabet — Φ or ϕ

phi·al \ˈfī-əl, ˈfīl\ *n* **:** VIAL [Latin *phiala,* from Greek *phialē*]

phil- *or* **philo-** *combining form* **:** loving **:** having an affinity for [Greek, from *philos* "dear, friendly"]

[1]**-phil** \ˌfil\ *or* **-phile** \ˌfīl\ *n combining form* **:** lover **:** one having an affinity for ⟨Franco*phile*⟩ [Greek *philos*]

[2]**-phil** *or* **-phile** *adj combining form* **:** being strongly attracted to

phil·a·del·phus \ˌfil-ə-ˈdel-fəs\ *n* **:** MOCK ORANGE [Greek *philadelphos* "brotherly," from *phil-* + *adelphos* "brother"]

phi·lan·der \fə-ˈlan-dər\ *vi* **phi·lan·dered; phi·lan·der·ing** \-də-ring, -dring\ **:** to be sexually unfaithful to one's wife [from obsolete *philander* "lover, philanderer," probably from the name *Philander*] — **phi·lan·der·er** \-dər-ər\ *n*

phil·an·throp·ic \ˌfil-ən-ˈthräp-ik\ *also* **phil·an·throp·i·cal** \-ˈthräp-i-kəl\ *adj* **:** of, relating to, or characterized by philanthropy **:** CHARITABLE — **phil·an·throp·i·cal·ly** \-i-kə-lē, -klē\ *adv*

phi·lan·thro·pist \fə-ˈlan-thrə-pəst, -ˈlant-\ *n* **:** one who practices philanthropy

phi·lan·thro·py \-pē\ *n, pl* **-pies 1 :** goodwill to all people; *esp* **:** effort to promote human welfare **2 a :** a philanthropic act or gift **b :** a group distributing or supported by philanthropic funds [derived from Greek *philanthrōpia,* from *philanthrōpos* "loving people," from *phil-* + *anthrōpos* "human being"]

phi·lat·e·ly \fə-ˈlat-l-ē\ *n* **:** the collection and study of postage and imprinted stamps [French *philatélie,* from Greek *phil-* + *atelia* "tax exemption," derived from *a-* + *telos* "tax"; from the fact that a stamped letter frees the recipient from paying the mailing charges] — **phil·a·tel·ic** \ˌfil-ə-ˈtel-ik\ *adj* — **phi·lat·e·list** \fə-ˈlat-l-əst\ *n*

Phi·le·mon \fə-ˈlē-mən, fī-\ *n* **:** a letter written by Saint Paul to a Christian living in the area of Colossae and included as a book in the New Testament — see BIBLE table

Phi·lip·pi·ans \fə-ˈlip-ē-ənz\ *n* **:** a letter written by Saint Paul to the Christians of Philippi and included as a book in the New Testament — see BIBLE table

phi·lip·pic \fə-ˈlip-ik\ *n* **:** TIRADE [Middle French *philippique,* from Greek *philippikoi logoi,* speeches of Demosthenes against Philip II of Macedon, literally, "speeches relating to Philip"]

Phil·ip·pine mahogany \ˌfil-ə-ˌpēn-\ *n* **:** any of several Philippine timber trees with wood resembling that of the true mahoganies; *also* **:** this wood

phi·lis·tine \ˈfil-ə-ˌstēn; fə-ˈlis-tən, -ˌtēn\ *n* **1** *cap* **:** a native or inhabitant of ancient Philistia **2** *often cap* **a :** a person who does not understand or care about art or culture **b :** someone uninformed in an area of knowledge — **philistine** *adj, often cap* — **phi·lis·tin·ism** \-ˌstē-ˌniz-əm; -tə-ˌniz-, -ˌtē-\ *n, often cap*

phil·o·den·dron \ˌfil-ə-ˈden-drən\ *n, pl* **-drons** *also* **-dra** \-drə\ **:** any of various plants of the arum family grown for their showy usually shiny leaves [Greek *philodendros* "loving trees," from *phil-* + *dendron* "tree"]

phi·lol·o·gy \fə-ˈläl-ə-jē\ *n* **1 :** the study of literature and of relevant fields **2 :** LINGUISTICS; *esp* **:** historical and comparative linguistics [French *philologie,* from Latin *philologia* "love of learning and literature," from Greek, from *phil-* + *logos* "word, speech"] — **phil·o·log·i·cal** \ˌfil-ə-ˈläj-i-kəl\ *adj* — **phil·o·log·i·cal·ly** \-ˈläj-i-kə-lē, -klē\ *adv* — **phi·lol·o·gist** \fə-ˈläl-ə-jəst\ *n*

phi·los·o·pher \fə-ˈläs-ə-fər\ *n* **1 a :** a person who seeks wisdom or enlightenment **b :** a student of philosophy **2 :** a person who faces trouble calmly, wisely, and bravely

philosopher's stone *n* **1 :** an imaginary stone, substance, or chemical preparation believed to have the power of transmuting base metals into gold and sought for by alchemists **2 :** an elusive or imaginary key to success

phil·o·soph·i·cal \ˌfil-ə-ˈsäf-i-kəl\ *also* **phil·o·soph·ic** \-ik\ *adj* **1 :** of, relating to, or based on philosophy **2 :** characterized by the attitude of a philosopher; *esp* **:** calm in the face of trouble, defeat, or loss — **phil·o·soph·i·cal·ly** \-i-kə-lē, -klē\ *adv*

phi·los·o·phize \fə-ˈläs-ə-ˌfīz\ *vi* **1 :** to reason in the manner of a philosopher **2 :** to expound a philosophy **:** MORALIZE — **phi·los·o·phiz·er** *n*

phi·los·o·phy \fə-ˈläs-ə-fē\ *n, pl* **-phies 1 :** the study of the nature of knowledge and existence and the principles of moral and esthetic value **2 :** the philosophical teachings or principles of a person or group ⟨Greek *philosophy*⟩ **3 :** the general principles of a field of study ⟨the *philosophy* of history⟩ ⟨the *philosophy* of cooking⟩ **4 :** the most basic beliefs, concepts, and attitudes of an individual or group [Medieval French *philosophie,* from Latin *philosophia,* from Greek, from *philosophos* "philosopher," from *phil-* + *sophia* "wisdom," from *sophos* "wise"]

phil·ter *n* **1 :** a potion, drug, or charm held to have the power to excite sexual passion **2 :** a magic potion [Middle French *philtre,* from Latin *philtrum,* from Greek *philtron*]

phil·tre *chiefly British variant of* PHILTER

phish·ing \ˈfish-iŋ\ *n* **:** a scam by which an e-mail user is fooled into revealing personal or confidential information which can be used illegally [alteration of *fishing*]

phle·bi·tis \fli-ˈbīt-əs\ *n* **:** inflammation of a vein [Greek *phleb-, phleps* "vein"]

phle·bot·o·my \fli-ˈbät-ə-mē\ *n* **:** the drawing of blood (as by incision or puncture) from a vein for transfusion, diagnosis, or experiment, and especially formerly in the treatment of disease [derived from Greek *phlebotomia,* from *phleb-, phleps* "vein" + *-tomia* "-tomy"] — **phle·bot·o·mist** \-mist\ *n*

phlegm \ˈflem\ *n* **1 :** viscid mucus secreted in abnormal quantity in the respiratory passages **2 a :** dull or apathetic coldness or indifference **b :** intrepid coolness or calm fortitude [Medieval French *fleume,* from Late Latin *phlegmat-, phlegma,* from Greek, "flame, inflammation, phlegm," from *phlegein* "to burn"] — **phlegmy** \ˈflem-ē\ *adj*

phleg·mat·ic \fleg-ˈmat-ik\ *adj* **:** having or showing a slow and stolid temperament ***synonyms*** see IMPASSIVE — **phleg·mat·i·cal·ly** \-i-kə-lē, -klē\ *adv*

phlo·em \ˈflō-ˌem\ *n* **:** a vascular tissue of higher plants that contains sieve tubes and functions in the transport of dissolved food material and lies mostly external to the cambium — compare XYLEM [German, from Greek *phloios* "bark"]

phloem ray *n* **:** a vascular ray or part of a vascular ray that is located in phloem — compare XYLEM RAY

phlo·gis·ton \flō-ˈjis-tən\ *n* **:** the hypothetical principle of fire regarded formerly as a material substance [Greek *phlogistos* "inflammable," from *phlogizein* "to set on fire," from *phlog-, phlox* "flame," from *phlegein* "to burn"]

phlox \ˈfläks\ *n, pl* **phlox** *or* **phlox·es :** any of a genus of American annual or perennial herbs widely grown for their showy clusters of usually pink, purplish, or white flowers [Greek, "flame, wallflower"]

pH meter *n* **:** an apparatus for determining the pH of a solution

-phobe \ˌfōb\ *n combining form* **:** one fearing or averse to (something specified) ⟨anglo*phobe*⟩ [Greek *phobos* "fear"] — **-phobic** \ˈfō-bik\ *adj combining form*

pho·bia \ˈfō-bē-ə\ *n* **:** an unreasonable persistent fear of a particular thing [Greek *-phobia,* from *phobos* "fear"] — **pho·bic** \ˈfō-bik\ *adj*

phoe·be \ˈfē-bē\ *n* **:** any of several American flycatchers; *esp* **:** one of the eastern U.S. that has a slight crest and is plain grayish brown above and yellowish white below [imitative]

Phoe·ni·cian \fi-ˈnēsh-ən\ *n* **1 :** a native or inhabitant of ancient Phoenicia **2 :** the Semitic language of ancient Phoenicia — **Phoenician** *adj*

phoe·nix \ˈfē-niks\ *n* **:** a legendary bird that according to one account lived 500 years, burned itself to death, and rose alive from the ashes to live another period [Old English *fenix,* from Latin *phoenix,* from Greek *phoinix*]

phon- *or* **phono-** *combining form* **:** sound **:** voice **:** speech ⟨*phon*ation⟩ ⟨*phono*graph⟩ [Greek *phōnē* "voice, sound"]

pho·na·tion \fō-ˈnā-shən\ *n* **:** the act or process of producing speech sounds ⟨organs of *phonation*⟩ — **pho·nate** \ˈfō-ˌnāt\ *vi*

[1]**phone** \ˈfōn\ *n* **:** a speech sound considered as a physical event without regard to its status in the structure of a language [Greek *phōnē*]

[2]**phone** *n* **1 :** EARPHONE **2 :** TELEPHONE

[3]**phone** *vb* **:** TELEPHONE

-phone \ˌfōn\ *n combining form* **:** sound ⟨homo*phone*⟩ — often in names of musical instruments and sound-transmitting and sound-receiving devices ⟨tele*phone*⟩ ⟨xylo*phone*⟩ [Greek *phōnē* "voice, sound"]

phone card *n* **:** a prepaid card used for making telephone calls

pho·neme \ˈfō-ˌnēm\ *n* **:** a member of the set of the smallest units of speech that serve to distinguish one utterance from another in a language or dialect ⟨\n\ and \t\ in *pin* and *pit* are different *phonemes*⟩ — compare ALLOPHONE [French *phonème,* from Greek *phōnēma* "speech sound," from *phōnein* "to sound"]

pho·ne·mic \fə-ˈnē-mik\ *adj* **1 :** of, relating to, or having the characteristics of a phoneme **2 :** being different phonemes ⟨in English \n\ and \m\ are *phonemic*⟩ — **pho·ne·mi·cal·ly** \-mi-kə-lē, -klē\ *adv*

pho·net·ic \fə-ˈnet-ik\ *adj* **1 a :** of or relating to spoken language or speech sounds ⟨*phonetic* differences in Old English and Modern English⟩ **b :** of or relating to phonetics ⟨a *phonetic* study⟩ **2 :** representing speech sounds ⟨a *phonetic* system⟩ [Greek *phōnētikos,* from *phōnein* "to sound," from *phōnē* "voice"] — **pho·net·i·cal·ly** \-i-kə-lē, -klē\ *adv*

phonetic alphabet *n* **:** a set of symbols used for phonetic transcription

pho·ne·ti·cian \ˌfō-nə-ˈtish-ən\ *n* **:** a specialist in phonetics

pho·net·ics \fə-ˈnet-iks\ *n* **1 :** the study and classification of speech sounds **2 :** the system of speech sounds of a language or group of languages

phon·ic \ˈfän-ik\ *adj* **1 :** of, relating to, or producing sound **2 :** of or relating to the sounds of speech or to phonics — **phon·i·cal·ly** \-i-kə-lē, -klē\ *adv*

phon·ics \ˈfän-iks\ *n* **:** a method of teaching beginners to read and pronounce words by learning the phonetic value of letters, letter groups, and especially syllables

pho·no·gram \ˈfō-nə-ˌgram\ *n* **:** a character or symbol used to represent a word, syllable, or phoneme

pho·no·graph \ˈfō-nə-ˌgraf\ *n* **:** an instrument for reproducing sounds by means of the vibration of a needle following a spiral groove on a revolving disc

pho·no·graph·ic \ˌfō-nə-ˈgraf-ik\ *adj* **1 :** of or relating to phonography **2 :** of or relating to a phonograph — **pho·no·graph·i·cal·ly** \-i-kə-lē, -klē\ *adv*

pho·nog·ra·phy \fō-ˈnäg-rə-fē\ *n* **:** spelling based on pronunciation

pho·nol·o·gy \fə-ˈnäl-ə-jē, fō-\ *n* **:** the science of speech sounds including especially the history and theory of sound changes in a language or in two or more related languages — **pho·no·log·i·cal** \ˌfōn-l-ˈäj-i-kəl *also* ˌfän-l-\ *adj* — **pho·no·log·i·cal·ly** \-kə-lē, -klē\ *adv* — **pho·nol·o·gist** \fə-ˈnäl-ə-jəst, fō-\ *n*

[1]**pho·ny** *also* **pho·ney** \ˈfō-nē\ *adj* **pho·ni·er; -est :** not genuine or real: as **a** (1) **:** intended to deceive or mislead (2) **:** COUNTERFEIT 1 **b :** probably dishonest ⟨a *phony* alibi⟩ **c :** FICTITIOUS ⟨*phony* stories⟩ **d :** FALSE [perhaps from *fawney,* a gilded brass ring used in the "fawney rig," a confidence game, from Irish *fáinne* "ring"] — **pho·ni·ness** \ˈfō-nē-nəs\ *n*

[2]**phony** *also* **phoney** *n, pl* **phonies** *also* **phoneys :** one that is phony

phoo·ey \ˈfü-ē\ *interj* — used to express repudiation or disgust

-phore \ˌfōr, ˌfȯr\ *n combining form* **:** carrier ⟨sema*phore*⟩ [Greek *-phoros,* from *pherein* "to carry"]

phos·gene \ˈfäz-ˌjēn\ *n* **:** a colorless gas of unpleasant odor that

\ə\ **abut**	\au̇\ **out**	\i\ **tip**	\ȯ\ **saw**	\u̇\ **foot**
\ər\ **further**	\ch\ **chin**	\ī\ **life**	\ȯi\ **coin**	\y\ **yet**
\a\ **mat**	\e\ **pet**	\j\ **job**	\th\ **thin**	\yü\ **few**
\ā\ **take**	\ē\ **easy**	\ng\ **sing**	\t͟h\ **this**	\yu̇\ **cure**
\ä\ **cot, cart**	\g\ **go**	\ō\ **bone**	\ü\ **food**	\zh\ **vision**

is a severe irritant of the respiratory system and has been used in chemical warfare [Greek *phōs* "light" + *-genēs* "born, produced"; from its originally having been obtained by the action of sunlight]

phosph- *or* **phospho-** *combining form* : phosphorus ⟨*phosphide*⟩ ⟨*phospholipid*⟩

phos·pha·tase \ˈfäs-fə-ˌtās, -ˌtāz\ *n* : any of various enzymes that accelerate the hydrolysis and synthesis of organic phosphates or the transfer of phosphate groups

phos·phate \ˈfäs-ˌfāt\ *n* **1 a :** a salt, ester, or compound of a phosphoric acid **b :** the anion PO_4^{3-} derived from phosphoric acid **2 :** an effervescent drink of carbonated water with a small amount of phosphoric acid or an acid phosphate flavored with fruit syrup **3 :** a phosphatic material used for fertilizers

phos·phat·ic \fäs-ˈfat-ik, -ˈfāt-\ *adj* : of, relating to, or containing phosphoric acid or phosphates ⟨*phosphatic* fertilizers⟩

phos·pha·tide \ˈfäs-fə-ˌtīd\ *n* : PHOSPHOLIPID — **phos·pha·tid·ic** \ˌfäs-fə-ˈtid-ik\ *adj*

phos·phide \ˈfäs-ˌfīd\ *n* : a compound of phosphorus usually with a more electropositive element or radical

phos·phite \-ˌfīt\ *n* : a salt or ester of phosphorous acid

phos·pho·glyc·er·al·de·hyde \ˈfäs-fō-ˌglis-ə-ˈral-də-ˌhīd\ *n* : a phosphate of glyceraldehyde $C_3H_7PO_6$ formed especially in the anaerobic metabolism of carbohydrates by the splitting of a phosphate of fructose containing two phosphate groups

phos·pho·gly·cer·ic acid \-glis-ˌer-ik-\ *n* : either of two acid phosphates $C_3H_7PO_7$ of glyceric acid that are formed as intermediates in photosynthesis and in carbohydrate metabolism

phos·pho·lip·id \ˌfäs-fō-ˈlip-əd\ *n* : a complex phosphoric ester lipid found in all living cells in association with stored fats

phos·phor \ˈfäs-fər, -ˌfȯr\ *n* **1 :** a phosphorescent substance **2 :** a luminescent substance that emits light when excited by radiation [derived from Greek *phōsphoros* "light-bearing," from *phōs* "light" + *pherein* "to carry, bring"]

phosphor bronze *n* : a bronze of great hardness, elasticity, and toughness that contains a small amount of phosphorus

phos·pho·res·cence \ˌfäs-fə-ˈres-ns\ *n* **1 :** luminescence caused by the absorption of radiations (as electrons or ultraviolet light) and continuing for a noticeable time after these radiations have stopped **2 :** luminescence without easily perceptible heat shown by phosphorus or living organisms (as various bacteria and fungi) — **phos·pho·resce** \ˌfäs-fə-ˈres\ *vi* — **phos·pho·res·cent** \-nt\ *adj*

phos·phor·ic \fäs-ˈfȯr-ik, -ˈfär-\ *adj* : of, relating to, or containing phosphorus especially with a valence higher than in phosphorous compounds

phosphoric acid *n* : an oxygen-containing acid of phosphorus; *esp* : a syrupy or crystalline acid H_3PO_4 used in making fertilizers and as a flavoring in soft drinks

phos·pho·rous \ˈfäs-fə-rəs, -frəs; fäs-ˈfōr-əs, -ˈfȯr-\ *adj* : of, relating to, or containing phosphorus especially with a valence lower than in phosphoric compounds

phosphorous acid *n* : a deliquescent crystalline acid H_3PO_3 used especially as a reducing agent and in making phosphites

phos·pho·rus \ˈfäs-fə-rəs, -frəs\ *n* **1 :** a phosphorescent substance; *esp* : one that glows in the dark **2 :** a nonmetallic chemical element that occurs widely especially as phosphates — see ELEMENT table [New Latin, from Greek *phōsphoros* "light-bearing," from *phōs* "light" + *pherein* "to carry"]

phos·phor·y·late \fäs-ˈfȯr-ə-ˌlāt\ *vt* : to cause (an organic compound) to take up or combine with phosphoric acid or a phosphorus-containing group — **phos·phor·y·la·tion** \ˌfäs-ˌfȯr-ə-ˈlā-shən\ *n* — **phos·phor·y·la·tive** \fäs-ˈfȯr-ə-ˌlāt-iv\ *adj*

phot- *or* **photo-** *combining form* **1 :** light ⟨*photo*graph⟩ ⟨*photon*⟩ **2 :** photograph : photographic ⟨*photo*engraving⟩ **3 :** photoelectric ⟨*photo*cell⟩ [Greek *phōt-, phōs*]

pho·tic \ˈfōt-ik\ *adj* **1 :** of, relating to, or involving light especially in relation to organisms ⟨a *photic* response⟩ **2 :** penetrated by light especially of the sun ⟨*photic* layers of the sea⟩

pho·to \ˈfōt-ō\ *n, pl* **photos** : PHOTOGRAPH — **photo** *vb* — **photo** *adj*

pho·to·cell \ˈfōt-ə-ˌsel\ *n* : PHOTOELECTRIC CELL

pho·to·chem·is·try \ˌfōt-ō-ˈkem-ə-strē\ *n* **1 :** a branch of chemistry that deals with the effect of radiant energy in producing chemical changes **2 :** photochemical properties or processes — **pho·to·chem·i·cal** \-ˈkem-i-kəl\ *adj*

pho·to·com·pose \-kəm-ˈpōz\ *vt* : to set (as reading matter) by photocomposition — **pho·to·com·pos·er** *n*

pho·to·com·po·si·tion \-ˌkäm-pə-ˈzish-ən\ *n* : composition of reading matter directly on film or photosensitive paper for reproduction

pho·to·copy \ˈfōt-ə-ˌkäp-ē\ *n* : a copy of usually printed matter made using a process in which an image is formed by the action of light on an electrically charged surface — **photocopy** *vb*

pho·to·du·pli·cate \ˌfōt-ō-ˈdü-plə-ˌkāt, -ˈdyü-\ *vb* : PHOTOCOPY — **pho·to·du·pli·cate** \-pli-kət\ *n*

pho·to·elec·tric \ˌfōt-ō-i-ˈlek-trik\ *adj* : relating to or utilizing electrical effects due to the interaction of light with matter — **pho·to·elec·tri·cal·ly** \-tri-kə-lē, -klē\ *adv*

photoelectric cell *n* : a device whose electrical properties are modified by the action of light

photoelectric effect *n* : the emission of free electrons from a metal surface when light strikes it

pho·to·elec·tron \ˌfōt-ō-i-ˈlek-ˌträn\ *n* : an electron released in the photoelectric effect

pho·to·emis·sive \-i-ˈmis-iv\ *adj* : emitting electrons when exposed to radiation (as light)

pho·to·en·grave \-in-ˈgrāv\ *vt* : to make a photoengraving of — **pho·to·en·grav·er** *n*

pho·to·en·grav·ing \-ˈgrā-ving\ *n* **1 :** a process for making linecuts and halftone cuts by photographing an image on a metal plate and then etching **2 a :** a plate made by photoengraving **b :** a print made from such a plate

photo finish *n* **1 :** a race or finish in which contestants are so close that a photograph of them as they cross the finish line has to be examined to determine the winner **2 :** a close contest

pho·to·flash \ˈfōt-ə-flash\ *n* : FLASHBULB

pho·to·flood \-ˌfləd\ *n* : a high-intensity electric lamp used in taking photographs

pho·to·ge·nic \ˌfōt-ə-ˈjen-ik, -ˈjēn-\ *adj* : suitable for being photographed : likely to photograph well ⟨a *photogenic* child⟩ — **pho·to·ge·ni·cal·ly** \-i-kə-lē, -klē\ *adv*

pho·to·gram·me·try \ˌfōt-ə-ˈgram-ə-trē\ *n* : the science of making reliable measurements by the use of usually aerial photographs in surveying and map making

[1]**pho·to·graph** \ˈfōt-ə-ˌgraf\ *n* : a picture or likeness obtained by photography

[2]**photograph** *vb* **1 :** to take a photograph of **2 :** to take photographs **3 :** to be photographed

pho·tog·ra·pher \fə-ˈtäg-rə-fər\ *n* : one that practices or is skilled in photography; *esp* : one who takes photographs as a business

pho·to·graph·ic \ˌfōt-ə-ˈgraf-ik\ *adj* **1 :** relating to, obtained by, or used in photography ⟨*photographic* supplies⟩ **2 :** representing nature and humans with the exactness of a photograph **3 :** capable of retaining vivid impressions ⟨a *photographic* memory⟩ — **pho·to·graph·i·cal·ly** \-i-kə-lē, -klē\ *adv*

pho·tog·ra·phy \fə-ˈtäg-rə-fē\ *n* : the art or process of producing images by the action of light or other radiant energy on a sensitive surface (as film or a CCD chip)

pho·to·gra·vure \ˌfōt-ə-grə-ˈvyu̇r\ *n* : a process for making prints from an engraved plate prepared by photographic methods — **photogravure** *vt*

pho·to·jour·nal·ism \ˌfōt-ō-ˈjər-nə-ˌliz-əm\ *n* : journalism in which written copy is subordinate to pictorial usually photographic presentation of news stories; *also* : news photography — **pho·to·jour·nal·ist** \-list\ *n* — **pho·to·jour·nal·is·tic** \-ˌjər-nə-ˈlis-tik\ *adj*

pho·to·li·thog·ra·phy \ˌfōt-ō-lith-ˈäg-rə-fē\ *n* : lithography in which photographically prepared plates are used — **pho·to·litho·graph·ic** \-ˌlith-ə-ˈgraf-ik\ *adj*

pho·tol·y·sis \fō-ˈtäl-ə-səs\ *n* : chemical decomposition by the action of radiant energy (as light)

pho·to·me·chan·i·cal \ˌfōt-ō-mi-ˈkan-i-kəl\ *adj* : relating to or involving any of various processes for producing printed matter from photographically prepared plates

pho·tom·e·ter \fō-ˈtäm-ət-ər\ *n* : an instrument for measuring luminous intensity, illumination, or brightness

pho·to·met·ric \ˌfōt-ə-ˈme-trik\ *adj* : of or relating to photometry or the photometer — **pho·to·met·ri·cal·ly** \-tri-kə-lē, -klē\ *adv*

pho·tom·e·try \fō-ˈtäm-ə-trē\ *n* : a branch of science that deals with measurement of the intensity of light

pho·to·mi·cro·graph \ˌfōt-ə-ˈmī-krə-ˌgraf\ *n* : a photograph of a microscope image — **pho·to·mi·cro·graph·ic** \-ˌmī-krə-ˈgraf-ik\ *adj* — **pho·to·mi·crog·ra·phy** \-mī-ˈkräg-rə-fē\ *n*

pho·to·mon·tage \-män-ˈtäzh, -mōⁿ-, -ˈtȧzh\ *n* : montage using photographic images; *also* : a picture made by photomontage

pho·to·mu·ral \ˌfōt-ō-ˈmyu̇r-əl\ *n* **:** a greatly enlarged photograph used on walls especially as decoration
pho·ton \ˈfō-ˌtän\ *n* **:** a quantum of electromagnetic radiation
pho·ton·ics \fō-ˈtän-iks\ *n* **:** a branch of physics that deals with the properties and applications of photons especially as used to transmit information
pho·to–off·set \ˌfōt-ō-ˈȯf-ˌset\ *n* **:** offset printing from photolithographic printing plates
photo opportunity *n* **:** a situation or event that lends itself to and is often arranged expressly for the taking of pictures that give favorable publicity to the individuals photographed
pho·to·pe·ri·od \ˌfōt-ə-ˈpir-ē-əd\ *n* **:** the recurring cycle of alternating periods of lightness and darkness as it affects the growth and functioning of an organism — **pho·to·pe·ri·od·ic** \-ˌpir-ē-ˈäd-ik\ *adj* — **pho·to·pe·ri·od·i·cal·ly** \-i-kə-lē, -klē\ *adv*
pho·to·pe·ri·od·ism \-ˈpir-ē-ə-ˌdiz-əm\ *n* **:** a plant's or animal's response or capacity to respond to photoperiod
pho·to·phos·phor·y·la·tion \ˈfōt-ō-ˌfäs-ˌfȯr-ə-ˈlā-shən\ *n* **:** the formation of ATP from ADP and phosphate in photosynthesis using radiant energy
pho·to·play \ˈfōt-ō-ˌplā\ *n* **:** MOVIE 2
pho·to·poly·mer \ˌfōt-ō-ˈpäl-ə-mər\ *n* **:** a photosensitive plastic used to make printing plates
pho·to·re·cep·tor \ˌfōt-ō-ri-ˈsep-tər\ *n* **:** a receptor for light stimuli — **pho·to·re·cep·tion** \-ˈsep-shən\ *n* — **pho·to·re·cep·tive** \-ˈsep-tiv\ *adj*
pho·to·sen·si·tive \-ˈsen-sət-iv, -ˈsen-stiv\ *adj* **:** sensitive or sensitized to the action of radiant energy (as light) ⟨*photosensitive* paper⟩ — **pho·to·sen·si·tiv·i·ty** \-ˌsen-sə-ˈtiv-ət-ē\ *n*
pho·to·sen·si·tize \-ˈsen-sə-ˌtīz\ *vt* **:** to make photosensitive — **pho·to·sen·si·ti·za·tion** \-ˌsen-sət-ə-ˈzā-shən\ *n*
pho·to·shop \ˈfōt-ō-ˌshäp\ *vt* **-shopped; -shop·ping** *often cap* **:** to alter (as a digital image) with computer software [*Photoshop*, trademark for image manipulation software]
pho·to·sphere \ˈfōt-ə-ˌsfiər\ *n* **:** the luminous surface of the sun or a star — **pho·to·spher·ic** \ˌfōt-ə-ˈsfiər-ik, -ˈsfer-\ *adj*
[1]**pho·to·stat** \ˈfōt-ə-ˌstat\ *n* **:** a device for making a photographic copy of graphic matter; *also* **:** a copy made by a photostat
[2]**photostat** *vb* **:** to copy by a photostat — **pho·to·stat·ic** \ˌfōt-ə-ˈstat-ik\ *adj*
pho·to·syn·the·sis \ˌfōt-ə-ˈsin-thə-səs, -ˈsint-\ *n* **:** the process by which plants and some bacteria and protists that contain chlorophyll make carbohydrates from water and from carbon dioxide in the air in the presence of light — **pho·to·syn·the·size** \-ˌsīz\ *vb* — **pho·to·syn·thet·ic** \-sin-ˈthet-ik\ *adj* — **pho·to·syn·thet·i·cal·ly** \-ˈthet-i-kə-lē, -klē\ *adv*
pho·to·sys·tem \ˈfōt-ō-ˌsis-təm\ *n* **:** either of two photochemical reaction sites occurring in chloroplasts: **a :** one that absorbs light with a wavelength of about 700 nanometers — called also *photosystem I* **b :** one that absorbs light with a wavelength of about 680 nanometers — called also *photosystem II*
pho·to·tax·is \ˌfōt-ə-ˈtak-səs\ *n* **:** a taxis in which light is the directive factor — **pho·to·tac·tic** \-ˈtak-tik\ *adj*
pho·tot·ro·pism \fō-ˈtä-trə-ˌpiz-əm\ *n* **:** a tropism in which light is the orienting stimulus — **pho·to·trop·ic** \ˌfōt-ə-ˈträp-ik\ *adj*
phrag·mi·tes \frag-ˈmī-ˌtēz\ *n* **:** any of a genus of tall reeds with large feathery flower clusters [New Latin, from Greek *phragmitēs* "growing in hedges," from *phragma* "fence, hedge"]
phras·al \ˈfrā-zəl\ *adj* **:** of, relating to, or consisting of a phrase
[1]**phrase** \ˈfrāz\ *n* **1 :** a manner of expression **:** DICTION **2 :** a brief expression; *esp* **:** one commonly used **3 :** a musical unit typically two to four measures long and closing with a cadence **4 :** a group of two or more words that express a single idea but do not by themselves make up a complete sentence ⟨"over the fence" in "hit it over the fence" is an adverbial *phrase*⟩ [Latin *phrasis*, from Greek, from *phrazein* "to point out, explain, tell"]
[2]**phrase** *vt* **1 a :** to express in words **:** WORD ⟨*phrased* his thoughts well⟩ **b :** to designate by a descriptive word or phrase **:** TERM **2 :** to divide into melodic phrases
phrase·ol·o·gy \ˌfrā-zē-ˈäl-ə-jē\ *n* **1 :** manner of organizing words and phrases into longer elements **2 :** choice of words
phras·ing \ˈfrā-ziŋ\ *n* **1 :** PHRASEOLOGY 1 **2 :** the act, method, or result of grouping notes into musical phrases
phre·net·ic *archaic variant of* FRENETIC
phre·nol·o·gy \fri-ˈnäl-ə-jē\ *n* **:** the study of the conformation of the skull based on the belief that it is indicative of mental faculties and character [Greek *phrēn* "diaphragm, mind"] — **phre·no·log·i·cal** \ˌfren-l-ˈäj-i-kəl, ˌfrēn-\ *adj* — **phre·nol·o·gist** \fri-ˈnäl-ə-jəst\ *n*

phy·co·cy·a·nin \ˌfī-kō-ˈsī-ə-nən\ *n* **:** any of the bluish green protein pigments of blue-green algae [Greek *phykos* "seaweed"]
phy·co·er·y·thrin \-ˈer-ə-thrən\ *n* **:** any of the red protein pigments of red algae [derived from Greek *phykos* "seaweed" + *erythros* "red"]
phy·col·o·gy \fī-ˈkäl-ə-jē\ *n* **:** the study or science of algae [Greek *phykos* "seaweed"] — **phy·co·log·i·cal** \ˌfī-kə-ˈläj-i-kəl\ *adj*
phy·co·my·cete \-ˈmī-ˌsēt, -mī-ˈsēt\ *n* **:** any of a large class (Phycomycetes) of lower fungi that are in many respects similar to algae [derived from Greek *phykos* "seaweed" + *mykēs* "fungus"] — **phy·co·my·ce·tous** \-mī-ˈsēt-əs\ *adj*
phyl- *or* **phylo-** *combining form* **:** tribe **:** race **:** phylum ⟨*phylogeny*⟩ [Greek *phylē, phylon* "race, tribe"]
phy·lac·tery \fə-ˈlak-tə-rē, -trē\ *n, pl* **-ter·ies 1 :** one of two small square leather boxes containing slips inscribed with scripture passages and worn by observant Jewish men and especially adherents of Orthodox Judaism during morning weekday prayers **2 :** CHARM 2, AMULET [derived from Greek *phylaktērion* "amulet, phylactery," from *phylassein* "to guard," from *phylax* "guard"]
phy·let·ic \fī-ˈlet-ik\ *adj* **:** of or relating to evolutionary change in a single line of descent without branching [derived from *phyl-*] — **phy·let·i·cal·ly** \-ˈlet-i-kə-lē, -klē\ *adv*
-phyll \ˌfil\ *n combining form* **:** leaf ⟨sporo*phyll*⟩ [Greek *phyllon* "leaf"]
phyl·lo \ˈfē-lō, ˈfī-\ *n* **:** extremely thin dough that is layered to produce a flaky pastry [Modern Greek, "sheet of pastry dough," literally, "leaf," from Greek *phyllon*]
phyl·lo·tax·is \ˌfil-ə-ˈtak-səs\ *also* **phyl·lo·taxy** \ˈfil-ə-ˌtak-sē\ *n* **:** the arrangement of leaves on a stem and in relation to one another [derived from Greek *phyllon* "leaf" + *taxis* "arrangement, order," from *tassein* "to arrange"]
phyl·lox·e·ra \ˌfil-ˌäk-ˈsir-ə, fə-ˈläk-sə-rə\ *n* **:** any of various plant lice; *esp* **:** one destructive to grapevines [derived from Greek *phyllon* "leaf" + *xēros* "dry"]

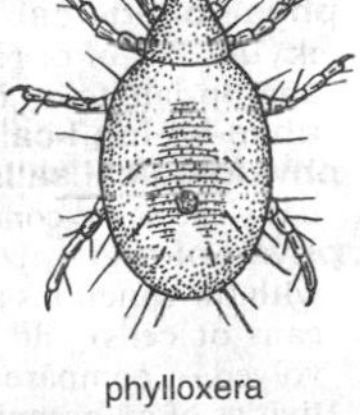
phylloxera

phy·log·e·ny \fī-ˈläj-ə-nē\ *n, pl* **-nies :** the evolutionary development of a group of related organisms as distinguished from the development of an individual organism — **phy·lo·ge·net·ic** \ˌfī-lə-jə-ˈnet-ik\ *adj* — **phy·lo·ge·net·i·cal·ly** \-i-kə-lē, -klē\ *adv*
phy·lum \ˈfī-ləm\ *n, pl* **phy·la** \-lə\ **:** a group of animals or in some classifications plants sharing one or more fundamental characteristics that set them apart from all other animals and plants and forming a primary category in biological classification that ranks above the class and below the kingdom — compare DIVISION [New Latin, from Greek *phylon* "tribe, race"]
phys ed \ˈfiz-ˈed\ *n* **:** PHYSICAL EDUCATION
physi- *or* **physio-** *combining form* **1 :** nature ⟨*physio*graphy⟩ **2 :** physical ⟨*physio*therapy⟩ [Greek *physis*]
[1]**phys·ic** \ˈfiz-ik\ *n* **1 :** the practice or profession of medicine **2 :** a medicinal agent or preparation; *esp* **:** PURGATIVE
[2]**physic** *vt* **phys·icked** \-ikt\; **phys·ick·ing** \-i-kiŋ\; **phys·ics** *or* **phys·icks :** to treat with or administer medicine to; *esp* **:** PURGE
phys·i·cal \ˈfiz-i-kəl\ *adj* **1 :** of or relating to nature or the laws of nature **2 :** of or relating to material things **:** not mental or spiritual **3 :** of or relating to natural science **4 :** of or relating to physics **5 a :** of or relating to the body **:** BODILY ⟨*physical* abuse⟩ **b :** preoccupied with the body or its needs ⟨*physical* appetites⟩ **c :** SEXUAL ⟨*physical* attraction⟩ ***synonyms*** see MATERIAL — **phys·i·cal·ly** \-kə-lē, -klē\ *adv*
physical anthropology *n* **:** a division of anthropology concerned with the study of human biological evolution and variation — compare CULTURAL ANTHROPOLOGY
physical education *n* **:** instruction in the care and development of the body including training in hygiene, exercises, and athletic games

\ə\ **abut**	\au̇\ **out**	\i\ **tip**	\ȯ\ **saw**	\u̇\ **foot**
\ər\ **further**	\ch\ **chin**	\ī\ **life**	\ȯi\ **coin**	\y\ **yet**
\a\ **mat**	\e\ **pet**	\j\ **job**	\th\ **thin**	\yü\ **few**
\ā\ **take**	\ē\ **easy**	\ŋ\ **sing**	\t͟h\ **this**	\yu̇\ **cure**
\ä\ **cot, cart**	\g\ **go**	\ō\ **bone**	\ü\ **food**	\zh\ **vision**

physical examination *n* : an examination of the bodily functions and condition of a person

physical geography *n* : a branch of geography that deals with the physical features and changes of the earth

physical science *n* : any of the natural sciences (as physics, geology, or astronomy) that deal primarily with nonliving materials

physical therapy *n* : the treatment of disease, injury, or disability by physical and mechanical means (as massage, exercise, water, or heat) — **physical therapist** *n*

phy·si·cian \fə-ˈzish-ən\ *n* : a person skilled in the art of healing; *esp* : one educated and licensed to practice medicine

physician assistant *n* : a person certified to provide basic medical services usually under the supervision of a licensed physician — called also *physician's assistant*

phys·i·cist \ˈfiz-ə-səst\ *n* : a specialist in the science of physics

phys·ics \ˈfiz-iks\ *n* **1** : a science that deals with matter and energy and their interactions in the fields of mechanics, heat, light, electricity, sound, and nuclear phenomena **2** : physical composition, properties, or processes ⟨the *physics* of sound⟩ [Latin *physica,* pl., "natural science," from Greek *physika,* from *physikos* "of nature," from *physis* "growth, nature," from *phyein* "to bring forth"]

phys·i·og·no·my \ˌfiz-ē-ˈäg-nə-mē, -ˈä-nə-\ *n, pl* **-mies** **1** : the art of discovering temperament and character from outward appearance **2** : the facial features held to show qualities of mind or character **3** : external aspect; *also* : inner character or quality revealed outwardly [derived from Greek *physiognōmonia,* from *physiognōmōn* "judging character by the features," from *physis* "nature, physique, appearance" + *gnōmōn* "interpreter," from *gignōskein* "to know"] — **phys·i·og·nom·ic** \-ē-əg-ˈnäm-ik, -ə-ˈnäm-\ *also* **phys·i·og·nom·i·cal** \-i-kəl\ *adj* — **phys·i·og·nom·i·cal·ly** \-i-kə-lē, -klē\ *adv*

phys·i·og·ra·phy \ˌfiz-ē-ˈäg-rə-fē\ *n* : the study of landforms : PHYSICAL GEOGRAPHY — **phys·i·og·ra·pher** \-rə-fər\ *n* — **phys·io·graph·ic** \ˌfiz-ē-ə-ˈgraf-ik\ *adj*

phys·i·o·log·i·cal \ˌfiz-ē-ə-ˈläj-i-kəl\ *or* **phys·i·o·log·ic** \-ˈläj-ik\ *adj* **1** : of or relating to physiology **2** : characteristic of or appropriate to an organism's healthy or normal functioning — **phys·i·o·log·i·cal·ly** \-i-kə-lē, -klē\ *adv*

physiological saline *n* : a solution of a salt or salts with essentially the same concentration of ions as tissue fluids or blood

phys·i·ol·o·gy \ˌfiz-ē-ˈäl-ə-jē\ *n* **1** : a branch of biology dealing with the functions and activities of life or of living matter (as organs or cells) and of the physical and chemical processes involved — compare ANATOMY **2** : the organic functions and activities of an organism or any of its parts or of a particular bodily process — **phys·i·ol·o·gist** \ˌfiz-ē-ˈäl-ə-jəst\ *n*

phys·io·ther·a·py \ˌfiz-ē-ō-ˈther-ə-pē\ *n* : PHYSICAL THERAPY

phy·sique \fə-ˈzēk\ *n* : the build of a person's body : physical constitution [French, from *physique* "physical"]

phyt- *or* **phyto-** *combining form* : plant ⟨*phyto*plankton⟩ [Greek *phyton,* from *phyein* "to bring forth"]

-phyte \ˌfīt\ *n combining form* **1** : plant having a (specified) characteristic or habitat ⟨xero*phyte*⟩ **2** : pathological growth

phy·to·chrome \ˈfī-tə-ˌkrōm\ *n* : a light-sensitive pigmented plant protein that controls many plant processes (as flowering and seed germination)

phy·to·plank·ton \ˌfīt-ō-ˈplang-tən, -ˈplangk-, -ˌtän\ *n* : plankton that is composed of plants — **phy·to·plank·ton·ic** \-plang-ˈtän-ik, -plangk-\ *adj*

[1]pi \ˈpī\ *n, pl* **pis** \ˈpīz\ **1** : the 16th letter of the Greek alphabet — Π or π **2 a** : the symbol π denoting the ratio of the circumference of a circle to its diameter **b** : the ratio itself having a value rounded to eight decimal places of 3.14159265

[2]pi *vb* **pied; pi·ing** **1** : to spill or throw (type or type matter) into disorder **2** : to become pied [origin unknown]

pia ma·ter \ˈpī-ə-ˌmāt-ər, ˈpē-ə-ˌmät-\ *n* : the innermost and thin vascular membrane investing the brain and spinal cord [Medieval Latin, from Latin, "tender mother"]

pi·a·nis·si·mo \ˌpē-ə-ˈnis-ə-ˌmō\ *adv or adj* : very softly — used as a direction in music [Italian, from *piano* "softly"]

pi·an·ist \pē-ˈan-əst, ˈpē-ə-nəst\ *n* : a person who plays the piano

[1]pi·a·no \pē-ˈän-ō\ *adv or adj* : in a soft or quiet manner — used as a direction in music [Italian, from Late Latin *planus* "smooth," from Latin, "level"]

[2]pi·ano \pē-ˈan-ō\ *n, pl* **-an·os** : a musical instrument having steel-wire strings that sound when struck by felt-covered hammers operated from a keyboard [Italian, short for *pianoforte,* from *piano e forte* "soft and loud"; from the fact that its tones could be varied in loudness]

Word History A harpsichord is played by means of a mechanism that plucks the strings, so it is not possible to achieve fine gradations of loudness. Feeling the need to overcome this drawback in the harpsichord, a Florentine named Bartolommeo Cristofori around the year 1709 invented a mechanism by means of which the strings of the instrument are struck by felt-covered hammers. This device allows the player more control over the loudness of his playing. Cristofori called his new instrument a *gravicembalo col piano e forte,* that is "a harpsichord with soft and loud." The instrument came to be designated by the term *piano e forte* or by contraction *pianoforte,* which was subsequently shortened to *piano.*

pi·ano·forte \pē-ˈan-ə-ˌfōrt, -ˌfȯrt, -ˌfȯrt-ē\ *n* : PIANO [Italian]

pi·as·tre *also* **pi·as·ter** \pē-ˈas-tər, -ˈäs-\ *n* **1** : PIECE OF EIGHT **2 a** : a monetary unit of Egypt, Lebanon, and Syria equal to $\frac{1}{100}$ pound **b** : a coin representing one piastre [French *piastre*]

pi·az·za \pē-ˈaz-ə, *1 is usually* -ˈat-sə, -ˈät-\ *n, pl* **piazzas** *or* **pi·az·ze** \-ˈat-sā, -ˈät-\ **1** *pl piazze* : an open square especially in an Italian town **2 a** : an arcaded and roofed gallery **b** *dialect* : VERANDA, PORCH [Italian, from Latin *platea* "broad street," from Greek *plateia,* from *platys* "broad, flat"]

pi·broch \ˈpē-ˌbräk, -ˌbräk\ *n* : a set of martial or mournful variations for the Scottish bagpipe [Scottish Gaelic *pìobaireachd* "pipe music"]

[1]pi·ca \ˈpī-kə\ *n* : an abnormal desire to eat substances (as chalk or ashes) not normally eaten [New Latin, from Latin, "magpie"]

[2]pica *n* **1** : 12-point type **2** : a unit equal to 12 points or about $\frac{1}{6}$ inch (about 4.2 millimeters) used in measuring typographical material **3** : a typewriter type providing 10 characters to the inch [probably from Medieval Latin, "collection of church rules"]

pic·a·dor \ˈpik-ə-ˌdȯr, ˌpik-ə-ˈ\ *n, pl* **picadors** \-ˌdȯrz, -ˈdȯrz\ *or* **pic·a·do·res** \ˌpik-ə-ˈdōr-ēz, -ˈdȯr-\ : a horseman in a bullfight who prods the bull with a lance to weaken its neck and shoulder muscles [Spanish, from *picar* "to prick"]

pi·ca·resque \ˌpik-ə-ˈresk, ˌpē-kə-\ *adj* : of or relating to rogues or rascals; *also* : of, relating to, suggesting, or being a type of fiction dealing with the adventures of a usually mischievous or dishonest character [Spanish *picaresco,* from *pícaro* "rogue"]

[1]pic·a·yune \ˌpik-ē-ˈün, -ˈyün\ *n* **1** : a Spanish half real piece formerly current in the southern U.S. **2** : something trivial [French *picaillon* "halfpenny," from Occitan *picaion,* from *picaio* "money," from *pica* "to jingle"]

[2]picayune *adj* : of little value : PALTRY; *also* : PETTY 3

pic·ca·lil·li \ˌpik-ə-ˈlil-ē\ *n* : a relish of chopped vegetables and spices [probably alteration of *pickle*]

pic·co·lo \ˈpik-ə-ˌlō\ *n, pl* **-los** : a small shrill flute pitched an octave higher than an ordinary flute [Italian, short for *piccolo flauto* "small flute"] — **pic·co·lo·ist** \-əst\ *n*

[1]pick \ˈpik\ *vb* **1** : to pierce, penetrate, or break up with a pointed tool **2 a** : to clear or free from something by or as if by plucking ⟨*pick* meat from a bone⟩ **b** : to gather by plucking ⟨*pick* berries⟩ **c** : to pluck with a pick or with the fingers ⟨*pick* a guitar⟩ ⟨*pick* a tune on the banjo⟩ **3 a** : CHOOSE 1, SELECT ⟨*pick* out a suit⟩ ⟨*pick* a book⟩ **b** : to make (one's way) slowly and carefully ⟨*picked* their way through the rubble⟩ **4** : to steal or pilfer from ⟨*pick* pockets⟩ **5** : PROVOKE ⟨*pick* a quarrel⟩ **6** : to dig at or into ⟨*picking* his teeth⟩ **7** : to eat sparingly or in a finicky manner ⟨*picked* at her dinner⟩ **8** : to unlock without a key ⟨*pick* a lock⟩ [Middle French *piquer* "to prick," perhaps derived from Latin *picus* "woodpecker"] — **pick·er** *n* — **pick and choose** : to select carefully and deliberately — **pick on** **1** : TEASE, HARASS ⟨*pick on* a smaller child⟩ **2** : to single out for a special purpose or for particular attention

[2]pick *n* **1** : a blow or stroke with a pointed instrument **2 a** : the act or privilege of choosing or selecting ⟨take your *pick*⟩ **b** : the best or choicest one ⟨the *pick* of the crop⟩ **c** : one that is picked ⟨his *pick* for vice president⟩

[3]pick *n* **1** : PICKAX **2** : any of several slender pointed implements for picking or chipping **3** : a small thin piece (as of plastic or metal) used to pluck a stringed instrument **4** : a comb with long widely spaced teeth used to give height to a hairstyle [Middle English *pik*]

pickaback *variant of* PIGGYBACK

pick·ax \ˈpik-ˌaks\ *n* : a heavy tool with a wooden handle and a curved or straight blade pointed at one or both ends that is used especially in loosening or breaking up soil or rock [Middle English *pecaxe, pikois,* from Medieval French *picois,* from *pic* "pick"]

pick·er·el \ˈpik-rəl, -ə-rəl\ *n, pl* **pickerel** *or* **pickerels** **1 :** either of two fishes resembling but smaller than the related pike **2 :** WALLEYE 2 [Middle English *pikerel,* from *pike*]

pick·er·el·weed \-ˌwēd\ *n* **:** a blue-flowered shallow-water herb chiefly of the eastern U.S. and Canada with large arrow-shaped leaves

pickerelweed

[1]pick·et \ˈpik-ət\ *n* **1 :** a pointed stake or post (as for a fence) **2 :** a soldier or a detachment of soldiers posted as a guard against surprise attack **3 :** a person posted by a labor organization at a place of work affected by a strike; *also* **:** a person posted for a demonstration or protest [French *piquet,* from *piquer* "to prick"]

[2]picket *vb* **1 :** to enclose, fence, or fortify with pickets **2 a :** to guard with a picket **b :** to post as a picket **3 :** TETHER **4 a :** to post pickets or act as a picket at ⟨*picket* a factory⟩ **b :** to serve as a picket — **pick·et·er** *n*

picket line *n* **:** a line of persons picketing a business, organization, or institution

pick·ings \ˈpik-iŋz, -ənz\ *n pl* **1 :** something available or left over; *esp* **:** eatable remains **2 :** yield or return for effort expended ⟨easy *pickings*⟩ ⟨slim *pickings*⟩

[1]pick·le \ˈpik-əl\ *n* **1 :** a solution or bath for preserving or cleaning; *esp* **:** a brine or vinegar solution in which foods are preserved **2 :** a difficult situation **:** PLIGHT **3 :** a food item (as a cucumber) preserved in brine or vinegar [Middle English *pekille*]

[2]pickle *vt* **pick·led; pick·ling** \ˈpik-liŋ, -ə-liŋ\ **:** to treat, preserve, or clean in or with a pickle

pickled *adj* **1 :** preserved with pickle ⟨*pickled* herring⟩ **2 :** DRUNK 1

pick·lock \ˈpik-ˌläk\ *n* **1 :** a tool for picking locks **2 :** BURGLAR

pick off *vt* **1 :** to shoot or bring down one by one **2 :** to catch (a base runner) off base with a quick throw by the pitcher or catcher

pick out *vt* **1 :** to make out **:** DISTINGUISH **2 :** to play the notes of by ear or one by one ⟨*picking out* tunes on the piano⟩

pick over *vt* **:** to examine in order to select the best or remove the unwanted

pick·pock·et \ˈpik-ˌpäk-ət\ *n* **:** a person who steals from pockets

pick·up \ˈpik-ˌəp\ *n* **1 a :** a revival of activity ⟨a business *pickup*⟩ **b :** ACCELERATION **2 :** a temporary chance acquaintance **3 :** the conversion of mechanical movements into electrical impulses in the reproduction of sound; *also* **:** a device (as on a phonograph) for making such conversion **4 a :** the reception of sound or an image into a radio or television transmitting apparatus for conversion into electrical signals **b :** a device (as a microphone or a television camera) for converting sound or the image of a scene into electrical signals **5 :** a light truck having an open body with low sides — called also *pickup truck*

pick up \pik-ˈəp, ˈpik-\ *vb* **1 a :** to take hold of and lift ⟨*pick up* sticks⟩ **b :** to gather together **:** COLLECT ⟨*picked up* every piece⟩ **c :** to clean up **:** TIDY **2 :** to take into a vehicle ⟨the bus *picked up* passengers⟩ **3 a :** to acquire casually or by chance ⟨*pick up* a habit⟩ **b :** to acquire by study or experience **:** LEARN ⟨*picked up* a new language while abroad⟩ **c :** to obtain especially by payment **:** BUY ⟨*picked up* some groceries⟩ **d :** to accept for the purpose of paying ⟨*pick up* the tab⟩ **4 a :** to strike up a casual acquaintance with (a previously unknown person) **b :** to take into custody ⟨was *picked up* by the police⟩ **5 :** to bring within range of sight or hearing **6 :** to resume after a break **:** CONTINUE ⟨*pick up* the discussion tomorrow⟩ **7 :** to recover or increase speed, vigor, or activity ⟨business is *picking up*⟩ **8 :** to pack up one's belongings ⟨*pick up* and leave⟩

picky \ˈpik-ē\ *adj* **pick·i·er; -est :** FUSSY 2b, FINICKY

[1]pic·nic \ˈpik-nik, -ˌnik\ *n* **1 :** an excursion or outing with food usually taken along and eaten in the open **2 :** something pleasant or easy **3 :** a shoulder of pork that is often smoked and boned [French *pique-nique*] — **pic·nic·ky** \-ē\ *adj*

[2]picnic *vi* **pic·nicked; pic·nick·ing :** to go on a picnic **:** eat in picnic fashion — **pic·nick·er** *n*

pi·co- \ˈpē-kō, -kə\ *combining form* **:** one trillionth part of [probably from Spanish *pico* "small amount"]

[1]pi·cot \ˈpē-kō, pē-ˈ\ *n* **:** one of a series of small ornamental loops forming an edging on ribbon or lace [French, literally, "small point," from Middle French *pic* "prick," from *piquer* "to prick"]

[2]picot *vt* **pi·coted** \-kōd, -ˈkōd\; **pi·cot·ing** \-kō-iŋ, -ˈkō-\ **:** to finish with a picot

pic·ric acid \ˌpik-rik-\ *n* **:** a bitter toxic explosive yellow crystalline strong acid used especially in high explosives, as a dye, or in medicine [Greek *pikros* "bitter"]

Pict \ˈpikt\ *n* **:** a member of a people of the north of Scotland who are first noted in historical records in the late 3rd century and who became amalgamated with the Scots in the mid-8th century [Late Latin *Picti* "Picts"] — **Pict·ish** \ˈpik-tish\ *adj or n*

pic·to·gram \ˈpik-tə-ˌgram\ *n* **:** PICTOGRAPH

pic·to·graph \-ˌgraf\ *n* **1 :** an ancient or prehistoric drawing or painting on a rock wall **2 :** one of the symbols belonging to a system of picture writing **3 :** a diagram representing statistical data by pictorial forms [Latin *pictus,* past participle of *pingere* "to paint" + English *-o-* + *-graph*] — **pic·to·graph·ic** \ˌpik-tə-ˈgraf-ik\ *adj*

pictograph 1

pic·tog·ra·phy \pik-ˈtäg-rə-fē\ *n* **:** PICTURE WRITING 1

pic·to·ri·al \pik-ˈtōr-ē-əl, -ˈtȯr-\ *adj* **1 :** of or relating to a painter, a painting, or the painting or drawing of pictures ⟨*pictorial* perspective⟩ ⟨*pictorial* art⟩ **2 a :** of, relating to, or consisting of pictures ⟨*pictorial* records⟩ **b :** illustrated by pictures ⟨*pictorial* magazines⟩ **3 :** suggesting or communicating visual images ⟨*pictorial* poetry⟩ [Late Latin *pictorius,* from Latin *pictor* "painter," from *pingere* "to paint"] — **pic·to·ri·al·ly** \-ē-ə-lē\ *adv*

[1]pic·ture \ˈpik-chər\ *n* **1 :** a representation made on a surface (as by painting, drawing, or photography) **2 a :** a very vivid description **b :** a mental image **3 a :** an exact likeness **:** COPY **b :** a tangible or visible representation **:** EMBODIMENT ⟨the *picture* of health⟩ **4 a :** a transitory visible image (as on a television screen) **b :** MOTION PICTURE 1 **5 :** a state of affairs **:** SITUATION ⟨the bleak economic *picture*⟩ [Latin *pictura,* from *pictus,* past participle of *pingere* "to paint"]

[2]picture *vt* **pic·tured; pic·tur·ing** \ˈpik-chə-riŋ, ˈpik-shriŋ\ **1 :** to make a picture of (as by drawing) **:** DEPICT **2 :** to describe vividly **3 :** to form a mental image of **:** IMAGINE

picture hat *n* **:** a woman's dressy hat with a broad brim

picture–perfect *adj* **:** completely flawless **:** PERFECT ⟨made a *picture-perfect* landing⟩

picture–postcard *adj* **:** PICTURESQUE ⟨a *picture-postcard* village⟩

pic·tur·esque \ˌpik-chə-ˈresk\ *adj* **1 :** resembling a picture **:** suggesting a painted scene ⟨*picturesque* scenery⟩ **2 :** CHARMING, QUAINT ⟨a *picturesque* village⟩ **3 :** evoking striking mental images ⟨a *picturesque* account of the event⟩ ***synonyms*** see GRAPHIC — **pic·tur·esque·ly** *adv* — **pic·tur·esque·ness** *n*

picture tube *n* **:** a cathode-ray tube on which the picture appears in a television

picture window *n* **:** an outsize window designed to frame a desirable exterior view

picture writing *n* **1 :** the recording of events or messages by pictures representing actions or facts **2 :** the record or message represented by picture writing

pid·dle \ˈpid-l\ *vi* **pid·dled; pid·dling** \ˈpid-liŋ, -l-iŋ\ **:** DAWDLE 1 [origin unknown]

pid·dling \ˈpid-lən, -l-ən, -liŋ, -l-iŋ\ *adj* **:** TRIVIAL 2, PALTRY

pid·dock \ˈpid-ək\ *n* **:** a marine bivalve mollusk that bores holes in stone, wood, or clay [origin unknown]

pid·gin \ˈpij-ən\ *n* **:** a simplified speech used for communication between people with different languages; *esp* **:** an English-based pidgin used in parts of east Asia [from *Pidgin English,* an

English-based pidgin of east Asia, from Chinese Pidgin English *pidgin* "business"]

Word History *Pidgin,* alluding to a makeshift language used between peoples with no language in common, comes from *Pidgin English,* the name for a particular pidgin based on English that was formerly used along the China coast in commercial transactions between Chinese and foreigners. (Linguists usually call it *Chinese Pidgin English* to distinguish it from other pidgins based on English.) The origin of *pidgin* in *Pidgin English* is mysterious. In Chinese Pidgin English the word *pidgin* means "business, affair, occupation," so that *pidgin English* presumably meant simply "business English," the language used to carry on trade. Consequently, *pidgin* has been explained with little phonetic plausability as a Chinese mispronunciation of *business* or, alternatively, of Portuguese *ocupação,* "occupation." Another theory is that *pidgin* meant originally "pidgin language" and ultimately draws its origin from the *Pidians,* supposedly an American Indian group of Guiana with whom inhabitants of a short-lived English colony were in contact in 1605-06. But while the phonetic shift from *Pidian* to *pidgin* is natural—compare *Cajun* from *Acadian*—the shift of sense and the transfer from Guiana to China two centuries later are entirely hypothetical.

[1]**pie** \ˈpī\ *n* : MAGPIE [Medieval French, from Latin *pica*]

[2]**pie** *n* : a dish consisting of a pastry crust and a filling (as of fruit or meat) [Middle English]

[1]**pie·bald** \ˈpī-ˌbȯld\ *adj* : of two colors; *esp* : spotted or blotched with black and white ⟨a *piebald* horse⟩ [[1]*pie* + *bald*]

[2]**piebald** *n* : a piebald animal (as a horse)

[1]**piece** \ˈpēs\ *n* **1** : a usually separated part of a whole ⟨a *piece* of the pie⟩ **2** : one of a group, set, or class of things ⟨a 3-*piece* suit⟩ ⟨a chess *piece*⟩ ⟨a *piece* of mail⟩ **3** : a usually unspecified distance ⟨down the road a *piece*⟩ **4** : a portion marked off ⟨a *piece* of land⟩ **5** : a single item, example, instance, or unit ⟨a *piece* of news⟩ **6** : a standard quantity (as of length, weight, or size) in which something is made or sold ⟨buy lumber by the *piece*⟩ **7** : a literary, artistic, or musical composition **8** : FIREARM **9** : COIN ⟨a gold *piece*⟩ **10** : INSTANCE 2, EXAMPLE ⟨a nice *piece* of acting⟩ [Medieval French, of Celtic origin] ***synonyms*** see PART — **of a piece** : of the same sort : ALIKE — **piece of one's mind** : a severe scolding : TONGUE-LASHING — **piece of the action** : a share in activity or profit — **to pieces** **1** : without reserve or restraint : COMPLETELY **2** : out of control : CRAZY ⟨went *to pieces* after the accident⟩

[2]**piece** *vt* **1** : to repair, renew, or complete by adding pieces : PATCH **2** : to join into a whole ⟨*pieced* their stories together⟩ — **piec·er** *n*

piece by piece *adv* : by degrees : PIECEMEAL

pièce de ré·sis·tance \pē-ˌes-də-rə-ˌzē-ˈstäns\ *n, pl* **pièces de ré·sis·tance** *same*\ **1** : the chief dish of a meal **2** : an outstanding item [French, literally, "piece of resistance"]

piece goods *n pl* : cloth fabrics sold from the bolt at retail in lengths specified by the customer

[1]**piece·meal** \ˈpē-ˌsmēl\ *adv* **1** : one piece at a time : GRADUALLY **2** : in pieces or fragments : APART [Middle English *pecemele,* from *pece* "piece" + *-mele* (from Old English *mǣl* "appointed time")]

[2]**piecemeal** *adj* : done, made, or accomplished piece by piece or in a fragmentary way : GRADUAL

piece of cake : something easily done : CINCH, BREEZE

piece of eight : an old Spanish peso of eight reals

piece of work : a complicated, difficult, or eccentric person

piece·work \ˈpē-ˌswərk\ *n* : work done by the piece and paid for at a set rate per unit — **piece·work·er** \-ˌswər-kər\ *n*

pie chart *n* : a circular chart that is divided into wedge-shaped pieces in such a way that the size of each piece represents the relative quantity or frequency of something — called also *circle graph*

pied \ˈpīd\ *adj* : of two or more colors in blotches [[1]*pie*]

pied–à–terre \pē-ˌād-ə-ˈteər\ *n, pl* **pieds–à–terre** *same*\ : a temporary or second lodging [French, literally, "foot to the ground"]

pied·mont \ˈpēd-ˌmänt\ *adj* : lying or formed at the base of mountains [*Piedmont,* region of Italy] — **piedmont** *n*

pie·plant \ˈpī-ˌplant\ *n* : garden rhubarb

pier \ˈpiər\ *n* **1** : a support for a bridge span **2** : a structure built out into the water for use as a landing place or walk or to protect or form a harbor **3** : a single pillar or a structure used to support something **4** : a mass of masonry (as a buttress) used to strengthen a wall [Old English *per,* from Medieval Latin *pera*]

pierce \ˈpiərs\ *vb* **1** : to run into or through as a pointed weapon does : STAB **2** : to make a hole through : PERFORATE; *esp* : to puncture (the flesh) for the purpose of inserting jewelry **3** : to force or make a way into or through something **4** : to penetrate with the eye or mind : DISCERN **5** : to penetrate so as to move or touch the emotions of [Medieval French *percer,* derived from Latin *pertusus,* past participle of *pertundere* "to perforate"] ***synonyms*** see ENTER — **pierc·er** *n*

pierced \ˈpiərst\ *adj* **1** : having holes **2** : having the flesh punctured for the attachment of a piece of jewelry ⟨*pierced* ears⟩ ⟨a *pierced* tongue⟩ **3** : designed for pierced ears ⟨*pierced* earrings⟩

[1]**pierc·ing** \ˈpir-sing\ *adj* : having the ability to enter, pierce, or penetrate: as **a** : loud and shrill ⟨*piercing* cries⟩ **b** : PERCEPTIVE 2 ⟨*piercing* eyes⟩ **c** : very cold ⟨a *piercing* wind⟩ **d** : INCISIVE ⟨*piercing* sarcasm⟩ — **pierc·ing·ly** *adv*

[2]**piercing** *n* : a piece of jewelry (as a ring or stud) that is attached to pierced flesh

pier glass *n* : a tall mirror; *esp* : one designed to occupy the wall space between windows

pie·ro·gi *also* **pi·ro·gi** \pə-ˈrō-gē\ *n, pl* **-gi** *also* **-gies** : a case of dough filled with meat, cheese, or vegetables and cooked by boiling and then panfrying [Polish, plural of *pieróg* "dumpling, pierogi"]

Pier·rot \ˈpē-ə-ˌrō\ *n* : a standard comic character of old French pantomime usually with whitened face and loose white clothes

pier table *n* : a table to be placed under a pier glass

pie·tà \ˌpē-ā-ˈtä, pyā-\ *n, often cap* : a representation of the Virgin Mary mourning over the dead body of Christ [Italian, literally, "pity," from Latin *pietas*]

pi·etism \ˈpī-ə-ˌtiz-əm\ *n* **1** : emphasis in religion on devotional experience and practices **2** : affected piety — **pi·etist** \ˈpī-ət-əst\ *n, often cap* — **pi·etis·tic** \ˌpī-ə-ˈtis-tik\ *adj* — **pi·etis·ti·cal·ly** \-ˈtis-ti-kə-lē, -klē\ *adv*

pi·ety \ˈpī-ət-ē\ *n, pl* **-eties** **1** : the quality or state of being pious: as **a** : loyalty to natural obligations (as to one's parents) **b** : dutifulness in religion : DEVOUTNESS **2** : an act inspired by piety [French *pieté* "piety, pity," from Latin *pietas,* from *pius* "dutiful, pious"]

pi·ezo·elec·tric·i·ty \pē-ˌā-zō-ə-ˌlek-ˈtris-ət-ē, -ˌāt-sō-, -ˈtris-tē\ *n* : electricity or electric polarity resulting from the application of mechanical force to certain crystals (as quartz) [Greek *piezein* "to press"] — **pi·ezo·elec·tric** \-ˈlek-trik\ *adj* — **pi·ezo·elec·tri·cal·ly** \-ˈlek-tri-kə-lē, -klē\ *adv*

[1]**pif·fle** \ˈpif-əl\ *vi* **pif·fled; pif·fling** \ˈpif-ling, -ə-ling\ : to talk or act in a trivial, inept, or ineffective way [perhaps blend of *piddle* and *trifle*]

[2]**piffle** *n* : trivial nonsense

[1]**pig** \ˈpig\ *n* **1 a** : a young domesticated swine usually weighing less than 120 pounds (54 kilograms) — compare HOG 1a **b** : a wild or domesticated swine regardless of age or weight **2 a** : PORK **b** : PIGSKIN 1 **3** : a dirty, gluttonous, or repulsive person **4** : a crude casting of metal (as iron or lead) [Middle English *pigge*] — **pig** *adj*

pig 1b

[2]**pig** *vb* **pigged; pig·ging** **1** : FARROW **2** : to live like a pig ⟨*pig* it⟩

pi·geon \ˈpij-ən\ *n* **1** : any of numerous birds (family Columbidae) with a stout body, usually short legs, and smooth and compact plumage; *esp* : any of numerous varieties of the rock dove that exist in domestication and in the feral state in cities and towns throughout most of the world **2** : an easy mark : DUPE [Medieval French *pijun,* from Late Latin *pipio* "young bird," from Latin *pipere* "to chirp"]

[1]**pi·geon·hole** \ˈpij-ən-ˌhōl\ *n* **1** : a hole or small place for pigeons to nest **2** : a small open compartment (as in a desk) for keeping letters or papers

[2]**pigeonhole** *vt* : to place in or as if in the pigeonhole of a desk: as **a** : to lay aside : SHELVE **b** : to assign to an often restrictive category : CLASSIFY

pi·geon–toed \ˌpij-ən-ˈtōd\ *adj* : having the toes and forefoot turned inward

pig·gery \ˈpig-rē, -ə-rē\ *n, pl* **-ger·ies** : a place where pigs are kept
pig·gish \ˈpig-ish\ *adj* : suggesting a pig (as in greed, dirtiness, or stubbornness) — **pig·gish·ly** *adv* — **pig·gish·ness** *n*
[1]**pig·gy·back** \ˈpig-ē-ˌbak\ *also* **pick·a·back** \ˈpig-ē-, ˈpik-ə-\ *adv or adj* **1** : on the back or shoulders **2** : on a railroad flatcar [alteration of earlier *a pick pack,* of unknown origin]
[2]**piggyback** *n* : the act of carrying piggyback
piggy bank *n* : a coin bank often in the shape of a pig
pig·head·ed \ˈpig-ˈhed-əd\ *adj* : STUBBORN 1a, OBSTINATE
pig in a blanket *n, pl* **pigs in a blanket** *or* **pigs in blankets** : a frankfurter served in a wrapper of baked dough
pig iron *n* : iron that is the direct product of the blast furnace and is refined to produce steel, wrought iron, or high-purity iron
pig latin *n, often cap L* : a jargon that is made by systematic alteration of English (as "amsray" for "scram")
piglet \ˈpig-lət\ *n* : a small usually young pig
[1]**pig·ment** \ˈpig-mənt\ *n* **1** : a substance that imparts black or white or a color to other materials; *esp* : a powdered substance mixed with a liquid in which it is relatively insoluble to impart color **2** : a natural coloring matter in animals and plants; *also* : any of various related colorless substances [Latin *pigmentum,* from *pingere* "to paint"] — **pig·men·tary** \-mən-ˌter-ē\ *adj*
[2]**pig·ment** \-mənt, -ˌment\ *vt* : to color with or as if with pigment
pig·men·ta·tion \ˌpig-mən-ˈtā-shən, -ˌmen-\ *n* : coloration with or deposition of pigment; *esp* : excessive pigment in bodily cells or tissues
pigmy *variant of* PYGMY
pig·nut \ˈpig-ˌnət\ *n* : any of several bitter-flavored hickory nuts; *also* : a tree bearing pignuts
pig out *vi* : to eat greedily : GORGE — **pig–out** \ˈpig-ˌau̇t\ *n*
pig·pen \-ˌpen\ *n* **1** : a pen for pigs **2** : a filthy or messy place
pig·skin \-ˌskin\ *n* **1** : the skin of a swine or leather made of it **2** : FOOTBALL 2
pig·sty \ˈpig-ˌstī\ *n* : PIGPEN
pig·tail \-ˌtāl\ *n* **1** : tobacco in small twisted strands or rolls **2** : a tight braid of hair
pig–tailed \-ˌtāld\ *adj* : wearing a pigtail or pigtails
pig·weed \-ˌwēd\ *n* : any of various weedy plants especially of the two families to which the goosefoots and amaranths belong
pi·ka \ˈpē-kə\ *n* : any of various small short-eared mammals of rocky areas in the mountains of Asia and western North America that are related to the rabbits — called also *coney* [perhaps from Evenki (Tungusic language of Siberia)]
[1]**pike** \ˈpīk\ *n* **1** : PIKESTAFF 1 **2** : a sharp point or spike; *also* : the tip of a spear [Old English *pīc* "pickax"] — **piked** \ˈpīkt\ *adj*
[2]**pike** *n, pl* **pike** *or* **pikes** : a large long-bodied and long-snouted freshwater fish valued for food and sport and widely distributed in cool northern waters; *also* : any of various related or similar fishes [Middle English, from [1]*pike*]

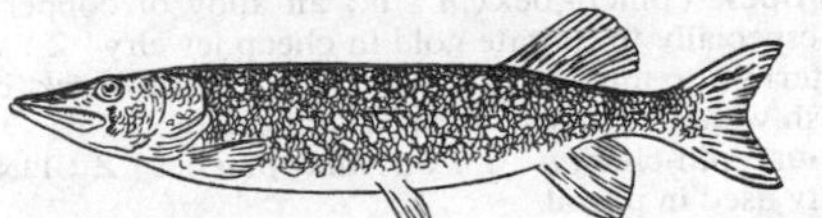

[2]pike

[3]**pike** *n* : a long wooden shaft with a pointed steel head formerly used as a weapon by infantry [Middle French *pique,* from *piquer* "to prick," perhaps derived from Latin *picus* "woodpecker"]
[4]**pike** *n* : TURNPIKE 2
[5]**pike** *n* : a body position (as in diving or gymnastics) in which the body is bent at the waist in the shape of a V [probably from [2]*pike*]
pike perch *n* : a fish (as a walleye) related to the perches but resembling the pike
pik·er \ˈpī-kər\ *n* **1** : one who gambles or speculates with small amounts of money **2** : one who does things in a small way; *also* : TIGHTWAD, CHEAPSKATE [*pike* "to play cautiously," of unknown origin]
pike·staff \ˈpīk-ˌstaf\ *n* **1** : a spiked staff for use on slippery ground **2** : the shaft of a soldier's pike
pi·laf *also* **pi·laff** \pi-ˈläf, ˈpē-ˌ\ *or* **pi·lau** \pi-ˈlō, -ˈlȯ, ˈpē-ˌ, *South often* ˈpər-lü, -lō\ *n* : a dish made of seasoned rice and often meat [Turkish *pilav,* from Persian *pilāv*]
pi·las·ter \ˈpī-ˌlas-tər\ *n* : a rectangular slightly projecting column that ornaments or helps to support a wall [Middle French *pilastre,* from Italian *pilastro*]
pil·chard \ˈpil-chərd\ *n* **1** : a fish resembling the related herring and occurring in great schools along the coasts of Europe — compare SARDINE 1 **2** : any of several fishes related to the pilchard [origin unknown]
[1]**pile** \ˈpīl\ *n* : a long slender column usually of timber, steel, or reinforced concrete driven into the ground to carry a vertical load [Old English *pīl* "dart, pole driven into the ground," from Latin *pilum* "javelin"]
[2]**pile** *vt* : to drive piles into
[3]**pile** *n* **1 a** : a quantity of things heaped together **b** : a heap of wood for burning a corpse or a sacrifice : PYRE **2** : a great amount (as of money) **3** : REACTOR 2b [Middle English, "pier of a bridge, stack, heap," from Medieval French *pille* "pier of a bridge," from Latin *pila* "pillar"]
[4]**pile** *vb* **1** : to lay or place in a pile : STACK **2** : to heap in abundance : LOAD **3** : to move or press forward in or as if in a mass : CROWD ⟨*pile* into the car⟩
[5]**pile** *n* **1** : a coat or surface of usually short close fine furry hairs **2** : a velvety surface produced on textile by an extra set of filling yarns that form raised loops which are cut and sheared [Medieval French *peil, pil* "hair, coat with thick nap," from Latin *pilus* "hair"] — **piled** \ˈpīld\ *adj*
pi·le·at·ed woodpecker \ˌpī-lē-ˌāt-əd-\ *n* : a North American woodpecker that is black with a red crest and white on the wings and sides of the neck [derived from Latin *pileus, pileum* "felt cap"]
pile driver *n* : a machine for driving or hammering piles into place
piles \ˈpīlz\ *n pl* : HEMORRHOIDS; *also* : the condition of one affected with hemorrhoids [Medieval Latin *pili,* pl., perhaps from Latin *pila* "ball"]
pi·le·us \ˈpī-lē-əs\ *n, pl* **pi·lei** \-lē-ˌī\ : CAP 3a [Latin, "felt cap"]
pil·fer \ˈpil-fər\ *vb* **pil·fered; pil·fer·ing** \-fə-ring, -fring\ : to steal articles of small value or in small amounts [Middle French *pelfrer,* from *pelfre* "booty"] — **pil·fer·age** \-fə-rij, -frij\ *n* — **pil·fer·er** \-fər-ər\ *n*
pil·grim \ˈpil-grəm\ *n* **1** : one who travels in foreign lands : WANDERER **2** : one who travels to a shrine or holy place as a devotee **3** *cap* : one of the English colonists founding the first permanent settlement in New England at Plymouth in 1620 [Medieval French *pelerin, pilegrin,* from Late Latin *pelegrinus,* from Latin *peregrinus* "foreigner," from *pereger* "abroad," from *per* "through" + *ager* "land"]
pil·grim·age \ˈpil-grə-mij\ *n* : a journey of a pilgrim — **pilgrimage** *vi*
pil·ing \ˈpī-ling\ *n* : a structure of piles
Pi·li·pi·no \ˌpil-ə-ˈpē-nō, ˌpēl-\ *n* : the Tagalog-based official language of the Republic of the Philippines [Tagalog, literally, "Philippine," from Spanish *Filipino*]
pill \ˈpil\ *n* **1 a** : a usually medicinal or dietary preparation in a small rounded mass to be swallowed whole **b** : BIRTH CONTROL PILL — usually used with *the* **2** : something unpleasant that must be accepted or endured **3** : something resembling a pill in size or shape **4** : a disagreeable or tiresome person [derived from Latin *pilula,* from *pila* "ball"]
[1]**pil·lage** \ˈpil-ij\ *n* **1** : the act of looting or plundering especially in war **2** : BOOTY 1 [Medieval French *pilage,* from *piler* "to rob, plunder"]
[2]**pillage** *vb* : to take booty : PLUNDER, LOOT — **pil·lag·er** *n*
pil·lar \ˈpil-ər\ *n* **1** : a comparatively slender upright support (as for a roof) **2** : a column or shaft standing alone (as for a monument) **3 a** : a supporting or important member or part ⟨a *pillar* of society⟩ **b** : a fundamental principle ⟨the five *pillars* of Islam⟩ [Medieval French *piler,* from Medieval Latin *pilare,* from Latin *pila* "pillar"] — **pil·lared** \-ərd\ *adj* — **from pillar to post** : from one place or situation to another
pill·box \ˈpil-ˌbäks\ *n* **1** : a small usually shallow round box for pills **2** : a small low concrete emplacement for machine guns and antitank weapons **3** : a small round hat without a brim

\ə\ **abut**	\au̇\ **out**	\i\ **tip**	\ȯ\ **saw**	\u̇\ **foot**
\ər\ **further**	\ch\ **chin**	\ī\ **life**	\ȯi\ **coin**	\y\ **yet**
\a\ **mat**	\e\ **pet**	\j\ **job**	\th\ **thin**	\yü\ **few**
\ā\ **take**	\ē\ **easy**	\ng\ **sing**	\t͟h\ **this**	\yu̇\ **cure**
\ä\ **cot, cart**	\g\ **go**	\ō\ **bone**	\ü\ **food**	\zh\ **vision**

pill bug *n* : WOOD LOUSE; *esp* : a wood louse capable of curling itself into a ball

[1]**pil·lion** \'pil-yən\ *n* **1** : a cushion or pad placed behind a saddle for an extra rider **2** : a passenger's saddle (as on a motorcycle) [Scottish Gaelic *pillean* or Irish *pillín*]

[2]**pillion** *adv* : on or as if on a pillion ⟨ride *pillion*⟩

pil·lo·ry \'pil-rē, -ə-rē\ *n, pl* **-ries** **1** : a device for publicly punishing offenders that consists of a wooden frame with holes in which the head and hands can be locked — compare STOCK **2** : a means for exposing to public scorn or ridicule [Medieval French *pilori*] — **pillory** *vt*

[1]**pil·low** \'pil-ō\ *n* : a support for the head of a person that consists usually of a bag filled with resilient material (as feathers or sponge rubber) [Old English *pyle, pylu,* from Latin *pulvinus*]

[2]**pillow** *vt* **1** : to place on or as if on a pillow **2** : to serve as a pillow for

pil·low·case \-ˌkās\ *n* : a removable covering for a pillow — called also *pillow slip*

[1]**pi·lot** \'pī-lət\ *n* **1 a** : one employed to steer a ship **b** : a person qualified and usually licensed to conduct a ship into and out of a port or in specified waters **2** : someone who provides guidance and direction : LEADER **3** : COWCATCHER **4** : a person who flies or is qualified to fly an aircraft or spacecraft **5** : a piece that guides a tool or machine part **6** : a television show produced as a sample of a proposed series **7** : PILOT LIGHT 2 [Middle French *pilote,* from Italian *pilota,* alteration of *pedota,* derived from Greek *pēdon* "oar"] — **pi·lot·less** \-ləs\ *adj*

[2]**pilot** *vt* **1** : GUIDE 1, CONDUCT **2 a** : to direct the navigation of : STEER ⟨*pilot* the ship through the canal⟩ **b** : to act as pilot of : FLY ⟨*pilot* the plane to the west coast⟩ ***synonyms*** see GUIDE

[3]**pilot** *adj* : serving as a guiding or tracing device, an activating or auxiliary unit, or a trial apparatus or operation ⟨a *pilot* study⟩ ⟨a *pilot* plant⟩

pi·lot·age \'pī-lət-ij\ *n* **1** : the act or business of piloting **2** : the compensation paid to a pilot

pilot balloon *n* : a small unmanned balloon sent up to show the direction and speed of the wind

pilot biscuit *n* : HARDTACK — called also *pilot bread*

pilot engine *n* : a locomotive going in advance of a train to make sure that the way is clear

pilot fish *n* : a fish with a narrow body, dark stripes, and a widely forked tail that often swims in company with a shark

pi·lot·house \'pī-lət-ˌhau̇s\ *n* : an enclosed area on the upper deck of a ship that contains the steering and navigating equipment

pilot light *n* **1** : a light indicating location (as of a switch) or operational state (as of a motor) **2** : a small permanent flame used to ignite gas at a burner

pilot whale *n* : either of two chiefly black medium-sized toothed whales related to the dolphins — called also *blackfish*

Pilt·down man \ˌpilt-ˌdau̇n-\ *n* : a supposedly very early hominid mistakenly reconstructed from comparatively recent human and animal skeletal remains found in a gravel pit at Piltdown, England, and later discovered to have been planted there as an elaborate hoax

Pi·ma cotton \ˌpē-mə-, ˌpim-ə-\ *n* : a cotton with fiber of exceptional strength and firmness that was developed in the U.S. from Egyptian cottons [*Pima* County, Arizona]

pi·men·to \pə-'ment-ō\ *n, pl* **-tos** *or* **-to** **1** : PIMIENTO **2** : ALLSPICE [Spanish *pimiento,* from *pimienta* "allspice, pepper," from Late Latin *pigmentum* "plant juice," from Latin, "pigment"]

pi·mien·to \pə-'ment-ō, pəm-'yent-\ *n, pl* **-tos** : any of various thick-fleshed sweet peppers of mild flavor used especially as a garnish, as a stuffing for olives, and as a source of paprika [Spanish]

[1]**pimp** \'pimp\ *n* : a man who solicits clients for a prostitute [origin unknown]

[2]**pimp** *vi* : to work as a pimp

pim·per·nel \'pim-pər-ˌnel\ *n* : any of a genus of herbs related to the primroses; *esp* : SCARLET PIMPERNEL [Medieval French *pimprenelle,* from Late Latin *pimpinella,* a medicinal herb]

pim·ple \'pim-pəl\ *n* : a small inflamed swelling of the skin often containing pus : PUSTULE [Middle English *pymple*] — **pimpled** \-pəld\ *adj* — **pim·ply** \-pə-lē, -plē\ *adj*

[1]**pin** \'pin\ *n* **1 a** : a piece of wood, metal, or plastic used especially for fastening things together or for hanging one thing from another **b** : one of the pieces constituting the target in various games (as bowling) **c** : the staff of the flag marking a hole on a golf course **d** : a peg for regulating the tension of the strings of a musical instrument **2 a** : a very thin small pointed metal pin with a head used especially for fastening cloth **b** : an ornament or emblem fastened to clothing with a pin **c** : a device (as a hairpin or a safety pin) used for fastening **3** : LEG 1 — usually used in plural ⟨wobbly on his *pins*⟩ **4** : LITTLE 1, TRIFLE ⟨doesn't care a *pin* for it⟩ [Old English *pinn*]

[2]**pin** *vt* **pinned; pin·ning** **1** : to fasten, join, or pierce with or as if with a pin **2 a** : FASTEN 1 ⟨*pinned* their hopes on a miracle⟩ **b** : to assign the blame or responsibility for ⟨*pinned* the robbery on the butler⟩ **c** : to define or determine clearly or precisely ⟨hard to *pin* down the main idea of the essay⟩ **3** : to hold (a wrestling opponent) down on the mat in a required position for a required length of time to win a match

pin·a·fore \'pin-ə-ˌfōr, -ˌfȯr\ *n* : a low-necked sleeveless garment worn by women and girls [[2]*pin* + *afore*]

pi·ña·ta *or* **pi·na·ta** \pēn-'yät-ə\ *n* : a decorated container (as of papier-mâché) filled with candies, fruits, and gifts and hung up to be broken with sticks by blindfolded persons as part of especially Latin-American festivities (as at Christmas or for a birthday party) [Spanish, literally, "pot"]

pin·ball \'pin-ˌbȯl\ *vi* : to move suddenly from one place to another

pinball machine *n* : an amusement device in which a ball propelled by a plunger scores points as it rolls down a slanting surface among pins and targets

pince–nez \pa^{n}-'snā, pan-\ *n, pl* **pince–nez** \-'snā, -'snāz\ : eyeglasses clipped to the nose by a spring [French, from *pincer* "to pinch" + *nez* "nose"]

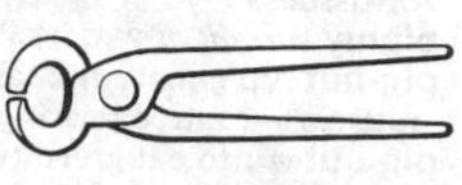

pincer 1a

pin·cer \'pin-chər, 'pin-sər\ *n* **1 a** *pl* : an instrument with two short handles and two pivoting jaws that is used for gripping things **b** : a claw (as of a lobster) resembling a pair of pincers : CHELA **2** : PINCER MOVEMENT [Middle English *pinceour*] — **pin·cer·like** \-ˌlīk\ *adj*

pincer movement *n* **1** : a military attack by two forces that close in on an enemy position from different directions **2** : a combination of two forces acting against an opposing force

[1]**pinch** \'pinch\ *vb* **1 a** : to squeeze between the finger and thumb or between the jaws of an instrument **b** : to prune the tip of (a plant or shoot) usually to induce branching **c** : to squeeze painfully **d** : to cause to appear thin, haggard, or shrunken ⟨a face *pinched* with hunger⟩ **2 a** : to subject to or practice strict economy **b** : to restrain or limit narrowly **3 a** : STEAL 2a **b** : ARREST 2 [Middle English]

[2]**pinch** *n* **1 a** : a critical point : EMERGENCY **b** : a painful pressure or stress : HARDSHIP ⟨the *pinch* of hunger⟩ **2 a** : an act of pinching **b** : as much as may be taken between the finger and thumb ⟨a *pinch* of salt⟩ **3 a** : the act of stealing : THEFT **b** : a police raid; *also* : ARREST 2

pinch bar *n* : a lever with a wedge-shaped end

pinch·beck \'pinch-ˌbek\ *n* **1** : an alloy of copper and zinc used especially to imitate gold in cheap jewelry **2** : something counterfeit or unauthentic [Christopher *Pinchbeck,* died 1732, English watchmaker] — **pinchbeck** *adj*

pinch·er \'pin-chər\ *n* **1** : one that pinches **2** : PINCER 1 — usually used in plural

pinch hitter *n* **1** : a baseball player sent in to bat for another especially when a hit is particularly needed **2** : a person called on to do another's work in an emergency — **pinch–hit** \'pinch-'hit\ *vi*

pin curl *n* : a curl made usually by dampening a strand of hair, coiling it, and securing it with a hairpin or clip

pin·cush·ion \'pin-ˌku̇sh-ən\ *n* : a small cushion in which pins may be stuck

Pin·dar·ic \pin-'dar-ik\ *adj* : of, relating to, or written in a manner or style characteristic of the poet Pindar

[1]**pine** \'pīn\ *vi* **1** : to lose vigor, health, or weight through grief, worry, or distress ⟨*pine* away⟩ **2** : to have a continuing fruitless desire : YEARN ⟨*pine* for home⟩ [Old English *pīnian,* derived from Latin *poena* "punishment, pain"] ***synonyms*** see LONG

[2]**pine** *n* **1** : any of a genus of cone-bearing evergreen trees having slender elongated needles and including valuable timber trees as well as many ornamentals **2** : the straight-grained white or yellow usually durable and resinous wood of a pine **3** : any of various Australian cone-bearing trees [Old English *pīn,* from Latin *pinus*] — **pin·ey** *also* **piny** \'pī-nē\ *adj*

pi•ne•al \ˈpin-ē-əl, ˈpī-nē-\ *adj* **:** of, relating to, or produced by the pineal gland [French *pinéal,* from Latin *pinea* "pine cone," from *pinus* "pine"]
pineal gland *n* **:** a small usually conical appendage of the brain of most vertebrates that has an eyelike structure in reptiles and produces melatonin especially in response to darkness — called also *pineal body*
pine•ap•ple \ˈpī-ˌnap-əl\ *n* **:** a tropical plant that is a monocotyledon with stiff spiny sword-shaped leaves and a short flowering stalk that develops into an edible fruit with usually pale yellow sweet juicy flesh and very thick skin; *also* **:** this fruit

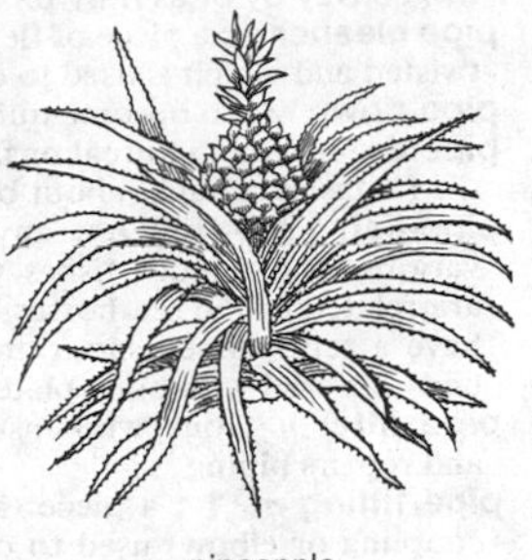
pineapple

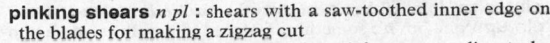

pine cone *n* **:** the cone of a pine tree
pine nut *n* **:** the edible seed of any of several chiefly western North American pines
pine tar *n* **:** tar obtained by distillation of pinewood and used especially in roofing and soaps and in the treatment of skin diseases
pine•wood \ˈpīn-ˌwu̇d\ *n* **1 :** the wood of a pine tree **2 :** a wood or growth of pines
pin•feath•er \ˈpin-ˌfe*th*-ər\ *n* **:** an incompletely developed feather just breaking through the skin
ping \ˈping\ *n* **1 :** a sharp sound like that of a bullet striking **2 :** KNOCK 2b ⟨kept hearing a *ping* in the car engine⟩ [imitative] — **ping** *vi*
Ping–Pong \ˈping-ˌpäng, -ˌpȯng\ *trademark* — used for table tennis
pin•head \ˈpin-ˌhed\ *n* **1 :** the head of a pin **2 :** something very small or insignificant **3 :** a very dull or stupid person **:** FOOL
pin•head•ed \ˈpin-ˈhed-əd\ *adj* **:** lacking intelligence or understanding **:** STUPID — **pin•head•ed•ness** *n*
pin•hole \-ˌhōl\ *n* **:** a small hole made by, for, or as if by a pin
[1]pin•ion \ˈpin-yən\ *n* **1 :** the end part of a bird's wing; *also* **:** a bird's wing **2 :** a feather of a bird's pinion [Medieval French *pignon*] — **pinioned** \-yənd\ *adj*
[2]pinion *vt* **1 a :** to disable or restrain by binding the arms **b :** to bind fast **:** SHACKLE **2 :** to restrain (a bird) from flight especially by cutting off the pinion of one wing
[3]pinion *n* **1 :** a gear with a small number of teeth designed to mesh with a larger wheel or rack **2 :** the smallest of a train or set of gears [French *pignon,* from Medieval French *peignon,* from *peigne* "comb," from Latin *pecten*]

P→
P [3]pinion 1

[1]pink \ˈpingk\ *vt* **1 :** PIERCE 1, STAB **2 a :** to perforate in an ornamental pattern **b :** to cut a saw-toothed edge on [Middle English]
[2]pink *n* **1 :** any of a genus of annual or perennial chiefly Eurasian herbs that have narrow leaves and are often grown for their showy usually pink flowers borne singly or in clusters **2 :** highest degree possible ⟨a house decorated in the *pink* of style⟩ [origin unknown] — **in the pink :** in the best of health or condition ⟨athletes *in the pink*⟩
[3]pink *adj* **1 :** of the color pink **2 :** holding moderately radical and usually socialistic political or economic views [[2]*pink*] — **pink•ly** *adv* — **pink•ness** *n*
[4]pink *n* **1 :** a pale red **2 a :** the scarlet color of a fox hunter's coat; *also* **:** a coat of this color **b** *pl* **:** light-colored trousers formerly worn by army officers **3 :** a person who holds moderately radical political or economic views [sense 3 from the viewing of pink as a weak form of red]
pink•eye \ˈping-ˌkī\ *n* **:** a contagious disease in which the inner surface of the eyelid and part of the eyeball become pinkish and sore
pin•kie *or* **pin•ky** \ˈping-kē\ *n, pl* **pinkies :** LITTLE FINGER [probably from Dutch *pinkje,* from *pink* "little finger"]
pinking shears *n pl* **:** shears with a saw-toothed inner edge on the blades for making a zigzag cut
pink•ish \ˈping-kish\ *adj* **:** somewhat pink; *esp* **:** tending to be pink in politics — **pink•ish•ness** *n*
pinko \ˈping-kō\ *n, pl* **pink•os** *also* **pink•oes :** [4]PINK 3
pink slip *n* **:** a notice from an employer that a recipient's employment is being terminated — **pink–slip** *vt*
pin money *n* **:** money for incidental expenses
pin•na \ˈpin-ə\ *n, pl* **pin•nae** \ˈpin-ˌē, -ˌī\ *or* **pinnas 1 a :** a projecting body part (as a wing or fin) **b :** the largely cartilaginous projecting portion of the external ear **2 :** a primary division of a pinnate leaf or frond [Latin, "feather, wing"]
pin•nace \ˈpin-əs\ *n* **1 :** a light sailing ship used largely as a tender **2 :** any of various ship's boats [Middle French *pinace*]
pin•na•cle \ˈpin-i-kəl\ *n* **1 :** an upright structure (as on a tower) generally ending in a small spire **2 :** a lofty peak **3 :** the highest point of achievement or development [Medieval French *pinacle,* from Late Latin *pinnaculum* "small wing, gable," from Latin *pinna* "wing, battlement"] ***synonyms*** see SUMMIT
pin•nate \ˈpin-ˌāt\ *adj* **:** resembling a feather especially in having similar parts arranged on opposite sides of an axis ⟨a *pinnate* leaf⟩ [Latin *pinnatus* "feathered," from *pinna* "feather"] — **pinnate•ly** *adv*
pin•ni•ped \ˈpin-ə-ˌped\ *n* **:** any of a group (Pinnipedia) of mammals (as seals, sea lions, and walruses) that typically live in oceans but bear their young on land or ice floes, feed on other animals (as fish), and have all four limbs modified in flippers [derived from Latin *pinna* "wing, fin" + *ped-, pes* "foot"] — **pinniped** *adj*
pi•noch•le \ˈpē-ˌnək-əl\ *n* **:** a card game played with a 48-card pack containing two of each suit of A, K, Q, J, 10, 9; *also* **:** the combination of queen of spades and jack of diamonds which scores 40 points in this game [probably from German dialect *Binokel,* a card game, from French dialect *binocle*]
pi•no•cy•to•sis \ˌpin-ə-sə-ˈtō-səs, ˌpīn-, -ˌsī-\ *n, pl* **-to•ses** \-ˌsēz\ **:** the uptake of fluid and dissolved substances by a cell by infolding and pinching off of the cell membrane [Greek *pinein* "to drink"]
pi•ñon *or* **pin•yon** \ˈpin-yōn, -ˌyän, -yən; pin-ˈyōn\ *n, pl* **piñons** *or* **pi•ño•nes** \pin-ˈyō-nēz\ *or* **pin•yons :** any of various small pines of western North America with edible seeds that are pine nuts; *also* **:** the seed of a piñon [American Spanish *piñón,* from Spanish, "pine nut," from *piña* "pine cone," from Latin *pinea,* from *pinus* "pine"]
[1]pin•point \ˈpin-ˌpȯint\ *vt* **1 :** to locate or determine with precision **2 :** to cause to stand out clearly **:** HIGHLIGHT
[2]pinpoint *adj* **1 :** extremely fine or precise **2 :** located, fixed, or directed with extreme precision
pin•prick \ˈpin-ˌprik\ *n* **1 :** a small puncture made by or as if by a pin **2 :** a petty irritation or annoyance — **pinprick** *vb*
pins and needles *n pl* **:** a pricking tingling sensation in a limb recovering from numbness — **on pins and needles :** in a nervous or jumpy state of anticipation
pin•set•ter \ˈpin-ˌset-ər\ *n* **:** one that sets up pins in a bowling alley
pin•spot•ter \-ˌspät-ər\ *n* **:** PINSETTER
pin•stripe \-ˌstrīp\ *n* **:** a very thin stripe on a fabric; *also* **:** a suit with such stripes — **pin–striped** \-ˌstrīpt\ *adj*
pint \ˈpīnt\ *n* **1 :** a unit of capacity equal to ½ quart — see MEASURE table **2 :** a pint vessel [Medieval French *pinte,* from Medieval Latin *pincta,* probably derived from Latin *pingere* "to paint"]
pin•tail \ˈpin-ˌtāl\ *n, pl* **pintail** *or* **pintails :** a bird (as a duck or grouse) with long central tail feathers
pin•tailed \-ˌtāld\ *adj* **1 :** having a tapered tail with the middle feathers longest **2 :** having the tail feathers spiny
[1]pin•to \ˈpin-tō\ *n, pl* **pintos** *also* **pintoes :** a horse or pony marked with patches of white and another color [American Spanish, from obsolete Spanish *pinto* "spotted," derived from Latin *pingere* "to paint"]
[2]pinto *adj* **:** PIED, MOTTLED
pinto bean *n* **:** a mottled kidney bean used for food; *also* **:** a plant producing pinto beans that is often used to feed livestock

\ə\ **abut**	\au̇\ **out**	\i\ **tip**	\ȯ\ **saw**	\u̇\ **foot**
\ər\ **further**	\ch\ **chin**	\ī\ **life**	\ȯi\ **coin**	\y\ **yet**
\a\ **mat**	\e\ **pet**	\j\ **job**	\th\ **thin**	\yü\ **few**
\ā\ **take**	\ē\ **easy**	\ng\ **sing**	\th\ **this**	\yu̇\ **cure**
\ä\ **cot, cart**	\g\ **go**	\ō\ **bone**	\ü\ **food**	\zh\ **vision**

pint–size \ˈpīnt-ˌsīz\ *or* **pint–sized** \-ˌsīzd\ *adj* : DIMINUTIVE 2

1**pin-up** \ˈpin-ˌəp\ *n* : something fastened to a wall: as **a** : a photograph or poster of a person considered to have glamorous qualities **b** : something (as a lamp) attached to a wall

2**pinup** *adj* **1** : of or relating to pinups ⟨male *pinup* calendars⟩ **2** : designed for hanging on a wall ⟨a *pinup* lamp⟩

pin·wale \ˈpin-ˌwāl\ *adj* : made with narrow wales ⟨*pinwale* corduroy⟩

pin·wheel \-ˌhwēl, -ˌwēl\ *n* **1** : a toy consisting of lightweight vanes that revolve at the end of a stick **2** : a fireworks device in the form of a revolving wheel of colored fire

pin·worm \-ˌwərm\ *n* : any of numerous small nematode worms that infest the intestines and usually the cecum of various vertebrates; *esp* : one parasitic in humans

pin·yin \ˈpin-ˈyin\ *n, often cap* : a system for writing Chinese using the Latin alphabet in which tones are indicated by diacritics, the letters *p, t,* and *k* are restricted to aspirates resembling English \p, t, k\, and *b, d,* and *g* are used to represent corresponding sounds without aspiration [Chinese (Beijing dialect) *pīnyīn,* from *pīn* "arrange" + *yīn* "sound, pronunciation"]

pinyon *variant of* PIÑON

pi·on \ˈpī-ˌän\ *n* : a meson that has a mass about 270 times that of an electron [contraction of *pi-meson* "pion," from 1*pi* + *meson*]

1**pi·o·neer** \ˌpī-ə-ˈniər\ *n* **1** : a person or group that originates or helps open up a new line of thought or activity or a new method or technical development ⟨*pioneers* of American medicine⟩ **2** : one of the first to settle in an area : COLONIST **3** : a plant or animal capable of establishing itself in a bare or barren area [Middle French *pionier* "soldier tasked with constructing earthworks," from Medieval French, "foot soldier," from *peon* "foot soldier," from Medieval Latin *pedon-, pedo,* from Latin *ped-, pes* "foot"] — **pioneer** *adj*

Word History Daniel Boone and the other pioneers who opened the American frontier are heroic figures to some, but the origins of the word *pioneer* are somewhat less than grand. Medieval French *peonier* or *pionier,* a derivative of *peon* "foot soldier," also originally meant "foot soldier," but later appeared in the sense "digger, excavator" and by the 14th century designated a soldier who dug earthworks and prepared fortifications in advance of the troops who would occupy them. The word was borrowed by English in the latter sense in the 16th century. With the modern spelling *pioneer* it sometimes still refers to troops who build fortifications, roads, and bridges, though in the 20th century American army "engineer" replaced it. In the sense "forerunner" or "initiator," however, the English word has gone beyond its French source. Its specific application to a frontiersman first appeared in American English in the early 19th century, notably in the title of *The Pioneers,* a novel by James Fenimore Cooper published in 1823.

2**pioneer** *vb* **1** : to act as a pioneer **2** : to open or prepare for others to follow; *esp* : SETTLE **3** : to originate or take part in the development of

pi·ous \ˈpī-əs\ *adj* **1** : having or showing reverence for deity : DEVOUT **2** : showing loyal reverence for a person or thing : DUTIFUL **3** : marked by sham or hypocrisy ⟨a *pious* fraud⟩ **4** : deserving praise : WORTHY ⟨a *pious* effort⟩ [Latin *pius*] — **pi·ous·ly** *adv* — **pi·ous·ness** *n*

1**pip** \ˈpip\ *n* : a disorder of a bird marked by formation of a scale or crust on the tongue; *also* : this scale or crust [Dutch *pippe,* derived from Latin *pituita* "phlegm, pip"]

2**pip** *vi* **pipped; pip·ping** **1** : 1PEEP 1 **2 a** : to break the shell of the egg in hatching **b** : to be broken by a pipping bird ⟨eggs starting to *pip*⟩ [imitative]

3**pip** *n* **1** : a dot or spot (as on dice or playing cards) to indicate numerical value **2** : 1SPIKE 6; *also* : BLIP [origin unknown]

4**pip** *n* **1** : a small fruit seed ⟨orange *pips*⟩ **2** : something very good of its kind [short for *pippin*]

5**pip** *n, chiefly British* : a short high-pitched tone ⟨broadcast six *pips* as a time signal⟩ [imitative]

1**pipe** \ˈpīp\ *n* **1 a** : a musical instrument consisting of a tube of reed, wood, or metal that is played by blowing **b** : a tube producing a musical sound ⟨an organ *pipe*⟩ **c** : BAGPIPE — usually used in plural **d** : the whistle, call, or note especially of a bird or an insect **2 a** : a long tube or hollow body used especially to conduct a substance (as water, steam, or gas) **b** : a cylindrical object, part, or passage **3** : a tube with a small bowl at one end used for smoking tobacco **4 a** : a large cask used especially for wine and oil **b** : any of various units of liquid capacity based on the size of a pipe; *esp* : a unit equal to 2 hogsheads [Old English *pīpa,* derived from Latin *pipare* "to peep"] — **pipe·less** \ˈpī-pləs\ *adj*

2**pipe** *vb* **1 a** : to play on a pipe **b** : to convey orders or direct by signals on a boatswain's pipe **c** : to receive aboard or attend the departure of by sounding a boatswain's pipe **2** : to speak in or have a high shrill tone **3** : to furnish or trim with piping **4** : to convey by or as if by pipes — **pip·er** *n*

pipe cleaner *n* : a piece of flexible wire in which tufted fabric is twisted and which is used to clean the stem of a tobacco pipe

pipe down *vi* : to become quiet : stop talking

pipe dream *n* : an unreal or fantastic plan, hope, or story [from the fantasies brought about by the smoking of opium]

pipe·fish \ˈpīp-ˌfish\ *n* : any of various long slender fishes that are related to the sea horses and have a tube-shaped snout and a body covered with bony plates

pipefish

pipe fitter *n* : one who installs and repairs piping

pipe fitting *n* **1** : a piece (as a coupling or elbow) used to connect pipe or as accessory to a pipe **2** : the work of a pipe fitter

pipe·ful \ˈpīp-ˌfu̇l\ *n* : a quantity of tobacco smoked in a pipe at one time

pipe·line \ˈpī-ˌplīn\ *n* **1** : a line of pipe with pumps, valves, and control devices for conveying liquids, gases, or finely divided solids **2** : a direct channel for information or supplies

pipe organ *n* : ORGAN 1a

pi·pette *also* **pi·pet** \pī-ˈpet\ *n* : a device for measuring and transferring small volumes of liquid that typically consists of a narrow glass tube into which the liquid is drawn by suction and retained by closing the upper end [French *pipette,* from *pipe* "pipe, cask"] — **pipette** *also* **pipet** *vb*

pipe up *vi* : to speak loudly and distinctly

pip·ing \ˈpī-ping\ *n* **1 a** : the music of a pipe **b** : a shrill sound or call ⟨the *piping* of frogs⟩ **2** : a quantity or system of pipes **3** : a narrow decorative fold stitched in seams or along edges (as of clothing or slipcovers)

piping hot *adj* : very hot

pip·it \ˈpip-ət\ *n* : any of various small songbirds resembling the lark [imitative]

pip·kin \ˈpip-kən\ *n* : a small earthenware or metal pot usually with a horizontal handle [perhaps from *pipe*]

pip·pin \ˈpip-ən\ *n* **1** : a crisp tart apple having usually yellow or greenish yellow skin strongly flushed with red and used especially for cooking **2** : someone or something greatly admired [Medieval French *pepin*]

pip·sis·se·wa \pip-ˈsis-ə-ˌwȯ\ *n* : a low evergreen herb related to the wintergreens that has astringent leaves used medicinally [perhaps from Eastern Abenaki (Algonquian language of northern New England) *kpipskʷáhsawe,* literally, "flower of the woods"]

pip–squeak \ˈpip-ˌskwēk\ *n* : one that is small or insignificant

pi·quant \ˈpē-kənt, -ˌkänt\ *adj* **1** : agreeably stimulating to the sense of taste **2** : pleasingly exciting ⟨a *piquant* bit of gossip⟩ **3** : engagingly provocative; *also* : having a lively roguish charm ⟨a *piquant* face⟩ [French, from *piquer* "to prick"] — **pi·quan·cy** \-kən-sē\ *n* — **pi·quant·ly** *adv* — **pi·quant·ness** *n*

1**pique** \ˈpēk\ *n* : offense taken by one slighted : RESENTMENT ⟨a fit of *pique*⟩

2**pique** *vt* **1** : to arouse anger or resentment in : IRRITATE; *esp* : to offend by slighting **2** : EXCITE 1b, AROUSE ⟨the package *piqued* my curiosity⟩ [French *piquer,* literally, "to prick"]

pi·qué *or* **pi·que** \pi-ˈkā, ˈpē-ˌ\ *n* : a durable ribbed fabric [French *piqué,* from *piquer* "to prick, quilt"]

pi·quet \pi-ˈkā, pik-ˈet\ *n* : a two-handed card game played with 32 cards in which players score points for certain combinations and for winning tricks [French]

pi·ra·cy \ˈpī-rə-sē\ *n, pl* **-cies** **1** : robbery on the high seas **2** : the unauthorized use of another's production or invention especially in violation of a copyright

pi·ra·nha \pə-ˈran-yə; -ˈrän-ə, -yə\ *n* : any of various usually small flesh-eating South American fishes that have very sharp teeth, often occur in schools, and include some that may attack and inflict dangerous wounds upon humans and large animals

— called also *caribe* [Portuguese, from Tupi *pirânya,* from *pirá* "fish" + *ânya* "tooth"]

¹pi·rate \ˈpī-rət\ *n* **:** a person who commits or practices piracy [Medieval French, from Latin *pirata,* from Greek *peiratēs,* from *peiran* "to attempt"] — **pi·rat·i·cal** \pə-ˈrat-i-kəl, pī-\ *adj*

²pirate *vt* **:** to take or make use of by piracy ⟨*pirate* an invention⟩

pi·rogue \ˈpē-ˌrōg\ *n* **1 :** DUGOUT 1 **2 :** a boat like a canoe [French, from Spanish *piragua*]

pir·ou·ette \ˌpir-ə-ˈwet\ *n* **:** a rapid whirling about of the body; *esp* **:** a full turn on the toe or ball of one foot in ballet [French] — **pirouette** *vi*

pis *plural of* PI

Pi·sces \ˈpī-ˌsēz, ˈpis-ˌēz\ *n* **1 :** a zodiacal constellation directly south of Andromeda **2 :** the 12th sign of the zodiac; *also* **:** one born under this sign [Latin, from pl. of *piscis* "fish"]

pi·scine \ˈpī-ˌsēn; ˈpis-ˌīn, -ˌkīn\ *adj* **:** of, relating to, or characteristic of fish [Latin *piscinus,* from *piscis* "fish"]

pis·mire \ˈpis-ˌmīr, ˈpiz-\ *n* **:** ANT [Middle English *pissemire,* from *pisse* "urine" + *mire* "ant," of Scandinavian origin]

pi·so \ˈpē-sō\ *n, pl* **pisos :** the peso of the Philippines [probably from Tagalog, from Spanish *peso*]

pis·tach·io \pə-ˈstash-ē-ˌō, -ˈstash-ō, -ˈstäsh-\ *n, pl* **-chios :** a small Asian tree related to the sumacs whose fruit contains a greenish edible seed; *also* **:** its seed [Italian *pistacchio,* from Latin *pistacium* "pistachio nut," from Greek *pistakion,* from *pistakē* "pistachio tree," of Iranian origin]

pis·til \ˈpis-tl\ *n* **:** the seed-producing part and female reproductive organ of a flower consisting usually of stigma, style, and ovary [Latin *pistillum* "pestle"]

pis·til·late \ˈpis-tə-ˌlāt\ *adj* **:** having pistils; *esp* **:** having pistils but no stamens

pis·tol \ˈpis-tl\ *n* **1 :** a short firearm intended to be aimed and fired with one hand **2 :** a notably sharp, spirited, or energetic person [Middle French *pistole,* from German, from Czech *píšťala,* literally, "pipe"] — **pistol** *vt*

pis·to·le·ro \ˌpis-tə-ˈler-ō\ *n, pl* **-ros :** GUNMAN

pis·tol–whip \-ˌhwip, -ˌwip\ *vt* **:** to beat with a pistol

pis·ton \ˈpis-tən\ *n* **1 :** a sliding piece moved by or moving against fluid pressure that usually consists of a short cylindrical body fitting within a cylindrical chamber or vessel along which it moves back and forth **2 :** a sliding valve in a brass wind instrument which when depressed lowers its pitch [French, from Italian *pistone,* from *pistare* "to pound," from Medieval Latin, from Latin *pistus,* past participle of *pinsere* "to crush"]

piston ring *n* **:** a springy split metal ring around a piston for making a tight fit

piston rod *n* **:** a rod by which a piston is moved or by which it transmits motion

¹pit \ˈpit\ *n* **1 :** a hole, shaft, or cavity in the ground ⟨a gravel *pit*⟩ **2 :** an area set off from and often lower than adjacent areas: as **a :** an enclosure where animals (as cocks) are set to fight **b :** the space occupied by an orchestra in a theater **3 a :** a hollowed or indented area especially in the surface of the body **b :** an indented scar (as from a boil) **c :** a thin area in a plant cell wall through which water and dissolved materials can pass **4** *pl* **:** WORST ⟨it's the *pits*⟩ **5 :** an area alongside an auto racetrack where cars are refueled and repaired during a race — often used in plural with *the* [Old English *pytt,* derived from Latin *puteus* "well, pit"]

²pit *vb* **pit·ted; pit·ting 1 a :** to put into or store in a pit **b :** to make pits in; *esp* **:** to scar with pits **2 :** to place in opposition or rivalry **3 :** to become marked with pits

³pit *n* **:** the stone of a fruit (as the cherry or peach) that is a drupe [Dutch] — **pit·less** \ˈpit-ləs\ *adj*

⁴pit *vt* **pit·ted; pit·ting :** to remove the pit from

pi·ta \ˈpēt-ə\ *n* **:** a thin flat bread that can be separated easily into two layers to form a pocket — called also *pita bread* [Modern Greek]

pit–a–pat \ˌpit-i-ˈpat\ *n* **:** PITTER-PATTER [imitative] — **pit–a–pat** *adv or adj* — **pit–a–pat** *vi*

pit bull *n* **1 :** a dog (as an American Staffordshire terrier) of any of several breeds originally developed for fighting and noted for strength and stamina **2 :** an aggressive and tenacious person ⟨a political *pit bull*⟩

pit bull terrier *n* **1 :** PIT BULL 1 **2 :** AMERICAN PIT BULL TERRIER

¹pitch \ˈpich\ *n* **1 :** a dark sticky substance obtained as a residue in the distillation of organic materials (as tars) **2 :** resin from various conifers [Old English *pic,* from Latin *pix*]

²pitch *vt* **:** to cover, smear, or treat with or as if with pitch

³pitch *vb* **1 :** to erect and fix firmly in place ⟨*pitch* a tent⟩ **2 :** to throw usually toward a certain point ⟨*pitch* hay into a wagon⟩ **3 :** to present or advertise especially in a high-pressure way **4 a :** to cause to be at a particular pitch or level ⟨*pitch* a tune too high⟩ ⟨a test *pitched* at a 5th-grade reading level⟩ **b :** to incline or cause to incline at a particular angle **5 a :** to fall headlong **b :** to have the bow alternately plunge and rise abruptly ⟨a ship *pitching* in heavy seas⟩ **c :** BUCK 1a ⟨a *pitching* horse⟩ **6 a :** to throw a ball to a batter **b :** to play ball as a pitcher [Middle English *pichen*]

⁴pitch *n* **1 :** the action or a manner of pitching; *esp* **:** an up-and-down movement **2 a :** SLOPE 2; *also* **:** degree of slope **b (1) :** distance between one point on a gear tooth and the corresponding point on the next tooth **(2) :** distance from any point on the thread of a screw to the corresponding point on an adjacent thread measured parallel to the axis **c :** the distance advanced by an aircraft with one revolution of its propeller **3 :** the relative level, intensity, or extent of some quality or state ⟨tensions rose to a feverish *pitch*⟩ **4 a :** the property of a tone that is determined by the frequency of the sound waves producing it **:** highness or lowness of sound **b :** a standard frequency for tuning instruments **c :** the phonemic change of vibrational frequency in human speech **5 a :** a high-pressure sales talk **b :** ADVERTISEMENT 1 **c :** RECOMMENDATION 1 ⟨made a *pitch* for tax cuts⟩ **6 a :** the delivery of a baseball by a pitcher to a batter **b :** a baseball so thrown — **pitched** \ˈpicht\ *adj*

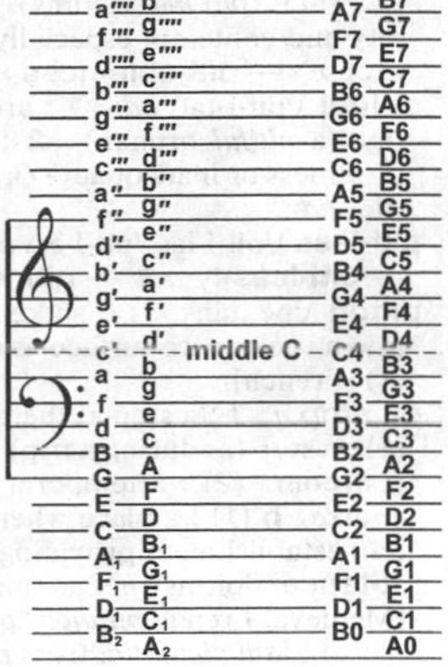

⁴pitch 4a: two systems of staff notation of pitch

pitch–black \ˈpich-ˈblak\ *adj* **:** extremely dark or black

pitch·blende \ˈpich-ˌblend\ *n* **:** a brown to black mineral that consists essentially of an oxide of uranium, often contains radium, and is a source of uranium [German *Pechblende,* from *Pech* "pitch" + *Blende* "sphalerite"]

pitch–dark \-ˈdärk\ *adj* **:** extremely dark

pitched battle \ˈpicht-, ˈpich-\ *n* **:** an intensely fought battle in which the opposing forces are locked in close combat

¹pitch·er \ˈpich-ər\ *n* **:** a container for holding and pouring liquids that usually has a lip or spout and a handle [Medieval French *picher,* from Medieval Latin *bicarius* "goblet"]

²pitcher *n* **:** one that pitches; *esp* **:** the player who pitches in a game of baseball

pitcher plant *n* **:** any of various plants with leaves modified into tubes resembling pitchers in which insects are trapped and digested by the plant

pitch·fork \ˈpich-ˌfȯrk\ *n* **:** a usually long-handled fork used in pitching hay or straw — **pitchfork** *vt*

pitch in *vi* **1 :** to begin to work energetically **2 :** to contribute to a common activity

pitch·out \ˈpich-ˌau̇t\ *n* **1 :** a pitch in baseball deliberately out of reach of the batter to enable the catcher to check or put out a base runner **2 :** a lateral pass in football between two backs behind the line of scrimmage

pitch pipe *n* **:** a small pipe blown to indicate musical pitch especially for singers or for tuning an instrument

pitchy \ˈpich-ē\ *adj* **1 :** full of pitch **:** TARRY **2 :** of, relating to, or having the qualities of pitch

pit·e·ous \ˈpit-ē-əs\ *adj* **:** of a kind to move to pity or compassion — **pit·e·ous·ly** *adv* — **pit·e·ous·ness** *n*

pit·fall \ˈpit-ˌfȯl\ *n* **1 :** TRAP 1, SNARE; *esp* **:** a covered or camouflaged pit used to capture and hold an animal or person **2 :** a hidden or not easily recognized danger or difficulty

[1]**pith** \ˈpith\ *n* **1 a :** a central strand of spongy tissue in the stems of most vascular plants that probably functions chiefly in storage **b :** any of various loose spongy internal tissues or parts (as of a bone or feather) **2 :** the essential part : CORE [Old English *pitha*]

[2]**pith** *vt* **:** to destroy the spinal cord or central nervous system of (as a frog) by passing a wire or needle up and down the vertebral canal

pithy \ˈpith-ē\ *adj* **pith·i·er; -est 1 :** consisting of or filled with pith **2 :** being short and to the point ⟨a *pithy* comment⟩ — **pith·i·ly** \ˈpith-ə-lē\ *adv* — **pith·i·ness** \ˈpith-ē-nəs\ *n*

piti·able \ˈpit-ē-ə-bəl\ *adj* **1 :** deserving or exciting pity : LAMENTABLE ⟨*pitiable* victims⟩ **2 :** of a kind to bring about mixed pity and contempt especially because of inadequacy ⟨a *pitiable* excuse⟩ — **piti·able·ness** *n* — **piti·ably** \-blē\ *adv*

piti·ful \ˈpit-i-fəl\ *adj* **1 :** arousing or deserving pity or sympathy ⟨a *pitiful* orphan⟩ **2 :** exciting pitying contempt (as by meanness or inadequacy) ⟨a *pitiful* excuse⟩ — **piti·ful·ly** \-fə-lē, -flē\ *adv*

piti·less \ˈpit-i-ləs, ˈpit-l-əs\ *adj* **:** having no pity : HARSH, CRUEL — **piti·less·ly** *adv* — **piti·less·ness** *n*

pi·ton \ˈpē-ˌtän\ *n* **:** a spike, wedge, or peg that can be driven into a rock or ice surface as a support (as for a mountain climber) [French]

pit stop *n* **1 :** a stop at the pits during an automobile race **2 a** (1) **:** a stop (as during a trip) for fuel, food, or rest or for use of a restroom (2) **:** a temporary deviation from a direct or usual course **b** (1) **:** a place where a pit stop is or can be made (2) **:** an establishment providing food or drink

pit·tance \ˈpit-ns\ *n* **:** a small portion, amount, or allowance [Medieval French *pitance* "piety, pity, dole, portion," from Medieval Latin *pietantia,* from *pietare* "to be charitable," from Latin *pietas* "piety, pity"]

pitted *adj* **:** marked by pits

pit·ter–pat·ter \ˈpit-ər-ˌpat-ər, ˈpit-ē-ˌpat-\ *n* **:** a rapid succession of light sounds or beats — **pit·ter–pat·ter** \ˌpit-ər-ˈ, ˌpit-ē-ˈ\ *adv or adj* — **pit·ter–pat·ter** \ˌpit-ər-ˈ, ˌpit-ē-ˈ\ *vi*

[1]**pi·tu·i·tary** \pə-ˈtü-ə-ˌter-ē, -ˈtyü-\ *adj* **:** of, relating to, or being the pituitary gland [Latin *pituita* "phlegm"; from the former belief that the pituitary gland secreted phlegm]

[2]**pituitary** *n, pl* **-tar·ies :** PITUITARY GLAND

pituitary gland *n* **:** a small oval endocrine organ attached to the base of the brain that produces various internal secretions with a direct or indirect regulatory action on most basic body functions and especially on growth and reproduction — called also *pituitary body*

pit viper *n* **:** any of various mostly New World venomous snakes with a sensory pit on each side of the head and hollow perforated fangs

[1]**pity** \ˈpit-ē\ *n, pl* **pit·ies 1 :** sympathetic sorrow for one suffering, distressed, or unhappy : COMPASSION **2 :** something to be regretted ⟨it's a *pity* you can't go⟩ [Medieval French *pité,* from Latin *pietas* "piety, pity," from *pius* "pious"]

[2]**pity** *vb* **pit·ied; pity·ing :** to feel pity or pity for — **piti·er** *n*

pity·ing *adj* **:** expressing or feeling pity ⟨a *pitying* glance⟩ — **pity·ing·ly** \-ing-lē\ *adv*

[1]**piv·ot** \ˈpiv-ət\ *n* **1 :** a shaft or pin on which something turns **2 :** something upon which something else turns or depends **:** a central member, part, or point [French]

[2]**pivot** *vb* **1 :** to turn on or as if on a pivot **2 :** to provide with, mount on, or attach by a pivot **3 :** to cause to pivot

piv·ot·al \ˈpiv-ət-l\ *adj* **1 :** of, relating to, or functioning as a pivot **2 :** vitally important : CRITICAL — **piv·ot·al·ly** \-l-ē\ *adv*

pivot joint *n* **:** an anatomical joint (as that of the skull and spine) that consists of a bony pivot in a ring of bone and cartilage and that permits rotatory movement only

pix·el \ˈpik-səl, -ˌsel\ *n* **:** any of the small elements that together make up an image (as on a television or computer screen) or optical sensor (as for a camera) [*pix* (plural of *pic,* short for *picture*) + *el*ement]

pix·ie *also* **pixy** \ˈpik-sē\ *n, pl* **pix·ies :** a mischievous sprite or fairy [origin unknown] — **pix·ie·ish** \-sē-ish\ *adj*

piz·za \ˈpēt-sə\ *n* **:** a dish made typically of flattened bread dough spread with a spiced mixture usually including tomatoes and cheese and often other toppings and baked — called also *pizza pie* [Italian, perhaps of Germanic origin]

piz·ze·ria \ˌpēt-sə-ˈrē-ə\ *n* **:** an establishment where pizzas are made or sold [Italian, from *pizza*]

piz·zi·ca·to \ˌpit-si-ˈkät-ō\ *adv or adj* **:** by means of plucking by the fingers instead of bowing — used as a direction in music [Italian, past participle of *pizzicare* "to pluck"]

pj's \ˈpē-ˈjāz\ *n pl* **:** PAJAMAS

pla·ca·ble \ˈplak-ə-bəl, ˈplā-kə-\ *adj* **:** easily placated — **pla·ca·bil·i·ty** \ˌplak-ə-ˈbil-ət-ē, ˌplā-kə-\ *n* — **pla·ca·bly** \ˈplak-ə-blē, ˈplā-kə-\ *adv*

[1]**plac·ard** \ˈplak-ərd, -ˌärd\ *n* **:** a notice posted or carried in a public place : POSTER [Middle French, from *plaquer* "to plate, make adhere"]

[2]**plac·ard** \ˈplak-ˌärd, -ərd\ *vt* **1 :** to post placards on or in **2 :** to anounce by or as if by posting

pla·cate \ˈplāk-ˌāt, ˈplak-\ *vt* **:** to calm the anger of especially by concessions : SOOTHE [Latin *placare*] ***synonyms*** see PACIFY — **pla·ca·tion** \plā-ˈkā-shən\ *n* — **pla·ca·tive** \ˈplāk-ˌāt-iv, ˈplak-\ *adj* — **pla·ca·to·ry** \ˈplāk-ə-ˌtōr-ē, ˈplak-, -ˌtór-\ *adj*

[1]**place** \ˈplās\ *n* **1 a :** physical extension : SPACE ⟨considerations of time and *place*⟩ **b :** a particular but often unspecified location : LOCALITY ⟨stopped several days at each *place*⟩ **c :** a certain region or center of population ⟨a nice *place* to visit⟩ **2 a :** DWELLING ⟨came over to my *place*⟩ **b :** a building or locality used for a particular purpose ⟨a *place* of learning⟩ **c :** an indefinite region or expanse ⟨all over the *place*⟩ **3 :** a particular part of a surface or body : SPOT ⟨a sore *place* on the shoulder⟩ ⟨lost my *place* in the book⟩ **4 a :** position in an ordering ⟨in the first *place*⟩ **b :** second position at the finish (as at a horse race) **c :** a position at the conclusion of a competition ⟨finished in third *place*⟩ **d :** position in a social scale ⟨put them in their *place*⟩ **e :** the position of a digit in a numeral ⟨in 2.718 the digit 1 is two *places* after the decimal point⟩ **5 a :** suitable or assigned location, position, or moment ⟨not the *place* for an active person⟩ **b :** an accommodation occupied by or available for one person ⟨set 12 *places* at table⟩ **c :** space or situation customarily or formerly occupied ⟨paper towels taking the *place* of linen⟩ **d :** JOB 3b, POSITION ⟨lose one's *place* at the office⟩ **6 :** a public square **7 :** a short street [Medieval French, "open space," from Latin *platea* "broad street," from Greek *plateia,* from *platys* "broad"] — **place·less** \ˈplā-sləs\ *adj* — **in place 1 a :** in an original or proper position **b :** established, instituted, or operational ⟨systems *in place*⟩ **2 :** in the same spot without forward or backward movement ⟨run *in place*⟩ — **in place of :** as a substitute or replacement for : INSTEAD OF — **out of place 1 :** not in the proper or usual location **2 :** IMPROPER, INAPPROPRIATE

[2]**place** *vb* **1 :** to distribute in an orderly manner : ARRANGE **2 a :** to put in or direct to a particular place **b :** to present for consideration ⟨a question *placed* before the group⟩ **c :** to put in a particular state **3 a :** to appoint to a position ⟨was *placed* in command⟩ **b :** to find employment or a home for **4 a :** to assign to or hold a position in a series : RANK **b :** ESTIMATE ⟨*placed* the value of the estate too high⟩ **c :** to identify by association ⟨couldn't quite *place* her face⟩ **5 :** to give an order for ⟨*place* a bet⟩ **6 :** to come in second (as in a horse race) — **place·able** \ˈplā-sə-bəl\ *adj*

pla·ce·bo \plə-ˈsē-bō\ *n, pl* **-bos :** an inert preparation prescribed more for the mental relief of the patient than for its actual effect on a disorder; *also* **:** an inert substance used as a control in experiments testing the effectiveness of another substance (as a new medicine) [Latin, "I shall please," from *placēre* "to please"]

placebo effect *n* **:** improvement in the condition of a patient that occurs in response to treatment but cannot be considered due to the specific treatment used

place·hold·er \ˈplās-ˌhōl-dər\ *n* **:** a symbol in a mathematical or logical expression that may be replaced by the name of any element of a given set

place·kick \ˈplā-ˌskik\ *n* **:** the kicking of a ball placed or held in a stationary position on the ground — **placekick** *vt*

place mat *n* **:** a small table mat on which a place setting is laid

place·ment \ˈplā-smənt\ *n* **1 :** an act or instance of placing; *esp* **:** the assignment of a person to a suitable place (as a class in school or a job) **2 :** PLACEKICK

pla·cen·ta \plə-ˈsent-ə\ *n, pl* **-centas** *or* **-cen·tae** \-ˈsent-ē\ **1 :** the vascular organ in most mammals by which the fetus is joined to the uterus of the mother and nourished; *also* **:** an analogous organ in another animal **2 :** a part of a plant ovary that bears ovules [Latin, "flat cake," from Greek *placoenta,* from *plak-, plax* "flat surface"] — **pla·cen·tal** \-ˈsent-l\ *adj or n* — **pla·cen·ta·tion** \ˌplas-n-ˈtā-shən, plə-ˌsen-\ *n*

plac·er \ˈplas-ər\ *n* **:** an alluvial or glacial deposit containing particles of valuable mineral (as gold) [Spanish, from Catalan, "submarine plain," from *plaza* "place," from Latin *platea* "broad street"]

place setting *n* : a set of dishes and silverware for one person

place value *n* : the value of the location of a digit in a numeral ⟨in 425 the location of the digit 2 has a *place value* of ten while the digit itself indicates that there are two tens⟩

plac·id \ˈplas-əd\ *adj* : peacefully free of interruption or disturbance : QUIET [Latin *placidus,* from *placēre* "to please"] ***synonyms*** see CALM — **pla·cid·i·ty** \pla-ˈsid-ət-ē, plə-\ *n* — **plac·id·ly** \ˈplas-əd-lē\ *adv* — **plac·id·ness** *n*

plack·et \ˈplak-ət\ *n* : a slit or opening in a garment (as a skirt) often forming the closure [origin unknown]

plac·o·derm \ˈplak-ə-ˌdərm\ *n* : any of a class (Placodermi) of extinct fishes chiefly of the Devonian period with an armor of bony plates and primitive jaw structures [Greek *plak-, plax* "flat surface"]

plac·oid \ˈplak-ˌȯid\ *adj* : of, relating to, or being a fish scale (as of a shark) of dermal origin with an enamel-tipped spine [Greek *plak-, plax* "flat surface"]

pla·gia·rism \ˈplā-jə-ˌriz-əm\ *n* **1** : an act of plagiarizing **2** : something plagiarized [derived from Latin *plagiarius,* literally, "kidnapper," from *plagium* "netting of game, kidnapping," from *plaga* "net"] — **pla·gia·rist** \-rəst\ *n* — **pla·gia·ris·tic** \ˌplā-jə-ˈris-tik\ *adj*

pla·gia·rize \ˈplā-jə-ˌrīz\ *vb* : to steal and pass off as one's own (the ideas or work of another) : commit literary theft — **pla·gia·riz·er** *n*

pla·gio·clase \ˈplā-jē-ə-ˌklās, ˈplā-jə-; ˈplaj-ē-ə-, ˈplaj-ə-; -ˌklāz\ *n* : a feldspar having calcium or sodium in its composition [Greek *plagios* "oblique" + *klasis* "breaking," from *klan* "to break"]

[1]**plague** \ˈplāg\ *n* **1** : a disastrous evil or destructively numerous influx ⟨a *plague* of locusts⟩; *also* : a cause or occasion of annoyance **2 a** : an epidemic disease causing a high rate of mortality : PESTILENCE **b** : a virulent contagious disease that is caused by a bacterium, occurs or has occurred in several forms including bubonic plague, and is usually passed to human beings from infected rodents and especially rats by the bite of a flea or is passed directly from person to person — called also *black death* [Late Latin *plaga,* from Latin, "blow"]

[2]**plague** *vt* **1** : to strike or afflict with or as if with disease, calamity, or natural evil **2** : TEASE 2a, TORMENT — **plagu·er** *n*

plagu·ey *also* **plaguy** \ˈplā-gē, ˈpleg-ē\ *adj* : causing irritation or annoyance : TROUBLESOME — **plaguey** *adv* — **plagu·i·ly** \ˈplā-gə-lē, ˈpleg-ə-\ *adv*

plaid \ˈplad\ *n* **1** : a rectangular length of tartan worn over the left shoulder as part of the Scottish national costume **2** : a fabric with a pattern of tartan or imitative of tartan **3 a** : TARTAN 1 **b** : a pattern of unevenly spaced repeated stripes crossing at right angles [Scottish Gaelic *plaide*] — **plaid** *adj* — **plaid·ed** \-əd\ *adj*

[1]**plain** \ˈplān\ *n* : an extensive area of level or rolling treeless country; *also* : a broad unbroken expanse [Medieval French, from Latin *planum,* from *planus* "flat, level"]

[2]**plain** *adj* **1** : lacking ornament or pattern ⟨the dress was *plain*⟩ **2** : free of added or extraneous matter : PURE ⟨a glass of *plain* water⟩ **3** : free of impediments to view ⟨in *plain* sight⟩ **4 a** : clear to the mind or senses ⟨the trouble was *plain* to the mechanic⟩ **b** : marked by candor : BLUNT ⟨*plain* speaking⟩ **5 a** : of common or average attainments or status : neither notable nor lowly : ORDINARY ⟨*plain* people⟩ **b** : free from complexity : SIMPLE ⟨a *plain* explanation⟩ ⟨*plain* cooking⟩ **c** : lacking beauty or ugliness [Medieval French, "level," from Latin *planus*] ***synonyms*** see FRANK — **plain·ly** *adv* — **plain·ness** \ˈplān-nəs\ *n*

[3]**plain** *adv* : in a plain manner ⟨if I may speak *plain*⟩

[4]**plain** *adv* : to a complete degree : TOTALLY ⟨were *plain* overcome by all the problems⟩ [partly from Middle English *plein* "entire, complete," from Medieval French, "full," from Latin *plenus*; partly from [3]*plain*]

plain·clothes·man \ˈplān-ˈklōz-mən, -ˈklōthz-, -ˌman\ *n* : a police officer who does not wear a uniform while on duty

Plains \ˈplānz\ *adj* : of or relating to North American Indians of the Great Plains or to their culture

plain sailing *n* : easy progress over an unobstructed course

plains·man \ˈplānz-mən\ *n* : an inhabitant of plains

plain·song \ˈplān-ˌsȯng\ *n* : rhythmic but not metrical chant of worship sung in unison in various Christian rites; *esp* : GREGORIAN CHANT

plain·spo·ken \ˈplān-ˈspō-kən\ *adj* : speaking or spoken plainly and especially bluntly ⟨a *plainspoken* teacher⟩ — **plain·spo·ken·ness** \-kən-nəs\ *n*

plaint \ˈplānt\ *n* **1** : LAMENTATION, WAIL **2** : PROTEST 3, COMPLAINT [Medieval French, from Latin *planctus,* from *plangere* "to strike, beat one's breast, lament"]

plain·tiff \ˈplānt-əf\ *n* : a person who begins a lawsuit to enforce a claim — compare DEFENDANT [Medieval French *plaintif,* from *plaintif* "complaining, plaintive"]

plain·tive \ˈplānt-iv\ *adj* : expressive of suffering or woe : MELANCHOLY [Middle French *plaintif* "grieving," from *plaint* "plaint"] — **plain·tive·ly** *adv* — **plain·tive·ness** *n*

plain weave *n* : a weave in which the threads interlace alternately — **plain–wo·ven** \ˌplān-ˈwō-vən\ *adj*

[1]**plait** \ˈplāt, ˈplat\ *n* **1** : PLEAT **2** : a braid of material (as hair or straw) [Medieval French *pleit,* derived from Latin *plicare* "to fold"]

[2]**plait** *vt* **1** : PLEAT 1 **2 a** : to interweave the strands or locks of : BRAID **b** : to make by plaiting ⟨*plait* a basket⟩ — **plait·er** *n*

[1]**plan** \ˈplan\ *n* **1** : a drawing or diagram showing the parts or outline of something **2** : a method or scheme of acting, doing, or arranging ⟨a civil defense *plan*⟩ ⟨vacation *plans*⟩ **3** : INTENT 1, AIM ⟨the *plan* was to stop them at the bridge⟩ [French, "plane, foundation, ground plan"; partly from Latin *planum* "level ground"; from *planus* "level," partly from French *planter* "to plant, fix in place," from Late Latin *plantare*] — **plan·less** \-ləs\ *adj* — **plan·less·ly** *adv* — **plan·less·ness** *n*

synonyms PLAN, DESIGN, PLOT, SCHEME mean a method of making or doing something or achieving an end. PLAN implies mental formulation and often graphic representation ⟨studied the *plans* for the stage sets⟩. DESIGN suggests a pattern and a degree of order or harmony ⟨*designs* for three new gowns⟩. PLOT implies a laying out in clearly distinguished sections with attention to their relations and proportions ⟨outlined the *plot* of the new play⟩. SCHEME stresses systematic choice and ordering of detail for the end in view and may suggest a plan motivated by craftiness and self-interest ⟨a *scheme* to swindle a neighbor⟩.

[2]**plan** *vb* **planned; plan·ning** **1** : to form a plan of or for : arrange the parts or details of in advance ⟨*plan* a party⟩ **2** : to have in mind : INTEND **3** : to make plans — **plan·ner** *n*

plan- *or* **plano-** *combining form* : flat : flat and ⟨*plano*-convex⟩ [Latin *planus*]

pla·nar \ˈplā-nər, -ˌnär\ *adj* : of, relating to, or lying in a plane

pla·nar·ia \plə-ˈnar-ē-ə, -ˈner-\ *n* : PLANARIAN; *esp* : one of a common freshwater genus [derived from Late Latin *planarius* "lying on a plane," from Latin *planum* "plane"]

pla·nar·i·an \-ē-ən\ *n* : any of an order (Tricladida) of small soft-bodied ciliated mostly aquatic flatworms; *esp* : one inhabiting fresh water and having two eyespots and a triangular head — **planarian** *adj*

[1]**plane** \ˈplān\ *vt* **1** : to make smooth or even especially with a plane **2** : to remove by or as if by planing — often used with *away* or *off* [Medieval French *planer,* from Late Latin *planare,* from Latin *planus* "level"] — **plan·er** *n*

[2]**plane** *n* : PLANE TREE [Medieval French, from Latin *platanus,* from Greek *platanos*]

[3]**plane** *n* : a tool for smoothing or shaping a wood surface

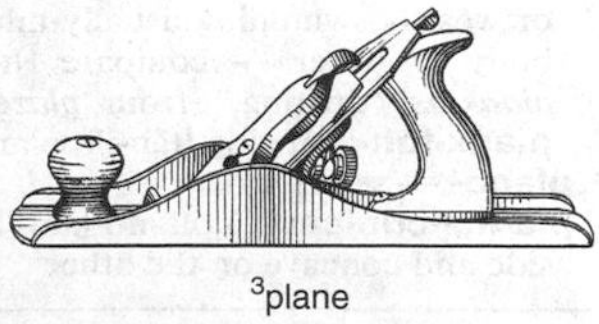
[3]plane

[4]**plane** *n* **1 a** : a surface in which a straight line joining any two points on the surface also lies completely on the surface **b** : a flat or level material surface **2** : a level of existence, consciousness, or development **3 a** : one of the main supporting surfaces of an airplane **b** : AIRPLANE [Latin *planum,* from *planus* "level"]

[5]**plane** *adj* **1** : lacking elevations or depressions : FLAT, LEVEL **2 a** : of, relating to, or dealing with geometric planes **b** : lying in a plane ⟨*plane* curves⟩ [Latin *planus*]

[6]**plane** *vi* **1** : to fly while keeping the wings motionless **2** : to

\ə\ **abut**	\au̇\ **out**	\i\ **tip**	\ȯ\ **saw**	\u̇\ **foot**
\ər\ **further**	\ch\ **chin**	\ī\ **life**	\ȯi\ **coin**	\y\ **yet**
\a\ **mat**	\e\ **pet**	\j\ **job**	\th\ **thin**	\yü\ **few**
\ā\ **take**	\ē\ **easy**	\ng\ **sing**	\th\ **this**	\yu̇\ **cure**
\ä\ **cot, cart**	\g\ **go**	\ō\ **bone**	\ü\ **food**	\zh\ **vision**

travel by airplane [Medieval French *planer,* from *plain* "level, plain," from Latin *planus*]

plane angle *n* **:** an angle that lies in a single plane

plane geometry *n* **:** a branch of geometry that deals with figures that lie in a single plane — compare SOLID GEOMETRY

plane–polarized *adj* **:** vibrating in a single plane ⟨*plane-polarized* light waves⟩

plan·et \ˈplan-ət\ *n* **:** a celestial body other than a comet, meteor, asteroid, or satellite that revolves around the sun; *also* **:** such a body orbiting another star [Medieval French *planete,* from Late Latin *planeta,* from Greek *planēt-, planēs,* literally, "wanderer," from *planasthai* "to wander"]

Word History In studying the sky ancient astronomers observed that while most of the stars maintain fixed relative positions there are a few celestial bodies that quite obviously change their positions in relation to each other and to the greater number of fixed stars. The most notable of these, of course, were the sun and moon, but five others were also observed — Mercury, Venus, Mars, Jupiter, and Saturn. The Greek name for these was *planēs,* whose literal meaning is "wanderer." This is the ancestor of English *planet.* Since ancient times more planets have been discovered, including Uranus in the 18th century and Neptune in the 19th. Pluto was discovered in the 20th century and treated as the ninth planet until 2006, when it was reclassified as a dwarf planet.

plan·e·tar·i·um \ˌplan-ə-ˈter-ē-əm\ *n, pl* **-i·ums** *or* **-ia** \-ē-ə\ **1 :** a model or representation of the solar system **2 a :** an optical device to project various celestial images and effects **b :** a building or room housing such a device

plan·e·tary \ˈplan-ə-ˌter-ē\ *adj* **1 a :** of or relating to a planet **b :** having a motion like that of a planet ⟨*planetary* electrons of the atomic nucleus⟩ **2 :** WORLDWIDE ⟨a *planetary* issue⟩

plan·e·tes·i·mal \ˌplan-ə-ˈtes-ə-məl, -ˈtez-\ *n* **:** any of numerous small solid celestial bodies which may have existed at an early stage of the development of the solar system and from which the planets may have been formed [*planet* + *-esimal* (as in *infinitesimal*)]

plan·e·toid \ˈplan-ə-ˌtȯid\ *n* **1 :** a body resembling a planet **2 :** ASTEROID

plane tree *n* **:** any of a genus of trees (as the sycamore) with large lobed leaves, flowers in globe-shaped heads, and usually scaling bark — called also *plane*

plan·gent \ˈplan-jənt\ *adj* **1 :** having a loud reverberating sound **2 :** having an expressive especially plaintive quality [Latin *plangens,* present participle of *plangere* "to strike, lament"] — **plan·gen·cy** *n* — **plan·gent·ly** *adv*

[1]**plank** \ˈplangk\ *n* **1 :** a heavy thick board **2 :** an article in the platform of a political party [Medieval French *plaunke, planche,* from Latin *planca*]

[2]**plank** *vt* **1 :** to cover or floor with planks **2 :** to set down forcefully ⟨*planked* the book onto the shelf⟩ **3 :** to cook and serve on a board usually with an elaborate garnish

plank·ing *n* **:** a quantity or covering of planks ⟨deck *planking*⟩

plank·ter \ˈplang-tər, ˈplangk-\ *n* **:** a planktonic organism [Greek *planktēr* "wanderer," from *plazesthai* "to wander"]

plank·ton \ˈplang-tən, ˈplangk-, -ˌtän\ *n* **:** the passively floating or weakly swimming usually minute animal and plant life of a body of water — compare NEKTON [German, from Greek *planktos* "drifting," from *plazesthai* "to wander, drift"] — **plank·ton·ic** \plang-ˈtän-ik, plangk-\ *adj*

plano- — see PLAN-

pla·no–con·cave \ˌplā-nō-kän-ˈkāv, -ˈkän-ˌ\ *adj* **:** flat on one side and concave on the other

pla·no–con·vex \-kän-ˈveks, -ˈkän-ˌ, -kən-ˈ\ *adj* **:** flat on one side and convex on the other

pla·nog·ra·phy \plā-ˈnäg-rə-fē, plə-\ *n* **:** a process (as lithography) for printing from a plane surface — **pla·no·graph·ic** \ˌplā-nə-ˈgraf-ik\ *adj*

[1]**plant** \ˈplant\ *vb* **1 a :** to put or set in the ground to grow ⟨*plant* seeds⟩ **b :** to set permanently in the consciousness of **:** IMPLANT ⟨*planted* the idea in his head⟩ ⟨*plant* good habits⟩ **2 a :** to cause to become established ⟨*plant* colonies⟩ **b :** to stock, set, or sow with something usually to grow or increase ⟨*plant* fields to corn⟩ ⟨*plant* a stream with trout⟩ **3 a :** to place or fix in the ground ⟨*planted* stakes to hold the vines⟩ **b :** to place firmly or forcibly ⟨*planted* a hard blow on his chin⟩ **4 :** to hide, place secretly, or prearrange with intent to mislead ⟨*planted* nuggets in a worthless mine⟩ ⟨*plant* a spy in an office⟩ ⟨*plant* a rumor⟩ **5 :** to plant something [Old English *plantian,* from Late Latin *plantare* "to plant, fix in place," from Latin, "to plant," from *planta* "plant"] — **plant·able** \-ə-bəl\ *adj*

[2]**plant** *n* **1 :** any of a kingdom (Plantae) of multicellular mostly photosynthetic living things typically lacking the ability to move from place to place under their own power, having no obvious nervous or sensory organs, and possessing cellulose cell walls and capacity for indefinite growth — compare ANIMAL **2 a :** land, buildings, and equipment of a business, institution, or organization ⟨the college *plant*⟩ **b :** a factory or workshop for the manufacture of a product ⟨an automobile *plant*⟩ **c :** POWER PLANT **3 :** something or someone planted ⟨the new clerk was a police *plant*⟩ [Old English *plante,* from Latin *planta*] — **plant·like** \-ˌlīk\ *adj*

Plan·tag·e·net \plan-ˈtaj-nət, -ə-nət\ *adj* **:** of or relating to a royal house ruling England from 1154 to 1485 [*Plantagenet,* nickname of the family adopted as a surname] — **Plantagenet** *n*

[1]**plan·tain** \ˈplant-n\ *n* **:** any of several common short-stemmed or stemless weedy herbs with parallel-veined leaves and a long spike of tiny greenish flowers [Medieval French, from Latin *plantago,* from *planta* "sole of the foot," from its broad leaves]

[2]**plantain** *n* **:** a banana plant with large greenish starchy fruit that is eaten cooked and is a staple food in the tropics; *also* **:** this fruit [Spanish *plántano, platano* "plane tree, banana tree," from Medieval Latin *plantanus* "plane tree," from Latin *platanus*]

plantain lily *n* **:** HOSTA

plan·tar \ˈplant-ər, ˈplan-ˌtär\ *adj* **:** of or relating to the sole of the foot [Latin *plantaris,* from *planta* "sole"]

plan·ta·tion \plan-ˈtā-shən\ *n* **1 :** a usually large group of plants and especially trees under cultivation **2 :** a settlement in a new country or region **:** COLONY **3 :** a planted area; *esp* **:** an agricultural estate worked by resident labor

plant·er \ˈplant-ər\ *n* **1 :** one that plants or cultivates ⟨a mechanical *planter*⟩; *esp* **:** an owner or operator of a plantation **2 :** one who settles or founds a colony **3 :** a container in which ornamental plants are grown

plant food *n* **1 :** FOOD 1b **2 :** soil fertilizer

plant hormone *n* **:** a substance that is not a nutrient and that in minute amounts modifies a plant physiological process; *esp* **:** one produced by a plant and active elsewhere than at the site of production

plan·ti·grade \ˈplant-ə-ˌgrād\ *adj* **:** walking on the sole with the heel touching the ground ⟨humans are *plantigrade* animals⟩ [French, from Latin *planta* "sole" + *gradi* "to step"] — **plantigrade** *n*

plant·ing *n* **:** an area where plants are grown for commercial or decorative purposes

plant kingdom *n* **:** a basic group of natural objects that includes

PLANETS

NAME	SYMBOL	MEAN DISTANCE FROM THE SUN *astronomical units*	*million miles*	*million kilometers*	PERIOD OF REVOLUTION *days or years*	PERIOD OF ROTATION *hours or days*	EQUATORIAL DIAMETER *miles*	*kilometers*	MASS *relative to Earth*
Mercury	☿	0.39	35.99	57.91	87.97 d.	58.65 d.	3,033	4,879	0.06
Venus	♀	0.72	67.25	108.21	224.70 d.	243.02 d.	7,522	12,104	0.82
Earth	⊕	1.00	92.98	149.60	365.26 d.	23.93 h.	7,928	12,756	1.00
Mars	♂	1.52	141.67	227.94	686.99 d.	24.62 h.	4,222	6,794	0.11
Jupiter	♃	5.20	483.78	778.41	11.86 y.	9.92 h.	88,865	142,984	317.82
Saturn	♄	9.54	886.72	1,426.73	29.47 y.	10.66 h.	74,914	120,536	95.16
Uranus	⛢	19.19	1,784.32	2,870.97	84.02 y.	17.24 h.	31,770	51,118	14.54
Neptune	♆	30.07	2,795.68	4,498.25	164.79 y.	16.11 h.	30,782	49,528	17.15

all living and extinct plants — compare ANIMAL KINGDOM, MINERAL KINGDOM

plant louse *n* : APHID; *also* : a similar insect

plan·u·la \ˈplan-yə-lə\ *n, pl* **-lae** \-ˌlē, -ˌlī\ : the young usually flattened oval or oblong free-swimming ciliated larva of some coelenterates [New Latin, from Latin *planus* "level, flat"]

plaque \ˈplak\ *n* **1** : an ornamental brooch; *esp* : the badge of an honorary order **2** : a flat thin piece (as of metal) used for decoration; *also* : a commemorative or identifying inscribed tablet **3 a** : a sticky usually colorless film on teeth that is formed by and contains bacteria **b** : a fatty deposit characteristic of atherosclerosis **4** : a clear area in a bacterial culture produced by destruction of cells by a virus [French, from Middle French, "metal sheet," from *plaquer* "to plate," from Dutch *placken* "to piece, patch"]

plash \ˈplash\ *n* : SPLASH [probably imitative] — **plash** *vb*

-pla·sia \ˈplā-zhə\ *n combining form* : development : formation ⟨hyper*plasia*⟩ [Greek *plasis* "molding," from *plassein* "to mold"]

-plasm \ˌplaz-əm\ *n combining form* : formative or formed material (as of a cell or tissue) ⟨endo*plasm*⟩ [New Latin *plasma*, from Greek *plassein* "to mold"]

plas·ma \ˈplaz-mə\ *n* **1** : the fluid part of blood, lymph, or milk as distinguished from suspended material; *esp* : BLOOD PLASMA **2** : a collection of charged particles that shows some properties of a gas but that differs from a gas in being a good conductor of electricity and in being affected by a magnetic field [German, from Late Latin, "something molded," from Greek, from *plassein* "to mold"] — **plas·mat·ic** \plaz-ˈmat-ik\ *adj*

plas·ma·lem·ma \ˌplaz-mə-ˈlem-ə\ *n* : CELL MEMBRANE [*plasma* + Greek *lemma* "husk"]

plasma membrane *n* : CELL MEMBRANE

plas·mid \ˈplaz-məd\ *n* : a ring of DNA found in certain bacteria that replicates independently of chromosomal DNA [*plasma* + *-id* "body, particle," from Greek]

plas·min·o·gen \plaz-ˈmin-ə-jən\ *n* : a substance that is found in blood plasma and serum and is the precursor of an enzyme that dissolves the fibrin of blood clots [*plasmin* "an enzyme that dissolves the fibrin of blood clots" + *-gen*]

plas·mo·di·um \plaz-ˈmōd-ē-əm\ *n, pl* **-dia** \-ē-ə\ **1** : a motile mass of protoplasm that is the nonreproductive stage of a slime mold and contains many nuclei without dividing cell walls **2** : an individual malaria parasite [New Latin, from *plasma*] — **plas·mo·di·al** \-ē-əl\ *adj*

plas·mol·y·sis \plaz-ˈmäl-ə-səs\ *n* : shrinking of the cytoplasm away from the wall of a living cell — **plas·mo·lyt·ic** \ˌplaz-mə-ˈlit-ik\ *adj* — **plas·mo·lyze** \ˈplaz-mə-ˌlīz\ *vb*

1**plas·ter** \ˈplas-tər\ *n* **1** : a medicated or protective dressing consisting of a film (as of cloth or plastic) spread with an often medicated substance ⟨adhesive *plaster*⟩ **2** : a pasty composition (as of lime, water, and sand) that hardens on drying and is used for coating walls, ceilings, and partitions [Old English, from Latin *emplastrum*, from Greek *emplastron*, from *emplassein* "to plaster on," from *en-* + *plassein* "to mold, plaster"] — **plas·tery** \-tə-rē, -trē\ *adj*

2**plaster** *vb* **plas·tered; plas·ter·ing** \-tə-ring, -tring\ **1** : to apply plaster : overlay or cover with plaster **2** : to apply a plaster to **3 a** : to cover over or conceal as if with a coat of plaster **b** : to smooth down with a sticky substance ⟨*plastered* my hair down⟩ **4** : to fasten or apply to another surface : stick tightly ⟨rain *plastered* the clothes to our backs⟩ **5** : to affix or place on especially in large numbers ⟨*plaster* a wall with signs⟩ — **plas·ter·er** \-tər-ər\ *n*

plas·ter·board \ˈplas-tər-ˌbōrd, -ˌbȯrd\ *n* : DRYWALL

plaster cast *n* : a rigid dressing of gauze filled with plaster of paris

plaster of par·is \-ˈpar-əs\ *often cap 2nd P* : a white powdery slightly hydrated calcium sulfate made by calcining gypsum and used chiefly for casts and molds in the form of a quick-setting paste with water [*Paris*, France]

1**plas·tic** \ˈplas-tik\ *adj* **1** : FORMATIVE, CREATIVE ⟨*plastic* forces in nature⟩ **2 a** : capable of being molded or modeled ⟨*plastic* clay⟩ **b** : capable of adapting to varying conditions ⟨*plastic* species⟩ ⟨a *plastic* tissue⟩ **3** : marked by or using modeling : SCULPTURAL **4** : made or consisting of a plastic **5** : capable of being deformed continuously and permanently in any direction without rupture **6** : of, relating to, or involving plastic surgery [Latin *plasticus* "of molding," from Greek *plastikos*, from *plassein* "to mold, form"] — **plas·ti·cal·ly** \-ti-kə-lē, -klē\ *adv*

synonyms PLASTIC, PLIABLE, PLIANT mean subject to being modified in form or nature and are applied to materials or to persons perceived as workable material. PLASTIC applies to substances soft enough to mold into any desired form or to beings that readily adapt to circumstance ⟨*plastic* materials allow the sculptor greater freedom⟩. PLIABLE implies lack of resistance to bending, folding, or manipulating and when applied to persons suggests obedience to another's will ⟨*pliable* rubber tubing⟩. PLIANT may stress flexibility and springiness and so suggest ready responsiveness either in material or individuals ⟨a sneaker with a *pliant* sole⟩.

2**plastic** *n* : a plastic substance; *esp* : any of numerous organic synthetic or processed materials (as polymers) that can be formed into objects, films, or filaments

plas·tic·i·ty \pla-ˈstis-ət-ē\ *n* : the quality or state of being plastic; *esp* : capacity for being molded or changed

plas·ti·ciz·er \ˈplas-tə-ˌsī-zər\ *n* : a chemical added to rubbers and resins to impart flexibility, workability, or stretchability

plastic surgery *n* : surgery concerned with the repair, restoration, or improvement of lost, injured, defective, or misshapen parts of the body — **plastic surgeon** *n*

plas·tid \ˈplas-təd\ *n* : any of various cytoplasmic organelles (as chloroplasts) of photosynthetic organisms (as plants) that often serve as centers for special metabolic activities (as starch storage) [German, from Greek *plastos* "molded"]

plas·tron \ˈplas-trən\ *n* **1** : a metal breastplate **2** : the lower part of the shell of a turtle **3** : a trimming like a bib for a woman's dress [Middle French, from Italian *piastrone*, from *piastra*, "thin metal plate," from Latin *emplastra*, *emplastrum* "plaster"] — **plas·tral** \-trəl\ *adj*

-plas·ty \ˌplas-tē\ *n combining form, pl* **-plasties** : plastic surgery

1**plat** \ˈplat\ *n* **1** : a small piece of ground : PLOT **2** : a plan or map of a piece of land (as a town) with lots and landmarks marked out [probably alteration of *plot*]

2**plat** *vt* **plat·ted; plat·ting** : to make a plat of

1**plate** \ˈplāt\ *n* **1** : a flat, thin, and usually smooth piece of material ⟨mica splits easily into *plates*⟩: as **a** : metal in sheets usually thicker than about ¼ inch (6 millimeters) ⟨steel *plate*⟩ **b** : a thin layer of one metal deposited on another usually by electrical means **c** : one of the broad metal pieces used in medieval armor; *also* : armor made of plates **d** : a usually flat bony or horny outgrowth forming part of a covering of an animal (as some fishes or reptiles) **e** : HOME PLATE **f** : the thin fatty underpart of a forequarter of beef or the back part of this cut **g** : any of the large movable segments into which the earth's lithosphere is held to be divided **2** : precious metal; *esp* : silver bullion **3 a** : domestic vessels (as bowls or cups) usually of or plated with precious metal (as silver) **b** : a shallow usually circular dish from which food is eaten or served **c (1)** : a main course served on a plate; *also* : food and service for one person ⟨ten dollars a *plate*⟩ **(2)** : PLATEFUL **d** : a dish or pouch used in taking a collection (as in a church) **e** : a flat glass or plastic dish used chiefly for culturing microorganisms **4 a** : LICENSE PLATE **b** : a sheet of material (as metal or plastic) with a specially prepared surface for printing **c** : a sheet of material (as glass) coated with a light-sensitive photographic emulsion **5** : a horizontal truss that supports the roof trusses or rafters of a building **6 a** : the electrode to which the electrons flow in an electron tube **b** : a metallic grid with its interstices filled with active material that forms one of the structural units of a storage cell or battery **7** : the part of a denture that bears the teeth and fits to the mouth; *also* : DENTURE 2 **8** : a full-page illustration often on special paper ⟨a book with color *plates*⟩ [Medieval French, from *plat* "flat"] — **platelike** \-ˌlīk\ *adj*

2**plate** *vt* **1** : to cover or equip with plate: as **a** : to arm with armor plate **b** : to cover with an adherent layer (as of metal) ⟨had the teapot *plated* with silver⟩ **c** : to deposit (as a layer of metal) on a surface ⟨*plate* silver onto copper⟩ **2** : to make a printing surface from or for

1**pla·teau** \pla-ˈtō, ˈpla-ˌ\ *n, pl* **plateaus** *or* **plateaux** \-ˈtōz, -ˌtōz\

\ə\ **abut**	\au̇\ **out**	\i\ **tip**	\ȯ\ **saw**	\u̇\ **foot**
\ər\ **further**	\ch\ **chin**	\ī\ **life**	\ȯi\ **coin**	\y\ **yet**
\a\ **mat**	\e\ **pet**	\j\ **job**	\th\ **thin**	\yü\ **few**
\ā\ **take**	\ē\ **easy**	\ng\ **sing**	\t͟h\ **this**	\yu̇\ **cure**
\ä\ **cot, cart**	\g\ **go**	\ō\ **bone**	\ü\ **food**	\zh\ **vision**

1 : a usually large relatively level land area raised above adjacent land on at least one side : TABLELAND **2** : a relatively stable level, period, or condition [French, from Medieval French, "platter," from *plat* "flat"]

[2]**plateau** *vi* : to reach a level, period, or condition of stability or maximum achievement

plate·ful \ˈplāt-ˌfu̇l\ *n* **1** : the amount a plate will hold; *also* : a generous helping **2** : a large number or amount ⟨a *plateful* of problems⟩

plate glass *n* : fine rolled, ground, and polished sheet glass

plate·let \ˈplāt-lət\ *n* : one of the minute colorless disk-shaped bodies of mammalian blood that assist in blood clotting by adhering to other platelets and to damaged tissue

plat·en \ˈplat-ⁿn\ *n* **1** : a flat plate of metal that exerts or receives pressure; *esp* : one in some printing presses that presses the paper against the type **2** : the roller of a typewriter [Medieval French *plateine,* from *plate* "plate"]

plat·er \ˈplāt-ər\ *n* : one that plates

plate tec·ton·ics \-tek-ˈtän-iks\ *n* **1** : a theory in geology: the lithosphere of the earth is divided into a small number of movable plates which float on the mantle and whose movements cause seismic activity **2** : the process and dynamics of plate movement [*tectonics* "science or art of construction, branch of geology concerned with structure," derived from Greek *tektonikos* "of a builder," from *tektōn* "builder"] — **plate–tec·ton·ic** \-ik\ *adj*

plat·form \ˈplat-ˌfȯrm\ *n* **1** : a declaration of principles; *esp* : a declaration of principles and policies adopted by a political party or a candidate **2** : a horizontal flat surface usually higher than the adjoining area; *esp* : a raised flooring (as for speakers or performers) **3** : a thick layered sole for a shoe; *also* : a shoe with such a sole **4** : OPERATING SYSTEM [Middle French *plate-forme* "diagram, map," literally, "flat form"]

platform rocker *n* : a chair that rocks on a stable platform

platform tennis *n* : a variation of paddle tennis played on a wooden platform enclosed by a wire fence

plat·ing \ˈplāt-iŋ\ *n* **1** : the act or process of covering especially with metal plate **2** : a coating of metal plates or plate ⟨the *plating* of a ship⟩ ⟨the *plating* wore off the spoons⟩

[1]**plat·i·num** \ˈplat-nəm, -ⁿn-əm\ *n* : a heavy precious grayish white ductile malleable metallic element that is used especially in chemical ware and apparatus, as a catalyst, and in jewelry — see ELEMENT table [New Latin, from Spanish *platina,* from *plata* "silver"]

[2]**platinum** *adj* : qualifying for a platinum record — **go platinum** : to have enough sales to qualify for a platinum record

platinum blonde *n* : a pale silvery blonde color; *also* : a person with hair of this color

platinum record *n* : a platinum phonograph record awarded to a singer or group whose album has sold at least one million copies

plat·i·tude \ˈplat-ə-ˌtüd, -ˌtyüd\ *n* **1** : the quality or state of being dull or trite **2** : a flat or trite remark [French, from *plat* "flat, dull"] — **plat·i·tu·di·nous** \ˌplat-ə-ˈtüd-nəs, -ˈtyüd-, -ⁿn-əs\ *adj*

pla·ton·ic \plə-ˈtän-ik, plā-\ *adj* **1** *cap* : of, relating to, or characteristic of Plato or Platonism **2** : of or relating to love free of sexual desire [Latin, *platonicus* "of Plato," from Greek *platōnikos,* from *Platōn* "Plato"] — **pla·ton·i·cal·ly** \-ˈtän-i-kə-lē, klē\ *adv*

Pla·to·nism \ˈplāt-ⁿn-ˌiz-əm\ *n* : the philosophy of Plato stressing especially that actual things and ideas (as of truth or beauty) are only copies of transcendent ideas which are the objects of true knowledge — **Pla·to·nist** \-ⁿn-əst\ *n*

pla·toon \plə-ˈtün, pla-\ *n* **1** : a subdivision of a military company normally consisting of a headquarters and two or more squads **2** : a group of persons sharing a common characteristic or activity ⟨a *platoon* of waiters⟩; *esp* : a group of football players who are trained for either offense or defense and are sent into or withdrawn from the game as a body [French *peloton* "small detachment," literally, "ball," from Medieval French *pelote* "little ball, pellet"]

platoon sergeant *n* : an enlisted rank in the Army above staff sergeant and below first sergeant

plat·ter \ˈplat-ər\ *n* **1** : a large plate used especially for serving meat **2** : a phonograph record [Medieval French *plater,* from Middle French *plat* "plate, dish"]

platy \ˈplat-ē\ *n, pl* **platy** *or* **plat·ys** *or* **plat·ies** : either of two freshwater live-bearers that are popular for tropical aquariums and are noted for their varied and brilliant colors [New Latin *Platypoecilus,* genus name, from Greek *platys* "broad, flat" + *poikilos* "many-colored"]

platy·pus \ˈplat-i-pəs, -ˌpu̇s\ *n, pl* **platy·pus·es** *also* **platy·pi** \-ˌpī, -ˌpē\ : a small aquatic egg-laying mammal of eastern Australia and Tasmania that eats small animals (as shrimp and insects) and has a fleshy bill resembling that of a duck, webbed feet, and a broad flattened tail [Greek *platypous* "flat-footed," from *platys* "broad, flat" + *pous* "foot"]

platypus

plau·dit \ˈplȯd-ət\ *n* **1** : APPLAUSE **2** : enthusiastic approval — usually used in plural ⟨received the *plaudits* of the critics⟩ [Latin, *plaudite* "applaud," pl. imperative of *plaudere* "to applaud"]

plau·si·bil·i·ty \ˌplȯ-zə-ˈbil-ət-ē\ *n, pl* **-ties** **1** : the quality or state of being plausible **2** : something plausible

plau·si·ble \ˈplȯ-zə-bəl\ *adj* **1** : apparently reasonable, fair, or valuable but often not so ⟨a *plausible* excuse⟩ **2** : appearing worthy of belief ⟨the argument was both powerful and *plausible*⟩ [Latin *plausibilis* "worthy of applause," from *plaudere* "to applaud"] — **plau·si·ble·ness** *n* — **plau·si·bly** \ˈplȯ-zə-blē\ *adv*

synonyms PLAUSIBLE, CREDIBLE, SPECIOUS mean outwardly acceptable as true or genuine. PLAUSIBLE implies reasonableness at first sight or hearing usually with a hint of a possibility of being deceived ⟨a *plausible* excuse⟩. CREDIBLE stresses worthiness of belief ⟨testimony given by a *credible* witness⟩. SPECIOUS stresses surface plausibility clearly with the implication of deceit or fraud ⟨*specious* reasoning⟩ ⟨*specious* claims for damage⟩.

[1]**play** \ˈplā\ *n* **1 a** : a brisk handling or using (as of a weapon) **b** : the conduct, course, or action of or a particular act or maneuver in a game; *also* : one's turn to participate in a game **2 a** : recreational activity; *esp* : the spontaneous activity of children **b** : JEST ⟨said it in *play*⟩ **c** : PUN ⟨a *play* on words⟩ **d** : the act of playing a game and risking something on an uncertain event : GAMBLING **3 a** : a way or manner of acting or proceeding ⟨fair *play*⟩ **b** : OPERATION, ACTIVITY ⟨the normal *play* of economic pressures⟩ **c** : brisk, fitful, or light movement ⟨the light *play* of a breeze⟩ **d** : free or unhindered motion ⟨a jacket that gave *play* in the shoulders⟩ **e** : scope or opportunity for action ⟨the new job gave *play* to their talents⟩ **4 a** : the stage representation of an action or story **b** : a dramatic composition : DRAMA [Old English *plega*] — **in play** : in condition or position to be legitimately played — **out of play** : not in play

[2]**play** *vb* **1 a** : to move swiftly, aimlessly, or lightly ⟨shadows *playing* on the wall⟩ **b** : to move freely within limits **c** : to treat or behave frivolously or lightly ⟨*played* with the idea of getting a job⟩ ⟨*play* a person for a fool⟩ **d** : to make use of double meaning or of the similarity of sound of two words usually for humorous effect **2 a** : to take advantage ⟨were *playing* upon fears⟩ **b** : to finger or trifle with something ⟨*played* with the pencil⟩ **c** : to discharge in a stream ⟨hoses *playing* on the fire⟩ **3 a** : to engage in sport or recreation and especially in spontaneous activity for amusement **b** : to imitate in playing ⟨*play* house⟩ **c** : to take part or engage in (as a game) ⟨*play* cards⟩ ⟨*play* ball⟩ **d** : to compete against in a game ⟨Pittsburgh *plays* Chicago today⟩ **e** : to bet on : WAGER ⟨*play* the horses⟩ **4 a** : to perform on a musical instrument ⟨*play* the piano⟩ **b** : to cause (as a radio) to emit sound **c** : to cause the recorded sound or image of (as a CD or videotape) to be reproduced **d** : to produce music ⟨listen to an organ *playing*⟩ **5** : to be staged or presented ⟨a new show *playing* for one week⟩ **6 a** : to conduct oneself in a particular way ⟨*play* safe⟩ **b** : to perform on or as if on the stage ⟨*play* a part⟩; *also* : to act the part of ⟨*play* the fool⟩ **c** : to put or keep in action ⟨*play* a card in a game⟩ ⟨*play* a fish on a line⟩ **d** : to do for amusement or from mischief ⟨*play* a trick on someone⟩; *also* : to bring about : WREAK ⟨the wind *played* havoc with the garden⟩ **e** : to pretend to be in a specified state ⟨*play* dead⟩ — **play·able** \-ə-bəl\ *adj* — **play ball** : COOPERATE — **play by ear** : to deal with something without previous planning or instructions — **play second fiddle** : to take a subordinate position

pla·ya \ˈplī-ə\ *n* : the flat-floored bottom of an undrained desert basin that becomes at times a shallow lake [Spanish, literally, "beach"]

play·act·ing \ˈplā-ˌak-ting\ *n* **1** : performance in theatrical productions **2** : insincere or artificial behavior

play–action pass *n* : a pass play in football in which the quarterback fakes a handoff before passing the ball — called also *play-action*

play·back \ˈplā-ˌbak\ *n* : an act of reproducing recorded sound or pictures often immediately after recording

play back \plā-ˈbak, ˈplā-\ *vt* : to perform a playback of (a disc or tape)

play·bill \ˈplā-ˌbil\ *n* : a poster advertising a play

Playbill *trademark* — used for a theater program

play·boy \-ˌbȯi\ *n* : a man whose chief interest is the pursuit of pleasure

play–by–play \ˌplā-bə-ˌplā, -bī-\ *adj* **1** : being a running commentary on a sports event **2** : relating each event as it occurs

play down *vt* : to refrain from emphasizing

play·er \ˈplā-ər\ *n* : one that plays: as **a** : a person who plays a game **b** : MUSICIAN **c** : ACTOR 1b **d** : a device for reproducing recorded material ⟨a CD *player*⟩ ⟨a tape *player*⟩

player piano *n* : a piano containing an automatic playing mechanism

play·fel·low \ˈplā-ˌfel-ō\ *n* : PLAYMATE

play·ful \-fəl\ *adj* **1** : full of play : SPORTIVE **2** : HUMOROUS, JOCULAR — **play·ful·ly** \-fə-lē\ *adv* — **play·ful·ness** *n*

play·girl \-ˌgərl\ *n* : a woman whose chief interest is the pursuit of pleasure

play·go·er \-ˌgō-ər, -ˌgōr\ *n* : a person who frequently attends plays

play·ground \-ˌgrau̇nd\ *n* : a piece of land used for games and recreation especially by children

play·house \-ˌhau̇s\ *n* **1** : THEATER 1 **2** : a small house for children to play in

playing card *n* : one of a set of usually 32, 48, or 52 thin rectangular pieces of cardboard or plastic marked on one side to show rank and suit (as spades, hearts, diamonds, or clubs) and used in playing various games

playing field *n* : a field for various games; *esp* : the part of a field officially marked off for play

play·let \ˈplā-lət\ *n* : a short play

play·mate \-ˌmāt\ *n* : a companion in play

play–off \ˈplā-ˌȯf\ *n* **1** : a final contest or series of contests to determine the winner between contestants or teams that have tied **2** : a series of contests played after the end of the regular season to determine a championship — often used in plural

play off \plā-ˈȯf, ˈplā-\ *vt* **1** : to complete the playing of (an interrupted contest) **2** : to break (a tie) by a play-off

play out *vb* **1** : to perform to the end **2 a** : to use up or become used up **b** : to become spent or exhausted **3** : UNREEL, UNFOLD

play·pen \ˈplā-ˌpen\ *n* : a portable enclosure in which a baby or young child may play

play·thing \-ˌthing\ *n* : TOY 2

play·time \-ˌtīm\ *n* : a time for play or diversion

play up *vt* : to give emphasis or prominence to

play·wright \ˈplā-ˌrīt\ *n* : a person who writes plays [obsolete *wright* "maker," from Old English *wryhta*]

pla·za \ˈplaz-ə, ˈpläz-\ *n* **1** : a public square in a city or town **2** : SHOPPING CENTER [Spanish, from Latin *platea* "broad street," from Greek *plateia*, from *platys* "broad"]

plea \ˈplē\ *n* **1** : a defendant's answer to a lawsuit or a criminal charge ⟨a *plea* of guilty⟩ **2** : something offered as an excuse **3** : an earnest request : APPEAL [Medieval French *plai, pleit* "lawsuit," from Medieval Latin *placitum*, from Latin, "decision, decree," from *placēre* "to please, be decided"]

plead \ˈplēd\ *vb* **plead·ed** \ˈplēd-əd\ *or* **pled** \ˈpled\; **plead·ing** **1** : to argue a case in a court of law **2** : to make a plea of a specified nature ⟨*plead* not guilty⟩ **3 a** : to argue for or against a claim **b** : to appeal earnestly : IMPLORE **4** : to offer in defense, apology, or excuse [Medieval French *plaider*, from *plai* "plea"] — **plead·able** \ˈplēd-ə-bəl\ *adj* — **plead·er** *n*

pleas·ant \ˈplez-nt\ *adj* **1** : giving pleasure : AGREEABLE **2** : having or characterized by pleasing manners, behavior, or appearance — **pleas·ant·ly** *adv* — **pleas·ant·ness** *n*

pleas·ant·ry \-n-trē\ *n, pl* **-ries** **1** : agreeable playfulness especially in conversation **2** : a humorous act or speech : JEST **3** : a polite social remark ⟨exchanged *pleasantries*⟩

[1]please \ˈplēz\ *vb* **1** : to give pleasure or satisfaction : GRATIFY **2** : to feel the desire or inclination : LIKE ⟨do as you *please*⟩ [Medieval French *plaisir*, from Latin *placēre*]

[2]please *adv* **1** — used as a function word to express politeness or emphasis in a request ⟨*please* come in⟩ **2** — used as a function word to express polite affirmation ⟨Have some tea? *Please.*⟩

pleas·ing \ˈplē-zing\ *adj* : giving pleasure : AGREEABLE — **pleas·ing·ly** \-zing-lē\ *adv* — **pleas·ing·ness** *n*

plea·sur·able \ˈplezh-rə-bəl, ˈplāzh-, -ə-rə-\ *adj* : PLEASANT 1, GRATIFYING — **plea·sur·able·ness** \ˈplezh-rə-bəl-nəs, ˈplāzh-, -ə-rə-\ *n* — **plea·sur·ably** \-blē\ *adv*

plea·sure \ˈplezh-ər, ˈplāzh-\ *n* **1** : DESIRE, INCLINATION ⟨what's your *pleasure*⟩ **2** : a state of gratification : ENJOYMENT **3** : a source of delight or joy

[1]pleat \ˈplēt\ *vt* **1** : FOLD 1; *esp* : to arrange in pleats **2** : PLAIT 2 [Middle English *pleten*, from *plete, pleit* "plait"] — **pleat·er** *n*

[2]pleat *n* : a fold in cloth made by doubling material over on itself

plebe \ˈplēb\ *n* : a freshman at a military or naval academy [obsolete *plebe* "common people," from French *plèbe*, from Latin *plebs*]

[1]ple·be·ian \pli-ˈbē-ən, -yən\ *n* **1** : a member of the Roman plebs **2** : one of the common people [Latin *plebeius* "of the common people," from *plebs* "common people"] — **ple·be·ian·ism** \-ə-ˌniz-əm, -yə-\ *n*

[2]plebeian *adj* **1** : of or relating to plebeians **2** : crude or coarse in manner or style : COMMON — **ple·be·ian·ly** *adv*

pleb·i·scite \ˈpleb-ə-ˌsīt, -sət\ *n* : a popular vote by which the people of an entire country or district indicate their wishes on a measure especially on a choice of government or ruler [Latin *plebis scitum* "decree of the common people"]

plebs \ˈplebz\ *n, pl* **ple·bes** \ˈplē-ˌbēz, ˈplā-ˌbās\ **1** : the common people of ancient Rome **2** : the general populace [Latin]

plec·trum \ˈplek-trəm\ *n, pl* **plec·tra** \-trə\ *or* **plectrums** : [3]PICK 3 [Latin, from Greek *plēktron*, from *plēssein* "to strike"]

[1]pledge \ˈplej\ *n* **1 a** : the handing over of something to another as security for an obligation without transfer of title; *also* : the thing so delivered **b** : the state of being held as a security ⟨given in *pledge*⟩ **2 a** : something given as security for the performance of an act **b** : a token, sign, or evidence of something else ⟨shake hands as a *pledge* of friendship⟩ **3 a** : TOAST 3 **b** : a binding promise or agreement **4 a** : a person pledged to join an organization (as a fraternity) **b** : a gift promised (as to a charity) [Medieval French *plege* "security," from Late Latin *plebium*]

[2]pledge *vt* **1** : to deposit as a pledge **2** : to drink the health of : TOAST **3** : to bind by a pledge ⟨*pledge* oneself⟩ **4** : to promise by a pledge ⟨*pledge* money to charity⟩ — **pledg·ee** \ple-ˈjē\ *n* — **pledg·er** \ˈplej-ər\ *n* — **pled·gor** \ˈplej-ər, ple-ˈjȯr\ *n*

Ple·ia·des \ˈplē-ə-ˌdēz\ *n pl* : a conspicuous loose cluster of stars in the constellation Taurus consisting of six stars visible to the average eye [Latin, the seven daughters of Atlas, who were transformed into a group of stars, from Greek]

pleio·tro·pic \ˌplī-ə-ˈtrō-pik, -ˈträp-\ *adj* : affecting the phenotype in more than one way ⟨*pleiotropic* genes⟩ [Greek *pleiōn* "more" + *tropos* "turn, way"]

Pleis·to·cene \ˈplī-stə-ˌsēn\ *n* : the earlier epoch of the Quaternary; *also* : the corresponding series of rocks [Greek *pleistos* "most"] — **Pleistocene** *adj*

ple·na·ry \ˈplē-nə-rē, ˈplen-ə-\ *adj* **1** : COMPLETE, FULL ⟨*plenary* powers⟩ **2** : including all entitled to attend ⟨a *plenary* session of an assembly⟩ [Late Latin *plenarius*, from Latin *plenus* "full"]

plen·i·po·ten·tia·ry \ˌplen-ə-pə-ˈtench-rē, -ə-rē; -ˈten-chē-ˌer-ē\ *n, pl* **-ries** : a person and especially a diplomatic agent having full power to transact any business [Medieval Latin *plenipotentiarius*, derived from Latin *plenus* "full" + *potens* "powerful, potent"] — **plenipotentiary** *adj*

plen·i·tude \ˈplen-ə-ˌtüd, -ˌtyüd\ *n* : the quality or state of being full or plentiful : ABUNDANCE [Latin *plenitudo*, from *plenus* "full"]

plen·te·ous \ˈplent-ē-əs\ *adj* : PLENTIFUL — **plen·te·ous·ly** *adv* — **plen·te·ous·ness** *n*

\ə\ **a**but	\au̇\ **ou**t	\i\ t**i**p	\ȯ\ s**aw**	\u̇\ f**oo**t
\ər\ f**ur**ther	\ch\ **ch**in	\ī\ l**i**fe	\ȯi\ c**oi**n	\y\ **y**et
\a\ m**a**t	\e\ p**e**t	\j\ **j**ob	\th\ **th**in	\yü\ f**ew**
\ā\ t**a**ke	\ē\ **ea**sy	\ng\ si**ng**	\t͟h\ **th**is	\yu̇\ c**u**re
\ä\ c**o**t, c**a**rt	\g\ **g**o	\ō\ b**o**ne	\ü\ f**oo**d	\zh\ vi**s**ion

plen·ti·ful \'plent-i-fəl\ *adj* **1 :** containing or yielding plenty : FRUITFUL **2 :** characterized by, constituting, or existing in plenty — **plen·ti·ful·ly** \-fə-lē\ *adv* — **plen·ti·ful·ness** *n*

synonyms PLENTIFUL, AMPLE, ABUNDANT, COPIOUS mean more than sufficient yet not in excess. PLENTIFUL suggests a great or rich supply ⟨eggs are cheap when *plentiful*⟩. AMPLE implies a generous sufficiency to satisfy a particular requirement ⟨an income *ample* for one's needs⟩. ABUNDANT suggests an even greater or richer supply than does PLENTIFUL ⟨*abundant* harvests⟩. COPIOUS stresses largeness in quantity or number rather than fullness or richness ⟨shed *copious* tears⟩ ⟨took *copious* notes at the lecture⟩.

plen·ti·tude \-ˌtüd, -ˌtyüd\ *n* : PLENITUDE [by alteration, influenced by *plenty*]

[1]**plen·ty** \'plent-ē\ *n* **1 a :** a full or abundant supply : a sufficient number or amount ⟨*plenty* to choose from⟩ ⟨*plenty* of time⟩ **b :** a large amount or number ⟨in *plenty* of trouble⟩ **2 :** ABUNDANCE ⟨in times of *plenty*⟩ [Medieval French *plenté,* from Late Latin *plenitas,* from Latin, "fullness," from *plenus* "full"]

[2]**plenty** *adj* : PLENTIFUL, ABUNDANT ⟨had *plenty* help⟩

[3]**plenty** *adv* : ABUNDANTLY, QUITE ⟨a *plenty* exciting trip⟩

ple·num \'plen-əm, 'plēn-əm\ *n, pl* **-nums** *or* **-na** \-ə\ : a general assembly of all members of a public body [New Latin, from Latin *plenus* "full"]

ple·sio·saur \'plē-sē-ə-ˌsȯr, 'plē-zē-\ *n* : any of a group (Plesiosauria) of large Mesozoic marine reptiles with flattened bodies and limbs modified into flippers [derived from Greek *plēsios* "close" + *sauros* "lizard"]

pleth·o·ra \'pleth-ə-rə\ *n* : an excessive quantity or fullness [Medieval Latin, from Greek *plēthōra,* literally, "fullness," from *plēthein* "to be full"] — **ple·tho·ric** \plə-'thȯr-ik, -'thär-; 'pleth-ə-rik\ *adj*

pleu·ra \'plu̇r-ə\ *n, pl* **pleu·rae** \'plu̇r-ˌē, -ˌī\ *or* **pleuras :** the delicate membrane that lines each half of the chest of mammals and is folded back over the surface of a lung of the same side [Greek, "rib, side"] — **pleu·ral** \'plu̇r-əl\ *adj*

pleu·ri·sy \'plu̇r-ə-sē\ *n* : inflammation of the pleura usually with fever, painful breathing, and coughing [Middle French *pleuresie,* derived from Greek *pleura* "side"] — **pleu·rit·ic** \plü-'rit-ic\ *adj*

pleu·ro·pneu·mo·nia \ˌplu̇r-ō-nu̇-'mō-nyə, -nyu̇-\ *n* : combined inflammation of the lungs and pleura; *also* : a disease (as of cattle) marked by this

Plexi·glas \'plek-si-ˌglas\ *trademark* — used for plastic sheets

plex·i·glass \'plek-si-ˌglas\ *n* : a transparent acrylic plastic often used in place of glass [alteration of *Plexiglas*]

plex·us \'plek-səs\ *n* : an interlacing network especially of blood vessels or nerves [New Latin, from Latin *plectere* "to braid"]

pli·able \'plī-ə-bəl\ *adj* **1 :** capable of being bent or folded without damage : FLEXIBLE **2 :** easily influenced [Medieval French, from *plier* "to bend, fold," from Latin *plicare* "to fold"] ***synonyms*** see PLASTIC — **pli·abil·i·ty** \ˌplī-ə-'bil-ət-ē\ *n* — **pli·able·ness** \'plī-ə-bəl-nəs\ *n* — **pli·ably** \-blē\ *adv*

pli·an·cy \'plī-ən-sē\ *n* : the quality or state of being pliant

pli·ant \'plī-ənt\ *adj* **1 :** readily yielding without breaking : FLEXIBLE ⟨*pliant* willow twigs⟩ **2 :** PLIABLE 2 **3 :** suitable for varied uses : ADAPTABLE ***synonyms*** see PLASTIC — **pli·ant·ly** *adv*

pli·cate \'plī-ˌkāt\ *adj* : having lengthwise folds or ridges ⟨a *plicate* leaf⟩ [Latin *plicatus,* past participle of *plicare* "to fold"]

pli·ers \'plī-ərz, 'plīrz\ *n pl* : a small pincers with long jaws for holding small objects or for bending and cutting wire

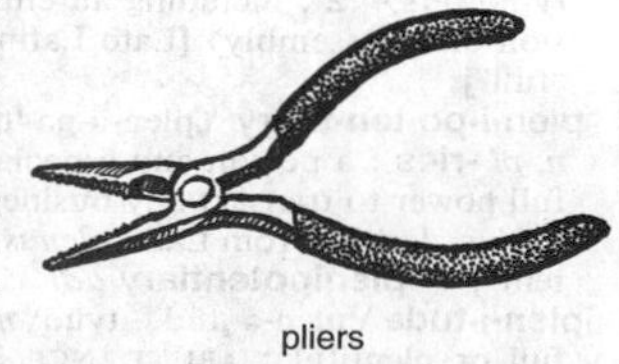

pliers

[1]**plight** \'plīt\ *vt* : to put or give in pledge : ENGAGE [Old English *plihtan* "to endanger," from *pliht* "danger"] — **plight·er** *n*

[2]**plight** *n* : a difficult or bad state or condition ⟨the *plight* of the unemployed⟩ [Middle English *plight, pliht* "danger, condition," in part from Old English *pliht*; in part from Medieval French *plit, pleit, pli* "condition, plight," literally, "bending, fold"; derived from Latin *plicare* "to fold"]

Plim·soll mark \ˌplim-səl-, ˌplimp-, -ˌsȯl-\ *n* : a load line or a set of load-line markings on an oceangoing cargo ship — called also *Plimsoll line* [Samuel *Plimsoll,* died 1898, English shipping reformer]

plink \'plingk\ *vb* **1 :** to make or cause to make a tinkling sound **2 :** to shoot at especially in a casual manner [imitative] — **plink** *n*

plinth \'plinth, 'plintth\ *n* **1 :** the lowest part of the base of an architectural column **2 :** a block used as a base (as for a statue or vase) [Latin *plinthus,* from Greek *plinthos*]

Plio·cene \'plī-ə-ˌsēn\ *n* : the latest epoch of the Tertiary; *also* : the corresponding series of rocks [Greek *pleiōn* "more"] — **Pliocene** *adj*

plod \'pläd\ *vi* **plod·ded; plod·ding 1 :** to walk heavily or slowly : TRUDGE **2 :** to work or study laboriously : DRUDGE **3 :** to proceed slowly or tediously [imitative] — **plod** *n* — **plod·der** *n* — **plod·ding·ly** \-ing-lē\ *adv*

ploi·dy \'plȯid-ē\ *n* : degree of repetition of the basic number of chromosomes [from such words as *diploidy, triploidy*]

plonk *variant of* PLUNK

plop \'pläp\ *vb* **plopped; plop·ping 1 :** to fall, drop, or move suddenly with a sound like that of something dropping into water **2 :** to allow the body to drop heavily ⟨*plopped* down on the couch⟩ **3 :** to set, drop, or throw heavily [imitative] — **plop** *n*

[1]**plot** \'plät\ *n* **1 :** a small area of land : LOT **2 :** GROUND PLAN 1 **3 :** the main story (as of a literary work or movie) **4 :** a secret plan for accomplishing a usually evil or unlawful end **5 :** a graphic representation : CHART, DIAGRAM [Old English]

synonyms PLOT, INTRIGUE, CONSPIRACY mean a plan secretly devised to accomplish an evil purpose. PLOT implies careful foresight in planning a complex scheme ⟨an elaborate kidnapping *plot*⟩. INTRIGUE suggests secret maneuvering ⟨the court thrived on *intrigues*⟩. CONSPIRACY implies a secret agreement among a number of persons usually involving treachery or criminal acts ⟨a *conspiracy* to fix prices⟩. ***synonyms*** see in addition PLAN

[2]**plot** *vb* **plot·ted; plot·ting 1 a :** to make a plot, map, or plan of **b :** to mark or note on or as if on a map or chart **2 a :** to locate and mark (a point) by means of coordinates **b :** to make (a curve) by marking out a number of plotted points **3 :** to plan or contrive especially secretly : SCHEME — **plot·ter** *n*

plough *chiefly British variant of* PLOW

plo·ver \'pləv-ər, 'plō-vər\ *n, pl* **plover** *or* **plovers :** any of numerous shorebirds differing from the related sandpipers in having shorter bills [Medieval French *plover, pluvier,* derived from Latin *pluvia* "rain"]

[1]**plow** \'plau̇\ *n* **1 :** an implement used to cut, lift, and turn over soil especially in preparing a seedbed **2 :** any of various devices (as for spreading or opening something) that operate like a plow; *esp* : SNOWPLOW [Old English *plōh* "land a yoke of oxen could plow in one day"]

[2]**plow** *vb* **1 :** to open, break up, or work with a plow ⟨*plow* a straight furrow⟩ ⟨*plow* the soil⟩ **2 a :** to move forcefully into or through ⟨a ship *plowing* the waves⟩ **b :** to proceed steadily and laboriously ⟨*plow* through a report⟩ **3 :** to clear away snow from with a snowplow ⟨*plow* the road⟩ — **plow·able** \-ə-bəl\ *adj* — **plow·er** \'plau̇-ər, 'plau̇r\ *n*

plow back *vt* : to reinvest (profits) in a business

plow·boy \'plau̇-ˌbȯi\ *n* : a boy who guides a plow or leads the horse drawing it

plow·man \-mən\ *n* **1 :** one that plows **2 :** a farm laborer

plow·share \-ˌsheər, -ˌshaər\ *n* : the part of a plow that cuts the earth

ploy \'plȯi\ *n* : a tactic intended to embarrass or baffle an opponent [probably from *employ*]

[1]**pluck** \'plək\ *vb* **1 a :** to pull or pick off or out ⟨*pluck* a flower⟩ **b :** to remove something and especially hair or feathers from by or as if by plucking ⟨*pluck* a fowl⟩ **2 :** ROB 1, FLEECE **3 :** to move or separate forcibly : TUG, SNATCH ⟨*plucked* the child from danger⟩ **4 a :** to pick, pull, or grasp at **b :** to play by sounding the strings with the fingers or a pick ⟨*pluck* a guitar⟩ **5 :** to make a sharp pull or twitch ⟨a briar *plucked* at my sleeve⟩ [Old English *pluccian*] — **pluck·er** *n*

[2]**pluck** *n* **1 :** a sharp pull : TUG **2 :** the heart, liver, lungs, and trachea of a slaughtered animal **3 :** courageous readiness to fight or continue against odds : SPIRIT

plucky \'plək-ē\ *adj* **pluck·i·er; -est :** COURAGEOUS — **pluck·i·ly** \'plək-ə-lē\ *adv* — **pluck·i·ness** \'plək-ē-nəs\ *n*

[1]**plug** \'pləg\ *n* **1 a :** a piece (as of wood or metal) used to stop or fill a hole : STOPPER **b :** an obtruding or obstructing mass of material (as in rock or tissue) resembling a stopper **2 :** something of lesser quality; *esp* : a worn-out horse **3 a :** HYDRANT, FIREPLUG **b :** SPARK PLUG 1 **4 :** a device for making an elec-

trical connection by insertion into a receptacle **5 :** a flat cake of tightly pressed tobacco leaves **6 :** a fishing lure with two or more hooks **7 :** a piece of favorable publicity usually placed in general material [Dutch]

[2]**plug** *vb* **plugged; plug·ging** **1 :** to stop, make tight, or secure with or as if with a plug **2 :** to hit with a bullet **3 :** to advertise or publicize insistently **4 :** to become plugged — usually used with *up* **5 :** to keep steadily at work or in action ⟨*plugged* away at my homework⟩ — **plug·ger** *n* — **plug into :** to connect or become connected by or as if by means of a plug

plug and play *n* **:** a feature of a computer system that allows attachments to be automatically detected and configured by the operating system

plug–in \'pləg-ˌin\ *n* **1 :** something that plugs in **2 :** software that supplements a larger program (as a browser)

plug in *vb* **:** to establish or connect to an electric circuit by inserting a plug

plug–ugly \'pləg-ˌəg-lē\ *n, pl* **-ug·lies :** THUG, TOUGH

plum \'pləm\ *n* **1 a :** any of various trees and shrubs related to the peach and cherries and having round to oval smooth-skinned edible fruits with oblong pits **b :** the fruit of a plum **2 a :** a raisin when used in desserts (as puddings or cake) **b :** SUGARPLUM **3 :** something excellent or superior; *esp* **:** something given in return for a favor **4 :** a dark reddish purple [Old English *plūme,* from Latin *prunum,* from Greek *proumnon*] — **plum·like** \-ˌlīk\ *adj*

plum·age \'plü-mij\ *n* **:** the feathers of a bird

[1]**plumb** \'pləm\ *n* **:** a weight often of lead used on a line especially to determine a vertical direction or distance [derived from Latin *plumbum* "lead"] — **out of plumb** *or* **off plumb :** out of vertical or true

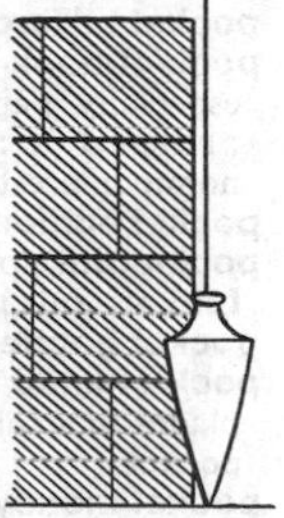
plumb

[2]**plumb** *adv* **1 :** straight down or up **:** VERTICALLY **2** *chiefly dialect* **:** WHOLLY 1, ABSOLUTELY **3 :** in a direct manner **:** EXACTLY

[3]**plumb** *vb* **1 :** to measure, adjust, or test with a plumb ⟨*plumb* a wall⟩ ⟨*plumb* the depth of the well⟩ **2 :** to examine and determine hidden aspects of ⟨*plumbed* their motives⟩ **3 :** to supply with or install as plumbing; *also* **:** to work as a plumber

[4]**plumb** *adj* **1 :** exactly vertical or true **2 :** ABSOLUTE 4, COMPLETE ***synonyms*** see VERTICAL

plum·ba·go \ˌpləm-'bā-gō\ *n* **:** GRAPHITE 1 [Latin, "galena," from *plumbum* "lead"]

plumb bob *n* **:** the metal bob of a plumb line

plumb·er \'pləm-ər\ *n* **:** one that installs, repairs, and maintains piping, fittings, and fixtures involved in the distribution and use of water in a building [derived from Latin *plumbum* "lead"]

plumber's helper *n* **:** PLUNGER 2b

plumb·ing \'pləm-ing\ *n* **1 :** a plumber's occupation or trade **2 :** the apparatus (as pipes and fixtures) concerned in the distribution and use of water in a building

plumb line *n* **:** a line or cord having at one end a weight (as a plumb bob) and serving especially to determine whether something is vertical or to measure depth

[1]**plume** \'plüm\ *n* **1 :** a feather of a bird; *esp* **:** a large conspicuous or showy feather **2 a :** a feather, cluster of feathers, tuft of hair, or similar object worn as an ornament **b :** a token of honor or victory **:** PRIZE **3 :** something (as a trail of smoke or a bushy tail of a dog) that resembles a plume [Medieval French, from Latin *pluma* "small soft feather, down"] — **plumed** \'plümd\ *adj* — **plumy** \'plü-mē\ *adj*

[2]**plume** *vt* **1 :** to provide or deck with plumes **2 :** to pride (oneself) on something **3 :** PREEN 1 ⟨a bird *pluming* itself⟩

[1]**plum·met** \'pləm-ət\ *n* **:** [1]PLUMB; *also* **:** PLUMB LINE [Medieval French *plumet, plomet,* from *plum* "lead, lead weight," derived from Latin *plumbum* "lead"]

[2]**plummet** *vi* **:** to drop straight down or sharply and abruptly

plu·mose \'plü-ˌmōs\ *adj* **:** FEATHERY, FEATHERED

[1]**plump** \'pləmp\ *vb* **1 :** to drop, sink, or come in contact suddenly or heavily ⟨*plumped* down into the chair⟩ **2 :** to favor someone or something strongly — used with *for* [Middle English *plumpen*]

[2]**plump** *n* **:** a sudden plunge, fall, or blow; *also* **:** the sound accompanying such an act

[3]**plump** *adv* **1 :** with a sudden or heavy drop **2 :** STRAIGHT, DIRECTLY ⟨ran *plump* into the wall⟩

[4]**plump** *vb* **:** to make or become plump

[5]**plump** *adj* **:** having a full rounded usually pleasing form [Middle English, "dull, blunt," from Dutch *plomp*] — **plump·ness** *n*

plum pudding *n* **:** a boiled or steamed pudding containing fruits (as raisins) and spices

plum tomato *n* **:** a small oblong tomato

plu·mule \'plü-myül\ *n* **1 :** the shoot or bud of a plant embryo or seedling that is located between the cotyledons and grows into the stem and leaves **2 :** a down feather [Latin *plumula* "small feather," from *pluma* "feather, down"]

[1]**plun·der** \'plən-dər\ *vb* **plun·dered; plun·der·ing** \-də-ring, -dring\ **:** to rob especially openly and by force (as in a raid) [German *plündern*] — **plun·der·er** \-dər-ər\ *n*

[2]**plunder** *n* **1 :** an act of plundering **2 :** something taken by force or theft **:** LOOT

[1]**plunge** \'plənj\ *vb* **1 :** to thrust or force quickly into something ⟨*plunging* a knife⟩ **2 :** to thrust or cast oneself into or as if into water **:** DIVE **3 a :** to throw oneself or move suddenly and sharply forward and downward ⟨the horse reared and *plunged*⟩ **b :** to move rapidly or suddenly downward ⟨the stock market *plunged*⟩ **4 a :** to rush or act with reckless haste ⟨*plunged* into another project⟩; *also* **:** to bring to a state or course of action suddenly or unexpectedly ⟨*plunged* the nation into recession⟩ **b :** to speculate or gamble recklessly [Medieval French *plunger,* derived from Latin *plumbum* "lead"]

[2]**plunge** *n* **:** a sudden dive, leap, or rush

plung·er \'plən-jər\ *n* **1 :** a person (as a diver or a reckless gambler) that plunges **2 a :** a device (as a piston in a pump) that acts with a plunging motion **b :** a device consisting of a rubber suction cup on a handle used to free plumbing traps and waste outlets of obstructions

plunk \'pləngk\ *or* **plonk** \'pläŋk, 'plȯngk\ *vb* **1 :** to pluck or hit so as to produce a hollow metallic sound **2 :** to set down suddenly ⟨*plunked* the money down⟩ **3 :** to publicly favor someone or something — used with *for* [imitative] — **plunk** *n*

plu·per·fect \plü-'pər-fikt, 'plü-\ *adj* **:** PAST PERFECT [Late Latin *plusquamperfectus,* literally, "more than perfect"] — **pluperfect** *n*

plu·ral \'plu̇r-əl\ *adj* **1 :** belonging to a class of grammatical forms used to denote more than one ⟨a *plural* suffix⟩ **2 :** relating to, consisting of, or containing more than one [Latin *pluralis,* from *plur-, plus* "more"] — **plural** *n* — **plu·ral·ly** \-ə-lē\ *adv*

plu·ral·ism \'plu̇r-ə-ˌliz-əm\ *n* **:** a state of society in which different (as ethnic or social) groups maintain their traditional cultures or special interests within the confines of a common civilization

plu·ral·i·ty \plu̇-'ral-ət-ē\ *n, pl* **-ties** **1 :** the state of being plural or numerous **2 :** the greater number or part ⟨a *plurality* of the nations want peace⟩ **3 a :** a number of votes cast for a candidate in a contest of three or more candidates that is more than the number cast for any other candidate but not more than half the total vote **b :** the excess of the number of votes received by one candidate over another ***synonyms*** see MAJORITY

plu·ral·ize \'plu̇r-ə-ˌlīz\ *vt* **:** to make plural or express in the plural form — **plu·ral·i·za·tion** \ˌplu̇r-ə-lə-'zā-shən\ *n*

plu·rip·o·tent \plu̇-'rip-ət-ənt\ *adj* **:** capable of developing into one of many cell types [Latin *plur-, plus* "more" + English *potent*]

[1]**plus** \'pləs\ *adj* **1 :** algebraically positive ⟨a *plus* quantity⟩ **2 :** having, receiving, or being in addition to what is expected **3 a :** falling high in a specified range ⟨a grade of C *plus*⟩ **b :** greater than that specified **4 :** electrically positive **5 :** relating to or being a particular one of the two mating types that are required for successful fertilization in sexual reproduction in some plantlike organisms (as a fungus)

[2]**plus** *n, pl* **plus·es** *also* **plus·ses** **1 :** an added quantity **2 :** a positive quality **:** ADVANTAGE **3 :** the amount that remains when use or need is satisfied

[3]**plus** *prep* **:** increased by **:** with the addition of ⟨four *plus* five is nine⟩ ⟨the debt *plus* interest⟩ [Latin, "more"]

[1]**plush** \'pləsh\ *n* **:** a fabric with pile longer and less dense than that of velvet [Middle French *peluche*] — **plushy** \-ē\ *adj*

\ə\ **abut**	\au̇\ **out**	\i\ **tip**	\ȯ\ **saw**	\u̇\ **foot**
\ər\ **further**	\ch\ **chin**	\ī\ **life**	\ȯi\ **coin**	\y\ **yet**
\a\ **mat**	\e\ **pet**	\j\ **job**	\th\ **thin**	\yü\ **few**
\ā\ **take**	\ē\ **easy**	\ng\ **sing**	\t͟h\ **this**	\yu̇\ **cure**
\ä\ **cot, cart**	\g\ **go**	\ō\ **bone**	\ü\ **food**	\zh\ **vision**

[2]**plush** *adj* **1 :** relating to, resembling, or made of plush **2 :** very luxurious or satisfactory

plus/minus sign *n* **:** the sign ± used to mean that a quantity (as 2 in "the square root of 4 is ±2") takes on both a positive and a negative value or to indicate a plus or minus quantity (as 5 in "the scale was accurate to ±5 grams") — called also *plus/minus symbol*

plus or minus *adj* **:** indicating a quantity whose positive and negative values establish the limits of a range of values ⟨measured with an accuracy of *plus or minus* 3 millimeters⟩ ⟨a mummy aged 3500 *plus or minus* 150 years⟩

plus sign *n* **:** a sign + denoting addition or a positive quantity

Plu·to \ˈplüt-ō\ *n* **:** a dwarf planet occupying an orbit that crosses the orbit of Neptune [*Pluto,* Greek god of the dead]

usage In 2006 the International Astronomical Union defined *planet* in such a way as to exclude Pluto, reclassifying it instead as a *dwarf planet*. Although still discussed, the change has been widely accepted.

plu·toc·ra·cy \plü-ˈtäk-rə-sē\ *n, pl* **-cies 1 :** government by the wealthy **2 :** a controlling class of rich people [Greek *ploutokratia,* from *ploutos* "wealth"] — **plu·to·crat** \ˈplüt-ə-ˌkrat\ *n* — **plu·to·crat·ic** \ˌplüt-ə-ˈkrat-ik\ *adj* — **plu·to·crat·i·cal·ly** \-ˈkrat-i-kə-lē, -klē\ *adv*

plu·to·ni·an \plü-ˈtō-nē-ən\ *adj, often cap* **:** of, relating to, or like the Greek god Pluto or the lower world **:** INFERNAL

plu·ton·ic \plü-ˈtän-ik\ *adj* **:** formed by solidification of magma deep within the earth and crystalline throughout ⟨*plutonic* rock⟩ [Latin *Pluton-, Pluto,* god of the dead, from Greek *Ploutōn*]

plu·to·ni·um \plü-ˈtō-nē-əm\ *n* **:** a radioactive metallic chemical element that is formed by decay of neptunium and found in minute quantities in pitchblende and that is fissionable to yield atomic energy — see ELEMENT table [New Latin, from *Pluton-, Pluto,* the planet Pluto]

plu·vi·al \ˈplü-vē-əl\ *adj* **1 :** of or relating to rain **2 :** characterized by or resulting from the action of abundant rain ⟨a *pluvial* period⟩ [Latin *pluvialis,* from *pluvia* "rain," from *pluere* "to rain"]

[1]**ply** \ˈplī\ *vt* **plied; ply·ing :** to twist together ⟨*ply* yarns⟩ [Medieval French *plier* "to fold," from Latin *plicare*]

[2]**ply** *n, pl* **plies :** one of the folds, thicknesses, layers, or strands of which something (as yarn or plywood) is made up

[3]**ply** *vb* **plied; ply·ing 1 a :** to use or wield diligently ⟨*ply* an ax⟩ **b :** to practice or perform diligently ⟨*ply* a trade⟩ **2 :** to keep supplying ⟨*ply* a guest with delicacies⟩ **3 :** to go or travel regularly [Middle English *plien,* short for *applien* "to apply"]

Plym·outh Rock \ˌplim-əth-\ *n* **:** any of a U.S. breed of medium-sized single-combed domestic chickens raised for meat and eggs [from *Plymouth Rock,* on which the Pilgrims are supposed to have landed in 1620]

plyo·met·rics \ˌplī-ə-ˈme-triks\ *n sing or pl* **:** exercise involving repeated rapid stretching and contracting of muscles (as by jumping down from a height and jumping back up again) to increase muscle power [probably from *plio-* "more" (from Greek *pleion*) + *-metrics* (as in *isometrics*)]

ply·wood \ˈplī-ˌwu̇d\ *n* **:** a structural material consisting of thin sheets of wood glued or cemented together under heat and pressure with the grains of adjacent layers arranged at right angles or at a wide angle

PMS \ˌpē-ˌem-ˈes\ *n* **:** PREMENSTRUAL SYNDROME

pneu·mat·ic \nu̇-ˈmat-ik, nyu̇-\ *adj* **1 :** of, relating to, or using air, wind, or other gas **2 :** moved or worked by air pressure ⟨a *pneumatic* drill⟩ **3 :** adapted for holding or inflated with compressed air ⟨*pneumatic* tires⟩ [Latin *pneumaticus,* from Greek *pneumatikos,* from *pneuma* "air, breath, spirit," from *pnein* "to breathe"] — **pneu·mat·i·cal·ly** \-ˈmat-i-kə-lē, -klē\ *adv*

pneu·mo·coc·cus \ˌnü-mə-ˈkäk-əs, ˌnyü-\ *n, pl* **-coc·ci** \-ˈkäk-ˌī, -ˌsī, -ˌē, -ˌsē\ **:** a bacterium that causes pneumonia [Greek *pneuma* "air, breath, spirit" + *kokkos* "grain, seed"] — **pneu·mo·coc·cal** \-ˈkäk-əl\ *adj*

pneu·mo·nia \nu̇-ˈmō-nyə, nyu̇-\ *n* **:** a disease of the lungs characterized by inflammation, congestion, fever, cough, and difficulty in breathing and caused especially by infection [Greek, from *pneumōn* "lung," alteration of *pleumōn*]

pneu·mon·ic \nu̇-ˈmän-ik, nyu̇-\ *adj* **1 :** of or relating to the lungs ⟨*pneumonic* plague⟩ **2 :** of, relating to, or affected with pneumonia

pneu·mo·tho·rax \ˌnü-mə-ˈthōr-ˌaks, ˌnyü-, -ˈthȯr-\ *n* **:** a state in which gas is present in the pleural cavity and which may occur in disease or injury or be induced surgically to collapse a lung for therapeutic reasons [Greek *pneuma* "air, breath"]

[1]**poach** \ˈpōch\ *vt* **:** to cook in simmering liquid ⟨*poach* an egg⟩ [Medieval French *pocher,* literally, "to put into a bag," from *poche* "bag, pocket," of Germanic origin]

[2]**poach** *vb* **:** to hunt or fish unlawfully [Middle French *pocher,* of Germanic origin] — **poach·er** *n*

po'·boy \ˈpō-ˌbȯi\ *also* **poor boy** *n* **:** SUBMARINE 2

po·chard \ˈpō-chərd\ *n* **:** any of several large-bodied large-headed diving ducks [origin unknown]

pock \ˈpäk\ *n* **:** a small swelling on the skin (as in chicken pox or smallpox) similar to a pimple; *also* **:** the scar it leaves [Old English *pocc*] — **pock** *vt* — **pocky** \-ē\ *adj*

[1]**pock·et** \ˈpäk-ət\ *n* **1 a :** a small bag carried by a person **:** PURSE **b :** a small bag open at the top or side inserted in a garment **2 :** supply of money **:** MEANS ⟨out of *pocket*⟩ **3 a :** CONTAINER **b :** a hole at the corner or side of a billiard table **4 :** a small isolated area or group: as **a :** a cavity containing a deposit (as of gold or water) **b :** AIR POCKET [Medieval French *poket, pochete,* from *poke, pouche* "bag," of Germanic origin]

[2]**pocket** *vt* **1 a :** to put or enclose in or as if in one's pocket ⟨*pocketed* the change⟩ **b :** to take for one's own use especially dishonestly ⟨*pocket* the profits⟩ **2 :** to put up with ⟨*pocket* an insult⟩ **3 :** to set aside **:** forget about ⟨*pocket* one's pride⟩ **4 a :** to hem in **b :** to drive (a ball) into a pocket of a pool table **5 :** to cover or supply with pockets

[3]**pocket** *adj* **1 a :** small enough to be carried in the pocket ⟨a *pocket* dictionary⟩ **b :** SMALL, MINIATURE **2 a :** of or relating to money **b :** carried in or paid from one's pocket

pocket billiards *n* **:** [3]POOL 2

pock·et·book \ˈpäk-ət-ˌbu̇k\ *n* **1** *often* **pocket book :** a small especially paperback book **2 a :** BILLFOLD, WALLET **b :** PURSE 1 **c :** HANDBAG 2 **3 a :** financial resources **b :** economic interests

pocket edition *n* **:** a miniature form of something

pock·et·ful \ˈpäk-ət-ˌfu̇l\ *n, pl* **pocketfuls** \-ˌfu̇lz\ *or* **pock·ets·ful** \-əts-ˌfu̇l\ **:** as much or as many as the pocket will contain

pocket gopher *n* **:** GOPHER 2a

pock·et·knife \ˈpäk-ət-ˌnīf\ *n* **:** a knife that has one or more blades that fold into the handle and that can be carried in the pocket

pocket money *n* **:** money for small personal expenses

pock·et–size \-ˌsīz\ *also* **pock·et·sized** \-ˌsīzd\ *adj* **1 :** of a size convenient for carrying in the pocket **2 :** SMALL ⟨a *pocket-size* country⟩

pocket veto *n* **:** an indirect veto of a legislative bill by an executive by failing to sign it before adjournment of the legislature

pock·mark \ˈpäk-ˌmärk\ *n* **:** the depressed scar caused by smallpox or acne; *also* **:** an imperfection or depression like a pockmark — **pockmark** *vt*

po·co \ˌpō-kō, ˌpȯ-\ *adv* **:** SOMEWHAT — used to qualify a direction in music [Italian, "little," from Latin *paucus*]

po·co a po·co \ˌpō-kō-ä-ˈpō-kō, ˌpȯ-kō-ä-ˈpȯ-kō\ *adv* **:** little by little **:** GRADUALLY — used as a direction in music [Italian]

po·co·sin \pə-ˈkōs-n\ *n* **:** an upland swamp of the coastal plain of the southeastern U.S. [probably from Virginia or North Carolina Algonquian]

[1]**pod** \ˈpäd\ *n* **1 :** a fruit or seed vessel that splits open when ripe; *esp* **:** LEGUME **2 :** any of various natural protective coverings or cases (as for grasshopper eggs) **3 :** a streamlined compartment under the wings or fuselage of an airplane used as a container (as for fuel or a jet engine) **4 :** a detachable compartment (as for instruments) on a spacecraft [probably alteration of *cod* "bag," from Old English *codd*]

[2]**pod** *n* **:** a number of animals (as whales) assembled together [origin unknown]

-pod \ˌpäd\ *n combining form* **:** foot **:** part resembling a foot ⟨uro*pod*⟩ [Greek *pod-, pous* "foot"]

pod·cast \ˈpäd-ˌkast\ *n* **:** a program (as of music or talk) made available in digital format for automatic download over the Internet [*iPod,* trademark for a portable media player + broad*cast*] — **podcast** *vb* — **pod·cast·er** *n*

podgy \ˈpäj-ē\ *adj* **podg·i·er; -est** *chiefly British* **:** PUDGY

po·di·a·try \pə-ˈdī-ə-trē\ *n* **:** the medical care and treatment of the human foot in health and disease — called also *chiropody* [Greek *pod-, pous* "foot" + English *-iatry*] — **po·di·a·trist** \-trəst\ *n*

po·di·um \ˈpōd-ē-əm\ *n, pl* **-di·ums** *or* **-dia** \-ē-ə\ **1 :** a low wall serving as a foundation or terrace wall: as **a :** one around the arena of an ancient amphitheater serving as a base for the tiers of seats **b** : the masonry under the stylobate of a temple **2 a** : a raised platform especially for an orchestral conductor **b** : LECTERN [Latin, from Greek *podion* "base," from *pod-, pous* "foot"]

Po•dunk \ˈpō-ˌdəŋk\ *n* : a small, unimportant, and isolated town [*Podunk,* village in Massachusetts or locality in Connecticut]

po•em \ˈpō-əm, -im, ˈpōm *also* ˈpō-ˌem\ *n* **1** : a composition in verse **2** : a creation, experience, or object likened to a poem [Medieval French *poeme,* from Latin *poema,* from Greek *poiēma, from poiein* "to make, create"]

po•e•sy \ˈpō-ə-zē, -sē\ *n, pl* **-sies** **1 a** : a poem or body of poems **b** : poetic form or composition : POETRY **2** : poetic inspiration [Medieval French *poesie,* from Latin *poesis,* from Greek *poiēsis,* literally, "creation," from *poiein* "to make, create"]

po•et \ˈpō-ət\ *n* **1** : a writer of poetry **2** : a creative artist of great imaginative and expressive gifts and special sensitivity to the medium [Medieval French *poete,* from Latin *poeta,* from Greek *poiētēs* "maker, poet," from *poiein* "to make, create"]

po•et•as•ter \ˈpō-ət-ˌas-tər\ *n* : an inferior poet [Latin *poeta* "poet" + *-aster,* suffix denoting partial resemblance]

po•et•ess \ˈpō-ət-əs\ *n* : a woman who is a poet

po•et•ic \pō-ˈet-ik\ *adj* **1 a** : of, relating to, or characteristic of poets or poetry ⟨*poetic* words⟩ **b** : given to writing poetry **2** : written in verse

po•et•i•cal \pō-ˈet-i-kəl\ *adj* **1** : POETIC 1 **2** : highly and usually splendidly imaginative — **po•et•i•cal•ly** \-kə-lē, -klē\ *adv*

poetic justice *n* : an outcome in which vice is punished and virtue rewarded in a manner peculiarly or ironically appropriate

poetic license *n* : LICENSE 4

po•et•ics \pō-ˈet-iks\ *n sing or pl* **1 a** : a treatise on poetry or aesthetics **b** : poetic theory or practice **2** : poetic feelings or expression

poet laureate *n, pl* **poets laureate** *or* **poet laureates** **1** : a poet honored for achievement **2 a** : a poet appointed by a British sovereign as a member of the royal household to write poems for state occasions **b** : a poet appointed annually by the U.S. Library of Congress as a consultant and typically involved in the promotion of poetry **3** : one regarded by a country or region as its most eminent or representative poet

po•et•ry \ˈpō-ə-trē\ *n* **1 a** : metrical writing : VERSE **b** : the productions of a poet : POEMS **2** : writing in language chosen and arranged to create a particular emotional response through meaning, sound, and rhythm **3** : poetic quality or aspect ⟨the *poetry* of dance⟩

po•go stick \ˈpō-gō\ *n* : a pole with a strong spring at the bottom and two footrests on which a person stands and moves along the ground by jumping [*pogo,* of unknown origin]

po•grom \ˈpō-grəm; pō-ˈgräm, pə-\ *n* : an organized slaughter of helpless people and especially of Jews [Yiddish, from Russian, literally, "devastation"]

po•gy \ˈpō-gē\ *n, pl* **pogies** : MENHADEN [from *poghaden,* perhaps from Eastern Abenaki (an Algonquian language of northern New England and Quebec)]

poi \ˈpȯi\ *n, pl* **poi** *or* **pois** : a Hawaiian food made of cooked taro root pounded to a paste and often fermented [Hawaiian and Samoan]

poi•gnant \ˈpȯi-nyənt\ *adj* **1** : PUNGENT **2 a** (1) : painfully affecting the feelings : PIERCING ⟨*poignant* grief⟩ (2) : deeply affecting : TOUCHING **b** : SARCASTIC, INCISIVE ⟨*poignant* satire⟩ **3 a** : pleasurably exciting **b** : being to the point : APT ⟨*poignant* remarks⟩ [Medieval French *poinant, poignant,* present participle of *poindre* "to prick, sting," from Latin *pungere*] — **poi•gnan•cy** \-nyən-sē\ *n* — **poi•gnant•ly** *adv*

poi•ki•lo•therm \pȯi-ˈkē-lə-ˌthərm, -ˈkil-ə-\ *n* : an organism (as a frog) with a variable temperature that tends to fluctuate with and is similar to or slightly higher than the environment : a cold-blooded organism [Greek *poikilos* "variegated" + *thermē* "heat"] — **poi•ki•lo•ther•mic** \ˌpȯi-kə-lō-ˈthər-mik\ *adj*

poin•ci•ana \ˌpȯin-sē-ˈan-ə, ˌpwän-\ *n* : any of several showy tropical trees or shrubs of the legume family with bright orange or red flowers [De *Poinci,* 17th century governor of part of the French West Indies]

poin•set•tia \pȯin-ˈset-ē-ə, -ˈset-ə\ *n* : a showy Mexican and Central American plant of the spurge family with tapering scarlet bracts that grow like petals about its small yellow flowers [Joel R. *Poinsett,* died 1851, American diplomat]

¹point \ˈpȯint\ *n* **1 a** (1) : an individual detail : ITEM ⟨interesting *points* in the proposal⟩ (2) : a distinguishing detail : CHARACTERISTIC ⟨tact isn't my strong *point*⟩ **b** : the most important essential in a discussion or matter ⟨the *point* of the joke⟩ **c** : FORCE 1c, COGENCY **2** : an end or object to be achieved : PURPOSE ⟨there's no *point* in continuing⟩ **3 a** : a geometric element that has position but no dimensions and is pictured as a small dot **b** (1) : a narrowly localized place having a precisely indicated position ⟨a *point* 50 feet north of the tree⟩ (2) : a particular place : LOCALITY ⟨visited many *points* of interest⟩ **c** (1) : an exact moment ⟨at this *point* in time⟩ (2) : a time interval immediately before something indicated : VERGE ⟨at the *point* of death⟩ **d** (1) : a particular step, stage, or degree in development ⟨at the *point* where I no longer cared⟩ (2) : a definite position in a scale **4 a** : the terminal usually sharp or narrowly rounded part of something (as a fin, sword, or pencil) : TIP **b** : a weapon or tool having such a part and used for stabbing or piercing **c** : either of two metal pieces in a distributor through which the circuit is made or broken **5 a** : a projecting usually tapering piece of land or a sharp prominence **b** (1) : the tip of a projecting body part (2) *pl* : terminal bodily projections or their markings especially when differing from the rest of the body in color **6** : a short musical phrase; *esp* : a phrase in contrapuntal music **7 a** : a very small mark **b** (1) : PUNCTUATION MARK; *esp* : PERIOD 3 (2) : DECIMAL POINT **8 a** : one of the 32 pointed marks indicating direction on a compass **b** : the difference of 11¼ degrees between two such adjacent points **9 a** : NEEDLEPOINT 1 **b** : lace made with a bobbin **10** : one of 12 spaces marked off on each side of a backgammon board **11** : a unit in a scale of measurement: as **a** : a unit of counting in the scoring of a game or contest **b** : a unit of academic credit **c** : a unit of about $^{1}/_{72}$ inch (about 0.35 millimeter) used to measure the size of printing type **12** : the action of pointing; *esp* : the action in dancing of extending one leg so that only the tips of the toes touch the floor [Medieval French, "puncture, small spot, point in time or space," from Latin *punctum,* from *pungere* "to prick"] — **beside the point** : IRRELEVANT — **in point of** : with regard to : in the matter of ⟨*in point of* fact⟩ — **to the point** : RELEVANT, PERTINENT, APT ⟨a remark that was quite *to the point*⟩

²point *vb* **1 a** : to furnish with a point **b** : to give added force, emphasis, or piquancy to ⟨*point* up a remark⟩ **2** : to scratch out the old mortar from the joints of (as a brick wall) and fill in with new material **3 a** (1) : PUNCTUATE 1 (2) : to separate (a decimal fraction) from a whole number by a decimal point ⟨*point* off three decimal places⟩ **b** : to mark the vowels in (as Hebrew words) **4 a** (1) : to direct someone's attention to ⟨*point* out a mistake⟩ (2) : to indicate game by stiffening into a fixed position with head and gaze directed toward the object hunted ⟨a dog that *points* well⟩ **b** : to indicate the position or direction of especially by extending a finger ⟨*point* the way home⟩ **5 a** : to turn, face, or cause to be turned in a particular direction : AIM ⟨*point* the boat upstream⟩ **b** : to extend (a leg) in executing a point in dancing **6** : to indicate the fact or probability of something specified ⟨everything *points* to success⟩

point–and–click *adj* : allowing activation of computer files or functions by pointing with a control device (as a mouse) and clicking a button ⟨a *point-and-click* interface⟩

point–and–shoot *adj* : having or using preset or automatic controls (as for focus) ⟨a *point-and-shoot* camera⟩

point–blank \ˈpȯint-ˈblaŋk\ *adj* **1 a** : marked by no noticeable drop below initial horizontal line of flight **b** : so close to a target that a missile fired will travel in a straight line to the mark ⟨fired from *point-blank* range⟩ **2** : DIRECT, BLUNT ⟨a *point-blank* refusal⟩ — **point–blank** *adv*

pointe \ˈpwaⁿt, ˈpwaⁿnt\ *n* : a position of balance in ballet on the extreme tip of the toe [French *pointe (du pied),* literally, "tiptoe"]

point•ed \ˈpȯint-əd\ *adj* **1 a** : having a point **b** : having a crown tapering to a point ⟨a *pointed* arch⟩ **2 a** : being to the point : TERSE **b** : aimed at a particular person or group ⟨*pointed* remarks⟩ **3** : CONSPICUOUS 1, MARKED ⟨*pointed* indifference⟩ — **point•ed•ly** *adv* — **point•ed•ness** *n*

\ə\ **abut**	\au̇\ **out**	\i\ **tip**	\ȯ\ **saw**	\u̇\ **foot**
\ər\ **further**	\ch\ **chin**	\ī\ **life**	\ȯi\ **coin**	\y\ **yet**
\a\ **mat**	\e\ **pet**	\j\ **job**	\th\ **thin**	\yü\ **few**
\ā\ **take**	\ē\ **easy**	\ng\ **sing**	\t͟h\ **this**	\yu̇\ **cure**
\ä\ **cot, cart**	\g\ **go**	\ō\ **bone**	\ü\ **food**	\zh\ **vision**

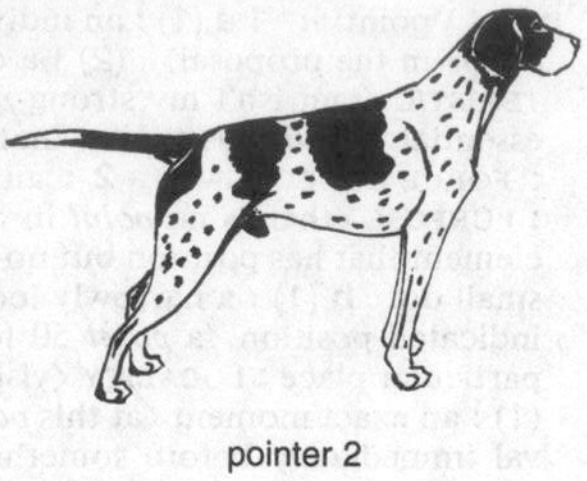
pointer 2

point·er \ˈpȯint-ər\ *n* **1 a :** one that points out; *esp* **:** a rod used to direct attention **b** *pl, cap* **:** the two stars in Ursa Major a line through which points to the North Star **2 :** a large strong slender smooth-haired hunting dog that hunts by scent and indicates the presence of game by pointing **3 :** a useful suggestion or hint **:** TIP ⟨gave a few *pointers* on how to study⟩

poin·til·lism \ˈpwa^{n}-tē-ˌiz-əm, ˈpwa^{n}n-\ *n* **:** the practice or technique of applying dots of color to a surface so that from a distance they blend together [French *pointillisme,* from *pointiller* "to stipple," from *point* "spot, point"] — **poin·til·list** \-tē-əst\ *n* — **poin·til·lis·tic** \ˌpwa^{n}-tē-ˈis-tik, ˌpwa^{n}n-\ *adj*

point·less \ˈpȯint-ləs\ *adj* **1 :** lacking meaning ⟨a *pointless* remark⟩ **2 :** INEFFECTIVE ⟨a *pointless* effort to help⟩ — **point·less·ly** *adv* — **point·less·ness** *n*

point of honor : a matter seriously affecting one's honor

point of view : a way of thinking about or looking at things **:** STANDPOINT

point spread *n* **:** the number of points by which a person who sets odds expects a favorite to defeat an underdog

pointy \ˈpȯin-tē\ *adj* **point·i·er; -est 1 :** coming to a rather sharp point **2 :** having parts that stick out sharply here and there

[1]**poise** \ˈpȯiz\ *vb* **1 a :** BALANCE; *esp* **:** to hold or carry in equilibrium **b :** to hold or be supported or suspended without motion in a steady position ⟨a bird *poised* in the air⟩ **2 :** to hold or carry (the head) in a particular way **3 :** to put into readiness **:** BRACE ⟨*poised* for action⟩ [Medieval French *peiser, poiser* "to ponder," from Latin *pensare,* from *pensus,* past participle of *pendere* "to weigh"]

[2]**poise** *n* **1 :** BALANCE 4a, EQUILIBRIUM **2 a (1) :** self-possessed composure, assurance, and dignity **(2) :** peaceful state **:** CALM **b :** a particular way of carrying oneself **:** BEARING

poised \ˈpȯizd\ *adj* **:** showing an easy composure in bearing and manner

[1]**poi·son** \ˈpȯiz-ⁿ\ *n* **1 a :** a substance that through its chemical action is able to kill, injure, or impair an organism **b (1) :** something destructive or harmful **(2) :** an object of aversion or abhorrence **2 :** a substance that inhibits the activity of another substance or the course of a reaction or process ⟨a catalyst *poison*⟩ [Medieval French, "drink, potion, poison," from Latin *potio* "drink, potion"]

[2]**poison** *vt* **poi·soned; poi·son·ing** \ˈpȯiz-ning, -n-ing\ **1 a :** to injure or kill with poison **b :** to treat, taint, or impregnate with or as if with poison ⟨*poisoned* the air with its fumes⟩ **2 :** to exert a destructive influence on **:** CORRUPT ⟨*poisoned* their minds⟩ **3 :** to inhibit the activity, course, or occurrence of — **poi·son·er** \ˈpȯiz-nər, -n-ər\ *n*

[3]**poison** *adj* **1 :** POISONOUS, VENOMOUS ⟨a *poison* plant⟩ ⟨a *poison* tongue⟩ **2 :** impregnated with poison ⟨a *poison* arrow⟩

poison gas *n* **:** a poisonous gas or a liquid or a solid giving off poisonous vapors designed (as in chemical warfare) to kill, injure, or disable by inhalation or contact

poison hemlock *n* **:** a biennial poisonous herb related to the carrot and having finely divided leaves and white flowers

poison ivy *n* **1 :** a usually climbing plant related to the sumacs and having three leaflets, greenish flowers, white berries, and foliage and stems that when bruised and touched may cause an itching rash on the skin **2 :** a rash caused by poison ivy

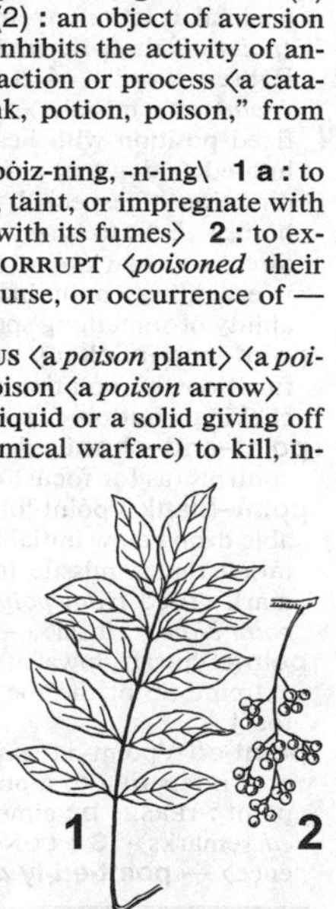

poison sumac: *1* leaf, *2* berries

poison oak *n* **:** any of several shrubby plants related to poison ivy and causing a similar rash

poi·son·ous \ˈpȯiz-nəs, -n-əs\ *adj* **:** having the properties or effects of poison **:** VENOMOUS — **poi·son·ous·ly** *adv*

poison sumac *n* **:** a swamp shrub that is related to poison ivy and causes a similar rash but has compound leaves with 7 to 13 leaflets

[1]**poke** \ˈpōk\ *n, chiefly Southern & Midland* **:** BAG 1a, SACK [Medieval French, of Germanic origin]

[2]**poke** *vb* **1 a (1) :** PROD, JAB ⟨*poked* me in the ribs⟩ **(2) :** to urge or stir by prodding or jabbing ⟨*poke* up the fire⟩ **(3) :** to cause to prod ⟨*poke* a stick at the snake⟩ **b (1) :** PIERCE 1, STAB **(2) :** to produce by piercing or jabbing ⟨*poke* a hole⟩ **c :** HIT 1a, PUNCH **2 a :** to cause to project ⟨*poked* its head out of the hole⟩ **b (1) :** to thrust forward so as to intrude or meddle ⟨don't *poke* your nose into our affairs⟩ **(2) :** MEDDLE ⟨*poking* about in other people's business⟩ **3 :** to look about or through something without system **:** RUMMAGE ⟨*poke* around in the attic⟩ **4 :** to move or act slowly or aimlessly **:** DAWDLE ⟨*poke* along⟩ [Middle English *poken*] — **poke fun at :** RIDICULE, MOCK

[3]**poke** *n* **1 a :** a quick thrust **:** JAB **b :** a blow with the fist **:** PUNCH **2 :** a projecting brim on the front of a woman's bonnet **3 :** a cutting remark **:** DIG

poke·ber·ry \ˈpōk-ˌber-ē\ *n* **:** the berry of the pokeweed; *also* **:** POKEWEED

[1]**pok·er** \ˈpō-kər\ *n* **:** one that pokes; *esp* **:** a metal rod for stirring a fire

[2]**po·ker** \ˈpō-kər\ *n* **:** any of several card games in which players bet on the value of their hands [probably from French *poque,* a card game similar to poker]

poker face *n* **:** a face that does not reveal what a person thinks or feels [from the need of poker players to conceal the quality of their hands] — **po·ker–faced** \ˌpō-kər-ˈfāst\ *adj*

poke·weed \ˈpō-ˌkwēd\ *n* **:** an American perennial herb with spikes of white flowers, dark purple juicy berries, a poisonous root, and young shoots sometimes used as potherbs [*poke,* perhaps from Virginia Algonquian *pocone, poughkone* "puccoon"]

poky *or* **pok·ey** \ˈpō-kē\ *adj* **pok·i·er; -est 1 :** being small and cramped ⟨a *poky* room⟩ **2 :** SHABBY, DULL ⟨a *poky* way of writing⟩ **3 :** annoyingly slow ⟨a *poky* horse⟩ [[2]*poke*] — **pok·i·ly** \-kə-lē\ *adv* — **pok·i·ness** \-kē-nəs\ *n*

Po·land Chi·na \ˌpō-lənd-ˈchī-nə, -lən-\ *n* **:** any of a breed of large white-marked black swine adapted to converting feed into fat [*Poland,* Europe + *China,* Asia]

po·lar \ˈpō-lər\ *adj* **1 :** of or relating to a geographical pole or the region around it; *also* **:** coming from or having the characteristics of such a region **2 a :** of or relating to one or more poles (as of a magnet) **b :** having a dipole or characterized by molecules having dipoles ⟨a *polar* molecule⟩ **3 :** serving as a guide ⟨a *polar* idea⟩ **4 :** diametrically opposite **5 :** PIVOTAL 2, CRUCIAL ⟨*polar* events⟩

polar bear *n* **:** a large creamy-white bear of arctic regions that is a powerful swimmer and eats flesh

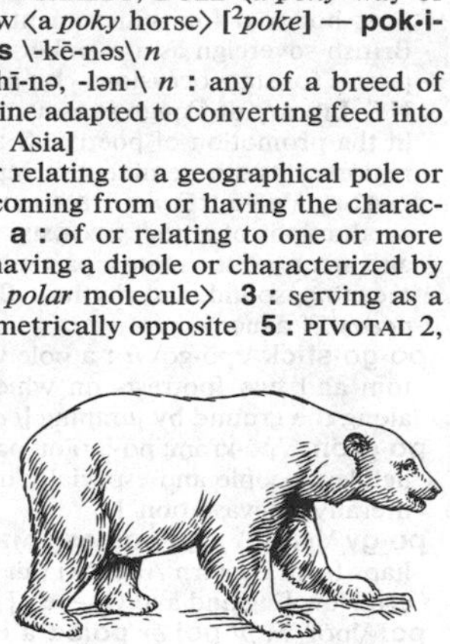
polar bear

polar body *n* **:** a cell that separates from an oocyte during meiosis and that contains a nucleus produced in the first or second meiotic division but very little cytoplasm

polar circle *n* **:** one of the two parallels of latitude each at a distance from a pole of the earth equal to about 23 degrees 27 minutes

polar coordinate *n* **:** either of two numbers that locate a point in a plane by its distance from a fixed point and the angle a line joining the two points makes with a fixed line

Po·lar·is \pə-ˈlar-əs, -ˈlär-\ *n* **:** NORTH STAR [New Latin, from *polaris* "polar"]

po·lari·scope \pō-ˈlar-ə-ˌskōp\ *n* **:** an instrument for studying the properties of substances in polarized light

po·lar·i·ty \pō-ˈlar-ət-ē, pə-\ *n, pl* **-ties 1 :** the quality or condition of being polar **:** having poles **2 :** attraction toward a particular object or in a specific direction **3 :** the particular state either positive or negative with reference to magnetic or electrical poles **4 a :** diametrical opposition **b :** an instance of diametrical opposition

po·lar·i·za·tion \ˌpō-lə-rə-ˈzā-shən\ *n* **1 :** the action of polarizing or state of being polarized: as **a :** the action of affecting radiation (as light) so that the vibrations of the wave assume a definite direction (as in one plane) **b :** the deposition of gas on one or both electrodes of an electrolytic cell increasing the resistance and setting up a counter electromotive force **c** : MAGNETIZATION **2 a** : division into two opposites ⟨*polarization* of views⟩ **b** : concentration about opposing extremes ⟨*polarization* of political factions⟩

po·lar·ize \ˈpō-lə-ˌrīz\ *vb* **1** : to cause to undergo polarization **2** : to give polarity to **3** : to break up into opposing groups **4** : to become polarized — **po·lar·iz·able** \-ˌrī-zə-bəl\ *adj* — **po·lar·iz·er** *n*

polar nucleus *n* : either of the two nuclei of a seed plant embryo sac that are destined to form endosperm — compare DOUBLE FERTILIZATION

Po·lar·oid \ˈpō-lə-ˌrȯid\ *trademark* — used for a light-polarizing material or for a camera

pol·der \ˈpōl-dər, ˈpäl-\ *n* : a tract of low land reclaimed from a body of water (as the sea) [Dutch]

[1]**pole** \ˈpōl\ *n* **1** : a long slender usually cylindrical piece of material (as wood or metal) ⟨telephone *poles*⟩ **2** : a unit of length usually equal to a rod (16½ feet or about 5 meters) **3** : the inside front row position on the starting line for a race [Old English *pāl* "stake, pole," from Latin *palus* "stake"]

[2]**pole** *vb* **1** : to act upon, impel, or push with a pole **2 a** : to propel a boat with a pole **b** : to use ski poles to gain speed — **poler** *n*

[3]**pole** *n* **1** : either end of an axis of a sphere and especially of the earth's axis **2 a** : either of two related opposites **b** : a point of guidance or attraction **3 a** : one of the two terminals of an electric cell, battery, or dynamo **b** : one of two or more regions in a magnetized body at which the magnetism is concentrated **4** : either of the two specialized areas at opposite ends of an axis in an organism or cell ⟨chromosomes moving toward the *poles* of a dividing cell⟩ [Latin *polus,* from Greek *polos* "pivot, pole"]

Pole \ˈpōl\ *n* **1** : a native or inhabitant of Poland **2** : a person of Polish descent [German, of Slavic origin]

pole·ax \ˈpō-ˌlaks\ *n* : a battle-ax with a short handle and often with a hook or point opposite the blade [Middle English *pollax,* from *polle* "poll" + *ax*]

pole bean *n* : a cultivated bean having twining stems and usually trained to grow upright on supports

pole·cat \ˈpōl-ˌkat\ *n, pl* **polecats** *or* **polecat** **1** : a brown to black European flesh-eating mammal related to the weasels from which the ferret is derived **2** : SKUNK 1 [Middle English *polcat,* probably from Middle French *poul, pol* "cock" + Middle English *cat*; probably from its preying on poultry]

po·lem·ic \pə-ˈlem-ik\ *n* **1 a** : an aggressive attack on or refutation of the opinions or principles of another **b** : the art or practice of disputation or controversy — usually used in plural **2** : an aggressive controversialist : DISPUTANT [French *polémique,* derived from Greek *polemikos* "warlike, hostile," from *polemos* "war"] — **po·lem·i·cal** \-ˈlem-i-kəl\ *also* **polemic** *adj* — **po·lem·i·cal·ly** \-i-kə-lē, -klē\ *adv* — **po·lem·i·cist** \-ˈlem-ə-səst\ *n*

po·len·ta \pō-ˈlen-tə\ *n* : mush made of chestnut meal, cornmeal, semolina, or farina [Italian, from Latin, "crushed and hulled barley"]

pole·star \ˈpōl-ˌstär\ *n* **1** : NORTH STAR **2 a** : a directing principle : GUIDE **b** : a center of attraction

pole vault *n* : a field event consisting of a vault for height over a crossbar with the aid of a pole — **pole–vault** \ˈpōl-ˌvȯlt\ *vi* — **pole–vault·er** *n*

[1]**po·lice** \pə-ˈlēs\ *n, pl* **police** **1** : the department of government that keeps order and enforces laws, investigates crimes, and makes arrests **2 a** : POLICE FORCE **b** *pl* : members of a police force **3** : a private organization resembling a police force ⟨railroad *police*⟩ **4** : one attempting to regulate or censor a specified field or activity ⟨the fashion *police*⟩ [French, "government," from Late Latin *politia,* from Greek *politeia,* from *politēs* "citizen," from *polis* "city, state"]

[2]**police** *vt* **1** : to control, regulate, or keep in order by use or as if by use of police **2** : to make clean and put in order : clean up ⟨*police* an area⟩ **3** : to supervise the operation, execution, or administration of

police action *n* : a military action undertaken without formal declaration of war by regular forces against persons held to be violators of international peace and order

police court *n* : a court having jurisdiction over various minor offenses and authority to send cases involving serious offenses to a superior court

police dog *n* **1** : a dog trained to assist police (as in detecting drugs) **2** : GERMAN SHEPHERD

police force *n* : a body of trained officers entrusted by a government with maintenance of public peace and order, enforcement of laws, and prevention and detection of crime

po·lice·man \pə-ˈlē-smən\ *n* : POLICE OFFICER

police officer *n* : a member of a police force

police power *n* : the inherent power of a government to exercise reasonable control over persons and property within its jurisdiction in the interest of the general security, health, safety, morals, and welfare

police reporter *n* : a reporter assigned to cover police news (as crimes, accidents, and arrests)

police state *n* : a state in which the social, economic, and political activities of the people are under the arbitrary power of the government often acting through a secret police force

police station *n* : the headquarters of the police for a particular locality

po·lice·wom·an \pə-ˈlē-ˌswu̇m-ən\ *n* : a female police officer

[1]**pol·i·cy** \ˈpäl-ə-sē\ *n, pl* **-cies** **1 a** : prudence or wisdom in the management of affairs : SAGACITY **b** : management or procedure based primarily on material interest **2** : a frame of reference or a set of principles or rules determining what and how things are done by a person or group ⟨it's our *policy* not to give refunds⟩ [Medieval French *police, policie* "government, regulation," from Late Latin *politia*]

[2]**policy** *n, pl* **-cies** **1** : a writing embodying a contract of insurance **2 a** : a daily lottery in which participants bet that certain numbers will be drawn **b** : NUMBER 8 [Medieval French *police* "certificate," from Italian *polizza,* from Medieval Latin *apodixa* "receipt," from Greek *apodeixis* "proof," from *apodeiknynai* "to demonstrate"]

pol·i·cy·hold·er \-ˌhōl-dər\ *n* : the owner of an insurance policy

po·lio \ˈpō-lē-ˌō\ *n* : POLIOMYELITIS — **polio** *adj*

po·lio·my·e·li·tis \ˌpō-lē-ˌō-ˌmī-ə-ˈlīt-əs\ *n* : an acute infectious virus disease marked by inflammation of neurons in the spinal cord accompanied by fever and often paralysis and wasting of muscles — called also *infantile paralysis* [Greek *polios* "gray" + *myelos* "marrow"]

po·lio·vi·rus \ˈpō-lē-ō-ˌvī-rəs\ *n* : a virus that causes human poliomyelitis and occurs in several distinct forms

[1]**pol·ish** \ˈpäl-ish\ *vb* **1** : to make smooth and glossy usually by friction ⟨*polish* furniture⟩ **2** : to smooth or refine in manners or condition **3** : to bring to a highly developed, finished, or refined state ⟨*polish* a technique⟩ [Medieval French *poliss-,* stem of *polir* "to polish," from Latin *polire*] — **pol·ish·er** *n*

[2]**polish** *n* **1 a** : a smooth glossy surface : LUSTER **b** : freedom from rudeness or coarseness : CULTURE **c** : a state of high development or refinement **2** : the action or process of polishing **3** : a preparation used in polishing

[1]**Pol·ish** \ˈpō-lish\ *adj* : of, relating to, or characteristic of Poland, the Poles, or Polish

[2]**Polish** *n* : the Slavic language of the Poles

polish off *vt* : to finish off or dispose of rapidly or completely

po·lit·bu·ro \ˈpäl-ət-ˌbyu̇r-ō, ˈpō-lət-, pə-ˈlit-\ *n* : the principal policy-making body of a Communist party [Russian *politbyuro,* from *politicheskoe byuro* "political bureau"]

po·lite \pə-ˈlīt\ *adj* **po·lit·er; -est** **1** : of, relating to, or having the characteristics of advanced culture ⟨customs of *polite* society⟩ **2 a** : showing or characterized by correct social usage ⟨*polite* forms of address⟩ **b** : marked by consideration, tact, deference, or courtesy : COURTEOUS [Latin *politus,* from *polire* "to polish"] ***synonyms*** see CIVIL — **po·lite·ly** *adv* — **po·lite·ness** *n*

po·li·tesse \ˌpäl-ē-ˈtes, ˌpȯ-li-\ *n* : formal politeness [French]

pol·i·tic \ˈpäl-ə-ˌtik\ *adj* **1** : characterized by shrewdness in managing, contriving, or dealing **2** : sagacious in promoting a policy **3** : shrewdly tactful ⟨a *politic* answer⟩ [Medieval French *politique* "political," from Latin *politicus,* from Greek *politikos,* from *politēs* "citizen," from *polis* "citizen"] ***synonyms*** see EXPEDIENT

po·lit·i·cal \pə-ˈlit-i-kəl\ *adj* **1** : of or relating to government, a government, or the conduct of government **2** : of or relating to politics **3** : organized in governmental terms ⟨*political* units⟩ **4** : involving or charged or concerned with acts against a government or political system ⟨*political* crimes⟩ ⟨*political* police⟩ — **po·lit·i·cal·ly** \-kə-lē, -klē\ *adv*

political action committee *n* : a group formed (as by an industry or an issue-oriented organization) to raise money for the campaigns of candidates likely to advance the group's interests

political economy *n* : the theory or study of the role of public policy in influencing the economic and social welfare of a political unit — **political economist** *n*

politically correct *adj* : conforming to a belief that language and practices which could offend political sensibilities (as in matters of sex or race) should be eliminated — **political correctness** *n*

political science *n* : a social science concerned chiefly with the description and analysis of political institutions and processes — **political scientist** *n*

pol·i·ti·cian \ˌpäl-ə-ˈtish-ən\ *n* **1** : one experienced in the art or science of government; *esp* : one actively conducting governmental affairs **2** : one engaged in party politics as a profession

pol·i·tick \ˈpäl-ə-ˌtik\ *vi* : to engage in political discussion or activity — **pol·i·tick·er** *n*

po·lit·i·co \pə-ˈlit-i-ˌkō\ *n, pl* **-cos** *also* **-coes** : POLITICIAN [Italian *politico* or Spanish *político,* derived from Latin *politicus* "political"]

pol·i·tics \ˈpäl-ə-ˌtiks\ *n sing or pl* **1 a** : the art or science of government **b** : the art or science of guiding or influencing governmental policy **c** : the art or science of winning and holding control over a government **2 a** : political affairs or business; *esp* : competition between groups or individuals for power and leadership **b** : political life especially as a profession **3** : political opinions

pol·i·ty \ˈpäl-ət-ē\ *n, pl* **-ties** **1** : political organization **2** : a form of political organization ⟨a republican *polity*⟩ **3** : a politically organized unit **4** : the form of government of a religious denomination

pol·ka \ˈpōl-kə\ *n* **1** : a vivacious couple dance of Bohemian origin with three steps and a hop in duple time **2** : a lively originally Bohemian dance tune in ²⁄₄ time [Czech, from *Polka* "Polish woman"] — **polka** *vi*

pol·ka dot \ˈpō-kə-ˌdät\ *n* : a dot in a pattern of regularly distributed dots in textile design — **polka–dot** *or* **polka–dot·ted** \-dät-əd\ *adj*

¹poll \ˈpōl\ *n* **1 a** : HEAD 1 **b** : the top or back of the head **c** : NAPE **2** : the broad or flat end of a hammer or similar tool **3 a** : a casting or recording of votes **b** : a place where votes are cast or recorded — usually used in plural **4 a** : a questioning of persons to obtain information or opinions **b** : the information so obtained [Low German *polle*]

²poll *vb* **1 a** : to cut off or cut short the hair or wool of : CROP, SHEAR **b** : to cut off or cut short (as wool) **c** : to cut off or cut short the horns of (cattle) **2 a** : to receive and record the votes of **b** : to request each member of to declare his or her vote individually ⟨*poll* a jury⟩ **3** : to receive (as votes) in an election **4** : to question or canvass in a poll **5** : to cast one's vote at a poll — **poll·ee** \pō-ˈlē\ *n* — **poll·er** \ˈpō-lər\ *n*

pol·lack *or* **pol·lock** \ˈpäl-ək\ *n, pl* **pollack** *or* **pollock** **1** : a commercially important northern Atlantic food fish resembling the related cods but darker **2** : a commercially important food fish of the northern Pacific that is related to and resembles the pollack [Scottish *podlok*]

polled \ˈpōld\ *adj* : having no horns

pol·len \ˈpäl-ən\ *n* : a mass of microspores in a seed plant that usually appears as a fine yellow dust [Latin *pollin-, pollen* "fine flour"]

pollen basket *n* : a flat or hollow area bordered with stiff hairs on the hind leg of a bee in which it carries pollen

pollen grain *n* : one of the granular microspores in pollen that give rise to the male gametophyte of a seed plant

pol·len·iz·er \ˈpäl-ə-ˌnī-zər\ *n* **1** : a plant that is a source of pollen **2** : POLLINATOR 1

pollen sac *n* : one of the pouches of a seed plant anther in which pollen is formed

pollen tube *n* : a tube formed by the pollen grain that passes down the style and conveys the sperm nuclei to the embryo sac of a flower

pol·lex \ˈpäl-ˌeks\ *n, pl* **pol·li·ces** \ˈpäl-ə-ˌsēz\ : the first digit of the forelimb : THUMB 1 [Latin, "thumb, big toe"]

pol·li·nate \ˈpäl-ə-ˌnāt\ *vt* : to place pollen on the stigma of — **pol·li·na·tion** \ˌpäl-ə-ˈnā-shən\ *n*

pol·li·na·tor \ˈpäl-ə-ˌnāt-ər\ *n* **1** : an agent that pollinates flowers **2** : POLLENIZER 1

pol·li·no·sis *or* **pol·len·osis** \ˌpäl-ə-ˈnō-səs\ *n* : HAY FEVER

poll·ster \ˈpōl-stər\ *n* : one that conducts a poll or compiles data obtained by a poll

poll tax *n* : a tax of a fixed amount per person levied on adults

pol·lu·tant \pə-ˈlüt-nt\ *n* : something that pollutes

pol·lute \pə-ˈlüt\ *vt* : to make impure; *esp* : to contaminate (as a natural resource) with man-made waste ⟨industrial wastes *polluted* the river⟩ [Latin *pollutus,* past participle of *polluere* "to pollute"] — **pol·lut·er** *n*

pol·lu·tion \pə-ˈlü-shən\ *n* **1** : the action of polluting : the state of being polluted **2** : POLLUTANT

Pol·lux \ˈpäl-əks\ *n* : a first-magnitude star in the constellation Gemini [*Pollux,* twin of Castor]

Pol·ly·an·na \ˌpäl-ē-ˈan-ə\ *n* : one characterized by unshakable optimism and a tendency to find good in everything [*Pollyanna,* heroine of the novel *Pollyanna* (1913) by Eleanor Porter, died 1920, American fiction writer]

pol·ly·wog *or* **pol·li·wog** \ˈpäl-ē-ˌwäg, -ˌwȯg\ *n* : TADPOLE [Middle English *polwygle,* probably from *pol* "poll" + *wiglen* "to wiggle"]

po·lo \ˈpō-lō\ *n* **1** : a game played by teams of players on horseback using mallets with long flexible handles to drive a wooden ball **2** : WATER POLO [Balti (language of northern Kashmir) "ball"] — **po·lo·ist** \ˈpō-lə-wəst\ *n*

polo coat *n* : a tailored casual overcoat made especially of camel's hair

po·lo·naise \ˌpäl-ə-ˈnāz, ˌpō-lə-\ *n* **1** : an elaborate 18th century short-sleeved overdress with fitted waist and draped cutaway overskirt **2 a** : a stately 19th century Polish processional dance **b** : music for this dance in moderate ¾ time [French, from *polonais* "Polish"]

po·lo·ni·um \pə-ˈlō-nē-əm\ *n* : a radioactive metallic element that is found in pitchblende and decays to form an isotope of lead — see ELEMENT table [New Latin, from Medieval Latin *Polonia* "Poland"]

polo shirt *n* : a close-fitting knitted cotton pullover shirt with a turnover collar or round banded neck

pol·ter·geist \ˈpōl-tər-ˌgīst\ *n* : a noisy usually mischievous ghost held to be responsible for unexplained noises (as rappings) [German, from *poltern* "to knock" + *Geist* "spirit"]

¹pol·troon \päl-ˈtrün\ *n* : a spiritless coward : CRAVEN [Middle French *poultron,* from Italian *poltrone,* probably related to *poltro* "colt," derived from Latin *pullus* "young of an animal"]

²poltroon *adj* : characterized by complete cowardice

poly- *combining form* **1** : many : several : much : MULTI- ⟨*polygyny*⟩ **2 a** : containing more than one of a (specified) substance ⟨*poly*nucleotide⟩ **b** : polymeric ⟨*poly*ethylene⟩ [Greek, from *polys*]

poly·an·dry \ˈpäl-ē-ˌan-drē\ *n* : the practice of having more than one husband or male mate at one time — compare POLYGYNY [Greek *polyandros* "having many husbands," from *poly-* + *andr-, anēr* "man, husband"] — **poly·an·drous** \ˌpäl-ē-ˈan-drəs\ *adj*

poly·atom·ic \ˌpäl-ē-ə-ˈtäm-ik\ *adj* : containing more than one atom

poly·chaete \ˈpäl-i-ˌkēt\ *n* : any of a class (Polychaeta) of chiefly marine annelid worms that usually have paired segmental appendages [derived from Greek *polychaitēs* "having much hair," from *poly-* + *chaitē* "long hair"] — **polychaete** *adj*

poly·chlo·ri·nat·ed biphenyl \ˌpäl-i-ˈklōr-ə-ˌnāt-əd-, -ˈklȯr-\ *n* : any of several compounds that have various industrial applications and are poisonous environmental pollutants which tend to accumulate in animal tissues

poly·chro·mat·ic \ˌpäl-i-krō-ˈmat-ik\ *adj* : showing a variety or a change of colors : MULTICOLORED

poly·chrome \ˈpäl-i-ˌkrōm\ *adj* : relating to, made with, or decorated in several colors ⟨*polychrome* pottery⟩

poly·clin·ic \ˌpäl-i-ˈklin-ik\ *n* : a clinic or hospital treating diseases of many sorts

poly·dac·ty·ly \ˌpäl-i-ˈdak-tə-lē\ *n* : the condition of having more than the normal number of toes or fingers [*poly-* + Greek *daktylos* "finger, toe"] — **poly·dac·tyl** \-ˈdak-tl\ *adj*

poly·es·ter \ˈpäl-ē-ˌes-tər\ *n* : any of a group of polymers that consist basically of repeated units of an ester and are used especially in making fibers or plastics

poly·eth·yl·ene \ˌpäl-ē-ˈeth-ə-ˌlēn\ *n* **:** one of various lightweight plastics resistant to chemicals and moisture that are used especially in packaging and electrical insulation

po·lyg·a·mous \pə-ˈlig-ə-məs\ *adj* **1 :** of, relating to, or being a marriage form in which a spouse of either sex has more than one mate at one time **2 :** having more than one spouse or mate at one time — **po·lyg·a·mist** \-məst\ *n* — **po·lyg·a·my** \-mē\ *n*

poly·gene \ˈpäl-i-ˌjēn\ *n* **:** any of a group of genes that collectively control or modify the expression of a particular character — **poly·gen·ic** \ˌpäl-i-ˈjē-nik\ *adj*

poly·glot \ˈpäl-i-ˌglät\ *adj* **1 :** speaking or writing several languages **2 :** containing matter in or derived from several languages [Greek *polyglōttos,* from *poly-* + *glōtta* "language"] — **polyglot** *n*

poly·gon \ˈpäl-i-ˌgän\ *n* **:** a geometric figure that is closed, that lies in a plane, and whose edges are all straight lines ⟨triangles, squares, and pentagons are all *polygons*⟩ — **po·lyg·o·nal** \pə-ˈlig-ən-l\ *adj*

poly·graph \ˈpäl-i-ˌgraf\ *n* **:** an instrument for recording tracings of several different pulsations simultaneously — compare LIE DETECTOR — **poly·graph·ic** \ˌpäl-i-ˈgraf-ik\ *adj*

po·lyg·y·ny \pə-ˈlij-ə-nē\ *n* **:** the practice of having more than one wife or female mate at one time — compare POLYANDRY [*poly-* + Greek *gynē* "woman, wife"] — **po·lyg·y·nous** \-nəs\ *adj*

poly·he·dron \ˌpäl-i-ˈhē-drən\ *n, pl* **-drons** *or* **-dra** \-drə\ **:** a geometric solid whose faces are each flat polygons formed by plane faces — **poly·he·dral** \-drəl\ *adj*

poly·math \ˈpäl-i-ˌmath\ *n* **:** one of encyclopedic learning [Greek *polymathēs* "very learned," from *poly-* + *manthanein* "to learn"]

poly·mer \ˈpäl-ə-mər\ *n* **:** a chemical compound or mixture of compounds that is formed by polymerization and consists essentially of repeating structural units [back-formation from *polymeric,* from Greek *polymerēs* "having many parts," from *poly-* + *meros* "part"] — **poly·mer·ic** \ˌpäl-ə-ˈmer-ik\ *adj*

po·ly·mer·ase \pə-ˈlim-ə-ˌrās, ˈpäl ə mə \ *n* **:** any of several enzymes that promote the formation of DNA or RNA using preexisting strands of DNA or RNA as templates

polymerase chain reaction *n* **:** a laboratory technique for rapidly producing large quantities of a specific DNA segment that involves the repeated use of polymerase to synthesize two-stranded DNA from a single DNA strand

po·ly·mer·i·za·tion \pə-ˌlim-ə-rə-ˈzā-shən, ˌpäl-ə-mə-rə-\ *n* **:** a chemical reaction in which two or more small molecules combine to form larger molecules — **po·ly·mer·ize** \pə-ˈlim-ə-ˌrīz, ˈpäl-ə-mə-\ *vb*

poly·morph \ˈpäl-i-ˌmȯrf\ *n* **:** a polymorphic organism; *also* **:** one of the several forms of such an organism

poly·mor·phic \ˌpäl-i-ˈmȯr-fik\ *or* **poly·mor·phous** \-fəs\ *adj* **:** having, assuming, or occurring in various forms, characters, or styles ⟨a *polymorphic* butterfly⟩ — **poly·mor·phism** \-ˌfiz-əm\ *n*

poly·mor·pho·nu·cle·ar \-ˌmȯr-fə-ˈnü-klē-ər, -ˈnyü-\ *adj* **:** having the nucleus complexly lobed ⟨*polymorphonuclear* white blood cells⟩ — **polymorphonuclear** *n*

Poly·ne·sian \ˌpäl-ə-ˈnē-zhən, -shən\ *n* **1 :** a member of any of the native peoples of Polynesia **2 :** a group of Austronesian languages spoken in Polynesia — **Polynesian** *adj*

poly·no·mi·al \ˌpäl-i-ˈnō-mē-əl\ *n* **:** a mathematical expression of two or more terms each of which is the product of a constant and one or more variables raised to a power ⟨$6 + 3x + 5x^2$ is a *polynomial*⟩ — compare MONOMIAL [*poly-* + *-nomial* (as in *binomial*)] — **polynomial** *adj*

poly·nu·cle·o·tide \ˌpäl-i-ˈnü-klē-ə-ˌtīd, -ˈnyü-\ *n* **:** a long chain of linked nucleotides

pol·yp \ˈpäl-əp\ *n* **1 :** a coelenterate (as a sea anemone or coral) having a hollow cylindrical body closed and attached at one end and opening at the other by a central mouth surrounded by tentacles armed with minute stinging organs **2 :** a growth that projects from a mucous membrane (as of the colon or vocal cords) [French *polype* "octopus, nasal tumor," from Latin *polypus,* from Greek *polypous,* from *poly-* + *pous* "foot"] — **pol·yp·oid** \ˈpäl-ə-ˌpȯid\ *adj*

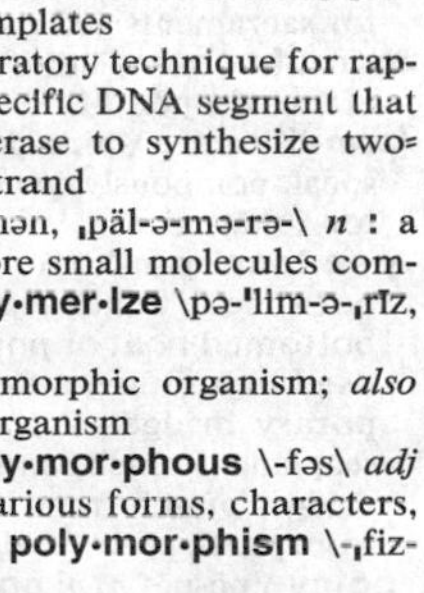

polyp 1

poly·pep·tide \ˌpäl-i-ˈpep-ˌtīd\ *n* **:** a chain of amino acids that contributes to the structure of a protein

poly·phase \ˈpäl-i-ˌfāz\ *or* **poly·pha·sic** \ˌpäl-i-ˈfā-zik\ *adj* **:** having or producing two or more phases ⟨a *polyphase* machine⟩ ⟨a *polyphase* current⟩

po·lyph·o·ny \pə-ˈlif-ə-nē\ *n* **:** music consisting of two or more independent but harmonious melodies [Greek *polyphōnia* "variety of tones," derived from *poly-* + *phōnē* "voice"] — **poly·phon·ic** \ˌpäl-i-ˈfän-ik\ *adj* — **poly·phon·i·cal·ly** \-i-kə-lē, -klē\ *or* **po·lyph·o·nous·ly** \pə-ˈlif-ə-nəs-lē\ *adv*

poly·ploid \ˈpäl-i-ˌplȯid\ *adj* **:** having or being a chromosome number that is a multiple greater than two of the basic haploid chromosome number [*poly-* + *-ploid* (as in *diploid*)] — **polyploid** *n* — **poly·ploi·dy** \-ˌplȯid-ē\ *n*

poly·po·dy \ˈpäl-ə-ˌpōd-ē\ *n, pl* **-dies :** a widely distributed fern with creeping rhizomes and usually deeply cleft fronds [Latin *polypodium,* from Greek *polypodion,* from *poly-* + *pod-, pous* "foot"]

poly·sac·cha·ride \ˌpäl-i-ˈsak-ə-ˌrīd\ *n* **:** a carbohydrate that can be decomposed by hydrolysis into two or more molecules of monosaccharides; *esp* **:** one (as cellulose, starch, or glycogen) containing a great number of monosaccharide units in a complex arrangement

poly·sty·rene \-ˈstīr-ˌēn\ *n* **:** a clear rigid plastic used especially in molded products, foams, and sheet materials

poly·syl·lab·ic \ˌpäl-i-sə-ˈlab-ik\ *adj* **1 :** having more than one and usually more than three syllables **2 :** using polysyllabic words — **poly·syl·lab·i·cal·ly** \-ˈlab-i-kə-lē, -klē\ *adv*

poly·syl·la·ble \ˈpäl-i-ˌsil-ə-bəl, ˌpäl-i-ˈ\ *n* **:** a polysyllabic word [Medieval Latin *polysyllaba,* from Greek *poly-* + *syllabē* "syllable"]

poly·syn·de·ton \ˌpäl-i-ˈsin-də-ˌtän\ *n* **:** repetition of conjunctions in close succession (as in "paper and pencils and books") [Late Greek, neuter of *polysyndetos* "using many conjunctions," from Greek *poly-* + *syndetos* "bound together"]

¹poly·tech·nic \ˌpäl-i-ˈtek-nik\ *adj* **:** relating to or devoted to instruction in many technical arts or applied sciences ⟨a *polytechnic* school⟩ [French *polytechnique,* from Greek *polytechnos* "skilled in many arts," from *poly-* + *technē* "art"]

²polytechnic *n* **:** a polytechnic school

poly·the·ism \ˈpäl-i-ˌthē-ˌiz-əm\ *n* **:** belief in or worship of more than one god — **poly·the·ist** \-ˌthē-əst\ *adj or n* — **poly·the·is·tic** \ˌpäl-i-thē-ˈis-tik\ *adj*

poly·to·nal·i·ty \ˌpäl-i-tō-ˈnal-ət-ē\ *n* **:** the simultaneous use of two or more musical keys — **poly·ton·al** \-ˈtōn-l\ *adj*

poly·un·sat·u·rat·ed \ˌpäl-ē-ˌən-ˈsach-ə-ˌrāt-əd\ *adj, of an oil or fatty acid* **:** having many double or triple bonds in a molecule

poly·va·lent \ˌpäl-i-ˈvā-lənt\ *adj* **1 a :** having a valence greater usually than two **b :** having variable valence **2 :** effective against or sensitive toward more than one exciting agent (as a toxin or antigen) — **poly·va·lence** \-ləns\ *n*

poly·vi·nyl chloride \ˌpä-lē-ˈvīn-l-\ *n* **:** a polymer of chlorinated vinyl used especially for pipes

pom·ace \ˈpəm-əs, ˈpäm-\ *n* **:** the dry or pulpy residue of plant material (as fruit or seeds) from which a liquid (as a juice or oil) has been pressed or extracted [probably from Medieval Latin *pomacium* "cider," from Late Latin *pomum* "apple," from Latin, "fruit"]

po·made \pō-ˈmād, -ˈmäd\ *n* **:** a perfumed ointment especially for the hair or scalp [Middle French *pommade* "ointment formerly made from apples," from Italian *pomata,* from *pomo* "apple," from Late Latin *pomum*] — **pomade** *vt*

po·man·der \ˈpō-ˌman-dər, pō-ˈ\ *n* **:** a mixture of aromatic substances enclosed in a perforated bag or box and formerly carried as a guard against infection [Medieval French *pome de ambre,* literally, "apple or ball of amber"]

pome \ˈpōm\ *n* **:** a fleshy fruit (as an apple or pear) consisting of a central core with usually five seeds enclosed in a capsule and surrounded by a thick fleshy outer layer [Medieval French *pume, pomme* "apple, fruit," from Late Latin *pomum* "apple," from Latin, "fruit"]

pome·gran·ate \ˈpäm-ˌgran-ət, ˈpäm-ə-ˌgran-, ˈpəm-ˌgran-\ *n* **:** a reddish fruit about the size of an orange having a thick leathery skin and many seeds in a tart crimson pulp; *also* : a tropical Asian tree that bears pomegranates [Medieval French *pomme garnette,* literally, "seedy fruit"]

pom·e·lo \ˈpäm-ə-ˌlō\ *n* **1** : GRAPEFRUIT **2** : a very large pear-shaped fruit that is related to the grapefruit and has thick rind and often dry pulp; *also* : a tropical Asian tree that bears this fruit [probably alteration of earlier *pompelmous,* from Dutch *pompelmoes*]

Pom·er·a·nian \ˌpäm-ə-ˈrā-nē-ən, -nyən\ *n* **1** : any of a breed of very small compact long-haired dogs **2** : a native or inhabitant of Pomerania — **Pomeranian** *adj*

1pom·mel \ˈpəm-əl, ˈpäm-\ *n* **1** : the knob on the hilt of a sword or saber **2** : the projection at the front and top of a saddlebow **3** : either of a pair of removable rounded or U-shaped handles on a pommel horse [Medieval French *pomel,* derived from Latin *pomum* "fruit"]

2pom·mel \ˈpəm-əl\ *vt* **-meled** *or* **-melled; -mel·ing** *or* **-mel·ling** \ˈpəm-ling, -ə-ling\ : POUND 2a, PUMMEL [*1pommel*]

pommel horse *n* : a padded horizontal rectangular or cylindrical form with two pommels on the top that is used for swinging and balancing feats in gymnastics

pomp \ˈpämp\ *n* **1** : a show of magnificence : SPLENDOR ⟨the *pomp* of a coronation ceremony⟩ **2** : a showy display [Medieval French *pompe,* from Latin *pompa* "procession, pomp," from Greek *pompē* "act of sending, escort, procession, pomp"]

pom·pa·dour \ˈpäm-pə-ˌdōr, -ˌdȯr\ *n* : a style of dressing the hair high over the forehead; *also* : hair dressed in this style [Marquise de *Pompadour*]

pom·pa·no \ˈpäm-pə-ˌnō, ˈpəm-\ *n, pl* **-no** *or* **-nos** : a food fish of the western Atlantic and Gulf of Mexico having a narrow body and forked tail; *also* : any of several related or similar fishes [Spanish *pámpano,* a kind of fish]

1pom–pom \ˈpäm-ˌpäm\ *n* **1** : an ornamental ball or tuft used on clothing, caps, and costumes **2** : a handheld usually brightly colored fluffy ball waved by cheerleaders [alteration of *pompon*]

2pom–pom *n* : an automatic antiaircraft gun of 20 to 40 millimeters mounted especially on ships [imitative]

pom·pon \ˈpäm-ˌpän\ *n* **1** : 1POM-POM 1 **2** : a chrysanthemum or dahlia with small rounded flower heads [French]

pom·pos·i·ty \päm-ˈpäs-ət-ē\ *n, pl* **-ties** **1** : the quality or state of being pompous **2** : a pompous gesture or act

pomp·ous \ˈpäm-pəs\ *adj* **1** : marked by stately show ⟨a *pompous* procession⟩ **2** : SELF-IMPORTANT ⟨a very *pompous* person⟩ **3** : too elevated or ornate ⟨*pompous* prose⟩ — **pomp·ous·ly** *adv* — **pomp·ous·ness** *n*

pon·cho \ˈpän-chō\ *n, pl* **ponchos** : a cloak resembling a blanket with a slit in the middle for the head; *also* : a waterproof garment of similar style worn chiefly as a raincoat [American Spanish, from Mapuche (the language of an American Indian people of southern Chile)]

pond \ˈpänd\ *n* : a body of standing water usually smaller than a lake [Middle English *ponde* "artificially confined body of water," probably alteration of *pounde* "enclosure"]

pon·der \ˈpän-dər\ *vb* **pon·dered; pon·der·ing** \ˈpän-dring, -də-ring\ : to consider carefully [Medieval French *ponderer,* from Latin *ponderare* "to weigh, ponder," from *ponder-, pondus* "weight"] — **pon·der·er** \-dər-ər\ *n*

synonyms PONDER, MEDITATE, RUMINATE mean to consider or examine closely or deliberately. PONDER implies prolonged thinking about a matter often with a careful consideration and weighing of different aspects or alternatives ⟨*pondered* her next chess move⟩. MEDITATE implies a definite focusing of one's thoughts on something so as to understand it deeply ⟨*meditated* on the meaning of life⟩. RUMINATE implies going over the same matter in one's thoughts again and again but suggests a more casual and less focused approach ⟨*ruminating* on the possibilities the future might hold⟩.

pon·der·a·ble \ˈpän-də-rə-bəl, -drə-bəl\ *adj* : capable of being weighed or appraised : APPRECIABLE [Late Latin *ponderabilis,* from Latin *ponderare* "to weigh, ponder"]

pon·der·o·sa pine \ˌpän-də-ˌrō-sə, -zə-\ *n* : a tall timber pine of western North America with long needles in bundles of 2 or 3; *also* : its strong reddish straight-grained wood [Latin *ponderosa,* feminine of *ponderosus* "ponderous"]

pon·der·ous \ˈpän-də-rəs, -drəs\ *adj* **1** : very heavy **2** : unwieldy or clumsy because of weight and size **3** : unpleasantly or oppressively dull ⟨*ponderous* prose⟩ [Medieval French *ponderus,* from Latin *ponderosus,* from *ponder-, pondus* "weight"] — **pon·der·ous·ly** *adv* — **pon·der·ous·ness** *n*

pond lily *n* : WATER LILY

pond scum *n* **1** : SPIROGYRA; *also* : any of various related algae **2** : a mass of tangled algal filaments in stagnant water

pond·weed \ˈpän-ˌdwēd\ *n* : any of several water plants with both submerged and floating leaves and spikes of greenish flowers

pone \ˈpōn\ *n, Southern & Midland* : CORN PONE [Virginia Algonquian *appone*]

pon·gee \pän-ˈjē, ˈpän-ˌ\ *n* : a thin soft fabric of Chinese origin woven from raw silk; *also* : an imitation of this fabric in cotton or a synthetic fiber [Chinese (Beijing dialect) *běnjī,* from *běn* "own" + *jī* "loom"]

pon·gid \ˈpän-jəd, ˈpäng-gəd\ *n* : any of a family of apes that includes the chimpanzee, gorilla, and orangutan [derived from Kongo (a language of western Africa) *mpongi* "ape"] — **pongid** *adj*

1pon·iard \ˈpän-yərd\ *n* : a slender dagger [Middle French *poignard,* from *poing* "fist," from Latin *pugnus*]

2poniard *vt* : to stab or kill with a poniard

pons \ˈpänz\ *n, pl* **pon·tes** \ˈpän-ˌtēz\ : a broad mass of nerve fibers on the ventral surface of the brain at the anterior end of the medulla oblongata [New Latin *pons Varolii,* literally, "bridge of Varoli," from Costanzo *Varoli,* died 1575, Italian surgeon and anatomist]

pon·ti·fex \ˈpänt-ə-ˌfeks\ *n, pl* **pon·tif·i·ces** \pän-ˈtif-ə-ˌsēz\ : a member of the ancient Roman council of priests [Latin *pontific-, pontifex,* literally, "bridge maker," from *pont-, pons* "bridge" + *facere* "to make"]

pon·tiff \ˈpänt-əf\ *n* **1** : PONTIFEX **2** : BISHOP 1; *esp, often cap* : POPE [French *pontif,* from Latin *pontifex*]

1pon·tif·i·cal \pän-ˈtif-i-kəl\ *adj* **1** : of or relating to a pontiff or pontifex **2** : celebrated by a prelate of episcopal rank with distinctive ceremonies ⟨a *pontifical* mass⟩ **3** : POMPOUS 2 **4** : POMPOUS 3 — **pon·tif·i·cal·ly** \-kə-lē, -klē\ *adv*

2pontifical *n* **1** : episcopal attire; *esp* : the insignia of the episcopal order worn by a prelate when celebrating a pontifical service — usually used in plural **2** : a book containing the forms for sacraments and rites performed by a bishop

1pon·tif·i·cate \pän-ˈtif-i-ket, -ˈtif-ə-ˌkāt\ *n* : the office or term of office of a pontiff

2pon·tif·i·cate \-ˈtif-ə-ˌkāt\ *vi* **1** : to officiate as a pontiff **2** : to speak pompously ⟨*pontificating* on the subject⟩ — **pon·tif·i·ca·tor** \-ˌkāt-ər\ *n*

pon·toon \pän-ˈtün\ *n* **1** : a flat-bottomed boat; *esp* : a flat-bottomed boat or portable float used in building a floating temporary bridge **2** : a float of a seaplane [French *ponton* "floating bridge, punt," from Latin *ponto,* from *pont-, pons* "bridge"]

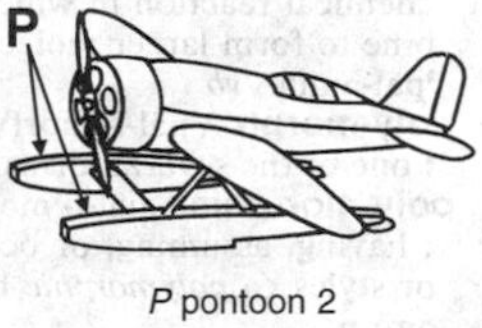

P pontoon 2

po·ny \ˈpō-nē\ *n, pl* **ponies** **1** : a small horse; *esp* : one of any of several breeds of very small stocky animals **2** : a small glass for an alcoholic drink or the amount it will hold **3** : a literal translation of a foreign language text [probably from obsolete French *poulenet,* from French *poulain* "colt," derived from Latin *pullus* "young of an animal, foal"]

pony express *n, often cap P&E* : a rapid postal and express system across the western United States in 1860-61 operating by relays of horses

po·ny·tail \ˈpō-nē-ˌtāl\ *n* : a hairstyle in which the hair is pulled together and banded usually at the back of the head so as to resemble the tail of a pony

po·ny up \ˌpō-nē-ˈəp\ *vb* : to pay especially in settlement of an account [origin unknown]

pooch \ˈpüch\ *n* : DOG 1 [origin unknown]

poo·dle \ˈpüd-l\ *n* : any of a breed of active intelligent dogs that have a thick curly solid-colored coat and that occur in three sizes [German *Pudel,* short for *Pudelhund,* from *pudeln* "to splash" (from *Pudel* "puddle") + *Hund* "dog"]

pooh \ˈpü, ˈpu̇\ *interj* — used to express contempt or disapproval [imitative]

pooh–pooh \ˈpü-pü, pü-ˈpü\ *also* **pooh** \ˈpü\ *vb* **1** : to express contempt or impatience **2** : to make fun of : SCORN ⟨*pooh-poohed* the idea that the house is haunted⟩

1pool \ˈpül\ *n* **1** : a small and rather deep natural or artificial body of usually fresh water **2** : a small body of standing liquid : PUDDLE **3** : SWIMMING POOL [Old English *pōl*]

[2]**pool** *vi* **1** : to form a pool **2** : to accumulate or become stationary ⟨blood *pooled* near the injury⟩

[3]**pool** *n* **1 a** : a stake to which each player of a game has contributed **b** : all the money bet by a number of persons on an event **2** : a game of billiards played with usually 15 object balls on a table having 6 pockets **3** : a common fund for buying or selling especially securities or commodities **4 a** : a group of people whose services or skills are available for use ⟨a *pool* of talent⟩ **b** : a group whose members share or take turns providing a facility ⟨car *pool*⟩ [French *poule,* literally, "hen"]

[4]**pool** *vt* : to combine in a common fund, sample, or effort

pool·room \ˈpül-ˌrüm, -ˌrům\ *n* : a room for the playing of pool

[1]**poop** \ˈpüp\ *n* **1** *obsolete* : STERN 1 **2** : an enclosed superstructure at the stern of a ship above the main deck [Medieval French *pope* "stern," from Latin *puppis*]

[2]**poop** *vt* **1** : to break over the stern of **2** : to ship (a sea or wave) over the stern

[3]**poop** *vb, slang* : to become or cause to become exhausted or worn out — often used with *out* [earlier, "to break wind," from Middle English *poupen* "to make a gulping sound," of imitative origin]

poop deck *n* : a partial deck above the main deck at the stern of a ship

[1]**poor** \ˈpůr, ˈpōr\ *adj* **1** : lacking riches or possessions **2** : SCANTY, INSUFFICIENT ⟨a *poor* crop⟩ **3** : meriting pity ⟨the *poor* soul is lost⟩ **4** : inferior in quality or value ⟨*poor* workmanship⟩ **5** : lacking fertility ⟨*poor* land⟩ **6** : not good : UNFAVORABLE ⟨had a *poor* opinion of the child⟩ **7** : lacking in signs of wealth or good taste ⟨*poor* furnishings⟩ **8** : lacking a normal or adequate supply of something specified ⟨oil-*poor* countries⟩ [Medieval French *povre, pore,* from Latin *pauper*] — **poor·ly** *adv* — **poor·ness** *n*

[2]**poor** *n pl* : people who lack money or material riches

poor box *n* : a box for alms for the poor; *esp* : one placed near the door of a church

poor boy *variant of* PO'BOY

poor farm \ˈpůr-ˌfärm, ˈpōr-\ *n* : a farm maintained at public expense for the support and employment of poor people

poor·house \-ˌhau̇s\ *n* : a place formerly maintained at public expense to house needy or dependent persons

poor·ly \-lē\ *adj* : somewhat ill : INDISPOSED

poor–spir·it·ed \-ˈspir-ət-əd\ *adj* : lacking confidence or courage — **poor–spir·it·ed·ly** *adv* — **poor–spir·it·ed·ness** *n*

[1]**pop** \ˈpäp\ *vb* **popped; pop·ping** **1** : to burst or cause to burst with a pop ⟨the balloon *popped*⟩ ⟨*popped* corn⟩ **2** : to go, come, push, or enter quickly or unexpectedly **3** : to shoot with a gun **4** : to bulge from the sockets ⟨eyes *popping* with surprise⟩ **5** : to hit a pop fly [Middle English *poppen*] — **pop the question** : to propose marriage

[2]**pop** *n* **1** : a sharp explosive sound **2** : a shot from a gun **3** : a flavored carbonated beverage

[3]**pop** *adv* : like or with a pop : SUDDENLY

[4]**pop** *adj* **1** : POPULAR ⟨*pop* music⟩ **2** : of or relating to pop music ⟨*pop* singer⟩ **3** : of or relating to pop art **4** : of or relating to the popular culture portrayed in and spread by the mass media ⟨*pop* psychology⟩

[5]**pop** *n* : popular music ⟨listens to *pop*⟩

[6]**pop** *n* : FATHER 1a [short for *poppa*]

pop art *n, often cap P* : art in which commonplace objects are used as subject matter

pop·corn \ˈpäp-ˌkȯrn\ *n* : corn with kernels that burst open to form a white starchy mass when heated; *also* : the popped kernels

pope \ˈpōp\ *n, often cap* : the head of the Roman Catholic Church [Old English *pāpa,* from Late Latin *papa,* from Greek *pappas, papas* title of bishops, literally, "papa"]

pop·ery \ˈpō-pə-rē, ˈpō-prē\ *n, usually disparaging* : ROMAN CATHOLICISM

pop·eyed \ˈpäp-ˈīd\ *adj* : having eyes that bulge (as from excitement)

pop fly *n* : a short high fly in baseball

pop·gun \ˈpäp-ˌgən\ *n* : a toy gun that usually shoots a cork and makes a popping sound

pop·in·jay \ˈpäp-ən-ˌjā\ *n* : a vain talkative thoughtless person [Middle English *papejay* "parrot," from Middle French *papegai, papejai,* from Arabic *babghā'*]

pop·ish \ˈpō-pish\ *adj, often disparaging* : Roman Catholic

pop·lar \ˈpäp-lər\ *n* **1** : any of a genus of slender quick growing trees (as an aspen or cottonwood) that are related to the willows and bear catkins **2** : the wood of a poplar [Medieval French *popler,* from Latin *populus*]

pop·lin \ˈpäp-lən\ *n* : a strong ribbed fabric in plain weave [French *papeline*]

pop·over \ˈpäp-ˌō-vər\ *n* : a quick bread made from a thin batter of eggs, milk, and flour which bakes into a hollow shell

poppa *variant of* PAPA

pop·per \ˈpäp-ər\ *n* : one that pops; *esp* : a utensil for popping corn

pop·ple \ˈpäp-əl\ *n, chiefly dialect* : POPLAR 1 [Old English *popul,* from Latin *populus*]

pop·py \ˈpäp-ē\ *n, pl* **poppies** : any of a genus of herbs with milky juice, showy flowers, and capsular fruits including one that is the source of opium and several that are grown as ornamentals [Old English *popæg, popig,* from Latin *papaver*]

pop·py·cock \ˈpäp-ē-ˌkäk\ *n* : empty talk : NONSENSE [Dutch dialect *pappekak, literally,* "soft dung," from Dutch *pap* "pap" + *kak* "dung"]

Pop·si·cle \ˈpäp-ˌsik-əl\ *trademark* — used for flavored and colored water frozen on a stick

pop·u·lace \ˈpäp-yə-ləs\ *n* **1** : the common people **2** : POPULATION 1 [Middle French, from Italian *popolaccio* "rabble," from *popolo* "the people," from Latin *populus*]

pop·u·lar \ˈpäp-yə-lər\ *adj* **1** : of, relating to, or coming from the whole body of people ⟨*popular* government⟩ **2** : suitable to the majority: as **a** : easy to understand ⟨*popular* science⟩ **b** : suited to the means of the majority : INEXPENSIVE ⟨*popular* prices⟩ **3** : generally current : PREVALENT ⟨*popular* opinion⟩ **4** : commonly liked or approved ⟨voted the most *popular* person in the class⟩ [Latin *popularis,* from *populus* "the people, a people"] — **pop·u·lar·ly** *adv*

pop·u·lar·i·ty \ˌpäp-yə-ˈlar-ət-ē\ *n* : the quality or state of being popular

pop·u·lar·ize \ˈpäp-yə-lə-ˌrīz\ *vt* : to make popular — **pop·u·lar·i·za·tion** \ˌpäp-yə-lə-rə-ˈzā-shən\ *n* — **pop·u·lar·iz·er** \ˈpäp-yə-lə-ˌrī-zər\ *n*

pop·u·late \ˈpäp-yə-ˌlāt\ *vt* **1** : to have a place in : OCCUPY **2** : to provide with inhabitants

pop·u·la·tion \ˌpäp-yə-ˈlā-shən\ *n* **1** : the whole number of people or inhabitants in a country or region **2** : the act or process of populating **3** : the organisms inhabiting a particular area or habitat **4** : a group of persons or objects from which samples are taken for statistical measurement

population explosion *n* : the recent great increase in human numbers that is usually related to both increased survival and increased reproduction

pop·u·list \ˈpäp-yə-ləst\ *n* **1** *often cap* : a member of a U.S. political party formed in 1891 primarily to represent agrarian interests and to advocate the free coinage of silver and government control of monopolies **2** : a member of any of various popular or agrarian political parties — **pop·u·lism** \-ˌliz-əm\ *n, often cap* — **populist** *adj, often cap*

pop·u·lous \ˈpäp-yə-ləs\ *adj* **1** : densely populated **2** : having a large population — **pop·u·lous·ly** *adv* — **pop·u·lous·ness** *n*

[1]**pop–up** \ˈpäp-ˌəp\ *n* **1** : POP FLY **2** : a pop-up window on a computer screen

[2]**pop–up** *adj* **1** : of, relating to, or having a part or device that pops up ⟨a *pop-up* book⟩ ⟨a *pop-up* menu⟩ **2** : appearing suddenly on a computer screen ⟨a *pop-up* window⟩

por·bea·gle \ˈpȯr-ˌbē-gəl\ *n* : a small viviparous shark with a pointed snout and crescent-shaped tail [Cornish *porgh-bugel*]

por·ce·lain \ˈpōr-sə-lən, ˈpȯr-, -slən\ *n* : a hard, fine-grained, nonporous, and usually translucent and white ceramic ware that consists essentially of kaolin, quartz, and feldspar and is used for dishes and chemical utensils [Middle French *porcelaine* "cowrie shell, porcelain," from Italian *porcellana,* from *porcello* "vulva," literally, "little pig," from Latin *porcellus,* from *porcus* "pig, vulva"] — **por·ce·lain·like** \-ˌlīk\ *adj*

\ə\ **abut**	\au̇\ **out**	\i\ **tip**	\ȯ\ **saw**	\u̇\ **foot**
\ər\ **further**	\ch\ **chin**	\ī\ **life**	\ȯi\ **coin**	\y\ **yet**
\a\ **mat**	\e\ **pet**	\j\ **job**	\th\ **thin**	\yü\ **few**
\ā\ **take**	\ē\ **easy**	\ng\ **sing**	\t͟h\ **this**	\yu̇\ **cure**
\ä\ **cot, cart**	\g\ **go**	\ō\ **bone**	\ü\ **food**	\zh\ **vision**

porch \ˈpōrch, ˈpȯrch\ *n* : a covered entrance to a building usually with a separate roof [Medieval French *porche,* from Latin *porticus* "portico," from *porta* "gate"]

porch

por·cine \ˈpȯr-ˌsīn\ *adj* : of, relating to, or suggesting swine [Latin *porcinus,* from *porcus* "pig"]

por·cu·pine \ˈpȯr-kyə-ˌpīn\ *n* : any of various rather large slow-moving chiefly plant-eating rodents with stiff sharp quills mingled with the hair [Medieval French *porc espin,* from Italian *porcospino,* from Latin *porcus* "pig" + *spina* "spine, prickle"]

porcupine fish *n* : any of several fish chiefly of tropical seas that have the body covered with spines and that can puff themselves up with air or water like a balloon when threatened

[1]**pore** \ˈpōr, ˈpȯr\ *vi* : to gaze, study, or think long or earnestly ⟨*pore* over a book⟩ [Middle English *pouren*]

[2]**pore** *n* : a tiny opening or space (as in the skin or the soil) often giving passage to a fluid [Medieval French, from Latin *porus,* from Greek *poros* "passage, pore"] — **pored** \ˈpōrd, ˈpȯrd\ *adj*

por·gy \ˈpȯr-gē\ *n, pl* **porgies** *also* **porgy** : a blue-spotted silvery red food fish of the coasts of Europe and America; *also* : any of various other related or similar fishes [Spanish and Portuguese *pargo,* from Latin *phager,* from Greek *phagros*]

pork \ˈpōrk, ˈpȯrk\ *n* : the fresh or salted flesh of swine when used for food [Medieval French *porc* "pig," from Latin *porcus*]

pork barrel *n* : a government project or appropriation yielding rich patronage benefits

pork·er \ˈpōr-kər, ˈpȯr-\ *n* : a domesticated swine and especially a young pig fattened for use as fresh pork

por·nog·ra·phy \pȯr-ˈnäg-rə-fē\ *n* : pictures or writings describing erotic behavior and intended to cause sexual excitement [Greek *pornographos,* adj., "writing about prostitutes," from *pornē* "prostitute" + *graphein* "to write"] — **por·nog·ra·pher** \-fər\ *n* — **por·no·graph·ic** \ˌpȯr-nə-ˈgraf-ik\ *adj* — **por·no·graph·i·cal·ly** \-ˈgraf-i-kə-lē, -klē\ *adv*

po·ros·i·ty \pə-ˈräs-ət-ē, pōr-ˈäs-, pȯ-ˈräs-\ *n, pl* **-ties** **1** : the quality or state of being porous **2** : PORE

po·rous \ˈpōr-əs, ˈpȯr-\ *adj* **1** : full of pores **2** : capable of absorbing liquids : permeable to fluids — **po·rous·ly** *adv* — **po·rous·ness** *n*

por·phy·ry \ˈpȯr-fə-rē, -frē\ *n, pl* **-ries** **1** : a rock consisting of feldspar crystals embedded in a compact dark red or purple groundmass **2** : an igneous rock having distinct crystals in a relatively fine-grained base [Medieval Latin *porphyrium,* from Latin *porphyrites,* from Greek *porphyritēs lithos,* literally, "purple-colored stone," from *porphyra* "purple"] — **por·phy·rit·ic** \ˌpȯr-fə-ˈrit-ik\ *adj*

por·poise \ˈpȯr-pəs\ *n* **1** : any of several small blunt-snouted toothed whales that live and travel in groups **2** : DOLPHIN 1a [Medieval French *porpeis,* from Medieval Latin *porcopiscis,* from Latin *porcus* "pig" + *piscis* "fish"]

por·ridge \ˈpȯr-ij, ˈpär-\ *n* : a soft food made by boiling meal of grains or legumes in milk or water until thick [alteration of *pottage*]

por·rin·ger \ˈpȯr-ən-jər, ˈpär-\ *n* : a low usually metal bowl with a single and usually flat handle [alteration of Middle English *potager, potynger,* from Medieval French *potageer,* from *potage* "pottage"]

[1]**port** \ˈpōrt, ˈpȯrt\ *n* **1** : a place where ships may ride secure from storms **2 a** : a harbor town or city where ships may take on or discharge cargo **b** : AIRPORT [Old English and Medieval French, both from Latin *portus* "house, door, port"]

[2]**port** *n* **1 a** : an opening (as in machinery) for intake or exhaust of a fluid **b** : a place of entry into a system **2** : PORTHOLE **3** : an electrical jack by which two devices are connected (as a printer or mouse to a computer) [Medieval French *porte* "gate, door," from Latin *porta* "passage, gate"]

[3]**port** *vt* : to turn or put (a helm) to the left — used chiefly as a command [[4]*port*]

[4]**port** *n* : the left side of a ship or airplane looking forward — called also *larboard*; compare STARBOARD [probably from [1]*port* or [2]*port*] — **port** *adj*

[5]**port** *n* : a rich sweet wine [*Oporto,* Portugal]

portabella *or* **portabello** *variant of* PORTOBELLO

[1]**por·ta·ble** \ˈpōrt-ə-bəl, ˈpȯrt-\ *adj* : capable of being carried : easily moved from place to place ⟨a *portable* TV⟩ [Medieval French, from Late Latin *portabilis,* from Latin *portare* "to carry"] — **por·ta·bil·i·ty** \ˌpōrt-ə-ˈbil-ət-ē, ˌpȯrt-\ *n*

[2]**portable** *n* : something that is portable

[1]**por·tage** \ˈpōrt-ij, ˈpȯrt-, *2 is also* pȯr-ˈtäzh\ *n* **1** : the labor of carrying or transporting **2** : the carrying of boats or goods overland from one body of water to another; *also* : a regular route for such carrying [Medieval French, from *porter* "to carry," from Latin *portare*]

[2]**por·tage** \ˈpōrt-ij, ˈpȯrt-; pȯr-ˈtäzh\ *vb* **1** : to carry over a portage ⟨a canoe light enough to *portage*⟩ **2** : to move gear over a portage ⟨we *portaged* around the falls⟩

[1]**por·tal** \ˈpōrt-l, ˈpȯrt-\ *n* **1** : DOOR 1a, ENTRANCE; *esp* : a grand or imposing one **2** : the point at which something (as an infection) enters the body of an organism [Medieval French, from Medieval Latin *portale* "city gate, porch," derived from Latin *porta* "gate"]

[2]**portal** *adj* : of, relating to, or being a portal vein [derived from Latin *porta* "gate"]

portal–to–portal *adj* : of or relating to the time spent by a worker in traveling from the entrance to the employer's property to the actual working place (as in a mine) and in returning after the work shift

portal vein *n* : a vein that collects blood from one part of the body and distributes it in another through capillaries; *esp* : one carrying blood from the digestive organs and spleen to the liver

por·ta·men·to \ˌpōrt-ə-ˈmen-tō, ˌpȯrt-\ *n, pl* **-ti** \-tē\ : a continuous gliding movement from one tone to another (as by the voice) [Italian, literally, "act of carrying," from *portare* "to carry," from Latin]

port·cul·lis \pōrt-ˈkəl-əs, pȯrt-\ *n* : a grating at the gateway of a castle or fortress that can be lowered to prevent entrance [Medieval French *porte coliz,* literally, "sliding door"]

porte co·chere \ˌpōrt-kō-ˈsheər, ˌpȯrt-\ *n* : a roofed structure extending from the entrance to a building over an adjacent driveway and sheltering those getting in or out of vehicles [French *porte cochère,* literally, "coach door"]

por·tend \pȯr-ˈtend, pōr-\ *vt* : to give a sign or warning of beforehand ⟨the distant thunder *portended* a storm⟩ [Latin *portendere,* from *por-* "forward" + *tendere* "to stretch"]

por·tent \ˈpȯr-ˌtent, ˈpōr-\ *n* : a sign or warning that foreshadows something usually evil : OMEN [Latin *portentum,* from *portendere* "to portend"]

por·ten·tous \pȯr-ˈtent-əs, pōr-\ *adj* **1** : being a portent ⟨*portentous* signs⟩ **2** : AMAZING, MARVELOUS ⟨a *portentous* effort⟩ **3** : self-consciously weighty : POMPOUS ⟨a *portentous* voice⟩ — **por·ten·tous·ly** *adv* — **por·ten·tous·ness** *n*

[1]**por·ter** \ˈpōrt-ər, ˈpȯrt-\ *n, chiefly British* : DOORKEEPER [Medieval French, from Late Latin *portarius,* from Latin *porta* "gate"]

[2]**porter** *n* **1** : one that carries burdens; *esp* : one employed to carry baggage for patrons at a hotel or transportation terminal **2** : a parlor-car or sleeping-car attendant **3** : a dark heavy ale [Medieval French *porteour,* from Late Latin *portator,* from Latin *portare* "to carry"; sense 3 short for *porter's beer*]

por·ter·house \-ˌhau̇s\ *n* : a beefsteak with a large piece of tenderloin on a T-shaped bone [earlier *porterhouse* "house where porter is sold"]

port·fo·lio \pōrt-ˈfō-lē-ˌō, pȯrt-\ *n, pl* **-lios** **1** : a case for carrying papers or drawings **2** : the office and functions of a minister of state or member of a cabinet **3** : the securities held by an investor or a financial house **4** : a selection of a student's work (as papers or art) compiled over a period of time and used for assessing performance or progress [Italian *portafoglio,* from *portare* "to carry" (from Latin) + *foglio* "leaf, sheet," from Latin *folium;* sense 2 from the use of such a case to carry documents of state]

port·hole \ˈpōrt-ˌhōl, ˈpȯrt-\ *n* **1** : an opening (as a window) in the side of a ship or airplane **2** : an opening (as in a wall) to shoot through **3** : [2]PORT 1

por·ti·co \ˈpōrt-i-ˌkō, ˈpȯrt-\ *n, pl* **-coes** *or* **-cos** : a colonnade or covered walkway around or at the entrance of a building [Italian, from Latin *porticus,* from *porta* "gate"]

[1]**por·tion** \ˈpōr-shən, ˈpȯr-\ *n* **1 a** : an individual's share of something ⟨a *portion* of food⟩ **b** : DOWRY **2** : one's lot, fate, or fortune **3** : an element, section, or division of a whole [Medieval French, from Latin *portio*] ***synonyms*** see PART

[2]**portion** *vt* **por·tioned; por·tion·ing** \ˈpōr-shə-ning, ˈpȯr-, -shning\ : to divide into portions : DISTRIBUTE

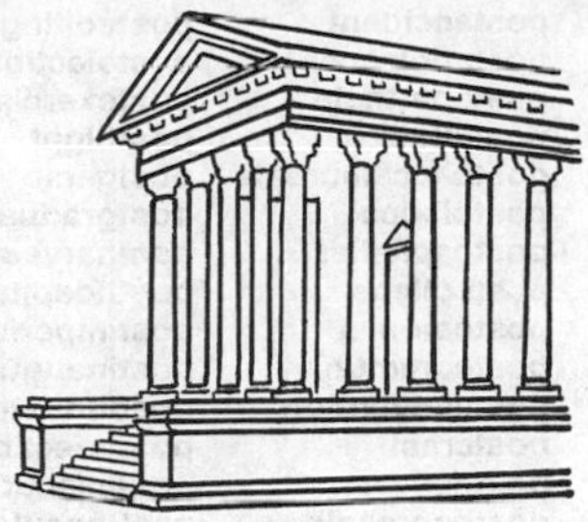
portico

port·land cement \ˌpōrt-lənd-, ˌpȯrt-, -lən-\ *n* : a cement made by burning and grinding a mixture of clay and limestone or a mixture of similar materials [Isle of *Portland,* England; from its resemblance to a limestone found there]

port·ly \ˈpōrt-lē, ˈpȯrt-\ *adj* **port·li·er; -est** : heavy of body : STOUT [derived from Latin *portare* "to carry"] — **port·li·ness** *n*

port·man·teau \pōrt-ˈman-tō, pȯrt\ *n, pl* **-teaus** *or* **-teaux** \-tōz\ : a large traveling bag [Middle French *portemanteau,* from *porter* "to carry" + *manteau* "mantle," from Latin *mantellum*]

por·to·bel·lo \ˌpȯr-tə-ˈbel-ō\ *also* **por·ta·bel·la** \-ə\ *or* **por·ta·bel·lo** \-ō\ *n* : a large dark mature cultivated mushroom noted for its meaty texture that is a variety of button mushroom [perhaps alteration of Italian *prataiollo, prataiuollo* or Italian dialect *pratarolo* "meadow mushroom," from *prato* "meadow," from Latin *pratum*]

port of call : an intermediate port where ships customarily stop for supplies, repairs, or transferring of cargo

port of entry **1** : a place where foreign goods may be cleared through a customhouse **2** : a place where an alien may enter a country

por·trait \ˈpōr-trət, ˈpȯr-, -ˌtrāt\ *n* **1** : a pictorial representation (as a painting) of a person usually showing the face **2** : a portrayal in words [Middle French, from *portraire* "to portray"]

por·trait·ist \-əst\ *n* : a maker of portraits

por·trai·ture \ˈpōr-trə-ˌchu̇r, ˈpȯr-, -chər\ *n* **1** : the making of portraits : PORTRAYAL **2** : PORTRAIT

por·tray \pōr-ˈtrā, pȯr-\ *vt* **1** : to make a picture of **2 a** : to describe in words **b** : to play the role of : ENACT [Medieval French *purtraire,* from Latin *protrahere* "to draw forth, reveal," from *pro-* "forth" + *trahere* "to draw, drag"] — **por·tray·er** *n*

por·tray·al \-ˈtrā-əl, -ˈtrāl\ *n* **1** : the act or process of portraying : REPRESENTATION **2** : PORTRAIT

Por·tu·guese \ˈpōr-chə-ˌgēz, ˈpȯr-, -ˌgēs; ˌpōr-chə-ˈgēz, ˌpȯr-, -ˈgēs\ *n, pl* **Portuguese** **1 a** : a native or inhabitant of Portugal **b** : a person of Portuguese descent **2** : the Romance language of Portugal and Brazil — **Portuguese** *adj*

Portuguese man–of–war *n, pl* **Portuguese man–of–wars** *also* **Portuguese men–of–war** : any of several large colonial hydrozoans having a large crested bladder by means of which the colony floats at the surface of the sea and long tentacles capable of inflicting a painful sting

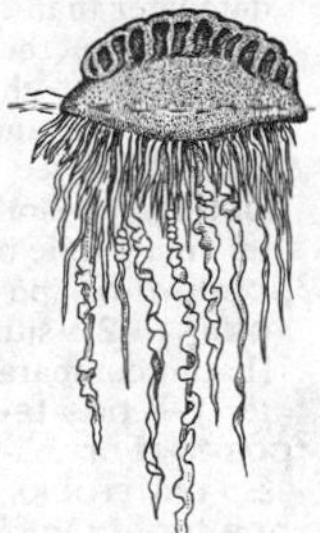
Portuguese man-of-war

por·tu·laca \ˌpōr-chə-ˈlak-ə, ˌpȯr-\ *n* : any of a genus of mostly tropical succulent herbs; *esp* : one of South America cultivated for its showy flowers [Latin, "purslane," derived from *porta* "gate"; from the lid of its capsule]

[1]**pose** \ˈpōz\ *vb* **1 a** : to hold or cause to hold a special posture ⟨*posed* for fashion photographers⟩ **b** : to pretend to be what one is not ⟨*pose* as a hero⟩ **2** : to put forth : PROPOSE ⟨*pose* a question⟩ [Medieval French *poser* "to put, place," from Late Latin *pausare* "to stop, rest, pause," from Latin *pausa* "pause"]

[2]**pose** *n* **1** : a sustained posture; *esp* : one assumed for artistic effect **2** : an assumed attitude ⟨her cheerfulness is just a *pose*⟩ ***synonyms*** see AFFECTATION

[1]**po·ser** \ˈpō-zer\ *n* : a puzzling or baffling question [from earlier *pose* "to puzzle," derived from Middle English *opposen* "to oppose"]

[2]**pos·er** \ˈpō-zər\ *n* : a person who poses

po·seur \pō-ˈzər\ *n* : an affected or insincere person : a person who pretends to be what he or she is not [French, from *poser* "to put, pose"]

posh \ˈpäsh\ *adj* : ELEGANT 1, FASHIONABLE [origin unknown]

pos·it \ˈpäz-ət\ *vt* : to assume the existence of [Latin *positus,* past participle of *ponere* "to put, place, assume"]

[1]**po·si·tion** \pə-ˈzish-ən\ *n* **1** : the manner in which something is placed or arranged **2** : the stand taken on a question **3** : the point or area occupied by something ⟨the *position* of the heart⟩ **4 a** : social or official rank or status **b** : EMPLOYMENT 2b, JOB **c** : a situation that confers advantage or preference ⟨jockeyed for *position* in the race⟩ [Medieval French *posicioun,* from Latin *positio,* from *ponere* "to lay down, put, place"] — **po·si·tion·al** \-ˈzish-nəl, -ən-l\ *adj*

[2]**position** *vt* **po·si·tioned; po·si·tion·ing** \-ˈzish-ning, -ə-ning\ : to put in a certain position

positional notation *n* : a system of expressing numbers in which the digits are arranged in succession, the position of each digit has a place value, and the number is equal to the sum of the products of each digit by its place value

[1]**pos·i·tive** \ˈpäz-ət-iv, ˈpäz-tiv\ *adj* **1 a** : formally laid down or imposed ⟨*positive* laws⟩ **b** : clearly or definitely stated ⟨*positive* orders⟩ **c** : fully assured : CONFIDENT ⟨were *positive* they'd win⟩ **2 a** : of the degree of comparison expressed by the unmodified and uninflected form of an adjective or adverb **b** : definite, accurate, or certain in its action ⟨*positive* traction of a sprocket chain⟩ **c** : UNQUALIFIED 2 ⟨a *positive* disgrace⟩ **3 a** : not fictitious : REAL ⟨a *positive* influence for good⟩ **b** : active in the social or economic sphere ⟨a *positive* government⟩ **4 a** : indicating, relating to, or characterized by affirmation, addition, inclusion, or presence rather than negation, withholding, or absence ⟨a *positive* change in temperature⟩ **b** : showing light and shade similar in tone to the tones of the original subject ⟨a *positive* photographic image⟩ **c** : being a real number numerically greater than zero ⟨+2 is a *positive* number⟩ **d** (1) : reckoned or proceeding in a direction taken as that of increase or progression (2) : directed or moving toward a source of stimulation ⟨a *positive* taxis⟩ **5 a** : of, being, or relating to electricity of which the proton is the smallest unit and which predominates in a glass rod after being rubbed with silk ⟨a *positive* charge⟩ **b** : charged with positive electricity : having a deficiency of electrons ⟨a *positive* particle⟩ **c** : being the part from which the current flows to the external circuit ⟨the *positive* pole of a discharging storage battery⟩ **d** : electron-collecting — used of an electrode in an electron tube **6 a** : marked by or indicating agreement or affirmation ⟨a *positive* response⟩ **b** : affirming the presence especially of a condition, substance, or organism suspected to be present ⟨a *positive* test for blood⟩ [Medieval French, from Latin *positivus,* from *positus,* past participle of *ponere* "to lay down, put, place"] ***synonyms*** see SURE — **pos·i·tive·ly** \-lē, *for emphasis often* ˌpäz-ə-ˈtiv-lē\ *adv* — **pos·i·tive·ness** *n*

[2]**positive** *n* : something positive: as **a** : the positive degree or a positive form in a language **b** : a positive photograph or a print from a negative **c** : a positive result (as of a test); *also* : a test yielding such a result

pos·i·tron \ˈpäz-ə-ˌträn\ *n* : a positively charged particle having the same mass and magnitude of charge as the electron [*posi*tive + *-tron* (as in *electron*)]

pos·se \ˈpäs-ē\ *n* **1** : a group of people called upon by a sheriff to aid in law enforcement ⟨a *posse* pursued the robber⟩ **2** : a number of people organized to make a search (as for a lost child) **3** : ENTOURAGE [Medieval Latin *posse comitatus,* literally, "power or authority of the county"]

pos·sess \pə-ˈzes\ *vt* **1** : to make (as a person) the owner or holder (as of property or power) ⟨*possessed* of knowledge⟩ **2 a** : to have and hold as property : OWN **b** : to have as an attribute, knowledge, or skill ⟨*possesses* a keen wit⟩ **3 a** : to make one's own **b** : to enter into and control firmly : DOMINATE ⟨what *possessed* you to do that⟩ [Middle French *possesser* "to have or take possession of," from Latin *possidēre,* from *potis* "able, having the power" + *sedēre* "to sit"] — **pos·ses·sor** \-ər\ *n*

pos·ses·sion \pə-ˈzesh-ən\ *n* **1 a** : the act of possessing or holding as one's own : OWNERSHIP **b** : physical control of property without regard to ownership **2** : something held as

\ə\ **abut**	\au̇\ **out**	\i\ **tip**	\ȯ\ **saw**	\u̇\ **foot**
\ər\ **further**	\ch\ **chin**	\ī\ **life**	\ȯi\ **coin**	\y\ **yet**
\a\ **mat**	\e\ **pet**	\j\ **job**	\th\ **thin**	\yü\ **few**
\ā\ **take**	\ē\ **easy**	\ng\ **sing**	\t͟h\ **this**	\yu̇\ **cure**
\ä\ **cot, cart**	\g\ **go**	\ō\ **bone**	\ü\ **food**	\zh\ **vision**

one's own : PROPERTY ⟨all my worldly *possessions*⟩ **3 a** : domination by something (as an evil spirit, an idea, or a passion) **b** : the fact or condition of being self-controlled — **pos·ses·sion·al** \-'zesh-nəl, -ən-l\ *adj*

[1]**pos·ses·sive** \pə-'zes-iv\ *adj* **1** : of, relating to, or being a grammatical case that denotes ownership or a similar relation — compare GENITIVE **2** : showing the desire to possess or keep ⟨a *possessive* attitude⟩ — **pos·ses·sive·ly** *adv* — **pos·ses·sive·ness** *n*

[2]**possessive** *n* **1** : the possessive case **2** : a word in the possessive case

possessive adjective *n* : a pronominal adjective expressing possession

possessive pronoun *n* : a pronoun that derives from a personal pronoun and expresses possession

pos·set \'päs-ət\ *n* : a hot drink of sweetened and spiced milk curdled with ale or wine [Middle English *poshet, possot*]

pos·si·bil·i·ty \ˌpäs-ə-'bil-ət-ē\ *n, pl* **-ties** **1** : the condition or fact of being possible **2** : something possible

pos·si·ble \'päs-ə-bəl\ *adj* **1** : being something that can be done or brought about **2** : being something that may or may not occur ⟨*possible* dangers⟩ **3** : able or fitted to be or to become ⟨a *possible* camp site⟩ [Medieval French, from Latin *possibilis,* from *posse* "to be able," from *potis* "able" + *esse* "to be"]

synonyms POSSIBLE, PRACTICABLE, FEASIBLE mean capable of being realized. POSSIBLE implies that a thing may exist or occur given the proper conditions ⟨a *possible* route up the mountain⟩. PRACTICABLE implies that something may be easily or readily put into operation by current available means ⟨a solution not *practicable* in the time available⟩. FEASIBLE applies to what is likely to work or be useful in attaining an end ⟨commercially *feasible* for mass production⟩. ***synonyms*** see in addition PROBABLE

pos·si·bly \-blē\ *adv* **1** : by possible means : by any possibility ⟨that cannot *possibly* be true⟩ **2** : PERHAPS ⟨may *possibly* recover⟩

pos·sum \'päs-əm\ *n* : OPOSSUM

[1]**post** \'pōst\ *n* **1** : a piece of timber or metal fixed firmly in an upright position especially as a stay or support : PILLAR, COLUMN **2** : a pole or stake set up to mark or indicate something ⟨starting *post*⟩ **3** : a metallic fixture attached to an electrical device (as a battery) for making connections [Old English, from Latin *postis*]

[2]**post** *vt* **1** : to fasten to a place (as a wall) for public notices **2 a** : to publish or announce by or as if by a placard **b** : to enter on a public listing ⟨*post* all daily flights⟩ **c** : to write a message and place it online ⟨she *posted* a response on her Web site⟩ **3** : to forbid persons from entering or using by putting up warning notices ⟨*post* a trout stream⟩ **4** : SCORE 1a ⟨*posted* 30 points in the first quarter of play⟩

[3]**post** *n* **1** *obsolete* : one that carries messages : COURIER **2** *archaic* : one of a series of stations for keeping horses for relays **3** *chiefly British* **a** : a nation's organization for handling mail; *also* : the mail handled **b** : a single dispatch of mail **c** : POST OFFICE **d** : MAILBOX **4** : something (as a message) that is published online [Middle French *poste* "relay station, courier," from Italian *posta* "relay station," from *posto,* past participle of *porre* "to place," from Latin *ponere*]

[4]**post** *vb* **1** : to ride or travel with haste : HURRY **2** : MAIL ⟨*post* a letter⟩ **3 a** : to transfer (a bookkeeping item) from a book of original entry to a ledger **b** : to make transfer entries in **4** : to make familiar with a subject : INFORM ⟨kept *posted* on the latest news⟩ [earlier *post* "to travel with post-horses"]

[5]**post** *adv* : with post-horses : EXPRESS

[6]**post** *n* **1 a** : the place at which a soldier is stationed; *esp* : a sentry's beat or station **b** : a station or task to which one is assigned **c** : a place to which troops are assigned **d** : a local subdivision of a veterans' organization **2** : an office or position to which a person is appointed **3** : TRADING POST; *also* : SETTLEMENT 3a ⟨sent supplies to the frontier *posts*⟩ [Middle French, from Italian *posto,* from *porre* "to place"]

[7]**post** *vt* **1 a** : to station in a given place ⟨*post* a guard⟩ **b** : to carry ceremoniously to a position ⟨*posting* the colors⟩ **2** : to put up as security ⟨*post* bond⟩

post- *prefix* **1 a** : after : subsequent : later ⟨*post*date⟩ **b** : behind : posterior : following after ⟨*post*consonantal⟩ **2 a** : subsequent to : later than ⟨*post*operative⟩ **b** : posterior to [Latin, from *post*]

postaccident	**postediting**	**postmarital**
postadolescent	**postelection**	**postpuberty**
postapartheid	**postexercise**	**postpubescent**
postattack	**postflight**	**postrace**
postbaccalaureate	**postgame**	**postrecession**
postbiblical	**postgraduation**	**postretirement**
postcapitalist	**postharvest**	**postrevolutionary**
postcollege	**posthospital**	**postseason**
postcolonial	**postimperial**	**postsecondary**
postcommunist	**postinaugural**	**post–Soviet**
postconvention	**postindustrial**	**postteen**
postcrash	**postinfection**	**posttreatment**
postdelivery	**postinjection**	**posttrial**
postdepression	**postinoculation**	**postvaccination**
postdrug	**postliberation**	

post·age \'pō-stij\ *n* : the charge imposed for carrying an article by mail

postage meter *n* : a machine that prints postal markings on pieces of mail, records the amount of postage given in the markings, and subtracts it from a total amount which has been paid at the post office and for which the machine has been set

postage stamp *n* : a government stamp used on mail to show that postage has been paid

post·al \'pōst-l\ *adj* : of or relating to mail or to the post office

postal card *n* **1** : a card officially stamped and issued by the government for use in the mail **2** : POSTCARD 2

postal service *n* : POST OFFICE 1

postal union *n* : an association of governments setting up uniform regulations and practices for international mail

[1]**post·card** \'pōst-ˌkärd, 'pōs-\ *n* **1** : POSTAL CARD 1 **2** : a card on which a message may be written for mailing without an envelope

[2]**postcard** *adj* : PICTURESQUE, PICTURE-POSTCARD ⟨a *postcard* village⟩

post chaise *n* : a carriage usually having a closed body on four wheels and seating two or four persons [[3]*post*]

post·clas·si·cal \pōst-'klas-i-kəl, 'pōst-, pōs-, 'pōs-\ *or* **post·clas·sic** \-ik\ *adj* : of or relating to a period (as in art, literature, or civilization) following a classical one

post–com·mu·nion \ˌpōst-kə-'myü-nyən, ˌpōs-\ *n, often cap P&C* : a prayer formerly following the communion at Mass

post·con·so·nan·tal \ˌpōst-ˌkän-sə-'nant-l, ˌpōs-\ *adj* : immediately following a consonant

post·con·sum·er \-kən-'sü-mər\ *adj* **1** : discarded by a consumer ⟨*postconsumer* waste⟩ **2** : having been used and recycled for reuse in another consumer product ⟨*postconsumer* plastics⟩

post·date \pōst-'dāt, 'pōst-, pōs-, 'pōs-\ *vt* **1** : to date with a date later than that of execution ⟨*postdate* a check⟩ **2** : to follow in time ⟨the text changes *postdated* the first printing⟩

post·doc·tor·al \-'däk-tə-rəl, -trəl\ *adj* : of, relating to, or engaged in advanced academic or professional work beyond a doctor's degree

post·er \'pō-stər\ *n* : a notice or advertisement to be posted often in a public place; *esp* : one that is decorative or pictorial

[1]**pos·te·ri·or** \pō-'stir-ē-ər, pä-\ *adj* **1** : later in time : SUBSEQUENT **2** : situated behind : situated toward or on the back [Latin, comparative of *posterus* "coming after," from *post* "after"] — **pos·te·ri·or·ly** *adv*

[2]**pos·te·ri·or** \pä-'stir-ē-ər, pō-\ *n* : the hinder parts of the body; *esp* : BUTTOCKS

pos·ter·i·ty \pä-'ster-ət-ē\ *n* **1** : the line of individuals descended from one ancestor **2** : those who come after in time ⟨leave a record for *posterity*⟩ [Medieval French *pusterité,* from Latin *posteritas,* from *posterus* "coming after"]

pos·tern \'pōs-tərn, 'päs-\ *n* **1** : a back door or gate **2** : a private or side entrance or way [Medieval French *posterne,* alteration of *posterle,* from Late Latin *posterula,* from *postera* "back door," from Latin *posterus* "coming after"] — **postern** *adj*

post exchange *n* : a store at a military post that sells to military personnel and authorized civilians

post·gan·gli·on·ic \ˌpōst-ˌgang-glē-'än-ik, ˌpōs-\ *adj* : distal to a ganglion; *also* : of, relating to, or being an axon arising from a cell body within an autonomic ganglion

post·gla·cial \pōst-'glā-shəl, 'pōst-, pōs-, 'pōs-\ *adj* : coming or occurring after a period of glaciation

[1]**post·grad·u·ate** \-'graj-wət, -ə-wət, -ə-ˌwāt\ *adj* : of, relating to, or engaged in formal studies after graduation : GRADUATE 2

[2]postgraduate *n* : a student continuing his or her education after graduation from high school or college
post·haste \ˈpōst-ˈhāst\ *adv* : with all possible speed ⟨sent *posthaste* for the doctor⟩ [[3]*post*]
post·hole \ˈpōst-ˌhōl\ *n* : a hole dug for a post
post–horse \-ˌhȯrs\ *n* : a horse for use especially by couriers or mail carriers [[3]*post*]
post·hu·mous \ˈpäs-chə-məs\ *adj* **1** : born after the death of the father ⟨*posthumous* twins⟩ **2** : published after the death of the author ⟨a *posthumous* novel⟩ **3** : following or occurring after one's death ⟨a *posthumous* award⟩ [Latin *posthumus,* alteration of *postumus* "late-born, posthumous," from *posterus* "coming after"] — **post·hu·mous·ly** *adv*
post·hyp·not·ic \ˌpōst-hip-ˈnät-ik, ˌpōst-ip-\ *adj* : of, relating to, or characteristic of the period following a hypnotic trance
pos·til·ion *or* **pos·til·lion** \pō-ˈstil-yən, pə-\ *n* : a person who rides as a guide on the left-hand horse of a pair drawing a coach [Middle French *postillon* "mail carrier using post-horses," from Italian *postiglione,* from *posta* "post"]
Post·im·pres·sion·ism \ˌpō-stim-ˈpresh-ə-ˌniz-əm\ *n* : a theory or practice of art originating in France in the last quarter of the 19th century that in revolt against impressionism stresses variously volume, picture structure, or expressionism
post·lude \ˈpōst-ˌlüd\ *n* : a closing piece of music; *esp* : an organ voluntary at the end of a church service [*post-* + *-lude* (as in *prelude*)]
post·man \ˈpōst-mən, ˈpōs-, -ˌman\ *n* : LETTER CARRIER
post·mark \-ˌmärk\ *n* : an official postal marking on a piece of mail; *esp* : a cancellation of the postage stamp that gives the date and place of mailing — **postmark** *vt*
post·mas·ter \-ˌmas-tər\ *n* : an official in charge of a post office
postmaster general *n, pl* **postmasters general** : an official in charge of a national post office department
post me·ri·di·em \ˈpōst-mə-ˈrid-ē-əm, ˈpōs-, -ē-ˌem\ *adj* : being after noon — abbreviation *p.m.* [Latin]
post·mis·tress \-ˌmis-trəs\ *n* : a woman in charge of a post office
[1]post·mor·tem \pōst-ˈmȯrt-əm, pōs-\ *adj* **1** : done, occurring, or collected after death **2** : following the event ⟨a *postmortem* analysis of the game⟩ [Latin *post mortem* "after death"]
[2]postmortem *n* **1** : AUTOPSY **2** : an analysis or discussion of an event after it is over
postmortem examination *n* : AUTOPSY
post·na·sal drip \pōst-ˈnā-zəl-, ˈpōst-, pōs-, ˈpōs-\ *n* : a flow of mucous secretion from the nasal passages onto the back of the throat that occurs especially in some allergic states (as hay fever)
post·na·tal \-ˈnāt-l\ *adj* : occurring or being after birth; *also* : of or relating to a newborn child ⟨*postnatal* care⟩ — **post·na·tal·ly** \-l-ē\ *adv*
post·nup·tial \ˌpōst-ˈnəp-shəl, -chəl\ *adj* : made or occuring after marriage or mating
post office *n* **1** : a government department handling the transmission of mail **2** : a local branch of a post office department handling the mail for a particular place **3** : a kissing game in which the one pretending to deliver a letter may demand a kiss as payment
post·op·er·a·tive \pōst-ˈäp-rət-iv, ˈpōst-, -ə-rət-, -ə-ˌrāt-\ *adj* **1** : following a surgical operation ⟨*postoperative* care⟩ **2** : having recently undergone a surgical operation ⟨a *postoperative* patient⟩ — **post·op·er·a·tive·ly** *adv*
post·paid \ˈpōst-ˈpād, ˈpōs-\ *adv* : with postage paid by the sender and not chargeable to the receiver [[3]*post*]
post·par·tum \pōst-ˈpärt-əm, pōs-\ *adj* : occurring in or being the period following childbirth [New Latin *post partum* "after birth"]
post·pone \-ˈpōn\ *vt* : to put off (as an action or event) to a later time : DEFER ⟨rain caused us to *postpone* the picnic⟩ [Latin *postponere* "to place after, postpone," from *post-* + *ponere* "to place"] ***synonyms*** see DEFER — **post·pone·ment** \-mənt\ *n* — **post·pon·er** *n*
post·pran·di·al \-ˈpran-dē-əl\ *adj* : following a meal ⟨taking a *postprandial* nap⟩ — **post·pran·di·al·ly** \-ə-lē\ *adv*
post·script \ˈpōs-ˌskript, ˈpō-\ *n* : a note or series of notes added at the end of a letter, article, or book [Latin *postscriptus,* past participle of *postscribere* "to write after," from *post-* + *scribere* "to write"]
post·sur·gi·cal \ˌpōst-ˈsər-ji-kəl\ *adj* : POSTOPERATIVE
pos·tu·lant \ˈpäs-chə-lənt\ *n* **1** : a person admitted to a religious community as a probationary candidate for membership **2** : a person on probation before being admitted as a candidate for holy orders in the Episcopal Church [French, "petitioner, candidate, postulant," from *postuler* "to demand, solicit," from Latin *postulare*] — **pos·tu·lan·cy** \-lən-sē\ *n*
[1]pos·tu·late \ˈpäs-chə-ˌlāt\ *vt* : to claim as true : assume as a postulate [Latin *postulare* "to demand"] — **pos·tu·la·tion** \ˌpäs-chə-ˈlā-shən\ *n*
[2]pos·tu·late \ˈpäs-chə-lət, -ˌlāt\ *n* **1** : a hypothesis advanced as an essential basis of a system of thought or premise of a train of reasoning **2** : a statement (as in logic or mathematics) that often cannot be proved to be true or false but that is assumed to be true without proof; *also* : AXIOM 2a
[1]pos·ture \ˈpäs-chər\ *n* **1** : the position or bearing of the body or of a body part ⟨an erect *posture*⟩ **2** : relative place or position : SITUATION **3** : a particular state with reference to something else ⟨a country's defense *posture*⟩ **4** : frame of mind : ATTITUDE ⟨a *posture* of arrogance⟩ [French, from Italian *postura,* from Latin *positura,* from *positus,* past participle of *ponere* "to place"] — **pos·tur·al** \-chə-rəl\ *adj*
[2]posture *vb* : to assume or cause to assume a given posture; *esp* : to strike a pose for effect — **pos·tur·er** *n*
post·vo·cal·ic \ˌpōst-vō-ˈkal-ik\ *adj* : immediately following a vowel
post·war \ˈpōst-ˈwȯr\ *adj* : of, relating to, or being a period after a war
po·sy \ˈpō-zē\ *n, pl* **posies** **1** : a brief motto **2 a** : FLOWER 1c **b** : a bunch of flowers : BOUQUET [alteration of *poesy*]
[1]pot \ˈpät\ *n* **1 a** : a rounded metal or earthen container used chiefly for domestic purposes **b** : the quantity held by a pot **2** : an enclosed framework for catching fish or lobsters **3 a** : a large quantity or sum **b** : the total of the bets at stake at one time **4** : RUIN 1, DETERIORATION ⟨their business went to *pot*⟩ [Old English *pott*] — **pot·ful** *n*
[2]pot *vt* **pot·ted; pot·ting** **1** : to preserve in a sealed pot, jar, or can ⟨*potted* chicken⟩ **2** : to plant or grow in a pot ⟨*potted* plants⟩ **3** : to shoot with a potshot ⟨*pot* a rabbit⟩
[3]pot *n* : MARIJUANA [perhaps from Mexican Spanish *potiguaya*]
po·ta·ble \ˈpōt-ə-bəl\ *adj* : suitable for drinking [Late Latin *potabilis,* from Latin *potare* "to drink"] — **po·ta·bil·i·ty** \ˌpōt-ə-ˈbil-ət-ē\ *n* — **po·ta·ble·ness** \ˈpōt-ə-bəl-nəs\ *n*
po·tage \pȯ-ˈtäzh\ *n* : a thick soup [Middle French, from Medieval French, "pottage"]
pot·ash \ˈpät-ˌash\ *n* **1 a** : potassium carbonate especially from wood ashes **b** : POTASSIUM HYDROXIDE **2** : potassium or a potassium compound especially as used in agriculture or industry [singular of *pot ashes*]
po·tas·si·um \pə-ˈtas-ē-əm\ *n* : a silver-white soft light low-melting univalent metallic chemical element that occurs abundantly in nature especially combined in minerals — see ELEMENT table [New Latin, from *potassa* "potash," from English *potash*]
potassium bromide *n* : a crystalline salt KBr with a saline taste used especially as a sedative and in photography
potassium carbonate *n* : a white salt K_2CO_3 that forms a strongly alkaline solution and is used in making glass and soap
potassium chlorate *n* : a crystalline salt $KClO_3$ that is used as an oxidizing agent in matches, fireworks, and explosives
potassium chloride *n* : a crystalline salt KCl that occurs as a mineral and in natural waters and is used as a fertilizer
potassium cyanide *n* : a very poisonous crystalline salt KCN used especially in extracting gold and silver from ore
potassium dichromate *n* : a soluble salt $K_2Cr_2O_7$ forming large orange-red crystals used in dyeing, in photography, and as an oxidizing agent
potassium hydroxide *n* : a white deliquescent solid KOH that dissolves in water with much heat to form a strongly alkaline and caustic liquid and is used in making soap and as a reagent
potassium nitrate *n* : a crystalline salt KNO_3 that occurs as a product of nitrification in soil, is a strong oxidizer, and is used in making gunpowder, as a fertilizer, and in medicine — called also *saltpeter*

potassium permanganate *n* : a dark purple salt $KMnO_4$ used as an oxidizer and disinfectant
potassium sulfate *n* : a white crystalline compound K_2SO_4 used especially as a fertilizer
po·ta·tion \pō-ˈtā-shən\ *n* **1** : a usually alcoholic drink or brew **2 a** : the act of drinking **b** : DRAFT 4a [Medieval French, from Latin *potatio* "act of drinking," from *potare* "to drink"]
po·ta·to \pə-ˈtāt-ō, pət-ˈāt-\ *n, pl* **-toes** **1** : SWEET POTATO **2 a** : an erect South American herb of the nightshade family widely cultivated for its thick edible starchy tuber **b** : the tuber of a potato — called also *Irish potato, spud, white potato* [Spanish *batata,* from Taino (aboriginal language of the Greater Antilles and the Bahamas)]
potato beetle *n* : COLORADO POTATO BEETLE
potato blight *n* : any of several destructive fungus diseases of the potato
potato bug *n* : COLORADO POTATO BEETLE
potato chip *n* : a thin slice of potato fried crisp and salted
potbellied pig *n* : any of a breed of small pigs originating in southeastern Asia and having a straight tail, potbelly, and black, white, or black and white coat
potbellied stove *n* : a stove with a rounded or bulging body — called also *potbelly stove*

potbellied stove

pot·bel·ly \ˈpät-ˌbel-ē\ *n* **1** : an enlarged, swollen, or protruding abdomen **2** : POTBELLIED STOVE — **pot·bel·lied** \-ēd\ *adj*
pot·boil·er \-ˌbȯi-lər\ *n* : a usually inferior work of art or literature produced only to earn money
pot cheese *n* : COTTAGE CHEESE
po·teen \pə-ˈtēn\ *n* : illicitly distilled whiskey of Ireland [Irish Gaelic *poitín*]
po·ten·cy \ˈpōt-n-sē\ *n, pl* **-cies** : the quality or condition of being potent; *esp* : power to bring about a given result
po·tent \ˈpōt-nt\ *adj* **1** : having or exercising force, authority, or influence : POWERFUL **2** : producing a given effect **3 a** : chemically or medicinally effective ⟨a *potent* vaccine⟩ **b** : rich in a constituent : STRONG ⟨*potent* tea⟩ **4** : able to copulate [Latin *potens,* derived from *potis, pote* "able"] — **po·tent·ly** *adv*
po·ten·tate \ˈpōt-n-ˌtāt\ *n* : one who exercises controlling power
[1]**po·ten·tial** \pə-ˈten-chəl\ *adj* : capable of becoming real : POSSIBLE ⟨the *potential* dangers in the scheme⟩ [Late Latin *potentialis,* from Latin *potentia* "power," from *potens* "potent"] — **po·ten·tial·ly** \-ˈtench-lē, -ə-lē\ *adv*
[2]**potential** *n* **1 a** : something that can develop or become actual : POSSIBILITY ⟨a *potential* for injury⟩ **b** : PROMISE ⟨a technology with great *potential*⟩ **2 a** : the work required to move a single positive charge from a reference point (as at infinity) to a point in question **b** : POTENTIAL DIFFERENCE
potential difference *n* : the difference in electrical potential between two points that represents the work involved or the energy released in the transfer of a unit quantity of electricity from one point to the other
potential energy *n* : the amount of energy a thing (as a weight raised to a height or a coiled spring) has because of its position or because of the arrangement of its parts
po·ten·ti·al·i·ty \pə-ˌten-chē-ˈal-ət-ē\ *n, pl* **-ties** **1** : the ability to develop or to come into existence **2** : POTENTIAL 1
po·ten·ti·ate \pə-ˈten-chē-ˌāt\ *vt* : to make potent; *esp* : to increase (the effect of a drug or treatment) synergistically — **po·ten·ti·a·tion** \-ˌten-chē-ˈā-shən\ *n* — **po·ten·ti·a·tor** \-ˈten-chē-ˌāt-ər\ *n*
po·ten·ti·om·e·ter \pə-ˌten-chē-ˈäm-ət-ər\ *n* **1** : an instrument for measuring electromotive forces **2** : VOLTAGE DIVIDER [*potential* + *-o-* + *-meter*]
pot·head \ˈpät-ˌhed\ *n* : a person who frequently smokes marijuana
[1]**poth·er** \ˈpät͟h-ər\ *n* **1 a** : COMMOTION **b** : FUSS 2 **2** : a choking cloud of dust or smoke **3** : mental turmoil [origin unknown]
[2]**pother** *vb* **poth·ered; poth·er·ing** \ˈpät͟h-ring, -ə-ring\ : to put into or be in a pother
pot·herb \ˈpät-ˌərb, -ˌhərb\ *n* : an herb whose leaves or stems are cooked for use as greens; *also* : one (as mint) used to season food
pot·hole \-ˌhōl\ *n* : a large pit or hole (as in the bed of a river or in a road surface)
pot·hook \-ˌhu̇k\ *n* **1** : an S-shaped hook for hanging pots and kettles over an open fire **2** : an S-shaped stroke in writing
pot·hunt·er \-ˌhənt-ər\ *n* : one who hunts game for food — **pot·hunt·ing** \-ˌhənt-ing\ *n*
po·tion \ˈpō-shən\ *n* : a mixture of liquids (as liquor or medicine) [Medieval French *poisun, pocioun* "drink, potion," from Latin, from *potare* "to drink"]
pot·latch \ˈpät-ˌlach\ *n* **1** : a ceremonial feast of the American Indians of the northwest coast in which the host distributes gifts lavishly and the guests must reciprocate **2** *Northwest* : a social event or celebration [Chinook Jargon (a pidgin language based on Chinook and other American Indian languages, French, and English) *patlač*]
pot liquor *n* : the liquid left in a pot after cooking
pot·luck \ˈpät-ˈlək\ *n* **1 a** : the regular meal available to a guest for whom no special preparations have been made **b** : a communal meal to which people bring food to share **2** : whatever is offered or available in given circumstances or at a given time
pot marigold *n* : a variable hardy calendula widely grown especially for ornament
pot·pie \ˈpät-ˈpī\ *n* : a stew of meat or poultry usually with vegetables and served with a crust or dumplings
pot·pour·ri \ˌpō-pu̇-ˈrē\ *n* **1** : a jar of flower petals and spices used for scent **2** : a miscellaneous collection : MEDLEY [French *pot pourri,* literally, "rotten pot"]
pot roast *n* : a piece of beef cooked by braising usually on top of the stove
pot·sherd \ˈpät-ˌshərd\ *n* : a pottery fragment
pot·shot \-ˌshät\ *n* **1** : a shot taken in a casual manner or at an easy target **2** : a critical remark made in a random or sporadic way [from the notion that such a shot is unsportsmanlike and worthy only of one whose object is to fill the cooking pot] — **potshot** *vb*
pot·tage \ˈpät-ij\ *n* : a thick soup of vegetables or vegetables and meat [Medieval French *potage,* from *pot* "pot," of Germanic origin]
[1]**pot·ter** \ˈpät-ər\ *n* : one that makes pottery
[2]**potter** *vi* : FIDDLE 2b, PUTTER [probably from English dialect *pote* "to poke"] — **pot·ter·er** *n*
potter's clay *n* : a plastic clay suitable for making pottery — called also *potter's earth*
potter's field *n* : a public burial place for paupers, unknown persons, and criminals [from the mention in Matthew 27:7 of the purchase of a potter's field for use as a graveyard]
potter's wheel *n* : a horizontal disk revolving on a spindle and carrying the clay being shaped by a potter

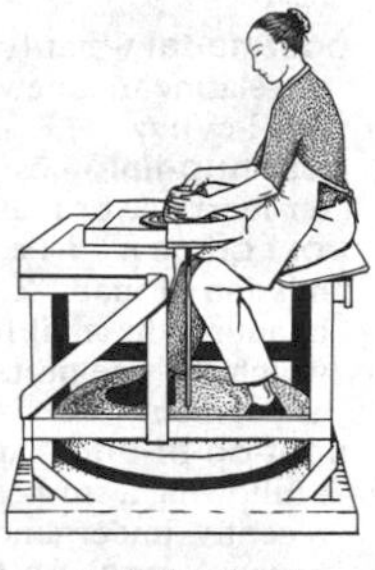
potter's wheel

pot·tery \ˈpät-ə-rē\ *n, pl* **-ter·ies** **1** : a place where earthen vessels are made **2** : the art of the potter : CERAMICS **3** : ware made usually from clay that is shaped while moist and soft and hardened by heat; *esp* : coarser ware so made
pot·to \ˈpät-ō\ *n, pl* **pottos** : any of several African primates; *esp* : a slow-moving primate that dwells in trees, is active at night, and has woolly brownish fur [perhaps from Wolof (Niger-Congo language of Senegambia) "speaker of Wolof, the Wolof language"]
[1]**pot·ty** \ˈpät-ē\ *adj, chiefly British* : slightly crazy [probably from [1]*pot*]
[2]**potty** *n, pl* **potties** **1** : a small child's pot for urinating or defecating; *also* : POTTY-CHAIR **2** : TOILET 2b, BATHROOM
pot·ty–chair \-ˌcheər, -ˌchaər\ *n* : a child's chair having an open seat under which a pot is placed for toilet training
[1]**pouch** \ˈpau̇ch\ *n* **1** : a small drawstring bag carried on the person **2** : a bag of small or moderate size for storing or carrying goods; *esp* : a bag with a lock for first class mail or diplomatic dispatches **3** : an anatomical structure in the form of a bag or sac; *esp* : one for carrying the young on the abdomen of a female marsupial (as a kangaroo or opossum) [Medieval French *pouche,* of Germanic origin] — **pouched** \ˈpau̇cht\ *adj*
[2]**pouch** *vb* : to put or form into or as if into a pouch
pouchy \ˈpau̇-chē\ *adj* **pouch·i·er; -est** : having, tending to have, or resembling a pouch

poult \ˈpōlt\ *n* **:** a young fowl; *esp* **:** a young turkey [Middle English *polet, pulte* "young fowl, pullet"]
poul·ter·er \ˈpōl-tər-ər\ *n* **:** one that deals in poultry [Middle French *pulleter*]
poul·tice \ˈpōl-təs\ *n* **:** a soft usually heated and often medicated mass spread on cloth and applied to lesions (as sores) [Medieval Latin *pultes* "pap," from Latin *pult-, puls* "porridge"] — **poultice** *vt*
poul·try \ˈpōl-trē\ *n* **:** domesticated birds kept for eggs or meat [Medieval French *pouleterie,* from *pulleter* "poulterer," from *pullet* "chicken"]
poul·try·man \-mən\ *n* **1 :** one that raises domestic fowls especially on a commercial scale **2 :** a dealer in poultry or poultry products
[1]**pounce** \ˈpau̇ns\ *vi* **1 :** to swoop upon and seize something with or as if with talons ⟨the cat *pounced*⟩ **2 :** to make an abrupt assault or approach [Middle English *pounce* "talon"]
[2]**pounce** *n* **:** the act of pouncing
[3]**pounce** *vt* **:** to dust, rub, finish, or stencil with pounce
[4]**pounce** *n* **1 :** a fine powder formerly used to prevent ink from spreading **2 :** a fine powder for making stenciled patterns [French *ponce* "pumice," from Latin *pumex*]
[1]**pound** \ˈpau̇nd\ *n, pl* **pounds** *also* **pound 1 :** any of various units of mass and weight; *esp* **:** a unit in general use among English-speaking peoples equal to 16 ounces (about 0.454 kilogram) — see MEASURE table **2 a :** the basic monetary unit of the United Kingdom — called also *pound sterling* **b :** the basic monetary unit of Egypt, Lebanon, and Syria **c :** a coin or note representing one pound [Old English *pund,* from Latin *pondo*]
[2]**pound** *n* **1 :** an enclosure for animals; *esp* **:** a public enclosure for stray or unlicensed animals **2 a :** an enclosure within which fish or crustaceans (as lobsters) are kept or caught; *esp* **:** the inner compartment of a fish trap **b :** an establishment selling live lobsters [Middle English, "enclosure," from Old English *pund-*]
[3]**pound** *vb* **1 :** to reduce to powder or pulp by beating **2 a :** to strike heavily or repeatedly ⟨*pound* the piano⟩ **b :** to produce by means of repeated vigorous strokes ⟨*pound* out a story on the typewriter⟩ **c :** DRIVE 5b **3 :** to move heavily or persistently ⟨the horses *pounded* along the lane⟩ [Old English *pūnian*]
[4]**pound** *n* **:** an act or sound of pounding
pound·al \ˈpau̇n-dl\ *n* **:** a unit of force equal to the force that would give a free mass of one pound an acceleration of one foot per second per second [[1]*pound* + *-al* (as in *quintal*)]
pound cake *n* **:** a rich butter cake made with a large amount of eggs and shortening [from the original recipe calling for a pound of each of the principal ingredients]
[1]**pound·er** \ˈpau̇n-dər\ *n* **:** one that pounds
[2]**pounder** *n* **1 :** one having a specified weight or value in pounds **2 :** a gun throwing a projectile of a specified weight in pounds
pound–fool·ish \ˈpau̇nd-ˈfü-lish, ˈpau̇n-\ *adj* **:** imprudent in dealing with large sums or weighty matters [from the phrase *penny-wise and pound-foolish*]
[1]**pour** \ˈpōr, ˈpȯr\ *vb* **1 :** to flow or to cause to flow in a stream ⟨*pour* the tea⟩ ⟨tears *pouring* down my cheeks⟩ **2 :** to supply or produce copiously **3 :** to rain hard [Middle English *pouren*] — **pour·able** \-ə-bəl\ *adj* — **pour·er** *n*
[2]**pour** *n* **:** the action of pouring; *esp* **:** a heavy rainfall
[1]**pout** \ˈpau̇t\ *vb* **1 a :** to show displeasure by thrusting out the lips or wearing a sullen expression **b :** SULK **2 :** to protrude or cause to protrude ⟨*pouted* her lips⟩ [Middle English *pouten*]
[2]**pout** *n* **1 :** a thrusting out of the lips expressing displeasure **2** *pl* **:** a fit of bad humor
[3]**pout** *n, pl* **pout** *or* **pouts :** any of several large-headed fishes (as a bullhead) [Old English *-pūte*]
pout·er \ˈpau̇t-ər\ *n* **1 :** one that pouts **2 :** a domestic pigeon of erect carriage with an inflatable crop
pouty \ˈpau̇t-ē\ *adj* **:** SULKY 1
pov·er·ty \ˈpäv-ərt-ē\ *n* **1 :** the state of being poor **:** lack of money or material possessions **:** WANT **2 :** an inadequate supply **3 :** lack of fertility ⟨*poverty* of the soil⟩ [Medieval French *poverté,* from Latin *paupertas,* from *pauper* "poor"]
pov·er·ty–strick·en \-ˌstrik-ən\ *adj* **:** very poor **:** DESTITUTE
POW \ˌpē-ˌō-ˈdəb-əl-ˌyü\ *n* **:** PRISONER OF WAR
[1]**pow·der** \ˈpau̇d-ər\ *n* **1 :** dry material made up of fine particles; *also* **:** a medicinal or cosmetic preparation in this form **2 :** any of various solid explosives used chiefly in gunnery and blasting [Medieval French *pudre, podre,* from Latin *pulver-, pulvis* "dust"]
[2]**powder** *vb* **1 :** to sprinkle or cover with or as if with powder **2 :** to reduce to or become powder — **pow·der·er** \-ər-ər\ *n*
powder blue *n* **:** a pale blue
powder horn *n* **:** a flask for carrying gunpowder; *esp* **:** one made of the horn of an ox or cow
powder keg *n* **1 :** a small usually metal cask for holding gunpowder or blasting powder **2 :** something (as an unstable political situation) liable to explode
powder puff *n* **:** a soft pad for applying cosmetic powder

powder horn

powder room *n* **:** a restroom for women
pow·dery \ˈpau̇d-ə-rē\ *adj* **1 a :** resembling or consisting of powder **b :** easily reduced to powder **:** CRUMBLY **2 :** covered with or as if with powder
powdery mildew *n* **:** a parasitic fungus producing abundant powdery spores on the host; *also* **:** a plant disease caused by such a fungus
[1]**pow·er** \ˈpau̇-ər, ˈpau̇r\ *n* **1 a :** possession of control, authority, or influence over others **b :** one having such power; *esp* **:** a sovereign state **2 a :** ability to act or do ⟨lose the *power* of speech⟩ **b :** legal or official authority, capacity, or right **3 a :** physical might **b :** mental strength and effectiveness **4 a :** the number of times as indicated by an exponent a number or expression is to be multiplied by itself ⟨5 to the third *power* is 125⟩ **b :** the product obtained by raising a number or expression to a power ⟨8 is a *power* of 2⟩ **5 a :** force or energy that is or can be applied to work; *esp* **:** mechanical or electrical force or energy **b :** the time rate at which work is done or energy emitted or transferred **6 :** MAGNIFICATION 2b [Medieval French *poer, pouer,* from *poer* "to be able," derived from Latin *potis, pote* "able"]
synonyms POWER, FORCE, ENERGY, STRENGTH mean the ability to exert effort. POWER may imply latent or exerted physical, mental, or spiritual ability to act or be acted upon ⟨the king had the *power* to pardon the prisoners⟩. FORCE implies the actual effective exercise of power ⟨pushed with enough *force* to overturn the chair⟩ ⟨a wind of intense *force*⟩. ENERGY applies to power expended or capable of being transformed into work ⟨a crusader of untiring *energy*⟩. STRENGTH applies to the quality or characteristic that enables one to exert force or withstand pressure or attack ⟨a mind of *strength* and decisiveness⟩.
[2]**power** *adj* **:** relating to, supplying, or utilizing power; *esp* **:** utilizing mechanical or electrical energy ⟨a *power* drill⟩ ⟨*power* steering⟩
[3]**power** *vt* **:** to supply with power
pow·er·boat \-ˈbōt\ *n* **:** MOTORBOAT
power dive *n* **:** a dive of an airplane accelerated by the power of the engine — **power–dive** *vb*
pow·er·ful \ˈpau̇-ər-fəl, ˈpau̇r-\ *adj* **:** having great power, strength, or influence — **pow·er·ful·ly** \-fə-lē, -flē\ *adv*
pow·er·house \-ˌhau̇s\ *n* **1 a :** POWER PLANT 1 **b :** a source of influence or inspiration **2 :** one that has great power or unusual energy or strength
pow·er·less \-ləs\ *adj* **1 :** lacking power, force, or energy **:** unable to produce an effect **2 :** lacking authority to act — **pow·er·less·ly** *adv* — **pow·er·less·ness** *n*
power of attorney : a legal instrument authorizing a person to act as the attorney or agent of another
power pack *n* **:** a unit for converting a power supply to a voltage suitable for an electronic device
power plant *n* **1 :** an electric utility generating station **2 :** an engine and related parts supplying the motive power of a self-propelled vehicle
power play *n* **:** a situation in ice hockey in which the players on the ice for one team outnumber those for the other team because of a penalty
power politics *n sing or pl* **:** politics characterized by attempts

\ə\ **abut**	\au̇\ **out**	\i\ **tip**	\ȯ\ **saw**	\u̇\ **foot**
\ər\ **further**	\ch\ **chin**	\ī\ **life**	\ȯi\ **coin**	\y\ **yet**
\a\ **mat**	\e\ **pet**	\j\ **job**	\th\ **thin**	\yü\ **few**
\ā\ **take**	\ē\ **easy**	\ng\ **sing**	\t͟h\ **this**	\yu̇\ **cure**
\ä\ **cot, cart**	\g\ **go**	\ō\ **bone**	\ü\ **food**	\zh\ **vision**

to advance national interests through military and economic coercion

power shovel *n* : a power-operated excavating machine consisting of a boom or crane that supports a dipper handle with a dipper at the end of it

power station *n* : POWER PLANT 1

power strip *n* : an electrical device that plugs into an outlet and contains several receptacles for powering additional devices

power train *n* : the mechanism that transmits power from an engine to a propeller or axle

power up *vt* : to cause to operate ⟨*power up* the computer⟩

[1]**pow·wow** \ˈpau̇-ˌwau̇\ *n* **1** : an American Indian medicine man **2 a** : an American Indian ceremony (as for victory in war) **b** : an American Indian social gathering or fair including competitive dancing **3 a** : a social get-together **b** : a meeting for discussion [Narragansett *powwaw* or Massachusett *pauwau*]

[2]**powwow** *vi* : to hold a powwow

pox \ˈpäks\ *n* : a disease (as chicken pox) that is caused by a virus and is characterized by a rash on the skin [alteration of *pocks,* pl. of *pock*]

PR \ˈpē-ˈär\ *n* : PUBLIC RELATIONS

prac·ti·ca·ble \ˈprak-ti-kə-bəl\ *adj* **1** : capable of being done, put into practice, or accomplished : FEASIBLE ⟨a *practicable* plan⟩ **2** : USABLE ⟨a *practicable* substitute⟩ ***synonyms*** see POSSIBLE — **prac·ti·ca·bil·i·ty** \ˌprak-ti-kə-ˈbil-ət-ē\ *n* — **prac·ti·ca·ble·ness** \ˈprak-ti-kə-bəl-nəs\ *n* — **prac·ti·ca·bly** \-blē\ *adv*

prac·ti·cal \ˈprak-ti-kəl\ *adj* **1** : actively engaged in an action or occupation ⟨a *practical* farmer⟩ **2 a** : of, relating to, or manifested in practice or action ⟨for *practical* purposes⟩ **b** : being such in practice or effect : VIRTUAL ⟨a *practical* failure⟩ **3** : capable of being put to use or account : USEFUL **4 a** : inclined to action rather than planning or theorizing ⟨a *practical* person⟩ **b (1)** : qualified by practice or practical training **(2)** : designed to supplement theoretical training by experience [Late Latin *practicus,* from Greek *praktikos,* from *prassein* "to pass over, act, do"] — **prac·ti·cal·i·ty** \ˌprak-ti-ˈkal-ət-ē\ *n* — **prac·ti·cal·ness** \ˈprak-ti-kəl-nəs\ *n*

practical joke *n* : a joke that depends on the tricking or abuse of a person at a disadvantage — **practical joker** *n*

prac·ti·cal·ly \ˈprak-ti-kə-lē, -klē\ *adv* **1** : in a practical manner ⟨talked *practically* about the problem⟩ **2** : NEARLY, ALMOST ⟨*practically* everyone was there⟩

practical nurse *n* : a nurse that cares for the sick professionally without having the training or experience required of a registered nurse; *esp* : LICENSED PRACTICAL NURSE

[1]**prac·tice** *also* **prac·tise** \ˈprak-təs\ *vb* **1 a** : to perform or work at repeatedly so as to become skilled ⟨*practiced* their act⟩ **b** : to train by repeated exercises ⟨*practice* pupils in writing⟩ **2 a** : to carry out : APPLY ⟨*practice* what you preach⟩ **b** : to do or perform often, customarily, or habitually ⟨*practice* politeness⟩ **c** : to be professionally engaged in ⟨*practice* law⟩ [Medieval French *practiser,* derived from Medieval Latin *practicare,* from *practica* "practice," noun, from Late Latin *practice,* from Greek *praktikē,* from *praktikos* "practical"] — **prac·tic·er** *n*

[2]**practice** *also* **practise** *n* **1 a** : actual performance or application **b** : a repeated or customary action **c** : the usual way of doing something ⟨local *practices*⟩ **d** : an established manner of conducting legal proceedings **2 a** : systematic exercise for gaining skill ⟨*practice* makes perfect⟩ **b** : the condition of being skilled through systematic exercise ⟨get in *practice*⟩ ⟨team members out of *practice* after a long winter⟩ **3 a** : the exercise of a profession ⟨the *practice* of law⟩ **b** : a professional business ***synonyms*** see HABIT — **in practice** : in actual or accepted usage

prac·ticed *also* **prac·tised** \ˈprak-təst\ *adj* **1** : EXPERIENCED, SKILLED ⟨a *practiced* welder⟩ **2** : learned by practice

prac·tice–teach \ˌprak-təs-ˈtēch\ *vi* : to engage in practice teaching — **practice teacher** *n*

practice teaching *n* : teaching in which a student practices educational skills and methods under the supervision of an experienced teacher in preparation for professional teaching

prac·ti·tio·ner \prak-ˈtish-nər, -ə-nər\ *n* **1** : a person who practices a profession and especially law or medicine **2** : a Christian Scientist who is an authorized healer [from earlier *practician,* from Middle French *praticien,* from *pratique* "practice"]

prae·no·men \prē-ˈnō-mən\ *n, pl* **-nomens** *or* **-no·mi·na** \-ˈnäm-ə-nə, -ˈnō-mə-\ : the first of the usual three names of an ancient Roman [Latin, from *prae-* "pre" + *nomen* "name"]

prae·tor \ˈprēt-ər\ *n* : an ancient Roman magistrate ranking below a consul and having chiefly judicial duties [Latin]

prae·to·ri·an \prē-ˈtōr-ē-ən, -ˈtȯr-\ *adj* **1** : of or relating to a praetor **2** *often cap* : of, forming, or resembling the Roman imperial bodyguard — **praetorian** *n, often cap*

prag·mat·ic \prag-ˈmat-ik\ *also* **prag·mat·i·cal** \-ˈmat-i-kəl\ *adj* **1 a** : concerned with practical rather than intellectual or artistic matters **b** : practical as opposed to idealistic **2** : relating to or in accordance with pragmatism [Latin *pragmaticus* "skilled in law or business," from Greek *pragmatikos,* from *pragma* "deed, action," from *prassein* "to do"] — **prag·mat·i·cal·ly** \-i-kə-lē, -klē\ *adv*

pragmatic sanction *n* : a solemn decree of a sovereign on a matter of primary importance and with the force of fundamental law

prag·ma·tism \ˈprag-mə-ˌtiz-əm\ *n* **1** : a practical approach to problems and affairs **2** : philosophical doctrine holding that the meaning of an idea is to be sought in its practical bearings, that the function of thought is to guide action, and that truth is to be tested by the practical consequences of belief — **prag·ma·tist** \-mət-əst\ *adj or n* — **prag·ma·tis·tic** \ˌprag-mə-ˈtis-tik\ *adj*

prai·rie \ˈpreər-ē\ *n* : a tract of grassland; *esp* : a large area of level or rolling land (as in the central U.S.) with deep fertile soil, a cover of tall coarse grasses, and few trees [French, derived from Latin *pratum* "meadow"]

prairie chicken *n* : a grouse of the central U.S. prairies with the male having a patch of bare skin on either side of the neck which is inflated during courtship displays

prairie dog *n* : a black-tailed buff or grayish rodent of central and western U.S. prairies that is related to the squirrels and usually lives in extensive colonial burrows

prairie schooner *n* : a covered wagon used by pioneers in cross-country travel — called also *prairie wagon*

prairie wolf *n* : COYOTE

prairie schooner

[1]**praise** \ˈprāz\ *vb* **1** : to express approval : COMMEND **2** : to glorify (a god or a saint) especially in song : EXTOL [Medieval French *preiser, priser* "to appraise, esteem," from Late Latin *pretiare* "to prize," from Latin *pretium* "price"] — **prais·er** *n*

[2]**praise** *n* **1** : an act of praising : COMMENDATION **2** : WORSHIP ⟨in *praise* of the Lord⟩

praise·wor·thy \-ˌwər-t͟hē\ *adj* : worthy of praise : LAUDABLE — **praise·wor·thi·ly** \-t͟hə-lē\ *adv* — **praise·wor·thi·ness** \-t͟hē-nəs\ *n*

Pra·krit \ˈpräk-ˌrit, -rət\ *n* **1** : any or all of the ancient Indic languages or dialects other than Sanskrit **2** : any of the modern Indic languages [Sanskrit *prākṛta,* from *prākṛta* "natural, vulgar"]

pra·line \ˈprä-ˌlēn, ˈprā-\ *n* : a candy of nut kernels embedded in boiled brown sugar or maple sugar [French, from Count Plessis-*Praslin,* died 1675, French soldier]

pram \ˈpram\ *n, chiefly British* : a baby carriage [short for *perambulator*]

prance \ˈprans\ *vi* **1** : to spring from the hind legs or move by so doing **2** : to ride on a prancing horse **3** : to move in a spirited manner : STRUT; *also* : CAPER [Middle English *prauncen*] — **prance** *n* — **pranc·er** \ˈpran-sər\ *n* — **pranc·ing·ly** \-sing-lē\ *adv*

pran·di·al \ˈpran-dē-əl\ *adj* : of or relating to a meal [Latin *prandium* "late breakfast, luncheon"]

[1]**prank** \ˈprangk\ *n* : a playful or mischievous act: as **a** : PRACTICAL JOKE ⟨Halloween *pranks*⟩ **b** : a ludicrous act [obsolete *prank* "to play tricks"] — **prank·ish** \ˈprang-kish\ *adj* — **prank·ish·ly** *adv* — **prank·ish·ness** *n*

[2]**prank** *vt* : to dress or adorn (as oneself) gaily or showily [probably from Dutch *pronken* "to strut"]

prank·ster \ˈprang-stər, ˈprangk-\ *n* : one that plays pranks

pra·seo·dym·i·um \ˌprā-zē-ō-ˈdim-ē-əm\ *n* : a yellowish white metallic chemical element used especially in alloys and in the form of its salts in coloring glass greenish yellow — see ELEMENT table [derived from Greek *prasios* "light green" + New Latin *didymium,* a mixture of rare earth elements, from Greek *didymos* "double"]

[1]**prate** \ˈprāt\ *vb* : to talk long and idly or foolishly [Dutch *praten*] — **prat·er** *n* — **prat·ing·ly** \ˈprāt-ing-lē\ *adv*

[2]**prate** *n* : idle or foolish talk

prat·fall \ˈprat-ˌfȯl\ *n* **1** : a fall on the buttocks **2** : a humiliating mishap or blunder [earlier *prat* "buttocks"]

pra·tique \pra-ˈtēk\ *n* : clearance given an incoming ship by the health authority of a port [French, literally, "practice"]

[1]**prat·tle** \ˈprat-l\ *vb* **prat·tled; prat·tling** \ˈprat-ling, -l-ing\ **1** : PRATE **2** : to utter meaningless sounds suggestive of the chatter of children [Low German *pratelen*] — **prat·tler** \ˈprat-lər, -l-ər\ *n* — **prat·tling·ly** \ˈprat-ling-lē\ *adv*

[2]**prattle** *n* **1** : PRATE **2** : a sound that is meaningless, repetitive, and suggestive of the chatter of children

prau \ˈprau̇\ *or* **proa** \ˈprō-ə\ *n* : any of several usually undecked Indonesian boats propelled by sails, oars, or paddles [Malay *pĕrahu*]

prawn \ˈprȯn, ˈprän\ *n* **1** : any of various widely distributed edible decapod crustaceans resembling shrimps with large compressed abdomens **2** : SHRIMP; *esp* : a large shrimp [Middle English *prane*]

pray \ˈprā\ *vb* **1** : ENTREAT, IMPLORE ⟨*pray* tell me the time⟩ **2** : to get or bring by praying **3** : to make entreaty or supplication : PLEAD **4** : to address God with adoration, confession, supplication, or thanksgiving [Medieval French *prier, praer, preier,* from Latin *precari,* from *prec-, prex* "request, prayer"]

[1]**prayer** \ˈpraər, ˈpreər\ *n* **1** : the act or practice of praying to God ⟨a moment of silent *prayer*⟩ **2 a** : a supplication or expression addressed to God ⟨a *prayer* of thanksgiving⟩ **b** : an earnest request or wish : PLEA **3** : a religious service consisting chiefly of prayers ⟨had regular family *prayers*⟩ **4** : a set form of words used in praying ⟨a book of *prayers*⟩ [Medieval French *priere, praiere, preiere,* from Medieval Latin *precaria,* from Latin *precarius* "obtained by entreaty," from *prec-, prex* "request, entreaty"]

[2]**pray·er** \ˈprā-ər\ *n* : one that prays : SUPPLIANT

prayer book *n* : a book containing prayers and often other forms and directions for worship

prayer·ful \ˈpraər-fəl, ˈpreər-\ *adj* **1** : given to or characterized by prayer : DEVOUT **2** : EARNEST 1 — **prayer·ful·ly** \-fə-lē\ *adv* — **prayer·ful·ness** *n*

prayer meeting *n* : a Protestant Christian service of evangelical worship usually held regularly on a weeknight — called also *prayer service*

prayer plant *n* : a Brazilian plant with oval leaves folding upward at night as if in prayer that is widely grown as an ornamental foliage plant

praying mantis *n* : MANTIS; *esp* : a European mantis that has been introduced into the U.S.

pre- *prefix* **1 a (1)** : earlier than : prior to : before ⟨*pre*historic⟩ **(2)** : preparatory or prerequisite to ⟨*pre*medical⟩ **b** : in advance : beforehand ⟨*pre*cancel⟩ **2 a** : in front of : anterior to ⟨*pre*molar⟩ **b** : front : anterior [Latin *prae-,* from *prae* "in front of, before"]

preadmission	**predefine**	**prelife**
preadult	**predelivery**	**prelunch**
preagricultural	**predeparture**	**premade**
preannounce	**predesignate**	**premarital**
preapprove	**predevelopment**	**premaritally**
prearrange	**predischarge**	**premarriage**
prearrangement	**prediscovery**	**premigration**
preassign	**predrill**	**premodern**
prebattle	**preelection**	**premodification**
prebiblical	**preelectric**	**premodify**
prebreakfast	**preelectronic**	**premoisten**
precapitalist	**preemployment**	**premold**
preclear	**preestablish**	**prenoon**
preclearance	**preexperiment**	**prenotification**
precode	**prefeudal**	**prenotify**
precollege	**prefight**	**preopening**
precolonial	**prefile**	**preoperational**
precombustion	**prefire**	**preorder**
precommitment	**pregame**	**preplan**
precompute	**preharvest**	**preprepared**
precomputer	**preinaugural**	**preproduction**
preconvention	**preindustrial**	**preprogram**
precool	**preinterview**	**prepublication**
precrash	**preinvasion**	**prepunch**
predawn	**prelaunch**	**prepurchase**
prequalification	**presale**	**pretreat**
prequalify	**preseason**	**pretreatment**
prerace	**prestamp**	**preuniversity**
prerehearsal	**presterilize**	**prewar**
prerelease	**prestrike**	**prewash**
preretirement	**presurgery**	**prework**
prerevolution	**pretape**	**prewrap**
prerevolutionary	**pretelevision**	
preriot	**pretournament**	

preach \ˈprēch\ *vb* **1 a** : to deliver a sermon : utter publicly **b** : to set forth in a sermon ⟨*preach* the gospel⟩ **2** : to urge acceptance or abandonment of an idea or course of action : ADVOCATE ⟨*preach* patience⟩; *esp* : to exhort in an officious or tiresome manner **3** : to bring, put, or affect by preaching [Medieval French *precher,* from Late Latin *praedicare,* from Latin, "to proclaim publicly," from *prae-* "pre-" + *dicare* "to proclaim"] — **preach·er** *n* — **preach·ing·ly** \ˈprē-ching-lē\ *adv*

preach·ify \ˈprē-chə-ˌfī\ *vi* **-fied; -fy·ing** : to preach ineptly or tediously

preach·ment \ˈprēch-mənt\ *n* **1** : the act or practice of preaching **2** : SERMON, EXHORTATION; *esp* : a tedious or unwelcome exhortation

preachy \ˈprē-chē\ *adj* **preach·i·er; -est** : marked by obvious moralizing ⟨put off by the speaker's *preachy* tone⟩ — **preach·i·ly** \-chə-lē\ *adv* — **preach·i·ness** \-chē-nəs\ *n*

pre·ad·o·les·cence \ˌprē-ˌad-l-ˈes-ns\ *n* : the period of human development just preceding adolescence — **pre·ad·o·les·cent** \-nt\ *adj or n*

pre·am·ble \ˈprē-ˌam-bəl, prē-ˈ\ *n* **1** : an introductory statement; *esp* : the usually explanatory introductory part of a constitution or statute **2** : an introductory fact or circumstance : PRELIMINARY; *esp* : one indicating what is to follow [Medieval French *preambule,* from Medieval Latin *praeambulum,* from Late Latin *praeambulus* "walking in front of," from Latin *prae-* "pre-" + *ambulare* "to walk"]

preb·end \ˈpreb-ənd\ *n* **1 a** : an endowment held by a cathedral or collegiate church for the maintenance of a prebendary **b** : the stipend paid from this endowment **2** : PREBENDARY [Medieval French *prebende,* from Medieval Latin *praebenda,* from Late Latin, "subsistence allowance granted by the state," from Latin *praebēre* "to offer," from *prae-* "pre-" + *habēre* "to have, hold"]

preb·en·dary \ˈpreb-ən-ˌder-ē\ *n, pl* **-dar·ies** **1** : a clergyman receiving a prebend for officiating at stated times in the church **2** : an honorary canon

Pre·cam·bri·an \prē-ˈkam-brē-ən, ˈprē-\ *n* : the earliest era of geological history consisting of the eons prior to the Phanerozoic; *also* : the corresponding system of rocks — **Precambrian** *adj*

pre·can·cel \prē-ˈkan-səl, ˈprē-\ *vt* : to cancel (a postage stamp) in advance of use — **pre·can·cel·la·tion** \ˌprē-ˌkan-sə-ˈlā-shən\ *n*

pre·can·cer·ous \prē-ˈkans-rəs, ˈprē-, -ə-rəs\ *adj* : likely to become cancerous ⟨a *precancerous* lesion⟩

pre·car·i·ous \pri-ˈkar-ē-əs, -ˈker-\ *adj* **1** : dependent upon uncertain premises ⟨*precarious* theories⟩ **2 a** : dependent on chance circumstances, unknown conditions, or uncertain developments **b** : characterized by a lack of security or stability that threatens with danger ⟨a *precarious* state of health⟩ [Latin *precarius* "obtained by entreaty, uncertain," from *prec-, prex* "request, entreaty"] — **pre·car·i·ous·ly** *adv* — **pre·car·i·ous·ness** *n*

pre·cau·tion \pri-ˈkȯ-shən\ *n* **1** : care taken in advance : FORESIGHT **2** : a measure taken beforehand to prevent harm or secure good : SAFEGUARD ⟨*precautions* against fire⟩ — **pre·cau·tion·ary** \-shə-ˌner-ē\ *adj*

pre·cede \pri-ˈsēd\ *vb* **1** : to surpass in rank, dignity, or importance **2** : to be, go, or come before or in front of in position or time **3** : to cause to be preceded : PREFACE ⟨*preceded* the speech with a welcome to the visitors⟩ [Middle French *preceder,* from *praecedere,* from *prae-* "pre-" + *cedere* "to go"]

pre·ce·dence \ˈpres-əd-əns, pri-ˈsēd-ns\ *n* **1** : the act or fact of preceding (as in time) **2 :** consideration based on order of importance : PRIORITY ⟨your safety takes *precedence*⟩

pre·ce·den·cy \-ən-sē, -n-sē\ *n* **:** PRECEDENCE

[1]**pre·ce·dent** \pri-ˈsēd-nt, ˈpres-əd-ənt\ *adj* **:** prior in time, order, arrangement, or significance [Medieval French, from Latin *praecedens,* present participle of *praecedere* "to precede"]

[2]**prec·e·dent** \ˈpres-əd-ənt\ *n* **1 :** an earlier occurrence of something similar **2 :** something that may serve as an example or rule to authorize or justify a similar future act or statement ⟨this decision will set a *precedent*⟩

pre·ced·ing \pri-ˈsēd-ing\ *adj* **:** going before in time or place

synonyms PRECEDING, ANTECEDENT, FOREGOING mean being before. PRECEDING usually implies being immediately before in time or place ⟨on the *preceding* day⟩ ⟨the last line in the *preceding* stanza⟩. ANTECEDENT applies to order in time and may suggest a causal relation ⟨study the revolution and *antecedent* economic distress⟩. FOREGOING applies to what has preceded especially in a discourse ⟨the *foregoing* remarks⟩.

pre·cen·tor \pri-ˈsent-ər\ *n* **:** a leader of the singing of a choir or congregation [Latin *praecentor,* from *praecinere* "to lead in singing," from *prae-* "pre-" + *canere* "to sing"] — **pre·cen·to·ri·al** \ˌprē-ˌsen-ˈtōr-ē-əl, -ˈtȯr-\ *adj* — **pre·cen·tor·ship** \pri-ˈsent-ər-ˌship\ *n*

pre·cept \ˈprē-ˌsept\ *n* **:** a command or principle intended as a general rule of action [Latin *praeceptum,* from *praeceptus,* past participle of *praecipere* "to take beforehand, instruct," from *prae-* "pre-" + *capere* "to take"]

pre·cep·tor \pri-ˈsep-tər, ˈprē-ˌ\ *n* **1 :** TEACHER, TUTOR **2 :** the principal of a school — **pre·cep·to·ri·al** \pri-ˌsep-ˈtōr-ē-əl, ˌprē-, -ˈtȯr-\ *adj* — **pre·cep·tor·ship** \pri-ˈsep-tər-ˌship, ˈprē-ˌ\ *n*

pre·ces·sion \prē-ˈsesh-ən\ *n* **:** a comparatively slow circling of the rotation axis of a spinning body about another line intersecting the axis [Medieval Latin *praecessio* "act of preceding," from Latin *praecedere* "to precede"]

pre·cinct \ˈprē-ˌsingt, -ˌsingkt\ *n* **1 :** an administrative subdivision of a territory: as **a :** a subdivision of a county, town, city, or ward for election purposes **b :** a division of a city for police control **2 :** the enclosure bounded by the walls or limits of a building or place ⟨within the *precincts* of the college⟩ **3** *pl* **:** the region immediately surrounding a place : ENVIRONS ⟨the *precincts* of the city⟩ [Medieval Latin *praecinctum* "bounded district," from Latin *praecinctus,* past participle of *praecingere* "to gird about," from *prae-* "pre-" + *cingere* "to gird"]

pre·ci·os·i·ty \ˌpresh-ē-ˈäs-ət-ē, ˌpres-\ *n, pl* **-ties :** often excessive fastidious refinement (as in language)

[1]**pre·cious** \ˈpresh-əs\ *adj* **1 :** of great value or high price ⟨diamonds, emeralds, and other *precious* stones⟩ **2 :** highly esteemed or cherished ⟨*precious* memories⟩ **3 :** excessively refined : AFFECTED ⟨*precious* language⟩ **4 :** THOROUGHGOING, UTTER ⟨a *precious* scoundrel⟩ [Medieval French *precios,* from Latin *pretiosus,* from *pretium* "price"] — **pre·cious·ly** *adv* — **pre·cious·ness** *n*

[2]**precious** *adv* **:** EXTREMELY, VERY ⟨they had *precious* little to say⟩

prec·i·pice \ˈpres-ə-pəs\ *n* **1 :** a very steep or overhanging place (as the face of a cliff) **2 :** the brink of disaster [Middle French, from Latin *praecipitium,* from *praecipit-, praeceps* "headlong," from *prae-* "pre-" + *caput* "head"]

pre·cip·i·tance \pri-ˈsip-ət-əns\ *n* **:** rash haste

pre·cip·i·tan·cy \-ən-sē\ *n, pl* **-cies :** PRECIPITANCE

pre·cip·i·tant \-ənt\ *adj* **:** PRECIPITATE — **pre·cip·i·tant·ly** *adv* — **pre·cip·i·tant·ness** *n*

[1]**pre·cip·i·tate** \pri-ˈsip-ə-ˌtāt\ *vb* **1 a :** to throw violently : HURL **b :** to fall headlong **c :** to fall or come suddenly into some condition **2 a :** to move, urge, or press on with haste or violence **b :** to bring on abruptly ⟨the tactless remark *precipitated* a long, bitter quarrel⟩ **3 a :** to separate or cause to separate from solution or suspension **b :** to condense from a vapor and fall as rain or snow [Latin *praecipitare,* from *praecipit-, praeceps* "headlong"] — **pre·cip·i·ta·tor** \-ˌtāt-ər\ *n*

[2]**pre·cip·i·tate** \pri-ˈsip-ət-ət, -ə-ˌtāt\ *n* **:** a usually solid substance separated from a solution or suspension by chemical or physical change

[3]**pre·cip·i·tate** \pri-ˈsip-ət-ət\ *adj* **1 :** exhibiting violent or unwise speed ⟨a *precipitate* attack⟩ **2 :** falling, flowing, or rushing with steep descent — **pre·cip·i·tate·ly** *adv* — **pre·cip·i·tate·ness** *n*

pre·cip·i·ta·tion \pri-ˌsip-ə-ˈtā-shən\ *n* **1 :** the quality or state of being precipitate : HASTE **2 :** the process of precipitating or of forming a precipitate **3 a :** a deposit on the earth of hail, mist, rain, sleet, or snow; *also* **:** the quantity of water deposited **b :** PRECIPITATE

pre·cip·i·tin \pri-ˈsip-ət-ən\ *n* **:** an antibody that forms an insoluble precipitate when it unites with its antigen

pre·cip·i·tous \pri-ˈsip-ət-əs\ *adj* **1 :** HASTY 2, RASH ⟨a *precipitous* act⟩ **2 a :** very steep, perpendicular, or overhanging ⟨a *precipitous* slope⟩ **b :** having precipices ⟨a *precipitous* ledge⟩ ***synonyms*** see STEEP — **pre·cip·i·tous·ly** *adv* — **pre·cip·i·tous·ness** *n*

pré·cis \prā-ˈsē, ˈprā-ˌsē\ *n, pl* **pré·cis** \-ˈsēz, -ˌsēz\ **:** a concise summary of essential points, statements, or facts [French, from *précis* "precise"]

pre·cise \pri-ˈsīs\ *adj* **1 :** free from vagueness or inaccuracy **2 :** very exact : ACCURATE ⟨*precise* scales⟩ ⟨*precise* time of arrival⟩ **3 :** clear and sharp in enunciation : DISTINCT ⟨a low *precise* voice⟩ **4 :** strictly conforming to rule or convention ⟨*precise* habits⟩ **5 :** distinguished from every other ⟨at that *precise* moment⟩ [Medieval French *precis,* from Latin *praecisus,* past participle of *praecidere* "to cut off," from *prae-* "pre-" + *caedere* "to cut"] ***synonyms*** see CORRECT — **pre·cise·ly** *adv* — **pre·cise·ness** *n*

pre·ci·sian \pri-ˈsizh-ən\ *n* **:** a person who stresses or practices scrupulous adherence to a strict standard especially of religious observance or morality

[1]**pre·ci·sion** \pri-ˈsizh-ən\ *n* **:** the quality or state of being precise; *esp* **:** the degree of refinement with which an operation is performed or a measurement stated — **pre·ci·sion·ist** \-ˈsizh-nəst, -ə-nəst\ *n*

[2]**precision** *adj* **1 :** adapted for extremely accurate measurement or operation ⟨a *precision* gauge⟩ **2 :** marked by precision of execution ⟨a *precision* drill team⟩

pre·clin·i·cal \prē-ˈklin-i-kəl, ˈprē-\ *adj* **:** of or relating to the period preceding clinical manifestations ⟨*preclinical* infection⟩

pre·clude \pri-ˈklüd\ *vt* **:** to prevent or make impossible by acting, existing, or occurring beforehand [Latin *praecludere,* literally, "to shut out," from *prae-* "pre-" + *claudere* "to close"] — **pre·clu·sion** \-ˈklü-zhən\ *n* — **pre·clu·sive** \-ˈklü-siv, -ziv\ *adj* — **pre·clu·sive·ly** *adv*

pre·co·cial \pri-ˈkō-shəl\ *adj* **:** capable of a high degree of independent activity from birth ⟨*precocial* birds⟩ — compare ALTRICIAL

pre·co·cious \pri-ˈkō-shəs\ *adj* **1 :** exceptionally early in development or occurrence ⟨*precocious* behavior⟩ **2 :** exhibiting mature qualities at an unusually early age ⟨a *precocious* child⟩ [Latin *praecoc-, praecox* "early ripening, precocious," from *prae-* "pre-" + *coquere* "to cook"] — **pre·co·cious·ly** *adv* — **pre·co·cious·ness** *n* — **pre·coc·i·ty** \pri-ˈkäs-ət-ē\ *n*

pre·cog·ni·tion \ˌprē-käg-ˈnish-ən\ *n* **:** clairvoyance concerning something not yet experienced

pre·con·ceive \ˌprē-kən-ˈsēv\ *vt* **:** to form an opinion of prior to knowledge or experience ⟨*preconceived* ideas about foreigners⟩ — **pre·con·cep·tion** \-ˈsep-shən\ *n*

pre·con·cert·ed \ˌprē-kən-ˈsərt-əd\ *adj* **:** arranged or agreed upon in advance ⟨a *preconcerted* plan of attack⟩

pre·con·di·tion \ˌprē-kən-ˈdish-ən\ *vt* **:** to put in proper or desired condition or frame of mind in advance

pre·con·scious \prē-ˈkän-chəs, ˈprē-\ *adj* **:** not present in consciousness but capable of being readily recalled — **pre·con·scious·ly** *adv*

pre·cook \prē-ˈku̇k, ˈprē-\ *vt* **:** to cook partially or entirely in advance

pre·cur·sor \pri-ˈkər-sər, ˈprē-ˌ\ *n* **1 a :** one that precedes and indicates the approach of another : FORERUNNER **b :** PREDECESSOR 1 **2 :** a substance or cell from which another substance or cell is formed [Latin *praecursor,* from *praecurrere* "to run before," from *prae-* "pre-" + *currere* "to run"]

pre·cur·so·ry \pri-ˈkərs-rē, -ə-rē\ *adj* **:** having the character of a precursor : PRELIMINARY, PREMONITORY ⟨*precursory* symptoms of a fever⟩

pre·da·ceous *or* **pre·da·cious** \pri-ˈdā-shəs\ *adj* **:** living by preying on others : PREDATORY — **pre·da·ceous·ness** *n* — **pre·dac·i·ty** \-ˈdas-ət-ē\ *n*

pre·date \prē-ˈdāt, ˈprē-\ *vt* **:** ANTEDATE

pre·da·tion \pri-ˈdā-shən\ *n* **1 :** the act of preying or plundering : DEPREDATION **2 :** a mode of life in which food is primarily obtained by killing and consuming animals [Latin *praedatio,* from *praedari* "to prey upon," from *praeda* "prey"]

pred·a·tor \ˈpred-ət-ər\ *n* **1 :** one that preys, destroys, or devours **2 :** an animal that obtains food primarily by killing and consuming animals

pred·a·to·ry \ˈpred-ə-ˌtōr-ē, -ˌtȯr-\ *adj* **1 :** of, relating to, or marked by plundering ⟨*predatory* raids⟩ **2 :** living by predation : PREDACEOUS; *also* **:** adapted to predation — **pred·a·to·ri·ly** \ˌpred-ə-ˈtōr-ə-lē, -ˈtȯr-\ *adv*

pre·de·cease \ˌprēd-i-sēs\ *vb* **:** to die before another person

pre·de·ces·sor \ˈpred-ə-ˌses-ər, ˈprēd-\ *n* **1 :** one that precedes; *esp* **:** a person who has held a position or office before another **2** *archaic* **:** ANCESTOR 1 [Medieval French *predecesseur,* from Late Latin *praedecessor,* from Latin *prae-* "pre-" + *decessor* "retiring governor," from *decedere* "to depart, retire from office," from *de-* + *cedere* "to go"]

pre·des·ti·nate \prē-ˈdes-tə-ˌnāt\ *vt* **1 :** to foreordain to an earthly or eternal destiny by divine decree **2** *archaic* **:** PREDETERMINE 1b

pre·des·ti·na·tion \ˌprē-ˌdes-tə-ˈnā-shən\ *n* **:** the act of predestinating **:** the state of being predestinated

pre·des·tine \prē-ˈdes-tən, ˈprē-\ *vt* **:** to destine, decree, determine, appoint, or settle beforehand; *esp* **:** PREDESTINATE 1

pre·de·ter·mine \ˌprēd-i-ˈtər-mən\ *vt* **1 a :** FOREORDAIN, PREDESTINE **b :** to determine or settle beforehand ⟨meet at a *predetermined* place⟩ **2 :** to impose a direction or tendency on beforehand — **pre·de·ter·mi·na·tion** \-ˌtər-mə-ˈnā-shən\ *n*

pred·i·ca·ble \ˈpred-i-kə-bəl\ *adj* **:** capable of being predicated or affirmed

pre·dic·a·ment \pri-ˈdik-ə-mənt\ *n* **:** a difficult, perplexing, or trying situation **:** FIX [Late Latin *praedicamentum* "that which is predicated, category," from *praedicare* "to predicate"]

synonyms PREDICAMENT, DILEMMA, QUANDARY mean a difficult and perplexing situation. PREDICAMENT suggests a difficult situation offering no satisfactory solution ⟨appeared to be no way out of this awkward *predicament*⟩. DILEMMA implies the need to choose between two alternatives offering essentially equal advantages or disadvantages ⟨in a *dilemma* about a choice of careers⟩. QUANDARY stresses puzzlement and perplexity ⟨in a *quandary* as to what excuse to make⟩.

¹pred·i·cate \ˈpred-i-kət\ *n* **1 :** something that is affirmed or denied of the subject in a proposition in logic ⟨in "paper is white," whiteness is the *predicate*⟩ **2 :** the part of a sentence or clause that expresses what is said of the subject and that usually consists of a verb with or without objects, complements, or adverbial modifiers [Late Latin *praedicatum,* from *praedicare* "to assert, predicate"] — **pred·i·ca·tive** \ˈpred-i-kət-iv, ˈpred-ə-ˌkāt-\ *adj* — **pred·i·ca·tive·ly** *adv*

²predicate *adj* **:** belonging to the predicate; *esp* **:** completing the meaning of a linking verb ⟨*hot* in "the sun is hot" is a *predicate* adjective⟩ — compare ATTRIBUTIVE

³pred·i·cate \ˈpred-ə-ˌkāt\ *vt* **1 :** AFFIRM 1b, DECLARE **2 a :** to assert as a predicate in a proposition **b :** to assert to be a quality or property ⟨*predicate* sweetness of sugar⟩ **3 :** BASE, FOUND ⟨a proposal *predicated* upon the belief that sufficient support could be obtained⟩ [Late Latin *praedicare* "to assert, predicate, preach"]

predicate nominative *n* **:** a noun or pronoun in the nominative case completing the meaning of a linking verb

pred·i·ca·tion \ˌpred-ə-ˈkā-shən\ *n* **:** an act or instance of predicating; *esp* **:** the expression of action, state, or quality by a grammatical predicate

pre·dict \pri-ˈdikt\ *vt* **:** to declare in advance **:** foretell on the basis of observation, experience, or scientific reasoning [Latin *praedictus,* past participle of *praedicere* "to predict," from *prae-* "pre-" + *dicere* "to say"] ***synonyms*** see FORETELL — **pre·dict·able** \-ˈdik-tə-bəl\ *adj* — **pre·dict·ably** \-blē\ *adv*

pre·dic·tion \pri-ˈdik-shən\ *n* **1 :** an act of predicting **2 :** something that is predicted **:** FORECAST — **pre·dic·tive** \-ˈdik-tiv\ *adj* — **pre·dic·tive·ly** *adv*

pre·di·gest \ˌprēd-ī-ˈjest, ˌprēd-ə-\ *vt* **:** to subject to predigestion

pre·di·ges·tion \-ˈjes-chən, -ˈjesh-chən\ *n* **:** artificial or natural partial digestion of food ⟨enzymatic *predigestion*⟩

pre·di·lec·tion \ˌpred-l-ˈek-shən-, ˌprēd-\ *n* **:** an inclination in favor of something **:** PREFERENCE, PARTIALITY [French *prédilection,* from Medieval Latin *praediligere* "to prefer," from Latin *prae-* "pre-" + *diligere* "to love," from *dis-* "apart" + *legere* "to pick, choose"]

pre·dis·pose \ˌprēd-is-ˈpōz\ *vt* **:** to dispose in advance **:** make susceptible ⟨malnutrition *predisposes* one to certain diseases⟩ ***synonyms*** see INCLINE

pre·dis·po·si·tion \ˌprē-ˌdis-pə-ˈzish-ən\ *n* **:** a condition of being predisposed **:** INCLINATION

pre·dom·i·nance \pri-ˈdäm-ə-nəns\ *also* **pre·dom·i·nan·cy** \-nən-sē\ *n* **:** the quality or state of being predominant

pre·dom·i·nant \-nənt\ *adj* **:** having superior strength, influence, or authority ⟨the *predominant* color in a painting⟩ — **pre·dom·i·nant·ly** *adv*

pre·dom·i·nate \pri-ˈdäm-ə-ˌnāt\ *vb* **1 :** to exert controlling power or influence **:** PREVAIL **2 :** to hold advantage in numbers or quantity — **pre·dom·i·na·tion** \-ˌdäm-ə-ˈnā-shən\ *n*

pre·em·i·nence \prē-ˈem-ə-nəns\ *n* **:** the quality or state of being preeminent **:** SUPERIORITY

pre·em·i·nent \-nənt\ *adj* **:** of the highest rank, dignity, or importance **:** OUTSTANDING — **pre·em·i·nent·ly** *adv*

pre·empt \prē-ˈemt, -ˈempt\ *vt* **1 :** to settle upon (as public land) with the right to purchase before others; *also* **:** to take by such a right **2 :** to take before someone else can ⟨*preempt* a seat at the stadium⟩ [back-formation from *preemption,* from Medieval Latin *praeemptus,* past participle of *praeemere* "to buy before," from Latin *prae-* "pre-" + *emere* "to buy"] — **pre·emp·tion** \-ˈem-shən, -ˈemp-\ *n* — **pre·emp·tive** \-ˈem-tiv, -ˈemp-\ *adj* — **pre·emp·tive·ly** *adv* — **pre·emp·tor** \-tər\ *n*

preen \ˈprēn\ *vb* **1 :** to groom with the bill ⟨a bird *preening* its feathers⟩ **2 :** to dress or smooth oneself up **:** PRIMP **3 :** to indulge oneself in pride **:** congratulate oneself **:** GLOAT [Middle English *prenen,* alteration of *proynen, prunen,* from Medieval French *puroindre, proindre,* from *pur-* "thoroughly" + *uindre, oindre* "to anoint, rub," from Latin *unguere*] — **preen·er** *n*

pre·ex·ist \ˌprē-ig-ˈzist\ *vb* **:** to exist earlier or before something

pre·ex·ist·ence \-ˈzis-təns\ *n* **:** existence in a former state or previous to something else; *esp* **:** existence of the soul before its union with the body — **pre·ex·ist·ent** \-tənt\ *adj*

pre·fab \prē-ˈfab, ˈprē-ˌ\ *n* **:** a prefabricated structure — **prefab** *adj*

pre·fab·ri·cate \prē-ˈfab-ri-ˌkāt, ˈprē-\ *vt* **1 :** to make the parts of at a factory so that construction consists mainly of assembling and uniting standardized parts **2 :** to produce artificially — **pre·fab·ri·ca·tion** \ˌprē-ˌfab-ri-ˈkā-shən\ *n*

¹pref·ace \ˈpref-əs\ *n* **1** *often cap* **:** a prayer introducing the central part of the eucharistic service **2 :** the introductory remarks of a speaker or author **:** PROLOGUE [Medieval French, from Latin *prefatio* "foreword," from *praefari* "to say beforehand," from *prae-* "pre-" + *fari* "to say"]

²preface *vb* **1 :** to say or write as a preface ⟨a note *prefaced* to the manuscript⟩ **2 :** PRECEDE 2, HERALD **3 :** to introduce by or begin with a preface **4 :** to locate in front of **5 :** to be a preliminary to — **pref·ac·er** *n*

pref·a·to·ri·al \ˌpref-ə-ˈtōr-ē-əl, -ˈtȯr-\ *adj* **:** PREFATORY — **pref·a·to·ri·al·ly** \-ē-ə-lē\ *adv*

pref·a·to·ry \ˈpref-ə-ˌtōr-ē, -ˌtȯr-\ *adj* **:** of, relating to, or constituting a preface ⟨*prefatory* remarks⟩

pre·fect \ˈprē-ˌfekt\ *n* **1 :** a high official or magistrate (as of ancient Rome or France) **2 :** a presiding or chief officer or magistrate **3 :** a student monitor in a private school [Medieval French, from Latin *praefectus,* from *praeficere* "to place at the head of," from *prae-* "pre-" + *facere* "to make"]

prefect apostolic *n* **:** a Roman Catholic priest functioning like a bishop over a district of a missionary territory

pre·fec·ture \ˈprē-ˌfek-chər\ *n* **1 :** the office or term of office of a prefect **2 :** the district governed by a prefect — **pre·fec·tur·al** \prē-ˈfek-chə-rəl\ *adj*

pre·fer \pri-ˈfər\ *vt* **pre·ferred; pre·fer·ring 1 :** to choose or like above another ⟨*prefer* dark clothes⟩ **2** *archaic* **:** to put or set forward or before someone **:** RECOMMEND **3 :** to present for action or consideration ⟨*prefer* charges against a person⟩ [Medieval French *preferer,* from Latin *praeferre* "to put before, prefer," from *prae-* "pre-" + *ferre* "to carry"] — **pre·fer·rer** *n*

pref·er·a·ble \ˈpref-rə-bəl, -ə-rə-; ˈpref-ər-bəl\ *adj* **:** worthy to be preferred **:** more desirable — **pref·er·a·bil·i·ty** \ˌpref-rə-ˈbil-ət-ē, -ə-rə-\ *n* — **pref·er·a·ble·ness** \ˈpref-rə-bəl-nəs, -ə-rə-; -ər-bəl-nəs\ *n* — **pref·er·a·bly** \-blē\ *adv*

\ə\ **a**but	\au̇\ **ou**t	\i\ t**i**p	\ȯ\ s**aw**	\u̇\ f**oo**t
\ər\ furth**er**	\ch\ **ch**in	\ī\ l**i**fe	\ȯi\ c**oi**n	\y\ **y**et
\a\ m**a**t	\e\ p**e**t	\j\ **j**ob	\th\ **th**in	\yü\ f**ew**
\ā\ t**a**ke	\ē\ **ea**sy	\ng\ si**ng**	\t͟h\ **th**is	\yu̇\ c**u**re
\ä\ c**o**t, c**ar**t	\g\ **g**o	\ō\ b**o**ne	\ü\ f**oo**d	\zh\ vi**si**on

pref•er•ence \ˈpref-ərns; ˈpref-rəns, -ə-rəns\ *n* **1 a :** the act of preferring **:** the state of being preferred **b :** the power or opportunity of choosing ⟨gave us our *preference*⟩ **2 :** one that is preferred **:** FAVORITE, CHOICE **3 :** the act, fact, or principle of giving advantages to some over others ⟨show *preference*⟩ [Medieval French *préférence,* from Medieval Latin *praeferentia,* from Latin *praeferre* "to prefer"] ***synonyms*** see CHOICE

pref•er•en•tial \ˌpref-ə-ˈren-chəl\ *adj* **1 :** showing preference ⟨*preferential* treatment⟩ **2 :** creating or using preference ⟨a *preferential* tariff⟩ **3 :** permitting the showing of preference or order of choice (as of candidates in an election) ⟨a *preferential* ballot⟩ **4 :** giving preference in hiring to union members ⟨a *preferential* shop⟩ — **pref•er•en•tial•ly** \-ˈrench-lē, -ə-lē\ *adv*

pre•fer•ment \pri-ˈfər-mənt\ *n* **1 a :** advancement or promotion in dignity, office, or station **b :** a position or office of honor or profit **2 :** the act of bringing forward (as charges)

preferred stock *n* **:** stock guaranteed priority by a corporation's charter over common stock in the payment of dividends and usually in the distribution of assets

pre•fig•ure \prē-ˈfig-yər, ˈprē-, *especially British* -ˈfig-ər\ *vt* **1 :** to show, suggest, or announce by an earlier type, image, or likeness ⟨other religions *prefigured* the Christian Easter⟩ **2 :** to picture or imagine beforehand **:** FORESEE ⟨*prefigure* the outcome of a ball game⟩ — **pre•fig•u•ra•tion** \prē-ˌfig-yə-ˈrā-shən, -ˌfig-ə-\ *n* — **pre•fig•u•ra•tive** \prē-ˈfig-yə-rət-iv, ˈprē-, -ˈfig-ə-; -ˈfig-yərt-iv, -ərt-\ *adj* — **pre•fig•u•ra•tive•ly** *adv* — **pre•fig•u•ra•tive•ness** *n* — **pre•fig•ure•ment** \prē-ˈfig-yər-mənt, ˈprē-, *especially British* -ˈfig-ər-\ *n*

[1]**pre•fix** *vt* **1** \prē-ˈfiks, ˈprē-\ *archaic* **:** to fix or appoint beforehand **2** \ˈprē-ˌ, prē-ˈ\ **:** to place in front **:** add as a prefix ⟨*prefix* a syllable to a word⟩

[2]**pre•fix** \ˈprē-ˌfiks\ *n* **:** a sound or sequence of sounds or a letter or sequence of letters occurring as a bound form attached to the beginning of a word and serving to produce a derivative word [New Latin *praefixum,* from Latin *praefixus,* past participle of *praefigere* "to fasten before," from *prae-* "pre-" + *figere* "to fasten"] — **pre•fix•al** \ˈprē-ˌfik-səl, prē-ˈ\ *adj* — **pre•fix•al•ly** \-sə-lē\ *adv*

pre•flight \ˈprē-ˈflīt\ *adj* **:** preparing for or preliminary to flight ⟨*preflight* training⟩

pre•form \ˈprē-ˈfȯrm\ *vt* **:** to form or shape beforehand

pre•for•ma•tion \ˌprē-fȯr-ˈmā-shən\ *n* **1 :** previous formation **2 :** a discredited biological theory holding that every germ cell contains the organism of its kind fully formed and that development consists merely in increase in size — **pre•for•ma•tion•ist** \-shə-nəst\ *n*

pre•fron•tal \prē-ˈfrənt-l, ˈprē-\ *adj* **:** anterior to or involving the anterior part of a frontal structure ⟨a *prefrontal* bone⟩

prefrontal cortex *n* **:** the gray matter of the front part of the frontal lobe that is highly developed in humans and plays a role in the regulation of complex intellectual, emotional, and behavioral functioning

pre•gan•gli•on•ic \ˌprē-ˌgang-glē-ˈän-ik\ *adj* **:** situated proximal to or preceding a ganglion; *also* **:** of, relating to, or being an axon passing from the central nervous system into an autonomic ganglion

preg•na•ble \ˈpreg-nə-bəl\ *adj* **:** capable of being taken or captured **:** VULNERABLE ⟨a *pregnable* fort⟩ [Medieval French *prenable,* from *prendre* "to take," from Latin *prehendere*] — **preg•na•bil•i•ty** \ˌpreg-nə-ˈbil-ət-ē\ *n*

preg•nan•cy \ˈpreg-nən-sē\ *n, pl* **-cies :** the condition or quality of being pregnant **:** GESTATION

preg•nant \ˈpreg-nənt\ *adj* **1 :** abounding in fancy, wit, or resourcefulness **:** INVENTIVE ⟨a *pregnant* mind⟩ **2 :** rich in significance or implication **:** MEANINGFUL ⟨a *pregnant* pause⟩ **3 :** containing a developing embryo, fetus, or unborn offspring within the body **4 :** having possibilities of development or consequence **:** MOMENTOUS ⟨*pregnant* years⟩ **5 :** FULL, TEEMING ⟨nature was *pregnant* with life⟩ [Latin *praegnans,* alteration of *praegnas*] — **preg•nant•ly** *adv*

pre•heat \prē-ˈhēt, ˈprē-\ *vb* **:** to heat beforehand; *esp* **:** to heat (an oven) to a designated temperature before using for cooking — **pre•heat•er** *n*

pre•hen•sile \prē-ˈhen-səl\ *adj* **:** adapted for grasping especially by wrapping around ⟨a *prehensile* tail⟩ [French *préhensile,* from Latin *prehensus,* past participle of *prehendere* "to grasp, take"]

pre•hen•sion \-ˈhen-chən\ *n* **:** the act of taking hold, seizing, or grasping

pre–His•pan•ic \ˌprē-is-ˈpan-ik, -his-\ *adj* **:** of, relating to, or being the time prior to Spanish conquests in the western hemisphere

pre•his•tor•ic \ˌprē-is-ˈtȯr-ik, -his-, -ˈtär-\ *adj* **:** of, relating to, or existing in times before written history — **pre•his•tor•i•cal** \-i-kəl\ *adj* — **pre•his•tor•i•cal•ly** \-i-kə-lē, -klē\ *adv*

pre•his•to•ry \prē-ˈhis-tə-rē, ˈprē-, -trē\ *n* **1 :** the study of prehistoric humans **2 :** a history of what leads up to an event or situation — **pre•his•to•ri•an** \ˌprē-is-ˈtōr-ē-ən, -his-, -ˈtȯr-\ *n*

pre•hu•man \ˈprē-ˈhyü-mən, -ˈyü-\ *n* **:** an extinct primate and especially an extinct hominid that resembles or is ancestral to humans — **prehuman** *adj*

pre•judge \prē-ˈjəj, ˈprē-\ *vt* **:** to judge before hearing or before full and sufficient examination — **pre•judg•ment** \-ˈjəj-mənt\ *n*

[1]**prej•u•dice** \ˈprej-əd-əs\ *n* **1 :** injury resulting from an unfair judgment or action of another; *esp* **:** an infringing of one's legal rights **2 a** (1) **:** a judgment or opinion formed before considering or without knowing the facts (2) **:** a favoring or dislike of something without grounds or before sufficient knowledge **b :** an irrational attitude of hostility directed against an individual, a group, or a race [Medieval French, from Latin *praejudicium* "previous judgment, damage," from *prae-* "pre-" + *judicium* "judgment"]

synonyms PREJUDICE, BIAS mean an attitude that predisposes one to favor or dislike something. PREJUDICE implies usually but not always an unfavorable view or fixed dislike and suggests a feeling rooted in suspicion, fear, or intolerance ⟨a mindless *prejudice* against the unfamiliar⟩. BIAS implies partiality or distortion of individual judgments in favor of or against persons or things of a particular kind or class ⟨a strong *bias* toward abstract art⟩.

[2]**prejudice** *vt* **1 :** to injure by an unfair judgment or action **2 :** to cause to have predjudice **:** BIAS ⟨the incident *prejudiced* them against me⟩

prej•u•di•cial \ˌprej-ə-ˈdish-əl\ *adj* **1 :** tending to injure or impair **:** DETRIMENTAL **2 :** leading to premature judgment or unwarranted opinion — **prej•u•di•cial•ly** \-ˈdish-lē, -ə-lē\ *adv* — **prej•u•di•cial•ness** \-ˈdish-əl-nəs\ *n*

prej•u•di•cious \ˌprej-ə-ˈdish-əs\ *adj* **:** PREJUDICIAL — **prej•u•di•cious•ly** *adv*

prel•a•cy \ˈprel-ə-sē\ *n, pl* **-cies 1 :** the office or dignity of a prelate **2 :** church government by prelates

prel•ate \ˈprel-ət\ *n* **:** a high-ranking clergyman (as a bishop) [Medieval French *prelat,* from Medieval Latin *praelatus,* literally, "one receiving preferment," from Latin, past participle of *praeferre* "to prefer"]

pre•lim \ˈprē-ˌlim, pri-ˈ\ *n or adj* **:** PRELIMINARY

[1]**pre•lim•i•nary** \pri-ˈlim-ə-ˌner-ē\ *n, pl* **-nar•ies :** something that precedes or is introductory or preparatory: as **a :** a preliminary scholastic examination ⟨pass the *preliminaries*⟩ **b :** a minor match preceding the main event [French *préliminaires,* pl., from Medieval Latin *praeliminaris,* adj., "preliminary," from Latin *prae-* "pre-" + *limin-, limen* "threshold"]

[2]**preliminary** *adj* **:** coming before the main part **:** INTRODUCTORY — **pre•lim•i•nar•i•ly** \-ˌlim-ə-ˈner-ə-lē\ *adv*

pre•lit•er•ate \prē-ˈlit-ə-rət, ˈprē-, -ˈli-trət\ *adj* **1 :** not yet using writing as a cultural medium **2 :** lacking the use of writing

[1]**pre•lude** \ˈprel-ˌyüd, ˈprā-ˌlüd\ *n* **1 :** an introductory performance, action, or event preceding and preparing for a principal matter **:** INTRODUCTION ⟨the wind was a *prelude* to the storm⟩ **2 a :** a musical movement introducing the chief subject (as of a fugue) or serving as an introduction to an opera or oratorio **b :** a short musical piece (as an organ solo) played at the beginning of a church service **c :** a separate concert piece usually for piano or orchestra and based entirely on a short motif [Middle French, from Medieval Latin *praeludium,* from Latin *praeludere* "to play beforehand," from *prae-* "pre-" + *ludere* "to play"]

[2]**prelude** *vb* **1 :** to give, play, or serve as a prelude; *esp* **:** to play a musical introduction **2 :** FORESHADOW ⟨the gray dawn *preluded* a gloomy day⟩ — **pre•lud•er** *n*

pre•man \ˈprē-ˈman\ *n* **:** PREHUMAN

pre•ma•ture \ˌprē-mə-ˈtu̇r, -ˈtyu̇r, -ˈchu̇r\ *adj* **:** happening, arriving, existing, or performed before the proper or usual time; *esp* **:** born after a gestation period of less than 37 weeks ⟨*premature* babies⟩ — **premature** *n* — **pre•ma•ture•ly** *adv* — **pre•ma•tu•ri•ty** \-ˈtu̇r-ət-ē, -ˈtyu̇r-, -ˈchu̇r-\ *n*

[1]**pre•med** \ˈprē-ˈmed\ *adj* **:** PREMEDICAL

[2]**premed** *n* **:** a premedical student or course of study

pre·med·i·cal \prē-ˈmed-i-kəl, ˈprē-\ *adj* : preceding and preparing for the professional study of medicine

pre·med·i·tate \pri-ˈmed-ə-ˌtāt, ˈprē-\ *vt* : to think about and plan beforehand ⟨*premeditate* murder⟩ — **pre·med·i·tat·ed·ly** \-ˌtāt-əd-lē\ *adv* — **pre·med·i·ta·tion** \pri-ˌmed-ə-ˈtā-shən, ˌprē-\ *n*

pre·men·stru·al \prē-ˈmen-strə-wəl, ˈprē-, -strəl\ *adj* : of, relating to, occurring in, or being the time period just preceding menstruation ⟨*premenstrual* symptoms⟩ — **pre·men·stru·al·ly** *adv*

premenstrual syndrome *n* : a varying group of symptoms manifested by some women prior to menstruation that may include irritability, insomnia, fatigue, anxiety, depression, headache, edema, and abdominal pain — called also *PMS*

¹pre·mier \pri-ˈmiər, -ˈmyiər; ˈprē-mē-ər, ˈprem-ē-\ *adj* **1** : first in position, rank, or importance : PRINCIPAL **2** : first in time : EARLIEST [Medieval French, *primer, primier* "first, chief," from Latin *primarius* "of the first rank," from *primus* "first"]

²premier *n* : the chief minister and head of government : PRIME MINISTER [French, from *premier,* adjective, from Medieval French] — **pre·mier·ship** \-ˌship\ *n*

¹pre·miere \pri-ˈmyeər, -ˈmiər\ *adj* : most eminent ⟨the nation's *premiere* author⟩ [alteration of ¹*premier*]

²premiere *n* : a first performance or exhibition ⟨the *premiere* of a play⟩ [French *première,* from *premier* "first"]

³premiere *vb* : to present or appear in a first public performance

¹prem·ise \ˈprem-əs\ *n* **1** : a proposition assumed as a basis of argument or inference; *esp* : either of the first two propositions of a syllogism from which the conclusion is drawn **2** *pl* : matters previously stated **3** *pl* **a** : a tract of land with the buildings thereon **b** : a building or part of a building usually with its grounds [Medieval Latin *praemissa,* from Latin *praemittere* "to place ahead," from *prae-* "pre-" + *mittere* "to send"; sense 3 from its being identified in the premises of the deed]

²premise *vt* **1** : to set forth beforehand as introductory or as postulated : POSTULATE **2** : to offer as a premise in an argument

¹pre·mi·um \ˈprē-mē-əm\ *n* **1 a** : a reward or recompense for a particular act **b** : a sum over and above a regular price or a face or par value **c** : something given free or at a reduced price with a purchase **2** : the amount paid for a contract of insurance **3** : a high value or a value in excess of that normally or usually expected ⟨put a *premium* on accuracy⟩ [Latin *praemium* "booty, profit, reward," from *prae-* "pre-" + *emere* "to take, buy"] — **at a premium** : usually valuable because of demand ⟨housing was *at a premium*⟩

²premium *adj* : of exceptional quality, value, or price

pre·mix \prē-ˈmiks, ˈprē-\ *vb* : to mix before use

pre·mo·lar \prē-ˈmō-lər, ˈprē-\ *n* : any of the double-pointed grinding teeth which occur between the true molars and the canines and of which in humans there are two on each side of each jaw — compare BICUSPID — **premolar** *adj*

pre·mo·ni·tion \ˌprē-mə-ˈnish-ən, ˌprem-ə-\ *n* **1** : previous warning or notice **2** : anticipation of an event without conscious reason : PRESENTIMENT [Medieval French *premunition,* from Late Latin *praemonitio,* from Latin *praemonēre* "to warn in advance," from *prae-* "pre-" + *monēre* "to warn"] — **pre·mon·i·to·ry** \prē-ˈmän-ə-ˌtōr-ē, -ˌtȯr-\ *adj*

pre·name \ˈprē-ˌnām\ *n* : FORENAME

pre·na·tal \prē-ˈnāt-l, ˈprē-\ *adj* : occurring or existing before birth ⟨*prenatal* care⟩ — **pre·na·tal·ly** \-l-ē\ *adv*

pren·tice \ˈprent-əs\ *n* : APPRENTICE 1, LEARNER — **prentice** *adj*

pre·oc·cu·pied \prē-ˈäk-yə-ˌpīd\ *adj* **1** : lost in thought ⟨too much *preoccupied* to notice⟩ **2** : already occupied

pre·oc·cu·py *vt* **-pied; -py·ing** **1** \prē-ˈäk-yə-ˌpī\ : to engage or absorb the attention of beforehand **2** \prē-, ˈprē-\ : to take possession of or fill beforehand or before another — **pre·oc·cu·pa·tion** \prē-ˌäk-yə-ˈpā-shən\ *n*

pre·op·er·a·tive \prē-ˈäp-rət-iv, ˈprē-, -ˈäp-ə-rət-, -ˈäp-ə-ˌrāt-\ *adj* : occurring before a surgical operation — **pre·op·er·a·tive·ly** *adv*

pre·or·dain \ˌprē-ȯr-ˈdān\ *vt* : to decree in advance : FOREORDAIN — **pre·or·di·na·tion** \prē-ˌȯrd-n-ˈā-shən\ *n*

¹prep \ˈprep\ *n* : PREPARATORY SCHOOL

²prep *vb* **prepped; prep·ping** **1** : to engage in preparatory study or training **2** : to get ready : PREPARE ⟨*prepped* the patient for the operation⟩

prep·a·ra·tion \ˌprep-ə-ˈrā-shən\ *n* **1** : the action or process of getting something ready (as for use or service) or of getting ready for some occasion, test, or duty **2** : a state of being prepared **3** : a preparatory act or measure **4** : something that is prepared; *esp* : a medicinal material made ready for use

pre·par·a·to·ry \pri-ˈpar-ə-ˌtōr-ē, -ˌtȯr-\ *adj* : preparing or serving to prepare for something : INTRODUCTORY — **pre·par·a·to·ri·ly** \-ˌpar-ə-ˈtōr-ə-lē, -ˈtȯr-\ *adv*

preparatory school *n* **1** : a usually private school preparing students primarily for college **2** *British* : a private elementary school preparing students primarily for public schools

pre·pare \pri-ˈpaər, -ˈpeər\ *vb* **1** : to make or get ready ⟨*prepared* them for the shocking news⟩ ⟨*prepare* for a test⟩ **2** : to put together : COMPOUND ⟨*prepare* a vaccine⟩ ⟨*prepare* a prescription⟩ [Medieval French *preparer,* from Latin *praeparare,* from *prae-* "pre-" + *parare* "to procure, prepare"] — **pre·par·er** *n*

pre·par·ed·ness \pri-ˈpar-əd-nəs, -ˈper-; -ˈpaərd-nəs, -ˈpeərd-\ *n* : the quality or state of being prepared

pre·pay \prē-ˈpā, ˈprē-\ *vt* **pre·paid** \-ˈpād\; **pre·pay·ing** : to pay or pay for in advance — **pre·pay·ment** \-ˈpā-mənt\ *n*

pre·pon·der·ance \pri-ˈpän-də-rəns, -drəns\ *n* **1** : a superiority in weight or in power, importance, or strength ⟨the *preponderance* of the evidence⟩ **2** : a superiority or excess in number or quantity ⟨the *preponderance* of lawyers in the legislature⟩

pre·pon·der·ant \pri-ˈpän-də-rənt, -drənt\ *adj* **1** : outweighing others : PREDOMINANT **2** : having greater frequency or prevalence — **pre·pon·der·ant·ly** *adv*

pre·pon·der·ate \pri-ˈpän-də-ˌrāt\ *vi* **1** : to exceed in weight, power, or importance : PREDOMINATE **2** : to exceed in numbers [Latin *praeponderare,* literally, "to outweigh," from *prae-* "pre-" + *ponder-, pondus* "weight"] — **pre·pon·der·a·tion** \-ˌpän-də-ˈrā-shən\ *n*

prep·o·si·tion \ˌprep-ə-ˈzish-ən\ *n* : a linguistic form that combines with a noun, pronoun, or nominal to form a phrase that typically has an adverbial, adjectival, or substantival relation to some other word [Latin *praepositio,* from *praeponere* "to put in front," from *prae* "pre-" + *ponere* "to put, place"] — **prep·o·si·tion·al** \-ˈzish-nəl, -ən-l\ *adj* — **prep·o·si·tion·al·ly** \-ē\ *adv*

pre·pos·sess \ˌprē-pə-ˈzes\ *vt* **1** : to cause to be preoccupied (as with an idea or belief) **2** : to influence beforehand; *esp* : to move to a favorable opinion beforehand

pre·pos·sess·ing *adj* : tending to create a favorable impression : ATTRACTIVE ⟨a *prepossessing* appearance⟩ — **pre·pos·sess·ing·ly** \-ing-lē\ *adv* — **pre·pos·sess·ing·ness** *n*

pre·pos·ses·sion \ˌprē-pə-ˈzesh-ən\ *n* **1** : an attitude, belief, or impression formed beforehand : PREJUDICE **2** : an exclusive concern with one idea or object

pre·pos·ter·ous \pri-ˈpäs-tə-rəs, -trəs\ *adj* : contrary to nature, reason, or common sense : ABSURD [Latin *praeposterus,* literally, "with the back part in front," from *prae-* "pre-" + *posterus* "hinder, posterior"] — **pre·pos·ter·ous·ly** *adv* — **pre·pos·ter·ous·ness** *n*

pre·po·tent \prē-ˈpōt-nt, ˈprē-\ *adj* : having an unusual ability to transmit characters to offspring ⟨a *prepotent* sire⟩ — **pre·po·ten·cy** \-n-sē\ *n*

prep school *n* : PREPARATORY SCHOOL

pre·pu·ber·ty \-ˈpyü-bərt-ē\ *n* : the period of development immediately preceding puberty — **pre·pu·ber·tal** \-bərt-l\ *adj*

pre·puce \ˈprē-ˌpyüs\ *n* : FORESKIN; *also* : a similar fold of skin investing the clitoris [Medieval French, from Latin *praeputium*] — **pre·pu·tial** \prē-ˈpyü-shəl\ *n*

pre·re·cord·ed \ˌprē-ri-ˈkȯrd-əd\ *adj* : recorded in advance of presentation or use ⟨a *prerecorded* television program⟩

pre·reg·is·tra·tion \ˌprē-ˌrej-ə-ˈstrā-shən\ *n* : a special registration prior to an official registration period ⟨preregistration for spring semester courses⟩; *also* : a registration prior to an event, activity or program ⟨*preregistration* for basketball was held last month⟩ — **pre·reg·is·ter** *vb*

pre·req·ui·site \prē-ˈrek-wə-zət, ˈprē-\ *n* : something that is required beforehand or is necessary as a preliminary to something else ⟨the course is a *prerequisite* for more advanced study⟩ — **prerequisite** *adj*

pre·rog·a·tive \pri-ˈräg-ət-iv\ *n* : a special privilege or advantage; *esp* : a right attached to an office, rank, or status ⟨a royal *prerogative*⟩ [Latin *praerogativa* "Roman century voting first in the assembly, privilege," from *praerogativus* "voting first," from *praerogare* "to ask for an opinion before another," from *prae-* "pre-" + *rogare* "to ask"]

[1]**pres·age** \ˈpres-ij\ *n* **1** : something that foreshadows or portends a future event : OMEN **2** : FOREBODING, PRESENTIMENT [Latin *praesagium,* from *praesagus* "having a foreboding," from *prae-* "pre-" + *sagus* "prophetic"] — **pre·sage·ful** \pri-ˈsāj-fəl\ *adj*

[2]**pre·sage** \ˈpres-ij, pri-ˈsāj\ *vt* **1** : to give an omen or warning of : FORESHADOW, PORTEND **2** : FORETELL, PREDICT

pre·sanc·ti·fied \prē-ˈsang-ti-ˌfīd, ˈprē-, -ˈsangk-\ *adj* : consecrated at a previous service — used of eucharistic elements

pres·by·o·pia \ˌprez-bē-ˈō-pē-ə, ˌpres-\ *n* : a visual condition usually beginning in middle age in which loss of elasticity of the lens of the eye causes defective accommodation and inability to focus sharply for near vision [Greek *presbys* "old man"] — **pres·by·opic** \-ˈō-pik, -ˈäp-ik\ *adj or n*

pres·by·ter \ˈprez-bət-ər, ˈpres-\ *n* **1** : a member of the governing body of an early Christian church **2** : a Christian priest [Late Latin, "elder, priest," from Greek *presbyteros,* from *presbys* "old man"] — **pres·byt·er·ate** \prez-ˈbit-ə-rət, pres-\ *n*

Pres·by·te·ri·an \ˌprez-bə-ˈtir-ē-ən, ˌpres-\ *adj* **1** *often not cap* : characterized by a system of representative governing councils of ministers and elders **2** : of, relating to, or constituting a Protestant Christian church that is presbyterian in government and traditionally Calvinistic in doctrine — **Presbyterian** *n* — **Pres·by·te·ri·an·ism** \-ē-ə-ˌniz-əm\ *n*

pres·by·tery \ˈprez-bə-ˌter-ē, ˈpres-\ *n, pl* **-ter·ies** **1** : the part of a church reserved for the officiating clergy **2** : a ruling body in presbyterian churches consisting of the ministers and representative elders from congregations within a district **3** : the territorial jurisdiction of a presbytery

[1]**pre·school** \ˈprē-ˌskül\ *adj* : of, relating to, or being the period in a child's life from infancy to the age of five or six

[2]**preschool** *n* : NURSERY SCHOOL

pre·science \ˈprēsh-əns, ˈpresh-, -ē-əns\ *n* : foreknowledge of events: **a** : omniscience with regard to the future **b** : FORESIGHT 1 [Late Latin *praescientia,* from Latin *praescire* "to know beforehand," from *prae-* "pre"- + *scire* "to know"] — **prescient** \-ənt\ *adj* — **pre·scient·ly** *adv*

pre·scribe \pri-ˈskrīb\ *vb* **1 a** : to lay down as a guide, direction, or rule of action : ORDAIN ⟨*prescribe* a way of life⟩ **b** : to specify with authority ⟨*prescribed* the courses for freshmen⟩ **2** : to order or direct the use of something as a remedy ⟨the doctor *prescribed* an antibiotic⟩ [Latin *praescribere* "to write at the beginning, dictate, order," from *prae-* "pre-" + *scribere* "to write"] — **pre·scrib·er** *n*

pre·script \ˈprē-ˌskript\ *n* : something prescribed — **prescript** *adj*

pre·scrip·tion \pri-ˈskrip-shən\ *n* **1 a** : the establishment of a claim of title to something usually by use and enjoyment for a fixed period **b** : the right or title acquired by possession **2** : the action of laying down authoritative rules or directions **3 a** : a written direction or order for the preparation and use of a medicine **b** : a medicine prescribed [Latin *praescriptio* "writing at the beginning, order," from *praescriptus,* past participle of *praescribere* "to write at the beginning, order"] — **pre·scrip·tive** \-ˈskrip-tiv\ *adj* — **pre·scrip·tive·ly** *adv*

pre·se·lect \ˌprē-sə-ˈlekt\ *vt* : to choose in advance usually on the basis of a particular criterion — **pre·se·lec·tion** \-ˈlek-shən\ *n*

pres·ence \ˈprez-ns\ *n* **1** : the fact or condition of being present ⟨no one noticed my *presence*⟩ **2 a** : the part of space within one's immediate vicinity ⟨felt awkward in their *presence*⟩ **b** : the neighborhood of one of superior and especially royal rank **3** : one that is present ⟨an influential *presence* in the group⟩ **4** : the bearing or air of a person; *esp* : stately or distinguished bearing **5** : something (as a spirit) felt to be present

presence chamber *n* : the room where a dignitary receives those entitled to come into his or her presence

presence of mind : self-control in an emergency such that one can say and do the right thing

[1]**pres·ent** \ˈprez-nt\ *n* : something presented : GIFT [Medieval French, from *presenter,* "to present," from Latin *praesentare*]

[2]**pre·sent** \pri-ˈzent\ *vt* **1 a** : to bring or introduce into the presence of someone; *esp* : to introduce socially **b** : to bring (as a play) before the public **2** : to make a gift to **3** : to give or bestow formally **4** : to lay (a charge) against a person **5** : to offer to view : DISPLAY, SHOW **6** : to aim, point, or direct (as a weapon) so as to face something or in a particular direction [Medieval French *presenter,* from Latin *praesentare,* from *praesens,* adj., "present"] ***synonyms*** see GIVE — **pre·sent·er** *n*

[3]**pres·ent** \ˈprez-nt\ *adj* **1** : now existing or in progress **2 a** : being in view or at hand **b** : existing in something mentioned or under consideration **3** : of, relating to, or being a verb tense that expresses present time or the time of speaking [Medieval French, from Latin *praesens,* from *praeesse* "to be before one," from *prae-* "pre-" + *esse* "to be"]

[4]**pres·ent** \ˈprez-nt\ *n* **1** *pl* : the present words or statements; *also* : the document in which these words are used ⟨know all men by these *presents*⟩ **2 a** : PRESENT TENSE **b** : a verb form in the present tense **3** : the present time

pre·sent·able \pri-ˈzent-ə-bəl\ *adj* **1** : capable of being presented ⟨whipped the speech into *presentable* form⟩ **2** : being in condition to be seen or inspected especially by the critical ⟨made the room *presentable*⟩ — **pre·sent·abil·i·ty** \-ˌzent-ə-ˈbil-ət-ē\ *n* — **pre·sent·able·ness** \-ˈzent-ə-bəl-nəs\ *n* — **pre·sent·ably** \-blē\ *adv*

pre·sen·ta·tion \ˌprē-ˌzen-ˈtā-shən, ˌprez-n-\ *n* **1** : the act of presenting **2** : something presented: as **a** : something offered or given : GIFT **b** : something set forth for one's attention **3** : the position in which the fetus lies in the uterus in labor with respect to the opening through which it passes in birth — **pre·sen·ta·tion·al** \-shnəl, -shən-l\ *adj*

pres·ent–day \ˌprez-nt-ˌdā\ *adj* : now existing or occurring

pre·sen·ti·ment \pri-ˈzent-ə-mənt\ *n* : a feeling that something will or is about to happen : PREMONITION [French *pressentiment,* from *pressentir* "to have a presentiment," from Latin *praesentire* "to feel beforehand," from *prae-* "pre-" + *sentire* "to feel"]

pres·ent·ly \ˈprez-nt-lē\ *adv* **1** *archaic* : at once **2** : before long : SOON ⟨*presently* they arrived⟩ **3** : at the present time : NOW ⟨*presently* we have none⟩

usage Both the sense of *presently* meaning "before long" and the sense meaning "now" are currently flourishing, though objections are often made to the second sense. Since this sense has been in continuous use since the 15th century, the reason it is objectionable is not entirely clear. Both are standard, the "now" sense most common in contexts relating to business and politics.

pre·sent·ment \pri-ˈzent-mənt\ *n* **1** : the act of presenting; *esp* : the act of offering a draft or a promissory note at the proper time and place to be paid by another **2 a** : the act of presenting to view or consciousness **b** : something set forth, presented, or exhibited

present participle *n* : a participle that expresses present action in relation to the time expressed by the finite verb in its clause and that in English is formed with the suffix *-ing* and is used in the formation of the progressive tenses

present perfect *adj* : of, relating to, or constituting a verb tense formed in English with *have* and expressing action or state completed at the time of speaking — **present perfect** *n*

present tense *n* : the tense of a verb that expresses action or state in the present time and is used of what occurs or is true at the time of speaking and of what is habitual or characteristic or is always or necessarily true, that is sometimes used to refer to action in the past (as in the historical present), and that is sometimes used for future events

[1]**pre·ser·va·tive** \pri-ˈzər-vət-iv\ *adj* : having the power of preserving

[2]**preservative** *n* : something that preserves; *esp* : an additive used to protect against decay, discoloration, or spoilage

[1]**pre·serve** \pri-ˈzərv\ *vt* **1** : to keep safe from harm or destruction : PROTECT ⟨*preserve* the republic⟩ **2 a** : to keep alive, intact, or free from decay ⟨*preserve* laboratory specimens⟩ **b** : to keep up : MAINTAIN **3 a** : to keep from decomposition **b** : to prepare (as by canning or pickling) for future use ⟨*preserve* beets⟩ [Medieval Latin *praeservare,* from Late Latin, "to observe beforehand," from Latin *prae-* "pre-" + *servare* "to keep, guard, observe"] — **pre·serv·able** \pri-ˈzər-və-bəl\ *adj* — **pres·er·va·tion** \ˌprez-ər-ˈvā-shən\ *n* — **pre·serv·er** *n*

[2]**preserve** *n* **1** : fruit canned or made into jams or jellies or cooked whole or in large pieces in a syrup so as to keep its shape — often used in plural ⟨strawberry *preserves*⟩ **2** : an area restricted for the protection and preservation of natural resources (as animals and plants) ⟨a game *preserve* for regulated

hunting or fishing› ‹nature *preserves*› **3 :** something regarded as reserved for certain persons

[1]**pre·set** \ˌprē-ˈset\ *vt* **-set; -set·ting :** to set in advance ‹*preset* an oven to 350 degrees›

[2]**preset** *n* **:** something (as a radio station) preprogrammed into a device

pre·shrink \ˈprē-ˈshringk\ *vt* **pre·shrank; pre·shrunk :** to shrink (as a fabric) before making into a garment so that the garment will not shrink much when washed

pre·side \pri-ˈzīd\ *vi* **1 a :** to occupy the place of authority **:** act as chairman **b :** to occupy a position similar to that of a president or chairman ‹*preside* over a ceremony› **2 :** to exercise guidance or control ‹*presided* over the destinies of the empire› **3 :** to occupy a position of featured instrumental performer [Latin *praesidēre,* "to guard, preside over," literally, "to sit at the head of," from *prae-* "pre-" + *sedēre* "to sit"] — **pre·sid·er** *n*

pres·i·den·cy \ˈprez-əd-ən-sē, ˈprez-dən-; ˈprez-ə-ˌden-sē\ *n, pl* **-cies 1 :** the office or term of a president **2 :** an executive council in the Mormon Church

pres·i·dent \ˈprez-əd-ənt, ˈprez-dənt, ˈprez-ə-ˌdent\ *n* **1 :** one who presides over a meeting or assembly **2 :** an appointed governor of a subordinate political unit **3 :** the chief officer of an organization (as a corporation) **4 :** the presiding officer of a governmental body **5 a :** an elected official serving as both chief of state and chief political executive in a republic having a presidential government **b :** an elected official having the position of chief of state but usually only minimal political powers in a republic having a parliamentary government [Medieval French, from Latin *praesidens,* from *praesidēre* "to preside"] — **pres·i·den·tial** \ˌprez-ə-ˈden-chəl\ *adj*

Presidents' Day *n* **:** WASHINGTON'S BIRTHDAY 2

pre·si·dio \pri-ˈsēd-ē-ˌō, -ˈsid-, -ˈzēd-, -ˈzid-\ *n, pl* **-di·os :** a garrisoned place; *esp* **:** a military post or fortified settlement in areas currently or originally under Spanish control [Spanish, from Latin *praesidium*]

pre·sid·i·um \pri-ˈsid-ē-əm, -ˈzid-\ *n, pl* **-ia** \-ē-ə\ *or* **-i·ums :** a permanent executive committee selected especially in Communist countries to act for a larger body [Russian *prezidium,* from Latin *praesidium* "garrison," from *praesid-, praeses* "guard, governor," from *praesidēre* "to guard, preside"]

[1]**pre·soak** \prē-ˈsōk\ *vt* **:** to soak before washing

[2]**pre·soak** \ˈprē-ˈsōk\ *n* **1 :** an instance of presoaking **2 :** a product used for presoaking clothes

pre·sort \prē-ˈsȯrt\ *vb* **:** to sort (outgoing mail) by zip code usually before delivery to a post office

[1]**press** \ˈpres\ *n* **1 :** a crowd or a crowded condition **2 :** an apparatus or machine for exerting pressure (as for shaping material, extracting liquid, drilling, or preventing something from warping) **3 :** CLOSET 2 **4 a :** an act of pressing or pushing **:** PRESSURE **b :** an aggressive defense in basketball **5 :** the properly smoothed and creased condition of a freshly pressed garment **6 a :** PRINTING PRESS **b :** the act or the process of printing **c :** a printing or publishing establishment **7 a :** the gathering and publishing of news **:** JOURNALISM **b :** newspapers, periodicals, and often radio and television news broadcasting **c :** news reporters, publishers, and broadcasters **d :** comment or notice in newspapers and periodicals ‹is getting good *press*› [Medieval French *presse,* from *presser* "to press"]

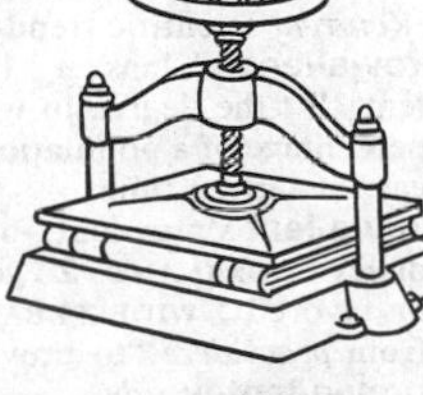

press 2

[2]**press** *vb* **1 :** to act upon through steady pushing or thrusting force exerted in contact **:** SQUEEZE **2 a :** ASSAIL **b :** OPPRESS 1 **3 a :** to squeeze out the juice or contents of ‹*press* grapes› **b :** to squeeze out ‹*press* juice from grapes› **4 a :** to shape by pressure (as with an apparatus) **b :** to smooth by pressure and especially by ironing **5 :** to urge strongly or forcefully **:** CONSTRAIN ‹*pressed* them to attend› **6 a :** to present earnestly or insistently ‹*press* a claim› **b :** to follow through (a course of action) **7 :** to clasp in affection or courtesy **:** EMBRACE **8 a :** to crowd closely **:** MASS ‹reporters *pressed* around the celebrity› **b :** to force or push one's way ‹*pressed* forward through the throng› **9 :** to seek urgently **:** CONTEND ‹*pressed* for higher salaries› [Medieval French *presser,* from Latin *pressare,* from *premere* "to press"] — **press·er** *n*

[3]**press** *vt* **:** to force into service especially in an army or navy **:** IMPRESS [obsolete *prest* "to enlist by giving pay in advance"]

press agent *n* **:** an agent employed to establish and maintain good public relations through publicity

press box *n* **:** a space reserved for reporters (as at a baseball or football game)

press conference *n* **:** an interview given by a public figure to the press by appointment

presser foot *n* **:** a piece on a sewing machine that holds the fabric down while stitching

press–gang \ˈpres-ˌgang\ *n* **:** a detachment of men formerly empowered to force men into military or naval service [[3]*press*]

press·ing *adj* **1 :** urgently important **:** CRITICAL ‹the *pressing* national interest› ‹a *pressing* issue› **2 :** EARNEST, WARM ‹a *pressing* invitation› — **press·ing·ly** \-ing-lē\ *adv*

press·man \ˈpres-mən, -ˌman\ *n* **1 :** an operator of a press; *esp* **:** the operator of a printing press **2** *British* **:** NEWSPAPERMAN

pres·sor \ˈpres-ˌȯr, -ər\ *adj* **:** raising or tending to raise blood pressure [Late Latin, "one that presses," from Latin *premere* "to press"]

press release *n* **:** material given in advance to a newspaper for publication at a future date

press·room \ˈpres-ˌrüm, -ˌru̇m\ *n* **:** a room in a printing plant containing the printing presses

press secretary *n* **:** a person officially in charge of press relations for a prominent public figure

[1]**pres·sure** \ˈpresh-ər\ *n* **1 a :** a painful feeling of weight or burden **:** OPPRESSION, DISTRESS **b :** a burdensome or restricting force or influence ‹the *pressure* of taxes› ‹the constant *pressures* of modern life› **2 a :** the action of pressing ‹use steady *pressure*› **b :** the condition of being pressed ‹kept under *pressure*› **3 a :** the action of a force against an opposing force **b :** the force exerted over a surface divided by its area **c :** the force exerted by the weight of the atmosphere **d :** ELECTROMOTIVE FORCE **4 :** the stress of matters demanding attention **:** URGENCY

[2]**pressure** *vt* **pres·sured; pres·sur·ing** \ˈpresh-ring, -ə-ring\ **1 :** to apply pressure to **:** CONSTRAIN **2 :** PRESSURIZE **3 :** to cook in a pressure cooker

pressure cooker *n* **:** an airtight utensil for quick cooking or preserving of foods by means of steam under pressure — **pressure–cook** \ˌpresh-ər-ˈku̇k\ *vb*

pressure group *n* **:** an interest group that seeks to influence governmental policy but not to elect candidates to office

pressure point *n* **:** a point where a blood vessel runs near a bone and can be compressed (as to stop bleeding) by applying pressure against the bone

pressure suit *n* **:** an inflatable suit for high-altitude or space flight to protect the body from low pressure

pressure wave *n* **:** a wave that travels as a variation of pressure in a material — called also *P-wave*

pres·sur·ize \ˈpresh-ə-ˌrīz\ *vt* **1 :** to maintain near-normal atmospheric pressure in (as an airplane cabin) during high-altitude or space flight **2 :** to apply pressure to — **pres·sur·i·za·tion** \ˌpresh-ə-rə-ˈzā-shən\ *n* — **pres·sur·iz·er** *n*

pres·ti·dig·i·ta·tion \ˌpres-tə-ˌdij-ə-ˈtā-shən\ *n* **:** SLEIGHT OF HAND 1, LEGERDEMAIN [French, from *prestidigitateur* "prestidigitator," from *preste* "nimble, quick," (from Italian *presto*) + Latin *digitus* "finger"] — **pres·ti·dig·i·ta·tor** \-ˈdij-ə-ˌtāt-ər\ *n*

pres·tige \pre-ˈstēzh, -ˈstēj\ *n* **:** usually high standing or fine reputation based on past performance or merit [French, from Middle French, "conjuror's trick, illusion," from Latin *praestigiae,* pl., "conjuror's tricks," from *praestringere* "to graze, blunt, constrict," from *prae-* "pre-" + *stringere* "to bind tight"] — **pres·ti·gious** \-ˈstij-əs\ *adj* — **pres·ti·gious·ly** *adv* — **pres·ti·gious·ness** *n*

pres·to \ˈpres-tō\ *adv or adj* **1 :** suddenly as if by magic ‹*presto,* it's gone› **2 :** at a rapid tempo — used as a direction in music [Italian, "quick, quickly," from Latin *praestus* "ready," from *praesto,* adv., "on hand"]

pre·sum·ably \pri-ˈzü-mə-blē\ *adv* **:** one would presume **:** it seems likely **:** PROBABLY

pre·sume \pri-ˈzüm\ *vb* **1 :** to undertake without leave or clear

\ə\ **abut**	\au̇\ **out**	\i\ **tip**	\ȯ\ **saw**	\u̇\ **foot**
\ər\ **further**	\ch\ **chin**	\ī\ **life**	\ȯi\ **coin**	\y\ **yet**
\a\ **mat**	\e\ **pet**	\j\ **job**	\th\ **thin**	\yü\ **few**
\ā\ **take**	\ē\ **easy**	\ng\ **sing**	\th\ **this**	\yu̇\ **cure**
\ä\ **cot, cart**	\g\ **go**	\ō\ **bone**	\ü\ **food**	\zh\ **vision**

justification : DARE ⟨*presume* to question the authority of a superior⟩ **2** : to expect or assume especially with confidence **3** : to suppose to be true without proof ⟨*presumed* innocent until proved guilty⟩ **4** : to act or behave boldly without reason [Late Latin *praesumere* "to dare," from Latin, "to anticipate, assume," from *prae-* "pre-" + *sumere* "to take"] — **pre·sum·able** \-ˈzü-mə-bəl\ *adj* — **pre·sum·er** *n*

pre·sum·ing *adj* : PRESUMPTUOUS — **pre·sum·ing·ly** \-ˈzü-ming-lē\ *adv*

pre·sump·tion \pri-ˈzəm-shən, -ˈzəmp-\ *n* **1** : presumptuous attitude or conduct : AUDACITY **2 a** : a conclusion reached on strong grounds of belief : something believed to be so but not proved **b** : the grounds or evidence leading one to believe something [Medieval French, from Latin *praesumptio* "assumption," from *praesumere* "to assume"]

pre·sump·tive \-ˈzəm-tiv, -ˈzəmp-\ *adj* **1** : giving grounds for reasonable opinion or belief ⟨*presumptive* evidence⟩ **2** : based on probability or presumption ⟨the *presumptive* heir⟩ — **pre·sump·tive·ly** *adv*

pre·sump·tu·ous \pri-ˈzəm-chə-wəs, -ˈzəmp-, -chəs, -shəs\ *adj* : overstepping due bounds : taking liberties — **pre·sump·tu·ous·ly** *adv* — **pre·sump·tu·ous·ness** *n*

pre·sup·pose \ˌprē-sə-ˈpōz\ *vt* : to suppose beforehand ⟨a book that *presupposes* wide knowledge in its readers⟩ — **pre·sup·po·si·tion** \prē-ˌsəp-ə-ˈzish-ən\ *n*

pre·sweet·ened \ˈprē-ˈswēt-ənd\ *adj* : sweetened by the manufacturer ⟨*presweetened* cereal⟩

[1]**pre·teen** \ˈprē-ˈtēn\ *n* : a boy or girl not yet 13 years old

[2]**preteen** *adj* **1** : relating to or produced for children especially in the 9 to 12 year-old age group ⟨*preteen* fashions⟩ **2** : being younger than 13

[1]**pre·tend** \pri-ˈtend\ *vb* **1** : to give a false appearance of being, possessing, or performing : PROFESS **2 a** : to make believe : FEIGN **b** : to claim, represent, or assert falsely **3** : to put in a claim (as to a throne or title) [Latin *praetendere* "to allege as an excuse," literally, "to stretch out," from *prae-* "pre-" + *tendere* "to stretch"] ***synonyms*** see ASSUME

[2]**pretend** *adj* : IMAGINARY, MAKE-BELIEVE

pre·tend·ed *adj* : professed or avowed but not genuine ⟨*pretended* affection⟩ — **pre·tend·ed·ly** *adv*

pre·tend·er \pri-ˈten-dər\ *n* : one that pretends; *esp* : a claimant to a throne who has no just title

pre·tense *or* **pre·tence** \ˈprē-ˌtens, pri-ˈ\ *n* **1** : a claim made or implied and usually not supported by fact **2 a** : mere show : OSTENTATION **b** : a pretentious act or assertion **3** : an insincere attempt to attain a condition or quality ⟨let's have some *pretense* of order here⟩ **4** : professed rather than real intention or purpose : PRETEXT ⟨was there under false *pretenses*⟩ **5** : MAKE-BELIEVE, FICTION **6** : false show : SIMULATION ⟨saw through your *pretense* of indifference⟩ [probably a modification of Medieval Latin *pretensio,* from Latin *praetendere* "to allege as an excuse"]

pre·ten·sion \pri-ˈten-chən\ *n* **1** : PRETEXT **2** : an effort to establish a claim **3** : a claim or right to attention or honor because of merit **4** : VANITY 3 — **pre·ten·sion·less** \-ləs\ *adj*

pre·ten·tious \-chəs\ *adj* **1** : making or having claims especially as to excellence or worth : SHOWY ⟨living in a *pretentious* style⟩ **2** : making demands on one's skill, ability, or means : AMBITIOUS ⟨*pretentious* plans⟩ [French *prétentieux,* derived from Latin *praetendere* "to allege as an excuse"] — **pre·ten·tious·ly** *adv* — **pre·ten·tious·ness** *n*

pret·er·it *or* **pret·er·ite** \ˈpret-ə-rət\ *n* : PAST TENSE [Medieval French *preterit,* from Latin *praeteritus,* from *praeterire* "to go by, pass," from *praeter* "beyond, past," + *ire* "to go"]

pre·ter·nat·u·ral \ˌprēt-ər-ˈnach-rəl, -ə-rəl\ *adj* **1** : not conforming to what is natural or regular in nature : ABNORMAL **2** : inexplicable by ordinary means; *esp* : PSYCHIC [Medieval Latin *praeternaturalis,* from Latin *praeter naturam* "beyond nature"] — **pre·ter·nat·u·ral·ly** \-ˈnach-rə-lē, -ə-rə-; -ˈnach-ər-lē\ *adv* — **pre·ter·nat·u·ral·ness** \-ˈnach-rəl-nəs, -ə-rəl-\ *n*

pre·test \ˈprē-ˌtest, prē-ˈ\ *n* : a preliminary test serving for exploration rather than evaluation — **pretest** *vt*

pre·text \ˈprē-ˌtekst\ *n* : a purpose or motive put forward in order to conceal a real intention or state of affairs [Latin *praetextus,* from *praetexere* "to assign as a pretext," literally, "to weave in front," from *prae-* "pre-" + *texere* "to weave"]

pret·ti·fy \ˈprit-i-ˌfī, ˈpu̇rt-\ *vt* **-fied; -fy·ing** : to make pretty — **pret·ti·fi·ca·tion** \ˌprit-i-fə-ˈkā-shən, ˌpu̇rt-\ *n*

[1]**pret·ty** \ˈprit-ē, ˈpu̇rt-\ *adj* **pret·ti·er; -est** **1 a** : ARTFUL 1, CLEVER **b** : PAT 1a, APT **2** : pleasing by delicacy or grace especially of appearance or sound : conventionally attractive but without elements of grandeur, stateliness, and excellence usually associated with true beauty ⟨a *pretty* face⟩ ⟨light *pretty* tunes⟩ ⟨a *pretty* manner⟩ **3** : MISERABLE ⟨a *pretty* mess we're in⟩ **4** : moderately large : CONSIDERABLE ⟨a very *pretty* profit⟩ [Old English *prættig* "tricky," from *prætt* "trick"] ***synonyms*** see BEAUTIFUL — **pret·ti·ly** \ˈprit-l-ē, ˈpu̇rt-\ *adv* — **pret·ti·ness** \ˈprit-ē-nəs, ˈpu̇rt-\ *n* — **pret·ty·ish** \-ē-ish\ *adj*

[2]**pret·ty** \ˈprit-ē, pərt-ē\ *adv* : in some degree : MODERATELY ⟨*pretty* cold weather⟩

usage Some handbooks complain that *pretty* is overworked and recommend the selection of a more specific word or restrict *pretty* to informal or colloquial contexts. *Pretty* is used to tone down a statement and is in wide use across the whole spectrum of English. It is common in informal speech and writing but is neither rare nor wrong in serious discourse.

[3]**pretty** *like* [1]\ *n, pl* **pretties** **1** : a pretty person or thing **2** *pl* : dainty clothes

pret·zel \ˈpret-səl\ *n* : a brittle glazed and salted cracker typically shaped like a loose knot [German *Brezel,* derived from Latin *brachiatus* "having branches like arms," from *brachium* "arm"]

Word History Pretzels were most likely introduced into the United States during the 19th century by German immigrants. Our word *pretzel* comes from the German *Brezel,* The familiar knot-shaped pretzel has been known, at least in Germanic countries, for centuries. Its name is derived from Latin *brachiatus,* which means "having branches like arms." Apparently the pretzel is so called because of the similarity between its knot shape and a pair of folded arms.

pre·vail \pri-ˈvāl\ *vi* **1** : to gain ascendancy through strength or superiority : TRIUMPH **2** : to be or become effective or effectual **3** : to urge successfully ⟨was *prevailed* upon to sing⟩ **4** : to be frequent : PREDOMINATE ⟨the west winds that *prevail* in the mountains⟩ **5** : to be or continue in use or fashion : PERSIST ⟨a custom that still *prevails*⟩ [Latin *praevalēre,* from *prae-* "pre-" + *valēre* "to be strong"]

pre·vail·ing *adj* **1** : having superior force or influence **2 a** : most frequent ⟨*prevailing* winds⟩ **b** : generally current : COMMON — **pre·vail·ing·ly** \-ˈvā-ling-lē\ *adv*

synonyms PREVAILING, PREVALENT, CURRENT mean generally circulated, accepted, or used in a certain time or place. PREVAILING applies especially to something that is predominant ⟨*prevailing* opinion⟩. PREVALENT implies widespread frequency ⟨a *prevalent* custom⟩ ⟨a disease that is *prevalent* in many countries⟩. CURRENT applies to things subject to change and implies *prevalence* at the present time ⟨*current* fashions⟩ ⟨*current* scientific trends⟩.

prev·a·lence \-ləns\ *n* **1** : the quality or state of being prevalent **2** : the degree to which something is prevalent; *esp* : the percentage of a population that is affected with a particular disease at a given time

prev·a·lent \ˈprev-lənt, -ə-lənt\ *adj* **1** *archaic* : being in ascendancy : DOMINANT **2** : generally or widely accepted, practiced, or favored : WIDESPREAD [Latin *praevalens* "very powerful," from *praevalēre* "to prevail"] ***synonyms*** see PREVAILING — **prev·a·lent·ly** *adv*

pre·var·i·cate \pri-ˈvar-ə-ˌkāt\ *vi* : to avoid telling the truth [Latin *praevaricari* "to act in collusion," literally, "to straddle," from *prae-* "pre-" + *varicare* "to straddle," from *varus* "bow-legged"] ***synonyms*** see [3]LIE — **pre·var·i·ca·tion** \-ˌvar-ə-ˈkā-shən\ *n* — **pre·var·i·ca·tor** \-ˈvar-ə-ˌkāt-ər\ *n*

pre·vent \pri-ˈvent\ *vt* **1** : to keep from happening or existing ⟨steps to *prevent* war⟩ **2** : to hold or keep back : STOP, HINDER ⟨there's nothing to *prevent* us from going⟩ [Latin *praeventus,* past participle of *praevenire* "to come before, anticipate, forestall," from *prae-* "pre-" + *venire* "to come"] — **pre·vent·able** *also* **pre·vent·ible** \-ə-bəl\ *adj* — **pre·vent·er** *n*

synonyms PREVENT, AVERT, FORESTALL mean to stop something from coming or occurring. PREVENT implies placing an insurmountable obstacle or impediment ⟨took measures to *prevent* an epidemic⟩. AVERT implies taking immediate or effective measures to force back, avoid, or counteract a threatening evil ⟨efforts to *avert* a revolution⟩. FORESTALL implies forehanded action to stop or interrupt something in its course ⟨radar helped *forestall* surprise attacks⟩.

pre·ven·ta·tive \-ˈvent-ət-iv\ *adj or n* : PREVENTIVE

pre·ven·tion \pri-ˈven-chən\ *n* : the act of preventing

[1]**pre·ven·tive** \-'vent-iv\ *n* : something that prevents; *esp* : something used to prevent disease

[2]**preventive** *adj* : devoted to, concerned with, or undertaken for prevention ⟨*preventive* measures⟩ ⟨*preventive* medicine⟩ — **pre·ven·tive·ly** *adv* — **pre·ven·tive·ness** *n*

[1]**pre·view** \'prē-ˌvyü\ *vt* : to view or to show in advance

[2]**preview** *n* **1** : an advance showing or performance **2** *also* **pre·vue** \-ˌvyü\ : a showing of snatches from a motion picture advertised for appearance in the near future **3** : an advance statement, sample, or survey

pre·vi·ous \'prē-vē-əs\ *adj* **1** : going before in time or order ⟨the *previous* lesson⟩ **2** : acting too soon : PREMATURE ⟨was a bit *previous* with the answer⟩ [Latin *praevius* "leading the way," from *prae-* "pre-" + *via* "way"] — **pre·vi·ous·ly** *adv* — **pre·vi·ous·ness** *n*

previous question *n* : a parliamentary motion that the pending question be put to an immediate vote without further debate or amendment

previous to *prep* : prior to : BEFORE

[1]**pre·vi·sion** \prē-'vizh-ən\ *n* **1** : FORESIGHT 1, PRESCIENCE **2** : FORECAST, PREDICTION — **pre·vi·sion·al** \-'vizh-nəl, -ən-l\ *adj* — **pre·vi·sion·ary** \-'vizh-ə-ˌner-ē\ *adj*

[2]**prevision** *vt* : FORESEE

pre·vo·cal·ic \ˌprē-vō-'kal-ik\ *adj* : immediately preceding a vowel

pre·writ·ing \'prē-ˌrīt-ing\ *n* : planning and getting ideas in order before writing

[1]**prey** \'prā\ *n* **1 a** : an animal taken by a predator as food **b** : a person who is helpless or unable to resist attack : VICTIM **2** : the act or habit of preying [Medieval French *preie* "booty, prey," from Latin *praeda*]

[2]**prey** *vi* **1** : to raid for booty **2** : to seize and devour something as prey **3** : to have an injurious, destructive, or wasting effect ⟨fears that *prey* on the mind⟩ — **prey·er** *n*

[1]**price** \'prīs\ *n* **1 a** : the quantity of one thing that is exchanged or sought in barter or sale for another **b** : the amount of money given or asked for a specified thing **2** : the terms for the sake of which something is done or undertaken: as **a** : an amount sufficient to bribe one **b** : a reward for the apprehension or death of a person **3** : the cost at which something is obtainable ⟨the *price* of freedom⟩ [Medieval French *pris* "value," from Latin *pretium* "price, money"] ***synonyms*** see WORTH

[2]**price** *vt* **1** : to set a price on **2** : to ask the price of **3** : to drive by raising prices excessively — **pric·er** *n*

price–cut·ter \'prī-ˌskət-ər\ *n* : one that reduces prices especially to a level designed to cripple competition

price·less \'prī-sləs\ *adj* **1** : having a value beyond any price : INVALUABLE **2** : surprisingly amusing, odd, or absurd

price support *n* : artificial maintenance of prices of a commodity at a level usually fixed through government action

price tag *n* **1** : a tag on merchandise showing the price at which it is offered for sale **2** : PRICE 1b, COST

price war *n* : a period of commercial competition in which prices are repeatedly cut below those of competitors

[1]**prick** \'prik\ *n* **1** : a mark or shallow hole made by a pointed instrument **2** : a pointed instrument or part **3** : an instance of pricking or the sensation of being pricked [Old English *prica*]

[2]**prick** *vb* **1 a** : to pierce slightly with a sharp point **b** : to have or cause a pricking sensation **2** : to cause to feel anguish, grief, or remorse ⟨if your conscience *pricks* you⟩ **3** : to urge a horse with spurs **4** : to mark or outline with or as if with pricks ⟨*prick* a design on paper⟩ **5** : to make or become erect ⟨the dog *pricked* its ears⟩ — **prick up one's ears** : to listen intently

prick·er \'prik-ər\ *n* **1** : one that pricks **2** : PRICKLE 1, THORN

[1]**prick·le** \'prik-əl\ *n* **1** : a fine sharp projection; *esp* : a sharp pointed process of the epidermis or bark of a plant **2** : a slight stinging or tingling sensation [Old English *pricle*]

[2]**prickle** *vb* **prickled; prick·ling** \'prik-ling, -ə-ling\ **1** : to prick slightly **2** : to cause or feel a slight stinging or tingling sensation

prick·ly \'prik-lē\ *adj* **prick·li·er; -est** **1** : full of or covered with prickles ⟨*prickly* plants⟩ **2** : marked by prickling ⟨a *prickly* sensation⟩ — **prick·li·ness** *n*

prickly heat *n* : a skin eruption of red pimples with intense itching and tingling caused by inflammation around the sweat ducts

prickly pear *n* **1** : OPUNTIA; *esp* : an opuntia with flat spiny stem segments **2** : the pear-shaped edible pulpy fruit of a prickly pear

[1]**pride** \'prīd\ *n* **1** : the quality or state of being proud: as **a** : excessive self-esteem : CONCEIT **b** : a reasonable or justifiable self-respect **c** : pleasure or satisfaction taken in some act, accomplishment, or possession **2** : proud or disdainful behavior or treatment : DISDAIN **3** : something that is or is fit to be a source of pride ⟨this pup is the *pride* of the litter⟩ **4** : a group of lions [Old English *prȳde,* from *prūd* "proud"]

prickly pear 1

[2]**pride** *vt* : to indulge in pride : PLUME ⟨*pride* oneself on one's skill⟩

pride·ful \'prīd-fəl\ *adj* : full of pride: as **a** : HAUGHTY **b** : ELATED — **pride·ful·ly** \-fə-lē\ *adv* — **pride·ful·ness** *n*

prie–dieu \prēd-'yər, -'yü, -'yœ\ *n, pl* **prie–dieux** *same or* -'yərz, -'yüz, -'yœz\ : a small kneeling bench designed for use by a person at prayer and fitted with a raised shelf on which the elbows or a book may be rested [French, literally, "pray God"]

priest \'prēst\ *n* : a person who has the authority to conduct religious rites [Old English *prēost,* derived from Late Latin *presbyter* "elder, priest," from Greek *presbyteros,* from *presbys* "old man"]

priest·ess \'prē-stəs\ *n* : a woman who is a priest ⟨ancient Roman *priestesses*⟩

priest·hood \'prēst-ˌhu̇d, 'prē-ˌstu̇d\ *n* **1** : the office, dignity, or status of a priest **2** : the whole group of priests

priest·ly \'prēst-lē\ *adj* **priest·li·er; -est** **1** : of or relating to a priest or the priesthood **2** : characteristic of or befitting a priest — **priest·li·ness** *n*

prig \'prig\ *n* : a person who annoys others by a too careful or rigid observance of niceties and proprieties (as of speech or manners) [from earlier *prig* "fellow, person," probably from *prig* "to steal"] — **prig·gery** \'prig-ə-rē\ *n* — **prig·gish** \'prig-ish\ *adj* — **prig·gish·ly** *adv* — **prig·gish·ness** *n*

prim \'prim\ *adj* **prim·mer; prim·mest** : very or excessively formal and precise (as in conduct or dress) ⟨a *prim* scholar⟩ ⟨*prim* remarks⟩ [from earlier *prim* "to give a prim expression to," of unknown origin] — **prim·ly** *adv* — **prim·ness** *n*

pri·ma ballerina \ˌprē-mə-\ *n* : the principal female dancer in a ballet company [Italian, "leading ballerina"]

pri·ma·cy \'prī-mə-sē\ *n* **1** : the condition of being first (as in time, place, or rank) **2** : the office, status, or dignity of a bishop of the highest rank

pri·ma don·na \ˌprim-ə-'dän-ə, ˌprē-mə-\ *n, pl* **prima donnas** **1** : a principal female singer (as in an opera) **2** : an extremely sensitive, vain, or undisciplined person [Italian, literally, "first lady"]

[1]**pri·ma fa·cie** \ˌprī-mə-'fā-shə, -shē, -sē\ *adv* : at first view : on the first appearance [Latin]

[2]**prima facie** *adj* **1** : APPARENT, SEEMING ⟨a *prima facie* solution to a problem⟩ **2** : adequate to legally establish a fact or case unless disproved ⟨*prima facie* evidence⟩

pri·mal \'prī-məl\ *adj* **1** : ORIGINAL 1, PRIMITIVE **2** : first in importance : CHIEF [Medieval Latin *primalis,* from Latin *primus* "first"]

pri·mar·i·ly \prī-'mer-ə-lē\ *adv* **1** : for the most part : CHIEFLY **2** : in the first place : ORIGINALLY

[1]**pri·mary** \'prī-ˌmer-ē; 'prīm-rē, -ə-rē\ *adj* **1** : first in order of time or development : INITIAL, PRIMITIVE ⟨the *primary* stages of a process⟩ **2 a** : of first rank, importance, or value : CHIEF ⟨the *primary* elective officer is the president⟩ **b** : BASIC, FUNDAMENTAL ⟨our *primary* duty⟩ **c** : of, relating to, or being one of the principal flight feathers of a bird's wing **d** : expressive of present or future time ⟨*primary* tense⟩ **e** : of, relating to, or constituting the strongest of the three or four degrees of stress ⟨the first syllable of *basketball* carries *primary* stress⟩ **3 a** : not derived from or dependent on something else ⟨a *primary* source of information⟩ **b** : not derivable from other colors, odors, or tastes **c** : coming before and usually preparatory to something else ⟨*primary* instruction⟩ **4** : of, relating to, or being the current or circuit that is connected to the source of electricity in an

\ə\ **abut**	\au̇\ **out**	\i\ **tip**	\ȯ\ **saw**	\u̇\ **foot**
\ər\ **further**	\ch\ **chin**	\ī\ **life**	\ȯi\ **coin**	\y\ **yet**
\a\ **mat**	\e\ **pet**	\j\ **job**	\th\ **thin**	\yü\ **few**
\ā\ **take**	\ē\ **easy**	\ng\ **sing**	\t͟h\ **this**	\yu̇\ **cure**
\ä\ **cot, cart**	\g\ **go**	\ō\ **bone**	\ü\ **food**	\zh\ **vision**

induction coil or transformer **5** : of, relating to, or derived from primary meristem **6** : of, relating to, or involved in the production of organic substances by green plants [Late Latin *primarius* "basic, primary," from Latin, "principal," from *primus* "first"]

[2]**primary** *n, pl* **-mar·ies** **1** : something that is primary: as **a** : a planet as distinguished from its satellites **b** : one of the usually nine or ten strong flight feathers on the outer joint of a bird's wing **c** : any of a set of colors (as red, yellow, or blue) from which all other colors may be derived **2** : an election in which voters select party candidates for political office, choose party officials, or select delegates for a party convention **3** : the coil that is connected to the source of electricity in an induction coil or transformer — called also *primary coil*

primary care *n* : health care provided by a medical professional (as a doctor or nurse) with whom a patient has initial contact and by whom the patient may be referred to a specialist

primary cell *n* : a cell that converts chemical energy into electrical energy by irreversible chemical reactions

primary germ layer *n* : GERM LAYER

primary meristem *n* : meristem (as procambium) that is derived from meristem at the tip of a root or shoot and functions in increasing length

primary root *n* : the root of a plant that develops first and originates from the radicle

primary school *n* : ELEMENTARY SCHOOL

pri·mate \ˈprī-ˌmāt *or especially for 1* -mət\ *n* **1** : a bishop or archbishop governing or having highest status in a district, nation, or church **2** : any of an order (Primates) of mammals that are characterized by hands and feet that grasp, a relatively large complex brain, and stereoscopic vision and that includes humans, apes, monkeys, and related forms (as lemurs and tarsiers) [Medieval French *primat,* from Medieval Latin *primat-, primas* "archbishop," from Latin, "leader," from *primus* "first"]

pri·ma·tol·o·gy \ˌprī-mə-ˈtäl-ə-jē\ *n* : the study of primates and especially nonhuman primates — **pri·ma·tol·o·gist** \-jist\ *n*

[1]**prime** \ˈprīm\ *n* **1** *often cap* : the second of the canonical hours **2** : the first part : earliest stage **3** : the most vigorous, prosperous, or satisfying stage or period ⟨in the *prime* of one's life⟩ **4** : the chief or best individual or part : PICK **5** : PRIME NUMBER **6** : the symbol ′ [Old English *prīm,* from Latin *prima hora* "first hour"]

[2]**prime** *adj* **1** : first in time : ORIGINAL **2 a** : of, relating to, or being a prime number **b** : having no polynomial factors other than itself and no monomial factors other than 1 ⟨a *prime* polynomial⟩ **c** : expressed as a product of prime factors (as prime numbers and prime polynomials) ⟨a *prime* factorization⟩ **3 a** : first in rank, authority, or significance : PRINCIPAL **b** : first in excellence, quality, or value **c** : of the highest grade regularly marketed ⟨*prime* rib of beef⟩ [Medieval French, feminine of *prim* "first," from Latin *primus*] — **prime·ly** *adv* — **prime·ness** *n*

[3]**prime** *vt* **1** : to prepare for firing by supplying with priming or a primer **2** : to apply (as in painting) a first color, coating, or preparation to **3** : to put into working order by filling or charging with something ⟨*prime* a pump with water⟩ **4** : to instruct beforehand : COACH [probably from [1]*prime*]

prime meridian *n* : the meridian of 0° longitude which runs through the original site of the Royal Observatory at Greenwich, England, and from which other longitudes are reckoned east and west

prime minister *n* **1** : the chief minister of a ruler or state **2** : the head of a cabinet or ministry; *esp* : the chief executive of a parliamentary government — **prime ministry** *n*

prime number *n* : a whole number other than 0 or ±1 that is not divisible without remainder by any other whole numbers except ±1 and ± itself

[1]**prim·er** \ˈprim-ər, *especially British* ˈprī-mər\ *n* **1** : a small book for teaching children to read **2** : a usually small introductory book on a subject ⟨a *primer* of chemistry⟩ **3** : a short informative piece of writing ⟨a *primer* on the relation between economic conditions and interest rates⟩ [Medieval Latin *primarium* "layperson's prayer book," from Late Latin *primarius* "primary"]

[2]**prim·er** \ˈprī-mər\ *n* **1** : a device (as a cap, tube, or wafer) containing a substance that ignites an explosive charge **2** : material used in priming a surface [[3]*prime*]

prime time *n* : the evening period during which television has its largest number of viewers

pri·me·val \prī-ˈmē-vəl\ *adj* : of or relating to the earliest ages : PRIMITIVE [Latin *primaevus,* from *primus* "first" + *aevum* "age"] — **pri·me·val·ly** \-və-lē\ *adv*

prim·ing *n* **1** : the explosive used in priming a charge **2** : [2]PRIMER 2

[1]**prim·i·tive** \ˈprim-ət-iv\ *adj* **1** : not derived : ORIGINAL, PRIMARY ⟨nature, the *primitive* source of art⟩ **2 a** : of or relating to the earliest age or period : PRIMEVAL ⟨*primitive* forests⟩ ⟨the *primitive* church⟩ **b** : little evolved and closely approximating an early ancestral type ⟨a *primitive* fish⟩ **c** : belonging to or characteristic of an early stage of development ⟨*primitive* building techniques⟩ **3 a** : of or relating to a people or culture that lacks a written language and advanced technologies ⟨*primitive* societies⟩ **b** (1) : lacking formal or technical training ⟨*primitive* craftsmen⟩ (2) : produced by a self-taught artist ⟨a *primitive* painting⟩ [Latin *primitivus* "first formed," from *primitus* "originally," from *primus* "first"] — **prim·i·tive·ly** *adv* — **prim·i·tive·ness** *n*

[2]**primitive** *n* **1 a** : something primitive; *esp* : a primitive idea, term, or proposition **b** : a root word **2 a** (1) : an artist of an early period of a culture or artistic movement (2) : a later imitator or follower of such an artist **b** : a work of art produced by a primitive artist **3** : a member of a primitive people

pri·mo·gen·i·tor \ˌprī-mō-ˈjen-ət-ər\ *n* : ANCESTOR 1, FOREFATHER [Late Latin, from Latin *primus* "first" + *genitor* "begetter," from *gignere* "to beget"]

pri·mo·gen·i·ture \-ˈjen-ə-ˌchu̇r, -ˈjen-i-chər\ *n* **1** : the state of being the firstborn of the children of the same parents **2** : an exclusive right of inheritance belonging to the eldest son [Late Latin *primogenitura,* from Latin *primus* "first" + *genitura* "birth," from *genitus,* past participle of *gignere* "to beget"]

pri·mor·di·al \prī-ˈmȯrd-ē-əl\ *adj* **1 a** : first created or developed : PRIMEVAL **b** : earliest formed in the growth of an individual or organ : PRIMITIVE ⟨*primordial* cells⟩ **2** : FUNDAMENTAL 1, PRIMARY [Late Latin *primordialis,* from Latin *primordium* "origin," from *primus* "first" + *ordiri* "to begin"] — **pri·mor·di·al·ly** \-ē-ə-lē\ *adv*

primordial soup *n* : a mixture of organic molecules in evolutionary theory from which life on earth originated

pri·mor·di·um \-ē-əm\ *n, pl* **-dia** \-ē-ə\ : the first-formed rudiment of a part or organ [Latin, "origin"]

primp \ˈprimp\ *vb* : to dress, adorn, or arrange in a careful or finicky manner [perhaps alteration of *prim* "to give a prim expression to, dress primly"]

prim·rose \ˈprim-ˌrōz\ *n* : any of a genus of perennial herbs with large tufted basal leaves and showy variously colored flowers borne in clusters on leafless stalks [Medieval French *primerose*]

primrose

primrose path *n* : a path of ease or pleasure and especially sensual pleasure

primrose yellow *n* : a light to moderate yellow

prim·u·la \ˈprim-yə-lə\ *n* : PRIMROSE [Medieval Latin, from *primula veris,* literally, "first fruit of spring"]

prince \ˈprins\ *n* **1 a** : MONARCH 1, SOVEREIGN **b** : the ruler of a principality or state **2** : a male member of a royal family; *esp* : a son of a king **3** : a nobleman of varying rank **4** : a person of high standing in a class or profession [Medieval French, from Latin *princeps* "leader, initiator," literally, "one who takes the first part," from *primus* "first" + *capere* "to take"] — **prince·dom** \-dəm\ *n* — **prince·ship** \-ˌship\ *n*

Prince Al·bert \prin-ˈsal-bərt\ *n* : a long double-breasted frock coat [*Prince Albert* Edward (later Edward VII, king of England), died 1910]

prince charming *n* : a suitor who fulfills the dreams of his beloved; *also* : a man deceptively charming and attractive to women [*Prince Charming,* hero of the fairy tale *Cinderella* by Charles Perrault, died 1703, French writer]

prince consort *n, pl* **princes consort** : the husband of a reigning female sovereign

prince·ling \ˈprins-ling\ *n* : a petty or insignificant prince

prince·ly \ˈprins-lē\ *adj* **prince·li·er; -li·est** **1** : of or relating to a prince : ROYAL **2** : befitting a prince : REGAL, MAGNIFICENT ⟨*princely* manners⟩ ⟨a *princely* sum⟩ — **prince·li·ness** *n*

Prince of Wales \-ˈwālz\ : the male heir apparent to the British throne — used as a title only after it has been specifically conferred by the sovereign

prince's feather *n* **:** a showy annual amaranth often grown for its dense spikes of usually red flowers

^{1}**prin·cess** \ˈprin-səs, ˈprin-ˌses, prin-ˈses\ *n* **1** *archaic* **:** a woman having sovereign power **2 :** a female member of a royal family; *esp* **:** a daughter or granddaughter of a sovereign **3 :** the wife of a prince **4 :** a woman of outstanding merit

^{2}**princess** *like* ^{1}\ *or* **prin·cesse** \prin-ˈses\ *adj* **:** close-fitting and usually with gores from neck to flaring hemline ⟨a *princess* gown⟩

princess royal *n, pl* **princesses royal :** the eldest daughter of a sovereign

^{1}**prin·ci·pal** \ˈprin-sə-pəl, -sə bəl\ *adj* **1 :** most important or influential **:** CHIEF **2 :** of, relating to, or being principal or a principal [Medieval French, from Latin *principalis,* from *princip-, princeps* "one who takes the first part"] ***usage*** see PRINCIPLE — **prin·ci·pal·ly** \-ē, ˈprin-splē\ *adv*

^{2}**principal** *n* **1 a :** a person (as a ruler or employer) who exercises authority **:** HEAD, CHIEF **b :** the chief executive officer of a school **c :** one who engages another to act as his or her agent **d :** an actual participant in a crime **e :** the person primarily liable on a legal obligation **f :** a leading performer **:** STAR **2 a :** a capital sum placed at interest, due as a debt, or used as a fund **b :** the main body of an estate or bequest left by will — **prin·ci·pal·ship** \-ˌship\ *n*

prin·ci·pal·i·ty \ˌprin-sə-ˈpal-ət-ē\ *n, pl* **-ties 1 :** the office or position of a prince or principal **2 :** the territory or jurisdiction of a prince

principal parts *n pl* **:** a series of verb forms from which all the other forms of a verb can be derived including in English the present infinitive, the past tense, the past participle, and sometimes the present participle

prin·ci·ple \ˈprin-sə-pəl, -sə-bəl\ *n* **1 a :** a fundamental law or doctrine **b :** a rule or code of conduct **c :** devotion to right principles **d :** the laws or facts of nature underlying the working of an artificial device ⟨trying to grasp the *principles* of radar⟩ **2 a :** a primary source **:** ORIGIN **b :** an underlying faculty or endowment ⟨such *principles* of human nature as greed and curiosity⟩ **3 :** a constituent that exhibits or imparts a characteristic quality ⟨quinine is the active *principle* of cinchona bark⟩ [Medieval French *principe, principle,* from Latin *principium* "beginning," from *princip-, princeps* "initiator, one taking the first part"]

usage Although nearly every handbook and many dictionaries warn against confusing *principle* and *principal,* many people still do. *Principle* is only a noun; *principal* is both adjective and noun. If you are unsure which noun you want, read the definitions in this dictionary.

prin·ci·pled \-sə-pəld, -sə-bəld, -spəld\ *adj* **:** exhibiting, based on, or characterized by principle ⟨high-*principled*⟩

prink \ˈpringk\ *vb* **:** PRIMP [probably alteration of ^{2}*prank*] — **prink·er** *n*

^{1}**print** \ˈprint\ *n* **1 a :** a mark made by pressure **:** IMPRESSION **b :** something impressed with a print or formed in a mold **2 :** a device or instrument for impressing or forming a print **3 a :** printed state or form ⟨put a manuscript into *print*⟩ **b :** printed matter **c :** printed letters **:** TYPE **4 a :** a copy made by printing (as from a photographic negative) **b :** cloth with a pattern applied by printing; *also* **:** an article of such cloth [Medieval French *preint, prient,* from *preindre* "to press," from Latin *premere*] — **in print :** available from the publisher — **out of print :** not available from the publisher

^{2}**print** *vb* **1 a :** to make an impression in or on **b :** to cause (as a mark) to be stamped **2 a :** to make a copy of especially by pressing paper against an inked surface **b :** to impress (a surface) with a design by pressure ⟨*print* wallpaper⟩ **c :** to publish in printed form **d :** to write on a surface (as a computer display screen) for viewing **e :** PRINT OUT **3 :** to write in unconnected letters like those made by a printing press **4 :** to make (a positive picture) on a sensitized photographic surface

print·able \ˈprint-ə-bəl\ *adj* **1 :** capable of being printed or of being printed from **2 :** worthy or fit to be published — **print·abil·i·ty** \ˌprint-ə-ˈbil-ət-ē\ *n*

printed circuit *n* **:** a circuit for electronic apparatus made by depositing conductive material on an insulating surface

printed matter *n* **:** matter mechanically printed that is eligible for mailing at a special rate

print·er \ˈprint-ər\ *n* **:** one that prints: as **a :** a person whose business or occupation is printing **b :** a device used for printing or for making printouts

printer's devil *n* **:** an apprentice in a printing office

print·ery \ˈprint-ə-rē\ *n, pl* **-er·ies :** an establishment where printing is done

print·ing *n* **1 :** reproduction in printed form **2 :** the art, practice, or business of a printer **3 :** IMPRESSION 4b

printing press *n* **:** a machine that produces printed copies

print·mak·er \ˈprint-ˌmā-kər\ *n* **:** an artist who makes prints

print·out \ˈprint-ˌau̇t\ *n* **:** a printed record produced by a computer

print out *vt* **:** to make a printout of

pri·on \ˈprē-ˌän\ *n* **:** a protein particle that lacks nucleic acid and has been implicated as the cause of several diseases (as mad cow disease) marked by deterioration of nervous tissue [*pro*teinaceous + *in*fectious + *-on*]

^{1}**pri·or** \ˈprī-ər, ˈprīr\ *n* **1 :** the deputy head of an abbey **2 :** the head of a monastic house, province, or order [Old English and Medieval French, both from Medieval Latin, from Late Latin, "administrator," from Latin, "former, superior"] — **pri·or·ate** \ˈprī-ə-rət\ *n* — **pri·or·ship** \ˈprī-ər-ˌship\ *n*

^{2}**prior** *adj* **1 :** earlier in time or order **2 :** taking precedence logically or in importance or value ⟨a *prior* responsibility⟩ [Latin, "former, superior"] — **pri·or·ly** *adv*

pri·or·ess \ˈprī-ə-rəs\ *n* **:** a nun who is the head of a religious house or order

pri·or·i·ty \prī-ˈor-ət-ē, -ˈär-\ *n, pl* **-ties 1 :** the quality or state of coming before another in time or importance: as **a :** superiority in rank, position, or privilege **b :** order of preference based on urgency, importance, or merit **2 :** something deserving or requiring attention before others of its kind ⟨it's high on our list of *priorities*⟩

prior to *prep* **:** in advance of **:** BEFORE

pri·o·ry \ˈprī-rē, -ə-rē\ *n, pl* **-ries :** a religious house under a prioress or prior

prise *chiefly British variant of* ^{5}PRIZE

prism \ˈpriz-əm\ *n* **1 :** a polyhedron with two opposite ends that are parallel polygons and faces that are each parallelograms **2 a :** a transparent body bounded in part by two plane faces that are not parallel used to deviate or disperse a beam of light **b :** a prism-shaped decorative glass pendant [Late Latin *prismat-, prisma,* literally, "anything sawn," from *priein* "to saw"]

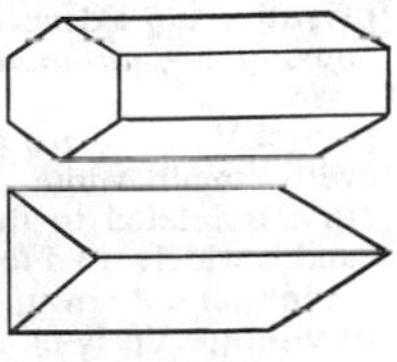

prism 1

pris·mat·ic \priz-ˈmat-ik\ *adj* **1 :** relating to, resembling, or being a prism **2 :** formed by refraction of light through a transparent prism ⟨*prismatic* colors⟩ **3 :** highly colored **:** BRILLIANT — **pris·mat·i·cal·ly** \-ˈmat-i-kə-lē, -klē\ *adv*

pris·ma·toid \ˈpriz-mə-ˌtȯid\ *n* **:** a polyhedron in which every vertex lies in one or the other of two parallel planes

pris·on \ˈpriz-n\ *n* **1 :** a state of confinement for criminals ⟨sentenced to *prison*⟩ **2 :** a place in which persons are locked up while awaiting or on trial or as punishment after conviction; *esp* **:** PENITENTIARY [Medieval French, from Latin *prehension-, prehensio* "act of seizing," from *prehendere* "to seize"]

pris·on·er \ˈpriz-nər, -n-ər\ *n* **:** a person kept under involuntary restraint, confinement, or custody; *esp* **:** one in prison

prisoner of war : a person captured in war; *esp* **:** a member of the armed forces of a nation taken by the enemy during combat

prisoner's base *n* **:** a children's game in which players of one team seek to tag and imprison players of the other team who have ventured out of their home territory

pris·sy \ˈpris-ē\ *adj* **pris·si·er; -est :** overly prim and finicky [probably blend of *prim* and *sissy*] — **pris·si·ly** \ˈpris-ə-lē\ *adv* — **pris·si·ness** \ˈpris-ē-nəs\ *n*

pris·tine \ˈpris-ˌtēn\ *adj* **:** of or relating to the earliest period or condition **:** ORIGINAL, PRIMITIVE ⟨*pristine* forest⟩; *esp* **:** having the purity or freshness of an original state ⟨*pristine* new uniforms⟩ [Latin *pristinus*] — **pris·tine·ly** *adv*

\ə\ **abut**	\au̇\ **out**	\i\ **tip**	\ȯ\ **saw**	\u̇\ **foot**
\ər\ **further**	\ch\ **chin**	\ī\ **life**	\ȯi\ **coin**	\y\ **yet**
\a\ **mat**	\e\ **pet**	\j\ **job**	\th\ **thin**	\yü\ **few**
\ā\ **take**	\ē\ **easy**	\ng\ **sing**	\t͟h\ **this**	\yu̇\ **cure**
\ä\ **cot, cart**	\g\ **go**	\ō\ **bone**	\ü\ **food**	\zh\ **vision**

prith·ee \'prith-ē, 'prith-\ *interj, archaic* — used to express a wish or request [alteration of *(I) pray thee*]

pri·va·cy \'prī-və-sē\ *n, pl* **-cies** **1** : the condition of being apart from company or observation : SECLUSION ⟨a yard with lots of *privacy*⟩ **2** : freedom from unauthorized intrusion ⟨a person's right to *privacy*⟩

1pri·vate \'prī-vət\ *adj* **1 a** : belonging to, concerning, or reserved for the use of a particular person or group : not public ⟨*private* property⟩ ⟨a *private* beach⟩ **b** : not under public control ⟨a *private* school⟩ **2** : not holding public office or employment ⟨a *private* citizen⟩ **3 a** : offering privacy : SECLUDED ⟨a *private* office⟩ **b** : not publicly known : SECRET ⟨*private* agreements⟩ [Latin *privatus* "not holding public office, private," from *privare* "to deprive," from *privus* "private, individual"] — **pri·vate·ly** *adv* — **pri·vate·ness** *n*

2private *n* **1** *pl* : PRIVATE PARTS **2 a** : a person of low or lowest rank in an organized group (as a police or fire department) **b** : an enlisted person of the lowest rank in the marine corps or of one of the two lowest ranks in the army — **in private** : PRIVATELY, SECRETLY

private detective *n* : PRIVATE INVESTIGATOR

private enterprise *n* : FREE ENTERPRISE

1pri·va·teer \,prī-və-'tiər\ *n* **1** : an armed private ship commissioned to cruise against the commerce or warships of an enemy **2** : the commander or one of the crew of a privateer

2privateer *vi* : to cruise in or as a privateer

private first class *n* : an enlisted person ranking above private and below corporal in the army and above private and below lance corporal in the marine corps

private investigator *n* : a person who does detective work and is not a member of a police force

private parts *n pl* : the external genital organs

pri·va·tion \prī-'vā-shən\ *n* **1** : an act or instance of depriving : DEPRIVATION **2** : the state of being deprived especially of what is needed for existence : WANT [Medieval French *privacion,* from Latin *privatio,* from *privare* "to deprive"]

1priv·a·tive \'priv-ət-iv\ *n* : a privative prefix or suffix

2privative *adj* : denoting or signifying privation or absence of a quality ⟨*a-, un-, non-* are *privative* prefixes⟩ — **priv·a·tive·ly** *adv*

priv·et \'priv-ət\ *n* : a shrub with small white flowers that is related to the olive and is widely used for hedges [origin unknown]

privet

priv·i·lege \'priv-lij, -ə-lij\ *n* : something special one is allowed to have, be, or do [Medieval French, from Latin *privilegium* "law for or against a private person," from *privus* "private" + *leg-, lex* "law"]

priv·i·leged \-lijd\ *adj* **1** : having or enjoying one or more privileges ⟨*privileged* classes⟩ **2** : not required to be disclosed in a court of law ⟨a *privileged* communication⟩

priv·i·ly \'priv-ə-lē\ *adv* : PRIVATELY, SECRETLY

1privy \'priv-ē\ *adj* **1** : belonging or relating to a person in his individual rather than his official capacity **2** : PRIVATE 3a ⟨a *privy* place⟩ **3** : sharing in a secret ⟨*privy* to the conspiracy⟩ [Medieval French *privé,* from Latin *privatus* "private"]

2privy *n, pl* **priv·ies** : a small building without plumbing that is used as a toilet; *also* : TOILET 2b

privy council *n* **1** *cap P&C* : an advisory council to the British crown which usually functions through committees **2** : a usually appointive advisory council to an executive — **privy councillor** *n*

privy purse *n* : an allowance for the private expenses of the British sovereign

1prize \'prīz\ *n* **1** : something won or to be won in competition or in contests of chance; *also* : a premium given as an inducement to buy **2** : something exceptionally desirable [Middle English *pris* "prize, price," from Medieval French, "price"]

2prize *adj* **1 a** : awarded a prize ⟨a *prize* essay⟩ **b** : awarded as a prize ⟨*prize* money⟩ **2** : outstanding of its kind ⟨*prize* hogs⟩

3prize *vt* **1** : to estimate the value of : RATE **2** : to value highly : ESTEEM [Medieval French *priser* to appraise, esteem, from Late Latin *pretiare,* from Latin *pretium* "price, value"]

4prize *n* **1** : something taken by force, stratagem, or threat; *esp* : property lawfully captured in time of war **2** : an act of capturing or taking; *esp* : the wartime capture of a ship and its cargo at sea [Medieval French *prise* "taking, seizure," from *prendre* "to take," from Latin *prehendere*]

5prize *vb* : to press, force, or move with or as if with a lever : PRY [from earlier *prize* "lever"]

prize·fight \'prīz-,fīt\ *n* : a professional boxing match — **prize·fight·er** \-ər\ *n* — **prize·fight·ing** \-ing\ *n*

prize ring *n* : a boxing ring where a prizefight takes place

prize·win·ner \-,win-ər\ *n* : a winner of a prize — **prize·win·ning** \-,win-ing\ *adj*

1pro \'prō\ *n, pl* **pros** \'prōz\ **1** : a favorable argument or piece of evidence ⟨*pros* and cons⟩ **2** : the affirmative position or one holding it [Latin, prep., "for"]

2pro *adv* : on the affirmative side

3pro *n or adj* : PROFESSIONAL

1pro- *prefix* **1 a** : prior to : prior ⟨*pro*gestational⟩ **b** : rudimentary : PROT- 2 ⟨*pro*nucleus⟩ **c** : precursory ⟨*pro*enzyme⟩ **2** : located in front of or at the front of ⟨*pro*thorax⟩ **3** : projecting ⟨*pro*gnathous⟩ [Latin, from Greek, from *pro* "before, forward, forth, for"]

2pro- *prefix* **1** : taking the place of : substituting for ⟨*pro*cathedral⟩ **2** : favoring : supporting : championing ⟨*pro*-American⟩ [Latin *pro* "in front of, before, for"]

proa *variant of* PRAU

prob·a·bil·i·ty \,präb-ə-'bil-ət-ē\ *n, pl* **-ties** **1** : the quality, state, or degree of being probable ⟨some *probability* of rain⟩ **2** : something probable **3** : a measure of the chance of one particular event occurring out of a set of equally likely events and equaling the ratio of the number of different ways that event could occur to the number of different ways any of the events could occur ⟨the *probability* of a coin coming up heads is ½⟩

prob·a·ble \'präb-ə-bəl, 'präb-bəl\ *adj* **1** : supported by evidence strong enough to make it likely though not certain to be true ⟨a *probable* explanation⟩ **2** : likely to happen or to have happened ⟨the *probable* outcome of the game⟩ [Latin *probabilis* "commendable, probable," from *probare* "to test, approve, prove," from *probus* "good, honest," from *pro* "for, in favor of"] — **prob·a·bly** \'präb-ə-blē, 'präb-lē\ *adv*

synonyms PROBABLE, POSSIBLE mean such as may be or may become true or actual. PROBABLE applies to what is supported by strong but not necessarily conclusive evidence ⟨the *probable* cause of the accident⟩. POSSIBLE refers to something which is within the limit of what may happen or of what a person or thing may do regardless of likelihood ⟨*possible* test questions⟩.

probable cause *n* : a reasonable ground for supposing that a criminal charge is well-founded

1pro·bate \'prō-,bāt\ *n* **1** : proof before a probate court that the last will and testament of a deceased person is genuine **2** : judicial determination of the validity of a will [Latin *probatus,* past participle of *probare* "to test, prove, approve"]

2probate *vt* : to establish (a will) by probate as valid

probate court *n* : a court having jurisdiction chiefly over the probate of wills and the administration of estates of deceased persons

pro·ba·tion \prō-'bā-shən\ *n* **1** : critical examination and evaluation or subjection to such examination and evaluation **2 a** : subjection of an individual to a period of testing and trial to ascertain fitness (as for a job or school) **b** : the suspending of a convicted offender's sentence during good behavior under the supervision of a probation officer **c** : the state or a period of being subject to probation — **pro·ba·tion·al** \-shnəl, -shən-l\ *adj* — **pro·ba·tion·al·ly** \-ē\ *adv* — **pro·ba·tion·ary** \-shə-,ner-ē\ *adj*

pro·ba·tion·er \prō-'bā-shə-nər, -shnər\ *n* : a person (as a new student nurse or a convict on a suspended sentence) who is undergoing probation

probation officer *n* : an officer appointed to investigate, report on, and supervise the conduct of convicted offenders on probation

pro·ba·tive \'prō-bət-iv\ *adj* **1** : serving to test or try **2** : serving to prove

pro·ba·to·ry \'prō-bə-,tōr-ē\ *adj* : PROBATIVE

1probe \'prōb\ *n* **1** : a slender medical instrument especially for examining a cavity (as a wound) **2 a** : a pointed metal tip for making electrical contact with a circuit element being checked **b** : a device used to penetrate or send back information especially from outer space **c** : a device (as an ultrasound generator) or a substance (as a radioactive molecule) used to obtain specific information for diagnostic or experimental purposes **3** : a searching examination; *esp* : an inquiry to discover evidence of wrongdoing ⟨a congressional *probe*⟩ [Medieval Latin *proba* "examination," from Latin *probare* "to test, prove"]

[2]**probe** *vb* **1** : to examine with or as if with a probe **2** : to investigate thoroughly **3** : to make an exploratory investigation — **prob·er** *n*

pro·bi·ty \'prō-bət-ē\ *n* : adherence to the highest principles and ideals : UPRIGHTNESS [Latin *probitas,* from *probus* "honest"]

[1]**prob·lem** \'präb-ləm\ *n* **1 a** : a question raised for inquiry, consideration, or solution **b** : a proposition in mathematics or physics stating something to be done **2 a** : an intricate unsettled question **b** : a source of perplexity or vexation [Latin *problema,* from Greek *problēma,* literally, "obstacle," from *proballein* "to throw forward," from *pro-* "forward" + *ballein* "to throw"]

[2]**problem** *adj* **1** : dealing with a problem of human conduct or social relationship ⟨a *problem* play⟩ **2** : difficult to deal with ⟨a *problem* child⟩

prob·lem·at·ic \ˌpräb-lə-'mat-ik\ *or* **prob·lem·at·i·cal** \-'mat-i-kəl\ *adj* : having the nature of a problem : difficult and uncertain : PUZZLING — **prob·lem·at·i·cal·ly** \-i-kə-lē, -klē\ *adv*

pro·bos·ci·de·an \prə-ˌbäs-ə-'dē-ən\ *or* **pro·bos·cid·i·an** \prə-ˌbäs-'id-ē-ən\ *n* : any of an order (Proboscidea) of large mammals comprising the elephants and extinct related forms (as mastodons) [derived from Latin *proboscid-, proboscis* "proboscis"] — **pro·boscidean** *adj*

pro·bos·cis \prə-'bäs-əs, -kəs\ *n, pl* **-bos·cis·es** *also* **-bos·ci·des** \-'bäs-ə-ˌdēz\ **1** : a long flexible snout; *esp* : the trunk of an elephant **2** : an elongated sometimes extensible tubular process (as the sucking organ of a butterfly) of the mouth region of an invertebrate [Latin, from Greek *proboskis,* from *pro-* + *boskein* "to feed"]

proboscis monkey *n* : a large monkey of Borneo with the males having a long fleshy nose hanging down from the face

pro·caine \'prō-ˌkān\ *n* : a drug used as a local anesthetic [[2]*pro-* + co*caine*]

pro·cam·bi·um \prō-'kam-bē-əm, 'prō-\ *n* : the part of the primary meristem of a plant that forms cambium and other primary vascular tissues — **pro·cam·bi·al** \-bē-əl\ *adj*

procaryote *variant of* PROKARYOTE

pro·ca·the·dral \ˌprō-kə-'thē-drəl\ *n* : a parish church used as a cathedral

pro·ce·dure \prə-'sē-jər\ *n* **1 a** : a particular way of accomplishing something or of acting **b** : a step in a procedure ⟨the first *procedure* was to line up alphabetically⟩ **2 a** : a series of steps followed in a regular definite order ⟨legal *procedure*⟩ ⟨a surgical *procedure*⟩ **b** : a series of instructions for a computer that has a name by which it can be called into action **3** : a traditional or established way of doing things — **pro·ce·dur·al** \prə-'sēj-rəl, -ə-rəl\ *adj* — **pro·ce·dur·al·ly** \-ē\ *adv*

pro·ceed \prō-'sēd, prə-\ *vi* **1** : to come forth from a source : ISSUE ⟨strange sounds *proceeded* from the room⟩ **2 a** : to continue after a pause or interruption **b** : to go on in an orderly regulated way **3 a** : to begin and carry on an action, process, or movement ⟨*proceeded* to tell her version⟩ **b** : to be in the process of being accomplished ⟨the work is *proceeding* well⟩ **4** : to move along a course [Middle French *proceder,* from Latin *procedere,* from *pro-* "forward" + *cedere* "to go"]

pro·ceed·ing *n* **1** : PROCEDURE 2 **2** *pl* : things that take place ⟨talked over the day's *proceedings*⟩ **3** : legal action ⟨a probate *proceeding*⟩ **4** : a thing done **5** *pl* : an official record of things said or done

pro·ceeds \'prō-ˌsēdz\ *n pl* : the total amount or the profit arising (as from a business or tax) : RETURN

[1]**pro·cess** \'präs-ˌes, 'prōs-, -əs\ *n, pl* **pro·cess·es** \-ˌes-əz, -ə-səz, -ə-ˌsēz\ **1 a** : PROGRESS, ADVANCE ⟨the *process* of time⟩ **b** : something going on **2 a** (1) : a natural phenomenon marked by gradual changes that lead toward a particular result ⟨the *process* of growth⟩ (2) : a continuing natural or biological activity or function ⟨breathing and other life *processes*⟩ **b** : a series of actions, operations, or changes leading to an end ⟨education is a long *process*⟩ **3 a** : the proceedings or manner of proceeding in a legal action ⟨due *process* of law⟩ **b** : a legal summons or writ used by a court to compel the appearance of the defendant or obedience to its orders **4** : a prominent or projecting bodily part : OUTGROWTH ⟨a bony *process*⟩ [Medieval French *procés,* from Latin *processus,* from *procedere* "to proceed"]

[2]**process** *vt* **1** : to change or prepare by special treatment ⟨*process* foods⟩ **2 a** : to take care of according to a routine ⟨*process* insurance claims⟩ **b** (1) : to take in and organize to be used in a variety of useful ways ⟨computers *process* data⟩ (2) : to integrate sensory information received so that an action or response is generated ⟨the brain *processes* visual images relayed from the retina⟩

process cheese *n* : cheese made by blending several lots of cheese

pro·ces·sion \prə-'sesh-ən\ *n* **1** : continuous forward movement : PROGRESSION **2** : a group of individuals moving along in an orderly often ceremonial way ⟨a funeral *procession*⟩

[1]**pro·ces·sion·al** \prə-'sesh-nəl, -ən-l\ *n* **1** : a hymn sung during a procession (as of a choir entering the church at the beginning of a service) **2** : a ceremonial procession

[2]**processional** *adj* : of, relating to, or moving in a procession — **pro·ces·sion·al·ly** \-ē\ *adv*

pro·ces·sor \'präs-ˌes-ər, 'prōs-\ *n* **1** : one that processes **2** : a part of a computer that processes data; *esp* : CPU

pro–choice \prō-'chȯis\ *adj* : favoring the legalization of abortion

pro·claim \prō-'klām\ *vt* **1** : to announce publicly ⟨*proclaimed* his belief in their innocence⟩ **2** : to declare officially or formally ⟨*proclaim* a holiday⟩ [Latin *proclamare,* from *pro-* "before" + *clamare* "to cry out"] ***synonyms*** see DECLARE — **pro·claim·er** *n*

proc·la·ma·tion \ˌpräk-lə-'mā-shən\ *n* **1** : the action of proclaiming : an official publication ⟨*proclamation* of a new law⟩ **2** : something proclaimed [Medieval French *proclamacion,* from Latin *proclamatio,* from *proclamare* "to proclaim"]

pro·cliv·i·ty \prō-'kliv-ət-ē\ *n, pl* **-ties** : a tendency or inclination of the mind or temperament : DISPOSITION ⟨a *proclivity* to procrastinate⟩ [Latin *proclivitas,* from *proclivis* "sloping, prone," from *pro-* "forward" + *clivus* "hill"]

pro·con·sul \prō-'kän-səl, 'prō-\ *n* **1** : a governor or military commander of an ancient Roman province **2** : an administrator in a modern colony, dependency, or occupied area [Latin, from *pro consule* "for a consul"] — **pro·con·sul·ar** \-sə-lər, -slər\ *adj* — **pro·con·sul·ate** \-sə-lət, -slət\ *n* — **pro·con·sul·ship** \-səl-ˌship\ *n*

pro·cras·ti·nate \prə-'kras-tə-ˌnāt\ *vb* **1** : to put off repeatedly **2** : to keep postponing something supposed to be done [Latin *procrastinare,* from *pro-* "forward" + *crastinus* "of tomorrow," from *cras* "tomorrow"] — **pro·cras·ti·na·tion** \-ˌkras-tə-'nā-shən\ *n* — **pro·cras·ti·na·tor** \-'kras-tə-ˌnāt-ər\ *n*

pro·cre·ate \'prō-krē-ˌāt\ *vb* : to beget or bring forth offspring : REPRODUCE [Latin *procreare,* from *pro-* "forth" + *creare* "to create"] — **pro·cre·a·tion** \ˌprō-krē-'ā-shən\ *n* — **pro·cre·a·tive** \'prō-krē-ˌāt-iv\ *adj* — **pro·cre·a·tor** \-ˌāt-ər\ *n*

pro·crus·te·an \prə-'krəs-tē-ən\ *adj, often cap* : marked by arbitrary often ruthless disregard of individual differences or special circumstances [*Procrustes,* legendary Greek robber who made his victims fit a certain bed by stretching or lopping off their legs]

procrustean bed *n, often cap P* : a scheme or pattern into which someone or something is arbitrarily forced

proc·tor \'präk-tər\ *n* : SUPERVISOR, MONITOR; *esp* : one appointed to supervise students (as at an examination) [Middle English *procutour* "procurator, proctor," alteration of *procuratour*] — **proctor** *vb* — **proc·to·ri·al** \präk-'tōr-ē-əl, -'tȯr-\ *adj* — **proc·tor·ship** \'präk-tər-ˌship\ *n*

pro·cum·bent \prō-'kəm-bənt\ *adj* **1** : being or having stems that trail along the ground **2** : lying face down [Latin *procumbens,* present participle of *procumbere* "to fall or lean forward"]

proc·u·ra·tor \'präk-yə-ˌrāt-ər\ *n* **1** : one that manages another's affairs : AGENT **2** : a Roman provincial administrator and financial manager **3** : a criminal prosecutor in various countries [Medieval French *procuratour,* from Latin *procurator,* from *procurare* "to take care of"] — **proc·u·ra·to·ri·al** \ˌpräk-yə-rə-'tōr-ē-əl, -'tȯr-\ *adj*

pro·cure \prə-'kyu̇r\ *vb* **1 a** : to get possession of : OBTAIN **b**

\ə\ **abut**	\au̇\ **out**	\i\ **tip**	\ȯ\ **saw**	\u̇\ **foot**
\ər\ **further**	\ch\ **chin**	\ī\ **life**	\ȯi\ **coin**	\y\ **yet**
\a\ **mat**	\e\ **pet**	\j\ **job**	\th\ **thin**	\yü\ **few**
\ā\ **take**	\ē\ **easy**	\ng\ **sing**	\th\ **this**	\yu̇\ **cure**
\ä\ **cot, cart**	\g\ **go**	\ō\ **bone**	\ü\ **food**	\zh\ **vision**

: to make women available for promiscuous sexual intercourse **2** : to bring about : ACHIEVE [Late Latin *procurare,* from Latin, "to take care of," from *pro-* "for" + *cura* "care"] — **pro•cur•able** \-ˈkyu̇r-ə-bəl\ *adj* — **pro•cure•ment** \-ˈkyu̇r-mənt\ *n*

pro•cur•er \-ˈkyu̇r-ər\ *n* : one that procures; *esp* : PANDER 1b

Pro•cy•on \ˈprō-sē-ˌän, ˈpräs-ē-\ *n* : the brightest star in Canis Minor [Latin, from Greek *Prokyōn,* literally, "fore-dog"; from its rising before the Dog Star]

[1]**prod** \ˈpräd\ *vt* **prod•ded; prod•ding** **1 a** : to thrust a pointed instrument into **b** : to move to action : STIR **2** : to poke or stir as if with a prod [origin unknown] — **prod•der** *n*

[2]**prod** *n* **1** : a pointed instrument used to prod **2** : something that moves one to act

[1]**prod•i•gal** \ˈpräd-i-gəl\ *adj* **1** : recklessly extravagant ⟨a *prodigal* spender⟩ **2** : wastefully lavish ⟨*prodigal* entertainment⟩ [Latin *prodigus,* from *prodigere* "to drive away, squander," from *pro-, prod-* "forth" + *agere* "to drive"] — **prod•i•gal•i•ty** \ˌpräd-ə-ˈgal-ət-ē\ *n* — **prod•i•gal•ly** \ˈpräd-i-gə-lē, -glē\ *adv*

[2]**prodigal** *n* **1** : a person who spends prodigally : SPENDTHRIFT **2** : one who has returned after an absence

pro•di•gious \prə-ˈdij-əs\ *adj* **1** : exciting amazement or wonder **2** : extraordinary in bulk, quantity, or degree : ENORMOUS ***synonyms*** see MONSTROUS — **pro•di•gious•ly** *adv* — **pro•di•gious•ness** *n*

prod•i•gy \ˈpräd-ə-jē\ *n, pl* **-gies** **1** : something extraordinary or unexplainable **2** : an amazing instance, deed, or performance ⟨a *prodigy* of strength and skill⟩ **3** : a highly talented child [Latin *prodigium* "omen, monster"]

[1]**pro•duce** \prə-ˈdüs, -ˈdyüs\ *vb* **1** : to offer to view or notice : EXHIBIT ⟨*produce* evidence⟩ **2** : to give birth or rise to ⟨a tree *producing* good fruit⟩ **3** : to extend in length, area, or volume ⟨*produce* a side of a triangle⟩ **4** : to provide funding for or oversee the production of (as a play) **5** : to give being, form, or shape to : MAKE; *esp* : MANUFACTURE **6** : to bring in as profit ⟨investments *producing* an income⟩ **7** : to produce something ⟨a pear tree that never *produced*⟩ [Latin *producere,* from *pro-* "forward" + *ducere* "to lead"]

[2]**pro•duce** \ˈpräd-ˌüs, ˈprōd- *also* -ˌyüs\ *n* **1** : something produced **2** : agricultural products; *esp* : fresh fruits and vegetables as distinguished from staple crops (as grain)

pro•duc•er \prə-ˈdü-sər, -ˈdyü-\ *n* **1** : one that produces; *esp* : one that grows agricultural products or manufactures articles **2** : a person who supervises or finances a stage or screen production or radio or television program **3** : an autotrophic organism (as a green plant) which produces its own organic compounds from simple precursors (as carbon dioxide and inorganic nitrogen) and many of which are food sources for other organisms — compare CONSUMER b

producer gas *n* : a manufactured fuel gas consisting chiefly of carbon monoxide, hydrogen, and nitrogen

producer goods *n pl* : goods (as tools) that are used to produce other goods

pro•duc•ible \prə-ˈdü-sə-bəl, -ˈdyü-\ *adj* : capable of being produced

prod•uct \ˈpräd-əkt, -ˌəkt\ *n* **1** : the number or expression resulting from the multiplication of two or more numbers or expressions **2** : something produced **3** : the amount, quantity, or total produced [Latin *productum* "something produced," from *productus,* past participle of *producere* "to produce"]

pro•duc•tion \prə-ˈdək-shən\ *n* **1 a** : something produced : PRODUCT **b** (1) : a literary or artistic work (2) : a work presented on the stage or screen or over the air **c** : something exaggerated out of proportion to its importance **2 a** : the act or process of producing **b** : the making of goods available for human wants **3** : total output

pro•duc•tive \prə-ˈdək-tiv\ *adj* **1** : having the power to produce especially in abundance ⟨*productive* fishing waters⟩ **2** : effective in or bringing about a production ⟨an age *productive* of great men⟩ **3** : yielding or furnishing results, benefits, or profits ⟨a *productive* training program⟩ **4** : yielding or devoted to the satisfaction of wants or the creation of utilities ⟨the *productive* labor force⟩ **5** : continuing to be used in the formation of new words or constructions ⟨*un-* is a *productive* English prefix⟩ — **pro•duc•tive•ly** *adv* — **pro•duc•tive•ness** *n*

pro•duc•tiv•i•ty \ˌprō-ˌdək-ˈtiv-ət-ē, ˌpräd-ək-, prə-ˌdək-\ *n* **1** : the quality or state of being productive **2** : the rate of production at which living matter consumable as food by other organisms is made by producer organisms

pro•em \ˈprō-ˌem\ *n* **1** : PREFACE 2 **2** : PRELUDE 1 [Medieval French *proeme,* from Latin *prooemium,* from Greek *prooimion,* from *pro-* + *oimē* "song"]

pro•en•zyme \prō-ˈen-ˌzīm\ *n* : ZYMOGEN

prof \ˈpräf\ *n* : PROFESSOR 2

prof•a•na•tion \ˌpräf-ə-ˈnā-shən, ˌprō-fə-\ *n* : the act of profaning

pro•fa•na•to•ry \prō-ˈfan-ə-ˌtōr-ē, -ˈfā-nə-, -ˌtȯr-\ *adj* : tending to profane

[1]**pro•fane** \prō-ˈfān, prə-\ *vt* **1** : to treat (something sacred) with irreverence, abuse, or contempt **2** : to put to a wrong, unworthy, or vulgar use — **pro•fan•er** *n*

[2]**profane** *adj* **1** : not concerned with religion or religious purposes **2** : not holy : not fit for religious uses **3** : serving to debase or defile what is holy : IRREVERENT [Medieval French *prophane,* from Latin *profanus,* from *pro-* "before" + *fanum* "temple"] — **pro•fane•ly** *adv* — **pro•fane•ness** \-ˈfān-nəs\ *n*

pro•fan•i•ty \prō-ˈfan-ət-ē\ *n, pl* **-ties** **1 a** : the quality or state of being profane **b** : the use of profane language **2** : profane language

pro•fess \prə-ˈfes\ *vt* **1** : to receive formally into a religious community following a novitiate by acceptance of the required vows **2 a** : to declare openly or freely ⟨*profess* confidence in a friend's honesty⟩ **b** : PRETEND, CLAIM ⟨*professed* to be a friend of mine⟩ **3** : to confess one's faith in or allegiance to ⟨*profess* Christianity⟩ **4** : to practice or claim to be versed in (a calling or profession) [derived from Latin *professus,* past participle of *profiteri* "to profess, confess," from *pro-* "before" + *fateri* "to acknowledge"]

pro•fessed \-ˈfest\ *adj* : openly declared whether truly or falsely

pro•fessed•ly \prə-ˈfes-əd-lē, -ˈfest-lē\ *adv* **1** : by one's own account **2** : supposedly but not really

pro•fes•sion \prə-ˈfesh-ən\ *n* **1** : the act of taking the vows of a religious community **2** : an act of openly declaring or publicly claiming a belief, faith, or opinion **3** : an avowed religious faith **4 a** : a calling requiring specialized knowledge and academic preparation ⟨the teaching *profession*⟩ **b** : a principal employment **c** : the whole body of persons engaged in a calling

[1]**pro•fes•sion•al** \prə-ˈfesh-nəl, -ən-l\ *adj* **1 a** : of, relating to, or characteristic of a profession ⟨*professional* publications⟩ **b** : engaged in one of the learned professions **2 a** : participating for gain or livelihood in an activity often engaged in by amateurs ⟨a *professional* golfer⟩ **b** : having a particular profession as a permanent career ⟨a *professional* soldier⟩ **c** : engaged in by persons receiving financial return ⟨*professional* football⟩ **3** : following a line of conduct as though it were a profession ⟨a *professional* patriot⟩ — **pro•fes•sion•al•ly** \-ē\ *adv*

[2]**professional** *n* : one that engages in an activity professionally

pro•fes•sion•al•ism \-ˌiz-əm\ *n* **1** : the conduct, aims, or qualities that mark a profession or a professional person **2** : the following of a profession (as athletics) for gain or livelihood

pro•fes•sion•al•ize \-ˌīz\ *vt* : to give a professional character to

pro•fes•sor \prə-ˈfes-ər\ *n* **1** : one that professes, avows, or declares **2 a** : a faculty member of the highest academic rank at an institution of higher education **b** : a teacher at a university, college, or sometimes secondary school — **pro•fes•so•ri•al** \ˌprō-fə-ˈsōr-ē-əl, ˌpräf-ə-, -ˈsȯr-\ *adj* — **pro•fes•so•ri•al•ly** \-ē-ə-lē\ *adv*

pro•fes•sor•ship \prə-ˈfes-ər-ˌship\ *n* : the office, duties, or position of an academic professor

[1]**prof•fer** \ˈpräf-ər\ *vt* **prof•fered; prof•fer•ing** \ˈpräf-ring, -ə-ring\ : to present for acceptance : TENDER, OFFER [Medieval French *profrer, porofrir,* from *por-* "forth" (from Latin *pro-*) + *offrir* "to offer"]

[2]**proffer** *n* : something proffered : OFFER

pro•fi•cien•cy \prə-ˈfish-ən-sē\ *n, pl* **-cies** **1** : advancement in knowledge or skill **2** : the quality or state of being proficient

pro•fi•cient \prə-ˈfish-ənt\ *adj* : well advanced in an art, occupation, or branch of knowledge [Latin *proficiens,* present participle of *proficere* "to go forward, accomplish," from *pro-* "forward" + *facere* "to make"] — **pro•fi•cient•ly** *adv*

synonyms PROFICIENT, ADEPT, SKILLFUL, EXPERT mean having great knowledge and experience in a trade or profession. PROFICIENT stresses competence derived from training and practice ⟨a *proficient* typist⟩. ADEPT adds to proficiency the implication of aptitude or cleverness ⟨an *adept* writer of dialogue⟩. SKILLFUL stresses dexterity in execution or performance ⟨*skillful* drivers⟩. EXPERT implies extraordinary proficiency and often connotes knowledge and technical skill ⟨an *expert* chef⟩.

[1]**pro·file** \ˈprō-ˌfīl\ *n* **1 :** a representation of something in outline; *esp* **:** a human head or face represented or seen in a side view **2 :** an outline seen or represented in sharp relief **3 :** a brief biographical sketch **4 :** a vertical section of soil that shows the various zones **5 :** degree or level of public exposure ⟨keep a low *profile*⟩ [Italian *profilo,* from *profilare* "to draw in outline," from *pro-* "forward" + *filare* "to spin"]

profile 1

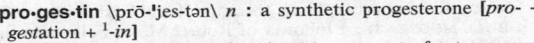

[2]**profile** *vt* **1 :** to represent in profile **:** draw or write a profile of **2 :** to shape the outline of by passing a cutter around

[1]**prof·it** \ˈpräf-ət\ *n* **1 :** a valuable return **:** GAIN **2 :** the gain after all expenses are subtracted from the total amount received **3 :** the return coming to those who assume the risks of a business as distinguished from wages or rent [Medieval French, from Latin *profectus* "advance, profit," from *proficere* "to go forward"] — **prof·it·less** \-ləs\ *adj*

[2]**profit** *vb* **1 :** to be of service or advantage **2 :** to derive benefit **:** GAIN ⟨*profit* by experience⟩ **3 :** BENEFIT ⟨a business deal that *profited* no one⟩

prof·it·able \ˈpräf-ət-ə-bəl, ˈpräf-tə-bəl\ *adj* **:** yielding profits **:** PRODUCTIVE ***synonyms*** see BENEFICIAL — **prof·it·abil·i·ty** \ˌpräf-ət-ə-ˈbil-ət-ē, ˌpräf-tə-ˈbil-\ *n* — **prof·it·able·ness** \ˈpräf-ət-ə-bəl-nəs, ˈpräf-tə-bəl-\ *n* — **prof·it·ably** \-blē\ *adv*

prof·i·teer \ˌpräf-ə-ˈtiər\ *n* **:** one who makes an unreasonable profit especially on the sale of essential goods during an emergency — **profiteer** *vi*

profit sharing *n* **:** the sharing with employees of a part of the profits of an enterprise

prof·li·ga·cy \ˈpräf-li-gə-sē\ *n* **:** the quality or state of being profligate

prof·li·gate \ˈpräf-li-gət\ *adj* **1 :** loose in character or morals **2 :** extremely wasteful ⟨*profligate* use of natural resources⟩ [Latin *profligatus,* from *profligare* "to strike down, ruin"] — **profligate** *n* — **prof·li·gate·ly** *adv*

pro for·ma \prō-ˈfȯr-mə, ˈprō-\ *adj* **:** for the sake of or as a matter of form [Latin]

pro·found \prə-ˈfau̇nd\ *adj* **1 a :** having intellectual depth and insight ⟨a *profound* scholar⟩ **b :** difficult to understand ⟨a *profound* work⟩ **2 a :** extending far below the surface **b :** coming from, reaching to, or situated at a depth ⟨a *profound* sigh⟩ **3 a :** deeply felt **:** INTENSE ⟨*profound* regret⟩ **b :** COMPLETE ⟨*profound* silence⟩ [Medieval French *profond* "deep," from Latin *profundus,* from *pro-* "before" + *fundus* "bottom"] — **pro·found·ly** *adv* — **pro·found·ness** \-ˈfau̇nd-nəs, -ˈfau̇n-\ *n*

pro·fun·di·ty \prə-ˈfən-dət-ē\ *n, pl* **-ties** **1 a :** intellectual depth **b :** something profound or hard to understand **2 :** the quality or state of being very profound or deep [Latin *profunditas* "depth," from *profundus* "deep"]

pro·fuse \prə-ˈfyüs\ *adj* **1 :** pouring forth in great amounts ⟨*profuse* in their thanks⟩ ⟨*profuse* spending⟩ **2 :** exhibiting great abundance ⟨*profuse* blooms⟩ [Latin *profusus,* past participle of *profundere* "to pour forth," from *pro-* "forth" + *fundere* "to pour"] — **pro·fuse·ly** *adv* — **pro·fuse·ness** *n*

pro·fu·sion \prə-ˈfyü-zhən\ *n* **1 :** profuse expenditure **2 :** lavish display or supply ⟨*profusion* of flowers⟩

pro·gen·i·tor \prō-ˈjen-ət-ər\ *n* **1 a :** a direct ancestor **b :** a biologically ancestral form **2 :** one that originates or precedes [Medieval French *progenitour,* from Latin *progenitor,* from *progenitus,* past participle of *progignere* "to beget"]

prog·e·ny \ˈpräj-ə-nē\ *n, pl* **-nies** **1 :** human descendents **:** CHILDREN **2 :** offspring of animals or plants [Medieval French *progenie,* from Latin *progenies,* from *progignere* "to beget," from *pro-* "forth" + *gignere* "to beget"]

pro·ges·ta·tion·al \ˌprō-ˌjes-ˈtā-shnəl, -shən-l\ *adj* **:** preceding pregnancy or gestation; *esp* **:** of, relating to, inducing, or being the changes in a female mammal associated with ovulation and corpus luteum formation ⟨*progestational* hormones⟩

pro·ges·ter·one \prō-ˈjes-tə-ˌrōn\ *n* **:** a female steroid sex hormone $C_{21}H_{30}O_2$ that is produced by the corpus luteum and induces and maintains changes in the uterus to provide a suitable environment for a fertilized egg [*proge*stin + *ster*ol + *-one,* alteration of *-ene*]

pro·ges·tin \prō-ˈjes-tən\ *n* **:** a synthetic progesterone [*pro-* + *gestation* + [1]*-in*]

pro·glot·tid \prō-ˈglät-əd, ˈprō-\ *n* **:** a segment of a tapeworm containing both male and female reproductive organs [New Latin *proglottid-, proglottis,* from Greek *proglōttis,* "tip of the tongue," from *pro-* + *glōtta* "tongue"]

prog·na·thous \ˈpräg-nə-thəs, präg-ˈnā-\ *adj* **:** being or having the lower jaw projecting beyond the upper part of the face [*pro-* + Greek *gnathos* "jaw"] — **prog·na·thism** \-ˌthiz-əm\ *n*

prog·no·sis \präg-ˈnō-səs\ *n, pl* **-no·ses** \-ˈnō-ˌsēz\ **1 :** the prospect of recovery of an individual who has a disease based on the usual course of the disease and the characteristics of the individual who is sick **2 :** FORECAST [Late Latin, from Greek *prognōsis,* literally, "foreknowledge," from *progignōskein* "to know before," from *pro-* + *gignōskein* "to know"]

prog·nos·tic \präg-ˈnäs-tik\ *n* **1 :** something that foretells **2 :** PROPHECY 2 [Medieval French *pronostique,* from Latin *prognosticum,* from Greek *prognōstikon,* from *prognōstikos* "foretelling," from *progignōskein* "to know before"] — **prognostic** *adj*

prog·nos·ti·cate \präg-ˈnäs-tə-ˌkāt\ *vt* **1 :** to foretell from signs or symptoms **:** PREDICT **2 :** to give an indication of in advance **:** FORESHADOW — **prog·nos·ti·ca·tive** \-ˌkāt-iv\ *adj* — **prog·nos·ti·ca·tor** \-ˌkāt-ər\ *n*

prog·nos·ti·ca·tion \präg-ˌnäs-tə-ˈkā-shən\ *n* **1 :** an indication in advance **:** FORETOKEN **2 :** FORECAST

[1]**pro·gram** \ˈprō-ˌgram, -grəm\ *n* **1 :** a brief usually written outline describing a presentation (as of a concert) **2 :** the performance of a program; *esp* **:** a performance that is broadcast ⟨a television *program*⟩ **3 :** a plan of action **4 :** a sequence of coded instructions for a computer [French *programme* "agenda, public notice," from Greek *programma,* from *prographein* "to write before," from *pro* + *graphein* "to write"]

[2]**program** *vt* **pro·grammed** *or* **pro·gramed** \-ˌgramd, -grəmd\; **pro·gram·ming** *or* **pro·gram·ing** **1 a :** to arrange or furnish a program of or for **b :** to enter in a program **2 :** to provide (as a computer) with a program **3 :** to direct the thinking or behavior of as if by a computer program ⟨kids *programmed* to expect success⟩ — **pro·gram·ma·ble** \ˈprō-ˌgram-ə-bəl\ *adj*

programme *chiefly British variant of* PROGRAM

programmed instruction *n* **:** instruction through information given in small steps with each step requiring a correct response before the learner can go on to the next

pro·gram·mer *also* **pro·gram·er** \ˈprō-ˌgram-ər\ *n* **:** a person who writes computer programs

[1]**prog·ress** \ˈpräg-rəs, -ˌres, *chiefly British* ˈprō-ˌgres\ *n* **1 a :** a royal journey or tour **b :** an official journey **c :** an expedition or tour through a region **2 :** a forward movement **:** ADVANCE ⟨the ship's *progress*⟩ **3 :** gradual improvement; *esp* **:** the progressive development of humankind [Medieval French *progrés,* from Latin *progressus* "advance," from *progredi* "to go forth," from *pro-* "forward" + *gradi* "to go"]

[2]**pro·gress** \prə-ˈgres\ *vi* **1 :** to move forward **:** PROCEED **2 :** to develop to a higher, better, or more advanced stage

pro·gres·sion \prə-ˈgresh-ən\ *n* **1 :** a sequence of numbers in which each term is related to its predecessor by a uniform law **2 a :** the action of progressing **b :** a connected series ⟨the rapid *progression* of incidents in a play⟩ **3 a :** series of musical chords **b :** the movement of voice parts in harmony — **pro·gres·sion·al** \-ˈgresh-nəl, -ən-l\ *adj*

[1]**pro·gres·sive** \prə-ˈgres-iv\ *adj* **1 a :** of, relating to, or characterized by progress or progression **b :** gradually increasing ⟨*progressive* income tax⟩ **2 :** of, relating to, or constituting an educational theory marked by emphasis on the individual child, informal classroom procedure, and encouragement of self-expression **3 :** moving forward or onward **4 :** increasing in extent or severity ⟨a *progressive* disease⟩ **5** *often cap* **:** of or relating to political Progressives **6 :** of, relating to, or constituting a verb form that expresses action or state in progress at the time of speaking or a time spoken of — **pro·gres·sive·ly** *adv* — **pro·gres·sive·ness** *n*

[2]**progressive** *n* **1 a :** one that is progressive **b :** one believing in moderate political change and social improvement by governmental action **2** *cap* **a :** a member of a minor United

\ə\ abut	\au̇\ **out**	\i\ **tip**	\ȯ\ **saw**	\u̇\ **foot**
\ər\ **further**	\ch\ **chin**	\ī\ **life**	\ȯi\ **coin**	\y\ **yet**
\a\ **mat**	\e\ **pet**	\j\ **job**	\th\ **thin**	\yü\ **few**
\ā\ **take**	\ē\ **easy**	\ng\ **sing**	\th\ **this**	\yu̇\ **cure**
\ä\ **cot, cart**	\g\ **go**	\ō\ **bone**	\ü\ **food**	\zh\ **vision**

States political party split off from the Republicans about 1912 : BULL MOOSE **b** : a follower of Robert M. La Follette in the presidential campaign of 1924 **c** : a follower of Henry A. Wallace in the presidential campaign of 1948

pro•gres•siv•ism \prə-ˈgres-iv-ˌiz-əm\ *n* **1** *often cap* : the principles or beliefs of progressives or of Progressives **2** : the theories of progressive education — **pro•gres•siv•ist** \-i-vəst\ *n or adj*

pro•hib•it \prō-ˈhib-ət\ *vt* **1** : to forbid by authority ⟨*prohibit* all-day parking⟩ **2 a** : to prevent from doing something ⟨common courtesy *prohibits* my saying anything⟩ **b** : to make impossible ⟨the high walls *prohibit* escape⟩ [Latin *prohibitus,* past participle of *prohibēre* "to hold away," from *pro-* "forward" + *habēre* "to hold"] ***synonyms*** see FORBID

pro•hi•bi•tion \ˌprō-ə-ˈbish-ən\ *n* **1** : the act of prohibiting **2** : an order forbidding something **3** *often cap* : the forbidding by law of the sale and sometimes the manufacture and transportation of alcoholic liquors as beverages

pro•hi•bi•tion•ist \-ˈbish-nəst, -ə-nəst\ *n* : a person who is in favor of prohibiting the manufacture and sale of alcoholic liquors as beverages; *esp, cap* : a member of a minor U.S. political party advocating prohibition

pro•hib•i•tive \prō-ˈhib-ət-iv\ *adj* : serving or tending to prohibit ⟨*prohibitive* prices⟩ — **pro•hib•i•tive•ly** *adv*

pro•hib•i•to•ry \prō-ˈhib-ə-ˌtōr-ē, -ˌtȯr-\ *adj* : PROHIBITIVE

¹proj•ect \ˈpräj-ˌekt, -ikt\ *n* **1** : a particular plan or design : SCHEME **2** : a planned undertaking: as **a** : a definitely formulated piece of research **b** : a large usually government-supported undertaking **c** : a task or problem engaged in usually by a group of students to supplement and apply classroom studies **3** : a group of houses or apartment buildings constructed and arranged according to a single plan; *esp* : one built with government help to provide low-cost housing [Medieval Latin *projectum,* from Latin *projectus,* past participle of *proicere* "to throw forward," from *pro-* + *jacere* "to throw"]

²pro•ject \prə-ˈjekt\ *vb* **1** : to devise in the mind : DESIGN ⟨*project* civic improvements⟩ **2** : to throw forward, upward, or outward **3** : to stick out ⟨a stone jetty *projecting* into the bay⟩ **4** : to cause (light or shadow) to fall into space or (an image) to fall on a surface ⟨*project* a beam of light⟩ ⟨*project* motion pictures on a screen⟩ **5** : to reproduce (as a point, line, or area) on a surface by motion in a prescribed manner [Medieval French *projecter,* from Medieval Latin *projectum*] — **pro•ject•able** \-ˈjek-tə-bəl\ *adj*

¹pro•jec•tile \prə-ˈjek-tl\ *n* **1** : a body projected by external force and continuing in motion by its own inertia; *esp* : a missile for a weapon (as a firearm or cannon) **2** : a self-propelling weapon (as a guided missile)

²projectile *adj* **1** : projecting or impelling forward ⟨a *projectile* force⟩ **2** : capable of being thrust forward

pro•jec•tion \prə-ˈjek-shən\ *n* **1 a** : a method of mapping a curved surface (as of the earth or the celestial sphere) on a flat surface based on a systematic presentation of intersecting coordinate lines **b** (1) : the process of reproducing a spatial object upon a surface by projecting its points; *also* : the graphic reproduction so formed (2) : a set of points obtained by projecting another set of points onto a line, plane, or surface **2** : the act of throwing or shooting forward : EJECTION **3** : the forming of a plan **4 a** : a jutting out **b** : a part that juts out **5** : attribution of one's own feelings or attitudes to another **6** : the display of motion pictures by projecting an image from them upon a screen **7** : an estimate of future possibilities based on a current trend — **pro•jec•tion•al** \-shnəl, -shən-l\ *adj*

synonyms PROJECTION, PROTRUSION, PROTUBERANCE, BULGE mean an extension beyond the normal line or surface. PROJECTION implies a jutting out especially at a sharp angle ⟨those *projections* along the wall are safety hazards⟩. PROTRUSION suggests a thrusting out so that the extension seems like a deformity ⟨the bizarre *protrusions* of a coral reef⟩. PROTUBERANCE implies a growing or swelling out in rounded form ⟨a skin disease marked by warty *protuberances*⟩. BULGE suggests an expansion caused by internal pressure ⟨*bulges* in the tile floor⟩.

pro•jec•tion•ist \-shə-nəst, -shnəst\ *n* : one that makes projections; *esp* : one that operates a motion-picture projector or television equipment

pro•jec•tive \prə-ˈjek-tiv\ *adj* : of, relating to, or involving geometric projection

projective geometry *n* : a branch of mathematics concerned with the properties of geometric figures that remain unchanged by projection

pro•jec•tor \prə-ˈjek-tər\ *n* **1** : one that plans a project; *esp* : PROMOTER **2** : one that projects: as **a** : a device for projecting a beam of light **b** : an optical instrument or machine for projecting an image or pictures upon a surface

pro•kary•ote *also* **pro•cary•ote** \prō-ˈkar-ē-ˌōt, ˈprō-\ *n* : a typically unicellular microorganism (as a bacterium or a blue-green alga) that does not have a nucleus or membrane-bound organelles (as mitochondria) characteristic of eukaryotes [New Latin *Prokaryotes,* derived from Greek *pro-* "before" + *karyon* "nut, kernel" (referring to a cell nucleus)] — **pro•kary•ot•ic** \ˌprō-ˌkar-ē-ˈät-ik\ *adj*

pro•lac•tin \prō-ˈlak-tən\ *n* : a protein hormone produced by the pituitary gland that induces lactation

pro•lapse \prō-ˈlaps\ *n* : the slipping of a body part from its usual position or relations [Late Latin *prolapsus* "fall," from Latin *prolabi* "to fall or slide forward," from *pro-* "forward" + *labi* "to slide"] — **prolapse** *vi*

pro•leg \ˈprō-ˌleg\ *n* : a fleshy leg on an abdominal segment of some insect larvae

pro•le•gom•e•non \ˌprō-li-ˈgäm-ə-ˌnän\ *n, pl* **-na** \-nə\ : introductory remarks; *esp* : a formal essay or critical discussion serving to introduce and interpret an extended work [Greek, neuter present passive participle of *prolegein* "to say beforehand," from *pro-* + *legein* "to say"] — **pro•le•gom•e•nous** \-nəs\ *adj*

¹pro•le•tar•i•an \ˌprō-lə-ˈter-ē-ən\ *n* : a member of the proletariat [Latin *proletarius,* from *proles* "progeny"]

²proletarian *adj* : of, relating to, or representative of the proletariat

pro•le•tar•i•at \ˌprō-lə-ˈter-ē-ət, -ˈtar-, -ē-ˌat\ *n* **1** : the lowest social or economic class of a community **2** : industrial workers who sell their labor to live [French *prolétariat,* from Latin *proletarius* "proletarian"]

pro–life \prō-ˈlīf\ *adj* : opposed to abortion and especially to the legalization of abortion

pro•lif•er•ate \prə-ˈlif-ə-ˌrāt\ *vi* : to grow or increase by rapid production of new units (as cells or offspring) [back-formation from *proliferation,* from French *prolifération,* from *proliférer* "to proliferate," from *prolifère* "reproducing freely," from Latin *proles* "progeny" + *-fer* "-ferous"] — **pro•lif•er•a•tion** \-ˌlif-ə-ˈrā-shən\ *n* — **pro•lif•er•a•tive** \-ˈlif-ə-ˌrāt-iv\ *adj*

pro•lif•ic \prə-ˈlif-ik\ *adj* **1** : producing young or fruit abundantly ⟨a *prolific* orchard⟩ **2** : highly inventive : PRODUCTIVE ⟨a *prolific* mind⟩ **3** : causing or characterized by fruitfulness ⟨*prolific* growing season⟩ [French *prolifique,* from Latin *proles* "progeny" + French *-fique* "-fic"] ***synonyms*** see FERTILE — **pro•lif•i•cal•ly** \-ˈlif-i-kə-lē,-klē\ *adv* — **pro•lif•ic•ness** *n*

pro•line \ˈprō-ˌlēn\ *n* : an amino acid $C_5H_9NO_2$ that can be synthesized by animals from glutamate [German *Prolin*]

pro•lix \prō-ˈliks, ˈprō-ˌliks\ *adj* : using or containing too many words : WORDY, LONG-WINDED [Latin *prolixus* "extended," from *pro-* "forward" + *liquēre* "to be fluid"] — **pro•lix•i•ty** \prō-ˈlik-sət-ē\ *n* — **pro•lix•ly** \prō-ˈliks-lē, ˈprō-ˌ\ *adv*

pro•logue \ˈprō-ˌlȯg\ *n* **1** : the preface or introduction to a literary work **2 a** : a speech often in verse addressed to the audience by an actor at the beginning of a play **b** : the actor speaking such a prologue **3** : an introductory or preceding event or development [Medieval French, from Latin *prologus* "preface to a play," from Greek *prologos,* from *pro-* + *legein* "to speak"]

pro•long \prə-ˈlȯŋ\ *vt* **1** : to make longer than usual : continue or lengthen in time ⟨a *prolonged* stay in the hospital⟩ **2** : to lengthen in extent or range ⟨*prolong* a boundary line⟩ [Medieval French *prolonguer,* from Late Latin *prolongare,* from Latin *pro-* "forward" + *longus* "long"] ***synonyms*** see EXTEND

pro•lon•ga•tion \prō-ˌlȯŋ-ˈgā-shən\ *n* **1** : a lengthening in space or time **2** : something that prolongs or is prolonged

prom \ˈpräm\ *n* : a formal dance given by a high school or college class [short for *promenade*]

¹prom•e•nade \ˌpräm-ə-ˈnād, -ˈnäd\ *n* **1** : a leisurely walk or ride especially in a public place for pleasure or display **2** : a place for strolling **3 a** : a ceremonious opening of a formal ball consisting of a grand march of all the guests **b** : a figure in a square dance in which couples move counterclockwise in a circle [French, from *promener* "to take for a walk," from Medieval French, alteration of *pourmener,* from *pour-* "completely" + *mener* "to lead," from Late Latin *minare* "to drive," from Latin *minari* "to threaten"]

²promenade *vb* **1** : to take or go on a promenade **2** : to perform a promenade in a dance **3** : to walk about in or on ⟨*promenading* the sun deck⟩ — **prom·e·nad·er** *n*

promenade deck *n* : an upper deck of a passenger ship where passengers stroll

Pro·me·the·an \prə-ˈmē-thē-ən\ *adj* : of, relating to, or resembling Prometheus; *esp* : daringly original or creative

pro·me·thi·um \-thē-əm\ *n* : a metallic chemical element obtained as a fission product of uranium or from neutron-irradiated neodymium — see ELEMENT table [New Latin, from *Prometheus,* a Titan]

prom·i·nence \ˈpräm-ə-nəns\ *n* **1** : the quality, state, or fact of being prominent or conspicuous ⟨a person of *prominence*⟩ **2** : PROJECTION 4b **3** : a mass or stream of gas resembling a cloud that arises from the chromosphere of the sun

prom·i·nent \-nənt\ *adj* **1** : standing out or projecting beyond a surface or line : PROTUBERANT **2** : readily noticeable : CONSPICUOUS **3** : EMINENT, NOTABLE [Latin *prominens,* from *prominēre* "to jut forward"] ***synonyms*** see NOTICEABLE — **prom·i·nent·ly** *adv*

prom·is·cu·i·ty \ˌpräm-əs-ˈkyü-ət-ē, ˌprō-məs-\ *n, pl* **-ties** **1** : a miscellaneous mingling of persons or things **2** : promiscuous sexual behavior

pro·mis·cu·ous \prə-ˈmis-kyə-wəs\ *adj* **1** : composed of all sorts of persons or things ⟨a *promiscuous* crowd of onlookers⟩ **2** : not restricted to one person or class ⟨give *promiscuous* praise⟩; *esp* : not restricted to one sexual partner **3** : HAPHAZARD, IRREGULAR ⟨*promiscuous* eating habits⟩ [Latin *promiscuus,* from *pro-* "forth" + *miscēre* "to mix"] — **pro·mis·cu·ous·ly** *adv* — **pro·mis·cu·ous·ness** *n*

[1]**prom·ise** \ˈpräm-əs\ *n* **1** : a statement assuring someone that the person making the statement will do or not do something : PLEDGE ⟨a *promise* to pay⟩ **2** : a cause or ground for hope or expectation especially of success or distinction ⟨the child shows *promise*⟩ **3** : something promised [Latin *promissum,* from *promissus,* past participle of *promittere* "to send forth, promise," from *pro-* "forth" + *mittere* "to send"]

[2]**promise** *vb* **1 a** : to pledge onself to do, bring about, or provide ⟨*promise* aid⟩ **b** : to tell as a promise ⟨*promised* them we'd wait⟩ **c** : to make a promise **2** : to suggest beforehand : FORETOKEN ⟨dark clouds *promising* rain⟩ — **prom·i·sor** \ˌpräm-ə-ˈsȯr\ *n*

promised land *n* : a better place that one hopes to reach or a better condition that one hopes to attain

prom·is·ing *adj* : full of promise : giving hope or assurance (as of success) ⟨a very *promising* pupil⟩ — **prom·is·ing·ly** \ˈpräm-ə-sing-lē\ *adv*

prom·is·so·ry \ˈpräm-ə-ˌsōr-ē, -ˌsȯr-\ *adj* : containing or conveying a promise or assurance

promissory note *n* : a written promise to pay at a fixed or determinable time a sum of money to a specified individual or to bearer

prom·on·to·ry \ˈpräm-ən-ˌtōr-ē, -ˌtȯr-\ *n, pl* **-ries** : a high point of land or rock jutting out into a body of water : HEADLAND [Latin *promunturium*]

pro·mote \prə-ˈmōt\ *vt* **1** : to advance in position, rank, or honor : ELEVATE ⟨*promote* pupils to a higher grade⟩ **2 a** : to contribute to the growth, success, or development of : FURTHER ⟨good food *promotes* health⟩ **b** : to present (merchandise) for buyer acceptance through advertising, publicity, or discounting ⟨*promoted* his new book⟩ **3** : to take the first steps in organizing (as a business) [Latin *promotus,* past participle of *promovēre,* literally, "to move forward," from *pro-* "forward" + *movēre* "to move"] — **pro·mot·able** \-ə-bəl\ *adj*

pro·mot·er \prə-ˈmōt-ər\ *n* : one that promotes; *esp* : one taking on the financial responsibilities of a sporting event

pro·mo·tion \prə-ˈmō-shən\ *n* **1** : the act or fact of being raised in position or rank **2** : the act of furthering the growth, development, or acceptance of something — **pro·mo·tion·al** \-shnəl, -shən-l\ *adj*

[1]**prompt** \ˈprämt, ˈprämpt\ *vt* **1** : to move to action : CAUSE ⟨curiosity *prompted* me to ask the question⟩ **2** : to remind of something forgotten or poorly learned (as by suggesting the next few words in a speech) ⟨*prompt* an actor⟩ **3** : SUGGEST, INSPIRE ⟨pride *prompted* the act⟩ [Medieval Latin *promptare,* from Latin *promptus* "ready, prompt"]

[2]**prompt** *adj* **1 a** : being ready and quick as occasion demands ⟨*prompt* to answer⟩ **b** : PUNCTUAL ⟨*prompt* in arriving⟩ **2** : performed readily or immediately ⟨*prompt* assistance⟩ [Latin *promptus* "ready, prompt," from past participle of *promere* "to bring forth," from *pro-* "forth" + *emere* "to take"] — **prompt·ly** *adv* — **prompt·ness** *n*

prompt·book \ˈprämt-ˌbu̇k, ˈprämp-\ *n* : a copy of a play with directions for performance used by a theater prompter

prompt·er \ˈpräm-tər, ˈprämp-\ *n* : a person who reminds another of the words to be spoken next (as in a play)

promp·ti·tude \ˈpräm-tə-ˌtüd, ˈprämp-, -ˌtyüd\ *n* : the quality or habit of being prompt : PROMPTNESS

prom·ul·gate \ˈpräm-əl-ˌgāt; prō-ˈməl-\ *vt* **1** : to make (as a doctrine) known by open declaration : PROCLAIM **2 a** : to make public the terms of (a proposed law) **b** : to put (a law) into action or force [Latin *promulgare*] — **prom·ul·ga·tion** \ˌpräm-əl-ˈgā-shən, ˌprō-məl-\ *n* — **prom·ul·ga·tor** \ˈpräm-əl-ˌgāt-ər, prō-ˈməl-\ *n*

pro·na·tion \prō-ˈnā-shən\ *n* : rotation of the hand or forearm so as to bring the palm facing downward or backward; *also* : rotation of the bones in the foot inward and downward so that in walking the foot tends to come down on its inner surface [from *pronate,* from Late Latin *pronatus,* past participle of *pronare* "to bend forward," from Latin *pronus* "bent forward"] — **pro·nate** \ˈprō-ˌnāt\ *vt*

pro·na·tor \ˈprō-ˌnāt-ər\ *n* : a muscle that produces pronation

prone \ˈprōn\ *adj* **1** : having a tendency or inclination ⟨*prone* to laziness⟩ **2** : having the front surface downward : lying belly or face downward ⟨shoot from a *prone* position⟩; *also* : lying flat [Latin *pronus* "bent forward, tending"] — **prone** *adv* — **prone·ness** \ˈprōn-nəs\ *n*

synonyms PRONE, PROSTRATE, SUPINE mean lying down. PRONE implies a position with the front of the body turned toward the supporting surface ⟨saw him *prone* on the deck⟩. PROSTRATE implies lying at full length as in submission or physical collapse ⟨the runner fell *prostrate* at the finish line⟩. SUPINE implies lying on one's back and may connote laziness or inertness ⟨lying *supine* on the couch⟩.

[1]**prong** \ˈprȯng, ˈpräng\ *n* **1** : a tine of a fork **2** : a slender pointed or projecting part (as of a tooth or an antler) [Middle English *pronge*] — **pronged** \ˈprȯngd, ˈprängd\ *adj*

[2]**prong** *vt* : to stab, pierce, or break up with a pronged device

prong·horn \ˈprȯng-ˌhȯrn, ˈpräng-\ *n, pl* **pronghorn** *or* **pronghorns** : a cud-chewing horned mammal of treeless parts of western North America that resembles an antelope — called also *pronghorn antelope*

pronghorn

pro·nom·i·nal \prō-ˈnäm-ən-l\ *adj* **1** : of, relating to, or being a pronoun **2** : resembling a pronoun in identifying or specifying without describing ⟨the *pronominal* adjective *this* in "this dog"⟩ [Late Latin *pronominalis,* from Latin *pronomen* "pronoun"] — **pro·nom·i·nal·ly** \-l-ē\ *adv*

pro·noun \ˈprō-ˌnau̇n\ *n* : a word that is used as a substitute for a noun or a noun phrase, takes noun constructions, and refers to persons or things named or understood in the context [Medieval French, from Latin *pronomen,* from *pro-* "for" + *nomen* "name"]

pro·nounce \prə-ˈnau̇ns\ *vt* **1** : to declare officially or solemnly ⟨the minister *pronounced* them husband and wife⟩ ⟨the judge *pronounced* sentence⟩ **2** : to assert as an opinion ⟨*pronounce* the book a success⟩ **3** : to utter the sounds of : speak aloud ⟨practice *pronouncing* foreign words⟩; *esp* : to say or speak correctly ⟨can't *pronounce* your name⟩ [Medieval French *pronuncier,* from Latin *pronuntiare,* from *pro-* "forth" + *nuntiare* "to report," from *nuntius* "messenger"] — **pro·nounce·able** \-ˈnau̇n-sə-bəl\ *adj* — **pro·nounc·er** *n*

pro·nounced \-ˈnau̇nst\ *adj* : strongly marked : DECIDED ⟨a *pronounced* change for the better⟩ — **pro·nounc·ed·ly** \-ˈnau̇n-səd-lē\ *adv*

\ə\ **abut**	\au̇\ **out**	\i\ **tip**	\ȯ\ **saw**	\u̇\ **foot**
\ər\ **further**	\ch\ **chin**	\ī\ **life**	\ȯi\ **coin**	\y\ **yet**
\a\ **mat**	\e\ **pet**	\j\ **job**	\th\ **thin**	\yü\ **few**
\ā\ **take**	\ē\ **easy**	\ng\ **sing**	\th\ **this**	\yu̇\ **cure**
\ä\ **cot, cart**	\g\ **go**	\ō\ **bone**	\ü\ **food**	\zh\ **vision**

pro·nounce·ment \prə-ˈnau̇ns-mənt\ *n* **1 :** a formal declaration of opinion **2 :** an authoritative announcement

pron·to \ˈprän-ˌtō\ *adv* **:** right away **:** QUICKLY, PROMPTLY [Spanish, from Latin *promptus* "prompt"]

pro·nu·cle·us \prō-ˈnü-klē-əs, -ˈnyü-\ *n* **:** the haploid nucleus of a male or female gamete (as an egg or sperm) up until the time it unites with another gamete in fertilization

pro·nun·ci·a·men·to \prō-ˌnən-sē-ə-ˈment-ō\ *n, pl* **-tos** *or* **-toes :** PROCLAMATION 1, PRONOUNCEMENT [Spanish *pronunciamiento,* from *pronunciar* "to pronounce," from Latin *pronuntiare*]

pro·nun·ci·a·tion \prə-ˌnən-sē-ˈā-shən\ *n* **:** the act or manner of pronouncing something [Medieval French, from Latin *pronuntiatio,* from *pronuntiare* "to pronounce"] — **pro·nun·ci·a·tion·al** \-shnəl, -shən-l\ *adj*

[1]**proof** \ˈprüf\ *n* **1 a** (1) **:** evidence of truth or correctness ⟨gave *proof* of their statement⟩ (2) **:** the process of or an instance of establishing the validity of a statement (as a mathematical theorem) especially by derivation from other statements by accepted rules of reasoning **b :** a test to find out or show the essential facts or truth ⟨put the theory to the *proof*⟩ **2 a :** a copy (as of composed text) made for correction or examination **b :** a test photographic print made from a negative **3 :** alcoholic content (as of a beverage) indicated by a number that is twice the percent by volume of alcohol present ⟨whiskey of 90 *proof* is 45 percent alcohol⟩ [Middle English *prof, prove,* alteration of *preve,* from Medieval French *preove,* from Late Latin *proba,* from Latin *probare* "to prove"]

[2]**proof** *adj* **1 :** successful in repelling, resisting, or withstanding ⟨*proof* against tampering⟩ — often used in combination ⟨water*proof*⟩ **2 :** used in proving or testing or as a standard of comparison ⟨*proof* gold⟩

[3]**proof** *vt* **:** to activate (yeast) by mixing with water

proof·read \ˈprü-ˌfrēd\ *vb* **:** to read and make corrections in ⟨*proofread* a composition⟩

proof·read·er \-ˌfrēd-ər\ *n* **:** a person who proofreads

[1]**prop** \ˈpräp\ *n* **:** something that props or sustains **:** SUPPORT [Dutch *proppe* "stopper"]

[2]**prop** *vt* **propped; prop·ping 1 a :** to hold up or keep from falling or slipping by placing something under or against ⟨*prop* up the table⟩ **b :** to support by placing against something ⟨*propped* the rake against the tree⟩ **2 :** SUSTAIN, STRENGTHEN ⟨*propped* up by faith in times of crisis⟩

[3]**prop** *n* **:** PROPERTY 5

[4]**prop** *n* **:** PROPELLER

pro·pa·gan·da \ˌpräp-ə-ˈgan-də, ˌprō-pə-\ *n* **:** the spreading of ideas, information, or rumor for the purpose of helping or injuring a cause; *also* **:** the ideas, facts, or allegations so spread [New Latin, from *Congregatio de propaganda fide* "congregation for propagating the faith," organization established by Pope Gregory XV] — **pro·pa·gan·dist** \-dəst\ *n or adj* — **pro·pa·gan·dis·tic** \-ˌgan-ˈdis-tik\ *adj* — **pro·pa·gan·dis·ti·cal·ly** \-ti-kə-lē, -klē\ *adv*

pro·pa·gan·dize \-ˈgan-ˌdīz\ *vb* **1 :** to spread propaganda **2 :** to influence or attempt to influence by propaganda

prop·a·gate \ˈpräp-ə-ˌgāt\ *vb* **1 :** to reproduce or increase by sexual or asexual means **:** MULTIPLY ⟨*propagate* an apple by grafting⟩ **2 :** to pass along to offspring **3 a :** to cause to spread out and affect a greater number or greater area **b :** PUBLICIZE **c :** TRANSMIT 2 **4 :** to increase in extent, number, or influence **:** EXTEND [Latin *propagare* "to set slips, propagate," from *propages* "slip, offspring," from *pro-* "before" + *pangere* "to fasten"] — **prop·a·ga·tive** \-ˌgāt-iv\ *adj* — **prop·a·ga·tor** \-ˌgāt-ər\ *n*

prop·a·ga·tion \ˌpräp-ə-ˈgā-shən\ *n* **:** the act or process of propagating: as **a :** multiplication (as of a kind of organism) in number of individuals **b :** the spreading of something (as a belief) abroad or into new regions **:** DISSEMINATION ⟨*propagation* of a faith⟩ — **prop·a·ga·tion·al** \-shnəl, -shən-l\ *adj*

pro·pane \ˈprō-ˌpān\ *n* **:** a heavy flammable gaseous hydrocarbon C_3H_8 found in crude petroleum and natural gas and used especially as fuel and in chemical synthesis [*prop*ionic acid + *-ane*]

pro·pel \prə-ˈpel\ *vt* **pro·pelled; pro·pel·ling 1 :** to push or drive usually forward or onward ⟨a bicycle is *propelled* by pedals⟩ **2 :** to give an impelling motive to **:** urge ahead ⟨people *propelled* by ambition⟩ [Latin *propellere,* from *pro-* "before" + *pellere* "to drive"] ***synonyms*** see PUSH

[1]**pro·pel·lant** *also* **pro·pel·lent** \-ˈpel-ənt\ *adj* **:** capable of propelling

[2]**propellant** *also* **propellent** *n* **:** something that propels: as **a :** an explosive for propelling projectiles **b :** fuel plus oxidizer used by a rocket engine **c :** a gas in a specially made container for expelling the contents when the pressure is released

pro·pel·ler *also* **pro·pel·lor** \prə-ˈpel-ər\ *n* **:** one that propels; *esp* **:** a device consisting of a hub with radiating blades that is used for propelling aircraft and boats

pro·pen·si·ty \prə-ˈpen-sət-ē\ *n, pl* **-ties :** a natural inclination or liking **:** BENT ⟨a *propensity* for drawing⟩ [derived from Latin *propensus,* past participle of *propendēre* "to incline," from *pro-* "before" + *pendēre* "to hang"]

[1]**prop·er** \ˈpräp-ər\ *adj* **1 :** suitable by reason of essential nature or condition **2 a :** appointed for the liturgy of a particular day **b :** belonging to one **:** OWN **3 :** belonging characteristically to a species or individual **:** PECULIAR **4 :** strictly limited to a specified thing, place, or idea ⟨outside the city *proper*⟩ **5 a :** strictly accurate **:** CORRECT ⟨the *proper* pronunciation⟩ **b :** strictly decorous **:** GENTEEL ⟨the *proper* attire⟩ [Medieval French *propre* "proper, own," from Latin *proprius* "own"] ***synonyms*** see FIT — **prop·er·ness** *n*

[2]**proper** *n* **:** the parts of the Mass or Divine Office that vary according to the day or feast

proper adjective *n* **:** an adjective formed from a proper noun

proper fraction *n* **:** a fraction in which the numerator is less or of lower degree than the denominator

prop·er·ly \ˈpräp-ər-lē\ *adv* **1 :** in a suitable or fit manner ⟨behave *properly* in church⟩ **2 :** strictly in accordance with fact **:** CORRECTLY ⟨goods not *properly* labeled⟩ ⟨*properly* speaking, whales are not fish⟩

proper noun *n* **:** a noun that designates a particular being or thing and in English is usually capitalized — called also *proper name*

proper subset *n* **:** a subset containing fewer elements than the set to which it belongs

prop·er·tied \ˈpräp-ərt-ēd\ *adj* **:** owning property and especially much property

prop·er·ty \ˈpräp-ərt-ē\ *n, pl* **-ties 1 :** a special quality or trait characteristic of a thing ⟨sweetness is a *property* of sugar⟩ **2 :** anything that is owned; *esp* **:** a piece of real estate ⟨a business *property*⟩ **3 :** the legal right to property **:** OWNERSHIP **4 :** any article used on the stage during a play or on the set of a motion picture except painted scenery and actors' costumes [Medieval French *proprete,* from Latin *proprietas,* from *proprius* "own"] ***synonyms*** see QUALITY

prop·er·ty·less \-ləs\ *adj* **:** lacking property especially in the form of real estate ⟨the *propertyless* classes⟩

pro·phage \ˈprō-ˌfāj, -ˌfäzh\ *n* **:** an intracellular form of a bacteriophage in which it is harmless to the host, is usually integrated into the hereditary material of the host, and reproduces when the host does

pro·phase \ˈprō-ˌfāz\ *n* **1 :** the initial phase of mitosis and of the second division of meiosis in which chromosomes consisting of paired chromatids condense from the resting form into tightly coiled dense bodies **2 :** the initial stage of the first division of meiosis in which individual chromosomes become visibly double as paired chromatids, pairs of homologous chromosomes undergo synapsis and crossing over, and the nuclear membrane disappears

proph·e·cy \ˈpräf-ə-sē\ *n, pl* **-cies 1 :** the divinely inspired work or revelation of a prophet **2 :** the foretelling of the future ⟨the gift of *prophecy*⟩ **3 :** something foretold of the future **:** PREDICTION [Medieval French *prophecie,* from Late Latin *prophetia,* from Greek *prophēteia,* from *prophētēs* "prophet"]

proph·e·sy \ˈpräf-ə-ˌsī\ *vb* **-sied; -sy·ing 1 a :** to speak or write as a prophet **b :** to utter by divine inspiration **2 :** to predict on or as if on the basis of mystic knowledge ⟨*prophesy* bad weather⟩ [Medieval French *prophecier,* from *prophecie* "prophecy"] ***synonyms*** see FORETELL — **proph·e·si·er** \-ˌsī-ər, -ˌsīr\ *n*

proph·et \ˈpräf-ət\ *n* **1 :** a person who declares publicly a message that he or she believes has been divinely inspired; *esp, often cap* **:** the writer of one of the prophetic books of the Old Testament **2 :** one gifted with more than ordinary spiritual and moral insight; *esp* **:** an inspired poet **3 :** one who foretells future events **4 :** an effective or leading spokesman for a cause, doctrine, or group ⟨a *prophet* of the revolution⟩ [Medieval

French *prophete,* from Latin *propheta,* from Greek *prophētēs,* from *pro* "for" + *phanai* "to speak"]

proph·et·ess \-ət-əs\ *n* **:** a woman who is a prophet

pro·phet·ic \prə-ˈfet-ik\ *adj* **1 :** of, relating to, or characteristic of a prophet or prophecy ⟨*prophetic* insight⟩ **2 :** foretelling events **:** PREDICTIVE ⟨a *prophetic* statement⟩ — **pro·phet·i·cal** \-ˈfet-i-kəl\ *adj* — **pro·phet·i·cal·ly** \-i-kə-lē, -klē\ *adv*

Proph·ets \ˈpräf-əts\ *n pl* **:** the second part of the Hebrew Bible — see BIBLE table; compare LAW 3b, WRITINGS

1pro·phy·lac·tic \ˌprō-fə-ˈlak-tik\ *adj* **1 :** guarding from or preventing the spread or occurrence of disease or infection **2 :** tending to prevent or ward off **:** PREVENTIVE [Greek *prophylaktikos,* from *prophylassein* "to be on guard," from *pro-* "before" + *phylassein* "to guard," from *phylax* "guard"] — **pro·phy·lac·ti·cal·ly** \-ti-kə-lē, -klē\ *adv*

2prophylactic *n* **:** something prophylactic; *esp* **:** a device and especially a condom for preventing venereal infection or conception

pro·phy·lax·is \-ˈlak-səs\ *n, pl* **-lax·es** \-ˈlak-ˌsēz\ **:** measures designed to preserve health and prevent the spread of disease [New Latin, from Greek *prophylaktikos* "prophylactic"]

pro·pin·qui·ty \prō-ˈping-kwət-ē\ *n* **1 :** nearness of blood **:** KINSHIP **2 :** nearness in place or time [Latin *propinquitas* "kinship, proximity," from *propinquus* "near, akin," from *prope* "near"]

pro·pi·on·ic acid \ˌprō-pē-ˌän-ik-\ *n* **:** a liquid sharp-odored fatty acid $C_3H_6O_2$ found in milk and distillates of wood, coal, and petroleum and used especially as a mold inhibitor and flavoring agent [*pro-* + Greek *piōn* "fat"]

pro·pi·ti·ate \prō-ˈpish-ē-ˌāt\ *vt* **:** to gain or regain the favor or goodwill of **:** APPEASE, CONCILIATE ⟨*propitiate* the angry gods with sacrifices⟩ [Latin *propitiare,* from *propitius* "propitious"] — **pro·pi·ti·a·tion** \-ˌpish-ē-ˈā-shən\ *n* — **pro·pi·ti·ator** \-ˈpish-ē-ˌāt-ər\ *n* — **pro·pi·tia·to·ry** \-ˈpish-ē-ə-ˌtōr-ē, -ˈpish-ə-, -ˌtȯr-\ *adj*

pro·pi·tious \prə-ˈpish-əs\ *adj* **1 :** favorably disposed **2 :** of good omen **:** PROMISING ⟨*propitious* signs⟩ **3 :** likely to produce good results **:** OPPORTUNE ⟨the *propitious* moment for asking a favor⟩ [Latin *propitius,* probably from *pro-* "for" + *petere* "to seek"] — **pro·pi·tious·ly** *adv* — **pro·pi·tious·ness** *n*

prop·jet engine \ˈpräp-ˌjet-\ *n* **:** TURBO-PROPELLER ENGINE

prop·man \ˈpräp-ˌman\ *n* **:** a person in charge of stage properties

prop·o·lis \ˈpräp-ə-ləs\ *n* **:** a brownish waxy resinous material collected by bees from the buds of trees and used as a cement in repairing and maintaining the hive [Latin, from Greek, from *pro-* "for" + *polis* "city"]

pro·po·nent \prə-ˈpō-nənt, ˈprō-ˌ\ *n* **:** one who argues in favor of something **:** ADVOCATE ⟨a *proponent* of year-round school⟩ [Latin *proponens,* present participle of *proponere* "to propound"]

1pro·por·tion \prə-ˈpōr-shən, pə-, -ˈpȯr-\ *n* **1 :** the relation of one part to another or to the whole with respect to magnitude, quantity, or degree **:** RATIO **2 :** balanced or pleasing arrangement **3 :** a statement of the equality of two ratios (as $\frac{4}{2} = \frac{10}{5}$) — compare EXTREME 1b, MEAN 2b **4 a :** fair or equal share **b :** QUOTA 1, PERCENTAGE **5 :** relative dimensions **:** SIZE [Medieval French *proporcion,* from Latin *proportio,* from *pro* "for" + *portio* "portion"] — **pro·por·tioned** \-shənd\ *adj* — **in proportion :** PROPORTIONAL 1

2proportion *vt* **-tioned; -tion·ing** \-shə-ning, -shning\ **1 :** to adjust (a part or thing) in size relative to other parts or things **2 :** to make the parts of harmonious or symmetrical

1pro·por·tion·al \prə-ˈpōr-shnəl, pə-, -ˈpȯr-, -shən-l\ *adj* **1 a :** corresponding in size, degree, or intensity ⟨salary *proportional* to ability⟩ **b :** having the same or a constant ratio ⟨corresponding sides of similar triangles are *proportional*⟩ **2 :** determined in size or degree with reference to proportions — **pro·por·tion·al·i·ty** \-ˌpōr-shə-ˈnal-ət-ē, -ˌpȯr-\ *n* — **pro·por·tion·al·ly** \-ˈpōr-shnə-lē, -ˈpȯr-, -shən-l-ē\ *adv*

2proportional *n* **:** a number or quantity in a proportion

proportional parts *n pl* **:** fractional parts of the difference between successive entries in a table for use in linear interpolation

proportional representation *n* **:** an electoral system designed to represent in a legislative body each political group or party in proportion to its actual voting strength in the electorate

1pro·por·tion·ate \prə-ˈpōr-shə-nət, pə-, -ˈpȯr-, -shnət\ *adj* **:** PROPORTIONAL 1 — **pro·por·tion·ate·ly** *adv*

2pro·por·tion·ate \-shə-ˌnāt\ *vt* **:** to make proportionate

pro·pos·al \prə-ˈpō-zəl\ *n* **1 :** an act of offering something for consideration **2 a :** something proposed **:** SUGGESTION **b :** OFFER 1b; *esp* **:** an offer of marriage

pro·pose \prə-ˈpōz\ *vb* **1 :** to offer for consideration or discussion **:** SUGGEST ⟨*propose* terms of peace⟩ **2 :** to make plans **:** INTEND ⟨*propose* to buy a new house⟩ **3 :** to offer as a toast **:** suggest drinking to ⟨*propose* the health of a friend⟩ **4 :** NAME, NOMINATE ⟨*propose* one for membership⟩ **5 :** to make an offer of marriage [Medieval French *purposer, proposer,* from Latin *proponere* "to propound"] — **pro·pos·er** *n*

prop·o·si·tion \ˌpräp-ə-ˈzish-ən\ *n* **1 a :** something offered for consideration or acceptance **:** PROPOSAL **b :** a theorem or problem to be demonstrated or performed **2 :** a declarative sentence **:** an expression in language or signs of something that can be either true or false **3 :** a project or situation of an indicated kind to be dealt with ⟨writing this paper is going to be an all-day *proposition*⟩ — **prop·o·si·tion·al** \-ˈzish-nəl, -ən-l\ *adj*

pro·pound \prə-ˈpau̇nd\ *vt* **:** to offer for consideration **:** PROPOSE [alteration of earlier *propone,* from Latin *proponere* "to display, propound," from *pro-* "before" + *ponere* "to put, place"] — **pro·pound·er** *n*

1pro·pri·etary \prə-ˈprī-ə-ˌter-ē\ *n, pl* **-tar·ies 1 :** PROPRIETOR 1 **2 :** a drug whose name, composition, or process of manufacture is protected by secrecy, patent, or copyright against free competition **:** PATENT MEDICINE **3 :** a business secretly owned and run as a cover for an intelligence organization

2proprietary *adj* **1 :** of, relating to, or characteristic of a proprietor ⟨*proprietary* rights⟩ **2 :** made and marketed by one having the exclusive right to manufacture and sell ⟨*proprietary* software⟩ **3 :** privately owned and managed ⟨a *proprietary* clinic⟩ [Late Latin *proprietarius,* from Latin *proprietas* "property"]

proprietary colony *n* **:** a colony granted to a proprietor

pro·pri·etor \prə-ˈprī-ət-ər\ *n* **1 :** one granted ownership of a colony and given full rights to establish a government and distribute land **2 :** one who holds something as property or a possession **:** OWNER ⟨*proprietor* of a store⟩ — **pro·pri·etor·ship** \-ˌship\ *n*

pro·pri·etress \-ˈprī-ə-trəs\ *n* **:** a woman who is a proprietor

pro·pri·ety \prə-ˈprī-ət-ē\ *n, pl* **-ties 1 :** the quality or state of being proper **2 :** correctness in manners or behavior **:** POLITENESS **3** *pl* **:** the rules and customs of polite society [Medieval French *proprieté, propreté* "property"] ***synonyms*** see DECORUM

pro·prio·cep·tor \ˌprō-prē-ō-ˈsep-tər\ *n* **:** a sensory receptor (as in a muscle) excited by stimuli (as changes in limb position) arising within the organism [Latin *proprius* "own" + English *-ceptor* (as in *receptor*)] — **pro·prio·cep·tive** \-tiv\ *adj*

prop root *n* **:** a root that braces or supports a plant

pro·pul·sion \prə-ˈpəl-shən\ *n* **1 :** the action or process of propelling **2 :** something that propels [Latin *propulsus,* past participle of *propellere* "to propel"]

pro·pul·sive \-ˈpəl-siv\ *adj* **:** tending or having power to propel

pro·pyl \ˈprō-pəl\ *n* **:** either of two isomeric radicals C_3H_7– derived from propane [*prop*ionic + *-yl*]

pro·pyl·ene gly·col \ˌprō-pə-ˌlēn-ˈglī-ˌkȯl, -ˌkōl\ *n* **:** a sweet viscous liquid $C_3H_8O_2$ used as an antifreeze, solvent, and food preservative [*propylene* from *prop*ionic acid + *-yl* + *-ene; glycol* from Greek *glykys* "sweet" + English *-ol*]

pro ra·ta \prō-ˈrāt-ə, ˈprō-, -ˈrät-ə\ *adv* **:** according to share or liability **:** PROPORTIONATELY [Latin] — **pro rata** *adj*

pro·rate \prō-ˈrāt, ˈprō-\ *vb* **:** to divide, distribute, or assess proportionately [*pro rata*] — **pro·ra·tion** \prō-ˈrā-shən\ *n*

pro·rogue \prə-ˈrōg, pə-ˈrōg\ *vb* **1 :** DEFER, POSTPONE **2 :** to suspend or end a legislative session [Medieval French *proroger* "to prolong, defer," from Latin *prorogare,* from *pro-* "before" + *rogare* "to ask"] — **pro·ro·ga·tion** \ˌprōr-ō-ˈgā-shən, ˌprȯr-\ *n*

pros *plural of* PRO

pro·sa·ic \prō-ˈzā-ik\ *adj* **1 a :** characteristic of prose as distinguished from poetry **b :** unimaginative in style or expression **2 :** belonging to the everyday world **:** COMMONPLACE [Late Latin *prosaicus,* from Latin *prosa* "prose"] — **pro·sa·i·cal·ly** \-ˈzā-ə-kə-lē, -klē\ *adv*

\ə\ **abut**	\au̇\ **out**	\i\ **tip**	\ȯ\ **saw**	\u̇\ **foot**
\ər\ **further**	\ch\ **chin**	\ī\ **life**	\ȯi\ **coin**	\y\ **yet**
\a\ **mat**	\e\ **pet**	\j\ **job**	\th\ **thin**	\yü\ **few**
\ā\ **take**	\ē\ **easy**	\ng\ **sing**	\th\ **this**	\yu̇\ **cure**
\ä\ **cot, cart**	\g\ **go**	\ō\ **bone**	\ü\ **food**	\zh\ **vision**

pro·sce·ni·um \prō-ˈsē-nē-əm\ *n* **1 :** the stage of an ancient Greek or Roman theater **2 :** the part of a modern stage in front of the curtain **3 :** the wall that separates the stage from the auditorium and provides the arch that frames it [Latin, from Greek *proskēnion* "front of the building forming the background for a dramatic performance, stage," from *pro-* + *skēnē* "building forming the background for a dramatic performance"]

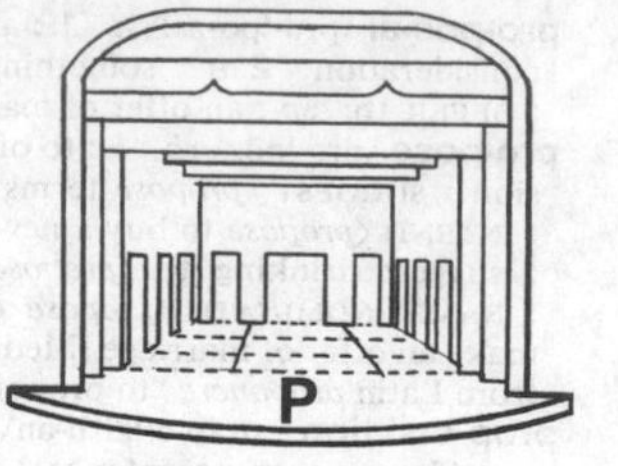

P proscenium 2

pro·scribe \prō-ˈskrīb\ *vt* **:** to condemn or forbid as harmful **:** PROHIBIT [Latin *proscribere* (past participle *proscriptus*) "to publish, proscribe," from *pro-* "before" + *scribere* "to write"] — **pro·scrib·er** *n* — **pro·scrip·tion** \-ˈskrip-shən\ *n* — **pro·scrip·tive** \-ˈskrip-tiv\ *adj* — **pro·scrip·tive·ly** *adv*

[1]**prose** \ˈprōz\ *n* **1 a :** the ordinary language people use in speaking or writing **b :** a literary medium distinguished from poetry especially by its greater irregularity and variety of rhythm and its closer correspondence to the patterns of everyday speech **2 :** a prosaic style, quality, character, or condition ⟨the *prose* of everyday life⟩ [Medieval French, from Latin *prosa,* from *prorsus, prosus* "straightforward," from *proversus,* past participle of *provertere* "to turn forward," from *pro-* "forward" + *vertere* "to turn"] — **prose** *adj*

[2]**prose** *vi* **1 :** to write prose **2 :** to write or speak in a prosaic manner

pros·e·cute \ˈpräs-i-ˌkyüt\ *vb* **1 :** to press on with **:** carry on to the end ⟨*prosecute* a war⟩ **2 a :** to carry on a legal action against (an accused person) in order to prove guilt **b :** to start legal proceedings with respect to ⟨*prosecute* a crime⟩ **c :** to start and carry on a legal suit or prosecution [Latin *prosecutus,* past participle of *prosequi* "to pursue"] — **pros·e·cut·able** \-ˌkyüt-ə-bəl\ *adj*

pros·e·cu·tion \ˌpräs-i-ˈkyü-shən\ *n* **1 :** the act or process of prosecuting; *esp* **:** the starting and continuing of a criminal suit in court **2 :** the party by whom criminal proceedings are begun or conducted

pros·e·cu·tor \ˈpräs-i-ˌkyüt-ər\ *n* **1 :** a person who institutes an official prosecution before a court **2 :** an attorney who conducts proceedings in a court on behalf of the government **:** DISTRICT ATTORNEY

[1]**pros·e·lyte** \ˈpräs-ə-ˌlīt\ *n* **:** a new convert [Late Latin *proselytus* "proselyte, alien resident," from Greek *prosēlytos*]

[2]**proselyte** *vt* **:** PROSELYTIZE — **pros·e·ly·tism** \-ˌlīt-ˌiz-əm, -lə-ˌtiz-\ *n*

pros·e·ly·tize \-lə-ˌtīz\ *vt* **:** to convert from one religion, belief, or party to another

pro·sim·i·an \prō-ˈsim-ē-ən, ˈprō-\ *n* **:** any of a group (Prosimii) of lower primates (as lemurs and tarsiers) [derived from Latin *pro-* "before" + *simia* "ape"] — **prosimian** *adj*

pros·i·ness \ˈprō-zē-nəs\ *n* **:** the quality or state of being prosy

pro·sit \ˈprō-zət, -sət\ *or* **prost** \ˈprōst\ *interj* — used to wish good health especially before drinking [German, from Latin *prosit* "may it be beneficial," from *prodesse* "to be useful"]

pros·o·dist \ˈpräs-əd-əst\ *n* **:** a specialist in prosody

pros·o·dy \ˈpräs-əd-ē\ *n, pl* **-dies** **1 :** the study of versification; *esp* **:** METRICS **2 :** a particular system, theory, or style of versification [Latin *prosodia* "accent of a syllable," from Greek *prosōidia* "song sung to instrumental music, accent," from *pros* "in addition to" + *ōidē* "song"] — **pro·sod·ic** \prə-ˈsäd-ik\ *adj* — **pro·sod·i·cal·ly** \-i-kə-lē, -klē\ *adv*

[1]**pros·pect** \ˈpräs-ˌpekt\ *n* **1 a :** a wide view **b :** a viewing with the mind **2 :** something extended to the view **:** SCENE **3 a :** the act of looking forward **:** ANTICIPATION **b :** something that is awaited or expected **:** POSSIBILITY ⟨the *prospect* of a peaceful solution⟩ **c** *pl* (1) **:** financial expectations (2) **:** CHANCE 4a ⟨what are his *prospects* of winning?⟩ **4 a :** a potential buyer or customer **b :** a candidate or a person likely to become a candidate ⟨presidential *prospects*⟩ [Latin *prospectus* "view, prospect," from *prospicere* "to look forward, exercise foresight," from *pro-* "forward" + *specere* "to look"]

[2]**prospect** *vb* **:** to explore an area especially for mineral deposits — **pros·pec·tor** \-ˌpek-tər\ *n*

pro·spec·tive \prə-ˈspek-tiv also ˈprä-ˌ, prō-ˈ, prä-ˈ\ *adj* **1 :** likely to come about **:** EXPECTED ⟨the *prospective* benefits of a law⟩ **2 :** likely to be or become ⟨a *prospective* athlete⟩ — **pro·spec·tive·ly** *adv*

pro·spec·tus \prə-ˈspek-təs, prä-\ *n, pl* **-tus·es** **:** a printed statement describing an enterprise and distributed to prospective investors [Latin, "prospect"]

pros·per \ˈpräs-pər\ *vb* **pros·pered; pros·per·ing** \-pə-ring, -pring\ **1 :** SUCCEED; *esp* **:** to succeed financially **2 :** FLOURISH 1, THRIVE **3 :** to cause to succeed or thrive [Medieval French *prosperer,* from Latin *prosperare* "to cause to succeed," from *prosperus* "favorable"]

pros·per·i·ty \prä-ˈsper-ət-ē\ *n* **:** the condition of being successful or thriving; *esp* **:** economic well-being

pros·per·ous \ˈpräs-pə-rəs, -prəs\ *adj* **1 :** AUSPICIOUS 1 **2 :** marked by success or economic well-being — **pros·per·ous·ly** *adv* — **pros·per·ous·ness** *n*

pros·ta·glan·din \ˌpräs-tə-ˈglan-dən\ *n* **:** any of various fatty acids of animals that may perform a variety of physiological actions (as controlling blood pressure or smooth muscle contraction) [*prosta*te *gland* + *-in*; from its occurrence in the sexual glands of animals]

pros·tate \ˈpräs-ˌtāt\ *n* **:** PROSTATE GLAND [Greek *prostatēs* "prostate gland," from *proïstanai* "to put in front," from *pro-* + *histanai* "to cause to stand"] — **pros·tat·ic** \präs-ˈtat-ik\ *adj*

prostate gland *n* **:** a firm partly muscular partly glandular body about the base of the mammalian male urethra that secretes a whitish fluid which is a major component of semen

pros·the·sis \präs-ˈthē-səs, ˈpräs-thə-\ *n, pl* **-the·ses** \-ˌsēz\ **:** an artificial device to replace a missing part of the body [Greek, "addition," from *prostithenai* "to add to," from *pros-* "in addition to" + *tithenai* "to put"] — **pros·thet·ic** \präs-ˈthet-ik\ *adj* — **pros·thet·i·cal·ly** \-ˈthet-i-kə-lē, -klē\ *adv*

prosthetic group *n* **:** a nonprotein group of a conjugated protein

pros·thet·ics \präs-ˈthet-iks\ *n sing or pl* **:** a medical specialty concerned with the design, construction, and fitting of prostheses

[1]**pros·ti·tute** \ˈpräs-tə-ˌtüt, -ˌtyüt\ *vt* **:** to devote to corrupt or unworthy purposes **:** DEBASE ⟨*prostitute* one's talents⟩ [Latin *prostitutus,* past participle of *prostituere* "to offer for prostitution," from *pro-* "before" + *statuere* "to set up, station," from *status* "position, state"]

[2]**prostitute** *n* **:** a person who engages in sexual activities for money

pros·ti·tu·tion \ˌpräs-tə-ˈtü-shən, -ˈtyü-\ *n* **1 :** the acts or practices of a prostitute **2 :** the state of being prostituted

pro·sto·mi·um \prō-ˈstō-mē-əm\ *n, pl* **-mia** \-mē-ə\ **:** the portion of the head of an annelid worm (as an earthworm) that is situated in front of the mouth [New Latin, from Greek *pro-* + *stoma* "mouth"] — **pro·sto·mi·al** \-mē-al\ *adj*

[1]**pros·trate** \ˈpräs-ˌtrāt\ *adj* **1 a :** stretched out with face on the ground (as in adoration or submission) **b :** lying flat and stretched out **2 :** lacking in vitality or will **:** OVERCOME ⟨*prostrate* from the heat⟩ **3 :** trailing on the ground ⟨a *prostrate* shrub⟩ [Latin *prostratus,* past participle of *prosternere* "to prostrate," from *pro-* "before" + *sternere* "to spread out, throw down"] ***synonyms*** see PRONE

[2]**prostrate** *vt* **1 :** to throw or put into a prostrate position **2 :** to make helpless or exhausted **:** OVERCOME

pros·tra·tion \prä-ˈstrā-shən\ *n* **1 :** the act of assuming or state of being in a prostrate position **2 :** complete physical or mental exhaustion **:** COLLAPSE

prosy \ˈprō-zē\ *adj* **pros·i·er; -est** **1 :** PROSAIC 1 **2 :** TEDIOUS

prot- *or* **proto-** *combining form* **1 :** first in time ⟨*proto*history⟩ **2 :** first formed **:** primary ⟨*proto*nema⟩ **3** *cap* **:** relating to or constituting the recorded or assumed language that is ancestral to a language or to a group of related languages or dialects [Greek *prōtos* "foremost, first"]

prot·ac·tin·i·um \ˌprōt-ˌak-ˈtin-ē-əm\ *n* **:** a shiny metallic radioactive chemical element of relatively short life — see ELEMENT table

pro·tag·o·nist \prō-ˈtag-ə-nəst\ *n* **1 :** the main character in a literary work **2 :** one who takes the leading part in an event **3 :** the leader of a cause **:** CHAMPION [Greek *prōtagōnistēs,* from *prōtos* "first" + *agōnistēs* "competitor at games, actor," derived from *agōn* "contest"]

prot·amine \ˈprōt-ə-ˌmēn\ *n* **:** any of various simple strongly basic proteins that are rich in arginine

prote- *or* **proteo-** *combining form* : protein ⟨*protease*⟩ ⟨*proteolytic*⟩ [derived from French *protéine* "protein"]

pro·te·an \ˈprōt-ē-ən\ *adj* : readily assuming different shapes or roles ⟨the *protean* amoeba⟩ ⟨a *protean* actor⟩ [*Proteus,* Greek sea god]

pro·te·ase \ˈprōt-ē-ˌās\ *n* : any of numerous enzymes that hydrolyze proteins especially to peptides — called also *proteinase* [derived from *prote-* + *-ase*]

pro·tect \prə-ˈtekt\ *vt* **1** : to cover or shield from injury or destruction : GUARD **2** : to shield or foster (an industry) by trade controls [Latin *protectus,* past participle of *protegere* "to protect," from *pro-* "in front" + *tegere* "to cover"] ***synonyms*** see DEFEND

pro·tec·tion \prə-ˈtek-shən\ *n* **1** : the act of protecting : the state of being protected **2 a** : one that protects **b** : the oversight or support of one that is smaller and weaker **3** : the freeing of the producers of a country from foreign competition especially by high duties on competing foreign goods **4** : money extorted by racketeers posing as a protective agency **5** : COVERAGE 2b — **pro·tec·tive** \-ˈtek-tiv\ *adj* — **pro·tec·tive·ly** *adv*

pro·tec·tion·ist \-shə-nəst, -shnəst\ *n* : an advocate of government economic protection for domestic producers through restrictions on foreign competitors — **pro·tec·tion·ism** \-shə-ˌniz-əm\ *n* — **protectionist** *adj*

protective coloration *n* : coloration that makes an organism appear less visible or less attractive to predators

protective tariff *n* : a tariff intended primarily to protect domestic producers rather than to yield revenue

pro·tec·tor \prə-ˈtek-tər\ *n* **1 a** : one that protects : GUARDIAN **b** : a device used to prevent injury : GUARD **2** : one having the care of a kingdom (as during a king's minority) : REGENT — **pro·tec·tor·ship** \-ˌship\ *n*

pro·tec·tor·ate \prə-ˈtek-tə-rət, -trət\ *n* **1 a** : government by a protector **b** *cap* : the government of England (1653–59) under Oliver Cromwell and his son **c** : the rank, office, or period of rule of a protector **2 a** : the relationship of superior authority assumed by one state over a dependent one **b** : the dependent state in such a relationship

pro·té·gé \ˈprōt-ə-ˌzhā\ *n* : one under the care and protection of someone influential especially for the furthering of his or her career [French, from *protéger* "to protect," from Latin *protegere*]

pro·té·gée \-ˌzhā\ *n* : a girl or woman who is a protégé [French, feminine of *protégé*]

pro·tein \ˈprō-ˌtēn, ˈprōt-ē-ən\ *n* **1** : any of various naturally occurring substances that consist of chains of amino acids, contain the elements carbon, hydrogen, nitrogen, oxygen, and often sulfur, include many essential biological compounds (as enzymes, hormones, and antibodies), and are supplied by various foods (as meat, eggs, milk, nuts, and beans) **2** : the total nitrogenous material in plant or animal substances [French *protéine,* derived from Greek *prōtos* "first"] — **pro·tein·aceous** \ˌprō-ˌtē-ˈnā-shəs, ˌprōt-ē-ə-ˈnā-\ *adj*

pro·tein·ase \ˈprō-ˌtē-ˌnās, ˈprōt-ē-ə-\ *n* : PROTEASE

pro tem \prō-ˈtem\ *adv* : pro tempore

pro tem·po·re \prō-ˈtem-pə-rē\ *adv* : for the present : TEMPORARILY [Latin]

pro·teo·lyt·ic \ˌprōt-ē-ə-ˈlit-ik\ *adj* : of, relating to, or producing the hydrolysis of proteins or peptides to simpler and soluble products ⟨*proteolytic* enzymes⟩ — **pro·te·ol·y·sis** \ˌprōt-ē-ˈäl-ə-səs\ *n*

pro·te·ome \ˈprōt-ē-ˌōm\ *n* : all the proteins expressed in a cell, tissue, or organism by a set of genes [*prote-* + *-ome* (as in *genome*)]

pro·te·o·mics \ˌprōt-ē-ˈō-miks\ *n* : a branch of science concerned with analyzing the structure, function, and interactions of the proteins produced by the genes of a particular cell, tissue, or organism

pro·te·ose \ˈprōt-ē-ˌōs, -ˌōz\ *n* : any of various water-soluble protein derivatives formed by partial hydrolysis

Prot·ero·zo·ic \ˌprät-ə-rə-ˈzō-ik, ˌprōt-\ *n* : the eon of geologic time between the Archean and Phanerozoic eons that exceeds in length all of subsequent geologic time and is marked by rocks that contain fossils indicating the first appearance of eukaryotic organisms (as algae); *also* : the corresponding system of rocks — see GEOLOGIC TIME table [Greek *proteros* "former, earlier," from *pro* "before"] — **Proterozoic** *adj*

[1]**pro·test** \ˈprō-ˌtest\ *n* **1** : a formal declaration of opinion and usually of objection or complaint **2** : a declaration that payment of a note or bill has been refused and that all endorsers are liable for damages **3** : a complaint, objection, or display of unwillingness or disapproval

[2]**pro·test** \prə-ˈtest, ˈprō-ˌtest, prō-ˈ\ *vb* **1 a** : to make solemn declaration of : ASSERT ⟨*protest* one's innocence⟩ **b** : to make a protestation **2 a** : to make a protest against ⟨*protested* the higher tax rate⟩ **b** : to object strongly ⟨*protest* against an arbitrary ruling⟩ [Medieval French *protester,* from Latin *protestari,* from *pro-* "forth" + *testari* "to call to witness"] — **pro·test·er** \-ˈtes-tər, -ˌtes-\ *n*

prot·es·tant \ˈprät-əs-tənt, *2 is also* prə-ˈtes-\ *n* **1** *cap* **a** : one of a group of German princes and cities presenting a defense of freedom of conscience against an edict of the Diet of Spires in 1529 intended to suppress the Lutheran movement **b** : a Christian denying the universal authority of the Pope and affirming the Reformation principles of justification by faith, the priesthood of all believers, and the primacy of the Bible **c** : a Christian not of a Catholic or Eastern church **2** : one who makes or enters a protest — **protestant** *adj, often cap* — **Prot·es·tant·ism** \ˈprät-əs-tənt-ˌiz-əm\ *n*

prot·es·ta·tion \ˌprät-əs-ˈtā-shən, ˌprō-ˌtes-\ *n* : the act of protesting : a solemn declaration or avowal

pro·thal·li·um \prō-ˈthal-ē-əm\ *n, pl* **-thal·lia** \-ˈthal-ē-ə\ : PROTHALLUS

pro·thal·lus \prō-ˈthal-əs\ *n, pl* **-li** \-ˌī, -ˌē\ : a small flat green thallus attached to the soil by rhizoids that is the gametophyte of a pteridophyte (as a fern) [New Latin, from *pro-* + *thallus*]

pro·tho·rax \prō-ˈthōr-ˌaks, ˈprō-, -ˈthȯr-\ *n* : the first segment of the thorax of an insect — **pro·tho·rac·ic** \ˌprō-thə-ˈras-ik\ *adj*

pro·throm·bin \prō-ˈthräm-bən, ˈprō-\ *n* : a plasma protein produced in the liver in the presence of vitamin K and converted into thrombin in the clotting of blood

pro·tist \ˈprōt-əst\ *n* : any of a diverse taxonomic group and especially a kingdom (Protista) of organisms that are eukaryotes and are unicellular and sometimes colonial or less often multicellular and that typically include the protozoans, most algae, and often some fungi (as slime molds) [derived from Greek *prōtistos* "very first, primal," from *prōtos* "first"] — **pro·tis·tan** \prō-ˈtis-tən\ *adj or n*

pro·ti·um \ˈprōt-ē-əm, ˈprō-shē-\ *n* : the ordinary light hydrogen isotope of atomic mass 1 [New Latin, from Greek *prōtos* "first"]

proto- — see PROT-

pro·to·cer·a·tops \ˌprōt-ō-ˈser-ə-ˌtäps\ *n* : any of several relatively small plant-eating dinosaurs of the Cretaceous period with a bony ridge projecting from the back of the skull [New Latin, from Greek *prot-* + *kerat-, keras* "horn" + *ōps* "face"]

pro·to·col \ˈprōt-ə-ˌkȯl\ *n* **1** : an original draft, minute, or record of a document or transaction : MEMORANDUM **2** : a code of diplomatic or military etiquette and precedence **3** : a set of rules which governs the format of data and its exchange between electronic devices (as computers) ⟨network *protocols*⟩ **4** : a detailed plan of a scientific or medical experiment, treatment, or procedure [Middle French *prothocole,* from Medieval Latin *protocollum,* from Late Greek *prōtokollon* "first sheet of a papyrus roll bearing date of manufacture," from Greek *prōtos* "first" + *kollan* "to glue," from *kolla* "glue"]

pro·to·his·to·ry \ˌprōt-ō-ˈhis-tə-rē, -trē\ *n* : the study of humanity of the period that just antedates recorded history — **pro·to·his·tor·ic** \-his-ˈtȯr-ik, -ˈtär-\ *adj*

pro·ton \ˈprō-ˌtän\ *n* : an elementary particle identical with the nucleus of the hydrogen atom that along with the neutron is a constituent of all other atomic nuclei and carries a positive charge numerically equal to the negative charge of an electron [Greek *prōton,* neuter of *prōtos* "first"] — **pro·ton·ic** \prō-ˈtän-ik\ *adj*

pro·to·ne·ma \ˌprōt-ə-ˈnē-mə\ *n, pl* **-ne·ma·ta** \-ˈnē-mət-ə, -ˈnem-ət-\ : the primary usually filamentous stage of the gametophyte in mosses and some liverworts that is comparable to the prothallus in ferns [*prot-* + Greek *nēmat-, nēma* "thread"] — **pro·to·ne·mal** \-ˈnē-məl\ *adj* — **pro·to·ne·ma·tal** \-ˈnē-mət-l, -ˈnem-ət-\ *adj*

\ə\ **abut**	\au̇\ **out**	\i\ **tip**	\ȯ\ **saw**	\u̇\ **foot**
\ər\ **further**	\ch\ **chin**	\ī\ **life**	\ȯi\ **coin**	\y\ **yet**
\a\ **mat**	\e\ **pet**	\j\ **job**	\th\ **thin**	\yü\ **few**
\ā\ **take**	\ē\ **easy**	\ng\ **sing**	\t͟h\ **this**	\yu̇\ **cure**
\ä\ **cot, cart**	\g\ **go**	\ō\ **bone**	\ü\ **food**	\zh\ **vision**

pro·to·plan·et \ˈprōt-ō-ˌplan-ət\ *n* : a whirling mass of gas and dust that rotates around a star and that is held to give rise to a planet — **pro·to·plan·e·tary** \ˌprōt-ō-ˈplan-ə-ˌter-ē\ *adj*

pro·to·plasm \ˈprōt-ə-ˌplaz-əm\ *n* **1** : a colloidal complex of various organic and inorganic substances (as proteins and water) that constitutes the living nucleus, cytoplasm, plastids, and mitochondria of the cell and is held to be the physical basis of life **2** : CYTOPLASM [German *Protoplasma,* from *prot-* "prot-" + *Plasma* "plasma"] — **pro·to·plas·mic** \ˌprōt-ə-ˈplaz-mik\ *adj*

pro·to·plast \ˈprōt-ə-ˌplast\ *n* : the nucleus, cytoplasm, and cell membrane of a cell constituting a living unit distinct from inert walls and inclusions [Middle French *protoplaste* "prototype, something formed first," from Late Latin *protoplastos* "first human," from Greek *prōtoplastos* "first formed," from *prōtos* "first" + *plastos* "formed," from *plassein* "to mold"]

pro·to·type \ˈprōt-ə-ˌtīp\ *n* **1** : an original model on which something is patterned **2** : an individual that exhibits the essential features of a later type — **pro·to·typ·al** \ˌprōt-ə-ˈtī-pəl\ *adj* — **pro·to·typ·i·cal** \-ˈtip-i-kəl\ *adj*

pro·to·zoa \ˌprōt-ə-ˈzō-ə\ *n pl* : organisms that are protozoans

pro·to·zo·an \ˌprōt-ə-ˈzō-ən\ *n* : any of a phylum or group (Protozoa) of microorganisms (as amoebas and paramecia) that are single-celled protists, have varied structure and physiology and often complex life cycles, are represented in almost every kind of habitat, and include some which are serious parasites of human and domestic animals [derived from *prot-* + Greek *zōion* "animal"] — **protozoan** *adj*

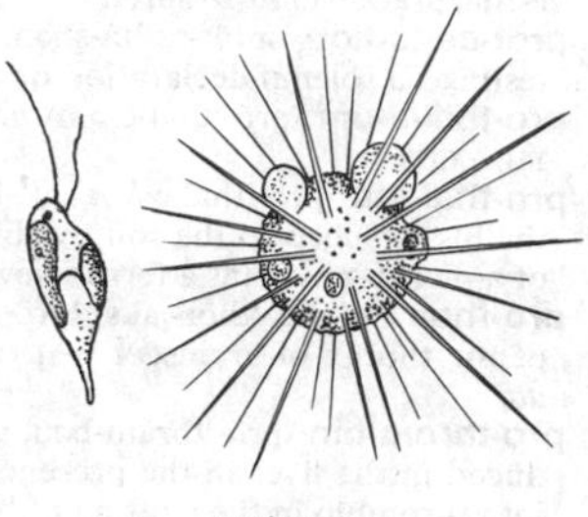
protozoan

pro·to·zo·ol·o·gy \-zō-ˈäl-ə-jē, -zə-ˈwäl-\ *n* : a branch of zoology dealing with protozoans — **pro·to·zo·ol·o·gist** \-jəst\ *n*

pro·tract \prō-ˈtrakt\ *vt* : to prolong in time or space [Latin *protractus,* past participle of *protrahere* "to draw forward, prolong," from *pro-* "forward" + *trahere* "to draw"] ***synonyms*** see EXTEND — **pro·trac·tion** \-ˈtrak-shən\ *n*

pro·trac·tor \prō-ˈtrak-tər, ˈprō-ˌ\ *n* **1 a** : one that protracts, prolongs, or delays **b** : a muscle that extends a part — compare RETRACTOR **2** : an instrument for laying down and measuring angles that is used in drawing and plotting

pro·trude \prō-ˈtrüd\ *vb* **1** : to cause to stick out : PROJECT **2** : to jut out from the surroundings [Latin *protrudere* (past participle *protrusus*) "to thrust forward," from *pro-* "forward" + *trudere* "to thrust"] — **pro·tru·si·ble** \-ˈtrü-sə-bəl, -zə-\ *adj*

pro·tru·sion \prō-ˈtrü-zhən\ *n* **1** : the act of protruding : the state of being protruded **2** : something that protrudes ***synonyms*** see PROJECTION

pro·tu·ber·ance \prō-ˈtü-bə-rəns, -ˈtyü-, -brəns\ *n* **1** : the quality or state of being protuberant **2** : something that is protuberant : BULGE ***synonyms*** see PROJECTION

pro·tu·ber·ant \-bə-rənt, -brənt\ *adj* : bulging beyond the surrounding surface : PROMINENT [Late Latin *protuberans,* present participle of *protuberare* "to bulge out," from Latin *pro-* "forward" + *tuber* "hump, swelling"] — **pro·tu·ber·ant·ly** *adv*

proud \ˈpraủd\ *adj* **1** : feeling or showing pride: as **a** : having or displaying excessive self-esteem **b** : very pleased ⟨*proud* parents of the valedictorian⟩ **c** : having proper self-respect ⟨too *proud* to beg⟩ **2 a** : MAGNIFICENT 1, STATELY ⟨*proud* palaces⟩ **b** : giving reason for pride ⟨a *proud* moment⟩ **3** : strong and spirited ⟨a *proud* steed⟩ [Old English *prūd*] — **proud·ly** *adv*

synonyms PROUD, ARROGANT, HAUGHTY, INSOLENT, DISDAINFUL mean showing scorn for inferiors. PROUD may suggest an assumed superiority or loftiness ⟨too *proud* to take charity⟩. ARROGANT implies a claiming for oneself of more consideration or importance than is warranted ⟨a conceited and *arrogant* executive⟩. HAUGHTY suggests a consciousness of superior birth or position ⟨a *haughty* aristocrat⟩. INSOLENT implies contemptuous haughtiness ⟨ignored by an *insolent* waiter⟩. DISDAINFUL suggests an openly scornful and patronizing haughtiness ⟨*disdainful* of their social inferiors⟩.

prove \ˈprüv\ *vb* **proved; proved** *or* **prov·en** \ˈprü-vən\; **prov·ing 1** : to test by an experiment or a standard ⟨*prove* gold⟩ **2 a** : to establish the truth or validity of by evidence or demonstration ⟨*prove* the charges⟩ **b** : to check the correctness of (as an arithmetic operation) **3** : to ascertain the genuineness of : VERIFY ⟨*prove* a will⟩ **4** : to turn out especially after trial or test ⟨the new drug *proved* effective⟩ **5** : to show oneself to be capable ⟨could finally *prove* himself⟩ [Medieval French *prover, pruver,* from Latin *probare* "to test, approve, demonstrate," from *probus* "good, honest"] — **prov·able** \ˈprü-və-bəl\ *adj*

prov·e·nance \ˈpräv-nəns, -ə-nəns\ *n* : ORIGIN 2b, SOURCE [French, from *provenir* "to come forth, originate," from Latin *provenire,* from *pro-* "forth" + *venire* "to come"]

Pro·ven·çal \ˌprōv-ən-ˈsäl, ˌpräv-, -ˌä^{n}-\ *n* **1** : a native or inhabitant of Provence **2** : OCCITAN [Middle French, from *provençal* "of Provence," from *Provence*] — **Provençal** *adj*

prov·en·der \ˈpräv-ən-dər\ *n* **1** : dry food for domestic animals : FEED **2** : FOOD 2, VICTUALS [Medieval French *provende, provendre,* from Medieval Latin *provenda,* alteration of *praebenda* "prebend"]

pro·ve·nience \prə-ˈvē-nyəns\ *n* : ORIGIN 2b, SOURCE [alteration of *provenance*]

pro·ven·tric·u·lus \ˌprō-ven-ˈtrik-yə-ləs\ *n, pl* **-li** \-ˌlī, -ˌlē\ **1** : the glandular stomach of a bird situated between the crop and gizzard **2** : a muscular pouch of the digestive tract of insects with mandibles that grinds food into smaller pieces [[1]*pro-* + Latin *ventriculus* "stomach, ventricle"]

prov·erb \ˈpräv-ˌərb\ *n* : a brief popular saying or maxim : ADAGE [Medieval French *proverbe,* from Latin *proverbium,* from *pro-* + *verbum* "word"]

pro·ver·bi·al \prə-ˈvər-bē-əl\ *adj* **1** : of, relating to, or resembling a proverb ⟨*proverbial* wisdom⟩ **2** : commonly spoken of ⟨the *proverbial* beginner's luck⟩ — **pro·ver·bi·al·ly** \-bē-ə-lē\ *adv*

Prov·erbs \ˈpräv-ˌərbz\ *n* : a collection of moral sayings and counsels forming a book of canonical Jewish and Christian Scriptures — see BIBLE table

pro·vide \prə-ˈvīd\ *vb* **1** : to take precautionary measures ⟨*provide* against a possible shortage⟩ **2** : to include a condition or stipulation ⟨the contract *provided* for 10 paid holidays⟩ **3** : to supply what is needed for sustenance or support ⟨*provides* for a large family⟩ **4 a** : OUTFIT, EQUIP ⟨*provide* the children with new shoes⟩ **b** : to supply or furnish (something needed, useful, or desirable) ⟨cows *provide* milk⟩ ⟨curtains *provide* some privacy⟩ [Latin *providēre,* literally, "to see ahead," from *pro-* "forward" + *vidēre* "to see"] — **pro·vid·er** *n*

pro·vid·ed *conj* : on condition : IF — sometimes followed by *that*

prov·i·dence \ˈpräv-əd-əns, -ə-ˌdens\ *n* **1 a** *often cap* : divine guidance or care **b** *cap* : God conceived as the power sustaining and guiding human destiny **2** : the quality or state of being provident : PRUDENCE [Medieval French, from Latin *providentia,* from *providens* "provident"]

prov·i·dent \-əd-ənt, -ə-ˌdent\ *adj* **1** : making provision for the future : PRUDENT **2** : FRUGAL, THRIFTY [Latin *providens,* from *providēre* "to provide"] — **prov·i·dent·ly** *adv*

prov·i·den·tial \ˌpräv-ə-ˈden-chəl\ *adj* **1** : of, relating to, or determined by Providence **2** : occurring by or as if by an intervention of Providence : FORTUNATE ⟨a *providential* escape⟩ — **prov·i·den·tial·ly** \-ˈdench-lē, -ə-lē\ *adv*

pro·vid·ing \prə-ˈvīd-ing\ *conj* : PROVIDED

prov·ince \ˈpräv-əns\ *n* **1 a** : a country or region brought under the control of the ancient Roman government **b** : an administrative district or division of a country **c** *pl* : all of a country except the metropolises **2** : a division of a country forming the jurisdiction of an archbishop or metropolitan **3** : proper or appropriate business or scope : SPHERE ⟨a legal question outside the physician's *province*⟩ [Medieval French, from Latin *provincia*]

[1]**pro·vin·cial** \prə-ˈvin-chəl\ *n* **1** : one living in or coming from a province **2 a** : a person of local or restricted outlook **b** : a person lacking urban polish or refinement

[2]**provincial** *adj* **1** : of, relating to, or coming from a province **2 a** : limited in outlook : NARROW **b** : lacking the polish of urban society : UNSOPHISTICATED **3** : of or relating to a decorative style (as in furniture) marked by simplicity and relative plainness — **pro·vin·ci·al·i·ty** \-ˌvin-chē-ˈal-ət-ē\ *n* — **pro·vin·cial·ly** \-ˈvinch-lē, -ə-lē\ *adv*

pro·vin·cial·ism \prə-ˈvin-chə-ˌliz-əm\ *n* **1** : a dialectal or local word, phrase, or idiom **2** : the quality or state of being provincial

proving ground *n* **1 :** a place for scientific experimentation or testing **2 :** a place where something new is tried out

pro·vi·rus \prō-ˈvī-rəs\ *n* **:** an inactive form of a virus that has become part of the genetic material of a host cell and replicates with it to be transmitted from one cell generation to the next

[1]**pro·vi·sion** \prə-ˈvizh-ən\ *n* **1 a :** the act or process of providing ⟨*provision* of transportation for the trip⟩ **b :** a measure taken beforehand **:** PREPARATION ⟨make *provision* for emergencies⟩ **2 :** a stock of needed materials or supplies; *esp* **:** a stock of food — usually used in plural **3 :** PROVISO 2, STIPULATION [Medieval French, from Latin *provisio* "foresight," from *providēre* "to see ahead, provide"]

[2]**provision** *vt* **pro·vi·sioned; pro·vi·sion·ing** \-ˈvizh-ning, -ə-ning\ **:** to supply with provisions ⟨*provision* a military garrison⟩

pro·vi·sion·al \prə-ˈvizh-nəl, -ən-l\ *adj* **:** serving for the time being ⟨a *provisional* government⟩ — **pro·vi·sion·al·ly** \-ē\ *adv*

pro·vi·so \prə-ˈvī-zō\ *n, pl* **-sos** *or* **-soes 1 :** a part of a legal document that states a condition **2 :** a requirement that is a condition ⟨given a bicycle with the *proviso* that it be kept in good repair⟩ [Medieval Latin *proviso quod* "provided that"]

pro·vi·ta·min \prō-ˈvīt-ə-mən, ˈprō-\ *n* **:** a precursor of a vitamin convertible into the vitamin in an organism

pro·vo·ca·teur \prō-ˌvä-kə-ˈtər\ *n* **:** one who provokes ⟨a political *provocateur*⟩ [short for *agent provocateur*]

prov·o·ca·tion \ˌpräv-ə-ˈkā-shən\ *n* **1 :** the act of provoking **:** INCITEMENT **2 :** something that provokes, arouses, or stimulates [Medieval French *provocacion,* from Latin *provocatio,* from *provocare* "to provoke"]

pro·voc·a·tive \prə-ˈväk-ət-iv\ *adj* **:** serving as a provocation ⟨*provocative* comments⟩ — **pro·voc·a·tive·ly** *adv* — **pro·voc·a·tive·ness** *n*

pro·voke \prə-ˈvōk\ *vt* **1 :** to excite to anger **2 a :** to call forth **:** EVOKE **b :** to stir up purposely **c :** to provide the needed stimulus for ⟨*provoke* a response from a nerve⟩ [Medieval French *provoquer,* from Latin *provocare,* from *pro-* "forth" + *vocare* "to call"]

synonyms PROVOKE, EXCITE, STIMULATE mean to arouse as if by pricking. PROVOKE directs attention to the response called forth ⟨a joke that failed to *provoke* laughter⟩ ⟨diplomatic moves that *provoke* war⟩. EXCITE implies a stirring up or moving profoundly ⟨a performance that *excited* admiration⟩. STIMULATE suggests a rousing out of lethargy, inactivity, or indifference ⟨the need to *stimulate* the economy⟩.

pro·vok·ing \-ˈvō-king\ *adj* **:** causing mild anger **:** ANNOYING ⟨a *provoking* delay⟩ — **pro·vok·ing·ly** \-king-lē\ *adv*

pro·vo·lo·ne \ˌprō-və-ˈlō-nē, ˈprō-və-ˌlōn\ *n* **:** a firm pliant cheese of Italian origin [Italian, from *provola,* a kind of cheese]

pro·vost \ˈprō-ˌvōst, ˈpräv-əst\ *n* **:** a high-ranking university administrative officer [Old English *profost* and Medieval French *provost,* both from Medieval Latin *propositus,* from Latin *praepositus* "one in charge," from *praeponere* "to place at the head"]

provost marshal \ˈprō-ˌvōst, ˈpräv-əst *also* ˌprō-vō\ *n* **:** the head of the military police of a command

prow \ˈprau̇\ *n* **1 :** the bow of a ship **:** STEM **2 :** a pointed projecting front part [Middle French *proue,* probably from Italian dialect *prua,* from Latin *prora,* from Greek *prōira*]

prow·ess \ˈprau̇-əs\ *n* **1 :** distinguished bravery; *esp* **:** military valor and skill **2 :** extraordinary ability ⟨athletic *prowess*⟩ [Medieval French *proesse,* from *prou* "valiant," from Late Latin *prode* "advantageous," from Latin *prodesse* "to be advantageous"]

prowl \ˈprau̇l\ *vb* **1 :** to move about or wander stealthily in or as if in search of prey **2 :** to roam over in a predatory manner ⟨*prowled* the streets⟩ [Middle English *prollen*] — **prowl** *n* — **prowl·er** *n*

prowl car *n* **:** SQUAD CAR

prox·i·mal \ˈpräk-sə-məl\ *adj* **1 :** being nearest **:** PROXIMATE **2 :** near or next to the point of attachment or origin; *esp* **:** located toward the center of the body ⟨the *proximal* end of a bone⟩ — compare DISTAL **3 :** of, relating to, or being the mesial and distal surfaces of a tooth [Latin *proximus*] — **prox·i·mal·ly** \-mə-lē\ *adv*

proximal convoluted tubule *n* **:** the convoluted portion of the vertebrate nephron that lies between Bowman's capsule and the loop of Henle and functions especially in the resorption of sugar, sodium and chloride ions, and water — called also *proximal tubule*

prox·i·mate \-mət\ *adj* **1 a :** very near **:** CLOSE **b :** soon forthcoming **2 :** next preceding or following **:** DIRECT ⟨the *proximate* cause⟩ [Latin *proximatus,* past participle of *proximare* "to approach," from *proximus* "nearest, next," superlative of *prope* "near"] — **prox·i·mate·ly** *adv* — **prox·i·mate·ness** *n*

prox·im·i·ty \präk-ˈsim-ət-ē\ *n* **:** the quality or state of being proximate

prox·i·mo \ˈpräk-sə-ˌmō\ *adj* **:** of or occurring in the next month after the present [Latin *proximo mense* "in the next month"]

proxy \ˈpräk-sē\ *n, pl* **prox·ies 1 a :** authority to act for another (as in voting) **b :** a document giving such authority **2 :** a person authorized to act for another [Middle English *proxi, procucie,* contraction of *procuracie,* from Medieval French, from Medieval Latin *procuratia,* from Latin *procuratio* "management, act of taking charge," from *procurare* "to take care of"] — **proxy** *adj*

prude \ˈprüd\ *n* **:** a person overly or priggishly concerned with modesty and decorum [French, "good woman, prudish woman," short for *prudefemme* "good woman"] — **prud·ish** \ˈprüd-ish\ *adj* — **prud·ish·ly** *adv* — **prud·ish·ness** *n*

pru·dence \ˈprüd-ns\ *n* **1 :** the ability to govern and discipline oneself by the use of reason **2 :** discretion and shrewdness in the management of affairs **3 :** skill and good judgment in the use of resources **4 :** CAUTION 2, CIRCUMSPECTION

pru·dent \-nt\ *adj* **1 :** marked by wisdom **2 :** shrewdly practical **3 :** CIRCUMSPECT, DISCREET **4 :** FRUGAL, PROVIDENT [Medieval French, from Latin *prudens,* from *providens* "provident"] ***synonyms*** see WISE — **pru·dent·ly** *adv*

pru·den·tial \prü-ˈden-chəl\ *adj* **1 :** of, relating to, or resulting from prudence **2 :** using prudence — **pru·den·tial·ly** \-chə-lē\ *adv*

prud·ery \ˈprüd-rē, -ə-rē\ *n, pl* **-er·ies 1 :** the quality or state of being prudish **:** exaggerated or priggish modesty **2 :** a prudish remark or act

[1]**prune** \ˈprün\ *n* **:** a plum dried or capable of drying without fermentation [Medieval French, "plum," from Latin *prunum*]

[2]**prune** *vt* **1 a :** to reduce by eliminating superfluous matter ⟨*prune* an essay⟩ **b :** to remove as superfluous **2 :** to cut off the dead or unwanted parts of (a woody plant) ⟨*prune* the hedge⟩ [Middle English *prouynen*] — **prun·er** *n*

pru·ri·ent \ˈpru̇r-ē-ənt\ *adj* **1 :** having indecent desires or thoughts **:** LEWD **2 :** inclined to or characterized by lasciviousness [Latin *pruriens,* present participle of *prurire* "to itch, crave, be wanton"] — **pru·ri·ence** \-ē-əns\ *n* — **pru·ri·ent·ly** *adv*

pru·ri·tus \prü-ˈrīt-əs, -ˈrēt-\ *n* **:** ITCH 1a [Latin, from *prurire* "to itch"] — **pru·rit·ic** \-ˈrit-ik\ *adj*

prus·sic acid \ˌprəs-ik-\ *n* **:** HYDROCYANIC ACID [French *prussique,* from *(bleu de) Prusse* "Prussian blue"]

[1]**pry** \ˈprī\ *vi* **pried; pry·ing :** to look closely or inquisitively; *esp* **:** to invade another's privacy ⟨*pry* into other people's affairs⟩ [Middle English *prien*]

[2]**pry** *vt* **pried; pry·ing 1 :** to raise, move, or pull apart with a tool or lever **2 :** to extract, detach, or open with difficulty ⟨*pry* a secret out of a person⟩ [probably back-formation from [5]*prize*]

[3]**pry** *n* **:** a tool for prying

pry·ing *adj* **:** inquisitive in an annoying or meddlesome way ***synonyms*** see CURIOUS — **pry·ing·ly** \-ing-lē\ *adv*

psalm \ˈsäm, ˈsälm\ *n* **:** a sacred song or poem; *esp* **:** one of the hymns that make up the Old Testament Book of Psalms [Old English *psealm,* from Late Latin *psalmus,* from Greek *psalmos,* literally, "twanging of a harp," from *psallein* "to pluck"]

psalm·ist \-əst\ *n* **:** a writer or composer of psalms

psalm·o·dy \-əd-ē\ *n, pl* **-dies 1 :** the art or practice of singing psalms in worship **2 :** a collection of psalms [Late Latin *psalmodia,* from Late Greek *psalmōidia,* literally, "singing to the harp," from Greek *psalmos* "psalm, twanging of a harp" + *aidein* "to sing"]

Psalms \ˈsämz, ˈsälmz\ *n* **:** a collection of sacred poems forming a book of canonical Jewish and Christian Scriptures — see BIBLE table

Psal·ter \ˈsȯl-tər\ *n* **:** the Book of Psalms; *also* **:** a collection of Psalms for liturgical or devotional use [Old English *psalter,* from Late Latin *psalterium,* from Late Greek *psaltērion,* from Greek, "psaltery"]

\ə\ **abut**	\au̇\ **out**	\i\ **tip**	\ȯ\ **saw**	\u̇\ **foot**
\ər\ **further**	\ch\ **chin**	\ī\ **life**	\ȯi\ **coin**	\y\ **yet**
\a\ **mat**	\e\ **pet**	\j\ **job**	\th\ **thin**	\yü\ **few**
\ā\ **take**	\ē\ **easy**	\ng\ **sing**	\t͟h\ **this**	\yu̇\ **cure**
\ä\ **cot, cart**	\g\ **go**	\ō\ **bone**	\ü\ **food**	\zh\ **vision**

psal·tery *also* **psal·try** \ˈsȯl-tə-rē, -trē\ *n, pl* **-ter·ies** *also* **-tries** : an ancient stringed musical instrument resembling the zither [Medieval French *psalterie,* from Latin *psalterium,* from Greek *psaltērion,* from *psallein* "to pluck, play on a stringed instrument"]

PSAT \ˌpē-ˌes-ˌā-ˈtē\ *trademark* — used for a standardized test designed to prepare students for the SAT

pseud- *or* **pseudo-** *combining form* : false : sham : spurious ⟨*pseudo*coel⟩ [Greek, from *pseudēs*]

pseu·do \ˈsüd-ō\ *adj* : SHAM 1, FALSE ⟨distinguishing between true and *pseudo* intellectualism⟩ [*pseudo-*]

pseu·do·coel \ˈsüd-ə-ˌsēl\ *or* **pseu·do·coe·lom** \-ˌsē-ləm\ *n* : a body cavity of an invertebrate that is not structurally or in origin a true coelom — **pseu·do·coe·lo·mate** \ˌsüd-ə-ˈsē-lə-ˌmāt\ *adj or n*

pseu·do·nym \ˈsüd-n-ˌim\ *n* : a fictitious name; *esp* : PEN NAME [French *pseudonyme,* from Greek *pseudōnymos* "bearing a false name," from *pseud-* + *onyma* "name"]

pseu·do·pod \ˈsüd-ə-ˌpäd\ *n* : PSEUDOPODIUM — **pseu·dop·o·dal** \sü-ˈdäp-əd-l\ *or* **pseu·do·po·di·al** \ˌsüd-ə-ˈpōd-ē-əl\ *adj*

pseu·do·po·di·um \ˌsüd-ə-ˈpōd-ē-əm\ *n, pl* **-po·dia** \-ē-ə\ : a part of a cell that is temporarily protruded by moving cytoplasm (as in the amoeba) and that helps to move the cell and to take in its food [New Latin, from Greek *pseud-* + *podion* "little foot," from *pod-, pous* "foot"]

pseu·do·sci·ence \ˌsü-dō-ˈsī-əns\ *n* : a system of theories, assumptions, and methods mistakenly regarded as scientific — **pseu·do·sci·en·tif·ic** \-ˌsī-ən-ˈtif-ik\ *adj*

pshaw \ˈshȯ\ *interj* — used to express irritation, disapproval, contempt, or disbelief

psi \ˈsī, ˈpsī\ *n* : the 23rd letter of the Greek alphabet — Ψ or ψ

psi·lo·cy·bin \ˌsī-lə-ˈsī-bən\ *n* : a hallucinogenic compound $C_{12}H_{17}N_2O_4P$ obtained from a fungus [New Latin *Psilocybe,* genus name]

psit·ta·cine \ˈsit-ə-ˌsīn\ *adj* : of or relating to the parrots [Latin *psittacinus,* from *psittacus* "parrot," from Greek *psittakos*] — **psittacine** *n*

psit·ta·co·sis \ˌsit-ə-ˈkō-səs\ *n* : an infectious disease of birds caused by a bacterium, marked by diarrhea and loss of weight and strength, and capable of being passed on to humans — called also *parrot fever*

pso·ri·a·sis \sə-ˈrī-ə-səs\ *n* : a chronic skin disease characterized by red patches often covered with white scales [Greek *psōriasis,* from *psōrian* "to have the itch," from *psōra* "itch"] — **pso·ri·at·ic** \ˌsōr-ē-ˈat-ik, ˌsȯr-\ *adj or n*

psych *or* **psyche** \ˈsīk\ *vt* **psyched; psych·ing** **1** : to make psychologically uneasy — often used with *out* ⟨*psych* out an opponent⟩ **2** : to make psychologically ready — often used with *up* ⟨*psyched* myself up for the test⟩ [short for *psychoanalyze*]

psych- *or* **psycho-** *combining form* **1** : mind : mental processes and activities ⟨*psycho*logy⟩ **2** : psychological methods ⟨*psycho*therapy⟩ **3** : brain ⟨*psycho*surgery⟩ **4** : mental and ⟨*psycho*somatic⟩ [Greek, from *psychē* "breath, principle of life, soul"]

psy·che \ˈsī-kē\ *n* : SOUL 1, SELF; *also* : MIND 2a [Greek *psychē* "soul"]

[1]**psy·che·del·ic** \ˌsī-kə-ˈdel-ik\ *adj* **1 a** : of, relating to, or being a drug (as LSD) that produces abnormal often extreme mental effects (as hallucinations) **b** : produced by or relating to the use of psychedelic drugs ⟨a *psychedelic* experience⟩ **2 a** : imitating the effect of psychedelic drugs ⟨*psychedelic* art⟩ **b** : bright and glowing as a result of fluorescence ⟨*psychedelic* colors⟩ [Greek *psychē* "soul" + *dēloun* "to show"]

[2]**psychedelic** *n* : a psychedelic drug

psy·chi·a·try \sə-ˈkī-ə-trē, sī-\ *n* : a branch of medicine that deals with mental, emotional, or behavioral disorders — **psy·chi·at·ric** \ˌsī-kē-ˈa-trik\ *adj* — **psy·chi·at·ri·cal·ly** \-tri-kə-lē, -klē\ *adv* — **psy·chi·a·trist** \sə-ˈkī-ə-trəst, sī-\ *n*

[1]**psy·chic** \ˈsī-kik\ *adj* **1** : of, relating to, affecting, or originating in the mind **2** : not physical; *esp* : not to be explained by knowledge of natural laws **3** : sensitive to influences or forces supposedly exerted from beyond the natural world — **psy·chi·cal** \-ki-kəl\ *adj* — **psy·chi·cal·ly** \-ki-kə-lē, -klē\ *adv*

[2]**psychic** *n* : a person (as a medium) apparently sensitive to nonphysical forces

psy·cho \ˈsī-kō\ *n* : a mentally disordered or psychopathic person — not used technically [short for *psychopath*]

psy·cho·ac·tive \ˌsī-kō-ˈak-tiv\ *adj* : affecting the mind or behavior ⟨*psychoactive* drugs⟩

psy·cho·anal·y·sis \ˌsī-kō-ə-ˈnal-ə-səs\ *n, pl* **-y·ses** \-ˌsēz\ : a method of explaining and treating mental and emotional disorders that emphasizes the importance of the patient's talking freely about himself or herself while under treatment and especially about dreams and early childhood memories and experiences — **psy·cho·an·a·lyst** \-ˈan-l-əst\ *n* — **psy·cho·an·a·lyt·ic** \-ˌan-l-ˈit-ik\ *also* **psy·cho·an·a·lyt·i·cal** \-ˈit-i-kəl\ *adj* — **psy·cho·an·a·lyt·i·cal·ly** \-ˈit-i-kə-lē, -klē\ *adv* — **psy·cho·an·a·lyze** \-ˈan-l-ˌīz\ *vb*

psy·cho·gen·ic \ˌsī-kə-ˈjen-ik\ *adj* : originating in the mind or in mental or emotional conflict

psy·cho·log·i·cal \ˌsī-kə-ˈläj-i-kəl\ *also* **psy·cho·log·ic** \-ˈläj-ik\ *adj* **1 a** : of or relating to psychology **b** : relating to, characteristic of, arising in, or acting through the mind : MENTAL **2** : intended to influence the will or mind ⟨*psychological* warfare⟩ — **psy·cho·log·i·cal·ly** \-i-kə-lē, -klē\ *adv*

psy·chol·o·gy \sī-ˈkäl-ə-jē\ *n, pl* **-gies** **1** : the science or study of mind and behavior **2** : the mental or behavioral characteristics of an individual or group — **psy·chol·o·gist** \-jəst\ *n*

psy·cho·neu·ro·sis \ˌsī-kō-nu̇-ˈrō-səs, -nyu̇-\ *n* : NEUROSIS — **psy·cho·neu·rot·ic** \-ˈrät-ik\ *adj or n*

psy·cho·path \ˈsī-kə-ˌpath\ *n* : a mentally ill or unstable person; *esp* : a person with a clear perception of reality but lacking a sense of social and moral obligation so that personal gain is sought by criminal acts, drug addiction, or sexual perversion without marked feelings of guilt — **psy·cho·path·ic** \ˌsī-kə-ˈpath-ik\ *adj* — **psy·cho·path·i·cal·ly** \-i-kə-lē, -klē\ *adv*

psy·cho·pa·thol·o·gy \ˌsī-kō-pə-ˈthäl-ə-jē\ *n* : the study of the abnormal psychological and behavioral functioning associated with mental disorders; *also* : such abnormal functioning — **psy·cho·path·o·log·i·cal** \-ˌpath-ə-ˈläj-i-kəl\ *adj* — **psy·cho·path·o·log·i·cal·ly** \-i-kə-lē, -klē\ *adv* — **psy·cho·pa·thol·o·gist** \-pə-ˈthäl-ə-jəst\ *n*

psy·cho·sis \sī-ˈkō-səs\ *n, pl* **-cho·ses** \-ˈkō-ˌsēz\ : fundamental or severe personality disorder characterized by defective or lost contact with reality and often by delusions and hallucinations

psy·cho·so·mat·ic \ˌsī-kə-sə-ˈmat-ik\ *adj* : of, relating to, or being bodily symptoms caused by mental or emotional disturbance (as stress and anxiety) ⟨*psychosomatic* illness⟩ — **psy·cho·so·mat·i·cal·ly** \-i-kə-lē, -klē\ *adv*

psy·cho·sur·gery \ˌsī-kō-ˈsərj-rē, -ə-rē\ *n* : brain surgery employed in treating the symptoms of mental illness — **psy·cho·sur·geon** \-ˈsər-jən\ *n* — **psy·cho·sur·gi·cal** \-ˈsər-ji-kəl\ *adj*

psy·cho·ther·a·py \ˌsī-kō-ˈther-ə-pē\ *n* : treatment of mental or emotional disorder or of related bodily ills by psychological means — **psy·cho·ther·a·pist** \-pəst\ *n*

psy·chot·ic \sī-ˈkät-ik\ *adj* : of, relating to, marked by, or affected with psychosis — **psychotic** *n* — **psy·chot·i·cal·ly** \-i-kə-lē, -klē\ *adv*

psy·chrom·e·ter \sī-ˈkräm-ət-ər\ *n* : an instrument for measuring the water vapor in the atmosphere by means of the difference in the readings of two thermometers when one of them is kept wet so that it is cooled by evaporation [Greek *psychros* "cold"] — **psy·chro·met·ric** \ˌsī-krō-ˈme-trik\ *adj*

psyl·la \ˈsil-ə\ *n* : any of various plant lice including many economic pests [Greek, "flea"] — **psyl·lid** \-əd\ *adj or n*

psyl·li·um \ˈsil-ē-əm\ *n* : the seed of a weedy herb that swells up and becomes gelatinous when moist and is used as a mild laxative [New Latin, from Greek *psyllion* "a variety of the herb plantain," from *psylla*]

ptar·mi·gan \ˈtär-mi-gən\ *n, pl* **ptarmigan** *or* **ptarmigans** : any of various grouse of northern regions with completely feathered feet [Scottish Gaelic *tarmachan*]

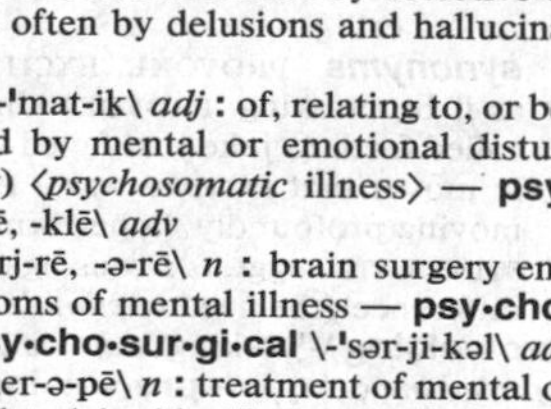
ptarmigan

P T boat \ˈpē-ˈtē-\ *n* : a high-speed motorboat usually equipped with torpedoes, machine guns, and depth charges [*p*atrol *t*orpedo]

PTC \ˌpē-ˌtē-ˈsē\ *n* : PHENYLTHIOCARBAMIDE

pter·an·o·don \tə-ˈran-ə-ˌdän\ *n* : any of a genus of extinct flying reptiles of the Cretaceous period with a wingspread of about 25 feet (8 meters) [Greek *pteron* "wing, feather" + *anodōn* "toothless," from *an-* + *odōn* "tooth"]

pte·rid·o·phyte \tə-ˈrid-ə-ˌfīt\ *n* : any of a division (Pteridophyta) of vascular plants that have roots, stems, and leaves, reproduce by spores instead of by flowers and seeds, and include the ferns, club mosses, horsetails, and their extinct relatives [derived from Greek *pterid-, pteris* "fern" + *phyton* "plant"]

ptero·dac·tyl \ˌter-ə-ˈdak-tl\ *n* : any of various extinct flying reptiles of the Mesozoic era with a featherless membrane extending from the body along the arms and forming the supporting surface of the wings [Greek *pteron* "wing" + *daktylos* "finger"]

ptero·saur \ˈter-ə-ˌsȯr\ *n* : PTERODACTYL [derived from Greek *pteron* "wing" + *sauros* "lizard"]

Ptol·e·ma·ic \ˌtäl-ə-ˈmā-ik\ *adj* : of, relating to, or characteristic of the astronomer Ptolemy and especially to his belief that the earth is at the center of the universe with the sun, moon, and planets revolving around it [Greek *Ptolemaikos,* from *Ptolemaios* "Ptolemy"]

pto·maine \ˈtō-ˌmān, tō-ˈ\ *n* : any of various often poisonous organic compounds formed by bacteria-induced rotting of nitrogenous matter (as proteins) [Italian *ptomaina,* from Greek *ptōma* "fall, fallen body, corpse," from *piptein* "to fall"]

ptomaine poisoning *n* : food poisoning caused by bacteria or bacterial products

pty·a·lin \ˈtī-ə-lən\ *n* : an amylase found in the saliva of many animals that converts starch into sugar [Greek *ptyalon* "saliva," from *ptyein* "to spit"]

pub \ˈpəb\ *n, chiefly British* : PUBLIC HOUSE

pub crawler *n* : one that goes from bar to bar

pu·ber·ty \ˈpyü-bərt-ē\ *n* **1** : the condition of being or the period of becoming first capable of reproducing sexually that is brought on by the production of sex hormones and the maturing of the sex organs (as the testes and ovaries) and is marked by the development of secondary sex characteristics (as male facial hair growth and female breast development) and by the occurrence of the first menstruation in the female **2** : the age at which puberty occurs often defined legally as 14 in boys and 12 in girls [Latin *pubertas,* from *puber* "pubescent"] — **pu·ber·tal** \-bərt-l\ *adj*

pu·bes·cent \pyü-ˈbes-nt\ *adj* **1** : arriving at or having reached puberty **2** : covered with fine soft short hairs — **pu·bes·cence** \-ns\ *n*

pu·bic \ˈpyü-bik\ *adj* : of, relating to, or situated near the pubis [Latin *pubes* "pubic hair, pubic region"]

pu·bis \ˈpyü-bəs\ *n, pl* **pu·bes** \-ˌbēz\ : the ventral and anterior of the three principal bones composing each half of the pelvis — called also *pubic bone* [New Latin *os pubis,* literally, "bone of the pubic region"]

[1]**pub·lic** \ˈpəb-lik\ *adj* **1 a** : of, relating to, or affecting all the people ⟨*public* law⟩ **b** : of or relating to government **c** : relating to or engaged in the service of the community or nation ⟨*public* life⟩ **2** : of or relating to humankind in general : UNIVERSAL **3** : of or relating to business or community interests as opposed to private affairs **4** : devoted to the general welfare : HUMANITARIAN ⟨*public* spirit⟩ **5** : accessible to or shared by all members of the community **6 a** : exposed to general view : OPEN **b** : WELL-KNOWN, PROMINENT ⟨a *public* figure⟩ **7** : supported by income from public funds and private contributions rather than by commercials ⟨*public* television⟩ [Medieval French *publique,* from Latin *publicus*] — **pub·lic·ly** *adv* — **pub·lic·ness** *n*

[2]**public** *n* **1** : a place accessible or visible to the public ⟨seen together in *public*⟩ **2** : the people as a whole : POPULACE ⟨a lecture open to the *public*⟩ **3** : a particular group of people ⟨a writer's *public*⟩

public address system *n* : an apparatus including one or more loudspeakers for reproducing sound so that it may be heard by a large audience in an auditorium or outdoors

pub·li·can \ˈpəb-li-kən\ *n* **1** : a provincial tax collector for the ancient Romans **2** *chiefly British* : a keeper of a public house [Medieval French, from Latin *publicanus,* from *publicum* "public revenue," from *publicus* "public"]

pub·li·ca·tion \ˌpəb-lə-ˈkā-shen\ *n* **1** : the act or process or an instance of publishing **2** : a published work [Medieval French, from Late Latin *publicatio,* from Latin *publicare* "to publish," from *publicus* "public"]

public domain *n* **1** : land owned directly by the government **2** : property rights that belong to the community at large, are unprotected by copyright or patent, and may be used by anyone

public house *n* **1** : INN 1, HOSTELRY **2** *chiefly British* : a licensed saloon or bar

pub·li·cist \ˈpəb-lə-səst\ *n* **1 a** : an expert in international law **b** : an expert or commentator on public affairs **2** : one that publicizes; *esp* : PRESS AGENT

pub·lic·i·ty \pə-ˈblis-ət-ē, ˌpə-\ *n* **1** : the condition of being public or publicly known **2** : something meant to attract attention; *esp* : information with a news value designed to further the interests of a place, person, or cause **3** : attention from the public and especially the communications media

pub·li·cize \ˈpəb-lə-ˌsīz\ *vt* : to give publicity to : ADVERTISE, PROMOTE

public opinion *n* : the general attitude of the public on some issue or the expression of this attitude ⟨*public opinion* favored the government's policy⟩

public relations *n* : the business of inducing the public to have understanding and goodwill for a person, firm, or institution; *also* : the degree of understanding and goodwill achieved

public school *n* **1** : any of various select endowed British schools that give a liberal education and prepare students for the universities **2** : an elementary or secondary school maintained by a local government

public servant *n* : a governmental official or employee

public service *n* **1** : the business of supplying a commodity (as electricity or gas) or service (as transportation) to any or all members of a community **2** : governmental employment; *esp* : CIVIL SERVICE

public speaking *n* **1** : the act or process of making speeches in public **2** : the art or science of effective oral communication with an audience

pub·lic–spir·it·ed \ˌpəb-lik-ˈspir-ət-əd\ *adj* : motivated by devotion to the general or national welfare — **pub·lic–spir·it·ed·ness** *n*

public utility *n* : a business organization (as a gas company) performing a public service and subject to special governmental regulation

public works *n pl* : works (as schools or highways) constructed for public use or enjoyment and financed and owned by the government

pub·lish \ˈpəb-lish\ *vb* **1** : to make generally known : make public announcement of ⟨*publish* a libel⟩ **2 a** : to produce or release for publication; *esp* : PRINT **b** : to issue the work of (an author) **3** : to have one's work accepted for publication ⟨a *publishing* scholar⟩ [Middle English *publishen,* from Medieval French *publier,* from Latin *publicare,* from *publicus* "public"] ***synonyms*** see DECLARE — **pub·lish·able** \-ə-bəl\ *adj*

pub·lish·er \-ər\ *n* : one that publishes; *esp* : one that issues and offers for sale printed matter (as books, periodicals, or newspapers)

puc·coon \pə-ˈkün\ *n* : any of several American plants (as the bloodroot) that yield a red or yellow pigment [Virginia Algonquian *poughkone*]

[1]**puck** \ˈpək\ *n* **1** *archaic* : an evil spirit : DEMON **2** : a mischievous sprite : HOBGOBLIN 1 [Old English *pūca*]

[2]**puck** *n* : a hard rubber disk used in ice hockey [English dialect *puck* "to poke," probably from Irish *poc* "butt, stroke in hurling," literally, "buck (male deer)"]

pucka *variant of* PUKKA

[1]**puck·er** \ˈpək-ər\ *vb* **puck·ered; puck·er·ing** \ˈpək-ring, -ə-ring\ : to contract into folds or wrinkles ⟨the cloth *puckered* in shrinking⟩ [probably derived from [1]*poke*]

[2]**pucker** *n* : a fold or wrinkle in a normally even surface — **puck·ered** \ˈpək-ərd\ *adj* — **puck·ery** \ˈpək-rē, -ə-rē\ *adj*

puck·ish \ˈpək-ish\ *adj* : IMPISH, MISCHIEVOUS ⟨*puckish* humor⟩ [[1]*puck*] — **puck·ish·ly** *adv* — **puck·ish·ness** *n*

pud·ding \ˈpu̇d-ing\ *n* **1** : a boiled or baked soft food usually with a cereal base ⟨corn *pudding*⟩ **2** : a dessert of a soft, spongy, or thick creamy consistency ⟨bread *pudding*⟩ **3** : a dish often containing suet or having a suet crust ⟨kidney *pudding*⟩ ⟨fig *pudding*⟩ [Middle English]

pudding stone *n* : conglomerate rock

[1]**pud·dle** \ˈpəd-l\ *n* **1** : a very small pool of usually dirty or muddy water **2** : an earthy mixture (as of clay, sand, and gravel)

\ə\ **abut**	\au̇\ **out**	\i\ **tip**	\ȯ\ **saw**	\u̇\ **foot**
\ər\ **further**	\ch\ **chin**	\ī\ **life**	\ȯi\ **coin**	\y\ **yet**
\a\ **mat**	\e\ **pet**	\j\ **job**	\th\ **thin**	\yü\ **few**
\ā\ **take**	\ē\ **easy**	\ng\ **sing**	\t͟h\ **this**	\yu̇\ **cure**
\ä\ **cot, cart**	\g\ **go**	\ō\ **bone**	\ü\ **food**	\zh\ **vision**

worked while wet into a compact mass that becomes impervious to water when dry [Middle English *podel*]

[2]**puddle** *vt* **pud·dled; pud·dling** \'pəd-ling, -l-ing\ **1 :** to make muddy or turbid **2 a :** to make a puddle of (as clay) **b :** to convert (melted pig iron) into wrought iron by stirring in the presence of an oxidizer **3 :** to strew with puddles — **pud·dler** \-ler, -l-ər\ *n*

pu·den·cy \'pyüd-n-sē\ *n* **:** MODESTY [Latin *pudentia,* from *pudēre* "to be ashamed"]

pu·den·dum \pyu̇-'den-dəm\ *n, pl* **-den·da** \-'den-də\ **:** the external genital organs especially of a woman [New Latin, sing. of Latin *pudenda,* from *pudendus* "shameful," from *pudēre* "to be ashamed"] — **pu·den·dal** \-'den-dl\ *adj*

pudgy \'pəj-ē\ *adj* **pudg·i·er; -est :** short and plump **:** CHUBBY [origin unknown] — **pudg·i·ness** *n*

pu·eb·lo \pü-'eb-lō, 'pweb-, pyü-'eb-\ *n, pl* **-los 1 :** an American Indian village of Arizona or New Mexico consisting of flat-roofed stone or adobe houses joined in groups sometimes several stories high **2** *cap* **:** a member of any of several American Indian peoples of the Southwest [Spanish, "village," literally, "people," from Latin *populus*]

pu·er·ile \'pyu̇-ər-əl, 'pyu̇r-, -ˌīl\ *adj* **1 :** JUVENILE 3 **2 :** CHILDISH, SILLY ⟨*puerile* remarks⟩ [Latin *puerilis,* from *puer* "boy, child"] — **pu·er·il·i·ty** \ˌpyu̇-ər-'il-ət-ē, ˌpyu̇r-\ *n*

pu·er·per·al \pyü-'ər-pə-rəl, -prəl\ *adj* **:** of, relating to, or occurring during childbirth or the period immediately following ⟨*puerperal* infection⟩ [Latin *puerpera* "woman in childbirth," from *puer* "child" + *parere* "to give birth to"]

puerperal fever *n* **:** an abnormal condition that results from infection of the placental site following delivery or abortion and is characterized in mild form by fever but in serious cases may spread through the wall of the uterus or into the bloodstream — called also *childbed fever*

[1]**puff** \'pəf\ *vb* **1 a** (1) **:** to blow in short gusts (2) **:** to exhale forcibly **b :** to breathe hard **:** PANT ⟨*puffed* as we climbed the hill⟩ **c :** to emit, propel, blow, or expel by or as if by small whiffs or clouds (as of smoke) ⟨*puff* at a pipe⟩ ⟨a brisk breeze *puffed* the clouds away⟩ **2 a :** to speak or act in a scornful, conceited, or affected manner **b :** to make proud or conceited **:** ELATE **c :** to praise extravagantly (as in advertising) **3 a :** to distend or become distended with or as if with gas **:** SWELL ⟨the sprained ankle *puffed* up⟩ **b :** to open or appear in or as if in a puff [Old English *pyffan,* of imitative origin]

[2]**puff** *n* **1 a :** an act or instance of puffing **:** WHIFF, GUST **b :** a slight explosive sound accompanying a puff **c :** a perceptible cloud (as of smoke or steam) emitted in a puff **2 :** a light pastry that rises high in baking **3 a :** a slight swelling **:** PROTUBERANCE **b :** a fluffy mass: as (1) **:** a small fluffy pad for applying cosmetic powder (2) **:** a soft loose roll of hair (3) **:** a quilted bed covering **4 :** a commendatory notice or review — **puff·i·ness** \'pəf-ē-nəs\ *n* — **puffy** \'pəf-ē\ *adj*

[3]**puff** *adj* **:** of, relating to, or designed for promotion or flattery ⟨a *puff* piece⟩

puff adder *n* **:** HOGNOSE SNAKE

puff·ball \'pəf-ˌbȯl\ *n* **:** any of various often edible globe-shaped fungi that discharge mature spores in a cloud resembling smoke when they are touched

puff·er \'pəf-ər\ *n* **1 :** one that puffs **2 :** PUFFER FISH

puffer fish *n* **:** any of various scaleless fishes chiefly of tropical seas which can puff themselves up with water or air when threatened and most of which are highly poisonous — called also *blowfish, globefish, puffer*

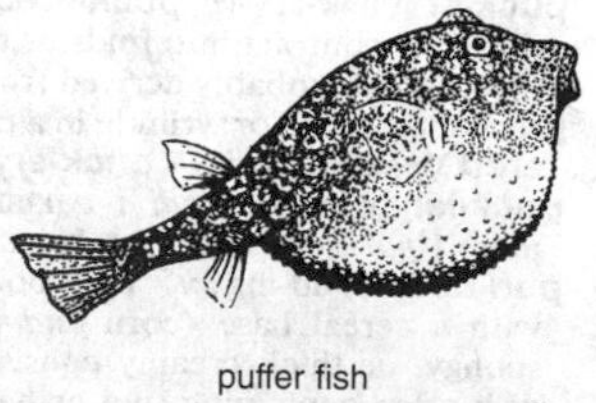
puffer fish

puf·fin \'pəf-ən\ *n* **:** any of several short-necked northern seabirds that are related to the auks and have a deep grooved bill marked with different colors [Middle English *pophyn*]

puff paste *n* **:** dough used in making light flaky pastries

pug \'pəg\ *n* **1 :** any of a breed of small sturdy compact dogs of Asian origin with a smooth, short coat, tightly curled tail, and broad wrinkled face **2 a :** PUG NOSE **b :** a close knot or coil of hair **:** BUN [obsolete *pug* "hobgoblin, monkey"]

pu·gi·list \'pyü-jə-ləst\ *n* **:** [1]BOXER [Latin *pugil* "boxer"] — **pu·gi·lism** \-ˌliz-əm\ *n* — **pu·gi·lis·tic** \ˌpyü-jə-'lis-tik\ *adj*

pug·na·cious \ˌpəg-'nā-shəs\ *adj* **:** having a quarrelsome or belligerent nature **:** TRUCULENT, COMBATIVE [Latin *pugnac-, pugnax,* from *pugnare* "to fight"] ***synonyms*** see BELLIGERENT — **pug·na·cious·ly** *adv* — **pug·na·cious·ness** *n* — **pug·nac·i·ty** \-'nas-ət-ē\ *n*

pug nose *n* **:** a nose having a slightly concave bridge and flattened nostrils — **pug–nosed** \'pəg-'nōzd\ *adj*

puis·ne \'pyü-nē\ *adj, chiefly British* **:** inferior in rank ⟨a *puisne* judge⟩ [Middle French *puisné* "younger," literally, "born afterward"]

puis·sance \'pwis-ns, 'pyü-ə-səns\ *n* **:** ability to dominate or sway **:** MIGHT [Medieval French *pussance, puissance,* from *pussant* "powerful," from *poer* "to be able, be powerful"] — **puis·sant** \-nt, -sənt\ *adj* — **puis·sant·ly** *adv*

puke \'pyük\ *vb* **:** VOMIT 1 [origin unknown] — **puke** *n*

puk·ka *or* **puc·ka** \'pək-ə\ *adj* **:** being genuine and authentic; *also* **:** FIRST-CLASS [Hindi and Urdu *pakkā* "cooked, ripe, solid," from Sanskrit *pakva*]

pul·chri·tude \'pəl-krə-ˌtüd, -ˌtyüd\ *n* **:** physical comeliness **:** BEAUTY [Latin *pulchritudin-, pulchritudo,* from *pulcher* "beautiful"] — **pul·chri·tu·di·nous** \ˌpəl-krə-'tüd-n-əs, -'tyüd-\ *adj*

pule \'pyül\ *vi* **:** WHINE 1, WHIMPER ⟨a *puling* infant⟩ [probably imitative]

[1]**pull** \'pu̇l\ *vb* **1 :** to separate forcibly from a natural or firm attachment **:** PLUCK, EXTRACT ⟨*pull* a tooth⟩; *also* **:** to admit of being pulled ⟨the stump *pulled* hard⟩ **2 a :** to exert force upon so as to cause or tend to cause motion toward the force ⟨*pull* a wagon⟩ **b :** to stretch (cooling candy) repeatedly **c :** to strain by stretching abnormally ⟨*pull* a tendon⟩ **d** (1) **:** to use force in drawing, dragging, or tugging ⟨*pull* on that rope⟩ (2) **:** MOVE ⟨the car *pulled* away from the curb⟩ (3) **:** to take a drink (4) **:** to draw hard in smoking ⟨*pulled* at my pipe⟩ **e :** to work (an oar) by drawing back strongly **3 :** to hit (a ball) to the left side of the field from a right-handed stance or to the right side from a left-handed stance **4 :** to draw apart **:** REND, TEAR **5 :** to print (as a proof) by impression **6 :** REMOVE ⟨*pull* a crankshaft⟩ ⟨*pulled* the pitcher in the third inning⟩ **7 :** to bring (a weapon) into the open ⟨*pulled* a knife⟩ **8 :** to carry out with skill or daring **:** COMMIT ⟨*pull* a robbery⟩ **9 :** ATTRACT ⟨*pull* votes⟩ **10 :** to feel or express strong sympathy **:** ROOT ⟨*pulling* for their team to win⟩ [Old English *pullian*] — **pull·er** *n* — **pull oneself together :** to regain one's self-possession — **pull one's leg :** to deceive someone playfully **:** HOAX — **pull stakes** *or* **pull up stakes :** to move out **:** LEAVE — **pull strings** *or* **pull wires :** to exert secret influence or control — **pull together :** to work in harmony **:** COOPERATE

[2]**pull** *n* **1 a :** the act or an instance of pulling **b** (1) **:** a draft of liquid (2) **:** an inhalation of smoke **c :** a route, journey, or climb requiring effort ⟨a long *pull* uphill⟩ **d :** force required to overcome resistance to pulling **2 a :** ADVANTAGE ⟨the *pull* of a good family name⟩ **b :** special influence ⟨got a job through *pull*⟩ **3 :** PROOF 2a **4 :** a device for pulling something or for operating by pulling ⟨a bell *pull*⟩ **5 :** a force that attracts, compels, or influences **:** ATTRACTION ⟨the *pull* of gravity⟩ **6 :** an injury resulting from abnormal straining or stretching ⟨a muscle *pull*⟩

pull away *vi* **:** to draw oneself back or away **:** WITHDRAW

pull·back \'pu̇l-ˌbak\ *n* **:** a pulling back; *esp* **:** an orderly withdrawal of troops from a position

pull–down *adj* **:** appearing below a selected item on a computer display ⟨a *pull-down* menu⟩

pull down *vt* **1 :** to tear down **:** WRECK **2 a :** to bring to a lower level **:** REDUCE **b :** to depress in health, strength, or spirits **3 :** to draw as wages or salary

pul·let \'pu̇l-ət\ *n* **:** a young hen; *esp* **:** a hen of the common domestic chicken less than a year old [Middle English *polet* "young fowl," from Medieval French *pullet,* from *pulle, poule* "young animal," from Late Latin *pullus,* from Latin, "young of an animal, chicken, sprout"]

pul·ley \'pu̇l-ē\ *n, pl* **pulleys 1 :** a small wheel with a grooved rim used singly with a rope or chain to change the direction and point of application of a pulling force and in combinations to increase the applied force especially for lifting

pulley 1

weights; *also* **:** the simple machine constituted by such a pulley with ropes **2 :** a wheel used to transmit power by means of a band, belt, cord, rope, or chain [Medieval French *poulie,* probably derived from Greek *polos* "axis, pole"]

pull in *vb* **1 :** CHECK, RESTRAIN ⟨*pull* a horse *in*⟩ **2 :** ARREST ⟨*pull in* a suspect⟩ **3 :** to arrive at a destination ⟨the train *pulled in* on time⟩

Pull·man \ˈpu̇l-mən\ *n* **:** a railroad passenger car with specially comfortable furnishings; *esp* **:** SLEEPING CAR [George M. *Pullman,* died 1897, American inventor]

pull off *vt* **:** to accomplish successfully especially against odds

pull·out \ˈpu̇l-ˌau̇t\ *n* **1 :** something that can be pulled out **2 :** the action in which an airplane goes from a dive to horizontal flight **3 :** PULLBACK

pull out \pu̇l-ˈau̇t, ˈpu̇l-\ *vi* **1 :** LEAVE, DEPART ⟨the ship finally *pulled out*⟩ **2 :** WITHDRAW ⟨*pulled out* at the last minute and left us a player short⟩

[1]**pull·over** \ˌpu̇l-ˌō-vər\ *adj* **:** put on by being pulled over the head

[2]**pullover** \ˈpu̇l-ˌō-vər\ *n* **:** a pullover garment

pull over \pu̇l-ˈō-vər, ˈpu̇l-\ *vi* **:** to steer one's vehicle to the side of the road

pull through *vb* **:** to survive or help through a dangerous or difficult period or situation

pull up *vb* **1 :** CHECK, REBUKE ⟨was *pulled up* for my bad manners⟩ **2 :** to bring or come to a stop **:** HALT ⟨*pulled* the car *up* in front of the hotel⟩ **3 :** to draw even with others in a race

pul·mo·nary \ˈpu̇l-mə-ˌner-ē, ˈpəl-\ *adj* **1 :** relating to, affecting, or occurring in the lungs ⟨*pulmonary* tissue⟩ **2 :** carried on by the lungs ⟨*pulmonary* respiration⟩ [Latin *pulmonarius,* from *pulmon-, pulmo* "lung"]

pulmonary artery *n* **:** an artery that carries oxygen-poor blood containing carbon dioxide from the right side of the heart to the lungs

pulmonary circulation *n* **:** the passage of blood from the right side of the heart through arteries to the lungs where it picks up oxygen and is returned to the left side of the heart by veins

pulmonary vein *n* **:** a vein that returns oxygenated blood from the lungs to the left side of the heart

pul·mo·nate \ˈpu̇l-mə-nāt, ˈpəl-\ *adj* **:** having lungs or organs resembling lungs; *also* **:** air-breathing ⟨*pulmonate* snails⟩

pul·mo·tor \ˈpu̇l-ˌmōt-ər, ˈpəl-\ *n* **:** a respiratory apparatus for pumping oxygen or air into and out of the lungs (as of an asphyxiated person) [from *Pulmotor,* a former trademark]

[1]**pulp** \ˈpəlp\ *n* **1 a :** the soft juicy or fleshy part of a fruit or vegetable ⟨the *pulp* of an apple⟩ **b :** a mass of vegetable matter from which the juice or moisture has been pressed **2 :** the soft sensitive tissue that fills the central cavity of a tooth **3 :** a material prepared by chemical or mechanical means chiefly from wood and used in making paper and cellulose products **4 a :** pulpy condition **b :** something in a pulpy condition **5 :** a magazine or book using rough-surfaced paper made of wood pulp and often dealing with sensational material [Latin *pulpa* "flesh, pulp"] — **pulp·i·ness** \ˈpəl-pē-nəs\ *n* — **pulpy** \ˈpəl-pē\ *adj*

[2]**pulp** *vb* **:** to reduce to pulp **:** make or become pulpy — **pulp·er** *n*

pul·pit \ˈpu̇l-ˌpit, ˈpəl-, -pət\ *n* **1 :** an elevated platform or high reading desk used in preaching or conducting a worship service **2 a :** the preaching profession **b :** a position as a preacher [Late Latin *pulpitum,* from Latin, "staging, platform"]

pulp·wood \ˈpəlp-ˌwu̇d\ *n* **:** a wood (as aspen, hemlock, pine, or spruce) used in making pulp for paper

pul·que \ˈpül-ˌkā\ *n* **:** an alcoholic drink made in Mexico from the fermented juice of various agaves [Mexican Spanish]

pul·sar \ˈpəl-ˌsär\ *n* **:** a celestial source of pulsating radio waves characterized by a short nearly constant interval (as .033 second) between pulses that is held to be a rotating neutron star [*pulse* + *-ar* (as in *quasar*)]

pul·sate \ˈpəl-ˌsāt\ *vi* **1 :** to vibrate or expand and contract in a rhythmic manner **:** PULSE ⟨my heart *pulsated*⟩ ⟨*pulsating* drums⟩ **2 :** to be vibrant (as with life, activity, or feeling) ⟨a busy *pulsating* city⟩ [Latin *pulsare,* from *pellere* "to drive, beat"]

pul·sa·tile \ˈpəl-sət-l, -sə-ˌtīl\ *adj* **:** of or marked by pulsation

pul·sa·tion \ˌpəl-ˈsā-shən\ *n* **:** a pulsating movement or action (as of an artery); *also* **:** a single throb of such movement

[1]**pulse** \ˈpəls\ *n* **:** the edible seeds of several crops (as peas, beans, or lentils) of the legume family; *also* **:** a plant yielding pulse [probably from Medieval French *puuiz* "porridge," from Latin *puls*]

[2]**pulse** *n* **1 :** a regular throbbing caused in the arteries by the contractions of the heart **2 a :** rhythmical beating, vibrating, or sounding **b :** BEAT 1c, THROB **3 a :** a transient variation of a quantity (as electrical current or voltage) whose value is normally constant **b :** an electromagnetic wave or a sound wave of brief duration [Medieval French *pouls,* from Latin *pulsus,* literally, "beating," from *pellere* "to drive, beat"]

[3]**pulse** *vb* **1 :** to exhibit a pulse or pulsation **:** THROB **2 :** to drive by or as if by a pulsation **3 :** to cause to pulsate **4 :** to produce or modulate (as electromagnetic waves) in the form of pulses ⟨*pulsed* waves⟩

pul·ver·ize \ˈpəl-və-ˌrīz\ *vb* **1 :** to reduce or become reduced (as by beating or grinding) into a powder **2 :** to demolish as if by pulverizing **:** SMASH, ANNIHILATE [Late Latin *pulverizare,* from Latin *pulver-, pulvis* "dust, powder"] — **pul·ver·iz·er** *n*

pu·ma \ˈpü-mə, ˈpyü-\ *n, pl* **pumas** *also* **puma :** COUGAR [Spanish, from Quechua]

pum·ice \ˈpəm-əs\ *n* **:** a volcanic glass full of cavities and very light in weight used especially in powder form for smoothing and polishing — called also *pumice stone* [Medieval French *pomice,* from Latin *pumic-, pumex*]

pum·mel \ˈpəm-əl\ *vb* **-meled** *or* **-melled; -mel·ing** *or* **-mel·ling 1 :** POUND 2a, BEAT ⟨knead and *pummel* the dough⟩ **2 :** to defeat decisively ⟨*pummeled* the competition⟩ [alteration of *pommel*]

[1]**pump** \ˈpəmp\ *n* **1 :** a device that raises, transfers, delivers, or compresses fluids especially by suction or pressure or both ⟨a water *pump*⟩ **2 :** a biological mechanism by which atoms, ions, or molecules are transported across cell membranes [Middle English *pumpe, pompe*]

[2]**pump** *vb* **1 :** to raise, transfer, or compress by means of a pump ⟨*pump* water⟩ **2 :** to draw fluid from by the use of a pump ⟨*pump* a boat dry⟩ **3 :** to draw, force, or drive onward in the manner of a pump ⟨the heart *pumps* blood into the arteries⟩ **4 a :** to question persistently **b :** to draw out by persistent questioning **5 :** to move up and down like a pump handle ⟨*pump* the hand of a friend⟩ **6 :** to fill by means of a pump ⟨*pump* up a tire⟩ **7 :** to spurt out intermittently — **pump·er** *n*

[3]**pump** *n* **:** a low shoe without a fastening that grips the foot chiefly at the toe and heel [origin unknown]

pum·per·nick·el \ˈpəm-pər-ˌnik-əl\ *n* **:** a dark coarse sourdough rye bread [German]

pump·kin \ˈpəng-kən, ˈpəm-, ˈpəmp-\ *n* **1 :** the usually round orange fruit of an annual vine of the gourd family widely grown as food; *also* **:** a fruit (as a crookneck squash) of a closely related vine **2 :** a usually hairy prickly vine that produces pumpkins **3 :** a strong orange color [French *popon, pompon* "melon, pumpkin," from Latin *pepon-, pepo,* from Greek *pepōn,* from *pepōn* "ripened"]

pump·kin·seed \-ˌsēd\ *n* **:** a small brightly colored North American freshwater sunfish

[1]**pun** \ˈpən\ *n* **:** the humorous use of a word in such a way as to suggest different meanings or applications or of words having the same or nearly the same sound but different meanings [perhaps from Italian *puntiglio* "fine point, quibble"]

[2]**pun** *vi* **punned; pun·ning :** to make puns

[1]**punch** \ˈpənch\ *n* **1 :** a tool or machine for piercing, cutting (as a hole or notch), forming, driving the head of a nail below a surface or a bolt out of a hole, or impressing a design in a softer material **2 :** a hole or notch resulting from a perforating operation [probably short for *puncheon*]

[2]**punch** *vb* **1 a :** PROD 2, POKE **b :** to act as herdsman of (range cattle) **2 a :** to strike with a forward thrust of the fist **b :** to drive or push forcibly by or as if by a punch **3 :** to emboss, cut, perforate, or make with a punch **4 :** to strike or press sharply the operating mechanism of **5 :** to enter (as data) by punching keys [Middle English *pouncen, punchen* "to emboss, pierce," probably from *pounce* "punching tool, dagger, talon"] — **punch·er** *n*

[3]**punch** *n* **1 :** the action of punching **2 :** a quick blow with or as if with the fist **3 :** energy or vigor that commands attention ⟨they lacked political *punch*⟩

[4]**punch** *n* **:** a drink made of several ingredients (as fruit juices and

spices) and often flavored with wine or distilled liquor [perhaps from Hindi and Urdu *pāc* "five," from Sanskrit *pañca*; from the number of ingredients]

Punch–and–Judy show \ˌpən-chən-ˈjüd-ē-\ *n* **:** a traditional puppet show in which the hook-nosed and hunchbacked Punch fights comically with his wife Judy

punch bowl *n* **:** a large bowl from which a beverage (as punch) is served

punch card *n* **:** a card with holes punched in particular positions each with its own signification for use in data processing — called also *punched card*

punch–drunk \ˈpənch-ˌdrəngk\ *adj* **1 :** suffering from brain injury that is a result of repeated blows to the head received in boxing **2 :** GROGGY ⟨*punch-drunk* with fatigue⟩ [[3]*punch*]

[1]pun·cheon \ˈpən-chən\ *n* **1 :** a pointed tool for piercing **2 a :** a short upright framing timber **b :** a split log or slab with the face smoothed **3 :** a figured stamp die or punch used especially by goldsmiths and engravers [Medieval French *ponchon* "pointed tool, support," derived from Latin *pungere* "to prick"]

[2]puncheon *n* **1 :** a large cask of varying capacity **2 :** any of various units of liquid capacity [Medieval French *ponchon*]

punch in *vi* **:** to record the time of one's arrival or beginning work by punching a time clock

pun·chi·nel·lo \ˌpən-chə-ˈnel-ō\ *n* **1** *cap* **:** a fat short humpbacked clown or buffoon in Italian puppet shows **2** *pl* **-los :** a squat grotesque person [Italian dialect *polecenella*]

punching bag *n* **:** a usually suspended stuffed or inflated bag to be punched for exercise or for training in boxing

punch line *n* **:** the sentence, statement, or phrase (as in a joke) that makes the point

punch out *vi* **:** to record the time of one's stopping work or departure by punching a time clock

punch press *n* **:** a press for working on material (as metal) by the use of cutting, shaping, or combination dies

punchy \ˈpən-chē\ *adj* **punch·i·er; -est :** PUNCH-DRUNK

punc·tate \ˈpəng-ˌtāt, ˈpəngk-\ *adj* **1 :** ending in or resembling a point **2 :** marked with minute spots or depressions ⟨a *punctate* leaf⟩ [Latin *punctum* "point"] — **punc·ta·tion** \ˌpəng-ˈtā-shən, ˌpəngk-\ *n*

punc·til·io \ˌpəng-ˈtil-ē-ˌō, ˌpəngk-\ *n, pl* **-i·os 1 :** a minute detail of conduct in a ceremony or in observance of a code **2 :** careful observance of forms (as in social conduct) [Italian *puntiglio* "point of honor, scruple, quibble," from Spanish *puntillo,* from *punto* "point," from Latin *punctum*]

punc·til·i·ous \-ē-əs\ *adj* **:** marked by precise exact accordance with the details of codes or conventions ***synonyms*** see CAREFUL — **punc·til·i·ous·ly** *adv* — **punc·til·i·ous·ness** *n*

punc·tu·al \ˈpəng-chə-wəl, ˈpəngk-\ *adj* **1 :** PUNCTILIOUS **2 a :** being on time **:** PROMPT **b :** characterized by regular occurrence [Medieval Latin *punctualis* "of a point," from Latin *punctus* "pricking, point," from *pungere* "to prick"] — **punc·tu·al·i·ty** \ˌpəng-chə-ˈwal-ət-ē, ˌpəngk-\ *n* — **punc·tu·al·ly** \ˈpəng-chə-wə-lē, ˈpəngk-\ *adv* — **punc·tu·al·ness** \-wəl-nəs\ *n*

punc·tu·ate \ˈpəng-chə-ˌwāt, ˈpəngk-\ *vt* **1 :** to mark or divide with punctuation marks **2 :** to break into or interrupt at intervals ⟨a speech *punctuated* by coughs⟩ [Medieval Latin *punctuare,* from Latin *punctus* "point"] — **punc·tu·a·tor** \-ˌwāt-ər\ *n*

punctuated equilibrium *n* **:** evolution that is characterized by long periods of stability in the characteristics of an organism and short periods of rapid change during which new forms appear

punc·tu·a·tion \ˌpəng-chə-ˈwā-shən, ˌpəngk-\ *n* **:** the act, practice, or system of inserting standardized marks or signs in written matter to clarify the meaning and separate structural units

punctuation mark *n* **:** any of the standardized marks or signs used in punctuation

[1]punc·ture \ˈpəng-chər, ˈpəngk-\ *n* **1 :** the act of puncturing **2 :** a hole or a narrow wound resulting from puncturing ⟨a *puncture* of the abdomen⟩ ⟨a tire with a *puncture*⟩ [Latin *punctura,* from *punctus,* past participle of *pungere* "to prick"]

[2]puncture *vb* **punc·tured; punc·tur·ing** \ˈpəng-chə-ring, ˈpəngshring, ˈpəngk-\ **1 :** to pierce with a pointed instrument or object **2 :** to suffer a puncture of **3 :** to become punctured **4 :** to make useless or absurd as if by a puncture ⟨*puncture* an argument⟩

pun·dit \ˈpən-dət\ *n* **1 :** a wise or learned person **2 :** a person who gives opinions in an authoritative manner usually through the mass media [Hindi *paṇḍit,* from Sanskrit *paṇḍita,* from *paṇḍita* "learned"]

pun·gen·cy \ˈpən-jən-sē\ *n* **:** the quality or state of being pungent

pun·gent \ˈpən-jənt\ *adj* **1 :** sharply stimulating to the mind ⟨*pungent* criticism⟩ ⟨*pungent* wit⟩ **2 :** causing a sharp or irritating sensation; *esp* **:** ACRID [Latin *pungens,* present participle of *pungere* "to prick, sting"] — **pun·gent·ly** *adv*

Pu·nic \ˈpyü-nik\ *adj* **:** of or relating to Carthage or the Carthaginians [Latin *punicus,* from *Poenus* "inhabitant of Carthage"]

pun·ish \ˈpən-ish\ *vb* **1 :** impose punishment on for a fault or offense ⟨*punish* the children for disobeying⟩ **2 :** to inflict punishment for (as a crime) ⟨*punish* treason with death⟩ **3 :** to deal with severely or roughly ⟨badly *punished* by my opponent⟩ **4 :** to inflict punishment [Middle French *puniss-,* stem of *punir* "to punish," from Latin *punire,* from *poena* "penalty, pain"] — **pun·ish·abil·i·ty** \ˌpən-ish-ə-ˈbil-ət-ē\ *n* — **pun·ish·able** \ˈpən-ish-ə-bəl\ *adj* — **pun·ish·er** *n*

synonyms PUNISH, CHASTISE, DISCIPLINE mean to impose a penalty on someone for doing wrong. PUNISH implies subjection to penalty for wrongdoing ⟨*punished* for stealing⟩. CHASTISE may apply to either the infliction of corporal punishment or to verbal censure or denunciation ⟨*chastised* his son for neglecting his studies⟩. DISCIPLINE may involve punishment but suggests action with the intent of bringing under control ⟨parents must *discipline* their children⟩.

pun·ish·ing \ˈpən-ish-ing\ *adj* **:** very arduous, demanding, or painful ⟨a *punishing* race⟩ — **pun·ish·ing·ly** *adv*

pun·ish·ment \ˈpən-ish-mənt\ *n* **1 :** the act of punishing **2 a :** suffering or pain that serves as retribution **b :** the penalty for a fault or crime ⟨the *punishment* for speeding⟩ **3 :** severe, rough, or disastrous treatment ⟨trees showing the effects of *punishment* by a heavy storm⟩

pu·ni·tive \ˈpyü-nət-iv\ *adj* **:** inflicting, involving, or aiming at punishment [French *punitif,* from Medieval Latin *punitivus,* from Latin *punitus,* past participle of *punire* "to punish"] — **pu·ni·tive·ly** *adv* — **pu·ni·tive·ness** *n*

Pun·jabi \ˌpən-ˈjäb-ē, -ˈjab-\ *n* **1 :** a native or inhabitant of the Punjab region of the northwestern Indian subcontinent **2 :** an Indo-Aryan language of the Punjab [Hindi and Urdu *pañjābī,* from *pañjābī* "of Punjab," from Persian *pañjābī,* from Panjāb "Punjab"] — **Punjabi** *adj*

[1]punk \ˈpəngk\ *n* **1 :** a young inexperienced man **2 :** a petty hoodlum or gangster **3 a :** PUNK ROCK **b :** a punk rock musician **c :** a person who wears punk styles [origin unknown]

[2]punk *adj* **1 :** very poor in quality ⟨played a *punk* game⟩ **2 :** being in poor health ⟨feeling *punk* today⟩ **3 :** of or relating to a style (as of clothing or hair) originally inspired by punk rock

[3]punk *n* **1 :** wood so decayed as to be dry, crumbly, and useful for tinder **2 :** a preparation (as of a stick of coated wood) that burns slowly and is used to ignite fuses especially of fireworks [perhaps alteration of *spunk* "tinder"]

pun·kah \ˈpəng-kə\ *n* **:** a large fan or a canvas-covered frame suspended from the ceiling and used especially in India for fanning a room [Hindi *pākhā*]

pun·kie *also* **pun·ky** \ˈpəng-kē\ *n, pl* **punkies :** a tiny biting fly [Dutch dialect *punki,* from Delaware *punk,* literally, "fine ashes, powder"]

punk rock *n* **:** rock music marked by extreme and often deliberately offensive expressions of alienation and discontent — **punk rocker** *n*

Pun·nett square \ˈpə-nət-\ *n* **:** a table in the form of a grid that is used in genetics for calculating the ratio of the different genotypes and phenotypes among the offspring of a cross and in which each allele of one or more gene pairs contributed by each parent and the resulting allelic combinations of the offspring are listed [Reginald C. *Punnett,* died 1967, English geneticist]

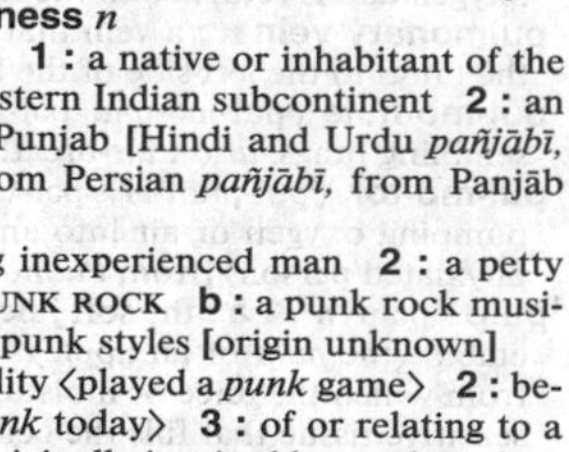

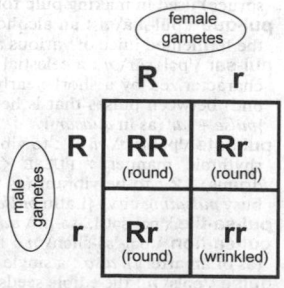

Punnett square: *R* round seed shape, *r* wrinkled seed shape

pun·ster \ˈpən-stər\ *n* **:** one given to making puns

[1]punt \ˈpənt\ *n* **:** a long narrow flat-bottomed square-ended boat usually propelled with a pole [Old English, from Latin *ponto,* from *pont-, pons* "bridge"]

[2]**punt** *vb* **:** to propel (a boat) by pushing with a pole against the bottom of a body of water

[3]**punt** *vi* **:** to play at a gambling game against the banker [French *ponter,* from *ponte* "point in some games," from Spanish *punto* "point," from Latin *punctum*]

[4]**punt** *vb* **1 :** to make a punt **2 :** to kick (a ball) by means of a punt [origin unknown]

[5]**punt** *n* **:** a kick of a ball which is dropped from the hands and hit before it touches the ground

punt·er \ˈpənt-ər\ *n* **:** one that punts

punt formation *n* **:** an offensive football formation in which a back making a punt stands approximately 10 yards behind the line and the other backs are in blocking position close to the line of scrimmage

pu·ny \ˈpyü-nē\ *adj* **pu·ni·er; -est :** slight or inferior in power, size, or importance **:** WEAK [Middle French *puisné* "younger," from *puis* "afterward" + *né* "born"] — **pu·ni·ness** *n*

Word History *Puny* is a spelling adopted to reflect the pronunciation of *puisne,* from the Middle French *puisné,* "younger." The literal meaning of the French *puisné* is "born afterward," and in their earliest uses in English *puisne* and *puny* referred to someone younger than, or of inferior position to, someone else. In this sense it developed a specific legal meaning: a *puisne* (or *puny*) judge is a junior or subordinate judge in the superior courts. Very soon after being borrowed into English *puny* developed from its literal meaning the sense of "slight or inferior in power, vigor, size, or importance."

pup \ˈpəp\ *n* **:** a young dog **:** PUPPY; *also* **:** one of the young of various animals (as seals) [short for *puppy*]

pu·pa \ˈpyü-pə\ *n, pl* **pu·pae** \-ˌpē, -ˌpī\ *or* **pu·pas :** the stage of an insect (as a bee, moth, or beetle) having complete metamorphosis that occurs between the larva and the adult, is usually enclosed in a cocoon or case, and undergoes internal changes by which larval structures are replaced by those of the adult [Latin, "girl, doll"] — **pu·pal** \ˈpyü-pəl\ *adj*

pupa

pu·par·i·um \pyü-ˈpar-ē-əm, -ˈper-\ *n, pl* **pu·par·ia** \-ē-ə\ **:** an outer shell that covers the pupae of some insects (as a fly) and is formed from the skin of the larva [New Latin, from *pupa*]

pu·pate \ˈpyü-ˌpāt\ *vi* **:** to become a pupa **:** pass through a pupal stage — **pu·pa·tion** \pyü-ˈpā-shən\ *n*

[1]**pu·pil** \ˈpyü-pəl\ *n* **1 :** a child or young person in school or in the charge of a tutor **:** STUDENT **2 :** one who has been taught or influenced by a famous or distinguished person [Middle French *pupille* "minor ward," from Latin *pupillus* "male ward" (from *pupus* "boy") and *pupilla* "female ward," from *pupa* "girl, doll"]

Word History In Latin a *pupa* was either a girl or a doll. Its diminutive *pupilla* had two senses. A person can see himself or herself reflected in miniature, like a little doll, in the eye of another. For this reason the opening in the iris which seems to hold this image was called a *pupilla.* Our English *pupil* was borrowed from the Middle French descendent of the Latin word. In Latin a little girl who was an orphan and a ward was also called a *pupilla,* her masculine counterpart being a *pupillus.* Middle French *pupille* served for both sexes. English *pupil* was originally used for a ward, but in the 16th century the word developed a new meaning, and a *pupil* became a student in the charge of a tutor or in school.

[2]**pupil** *n* **:** the usually round opening in the iris of the eye that contracts and expands to control the amount of light falling on the retina [Middle French *pupille,* from Latin *pupilla,* from *pupa* "girl, doll"; from the tiny image of oneself seen reflected in another's eye]

pu·pil·age *or* **pu·pil·lage** \ˈpyü-pə-lij\ *n* **:** the state or period of being a pupil

pup·pet \ˈpəp-ət\ *n* **1 a :** a small-scale figure (as of a person) usually with a cloth body and hollow head that fits over and is moved by the hand **b :** MARIONETTE **2 :** DOLL 1 **3 :** one whose acts are controlled by an outside force or influence [Middle French *poupette,* derived from Latin *pupa* "doll"]

pup·pe·teer \ˌpəp-ə-ˈtiər\ *n* **:** one who manipulates puppets

pup·pet·ry \ˈpəp-ə-trē\ *n, pl* **-ries :** the production or creation of puppets or puppet shows

pup·py \ˈpəp-ē\ *n, pl* **puppies :** a young domestic dog; *esp* **:** one less than a year old [Middle French *poupée* "doll, toy," derived from Latin *pupa* "doll"] — **pup·py·ish** \-ē-ish\ *adj*

pup tent *n* **:** a small low tent for two persons usually consisting of two halves fastened together

pur·blind \ˈpər-ˌblīnd\ *adj* **1 :** partly blind **2 :** lacking in vision, insight, or understanding **:** OBTUSE [obsolete *purblind* "wholly blind," from Middle English *pur blind,* from *pur* "purely, wholly," from *pur* "pure"] — **pur·blind·ly** *adv* — **pur·blind·ness** \-ˌblīnd-nəs, -ˌblīn-nəs\ *n*

[1]**pur·chase** \ˈpər-chəs\ *vt* **1 a :** to obtain by paying money or its equivalent **:** BUY ⟨*purchase* a house⟩ **b :** to obtain by labor, danger, or sacrifice **:** EARN ⟨*purchase* one's life at the expense of one's honor⟩ **2 :** to constitute the means for buying ⟨our dollars *purchase* less each year⟩ [Medieval French *purchacer* "to seek to obtain," from *por-, pur-* "thoroughly, to a conclusion" (from Latin *pro-* "forward, for") + *chacer* "to chase"] — **pur·chas·able** \-chə-sə-bəl\ *adj* — **pur·chas·er** *n*

[2]**purchase** *n* **1 :** an act or instance of purchasing **2 :** something purchased **3 a :** a mechanical hold or advantage applied to the raising or moving of heavy bodies **b :** an apparatus or device by which advantage is gained **4 :** a secure hold, grasp, or place to stand ⟨could not get a *purchase* on the ledge⟩

pur·dah \ˈpərd-ə\ *n* **:** seclusion of women from public observation among Muslims and some Hindus especially in India [Hindi and Urdu *parda,* literally, "screen, veil"]

pure \ˈpyu̇r\ *adj* **1 a :** not mixed with anything else ⟨*pure* gold⟩ **b :** free from dust, dirt, or taint ⟨*pure* water⟩ **2 a :** nothing other than **:** SHEER ⟨*pure* nonsense⟩ **b :** ABSTRACT 3a, THEORETICAL ⟨*pure* science⟩ ⟨*pure* mathematics⟩ **3 a :** free from sin or moral guilt; *esp* **:** marked by chastity **b :** of unmixed ancestry **c :** producing offspring which do not vary from the type of the parents or among themselves with respect to one or more characters [Medieval French *pur,* from Latin *purus*] ***synonyms*** see CHASTE — **pure·ness** *n*

pure–blood·ed \-ˈbləd-əd\ *or* **pure·blood** \-ˌbləd\ *adj* **:** of unmixed ancestry **:** PUREBRED — **pureblood** *n*

pure·bred \-ˈbred\ *adj* **:** bred from members of a recognized breed, strain, or kind without cross-breeding over many generations — **pure·bred** \-ˌbred\ *n*

[1]**pu·ree** \pyu̇-ˈrā, -ˈrē\ *n* **1 :** a paste or thick liquid suspension usually made from cooked food ground finely **2 :** a thick soup made of pureed vegetables [French *purée,* from *purer* "to purify, strain," from Latin *purare* "to purify," from *purus* "pure"]

[2]**puree** *vt* **pu·reed; pu·ree·ing :** to make a puree of

pure·ly \ˈpyu̇r-lē\ *adv* **1 :** without admixture of anything injurious or foreign **2 :** MERELY ⟨read *purely* for relaxation⟩ **3 :** in a chaste manner **4 :** WHOLLY 1

[1]**pur·ga·tive** \ˈpər-gət-iv\ *adj* **:** purging or tending to purge

[2]**purgative** *n* **:** a strong laxative

pur·ga·to·ri·al \ˌpər-gə-ˈtōr-ē-əl, -ˈtȯr-\ *adj* **1 :** cleansing of sin **:** EXPIATORY **2 :** of or relating to purgatory

pur·ga·to·ry \ˈpər-gə-ˌtōr-ē, -ˌtȯr-\ *n, pl* **-ries 1 :** an intermediate state after death in which according to Roman Catholic doctrine the souls of those who die in God's grace but without having made full satisfaction for their sins are purified by suffering **2 :** a place or state of temporary punishment [Medieval Latin *purgatorium,* from Late Latin *purgatorius* "purging," from Latin *purgare* "to purge"]

[1]**purge** \ˈpərj\ *vb* **1 a :** to clear of sin or guilt **b :** to cleanse or purify by separating and carrying off impurities **2 :** to become free of impurities or excess matter through a cleansing process **3 :** to remove by cleansing **4 :** to have or cause vigorous and usually repeated evacuation of the bowels **5 :** to get rid of (as undesirable persons) [Medieval French *purger,* from Latin *purigare, purgare* "to purify, purge," from *purus* "pure"] — **purga·tion** \ˌpər-ˈgā-shən\ *n* — **purg·er** *n*

[2]**purge** *n* **1 a :** an act or instance of purging **b :** a ridding of persons regarded as treacherous or disloyal **2 :** something that purges; *esp* **:** PURGATIVE

pu·ri·fi·ca·tion \ˌpyu̇r-ə-fə-ˈkā-shən\ *n* **:** an act or instance of purifying or of being purified

pu·ri·fi·ca·tor \ˈpyru̇r-ə-fə-ˌkāt-ər\ *n* **1 :** one that purifies **2 :** a

\ə\ **abut**	\au̇\ **out**	\i\ **tip**	\ȯ\ **saw**	\u̇\ **foot**
\ər\ **further**	\ch\ **chin**	\ī\ **life**	\ȯi\ **coin**	\y\ **yet**
\a\ **mat**	\e\ **pet**	\j\ **job**	\th\ **thin**	\yü\ **few**
\ā\ **take**	\ē\ **easy**	\ng\ **sing**	\t͟h\ **this**	\yu̇\ **cure**
\ä\ **cot, cart**	\g\ **go**	\ō\ **bone**	\ü\ **food**	\zh\ **vision**

linen cloth used to wipe the chalice after celebration of the Eucharist

pu•rif•i•ca•to•ry \pyu̇r-ˈif-i-kə-ˌtōr-ē, ˈpyu̇r-ə-fə-kə-, -ˌtȯr-\ *adj* : serving, tending, or intended to purify

pu•ri•fy \ˈpyu̇r-ə-ˌfī\ *vb* **-fied; -fy•ing** **1** : to make pure : free from anything alien, extraneous, corrupting, polluting, or damaging **2** : to grow or become pure or clean — **pu•ri•fi•er** \-ˌfī-ər, -ˌfīr\ *n*

Pu•rim \ˈpu̇r-ˌim, pu̇r-ˈ\ *n* : a Jewish holiday celebrated in February or March in commemoration of the deliverance of the Jews from the massacre plotted by Haman [Hebrew *pūrīm*, literally, "lots"; from the casting of lots by Haman (Esther 9:24-26)]

pu•rine \ˈpyu̇r-ˌēn\ *n* : any of a group of bases including several (as adenine and guanine) that are fundamental constituents of DNA and RNA [German *Purin*, from Latin *purus* "pure" + New Latin *uricus* "uric" + German *-in* "ine"]

pur•ism \ˈpyu̇r-ˌiz-əm\ *n* : rigid adherence to or insistence of nicety especially in use of words — **pur•ist** \-əst\ *n* — **pu•ris•tic** \pyu̇r-ˈis-tik\ *adj*

pu•ri•tan \ˈpyu̇r-ət-n\ *n* **1** *cap* : a member of a 16th and 17th century Protestant group in England and New England opposing as unscriptural many traditional customs of the Church of England **2** : one who practices or preaches or follows a stricter moral code than that which prevails [probably from Late Latin *puritas* "purity"] — **puritan** *adj, often cap* — **pu•ri•tan•i•cal** \ˌpyu̇r-ə-ˈtan-i-kəl\ *adj* — **pu•ri•tan•i•cal•ly** \-kə-lē, -klē\ *adv* — **pu•ri•tan•ism** \ˈpyu̇r-ət-n-ˌiz-əm\ *n, often cap*

pu•ri•ty \ˈpyu̇r-ət-ē\ *n* : the quality or state of being pure [Medieval French *purité*, from Late Latin *puritas*, from Latin *purus* "pure"]

[1]purl \ˈpərl\ *n* : an intertwining of thread through the loop of a stitch along an edge (as in buttonholing) [obsolete *pirl* "to twist"]

[2]purl *vb* : to knit in purl stitch

[3]purl *n* **1** : a purling or swirling stream or rill **2** : a gentle murmur or movement (as of purling water) [perhaps of Scandinavian origin]

[4]purl *vi* **1** : EDDY, SWIRL **2** : to make a soft murmuring sound like that of a purling stream

pur•lieu \ˈpərl-ˌyü\ *n* **1 a** : a place of resort : HAUNT **b** *pl* : [2]BOUND 3 **2 a** : an outlying or adjacent district **b** *pl* : ENVIRONMENT 1 [Middle English *purlewe* "land severed from a royal forest by perambulation," from Medieval French *puralé* "perambulation," from *puraler* "to travel through," from *pur-* "thoroughly" + *aler* "to go"]

pur•lin \ˈpər-lən\ *n* : a horizontal member in a roof supporting the rafters [origin unknown]

pur•loin \pər-ˈlȯin, ˌpər-ˈ, ˈpər-ˌ\ *vt* : STEAL 2a, FILCH [Medieval French *purluigner* "to put off, delay, put aside," from *pur-* "forward" + *luin, loing* "at a distance," from Latin *longe*, from *longus* "long"] — **pur•loin•er** *n*

purl stitch *n* : a knitting stitch usually made with the yarn at the front of the work by inserting the right needle into the front of a loop on the left needle from the right, catching the yarn with the right needle, and bringing it through to form a new loop — compare KNIT STITCH

[1]pur•ple \ˈpər-pəl\ *adj* **1** : of the color purple **2** : highly rhetorical : ORNATE ⟨*purple* prose⟩ [Middle English *purpel*, alteration of *purper*, from Old English *purpuran* "of purple," from *purpure* "purple color," from Latin *purpura*, from Greek *porphyra*]

[2]purple *n* **1 a** : TYRIAN PURPLE **b** : a color about midway between red and blue **2 a** : cloth dyed purple **b** : a garment of purple cloth; *esp* : a robe worn as an emblem of rank or authority **3** : a gastropod mollusk yielding a purple dye and especially the Tyrian purple of ancient times **4** : a pigment or dye that colors purple **5** : imperial or regal rank or power : exalted station

[3]purple *vb* **pur•pled; pur•pling** \ˈpər-pə-liŋ, -pliŋ\ : to turn purple

Purple Heart *n* : a U.S. military decoration awarded to any member of the armed forces wounded or killed in action

purple loosestrife *n* : a perennial Eurasian marsh herb that is naturalized in eastern North America and has long spikes of purple flowers

pur•plish \ˈpər-pə-lish, -plish\ *adj* : somewhat purple

[1]pur•port \ˈpər-ˌpōrt, -ˌpȯrt\ *n* : meaning conveyed, professed, or implied : IMPORT; *also* : SUBSTANCE 1b, GIST [Medieval French, "content, tenor," from *purporter* "to carry, mean, purport," from *pur-* "thoroughly" + *porter* "to carry"]

[2]pur•port \pər-ˈpōrt, ˌpər-ˈ, -ˈpȯrt\ *vt* : to profess outwardly but often deceptively : CLAIM

pur•port•ed *adj* : REPUTED 2, RUMORED — **pur•port•ed•ly** *adv*

[1]pur•pose \ˈpər-pəs\ *n* **1 a** : something set up as an end to be attained : INTENTION **b** : RESOLUTION 5b, DETERMINATION **2** : an object or result aimed at or achieved **3** : a subject under discussion [Medieval French *purpos*, from *purposer* "to intend, propose," from Latin *proponere* "to propose"] ***synonyms*** see INTENTION — **pur•pose•ful** \-fəl\ *adj* — **pur•pose•ful•ly** \-fə-lē\ *adv* — **pur•pose•ful•ness** \-fəl-nəs\ *n* — **pur•pose•less** \-ləs\ *adj* — **on purpose** : by intent : INTENTIONALLY

[2]purpose *vt* : to have in mind as a purpose : INTEND, PROPOSE

pur•pose•ly \ˈpər-pəs-lē\ *adv* : with a deliberate or express purpose

pur•pos•ive \ˈpər-pə-siv\ *adj* **1** : serving or effecting a useful end though not clearly as a result of design **2** : having or tending to fulfill a conscious purpose or design : PURPOSEFUL — **pur•pos•ive•ly** *adv* — **pur•pos•ive•ness** *n*

purr \ˈpər\ *n* : the characteristic low vibrating murmur of an apparently contented or pleased cat [imitative] — **purr** *vb*

[1]purse \ˈpərs\ *n* **1 a** : a small bag or pouch usually closed with a drawstring or snap and used to carry money **b** : a container (as a handbag) used to carry money and often small objects **2 a** : FUND 2b, RESOURCES **b** : a sum of money offered as a prize or present [Old English *purs*, from Medieval Latin *bursa*, from Late Latin, "hide of an ox," from Greek *byrsa*]

[2]purse *vt* **1** : to put into a purse **2** : PUCKER, KNIT ⟨*purse* one's lips⟩

purse–proud \-ˌprau̇d\ *adj* : proud of one's wealth

purs•er \ˈpər-sər\ *n* : an official on a ship who keeps accounts and supervises the care of passengers

purs•lane \ˈpər-slən, -ˌslān\ *n* : a fleshy-leaved trailing plant with tiny bright yellow flowers that is a common troublesome weed but is sometimes used as a potherb or in salads [Medieval French *porsulaigne*, from Late Latin *porcillago*, from Latin *porcillaca*, alteration of *portulaca*]

purslane

pur•su•ance \pər-ˈsü-əns\ *n* : the act of pursuing or carrying out ⟨in *pursuance* of their plans⟩

pur•su•ant to \-ənt-\ *prep* : in carrying out : in conformance to : according to

pur•sue \pər-ˈsü\ *vt* **1** : to follow in order to overtake and capture or destroy **2** : to try to obtain or accomplish : SEEK ⟨*pursue* a goal⟩ **3** : to proceed along : FOLLOW ⟨*pursue* a northerly course⟩ **4** : to engage in : PRACTICE ⟨*pursue* a hobby⟩ **5** : to continue to afflict : HAUNT ⟨*pursued* by fears of bankruptcy⟩ **6** : COURT 2, WOO [Medieval French *pursure, pursuire*, from Latin *prosequi*, from *pro-* "forward" + *sequi* "to follow"] ***synonyms*** see CHASE — **pur•su•er** *n*

pur•suit \pər-ˈsüt\ *n* **1** : the act of pursuing **2** : an activity that one engages in especially as a vocation [Medieval French *poursute*, from *pursure* "to pursue"]

pur•sui•vant \ˈpər-swi-vənt, -si-\ *n* : a person ranking below a herald but having similar duties [Medieval French *pursevaunt, pursuant*, literally, "follower," from *pursure* "to pursue"]

pur•sy \ˈpəs-ē, ˈpər-sē\ *or* **pus•sy** \ˈpəs-ē\ *adj* **pur•si•er** *or* **pus•si•er; -est** **1** : short-winded especially because of corpulence **2** : too fat especially from self-indulgent or luxurious living [Medieval French *porsif*, from *pousser* "to exert pressure, breathe heavily"] — **pur•si•ness** *n*

pu•ru•lent \ˈpyu̇r-yə-lənt, ˈpyu̇r-ə-\ *adj* : containing, consisting of, or accompanied by the formation of pus ⟨a *purulent* discharge⟩ [Latin *purulentus*, from *pur-, pus* "pus"] — **pu•ru•lence** \-ləns\ *n*

pur•vey \pər-ˈvā, ˌpər-ˈ, ˈpər-ˌ\ *vt* **1** : to supply (as provisions) usually as a business **2** : CIRCULATE 2b [Medieval French *purveier, purveer* "to look at, foresee," from Latin *providēre* "to provide"] — **pur•vey•ance** \-əns\ *n*

pur•vey•or \-ər\ *n* : one that purveys something (as provisions or news); *esp* : CATERER

pur•view \ˈpər-ˌvyü\ *n* **1** : the range or limit of authority, competence, responsibility, concern, or intention **2** : range of vision, understanding, or awareness [Middle English *purveu* "provision of a statute," from Medieval French *purveu est* "it is provided" (opening phrase of a statute)]

pus \ˈpəs\ *n* **:** thick cloudy usually yellowish white fluid matter formed at a place of inflammation and infection (as an abscess) and containing white blood cells, tissue debris, and microorganisms [Latin]

[1]**push** \ˈpu̇sh\ *vb* **1 a :** to press against with force in order to drive or impel **b :** to exert or use pressure ⟨*push* on the door⟩ **2 :** to thrust forward, downward, or outward ⟨plants *pushing* roots into the soil⟩ **3 a :** to press or urge forward **b :** to carry on with vigor or effectiveness ⟨*push* a campaign⟩ **4 :** to bear hard upon so as to involve in difficulty ⟨was *pushed* for money⟩ **5 :** to exert oneself continuously, vigorously, or obtrusively to gain an end (as social advancement) **6 :** to engage in the sale of (illicit drugs) [Medieval French *pousser* "to exert pressure," from Latin *pulsare,* from *pellere* "to drive, strike"]

synonyms PUSH, SHOVE, THRUST, PROPEL mean to cause to move ahead or aside by force. PUSH implies application of force by a body already in contact with the body to be moved ⟨*pushed* me on the swing⟩. SHOVE implies a fast or rough pushing of something usually along a surface ⟨*shove* the box out of your way⟩. THRUST suggests less steadiness and greater violence than PUSH ⟨*thrust* a knife into the crack⟩. PROPEL suggests rapidly driving forward or onward by force applied in any manner ⟨boats *propelled* by the wind⟩.

[2]**push** *n* **1 :** a vigorous advance against obstacles **2 :** a condition or occasion of stress **:** EMERGENCY **3 :** an act of pushing: as **a :** a sudden thrust **:** SHOVE **b :** a steady application of physical force in a direction away from the body exerting it **c :** a stimulating effect or action ⟨the holiday business gave retail trade a *push*⟩

push–but·ton \ˌpu̇sh-ˌbət-n\ *adj* **1 :** operated or done by means of push bottons ⟨a *push-button* phone⟩ **2 :** using or dependent on complex and more or less automatic mechanisms ⟨*push-button* warfare⟩

push button *n* **:** a small button or knob that when pushed operates something especially by closing an electric circuit

push·cart \ˈpu̇sh-ˌkärt\ *n* **:** a cart or barrow pushed by hand

push·er \ˈpu̇sh-ər\ *n* **1 :** one that pushes **2 :** a seller of illegal drugs

push·ing *adj* **1 :** ENTERPRISING **2 :** tactlessly forward **:** PUSHY

push off *vi* **:** to set out **:** LEAVE

push·over \ˈpu̇sh-ˌō-vər\ *n* **1 :** an opponent easy to defeat or a victim incapable of effective resistance **2 :** someone unwilling or unable to resist the power of a particular attraction or appeal **3 :** something accomplished without difficulty **:** SNAP ⟨the test was a *pushover*⟩

push·rod \ˈpu̇sh-ˌräd\ *n* **:** a rod that opens or closes a valve in an internal combustion engine

Pushtu *variant of* PASHTO

Pushtun *variant of* PASHTUN

push–up \ˈpu̇sh-ˌəp\ *n* **:** a conditioning exercise performed in a prone position by bending and straightening the arms while keeping the body straight supported on the hands and toes

pushy \ˈpu̇sh-ē\ *adj* **push·i·er; -est :** aggressive often to an objectionable degree **:** FORWARD — **push·i·ly** \ˈpu̇sh-ə-lē\ *adv* — **push·i·ness** \ˈpu̇sh-ē-nəs\ *n*

pu·sil·la·nim·i·ty \ˌpyü-sə-lə-ˈnim-ət-ē\ *n* **:** the quality or state of being pusillanimous

pu·sil·lan·i·mous \ˌpyü-sə-ˈlan-ə-məs\ *adj* **:** lacking courage and resolution **:** COWARDLY [Late Latin *pusillanimis,* from Latin *pusillus* "very small" (from *pusus* "small child") + *animus* "spirit"] — **pu·sil·lan·i·mous·ly** *adv*

[1]**puss** \ˈpu̇s\ *n* **1 :** CAT 1a **2 :** GIRL 1 [origin unknown]

[2]**puss** *n, slang* **:** FACE 1 [Irish *pus* "mouth"]

puss·ley \ˈpəs-lē\ *n* **:** PURSLANE [by alteration]

[1]**pussy** \ˈpu̇s-ē\ *n, pl* **puss·ies 1 :** CAT 1a **2 :** a catkin of the pussy willow

[2]**pus·sy** \ˈpəs-ē\ *adj* **pus·si·er; -est :** full of or resembling pus ⟨a *pussy* wound⟩

[3]**pussy** *variant of* PURSY

pussy·foot \ˈpu̇s-ē-ˌfu̇t\ *vi* **1 :** to tread or move warily or stealthily **2 :** to avoid committing oneself **:** HEDGE

pussy willow \ˌpu̇s-ē-\ *n* **:** a willow having large cylindrical silky catkins

pus·tu·lar \ˈpəs-chə-lər\ *adj* **1 :** of, relating to, marked by, or resembling pustules ⟨a *pustular* eruption⟩ **2 :** covered with pustules ⟨a *pustular* leaf⟩

pus·tule \ˈpəs-chül\ *n* **1 :** a small elevation of the skin having an inflamed base and containing pus **2 :** a small elevation resembling a pimple or blister [Latin *pustula*]

[1]**put** \ˈpu̇t\ *vb* **put; put·ting 1 a :** to place in a particular position or relationship ⟨*put* the book down⟩ **b :** to cause to move or go ⟨*put* a fist through the window⟩ ⟨*put* the ball into right field⟩ **c :** to throw with an overhand pushing motion ⟨*put* the shot⟩ **d :** to bring into a specified state or condition ⟨*put* it to use⟩ ⟨*put* the matter right⟩ **2 a :** to cause to suffer something ⟨*put* them to death⟩ **b :** IMPOSE, INFLICT ⟨*put* a special tax on luxuries⟩ **c :** to apply to some end ⟨*put* their skills to use⟩ **3 :** to set before one for judgment or decision (as by a formal vote) **4 :** to give expression to especially in intelligible language **:** TRANSLATE ⟨*put* your feelings into words⟩ ⟨*put* the poem into English⟩ **5 a :** to devote or urge to an activity or end ⟨*put* your mind to the problem⟩ ⟨*put* them to work⟩ **b :** INVEST ⟨*put* money in land⟩ **6 a :** to give as an estimate ⟨*put* the time at about eleven⟩ **b :** ATTACH, ATTRIBUTE ⟨*puts* a high value on friendship⟩ **c :** IMPUTE ⟨*put* the blame on your partner⟩ **7 a :** to commence a voyage ⟨the ship *put* to sea shorthanded⟩ **b :** to take a course ⟨*put* into a sheltered bay⟩ [Middle English *putten*] — **put forth 1 :** to bring into action **:** EXERT **2 :** to produce or send out by growth ⟨*put forth* leaves⟩ **3 :** to start out — **put forward :** PROPOSE ⟨*put forward* a theory⟩ — **put in mind :** REMIND — **put to it :** to give difficulty to ⟨had been *put to it* to keep up⟩ — **put up with :** TOLERATE 1, ENDURE

[2]**put** *n* **:** a throw made usually with an overhand pushing motion

put about *vb* **:** to change or cause to change course or direction ⟨*put* the ship *about*⟩

put across *vt* **:** to achieve or convey successfully ⟨*put across* a plan⟩ ⟨*put* an idea *across*⟩

pu·ta·tive \ˈpyüt-ət-iv\ *adj* **:** commonly accepted or supposed to exist ⟨*putative* racial superiority⟩ ⟨a *putative* conspiracy⟩ [Late Latin *putativus,* from Latin *putare* "to think"] — **pu·ta·tive·ly** *adv*

put away *vt* **1 :** DISCARD 2, RENOUNCE **2 :** to consume by eating or drinking **3 :** to confine especially in a mental institution

put by *vt* **:** to lay aside **:** SAVE ⟨had some money *put by*⟩

put down *vt* **1 :** to bring to an end by force ⟨*put down* a riot⟩ **2 a :** DEPOSE 1, DEGRADE **b :** DISPARAGE, BELITTLE ⟨mentioned my poetry only to *put* it *down*⟩ **c :** DISAPPROVE, CRITICIZE ⟨were *put down* for the way they dressed⟩ **d :** HUMILIATE, SQUELCH ⟨was *put down* with a sharp retort⟩ **3 :** to make ineffective **:** CHECK **4 a :** to write down (as in a list) **b :** to assign to a particular category or cause **5 :** to preserve for future use ⟨*put down* a cask of pickles⟩

put in *vb* **1 :** to make or make as a request, offer, or declaration ⟨*put in* a plea of not guilty⟩ ⟨*put in* for a job at the store⟩ **2 :** to spend (time) at some activity or place ⟨*put in* six hours at the office⟩ **3 :** PLANT ⟨*put in* a crop⟩ **4 :** to call at or enter a place; *esp* **:** to enter a harbor or port

put off *vt* **1 :** DISCONCERT, REPEL ⟨*put off* by their indifference⟩ **2 a :** to hold back to a later time **:** DEFER ⟨*put off* a visit to the dentist⟩ **b :** to induce to wait ⟨*put* the bill collector *off*⟩ **3 :** to rid oneself of

put on *vt* **1 a :** to dress oneself in **b :** to assume as if a garment **:** ADOPT ⟨*put on* airs⟩; *also* **:** FEIGN ⟨*put on* a show of anger⟩ **2 :** EXAGGERATE 1 ⟨they are *putting* it *on* when they make such claims⟩ **3 :** PERFORM, PRODUCE ⟨*put on* an entertaining act⟩ **4 :** to mislead deliberately especially for amusement ⟨you're *putting* me *on*⟩ — **put–on** *adj*

put·out \ˈpu̇t-ˌau̇t\ *n* **:** the act or an instance of causing a base runner or batter to be out in baseball

put out \pu̇t-ˈau̇t, ˈpu̇t-\ *vb* **1 :** EXERT, USE ⟨*put out* all their strength to move the piano⟩ **2 :** to cause to cease to burn or glow **3 :** PRODUCE ⟨*puts out* a lot of work in eight hours⟩ **4 a :** IRRITATE, PROVOKE ⟨*put out* by our tardiness⟩ **b :** INCONVENIENCE ⟨don't *put* yourself *out* for us⟩ **5 :** to cause to be out (as in baseball) **6 :** to set out from shore ⟨Columbus *put out* for the New World⟩

put over *vt* **:** to put across ⟨*put over* a scheme⟩ ⟨they're always trying to *put* something *over* on me⟩

pu·tre·fac·tion \ˌpyü-trə-ˈfak-shən\ *n* **1 :** the rotting of organic matter; *esp* : bacterial or fungal decay of proteins with the formation of foul-smelling incompletely oxidized products **2** : the state of being putrefied : CORRUPTION [Late Latin *putrefactio,* from Latin *putrefacere* "to putrefy"] — **pu·tre·fac·tive** \-ˈfak-tiv\ *adj*

pu·tre·fy \ˈpyü-trə-ˌfī\ *vb* **-fied; -fy·ing** : to make or become putrid : DECOMPOSE, ROT [Latin *putrefacere,* from *putrēre* "to be rotten" + *facere* "to make"]

pu·tres·cent \pyü-ˈtres-nt\ *adj* : becoming putrid : ROTTING — **pu·tres·cence** \-ns\ *n*

pu·trid \ˈpyü-trəd\ *adj* **1 a** : being in a state of putrefaction : ROTTEN ⟨*putrid* meat⟩ **b** : characteristic of putrefaction : FOUL ⟨a *putrid* odor⟩ **2 a** : morally corrupt **b** : totally disagreeable or objectionable : VILE [Latin *putridus,* from *putrēre* "to be rotten," from *puter, putris* "rotten"] — **pu·trid·i·ty** \pyü-ˈtrid-ət-ē\ *n* — **pu·trid·ly** \ˈpyü-trəd-lē\ *adv* — **pu·trid·ness** *n*

putsch \ˈpu̇ch\ *n* : a secretly plotted and suddenly executed attempt to overthrow a government [German]

putt \ˈpət\ *n* : a golf stroke made on a putting green to cause the ball to roll toward the hole [Scottish, literally, "shove, gentle push," from *putt, put* "to put"] — **putt** *vb*

put·tee \ˌpə-ˈtē, pu̇-; ˈpət-ē\ *n* **1** : a cloth strip wrapped around the leg from ankle to knee **2** : a leather legging secured by a strap or catch or by laces [Hindi and Urdu *paṭṭī* "strip of cloth," from Sanskrit *paṭṭikā*]

[1]**put·ter** \ˈpu̇t-ər\ *n* : one that puts

[2]**putt·er** \ˈpət-ər\ *n* : a golf club used in putting

[3]**put·ter** \ˈpət-ər\ *vi* **1** : to move or act aimlessly or idly : DAWDLE **2** : to work at random : TINKER [alteration of *potter*] — **put·ter·er** \-ər-ər\ *n*

put through *vt* : to carry to a successful conclusion : EFFECT ⟨*put* a reform *through*⟩

putt·ing green \ˈpət-ing-\ *n* : a smooth usually grassy area around the hole into which the ball must be played in golf

put to *vi* : to put in to shore (as for shelter)

[1]**put·ty** \ˈpət-ē\ *n, pl* **putties** : a cement usually made of whiting and boiled linseed oil beaten or kneaded to the consistency of dough and used in fastening glass in sashes and stopping crevices in woodwork; *also* : any of various substances resembling such cement in appearance, consistency, or use [French *potée,* literally, "potful," from *pot* "pot"]

[2]**putty** *vt* **put·tied; put·ty·ing** : to cement or seal with putty

putty knife *n* : a tool with a broad flat metal blade used especially for applying putty and for scraping

put–up \ˌpu̇t-ˌəp\ *adj* : arranged secretly beforehand ⟨a *put-up* job⟩

put up \pu̇t-ˈəp, ˈpu̇t-\ *vb* **1 a** : to prepare for later use ⟨*put up* a lunch⟩; *esp* : CAN ⟨*put up* peaches⟩ **b** : to put away out of use ⟨*put up* your sword⟩ **2** : to nominate for election **3** : to offer for public sale ⟨*put* the furniture *up* for auction⟩ **4** : to give or obtain food and shelter : LODGE ⟨*put* us *up* overnight⟩ **5** : BUILD 1, ERECT **6** : CARRY ON 2 ⟨*put up* a struggle against odds⟩ **7** : to offer as a prize or stake — **put up to** : INCITE, INSTIGATE — **put up with** : to endure or tolerate without complaint or attempt at retaliation ⟨*put up with* their insults⟩

[1]**puz·zle** \ˈpəz-əl\ *vb* **puz·zled; puz·zling** \ˈpəz-ling, -ə-ling\ **1** : to confuse the understanding of : PERPLEX, BEWILDER **2** : to solve with difficulty or ingenuity ⟨*puzzled* out the mystery⟩ **3** : to be uncertain as to action or choice **4** : to seek for or grope after something in a confused or uncertain manner ⟨*puzzle* over a problem⟩ [origin unknown] — **puz·zler** \ˈpəz-lər, -ə-lər\ *n*

synonyms PUZZLE, PERPLEX, MYSTIFY mean to baffle and disturb mentally. PUZZLE suggests existence of a problem difficult to solve ⟨the patient's symptoms *puzzled* the doctor⟩. PERPLEX usually adds an implication of worry and uncertainty ⟨*perplexed* by the sudden departure of their friend⟩. MYSTIFY implies puzzling or perplexing thoroughly often by deliberate intent ⟨the magic trick *mystified* the audience⟩.

[2]**puzzle** *n* **1** : PUZZLEMENT 1 **2 a** : something that puzzles **b** : a question, problem, or contrivance designed for testing ingenuity ***synonyms*** see MYSTERY

puz·zle·ment \ˈpəz-əl-mənt\ *n* **1** : the state of being puzzled : PERPLEXITY **2** : PUZZLE 2a

P–wave \ˈpē-ˌwāv\ *n* : PRESSURE WAVE

py- *or* **pyo-** *combining form* : pus ⟨pyemia⟩ ⟨pyorrhea⟩ [Greek *pyon*]

pyc·nom·e·ter \pik-ˈnäm-ət-ər\ *n* : a standard vessel for measuring and comparing the densities of liquids or solids [Greek *pyknos* "dense"]

py·emia \pī-ˈē-mē-ə\ *n* : infection of the blood with pus-forming bacteria accompanied by multiple abscesses

py·gid·i·um \pī-ˈjid-ē-əm\ *n, pl* **-ia** \-ē-ə\ : a tail or terminal body region of an invertebrate [New Latin, from Greek *pygidion* "small rump," from *pygē* "rump"] — **py·gid·i·al** \-ē-əl\ *adj*

pyg·my *also* **pig·my** \ˈpig-mē\ *n, pl* **pygmies** **1** *often cap* : one of a race of dwarfs described by ancient Greek authors **2** *cap* : one of a small people of equatorial Africa ranging under five feet (1.5 meters) in height **3** : a person or thing very small for its kind : DWARF [Latin *pygmaeus* "of a pygmy, dwarfish," from Greek *pygmaios,* from *pygmē,* a measure of length, literally, "fist"] — **pygmy** *adj*

py·ja·mas \pə-ˈjä-məz\ *chiefly British variant of* PAJAMAS

py·lon \ˈpī-ˌlän, -lən\ *n* **1** : a usually massive gateway; *esp* : an ancient Egyptian one composed of two flat-topped pyramids and a crosspiece **2** : a tower for supporting either end of a wire over a long span **3** : a projection (as a post or tower) marking a prescribed course of flight for an airplane [Greek *pylōn,* from *pylē* "gate"]

py·lo·ric \pī-ˈlōr-ik, pə-, -ˈlȯr-\ *adj* : of or relating to the pylorus; *also* : of, relating to, or situated in or near the posterior part of the stomach

py·lo·rus \-ˈlōr-əs, -ˈlȯr-\ *n, pl* **-lo·ri** \-ˈlōr-ˌī, -ˈlȯr-, -ˌē\ : the muscular opening from the stomach into the intestine of a vertebrate [Late Latin, from Greek *pylōros,* literally, "one who guards a gate," from *pylē* "gate"]

pyo·gen·ic \ˌpī-ə-ˈjen-ik\ *adj* : producing pus : marked by pus production

py·or·rhea \ˌpī-ə-ˈrē-ə\ *n* : a pussy inflammation of the sockets of the teeth leading usually to loosening of the teeth

pyr- *or* **pyro-** *combining form* : fire : heat ⟨*pyro*mania⟩ [Greek *pyr* "fire"]

[1]**pyr·a·mid** \ˈpir-ə-ˌmid\ *n* **1** : a massive structure built especially in ancient Egypt that usually has a square base and four triangular faces meeting at a point and contains tombs **2 a** : something felt to resemble a pyramid (as in shape or in broad-based organization) ⟨the social *pyramid*⟩ **b** : one of the conical masses that project from the medulla into the cavity of the kidney pelvis **3** : a polyhedron that has a polygon for its base and triangles that meet at a point at the top for its sides [Latin *pyramid-, pyramis,* from Greek] — **py·ram·i·dal** \pə-ˈram-əd-l, ˌpir-ə-ˈmid-l\ *adj* — **py·ram·i·dal·ly** \-ē\ *adv* — **pyr·a·mid·i·cal** \ˌpir-ə-ˈmid-i-kəl\ *adj*

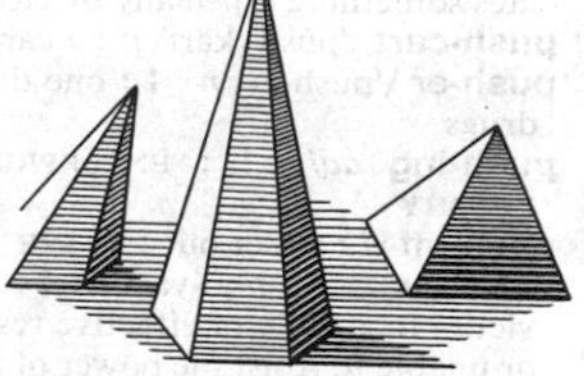

pyramid 3

[2]**pyramid** *vb* **1** : to increase rapidly and progressively step by step on a broad base **2** : to arrange or build up as if on the base of a pyramid

pyre \ˈpīr\ *n* : a combustible heap for burning a dead body as a funeral rite; *also* : a pile of material to be burned [Latin *pyra,* from Greek, from *pyr* "fire"]

py·re·noid \pī-ˈrē-ˌnȯid, ˈpī-rə-\ *n* : one of the protein bodies in the chloroplasts of various lower organisms (as some algae) that are involved in starch production and deposition [Greek *pyrēn* "stone of a fruit"]

py·re·thrin \pī-ˈrē-thrən, -ˈreth-rən\ *n* : either of two oily liquid esters having insecticidal properties and occurring especially in pyrethrum flowers

py·re·thrum \-ˈrē-thrəm, -ˈreth-rəm\ *n* **1** : any of several chrysanthemums with finely divided often aromatic leaves including ornamentals as well as important sources of insecticides **2** : an insecticide made from the dried heads of any of several Old World pyrethrums [Latin, a plant resembling yarrow, from Greek *pyrethron,* from *pyr* "fire"]

Py·rex \ˈpī-ˌreks\ *trademark* — used for glass and glassware resistant to heat, chemicals, or electricity

pyr·i·dine \ˈpir-ə-ˌdēn\ *n* : a toxic water-soluble flammable liquid organic base C_5H_5N of pungent odor used as a solvent and in the manufacture of pharmaceuticals [derived from Greek *pyr* "fire"]

pyr·i·dox·ine *also* **pyr·i·dox·in** \ˌpir-ə-ˈdäk-ˌsēn, -sən\ *n* : a crystalline alcohol of the vitamin B_6 group found especially in cereals and convertible in the body into phosphate compounds that are essential coenzymes [*pyridine* + *ox-* + *-ine*]

pyr·i·form \ˈpir-ə-ˌfȯrm\ *adj* : having the form of a pear [Medieval Latin *pyrum* "pear," from Latin *pirum*]

py·rim·i·dine \pī-ˈrim-ə-ˌdēn, pə-\ *n* : any of a group of bases including several (as cytosine or thymine) that are fundamental constituents of DNA and RNA [alteration of *pyridine*]

py·rite \ˈpī-ˌrīt\ *n* : a common mineral FeS_2 that consists of iron disulfide, has a pale brass-yellow color and metallic luster, and is burned in making sulfur dioxide and sulfuric acid [Latin *pyrites* "flint"]

py·rites \pə-ˈrīt-ēz, pī-; ˈpī-ˌrīts\ *n, pl* **pyrites** : any of various metallic-looking sulfides of which pyrite is the commonest [Latin, "flint," from Greek *pyritēs* "of fire," from *pyr* "fire"]

py·ro·lu·site \ˌpī-rō-ˈlü-ˌsīt\ *n* : a mineral MnO_2 consisting of manganese dioxide that is of an iron-black or dark steel-gray color and metallic luster, is usually soft, and is the most important ore of manganese [German *Pyrolusit,* from Greek *pyr* "fire" + *lousis* "washing," from *louein* "to wash"]

py·rol·y·sis \pī-ˈräl-ə-səs\ *n* : chemical change brought about by the action of heat

py·ro·ma·nia \ˌpī-rō-ˈmā-nē-ə, -nyə\ *n* : a persistent abnormal urge to start fires — **py·ro·ma·ni·ac** \-nē-ˌak\ *n*

py·rom·e·ter \pī-ˈräm-ət-ər\ *n* : an instrument for measuring temperatures especially when above the range of mercurial thermometers — **py·ro·met·ric** \ˌpī-rə-ˈme-trik\ *adj* — **py·ro·met·ri·cal·ly** \-tri-kə-lē, -klē\ *adv* — **py·rom·e·try** \pī-ˈräm-ə-trē\ *n*

py·rope \ˈpī-ˌrōp\ *n* : a magnesium-aluminum garnet that is deep red in color and is frequently used as a gem [Middle French *pirope,* a red gem, from Latin *pyropus,* a red bronze, from Greek *pyrōpos,* literally, "fiery-eyed," from *pyr* "fire" + *ōps* "eye"]

py·ro·phor·ic \ˌpī-rə-ˈfȯr-ik, -ˈfär-\ *adj* **1** : igniting spontaneously **2** : emitting sparks when scratched or struck especially with steel [Greek *pyrophoros* "fire-bearing," from *pyr* "fire" + *-phoros* "carrying," from *pherein* "to carry"]

py·ro·tech·nic \ˌpī-rə-ˈtek-nik\ *n* **1** *pl* : the art of making or the manufacture and use of fireworks **2** *pl* **a** : materials (as fireworks) for flares or signals **b** : a display of fireworks **3** : a spectacular display (as of oratory) — usually used in plural [derived from Greek *pyr* "fire" + *technē* "art"] — **pyrotechnic** *also* **py·ro·tech·ni·cal** \-ni-kəl\ *adj* — **py·ro·tech·ni·cal·ly** \-ni-kə-lē, -klē\ *adv* — **py·ro·tech·ni·cian** \-tek-ˈnish-ən\ *n* — **py·ro·tech·nist** \-ˈtek-nəst\ *n*

py·rox·ene \pī-ˈräk-ˌsēn\ *n* : any of various silicate minerals that usually contain magnesium or iron [French *pyroxène,* from Greek *pyr* "fire" + *xenos* "stranger"] — **py·rox·e·nic** \ˌpī-ˌrak-ˈsē-nik\ *adj*

py·rox·y·lin \pī-ˈräk-sə-lən\ *n* : a flammable substance resembling cotton that is produced chemically from cellulose and used in the manufacture of various products (as celluloid, lacquer, and some explosives) [*pyr-* + Greek *xylon* "wood"]

Pyr·rhic victory \ˌpir-ik-\ *n* : a victory won at excessive cost [*Pyrrhus,* died 272 B.C., king of Epirus who sustained heavy losses in defeating the Romans]

py·ru·vate \pī-ˈrü-ˌvāt\ *n* : a salt or ester of pyruvic acid

py·ru·vic acid \pī-ˌrü-vik-\ *n* : a 3-carbon liquid organic acid $C_3H_4O_3$ that is an important intermediate in carbohydrate metabolism and can be formed from either glucose or glycogen [*pyr-* + Latin *uva* "grapes"; from its importance in fermentation]

Py·thag·o·re·an \pə-ˌthag-ə-ˈrē-ən, pī-\ *adj* : of, relating to, or associated with the Greek philosopher Pythagoras — **Pythagorean** *n*

Pythagorean theorem *n* : a theorem in geometry: the square of the length of the hypotenuse of a right triangle equals the sum of the squares of the lengths of the other two sides

Pyth·i·an \ˈpith-ē-ən\ *adj* : of or relating to the ancient Greek god Apollo especially as patron deity of Delphi [Latin *pythius* "of Delphi," from Greek *pythios,* from *Pythō* "Pytho," former name of Delphi]

Pythian Games *n pl* : an ancient Panhellenic festival similar to the Olympic Games celebrated at Delphi every four years in honor of Apollo

py·thon \ˈpī-ˌthän, -thən\ *n* : any of various large nonpoisonous snakes especially of Africa, Asia, and Australia that squeeze and suffocate their prey and include some of the largest snakes living at the present time [Latin *Python,* a monstrous serpent killed by Apollo, from Greek *Pythōn*] — **py·tho·nine** \ˈpī-thə-ˌnīn\ *adj*

py·tho·ness \ˈpī-thə-nəs, ˈpith-ə-\ *n* : a woman supposed to have a spirit of divination; *esp* : a priestess of Apollo held to have prophetic powers [Middle French *pithonisse,* from Late Latin *pythonissa,* from Greek *Pythōn,* spirit of divination, from *Pythō,* seat of the Delphic oracle] — **py·thon·ic** \pī-ˈthän-ik\ *adj*

pyx \ˈpiks\ *n* : a small round case used to carry the Eucharist to the sick [Medieval Latin *pyxis,* from Latin, "box," from Greek]

Q

q \ˈkyü\ *n, pl* **q's** *or* **qs** \ˈkyüz\ *often cap* : the seventeenth letter of the English alphabet

Q fever \ˈkyü-\ *n* : a disease that is marked by high fever, chills, and muscular pains, is caused by a bacterium, and is transmitted from infected domestic animals to humans especially by inhalation of airborne bacteria [*query*]

qt \ˈkyü-ˈtē\ *n, often cap Q&T* : QUIET — usually used in the phrase *on the qt* [abbreviation]

Q–tip \ˈkyü-ˌtip\ *trademark* — used for a cotton-tipped swab

¹quack \ˈkwak\ *vi* : to utter the characteristic cry of a duck [imitative]

²quack *n* : a cry made by or as if by quacking

³quack *n* **1** : CHARLATAN **2** : a person who pretends to have medical skill [short for earlier *quacksalver,* from obsolete Dutch] — **quack·ery** \ˈkwak-rē, -ə-rē\ *n*

⁴quack *adj* : of, relating to, or used by a person who is a quack

quack grass *n* : a European grass that is naturalized throughout North America as a weed and spreads by creeping rhizomes — called also *couch grass, witchgrass* [derived from Old English *cwice*]

¹quad \ˈkwäd\ *n* : QUADRANGLE

²quad *n* : a type-metal space that is 1 en or more in width [derived from *quadrate*]

³quad *n* : QUADRUPLET

quad·ran·gle \ˈkwäd-ˌrang-gəl\ *n* **1** : QUADRILATERAL **2 a** : a 4-sided enclosure especially when surrounded by buildings **b** : the buildings enclosing a quadrangle — **qua·dran·gu·lar** \kwä-ˈdrang-gyə-lər\ *adj*

quad·rant \ˈkwäd-rənt\ *n* **1** : an instrument for measuring altitudes (as in astronomy or surveying) **2**

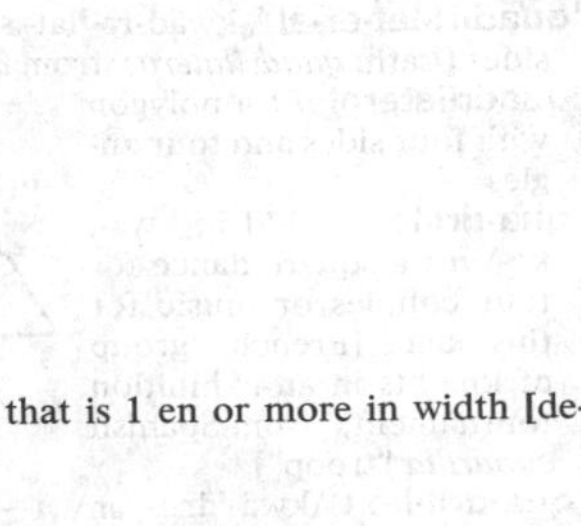

quadrant 2a

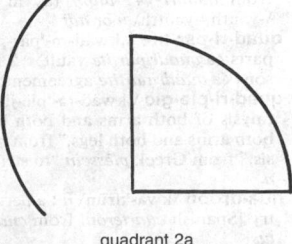

\ə\ **abut**	\au̇\ **out**	\i\ **tip**	\ȯ\ **saw**	\u̇\ **foot**
\ər\ **further**	\ch\ **chin**	\ī\ **life**	\ȯi\ **coin**	\y\ **yet**
\a\ **mat**	\e\ **pet**	\j\ **job**	\th\ **thin**	\yü\ **few**
\ā\ **take**	\ē\ **easy**	\ng\ **sing**	\t͟h\ **this**	\yu̇\ **cure**
\ä\ **cot, cart**	\g\ **go**	\ō\ **bone**	\ü\ **food**	\zh\ **vision**

a : an arc of 90° : one quarter of a circle **b** : the area enclosed by a quadrant and two radii **3 a** : any of the four parts into which a plane is divided by rectangular coordinate axes lying in that plane **b** : any of the four quarters into which something is divided by two real or imaginary lines that intersect each other at right angles [Latin *quadrans* "fourth part"] — **qua·dran·tal** \kwä-ˈdrant-l\ *adj*

qua·draph·o·ny \kwä-ˈdraf-ə-nē\ *n* : the transmission, recording, or reproduction of sound by techniques that utilize four transmission channels [derived from *quadri-* + *-phone*] — **quad·ra·phon·ic** \ˌkwäd-rə-ˈfän-ik\ *adj*

quad·rat \ˈkwäd-rət, -ˌrat\ *n* : a usually rectangular plot used for ecological or population studies [alteration of *quadrate* "square or cubical area or object"]

quad·rate \ˈkwäd-ˌrāt, -rət\ *n* : a bony or cartilaginous element on each side of the skull to which the lower jaw is attached in most vertebrates that are not mammals [earlier *quadrate* "square or cubical area or object," from Latin *quadratus,* past participle of *quadrare* "to make square"] — **quadrate** *adj*

qua·drat·ic \kwä-ˈdrat-ik\ *adj* : involving or consisting of terms in which no variable is raised to a power higher than 2 ⟨a *quadratic* polynomial⟩ — **quadratic** *n*

quadratic equation *n* : an equation containing one term in which the unknown is squared and no term in which it is raised to a higher power ⟨solve for x in the *quadratic equation* $x^2 + 4x + 4 = 0$⟩

quadratic formula *n* : a formula that gives the solutions of the general quadratic equation $ax^2 + bx + c = 0$ and that is usually written in the form

$$x = \frac{-b \pm \sqrt{b^2 - 4ac}}{2a}$$

quad·ra·ture \ˈkwäd-rə-ˌchu̇r, -chər\ *n* **1** : the process of finding a square equal in area to a given area ⟨*quadrature* of the circle is impossible with ruler and compass⟩ **2** : a configuration in which two celestial bodies have a separation of 90 degrees ⟨Mars in *quadrature* with the sun⟩

qua·dren·ni·al \kwä-ˈdren-ē-əl\ *adj* **1** : consisting of or lasting for four years **2** : occurring or being done every four years [Latin *quadriennium* "period of four years," from *quadri-* + *annus* "year"] — **qua·dren·ni·al·ly** \-ē-ə-lē\ *adv*

quadri- *or* **quadr-** *or* **quadru-** *combining form* **1** : four **2** : fourth [Latin]

quad·ri·ceps \ˈkwäd-rə-ˌseps\ *n, pl* **quadriceps** *also* **quad·ri·ceps·es** : the great extensor muscle of the front of the thigh [*quadri-* + *-ceps* (as in *biceps*)]

[1]**quad·ri·lat·er·al** \ˌkwäd-rə-ˈlat-ə-rəl, -ˈla-trəl\ *adj* : having four sides [Latin *quadrilaterus,* from *quadri-* + *later-, latus* "side"]

[2]**quadrilateral** *n* : a polygon with four sides and four angles

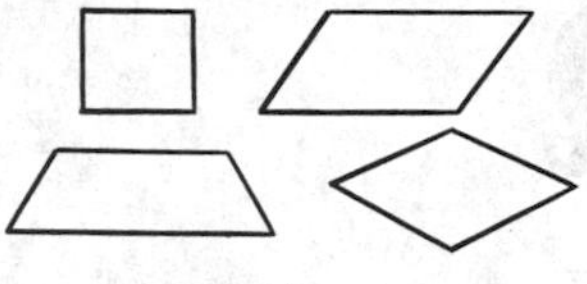

quadrilateral

qua·drille \kwä-ˈdril, kwə-, kə-\ *n* : a square dance for four couples or music for this dance [French, "group of knights in an exhibition tournament," from Spanish *cuadrilla* "troop"]

qua·dril·lion \kwä-ˈdril-yən\ *n* — see NUMBER table [French, from *quadri-* + *-illion* (as in *million*)] — **qua·dril·lion·th** \-yənth, -yəntth\ *n or adj*

quad·ri·par·tite \ˌkwäd-rə-ˈpär-ˌtīt\ *adj* **1** : consisting of four parts ⟨a *quadripartite* vault⟩ **2** : shared by four parties or persons ⟨a *quadripartite* agreement⟩

quad·ri·ple·gic \ˌkwäd-rə-ˈplē-jik\ *n* : a person affected with paralysis of both arms and both legs [*quadriplegia,* "paralysis of both arms and both legs," from *quadri-* "four" + *-plegia* "paralysis," from Greek *plēssein* "to strike"] — **quad·ri·ple·gia** \-jē-ə\ *n*

qua·droon \kwä-ˈdrün\ *n* : a person of one-quarter black ancestry [Spanish *cuarterón,* from *cuarto* "fourth," from Latin *quartus*]

quad·ru·ped \ˈkwäd-rə-ˌped\ *n* : an animal having four feet — **quadruped** *or* **qua·dru·pe·dal** \kwä-ˈdrü-pəd-l, ˌkwäd-rə-ˈped-\ *adj*

[1]**qua·dru·ple** \kwä-ˈdrüp-əl, -ˈdrəp-; ˈkwäd-rəp-\ *vb* **qua·dru·pled; qua·dru·pling** \-ling, -ə-ling\ : to make or become four times as great or as many

[2]**quadruple** *adj* **1** : having four units or members **2** : being four times as great or as many **3** : marked by four beats per measure ⟨*quadruple* meter⟩ [Latin *quadruplus,* from *quadri-* + *-plus* "multiplied by"] — **quadruple** *n*

qua·drup·let \kwä-ˈdrəp-lət, -ˈdrüp-; ˈkwäd-rəp-\ *n* **1** : a combination of four of a kind **2** : one of four offspring born at one birth

[1]**qua·dru·pli·cate** \kwä-ˈdrü-pli-kət\ *adj* : having or being four corresponding or identical parts or examples [Latin *quadruplicatus,* past participle of *quadruplicare* "to quadruple," from *quadruplic-, quadruplex* "fourfold"]

[2]**qua·dru·pli·cate** \-plə-ˌkāt\ *vt* **1** : QUADRUPLE **2** : to prepare in quadruplicate — **qua·dru·pli·ca·tion** \kwä-ˌdrü-plə-ˈkā-shən\ *n*

[3]**qua·dru·pli·cate** \kwä-ˈdrü-pli-kət\ *n* **1** : one of four like things **2** : four copies all alike ⟨typed in *quadruplicate*⟩

quaes·tor \ˈkwes-tər\ *n* : one of numerous ancient Roman officials concerned chiefly with financial administration [Latin, from *quaerere* "to seek, ask"]

quaff \ˈkwäf, ˈkwaf\ *vb* : to drink deeply or repeatedly [origin unknown] — **quaff** *n*

quag \ˈkwag, ˈkwäg\ *n* : MARSH, BOG [origin unknown]

quag·ga \ˈkwag-ə, ˈkwäg-\ *n* : an extinct mammal of southern Africa that resembled and was related to the zebras [obsolete Afrikaans]

quag·mire \ˈkwag-ˌmīr, ˈkwäg-\ *n* **1** : soft spongy wet land that shakes or gives way under the feet **2** : a complex or uncertain position : PREDICAMENT

qua·hog \ˈkwȯ-ˌhȯg, ˈkwō-, ˈkō-, -ˌhäg\ *n* : a thick-shelled edible clam of the U.S. [modification of Narragansett (Algonquian language of Rhode Island) *poquaûhock*]

quai \ˈkā\ *n* : QUAY [French]

[1]**quail** \ˈkwāl\ *n, pl* **quail** *or* **quails** : any of various mostly small plump game birds (as the bobwhite) that are related to the common domestic chicken [Medieval French *quaile,* from Medieval Latin *quaccula*]

[2]**quail** *vi* : to shrink in dread or terror : COWER [Dutch *quelen* "wither, decline"]

quaint \ˈkwānt\ *adj* **1** : unusual or different in character or appearance : ODD **2** : pleasingly old-fashioned or unfamiliar [Medieval French *queinte, cointe* "clever, expert," from Latin *cognitus,* past participle of *cognoscere* "to know"] — **quaint·ly** *adv* — **quaint·ness** *n*

[1]**quake** \ˈkwāk\ *vi* **1** : to shake or vibrate usually from shock or instability **2** : to tremble or shudder usually from cold or fear [Old English *cwacian*]

[2]**quake** *n* : a shaking or trembling; *esp* : EARTHQUAKE

quak·er \ˈkwā-kər\ *n* **1** : one that quakes **2** *cap* : FRIEND 4

Quaker meeting *n* : a meeting of Friends for worship marked often by long periods of silence

quaking aspen *n* : an aspen chiefly of the U.S. and Canada with roundish leaves that flutter in the slightest breeze

qual·i·fi·ca·tion \ˌkwäl-ə-fə-ˈkā-shən\ *n* **1** : something that limits or restricts ⟨agreed without *qualification*⟩ **2 a** : a quality or skill that fits a person (as for an office) ⟨the applicant with the best *qualifications*⟩ **b** : a condition that must be met ⟨a *qualification* for membership⟩

qual·i·fied \ˈkwäl-ə-ˌfīd\ *adj* **1** : having the necessary skill, knowledge, or ability to do something ⟨a *qualified* accountant⟩ **2** : limited or modified in some way ⟨*qualified* agreement⟩ — **qual·i·fied·ly** \-ˌfī-əd-lē, -ˌfīd-lē\ *adv*

qual·i·fi·er \-ˌfī-ər, -ˌfīr\ *n* : one that qualifies: as **a** : one that satisfies specified requirements **b** : a word or word group that limits the meaning of another word or word group : MODIFIER

qual·i·fy \ˈkwäl-ə-ˌfī\ *vb* **-fied; -fy·ing** **1 a** : to make less general and more restricted : LIMIT **b** : to make less harsh or strict : MODERATE **c** : to alter the strength or flavor of ⟨*qualify* a liquor⟩ **d** : to limit the meaning of (as a noun) **2** : to characterize by naming a quality : DESCRIBE **3 a** : to fit by training, skill, or ability for a special purpose **b** : CERTIFY, LICENSE ⟨*qualified* to practice law⟩ **4** : to exhibit needed fitness, skill, or ability for some end [Middle French *qualifier,* from Medieval Latin *qualificare,* from Latin *qualis* "of what kind"]

qual·i·ta·tive \ˈkwäl-ə-ˌtāt-iv\ *adj* : of, relating to, or involving quality or kind — **qual·i·ta·tive·ly** *adj*

qualitative analysis *n* : chemical analysis designed to identify the components of a substance or mixture

qual·i·ty \ˈkwäl-ət-ē\ *n, pl* **-ties** **1 a** : peculiar and essential character : NATURE **b** : an inherent feature : PROPERTY

⟨hardness is a *quality* of steel⟩ **2 :** degree of excellence **:** GRADE **3 :** usually high social status **:** RANK **4 :** a distinguishing attribute **:** CHARACTERISTIC **5 a :** vividness of hue **b :** TIMBRE [Medieval French *qualité,* from Latin *qualitas,* from *qualis* "of what kind"]

synonyms QUALITY, PROPERTY, ATTRIBUTE mean a feature by which a thing may be identified. QUALITY is a general term applying to any trait, mark, or character of an individual or of a type ⟨material with a silky *quality*⟩. PROPERTY applies to a quality belonging to a thing's essential nature and helping to distinguish and identify its type or class ⟨the *property* of not conducting electricity⟩. ATTRIBUTE implies a quality inherent to a thing or being ⟨the traditional *attributes* of a hero⟩.

quality point *n* **:** GRADE POINT

quality point average *n* **:** GRADE POINT AVERAGE

qualm \ˈkwäm, ˈkwälm *also* ˈkwȯm\ *n* **1 :** a sudden attack of illness, faintness, or nausea **2 :** a sudden fear or misgiving **3 :** a feeling of doubt or hesitation in matters of conscience ⟨had no *qualms* about lying⟩ [origin unknown] — **qualmy** \-ē\ *adj*

synonyms QUALM, SCRUPLE, COMPUNCTION mean a misgiving about what one is doing or going to do. QUALM implies an uneasy fear that one is not following one's conscience or better judgment ⟨had no *qualms* about plagiarizing⟩. SCRUPLE implies doubt of the rightness of an act on grounds of principle ⟨no *scruples* against endorsing his opponent⟩. COMPUNCTION implies a spontaneous feeling that one is inflicting a wrong or injustice on someone ⟨had *compunctions* about lying to her friend⟩.

qualm·ish \-ish\ *adj* **1 a :** feeling qualms **:** NAUSEATED **b :** overly scrupulous **2 :** of, relating to, or producing qualms — **qualm·ish·ly** *adv* — **qualm·ish·ness** *n*

quan·da·ry \ˈkwän-də-rē, -drē\ *n, pl* **-ries :** a state of puzzlement or doubt **:** DILEMMA [origin unknown] ***synonyms*** see PREDICAMENT

quan·ti·fi·er \ˈkwänt-ə-ˌfī-ər, -ˌfīr\ *n* **:** a term (as *two, all, most,* or *no*) expressive of quantity; *esp* **:** one that binds the variables in a logical formula

quan·ti·ta·tive \ˈkwänt-ə-ˌtāt-iv, ˈkwän-\ *adj* **:** of, relating to, expressible as, or involving the measurement of quantity — **quan·ti·ta·tive·ly** *adv* — **quan·ti·ta·tive·ness** *n*

quantitative analysis *n* **:** chemical analysis designed to determine the amounts or proportions of the components of a substance or mixture

quantitative inheritance *n* **:** inheritance of a character (as height or skin color in humans) controlled by a group of gene pairs at different chromosomal locations with each pair having a specific quantitative effect

quan·ti·ty \ˈkwänt-ət-ē, ˈkwän-\ *n, pl* **-ties 1 a :** an indefinite amount or number **b :** a large amount or number — often used in plural **2 a :** the aspect in which a thing is measurable in terms of degree or magnitude **b :** something on which a mathematical operation can be performed ⟨multiply the *quantity x* by *y*⟩ **3 :** duration of a speech sound as distinct from individual quality [Medieval French *quantité,* from Latin *quantitas,* from *quantus* "how much, how large"]

quan·tize \ˈkwän-ˌtīz\ *vt* **1 :** to subdivide (as energy) into small units or amounts **2 :** to calculate or express in terms of quantum mechanics — **quan·ti·za·tion** \ˌkwänt-ə-ˈzā-shən\ *n*

[1]quan·tum \ˈkwänt-əm\ *n, pl* **quan·ta** \ˈkwänt-ə\ **1 :** QUANTITY 1a, AMOUNT **2 :** one of the very small parcels into which many forms of energy are subdivided [Latin, neuter of *quantus* "how much"]

[2]quantum *adj* **:** of or relating to the principles of quantum mechanics ⟨*quantum* physics⟩

quantum mechanics *n* **:** a general mathematical theory dealing with the interactions of matter and radiation in terms of observable quantities only — **quantum mechanical** *adj*

quantum theory *n* **:** a branch of physical theory based on the concept of the subdivision of radiant energy into finite quanta and applied to numerous processes involving transference or transformation of energy on an atomic or molecular scale

[1]quar·an·tine \ˈkwȯr-ən-ˌtēn, ˈkwär-\ *n* **1 :** a term during which a ship arriving in port and suspected of carrying contagious disease is forbidden contact with the shore **2 :** a restraint upon the activities or movements of persons or the transport of goods designed to prevent the spread of disease or pests **3 :** the period during which a person with a contagious disease is under quarantine **4 :** a place (as a hospital) where individuals under quarantine are kept [Italian *quarantena* "quarantine of a ship," from *quaranta* "forty," from Latin *quadraginta*]

[2]quarantine *vt* **:** to detain in or exclude by or as if by quarantine **:** ISOLATE — **quar·an·tin·able** \-ˌtē-nə-bəl\ *adj*

quark \ˈkwȯrk, ˈkwärk\ *n* **:** any of several elementary particles that are believed to be components of heavier particles (as protons and neutrons) [coined by Murray Gell-Mann, American physicist]

[1]quar·rel \ˈkwȯr-əl, ˈkwär-əl, ˈkwȯrl, ˈkwärl\ *n* **1 :** a cause of dispute or complaint **2 :** a usually angry verbal dispute [Medieval French *querele* "complaint," from Latin *querela* "grievance, complaint," from *queri* "to complain"]

[2]quarrel *vi* **-reled** *or* **-relled; -rel·ing** *or* **-rel·ling 1 :** to find fault ⟨*quarrel* with an idea⟩ **2 :** to contend or dispute actively **:** SQUABBLE — **quar·rel·er** *or* **quar·rel·ler** *n*

quar·rel·some \ˈkwȯr-əl-səm, ˈkwär-əl-, ˈkwȯrl-, ˈkwärl-\ *adj* **:** apt or inclined to quarrel **:** CONTENTIOUS — **quar·rel·some·ly** *adv* — **quar·rel·some·ness** *n*

[1]quar·ry \ˈkwȯr-ē, ˈkwär-\ *n, pl* **quarries 1 :** the object of a chase **:** GAME; *esp* **:** game hunted with hawks **2 :** PREY 1 [Middle English *quirre, querre* "entrails of game given to the hounds," from Medieval French *cureie, quereie,* from *quir, cuir* "skin, hide (on which the entrails were placed)"]

Word History The *quarry* the hunter stalks is not related to the stonecutter's quarry. The first can be traced to a minor ceremony that was once part of every successful hunt. The hounds were rewarded after the kill with a part of the slain animal's entrails. The French word for this hounds' portion was *cureie* or *quereie. Cureie/quereie* was borrowed into Middle English as *quirre or querre.* The word for the entrails of an animal was later transferred to the animal itself, when considered in the character of game pursued. Now anything pursued is its pursuer's *quarry.*

[2]quarry *n, pl* **quarries :** an open excavation usually for obtaining building stone, slate, or limestone [Medieval French *quarrere,* derived from Late Latin *quadrus* "hewn stone," literally, "squared stone," from Latin *quadrum* "square"]

Word History The stone *quarry* is not so called because it is sought after, as is game by a hunter, but rather takes its name from the building stones it provides. *Quarrere* was the Medieval French word for a quarry, a source of squared stones. Its ultimate source was Latin *quadrum,* which means "square."

[3]quarry *vt* **quar·ried; quar·ry·ing 1 :** to dig or take from or as if from a quarry **2 :** to make a quarry in — **quar·ri·er** *n*

quart \ˈkwȯrt\ *n* **1 :** a unit of measure equal to ¼ gallon — see MEASURE table **2 :** a vessel or measure having a capacity of one quart [Medieval French *quarte* "fourth of a gallon," from *quart* "fourth," from Latin *quartus*]

[1]quar·tan \ˈkwȯrt-n\ *adj* **:** recurring at approximately 72-hour intervals [Medieval French *(fevre) quartaine* "quartan fever," from Latin *(febris) quartana,* from *quartanus* "of the fourth," from *quartus* "fourth"]

[2]quartan *n* **:** a quartan fever

[1]quar·ter \ˈkwȯrt-ər, ˈkwȯt-\ *n* **1 :** one of four equal parts **2 :** a unit (as of weight or length) that equals one fourth of some larger unit **3 a :** any of four 3-month divisions of a year **b :** a school term of about 12 weeks **c :** QUARTER HOUR **d :** a coin worth a fourth of a dollar; *also* **:** the sum of 25 cents **e :** one limb of a 4-limbed animal or carcass with the parts near it ⟨a *quarter* of beef⟩ **f :** a fourth part of the moon's period ⟨a moon in its first *quarter*⟩ **g :** one of the four parts into which the horizon may be divided; *also* **:** a region or direction under such a part **h :** one of the four cardinal points corresponding to the four parts of the horizon; *also* **:** a compass point **4 :** someone or something (as a place, direction, or group) not specified ⟨expecting trouble from another *quarter*⟩ **5 a :** a particular division or district of a city ⟨the foreign *quarter*⟩ **b :** an assigned place or duty station especially of a member of a naval crew ⟨a call to *quarters*⟩ **c** *pl* **:** living accommodations **:** LODGING **6 :** MERCY; *esp* **:** a refraining from destroying a defeated enemy **7 :** the stern area of a ship's side [Medieval French *quarter,* from Latin *quartarius,* from *quartus* "fourth"] — **at close quarters :** at close range or in immediate contact

\ə\ **abut**	\au̇\ **out**	\i\ **tip**	\ȯ\ **saw**	\u̇\ **foot**
\ər\ **further**	\ch\ **chin**	\ī\ **life**	\ȯi\ **coin**	\y\ **yet**
\a\ **mat**	\e\ **pet**	\j\ **job**	\th\ **thin**	\yü\ **few**
\ā\ **take**	\ē\ **easy**	\ng\ **sing**	\t͟h\ **this**	\yu̇\ **cure**
\ä\ **cot, cart**	\g\ **go**	\ō\ **bone**	\ü\ **food**	\zh\ **vision**

[2]**quarter** *vb* **1 a :** to divide into four equal parts **b :** to separate into parts ⟨peel and *quarter* an orange⟩ **c :** DISMEMBER 1 **2 :** to provide with or occupy a lodging **3 :** to crisscross an area in many directions ⟨*quartered* the hills looking for the child⟩

[3]**quarter** *adj* **:** consisting of or equal to a quarter

[1]**quar·ter·back** \-ˌbak\ *n* **:** an offensive football back who calls the signals and directs the offensive play of the team

[2]**quarterback** *vt* **:** to act as quarterback of (a football team)

quarter day *n, chiefly British* **:** the day which begins a quarter of the year and on which a quarterly payment falls due

quar·ter·deck \-ˌdek\ *n* **1 :** the stern area of a ship's upper deck **2 :** a part of a deck on a naval vessel set aside for ceremonial and official use

quarter horse *n* **:** any of a breed of alert stocky muscular horses capable of high speed for short distances and of great endurance under the saddle [from its high speed for distances up to a quarter of a mile]

quarter horse

quarter hour *n* **1 :** 15 minutes **2 :** any of the quarter points of an hour

quar·ter·ing *adj* **:** coming from a point well abaft the beam of a ship but not directly astern ⟨a *quartering* wind⟩

[1]**quar·ter·ly** \ˈkwȯrt-ər-lē, ˈkwȯt-\ *adv* **:** at 3-month intervals ⟨interest compounded *quarterly*⟩

[2]**quarterly** *adj* **:** coming during or at the end of each 3-month interval ⟨*quarterly* premium⟩ ⟨*quarterly* meeting⟩

[3]**quarterly** *n, pl* **-lies :** a periodical published four times a year

quar·ter·mas·ter \ˈkwȯrt-ər-ˌmas-tər, ˈkwȯt-\ *n* **1 :** a petty officer who attends to a ship's steering and signals **2 :** an army officer responsible for the clothing and subsistence of a body of troops

quar·tern \ˈkwȯrt-ərn, ˈkwȯt-\ *n* **:** a fourth part **:** QUARTER [Medieval French *quarteron* "quarter of a hundred," from *quarter* "quarter"]

quarter note *n* **:** a musical note equal in value to one fourth of a whole note

quarter rest *n* **:** a musical rest equal in time value to a quarter note

quar·ter·saw \ˈkwȯrt-ər-ˌsȯ, ˈkwȯt-\ *vt* **-sawed; -sawed** *or* **-sawn** \-ˌsȯn\; **-saw·ing :** to saw (a log) into quarters and then into planks in which the annual rings are nearly at right angles to the wide face

quarter section *n* **:** a tract of land that is half a mile square and contains 160 acres (about 0.65 square kilometer or 65 hectares) in the U.S. government system of land surveying

quar·ter·staff \ˈkwȯrt-ər-ˌstaf\ *n, pl* **-staves** \-ˌstavz, -ˌstāvz\ **:** a long stout staff formerly used as a weapon

quar·tet *also* **quar·tette** \kwȯr-ˈtet\ *n* **1 :** a musical composition for four instruments or voices **2 :** a group or set of four [Italian *quartetto,* from *quarto* "fourth," from Latin *quartus*]

quar·tile \ˈkwȯr-ˌtīl, ˈkwȯrt-l\ *n* **:** one of three values that divide a frequency distribution into four equal intervals [derived from Latin *quartus* "fourth"]

quar·to \ˈkwȯrt-ō\ *n, pl* **quartos :** a book made of sheets of paper each folded twice to make four leaves or eight pages [Latin, ablative of *quartus* "fourth"]

quartz \ˈkwȯrts\ *n* **1 :** a common mineral SiO_2 consisting of silica often found in the form of colorless transparent crystals but sometimes (as in amethysts, agates, and jaspers) brightly colored **2 :** a quartz crystal that when placed in an electric field oscillates at a constant frequency and is used to control devices which require precise regulation ⟨a *quartz* watch⟩ [German *Quarz*] — **quartz·ose** \ˈkwȯrt-ˌsōs\ *adj*

quartz glass *n* **:** vitreous silica prepared from pure quartz and noted for its transparency to ultraviolet radiation

quartz·ite \ˈkwȯrt-ˌsīt\ *n* **:** a compact granular rock composed of quartz and derived from sandstone

qua·sar \ˈkwā-ˌzär *also* -ˌsär\ *n* **:** any of various distant celestial objects that resemble stars but emit unusually bright blue and ultraviolet light and radio waves [*quasi*-stell*ar* radio source]

[1]**quash** \ˈkwäsh, ˈkwȯsh\ *vt* **:** to suppress completely **:** QUELL ⟨*quash* a rebellion⟩ [Middle English *quashen* "to smash," from Medieval French *quasser, casser,* from Latin *quassare* "to shake violently, shatter," from *quatere* "to shake"]

[2]**quash** *vt* **:** to make void by judicial action ⟨*quash* an indictment⟩ [Medieval French *casser, quasser* "to annul," from Late Latin *cassare,* from Latin *cassus* "void"]

qua·si \ˈkwā-ˌzī, -ˌsī; ˈkwäz-ē, ˈkwäs-; ˈkwā-zē\ *adj* **:** having or legally held to have a likeness to something else ⟨a *quasi* contract⟩

qua·si- \ˈkwā-ˌzī, -ˌsī; ˈkwäz-ē, ˈkwäs-; ˈkwā-zē\ *combining form* **:** in some sense or degree **:** SEEMINGLY ⟨*quasi*-judicial⟩ [Latin *quasi* "as if, as it were, approximately," from *quam* "as" + *si* "if"]

qua·si–gov·ern·men·tal \-gəv-ərn-ˈment-l\ *adj* **:** supported by the government but managed privately ⟨a *quasi-governmental* health-care agency⟩

qua·si–ju·di·cial \-jü-ˈdish-əl\ *adj* **1 :** having a partly judicial character by possession of the right to hold hearings and conduct investigations and to make decisions in the general manner of the courts ⟨*quasi-judicial* bodies⟩ **2 :** essentially judicial in character but not within the judicial power or function especially as constitutionally defined ⟨*quasi-judicial* review⟩

qua·si–leg·is·la·tive \-ˈlej-ə-ˌslāt-iv\ *adj* **1 :** having a partly legislative character by possession of the right to make rules and regulations having the force of law ⟨a *quasi-legislative* agency⟩ **2 :** essentially legislative in character but not within the legislative power or function especially as constitutionally defined ⟨*quasi-legislative* powers⟩

qua·si–pub·lic \-ˈpəb-lik\ *adj* **:** essentially public (as in services rendered) although under private ownership or control

qua·si–stel·lar radio source \-ˈstel-ər-\ *n* **:** QUASAR

quas·sia \ˈkwäsh-ə\ *n* **:** a bitter drug from the heartwood and bark of several tropical trees related to the ailanthus and sometimes used as a remedy against parasitic worms or as an insecticide [*Quassi,* 18th century Surinam slave who discovered the medicinal value of quassia]

Qua·ter·na·ry \ˈkwät-ər-ˌner-ē, kwə-ˈtər-nə-rē\ *n* **:** the period of the Cenozoic era from the end of the Tertiary to the present time; *also* **:** the corresponding system of rocks — see GEOLOGIC TIME table [Latin *quaternarius* "consisting of four each," from *quaterni* "four each"] — **Quaternary** *adj*

qua·train \ˈkwä-ˌtrān\ *n* **:** a unit or group of four lines of verse [Middle French, from *quatre* "four," from Latin *quattuor*]

qua·tre·foil \ˈkat-ər-ˌfoil, ˈka-trə-\ *n* **1 :** a conventionalized representation of a flower with four petals or of a leaf with four leaflets **2 :** a 4-lobed foliation in architecture [Middle English *quaterfoil* "set of four leaves," from Medieval French *quatre* "four" + Middle English *-foil* (as in *trefoil*)]

quatrefoil 2

[1]**qua·ver** \ˈkwā-vər\ *vb* **qua·vered; qua·ver·ing** \ˈkwāv-ring, -ə-ring\ **1 :** TREMBLE, SHAKE ⟨*quavering* inwardly⟩ **2 :** TRILL 2 **3 :** to utter sound in tremulous uncertain tones ⟨a voice that *quavered*⟩ **4 :** to utter quaveringly [Middle English *quaveren,* from *quaven* "to tremble"] — **qua·ver·ing·ly** \ˈkwāv-ring-lē, -ə-ring-\ *adv* — **qua·very** \ˈkwāv-rē, -ə-rē\ *adj*

[2]**quaver** *n* **1 :** TRILL 1 **2 :** a tremulous sound

quay \ˈkē, ˈkā, ˈkwā\ *n* **:** a paved bank or a solid artificial landing place beside water for convenience in loading and unloading ships [alteration of earlier *key,* from Middle French *kay,* probably of Celtic origin]

quean \ˈkwēn\ *n* **:** a disreputable woman [Old English *cwene*]

quea·sy *also* **quea·zy** \ˈkwē-zē\ *adj* **quea·si·er; -est 1 a :** causing nausea ⟨*queasy* motion⟩ **b :** suffering from nausea **2 :** full of doubt **:** HAZARDOUS **3 a :** causing uneasiness **b** (1) **:** DELICATE, SQUEAMISH ⟨a *queasy* conscience⟩ (2) **:** ill at ease ⟨*queasy* about our debts⟩ [Middle English *coysy, qwesye*] — **quea·si·ly** \-zə-lē\ *adv* — **quea·si·ness** \-zē-nəs\ *n*

que·bra·cho \kā-ˈbräch-ō, ki-\ *n, pl* **-chos :** a South American tree that is related to the cashews and has dense wood rich in tannins; *also* **:** its wood or a tannin-rich extract of this used in tanning [American Spanish, alteration of *quiebracha,* from Spanish *quiebra* "it breaks" + *hacha* "ax"]

Que·chua \ˈkech-wə, -ə-wə\ *n* **1 a :** a member of an Indian people of central Peru **b :** a group of peoples constituting the dominant element of the Inca Empire **2 :** the language of the Quechua people widely spoken by other Indian peoples of southern and western South America [Spanish, probably from Southern Peruvian Quechua *qheswa* (*simi*), literally, "valley speech"] — **Que·chu·an** \-wən\ *adj or n*

[1]**queen** \ˈkwēn\ *n* **1 :** the wife or widow of a king **2 :** a woman who is a monarch **3 a :** a woman eminent in rank, power, or attractions ⟨a society *queen*⟩ **b :** something that is thought of as female and that is considered better than all others ⟨*queen* of the ocean liners⟩ **c :** an attractive girl or woman; *esp* **:** a beauty contest winner **4 :** the most privileged piece in chess having the power to move in any direction any number of unobstructed squares **5 :** a playing card bearing the stylized figure of a queen **6 a :** the fertile fully developed female of social bees, ants, and termites whose function is to lay eggs **b :** a mature female cat [Old English *cwēn* "woman, wife, queen"] — **queen·like** \-ˌlīk\ *adj* — **queen·li·ness** \-lē-nəs\ *n* — **queen·ly** \-lē\ *adv or adj*

[2]**queen** *vb* **1 :** to act like a queen; *esp* **:** to put on airs — usually used with *it* **2 :** to become or promote to a queen in chess

Queen Anne \kwē-ˈnan\ *adj* **1 :** of or relating to an early 18th century style of furniture characterized by extensive use of upholstery, marquetry, and Asian fabrics **2 :** of or relating to an early 18th century English style of building characterized by modified classic ornament and red brickwork in which relief ornament is carved [*Queen Anne* of England]

Queen Anne's lace *n* **:** a widely naturalized Eurasian biennial herb which has a whitish root and flat lacelike clusters of tiny white flowers and from which the cultivated carrot originated — called also *wild carrot*

queen consort *n, pl* **queens consort :** the wife of a reigning king

queen mother *n* **:** a dowager queen who is mother of the reigning sovereign

queen post *n* **:** one of two vertical tie posts in a truss (as of a roof)

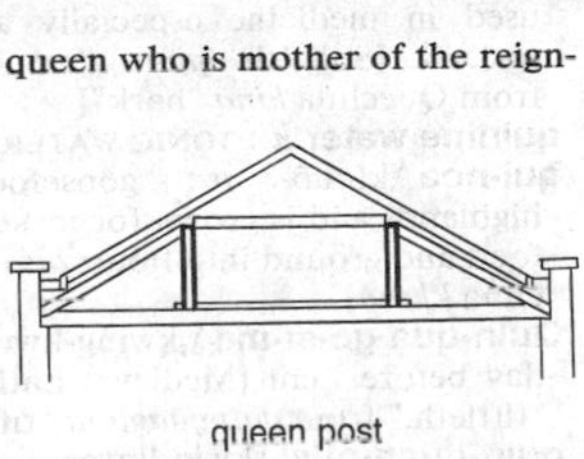

queen post

queen–size *adj* **:** having the size of about 60 inches by 80 inches (about 1.5 by 1.9 meters) ⟨a *queen–size* bed⟩

[1]**queer** \ˈkwiər\ *adj* **1 a :** differing from what is usual or normal **:** ODD **b** (1) **:** ECCENTRIC 2, UNCONVENTIONAL (2) **:** mildly insane **2 a :** WORTHLESS 1a, COUNTERFEIT ⟨*queer* money⟩ **b :** QUESTIONABLE 2, SUSPICIOUS **3 :** not quite well **:** QUEASY [origin unknown] — **queer·ish** \-ish\ *adj* — **queer·ly** *adv* — **queer·ness** *n*

[2]**queer** *vt* **1 :** to spoil the effect or success of **:** DISRUPT ⟨*queer* one's plans⟩ **2 :** to put or get into an embarrassing or unfavorable situation

quell \ˈkwel\ *vt* **1 :** to put down **:** SUPPRESS ⟨*quell* a riot⟩ **2 :** QUIET 1, PACIFY ⟨*quell* fears⟩ [Old English *cwellan* "to kill"] — **quell·er** *n*

quench \ˈkwench\ *vt* **1 :** to put out ⟨*quench* a fire⟩ ⟨*quench* a lamp⟩ **2 :** to bring to an end: as **a :** OVERCOME 1 ⟨*quench* anger⟩ **b :** REPRESS 3 ⟨*quench* rebellion⟩ **c :** SLAKE 2, SATISFY ⟨*quench* thirst⟩ **3 :** to cool (as heated steel) suddenly by immersion (as in water or oil) [Old English *-cwencan*] — **quench·able** \ˈkwen-chə-bəl\ *adj* — **quench·er** *n* — **quench·less** \ˈkwench-ləs\ *adj*

quern \ˈkwərn\ *n* **:** a primitive hand mill for grinding grain [Old English *cweorn*]

quer·u·lous \ˈkwer-ə-ləs, -yə-ləs\ *adj* **1 :** habitually complaining **2 :** FRETFUL, PETULANT ⟨a *querulous* voice⟩ [Latin *querulus,* from *queri* "to complain"] — **quer·u·lous·ly** *adv* — **quer·u·lous·ness** *n*

[1]**que·ry** \ˈkwiər-ē, ˈkweər-\ *n, pl* **queries 1 :** QUESTION 1a(1), INQUIRY **2 :** a question in the mind **:** DOUBT **3 :** QUESTION MARK [Latin *quaere,* imperative of *quaerere* "to ask"]

[2]**query** *vt* **que·ried; que·ry·ing 1 :** to put as a question ⟨"When can I leave?" I *queried*⟩ **2 :** to ask questions about especially in order to resolve a doubt ⟨*queried* a statement⟩ **3 :** to ask questions of especially with a desire for authoritative information ⟨*queried* the professor about the lesson⟩ **4 :** to mark with a query

[1]**quest** \ˈkwest\ *n* **1 :** an act or instance of seeking: **a :** PURSUIT, SEARCH ⟨in *quest* of game⟩ **b :** a chivalrous enterprise in medieval romance ⟨the *quest* of the Holy Grail⟩ **2** *obs* **:** a person or group of persons who search or make inquiry [Medieval French *queste* "search, pursuit," from Latin *quaestus,* past participle of *quaerere* "to seek, ask"]

[2]**quest** *vb* **1 :** to go on a quest **2 :** to search for **:** SEEK, PURSUE **3 :** to ask for **:** DEMAND

[1]**ques·tion** \ˈkwes-chən, ˈkwesh-\ *n* **1 a** (1) **:** an interrogative expression often used to test knowledge (2) **:** an interrogative sentence or clause **b :** a subject or aspect in dispute or open for discussion **:** ISSUE; *also* **:** MATTER 1b **c** (1) **:** a subject or point of debate or a proposition to be voted on in a meeting ⟨put the *question* to the members⟩ (2) **:** the bringing of this to a vote **d :** the specific point at issue **2 a :** an act or instance of asking **:** INQUIRY **b** (1) **:** OBJECTION, DISPUTE ⟨obey without *question*⟩ (2) **:** room for doubt or objection ⟨there's no *question* about their honesty⟩ (3) **:** CHANCE, POSSIBILITY ⟨no *question* of escape⟩ [Medieval French, from Latin *quaestio,* from *quaerere* "to seek, ask"]

[2]**question** *vb* **1 a :** to ask questions of or about **b :** INQUIRE 2 ⟨a *questioning* mind⟩ **2 :** CROSS-EXAMINE ⟨*question* a witness⟩ **3 a :** DOUBT, DISPUTE ⟨*question* a decision⟩ **b :** to subject to analysis **:** EXAMINE — **ques·tion·er** *n* — **ques·tion·ing·ly** \-chə-ning-lē\ *adv*

ques·tion·able \ˈkwes-chə-nə-bəl, ˈkwesh-, *rapid* ˈkwesh-nə-\ *adj* **1 :** affording reason for being doubted, questioned, or challenged **:** PROBLEMATIC ⟨milk of *questionable* purity⟩ ⟨a *questionable* decision⟩ **2 :** attended by well-grounded suspicions of being immoral, crude, false, or unsound **:** DUBIOUS ⟨*questionable* motives⟩ — **ques·tion·ably** \-blē\ *adv*

question mark *n* **:** a punctuation mark ? used chiefly at the end of a sentence to indicate a direct question

ques·tion·naire \ˌkwes-chə-ˈnaər, -ˈneər\ *n* **:** a set of questions that are given to people in order to collect facts or opinions [French, from *questionner* "to question"]

quet·zal \ket-ˈsäl, -ˈsal\ *n, pl* **quet·zals** *or* **quet·za·les** \-ˈsäl-ās\ **1 :** a brightly colored Central American bird with green plumage, a red breast, and in the male tail feathers often more than two feet (60 centimeters) in length **2** *pl usually* **quetzales a :** the basic monetary unit of Guatemala **b :** a coin or note representing one quetzal [American Spanish, from Nahuatl *quetzalli* "tail coverts of the quetzal"]

[1]**queue** \ˈkyü\ *n* **1 :** a braid of hair usually worn hanging at the back of the head **2 :** a line especially of persons or vehicles **3 a :** a sequence of messages or jobs held in temporary storage in a computer awaiting transmission or processing **b :** a data structure that consists of a list of records such that records are added at one end and removed from the other [French, literally, "tail," from Latin *cauda*]

[2]**queue** *vb* **queued; queu·ing** *or* **queue·ing 1 :** to arrange or form in a queue **2 :** to line up or wait in a queue ⟨the crowd *queued* up for tickets⟩ — **queu·er** *n*

[1]**quib·ble** \ˈkwib-əl\ *n* **1 :** an evasion of or shift from the point **:** EQUIVOCATION **2 :** a trivial objection or criticism [probably from obsolete *quib* "quibble"]

[2]**quibble** *vi* **quib·bled; quib·bling** \ˈkwib-ling, -ə-ling\ **1 :** to evade the issue **:** EQUIVOCATE **2 :** to argue or complain about small unimportant things — **quib·bler** \ˈkwib-lər, -ə-lər\ *n*

[1]**quick** \ˈkwik\ *adj* **1** *archaic* **:** not dead **:** LIVING, ALIVE **2 :** RAPID, SPEEDY: as **a :** fast in understanding, thinking, or learning **:** mentally agile **b :** reacting with speed and sensitivity **c :** aroused immediately and intensely ⟨*quick* temper⟩ **d :** fast in development or occurrence ⟨a *quick* succession of events⟩ ⟨gave them a *quick* look⟩ **e :** marked by speed, readiness, or promptness of physical movement ⟨walked with *quick* steps⟩ **f :** capable of being speedily prepared ⟨a *quick* dinner⟩ **3 :** having a sharp angle ⟨a *quick* turn in the road⟩ [Old English *cwic*] — **quick·ly** *adv* — **quick·ness** *n*

synonyms QUICK, SPEEDY mean able to respond without delay or hesitation. QUICK stresses promptness and the shortness of time in which response, movement, or action takes place ⟨saved by *quick* thinking⟩ ⟨a *quick* answer⟩. SPEEDY implies quickness of successful accomplishment ⟨found a *speedy* solution to the problems⟩ or unusual velocity ⟨a *speedy* runner⟩.

[2]**quick** *adv* : in a quick manner

[3]**quick** *n* **1** : a very sensitive area of flesh (as under a fingernail) **2** : the innermost sensibilities ⟨hurt to the *quick* by the remark⟩ **3** : the very center of something : HEART ⟨the *quick* of the matter⟩ [probably of Scandinavian origin]

quick bread *n* : a bread made with a leavening agent that permits immediate baking of the dough or batter mixture

quick·en \ˈkwik-ən\ *vb* **quick·ened; quick·en·ing** \ˈkwik-ning, -ə-ning\ **1 a** : to make or become alive : REVIVE **b** : to cause to be enlivened : STIMULATE ⟨curiosity *quickened* my interest⟩ **2** : to make or become more rapid : HASTEN, ACCELERATE ⟨*quickened* their steps⟩ ⟨my pulse *quickened* at the sight⟩ **3** : to show vitality or animation: as **a** : to commence active growth and development ⟨seeds *quickening* in the soil⟩ **b** : to reach the stage of fetal growth at which motion is felt by the mother **4** : to shine more brightly ⟨watched the dawn *quickening* in the east⟩ — **quick·en·er** \ˈkwik-nər, -ə-nər\ *n*

quick–freeze \ˈkwik-ˈfrēz\ *vt* **-froze** \-ˈfrōz\; **-fro·zen** \-ˈfrōz-n\; **-freez·ing** : to freeze (food) for preservation so rapidly that ice crystals formed are too small to rupture the cells and the natural juices and flavor are preserved

quick·ie \ˈkwik-ē\ *n* : something done or made in a hurry

quick·lime \ˈkwik-ˌlīm\ *n* : [1]LIME 2a

quick·sand \-ˌsand\ *n* : a deep mass of mixed loose sand and water into which heavy objects sink

quick·sil·ver \-ˌsil-vər\ *n* : MERCURY 1a [Old English *cwicseolfor,* from *cwic* "alive" + *seolfor* "silver"]

Word History The metal mercury resembles silver in color, but, unlike silver, mercury is liquid at normal temperatures. It moves, then, like a living thing. The Old English word for mercury was *cwicseolfor,* a compound of *cwic* "alive" and *seolfor* "silver." The descriptive nature of the word *quicksilver,* however, is not native to English. The compound is a translation of the Latin *argentum vivum* found in Pliny and literally meaning "living silver."

quick·step \ˈkwik-ˌstep\ *n* : a spirited march tune usually accompanying a march in quick time

quick–tem·pered \ˈkwik-ˈtem-pərd\ *adj* : easily angered

quick time *n* : a rate of marching in which 120 steps each 30 inches in length are taken in one minute

quick–wit·ted \-ˈwit-əd\ *adj* : quick in perception and understanding : mentally alert — **quick–wit·ted·ness** *n*

[1]**quid** \ˈkwid\ *n, pl* **quid** *also* **quids** *British* : a pound sterling : SOVEREIGN [origin unknown]

[2]**quid** *n* : a wad of something chewable ⟨a *quid* of tobacco⟩ [Old English *cwidu* "cud"]

quid pro quo \ˌkwid-ˌprō-ˈkwō\ *n* : something given or received for something else [New Latin, "something for something"]

qui·es·cent \kwī-ˈes-nt, kwē-\ *adj* **1** : being at rest : INACTIVE **2** : causing no trouble or symptoms [Latin *quiescens,* present participle of *quiescere* "to become quiet, rest," from *quies* "quiet"] ***synonyms*** see LATENT — **qui·es·cence** \-ns\ *n* — **qui·es·cent·ly** *adv*

[1]**qui·et** \ˈkwī-ət\ *n* : the quality or state of being quiet : TRANQUILLITY [Latin *quiet-, quies* "rest, quiet"] — **on the quiet** : in a secretive manner

[2]**quiet** *adj* **1 a** : marked by little or no motion or activity : CALM **b** : GENTLE, EASYGOING ⟨a *quiet* temperament⟩ **c** : not disturbed ⟨*quiet* reading⟩ **d** : enjoyed in peace and relaxation ⟨a *quiet* cup of tea⟩ **2 a** : free from noise or uproar : STILL **b** : UNOBTRUSIVE, CONSERVATIVE ⟨*quiet* clothes⟩ **3** : SECLUDED 1 ⟨a *quiet* nook⟩ [Medieval French *quiete,* from Latin *quietus,* from past participle of *quiescere* "to become quiet, rest," from *quies* "rest, quiet"] — **qui·et·ly** *adv* — **qui·et·ness** *n*

[3]**quiet** *adv* : in a quiet manner ⟨*quiet*-running engine⟩

[4]**quiet** *vb* **1** : to cause to be quiet : CALM **2** : to become quiet ⟨the audience *quieted* as the curtain rose⟩ — **qui·et·er** *n*

qui·etude \ˈkwī-ə-ˌtüd, -ˌtyüd\ *n* : a quiet state : REPOSE

qui·etus \kwī-ˈēt-əs\ *n* **1** : a final freeing from something (as a debt or duty) **2** : removal from activity; *esp* : DEATH **3** : something that quiets or represses ⟨put the *quietus* on their celebration⟩ [Medieval Latin *quietus est* "he is quit," formula of discharge from obligation]

[1]**quill** \ˈkwil\ *n* **1 a** : a bobbin, spool, or spindle on which filling yarn is wound **b** : a roll of dried bark ⟨cinnamon *quills*⟩ **c** : a hollow shaft often surrounding another shaft and used in various mechanical devices **2 a** : the hollow horny shaft of a feather; *also* : one of the large stiff feathers of a bird's wing or tail **b** : one of the hollow sharp spines of a porcupine or hedgehog **3** : an article made from or resembling the quill of a feather: as **a** : a pen for writing **b** : a float for a fishing line [Middle English *quil* "hollow reed, bobbin"]

[2]**quill** *vt* : to pierce with quills ⟨a dog *quilled* by a porcupine⟩

[1]**quilt** \ˈkwilt\ *n* **1** : a bed coverlet having two layers of cloth filled with wool, cotton, or down held in place by patterned stitching **2** : something that is quilted or resembles a quilt [Middle English *quilte* "mattress, quilt," from Medieval French *coilte,* from Latin *culcita* "mattress"]

[2]**quilt** *vb* **1 a** : to fill, pad, or line like a quilt **b** : to stitch, sew, or cover with lines or patterns like those used in quilts **c** : to fasten between two pieces of material **2** : to stitch or sew in layers with padding in between **3 a** : to make quilts **b** : to do quilted work — **quilt·er** *n*

quilt·ing *n* **1** : the act of one who quilts something **2** : material that is quilted or used for making quilts

quince \ˈkwins\ *n* : the fruit of an Asian tree related to the roses that resembles a hard-fleshed yellow apple and is used especially for marmalade, jelly, and preserves; *also* : a tree that bears quinces [Middle English *quynce* "quinces," pl. of *coyn, quyn* "quince," from Medieval French *coign,* from Latin *cydonium,* from Greek *kydōnion*]

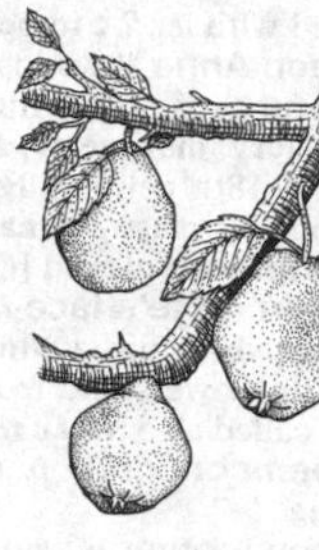

quince

qui·nine \ˈkwī-ˌnīn *also* ˈkwin-ˌīn\ *n* : a bitter crystalline alkaloid from cinchona bark; *also* : a salt of quinine used in medicine especially against malaria [Spanish *quina* "cinchona," from Quechua *kina* "bark"]

quinine water *n* : TONIC WATER

qui·noa \ki-ˈnō-ə\ *n* : a goosefoot that is native to the Andean highlands and is grown for its starchy seeds which are used for food and ground into flour; *also* : its seeds [Spanish, from Quechua *kinua*]

Quin·qua·ge·si·ma \ˌkwing-kwə-ˈjes-ə-mə, -ˈjā-zə-\ *n* : the Sunday before Lent [Medieval Latin, from Latin *quinquagesimus* "fiftieth," from *quinquaginta* "fifty"]

quin·quen·ni·al \kwin-ˈkwen-ē-əl\ *adj* **1** : consisting of or lasting for five years **2** : occurring or being done every five years [Middle French, from Latin *quinquennium* "period of five years," from *quinque* "five" + *annus* "year"] — **quinquennial** *n* — **quin·quen·ni·al·ly** \-ē-ə-lē\ *adv*

quin·sy \ˈkwin-zē\ *n* : severe inflammation around a tonsil that is accompanied by pain and fever [Medieval French *esquinauncy, quinancie,* from Late Latin *cynanche,* from Greek *kynanchē,* from *kyn-, kyōn* "dog" + *anchein* "to strangle"]

quint \ˈkwint\ *n* : QUINTUPLET

quin·tain \ˈkwint-n\ *n* : an object to be tilted at; *esp* : a post with a revolving crosspiece that has a target at one end and a sandbag at the other [Medieval French *quintaine,* perhaps from Latin *quintana* "street in a Roman camp separating the 5th maniple from the 6th where a market was held," from *quintanus* "5th in rank," from *quintus* "fifth"]

quin·tes·sence \kwin-ˈtes-ns\ *n* **1** : the purest form of something ⟨melody is the *quintessence* of music⟩ **2** : the most typical example or representative ⟨manners that were the *quintessence* of courtesy⟩ [derived from Medieval Latin *quinta essentia* "fifth essence, supposed fifth element more subtle than earth, air, fire, or water"] — **quint·es·sen·tial** \ˌkwint-ə-ˈsen-chəl\ *adj*

quin·tet *also* **quin·tette** \kwin-ˈtet\ *n* **1** : a musical composition or movement for five instruments or voices **2** : a group or set of five (as musicians or basketball players) [Italian *quintetto,* from *quinto* "fifth," from Latin *quintus*]

quin·til·lion \kwin-ˈtil-yən\ *n* — see NUMBER table [Latin *quintus* "fifth" + English *-illion* (as in *million*)] — **quin·til·lionth** \-yənth, -yəntth\ *adj or n*

[1]**quin·tu·ple** \kwin-ˈtüp-əl, -ˈtyüp-, -ˈtəp-; ˈkwint-əp-\ *adj* **1** : having five units or members **2** : being five times as great or as many [Middle French, from Medieval Latin *quintuplus,* from Latin *quintus* "fifth" + *-plex* "fold"] — **quintuple** *n*

[2]**quintuple** *vb* **quin·tu·pled; quin·tu·pling** \-ling, -ə-ling\ : to make or become five times as great or as many

quin·tup·let \kwin-ˈtəp-lət, -ˈtüp-, -ˈtyüp-; ˈkwint-əp-\ *n* **1** : a combination of five of a kind **2 :** one of five offspring born at one birth

[1]**quin·tu·pli·cate** \kwin-ˈtü-pli-kət, -ˈtyü-\ *adj* **:** having or being five corresponding or identical parts or examples [Medieval Latin *quintuplicatus,* past participle of *quintuplicare* "to quintuple," from *quintuplus* "quintuple"]

[2]**quin·tu·pli·cate** \-pli-kət\ *n* **1 :** one of five like things **2 :** five copies all alike ⟨typed in *quintuplicate*⟩

[3]**quin·tu·pli·cate** \-plə-ˌkāt\ *vt* **1 :** QUINTUPLE **2 :** to provide in quintuplicate

[1]**quip** \ˈkwip\ *n* **1 a :** a clever usually taunting remark **:** GIBE **b :** a witty or funny observation or response **2 :** something strange or eccentric **:** ODDITY [earlier *quippy,* perhaps from Latin *quippe* "indeed," from *quid* "what"] ***synonyms*** see JEST — **quip·ster** \-stər\ *n*

[2]**quip** *vb* **quipped; quip·ping :** to make quips; *also* **:** to make quips at

quire \ˈkwīr\ *n* **:** a collection of 24 or sometimes 25 sheets of paper of the same size and quality **:** 1/20 ream [Medieval French *quaier* "four sheets of paper folded once, collection of sheets," derived from Latin *quaterni* "four each, set of four"]

quirk \ˈkwərk\ *n* **1 :** an abrupt turn, twist, or curve ⟨some *quirk* of fate threw us together⟩ **2 :** a peculiar trait **:** MANNERISM, IDIOSYNCRASY ⟨human beings with their *quirks* and foibles⟩ [origin unknown] — **quirk·i·ly** \ˈkwər-kə-lē\ *adv* — **quirk·i·ness** \-kē-nəs\ *n* — **quirky** \-kē\ *adj*

quirt \ˈkwərt\ *n* **:** a riding whip with a short handle and a rawhide lash [Mexican Spanish *cuarta*]

quis·ling \ˈkwiz-liŋ\ *n* **:** a traitor who collaborates with the invaders of his or her country especially by serving in a puppet government [Vidkun *Quisling,* died 1945, Norwegian politician who collaborated with the Nazis]

[1]**quit** \ˈkwit\ *adj* **:** released from obligation, charge, or penalty; *esp* **:** FREE ⟨*quit* of unnecessary fears⟩ [Medieval French *quite,* literally, "at rest," from Latin *quietus* "quiet, at rest"]

[2]**quit** *vb* **quit** *also* **quit·ted; quit·ting 1 :** to make full payment of ⟨*quit* a debt⟩ **2 :** ACQUIT ⟨the youths *quit* themselves like adults⟩ **3 a :** to depart from or out of **b :** to bring (as a way of thought, acting, or living) to an end **:** STOP ⟨*quit* horsing around⟩ **c :** to give up (an action, activity, or employment) for good ⟨*quit* smoking⟩ ⟨*quit* a job⟩ **4 :** to admit defeat **:** SURRENDER ***synonyms*** see STOP

quit·claim \ˈkwit-ˌklām\ *vt* **:** to release or relinquish a legal claim to especially by a quitclaim deed — **quitclaim** *n*

quitclaim deed *n* **:** a legal instrument used to release a right, title, or interest in property to another without warranting the title

quite \ˈkwīt\ *adv* **1 :** WHOLLY 1, COMPLETELY ⟨not *quite* all⟩ **2 :** to an extreme **:** POSITIVELY ⟨not *quite* sure⟩ **3 :** to a considerable extent **:** RATHER ⟨*quite* near⟩ [Middle English, from *quite* "free, quit"]

quit·rent \ˈkwit-ˌrent\ *n* **:** a fixed rent; *esp* **:** one payable to a feudal superior in the place of services

quits \ˈkwits\ *adj* **:** even or equal with another (as by repaying a debt or returning a favor)

quit·tance \ˈkwit-ns\ *n* **1 a :** discharge from a debt or an obligation **b :** a document evidencing quittance **2 :** RECOMPENSE, REQUITAL

quit·ter \ˈkwit-ər\ *n* **:** one that quits; *esp* **:** one that gives up too easily

[1]**quiv·er** \ˈkwiv-ər\ *n* **:** a case for holding arrows [Medieval French *quivre,* of Germanic origin]

[2]**quiver** *vi* **quiv·ered; quiv·er·ing** \ˈkwiv-riŋ, -ə-riŋ\ **:** to move with a slight trembling motion ⟨tall grass *quivering* in the breeze⟩ [Middle English *quiveren*]

[3]**quiver** *n* **:** the act or action of quivering

qui vive \kē-ˈvēv, ˈkē-\ *n* **1 :** CHALLENGE 2 **2 :** ALERT, LOOKOUT ⟨on the *qui vive* for prowlers⟩ [French *qui vive?* "long live who?," challenge of a French sentry]

quix·ot·ic \kwik-ˈsät-ik\ *adj* **:** idealistic to an impractical degree; *esp* **:** marked by rash lofty romantic ideas or extravagantly chivalrous action [Don *Quixote,* hero of the novel *Don Quixote de la Mancha* by Cervantes] — **quix·ot·i·cal·ly** \-ˈsät-i-kə-lē, -klē\ *adv* — **quix·o·tism** \ˈkwik-sə-ˌtiz-əm\ *n*

[1]**quiz** \ˈkwiz\ *n, pl* **quiz·zes 1 :** an eccentric or mocking person **2 :** PRACTICAL JOKE **3 :** the act or action of quizzing; *esp* **:** a short oral or written test [origin unknown]

[2]**quiz** *vt* **quizzed; quiz·zing 1 :** to make fun of **:** MOCK **2 :** to look at inquisitively **3 :** to question closely **:** EXAMINE — **quiz·zer** *n*

quiz·zi·cal \ˈkwiz-i-kəl\ *adj* **1 :** slightly eccentric **:** ODD **2 :** marked by bantering or teasing **3 :** INQUISITIVE ⟨a *quizzical* look⟩ — **quiz·zi·cal·ly** \-kə-lē, -klē\ *adv*

quoin \ˈkȯin, ˈkwȯin\ *n* **:** a solid exterior angle (as of a building); *also* **:** one of the blocks forming it [alteration of earlier *coin* "corner, coin"]

quoin

quoit \ˈkwȯit, ˈkwāt, ˈkȯit\ *n* **1 :** a flattened ring of iron or circle of rope used in quoits **2** *pl* **:** a game in which quoits are tossed in an attempt to encircle a peg or come closer than one's opponent [Middle English *coite*]

quon·dam \ˈkwän-dəm, -ˌdam\ *adj* **:** FORMER 1, SOMETIME ⟨a *quondam* friend⟩ [Latin, "at one time, formerly"]

Quon·set \ˈkwän-sət\ *trademark* — used for a prefabricated shelter having a semicircular arching roof of corrugated metal

quo·rum \ˈkwōr-əm, ˈkwȯr-\ *n* **:** the number of officers or members of a body that when duly assembled is legally competent to transact business [Latin, "of whom"]

quo·ta \ˈkwōt-ə\ *n* **1 :** a proportional part or share; *esp* **:** the share or proportion assigned to each member of a body **2 :** the number or amount constituting a proportional share [Medieval Latin, from Latin *quota pars* "how great a part"]

quot·able \ˈkwōt-ə-bəl\ *adj* **:** fit for or worth quoting

quo·ta·tion \kwō-ˈtā-shən\ *n* **1 :** something that is quoted; *esp* **:** a passage referred to or repeated **2 a :** the act or process of quoting **b :** the naming or publishing of current bids and offers or prices of securities or commodities; *also* **:** the bids, offers, or prices so named or published

quotation mark *n* **:** one of a pair of punctuation marks " " or ' ' used chiefly to indicate the beginning and the end of a quotation in which the exact phraseology of another or of a text is directly cited

[1]**quote** \ˈkwōt\ *vb* **1 a :** to speak or write (a passage) from another usually with credit acknowledgment **b :** to repeat a passage from especially as authority or illustration ⟨*quote* Shakespeare⟩ **2 :** to cite in illustration ⟨*quote* cases⟩ **3 a :** to name (the current price) of a commodity, stock, or bond **b :** to give exact information on **4 :** to set off by quotation marks **5 :** to give a quotation ⟨the defendant said, and I *quote,* . . .⟩ ⟨*quoted* from the Bible⟩ [Medieval Latin *quotare* "to mark the number of, number references," derived from Latin *quot* "how many"]

[2]**quote** *n* **1 :** QUOTATION 1 **2 :** QUOTATION MARK

quoth \kwōth, ˈkwōth\ *vb past, archaic* **:** SAID — used chiefly in the first and third persons and placed before the subject [Old English *cwæth,* past of *cwethan* "to say"]

quo·tid·i·an \kwō-ˈtid-ē-ən\ *adj* **1 :** belonging to each day ⟨*quotidian* routine⟩ **2 :** COMMONPLACE, ORDINARY ⟨*quotidian* drabness⟩ [Medieval French *cotidian,* from Latin *quotidianus, cotidianus,* from *quotidie* "every day," from *quot* "(as) many as" + *dies* "day"]

quo·tient \ˈkwō-shənt\ *n* **:** the number resulting from the division of one number by another ⟨dividing 10 by 5 gives a *quotient* of 2⟩ [Latin *quotiens* "how many times," from *quot* "how many"]

\ə\ **abut**	\au̇\ **out**	\i\ **tip**	\ȯ\ **saw**	\u̇\ **foot**
\ər\ **further**	\ch\ **chin**	\ī\ **life**	\ȯi\ **coin**	\y\ **yet**
\a\ **mat**	\e\ **pet**	\j\ **job**	\th\ **thin**	\yü\ **few**
\ā\ **take**	\ē\ **easy**	\ŋ\ **sing**	\t͟h\ **this**	\yu̇\ **cure**
\ä\ **cot, cart**	\g\ **go**	\ō\ **bone**	\ü\ **food**	\zh\ **vision**

R

r \'är\ *n, pl* **r's** *or* **rs** \'ärz\ *often cap* **:** the 18th letter of the English alphabet

R *certification mark* — used to certify that a motion picture is of such a nature that admission is restricted to persons over a specified age (as 17) unless accompanied by a parent or guardian; compare G, NC-17, PG, PG-13

rab·at \'rab-ē, 'rab-ət\ *n* **:** a black shirtfront often worn with a clerical collar [Middle French]

[1]**rab·bet** \'rab-ət\ *n* **:** a groove or recess cut in the edge or face of a surface especially to receive the edge of another surface (as a panel) [Medieval French *rabat* "act of forcing down," from *rabattre* "to force down"]

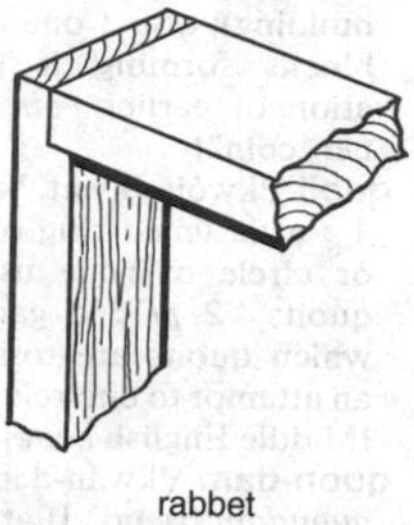
rabbet

[2]**rabbet** *vt* **1 :** to cut a rabbet in **2 :** to join the edges of (as boards) by a rabbet

rab·bi \'rab-ˌī\ *n* **1 :** MASTER, TEACHER — used as a term of address for Jewish religious leaders **2 :** a Jew qualified to expound and apply the halakah and other Jewish law **3 a :** a Jew trained and ordained for professional religious leadership **b :** the official leader of a Jewish congregation [Late Latin, from Greek *rhabbi,* from Hebrew *rabbī* "my master," from *rabh* "master" + *-ī* "my"]

rab·bin·ate \'rab-ə-nət, -ˌnāt\ *n* **1 :** the office or tenure of a rabbi **2 :** the whole body of rabbis

rab·bin·ic \rə-'bin-ik, ra-\ *or* **rab·bin·i·cal** \-'bin-i-kəl\ *adj* **1 :** of or relating to rabbis or their writings **2 :** of or preparing for the rabbinate — **rab·bin·i·cal·ly** \-i-kə-lē, -klē\ *adv*

rab·bin·ism \'rab-ə-ˌniz-əm\ *n* **:** rabbinic teachings and traditions

[1]**rab·bit** \'rab-ət\ *n, pl* **rabbit** *or* **rabbits :** any of various small burrowing mammals with long ears and short tails that differ from the related hares especially in being born with the eyes closed and without fur; *also* **:** the pelt of a rabbit [Middle English *rabet*]

[2]**rab·bit** *vi* **:** to hunt rabbits — **rab·bit·er** *n*

rabbit fever *n* **:** TULAREMIA

rabbit punch *n* **:** a short chopping blow delivered to the back of the neck or the base of the skull [from the way a rabbit is stunned before being killed and butchered] — **rabbit–punch** *vt*

rab·ble \'rab-əl\ *n* **1 :** a noisy and unruly crowd **:** MOB **2 :** a body of people looked down upon as ignorant and disorderly [Middle English *rabel* "pack of animals"]

rab·ble–rous·er \-ˌraú-zər\ *n* **:** one that stirs up the masses of the people especially to hatred or violence

Ra·be·lai·sian \ˌrab-ə-'lā-zhən, -zē-ən\ *adj* **1 :** of, relating to, or characteristic of Rabelais or his works **2 :** marked by gross robust humor or extravagant caricature

rab·id \'rab-əd\ *adj* **1 :** extremely violent **:** FURIOUS **2 :** going to extreme lengths in expressing or pursuing a feeling, interest, or opinion ⟨a *rabid* sports fan⟩ **3 :** affected with rabies ⟨a *rabid* dog⟩ [Latin *rabidus* "mad," from *rabere* "to rage, rave"] — **rab·id·ly** *adv* — **rab·id·ness** *n*

ra·bies \'rā-bēz\ *n* **:** an acute virus disease of the central nervous system of mammals usually transmitted by the bite of an infected animal and always fatal when untreated [Latin "madness," from *rabere* "to rage, rave"] — **ra·bic** \'rā-bik\ *adj*

rac·coon *also* **ra·coon** \ra-'kün\ *n, pl* **raccoon** *or* **raccoons** *also* **racoon** *or* **racoons :** a small mammal of North America that is active at night and lives chiefly in trees, is mostly gray with a black mask, has a bushy ringed tail, and has a varied diet including insects, eggs, fruits, and small animals; *also* **:** the pelt of a raccoon [Virginia Algonquian *raugroughcun, araucoun*]

raccoon

[1]**race** \'rās\ *n* **1 :** a strong or rapid current of water or its channel or passage; *esp* **:** a current of water used for industrial purposes (as turning a mill wheel) **2 a :** a set course or duration of time **b :** the course of life **3 a :** a running in competition **b** *pl* **:** a meeting for contests in the running especially of horses ⟨off to the *races*⟩ **c :** a contest involving progress toward a goal ⟨the *race* for governor⟩ **4 :** a track or channel in which something rolls or slides; *esp* **:** a groove for the balls in a bearing [Old Norse *rās*]

[2]**race** *vb* **1 :** to run in a race **2 :** to go, move, or function at top speed or out of control ⟨the flood *raced* through the valley⟩ ⟨a heart *racing* from excitement⟩ **3 a :** to engage in a race with ⟨*race* the champion⟩ **b :** to enter in a race ⟨had a new horse to *race*⟩ **4 :** to run (as an engine) at high speed without a load or with the transmission disengaged

[3]**race** *n* **1 a :** a group of people of common ancestry or stock ⟨the English *race*⟩ ⟨scion of a noble *race*⟩ **b :** a class or kind of people unified by common interests, habits, or characteristics ⟨a new *race* of scientists⟩ **2 a :** a variety or breed of animals or plants **b :** a category of humankind that shares certain distinctive physical traits **3 :** a major group of living things ⟨the human *race*⟩ [Middle French, "generation," from Italian *razza*]

race·course \'rā-ˌskōrs, -ˌskȯrs\ *n* **:** a course for racing

race·horse \'rās-ˌhȯrs\ *n* **:** a horse bred or kept for racing

ra·ceme \rā-'sēm\ *n* **:** a simple inflorescence with a long axis bearing short-stemmed flowers which open in succession toward the apex [Latin *racemus* "bunch of grapes"] — **ra·ce·mose** \'ras-ə-ˌmōs, rā-'sē-\ *adj*

rac·er \'rā-sər\ *n* **1 :** one that races **2 :** any of various active American snakes: as **a :** BLACK RACER **b :** BLUE RACER

race·run·ner \-ˌrən-ər\ *n* **:** a North American lizard that has six narrow stripes down the back and moves swiftly

race·track \'rā-ˌstrak\ *n* **:** a usually oval course for races

race·way \'rās-ˌwā\ *n* **1 :** a channel for a current of water **2 :** RACETRACK; *esp* **:** one for harness racing

ra·chis \'rā-kəs, 'rak-əs\ *n, pl* **ra·chis·es** *also* **ra·chi·des** \'rak-ə-ˌdēz, 'rā-kə-\ **1 :** the axis of an inflorescence **2 :** an extension of the petiole of a compound leaf that bears the leaflets **3 :** the distal part of the shaft of a feather [Greek *rhachis* "spine, backbone"]

ra·cial \'rā-shəl\ *adj* **1 :** of, relating to, or based on race **2 :** existing or occurring between human races ⟨*racial* equality⟩ — **ra·cial·ly** \-shə-lē\ *adv*

ra·cial·ism \'rā-shə-ˌliz-əm\ *n* **:** RACISM — **ra·cial·ist** \'rāsh-ləst, -ə-ləst\ *n or adj* — **ra·cial·is·tic** \ˌrā-shə-'lis-tik\ *adj*

ra·cial·ize \'rā-shə-ˌlīz\ *vt* **-ized; -iz·ing :** to give a racial character to

rac·i·ly \'rā-sə-lē\ *adv* **:** in a racy manner

rac·i·ness \-sē-nəs\ *n* **:** the quality or state of being racy

rac·ism \'rā-ˌsiz-əm\ *n* **1 :** belief that certain races of people are by birth and nature superior to others **2 :** discrimination or prejudice based on race — **rac·ist** \'rā-səst\ *n*

[1]**rack** \'rak\ *n* **1 :** a framework for holding fodder for livestock **2 :** an instrument of torture on which a body is stretched **3 :** a framework, stand, or grating on or in which articles are placed ⟨clothes *rack*⟩ ⟨bicycle *rack*⟩ **4 :** a bar with teeth on one face for gearing with a pinion or worm gear **5 :** a pair of antlers **6 :** a triangular frame used to set up the balls in a pool game; *also* **:** the balls as set up [Middle English] — **on the rack :** under great mental or emotional stress

[2]**rack** *vt* **1 :** to torture on the rack **2 :** to cause to suffer torture, pain, anguish, or ruin ⟨*racked* by a cough⟩ **3 :** to stretch or strain violently ⟨*racking* his brains for an answer⟩ ***synonyms*** see AFFLICT

[3]**rack** *vi* **:** to go at a rack [probably alteration of [1]*rock*]

[4]**rack** *n* **:** either of two gaits of a horse: **a :** PACE 2b **b :** a fast showy 4-beat gait similar to the pace but in which the feet of the same side do not touch down at the same time

[6]**rack** *n* : a cut of meat that includes the rib section of a lamb's forequarters used for chops or as a roast [perhaps from [1]*rack*]

[6]**rack** *n* : DESTRUCTION ⟨went to *rack* and ruin⟩ [alteration of *wrack*]

[1]**rack•et** *or* **rac•quet** \ˈrak-ət\ *n* : a usually long-handled implement used for hitting a ball or shuttlecock (as in tennis or badminton) that consists of an oval open frame strung with a netting (as of nylon) [Middle French *raquette,* derived from Medieval Latin *rasceta* "wrist," from Arabic *rusgh*]

[1]racket: *left* tennis, *right* badminton

[2]**racket** *n* **1** : confused clattering noise : DIN **2 a** : a dishonest scheme; *esp* : one for obtaining money by cheating or through threats of violence **b** : an easy and profitable means of livelihood **c** *slang* : OCCUPATION [origin unknown]

[3]**racket** *vi* **1** : to engage in active social life **2** : to move with or make a racket

[1]**rack•e•teer** \ˌrak-ə-ˈtiər\ *n* : a person who engages in an illegal activity for getting money especially by extortion

[2]**racketeer** *vi* : to operate an illegal racket

rack up *vt* : ACHIEVE 2, GAIN ⟨*racked up* their 10th victory⟩

ra•con•teur \ˌrak-ˌän-ˈtər, ˌrak-ən-\ *n* : one who excels in telling anecdotes [French, from *raconter* "to tell," from Medieval French, from *re-* "re-" + *aconter, acompter* "to tell, count"]

racoon *variant of* RACCOON

rac•quet•ball \ˈrak-ət-ˌbȯl\ *n* : a game similar to handball that is played on a 4-walled court with a short-handled racket and a larger ball; *also* : the ball used in this game

[1]**racy** \ˈrā-sē\ *adj* **rac•i•er; -est 1 a** : full of zest or vigor : LIVELY **b** : slightly indecent or improper : RISQUÉ, SUGGESTIVE ⟨*racy* stories⟩ **2** : having the distinctive quality of something in its original or most characteristic form [[3]*race*]

[2]**racy** *adj* **rac•i•er; -est** : being long-bodied and lean ⟨a *racy* dog⟩

ra•dar \ˈrā-ˌdär\ *n* **1** : a device or system that sends out radio waves for detecting and locating an object by the reflection of the radio waves and that may use this reflection to find out the position and speed of the object **2** : range of notice ⟨fell off the *radar* after losing their first three games⟩ [*ra*dio *d*etecting *a*nd *r*anging]

radar gun *n* : a handheld device that uses radar to measure the speed of a moving object (as a car)

ra•dar•scope \-ˌskōp\ *n* : the part of a radar apparatus on which the spots of light appear that indicate the position and direction of motion of a distant object [*radar* + oscillo*scope*]

[1]**ra•di•al** \ˈrād-ē-əl\ *adj* **1** : arranged or having parts arranged like rays coming from a common center **2** : relating to, placed like, or moving along a radius [Medieval Latin *radialis,* from Latin *radius* "spoke, radius, ray"] — **ra•di•al•ly** \-ē-ə-lē\ *adv*

[2]**radial** *n* **1** : a radial part **2** : a pneumatic tire in which the ply cords are laid at approximately 90° to the center line of the tread — called also *radial tire*

radial engine *n* : a usually internal-combustion engine with cylinders arranged radially like the spokes of a wheel

radial symmetry *n* : the condition of having similar parts regularly arranged around a central axis ⟨*radial* symmetry of the starfish⟩ — compare BILATERAL SYMMETRY — **radially symmetrical** *adj*

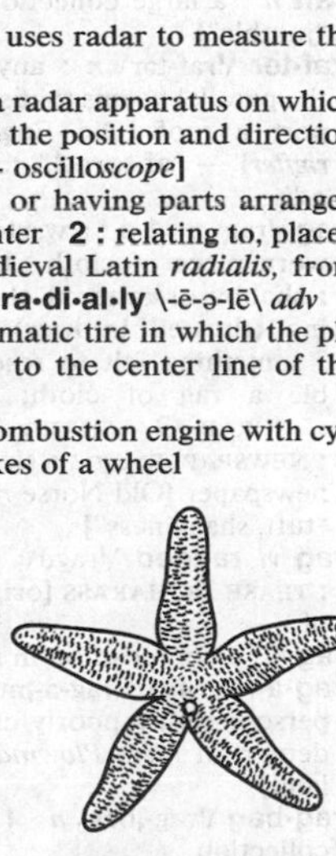
radial symmetry

ra•di•an \ˈrād-ē-ən\ *n* : a unit of measure for angles equal to approximately 57.25 degrees or to an angle with its vertex at the center of a circle and its sides cutting off an arc of the circumference that has the same length as the circle's radius [*radius* + *-an*]

ra•di•ance \ˈrād-ē-əns\ *n* : the quality or state of being radiant : SPLENDOR

ra•di•ant \ˈrād-ē-ənt\ *adj* **1 a** : giving out or reflecting rays of light ⟨the *radiant* sun⟩ ⟨a *radiant* jewel⟩ **b** : vividly bright and shining ⟨*radiant* eyes⟩ **2** : marked by or expressive of love, confidence, or happiness **3 a** : emitted or transmitted by radiation ⟨*radiant* heat from the sun⟩ **b** : emitting or relating to radiant heat ⟨a *radiant* lamp⟩ — **ra•di•ant•ly** *adv*

radiant energy *n* : energy transmitted in the form of electromagnetic waves (as heat waves, light waves, radio waves, or X-rays)

ra•di•ate \ˈrād-ē-ˌāt\ *vb* **1** : to send out rays : shine brightly **2 a** : to come or be sent out from a center in or as if in rays ⟨heat *radiates*⟩ ⟨a story that *radiated* widely⟩ **b** : to send out in rays or as if in rays ⟨stars *radiate* energy⟩ **3** : IRRADIATE 1a, ILLUMINATE **4** : to spread abroad or around : DISSEMINATE [Latin *radiare,* from *radius* "ray"]

ra•di•a•tion \ˌrād-ē-ˈā-shən\ *n* **1** : the action or process of radiating; *esp* : the process of emitting radiant energy in the form of waves or particles **2** : something that is radiated: as **a** : energy radiated in the form of waves or particles **b** : biological evolution in a group of organisms that is characterized by spreading into different environments and by divergence of structure ⟨the Devonian *radiation* of fishes⟩ — **ra•di•a•tion•al** \-shnəl, -shən-l\ *adj* — **ra•di•a•tive** \ˈrād-ē-ˌāt-iv\ *adj*

radiation sickness *n* : sickness that results from exposure to radiation and is commonly marked by fatigue, nausea, vomiting, loss of teeth and hair, and in more severe cases by damage to blood-forming tissue with decrease in red and white blood cells and bleeding

ra•di•a•tor \ˈrād-ē-ˌāt-ər\ *n* : one that radiates; *esp* : any of various devices (as a set of pipes or tubes) for transferring heat from a fluid within to an area or object outside

[1]**rad•i•cal** \ˈrad-i-kəl\ *adj* **1** : of, relating to, or proceeding from a root **2** : of or relating to the origin : FUNDAMENTAL ⟨*radical* differences⟩ **3 a** : marked by a sharp departure from the usual or traditional : EXTREME **b** : of, relating to, or disposed to the making of extreme changes in existing views, habits, conditions, or institutions ⟨*radical* ideas⟩; *esp* : of, relating to, or constituting a political group associated with views, practices, and policies of extreme change [Late Latin *radicalis,* from Latin *radic-, radix* "root"] — **rad•i•cal•ness** *n*

[2]**radical** *n* **1** : ROOT 5 **2** : one who is radical **3** : a group of atoms that is replaceable by a single atom and is capable of remaining unchanged during a series of reactions **4 a** : a mathematical expression (as $\sqrt{2x}$) indicating a root by means of a radical sign **b** : RADICAL SIGN

rad•i•cal•ism \ˈrad-i-kə-ˌliz-əm\ *n* **1** : the quality or state of being radical **2** : the doctrines or principles of radicals

rad•i•cal•ize \-kə-ˌlīz\ *vt* : to make radical especially in politics — **rad•i•cal•i•za•tion** \ˌrad-i-kə-lə-ˈzā-shən\ *n*

rad•i•cal•ly \ˈrad-i-kə-lē, -klē\ *adv* **1** : in origin or essence : NATURALLY **2** : in a radical or extreme manner

radical sign *n* : the sign √ placed before an expression in mathematics to indicate that its root is to be found

rad•i•cand \ˌrad-ə-ˈkand\ *n* : the expression under a radical sign [derived from Latin *radicari* "to take root," from *radic-, radix* "root"]

ra•dic•chio \ra-ˈdik-ē-ō\ *n* : a chicory of a red variety with variegated leaves that is used as a salad green [Italian, "chicory," from Latin *radicula*]

radices *plural of* RADIX

rad•i•cle \ˈrad-i-kəl\ *n* : the lower part of the axis of a plant embryo or seedling; *esp* : the root of a plant embryo [Latin *radicula* "small root," from *radic-, radix* "root"] — **ra•dic•u•lar** \ra-ˈdik-yə-lər\ *adj*

radii *plural of* RADIUS

[1]**ra•dio** \ˈrād-ē-ˌō\ *n, pl* **ra•di•os 1** : the sending or receiving of signals by means of electromagnetic waves without a connecting wire; *esp* : the use of these waves to carry sound that has been converted into electrical impulses **2** : a radio message **3** : a radio receiving set **4 a** : a radio transmitting station **b** : a radio broadcasting organization **c** : the radio broadcasting industry [short for *radiotelegraphy*]

[2]**radio** *adj* **1** : of, relating to, using, or operated by radiant energy ⟨*radio* communication⟩ **2** : of or relating to electric currents or phenomena of frequencies between about 3000 hertz

\ə\ abut	\au̇\ out	\i\ tip	\ȯ\ saw	\u̇\ foot
\ər\ further	\ch\ chin	\ī\ life	\ȯi\ coin	\y\ yet
\a\ mat	\e\ pet	\j\ job	\th\ thin	\yü\ few
\ā\ take	\ē\ easy	\ng\ sing	\th̲\ this	\yu̇\ cure
\ä\ cot, cart	\g\ go	\ō\ bone	\ü\ food	\zh\ vision

and 300 gigahertz **3 a** : of, relating to, or used in radio or a radio set **b** : controlled or directed by radio

[3]radio *vb* **1** : to send or communicate by radio **2** : to send a radio message to

radio- *combining form* **1** : radial : radially ⟨*radio*symmetrical⟩ **2 a** : radiant energy : radiation ⟨*radio*active⟩ **b** : radioactive ⟨*radio*carbon⟩ **c** : radio ⟨*radio*telegraph⟩ [French, from Latin *radius* "spoke, radius, ray"]

ra·dio·ac·tive \ˌrād-ē-ō-ˈak-tiv\ *adj* : of, caused by, or exhibiting radioactivity — **ra·dio·ac·tive·ly** *adv*

ra·dio·ac·tiv·i·ty \-ˌak-ˈtiv-ət-ē\ *n* : the property possessed by some elements (as uranium) of spontaneously emitting particles (as electrons or alpha particles) by the disintegration of their atomic nuclei

radio astronomy *n* : astronomy dealing with electromagnetic radiations of radio frequency received from outside the earth's atmosphere — **radio astronomer** *n*

ra·dio·au·to·graph \ˌrād-ē-ō-ˈȯt-ə-ˌgraf\ *n* : AUTORADIOGRAPH — **ra·dio·au·tog·ra·phy** \-ȯ-ˈtäg-rə-fē\ *n*

radio beacon *n* : a radio transmitting station that transmits radio signals for use (as on a landing field) in determining the direction or position of those receiving them

radio car *n* : an automobile (as a police car) equipped with two-way radio communications

ra·dio·car·bon \-ˈkär-bən\ *n* : radioactive carbon; *esp* : CARBON 14

radiocarbon dating *n* : CARBON DATING

ra·dio·el·e·ment \ˌrād-ē-ō-ˈel-ə-mənt\ *n* : a radioactive element

radio frequency *n* : any of the electromagnetic wave frequencies that lie in a range from below 3 kilohertz to about 300 gigahertz used especially in radio and television transmission and for radar signals

ra·dio·gram \ˈrād-ē-ō-ˌgram\ *n* **1** : RADIOGRAPH **2** : a message sent by radiotelegraphy

[1]ra·dio·graph \-ˌgraf\ *n* : a picture produced on a sensitive surface by a form of radiation other than visible light; *esp* : an X-ray photograph — **ra·dio·graph·ic** \ˌrād-ē-ō-ˈgraf-ik\ *adj* — **ra·dio·graph·i·cal·ly** \-ˈgraf-i-kə-lē, -klē\ *adv* — **ra·di·og·ra·phy** \ˌrād-ē-ˈäg-rə-fē\ *n*

[2]radiograph *vt* : to make a radiograph of

ra·dio·iso·tope \ˌrād-ē-ō-ˈī-sə-ˌtōp\ *n* : a radioactive isotope

ra·di·o·lar·i·an \ˌrād-ē-ō-ˈlar-ē-ən, -ˈler-\ *n* : any of various usually spherical marine protozoans with radiating threadlike pseudopodia and a siliceous skeleton of spicules [derived from Late Latin *radiolus* "small sunbeam," from Latin *radius* "ray"]

ra·di·ol·o·gy \ˌrād-ē-ˈäl-ə-jē\ *n* : a branch of medicine concerned with the use of radiant energy (as X-rays) or radioactive material in the diagnosis and treatment of disease — **ra·dio·log·i·cal** \ˌrād-ē-ə-ˈläj-i-kəl\ *or* **ra·dio·log·i·c** \-ik\ *adj* — **ra·di·ol·o·gist** \ˌrād-ē-ˈäl-ə-jəst\ *n*

ra·dio·man \ˈrād-ē-ō-ˌman\ *n* : a radio operator or technician

ra·di·om·e·ter \ˌrād-ē-ˈäm-ət-ər\ *n* : an instrument for measuring the intensity of radiant energy — **ra·dio·met·ric** \ˌrād-ē-ō-ˈme-trik\ *adj* — **ra·di·om·e·try** \-ˈäm-ə-trē\ *n*

ra·dio·nu·clide \ˌrād-ē-ō-ˈnü-ˌklīd, -ˈnyü-\ *n* : a radioactive nuclide

ra·dio·phone \ˈrād-ē-ə-ˌfōn\ *n* : RADIOTELEPHONE

ra·dio·pho·to \ˌrād-ē-ō-ˈfōt-ō\ *n* **1** : a picture transmitted by radio **2** : the process of transmitting a picture by radio

ra·dio·sonde \ˈrād-ē-ō-ˌsänd\ *n* : a miniature radio transmitter that is carried (as by a balloon) aloft with instruments for sensing and broadcasting atmospheric conditions [French *sonde* "sounding line"]

ra·dio·tel·e·graph \ˌrād-ē-ō-ˈtel-ə-ˌgraf\ *n* : WIRELESS TELEGRAPHY

ra·dio·te·leg·ra·phy \-tə-ˈleg-rə-fē\ *n* : WIRELESS TELEGRAPHY

ra·dio·tel·e·phone \-ˈtel-ə-ˌfōn\ *n* : a telephone that uses radio waves wholly or partly instead of connecting wires — **ra·dio·te·le·pho·ny** \-tə-ˈlef-ə-nē, -ˈtel-ə-ˌfō-nē\ *n*

radio telescope *n* : a radio receiver-antenna combination used for observation in radio astronomy

ra·dio·ther·a·py \ˌrād-ē-ō-ˈther-ə-pē\ *n* : the treatment of disease by means of X-rays or radioactive substances — **ra·dio·ther·a·pist** \-pəst\ *n*

ra·dio–ul·na \ˌrād-ē-ō-ˈəl-nə\ *n* : a single bone in the forelimb of an amphibian (as a frog) equivalent to the separate radius and ulna of higher vertebrate forms

radio wave *n* : an electromagnetic wave with radio frequency

rad·ish \ˈrad-ish, ˈred-\ *n* : the crisp edible pungent root of a plant related to the mustards that is usually eaten raw as a vegetable; *also* : a plant that produces radishes [Old English *rædic,* from Latin *radix* "root, radish"]

ra·di·um \ˈrād-ē-əm\ *n* : an intensely radioactive shining white metallic chemical element that occurs in combination in minute quantities in minerals (as pitchblende), emits alpha particles and gamma rays to form radon, and is used chiefly in luminous materials and in the treatment of cancer — see ELEMENT table [New Latin, from Latin *radius* "ray"]

ra·di·us \ˈrād-ē-əs\ *n, pl* **-dii** \-ē-ˌī\ *also* **-di·us·es** **1** : the bone on the thumb side of the human forearm; *also* : a corresponding part of other vertebrates **2 a** : a line segment extending from the center of a circle or sphere to the circumference or surface; *also* : its length **b** : a circular area defined by a radius ⟨deer may wander within a *radius* of several miles⟩ **3** : a radial part or plane [Latin, "spoke, ray, radius"]

ra·dix \ˈrād-iks\ *n, pl* **ra·di·ces** \ˈrād-ə-ˌsēz, ˈrad-\ *or* **ra·dix·es** : the base of a number system [Latin, "root"]

ra·dome \ˈrā-ˌdōm\ *n* : a usually plastic housing sheltering the antenna assembly of a radar set [*radar dome*]

ra·don \ˈrā-ˌdän\ *n* : a heavy radioactive gaseous chemical element formed by disintegration of radium — see ELEMENT table [derived from *radium*]

rad·u·la \ˈraj-ə-lə\ *n, pl* **-lae** \-ˌlē, -ˌlī\ *also* **-las** : a toothed horny band in mollusks (as snails and slugs) other than bivalves used to scrape or tear off food and draw it into the mouth [Latin, "scraper," from *radere* "to scrape"] — **rad·u·lar** \-lər\ *adj*

raf·fia \ˈraf-ē-ə\ *n* : fiber from a pinnate-leaved palm of Madagascar and tropical Africa used especially for weaving various articles (as baskets and hats) and for tying [Malagasy *rafia*]

raff·ish \ˈraf-ish\ *adj* **1** : vulgarly crude or flashy ⟨*raffish* language⟩ **2** : marked by a carefree unconventionality : RAKISH [Middle English *raf* "rubbish"] — **raff·ish·ly** *adv* — **raff·ish·ness** *n*

[1]raf·fle \ˈraf-əl\ *n* : a lottery in which the prize is won by one of the persons buying chances [Middle French *rafle,* a dice game]

[2]raffle *vt* **raf·fled; raf·fling** \ˈraf-ling, -ə-ling\ : to offer as a prize in a raffle ⟨*raffle* off a turkey⟩

[1]raft \ˈraft\ *n* **1** : a collection of logs or timber fastened together for transportation by water **2** : a flat structure for support or transportation on water [Middle English *rafte* "rafter, raft," from Old Norse *raptr* "rafter"]

[2]raft *vb* **1** : to transport or move in or by means of a raft **2** : to make into a raft

[3]raft *n* : a large collection or number [alteration of earlier *raff* "jumble"]

raf·ter \ˈraf-tər\ *n* : any of the parallel beams that support a roof [Old English *ræfter*] — **raf·tered** \-tərd\ *adj*

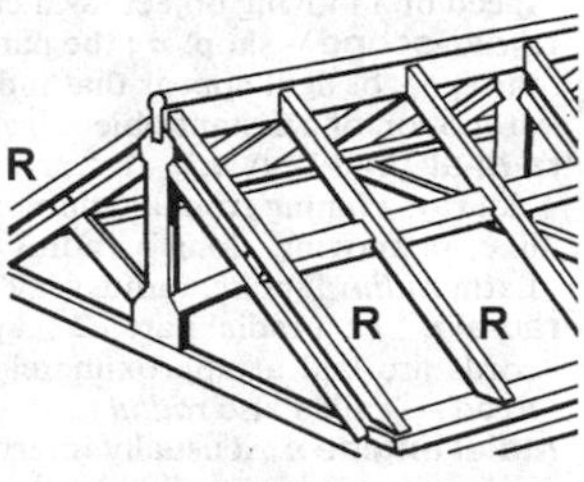

R rafter

[1]rag \ˈrag\ *n* **1 a** : a waste or worn piece of cloth **b** *pl* : shabby or tattered clothing ⟨dressed in *rags*⟩ **2** : something felt to resemble a rag of cloth; *esp* : SCRAP 2, SHRED **3** : NEWSPAPER; *esp* : a sleazy newspaper [Old Norse *rögg* "tuft, shagginess"]

[2]rag *vt* **ragged** \ˈragd\; **rag·ging** **1** : to rail at : SCOLD **2** : TEASE 2a, HARASS [origin unknown] — **rag on** : to make fun of

[3]rag *n* : a composition in ragtime

rag·a·muf·fin \ˈrag-ə-ˌməf-ən\ *n* : a ragged often disreputable person; *esp* : a poorly clothed often dirty child [*Ragamoffyn,* a demon in *Piers Plowman* (1393), attributed to William Langland]

rag·bag \ˈrag-ˌbag\ *n* **1** : a bag for scraps **2** : a miscellaneous collection

rag doll *n* : a stuffed usually painted cloth doll

[1]rage \ˈrāj\ *n* **1 a** : violent and uncontrolled anger : FURY **b** : a fit of violent anger **2** : violent action (as of wind or sea) **3** : CRAZE, VOGUE ⟨was all the *rage*⟩ [Medieval French, derived from Latin *rabies* "madness, rage," from *rabere* "to rage, be mad"] ***synonyms*** see ANGER

[2]**rage** *vi* **1 :** to be in a rage **2 :** to be in tumult ⟨the storm *raged*⟩ **3 :** to persist or spread uncontrollably ⟨a *raging* epidemic⟩

rag·ged \'rag-əd\ *adj* **1 :** roughly unkempt : STRAGGLY ⟨a *ragged* lawn⟩ **2 :** having an irregular edge or outline : JAGGED ⟨*ragged* cliffs⟩ **3 a :** torn or worn to or as if to tatters ⟨a *ragged* dress⟩ **b :** wearing tattered clothes ⟨a *ragged* child⟩ **4 :** executed in an irregular or uneven manner ⟨played *ragged* defense⟩ — **rag·ged·ly** *adv* — **rag·ged·ness** *n*

rag·gedy \-əd-ē\ *adj* **-ged·i·er; -est :** somewhat ragged

rag·gle–tag·gle \'rag-əl-ˌtag-əl\ *adj* **:** MOTLEY [derived from *ragtag*]

rag·ing \'rā-jing\ *adj* **1 :** causing great pain or distress **2 :** VIOLENT 1, WILD ⟨a *raging* fire⟩ **3 :** EXTRAORDINARY 1, TREMENDOUS ⟨a *raging* success⟩

rag·lan sleeve \'rag-lən-\ *n* **:** a sleeve that extends to the neckline with slanted seams from the underarm to the neck [F. J. H. Somerset, Baron *Raglan,* died 1855, British field marshal]

rag·man \'rag-ˌman\ *n* **:** a collector of or dealer in rags

ra·gout \ra-'gü\ *n* **:** a highly seasoned meat stew with vegetables [French *ragoût*]

rag·pick·er \'rag-ˌpik-ər\ *n* **:** a person who collects rags and refuse for a living

rag·tag \'rag-ˌtag\ *adj* **:** RAGGED 1

rag·tag and bob·tail \ˌrag-ˌtag-ən-'bäb-ˌtāl\ *n* **:** RABBLE

rag·time \'rag-ˌtīm\ *n* **1 :** musical rhythm in which the melody has the accented notes falling on beats that are not usually accented **2 :** music with ragtime rhythm [probably from *ragged* + *time*]

rag·top \-ˌtäp\ *n* **:** a convertible automobile

rag·weed \'rag-ˌwēd\ *n* **:** any of various chiefly North American weedy herbs related to the daisies that produce pollen highly irritating to the eyes and nasal passages of some persons

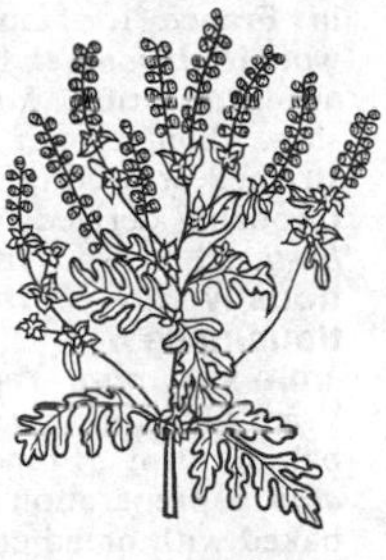

ragweed

rah \'rä, 'ró\ *interj* **:** HOORAY — used especially to cheer on a team

[1]**raid** \'rād\ *n* **1 a :** an entering of something hostile or predatory **b :** a surprise attack by a small military force **2 :** a sudden entry of officers of the law [Scottish dialect, from Old English *rād* "ride, raid"]

[2]**raid** *vt* **:** to make a raid on — **raid·er** *n*

[1]**rail** \'rāl\ *n* **1 a :** a bar extending from one post or support to another and serving as a guard or barrier **b :** RAILING 1 **2 a :** a bar of rolled steel forming a track for wheeled vehicles **b :** TRACK 1c (2) **c :** RAILROAD [Middle French *raille, reille* "ruler, bar," from Latin *regula* "ruler," from *regere* "to keep straight, rule"]

[2]**rail** *vt* **:** to provide with a railing

[3]**rail** *n, pl* **rails** *or* **rail :** any of various small wading birds related to the cranes [Middle French *raalle*]

[4]**rail** *vi* **:** to criticize or scold in harsh or abusive language [Middle French *railler* "to mock"] — **rail·er** *n*

rail·car \-ˌkär\ *n* **:** a railroad car

rail·ing \'rā-ling\ *n* **1 :** a barrier (as a fence or balustrade) consisting of rails and their supports **2 :** material for making rails **:** RAILS

rail·lery \'rā-lə-rē\ *n, pl* **-ler·ies :** good-natured ridicule **:** BANTER [French *raillerie,* from *railler* "to mock"]

[1]**rail·road** \'rāl-ˌrōd\ *n* **:** a permanent road having a line of rails fixed to ties and laid on a roadbed and providing a track for cars and equipment drawn by locomotives or propelled by self-contained motors; *also* **:** such a road and its assets constituting a single property **:** a railroad company

[2]**railroad** *vb* **1 a :** to transport by railroad **b :** to work for a railroad company **2 a :** to push through hastily or without due consideration ⟨*railroad* a bill into law⟩ **b :** to convict with undue haste and by means of false charges or insufficient evidence — **rail·road·er** *n*

rail·road·ing *n* **:** construction or operation of a railroad

rail·way \'rāl-ˌwā\ *n* **:** RAILROAD; *esp* **:** a railroad operating with light equipment or within a small area

rai·ment \'rā-mənt\ *n* **:** CLOTHING, GARMENTS [Middle English *rayment,* short for *arrayment,* from *arrayen* "to array"]

[1]**rain** \'rān\ *n* **1 a :** water falling in drops condensed from vapor in the atmosphere; *also* **:** the descent of such water **b :** RAINWATER **2 a :** a fall of rain **:** RAINSTORM **b** *pl* **:** the rainy season **3 :** rainy weather **4 :** a heavy fall ⟨a *rain* of arrows⟩; *also* **:** a large outpouring ⟨a *rain* of abuse⟩ [Old English *regn*] — **rain·less** \-ləs\ *adj*

[2]**rain** *vb* **1 :** to fall as water in drops from the clouds **2 :** to send down rain **3 :** to fall like rain ⟨soot and ash *rained* down⟩ **4 :** to give or administer abundantly ⟨*rained* praises on the returning heroes⟩ — **rain cats and dogs :** to rain very hard **:** POUR

[1]**rain·bow** \-ˌbō\ *n* **1 :** an arc or circle that exhibits in concentric bands the colors of the spectrum and that is formed opposite the sun by the refraction and reflection of the sun's rays in raindrops, spray, or mist **2 :** a multicolored array

[2]**rainbow** *adj* **1 :** having many colors **2 :** of, relating to, or being people of different races or cultural backgrounds ⟨a *rainbow* coalition⟩

rainbow runner *n* **:** a large brightly marked blue and yellow food and sport fish of warm seas

rainbow trout *n* **:** a large stout-bodied trout native to western North America that usually has red or pink stripes with black dots on its side — called also *rainbow;* compare STEELHEAD

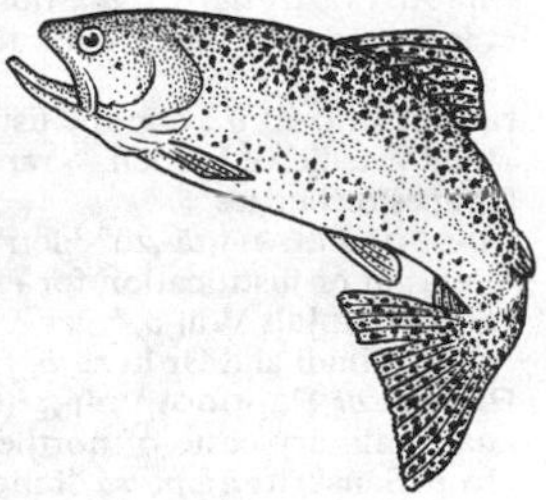

rainbow trout

rain check *n* **1 :** a ticket stub good for a later performance when the scheduled one is rained out **2 :** an assurance of an offer at a later time; *esp* **:** a document assuring that a customer can take advantage of a sale later if the item or service offered is not available (as by being sold out)

rain·coat \'rān-ˌkōt\ *n* **:** a coat of waterproof or water-resistant material

rain date *n* **:** an alternative date set aside for use if a scheduled event must be postponed due to rain

rain·drop \-ˌdräp\ *n* **:** a drop of rain

rain·fall \-ˌfól\ *n* **1 :** RAIN 2a **2 :** amount of precipitation ⟨an annual *rainfall* of 20 inches⟩

rain forest *n* **1 :** a usually tropical woodland with an annual rainfall of at least 100 inches (254 centimeters) and lofty trees forming a continuous canopy **2 :** TEMPERATE RAIN FOREST

rain gauge *n* **:** an instrument for measuring rainfall

rain·mak·ing \'rān-ˌmā-king\ *n* **:** the act or process of producing or attempting to produce rain by artificial means — **rain·mak·er** \-kər\ *n*

rain out *vt* **:** to interrupt or prevent (as a sports event) by rain — **rain·out** \'rān-ˌaút\ *n*

rain·proof \'rān-'prüf\ *adj* **:** impervious to rain

rain·storm \-ˌstórm\ *n* **:** a storm of or with rain

rain·wa·ter \-ˌwót-ər, -ˌwät-\ *n* **:** water fallen as rain

rain·wear \-ˌwaər, -ˌweər\ *n* **:** waterproof or water-resistant clothing — called also *rain gear*

rainy \'rā-nē\ *adj* **rain·i·er; -est :** having much rain **:** SHOWERY ⟨a *rainy* season⟩

rainy day *n* **:** a period of want or need ⟨saving for a *rainy day*⟩ — **rainy–day** *adj*

[1]**raise** \'rāz\ *vb* **1 :** to cause or help to rise ⟨*raise* dust⟩ **2 a :** to rouse from sleep **:** AROUSE **b :** to stir up **:** INCITE ⟨*raise* a rebellion⟩ **c :** to recall from or as if from death ⟨enough noise to *raise* the dead⟩ **3 a :** to set upright by lifting or building ⟨*raise* a monument⟩ **b :** to lift up ⟨*raise* your hand⟩ **c :** to place higher in rank or dignity **:** ELEVATE ⟨was *raised* to captain⟩ **d :** HEIGHTEN 1a, INVIGORATE ⟨*raise* the spirits⟩ **e :** to end or suspend the operation or validity of ⟨*raise* a siege⟩ **4 :** COLLECT 1b ⟨*raise* funds⟩ **5 a :** to foster the growth and development of **:** GROW ⟨*raise* corn⟩ ⟨*raise* pigs⟩ **b :** BRING UP 1, REAR ⟨*raise* a child⟩ ⟨was *raised* in the city⟩ **6 a :** to give rise to **:** PROVOKE ⟨*raise* a commotion⟩ **b :** to give voice to ⟨*raise* a cheer⟩ **7 :** to bring up for consideration or debate ⟨*raise* an issue⟩ **8 a :** to increase the strength, intensity, or pitch of ⟨don't

raise your voice⟩ **b** : to increase the degree or rate of ⟨*raise* the rent⟩ **c** : to increase a bid or bet **d** : to multiply (a quantity) by itself a specified number of times ⟨*raise* two to the fourth power⟩ **9** : to make light and porous ⟨*raise* dough⟩ **10** : to bring in sight on the horizon by approaching ⟨*raise* land⟩ **11** : to cause (an elevated injury) to form on the skin ⟨the blow *raised* a welt⟩ **12** : to establish radio communication with [Old Norse *reisa*] ***synonyms*** see LIFT — **rais•er** *n* — **raise Cain** *or* **raise hell** **1** : to act wildly : create a disturbance **2** : to scold or criticize someone especially loudly ⟨*raised hell* with the umpire⟩ — **raise eyebrows** : to cause surprise or mild disapproval ⟨*raised eyebrows* by turning down the award⟩ — **raise the bar** : to set a higher standard ⟨new software that *raises the bar* for competitors⟩

^{2}**raise** *n* **1** : an act or method of raising or lifting **2** : an upward grade : RISE **3 a** : an increase in amount (as of a bet or bid) **b** : an increase in pay

raised \ˈrāzd\ *adj* **1 a** : done in relief **b** : having a nap **2** : leavened with yeast rather than with baking powder or baking soda

rai•sin \ˈrāz-ⁿn\ *n* : a grape usually rich in sugar that is dried for food [Medieval French, "grape," from Latin *racemus* "cluster of grapes or berries"]

rai•son d'être \ˌrā-ˌzō^{n}-ˈdetr\ *n, pl* **rai•sons d'être** \-ˌzō^{n}z-\ : reason or justification for existence [French]

ra•ja *or* **ra•jah** \ˈräj-ə, ˈräzh-\ *n* : an Indian or Malay prince or chief [Hindi and Urdu *rājā,* from Sanskrit *rājan* "king"]

Raj•put *or* **Raj•poot** \ˈräj-ˌpu̇t, ˈräzh-\ *n* : a member of a dominant military caste of northern India [Hindi and Urdu *rājpūt,* from Sanskrit *rājaputra* "king's son," from *rājan* "king" + *putra* "son"]

^{1}**rake** \ˈrāk\ *n* **1** : a long-handled garden tool having prongs at the end **2** : a machine for gathering hay [Old English *racu*]

^{2}**rake** *vt* **1** : to gather, loosen, or smooth with or as if with a rake **2** : to gain (as money) quickly and in abundance **3 a** : to touch in passing over lightly **b** : SCRATCH 1, SCRAPE **4** : to search through : RANSACK **5** : to sweep the length of especially with gunfire **6** : to glance over rapidly — **rak•er** *n*

^{3}**rake** *vi* : to incline from the perpendicular : SLANT [origin unknown]

^{4}**rake** *n* : a slant or slope away from the perpendicular

^{5}**rake** *n* : a dissolute person : LIBERTINE [short for earlier *rakehell*]

rake–off \ˈrā-ˌkȯf\ *n* : an improper or unlawful commission or profit received by one party in a business deal

^{1}**rak•ish** \ˈrā-kish\ *adj* : of, relating to, or characteristic of a rake : DISSOLUTE — **rak•ish•ly** *adv* — **rak•ish•ness** *n*

^{2}**rakish** *adj* **1** : having a trim or streamlined appearance suggestive of speed ⟨a *rakish* ship⟩ **2** : dashingly or carelessly unconventional : JAUNTY ⟨*rakish* clothes⟩ [probably from ^{3}*rake;* from the raking masts of pirate ships] — **rak•ish•ly** *adv* — **rak•ish•ness** *n*

ra•ku \ˈrä-kü\ *n* : Japanese hand-modeled pottery that is fired at a low temperature and rapidly cooled [Japanese, literally, "pleasure"; from the use of the character for this word on the family seal of the potter who introduced the style]

rale \ˈral, ˈräl\ *n* : an abnormal sound accompanying the sounds of normal breathing (as in pneumonia) [French *râle*]

ral•len•tan•do \ˌräl-ən-ˈtän-dō\ *adv or adj* : with a gradual decrease in tempo — used as a direction in music [Italian, literally, "slowing down"]

^{1}**ral•ly** \ˈral-ē\ *vb* **ral•lied; ral•ly•ing** **1 a** : to bring together for a common purpose **b** : to bring back to order ⟨*rallying* the forces for a second assault⟩ **2** : to rouse for action or from depression or weakness ⟨the medicine *rallied* the patient⟩ **3** : to come together to renew an effort **4** : to join in a common cause **5** : RECOVER, REBOUND ⟨the market *rallied* after a slump⟩ **6** : to engage in a rally (as in tennis) [French *rallier,* from Medieval French *ralier,* from *re-* "re-" + *alier* "to unite, ally"]

^{2}**rally** *n, pl* **rallies** **1** : the action of rallying **2** : a mass meeting intended to arouse group enthusiasm **3** : a series of shots interchanged between players (as in tennis) before a point is won

^{3}**rally** *vt* **ral•lied; ral•ly•ing** : to tease with good-natured or friendly ridicule [French *railler* "to mock, rally," probably from Medieval French *reillier* "to growl, mutter," derived from Late Latin *ragere* "to neigh"]

rallying cry *n* : WAR CRY

^{1}**ram** \ˈram\ *n* **1** : a male sheep **2** : BATTERING RAM **3** : a pointed beak on the prow of a ship for piercing an enemy ship **4** : a guided piece for exerting pressure or for driving or forcing something by impact [Old English *ramm*]

^{2}**ram** *vb* **rammed; ram•ming** **1** : to strike or strike against with violence : CRASH **2** : to move with extreme rapidity **3** : to force in, down, or together by or as if by driving or pressing **4** : to force passage or acceptance of ⟨*ram* a bill through Congress⟩ [Middle English *rammen,* probably from *ram,* n.] — **ram•mer** *n*

RAM \ˈram\ *n* : a computer memory that acts as the main storage available to the user for programs and data — compare ROM

Ram•a•dan \ˈram-ə-ˌdän, ˌräm-ə-ˈ\ *n* : the 9th month of the Islamic year observed as sacred with daily fasting from dawn to sunset [Arabic *Ramaḍān*]

^{1}**ram•ble** \ˈram-bəl\ *vb* **ram•bled; ram•bling** \-bə-ling, -bling\ **1 a** : to move aimlessly from place to place : WANDER, ROAM **b** : to explore idly **2** : to talk or write in a disjointed or long-winded fashion **3** : to grow or extend irregularly [perhaps from Middle English *romblen,* from *romen* "to roam"] ***synonyms*** see WANDER — **ram•bling•ly** \-bling-lē\ *adv*

^{2}**ramble** *n* **1** : a leisurely excursion for pleasure; *esp* : a leisurely or aimless walk **2** : a rambling story or discussion

ram•bler \ˈram-blər\ *n* **1** : one that rambles **2** : a climbing rose with flexible stems and rather small flowers in large clusters

ram•bouil•let \ˌram-bə-ˈlā\ *n, often cap* : any of a breed of large sturdy sheep developed in France for mutton and wool [*Rambouillet,* France]

rambouillet

ram•bunc•tious \ram-ˈbəng-shəs, -ˈbəngk-\ *adj* : not restrained or orderly : UNRULY [probably derived from *rumbustious*] — **ram•bunc•tious•ly** *adv* — **ram•bunc•tious•ness** *n*

ram•e•kin *also* **ram•e•quin** \ˈram-i-kən\ *n* : an individual baking dish [French *ramequin,* a preparation of cheese baked with bread crumbs or eggs, from Low German *ramken,* from *ram* "cream"]

ra•mie \ˈrā-mē, ˈram-ē\ *n* : an Asian perennial plant related to the nettles; *also* : its strong lustrous bast fiber used especially in making cloth [Malay *rami*]

ram•i•fi•ca•tion \ˌram-ə-fə-ˈkā-shən\ *n* **1** : the act or process of branching **2** : BRANCH 2, OFFSHOOT **3** : OUTGROWTH, CONSEQUENCE ⟨the *ramifications* of the decision⟩

ram•i•fy \ˈram-ə-ˌfī\ *vb* **-fied; -fy•ing** : to spread out or split up into branches or divisions [Medieval French *ramifier,* from Medieval Latin *ramificare,* from Latin *ramus* "branch"]

ram•jet \ˌram-ˌjet\ *n* : a jet engine having in its forward end a continuous inlet of air so that there is a compressing effect produced on the air taken in while the engine is in motion

^{1}**ramp** \ˈramp\ *vi* **1** : to stand or advance menacingly with forelegs or with arms raised **2** : to move or act furiously : STORM **3** : to increase, expand, or decrease especially quickly or at a constant rate — usually used with *up* or *down* ⟨*ramp* up production⟩ [Medieval French *ramper* "to crawl, rear," of Germanic origin]

^{2}**ramp** *n* : a sloping way or plane: as **a** : a sloping passage or roadway connecting different levels **b** : a slope for launching boats [French *rampe, from ramper* "to crawl, rear"]

^{1}**ram•page** \ˈram-ˌpāj, ram-ˈ, ˈram-ˈ\ *vi* : to rush wildly about : STORM [Scottish]

^{2}**ram•page** \ˈram-ˌpāj\ *n* : a course of violent, riotous, or reckless action or behavior — **ram•pa•geous** \ram-ˈpā-jəs\ *adj* — **ram•pa•geous•ly** *adv* — **ram•pa•geous•ness** *n*

ram•pant \ˈram-pənt, -ˌpant\ *adj* **1** : rearing upon one or both hind legs with forelegs extended **2 a** : marked by a menacing wildness, extravagance, or absence of restraint ⟨rumors ran *rampant*⟩ **b** : profusely widespread ⟨*rampant* weeds⟩ [Medieval French, present participle of *ramper* "to crawl, rear"] — **ram•pant•ly** *adv*

ram•part \ˈram-ˌpärt, -pərt\ *n* : a broad wall or mound of earth raised as a fortification or protective barrier [Middle French, from *ramparer* "to fortify," from *re-* + *emporer* "to defend," derived from Latin [2]*in-* + *parare* "to prepare"]

[1]**ram·rod** \'ram-ˌräd\ *n* **1** : a rod for ramming home the charge in a muzzle-loading firearm **2** : a cleaning rod for small arms

[2]**ramrod** *adj* : marked by rigidity, severity, or stiffness

[3]**ramrod** *adv* : in a fully upright position : RIGIDLY ⟨sat *ramrod* straight⟩

ram·shack·le \'ram-ˌshak-əl\ *adj* : appearing ready to collapse: as **a** : DILAPIDATED ⟨a *ramshackle* old barn⟩ **b** : carelessly or loosely constructed ⟨the story had a *ramshackle* plot⟩ [alteration of earlier *ransackled,* derived from *ransack*]

ra·mus \'rā-məs\ *n, pl* **ra·mi** \-ˌmī\ : a projecting part or elongated process : BRANCH ⟨the upward extending *rami* of the lower back jaw⟩ [Latin, "branch"]

ran *past of* RUN

[1]**ranch** \'ranch\ *n* **1** : an establishment for raising horses, cattle, or sheep **2** : a farm devoted to raising a specific crop or kind of animal ⟨a fruit *ranch*⟩ ⟨a mink *ranch*⟩ **3** : RANCH HOUSE 2 [Mexican Spanish *rancho* "small ranch," from Spanish, "camp, hut," and Spanish dialect, "small farm," from *ranchearse* "to take up quarters," from Medieval French *se ranger* "to take up a position," from *ranger* "to set in a row"]

[2]**ranch** *vi* **1** : to live or work on a ranch **2** : to raise on a ranch ⟨*ranched* horses⟩

ranch·er \'ran-chər\ *n* : one who owns or works on a ranch

ran·che·ro \ran-'cheər-ō, rän-\ *n, pl* **-ros** : RANCHER [Mexican Spanish, from *rancho* "small ranch"]

ranch house *n* **1** : the main dwelling house on a ranch **2** : a one-story house typically with a low-pitched roof

ranch·man \'ranch-mən\ *n* : RANCHER

ran·cho \'ran-chō, 'rän-\ *n, pl* **ranchos** : RANCH 1 [Mexican Spanish, "small ranch"]

ran·cid \'ran-səd\ *adj* **1** : having an unpleasant smell or taste ⟨*rancid* butter⟩ **2** : distinctly unpleasant or distasteful; *also* : CORRUPT [Latin *rancidus,* from *rancēre* "to be rancid"] — **ran·cid·i·ty** \ran-'sid-ət-ē\ *n* — **ran·cid·ness** \'ran-səd-nəs\ *n*

ran·cor \'rang-kər\ *n* : intense hatred or spite [Medieval French *rancur,* from Late Latin *rancor* "rancidity, rancor," from Latin *rancēre* "to be rancid"] — **ran·cor·ous** \-kə-rəs, -krəs\ *adj* — **ran·cor·ous·ly** *adv*

rand \'rand, 'ränd, 'ränt\ *n, pl* **rand** **1** : the basic monetary unit of South Africa **2** : a coin or note representing one rand [the *Rand,* South Africa]

[1]**ran·dom** \'ran-dəm\ *n* : a haphazard course [Medieval French *randun* "succession, surge," from *randir* "to run," of Germanic origin] — **at random** : without definite aim, direction, rule, or method ⟨subjects chosen *at random*⟩

[2]**random** *adj* **1** : lacking a definite plan, purpose, or pattern **2** : having a definite and especially an equal probability of occurring ⟨a *random* number⟩; *also* : consisting of or relating to such elements each selected mathematically independently from the others ⟨*random* samples⟩ — **ran·dom·ly** *adv* — **ran·dom·ness** *n*

synonyms RANDOM, HAPHAZARD, CASUAL mean determined by accident rather than design. RANDOM stresses lack of definite aim or fixed goal or avoidance of regular procedure ⟨a *random* selection of books⟩. HAPHAZARD applies to what is done without regard for regularity or fitness or ultimate consequences ⟨*haphazard* arrangement of furniture⟩. CASUAL suggests working or acting without deliberation, intention, or purpose ⟨a *casual* collector⟩.

[3]**random** *adv* : in a random manner

ran·dom–ac·cess \ˌran-dəm-'ak-ˌses\ *adj* : permitting access to stored data in any order the user desires

random–access memory *n* : RAM

ran·dom·ize \'ran-də-ˌmīz\ *vt* : to make random ⟨a *randomized* sampling⟩ — **ran·dom·i·za·tion** \ˌran-də-mə-'zā-shən\ *n*

rang *past of* RING

[1]**range** \'rānj\ *n* **1 a** : a series of things in a line : ROW ⟨a *range* of mountains⟩ **b** : an aggregate of individuals in one rank : CLASS, ORDER **2** : a cooking stove that has an oven and a flat top with burners or heating elements **3 a** : a place that may be ranged over **b** : open land over which livestock may roam and feed **c** : the region throughout which a kind of organism or ecological community naturally occurs **4** : the act of ranging about **5 a** (1) : the horizontal distance to which a projectile can be propelled (2) : the maximum distance a vehicle can travel without refueling **b** : a place where shooting is practiced; *also* : a special course (as over water) where missiles are tested **6 a** : the space or extent included, covered, or used : SCOPE **b** : the extent of pitch covered by a voice or instrument or a melody **7 a** : a sequence, series, or scale between limits ⟨a wide *range* of patterns⟩ **b** : the limits of a series : the distance or extent between possible extremes **c** : the difference between the least and greatest of a set of values **8** : the set of values a function may take on; *esp* : the set of values that the dependent variable may take on — compare DOMAIN 4 [Middle English, "row of persons," from Medieval French *range, renge,* from *renger* "to range"]

[2]**range** *vb* **1 a** : to set in a row or in the proper order **b** : to place among others in a position or situation **c** : to assign to a category : CLASSIFY **2** : to rove over or through : roam at large or freely **3** : to raise (livestock) on a range **4 a** : to correspond in direction or line : ALIGN **b** : to extend in a particular direction **5** : to vary within limits **6** : to live or occur in or be native to a region [Medieval French *renger,* from *renc, reng* "line, place, row, rank"]

range finder *n* : a device used to determine the distance of an object (as a target)

range·land \'rānj-ˌland\ *n* : land used or suitable for range

rang·er \'rān-jər\ *n* **1 a** : the keeper of a British royal park or forest **b** : FOREST RANGER **2** : an animal that ranges **3 a** : one of a body of organized armed men who range over a region **b** : a soldier in an army unit with special training (as parachute jumping and scuba diving) for carrying out surprise attacks and raids

rangy \'rān-jē\ *adj* **rang·i·er; -est** **1** : able to range for considerable distances **2 a** : being long-limbed and long-bodied ⟨*rangy* cattle⟩ **b** : tall and slender in body build ⟨*rangy* athletes⟩ **3** : having room for ranging — **rang·i·ness** *n*

ra·ni *or* **ra·nee** \rä-'nē, 'rän-ē\ *n* : a Hindu queen : a raja's wife [Hindi and Urdu *rānī,* from Sanskrit *rājñī,* feminine of *rājan* "king"]

[1]**rank** \'rangk\ *adj* **1** : strong and vigorous in growth ⟨*rank* weeds⟩ **2** : offensively gross or coarse ⟨*rank* language⟩ **3 a** : shockingly conspicuous ⟨*rank* cowardice⟩ **b** : OUTRIGHT 1 ⟨a *rank* amateur⟩ **4** : offensive in odor or flavor [Old English *ranc* "overbearing, strong"] ***synonyms*** see FLAGRANT — **rank·ness** *n*

[2]**rank** *n* **1** : ROW, SERIES ⟨*ranks* of houses⟩ **2** : a line of soldiers in close order side by side **3** : a group of individuals classed together — usually used in plural ⟨in the *ranks* of the unemployed⟩ **4** : relative position or order : STANDING **5** : official grade or status (as in the army or navy) ⟨the *rank* of general⟩ **6** : position in regard to merit ⟨a musician of the highest *rank*⟩ **7** : a high social position **8** *pl* : the body of enlisted personnel (as in an army) [Medieval French *renc, reng,* of Germanic origin]

[3]**rank** *vb* **1** : to arrange in lines or in a regular formation **2** : to determine the relative position of : RATE ⟨a highly *ranked* player⟩ **3** : to take precedence of ⟨a captain *ranks* a lieutenant⟩ **4** : to take or have a position in relation to others : be in a class ⟨*ranks* first in her class⟩

rank and file *n* **1** : the enlisted personnel of an armed force **2** : the ordinary body of an organization or society as distinguished from the leaders

rank·er \'rang-kər\ *n* : one who serves or has served in the ranks; *esp* : a commissioned officer promoted from the ranks

rank·ing *adj* : having the highest rank or a high position ⟨the *ranking* officer⟩

ran·kle \'rang-kəl\ *vb* **ran·kled; ran·kling** \-kə-ling, -kling\ **1** : to cause anger, irritation, or deep bitterness **2** : to cause resentment or bitterness in : irritate deeply [Medieval French *rancler* "to fester," alteration of *draoncler, raoncler,* from *draoncle, raoncle* "festering sore," from Medieval Latin *dracunculus,* from Latin, "small serpent"]

Word History The modern senses of the verb *rankle* are figurative extensions of an earlier meaning, "to fester." The word was borrowed from Medieval French *rancler.* The Medieval French noun *raoncle,* or *draoncle,* from which the verb is derived, means "a festering sore" and comes ultimately from Latin *dracunculus.* This word means literally "small serpent or dragon." In Medieval Latin *dracunculus* was used for a cancerous tumor or ulcer, probably because the form of a tumor was thought to be like that of a small serpent.

ran·sack \ˈran-ˌsak, ran-ˈ, ˈran-ˈ\ *vt* **:** to search thoroughly **:** RUMMAGE; *esp* **:** to search through and steal things of value [Old Norse *rannsaka*] — **ran·sack·er** *n*

[1]**ran·som** \ˈran-səm\ *n* **1 :** something (as money) paid or demanded for the freedom of a captured person **2 :** the act of ransoming [Medieval French *rançun,* from Latin *redemptio* "redemption"]

[2]**ransom** *vt* **:** to free from captivity or punishment by paying a price ***synonyms*** see RESCUE — **ran·som·er** *n*

[1]**rant** \ˈrant\ *vi* **1 :** to talk noisily, excitedly, or wildly ‹*rant* and rave in anger› **2 :** to scold violently [obsolete Dutch *ranten*] — **rant·er** *n*

[2]**rant** *n* **:** ranting speech **:** wild unrestrained language

[1]**rap** \ˈrap\ *n* **1 :** a sharp blow or knock **2 a :** a sharp rebuke or criticism **b :** a negative and often undeserved reputation ‹given a bad *rap* by the press› **3 a :** the blame for or unfavorable consequences of an action ‹took the *rap*› **b :** a criminal charge ‹a murder *rap*› **c :** a prison sentence [Middle English *rappe*]

[2]**rap** *vb* **rapped; rap·ping 1 :** to give a quick sharp blow **:** KNOCK ‹*rap* on the door› **2 :** to utter suddenly with force ‹*rap* out an order›

[3]**rap** *n* **:** the least bit ‹don't care a *rap*› [perhaps from [1]*rap*]

[4]**rap** *n* **1 :** CONVERSATION, TALK **2 :** a rhythmic chanting often in unison of usually rhymed couplets to a musical accompaniment; *also* **:** a musical piece so performed [perhaps from [1]*rap*]

[5]**rap** *vi* **rapped; rap·ping 1 :** to talk freely and frankly **2 :** to perform rap

ra·pa·cious \rə-ˈpā-shəs\ *adj* **1 :** very grasping or greedy **2 :** living on prey **:** PREDATORY **3 :** RAVENOUS [Latin *rapac-, rapax,* from *rapere* "to seize"] — **ra·pa·cious·ly** *adv* — **ra·pa·cious·ness** *n* — **ra·pac·i·ty** \-ˈpas-ət-ē\ *n*

[1]**rape** \ˈrāp\ *n* **:** a European herb related to the mustards and grown as a forage crop and for its seeds which are used as a source of oil and as a bird food — compare CANOLA [Latin *rapa, rapum* "turnip, rape"]

[2]**rape** *vt* **1** *archaic* **:** to seize and take away by force **2 :** to commit rape on **:** RAVISH [Latin *rapere*] — **rap·er** *n* — **rap·ist** \ˈrā-pəst\ *n*

[3]**rape** *n* **1 :** a seizing by force **2 :** unlawful sexual activity and especially sexual intercourse carried out forcibly or under threat of injury against the will usually of a female or with a person who is beneath an age set by law or incapable of valid consent **3 :** an outrageous violation

ra·phe \ˈrā-fē, -ˌfē\ *n* **:** a seam or ridge (as at the union of the two lateral halves of an organ or on a seed) [Greek *rhaphē* "seam," from *rhaptein* "to sew"]

[1]**rap·id** \ˈrap-əd\ *adj* **:** marked by a fast rate of motion, activity, succession, or occurrence **:** SWIFT [Latin *rapidus* "seizing, sweeping, rapid," from *rapere* "to seize, sweep away"] ***synonyms*** see FAST — **rap·id·ly** *adv* — **rap·id·ness** *n*

[2]**rapid** *n* **:** a part of a river where the current is fast and the surface is usually broken by obstructions — usually used in plural

rapid eye movement *n* **:** rapid movement of the eyes which occurs during the dreaming period of sleep

rap·id–fire \ˌrap-əd-ˈfīr\ *adj* **1 :** firing or adapted for firing shots in rapid succession **2 :** marked by rapidity, liveliness, or sharpness ‹*rapid-fire* questions›

ra·pid·i·ty \rə-ˈpid-ət-ē, ra-\ *n* **:** the quality or state of being rapid

rapid transit *n* **:** fast public passenger transportation (as by subway) in urban areas

ra·pi·er \ˈrā-pē-ər\ *n* **:** a straight 2-edged sword with a narrow pointed blade [Middle French *(espee) rapiere*]

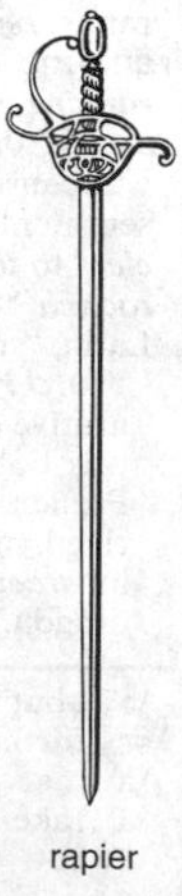

rapier

rap·ine \ˈrap-ən, -ˌīn\ *n* **:** the seizing and carrying away of something by force **:** PILLAGE, PLUNDER [Latin *rapina,* from *rapere* "to seize"]

rap·pel \rə-ˈpel, ra-\ *vi* **-pelled** *also* **-peled; -pel·ling** *also* **-pel·ing :** to descend (as from a cliff) by sliding down a rope [French, literally, "recall," from *rapeler* "to recall," from *re-* "re-" + *apeler* "to appeal, call"]

rap·pen \ˈräp-ən\ *n, pl* **rappen :** the centime of Switzerland [German, from German dialect, literally, "raven"]

rap·per \ˈrap-ər\ *n* **:** one that raps or is used for rapping: as **a :** a door knocker **b :** a performer of rap music

rap·port \ra-ˈpōr, -ˈpȯr\ *n* **:** harmonious accord or relation that makes communication possible or easy ‹the teacher had good *rapport* with the pupils› [French, from *rapporter* "to bring back, refer"]

rap·proche·ment \ˌrap-ˌrōsh-ˈmä^{n}\ *n* **:** establishment of or state of having cordial relations [French, from *rapprocher* "to bring together," from *re-* "re-" + *approcher* "to approach"]

rap·scal·lion \rap-ˈskal-yən\ *n* **:** RASCAL 1, SCAMP [alteration of earlier *rascallion,* from *rascal*]

rap sheet *n* **:** a police arrest record especially for an individual

rapt \ˈrapt\ *adj* **1 :** carried away with emotion ‹a *rapt* audience› **2 :** wholly absorbed ‹listened with *rapt* attention› [Latin *raptus,* past participle of *rapere* "to seize, sweep away"] — **rapt·ly** *adv* — **rapt·ness** \ˈrapt-nəs, ˈrap-\ *n*

rap·tor \ˈrap-tər, -ˌtȯr\ *n* **:** BIRD OF PREY [derived from Latin *raptor* "plunderer," from *rapere* "to seize"]

rap·to·ri·al \rap-ˈtōr-ē-əl, -ˈtȯr-\ *adj* **1 :** adapted to seize prey **2 :** of, relating to, or being a bird of prey

rap·ture \ˈrap-chər\ *n* **:** a deeply moving sense of joy, delight, or love — **rap·tur·ous** \ˈrap-chə-rəs, ˈrap-shrəs\ *adj* — **rap·tur·ous·ly** *adv* — **rap·tur·ous·ness** *n*

ra·ra avis \ˌrar-ə-ˈā-vəs, ˌrer-; ˌrär-ə-ˈäwəs\ *n, pl* **ra·ra avis·es** \-ˈā-və-səz\ *or* **ra·rae aves** \ˌrär-ˌī-ˈä-ˌwās\ **:** a rare person or thing **:** RARITY [Latin, "rare bird"]

[1]**rare** \ˈraər, ˈreər\ *adj* **1 :** not thick or dense **:** THIN ‹the *rare* atmosphere at high altitudes› **2 :** unusually fine **:** EXCELLENT, SPLENDID ‹a person of *rare* charm› **3 :** seldom occurring or found **:** very uncommon **4 :** valuable because of scarcity ‹a collection of *rare* books› [Latin *rarus*] — **rare·ness** *n*

[2]**rare** *adj* **:** cooked so that the inside is still red ‹*rare* roast beef› [Old English *hrēre* "lightly boiled"]

rare bird *n* **:** RARA AVIS

rare·bit \ˈraər-bət, ˈreər-\ *n* **:** WELSH RABBIT [by alteration]

rare earth element *n* **:** any of a series of metallic elements that include the lanthanides and sometimes yttrium and scandium

rar·e·fac·tion \ˌrar-ə-ˈfak-shən, ˌrer-\ *n* **:** the act or process of rarefying **:** the state of being rarefied [Medieval Latin *rarefactio,* from Latin *rarefacere* "to rarefy"] — **rar·e·fac·tion·al** \-shnəl, -shən-l\ *adj*

rar·e·fy *also* **rar·i·fy** \ˈrar-ə-ˌfī, ˈrer-\ *vb* **-fied; -fy·ing 1 :** to make or become thin, porous, or less dense **2 :** to make or become more spiritual, refined, or abstruse [Latin *rarefacere,* from *rarus* "rare" + *facere* "to make"]

rare·ly \ˈraər-lē, ˈreər-\ *adv* **1 :** not often **:** SELDOM **2 :** with rare skill **:** EXCELLENTLY **3 :** UNUSUALLY ‹a *rarely* fine view›

rare·ripe \-ˌrīp\ *n* **:** an early ripening fruit or vegetable [English dialect *rare* "early" + *ripe*]

rar·ing \-ing\ *adj* **:** full of enthusiasm or eagerness ‹ready and *raring* to go› [from English dialect *rare* "to rear," alteration of English *rear*]

rar·i·ty \ˈrar-ət-ē, ˈrer-\ *n, pl* **-ties 1 :** the quality, state, or fact of being rare **2 :** one that is rare ‹black pearls are *rarities*›

ras·cal \ˈras-kəl\ *n* **1 :** a mean, unprincipled, or dishonest person **:** ROGUE **2 :** a mischievous person or animal [Middle English *rascaile* "foot soldiers, commoners, worthless person," from Medieval French *rascaille*]

ras·cal·i·ty \ra-ˈskal-ət-ē\ *n, pl* **-ties :** the act, actions, or character of a rascal

ras·cal·ly \ˈras-kə-lē\ *adj* **:** of or characteristic of a rascal ‹a *rascally* trick› — **rascally** *adv*

[1]**rash** \ˈrash\ *adj* **:** marked by or resulting from being too hasty or reckless ‹a *rash* decision› [Middle English, *rasch* "quick"] ***synonyms*** see DARING — **rash·ly** *adv* — **rash·ness** *n*

[2]**rash** *n* **:** a breaking out of the skin with red spots **:** ERUPTION [obsolete French *rache* "scurf," derived from Latin *rasus,* past participle of *radere* "to scrape, shave"]

rash·er \ˈrash-ər\ *n* **:** a thin slice of bacon or ham cut for broiling or frying; *also* **:** a portion consisting of several such slices [perhaps from obsolete *rash* "to cut," from Middle English *rashen*]

[1]**rasp** \ˈrasp\ *vb* **1 :** to rub with or as if with a rough file ‹*rasp* off a rough edge› **2 :** to grate harshly upon **:** IRRITATE ‹a voice that *rasps* the ear› **3 :** to speak or utter in a grating tone ‹*rasp* out a complaint› **4 :** to produce a grating sound [Middle English *raspen*] — **rasp·er** *n*

[2]**rasp** *n* **1 :** a coarse file with cutting points instead of lines **2 a :** an act of rasping **b :** a rasping sound, sensation, or effect

rasp·ber·ry \ˈraz-ˌber-ē, -bə-rē, -brē\ *n* **1 a :** any of various black or red edible berries that consist of numerous small drupes on a fleshy receptacle and are rounder and smaller than the related blackberries **b :** a usually prickly plant that bears raspberries **2 :** a sound of contempt made by protruding the tongue between the lips and expelling air so forcibly as to produce a vibration [English dialect *rasp* "raspberry" + English *berry*]

raspberry 1a

raspy \ˈras-pē\ *adj* **rasp·i·er; -est** **1 :** HARSH, GRATING ⟨spoke with a *raspy* twang⟩ **2 :** IRRITABLE 1

¹rat \ˈrat\ *n* **1 :** any of various gnawing rodents that have a long usually nearly hairless tail and are distinguished from the related mice chiefly by larger size **2 :** a person who betrays or deserts friends or associates **3 :** a person who spends much time in a specified place ⟨a mall *rat*⟩ [Old English *ræt*] — **rat-like** \-ˌlīk\ *adj*

²rat *vb* **rat·ted; rat·ting** **1 :** to desert, betray, or inform on one's associates **2 :** to catch or hunt rats

rat·able *or* **rate·able** \ˈrāt-ə-bəl\ *adj* **:** capable of being rated, estimated, or apportioned — **rat·ably** \-blē\ *adv*

rat cheese *n* **:** CHEDDAR

¹ratch·et \ˈrach-ət\ *n* **1 :** a mechanism that consists of a bar or wheel having inclined teeth into which a pawl drops so as to allow motion in one direction only **2 :** a pawl or detent for holding or propelling a ratchet wheel [alteration of earlier *rochet,* from French, from Middle French *rocquet* "ratchet, bobbin," of Germanic origin]

R ratchet 1

²ratchet *vb* **:** to move or cause to move by steps or degrees ⟨tried to *ratchet* down the debt⟩

¹rate \ˈrāt\ *vt* **:** to scold violently **:** BERATE [Middle English *raten*]

²rate *n* **1 :** reckoned value **:** VALUATION **2 a :** a fixed ratio between two things **b** (1) **:** a charge, payment, or price fixed according to a ratio, scale, or standard ⟨the tax *rate*⟩ (2) *British* **:** a local tax **3 a :** a quantity, amount, or degree of something measured per unit of something else ⟨the unemployment *rate*⟩ **b :** an amount of payment or charge based on another amount ⟨interest at the *rate* of six percent⟩ **4 :** relative condition or quality **:** CLASS [Medieval French, from Medieval Latin *rata,* from Latin *pro rata parte* "according to a fixed proportion"] — **at any rate :** in any case **:** at least

³rate *vb* **1 :** CONSIDER, REGARD ⟨was *rated* a good pianist⟩ **2 :** to set an estimate or value on ⟨*rate* houses for tax purposes⟩ **3 :** to determine the rank, class, or position of **:** GRADE ⟨*rate* a movie⟩ **4 :** to have a rating or rank **:** be classed ⟨*rates* high in math⟩ **5 :** to set a rate on **6 :** to have a right to **:** DESERVE ⟨she *rated* special privileges⟩

rate of exchange : the amount of one currency that will buy a given amount of another

rate·pay·er \ˈrāt-ˌpā-ər\ *n, British* **:** TAXPAYER

rat·er \ˈrāt-ər\ *n* **1 :** one that rates; *esp* **:** a person who estimates or determines a rating **2 :** one having a specified rating or class — usually used in combination ⟨first-*rater*⟩

rath·er \ˈrath-ər, ˈrəth-, ˈräth-\ *adv* **1 :** with better reason **:** more properly ⟨to be pitied *rather* than blamed⟩ **2 :** more willingly **:** PREFERABLY ⟨I would *rather* not go⟩ **3 :** more correctly speaking ⟨my father, or *rather* my stepfather⟩ **4 :** on the contrary **:** INSTEAD ⟨things did not turn out well; *rather,* they turned out very badly⟩ **5 :** in some degree **:** SOMEWHAT ⟨*rather* cold today⟩ [Old English *hrathor,* comparative of *hrathe* "quickly"]

¹rather than *conj* **1** — used with the infinitive form of a verb to indicate negation or a contrary choice or wish ⟨*rather than* continue the argument, he walked away⟩ ⟨chose to sing *rather than* play violin⟩ **2 :** and not ⟨happy *rather than* sad⟩

²rather than *prep* **:** INSTEAD OF ⟨*rather than* being pleased, she was angry⟩

raths·kel·ler \ˈräts-ˌkel-ər, ˈrats-, ˈraths-\ *n* **:** a usually basement tavern or restaurant [obsolete German (now *Ratskeller*), "city-hall basement restaurant," from *Rat* "council" + *Keller* "cellar"]

rat·i·fy \ˈrat-ə-ˌfī\ *vt* **-fied; -fy·ing :** to approve and sanction formally **:** CONFIRM ⟨*ratify* a treaty⟩ ⟨*ratify* the decision of a subordinate⟩ [Medieval French *ratifier,* from Medieval Latin *ratificare,* from Latin *ratus* "determined," from past participle of *reri* "to calculate"] — **rat·i·fi·ca·tion** \ˌrat-ə-fə-ˈkā-shən\ *n* — **rat·i·fi·er** \ˈrat-ə-ˌfī-ər, -ˌfīr\ *n*

rat·ing \ˈrāt-ing\ *n* **1 a :** a classification according to grade or rank **b :** a naval specialist classification **2** *chiefly British* **:** a naval enlisted man **3 :** a relative estimate or evaluation **:** STANDING ⟨a good credit *rating*⟩

ra·tio \ˈrā-shō, -shē-ˌō\ *n, pl* **ra·tios** **1 :** the quotient of two numbers or mathematical expressions ⟨the *ratio* of 6 to 3 may be expressed as 6:3, $\frac{6}{3}$, and 2⟩ **2 :** the relationship in quantity, amount, or size between two or more things ⟨women outnumbered men in the *ratio* of three to one⟩ [Latin, "computation, reason"]

ra·ti·o·ci·na·tion \ˌrat-ē-ˌōs-n-ˈā-shən, ˌrash-ē-, -ˌäs-\ *n* **1 :** the process of exact thinking **:** REASONING **2 :** a reasoned train of thought [Latin *ratiocinatio,* from *ratiocinari* "to reckon," from *ratio* "computation, reason"] — **ra·ti·o·ci·na·tive** \-ˈōs-n-ˌāt-iv, -ˈäs-\ *adj*

¹ra·tion \ˈrash-ən, ˈrā-shən\ *n* **1 a :** a food allowance for one day **b :** FOOD, PROVISIONS — usually used in plural ⟨had to pack supplies and *rations* on their backs⟩ **2 :** a share especially as determined by supply or allotment by authority ⟨a wartime meat *ration*⟩ [French, from Latin *ratio* "computation, reason"]

²ration *vt* **ra·tioned; ra·tion·ing** \ˈrash-ning, ˈrāsh-, -ə-ning\ **1 :** to supply with rations ⟨*ration* cattle⟩ **2 a :** to distribute or allot as a ration ⟨the government *rationed* gas⟩ **b :** to use or allot sparingly ⟨the doctor *rations* a diabetic's sugar intake⟩

¹ra·tio·nal \ˈrash-nəl, -ən-l\ *adj* **1 a :** having reason or understanding ⟨*rational* beings⟩ **b :** relating to, based on, or agreeable to reason **:** REASONABLE ⟨*rational* behavior⟩ **2 :** relating to, consisting of, or being rational numbers ⟨a *rational* root to the equation⟩ [Latin *rationalis,* from *ratio* "computation, reason"] — **ra·tio·nal·i·ty** \ˌrash-ə-ˈnal-ət-ē\ *n* — **ra·tio·nal·ly** \ˈrash-nə-lē, -ən-l-ē\ *adv*

²rational *n* **:** something rational; *esp* **:** RATIONAL NUMBER

ra·tio·nale \ˌrash-ə-ˈnal\ *n* **:** a basic reason or explanation [Latin, neuter of *rationalis* "rational"]

ra·tio·nal·ism \ˈrash-nə-ˌliz-əm, -ən-l-ˌiz-\ *n* **:** the theory or practice of guiding one's actions and opinions solely by what seems reasonable — **ra·tio·nal·ist** \-nə-ləst, -ən-l-əst\ *n* — **rationalist** *or* **ra·tio·nal·is·tic** \ˌrash-nə-ˈlis-tik, -ən-l-ˈis-\ *adj* — **ra·tio·nal·is·ti·cal·ly** \-ti-kə-lē, -klē\ *adv*

ra·tio·nal·ize \ˈrash-nə-ˌlīz, -ən-l-ˌīz\ *vb* **1 a :** to bring into agreement with reason or cause something to seem reasonable **b :** to create an excuse or more attractive reason for ⟨*rationalized* his inability to complete the job⟩ **2 :** to free (a mathematical equation) from irrational expressions ⟨*rationalize* a denominator⟩ — **ra·tio·nal·i·za·tion** \ˌrash-nə-lə-ˈzā-shən, -ən-l-ə-\ *n*

rational number *n* **:** a number that can be expressed as a whole number or the quotient of two whole numbers

rat·line \ˈrat-lən\ *n* **:** one of the small cross ropes attached to the shrouds of a ship so as to form the steps of a rope ladder [Middle English *radelyng*]

ratline

rat snake *n* **:** any of various large nonpoisonous snakes that eat rodents and birds and that kill their prey by squeezing and suffocating it

rat·tan \ra-ˈtan, rə-\ *n* **1 a** : a climbing palm with very long tough stems **b** : a part of the stem used especially for furniture, wickerwork, and walking sticks **2** : a rattan cane or switch [Malay *rotan*]

rat·ter \ˈrat-ər\ *n* : one that catches rats; *esp* : a rat-catching dog or cat

[1]**rat·tle** \ˈrat-l\ *vb* **rat·tled; rat·tling** \ˈrat-ling, -l-ing\ **1** : to make or cause to make a rattle **2** : to chatter incessantly and aimlessly **3** : to say or do in a brisk lively fashion ⟨*rattled* off the answers⟩ **4** : to disturb the composure of : UPSET ⟨*rattled* the speaker with questions⟩ [Middle English *ratelen*]

[2]**rattle** *n* **1** : a series of short sharp sounds : CLATTER ⟨the *rattle* of hail on a roof⟩ **2** : a device (as a toy) for making a rattling sound **3** : a rattling organ at the end of a rattlesnake's tail made up of horny joints **4** : DEATH RATTLE

rat·tler \ˈrat-lər, -l-ər\ *n* **1** : one that rattles **2** : RATTLESNAKE

rat·tle·snake \ˈrat-l-ˌsnāk\ *n* : any of several venomous American snakes that are pit vipers and have horny interlocking joints at the end of the tail that rattle when shaken

rat·tle·trap \-ˌtrap\ *n* : something rattly or rickety; *esp* : an old car — **rattletrap** *adj*

rat·tling \ˈrat-ling, -l-ing\ *adj* : LIVELY, BRISK ⟨moved at a *rattling* pace⟩ — **rat·tling·ly** \ˈrat-ling-lē\ *adv*

rat·tly \ˈrat-lē, -l-ē\ *adj* : likely to rattle : making a rattle ⟨a *rattly* old car⟩

rat·ty \ˈrat-ē\ *adj* **rat·ti·er; -est** **1** : infested with or suggestive of rats **2** : SHABBY, UNKEMPT ⟨a *ratty* old overcoat⟩

rau·cous \ˈrȯ-kəs\ *adj* **1** : disagreeably harsh or strident ⟨a *raucous* voice⟩ **2** : boisterously disorderly ⟨a *raucous* party⟩ [Latin *raucus* "hoarse"] — **rau·cous·ly** *adv* — **rau·cous·ness** *n*

rau·wol·fia \rau̇-ˈwu̇l-fē-ə, rȯ-\ *n* : the root of an Indian tree related to the dogbanes from which medicinal substances (as reserpine) are obtained; *also* : an extract of the root **2** : the tree that yields rauwolfia [New Latin, a genus of trees, from Leonhard *Rauwolf,* died 1596, German botanist]

[1]**rav·age** \ˈrav-ij\ *n* **1** : an act or practice of ravaging **2** : damage resulting from ravaging ⟨the *ravage* of time⟩ [French, from *ravir* "to ravish"]

[2]**ravage** *vb* **rav·aged; rav·ag·ing** **1** : to wreak havoc on : affect destructively ⟨a land *ravaged* by war⟩ **2** : to commit destructive actions — **rav·age·ment** \-mənt\ *n* — **rav·ag·er** *n*

synonyms RAVAGE, DEVASTATE, WASTE mean to lay waste by plundering or destroying. RAVAGE suggests violent often repeated or continuing pillaging and destruction ⟨a destructive pest *ravaging* the crops⟩. DEVASTATE implies causing complete ruin and desolation over a wide area ⟨an earthquake *devastated* the city⟩. WASTE may suggest destruction as a result of a slow process rather than sudden and violent action ⟨years of drought had *wasted* the area⟩.

[1]**rave** \ˈrāv\ *vb* **1** : to talk irrationally in or as if in delirium **2** : to declaim wildly **3** : to talk or utter with extreme enthusiasm [Middle English *raven*] — **rav·er** *n*

[2]**rave** *n* **1** : an act or instance of raving **2** : an extravagantly favorable criticism

[1]**rav·el** \ˈrav-əl\ *vb* **rav·eled** *or* **rav·elled; rav·el·ing** *or* **rav·el·ling** \ˈrav-ling, -ə-ling\ **1** : to separate or undo the texture of : UNRAVEL **2** : to make plain : SIMPLIFY **3** : ENTANGLE, CONFUSE [Dutch *rafelen,* from *rafel* "loose thread"] — **rav·el·er** *or* **rav·el·ler** \ˈrav-lər, -ə-lər\ *n*

[2]**ravel** *n* : something that is raveled

rav·el·ing *or* **rav·el·ling** \ˈrav-ling, -ə-ling, -lən\ *n* : something raveled or frayed; *esp* : a thread raveled out of a fabric

[1]**ra·ven** \ˈrā-vən\ *n* : a bird of Europe, Asia, northern Africa, and America that has glossy black feathers and is larger than the related crow [Old English *hræfn*]

[2]**raven** *adj* : black or glossy like a raven ⟨*raven* hair⟩

rav·en·ous \ˈrav-ə-nəs\ *adj* : very eager for food, satisfaction, or gratification ⟨a *ravenous* appetite⟩ [Medieval French *ravineus* "rushing, rapacious," from *raviner* "to rush forward, ravish," from *ravine* "rapine," from Latin *rapina*] — **rav·en·ous·ly** *adv* — **rav·en·ous·ness** *n*

ra·vine \rə-ˈvēn\ *n* : a small narrow steep-sided valley larger than a gully, smaller than a canyon, and usually worn by running water [French, "mountain torrent," from Middle French, "rapine, rush," from Latin *rapina* "rapine"]

rav·i·o·li \ˌrav-ē-ˈō-lē, ˌräv-\ *n, pl* **ravioli** *also* **raviolis** : little cases of dough containing a filling (as of meat or cheese) [Italian, from Italian dialect *raviolo* "little turnip," from *rava* "turnip," from Latin *rapa*]

rav·ish \ˈrav-ish\ *vt* **1** : to seize and take away by violence **2** : to overcome with emotion **3** : RAPE 2 **4** : PLUNDER, ROB [Medieval French *raviss-,* stem of *ravir* "to ravish," from Latin *rapere* "to seize"] — **rav·ish·er** *n* — **rav·ish·ment** \-mənt\ *n*

rav·ish·ing \ˈrav-i-shing\ *adj* : unusually attractive, pleasing, or striking — **rav·ish·ing·ly** \-shing-lē\ *adv*

[1]**raw** \ˈrȯ\ *adj* **raw·er** \ˈrȯ-ər, ˈrȯr\; **raw·est** \ˈrȯ-əst\ **1** : not cooked **2 a** : being in or nearly in the natural state ⟨*raw* furs⟩: not processed or manufactured ⟨*raw* milk⟩ **b** : not being in polished, finished, or processed form ⟨*raw* data⟩ **c** : not diluted or blended ⟨*raw* spirits⟩ **3 a** : having the surface abraded or chafed ⟨*raw* red hands⟩ **b** : very sore or irritated ⟨a *raw* sore throat⟩ **4 a** : lacking experience or understanding : GREEN ⟨a *raw* recruit⟩ **b** : lacking comforts or refinements ⟨a *raw* frontier village⟩ **c** : VULGAR, COARSE ⟨a *raw* story⟩ **5** : disagreeably damp or cold ⟨a *raw* blustery day⟩ [Old English *hrēaw*] — **raw·ly** \ˈrȯ-lē\ *adv* — **raw·ness** *n*

[2]**raw** *n* : a raw place or state — **in the raw** **1** : in a natural or crude state ⟨life *in the raw*⟩ **2** : NAKED ⟨slept *in the raw*⟩

raw·boned \ˈrȯ-ˈbōnd\ *adj* : extremely thin : GAUNT ***synonyms*** see LANK

raw deal *n* : an instance of unfair treatment

[1]**raw·hide** \ˈrȯ-ˌhīd\ *n* **1** : a whip of untanned hide **2** : untanned cattle skin

[2]**rawhide** *vt* **-hid·ed; -hid·ing** : to whip or drive with or as if with a rawhide

raw material *n* : material (as natural resources in an unprocessed state) from which useful things can be produced or manufactured; *also* : something that can be improved, developed, or elaborated ⟨collect *raw material* for writing a story⟩

[1]**ray** \ˈrā\ *n* : any of numerous flat broad cartilaginous fishes (as sting rays and skates) that typically live on the sea bottom and have a long narrow tail and their eyes on the upper surface of their bodies [Medieval French *raie,* from Latin *raia*]

[2]**ray** *n* **1 a** : one of the lines of light that appear to radiate from a bright object **b** : a thin beam of radiant energy (as light) **c** : a stream of particles traveling (as in radioactive phenomena) in the same line **2** : light cast by rays : RADIANCE **3** : a thin line suggesting a ray: as **a** : any of a group of lines diverging from a common center **b** : HALF LINE **4** : a plant or animal structure that resembles a ray: as **a** : VASCULAR RAY **b** : RAY FLOWER **c** : one of the bony rods in the fin of a fish **5** : PARTICLE, TRACE ⟨a *ray* of hope⟩ [Medieval French *rai,* from Latin *radius* "rod, spoke, ray"]

[3]**ray** *vb* **1** : to send out rays of or as if of light **2** : RADIATE 4 **3** : to subject to radiation

rayed \ˈrād\ *adj* : having rays or ray flowers

ray flower *n* : one of the flowers with long flat petals that grow on the outer edge of the head of a plant (as a daisy) of the composite family — called also *ray floret*; compare DISK FLOWER

ray·less \ˈrā-ləs\ *adj* : lacking rays or ray flowers

ray·on \ˈrā-ˌän\ *n* **1** : any of a group of smooth textile fibers made from cellulosic material by extrusion through minute holes **2** : a rayon yarn, thread, or fabric [derived from [2]*ray*]

raze \ˈrāz\ *vt* : to destroy utterly by tearing down : DEMOLISH ⟨*raze* a building⟩ [Middle English *rasen* "to erase," from Medieval French *raser* "to scrape, erase," from Latin *rasus,* past participle of *radere* "to scrape, shave"]

ra·zor \ˈrā-zər\ *n* : a sharp cutting instrument used especially to shave off hair [Medieval French *rasur,* from *raser,* "to scrape, shave, erase"] — **razor** *adj*

ra·zor·back \-ˌbak\ *n* : a thin-bodied long-legged feral hog chiefly of the southeastern U.S. having long stiff hairs down the center of its back

razor clam *n* : any of numerous marine bivalve mollusks having a long narrow thin shell

razz \ˈraz\ *vt* : to tease mockingly : KID [*raspberry*]

raz·zle–daz·zle \ˌraz-əl-ˈdaz-əl\ *n* **1** : a state of confusion or hilarity **2** : a complex maneuver (as in sports) designed to confuse an opponent **3** : a confusing or colorful often gaudy action or display [reduplication of *dazzle*] — **razzle–dazzle** *adj*

RBI \ˌär-ˌbē-ˈī, ˈrib-ē\ *n, pl* **RBIs** *or* **RBI** : a run in baseball that is driven in by a batter

-rd *symbol* — used after the figure 3 to indicate the ordinal number third ⟨3*rd*⟩ ⟨53*rd*⟩

[1]**re** \ˈrā\ *n* : the 2nd note of the diatonic scale [Medieval Latin]

²re \ˈrā, ˈrē\ *prep* **:** with regard to **:** IN RE [Latin, ablative of *res* "thing"]

re- *prefix* **1 :** again **:** anew ⟨*re*appear⟩ **2 :** back **:** backward ⟨*re*call⟩ [Latin *re-, red-* "back, again, against"]

reaccelerate
reaccept
reacclimatize
reaccredit
reaccreditation
reacquaint
reacquire
reacquisition
reactivate
reactivation
readdress
readjust
readjustment
readmission
readmit
readopt
reaffirm
reaffirmation
reaffix
reallocate
reallocation
reanalysis
reanalyze
reanimate
reanimation
reannex
reannexation
reappear
reappearance
reapplication
reapply
reappoint
reappointment
reappraisal
reappraise
reappropriate
reapprove
reargue
reargument
rearousal
rearouse
rearrest
reascend
reascent
reassemble
reassembly
reassert
reassertion
reassess
reassessment
reassign
reassignment
reassume
reattach
reattachment
reattain
reattempt
reattribute
reattribution
reauthorize
reawaken
rebait
rebalance
rebaptism
rebaptize
rebid
rebind
reboard
reboil
rebook
reboot
reburial
rebury
rebuy
recalculate
recalculation
recalibrate
recalibration
recentralization
recertification
recertify
rechannel
recheck
rechristen
recirculate
recirculation
reclassification
reclassify
recodification
recodify
recolonization
recolonize
recolor
recommence
recommencement
recommission
recompilation
recompile
recomputation
recompute
reconceive
reconception
recondense
reconnect
reconnection
reconquer
reconquest
reconsecrate
reconsecration
reconsolidate
recontact
recontaminate
recontamination
recontour
reconvene
reconvict
reconviction
reconvince
recopy
recross
recultivate
rededicate
rededication
redeliver
redelivery
redeposit
redetermination
redetermine
redigestion
rediscover
rediscovery
redissolve
redistill
redivide
redivision
redraft
redraw
reeligibility
reeligible
reemerge
reemergence
reemission
reemit
reemphasis
reemphasize
reemploy
reengage
reengagement
reengrave
reenlist
reenlistment
reenroll
reequip
reerect
reescalate
reescalation
reestablish
reestablishment
reestimate
reevaluate
reevaluation
reexamination
reexamine
reexperience
reexplore
reexport
reexportation
reface
refeed
refight
refind
refire
refix
refloat
refold
reformat
reformulate
reformulation
refortification
refortify
reframe
refreeze
refry
regather
regild
reglaze
regrind
regroove
reheat
rehire
rehospitalization
rehospitalize
rehumanize
reidentify
reignite
reignition
reimmerse
reimplant
reimplantation
reimpose
reimposition
reincorporate
reincorporation
reindict
reindictment
reinfestation
reinflate
reinflation
reinitiate
reinject
reinjection
reinjure
reinoculate
reinoculation
reinsert
reinsertion
reinspect
reinspection
reinstall
reinstallation
reinstitute
reinstitutionalize
reinter
reinterment
reintroduce
reintroduction
reinvade
reinvasion
reinvestigate
reinvestigation
reinvigorate
reinvigoration
rejudge
rekey
rekeyboard
rekindle
reknit
relabel
relandscape
relaunch
relearn
relend
relicense
relight
reload
reloadable
relock
relubricate
relubrication
remeasure
remeasurement
remeet
remelt
remigration
remilitarization
remilitarize
remobilization
remobilize
remoisten
remold
remotivate
remotivation
rename
renationalization
renationalize
renumber
reobserve
reoccupation
reoccupy
reoccur
reoccurrence
reoperate
reoperation
reorchestrate
reorchestration
reorient
reorientate
reorientation
repack
repaint
repattern
repave
rephotograph
rephrase
replan
replaster
replot
repolish
repoll
repopularize
repopulate
repopulation
repressurize
reprice
repurchase
reread
rereading
rerecord
reregister
reregistration
reroof
reroute
resample
resaw
reschool
rescore
rescreen
reseal
resealable
reseat
resee
resegregate
resegregation
resell
reseller
resentence
resettle
resettlement
resew
reshipment
reshoot
reshow
resilver
resoak
resocialization
resocialize
resod
resolder
resolidification
resolidify
resow
respray
restage
restamp
restimulate
restimulation
restock
restrengthen
restudy
restyle
resubmission
resubmit
resummon
resupply
resurvey
resynthesis
resynthesize
retag
retarget
retaste
reteach
retest
rethread
retie
retighten
retransfer
retransform
retransformation
retransmission
retransmit
retry
retune
retype
reunification
reunify
reupholster
reutilization
reutilize
revaccinate
revaccination
revalidate
revalidation
rewarm
rewash
reweave
reweigh
rewet
rewire
rewrap

're \ər, r\ *vb* **:** ARE ⟨what*'re* you doing⟩ ⟨they*'re* very nice⟩

re·ab·sorb \ˌrē-əb-ˈsȯrb, -ˈzȯrb\ *vt* **:** to absorb again; *esp* **:** RESORB — **re·ab·sorp·tion** \-ˈsȯrp-shən, -ˈzȯrp-\ *n* — **re·ab·sorp·tive** \-ˈsȯrp-tiv, -ˈzȯrp-\ *adj*

¹reach \ˈrēch\ *vb* **1 a :** to stretch out **:** EXTEND ⟨*reach* out your hand⟩ **b :** to move the arm so as to make a grab ⟨*reached* for a knife⟩ **c :** to touch or grasp by extending a part of the body or an object ⟨couldn't *reach* the apple on the tree⟩ **2 a :** to go as far as ⟨the shadow *reached* the wall⟩ **b :** to extend continuously ⟨the field *reaches* to the highway⟩ **c :** to go or function effectively ⟨as far as the eye can *reach*⟩ **3 a :** to arrive at **:** come to ⟨*reached* home late⟩; *also* **:** ACHIEVE ⟨*reached* an understanding⟩ **b :** to get or be delivered to ⟨your message *reached* me⟩ **4 :** to communicate with ⟨tried to *reach* you by phone⟩; *also* **:** to make an impression on **:** INFLUENCE ⟨couldn't *reach* his audience⟩ **5 :** to hand over **:** PASS ⟨*reach* me the salt⟩ **6 :** to sail on a reach [Old English *rǣcan*] — **reach·able** \ˈrē-chə-bəl\ *adj* — **reach·er** *n*

²reach *n* **1 :** a continuous unbroken stretch or expanse; *esp* **:** a

\ə\ abut	\au̇\ out	\i\ tip	\ȯ\ saw	\u̇\ foot
\ər\ further	\ch\ chin	\ī\ life	\ȯi\ coin	\y\ yet
\a\ mat	\e\ pet	\j\ job	\th\ thin	\yü\ few
\ā\ take	\ē\ easy	\ng\ sing	\th\ this	\yu̇\ cure
\ä\ cot, cart	\g\ go	\ō\ bone	\ü\ food	\zh\ vision

straight portion of a stream or river **2 a :** the action or an act of reaching **b :** the distance one can reach ⟨kept it in easy *reach*⟩ **c :** ability to stretch so as touch something ⟨you have a long *reach*⟩ **d :** the ability to reach something as if with the hands ⟨a new car is beyond our *reach*⟩ **3 :** a course sailed approximately at right angles to the wind **4 :** LEVEL 4 ⟨the upper *reaches* of government⟩

re•act \rē-ˈakt\ *vb* **1 :** to exert a reciprocal or counteracting force or influence — often used with *on* or *upon* **2 :** to change in response to a stimulus **3 :** to act in opposition to a force or influence — usually used with *against* ⟨*reacted* against unfair treatment⟩ **4 :** to move or tend in a reverse direction ⟨prices *reacted* strongly after a brief drop⟩ **5 :** to undergo or cause to undergo chemical reaction [New Latin *reactus,* past participle of *reagere* "to react," from Latin *re-* + *agere* "to act"]

re•ac•tance \rē-ˈak-təns\ *n* **:** the part of the impedance of an alternating-current circuit due to capacitance and inductance and expressed in ohms

re•ac•tant \-tənt\ *n* **:** a substance that enters into and is changed by a chemical reaction

re•ac•tion \rē-ˈak-shən\ *n* **1 a :** the act or process or an instance of reacting **b :** tendency toward a former especially outmoded political or social order or policy **2 a :** a response to some treatment, situation, or stimulus ⟨her angry *reaction* to the news⟩ **b :** bodily response to or activity aroused by a stimulus; *esp* **:** the response of tissues to a foreign substance (as an allergen or infective agent) **3 :** the force that a body subjected to the action of a force from another body exerts in the opposite direction **4 a :** chemical transformation or change **:** the action between atoms or molecules to form one or more new substances **b :** a process involving change in atomic nuclei — **re•ac•tion•al** \-shnəl, -shən-l\ *adj* — **re•ac•tion•al•ly** \-ē\ *adv*

[1]**re•ac•tion•ary** \rē-ˈak-shə-ˌner-ē\ *adj* **:** relating to, marked by, or favoring reaction; *esp* **:** ultraconservative in politics

[2]**reactionary** *n, pl* **-ar•ies :** a reactionary person

reaction time *n* **:** the time between the beginning of a stimulus and an individual's reaction to it

re•ac•ti•vate \rē-ˈak-tə-ˌvāt, ˈrē-\ *vb* **:** to make or become activated again — **re•ac•ti•va•tion** \ˌrē-ˌak-tə-ˈvā-shən\ *n*

re•ac•tive \rē-ˈak-tiv\ *adj* **1 :** of or relating to reaction or reactance **2 :** reacting or tending to react — **re•ac•tive•ly** *adv* — **re•ac•tive•ness** *n* — **re•ac•tiv•i•ty** \ˌrē-ˌak-ˈtiv-ət-ē\ *n*

re•ac•tor \rē-ˈak-tər\ *n* **1 :** one that reacts **2 a :** a vat for an industrial chemical reaction **b :** a device for the controlled release of nuclear energy (as for producing heat)

[1]**read** \ˈrēd\ *vb* **read** \ˈred\; **read•ing** \ˈrēd-ing\ **1 a** (1) **:** to go over systematically by sight or touch to take in and understand the meaning of (as letters or symbols) (2) **:** to study the movements of (a speaker's lips) and so understand what is being said (3) **:** to utter aloud the printed or written words of (4) **:** to understand the written form of ⟨*reads* French⟩ **b :** to learn from what one has seen in writing or printing ⟨*read* that they got married⟩ ⟨*read* about your promotion⟩ **c :** to deliver aloud by or as if by reading **d :** to make a study of ⟨*read* law⟩ **e :** PROOFREAD **f :** to hear and understand (a speaker or a transmission) in radio communications ⟨how do you *read* me — over⟩ **2 a :** to interpret the meaning or significance of ⟨*read* palms⟩ **b :** FORETELL, PREDICT ⟨able to *read* his fortune⟩ **3 a :** to discover by interpreting outward expression or signs ⟨*read* guilt in their faces⟩ **b :** to note the action or characteristic of in order to anticipate what will happen ⟨a good canoeist *reads* the rapids⟩ **4 a :** to attribute a meaning to **:** UNDERSTAND ⟨how do you *read* this passage⟩ **b :** to attribute as an assumption or conjecture ⟨*read* a nonexistent meaning into my words⟩ **5 :** to use as a substitute for or in preference to another word or phrase in a particular passage, text, or version ⟨*read* "hurry" for "harry"⟩ **6 :** INDICATE ⟨the thermometer *reads* zero⟩ **7 a :** to sense the meaning of (coded information) ⟨data must be *read* before it can be processed⟩ **b :** to sense the coded information on ⟨*read* a CD-ROM⟩ **c :** to cause to be read and transferred to storage ⟨*read* data into memory⟩ **8 :** to consist of specific words, phrases, or symbols ⟨the passage *reads* differently in older versions⟩ [Old English *rǣdan* "to advise, interpret, read"] — **read•abil•i•ty** \ˌrēd-ə-ˈbil-ət-ē\ *n* — **read•able** \ˈrēd-ə-bəl\ *adj* — **read•able•ness** *n* — **read•ably** \-blē\ *adv* — **read between the lines :** to understand more than is directly stated — **read the riot act 1 :** to give an order or warning to cease something **2 :** to give a severe reprimand

[2]**read** \ˈred\ *adj* **:** taught or informed by reading

read•er \ˈrēd-ər\ *n* **1 :** one that reads **2 a :** a device that makes a readable image ⟨a microfiche *reader*⟩ **b :** a device that scans recorded data for input ⟨a card *reader*⟩ **3 :** a book for instruction and practice especially in reading

read•er•ship \-ˌship\ *n* **1 :** the office or position of a reader **2 :** the mass or a particular group of readers

read•i•ly \ˈred-l-ē\ *adv* **:** in a ready manner: as **a :** WILLINGLY ⟨*readily* accepted advice⟩ **b :** EASILY ⟨reasons that were *readily* understood⟩

read•ing \ˈrēd-ing\ *n* **1 a :** material read or for reading **b :** extent of material read ⟨a person of vast *reading*⟩ **2 a :** a particular version **b :** data indicated by an instrument ⟨the thermometer *reading* was 70 degrees⟩ **3 a :** a particular interpretation of something (as a law) **b :** a particular performance of something (as a musical work) **4 :** an indication of a certain state of affairs ⟨a study to get some *reading* of shoppers' preferences⟩

reading desk *n* **:** a desk to support a book in a convenient position for a standing reader

read–only memory *n* **:** ROM

read•out \ˈrēd-ˌau̇t\ *n* **1 :** the process of removing information from an automatic device (as a computer) and displaying it in an understandable form **2 :** an electronic device that displays information (as data from a calculator); *also* **:** the information displayed

[1]**ready** \ˈred-ē\ *adj* **read•i•er; -est 1 :** prepared for use or action ⟨dinner is *ready*⟩ **2 :** likely to do something indicated ⟨*ready* to cry⟩ **3 :** WILLING ⟨*ready* to give aid⟩ **4 :** notably dexterous, adroit, or skilled ⟨a *ready* wit⟩ **5 :** PROMPT ⟨a *ready* answer⟩ **6 :** AVAILABLE, HANDY ⟨*ready* money⟩ [Middle English *redy*] — **read•i•ness** \-nəs\ *n*

[2]**ready** *vt* **read•ied; ready•ing :** to make ready

[3]**ready** *n* **:** the state of being ready; *esp* **:** preparation of a gun for immediate aiming or firing

[1]**ready–made** \ˌred-ē-ˈmād\ *adj* **1 :** made beforehand for general sale ⟨*ready-made* clothes⟩ **2 :** lacking individuality

[2]**ready–made** *n* **:** something (as a garment) that is ready-made

ready room *n* **:** a room in which pilots or astronauts are briefed and await takeoff orders

ready–to–wear \ˌred-ēt-ə-ˈwaər, -ˈweər\ *adj* **:** READY-MADE 1

re•agent \rē-ˈā-jənt\ *n* **:** one that reacts or induces a reaction; *esp* **:** a substance that takes part in or brings about a particular chemical reaction ⟨a fixing *reagent* for tissues⟩ ⟨a *reagent* for etching steel⟩ [New Latin *reagens,* present participle of *reagere* "to react"]

[1]**re•al** \ˈri-əl, ˈril, ˈrē-əl, ˈrēl\ *adj* **1 :** of or relating to fixed, permanent, or immovable things (as land or buildings) **2 a :** not artificial, deceptive, or false **:** GENUINE ⟨*real* gold⟩; *also* **:** being exactly what the name implies ⟨a *real* professional⟩ **b** (1) **:** occurring or existing in actuality ⟨a story of *real* life⟩ ⟨saw a *real* live celebrity⟩ (2) **:** of or relating to practical or everyday concerns or activities ⟨left school to live in the *real* world⟩ **c** (1) **:** belonging to or having elements that belong to the set of real numbers ⟨the *real* roots of an equation⟩ (2) **:** taking on only real numbers for values ⟨a *real* variable⟩ **3 :** measured by purchasing power ⟨*real* income⟩ **4 :** ABSOLUTE 4, UTTER ⟨a *real* fiasco⟩ [Medieval French, from Medieval Latin *realis* "relating to things (in law)" and Late Latin *realis* "real, actual," from Latin *res* "thing, fact"] — **re•al•ness** *n* — **for real 1 :** in earnest **:** SERIOUSLY ⟨arguing *for real*⟩ **2 :** free from pretense **:** SINCERE ⟨couldn't believe the offers were *for real*⟩ **3 :** genuinely good or capable of success ⟨not yet sure if this team is *for real*⟩

synonyms REAL, ACTUAL, TRUE mean corresponding to known facts. REAL implies an agreement between what a thing seems to be and what it is ⟨this is a *real* diamond⟩. ACTUAL stresses occurrence or existence as action or fact ⟨the *actual* temperature today is higher than predicted⟩. TRUE implies conforming to what is real or actual ⟨a *true* account of the incident⟩ or to a model or standard ⟨prove oneself a *true* friend⟩.

[2]**real** *n* **:** a real thing; *esp* **:** REAL NUMBER

[3]**real** *adv* **:** VERY ⟨we had a *real* good time⟩

usage *Real* is generally informal and more suitable to speech than writing. It is becoming more common in writing of an informal, conversational style. *Real* is used as an intensifier only and is not interchangeable with *really* except in that use.

[4]**re•al** \rā-ˈäl\ *n, pl* **re•als** *or* **re•ales** \-ˈäl-ās\ **:** the chief former

monetary unit of Spain [Spanish, from *real* "royal," from Latin *regalis*]

[5]**re·al** \rā-ˈäl\ *n, pl* **reals** *or* **reis** \ˈrāsh\ **1 :** the basic monetary unit of Brazil **2 :** a coin or note representing one real [Portuguese, from *real* "royal," from Latin *regalis*]

real estate *n* **:** property in houses and land

re·al·gar \rē-ˈal-ˌgär, -gər\ *n* **:** an orange-red mineral As_4S_4 or AsS consisting of a sulfide of arsenic and having a resinous luster [Medieval Latin, from Catalan, from Arabic *rahj al-ghār* "powder of the mine"]

re·align \ˌrē-ə-ˈlīn\ *vt* **:** to align again; *esp* **:** to reorganize or make new groupings of — **re·align·ment** \-mənt\ *n*

real image *n* **:** an image of an object formed by rays of light coming to a focus (as after passing through a lens or after being reflected by a concave mirror)

re·al·ism \ˈri-ə-ˌliz-əm, ˈrē-ə-\ *n* **1 :** the belief that objects we perceive through our senses are real and have an existence outside our own minds **2 :** the tendency to see situations or difficulties in the light of facts and to deal with them practically **3 :** the representation in literature and art of things as they are in life — **re·al·ist** \-ləst\ *adj or n*

re·al·is·tic \ˌri-ə-ˈlis-tik, ˌrē-ə-\ *adj* **1 :** true to life or nature ⟨a *realistic* painting⟩ **2 :** having or showing an inclination to face facts and to deal with them sensibly ⟨a *realistic* approach⟩ — **re·al·is·ti·cal·ly** \-ti-kə-lē, -klē\ *adv*

re·al·i·ty \rē-ˈal-ət-ē\ *n, pl* **-ties** **1 :** the quality or state of being real **2 a :** someone or something real or actual ⟨our dream became a *reality*⟩ **b :** all real things and events as a totality ⟨trying to escape *reality*⟩ **3 :** television programming that features videos of actual occurrences (as a police chase, stunt, or natural disaster) — **in reality :** in actual fact

re·al·ize \ˈri-ə-ˌlīz, ˈrē-ə-\ *vt* **1 :** to make actual **:** ACCOMPLISH ⟨*realize* a lifelong ambition⟩ **2 :** to convert into money ⟨*realized* their assets⟩ **3 :** to bring or get by sale, investment, or effort **:** GAIN ⟨*realize* a large profit⟩ **4 :** to be aware of ⟨*realized* the danger⟩ — **re·al·iz·able** \ˈri-ə-ˌlī-zə-bəl, ˈrē-ə-\ *adj* — **re·al·i·za·tion** \ˌri-ə-lə-ˈzā-shən, ˌrē-ə-\ *n* — **re·al·iz·er** *n*

real–life *adj* **:** happening in reality **:** based on actual events or situations ⟨*real-life* problems⟩ ⟨a *real-life* drama⟩

re·al·ly \ˈril-ē, ˈrēl-ē, ˈri-ə-lē, ˈrē-ə-lē\ *adv* **1 :** in reality **:** ACTUALLY ⟨didn't *really* mean what I said⟩ **2 :** without question **:** TRULY ⟨a *really* beautiful day⟩ **3 :** VERY 1 ⟨look *really* close⟩ **4 :** to be honest **:** FRANKLY ⟨*really,* you're being ridiculous⟩

realm \ˈrelm\ *n* **1 :** KINGDOM 1 **2 :** SPHERE, DOMAIN ⟨the *realm* of fancy⟩ [Medieval French *realme,* from Latin *regimen* "control"]

real number *n* **:** any of the set of numbers (as –2, 3, ⅞, .25, $\sqrt{2}$, π) that includes the rational numbers and the irrational numbers but not the imaginary numbers

Re·al·tor \ˈrē-əl-tər, ˈrēl-, -ˌtȯr\ *collective mark* — used for a real estate agent who is a member of the National Association of Realtors

re·al·ty \ˈrē-əl-tē, ˈrēl-\ *n* **:** REAL ESTATE [*real* + *-ty* (as in *property*)]

[1]**ream** \ˈrēm\ *n* **1 :** a quantity of paper being variously 480, 500, or 516 sheets **2 :** a great amount — usually used in plural ⟨*reams* of information⟩ [Medieval French *reme,* from Arabic *rizmah,* literally, "bundle"]

[2]**ream** *vt* **1 :** to widen the opening of (a hole) **:** COUNTERSINK **2 :** to shape, enlarge, or smooth out (a hole) with a reamer **3 :** to remove by reaming **4 a :** to press out with a reamer **b :** to press out the juice of (as an orange) with a reamer **5 :** CHEAT 1, VICTIMIZE **6 :** REPRIMAND — often used with *out* [perhaps from Old English *rēman*]

ream·er \ˈrē-mər\ *n* **1 :** a rotating tool with cutting edges for enlarging or shaping a hole **2 :** a juice extractor with a ridged and pointed center rising from a shallow dish

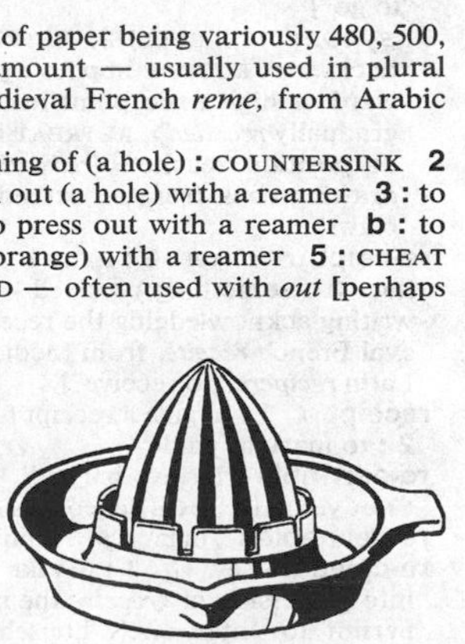

reamer 2

reap \ˈrēp\ *vb* **1 a** (1) **:** to cut with a sickle, scythe, or reaping machine ⟨*reap* rye⟩ (2) **:** to clear (as a field) of a crop by so cutting **b :** to gather (a crop) by so cutting **:** HARVEST **2 :** to gain as a reward ⟨*reap* the benefit of hard work⟩ [Old English *reopan*]

reap·er \ˈrē-pər\ *n* **:** one that reaps; *esp* **:** a machine for reaping grain

re·ap·por·tion \ˌrē-ə-ˈpȯr-shən\ *vb* **1 :** to apportion (as a house of representatives) anew **2 :** to make a new apportionment — **re·ap·por·tion·ment** \-mənt\ *n*

[1]**rear** \ˈriər\ *vb* **1 :** to erect by building **:** CONSTRUCT **2 a :** to raise upright **b :** to rise high ⟨skyscrapers *rearing* above the city⟩ **c :** to rise up on the hind legs ⟨the horse *reared* in fright⟩ **3 a :** to undertake the breeding and raising of ⟨*rear* cattle⟩ **b :** to bring to maturity or self-sufficiency through continuing care ⟨*reared* five children⟩ [Old English *rǣran*]

[2]**rear** *n* **1 :** the back part of something: as **a :** the unit (as of an army) or area farthest from the enemy **b :** BUTTOCK 2a **2 :** the space or position at the back ⟨the *rear* of a building⟩ [probably from *rear-* (in such terms as *rear guard*)]

[3]**rear** *adj* **:** being at the back

rear admiral *n* **:** an officer rank in the navy and coast guard above captain and below vice admiral

rear guard *n* **:** a military detachment detailed to bring up and protect the rear of a main body or force [Medieval French *reregarde,* from *rere* "backward, behind" (from Latin *retro*) + *garde* "guard"]

re·arm \rē-ˈärm, ˈrē-\ *vb* **:** to arm again especially with new or better weapons — **re·ar·ma·ment** \-ˈär-mə-mənt\ *n*

rear·most \ˈriər-ˌmōst\ *adj* **:** farthest in the rear

re·ar·range \ˌrē-ə-ˈrānj\ *vt* **:** to arrange again especially in a different way — **re·ar·range·able** \-ˈrān-jə-bəl\ *adj* — **re·ar·range·ment** \-ˈrānj-mənt\ *n*

rear·view mirror \ˌriər-ˌvyü-\ *n* **:** a mirror (as in a car) that gives a view to the rear

[1]**rear·ward** \ˈriər-wərd\ *adj* **1 :** located at, near, or toward the rear **2 :** directed toward the rear — **rear·ward·ly** *adv*

[2]**rearward** *also* **rear·wards** \-wərdz\ *adv* **:** at, near, or toward the rear **:** BACKWARD

[1]**rea·son** \ˈrēz-n\ *n* **1 a :** a statement offered in explanation or justification **b :** a rational ground or motive ⟨*reasons* for thinking life may exist on Mars⟩ **c :** the thing that makes some fact intelligible **:** CAUSE **2 a :** the power of comprehending, inferring, or thinking especially in orderly logical ways **:** INTELLIGENCE **b :** SANITY ⟨almost lost my *reason*⟩ [Medieval French *raisun,* from Latin *ratio* "computation, reason"] ***synonyms*** see CAUSE — **in reason :** with reason — **within reason :** within reasonable limits — **with reason :** with good cause **:** JUSTIFIABLY

[2]**reason** *vb* **rea·soned; rea·son·ing** \ˈrēz-ning, -n-ing\ **1 :** to talk persuasively or to present reasons in order to cause a change of mind ⟨*reason* with someone⟩ **2 a :** to use one's reason or to think in a logical way or manner **b :** to state, formulate, or conclude by use of reason ⟨*reasoned* that both statements couldn't be true⟩ ***synonyms*** see THINK

rea·son·able \ˈrēz-nə-bəl, -n-ə-bəl\ *adj* **1 a :** agreeable to reason ⟨a *reasonable* theory⟩ **b :** not extreme or excessive **:** MODERATE ⟨a *reasonable* request⟩ **c :** not expensive ⟨*reasonable* prices⟩ **2 a :** having the faculty of reason **:** RATIONAL ⟨a *reasonable* person⟩ **b :** possessing sound judgment — **rea·son·abil·i·ty** \ˌrēz-nə-ˈbil-ət-ē, -n-ə-\ *n* — **rea·son·able·ness** \ˈrēz-nə-bəl-nəs, -n-ə-\ *n* — **rea·son·ably** \-blē\ *adv*

rea·son·ing *n* **1 :** the use of reason; *esp* **:** the drawing of inferences or conclusions through the use of reason **2 :** the reasons used in and the proofs that result from thought

re·as·sur·ance \ˌrē-ə-ˈshu̇r-əns\ *n* **:** the action of reassuring **:** the state of being reassured

re·as·sure \ˌrē-ə-ˈshu̇r\ *vt* **1 :** to assure anew **2 :** to restore to confidence — **re·as·sur·ing·ly** \-ˈshu̇r-ing-lē\ *adv*

re·ata \rē-ˈat-ə, -ˈät-\ *n* **:** LARIAT [American Spanish]

Ré·au·mur \ˌrā-ō-ˈmyu̇r\ *adj* **:** relating or conforming to a temperature scale on which the boiling point of water is at 80° above the zero of the scale and the freezing point is at zero [René Antoine Ferchault de *Réaumur,* died 1757, French physicist]

reave \ˈrēv\ *vb* **reaved** *or* **reft** \ˈreft\; **reav·ing** *archaic* **:** PLUNDER, ROB [Old English *rēafian*] — **reav·er** *n*

reb \ˈreb\ *n* **:** JOHNNY REB [short for *rebel*]

\ə\ **abut**	\au̇\ **out**	\i\ **tip**	\ȯ\ **saw**	\u̇\ **foot**
\ər\ **further**	\ch\ **chin**	\ī\ **life**	\ȯi\ **coin**	\y\ **yet**
\a\ **mat**	\e\ **pet**	\j\ **job**	\th\ **thin**	\yü\ **few**
\ā\ **take**	\ē\ **easy**	\ng\ **sing**	\t͟h\ **this**	\yu̇\ **cure**
\ä\ **cot, cart**	\g\ **go**	\ō\ **bone**	\ü\ **food**	\zh\ **vision**

re·bar \rē-ˌbär\ *n* : a steel bar for use in reinforced concrete [*re*inforcing *bar*]

[1]**re·bate** \ˈrē-ˌbāt, ri-ˈ\ *vt* : to make a rebate of : give as a rebate [Medieval French *rebatre, rabatre* "to beat back, deduct," from *re-* "re-" + *abatre* "to strike down"] — **re·bat·er** *n*

[2]**re·bate** \ˈrē-ˌbāt\ *n* : a return of a portion of a payment

[1]**reb·el** \ˈreb-əl\ *adj* **1 a** : opposing or taking arms against the government or ruler **b** : of or relating to rebels **2** : REBELLIOUS 2, DISOBEDIENT [Medieval French, from Latin *rebellis,* from *re-* "re-, against" + *bellum* "war"]

[2]**rebel** *n* : one who rebels or participates in a rebellion

[3]**re·bel** \ri-ˈbel\ *vi* **re·belled; re·bel·ling** **1 a** : to oppose or resist authority or control **b** : to renounce and resist by force the authority of one's government **2** : to feel or exhibit anger or revulsion

re·bel·lion \ri-ˈbel-yən\ *n* **1** : opposition to one in authority or dominance **2 a** : open defiance of or resistance to an established government **b** : an instance of such defiance or resistance : REVOLT, UPRISING

synonyms REBELLION, UPRISING, REVOLT, REVOLUTION mean an outbreak against authority. REBELLION implies open, organized resistance that is often unsuccessful ⟨the *rebellion* lasted a year before the government put it down⟩. UPRISING implies rebellion that quickly fails ⟨*uprisings* on the frontier⟩. REVOLT suggests an armed uprising that quickly succeeds or fails ⟨a *revolt* that surprised party leaders⟩. REVOLUTION applies to a successful rebellion resulting in a major change (as in government) ⟨the American *Revolution* brought about the creation of a new country⟩.

re·bel·lious \ri-ˈbel-yəs\ *adj* **1** : engaged in rebellion **2** : inclined to resist or disobey authority : INSUBORDINATE — **re·bel·lious·ly** *adv* — **re·bel·lious·ness** *n*

re·birth \rē-ˈbərth, ˈrē-ˌ\ *n* **1** : a new or second birth **2** : RENAISSANCE 2, REVIVAL

re·born \-ˈbȯrn\ *adj* : experiencing a rebirth

[1]**re·bound** \ri-ˈbau̇nd\ *vi* **1** : to spring back on striking something **2** : to recover from setback or frustration [Medieval French *rebundir,* from *re-* "re-" + *bondir* "to leap, bound"]

[2]**re·bound** \ˈrē-ˌbau̇nd, ri-ˈ\ *n* **1 a** : the action of rebounding : RECOIL **b** : an upward leap or movement ⟨a sharp *rebound* of the market⟩ **2** : a basketball or hockey puck that rebounds **3** : a reaction to setback, frustration, or crisis

re·bo·zo \ri-ˈbō-ˌzō, -ˌsō\ *n, pl* **-zos** : a long scarf worn chiefly by Mexican women [Spanish, shawl, from *rebozar* to muffle]

re·branch \rē-ˈbranch, ˈrē-\ *vi* : to form secondary branches : to branch again ⟨the stream branched and *rebranched*⟩

re·broad·cast \rē-ˈbrȯd-ˌkast, ˈrē-\ *vt* **-cast** *also* **-cast·ed; -cast·ing** **1** : to broadcast again (a radio or television program being simultaneously received from another source) **2** : to repeat (a broadcast) at a later time — **rebroadcast** *n*

re·buff \ri-ˈbəf\ *vt* : to refuse or check sharply : SNUB [Middle French *rebuffer,* from obsolete Italian *ribuffare* "to reprimand"] — **rebuff** *n*

re·build \rē-ˈbild\ *vb* **-built** \-ˈbilt\; **-build·ing** **1 a** : to make extensive repairs to **b** : to restore to a previous state **2** : to make extensive changes in : REMODEL **3** : to build again ⟨planned to *rebuild* after the fire⟩

[1]**re·buke** \ri-ˈbyük\ *vt* : to scold or criticize sharply : REPRIMAND [Medieval French *rebucher, rebouker* "to blunt, check, reprimand"] ***synonyms*** see REPROVE — **re·buk·er** *n*

[2]**rebuke** *n* : REPRIMAND, REPROOF

re·bus \ˈrē-bəs\ *n* : a representation of words or syllables by pictures of objects whose names resemble the intended words or syllables in sound; *also* : a riddle made up of such pictures or symbols [Latin, "by things," from *res* "thing"]

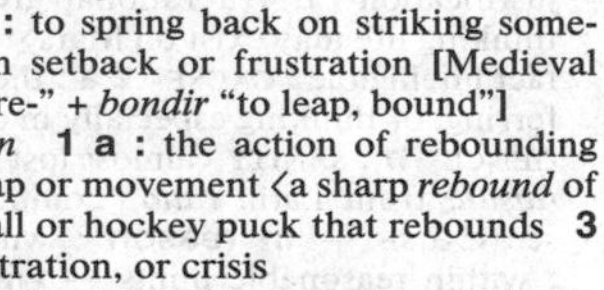

rebus

re·but \ri-ˈbət\ *vt* **re·but·ted; re·but·ting** **1** : to contradict or oppose by formal argument, plea, or contrary proof **2** : to expose the falsity of : REFUTE ⟨*rebut* a theory⟩ [Medieval French *reboter* "to drive back," from *re-* "re-" + *boter* "to butt"] — **re·but·ta·ble** \-ˈbət-ə-bəl\ *adj*

re·but·tal \ri-ˈbət-l\ *n* : the act of rebutting; *also* : argument or proof that rebuts

re·cal·ci·trance \ri-ˈkal-sə-trəns\ *n* : the state of being recalcitrant

re·cal·ci·tran·cy \-trən-sē\ *n* : RECALCITRANCE

re·cal·ci·trant \-trənt\ *adj* **1** : obstinately defiant of authority or restraint **2** : not responsive to handling or treatment [Late Latin *recalcitrare* "to be stubbornly disobedient," from Latin, "to kick back," from *re-* + *calcitrare* "to kick," from *calc-, calx* "heel"] ***synonyms*** see UNRULY — **recalcitrant** *n*

[1]**re·call** \ri-ˈkȯl\ *vt* **1** : CANCEL 2a, REVOKE ⟨*recalled* the order⟩ **2 a** : to call back ⟨*recalled* to duty⟩ ⟨*recall* a defective product⟩ **b** : to bring back to mind usually with some effort ⟨*recalled* seeing her somewhere before⟩ **3 a** : to bring back into existence **b** : to restore to consciousness or awareness ***synonyms*** see REMEMBER — **re·call·able** \-ˈkȯ-lə-bəl\ *adj*

[2]**re·call** \ri-ˈkȯl, ˈrē-ˌ\ *n* **1** : a summons to return **2** : the right or procedure by which an official may be removed by vote of the people on petition **3** : remembrance of what has been learned or experienced **4** : the act of revoking **5** : a public call by a manufacturer for the return of a product that may be defective or contaminated

re·cant \ri-ˈkant\ *vb* : to withdraw or repudiate a statement of opinion or belief formally and publicly : make an open confession of error [Latin *recantare,* from *re-* + *cantare* "to sing"] — **re·can·ta·tion** \ˌrē-ˌkan-ˈtā-shən\ *n*

synonyms RECANT, RETRACT mean to withdraw publicly something declared or professed. RECANT implies admission of error in something one has openly professed or taught ⟨the candidate *recanted* the challenged position⟩. RETRACT stresses the repudiation of something (as an accusation or an offer) previously put forward ⟨*retracted* their earlier offer⟩.

[1]**re·cap** \rē-ˈkap, ˈrē-\ *vt* **re·capped; re·cap·ping** : [1]RETREAD

[2]**re·cap** \ˈrē-ˌkap\ *n* : a recapped tire : [2]RETREAD 2

[3]**re·cap** \ri-ˈkap, ˈrē-\ *vt* **re·capped; re·cap·ping** : RECAPITULATE ⟨now, to *recap* the news⟩

[4]**re·cap** \ˈrē-ˌkap, ri-ˈ\ *n* : RECAPITULATION

re·ca·pit·u·late \ˌrē-kə-ˈpich-ə-ˌlāt\ *vb* : to repeat briefly : SUMMARIZE [Late Latin *recapitulare* "to restate by heads, sum up," from Latin *re-* + *capitulum* "division of a book," from *caput* "head"]

re·ca·pit·u·la·tion \-ˌpich-ə-ˈlā-shən\ *n* **1** : a concise summary **2** : the hypothetical repetition in the development of an individual of the evolutionary stages represented in its ancestral types **3** : the third section of a sonata form — **re·ca·pit·u·la·to·ry** \-ˈpich-ə-lə-ˌtōr-ē, -ˌtȯr-\ *adj*

re·cap·ture \rē-ˈkap-chər, ˈrē-\ *n* : the act of retaking : the fact of being retaken : RECOVERY — **recapture** *vt*

re·cast \rē-ˈkast\ *vt* **1** : to cast again ⟨*recast* a cannon⟩ ⟨*recast* a play⟩ **2** : to give a different form or quality to : REFASHION, REMODEL ⟨*recast* her image⟩ ⟨*recast* the poem⟩

re·cede \ri-ˈsēd\ *vi* **1 a** : to move back or away : WITHDRAW ⟨the *receding* tide⟩ **b** : to slant backward ⟨a *receding* forehead⟩ **2** : to grow less or smaller : DIMINISH, DECREASE ⟨a *receding* deficit⟩ [Latin *recedere* "to go back," from *re-* + *cedere* "to go"]

synonyms RECEDE, RETREAT, RETRACT mean to move backward. RECEDE implies a gradual withdrawing from a forward or high fixed point in time or space ⟨the flood waters gradually *receded*⟩. RETREAT implies withdrawal from a point or position reached ⟨*retreating* soldiers⟩. RETRACT implies drawing back from an extended position ⟨a cat *retracting* its claws⟩.

[1]**re·ceipt** \ri-ˈsēt\ *n* **1** : RECIPE **2** : the act or process of receiving **3** : something received — usually used in plural **4** : a writing acknowledging the receiving of goods or money [Medieval French *receite,* from Medieval Latin *recepta,* derived from Latin *recipere* "to receive"]

[2]**receipt** *vt* **1** : to give a receipt for or acknowledge the receipt of **2** : to mark as paid

re·ceiv·able \ri-ˈsē-və-bəl\ *adj* **1** : capable of being received **2** : not yet paid : DUE ⟨accounts *receivable*⟩

re·ceiv·ables \-bəlz\ *n pl* : amounts of money receivable

re·ceive \ri-ˈsēv\ *vb* **1** : to take possession or delivery of : come into possession of ⟨*receive* the money⟩ ⟨*receive* a letter⟩ **2** : to permit to enter one's household or company : WELCOME, GREET ⟨*receive* friends⟩ **3** : to hold a reception ⟨*receive* from four to six o'clock⟩ **4** : to undergo or be subjected to (an experience or treatment) ⟨*receive* a shock⟩ **5** : to change incoming radio waves into sounds or pictures [Medieval French *receivre,* from Latin *recipere,* from *re-* + *capere* "to take"]

re·ceiv·er \ri-ˈsē-vər\ *n* **:** one that receives: as **a :** a person appointed to take control of property that is involved in a lawsuit or of a business that is bankrupt or is being reorganized **b** (1) **:** an apparatus for receiving radio or television broadcasts (2) **:** the portion of a telegraphic or telephonic apparatus that converts electric currents or waves into visible or audible signals **c :** an offensive football player who is eligible to catch a forward pass

re·ceiv·er·ship \-ˌship\ *n* **1 :** the office or function of a receiver **2 :** the state of being in the hands of a receiver

re·cen·cy \ˈrēs-n-sē\ *n* **:** the quality or state of being recent

re·cent \ˈrēs-nt\ *adj* **1 a :** of or relating to a time not long past **b :** having lately appeared or come into being **2** *cap* **:** HOLOCENE — **re·cent·ly** *adv* — **re·cent·ness** *n*

synonyms RECENT, MODERN, LATE mean having taken place, existed, or developed in times close to the present. RECENT is the least precise, suggesting only comparative nearness to the present ⟨*recent* medical advances⟩. MODERN implies being characteristic of the present age ⟨*modern* methods of teaching⟩. LATE usually implies a series or succession of which the one described is the most recent ⟨the *late* war⟩.

re·cep·ta·cle \ri-ˈsep-ti-kəl\ *n* **1 :** something used to receive and contain smaller objects **:** CONTAINER **2 :** the enlarged end of the flower stalk upon which the floral organs are borne **3 :** an electrical fitting (as a socket) into which another fitting may be pushed or screwed for making an electrical connection [Latin *receptaculum,* from *receptare* "to receive," from *recipere* "to receive"]

re·cep·tion \ri-ˈsep-shən\ *n* **1 :** the act or process of receiving, welcoming, or accepting ⟨our *reception* of the news⟩ ⟨got a cool *reception*⟩ **2 :** the state or fact of being received (as into shelter or membership) **3 :** the receiving of a radio or television broadcast **4 :** a social gathering ⟨a wedding *reception*⟩ [Latin *receptio,* from *recipere* "to receive"]

re·cep·tion·ist \ri-ˈsep-shə-nəst, -shnəst\ *n* **:** an office employee who greets and assists callers

re·cep·tive \ri-ˈsep-tiv\ *adj* **1 :** open and responsive to ideas **2 :** able to receive and transmit stimuli ⟨the *receptive* part of the retina⟩ — **re·cep·tive·ly** *adv* — **re·cep·tive·ness** *n* — **re·cep·tiv·i·ty** \ˌrē-ˌsep-ˈtiv-ət-ē, ri-\ *n*

re·cep·tor \ri-ˈsep-tər\ *n* **1 :** a cell or group of cells that receives stimuli **:** SENSE ORGAN **2 :** a chemical group or molecule (as a protein) on the surface or in the interior of a cell that recognizes and binds to a specific chemical group or molecule whereupon a signal is transmitted to the interior of the cell or an activity within the cell is initiated

[1]**re·cess** \ˈrē-ˌses, ri-ˈ\ *n* **1 :** a hidden, secret, or secluded place **2 a :** a space or little hollow set back (as from the main line of a coast) **:** INDENTATION **b :** ALCOVE 1 **3 :** a suspension of business or procedure; *esp* **:** a brief period for relaxation between class or study periods of a school day [Latin *recessus,* from *recedere* "to recede"]

[2]**recess** *vb* **1 :** to put into a recess ⟨*recessed* lighting⟩ **2 :** to make a recess in **3 :** to interrupt for or take a recess

re·ces·sion \ri-ˈsesh-ən\ *n* **1 :** the act or fact of receding **2 :** a departing procession (as of clergy and choir at the end of a church service) **3 :** a downturn in business activity; *also* **:** the period of such a downturn

re·ces·sion·al \ri-ˈsesh-nəl, -ən-l\ *n* **:** a hymn or musical piece at the conclusion of a service or program; *also* **:** RECESSION 2

[1]**re·ces·sive** \ri-ˈses-iv\ *adj* **1 :** tending to go back **2 a :** producing an effect on a bodily characteristic (as eye color) when homozygous and not masked by a copy of the gene that is dominant ⟨*recessive* genes⟩ **b :** exhibited by the body only when the determining gene is homozygous ⟨blue eye color is a *recessive* trait⟩ — **re·ces·sive·ly** *adv* — **re·ces·sive·ness** *n*

[2]**recessive** *n* **:** a recessive trait or gene; *also* **:** an organism expressing one or more recessive characters

re·charge \rē-ˈchärj\ *vb* **1 :** to make a new attack **2 :** to charge again; *esp* **:** to restore the chemical energy of (a storage battery) so it may be used again **3 :** to regain energy or spirit ⟨needed some time to relax and *recharge*⟩ **4 :** to inspire or invigorate anew **:** RENEW ⟨the speech *recharged* their determination⟩ — **re·charge·able** \-ˈchär-jə-bəl\ *adj*

re·cher·ché \rə-ˌsher-ˈshā\ *adj* **1 :** being rare or exotic **2 :** excessively refined **:** PRECIOUS [French, from *rechercher* "to seek out, research"]

rec·i·pe \ˈres-ə-pē, -ˌpē\ *n* **1 :** PRESCRIPTION 3a **2 :** a set of instructions for making something (as a food dish) from various ingredients **3 :** method of procedure ⟨a *recipe* for happiness⟩ [Latin, "take," imperative of *recipere* "to take, receive"]

re·cip·i·ent \ri-ˈsip-ē-ənt\ *n* **:** one that receives ⟨the *recipient* of many honors⟩ [Latin *recipiens,* present participle of *recipere* "to receive"] — **recipient** *adj*

[1]**re·cip·ro·cal** \ri-ˈsip-rə-kəl\ *adj* **1 :** done or felt equally by both sides ⟨*reciprocal* affection⟩ **2 :** related to each other in such a way that one completes the other or is the equivalent of the other **:** mutually corresponding ⟨*reciprocal* agreements⟩ **3 :** of, constituting, or resulting from paired crosses in which the kind that supplies the male parent of the first cross supplies the female parent of the second cross and vice versa [Latin *reciprocus* "returning the same way, alternating," derived from *re-* "back" + *pro-* "forward"] — **re·cip·ro·cal·ly** \-kə-lē, -klē\ *adv*

synonyms RECIPROCAL, MUTUAL, COMMON mean shared or experienced by each of those involved. RECIPROCAL implies an equal return or counteraction by each of two sides ⟨*reciprocal* lowering of tariffs⟩. MUTUAL applies to feelings or effects shared by two jointly ⟨*mutual* affection⟩. COMMON implies only being shared by others ⟨united in a *common* purpose⟩.

[2]**reciprocal** *n* **1 :** something in a reciprocal relationship to another **2 :** either of a pair of numbers (as ⅔ and 3/2 or 9 and ⅑) whose product is one; *also* **:** MULTIPLICATIVE INVERSE

re·cip·ro·cate \ri-ˈsip-rə-ˌkāt\ *vb* **1 :** to give and take mutually **:** EXCHANGE **2 :** to make a return for something **3 :** to move forward and backward alternately ⟨a *reciprocating* mechanical part⟩ — **re·cip·ro·ca·tion** \-ˌsip-rə-ˈkā-shən\ *n* — **re·cip·ro·ca·tor** \-ˈsip-rə-ˌkāt-ər\ *n*

reciprocating engine *n* **:** an engine in which the to-and-fro motion of a piston is transformed into circular motion of the crankshaft

rec·i·proc·i·ty \ˌres-ə-ˈpräs-ət-ē\ *n, pl* **-ties 1 :** mutual dependence, cooperation, or exchange between persons, groups or states **2 :** a mutual exchange of privileges; *esp* **:** a recognition by one of two countries or institutions of the validity of licenses or privileges granted by the other

re·cit·al \ri-ˈsīt-l\ *n* **1 :** a reciting of something; *esp* **:** a story told in detail ⟨the *recital* of their troubles⟩ **2 :** a program of one kind of music ⟨a piano *recital*⟩ **3 :** a public performance by pupils (as music or dancing pupils) — **re·cit·al·ist** \-l-əst\ *n*

rec·i·ta·tion \ˌres-ə-ˈtā-shən\ *n* **1 :** an enumeration or telling in detail **2 :** the act or an instance of reading or repeating aloud especially publicly **3 a :** a student's oral reply to questions **b :** a class period

rec·i·ta·tive \ˌres-tə-ˈtēv, -ət-ə-\ *n* **:** a rhythmically free vocal style that imitates the natural inflections of speech and that is used for dialogue and narrative in operas and oratorios; *also* **:** a passage in this style [Italian] — **recitative** *adj*

re·cite \ri-ˈsīt\ *vb* **1 :** to repeat from memory or read aloud publicly ⟨*recite* a poem⟩ **2 a :** to give a detailed narration of **b :** STATE 2 **3 :** to answer (as to a teacher) questions about a lesson [Latin *recitare,* from *re-* + *citare* "to summon"] — **re·cit·er** *n*

reck \ˈrek\ *vi* **1 :** CARE 1a, MIND **2** *archaic* **:** to be of interest **:** MATTER [Old English *reccan* "to take heed"]

reck·less \ˈrek-ləs\ *adj* **1 :** marked by lack of caution **:** RASH **2 :** NEGLIGENT 1a, IRRESPONSIBLE ⟨*reckless* driving⟩ ***synonyms*** see DARING — **reck·less·ly** *adv* — **reck·less·ness** *n*

reck·on \ˈrek-ən\ *vb* **reck·oned; reck·on·ing** \ˈrek-ning, -ə-ning\ **1 a :** COUNT 1a, COMPUTE ⟨*reckon* the days till her birthday⟩ **b :** to estimate by calculation ⟨*reckon* the height of a building⟩ **2 :** CONSIDER 3, REGARD ⟨was *reckoned* among the leaders⟩ **3** *chiefly dialect* **:** THINK, SUPPOSE ⟨*reckoned* they might win⟩ **4 :** to make up or settle an account **5 :** to count on **:** DEPEND ⟨*reckon* on support⟩ [Old English *-recenian* (as in *gerecenian* "to narrate")] — **reck·on·er** \ˈrek-nər, -ə-nər\ *n* — **reckon with :** to take into account — **reckon without :** to fail to take into account

reck·on·ing *n* **1 :** the act or an instance of reckoning: as **a :** [4]BILL 4, ACCOUNT **b :** COMPUTATION **c :** calculation of a ship's position **2 :** a settling of accounts ⟨a day of *reckoning*⟩ **3 :** a summing up **:** APPRAISAL

\ə\ **abut**	\au̇\ **out**	\i\ **tip**	\ȯ\ **saw**	\u̇\ **foot**
\ər\ **further**	\ch\ **chin**	\ī\ **life**	\ȯi\ **coin**	\y\ **yet**
\a\ **mat**	\e\ **pet**	\j\ **job**	\th\ **thin**	\yü\ **few**
\ā\ **take**	\ē\ **easy**	\ng\ **sing**	\t͟h\ **this**	\yu̇\ **cure**
\ä\ **cot, cart**	\g\ **go**	\ō\ **bone**	\ü\ **food**	\zh\ **vision**

re·claim \ri-ˈklām\ *vt* **1 :** to recall from wrong or improper conduct : REFORM **2 :** to alter from an undesirable or uncultivated state ⟨*reclaim* desert for agriculture⟩; *also* : to restore to a previous natural state ⟨*reclaim* mining sites⟩ **3 :** to obtain from a waste product or by-product : RECOVER ⟨*reclaimed* wool⟩ [Medieval French *reclamer* "to call back," from Latin *reclamare* "to cry out against," from *re-* + *clamare* "to cry out"] — **re·claim·able** \-ˈklā-mə-bəl\ *adj* — **re·claim·er** *n*

rec·la·ma·tion \ˌrek-lə-ˈmā-shən\ *n* **:** the act or process of reclaiming : the state of being reclaimed

re·cline \ri-ˈklīn\ *vb* **1 :** to lean or cause to lean backwards **2 :** REPOSE, LIE ⟨*reclining* on the sofa⟩ [Latin *reclinare,* from *re-* + *clinare* "to bend"]

[1]**re·cluse** \ˈrek-ˌlüs, ri-ˈklüs\ *adj* **:** marked by withdrawal from society : SOLITARY [Medieval French *reclus,* literally, "shut up," from Late Latin *reclusus,* past participle of *recludere* "to shut up," from Latin *re-* + *claudere* "to close"] — **re·clu·sive** \ri-ˈklü-siv, -ziv\ *adj*

[2]**recluse** *n* **:** a person (as a hermit) who lives away from others

rec·og·ni·tion \ˌrek-ig-ˈnish-ən, ˌrek-əg-\ *n* **1 :** the act of recognizing ⟨their *recognition* of me⟩ **2 :** special attention or notice **3 :** formal acknowledgment of the political existence of a government or nation **4 :** acknowledgment of something done or given (as by making an award) ⟨got a medal in *recognition* of bravery⟩ [Latin *recognitio,* from *recognoscere* "to recognize"]

rec·og·niz·able \ˈrek-ig-ˌnī-zə-bəl, ˈrek-əg-\ *adj* **:** capable of being recognized — **rec·og·niz·abil·i·ty** \ˌrek-ig-ˌnī-zə-ˈbil-ət-ē, ˌrek-əg-\ *n* — **rec·og·niz·ably** \ˈrek-ig-ˌnī-zə-blē, -əg-\ *adv*

re·cog·ni·zance \ri-ˈkäg-nə-zəns, -ˈkän-ə-\ *n* **:** a recorded legal promise to do something (as to appear in court)

rec·og·nize \ˈrek-ig-ˌnīz, ˈrek-əg-\ *vt* **1 :** to know and remember upon seeing ⟨*recognize* a person⟩ **2 :** to consent to admit : ACKNOWLEDGE ⟨*recognize* one's faults⟩ **3 :** to take approving notice of ⟨*recognize* an act of bravery⟩ **4 :** to acknowledge acquaintance with ⟨*recognize* someone with a nod⟩ **5 :** to acknowledge as entitled to be heard at a meeting ⟨the chair *recognizes* the delegate from Illinois⟩ **6 :** to grant diplomatic recognition to ⟨*recognized* the new government⟩ [Middle French *reconois-,* stem of *reconoistre* "to recognize," from Latin *recognoscere,* from *re-* + *cognoscere* "to know," from *co-* + *gnoscere* "to come to know"]

[1]**re·coil** \ri-ˈkȯil\ *vi* **1 a :** to fall back under pressure ⟨the soldiers *recoiled* before the enemy attack⟩ **b :** to shrink back ⟨*recoil* in horror⟩ **2 :** to spring back to or as if to a starting point ⟨the spring *recoiled* upon release⟩ [Medieval French *reculer, reculer,* from *re-* "re-" + *cul* "backside," from Latin *culus*]

[2]**re·coil** \ri-ˈkȯil, ˈrē-ˌ\ *n* **1 :** REBOUND 1 **2 :** a springing back **3 :** the distance through which something (as a spring) recoils

re·coil·less \ri-ˈkȯil-ləs, ˈrē-ˌ\ *adj* **:** having a minimum of recoil ⟨a *recoilless* gun⟩

rec·ol·lect \ˌrek-ə-ˈlekt\ *vb* **1 :** to bring back to the level of conscious awareness **2 :** to recall to (oneself) something forgotten or overlooked ⟨*recollected* myself and apologized⟩ [Medieval Latin *recollectus,* past participle of *recolligere* "to recollect," from Latin, "to gather again"] ***synonyms*** see REMEMBER

re–col·lect \ˌrē-kə-ˈlekt\ *vt* **:** to collect again; *esp* : RECOVER ⟨*re-collect* one's drooping spirits⟩

rec·ol·lec·tion \ˌrek-ə-ˈlek-shən\ *n* **1 :** the action or power of recalling to mind : REMEMBRANCE **2 :** something recalled to the mind ***synonyms*** see MEMORY

re·com·bi·nant \rē-ˈkäm-bə-nənt, ˈrē-\ *adj* **1 :** relating to or exhibiting genetic recombination ⟨*recombinant* offspring⟩ **2 :** relating to, containing, or produced by recombinant DNA ⟨*recombinant* strains of bacteria⟩ — **recombinant** *n*

recombinant DNA *n* **:** DNA prepared in the laboratory by breaking up and joining together DNA from several different species of organisms

re·com·bi·na·tion \ˌrē-ˌkäm-bə-ˈnā-shən\ *n* **:** the production of new combinations of genes especially through genetic crossing-over and the operation of the law of independent assortment

re·com·bine \ˌrē-kəm-ˈbīn\ *vb* **1 :** to combine again or anew **2 :** to undergo or cause to undergo recombination

rec·om·mend \ˌrek-ə-ˈmend\ *vt* **1 :** to make a statement in praise of; *esp* : to endorse as fit, worthy, or competent ⟨*recommend* a person for a position⟩ **2 :** to put forward or suggest as one's advice, as one's choice, or as having one's support ⟨*recommend* that the matter be dropped⟩ **3 :** to cause to receive favorable attention [Medieval Latin *recommendare* "to present as worthy of acceptance or trial," from Latin *re-* + *commendare* "to commend"] — **rec·om·mend·able** \-ˈmen-də-bəl\ *adj* — **rec·om·mend·er** *n*

rec·om·men·da·tion \ˌrek-ə-mən-ˈdā-shən, -ˌmen-\ *n* **1 :** the act of recommending **2 :** something that recommends **3 :** a thing or course of action recommended

re·com·mit \ˌrē-kə-ˈmit\ *vt* **1 :** to refer (as a bill) again to a committee **2 :** to commit again — **re·com·mit·ment** \-mənt\ *n* — **re·com·mit·al** \-ˈmit-l\ *n*

[1]**rec·om·pense** \ˈrek-əm-ˌpens\ *vt* **:** to give compensation to or for [Medieval French *recompenser,* from Late Latin *recompensare,* from Latin *re-* + *compensare* "to compensate"]

[2]**recompense** *n* **:** a return for something done, suffered, or given

rec·on·cil·abil·i·ty \ˌrek-ən-ˌsī-lə-ˈbil-ət-ē\ *n* **:** the quality or state of being reconcilable

rec·on·cil·able \ˌrek-ən-ˈsī-lə-bəl\ *adj* **:** capable of being reconciled — **rec·on·cil·able·ness** *n*

rec·on·cile \ˈrek-ən-ˌsīl\ *vt* **1 :** to make friendly again ⟨*reconcile* friends who have quarreled⟩ **2 :** SETTLE, ADJUST ⟨*reconcile* differences of opinion⟩ **3 :** to make agree ⟨a story that cannot be *reconciled* with the facts⟩ **4 :** to cause to submit or accept ⟨*reconciled* to hardship⟩ [Latin *reconciliare,* from *re-* + *conciliare* "to conciliate"] — **rec·on·cile·ment** \-mənt\ *n* — **rec·on·cil·er** *n* — **rec·on·cil·ia·to·ry** \ˌrek-ən-ˈsil-yə-ˌtōr-ē, -ˌtȯr-\ *adj*

rec·on·cil·i·a·tion \ˌrek-ən-ˌsil-ē-ˈā-shən\ *n* **1 :** the action of reconciling : the state of being reconciled **2 :** the Roman Catholic sacrament of penance

rec·on·dite \ˈrek-ən-ˌdīt, ri-ˈkän-\ *adj* **1 :** hidden from sight : CONCEALED **2 :** difficult to understand : DEEP ⟨a *recondite* subject⟩ **3 :** of, relating to, or dealing with something little known [Latin *reconditus,* past participle of *recondere* "to conceal," from *re-* + *condere* "to store up"] — **rec·on·dite·ly** *adv* — **rec·on·dite·ness** *n*

re·con·di·tion \ˌrē-kən-ˈdish-ən\ *vt* **:** to restore to good condition (as by repairing or replacing parts) ⟨*recondition* a house⟩

re·con·firm \ˌrē-kən-ˈfərm\ *vt* **:** to confirm again; *also* : to establish more strongly — **re·con·fir·ma·tion** \ˌrē-ˌkän-fər-ˈmā-shən\ *n*

re·con·nais·sance \ri-ˈkän-ə-zəns\ *n* **:** a preliminary survey to gain information; *esp* : an exploratory military survey of enemy territory [French, literally, "recognition," from Medieval French *reconoissance,* from *reconoistre* "to recognize"]

re·con·noi·ter \ˌrē-kə-ˈnȯit-ər, ˌrek-ə-\ *vb* **:** to make a reconnaissance; *esp* : to survey in preparation for military action ⟨*reconnoiter* enemy territory⟩ [obsolete French *reconnoître,* literally, "to recognize," from Medieval French *reconoistre*]

re·con·sid·er \ˌrē-kən-ˈsid-ər\ *vb* **:** to consider again especially with a view to change or reversal — **re·con·sid·er·a·tion** \-ˌsid-ə-ˈrā-shən\ *n*

re·con·sti·tute \rē-ˈkän-stə-ˌtüt, ˈrē-, -ˌtyüt\ *vt* **:** to restore to a former condition by adding water

re·con·struct \ˌrē-kən-ˈstrəkt\ *vt* **1 :** to construct again : REBUILD, REMODEL **2 :** to subject (a body part) to surgery to re-form its structure or correct a defect — **re·con·struc·tive** \-ˈstrək-tiv\ *adj*

re·con·struc·tion \ˌrē-kən-ˈstrək-shən\ *n* **1 a :** the action of reconstructing : the state of being reconstructed **b** *often cap* **:** the reorganization and reestablishment of the seceded states in the Union after the American Civil War **2 :** something reconstructed

re·con·ver·sion \ˌrē-kən-ˈvər-zhən\ *n* **:** conversion back to a previous state

re·con·vert \ˌrē-kən-ˈvərt\ *vb* **:** to convert back

[1]**re·cord** \ri-ˈkȯrd\ *vb* **1 a** (1) **:** to set down in writing (2) **:** to deposit an authentic official copy of ⟨*record* a deed⟩ **b** (1) **:** to register permanently (2) **:** INDICATE, READ ⟨the thermometer *recorded* 90°⟩ **2 :** to cause (as sound or visual images) to be registered (as on an optical disk or magnetic tape) in reproducible form **3 :** REPRODUCE 2 ⟨a voice that *records* well⟩ **4 :** to give evidence of [Medieval French *recorder* "to recall to mind," from Latin *recordari,* from *re-* + *cord-, cor* "heart"]

[2]**rec·ord** \ˈrek-ərd, -ˌȯrd\ *n* **1 :** the state or fact of being recorded **2 :** something that records: as **a :** something (as a monument) that recalls or reports past events **b :** an official writing that records the proceedings or acts of a group, organization, or official **c :** an authentic official copy of a document **3 a :** the known or recorded facts regarding something or someone ⟨my school *record*⟩ **b :** the best that has ever been done (as in a par-

ticular competition) ⟨broke the long jump *record*⟩ **4** : something on which sound or visual images have been recorded for later reproduction; *esp* : a disc with a spiral groove carrying recorded sound for phonograph reproduction — **off the record** : not for publication — **on record** **1** : in the position of having publicly declared oneself **2** : in the status of being known, published, or documented

[3]**rec·ord** \ˈrek-ərd\ *adj* : setting a record : outstanding among other like things ⟨a *record* crop⟩

re·cord·er \ri-ˈkȯrd-ər\ *n* **1** : one that records **2** : a municipal judge with criminal and sometimes limited civil jurisdiction **3** : any of a group of wind instruments ranging from soprano to bass that are characterized by a conical tube, a whistle mouthpiece, and eight finger holes

recorder 3

re·cord·ing \ri-ˈkȯrd-ing\ *n* : RECORD 4

re·cord·ist \ri-ˈkȯrd-əst\ *n* : one who records sound especially on film

rec·ord player \ˈrek-ərd-\ *n* : an instrument for playing phonograph records through a loudspeaker

[1]**re·count** \ri-ˈkau̇nt\ *vt* : to relate in detail ⟨*recount* an adventure⟩ [Middle French *reconter,* from *re-* "re-" + *conter* "to count, relate"]

[2]**re·count** \rē-ˈkau̇nt, ˈrē-\ *vb* : to count again

[3]**re·count** \rē-ˈkau̇nt, ˈrē-ˌ\ *n* : a second or fresh count

re·coup \ri-ˈküp\ *vt* **1** : to make up for : RECOVER ⟨*recoup* a loss⟩ **2** : REIMBURSE, COMPENSATE ⟨*recoup* a person for losses⟩ [French *recouper* "to cut back," from Medieval French, from *re-* "re-" + *couper* "to cut"] — **re·coup·able** \-ˈkü-pə-bəl\ *adj* — **re·coup·ment** \-ˈküp-mənt\ *n*

re·course \ˈrē-ˌkōrs, -ˌkȯrs, ri-ˈ\ *n* **1** : a turning for assistance or protection ⟨have *recourse* to the law⟩ **2** : a source of help or strength [Medieval French *recours,* from Late Latin *recursus,* from Latin, "act of running back," from *recurrere* "to run back," from *re-* + *currere* "to run"]

re·cov·er \ri-ˈkəv-ər\ *vb* **-cov·ered; -cov·er·ing** \-ˈkəv-ring, -ə-ring\ **1** : to get back : REGAIN ⟨*recover* a lost wallet⟩ **2** : to bring back to normal position or condition ⟨stumbled, then *recovered* myself⟩ **3 a** : to make up for ⟨*recover* lost time⟩ **b** : to gain by legal process ⟨*recover* damages⟩; *also* : to win damages at law **4** *archaic* : to come or return to : REACH **5** : RECLAIM ⟨*recover* gold from ore⟩ **6** : to regain health, consciousness, or self-control [Medieval French *recoverer,* from Latin *recuperare*] — **re·cov·er·able** \-ˈkəv-rə-bəl, -ə-rə-\ *adj*

re–cov·er \rē-ˈkəv-ər, ˈrē-\ *vt* : to cover again or anew

re·cov·ery \ri-ˈkəv-rē, -ə-rē\ *n, pl* **-er·ies** : the act or process or an instance of recovering; *esp* : return to a former normal state

recovery room *n* : a hospital room equipped for meeting emergencies following surgery or childbirth

[1]**rec·re·ant** \ˈrek-rē-ənt\ *adj* **1** : crying for mercy : COWARDLY **2** : unfaithful to duty or allegiance [Medieval French, from *(se) recreire* "to give up, yield," from Medieval Latin *(se) recredere* "to resign oneself (to a judgment)," from Latin *re-* + *credere* "to believe"]

[2]**recreant** *n* **1** : COWARD **2** : one that is unfaithful : TRAITOR

rec·re·ate \ˈrek-rē-ˌāt\ *vt* **1** : to give new life or freshness to **2** : to take recreation [Latin *recreare* "to create anew, restore, refresh," from *re-* + *creare* "to create"] — **rec·re·ative** \-ˌāt-iv\ *adj*

re–cre·ate \ˌrē-krē-ˈāt\ *vt* : to create anew especially in the imagination — **re–cre·a·tion** \-ˈā-shən\ *n* — **re–cre·ative** \-ˈāt-iv\ *adj*

rec·re·ation \ˌrek-rē-ˈā-shən\ *n* : refreshment of strength and spirits after toil : DIVERSION; *also* : a means of refreshment or diversion (as a game or exercise) [Medieval French *recreacion,* from Latin *recreatio* "restoration to health," from *recreare* "to restore, refresh"] — **rec·re·ation·al** \-shnəl, -shən-l\ *adj*

recreational vehicle *n* : a vehicle designed for recreational use (as in camping); *esp* : MOTOR HOME

re·crim·i·nate \ri-ˈkrim-ə-ˌnāt\ *vb* **1** : to make a return charge against an accuser **2** : to retort bitterly [Medieval Latin *recriminare,* from Latin *re-* + *criminari* "to accuse," from *crimen* "accusation, crime"] — **re·crim·i·na·tion** \-ˌkrim-ə-ˈnā-shən\ *n* — **re·crim·i·na·to·ry** \-ˈkrim-ə-nə-ˌtōr-ē, -ˌtȯr-\ *adj*

re·cru·des·cence \ˌrē-krü-ˈdes-ns\ *n* : a renewal or breaking out again especially of something unhealthful or dangerous [Latin *recrudescere* "to become raw again," from *re-* + *crudescere* "to become raw," from *crudus* "raw"] — **re·cru·desce** \-ˈdes\ *vi* — **re·cru·des·cent** \-ˈdes-nt\ *adj*

[1]**re·cruit** \ri-ˈkrüt\ *n* : a newcomer to a field or activity; *esp* : a newly enlisted or drafted member of the armed forces [French *recrute, recrue* "fresh growth, new levy of soldiers," from Middle French, from *recroistre* "to grow up again," from Latin *recrescere,* from *re-* + *crescere* "to grow"]

[2]**recruit** *vb* **1 a** : to fill up the number of (as an army) with new members **b** : to enlist new members **c** : to secure the services of : ENGAGE **2** : REPLENISH **3** : to restore or increase the health, vigor, or intensity of — **re·cruit·er** *n* — **re·cruit·ment** \-ˈkrüt-mənt\ *n*

re·crys·tal·lize \rē-ˈkris-tə-ˌlīz, ˈrē-\ *vb* : to form or cause to form crystals after being dissolved or melted — **re·crys·tal·li·za·tion** \rē-ˌkris-tə-lə-ˈzā-shən\ *n*

rect·an·gle \ˈrek-ˌtang-gəl\ *n* : a four-sided polygon that has four right angles and each pair of opposite sides parallel and of the same length [Medieval Latin *rectangulus* "having a right angle," from Latin *rectus* "right" + *angulus* "angle"]

rect·an·gu·lar \rek-ˈtang-gyə-lər\ *adj* **1** : shaped like a rectangle ⟨a *rectangular* building⟩ **2 a** : crossing, lying, or meeting at a right angle ⟨*rectangular* axes⟩ **b** : having edges, surfaces, or faces that meet at right angles : having faces that are shaped like rectangles ⟨a *rectangular* solid⟩ ⟨*rectangular* blocks⟩ — **rect·an·gu·lar·i·ty** \rek-ˌtang-gyə-ˈlar-ət-ē\ *n* — **rect·an·gu·lar·ly** \rek-ˈtang-gyə-lər-lē\ *adv*

rectangular coordinate *n* : a Cartesian coordinate of a Cartesian coordinate system whose straight-line axes are perpendicular

rec·ti·fi·er \ˈrek-tə-ˌfī-ər, -ˌfīr\ *n* : one that rectifies; *esp* : a device for converting alternating current into direct current

rec·ti·fy \ˈrek-tə-ˌfī\ *vt* **-fied; -fy·ing** **1** : to set right : REMEDY **2** : to purify (as alcohol) especially by repeated or fractional distillation **3** : to correct by removing errors : ADJUST ⟨*rectify* the calendar⟩ **4** : to convert (an alternating current) into a direct current [Medieval French *rectifier,* from Medieval Latin *rectificare,* from Latin *rectus* "right"] ***synonyms*** see CORRECT — **rec·ti·fi·able** \ˈrek-tə-ˌfī-ə-bəl\ *adj* — **rec·ti·fi·ca·tion** \ˌrek-tə-fə-ˈkā-shən\ *n*

rec·ti·lin·e·ar \ˌrek-tə-ˈlin-ē-ər\ *adj* **1** : moving in, being in, or forming a straight line ⟨*rectilinear* motion⟩ **2** : characterized by straight lines [Late Latin *rectilineus,* from Latin *rectus* "straight, right" + *linea* "line"] — **rec·ti·lin·e·ar·ly** *adv*

rec·ti·tude \ˈrek-tə-ˌtüd, -ˌtyüd\ *n* **1** : the quality or state of being straight **2** : moral integrity [Medieval French, from Late Latin *rectitudo,* from Latin *rectus* "straight, right"]

rec·to \ˈrek-tō\ *n, pl* **rectos** : a right-hand page — compare VERSO [New Latin *recto folio* "on the right-hand leaf"]

rec·tor \ˈrek-tər\ *n* **1** : a clergyman in charge of a church or parish **2** : the priest in charge of certain Roman Catholic religious houses for men **3** : the head of a university or school [Latin, "guide, director," from *regere* "to direct"]

rec·to·ry \ˈrek-tə-rē, -trē\ *n, pl* **-ries** : a rector's residence

rec·tum \ˈrek-təm\ *n, pl* **rectums** *or* **rec·ta** \-tə\ : the last part of the intestine linking the colon to the anus [Medieval Latin, from *rectum intestinum,* literally, "straight intestine"] — **rec·tal** \-tl\ *adj*

rec·tus \ˈrek-təs\ *n, pl* **rec·ti** \-ˌtī, -ˌtē\ : any of several straight muscles (as of the abdomen) [New Latin, from *rectus musculus* "straight muscle"]

re·cum·bent \ri-ˈkəm-bənt\ *adj* **1** : being in a state of rest **2** : lying down [Latin *recumbens,* present participle of *recumbere* "to lie down"] — **re·cum·bent·ly** *adv*

re·cu·per·ate \ri-ˈkü-pə-ˌrāt, -ˈkyü-\ *vb* : to get back : RECOVER; *esp* : to regain health or strength [Latin *recuperare*] — **re·cu·per·a·tion** \-ˌkü-pə-ˈrā-shən, -ˌkyü-\ *n*

re·cu·per·a·tive \ri-ˈkü-pə-ˌrāt-iv, -ˈkyü-, -pə-rət-, -prət-\ *adj* : of, relating to, or promoting recuperation

re·cur \ri-ˈkər\ *vi* **re·curred; re·cur·ring** **1** : to go or come back in thought or discussion ‹*recur* to a subject in conversation› **2** : to come again into the mind ‹a memory that *recurred* over and over› **3** : to occur again ‹the fever *recurred*› [Latin *recurrere* "to run back, return," from *re-* + *currere* "to run"] — **re·cur·rence** \-ˈkər-əns, -ˈkə-rəns\ *n*

re·cur·rent \ri-ˈkər-ənt, -ˈkə-rənt\ *adj* **1** : running or turning back in direction ‹a *recurrent* vein› **2** : happening time after time ‹*recurrent* complaints› [Latin *recurrens,* present participle of *recurrere* "to return"] — **re·cur·rent·ly** *adv*

re·curved \rē-ˈkərvd, ˈrē-\ *adj* : curved backward or inward ‹*recurved* claws›

re·cut \rē-ˈkət\ *vt* **1** : to cut again **2** : to edit anew ‹*recut* a film›

re·cy·cle \rē-ˈsī-kəl, ˈrē-\ *vt* : to process (as liquid body waste, glass, or cans) in order to regain for use — **re·cy·cla·ble** \-kə-lə-bəl, -klə-bəl\ *adj*

[1]**red** \ˈred\ *adj* **red·der; red·dest** **1 a** : of the color red **b** : having red as a distinguishing color **2 a (1)** : flushed usually from emotion **(2)** : RUDDY 1 **(3)** : BLOODSHOT **b** : of a coppery hue **c** : being in the color range between a moderate orange and russet or bay **d** : REDDISH **3 a** : stirring up or approving extreme social or political change especially by force **b** *cap* : COMMUNIST **c** : of or relating to a Communist country (as the former Soviet Union) [Old English *rēad*] — **red·ly** *adv* — **red·ness** *n*

[2]**red** *n* **1** : a color whose hue resembles that of fresh blood or the ruby or is that of the long-wave extreme of the visible spectrum **2** : one that is of a red or reddish color **3** : a pigment or dye that colors red **4 a** : a person who seeks the overthrow of an existing social or political order **b** *cap* : COMMUNIST **5** : the condition of showing a loss ‹in the *red*› [sense 5 from the bookkeeping practice of entering debit items in red ink]

re·dact \ri-ˈdakt\ *vt* **1** : to put in writing : FRAME **2** : to select or adapt for publication [Latin *redactus,* past participle of *redigere* "to bring back, reduce"] — **re·dac·tor** \-ˈdak-tər\ *n*

re·dac·tion \ri-ˈdak-shən\ *n* **1** : an act or instance of redacting **2** : EDITION 1 [French *rédaction,* derived from Latin *redigere* "to bring back, reduce," from *re-, red-* "re-" + *agere* "to lead"] — **re·dac·tion·al** \-shnəl, -shən-l\ *adj*

red alga *n* : any of a group (division Rhodophyta) of chiefly marine algae having predominantly red pigmentation

re·date \rē-ˈdāt\ *vt* **1** : to date again or anew **2** : to change the date of : give a different date to

red·bird \ˈred-ˌbərd\ *n* : any of several birds (as a cardinal or scarlet tanager) with predominantly red plumage

red blood cell *n* : one of the hemoglobin-containing cells that carry oxygen to the tissues and are responsible for the red color of vertebrate blood — called also *erythrocyte, red blood corpuscle, red cell, red corpuscle*

red–blood·ed \ˈred-ˈbləd-əd\ *adj* : full of spirit and vigor

red·bone \ˈred-ˌbōn\ *n* : any of a breed of speedy usually dark red hounds of U.S. origin used especially for hunting raccoons

red·breast \-ˌbrest\ *n* : a bird (as a robin) with a reddish breast

red·bud \-ˌbəd\ *n* : an American tree of the legume family with usually pale rosy pink flowers and heart-shaped leaves

red·cap \-ˌkap\ *n* : a baggage porter

red–car·pet \ˈred-ˈkär-pət\ *adj* : marked by ceremonial courtesy ‹*red-carpet* treatment› [from the traditional laying down of a red carpet for important guests to walk on]

red cedar *n* **1** : any of several coniferous evergreen trees of the U.S. with scalelike leaves and fragrant red or reddish brown wood: as **a** : a common juniper chiefly of the eastern U.S. **b** : a large arborvitae of the Pacific Northwest **2** : the wood of a red cedar

red cell *n* : RED BLOOD CELL

red cent *n* : a trivial amount

red clover *n* : a European clover with globe-shaped heads of reddish purple flowers widely grown as a hay, forage, and cover crop

red·coat \ˈred-ˌkōt\ *n* : a British soldier especially during the American Revolution

red corpuscle *n* : RED BLOOD CELL

red cross *n* : a red-colored cross on a white background used as a badge for hospitals and for members of an international organization that helps the suffering especially in war or disaster areas

[1]**redd** \ˈred\ *vb* **redd·ed** *or* **redd; redd·ing** **1** *chiefly dialect* : to set in order **2** *chiefly dialect* : to make things tidy [Middle English *redden* "to clear"]

[2]**redd** *n* : the spawning place or nest of a fish [origin unknown]

red deer *n* : ELK 1b — used for one of the Old World

Red Delicious *n* : a usually large apple with sweet crisp juicy flesh and dark red skin

red·den \ˈred-n\ *vb* **red·dened; red·den·ing** \ˈred-ning, -n-ing\ : to make or become red or reddish; *esp* : BLUSH 1

red·dish \ˈred-ish\ *adj* : somewhat red — **red·dish·ness** *n*

red dwarf *n* : a star having much lower surface temperature, intrinsic luminosity, mass, and size than the sun

rede \ˈrēd\ *vt* **1** *archaic* : to give counsel to : ADVISE **2** *archaic* : INTERPRET 1, EXPLAIN [Old English *rǣdan* "to advise, interpret, read"]

red·ear \ˈred-ˌiər\ *n* : a common sunfish of the southern and eastern U.S. with orange-red marks on the gill cover

re·dec·o·rate \rē-ˈdek-ə-ˌrāt, ˈrē-\ *vb* **1** : to freshen or change in appearance : REFURBISH **2** : to freshen or change a decorative scheme — **re·dec·o·ra·tion** \ˌrē-ˌdek-ə-ˈrā-shən\ *n*

re·deem \ri-ˈdēm\ *vt* **1 a** : to buy back : REPURCHASE **b** : to get or win back **2 a** : to free from captivity usually by paying a ransom **b** : LIBERATE 1 **c** : to free from the bondage of sin **3** : to change for the better : REFORM **4** : REPAIR 1, RESTORE **5 a** : to get back (a pledge) by payment of an amount secured thereby **b** : to remove the obligation of by payment ‹the U.S. Treasury *redeems* savings bonds on demand› **c** : to change into something of value **6** : to make good : FULFILL ‹*redeem* a promise› **7 a** : to atone for : EXPIATE **b** : to offset the bad effect of [Medieval French *redemer,* from Latin *redimere,* from *re-, red-* "re-" + *emere* "to take, buy"] ***synonyms*** see RESCUE — **re·deem·able** \-ˈdē-mə-bəl\ *adj* — **re·deem·er** \-ˈdē-mər\ *n*

re·de·fine \ˌrē-di-ˈfīn\ *vt* **1** : to define (as a concept) again ‹*redefined* their terms› **2 a** : to reexamine or reevaluate especially with a view to change ‹*redefine* our goals› **b** : TRANSFORM 1a ‹new car models claim to *redefine* driving› — **re·def·i·ni·tion** \rē-ˌdef-ə-ˈnish-ən\ *n*

re·demp·tion \ri-ˈdem-shən, -ˈdemp-\ *n* : the act or process or an instance of redeeming [Medieval French *redempcion,* from Latin *redemptio,* from *redimere* "to redeem"] — **re·demp·tion·al** \-shnəl, -shən-l\ *adj* — **re·demp·tive** \-ˈdem-tiv, -ˈdemp-\ *adj*

Re·demp·tor·ist \ri-ˈdem-tə-rəst, -ˈdemp-, -trəst\ *n* : a member of the Roman Catholic Congregation of the Most Holy Redeemer [French *rédemptoriste,* from Late Latin *redemptor* "redeemer," derived from Latin *redimere* "to redeem"]

re·de·sign \ˌrēd-i-ˈzīn\ *vt* : to revise in appearance, function, or content — **redesign** *n*

re·de·vel·op \ˌrē-di-ˈvel-əp\ *vt* : to develop again; *esp* : REDESIGN, REBUILD — **redeveloper** *n*

re·de·vel·op·ment \ˌrēd-i-ˈvel-əp-mənt\ *n* : the act or process of redeveloping; *esp* : renewal of a blighted area

red–eye *n* **1** : the phenomenon of a subject's eyes appearing red in a color photograph taken with a flash **2** : a late night or overnight flight

red·fish \ˈred-ˌfish\ *n* : any of various reddish fishes

red fox *n* : a usually orange-red to reddish brown fox with a white-tipped tail — compare SILVER FOX

red fox

red giant *n* : a very large star with a relatively low surface temperature

red–green color blindness *n* : a deficiency of color vision that ranges from seeing red and green imperfectly to seeing only tones of yellow, blue, and gray

red gum *n* : SWEET GUM

red–hand·ed \ˈred-ˈhan-dəd\ *adv or adj* : in the act of committing a crime or misdeed

red·head \ˈred-ˌhed\ *n* **1** : a person having red hair **2** : a North American duck related to the canvasback but having a shorter bill with a black tip and in the male a brighter reddish head

red·head·ed \-ˌhed-əd\ *adj* : having red hair or a red head

redheaded woodpecker *n* : a large North American woodpecker that has a red head, a black back, and white patches on the wings

red heat *n* : the state of being red-hot; *also* : the temperature at which a substance is red-hot

red herring *n* **1** : a herring cured by salting and slow smoking to a dark brown color **2** : something intended to distract attention from the real issue [sense 2 from the practice of drawing a red herring across a trail to confuse hunting dogs]

red–hot \ˈred-ˈhät\ *adj* **1** : glowing red with heat **2** : exhibiting or marked by intense emotion, enthusiasm, or energy ⟨a *red-hot* political campaign⟩ **3** : FRESH, NEW ⟨*red-hot* news⟩

re·dia \ˈrēd-ē-ə\ *n, pl* **re·di·ae** \-ē-ˌē\ *also* **re·di·as** : a larva produced within the sporocyst of many trematodes that produces another generation of rediae or develops into a cercaria [Francesco *Redi*, died 1698?, Italian naturalist] — **re·di·al** \-ē-əl\ *adj*

Red Indian *n, chiefly British* : AMERICAN INDIAN

red·in·gote \ˈred-ing-ˌgōt\ *n* : a fitted outer garment: as **a** : a woman's lightweight coat open at the front **b** : a dress with a front gore of contrasting material [French, from English *riding coat*]

red·in·te·grate \ri-ˈdint-ə-ˌgrāt, re-\ *vt, archaic* : to restore to a former or sound state [Latin *redintegrare,* from *re-, red-* "re-" + *integrare* "to make complete"] — **red·in·te·gra·tion** \-ˌdint-ə-ˈgrā-shən, ˌrē-, ˌre-\ *n, archaic*

re·di·rect \ˌrēd-ə-ˈrekt, ˌrē-dī-\ *vt* : to change the course or direction of — **re·di·rec·tion** \-ˈrek-shən\ *n*

[1]re·dis·count \rē-ˈdis-ˌkau̇nt, ˈrē-; ˌrē-dis-ˈ\ *vt* : to discount again — **re·dis·count·able** \-ə-bəl\ *adj*

[2]re·dis·count \rē-ˈdis-ˌkau̇nt, ˈrē-\ *n* : the act or process of rediscounting

re·dis·trib·ute \ˌrē-dis-ˈtrib-yət\ *vt* **1** : to alter the distribution of **2** : to spread to other areas — **re·dis·tri·bu·tion** \-ˌdis-trə-ˈbyü-shən\ *n*

re·dis·trict \rē-ˈdis-trikt, ˈrē-\ *vt* : to divide anew into districts; *esp* : to revise the legislative districts of

red lead *n* : a red lead oxide Pb_3O_4 used in storage-battery plates, in glass and ceramics, and as a paint pigment

red–let·ter \ˈred-ˈlet-ər\ *adj* : memorable especially in a happy or joyful way ⟨a *red-letter* day⟩ [from the practice of marking holy days in red letters in church calendars]

red·line \ˈred-ˌlīn\ *vb* : to withhold home-loan funds or insurance from neighborhoods held to be poor economic risks : discriminate against in lending or insuring — **red·lin·ing** \-ing\ *n*

red man *n* : AMERICAN INDIAN

red maple *n* : a common North American maple that has reddish twigs and rather soft wood and grows chiefly in moist soils

red marrow *n* : BONE MARROW b

red meat *n* : meat (as beef) that is reddish in color when raw

red mullet *n* : either of two red or reddish goatfishes of warm seas that are used as food

red·neck \ˈred-ˌnek\ *n, sometimes disparaging* : a member of the white Southern rural laboring class

re·do \rē-ˈdü, ˈrē-\ *vt* **-did** \-ˈdid\; **-done** \-ˈdən\; **-do·ing** : to do over or again; *esp* : REDECORATE ⟨*redid* the bedroom in blue⟩

red oak *n* **1** : any of various North American oaks that have acorns that take two years to mature and leaves with bristles on the edges **2** : the wood of a red oak

red ocher *n* : a red earthy hematite used as a pigment

red·o·lence \ˈred-l-əns\ *n* **1** : SCENT 1b, AROMA **2** : the quality or state of being redolent

red·o·lent \-ənt\ *adj* **1** : exuding fragrance : AROMATIC **2 a** : full of a specified fragrance ⟨a room *redolent* of tobacco smoke⟩ **b** : tending to suggest ⟨a city *redolent* of ancient times⟩ [Middle French, from Latin *redolens,* present participle of *redolēre* "to emit a scent," from *re-, red-* "re-" + *olere* "to smell"] — **red·o·lent·ly** *adv*

re·dou·ble \rē-ˈdəb-əl, ˈrē-\ *vb* **1** : to make or become doubled (as in size, amount, or degree) ⟨*redouble* one's efforts⟩ **2** : to double back ⟨the fox *redoubled* on its tracks⟩ **3** : to double again

re·doubt \ri-ˈdau̇t\ *n* : a small often temporary fortification (as for defending a hilltop) [French *redoute,* from Italian *ridotto,* from Medieval Latin *reductus* "secret place," from Latin, "withdrawn," from *reducere* "to lead back"]

re·doubt·able \ri-ˈdau̇t-ə-bəl\ *adj* **1** : arousing fear or dread : FORMIDABLE ⟨a *redoubtable* enemy⟩ **2** : arousing admiring respect : EMINENT ⟨a *redoubtable* scholar⟩ [Medieval French *redoubtable,* from *redouter* "to dread," from *re-* "re-" + *douter* "to doubt"] — **re·doubt·ably** \-blē\ *adv*

re·dound \ri-ˈdau̇nd\ *vi* **1** : to become reflected back especially so as to bring credit or discredit ⟨actions that *redound* to one's credit⟩ **2** : to become transferred or added : ACCRUE ⟨additions that *redound* to the benefit of the library⟩ [Medieval French *redunder* "to overflow," from Latin *redundare,* from *re-, red-* "re-" + *unda* "wave"]

re·dox \ˈrē-ˌdäks\ *n* : OXIDATION-REDUCTION [*red*uction + *ox*idation]

red panda *n* : a long-tailed chiefly tree-dwelling mammal that is related to and resembles the raccoon, has long reddish brown fur and a ringed tail, feeds especially on bamboo leaves, and is found from the Himalayas to China — called also *lesser panda*

red–pen·cil \ˈred-ˈpen-səl\ *vt* **1** : CENSOR **2** : EDIT 1a, CORRECT, REVISE

red pepper *n* **1** : a mature red sweet pepper or hot pepper **2** : CAYENNE

red·poll \ˈred-ˌpōl\ *n* : either of two small finches with a red or rosy crown

[1]re·dress \ri-ˈdres\ *vt* **1** : to set (as a wrong) right : make amends for : REMEDY, RELIEVE **2** : to correct or amend the faults of [Medieval French *redresser,* "to set upright, restore, redress," from *re-* "re-" + *dresser* "to set straight," from Latin *directus* "direct"]

[2]re·dress \ri-ˈdres, ˈrē-ˌ\ *n* **1 a** : relief from distress **b** : means or possibility of seeking a remedy **2** : compensation for wrong or loss **3 a** : an act or instance of redressing **b** : CORRECTION 1, RETRIBUTION

red salmon *n* : SOCKEYE SALMON

red–shaft·ed flicker \ˈred-ˈshaf-təd-\ *n* : a flicker of western North America with light red on the underside of the tail and wings and in the male a red streak on each side of the base of the bill

red·shift \ˈred-ˈshift\ *n* : a displacement of the spectrum of a celestial body toward longer wavelengths that is a consequence of the Doppler effect or the gravitational field of the source; *also* : a measurement of a celestial body's redshift used to calculate the body's distance from earth — **red·shift·ed** *adj*

red snapper *n* : any of several reddish sea fishes including some used for food or sport

red snow *n* : snow reddened by various airborne dusts or especially by a growth of reddish algae

red spider *n* : SPIDER MITE

red spruce *n* : a spruce of the eastern U.S. and Canada that is an important source of lumber and pulpwood

red squirrel *n* : a common North American squirrel that has reddish upper parts and is smaller than the gray squirrel

red star *n* : a star having a low surface temperature and a red color

red·start \ˈred-ˌstärt\ *n* **1** : a small European thrush with a red breast and tail **2** : an American warbler with a black and orange male [*red* + obsolete *start* "tail," from Old English *steort*]

redstart 2

red–tailed hawk \ˈred-ˌtāld-\ *n* : an American hawk that has a rather short usually reddish tail and feeds chiefly on small rodents (as mice) — called also *redtail*

red tape *n* : official routine or procedure especially as marked by delay or inaction [from the red tape formerly used to bind legal documents in England]

red tide *n* : seawater discolored and made toxic by the presence of large numbers of dinoflagellates

red·top \ˈred-ˌtäp\ *n* : any of several grasses with reddish panicles including an important forage and lawn grass of eastern North America

re·duce \ri-ˈdüs, -ˈdyüs\ *vb* **1 a** : to draw together or cause to converge : CONSOLIDATE **b** : to diminish in size, amount, ex-

\ə\ abut	\au̇\ out	\i\ tip	\ȯ\ saw	\u̇\ foot
\ər\ further	\ch\ chin	\ī\ life	\ȯi\ coin	\y\ yet
\a\ mat	\e\ pet	\j\ job	\th\ thin	\yü\ few
\ā\ take	\ē\ easy	\ng\ sing	\t͟h\ this	\yu̇\ cure
\ä\ cot, cart	\g\ go	\ō\ bone	\ü\ food	\zh\ vision

tent, or number ⟨*reduce* the number of accidents⟩; *esp* : to lose weight by dieting **2** : to bring to a specified state or condition ⟨*reduce* anarchy to order⟩ **3** : to force to surrender **4 a** : to bring to a systematic form or character ⟨*reduce* language to writing⟩ ⟨*reduced* their observations to a theorem⟩ **b** : to become converted or equated ⟨their differences *reduced* to a question of semantics⟩ **5** : to correct (as a fracture) by bringing displaced or broken parts back into normal position **6 a** : to lower in grade or rank : DEMOTE **b** : to lower in condition or status ⟨*reduced* to panhandling⟩ **c** : to diminish in strength or intensity **d** : to diminish in value **7 a** : to change the denominations or form of without changing the value **b** : to transpose from one form into another **c** : to change (a mathematical expression) to a simpler form without changing the value ⟨*reduce* a fraction⟩ **8** : to break down (as by crushing or grinding) ⟨*reduce* metal from its ore⟩ **9 a** : to bring to the metallic state by removal of nonmetallic elements **b** : DEOXIDIZE **c** : to combine with or subject to the action of hydrogen **d** (1) : to change (an element or ion) from a higher to a lower oxidation state (2) : to add one or more electrons to (an atom or ion or molecule) [Latin *reducere* "to lead back," from *re-* + *ducere* "to lead"] — **re·duc·er** *n* — **re·duc·ibil·i·ty** \-ˌdü-sə-ˈbil-ət-ē, -ˌdyü-\ *n* — **re·duc·ible** \-ˈdü-sə-bəl, -ˈdyü-\ *adj* — **re·duc·ibly** \-blē\ *adv*

reducing agent *n* : a substance that reduces a chemical compound usually by donating electrons

re·duc·tase \ri-ˈdək-ˌtās, -ˌtāz\ *n* : an enzyme that catalyzes a chemical reduction

re·duc·tio ad ab·sur·dum \ri-ˈdək-tē-ˌō-ˌad-əb-ˈsərd-əm, -ˈzərd-\ *n* : disproof of a proposition by showing that it contradicts accepted propositions when carried to its logical conclusion [Late Latin, literally, "reduction to the absurd"]

re·duc·tion \ri-ˈdək-shən\ *n* **1** : the act or process of reducing : the state of being reduced **2 a** : the amount by which something is reduced in price **b** : something made by reducing **3** : a South American Indian settlement directed by Spanish missionaries **4** : MEIOSIS; *esp* : halving of the chromosome number usually in the first meiotic division [Medieval French *reducion,* from Latin *reductio* "restoration," from *reducere* "to lead back"] — **re·duc·tion·al** \-shnəl, -shən-l\ *adj* — **re·duc·tive** \-ˈdək-tiv\ *adj*

reduction division *n* : the first meiotic cell division in the formation of gametes in which the number of chromosomes in each cell is halved; *also* : MEIOSIS

re·dun·dan·cy \ri-ˈdən-dən-sē\ *n, pl* **-cies** **1** : the quality or state of being redundant **2** : a lavish or excessive amount **3 a** : unnecessary repetition : PROLIXITY **b** : an act or instance of needless repetition

re·dun·dant \ri-ˈdən-dənt\ *adj* **1 a** : exceeding what is necessary or normal **b** : using more words than necessary : REPETITIOUS **2** : ABUNDANT, PROFUSE [Latin *redundare* "to overflow," from *re-, red-* "re-" + *unda* "wave"] — **re·dun·dant·ly** *adv*

re·du·pli·cate \ri-ˈdü-pli-ˌkāt, ˈrē-, -ˈdyü-\ *vt* **1** : to make or perform again : COPY **2** : to form (a word) by reduplication — **re·du·pli·cate** \-kət\ *adj*

re·du·pli·ca·tion \ri-ˌdü-pli-ˈkā-shən, ˌrē-, -ˌdyü-\ *n* **1** : an act or instance of doubling or reiterating : DUPLICATION **2** : repetition of a radical element or a part of it occurring usually at the beginning of a word and often accompanied by change of the radical vowel — **re·du·pli·ca·tive** \ri-ˈdü-pli-ˌkāt-iv, ˈrē-, -ˈdyü-\ *adj* — **re·du·pli·ca·tive·ly** *adv*

red·wing \ˈred-ˌwing\ *n* **1** : a red-winged European thrush **2** : RED-WINGED BLACKBIRD

red–winged blackbird \ˌred-ˌwingd-, -ˌwing-\ *n* : a North American blackbird of which the adult male is black with a patch of bright scarlet on each wing — called also *redwing blackbird*

red-winged blackbird

red·wood \ˈred-ˌwu̇d\ *n* : a tall coniferous evergreen tree chiefly of coastal California that is related to the bald cypresses and sometimes reaches a height of 360 feet (110 meters); *also* : its durable brownish red wood

re·echo \rē-ˈek-ō, ˈrē-\ *vb* : to echo back : REVERBERATE ⟨thunder *reechoed* through the valley⟩

reed \ˈrēd\ *n* **1 a** : any of various tall grasses (as phragmites) having slender often prominently jointed stems and growing especially in wet areas **b** : a stem of such a grass **c** : a mass or growth of reeds **2** : ARROW 1 **3** : a musical instrument made of the hollow joint of a plant **4** : an ancient Hebrew unit of length equal to 6 cubits **5 a** : a thin elastic tongue (as of cane, wood, metal, or plastic) fastened at one end to the mouthpiece of a musical instrument (as a clarinet) or to a fixture (as a reed block) over an air opening (as in an accordion) and set in vibration by an air current (as the breath) **b** : a reed instrument ⟨the *reeds* of an orchestra⟩ **6** : a device on a loom resembling a comb and used to space warp yarns evenly [Old English *hrēod*]

reed·buck \-ˌbək\ *n, pl* **reedbuck** *also* **reedbucks** : any of several fawn-colored African antelopes with the males having curved and ridged horns

reed organ *n* : a keyboard wind instrument in which the wind acts on a set of metal reeds

re·ed·u·cate \rē-ˈej-ə-ˌkāt, ˈrē-\ *vt* : to train again; *esp* : to rehabilitate through education — **re·ed·u·ca·tion** \ˌrē-ˌej-ə-ˈkā-shən\ *n* — **re·ed·u·ca·tive** \rē-ˈej-ə-ˌkāt-iv, ˈrē-\ *adj*

reedy \ˈrēd-ē\ *adj* **reed·i·er; -est** **1** : abounding in or covered with reeds ⟨a *reedy* marsh⟩ **2** : made of or resembling reeds; *esp* : SLENDER, FRAIL ⟨*reedy* arms⟩ ⟨the *reedy* stem of a goblet⟩ **3** : having the tone quality of a reed instrument ⟨a *reedy* tenor voice⟩ — **reed·i·ly** \ˈrēd-l-ē\ *adv* — **reed·i·ness** \ˈrēd-ē-nəs\ *n*

[1]**reef** \ˈrēf\ *n* **1** : a part of a sail taken in or let out in regulating size **2** : the reduction in sail area made by reefing [Old Norse *rif*]

[2]**reef** *vt* : to reduce the area of (a sail) by rolling or folding and tying a portion

[3]**reef** *n* **1** : a chain of rocks or coral or ridge of sand at or near the surface of water **2** : LODE [Dutch *rif*]

[1]**reef·er** \ˈrē-fər\ *n* **1** : one that reefs **2** : a close-fitting usually double-breasted jacket of thick cloth

[2]**reefer** *n* : REFRIGERATOR; *also* : a refrigerator car, truck, trailer, or ship [by alteration]

[3]**reefer** *n* : a marijuana cigarette [probably from Mexican Spanish *grifa*]

reef knot *n* : a square knot used in reefing a sail

[1]**reek** \ˈrēk\ *n* **1** : VAPOR 1 **2** : a strong or disagreeable odor [Old English *rēc* "smoke"] — **reeky** \ˈrē-kē\ *adj*

[2]**reek** *vi* **1** : to emit smoke or vapor **2** : to have or give off a strong or unpleasant smell ⟨clothes *reeking* of tobacco smoke⟩ **3** : to give a strong impression of some quality or feature ⟨she *reeks* of hypocrisy⟩

[1]**reel** \ˈrēl\ *n* **1** : a revolvable device on which something flexible is wound: as **a** : a small windlass at the butt of a fishing rod for the line **b** : a flanged spool especially for photographic film **2** : a quantity of something wound on a reel [Old English *hrēol*]

[2]**reel** *vb* **1** : to wind on or as if on a reel **2** : to bring in (as a hooked fish) by reeling a fishing line : to wind or turn a reel — **reel·able** \ˈrē-lə-bəl\ *adj* — **reel·er** *n*

[3]**reel** *vi* **1 a** : to whirl around ⟨*reeling* in a dance⟩ **b** : to be in a whirl ⟨heads *reeling* with excitement⟩ **2** : to give way : fall back ⟨soldiers *reeling* in defeat⟩ **3** : STAGGER 1a [Middle English *relen,* probably from [1]*reel*]

[4]**reel** *n* : a reeling motion

[5]**reel** *n* : a lively dance originally of the Scottish Highlands; *also* : its music [probably from [4]*reel*]

re·elect \ˌrē-ə-ˈlekt\ *vt* : to elect for another term in office — **re·elec·tion** \-ˈlek-shən\ *n*

reel off *vt* : to recite fluently ⟨*reeled off* the statistics⟩

re·en·act \ˌrē-ə-ˈnakt\ *vt* **1** : to enact again **2** : to perform again — **re·en·act·ment** \-ˈnakt-mənt, -ˈnak-\ *n*

re·en·ter \rē-ˈent-ər\ *vb* **1** : to enter again ⟨*reenter* the data into the computer⟩ **2** : to return to and enter ⟨*reenter* the labor force⟩

re·en·trance \rē-ˈen-trəns, ˈrē-\ *n* **1** : REENTRY 2 **2** : REENTRY 3

re·en·trant \rē-ˈen-trənt\ *n* : one that reenters ⟨*reentrants* to the labor force⟩

re·en·try \rē-ˈen-trē, ˈrē-\ *n* **1** : a retaking possession especially from a tenant **2** : a second or new entry **3** : the action of reentering the earth's atmosphere after travel in space

[1]**reeve** \ˈrēv\ *n* : a medieval English manor officer responsible chiefly for enforcing the discharge of feudal obligations [Old English *gerēfa*]

[2]reeve *vt* **rove** \'rōv\ *or* **reeved; reev·ing 1 :** to pass (as a rope) through a hole or opening **2 :** to rig for operation by passing a rope through ‹*reeve* up a set of blocks› [origin unknown]

[3]reeve *n* **:** the female of the ruff [origin unknown]

ref \'ref\ *n* **:** REFEREE 2

re·fash·ion \rē-'fash-ən, 'rē-\ *vt* **:** to make over **:** ALTER

re·fec·tion \ri-'fek-shən\ *n* **1 :** refreshment of mind, spirit, or body; *esp* **:** NOURISHMENT **2 a :** the taking of refreshment **b :** food and drink together **:** REPAST [Medieval French *refectiun,* from Latin *refectio,* from *reficere* "to restore," from *re-* + *facere* "to make"]

re·fec·to·ry \ri-'fek-tə-rē, -trē\ *n, pl* **-ries :** a dining hall especially in a monastery or convent [Late Latin *refectorium,* from Latin *reficere* "to restore"]

refectory table *n* **:** a long narrow table with heavy legs

re·fer \ri-'fər\ *vb* **re·ferred; re·fer·ring 1 :** to place in a certain class so far as cause, relationship, or source is concerned ‹*referred* the defeat to poor training› **2 :** to send or direct to a person or place for treatment, help, or information ‹*refer* a child to a dictionary› ‹*refer* a patient to a specialist› **3 :** to go for information, advice, or aid ‹*refer* to the dictionary for the meaning of a word› **4 :** to have relation or connection **:** RELATE ‹the asterisk *refers* to a footnote› **5 :** to direct attention **:** make reference ‹no one *referred* to yesterday's quarrel› [Latin *referre* "to bring back, report, refer," from *re-* + *ferre* "to carry"] — **re·fer·able** \'ref-rə-bəl, -ə-rə-; ri-'fər-ə-\ *adj* — **re·fer·rer** \ri-'fər-ər\ *n*

synonyms REFER, ALLUDE mean to direct attention to something. REFER implies intentional introduction and distinct mention as by direct naming ‹the story *referred* to the suspect by name›. ALLUDE suggests such indirect mention as is conveyed in a hint, a figure of speech, or other roundabout expression ‹*alluded* to inconsistencies in her explanation›.

[1]ref·er·ee \ˌref-ə-'rē\ *n* **1 a :** a person to whom a legal matter is referred for investigation and report or for settlement **b :** a person who reviews a usually technical paper and recommends whether it should be published **2 :** a sports official usually having final authority in administering a game

[2]referee *vb* **-eed; -ee·ing :** to act or supervise as a referee

ref·er·ence \'ref-ərns, 'ref-rəns, -ə-rəns\ *n* **1 :** the act of referring or consulting **2 :** a bearing on a matter **:** RELATION ‹with *reference* to what was said› **3 a :** a remark referring to something **:** ALLUSION ‹made *reference* to our agreement› **b :** a sign or indication referring a reader to another passage or book **c :** consultation of information sources ‹books for ready *reference*› **4 a :** a person to whom inquiries as to the character or ability of another can be made **b :** a statement as to a person's character or ability given by someone familiar with them **c :** a book, passage, or document to which a reader is referred

reference book *n* **:** a book (as a dictionary, encyclopedia, or almanac) containing useful facts or information

reference mark *n* **:** a conventional mark (as *, †, or ‡) used in printing or writing to mark a reference

ref·er·en·dum \ˌref-ə-'ren-dəm\ *n, pl* **-da** \-də\ *or* **-dums :** the principle or practice of submitting to popular vote a measure proposed or passed on by a legislative body or by popular initiative; *also* **:** a vote on such a measure [Latin, neuter of *referendus* "to be referred," from *referre* "to refer"]

ref·er·ent \'ref-rənt, -ə-rənt\ *n* **:** something that refers or is referred to; *esp* **:** the thing a word stands for [Latin *referens,* present participle of *referre* "to refer"] — **referent** *adj*

re·fer·ral \ri-'fər-əl\ *n* **1 :** the act or an instance of referring **2 :** one that is referred

re·fig·ure \rē-'fig-yər\ *vt* **1 :** to figure again or anew ‹*refigure* the shipping charges› **2 :** to give new meaning or use to ‹*refigure* old fashion styles›

[1]re·fill \rē-'fil, 'rē-\ *vb* **:** to fill or become filled again — **re·fill·able** \-'fil-ə-bəl\ *adj*

[2]re·fill \'rē-ˌfil\ *n* **1 :** material used to replace the exhausted supply of a device ‹a lipstick *refill*› **2 :** something provided again; *esp* **:** a second or later filling of a medical prescription

re·fi·nance \ˌrē-fə-'nans, -'fī-ˌ, -fī-'\ *vb* **1 :** to renew or reorganize the financing of **2 :** to finance something anew

re·fine \ri-'fīn\ *vb* **1 a :** to come or bring to a pure state ‹*refine* sugar› **b :** to distill (crude oil) and purify the resulting products **2 :** to make or become improved or perfected by pruning or polishing **3 :** to free from what is coarse, vulgar, or uncouth **4 :** to make improvement by introducing subtleties or distinctions ‹*refined* upon the older methods› — **re·fin·er** *n*

re·fined \ri-'fīnd\ *adj* **1 :** freed from impurities **:** PURE ‹*refined* sugar› **2 :** socially well trained **:** WELL-BRED, CULTIVATED ‹very *refined* manners› **3 :** carried to a fine point **:** EXACT ‹*refined* measurements›

re·fine·ment \ri-'fīn-mənt\ *n* **1 :** the act or process of refining **2 :** the quality or state of being refined **:** CULTIVATION **3 a :** a refined feature or method **b :** SUBTLETY 2 **c :** a feature or device intended to improve or perfect

re·fin·ery \ri-'fīn-rē, -ə-rē\ *n, pl* **-er·ies :** a building and equipment for refining or purifying metals, oil, or sugar

re·fin·ish \rē-'fin-ish, 'rē-\ *vt* **:** to give (as furniture) a new surface — **re·fin·ish·er** *n*

re·fit \rē-'fit, 'rē-\ *vb* **re·fit·ted; re·fit·ting :** to get ready for use again **:** fit out or equip again ‹*refit* a ship for service› — **re·fit** \'rē-ˌfit, rē-', 'rē-'\ *n*

re·flect \ri-'flekt\ *vb* **1 :** to bend or throw back waves of light, sound, or heat ‹a polished surface *reflects* light› **2 :** to give back an image or likeness of as if by a mirror **3 :** to bring as a result ‹your scholarship *reflects* credit on your school› **4 :** to cast reproach or blame ‹our bad conduct *reflects* on our training› **5 :** to think seriously and carefully **:** MEDITATE [Latin *reflectere* "to bend back," from *re-* + *flectere* "to bend"]

synonyms see THINK

re·flec·tance \ri-'flek-təns\ *n* **:** the part of the light falling upon a surface that is reflected

reflecting telescope *n* **:** REFLECTOR 2

re·flec·tion \ri-'flek-shən\ *n* **1 :** an instance of reflecting; *esp* **:** the return of light or sound waves from a surface **2 :** the production of an image by or as if by a mirror **3 a :** the action of bending or folding back **b :** a reflected part **:** FOLD **4 :** something produced by reflecting; *esp* **:** an image given back by a reflecting surface **5 :** an often obscure or indirect criticism **:** REPROACH **6 :** a thought, idea, or opinion formed or a remark made as a result of careful thinking **7 :** consideration of some subject matter, idea, or purpose **8 :** a geometric figure or a graph of an equation that is symmetric to another geometric figure or graph with respect to a line (as an axis of a coordinate system) — **re·flec·tion·al** \-shnəl, -shən-l\ *adj*

re·flec·tive \ri-'flek-tiv\ *adj* **1 :** capable of reflecting light, images, or sound waves **2 :** marked by reflection **:** THOUGHTFUL **3 :** of, relating to, or caused by reflection — **re·flec·tive·ly** *adv* — **re·flec·tive·ness** *n* — **re·flec·tiv·i·ty** \ˌrē-ˌflek-'tiv-ət-ē, ri-\ *n*

re·flec·tor \ri-'flek-tər\ *n* **1 :** one that reflects; *esp* **:** a polished surface for reflecting light or heat **2 :** a telescope in which the principal focusing element is a mirror

[1]re·flex \'rē-ˌfleks\ *n* **1 a :** reflected heat, light, or color **b :** a mirrored image **c :** a copy exact in essential or peculiar features **2 a :** an automatic response to a stimulus in which a nerve impulse passes inward from a receptor to the spinal cord and thence outward to an effector (as a muscle or gland) without reaching the level of consciousness and often without first passing to the brain ‹the knee-jerk *reflex*› — compare HABIT 5a **b** *pl* **:** the power of acting or responding with adequate speed ‹an athlete with great *reflexes*› [Latin *reflexus,* past participle of *reflectere* "to reflect"]

[2]reflex *adj* **1 :** produced in reaction, resistance, or return **2 :** of, relating to, or produced by a reflex of the nervous system ‹*reflex* action› — **re·flex·ly** *adv*

reflex arc *n* **:** the complete nervous path involved in a reflex

reflex camera *n* **:** a single- or double-lens camera in which the image formed by the focusing lens is reflected onto a usually ground-glass screen for viewing

re·flexed \'rē-ˌflekst, ri-'\ *adj* **:** bent or curved backward or downward ‹*reflexed* petals›

re·flex·ion \ri-'flek-shən\ *chiefly British variant of* REFLECTION

[1]re·flex·ive \ri-'flek-siv\ *adj* **1 :** REFLEXED **2 :** relating to, characterized by, or being a relation that exists between an entity and itself ‹the relation "is equal to" is *reflexive* but the relation "is the parent of" is not› **3 :** of, relating to, or being an action directed back upon the doer or the grammatical subject ‹*myself* in "I hurt myself" is a *reflexive* pronoun› **4 :** characterized by habitual behavior that occurs automatically without thinking ⟨a *reflexive* response⟩ — **re·flex·ive·ly** *adv* — **re·flex·ive·ness** *n* — **re·flex·iv·i·ty** \ˌrē-ˌflek-ˈsiv-ət-ē, ri-\ *n*

[2]**reflexive** *n* : a reflexive pronoun or verb

re·flux \ˈrē-ˌfləks\ *n* : a flowing back : EBB

re·fo·cus \rē-ˈfō-kəs\ *vb* **1** : to focus again ⟨*refocus* the camera lens⟩ **2** : to change or cause to change emphasis or direction ⟨*refocused* the discussion⟩

re·for·es·ta·tion \rē-ˌfȯr-ə-ˈstā-shən, -ˌfär-\ *n* : the action of renewing a forest by planting seeds or young trees — **re·for·est** \-ˈfȯr-əst, -ˈfär-\ *vt*

[1]**re·form** \ri-ˈfȯrm\ *vb* **1** : to make better by removal of faults ⟨*reform* the penal system⟩ **2** : to correct or improve one's own character or habits [Medieval French *refurmer,* from Latin *reformare,* from *re-* + *formare* "to form"] — **re·form·able** \-ˈfȯr-mə-bəl\ *adj*

[2]**reform** *n* **1** : improvement of what is bad or corrupt **2** : a removal or correction of an abuse, a wrong, or errors

re–form \rē-ˈfȯrm, ˈrē-\ *vt* : to form or take form again

ref·or·ma·tion \ˌref-ər-ˈmā-shən\ *n* **1** : the act of reforming : the state of being reformed **2** *cap* : a 16th century religious movement marked by rejection or modification of much of the Roman Catholic doctrine and practice and establishment of the Protestant churches — **ref·or·ma·tion·al** \-shnəl, -shən-l\ *adj*

re·for·ma·tive \ri-ˈfȯr-mət-iv\ *adj* : tending or inclined to reform

[1]**re·for·ma·to·ry** \ri-ˈfȯr-mə-ˌtōr-ē, -ˌtȯr-\ *adj* : tending or intended to reform ⟨*reformatory* measures⟩

[2]**reformatory** *n, pl* **-ries** : a penal institution to which youthful or first offenders or women are committed for training and rehabilitation

re·formed *adj* **1** : changed for the better **2** *cap* : PROTESTANT; *esp* : of or relating to the Calvinist churches of continental Europe

reformed spelling *n* : any of several methods of spelling English words that use letters with more phonetic consistency than conventional spelling and usually discard some silent letters (as in *thoro* for thorough)

re·form·er \ri-ˈfȯr-mər\ *n* **1** : one that works for or urges reform **2** *cap* : a leader of the Reformation

re·form·ism \ri-ˈfȯr-ˌmiz-əm\ *n* : a doctrine, policy, or movement of reform — **re·form·ist** \-məst\ *n*

Reform Judaism *n* : a 19th and 20th century development of Judaism marked by rationalization of belief, simplification of many observances, and affirmation of the religious rather than the national character of Judaism

reform school *n* : a reformatory for youthful offenders

re·fract \ri-ˈfrakt\ *vt* : to subject to refraction [Latin *refractus,* past participle of *refringere* "to break open, break up," from *re-* + *frangere* "to break"]

refracting telescope *n* : REFRACTOR

re·frac·tion \ri-ˈfrak-shən\ *n* : the bending of a ray when it passes at an angle from one medium (as air) into another (as glass) in which its speed is different — **re·frac·tive** \-ˈfrak-tiv\ *adj* — **re·frac·tiv·i·ty** \ˌrē-ˌfrak-ˈtiv-ət-ē, ri-\ *n*

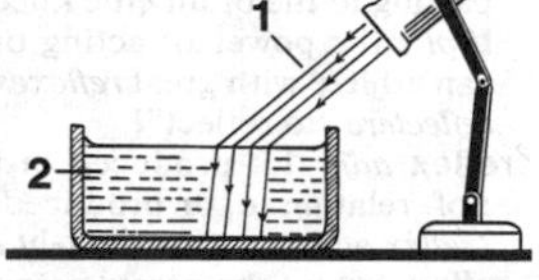

refraction: *1* light rays, *2* water

refractive index *n* : the ratio of the speed of light in one medium (as air or glass) to that in another medium

re·frac·tor \ri-ˈfrak-tər\ *n* : a telescope whose principal focusing element is a lens

[1]**re·frac·to·ry** \ri-ˈfrak-tə-rē, -trē\ *adj* **1** : resisting control or authority : STUBBORN ⟨a *refractory* child⟩ **2 a** : resistant to treatment or cure **b** : unresponsive to stimulus **3** : difficult to fuse, corrode, or draw out; *esp* : capable of enduring high temperature [Latin *refractarius,* from *refragari* "to oppose"] ***synonyms*** see UNRULY — **re·frac·to·ri·ly** \-tə-rə-lē, -trə-\ *adv* — **re·frac·to·ri·ness** \-tə-rē-nəs, -trē-\ *n*

[2]**refractory** *n, pl* **-ries** : something refractory; *esp* : a heat-resisting ceramic material

[1]**re·frain** \ri-ˈfrān\ *vi* : to hold oneself back from some often impulsive course of action ⟨*refrain* from laughing⟩ [Medieval French *refreiner, refreindre* "to restrain," from Latin *refrenare,* from *re-* + *frenum* "bridle"] — **re·frain·ment** \-mənt\ *n*

synonyms REFRAIN, ABSTAIN, FORBEAR mean to keep oneself from doing or indulging in something. REFRAIN suggests the checking of a momentary impulse or inclination ⟨*refrain* from smiling⟩. ABSTAIN implies deliberate renunciation or self-denial on principle ⟨*abstained* from alcohol in any form⟩. FORBEAR suggests self-restraint motivated by compassion, charity, or stoicism ⟨could not *forbear* from expressing my distress⟩.

[2]**refrain** *n* : a regularly recurring phrase or verse especially at the end of each stanza of a poem or song : CHORUS; *also* : the melody of a refrain [Medieval French, from *refraindre* "to break up, moderate," from Latin *refringere* "to break up, refract"]

re·fran·gi·ble \ri-ˈfran-jə-bəl\ *adj* : capable of being refracted [derived from Latin *refringere* "to break up"] — **re·fran·gi·bil·i·ty** \-ˌfran-jə-ˈbil-ət-ē\ *n* — **re·fran·gi·ble·ness** *n*

re·fresh \ri-ˈfresh\ *vb* **1** : to restore strength and animation to : REVIVE ⟨sleep *refreshes* the body⟩ **2 a** : to restore or maintain by renewing supply : REPLENISH **b** : STIMULATE ⟨let me *refresh* your memory⟩ **3** : to restore water to **4** : to take refreshment **5** : to update or renew (as an image, a display, or a computer memory) especially by sending a new signal ***synonyms*** see RENEW

re·fresh·en \-ˈfresh-ən\ *vt* **1** : REFRESH 1 **2** : REFRESH 2

re·fresh·er \ri-ˈfresh-ər\ *n* **1** : something that refreshes **2** : review or instruction designed especially to keep one up-to-date on professional developments

re·fresh·ing \-ing\ *adj* : serving to refresh; *esp* : agreeably stimulating because of freshness or newness — **re·fresh·ing·ly** \-ing-lē\ *adv*

re·fresh·ment \ri-ˈfresh-mənt\ *n* **1** : the act of refreshing : the state of being refreshed **2 a** : something that refreshes **b** *pl* : a light meal

re·fried beans \ˈrē-ˌfrīd-\ *n* : beans cooked with seasonings, fried, then mashed and fried again

re·frig·er·ant \ri-ˈfrij-rənt, -ə-rənt\ *n* : a substance used in refrigeration

re·frig·er·ate \ri-ˈfrij-ə-ˌrāt\ *vt* : to make or keep cold or cool; *esp* : to freeze or chill (food) for preservation [Latin *refrigerare,* from *re-* + *frigerare* "to cool," from *frigor-, frigus* "cold"] — **re·frig·er·a·tion** \ri-ˌfrij-ə-ˈrā-shən\ *n*

re·frig·er·a·tor \ri-ˈfrij-ə-ˌrāt-ər\ *n* : a cabinet or room for keeping articles (as food) cool especially by means of a mechanical device

reft *past of* REAVE

re·fu·el \rē-ˈfyü-əl, ˈrē-\ *vb* : to provide with or take on additional fuel

ref·uge \ˈref-yüj, -ˌyüj\ *n* **1** : shelter or protection from danger or distress **2** : a place that provides shelter or protection ⟨a wildlife *refuge*⟩ [Medieval French, from Latin *refugium,* from *refugere* "to escape," from *re-* + *fugere* "to flee"]

ref·u·gee \ˌref-yu̇-ˈjē\ *n* : a person who flees for safety especially to a foreign country

re·ful·gence \ri-ˈfu̇l-jəns, -ˈfəl-\ *n* : a radiant or resplendent quality or state : BRILLIANCE [Latin *refulgentia,* from *refulgēre* "to shine brightly," from *re-* + *fulgēre* "to shine"] — **re·ful·gent** \-jənt\ *adj*

[1]**re·fund** \ri-ˈfənd, ˈrē-ˌfənd\ *vt* : to return (money) in restitution or repayment [Latin *refundere,* literally, "to pour back," from *re-* + *fundere* "to pour"] — **re·fund·able** \-ə-bəl\ *adj*

[2]**re·fund** \ˈrē-ˌfənd\ *n* **1** : the act of refunding **2** : a sum refunded

[3]**re·fund** \rē-ˈfənd, ˈrē-\ *vt* : to fund (a debt) again or anew

re·fur·bish \rē-ˈfər-bish, ˈrē-\ *vt* : to brighten or freshen up : RENOVATE — **re·fur·bish·ment** \-mənt\ *n*

re·fus·al \ri-ˈfyü-zəl\ *n* **1** : the act of refusing **2** : the opportunity or right of refusing or taking before others

[1]**re·fuse** \ri-ˈfyüz\ *vb* **1** : to decline to accept : REJECT ⟨*refused* the money⟩ **2 a** : to show or express positive unwillingness : fail deliberately ⟨*refused* to act⟩ **b** : DENY ⟨was *refused* entrance⟩ **3** : to withhold acceptance, compliance, or permission [Medieval French *refuser*] — **re·fus·er** *n*

[2]**ref·use** \ˈref-ˌyüs, -ˌyüz\ *n* **1** : worthless material **2** : RUBBISH, TRASH [Medieval French *refus* "leavings," from *refuser* "to refuse"]

ref·u·ta·tion \ˌref-yu̇-ˈtā-shən\ *n* : the act or process of refuting : DISPROOF

re·fute \ri-ˈfyüt\ *vt* : to prove wrong by argument or evidence : show to be false ⟨*refute* a witness's testimony⟩ [Latin *refutare* "to check, suppress, refute"] — **re·fut·able** \-ˈfyüt-ə-bəl\ *adj* — **re·fut·ably** \-blē\ *adv* — **re·fut·er** *n*

reg \ˈreg\ *n* : REGULATION ⟨government *regs*⟩

re·gain \ri-ˈgān\ *vt* **1** : to gain again : RECOVER ⟨*regained* my health⟩ **2** : to get back to : reach again ⟨*regain* the shore⟩

re·gal \ˈrē-gəl\ *adj* **1** : of, relating to, or suitable for a sovereign **2** : notably excellent or magnificent : SPLENDID [Latin *regalis,* from *reg-, rex* "king"] — **re·gal·i·ty** \ri-ˈgal-ət-ē\ *n* — **re·gal·ly** \ˈrē-gə-lē\ *adv*

re·gale \ri-ˈgāl\ *vb* **1** : to treat or entertain lavishly **2** : to give pleasure and amusement to ⟨*regaled* us with stories⟩ **3** : to feast oneself : FEED [French *régaler,* from Middle French *regale* "sumptuous feast," from *re-* + *galer* "to have a good time"] — **re·gale·ment** \-mənt\ *n*

re·ga·lia \ri-ˈgāl-yə\ *n sing or pl* **1** : the emblems and symbols (as the crown and scepter) of royalty **2** : the insignia of an office or order **3** : special or official dress [Medieval Latin, from Latin *regalis* "regal"]

[1]**re·gard** \ri-ˈgärd\ *n* **1 a** : CONSIDERATION 1, HEED **b** : LOOK 1, GAZE **2 a** : the worth or estimation in which something is held **b** (1) : a feeling of respect and affection : ESTEEM (2) *pl* : friendly greetings implying such feeling ⟨give them my *regards*⟩ **3** : REFERENCE, RESPECT ⟨this is in *regard* to your unpaid balance⟩ **4** : an aspect to be considered ⟨nothing to worry about in that *regard*⟩ [Medieval French *regarder* "to look back at, regard," from *re-* + *garder* "to guard, look at"]

[2]**regard** *vt* **1** : to pay attention to **2 a** : to show respect or consideration for **b** : to hold in high esteem **3** : to look at steadily or attentively **4** : to take into consideration or account **5** : CONSIDER 3 ⟨*regarded* you as a friend⟩ — **as regards** : with respect to : REGARDING

synonyms REGARD, RESPECT, ESTEEM, ADMIRE mean to recognize the worth of. REGARD is a general term and requires some qualification ⟨one highly *regarded* in literary circles⟩. RESPECT implies having a good opinion of without suggesting real liking or warmth of feeling ⟨*respected* her views⟩. ESTEEM implies high evaluation together with warmth of feeling ⟨no citizen of the town was more highly *esteemed*⟩. ADMIRE implies enthusiastic and often uncritical appreciation ⟨a musician that I truly *admire*⟩.

re·gard·ful \ri-ˈgärd-fəl\ *adj* **1** : OBSERVANT 3, HEEDFUL **2** : full of or expressing regard : RESPECTFUL — **re·gard·ful·ly** \-fə-lē\ *adv* — **re·gard·ful·ness** *n*

re·gard·ing *prep* : with respect to : CONCERNING

[1]**re·gard·less** \ri-ˈgärd-ləs\ *adj* : having or taking no regard : HEEDLESS — **re·gard·less·ly** *adv* — **re·gard·less·ness** *n*

[2]**regardless** *adv* : despite everything ⟨we are going there *regardless*⟩

re·gat·ta \ri-ˈgät-ə, -ˈgat-\ *n* : a boat race or a series of such races [Italian *regata*]

re·gen·cy \ˈrē-jən-sē\ *n, pl* **-cies** **1** : the office, jurisdiction, or government of a regent or body of regents **2** : the period of rule of a regent or body of regents

Regency *adj* : of, relating to, or resembling the furniture or the dress of the regency (1811–20) of George, Prince of Wales

re·gen·er·a·cy \ri-ˈjen-rə-sē, -ə-rə-\ *n* : the state of being regenerated

[1]**re·gen·er·ate** \ri-ˈjen-rət, -ə-rət\ *adj* : having been regenerated; *esp* : spiritually reborn or converted — **re·gen·er·ate·ly** *adv* — **re·gen·er·ate·ness** *n*

[2]**re·gen·er·ate** \ri-ˈjen-ə-ˌrāt\ *vb* **1** : to cause to be reborn spiritually **2** : to reform radically for the better ⟨*regenerating* criminals⟩ **3** : to generate or produce anew; *esp* : to replace (a lost or damaged body part) by a new growth of tissue **4** : to restore to original strength or properties — **re·gen·er·a·tor** \-ˌrāt-ər\ *n*

re·gen·er·a·tion \ri-ˌjen-ə-ˈrā-shən, ˌrē-\ *n* **1** : an act or the process of regenerating : the state of being regenerated **2** : spiritual renewal or revival

re·gen·er·a·tive \ri-ˈjen-ə-ˌrāt-iv\ *adj* **1** : of, relating to, or marked by regeneration **2** : tending to regenerate

re·gent \ˈrē-jənt\ *n* **1** : a person who governs a kingdom during the minority, absence, or disability of the sovereign **2** : a member of a governing board (as of a state university) [Medieval Latin *regens,* from Latin *regere* "to direct, rule"] — **regent** *adj*

reg·gae \ˈreg-ˌā, ˈrā-ˌgā\ *n* : popular music of Jamaican origin that combines native styles with elements of U.S. black popular music and is performed at moderate tempos with the accent on the offbeat [origin unknown]

reg·i·cide \ˈrej-ə-ˌsīd\ *n* **1** : a person who murders a king or assists in his death **2** : the murdering of a king [Latin *reg-, rex* "king" + English *-cide* "killer"] — **reg·i·cid·al** \ˌrej-ə-ˈsīd-l\ *adj*

re·gime *also* **ré·gime** \rā-ˈzhēm, ri-\ *n* **1 a** : REGIMEN 1 **b** : a regular pattern of occurrence or action **2 a** : mode of rule or management **b** : a form of government ⟨a socialist *regime*⟩ **c** : a government in power **d** : a period of rule ⟨during the last *regime*⟩ [French *régime,* from Latin *regimen* "steering, control, guidance"]

reg·i·men \ˈrej-ə-mən, -ˌmen\ *n* **1** : a systematic course of treatment ⟨a strict dietary *regimen*⟩ **2** : REGIME 2b [Medieval Latin, "set of rules," from Latin, "steering, control," from *regere* "to direct"]

[1]**reg·i·ment** \ˈrej-mənt, -ə-mənt\ *n* : a military unit consisting of a number of battalions [Medieval French, "rule, government," from Late Latin *regimentum,* derived from Latin *regere* "to guide, direct, command (a military unit)"] — **reg·i·men·tal** \ˌrej-ə-ˈment-l\ *adj* — **reg·i·men·tal·ly** \-l-ē\ *adv*

[2]**reg·i·ment** \ˈrej-ə-ˌment\ *vt* **1** : to organize rigidly so as to regulate or control **2** : to subject to order or uniformity — **reg·i·men·ta·tion** \ˌrej-ə-mən-ˈtā-shən, -ˌmen-\ *n*

reg·i·men·tals \ˌrej-ə-ˈment-lz\ *n pl* **1** : a regimental uniform **2** : military dress

re·gion \ˈrē-jən\ *n* **1** : an administrative area, division, or district **2 a** : an often indefinite part, portion, or area ⟨cloudy *regions* of the sky⟩ **b** : a broad geographic area ⟨arctic *regions*⟩ **3** : an indefinite area surrounding a specified body part ⟨a pain in the *region* of the heart⟩ **4** : FIELD 2a **5** : a set of points any two points of which can be connected by a line lying wholly within the set together with none, some, or all of the points on its boundary ⟨a rectangular *region*⟩ [Medieval French *regiun,* from Latin *regio,* from *regere* "to direct, rule"]

re·gion·al \ˈrēj-nəl, -ən-l\ *adj* **1** : of, relating to, or characteristic of a region ⟨a *regional* dialect⟩ **2** : affecting a particular region : LOCAL ⟨*regional* pain⟩ — **re·gion·al·ly** \-ē\ *adv*

re·gion·al·ism \ˈrēj-nəl-ˌiz-əm, -ən-l-\ *n* **1** : consciousness of and loyalty to a distinct geographical region **2** : emphasis on regional locale and characteristics in art or literature — **re·gion·al·ist** \-əst\ *n or adj* — **re·gion·al·is·tic** \ˌrēj-nəl-ˈis-tik, -ən-l-\ *adj*

[1]**reg·is·ter** \ˈrej-ə-stər\ *n* **1 a** : a written record containing regular entries of items or details **b** : a book for such a record ⟨a *register* of voters⟩ **2 a** : a set of organ pipes of like quality : STOP **b** : the range or a part of the range of a human voice or a musical instrument comprising tones similarly produced or of the same quality **3** : a device (as in a floor or a wall) usually with a grille and shutters that regulate the flow of heated air from a furnace **4** : REGISTRATION, REGISTRY ⟨a port of *register*⟩ **5 a** : an automatic device registering a number or a quantity **b** : a number or quantity so registered **6** : a condition of correct alignment or proper relative position [Medieval French *registre,* from Medieval Latin *registrum,* from Late Latin *regesta,* pl., "register," from Latin *regerere* "to bring back, pile up, collect," from *re-* + *gerere* "to carry"]

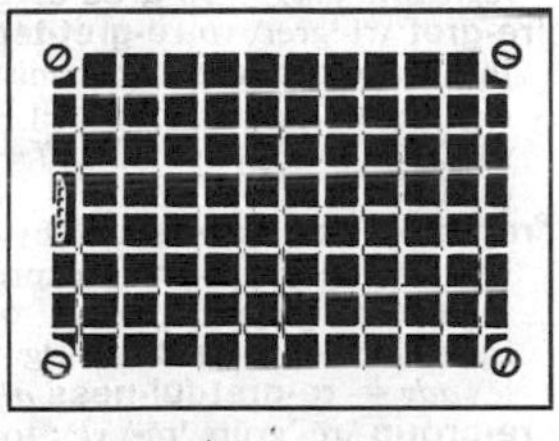
[1]register 3

[2]**register** *vb* **reg·is·tered; reg·is·ter·ing** \-stə-ring, -string\ **1 a** : to make or secure official entry of in a register : RECORD ⟨*register* a deed⟩ **b** : to enroll formally especially as a voter or student **c** : to record automatically ⟨the thermometer *registered* zero⟩ **2** : to make or adjust so as to correspond exactly **3** : to obtain special protection for (a piece of mail) by prepayment of a fee **4** : to convey an impression of ⟨your face *registered* fear⟩ **5** : to be in correct alignment or register **6** : to make an impression ⟨the name didn't *register*⟩

[3]**register** *n* : REGISTRAR

reg·is·tered *adj* **1** : having the owner's name entered in a register ⟨a *registered* security⟩ **2** : recorded on the basis of pedigree or breed characteristics in the studbook of a breed association

registered nurse *n* : a graduate trained nurse licensed by a state authority — called also *RN*

\ə\ **abut**	\au̇\ **out**	\i\ **tip**	\ȯ\ **saw**	\u̇\ **foot**
\ər\ **further**	\ch\ **chin**	\ī\ **life**	\ȯi\ **coin**	\y\ **yet**
\a\ **mat**	\e\ **pet**	\j\ **job**	\th\ **thin**	\yü\ **few**
\ā\ **take**	\ē\ **easy**	\ng\ **sing**	\t͟h\ **this**	\yu̇\ **cure**
\ä\ **cot, cart**	\g\ **go**	\ō\ **bone**	\ü\ **food**	\zh\ **vision**

reg·is·tra·ble \'rej-ə-strə-bəl\ *also* **reg·is·ter·able** \-stə-rə-bəl, -strə-bəl\ *adj* : that can be registered

reg·is·trant \'rej-ə-strənt\ *n* : one that registers or is registered

reg·is·trar \'rej-ə-ˌsträr\ *n* : an official recorder or keeper of records [alteration of Middle English *registrer,* from Medieval French *registrer* "to register," from Medieval Latin *registrare,* from *registrum* "register"]

reg·is·tra·tion \ˌrej-ə-'strā-shən\ *n* **1** : the act of registering **2** : an entry in a register **3** : the number of individuals registered : ENROLLMENT **4** : a document certifying an act of registering ⟨an automobile *registration*⟩

reg·is·try \'rej-ə-strē\ *n, pl* **-tries** **1** : REGISTRATION 3, ENROLLMENT **2** : a ship's nationality as proved by its entry in a register **3** : a place of registration **4** : an official record book or an entry in one

reg·nal \'reg-nl\ *adj* : of or relating to a reign; *esp* : calculated from a monarch's accession to the throne ⟨during the second *regnal* year⟩ [Medieval Latin *regnalis,* from Latin *regnum* "reign"]

reg·nant \'reg-nənt\ *adj* **1** : exercising rule ⟨the queen *regnant*⟩ **2** : having the chief power [Latin *regnare* "to reign," from *regnum* "reign"]

reg·o·lith \'reg-ə-ˌlith\ *n* : MANTLEROCK [Greek *rhēgos* "blanket" + English *-lith*]

¹**re·gress** \'rē-ˌgres\ *n* **1** : an act or the privilege of going or coming back **2** : REENTRY 1 [Latin *regressus,* from *regredi* "to go back," from *re-* + *gradi* "to go"]

²**re·gress** \ri-'gres\ *vb* : to go or cause to go back especially to a former level or condition — **re·gres·sor** \-'gres-ər\ *n*

re·gres·sion \ri-'gresh-ən\ *n* : an act or the fact of regressing: as **a** : progressive decline of something (as a symptom of disease) **b** : gradual loss of differentiation and function by a body part **c** : reversion of thought or behavior to that characteristic of an earlier level of development

re·gres·sive \ri-'gres-iv\ *adj* **1** : of, relating to, or tending toward regression **2** : decreasing in rate as the base increases ⟨a *regressive* tax⟩ — **re·gres·sive·ly** *adv* — **re·gres·sive·ness** *n*

¹**re·gret** \ri-'gret\ *vb* **re·gret·ted; re·gret·ting** **1 a** : to mourn the loss or death of **b** : to miss very much **2** : to be very sorry for **3** : to experience regret [Medieval French *regreter*] — **re·gret·ta·ble** \-'gret-ə-bəl\ *adj* — **re·gret·ta·bly** \-blē\ *adv* — **re·gret·ter** *n*

²**regret** *n* **1** : sorrow caused by circumstances beyond one's ability to remedy **2 a** : an expression of distressing emotion (as sorrow or disappointment) **b** *pl* : a note politely declining an invitation — **re·gret·ful** \-'gret-fəl\ *adj* — **re·gret·ful·ly** \-fə-lē\ *adv* — **re·gret·ful·ness** *n*

re·group \rē-'grüp, 'rē-\ *vb* : to form into a new group ⟨in order to subtract 129 from 531 *regroup* 531 into 5 hundreds, 2 tens, and 11 ones⟩ — **re·group·ment** \-mənt\ *n*

re·grow \rē-'grō\ *vb* **-grew** \-'grü\; **-grown** \-'grōn\; **-grow·ing** : to grow (as a missing part) again

re·growth \rē-'grōth\ *n* : the process of regrowing ⟨conditions affecting forest *regrowth*⟩; *also* : a result or product of regrowing ⟨cattle grazing on pasture *regrowth*⟩

¹**reg·u·lar** \'reg-yə-lər\ *adj* **1** : belonging to a religious order ⟨*regular* clergy⟩ **2 a** : formed, built, arranged, or ordered according to an established rule, law, principle, or type **b** (1) : having all sides and all angles equal ⟨a square is a *regular* polygon⟩ (2) : having faces that are regular polygons of the same size and shape and angles that are all equal ⟨a cube is a *regular* polyhedron⟩ **c** : perfectly symmetrical or even; *esp* : having radial symmetry ⟨*regular* flowers⟩ **d** : having or constituting an isometric system ⟨*regular* crystals⟩ **3 a** : ORDERLY, METHODICAL ⟨*regular* habits⟩ **b** : recurring or functioning at fixed, uniform, or regular intervals **4 a** : following established or prescribed usages, rules, or discipline **b** : NORMAL 2, CORRECT: as (1) : COMPLETE, ABSOLUTE ⟨a *regular* scoundrel⟩ (2) : thinking or behaving in an acceptable manner **c** : conforming to the normal or usual manner of inflection ⟨*regular* verbs⟩ **5** : of, relating to, or constituting a regular army [Medieval French *reguler,* from Late Latin *regularis,* derived from Latin *regula* "straightedge, rule"] — **reg·u·lar·i·ty** \ˌreg-yə-'lar-ət-ē\ *n* — **reg·u·lar·ly** \'reg-yə-lər-lē\ *adv*

synonyms REGULAR, NORMAL, TYPICAL mean being of the sort or kind that is expected as usual, ordinary, or average. REGULAR stresses conformity to a rule, standard, or pattern ⟨the club's *regular* monthly meeting⟩. NORMAL implies lack of deviation from what has been established as the most usual or expected ⟨*normal* behavior for a two-year-old⟩. TYPICAL implies showing all the important traits of a type, class, or group and may suggest lack of strong individuality ⟨a *typical* small town⟩.

²**regular** *n* : one who is regular: as **a** : one of the regular clergy **b** : a soldier in a regular army **c** : a player on an athletic team who usually starts every game

regular army *n* : a permanently organized body that is the standing army of a state

reg·u·lar·ize \'reg-yə-lə-ˌrīz\ *vt* : to make regular — **reg·u·lar·iz·er** *n*

reg·u·late \'reg-yə-ˌlāt\ *vt* **1 a** : to govern or direct according to rule **b** : to bring under the control of law or established authority **2** : to reduce to order, method, or uniformity ⟨*regulated* their habits⟩ **3** : to adjust for accurate functioning ⟨*regulate* a clock⟩ [Late Latin *regulare,* from Latin *regula* "rule"] — **reg·u·la·tive** \-ˌlāt-iv\ *adj* — **reg·u·la·tor** \-ˌlāt-ər\ *n* — **reg·u·la·to·ry** \-lə-ˌtōr-ē, -ˌtȯr-\ *adj*

¹**reg·u·la·tion** \ˌreg-yə-'lā-shən\ *n* **1** : the act of regulating : the state of being regulated **2 a** : an authoritative rule dealing with details **b** : a rule or order having the force of law issued by an executive authority ***synonyms*** see LAW

²**regulation** *adj* : conforming to regulations : OFFICIAL

regulatory gene *or* **regulator gene** *n* : a gene that regulates the expression of one or more other genes especially by controlling the production of a genetic repressor

Reg·u·lus \'reg-yə-ləs\ *n* : a bright star in the constellation Leo [Latin, "petty king," from *reg-, rex* "king"]

re·gur·gi·tate \rē-'gər-jə-ˌtāt, 'rē-\ *vb* : to throw or be thrown back or out again ⟨*regurgitate* undigested food⟩ [Medieval Latin *regurgitare,* from Latin *re-* + Late Latin *gurgitare* "to engulf," from Latin *gurgit-, gurges* "whirlpool"] — **re·gur·gi·ta·tion** \rē-ˌgər-jə-'tā-shən\ *n*

re·ha·bil·i·tate \ˌrē-ə-'bil-ə-ˌtāt, ˌrē-hə-'bil-\ *vt* **1 a** : to restore to a former status : REINSTATE **b** : to restore to good repute : reestablish the good name of **2 a** : to restore to a state of efficiency, good management, or repair **b** : to restore to a condition of health or useful and constructive activity [Medieval Latin *rehabilitare,* derived from Latin *re-* + *habilitas* "aptness, ability," from *habilis* "handy, apt," from *habēre* "to have, hold"] — **re·ha·bil·i·ta·tion** \-ˌbil-ə-'tā-shən\ *n* — **re·ha·bil·i·ta·tive** \-'bil-ə-ˌtāt-iv\ *adj*

re·hash \rē-'hash, 'rē-\ *vt* : to present or use (as an argument) again in another form without substantial change or improvement — **re·hash** \'rē-ˌhash\ *n*

re·hear \rē-'hir\ *vt* : to hear again especially judiciously ⟨the court agreed to *rehear* the case⟩

re·hears·al \ri-'hər-səl\ *n* : a rehearsing of something: as **a** : a private performance or practice session preparatory to a public appearance **b** : a practice exercise : TRIAL

re·hearse \ri-'hərs\ *vb* **1 a** : to say again : REPEAT **b** : to recount in order : ENUMERATE **2 a** : to practice (as a play or scene) for public performance **b** : to train or make proficient (as actors) by rehearsal **3** : to engage in a rehearsal [Medieval French *rehercer,* literally, "to harrow again," from *re-* "re-" + *hercer* "to harrow," from *herce* "harrow," from Latin *hirpex*] — **re·hears·er** *n*

re·house \rē-'hau̇z\ *vt* : to house again or anew; *esp* : to establish in a new or different housing unit of a better quality ⟨*rehoused* 30 tenants⟩

re·hy·drate \rē-'hī-ˌdrāt, 'rē-\ *vt* : to restore fluid to (something dehydrated) — **re·hy·dra·tion** \ˌrē-ˌhī-'drā-shən\ *n*

reichs·mark \'rīk-ˌsmärk\ *n, pl* **reichsmarks** *also* **reichsmark** : the German mark from 1925 to 1948 [German, from *Reich* "empire" + *Mark* "mark"]

¹**reign** \'rān\ *n* **1 a** : royal authority : SOVEREIGNTY **b** : the domination or influence of one resembling a monarch **2** : the time during which a monarch rules [Medieval French *regne,* from Latin *regnum,* from *reg-, rex* "king"]

²**reign** *vi* **1 a** : to have or exercise sovereign power : RULE **b** : to hold office as chief of state with only slight governing powers **2** : to exercise authority in the manner of a monarch **3** : to be predominant or prevalent

reign of terror : a period marked by violence that is often committed by those in power and produces widespread terror

re·im·burse \ˌrē-əm-'bərs\ *vt* : to pay back : REPAY [*re-* + obsolete *imburse* "to put in the pocket, pay," from Medieval Latin *imbursare,* from Latin *in-* + Medieval Latin *bursa* "purse"] —

re·im·burs·able \-'bər-sə-bəl\ *adj* — **re·im·burse·ment** \-'bərs-mənt\ *n*

¹rein \'rān\ *n* **1** : a line or strap fastened to a bit on each side for controlling an animal — usually used in plural **2 a** : a restraining influence : CHECK ⟨kept the child under a tight *rein*⟩ **b** : controlling or guiding power — usually used in plural ⟨seize the *reins* of government⟩ **3** : complete freedom : SCOPE — usually used in the phrase *give rein to* [Medieval French *resne, reine,* derived from Latin *retinēre* "to hold back, restrain," from *re-* + *tenēre* "to hold"]

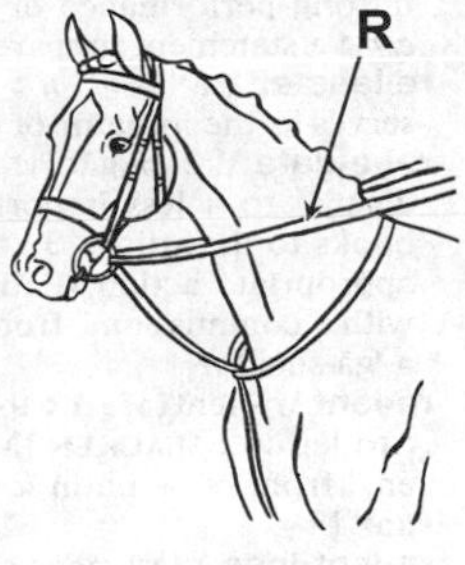

R rein 1

²rein *vb* : to check, control, or stop by or as if by reins

re·in·car·nate \ˌrē-ən-'kär-ˌnāt\ *vt* : to give a new or different body or form to

re·in·car·na·tion \rē-ˌin-ˌkär-'nā-shən\ *n* **1** : the action of reincarnating : the state of being reincarnated **2** : rebirth in new bodies or forms of life; *esp* : a rebirth of a soul in a new human body

rein·deer \'rān-ˌdiər\ *n, pl* **reindeer** *also* **reindeers** : CARIBOU — used especially for one of the Old World [Middle English *reindere,* from Old Norse *hreinn* "reindeer" + Middle English *deer* "deer"]

reindeer moss *n* : a gray, erect, and much-branched lichen of northern and arctic regions important as food for caribou

re·in·fec·tion \ˌrē-ən-'fek-shən\ *n* : infection following recovery from another infection of the same type — **re·in·fect** \-'fekt\ *vt*

re·in·force \ˌrē-ən-'fōrs, -'fȯrs\ *vt* **1** : to strengthen by additional assistance, material, or support ⟨*reinforce* a wall⟩ ⟨*reinforce* an argument⟩ **2** : to strengthen or increase by fresh additions ⟨*reinforce* our troops⟩ ⟨were *reinforcing* their pitching staff⟩ **3** : to stimulate (a person or animal) with a reinforcer; *also* : to increase the frequency of (a response) with a reinforcer [*re-* + *inforce,* alteration of *enforce*]

reinforced concrete *n* : concrete in which metal rods, bars, or mesh are embedded for strengthening

re·in·force·ment \ˌrē-ən-'fōr-smənt, -'fȯr-\ *n* **1** : the action of reinforcing : the state of being reinforced **2** : something that reinforces

re·in·forc·er \-sər\ *n* **1** : one that reinforces **2** : a stimulus (as a reward or the removal of something unpleasant) given after a desired action or reply that helps to make the individual act or reply in the same way when the conditions are repeated

reins \'rānz\ *n pl* **1** : the kidneys or the region of the kidneys **2** : the seat of the feelings or passions [Medieval French, from Latin *renes*]

re·in·state \ˌrē-ən-'stāt\ *vt* : to restore to possession or to a former position, condition, or capacity ⟨*reinstate* an official⟩ — **re·in·state·ment** \-mənt\ *n*

re·in·te·grate \rē-'int-ə-ˌgrāt\ *vt* : to integrate again into an entity : restore to unity — **re·in·te·gra·tion** \-ˌint-ə-'grā-shən\ *n*

re·in·ter·pret \ˌrē-ən-'tər-prət\ *vt* : to interpret again; *esp* : to give a new or different interpretation to — **re·in·ter·pre·ta·tion** \-ˌtər-prə-'tā-shən\ *n*

re·in·vent \ˌrē-ən-'vent\ *vt* **1** : to make as if for the first time something already invented ⟨*reinvent* the wheel⟩ **2** : to remake or redo completely ⟨the designer *reinvented* fashion⟩ — **re·in·ven·tion** \ˌrē-ən-'ven-chən\ *n*

re·in·vest \ˌrē-ən-'vest\ *vt* **1** : to invest again or anew **2 a** : to invest (as income from investments) in additional securities **b** : to invest (as earnings) in a business rather than distribute as dividends or profits — **re·in·vest·ment** \-'vest-mənt, -'ves-\ *n*

reis *pl of* ⁵REAL

re·is·sue \rē-'ish-ü, 'rē-\ *vb* : to issue again; *esp* : to cause to become available again ⟨*reissued* the book in paperback form⟩ — **reissue** *n*

re·it·er·ate \rē-'it-ə-ˌrāt\ *vt* : to say or do over again or repeatedly — **re·it·er·a·tion** \rē-ˌit-ə-'rā-shən\ *n* — **re·it·er·a·tive** \rē-'it-ə-ˌrāt-iv, -rət-\ *adj* — **re·it·er·a·tive·ly** *adv*

¹re·ject \ri-'jekt\ *vt* **1** : to refuse to accept, submit to, or deal with **2** : DISCARD 2 **3** : to refuse to grant or consider **4** : to subject to immunological rejection ⟨*reject* a heart transplant⟩ [Latin *rejectus,* past participle of *reicere* "to reject," from *re-* + *jacere* "to throw"]

synonyms REJECT, REPUDIATE, SPURN mean to refuse to accept, receive, or consider something proposed or offered. REJECT stresses a casting back on the source and implies firmness and finality ⟨*rejected* all proposals for a truce⟩. REPUDIATE implies a usually scornful and public thrusting away as unworthy, untrue, or unjustified ⟨now *repudiate* former beliefs⟩. SPURN implies disdain or contempt more strongly than REJECT ⟨*spurned* all offers of assistance⟩.

²re·ject \'rē-ˌjekt\ *n* : a rejected person or thing

re·jec·tion \ri-'jek-shən\ *n* **1 a** : the act of rejecting : the state of being rejected **b** : the process by which the immune system causes foreign tissue (as of a skin graft or transplanted organ) to separate from and stop functioning with the tissues of the human or animal that has received it **2** : something rejected

re·joice \ri-'jȯis\ *vb* **1** : to give joy to ⟨news that *rejoices* the heart⟩ **2** : to feel joy ⟨*rejoice* over a friend's good fortune⟩ [Medieval French *rejois-,* stem of *rejoier, rejoir* "to rejoice," from *re-* "re-" + *joir* "to welcome, enjoy," from Latin *gaudēre* "to be glad"] — **re·joic·er** *n* — **re·joic·ing·ly** \-'jȯi-sing-lē\ *adv*

re·joic·ing \-'jȯi-sing\ *n* **1** : the action of one that rejoices **2** : an instance, occasion, or expression of joy : FESTIVITY

re·join *vt* **1** \rē-'jȯin, 'rē-\ : to join again : return to ⟨*rejoined* my family after a trip⟩ **2** \ri-\ : ANSWER 1, REPLY

re·join·der \ri-'jȯin-dər\ *n* : REPLY; *esp* : an answer to a reply [Middle English *rejoiner,* from Medieval French *rejoinder* "to rejoin"]

re·ju·ve·nate \ri-'jü-və-ˌnāt\ *vt* : to make young or youthful again : give new vigor to [*re-* + Latin *juvenis* "young"] — **re·ju·ve·na·tion** \-ˌjü-və-'nā-shən\ *n* — **re·ju·ve·na·tor** \-'jü-və-ˌnāt-ər\ *n*

¹re·lapse \ri-'laps, 'rē-ˌ\ *n* : the act or fact of relapsing; *esp* : a recurrence of illness after a period of improvement [Latin *relapsus,* from *relabi* "to slide back," from *re-* + *labi* "to slide"]

²relapse *vi* **1** : to slip or fall back into a former worse state **2** : SINK, SUBSIDE ⟨*relapsed* into thought⟩ — **re·laps·er** *n*

relapsing fever *n* : an epidemic disease marked by recurring high fever usually lasting three to seven days and caused by a spirochete transmitted by the bites of lice or ticks

re·late \ri-'lāt\ *vb* **1** : to give an account of : NARRATE ⟨*relate* a story⟩ **2** : to show or establish a relationship between ⟨*relate* cause and effect⟩ **3** : to have relationship or connection : REFER **4** : to have meaningful social relationships [Latin *relatus,* past participle of *referre* "to carry back"] — **re·lat·able** \-'lāt-ə-bəl\ *adj* — **re·lat·er** *or* **re·la·tor** \-'lāt-ər\ *n*

re·lat·ed *adj* : belonging to the same group on the basis of known or determinable qualities ⟨*related* phenomena⟩: as **a** (1) : having a common ancestry (2) : belonging to the same family by blood or marriage **b** : having close harmonic connection ⟨*related* chords⟩ — **re·lat·ed·ness** *n*

re·la·tion \ri-'lā-shən\ *n* **1** : the act of telling or recounting : ACCOUNT **2** : an aspect or quality (as resemblance) that connects two or more things or parts as being or belonging or working together or as being of the same kind ⟨the *relation* of time and space⟩; *also* : a property (as one expressed by *is equal to* or *is less than*) that holds between an ordered pair of objects **3 a** : RELATIVE 3 **b** : relationship by blood or marriage : KINSHIP **4** : REFERENCE 2, RESPECT ⟨in *relation* to this⟩ **5** : the attitude which two or more individuals assume toward one another ⟨race *relations*⟩ **6 a** : the state of being mutually or reciprocally interested (as in social or commercial matters) **b** *pl* (1) : AFFAIR 1a, DEALINGS ⟨foreign *relations*⟩ (2) : INTERCOURSE 1 — **re·la·tion·al** \-shnəl, -shən-l\ *adj*

re·la·tion·ship \-shən-ˌship\ *n* **1** : the state or character of being related or interrelated ⟨the mathematical *relationship* between two variables⟩ ⟨study language *relationships*⟩ **2** : KINSHIP ⟨claimed a *relationship* with the deceased⟩; *also* : a specific instance or type of kinship ⟨family *relationships*⟩ **3** : a state of affairs existing between those having shared dealings ⟨good doctor-patient *relationships*⟩

¹rel·a·tive \'rel-ət-iv\ *n* **1** : a word referring grammatically to an antecedent **2** : a thing having a relation to or connection with or necessary dependence upon another thing **3** : an individual connected with another by blood or marriage

\ə\ **abut**	\au̇\ **out**	\i\ **tip**	\ȯ\ **saw**	\u̇\ **foot**
\ər\ **further**	\ch\ **chin**	\ī\ **life**	\ȯi\ **coin**	\y\ **yet**
\a\ **mat**	\e\ **pet**	\j\ **job**	\th\ **thin**	\yü\ **few**
\ā\ **take**	\ē\ **easy**	\ng\ **sing**	\t͟h\ **this**	\yu̇\ **cure**
\ä\ **cot, cart**	\g\ **go**	\ō\ **bone**	\ü\ **food**	\zh\ **vision**

[2]relative *adj* **1 :** introducing a subordinate clause that qualifies an expressed or implied antecedent ⟨*relative* pronouns⟩; *also* **:** introduced by a connective having such an antecedent ⟨a *relative* clause⟩ **2 :** RELEVANT, PERTINENT ⟨questions *relative* to the topic⟩ **3 :** not absolute or independent **:** COMPARATIVE ⟨lived in *relative* isolation⟩ **4 :** having the same key signature — used of major and minor keys and scales — **rel•a•tive•ly** *adv* — **rel•a•tive•ness** *n*

relative error *n* **:** the ratio of an error in a measured or calculated quantity to the magnitude of that quantity

relative humidity *n* **:** the ratio of the amount of water vapor actually present in the air to the greatest amount possible at the same temperature

relative to *prep* **:** with regard to **:** in connection with

rel•a•tiv•ism \ˈrel-ət-iv-ˌiz-əm\ *n* **1 a :** a theory that knowledge is relative to the limited nature of the mind and the conditions of knowing **b :** a view that ethical truths depend on the individuals and groups holding them **2 :** RELATIVITY — **rel•a•tiv•ist** \-əst\ *n*

rel•a•tiv•is•tic \ˌrel-ət-iv-ˈis-tik\ *adj* **1 :** of, relating to, or characterized by relativity or relativism **2 :** moving at a velocity such that there is a significant change in properties (as mass) in accordance with the theory of relativity ⟨a *relativistic* electron⟩ — **rel•a•tiv•is•tic•al•ly** *adv*

rel•a•tiv•i•ty \ˌrel-ə-ˈtiv-ət-ē\ *n* **1 :** the quality or state of being relative; *esp* **:** dependence on something else **2 a :** a theory in physics that equates mass and energy and that describes changes in mass, dimension, and time which are related to velocities approaching the speed of light **b :** an extension of relativity theory to include gravity and related acceleration phenomena

re•lax \ri-ˈlaks\ *vb* **1 :** to make or become less tense or rigid **:** EASE **2 :** to make or become less severe or rigid ⟨*relax* immigration laws⟩ **3 :** to cast off social restraint, nervous tension, anxiety, or suspicion ⟨couldn't *relax* in crowds⟩ **4 :** to seek rest or recreation [Latin *relaxare,* from *re-* + *laxare* "to loosen," from *laxus* "loose"] — **re•lax•er** *n*

[1]re•lax•ant \ri-ˈlak-sənt\ *adj* **:** producing relaxation

[2]relaxant *n* **:** a relaxing agent; *esp* **:** a drug causing muscular relaxation

re•lax•a•tion \ˌrē-ˌlak-ˈsā-shən, ri-\ *n* **1 :** the act or fact of relaxing or being relaxed **2 :** a relaxing state, activity, or pastime **3 :** the lengthening that characterizes inactive muscles

re•laxed \ri-ˈlakst\ *adj* **1 :** lacking in precision or strictness **2 :** set at rest or at ease **3 :** easy of manner **:** INFORMAL **4 :** somewhat loose-fitting and usually casual in style ⟨*relaxed* jeans⟩ — **re•laxed•ly** \-ˈlak-səd-lē, -ˈlaks-tlē\ *adv* — **re•laxed•ness** \-ˈlak-səd-nəs, -ˈlakst-nəs, -ˈlaks-nəs\ *n*

re•lax•in \ri-ˈlak-sən\ *n* **:** a hormone of the corpus luteum that relaxes pelvic ligaments and facilitates childbirth

[1]re•lay \ˈrē-ˌlā\ *n* **1 :** a fresh supply (as of horses or men) arranged to relieve others at various stages especially of a journey or race **2 a :** a race between teams in which each team member successively covers a specified portion of the course or of the total distance **b :** one of the divisions of a relay **3 a :** an electromagnetic device in which the opening or closing of a circuit operates another device **b :** SERVOMOTOR **4 :** the act of passing along by stages; *also* **:** one of such stages [Middle English, "set of fresh hounds," from Medieval French *relaier* "to release a set of fresh hounds, take a fresh horse," from *re-* "re-" + *laier* "to let go, leave," derived from Latin *laxare* "to loosen"]

[2]re•lay \ˈrē-ˌlā, ri-ˈlā\ *vt* **re•layed; re•lay•ing 1 :** to place in or provide with relays **2 :** to pass along by relays **3 :** to control or operate by a relay

[3]re•lay \rē-ˈlā, ˈrē-\ *vt* **-laid** \-ˈlād\; **-lay•ing :** to lay again ⟨*relay* the patio flagstones⟩

[1]re•lease \ri-ˈlēs\ *vt* **1 :** to set free from restraint, confinement, or servitude **2 :** to relieve from something that holds, burdens, or oppresses **3 :** to give up in favor of another ⟨*release* a claim to property⟩ **4 :** to give permission for publication, performance, exhibition, or sale of at a specified date [Medieval French *relesser,* from Latin *relaxare* "to relax"] ***synonyms*** see FREE — **re•leas•able** \-ˈlē-sə-bəl\ *adj*

[2]release *n* **1 :** relief or deliverance from sorrow, suffering, or trouble **2 a :** a discharge from an obligation (as a debt) **b :** a relinquishment of a right or claim; *esp* **:** a conveyance of a right in real property to another **c :** a document embodying a release **3 a :** the act or an instance of liberating or freeing (as from physical restraint) **b :** the act or manner of ending a speech sound **4 :** the state of being freed **5 :** a device adapted to hold or release a mechanism as required **6 a :** the act of permitting performance or publication **b :** the matter released; *esp* **:** a statement prepared for the press ⟨a news *release*⟩

re•leas•er \ri-ˈlē-sər\ *n* **:** one that releases; *esp* **:** a stimulus that serves as the initiator of complex reflex behavior

rel•e•gate \ˈrel-ə-ˌgāt\ *vt* **1 :** EXILE, BANISH **2 :** to remove or dismiss to a less important or prominent place ⟨*relegate* old books to the attic⟩ **3 :** to submit to someone or something for appropriate action [Latin *relegare,* from *re-* + *legare* "to send with a commission," from *leg-, lex* "law"] — **rel•e•ga•tion** \ˌrel-ə-ˈgā-shən\ *n*

re•lent \ri-ˈlent\ *vi* **1 :** to become less severe, harsh, or strict **2 :** to let up **:** SLACKEN [Medieval French *relenter* "to melt, soften," from *re-* + Latin *lentare* "to bend," from *lentus* "soft, pliant"]

re•lent•less \-ləs\ *adj* **:** showing or promising no abatement of severity, intensity, strength, or pace **:** UNRELENTING ⟨*relentless* criticism⟩ — **re•lent•less•ly** *adv* — **re•lent•less•ness** *n*

rel•e•vance \ˈrel-ə-vəns\ *n* **:** relation to the matter at hand **:** PERTINENCE

rel•e•van•cy \-vən-sē\ *n, pl* **-cies :** RELEVANCE; *also* **:** something relevant

rel•e•vant \-vənt\ *adj* **:** having relevance ⟨a *relevant* question⟩ [Medieval Latin *relevans,* from Latin *relevare* "to raise up"] — **rel•e•vant•ly** *adv*

re•li•abil•i•ty \ri-ˌlī-ə-ˈbil-ət-ē\ *n* **:** the quality or state of being reliable

re•li•able \ri-ˈlī-ə-bəl\ *adj* **:** that can be relied on **:** DEPENDABLE — **re•li•able•ness** *n* — **re•li•ably** \-blē\ *adv*

re•li•ance \ri-ˈlī-əns\ *n* **1 :** the act of relying **2 :** the condition of being reliant **3 :** something or someone relied on

re•li•ant \-ənt\ *adj* **:** having reliance on something or someone **:** TRUSTING — **re•li•ant•ly** *adv*

rel•ic \ˈrel-ik\ *n* **1 :** an object venerated because of association with a saint or martyr **2 :** a surviving ruin or remnant ⟨*relics* of ancient cities⟩ **3 :** a trace of some past or outmoded practice, custom, or belief **:** VESTIGE [Medieval French *relike,* derived from Late Latin *reliquiae* "remains of a martyr," from Latin, "remains," from *relinquere* "to leave behind"]

rel•ict \ˈrel-ikt\ *n* **1 :** WIDOW **2 :** a persistent small surviving group of a formerly widespread plant or animal species that continues to exist in an isolated area [derived from Latin *relictus,* past participle of *relinquere* "to leave behind"]

re•lief \ri-ˈlēf\ *n* **1 a :** removal or lightening of something oppressive, painful, or distressing **b :** WELFARE 2a **c :** military assistance to a post or force in extreme danger **d :** means of breaking monotony or boredom **:** DIVERSION **2 a :** release from sentry or other duty **b :** one that takes the place of another on duty **3 :** legal remedy or redress **4 a :** projection from the background (as of figures in sculpture) **b :** a work of art with such raised figures **c :** vividness or sharpness of outline due to contrast (as of color or shading) **5 :** the elevations or inequalities of a land surface [Medieval French, from *relever* "to relieve"]

relief 4b

relief map *n* **:** a map representing topographic relief

relief pitcher *n* **:** a baseball pitcher who takes over for another during a game

re•lieve \ri-ˈlēv\ *vb* **1 :** to free from pain, discomfort, or distress **:** give aid or help to ⟨*relieve* the poor⟩ ⟨*relieved* by the news⟩ **2 :** to bring about the removal or reduction of ⟨efforts to *relieve* world hunger⟩ **3 :** to release from a post or duty especially by taking the place of ⟨*relieve* a sentry⟩ **4 :** to remove or lessen the monotony of ⟨a black dress *relieved* by a white collar⟩ **5 :** to put in or stand out in relief **:** give prominence to or set off by contrast (as in sculpture or painting) **6 :** to discharge the bladder or bowels of (oneself) [Middle French *relever* "to raise up, relieve," from Latin *relevare,* from *re-* + *levare* "to raise"] — **re•liev•er** *n*

synonyms RELIEVE, ALLEVIATE, LIGHTEN mean to make something less grievous or more bearable. RELIEVE implies either removing entirely or lifting enough of a burden to make it tolerable ⟨was able to *relieve* my fatigue with a short rest⟩. ALLEVIATE suggests temporary or partial lessening of pain or distress ⟨took medication to *alleviate* her symptoms⟩. LIGHTEN implies reducing a burdensome or depressing weight ⟨the good news *lightened* their minds⟩.

re·li·gion \ri-ˈlij-ən\ *n* **1 a :** the service and worship of God or the supernatural **b :** belief in or devotion to religious faith or observance **c :** the state of a religious **2 :** a set or system of religious attitudes, beliefs, and practices **3 :** a cause, principle, or system of beliefs held to with zeal and faith [Latin *religio* "supernatural constraint, sanction, religious practice," perhaps from *religare* "to restrain, tie back"]

re·li·gion·ist \ri-ˈlij-nəst, -ə-nəst\ *n* **:** a person adhering to a religion

1re·li·gious \ri-ˈlij-əs\ *adj* **1 a :** devoted to God or to the powers or principles believed to govern life ⟨a very *religious* person⟩ **b :** belonging to a religious order ⟨a *religious* house⟩ **2 :** of or relating to religion ⟨*religious* beliefs⟩ **3 :** DEPENDABLE, FAITHFUL — **re·li·gious·ly** *adv* — **re·li·gious·ness** *n*

2religious *n, pl* **religious :** a member of a religious order

re·line \rē-ˈlīn\ *vt* **:** to put new lines on or a new lining in

re·lin·quish \ri-ˈling-kwish\ *vt* **1 :** to withdraw or retreat from **:** ABANDON **2 a :** to desist from **b :** to release a claim to or possession or control of **:** RENOUNCE **3 :** to release or let go (as a grip or hold) [Medieval French *relinquiss-,* stem of *relinquir* "to relinquish," from Latin *relinquere* "to leave behind," from *re-* + *linquere* "to leave"] — **re·lin·quish·ment** \-mənt\ *n*

synonyms RELINQUISH, YIELD, RESIGN, SURRENDER mean to give up completely. RELINQUISH suggests that some regret, reluctance, or weakness is involved ⟨*relinquished* her secret after much coaxing from us⟩. YIELD implies concession or compliance or submission to force ⟨the troops *yielded* ground⟩. RESIGN emphasizes voluntary and usually formal relinquishment ⟨*resigned* her position⟩. SURRENDER implies a giving up after a struggle to retain or resist ⟨the enemy *surrendered* after a long battle⟩.

rel·i·quary \ˈrel-ə-ˌkwer-ē\ *n, pl* **-quar·ies :** a small box or shrine in which sacred relics are kept

1rel·ish \ˈrel-ish\ *n* **1 :** a pleasing appetizing taste **2 :** a small bit added for flavor **:** DASH **3 :** personal liking ⟨*relish* for hard work⟩ **4 :** keen enjoyment of something that satisfies one's tastes, inclination, or desires **5 :** a highly seasoned sauce (as of pickles or mustard) eaten with other food to add flavor [Middle English *reles* "taste," from Medieval French, "something left behind," from *relesser* "to release"] ***synonyms*** see TASTE

2relish *vt* **1 :** to add relish to **2 :** to be pleased or gratified by **:** ENJOY **3 :** to eat or drink with pleasure — **rel·ish·able** \-ə-bəl\ *adj*

re·live \rē-ˈliv, ˈrē-\ *vb* **:** to live again or over; *esp* **:** to experience again in imagination

re·lo·cate \rē-ˈlō-ˌkāt, ˈrē-; ˌrē-lō-ˈkāt\ *vb* **1 :** to locate again **2 :** to move to a new location ⟨*relocate* a factory⟩ — **re·lo·cat·able** \-ə-bəl\ *adj* — **re·lo·ca·tion** \ˌrē-lō-ˈkā-shən\ *n*

re·luc·tance \ri-ˈlək-təns\ *n* **:** the quality or state of being reluctant

re·luc·tan·cy \-tən-sē\ *n, pl* **-cies :** RELUCTANCE

re·luc·tant \ri-ˈlək-tənt\ *adj* **:** not willing ⟨*reluctant* to go⟩ [Latin *reluctari* "to struggle against," from *re-* + *luctari* "to struggle"] — **re·luc·tant·ly** *adv*

re·ly \ri-ˈlī\ *vi* **re·lied; re·ly·ing 1 :** to depend confidently ⟨I know I can *rely* on you⟩ **2 :** to be dependent ⟨*relied* on a spring for water⟩ [Medieval French *relier* "to retie, gather, rally," from Latin *religare* "to tie back," from *re-* + *ligare* "to tie"]

rem \ˈrem\ *n* **:** the dosage of an ionizing radiation that will cause the same biological effect as one roentgen of exposure [*r*oentgen *e*quivalent *m*an]

REM \ˈrem\ *n* **:** RAPID EYE MOVEMENT

1re·main \ri-ˈmān\ *vi* **1 a :** to be a part not destroyed, taken, or used up ⟨little *remained* after the fire⟩ **b :** to be something yet to be shown, done, or treated ⟨that *remains* to be proved⟩ **2 :** to stay in the same place or with the same person or group; *esp* **:** to stay behind **3 :** to continue unchanged ⟨the weather *remained* cold⟩ [Medieval French *remaindre,* from Latin *remanēre,* from *re-* + *manēre* "to stay, remain"] ***synonyms*** see STAY

2remain *n* **1 :** a remaining part or trace — usually used in plural **2** *pl* **:** a dead body

1re·main·der \ri-ˈmān-dər\ *n* **1 a :** a remaining group, part, or trace **b** (1) **:** the number left after a subtraction (2) **:** the final undivided part after division that is less than or of lower degree than the divisor **2 :** a book sold at a reduced price by the publisher after sales have slowed [Medieval French, from *remaindre* "to remain"] ***synonyms*** see BALANCE

2remainder *vt* **re·main·dered; re·main·der·ing** \-də-ring, -dring\ **:** to dispose of (books) as remainders

re·make \rē-ˈmāk, ˈrē-\ *vt* **-made** \-ˈmād\; **-mak·ing :** to make anew or in a different form — **re·make** \ˈrē-ˌmāk\ *n*

1re·mand \ri-ˈmand\ *vt* **:** to order back: as **a :** to send back (a case) to a lower court for further action **b :** to return to custody pending trial or for further detention [Medieval French *remander,* from Late Latin *remandare* "to send back word," from Latin *re-* + *mandare* "to order"]

2remand *n* **:** the act of remanding **:** the state of being remanded

re·man·u·fac·ture \rē-ˌman-yə-ˈfak-chər, -ˌman-ə-\ *vb* **:** to manufacture into a new product — **remanufacture** *n* — **re·man·u·fac·tur·er** *n*

1re·mark \ri-ˈmärk\ *n* **1 :** the act of remarking **:** NOTICE **2 :** mention of that which deserves attention or notice **3 :** an expression of opinion or judgment [French *remarque,* from Medieval French, from *remarquer* "to remark," from *re-* + *marquer* "to mark"]

2remark *vb* **1 :** to take notice of **:** OBSERVE ⟨*remarked* his strange manner⟩ **2 :** to express as an observation or comment **:** SAY ⟨"Nice day," she *remarked*⟩ **3 :** to make an observation or comment ⟨*remarked* on how well the team was doing⟩

re·mark·able \ri-ˈmär-kə-bəl\ *adj* **1 :** worthy of being or likely to be noticed **2 :** UNCOMMON, EXTRAORDINARY ⟨a *remarkable* career⟩ ***synonyms*** see NOTICEABLE — **re·mark·able·ness** *n* — **re·mark·ably** \-blē\ *adv*

re·mar·ry \re-ˈmar-ē\ *vb* **:** to marry again **:** marry after an earlier marriage — **re·mar·riage** \rē-ˈmar-ij, ˈrē-\ *n*

re·match \rē-ˈmach, ˈrē-ˌ\ *n* **:** a second match between the same contestants or teams

re·me·di·a·ble \ri-ˈmēd-ē-ə-bəl\ *adj* **:** capable of being remedied

re·me·di·al \ri-ˈmed-ē-əl\ *adj* **:** intended to remedy or improve ⟨*remedial* measures⟩ ⟨*remedial* reading courses⟩ — **re·me·di·al·ly** \-ē-ə-lē\ *adv*

re·me·di·a·tion \ri-ˌmed-ē-ˈā-shən\ *n* **:** the act or process of remedying ⟨*remediation* of environmental pollution⟩ — **re·me·di·ate** \-ˈmēd-ē-ˌāt\ *vt*

1rem·e·dy \ˈrem-əd-ē\ *n, pl* **-dies 1 :** a medicine or treatment that cures or relieves **2 :** something that corrects an evil, rights a wrong, or makes up for a loss [Medieval French *remedie,* from Latin *remedium,* from *re-* + *mederi* "to heal"]

2remedy *vt* **-died; -dy·ing :** to provide or serve as a remedy for **:** RELIEVE ***synonyms*** see CURE

re·mem·ber \ri-ˈmem-bər\ *vb* **-bered; -ber·ing** \-bə-ring, -bring\ **1 :** to bring to mind or think of again **2 a :** to keep in mind for attention or consideration **b :** to show remembrance of usually by kindness or giving ⟨*remembered* in the will⟩ **3 :** to retain in the memory **4 :** to convey greetings from [Medieval French *remembrer,* from Late Latin *rememorari,* from *re-* + *memorari* "to be mindful of," from Latin *memor* "mindful"] — **re·mem·ber·able** \-bə-rə-bəl, -brə-bəl\ *adj* — **re·mem·ber·er** \-bər-ər\ *n*

synonyms REMEMBER, RECOLLECT, RECALL, REMINISCE mean to bring an image or idea from the past into the mind. REMEMBER implies a keeping in memory that may be effortless or unwilled ⟨*remembers* that day as if it were yesterday⟩. RECOLLECT implies bringing back to mind what is lost or scattered ⟨as near as I can *recollect*⟩. RECALL suggests an effort to bring back to mind and often to recreate in speech ⟨can't *recall* the words of the song⟩. REMINISCE implies a casual often nostalgic recalling of experiences from long ago ⟨old high school friends like to *reminisce*⟩.

re·mem·brance \ri-ˈmem-brəns\ *n* **1 :** the state of bearing in mind ⟨let us live in constant *remembrance* of our faults⟩ **2 :** ability to remember **:** MEMORY **3 :** an act of calling to mind ⟨*remembrance* of past wrongs⟩ **4 :** a memory of something ⟨had no *remembrance* of that day⟩ **5 a :** something that serves to keep in or bring to mind **b :** something (as a gift or greeting) expressive of friendly remembrance ***synonyms*** see MEMORY

re·mind \ri-ˈmīnd\ *vt* **:** to cause to remember something ⟨*remind* a child that it is bedtime⟩ — **re·mind·er** *n*

rem·i·nisce \ˌrem-ə-ˈnis\ *vi* **:** to engage in reminiscence ⟨*reminisced* about old times⟩ ***synonyms*** see REMEMBER

rem·i·nis·cence \ˌrem-ə-ˈnis-ns\ *n* **1 a :** a recalling to mind of past experience ⟨had a pleasant *reminiscence* of a favorite childhood game⟩ **b :** the process or practice of thinking or telling about past experiences ⟨spent an hour in *reminiscence*⟩ **2 :** an account of a memorable experience — often used in plural ***synonyms*** see MEMORY

rem·i·nis·cent \-nt\ *adj* **1 :** of or relating to reminiscence **2 :** marked by or given to reminiscence **3 :** tending to remind **:** SUGGESTIVE [Latin *reminiscens,* present participle of *reminisci* "to remember"]

re·miss \ri-ˈmis\ *adj* **1 :** negligent in the performance of work or duty **:** CARELESS ⟨*remiss* in paying the bills⟩ **2 :** showing neglect or inattention **:** LAX ⟨service at the restaurant was *remiss*⟩ [Latin *remissus,* from *remittere* "to send back, relax"] ***synonyms*** see NEGLIGENT — **re·miss·ly** *adv* — **re·miss·ness** *n*

re·mis·si·ble \ri-ˈmis-ə-bəl\ *adj* **:** capable of being forgiven ⟨*remissible* sins⟩ — **re·mis·si·bly** \-blē\ *adv*

re·mis·sion \ri-ˈmish-ən\ *n* **1 :** the act or process of remitting **2 :** a state or period during which something is remitted

[1]**re·mit** \ri-ˈmit\ *vb* **re·mit·ted; re·mit·ting** **1 a :** to put aside (a mood or disposition) **b :** to desist from **c :** to let (as attention or care) slacken **:** RELAX **2 a :** to release from the guilt or penalty of ⟨*remit* sins⟩ **b :** to refrain from exacting ⟨*remit* a tax⟩ **c :** to give relief from (suffering) **3 :** to submit or refer for consideration, judgment, decision, or action **4 :** to restore or consign to a former status or condition **5 :** POSTPONE, DEFER **6 :** to send (money) especially in payment **7 :** to lessen in force, intensity, or severity often temporarily [Latin *remittere* "to send back," from *re-* + *mittere* "to send"] — **re·mit·ment** \-ˈmit-mənt\ *n* — **re·mit·ta·ble** \-ˈmit-ə-bəl\ *adj* — **re·mit·ter** *n*

[2]**remit** *n* **1 :** an act of remitting **2 :** something remitted to another person or authority

re·mit·tal \ri-ˈmit-l\ *n* **:** REMISSION

re·mit·tance \ri-ˈmit-ns\ *n* **1 :** a sum of money remitted **2 :** a sending of money (as to a distant place)

re·mit·tent \ri-ˈmit-nt\ *adj* **:** marked by alternating periods of abatement and increase of symptoms ⟨a *remittent* fever⟩ [Latin *remittens,* present participle of *remittere* "to remit"]

rem·nant \ˈrem-nənt\ *n* **1 :** a usually small surviving part or trace ⟨the *remnants* of a great civilization⟩ **2 :** something unused and left over ⟨a *remnant* of cloth⟩ [Middle French *remenant,* from *remenoir* "to remain," from Latin *remanēre*]

re·mod·el \rē-ˈmäd-l, ˈrē-\ *vt* **:** to alter the structure of **:** REMAKE

re·mon·strance \ri-ˈmän-strəns\ *n* **:** an act or instance of remonstrating **:** PROTEST

re·mon·strant \-strənt\ *adj* **:** vigorously objecting or opposing — **remonstrant** *n* — **re·mon·strant·ly** *adv*

re·mon·strate \ri-ˈmän-ˌstrāt\ *vb* **1 :** to present and urge reasons in opposition ⟨*remonstrate* with the students over their unruly behavior⟩ **2 :** to say or plead in protest or reproof ⟨*remonstrated* that his decision was unwise⟩ [Medieval Latin *remonstrare* "to demonstrate," from Latin *re-* + *monstrare* "to show"] — **re·mon·stra·tion** \ri-ˌmän-ˈstrā-shən\ *n* — **re·mon·stra·tive** \ri-ˈmän-strət-iv\ *adj*

rem·o·ra \ˈrem-ə-rə\ *n* **:** any of a family of marine fishes having the front upper fin modified into a disk on the head by means of which it adheres especially to other fishes [Latin, literally, "delay"]

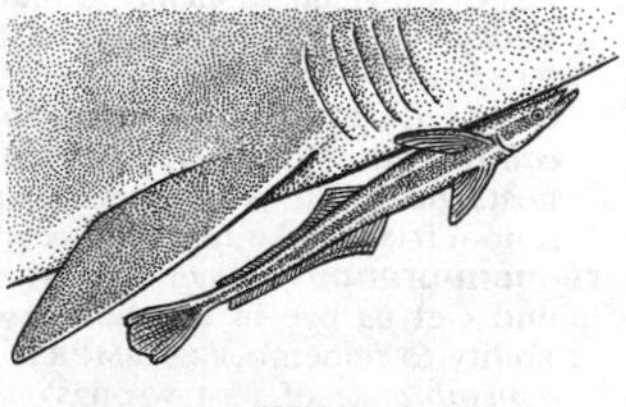

remora

re·morse \ri-ˈmȯrs\ *n* **:** a deep regret arising from a sense of guilt for past wrongs **:** SELF-REPROACH [Medieval French *remors,* from Medieval Latin *remorsus,* from Latin *remordēre* "to bite again," from *re-* + *mordēre* "to bite"]

re·morse·ful \-fəl\ *adj* **:** arising from or marked by remorse — **re·morse·ful·ly** \-fə-lē\ *adv* — **re·morse·ful·ness** *n*

re·morse·less \-ləs\ *adj* **1 :** being without remorse **:** MERCILESS **2 :** showing or promising no lessening of intensity, severity, or strength ⟨a *remorseless* work schedule⟩ — **remorse·less·ly** *adv* — **re·morse·less·ness** *n*

[1]**re·mote** \ri-ˈmōt\ *adj* **1 :** far removed in space, time, or relation ⟨the *remote* past⟩ **2 :** OUT-OF-THE-WAY, SECLUDED ⟨a *remote* valley⟩ **3 :** acting, acted on, or controlled indirectly or from a distance ⟨*remote* computer operation⟩ **4 :** small in degree **:** SLIGHT ⟨*remote* possibility⟩ **5 :** distant in manner **:** ALOOF ⟨he is often very *remote*⟩ [Latin *remotus,* from *removēre* "to remove"] ***synonyms*** see DISTANT — **re·mote·ly** *adv* — **re·mote·ness** *n*

[2]**remote** *n* **:** REMOTE CONTROL 2

remote control *n* **1 :** control (as by a radio signal) of operation from a point some distance away ⟨operated by *remote control*⟩ **2 :** a device for controlling something from a distance ⟨a *remote control* for a VCR⟩

[1]**re·mount** \rē-ˈmau̇nt, ˈrē-\ *vb* **1 :** to mount (something) again ⟨*remount* a picture⟩ **2 :** to mount again ⟨*remount* and ride back to the stables⟩

[2]**re·mount** \ˈrē-ˌmau̇nt, rē-ˈ\ *n* **:** a fresh horse to take the place of one no longer available

re·mov·able *also* **re·move·able** \ri-ˈmü-və-bəl\ *adj* **:** that can be removed — **re·mov·abil·i·ty** \ri-ˌmü-və-ˈbil-ət-ē\ *n* — **re·mov·able·ness** \-ˈmü-və-bəl-nəs\ *n* — **re·mov·ably** \-blē\ *adv*

re·mov·al \ri-ˈmü-vəl\ *n* **:** the act of removing **:** the fact of being removed

[1]**re·move** \ri-ˈmüv\ *vb* **1 a :** to change or cause to change to another location, position, station, or residence **b :** to go away **2 a :** to move by lifting, pushing aside, or taking away or off **b :** to yield to being so moved ⟨this cap should *remove* easily⟩ **3 :** to dismiss from office **4 :** to get rid of **:** ELIMINATE ⟨*remove* a tumor surgically⟩ [Medieval French *remuver, removeir,* from Latin *removēre,* from *re-* + *movēre* "to move"]

[2]**remove** *n* **1 :** REMOVAL; *esp* **:** a change of residence or location **2 a :** a distance or interval separating one thing from another **b :** a degree or stage of separation ⟨at one *remove*⟩

re·moved \ri-ˈmüvd\ *adj* **1 a :** distant in degree of relationship **b :** of a younger or older generation ⟨the children of your first cousin are your first cousins once *removed*⟩ **2 :** separate or remote in space, time, or character ⟨a home far *removed* from cities⟩ ***synonyms*** see DISTANT

re·mov·er \-ˈmü-vər\ *n* **:** something (as a chemical) used in removing a substance ⟨paint *remover*⟩ ⟨nail polish *remover*⟩

re·mu·da \ri-ˈmüd-ə\ *n* **:** a herd of horses from which those to be used (as on a ranch) for the day are chosen [American Spanish, "relay of horses," from Spanish, "exchange," from *remudar* "to exchange," from *re-* "re-" + *mudar* "to change," from Latin *mutare*]

re·mu·ner·ate \ri-ˈmyü-nə-ˌrāt\ *vt* **:** to pay an equivalent to for a service, loss, or expense **:** COMPENSATE [Latin *remunerare,* from *re-* + *munerare* "to give," from *muner-, munus* "gift"] ***synonyms*** see PAY — **re·mu·ner·a·tor** \-ˌrāt-ər\ *n* — **re·mu·ner·a·to·ry** \ri-ˈmyü-nə-rə-ˌtōr-ē, -ˌtȯr-\ *adj*

re·mu·ner·a·tion \ri-ˌmyü-nə-ˈrā-shən\ *n* **1 :** something that remunerates **:** COMPENSATION **2 :** an act or fact of remunerating

re·mu·ner·a·tive \ri-ˈmyü-nə-ˌrāt-iv\ *adj* **1 :** serving to remunerate **2 :** PROFITABLE ⟨made a *remunerative* investment⟩ — **re·mu·ner·a·tive·ly** *adv* — **re·mu·ner·a·tive·ness** *n*

re·nais·sance \ˌren-ə-ˈsäns, -ˈzäns\ *n* **1** *cap* **a :** the movement or period in Europe between the 14th and 17th centuries marked by a flourishing of classically-influenced arts and literature and by the beginnings of modern science **b :** the period of the Renaissance **c :** the neoclassic style of architecture prevailing during the Renaissance **2** *often cap* **:** a movement or period marked by a revival of vigorous artistic and intellectual activity **3 :** REVIVAL [French, from Medieval French, "rebirth," from *renaistre* "to be born again," from Latin *renasci,* from *re-* + *nasci* "to be born"]

re·nal \ˈrēn-l\ *adj* **:** of, relating to, or located in or near the kidneys [Late Latin *renalis,* from Latin *renes* "kidneys"]

re·na·scence \ri-ˈnas-ns, -ˈnās-\ *n, often cap* **:** RENAISSANCE

re·na·scent \-nt\ *adj* **:** rising again into existence or vigor [Latin *renascent-, renascens,* present participle of *renasci* "to be born again"]

rend \ˈrend\ *vt* **rent** \ˈrent\ *also* **rend·ed; rend·ing** **1 :** to remove from place by violence **:** WREST **2 :** to split or tear apart or in pieces by violence **3 :** to tear (the hair or clothing) as a sign of anger, grief, or despair **4 a :** to hurt mentally or emotionally **b :** to pierce with sound **c :** to divide (as a nation) into parties [Old English *rendan*]

ren·der \ˈren-dər\ *vt* **ren·dered; ren·der·ing** \-də-riŋ, -driŋ\ **1 a :** to give to another : DELIVER ⟨*render* a report⟩ **b :** to furnish or offer for consideration, approval, or information ⟨*render* a judgment⟩ **2 :** to melt down : extract by heating ⟨*render* lard⟩ **3 :** to give up : SURRENDER ⟨*render* one's life for a cause⟩ **4 a :** to give in return ⟨*render* thanks⟩ **b :** to give compensation ⟨will *render* according to work done⟩ **5 :** to give in acknowledgment of dependence or obligation : PAY ⟨*render* a bill⟩ **6 :** to cause to be or become : MAKE ⟨*render* a person helpless⟩ **7 a :** to express in an artistic or verbal way ⟨*render* the scene in oil pastels⟩ ⟨*render* a play⟩ **b :** to produce a copy or version of ⟨*render* it in the original German⟩ **8 :** TRANSLATE ⟨*rendered* the Latin into English⟩ **9 :** ADMINISTER ⟨*render* justice⟩ [Middle French *rendre* "to give back, yield," derived from Latin *reddere*] — **ren·der·able** \-də-rə-bəl, -drə-bəl\ *adj* — **ren·der·er** \-dər-ər\ *n*

[1]**ren·dez·vous** \ˈrän-di-ˌvü, -dā-\ *n, pl* **ren·dez·vous** \-ˌvüz\ **1 a :** a place appointed for assembling or meeting **b :** a place where people get together : HAUNT **2 :** an appointed meeting **3 :** the process of bringing two spacecraft together [Middle French, from *rendez vous* "present yourselves"]

[2]**rendezvous** *vb* **ren·dez·voused** \-ˌvüd\; **ren·dez·vous·ing** \-ˌvü-iŋ\; **ren·dez·vouses** \-ˌvüz\ **:** to come or bring together at a rendezvous

ren·di·tion \ren-ˈdish-ən\ *n* **:** the act or result of rendering: as **a :** SURRENDER ⟨forbade the *rendition* of fugitives⟩ **b :** TRANSLATION ⟨an accurate *rendition* of the Greek⟩ **c :** PERFORMANCE 3, INTERPRETATION ⟨his *rendition* of that song⟩ [obsolete French, from Middle French *reddition,* from Late Latin *redditio,* from Latin *reddere* "to give back, return"]

[1]**ren·e·gade** \ˈren-i-ˌgād\ *n* **1 :** a deserter from one faith, cause, or allegiance to another **2 :** one who rejects lawful or conventional behavior [Spanish *renegado,* from Medieval Latin *renegatus,* from *renegare* "to deny," from Latin *re-* + *negare* "to deny"]

[2]**renegade** *vi* **:** to become a renegade

[3]**renegade** *adj* **1 :** having deserted a faith, cause, or religion **2 :** having rejected tradition : UNCONVENTIONAL

re·nege \ri-ˈnig, -ˈneg, -ˈnēg, -ˈnāg\ *vb* **re·neged; re·neg·ing 1 :** DENY **2 :** to go back on a promise or commitment [Medieval Latin *renegare* "to deny"] — **re·neg·er** *n*

re·ne·go·tia·ble \ˌrē-ni-ˈgō-shə-bəl, -shē-ə-bəl\ *adj* **:** subject to renegotiation ⟨*renegotiable* interest rates⟩

re·ne·go·ti·ate \ˌrē-ni-ˈgō-shē-ˌāt\ *vt* **:** to negotiate again ⟨*renegotiate* a loan to reduce payments⟩

re·new \ri-ˈnü, -ˈnyü\ *vt* **1 :** to make or become like new again : restore to freshness or vigor ⟨strength *renewed* by a night's rest⟩ **2 :** to restore to existence ⟨*renewed* business in the old downtown⟩ **3 :** to do or make again : REPEAT ⟨*renew* a complaint⟩ **4 :** to begin again : RESUME ⟨*renewed* efforts to make peace⟩ **5 :** to put in a fresh supply of : REPLACE ⟨*renew* the water in a tank⟩ **6 :** to grant or obtain an extension of ⟨*renew* a lease⟩

synonyms RENEW, RESTORE, REFRESH, RENOVATE mean to make like new. RENEW implies a restoration of something faded or disintegrated so that it seems like new ⟨*renew* the splendor of the old castle⟩. RESTORE implies a return to an original state after depletion or loss ⟨*restore* a piece of furniture⟩. REFRESH implies the supplying of something necessary to restore lost strength, animation, or power ⟨*refreshed* by a short nap⟩. RENOVATE applies chiefly to material things and suggests making like new by cleansing, repairing, or rebuilding ⟨*renovate* the upstairs rooms⟩.

re·new·able \ri-ˈnü-ə-bəl, -ˈnyü-\ *adj* **1 :** capable of being renewed **2 :** capable of being replaced by natural ecological cycles or sound management procedures ⟨*renewable* resources like water, wildlife, forests, and grasslands⟩ — **re·new·abil·i·ty** \-ˌnü-ə-ˈbil-ət-ē, -ˌnyü-\ *n* — **renewable** *n*

re·new·al \ri-ˈnü-əl, -ˈnyü-\ *n* **1 a :** the act of renewing **b :** the state of being renewed **2 :** something renewed **3 :** the rebuilding of a large area (as of a city) by a public authority ⟨urban *renewal*⟩

re·ni·form \ˈren-ə-ˌfȯrm, ˈrē-nə-\ *adj* **:** suggesting a kidney in outline ⟨a *reniform* leaf⟩ [Latin *renes* "kidneys"]

ren·net \ˈren-ət\ *n* **1 a :** the contents of the stomach of an unweaned animal and especially a calf **b :** the lining membrane of the stomach used for curdling milk **2 :** rennin or a substitute used to curdle milk [Middle English, from Old English *gerennan* "to cause to coagulate"]

ren·nin \ˈren-ən\ *n* **:** a stomach enzyme that curdles milk and is used in the making of cheese

re·nom·i·nate \rē-ˈnäm-ə-ˌnāt, ˈrē-\ *vt* **:** to nominate again especially for a succeeding term — **re·nom·i·na·tion** \rē-ˌnäm-ə-ˈnā-shən\ *n*

re·nounce \ri-ˈnau̇ns\ *vt* **1 :** to give up, refuse, or resign usually by formal declaration ⟨*renounced* the throne⟩ ⟨*renounce* one's errors⟩ **2 :** to refuse to follow, obey, or recognize any further : REPUDIATE ⟨*renounce* one's allegiance⟩ [Medieval French *renuncer,* from Latin *renuntiare,* from *re-* + *nuntiare* "to report, announce," from *nuntius* "messenger"] — **re·nounce·ment** \-mənt\ *n* — **re·nounc·er** *n*

ren·o·vate \ˈren-ə-ˌvāt\ *vt* **1 :** to restore to a former state or to good condition **2 :** REVIVE [Latin *renovare,* from *re-* + *novare* "to make new," from *novus* "new"] ***synonyms*** see RENEW — **ren·o·va·tion** \ˌren-ə-ˈvā-shən\ *n* — **ren·o·va·tor** \ˈren-ə-ˌvāt-ər\ *n*

re·nown \ri-ˈnau̇n\ *n* **:** a state of being widely known and highly honored : FAME [Medieval French *renum, renoun,* from *renomer* "to report, speak of," from *re-* + *nomer* "to name," from Latin *nominare,* from *nomen* "name"]

re·nowned \-ˈnau̇nd\ *adj* **:** having renown : CELEBRATED ***synonyms*** see FAMOUS

[1]**rent** \ˈrent\ *n* **1 :** property (as a house) rented or for rent **2 :** money paid for the use of property : a periodic payment made by a tenant to the owner for the possession and use of property **3 :** the portion of the national income attributable to land as a factor of production [Medieval French *rente* "income from a property," derived from Latin *reddere* "to give back, yield"] — **for rent :** available for use or service in return for payment

[2]**rent** *vb* **1 :** to take and hold property under an agreement to pay rent **2 :** to grant the possession and enjoyment of for rent : LET **3 :** to be for rent ***synonyms*** see HIRE — **rent·able** \-ə-bəl\ *adj*

[3]**rent** *past of* REND

[4]**rent** *n* **1 a :** an opening made by or as if by rending **b :** a split in a party or organized group **2 :** an act or instance of rending

rent–a–car \ˈrent-ə-ˌkär\ *n* **:** a rented car

[1]**rent·al** \ˈrent-l\ *n* **1 :** an amount paid or collected as rent **2 :** something rented **3 :** an act of renting

[2]**rental** *adj* **1 :** of, relating to, or available for rent **2 :** dealing in rental property ⟨a *rental* agency⟩

rental library *n* **:** a commercially operated library (as in a store) that lends books at a fixed charge per book per day

rent control *n* **:** government regulation of the amount of rent charged for housing and also of eviction — **rent–controlled** *adj*

rent·er \ˈrent-ər\ *n* **:** one that rents; *esp* **:** TENANT

rent·tier \rä^{n}-ˈtyā\ *n* **:** a person who receives a fixed income from property or investments [French, from *rente* "income from a property"]

re·nun·ci·a·tion \ri-ˌnən-sē-ˈā-shən\ *n* **:** the act or practice of renouncing [Latin *renuntiatio,* from *renuntiare* "to renounce"] — **re·nun·ci·a·tive** \-ˈnən-sē-ˌāt-iv\ *adj* — **re·nun·ci·a·to·ry** \-sē-ə-ˌtōr-ē, -ˌtȯr-\ *adj*

re·of·fer \rē-ˈȯf-ər, -ˈäf-\ *vt* **:** to offer (as a security) for public sale ⟨*reoffer* that stock⟩

re·open \rē-ˈō-pən, ˈrē-, -ˈōp-m\ *vb* **1 a :** to open again **b :** to resume discussion or consideration of ⟨*reopen* a contract⟩ **2 :** to take up again : RESUME

[1]**re·or·der** \rē-ˈȯrd-ər, ˈrē-\ *vb* **1 :** REORGANIZE **2 :** to place a reorder or a reorder for

[2]**reorder** *n* **:** an order like a previous order placed with the same supplier

re·or·ga·ni·za·tion \rē-ˌȯrg-nə-ˈzā-shən, ˌrē-, -ə-nə-\ *n* **:** the act of reorganizing : the state of being reorganized; *esp* **:** the financial reconstruction of a business concern — **re·or·ga·ni·za·tion·al** \-shnəl, -shən-l\ *adj*

re·or·ga·nize \rē-ˈȯr-gə-ˌnīz, ˈrē-\ *vb* **:** to organize again or anew; *esp* **:** to bring about a reorganization (as of a business concern) — **re·or·ga·niz·er** *n*

\ə\ **abut**	\au̇\ **out**	\i\ **tip**	\ȯ\ **saw**	\u̇\ **foot**
\ər\ **further**	\ch\ **chin**	\ī\ **life**	\ȯi\ **coin**	\y\ **yet**
\a\ **mat**	\e\ **pet**	\j\ **job**	\th\ **thin**	\yü\ **few**
\ā\ **take**	\ē\ **easy**	\ŋ\ **sing**	\t͟h\ **this**	\yu̇\ **cure**
\ä\ **cot, cart**	\g\ **go**	\ō\ **bone**	\ü\ **food**	\zh\ **vision**

[1]**rep** \ˈrep\ *n* : REPRESENTATIVE ⟨sales *reps*⟩
[2]**rep** *or* **repp** \ˈrep\ *n* : a plain-woven fabric with prominent rounded crosswise ribs [French *reps,* from English *ribs,* pl. of *rib*]
[3]**rep** *n* : REPETITION 1b
re·pack·age \rē-ˈpak-ij, ˈrē-\ *vt* : to package again; *esp* : to put into a more efficient or attractive form
[1]**re·pair** \ri-ˈpaər, -ˈpeər\ *vi* : to make one's way : GO ⟨*repair* to an inner office⟩ [Medieval French *repairer* "to go back, return," from Late Latin *repatriare* "to go home again," from Latin *re-* + *patria* "native country"]
[2]**repair** *vb* **1 a :** to restore by replacing a part or putting together what is damaged : FIX **b :** to restore to a sound or healthy state : RENEW **2 :** to compensate for : REMEDY [Medieval French *reparer,* from Latin *reparare,* from *re-* + *parare* "to prepare"] ***synonyms*** see MEND — **re·pair·abil·i·ty** \-ˌpar-ə-ˈbil-ət-ē, -ˌper-\ *n* — **re·pair·able** \-ˈpar-ə-bəl, -ˈper-\ *adj* — **re·pair·er** \-ər\ *n*
[3]**repair** *n* **1 :** the action or process of repairing ⟨make *repairs*⟩ **2 :** the result of repairing ⟨a tire with three *repairs*⟩ **3 :** good or sound condition ⟨a house in *repair*⟩ **4 :** condition with respect to soundness or need of repairing ⟨a house in bad *repair*⟩
re·pair·man \ri-ˈpaər-ˌman, -ˈpeər-, -mən\ *n* : one whose occupation is making repairs ⟨a TV *repairman*⟩
rep·a·ra·ble \ˈrep-rə-bəl, -ə-rə-\ *adj* : capable of being repaired
rep·a·ra·tion \ˌrep-ə-ˈrā-shən\ *n* **1 :** the action or process of repairing or keeping in repair **2 a :** a making amends for a wrong or injury done : COMPENSATION **b :** something done or given as amends or satisfaction ⟨gave me his watch as *reparation* for breaking mine⟩ **3 :** the payment of damages; *esp* : money paid (as by one country to another) in compensation (as for damages in war) [Medieval French, from Late Latin *reparatio,* from Latin *reparare* "to repair"]
re·par·a·tive \ri-ˈpar-ət-iv\ *adj* **1 :** of, relating to, or effecting repair **2 :** serving to make amends
rep·ar·tee \ˌrep-ər-ˈtē, -är-, -ˈtā\ *n* **1 :** a clever witty reply **2 :** skill in making clever replies [French *repartie,* from *repartir* "to retort," from *re-* "re-" + *partir* "to divide, part"]
re·pass \rē-ˈpas, ˈrē-\ *vb* **1 :** to pass again especially in the opposite direction : RETURN **2 :** to cause to pass again **3 :** to adopt again — **re·pas·sage** \-ˈpas-ij\ *n*
re·past \ri-ˈpast\ *n* **1 :** something taken as food : MEAL **2 :** the act or time of taking food [Medieval French, from *repaistre* "to feed," from *re-* "re-" + *paistre* "to feed," from Latin *pascere*]
re·pa·tri·ate \rē-ˈpā-trē-ˌāt, ˈrē-, -ˈpa-\ *vt* : to send or bring back to the country of origin, allegiance, or citizenship ⟨*repatriate* prisoners of war⟩ [Late Latin *repatriare* "to go home again," from Latin *re-* + *patria* "native country"] — **re·pa·tri·ate** \-trē-ət, -trē-ˌāt\ *n* — **re·pa·tri·a·tion** \ˌrē-ˌpā-trē-ˈā-shən, -ˌpa-\ *n*
re·pay \rē-ˈpā, ˈrē-\ *vb* **-paid; -pay·ing 1 a :** to pay back ⟨I've already been *repaid*⟩ ⟨*repay* a loan⟩ **b :** to give or inflict in return ⟨*repay* evil with evil⟩ **2 :** to make return payment ⟨a lending bank requires proof of ability to *repay*⟩ — **re·pay·able** \-ə-bəl\ *adj* — **re·pay·ment** \-mənt\ *n*
re·peal \ri-ˈpēl\ *vt* : REVOKE, ANNUL; *esp* : to do away with by legislative enactment [Medieval French *repeler,* from *re-* + *apeler* "to call, appeal"] — **repeal** *n* — **re·peal·able** \-ˈpē-lə-bəl\ *adj*
re·peal·er \ri-ˈpē-lər\ *n* : one that repeals; *esp* : a legislative act that cancels or does away with an earlier act
[1]**re·peat** \ri-ˈpēt\ *vt* **1 a :** to say or state again : REITERATE **b :** to say over from memory : RECITE **c :** to say after another **2 a :** to make, do, or perform again ⟨*repeat* a mistake⟩ **b :** to go through an experience again ⟨the cycle *repeats* itself indefinitely⟩ **3 :** to express or present (oneself) again in the same words, terms, or form ⟨I hate *repeating* myself⟩ [Medieval French *repeter,* from Latin *repetere,* from *re-* + *petere* "to go to, seek"] — **re·peat·able** \-ə-bəl\ *adj*
[2]**re·peat** \ri-ˈpēt, ˈrē-ˌ\ *n* **1 :** the act of repeating **2 a :** something repeated **b** (1) **:** a musical passage to be repeated in performance (2) **:** a sign consisting of vertical dots placed before and after a passage to be repeated **c :** a repetition of a radio or television program

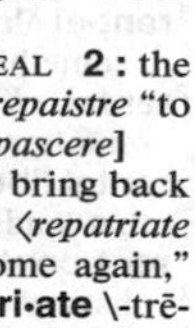

repeat 2b(2)

[3]**re·peat** \ri-ˈpēt\ *adj* : of, relating to, or being one that repeats an offense, achievement, or action ⟨a *repeat* customer⟩
re·peat·ed \ri-ˈpēt-əd\ *adj* : done or happening again and again : FREQUENT
re·peat·ed·ly *adv* : at frequent intervals : OFTEN
re·peat·er \ri-ˈpēt-ər\ *n* : one that repeats: as **a :** a watch that strikes the time when a spring is pressed **b :** a firearm that fires several times without reloading **c :** a habitual violator of the laws **d :** a student repeating a class or course
repeating decimal *n* : a decimal in which after a certain point a particular digit or sequence of digits repeats itself indefinitely — compare TERMINATING DECIMAL
re·pel \ri-ˈpel\ *vb* **re·pelled; re·pel·ling 1 a :** to drive back : REPULSE **b :** to fight against : RESIST **2 :** to turn away : REJECT ⟨*repelled* the insinuation⟩ **3 a :** to drive away : DISCOURAGE **b :** to be incapable of adhering to, mixing with, taking up, or holding **c :** to force away or apart or tend to do so by mutual action at a distance **4 :** to cause aversion : DISGUST [Latin *repellere,* from *re-* + *pellere* "to drive"] — **re·pel·ler** *n*
re·pel·len·cy \-ən-sē\ *n* : the quality of or capacity for repelling
[1]**re·pel·lent** *also* **re·pel·lant** \-ənt\ *adj* **1 :** serving or tending to drive away or ward off **2 :** arousing aversion or disgust : REPULSIVE [Latin *repellens,* present participle of *repellere* "to repel"] ***synonyms*** see REPUGNANT — **re·pel·lent·ly** *adv*
[2]**repellent** *also* **repellant** *n* : something that repels; *esp* : a substance used to prevent insect attacks
re·pent \ri-ˈpent\ *vb* **1 :** to turn from sin and determine to do what is right **2 :** to feel or cause to feel sorrow for or dissatisfaction with : REGRET ⟨*repent* a rash decision⟩ [Medieval French *repentir,* from Latin *re-* "re-" + Late Latin *poenitēre* "to feel regret," from Latin *paenitēre*] — **re·pent·er** *n*
re·pent·ance \ri-ˈpent-ns\ *n* : the action or process of repenting especially for misdeeds or moral shortcomings ***synonyms*** see PENITENCE
re·pent·ant \ri-ˈpent-nt\ *adj* : feeling or showing repentance — **re·pent·ant·ly** *adv*
re·per·cus·sion \ˌrē-pər-ˈkəsh-ən, ˌrep-ər-\ *n* **1 :** REFLECTION 1, REVERBERATION **2 a :** a reciprocal action or effect **b :** a widespread, indirect, or unforeseen effect of an act, action, or event — usually used in plural — **re·per·cus·sive** \-ˈkəs-iv\ *adj*
rep·er·toire \ˈrep-ə-ˌtwär, -ər-\ *n* **1 a :** a list or supply of dramas, operas, pieces, or parts that a company or person is prepared to perform **b :** a supply of skills, devices, or expedients ⟨part of the *repertoire* of a quarterback⟩ **2 a :** the complete list or supply of dramas, operas, or musical works available for performance **b :** the complete list or supply of skills, devices, or ingredients used in a particular field, occupation, or practice [French *répertoire,* from Late Latin *repertorium* "list"]
rep·er·to·ry \ˈrep-ər-ˌtōr-ē, -ə-, -ˌtȯr-\ *n, pl* **-ries 1 :** a place where something may be found : REPOSITORY **2 a :** REPERTOIRE **b :** a company that presents several different plays, operas, or pieces in the course of a season at one theater **c :** a theater housing such a company [Late Latin *repertorium* "list," from Latin *reperire* "to find," from *re-* + *parere* "to produce"]
rep·e·ti·tion \ˌrep-ə-ˈtish-ən\ *n* **1 a :** the act or an instance of repeating **b :** a motion or exercise (as a push-up) that is repeated and usually counted **2 :** the fact of being repeated **3 :** something repeated [Latin *repetitio,* from *repetere* "to repeat"]
rep·e·ti·tious \-ˈtish-əs\ *adj* : marked by repetition; *esp* : tediously repeating — **rep·e·ti·tious·ly** *adv* — **rep·e·ti·tious·ness** *n*
re·pet·i·tive \ri-ˈpet-ət-iv\ *adj* **1 :** REPETITIOUS **2 :** containing repetition — **re·pet·i·tive·ly** *adv* — **re·pet·i·tive·ness** *n*
re·pine \ri-ˈpīn\ *vi* **1 :** to feel or express dejection or discontent : COMPLAIN **2 :** to long for something — **re·pin·er** *n*
re·place \ri-ˈplās\ *vt* **1 :** to put back in a proper or former place ⟨*replace* a card in a file⟩ **2 :** to take the place of : SUPPLANT ⟨paper money has *replaced* gold coins⟩ **3 :** to put something new in the place of ⟨*replace* a broken dish⟩ — **re·place·able** \-ˈplā-sə-bəl\ *adj*

synonyms REPLACE, SUPPLANT, SUPERSEDE mean to put out of a usual or proper place or into the place of another. REPLACE implies a supplying of a substitute or equivalent for something lost, destroyed, or no longer usable or adequate ⟨*replace* a broken window⟩. SUPPLANT implies taking the place of one forced out or the replacing of a thing with another newer or better ⟨was suddenly *supplanted* in her affections by another⟩. SUPERSEDE implies taking the place of one that has become outmoded, obsolete, or inferior ⟨the new edition *supersedes* all previous ones⟩.

re·place·ment \ri-ˈplā-smənt\ *n* **1 :** the act of replacing : the state of being replaced **2 :** one that replaces another

replacement set *n* : a set of elements any one of which may be used to replace a given variable or placeholder in a mathematical sentence or expression (as an equation)

re·plant \rē-ˈplant, ˈrē-\ *vt* **1** : to set (a plant) to grow again or anew **2** : to provide with new plants ⟨*replanted* the park⟩

¹re·play \rē-ˈplā\ *vt* : to play again or over

²re·play \ˈrē-ˌplā\ *n* **1 a** : an act or instance of replaying **b** : the playing of a tape (as a videotape) **2** : REPETITION ⟨don't want a *replay* of our old mistakes⟩

re·plen·ish \ri-ˈplen-ish\ *vt* : to fill again : bring back to a condition of being full or complete [Medieval French *repleniss-*, stem of *replenir* "to fill," from *re-* "re-" + *plein* "full," from Latin *plenus*] — **re·plen·ish·able** \-i-shə-bəl\ *adj* — **re·plen·ish·er** *n* — **re·plen·ish·ment** \-ish-mənt\ *n*

re·plete \ri-ˈplēt\ *adj* **1** : well fed **2** : fully supplied or provided ⟨a book *replete* with illustrations⟩ **3** : COMPLETE 1a [Latin *repletus,* past participle of *replēre* "to fill up," from *re-* + *plēre* "to fill"] — **re·plete·ness** *n*

re·ple·tion \ri-ˈplē-shən\ *n* **1** : the act of eating to excess : the state of being fed to excess **2** : the condition of being filled up or overcrowded **3** : fulfillment of a need or desire : SATISFACTION

rep·li·ca \ˈrep-li-kə\ *n* **1** : a close reproduction or facsimile especially by the maker of the original **2** : a copy exact in all details : DUPLICATE [Italian, "repetition," from *replicare* "to repeat," from Late Latin, from Latin, "to fold back"]

rep·li·ca·ble \ˈrep-lə-kə-bəl\ *adj* : capable of replication ⟨*replicable* experimental results⟩ — **rep·li·ca·bil·i·ty** \ˌrep-lə-kə-ˈbil-ət-ē\ *n*

¹rep·li·cate \ˈrep-lə-ˌkāt\ *vb* **1** : DUPLICATE 1, REPEAT ⟨*replicate* an experiment⟩ **2** : to undergo replication ⟨*replicating* DNA⟩

²rep·li·cate \-li-kət\ *n* : one of several identical experiments, procedures, or samples

rep·li·ca·tion \ˌrep-lə-ˈkā-shən\ *n* **1** : ANSWER 1a, REPLY **2** : precise copying, duplication, or reproduction; *also* : an act or process of this

¹re·ply \ri-ˈplī\ *vb* **re·plied; re·ply·ing** **1 a** : to respond in speech or writing **b** : to give as an answer **2** : to do something in response; *esp* : to return an attack [Medieval French *replier* "to fold again," from Latin *replicare* "to fold back," from *re-* + *plicare* "to fold"] — **re·pli·er** \-ˈplī-ər, -ˈplīr\ *n*

²reply *n, pl* **replies** : something said, written, or done in response

re·po·lar·i·za·tion \rē-ˌpō-lə-rə-ˈzā-shən\ *n* : restoration of the difference in electrical charge between the inside and outside of the cell membrane following depolarization — **re·po·lar·ize** \-ˈpō-lə-ˌrīz\ *vb*

¹re·port \ri-ˈpōrt, -ˈpȯrt\ *n* **1 a** : common talk or an account spread by common talk : RUMOR **b** : REPUTATION ⟨a person of good *report*⟩ **2** : a usually detailed account or statement ⟨a news *report*⟩ **3** : an explosive noise ⟨the *report* of a gun⟩ [Medieval French, from *reporter* "to bring back, report," from Latin *reportare,* from *re-* + *portare* "to carry"]

²report *vb* **1** : to give an account (as of an incident or of one's activities) **2 a** : to give an account of **b** : to write or present an account of for the news media ⟨*reported* the hurricane's movement on the news⟩ **c** : to act in the capacity of a reporter ⟨*reported* on the latest developments⟩ **3** : to make a charge of misconduct against ⟨*report* a schoolmate⟩ **4 a** : to present oneself ⟨*report* for duty⟩ ⟨*report* at the office⟩ **b** : to account for oneself ⟨*reported* sick on Friday⟩ **c** : to work as a subordinate ⟨*reports* to the vice president⟩ **5** : to make known to the proper authorities ⟨*report* a fire⟩ **6** : to return or present (as a matter officially referred to a committee) with conclusions and recommendations

re·port·able \ri-ˈpōrt-ə-bəl\ *adj* **1** : worth reporting **2** : required by law to be reported ⟨*reportable* income⟩

re·port·age \ri-ˈpōrt-ij, -ˈpȯrt-, *especially for 2* ˌrep-ər-ˈtäzh\ *n* **1** : the act or process of reporting news **2** : writing intended to report observed or documented events [French, from *reporter* "to report"]

report card *n* : a report on a student's grades that is periodically submitted by a school to the student's parents or guardian

re·port·ed·ly \ri-ˈpōrt-əd-lē, -ˈpȯrt-\ *adv* : according to report

re·port·er \ri-ˈpōrt-ər, -ˈpȯrt-\ *n* : one that reports: as **a** : a person that makes authorized statements of law decisions or legislative proceedings **b** : a person employed by a newspaper, magazine, or television company to gather and write news **c** : a person that broadcasts news — **rep·or·to·ri·al** \ˌrep-ər-ˈtōr-ē-əl, ˌrēp-, -ə-ˈtōr-, -ˈtȯr-\ *adj* — **rep·or·to·ri·al·ly** \-ē-ə-lē\ *adv*

¹re·pose \ri-ˈpōz\ *vt* **1** : to place unquestioningly : SET ⟨*repose* trust in a friend⟩ **2** : to place for control, management, or use [derived from Latin *reponere* "to put back, put away, place," from *re-* + *ponere* "to put"]

²repose *vb* **1** : to lay at rest : put in a restful position ⟨*reposed* my head on a cushion⟩ **2** : to lie at rest : take rest ⟨*reposing* on the couch⟩ [Medieval French, *reposer,* from Late Latin *repausare,* from *re-* + *pausare* "to stop," from Latin *pausa* "pause"]

³repose *n* **1** : a state of resting after exertion or strain; *esp* : rest in sleep **2** : CALM 2, PEACE ⟨the *repose* of the quiet forests⟩ **3** : cessation or absence of activity, movement, or animation ⟨a face in *repose*⟩

re·pose·ful \ri-ˈpōz-fəl\ *adj* : likely to induce repose — **re·pose·ful·ly** \-fə-lē\ *adv* — **re·pose·ful·ness** *n*

re·po·si·tion \ˌrē-pə-ˈzish-ən\ *vt* : to change or restore the position of

re·pos·i·to·ry \ri-ˈpäz-ə-ˌtōr-ē, -ˌtȯr-\ *n, pl* **-ries** **1** : a place or container where something is deposited or stored **2** : a side altar in a Roman Catholic church where the consecrated Host is reserved from Maundy Thursday until Good Friday **3** : one that contains or stores something nonmaterial ⟨libraries are *repositories* of knowledge⟩ **4** : a person to whom something is confided or entrusted [Latin *repositorium,* from *repositus,* past participle of *reponere* "to put away"]

re·pos·sess \ˌrē-pə-ˈzes\ *vt* **1 a** : to regain possession of **b** : to take possession of (something bought) from a buyer in default of the payment of installments due **2** : to restore to possession — **re·pos·ses·sion** \-ˈzesh-ən\ *n*

re·pous·sé \rə-ˌpü-ˈsā\ *adj* **1** : shaped or ornamented with patterns in relief made by hammering or pressing on the reverse side — used especially of metal **2** : formed in relief [French, literally, "pushed back"]

repp *variant of* ²REP

rep·re·hend \ˌrep-ri-ˈhend\ *vt* : to voice disapproval of : CENSURE [Latin *reprehendere,* literally, "to hold back," from *re-* + *prehendere* "to grasp"]

rep·re·hen·si·ble \ˌrep-ri-ˈhen-sə-bəl\ *adj* : worthy of or deserving censure or blame : CULPABLE — **rep·re·hen·si·bil·i·ty** \-ˌhen-sə-ˈbil-ət-ē\ *n* — **rep·re·hen·si·ble·ness** *n* — **rep·re·hen·si·bly** \-blē\ *adv*

rep·re·hen·sion \-ˈhen-chən\ *n* : the act of reprehending : REPROOF [Latin *reprehensio,* from *reprehendere* "to reprehend"]

rep·re·hen·sive \-ˈhen-siv\ *adj* : serving to reprehend : conveying reprehension or reproof

rep·re·sent \ˌrep-ri-ˈzent\ *vt* **1** : to present a picture, image, or likeness of : PORTRAY ⟨this picture *represents* a scene at King Arthur's court⟩ **2** : to serve as a sign or symbol of ⟨the flag *represents* our country⟩ **3** : to serve as the counterpart or image of ⟨a hero that *represents* the ideals of the culture⟩ **4 a** : to take the place of in some respect **b** : to act for or in the place of (as in a legislative body) **c** : to manage the legal and business affairs of ⟨an athlete *represented* by top agents⟩ **5** : to describe as having a specified character or quality **6** : to give one's impression and judgment of ⟨I *represented* him in the best light⟩ **7** : to serve as a specimen, example, or instance of [Medieval French *representer,* from Latin *repraesentare,* from *re-* + *praesentare* "to present"] — **rep·re·sent·able** \-ə-bəl\ *adj* — **rep·re·sent·er** *n*

re–pre·sent \ˌrē-pri-ˈzent\ *vt* : to present again or anew — **re–pre·sen·ta·tion** \-ˌprē-ˌzen-ˈtā-shən, -ˌprez-n-\ *n*

rep·re·sen·ta·tion \ˌrep-ri-ˌzen-ˈtā-shən\ *n* **1** : one that represents: as **a** : an artistic likeness or image **b** : a statement or account made to influence action or opinion **c** : a sign or symbol of something **2** : a usually formal protest **3** : the act or action of representing or state of being represented (as in a legislative body) **4** : the body of persons representing a constituency — **rep·re·sen·ta·tion·al** \-shnəl, -shən-l\ *adj*

¹rep·re·sen·ta·tive \ˌrep-ri-ˈzent-ət-iv\ *adj* **1** : serving to represent ⟨a painting *representative* of a battle⟩ **2** : standing or acting for another especially through delegated authority **3** : of, based upon, or being a government in which the people are represented by persons chosen from among them usually by election **4** : serving as a typical or characteristic example ⟨a *repre-*

\ə\ **abut**	\au̇\ **out**	\i\ **tip**	\ȯ\ **saw**	\u̇\ **foot**
\ər\ **further**	\ch\ **chin**	\ī\ **life**	\ȯi\ **coin**	\y\ **yet**
\a\ **mat**	\e\ **pet**	\j\ **job**	\th\ **thin**	\yü\ **few**
\ā\ **take**	\ē\ **easy**	\ng\ **sing**	\t͟h\ **this**	\yu̇\ **cure**
\ä\ **cot, cart**	\g\ **go**	\ō\ **bone**	\ü\ **food**	\zh\ **vision**

sentative sample⟩ — **rep·re·sen·ta·tive·ly** *adv* — **rep·re·sen·ta·tive·ness** *n*

[2]**representative** *n* **1 :** a typical example of a group, class, or quality : SPECIMEN **2 :** one that represents another or others: as **a :** one that represents another or others as agent, deputy, substitute, or delegate usually being invested with the authority of the principal **b :** a member of the house of representatives of the U.S. Congress or a state legislature

re·press \ri-ˈpres\ *vt* **1 :** to check by or as if by pressure : CURB **2 :** to hold in by self-control ⟨*repress* a laugh⟩ **3 :** to put down by force : SUBDUE ⟨*repress* a disturbance⟩ **4 :** to prevent the natural or normal expression, activity, or development of ⟨*repress* one's anger⟩ **5 :** to exclude from consciousness ⟨*repressed* painful past experiences⟩ [Latin *repressus,* past participle of *reprimere* "to check, repress," from *re-* + *premere* "to press"] — **re·press·ible** \-ˈpres-ə-bəl\ *adj* — **re·pres·sive** \-ˈpres-iv\ *adj* — **re·pres·sive·ly** *adv* — **re·pres·sive·ness** *n* — **re·pres·sor** \-ˈpres-ər\ *n*

re·pressed *adj* **1 :** subjected to or marked by repression **2 :** characterized by restraint

re·pres·sion \ri-ˈpresh-ən\ *n* **1 :** the act of repressing : the state of being repressed **2 :** a mental process by which painful or disturbing thoughts, memories, or desires are kept from conscious awareness

re·pres·sor \ri-ˈpres-ər\ *n* **:** a protein that binds to a genetic operator to inhibit its function

[1]**re·prieve** \ri-ˈprēv\ *vt* **1 :** to delay the punishment of (as a condemned prisoner) **2 :** to give relief or deliverance to for a time [perhaps from Middle French *repris,* past participle of *reprendre* "to take back"]

[2]**reprieve** *n* **1 a :** the act of reprieving : the state of being reprieved **b :** a formal temporary suspension of the execution of a sentence **2 :** a temporary respite (as from pain or trouble)

[1]**rep·ri·mand** \ˈrep-rə-ˌmand\ *n* **:** a severe or formal reproof [French *réprimande,* from Latin *reprimendus* "to be checked," from *reprimere* "to check, repress"]

[2]**reprimand** *vt* **:** to reprove severely and usually formally from a position of authority ***synonyms*** see REPROVE

[1]**re·print** \rē-ˈprint, ˈrē-\ *vt* **:** to print again : make a reprint of — **re·print·er** *n*

[2]**re·print** \ˈrē-ˌprint\ *n* **1 :** a new or additional printing without any change in the text of a book already published **2 :** a separately printed text or excerpt

re·pri·sal \ri-ˈprī-zəl\ *n* **1 a :** the use of force short of war by one nation against another in retaliation for damage or loss suffered ⟨economic *reprisals*⟩ **b :** an instance of such use **2 :** a retaliatory act [Medieval French *reprisaile,* from obsolete Italian *rappresaglia,* from *ripreso,* past participle of *riprendere* "to take back," from *ri-* "re-" + *prendere* "to take," from Latin *prehendere*]

re·prise \ri-ˈprēz\ *n* **1 :** a recurrence, renewal, or resumption of an action **2 :** a repetition of a musical passage or theme [Medieval French, "seizure, repossession, expense," from *reprendre* "to take back," from *re-* "re-" + *prendre* "to take," from Latin *prehendere*]

re·pro \ˈrē-prō\ *n, pl* **repros** **1 :** a clear sharp proof made especially from a letterpress printing surface to serve as photographic copy for a printing plate **2 :** REPRODUCTION 2 [short for *reproduction*]

[1]**re·proach** \ri-ˈprōch\ *n* **1 a :** a cause or occasion of blame, discredit, or disgrace **b :** loss of credit or reputation : DISGRACE **2 a :** the act or action of reproaching : REBUKE **b :** an expression of rebuke or disapproval [Medieval French *reproche,* from *reprocher* "to reproach," derived from Latin *re-* + *prope* "near"] — **re·proach·ful** \-fəl\ *adj* — **re·proach·ful·ly** \-fə-lē\ *adv* — **re·proach·ful·ness** *n*

[2]**reproach** *vt* **1 :** to find fault with : blame for a mistake or failure ⟨*reproached* me for my carelessness⟩ **2 :** to bring into discredit ***synonyms*** see REPROVE — **re·proach·able** \-ˈprō-chə-bəl\ *adj* — **re·proach·er** *n* — **re·proach·ing·ly** \-ˈprō-ching-lē\ *adv*

[1]**rep·ro·bate** \ˈrep-rə-ˌbāt\ *vt* **:** to condemn as unworthy or evil [Late Latin *reprobare,* from Latin *re-* + *probare* "to test, approve"] — **rep·ro·ba·tion** \ˌrep-rə-ˈbā-shən\ *n* — **rep·ro·ba·tive** \ˈrep-rə-ˌbāt-iv\ *adj* — **rep·ro·ba·to·ry** \-bə-ˌtōr-ē, -ˌtȯr-\ *adj*

[2]**reprobate** *adj* **1 :** doomed to damnation **2 :** morally corrupt **3 :** of, relating to, or characteristic of a wicked person

[3]**reprobate** *n* **:** a reprobate person

re·pro·cess \rē-ˈpräs-ˌes, -ˈprōs-, -əs\ *vt* **:** to subject to a special process or treatment in preparation for reuse

re·pro·duce \ˌrē-prə-ˈdüs, -ˈdyüs\ *vb* **1 :** to produce again: as **a :** to give rise to (new individuals of the same kind) by a sexual or asexual process **b :** to cause to exist again or anew ⟨*reproduce* water from steam⟩ **c :** to imitate closely ⟨*reproduce* the sound of thunder and footsteps by sound effects⟩ **d :** to present again **e :** to make a representation (as an image or copy) of **f :** to translate (a recording) into sound **2 :** to undergo reproduction ⟨your voice *reproduces* well⟩ **3 :** to produce offspring — **re·pro·duc·er** *n* — **re·pro·duc·ibil·i·ty** \-ˌdü-sə-ˈbil-ət-ē, -ˌdyü-\ *n* — **re·pro·duc·ible** \-ˈdü-sə-bəl, -ˈdyü-\ *adj*

re·pro·duc·tion \ˌrē-prə-ˈdək-shən\ *n* **1 :** the act or process of reproducing; *esp* **:** the process by which plants and animals give rise to offspring **2 :** something reproduced : COPY ***synonyms*** see DUPLICATE

re·pro·duc·tive \ˌrē-prə-ˈdək-tiv\ *adj* **:** of, relating to, or capable of reproduction — **re·pro·duc·tive·ly** *adv*

re·pro·gram \rē-ˈprō-ˌgram\ *vb* **1 :** to program anew; *esp* **:** to revise or write new programs for **2 :** to rewrite or revise a program — **re·pro·gram·ma·ble** \-ə-bəl\ *adj*

re·proof \ri-ˈprüf\ *n* **:** censure for a fault : REBUKE [Medieval French *reproefe,* from *reprover* "to reprove"]

re·prove \ri-ˈprüv\ *vt* **1 :** to scold usually gently or with kindly intent **2 :** to express disapproval of : CENSURE [Medieval French *reprover,* from Late Latin *reprobare* "to disapprove, condemn," from Latin *re-* "re-" + *probare* "to test, approve"] — **re·prov·er** *n*

synonyms REPROVE, REBUKE, REPRIMAND, REPROACH mean to criticize for faulty behavior. REPROVE may imply a kindly intent and lack of harshness ⟨gently *reproved* my table manners⟩. REBUKE implies a stern or sharp reproving ⟨was *rebuked* for his role in the rebellion⟩. REPRIMAND implies a severe, formal, often public or official rebuke ⟨*reprimanded* by the ethics committee⟩. REPROACH often suggests displeasure or disappointment expressed in mild scolding ⟨*reproached* him for his tardiness⟩.

[1]**rep·tile** \ˈrep-tl, -ˌtīl\ *n* **1 :** any of a class (Reptilia) of cold-blooded air-breathing vertebrates including the alligators and crocodiles, lizards, snakes, turtles, and extinct related forms (as dinosaurs) that have a bony skeleton and a body usually covered with scales or bony plates and usually lay eggs **2 :** a groveling or despicable person [Late Latin, from *reptilis* "creeping," from *repere* "to crawl"]

[2]**reptile** *adj* **:** characteristic of a reptile : REPTILIAN

[1]**rep·til·i·an** \rep-ˈtil-ē-ən\ *adj* **1 :** of, relating to, characteristic of, or resembling reptiles **2 :** cold-bloodedly treacherous

[2]**reptilian** *n* **:** REPTILE 1

re·pub·lic \ri-ˈpəb-lik\ *n* **1 a :** a government having a chief of state who is not a monarch and who in modern times is usually a president **b :** a political unit having such a form of government **2 a :** a government in which supreme power resides in a body of citizens entitled to vote and is exercised by elected officers and representatives responsible to them and governing according to law **b :** a political unit (as a nation) having such a form of government **3 :** a constituent political and territorial unit of the former nations of Czechoslovakia, the U.S.S.R., or Yugoslavia [French *république,* from Latin *respublica,* from *res* "thing, wealth" + *publica,* feminine of *publicus* "public"]

[1]**re·pub·li·can** \ri-ˈpəb-li-kən\ *adj* **1 a :** of, relating to, or having the characteristics of a republic **b :** favoring, supporting, or advocating a republic **2** *cap* **a :** DEMOCRATIC-REPUBLICAN **b :** of, relating to, or constituting one of the two major political parties evolving in the U.S. in the mid-19th century that is usually primarily associated with business, financial, and some agricultural interests and is held to favor a restricted governmental role in economic life

[2]**republican** *n* **1 :** one that favors or supports a republican form of government **2** *cap* **a :** a member of a political party advocating republicanism **b :** a member of the Democratic-Republican party or the Republican party of the U.S.

re·pub·li·can·ism \-kə-ˌniz-əm\ *n* **1 :** adherence to or sympathy for a republican form of government **2 :** the principles or theory of republican government **3** *cap* **:** the principles, policy, or practices of the Republican party of the U.S.

re·pub·li·ca·tion \rē-ˌpəb-lə-ˈkā-shən\ *n* **1 :** the act or action of republishing : the state of being republished **2 :** something that has been republished

re·pub·lish \rē-ˈpəb-lish\ *vt* : to publish again or anew — **re·pub·lish·er** \-ər\ *n*

re·pu·di·ate \ri-ˈpyüd-ē-ˌāt\ *vt* **1** : to divorce or separate formally from (a woman) **2** : to refuse to have anything to do with : DISOWN **3 a** : to refuse to accept; *esp* : to reject as unauthorized or having no binding force ⟨*repudiate* a contract⟩ **b** : to reject as untrue or unjust ⟨*repudiate* a charge of favoritism⟩ **4** : to refuse to acknowledge or pay ⟨*repudiate* a debt⟩ [Latin *repudiare,* from *repudium* "divorce"] ***synonyms*** see REJECT — **re·pu·di·a·tion** \-ˌpyüd-ē-ˈā-shən\ *n* — **re·pu·di·a·tor** \-ˈpyüd-ē-ˌāt-ər\ *n*

re·pug·nance \ri-ˈpəg-nəns\ *n* : strong dislike, distaste, or antagonism

re·pug·nant \-nənt\ *adj* **1** : CONTRARY, INCOMPATIBLE ⟨punishments *repugnant* to the spirit of the law⟩ **2** : arousing distaste or aversion ⟨a *repugnant* idea⟩ [Medieval French, "opposed, incompatible," from Latin *repugnare* "to fight against," from *re-* + *pugnare* "to fight"] — **re·pug·nant·ly** *adv*

synonyms REPUGNANT, REPELLENT, ABHORRENT, HATEFUL mean so different or unlikable as to arouse aversion. REPUGNANT implies arousing one's resistance or loathing by being alien to one's ideas, principles, or tastes ⟨avoids using such *repugnant* language at home⟩. REPELLENT suggests a generally forbidding or unlovely quality that makes one back away ⟨thought that eating insects was *repellent*⟩. ABHORRENT is applied to something that is so detestable as to evoke horror or disgust ⟨brutal crimes *abhorrent* to the public⟩. HATEFUL suggests something arousing or deserving of hatred ⟨*hateful* acts of vandalism⟩.

1re·pulse \ri-ˈpəls\ *vt* **1** : to drive or beat back : REPEL ⟨*repulse* an attack⟩ **2** : to repel by discourtesy, coldness, or denial : REBUFF ⟨*repulsed* their advances⟩ **3** : to cause repulsion in : DISGUST ⟨*repulsed* at the sight⟩ [Latin *repulsus,* past participle of *repellere* "to repel"]

2repulse *n* **1** : a cold discourteous rebuff **2 a** : the action of repelling an attacker **b** : the fact of being repelled

re·pul·sion \ri-ˈpəl-shən\ *n* **1** : the action of repulsing : the state of being repulsed **2** : the action of repelling : the force with which bodies, particles, or like forces repel one another **3** : a feeling of aversion : REPUGNANCE

re·pul·sive \ri-ˈpəl-siv\ *adj* **1** : tending or serving to repulse **2** : arousing aversion or disgust — **re·pul·sive·ly** *adv* — **re·pul·sive·ness** *n*

rep·u·ta·ble \ˈrep-yət-ə-bəl\ *adj* : having a good reputation : RESPECTABLE — **rep·u·ta·bil·i·ty** \ˌrep-yət-ə-ˈbil-ət-ē\ *n* — **rep·u·ta·bly** \ˈrep-yət-ə-blē\ *adv*

rep·u·ta·tion \ˌrep-yə-ˈtā-shən\ *n* **1** : overall quality or character as seen or judged by people in general ⟨has a bad *reputation*⟩ **2** : recognition by other people of some characteristic or ability ⟨has the *reputation* of being clever⟩ **3** : good name : a place in public esteem ⟨lose one's *reputation*⟩

1re·pute \ri-ˈpyüt\ *vt* : to hold as a belief : CONSIDER ⟨is *reputed* to be a shrewd negotiator⟩ [Medieval French *reputer,* from Latin *reputare* "to reckon up, think over," from *re-* + *putare* "to reckon"]

2repute *n* **1** : REPUTATION ⟨know a person by *repute*⟩ **2** : the state of being favorably known, spoken of, or esteemed ⟨a scientist of *repute*⟩

re·put·ed \ri-ˈpyüt-əd\ *adj* **1** : having a good repute ⟨a highly *reputed* lawyer⟩ **2** : being such according to reputation or general belief ⟨a *reputed* success⟩ — **re·put·ed·ly** *adv*

1re·quest \ri-ˈkwest\ *n* **1** : an asking for something ⟨a *request* for help⟩ **2** : something asked for ⟨grant every *request*⟩ **3** : the condition of being requested ⟨tickets are available upon *request*⟩ **4** : DEMAND ⟨that book is in great *request*⟩ [Medieval French *requeste,* derived from Latin *requaerere* "to seek for, require"]

2request *vt* **1** : to make a request to or of **2** : to ask for ⟨*request* a loan⟩ ***synonyms*** see ASK — **re·quest·er** *or* **re·quest·or** *n*

re·qui·em \ˈrek-wē-əm *also* ˈrāk- *or* ˈrēk-\ *n* **1** : a mass for the dead **2 a** : a musical setting of the mass for the dead **b** : a musical composition in honor of the dead [Latin, accusative of *requies* "rest"; first word of the introit of the requiem mass]

requiem shark *n* : any of a family of large sharks (as the tiger shark) typically of warm seas [obsolete French *requiem* "shark," alteration of French *requin*]

req·ui·es·cat \ˌrek-wē-ˈes-ˌkät, ˌrā-kwē-\ *n* : a prayer for the repose of a dead person [Latin, "may he (or she) rest," from *requiescere* "to rest," from *re-* + *quiescere* "to be quiet," from *quies* "quiet"]

re·quire \ri-ˈkwīr\ *vt* **1** : COMMAND ⟨the law *requires* drivers to observe traffic lights⟩ **2 a** : to call for as suitable or appropriate ⟨the occasion *requires* formal dress⟩ **b** : to demand as necessary or essential ⟨all living beings *require* food⟩ [Medieval French *requere,* derived from Latin *requirere,* from *re-* + *quaerere* "to seek, ask"] ***synonyms*** see DEMAND

re·quire·ment \-mənt\ *n* **1** : something needed ⟨sleep is a *requirement* for health⟩ **2** : something essential to the existence or occurrence of something else : CONDITION ⟨met all the *requirements* for graduation⟩

req·ui·site \ˈrek-wə-zət\ *adj* : absolutely needed : ESSENTIAL [Latin *requisitus,* past participle of *requirere* "to require"] ***synonyms*** see NECESSARY — **requisite** *n* — **req·ui·site·ness** *n*

1req·ui·si·tion \ˌrek-wə-ˈzish-ən\ *n* **1** : the act of requiring or demanding **2** : a demand or application made with authority ⟨a *requisition* for army supplies⟩ **3** : the state of being in demand or use ⟨every car was in *requisition*⟩

2requisition *vt* **-si·tioned; -si·tion·ing** \-ˈzish-ning, -ə-ning\ : to take or get with a requisition ⟨*requisition* fresh supplies⟩

re·quit·al \ri-ˈkwīt-l\ *n* **1** : the act or action of requiting : the state of being requited **2** : something given in return, compensation, or retaliation

re·quite \ri-ˈkwīt\ *vt* **1 a** : to make return for : REPAY **b** : to retaliate for : AVENGE **2** : to give something to in return for a benefit or service or for an injury [*re-* + obsolete *quite* "to quit, pay"] — **re·quit·er** *n*

re·ra·di·ate \rē-ˈrād-ē-ˌāt\ *vb* : to radiate anew ⟨the ground *reradiates* the heat absorbed from the sun⟩ — **re·ra·di·a·tion** \-ˌrād-ē-ˈā-shən\ *n*

1re·run \rē-ˈrən, ˈrē-\ *vt* : to run again or anew

2re·run \ˈrē-ˌrən, rē-ˈ, ˈrē-ˈ\ *n* : the act or action or an instance of rerunning; *esp* : a movie or television show that is rerun

re·sale \ˈrē-ˌsāl, rē-ˈ, ˈrē-ˈ\ *n* **1** : the act or an instance of selling again **2** : a secondhand sale

re·sched·ule \rē-ˈskej-ül, -əl, *Canadian also* ˈshej-, *British usually* ˈshed-yül\ *vt* : to schedule or plan again according to a different timetable

re·scind \ri-ˈsind\ *vt* **1** : to make void : CANCEL ⟨*rescind* a contract⟩ **2** : REPEAL ⟨*rescind* a law⟩ [Latin *rescindere* "to cut apart, annul," from *re-* + *scindere* "to cut"] — **re·scind·er** *n* — **re·scind·ment** \-mənt\ *n*

re·scis·sion \ri-ˈsizh-ən\ *n* : an act of rescinding [Late Latin *rescissio,* from Latin *rescindere* "to annul"]

res·cue \ˈres-kyü\ *vt* : to free from confinement, danger, or evil : SAVE [Medieval French *rescure,* from *re-* + *escure* "to shake out, wrest away," from Latin *excutere,* from *ex-* + *quatere* "to shake"] — **re·scu·able** \-ə-bəl\ *adj* — **rescue** *n* — **res·cu·er** *n*

synonyms RESCUE, DELIVER, REDEEM, RANSOM mean to set free from confinement or danger. RESCUE implies freeing from imminent danger by prompt or vigorous action ⟨*rescued* the crew of a sinking ship⟩. DELIVER implies releasing from confinement, temptation, slavery, or suffering ⟨*delivered* his people from bondage⟩. REDEEM implies releasing from bondage or penalties by giving what is demanded or necessary ⟨job training designed to *redeem* school dropouts from unemployment⟩. RANSOM applies specifically to buying out of captivity ⟨*ransom* the kidnapping victim⟩.

1re·search \ri-ˈsərch, ˈrē-ˌ\ *n* **1** : careful or diligent search **2** : studious inquiry or examination; *esp* : investigation or experimentation aimed at the discovery and interpretation of facts, revision of accepted theories or laws in the light of new facts, or practical application of such new or revised theories or laws **3** : the collecting of information about a particular subject [Middle French *recerche,* from *recerchier* "to investigate thoroughly," from *re-* + *cerchier* "to search"]

2research *vb* **1** : to search or investigate thoroughly ⟨*research* a problem⟩ **2** : to do research for ⟨*research* a book⟩ **3** : to engage in research — **re·search·able** \ri-ˈsər-chə-bəl, ˈrē-ˌ\ *adj* — **re·search·er** *n*

\ə\ **abut**	\au̇\ **out**	\i\ **tip**	\ȯ\ **saw**	\u̇\ **foot**
\ər\ **further**	\ch\ **chin**	\ī\ **life**	\ȯi\ **coin**	\y\ **yet**
\a\ **mat**	\e\ **pet**	\j\ **job**	\th\ **thin**	\yü\ **few**
\ā\ **take**	\ē\ **easy**	\ng\ **sing**	\th\ **this**	\yu̇\ **cure**
\ä\ **cot, cart**	\g\ **go**	\ō\ **bone**	\ü\ **food**	\zh\ **vision**

re·sec·tion \ri-ˈsek-shən\ *n* : the surgical removal of part of an organ or structure [Latin *resectio* "act of cutting off," from *resecare* "to cut off," from *re-* + *secare* "to cut"] — **re·sect** \-ˈsekt\ *vt*

re·seed \rē-ˈsēd, ˈrē-\ *vb* **1** : to sow seed on again or anew **2** : to maintain itself by self-sown seed

re·sem·blance \ri-ˈzem-bləns\ *n* **1 a** : the quality or state of resembling; *esp* : correspondence in appearance or superficial qualities **b** : a point of likeness **2** : an artistic likeness : IMAGE ***synonyms*** see LIKENESS

re·sem·ble \ri-ˈzem-bəl\ *vt* **-bled; -bling** \-bə-ling, -bling\ : to be like or similar to [Medieval French *resembler*, from *re-* "re-" + *sembler* "to be like, seem," from Latin *similare* "to copy," from *similis* "like"]

re·send \rē-ˈsend\ *vt* **-sent** \-ˈsent\; **-send·ing** : to send again or back ⟨*resent* a returned letter⟩

re·sent \ri-ˈzent\ *vt* : to feel or show annoyance or ill will at ⟨*resent* criticism⟩ [French *ressentir* "to be emotionally sensible of," from *re-* "re-" + *sentir* "to feel," from Latin *sentire*]

re·sent·ful \-fəl\ *adj* **1** : full of resentment : inclined to resent ⟨felt *resentful* of their success⟩ **2** : caused or marked by resentment ⟨*resentful* anger⟩ — **re·sent·ful·ly** \-fə-lē\ *adv* — **re·sent·ful·ness** *n*

re·sent·ment \ri-ˈzent-mənt\ *n* : a feeling of angry displeasure at something regarded as a wrong, insult, or injury

re·ser·pine \ri-ˈsər-ˌpēn, -pən\ *n* : a drug obtained from the root of rauwolfia and used chiefly in the treatment of high blood pressure [German *Reserpin*, probably derived from New Latin *Rauwolfia serpentina*, a species of rauwolfia]

res·er·va·tion \ˌrez-ər-ˈvā-shən\ *n* **1** : the act of reserving **2** : an arrangement to have something (as a hotel room) held for one's use **3** : something reserved for a special use; *esp* : a tract of public lands so reserved (as for use by American Indians) **4 a** : a limiting condition : EXCEPTION ⟨agree without *reservations*⟩ **b** : MISGIVING ⟨had *reservations* about taking the job⟩

[1]**re·serve** \ri-ˈzərv\ *vt* **1** : to keep in store for future or special use **2** : to retain or hold over to a future time or place : DEFER ⟨*reserve* one's comments on a plan⟩ **3** : to set or have set aside or apart ⟨*reserve* a hotel room⟩ [Medieval French *reserver*, from Latin *reservare*, literally, "to keep back," from *servare* "to keep, save"] — **re·serv·able** \-ˈzər-və-bəl\ *adj*

[2]**reserve** *n* **1** : something stored or available for future use : STOCK ⟨oil *reserves*⟩ **2** : something reserved for a particular use: as **a** : military forces withheld for later use — usually used in plural **b** : the military forces of a country not part of the regular services; *also* : RESERVIST **c** : a tract (as of public land) set apart : RESERVATION ⟨a wild game *reserve*⟩ **3** : an act of reserving : EXCEPTION **4** : restraint, closeness, or caution in one's words and bearing **5** : money or its equivalent kept on hand or set apart usually to meet obligations **6** : SUBSTITUTE ⟨the *reserves* on the football team⟩ — **in reserve** : held back for future or special use

reserve bank *n* : a central bank holding reserves of other banks

re·served \ri-ˈzərvd\ *adj* **1** : restrained in words and actions ⟨very *reserved* in public⟩ **2** : set aside for future or special use ***synonyms*** see SILENT — **re·serv·ed·ly** \-ˈzər-vəd-lē\ *adv* — **re·served·ness** \-ˈzər-vəd-nəs, -ˈzərvd-nəs, -ˈzerv-nəs\ *n*

re·serv·ist \ri-ˈzər-vəst\ *n* : a member of a military reserve

res·er·voir \ˈrez-ərv-ˌwär, -əv-, -ˌwȯr, -ˌȯr\ *n* **1** : a place where something is kept in store; *esp* : an artificial lake where water is collected and kept in quantity for use **2** : an extra supply : RESERVE **3** : an organism (as a fly or mouse) in which a parasite (as a bacterium) that is harmful to some other species lives and multiplies usually without damaging its host [French *réservoir*, from *réserver* "to reserve"]

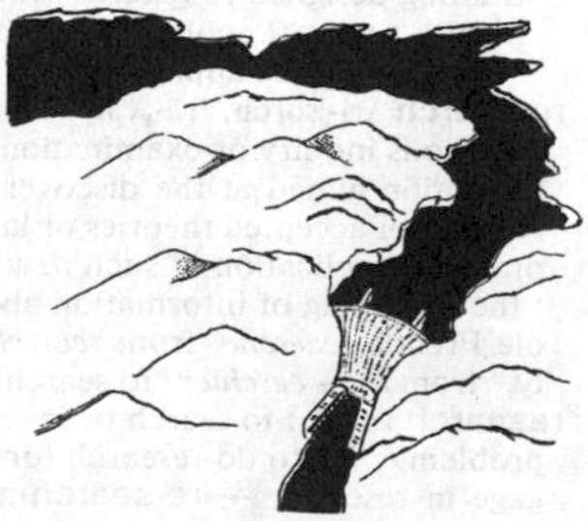
reservoir 1

re·set \rē-ˈset\ *vt* **-set; -set·ting** **1** : to set again or anew ⟨*reset* a circuit breaker⟩ ⟨*reset* a diamond⟩ **2** : to change the reading of often to zero ⟨*reset* a stopwatch⟩ — **reset** \ˈrē-ˌset\ *n* — **re·set·table** \-ˈset-ə-bəl\ *adj*

re·shape \rē-ˈshāp, ˈrē-\ *vt* : to give a new form to

re·shuf·fle \-ˈshəf-əl\ *vt* **1** : to shuffle again **2** : to reorganize usually by redistribution of existing elements ⟨the prime minister *reshuffled* the cabinet⟩ — **reshuffle** *n*

re·side \ri-ˈzīd\ *vi* **1** : to dwell permanently or continuously ⟨*reside* in St. Louis⟩ **2** : to be present as an element, quality, or right ⟨the power of veto *resides* in the president⟩ [Latin *residēre* "to sit back, abide," from *re-* + *sedēre* "to sit"] — **re·sid·er** *n*

res·i·dence \ˈrez-əd-əns, -ə-ˌdens\ *n* **1** : the act or fact of residing in a place as a dweller or in discharge of a duty ⟨physicians in *residence* in a hospital⟩ **2 a** : the place where one lives **b** : the status of a legal resident **3 a** : a building used as a home : DWELLING **b** : a unit of housing provided for students **4 a** : the period during which a person resides in a place **b** : a period of active study, research, or teaching at a college or university — **in residence** : engaged to live and work at a particular place often for a specified time ⟨a poet *in residence* at a university⟩

res·i·den·cy \ˈrez-əd-ən-sē, -ə-ˌden-\ *n, pl* **-cies** **1 a** : a usually official place of residence **b** : a state or period of residency ⟨a 20-year *residency* in the city⟩; *also* : RESIDENCE 2b ⟨applied for *residency*⟩ **2** : a territorial unit in which a political resident exercises authority **3 a** : a period of advanced training in a medical specialty that typically follows graduation from medical school **b** : RESIDENCE 4b

[1]**res·i·dent** \ˈrez-əd-ənt, -ə-ˌdent\ *adj* **1 a** : living in a place for some length of time **b** : serving in a regular or full-time capacity ⟨a *resident* engineer⟩; *also* : being in residence ⟨a *resident* artist⟩ **2** : PRESENT 2b ⟨energy *resident* in matter⟩ **3** : not migratory ⟨*resident* birds⟩ [Latin *residens*, present participle of *residēre* "to sit back, abide"]

[2]**resident** *n* **1** : one who resides in a place **2** : a diplomatic agent exercising authority in a protected state as representative of the protecting power **3** : a physician serving a residency

res·i·den·tial \ˌrez-ə-ˈden-chəl\ *adj* **1** : used as a residence or by residents ⟨a *residential* hotel⟩ **2** : restricted to or occupied by residences ⟨a *residential* neighborhood⟩ **3** : of or relating to residence or residences — **res·i·den·tial·ly** \-ˈdench-lē, -ə-lē\ *adv*

[1]**re·sid·u·al** \ri-ˈzij-ə-wəl, -ˈzij-wəl\ *adj* : of, relating to, being, or leaving a residue — **re·sid·u·al·ly** \-ē\ *adv*

[2]**residual** *n* **1** : REMAINDER **2** : a payment (as to an actor or writer) for each rerun after an initial showing

residual power *n* : power held to remain at the disposal of a government authority after the delegation of specified powers to other authorities

re·sid·u·ary \ri-ˈzij-ə-ˌwer-ē\ *adj* : of, relating to, or being a residue ⟨a *residuary* clause in a will⟩

res·i·due \ˈrez-ə-ˌdü, -ˌdyü\ *n* **1 a** : whatever remains after a part is taken, set apart, or lost or after the completion of a process : REMNANT, REMAINDER **b** : the part of an estate remaining after the payment of all debts and specific devises and bequests **2** : a constituent structural unit of a usually complex molecule ⟨amino acid *residues* from hydrolysis of protein⟩ [Medieval French *residue*, from Latin *residuum*, from *residuus* "left over," from *residēre* "to sit back, remain"]

re·sid·u·um \ri-ˈzij-ə-wəm\ *n, pl* **re·sid·ua** \-ə-wə\ : something residual : RESIDUE [Latin]

re·sign \ri-ˈzīn\ *vb* **1** : to give up by a formal or official act ⟨*resign* his position⟩ **2** : to give up an office or position : QUIT **3 a** : to submit (oneself) without resistance ⟨*resigned* herself to her fate⟩ **b** : to accept something as inevitable : SUBMIT ⟨is *resigned* to her fate⟩ [Medieval French *resigner*, from Latin *resignare* "to unseal, cancel, resign," from *re-* + *signare* "to sign, seal"] ***synonyms*** see RELINQUISH — **re·sign·ed·ly** \-ˈzī-nəd-lē\ *adv* — **re·sign·ed·ness** \-nəs\ *n* — **re·sign·er** *n*

res·ig·na·tion \ˌrez-ig-ˈnā-shən\ *n* **1 a** : an act of resigning **b** : a formal notification of resigning **2** : the quality or the feeling of a person who is resigned : SUBMISSION 2

re·sil·ience \ri-ˈzil-yəns\ *or* **re·sil·ien·cy** \-yən-sē\ *n* **1** : the ability of a strained body to recover its original size and shape after being compressed, bent, or stretched ⟨the *resilience* of rubber⟩ ⟨the *resiliency* of arteries⟩ **2** : the ability to recover from or adjust easily to misfortune or change

re·sil·ien·cy \-yən-sē\ *n* : RESILIENCE

re·sil·ient \-yənt\ *adj* : characterized or marked by resilience: as **a** : capable of withstanding shock without permanent deformation or rupture **b** : tending to recover readily from or adjust easily to misfortune or change [Latin *resiliens*, present participle of *resilire* "to jump back, recoil," from *re-* + *salire* "to leap"] ***synonyms*** see ELASTIC — **re·sil·ient·ly** *adv*

res·in \ˈrez-ⁿn\ *n* **1 a :** any of various solid or semisolid fusible natural organic substances that are usually transparent or translucent and yellowish to brown, are formed especially in plant secretions, are soluble in organic solvents but not in water, are electrical nonconductors, and are used chiefly in varnishes, printing inks, plastics, and sizes and in medicine **b :** ROSIN **2 :** any of a large class of synthetic products that have some of the physical properties of natural resins but are different chemically and are used chiefly in plastics [Medieval French *reisine,* from Latin *resina*] — **res·in·ous** \-əs\ *adj*

res·in·oid \-ˌȯid\ *n* **:** a somewhat resinous substance; *esp* **:** a thermosetting synthetic resin

[1]**re·sist** \ri-ˈzist\ *vb* **1 :** to withstand the force or effect of ‹*resist* disease› ‹silver *resists* acids› **2 :** to exert oneself to check or defeat ‹*resist* temptation› **3 :** to exert force in opposition [Latin *resistere,* from *re-* + *sistere* "to take a stand"] ***synonyms*** see OPPOSE

[2]**resist** *n* **:** something (as a coating) that resists or prevents a particular action

[1]**re·sis·tance** \ri-ˈzis-təns\ *n* **1 a :** an act or instance of resisting **:** OPPOSITION **b :** a means of resisting **2 :** the power or capacity to resist: as **a :** the ability of an organism to resist harmful influences (as infection) **b :** the capacity of a microorganism to survive exposure to a toxic agent (as a drug) that was formerly effective against it **3 :** an opposing or retarding force **4 a :** the opposition offered by a body or substance to the passage through it of an electric current **b :** a source of electrical resistance **5** *often cap* **:** an underground organization of a conquered or nearly conquered country engaging in sabotage and secret operations against occupation forces and collaborators

[2]**resistance** *adj* **:** of, relating to, or being exercise involving pushing or pulling against a source of resistance (as a weight) to increase muscle strength ‹*resistance* training›

re·sis·tant \-tənt\ *adj* **:** giving, capable of, or exhibiting resistance — often used in combination ‹wrinkle-*resistant* clothes›

re·sist·er \ri-ˈzis-tər\ *n* **:** one that resists; *esp* **:** one who actively opposes the policies of a government

re·sist·ibil·i·ty \ri-ˌzis-tə-ˈbil-ət-ē\ *n* **1 :** the quality or state of being resistible **2 :** ability to resist

re·sist·ible \ri-ˈzis-tə-bəl\ *adj* **:** capable of being resisted

re·sis·tive \ri-ˈzis-tiv\ *adj* **:** marked by resistance

re·sis·tiv·i·ty \ri-ˌzis-ˈtiv-ət-ē\ *n, pl* **-ties 1 :** capacity for resisting **:** RESISTANCE **2 :** the longitudinal electrical resistance of a uniform rod of unit length and unit cross-sectional area **:** the reciprocal of conductivity

re·sist·less \ri-ˈzist-ləs\ *adj* **1 :** too strong to be resisted **2 :** offering no resistance — **re·sist·less·ly** *adv* — **re·sist·less·ness** *n*

re·sis·tor \ri-ˈzis-tər\ *n* **:** a device offering electrical resistance

res·o·lute \ˈrez-ə-ˌlüt\ *adj* **1 :** marked by firm determination ‹a *resolute* leader› **2 :** BOLD 1, STEADY ‹a *resolute* gaze› [Latin *resolutus,* past participle of *resolvere* "to resolve, unloose"] — **res·o·lute·ly** *adv* — **res·o·lute·ness** *n*

res·o·lu·tion \ˌrez-ə-ˈlü-shən\ *n* **1 :** the act or process of resolving: as **a :** the act of analyzing a complex idea into simpler ones **b :** the act of answering **c :** the act of determining **2 :** the progression of a sound (as a voice or chord) from dissonance to consonance **3 a :** the process or capability of making distinguishable individual parts, closely adjacent optical images, or sources of light **b :** a measure of the sharpness of an image or of the fineness with which a device (as a video display, printer, or scanner) can produce or record such an image ‹a *resolution* of 1200 dots per inch› **4 :** the subsidence of inflammation especially in a lung **5 a :** something that is resolved ‹New Year's *resolutions*› **b :** firmness of resolve **6 :** a formal expression of the opinion, will, or intent of an official body or assembled group **7 :** the point in a literary work at which the chief dramatic complication is worked out

[1]**re·solve** \ri-ˈzälv, -ˈzȯlv\ *vb* **1 a :** to break up or separate into component parts; *also* **:** to change by disintegration **b :** to reduce by analysis ‹*resolve* the problem into simpler elements› **c :** to distinguish between or make independently visible adjacent parts of **2 a :** to clear up **:** DISPEL ‹*resolve* doubts› **b :** to find an answer or solution to **3 a :** to reach a firm decision about ‹*resolve* to get more sleep› **b :** to form a resolution **4 :** to declare or decide by a formal resolution and vote **5 :** to work out the resolution of (as a play) **6 :** to progress or cause to progress from dissonance to consonance [Latin *resolvere* "to unloose, break up, dissolve," from *re-* + *solvere* "to loosen"] — **re·solv·able** \-ˈzäl-və-bəl, -ˈzȯl-\ *adj* — **re·solv·er** *n*

[2]**resolve** *n* **1 :** something resolved **2 :** firmness of purpose **3 :** a legal or official determination; *esp* **:** a formal resolution

re·solved \ri-ˈzälvd, -ˈzȯlvd\ *adj* **:** RESOLUTE 1, DETERMINED — **re·solv·ed·ly** \-ˈzäl-vəd-lē, -ˈzȯl-\ *adv*

res·o·nance \ˈrez-ⁿn-əns\ *n* **1 a :** the quality or state of being resonant **b** (1) **:** a vibration of large amplitude in a mechanical or electrical system caused by a relatively small periodic stimulus of the same or nearly the same period as the natural vibration period of the system (as when a radio receiving circuit is tuned to a broadcast frequency) (2) **:** the state of adjustment that produces resonance in a mechanical or electrical system ‹two circuits in *resonance* with each other› **2 a :** the intensification and enriching of a musical tone by supplementary vibration **b :** a quality imparted to voiced sounds by the configuration of the mouth and pharynx and in some cases also of the nasal cavity **3 :** the state of a molecule, ion, or radical that is best understood as a combination or blend of two or more possible structures **4 :** a quality of evoking response ‹the tragedy has national *resonance*›

res·o·nant \-ⁿn-ənt\ *adj* **1 :** continuing to sound **:** ECHOING **2 :** of, relating to, or showing resonance **3 :** intensified and enriched by resonance — **res·o·nant·ly** *adv*

res·o·nate \ˈrez-ⁿn-ˌāt\ *vi* **1 :** to produce or exhibit resonance **2 a :** to respond as if by resonance ‹*resonate* to the music› **b :** to relate harmoniously **:** strike a chord ‹a message that *resonates* with voters› [Latin *resonare* "to resound"]

res·o·na·tor \-ˌāt-ər\ *n* **:** something (as a device for increasing the resonance of a musical instrument) that resounds or resonates

re·sorb \rē-ˈsȯrb, ˈrē-, -ˈzȯrb\ *vt* **:** to break down and assimilate (something previously produced) ‹the tadpole's tail is gradually *resorbed*› [Latin *resorbēre* "to swallow again," from *re-* + *sorbēre* "to suck up"] — **re·sorp·tion** \-ˈsȯrp-shən, -ˈzȯrp-\ *n*

[1]**re·sort** \ri-ˈzȯrt\ *n* **1 a :** one that is looked to for help **:** REFUGE, RESOURCE **b :** RECOURSE ‹have *resort* to force› **2 a :** frequent, habitual, or general visiting ‹a place of popular *resort*› **b** (1) **:** a frequently visited place (2) **:** a place providing recreation and entertainment especially to vacationers [Medieval French, "return, source of aid," from *resortir* "to rebound, resort," from *re-* + *sortir* "to go out, leave"] ***synonyms*** see RESOURCE

[2]**resort** *vi* **1 :** to go especially frequently or habitually **:** REPAIR **2 :** to have recourse ‹*resort* to violence›

re·sort·er \ri-ˈzȯrt-ər\ *n* **:** a frequenter of resorts

re·sound \ri-ˈzau̇nd\ *vb* **1 :** to become filled with sound **:** REVERBERATE **2 a :** to sound loudly ‹the gunshot *resounded*› **b :** to sound or utter in full resonant tones **3 :** to become renowned **4 :** to extol loudly or widely **:** CELEBRATE [Medieval French *resoner,* from Latin *resonare,* from *re-* + *sonare* "to sound"]

re·sound·ing *adj* **1 :** producing or characterized by resonant sound **:** RESONATING **2 a :** impressively sonorous ‹a *resounding* name› **b :** leaving no doubt **:** UNEQUIVOCAL ‹a *resounding* success› — **re·sound·ing·ly** \-ˈzau̇n-diŋ-lē\ *adv*

re·source \ˈrē-ˌsōrs, -ˌzōrs, -ˌsȯrs, -ˌzȯrs, ri-ˈ\ *n* **1 a :** a new or a reserve source of supply or support **b** *pl* **:** a usable stock or supply (as of money, products, power, or energy) ‹financial *resources*› **c :** NATURAL RESOURCE **2 :** a possibility of relief or recovery **3 :** the ability to meet and handle situations **:** RESOURCEFULNESS **4 :** a means of handling a situation or of getting out of difficulty **:** EXPEDIENT [French *ressource,* from Medieval French *ressourse* "relief, resource," from *resourdre* "to relieve," literally, "to rise again," from Latin *resurgere*]

synonyms RESOURCE, RESORT, EXPEDIENT, STOPGAP mean something one turns to in the absence of the usual means or source of supply. RESOURCE and RESORT apply to anything one falls back on ‹exhausted of all their *resources*› ‹a last *resort*›. EXPEDIENT may apply to any device or contrivance used when the usual one is not at hand or possible ‹a flimsy and poorly made *expedient*›. STOPGAP applies to something used

\ə\ **abut**	\au̇\ **out**	\i\ **tip**	\ȯ\ **saw**	\u̇\ **foot**
\ər\ **further**	\ch\ **chin**	\ī\ **life**	\ȯi\ **coin**	\y\ **yet**
\a\ **mat**	\e\ **pet**	\j\ **job**	\th\ **thin**	\yü\ **few**
\ā\ **take**	\ē\ **easy**	\ng\ **sing**	\t͟h\ **this**	\yu̇\ **cure**
\ä\ **cot, cart**	\g\ **go**	\ō\ **bone**	\ü\ **food**	\zh\ **vision**

temporarily as an emergency measure ⟨a new law intended only as a *stopgap*⟩.

re·source·ful \-fəl\ *adj* : able to meet and deal with difficult situations — **re·source·ful·ly** \-fə-lē\ *adv* — **re·source·ful·ness** *n*

[1]**re·spect** \ri-ˈspekt\ *n* **1** : a relation or reference to a particular thing or situation ⟨with *respect* to your last letter⟩ **2** : an act of giving particular attention : CONSIDERATION **3 a** : high or special regard : ESTEEM ⟨we've great *respect* for your opinion⟩ **b** : the quality or state of being esteemed : HONOR **c** *pl* : expressions of respect or deference ⟨pay one's *respects*⟩ **4** : an individual fact, detail, or item : DETAIL ⟨perfect in all *respects*⟩ [Latin *respectus,* literally, "act of looking back," from *respicere* "to look back, regard," from *re-* + *specere* "to look"] ***synonyms*** see DEFERENCE — **in respect to** : with respect to : CONCERNING — **with respect to** : with reference to : in relation to

[2]**respect** *vt* **1 a** : to consider worthy of high regard : ESTEEM **b** : to avoid interfering with ⟨*respected* their privacy⟩ **2** : to have reference to : CONCERN ***synonyms*** see REGARD — **re·spect·er** *n*

re·spect·able \ri-ˈspek-tə-bəl\ *adj* **1** : worthy of respect : ESTIMABLE **2** : decent or correct in character or behavior : PROPER ⟨*respectable* people⟩ **3 a** : fair in size or quantity ⟨a *respectable* amount⟩ **b** : moderately good : TOLERABLE **4** : fit to be seen : PRESENTABLE ⟨*respectable* clothes⟩ — **re·spect·abil·i·ty** \-ˌspek-tə-ˈbil-ət-ē\ *n* — **re·spect·able·ness** *n* — **re·spect·ably** \-blē\ *adv*

re·spect·ful \ri-ˈspekt-fəl\ *adj* : marked by or showing respect — **re·spect·ful·ly** \-fə-lē\ *adv* — **re·spect·ful·ness** *n*

re·spect·ing *prep* **1** : in view of : CONSIDERING ⟨*respecting* the evidence, we must acquit him⟩ **2** : with respect to : CONCERNING

re·spec·tive \ri-ˈspek-tiv\ *adj* **1** *obsolete* : inclined to favor one party more than the other : DISCRIMINATIVE **2** : OWN, SEPARATE ⟨their *respective* homes⟩ — **re·spec·tive·ness** *n*

re·spec·tive·ly \ri-ˈspek-tiv-lē\ *adv* **1** : in particular : SEPARATELY **2** : in the order given ⟨a son and daughter ages 12 and 16 *respectively*⟩

re·spell \rē-ˈspel, ˈrē-\ *vt* : to spell again or in another way; *esp* : to spell out according to a phonetic system ⟨*respelled* pronunciations⟩ — **re·spell·ing** *n*

re·spi·ra·ble \ˈres-pə-rə-bəl, -prə-bəl; ri-ˈspī-rə-\ *adj* : fit for breathing; *also* : capable of being taken in by breathing ⟨*respirable* particles of ash⟩

res·pi·ra·tion \ˌres-pə-ˈrā-shən\ *n* **1** : the act or process of breathing **2** : the physical processes (as breathing and diffusion) by which an organism supplies its cells and tissues with the oxygen needed for metabolism and relieves them of the carbon dioxide formed **3** : any of various chemical reactions (as oxidation) in cells that release energy from food molecules (as glucose)

res·pi·ra·tor \ˈres-pə-ˌrāt-ər\ *n* **1** : a device covering the mouth and nose especially to prevent the inhalation of harmful substances (as dusts or fumes) **2** : a device used in artificial respiration

res·pi·ra·to·ry \ˈres-pə-rə-ˌtōr-ē, -prə-tōr-; ri-ˈspī-rə-; -ˌtōr-\ *adj* : of or relating to respiration or the organs of respiration ⟨*respiratory* diseases⟩ ⟨*respiratory* enzymes⟩

respiratory pigment *n* : any of various permanently or intermittently colored complex proteins (as hemoglobin and cytochrome) that function in the transfer of oxygen in cellular respiration

respiratory system *n* : a system of organs that functions in respiration and in humans consists especially of the nose, nasal passages, pharynx, larynx, trachea, bronchi, and lungs

re·spire \ri-ˈspīr\ *vb* : to engage in respiration; *esp* : BREATHE [Latin *respirare,* from *re-* + *spirare* "to blow, breathe"]

[1]**res·pite** \ˈres-pət\ *n* **1** : a temporary delay : POSTPONEMENT **2** : an interval of rest or relief ⟨a *respite* from toil⟩ [Medieval French *respit,* from Medieval Latin *respectus,* from Latin, "act of looking back"]

[2]**respite** *vt* **1** : to grant a respite to **2** : PUT OFF, DELAY

re·splen·dence \ri-ˈsplen-dəns\ *n* : the quality or state of being resplendent : SPLENDOR

re·splen·den·cy \-dən-sē\ *n* : RESPLENDENCE

re·splen·dent \-dənt\ *adj* : shining brilliantly : marked by glowing splendor [Latin *resplendens,* present participle of *resplendēre* "to shine back," from *re-* + *splendēre* "to shine"] — **re·splen·dent·ly** *adv*

re·spond \ri-ˈspänd\ *vb* **1** : to say something in return : REPLY **2** : to react in response ⟨*responded* to a call for help⟩ **3** : to react especially favorably in response ⟨the patient is *responding* to the treatment⟩ [Middle French *respundre,* from Latin *respondēre* "to promise in return, answer," from *re-* + *spondēre* "to promise"] — **re·spond·er** *n*

[1]**re·spon·dent** \ri-ˈspän-dənt\ *n* : one who responds: as **a** : one who maintains a thesis in reply **b** : one who answers in various legal proceedings (as in equity or to an appeal) **c** : one who answers a poll [Latin *respondens,* present participle of *respondēre* "to answer"]

[2]**respondent** *adj* : RESPONSIVE 1; *esp* : being a respondent at law

re·sponse \ri-ˈspäns\ *n* **1** : the act of replying : ANSWER **2** : words said or sung by the congregation or choir in a religious service **3** : a reaction of an organism to stimulation [Latin *responsum,* from *responsus,* past participle of *respondēre* "to answer"]

re·spon·si·bil·i·ty \ri-ˌspän-sə-ˈbil-ət-ē\ *n, pl* **-ties** **1** : the quality or state of being responsible: as **a** : moral, legal, or mental accountability **b** : RELIABILITY, TRUSTWORTHINESS **2** : something for which one is responsible

re·spon·si·ble \ri-ˈspän-sə-bəl\ *adj* **1 a** : liable to be called upon to answer or account ⟨*responsible* for the damage⟩ **b** : being the cause or explanation ⟨the virus *responsible* for the illness⟩ **2 a** : able to answer for one's conduct and obligations : RELIABLE ⟨a *responsible* tenant⟩ **b** : able to choose for oneself between right and wrong **3** : marked by or requiring responsibility or accountability ⟨a *responsible* job⟩ ⟨*responsible* policies⟩ — **re·spon·si·ble·ness** *n* — **re·spon·si·bly** \-blē\ *adv*

re·spon·sive \ri-ˈspän-siv\ *adj* **1** : giving response : ANSWERING ⟨*responsive* glances⟩ **2** : quick to respond or react sympathetically : SENSITIVE **3** : using responses ⟨a *responsive* reading⟩ — **re·spon·sive·ly** *adv* — **re·spon·sive·ness** *n*

[1]**rest** \ˈrest\ *n* **1** : REPOSE, SLEEP; *esp* : a bodily state characterized by minimal functional and metabolic activities **2 a** : freedom from activity **b** : a state of motionlessness or inactivity **c** : the repose of death **3** : a place for resting or lodging **4** : peace of mind or spirit **5 a** (1) : a silence in music equivalent in duration to a note of the same value (2) : a character representing such a silence **b** : a brief pause in reading **6** : something used for support ⟨leaned against the back *rest*⟩ [Old English] — **at rest** **1** : resting or reposing especially in sleep or death **2** : not moving : MOTIONLESS **3** : free of anxieties

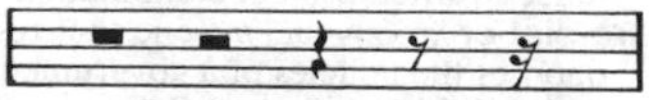

[1]rest 5a(2)

[2]**rest** *vb* **1 a** (1) : to get rest by lying down; *esp* : SLEEP (2) : to give rest to ⟨*rest* yourself on the couch⟩ **b** : to lie dead **2** : to refrain from work or activity **3** : to place or be placed for or as if for support ⟨*rest* one's feet on a footstool⟩ **4 a** : to remain for action or accomplishment ⟨the decision *rests* with you alone⟩ **b** : DEPEND ⟨the success of the flight *rests* on the wind⟩ **c** : to cause to be firmly fixed ⟨*rested* our hopes on their promise⟩ **5** : to stop voluntarily the introduction of evidence in a law case ⟨the defense *rests*⟩ — **rest·er** *n*

[3]**rest** *n* : something that is left over or behind : REMAINDER ⟨ate the *rest* of the candy⟩ [Medieval French *reste,* from *rester* "to remain," from Latin *restare,* literally, "to stand back," from *re-* + *stare* "to stand"] ***synonyms*** see BALANCE

re·start \rē-ˈstärt\ *vb* **1** : to start anew **2 a** : to resume after interruption ⟨*restart* our mail delivery after vacation⟩ **b** : to resume operation ⟨the ride will *restart* in one hour⟩ — **restart** *n* — **re·start·able** \-ˈstärt-ə-bəl\ *adj*

re·state \rē-ˈstāt, ˈrē-\ *vt* : to state again or in another way

re·state·ment \-mənt\ *n* **1** : something that is restated **2** : the act of restating

res·tau·rant \ˈres-tə-rənt, -trənt, -tə-ˌränt\ *n* : a business establishment where meals or refreshments may be purchased [French, from *restaurer* "to restore," from Latin *restaurare*]

res·tau·ra·teur \ˌres-tə-rə-ˈtər\ *also* **res·tau·ran·teur** \-ˌrän-\ *n* : the operator or proprietor of a restaurant [French *restaurateur,* from Late Latin *restaurator* "restorer," from Latin *restaurare* "to restore"]

rest·ed \ˈres-təd\ *adj* : having had sufficient rest or sleep

rest·ful \ˈrest-fəl\ *adj* **1** : marked by or suggesting rest ⟨a *restful* chair⟩ **2 :** being at rest **:** QUIET ⟨a *restful* child⟩ — **rest·ful·ly** \-fə-lē\ *adv* — **rest·ful·ness** *n*

rest home *n* **:** an establishment that provides housing and care for the aged or sick

rest house *n* **:** a building used for shelter by travelers

rest·ing *adj* **1 :** DORMANT 2b ⟨a *resting* spore⟩ **2 :** not undergoing division **:** VEGETATIVE 1a ⟨a *resting* nucleus⟩

res·ti·tu·tion \ˌres-tə-ˈtü-shən, -ˈtyü-\ *n* **1 :** the restoring of something to its rightful owner **2 :** a making good of or the giving of an equivalent (as for loss or damage) ⟨make *restitution* for personal injuries⟩ [Medieval French, from Latin *restitutio,* from *restituere* "to restore," from *re-* + *statuere* "to set up," from *status* "position, condition, state"]

res·tive \ˈres-tiv\ *adj* **1 :** stubbornly resisting control **:** BALKY ⟨a *restive* horse⟩ **2 :** marked by impatience or uneasiness ⟨a *restive* class⟩ [Medieval French *restif,* from *rester* "to stop, resist, remain," from Latin *restare* "to stand back"] — **res·tive·ly** *adv* — **res·tive·ness** *n*

synonyms RESTIVE, RESTLESS mean showing signs of unrest. RESTIVE implies unwillingness to submit to discipline or follow orders ⟨the colonies were becoming increasingly *restive*⟩. RESTLESS implies constant, aimless activity as from anxiety, boredom, discontent, or discomfort ⟨*restless* children in rainy weather⟩.

rest·less \ˈrest-ləs\ *adj* **1 :** lacking rest **:** giving no rest ⟨a *restless* night⟩ **2 :** continuously moving **:** UNQUIET ⟨the *restless* sea⟩ **3 :** marked by or showing unrest especially of mind ⟨*restless* pacing⟩ ***synonyms*** see RESTIVE — **rest·less·ly** *adv* — **rest·less·ness** *n*

rest mass *n* **:** the mass of a body exclusive of additional mass acquired by the body when in motion according to the theory of relativity

re·stor·able \ri-ˈstōr-ə-bəl, -ˈstȯr-\ *adj* **:** fit to be restored or reclaimed

res·to·ra·tion \ˌres-tə-ˈrā-shən\ *n* **1 :** an act of restoring or the condition of being restored: as **a :** a bringing back to a former position or condition ⟨the *restoration* of peace⟩ **b :** RESTITUTION 2 **c :** a restoring to an undamaged, fully functional, or improved condition ⟨the *restoration* of a painting⟩ **2 :** something that is restored; *esp* **:** a representation or reconstruction of the original form (as of a fossil or a building) **3** *cap* **a :** the reestablishment of the monarchy in England in 1660 under Charles II **b :** the period in English history usually held to coincide with the reign of Charles II but sometimes to extend through the reign of James II

[1]**re·stor·ative** \ri-ˈstōr-ət-iv, -ˈstȯr-\ *adj* **:** of or relating to restoration; *esp* **:** having power to restore ⟨*restorative* sleep⟩

[2]**restorative** *n* **:** something that serves to restore to consciousness or health

re·store \ri-ˈstōr, -ˈstȯr\ *vt* **1 :** RETURN 5 ⟨*restored* the package to its owner⟩ **2 :** to put or bring back into existence or use ⟨*restore* harmony to the club⟩ **3 :** to bring back to or put back into a former or original state **:** RENEW **4 :** to put again in possession of something [Medieval French *restorer,* from Latin *restaurare* "to renew, rebuild," alteration of *instaurare*] ***synonyms*** see RENEW — **re·stor·er** *n*

re·strain \ri-ˈstrān\ *vt* **1 a :** to prevent from doing, expressing, or exhibiting ⟨*restrain* the child from jumping⟩ **b :** to limit, restrict, or keep under control ⟨*restrain* your anger⟩ **2 :** to moderate or limit the force, effect, development, or full exercise of ⟨*restrain* trade⟩ **3 :** to deprive of liberty; *esp* **:** to place under arrest or restraint [Medieval French *restreindre,* from Latin *restringere* "to restrain, restrict," from *re-* + *stringere* "to bind tight"] — **re·strain·able** \-ˈstrā-nə-bəl\ *adj* — **re·strain·er** \-ˈstrā-nər\ *n*

re·strained \ri-ˈstrānd\ *adj* **:** marked by restraint **:** not excessive or extravagant — **re·strain·ed·ly** \-ˈstrā-nəd-lē\ *adv*

re·straint \ri-ˈstrānt\ *n* **1 :** the act of restraining **:** the state of being restrained ⟨held in *restraint*⟩ **2 a :** a means of restraining **:** a restraining force or influence ⟨place *restraints* on imports⟩ **b :** a device that restricts movement ⟨a *restraint* for children riding in cars⟩ **3 :** control over the expression of one's thoughts or feelings **:** RESERVE ⟨acted with admirable *restraint*⟩ [Medieval French *restreinte,* from *restreindre* "to restrain"]

re·strict \ri-ˈstrikt\ *vt* **1 :** to confine within bounds **:** RESTRAIN **2 :** to place under restrictions as to use [Latin *restrictus,* past participle of *restringere* "to restrain, restrict"] ***synonyms*** see LIMIT

re·strict·ed \ri-ˈstrik-təd\ *adj* **:** subject or subjected to restrictions or limits ⟨a *restricted* club⟩ — **re·strict·ed·ly** *adv*

re·stric·tion \ri-ˈstrik-shən\ *n* **1 :** something (as a law or rule) that restricts **2 :** an act of restricting **:** the condition of being restricted

restriction enzyme *n* **:** any of various enzymes that break DNA into fragments at specific sites in the interior of the molecule

re·stric·tive \ri-ˈstrik-tiv\ *adj* **1 :** serving or tending to restrict **2 :** limiting the reference of a modified word or phrase ⟨*restrictive* clause⟩ — **restrictive** *n* — **re·stric·tive·ly** *adv* — **re·stric·tive·ness** *n*

rest·room \ˈrest-ˌrüm, -ˌru̇m\ *n* **:** a room or suite of rooms providing personal facilities (as toilets)

re·struc·ture \rē-ˈstrək-chər\ *vb* **1 :** to change the makeup, organization, or pattern of **2 :** to restructure something

[1]**re·sult** \ri-ˈzəlt\ *vi* **1 :** to come about as an effect, consequence, or conclusion of something ⟨disease *results* from infection⟩ **2 :** to have something as an effect ⟨a disease that *results* in death⟩ [Medieval Latin *resultare,* from Latin, "to rebound," from *re-* + *saltare* "to leap," from *saltus,* past participle of *salire* "to leap"]

[2]**result** *n* **1 :** something that results as a consequence, issue, or conclusion **2 :** a beneficial or tangible effect ⟨this method gets *results*⟩ **3 :** something obtained by calculation or investigation ⟨the *result* of 2 × 2 is 4⟩ ***synonyms*** see EFFECT — **re·sult·ful** \-fəl\ *adj* — **re·sult·less** \-ləs\ *adj*

[1]**re·sult·ant** \ri-ˈzəlt-nt\ *adj* **:** derived from or resulting from something else — **re·sult·ant·ly** *adv*

[2]**resultant** *n* **:** something that results **:** OUTCOME; *esp* **:** the single vector that is the sum of a given set of vectors

re·sume \ri-ˈzüm\ *vb* **1 :** to take or occupy again ⟨*resume* your seats⟩ **2 :** to begin again or go back to (as after an interruption) ⟨*resume* speaking⟩ **3 :** SUMMARIZE [Latin *resumere,* from *re-* + *sumere* "to take up, take"]

ré·su·mé *or* **re·su·me** *also* **re·su·mé** \ˈrez-ə-ˌmā\ *n* **1 :** SUMMARY **2 :** a short account of one's career and qualifications prepared typically by someone applying for a job **3 :** a set of accomplishments ⟨a musical *résumé*⟩ [French *résumé,* from *résumer* "to resume, summarize," from Latin *resumere* "to resume"]

re·sump·tion \ri-ˈzəm-shən, -ˈzəmp-\ *n* **:** the action of resuming ⟨*resumption* of work⟩ [Late Latin *resumptio,* from Latin *resumere* "to resume"]

re·sur·face \rē-ˈsər-fəs\ *vb* **1 :** to provide with a fresh or new surface ⟨*resurface* the road⟩ **2 :** to come again to the surface **:** REAPPEAR — **re·sur·fac·er** *n*

re·surge \ri-ˈsərj\ *vi* **:** to undergo a resurgence

re·sur·gence \ri-ˈsər-jəns\ *n* **:** a rising again into life, activity, or prominence [derived from Latin *resurgens,* present participle of *resurgere* "to rise again"]

re·sur·gent \-jənt\ *adj* **:** undergoing or tending to produce resurgence

res·ur·rect \ˌrez-ə-ˈrekt\ *vt* **1 :** to raise from the dead **:** bring back to life **2 :** to bring to view or into use again ⟨*resurrect* an old song⟩ [back-formation from *resurrection*]

res·ur·rec·tion \ˌrez-ə-ˈrek-shən\ *n* **1 a** *cap* **:** the rising of Christ from the dead **b** *often cap* **:** the rising again to life of all the human dead before the final judgment **2 :** RESURGENCE, REVIVAL [Late Latin *resurrectio* "act of rising from the dead," from Latin *resurgere* "to rise again," from *re-* + *surgere* "to rise"] — **res·ur·rec·tion·al** \-shnəl, -shən-l\ *adj*

re·sus·ci·tate \ri-ˈsəs-ə-ˌtāt\ *vb* **:** to revive from apparent death or from unconsciousness; *also* **:** REVITALIZE [Latin *resuscitare* "to reawaken," from *re-* + *suscitare* "to rouse," from *sub-, sus-* "up" + *citare* "to put in motion, stir"] — **re·sus·ci·ta·tive** \-ˈsəs-ə-ˌtāt-iv\ *adj*

re·sus·ci·ta·tion \-ˌsəs-ə-ˈtā-shən\ *n* **:** an act or procedure that attempts to resuscitate; *also* **:** the state of being resuscitated — compare CARDIOPULMONARY RESUSCITATION

re·sus·ci·ta·tor \ri-ˈsəs-ə-ˌtāt-ər\ *n* **:** one that resuscitates; *esp* **:** an apparatus used to restore respiration (as to a person partially asphyxiated)

ret \ˈret\ *vb* **ret·ted; ret·ting :** to soak (as flax) so as to loosen the fiber from the woody tissue [Dutch *reten*]

[1]**re·tail** \ˈrē-ˌtāl, *especially for 2 also* ri-ˈ\ *vb* **1 :** to sell in small

\ə\ **abut**	\au̇\ **out**	\i\ **tip**	\ȯ\ **saw**	\u̇\ **foot**
\ər\ **further**	\ch\ **chin**	\ī\ **life**	\ȯi\ **coin**	\y\ **yet**
\a\ **mat**	\e\ **pet**	\j\ **job**	\th\ **thin**	\yü\ **few**
\ā\ **take**	\ē\ **easy**	\ng\ **sing**	\th\ **this**	\yu̇\ **cure**
\ä\ **cot, cart**	\g\ **go**	\ō\ **bone**	\ü\ **food**	\zh\ **vision**

quantities directly to the ultimate consumer **2** : TELL 2a, RETELL [Medieval French *retaillier* "to cut back, divide into pieces," from *re-* "re-" + *taillier* "to cut," from Late Latin *taliare,* from Latin *talea* "twig, cutting"] — **re·tail·er** *n*

[2]**re·tail** \ˈrē-ˌtāl\ *n* : the sale of commodities or goods in small quantities directly to consumers — **at retail 1** : at a retailer's price **2** : [4]RETAIL

[3]**re·tail** \ˈrē-ˌtāl\ *adj* : of, relating to, or engaged in the sale of commodities at retail ⟨*retail* trade⟩

[4]**re·tail** \ˈrē-ˌtāl\ *adv* **1** : in small quantities **2** : from a retailer

re·tain \ri-ˈtān\ *vt* **1 a** : to keep in possession or use ⟨*retain* knowledge⟩ **b** : to keep in one's employ or service; *esp* : to employ by paying a retainer **c** : to keep in mind or memory **2** : to hold secure or intact ⟨lead *retains* heat⟩ [Medieval French *retenir,* from Latin *retinēre* "to hold back, keep," from *re-* + *tenēre* "to hold"]

retained object *n* : an object of a verb in a passive construction (as *me* in "a book was given me" or *book* in "I was given a book")

[1]**re·tain·er** \ri-ˈtā-nər\ *n* : a fee paid (as to a lawyer) for advice or services or for a claim upon services in case of need [Middle English *reteigner,* literally, "retention," from Medieval French, from *reteigner* "to retain"]

[2]**retainer** *n* **1** : a servant or follower in a wealthy household **2** : one that retains **3** : a usually removable dental device used to hold teeth in correct position especially following orthodontic treatment (as with braces)— called also *bite plate*

[1]**re·take** \rē-ˈtāk, ˈrē-\ *vt* **-took** \-ˈtu̇k\; **-tak·en** \-ˈtā-kən\; **-tak·ing** : to take again; *esp* : to film again

[2]**re·take** \ˈrē-ˌtāk\ *n* : a second filming or photograph

re·tal·i·ate \ri-ˈtal-ē-ˌāt\ *vi* : to return like for like; *esp* : to get revenge [Late Latin *retaliare,* from Latin *re-* + *talio* "legal retaliation"] — **re·tal·i·a·tion** \-ˌtal-ē-ˈā-shən\ *n* — **re·tal·i·a·tive** \-ˈtal-ē-ˌāt-iv\ *adj* — **re·tal·ia·to·ry** \-ˈtal-yə-ˌtōr-ē, -ˌtȯr-\ *adj*

re·tard \ri-ˈtärd\ *vt* : to slow up especially by preventing progress : HINDER [Latin *retardare,* from *re-* + *tardus* "slow"] — **re·tard·er** *n*

re·tar·dant \ri-ˈtärd-nt\ *adj* : serving or tending to retard ⟨fire-*retardant* material⟩ — **retardant** *n*

re·tar·da·tion \ˌrē-ˌtär-ˈdā-shən\ *n* **1** : an act or instance of retarding **2** : the extent to which something is retarded **3** : an abnormal slowness especially of intellectual or bodily development; *esp* : MENTAL RETARDATION

re·tard·ed \ri-ˈtärd-əd\ *adj, sometimes offensive* : slow or limited in intellectual or emotional development or academic progress

retch \ˈrech, *especially British* ˈrēch\ *vb* : VOMIT 1; *also* : to try to vomit [Old English *hrǣcan* "to spit, clear the throat"]

re·te \ˈrēt-ē\ *n, pl* **re·tia** \-ē-ə\ : an anatomical network (as of nerves or blood vessels) [Latin, "net"]

re·tell \rē-ˈtel\ *vt* **-told** \-ˈtōld\; **-tell·ing 1** : to tell again or in another form **2** : to count again

re·ten·tion \ri-ˈten-chən\ *n* **1** : the act of retaining : the state of being retained **2** : power of or capacity for retaining **3** : something retained [Latin *retentio,* from *retinēre* "to retain"]

re·ten·tive \ri-ˈtent-iv\ *adj* : having ability to retain; *esp* : having a good memory — **re·ten·tive·ly** *adv* — **re·ten·tive·ness** *n*

re·ten·tiv·i·ty \ˌrē-ˌten-ˈtiv-ət-ē\ *n* : the power of retaining; *esp* : the capacity for retaining magnetism after the action of the magnetizing force has ceased

re·think \rē-ˈthingk\ *vb* **-thought** \-ˈthȯt\; **-think·ing** : to think about again : RECONSIDER

ret·i·cence \ˈret-ə-səns\ *n* **1** : the quality or state of being reticent **2** : an instance of being reticent **3** : RELUCTANCE

ret·i·cent \-sənt\ *adj* **1** : inclined to be silent or secretive : UNCOMMUNICATIVE **2** : restrained in expression or presentation **3** : RELUCTANT [Latin *reticens,* present participle of *reticēre* "to keep silent," from *re-* + *tacēre* "to be silent"] ***synonyms*** see SILENT — **ret·i·cent·ly** *adv*

re·tic·u·lar \ri-ˈtik-yə-lər\ *adj* : RETICULATE

[1]**re·tic·u·late** \-lət\ *adj* : resembling a net [Latin *reticulatus,* from *reticulum* "network," from *rete* "net"] — **re·tic·u·late·ly** *adv*

[2]**re·tic·u·late** \-ˌlāt\ *vb* **1** : to divide, mark, or construct so as to form a network **2** : to become reticulated

re·tic·u·la·tion \ri-ˌtik-yə-ˈlā-shən\ *n* : a reticulate formation : NETWORK

ret·i·cule \ˈret-i-ˌkyül\ *n* : a woman's drawstring bag used especially as a carryall [French *réticule,* from Latin *reticulum* "small net, mesh bag," from *rete* "net"]

re·tic·u·lo·en·do·the·li·al system \ri-ˈtik-yə-lō-ˌen-də-ˈthē-lē-əl-\ *n* : a system of scattered cells that includes all phagocytic cells (as macrophages) and their precursors in the body [*reticulum* + *endothelium*]

re·tic·u·lum \ri-ˈtik-yə-ləm\ *n, pl* **-la** \-lə\ **1** : the second compartment of the stomach of a ruminant mammal **2** : a netlike structure [Latin, "network," from *rete* "net"]

ret·i·na \ˈret-n-ə, ˈret-nə\ *n, pl* **retinas** *also* **ret·i·nae** \-n-ˌē, -n-ˌī\ : the light-sensitive inner layer lining the back of the eye that contains the rods and cones and converts the images formed by the lens into nerve impulses which reach the brain by way of the optic nerve [Medieval Latin, probably from *rete* "net"] — **ret·i·nal** \ˈret-n-əl, ˈret-nəl\ *adj*

ret·i·nal \ˈret-n-ˌal, -ˌȯl\ *n* : a yellowish to orange aldehyde derived from vitamin A that in combination with proteins forms the visual pigments of the retinal rods and cones [derived from *retina*]

ret·i·nene \ˈret-n-ˌēn\ *n* : RETINAL

ret·i·nol \ˈret-ə-ˌnȯl, -ˌnōl\ *n* : the most common form of vitamin A [*retina* + *ol*]

ret·i·nue \ˈret-n-ˌü, -ˌyü\ *n* : the body of retainers or attendants [Medieval French *retenue,* from *retenu,* past participle of *retenir* "to retain"]

re·tire \ri-ˈtīr\ *vb* **1** : to withdraw or cause to withdraw from action or danger : RETREAT **2** : to withdraw especially for privacy **3** : to give up or cause to give up one's position or occupation **4** : to go to bed **5 a** : to withdraw from circulation or from the market : RECALL **b** : to withdraw (as obsolete equipment) from usual use or service **6** : to put out (a batter or side) in baseball **7** : to win permanent possession of (as a trophy) **8** : to pay in full ⟨*retire* a debt⟩ [Middle French *retirer,* from *re-* "re-" + *tirer* "to draw"]

re·tired \ri-ˈtīrd\ *adj* **1** : HIDDEN, SECLUDED ⟨a *retired* spot in the woods⟩ **2** : having finished one's working or professional career **3** : received by or due to a person who has retired ⟨*retired* pay⟩ — **re·tired·ly** \-ˈtī-rəd-lē, -ˈtīrd-\ *adv* — **re·tired·ness** \-ˈtīrd-nəs\ *n*

re·tir·ee \ri-ˌtī-ˈrē\ *n* : a person who has retired from a working or professional career

[1]**re·tire·ment** \ri-ˈtīr-mənt\ *n* : an act of retiring : the state of being retired; *esp* : a giving up of one's position or occupation **2** : a place of seclusion or privacy

[2]**retirement** *adj* : of, relating to, or designed for retired persons ⟨a *retirement* community⟩

re·tir·ing \ri-ˈtīr-ing\ *adj* : RESERVED 1, SHY — **re·tir·ing·ly** \-ing-lē\ *adv* — **re·tir·ing·ness** *n*

re·tool \rē-ˈtül, ˈrē-\ *vt* **1** : to equip anew with new or different tools ⟨*retool* a factory for making a new product⟩ **2** : REORGANIZE **3** : to make changes or improvements to : REVISE

[1]**re·tort** \ri-ˈtȯrt\ *vb* **1** : to answer back : reply angrily or sharply **2** : to reply (as to an argument) with a counterargument [Latin *retortus,* past participle of *retorquēre* "to twist back, hurl back, retort," from *re-* + *torquēre* "to twist"]

[2]**retort** *n* : a quick, witty, or cutting reply; *esp* : one that turns the first speaker's words against him

[3]**re·tort** \ri-ˈtȯrt, ˈrē-ˌ\ *n* : a vessel in which substances are distilled or decomposed by heat [Middle French *retorte,* from Medieval Latin *retorta,* from Latin *retorquēre* "to twist back"; from its shape]

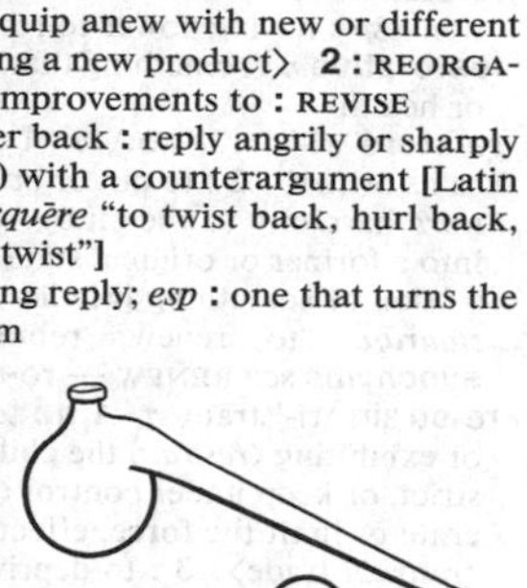
[3]retort

re·touch \rē-ˈtəch, ˈrē-\ *vt* **1** : TOUCH UP **2** : to alter (as a photographic negative) in order to produce a more desirable appearance **3** : to color (new hair growth) to match previous dyed, tinted, or bleached hair — **re·touch** \ˈrē-ˌtəch, rē-ˈ, ˈrē-ˈ\ *n* — **re·touch·er** \rē-ˈtəch-ər, ˈrē-\ *n*

re·trace \rē-ˈtrās, ˈrē-\ *vt* : to trace again or back

re·tract \ri-ˈtrakt\ *vt* **1** : to draw or pull back or in ⟨a cat can *retract* its claws⟩ **2** : to take back (as an offer or accusation) : WITHDRAW **3** : to deny responsibility for or knowledge of [Latin *retractus,* past participle of *retrahere* "to withdraw," from *re-* + *trahere* "to draw"] ***synonyms*** see RECANT, RECEDE — **re·tract·able** \-ˈtrak-tə-bəl\ *adj*

re·trac·tile \ri-ˈtrak-tl, -ˌtīl\ *adj* : capable of being drawn back or in ⟨the *retractile* claws of a cat⟩

re·trac·tion \ri-ˈtrak-shən\ *n* **1** : a statement retracting something previously said or published **2** : an act of retracting : the state of being retracted

re·trac·tor \ri-ˈtrak-tər\ *n* : one that retracts; *esp* : a muscle that draws an organ or part in or back — compare PROTRACTOR

re·train \rē-ˈtrān\ *vb* **1** : to train again or anew ⟨*retrain* the roses to climb the wall⟩ **2** : to become trained again — **re·train·able** \-ˈtrā-nə-bəl\ *adj*

re·trans·late \rē-trans-ˈlāt, -tranz-\ *vb* : to translate (a translation) into another language ⟨*retranslate* the German translation into English⟩; *also* : to give a new form to — **re·trans·la·tion** \-ˈlā-shən\ *n*

[1]**re·tread** \rē-ˈtred, ˈrē-\ *vt* **re·tread·ed; re·tread·ing** **1** : to put a new tread on (a worn tire) **2** : to make over as if new ⟨*retread* an old plot⟩

[2]**re·tread** \ˈrē-ˌtred\ *n* **1** : a retreaded tire **2** : something made or done again in a slightly altered form

[1]**re·treat** \ri-ˈtrēt\ *n* **1 a** : an act or process of withdrawing especially from what is difficult, dangerous, or disagreeable **b** : the usually forced withdrawal of troops from an enemy or from an advanced position **c** : a signal for retreating **d** : a signal given by bugle at the beginning of a military flag-lowering ceremony **e** : a military flag-lowering ceremony **2** : a place of privacy or safety : REFUGE **3** : a period of group withdrawal for prayer, meditation, or instruction under a director [Medieval French *retrait,* from *retraire* "to withdraw," from Latin *retrahere* "to retract, withdraw"]

[2]**retreat** *vi* **1** : to make a retreat **2** : to slope backward ***synonyms*** see REDEDE — **re·treat·er** *n*

re·trench \ri-ˈtrench\ *vb* **1** : to cut down (as expenses) : REDUCE **2** : to reduce expenses : ECONOMIZE [obsolete French *retrencher,* from Middle French *retrenchier,* from *re-* + *trenchier* "to cut"] — **re·trench·ment** \-mənt\ *n*

re·tri·al \rē-ˈtrī-əl, ˈrē-, -ˈtrīl\ *n* : a second trial, experiment, or test; *esp* : a second judicial trial

ret·ri·bu·tion \ˌre-trə-ˈbyü-shən\ *n* : something given or exacted in payment for an offense : PUNISHMENT [Medieval French, from Late Latin *retributio,* from Latin *retribuere* "to pay back," from *re-* + *tribuere* "to pay"]

re·trib·u·tive \ri-ˈtrib-yət-iv\ *adj* : of, relating to, or marked by retribution — **re·trib·u·tive·ly** *adv*

re·trib·u·to·ry \-yə-ˌtōr-ē, -ˌtȯr-\ *adj* : RETRIBUTIVE

re·triev·al \ri-ˈtrē-vəl\ *n* **1** : an act or process of retrieving **2** : possibility of being retrieved or of recovering

[1]**re·trieve** \ri-ˈtrēv\ *vb* **1** : to locate and bring in killed or wounded game ⟨a dog that *retrieves* well⟩ **2** : to call to mind again **3** : to get back again **4** : SALVAGE ⟨artifacts *retrieved* from the wreckage⟩ **5** : REVIVE ⟨writing that *retrieves* the past⟩ **6** : to remedy the evil consequences of : CORRECT **7** : to get and bring back ⟨*retrieve* that book from the stacks⟩ [Medieval French *retrover* "to find again," from *re-* "re-" + *trover* "to find"] — **re·triev·able** \-ˈtrē-və-bəl\ *adj*

[2]**retrieve** *n* **1** : RETRIEVAL **2** : the successful return of a ball that is difficult to reach or control (as in tennis)

re·triev·er \ri-ˈtrē-vər\ *n* : one that retrieves; *esp* : a dog (as a golden retriever) of any of several breeds having a heavy water-resistant coat and used especially for retrieving game

ret·ro \ˈre-ˌtrō\ *adj* : relating to, reviving, or being the styles and especially the fashions of the past : fashionably nostalgic or old-fashioned ⟨a *retro* look⟩

retro- *prefix* : backward : back ⟨*retro*rocket⟩ [Latin, from *retro,* from *re-* "re-" + *-tro* (as in *intro* "within")]

ret·ro·ac·tive \ˌre-trō-ˈak-tiv\ *adj* : intended to apply or take effect at a date in the past ⟨a *retroactive* pay raise⟩ — **ret·ro·ac·tive·ly** *adv*

ret·ro·cede \ˌre-trō-ˈsēd\ *vb* **1** : to go back : RECEDE **2** : to cede back (as a territory or jurisdiction) [Latin *retrocedere,* from *retro-* "backward" + *cedere* "to go, cede"] — **ret·ro·ces·sion** \-ˈsesh-ən\ *n*

ret·ro·fire \ˌre-trə-ˈfīr\ *vb* : to ignite a retro-rocket — **retrofire** *n*

ret·ro·fit \ˈre-trə-ˌfit\ *vt* **1** : to furnish (as a computer, airplane, or building) with new or modified parts or equipment not available or considered necessary at the time of manufacture **2** : to install (new or modified parts or equipment) in something previously manufactured or constructed — **retrofit** *n*

ret·ro·flex \ˈre-trə-ˌfleks\ *adj* **1** : turned or bent abruptly backward **2** : pronounced with the tongue tip turned up or curled back just under the hard palate [Latin *retro-* + *flexus,* past participle of *flectere* "to bend"]

ret·ro·flex·ion *or* **ret·ro·flec·tion** \ˌre-trə-ˈflek-shən\ *n* : the act or process of bending back : the state of being bent back

[1]**ret·ro·grade** \ˈre-trə-ˌgrād\ *adj* **1** : having a backward direction, motion, or tendency **2** : going or inclined to go from a better to a worse state [Latin *retrogradus,* past participle of *retrogradi* "to go back"]

[2]**retrograde** *vi* **1** : to go back : RETREAT ⟨a glacier *retrogrades*⟩ **2** : to decline to a worse condition [Latin *retrogradi,* from *retro-* "backward" + *gradi* "to go"] — **ret·ro·gra·da·tion** \ˌre-trō-grā-ˈdā-shən\ *n*

ret·ro·gress \ˌre-trə-ˈgres\ *vi* : to move backward : REVERT [Latin *retrogressus,* past participle of *retrogradi* "to turn back," from *retro-* "backward" + *gradi* "to go"]

ret·ro·gres·sion \ˌre-trə-ˈgresh-ən\ *n* **1** : movement backwards **2** : return to a former and less complex level of development or organization — **ret·ro·gres·sive** \-ˈgres-iv\ *adj* — **ret·ro·gres·sive·ly** *adv*

ret·ro–rock·et \ˈre-trō-ˌräk-ət\ *n* : an auxiliary rocket on an airplane, missile, or spacecraft that produces thrust in a direction opposite to or at an oblique angle to the motion of the object for deceleration

ret·ro·spect \ˈre-trə-ˌspekt\ *n* : a looking back or reflection on past events [probably from *retro-* + *-spect* (as in *prospect*)] — **in retrospect** : in considering the past or a past event

ret·ro·spec·tion \ˌre-trə-ˈspek-shən\ *n* : the act or process or an instance of reviewing the past

[1]**ret·ro·spec·tive** \-ˈspek-tiv\ *adj* **1** : of, relating to, characteristic of, or given to retrospection **2** : affecting things past : RETROACTIVE — **ret·ro·spec·tive·ly** *adv*

[2]**retrospective** *n* : a usually complete exhibition, compilation, or performance of the work of an artist over a span of years; *also* : REVIEW 6a

ret·ro·vi·rus \ˈre-trō-ˌvī-rəs\ *n* : any of a group of viruses (as HIV) containing a single strand of RNA that include numerous tumor-producing viruses and that replicate by becoming incorporated into the chromosomes of infected cells in the form of double-stranded DNA which is produced from the viral RNA by the use of reverse transcriptase

[1]**re·turn** \ri-ˈtərn\ *vb* **1 a** : to come or go back **b** : to go back in thought or practice : REVERT ⟨*returned* to his old ways⟩ **2** : REPLY, ANSWER **3** : to make (as a report) officially by submitting a statement ⟨the jury *returned* a verdict⟩ **4** *British* : to reelect to office ⟨a candidate *returned* by a large majority⟩ **5 a** : to bring, carry, send, or put back : RESTORE ⟨*return* a book to the library⟩ **b** : to restore to a former or normal condition **6** : to bring in (as profit) : YIELD **7 a** : REPAY ⟨*return* borrowed money⟩; *also* : to respond to in kind ⟨*return* kindness with kindness⟩ **b** : to give back to the owner ⟨need to *return* those clippers⟩ **8 a** : to hit back (a ball or shuttlecock) **b** : to run with (a football) after a change of possession (as by a punt or a fumble) [Medieval French *returner,* from *re-* "re-" + *turner, tourner* "to turn"] — **re·turn·er** *n*

[2]**return** *n* **1 a** : the act of coming back to or from a place or condition **b** : a regular or frequent returning : RECURRENCE ⟨the *return* of spring⟩ **2 a** : an account or formal report **b** : a report of the results of balloting — usually used in plural ⟨election *returns*⟩ **c** : a completed income tax form **3** : a means for conveying something (as water) back to its starting point **4 a** : the profit from labor, investment, or business : YIELD **b** : the rate of profit per unit of cost **5 a** : the act of returning something to a former place, condition, or ownership **b** : something returned **6 a** : something given in repayment or reciprocation ⟨a *return* on their years of hard work⟩ **b** : RETORT **7** : an action or an instance of returning a ball (as in football or tennis) — **in return** : in reciprocation, repayment, or compensation

[3]**return** *adj* **1 a** : played, delivered, or given in return ⟨a *return* call⟩ ⟨a *return* game⟩ **b** : taking place for the second time ⟨a *return* meeting for the two champions⟩ **2** : used or taken on returning ⟨the *return* road⟩ **3** : of, relating to, or causing a return to a place or condition ⟨use the *return* envelope⟩

\ə\ **abut**	\au̇\ **out**	\i\ **tip**	\ȯ\ **saw**	\u̇\ **foot**
\ər\ **further**	\ch\ **chin**	\ī\ **life**	\ȯi\ **coin**	\y\ **yet**
\a\ **mat**	\e\ **pet**	\j\ **job**	\th\ **thin**	\yü\ **few**
\ā\ **take**	\ē\ **easy**	\ng\ **sing**	\t͟h\ **this**	\yu̇\ **cure**
\ä\ **cot, cart**	\g\ **go**	\ō\ **bone**	\ü\ **food**	\zh\ **vision**

re·turn·able \ri-ˈtər-nə-bəl\ *adj* **1 :** that may be returned ⟨*returnable* bottles⟩ **2 :** that must be returned ⟨a library book *returnable* in two weeks⟩

re·turn·ee \ri-ˌtər-ˈnē\ *n* **:** one who returns; *esp* **:** one returning to the U.S. after military service abroad

re·union \rē-ˈyü-nyən, ˈrē-\ *n* **1 :** the act of reuniting **:** the state of being reunited **2 :** a reuniting of persons after separation ⟨a class *reunion*⟩

re·unite \ˌrē-yü-ˈnīt\ *vb* **:** to come or bring together again after a separation

re·us·able \rē-ˈyü-zə-bəl\ *adj* **:** capable of being used anew or repeatedly — **re·us·abil·i·ty** \-ˌyü-zə-ˈbil-ət-ē\ *n*

re·use \rē-ˈyüz, ˈrē-\ *vt* **:** to use again especially in a different way — **re·use** \-ˈyüs\ *n*

¹rev \ˈrev\ *n* **:** a revolution of a motor

²rev *vb* **revved; rev·ving 1 :** to operate or cause to operate at an increasing speed of revolution ⟨*rev* up a motor⟩ **2 :** to make more active or effective — used with *up* ⟨need to *rev* up the campaign⟩ **3 :** EXCITE — usually used with *up* ⟨the concert *revved* us up⟩

re·val·u·ate \rē-ˈval-yə-ˌwāt, ˈrē-\ *vt* **:** REVALUE — **re·val·u·a·tion** \rē-ˌval-yə-ˈwā-shən\ *n*

re·val·ue \rē-ˈval-yü, ˈrē-\ *vt* **1 :** to value (currency) anew **2 :** to make a new valuation of

re·vamp \rē-ˈvamp, ˈrē-\ *vt* **1 :** RENOVATE, RECONSTRUCT **2 :** to work over **:** REVISE

re·veal \ri-ˈvēl\ *vt* **1 :** to make known ⟨*reveal* a secret⟩ **2 :** to show plainly **:** DISPLAY [Medieval French *reveler,* from Latin *revelare* "to uncover, reveal," from *re-* + *velare* "to cover," from *velum* "veil"] — **re·veal·able** \-ˈvē-lə-bəl\ *adj* — **re·veal·er** *n*

re·veal·ment \-ˈvēl-mənt\ *n* **:** an act of revealing **:** REVELATION

rev·eil·le \ˈrev-ə-lē\ *n* **1 :** a signal to get up in the morning **2 :** a bugle call signaling the first military formation of the day [French *réveillez,* imperative pl. of *réveiller* "to awaken," from *re-* "re-" + *éveiller* "to awaken," derived from Latin *ex-* + *vigilare* "to keep watch, stay awake"]

¹rev·el \ˈrev-əl\ *vi* **rev·eled** *or* **rev·elled; rev·el·ing** *or* **rev·el·ling** \ˈrev-ling, -ə-ling\ **1 :** to take part in a revel **2 :** to take intense satisfaction ⟨*reveling* in success⟩ [Medieval French *reveler,* literally, "to rebel," from Latin *rebellare*] — **rev·el·er** *or* **rev·el·ler** \ˈrev-lər, -ə-lər\ *n*

²revel *n* **:** a noisy or merry celebration or party

rev·e·la·tion \ˌrev-ə-ˈlā-shən\ *n* **1 :** an act of revealing or communicating divine truth **2 a :** an act of revealing to view or making known **b :** something that is revealed; *esp* **:** an enlightening or astonishing disclosure [Medieval French, from Late Latin *revelatio,* from Latin *revelare* "to reveal"]

Rev·e·la·tion \ˌrev-ə-ˈlā-shən\ *n* **:** an apocalyptic writing addressed to early Christians of Asia Minor and included as a book in the New Testament — see BIBLE table

re·vel·a·to·ry \ˈrev-ə-lə-ˌtōr-ē, -ˌtór-, ri-ˈvel-ə-\ *adj* **:** of, relating to, or characteristic of revelation

rev·el·ry \ˈrev-əl-rē\ *n, pl* **-ries :** boisterous merrymaking

¹re·venge \ri-ˈvenj\ *vt* **1 :** to inflict injury in return for ⟨*revenge* an insult⟩ **2 :** to avenge for a wrong done ⟨able to *revenge* themselves on their former persecutors⟩ [Medieval French *revenger,* from *re-* + *venger* "to avenge," from Latin *vindicare*] ***synonyms*** see AVENGE — **re·veng·er** *n*

²revenge *n* **1 :** an act or instance of revenging ⟨plotted her *revenge*⟩ **2 :** a desire to repay injury for injury ⟨motivated by *revenge*⟩ **3 :** an opportunity for getting satisfaction

re·venge·ful \-fəl\ *adj* **:** full of or given to revenge **:** VINDICTIVE — **re·venge·ful·ly** \-fə-lē\ *adv* — **re·venge·ful·ness** *n*

rev·e·nue \ˈrev-ə-ˌnü, -ˌnyü\ *n* **1 :** the income from an investment **2 :** the income that a government collects for public use **3 :** the income produced by a given source [Medieval French, from *revenir* "to return," from Latin *revenire,* from *re-* + *venire* "to come"]

rev·e·nu·er \-ˌnü-ər, -ˌnyü-\ *n* **:** a revenue department officer

revenue stamp *n* **:** a stamp (as on a cigar box) for use as evidence of payment of a tax

re·ver·ber·ant \ri-ˈvər-brənt, -bə-rənt\ *adj* **:** tending to reverberate — **re·ver·ber·ant·ly** *adv*

re·ver·ber·ate \ri-ˈvər-bə-ˌrāt\ *vb* **:** RESOUND, ECHO ⟨the shot *reverberated* among the hills⟩ [Latin *reverberare* "to cause to rebound," from *re-* + *verberare* "to lash," from *verber* "rod"] — **re·ver·ber·a·tion** \-ˌvər-bə-ˈrā-shən\ *n* — **re·ver·ber·a·tive** \-ˈvər-bə-ˌrāt-iv\ *adj*

re·ver·ber·a·to·ry \ri-ˈvər-bə-rə-ˌtōr-ē, -brə-, -ˌtór-\ *adj* **:** acting by reverberation

reverberatory furnace *n* **:** a furnace or kiln in which heat is radiated from the roof onto the material treated

¹re·vere \ri-ˈviər\ *vt* **:** to show devotion and honor to [Latin *revereri,* from *re-* + *vereri* "to fear, respect"]

synonyms REVERE, REVERENCE, VENERATE, WORSHIP mean to hold in profound respect and honor. REVERE further implies deference and tenderness of feeling ⟨*revered* their grandparents⟩. REVERENCE suggests a self-denying acknowledging of what has a deep and inviolate claim to respect ⟨*reverence* truth⟩. VENERATE implies regarding as holy or sacrosanct especially because of age ⟨heroes still *venerated*⟩. WORSHIP implies paying homage to or as if to a divine being ⟨*worship* idols⟩.

²revere *n* **:** REVERS [by alteration]

¹rev·er·ence \ˈrev-rəns, ˈrev-ə-rəns, ˈrev-ərns\ *n* **1 a :** honor or respect felt or shown **:** DEFERENCE **b :** a feeling of worshipful respect **:** VENERATION **2 :** a gesture of respect (as a bow) **3 :** the state of being revered or honored **4 :** one held in reverence — used as a title for a member of the clergy ***synonyms*** see DEFERENCE

²reverence *vt* **:** to regard or treat with reverence ***synonyms*** see REVERE

¹rev·er·end \ˈrev-rənd, ˈrev-ə-rənd, ˈrev-ərnd\ *adj* **1 :** worthy of reverence **2 :** being a member of the clergy — used as a title usually preceded by *the* and followed by a title or a full name ⟨the *Reverend* Mr. Doe⟩ ⟨the *Reverend* Jane M. Doe⟩ [Medieval French, from Latin *reverendus,* from *revereri* "to revere"]

²reverend *n* **:** a member of the clergy ⟨spoke to the *reverend*⟩

rev·er·ent \ˈrev-rənt, ˈrev-ə-rənt, ˈrev-ərnt\ *adj* **:** very respectful **:** showing reverence [Latin *reverens,* present participle of *revereri* "to revere"] — **rev·er·ent·ly** *adv*

rev·er·en·tial \ˌrev-ə-ˈren-chəl\ *adj* **1 :** proceeding from or expressing reverence ⟨*reverential* awe⟩ **2 :** inspiring reverence — **rev·er·en·tial·ly** \-ˈrench-lē, -ə-lē\ *adv*

rev·er·ie *also* **rev·ery** \ˈrev-rē, -ə-rē\ *n, pl* **-er·ies 1 :** DAYDREAM **2 :** the condition of being lost in thought [French *rêverie,* from Medieval French, "delirium," from *resver, rever* "to wander, be delirious"]

re·vers \ri-ˈviər, -ˈveər\ *n, pl* **re·vers** \-ˈviərz, -ˈveərz\ **:** a lapel especially on a woman's garment [French, from Middle French *revers* "turned back, reversed"]

re·vers·al \ri-ˈvər-səl\ *n* **:** an act or the process of reversing

¹re·verse \ri-ˈvərs\ *adj* **1 :** opposite or contrary to a previous or normal condition ⟨*reverse* order⟩ **2 :** acting or operating in a manner contrary to the usual **3 :** effecting reverse movement ⟨*reverse* gear⟩ [Medieval French *revers,* from Latin *reversus,* past participle of *revertere* "to turn back"] — **re·verse·ly** *adv*

²reverse *vb* **1 a :** to turn completely about or upside down or inside out **b :** to cause to take an opposite point of view **2 :** NEGATE, UNDO: as **a :** to overthrow or set aside (a legal decision) by a contrary decision **b :** to undo the effect of (as a condition) ⟨face creams that promise to *reverse* the signs of aging⟩ **c :** to change to the contrary ⟨*reverse* a policy⟩ **3 a :** to go or cause to go in the opposite direction **b :** to put (as a car) into reverse — **re·vers·er** *n*

synonyms REVERSE, TRANSPOSE, INVERT mean to change to the opposite position. REVERSE may imply change in order, direction of motion, or meaning ⟨*reversed* her position on the issue⟩. TRANSPOSE implies a change in order or relative position of units often through exchange of position ⟨*transposed* the letters to form an anagram⟩. INVERT applies chiefly to turning upside down or inside out, less often end for end ⟨the magician *inverts* the bag to show it is empty⟩.

³reverse *n* **1 :** something directly contrary to something else **:** OPPOSITE **2 :** an act or instance of reversing; *esp* **:** a change for the worse ⟨financial *reverses*⟩ **3 :** the back part of something **4 a :** a gear that reverses something; *also* **:** the whole mechanism brought into play when such a gear is used **b :** movement in reverse

reverse tran·scrip·tase \-ˌtran-ˈskrip-ˌtās, -ˌtāz\ *n* **:** an enzyme especially of retroviruses (as HIV) that catalyzes the formation of DNA using RNA as a model

re·vers·ibil·i·ty \ri-ˌvər-sə-ˈbil-ət-ē\ *n* **:** the quality or state of being reversible

¹re·vers·ible \ri-ˈvər-sə-bəl\ *adj* **:** capable of being reversed or of reversing: as **a :** having two finished usable sides ⟨*reversible*

fabric⟩ **b** : wearable with either side out ⟨a *reversible* coat⟩ — **re·vers·ibly** \-blē\ *adv*

²reversible *n* : a reversible fabric or garment

re·ver·sion \ri-ˈvər-zhən\ *n* **1** : a right of future possession (as of property or a title) **2 a** : an act or the process of returning (as to a former condition) **b** : reappearance of an ancestral character **3** : an act or instance of turning the opposite way : the state of being so turned **4** : a product of reversion (as an organism with atavistic characteristics) [Medieval French, from Latin *reversio* "act of returning," from *revertere* "to turn back"]

re·ver·sion·ary \-zhə-ˌner-ē\ *adj* : of, relating to, constituting, or involving especially a legal reversion

re·vert \ri-ˈvərt\ *vi* **1** : to come or go back ⟨*reverted* to her old habits⟩ **2** : to undergo reversion [Medieval French *revertir,* from *revertere* "to turn back," from *re-* + *vertere* "to turn"] — **re·vert·er** *n* — **re·vert·ible** \-ˈvərt-ə-bəl\ *adj*

re·vet \ri-ˈvet\ *vt* **re·vet·ted; re·vet·ting** : to face (as an embankment) with a revetment [French *revêtir,* literally, "to clothe, put on," from Latin *revestire,* from *re-* + *vestire* "to clothe"]

re·vet·ment \-mənt\ *n* **1** : a facing (as of stone) to sustain an embankment **2** : EMBANKMENT; *esp* : a protective barricade (as against bomb splinters)

re·vict·ual \rē-ˈvit-l, ˈrē-\ *vb* : to resupply with provisions

¹re·view \ri-ˈvyü\ *n* **1 a** : a formal military inspection **b** : a military ceremony honoring a person or an event **2** : a general survey ⟨a *review* of the week's news⟩ **3** : an act of inspecting or examining ⟨the auditors' *review* was thorough⟩ **4** : judicial reexamination of the proceedings of a lower court **5 a** : a critical evaluation (as of a book or play) **b** : a magazine devoted chiefly to reviews and essays **6 a** : a retrospective view or survey **b** (1) : renewed study of material previously studied (2) : an exercise facilitating such study **7** : REVUE [Middle French *reveue,* from *revoir* "to see again, reexamine," from *re-* "re-" + *voir* "to see," from Latin *vidēre*]

²review *vb* **1** : to look at a thing again **2** : study or examine again ⟨*review* a lesson⟩; *esp* : to reexamine judicially **3** : to make a formal inspection of (as troops) **4** : to give a criticism of (as a book or play) **5** : to look back on ⟨*review* accomplishments⟩ — **re·view·er** *n*

re·vile \ri-ˈvīl\ *vb* **1** : to subject to verbal abuse **2** : to use abusive language : RAIL [Middle French *reviler* "to despise," from *re-* "re-" + *vil* "vile"] — **re·vile·ment** \-mənt\ *n* — **re·vil·er** *n*

re·vis·able \ri-ˈvī-zə-bəl\ *adj* : capable of being revised

re·vis·al \-zəl\ *n* : an act of revising : REVISION

¹re·vise \ri-ˈvīz\ *vt* **1** : to look over again in order to correct or improve ⟨*revise* a manuscript⟩ **2** : to make a new, amended, improved, or up-to-date version or arrangement of ⟨*revise* a dictionary⟩ [Middle French *reviser,* from Latin *revisere* "to look at again," from *revidēre* "to see again," from *re-* + *vidēre* "to see"] — **re·vis·er** *or* **re·vi·sor** \-ˈvī-zər\ *n*

²re·vise \ˈrē-ˌvīz, ri-ˈ\ *n* : an act of revising : REVISION

Revised Standard Version *n* : a revision of the American Standard Version of the Bible published in 1946 and 1952

Revised Version *n* : a British revision of the Authorized Version of the Bible published in 1881 and1885

re·vi·sion \ri-ˈvizh-ən\ *n* **1** : an act of revising (as a manuscript) **2** : a revised version — **re·vi·sion·ary** \-ˈvizh-ə-ˌner-ē\ *adj*

re·vi·sion·ism \ri-ˈvizh-ə-ˌniz-əm\ *n* : a movement in revolutionary Marxian socialism favoring an evolutionary spirit — **re·vi·sion·ist** \-ˈvizh-nəst, -ə-nəst\ *adj or n*

re·visit \rē-ˈviz-ət\ *vt* : to visit again : return to ⟨*revisit* the old neighborhood⟩; *also* : to consider or take up again ⟨reluctant to *revisit* past disputes⟩

re·vi·so·ry \ri-ˈvīz-rē, -ə-rē\ *adj* : having the power or purpose to revise ⟨*revisory* body⟩ ⟨a *revisory* function⟩

re·vi·tal·i·za·tion \rē-ˌvīt-l-ə-ˈzā-shən\ *n* **1** : an act or instance of revitalizing **2** : something revitalized

re·vi·tal·ize \rē-ˈvīt-l-ˌīz, ˈrē-\ *vt* : to give new life or vigor to

re·viv·al \ri-ˈvī-vəl\ *n* : an act or instance of reviving : the state of being revived: as **a** : renewed attention to or interest in something (as in art, literature, or religion) **b** : a new publication or presentation (as of a book or play) **c** : a renewed flourishing ⟨a *revival* of business⟩ **d** : a meeting or series of meetings conducted by a preacher to arouse religious emotions or to make converts

re·viv·al·ism \-ˈvī-və-ˌliz-əm\ *n* : the often highly emotional spirit or methods characteristic of religious revivals

re·viv·al·ist \ri-ˈvī-və-ləst\ *n* : one who conducts revivals — **re·viv·al·is·tic** \-ˌvī-və-ˈlis-tik\ *adj*

re·vive \ri-ˈvīv\ *vb* **1** : to bring back or come back to life, consciousness, or activity : make or become fresh or strong again **2** : to bring back into use ⟨trying to *revive* an old fashion⟩ [Medieval French *revivre,* from Latin *revivere* "to live again," from *re-* + *vivere* "to live"] — **re·viv·er** *n*

re·viv·i·fy \rē-ˈviv-ə-ˌfī\ *vt* **-fied; -fy·ing** : to give new life to : REVIVE — **re·viv·i·fi·ca·tion** \-ˌviv-ə-fə-ˈkā-shən\ *n*

rev·o·ca·ble \ˈrev-ə-kə-bəl\ *adj* : capable of being revoked ⟨a *revocable* privilege⟩ [Medieval French, from Latin *revocabilis,* from *revocare* "to revoke"]

rev·o·ca·tion \ˌrev-ə-ˈkā-shən\ *n* : an act or instance of revoking

re·voke \ri-ˈvōk\ *vb* : to put an end to (as a law, order, or privilege) by withdrawing, repealing, or canceling : ANNUL ⟨*revoke* a driver's license for speeding⟩ [Medieval French *revoquer,* from Latin *revocare,* literally, "to call back," from *re-* + *vocare* "to call"] — **re·vok·er** *n*

¹re·volt \ri-ˈvōlt\ *vb* **1** : to renounce allegiance or subjection (as to a government) : REBEL **2** : to experience disgust or shock ⟨my tender nature *revolts* against such treatment⟩ **3** : to turn or cause to turn away with disgust or abhorrence [Middle French *revolter,* from Italian *rivoltare* "to overthrow," derived from Latin *revolvere* "to revolve, roll back"] — **re·volt·er** *n*

²revolt *n* **1** : an act or instance of revolting **2** : a renunciation of allegiance to a government or other legitimate authority; *esp* : a determined armed uprising ***synonyms*** see REBELLION

re·volt·ing *adj* : extremely offensive : NAUSEATING — **re·volt·ing·ly** \-ˈvōl-ting-lē\ *adv*

rev·o·lu·tion \ˌrev-ə-ˈlü-shən\ *n* **1** : the action by a celestial body of going round in an orbit; *also* : the time taken to complete one such orbit **2** : completion of a course (as of years) ⟨a geologic *revolution*⟩ **3 a** : the action or motion of revolving : a turning round a center or axis : ROTATION **b** : a single complete turn (as of a wheel or a phonograph record) **4 a** : a sudden, radical, or complete change **b** : a fundamental change in political organization; *esp* : the overthrow of one government and the substitution of another by the governed [Medieval French, from Late Latin *revolutio,* from Latin *revolvere* "to revolve, roll back"] ***synonyms*** see REBELLION

¹rev·o·lu·tion·ary \-shə-ˌner-ē\ *adj* **1 a** : of, relating to, or constituting a revolution ⟨*revolutionary* war⟩ **b** : tending to or promoting revolution **c** : constituting or bringing about a major or fundamental change ⟨a *revolutionary* new product⟩ **2** *cap* : of or relating to the American Revolution

²revolutionary *n, pl* **-ar·ies** : REVOLUTIONIST

rev·o·lu·tion·ist \ˌrev-ə-ˈlü-shə-nəst, -shnəst\ *n* **1** : one engaged in a revolution **2** : one who holds or puts forward revolutionary doctrines — **revolutionist** *adj*

rev·o·lu·tion·ize \-shə-ˌnīz\ *vt* **1** : to overthrow the established government of **2** : to imbue with revolutionary doctrines **3** : to change fundamentally or completely ⟨*revolutionized* the industry⟩ — **rev·o·lu·tion·iz·er** *n*

re·volve \ri-ˈvälv, -ˈvȯlv\ *vb* **1** : to turn over at length in the mind ⟨*revolved* the story while I waited⟩ **2 a** : to go round in an orbit **b** : to turn round on or as if on an axis : ROTATE **3** : to happen again : RECUR **4** : to have or come to a specific focus ⟨the household *revolves* around the baby⟩ [Latin *revolvere* "to roll back, cause to return," from *re-* + *volvere* "to roll"] — **re·volv·able** \-ˈväl-və-bəl, -ˈvȯl-\ *adj*

re·volv·er \ri-ˈväl-vər, -ˈvȯl-\ *n* : a handgun with a cylinder of several chambers brought successively into line with the barrel and discharged with the same hammer

re·volv·ing *adj* **1** : tending to revolve or recur; *esp* : recurrently available **2** : of, relating to, or being credit that may be used repeatedly up to the specified limit and is usually repaid in regular proportional installments

re·vue \ri-ˈvyü\ *n* : a theatrical production consisting typically of brief often satirical sketches and songs — compare MUSICAL [French, literally, "review"]

re·vul·sion \ri-ˈvəl-shən\ *n* **1** : a strong pulling or drawing away : WITHDRAWAL **2 a** : a sudden or strong reaction or change **b** : a sense of utter repugnance : REPULSION [Latin *re-*

vulsio "act of tearing away," from *revellere* "to pluck away," from *re-* + *vellere* "to pluck"] — **re·vul·sive** \-ˈvəl-siv\ *adj*

re·wake \rē-ˈwāk, ˈrē-\ *vb* **-waked** *or* **-woke** \-ˈwōk\; **-waked** *or* **-wo·ken** \-ˈwō-kən\ *or* **-woke; -wak·ing :** to waken again or anew

re·wak·en \-ˈwā-kən\ *vb* **:** REWAKE

[1]**re·ward** \ri-ˈwȯrd\ *vt* **:** to give a reward to or for ⟨*rewarded* our honesty⟩ [Medieval French *rewarder* "to regard, reward," from *re-* "re-" + *warder* "to watch, guard," of Germanic origin] — **re·ward·able** \-ə-bəl\ *adj* — **re·ward·er** *n*

[2]**reward** *n* **1 :** something (as money) given or offered in return for a service ⟨a *reward* for finding the missing dog⟩ **2 :** a stimulus (as food) that serves to reinforce a desired response

re·ward·ing \-ˈwȯrd-iŋ\ *adj* **:** giving satisfaction ⟨a *rewarding* experience⟩

[1]**re·wind** \rē-ˈwīnd\ *vt* **-wound** \-ˈwau̇nd\; **-wind·ing :** to wind again; *esp* **:** to reverse the winding of (as a videotape)

[2]**re·wind** \ˈrē-ˌwīnd\ *n* **:** a function of an electronic device that reverses a recording to a previous portion

re·word \rē-ˈwərd, ˈrē-\ *vt* **:** to state in different words

re·work \rē-ˈwərk, ˈrē-\ *vt* **:** to work again or anew: as **a :** REVISE **b :** to process (used or scrap material) for further use

[1]**re·write** \rē-ˈrīt, ˈrē-\ *vt* **-wrote** \-ˈrōt\; **-writ·ten** \-ˈrit-n\; **-writ·ing 1 :** to write over again especially in a different form **2 :** to put (material turned in by a reporter) into form for publication in a newspaper — **re·writ·er** *n*

[2]**re·write** \ˈrē-ˌrīt\ *n* **:** something (as a newspaper article) rewritten

rex \ˈreks\ *n, pl* **rex·es** *or* **rex :** an animal (as a domestic rabbit or cat) characterized by a coat in which the normally longer and coarser guard hairs are shorter than the undercoat or lacking entirely [French *castorex,* a variety of rabbit, perhaps from Latin *castor* "beaver" + *rex* "king"]

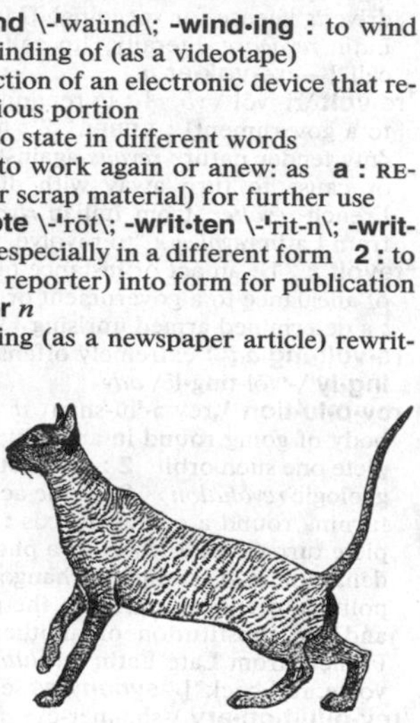
rex

rey·nard \ˈrān-ərd, ˈren-\ *n, often cap* **:** FOX 1a [Medieval French *Renart, Renard,* the fox who is hero of the French beast epic *Roman de Renart*]

re·zone \rē-ˈzōn, ˈrē-\ *vt* **:** to alter the zoning of

Rh \ˈär-ˈāch\ *adj* **:** of, relating to, or being an Rh factor

rhad·a·man·thine \ˌrad-ə-ˈman-thən, -ˈmant-\ *adj, often cap* **:** rigorously strict or just [*Rhadamanthus,* mythical judge in the lower world]

Rhae·to–Ro·mance \ˌrēt-ō-rō-ˈmans\ *also* **Rhae·to–Ro·man·ic** \ˌrēt-ō-rō-ˈman-ik\ *n* **:** a group of Romance languages of eastern Switzerland and northeastern Italy [Latin *Rhaetus* "of Rhaetia (ancient Roman province)"]

rhap·so·dize \ˈrap-sə-ˌdīz\ *vi* **:** to speak or write with great praise ⟨*rhapsodize* about a book⟩ — **rhap·so·dist** \-səd-əst\ *n*

rhap·so·dy \ˈrap-səd-ē\ *n, pl* **-dies 1 :** a written or spoken expression of great emotion **2 :** a musical composition of irregular form [Latin *rhapsodia* "portion of an epic poem adapted for recitation," from Greek *rhapsōidia* "recitation of selections from epic poetry," from *rhaptein* "to sew, stitch together" + *aidein* "to sing"] — **rhap·sod·ic** \rap-ˈsäd-ik\ *also* **rhap·sod·i·cal** \-i-kəl\ *adj* — **rhap·sod·i·cal·ly** \-i-kə-lē, -klē\ *adv*

rhea \ˈrē-ə\ *n* **:** either of two large tall flightless three-toed South American birds that resemble but are smaller than the ostrich [New Latin *Rhea,* genus name, probably from Latin, mother of Zeus, from Greek]

rhe·ni·um \ˈrē-nē-əm\ *n* **:** a rare heavy hard silvery white metallic chemical element that is used in catalysts and alloys — see ELEMENT table [New Latin, from Latin *Rhenus* "Rhine river"]

rhe·o·stat \ˈrē-ə-ˌstat\ *n* **:** a resistor for regulating an electric current by means of variable resistances [Greek *rhein* "to flow" + *-states* "one that stops or steadies," from *histanai* "to cause to stand"] — **rhe·o·stat·ic** \ˌrē-ə-ˈstat-ik\ *adj*

rhe·sus monkey \ˌrē-səs-\ *n* **:** a pale brown Asian monkey often used in medical research [New Latin *Rhesus,* genus of monkeys, from Latin, a mythical king of Thrace, from Greek *Rhēsos*]

rhet·o·ric \ˈret-ə-rik\ *n* **1 :** the art of speaking or writing effectively; *also* **:** the study of the principles and rules of composition **2 a :** skill in the effective use of speech **b :** insincere or pretentious language [Medieval French *rethorique,* from Latin *rhetorica,* from Greek *rhētorikē,* derived from *rhētōr* "orator, rhetorician," from *eirein* "to say, speak"]

rhe·tor·i·cal \ri-ˈtȯr-i-kəl, -ˈtär-\ *adj* **1 a :** of, relating to, or dealing with rhetoric ⟨*rhetorical* studies⟩ **b :** used for rhetorical effect ⟨a *rhetorical* question⟩; *esp* **:** asked merely for effect with no answer expected **2 :** using rhetoric **:** pretentious in language — **rhe·tor·i·cal·ly** \-kə-lē, -klē\ *adv*

rhet·o·ri·cian \ˌret-ə-ˈrish-ən\ *n* **1 a :** a master or teacher of rhetoric **b :** ORATOR **2 :** an eloquent or pretentious writer or speaker

rheum \ˈrüm\ *n* **:** a watery discharge from the mucous membranes especially of the eyes or nose [Medieval French *reume,* from Latin *rheuma,* from Greek, literally, "flow, flux," from *rhein* "to flow"] — **rheumy** \ˈrü-mē\ *adj*

[1]**rheu·mat·ic** \ru̇-ˈmat-ik\ *adj* **:** of, relating to, characteristic of, or affected with rheumatism — **rheu·mat·i·cal·ly** \-ˈmat-i-kə-lē, -klē\ *adv*

[2]**rheumatic** *n* **:** one affected with rheumatism

rheumatic fever *n* **:** an acute disease especially of young people characterized by fever, by inflammation and pain in and around the joints, and by inflammation of the pericardium and heart valves

rheu·ma·tism \ˈrü-mə-ˌtiz-əm\ *n* **1 :** any of various conditions characterized by inflammation or pain in muscles, joints, or fibrous tissue **2 :** RHEUMATOID ARTHRITIS [Latin *rheumatismus* "flux, rheum," from Greek *rheumatismos,* derived from *rheuma* "flux, rheum," from *rhein* "to flow"]

rheu·ma·toid arthritis \ˌrü-mə-ˌtȯid-\ *n* **:** a usually chronic disease characterized especially by pain, stiffness, inflammation, and swelling of joints

Rh factor \ˈär-ˈāch-\ *n* **:** a genetically determined protein on the red blood cells of some people that is one of the substances used to classify human blood as to compatibility for transfusion and that when present in a fetus but not in the mother causes a serious condition in which the mother produces antibodies that cross the placenta and attack the red blood cells of the fetus [*rh*esus monkey (in which it was first detected)]

rhine·stone \ˈrīn-ˌstōn\ *n* **:** a brilliant colorless imitation diamond made usually of glass or paste [*Rhine* river]

Rhine wine \ˈrīn-\ *n* **:** a usually white wine produced in the Rhine valley; *also* **:** a similar wine made elsewhere

rhi·ni·tis \rī-ˈnīt-əs\ *n* **:** inflammation of the mucous membrane of the nose [Greek *rhin-, rhis* "nose"]

rhi·no \ˈrī-nō\ *n, pl* **rhinos** *also* **rhino :** RHINOCEROS

rhi·noc·er·os \rī-ˈnäs-rəs, -ə-rəs\ *n, pl* **-noc·er·os·es** *also* **-noc·er·os :** any of several large plant-eating mammals of Africa and Asia that are related to the horse and tapir and have a thick skin with little hair, three toes on each foot, and one or two heavy upright horns on the snout [Latin *rhinoceros,* from Greek *rhinokerōs,* from *rhin-, rhis* "nose" + *keras* "horn"]

rhinoceros

rhi·no·vi·rus \ˌrī-nō-ˈvī-rəs\ *n* **:** any of a group of viruses containing RNA and including causative agents of respiratory tract disorders (as the common cold) [New Latin, from Greek *rhin-, rhis* "nose" + New Latin *virus*]

rhiz- *or* **rhizo-** *combining form* **:** root ⟨*rhizo*sphere⟩ [Greek *rhiza*]

rhi·zo·bi·um \rī-ˈzō-bē-əm\ *n, pl* **-bia** \-bē-ə\ **:** any of a genus of soil bacteria capable of forming symbiotic nodules on the roots of leguminous plants and of there fixing atmospheric nitrogen [*rhiz-* + Greek *bios* "life"]

rhi·zoid \ˈrī-ˌzȯid\ *n* **:** a structure (as a fungal hypha) that functions like a root in absorption or support — **rhi·zoi·dal** \rī-ˈzȯid-l\ *adj*

rhi·zome \ˈrī-ˌzōm\ *n* **:** a somewhat elongate, often thickened, and usually horizontal underground plant stem that produces shoots above and roots below [Greek *rhizōma* "mass of roots," derived from *rhiza* "root"]

rhi·zo·pod \ˈrī-zə-ˌpäd\ *n* **:** any of a group (Rhizopoda) of usually creeping protozoans having pseudopodia and including the typical amoebas and related forms

rhi·zo·pus \'rī-zə-pəs\ *n* **:** any of a genus of mold fungi including economic pests (as the common black mold of bread) causing decay [*rhiz-* + Greek *pous* "foot"]

rhi·zo·sphere \'rī-zə-ˌsfiər\ *n* **:** the soil immediately about and influenced by plant roots **:** the rooting zone of a soil

Rh–negative \ˌär-ˌāch-'neg-ət-iv\ *adj* **:** lacking Rh factor on the red blood cells

rho \'rō\ *n* **:** the 17th letter of the Greek alphabet — P or ρ

Rhode Is·land Red \rō-ˌdī-lənd-, -lən-\ *n* **:** any of a U.S. breed of domestic chickens that have rich brownish red plumage and are raised especially for eggs and meat [*Rhode Island,* United States]

rho·di·um \'rōd-ē-əm\ *n* **:** a rare silvery white hard ductile metallic chemical element used in platinum alloys — see ELEMENT table [New Latin, from Greek *rhodon* "rose"]

rho·do·den·dron \ˌrōd-ə-'den-drən\ *n* **:** any of a genus of widely grown shrubs and trees of the heath family with alternate leaves and showy clusters of flowers; *esp* **:** one with leathery evergreen leaves as distinguished from a deciduous azalea [Latin, "oleander," from Greek, from *rhodon* "rose" + *dendron* "tree"]

rho·dop·sin \rō-'däp-sən\ *n* **:** a red light-sensitive pigment in the retinal rods of the eyes of most vertebrates that is important in vision in dim light — called also *visual purple*; compare IODOPSIN [Greek *rhodon* "rose" + *opsis* "sight, vision"]

rhomb·en·ceph·a·lon \ˌräm-ˌben-'sef-ə-ˌlän\ *n* **:** HINDBRAIN [Greek *rhombos* "rhombus" + English *encephalon*]

rhom·bic \'räm-bik\ *adj* **1 :** having the form of a rhombus **2 :** ORTHORHOMBIC

rhom·bo·he·dron \ˌräm-bō-'hē-drən\ *n, pl* **-drons** *or* **-dra** \-drə\ **:** a parallelepiped whose faces are rhombuses — **rhom·bo·he·dral** \-drəl\ *adj*

rhom·boid \'räm-ˌbȯid\ *n* **:** a parallelogram with no right angles and with each side differing in length from its two adjacent sides — **rhomboid** *adj* — **rhom·boi·dal** \räm-'bȯid-l\ *adj*

rhom·bus \'räm-bəs\ *n, pl* **rhom·bus·es** *or* **rhom·bi** \-ˌbī, -ˌbē\ **:** a parallelogram with all four sides of equal length and usually with no right angles [Latin, from Greek *rhombos* "piece of wood whirled on a string, lozenge," from *rhembein* "to whirl"]

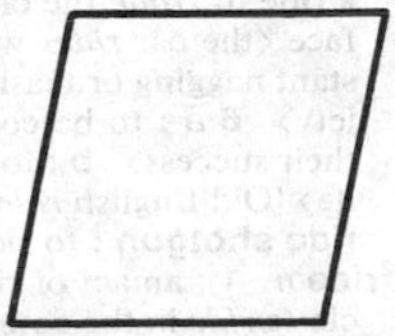
rhombus

Rh–pos·i·tive \ˌär-ˌāch-'päz-ət-iv, -'päz-tiv\ *adj* **:** having Rh factor on the red blood cells

rhu·barb \'rü-ˌbärb\ *n* **1 :** a plant related to buckwheat that has broad green leaves borne on thick juicy pinkish or red stems often used for food **2 :** a heated dispute or controversy ⟨the pitcher got into a *rhubarb* with the umpire⟩ [Medieval French *reubarbe,* from Medieval Latin *reubarbarum,* alteration of *rha barbarum,* literally, "barbarian rhubarb"]

rhumb line \'rəm-\ *n* **:** a line on the surface of the earth that makes equal oblique angles with all meridians [Spanish *rumbo*]

[1]**rhyme** *also* **rime** \'rīm\ *n* **1 a :** correspondence in terminal sounds of two or more words or lines of verse **b :** one of two or more words thus corresponding in sound **2 a :** rhyming verse **b :** a composition in verse that rhymes [Medieval French *rime*]

[2]**rhyme** *also* **rime** *vb* **1 :** to make rhymes **:** put into rhyme; *also* **:** to compose rhyming verse **2 :** to end in syllables that form rhymes ⟨words that *rhyme*⟩ **3 :** to be in accord **:** HARMONIZE ⟨colors that *rhyme* well⟩ **4 :** to cause to rhyme **:** use as rhyme ⟨*rhymed* "moon" with "June"⟩ — **rhym·er** *n*

rhyme scheme *n* **:** the arrangement of rhymes in a stanza or a poem

rhyme·ster *also* **rime·ster** \'rīm-stər\ *n* **:** an inferior poet **:** a maker of poor verse

rhy·o·lite \'rī-ə-ˌlīt\ *n* **:** a very acid volcanic rock that is the lava form of granite [German *Rhyolith,* from Greek *rhyax* "stream, stream of lava" (from *rhein* "to flow") + German *-lith* "-lite"] — **rhy·o·lit·ic** \ˌrī-ə-'lit-ik\ *adj*

rhythm \'rith-əm\ *n* **1 a :** a flow of rising and falling sounds in language that is produced in verse by a regular recurrence of stressed and unstressed syllables **:** CADENCE **b :** a particular example or form of rhythm ⟨iambic *rhythm*⟩ **2 a :** a flow of sound in music marked by accented beats coming at regular intervals **b :** a characteristic rhythmic pattern ⟨waltz *rhythm*⟩ **c :** the group of instruments in a band providing the rhythm — called also *rhythm section* **3 :** a movement or activity in which some action or element recurs regularly ⟨the *rhythm* of breathing⟩ [Latin *rhythmus,* from Greek *rhythmos,* probably from *rhein* "to flow"] — **rhyth·mic** \'rith-mik\ *or* **rhyth·mi·cal** \-mi-kəl\ *adj* — **rhyth·mi·cal·ly** \-mi-kə-lē, -klē\ *adv*

rhythm and blues *n* **:** popular music with elements of blues and African-American folk music

rhythm method *n* **:** a method of birth control in which a couple does not have sexual intercourse during the time when ovulation is most likely to occur

[1]**ri·al** \rē-'ȯl, -'äl\ *n* **1** *also* **ri·yal** \-'ȯl, -'yȯl, -'äl, -'yäl\ **:** the basic monetary unit of Iran, Oman, and Yemen **2 :** a coin or note representing one rial [Persian, from Arabic *riyāl* "riyal"]

[2]**rial** *variant of* RIYAL

ri·al·to \rē-'al-tō\ *n, pl* **-tos 1 :** a center of business or financial activity **2 :** a theater district [*Rialto,* island and district in Venice]

ri·ata \rē-'at-ə, -'ät-\ *n* **:** LARIAT [American Spanish *reata*]

[1]**rib** \'rib\ *n* **1 a :** one of the paired curved bony or partly cartilaginous rods that are joined to the spinal column, stiffen the walls of the body of most vertebrates, and protect the internal organs **b :** a cut of meat including a rib **2 :** something (as a structural member of a ship or airplane or a stiff strip supporting an umbrella's fabric) resembling a rib in shape or function **3 :** an elongated ridge: as **a :** a major vein of an insect's wing or of a leaf **b :** one of the ridges in some knitted or woven fabrics [Old English *ribb*]

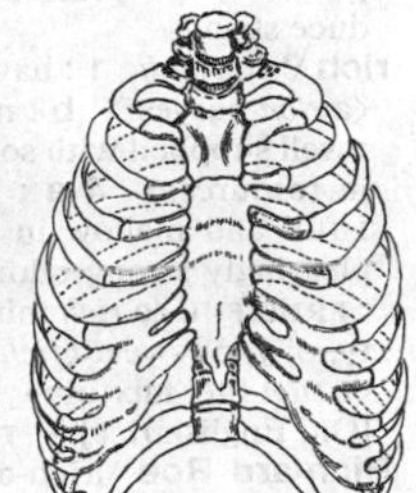
rib 1a

[2]**rib** *vt* **ribbed; rib·bing 1 :** to furnish or enclose with ribs **2 :** to form ribs in (a fabric) especially in knitting — **rib·ber** *n*

[3]**rib** *vt* **ribbed; rib·bing :** to poke fun at **:** KID [probably from [1]*rib,* from the tickling of the ribs to cause laughter] — **rib·ber** *n*

rib·ald \'rib-əld\ *adj* **:** marked by or inclined to coarse or indecent language or humor ⟨*ribald* jokes⟩ ⟨a *ribald* writer⟩ [Medieval French *ribaud* "rascal, wanton," from *riber* "to be wanton," of Germanic origin] ***synonyms*** see COARSE — **rib·ald·ry** \-əl-drē\ *n*

rib·and \'rib-ənd\ *n* **:** a ribbon used especially as a decoration [Middle English, alteration of *riban*]

rib·bon \'rib-ən\ *n* **1 a :** a narrow closely woven strip of fabric (as silk) used especially for trimming or for tying or ornamenting packages **b :** a piece of usually multicolored ribbon worn as a military decoration or as a symbol of a medal **c :** a strip of colored ribbon given for winning a place in competition **2 :** a strip of inked fabric (as in a typewriter) **3 :** SHRED, TATTER — usually used in plural ⟨torn to *ribbons*⟩ [Middle English *riban,* from Medieval French *ribane, rubane*] — **rib·bon·like** \-ˌlīk\ *adj*

rib·bon·fish \-ˌfish\ *n* **:** any of various long marine fishes with bodies that are thin from side to side

ribbon worm *n* **:** NEMERTEAN

rib·by \'rib-ē\ *adj* **:** showing or marked by ribs

rib cage *n* **:** the bony enclosing wall of the chest consisting chiefly of the ribs and the structures connecting them

ri·bo·fla·vin \ˌrī-bə-'flā-vən\ *n* **:** a yellow crystalline vitamin that is a growth-promoting member of the vitamin B complex occurring both free (as in milk) and combined (as in liver) — called also *vitamin* B_2 [*ribose* + Latin *flavus* "yellow"]

ri·bo·nu·cle·ase \ˌrī-bō-'nü-klē-ˌās, -'nyü-, -ˌāz\ *n* **:** an enzyme that catalyzes the hydrolysis of RNA — called also *RNase*

ri·bo·nu·cle·ic acid \ˌrī-bō-nu̇-ˌklē-ik-, -nyu̇-, -ˌklā-\ *n* **:** RNA [*ribose* + *nucleic acid*]

ri·bo·nu·cle·o·tide \-'nü-klē-ə-ˌtīd, -'nyü-\ *n* **:** a ribose-containing nucleotide that occurs especially in RNA

ri·bose \'rī-ˌbōs\ *n* **:** a pentose sugar $C_5H_{10}O_5$ found in the nucleotides of RNA [from *ribonic acid,* an acid obtained by oxidation of ribose]

\ə\ **abut**	\au̇\ **out**	\i\ **tip**	\ȯ\ **saw**	\u̇\ **foot**
\ər\ **further**	\ch\ **chin**	\ī\ **life**	\ȯi\ **coin**	\y\ **yet**
\a\ **mat**	\e\ **pet**	\j\ **job**	\th\ **thin**	\yü\ **few**
\ā\ **take**	\ē\ **easy**	\ng\ **sing**	\th\ **this**	\yu̇\ **cure**
\ä\ **cot, cart**	\g\ **go**	\ō\ **bone**	\ü\ **food**	\zh\ **vision**

ribosomal RNA *n* : RNA that is a basic structural element of ribosomes — called also *rRNA*

ri·bo·some \'rī-bə-ˌsōm\ *n* : any of the specialized parts of the cytoplasm of a cell that contain RNA and are sites of protein synthesis [*ribo*nucleic acid + *-some*] — **ri·bo·som·al** \ˌrī-bə-'sō-məl\ *adj*

rice \'rīs\ *n* : a southeast Asian cereal grass grown in warm wet areas especially for its starchy seeds which are used for food; *also* : the seeds [Medieval French *ris,* from Italian *riso,* from Greek *oryza*]

rice·bird \'rīs-ˌbərd\ *n* : any of several small birds common in rice fields; *esp* : BOBOLINK

rice paper *n* : a thin papery material made from the spongy inner part of the stem of an Asian shrub or small tree related to the ginseng

ric·er \'rī-sər\ *n* : a kitchen utensil in which soft foods (as boiled potatoes) are pressed through a perforated container to produce strings

rich \'rich\ *adj* **1** : having great wealth **2 a** : having great value ⟨a *rich* harvest⟩ **b** : magnificently impressive : SUMPTUOUS **3** : well supplied with something pleasing or desirable ⟨a land *rich* in resources⟩ **4 a** : vivid and deep in color ⟨a *rich* red⟩ **b** : full and mellow in tone and quality ⟨a *rich* voice⟩ **c** : of pleasingly strong odor ⟨*rich* perfumes⟩ **5** : highly productive : FRUITFUL ⟨a *rich* mine⟩ ⟨*rich* soil⟩ **6 a** : highly seasoned, fatty, oily, or sweet ⟨*rich* foods⟩ **b** : high in combustible content ⟨a *rich* fuel mixture⟩ **7** : giving amusement; *also* : LAUGHABLE [Old English *rīce*] — **rich·ness** *n*

Rich·ard Roe \ˌrich-ərd-'rō\ *n* : a party to legal proceedings whose true name is unknown — compare JOHN DOE

rich·en \'rich-ən\ *vt* **rich·ened; rich·en·ing** \'rich-ning, -ə-ning\ : to make rich or richer

rich·es \'rich-əz\ *n pl* : things that make one rich : WEALTH [Medieval French *richesce* "richness," from *riche* "rich," of Germanic origin]

rich·ly \'rich-lē\ *adv* **1** : in a rich manner **2** : in full measure : AMPLY ⟨praise *richly* deserved⟩

Rich·ter scale \'rik-ter-\ *n* : a logarithmic scale for expressing the intensity of a seismic disturbance (as an earthquake) in terms of the energy dissipated in it [Charles F. *Richter,* died 1985, American seismologist]

[1]**rick** \'rik\ *n* : a stack (as of hay) in the open air [Old English *hrēac*]

[2]**rick** *vt* : to pile (as hay) in ricks

rick·ets \'rik-əts\ *n* : a disease of young people and animals marked especially by soft and deformed bones due to failure to assimilate and use calcium and phosphorus normally and caused by inadequate vitamin D [origin unknown]

rick·ett·sia \rik-'et-sē-ə\ *n, pl* **-si·as** *or* **-si·ae** \-sē-ˌē, -sē-ˌī\ : any of various bacteria that are internal parasites of arthropods (as lice and ticks) including some that when transmitted to humans cause various diseases (as Rocky Mountain spotted fever and typhus) [Howard T. *Ricketts,* died 1910, American pathologist] — **rick·ett·si·al** \-sē-əl\ *adj*

rick·ety \'rik-ət-ē\ *adj* **1** : affected with rickets **2** : in weak physical condition ⟨a *rickety* old pensioner⟩ **3** : UNSOUND c, SHAKY ⟨a *rickety* wagon⟩

rick·ey \'rik-ē\ *n, pl* **rickeys** : a drink containing liquor, lime juice, sugar, and soda water; *also* : a similar drink without liquor [probably from the name *Rickey*]

rick·rack *or* **ric·rac** \'rik-ˌrak\ *n* : a flat braid woven to form zigzags and used especially as trimming on clothing [reduplication of [2]*rack*]

rick·shaw *also* **rick·sha** \'rik-ˌshȯ\ *n* : a small 2-wheeled covered vehicle pulled by one man and used originally in Japan [alteration of *jinrikisha*]

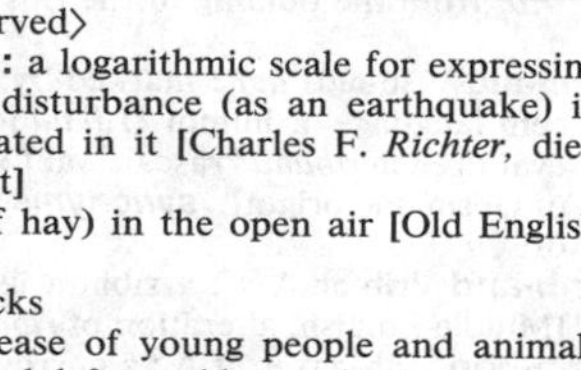
rickshaw

[1]**ric·o·chet** \'rik-ə-ˌshā, *British also* -ˌshet\ *n* : a glancing rebound (as of a bullet off a flat surface); *also* : an object that ricochets [French]

[2]**ricochet** *vi* **-cheted** \-ˌshād\ *also* **-chet·ted** \-ˌshet-əd\; **-chet·ing** \-ˌshā-ing\ *also* **-chet·ting** \-ˌshet-ing\ : to bounce or skip with or as if with glancing rebounds

ri·cot·ta \ri-'kȯt-ə\ *n* : a white unripened whey cheese of Italy that resembles cottage cheese [Italian, from *ricuocere* "to cook again," from Latin *recoquere,* from *re-* + *coquere* "to cook"]

ric·tus \'rik-təs\ *n* : a gaping grin or grimace [Latin, "open mouth," from *rictus,* past participle of *ringi* "to gape"]

rid \'rid\ *vt* **rid** *also* **rid·ded; rid·ding** : to make free : RELIEVE ⟨*rid* yourself of worries⟩ ⟨get *rid* of that junk⟩ [Middle English *ridden* "to clear"]

rid·dance \'rid-ns\ *n* : the act of ridding : the state of being rid of

rid·den \'rid-n\ *adj* : extremely concerned with or burdened by — usually used in combination ⟨guilt-*ridden*⟩ ⟨slum-*ridden*⟩

[1]**rid·dle** \'rid-l\ *n* **1** : a mystifying, misleading, or puzzling question posed as a problem to be solved or guessed : CONUNDRUM **2** : something or someone difficult to understand [Old English *rǣdelse* "opinion, conjecture, riddle"] ***synonyms*** see MYSTERY

[2]**riddle** *vb* **rid·dled; rid·dling** \'rid-ling, -l-ing\ **1** : to find the solution of **2** : to set a riddle for : PUZZLE **3** : to speak in riddles or set forth a riddle — **rid·dler** \-lər, -l-ər\ *n*

[3]**riddle** *n* : a coarse sieve [Old English *hriddel*]

[4]**riddle** *vt* **1** : to sift or separate (as grain from chaff) with or as if with a riddle **2 a** : to pierce with many holes ⟨a boat *riddled* with shot⟩ **b** : to spread through : PERMEATE ⟨a story *riddled* with lies⟩

[1]**ride** \'rīd\ *vb* **rode** \'rōd\; **rid·den** \'rid-n\; **rid·ing** \'rīd-ing\ **1 a** : to sit on and control so as to move from one place to another ⟨*ride* a horse⟩ ⟨*ride* a motorcycle⟩ **b** : to travel in or on as a means of transport ⟨*ride* a bus⟩ ⟨*ride* in an airplane⟩ **2** : to travel as if on a means of transport : be carried ⟨*rode* on a wave of popularity⟩ **3 a** : to be supported by and move with ⟨a ship *riding* the waves⟩ ⟨the bearings *ride* on a cushion of grease⟩ **b** : to float at anchor **c** : to remain afloat through : SURVIVE ⟨*ride* out a storm⟩ **4 a** : to convey in or as if in a vehicle : give a ride to ⟨*rode* the child on my back⟩ **b** : to travel over a surface ⟨the car *rides* well⟩ **5 a** : to torment by or as if by constant nagging or teasing **b** : OPPRESS 2, OBSESS ⟨*ridden* by anxiety⟩ **6 a** : to be contingent : DEPEND ⟨all our hopes *ride* on their success⟩ **b** : to be bet ⟨their money is *riding* on the favorite⟩ [Old English *rīdan*] — **ride for a fall** : to court disaster — **ride shotgun** : to ride in the front passenger seat of a vehicle

[2]**ride** *n* **1** : an act of riding; *esp* : a trip on horseback or by vehicle ⟨a *ride* in the country⟩ **2** : a way (as a road or path) for riding **3** : a mechanical device (as at an amusement park) for riding on **4 a** : a trip on which a gangster takes a victim in order to murder that person **b** : something likened to such a trip ⟨take the taxpayers for a *ride*⟩ **5** : a means of transportation ⟨needs a *ride* to work⟩

ride·able *also* **rid·able** \'rīd-ə-bəl\ *adj* : fit for riding on or over

rid·er \'rīd-ər\ *n* **1** : one that rides **2 a** : an addition to a document often attached on a separate piece of paper **b** : a clause added to a legislative bill to secure a usually distinct object **3** : something that lies over or moves along on another piece ⟨the scale has *riders* to measure weight⟩ — **rid·er·less** \-ləs\ *adj*

[1]**ridge** \'rij\ *n* **1** : a raised body part or structure **2** : a range of hills or mountains **3** : a raised strip (as of plowed ground) **4** : the line made where two sloping surfaces come together ⟨the *ridge* of a roof⟩ [Old English *hrycg*]

[2]**ridge** *vb* : to form into or extend in ridges

ridge·ling *or* **ridg·ling** \'rij-ling\ *n* : a male domestic animal that is imperfectly developed sexually [perhaps from [1]*ridge*]

ridge·pole \'rij-ˌpōl\ *n* **1** : the highest horizontal timber in a sloping roof to which the upper ends of the rafters are fastened **2** : a horizontal support for the top of a tent

ridgy \'rij-ē\ *adj* : having or rising in ridges

[1]**rid·i·cule** \'rid-ə-ˌkyül\ *n* : the act of exposing to laughter : DERISION, MOCKERY [Latin *ridiculum* "jest," from *ridiculus* "laughable," from *ridēre* "to laugh"]

[2]**ridicule** *vt* : to make fun of — **rid·i·cul·er** *n*

synonyms RIDICULE, DERIDE, MOCK, TAUNT mean to make an object of laughter or scorn. RIDICULE implies an often malicious belittling ⟨*ridiculed* everything she said⟩. DERIDE suggests contemptuous and often bitter ridicule ⟨*derided* their efforts to start their own business⟩. MOCK implies scorn often expressed ironically as by mimicry or sham deference ⟨*mocked* her brother at his recital⟩. TAUNT implies mockery and often jeering insults in an effort to challenge or reproach ⟨hometown fans *taunted* the visiting team⟩.

ri·dic·u·lous \rə-'dik-yə-ləs\ *adj* : arousing or deserving ridicule

: ABSURD, PREPOSTEROUS ***synonyms*** see LAUGHABLE — **ri·dic·u·lous·ly** *adv* — **ri·dic·u·lous·ness** *n*

[1]ri·ding \'rīd-iŋ\ *n* : one of the three administrative jurisdictions into which Yorkshire, England, was formerly divided [Middle English, derived from Old Norse *thrithjungr* "third part," from *thrithi* "third"]

[2]rid·ing \'rīd-iŋ\ *n* : the action or state of one that rides

[3]rid·ing *adj* **1** : used for or when riding ⟨a *riding* horse⟩ **2** : operated by a rider ⟨a *riding* plow⟩

rid·ley \'rid-lē\ *n* : either of two sea turtles: **a** : KEMP'S RIDLEY **b** : OLIVE RIDLEY [origin unknown]

rife \'rīf\ *adj* **1** : WIDESPREAD 2, PREVALENT ⟨lands where famine is *rife*⟩ **2** : well supplied ⟨the air was *rife* with rumors⟩ [Old English *rȳfe*] — **rife** *adv* — **rife·ly** *adv*

[1]riff \'rif\ *vb* : RIFFLE 3a, SKIM ⟨*riff* pages⟩ [short for *riffle*]

[2]riff *n* : a repeated musical phrase (as in jazz) typically supporting a solo improvisation [probably from *refrain*]

[3]riff *vi* : to perform a riff

[1]rif·fle \'rif-əl\ *n* **1 a** : a shallow extending across a stream bed and causing broken water **b** : a stretch of water flowing over a riffle **2** : a small wave or succession of small waves : RIPPLE **3** : the act or process of shuffling (as cards) [perhaps alteration of *ruffle*]

[2]riffle *vb* **rif·fled; rif·fling** \'rif-liŋ, -ə-liŋ\ **1** : to form, flow over, or move in riffles **2** : to ruffle slightly : RIPPLE **3 a** : to flip or leaf through hastily **b** : to shuffle (playing cards) by separating the deck into two parts and sliding the thumbs along the edges so that the cards intermix **4** : to manipulate idly between the fingers ⟨*riffle* a stack of coins⟩

riff·raff \'rif-ˌraf\ *n* **1 a** : disreputable persons **b** : a class of people who are looked down upon : RABBLE **2** : RUBBISH, REFUSE [Middle English *ryffe raffe,* from *rif* and *raf* "every single one," from Medieval French *rif et raf* "completely"] — **riffraff** *adj*

[1]ri·fle \'rī-fəl\ *vb* **ri·fled; ri·fling** \'rī-fliŋ, -fə-liŋ\ **1** : to ransack especially with the intent to steal ⟨*rifle* the mail⟩ **2** : to steal and carry away **3** : to engage in ransacking and stealing [Medieval French *rifler* "to scrape off, plunder," of Germanic origin] — **ri·fler** \'rī-flər, -fə-lər\ *n*

Word History The basic meaning of Middle French *rifler* was "to scratch or file." But it was in the extended sense "to plunder or ransack" that the Middle English borrowed the word from the French. Early in the 17th century the French word was borrowed again into English in something closer to its original sense, "to scratch." To *rifle* a gun was to cut spiral grooves into its bore. By functional shift *rifle* became a noun which named such a groove. And by the late 18th century a gun with a rifled bore was itself called a *rifle.*

[2]rifle *vt* **ri·fled; ri·fling** : to cut spiral grooves into the inside of the barrel of ⟨*rifled* arms⟩ ⟨*rifled* pipe⟩ [perhaps from French *rifler* "to scratch, file"]

[3]rifle *n* **1 a** : a weapon with a rifled bore intended to be fired from the shoulder **b** : a rifled artillery piece **2** *pl* : a body of soldiers armed with rifles

[4]rifle *vt* **ri·fled; ri·fling** : to propel (as a ball) with great force or speed

ri·fle·man \'rī-fəl-mən\ *n* **1** : a soldier armed with a rifle **2** : a person skilled in shooting with a rifle

ri·fle·ry \'rī-fəl-rē\ *n* : rifle shooting especially at targets

ri·fling \'rī-fliŋ, -fə-liŋ\ *n* **1** : the act or process of making spiral grooves **2** : a system of spiral grooves in the bore of a gun causing a projectile when fired to rotate about its longer axis

[1]rift \'rift\ *n* **1 a** : an opening (as a fissure or crevasse) made by splitting or separation **b** : FAULT 4 **2** : BREACH 3a, ESTRANGEMENT [of Scandinavian origin]

[2]rift *vb* : [2]CLEAVE 1a, DIVIDE

rift valley *n* : a long valley formed by the sinking of the earth's crust between two nearly parallel faults or groups of faults

[1]rig \'rig\ *vt* **rigged; rig·ging** **1** : to fit out (as a ship) with rigging **2** : CLOTHE, DRESS ⟨was *rigged* out in my Sunday clothes⟩ **3** : to furnish with special gear : EQUIP **4** : to set up or construct often for temporary use ⟨*rig* a temporary shelter⟩ [Middle English *riggen*] — **rig·ger** \-ər\ *n*

[2]rig *n* **1** : the distinctive shape, number, and arrangement of sails and masts of a ship ⟨a schooner *rig*⟩ **2** : EQUIPAGE; *esp* : a carriage with its horse **3** : CLOTHING, DRESS **4** : tackle, equipment, or machinery fitted for a specified purpose ⟨oil-drilling *rig*⟩

[3]rig *vt* **rigged; rig·ging** **1** : to manipulate or control usually by deceptive or dishonest means ⟨*rig* an election⟩ **2** : to fix in advance for a desired result ⟨*rig* the contest⟩ [from earlier *rig* "swindle"]

rig·a·doon \ˌrig-ə-'dün\ *or* **ri·gau·don** \rē-gō-'dōⁿ\ *n* : a lively dance of the 17th and 18th centuries; *also* : the music for a rigadoon [French *rigaudon*]

rigamarole *variant of* RIGMAROLE

Ri·gel \'rī-jəl, -gəl\ *n* : a bright star in the left foot of the constellation Orion [Arabic *Rijl,* literally, "foot"]

rig·ging \'rig-iŋ, -ən\ *n* **1 a** : the lines and chains used aboard a ship for supporting masts and spars and controlling sails **b** : a similar network (as in theater scenery) used for support and manipulation **2** : CLOTHING

[1]right \'rīt\ *adj* **1** : RIGHTEOUS 1, UPRIGHT **2** : being in accordance with what is just, good, or proper ⟨*right* conduct⟩ **3** : conforming to facts or truth : CORRECT ⟨the *right* answer⟩ **4** : SUITABLE, APPROPRIATE ⟨the *right* person for the job⟩ **5** : STRAIGHT ⟨a *right* line⟩ **6** : GENUINE 1, REAL **7 a** : of, relating to, situated on, or being the side of the body which is away from the side on which the heart is mostly located ⟨the *right* arm⟩ **b** : located in the same relative position as the right of the body when facing in the same direction as the observer : RIGHT-HAND ⟨the *right* side of the road⟩ **c** : done with the right hand ⟨a *right* hook to the jaw⟩ **8** : having its axis perpendicular to the base ⟨a *right* cone⟩ **9** : of, relating to, or being the principal or more prominent side of an object ⟨turn the *right* side out⟩ **10** : acting or judging in accordance with truth or fact ⟨time proved them *right*⟩ **11 a** : physically or mentally well ⟨did not feel *right*⟩ **b** : being in a correct or proper state ⟨put things *right*⟩ **12** : most favorable or desired : PREFERABLE ⟨live on the *right* side of town⟩ **13** *often cap* : of or adhering to the Right in politics [Old English *riht*] — **right·ness** *n*

[2]right *n* **1** : qualities (as adherence to duty and obedience to lawful authority) that together constitute the ideal of moral propriety **2** : something to which one has a just claim ⟨the *right* to decide⟩: as **a** : a power or privilege to which one is justly entitled ⟨one's *right* to vote⟩ **b** : an interest that one has in a property — often used in plural ⟨mineral *rights*⟩ ⟨film *rights* of a novel⟩ **3** : something that one may properly claim as due ⟨knowing the truth is her *right*⟩ **4** : the cause of truth or justice **5 a** : the location or direction of the right side ⟨the woods on my *right*⟩ **b** : the part on the right side **c** : a turn to the right ⟨take a *right* at the stop sign⟩ **6 a** : the true account or correct interpretation **b** : the quality or state of being factually correct **7** *often cap* **a** : the part of a legislative chamber located to the right of the presiding officer **b** : the members of a continental European legislative body occupying the right and holding more conservative political views than other members **8** *often cap* **a** : individuals professing opposition to change in the established order and favoring traditional attitudes and practices and conservative governmental policies **b** *often cap* : a conservative position — **by rights** : with reason or justice : PROPERLY — **to rights** : into proper order

[3]right *adv* **1** : according to right ⟨live *right*⟩ **2** : in the exact location, position, or moment : PRECISELY ⟨*right* at my fingertips⟩ **3** : in a suitable, proper, or desired manner ⟨hold your pen *right*⟩ **4** : in a direct line or course : DIRECTLY ⟨go *right* home⟩ **5** : according to fact or truth : TRULY ⟨guess *right*⟩ **6 a** : all the way ⟨windows *right* to the floor⟩ **b** : COMPLETELY ⟨felt *right* at home⟩ **7** : IMMEDIATELY ⟨*right* after lunch⟩ **8** : VERY ⟨a *right* pleasant day⟩ **9** : on or to the right ⟨looked *right* and left⟩

[4]right *vb* **1 a** : to relieve from wrong **b** : JUSTIFY 1a, VINDICATE ⟨felt the need to *right* himself in court⟩ **2 a** : to adjust or restore to the proper state or condition ⟨*right* the economy⟩ **b** : to bring or restore to an upright position ⟨*right* a capsized boat⟩ **3** : to become upright — **right·er** *n*

right angle *n* : the angle that is formed by two lines perpendicular to each other and measures 90 degrees — **right–an·gled** \'rīt-'aŋ-gəld\ *or* **right–an·gle** \-gəl\ *adj*

right away *adv* : without delay or hesitation : IMMEDIATELY

right circular cone *n* : CONE 2a

\ə\ **abut**	\au̇\ **out**	\i\ **tip**	\ȯ\ **saw**	\u̇\ **foot**
\ər\ **further**	\ch\ **chin**	\ī\ **life**	\ȯi\ **coin**	\y\ **yet**
\a\ **mat**	\e\ **pet**	\j\ **job**	\th\ **thin**	\yü\ **few**
\ā\ **take**	\ē\ **easy**	\ŋ\ **sing**	\t͟h\ **this**	\yu̇\ **cure**
\ä\ **cot, cart**	\g\ **go**	\ō\ **bone**	\ü\ **food**	\zh\ **vision**

right circular cylinder *n* **:** a cylinder with bases that are circles and with the line joining the centers of the two bases perpendicular to both bases

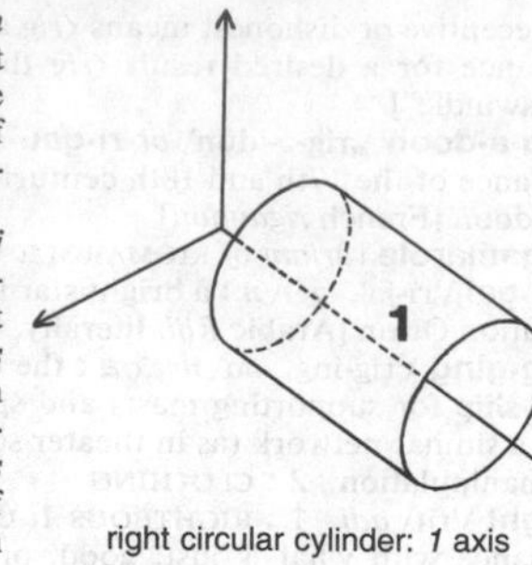

right circular cylinder: *1* axis

righ•teous \'rī-chəs\ *adj* **1 :** acting rightly **:** UPRIGHT **2 a :** morally right or justifiable ⟨*righteous* actions⟩ **b :** arising from an outraged sense of justice or morality ⟨*righteous* indignation⟩ [alteration of earlier *rightuous,* from Middle English *rightwise, rightwos,* from Old English *rihtwīs,* from *riht* "right" + *wīs* "wise"] ***synonyms*** see MORAL — **righ•teous•ly** *adv* — **righ•teous•ness** *n*

right field *n* **1 :** the part of the baseball outfield to the right looking out from the home plate **2 :** the position of the player defending right field — **right fielder** *n*

right•ful \'rīt-fəl\ *adj* **1 :** morally right or good **2 a :** having a just or legally enforceable claim **:** LEGITIMATE ⟨the *rightful* owner⟩ **b :** held by right or just claim **:** LEGAL ⟨*rightful* authority⟩ **3 :** PROPER 1, FITTING — **right•ful•ly** \-fə-lē\ *adv* — **right•ful•ness** *n*

right–hand \ˌrīt-ˌhand\ *adj* **1 :** situated on the right **2 a :** RIGHT-HANDED 1 **b :** RIGHT-HANDED 2 **3 :** chiefly relied on ⟨my *right-hand* man⟩

right hand *n* **1 a :** the hand on a person's right side **b :** a reliable or indispensable person **2 a :** the right side **b :** a place of honor

right–hand•ed \'rīt-'han-dəd\ *adj* **1 :** using the right hand more skillfully or freely than the left **2 :** done or made with or for the right hand **3 :** having or moving with a clockwise turn or twist — **right–hand•ed•ly** *or* **right–hand•ed** *adv* — **right–hand•ed•ness** *n*

right–hand•er \-'han-dər\ *n* **1 :** a blow struck with the right hand **2 :** a right-handed person

right•ist \'rīt-əst\ *n, often cap* **:** an advocate or adherent of the doctrines of the Right — **rightist** *adj, often cap*

right•ly \'rīt-lē\ *adv* **1 :** in agreement with right conduct **:** FAIRLY, JUSTLY **2 :** in the right or proper manner **:** PROPERLY **3 :** according to truth or fact

right–minded \'rīt-'mīnd-əd\ *adj* **:** likely to do what is right

right now *adv* **1 :** RIGHT AWAY **2 :** at the present time

right–of–way \ˌrīt-əv-'wā, -ə-\ *n, pl* **rights–of–way** *also* **right–of–ways 1 :** a legal right of passage over another person's ground **2 a :** the area over which a right-of-way exists **b :** the strip of land over which a public road is built **c :** the land occupied by a railroad especially for its main line **d :** the land used by a public utility (as for a transmission line) **3 :** the right of traffic to take precedence over other traffic **4 :** the right to take priority over others ⟨gave the problem *right-of-way*⟩

right on *adj* **:** exactly correct — often used interjectionally to express agreement

right prism *n* **:** a prism that has exactly two bases and whose other sides are all rectangles that are perpendicular to these bases

Right Reverend — used as a title for some high religious officials (as Episcopal bishops)

right–to–work law \ˌrīt-tə-'wərk-\ *n* **:** a law banning the union shop and the closed shop

right triangle *n* **:** a triangle having a right angle

right•ward \-wərd\ *adj or adv* **:** toward, at, or to the right — **rightward** *adj*

right whale *n* **:** a large baleen whale with no fin on the back, a very large head, and small eyes near the angles of the mouth

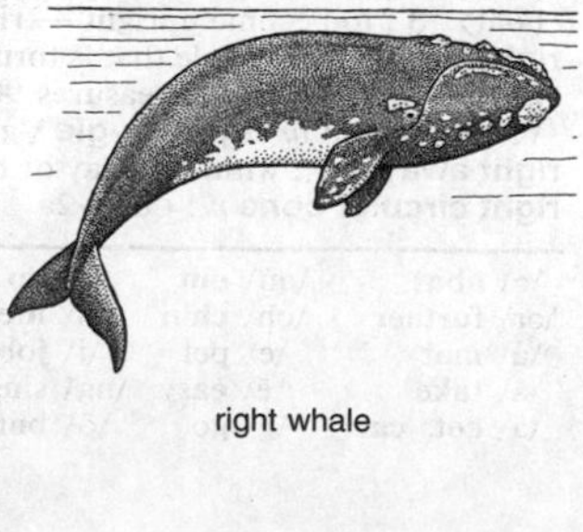
right whale

right wing *n* **1 :** the rightist division of a group **2 :** RIGHT 8 — **right–wing** \'rīt-'wing\ *adj* — **right–wing•er** \'rīt-'wing-ər\ *n*

rig•id \'rij-əd\ *adj* **1 :** lacking flexibility **:** STIFF, HARD **2 a :** inflexibly set in opinion **:** UNYIELDING **b :** strictly observed **:** ⟨follows a *rigid* schedule⟩ **3 :** HARSH, SEVERE ⟨*rigid* treatment⟩ **4 :** precise and accurate in procedure [Latin *rigidus,* from *rigēre* "to be stiff"] — **ri•gid•i•ty** \rə-'jid-ət-ē\ *n* — **rig•id•ly** \'rij-əd-lē\ *adv* — **rig•id•ness** *n*

synonyms RIGID, RIGOROUS, STRICT, STRINGENT mean very severe or stern. RIGID implies uncompromising inflexibility ⟨*rigid* and arbitrary rules⟩. RIGOROUS implies the imposing of hardship and difficulty ⟨*rigorous* training⟩. STRICT emphasizes close conformity to rules, standards, or requirements ⟨*strict* discipline⟩. STRINGENT suggests restrictions or limitations that curb or coerce ⟨*stringent* punishment⟩.

rig•ma•role *also* **rig•a•ma•role** \'rig-ə-mə-ˌrōl, 'rig-mə-\ *n* **1 :** confused or meaningless talk **2 :** a complex and often unnecessary procedure [alteration of obsolete *ragman roll* "long list, catalog"]

rig•or \'rig-ər, *2 is also* 'rī-ˌgȯr\ *n* **1 a :** harsh strictness **:** the quality of being unyielding **:** SEVERITY **b :** an act or instance of strictness, severity, or cruelty **2 :** a tremor caused by a chill **3 :** a condition that makes life difficult or uncomfortable ⟨the *rigors* of frontier life⟩ ⟨the *rigors* of winter⟩ **4 :** strict precision ⟨logical *rigor*⟩ [Medieval French *rigour,* from Latin *rigor,* literally, "stiffness," from *rigēre* "to be stiff"]

rig•or mor•tis \ˌrig-ər-'mȯrt-əs\ *n* **:** temporary rigidity of muscles occurring after death [New Latin, "stiffness of death"]

rig•or•ous \'rig-rəs, -ə-rəs\ *adj* **1 :** exercising or favoring rigor **:** very strict **2 :** marked by extremes of temperature or climate **:** HARSH, SEVERE **3 :** extremely accurate **:** PRECISE ***synonyms*** see RIGID — **rig•or•ous•ly** *adv* — **rig•or•ous•ness** *n*

rile \'rīl\ *vt* **1 :** ROIL 1 **2 :** to make angry [alteration of *roil*]

[1]**rill** \'ril\ *n* **:** a very small brook [Dutch *ril* or Low German *rille*]

[2]**rill** \'ril\ *or* **rille** \'ril, 'ril-ə\ *n* **:** any of several long narrow valleys on the moon's surface [German *rille,* literally, "channel made by a small stream," from Low German, "rill"]

[1]**rim** \'rim\ *n* **1 a :** the outer often curved or circular edge or border of something **b :** BRINK 2 **2 :** the outer part of a wheel joined to the hub usually by spokes [Old English *rima*] — **rim•less** \-ləs\ *adj*

synonyms RIM, BRIM mean the very edge of something often round or circular. RIM applies to the edge of something circular or curving ⟨*rim* of a plate⟩. BRIM applies to the upper inside rim of something hollow ⟨fill the cup to the *brim*⟩.

[2]**rim** *vb* **rimmed; rim•ming 1 :** to furnish with a rim **:** serve as a rim for **:** BORDER **2 :** to run around the rim of ⟨putts that *rim* the cup⟩ **3 :** to form or show a rim

[1]**rime** \'rīm\ *n* **1 :** FROST 1c **2 :** an accumulation of granular ice tufts on objects that resembles frost in appearance but is formed from supercooled fog or cloud **3 :** CRUST 3a, INCRUSTATION [Old English *hrīm*]

[2]**rime** *vt* **:** to cover with or as if with rime

[3]**rime, rimester** *variant of* RHYME, RHYMESTER

rim•rock \'rim-ˌräk\ *n* **1 :** the top layer or layers of rock on a plateau that remains as a vertical surface after the land near it is worn away **2 :** the edge or surface of a layer of rimrock

rimy \'rī-mē\ *adj* **rim•i•er; -est :** covered with rime **:** FROSTY

rind \'rīnd\ *n* **:** the bark of a tree; *also* **:** a usually hard or tough outer layer (as the skin of a fruit) [Old English] — **rind•ed** \'rīn-dəd\ *adj*

rin•der•pest \'rin-dər-ˌpest\ *n* **:** an acute usually fatal virus disease of cattle and sometimes sheep and goats [German, from *Rinder* "cattle" + *Pest* "pestilence"]

[1]**ring** \'ring\ *n* **1 :** a circular band for holding, connecting, hanging, pulling, packing, or sealing ⟨a curtain *ring*⟩ ⟨a key *ring*⟩ **2 :** a circlet often of precious metal worn especially on the finger **3 a :** a circular line, figure, or object **b :** an encircling arrangement ⟨a *ring* of suburbs⟩ **c :** a circular or spiral course **4 a :** an often circular space for exhibitions or competitions; *esp* **:** such a space at a circus **b :** a square enclosure in which fighting contests (as boxing matches) are held; *also* **:** the sport of boxing **5 :** ANNUAL RING **6 :** a combination of persons for a selfish and often corrupt purpose ⟨a drug *ring*⟩ **7 :** an arrangement of atoms represented in formulas or models as a ring **8** *pl* **:** a pair of usually rubber-covered metal rings suspended from above and used for hanging, swinging, and balancing feats in gymnastics [Old English *hring*] — **ringed** \'ringd\ *adj* — **ring•like** \'ring-ˌlīk\ *adj*

[2]**ring** *vb* **ringed; ring•ing** \'ring-ing\ **1 :** to place or form a ring

around : ENCIRCLE **2** : to provide with a ring **3** : GIRDLE 3 **4** : to throw a ring over (the mark) in a game where curved objects (as horseshoes) are tossed at a mark **5** : to form or take the shape of a ring

[3]**ring** *vb* **rang** \'raŋ\; **rung** \'rəŋ\; **ring·ing** \'riŋ-iŋ\ **1** : to sound clearly and reasonantly ⟨church bells *ringing*⟩ ⟨cheers *rang* out⟩ **2** : to cause to sound especially by striking ⟨*rang* the dinner bell⟩ **3** : to ring a bell as a signal **4** : to announce by or as if by ringing ⟨*ring* in the new year⟩ **5 a** : to be filled with reverberating sound : RESOUND ⟨the hall *rang* with cheers⟩ **b** : to have the sensation of being filled with a humming sound ⟨my ears were *ringing*⟩ **6** : to be filled with talk or report ⟨the whole town *rang* with the story⟩ **7** : to repeat often or loudly or earnestly **8** : to have a sound or character expressive of some quality ⟨the story *rings* true⟩ **9 a** : to summon especially by bell **b** *chiefly British* : TELEPHONE 3 — usually used with *up* [Old English *hringan*] — **ring a bell** : to arouse a response ⟨that name *rings a bell*⟩ — **ring down the curtain** : to end a performance or an action — **ring the changes** *or* **ring changes** : to run through a whole range of possibilities

[4]**ring** *n* **1** : a set of bells **2** : a clear resonant sound made by or as if by vibrating metal **3** : resonant tone : SONORITY **4** : a loud sound continued, repeated, or reverberated **5** : a sound or character expressive of a particular quality ⟨a story with the *ring* of truth⟩ **6 a** : the act or an instance of ringing **b** : a telephone call

ring·bolt \'riŋ-ˌbōlt\ *n* : a bolt with a ring through a loop at one end

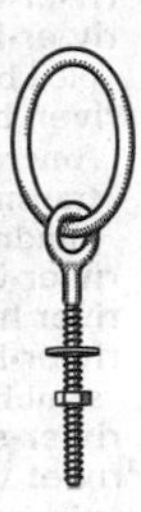

ringbolt

[1]**ring·er** \'riŋ-ər\ *n* **1** : one that sounds especially by ringing **2 a** : one that enters a competition under false representations ⟨charged that a *ringer* had won the feature race⟩ **b** : one that strongly resembles another ⟨you're a dead *ringer* for my cousin⟩

[2]**ringer** *n* : one (as a quoit or horseshoe) that encircles or puts a ring around a peg

Ring·er's solution \'riŋ-ərz-\ *n* : a balanced aqueous ionic solution that is used in physiological experiments to provide a medium essentially isotonic to many animal tissues [Sidney *Ringer*, died 1910, English physician]

ring finger *n* : the third finger of the hand counting the index finger as the first

ring·git \'riŋ-git\ *n, pl* **ringgit** *or* **ringgits** **1** : the basic monetary unit of Malaysia **2** : a coin or note representing one ringgit [Malay literally, "serration, coin with milled edge"]

ring·lead·er \'riŋ-ˌlēd-ər\ *n* : a leader of a group engaged especially in improper or unlawful activities

ring·let \'riŋ-lət\ *n* **1** : a small ring or circle **2** : CURL; *esp* : a long curl of hair

ring·mas·ter \'riŋ-ˌmas-tər\ *n* : one in charge of performances in a ring (as of a circus)

ring–necked \'riŋ-'nekt, -'nek, ˌriŋ-\ *or* **ring–neck** \ˌriŋ-ˌnek\ *adj* : having a ring of color about the neck

ring–necked pheasant *n* : a Eurasian pheasant that has a white neck ring in the male and that has been widely introduced in North America as a game bird

ring·side \'riŋ-ˌsīd\ *n* **1** : the area just outside a ring especially in which a contest occurs **2** : a place from which one may have a close view — **ringside** *adj*

ring stand *n* : a metal stand consisting of an upright rod on a rectangular base used with rings and clamps for supporting laboratory apparatus

ring–tailed \'riŋ-'tāld\ *adj* : having a tail marked with rings of differing colors

ring·tone \'riŋ-ˌtōn\ *n* : the sound made by a cell phone to signal an incoming call

ring·toss \-ˌtȯs, -ˌtäs\ *n* : a game the object of which is to toss a ring so that it will fall over an upright stick

ring up *vt* : to add up and record on a cash register

ring·worm \-ˌwərm\ *n* : a contagious skin disease caused by fungi and characterized by ring-shaped discolored patches

rink \'riŋk\ *n* **1 a** : a sheet of ice marked off for curling or ice hockey **b** : a usually artificial sheet of ice for ice-skating **c** : an enclosure for roller-skating **2** : a division of a bowling green large enough for a match **3** : a team in bowls or curling [Middle English *rinc* "area for a contest," from Middle French *renc* "row, rank, place"]

[1]**rinse** \'rins\ *vt* **1 a** : to cleanse with liquid (as water) ⟨*rinse* out your mouth⟩ **b** : to clean off with clear water the soap left over from washing ⟨*rinse* the dishes⟩ **2** : to treat (hair) with a rinse **3** : to remove (as dirt or impurities) by washing lightly or in water only [Medieval French *rincer*, derived from Latin *recens* "fresh, recent"] — **rins·er** *n*

[2]**rinse** *n* **1** : the act or process of rinsing **2 a** : liquid used for rinsing **b** : a solution that temporarily tints hair

[1]**ri·ot** \'rī-ət\ *n* **1** *archaic* **a** : DEBAUCHERY **b** : unrestrained revelry **2 a** : public violence, tumult, or disorder **b** : a tumultuous disturbance of the public peace by three or more persons assembled together **3** : a random or disorderly abundance especially of color **4** : one that is wildly amusing [Medieval French, "rash action, noise, disorder"]

[2]**riot** *vi* **1** : REVEL 1 **2** : to create or engage in a riot — **ri·ot·er** *n*

riot act *n* : a very strong reprimand or warning — used in the phrase *read the riot act* [the *Riot Act,* English law of 1715 providing for the dispersal of riots upon command of legal authority]

riot gun *n* : a small arm used to disperse rioters rather than to inflict serious injury; *esp* : a short-barreled shotgun

ri·ot·ous \'rī-ət-əs\ *adj* **1** : PROFUSE 2, ABUNDANT **2 a** : of the nature of a riot : TURBULENT **b** : taking part in a riot — **ri·ot·ous·ly** *adv* — **ri·ot·ous·ness** *n*

[1]**rip** \'rip\ *vb* **ripped; rip·ping** **1** : to tear or split apart or open **2** : to saw or split (wood) with the grain **3** : to slash or slit with or as if with a sharp blade **4** : to rush headlong [probably from Dutch *rippen* "to pull, jerk"] — **rip·per** *n* — **rip into** : to tear into : ATTACK

[2]**rip** *n* : a rent made by ripping : TEAR

[3]**rip** *n* **1** : a body of water made rough by the meeting of opposing currents or by passing over an irregular bottom **2** : RIP CURRENT [perhaps from [2]*rip*]

[4]**rip** *n* : a reckless or dissolute person [perhaps from *reprobate*]

ri·par·i·an \rə-'per-ē-ən, rī-\ *adj* : relating to or living or located on the bank of a natural watercourse (as a stream or river) or sometimes of a lake or a tidewater ⟨*riparian* trees⟩ [Latin *riparius*, from *ripa* "bank, shore"]

rip cord *n* : a cord or wire pulled in making a descent to release a parachute out of its container

rip current *n* : a strong surface current flowing outward from a shore

ripe \'rīp\ *adj* **1** : fully grown and developed : MATURE ⟨*ripe* fruit⟩ ⟨*ripe* wheat⟩ **2** : having mature knowledge, understanding, or judgment **3** : of advanced years ⟨a *ripe* old age⟩ **4 a** : fully arrived : SUITABLE ⟨the time seemed *ripe*⟩ **b** : fully prepared : READY ⟨*ripe* for action⟩ **5** : brought by aging to full flavor or the best state : MELLOW ⟨*ripe* cheese⟩ **6** : ruddy, plump, or full like ripened fruit [Old English *rīpe*] — **ripe·ly** *adv* — **ripe·ness** *n*

rip·en \'rī-pən\ *vb* **rip·ened; rip·en·ing** \'rīp-niŋ, -ə-niŋ\ : to grow or make ripe — **rip·en·er** \'rīp-nər, -ə-nər\ *n*

rip–off \'rip-ˌȯf\ *n* : an act or instance of stealing : THEFT; *also* : a financial exploitation

rip off \rip-'ȯf, 'rip-\ *vt* **1** : ROB 1; *also* : DEFRAUD **2** : STEAL 2a

ri·poste \ri-'pōst\ *n* **1** : a fencer's quick return thrust following a parry **2** : a quick retort **3** : a retaliatory maneuver or measure [French, from Italian *risposta*, literally, "answer," from *rispondere* "to answer, respond," from Latin *respondēre*] — **riposte** *vb*

rip·ping \'rip-iŋ\ *adj, chiefly British* : MARVELOUS 3, TERRIFIC [probably from [1]*rip*]

[1]**rip·ple** \'rip-əl\ *vb* **rip·pled; rip·pling** \'rip-liŋ, -ə-liŋ\ **1 a** : to become lightly ruffled or covered with small waves **b** : to flow in small waves **2** : to stir up small waves on ⟨wind *rippling* water⟩ **3** : to flow with a light rise and fall of sound or inflection ⟨laughter *rippling* over the audience⟩ **4** : to impart a wavy motion or appearance to [perhaps from [1]*rip*] — **rip·pler** \'rip-lər, -ə-lər\ *n*

[2]**ripple** *n* **1 a** : the ruffling of the surface of water **b** : a small wave or a mark like a small wave **2** : a sound like that of rippling water

rip·ply \'rip-lē, 'rip-ə-lē\ *adj* : having ripples

[1]**rip·rap** \'rip-ˌrap\ *n* **1** : a foundation or sustaining wall of stones thrown together without order (as in deep water or on an

embankment slope to prevent erosion) **2 :** stone used for riprap [obsolete *riprap* "sound of rapping"]

[2]**riprap** *vt* **rip·rapped; rip·rap·ping 1 :** to form a riprap in or on **2 :** to strengthen or support with a riprap

rip–roar·ing \ˈrip-ˈrōr-ing, -ˈrȯr-\ *adj* **:** noisily excited or exciting

rip·saw \ˈrip-ˌsȯ\ *n* **:** a coarse-toothed saw for cutting wood in the direction of the grain

rip·tide \ˈrip-ˌtīd\ *n* **:** RIP CURRENT

[1]**rise** \ˈrīz\ *vi* **rose** \ˈrōz\; **ris·en** \ˈriz-n\; **ris·ing** \ˈrī-zing\ **1 a :** to get up especially from lying, kneeling, or sitting **b :** to get up from sleep or from one's bed **2 :** to return from death **3 :** to take up arms ⟨*rise* in rebellion⟩ **4 :** to respond warmly **:** APPLAUD — usually used with *to* **5** *chiefly British* **:** to end a session **:** ADJOURN **6 :** to appear above the horizon ⟨the sun *rises* at six⟩ ⟨land *rose* to starboard⟩ **7 a :** to move upward **:** ASCEND ⟨smoke *rises*⟩ **b :** to extend upward ⟨the hill *rises* to a great height⟩ **8 :** to swell in size or volume ⟨the river is *rising*⟩ ⟨dough *rises*⟩ **9 a :** to become heartened or elated ⟨their spirits *rose*⟩ **b :** to increase in intensity ⟨felt my anger *rising*⟩ **10 a :** to go higher in rank **:** be promoted ⟨*rose* to colonel⟩ **b :** to increase in quantity or number ⟨production *rose* sharply⟩ ⟨*rising* costs⟩ **11 a :** to come about **:** HAPPEN ⟨an ugly rumor had *risen*⟩ **b :** to have a source **:** ORIGINATE ⟨that river *rises* in the hills⟩ **12 :** to exert oneself to meet a challenge ⟨*rise* to the occasion⟩ [Old English *rīsan*]

[2]**rise** \ˈrīz\ *n* **1 :** an act of rising **:** a state of having risen **2 :** ORIGIN 2a, BEGINNING **3 :** the distance or elevation of one point above another **4 :** an increase especially in amount, number, volume, or price **5 a :** an upward slope **b :** a spot higher than surrounding ground **6 :** an irritated or angry reaction ⟨got a *rise* out of you⟩

ris·er \ˈrī-zər\ *n* **1 :** one that rises (as from sleep) **2 :** the upright member between two stair treads

ris·i·bil·i·ty \ˌriz-ə-ˈbil-ət-ē\ *n, pl* **-ties 1 :** the ability or inclination to laugh — often used in plural **2 :** LAUGHTER

ris·i·ble \ˈriz-ə-bəl\ *adj* **1 :** able or inclined to laugh **2 :** provoking laughter **:** FUNNY [Late Latin *risibilis,* from Latin *risus,* past participle of *ridēre* "to laugh"] ***synonyms*** see LAUGHABLE

[1]**risk** \ˈrisk\ *n* **1 :** possibility of loss or injury **:** PERIL **2 :** someone or something that creates or suggests a hazard **3 a :** the chance of loss or the perils to a person or thing that is insured **b :** a person or thing that is a hazard to an insurer ⟨a poor *risk*⟩ [French *risque,* from Italian *risco*] ***synonyms*** see DANGER

[2]**risk** *vt* **1 :** to expose to hazard or danger ⟨*risked* my life⟩ **2 :** to take the risk or danger of ⟨*risked* breaking my neck⟩ — **risk·er** *n*

risk factor *n* **:** something that increases risk or susceptibility ⟨cigarette smoking is a *risk factor* for lung cancer⟩

risky \ˈris-kē\ *adj* **risk·i·er; -est :** involving risk or danger **:** HAZARDOUS — **risk·i·ness** *n*

ris·qué \ri-ˈskā\ *adj* **:** bordering on impropriety or indecency **:** OFF-COLOR [French, from *risquer* "to risk," from *risque* "risk"]

ri·tar·dan·do \ri-ˌtär-ˈdän-dō, ˌrē-\ *adv or adj* **:** with a gradual slackening in tempo — used as a direction in music [Italian, literally, "retarding"] — **ritardando** *n*

rite \ˈrīt\ *n* **1 a :** a prescribed form for a ceremony **b :** the ceremonial practices of a church or group of churches **2 :** a ceremonial act or action **3 :** a division of the Christian church using a distinctive liturgy [Latin *ritus*]

[1]**rit·u·al** \ˈrich-ə-wəl, ˈrich-əl\ *adj* **1 :** of or relating to rites or a ritual ⟨a *ritual* dance⟩ **2 :** according to religious law or social custom ⟨*ritual* purity⟩ — **rit·u·al·ly** \-ē\ *adv*

[2]**ritual** *n* **1 :** an established form for a ceremony **2 a :** ritual observance; *esp* **:** a system of rites **b :** RITE 2 **c :** a formal and customarily repeated act or series of acts

rit·u·al·ism \-ˌiz-əm\ *n* **1 :** the use of ritual **2 :** excessive devotion to ritual — **rit·u·al·ist** \-əst\ *n* — **rit·u·al·is·tic** \ˌrich-ə-wəl-ˈis-tik, ˌrich-əl-\ *adj* — **rit·u·al·is·ti·cal·ly** \-ti-kə-lē, -klē\ *adv*

ritzy \ˈrit-sē\ *adj* **ritz·i·er; -est 1 :** SNOBBISH **2 :** showily elegant **:** POSH [*Ritz* hotels, noted for their opulence]

[1]**ri·val** \ˈrī-vəl\ *n* **1 a :** one of two or more trying to reach or obtain something that only one can possess **b :** one who tries to excel in a competition **2 :** one that equals another in desired qualities **:** PEER [Latin *rivalis* "one using the same stream as another, rival in love," from *rivalis* "of a stream," from *rivus* "stream"]

Word History *Rival* is derived from Latin *rivalis,* which as an adjective means "of a brook or stream," from *rivus,* "brook or stream." As a noun *rivalis* (in its plural forms) refers literally to those who use the same stream as a source of water. Just as neighbors are likely to dispute each other's rights to a common source of water, so too contention is inevitable when two or more persons strive to obtain something that only one can possess. Latin *rivalis* developed a sense relating to rivalry in love, and in this sense it came into English.

[2]**rival** *adj* **:** having the same pretensions or claims

[3]**rival** *vt* **-valed** *or* **-valled; -val·ing** *or* **-val·ling** \ˈrīv-ling, -ə-ling\ **1 :** to be in competition with **2 :** to try to equal or excel **3 :** to possess qualities or aptitudes that approach or equal (those of another)

ri·val·ry \ˈrī-vəl-rē\ *n, pl* **-ries :** the act of rivaling **:** the state of being a rival **:** COMPETITION

rive \ˈrīv\ *vb* **rived** \ˈrīvd\; **riv·en** \ˈriv-ən\ *also* **rived; riv·ing** \ˈrī-ving\ **1 a :** to tear apart **:** REND **b :** to split with force or violence **2 a :** to divide into pieces or factions ⟨the church was *riven* with discord⟩ **b :** FRACTURE ⟨a country *riven* by earthquakes⟩ **3 :** to become split **:** CRACK [Old Norse *rīfa*]

riv·er \ˈriv-ər\ *n* **1 :** a natural stream of water larger than a brook or creek **2 :** a large stream or flow ⟨a *river* of oil⟩ [Medieval French *rivere,* derived from Latin *riparius* "of a bank or shore," from *ripa* "bank, shore"]

riv·er·bank \ˈriv-ər-ˌbangk\ *n* **:** the bank of a river

riv·er·bed \-ˌbed\ *n* **:** the channel occupied or formerly occupied by a river

river blindness *n* **:** a human disease of Africa and tropical America that is caused by a slender parasitic nematode worm transmitted by the bite of a blackfly and that typically results in blindness if untreated — called also *onchocerciasis*

riv·er·boat \-ˌbōt\ *n* **:** a boat for use on a river

river horse *n* **:** HIPPOPOTAMUS

riv·er·ine \ˈriv-ə-ˌrīn, -ˌrēn\ *adj* **1 :** relating to, formed by, or resembling a river **2 :** living or situated on the banks of a river

riv·er·side \ˈriv-ər-ˌsīd\ *n* **:** the side or bank of a river

[1]**riv·et** \ˈriv-ət\ *n* **:** a single-headed pin or bolt of metal used for uniting two or more pieces by passing the shank through a hole in each piece and then beating or pressing down the plain end so as to make a second head [Medieval French, from *river* "to attach, clinch," probably from *rive* "border, edge, bank," from Latin *ripa*]

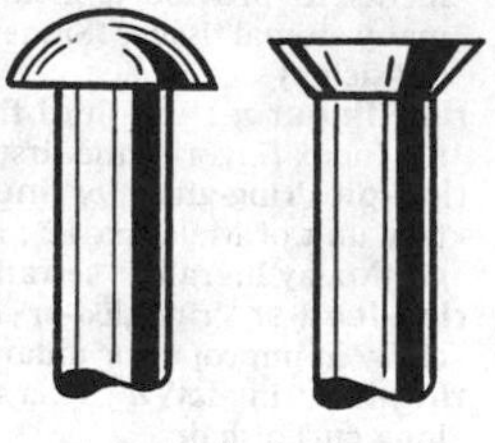
rivet

[2]**rivet** *vt* **1 :** to fasten with or as if with rivets **2 :** to beat or press the end or point of (as a metallic pin, rod, or bolt) so as to form a head **3 :** to attract and hold (as the attention) completely — **riv·et·er** *n*

ri·vi·era \ˌriv-ē-ˈer-ə, ri-ˈvyer-ə\ *n, often cap* **:** a coastal region frequented as a resort area and usually marked by a mild climate [*Riviera,* region in France and Italy]

riv·u·let \ˈriv-yə-lət, ˈriv-ə-lət\ *n* **:** a small stream [Italian *rivoletto,* from *rivolo,* from Latin *rivulus* "small stream," from *rivus* "brook, stream"]

[1]**ri·yal** \rē-ˈȯl, -ˈyȯl, -ˈäl, -ˈyäl\ *n* **1** *also* **ri·al** \-ˈȯl, -ˈäl\ **:** the basic monetary unit of Qatar and Saudi Arabia **2 :** a coin or note representing one riyal [Arabic *riyāl,* from Spanish *real* "real"]

[2]**riyal** *variant of* RIAL

RN \ˌär-ˈen\ *n* **:** REGISTERED NURSE

RNA \ˌär-ˌen-ˈā\ *n* **:** any of various nucleic acids that are typically composed of a single chain of nucleotides, that differ from DNA in containing ribose instead of deoxyribose and uracil instead of thymine as structural components, that function especially in protein synthesis, and that in some viruses (as retroviruses) replace DNA as the basic carrier of genetic information — compare MESSENGER RNA, RIBOSOMAL RNA, TRANSFER RNA [*ri*bo*n*ucleic *a*cid]

RN·ase \ˌär-ˈen-ˌās, -ˌāz\ *n* **:** RIBONUCLEASE [*RNA* + *-ase*]

[1]**roach** \ˈrōch\ *n, pl* **roach** *also* **roach·es :** a silver-white greenish-backed European freshwater fish related to the carp; *also* **:** any of several similar or related fishes [Medieval French *roche*]

[2]**roach** *vt* **:** to brush (the hair) into an arched roll — often used with *up* [origin unknown]

[3]**roach** *n* : COCKROACH

road \'rōd\ *n* **1** : a place less enclosed than a harbor where ships may ride at anchor — often used in plural **2 a** : an open way for vehicles, persons, and animals; *esp* : one lying outside an urban district **b** : ROADBED 2 **3** : a route or way to an end, conclusion, or circumstance ⟨the *road* to success⟩ **4** : RAILWAY **5** : a series of visits to several places or the travel necessary to get there ⟨the team is on the *road*⟩ ⟨on tour with the musical's *road* company⟩ [Old English *rād* "ride, journey"]

road·abil·i·ty \ˌrōd-ə-'bil-ət-ē\ *n* : the qualities (as steadiness and balance) desirable in an automobile on the road

road·bed \'rōd-ˌbed\ *n* **1** : the foundation of a road or railroad **2** : the part of the surface of a road traveled by vehicles

road·block \-ˌbläk\ *n* **1 a** : a barricade at a point on a road that can be covered by fire from a defending army **b** : a road barricade set up by law-enforcement officers **2** : an obstruction in a road **3** : something that hinders progress

road hog *n* : a motorist who obstructs others especially by occupying part of another's traffic lane

road·house \'rōd-ˌhau̇s\ *n* : a bar or inn usually outside a city

road metal *n* : broken stone or cinders used in making and repairing roads or ballasting railroads

road·run·ner \'rōd-ˌrən-ər\ *n* : a swift-running long-tailed bird of the southwestern U.S. that is related to the cuckoo and is chiefly ground-dwelling

roadrunner

[1]**road·side** \'rōd-ˌsīd\ *n* : the strip of land along a road : the side of a road

[2]**roadside** *adj* : situated at the side of a road

road·stead \'rōd-ˌsted\ *n* : ROAD 1

road·ster \'rōd-stər\ *n* : an automobile that seats two and has an open body and a folding fabric top

road test *n* : a test (as of a vehicle or a person's ability to drive) made on the road

road trip *n* **1** : a trip taken by a sports team to play one or more away games **2** : an extended trip in a motor vehicle — **road–trip** *vi*

road·way \'rōd-ˌwā\ *n* **1 a** : the strip of land over which a road passes **b** : ROAD; *esp* : ROADBED 2 **2** : a railroad right-of-way **3** : the part of a bridge used by vehicles

road·work \-ˌwərk\ *n* : conditioning for an athletic contest (as a boxing match) consisting mainly of long runs

roam \'rōm\ *vb* **1** : to go from place to place aimlessly : WANDER ⟨*roam* the hills⟩ **2** : to travel purposefully and unhindered through a wide area ⟨cattle *roaming* in search of water⟩ **3** : to use a cellular phone outside one's local calling area ⟨*roaming* charges⟩ [Middle English *romen*] ***synonyms*** see WANDER — **roam·er** *n*

[1]**roan** \'rōn\ *adj* : having the base color (as black, red, or brown) dulled and lightened by white hairs ⟨a *roan* horse⟩ [Middle French, from Old Spanish *roano*]

[2]**roan** *n* **1** : an animal (as a horse) with a roan coat **2** : the color of a roan horse

[1]**roar** \'rōr, 'rȯr\ *vb* **1** : to utter or emit a full loud prolonged sound ⟨the lion *roared*⟩ **2 a** : to make a loud confused sound (as rumbling) ⟨the engine *roared*⟩ **b** : to laugh loudly **3** : to be boisterous or disorderly **4** : to utter or proclaim with a roar **5** : to cause to roar ⟨*roar* a motor⟩ [Old English *rārian*] — **roar·er** \'rōr-ər, 'rȯr-\ *n*

[2]**roar** *n* **1 a** : the deep loud cry of a wild animal (as a lion) **b** : a loud deep cry (as of pain or anger) **2** : a loud continuous confused sound ⟨the *roar* of the crowd⟩

roar·ing *adj* : very strong or active ⟨a *roaring* fire⟩ ⟨a *roaring* headache⟩

[1]**roast** \'rōst\ *vb* **1 a** : to cook by exposing to dry heat (as in an oven) **b** : to dry and parch by exposure to heat ⟨*roast* coffee⟩ **2** : to heat (inorganic material) with access of air and without fusing to effect change (as expulsion of volatile matter) ⟨*roast* a sulfide ore⟩ **3** : to criticize severely in either a serious or joking way **4** : to undergo roasting **5** : to be or make very hot ⟨*roasted* by the summer sun⟩ [Medieval French *rostir*, of Germanic origin]

[2]**roast** *n* **1** : a piece of meat roasted or suitable for roasting **2** : an outing at which food is roasted **3** : an act of roasting; *esp* : severe banter or criticism

[3]**roast** *adj* : cooked by roasting ⟨*roast* beef⟩

roast·er \'rō-stər\ *n* **1** : one that roasts **2** : a pan or an appliance for roasting **3** : something (as a young chicken) suitable for roasting

rob \'räb\ *vb* **robbed; rob·bing** **1 a** : to take something away from (a person or place) by force, threat, stealth, or trickery ⟨*rob* a store⟩ ⟨*rob* a pedestrian⟩ **b** : to take away as loot : STEAL ⟨*rob* jewelry⟩ **c** : to commit robbery **2 a** : to deprive of something due, expected, or desired **b** : to withhold unjustly or injuriously [Medieval French *rober*, of Germanic origin] — **rob·ber** *n*

robber fly *n* : any of various two-winged flies that feed on other insects and are covered with coarse bristly hairs

rob·bery \'räb-rē, -ə-rē\ *n, pl* **-ber·ies** : the act or practice of robbing; *esp* : larceny from the person or presence of another by violence or threat

[1]**robe** \'rōb\ *n* **1** : a long loose or flowing garment: as **a** : one used for ceremonial occasions or as a symbol of office or profession **b** : a garment (as a dressing gown) replacing outer garments for informal wear **2** : a covering or wrap for the lower body ⟨wrapped the legs in a *robe* at the game⟩ [Medieval French, "plunder, clothing, robe," of Germanic origin]

[2]**robe** *vb* **1** : to clothe or cover with or as if with a robe **2** : to put on a robe **3** : DRESS 2a

rob·in \'räb-ən\ *n* **1** : a small European thrush with an olive-brown back and wings and orange-red face, throat, and breast **2** : a large North American thrush with a grayish back and head and brick red breast and underparts [related to Dutch *robijntje* "linnet" and Frisian *robyntsye*]

robin 2

ro·bot \'rō-ˌbät, -bət\ *n* **1 a** : a machine that looks like a human being and performs various complex acts (as walking or talking) of a human being **b** : an efficient insensitive person who functions automatically **2** : a device that automatically performs tasks that are complicated and often continuously repeated **3** : something guided by automatic controls ⟨a *robot* airplane⟩ ⟨a *robot* factory⟩ [Czech, from *robota* "forced labor"] — **ro·bot·ic** \rō-'bät-ik\ *adj* — **ro·bot·i·cal·ly** \-i-kə-lē, -klē\ *adv*

Word History In 1923 a play called *R.U.R.* opened in London and New York. The author, Karel C˘apek, coined the term *robot* from the Czech *robota*, meaning "forced labor." In *R.U.R.* (which stands for "Rossum's Universal Robots") mechanical men originally designed to perform manual labor become so sophisticated that some advanced models develop the capacity to feel and hate, and eventually they destroy mankind.

ro·bust \rō-'bəst, 'rō-ˌ\ *adj* **1** : strong and vigorously healthy : STURDY **2** : ROUGH, RUDE ⟨*robust* humor⟩ **3** : requiring strength or vigor ⟨*robust* work⟩ **4** : STRONG 7a, FULL-BODIED [Latin *robustus* "oaken, strong," from *robur* "oak, strength"] — **ro·bust·ly** *adv* — **ro·bust·ness** *n*

roc \'räk\ *n* : a legendary bird of great size and strength believed to inhabit the Indian Ocean area [Arabic *rukhkh*]

Ro·chelle salt \rō-ˌshel-\ *n* : a hydrated crystalline salt of potassium and sodium that is used as a laxative [La *Rochelle*, France]

roch·et \'räch-ət\ *n* : a white linen vestment resembling a surplice worn by bishops and privileged prelates [Medieval French]

[1]**rock** \'räk\ *vb* **1** : to move back and forth in or as if in a cradle **2 a** : to sway or cause to sway back and forth **b (1)** : DAZE 1, STUN **(2)** : DISTURB 2a, b, UPSET ⟨the news *rocked* the community⟩ [Old English *roccian*] ***synonyms*** see SHAKE

[2]**rock** *n* **1** : a rocking movement **2** : music usually played on

\ə\ **abut**	\au̇\ **out**	\i\ **tip**	\ȯ\ **saw**	\u̇\ **foot**
\ər\ **further**	\ch\ **chin**	\ī\ **life**	\ȯi\ **coin**	\y\ **yet**
\a\ **mat**	\e\ **pet**	\j\ **job**	\th\ **thin**	\yü\ **few**
\ā\ **take**	\ē\ **easy**	\ng\ **sing**	\t͟h\ **this**	\yu̇\ **cure**
\ä\ **cot, cart**	\g\ **go**	\ō\ **bone**	\ü\ **food**	\zh\ **vision**

amplified instruments and marked by a heavy beat, repetition of simple phrases, and often country, folk, and blues elements

[3]**rock** *n* **1 :** a large mass of stone forming a cliff, promontory, or peak **2 :** consolidated or unconsolidated solid mineral matter; *also* : a broken piece of it **3 :** something (as a support or refuge) like a rock in firmness **4** *slang* **a :** GEM 1 **b :** DIAMOND 1a [Medieval French *roke*] — **rock·like** \-ˌlīk\ *adj* — **on the rocks 1 :** in or into a state of destruction or wreckage ⟨a relationship *on the rocks*⟩ **2 :** on ice cubes ⟨bourbon *on the rocks*⟩

rock and roll *or* **rock 'n' roll** *n* : [2]ROCK 2 — **rock–and–roll** *or* **rock 'n' roll** *adj*

rock bass *n* : a brown-spotted sunfish found especially in the upper Mississippi valley and Great Lakes region

rock bottom *n* : the lowest or most basic part or level — **rock–bottom** *adj*

rock·bound \ˈräk-ˈbau̇nd\ *adj* : fringed, surrounded, or covered with rocks : ROCKY

rock candy *n* : sugar crystallized in large masses

rock crystal *n* : transparent quartz

rock dove *n* : a bluish gray Eurasian dove that is established in most of North America — compare PIGEON

rock·er \ˈräk-ər\ *n* **1 a :** a curving piece of wood or metal on which an object (as a cradle) rocks **b :** a structure or device (as a chair) that rocks upon rockers **2 :** a mechanism that works with a rocking motion **3 :** a rock performer, fan, or song — **off one's rocker** : in a state of extreme confusion or insanity

[1]**rock·et** \ˈräk-ət\ *n* **1 :** a firework consisting of a case containing a combustible composition fastened to a guiding stick and projected through the air by the reaction resulting from the rearward discharge of the gases liberated by combustion **2 :** a jet engine that operates on the same principle as the firework rocket, carries the fuel and oxygen needed for combustion and thus makes the engine independent of the oxygen of the air, and is used especially for the propulsion of a missile or a vehicle (as an airplane) — called also *rocket engine* **3 :** a rocket-propelled bomb, missile, vehicle, or projectile [Italian *rocchetta,* literally, "small distaff," from *rocca* "distaff," of Germanic origin]

[2]**rocket** *vb* **1 :** to convey by or as if by means of a rocket ⟨*rocket* a satellite into orbit⟩ **2 :** to rise up swiftly, spectacularly, and with force ⟨*rocketed* to great fame⟩ **3 :** to travel rapidly in or as if in a rocket

rock·e·teer \ˌräk-ə-ˈtiər\ *n* **1 :** one who fires, pilots, or rides in a rocket **2 :** a scientist who specializes in rocketry

rocket plane *n* : an airplane propelled by rockets

rock·et·ry \ˈräk-ə-trē\ *n* : the study of, experimentation with, or use of rockets

rocket ship *n* : a rocket-propelled spaceship

rocket sled *n* : a rocket-propelled vehicle that runs usually on a single rail and that is used especially in aviation research

rock·fish \ˈräk-ˌfish\ *n* : any of various fishes that live among rocks or on rocky bottoms

rock garden *n* : a garden laid out among rocks or decorated with rocks and adapted for the growth of particular kinds of plants (as alpines)

rock hound *n* : an amateur rock and mineral collector

rocking chair *n* : a chair mounted on rockers

rocking horse *n* : a toy horse mounted on rockers — called also *hobbyhorse*

rock lobster *n* : SPINY LOBSTER

rock 'n' roll *variant of* ROCK AND ROLL

rock pigeon *n* : ROCK DOVE

rock–ribbed \ˈräk-ˈribd\ *adj* **1 :** [1]ROCKY 1 **2 :** firm and inflexible in decisions or beliefs

rock salt *n* : common salt in large crystals or masses

rock·weed \ˈräk-ˌwēd\ *n* : any of various brown algae commonly growing attached to rocks along shores — called also *fucus*

rock wool *n* : mineral wool made by blowing a jet of steam through molten rock or through slag and used chiefly for heat and sound insulation

[1]**rocky** \ˈräk-ē\ *adj* **rock·i·er; -est 1 :** abounding in or consisting of rocks **2 :** difficult to impress or affect : INSENSITIVE **3 :** firmly held : STEADFAST — **rock·i·ness** *n*

[2]**rocky** *adj* **rock·i·er; -est 1 :** not stable : WOBBLY **2 :** physically upset or mentally confused **3 :** marked by obstacles or problems : DIFFICULT, ROUGH ⟨a *rocky* start⟩ — **rock·i·ness** *n*

Rocky Mountain goat *n* : MOUNTAIN GOAT [*Rocky Mountains,* North America]

Rocky Mountain sheep *n* : BIGHORN SHEEP

Rocky Mountain spotted fever *n* : an acute rickettsial disease marked by chills, fever, prostration, pains in muscles and joints, and a red to purple rash and caused by a bacterium transmitted by the bite of a tick

ro·co·co \rə-ˈkō-kō, ˌrō-kə-ˈkō\ *adj* **1 :** of or relating to an 18th century artistic style marked especially by fanciful curved forms and elaborate ornamentation **2 :** excessively ornate [French, from *rocaille* literally, "stone debris," from *roquailles,* pl., "rocky terrain," from *roc* "rock," from Medieval French *roche*] — **rococo** *n*

rod \ˈräd\ *n* **1 a :** a straight slender stick or bar ⟨a curtain *rod*⟩ **b :** a stick used to punish; *also* : PUNISHMENT **c :** a pole with a line and usually a reel attached for fishing **d :** a bar for measuring **2 a :** a unit of length — see MEASURE table **b :** a square rod **3 :** any of the rod-shaped light-sensitive cells in the retina responsive to faint light **4 :** a bacterium shaped like a rod **5** *slang* : PISTOL 1 [Old English *rodd*] — **rod·less** \-ləs\ *adj* — **rod·like** \-ˌlīk\ *adj*

rode *past of* RIDE

ro·dent \ˈrōd-nt\ *n* : any of an order (Rodentia) of relatively small gnawing mammals (as mice, squirrels, or beavers) having in both jaws a single pair of incisors with a chisel-shaped edge — compare LAGOMORPH [derived from Latin *rodens,* present participle of *rodere* "to gnaw"] — **rodent** *adj*

ro·den·ti·cide \rō-ˈdent-ə-ˌsīd\ *n* : an agent that kills or repels rodents — **ro·den·ti·cid·al** \-ˌdent-ə-ˈsīd-l\ *adj*

ro·deo \ˈrōd-ē-ˌō, rə-ˈdā-ō\ *n, pl* **-de·os 1 :** ROUNDUP 1 **2 :** a contest or exhibition of cowboy skills (as riding and roping) [Spanish, from *rodear* "to surround," from *rueda* "wheel," from Latin *rota*]

[1]**roe** \ˈrō\ *n, pl* **roe** *or* **roes** : DOE [Old English *rā*]

[2]**roe** *n* : the eggs of a fish especially while still bound together in a membrane [Middle English *roof, roughe, row*]

roe·buck \ˈrō-ˌbək\ *n, pl* **roebuck** *or* **roebucks** : ROE DEER; *esp* : the male roe deer

roe deer *n* : either of two small nimble deer of Europe and Asia that have erect antlers forked at the tip and are reddish brown in summer and grayish in winter

[1]**roent·gen** \ˈrent-gən, ˈrənt-, -jən\ *adj* : of or relating to X-rays [Wilhelm *Röntgen,* died 1923, German physicist]

[2]**roentgen** *n* : the international unit of x-radiation or gamma radiation equal to the amount of radiation that produces in one cubic centimeter of dry air ionization equal to one electrostatic unit of charge

roent·gen·i·um \rent-ˈgen-ē-əm, rənt-, -ˈjen-\ *n* : a short-lived radioactive element produced artificially — see ELEMENT table [New Latin, from Wilhelm *Röntgen*]

roentgen ray *n, often cap 1st R* : X-RAY

Ro·ga·tion Day \rō-ˈgā-shən-\ *n* : one of the Christian days of prayer especially for the harvest observed on the three days before Ascension Day and by Roman Catholics also on April 25 [Latin *rogatio* "questioning," from *rogare* "to ask"]

rogations *n pl* : the ceremonies of the Rogation Days

rog·er \ˈräj-ər\ *interj* — used especially in radio and signaling to indicate that a message has been received and understood [*Roger,* former communications code word for *r,* initial letter of *received*]

[1]**rogue** \ˈrōg\ *n* **1 a :** TRAMP 1, VAGRANT **b :** a dishonest or worthless person : SCOUNDREL **c :** a mischievous person : SCAMP **2 :** a vicious or lazy horse **3 :** an individual plant or animal with a chance and usually inferior biological variation [origin unknown] — **rogu·ish** \ˈrō-gish\ *adj* — **rogu·ish·ly** *adv* — **rogu·ish·ness** *n*

[2]**rogue** *vi* **rogued; rogu·ing** *or* **rogue·ing** : to weed out inferior individuals from a crop

[3]**rogue** *adj* **1 :** resembling or suggesting a rogue elephant in being isolated, dangerous or uncontrollable ⟨a *rogue* wave⟩ **2 :** CORRUPT, DISHONEST ⟨*rogue* cops⟩ **3 :** of or being a nation whose leaders defy international law ⟨*rogue* states⟩

rogue elephant *n* : a vicious elephant that separates from the herd and roams alone

rogu·ery \ˈrō-gə-rē, -grē\ *n, pl* **-er·ies 1 :** the practices or an act characteristic of a rogue **2 :** mischievous play

rogues' gallery *n* : a collection of pictures of persons arrested as criminals

roil \ˈrȯil, *2 is also* ˈrīl\ *vt* **1 :** to make cloudy or muddy by stirring up sediment **2 :** RILE 2 [origin unknown]

rois·ter \ˈrȯi-stər\ *vi* **rois·tered; rois·ter·ing** \-stə-ring, -string\ : REVEL 1 [from earlier *roister* "roisterer," from Middle French *rustre* "boor, lout," derived from Latin *rusticus* "rustic, rural"] — **rois·ter·er** \-stər-ər\ *n*

role *also* **rôle** \ˈrōl\ *n* **1 a** (1) **:** a character assigned or assumed (2) **:** a socially expected behavior pattern usually determined by an individual's status in a particular society **b :** a part played by an actor or singer **2 :** a function or part performed especially in a particular operation or process ⟨had a major *role* in the negotiations⟩ [French *rôle,* literally, "roll, scroll," from Medieval French *rolle*]

role model *n* **:** a person whose behavior in a particular role is imitated by others

role–play *vt* **:** to act out the role of ⟨*role-play* an interviewer⟩

[1]**roll** \ˈrōl\ *n* **1 a :** a written document that may be rolled up **:** SCROLL **b :** an official list especially of members of a body (as a legislature) **2 :** something that is rolled or rounded: as **a :** a quantity (as of fabric or paper) rolled up to form a single package **b :** a food preparation rolled up for cooking or serving; *esp* **:** a small piece of baked yeast dough **c :** paper money folded or rolled **3 :** something that rolls **:** ROLLER [Medieval French *rolle,* from Latin *rotula* "small wheel," from *rota* "wheel"]

[2]**roll** *vb* **1 a :** to move along a surface by rotation without sliding **b :** to turn over and over **c :** to move about or as if about an axis or point **2 a :** to put a wrapping around **b :** to form into a ball or roll **3 :** to press, spread, or level with a roller **:** to make smooth, even, or compact ⟨hulled and *rolled* oats⟩ ⟨*roll* paint⟩ — often used with *out* ⟨*roll* out the dough⟩ **4 a :** to move on rollers or wheels **b :** to begin operating or moving ⟨the new shop got *rolling*⟩ **5 a :** to make or cause to make a full reverberating or continuous beating sound ⟨*roll* a drum⟩ ⟨thunder *rolled*⟩ **b :** to utter with a trill ⟨you *roll* your *r*'s⟩ **6 :** to rob (as an unconscious person) usually by going through the pockets; *also* **:** ROB **7 :** to luxuriate in an abundant supply ⟨*rolling* in money⟩ **8 :** ELAPSE, PASS ⟨time *rolls* by⟩ **9 :** to flow in a continuous stream ⟨money was *rolling* in⟩ **10 :** to have a wavy surface ⟨*rolling* prairies⟩ **11 :** to sway from side to side **:** ROCK ⟨the ship heaved and *rolled*⟩ **12 :** to respond to rolling in a specified way ⟨a good paint *rolls* on smoothly⟩ **13 :** to move forward **:** develop and maintain impetus

[3]**roll** *n* **1 a :** a sound produced by rapid strokes on a drum **b :** a sonorous and often rhythmical flow of speech **c :** a heavy reverberating sound ⟨the *roll* of cannon⟩ **2 :** a rolling movement or an action or process involving such movement; *esp* **:** a swaying or side-to-side movement

roll bar *n* **:** an overhead metal bar on an automobile that is designed to protect the occupant in case of a turnover

roll call *n* **:** the act of calling off a list of names (as for checking attendance); *also* **:** a time for a roll call

[1]**roll·er** \ˈrō-lər\ *n* **1 a :** a revolving cylinder over or on which something is moved or which is used to press, shape, spread, or smooth something **b :** a rod on which something (as a map) is rolled up **c :** a small wheel (as of a roller skate) **2 :** a long heavy wave on the sea **3 :** one that rolls or rolls over

[2]**rol·ler** \ˈrō-lər\ *n* **:** a canary with a soft trilling song [German, from *rollen* "to roll, reverberate," from Middle French *roller,* derived from Latin *rotula* "small wheel"]

roller bearing *n* **:** a bearing in which a revolving part turns on rollers held in a circular frame or cage

roll·er coaster \ˈrō-lər-ˌkō-stər, ˈrō-lē-ˌkō-\ *n* **:** an amusement park ride consisting of an elevated railway with sharp curves and steep inclines on which cars roll

roller rink *n* **:** RINK 1c

roll·er skate *n* **:** a skate that has wheels instead of a runner — **roller–skate** *vi*

rol·lick \ˈräl-ik\ *vi* **:** FROLIC [origin unknown] — **rollick** *n* — **rol·lick·ing** *adj*

rolling mill *n* **:** an establishment where metal is rolled into plates and bars

rolling pin *n* **:** a cylinder (as of wood) for rolling out dough

rolling stock *n* **:** wheeled vehicles owned or used by a railroad or trucking company

roll·top desk \ˌrōl-ˌtäp-\ *n* **:** a writing desk with a cover that rolls back into the frame

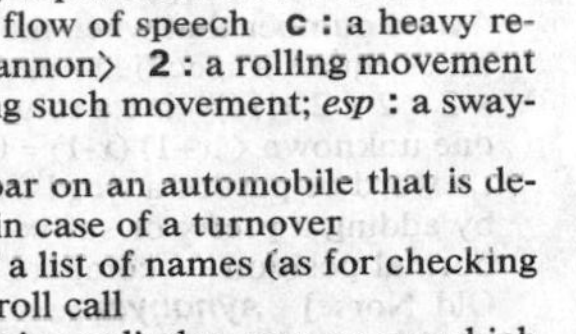

rolling pin

roll up *vb* **1 :** ACCUMULATE ⟨*rolled up* a majority⟩ **2 :** to arrive in a vehicle

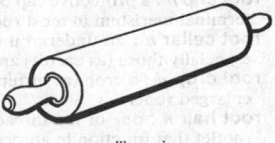

ro·ly–po·ly \ˌrō-lē-ˈpō-lē\ *n, pl* **-lies 1 :** a short stout person or thing **2 :** a pudding made of rolled-out dough spread with a filling, rolled up into a cylinder shape, and baked or steamed [reduplication of *roly,* from [2]*roll*] — **roly–poly** *adj*

ROM \ˈräm\ *n* **:** a usually small computer memory that contains special-purpose information (as a program) which cannot be altered — compare RAM

ro·maine \rō-ˈmān\ *n* **:** a lettuce with long crisp leaves and columnar heads [French, from *romain* "Roman," from Latin *Romanus*]

[1]**Ro·man** \ˈrō-mən\ *n* **1 a :** a native or resident of Rome **b :** a citizen of the Roman Empire **2** *often offensive* **:** ROMAN CATHOLIC **3** *not cap* **:** roman letters or type

[2]**Roman** *adj* **1 :** of or relating to ancient or modern Rome, the people of Rome, or the empire of which Rome was the original capital; *esp* **:** characteristic of the ancient Romans ⟨*Roman* fortitude⟩ **2 :** LATIN 2 **3** *not cap* **:** of or relating to a type style with upright characters (as in "these words are roman") **4 :** of or relating to the see of Rome or the Roman Catholic Church **5 :** having a prominent slightly aquiline bridge ⟨a *Roman* nose⟩

ro·man à clef \rō-ˌmä^{n}n-ä-ˈklā\ *n, pl* **ro·mans à clef** \-ˌmä^{n}z-ä-\ **:** a novel in which real persons or actual events figure under disguise [French, literally, "novel with a key"]

Roman candle *n* **:** a cylindrical firework that discharges at intervals balls or stars of fire

Roman Catholic *adj* **:** of or relating to the body of Christians having a hierarchy under the pope, a liturgy centered in the Mass, and a body of dogma formulated by the church as the infallible interpreter of revealed truth — **Roman Catholic** *n* — **Roman Catholicism** *n*

[1]**ro·mance** \rō-ˈmans, ˈrō-ˌ\ *n* **1 a :** a medieval tale based on legend, chivalrous love and adventure, and the supernatural **b :** a prose narrative dealing with imaginary characters involved in heroic, adventurous, or mysterious events remote in time or place **c :** a love story **2 :** something that lacks basis in fact **3 :** the adventurous or glamorous attractiveness of something ⟨the *romance* of the old West⟩ **4 :** a love affair **5** *cap* **:** the Romance languages [Medieval French *romanz* "French, something written in French," from Latin *romanice* "in a vernacular (as opposed to Latin)," from Late Latin *Romanus* "Gallic Romance speaker (as opposed to a Frank)," from *Romanus* "Roman"]

Word History In the last centuries of the Roman Empire the wide variety and distribution of the peoples recognized as Roman citizens led to the gradual change of the Latin language. The developing languages, which in their early stages were local dialects of Latin, were called *romanz* (to use the Medieval French term) to distinguish them from the formal and official language. Most serious literature was still written in Latin, but in France entertaining verse tales were often written in the more popular spoken language, *romanz.* The word *romanz* came to be used for such a tale and was borrowed, in this sense, into English. Because many of these tales dealt with love, *romance* came to mean simply "a love story."

[2]**romance** *vb* **1 :** to exaggerate or invent detail or incident **2 a :** to entertain romantic thoughts or ideas **b :** to carry on a love affair with ⟨a fine place in which to *romance* their girls⟩

Ro·mance \rō-ˈmans, ˈrō-ˌ\ *adj* **:** of, relating to, or being the languages (as French, Italian, or Spanish) developed from Latin

Roman collar *n* **:** CLERICAL COLLAR

Ro·man·esque \ˌrō-mə-ˈnesk\ *adj* **:** of or relating to an architectural style developed in Italy and western Europe and characterized in its development after 1000 A.D. by the use of the round arch and vault, decorative use of arcades, and profuse ornament — **Romanesque** *n*

Ro·ma·ni·an \rú-ˈmā-nē-ən, rō-, -nyən\ *also* **Ru·ma·ni·an** *or* **Rou·ma·ni·an** \rú-\ *n* **1 :** a native or inhabitant of Romania **2 :** the Romance language of the Romanians — **Romanian** *also* **Rumanian** *or* **Roumanian** *adj*

Ro·man·ic \rō-ˈman-ik\ *adj* **:** ROMANCE — **Romanic** *n*

Roman numeral *n* **:** a numeral in a system of notation based on the ancient Roman system — see NUMBER table

Ro·ma·no \rə-ˈmän-ō, rō-\ *n* **:** a sharp hard Italian cheese [Italian, "Roman," from Latin *Romanus*]

\ə\ **about**	\aù\ **out**	\i\ **tip**	\ò\ **saw**	\ù\ **foot**
\ər\ **further**	\ch\ **chin**	\ī\ **life**	\òi\ **coin**	\y\ **yet**
\a\ **mat**	\e\ **pet**	\j\ **job**	\th\ **thin**	\yü\ **few**
\ā\ **take**	\ē\ **easy**	\ng\ **sing**	\t͟h\ **this**	\yù\ **cure**
\ä\ **cot, cart**	\g\ **go**	\ō\ **bone**	\ü\ **food**	\zh\ **vision**

Ro·mans \ˈrō-mənz\ *n* : a letter on doctrine written by Saint Paul to the Christians of Rome and included as a book in the New Testament — see BIBLE table

Ro·mansh *or* **Ro·mansch** \rō-ˈmänch\ *n* : the Raeto-Romance dialects spoken in the Grisons, Switzerland, and adjacent parts of Italy [Romansh *romonsch*]

[1]ro·man·tic \rō-ˈmant-ik\ *adj* **1** : consisting of or resembling a romance ⟨a *romantic* novel⟩ **2** : having no basis in fact ⟨*romantic* notions of a famous ancestor⟩ **3** : UNREALISTIC, IMPRACTICAL **4 a** : marked by imaginative or emotional appeal (as of what is heroic or idealized) **b** *often cap* : of, relating to, or exhibiting romanticism **c** : of or relating to music of the 19th century characterized by emotion and freedom of form **5** : marked by or being passionate love [French *romantique,* from obsolete *romant* "romance," from Medieval French *romanz*] — **ro·man·ti·cal·ly** \-i-kə-lē, -klē\ *adv*

[2]romantic *n* **1** : a romantic person, trait, or component **2** *cap* : a romantic writer, artist, or composer

ro·man·ti·cism \rō-ˈmant-ə-ˌsiz-əm\ *n* **1** *often cap* : a literary, artistic, and philosophical movement marked by emphasis on the imagination and emotions and by an exaltation of the primitive and the common man, appreciation of nature, and interest in the remote or melancholy **2** : the quality or state of being romantic — **ro·man·ti·cist** \-səst\ *n, often cap*

ro·man·ti·cize \rō-ˈmant-ə-ˌsīz\ *vb* **1** : to make romantic : present romantically **2** : to have romantic ideas — **ro·man·ti·ci·za·tion** \-ˌmant-ə-sə-ˈzā-shən\ *n*

Ro·ma·ny \ˈräm-ə-nē, ˈrō-mə-\ *n* **1** : GYPSY 1 **2** : the Indic language of the Gypsies [Romany *romani,* adj., "gypsy," from *rom* "gypsy man," from Sanskrit *ḍomba* "man of a low caste of musicians"] — **Romany** *adj*

[1]romp \ˈrämp\ *n* **1** : ROMPER 1 **2** : boisterous play : FROLIC [derived from [1]*ramp*]

[2]romp *vi* : to play in a boisterous way : FROLIC

romp·er \ˈräm-pər\ *n* **1** : one that romps **2** : a child's one-piece garment including pants and a top — usually used in plural

ron·do \ˈrän-dō\ *n, pl* **rondos** : a musical composition or movement in which the principal theme recurs several times with contrasting themes in between [Italian *rondò,* from Middle French *rondeau* "song with frequent repetitions of its two themes, rondeau"]

rood \ˈrüd\ *n* **1** : CROSS 1b, CRUCIFIX **2** : any of various units of land area; *esp* : a British unit equal to $\frac{1}{4}$ acre (about $\frac{1}{10}$ hectare) [Old English *rōd* "rod, rood"]

[1]roof \ˈrüf, ˈru̇f\ *n, pl* **roofs** \ˈrüfs, ˈru̇fs *also* ˈrüvz, ˈru̇vz\ **1** : the upper covering part of a building; *also* : ROOFING **2** : the arched upper boundary of the mouth **3** : something resembling a roof in form, position, or function [Old English *hrōf*] — **roofed** \ˈrüft, ˈru̇ft\ *adj* — **roof·less** \-ləs\ *adj* — **roof·like** \-ˌlīk\ *adj*

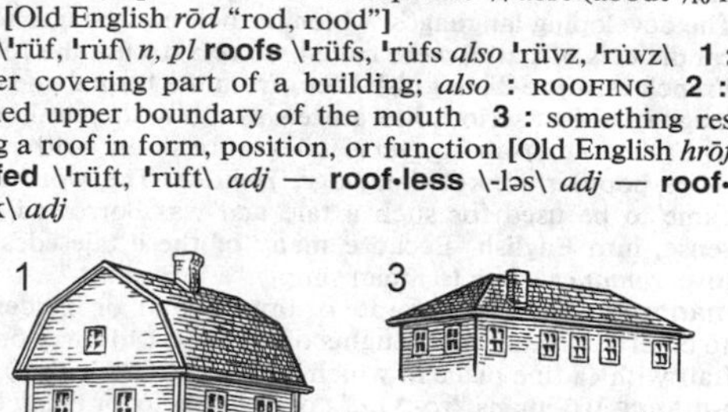

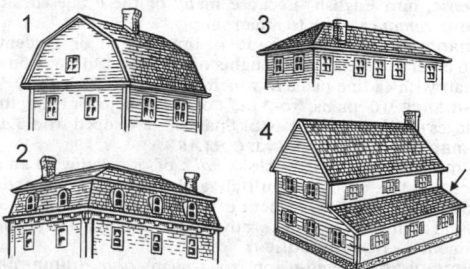

roof 1: *1* gambrel, *2* mansard, *3* hip, *4* lean-to

[2]roof *vt* : to cover with or as if with a roof — **roof·er** *n*

roof·ing *n* : material for a roof

roof·top \ˈrüf-ˌtäp, ˈru̇f-\ *n* : ROOF 1; *esp* : the outer surface of a usually flat roof ⟨sunning themselves on the *rooftop*⟩

roof·tree \-ˌtrē\ *n* : RIDGEPOLE 1

[1]rook \ˈru̇k\ *n* : a common Old World crow that nests and roosts in usually treetop colonies [Old English *hrōc*]

[2]rook *vt* : to defraud by cheating or swindling

[3]rook *n* : a chess piece that can move forward, backward, or sideways across any number of unoccupied squares — called also *castle* [Medieval French *roc,* from Arabic *rukhkh,* from Persian *rukh*]

rook·ery \ˈru̇k-ə-rē\ *n, pl* **-er·ies** **1** : the breeding place of a colony of gregarious birds or mammals (as penguins or seals); *also* : a colony of such birds or mammals **2** : a crowded dilapidated tenement or group of dwellings

rook·ie \ˈru̇k-ē\ *n* **1** : RECRUIT 1 **2** : a person who is in the first year of participation in a professional sport [perhaps alteration of *recruit*]

[1]room \ˈrüm, ˈru̇m\ *n* **1** : unoccupied area : SPACE ⟨*room* to turn the car⟩ **2 a** : a partitioned part of the inside of a building **b** : BEDROOM **c** : the people in a room **d** *pl* : LODGING 2 **3** : opportunity or occasion for something ⟨*room* for doubt⟩ [Old English *rūm*] — **roomed** \ˈrümd, ˈru̇md\ *adj*

[2]room *vb* : to provide with or occupy lodgings

room·er \ˈrü-mər, ˈru̇m-ər\ *n* : LODGER

room·ette \rü-ˈmet, ru̇m-ˈet\ *n* : a small private single room on a railroad sleeping car

room·ful \ˈrüm-ˌfu̇l, ˈru̇m-\ *n, pl* **roomfuls** \-ˌfu̇lz\ *or* **rooms·ful** \ˈrümz-ˌfu̇l, ˈru̇mz-\ : as much or as many as a room will hold; *also* : the persons or objects in a room

rooming house *n* : a house where rooms are rented to lodgers

room·mate \ˈrüm-ˌmāt, ˈru̇m-\ *n* : one of two or more persons occupying the same room

roomy \ˈrü-mē, ˈru̇m-ē\ *adj* **room·i·er; -est** : having plenty of room : SPACIOUS — **room·i·ness** *n*

[1]roost \ˈrüst\ *n* **1** : a support on which birds rest **2** : a place where winged animals and especially birds customarily roost [Old English *hrōst*]

[2]roost *vb* : to settle on or as if on a roost : PERCH

roost·er \ˈrü-stər\ *n* **1** : an adult male domestic chicken **2** : an adult male bird

[1]root \ˈrüt, ˈru̇t\ *n* **1 a** : the usually underground part of a seed plant body that functions as an organ of absorption, aeration, and food storage or as a means of anchorage and support and that differs from a stem especially in lacking nodes, buds, and leaves **b** : an undergound plant part especially when fleshy and edible **2 a** : the part of a tooth within the socket **b** : the enlarged basal part of a hair within the skin **c** : the base or end of a bodily part (as a nerve or fingernail) or the part by which it is attached **3 a** : the cause or origin of something : SOURCE **b** : an underlying support : BASIS **c** : the essential core : HEART **4 a** : a number that when multiplied by itself a given number of times equals a specified number ⟨2 is a 4th *root* of 16 because $2 \times 2 \times 2 \times 2 = 16$⟩ **b** : a solution of a polynomial equation with one unknown ⟨$(x+1)(x-1) = 0$ has the *roots* $x = -1$ and $x = 1$⟩ **5** : a word or part of a word from which other words are derived by adding a prefix or suffix **6** : the lowest tone of a chord in normal position — compare INVERSION [Old English *rōt,* from Old Norse] ***synonyms*** see ORIGIN — **root·ed** \-əd\ *adj* — **root·less** \-ləs\ *adj* — **root·like** \-ˌlīk\ *adj*

[2]root *vb* **1 a** : to form or enable to form roots **b** : to fix or become fixed by or as if by roots : take root **2** : to remove altogether often by force ⟨*root* out dissenters⟩

[3]root *vb* **1** : to turn up or dig in the earth with the snout ⟨pigs *rooting* for truffles⟩ **2** : to poke or dig about [Old English *wrōtan*]

[4]root \ˈrüt *also* ˈru̇t\ *vi* **1** : to applaud noisily : CHEER ⟨a group of students *rooting* for the football team⟩ **2** : to encourage or lend support to someone or something ⟨*rooted* for the reform candidate⟩ [perhaps from earlier *rout* "to bellow," from Old Norse *rauta*] — **root·er** *n*

root ball *n* : the compact mass of roots and soil formed by a plant especially in a container

root beer *n* : a sweetened carbonated beverage flavored with extracts of roots and herbs

root canal *n* : the space in the root of a tooth that contains soft sensitive tissue; *also* : a dental procedure to save a tooth by removing this tissue when diseased or injured and filling the space with a protective material

root cap *n* : a protective cap of parenchyma cells that covers the terminal meristem in most root tips

root cellar *n* : an underground storage area for vegetables and especially those (as carrots and turnips) with enlarged roots

root crop *n* : a crop (as turnips or sweet potatoes) grown for its enlarged roots

root hair *n* : one of the threadlike outgrowths near the tip of a rootlet that function in absorption of water and minerals

root·let \ˈrüt-lət, ˈru̇t-\ *n* : a small root

root pressure *n* : the chiefly osmotic pressure by which water rises into the stems of plants from the roots

root·stock \'rüt-ˌstäk, 'rút-\ *n* **1** : RHIZOME **2** : a stock for grafting consisting of a root or a piece of root

rooty \'rüt-ē, 'rút-\ *adj* **root·i·er; -est** : full or consisting of roots ⟨*rooty* soil⟩

[1]**rope** \'rōp\ *n* **1 a** : a large stout cord of strands (as of fiber or wire) twisted or braided together **b** : a length of material (as rope or rawhide) suitable for a use; *esp* : LARIAT **c** : a hangman's noose **2** : a row or string consisting of things united by or as if by braiding, twining, or threading ⟨a *rope* of daisies⟩ **3** *pl* : special techniques or procedures ⟨show them the *ropes*⟩ [Old English *rāp*] — **rope·like** \-ˌlīk\ *adj*

[2]**rope** *vb* **1 a** : to bind, fasten, or tie with a rope or cord **b** : to set off or divide by a rope ⟨*rope* off the street⟩ **c** : LASSO **2** : to draw as if with a rope : LURE **3** : to take the form of or twist in the manner of rope — **rop·er** *n*

rope·danc·er \'rōp-ˌdan-sər\ *n* : one that dances, walks, or performs acrobatic feats on a rope high in the air — **rope·danc·ing** \-siŋ\ *n*

rope·walk \-ˌwȯk\ *n* : a place where rope is made

rope·walk·er \-ˌwȯ-kər\ *n* : an acrobat who walks on a rope high in the air

ropy \'rō-pē\ *adj* **rop·i·er; -est** **1** : capable of being drawn into a sticky thread **2** : suggesting rope : STRINGY, SINEWY ⟨*ropy* muscles⟩ — **rop·i·ness** *n*

Roque·fort \'rōk-fərt\ *trademark* — used for a cheese made of ewes' milk and ripened in caves

ro·que·laure \ˌrō-kə-'lōr\ *n* : a knee-length cloak [French, from the Duc de *Roquelaure,* died 1738, French marshall]

ror·qual \'rȯr-kwəl, -ˌkwȯl\ *n* : any of several large baleen whales (as a humpback whale) having the skin of the throat marked with deep longitudinal furrows [French, from Norwegian *rørhval,* from Old Norse *reytharhvalr,* from *reythr* "rorqual" + *hvalr* "whale"]

Ror·schach test \ˌrȯr-ˌshäk-, ˌrōr-\ *n* : a psychological test in which a person is asked to interpret ink blots of varying designs and colors and which is used to reveal certain personality traits [Herman *Rorschach,* died 1922, Swiss psychiatrist]

ro·sar·i·an \rō-'zar-ē-ən, -'zer-\ *n* : a grower or fancier of roses

ro·sa·ry \'rōz-rē, -ə-rē\ *n, pl* **-ries** **1** : a string of beads used in counting prayers especially of the Roman Catholic rosary **2** *often cap* : a Roman Catholic devotion consisting of meditation on usually five sacred mysteries during recitation of five decades of Hail Marys of which each is preceded by the Lord's Prayer and followed by the Gloria Patri [Medieval Latin *rosarium,* from Latin, "rose garden," derived from *rosa* "rose"]

Word History *Rosary* comes from Medieval Latin *rosarium,* which in earlier Latin meant literally "a rose garden." It was used metaphorically to refer to a series of prayers, thought of perhaps as a garden of prayers and perhaps influenced by the association in Christian symbolism of the rose with the Virgin Mary and the rose garden with paradise. *Rosarium* was applied by extension to the string of beads as well as to the prayers themselves.

[1]**rose** *past of* RISE

[2]**rose** \'rōz\ *n* **1 a** : any of a genus of usually prickly shrubs with pinnate leaves and showy often fragrant flowers having five petals in the wild state but usually many petals arranged in several layers in cultivation **b** : the flower of a rose **2** : COMPASS CARD **3** : a moderate purplish red [Old English, from Latin *rosa*] — **rose·like** \-ˌlīk\ *adj*

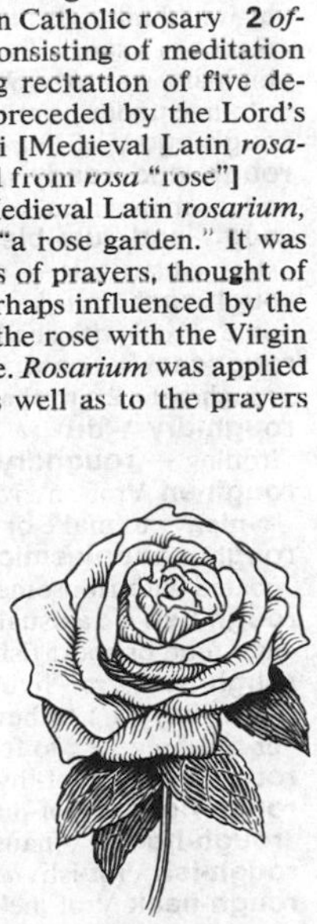
rose 1b

[3]**rose** *adj* **1** : of, relating to, resembling, or used for the rose **2** : of the color rose

ro·se·ate \'rō-zē-ət, -zē-ˌāt\ *adj* **1** : resembling a rose especially in color **2** : overly optimistic — **ro·se·ate·ly** *adv*

rose·bay \'rōz-ˌbā\ *n* : RHODODENDRON; *esp* : one of eastern North America with rosy bell-shaped flowers

rose–breast·ed grosbeak \ˌrōz-ˌbres-təd-\ *n* : a grosbeak of eastern North America that in the male is chiefly black and white with a rose red breast and in the female is grayish brown with a streaked breast

rose·bud \'rōz-ˌbəd\ *n* : the bud of a rose

rose·bush \-ˌbu̇sh\ *n* : a shrub that produces roses

rose–col·ored \'rōz-ˌkəl-ərd\ *adj* **1** : having a rose color **2** : seeing or seen in a promising light : OPTIMISTIC

rose fever *n* : hay fever occurring in the spring or early summer

rose·fish \'rōz-ˌfish\ *n* : a marine food fish of northern Atlantic coasts that is usually rosy red when adult

rose hip *n* : the ripened usually red or orange fruit of a rose

rose mallow *n* : a hibiscus with large usually rose-colored flowers

rose·mary \'rōz-ˌmer-ē\ *n* : a fragrant shrubby mint of the Mediterranean region having grayish-green needlelike leaves used as a seasoning; *also* : the leaves of rosemary [Latin *rosmarinus,* from *ros* "dew" + *marinus* "of the sea"]

rose of Shar·on \-'shar-ən, -'sher-\ : a commonly cultivated Asian small shrub or tree having showy rose, purple, or white flowers [Plain of *Sharon,* Palestine]

ro·se·o·la \ˌrō-zē-'ō-lə, rō-'zē-ə-lə\ *n* : a spotty rose-colored eruption or a condition marked by this [New Latin, from Latin *roseus* "rosy," from *rosa* "rose"] — **ro·se·o·lar** \-lər\ *adj*

Ro·set·ta stone \rō-'zet-ə-\ *n* : a stone found in 1799 that bears an inscription in hieroglyphics, demotic characters, and Greek and is known for giving the first clue in deciphering Egyptian hieroglyphics [*Rosetta,* Egypt]

ro·sette \rō-'zet\ *n* **1** : an ornament (as of cloth or paper) resembling a rose **2** : a cluster of leaves developed on a plant in crowded whorls either basally (as in a dandelion) or at the apex (as in palms)

rose water *n* : a watery solution of the fragrant constituents of the rose used as a perfume

rose·wood \'rōz-ˌwu̇d\ *n* **1** : any of various tropical trees with dark red or purplish wood streaked and variegated with black that is used especially for making furniture and musical instruments **2** : the wood of a rosewood

Rosh Ha·sha·nah \ˌrōsh-hə-'shō-nə, ˌrōsh-ə-, ˌräsh-, -'shän-ə\ *n* : the Jewish New Year observed as a religious holiday in September or October [Hebrew *rōsh hashshānāh,* literally, "beginning of the year"]

[1]**ros·in** \'räz-n, 'rȯz-\ *n* : a translucent amber-colored to almost black brittle resin that is obtained by chemical means from pine trees or from tall oil and is used in making varnish and on violin bows [Medieval French *reisine, roisine* "resin"] — **ros·in·ous** \'räz-n-əs, 'räz-nəs, 'rȯz-\ *adj*

[2]**rosin** *vt* : to rub (as the bow of a violin) with rosin

ros·ter \'räs-tər\ *n* : a list usually of personnel; *esp* : one assigning duties [Dutch *rooster,* literally, "gridiron," from the parallel lines]

ros·trum \'räs-trəm\ *n, pl* **ros·tra** \-trə\ *or* **rostrums** **1** : a stage or platform for public speaking **2** : a bodily part or process (as a snout or mouthpart) suggesting a bird's bill [Latin, "beak, ship's beak," from *rodere* "to gnaw"; sense 1 from Latin *Rostra,* speakers' platform in the Roman Forum, from pl. of *rostrum* "beak"] — **ros·tral** \-trəl\ *adj* — **ros·trate** \-ˌtrāt\ *adj*

Word History The Latin word *rostrum,* whose primary meaning is "beak," was derived from the verb *rodere,* "to gnaw." Eventually *rostrum* came to be used to refer to the prow or beak of a ship. In 338 B.C. the beaks of ships captured from the people of Antium (now called Anzio) were used to decorate the orators' platform in the Roman Forum. From this time on, this platform was called *Rostra,* the plural form of *rostrum.* Later *rostra* was used to refer to any platform from which a speaker addressed an assembly. In English the singular form *rostrum* is still so used.

rosy \'rō-zē\ *adj* **ros·i·er; -est** **1 a** : of the color rose **b** : having a healthy pink complexion **c** : marked by blushes **2** : characterized by or tending to promote optimism ⟨*rosy* prospects⟩ — **ros·i·ly** \-zə-lē\ *adv* — **ros·i·ness** \-zē-nəs\ *n*

[1]**rot** \'rät\ *vb* **rot·ted; rot·ting** **1 a** : to undergo decomposition from the action of bacteria or fungi **b** : to become unsound or weak (as from use or chemical action) **2 a** : to go to ruin : DETERIORATE **b** : to become morally corrupt : DEGENERATE **3** : to cause to decompose or deteriorate with or as if with rot [Old English *rotian*] ***synonyms*** see DECAY

[2]**rot** *n* **1 a** : the process of rotting : the state of being rotten **b** : something rotten or rotting **2** : a disease of plants or animals

\ə\ **abut**	\au̇\ **out**	\i\ **tip**	\ȯ\ **saw**	\u̇\ **foot**
\ər\ **further**	\ch\ **chin**	\ī\ **life**	\ȯi\ **coin**	\y\ **yet**
\a\ **mat**	\e\ **pet**	\j\ **job**	\th\ **thin**	\yü\ **few**
\ā\ **take**	\ē\ **easy**	\ŋ\ **sing**	\th\ **this**	\yu̇\ **cure**
\ä\ **cot, cart**	\g\ **go**	\ō\ **bone**	\ü\ **food**	\zh\ **vision**

marked by the decay of tissue; *also* : an area of decayed tissue **3** : NONSENSE 1 — often used interjectionally

Ro·ta \ˈrōt-ə\ *n* : a tribunal of the papal curia exercising jurisdiction especially in matrimonial cases appealed from diocesan courts [Medieval Latin, from Latin, "wheel"]

Ro·tar·i·an \rō-ˈter-ē-ən\ *n* : a member of one of the major service clubs [*Rotary (club)*]

1**ro·ta·ry** \ˈrōt-ə-rē\ *adj* **1 a** : turning on an axis like a wheel ⟨a *rotary* blade⟩ **b** : taking place about an axis ⟨*rotary* motion⟩ **2** : having an important part that turns on an axis ⟨a *rotary* cutter⟩ **3** : characterized by rotation [Medieval Latin *rotarius,* from Latin *rota* "wheel"]

2**rotary** *n, pl* **-ries** **1** : a rotary machine **2** : a road junction formed around a central circle about which traffic moves in one direction only

rotary engine *n* **1** : any of various engines (as a turbine) in which power is applied to vanes or similar parts that move in a circular path **2** : a radial engine in which the cylinders revolve about a stationary crankshaft

rotary–wing aircraft *n* : an aircraft supported in flight partially or wholly by rotating airfoils

ro·tate \ˈrō-ˌtāt\ *vb* **1** : to turn or cause to turn about an axis or a center : REVOLVE ⟨the earth *rotates*⟩ **2 a** : to do or cause to do something in turn : ALTERNATE ⟨*rotate* on the night shift⟩ **b** : to pass in a series ⟨the seasons *rotate*⟩ **3** : to cause to grow in succession on the same land ⟨*rotate* alfalfa and corn⟩ [Latin *rotare,* from *rota* "wheel"] — **ro·tat·able** \ˈrō-ˌtāt-ə-bəl *also* rō-ˈ\ *adj* — **ro·tat·or** \ˈrō-ˌtāt-ər *also* rō-ˈ\ *n*

ro·ta·tion \rō-ˈtā-shən\ *n* **1 a** : the act of rotating especially on or as if on an axis **b** : one complete turn **2 a** : return or succession in a recurring series ⟨*rotation* of the seasons⟩ **b** : CROP ROTATION — **ro·ta·tion·al** \-shnəl, -shən-l\ *adj* — **in rotation** : one after another in an orderly sequence

ro·ta·to·ry \ˈrōt-ə-ˌtōr-ē, -ˌtȯr-\ *adj* **1** : of, relating to, or producing rotation **2** : occurring in rotation

1**rote** \ˈrōt\ *n* **1** : the use of memory usually with little intelligence ⟨learn by *rote*⟩ **2** : routine or repetition carried out mechanically or without understanding [Middle English]

2**rote** *adj* : learned or memorized by rote

ro·te·none \ˈrōt-n-ˌōn\ *n* : a crystalline insecticide obtained from the roots of several tropical plants (as derris) that is of low toxicity to warm-blooded animals and is used especially in home gardens [Japanese *roten* "derris plant"]

ro·ti·fer \ˈrōt-ə-fər\ *n* : any of a class (Rotifera) of minute aquatic invertebrates having at one end a disk with circles of cilia which in motion look like revolving wheels [derived from Latin *rota* "wheel" + *ferre* "to bear, carry"]

rotifer

ro·tis·ser·ie \rō-ˈtis-rē, -ə-rē\ *n* : an appliance fitted with a spit on which food is rotated before or over a source of heat [French *rôtisserie* "restaurant," from Middle French *rostisserie,* from *rostir* "to roast"]

ro·to \ˈrōt-ō\ *n, pl* **rotos** : ROTOGRAVURE

ro·to·gra·vure \ˌrōt-ə-grə-ˈvyu̇r\ *n* **1** : PHOTOGRAVURE **2** : a section of a newspaper devoted to rotogravure pictures [German *Rotogravur,* blend of Latin *rota* "wheel" and German *Photogravur* "photogravure"]

ro·tor \ˈrōt-ər\ *n* **1** : a part that revolves in a stationary part (as in an electrical machine) **2** : a complete system of rotating blades that supplies the force supporting an aircraft in flight ⟨the *rotor* of a helicopter⟩ [contraction of *rotator*]

ro·to·till·er \ˈrōt-ə-ˌtil-ər\ *n* : a landscaping machine with rotating blades that lift and turn over soil [from *Rototiller,* a trademark]

rot·ten \ˈrät-n\ *adj* **1** : having rotted : PUTRID ⟨*rotten* fruit⟩ **2** : morally corrupt **3** : extremely unpleasant or inferior ⟨*rotten* weather⟩ [Old Norse *rotinn*] — **rot·ten·ly** *adv* — **rot·ten·ness** \-n-nəs\ *n*

rot·ten·stone \ˈrät-n-ˌstōn\ *n* : a decomposed siliceous limestone used for polishing

rot·ter \ˈrät-ər\ *n* : a thoroughly objectionable person

ro·tund \rō-ˈtənd, ˈrō-ˌ\ *adj* **1** : marked by roundness **2** : FULL, SONOROUS ⟨*rotund* voices⟩ **3** : PLUMP, CHUBBY [Latin *rotundus*] — **ro·tun·di·ty** \rō-ˈtən-dət-ē\ *n* — **ro·tund·ly** \rō-ˈtən-dlē, ˈrō-ˌ\ *adv* — **ro·tund·ness** \rō-ˈtənd-nəs, -ˈtən-, ˈrō-ˌ\ *n*

ro·tun·da \rō-ˈtən-də\ *or* **ro·ton·da** \-ˈtän-\ *n* **1** : a round building; *esp* : one covered by a dome **2 a** : a large round room **b** : a large central area (as in a hotel) [Italian *rotonda,* from Latin *rotundus* "round"]

roué \rü-ˈā\ *n* : a usually male libertine [French, literally, "broken on the wheel," from *rouer* "to break on the wheel," from Medieval Latin *rotare,* from Latin, "to rotate"; from the feeling that such a person deserves this punishment]

1**rouge** \ˈrüzh, *especially Southern* ˈrüj\ *n* **1** : any of various cosmetics to color the cheeks or lips red **2** : a red powder consisting essentially of ferric oxide used in polishing (as gems) and as a pigment [French, from *rouge* "red," from Latin *rubeus* "reddish"]

2**rouge** *vb* **1** : to apply rouge to **2** : to use rouge

1**rough** \ˈrəf\ *adj* **1 a** : having an uneven surface : not smooth **b** : covered with or made up of coarse and often shaggy hair or bristles ⟨a *rough*-coated terrier⟩ **c** : difficult to travel over or penetrate : WILD ⟨*rough* country⟩ **2 a** : characterized by harshness, violence, or force **b** : DIFFICULT, TRYING ⟨a *rough* day at the office⟩ **3** : coarse or rugged in character or appearance: as **a** : harsh to the ear **b** : crude in style or expression **c** : marked by a lack of refinement or grace : UNCOUTH **4** : marked by incompleteness or inexactness ⟨a *rough* draft⟩ ⟨*rough* estimates⟩ [Old English *rūh*] — **rough·ly** *adv* — **rough·ness** *n*

synonyms ROUGH, HARSH, RUGGED mean not smooth or even. ROUGH implies having points, bristles, ridges, or projections on the surface ⟨*rough* wood⟩. HARSH implies having a surface or texture that is unpleasant to the touch ⟨*harsh* sand⟩. RUGGED implies irregularity or unevenness of land surface and connotes difficulty of travel ⟨*rugged* mountain roads⟩.

2**rough** *n* **1** : uneven ground covered with high grass, brush, and stones; *esp* : such ground bordering a golf fairway **2** : the disagreeable side or aspect ⟨take the *rough* with the smooth⟩ **3** : something in a crude, unfinished, or preliminary state; *also* : such a state ⟨diamonds in the *rough*⟩ **c** : a hasty preliminary drawing or layout **4** : ROWDY, TOUGH ⟨a gang of *roughs*⟩

3**rough** *adv* : in a rough manner

4**rough** *vt* **1** : ROUGHEN **2 a** : MANHANDLE, BEAT ⟨*roughed* up by hoodlums⟩ **b** : to subject to unnecessary and intentional violence in a sport **3** : to shape, make, or dress in a rough or preliminary way ⟨*rough* out a plan⟩ — **rough·er** *n* — **rough it** : to live under primitive conditions

rough·age \ˈrəf-ij\ *n* : FIBER 1e

rough–and–ready \ˌrəf-ən-ˈred-ē\ *adj* : crude in nature, method, or manner but effective in action or use

rough–and–tum·ble \-ən-ˈtəm-bəl\ *n* : a rough disorderly unrestrained struggle — **rough–and–tumble** *adj*

1**rough·cast** \ˈrəf-ˌkast\ *n* **1** : a rough model **2** : a plaster of lime mixed with shells or pebbles used for covering buildings

2**roughcast** *vt* **-cast; -cast·ing** **1** : to plaster (as a wall) with roughcast **2** : to shape or form roughly

rough·dry \-ˈdrī\ *vt* : to dry (laundry) without smoothing or ironing — **roughdry** *adj*

rough·en \ˈrəf-ən\ *vb* **rough·ened; rough·en·ing** \ˈrəf-ning, -ə-ning\ : to make or become rough

rough endoplasmic reticulum *n* : endoplasmic reticulum coated with ribosomes

rough fish *n* : a usually freshwater fish considered undersirable as a food or sport fish

rough·hew \ˈrəf-ˈhyü\ *vt* **-hewed; -hewed** *or* **-hewn** \-ˈhyün\; **-hew·ing** **1** : to hew (as timber) coarsely without smoothing or finishing **2** : to form crudely

rough–hewn \ˈrəf-ˈhyün\ *adj* : lacking polish or social graces

rough·house \ˈrəf-ˌhau̇s\ *n* : violence or rough rowdy play — **rough·house** \-ˌhau̇s, -ˌhau̇z\ *vb* — **rough·house** \-ˌhau̇s\ *adj*

rough·ish \ˈrəf-ish\ *adj* : somewhat rough

rough·neck \ˈrəf-ˌnek\ *n* **1** : a rough person; *esp* : ROWDY, TOUGH **2** : a worker on an oil-drilling crew

Rough Rid·er *n* : a member of the 1st United States Volunteer Cavalry regiment in the Spanish-American War commanded by Theodore Roosevelt

1**rough·shod** \-ˈshäd\ *adj* **1** : shod with calked shoes **2** : marked by force without justice or consideration

2**roughshod** *adv* : in a roughshod manner

rou·lade \rü-ˈläd\ *n* : a slice of meat rolled with or without a stuffing [French, from *rouler* "to roll"]

1**rou·lette** \rü-ˈlet\ *n* **1** : a gambling game in which players bet on which compartment of a revolving wheel a small ball will come to rest in **2 a :** a toothed wheel or disk (as for producing rows of dots on engraved plates or for making short consecutive incisions in paper to facilitate subsequent division) **b :** tiny slits in a sheet of stamps made by a roulette [French, literally, "small wheel," from Medieval French *roelete,* from *roele* "wheel," from Late Latin *rotella* "small wheel," from Latin *rota* "wheel"]

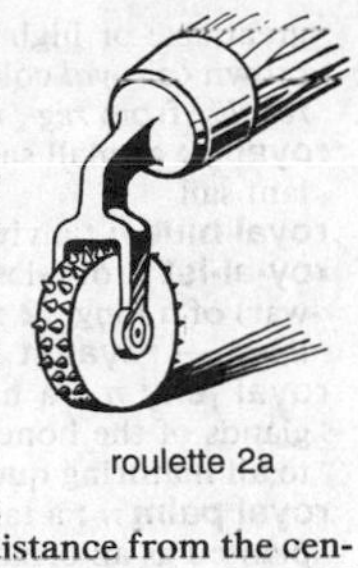
roulette 2a

²roulette *vt* **:** to make roulettes in

Roumanian *variant of* ROMANIAN

¹round \ˈrau̇nd\ *adj* **1 a :** having every part of the surface or circumference the same distance from the center **b :** CYLINDRICAL **c :** having a curved outline **2 :** well fleshed **:** PLUMP **3 a :** COMPLETE, FULL ⟨a *round* dozen⟩ **b :** approximately correct; *esp* **:** exact only to a specific decimal place ⟨use the *round* number 1400 for the exact figure 1411⟩ **c :** LARGE ⟨a good *round* sum⟩ **4 a :** BLUNT, OUTSPOKEN **b :** not restrained or toned down ⟨a *round* oath⟩ **5 :** moving in or forming a circle **6 a :** brought to completion or perfection **:** FINISHED **b :** presented with lifelike fullness or vividness **7 a :** having full or unimpeded resonance or tone **b :** pronounced with rounded lips **8 :** of or relating to handwriting predominantly curved rather than angular [Medieval French *rund, reund,* from Latin *rotundus*] — **round·ly** *adv* — **round·ness** \ˈrau̇nd-nəs, ˈrau̇n-\ *n*

²round *adv* **:** ¹AROUND

³round \ˈrau̇nd\ *n* **1 a :** something (as a circle, globe, or ring) that is round **b :** a knot or circle of people or things **2 :** ROUND DANCE 1 **3 :** a song in which three or four voices follow each other around and sing the same melody and words **4 a :** a rung of a ladder or a chair **b :** a rounded molding **5 a :** a circling path or course **b :** motion in a circle or a curving path **6 a :** a route or circuit habitually covered ⟨a watchman's *rounds*⟩ **b :** a series of calls or stops regularly made ⟨a doctor on her *rounds* in the hospital⟩ **7 :** a drink apiece served at one time to each person in a group **8 :** a series of recurring routine or repetitive actions or events ⟨the newest *round* of talks⟩ **9 :** a period of time that recurs in a fixed pattern ⟨the daily *round*⟩ **10 a :** one shot fired by a weapon or by each man in a military unit **b :** a unit of ammunition consisting of the parts necessary to fire one shot **11 :** a unit of action in a contest or game that occupies a stated period, covers a prescribed distance, includes a specified number of plays, or gives each player one turn **12 :** a demonstrative outpouring or burst ⟨a *round* of applause⟩ **13 :** a cut of beef especially between the rump and the lower leg **14 :** a rounded or curved part — **in the round 1 :** in full sculptured form unattached to a background **:** FREESTANDING **2 :** with a comprehensive view or representation **3 :** with a center stage surrounded by an audience on all sides ⟨theater *in the round*⟩ — **out of round :** not perfectly or adequately round or circular

⁴round \ˈrau̇nd\ *vb* **1 a :** to make round **b :** to become round or plump **c :** to pronounce (a sound) with rounding of the lips **2 a :** to go around **b :** to pass part of the way around **3 :** to form a circle around **4 a :** to bring to completion ⟨*round* out a career⟩ **b :** to become complete **c :** to bring to perfection of style **:** POLISH 3 **5 :** to express as a round number; *esp* **:** to drop any digits to the right of a given decimal place and increase the last remaining digit by 1 if the first dropped digit is 5 or greater ⟨4.57268 *rounded* off to three decimal places is 4.573⟩ **6 :** to follow a winding course ⟨horses *rounding* into the homestretch⟩ — **round on :** to turn against

⁵round \rau̇nd, ˈrau̇nd\ *prep* **:** ²AROUND

¹round·about \ˈrau̇n-də-ˌbau̇t\ *n* **1 :** an indirect route **:** DETOUR **2** *British* **a :** MERRY-GO-ROUND **b :** ROTARY 2

²round·about \ˌrau̇n-də-ˈbau̇t\ *adj* **:** not direct

round clam *n* **:** QUAHOG

round dance *n* **1 :** a folk dance in which dancers form a ring and move in a prescribed direction **2 :** a ballroom dance in which couples progress around the room **3 :** a series of movements performed by a bee to indicate that a source of food is nearby

round·ed \ˈrau̇n-dəd\ *adj* **1 :** curving or round in shape **2 :** fully developed — **round·ed·ness** *n*

roun·del \ˈrau̇n-dl\ *n* **:** a round figure or object; *esp* **:** a circular panel, window, or niche [Medieval French *rondel, roundel,* from *rund* "round"]

roun·de·lay \ˈrau̇n-də-ˌlā\ *n* **1 :** a simple song with a refrain **2 :** a poem with a refrain recurring frequently or at fixed intervals [Middle French *rondelet,* literally, "small circle," from *rondel* "small circle, roundel"]

round·er \ˈrau̇n-dər\ *n* **1 :** a person of loose morals or conduct **2** *pl* **:** an English game played with ball and bat somewhat resembling baseball **3 a :** one that rounds by hand or by machine **b :** a tool for making an edge or a surface round

Round·head \ˈrau̇nd-ˌhed\ *n* **:** a Puritan or member of the parliamentary party in England at the time of Charles I and Oliver Cromwell [from the Puritans' cutting their hair short in contrast to the Cavaliers]

round·head·ed \-ˈhed-əd\ *adj* **:** having a round head

round·house \ˈrau̇nd-ˌhau̇s\ *n* **1 :** a circular building for housing and repairing locomotives **2 :** a cabin or apartment on the after part of a quarterdeck **3 :** a blow in boxing delivered with a wide swing **4 :** a slow wide curve in baseball

round·ish \ˈrau̇n-dish\ *adj* **:** somewhat round

round robin *n* **1 a :** a written petition or protest with signatures in a circle so as not to indicate who signed first **b :** a letter sent in turn to the members of a group each of whom signs and forwards it sometimes after adding comment **2 :** a tournament in which every contestant meets every other contestant in turn **3 :** SERIES 1, ROUND [from the name *Robin*]

round–shoul·dered \ˈrau̇nd-ˈshōl-dərd, ˈrau̇n-\ *adj* **:** having the shoulders stooping or rounded

round table *n* **1** *cap R&T* **a :** a large circular table for King Arthur and his knights **b :** the knights of King Arthur **2 :** a meeting of a group of persons for discussion; *also* **:** the persons meeting

round–the–clock *adj* **:** being in effect, continuing, or lasting 24 hours a day

round trip *n* **:** a trip to a place and back usually over the same route

round·up \ˈrau̇n-ˌdəp\ *n* **1 :** the gathering together of animals (as cattle) on the range by riding around them and driving them in **2 :** a gathering together of scattered persons or things **3 :** SUMMARY, RÉSUMÉ ⟨the 6 o'clock news *roundup*⟩

round up \rau̇n-ˈdəp, ˈrau̇n-\ *vt* **1 :** to collect (as cattle) by means of a roundup **2 :** to gather in or bring together

round·worm \ˈrau̇n-ˌdwərm\ *n* **:** a nematode worm (as a hookworm or a trichina); *also* **:** a related round-bodied unsegmented worm as distinguished from a flatworm

¹rouse \ˈrau̇z\ *vb* **1 :** to arouse or become aroused from or as if from sleep **:** AWAKEN **2 :** to become stirred **3 :** to stir up **:** EXCITE [Middle English *rousen* "to shake the feathers"]

²rouse *n* **:** an act or instance of rousing; *esp* **:** an excited stir

³rouse *n, archaic* **:** CAROUSE

rous·ing \ˈrau̇-ziŋ\ *adj* **1 a :** EXCITING ⟨played a *rousing* march⟩ **b :** BRISK, LIVELY ⟨a *rousing* cheer⟩ **2 :** EXCEPTIONAL 2

roust·about \ˈrau̇-stə-ˌbau̇t\ *n* **:** one who does heavy or unskilled labor (as a deckhand or longshoreman, a laborer in an oil field, or a circus worker who erects and dismantles tents) [from *roust* "to rouse," alteration of *rouse*]

¹rout \ˈrau̇t\ *n* **1 :** a crowd of people; *esp* **:** RABBLE **2 :** DISTURBANCE 3 **3 :** a fashionable gathering **:** RECEPTION [Medieval French *route* "band, company of soldiers, crowd," derived from Latin *ruptus,* past participle of *rumpere* "to break"]

²rout *vb* **1 :** to poke around with the snout **:** ³ROOT 1 **2 :** to search haphazardly **:** RUMMAGE **3 :** to find or bring to light especially with difficulty **:** DISCOVER **4 :** to gouge out or make a furrow in (as wood or metal) **5 a :** to expel by force **:** EJECT ⟨*routed* out of their homes⟩ **b :** to cause to emerge especially from bed **:** ROUSE [alteration of ³*root*]

³rout *n* **1 :** a state of wild confusion and disorderly retreat **2 a :** a disastrous defeat **b :** an act or instance of routing [Middle French *route* "defeat," perhaps from *mettre en route* "to set going, put into motion"]

⁴rout *vt* **1 :** to disorganize or defeat completely **2 :** to drive out **:** DISPEL

¹route \ˈrüt, ˈrau̇t\ *n* **1 a :** a traveled way **:** HIGHWAY **b :** a means of access **:** CHANNEL **2 :** an established, selected, or as-

\ə\ **abut**	\au̇\ **out**	\i\ **tip**	\ȯ\ **saw**	\u̇\ **foot**
\ər\ **further**	\ch\ **chin**	\ī\ **life**	\ȯi\ **coin**	\y\ **yet**
\a\ **mat**	\e\ **pet**	\j\ **job**	\th\ **thin**	\yü\ **few**
\ā\ **take**	\ē\ **easy**	\ŋ\ **sing**	\th\ **this**	\yu̇\ **cure**
\ä\ **cot, cart**	\g\ **go**	\ō\ **bone**	\ü\ **food**	\zh\ **vision**

signed course of travel [Medieval French *rute,* derived from Latin *ruptus,* past participle of *rumpere* "to break"]

[2]route *vt* **1 :** to send, forward, or transport by a certain route ⟨*route* traffic around the city⟩ **2 :** to arrange and direct the order and carrying out of (as a series of operations in a factory)

[1]rout·er \ˈrau̇t-ər\ *n* **:** a machine with a revolving vertical spindle for milling out the surface of wood or metal

[2]rout·er \ˈrüt-ər, ˈrau̇t-\ *n* **:** one that routes; *esp* **:** a device that sends data from one place to another within a computer network or between computer networks

[1]rou·tine \rü-ˈtēn\ *n* **1 :** a regular or customary course of procedure **2 :** an often repeated speech **3 :** a fixed piece of entertainment often repeated **:** ACT; *esp* **:** a theatrical number **4 :** a sequence of computer instructions for performing a particular task [French, from *route* "traveled way"]

[2]routine *adj* **1 :** being commonplace or uninspired **2 :** done or happening regularly ⟨*routine* inspection⟩ — **rou·tine·ly** *adv*

[1]rove \ˈrōv\ *vb* **1 :** to move aimlessly **:** ROAM ⟨*rove* about the country⟩ **2 :** to wander through or over ⟨*rove* the seas⟩ [Middle English *roven* "to shoot arrows at marks chosen at random"]

[2]rove *past of* REEVE

rove beetle *n* **:** any of numerous often predatory active beetles with a long body and very short elytra [perhaps from [1]*rove*]

[1]ro·ver \ˈrō-vər\ *n* **:** PIRATE [Dutch, from *roven* "to rob"]

[2]rov·er \ˈrō-vər\ *n* **1 :** one that roves **:** WANDERER, ROAMER **2 :** a vehicle for exploring the surface of an extraterrestrial body (as the moon or Mars)

rov·ing \ˈrō-ving\ *n* **:** a twisted roll or strand of fibers

[1]row \ˈrō\ *vb* **1 :** to propel a boat by means of oars **2 :** to move by or as if by the propulsion of oars **3 :** to be equipped with (a specified number of oars) **4 :** to engage in rowing **5 :** to transport in or as if in a boat propelled by oars [Old English *rōwan*] — **row·er** \ˈrō-ər, ˈrōr\ *n*

[2]row *n* **:** an act or instance of rowing

[3]row *n* **1 :** a group forming a more or less straight line ⟨a *row* of bottles⟩ ⟨corn planted in *rows*⟩ **2 :** an urban street or district [Middle English *rawe*]

[4]row \ˈrau̇\ *n* **:** a noisy disturbance or quarrel **:** BRAWL [origin unknown]

[5]row \ˈrau̇\ *vi* **:** to engage in a row **:** FIGHT, QUARREL

row·an \ˈrau̇-ən, ˈrō-ən\ *n* **1 :** a mountain ash of Eurasia or one of the eastern U.S. and Canada with flat clusters of white flowers followed by small red fruits **2** *or* **row·an·ber·ry** \-ˌber-ē\ **:** the fruit of a rowan [of Scandinavian origin]

rowan

row·boat \ˈrō-ˌbōt\ *n* **:** a boat designed to be rowed

[1]row·dy \ˈrau̇d-ē\ *adj* **row·di·er; -est :** coarse or boisterous in behavior **:** ROUGH [perhaps from [4]*row*] — **row·di·ness** *n* — **row·dy·ish** \-ē-ish\ *adj* — **row·dy·ism** \-ē-ˌiz-əm\ *n*

[2]rowdy *n, pl* **rowdies :** a rowdy person **:** TOUGH

[1]row·el \ˈrau̇-əl, ˈrau̇l\ *n* **:** a revolving disk at the end of a spur with sharp points for goading a horse [Medieval French *roele* "small wheel," from Late Latin *rotella,* from Latin *rota* "wheel"]

[2]rowel *vt* **-eled** *or* **-elled; -el·ing** *or* **-el·ling :** to goad with or as if with a rowel **:** SPUR

row·en \ˈrau̇-ən\ *n* **1 :** a stubble field left unplowed for late grazing **2 :** AFTERMATH 1 — often used in plural [Middle English *rowein,* from Medieval French *regain, rewain,* from *re-* + *gain, wain* "arable land, produce, profit," from *gaaigner* "to till, earn, gain," of Germanic origin]

row house \ˈrō-\ *n* **:** one of a series of houses connected by common sidewalls

row·ing \ˈrō-ing\ *n* **:** the sport of racing long narrow boats propelled by oars

rowing boat *n, chiefly British* **:** ROWBOAT

row·lock \ˈräl-ək, ˈrəl-; ˈrō-ˌläk\ *n, chiefly British* **:** OARLOCK

[1]roy·al \ˈrȯi-əl, ˈrȯil\ *adj* **1 a :** of kingly ancestry **b :** of, relating to, or subject to the crown **c :** being in the crown's service ⟨*Royal* Navy⟩ **2 a :** suitable for royalty **:** MAGNIFICENT ⟨a *royal* welcome⟩ **b :** EASY 1 ⟨no *royal* road to victory⟩ **3 a :** of great size or high quality **b :** established or chartered by the crown ⟨a *royal* colony⟩ [Medieval French *real, roial,* from Latin *regalis,* from *reg-, rex* "king"] — **roy·al·ly** \ˈrȯi-ə-lē\ *adv*

[2]royal *n* **:** a small sail on the mast immediately above the topgallant sail

royal blue *n* **:** a vivid purplish blue

roy·al·ist \ˈrȯi-ə-ləst\ *n* **1 :** a supporter (as during a time of civil war) of a king **2 :** a believer in monarchy as a form of government — **royalist** *adj*

royal jelly *n* **:** a highly nutritious secretion of the pharyngeal glands of the honeybee that is fed to all very young larvae and to all maturing queen bees

royal palm *n* **:** a tall graceful palm native to Cuba that is widely planted as an ornamental tree in tropical regions

royal poinciana *n* **:** a showy tree of Madagascar widely planted for its immense clusters of scarlet and orange flowers

roy·al·ty \ˈrȯi-əl-tē, ˈrȯil-tē\ *n, pl* **-ties 1 a :** royal standing or power **b :** a right or privilege of a sovereign (as a percentage of gold or silver taken from mines) **2 :** regal character or bearing **:** NOBILITY **3 a :** persons of royal lineage **b :** a person of royal rank **c :** a privileged class **4 a :** a share of the product or profit reserved by the grantor especially of an oil or mining lease **b :** a payment made to the owner of a patent or copyright for the use of it

RPV \ˌär-ˌpē-ˈvē\ *n* **:** an unmanned aircraft flown by remote control and used especially for reconnaissance [*r*emotely *p*iloted *v*ehicle]

-rrhea *also* **-rrhoea** *n combining form* **:** flow **:** discharge ⟨*seborrhea*⟩ [Greek *-rrhoia,* from *rhoia,* from *rhein* "to flow"]

rRNA \ˌär-ˌär-ˌen-ˈā\ *n* **:** RIBOSOMAL RNA

RSS \ˈär-ˌes-ˈes\ *n* **:** a computer document format that enables updates to Web sites to be easily distributed [*R*DF (Resource Description Framework) *S*ite *S*ummary]

[1]rub \ˈrəb\ *vb* **rubbed; rub·bing 1 a :** to move or make move along the surface of a body with pressure **b** (1) **:** to fret or chafe with friction ⟨the new shoes *rubbed*⟩ (2) **:** to cause or cause to feel discontent, irritation, or anger ⟨*rubbed* me the wrong way⟩ **2 a :** to apply or spread by rubbing ⟨*rub* ointment on your chest⟩ **b :** to treat in some way by rubbing ⟨*rub* the surface clean⟩ [Middle English *rubben*]

[2]rub *n* **1 a :** DIFFICULTY ⟨that's the *rub*⟩ **b :** something (as sharp criticism) that grates the feelings **c :** something that mars or upsets serenity **2 :** the application of friction with pressure ⟨an alcohol *rub*⟩

ru·ba·to \rü-ˈbät-ō\ *n, pl* **-tos :** fluctuation of speed within a musical phrase typically against a rhythmically steady accompaniment [Italian, literally, "robbed"]

[1]rub·ber \ˈrəb-ər\ *n* **1 a :** one that rubs **b :** an instrument or object (as a rubber eraser) used in rubbing, polishing, scraping, or cleaning **c :** something that prevents rubbing or chafing **2 a :** an elastic substance obtained by coagulating the milky juice of various tropical plants **b :** any of various synthetic rubber-like substances **c :** natural or synthetic rubber modified by chemical treatment to increase its useful properties (as toughness and resistance to wear) and used in tires, electrical insulation, and waterproof materials **3 :** something made of or resembling rubber: as **a :** a rubber overshoe **b :** a rectangular slab of white rubber in the middle of a baseball infield from which a pitcher pitches **4 :** CONDOM [sense 2 from its use in erasers] — **rub·ber-like** \-ˌlīk\ *adj* — **rub·bery** \ˈrəb-rē, -ə-rē\ *adj*

[2]rubber *n* **1 :** a contest that consists of an odd number of games and is won by the side that takes a majority (as two out of three) **2 :** an extra game played to decide the winner of a tie [origin unknown]

rubber band *n* **:** a continuous band of rubber used in various ways (as to hold a bunch of things together)

rub·ber·ized \ˈrəb-ə-ˌrīzd\ *adj* **:** coated or saturated with rubber or a rubber preparation ⟨*rubberized* raincoats⟩

rub·ber·neck \ˈrəb-ər-ˌnek\ *n* **1 :** an inquisitive person **2 :** TOURIST; *esp* **:** one on a guided tour — **rubberneck** *vi*

rubber plant *n* **:** a plant that produces rubber; *esp* **:** a tall tropical Asian tree related to the mulberries that is often dwarfed in pots as a houseplant

rub·ber–stamp \ˌrəb-ər-ˈstamp\ *vt* **:** to approve, endorse, or dispose of as a matter of routine usually without exercise of judgment or at the command of another

rubber stamp *n* **1 :** a stamp of rubber for making imprints **2 a :** a person who echoes or imitates others **b :** a person or body given to rubber-stamping

rubber tree *n* **:** a tree that produces rubber; *esp* **:** a South American tree that is cultivated in plantations as a commercial source of rubber

rubber tree

rub•bing \ˈrəb-iŋ\ *n* **:** an image of a raised, indented, or textured surface obtained by placing paper over it and rubbing the paper with colored material

rubbing alcohol *n* **:** a watery solution of an alcohol used externally especially to soothe or refresh

rub•bish \ˈrəb-ish\ *n* **:** useless waste or rejected matter **:** TRASH [Middle English *robous*] — **rub•bishy** \ˈrəb-i-shē\ *adj*

rub•ble \ˈrəb-əl\ *n* **1 :** rough stone as it comes from the quarry **2 :** water-worn or rough broken stones or bricks used in coarse masonry or in filling courses of walls **3 :** a mass of rough irregular pieces ⟨a town bombed to *rubble*⟩ [Middle English *robyl*]

rub•down \ˈrəb-ˌdau̇n\ *n* **:** a brisk rubbing of the body (as to relax fatigued muscles)

rube \ˈrüb\ *n* **:** an uneducated person who is usually from the country [*Rube,* nickname for *Reuben*]

¹ru•be•fa•cient \ˌrü-bə-ˈfā-shənt\ *adj* **:** causing redness (as of the skin) [Latin *rubefaciens,* present participle of *rubefacere* "to make red," from *rubeus* "reddish" + *facere* "to make"]

²rubefacient *n* **:** a substance for external application that produces redness of the skin

ru•bel•la \rü-ˈbel-ə\ *n* **:** GERMAN MEASLES [New Latin, from Latin *rubellus* "reddish," from *ruber* "red"]

ru•be•o•la \rü-ˈbē-ə-lə, ˌrü-bē-ˈō-\ *n* **:** MEASLES [New Latin, from Latin *rubeus* "reddish"]

Ru•bi•con \ˈrü-bi-ˌkän\ *n* **:** a deliberate irrevocable step or act [Latin *Rubicon-, Rubico,* river of northern Italy forming part of the boundary between Cisalpine Gaul and Italy whose crossing by Julius Caesar in 49 B.C. was regarded by the Senate as an act of war]

ru•bi•cund \ˈrü-bi-ˌkənd, -kənd\ *adj* **:** somewhat red **:** RUDDY [Latin *rubicundus,* from *rubēre* "to be red"] — **ru•bi•cun•di•ty** \ˌrü-bi-ˈkən-dət-ē\ *n*

ru•bid•i•um \rü-ˈbid-ē-əm\ *n* **:** a soft silvery metallic chemical element that decomposes water with violence and bursts into flame spontaneously in air — see ELEMENT table [New Latin, from Latin *rubidus* "red," from *rubēre* "to be red"]

ru•big•i•nous \rü-ˈbij-ə-nəs\ *adj* **:** of a rusty red color [Latin *robiginosus, rubiginosus* "rusty," from *robigo* "rust"]

ru•ble \ˈrü-bəl\ *n* **1 :** the basic monetary unit of Russia and formerly of the Soviet Union **2 :** a coin or note representing one ruble [Russian *rubl'*]

rub out *vt* **1 :** to obliterate by rubbing **2 :** KILL 1

ru•bric \ˈrü-brik\ *n* **1 :** a heading of a part of a book or manuscript done or underlined in a color (as red) different from the rest **2 a** (1) **:** NAME, TITLE; *esp* **:** the title of a law (2) **:** something under which a thing is classed **:** CATEGORY **b :** an authoritative rule; *esp* **:** a rule for conduct of a liturgical service **c :** an explanatory or introductory comment or gloss; *esp* **:** an editorial interpolation **3 :** an established rule or custom **4 :** a guide listing specific criteria for grading or scoring academic papers, projects, or tests [Middle French *rubrique,* literally, "red ocher," from Latin *rubrica,* from *ruber* "red"] — **rubric** *or* **ru•bri•cal** \-bri-kəl\ *adj*

Word History Derived ultimately from Latin *ruber,* "red," *rubric* was originally used in Middle English to name red ocher, a red pigment. Yet in present-day English *rubric* is used to mean "a rule" or "an explanation." This semantic transformation is derived from the practice originated centuries ago of putting instructions or explanations in a manuscript or printed book in red ink to contrast with the black ink of the text.

¹ru•by \ˈrü-bē\ *n, pl* **rubies 1 :** a precious stone that is a deep red corundum **2 a :** the dark red color of the ruby **b :** something resembling a ruby in color [Medieval French *rubi, rubin,* from Latin *rubeus* "reddish"]

²ruby *adj* **:** of the color ruby

ruby glass *n* **:** glass of a deep red color containing selenium, an oxide of copper, or chloride of gold

ru•by–throat•ed hummingbird \ˈrü-bē-ˌthrōt-əd-\ *n* **:** a hummingbird of eastern North America that has a bright shiny green back, whitish underparts, and in the adult male a shiny red throat

ruck \ˈrək\ *n* **:** the usual run of persons or things [Middle English, "heap, pile," of Scandinavian origin]

ruck•sack \ˈrək-ˌsak, ˈru̇k-\ *n* **:** KNAPSACK [German, from German dialect *Rucken* "back" + *Sack* "sack"]

ruck•us \ˈrək-əs, ˈrük-, ˈru̇k-\ *n* **:** ⁴ROW, DISTURBANCE [probably blend of *ruction* and *rumpus*]

ruc•tion \ˈrək-shən\ *n* **1 :** a noisy fight **2 :** UPROAR [perhaps from *insurrection*]

rud•der \ˈrəd-ər\ *n* **:** a flat piece of wood or metal attached to the stern of a boat or the after end of the keel for steering a boat; *also* **:** a similar piece attached to the rear of an aircraft [Old English *rōther* "paddle"]

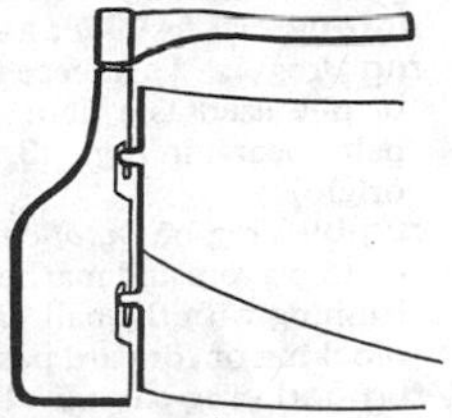
rudder

rud•dy \ˈrəd-ē\ *adj* **rud•di•er; -est 1 :** having a healthy reddish color **2 :** REDDISH [Old English *rudig,* from *rudu* "redness"] — **rud•di•ly** \ˈrəd-l-ē\ *adv* — **rud•di•ness** \ˈrəd-ē-nəs\ *n*

rude \ˈrüd\ *adj* **1 :** being in a rough or unfinished state **:** CRUDE **2 :** lacking refinement, delicacy, or culture **3 :** offensive in manner or action **:** DISCOURTEOUS **4 :** FORCEFUL, ABRUPT ⟨a *rude* awakening⟩ [Medieval French, from Latin *rudis*] — **rude•ly** *adv* — **rude•ness** *n*

ru•di•ment \ˈrüd-ə-mənt\ *n* **1 :** an elementary principle or skill — usually used in plural ⟨the *rudiments* of chess⟩ **2 :** something unformed or undeveloped **:** BEGINNING — usually used in plural **3 :** a body part so undeveloped in size or structure that it is unable to perform its normal function [Latin *rudimentum* "beginning," from *rudis* "raw, rude"]

ru•di•men•ta•ry \ˌrüd-ə-ˈment-ə-rē, -ˈmen-trē\ *adj* **1 :** ELEMENTARY 1a, FUNDAMENTAL **2 :** very imperfectly developed or represented only by a small part compared to the fully developed form ⟨a *rudimentary* tail⟩

¹rue \ˈrü\ *vt* **rued; ru•ing :** to feel penitence, remorse, or regret for [Old English *hrēowan*]

²rue *n* **:** REGRET 1, SORROW

³rue *n* **:** a European woody perennial herb with yellow flowers, a strong smell, and bitter-tasting leaves [Medieval French, from Latin *ruta,* from Greek *rhytē*]

rue anemone *n* **:** a delicate North American spring herb that is related to the buttercups and has white flowers

rue•ful \ˈrü-fəl\ *adj* **1 :** exciting pity or sympathy **:** PITIABLE ⟨a *rueful* tale⟩ **2 :** MOURNFUL, REGRETFUL ⟨took defeat with a *rueful* smile⟩ — **rue•ful•ly** \-fə-lē\ *adv* — **rue•ful•ness** *n*

ru•fes•cent \rü-ˈfes-nt\ *adj* **:** REDDISH [Latin *rufescens,* present participle of *rufescere* "to become red," from *rufus* "red"]

¹ruff \ˈrəf\ *n* **1 :** a large round collar of pleated muslin worn by men and women of the late 16th and early 17th centuries **2 a :** a fringe of long hairs or feathers growing around or on the neck of an animal **b :** a common Eurasian sandpiper of which the male during the breeding season has a large ruff [probably from *ruffle*] — **ruffed** \ˈrəft\ *adj*

²ruff *n* **:** the act of trumping [Middle French *roffle*] — **ruff** *vb*

ruffed grouse *n* **:** a grouse of the U.S. and Canada of which the male erects a ruff of shiny black feathers during breeding displays

ruffed grouse

ruf•fi•an \ˈrəf-ē-ən\ *n* **:** a coarse brutal person [Middle French *rufian*] — **ruffian**

\ə\ **abut**	\au̇\ **out**	\i\ **tip**	\ȯ\ **saw**	\u̇\ **foot**
\ər\ **further**	\ch\ **chin**	\ī\ **life**	\ȯi\ **coin**	\y\ **yet**
\a\ **mat**	\e\ **pet**	\j\ **job**	\th\ **thin**	\yü\ **few**
\ā\ **take**	\ē\ **easy**	\ŋ\ **sing**	\t͟h\ **this**	\yu̇\ **cure**
\ä\ **cot, cart**	\g\ **go**	\ō\ **bone**	\ü\ **food**	\zh\ **vision**

adj — **ruf·fi·an·ism** \-ē-ə-ˌniz-əm\ *n* — **ruf·fi·an·ly** \-ē-ən-lē\ *adj*

[1]ruf·fle \'rəf-əl\ *vb* **ruf·fled; ruf·fling** \'rəf-ling, -ə-ling\ **1 a :** to disturb the smoothness of : ROUGHEN ⟨*ruffle* the waters of a pond⟩ **b :** TROUBLE 1a, VEX **2 :** to erect (as feathers) in or like a ruff **3 :** RIFFLE 3, SHUFFLE **4 :** to make into a ruffle [Middle English *ruffelen*]

[2]ruffle *n* **1 :** a state or cause of irritation **2 :** an unevenness or disturbance of surface : RIPPLE **3 a :** a strip of lace or cloth gathered or pleated on one edge **b :** [1]RUFF 2a — **ruf·fly** \'rəf-lē, -ə-lē\ *adj*

[3]ruffle *n* **:** a low vibrating drumbeat that is less loud than a roll [from earlier *ruff* "drumbeat," of imitative origin]

ru·fous \'rü-fəs\ *adj* **:** REDDISH [Latin *rufus* "red"]

rug \'rəg\ *n* **1 :** a piece of thick heavy fabric usually with a nap or pile used as a floor covering **2 :** a floor mat of an animal pelt ⟨bearskin *rug*⟩ **3 :** a lap robe [probably of Scandinavian origin]

rug·by \'rəg-bē\ *n, often cap* **:** a football game played by teams of 15 players and marked by continuous play featuring kicking, running with the ball, lateral passing, and tackling but without blocking or forward passing [*Rugby* School, Rugby, England]

rug·ged \'rəg-əd\ *adj* **1 :** having a rough uneven surface : JAGGED ⟨*rugged* mountains⟩ **2 :** STORMY 2 **3 :** showing signs of strength : STURDY ⟨*rugged* pioneers⟩ **4 a :** STERN ⟨*rugged* times⟩ **b :** COARSE 3, RUDE **5 :** presenting a severe test of ability, endurance, or resolution ⟨*rugged* course of training⟩ [Middle English, "shaggy"] ***synonyms*** see ROUGH — **rug·ged·ly** *adv* — **rug·ged·ness** *n*

ru·gose \'rü-ˌgōs\ *adj* **:** full of folds or wrinkles ⟨*rugose* leaves⟩ [Latin *rugosus,* from *ruga* "wrinkle"] — **ru·gose·ly** *adv* — **ru·gos·i·ty** \rü-'gäs-ət-ē\ *n*

[1]ru·in \'rü-ən, -ˌin\ *n* **1 :** physical, moral, economic, or social collapse **2 a :** the state of being ruined **b :** the remains of something destroyed — usually used in plural ⟨the *ruins* of a city⟩ **3 :** a cause of destruction ⟨greed was my *ruin*⟩ **4 :** the action of destroying, laying waste, or wrecking **5 :** a ruined building, person, or object [Medieval French *ruine* "collapse," from Latin *ruina*]

[2]ruin *vt* **1 :** to reduce to ruins : DEVASTATE ⟨a *ruined* city⟩ **2 a :** to damage irreparably ⟨*ruined* our chances⟩ **b :** BANKRUPT, IMPOVERISH ⟨*ruined* by the depression⟩ — **ru·in·er** *n*

ru·in·ation \ˌrü-ə-'nā-shən\ *n* **:** RUIN 3

ru·in·ous \'rü-ə-nəs\ *adj* **1 :** DILAPIDATED **2 :** causing or tending to cause ruin : DESTRUCTIVE ⟨*ruinous* tax laws⟩ — **ru·in·ous·ly** *adv*

[1]rule \'rül\ *n* **1 a :** a prescribed guide for conduct or action **b :** the laws laid down by the founder of a religious order **c :** an accepted procedure, custom, or habit **d :** a legal precept or doctrine **e :** REGULATION, BYLAW ⟨the *rules* of the club⟩ **2 a :** a usually valid generalization **b :** a generally prevailing quality, state, or mode **c :** a regulating principle ⟨the *rules* of harmony⟩ **3 a :** the exercise of authority or control : DOMINION **b :** a period of such rule : REIGN ⟨during the *rule* of King George III⟩ **4 a :** RULER 2 **b (1) :** a metal strip that prints a linear design **(2) :** a linear design produced by or as if by such a strip [Medieval French *reule,* from Latin *regula* "straightedge, norm, rule," from *regere* "to keep straight, direct"]

[2]rule *vb* **1 a :** CONTROL 2a, DIRECT **b :** MANAGE 2 **2 a :** to exercise authority or power over : GOVERN **b :** to be preeminent in : DOMINATE **3 :** to declare authoritatively; *esp* **:** to lay down a legal rule **4 :** to mark with lines drawn along or as if along the straight edge of a ruler **5 a :** to exercise supreme authority **b :** PREDOMINATE 2, PREVAIL

rule·less \'rül-ləs\ *adj* **:** not restrained or regulated by law

rule of thumb 1 : a method based on experience and common sense **2 :** a general principle regarded as roughly correct but not scientifically accurate

rule out *vt* **1 :** to eliminate as a possibility **2 :** to make impossible : PREVENT

rul·er \'rü-lər\ *n* **1 :** one that rules; *esp* **:** SOVEREIGN **2 :** a smooth-edged strip (as of wood or metal) marked off in units and used as a guide in drawing lines or for measuring

[1]rul·ing \'rü-ling\ *n* **:** an official or authoritative decision or interpretation (as by a judge on a point of law)

[2]ruling *adj* **1 :** exerting power or authority **2 :** CHIEF ⟨a *ruling* ambition⟩

rum \'rəm\ *n* **1 :** an alcoholic liquor distilled from a fermented cane product (as molasses) **2 :** alcoholic liquor [probably from obsolete *rumbullion* "rum"]

Rumanian *variant of* ROMANIAN

rum·ba \'rəm-bə, 'rüm-\ *n* **:** a ballroom dance of Cuban origin in 2/4 or 4/4 time marked by pronounced hip movements; *also* **:** the music for this dance [American Spanish]

[1]rum·ble \'rəm-bəl\ *vb* **rum·bled; rum·bling** \-bə-ling, -bling\ **1 :** to make a low heavy rolling sound **2 :** to travel with a low reverberating sound **3 :** to speak or utter in a low rolling tone [Middle English *rumblen*]

[2]rumble *n* **:** a low heavy continuous reverberating often muffled sound

rumble seat *n* **:** a folding seat in the back of an automobile (as a coupe or roadster) not covered by the top

ru·men \'rü-mən\ *n, pl* **ru·mi·na** \-mə-nə\ *or* **rumens :** the large first compartment of the stomach of a ruminant in which cellulose is broken down by the action of symbiotic microorganisms [Latin *rumin-, rumen* "gullet"] — **ru·mi·nal** \-mən-l\ *adj*

[1]ru·mi·nant \'rü-mə-nənt\ *n* **:** a ruminant mammal

[2]ruminant *adj* **1 a :** chewing the cud **b :** of or relating to a group of even-toed hoofed mammals (as sheep, oxen, deer, and camels) that chew the cud and have a complex 3- or 4-chambered stomach **2 :** given to or engaged in contemplation : MEDITATIVE — **ru·mi·nant·ly** *adv*

ru·mi·nate \'rü-mə-ˌnāt\ *vb* **1 :** to engage in contemplation : MUSE, MEDITATE **2 :** to chew the cud : bring up and chew again what has been chewed slightly and swallowed [Latin *ruminari* "to chew the cud, muse upon," from *rumen* "gullet"] ***synonyms*** see PONDER — **ru·mi·na·tion** \ˌrü-mə-'nā-shən\ *n* — **ru·mi·na·tive** \'rü-mə-ˌnāt-iv\ *adj* — **ru·mi·na·tive·ly** *adv* — **ru·mi·na·tor** \-ˌnāt-ər\ *n*

[1]rum·mage \'rəm-ij\ *vb* **1 :** to make a thorough search especially by moving about, turning over, or looking through the contents of a place or receptacle ⟨*rummage* through the whole attic⟩ **2 :** to make a haphazard search ⟨*rummaging* around in the drawer⟩ **3 :** to discover by searching ⟨*rummaged* up a costume⟩

[2]rummage *n* **1 :** a confused miscellaneous collection **2 :** a thorough search especially among a confusion of objects [Middle French *arrimage* "act of stowing cargo," from *arrimer* "to stow," from *a-* (from Latin *ad-* "to") + *-rimer,* from Middle English *rimen* "to open up, make room for," from Old English *rȳman*]

rummage sale *n* **:** a sale of miscellaneous and often donated articles

rum·my \'rəm-ē\ *n* **:** a card game in which each player tries to be the first to play all cards held in the hand by laying them down in groups of three or more of the same kind or in sequence [derived from earlier *rum* "queer, odd"]

[1]ru·mor \'rü-mər\ *n* **1 :** talk or opinion widely current but having no known source : HEARSAY **2 :** a statement or report going around without known authority for its truth [Medieval French *rumour,* from Latin *rumor*]

[2]rumor *vt* **ru·mored; ru·mor·ing** \'rüm-ring, -ə-ring\ **:** to tell or spread by rumor

ru·mor·mon·ger \'rü-mər-ˌməng-gər, -ˌmäng-\ *n* **:** one who spreads rumors

rump \'rəmp\ *n* **1 a :** the upper rounded part of the hindquarters of a 4-legged animal **b :** BUTTOCK 2a **2 :** a cut of beef between the loin and round **3 :** a small fragment remaining after the separation of the larger part of a group or an area; *esp* **:** a group (as a parliament) carrying on in the name of the original body after the departure or expulsion of a large number of its members [of Scandinavian origin] — **rumped** \'rəmt, 'rəmpt\ *adj*

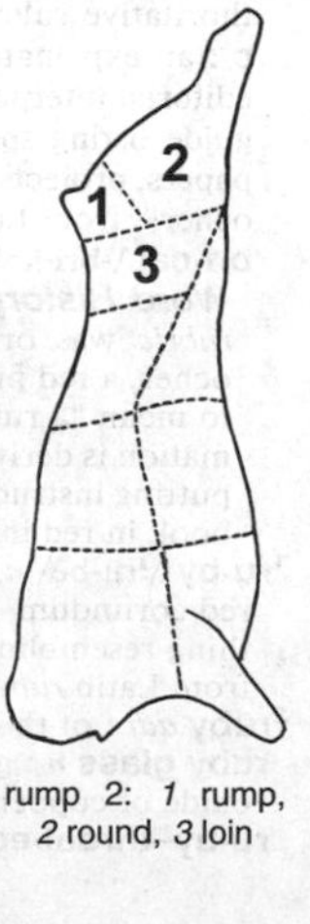

rump 2: *1* rump, *2* round, *3* loin

rum·ple \'rəm-pəl\ *vb* **rum·pled; rum·pling** \-pə-ling, -pling\ **1 :** WRINKLE, CRUMPLE ⟨*rumple* the bedclothes⟩ **2 :** to make unkempt : TOUSLE ⟨*rumpled* my hair⟩ [Dutch *rompelen*]

rum·pus \'rəm-pəs\ *n* **:** a noisy commotion [origin unknown]

rumpus room *n* **:** a room (as in the basement of a home) set apart for games, parties, and recreation

[1]run \'rən\ *vb* **ran** \'ran\; **run; run·ning 1 a**

: to go faster than a walk; *esp* : to go steadily by springing steps so that both feet leave the ground for an instant in each step **b** : to move at a fast gallop ⟨*running* horses⟩ **c** : FLEE 1, RETREAT, ESCAPE ⟨dropped the gun and *ran*⟩ **2 a** : to move freely about at will ⟨let the dog *run* loose⟩ **b** : to keep company ⟨*running* with a bad crowd⟩ **c** : to sail in the same direction the wind is blowing **d** : to go about ⟨*running* around without a coat⟩ **3 a** : to go or cause to go rapidly or hurriedly : HASTEN **b** : to do or accomplish by or as if by running ⟨*run* errands⟩ **4 a** : to compete in a race **b** : to enter or put forward as a contestant in an election contest **5 a** : to move on or as if on wheels : GLIDE ⟨file drawers *running* on ball bearings⟩ **b** : to roll forward rapidly or freely **c** : to ravel lengthwise **6** : to sing or play a musical passage quickly ⟨*run* up the scale⟩ **7 a** : to go back and forth : PLY **b** : to migrate or move in schools; *esp* : to ascend a river to spawn ⟨shad are *running* in the river⟩ **8 a** : FUNCTION, OPERATE ⟨keep the car *running*⟩ **b** : to cause to be treated or operated on : PROCESS ⟨*ran* my program on the computer⟩ **9** : to continue in force or operation ⟨the contract has two years to *run*⟩ **10** : to pass into a specified condition ⟨*run* into debt⟩ **11 a** : to move as a fluid : FLOW **b** : MELT ⟨solder *runs* at low heat⟩ **c** : to spread out : DISSOLVE ⟨colors guaranteed not to *run*⟩ **d** : to discharge a fluid ⟨a *running* sore⟩ **12** : to tend to develop a specified quality or feature ⟨they *run* to big noses in that family⟩ **13 a** : to extend through space or time ⟨the boundary line *runs* east⟩ ⟨a family line that *runs* back to a notorious horse thief⟩ **b** : to be in a certain form or expression ⟨the letter *runs* as follows⟩ or order of succession ⟨house numbers *run* in odd numbers from 3 to 57⟩ **14 a** : to occur persistently : RECUR ⟨musical talent *runs* in the family⟩ **b** : to exist or occur in a continuous range of variation ⟨the quality *runs* from good to terrible⟩ **c** : to play on stage ⟨the play *ran* for six months⟩ **15 a** : to spread or pass quickly from point to point ⟨chills *ran* up my spine⟩ **b** : to be current : CIRCULATE ⟨speculation *ran* rife on who it would be⟩ **16 a** : to bring to a specified condition by or as if by running ⟨*ran* themselves to death⟩ **b** : TRACE ⟨*ran* the rumor to its source⟩ **c** : to keep or maintain (livestock) on or as if on pasturage **17 a** : to pass over or traverse ⟨*ran* the whole range of emotions⟩ **b** : to slip through or past ⟨*run* a blockade⟩ **18 a** : to cause to penetrate or enter : THRUST ⟨*ran* a splinter into my toe⟩ **b** : STITCH ⟨*run* a basting⟩ **c** : to cause to pass : LEAD ⟨*run* a wire in from the antenna⟩ **d** : to cause to collide ⟨*ran* my head into a post⟩ **e** : SMUGGLE ⟨*run* guns⟩ **19** : to cause to pass lightly or quickly over, along, or into something ⟨*ran* my eye down the list⟩ **20 a** : to cause or allow to go in a specified manner or direction ⟨*ran* the car off the road⟩ **b** : to carry on : MANAGE ⟨*run* a factory⟩ **21 a** : to flow with ⟨streets *ran* blood⟩ **b** : ASSAY ⟨the ore *runs* high in silver⟩ **22** : to make oneself liable to : INCUR ⟨*ran* the risk of discovery⟩ **23** : to mark out : DRAW ⟨*run* a contour line on a map⟩ **24** : to permit charges to accumulate before settling ⟨*run* an account⟩ ⟨*ran* up a big bill⟩ **25** : PRINT ⟨*run* the advertisement for three days⟩ [Middle English *rinnen,* v.i., (from Old English *iernan, rinnan* and Old Norse *rinna*) and *rennen,* v.t., from Old Norse *renna*] — **run across** : to meet with or discover by chance — **run a fever** *or* **run a temperature** : to have a fever — **run foul of 1** : to collide with ⟨*ran foul of* a hidden reef⟩ **2** : to run into conflict with or hostility to ⟨*run foul of* the law⟩ — **run into 1** : to mount up to ⟨a boat like that one *runs into* money⟩ **2 a** : to collide with **b** : ENCOUNTER, MEET ⟨*ran into* an old friend⟩ — **run riot 1** : to act wildly or without restraint **2** : to occur in profusion — **run short** : to become insufficient

[2]run *n* **1 a** : an act or the action of running : continued rapid movement ⟨broke into a *run*⟩ **b** : a fast gallop **c** : an annual migration of fish up a river especially to spawn; *also* : such fish in the process of migration **d** : a running race ⟨a mile *run*⟩ **e** : a score made in baseball by a base runner reaching home plate **2 a** *chiefly Midland* : CREEK 2 **b** : something that flows in the course of an operation or during a particular time ⟨the first *run* of maple sap⟩ **3 a** : the horizontal distance from one point to another **b** : general tendency or direction **4** : a continuous series or unbroken period especially of things of identical or similar sort: as **a** : a rapid scale passage in vocal or instrumental music **b** : an unbroken course of theatrical performances **c** : an unbroken stretch ⟨a *run* of bad luck⟩ **d** : sudden heavy demands from depositors, creditors, or customers ⟨a *run* on a bank⟩ **5** : the quantity of work turned out in a continuous operation **6** : the usual or normal kind ⟨average *run* of college graduates⟩ **7 a** : the distance covered in a period of continuous traveling or sailing ⟨logged the day's *run*⟩ **b** : regular course : TRIP ⟨the bus makes four *runs* daily⟩ **c** : freedom of movement in or access to a place or area ⟨has the *run* of the house⟩ **8 a** : a way, track, or path frequented by animals ⟨a deer *run*⟩ **b** : an enclosure for domestic animals where they may feed or exercise **9 a** : an inclined course (as for skiing) **b** : a track or guide on which something runs **10** : a ravel in a knitted fabric (as in hosiery) caused by the breaking of stitches **11** *pl* : DIARRHEA ⟨had a bad case of the *runs*⟩ — **run·less** \-ləs\ *adj* — **on the run 1** : while running : without stopping ⟨had lunch *on the run*⟩ **2** : running away

run·about \ˈrən-ə-ˌbau̇t\ *n* **1** : one who wanders about : STRAY **2** : a light open wagon, roadster, or motorboat

run·a·gate \ˈrən-ə-ˌgāt\ *n* **1** : FUGITIVE 1, RUNAWAY **2** : VAGABOND [from obsolete *renegate* "renegade," from Medieval Latin *renegatus*]

run·around \ˈrən-ə-ˌrau̇nd\ *n* : deceptive or delaying action especially in response to a request

[1]run·away \ˈrən-ə-ˌwā\ *n* **1** : FUGITIVE 1 **2** : the act of running away out of control; *also* : a horse that is running out of control **3** : a one-sided victory

[2]runaway *adj* **1** : running away : FUGITIVE **2** : accomplished by elopement or during flight ⟨a *runaway* marriage⟩ **3** : won by or having a long lead **4** : subject to uncontrolled changes ⟨*runaway* inflation⟩

run away \ˌrən-ə-ˈwā\ *vi* **1** : FLEE 1, DESERT ⟨*ran away* from the fight⟩ **2** : to leave home; *esp* : ELOPE ⟨*ran away* to get married⟩ **3** : to run out of control : STAMPEDE, BOLT

run·down \ˈrən-ˌdau̇n\ *n* : an item-by-item report : SUMMARY

run–down \ˈrən-ˈdau̇n\ *adj* **1** : being in poor repair : DILAPIDATED **2** : being in poor health **3** : completely unwound ⟨a *run-down* clock⟩

run down \ˈrən-ˈdau̇n, ˌrən-\ *vb* **1 a** : to collide with and knock down **b** : to run against and cause to sink **2 a** : to chase until exhausted or captured **b** : to find by search : trace the source of **3** : DISPARAGE 2 **4** : to cease to operate because of the exhaustion of motive power **5** : to deteriorate in physical condition

rune \ˈrün\ *n* **1** : one of the characters of an alphabet used by the Germanic peoples from about the 3rd to the 13th centuries **2** : mystic utterance or inscription **3** : a Finnish or Old Norse poem [Old Norse and Old English *rūn* "mystery, runic character, writing"; sense 3 from Finnish *runo,* of Germanic origin] — **ru·nic** \ˈrü-nik\ *adj*

rune 1

[1]rung *past participle of* RING

[2]rung \ˈrəŋ\ *n* **1 a** : a rounded part placed as a crosspiece between the legs of a chair **b** : one of the crosspieces of a ladder **2** : STEP 5a, LEVEL ⟨down a few *rungs* in the social scale⟩ [Old English *hrung* "crossbar, spoke"]

run–in \ˈrən-ˌin\ *n* : ALTERCATION, QUARREL

run·let \ˈrən-lət\ *n* : RUNNEL

run·nel \ˈrən-l\ *n* : RIVULET, STREAMLET [Old English *rynel*]

run·ner \ˈrən-ər\ *n* **1 a** : one that runs : RACER **b** : BALLCARRIER **c** : BASE RUNNER **2** : MESSENGER ⟨was a *runner* on Wall Street⟩ **3** : any of various large active sea fishes **4 a** : either of the longitudinal pieces on which a sled or sleigh slides **b** : the blade of a skate **c** : the support of a drawer or a sliding door **5 a** : a slender creeping stem arising from the base of a plant; *esp* : STOLON 1 **b** : a plant (as a strawberry) that forms or spreads by runners **6 a** : a long narrow carpet **b** : a narrow decorative cloth cover for a table or dresser top

run·ner–up \ˈrən-ər-ˌəp\ *n* : the competitor in a contest that finishes next to the winner

[1]run·ning *n* : the action of running — **in the running** : having a chance to win a contest — **out of the running** : having no chance to win a contest

\ə\ abut	\au̇\ out	\i\ tip	\ȯ\ saw	\u̇\ foot
\ər\ further	\ch\ chin	\ī\ life	\ȯi\ coin	\y\ yet
\a\ mat	\e\ pet	\j\ job	\th\ thin	\yü\ few
\ā\ take	\ē\ easy	\ng\ sing	\th\ this	\yu̇\ cure
\ä\ cot, cart	\g\ go	\ō\ bone	\ü\ food	\zh\ vision

[2]**running** *adj* **1** : FLUID, RUNNY ⟨a *running* sore⟩ **2** : INCESSANT, CONTINUOUS ⟨a *running* battle⟩ **3** : measured in a straight line ⟨buy cloth by the *running* meter⟩ **4** : initiated or performed while running or with a running start ⟨a *running* leap⟩

[3]**running** *adv* : in succession ⟨four days *running*⟩

running board *n* : a footboard especially at the side of an automobile

running knot *n* : a knot that slips along the line round which it is tied

running light *n* : one of the lights carried by a vehicle (as a ship) under way at night that indicate position, size, and direction

running mate *n* : a candidate running for a subordinate office (as of vice president) who is paired with the candidate for the top office on the same ticket

running stitch *n* : a small even stitch run in and out in cloth

run·ny \ˈrən-ē\ *adj* **run·ni·er; -est** : having a tendency to run: as **a** : extremely or excessively soft and liquid ⟨*runny* scrambled eggs⟩ **b** : giving off a flow of mucus ⟨a *runny* nose⟩

run·off \ˈrən-ˌȯf\ *n* **1** : a final contest to decide a previous indecisive contest or series of contests **2** : water from rain or snow that eventually reaches streams by natural drainage

run off \ˈrən-ˈȯf, ˌrən-\ *vb* **1** : to produce by or as if by printing ⟨*ran off* a few more copies⟩ **2** : to cause to be run or played to a finish **3** : to steal (as cattle) by driving away **4** : to run away — **run off with** : to carry off : STEAL

run–of–the–mill \ˌrən-əv-t͟hə-ˈmil, ˌrən-ə-t͟hə-\ *adj* : not outstanding in quality or rarity : AVERAGE

[1]**run–on** \ˈrən-ˈȯn, -ˈän\ *adj* : continuing without rhetorical pause from one line of verse into another

[2]**run–on** \ˈrən-ˌȯn, -ˌän\ *n* **1** : something (as a dictionary entry) that is run on **2** : RUN-ON SENTENCE

run on \ˈrən-ˈȯn, ˌrən-, -ˈän\ *vb* **1** : PERSIST 2 **2** : to talk or narrate at length **3** : to continue (matter in type) without a break or a new paragraph **4** : to place or add (as an entry in a dictionary) at the end of a paragraphed item

run–on sentence *n* : a sentence containing a comma splice

run out *vi* **1** : to come to an end : EXPIRE **2** : to become exhausted or used up : FAIL — **run out of** : to use up the available supply of

run over *vb* **1 a** : OVERFLOW 2 **b** : OVERFLOW 3 **2** : to exceed a limit **3** : to go over, examine, repeat, or rehearse quickly **4** : to collide with, knock down, and often drive over

runt \ˈrənt\ *n* : an unusually small person or animal [origin unknown] — **runty** \-ē\ *adj*

run through *vt* **1** : PIERCE 1 **2** : to spend or consume wastefully and rapidly **3** : to read or rehearse without pausing

run·way \ˈrən-ˌwā\ *n* **1** : RUN 8a **2** : a paved strip of ground on a landing field for the landing and takeoff of airplanes **3** : a support (as a track, pipe, or trough) on which something runs

ru·pee \rü-ˈpē, ˈrü-ˌpē\ *n* **1** : the basic monetary unit of India, Mauritius, Nepal, Pakistan, Seychelles, and Sri Lanka **2** : a coin or note representing one rupee [Hindi and Urdu *rūpaiyā,* from Sanskrit *rūpya* "coined silver"]

ru·pi·ah \rü-ˈpē-ə\ *n* **1** : the basic monetary unit of Indonesia **2** : a coin representing one rupiah [Malay, from Hindi and Urdu *rūpaiyā* "rupee"]

[1]**rup·ture** \ˈrəp-chər\ *n* **1** : breach of peace or concord; *esp* : open hostility or war between nations **2** : a breaking or tearing apart (as of body tissue) or the resulting state **3** : HERNIA [Latin *ruptura* "fracture," from *ruptus,* past participle of *rumpere* "to break"] ***synonyms*** see FRACTURE

[2]**rupture** *vb* **rup·tured; rup·tur·ing** \-chə-ring, -shring\ **1** : to part by violence : BREAK **2** : to produce a rupture in **3** : to have or undergo a rupture

ru·ral \ˈru̇r-əl\ *adj* : of or relating to the country, country people or life, or agriculture [Medieval French, from Latin *ruralis,* from *rur-, rus* "open land, country"]

rural free delivery *n* : the free delivery of mail on routes in country districts — called also *rural delivery*

rural route *n* : a mail-delivery route in a rural free delivery area

rur·ban \ˈrər-bən, ˈru̇r-\ *adj* : of, relating to, or constituting an area which is chiefly residential but where some farming is carried on [blend of *rural* and *urban*]

ruse \ˈrüs, ˈrüz\ *n* : a deceptive stratagem : ARTIFICE, SUBTERFUGE [French, from Medieval French "roundabout path taken by fleeing game, trickery," from *reuser* "to dodge, deceive," from Latin *recusare* "to refuse"] ***synonyms*** see TRICK

[1]**rush** \ˈrəsh\ *n* : any of various monocotyledonous often tufted marsh plants with cylindrical often hollow stems sometimes used in chair seats and mats [Old English *rysc*] — **rushy** \-ē\ *adj*

[2]**rush** *vb* **1** : to move forward, progress, or act with haste or eagerness or without preparation ⟨*rush* out the door⟩ **2** : to push or impel on or forward with speed or violence ⟨*rush* them to the hospital⟩ **3** : to perform in a short time or at a high speed ⟨*rush* a job through⟩ **4** : CHARGE 4 ⟨*rushed* the enemy⟩ **5** : to carry the football in a running play **6** : to lavish attention on : COURT [Middle French *reuser, ruser, russher* "to drive back, repulse," from Latin *recusare* "to refuse"] — **rush·er** *n*

[3]**rush** *n* **1 a** : a violent forward motion ⟨a *rush* of wind⟩ **b** : CHARGE 7, ONSET ⟨led the *rush* on the enemy position⟩ **2** : a burst of activity, productivity, or speed **3** : a thronging of people usually to a new place and in search of wealth ⟨gold *rush*⟩ **4** : a running play in football **5** : a round of attention usually involving extensive social activity **6** : the first rapid excitation produced by a narcotic drug

[4]**rush** *adj* : requiring or marked by special speed or urgency ⟨*rush* orders⟩ ⟨the *rush* season⟩

rusk \ˈrəsk\ *n* : a sweet or plain bread baked, sliced, and baked again until dry and crisp [Spanish and Portuguese *rosca* "coil, twisted roll"]

Russ \ˈrəs\ *n, pl* **Russ** *or* **Russ·es** : RUSSIAN 1a [Russian *Rus'*] — **Russ** *adj*

[1]**rus·set** \ˈrəs-ət\ *n* **1** : coarse homespun usually reddish brown cloth **2** : a reddish brown **3** : any of various typically late-ripening apples with rough usually russet-colored skins [Medieval French *russet,* from *russet* "reddish brown," from *rus, rous* "red," from Latin *russus* "red"]

[2]**russet** *adj* : of the color russet

Rus·sian \ˈrəsh-ən\ *n* **1 a** : a native or inhabitant of Russia; *esp* : a member of the dominant Slavic-speaking ethnic group of Russia **b** : a person of Russian descent **2** : a Slavic language of the Russian people that is the official language of Russia and formerly of the Soviet Union — **Russian** *adj*

Russian olive *n* : a Eurasian shrub or small tree with usually silvery leaves that is widely grown as a hedge and shelter plant

Russian thistle *n* : a prickly European herb that is a serious weed in North America

Russian wolfhound *n* : BORZOI

Russo- *combining form* : Russian and ⟨the *Russo*-Japanese war⟩

[1]**rust** \ˈrəst\ *n* **1 a** : the reddish brittle coating chiefly of ferric oxide formed on iron especially when chemically attacked by moist air **b** : a comparable coating produced on other metals by corrosion **2** : corrosive or injurious influence or effect **3 a** : any of numerous destructive diseases of plants caused by fungi and marked by reddish brown lesions **b** : any of an order (Uredinales) of parasitic fungi that cause plant rusts **4** : a strong reddish brown [Old English *rūst*]

[2]**rust** *vb* **1** : to form or cause to form rust : become oxidized ⟨iron *rusts*⟩ **2** : to weaken or degenerate or cause to degenerate especially from inaction, lack of use, or passage of time : CORRODE ⟨diplomatic skill that had not *rusted*⟩ **3** : to turn the color of rust

[1]**rus·tic** \ˈrəs-tik\ *adj* **1** : of, relating to, or suitable for the country : RURAL ⟨*rustic* sports⟩ **2** : made of the rough limbs of trees ⟨*rustic* furniture⟩ **3** : AWKWARD, BOORISH ⟨*rustic* manners⟩ [Latin *rusticus,* from *rus* "open land, country"] — **rus·ti·cal·ly** \-ti-kə-lē, -klē\ *adv* — **rus·tic·i·ty** \ˌrəs-ˈtis-ət-ē\ *n*

[2]**rustic** *n* : an inhabitant of a rural area; *esp* : an unsophisticated one

rus·ti·cate \ˈrəs-ti-ˌkāt\ *vb* **1** : to go into or reside in the country **2** : to suspend from school or college — **rus·ti·ca·tion** \ˌrəs-ti-ˈkā-shən\ *n* — **rus·ti·ca·tor** \ˈrəs-ti-ˌkāt-ər\ *n*

[1]**rus·tle** \ˈrəs-əl\ *vb* **rus·tled; rus·tling** \ˈrəs-ling, -ə-ling\ **1** : to make or cause to make a rustle **2** : to act or move with energy or speed **3** : to get by or as if by foraging ⟨*rustle* up some food⟩ **4** : to steal (as cattle) from the range [Middle English *rustelen*]

[2]**rustle** *n* : a quick succession or confusion of small sounds ⟨the *rustle* of leaves⟩ ⟨the *rustle* among a theater audience⟩

rus·tler \ˈrəs-lər, -ə-lər\ *n* : one that rustles cattle

rust·proof \ˈrəst-ˈprüf\ *adj* : incapable of rusting

rusty \ˈrəs-tē\ *adj* **rust·i·er; -est** **1** : affected by or as if by rust; *esp* : stiff with or as if with rust **2** : inept and slow through lack of practice or old age **3 a** : of the color rust **b** : dulled in color or appearance by age and use — **rust·i·ly** \ˈrəs-tə-lē\ *adv* — **rust·i·ness** \-tē-nəs\ *n*

[1]**rut** \ˈrət\ *n* : a state of sexual excitement especially in the male

deer; *also* : a period in which this occurs [Middle French *rut, ruit* "rut, disturbance," from Late Latin *rugitus* "roar," from Latin *rugire* "to roar"]

[2]rut *vi* **rut·ted; rut·ting** : to be in or enter into a state of rut

[3]rut *n* **1** : a track worn by a wheel or by habitual passage **2** : a usual or fixed practice : a regular course; *esp* : a monotonous routine ⟨my life's in a *rut*⟩ [perhaps from Middle French *route* "way, route"] — **rut·ty** \ˈrət-ē\ *adj*

[4]rut *vt* **rut·ted; rut·ting** : to make a rut in : FURROW

ru·ta·ba·ga \ˌrüt-ə-ˈbā-gə, ˌru̇t-, -ˈbeg-ə\ *n* : a turnip with a large yellowish root that is eaten as a vegetable; *also* : the root [Swedish dialect *rotabagge,* from Swedish *rot* "root" + *bagge* "bag"]

ruth \ˈrüth\ *n* **1** : compassion for the misery of another : PITY **2** : REMORSE [Middle English *ruthe,* from *ruen* "to rue"]

Ruth \ˈrüth\ *n* : a short narrative book of canonical Jewish and Christian Scriptures — see BIBLE table

ru·the·ni·um \rü-ˈthē-nē-əm\ *n* : a hard brittle grayish rare metallic element used especially in alloys and catalysts — see ELEMENT table [New Latin, from Medieval Latin *Ruthenia* "Russia"]

ruth·er·ford·i·um \ˌrəth-ər-ˈfȯrd-ē-əm\ *n* : a short-lived radioactive element that is produced artificially — see ELEMENT table [New Latin, from Ernest *Rutherford,* died 1937, British physicist]

ruth·less \ˈrüth-ləs\ *adj* : having no pity : MERCILESS, CRUEL — **ruth·less·ly** *adv* — **ruth·less·ness** *n*

ru·tile \ˈrü-ˌtēl\ *n* : a mineral TiO_2 that consists of titanium dioxide usually with a little iron, is mostly of a reddish brown color, and is a major source of titanium [German *Rutil,* from Latin *rutilus* "reddish"]

RV \ˌär-ˈvē\ *n* : RECREATIONAL VEHICLE

Rx \ˌär-ˈeks\ *n* : PRESCRIPTION 3a [alteration of ℞ symbol used at the beginning of a prescription, abbreviation for Latin *recipe* "prescription," literally, "take"]

-ry \rē\ *n suffix, pl* **-ries** : -ERY ⟨citizen*ry*⟩ ⟨wizard*ry*⟩ [Medieval French *-erie, -rie* "-ery"]

rye \ˈrī\ *n* **1** : a hardy annual cereal grass widely grown for grain and as a cover crop; *also* : its seeds **2** : RYE BREAD **3** : whiskey distilled from rye or from rye and malt [Old English *ryge*]

rye bread *n* : bread made wholly or partly from rye flour

rye·grass \ˈrī-ˌgras\ *n* : either of two grasses that are used as lawn and pasture grass and as cover crops

rye 1

S

s \ˈes\ *n, pl* **s's** *or* **ss** \ˈes-əz\ *often cap* **1** : the 19th letter of the English alphabet **2** : a grade rating a student's work as satisfactory **3** : something shaped like the letter S

[1]-s \s *after a voiceless consonant sound,* z *after a voiced consonant sound or a vowel sound*\ *n pl suffix* — used to form the plural of most nouns that do not end in *s, z, sh, ch,* or *y* following a consonant ⟨head*s*⟩ ⟨book*s*⟩ ⟨boy*s*⟩ ⟨belief*s*⟩, to form the plural of proper nouns that end in *y* following a consonant ⟨Mary*s*⟩, and with or without a preceding apostrophe to form the plural of abbreviations, numbers, letters, and symbols used as nouns ⟨MC*s*⟩ ⟨4*s*⟩ ⟨#*s*⟩ ⟨B'*s*⟩; compare [1]-ES 1 [Old English *as,* nominative and accusative pl. ending of some masculine nouns]

[2]-s *adv suffix* — used to form adverbs denoting usual or repeated action or state ⟨always at home Sunday*s*⟩ ⟨morning*s* we stop by the newsstand⟩ ⟨goes to school night*s*⟩ [Old English *-es,* genitive sing. ending of nouns (functioning adverbially)]

[3]-s *vb suffix* — used to form the third person singular present of most verbs that do not end in *s, z, sh, ch,* or in *y* following a consonant ⟨fall*s*⟩ ⟨take*s*⟩ ⟨play*s*⟩; compare [2]-ES

[1]'s *like* -'s\ *vb* **1** : IS ⟨someone'*s* here⟩ **2** : HAS ⟨who'*s* seen them?⟩ **3** : DOES ⟨what'*s* it need?⟩

[2]'s \s\ *pron* : US — used with let ⟨let'*s*⟩

-'s \s *after voiceless consonant sounds other than* s, sh, ch; z *after vowel sounds or voiced consonant sounds other than* z, zh, j; əz *after* s, sh, ch, z, zh, j\ *n suffix or pron suffix* — used to form the possessive of singular nouns ⟨child'*s*⟩, of plural nouns not ending in s ⟨children'*s*⟩, of some pronouns ⟨anyone'*s*⟩, and of word groups functioning as nouns ⟨the book on the shelf'*s* cover⟩ or pronouns ⟨someone else'*s*⟩ [Old English *-es,* genitive singular ending]

sab·a·dil·la \ˌsab-ə-ˈdil-ə, -ˈdē-ə, -ˈdē-yə\ *n* : a Mexican plant related to the lilies; *also* : its seeds used in insecticides [Spanish *cebadilla*]

Sab·ba·tar·i·an \ˌsab-ə-ˈter-ē-ən\ *n* **1** : one who keeps the 7th day of the week as holy **2** : one who favors strict observance of the Sabbath [Latin *sabbatarius,* from *sabbatum* "Sabbath"] — **Sabbatarian** *adj* — **Sab·ba·tar·i·an·ism** \-ˌiz-əm\ *n*

Sab·bath \ˈsab-əth\ *n* **1** : the 7th day of the week observed from Friday evening to Saturday evening as a day of rest and worship by Jews and some Christians **2** : the day of the week (as among Christians) set aside in a religion for rest and worship [Medieval French and Old English *sabat,* from Latin *sabbatum,* from Greek *sabbaton,* from Hebrew *shabbāth,* literally, "rest"]

sab·bat·i·cal \sə-ˈbat-i-kəl\ *or* **sab·bat·ic** \-ˈbat-ik\ *adj* **1** : of or relating to the Sabbath **2** : of or relating to a sabbatical year

sabbatical year *n* : a leave granted (as to a professor) usually every 7th year for rest, travel, or research — called also *sabbatical leave*

[1]sa·ber *or* **sa·bre** \ˈsā-bər\ *n* **1** : a cavalry sword with a curved blade, thick back, and guard **2 a** : a fencing sword with an arched guard that covers the back of the hand and an imaginary full-length cutting edge **b** : the sport of fencing with a saber [French *sabre,* from German dialect *Sabel,* probably of Slavic origin]

[2]saber *or* **sabre** *vt* **sa·bered** *or* **sa·bred; sa·ber·ing** *or* **sa·bring** \-bə-ring, -bring\ : to strike, cut, or kill with a saber

saber rattling *n* : aggressive display of military power

sa·ber–toothed tiger \ˌsā-bər-ˌtüth-ˈtī-gər, -ˌtütht-\ *n* : any of various large prehistoric extinct cats with very long curved upper canine teeth — called also *saber-toothed cat*

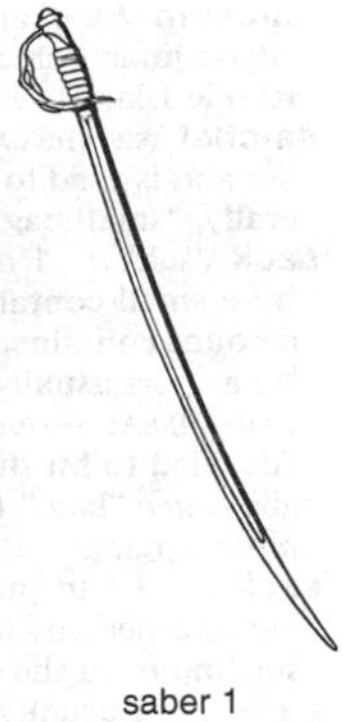

saber 1

Sa·bine \ˈsā-ˌbīn\ *n* : a member of an ancient people of the Apennines northeast of Latium conquered by Rome in 290 B.C. [Latin *Sabinus*] — **Sabine** *adj*

[1]sa·ble \ˈsā-bəl\ *n, pl* **sables** **1 a** : the color black **b** : black clothing worn in mourning — usually used in plural **2 a** *or pl* **sable** : a flesh-eating mammal of northern Europe and Asia related to the martens and valued for its soft rich brown fur; *also* : a related animal **b** : the fur or pelt of a sable [Medieval French, "sable or its fur, the heraldic color black," from Low German *sabel,* of Slavic origin]

[2]sable *adj* **1** : BLACK 1a **2** : DARK ⟨the *sable* sky⟩

sa·ble·fish \ˈsā-bəl-ˌfish\ *n* : BLACK COD

\ə\ **abut**	\au̇\ **out**	\i\ **tip**	\ȯ\ **saw**	\u̇\ **foot**
\ər\ **further**	\ch\ **chin**	\ī\ **life**	\ȯi\ **coin**	\y\ **yet**
\a\ **mat**	\e\ **pet**	\j\ **job**	\th\ **thin**	\yü\ **few**
\ā\ **take**	\ē\ **easy**	\ng\ **sing**	\th\ **this**	\yu̇\ **cure**
\ä\ **cot, cart**	\g\ **go**	\ō\ **bone**	\ü\ **food**	\zh\ **vision**

sa·bot \sa-ˈbō, ˈsab-ō\ *n* **:** a wooden shoe worn especially in various European countries [French]

[1]**sab·o·tage** \ˈsab-ə-ˌtäzh\ *n* **1 :** destruction of an employer's property (as tools or materials) or the hindering of manufacturing by discontented workers **2 :** destructive or obstructive action carried on by enemy agents or sympathizers to hinder a nation's war or defense effort [French, from *saboter* "to clatter with sabots, botch, sabotage," from *sabot* "sabot"]

[2]**sabotage** *vt* **:** to practice sabotage on ‹deliberately *sabotaging* the equipment›

sab·o·teur \ˌsab-ə-ˈtər, -ˈtu̇r\ *n* **:** a person who commits sabotage [French, from *saboter* "to sabotage"]

sa·bra \ˈsäb-rə\ *n, often cap* **:** a native Israeli [Modern Hebrew *ṣābhār,* literally, "prickly pear"]

sac \ˈsak\ *n* **:** a pouch within an animal or plant often containing a fluid ‹a synovial *sac*› [French, literally, "bag," from Latin *saccus*] — **sac·like** \ˈsak-ˌlīk\ *adj*

sac·cha·ride \ˈsak-ə-ˌrīd\ *n* **:** a monosaccharide sugar or combination of sugars

sac·cha·rim·e·ter \ˌsak-ə-ˈrim-ət-ər\ *n* **:** a device for measuring the amount of sugar in a solution

sac·cha·rin \ˈsak-rən, -ə-rən\ *n* **:** a very sweet white crystalline compound that is used as a calorie-free sweetener

sac·cha·rine \ˈsak-rən, -ə-rən, -ə-ˌrēn, -ə-ˌrīn\ *adj* **1 a :** of, relating to, or resembling that of sugar ‹*saccharine* taste› ‹*saccharine* fermentation› **b :** yielding or containing sugar ‹*saccharine* fluids› **2 :** overly or ingratiatingly sweet ‹a *saccharine* smile› [Latin *saccharum* "sugar," from Greek *sakcharon,* derived from Sanskrit *śarkarā* "gravel, sugar"] — **sac·cha·rin·i·ty** \ˌsak-ə-ˈrin-ət-ē\ *n*

sac·cule \ˈsak-yül\ *n* **:** a little sac; *esp* **:** the smaller chamber of the membranous labyrinth of the ear — compare UTRICLE [Latin *sacculus* "little bag," from *saccus* "bag"]

sac·cu·lus \ˈsak-yə-ləs\ *n, pl* **-li** \-ˌlī, -ˌlē\ **:** SACCULE

sac·er·do·tal \ˌsas-ər-ˈdōt-l, ˌsak-\ *adj* **:** PRIESTLY [Medieval French, from Latin *sacerdotalis,* from *sacerdos* "priest," from *sacer* "sacred"] — **sac·er·do·tal·ly** \-l-ē\ *adv*

sac·er·do·tal·ism \-l-ˌiz-əm\ *n* **:** religious belief emphasizing the powers of priests as essential mediators between God and humankind — **sac·er·do·tal·ist** \-l-əst\ *n*

sac fungus *n* **:** ASCOMYCETE

sa·chem \ˈsā-chəm\ *n* **:** a North American Indian chief; *esp* **:** an Algonquian chief [Narragansett (Algonquian language of Rhode Island) *sâchim*] — **sa·chem·ic** \sā-ˈchem-ik\ *adj*

sa·chet \sa-ˈshā\ *n* **:** a small bag that contains a perfumed powder and is used to scent clothes and linens [Medieval French, literally, "small bag," from *sac* "bag"]

[1]**sack** \ˈsak\ *n* **1 a :** a large bag made of coarse strong material **b :** a small container made of light material (as paper) **2 :** the amount contained in a sack **3 a :** a woman's loose-fitting dress **b :** a short usually loose-fitting coat for women and children **4 :** DISMISSAL — usually used with *get* or *give* **5 :** BUNK 2, BED ‹decided to hit the *sack* early after a long, tiring day› [Old English *sacc* "bag," from Latin *saccus,* from Greek *sakkos,* of Semitic origin]

[2]**sack** *vt* **1 :** to put in a sack **2 :** to dismiss (as from employment) especially in a summary manner ‹*sacked* the workers for stealing from the company›

[3]**sack** *n* **:** a usually dry and strong white wine imported to England from the south of Europe especially during the 16th and 17th centuries [Middle French *sec* "dry," from Latin *siccus*]

[4]**sack** *vt* **1 :** to plunder after capture **2 :** to strip of valuables **:** LOOT

[5]**sack** *n* **:** the plundering of a captured town [Middle French *sac,* from Italian *sacco* literally, "bag," from Latin *saccus*]

sack·but \ˈsak-ˌbət, -bət\ *n* **:** a medieval trombone [Middle French *saqueboute,* literally, "hooked lance," from *saquer* "to pull" + *boter* "to push"]

sack·cloth \ˈsak-ˌklȯth\ *n* **1 :** a coarse cloth suitable for sacks **:** SACKING **2 :** a garment of sackcloth worn as a sign of mourning or penitence

sack coat *n* **:** a man's jacket with a straight unfitted back

sack·ful \ˈsak-ˌfu̇l\ *n, pl* **sackfuls** \-ˌfu̇lz\ *or* **sacks·ful** \ˈsaks-ˌfu̇l\ **:** the quantity that fills a sack

sack·ing \ˈsak-ing\ *n* **:** strong coarse cloth (as burlap) from which sacks are made

sack race *n* **:** a jumping race in which the legs of each competitor are enclosed in a sack

sacque \ˈsak\ *n* **:** a loose lightweight jacket; *esp* **:** an infant's short jacket fastened at the neck [alteration of [1]*sack*]

sa·cral \ˈsak-rəl, ˈsā-krəl\ *adj* **:** of, relating to, or lying near the sacrum ‹the *sacral* region of the spinal cord›

sac·ra·ment \ˈsak-rə-mənt\ *n* **1 :** a formal religious act that is sacred as a sign or symbol of a spiritual reality; *esp* **:** one instituted by Jesus Christ as a means of grace **2** *cap* **:** BLESSED SACRAMENT [Late Latin *sacramentum,* from Latin, "oath of allegiance, obligation," from *sacrare* "to consecrate," from *sacer* "holy, sacred"] — **sac·ra·men·tal** \ˌsak-rə-ˈment-l\ *adj* — **sac·ra·men·tal·ly** \-l-ē\ *adv*

sac·ra·men·tal \ˌsak-rə-ˈment-l\ *n* **:** an action (as a rite) or object (as a rosary) originating in the church but serving as an indirect means of grace by producing devotion

sac·ra·men·tal·ism \-l-ˌiz-əm\ *n* **:** belief in or use of sacramental rites, acts, or objects; *esp* **:** belief that the sacraments are in themselves effective and necessary for salvation — **sac·ra·men·tal·ist** \-l-əst\ *n*

sa·cred \ˈsā-krəd\ *adj* **1 :** set apart in honor of someone ‹a monument *sacred* to the memory of our heroes› **2 :** worthy of religious veneration **:** HOLY ‹the *sacred* name of Jesus› **3 :** RELIGIOUS ‹*sacred* songs› **4 :** requiring or deserving to be held in highest esteem and protected from violation or encroachment ‹a *sacred* right› ‹one's *sacred* word› [Middle English, from past participle of *sacren* "to consecrate," from Medieval French *sacrer,* from Latin *sacrare,* from *sacer* "sacred, holy"] — **sa·cred·ly** *adv* — **sa·cred·ness** *n*

sacred cow *n* **:** a person or thing immune from criticism [from the veneration of the cow by Hindus]

[1]**sac·ri·fice** \ˈsak-rə-ˌfīs, -fəs\ *n* **1 :** an act of offering to a deity something precious; *esp* **:** the killing of a victim on an altar **2 :** something offered in sacrifice **3 :** a giving up of something for the sake of something else; *also* **:** something so given up ‹the *sacrifices* made by parents› **4 :** loss of something and especially of a profit ‹sell goods at a *sacrifice*› [Medieval French, from Latin *sacrificium,* from *sacer* "sacred" + *facere* "to make"]

[2]**sac·ri·fice** \-ˌfīs, -ˌfīz\ *vb* **1 :** to offer as a sacrifice or perform sacrificial rites **2 :** to give up for the sake of something else ‹*sacrifice* one's free time to help a friend› ‹*sacrificed* everything to win the election› **3 :** to sell at a loss **4 :** to make a sacrifice hit — **sac·ri·fic·er** *n*

sacrifice fly *n* **:** an outfield fly in baseball that is caught but that is long enough to permit a base runner to score

sacrifice hit *n* **:** a bunt in baseball that allows a base runner to advance one base while the batter is put out

sac·ri·fi·cial \ˌsak-rə-ˈfish-əl\ *adj* **:** of or relating to sacrifice — **sac·ri·fi·cial·ly** \-ˈfish-ə-lē\ *adv*

sac·ri·lege \ˈsak-rə-lij\ *n* **1 :** theft or violation of something consecrated to God **2 :** gross misuse or disrespect of something sacred or precious ‹it would be a *sacrilege* to cut such splendid trees› [Medieval French, from Latin *sacrilegium,* derived from *sacer* "sacred" + *legere* "to gather, steal"] — **sac·ri·le·gious** \ˌsak-rə-ˈlij-əs, -ˈlē-jəs\ *adj* — **sac·ri·le·gious·ly** *adv* — **sac·ri·le·gious·ness** *n*

sac·ris·tan \ˈsak-rə-stən\ *n* **:** an officer of a church in charge of the sacristy and ceremonial equipment; *also* **:** SEXTON

sac·ris·ty \ˈsak-rə-stē\ *n, pl* **-ties :** a room in a church where sacred utensils and vestments are kept [Medieval Latin *sacristia,* from *sacrista* "sacristan," from Latin *sacer* "sacred"]

sac·ro·il·i·ac \ˌsak-rō-ˈil-ē-ˌak, ˌsā-krō-\ *n* **:** the region in which the sacrum and ilium join — **sacroiliac** *adj*

sac·ro·sanct \ˈsak-rō-ˌsangt, -ˌsangkt\ *adj* **1 :** SACRED 4, INVIOLABLE **2 :** treated as if holy **:** immune from criticism or violation ‹a politically *sacrosanct* social program› [Latin *sacrosanctus,* probably from *sacro sanctus* "hallowed by a sacred rite"] — **sac·ro·sanc·ti·ty** \ˌsak-rō-ˈsang-tət-ē, -ˈsangk-\ *n*

sa·crum \ˈsak-rəm, ˈsā-krəm\ *n, pl* **sa·cra** \ˈsak-rə, ˈsā-krə\ **:** a triangular bone at the base of the spinal column that is directly connected with or forms a part of the pelvis and in humans consists of five fused vertebrae [Late Latin *os sacrum* "last bone of the spine," literally, "sacred bone"]

sad \ˈsad\ *adj* **sad·der; sad·dest 1 :** affected with or expressive of grief or unhappiness ‹*sad* at the loss› ‹*sad* songs› **2 a :** causing or associated with grief or unhappiness **:** DEPRESSING ‹*sad* news› **b :** DEPLORABLE, WRETCHED ‹a *sad* loss of confidence› [Old English *sæd* "sated"] — **sad·ly** *adv*

sad·den \ˈsad-n\ *vb* **sad·dened; sad·den·ing** \ˈsad-ning, -n-ing\ **:** to make or become sad

[1]sad·dle \ˈsad-ᵊl\ *n* **1 a :** a girthed usually padded and leather-covered seat for a rider on horseback; *also* **:** a comparable part of a driving harness **b :** a seat to be straddled on a vehicle (as a bicycle) **2 :** a ridge connecting two higher land elevations **3 :** a cut of meat consisting of both sides of the back including the loins **4 :** something like a saddle in shape, position, or use; *esp* **:** a support for an object **5 :** a piece of leather across the instep of a shoe [Old English *sadol*] — **in the saddle :** in control or command

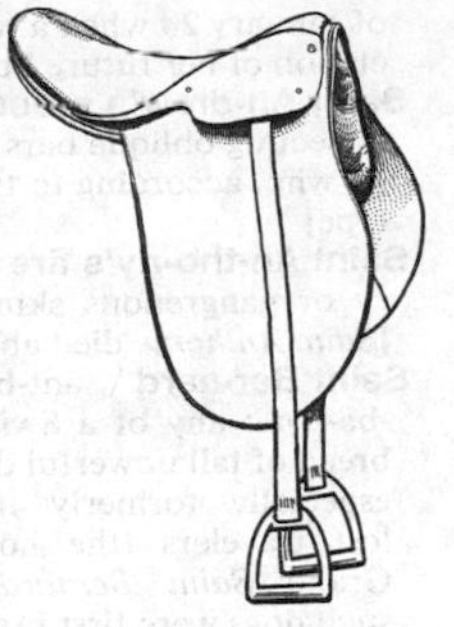
saddle 1a

[2]saddle *vb* **sad·dled; sad·dling** \ˈsad-ling, -ᵊl-ing\ **1 :** to put a saddle on or on a horse ⟨quickly *saddled* and rode off⟩ **2 :** ENCUMBER 1, BURDEN

sad·dle·bag \ˈsad-ᵊl-ˌbag\ *n* **:** a large pouch carried hanging from a saddle or over the rear wheel of a bicycle or motorcycle

saddle blanket *n* **:** a blanket or pad placed under a saddle

sad·dle·bow \ˈsad-ᵊl-ˌbō\ *n* **:** the arch in the front of a saddle

sad·dle·cloth \-ˌklȯth\ *n* **:** a cloth placed under or over a saddle

saddle horse *n* **:** a horse suited for or trained for riding

saddle leather *n* **:** vegetable-tanned leather from cattle hide that is used for saddlery; *also* **:** smooth polished leather simulating this

sad·dler \ˈsad-lər\ *n* **:** one that makes, repairs, or sells equipment for horses (as saddles)

sad·dlery \ˈsad-lə-rē, ˈsad-ᵊl-rē\ *n, pl* **-dler·ies :** the work, articles of trade, or shop of a saddler

saddle shoe *n* **:** an oxford-style shoe having a saddle of contrasting color or leather

saddle soap *n* **:** a mild soap used for cleansing and conditioning leather

saddle sore *n* **1 :** a sore on the back of a horse from an ill-fitting saddle **2 :** an irritation or sore on parts of a rider's body chafed by the saddle

sad·dle·tree \ˈsad-ᵊl-ˌtrē\ *n* **:** the frame of a saddle

Sad·du·cee \ˈsaj-ə-ˌsē, ˈsad-yə-\ *n* **:** a member of a Jewish party of the time of Christ that consisted largely of a priestly aristocracy and that rejected doctrines not in the Law [Old English *sadduce,* from Late Latin *sadducaeus,* from Greek *saddoukaios,* from Hebrew *ṣaddūqī*] — **Sad·du·ce·an** \ˌsaj-ə-ˈsē-ən, ˌsad-yə-\ *adj* — **Sad·du·cee·ism** \ˈsaj-ə-ˌsē-ˌiz-əm, ˈsad-yə-\ *n*

sad·iron \ˈsad-ˌī-ərn, -ˌīrn\ *n* **:** a flatiron pointed at both ends and having a removable handle [*sad* "compact, heavy" + *iron*]

sa·dism \ˈsād-ˌiz-əm, ˈsad-\ *n* **1 :** a perversion in which sexual pleasure is obtained by inflicting physical or mental pain upon another person **2 a :** pleasure taken in cruelty **b :** extreme cruelty [Marquis de *Sade,* died 1814, French erotic writer] — **sa·dist** \-əst\ *n* — **sa·dis·tic** \sə-ˈdis-tik, sā-\ *adj* — **sa·dis·ti·cal·ly** \-ti-kə-lē, -klē\ *adv*

sad·ness \ˈsad-nəs\ *n* **:** the quality, state, or fact of being sad ***synonyms*** see MELANCHOLY

sad sack *n* **:** a very inept person

sa·fa·ri \sə-ˈfär-ē, -ˈfar-\ *n* **1 :** the caravan and equipment of a hunting expedition especially in eastern Africa **2 :** a hunting expedition in eastern Africa **3 :** EXPEDITION 1a [Swahili, "journey," from Arabic *safarī* "of a trip"]

[1]safe \ˈsāf\ *adj* **1 :** freed from harm or risk **:** UNHURT **2 a :** secure from threat of danger, harm, or loss **b :** successful in reaching base in baseball **3 :** affording safety **4 :** not threatening danger **:** HARMLESS ⟨*safe* medicine⟩ **5 a :** CAUTIOUS ⟨a *safe* policy⟩ **b :** TRUSTWORTHY, RELIABLE ⟨a *safe* guide⟩ [Medieval French *salf, sauf,* from Latin *salvus* "safe, healthy"] — **safe·ly** *adv* — **safe·ness** *n*

[2]safe *n* **:** a place or container to keep articles (as valuables) safe

safe–con·duct \ˈsāf-ˈkän-ˌdəkt, -dəkt\ *n* **1 :** protection given a person passing through a military zone or occupied area **2 :** a document authorizing safe-conduct

safe·crack·er \ˈsāf-ˌkrak-ər\ *n* **:** one that breaks open safes to steal their contents

safe–de·pos·it box \ˌsāf-di-ˈpäz-ət-\ *n* **:** a box (as in the vault of a bank) for the safe storage of valuables

[1]safe·guard \ˈsāf-ˌgärd\ *n* **:** something that protects and gives safety **:** DEFENSE

[2]safeguard *vt* **:** to make safe or secure **:** PROTECT

safe·keep·ing \ˈsāf-ˈkē-ping\ *n* **:** a keeping or being kept in safety

safe·light \ˈsā-ˌflīt\ *n* **:** a darkroom lamp with a filter to screen out rays that are harmful to sensitive film or paper

safe sex *n* **:** sexual activity and especially sexual intercourse in which various measures (as the use of latex condoms or the practice of monogamy) are taken to avoid disease (as AIDS) transmitted by sexual contact — called also *safer sex*

safe·ty \ˈsāf-tē\ *n, pl* **safeties 1 :** the state or condition of being safe **:** freedom from hurt, injury, or loss **2 :** a protective device (as on a firearm) to prevent accidental operation **3 a :** a situation in football in which a member of the offensive team is tackled behind its own goal line and which counts two points for the defensive team — compare TOUCHBACK **b :** a defensive football back who plays the deepest position in the secondary

safety belt *n* **:** a belt fastening a person to an object to prevent falling or injury

safety glass *n* **:** glass that resists shattering and is formed of two sheets of glass with a sheet of transparent plastic between them

safety lamp *n* **:** a miner's lamp constructed to avoid explosion in an atmosphere containing flammable gas usually by enclosing the flame in fine wire gauze

safety match *n* **:** a match that can be ignited only by striking on a specially prepared surface

safety pin *n* **:** a pin in the form of a clasp with a guard covering its point

safety razor *n* **:** a razor with a guard for the blade to prevent deep cuts

safety valve *n* **1 :** a valve that opens automatically (as when steam pressure becomes too great) **2 :** OUTLET 2

saf·flow·er \ˈsaf-ˌlau̇-ər, -ˌlau̇r\ *n* **:** a widely grown Old World herb related to the daisies and having large orange or red flower heads yielding a dyestuff and seeds rich in edible oil [Middle French *saffleur,* from Italian *saffiore,* from Arabic *ʿaṣfar, ʿuṣfar,* a yellow plant]

safflower oil *n* **:** a polyunsaturated edible oil obtained from the seeds of the safflower

saf·fron \ˈsaf-rən\ *n* **1 a :** a purple-flowered crocus whose deep orange aromatic pungent dried stigmas are used especially to color and flavor foods **b :** the dried usually powdered stigmas of saffron **2 :** a moderate orange to orange yellow [Medieval French *safren,* from Medieval Latin *safranum,* from Arabic *zaʿfarān*]

saf·ra·nine *or* **saf·ra·nin** \ˈsaf-rə-ˌnēn, -nən\ *n* **:** any of various usually red synthetic dyes [from French or German *safran* "saffron"]

[1]sag \ˈsag\ *vi* **sagged; sag·ging 1 :** to droop, sink, or settle from or as if from pressure or loss of tautness **2 :** to lose firmness, resiliency, or vigor ⟨*sagging* spirits⟩ **3 :** to decline from a thriving position ⟨a *sagging* economy⟩ — **sag·gy** \ˈsag-ē\ *adj*

[2]sag *n* **:** a sagging part or area ⟨the *sag* in a rope⟩; *also* **:** an instance or amount of sagging

sa·ga \ˈsäg-ə\ *n* **1 :** a tale of historic or legendary figures and events of Norway and Iceland **2 :** a story of heroic deeds **3 :** a long detailed account [Old Norse]

sa·ga·cious \sə-ˈgā-shəs\ *adj* **:** keen and farsighted in understanding and judgment **:** DISCERNING ⟨a *sagacious* judge of character⟩ [Latin *sagac-, sagax,* from *sagire* "to perceive keenly"] ***synonyms*** see SHREWD — **sa·ga·cious·ly** *adv* — **sa·ga·cious·ness** *n* — **sa·gac·i·ty** \-ˈgas-ət-ē\ *n*

sag·a·more \ˈsag-ə-ˌmōr, -ˌmȯr\ *n* **1 :** an Algonquian Indian chief subordinate to a sachem **2 :** SACHEM [Eastern Abenaki (Algonquian language of northern New England) *sàkəma*]

[1]sage \ˈsāj\ *adj* **1 :** wise through reflection and experience **2 :** proceeding from or characterized by wisdom, prudence, and good judgment ⟨*sage* advice⟩ [Medieval French, derived from Latin *sapere* "to taste, have good taste, be wise"] ***synonyms*** see WISE — **sage·ly** *adv* — **sage·ness** *n*

\ə\ **abut**	\au̇\ **out**	\i\ **tip**	\ȯ\ **saw**	\u̇\ **foot**
\ər\ **further**	\ch\ **chin**	\ī\ **life**	\ȯi\ **coin**	\y\ **yet**
\a\ **mat**	\e\ **pet**	\j\ **job**	\th\ **thin**	\yü\ **few**
\ā\ **take**	\ē\ **easy**	\ng\ **sing**	\t͟h\ **this**	\yu̇\ **cure**
\ä\ **cot, cart**	\g\ **go**	\ō\ **bone**	\ü\ **food**	\zh\ **vision**

[2]**sage** *n* : a very wise person

[3]**sage** *n* **1** : a European mint with grayish green aromatic leaves used especially in flavoring meats; *also* : SALVIA **2** : SAGEBRUSH [Medieval French *sage, salge,* from Latin *salvia,* from *salvus* "healthy"; from its use as a medicinal herb]

sage·brush \'sāj-ˌbrəsh\ *n* : any of several low shrubby North American plants related to the daisies; *esp* : a common plant with a bitter juice and an odor resembling sage that is widespread on alkaline plains of the western U.S.

sagebrush

sag·it·tal \'saj-ət-l, sə-'jit-\ *adj* : of, relating to, or being the median longitudinal plane of the body or any plane parallel to it [Latin *sagitta* "arrow"] — **sag·it·tal·ly** \-l-ē\ *adv*

Sag·it·tar·i·us \ˌsaj-ə-'ter-ē-əs\ *n* **1** : a zodiacal southern constellation pictured as a centaur shooting an arrow **2** : the 9th sign of the zodiac; *also* : one born under this sign [Latin, literally, "archer," from *sagitta* "arrow"]

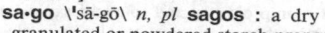

sa·go \'sā-gō\ *n, pl* **sagos** : a dry granulated or powdered starch prepared from spongy tissue inside the stem of a sago palm [Malay *sagu* "sago palm"]

sago palm *n* : a palm or cycad that yields sago; *esp* : any of various tall pinnate-leaved Malaysian palms

sa·gua·ro \sə-'wär-ə, -'wär-ō, -'gwär-ō\ *n, pl* **-ros** : a cactus of desert regions of the southwestern U.S. and Mexico that has a columnar spiny sparsely branched trunk, bears white flowers and edible reddish fruit, and may reach a height of up to 50 feet (16 meters) [Mexican Spanish]

sa·hib \'sä-ˌhib, -ˌib, -ˌhēb, -ˌēb, ˌsä-'\ *n* **1** : SIR, MASTER — used especially among Hindus and Muslims in colonial India when addressing or speaking of a European of some social or official status **2** : a European man of some social status living in India — compare MEMSAHIB [Hindi *sāhab* and Urdu *ṣāḥib, ṣāḥab* "companion, master," from Arabic *ṣāḥib*]

said \'sed\ *adj* : AFOREMENTIONED ⟨the *said* parties will abide by the terms of the contract⟩ [from past participle of *say*]

[1]**sail** \'sāl, *as last element in compounds often* səl\ *n* **1 a** : a usually rectangular or triangular piece of fabric by means of which wind is used to propel a wind-powered vessel or craft **b** : the sails of a ship **2** *pl usually* **sail** : a ship equipped with sails **3** : a passage by a sailing boat or ship ⟨go for a *sail*⟩ [Old English *segl*]

[2]**sail** *vb* **1 a** : to travel on water in a sailing vessel; *also* : to travel or begin a journey by water ⟨*sailed* for England on the first steamer⟩ **b** : to move or pass over by ship ⟨*sail* the seas⟩ **c** : to function in sailing ⟨a boat that *sails* well⟩; *also* : to handle or manage the sailing of ⟨experienced in *sailing* small craft⟩ **2** : to move effortlessly or gracefully — **sail into** : to attack vigorously or sharply ⟨*sailed into* their dinner⟩ ⟨*sailed into* me for being late⟩

sail·boat \'sāl-ˌbōt\ *n* : a boat equipped with sails

sail·cloth \-ˌklȯth\ *n* : a heavy canvas formerly much used for sails and tents

sail·er \'sā-lər\ *n* : a ship or boat especially having specified sailing qualities

sail·fish \'sāl-ˌfish\ *n* : any of a genus of large marine fishes that are related to the swordfish and marlins and have long slender jaws and a very large fin resembling a sail on the back

sail·ing \'sā-ling\ *n* **1** : the technical skill of managing a ship : NAVIGATION **2** : the sport of navigating or riding in a sailboat

sail·or \'sā-lər\ *n* **1** : one that sails: as **a** : a member of a ship's crew **b** : a person of the rank of seaman in the Navy **c** : a traveler by water **2** : a stiff straw hat with a low flat crown and straight circular brim

sail·plane \'sāl-ˌplān\ *n* : a glider designed to rise in an upward current of air

[1]**saint** \'sānt; *when a name follows* ˌsānt *or* sānt *or* sənt\ *n* **1** : a holy and godly person; *esp* : one who is canonized **2** *cap* : LATTER-DAY SAINT **3** : a very pious or virtuous person [Medieval French, from Late Latin *sanctus,* from Latin, "sacred," from *sancire* "to make sacred"]

[2]**saint** \'sānt\ *vt* : CANONIZE

Saint Ag·nes's Eve \-ˌag-nə-səz-'ēv, -ˌag-nəs-'ēv\ *n* : the night of January 20 when a woman is traditionally held to have a revelation of her future husband [*Saint Agnes*]

Saint An·drew's cross \-ˌan-ˌdrüz-\ *n* : a cross having two intersecting oblique bars [*Saint Andrew,* died about 60 A.D., apostle who, according to tradition, was crucified on a cross of this type]

Saint An·tho·ny's fire \-ˌan-thə-nēz-, -ˌant-\ *n* : an inflammatory or gangrenous skin condition (as erysipelas or ergotism) [*Saint Anthony,* died about 350, Egyptian monk]

Saint Ber·nard \ˌsānt-bər-'närd, -bə-\ *n* : any of a Swiss alpine breed of tall powerful dogs used especially formerly in aiding lost travelers [the hospice of Grand *Saint Bernard,* where such dogs were first bred]

Saint Bernard

saint·dom \'sānt-dəm\ *n* : SAINTHOOD 1

saint·ed \'sānt-əd\ *adj* **1** : SAINTLY, PIOUS **2** : DECEASED

Saint El·mo's fire \-ˌel-mōz-\ *n* : a luminous discharge of electricity sometimes seen in stormy weather at prominent points on an airplane or ship [*Saint Elmo (Erasmus),* died 303, Italian bishop and patron saint of sailors]

saint·hood \'sānt-ˌhu̇d\ *n* **1** : the quality or state of being a saint **2** : saints as a group

Saint–John's–wort \-'jänz-ˌwərt, -ˌwȯrt\ *n* : any of a large genus of herbs and shrubs with showy yellow flowers [*Saint John* the Baptist]

saint·ly \'sānt-lē\ *adj* **saint·li·er; -est** : relating to, resembling, or befitting a saint : HOLY — **saint·li·ness** *n*

Saint Mar·tin's summer \-ˌmärt-nz-'səm-ər, -ˌmärt-n-\ *n* : Indian summer when occurring in November [*Saint Martin's Day,* November 11]

Saint Pat·rick's Day \-'pa-triks-\ *n* : March 17 observed by the Roman Catholic Church in honor of St. Patrick and celebrated as a legal holiday in Ireland in commemoration of his death

saint·ship \'sānt-ˌship\ *n* : SAINTHOOD 1

Saint Valentine's Day *n* : VALENTINE'S DAY [*Saint Valentine,* died about 270, Italian priest]

Saint Vi·tus' dance *or* **Saint Vi·tus's dance** \-ˌvīt-əs-, -əs-əz-\ *n* : CHOREA [*Saint Vitus,* 3rd century Christian child martyr]

saith \seth, 'seth, 'sā-əth\ *archaic present 3rd singular of* SAY

[1]**sake** \'sāk\ *n* **1** : END, PURPOSE ⟨for the *sake* of argument⟩ **2** : GOOD, ADVANTAGE ⟨the *sake* of my country⟩ [Middle English, "dispute, guilt, purpose," from Old English *sacu* "guilt, action at law"]

[2]**sa·ke** *or* **sa·ki** \'säk-ē\ *n* : a Japanese alcoholic beverage of fermented rice usually served hot [Japanese *sake*]

sal \'sal\ *n* : SALT ⟨*sal* soda⟩ [Latin]

sa·laam \sə-'läm\ *n* **1** : a salutation or ceremonial greeting in the East **2** : deference shown by bowing very low and placing the right palm on the forehead [Arabic *salām,* literally, "peace"] — **salaam** *vb*

sal·able *or* **sale·able** \'sā-lə-bəl\ *adj* : capable of being or fit to be sold : MARKETABLE — **sal·abil·i·ty** \ˌsā-lə-'bil-ət-ē\ *n*

sa·la·cious \sə-'lā-shəs\ *adj* **1** : arousing sexual desire or imagination **2** : LUSTFUL, LECHEROUS [Latin *salac-, salax* "fond of leaping, lustful," from *salire* "to leap"] — **sa·la·cious·ly** *adv* — **sa·la·cious·ness** *n*

sal·ad \'sal-əd\ *n* **1** : a cooked or uncooked usually cold dish typically prepared or served with a savory dressing: as **a** : raw vegetables (as lettuce and tomatoes) served with dressing **b** : a cold dish (as of meat, shellfish, fruit, or vegetables) usually served with a dressing **2** : a green vegetable or herb grown for salad [Medieval French *salade,* from Italian dialect *salata, salada,* from *salar* "to salt," from *sal* "salt," from Latin]

salad bar *n* : a self-service counter in a restaurant featuring a selection of salad makings and dressings

salad days *n pl* : time of youthful inexperience or indiscretion

salad dressing *n* : a sauce for a salad

salad oil *n* : a vegetable oil suitable for use in salad dressings

sal·a·man·der \'sal-ə-ˌman-dər\ *n* **1** : a mythical being having the power to endure fire without harm **2** : any of an order (Caudata) of amphibians superficially resembling lizards but scaleless and covered with a soft moist skin and breathing by gills in the larval stage **3** : something (as a utensil for browning pastry or a portable stove or incinerator) used in connection with fire [Medieval French *salamandre,* from Latin *salamandra,* from Greek] — **sal·a·man·drine** \ˌsal-ə-ˈman-drən\ *adj*

salamander 2

sa·la·mi \sə-ˈläm-ē\ *n* **:** highly seasoned sausage of pork and beef often dried for storage [Italian, pl. of *salame* "salami," from *salare* "to salt," from *sale* "salt," from Latin *sal*]

sal am·mo·ni·ac \ˌsal-ə-ˈmō-nē-ˌak\ *n* **:** AMMONIUM CHLORIDE [Latin *sal ammoniacus,* literally, "salt of Ammon"]

sal·a·ried \ˈsal-rēd, -ə-rēd\ *adj* **:** receiving or yielding a salary

sal·a·ry \ˈsal-rē, -ə-rē\ *n, pl* **-ries :** money paid regularly (as by the year or month) for work or services [Latin *salarium* "salt money, pension, salary," derived from *sal* "salt"]

Word History In the Roman army soldiers were allowed a sum of money to buy salt with, since salt was not always easily come by and was important for more than increasing the savor of food in the days before refrigeration. Later *salarium,* the name for this money, came to be used for the stipend or pension paid to soldiers and still later for payments made to officials of the empire. Latin *salarium,* the source of English *salary,* is derived from *sal,* "salt."

sale \ˈsāl\ *n* **1 :** the act of selling; *esp* **:** the transfer of ownership of property from one person to another for a price **2 :** public disposal to the highest bidder **:** AUCTION **3 :** a selling of goods at bargain prices **4** *pl* **a :** the business of selling **b :** gross receipts ⟨*sales* are up⟩ [Old English *sala*] — **for sale :** available for purchase — **on sale 1 :** for sale **2 :** available for purchase at a reduced price

sales \ˈsālz\ *adj* **:** of, relating to, or used in selling

sales check *n* **:** a piece of paper used by retail stores as a memorandum, record, or receipt of a sale

sales·clerk \-ˌklərk\ *n* **:** a person employed to sell merchandise in a store

Sa·le·sian \sə-ˈlē-zhən, sā-\ *n* **:** a member of the Society of St. Francis de Sales founded by St. John Bosco in Turin, Italy in the 19th century and devoted chiefly to education

sales·man \ˈsālz-mən\ *n* **:** one who is employed to sell merchandise either in a territory or in a store — **sales·man·ship** \-ˌship\ *n*

sales·peo·ple \-ˌpē-pəl\ *n pl* **:** people employed to sell goods or services

sales·per·son \-ˌpər-sən\ *n* **:** a person employed to sell goods or services

sales register *n* **:** CASH REGISTER

sales·room \ˈsālz-ˌrüm, -ˌrům\ *n* **:** a place where goods are displayed for sale

sales tax *n* **:** a tax on the sale of goods and services that is usually calculated as a percentage of the purchase price and collected by the seller

sales·wom·an \ˈsālz-ˌwům-ən\ *n* **:** a woman employed to sell merchandise

Sa·lic \ˈsā-lik, ˈsal-ik\ *adj* **:** of, relating to, or being a Frankish people that settled on the IJssel river early in the 4th century [Medieval Latin *Salicus,* from Late Latin *Salii* "Salic Franks"]

sal·i·cin \ˈsal-ə-sən\ *n* **:** a bitter white crystalline compound found in the bark and leaves of several willows and poplars and used in medicine like salicylic acid [French *salicine,* from Latin *salic-, salix* "willow"]

sa·lic·y·late \sə-ˈlis-ə-ˌlāt\ *n* **:** a salt or ester of salicylic acid; *also* **:** SALICYLIC ACID

sal·i·cyl·ic acid \ˌsal-ə-ˌsil-ik-\ *n* **:** a crystalline organic acid $C_7H_6O_3$ used especially in the form of salts to relieve pain or fever [derived from Latin *salic-, salix* "willow"]

sa·lience \ˈsāl-yəns, ˈsā-lē-əns\ *n* **1 :** the quality or state of being salient **2 :** a striking point or feature **:** HIGHLIGHT

[1]**sa·lient** \ˈsāl-yənt, ˈsā-lē-ənt\ *adj* **1 :** jetting upward ⟨a *salient* fountain⟩ **2 a :** projecting beyond a line, surface, or level ⟨a *salient* angle⟩ **b :** standing out conspicuously **:** PROMINENT ⟨*salient* traits⟩ [Latin *saliens,* present participle of *salire* "to leap"] — **sa·lient·ly** *adv*

[2]**salient** *n* **:** something that projects outward; *esp* **:** an outwardly projecting part of a fortification or line of defense

[1]**sa·line** \ˈsā-ˌlēn, -ˌlīn\ *adj* **1 :** consisting of or containing salt ⟨a *saline* solution⟩ **2 :** of, relating to, or resembling salt **:** SALTY ⟨a *saline* taste⟩ ⟨*saline* compounds⟩ [Latin *salinus,* from *sal* "salt"] — **sa·lin·i·ty** \sā-ˈlin-ət-ē, sə-\ *n*

[2]**saline** *n* **1 :** a metallic salt; *esp* **:** a salt of potassium, sodium, or magnesium with a cathartic action **2 :** a saline solution

sal·i·nom·e·ter \ˌsal-ə-ˈnäm-ət-ər\ *n* **:** an instrument for measuring the amount of salt in a solution

Salis·bury steak \ˈsȯlz-ˌber-ē-, ˈsalz-, -bə-rē, -brē-\ *n* **:** ground beef mixed with egg, milk, bread crumbs, and seasoning and formed into large patties for cooking [J. H. *Salisbury,* died 1905, American physician]

sa·li·va \sə-ˈlī-və\ *n* **:** a slightly alkaline secretion of water, mucin, protein, salts, and often a starch-splitting enzyme secreted into the mouth by salivary glands [Latin]

sal·i·vary \ˈsal-ə-ˌver-ē\ *adj* **:** of or relating to saliva or the glands that secrete it; *esp* **:** producing or carrying saliva ⟨*salivary* glands⟩

sal·i·vate \ˈsal-ə-ˌvāt\ *vi* **:** to secrete saliva especially in large amounts — **sal·i·va·tion** \ˌsal-ə-ˈvā-shən\ *n*

Salk vaccine \ˈsȯk-, ˈsȯlk-\ *n* **:** a polio vaccine that contains virus inactivated with formaldehyde and is administered by injection [Jonas *Salk,* died 1985, American physician]

[1]**sal·low** \ˈsal-ō\ *n* **:** any of several Old World broad-leaved willows used especially as sources of charcoal and tanbark [Old English *sealh*]

[2]**sallow** *adj* **:** of a grayish greenish yellow color [Old English *salu*] — **sal·low·ish** \ˈsal-ə-wish\ *adj* — **sal·low·ness** \ˈsal-ō-nəs\ *n*

[3]**sallow** *vt* **:** to make sallow

[1]**sal·ly** \ˈsal-ē\ *n, pl* **sallies 1 :** an action of rushing or bursting forth; *esp* **:** a sortie of troops from a defensive position to attack the enemy **2 a :** a brief outbreak **:** OUTBURST **b :** a witty remark **:** QUIP **3 :** an excursion usually off the beaten track **:** JAUNT [Middle French *saillie,* from *saillir* "to rush forward," from Latin *salire* "to leap"]

[2]**sally** *vi* **sal·lied; sal·ly·ing 1 :** to leap out or burst forth suddenly **2 :** to set out **:** DEPART — usually used with *forth*

Sal·ly Lunn \ˌsal-ē-ˈlən\ *n* **:** a slightly sweetened yeast-leavened bread [*Sally Lunn,* 18th century English baker]

sal·ma·gun·di \ˌsal-mə-ˈgən-dē\ *n* **1 :** a salad of chopped meats, anchovies, eggs, and vegetables arranged in rows for contrast and served with dressing **2 :** a varied mixture **:** POTPOURRI [French *salmigondis*]

salm·on \ˈsam-ən\ *n, pl* **salmon** *also* **salmons 1 :** any of various large food and game fishes that are related to the trouts, have reddish or pinkish flesh, live in oceans or large lakes, and swim up rivers or streams to deposit or fertilize eggs: as **a :** one of the northern Atlantic that does not die after spawning — called also *Atlantic salmon* **b :** any of several closely related fishes (as the chinook salmon or coho) of the northern Pacific that typically die after spawning — called also *Pacific salmon* **2 :** a strong yellowish pink color resembling that of the flesh of some salmons [Medieval French, from Latin *salmo*] — **salm·on·oid** \ˈsam-ə-ˌnȯid\ *adj or n*

salm·on·ber·ry \-ˌber-ē\ *n* **:** a showy red-flowered raspberry of the Pacific coast of North America; *also* **:** its edible salmon-colored fruit

sal·mo·nel·la \ˌsal-mə-ˈnel-ə\ *n, pl* **-nel·lae** \-ˈnel-ˌē, -ˌī\ *or* **-nellas** *or* **-nella :** any of a genus of rod-shaped bacteria that cause food poisoning, gastrointestinal inflammation, typhoid fever, or blood poisoning of warm-blooded animals [New Latin, from Daniel E. *Salmon,* died 1914, American veterinarian]

sal·mo·nel·lo·sis \ˌsal-mə-ˌnel-ˈō-səs\ *n, pl* **-lo·ses** \-ˌsēz\ **:** infection with or disease caused by salmonellas

salmon pink *n* **:** a strong yellowish pink

sa·lon \sə-ˈlän, ˈsal-ˌän, sa-ˈlōⁿ\ *n* **1 :** an elegant apartment or living room **2 :** a fashionable gathering of notables customarily held at the home of a prominent person **3 a :** a place for the exhibition of art **b** *cap* **:** an annual art exhibition **4 :** a stylish business establishment [French]

sa·loon \sə-ˈlün\ *n* **1 :** an elaborately decorated public apartment or hall (as a large cabin for the social use of a ship's passengers) **2 :** a place in which alcoholic beverages are sold and consumed [French *salon,* from Italian *salone,* from *sala* "hall," of Germanic origin]

\ə\ **abut**	\au̇\ **out**	\i\ **tip**	\ȯ\ **saw**	\u̇\ **foot**
\ər\ **further**	\ch\ **chin**	\ī\ **life**	\ȯi\ **coin**	\y\ **yet**
\a\ **mat**	\e\ **pet**	\j\ **job**	\th\ **thin**	\yü\ **few**
\ā\ **take**	\ē\ **easy**	\ng\ **sing**	\t͟h\ **this**	\yu̇\ **cure**
\ä\ **cot, cart**	\g\ **go**	\ō\ **bone**	\ü\ **food**	\zh\ **vision**

sal·pi·glos·sis \ˌsal-pə-ˈgläs-əs\ *n* : any of a genus of Chilean herbs of the nightshade family that are sometimes grown for their large multicolored funnel-shaped flowers [New Latin, from Greek *salpinx* "trumpet" + *glōssa* "tongue"]

sal·sa \ˈsȯl-sə, ˈsäl-\ *n* **1** : a spicy sauce of tomatoes, onions, and hot peppers **2** : popular music of Latin American origin that has absorbed characteristics of rhythm and blues, jazz, and rock [Spanish, literally, "sauce," from Latin, feminine of *salsus* "salted"]

sal·si·fy \ˈsal-sə-fē, -ˌfī\ *n, pl* **-fies** : a purple-flowered European herb related to the daisies that is grown for its long fleshy edible root — called also *oyster plant* [French *salsifis,* from Italian *salsefica, sassefrica*]

[1]**salt** \ˈsȯlt\ *n* **1 a** : a compound in the form of crystals that consists of sodium chloride, is abundant in nature, and is used especially for seasoning or preserving food — called also *common salt* **b** *pl* (1) : a mineral or saline mixture (as Epsom salts) used as a laxative or carthartic (2) : SMELLING SALTS **c** : a compound formed by replacement of part or all of the acid hydrogen of an acid by a metal or a group acting like a metal **2 a** : an ingredient that gives savor, piquancy, or zest (as to one's life) : FLAVOR 4 **b** : sharpness of wit : PUNGENCY **c** : COMMON SENSE **d** : SKEPTICISM 1 — usually used in the phrases *with a grain of salt* and *with a pinch of salt* **e** : the sprinkling of people thought to set a model of excellence for or to give tone to the rest — usually used in the phrase *salt of the earth* **3** : SAILOR ⟨a tale told by an old *salt*⟩ [Old English *sealt*]

[2]**salt** *vt* **1 a** : to treat, flavor, or supply with salt ⟨*salt* a dish to taste⟩ **b** : to preserve (food) with salt **2** : to add flavor or zest to (as a story) **3** : to make (as a mine) appear richer by secretly adding valuable mineral

[3]**salt** *adj* **1 a** : SALINE, SALTY ⟨*salt* water⟩ **b** : being or inducing the one of the four basic taste sensations produced by table salt **2** : cured or seasoned with salt ⟨*salt* pork⟩ **3** : flooded by the sea ⟨a *salt* pond⟩ **4** : SALTY 3a — **salt·ness** *n*

salt–and–pepper *adj* : having black-and-white or dark and light color intermingled in small flecks

sal·ta·tion \sal-ˈtā-shən, sȯl-\ *n* : the action of leaping or jumping [Latin *saltatio,* from *saltare* "to leap, dance," from *salire* "to leap"]

salt away *vt* : to lay away (as money) safely : SAVE

salt·box \ˈsȯlt-ˌbäks\ *n* : a frame dwelling with two stories in front and one behind and a roof with a long rear slope

saltbox

salt·bush \ˈsȯlt-ˌbu̇sh\ *n* : any of various shrubby plants that are related to the goosefoots and thrive in dry salty soils

salt·cel·lar \-ˌsel-ər\ *n* : a small container for holding salt at the table [Middle English *salt saler,* from *salt* + *saler* "saltcellar," from Medieval French, from Latin *salarius* "of salt," from *sal* "salt"]

sal·tern \ˈsȯl-tərn\ *n* : a place where salt is made by boiling or evaporation [Old English *sealtern,* from *sealt* "salt" + *ærn* "house"]

salt flat *n* : an area of salt-encrusted land left by evaporation of water (as from a former lake)

salt gland *n* : a gland (as of a seabird) capable of excreting a concentrated salt solution

sal·tine \sȯl-ˈtēn\ *n* : a thin crisp cracker sprinkled with salt

salt lake *n* : a lake that has become salty through evaporation

salt lick *n* : LICK 3

salt marsh *n* : flat land subject to overflow by salt water

salt out *vt* : to precipitate, coagulate, or separate (a dissolved substance or sol) from a solution by adding salt

salt pan *n* : an undrained natural depression in which water gathers and leaves a deposit of salt on evaporation

salt·pe·ter \ˈsȯlt-ˈpēt-ər\ *n* **1** : POTASSIUM NITRATE **2** : SODIUM NITRATE [Medieval Latin *sal petrae,* literally, "salt of the rock"]

salt·shak·er \-ˌshā-kər\ *n* : a container with a perforated top for sprinkling salt

salt·wa·ter \ˈsȯlt-ˌwȯt-ər, -ˌwät-\ *adj* : relating to, living in, or consisting of salt water

salt·works \ˈsȯlt-ˌwərks\ *n sing or pl* : a plant where salt is prepared commercially

salty \ˈsȯl-tē\ *adj* **salt·i·er; -est** **1** : seasoned with or containing salt often to excess **2** : suggesting the sea or nautical life **3 a** : CAUSTIC ⟨*salty* wit⟩ **b** : SPICY 4, RACY — **salt·i·ness** *n*

sa·lu·bri·ous \sə-ˈlü-brē-əs\ *adj* : favorable to or promoting health [Latin *salubris*] ***synonyms*** see HEALTHFUL — **sa·lu·bri·ous·ly** *adv* — **sa·lu·bri·ous·ness** *n* — **sa·lu·bri·ty** \-brət-ē\ *n*

sa·lu·ki \sə-ˈlü-kē\ *n* : any of an old northern African and Asian breed of tall slender swift-footed keen-eyed hunting dogs having long narrow heads and a smooth silky coat [Arabic *salūqī* "of Saluq," from *Salūq* "Saluq (ancient city in Arabia)"]

saluki

sal·u·tary \ˈsal-yə-ˌter-ē\ *adj* **1** : producing a beneficial effect ⟨*salutary* influences⟩ **2** : promoting health : CURATIVE [Middle French *salutaire,* from Latin *salutaris,* from *salut-, salus* "health"] ***synonyms*** see HEALTHFUL — **sal·u·tar·i·ly** \ˌsal-yə-ˈter-ə-lē\ *adv* — **sal·u·tar·i·ness** \ˈsal-yə-ˌter-ē-nəs\ *n*

sal·u·ta·tion \ˌsal-yə-ˈtā-shən\ *n* **1 a** : an expression of greeting, goodwill, or courtesy **b** *pl* : REGARD 2b(2) **2** : the word or phrase of greeting that conventionally begins a letter — **sal·u·ta·tion·al** \-shnəl, -shən-l\ *adj*

sa·lu·ta·to·ri·an \sə-ˌlüt-ə-ˈtōr-ē-ən, -ˈtȯr-\ *n* : the graduating student usually second highest in rank who gives the salutatory address

[1]**sa·lu·ta·to·ry** \sə-ˈlüt-ə-ˌtōr-ē, -ˌtȯr-\ *adj* : expressing salutations or welcome

[2]**salutatory** *n, pl* **-ries** : a salutatory address given at a commencement exercise

[1]**sa·lute** \sə-ˈlüt\ *vb* **1** : to greet with courteous words or with a sign of respect or goodwill **2 a** : to honor by a conventional military ceremony **b** : to show respect and recognition by assuming a prescribed position or making a prescribed gesture ⟨*salute* an officer⟩ **c** : PRAISE 1 [Latin *salutare,* from *salut-, salus* "health, safety, greeting"] — **sa·lut·er** *n*

[2]**salute** *n* **1** : SALUTATION 1, GREETING **2 a** : a sign, token, or ceremony (as a kiss or a bow) expressing goodwill, compliment, or respect **b** : the position or gesture of a person saluting a superior

salv·able \ˈsal-və-bəl\ *adj* : capable of being saved or salvaged [Late Latin *salvare* "to save"]

[1]**sal·vage** \ˈsal-vij\ *n* **1** : money paid for saving a wrecked or endangered ship, its cargo, or its passengers **2 a** : the act of saving a ship **b** : the act of saving property in danger **3** : property saved or recovered (as from a wreck or fire) [French, from Middle French *salver* "to save," from Late Latin *salvare* "to save," from Latin *salvus* "safe"]

[2]**salvage** *vt* : to rescue or save especially from wreckage or ruin — **sal·vage·able** \-ə-bəl\ *adj* — **sal·vag·er** *n*

sal·var·san \ˈsal-vər-ˌsan\ *n* : ARSPHENAMINE

sal·va·tion \sal-ˈvā-shən\ *n* **1** : deliverance from sin **2** : something that saves ⟨the medicine was the patient's *salvation*⟩ **3** : preservation from destruction or failure [Medieval French, from Late Latin *salvatio,* from *salvare* "to save," from Latin *salvus* "safe"] — **sal·va·tion·al** \-shnəl, -shən-l\ *adj*

[1]**salve** \ˈsav, ˈsȧv\ *n* **1** : a healing ointment **2** : an influence or agent that remedies or soothes [Old English *sealf*]

[2]**salve** *vt* : to ease or soothe with or as if with a salve

sal·ver \ˈsal-vər\ *n* : a serving tray [French *salve,* from Spanish *salva* "sampling of food to detect poison, tray," from *salvar* "to save, sample food to detect poison," from Late Latin *salvare* "to save," from Latin *salvus* "safe"]

sal·via \ˈsal-vē-ə\ *n* : any of a large and widely distributed genus of herbs or shrubs of the mint family; *esp* : SCARLET SAGE [Latin]

sal·vo \ˈsal-vō\ *n, pl* **salvos** *or* **salvoes** **1 a** : a firing at one time of two or more guns in military action or as a salute **b** : the release all at once of a rack of bombs or rockets **c** : a discharge of one gun after another in a battery **d** : the bombs or projectiles released in a salvo **2** : SALUTE 2a, TRIBUTE **3** : a sudden burst (as of cheers) [Italian *salva,* from French *salve,* from Latin, "hail!," imperative of *salvēre* "to be healthy," from *salvus* "healthy, safe"]

SAM \ˈsam, ˌes-ˌā-ˈem\ *n* **:** a surface-to-air missile

sa·ma·ra \ˈsam-ə-rə; sə-ˈmar-ə, -ˈmär-\ *n* **:** a dry usually one-seeded winged fruit (as of an ash or elm tree) that does not split open when mature — called also *key* [Latin, "elm seed"]

Sa·mar·i·tan \sə-ˈmar-ət-n, -ˈmer-\ *n* **1 :** a native or inhabitant of Samaria **2** *often not cap* **:** one ready and generous in helping those in distress [Late Latin *samaritanus,* from Greek *samaritēs,* from *Samaria* "Samaria"; sense 2 from the parable of the good Samaritan, Luke 10:30-37] — **samaritan** *adj, often cap*

sa·mar·i·um \sə-ˈmer-ē-əm, -ˈmar-\ *n* **:** a pale gray lustrous metallic chemical element — see ELEMENT table [New Latin, from French *samarskite,* a mineral, from V. E. *Samarskiĭ*-Bykhovets, died 1870, Russian mining engineer]

sam·ba \ˈsam-bə, ˈsäm-\ *n* **:** a Brazilian dance characterized by a dip and spring upward at each beat of the music [Portuguese] — **samba** *vi*

Sam Browne belt \ˌsam-ˌbraůn-\ *n* **:** a leather belt for a dress uniform supported by a light strap passing over the right shoulder [Sir *Sam*uel James *Browne,* died 1901, British army officer]

[1]same \ˈsām\ *adj* **1 a :** resembling in every relevant respect **b :** conforming in every respect ⟨gave the *same* answer as before⟩ **2 a :** being one without addition, change, or discontinuance **:** IDENTICAL **b :** being the one under discussion or already referred to ⟨quoted from this *same* book⟩ **3 :** corresponding so closely as to be indistinguishable ⟨on the *same* day last year⟩ [Old Norse *samr*]

[2]same *pron* **1 :** something identical with or similar to another **2 :** something previously defined or described

[3]same *adv* **:** in the same manner

same·ness \ˈsām-nəs\ *n* **1 :** the quality or state of being the same **:** IDENTITY **2 :** lack of variety **:** MONOTONY

sam·i·sen \ˈsam-ə-ˌsen\ *n* **:** a 3-stringed Japanese musical instrument resembling a banjo [Japanese]

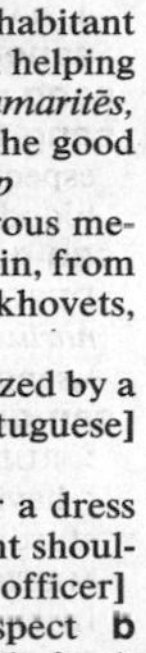
samisen

sa·mite \ˈsam-ˌīt, ˈsā-ˌmīt\ *n* **:** a rich medieval silk fabric interwoven with gold or silver [Medieval French *samit,* from Medieval Latin *examitum, samitum,* from Middle Greek *hexamiton,* from Greek *hexamitos* "of 6 threads," from *hex* "six" + *mitos* "warp thread"]

Samoa time *n* **:** the time of the 11th time zone west of Greenwich that includes American Samoa

sam·o·var \ˈsam-ə-ˌvär\ *n* **1 :** an urn with a spigot at its base used especially in Russia to boil water for tea **2 :** an urn similar to a Russian samovar with a device for heating the contents [Russian, from *samo-* "self" + *varit'* "to boil"]

Sam·o·yed \ˈsam-ə-ˌyed, -ˌói-ˌed\ *n* **:** any of a Siberian breed of medium-sized white or cream-colored sled dogs [Russian *samoed* "a people inhabiting the far north of European Russia and parts of northwestern Siberia"]

samp \ˈsamp\ *n* **:** coarse hominy or a boiled cereal made from it [Narragansett *nasàump* "corn mush"]

sam·pan \ˈsam-ˌpan\ *n* **:** a flat-bottomed Chinese skiff usually propelled by two short oars [Chinese (Guangdong dialect) *sàambáan,* from *sàam* "three" + *báan* "plank"]

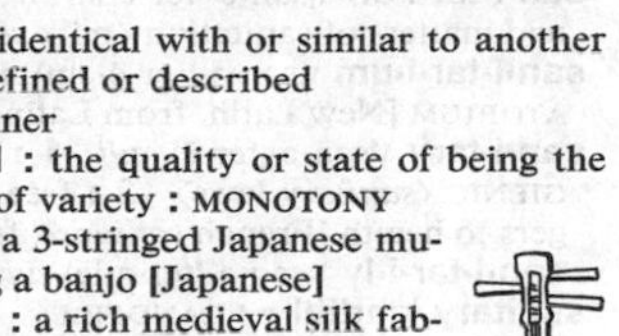
sampan

[1]sam·ple \ˈsam-pəl\ *n* **1 :** a representative part or a single item from a larger whole or group **:** SPECIMEN **2 :** a part of a statistical population whose properties are studied to gain information about the whole [Medieval French *essample* "example, sample," from Latin *exemplum*]

[2]sample *vt* **sam·pled; sam·pling** \-pə-ling, -pling\ **:** to take a sample of; *esp* **:** to judge the quality of by a sample

[1]sam·pler \ˈsam-plər\ *n* **:** a piece of embroidery typically having letters or verses in various stitches as an example of skill

[2]sampler *n* **1 :** one that collects, prepares, or examines samples **2 :** a collection of samples

sample room *n* **:** a room where samples of merchandise are displayed for the inspection of buyers for retail stores

sample space *n* **:** the set of all the possible outcomes of a statistical experiment ⟨if you flip a coin once, the *sample space* is {heads, tails}⟩

sam·pling *n* **1** \ˈsam-pə-ling, -pling\ **:** the act, process, or technique of selecting a suitable sample **2** \-pling\ **:** a small part selected as a sample for inspection or analysis

Sam·u·el \ˈsam-yə-wəl, ˈsam-yəl\ *n* **:** either of two narrative and historical books of canonical Jewish and Christian Scriptures — see BIBLE table

sam·u·rai \ˈsam-ə-ˌrī, -yə-ˌrī\ *n, pl* **samurai 1 :** a military retainer of a Japanese daimyo practicing the code of conduct of Bushido **2 :** the warrior aristocracy of Japan [Japanese]

san·a·to·ri·um \ˌsan-ə-ˈtōr-ē-əm, -ˈtȯr-\ *n, pl* **-ri·ums** *or* **-ria** \-ē-ə\ **:** an establishment for the care and treatment especially of convalescents or the chronically ill [New Latin, derived from Latin *sanare* "to heal, cure," from *sanus* "healthy"]

sanc·ti·fy \ˈsang-tə-ˌfī, ˈsangk-\ *vt* **-fied; -fy·ing 1 :** to set apart as sacred **:** CONSECRATE **2 :** to make free from sin **3 :** to give official sanction to [Medieval French *sanctifier,* from Late Latin *sanctificare,* from Latin *sanctus* "sacred," from *sancire* "to make sacred"] — **sanc·ti·fi·ca·tion** \ˌsang-tə-fə-ˈkā-shən, ˌsangk-\ *n* — **sanc·ti·fi·er** \ˈsang-tə-ˌfī-ər, ˈsangk-,-ˌfīr\ *n*

sanc·ti·mo·ni·ous \ˌsang-tə-ˈmō-nē-əs, ˌsangk-\ *adj* **:** hypocritically devout — **sanc·ti·mo·ni·ous·ly** *adv* — **sanc·ti·mo·ni·ous·ness** *n*

sanc·ti·mo·ny \ˈsang-tə-ˌmō-nē, ˈsangk-\ *n* **:** hypocritical piety [Middle French *sanctimonie* "holiness," from Latin *sanctimonia,* from *sanctus* "holy, sacred"]

[1]sanc·tion \ˈsang-shən, ˈsangk-\ *n* **1 :** a binding or compelling force; *esp* **:** one that determines action in accordance with morality **2 :** explicit or official permission or approval **3 :** an economic or military measure adopted usually by several nations against another nation violating international law [Latin *sanctio,* from *sancire* "to make sacred, sanction"]

[2]sanction *vt* **sanc·tioned; sanc·tion·ing** \-shə-ning, -shning\ **1 :** to make valid or binding usually by a formal procedure **2 :** to give effective or authoritative approval or consent to *synonyms* see APPROVE

sanc·ti·ty \ˈsang-tət-ē, ˈsangk-\ *n, pl* **-ties 1 :** holiness of life and character **2 a :** inviolable quality ⟨the *sanctity* of a promise⟩ **b** *pl* **:** sacred objects, obligations, or rights

sanc·tu·ary \ˈsang-chə-ˌwer-ē, ˈsangk-\ *n, pl* **-ar·ies 1 :** a holy or sacred place: as **a :** the most sacred part (as near the altar) of a place of worship **b :** a building or room for religious worship **2 a (1) :** a place of refuge and protection **(2) :** a refuge for wildlife where predators are controlled and hunting is illegal **b :** safety or protection afforded by a sanctuary [Middle French *saintuarie,* from Late Latin *sanctuarium,* from Latin *sanctus* "sacred"]

sanc·tum \ˈsang-təm, ˈsangk-\ *n, pl* **sanctums** *also* **sanc·ta** \-tə\ **1 :** a sacred place **2 :** a place where one is free from intrusion [Late Latin, from Latin *sanctus* "sacred"]

Sanc·tus \ˈsang-təs, ˈsangk-, ˈsäng-, ˈsängk-\ *n* **:** an ancient Christian hymn closing the preface of most Christian liturgies and commencing with the words *Sanctus, sanctus, sanctus* or *Holy, holy, holy*

[1]sand \ˈsand\ *n* **1 a :** a loose granular material resulting from the disintegration of rocks **b :** soil containing 85 percent or more of sand and a maximum of 10 percent of clay **2 :** a tract of sand **:** BEACH **3 :** the sand in an hourglass; *also* **:** the moments of a lifetime — usually used in plural **4 :** firm resolution **:** COURAGE ⟨hasn't the *sand* to object⟩ [Old English]

[2]sand *vt* **1 :** to sprinkle with or as if with sand **2 :** to cover or fill with sand **3 :** to smooth with an abrasive and especially with sandpaper

san·dal \ˈsan-dl\ *n* **1 :** a shoe with a bottom part or sole that is held in place with straps around the foot and sometimes the ankle **2 :** a rubber overshoe cut very low [Latin *sandalium,* from Greek *sandalion,* from *sandalon* "sandal"] — **san·daled** *or* **san·dalled** \ˈsan-dld\ *adj*

san·dal·wood \ˈsan-dl-ˌwůd\ *n* **:** the close-grained fragrant yellowish heartwood of a tree of southern Asia much used in ornamental carving and cabinetwork; *also* **:** the tree that yields this wood [Medieval French *sandali,* from Medieval Latin *san-*

\ə\ **abut**	\aů\ **out**	\i\ **tip**	\ȯ\ **saw**	\ů\ **foot**
\ər\ **further**	\ch\ **chin**	\ī\ **life**	\ȯi\ **coin**	\y\ **yet**
\a\ **mat**	\e\ **pet**	\j\ **job**	\th\ **thin**	\yü\ **few**
\ā\ **take**	\ē\ **easy**	\ng\ **sing**	\th\ **this**	\yů\ **cure**
\ä\ **cot, cart**	\g\ **go**	\ō\ **bone**	\ü\ **food**	\zh\ **vision**

dalum, from Late Greek *santalon,* derived from Sanskrit *candana*]

[1]**sand·bag** \ˈsand-ˌbag, ˈsan-\ *n* : a bag filled with sand (as for use as ballast or as a weapon or in a wall or fortification)

[2]**sandbag** *vt* **1** : to bank, stop up, or weight with sandbags **2 a** : to hit or stun with a sandbag **b** : to force by crude means — **sand·bag·ger** *n*

sand·bank \-ˌbangk\ *n* : a large deposit of sand

sand·bar \-ˌbär\ *n* : a ridge of sand formed in water by tides or currents

[1]**sand·blast** \-ˌblast\ *n* : a stream of sand projected by compressed air (as for engraving, cutting, or cleaning glass or stone)

[2]**sandblast** *vt* : to engrave, cut, or clean with a high-velocity stream of sand — **sand·blast·er** *n*

sand·box \-ˌbäks\ *n* : a box for holding sand especially for children to play in

sand·bur \-ˌbər\ *n* : any of a genus of grasses chiefly of warm sandy areas that produce small prickly dry fruits; *also* : one of these fruits

sand dollar *n* : any of various flat circular sea urchins that live chiefly in shallow water and on sandy bottoms

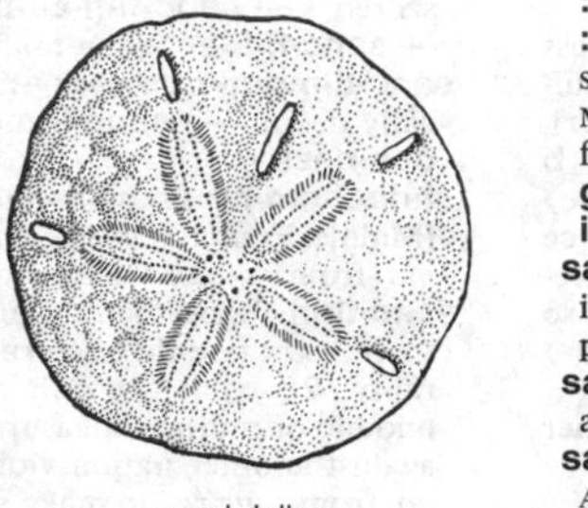
sand dollar

sand·er \ˈsan-dər\ *n* : one that sands: as **a** : a device for spreading sand (as on icy roads); *also* : a truck that carries such a device **b** : a power tool that smooths or polishes using a rough material (as sandpaper)

sand·er·ling \ˈsan-dər-ling\ *n* : a small largely gray and white sandpiper [*sand* + *-erling,* perhaps from Old English *yrthling* "kind of bird found in fields," literally, "plowman"]

sand flea *n* **1** : a flea found in sandy places **2** : any of numerous tiny leaping crustaceans common on ocean beaches

sand fly *n* : any of various small biting two-winged flies

sand·glass \ˈsand-ˌglas, ˈsan-\ *n* : an instrument like an hourglass for measuring time by the running of sand

sand·hill crane \ˈsand-ˌhil-\ *n* : a crane of North America and Siberia that has a red crown and is chiefly bluish gray

sand·hog \ˈsand-ˌhȯg, -ˌhäg\ *n* : a laborer who works in a caisson in driving underwater tunnels

sand·lot \ˈsan-ˌdlät, -ˌlät\ *n* : a vacant lot especially when used by youngsters for unorganized sports — **sandlot** *adj* — **sandlot·ter** *n*

sand·man \ˈsand-ˌman, ˈsan-\ *n* : a character in folklore who makes children sleepy supposedly by sprinkling sand in their eyes

[1]**sand·pa·per** \-ˌpā-pər\ *n* : paper covered on one side with abrasive material (as sand) glued fast and used for smoothing and polishing

[2]**sandpaper** *vt* : to rub with sandpaper

sand·pile \-ˌpīl\ *n* : a pile of sand especially for children to play in

sand·pip·er \-ˌpī-pər\ *n* : any of numerous small shorebirds with usually long slender bills and long legs

sand·stone \ˈsand-ˌstōn, ˈsan-\ *n* : a sedimentary rock consisting of usually quartz sand and a natural cement

sand·storm \-ˌstȯrm\ *n* : a storm of wind (as in a desert) that drives clouds of sand

sand trap *n* : an artificial hazard on a golf course consisting of a depression containing sand

[1]**sand·wich** \ˈsan-ˌdwich, -ˌwich\ *n* **1** : slices of bread with a filling (as of meat, cheese, or a spread) between them **2** : something resembling a sandwich [John Montagu, 4th Earl of *Sandwich,* died 1792, English diplomat]

[2]**sandwich** *vt* **1** : to insert between two or more things ⟨plastic *sandwiched* between layers of glass to make safety glass⟩ **2** : to make a place for : CROWD ⟨*sandwich* another activity into a busy schedule⟩

sandwich board *n* : two usually hinged boards designed for hanging from the shoulders with one board before and one behind and used especially for advertising

sandwich man *n* : a person who advertises or pickets a place of business by wearing a sandwich board

sand·worm \ˈsan-ˌdwərm, -ˌwərm\ *n* : any of various sand-dwelling polychaete worms; *esp* : any of several large burrowing worms often used as bait

sand·wort \ˈsan-ˌdwərt, -ˌwərt, -ˌdwȯrt, -ˌwȯrt\ *n* : any of various low tufted herbs that are related to the pinks and grow in sandy or gritty soil

sandy \ˈsan-dē\ *adj* **sand·i·er; -est** **1** : consisting of, containing, or sprinkled with sand **2** : of a yellowish gray color

sane \ˈsān\ *adj* **1** : mentally sound and healthy **2** : SENSIBLE 4, RATIONAL [Latin *sanus* "healthy, sane"] — **sane·ly** *adv* — **sane·ness** \ˈsān-nəs\ *n*

sang *past of* SING

sang·froid \ˈsäⁿ-ˈfrwä\ *n* : self-possession or imperturbability especially under strain [French *sang-froid,* literally, "cold blood"]

san·gui·nary \ˈsang-gwə-ˌner-ē\ *adj* **1** : BLOODTHIRSTY, MURDEROUS **2** : BLOODY ⟨a *sanguinary* battle⟩ [Latin *sanguinarius,* from *sanguin-, sanguis* "blood"] — **san·gui·nar·i·ly** \ˌsang-gwə-ˈner-ə-lē\ *adv*

san·guine \ˈsang-gwən\ *adj* **1 a** : having the color of blood **b** : RUDDY ⟨a *sanguine* complexion⟩ **2** : SANGUINARY 1 **3** : having a bodily conformation and temperament marked by sturdiness, high color, and cheerfulness **4** : CONFIDENT, OPTIMISTIC ⟨*sanguine* about the future⟩ [Medieval French *sanguin,* from Latin *sanguineus,* from *sanguin-, sanguis* "blood"] — **sanguine·ly** *adv* — **san·guine·ness** \-gwən-nəs\ *n* — **san·guin·i·ty** \sang-ˈgwin-ət-ē, san-\ *n*

san·i·cle \ˈsan-i-kəl\ *n* : any of several plants held to have healing powers [Medieval French, from Medieval Latin *sanicula,* probably from *sanus* "healthy"]

san·i·tar·i·an \ˌsan-ə-ˈter-ē-ən\ *n* : a specialist in public health and matters of sanitation ⟨milk *sanitarian*⟩

san·i·tar·i·um \ˌsan-ə-ˈter-ē-əm\ *n, pl* **-i·ums** *or* **-ia** \-ē-ə\ : SANATORIUM [New Latin, from Latin *sanitas* "health, sanity"]

san·i·tary \ˈsan-ə-ˌter-ē\ *adj* **1** : of or relating to health : HYGIENIC ⟨*sanitary* laws⟩ **2** : free from filth, infection, or dangers to health [French *sanitaire,* from Latin *sanitas* "health"] — **san·i·tar·i·ly** \ˌsan-ə-ˈter-ə-lē\ *adv*

sanitary landfill *n* : LANDFILL

sanitary napkin *n* : a disposable absorbent pad used to absorb the uterine flow (as during menstruation)

san·i·ta·tion \ˌsan-ə-ˈtā-shən\ *n* **1** : the act or process of making sanitary **2** : the promotion of community hygiene and disease prevention especially by supervision and maintenance of sewage disposal systems, collection and disposal of trash and garbage, and cleaning of streets

san·i·tize \ˈsan-ə-ˌtīz\ *vt* : to make sanitary (as by cleaning or sterilizing) — **san·i·ti·za·tion** \ˌsan-ət-ə-ˈzā-shən\ *n*

san·i·ty \ˈsan-ət-ē\ *n* : the quality or state of being sane [Latin *sanitas* "health, sanity," from *sanus* "healthy, sane"]

San Jo·se scale \ˌsan-ə-ˌzā-\ *n* : a scale insect that is naturalized in the U.S. probably from Asia and is a most damaging pest to fruit trees [*San Jose,* California]

sank *past of* SINK

sans \sanz, ˌsanz\ *prep* : WITHOUT [Medieval French, from Latin *sine*]

San·skrit \ˈsan-ˌskrit\ *n* : an ancient Indic language that is the classical language of India and of Hinduism [Sanskrit *saṁskṛta,* literally, "perfected"] — **Sanskrit** *adj*

sans ser·if *or* **san·ser·if** \san-ˈser-əf\ *n* : a letter or typeface with no serifs

san·se·vie·ria \ˌsan-sə-ˈvir-ē-ə\ *n* : any of a genus of tropical herbs related to the agaves and having showy mottled sword-shaped leaves — called also *snake plant* [Raimondo di Sangro, prince of *San Severo,* died 1774, Italian scholar]

sansevieria

San·ta Claus \ˈsant-ə-ˌklȯz, ˈsant-ē-\ *n* : the spirit of Christmas personified as a fat, jolly old man in a red suit who distributes toys to children [Dutch *Sinterklaas,* alteration of *Sint Nikolaas* "Saint Nicholas"]

San·ta Ger·tru·dis \ˌsant-ə-ˌgər-ˈtrüd-əs\ *n* : any of a U.S. breed of red beef cattle developed from a Brahman-shorthorn cross and noted for their ability to withstand heat and their resistance to insects [*Santa Gertrudis,* section of the King Ranch, Kingsville, Texas]

[1]**sap** \ˈsap\ *n* **1** : the fluid part of a plant; *esp* : a watery solution

that circulates through a vascular plant **2 :** bodily health and vigor : VITALITY **3 :** a foolish gullible person [Old English *sæp*]

[2]**sap** *vt* **sapped; sap·ping 1 :** UNDERMINE ⟨heavy waves *sapped* the seawall⟩ **2 :** to weaken gradually ⟨the heat *sapped* my strength⟩ [Middle French *sapper* "to dig a sap (extension of a trench to a point beneath an enemy's fortifications)," from Italian *zappare,* from *zappa* "hoe"]

sap·head \ˈsap-ˌhed\ *n* **:** a weak-minded or foolish person : SAP

sa·pi·ence \ˈsā-pē-əns, ˈsap-ē-\ *n* **:** WISDOM 1a

sa·pi·ent \ˈsā-pē-ənt, ˈsap-ē-\ *adj* **:** WISE 1, DISCERNING [Middle French, from Latin *sapiens,* from *sapere* "to taste, be wise"] — **sa·pi·ent·ly** *adv*

sap·less \ˈsap-ləs\ *adj* **1 :** destitute of sap : DRY **2 :** lacking vitality or vigor : FEEBLE — **sap·less·ness** *n*

sap·ling \ˈsap-liŋ\ *n* **:** a young tree usually not over four inches (about 10 centimeters) in diameter at breast height

sap·o·dil·la \ˌsap-ə-ˈdil-ə\ *n* **:** a tropical American evergreen tree with hard reddish wood, a rough-skinned brownish fruit with sweet flesh, and a latex that yields chicle [Spanish *zapotillo,* from *zapote* "sapodilla fruit," from Nahuatl *tzapotl*]

sap·o·na·ceous \ˌsap-ə-ˈnā-shəs\ *adj* **:** resembling or similar to soap [Latin *sapon-, sapo* "soap," of Germanic origin]

sa·pon·i·fy \sə-ˈpän-ə-ˌfī\ *vb* **-fied; -fy·ing 1 :** to convert (as fat) into soap; *specif* **:** to hydrolyze (a fat) with alkali to form a soap and glycerol **2 :** to undergo saponifying — **sa·pon·i·fi·able** \-ˌfī-ə-bəl\ *adj* — **sa·pon·i·fi·ca·tion** \-ˌpän-ə-fə-ˈkā-shən\ *n* — **sa·pon·i·fi·er** \-ˈpän-ə-ˌfī-ər, -ˌfīr\ *n*

sa·po·te \sə-ˈpōt-ē\ *n* **:** any of several roundish or egg-shaped sweet fruits of several trees of Mexico and Central America [Spanish *zapote* "sapodilla fruit"]

sap·per \ˈsap-ər\ *n* **1 :** a military engineer who constructs field fortifications **2 :** a military demolitions specialist

sap·phire \ˈsaf-ˌīr\ *n* **1 :** a gem variety of corundum occurring in transparent or translucent colorless or colored forms except red; *esp* **:** a transparent rich blue gemstone **2 :** a deep purplish blue [Medieval French *safir,* from Latin *sapphirus,* from Greek *sappheiros,* perhaps of Semitic origin] — **sapphire** *adj*

sap·py \ˈsap-ē\ *adj* **sap·pi·er; -est 1 :** abounding with sap **2 :** containing much sapwood **3 a :** foolishly sentimental **b :** lacking in good sense : SILLY — **sap·pi·ness** *n*

sapr- *or* **sapro-** *combining form* **1 :** rotten : putrid **2 :** dead or decaying organic matter ⟨*sapro*phyte⟩ [Greek *sapros*]

sap·ro·phyte \ˈsap-rə-ˌfīt\ *n* **:** a saprophytic organism

sap·ro·phyt·ic \ˌsap-rə-ˈfit-ik\ *adj* **:** obtaining food by absorbing dissolved organic material and especially the products of organic breakdown and decay ⟨*saprophytic* fungi⟩ — **sap·ro·phyt·i·cal·ly** \-ˈfit-i-kə-lē, -klē\ *adv*

sap·suck·er \ˈsap-ˌsək-ər\ *n* **:** any of various North American woodpeckers that drill holes in trees in order to obtain sap and insects for food

sapsucker

sap·wood \-ˌwu̇d\ *n* **:** the younger softer sap-containing and usually lighter-colored wood in the outer portion of a woody stem — compare HEARTWOOD

Sar·a·cen \ˈsar-ə-sən\ *n* **1 :** a member of a nomadic people of the deserts of Syria and northern Arabia **2 :** ARAB 1 [Late Latin *Saracenus,* from Late Greek *Sarakēnos*] — **Saracen** *adj* — **Sar·a·cen·ic** \ˌsar-ə-ˈsen-ik\ *adj*

sa·ran \sə-ˈran\ *n* **:** a tough flexible thermoplastic resin [from *Saran,* a trademark]

sarape *variant of* SERAPE

sarc- *or* **sarco-** *combining form* **:** flesh [Greek *sark-, sarx*]

sar·casm \ˈsär-ˌkaz-əm\ *n* **1 :** a cutting and often ironic remark ⟨tired of continual *sarcasms*⟩ **2 :** the use of sarcasms in speech or writing [French *sarcasme,* from Late Latin *sarcasmos,* from Greek *sarkasmos,* from *sarkazein* "to tear flesh, bite the lips in rage, sneer," from *sark-, sarx* "flesh"]

sar·cas·tic \sär-ˈkas-tik\ *adj* **1 :** containing sarcasm ⟨a *sarcastic* remark⟩ **2 :** given to sarcasm ⟨a *sarcastic* critic⟩ — **sar·cas·ti·cal·ly** \-ti-kə-lē, -klē\ *adv*

sar·co·dine \ˈsär-kə-ˌdīn\ *n* **:** any of a group (Sarcodina) of protozoans (as an amoeba, radiolarian, or foraminifera) that typically move by pseudopodia [New Latin *Sarcodina,* from Greek *sarkōdes* "fleshy part," from *sark-, sarx* "flesh"]

sar·co·lem·ma \ˌsär-kə-ˈlem-ə\ *n* **:** the membrane enclosing a striated muscle fiber [*sarc-* + Greek *lemma* "husk," from *lepein* "to peel"]

sar·co·ma \sär-ˈkō-mə\ *n* **:** a malignant tumor arising in tissue (as connective tissue or striated muscle) of mesodermal origin — **sar·co·ma·tous** \sär-ˈkäm-ət-əs, -ˈkōm-\ *adj*

sar·co·mere \ˈsär-kə-ˌmir\ *n* **:** one of the repeating structural units of a myofibril

sar·coph·a·gus \sär-ˈkäf-ə-gəs\ *n, pl* **-gi** \-ˌgī, -ˌjī, -ˌgē\ *or* **-gus·es :** a stone coffin; *esp* **:** one exposed to view in the open air or in a tomb [Latin *sarcophagus (lapis)* "limestone used for coffins," from Greek (lithos) *sarkophagos,* literally, "flesh-eating stone," from *sark-, sarx* "flesh" + *phagein* "to eat"]

sardar *variant of* SIRDAR

sar·dine \sär-ˈdēn\ *n, pl* **sardines** *also* **sardine 1 :** any of several small or immature fishes related to the herring; *esp* **:** the European pilchard especially when young and of a size suitable for preserving for food **2 :** any of various small fishes (as an anchovy) resembling the true sardines or similarly preserved for food [Medieval French *sardeine,* from Latin *sardina*]

sar·don·ic \sär-ˈdän-ik\ *adj* **:** bitterly scornful : CYNICAL [French *sardonique,* from Greek *sardonios*] — **sar·don·i·cal·ly** \-ˈdän-i-kə-lē, -klē\ *adv*

sard·on·yx \sär-ˈdän-iks, ˈsärd-n-\ *n* **:** onyx having layers of carnelian [Latin, from Greek]

sar·gas·so \sär-ˈgas-ō\ *n, pl* **-sos 1 :** GULFWEED, SARGASSUM **2 :** a mass of floating vegetation and especially sargassums [Portuguese *sargaço*]

sar·gas·sum \sär-ˈgas-əm\ *n* **:** any of a genus of brown algae that have a leafy branching body and air bladders and that often grow in free-floating masses in the ocean [New Latin, from *sargasso*]

sa·ri *or* **sa·ree** \ˈsär-ē\ *n* **:** a garment of Hindu women that consists of a long cloth draped so that one end forms a skirt and the other a head or shoulder covering [Hindi and Urdu *sāṛī,* from Sanskrit *śāṭī* "strip of cloth"]

sari

sa·rin \ˈsar-ən, ˈsar-; zä-ˈrēn\ *n* **:** an extremely toxic chemical weapon $C_4H_{10}FO_2P$ that is used as a lethal nerve gas [German]

sa·rong \sə-ˈrȯŋ, -ˈräŋ\ *n* **:** a loose skirt made of a long strip of cloth wrapped loosely around the body and worn by men and women of the Malay archipelago and the Pacific islands [Malay]

sar·sa·pa·ril·la \ˌsas-pə-ˈril-ə, ˌsärs-, -ə-pə-\ *n* **1 a :** any of various tropical American greenbriers **b :** the dried roots of a sarsaparilla plant used especially as a flavoring **2 :** a sweetened carbonated beverage flavored chiefly with birch oil and sassafras [Spanish *zarzaparilla*]

sar·to·ri·al \sär-ˈtōr-ē-əl, -ˈtȯr-\ *adj* **:** of or relating to a tailor or tailored clothes ⟨the *sartorial* appearence of a politician⟩ ⟨*sartorial* splendor⟩ [Latin *sartor* "tailor," from *sarcire* "to mend"] — **sar·to·ri·al·ly** \-ē-ə-lē\ *adv*

sar·to·ri·us \-ē-əs\ *n* **:** a muscle that crosses the front of the thigh obliquely and assists in rotating the leg outward to the position assumed in sitting cross-legged and in humans is the longest muscle [New Latin, from Medieval Latin *sartor* "tailor," from *sarcire* "to mend"]

[1]**sash** \ˈsash\ *n* **:** a broad band (as of silk) worn around the waist or over the shoulder [Arabic *shāsh* "muslin"]

[2]**sash** *n, pl* **sash** *or* **sash·es :** the framework in which panes of glass are set in a window or door; *also* **:** the movable part of a window ⟨raised the *sash* to let in air⟩ [probably from French *châssis* "chassis" (taken as plural)]

sa·shay \sa-ˈshā\ *vi* **1 :** to strut or move about in an ostentatious manner **2 :** to proceed in a diagonal or sideways manner [French *chassé,* a dance step, from *chasser* "to chase"]

sas·quatch \ˈsas-ˌkwach, -ˌkwäch\ *n* **:** BIG FOOT [Halkomelem (Salishan language of southwestern British Columbia) *sésq̓ec*]

[1]**sass** \ˈsas\ *n* **:** impudent speech [alteration of [1]*sauce*]

\ə\ **abut**	\au̇\ **out**	\i\ **tip**	\ȯ\ **saw**	\u̇\ **foot**
\ər\ **further**	\ch\ **chin**	\ī\ **life**	\ȯi\ **coin**	\y\ **yet**
\a\ **mat**	\e\ **pet**	\j\ **job**	\th\ **thin**	\yü\ **few**
\ā\ **take**	\ē\ **easy**	\ŋ\ **sing**	\t͟h\ **this**	\yu̇\ **cure**
\ä\ **cot, cart**	\g\ **go**	\ō\ **bone**	\ü\ **food**	\zh\ **vision**

[2]**sass** *vt* : to talk impudently or disrespectfully to
sas·sa·fras \'sas-ˌfras, -ə-ˌfras\ *n* : a tall eastern North American tree that is related to the laurels and has fragrant yellow flowers and bluish black berries; *also* : its dried root bark used formerly in medicine or as a flavoring agent [Spanish *sasafrás*]
sassy \'sas-ē\ *adj* **sass·i·er; -est** : given to back talk : IMPUDENT [alteration of *saucy*]
sat *past of* SIT
SAT \ˌes-ˌā-'tē\ *trademark* — used for a standardized test used to evaluate suitability for college admission
Sa·tan \'sāt-n\ *n* : DEVIL 1 [Old English, from Late Latin, from Greek, from Hebrew *śāṭān* "adversary"] — **sa·tan·ic** \sə-'tan-ik, sā-\ *adj* — **sa·tan·i·cal·ly** \-'tan-i-kə-lē, -klē\ *adv*
satch·el \'sach-əl\ *n* : a small bag for carrying clothes or books [Middle French *sachel, sacel,* derived from Latin *sacculus* "small bag," from *saccus* "bag"]
sate \'sāt\ *vt* **1** : to fill (as with food) beyond desire : GLUT **2** : to satisfy fully : SATIATE [probably from *satiate*]
sa·teen \sa-'tēn\ *n* : a glossy cotton fabric resembling satin [alteration of *satin*]
sat·el·lite \'sat-l-ˌīt\ *n* **1** : a servile follower **2 a** : a celestial body orbiting another of larger size **b** : a man-made object or vehicle intended to orbit the earth, the moon, or another celestial body **3** : one that is subordinate to or dependent on another; *esp* : a country dominated or controlled by another more powerful country [Middle French, from Latin *satellit-, satelles* "attendant"] — **satellite** *adj*
satellite dish *n* : a microwave dish for receiving usually television transmissions from an orbiting satellite
sa·tia·ble \'sā-shə-bəl\ *adj* : capable of being appeased or satisfied ⟨a *satiable* curiosity⟩
[1]**sa·tiate** \'sā-shē-ət, -shət\ *adj* : marked by or feeling satiety
[2]**sa·ti·ate** \'sā-shē-ˌāt\ *vt* : to satisfy (as a need or desire) fully or to excess [Latin *satiare,* from *satis* "enough"] — **sa·ti·a·tion** \ˌsā-shē-'ā-shən, ˌsā-sē-\ *n*
sa·ti·e·ty \sə-'tī-ət-ē\ *n* **1** : the quality or state of being fed or gratified to or beyond capacity : SURFEIT **2** : revulsion or disgust caused by overindulgence or excess [Middle French *satieté,* from Latin *satietas,* from *satis* "enough"]
sat·in \'sat-n\ *n* : a fabric (as of silk) in satin weave with lustrous face and dull back [Medieval French, probably from Arabic *zaytūnī*, literally, "of Zaytūn," seaport in China during the Middle Ages] — **satin** *adj*
sat·in·et *or* **sat·in·ette** \ˌsat-n-'et\ *n* : a usually thin silk satin
satin weave *n* : a weave in which warp threads interlace with filling threads to produce a smooth-faced fabric
sat·in·wood \'sat-n-ˌwu̇d\ *n* **1** : a hard yellowish brown wood with a satiny luster **2** : a tree yielding satinwood; *esp* : a tall tree native to India and Sri Lanka
sat·iny \'sat-n-ē\ *adj* : having the soft lustrous smoothness of satin : resembling satin ⟨*satiny* skin⟩
sat·ire \'sa-ˌtīr\ *n* **1** : a literary work holding up human vices and follies to ridicule or scorn **2** : biting wit, irony, or sarcasm used to expose and discredit vice or folly [Middle French, from Latin *satura, satira,* perhaps from *(lanx) satura* "full plate, dish of mixed ingredients," from *satur* "well fed"] — **sa·tir·ic** \sə-'tir-ik\ *or* **sa·tir·i·cal** \-'tir-i-kəl\ *adj* — **sa·tir·i·cal·ly** \-i-kə-lē, -klē\ *adv*

Word History English *satire* is derived from Latin *satira* and its earlier form *satura,* which in classical times meant "a satirical poem." Before the development of this style of satiric poetry, the *satura* was a poem dealing with a number of different subjects. It is this sense of "a poetic medley" that gives us a clue to the early development of the word. This sense of *satura* evolved from the phrase *lanx satura,* literally, "a full plate." *Satura* is a form of *satur,* which means "sated" or "full of food." *Lanx satura* once meant a plate filled with various fruits or a dish made from a mixture of many ingredients.

sat·i·rist \'sat-ə-rəst\ *n* : one that satirizes; *esp* : a satirical writer
sat·i·rize \-ˌrīz\ *vb* **1** : to utter or write satires **2** : to criticize or ridicule by means of satire
sat·is·fac·tion \ˌsat-əs-'fak-shən\ *n* **1 a** : fulfillment of a need or want **b** : the quality or state of being satisfied : CONTENTMENT **c** : a cause or means of enjoyment : GRATIFICATION **2** : compensation for a loss or injury : RESTITUTION **3** : convinced assurance or certainty ⟨proved to the *satisfaction* of the court⟩ [Medieval French, from Latin *satisfactio* "reparation, amends," from *satisfacere* "to satisfy," from *satis* "enough" + *facere* "to do, make"]
sat·is·fac·to·ry \ˌsat-əs-'fak-tə-rē, -trē\ *adj* : sufficient or adequate to satisfy : meeting what is asked or demanded — **sat·is·fac·to·ri·ly** \-tə-rə-lē, -trə-\ *adv*
sat·is·fy \'sat-əs-ˌfī\ *vb* **-fied; -fy·ing** **1 a** : to carry out the terms of ⟨*satisfy* a contract⟩ **b** : to meet a financial obligation to : PAY **2 a** : to make happy : PLEASE ⟨a vacation destination sure to *satisfy* everyone⟩ **b** : to gratify to the full : APPEASE ⟨*satisfied* my hunger⟩ **3 a** : CONVINCE ⟨*satisfied* that the defendant is innocent⟩ **b** : to put an end to : DISPEL ⟨*satisfied* all their objections⟩ **4 a** : to conform or be adequate to : MEET ⟨*satisfy* a need⟩ **b** : to make true by fulfilling a condition ⟨values that *satisfy* an equation⟩ ⟨*satisfy* a hypothesis⟩ [Medieval French *satisfier,* from Latin *satisfacere,* from *satis* "enough" + *facere* "to do, make"] — **sat·is·fi·able** \ˌsat-əs-'fī-ə-bəl\ *adj* — **sat·is·fy·ing·ly** \'sat-əs-ˌfī-ing-lē\ *adv*
sa·trap \'sā-ˌtrap, 'sa-\ *n* **1** : the governor of a province in ancient Persia **2** : a subordinate ruler; *esp* : a petty tyrant [Latin *satrapes,* from Greek *satrapēs,* from Persian *khshathrapāvan,* literally, "protector of the dominion"]
sa·tra·py \'sā-trə-pē, 'sa-, -ˌtrap-ē\ *n, pl* **-pies** : the territory or jurisdiction of a satrap
sat·u·rant \'sach-ə-rənt\ *n* : something that saturates
sat·u·rate \'sach-ə-ˌrāt\ *vt* **1** : to treat, furnish, or charge with something to the point where no more can be absorbed, dissolved, or retained ⟨water *saturated* with salt⟩ **2** : to fill completely with something that permeates or pervades [Latin *saturare,* from *satur* "well fed"] ***synonyms*** see SOAK — **sat·u·rable** \'sach-rə-bəl, -ə-rə-\ *adv*
sat·u·rat·ed \'sach-ə-ˌrāt-əd\ *adj* **1** : steeped in moisture : SOAKED **2 a** : being a solution that is unable to absorb or dissolve any more of a substance at a given temperature and pressure **b** : being a carbon compound having no double or triple bonds between carbon atoms ⟨*saturated* fats⟩ **3** : not diluted with white ⟨a *saturated* color⟩
sat·u·ra·tion \ˌsach-ə-'rā-shən\ *n* **1** : the act of saturating : the state of being saturated **2** : chromatic purity : freedom from dilution with white **3** : an overwhelming concentration of military forces or firepower
Sat·ur·day \'sat-ərd-ē\ *n* : the 7th day of the week [Old English *sæterndæg,* literally, "Saturn's day," derived from Latin *Saturnus* "the Roman god Saturn"]
Sat·urn \'sat-ərn\ *n* : the planet 6th in order from the sun — see PLANET table [Latin *Saturnus* "Roman god of agriculture"] — **Sa·tur·ni·an** \sa-'tər-nē-ən\ *adj*
sat·ur·na·lia \ˌsat-ər-'nāl-yə\ *n sing or pl* **1** *cap* : the festival of Saturn in ancient Rome beginning on December 17 **2** : an unrestrained often licentious celebration : ORGY [Latin, derived from *Saturnus* "the Roman god Saturn"] — **sat·ur·na·lian** \-yən\ *adj*
sat·ur·nine \'sat-ər-ˌnīn\ *adj* : having a sullen or sardonic aspect : GLOOMY, GRAVE [from the supposed character of those born under the planet Saturn] — **sat·ur·nine·ly** *adv*
sa·tyr \'sāt-ər, 'sat-\ *n* **1** : a forest god in Greek mythology often represented as having the ears and tail of a horse or goat and given to boisterous pleasures **2** : a man of lustful or lecherous habits **3** : any of a family of usually brown and gray butterflies often with eyespots on the wings [Latin *satyrus,* from Greek *satyros*] — **sa·tyr·ic** \sā-'tir-ik, sə-, sa-\ *adj*
[1]**sauce** \'sȯs\ *n* **1** : a condiment or relish for food; *esp* : one in the form of a liquid or semisolid : DRESSING **2** : something that adds zest or piquancy **3** : cooked fruit eaten with other food or as a dessert ⟨apple *sauce*⟩ **4** : pert or impudent language or actions [Medieval French, from Latin *salsus* "salted," from *sallere* "to salt," from *sal* "salt"]
[2]**sauce** *vt* **1** : to add relish or seasoning to **2** : to be rude or impudent to
sauce·pan \'sȯ-ˌspan\ *n* : a small deep cooking pan with a handle
sau·cer \'sȯ-sər\ *n* **1** : a small round shallow dish in which a cup is set at table **2** : something like a saucer especially in shape [Medieval French, "dish for sauce," from *sauce* "sauce"]
saucy \'sȯs-ē\ *adj* **sauc·i·er; -est** **1** : marked by bold rudeness or disrespect : IMPUDENT **2** : amusingly forward and flippant : IRREPRESSIBLE **3** : SMART, TRIM ⟨a *saucy* little hat⟩ — **sauc·i·ly** \-ə-lē\ *adv* — **sauc·i·ness** \-ē-nəs\ *n*
sau·er·bra·ten \'sau̇-ər-ˌbrät-n, 'sau̇r-\ *n* : pot-roasted beef marinated in vinegar with seasonings before cooking [German, from *sauer* "sour" + *Braten* "roast meat"]

sau·er·kraut \ˈsau̇-ər-ˌkrau̇t, ˈsau̇r-\ *n* : finely cut cabbage fermented in brine [German, from *sauer* "sour" + *Kraut* "greens"]

sau·ger \ˈsȯ-gər\ *n* : a pike perch of Canada and the U.S. similar to the walleye but smaller [origin unknown]

sau·na \ˈsȯ-nə, ˈsau̇-nə\ *n* : a Finnish steam bath; *also* : a bathhouse with steam provided usually by water thrown on hot stones [Finnish]

saun·ter \ˈsȯnt-ər, ˈsänt-\ *vi* : to walk along in an idle or leisurely manner : STROLL [probably from Middle English *santren* "to muse"] — **saunter** *n* — **saun·ter·er** \-ər-ər\ *n*

sau·ri·an \ˈsȯr-ē-ən\ *n* : any of a group (Sauria) of reptiles including the lizards and in older classifications the crocodiles and various extinct forms (as the dinosaurs) resembling lizards [derived from Greek *sauros* "lizard"] — **saurian** *adj*

saur·is·chi·an \sȯ-ˈris-kē-ən\ *n* : any of an order (Saurischia) of herbivorous or carnivorous dinosaurs that have the pubis of the pelvis typically pointed downward and forward and that include the sauropods and theropods — compare ORNITHISCHIAN [derived from Greek *sauros* "lizard" + *ischion* "hip joint"] — **saurischian** *adj*

sau·ro·pod \ˈsȯr-ə-ˌpäd\ *n* : any of a group (Sauropoda) of large four-footed plant-eating saurischian dinosaurs (as a brontosaurus) with a long neck and tail — **sauropod** *adj*

sau·sage \ˈsȯ-sij\ *n* : highly seasoned minced meat (as pork) usually stuffed in casings [Medieval French *sauseche, saucis,* from Late Latin *salsicia,* from Latin *salsus* "salted," from *sallere* "to salt," from *sal* "salt"]

1**sau·té** \sȯ-ˈtā, sō-\ *n* : a sautéed dish [French, "sautéed," from *sauter* "to jump," from Latin *saltare*] — **sauté** *adj*

2**sauté** *vt* **sau·téed** *or* **sau·téd; sau·té·ing** : to fry (food) in a small amount of fat

sau·terne \sō-ˈtərn, sȯ-, -ˈteərn\ *n* : a semisweet white wine [French, from *Sauternes,* commune in France]

1**sav·age** \ˈsav-ij\ *adj* **1** : not domesticated or under human control ⟨*savage* beasts⟩ **2** : very cruel and unrestrained ⟨a *savage* attack⟩ **3** : not cultivated : WILD ⟨*savage* wilderness⟩ **4** : lacking complex or advanced culture : not civilized ⟨*savage* customs⟩ **5** : very critical or harsh [Medieval French *salvage, savage,* derived from Latin *silvaticus* "of the woods, wild," from *silva* "wood, forest"] ***synonyms*** see BARBARIAN — **sav·age·ly** *adv* — **sav·age·ness** *n*

2**savage** *n* **1** : a person belonging to a primitive society **2** : a brutal person **3** : a rude or unmannerly person

3**savage** *vt* : to attack or treat violently or brutally

sav·age·ry \ˈsav-ij-rē, -ə-rē\ *n, pl* **-ries** **1** : the quality of being savage **2** : a cruel or violent act **3** : an uncivilized state

sa·van·na *also* **sa·van·nah** \sə-ˈvan-ə\ *n* : a tropical or subtropical grassland (as of eastern Africa or northern South America) containing scattered trees [Spanish *zavana,* from Taino *zabana*]

sa·vant \sa-ˈvänt, -ˈväⁿ; sə-ˈvant, ˈsav-ənt\ *n* : a learned person : SCHOLAR [French, from *savoir* "to know," from Latin *sapere* "to taste, be wise"]

1**save** \ˈsāv\ *vb* **1 a** : to deliver from sin **b** : to rescue from danger or harm ⟨*saved* his friend from drowning⟩ **c** : to preserve or guard from injury, destruction, or loss ⟨*save* the coat from damage by moths⟩ **d** : to store (data) in a computer, on a storage device (as a flash drive), or in the cloud **2 a** : to put aside as a store or reserve : ACCUMULATE ⟨*save* a little for later⟩ **b** : to put aside money ⟨*saved* up for a new car⟩ **3 a** : to make unnecessary : AVOID ⟨it *saves* an hour's driving time⟩ **b** : to prevent an opponent from scoring or winning ⟨a diving catch that *saved* a goal⟩ **4** : MAINTAIN, PRESERVE ⟨*save* appearances⟩ **5 a** : to avoid unnecessary waste or expense : ECONOMIZE **b** : to spend less money ⟨buy now and *save*⟩ **c** : to spend less by ⟨*save* 25 percent⟩ [Medieval French *salver,* from Late Latin *salvare,* from Latin *salvus* "safe"] — **sav·able** *or* **save·able** \ˈsā-və-bəl\ *adj* — **sav·er** *n* — **save the day** : to solve or avert a problem ⟨her quick thinking *saved the day*⟩

2**save** *n* **1** : a play that prevents an opponent from scoring or winning **2** : the action of a relief pitcher in baseball in successfully protecting a team's lead; *also* : official credit for a save

3**save** *prep* : EXCEPT ⟨no hope *save* one⟩ [Medieval French *sauf,* from *sauf,* adj., "safe"]

4**save** *conj* : except for the fact that : ONLY — used with *that* ⟨little is known about her, *save* that she is new to town⟩

sav·in \ˈsav-ən\ *n* : any of several mostly low-growing junipers [Medieval French *savine,* from Latin *(herba) sabina,* literally, "Sabine plant"]

1**sav·ing** \ˈsā-viŋ\ *n* **1** : the act of rescuing ⟨the *saving* of lives⟩ **2 a** : something saved ⟨made a *saving* of 50 percent⟩ **b** *pl* : money saved over a period of time

2**saving** *adj* **1** : ECONOMICAL 1, THRIFTY **2** : making up for something : COMPENSATORY ⟨a *saving* sense of humor⟩

3**saving** *prep* **1** : EXCEPT, SAVE **2** : without disrespect to

4**saving** *conj* : EXCEPT

savings account *n* : an interest-bearing account with a bank

savings bank *n* : a bank that receives and invests savings accounts and pays interest to depositors

savings bond *n* : a registered U.S. bond issued in denominations of $25 to $10,000

sav·ior *or* **sav·iour** \ˈsāv-yər\ *n* **1** : one that saves from harm **2** *cap* : a bringer of salvation; *esp* : MESSIAH 1b [Medieval French *saveour,* from Late Latin *salvator,* from *salvare* "to save"]

sa·voir faire \ˌsav-ˌwär-ˈfaər, -ˈfeər\ *n* : ability to do or say the right or graceful thing : TACT [French *savoir-faire,* literally, "knowing how to do"]

1**sa·vor** \ˈsā-vər\ *n* **1** : the taste and odor of something ⟨the *savor* of roast meat⟩ **2** : a distinctive quality [Medieval French, from Latin *sapor,* from *sapere* "to taste"] — **sa·vor·less** \-ləs\ *adj*

2**savor** *vb* **sa·vored; sa·vor·ing** \ˈsāv-riŋ, -ə-riŋ\ **1** : to have a specified smell or quality **2** : to give flavor to : SEASON **3 a** : to have experience of **b** : to taste or smell with pleasure : RELISH **c** : to delight in : ENJOY — **sa·vor·er** \ˈsā-vər-ər\ *n*

1**sa·vory** \ˈsāv-rē, -ə-rē\ *adj* **sa·vor·i·er; -est** : pleasing to the taste or smell : APPETIZING — **sa·vor·i·ness** *n*

2**sa·vo·ry** \ˈsāv-rē, -ə-rē\ *n, pl* **-ries** : either of two European mints with aromatic leaves used to season food [Middle English *saverey*]

savory

1**sav·vy** \ˈsav-ē\ *vb* **sav·vied; sav·vy·ing** : UNDERSTAND 1 ⟨you *savvy* what I mean?⟩ [alteration of *sabi* "know" (in English-based creoles and pidgins), from Portuguese *sabe* "he knows," from *saber* "to know," from Latin *sapere* "to taste, be wise"]

2**savvy** *n* : practical understanding ⟨political *savvy*⟩

3**savvy** *adj* : having practical understanding or knowledge of something ⟨a *savvy* investor⟩

1**saw** *past of* SEE

2**saw** \ˈsȯ\ *n* **1** : a hand or power tool used to cut hard material (as wood, metal, or bone) with a toothed blade or disk **2** : a machine mounting a saw (as a band saw or circular saw) [Old English *sagu*] — **saw·like** \-ˌlīk\ *adj*

3**saw** *vb* **sawed** \ˈsȯd\; **sawed** *or* **sawn** \ˈsȯn\; **saw·ing** \ˈsȯ-iŋ, ˈsȯiŋ\ **1** : to cut or form by cutting with a saw **2** : to slice as though with a saw **3** : to make motions as though using a saw ⟨*sawed* at the reins⟩ — **saw·er** \ˈsȯ-ər, ˈsȯr\ *n*

4**saw** *n* : a common saying : PROVERB [Old English *sagu* "talk"]

saw·buck \ˈsȯ-ˌbək\ *n* **1** *slang* : a 10-dollar bill **2** : SAWHORSE; *esp* : one with X-shaped ends

saw·dust \ˈsȯ-ˌdəst\ *n* : dust or fine particles of wood made by a saw in cutting

saw–edged \ˈsȯ-ˈejd\ *adj* : having a toothed or nicked edge

sawed–off \ˈsȯ-ˌdȯf\ *adj* **1** : having an end sawed off ⟨a *sawed-off* shotgun⟩ **2** : being of less than average height

saw·fish \ˈsȯ-ˌfish\ *n* : any of several mostly tropical rays that resemble sharks but have a long flattened snout bearing a row of stout toothlike structures along each edge

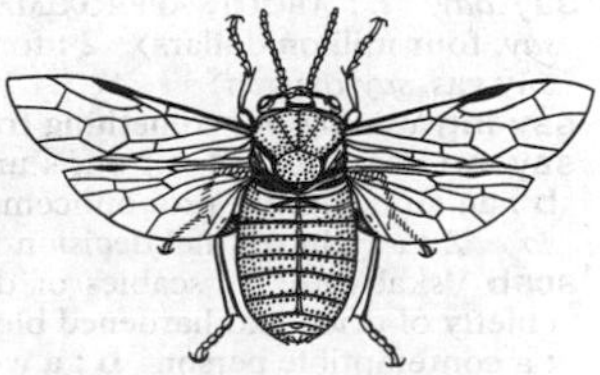
sawfly

saw·fly \-ˌflī\ *n* : any of numerous insects that are related to the wasps and bees and usually have in

\ə\ **abut**	\au̇\ **out**	\i\ **tip**	\ȯ\ **saw**	\u̇\ **foot**
\ər\ **further**	\ch\ **chin**	\ī\ **life**	\ȯi\ **coin**	\y\ **yet**
\a\ **mat**	\e\ **pet**	\j\ **job**	\th\ **thin**	\yü\ **few**
\ā\ **take**	\ē\ **easy**	\ŋ\ **sing**	\t͟h\ **this**	\yu̇\ **cure**
\ä\ **cot, cart**	\g\ **go**	\ō\ **bone**	\ü\ **food**	\zh\ **vision**

the female a pair of organs for making slits in plants into which eggs are laid

saw grass *n* : a sedge with leaves that have sharp jagged edges

saw·horse \ˈsȯ-ˌhȯrs\ *n* : a frame or rack on which wood is rested while being sawed by hand

saw·log \-ˌlȯg, -ˌläg\ *n* : a log fit for sawing into lumber

saw·mill \-ˌmil\ *n* : a mill or machine for sawing logs

saw palmetto *n* : a low-growing palm of the southeastern U.S. with a usually creeping stem and spiny-toothed petioles

saw·tim·ber \ˈsȯ-ˌtim-bər\ *n* : timber suitable for sawing into lumber

saw·tooth \-ˌtüth\ *adj* : SAW-TOOTHED

saw–toothed \-ˈtütht\ *adj* : having an edge or outline like the teeth of a saw

saw–whet owl \-ˌhwet-, -ˌwet-\ *n* : a very small harsh-voiced North American owl that is largely dark brown above and chestnut streaked with white beneath [from the resemblance of its cry to the sound of filing a saw]

saw·yer \ˈsȯ-yər, ˈsȯi-ər\ *n* **1** : one that saws timber **2** : any of several large beetles whose larvae bore large holes in timber

sax \ˈsaks\ *n* : SAXOPHONE

sax·horn \ˈsaks-ˌhȯrn\ *n* : one of a family of valved brass instruments having a conical tube, oval shape, and cup-shaped mouthpiece [Antoine J. *Sax,* died 1894, Belgian maker of musical instruments]

sax·i·frage \ˈsak-sə-frij, -ˌfrāj\ *n* : any of a genus of herbs with showy 5-parted flowers and usually with leaves growing in tufts close to the ground [Medieval French, from Late Latin *saxifraga,* derived from Latin *saxum* "rock" + *frangere* "to break"]

Sax·on \ˈsak-sən\ *n* **1** : a member of a Germanic people invading and conquering England with the Angles and Jutes in the 5th century A.D. and merging with them to form the Anglo-Saxon people **2** : a native or inhabitant of Saxony [Late Latin *Saxones* "Saxons," of Germanic origin] — **Saxon** *adj*

sax·o·phone \ˈsak-sə-ˌfōn\ *n* : a wind instrument with reed mouthpiece, curved conical metal tube, and finger keys [French, from Antoine J. *Sax,* died 1894, Belgian maker of musical instruments] — **sax·o·phon·ic** \ˌsak-sə-ˈfän-ik\ *adj* — **sax·o·phon·ist** \ˈsak-sə-ˌfō-nəst\ *n*

saxophone

sax·tu·ba \ˈsaks-ˈtü-bə, -ˈtyü-\ *n* : a bass saxhorn

[1]**say** \ˈsā\ *vt* **said** \ˈsed\; **say·ing** \ˈsā-iŋ\; **says** \ˈsez\ **1 a** : to express in words : STATE ⟨*say* what you mean using as few words as possible⟩ **b** : to state as opinion or belief : DECLARE ⟨*said* to be the best you can get⟩ **2 a** : UTTER 1b, PRONOUNCE ⟨can't *say* more than three words without laughing⟩ **b** : RECITE, REPEAT ⟨*said* their prayers⟩ **3 a** : INDICATE, SHOW ⟨the clock *says* five minutes after twelve⟩ **b** : to give expression to : COMMUNICATE ⟨a glance that *said* all that was necessary⟩ **4** : SUPPOSE, ASSUME ⟨let's *say* you're right⟩ [Old English *secgan*] — **say·er** \ˈsā-ər\ *n*

[2]**say** *n* **1** : an expression of opinion ⟨had my *say*⟩ **2** : the power to decide or help decide ⟨had no *say* in the decision⟩

[3]**say** *adv* **1** : ABOUT, APPROXIMATELY ⟨the property is worth, *say,* four million dollars⟩ **2** : for example : AS ⟨if we compress any gas, *say* oxygen⟩

say·ing \ˈsā-iŋ\ *n* : something frequently said : PROVERB

say–so \ˈsā-ˌsō\ *n* **1 a** : one's unsupported word or assurance **b** : an authoritative pronouncement ⟨acted on the doctor's *say-so*⟩ **2** : a right of final decision : AUTHORITY

[1]**scab** \ˈskab\ *n* **1** : scabies of domestic animals **2** : a crust chiefly of dried and hardened blood formed over a wound **3 a** : a contemptible person **b** : a worker who takes the place of a striking worker **4** : any of various plant diseases characterized by crusted spots [of Scandinavian origin]

[2]**scab** *vi* **scabbed; scab·bing 1** : to become covered with a scab **2** : to act as a scab

scab·bard \ˈskab-ərd\ *n* : a sheath for a sword, dagger, or bayonet [Medieval French *escalberc*] — **scabbard** *vt*

scab·by \ˈskab-ē\ *adj* **scab·bi·er; -est 1 a** : covered with or full of scabs ⟨*scabby* skin⟩ **b** : diseased with scab ⟨a *scabby* animal⟩ ⟨*scabby* potatoes⟩ **2** : MEAN, CONTEMPTIBLE ⟨a *scabby* trick⟩

sca·bies \ˈskā-bēz\ *n, pl* **scabies** : an itch or mange caused by mites living as parasites under the skin [Latin, from *scabere* to "scratch"]

sca·brous \ˈskab-rəs *also* ˈskāb-\ *adj* **1** : DIFFICULT, KNOTTY ⟨a *scabrous* problem⟩ **2** : rough to the touch ⟨a *scabrous* leaf⟩ **3** : unpleasant, repulsive, or reprehensible in some way [Latin *scaber* "rough, scurfy"] — **sca·brous·ly** *adv* — **sca·brous·ness** *n*

[1]**scad** \ˈskad\ *n, pl* **scad** *also* **scads** : any of several mostly small sea fishes related to the pompanos [origin unknown]

[2]**scad** *n* **1** : a large number or quantity **2** *pl* : a great abundance ⟨*scads* of money⟩ [probably from English dialect *scald* "a multitude"]

scaf·fold \ˈskaf-əld *also* -ˌōld\ *n* **1 a** : a temporary or movable platform for workmen **b** : a platform on which a criminal is executed (as by hanging) **2** : a supporting framework [Medieval French *scafald,* alteration of *escafaut*]

scaf·fold·ing \-iŋ\ *n* : a system of scaffolds; *also* : materials for scaffolds

scal·able \ˈskā-lə-bəl\ *adj* **1** : capable of being scaled **2** : capable of being easily expanded or upgraded on demand ⟨a *scalable* computer network⟩ — **scal·abil·i·ty** \ˌskā-lə-ˈbil-ət-ē\ *n*

[1]**sca·lar** \ˈskā-lər, -ˌlär\ *adj* **1** : arranged like a ladder : GRADUATED ⟨a *scalar* chain of authority⟩ **2 a** : capable of being represented by a point on a scale ⟨a *scalar* quantity⟩ **b** : of or relating to a scalar or a scalar product ⟨*scalar* multiplication⟩ [Latin *scalaris,* from *scalae* "stairs, ladders"]

[2]**scalar** *n* **1** : a real number rather than a vector **2** : a quantity (as mass or time) that has a magnitude describable by a real number and no direction

sca·la·re \skə-ˈlaər-ē, -ˈleər-, -ˈlär-\ *n* : ANGELFISH 2 [derived from Latin *scalaris* "scalar"; from the barred pattern on its body]

scalar product *n* : a real number that is the product of the lengths of two vectors and the cosine of the angle between them

scal·a·wag *or* **scal·ly·wag** \ˈskal-i-ˌwag\ *n* **1** : RASCAL 1, SCAMP **2** : a white Southerner acting as a Republican in the time of reconstruction after the American Civil War [origin unknown]

[1]**scald** \ˈskȯld\ *vt* **1** : to burn with or as if with hot liquid or steam **2 a** : to subject to the action of boiling water or steam ⟨*scald* dishes⟩ **b** : to bring to a temperature just below the boiling point ⟨*scald* milk⟩ **3** : SCORCH 1a [Medieval French *escalder,* from Late Latin *excaldare* "to wash in warm water," from Latin *ex-* + *calida, calda* "warm water," from *calidus* "warm"]

[2]**scald** *n* **1** : an injury to the body caused by scalding **2** : an act or process of scalding **3** : a plant disease marked especially by discoloration suggesting injury by heat

scald·ing \ˈskȯl-diŋ\ *adj* **1** : causing the sensation of scalding or burning **2** : BOILING ⟨*scalding* water⟩ **3** : very hot : SCORCHING ⟨the *scalding* sun⟩ **4** : SCATHING, CUTTING ⟨a *scalding* editorial⟩

[1]**scale** \ˈskāl\ *n* **1 a** : either pan of a balance **b** : BALANCE — usually used in plural **2** : a device for weighing ⟨a bathroom *scale*⟩ [Old Norse *skāl* "bowl, scale of a balance"]

[2]**scale** *vb* **1** : to weigh in scales **2** : to have a specified weight

[3]**scale** *n* **1 a** : one of the small stiff flattened plates forming an outer covering on the body especially of a fish or reptile **b** : a small thin part or structure suggesting a fish scale ⟨*scales* of mica⟩ ⟨the *scales* on a moth's wing⟩ **2** : a small dry flake of skin ⟨dandruff *scales*⟩ **3** : a thin layer, coating, or incrustation forming especially on metal (as iron) ⟨boiler *scale*⟩ **4** : a modified leaf covering a bud of a seed plant **5 a** : SCALE INSECT **b** : a disease of plants caused by a scale insect [Medieval French *escale,* of Germanic origin] — **scaled** \ˈskāld\ *adj* — **scale·less** \ˈskāl-ləs\ *adj* — **scale·like** \ˈskāl-ˌlīk\ *adj*

[4]**scale** *vb* **1** : to remove scale or the scales from ⟨*scale* a boiler⟩ ⟨*scale* fish⟩ **2** : to take off in scales or thin layers ⟨*scale* tartar from the teeth⟩ **3** : to come off in scales or shed scales : FLAKE **4** : to throw (a flat object) and cause to sail in the air or skip on the water ⟨*scaling* cards into a hat⟩

[5]**scale** *n* **1** : a graduated series of tones going up or down in pitch **2** : something graduated especially when used as a measure or rule: as **a** : a series of spaces marked by lines and used to measure distances or to register something (as the height of the mercury in a thermometer) **b** : a divided line on a map or

chart indicating the length (as an inch) used to represent a larger unit of measure (as a mile) **c :** an instrument consisting of a strip (as of wood, plastic, or metal) with one or more sets of spaces graduated and numbered on its surface for measuring or laying off distances or dimensions **3 :** a basis for a system of numbering ⟨the decimal *scale*⟩ **4 :** a graduated series ⟨the *scale* of prices⟩ **5 :** the size of a picture, plan, or model of a thing in proportion to the size of the thing itself **6 :** relative size or degree ⟨do things on a large *scale*⟩ **7 :** a standard by which something can be measured or judged [Late Latin *scala* "ladder, staircase," from Latin *scalae,* pl., "stairs, ladder"]

[6]**scale** *vb* **1 :** to climb by or as if by means of a ladder or rope ⟨*scale* a wall⟩ **2 a :** to arrange in a graduated series ⟨*scale* a test⟩ **b :** to measure by or as if by a scale **c :** to make, regulate, or estimate according to a rate or standard ⟨*scale* down a budget⟩ ***synonyms*** see ASCEND

scale insect *n* **:** any of numerous small insects that are related to aphids, include many destructive plant pests, and have winged males, scale-covered females often permanently attached to the host plant, and young that suck the juices of plants

sca·lene \ˈskā-ˌlēn, skā-ˈ\ *adj* **:** having sides that are each a different length ⟨a *scalene* triangle⟩ [Late Latin *scalenus,* from Greek *skalēnos,* literally, "uneven"]

scale·pan \ˈskāl-ˌpan\ *n* **:** a pan of a scale for weighing

scal·er \ˈskā-lər\ *n* **:** one that scales

scal·lion \ˈskal-yən\ *n* **:** GREEN ONION [Medieval French *scalun, escaloin,* derived from Latin *ascalonia caepa* "onion of Ascalon (a seaport in Palestine)"]

[1]**scal·lop** \ˈskäl-əp, ˈskal-\ *n* **1 a :** any of a family of marine bivalve mollusks with the shell radially ribbed **b :** the adductor muscle of a scallop used for food **2 :** a scallop-shell valve or a similarly shaped dish used for baking **3 :** one of a continuous series of circle segments or angular projections forming a border [Medieval French *escalope* "shell," of Germanic origin]

[2]**scallop** *vt* **1 :** to bake in a sauce usually covered with seasoned bread or cracker crumbs ⟨*scalloped* potatoes⟩ **2 :** to shape, cut, or finish in scallops — **scal·lop·er** *n*

scallywag *variant of* SCALAWAG

[1]**scalp** \ˈskalp\ *n* **1 :** the part of the skin and flesh of the head usually covered with hair **2 :** a part of the human scalp cut or torn from an enemy as a token of victory [of Scandinavian origin]

[2]**scalp** *vt* **1 a :** to deprive of the scalp **b :** to remove an upper or better part from **2 :** to buy and sell so as to make small quick profits; *esp* **:** to resell at greatly increased prices ⟨*scalp* theater tickets⟩ — **scalp·er** *n*

scal·pel \ˈskal-pəl *also* skal-ˈpel\ *n* **:** a small straight thin-bladed knife used especially in surgery [Latin *scalpellum* "small knife," from *scalprum* "chisel, knife," from *scalpere* "to carve"]

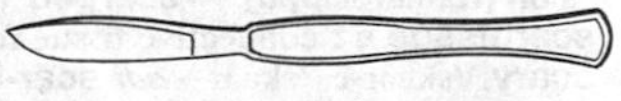
scalpel

scalp lock *n* **:** a long tuft of hair on the crown of the otherwise shaved head of a warrior of some American Indian tribes

scaly \ˈskā-lē\ *adj* **scal·i·er; -est 1 a :** covered with, composed of, or rich in scale or scales **b :** FLAKY 2 ⟨*scaly* skin⟩ **2 :** infested with scale insects ⟨*scaly* fruit⟩ — **scal·i·ness** *n*

scam \ˈskam\ *n* **:** a fraudulent or deceptive act or operation ⟨lost $500 in a business *scam*⟩ [origin unknown]

[1]**scamp** \ˈskamp\ *n* **1 :** RASCAL 1, ROGUE **2 :** an impish or playful young person [obsolete *scamp* "to roam about idly"]

[2]**scamp** *vt* **:** to perform in a hasty, neglectful, or imperfect manner **:** SKIMP ⟨*scamp* one's work⟩ [origin unknown]

scam·per \ˈskam-pər\ *vi* **scam·pered; scam·per·ing** \-pə-ring, -pring\ **:** to run nimbly and usually playfully about [perhaps from obsolete Dutch *schampen* "to flee," from Medieval French *escamper,* derived from Latin *ex-* + *campus* "field"] — **scamper** *n*

[1]**scan** \ˈskan\ *vb* **scanned; scan·ning 1 a :** to read or mark so as to show metrical structure ⟨*scan* poetry⟩ **b :** to conform to a metrical pattern ⟨this poem *scans* well⟩ **2 a :** to examine thoroughly ⟨*scanned* their faces for signs of anger⟩ **b :** to make a wide sweeping search of ⟨a fire lookout *scanning* the hills⟩ **c :** to look through or over hastily ⟨*scan* the headlines⟩ **d :** to examine systematically (as by passing a beam of radiation over or through) in order to obtain data especially for display or storage ⟨*scanned* the patient's heart⟩ ⟨*scan* the photos onto the computer⟩ **3 :** to move across in successive lines to form an image on a cathode-ray tube ⟨the electron beam *scans* the face of the picture tube⟩ [Late Latin *scandere,* from Latin, "to climb"] ***synonyms*** see SCRUTINIZE

[2]**scan** *n* **1 :** the act or process of scanning **2 :** an image formed by scanning something: as **a :** a picture of the distribution of radioactive material in something (as a bodily organ) **b :** a picture of part of the body produced (as by computer) by combining separate pictures taken from different angles or of different sections

scan·dal \ˈskan-dᵊl\ *n* **1 :** an offense against faith or morals that causes another to sin **2 :** loss of or damage to reputation caused by actual or apparent violation of morality or propriety **:** DISGRACE ⟨brought *scandal* on the school⟩ **3 a :** a circumstance or action that offends propriety or accepted moral standards or disgraces those associated with it ⟨their behavior is a *scandal*⟩ ⟨a bribery *scandal*⟩ **b :** a person whose conduct offends propriety or morality ⟨a *scandal* to the profession⟩ **4 :** malicious or defamatory gossip ⟨untouched by *scandal*⟩ [Late Latin *scandalum* "stumbling block, offense," from Greek *skandalon*]

scan·dal·ize \ˈskan-də-ˌlīz\ *vt* **1** *archaic* **:** to speak falsely or maliciously of **:** MALIGN **2 :** to offend the moral sense of **:** SHOCK ⟨their actions *scandalized* the neighbors⟩ — **scan·dal·i·za·tion** *n* — **scan·dal·iz·er** *n*

scan·dal·mon·ger \ˈskan-dᵊl-ˌməng-gər, -ˌmäng-\ *n* **:** a person who spreads scandal

scan·dal·ous \ˈskan-də-ləs, -dləs\ *adj* **1 :** DEFAMATORY ⟨a *scandalous* story⟩ **2 :** offensive to propriety or morality **:** SHOCKING ⟨*scandalous* behavior⟩ — **scan·dal·ous·ly** *adv* — **scan·dal·ous·ness** *n*

scandal sheet *n* **:** a newspaper or periodical dealing to a large extent in scandal and gossip

Scan·di·na·vian \ˌskan-də-ˈnā-vē-ən, -vyən\ *n* **1 a :** a native or inhabitant of Scandinavia **b :** a person of Scandinavian descent **2 :** the Germanic languages of the Scandinavian peoples including Icelandic, Norwegian, Swedish, and Danish — **Scandinavian** *adj*

scan·di·um \ˈskan-dē-əm\ *n* **:** a silvery white metallic chemical element — see ELEMENT table [New Latin, from Latin *Scandia,* southern part of the Scandinavian peninsula]

scan·ner \ˈskan-ər\ *n* **:** one that scans: as **a :** a device that senses recorded information **b :** a radio receiver that sequentially scans a range of frequencies for a signal **c :** a device that scans an image (as a photograph) or document (as a page of text) especially for use or storage on a computer **d :** a medical device for scanning a living body to collect diagnostic information

scanning electron microscope *n* **:** an electron microscope in which a beam of focused electrons moves across the object with the electrons produced or scattered by the object being collected to form a three-dimensional image on a display screen — called also *scanning microscope* — **scanning electron microscopy** *n*

scan·sion \ˈskan-chən\ *n* **:** the analysis of verse to show its meter [Late Latin *scansio,* from *scandere* "to scan"]

[1]**scant** \ˈskant\ *adj* **1** *dialect* **:** excessively frugal **:** PARSIMONIOUS **2 a :** barely or scarcely sufficient ⟨paid *scant* attention to me⟩; *esp* **:** not quite coming up to a stated measure ⟨a *scant* cup of milk⟩ **b :** lacking in amplitude or quantity **:** MEAGER, SCANTY ⟨*scant* growth⟩ **3 :** having a small or insufficient supply ⟨*scant* of breath⟩ [Old Norse *skamt,* neuter of *skammr* "short"] — **scant·ly** *adv* — **scant·ness** *n*

[2]**scant** *adv, dialect* **:** SCARCELY, HARDLY

[3]**scant** *vt* **1 :** to provide an incomplete supply of ⟨*scant* one's efforts⟩ **2 :** to make small, narrow, or meager **:** SKIMP **3 :** to give scant attention to **:** SLIGHT ⟨a subject *scanted* in textbooks⟩ **4 :** to provide with a meager or inadequate portion or share **:** STINT

scant·ling \ˈskant-ling, -lən\ *n* **:** a small piece of lumber; *esp* **:** one of the upright pieces in the frame of a house [Middle English *scantilon,* literally, "mason's or carpenter's measure," from Medieval French *escantilloun*]

scanty \ˈskant-ē\ *adj* **scant·i·er; -est :** limited or less than suf-

\ə\ **abut**	\au̇\ **out**	\i\ **tip**	\ȯ\ **saw**	\u̇\ **foot**
\ər\ **further**	\ch\ **chin**	\ī\ **life**	\ȯi\ **coin**	\y\ **yet**
\a\ **mat**	\e\ **pet**	\j\ **job**	\th\ **thin**	\yü\ **few**
\ā\ **take**	\ē\ **easy**	\ng\ **sing**	\t͟h\ **this**	\yu̇\ **cure**
\ä\ **cot, cart**	\g\ **go**	\ō\ **bone**	\ü\ **food**	\zh\ **vision**

ficient in degree, quantity, or extent *synonyms* see MEAGER — **scant·i·ly** \ˈskant-l-ē\ *adv* — **scant·i·ness** \ˈskant-ē-nəs\ *n*

[1]**scape** \ˈskāp\ *vb* : ESCAPE

[2]**scape** *n* **1** : a leafless flower stalk (as in the tulip) that begins at or beneath the surface of the ground **2** : the shaft of an animal part (as an antenna or a feather) [Latin *scapus* "shaft, stalk"]

[3]**scape** \ˌskāp\ *n* : a view or picture of a scene — usually used in combination ⟨moon*scape*⟩ [*landscape*]

scape·goat \ˈskāp-ˌgōt\ *n* **1** : a goat upon whose head are symbolically placed the sins of the people after which he is sent into the wilderness in the biblical ceremony for Yom Kippur **2** : a person or thing bearing the blame for others [[1]*scape*]

scape·grace \-ˌgrās\ *n* : an incorrigible rascal

scap·u·la \ˈskap-yə-lə\ *n, pl* **-lae** \-ˌlē, -ˌlī\ *or* **-las** : SHOULDER BLADE [Latin, "shoulder, shoulder blade"]

[1]**scap·u·lar** \ˈskap-yə-lər\ *n* **1 a** : a long wide band of cloth with an opening for the head worn front and back over the shoulders as part of a monastic habit **b** : a pair of small cloth squares joined by shoulder tapes and worn under the clothing on the breast and back as a sacramental and often also as a badge of a third order or confraternity **2** : one of the feathers covering the base of a bird's wing [Late Latin *scapulare,* from Latin *scapula* "shoulder"]

[2]**scapular** *adj* : of or relating to the shoulder or the shoulder blade

scapular medal *n* : a medal worn in place of a sacramental scapular

[1]**scar** \ˈskär\ *n* **1** : an isolated or protruding rock **2** : a steep rocky eminence : a bare place on the side of a mountain [Old Norse *sker* "skerry"]

[2]**scar** *n* **1 a** : a mark remaining (as on the skin) after injured tissue has healed **b** : a mark marking the former point of attachment of some other structure; *esp* : one on a stem where a leaf or fruit has separated **2** : a mark or indentation (as on furniture) resembling a scar **3** : a lasting moral or emotional injury [Medieval French *escare* "scab," from Late Latin *eschara,* from Greek, "hearth, scab"] — **scar·less** \-ləs\ *adj*

[3]**scar** *vb* **scarred; scar·ring** **1** : to mark with or form a scar **2** : to do lasting injury to **3** : to become scarred

scar·ab \ˈskar-əb\ *n* **1** : any of a family of large stout beetles (as a dung beetle) **2** : an ornament or a gem made to represent a scarab; *esp* : one used in ancient Egypt as a symbol of eternal life [Middle French *scarabee,* from Latin *scarabaeus*]

scarab 1

scar·a·mouch *or* **scar·a·mouche** \ˈskar-ə-ˌmüsh, -ˌmüch, -ˌmau̇ch\ *n* **1** : a cowardly buffoon **2** : RASCAL, SCAMP [French *Scaramouche,* a stock character in Italian comedy, from Italian *Scaramuccia,* from *scaramuccia* "skirmish"]

[1]**scarce** \ˈskeərs, ˈskaərs\ *adj* : deficient in quantity or number : not plentiful or abundant [Medieval French *escars* "narrow, stingy, deficient," derived from Latin *excerpere* "to pluck out, excerpt"] — **scarce·ness** *n*

[2]**scarce** *adv* : SCARCELY, HARDLY

scarce·ly \ˈsker-slē, ˈskar-\ *adv* **1 a** : by a narrow margin : only just ⟨had *scarcely* got there when they started the meeting⟩ **b** : almost not ⟨could *scarcely* see for the fog⟩ **2 a** : certainly not ⟨could *scarcely* tell them they were wrong⟩ **b** : probably not ⟨could *scarcely* have found a neater solution⟩

scar·ci·ty \ˈsker-sət-ē, ˈskar-\ *n, pl* **-ties** : the quality or state of being scarce; *esp* : want of provisions for the support of life

[1]**scare** \ˈskeər, ˈskaər\ *vb* **1** : to frighten suddenly : ALARM **2** : to become frightened ⟨they *scare* easily⟩ [Old Norse *skirra,* from *skjarr* "shy, timid"] — **scar·er** *n*

[2]**scare** *n* **1** : a sudden fright **2** : a widespread state of alarm : PANIC

scare·crow \ˈskeər-ˌkrō, ˈskaər-\ *n* **1 a** : an object usually suggesting a human figure that is set up to scare birds away from crops **b** : something frightening but harmless **2** : a skinny or ragged person

scare·head \-ˌhed\ *n* : a big, sensational, or alarming newspaper headline

scare·mon·ger \-ˌməng-gər, -ˌmäng-\ *n* : ALARMIST — **scare·mon·ger·ing** \-gər-ing\ *n*

scare up *vt* : to find or get together with considerable labor or difficulty ⟨managed to *scare up* the money⟩

[1]**scarf** \ˈskärf\ *n* **1** : either of the ends that fit together to form a scarf joint **2** : a joint made by beveling, halving, or notching two pieces to correspond and lapping and bolting them [Middle English *skarf*]

[2]**scarf** *also* **scarph** \ˈskärf\ *vt* : to unite by a scarf joint

[3]**scarf** *n, pl* **scarves** \ˈskärvz\ *or* **scarfs** \ˈskärfs\ **1** : a broad band (as of cloth) worn about the shoulders, around the neck, over the head, or about the waist **2** : TIPPET 3 **3** : RUNNER 6 [Medieval French *escherpe* "sash, sling"]

[4]**scarf** *vt* **1** : [3]SCOFF 1 ⟨*scarfed* down my sandwich⟩ **2** : SNAP 1c ⟨*scarfed* up the best seats⟩ [by alteration]

scarf·pin \ˈskärf-ˌpin\ *n* : TIEPIN

scarf·skin \ˈskärf-ˌskin\ *n* : EPIDERMIS 1, CUTICLE; *esp* : that about the base of a nail [[3]*scarf*]

scar·i·fy \ˈskar-ə-ˌfī, ˈsker-\ *vt* **-fied; -fy·ing** **1** : to make scratches or small cuts in ⟨*scarify* skin for vaccination⟩ ⟨*scarify* seeds to help them germinate⟩ **2** : to lacerate the feelings of : FLAY [Medieval French *scarefier,* from Late Latin *scarificare,* from Latin *scarifare,* from Greek *skariphasthai* "to scratch an outline, sketch"] — **scar·i·fi·ca·tion** \ˌskar-ə-fə-ˈkā-shən, ˌsker-\ *n* — **scar·i·fi·er** \ˈskar-ə-ˌfī-ər, ˈsker-, -ˌfīr\ *n*

scar·la·ti·na \ˌskär-lə-ˈtē-nə\ *n* : SCARLET FEVER [New Latin, from Medieval Latin *scarlata* "scarlet"]

[1]**scar·let** \ˈskär-lət\ *n* **1** : scarlet cloth or clothes **2** : a bright red [Medieval Latin *scarlata,* from Persian *saqalāt,* a kind of rich cloth]

[2]**scarlet** *adj* : of the color scarlet

scarlet fever *n* : an acute contagious disease that is marked by fever, by inflammation of the nose, throat, and mouth, and by a red rash and that is caused by a streptococcus which attacks red blood cells

scarlet pimpernel *n* : a European pimpernel having scarlet, white, or purplish flowers that close in cloudy weather

scarlet runner bean *n* : a tropical American high-climbing bean with large bright red flowers and red and black seeds that is grown for ornament and for its edible pods and seeds

scarlet sage *n* : a salvia native to Brazil that is widely grown for its spikes of typically scarlet flowers

scarlet tanager *n* : a common American tanager of which the male is scarlet with black wings during the breeding season and the female and young are chiefly olive

scarp \ˈskärp\ *n* **1** : a line of cliffs produced by faulting or erosion **2** : a low steep slope along a beach caused by wave erosion [Italian *scarpa*] — **scarped** \ˈskärpt\ *adj*

scar tissue *n* : connective tissue forming a bodily scar

scary \ˈskeər-ē, ˈskaər-\ *adj* **scar·i·er; -est** **1** : causing fright : ALARMING ⟨a *scary* movie⟩ **2** : easily scared : TIMID **3** : marked by fear ⟨a *scary* feeling⟩

[1]**scat** \ˈskat\ *vi* **scat·ted; scat·ting** **1** : to go away quickly **2** : to move fast : SCOOT [*scat,* interj. used to drive away a cat]

[2]**scat** *n* : the feces deposited by an animal ⟨bear *scat*⟩ [perhaps from Greek *skat-, skōr* "excrement"]

[3]**scat** *n* : jazz singing with nonsense syllables [origin unknown]

[4]**scat** *vi* **scat·ted; scat·ting** : to improvise nonsense syllables to an instrumental accompaniment : sing scat

[1]**scathe** \ˈskāth\ *n* : HARM, INJURY [Old Norse *skathi*] — **scathe·less** \-ləs\ *adj*

[2]**scathe** *vt* **1** : to do harm to; *esp* : to injure by fire **2** : to assail with withering denunciation

scath·ing \ˈskā-thing\ *adj* : bitterly severe ⟨a *scathing* rebuke⟩ — **scath·ing·ly** \-thing-lē\ *adv*

sca·tol·o·gy \skə-ˈtäl-ə-jē, ska-\ *n* : interest in or treatment of obscene matters especially in literature [Greek *skat-, skōr* "dung"] — **scat·o·log·i·cal** \ˌskat-l-ˈäj-i-kəl\ *adj*

scat·ter \ˈskat-ər\ *vb* **1** : to cause to separate widely **2** : to distribute irregularly **3** : to sow by casting in all directions : STREW **4** : to diffuse, disperse, or reflect (a beam of radiation) in a random manner **5** : to separate from each other and go in various directions ⟨we all *scattered* after graduation⟩ **6** : to occur or fall irregularly or at random [Middle English *scateren*] — **scat·ter·er** \-ər-ər\ *n*

synonyms SCATTER, DISPERSE, DISPEL, DISSIPATE mean to cause to separate or break up. SCATTER implies forcefully driving parts or units irregularly in many directions ⟨the bowling ball *scattered* the pins⟩. DISPERSE implies a wider separation and complete breaking up of mass or group ⟨police *dispersed* the crowd⟩. DISPEL stresses a driving away or getting rid of as if by scattering ⟨an official statement that *dispelled* any doubt⟩. DISSIPATE stresses complete disintegration or dissolution and final disappearance ⟨the fog was *dissipated* by the morning sun⟩.

scat·ter·brain \-ˌbrān\ *n* : a giddy heedless person incapable of concentration — **scat·ter·brained** \-ˌbrānd\ *adj*

[1]**scat·ter·ing** \ˈskat-ə-riŋ\ *n* **1** : an act or process in which something scatters or is scattered **2** : something scattered; *esp* : a small number or quantity interspersed here and there ⟨a *scattering* of visitors⟩

[2]**scattering** *adj* **1** : going in various directions **2** : found or placed far apart and in no order — **scat·ter·ing·ly** *adv*

scatter pin *n* : a small pin used as jewelry and worn usually in groups of two or more on a woman's dress

scatter rug *n* : THROW RUG

scaup \ˈskȯp\ *n, pl* **scaup** *or* **scaups** : either of two diving ducks with the male having a purplish or greenish head and a black breast and tail [perhaps from *scalp* "bed of shellfish"; from its fondness for shellfish]

scav·enge \ˈskav-inj\ *vb* **1** : to remove dirt or refuse from an area **2** : to salvage (usable material) from what has been discarded [back-formation from *scavenger*]

scav·en·ger \ˈskav-ən-jer\ *n* **1** *chiefly British* : a person employed to remove dirt and refuse from streets **2** : one that scavenges **3** : an organism (as a vulture or hyena) that typically feeds on refuse or carrion [Middle English *scavager* "collector of a toll on goods sold by nonresident merchants," from Medieval French *scawageour,* from *skawage* "toll on goods sold by nonresident merchants," from *escauver* "to inspect," from Dutch *scouwen*]

Word History In the 14th, 15th, and 16th centuries many English towns and cities levied a tax on goods shown for sale by nonresident merchants in order to put outsiders at a disadvantage in their trade in comparison with local merchants. Middle English *skawage,* the name for this tax, was borrowed from Medieval French *escauwage,* "inspection," a word of Germanic origin, related to English *show.* The *skawagers* (or later *scavengers*) of London were officers who collected the *skawage.* The responsibility for keeping the streets clean later fell on their shoulders as well. Now anyone who collects junk is a *scavenger.*

scavenger hunt *n* : a party contest in which players are sent out usually in pairs to obtain without buying unusual objects within a time limit

sce·nar·io \sə-ˈnar-ē-ˌō, -ˈner-\ *n, pl* **-i·os** **1 a** : an outline or synopsis of a play **b** : the libretto of an opera **2** : SCREENPLAY **3** : a sequence of events especially when imagined; *esp* : an account or synopsis of a possible course of action or events [Italian, from Latin *scaenarium,* from *scaena, scena* "stage, scene"]

sce·nar·ist \-ˈnar-əst, -ˈner-\ *n* : a writer of scenarios

scend \ˈsend\ *n* **1** : the lift of a wave **2** : the upward movement of a pitching ship [perhaps short for *ascend*]

scene \ˈsēn\ *n* **1** : one of the subdivisions of a play: as **a** : a division of an act presenting continuous action in one place **b** : a single situation or unit of dialogue in a play ⟨the love *scene*⟩ **c** : a motion picture or television episode or sequence **2 a** : a stage setting ⟨change *scenes*⟩ **b** : a view or sight having pictorial quality ⟨a winter *scene*⟩ **3** : the place of an occurrence or action : LOCALE ⟨the *scene* of the crime⟩ **4** : an exhibition of anger or indecorous behavior ⟨create a *scene*⟩ [Middle French, "stage," from Latin *scena* "stage, scene," from Greek *skēnē* "temporary shelter, tent, building forming the background for a dramatic performance, stage"] — **behind the scenes** **1** : out of public view : in secret **2** : in a position to see or control the hidden workings

scen·ery \ˈsēn-rē, -ə-rē\ *n* **1** : the painted scenes or hangings and accessories used on a theater stage **2** : a picturesque view or landscape ⟨mountain *scenery*⟩ **3** : one's usual surroundings ⟨needed a change of *scenery*⟩

scene·shift·er \ˈsēn-ˌshif-tər\ *n* : a worker who moves the scenes in a theater

scene–steal·er \-ˌstē-lər\ *n* : an actor who attracts attention when another is intended to be the center of attention

sce·nic \ˈsē-nik\ *also* **sce·ni·cal** \-ni-kəl\ *adj* **1** : of or relating to the stage, a stage setting, or stage representation ⟨*scenic* effects⟩ **2** : of, relating to, or marked by natural scenery ⟨a *scenic* route⟩ **3** : representing graphically an action, event, or episode ⟨*scenic* wallpaper⟩ — **sce·ni·cal·ly** \-ni-kə-lē, -klē\ *adv*

scenic railway *n, chiefly British* : a miniature railway (as in an amusement park) with artificial scenery along the way

[1]**scent** \ˈsent\ *n* **1 a** : an odor left by an animal on a surface passed over **b** : a characteristic or particular and usually agreeable odor **2 a** : sense of smell ⟨a keen *scent*⟩ **b** : power of detection : NOSE ⟨a *scent* for heresy⟩ **3** : a course of pursuit or discovery ⟨throw one off the *scent*⟩ **4** : INKLING, INTIMATION ⟨a *scent* of trouble⟩ **5** : PERFUME 2 **6** : bits of paper dropped in the game of hare and hounds **7** : a mixture prepared for use as a lure in hunting or fishing ***synonyms*** see SMELL

[2]**scent** *vt* **1 a** : to become aware of or follow through the sense of smell ⟨the dog *scented* a rabbit⟩ **b** : to get or have an inkling of ⟨*scent* trouble⟩ **2** : to imbue or fill with odor ⟨*scent* a handkerchief⟩ [Medieval French *sentir* "to feel, smell," from Latin *sentire* "to perceive, feel"]

scent·ed *adj* : having scent; *esp* : PERFUMED

scent·less \ˈsent-ləs\ *adj* : lacking scent; *esp* : ODORLESS — **scent·less·ness** *n*

scep·ter \ˈsep-tər\ *n* **1** : a staff or baton borne by a sovereign as an emblem of authority **2** : royal or imperial authority : SOVEREIGNTY [Medieval French *septre,* from Latin *sceptrum,* from Greek *skēptron*] — **scep·tered** \-tərd\ *adj*

scepter 1

scep·tic, scep·ti·cal, scep·ti·cism *chiefly British variant of* SKEPTIC, SKEPTICAL, SKEPTICISM

[1]**sched·ule** \ˈskej-ül, -əl, *Canadian also* ˈshej-, *British usually* ˈshed-yül\ *n* **1 a** : a written or printed list, catalog, or inventory **b** : TIMETABLE **2** : PROGRAM 3, AGENDA [Late Latin *schedula* "slip of paper," from Latin *schedium* "impromptu speech," from Greek *schedios* "casual"]

[2]**schedule** *vt* **1** : to place in or as if in a schedule ⟨*schedule* a meeting⟩ **2** : to make a schedule of

schee·lite \ˈshā-ˌlīt\ *n* : a calcium mineral that is an ore of tungsten [German *Scheelit,* from Karl W. *Scheele,* died 1786, Swedish chemist]

[1]**sche·mat·ic** \ski-ˈmat-ik\ *adj* : of, relating to, or forming a scheme, plan, or diagram — **sche·mat·i·cal·ly** \-ˈmat-i-kə-lē, -klē\ *adv*

[2]**schematic** *n* : a schematic drawing or diagram

sche·ma·tize \ˈskē-mə-ˌtīz\ *vt* **1** : to form or form into a scheme or systematic arrangement **2** : to express or depict schematically — **sche·ma·ti·za·tion** \ˌskē-mət-ə-ˈzā-shən\ *n*

[1]**scheme** \ˈskēm\ *n* **1** : a graphic sketch or outline **2** : a concise statement or table **3** : a plan or program of action; *esp* : a crafty or secret one **4** : a systematic or organized design or configuration ⟨the color *scheme* of a room⟩ ⟨their whole *scheme* of life⟩ [Latin *schemat-, schema* "arrangement, figure," from Greek *schēmat-, schēma,* from *echein* "to have, hold, be in (such) a condition"] ***synonyms*** see PLAN

[2]**scheme** *vb* **1** : to form a scheme for **2** : to form plans; *also* : to engage in intrigue : PLOT — **schem·er** *n*

schem·ing *adj* : given to forming schemes; *esp* : shrewdly devious and intriguing

scher·zan·do \skert-ˈsän-dō\ *adv or adj* : in a sportive manner : PLAYFULLY — used as a direction in music indicating style and tempo ⟨allegretto *scherzando*⟩ [Italian, from *scherzare* "to joke," of Germanic origin]

scher·zo \ˈskert-sō\ *n, pl* **scherzos** *or* **scher·zi** \-sē\ : a sprightly humorous instrumental musical composition or movement commonly in quick triple time [Italian, literally, "joke," from *scherzare* "to joke"]

schil·ler \ˈshil-ər\ *n* : a bronzy iridescent luster (as of a mineral) [German]

schil·ling \ˈshil-iŋ\ *n* : the basic monetary unit of Austria until 2002 [German]

\ə\ **abut**	\au̇\ **out**	\i\ **tip**	\ȯ\ **saw**	\u̇\ **foot**
\ər\ **further**	\ch\ **chin**	\ī\ **life**	\ȯi\ **coin**	\y\ **yet**
\a\ **mat**	\e\ **pet**	\j\ **job**	\th\ **thin**	\yü\ **few**
\ā\ **take**	\ē\ **easy**	\ŋ\ **sing**	\t͟h\ **this**	\yu̇\ **cure**
\ä\ **cot, cart**	\g\ **go**	\ō\ **bone**	\ü\ **food**	\zh\ **vision**

schism \ˈsiz-əm, ˈskiz-\ *n* **1** : DIVISION 5, SEPARATION; *also* : lack of harmony : DISCORD **2 a** : formal division in or separation from a church or religious body **b** : the religious offense of promoting schism [Medieval French *scisme, cisme,* from Late Latin *schismat-, schisma,* from Greek, "cleft, division," from *schizein* "to split"]

¹schis·mat·ic \siz-ˈmat-ik, skiz-\ *n* : one who creates or takes part in schism

²schismatic *adj* : of, relating to, or guilty of schism — **schis·mat·i·cal** \-ˈmat-i-kəl\ *adj* — **schis·mat·i·cal·ly** \-i-kə-lē, -klē\ *adv*

schis·ma·tist \ˈsiz-mət-əst, ˈskiz-\ *n* : SCHISMATIC

schis·ma·tize \-mə-ˌtīz\ *vb* : to take part in or induce into schism

schist \ˈshist\ *n* : a metamorphic crystalline rock that can be split along approximately parallel planes [French *schiste,* derived from Greek *schizein* "to split"] — **schis·tose** \ˈshis-ˌtōs\ *adj*

schis·to·some \ˈshis-tə-ˌsōm\ *n* : any of various elongated trematode worms with the sexes separate that mostly parasitize the blood vessels of birds and mammals and cause serious diseases in humans [Greek *schistos* "that may be split" (from *schizein* "to split") + *sōma* "body"] — **schistosome** *adj*

schis·to·so·mi·a·sis \ˌshis-tə-sə-ˈmī-ə-səs\ *n, pl* **-a·ses** \-ə-ˌsēz\ : infestation with or disease caused by schistosomes

schiz- *or* **schizo-** *combining form* **1** : split : cleft ⟨*schizo*carp⟩ **2** : characterized by or involving cleavage ⟨*schizo*gony⟩ [Greek *schizein* "to split"]

schiz·o·carp \ˈskiz-ə-ˌkärp, ˈskit-sə-\ *n* : a dry compound fruit that splits at maturity into several closed one-seeded carpels

schiz·oid \ˈskit-ˌsȯid\ *adj* : characterized by, resulting from, or suggestive of schizophrenia — **schizoid** *n*

schiz·o·phre·nia \ˌskit-sə-ˈfrē-nē-ə\ *n* : a psychosis characterized by abnormalities of thought, emotion, and behavior including distorted perception of reality, withdrawal from social interaction, greatly reduced ability to carry on one's daily tasks, delusions, and hallucinations [New Latin, from *schiz-* + Greek *phrēn* "mind"] — **schiz·o·phren·ic** \-ˈfren-ik\ *adj or n*

schle·miel *also* **shle·miel** \shlə-ˈmēl\ *n* : an unlucky bungler : CHUMP [Yiddish *shlemil*]

schlock \ˈshläk\ *or* **schlocky** \ˈshläk-ē\ *also* **shlock** *or* **shlocky** *adj* : of low quality or value ⟨*schlock* merchandise⟩ [Yiddish *shlak* "evil, nuisance," literally, "blow"] — **schlock** *n*

schm- *or* **shm-** \shm\ *prefix* — used to form a rhyming term of derision by replacing the initial consonant or consonant cluster of a word or by preceding the initial vowel ⟨art, *schm*art, that's just kitsch⟩ ⟨fancy, *schm*ancy, I prefer plain⟩ [Yiddish *shm-*]

schmaltz *also* **schmalz** \ˈshmȯlts\ *n* : sentimental or florid music or art [Yiddish *shmalts,* literally, "rendered fat"] — **schmaltzy** \ˈshmȯlt-sē\ *adj*

schmear *or* **schmeer** \ˈshmiər\ *n* : a mass or body of similar things ⟨the whole *schmear*⟩ [Yiddish *shmir* "smear," from *shmiren* "to smear," from Middle High German *smiren*]

¹schmooze *or* **shmooze** \ˈshmüz\ *vb* **schmoozed** *or* **shmoozed; schmooz·ing** *or* **shmooz·ing** **1** : to converse informally : CHAT; *also* : to chat in a friendly and persuasive manner especially so as to gain favor, business, or connections **2** : to engage in schmoozing with ⟨she *schmoozed* her teachers⟩ [Yiddish *shmuesn,* from *shmues* "talk," from Hebrew *shĕmuʿōth* "news, rumor"] — **schmooz·er** \ˈshmü-zər\ *n*

²schmooze *n* **1** : a gathering or time devoted to schmoozing **2** : casual talk that is often gossipy or intended to gain favor

schmoozy \ˈshmü-zē\ *adj* : of, relating to, characterized by, or given to schmoozing ⟨a *schmoozy* salesclerk⟩

schmuck \ˈshmək\ *n, slang* : an unlikable person; *esp* : one who is cruel, rude, or small-minded [Yiddish *shmok* "penis, fool"]

schnapps \ˈshnaps\ *n, pl* **schnapps** : any of various distilled liquors; *esp* : strong Holland gin [German *Schnaps*]

schnau·zer \ˈshnau̇t-sər; ˈshnau̇-zər, ˈsnau̇-\ *n* : a dog of any of three German breeds that are characterized by a long head, pointed ears, and wiry coat [German, from *Schnauze* "snout"]

schnit·zel \ˈshnit-səl, ˈsnit-\ *n* : a seasoned and garnished veal cutlet [German, "cutlet, shaving, chip"]

schnoz *or* **schnozz** \ˈshnäz\ *n, slang* : NOSE; *esp* : a large nose [probably modification of Yiddish *shnoitsl* "small snout," from *shnoits* "snout"]

schnoz·zle \ˈshnäz-əl, ˈsnäz-\ *n, slang* : SCHNOZ [probably from Yiddish *shnoitsl,* from *shnoits* "snout"]

scho·la can·to·rum \ˌskō-lə-ˌkan-ˈtōr-əm, -ˈtȯr-\ *n, pl* **scho·lae cantorum** \-ˌlē-, -ˌlā-, -ˌlī-\ : a liturgical choir or choir school [Medieval Latin, "school of singers"]

schol·ar \ˈskäl-ər\ *n* **1** : a person who attends a school or studies under a teacher : PUPIL **2 a** : a person who has done advanced study in a special field **b** : a learned person **3** : a holder of a scholarship [Old English *scolere* and Medieval French *escoler,* from Medieval Latin *scholaris,* derived from Latin *schola* "school"]

schol·ar·ly \-ər-lē\ *adj* : characteristic of or suitable to learned persons : LEARNED, ACADEMIC ⟨*scholarly* writing⟩

schol·ar·ship \-ər-ˌship\ *n* **1** : financial aid given to a student (as by a college or foundation) to assist in the cost of education **2** : the character, qualities, or attainments of a scholar : LEARNING

Scholarship level *n* : S LEVEL

¹scho·las·tic \skə-ˈlas-tik\ *adj* **1 a** *often cap* : of or relating to Scholasticism ⟨*scholastic* theology⟩ **b** : excessively dogmatic or formal in instruction : PEDANTIC ⟨dull *scholastic* reports⟩ **2** : of or relating to schools or scholars [Latin *scholasticus* "of a school," from Greek *scholastikos,* derived from *scholē* "school"] — **scho·las·ti·cal·ly** \-ti-kə-lē, -klē\ *adv*

²scholastic *n* **1** *cap* : a Scholastic philosopher **2** : a person who adopts academic or traditional methods in art

scho·las·ti·cism \skə-ˈlas-tə-ˌsiz-əm\ *n* **1** *cap* : a philosophical movement dominant from the 9th until the 17th century and typically using methods of reasoning adapted from Aristotle to interpret systematically the dogmas of Christian faith **2** : close adherence to the traditional teachings or methods of a school or sect

scho·li·ast \ˈskō-lē-ˌast, -lē-əst\ *n* : a maker of scholia : COMMENTATOR, ANNOTATOR [Middle Greek *scholiastēs,* derived from Greek *scholion* "scholium"]

scho·li·um \ˈskō-lē-əm\ *n, pl* **-lia** \-lē-ə\ *or* **-li·ums** **1** : a marginal annotation or comment (as on the text of a classic by an early grammarian) **2** : explanatory or elaborative matter appended to but not essential to a demonstration or a train of reasoning [New Latin, from Greek *scholion* "comment, scholium," from *scholē* "lecture, school"]

¹school \ˈskül\ *n* **1 a** : a place or establishment for teaching and learning ⟨driving *school*⟩ ⟨public *schools*⟩ **b** : a faculty or division of an institution of higher learning devoted to teaching, study, and research in a particular field of knowledge ⟨graduate *school*⟩ ⟨the *school* of law⟩ **2 a** : the process of learning or being instructed at a school ⟨found *school* very difficult⟩ **b** : attendance at a school ⟨my last year of *school*⟩ **c** : a session of school ⟨missed *school* yesterday⟩ **d** : the students or the students and faculty of a school ⟨the whole *school* was at the assembly⟩ **3** : SCHOOLHOUSE **4** : a group of persons holding the same opinions and beliefs or accepting the same intellectual methods or leadership; *also* : the shared opinions, beliefs, or methods of such a group ⟨certain *schools* of thought⟩ [Old English *scōl,* from Latin *schola,* from Greek *scholē* "leisure, discussion, lecture, school"]

Word History The original meaning of the Greek word *scholē,* from which our *school* is derived, was "leisure." To the Greeks it seemed only natural to occupy one's leisure with learning and thinking, and *scholē* came to mean "a place for learning" as well as "leisure." The Romans borrowed the Greek word as *schola* and employed Greek slaves as teachers. Christian missionaries later established schools throughout Europe, and Latin *schola* became Old English *scōl.*

²school *vt* **1** : to teach or drill in a specific knowledge or skill ⟨well *schooled* in languages⟩ **2** : to discipline or habituate to something ⟨*school* oneself in patience⟩

³school *n* : a large number of aquatic animals of one kind swimming together [Dutch *schole*]

⁴school *vi* : to swim or feed in a school ⟨bluefish are *schooling*⟩

school age *n* : the period of life during which a child is considered mentally and physically fit to attend school and is commonly required to do so by law

school·bag \ˈskül-ˌbag\ *n* : a bag for carrying schoolbooks and school supplies

school board *n* : a board in charge of local public schools

school·book \ˈskül-ˌbu̇k\ *n* : a school textbook

school·boy \-ˌbȯi\ *n* : a boy attending school

school bus *n* : a vehicle used for transporting children to or from school or on activities connected with school

school·child \ˈskül-ˌchīld\ *n* : a child attending school

school·fel·low \-ˌfel-ō\ *n* : SCHOOLMATE

school·girl \-ˌgərl\ *n* : a girl attending school
school·house \-ˌhau̇s\ *n* : a building used as a school
school·ing *n* **1** : instruction in school : EDUCATION **2** : the cost of instruction and maintenance at school **3** : the training of an animal and especially a horse to perform a certain function or act (as jumping over obstacles)
School·man \ˈskül-mən, -ˌman\ *n* : SCHOLASTIC 1
school·marm \-ˌmärm, -ˌmäm\ *or* **school·ma'am** \-ˌmäm, -ˌmam\ *n* **1** : a woman who is a schoolteacher especially in a rural or small-town school **2** : a person who exhibits characteristics attributed to schoolteachers (as strict adherence to arbitrary rules) [*school* + *marm,* alteration of *ma'am*]
school·mas·ter \-ˌmas-tər\ *n* : a man who teaches school
school·mate \-ˌmāt\ *n* : a companion at school
school·mis·tress \-ˌmis-trəs\ *n* : a woman who teaches school
school·room \-ˌrüm, -ˌru̇m\ *n* : CLASSROOM
school·teach·er \-ˌtē-chər\ *n* : a person who teaches school
school·time \-ˌtīm\ *n* **1** : the time for beginning a session of school or during which school is held **2** : the period of life spent in school or in study
school·work \-ˌwərk\ *n* : lessons done in classes at school or assigned to be done at home
school·yard \-ˌyärd\ *n* : the playground of a school
schoo·ner \ˈskü-nər\ *n* **1** : a fore-and-aft rigged sailing vessel with two masts; *also* : any large fore-and-aft rigged ship **2** : a large tall glass (as for beer) **3** : PRAIRIE SCHOONER [origin unknown]

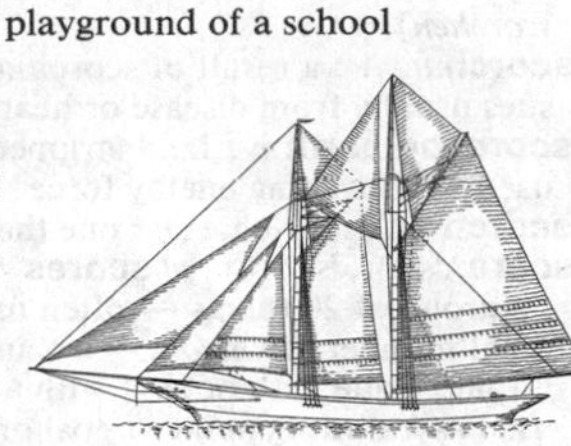
schooner 1

schot·tische \ˈshät-ish, shä-ˈtēsh\ *n* **1** : a round dance similar to but slower than the polka **2** : music for the schottische [German, from *schottisch* "Scottish"]
Schrö·ding·er equation \ˈshrā-ding-ər-, ˈshrœ-\ *n* : an equation that describes the wave nature of elementary particles and is fundamental to the description of the properties of all matter [Erwin *Schrödinger,* died 1961, Austrian physicist]
schuss \ˈshu̇s, ˈshüs\ *vi* : to ski directly down a slope at high speed [German, literally, "shot"] — **schuss** *n* — **schuss·er** *n*
schwa \ˈshwä\ *n* **1** : an unstressed vowel that is the usual sound of the first and last vowels of the English word *America* **2** : the symbol ə commonly used for a schwa and sometimes also for a similarly articulated stressed vowel (as in *cut*) [German, from Hebrew *shĕwā*]
Schwann cell \ˈshwän-\ *n* : a myelin-secreting cell that surrounds a myelinated nerve fiber between two nodes of Ranvier [Theodor *Schwann,* died 1882, German naturalist]
sci·at·ic \sī-ˈat-ik\ *adj* **1** : of, relating to, or situated near the hip **2** : of, relating to, or caused by sciatica ⟨*sciatic* pains⟩ [Middle French *sciatique,* from Late Latin *sciaticus,* from Latin *ischiadicus* "of sciatica," from Greek *ischiadikos,* from *ischiad-, ischias* "sciatica," from *ischion* "ischium"]
sci·at·i·ca \sī-ˈat-i-kə\ *n* : pain along the course of a sciatic nerve especially in the back of a thigh; *also* : pain in or near the hips [Medieval Latin, from Late Latin *sciaticus* "sciatic"]
sciatic nerve *n* : either of the pair of largest nerves in the body each of which supplies a leg and the pelvic region and passes out of the pelvis and down the back of the thigh
sci·ence \ˈsī-əns\ *n* **1 a** : a department of systematized knowledge that is an object of study ⟨the *science* of theology⟩; *esp* : one of the natural sciences (as biology, physics, or chemistry) **b** : something (as a sport or technique) that may be studied or learned like systematized knowledge ⟨have it down to a *science*⟩ **2** : knowledge covering general truths or the operation of general laws especially as obtained and tested through the scientific method [Medieval French, from Latin *scientia,* from *sciens* "having knowledge," from *scire* "to know"]
science fair *n* : an exhibition of science projects typically prepared and presented by schoolchildren
science fiction *n* : fiction dealing with the impact of actual or imagined science on society or individuals or having a scientific factor as an essential component of the plot — **sci·ence–fic·tion·al** \-ˈfik-shnəl, -shən-l\ *adj*
sci·en·tial \sī-ˈen-chəl\ *adj* **1** : relating to or producing knowledge or science **2** : having efficient knowledge : CAPABLE
sci·en·tif·ic \ˌsī-ən-ˈtif-ik\ *adj* : of, relating to, or exhibiting the methods or principles of science — **sci·en·tif·i·cal·ly** \-ˈtif-i-kə-lē, -klē\ *adv*
scientific method *n* : principles and procedures for the systematic pursuit of knowledge involving the recognition and formulation of a problem, the collection of data through observation and experiment, and the formulation and testing of hypotheses
scientific notation *n* : a system of writing numbers as the product of a number between 1 and 10 and a power of 10 ⟨999.9 expressed in *scientific notation* is 9.999×10^2⟩
sci·en·tism \ˈsī-ən-ˌtiz-əm\ *n* **1** : methods and attitudes typical of or attributed to the natural scientist **2** : an exaggerated trust in the effectiveness of the methods of natural science applied to all areas of investigation (as in philosophy, the social sciences, and the humanities)
sci·en·tist \ˈsī-ən-təst\ *n* **1** : one learned in science and especially natural science : a scientific investigator **2** *cap* : CHRISTIAN SCIENTIST
sci·en·tis·tic \ˌsī-ən-ˈtis-tik\ *adj* **1** : professedly scientific **2** : relating to or characterized by scientism
sci–fi \ˈsī-ˈfī\ *adj* : of, relating to, or being science fiction ⟨a *sci-fi* film⟩ — **sci–fi** *n*
scil·la \ˈsil-ə, ˈskil-ə\ *n* : any of a genus of Old World bulbous herbs related to the lilies and often grown for their clusters of purple, blue, or white flowers [Latin, "squill"]
scim·i·tar \ˈsim-ət-ər, -ə-ˌtär\ *n* : a curved sword used especially by Arabs and Turks [Italian *scimitarra*]

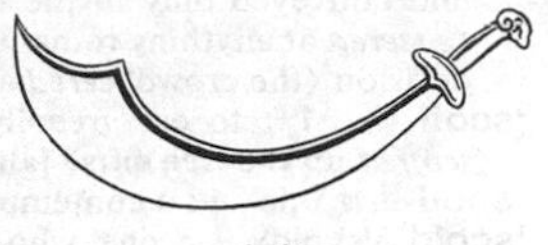
scimitar

scin·til·la \sin-ˈtil-ə\ *n* : a very small amount : IOTA, TRACE [Latin]
scin·til·late \ˈsint-l-ˌāt\ *vb* **-lat·ed; -lat·ing** **1** : to emit sparks : SPARK **2** : to emit quick flashes as if throwing off sparks : SPARKLE ⟨eyes *scintillating* with anger⟩ **3** : to throw off as a spark or as sparkling flashes ⟨*scintillate* witticisms⟩ [Latin *scintillare* "to sparkle," from *scintilla* "spark"] ***synonyms*** see GLISTEN — **scin·til·lant** \-l-ənt\ *adj* — **scin·til·lant·ly** *adv* — **scin·til·la·tion** \ˌsint-l-ˈā-shən\ *n* — **scin·til·la·tor** \ˈsint-l-ˌāt-ər\ *n*
scintillation counter *n* : a device for detecting and registering individual scintillations (as in radioactive emission)
sci·o·lism \ˈsī-ə-ˌliz-əm\ *n* : a superficial show of learning [Late Latin *sciolus* "one whose knowledge is superficial," from Latin *scius* "knowing," from *scire* "to know"] — **sci·o·list** \-ləst\ *n* — **sci·o·lis·tic** \ˌsī-ə-ˈlis-tik\ *adj*
sci·on \ˈsī-ən\ *n* **1** : a detached living portion of a plant (as a bud or shoot) joined to a stock in grafting and usually supplying only aerial parts to a graft **2 a** : DESCENDANT, CHILD; *esp* : a descendent of a wealthy, aristocratic, or influential family **b** : HEIR 1 ⟨a *scion* of a railroad empire⟩ [Medieval French, *cion,* of Germanic origin]
scis·sion \ˈsizh-ən\ *n* : a dividing of or split in a group or union [Late Latin *scissio,* from Latin *scindere* "to split"]
1**scis·sor** \ˈsiz-ər\ *n* : SCISSORS [Middle French *cisoire,* derived from Latin *caedere* "to cut"]
2**scissor** *vt* : to cut, cut up, or cut off with scissors ⟨*scissored* the paper into strips⟩
scis·sors \ˈsiz-ərz\ *n sing or pl* **1** : a cutting instrument having two blades whose cutting edges slide past each other **2 a** : a gymnastic feat in which the leg movements suggest the opening and closing of scissors **b** : SCISSORS HOLD
scissors hold *n* : a wrestling hold in which the legs are locked around the head and body of an opponent
scissors kick *n* : a swimming kick used especially in the sidestroke in which the legs move like scissors
scler- *or* **sclero-** *combining form* : hard ⟨*scler*ite⟩ [Greek *sklēros*]
sclera \ˈskler-ə\ *n* : the dense fibrous white or bluish white tissue that forms the outer covering of the back five-sixths of the eye and is replaced in front by the transparent cornea with which it is continuous [New Latin, from Greek *sklēros* "hard"]

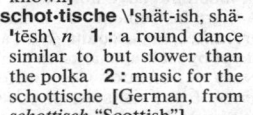

\ə\ **abut**	\au̇\ **out**	\i\ **tip**	\ȯ\ **saw**	\u̇\ **foot**
\ər\ **further**	\ch\ **chin**	\ī\ **life**	\ȯi\ **coin**	\y\ **yet**
\a\ **mat**	\e\ **pet**	\j\ **job**	\th\ **thin**	\yü\ **few**
\ā\ **take**	\ē\ **easy**	\ng\ **sing**	\t͟h\ **this**	\yu̇\ **cure**
\ä\ **cot, cart**	\g\ **go**	\ō\ **bone**	\ü\ **food**	\zh\ **vision**

scler•e•id \ˈskler-ē-əd\ *n* : a supporting cell of a plant that is lignified and often mineralized — called also *stone cell* [derived from Greek *sklēros* "hard"]

scle•ren•chy•ma \sklə-ˈreng-kə-mə\ *n* : a protective or supporting tissue in higher plants composed of cells with walls thickened and lignified and often mineralized — compare COLLENCHYMA [*scler-* + *-enchyma* (as in *parenchyma*)] — **scler•en•chy•ma•tous** \ˌskler-ən-ˈkim-ət-əs, -ˈkī-mət-\ *adj*

scler•ite \ˈskliər-ˌīt, ˈskleər-\ *n* : a hard chitinous or calcareous plate or piece (as of the exoskeleton of an insect)

scle•ro•sis \sklə-ˈrō-səs\ *n* : an abnormal hardening of tissue especially from increase of connective tissue; *also* : a disease characterized by sclerosis — compare *multiple sclerosis*

1**scle•rot•ic** \sklə-ˈrät-ik\ *adj* **1** : being or relating to the sclera **2** : of, relating to, or affected with or as if with sclerosis

2**sclerotic** *n* : SCLERA

sclerotic coat *n* : SCLERA

1**scoff** \ˈskäf, ˈskȯf\ *n* : an expression of scorn, derision, or contempt [Middle English *scof*]

2**scoff** *vb* : to show or treat with contempt by derisive acts or words : MOCK — **scoff•er** *n*

synonyms SCOFF, SNEER, JEER mean to show contempt in derision or mockery. SCOFF implies insolent or irreverent mockery or derision ⟨*scoffed* at the coach's training rules⟩. SNEER implies an ill-natured contempt often half concealed and conveyed only in the tone of voice or facial expression ⟨*sneered* at anything romantic⟩. JEER suggests coarse or vulgar derision ⟨the crowd *jeered* at the prisoners⟩.

3**scoff** *vb* **1** : to eat greedily ⟨*scoffed* dinner⟩ **2** : SNAP 1c ⟨*scoffed* up the free gifts⟩ [alteration of English dialect *scaff*]

scoff•law \-ˌlȯ\ *n* : a contemptuous law violator

1**scold** \ˈskōld\ *n* : one who scolds habitually or persistently [Middle English *scald, scold*]

2**scold** *vb* **1** : to find fault noisily or angrily **2** : to rebuke severely or angrily — **scold•er** *n*

sco•lex \ˈskō-ˌleks\ *n, pl* **sco•li•ces** *also* **sco•le•ces** \-lə-ˌsēz\ : the head of a tapeworm [Greek *skōlēx* "worm"]

sco•li•o•sis \ˌskō-lē-ˈō-səs, ˌskäl-ē-\ *n, pl* **-o•ses** \-ˌsēz\ : a lateral curvature of the spine — compare KYPHOSIS, LORDOSIS [Greek *skoliōsis* "crookedness of a bodily part," from *skolios* "crooked"] — **sco•li•ot•ic** \-ˈät-ik\ *adj*

sconce \ˈskäns\ *n* : a candlestick or group of candlesticks mounted on a plaque and fastened to a wall [Medieval French *sconse* "screened lantern," from *escondre* "to hide," from Latin *abscondere*]

sconce

scone \ˈskōn, ˈskän\ *n* : a quick bread cooked on a griddle or baked on a sheet [perhaps from Dutch *schoonbrood* "fine white bread," from *schoon* "pure, clean" + *brood* "bread"]

1**scoop** \ˈsküp\ *n* **1 a** : a large ladle **b** : a deep shovel or similar implement for digging, dipping, or shoveling **c** : a round utensil for dipping food ⟨an ice cream *scoop*⟩ **d** : a small spoon-shaped utensil or instrument for cutting or gouging **2** : an act or the action of scooping : a motion made with or as if with a scoop **3 a** : the amount held by a scoop ⟨a *scoop* of sugar⟩ **b** : a hole made by scooping **4** : information of immediate interest; *also* : an exclusive news report [Dutch *schope*] — **scoop•ful** \-ˌfu̇l\ *n*

2**scoop** *vt* **1** : to take out or up or empty with or as if with a scoop **2** : to make hollow : dig out **3** : BEAT 5a(2) — **scoop•er** *n*

scoot \ˈsküt\ *vi* **1** : to go suddenly and swiftly : DART **2** : to slide especially while seated ⟨*scoot* over and let me sit down⟩ [perhaps alteration of earlier *scout,* of unknown origin] — **scoot** *n*

scoot•er \ˈsküt-ər\ *n* **1** : a child's vehicle that consists of a narrow board mounted between two wheels one behind the other with an upright steering handle attached to the front wheel **2** : MOTOR SCOOTER

scop \ˈshōp, ˈskōp, ˈskäp\ *n* : an Old English bard or poet [Old English]

1**scope** \ˈskōp\ *n* **1** : space or opportunity for unhampered motion, activity, or thought ⟨given full *scope* to develop new solutions⟩ **2** : something sought : OBJECT **3** : extent covered, reached, or viewed : RANGE ⟨a subject broad in *scope*⟩ [Italian *scopo* "purpose, goal," from Greek *skopos*]

2**scope** *n* : any of various instruments for viewing: as **a** : MICROSCOPE **b** : TELESCOPE **c** : OSCILLOSCOPE **d** : RADARSCOPE [*-scope*]

-scope \ˌskōp\ *n combining form* : means (as an instrument) for viewing or observing ⟨micro*scope*⟩ [Greek *-skopion*]

sco•pol•amine \skō-ˈpäl-ə-ˌmēn, -mən\ *n* : a poisonous alkaloid found in some plants of the nightshade family that is used medically (as to prevent nausea or dilate the pupil of the eye) [German *Scopolamin,* from New Latin *Scopolia,* genus of plants + German *Amin* "amine"]

-s•co•py \s-kə-pē\ *n combining form, pl* **-pies** : viewing : observation ⟨stereo*scopy*⟩ [Greek *-skopia,* from *skeptesthai* "to watch, look at"]

scor•bu•tic \skȯr-ˈbyüt-ik\ *adj* : of, relating to, producing, or affected with scurvy [New Latin *scorbutus* "scurvy"]

1**scorch** \ˈskȯrch\ *vb* **1 a** : to burn superficially usually to the point of changing color, texture, or flavor ⟨*scorch* a roast⟩ ⟨linen *scorches* easily⟩ **b** : to parch and discolor with or as if with intense heat ⟨lawns *scorched* by summer suns⟩ **2** : to distress or embarrass with usually sarcastic censure [Middle English *scorchen*]

2**scorch** *n* **1** : a result of scorching **2** : a browning of plant tissues usually from disease or heat

scorched earth *n* : land stripped of anything that could be of use to an invading enemy force

scorch•er \ˈskȯr-chər\ *n* : one that scorches; *esp* : a very hot day

1**score** \ˈskōr, ˈskȯr\ *n, pl* **scores** **1** *or pl* **score** **a** : TWENTY **b** : a group of 20 things — often used in combination with a cardinal number ⟨five*score*⟩ **c** : an indefinite large number **2 a** : a line made with or as if with a sharp instrument **b** : a mark used as a starting point or goal or for keeping account **3 a** : an account or reckoning originally kept by making marks on a tally **b** : amount due : INDEBTEDNESS **4** : GRUDGE ⟨looking for an opportunity to settle the *score*⟩ **5 a** : REASON, GROUND ⟨you have nothing to fear on that *score*⟩ **b** : SUBJECT 3c, TOPIC ⟨has nothing to say on that *score*⟩ **6** : a musical composition in written or printed notation **7 a** : a number expressing accomplishment (as in a game or test) or quality (as of a product) ⟨a *score* of 80 out of a possible 100⟩ **b** : an act (as a goal, run, or touchdown) that gains points in any of various games or contests **8** : the true facts or prospects of a situation ⟨know the *score* on the unemployment situation⟩ [Old Norse *skor* "notch, tally, twenty"]

2**score** *vb* **1 a** : to record by or as if by notches on a tally **b** : to keep score in a game or contest **2** : to mark with lines, grooves, scratches, or notches **3** : BERATE, SCOLD **4 a** : to make a score in or as if in a game : TALLY ⟨*score* a run⟩ **b** : to enable (a base runner) to make a score ⟨*scored* the runner from second base with a single⟩ **c** : to have as a value in a game or contest : COUNT ⟨a touchdown *scores* six points⟩ **d** : ACHIEVE 2, ATTAIN ⟨*scored* a big success⟩ **e** : WIN 2a ⟨*scored* free tickets over the radio⟩ **5** : to determine the merit of : GRADE **6** : to write or arrange music for (a movie) **7 a** : to gain or have the advantage **b** : to be successful — **scor•er** *n* — **score points** : to gain favor, status, or advantage

score•board \ˈskōr-ˌbōrd, ˈskȯr-ˌbȯrd\ *n* : a large board for displaying the score of a game or match

score•card \-ˌkärd\ *n* : a card for recording the score (as of a game)

score•keep•er \-ˌkē-pər\ *n* : an official who records the score during the progress of a game or contest

score•less \-ləs\ *adj* : having no score; *esp* : involving no points or runs

sco•ria \ˈskōr-ē-ə, ˈskȯr-\ *n, pl* **-ri•ae** \-ē-ˌē, -ē-ˌī\ **1** : the refuse from melting of metals or reduction of ores : SLAG **2** : rough cindery lava [Latin, from Greek *skōria,* from *skōr* "excrement"] — **sco•re•a•ceous** \ˌskōr-ē-ˈā-shəs, ˌskȯr-\ *adj*

1**scorn** \ˈskȯrn\ *n* **1** : a feeling of contempt and loathing toward something considered inferior or unworthy **2** : an object of extreme disdain, contempt, or derision [Medieval French *escharne, escar,* of Germanic origin]

2**scorn** *vt* **1** : to treat with scorn : reject or dismiss as contemptible or unworthy ⟨*scorned* all weaklings⟩ ⟨*scorned* to reply to the charge⟩ **2** : to show disdain or derision : SCOFF ***synonyms*** see DESPISE — **scorn•er** *n*

scorn•ful \ˈskȯrn-fəl\ *adj* : full of scorn : CONTEMPTUOUS — scorn•ful•ly \-fə-lē\ *adv* — **scorn•ful•ness** *n*

Scor·pio \ˈskȯr-pē-ˌō\ *n* **1 :** a zodiacal southern constellation that is located partly in the Milky Way and adjoins Libra **2 :** the 8th sign of the zodiac; *also* **:** one born under this sign [Latin, from Greek *Skorpios,* literally, "scorpion"]

scor·pi·on \ˈskȯr-pē-ən\ *n* **:** any of an order (Scorpionida) of arachnids that are active at night and have an elongated body and a narrow segmented tail with a venomous sting at the tip [Medieval French *eskorpiun,* from Latin *scorpio,* from Greek *skorpios*]

scorpion fish *n* **:** any of various large-headed marine fishes usually with poisonous spines on the fins

Scor·pi·us \ˈskȯr-pē-əs\ *n* **:** SCORPIO 1 [Latin, from Greek *Skorpios,* literally, "scorpion"]

Scot \ˈskät\ *n* **1 :** a member of a Celtic people of northern Ireland settling in Scotland about A.D. 500 **2 a :** a native or inhabitant of Scotland **b :** a person of Scottish descent [Old English *Scottas* "Irishmen, Scotsmen," from Late Latin *Scotus*]

scotch \ˈskäch\ *vt* **1** *archaic* **:** to injure so as to make temporarily harmless **2 :** to stamp out **:** CRUSH ⟨*scotch* a rebellion⟩; *esp* **:** to end decisively by showing the falsity of ⟨*scotch* a rumor⟩ [Middle English *scocchen* "to gash"]

[1]**Scotch** \ˈskäch\ *adj* **1 :** SCOTTISH **2 :** ECONOMICAL 1, FRUGAL [contraction of *Scottish*]

[2]**Scotch** *n* **1 :** SCOTS **2** *pl in constr* **:** the people of Scotland **3** *often not cap* **:** whiskey distilled in Scotland especially from barley — called also *Scotch whisky*

Scotch broth *n* **:** a soup made from beef or mutton and vegetables and thickened with barley

Scotch–Irish *adj* **:** of, relating to, or descended from Scottish settlers in northern Ireland — **Scotch–Irish** *n*

Scotch·man \ˈskäch-mən\ *n* **:** SCOTSMAN

Scotch terrier *n* **:** SCOTTISH TERRIER

Scotch·wom·an \ˈskäch-ˌwu̇m-ən\ *n* **:** SCOTSWOMAN

sco·ter \ˈskōt-ər\ *n, pl* **scoters** *or* **scoter :** any of several sea ducks of coastal Eurasia, Canada, and the U.S. [origin unknown]

scoter

scot–free \ˈskät-ˈfrē\ *adj* **:** totally free from obligation, harm, or penalty [from *scot* "money assessed or paid," from Old Norse *skot* "shot, contribution"]

[1]**Scots** \ˈskäts\ *adj* **:** SCOTTISH [Middle English *Scottis,* alteration of *Scottish*]

[2]**Scots** *n* **:** the English language of Scotland

Scots–Irish *adj* **:** SCOTCH-IRISH

Scots·man \ˈskät-smən\ *n* **:** a native or inhabitant of Scotland

Scots·wom·an \-ˌswu̇m-ən\ *n* **:** a woman who is a native or inhabitant of Scotland

Scot·tie \ˈskät-ē\ *n* **:** SCOTTISH TERRIER

[1]**Scot·tish** \ˈskät-ish\ *adj* **:** of, relating to, or characteristic of Scotland, the people of Scotland, or Scots

[2]**Scottish** *n* **:** SCOTS

Scottish deerhound *n* **:** any of an old breed of dogs of Scottish origin that resemble a greyhound but are larger and taller with a shaggy harsh coat

Scottish Gaelic *n* **:** the Gaelic language of Scotland

Scottish terrier *n* **:** any of an old Scottish breed of terrier with short legs, a long head with small erect ears, a broad deep chest, and a hard coat of wiry hair

scoun·drel \ˈskau̇n-drəl\ *n* **:** a mean worthless person **:** VILLAIN [origin unknown] — **scoundrel** *adj* — **scoun·drel·ly** \-drə-lē\ *adj*

[1]**scour** \ˈskau̇r\ *vb* **1 :** to move about or through quickly especially in search **2 :** to examine minutely and rapidly [Middle English *scuren*]

[2]**scour** *vb* **1 a :** to rub hard in order to clean **b :** to remove by rubbing hard and washing ⟨*scour* spots from the stove⟩ **2 :** to free from foreign matter or impurities by or as if by washing ⟨*scour* wool⟩ **3 a :** to clear, dig, or remove by a powerful current of water **b :** to wear away (as by water) **:** ERODE ⟨a stream *scouring* its banks⟩ **4 :** to suffer from diarrhea or dysentery **5 :** to become clean and bright by rubbing [Middle English *scouren*] — **scour·er** *n*

[3]**scour** *n* **1 :** an action or result of scouring **2** *pl* **:** DIARRHEA, DYSENTERY

[1]**scourge** \ˈskərj\ *n* **1 :** WHIP 1, LASH **2 a :** an instrument of punishment or criticism **b :** a cause of widespread or great affliction [Medieval French *escorge,* derived from *es-* "ex-" + Latin *corrigia* "whip"]

[2]**scourge** *vt* **1 :** to whip severely **:** FLOG **2 :** to subject to affliction **:** DEVASTATE ⟨a region *scourged* by malaria⟩ — **scourg·er** *n*

scouring rush *n* **:** HORSETAIL; *esp* **:** one with harsh abrasive stems formerly used for scouring

[1]**scout** \ˈskau̇t\ *vb* **1 :** to go about and observe in search of information ⟨*scout* an area for minerals⟩ ⟨*scouted* around the enemy position⟩ **2 a :** to make a search ⟨*scout* about for firewood⟩ **b :** to find by searching [Medieval French *escouter* "to listen," from Latin *auscultare*]

[2]**scout** *n* **1 a :** one sent to obtain information and especially to reconnoiter in war **b :** LOOKOUT 1 **c :** a person who searches for talented newcomers **2 :** the act or an instance of scouting **:** RECONNAISSANCE **3** *often cap* **a :** BOY SCOUT **b :** GIRL SCOUT **4 :** FELLOW 4a, GUY

[3]**scout** *vb* **1 :** to make fun of **:** MOCK **2 :** to reject scornfully as absurd **:** SCOFF ⟨*scout* a theory⟩ [of Scandinavian origin]

scout car *n* **:** a fast armored military reconnaissance vehicle with four-wheel drive and open top

scout·craft \-ˌkraft\ *n* **:** the craft, skill, or practice of a scout

scout·er \-ər\ *n* **1 :** one that scouts **2** *often cap* **:** an adult leader of the Boy Scouts of America

scout·ing \ˈskau̇t-ing\ *n* **1 :** the action of one that scouts **2** *often cap* **:** the activities of the various organizations for youth intended to develop character, citizenship, and individual skills

scout·mas·ter \ˈskau̇t-ˌmas-tər\ *n* **:** the leader of a band of scouts and especially of a troop of Boy Scouts

scow \ˈskau̇\ *n* **:** a large flat-bottomed boat with broad square ends used chiefly for transporting sand, gravel, or refuse [Dutch *schouw*]

scow

[1]**scowl** \ˈskau̇l\ *vb* **1 :** FROWN 1, GLOWER ⟨*scowled* at my impudence⟩ **2 :** to exhibit or express with a scowl ⟨*scowl* one's displeasure⟩ [Middle English *skoulen*] — **scowl·er** *n*

[2]**scowl** *n* **:** a facial expression of displeasure **:** FROWN

[1]**scrab·ble** \ˈskrab-əl\ *vb* **scrab·bled; scrab·bling** \ˈskrab-ling, -ə-ling\ **1 :** SCRAWL, SCRIBBLE **2 :** to scratch or claw about clumsily or frantically **3 a :** to struggle for a foothold **:** SCRAMBLE **b :** to struggle by or as if by scraping or scratching ⟨*scrabble* for a living⟩ [Dutch *schrabbelen* "to scratch"] — **scrab·bler** \ˈskrab-lər, -ə-lər\ *n*

[2]**scrabble** *n* **:** an act or instance of scrabbling

scrab·bly \ˈskrab-lē, -ə-lē\ *adj* **scrab·bli·er; -est 1 :** RASPY 1, SCRATCHY **2 :** SPARSE, SCRUBBY ⟨a *scrabbly* garden⟩

[1]**scrag** \ˈskrag\ *n* **1 :** a rawboned or scrawny person or animal **2 :** the lean end of a neck of mutton or veal [perhaps from *crag* "neck, throat," from Dutch *crāghe*]

[2]**scrag** *vt* **scragged; scrag·ging :** KILL, MURDER

scrag·gly \ˈskrag-lē, -ə-lē\ *adj* **scrag·gli·er; -est :** irregular in form or growth ⟨*scraggly* hills⟩ ⟨a *scraggly* beard⟩; *also* **:** RAGGED, UNKEMPT

scrag·gy \ˈskrag-ē\ *adj* **scrag·gi·er; -est 1 :** ROUGH 1c, JAGGED **2 :** being lean and long **:** SCRAWNY

scram \ˈskram\ *vi* **scrammed; scram·ming :** to go away at once ⟨*scram,* you're not wanted⟩ [short for *scramble*]

[1]**scram·ble** \ˈskram-bəl\ *vb* **scram·bled; scram·bling** \-bə-ling, -bling\ **1 a :** to move with urgency or panic **b :** to move or climb hastily on all fours **2 a :** to struggle eagerly or unceremoniously for possession of something ⟨*scramble* for front seats⟩ **b :** to get or gather something with difficulty or in irregular ways ⟨*scramble* for a living⟩ **3 :** SPRAWL 3, STRAGGLE **4 a :** to toss or mix together **:** JUMBLE **b :** to prepare (eggs) by stirring during cooking [perhaps alteration of [1]*scrabble*] — **scram·bler** \-bə-lər, -blər\ *n*

[2]**scramble** *n* **1 :** the act or an instance of scrambling **2 :** a disordered mess **:** JUMBLE

\ə\ abut	\au̇\ out	\i\ tip	\ȯ\ saw	\u̇\ foot
\ər\ further	\ch\ chin	\ī\ life	\ȯi\ coin	\y\ yet
\a\ mat	\e\ pet	\j\ job	\th\ thin	\yü\ few
\ā\ take	\ē\ easy	\ng\ sing	\t͟h\ this	\yu̇\ cure
\ä\ cot, cart	\g\ go	\ō\ bone	\ü\ food	\zh\ vision

[1]**scrap** \ˈskrap\ *n* **1** *pl* : fragments of discarded or leftover food **2** : a small bit : FRAGMENT ⟨*scraps* of cloth⟩ ⟨not a *scrap* of truth in the story⟩ **3** : discarded or waste material (as metal) for reprocessing [Old Norse *skrap* "scraps"]
[2]**scrap** *vt* **scrapped; scrap·ping 1** : to break up into scrap ⟨*scrap* a battleship⟩ **2** : to discard as worthless
[3]**scrap** *n* : [1]QUARREL, FIGHT [origin unknown]
[4]**scrap** *vi* **scrapped; scrap·ping** : QUARREL 2, FIGHT — **scrap·per** *n*
scrap·book \ˈskrap-ˌbu̇k\ *n* : a blank book in which various items (as newspaper clippings or pictures) are collected and preserved
[1]**scrape** \ˈskrāp\ *vb* **1 a** : to remove by repeated strokes of an edged tool ⟨*scrape* off rust⟩ **b** : to clean or smooth by rubbing with an edged tool or abrasive **2 a** : to move along or over something with a grating noise : GRATE **b** : to damage or injure the surface of by contact with a rough surface ⟨*scraped* his knee on the pavement⟩ **3 a** : to gather with difficulty and little by little ⟨*scrape* together a few dollars⟩ **b** : to make one's way with difficulty : barely manage or succeed ⟨*scraped* through with low grades⟩ [Old Norse *skrapa*] — **scrap·er** *n*
[2]**scrape** *n* **1 a** : the act or process of scraping **b** : a sound, mark, or injury made by scraping : ABRASION **2** : a bow made by drawing back the foot **3 a** : a disagreeable predicament **b** : ALTERCATION, FIGHT
scrap·ple \ˈskrap-əl\ *n* : a seasoned ground mush of cornmeal and bits of meat set in a mold and served sliced and fried [derived from [1]*scrap*]
[1]**scrap·py** \ˈskrap-ē\ *adj* **scrap·pi·er; -est** : consisting of scraps
[2]**scrappy** *adj* **scrap·pi·er; -est 1** : likely or tending to quarrel : QUARRELSOME **2** : aggressive and determined in spirit — **scrap·pi·ness** *n*
[1]**scratch** \ˈskrach\ *vb* **1** : to scrape or dig with or as if with the claws or nails **2** : to rub and tear or mark the surface of with something sharp **3**: to act on (a desire) — used with *itch* ⟨*scratch* the itch to travel⟩ **4** : to scrape together : collect with difficulty or effort ⟨*scratch* out a living⟩ **5** : to write or draw on a surface especially hastily or carelessly : SCRAWL **6 a** : to cancel or erase by or as if by drawing a line through **b** : to withdraw (an entry) from competition **7 a** : to use the claws or nails in digging, tearing, or wounding **b** : to scrape or rub oneself lightly (as to relieve itching) **8** : to make a thin grating sound [Middle English *scracchen,* probably blend of *scratten* "to scratch" and *cracchen* "to scratch"] — **scratch·er** *n* — **scratch one's back** : to accommodate with a favor especially in expectation of like return — **scratch one's head** : to be or become confused or perplexed — **scratch the surface** : to make a modest effort or start
[2]**scratch** *n* **1** : a mark (as a line) or injury made by scratching; *also* : a slight wound **2** : the sound made by scratching **3** : the starting line in a race **4** : satisfactory condition or performance ⟨not up to *scratch*⟩ **5** : poultry feed scattered especially to induce birds to exercise **6** : a shot in billiards or pool that ends a player's turn; *esp* : a shot in pool in which the cue ball falls into a pocket — **from scratch 1** : from a point at which nothing has been done ahead of time ⟨made a new plan *from scratch*⟩ **2** : without using a prepared mixture of ingredients ⟨bake a cake *from scratch*⟩
[3]**scratch** *adj* **1** : arranged or put together with little selection : HAPHAZARD ⟨a *scratch* team⟩ **2** : made as or used for a tentative effort **3** : made or done by chance and not as intended ⟨a *scratch* shot⟩ **4** : having no handicap ⟨a *scratch* golfer⟩ **5** : made from scratch : made with basic ingredients ⟨a *scratch* cake⟩
scratch hit *n* : a batted ball not solidly hit or cleanly played yet credited to the batter as a base hit
scratch paper *n* : paper suitable for casual writing
scratch test *n* : a test for allergic susceptibility made by rubbing an extract of an allergy-producing substance into small breaks or scratches in the skin
scratchy \ˈskrach-ē\ *adj* **scratch·i·er; -est 1** : likely to scratch or irritate : PRICKLY ⟨*scratchy* woolens⟩ **2** : making a scratching noise **3** : marked or made with scratches ⟨a *scratchy* surface⟩ **4** : uneven in quality **5** : somewhat inflamed and sore ⟨a *scratchy* throat⟩ — **scratch·i·ly** \ˈskrach-ə-lē\ *adv* — **scratch·i·ness** \ˈskrach-ē-nəs\ *n*
scrawl \ˈskrȯl\ *vb* : to write or draw awkwardly, hastily, or carelessly : SCRIBBLE [origin unknown] — **scrawl** *n* — **scrawl·er** *n* — **scrawly** \ˈskrȯ-lē\ *adj*
scraw·ny \ˈskrȯ-nē\ *adj* **scraw·ni·er; -est** : ill-nourished : SKINNY ⟨*scrawny* cattle⟩ [origin unknown] — **scraw·ni·ness** *n*
[1]**scream** \ˈskrēm\ *vb* **1** : to utter a loud shrill prolonged cry or sound; *also* : to utter with such a sound ⟨*screamed* my name⟩ **2** : to move with great speed **3 a** : to produce or give a vivid, startling, or alarming effect ⟨a *screaming* red⟩ ⟨*screaming* headlines⟩ **b** : to protest, demand, or complain forcefully [Middle English *scremen*]
[2]**scream** *n* **1** : a loud shrill prolonged cry or sound **2** : a very funny person or thing ⟨you're a *scream*⟩
synonyms SCREAM, SHRIEK, SCREECH mean a sudden piercing cry. SCREAM is the general term for utterance that is sharpened and prolonged by intensity of feeling ⟨*screams* of distress⟩. SHRIEK may imply an intensified scream or suggest a degree of wildness or lack of control ⟨*shrieks* of dismay⟩ ⟨hysterical *shrieks* of laughter⟩. SCREECH implies a harsh shrillness painful to the hearer and suggesting an unearthly or, often, a comic effect ⟨the *screech* of an angry parrot⟩.
scream·er \ˈskrē-mər\ *n* **1** : one that screams **2** : a sensationally startling headline
scream·ing \ˈskrē-ming\ *adj* **1** : noticeable as if by screaming ⟨*screaming* headlines⟩ ⟨dressed in *screaming* red⟩ **2** : very funny **3** : extremely fast or powerful ⟨a *screaming* line drive⟩ — **scream·ing·ly** *adv*
[1]**screech** \ˈskrēch\ *n* **1** : a shrill harsh cry usually of terror or pain **2** : a sound like a screech ⟨the *screech* of brakes⟩ ***synonyms*** see SCREAM
[2]**screech** *vb* **1** : to utter a high shrill piercing cry usually in terror or pain; *also* : to utter with a screech ⟨*screeched* a warning⟩ **2** : to make a sound like a screech ⟨the car *screeched* to a halt⟩ [Middle English *scrichen*] — **screech·er** *n*
screech·ing \ˈskrē-ching\ *adj* : SUDDEN 1a ⟨her career came to a *screeching* halt⟩
screech owl *n* : any of various New World owls; *esp* : either of two small North American owls with a pair of tufts of lengthened feathers on the head that resemble ears

screech owl

screed \ˈskrēd\ *n* : a lengthy discourse [Old English *scrēade* "fragment, shred"]
[1]**screen** \ˈskrēn\ *n* **1 a** : a device or partition used to hide, restrain, protect, or decorate ⟨a window *screen*⟩; *also* : something that serves to shelter, protect, or conceal ⟨a *screen* of fighter planes⟩ ⟨used the store as a *screen* for illegal activities⟩ **b** : a maneuver in various sports (as basketball or ice hockey) whereby an opponent is legally impeded or the opponent's view of the play is momentarily blocked **2** : a sieve or perforated material set in a frame and used for separating finer parts from coarser parts (as of sand) **3 a** : a flat surface upon which a picture or series of pictures is projected **b** : the surface on which the image appears in an electronic display (as in a television set or computer terminal) **4** : the motion-picture industry [Middle French *escren,* from Dutch *scherm*]
[2]**screen** *vb* **1** : to guard from injury or danger **2 a** : to shelter, protect, or separate with or as if with a screen **b** : to pass (as coal, gravel, or ashes) through a screen to separate the fine part from the coarse; *also* : to remove by or as if by a screen **c** (1) : to examine systematically in order to separate into groups; *also* : to select or eliminate by this means ⟨*screened* the applicants⟩ (2) : to test or examine for the presence of something (as a disease) ⟨patients were *screened* for hepatitis⟩ **3** : to provide with a screen especially to keep out insects ⟨*screen* a porch⟩ **4 a** : to project (as a motion-picture film) on a screen **b** : to present in a motion picture **c** : to appear on a motion-picture screen **5** : to cut off an opponent from a play — **screen·able** \ˈskrē-nə-bəl\ *adj* — **screen·er** *n*
screen·ing \ˈskrē-ning\ *n* **1** *pl* : material (as fine coal) separated out by passage through or retention on a screen **2** : a mesh (as of metal or plastic) used especially for screens
screen pass *n* : a forward pass in football to a receiver who is protected by a screen of blockers
screen·play \ˈskrēn-ˌplā\ *n* : the written form of a story prepared for motion-picture or television production
screen saver *n* : a computer program that usually displays var-

ious images on the screen of a computer that is on but not in use [from its function of preventing damage to the screen's phosphors]

screen test *n* : a short film sequence testing the ability or suitability of a person for a motion-picture role — **screen–test** *vt*

screen·writ·er \ˈskrēn-ˌrīt-ər\ *n* : a writer of screenplays

[1]**screw** \ˈskrü\ *n* **1 a** : a simple machine consisting of a spirally grooved solid cylinder and a correspondingly grooved cylindrical hollow part into which it fits **b** : a nail-shaped or rod-shaped metal piece with a spiral groove and a slotted or recessed head used for fastening pieces of solid material together **2 a** : a screw-shaped form : SPIRAL **b** : a turn of a screw; *also* : a twist like the turn of a screw **c** : a screw-shaped device (as a corkscrew) **3** : PROPELLER **4** : THUMBSCREW 2 [Middle French *escroe* "screw, nut," from Medieval Latin *scrofa,* from Latin, "sow"] — **screw·like** \-ˌlīk\ *adj* — **have a screw loose** : to be mentally unbalanced

[2]**screw** *vb* **1 a** (1) : to attach, fasten, or close by means of a screw ⟨*screw* a hinge to a door⟩ (2) : to operate, tighten, or adjust by means of a screw **b** : to move or cause to move spirally as a screw does; *also* : to close or set in position by such an action ⟨*screw* on a lid⟩ ⟨*screw* a jar shut⟩ **2 a** : to twist out of shape : CONTORT ⟨a face *screwed* up in pain⟩ **b** : SQUINT 2 **3** : to increase in amount or capability ⟨*screwed* up my nerve⟩ **4** : to deprive of or cheat out of something due or expected ⟨*screwed* out of a job⟩ — **screw·er** *n*

screw around *vi* **1** : to waste time with unproductive activity : DALLY **2** : to have sexual relations with someone outside of a marriage or steady relationship

[1]**screw·ball** \ˈskrü-ˌbȯl\ *n* **1** : a baseball pitch that spins and breaks in the opposite direction to a curve **2** : NUT 4a

[2]**screwball** *adj* : NUTTY 2

screw·driv·er \ˈskrü-ˌdrī-vər\ *n* : a tool for turning screws

screw eye *n* : a screw having a head in the form of a loop

screw pine *n* : any of a genus of tropical trees or shrubs that are monocotyledons with slender palmlike stems, often huge prop roots, and terminal crowns of swordlike leaves — called also *pandanus*

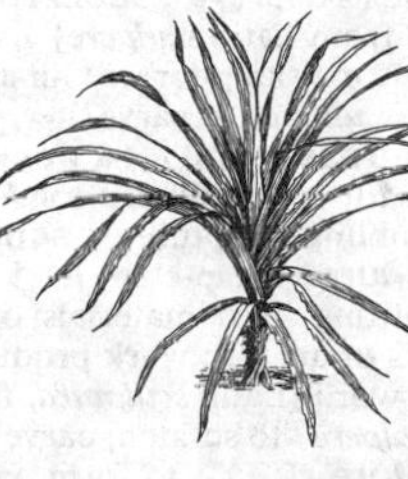

screw pine

screw propeller *n* : PROPELLER

screw thread *n* : the projecting spiral rib of a screw between the grooves

screw·up \ˈskrü-ˌəp\ *n* **1** : one who screws up **2** : BOTCH, BLUNDER

screw up *vb* **1** : to tighten, fasten, or lock by or as if by a screw **2 a** : BUNGLE **b** : to cause to act in a crazy or confused way

screw·worm \ˈskrü-ˌwərm\ *n* : a blowfly of warm parts of America whose larva develops in sores or wounds of mammals and may cause disease or death; *esp* : its larva

screwy \ˈskrü-ē\ *adj* **screw·i·er; -est** **1** : crazily absurd, eccentric, or unusual **2** : CRAZY 2a, INSANE — **screw·i·ness** *n*

scrib·al \ˈskrī-bəl\ *adj* : of, relating to, or due to a scribe ⟨a *scribal* error⟩

scrib·ble \ˈskrib-əl\ *vb* **scrib·bled; scrib·bling** \ˈskrib-ling, -ə-ling\ : to write or draw hastily or carelessly [Medieval Latin *scribillare,* from Latin *scribere* "to write"] — **scribble** *n*

scrib·bler \ˈskrib-lər\ *n* **1** : one that scribbles **2** : a minor or inferior author

[1]**scribe** \ˈskrīb\ *n* **1** : a scholar of the Jewish law in New Testament times **2 a** : an official or public secretary or clerk **b** : a copier of manuscripts **3** : AUTHOR 1; *esp* : JOURNALIST [Latin *scriba* "official writer," from *scribere* "to write"]

[2]**scribe** *vt* : to mark or make by cutting or scratching with a pointed instrument ⟨*scribe* a line on metal⟩ [probably short for *describe*]

scrib·er \ˈskrī-bər\ *n* : a sharp-pointed tool for marking off material (as wood or metal) to be cut

scrim \ˈskrim\ *n* : a durable plain-woven usually cotton fabric [origin unknown]

[1]**scrim·mage** \ˈskrim-ij\ *n* **1 a** : a minor battle : SKIRMISH **b** : a confused fight : SCUFFLE **2** : the interplay between two football teams that begins with the snap of the ball and continues until the ball is dead **3** : practice play between a team's squads or a practice game between two teams [alteration of [1]*skirmish*]

[2]**scrimmage** *vi* : to take part in a scrimmage — **scrim·mag·er** *n*

scrimp \ˈskrimp\ *vb* **1** : STINT 1, SKIMP **2** : ECONOMIZE 1 [perhaps of Scandinavian origin] — **scrimpy** \ˈskrim-pē\ *adj*

scrim·shaw \ˈskrim-ˌshȯ\ *n* : carved or engraved articles made originally by American whalers usually from baleen and whale teeth [origin unknown] — **scrimshaw** *vb*

scrip \ˈskrip\ *n* **1** : a document showing that the holder or bearer is entitled to something (as stock or land) **2** : paper currency or a token issued for temporary use in an emergency [short for *script*]

script \ˈskript\ *n* **1 a** : something written : TEXT **b** : an original or principal legal document **c** (1) : MANUSCRIPT 1 (2) : the written text of a stage play, screenplay, or broadcast **2 a** : printed lettering resembling handwritten lettering **b** : written characters : HANDWRITING **c** : ALPHABET 1 [Latin *scriptum* "thing written," from *scribere* "to write"]

scrip·to·ri·um \skrip-ˈtōr-ē-əm, -ˈtȯr-\ *n, pl* **-ria** \-ē-ə\ : a copying room in a medieval monastery set apart for the scribes [Medieval Latin, from Latin *scribere* "to write"]

scrip·tur·al \ˈskrip-chə-rəl, ˈskrip-shrəl\ *adj* : of, relating to, or being in accordance with a sacred writing; *esp* : BIBLICAL — **scrip·tur·al·ly** \-ē\ *adv*

scrip·ture \ˈskrip-chər\ *n* **1 a** *cap* : the books of the Old and New Testaments or of either of them : BIBLE — often used in plural **b** *often cap* : a passage from the Bible **2** : a body of writings considered sacred or authoritative [Latin *scriptura* "writing," from *scribere* "to write"]

script·writ·er \ˈskrip-ˌrīt-ər\ *n* : a person who writes scripts (as screenplays)

scriv·e·ner \ˈskriv-nər, -ə-nər\ *n* : a professional copyist or writer : SCRIBE [Middle French *escrivein,* derived from Latin *scriba* "scribe"]

scrod \ˈskräd\ *n* : a young fish (as a cod or haddock); *esp* : one split and boned for cooking [origin unknown]

scrof·u·la \ˈskrȯf-yə-lə, ˈskräf-\ *n* : tuberculosis of the lymph glands especially in the neck [New Latin, back-formation from Late Latin *scrofulae* "swellings of the lymph glands of the neck," from Latin *scrofa* "sow"] — **scrof·u·lous** \-ləs\ *adj*

[1]**scroll** \ˈskrōl\ *n* **1** : a roll (as of paper or parchment) providing a writing surface; *esp* : one on which something is written or engraved **2** : an ornament suggesting a loosely or partly rolled scroll [Middle English *scrowle,* blend of *rolle* "roll" and *scrowe* "scrap," from Medieval French *escroue,* of Germanic origin]

scroll 1

[2]**scroll** *vb* **1** : to move text or graphics across a display screen as if by unrolling a scroll **2** : to cause (text or graphics) to move in scrolling

scroll saw *n* : a saw with a thin blade for cutting curves or irregular designs

scroll·work \ˈskrōl-ˌwərk\ *n* : ornamental work (as in metal or wood) having a scroll or scrolls as its chief feature

scrooge \ˈskrüj\ *n, often cap* : a miserly person [Ebenezer *Scrooge,* character in *A Christmas Carol,* story by Charles Dickens]

scro·tum \ˈskrōt-əm\ *n, pl* **scro·ta** \ˈskrōt-ə\ *or* **scrotums** : the external pouch that in most male mammals contains the testes [Latin] — **scro·tal** \ˈskrōt-l\ *adj*

scrounge \ˈskrau̇nj\ *vb* **1** : to hunt or collect by or as if by foraging ⟨*scrounge* around for firewood⟩ **2** : CADGE, WHEEDLE ⟨*scrounge* a dollar from a friend⟩ [from English dialect *scrunge* "to wander about idly"] — **scroung·er** *n*

[1]**scrub** \ˈskrəb\ *n* **1 a** : a stunted tree or shrub **b** : vegetation consisting chiefly of a tract covered with scrubs **2** : a domestic animal of mixed or unknown parentage and usually inferior build **3 a** : a person of insignificant size or standing **b** : a player not on the first string **4** *pl* : loose-fitting clothing worn

\ə\ **abut**	\au̇\ **out**	\i\ **tip**	\ȯ\ **saw**	\u̇\ **foot**
\ər\ **further**	\ch\ **chin**	\ī\ **life**	\ȯi\ **coin**	\y\ **yet**
\a\ **mat**	\e\ **pet**	\j\ **job**	\th\ **thin**	\yü\ **few**
\ā\ **take**	\ē\ **easy**	\ng\ **sing**	\t͟h\ **this**	\yu̇\ **cure**
\ä\ **cot, cart**	\g\ **go**	\ō\ **bone**	\ü\ **food**	\zh\ **vision**

by hospital staff [Middle English, alteration of *schrobbe* "shrub," from Old English *scrybb* "brushwood"] — **scrub** *adj*

[2]**scrub** *vb* **scrubbed; scrub·bing 1 :** to clean with hard rubbing : SCOUR **b :** to remove by or as if by scrubbing **2 :** to subject to friction : RUB [of Low German or Scandinavian origin] — **scrub·ber** *n*

[3]**scrub** *n* **1 :** an act or instance of scrubbing **2 :** one that scrubs

scrub brush *n* **:** a brush with hard bristles for heavy cleaning

scrub·by \ˈskrəb-ē\ *adj* **scrub·bi·er; -est 1 :** inferior in size or quality : STUNTED ⟨*scrubby* cattle⟩ **2 :** covered with or consisting of vegetational scrub ⟨a *scrubby* hill⟩ **3 :** lacking distinction : SHABBY [[1]*scrub*]

scrub·land \ˈskrəb-ˌland\ *n* **:** land covered with scrub

scrub nurse *n* **:** a nurse who assists the surgeon in an operating room

scrub typhus *n* **:** an acute bacterial disease of the western Pacific area that resembles typhus and is transmitted by larval mites — called also *tsutsugamushi disease*

scrub·wom·an \ˈskrəb-ˌwu̇m-ən\ *n* **:** a woman who hires herself out for cleaning : CHARWOMAN

scruff \ˈskrəf\ *n* **:** the loose skin of the back of the neck : NAPE [alteration of earlier *scuff,* of unknown origin]

scruffy \-ē\ *adj* **scruff·i·er; -est :** dirty or shabby in appearance ⟨a *scruffy* beard⟩ [English dialect *scruff* "something worthless"]

scrump·tious \ˈskrəm-shəs, ˈskrəmp-\ *adj* **:** DELIGHTFUL, EXCELLENT; *esp* : DELICIOUS [perhaps alteration of *sumptuous*] — **scrump·tious·ly** *adv*

[1]**scrunch** \ˈskrənch\ *vb* **1 a :** CRUNCH, CRUSH **b :** to make or move with a crunching sound **2 a :** to draw or squeeze together tightly **b :** CRUMPLE 1 ⟨*scrunch* up a piece of paper⟩ **c :** to cause (as one's features) to draw together ⟨*scrunched* up his nose⟩ **3 :** CROUCH 1, HUNCH [alteration of [1]*crunch*]

[2]**scrunch** *n* **:** a crunching sound

scrunch·ie *or* **scrunchy** \ˈskrən-chē\ *n, pl* **scrunchies :** a fabric-covered elastic used for holding back hair (as in a ponytail)

[1]**scru·ple** \ˈskrü-pəl\ *n* **1 —** see MEASURE table **2 :** a tiny part or quantity [Latin *scrupulus,* a unit of weight, from *scrupus* "small sharp stone"]

[2]**scruple** *n* **1 :** an ethical consideration or principle that makes one uneasy or inhibits action **2 :** SCRUPULOSITY 1 **3 :** a sense of guilt felt when one does wrong [Medieval French *scrupule,* from Latin *scrupulus* "scruple," from *scrupus* "sharp stone"] ***synonyms*** see QUALM

[3]**scruple** *vi* **scru·pled; scru·pling** \-pə-liŋ, -pliŋ\ **:** to have scruples

scru·pu·los·i·ty \ˌskrü-pyə-ˈläs-ət-ē\ *n, pl* **-ties 1 :** the quality or state of being scrupulous **2 :** [2]SCRUPLE 1

scru·pu·lous \ˈskrü-pyə-ləs\ *adj* **1 :** having or full of scruples **2 :** PUNCTILIOUS ⟨working with *scrupulous* care⟩ ***synonyms*** see CAREFUL — **scru·pu·lous·ly** *adv* — **scru·pu·lous·ness** *n*

scru·ta·ble \ˈskrüt-ə-bəl\ *adj* **:** capable of being deciphered : COMPREHENSIBLE [Late Latin *scrutabilis* "searchable," from Latin *scrutari* "to search, examine"]

scru·ti·nize \ˈskrüt-n-ˌīz\ *vt* **:** to examine very closely or critically : INSPECT — **scru·ti·niz·er** *n*

synonyms SCRUTINIZE, SCAN, EXAMINE mean to look at searchingly and critically. SCRUTINIZE stresses close attention to minute detail ⟨*scrutinized* every line of the contract⟩. SCAN suggests a rapid but thorough covering of an entire surface or body of printed matter ⟨*scanned* the menu⟩. EXAMINE suggests scrutinizing in order to determine the nature, condition, or quality of a thing ⟨*examined* the gem for flaws⟩.

scru·ti·ny \ˈskrüt-n-ē, ˈskrüt-nē\ *n, pl* **-nies 1 :** a thorough study, inquiry, or inspection : EXAMINATION **2 :** a searching look [Latin *scrutinium,* from *scrutari* "to search, examine," probably from *scruta* "trash"]

scu·ba \ˈskü-bə, ˈskyü-\ *n* **:** an apparatus that provides air for breathing while swimming underwater [*s*elf-*c*ontained *u*nderwater *b*reathing *a*pparatus]

scuba diver *n* **:** a person who swims underwater with scuba gear — **scuba dive** *vi*

[1]**scud** \ˈskəd\ *vi* **scud·ded; scud·ding :** to move or run swiftly especially as if driven forward [probably of Scandinavian origin]

[2]**scud** *n* **1 :** the act of scudding **2 :** wind-driven clouds or water

[1]**scuff** \ˈskəf\ *vb* **1 :** to scrape the feet in walking : SHUFFLE ⟨*scuff* one's feet on the ground⟩ ⟨*scuffed* along the path⟩ **2 :** to become rough or scratched through wear ⟨some leathers *scuff* easily⟩ [probably of Scandinavian origin]

[2]**scuff** *n* **1 :** a noise or act of scuffing **2 :** a flat-soled house slipper

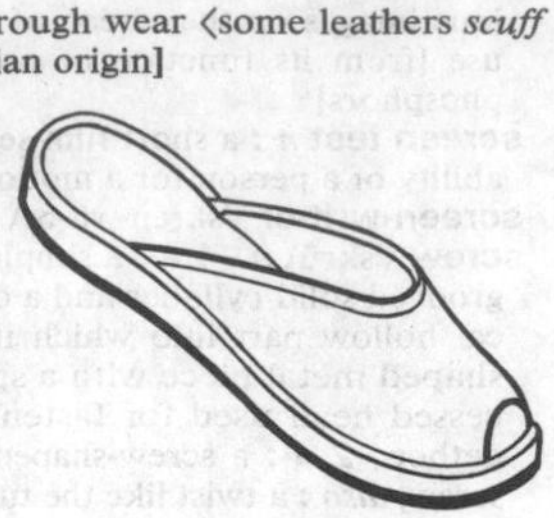
scuff 2

scuf·fle \ˈskəf-əl\ *vb* **scuf·fled; scuf·fling** \ˈskəf-liŋ, -ə-liŋ\ **1 :** to struggle in a confused way at close quarters **2 :** to move with a quick shuffling gait; *also* : SCUFF [probably of Scandinavian origin] — **scuffle** *n* — **scuf·fler** \ˈskəf-lər, -ə-lər\ *n*

[1]**scull** \ˈskəl\ *n* **1 a :** an oar used at the stern of a boat to propel it forward with a side-to-side motion **b :** one of a pair of short oars for use by one person **2 :** a long narrow boat usually for racing propelled by one or more persons using sculls [Middle English *sculle*]

[2]**scull** *vb* **1 :** to propel by a scull or sculls **2 :** to scull a boat — **scull·er** *n*

scul·lery \ˈskəl-rē, -ə-rē\ *n, pl* **-ler·ies :** a room for cleaning and storing dishes and culinary utensils, washing vegetables, and similar domestic work [Medieval French *escuelerie* "department of household in charge of dishes," from *escuelle* "bowl," from Latin *scutella* "drinking bowl, tray," from *scutra* "platter"]

scul·lion \ˈskəl-yən\ *n* **:** a kitchen helper [Middle French *escouillon* "dishcloth," from *escouve* "broom," from Latin *scopae,* literally, "twigs bound together"]

scul·pin \ˈskəl-pən\ *n, pl* **sculpins** *also* **sculpin 1 :** any of numerous spiny large-headed often scaleless fishes with large fanlike pectoral fins **2 :** a scorpion fish of the southern California coast caught for food and sport [origin unknown]

sculpt \ˈskəlpt\ *vb* **:** SCULPTURE 1, CARVE [French *sculpter,* derived from Latin *sculpere*]

sculp·tor \ˈskəlp-tər\ *n* **:** an artist who makes sculptures [Latin, from *sculpere* "to carve"]

sculp·tress \-trəs\ *n* **:** a woman who is a sculptor

sculp·tur·al \ˈskəlp-chə-rəl, ˈskəlp-shrəl\ *adj* **:** of, relating to, or resembling sculpture — **sculp·tur·al·ly** \-ē\ *adv*

[1]**sculp·ture** \ˈskəlp-chər\ *n* **1 :** the act, process, or art of carving or cutting hard materials or modeling plastic materials into works of art **2 :** work produced by sculpture; *also* : a piece of such work [Latin *sculptura,* from *sculpere* "to carve," alteration of *scalpere* "to scratch, carve"]

[2]**sculpture** *vb* **1 :** to form an image or representation of from solid material (as wood or metal) ⟨*sculpture* a model's head⟩ **2 :** to shape by or as if by carving or molding ⟨*sculpture* a statue⟩ ⟨*sculpture* marble⟩ **3 :** to work as a sculptor

[1]**scum** \ˈskəm\ *n* **1 a :** extraneous matter or impurities risen to or formed on the surface of a liquid often as a slimy covering — compare POND SCUM **b :** a film formed on a solid or gelatinous object ⟨soap *scum*⟩ **2 a :** foul or worthless things **b :** a loathsome or worthless person or group of people [Dutch *schum*] — **scum·my** \ˈskəm-ē\ *adj*

[2]**scum** *vi* **scummed; scum·ming :** to form or become covered with or as if with scum

scun·ner \ˈskən-ər\ *n* **:** an unreasonable or extreme dislike or prejudice [Middle English *skunniren* "to be disgusted"]

scup \ˈskəp\ *n, pl* **scup** *also* **scups :** a porgy of the Atlantic coast of the U.S. used as a panfish [short for *scuppaug,* modification of Narragansett *mishcùppaûog*]

scup·per \ˈskəp-ər\ *n* **:** an opening in the bulwarks of a boat through which water drains overboard [Middle English *skopper*]

scup·per·nong \-ˌnȯŋ, -ˌnäŋ\ *n* **1 :** MUSCADINE; *esp* : a cultivated muscadine with yellowish green plum-flavored grapes **2 :** a wine made from grapes of the scuppernong [*Scuppernong,* river and lake in North Carolina]

scurf \ˈskərf\ *n* **1 :** thin dry scales given off by the skin especially in an abnormal skin condition; *esp* : DANDRUFF **2 :** a substance that sticks to a surface in flakes **3 :** a scaly deposit or covering on plant parts; *also* : a plant disease characterized by scurf [of Scandinavian origin] — **scurfy** \ˈskər-fē\ *adj*

scur·ri·lous \ˈskər-ə-ləs, ˈskə-rə-\ *adj* **1 a :** using or given to coarse language **b :** vulgar and evil **2 :** containing obscenities, abuse, or slander ⟨*scurrilous* accusations⟩ [Latin *scurrilis,* from *scurra* "buffoon"] — **scur·ril·i·ty** \skə-ˈril-ət-ē\ *n* —

scur·ri·lous·ly \'skər-ə-ləs-lē, 'skə-rə-\ *adv* — **scur·ri·lous·ness** *n*

scur·ry \'skər-ē, 'skə-rē\ *vi* **scur·ried; scur·ry·ing** : to move briskly : SCAMPER [short for *hurry-scurry,* reduplication of *hurry*] — **scurry** *n*

1**scur·vy** \'skər-vē\ *n* : a disease that is caused by lack of vitamin C and is marked by loosening of the teeth, softening of the gums, and bleeding under the skin [2*scurvy*]

2**scurvy** *adj* **scur·vi·er; -est** : arousing disgust or scorn : CONTEMPTIBLE, DESPICABLE ⟨*scurvy* tricks⟩ [*scurf*] ***synonyms*** see CONTEMPTIBLE — **scur·vi·ly** \-və-lē\ *adv* — **scur·vi·ness** \-vē-nəs\ *n*

scut \'skət\ *n* : a short erect tail (as of a rabbit) [origin unknown]

1**scutch** \'skəch\ *vt* : to separate the woody fiber from (flax or hemp) by beating [obsolete French *escoucher,* derived from Latin *excutere* "to beat out," from *ex-* + *quatere* "to shake, strike"]

2**scutch** *n* : SCUTCHER

scutch·eon \'skəch-ən\ *n* : ESCUTCHEON

scutch·er \'skəch-ər\ *n* : an implement or machine for scutching

scute \'sküt, 'skyüt\ *n* : an external bony or horny plate or large scale (as of a turtle shell) [Latin *scutum* "shield"]

scu·tel·lum \skü-'tel-əm, skyü-\ *n, pl* **-tel·la** \-'tel-ə\ : a triangular or shield-shaped plant or animal structure (as the cotyledon of a grass or a plate on the thorax of an insect) [New Latin, from Latin *scutum* "shield"] — **scu·tel·late** \-'tel-ət\ *adj*

scut·ter \'skət-ər\ *vi* : SCURRY, SCUTTLE [alteration of 4*scuttle*]

1**scut·tle** \'skət-l\ *n* **1** : a shallow open basket (as for grain or garden produce) **2** : a metal pail for carrying coal [Latin *scutella* "drinking bowl, tray," from *scutra* "platter"]

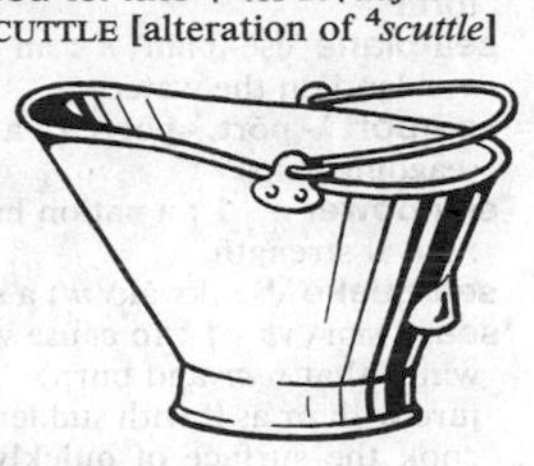

1scuttle 2

2**scuttle** *n* : a small opening (as in the side or deck of a ship or the roof of a house) furnished with a lid; *also* : its lid [Middle English *skottell*]

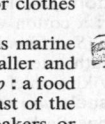

3**scuttle** *vt* **scut·tled; scut·tling** \'skət-ling, -l-ing\ **1** : to sink (a boat) intentionally by making holes in the sides or bottom **2** : to injure or end by a deliberate act ⟨*scuttle* a conference⟩

4**scuttle** *vi* **scut·tled; scut·tling** \'skət-ling, -l-ing\ : SCURRY [perhaps blend of *scud* and *shuttle*]

5**scuttle** *n* **1** : a quick shuffling pace **2** : a short swift run

scut·tle·butt \'skət-l-,bət\ *n* : RUMOR 1, GOSSIP [earlier *scuttlebutt* "cask fitted with a spigot to provide drinking water on shipboard, drinking fountain on a ship," from 2*scuttle* + 6*butt*]

scy·phis·to·ma \sī-'fis-tə-mə\ *n, pl* **-mae** \-,mē\ *also* **-mas** : a sexually produced scyphozoan larva that repeatedly constricts transversely to form free-swimming medusae [Latin *scyphus* "cup" + Greek *stoma* "mouth"]

scy·pho·zo·an \,sī-fə-'zō-ən\ *n* : any of a class (Scyphozoa) of coelenterates comprising mostly large jellyfishes that lack a true polyp stage [Latin *scyphus* "cup" + Greek *zōion* "animal"] — **scyphozoan** *adj*

1**scythe** \'sīth, 'sī\ *n* : an implement used for mowing (as grass) and composed of a long curving blade fastened at an angle to a long handle [Old English *sīthe*]

2**scythe** *vt* : to cut with or as if with a scythe : MOW

sea \'sē\ *n* **1 a** : the great body of salty water that covers much of the earth; *also* : the waters of the earth as distinguished from the land and air **b** : a body of salt water less extensive than an ocean ⟨the Mediterranean *sea*⟩ **c** : OCEAN 2 **d** : an inland body of water either salt or fresh ⟨the *Sea* of Galilee⟩ **2 a** : surface motion on a large body of water or its direction ⟨a following *sea*⟩ **b** : rough water : a heavy swell or wave ⟨a high *sea* swept the deck⟩ **3** : something suggesting the sea (as in vastness) ⟨a golden *sea* of wheat⟩ **4** : the seafaring life **5** : 2MARE [Old English *sǣ*] — **sea** *adj* — **at sea** **1** : on the sea; *esp* : on a sea voyage **2** : LOST 2c, BEWILDERED ⟨she was all *at sea* about how to proceed⟩ — **to sea** : to or on the open waters of the sea

sea anchor *n* : a drag typically of canvas thrown overboard to retard the drifting of a ship or seaplane and to keep its head to the wind

sea anemone *n* : any of numerous anthozoan coelenterates (order Actiniaria) that are solitary polyps having bright and varied colors and a cluster of tentacles and that superficially resemble a flower in form

sea anemone

sea·bag \'sē-,bag\ *n* : a cylindrical canvas bag used especially by a sailor for clothes and other gear

sea bass *n* **1** : any of numerous marine fishes related to but usually smaller and more active than the groupers; *esp* : a food and sport fish of the Atlantic coast of the U.S. **2** : any of numerous croakers or drums including noted sport and food fishes

sea·bed \'sē-,bed\ *n* : the floor of a sea or ocean

Sea·bee \'sē-,bē\ *n* : a member of one of the U.S. Navy construction battalions for building naval shore facilities in combat zones [alteration of *cee* + *bee;* from the initials of *construction battalion*]

sea·bird \'sē-,bərd\ *n* : a bird (as a gull or an albatross) frequenting the open ocean

sea biscuit *n* : HARDTACK

sea·board \'sē-,bōrd, -,bȯrd\ *n* : SEACOAST; *also* : the country bordering a seacoast — **seaboard** *adj*

sea·boot \'sē-,büt\ *n* : a very high waterproof boot used especially by sailors and fishermen

sea·borg·i·um \sē-'bȯr-gē-əm\ *n* : a short-lived radioactive element that is produced artificially — see ELEMENT table [New Latin, from Glenn T. *Seaborg,* died 1999, American chemist]

sea·borne \-,bōrn, -,bȯrn\ *adj* **1** : borne over or on the sea ⟨a *seaborne* invasion⟩ **2** : engaged in or carried on by overseas shipping ⟨*seaborne* trade⟩

sea bream *n* : BREAM 2

sea breeze *n* : a breeze blowing inland from the sea

sea change *n* **1** : a change brought about by the sea **2** : a marked change : TRANSFORMATION ⟨a *sea change* in court procedure⟩

sea chest *n* : a sailor's storage chest for personal property

sea·coast \'sē-,kōst\ *n* : the shore or border of the land adjacent to the sea

sea cow *n* : SIRENIAN

sea·craft \'sē-,kraft\ *n* **1** : seagoing ships **2** : skill in navigation

sea cucumber *n* : any of a class (Holothurioidea) of echinoderms with a long tough flexible muscular body resembling a cucumber and having tentacles surrounding the mouth at one end — called also *holothurian*

sea dog *n* : a veteran sailor

sea duck *n* : any of various ducks (as an eider or scoter) that typically frequent the sea and obtain their food by diving

sea duty *n* : duty in the U.S. Navy performed outside the continental U.S. or specified dependencies thereof

sea eagle *n* : any of various eagles that feed largely on fish

Sea Explorer *n* : an Explorer in a scouting program that teaches seamanship

sea fan *n* : a coelenterate that is related to the corals and sea anemones and forms colonies with a fan-shaped form

sea·far·er \'sē-,far-ər, -,fer-\ *n* : MARINER

sea·far·ing \-,far-ing, -,fer-\ *n* **1** : traveling over the sea **2** : the occupation of a sailor — **seafaring** *adj*

sea·floor \'sē-,flōr, -,flȯr\ *n* : SEABED

sea·food \'sē-,füd\ *n* : edible marine fish and shellfish

sea·front \-,frənt\ *n* : the waterfront of a seaside place

sea·girt \-,gərt\ *adj* : surrounded by the sea

sea·go·ing \-,gō-ing\ *adj* : adapted or used for sea travel ⟨*seagoing* ships⟩

sea green *n* **1** : a moderate green or bluish green **2** : a moderate yellow green

sea gull *n* : GULL; *esp* : one frequenting the sea

sea hare *n* : any of various large sea mollusks that have an arched back and two front tentacles and have the shell much reduced or missing

\ə\ abut	\aù\ out	\i\ tip	\ȯ\ saw	\ù\ foot
\ər\ further	\ch\ chin	\ī\ life	\ȯi\ coin	\y\ yet
\a\ mat	\e\ pet	\j\ job	\th\ thin	\yü\ few
\ā\ take	\ē\ easy	\ng\ sing	\th\ this	\yù\ cure
\ä\ cot, cart	\g\ go	\ō\ bone	\ü\ food	\zh\ vision

sea horse *n* **1 :** a mythical animal half horse and half fish **2 :** a small long-snouted fish that is covered with bony plates and has a head that looks like a horse's head

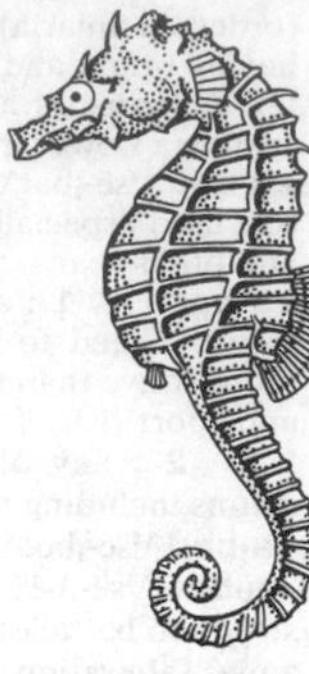

sea horse 2

sea is·land cotton \ˌsē-ˌī-lənd-, -ˌī-lən-\ *n, often cap S&I* **:** a cotton with especially long silky fiber [*Sea Islands,* chain of islands off the southeastern U.S. coast]

sea king *n* **:** a Viking chief

[1]**seal** \ˈsēl\ *n, pl* **seals** *also* **seal** **1 :** any of numerous marine flesh-eating mammals chiefly of cold regions that have limbs modified into webbed flippers adapted primarily to swimming and that mate and bear young on land **2 a :** the pelt of a seal **b :** leather made from the skin of a seal [Old English *seolh*]

[2]**seal** *vi* **:** to hunt seals

[3]**seal** *n* **1 a :** something (as a pledge) that makes safe or secure ⟨under *seal* of secrecy⟩ **b :** a device with an identifying design or words cut into or raised on its surface that can be pressed or stamped (as into paper or wax) to form a mark (as for certifying a signature or authenticating a document); *also* **:** a piece of wax or a wafer bearing such an impressed mark or the mark itself **c :** a usually ornamental adhesive stamp that may be used to close a letter or package; *esp* **:** one sold in a fund-raising campaign **2 a :** a closure that must be broken to be opened and that thus reveals tampering **b :** a tight and perfect closure ⟨test the *seal* of the jars⟩; *also* **:** a device or an arrangement of material designed to produce such a closure ⟨covered the joint with a thick *seal* of rosin⟩ ⟨the water *seal* of a toilet⟩ [Medieval French *seel,* from Latin *sigillum,* from *signum* "sign, seal"] — **under seal :** with an authenticating seal affixed

[4]**seal** *vt* **1 :** to mark with or certify or authenticate by or as if by a seal ⟨*seal* a deed⟩ **2 :** to close with or as if with a seal ⟨the sheriff *sealed* the premises⟩ ⟨ice *sealed* the ships into the harbor⟩ **3 :** to determine finally and irrevocably ⟨this answer *sealed* our fate⟩

sea lamprey *n* **:** a lamprey of the Atlantic coast that is also found in the Great Lakes and that attaches to and feeds on other fishes with its sucking disk-shaped mouth

sea–lane \ˈsē-ˌlān\ *n* **:** an established sea route

seal·ant \ˈsē-lənt\ *n* **:** a sealing agent ⟨radiator *sealant*⟩

sea lavender *n* **:** any of a genus of chiefly coastal plants with basal leaves and clusters of tiny usually lavender flowers

sea legs *n pl* **:** bodily adjustment to the motion of a ship at sea indicated especially by ability to walk steadily and by freedom from seasickness

[1]**seal·er** \ˈsē-lər\ *n* **1 :** an official who certifies conformity to a standard of correctness **2 :** a substance applied to a surface to prevent subsequent coats of paint or varnish from sinking in

[2]**sealer** *n* **:** a person or ship engaged in hunting seals

sea lettuce *n* **:** any of a genus of marine green algae with broad fronds sometimes eaten as salad or used in soups

sea level *n* **:** the height of the surface of the sea midway between the average high and low tides

sea·lift \ˈsē-ˌlift\ *n* **:** transport of military personnel and especially equipment by ship — **sealift** *vt*

sea lily *n* **:** CRINOID; *esp* **:** a stalked crinoid

sealing wax *n* **:** a resinous composition that is plastic when warm and is used for sealing (as letters or dry cells)

sea lion *n* **:** any of several large Pacific eared seals

seal off *vt* **:** to close tightly

seal·skin \ˈsēl-ˌskin\ *n* **1 :** the fur or pelt of a fur seal **2 :** a garment (as a coat) of sealskin — **sealskin** *adj*

[1]**seam** \ˈsēm\ *n* **1 :** the joining or the mark made by the joining of two pieces or edges of material by sewing **2 :** the space between adjacent planks of a ship **3 a :** a line, groove, or ridge formed between touching edges **b :** a layer or stratum (as of mineral) between distinctive layers ⟨coal *seams*⟩ **c :** a line left by a cut or wound; *also* **:** WRINKLE [Old English *sēam*] — **seam·less** \-ləs\ *adj* — **seam·like** \-ˌlīk\ *adj*

[2]**seam** *vt* **1 :** to join by or as if by sewing **2 :** to mark with lines suggesting seams **:** FURROW ⟨creeks *seam* the valley⟩ — **seam·er** *n*

sea·man \ˈsē-mən\ *n* **1 :** SAILOR 1a, MARINER **2 :** an enlisted rank in the navy and coast guard above seaman apprentice and below petty officer third class

seaman apprentice *n* **:** an enlisted rank in the navy and coast guard above seaman recruit and below seaman

seaman recruit *n* **:** the lowest enlisted rank in the navy and coast guard

sea·man·ship \ˈsē-mən-ˌship\ *n* **:** the art or skill of handling, working, and navigating a ship

sea·mark \-ˌmärk\ *n* **1 :** a line on a coast marking the tidal limit **2 :** an elevated object serving as a beacon to mariners

sea mile *n* **:** NAUTICAL MILE

sea monkey *n* **:** a brine shrimp that hatches from a dormant egg and is sometimes raised in aquariums

sea·mount \ˈsē-ˌmau̇nt\ *n* **:** a submarine mountain

seam·stress \ˈsēm-strəs, ˈsēmp-\ *n* **:** a woman who sews especially for a living [*seamster, sempster* "tailor" (from Old English *sēamestre,* from *sēam* "seam")]

seamy \ˈsē-mē\ *adj* **seam·i·er; -est :** UNPLEASANT, SORDID ⟨the *seamy* side of urban life⟩ — **seam·i·ness** *n*

sé·ance \ˈsā-ˌäns, -ˌäⁿs\ *n* **1 :** SESSION 1 **2 :** a meeting of persons seeking to communicate with spirits [French, literally, "sitting," from *seoir* "to sit," from Latin *sedēre*]

sea nettle *n* **:** a stinging jellyfish

sea otter *n* **:** a large marine otter of northern Pacific coasts that attains a maximum length of nearly six feet (two meters) and feeds largely on shellfish (as clams, crabs, and sea urchins)

sea pen *n* **:** any of numerous coelenterates that are related to the corals and sea anemones and form colonies with a feathery form

sea·plane \ˈsē-ˌplān\ *n* **:** an airplane designed to take off from and land on the water

sea·port \-ˌpōrt, -ˌpȯrt\ *n* **:** a port, harbor, or town accessible to seagoing ships

sea power *n* **1 :** a nation having formidable naval strength **2 :** naval strength

sea·quake \ˈsē-ˌkwāk\ *n* **:** a submarine earthquake

[1]**sear** \ˈsiər\ *vb* **1 :** to cause withering or drying **:** PARCH ⟨harsh winds that *sear* and burn⟩ **2 a :** to burn, scorch, mark, or injure with or as if with sudden application of intense heat **b :** to cook the surface of quickly with intense heat ⟨*sear* a steak⟩ [Old English *sēarian* "to become sere," from *sēar* "sere"]

[2]**sear** *n* **:** a mark or scar left by searing

[1]**search** \ˈsərch\ *vb* **1 a :** to go through or look carefully and thoroughly in an effort to find or discover something ⟨*search* a room⟩ ⟨*search* for a lost child⟩ **b :** to examine for articles concealed on the person **c :** to examine or explore with painstaking care often with a particular objective in view **:** PROBE ⟨*searching* for an answer⟩ **2 :** to find or come to know by or as if by careful investigation or scrutiny ⟨*searching* out an opponent's every weakness⟩ [Medieval French *cerchier,* from Late Latin *circare* "to go about," from Latin *circum* "round about," from circus "circle"] — **search·able** \ˈsər-chə-bəl\ *adj* — **search·er** \-chər\ *n* — **search·ing·ly** \-ching-lē\ *adv*

[2]**search** *n* **1 :** an act of searching ⟨a *search* for food⟩ ⟨go in *search* of help⟩ **2 :** an act of boarding and inspecting a ship on the high seas

search engine *n* **:** computer software used to search data (as text or a database) for specified information; *also* **:** a Web site that uses such software

search·light \ˈsərch-ˌlīt\ *n* **:** an apparatus for projecting a powerful beam of light; *also* **:** a beam of light projected by such an apparatus

search warrant *n* **:** a warrant authorizing a search of a specified place (as a house) for stolen goods or unlawful possessions

sea robin *n* **:** any of various chiefly bottom-dwelling marine fishes with large heads covered by bony plates and modified pectoral fins used especially as feelers or in crawling

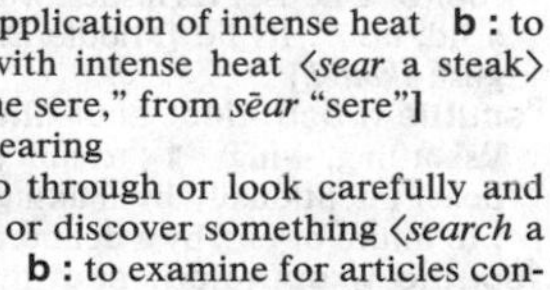

sea robin

sea–run \ˌsē-ˌrən\ *adj* **:** ANADROMOUS ⟨a *sea-run* salmon⟩

sea·scape \ˈsē-ˌskāp\ *n* **1 :** a view of the sea **2 :** a picture representing a scene at sea

sea scorpion *n* **:** SCULPIN

Sea Scout *n* **:** SEA EXPLORER

sea serpent *n* **:** a large marine animal resembling a snake often reported to have been seen but never proved to exist

sea·shell \'sē-ˌshel\ *n* : the shell of a marine animal and especially a mollusk
sea·shore \-ˌshōr, -ˌshȯr\ *n* **1** : land adjacent to the sea : SEACOAST **2** : the ground between the ordinary high-water and low-water marks
sea·sick \-ˌsik\ *adj* : affected with or suggestive of seasickness
sea·sick·ness \-nəs\ *n* : motion sickness experienced on the water
sea·side \'sē-ˌsīd\ *n* : country adjacent to the sea : SEASHORE
sea slug *n* **1** : SEA CUCUMBER **2** : a naked marine gastropod mollusk; *esp* : NUDIBRANCH
sea snake *n* **1** : SEA SERPENT **2** : any of numerous venomous aquatic snakes of warm seas
[1]**sea·son** \'sēz-ⁿn\ *n* **1 a** : a suitable or natural time or occasion ⟨a *season* for all things⟩ **b** : an indefinite period of time : WHILE ⟨willing to wait a *season*⟩ **2 a** : a period of the year associated with some recurrent phenomenon or activity ⟨the growing *season*⟩ **b** : a period characterized by a particular kind of weather ⟨a long dry *season*⟩ **c** : a period marked by special activity especially in some field ⟨tourist *season*⟩ ⟨hunting *season*⟩ **d** : a period in which a place is most frequented **e** : one of the four quarters into which the year is commonly divided — compare AUTUMN, SPRING, SUMMER, WINTER **f** : the time of a major holiday **3** : SEASONING **4** : the schedule of official games played or to be played by a sports team during a playing season ⟨got through the *season* undefeated⟩ [Medieval French *saison,* from Latin *satio* "act of sowing," from *serere* "to sow"] — **in season 1** : at the right or fitting time **2** : at the stage of greatest fitness (as for eating) ⟨peaches are *in season*⟩ **3** : legal to take by hunting or fishing — **out of season** : not in season ⟨fined for hunting *out of season*⟩
[2]**season** *vb* **sea·soned; sea·son·ing** \'sēz-ning, -ⁿn-ing\ **1** : to give food better flavor or more zest by adding seasoning ⟨a perfectly *seasoned* stew⟩; *also* : to add seasoning ⟨*season* to taste⟩ **2 a** : to treat so as to be fit for use; *esp* : to prepare (lumber) for use by controlled drying **b** : to make fit by experience ⟨*seasoned* veterans⟩ **3** : to become seasoned [Medieval French *assaisoner* "to ripen, season," from *a* "to, at" (from Latin *ad*) + *saison* "season"] — **sea·son·er** \'sēz-nər, -ⁿn-ər\ *n*
sea·son·able \'sēz-nə-bəl, -ⁿn-ə-bəl\ *adj* **1** : suitable to the season or circumstances : TIMELY ⟨a *seasonable* frost⟩ ⟨*seasonable* temperatures⟩ **2** : occurring in good or proper time : OPPORTUNE ⟨*seasonable* advice⟩ ⟨a *seasonable* time to open discussions⟩ — **sea·son·able·ness** *n* — **sea·son·ably** \-blē\ *adv*
sea·son·al \'sēz-nəl, -ⁿn-əl\ *adj* **1** : of, relating to, or varying in occurrence with the seasons ⟨*seasonal* storms⟩ **2** : affected or caused by seasonal need or availability ⟨*seasonal* industries⟩ ⟨*seasonal* unemployment⟩ — **sea·son·al·ly** \-ē\ *adv*
sea·son·ing \'sēz-ning, -ⁿn-ing\ *n* : an ingredient (as a condiment, spice, or herb) added to food primarily for savor
season ticket *n* : a ticket (as to all of a club's home games) valid during a specified time
sea spider *n* : any of a class (Pycnogonida) of small long-legged marine arthropods superficially resembling spiders
sea squirt *n* : ASCIDIAN
sea star *n* : STARFISH
sea stores *n pl* : supplies (as of foodstuffs) laid in before starting on a sea voyage
[1]**seat** \'sēt\ *n* **1 a** : something (as a chair) intended to be sat in or on **b** : the particular part of something on which one rests in sitting ⟨*seat* of the trousers⟩ ⟨a chair *seat*⟩ **c** : the part of the body that bears the weight in sitting : BUTTOCKS **2 a** : a seating accommodation ⟨had three *seats* for the game⟩ **b** : a right of sitting usually as a member ⟨a *seat* in the senate⟩ **c** : MEMBERSHIP ⟨a *seat* on the stock exchange⟩ **3** : a place or area where something is situated or centered ⟨*seats* of higher learning⟩; *esp* : a place (as a capital city) from which authority is exercised ⟨the new *seat* of the government⟩ **4** : posture in or way of sitting especially on horseback **5** : a part or surface on which another part or surface rests ⟨a valve *seat*⟩ [Old Norse *sæti*] — **seat·ed** \-əd\ *adj*
[2]**seat** *vb* **1 a** : to cause to sit or assist in finding a seat ⟨*seat* a guest⟩ **b** : to provide seats for ⟨a theater *seating* 1000 persons⟩ **c** : to put in a sitting position ⟨*seat* oneself at the table⟩ **2** : to repair the seat of or provide a new seat for **3** : to fit to, on, or with a seat ⟨*seat* a valve⟩ — **seat·er** *n*
seat belt *n* : straps designed to hold a person steady in a seat (as in an automobile or airplane)
sea·train \'sē-ˌtrān\ *n* : a seagoing ship equipped for carrying a train of railroad cars
sea trout *n* **1** : a trout or char that as an adult inhabits the sea but ascends rivers to spawn **2** : any of various sea fishes (as a weakfish) resembling trouts
sea turtle *n* : any of various large marine turtles (as the green turtle or the loggerhead) that have paddle-shaped feet to aid in swimming
sea urchin *n* : any of a class (Echinoidea) of echinoderms enclosed in shells that are usually flattened and globe-shaped and covered with movable spines

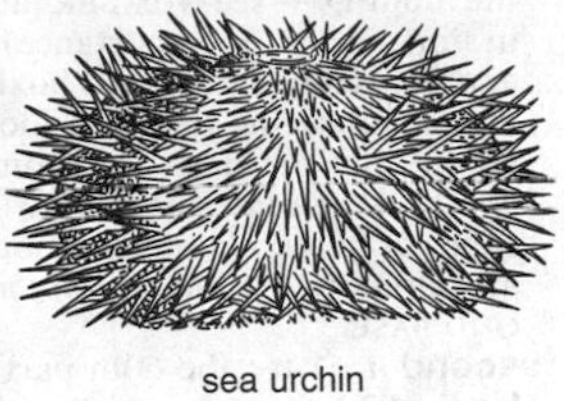
sea urchin

sea·wall \'sē-ˌwȯl\ *n* : a wall or embankment to protect the shore from erosion or to act as a breakwater
[1]**sea·ward** \'sē-wərd\ *n* : the direction or side away from land and toward the open sea
[2]**seaward** *also* **sea·wards** \-wərdz\ *adv or adj* : toward the sea
sea·wa·ter \'sē-ˌwȯt-ər, -ˌwät-\ *n* : water in or from the sea
sea·way \-ˌwā\ *n* **1** : a route for travel on the sea; *also* : an ocean traffic lane **2** : a moderate or rough sea **3** : a deep inland waterway that admits ocean shipping
sea·weed \-ˌwēd\ *n* : a plant growing in the sea; *esp* : a marine alga (as a kelp)
sea·wor·thy \-ˌwər-thē\ *adj* : fit or safe for a sea voyage ⟨a *seaworthy* ship⟩ — **sea·wor·thi·ness** *n*
sea wrack *n* : SEAWEED; *esp* : seaweed growing or washed ashore in large masses
se·ba·ceous gland \si-ˌbā-shəs-\ *n* : one of the skin glands that secrete an oily lubricating substance at the base of hairs or onto the skin [Latin *sebaceus* "made of tallow," from *sebum* "tallow"]
seb·or·rhea \ˌseb-ə-'rē-ə\ *n* : excessive secretion and discharge of sebum — **seb·or·rhe·ic** \-'rē-ik\ *adj*
se·bum \'sē-bəm\ *n* : fatty lubricant matter secreted by the sebaceous glands [Latin, "tallow, grease"]
se·cant \'sē-ˌkant, -kənt\ *n* **1** : a straight line that intersects a curve at two or more points **2** : a trigonometric function that for an acute angle considered as part of a right triangle is the ratio of the hypotenuse to the side adjacent to the angle — abbreviation *sec* **3** : a trigonometric function *sec* θ that is the reciprocal of the cosine for all real numbers θ for which cosine is not zero and that is exactly equal to the secant of an angle of measure θ in radians [Latin *secans,* present participle of *secare* "to cut"]
se·cede \si-'sēd\ *vi* : to withdraw from an organization (as a nation, church, or political party) [Latin *secedere,* from *se-* "apart" + *cedere* "to go"] — **se·ced·er** *n*
se·ces·sion \si-'sesh-ən\ *n* : the act of seceding : a formal withdrawal [Latin *secessio,* from *secedere* "to secede"]
se·ces·sion·ist \-'sesh-nəst, -ə-nəst\ *n* : one who joins in or supports a secession — **se·ces·sion·ism** \-ə-ˌniz-əm\ *n* — **secessionist** *adj*
se·clude \si-'klüd\ *vt* **1** : to keep away from others : SECRETE, HIDE ⟨*secluded* themselves⟩ **2** : to shut away : SCREEN, ISOLATE ⟨a cottage *secluded* by forests⟩ [Latin *secludere,* from *se-* "apart" + *claudere* "to close"]
se·clud·ed *adj* **1** : screened or hidden from view ⟨a *secluded* valley⟩ **2** : living in seclusion ⟨*secluded* monks⟩ — **se·clud·ed·ly** *adv* — **se·clud·ed·ness** *n*
se·clu·sion \si-'klü-zhən\ *n* **1** : the act of secluding : the condition of being secluded **2** : a secluded or isolated place [Medieval Latin *seclusio,* from Latin *secludere* "to seclude"] — **se·clu·sive** \-'klü-siv, -ziv\ *adj* — **se·clu·sive·ly** *adv* — **se·clu·sive·ness** *n*
seco·bar·bi·tal \ˌsek-ō-'bär-bə-ˌtȯl\ *n* : a barbiturate $C_{12}H_{18}N_2O_3$ used chiefly in the form of its sodium salt as a sedative and to induce sleep [*Seco*nal, a trademark + *barbital*]
Sec·o·nal \'sek-ə-ˌnȯl\ *trademark* — used for secobarbital
[1]**sec·ond** \'sek-ənd *also* -ənt\ *adj* **1** : being number two in a

\ə\ **abut**	\au̇\ **out**	\i\ **tip**	\ȯ\ **saw**	\u̇\ **foot**
\ər\ **further**	\ch\ **chin**	\ī\ **life**	\ȯi\ **coin**	\y\ **yet**
\a\ **mat**	\e\ **pet**	\j\ **job**	\th\ **thin**	\yü\ **few**
\ā\ **take**	\ē\ **easy**	\ng\ **sing**	\th\ **this**	\yu̇\ **cure**
\ä\ **cot, cart**	\g\ **go**	\ō\ **bone**	\ü\ **food**	\zh\ **vision**

countable series **2 :** being next after the first (as in order, time, or importance) **3 :** ALTERNATE, OTHER ⟨elects a mayor every *second* year⟩ **4 :** resembling or suggesting a prototype ⟨a *second* Thoreau⟩ **5 :** having a musical part lower in pitch than or subordinate to another of its kind ⟨*second* violin⟩ [Medieval French, from Latin *secundus* "following, second," from *sequi* "to follow"] — **second** *adv* — **sec·ond·ly** *adv*

[2]**second** *n* **1 a :** number two in a countable series ⟨the *second* of the month⟩ — see NUMBER table **b :** one next after the first (as in time, order, or importance) **2 :** one who assists or supports another (as in a duel or a boxing match) **3 a :** the musical interval embracing two diatonic degrees **b :** the tone at this interval **c :** the harmonic combination of two tones a second apart **4 :** an inferior or flawed article (as of merchandise) **5 :** the act of seconding a motion **6 :** the second gear or speed in an automotive vehicle **7** *pl* **:** a second helping of food **8 :** SECOND BASE

[3]**second** *n* **1 a :** the 60th part of a minute of angular measure **b :** the 60th part of a minute of time; *esp* **:** the international unit of time related to the period of the radiation corresponding to a change between the two levels of the ground state of a particular isotope of the cesium atom **2 :** an instant of time **:** MOMENT ⟨I'll be back in a *second*⟩ [Medieval Latin *secunda,* from Latin *secundus* "second"; from its being the second sexagesimal division of a unit, as a minute is the first]

[4]**second** *vt* **1 :** to give support or encouragement to **:** ASSIST **2 :** to endorse (a motion or a nomination) so that debate or voting may begin [Latin *secundare,* from *secundus* "second, favorable"] — **sec·ond·er** *n*

[1]**sec·ond·ary** \ˈsek-ən-ˌder-ē\ *adj* **1 a :** of second rank, importance, or value ⟨*secondary* streams⟩ **b :** of, relating to, or constituting the second strongest of the three or four degrees of stress ⟨the fourth syllable of "basketball team" carries *secondary* stress⟩ **2 a :** derived from something original, primary, or basic **b :** of, relating to, or being the current created by a change in the primary current or the circuit of the created current in an induction coil or transformer **c (1) :** not first in order of occurrence or development **(2) :** produced by activity of formative tissue and especially cambium other than that at the growing point ⟨*secondary* growth⟩ **3 a :** of, relating to, or being a second order or stage in a sequence or series **b :** of, relating to, or being the second segment of the wing of a bird or the quills of this segment **c :** of or relating to secondary school ⟨*secondary* education⟩ — **sec·ond·ar·i·ly** \ˌsek-ən-ˈder-ə-lē\ *adv* — **sec·ond·ar·i·ness** \ˈsek-ən-ˌder-ē-nəs\ *n*

[2]**secondary** *n, pl* **-ar·ies :** one that is secondary: as **a :** a defensive football backfield **b :** any of the flight feathers attached to the ulna of a bird's wing **c :** the coil through which the secondary current passes in an induction coil or transformer — called also *secondary coil*

secondary cell *n* **:** STORAGE CELL

secondary color *n* **:** a color formed by mixing two primary colors in equal or equivalent quantities

secondary emission *n* **:** the emission of electrons from a surface that is bombarded by charged particles

secondary road *n* **1 :** a road not of primary importance **2 :** a road that feeds traffic to a more important road (as a turnpike)

secondary school *n* **:** a school between elementary school and college

secondary sex characteristic *n* **:** a physical characteristic (as the growth of breasts in the human female or the showy feathers of a male bird) that appears in members of one sex at puberty or in seasonal breeders at the breeding season and is not directly concerned with reproduction

second base *n* **1 :** the base that must be touched second by a base runner in baseball **2 :** the position of the player defending the area to the right of second base

second base·man \-ˈbā-smən\ *n* **:** a player defending the area to the right of second base

sec·ond–best \ˌsek-ən-ˈbest\ *adj* **:** next to the best

second childhood *n* **:** a state of feebleness or childishness of mind caused by or accompanying old age

sec·ond–class \ˌsek-ng-ˈklas, -ən-, -ənd-\ *adj* **1 :** of or relating to a second class **2 a :** INFERIOR 3, MEDIOCRE **b :** socially or economically deprived ⟨*second-class* citizens⟩

second class *n* **1 :** the second and usually next to highest group in a classification **2 :** CABIN CLASS **3 :** a class of U.S. or Canadian mail comprising periodicals sent to subscribers

Second Coming *n* **:** the coming of Christ on Judgment Day

second cousin *n* **:** the child of one's parent's first cousin

second–degree burn *n* **:** a burn marked by pain, blistering, and superficial destruction of the skin with fluid infiltration and reddening of the tissues beneath the burn

second growth *n* **:** forest trees that come up naturally after removal of the first growth by cutting or by fire

sec·ond–guess \ˌsek-ng-ˈges, -ən-\ *vt* **1 :** to question or criticize actions or decisions of (someone) often after the results of those actions or decisions are known **2 :** PREDICT — **sec·ond–guess·er** *n*

sec·ond·hand \ˌsek-ən-ˈhand\ *adj* **1 :** taken from someone else ⟨*secondhand* information⟩ **2 :** having had a previous owner ⟨a *secondhand* car⟩ **3 :** selling used goods ⟨a *secondhand* store⟩ — **secondhand** *adv*

second hand \ˈsek-ən-ˌhand\ *n* **:** the hand marking seconds on a timepiece

secondhand smoke *n* **:** tobacco smoke that is exhaled by smokers or is given off by burning tobacco and is inhaled by persons nearby

second lieutenant *n* **:** the lowest officer rank in the army, marine corps, and air force

second nature *n* **:** an acquired deeply ingrained habit or skill ⟨once learned, riding a bike is *second nature*⟩

second person *n* **:** a set of words or forms (as verb forms or pronouns) referring to the person or thing addressed in the utterance in which they occur; *also* **:** a word or form belonging to such a set

sec·ond–rate \ˌsek-ən-ˈdrāt, -ˈrāt\ *adj* **:** of second or inferior quality or value **:** MEDIOCRE — **sec·ond–rate·ness** *n* — **sec·ond–rat·er** \-ˈdrāt-ər, -ˈrāt-\ *n*

second sight *n* **:** CLAIRVOYANCE 1

second–story man *n* **:** a burglar who enters a house by an upstairs window

sec·ond–string \ˌsek-ən-ˈstring, -ng-\ *adj* **:** being a substitute player as distinguished from a regular [from the reserve bowstring carried by an archer in case the first breaks]

se·cre·cy \ˈsē-krə-sē\ *n, pl* **-cies 1 :** the habit or practice of keeping secrets **2 :** the quality or state of being hidden or concealed [Medieval English *secretee,* from *secre* "secret," from Middle French *secré,* from Latin *secretus*]

[1]**se·cret** \ˈsē-krət\ *adj* **1 a :** hidden or kept from knowledge or view **b :** working with hidden aims or methods **:** UNDERCOVER ⟨a *secret* agent⟩ **2 :** SECLUDED 1 ⟨a *secret* valley⟩ [Medieval French, from Latin *secretus,* from *secernere* "to separate, distinguish," from *se-* "apart" + *cernere* "to sift"] — **se·cret·ly** *adv*

synonyms SECRET, COVERT, CLANDESTINE, SURREPTITIOUS mean done without attracting observation. SECRET may imply concealment on any grounds or for any reason ⟨*secret* diplomatic negotiations⟩. COVERT stresses the fact of not being open or declared ⟨*covert* intelligence gathering⟩. CLANDESTINE implies secrecy usually of a forbidden act ⟨*clandestine* drug trade⟩. SURREPTITIOUS stresses the careful and skillful avoidance of detection as in violating a law or custom or right ⟨*surreptitious* stockpiling of weapons⟩.

[2]**secret** *n* **1 a :** something kept hidden or unexplained **:** MYSTERY **b :** something kept from the knowledge of others or shared only confidentially with a few **2 :** something taken to be a key to a desired end ⟨the *secret* of longevity⟩ — **in secret :** in a private place or manner

sec·re·tar·i·at \ˌsek-rə-ˈter-ē-ət\ *n* **1 :** the clerical staff of an organization **2 :** the administrative department of a governmental organization ⟨the United Nations *secretariat*⟩ [French *secrétariat* "office of a secretary, secretariat," from Medieval Latin *secretariatus* "office of a secretary," from *secretarius* "secretary"]

sec·re·tary \ˈsek-rə-ˌter-ē\ *n, pl* **-taries 1 :** a person employed to handle correspondence and routine or detail work for a superior **2 :** an officer of a business corporation or society who has charge of the correspondence and records **3 :** a government official in charge of the affairs of a department ⟨*Secretary* of State⟩ **4 :** a writing

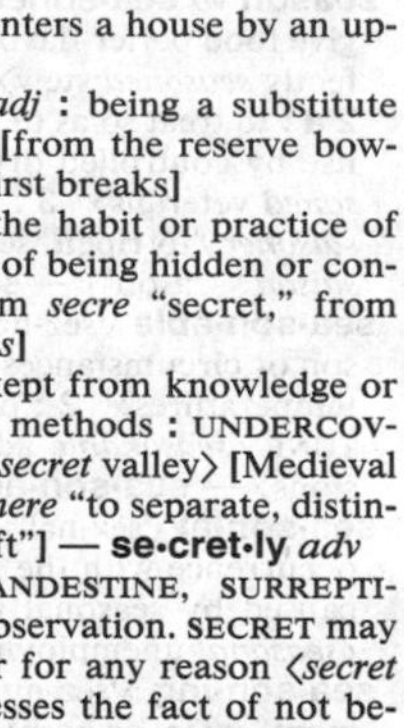

secretary 4

desk with a top section for books [Medieval Latin *secretarius* "confidential employee, secretary," derived from Latin *secretus* "secret"] — **sec·re·tari·al** \ˌsek-rə-ˈter-ē-əl\ *adj* — **sec·re·tary·ship** \ˈsek-rə-ˌter-ē-ˌship\ *n*

secretary–general *n, pl* **secretaries–general** : a principal administrative officer

secret ballot *n* : AUSTRALIAN BALLOT

[1]**se·crete** \si-ˈkrēt\ *vb* : to produce and give off a secretion ⟨glands that *secrete* intermittently⟩ [back-formation from *secretion*]

[2]**se·crete** \si-ˈkrēt, ˈsē-krət\ *vt* : to deposit or conceal in a hiding place [[1]*secret*] ***synonyms*** see HIDE

se·cre·tin \si-ˈkrēt-n\ *n* : an intestinal hormone capable of stimulating the pancreas and liver to secrete [*secret*ion + *-in*]

se·cre·tion \si-ˈkrē-shən\ *n* **1 a** : the process of giving off a glandular substance **b** : a product of glandular activity; *esp* : one (as a hormone or enzyme) that performs a specific useful function in the organism **2** : a concealing or hiding of something [sense 1 from French *sécrétion,* from Latin *secretio* "separation," from *secernere* "to separate," from *se-* "apart" + *cernere* "to sift"; sense 2 from [2]*secrete*] — **se·cre·tion·ary** \-shə-ˌner-ē\ *adj*

se·cre·tive \ˈsē-krət-iv, si-ˈkrēt-\ *adj* : disposed to secrecy or concealment : not frank or open — **se·cre·tive·ly** *adv* — **se·cre·tive·ness** *n*

se·cre·to·ry \si-ˈkrēt-ə-rē\ *adj* : of, relating to, or active in secretion

secret police *n* : a police organization operating largely in secrecy and especially to further the political purposes of its government often with terroristic methods

Secret Service *n* : a division of the U.S. Treasury Department charged chiefly with the suppression of counterfeiting and the protection of the president

sect \ˈsekt\ *n* **1 a** : a dissenting or schismatic religious body; *esp* : one regarded as extreme or heretical **b** : a religious denomination **2 a** : a group adhering to a distinctive doctrine or to a leader **b** : PARTY 1 **c** : FACTION 1 [Latin *secta* "course of action, way of life," probably from *sectari* "to pursue," from *sequi* "to follow"]

[1]**sec·tar·i·an** \sek-ˈter-ē-ən\ *adj* **1** : of, relating to, or characteristic of a sect or sectarian **2** : limited in character or scope : PAROCHIAL — **sec·tar·i·an·ism** \-ē-ə-ˌniz-əm\ *n*

[2]**sectarian** *n* **1** : a member of a sect **2** : a narrow or bigoted person

sec·tar·i·an·ize \sek-ˈter-ē-ə-ˌnīz\ *vb* **1** : to act as sectarians **2** : to make sectarian

sec·ta·ry \ˈsek-tə-rē\ *n, pl* **-ries** : a member of a sect

[1]**sec·tion** \ˈsek-shən\ *n* **1 a** : the action or an instance of cutting or separating by cutting **b** : a part set off by or as if by cutting : PORTION, SLICE **2** : a distinct part or portion of a writing: as **a** : a subdivision of a chapter **b** : a distinct component part of a newspaper ⟨the sports *section*⟩ **3** : CROSS SECTION 1b **4** : a character § used chiefly as a reference mark or to show the beginning of a section **5** : a piece of land one square mile (about 2.6 square kilometers) in area forming one of the 36 subdivisions of a township **6** : a distinct part of an area, community, or group of people ⟨the business *section* of town⟩ **7 a** : a division of a railroad sleeping car with an upper and a lower berth **b** : a part of a permanent railroad way under the care of a particular crew **c** : one of two or more vehicles that run on the same schedule **8** : one of several component parts (as of a bookcase) that may be assembled or reassembled **9** : a division of an orchestra composed of one class of instruments ⟨brass *section*⟩ [Latin *sectio,* from *secare* "to cut"]

[2]**section** *vb* **sec·tioned; sec·tion·ing** \-shə-ning, -shning\ **1** : to cut or separate into or become cut or separated into parts or sections **2** : to represent in sections (as by a drawing)

sec·tion·al \ˈsek-shnəl, -shən-l\ *adj* **1 a** : of or relating to a section **b** : local or regional rather than general in character ⟨*sectional* interests⟩ **2** : made up of or divided into sections ⟨a *sectional* sofa⟩ — **sec·tion·al·ly** \-ē\ *adv*

sec·tion·al·ism \ˈsek-shnə-ˌliz-əm, -shən-l-ˌiz-\ *n* : an exaggerated devotion to the interests of a region

sec·tor \ˈsek-tər, -ˌtȯr\ *n* **1** : the part of a circle enclosed by two radii and an arc of the circumference **2** : an area assigned to a military commander to defend **3** : a distinctive part (as of an economy) ⟨the industrial *sector*⟩ **4** : a subdivision of a track on a computer disk [Latin, "cutter," from *secare* "to cut"] — **sec·to·ri·al** \sek-ˈtōr-ē-əl, -ˈtȯr-\ *adj*

[1]**sec·u·lar** \ˈsek-yə-lər\ *adj* **1 a** : of or relating to the worldly or temporal ⟨*secular* concerns⟩ **b** : not openly or specifically religious ⟨*secular* music⟩ **c** : not ecclesiastical or clerical ⟨*secular* courts⟩ **2** : of or relating to clergy not belonging to a religious order ⟨a *secular* priest⟩ **3 a** : occurring once in an age or a century **b** : existing or continuing through ages or centuries ⟨*secular* oak trees⟩ [Medieval French *seculer,* from Late Latin *saecularis,* from Latin, "coming once in an age," from *saeculum* "breed, generation, age"] — **sec·u·lar·ly** *adv*

[2]**secular** *n* **1** : a secular ecclesiastic (as a parish priest) **2** : LAYMAN

sec·u·lar·ism \-lə-ˌriz-əm\ *n* : indifference to or rejection or exclusion of religion and religious considerations — **sec·u·lar·ist** \-rəst\ *n* — **secularist** *also* **sec·u·lar·is·tic** \ˌsek-yə-lə-ˈris-tik\ *adj*

sec·u·lar·ize \ˈsek-yə-lə-ˌrīz\ *vt* **1** : to make secular **2** : to transfer from ecclesiastical to civil or lay use, possession, or control — **sec·u·lar·i·za·tion** \ˌsek-yə-lə-rə-ˈzā-shən\ *n* — **sec·u·lar·iz·er** \ˈsek-yə-lə-ˌrī-zər\ *n*

se·cur·ance \si-ˈkyu̇r-əns\ *n* : the act of making secure

[1]**se·cure** \si-ˈkyu̇r\ *adj* **1 a** : easy in mind : CONFIDENT **b** : assured in opinion or expectation : having no doubt **2 a** : free from danger ⟨safety devices to keep children *secure*⟩ **b** : free from risk of loss **c** : affording safety : INVIOLABLE ⟨a *secure* hideaway⟩ **d** : TRUSTWORTHY, DEPENDABLE ⟨a *secure* foundation⟩ **3** : SURE 5a, CERTAIN ⟨our victory is *secure*⟩ [Latin *securus* "safe, secure," from *se* "without" + *cura* "care"] — **se·cure·ly** *adv* — **se·cure·ness** *n*

[2]**secure** *vb* **1 a** : to relieve from exposure to danger : GUARD, SHIELD ⟨*secure* a supply line from enemy raids⟩ **b** : to put beyond hazard of losing or of not receiving : GUARANTEE **c** : to give pledge of payment to (a creditor) or of (an obligation) ⟨*secure* a note with collateral⟩ **2 a** : to take (a person) into custody ⟨*secure* the prisoner⟩ **b** : to make fast : SEAL ⟨*secure* a door⟩ **c** : to tie up : BERTH ⟨*secure* a boat for the night⟩ **3 a** : to get secure possession of : PROCURE ⟨*secure* employment⟩ **b** : to bring about : EFFECT **4** : to release (naval personnel) from work or duty; *also* : to stop work — **se·cur·er** *n*

se·cure·ment \si-ˈkyu̇r-mənt\ *n* : the act or process of making secure

se·cu·ri·ty \si-ˈkyu̇r-ət-ē\ *n, pl* **-ties** **1** : the quality or state of being secure: as **a** : freedom from danger : SAFETY **b** : freedom from fear or anxiety **2 a** : something given, deposited, or pledged to make certain the fulfillment of an obligation ⟨*security* for a loan⟩ **b** : SURETY 3 **3** : an instrument of investment in the form of a document (as a stock certificate or bond) providing evidence of its ownership **4 a** : something that secures : PROTECTION **b** : measures taken especially to guard against espionage or sabotage, crime, attack, or escape ⟨concern over national *security*⟩

Security Council *n* : a permanent council of the United Nations having primary responsibility for maintaining peace and security

se·dan \si-ˈdan\ *n* **1** : a portable often covered chair that is designed to carry one person and is borne on poles by two people **2 a** : an enclosed automobile that seats four to seven persons including the driver in a single compartment and has a permanent top **b** : CRUISER 3 [origin unknown]

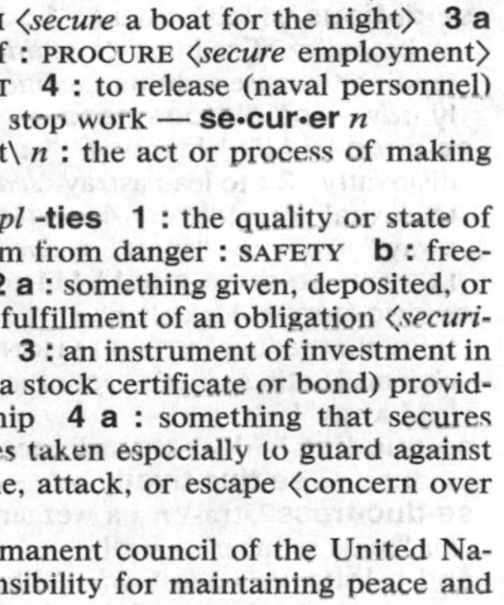

sedan 1

[1]**se·date** \si-ˈdāt\ *adj* : keeping a quiet steady attitude or pace : UNRUFFLED [Latin *sedatus,* from *sedare* "to calm"] — **se·date·ly** *adv* — **se·date·ness** *n*

[2]**sedate** *vt* : to put (a patient) under the influence of a sedative drug

se·da·tion \si-ˈdā-shən\ *n* **1** : the inducing of a relaxed easy

\ə\ abut	\au̇\ **out**	\i\ **tip**	\ȯ\ **saw**	\u̇\ **foot**
\ər\ **further**	\ch\ **chin**	\ī\ **life**	\ȯi\ **coin**	\y\ **yet**
\a\ **mat**	\e\ **pet**	\j\ **job**	\th\ **thin**	\yü\ **few**
\ā\ **take**	\ē\ **easy**	\ng\ **sing**	\th\ **this**	\yu̇\ **cure**
\ä\ **cot, cart**	\g\ **go**	\ō\ **bone**	\ü\ **food**	\zh\ **vision**

state especially by the use of sedatives **2 :** a state resulting from or like that resulting from sedation

[1]**sed·a·tive** \'sed-ət-iv\ *adj* **:** tending to calm, moderate, or relieve tension or irritability

[2]**sedative** *n* **:** a sedative agent or drug

sed·en·tary \'sed-n-ˌter-ē\ *adj* **1 :** not migratory **:** SETTLED ⟨*sedentary* birds⟩ **2 :** doing or requiring much sitting ⟨a *sedentary* job⟩ **3 :** permanently attached ⟨*sedentary* barnacles⟩ [Middle French *sedentaire,* from Latin *sedentarius,* from *sedens,* present participle of *sedēre* "to sit"]

se·der \'sād-ər\ *n, pl* **seders** *also* **se·da·rim** \si-'där-əm\ *often cap* **:** a Jewish home or community service and ceremonial dinner held on the first or first and second evenings of the Passover in commemoration of the exodus from Egypt [Hebrew *sēdher* "order"]

sedge \'sej\ *n* **:** any of a family of usually tufted marsh plants that are monocotyledons differing from the related grasses in having achenes and solid stems [Old English *secg*] — **sedgy** \'sej-ē\ *adj*

sed·i·ment \'sed-ə-mənt\ *n* **1 :** material that settles to the bottom of a liquid **2 :** material (as stones and sand) deposited by water, wind, or glaciers [Middle French, from Latin *sedimentum* "settling," from *sedēre* "to sit, sink down"] — **sed·i·ment** \-ˌment\ *vb*

sed·i·men·ta·ry \ˌsed-ə-'ment-ə-rē, -'men-trē\ *adj* **1 :** of, relating to, or containing sediment ⟨*sedimentary* deposits⟩ **2 :** formed by or from deposits of sediment ⟨limestone and sandstone are *sedimentary* rocks⟩

sed·i·men·ta·tion \ˌsed-ə-mən-'tā-shən, -ˌmen-\ *n* **:** the action or process of depositing sediment

se·di·tion \si-'dish-ən\ *n* **:** incitement of resistance to or of insurrection against lawful authority [Middle French, from Latin *seditio,* literally, "separation," from *sed-, se-* "apart" + *itio* "act of going," from *ire* "to go"]

se·di·tious \si-'dish-əs\ *adj* **1 :** disposed to arouse, take part in, or be guilty of sedition ⟨a *seditious* agitator⟩ **2 :** of, being, or tending to cause sedition ⟨*seditious* statements⟩ — **se·di·tious·ly** *adv* — **se·di·tious·ness** *n*

se·duce \si-'düs, -'dyüs\ *vt* **1 :** to persuade to disobedience or disloyalty **2 :** to lead astray ⟨*seduced* into crime⟩ **3 :** to entice to sexual intercourse **4 :** ATTRACT [Latin *seducere* "to lead away," from *se-* "apart" + *ducere* "to lead"] ***synonyms*** see LURE — **se·duce·ment** \-'dü-smənt, -'dyü-\ *n* — **se·duc·er** *n*

se·duc·tion \si-'dək-shən\ *n* **1 :** the act of seducing **2 :** something that seduces **:** TEMPTATION **3 :** something that attracts or charms [Latin *seductio* "act of leading aside," from *seducere* "to lead away"]

se·duc·tive \si-'dək-tiv\ *adj* **:** tending or having the qualities to seduce — **se·duc·tive·ly** *adv* — **se·duc·tive·ness** *n*

se·duc·tress \-trəs\ *n* **:** a woman who seduces [obsolete *seductor* "male seducer" + *-ess*]

sed·u·lous \'sej-ə-ləs\ *adj* **:** diligent in application or pursuit **:** ASSIDUOUS [Latin *sedulus,* from *sedulo* "sincerely, diligently," from *se* "without" + *dolus* "guile"] — **sed·u·lous·ly** *adv* — **sed·u·lous·ness** *n*

se·dum \'sēd-əm\ *n* **:** any of a genus of fleshy-leaved herbs including the orpine [Latin, a plant related to sedum]

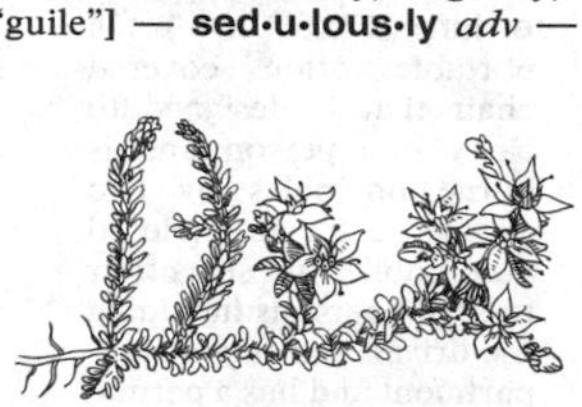

sedum

[1]**see** \'sē\ *vb* **saw** \'sȯ\; **seen** \'sēn\; **see·ing** \'sē-ing\ **1 a :** to perceive by the eye or have the power of sight ⟨*see* a bird⟩ ⟨a person who cannot *see*⟩ **b :** to give or pay attention ⟨*see,* the bus is coming⟩ **c :** to look about **2 a :** to have experience of **:** UNDERGO ⟨*see* army service⟩ **b :** to come to know **:** DISCOVER **c :** to acknowledge or consider something being pointed out ⟨*see,* I told you it would rain⟩ **3 a :** to form a mental picture of **:** VISUALIZE **b :** to perceive the meaning or importance of **:** UNDERSTAND **c :** to be aware of **:** RECOGNIZE ⟨*sees* only our faults⟩ **d :** to imagine as a possibility **:** SUPPOSE ⟨can't *see* how we can lose⟩ **4 a :** to make investigation or inquiry **:** EXAMINE, WATCH ⟨want to *see* how they handle the problem⟩ **b :** READ ⟨*saw* the story in the paper⟩ **c :** to attend as a spectator ⟨*see* a play⟩ **5 a :** to take care of **:** provide for ⟨enough money to *see* us through⟩ **b :** to make sure ⟨*see* that order is kept⟩ **6 a :** to regard as **:** JUDGE **b :** to prefer to have ⟨I'll *see* you dead before I accept your terms⟩ **c :** to find acceptable or attractive ⟨still can't *see* the design⟩ **7 a :** to call on **:** VISIT ⟨*see* a sick friend⟩ **b** (1) **:** to keep company with especially in courtship or dating ⟨had been *seeing* each other for a year⟩ (2) **:** to grant an interview to **:** RECEIVE ⟨the president will *see* you now⟩ **8 :** ACCOMPANY, ESCORT ⟨*see* the babysitter home⟩ **9 :** to meet (a bet) in poker or to equal the bet of (a player) **:** CALL [Old English *sēon*] — **see after :** to attend to **:** care for — **see eye to eye :** to have a common viewpoint **:** AGREE — **see red :** to become very angry — **see the light :** to discover or realize a usually obscured truth — **see the light of day :** to become publicly known or available (as through publication) ⟨manuscripts that will never *see the light of day*⟩ — **see things :** HALLUCINATE — **see through :** to learn the true nature of ⟨*saw through* the scheme⟩ — **see to :** to attend to **:** care for

[2]**see** *n* **1 :** the city in which a bishop's church is located **2 :** the jurisdiction of a bishop **:** DIOCESE [Medieval French *se,* from Latin *sedes* "seat"]

see·able \'sē-ə-bəl\ *adj* **:** capable of being seen

[1]**seed** \'sēd\ *n, pl* **seed** *or* **seeds 1 a :** the grains or ripened ovules of plants used for sowing **b :** the fertilized ripened ovule of a flowering plant containing an embryo and capable normally of germination to produce a new plant; *also* **:** a plant structure (as a spore or small dry fruit) capable of producing a new plant **2 a :** MILT, SEMEN **b :** a developmental form of a lower animal suitable for transplanting; *esp* **:** SPAT **3 :** PROGENY ⟨the *seed* of David⟩ **4 :** a source of development or growth **:** GERM ⟨sowed the *seeds* of discord⟩ **5 :** something (as a small bubble in glass) that resembles a seed in shape or size **6 :** a competitor who has been seeded in a tournament ⟨the top *seed*⟩ [Old English *sǣd*] — **seed** *adj* — **seed·ed** \-əd\ *adj* — **seed·like** \'sēd-ˌlīk\ *adj* — **go to seed** *or* **run to seed 1 :** to develop seed **2 :** to lose effectiveness **:** DECAY, DETERIORATE

[2]**seed** *vb* **1 a :** to bear or shed seeds ⟨weeds that *seed* freely⟩ **b :** to plant seeds in **:** SOW ⟨*seed* a lawn with grass⟩ **2 :** to supply with nuclei (as of crystallization or condensation); *esp* **:** to treat (a cloud) with solid particles to convert water droplets into ice crystals in an attempt to produce rain **3 :** to remove seeds from ⟨*seed* raisins⟩ **4 :** to rank (a contestant) relative to others in a tournament on the basis of previous record ⟨was *seeded* second in the state tournament⟩

seed·bed \'sēd-ˌbed\ *n* **:** soil or a bed of soil prepared for planting seed

seed·case \-ˌkās\ *n* **:** a dry hollow fruit (as a pod) enclosing seeds

seed coat *n* **:** the hard protective outer covering of a seed

seed·eat·er \'sēd-ˌēt-ər\ *n* **:** a bird (as a finch) whose diet consists mainly of seeds

seed·er \'sēd-ər\ *n* **1 :** a machine for planting or sowing seeds **2 :** a device for seeding fruit

seed fern *n* **:** any of an order (Pteridospermales) of extinct plants related to the cycads and having foliage like that of ferns and naked seeds

seed leaf *n* **:** COTYLEDON 2

seed·less \'sēd-ləs\ *adj* **:** having no seeds ⟨*seedless* grapes⟩

seed·ling \-ling\ *n* **1 :** a young plant grown from seed **2 :** a young tree before it becomes a sapling — **seedling** *adj*

seed oyster *n* **:** a young oyster especially of a size for transplantation

seed pearl *n* **:** a very small and often irregular pearl

seed plant *n* **:** a plant that bears seeds **:** SPERMATOPHYTE

seed·pod \'sēd-ˌpäd\ *n* **:** [1]POD 1

seeds·man \'sēdz-mən\ *n* **1 :** a person who sows seed **2 :** a dealer in seeds

seed·time \'sēd-ˌtīm\ *n* **:** the season of sowing

seedy \'sēd-ē\ *adj* **seed·i·er; -est 1 a :** containing or full of seeds ⟨a *seedy* fruit⟩ **b :** containing many small similar inclusions ⟨glass *seedy* with air bubbles⟩ **2 :** inferior in condition or quality: as **a :** SHABBY, RUN-DOWN ⟨*seedy* clothes⟩ **b :** somewhat disreputable **:** SQUALID ⟨a *seedy* district⟩ ⟨*seedy* entertainment⟩ **c :** slightly unwell ⟨felt *seedy* and went home early⟩ — **seed·i·ly** \'sēd-l-ē\ *adv* — **seed·i·ness** \'sēd-ē-nəs\ *n*

[1]**see·ing** \'sē-ing\ *conj* **:** in view of the fact **:** inasmuch as — often used with *that* or *as*

[2]**seeing** *n* **:** the quality of the images of heavenly bodies seen through a telescope ⟨had good *seeing* last night⟩

Seeing Eye *trademark* — used for a guide dog trained to lead the blind

seek \ˈsēk\ *vb* **sought** \ˈsȯt\; **seek·ing** **1 :** to resort to : go to ⟨*seek* the shade on a hot day⟩ **2 a :** to go in search of : look for ⟨*seek* a friend⟩ **b :** to make a search or inquiry **c :** to try to discover ⟨*seek* the truth⟩ **3 :** to ask for ⟨*seek* advice⟩ **4 :** to try to acquire or gain ⟨*seek* one's fortune⟩ **5 :** to make an attempt : TRY ⟨*seek* to find a way⟩ [Old English *sēcan*] — **seek·er** *n*

seel \ˈsēl\ *vt* : to close the eyes of (as a hawk) by drawing threads through the eyelids [Medieval French *ciller,* from Medieval Latin *ciliare,* from Latin *cilium* "eyelid"]

seem \ˈsēm\ *vi* **1 a** (1) **:** to give the impression of being : APPEAR ⟨*seem* reasonable⟩ (2) **:** to pretend to be **b :** to appear to the observation or understanding ⟨*seemed* to know⟩ **c :** to appear to one's own mind or opinion ⟨*seem* to feel no pain⟩ **2 :** to give evidence of existing or being present ⟨there *seems* no reason for worry⟩ [of Scandinavian origin]

1seem·ing \ˈsē-miŋ\ *n* : external appearance as distinguished from true character : LOOK

2seeming *adj* : apparent on superficial view : OSTENSIBLE ⟨*seeming* enthusiasm⟩ — **seem·ing·ly** \ˈsē-miŋ-lē\ *adv*

seem·ly \ˈsēm-lē\ *adj* **seem·li·er; -est** **1 :** good-looking : HANDSOME, ATTRACTIVE **2 :** conventionally proper : DECOROUS ⟨*seemly* behavior⟩ **3 :** suited to the occasion, purpose, or person : FIT ⟨a *seemly* reply⟩ [Old Norse *sœmiligr,* from *sœmr* "fitting"] — **seem·li·ness** *n* — **seemly** *adv*

seen *past participle of* SEE

seep \ˈsēp\ *vi* : to flow or pass slowly through fine pores or small openings : OOZE ⟨water *seeped* through the wall⟩ [Old English *sipian*]

seep·age \ˈsē-pij\ *n* **1 :** the process of seeping **2 :** fluid that has seeped through porous material

seer \ˈsiər, *esp for 1 also* ˈsē-ər\ *n* **1 :** one that sees **2 a :** one that predicts events or developments : PROPHET **b :** a person credited with extraordinary moral and spiritual insight

seer·ess \ˈsiər-əs\ *n* : a woman who is a seer

seer·suck·er \ˈsiər-ˌsək-ər\ *n* : a light fabric of linen, cotton, or rayon usually striped and slightly puckered [Hindi *śīrśakkar,* literally, "milk and sugar," from Persian *shīr-o-shakar*]

1see·saw \ˈsē-ˌsȯ\ *n* **1 :** an alternating up-and-down or backward-and-forward motion or movement; *also* **:** a contest or struggle in which now one side now the other has the lead **2 a :** a pastime in which two children or groups of children ride on opposite ends of a plank balanced in the middle so that one end goes up as the other goes down **b :** the plank or apparatus so used [probably from reduplication of 3*saw*] — **seesaw** *adj*

2seesaw *vb* **see·sawed; see·saw·ing** **1 a :** to move backward and forward or up and down **b :** to play on a seesaw **2 :** ALTERNATE

seethe \ˈsēth\ *vb* **1** *archaic* **:** BOIL, STEW **2 :** to soak or saturate in a liquid **3 a :** to be in a state of rapid agitated movement **b :** to churn or foam as if boiling ⟨the river rapids *seethed*⟩ **4 :** to suffer violent internal excitement ⟨*seethed* with rage⟩ [Old English *sēothan*]

1seg·ment \ˈseg-mənt\ *n* **1 :** any of the parts into which a thing is divided or naturally separates : SECTION, DIVISION **2 a :** a part cut off from a geometric figure (as a circle or sphere) by a line or plane; *esp* **:** the part of a circle enclosed by a chord and an arc **b :** a part of a straight line included between two points — called also *line segment* [Latin *segmentum,* from *secare* "to cut"] ***synonyms*** see PART — **seg·men·tary** \ˈseg-mən-ˌter-ē\ *adj* — **seg·ment·ed** \ˈseg-ˌment-əd, seg-ˈment-\ *adj*

2seg·ment \ˈseg-ˌment\ *vb* : to separate into segments : give off as segments

seg·men·tal \seg-ˈment-l\ *adj* **1 :** of, relating to, or having the form of a segment or sector of a circle ⟨*segmental* fanlight⟩ ⟨*segmental* pediment⟩ **2 :** METAMERIC **3 :** of, relating to, or resulting from segmentation : SUBSIDIARY ⟨*segmental* data⟩ — **seg·men·tal·ly** \-l-ē\ *adv*

seg·men·ta·tion \ˌseg-mən-ˈtā-shən, -ˌmen-\ *n* : the process of dividing into segments; *esp* **:** the formation of many cells from a single cell (as in a developing egg)

se·go lily \ˌsē-gō-\ *n* : a western North American perennial herb related to the lilies and having an edible bulb and bell-shaped flowers that are usually white with purple, yellow, and lilac markings [from a Southern Paiute word meaning "bulb of the sego lily"]

1seg·re·gate \ˈseg-ri-ˌgāt\ *vb* **1 :** to separate or set apart from others or from the general mass : ISOLATE **2 :** to cause or force the segregation of **3 :** to separate during meiosis ⟨genes *segregated* randomly⟩ [Latin *segregare,* from *se-* "apart" + *greg-, grex* "herd"] — **seg·re·ga·tive** \-ˌgāt-iv\ *adj*

2seg·re·gate \-gət, -ˌgāt\ *n* : a segregated individual or class of individuals

seg·re·gat·ed \-ˌgat-əd\ *adj* **1 a :** set apart or separated from others of the same kind or group **b :** divided in facilities or administered separately for members of different races **c :** restricted to one group or race by a policy of segregation ⟨*segregated* schools⟩ **2 :** practicing or maintaining segregation especially of races

seg·re·ga·tion \ˌseg-ri-ˈgā-shən\ *n* **1 :** the act or process of segregating : the state of being segregated **2 :** the separation or isolation of a race, class, or ethnic group by discriminatory means (as restriction to an area, barriers to social intercourse, or separate educational facilities)

seg·re·ga·tion·ist \-shə-nəst, -shnəst\ *n* : an advocate of segregation especially of races

1se·gue \ˈsāg-wā, ˈseg-\ *imperative verb* : proceed to what follows without pause — used as a direction in music [Italian, "there follows," from *seguire* "to follow," from Latin *sequi*]

2segue *vi* **se·gued; se·gue·ing** : to make a transition without pause or interruption ⟨*segued* from one story to the next⟩

sei·del \ˈsīd-l\ *n* : a large glass for beer [German, from Middle High German *sīdel,* from Latin *situla* "bucket"]

sei·gneur \sān-ˈyər\ *n, often cap* : a man of rank or authority; *esp* **:** the feudal lord of a manor [Medieval French, from Medieval Latin *senior,* from Latin, adj., "senior"] — **sei·gneur·ial** \-ē-əl\ *adj*

sei·gnior \sān-ˈyȯr, ˈsān-ˌ\ *n* : SEIGNEUR [Middle English *seygnour,* from Medieval French *seignur, seigneur*]

sei·gniory *or* **sei·gnory** \ˈsān-yə-rē\ *n, pl* **-gnior·ies** *or* **-gnor·ies** : the territory of a lord : DOMAIN

sei·gno·ri·al \sān-ˈyōr-ē-əl, -ˈyȯr-\ *adj* : of, relating to, or befitting a seignior : MANORIAL

1seine \ˈsān\ *n* : a large fishing net kept vertical in the water by weights and floats [Old English *segne,* from Latin *sagena,* from Greek *sagēnē*]

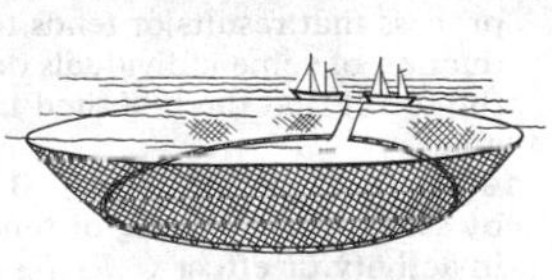

seine

2seine *vb* : to fish with or catch with a seine — **sein·er** *n*

seism- *or* **seismo-** *combining form* : earthquake : vibration ⟨*seismo*graph⟩ [Greek *seismos* "shock, earthquake," from *seiein* "to shake"]

seis·mic \ˈsīz-mik, ˈsīs-\ *adj* : of, subject to, or caused by an earthquake or an artificially produced earth vibration — **seis·mi·cal·ly** \-mi-kə-lē, -klē\ *adv*

seis·mic·i·ty \sīz-ˈmis-ət-ē, sīs-\ *n* : the relative frequency and distribution of earthquakes

seis·mo·gram \ˈsīz-mə-ˌgram, ˈsīs-\ *n* : the record of an earth tremor made by a seismograph

seis·mo·graph \-ˌgraf\ *n* : an apparatus for recording the intensity, direction, and duration of earthquakes or similar vibrations of the ground — **seis·mo·graph·ic** \ˌsīz-mə-ˈgraf-ik, ˌsīs-\ *adj* — **seis·mog·ra·phy** \sīz-ˈmäg-rə-fē, sīs-\ *n*

seis·mol·o·gy \sīz-ˈmäl-ə-jē, sīs-\ *n* : a science that deals with earthquakes and with artificially produced vibrations of the earth — **seis·mo·log·i·cal** \ˌsīz-mə-ˈläj-i-kəl, ˌsīs-\ *adj* — **seis·mo·log·i·cal·ly** \-k-lē, -klē\ *adv* — **seis·mol·o·gist** \sīz-ˈmäl-ə-jəst, sīs-\ *n*

seis·mom·e·ter \sīz-ˈmäm-ət-ər\ *n* : a seismograph that measures actual movements of the ground (as on the earth or the moon)

seize \ˈsēz\ *vb* **1 :** to take possession of : CONFISCATE **2 a :** to take possession of by force ⟨*seize* a fortress⟩ **b :** to take prisoner : ARREST **3 a :** to take hold of suddenly or with force : CLUTCH **b :** UNDERSTAND, COMPREHEND ⟨*seize* an idea quickly⟩ **4 :** to bind together by lashing (as with small cord) ⟨*seize* two ropes⟩ **5 :** to attack or overwhelm suddenly ⟨was *seized* with a fever⟩ **6 a :** to stick fast to or jam with a part in relative motion ⟨the piston *seized*⟩ **b :** to fail to operate due to the seizing of a part ⟨the engine *seized*⟩ [Medieval French *seisir* "to put in possession of," from Medieval Latin *sacire,* of Germanic origin] ***synonyms*** see TAKE — **seiz·er** *n*

seiz·ing \ˈsē-zing\ *n* **1 a** : the cord used in seizing **b** : the fastening so made **2** : the operation of fastening together or lashing with small rope or cord

sei·zure \ˈsē-zhər\ *n* **1** : the act or process of seizing : the state of being seized **2** : a sudden attack (as of disease); *esp* : the physical symptoms (as convulsions) resulting from abnormal electrical discharges in the brain (as in epilepsy)

se·lag·i·nel·la \sə-ˌlaj-ə-ˈnel-ə\ *n* : any of a genus of lower vascular plants that are related to the club mosses and have scalelike leaves [New Latin, from Latin *selagin-, selago,* a kind of plant]

se·lah \ˈsē-lə, -ˌlä\ *interj* — a term of uncertain meaning found in the Hebrew text of the Psalms and Habakkuk carried over untranslated into some English versions [Hebrew *selāh*]

sel·dom \ˈsel-dəm\ *adv* : in few instances : RARELY [Old English *seldan*]

1se·lect \sə-ˈlekt\ *adj* **1** : chosen from a number or group by fitness or preference **2 a** : of special value or excellence : SUPERIOR, CHOICE ⟨a *select* hotel⟩ **b** : carefully or fastidiously chosen often with regard to social, economic, or cultural characteristics ⟨a *select* membership⟩ **3** : judicious or restrictive in choice : DISCRIMINATING [Latin *selectus,* past participle of *seligere* "to select," from *se-* "apart" + *legere* "to gather, pick"] — **se·lect·ness** *n*

2select *vb* : to take by preference from a number or group : pick out : CHOOSE

se·lect·ee \sə-ˌlek-ˈtē\ *n* : one inducted into military service under selective service

se·lec·tion \sə-ˈlek-shən\ *n* **1** : the act or process of selecting : the state of being selected **2** : one that is selected : CHOICE; *also* : a collection of selected things **3** : a natural or artificial process that results or tends to result in the survival and reproduction of some individuals or organisms but not of others with the result that the inherited traits of the survivors are perpetuated

se·lec·tive \sə-ˈlek-tiv\ *adj* **1** : of, relating to, or characterized by selection : selecting or tending to select **2** : highly specific in activity or effect ⟨*selective* pesticides⟩ — **se·lec·tive·ly** *adv* — **se·lec·tive·ness** *n* — **se·lec·tiv·i·ty** \si-ˌlek-ˈtiv-ət-ē, ˌsē-\ *n*

selective service *n* : a system under which individuals are called up for military service : DRAFT

se·lect·man \sə-ˈlekt-ˌman, -ˈlek-, -mən; -ˌlekt-ˈman, -ˌlek-\ *n* : one of a board of elected town officials in all New England states except Rhode Island

se·lec·tor \sə-ˈlek-tər\ *n* : one that selects

sel·e·nite \ˈsel-ə-ˌnīt\ *n* : a variety of gypsum occurring in transparent colorless crystals or crystalline masses [Latin *selenites,* from Greek *selēnitēs lithos,* literally, "stone of the moon," from *selēnē* "moon"; from the belief that it waxed and waned with the moon]

se·le·ni·um \sə-ˈlē-nē-əm\ *n* : a photosensitive chemical element that is used chiefly in glass, alloys, and electronic devices — see ELEMENT table [New Latin, from Greek *selēnē* "moon"]

1self \ˈself, *South also* ˈsef\ *pron* : MYSELF, HIMSELF, HERSELF ⟨check payable to *self*⟩ [Old English, intensive pron.]

2self *adj* **1** : having a single character or quality throughout; *esp* : having one color only ⟨a *self* flower⟩ **2** : of the same kind (as in color, material, or pattern) as something with which it is used ⟨a *self* belt⟩ ⟨*self* trimming⟩

3self \ˈself\ *n, pl* **selves** \ˈselvz, *South also* ˈsevz\ **1** : a person regarded as an individual apart from everyone else **2** : a typical or particular aspect of one's behavior or character ⟨one's true *self*⟩ ⟨your better *self*⟩ **3** : personal interest or advantage ⟨without thought of *self*⟩ **4** : material that is part of an individual organism ⟨ability of the immune system to distinguish *self* from material that is foreign⟩

4self *vb* **1** : INBREED **2** : SELF-POLLINATE

self- *combining form* **1 a** : oneself or itself ⟨*self*-devouring⟩ **b** : of oneself or itself ⟨*self*-abasement⟩ **c** : by oneself or itself ⟨*self*-made⟩ **2 a** : to, with, for, or toward oneself or itself ⟨*self*-addressed⟩ ⟨*self*-satisfaction⟩ **b** : of or in oneself or itself inherently ⟨*self*-evident⟩ **c** : from or by means of oneself or itself ⟨*self*-fertile⟩

self–aban·doned \ˌsel-fə-ˈban-dənd\ *adj* : abandoned by oneself; *esp* : given up to one's impulses

self–abase·ment \ˌsel-fə-ˈbās-mənt\ *n* : humiliation of oneself based on feelings of inferiority, guilt, or shame

self–ab·ne·gat·ing \ˈsel-ˈfab-ni-ˌgāt-ing\ *adj* : SELF-DENYING

self–ab·ne·ga·tion \ˌsel-ˌfab-ni-ˈgā-shən\ *n* : SELF-DENIAL

self–ab·sorbed \ˌsel-fəb-ˈsȯrbd, -ˈzȯrbd\ *adj* : absorbed in one's own thoughts, activities, or interests

self–ab·sorp·tion \-ˈsȯrp-shən, -ˈzȯrp-\ *n* : preoccupation with oneself

self–abuse \ˌsel-fə-ˈbyüs\ *n* **1** : reproach of oneself **2** : abuse of one's body or health

self–ac·cu·sa·tion \ˌsel-ˌfak-yə-ˈzā-shən\ *n* : the act or an instance of accusing oneself

self–ac·quired \ˌsel-fə-ˈkwīrd\ *adj* : acquired by oneself

self–act·ing \ˈsel-ˈfak-ting\ *adj* : acting or capable of acting of or by itself

self–ac·tu·al·ize \-ˈfak-chə-wə-ˌlīz, -chə-ˌlīz; -ˈfaksh-wə-\ *vi* : to realize fully one's potential — **self–ac·tu·al·i·za·tion** \-ˌfak-chə-wə-lə-ˈzā-shən, -chə-lə-; -ˌfaksh-wə-\ *n*

self–ad·dressed \ˌsel-fə-ˈdrest, ˈsel-ˈfad-ˌrest\ *adj* : addressed for return to the sender ⟨*self-addressed* envelopes⟩

self–ad·just·ing \ˌsel-fə-ˈjəs-ting\ *adj* : adjusting by itself ⟨a *self-adjusting* wrench⟩

self–ad·min·is·tered \ˌsel-fəd-ˈmin-ə-stərd\ *adj* : administered, managed, or dispensed by oneself

self–ad·mi·ra·tion \ˌsel-ˌfad-mə-ˈrā-shən\ *n* : SELF-CONCEIT

self–ad·vance·ment \ˌsel-fəd-ˈvan-smənt\ *n* : the act of advancing oneself

self–af·fect·ed \ˌsel-fə-ˈfek-təd\ *adj* : VAIN 3, CONCEITED

self–ag·gran·dize·ment \ˌsel-fə-ˈgran-dəz-mənt, -ˌdīz-; ˌsel-ˌfag-rən-ˈdīz-\ *n* : the act or process of making oneself greater (as in power or influence)

self–ag·gran·diz·ing \ˌsel-fə-ˈgran-ˌdī-zing, ˈsel-ˈfag-rən-\ *adj* : acting or seeking to make oneself greater

self–anal·y·sis \ˌsel-fə-ˈnal-ə-səs\ *n* : a systematic attempt by an individual to understand his or her own personality without the aid of another person — **self–an·a·lyt·i·cal** \ˌsel-ˌfan-l-ˈit-i-kəl\ *adj*

self–ap·plause \ˌsel-fə-ˈplȯz\ *n* : an expression or feeling of approval of oneself

self–ap·point·ed \ˌsel-fə-ˈpȯint-əd\ *adj* : appointed by oneself usually without justification or qualifications ⟨a *self-appointed* censor⟩

self–ap·pro·ba·tion \ˌsel-ˌfap-rə-ˈbā-shən\ *n* : satisfaction with one's actions and achievements

self–as·sem·bly \-fə-ˈsem-blē\ *n* : the process by which a complex macromolecule (as a protein) assembles itself from its components — **self–as·sem·ble** \-bəl\ *vi*

self–as·sert·ing \ˌsel-fə-ˈsərt-ing\ *adj* **1** : asserting oneself or one's own rights, opinions, or claims **2** : putting oneself forward in a confident or arrogant manner

self–as·ser·tion \ˌsel-fə-ˈsər-shən\ *n* **1** : the act of asserting oneself or one's own rights, opinions, or claims **2** : the act of asserting one's superiority over others

self–as·ser·tive \-ˈsərt-iv\ *adj* : given to or marked by self-assertion — **self–as·ser·tive·ly** *adv* — **self–as·ser·tive·ness** *n*

self–as·sur·ance \ˌsel-fə-ˈshu̇r-əns\ *n* : SELF-CONFIDENCE

self–as·sured \-ˈshu̇rd\ *adj* : SELF-CONFIDENT — **self–as·sured·ness** \-ˈshu̇r-əd-nəs, -ˈshu̇rd-\ *n*

self–aware·ness \ˌsel-fə-ˈwaər-nəs, -ˈweər-\ *n* : an awareness of one's own personality or individuality

self–born \ˈself-ˈbȯrn\ *adj* **1** : arising within the self ⟨*self-born* sorrows⟩ **2** : springing from a prior self ⟨a phoenix rising *self-born* from the fire⟩

self–cen·tered \ˈself-ˈsent-ərd\ *adj* : interested chiefly in one's own self : SELFISH — **self–cen·tered·ly** *adv* — **self–cen·tered·ness** *n*

self–charg·ing \-ˈchär-jing\ *adj* : that charges itself

self–clos·ing \-ˈklō-zing\ *adj* : closing or shutting automatically after being opened

self–com·mand \ˌself-kə-ˈmand\ *n* : control of one's own behavior and emotions : SELF-CONTROL

self–com·pat·i·ble \ˌself-kəm-ˈpat-ə-bəl\ *adj* : capable of effective self-pollination — compare SELF-INCOMPATIBLE

self–com·pla·cent \ˌself-kəm-ˈplās-nt\ *adj* : SELF-SATISFIED, COMPLACENT — **self–com·pla·cen·cy** \-ˈplās-n-sē\ *n* — **self–com·pla·cent·ly** *adv*

self–com·posed \ˌself-kəm-ˈpōzd\ *adj* : having one's emotions under control — **self–com·pos·ed·ly** \-ˈpō-zəd-lē\ *adv*

self–con·ceit \ˌself-kən-ˈsēt\ *n* **:** too high an opinion of one's qualities or abilities — **self–con·ceit·ed** \-əd\ *adj*
self–con·cept \-ˈkän-ˌsept\ *n* **:** the mental image one has of oneself
self–con·cern \ˌself-kən-ˈsərn\ *n* **:** selfish or morbid concern for oneself — **self–con·cerned** \-ˈsərnd\ *adj*
self–con·dem·na·tion \ˌself-ˌkän-ˌdem-ˈnā-shən, -dəm-\ *n* **:** condemnation of one's own character or actions
self–con·fessed \ˌself-kən-ˈfest\ *adj* **:** openly acknowledged
self–con·fi·dence \ˈself-ˈkän-fəd-əns, -fə-ˌdens\ *n* **:** confidence in oneself and in one's powers and abilities — **self–con·fi·dent** \-fəd-ənt, -fə-ˌdent\ *adj* — **self–con·fi·dent·ly** *adv*
self–con·scious \ˈself-ˈkän-chəs\ *adj* **1 :** aware of oneself as an individual **2 :** uncomfortably conscious of oneself as an object of the observation of others **:** ill at ease — **self–con·scious·ly** *adv* — **self–con·scious·ness** *n*
self–con·sis·tent \ˌself-kən-ˈsis-tənt\ *adj* **:** having each part logically consistent with the rest — **self–con·sis·ten·cy** \-tən-sē\ *n*
self–con·sti·tut·ed \ˈself-ˈkän-stə-ˌtüt-əd, -ˌtyüt-\ *adj* **:** constituted by oneself
self–con·tained \ˌself-kən-ˈtānd\ *adj* **1 :** complete in itself **2 a :** showing self-control **b :** formal and reserved in manner — **self–con·tained·ly** \-ˈtā-nəd-lē, -ˈtān-dlē\ *adv* — **self–con·tained·ness** \-ˈtā-nəd-nəs, -ˈtānd-nəs, -ˈtān-nəs\ *n* — **self–con·tain·ment** \-ˈtān-mənt\ *n*
self–con·tempt \ˌself-kən-ˈtemt, -ˈtempt\ *n* **:** contempt for oneself
self–con·tent·ed \ˌself-kən-ˈtent-əd\ *adj* **:** SELF-SATISFIED, COMPLACENT — **self–con·tent** \-ˈtent\ *n* — **self–con·tent·ed·ly** *adv* — **self–con·tent·ed·ness** *n* — **self–con·tent·ment** \-ˈtent-mənt\ *n*
self–con·tra·dic·to·ry \ˌself-ˌkän-trə-ˈdik-tə-rē, -trē\ *adj* **:** consisting of two contradictory members or parts ⟨a *self-contradictory* statement⟩
self–con·trol \ˌself-kən-ˈtrōl\ *n* **:** control over one's own impulses, emotions, or acts — **self–con·trolled** \-ˈtrōld\ *adj*
self–cor·rect·ing \ˌself-kə-ˈrek-ting\ *adj* **:** correcting or compensating for one's own errors or weaknesses
self–cor·rec·tive \-ˈrek-tiv\ *adj* **:** SELF-CORRECTING
self–cre·at·ed \ˌself-krē-ˈāt-əd\ *adj* **:** created or appointed by oneself
self–crit·i·cism \ˈself-ˈkrit-ə-ˌsiz-əm\ *n* **:** the act of or capacity for criticizing one's own faults or shortcomings
self–de·ceiv·ing \ˌself-di-ˈsē-ving\ *adj* **1 :** given to self-deception ⟨a *self-deceiving* hypocrite⟩ **2 :** serving to deceive oneself ⟨*self-deceiving* excuses⟩
self–de·cep·tion \ˌself-di-ˈsep-shən\ *n* **:** the act of deceiving oneself **:** the state of being deceived by oneself — **self–de·cep·tive** \-ˈsep-tiv\ *adj*
self–ded·i·ca·tion \ˌself-ˌded-i-ˈkā-shən\ *n* **:** dedication of oneself to a cause or ideal
self–de·feat·ing \ˌself-di-ˈfēt-ing\ *adj* **:** acting to defeat its own purpose
self–de·fense \ˌself-di-ˈfens\ *n* **:** the act of defending oneself, one's property, or a close relative
self–de·ni·al \ˌself-di-ˈnī-əl, -ˈnīl\ *n* **:** the act of refraining from gratifying one's own desires — **self–de·ny·ing** \-ˈnī-ing\ *adj*
self–de·pen·dence \ˌself-di-ˈpen-dəns\ *n* **:** SELF-RELIANCE — **self–de·pen·dent** \-dənt\ *adj*
self–de·pre·ci·a·tion \ˌself-di-ˌprē-shē-ˈā-shən\ *n* **:** belittlement or undervaluation of oneself
self–de·spair \ˌself-di-ˈspaər, -ˈspeər\ *n* **:** despair of oneself **:** HOPELESSNESS
self–de·struct \ˌself-di-ˈstrəkt\ *vi* **:** to destroy itself
self–de·struc·tion \ˌself-di-ˈstrək-shən\ *n* **:** destruction of oneself; *esp* **:** SUICIDE — **self–de·struc·tive** \-ˈstrək-tiv\ *adj*
self–de·ter·mi·na·tion \ˌself-di-ˌtər-mə-ˈnā-shən\ *n* **1 :** the act or power of deciding things for oneself **2 :** the right of a people to determine the form of government they will have — **self–de·ter·min·ing** \-ˈtər-mə-ning\ *adj*
self–de·ter·mined \-ˈtər-mənd\ *adj* **:** determined by oneself
self–de·vel·op·ment \ˌself-di-ˈvel-əp-mənt\ *n* **:** development of one's own capabilities or possibilities
self–de·vo·tion \ˌself-di-ˈvō-shən\ *n* **:** devotion of oneself especially in service or sacrifice
self–de·vour·ing \ˌself-di-ˈvaůr-ing\ *adj* **:** devouring itself
self–di·rect·ed \ˌself-də-ˈrek-təd, -dī-\ *adj* **:** directed by oneself; *esp* **:** not guided or impelled by an outside force or agency ⟨a *self-directed* personality⟩
self–dis·ci·pline \ˈself-ˈdis-ə-plən\ *n* **:** correction or regulation of oneself for the sake of improvement — **self–dis·ci·plined** \-plənd\ *adj*
self–dis·cov·ery \ˌself-dis-ˈkəv-rē, -ə-rē\ *n* **:** the act or process of achieving self-knowledge
self–dis·trust \ˌself-dis-ˈtrəst\ *n* **:** a lack of confidence in oneself **:** DIFFIDENCE — **self–dis·trust·ful** \-fəl\ *adj*
self–doubt \ˈself-ˈdaůt\ *n* **:** a lack of faith in oneself — **self–doubt·ing** \-ing\ *adj*
self–ed·u·cat·ed \ˈsel-ˈfej-ə-ˌkāt-əd\ *adj* **:** educated by one's own efforts without formal instruction — **self–ed·u·ca·tion** \ˌsel-ˌfej-ə-ˈkā-shən\ *n*
self–ef·fac·ing \ˌsel-fə-ˈfā-sing\ *adj* **:** tending to keep oneself in the background **:** UNASSERTIVE — **self–ef·face·ment** \-ˈfā-smənt\ *n* — **self–ef·fac·ing·ly** \-ˈfā-sing-lē\ *adv*
self–em·ployed \ˌsel-fim-ˈplȯid\ *adj* **:** earning income directly from one's own business, trade, or profession rather than as salary or wages from an employer — **self–em·ploy·ment** \-ˈplȯi-mənt\ *n*
self–es·teem \ˌsel-fə-ˈstēm\ *n* **1 :** a proper satisfaction with one's own worth **2 :** an inflated opinion of one's own worth
self–ev·i·dent \ˈsel-ˈfev-əd-ənt, -ə-ˌdent\ *adj* **:** evident without proof or argument — **self–ev·i·dent·ly** *adv*
self–ex·am \ˌsel-fig-ˈzam\ *n* **:** SELF-EXAMINATION
self–ex·am·i·na·tion \ˌsel-fig-ˌzam-ə-ˈnā-shən\ *n* **:** an act of examining oneself: as **a :** INTROSPECTION **b :** examination of one's body especially for evidence of disease
self–ex·e·cut·ing \ˈsel-ˈfek-sə-ˌkyüt-ing\ *adj* **:** taking effect immediately without implementing legislation ⟨a *self-executing* treaty⟩
self–ex·plain·ing \ˌsel-fik-ˈsplā-ning\ *adj* **:** SELF-EXPLANATORY
self–ex·plan·a·to·ry \-ˈsplan-ə-ˌtōr-ē, -ˌtȯr-\ *adj* **:** understandable without explanation
self–ex·pres·sion \ˌsel-fik-ˈspresh-ən\ *n* **:** the expression of one's own personality **:** assertion of one's individual traits — **self–ex·pres·sive** \-ˈspres-iv\ *adj*
self–feed·er \ˈself-ˈfēd-ər\ *n* **:** a device for feeding livestock equipped with a feed hopper that automatically supplies a trough below
self–fer·tile \ˈself-ˈfərt-l\ *adj* **:** fertile by means of its own pollen or sperm — **self–fer·til·i·ty** \ˌself-fər-ˈtil-ət-ē\ *n*
self–fer·til·i·za·tion \ˌself-ˌfərt-l-ə-ˈzā-shən\ *n* **:** fertilization by pollen or sperm from the same individual — **self–fer·til·ize** \ˈself-ˈfərt-l-ˌīz\ *vb*
self–flat·tery \ˈself-ˈflat-ə-rē\ *n* **:** the glossing over of one's own weaknesses or mistakes and the exaggeration of one's own good qualities and achievements
self–for·get·ful \ˌself-fər-ˈget-fəl\ *adj* **:** having or showing no thought of self or selfish interests — **self–for·get·ful·ly** \-fə-lē\ *adv* — **self–for·get·ful·ness** *n*
self–formed \ˈself-ˈfȯrmd\ *adj* **:** formed or developed by one's own efforts
self–fruit·ful \ˈself-ˈfrüt-fəl\ *adj* **:** capable of setting a crop of self-pollinated fruit — **self–fruit·ful·ness** *n*
self–ful·fill·ing \ˌself-fůl-ˈfil-ing\ *adj* **:** marked by or achieving self-fulfillment
self–ful·fill·ment \-ˈfil-mənt\ *n* **:** fulfillment of oneself
self–giv·ing \ˈself-ˈgiv-ing\ *adj* **:** inclined to self-sacrifice **:** UNSELFISH
self–glo·ri·fi·ca·tion \ˌself-ˌglōr-ə-fə-ˈkā-shən, -ˌglȯr-\ *n* **:** a feeling or expression of one's own superiority
self–glo·ry \ˈself-ˈglōr-ē, -ˈglȯr-\ *n* **:** personal vanity **:** PRIDE
self–gov·ern·ment \ˈself-ˈgəv-ər-mənt; -ˈgəb-m-ənt, -ˈgəv-; -ˈgəv-ərn-mənt\ *n* **1 :** SELF-CONTROL **2 :** government of a political unit by action of its own people; *esp* **:** democratic government — **self–gov·erned** \-ˈgəv-ərnd\ *adj* — **self–gov·ern·ing** \-ər-ning\ *adj*
self–grat·i·fi·ca·tion \ˌself-ˌgrat-ə-fə-ˈkā-shən\ *n* **:** the act of pleasing oneself or of satisfying one's desires
self–heal \ˈself-ˌhēl\ *n* **:** a low-growing blue-flowered Eurasian mint that is held to have medicinal properties

\ə\ **abut**	\aů\ **out**	\i\ **tip**	\ȯ\ **saw**	\ů\ **foot**
\ər\ **further**	\ch\ **chin**	\ī\ **life**	\ȯi\ **coin**	\y\ **yet**
\a\ **mat**	\e\ **pet**	\j\ **job**	\th\ **thin**	\yü\ **few**
\ā\ **take**	\ē\ **easy**	\ng\ **sing**	\t͟h\ **this**	\yů\ **cure**
\ä\ **cot, cart**	\g\ **go**	\ō\ **bone**	\ü\ **food**	\zh\ **vision**

self–help \ˈself-ˈhelp\ *n* : the action or process of bettering oneself or overcoming one's problems without the aid of others; *esp* : the coping with one's personal or emotional problems without professional help — **self–help** *adj*
self•hood \ˈself-ˌhu̇d\ *n* : INDIVIDUALITY 1
self•hyp•no•sis \ˌself-hip-ˈnō-səs\ *n* : hypnosis of oneself
self–iden•ti•ty \ˌsel-fī-ˈdent-ət-ē\ *n* : INDIVIDUALITY 1
self•ie \ˈsel-fē\ *n, pl* **self•ies** : an image of oneself taken by oneself using a digital camera especially for posting on social networks
self–ig•nite \ˌsel-fig-ˈnīt\ *vi* : to become ignited without flame or spark (as under high compression) — **self–ig•ni•tion** \-ˈnish-ən\ *n*
self–im•age \ˈsel-ˈfim-ij\ *n* : one's conception of oneself or of one's role
self–im•mo•la•tion \ˌsel-ˌfim-ə-ˈlā-shən\ *n* : a deliberate and willing sacrifice of oneself
self–im•por•tance \ˌsel-fim-ˈpȯrt-ns, -əns\ *n* **1** : an exaggerated estimate of one's own importance : SELF-CONCEIT **2** : arrogant or pompous behavior — **self–im•por•tant** \-nt, -ənt\ *adj* — **self–im•por•tant•ly** *adv*
self–im•posed \ˌsel-fim-ˈpōzd\ *adj* : imposed on one by oneself : voluntarily assumed ⟨a *self-imposed* exile⟩
self–im•prove•ment \ˌsel-fim-ˈprüv-mənt\ *n* : improvement of oneself by one's own action
self–in•clu•sive \ˌsel-fin-ˈklü-siv, -ziv\ *adj* : SELF-CONTAINED 1
self–in•com•pat•i•ble \ˌsel-ˌfin-kəm-ˈpat-ə-bəl\ *adj* : incapable of effective self-pollination — compare SELF-COMPATIBLE
self–in•crim•i•na•tion \ˌsel-fin-ˌkrim-ə-ˈnā-shən\ *n* : incrimination of oneself; *esp* : the giving of evidence or answering of questions which could make one subject to criminal prosecution — **self–in•crim•i•nat•ing** \-ˈkrim-ə-ˌnāt-ing\ *adj*
self–in•duced \ˌsel-fin-ˈdüst, -ˈdyüst\ *adj* **1** : induced by oneself **2** : produced by self-induction ⟨a *self-induced* voltage⟩
self–in•duc•tance \-ˈdək-təns\ *n* : inductance in which an electromotive force is produced by self-induction
self–in•duc•tion \-ˈdək-shən\ *n* : induction of an electromotive force in a circuit by a varying current in the same circuit
self–in•dul•gence \ˌsel-fin-ˈdəl-jəns\ *n* : overindulgence of one's own appetites, desires, or whims — **self–in•dul•gent** \-jənt\ *adj* — **self–in•dul•gent•ly** *adv*
self–in•flict•ed \ˌsel-fin-ˈflik-təd\ *adj* : inflicted by oneself ⟨a *self-inflicted* wound⟩
self–in•struct•ed \ˌsel-fin-ˈstrək-təd\ *adj* : SELF-TAUGHT
self–in•ter•est \ˈsel-ˈfin-trəst, -ˈfint-ə-rəst\ *n* **1** : one's own interest or advantage **2** : a concern for one's own advantage and well-being — **self–in•ter•est•ed** \-əd\ *adj* — **self–in•ter•est•ed•ness** *n*
self–in•volved \ˌsel-fin-ˈvälvd, -ˈvȯlvd\ *adj* : SELF-ABSORBED
self•ish \ˈsel-fish\ *adj* **1** : concerned excessively or exclusively with oneself : seeking or concentrating on one's own advantage, pleasure, or well-being without regard for others **2** : arising from concern with one's own welfare or advantage in disregard of others ⟨a *selfish* act⟩ — **self•ish•ly** *adv* — **self•ish•ness** *n*
self–jus•ti•fi•ca•tion \ˌself-ˌjəs-tə-fə-ˈkā-shən\ *n* : the act or an instance of making excuses for oneself
self–knowl•edge \ˈself-ˈnäl-ij\ *n* : knowledge of one's own capabilities, character, feelings, or motivations
self•less \ˈsel-fləs\ *adj* : having or showing no concern for self : UNSELFISH — **self•less•ly** *adv* — **self•less•ness** *n*
self–lim•it•ing \ˈsel-ˈflim-ət-ing\ *adj* : limiting oneself or itself
self–lock•ing \ˈsel-ˈfläk-ing\ *adj* : locking by its own action
self–love \ˈsel-ˈfləv\ *n* : love of self: **a** : CONCEIT 1 **b** : regard for one's own happiness or advantage — **self–lov•ing** \-ing\ *adj*
self–lu•bri•cat•ing \ˈsel-ˈflü-brə-ˌkāt-ing\ *adj* : lubricating itself
self–lu•mi•nous \ˈsel-ˈflü-mə-nəs\ *adj* : having in itself the property of emitting light
self–made \ˈself-ˈmād\ *adj* **1** : made by oneself or itself **2** : raised from poverty or obscurity by one's own efforts
self–mas•tery \ˈself-ˈmas-tə-rē, -trē\ *n* : SELF-COMMAND, SELF-CONTROL
self–ob•ser•va•tion \ˌsel-ˌfäb-sər-ˈvā-shən, -zər-\ *n* **1** : INTROSPECTION **2** : observation of one's own appearance
self–op•er•at•ing \ˈsel-ˈfäp-ə-ˌrāt-ing\ *or* **self–op•er•a•tive** \-ˈfäp-rət-iv, -ə-rət-; -ˈfäp-ə-ˌrāt-\ *adj* : SELF-ACTING
self–opin•ion•at•ed \ˌsel-fə-ˈpin-yə-ˌnāt-əd\ *adj* **1** : CONCEITED **2** : stubbornly holding to one's own opinion
self–orig•i•nat•ed \ˌsel-fə-ˈrij-ə-ˌnāt-əd\ *adj* : originated by oneself or itself
self–per•pet•u•at•ing \ˌself-pər-ˈpech-ə-ˌwāt-ing\ *adj* : capable of continuing or renewing itself indefinitely
self–pity \ˈself-ˈpit-ē\ *n* : pity for oneself — **self–pity•ing** \-ē-ing\ *adj* — **self–pity•ing•ly** \-ing-lē\ *adv*
self–poised \ˈself-ˈpȯizd\ *adj* **1** : balanced without support **2** : having poise through self-command
self–pol•li•nate \ˈself-ˈpäl-ə-ˌnāt\ *vb* : to undergo or cause to undergo self-pollination
self–pol•li•na•tion \ˌself-ˌpäl-ə-ˈnā-shən\ *n* : the transfer of pollen from the anther of a flower to the stigma of the same flower or sometimes to that of a genetically identical flower (as of the same plant or clone)
self–por•trait \ˈself-ˈpōr-trət, -ˈpȯr-, -ˌtrāt\ *n* : a portrait of oneself done by oneself
self–pos•sessed \ˌself-pə-ˈzest\ *adj* : composed in mind or manner : CALM — **self–pos•sessed•ly** \-ˈzes-əd-lē, -ˈzest-lē\ *adv*
self–pos•ses•sion \ˌself-pə-ˈzesh-ən\ *n* : control of one's emotions or reactions : COMPOSURE
self–praise \ˈself-ˈprāz\ *n* : praise of oneself
self–pres•er•va•tion \ˌself-ˌprez-ər-ˈvā-shən\ *n* : the keeping of oneself from destruction, injury, or loss
self–pride \ˌself-ˈprīd\ *n* : pride in oneself or in that which relates to oneself
self–pro•claimed \ˌself-prō-ˈklāmd\ *adj* : SELF-STYLED ⟨a *self-proclaimed* genius⟩
self–pro•duced \ˌself-prə-ˈdüst, -ˈdyüst\ *adj* : produced by oneself or itself
self–pro•pelled \ˌself-prə-ˈpeld\ *adj* : containing within itself the means for its own propulsion
self–pro•pel•ling \-ˈpel-ing\ *adj* : SELF-PROPELLED
self–pro•tec•tion \ˌself-prə-ˈtek-shən\ *n* : protection of oneself : SELF-DEFENSE
self–pun•ish•ment \ˈself-ˈpən-ish-mənt\ *n* : punishment of oneself
self–pu•ri•fi•ca•tion \ˌself-ˌpyu̇r-ə-fə-ˈkā-shən\ *n* : purification of oneself ⟨moral *self-purification*⟩
self–ques•tion•ing \ˈself-ˈkwes-chə-ning\ *n* : INTROSPECTION
self–re•al•i•za•tion \ˌsel-ˌfrē-ə-lə-ˈzā-shən\ *n* : fulfillment by oneself of the possibilities of one's character or personality
self–re•cord•ing \ˌsel-fri-ˈkȯrd-ing\ *adj* : making a record automatically ⟨*self-recording* instruments⟩
self–re•gard \ˌsel-fri-ˈgärd\ *n* **1** : regard for or consideration of oneself or one's own interests **2** : SELF-RESPECT 1 — **self–re•gard•ing** \-ing\ *adj*
self–reg•u•lat•ing \ˈsel-ˈfreg-yə-ˌlāt-ing\ *adj* : regulating oneself or itself; *esp* : AUTOMATIC ⟨a *self-regulating* mechanism⟩ — **self–reg•u•la•tion** \ˌsel-ˌfreg-yə-ˈlā-shən\ *n*
self–re•li•ance \ˌsel-fri-ˈlī-ənts\ *n* : reliance on one's own efforts and abilities — **self–re•li•ant** \-ənt\ *adj*
self–re•nun•ci•a•tion \ˌsel-fri-ˌnən-sē-ˈā-shən\ *n* : renunciation of one's own desires or ambitions
self–rep•li•cat•ing \ˈsel-ˈfrep-lə-ˌkāt-ing\ *adj* : duplicating itself ⟨DNA is a *self-replicating* molecule⟩
self–re•proach \ˌsel-fri-ˈprōch\ *n* : the act of blaming or accusing oneself — **self–re•proach•ful** \-fəl\ *adj* — **self–re•proach•ing** \-ˈprō-ching\ *adj*
self–re•pro•duc•ing \ˈsel-ˌfrē-prə-ˈdü-sing, -ˈdyü-\ *adj* : SELF-REPLICATING
self–re•spect \ˌsel-fri-ˈspekt\ *n* **1** : a proper respect for oneself as a human being **2** : regard for one's own standing or position — **self–re•spect•ing** \-ˈspek-ting\ *adj*
self–re•straint \ˌsel-fri-ˈstrānt\ *n* : restraint imposed on oneself : SELF-CONTROL
self–re•veal•ing \ˌsel-fri-ˈvē-ling\ *adj* : marked by self-revelation
self–rev•e•la•tion \ˌsel-ˌfrev-ə-ˈlā-shən\ *n* : revelation of one's own thoughts, feelings, and attitudes especially without deliberate intent
self–re•ward•ing \ˌsel-fri-ˈwȯrd-ing\ *adj* : containing or producing its own reward ⟨a *self-rewarding* virtue⟩
self–righ•teous \ˈsel-ˈfrī-chəs\ *adj* : convinced of one's own righteousness especially in contrast with the actions and beliefs of others — **self–righ•teous•ly** *adv* — **self–righ•teous•ness** *n*
self–ris•ing flour \ˈsel-ˈfrī-zing\ *n* : a mixture of flour, salt, and a leavening agent — called also *self-raising flour*
self–rule \ˈsel-ˈfrül\ *n* : SELF-GOVERNMENT 2
self–sac•ri•fice \ˈself-ˈsak-rə-ˌfīs, -fəs\ *n* : sacrifice of oneself or

one's interest for others or for a cause or ideal — **self–sac·ri·fic·ing** \-ˌfī-sing\ *adj* — **self–sac·ri·fic·ing·ly** \-sing-lē\ *adv*

self·same \ˈself-ˌsām\ *adj* : precisely the same : IDENTICAL — **self·same·ness** *n*

self–sat·is·fac·tion \ˌself-ˌsat-əs-ˈfak-shən\ *n* : a usually smug satisfaction with oneself, one's position, or one's achievements

self–sat·is·fied \ˈself-ˈsat-əs-ˌfīd\ *adj* : feeling or showing self-satisfaction

self–sat·is·fy·ing \-ˌfī-ing\ *adj* : giving satisfaction to oneself

self–seal·ing \ˈself-ˈsē-ling\ *adj* : capable of sealing itself (as after puncture) ⟨a *self-sealing* tire⟩

self–search·ing \ˈself-ˈsər-ching\ *adj* : SELF-QUESTIONING

self–seek·er \ˈself-ˈsē-kər\ *n* : a person who is interested only in his or her own advantage or pleasure — **self–seek·ing** \-king\ *n or adj*

self–serve \ˈself-ˈsərv\ *adj* : permitting self-service

self–ser·vice \ˈself-ˈsər-vəs\ *n* : the serving of oneself (as in a cafeteria or market) with things to be paid for usually upon leaving — **self–service** *adj*

self–slaugh·ter \ˈself-ˈslȯt-ər\ *n* : SUICIDE 1a

self–sow \ˈself-ˈsō\ *vi* : to sow itself by dropping seeds or by natural action (as of wind or water)

self–start·er \ˈself-ˈstärt-ər\ *n* **1** : more or less automatic attachment for starting an internal combustion engine **2** : a person who has initiative

self–start·ing \-ˈstärt-ing\ *adj* : capable of starting by itself

self–ster·ile \ˈself-ˈster-əl\ *adj* : sterile to its own pollen or sperm — **self–ste·ril·i·ty** \ˌself-stə-ˈril-ət-ē\ *n*

self–styled \ˈself-ˈstīld\ *adj* : called by oneself ⟨*self-styled* experts⟩

self–suf·fi·cient \ˌself-sə-ˈfish-ənt\ *adj* **1** : able to take care of oneself without outside help **2** : having great confidence in one's own ability or worth : SECURE — **self–suf·fi·cien·cy** \-ən-sē\ *n*

self–sup·port \ˌself-sə-ˈpōrt, -ˈpȯrt\ *n* : independent support of oneself or itself — **self–sup·port·ed** \-əd\ *adj*

self–sup·port·ing \-ing\ *adj* : characterized by self-support: as **a** : meeting one's needs by one's own efforts or output **b** : supporting itself or its own weight ⟨a *self-supporting* wall⟩

self–sus·tained \ˌself-sə-ˈstānd\ *adj* : sustained by oneself

self–sus·tain·ing \-ˈstā-ning\ *adj* **1** : maintaining or able to maintain oneself by independent effort : SELF-SUPPORTING **2** : maintaining or able to maintain itself once started ⟨a *self-sustaining* nuclear reaction⟩

self–taught \ˈself-ˈtȯt\ *adj* **1** : having knowledge or skills acquired by one's own efforts without formal instruction **2** : learned by oneself ⟨*self-taught* knowledge⟩

self–treat·ment \ˈself-ˈtrēt-mənt\ *n* : medication of oneself or treatment of one's ailment without medical supervision

self–trust \ˈself-ˈtrəst\ *n* : SELF-CONFIDENCE

self–un·der·stand·ing \ˌsel-ˌfən-dər-ˈstan-ding\ *n* : SELF-KNOWLEDGE

self–will \ˈself-ˈwil\ *n* : stubborn or willful adherence to one's own desires or ideas : OBSTINACY — **self–willed** \-ˈwild\ *adj*

self–wind·ing \ˈself-ˈwīn-ding\ *adj* : not needing to be wound by hand : winding by itself ⟨a *self-winding* watch⟩

self–worth \-ˈwərth\ *n* : SELF-ESTEEM

Sel·juk \ˈsel-ˌjük, sel-ˈ\ *or* **Sel·ju·ki·an** \sel-ˈjü-kē-ən\ *adj* **1** : of or relating to any of several Turkish dynasties ruling in western Asia in the 11th, 12th, and 13th centuries **2** : of, relating to, or characteristic of a Turkish people ruled over by a Seljuk dynasty [derived from Turkish *Selçuk,* ancestor of the dynasties] — **Seljuk** *or* **Seljukian** *n*

[1]**sell** \ˈsel\ *vb* **sold** \ˈsōld\; **sell·ing** **1** : to deliver up in violation of duty, trust, or loyalty : BETRAY ⟨the traitors *sold* their king to the enemy⟩ **2 a** : to give in exchange especially for money ⟨they *sold* us some fish⟩; *also* : to give in exchange foolishly or dishonorably ⟨*sell* one's birthright for a mess of pottage⟩ **b** : to work at or deal in the sale of : have or offer for sale ⟨*sells* insurance⟩ ⟨that store *sells* imported foods⟩; *also* : to achieve the sale of ⟨tried *selling* encyclopedias for a while⟩ **3 a** : to find buyers : be bought ⟨that model didn't *sell* very well⟩ **b** : to be for sale ⟨they *sell* for $15 apiece⟩ **4 a** : to make acceptable, believable, or desirable by persuasion ⟨the President couldn't *sell* the program to Congress⟩ **b** : to bring around to a favorable way of thinking ⟨tried to *sell* me on the idea⟩ **c** : to gain acceptance or approval ⟨your idea won't *sell* with them⟩ [Old English *sellan*] — **sell·able** \ˈsel-ə-bəl\ *adj* — **sell short** **1** : to make a short sale of ⟨*sell* a stock short⟩ **2** : to underestimate the ability, strength, or importance of

[2]**sell** *n* **1** : a deliberate deception : HOAX **2** : the act or a type of selling : SALESMANSHIP

sell·er \ˈsel-ər\ *n* **1** : one that offers for sale or makes a sale **2** : a product selling well or to a specified extent ⟨a good *seller*⟩

seller's market *n* : a market with few goods at relatively high prices — compare BUYER'S MARKET

sell·out \ˈsel-ˌau̇t\ *n* **1** : the act or an instance of selling out **2** : a performance or exhibition for which all seats are sold

sell out \sel-ˈau̇t, ˈsel-\ *vb* **1 a** : to dispose of one's goods by sale **b** : to sell the goods of usually to meet an obligation **2** : to betray one's cause or associates

selt·zer \ˈselt-sər\ *n* : an artificially prepared water containing carbon dioxide [German *Selterser Wasser* "water of Selters," from Nieder *Selters,* Germany]

sel·vage *or* **sel·vedge** \ˈsel-vij\ *n* : the edge of cloth so woven that it will not ravel [Middle English *selfegge, selvage,* from *self* "self" + *egge* "edge" (modeled on Dutch *selfegghe*)]

selves *plural of* SELF

se·man·tic \si-ˈmant-ik\ *adj* **1** : of or relating to meaning in language **2** : of or relating to semantics [Greek *sēmantikos* "significant," from *sēmanein* "to signify, mean," from *sēma* "sign, token"] — **se·man·ti·cal·ly** \-ˈmant-i-kə-le, -klē\ *adv*

se·man·ti·cist \si-ˈmant-ə-səst\ *n* : a specialist in semantics

se·man·tics \si-ˈmant-iks\ *n* **1** : the study of meanings **2 a** : the meaning or relationship of meaning of a word or set of words ⟨it's just a question of *semantics*⟩ **b** : the careful use of words (as in advertising or political propaganda) to achieve a desired effect on an audience

[1]**sem·a·phore** \ˈsem-ə-ˌfōr, -ˌfȯr\ *n* **1** : an apparatus for visual signaling (as by the position of one or more movable arms) **2** : a system of visual signaling by two flags held one in each hand [Greek *sēma* "sign, signal" + *-phoros* "-phore"]

[2]**semaphore** *vb* : to signal by or as if by semaphore

sem·blance \ˈsem-bləns\ *n* **1** : outward appearance or show **2 a** : one that resembles another **b** : SIMILARITY 1 [Medieval French, from *sembler* "to be like, seem," from Latin *similare* "to copy," from *similis* "like, similar"]

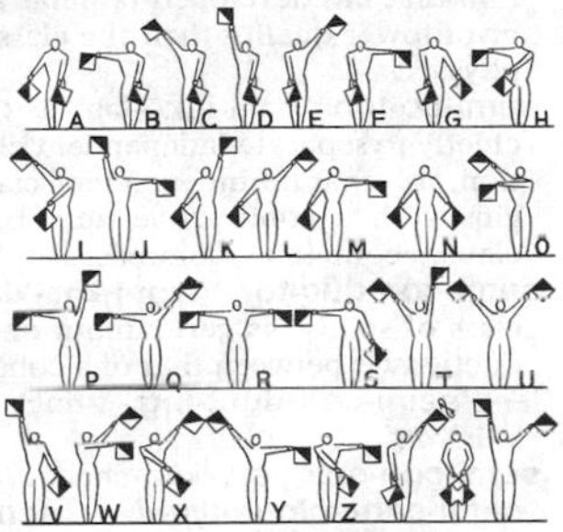

semaphore 2: alphabet; 3 positions following Z: error, end of word, numerals follow; numerals 1, 2, 3, 4, 5, 6, 7, 8, 9, 0 same as A through J

se·men \ˈsē-mən\ *n* : a sticky whitish fluid of the male reproductive tract consisting of spermatozoa suspended in secretions of accessory glands (as of the prostate and Cowper's glands) [Latin, "seed"]

se·mes·ter \sə-ˈmes-tər\ *n* : one of two usually 18-week terms into which an academic year is often divided [German, from Latin *semestris* "half-yearly," from *sex* "six" + *mensis* "month"] — **se·mes·tral** \-trəl\ *or* **se·mes·tri·al** \-trē-əl\ *adj*

semi- \ˌsem-i, ˈsem-, -ē, -ˌī\ *prefix* **1 a** : precisely half of **b** : half in quantity or value : half of or occurring halfway through a specified period of time ⟨*semi*annual⟩ ⟨*semi*centennial⟩ — compare BI- **2** : to some extent : partly : incompletely ⟨*semi*dry⟩ ⟨*semi*-independent⟩ — compare DEMI-, HEMI- **3 a** : partial : incomplete ⟨*semi*darkness⟩ **b** : having some of the characteristics of ⟨*semi*desert⟩ **c** : in some sense or degree ⟨*semi*governmental⟩ [Latin]

semi·ab·strac·tion \ˌsem-ē-ab-ˈstrak-shən, ˌsem-ˌī-\ *n* : a composition or creation (as in painting or sculpture) in which the subject matter is easily recognizable though the form is stylized — **semi·ab·stract** \-ab-ˈstrakt, -ˈab-ˌ\ *adj*

semi·an·nu·al \ˌsem-ē-ˈan-yə-wəl, ˌsem-ˌī-, -ˈan-yəl\ *adj* : occurring twice a year — **semi·an·nu·al·ly** \-ē\ *adv*

\ə\ **abut**	\au̇\ **out**	\i\ **tip**	\ȯ\ **saw**	\u̇\ **foot**
\ər\ **further**	\ch\ **chin**	\ī\ **life**	\ȯi\ **coin**	\y\ **yet**
\a\ **mat**	\e\ **pet**	\j\ **job**	\th\ **thin**	\yü\ **few**
\ā\ **take**	\ē\ **easy**	\ng\ **sing**	\t͟h\ **this**	\yu̇\ **cure**
\ä\ **cot, cart**	\g\ **go**	\ō\ **bone**	\ü\ **food**	\zh\ **vision**

semi·aquat·ic \-ə-ˈkwät-ik, -ˈkwat-\ *adj* : growing equally well in or adjacent to water ⟨*semiaquatic* plants⟩; *also* : frequenting but not living wholly in water ⟨the hippopotamus is a *semiaquatic* animal⟩
semi·ar·bo·re·al \-ˌär-ˈbōr-ē-əl, -ˈbȯr-\ *adj* : often inhabiting and frequenting trees but not completely arboreal ⟨*semiarboreal* snakes⟩
semi·ar·id \-ˈar-əd\ *adj* : characterized by light rainfall; *esp* : having from about 10 to 20 inches (25 to 51 centimeters) of annual precipitation
semi·au·to·mat·ic \-ˌȯt-ə-ˈmat-ik\ *adj* : not fully automatic — **semiautomatic** *n* — **semi·au·to·mat·i·cal·ly** \-ˈmat-i-kə-lē, -klē\ *adv*
semi·au·ton·o·mous \-ȯ-ˈtän-ə-məs\ *adj* : chiefly self-governing within a larger political or organizational entity
semi·cen·ten·a·ry \ˌsem-i-ˌsen-ˈten-ə-rē, ˌsem-ˌī-, -ˈsent-n-ˌer-ē\ *n or adj* : SEMICENTENNIAL
semi·cen·ten·ni·al \-ˌsen-ˈten-ē-əl\ *n* : a 50th anniversary or its celebration — **semicentennial** *adj*
semi·cir·cle \ˈsem-i-ˌsər-kəl\ *n* : a half of a circle — **semi·cir·cu·lar** \ˌsem-i-ˈsər-kyə-lər\ *adj*
semicircular canal *n* : any of the loop-shaped tubular parts in the inner ear of vertebrates that together constitute a sensory organ concerned with the maintenance of sense of balance
semi·civ·i·lized \ˌsem-i-ˈsiv-ə-ˌlīzd, ˌsem-ˌī-\ *adj* : partly civilized
semi·clas·si·cal \-ˈklas-i-kəl\ *adj* **1** : having some of the characteristics of the classical: as **a** : of, relating to, or being a musical composition that acts as a bridge between classical and popular music **b** : of, relating to, or being a classical composition that has developed popular appeal **2** : of less importance or of lower quality than the classical ⟨a *semiclassical* theory in physics⟩
semi·co·lon \ˈsem-i-ˌkō-lən\ *n* : a punctuation mark ; used chiefly to separate independent clauses not joined by a conjunction, to separate independent clauses the second of which begins with a conjunctive adverb, or to separate phrases and clauses containing commas
semi·con·duc·tor \ˌsem-i-kən-ˈdək-tər, ˌsem-ˌī-\ *n* : any of a class of solids (as germanium or silicon) whose electrical conductivity is between that of a conductor and that of an insulator — **semi·con·duct·ing** \-ting\ *adj* — **semi·con·duc·tive** \-tiv\ *adj*
semi·con·scious \-ˈkän-chəs\ *adj* : incompletely conscious — **semi·con·scious·ly** *adv* — **semi·con·scious·ness** *n*
semi·crys·tal·line \-ˈkris-tə-lən\ *adj* : partly crystalline
semi·dark·ness \-ˈdärk-nəs\ *n* : partial darkness
semi·des·ert \-ˈdez-ərt\ *n* : an area having some of the characteristics of a desert and often lying between a desert and grassland
semi·de·tached \-di-ˈtacht\ *adj* : forming one of a pair of residences joined into one building by a common sidewall
semi·di·vine \-də-ˈvīn\ *adj* : more than mortal but not fully divine
semi·do·mes·ti·cat·ed \-də-ˈmes-ti-ˌkāt-əd\ *adj* : of, relating to, or living in semidomestication
semi·do·mes·ti·ca·tion \-də-ˌmes-ti-ˈkā-shən\ *n* : a captive state of a wild animal in which its living conditions and often its breeding are controlled by humans
semi·dry \ˌsem-i-ˈdrī\ *adj* : fairly dry
semi·dry·ing \ˌsem-i-ˈdrī-ing\ *adj* : that dries imperfectly or slowly ⟨cottonseed oil is a *semidrying* oil⟩
[1]**semi·fi·nal** \ˌsem-i-ˈfīn-l\ *adj* **1** : being next to the last in an elimination tournament ⟨*semifinal* pairings⟩ **2** : of or participating in a semifinal
[2]**semi·fi·nal** \ˈsem-i-ˌfīn-l\ *n* : a semifinal match or round — **semi·fi·nal·ist** \ˌsem-i-ˈfīn-l-əst\ *n*
semi·fit·ted \ˌsem-i-ˈfit-əd, ˌsem-ˌī-\ *adj* : partly fitted
semi·flex·i·ble \-ˈflek-sə-bəl\ *adj* : somewhat flexible
semi·flu·id \ˌsem-i-ˈflü-əd, ˌsem-ˌī-\ *adj* : having the qualities of both a fluid and a solid : VISCOUS ⟨fluid and *semifluid* greases⟩ — **semifluid** *n*
semi·for·mal \-ˈfȯr-məl\ *adj* : being or suitable for an occasion of moderate formality ⟨a *semiformal* dinner⟩
semi·gloss \ˈsem-i-ˌgläs, ˈsem-ˌī-, -ˌglȯs\ *adj* : having a low luster ⟨*semigloss* paint⟩
semi·gov·ern·men·tal \ˌsem-i-ˌgəv-ər-ˈment-l, ˌsem-ˌī-, -ˌgəv-ərn-ˈment-l\ *adj* : having some governmental functions and powers
semi·hard \-ˈhärd\ *adj* : moderately hard
semi·hol·i·day \ˌsem-i-ˈhäl-ə-ˌdā, ˌsem-ˌī-\ *n* : a weekday during a religious festival (as Passover) on which ceremonial observances continue but activities forbidden on full festival days are permitted though discouraged
semi–in·de·pend·ent \ˌsem-ē-ˌin-də-ˈpen-dənt, ˌsem-ˌī-\ *adj* : partially independent; *esp* : SEMIAUTONOMOUS
semi·leg·end·ary \ˌsem-i-ˈlej-ən-ˌder-ē, ˌsem-ˌī-\ *adj* : elaborated in legend but having a possible historical existence
semi·liq·uid \ˌsem-i-ˈlik-wəd, ˌsem-ˌī-\ *adj* : having the qualities of both a liquid and a solid : SEMIFLUID ⟨*semiliquid* ice cream⟩ — **semiliquid** *n*
semi·lit·er·ate \-ˈlit-ə-rət, -ˈli-trət\ *adj* **1** : able to read and write on an elementary level **2** : able to read but unable to write
semi·log·a·rith·mic \-ˌlȯg-ə-ˈrith-mik, -ˌläg-\ *also* **semi·log** \ˈsem-i-ˌlȯg, ˈsem-ˌī-, -ˌläg\ *adj* : having one axis with a logarithmic scale and the other with an arithmetic scale ⟨*semilogarithmic* graph paper⟩
semi·lu·nar \ˌsem-i-ˈlü-nər, ˌsem-ˌī-\ *adj* : shaped like a crescent
semilunar valve *n* : either of two heart valves of which one occurs between the heart and the aorta and the other between the heart and pulmonary artery and that consist of three crescent-shaped flaps that prevent backward flow of blood into the ventricles
semi·lus·trous \ˌsem-i-ˈləs-trəs, ˌsem-ˌī-\ *adj* : slightly lustrous
semi·mat *or* **semi·matt** *or* **semi·matte** \ˌsem-i-ˈmat, ˌsem-ˌī-\ *adj* : having little luster
semi·moist \-ˈmȯist\ *adj* : slightly moist
semi·mo·nas·tic \-mə-ˈnas-tik\ *adj* : having some features characteristic of a monastic order
[1]**semi·month·ly** \-ˈmənth-lē, -ˈmən*t*th-\ *adj* : done, appearing, or occurring twice a month
[2]**semimonthly** *n* : a semimonthly publication
[3]**semimonthly** *adv* : twice a month
semi·mys·ti·cal \-ˈmis-ti-kəl\ *adj* : having some of the qualities of mysticism
sem·i·nal \ˈsem-ən-l\ *adj* **1** : of, relating to, or consisting of seed or semen **2** : having the character of a creative power, principle, or source : containing or contributing the seeds of later development [Latin *seminalis,* from *semin-, semen* "seed"] — **semi·nal·ly** \-l-ē\ *adv*
seminal vesicle *n* : a pouch on either side of the male reproductive tract secretes a sugar- and protein-containing fluid into the ejaculatory duct
sem·i·nar \ˈsem-ə-ˌnär\ *n* **1** : a course of study pursued by a group of advanced students doing original research under a professor and exchanging results and discussions **2** : a meeting of a seminar or a room for such meetings [German, from Latin *seminarium* "seedbed"]
sem·i·nar·i·an \ˌsem-ə-ˈner-ē-ən\ *n* : a student in a seminary especially of the Roman Catholic Church
sem·i·nary \ˈsem-ə-ˌner-ē\ *n, pl* **-nar·ies** **1** : an institution of secondary education; *esp* : an academy for girls **2** : an institution for training clergymen [Latin *seminarium* "seedbed," from *semin-, semen* "seed"]
sem·i·nif·er·ous \ˌsem-ə-ˈnif-rəs, -ə-rəs\ *adj* : producing or bearing seed or semen [Latin *semin-, semen* "seed" + English *-iferous*]
seminiferous tubule *n* : any of the coiled threadlike tubules that make up the bulk of the testis and are lined with a layer of epithelial cells from which the spermatozoa are produced
Sem·i·nole \ˈsem-ə-ˌnōl\ *n* : a member of an American Indian people of what is now Florida [Creek *simalóni, simanóli* "untamed, wild," from American Spanish *cimarrón*]
semi·no·mad \ˌsem-i-ˈnō-ˌmad, ˌsem-ˌī-\ *n* : a member of a people living usually in portable or temporary dwellings and practicing seasonal migration but having a base camp at which some crops are cultivated — **semi·no·mad·ic** \-nō-ˈmad-ik\ *adj*
semi·of·fi·cial \ˌsem-ē-ə-ˈfish-əl, ˌsem-ˌī-\ *adj* : having some official authority or standing ⟨a *semiofficial* statement⟩ — **semi·of·fi·cial·ly** \-ˈfish-lē, -ə-lē\ *adv*
semi·opaque \-ō-ˈpāk\ *adj* : nearly opaque
semi·pal·mat·ed \ˌsem-i-ˈpal-ˌmāt-əd, ˌsem-ˌī-, -ˈpäm-ˌāt-, -ˈpäl-ˌmāt-\ *adj* : having the toes joined only part way down with a web ⟨a plover with *semipalmated* feet⟩
semi·per·ma·nent \-ˈpər-mə-nənt\ *adj* **1** : permanent in some respects **2** : lasting for an indefinite time
semi·per·me·able \-ˈpər-mē-ə-bəl\ *adj* : partially but not freely

or wholly permeable; *esp* : permeable to some usually small molecules but not to other usually larger particles ⟨a *semipermeable* membrane⟩ — **semi·per·me·abil·i·ty** \-ˌpər-me-ə-ˈbil-ət-ē\ *n*

semi·po·lit·i·cal \-pə-ˈlit-i-kəl\ *adj* : of, relating to, or involving some political features or activity

semi·post·al \-ˈpōs-tl\ *n* : a postage stamp sold (as for various humanitarian purposes) at a premium over its postal value

semi·pre·cious \-ˈpresh-əs\ *adj* : of less commercial value than a precious stone ⟨*semiprecious* gemstones⟩

semi·pri·vate \-ˈprī-vət\ *adj* : shared with one other or a few others ⟨a *semiprivate* room in a hospital⟩

semi·pro \ˈsem-i-ˌprō, ˈsem-ˌī-\ *adj or n* : SEMIPROFESSIONAL

semi·pro·fes·sion·al \ˌsem-i-prə-ˈfesh-nəl, -ən-l, ˌsem-ˌī-\ *adj* 1 : engaging in an activity for pay or gain but not as a full-time occupation 2 : engaged in by semiprofessional players ⟨*semiprofessional* baseball⟩ — **semiprofessional** *n* — **semi·pro·fes·sion·al·ly** \-ē\ *adv*

semi·pub·lic \-ˈpəb-lik\ *adj* 1 : having some features of a public institution; *esp* : maintained as a public service by a private nonprofit organization 2 : open to some persons outside the regular membership

semi·re·li·gious \-ri-ˈlij-əs\ *adj* : somewhat religious in character

semi·rig·id \-ˈrij-əd\ *adj* 1 : rigid to some degree or in some parts 2 : having a flexible cylindrical gas container with an attached stiffening keel that carries the load ⟨*semirigid* airships⟩

semi·sa·cred \-ˈsā-krəd\ *adj* : SEMIRELIGIOUS

semi·skilled \ˌsem-i-ˈskild, ˌsem-ˌī-\ *adj* : having or requiring less training than skilled labor and more than unskilled labor

semi·soft \-ˈsȯft\ *adj* : fairly soft; *esp* : firm but easily cut ⟨*semisoft* cheese⟩

semi·sol·id \-ˈsäl-əd\ *adj* : having the qualities of both a solid and a liquid ⟨jelly is *semisolid*⟩ — **semisolid** *n*

semi·sweet \-ˈswēt\ *adj* : slightly sweetened ⟨*semisweet* chocolate⟩

semi·syn·thet·ic \-sin-ˈthet-ik\ *adj* : produced by chemical alteration of a natural starting material ⟨*semisynthetic* penicillins⟩

Sem·ite \ˈsem-ˌīt\ *n* 1 a : a member of any of a number of peoples of ancient southwestern Asia including the Akkadians, Phoenicians, Hebrews, and Arabs b : a descendant of these peoples 2 : a member of a modern people speaking a Semitic language [French *sémite,* from *Sem* "Shem (eldest son of Noah)," from Late Latin, from Greek *Sēm,* from Hebrew *Shēm*]

semi·ter·res·tri·al \ˌsem-i-tə-ˈres-trē-əl, ˌsem-ˌī-, -ˈres-chəl, -ˈresh-chəl\ *adj* 1 : growing on boggy ground ⟨*semiterrestrial* plants⟩ 2 : frequenting but not living wholly on land ⟨a *semiterrestrial* crab⟩

[1]**Se·mit·ic** \sə-ˈmit-ik\ *adj* 1 : of, relating to, or characteristic of the Semites; *esp* : JEWISH 2 : of, relating to, or constituting a branch of the Afro-Asiatic language family that includes Hebrew, Aramaic, Arabic, and Ethiopic

[2]**Semitic** *n* : any or all of the Semitic languages

Sem·i·tism \ˈsem-ə-ˌtiz-əm\ *n* 1 a : Semitic character or qualities b : a Semitic idiom or expression 2 : policy favorable to Jews : predisposition in favor of Jews

semi·ton·al \ˌsem-i-ˈtōn-l, ˌsem-ˌī-\ *adj* : CHROMATIC 2, SEMITONIC — **semi·ton·al·ly** \-l-ē\ *adv*

semi·tone \ˈsem-i-ˌtōn, ˈsem-ˌī-\ *n* : the tone at a half step; *also* : HALF STEP — **semi·ton·ic** \ˌsem-i-ˈtän-ik, ˌsem-ˌī-\ *adj* — **semi·ton·i·cal·ly** \-ˈtän-i-kə-lē, -klē\ *adv*

semi·trail·er \ˈsem-i-ˌtrā-lər, ˈsem-ˌī-\ *n* : a freight trailer that in use is supported at its forward end by the truck tractor; *also* : a semitrailer with attached tractor

semi·trans·lu·cent \ˌsem-i-ˌtrans-ˈlüs-nt, ˌsem-ˌī-, -ˌtranz-\ *adj* : partly translucent

semi·trans·par·ent \-ˈpar-ənt, -ˈper-\ *adj* : imperfectly transparent — **semi·trans·par·en·cy** \-ən-sē\ *n*

semi·trop·i·cal \-ˈträp-i-kəl\ *also* **semi·trop·ic** \-ik\ *adj* : SUBTROPICAL

semi·trop·ics \-ˈträp-iks\ *n pl* : SUBTROPICS

[1]**semi·week·ly** \-ˈwē-klē\ *adj* : done, appearing, or occurring twice a week — **semiweekly** *adv*

[2]**semiweekly** *n* : a semiweekly publication

semi·works \ˈsem-i-ˌwərks, ˈsem-ˌī-\ *n pl* : a manufacturing plant operating on a limited commercial scale to provide final tests of a new product or process

semi·year·ly \ˌsem-i-ˈyiər-lē, ˌsem-ˌī-\ *adj* : done, appearing, or occurring twice a year

sem·o·li·na \ˌsem-ə-ˈlē-nə\ *n* : a grainy powder milled from hard wheat (as durum) and often used to make pasta (as macaroni or spaghetti) [Italian *semolino,* from *semola* "bran," from Latin *simila* "finest wheat flour"]

sem·per·vi·vum \ˌsem-pər-ˈvī-vəm\ *n* : any of a genus of Old World fleshy herbs related to the orpine and often grown as ornamentals [New Latin, from Latin *sempervivus* "ever-living," from *semper* "ever" + *vivus* "living"]

sem·pi·ter·nal \ˌsem-pi-ˈtərn-l\ *adj* : of never-ending duration : ETERNAL [Late Latin *sempiternalis,* from Latin *sempiternus,* from *semper* "ever, always"] — **sem·pi·ter·nal·ly** \-l-ē\ *adv* — **sem·pi·ter·ni·ty** \-ˈtər-nət-ē\ *n*

sem·pre \ˈsem-prā\ *adv* : ALWAYS — used in music directions [Italian, from Latin *semper*]

sempstress *variant of* SEAMSTRESS

[1]**sen** \ˈsen\ *n, pl* **sen** 1 : a Japanese monetary unit equal to 1/100 yen 2 : an old coin representing one sen [Japanese]

[2]**sen** *n, pl* **sen** 1 : a monetary unit equal to 1/100 ringgit or 1/100 rupiah 2 : a coin representing one sen [Malay, probably from English *cent*]

sen·ate \ˈsen-ət\ *n* 1 a : the supreme council of the ancient Roman republic and empire b : the higher chamber in some bicameral legislatures 2 : the hall or chamber in which a senate meets 3 : a governing body of some universities charged with maintaining academic standards and regulations [Medieval French *senat,* from Latin *senatus,* from *senex* "old, old man"]

sen·a·tor \ˈsen-ət-ər\ *n* : a member of a senate — **sen·a·tor·ship** \-ˌship\ *n*

sen·a·to·ri·al \ˌsen-ə-ˈtōr-ē-əl, -ˈtȯr-\ *adj* : of, relating to, or befitting a senator or a senate ⟨*senatorial* office⟩ ⟨*senatorial* rank⟩

senatorial courtesy *n* : a custom of the U.S. Senate of refusing to confirm a presidential appointment of an official in or from a state when the appointment is opposed by the senators or senior senator of the president's party from that state

send \ˈsend\ *vb* **sent** \ˈsent\; **send·ing** 1 : to cause to go : DISPATCH ⟨*sent* the student home⟩ ⟨*send* a message⟩; *esp* : to drive or propel physically ⟨*sent* the ball into right field⟩ 2 : to cause to happen ⟨whatever fate may *send*⟩ 3 : to have an agent, order, or request go or be transmitted ⟨*send* out for coffee⟩ ⟨*sent* for their price list⟩; *esp* : to transmit an order or request to come or return ⟨the principal *sent* for me⟩ 4 : to put or bring into a certain condition ⟨the request *sent* them into a tizzy⟩ [Old English *sendan*] — **send·er** *n* — **send packing** : to send off roughly or in disgrace

send–off \ˈsen-ˌdȯf\ *n* : a demonstration of goodwill and enthusiasm for the beginning of a new venture (as a trip)

Sen·e·ca \ˈsen-i-kə\ *n, pl* **Seneca** *or* **Senecas** : a member of an Iroquoian people of what is now western New York [Dutch *Sennecaas* "the Seneca, Oneida, Onondaga, and Cayuga people"]

sen·e·schal \ˈsen-ə-shəl\ *n* : an agent or bailiff who managed a lord's estate in feudal times [Medieval French, of Germanic origin]

se·nes·cence \si-ˈnes-ns\ *n* 1 : the process of growing old 2 : the state of being old [Latin *senescens,* present participle of *senescere* "to grow old," from *senex* "old"] — **se·nesce** \si-ˈnes\ *vi* — **se·nes·cent** \-nt\ *adj*

se·nhor \si-ˈnyōr, -ˈnyȯr\ *n, pl* **senhors** *or* **se·nho·res** \-ˈnyōr-ēs, -ˈnyȯr-, -ēsh, -ēz, -ēzh\ : a Portuguese or Brazilian man — used as a title equivalent to *Mr.* [Portuguese, from Medieval Latin *senior* "lord, superior," from Latin, adj., "senior"]

se·nho·ra \si-ˈnyōr-ə, -ˈnyȯr-\ *n* : a married Portuguese or Brazilian woman — used as a title equivalent to *Mrs.* [Portuguese, feminine of *senhor*]

se·nho·ri·ta \ˌsē-nyə-ˈrēt-ə\ *n* : an unmarried Portuguese or Brazilian woman or girl — used as a title equivalent to *Miss* [Portuguese, from *senhora*]

se·nile \ˈsēn-ˌīl *also* ˈsen-\ *adj* : of, relating to, or characteristic of old age ⟨*senile* weakness⟩; *esp* : exhibiting a loss of mental abilities (as memory) that is associated with old age [Latin *senilis,* from *senex* "old, old man"] — **se·nile·ly** \-ˌīl-lē\ *adv*

se•nil•i•ty \si-ˈnil-ət-ē\ *n* : the quality or state of being senile; *esp* : the physical and mental weakness of old age

[1]**se•nior** \ˈsē-nyər\ *n* **1** : a person older or of higher rank than another **2** : a student in the last year before graduating from a school of secondary or higher level [Latin, from *senior,* adj.]

[2]**senior** *adj* **1 a** : OLDER — used chiefly to distinguish a father with the same given name as his son and usually placed in its abbreviated form after a surname ⟨John M. Doe, *Sr.*⟩ **b** : having reached the age of retirement ⟨*senior* citizens⟩ **2** : higher in standing or rank ⟨*senior* partner⟩ **3** : of or relating to seniors ⟨the *senior* class⟩ [Latin, "older, elder, senior," comparative of *senex* "old"]

senior airman *n* : a rank in the air force comparable to sergeant that is usually held temporarily by an airman before being appointed sergeant

senior chief petty officer *n* : an enlisted rank in the navy and coast guard above chief petty officer and below master chief petty officer

senior high school *n* : a school usually including grades 10-12

se•nior•i•ty \sēn-ˈyȯr-ət-ē, -ˈyär-\ *n* **1** : the quality or state of being senior **2** : a privileged status attained by length of service

senior master sergeant *n* : an enlisted rank in the air force above master sergeant and below chief master sergeant

sen•na \ˈsen-ə\ *n* **1** : CASSIA 2; *esp* : one used medicinally **2** : the dried leaflets of various cassias used as a strong laxative [Arabic *sanā*]

sen•net \ˈsen-ət\ *n* : a signal call on a trumpet or cornet for entrance or exit on the stage [probably from obsolete *signet* "signal"]

sen•night *also* **se'n•night** \ˈsen-ˌīt\ *n, archaic* : one week [Old English *seofon nihta* "seven nights"]

sen•nit \ˈsen-ət\ *n* **1** : a braided cord or fabric of plaited rope yarns or other small stuff **2** : a straw or grass braid for hats [origin unknown]

se•nor *or* **se•ñor** \sān-ˈyȯr\ *n, pl* **senors** *or* **se•ño•res** \-ˈyōr-ās, -ˈyȯr-\ : a Spanish or Spanish-speaking man — used as a title equivalent to *Mr.* [Spanish *señor,* from Medieval Latin *senior* "superior, lord," from Latin, adj., "senior"]

se•no•ra *or* **se•ño•ra** \sān-ˈyōr-ə, -ˈyȯr-\ *n* : a married Spanish or Spanish-speaking woman — used as a title equivalent to *Mrs.* [Spanish *señora,* feminine of *señor*]

se•no•ri•ta *or* **se•ño•ri•ta** \ˌsān-yə-ˈrēt-ə\ *n* : an unmarried Spanish or Spanish-speaking girl or woman — used as a title equivalent to *Miss* [Spanish *señorita,* from *señora*]

sen•sa•tion \sen-ˈsā-shən, sən-\ *n* **1 a** : a mental process (as seeing, hearing, or smelling) resulting from external stimulation of a sense organ **b** : awareness (as of heat or pain) due to stimulation of a sense organ **c** : an indefinite bodily feeling ⟨a *sensation* of buoyancy⟩ **2** : something that causes or is the object of sensation **3 a** : a state of excited interest or feeling **b** : a cause of such excitement ⟨the play was a *sensation*⟩

sen•sa•tion•al \-shnəl, -shən-l\ *adj* **1** : of or relating to sensation or the senses **2** : arousing or tending to arouse (as by lurid details) an intense and usually superficial interest or emotional reaction ⟨*sensational* news⟩ **3** : exceedingly or unexpectedly excellent or great ⟨a *sensational* diving catch⟩ — **sen•sa•tion•al•ly** \-ē\ *adv*

sen•sa•tion•al•ism \-ˌiz-əm\ *n* : the use or effect of sensational subject matter or treatment — **sen•sa•tion•al•ist** \-əst\ *n* — **sen•sa•tion•al•is•tic** \-ˌsā-shnəl-ˈis-tik, -shən-l-\ *adj*

[1]**sense** \ˈsens\ *n* **1** : a meaning conveyed or intended; *esp* : one of the meanings a word may bear **2 a** : the power to become aware of by means of sense organs **b** : a specialized function or mechanism (as sight, hearing, smell, taste, or touch) of the body that involves the action and effect of a stimulus on a sense organ **c** : the sensory mechanisms constituting a unit distinct from other functions (as movement or thought) **3** : conscious awareness or rationality ⟨finally came to his *senses*⟩ **4 a** : a particular sensation or kind or quality of sensation ⟨a good *sense* of balance⟩ **b** : a definite but often vague awareness ⟨a *sense* of danger⟩ **c** : intellectual appreciation ⟨a *sense* of humor⟩ **5** : INTELLIGENCE 1a, JUDGMENT; *esp* : good judgment **6** : one of two opposite directions describable by the motion of a point, line, or surface [Medieval French *sen, sens,* from Latin *sensus* "sensation, feeling, meaning," from *sentire* "to perceive, feel"] ***synonyms*** see MEANING

[2]**sense** *vt* **1 a** : to perceive by the senses **b** : to be or become conscious of ⟨*sense* danger⟩ **2** : UNDERSTAND 1 **3** : to detect automatically especially in response to a physical stimulus (as light or movement)

sense•less \ˈsen-sləs\ *adj* : destitute of, deficient in, or contrary to sense: as **a** : UNCONSCIOUS ⟨knocked *senseless*⟩ **b** : FOOLISH, STUPID **c** : MEANINGLESS, PURPOSELESS ⟨a *senseless* act⟩ — **sense•less•ly** *adv* — **sense•less•ness** *n*

sense organ *n* : a bodily structure that receives a stimulus (as heat or sound waves) and is affected in such a manner as to initiate excitation of associated sensory nerve fibers which convey impulses to the central nervous system where they are interpreted as corresponding sensations

sen•si•bil•i•ty \ˌsen-sə-ˈbil-ət-ē\ *n, pl* **-ties** **1** : ability to receive sensations : SENSITIVITY ⟨tactile *sensibility*⟩ **2** : peculiar susceptibility to a pleasurable or painful impression (as praise or a slight) — often used in plural **3** : awareness of and responsiveness toward something (as emotion in another) **4** : refined sensitiveness in emotion and taste

sen•si•ble \ˈsen-sə-bəl\ *adj* **1 a** : capable of being perceived by the senses or by reason or understanding **b** : perceptibly large : CONSIDERABLE ⟨a *sensible* error⟩ **2** : capable of receiving sense impressions ⟨*sensible* to pain⟩ **3** : COGNIZANT, AWARE **4** : having or containing good sense or reason : REASONABLE ⟨a *sensible* arrangement⟩ ***synonyms*** see WISE — **sen•si•ble•ness** *n* — **sen•si•bly** \-blē\ *adv*

sen•si•tive \ˈsen-sət-iv, ˈsen-stiv\ *adj* **1** : capable of being stimulated or excited by external agents **2 a** : easily or strongly affected or hurt ⟨a *sensitive* child⟩ **b** : excessively or abnormally susceptible : HYPERSENSITIVE ⟨*sensitive* to egg protein⟩ **3 a** : capable of indicating minute differences : DELICATE ⟨*sensitive* scales⟩ **b** : readily affected or changed by various agents or causes (as light or mechanical shock) **4** : concerned with or involving highly classified government information ⟨appointed to a *sensitive* government post⟩ [Medieval French, from Medieval Latin *sensitivus,* derived from Latin *sentire* "to feel"] — **sen•si•tive•ly** *adv* — **sen•si•tive•ness** *n*

sensitive fern *n* : a common fern with fronds very susceptible to frost injury

sensitive plant *n* : any of several mimosas having leaves that fold or droop when touched

sen•si•tiv•i•ty \ˌsen-sə-ˈtiv-ət-ē\ *n, pl* **-ties** : the quality or state of being sensitive: as **a** : the capacity of an organism or sense organ to respond to stimulation : IRRITABILITY **b** : the quality or state of being hypersensitive **c** : the degree to which a radio receiving set responds to incoming waves

sen•si•tize \ˈsen-sə-ˌtīz\ *vb* : to make or become sensitive or hypersensitive — **sen•si•ti•za•tion** \ˌsen-sət-ə-ˈzā-shən\ *n* — **sen•si•tiz•er** \ˈsen-sə-ˌtī-zər\ *n*

sen•si•tom•e•ter \ˌsen-sə-ˈtäm-ət-ər\ *n* : an instrument for measuring sensitivity of photographic material — **sen•si•to•met•ric** \ˌsen-sət-ə-ˈme-trik\ *adj* — **sen•si•tom•e•try** \ˌsen-sə-ˈtäm-ə-trē\ *n*

sen•sor \ˈsen-ˌsȯr, ˈsen-sər\ *n* : a device that responds to a physical stimulus (as heat or light) and transmits a resulting impulse (as for operating a control)

sen•so•ri•mo•tor \ˌsens-rē-ˈmōt-ər, -ə-rē-\ *adj* : of, relating to, or functioning in both sensory and motor aspects of bodily activity ⟨*sensorimotor* skills⟩

sen•so•ry \ˈsens-rē, -ə-rē\ *adj* **1** : of or relating to sensation or to the senses ⟨*sensory* stimulation⟩ **2** : conveying nerve impulses from the sense organs toward or to the brain : AFFERENT

sensory neuron *n* : a neuron that transmits nerve impulses from a sense organ (as an eye or nose) toward the central nervous system — compare MOTOR NEURON

sen•su•al \ˈsench-wəl, -ə-wəl; ˈsen-shəl\ *adj* **1** : SENSORY 1 **2** : relating to or consisting in the gratification of the senses or the indulgence of appetite **3 a** : devoted to or preoccupied with the senses or appetites **b** : VOLUPTUOUS 1 **c** : deficient in moral, spiritual, or intellectual interests : WORLDLY; *esp* : IRRELIGIOUS [Late Latin *sensualis,* from Latin *sensus* "sense"] — **sen•su•al•i•ty** \ˌsen-chə-ˈwal-ət-ē\ *n* — **sen•su•al•ly** \ˈsench-wə-lē, -ə-wə-; ˈsen-shə-lē\ *adv*

sen•su•al•ism \ˈsench-wə-ˌliz-əm, -ə-wə-, ˈsen-shə-ˌliz-\ *n* : persistent pursuit of sensual pleasures — **sen•su•al•ist** \-ləst\ *n* — **sen•su•al•is•tic** \ˌsench-wə-ˈlis-tik, -ə-wə-; ˌsen-shə-ˈlis-\ *adj*

sen•su•al•ize \ˈsench-wə-ˌlīz, -ə-wə-; ˈsen-shə-ˌlīz\ *vt* : to make sensual — **sen•su•al•i•za•tion** \ˌsench-wə-lə-ˈzā-shən, -ə-wə-; ˌsen-shə-lə-\ *n*

sen•su•ous \ˈsench-wəs, -ə-wəs\ *adj* **1 a** : of or relating to the senses **b** : having strong sensory appeal ⟨*sensuous* pleasure⟩

2 : characterized by sense impressions or imagery aimed at the senses ⟨*sensuous* description⟩ **3** : highly susceptible to influence through the senses — **sen·su·ous·ly** *adv* — **sen·su·ous·ness** *n*

sent *past of* SEND

¹sen·tence \ˈsent-ns, -nz\ *n* **1 a** : JUDGMENT 2a; *esp* : one formally pronounced by a court in a criminal proceeding and specifying the punishment to be inflicted **b** : the punishment so imposed ⟨serve a *sentence* for robbery⟩ **2** *archaic* : AXIOM 1 **3 a** : a grammatically self-contained speech unit that expresses an assertion, a question, a command, a wish, or an exclamation, that in writing usually begins with a capital letter and concludes with appropriate end punctuation, and that in speaking is phonetically distinguished by various patterns of stress, pitch, and pauses **b** : a mathematical or logical statement (as an equation or a proposition) in words or symbols [Medieval French, from Latin *sententia* "feeling, opinion," derived from *sentire* "to feel"] — **sen·ten·tial** \sen-ˈten-chəl\ *adj* — **sen·ten·tial·ly** \-chə-lē\ *adv*

²sentence *vt* **1** : to pronounce sentence on **2** : to condemn to a specified punishment

sentence fragment *n* : a word, phrase, or clause that lacks the grammatically self-contained structure of a sentence but has in speech the intonation of a sentence and is written and punctuated as if it were a complete sentence

sentence stress *n* : the manner in which stresses are distributed on the syllables of words assembled into sentences — called also *sentence accent*

sen·ten·tious \sen-ˈten-chəs\ *adj* **1** : being concise and forceful : PITHY **2** : containing, using, or inclined to use high-sounding empty phrases or pompous sayings [Latin *sententiosus*, from *sententia* "sentence, maxim, feeling"] — **sen·ten·tious·ly** *adv* — **sen·ten·tious·ness** *n*

sen·tient \ˈsen-chē-ənt, -chənt\ *adj* : capable of feeling : conscious of sense impressions ⟨the lowest of *sentient* creatures⟩ [Latin *sentiens*, present participle of *sentire* "to feel"] — **sen·tience** \-chē-ənts, -chəns\ *n* — **sen·tient·ly** *adv*

sen·ti·ment \ˈsent-ə-mənt\ *n* **1 a** : an attitude, thought, or judgment prompted by feeling **b** : a specific view or notion : OPINION **2 a** : EMOTION 2 **b** : refined feeling : delicate sensibility **c** : emotional idealism **d** : a romantic or nostalgic feeling [Medieval Latin *sentimentum*, from Latin *sentire* "to feel"] ***synonyms*** see FEELING

sen·ti·men·tal \ˌsent-ə-ˈment-l\ *adj* **1 a** : marked or governed by feeling, sensibility, or emotional idealism **b** : resulting from feeling rather than reason or thought **2** : having an excess or affectation of sentiment or sensibility — **sen·ti·men·tal·ly** \-l-ē\ *adv*

sen·ti·men·tal·ism \-l-ˌiz-əm\ *n* **1** : the disposition to favor or indulge in sentiment **2** : SENTIMENTALITY 2 — **sen·ti·men·tal·ist** \-l-əst\ *n*

sen·ti·men·tal·i·ty \ˌsent-ə-ˌmen-ˈtal-ət-ē, -mən-\ *n, pl* **-ties 1** : the quality or state of being sentimental especially to excess or in affectation **2** : a sentimental idea or its expression

sen·ti·men·tal·ize \-ˈment-l-ˌīz\ *vb* **1** : to indulge in sentiment **2** : to look upon or imbue with sentiment — **sen·ti·men·tal·i·za·tion** \-ˌment-l-ə-ˈzā-shən\ *n*

¹sen·ti·nel \ˈsent-nəl, -n-əl\ *n* : one that watches or guards [Middle French *sentinelle*, from Italian *sentinella*, from *sentina* "vigilance," from *sentire* "to perceive," from Latin]

²sentinel *vt* **-neled** *or* **-nelled; -nel·ing** *or* **-nel·ling 1** : to watch over as a sentinel **2** : to furnish with a sentinel **3** : to post as sentinel

sen·try \ˈsen-trē\ *n, pl* **sentries** : GUARD, WATCH; *esp* : a soldier standing guard at a point of passage [perhaps from obsolete *sentry* "sanctuary, watchtower"]

sentry box *n* : a shelter for a sentry on duty

se·pal \ˈsēp-əl, ˈsep-\ *n* : one of the modified leaves that form the calyx of a flower [New Latin *sepalum*, derived from Greek *skepē* "covering"]

sep·a·ra·ble \ˈsep-rə-bəl, -ə-rə-\ *adj* : capable of being separated or distinguished — **sep·a·ra·bil·i·ty** \ˌsep-rə-ˈbil-ət-ē, -ə-rə-\ *n* — **sep·a·ra·ble·ness** \ˈsep-rə-bəl-nəs, -ə-rə-\ *n*

¹sep·a·rate \ˈsep-ə-ˌrāt, ˈsep-ˌrāt\ *vb* **1 a** : to set or keep apart : DISCONNECT **b** : to keep distinct in the mind : DISTINGUISH ⟨*separate* religion from magic⟩ **c** : SORT ⟨*separate* mail⟩ **d** : to disperse in space or time : SCATTER ⟨widely *separated* homesteads⟩ **2** : to release officially : DISCHARGE ⟨was *separated* from the army⟩ **3** : to block off : SEGREGATE **4** : to isolate or become isolated from a mixture ⟨*separate* cream from milk⟩ **5** : to become divided or detached : come apart **6 a** : to break off an association : WITHDRAW **b** : to cease to be or live together especially as husband and wife **7** : to go in different directions [Latin *separare*, from *se-* "apart" + *parare* "to prepare, procure"]

synonyms SEPARATE, DIVIDE, SEVER mean to break or keep apart. SEPARATE may imply any one of several ways or causes such as dispersion, removal of one from others, or presence of an intervening thing ⟨a fence *separates* the yard⟩. DIVIDE implies separating by cutting or breaking into pieces or sections ⟨*divide* the pie into six equal servings⟩. SEVER implies violence especially in the removal of a part or member ⟨a *severed* limb⟩.

²sep·a·rate \ˈsep-rət, -ə-rət\ *adj* **1** : set or kept apart : DETACHED **2** : not shared with another : INDIVIDUAL ⟨*separate* rooms⟩ **3 a** : existing by itself **b** : dissimilar in nature or identity ⟨the *separate* pieces of a puzzle⟩ — **sep·a·rate·ly** \-rət-lē, ˈsep-ərt-lē\ *adv* — **sep·a·rate·ness** \-rət-nəs\ *n*

³sep·a·rate \ˈsep-rət, -ə-rət\ *n* : an article of dress designed to be worn interchangeably with others to form various costume combinations

sep·a·ra·tion \ˌsep-ə-ˈrā-shən\ *n* **1** : the act or process of separating : the state of being separated **2 a** : a point, line, or means of division **b** : an intervening space : GAP **3 a** : a formal separating of husband and wife by agreement but without divorce **b** : termination of a contractual relationship (as employment or military service)

sep·a·rat·ist \ˈsep-rət-əst, -ə-rət-\ *n, often cap* : one that favors separation: as **a** *cap* : one of a group of 16th and 17th century English Protestants preferring to separate from rather than to reform the Church of England **b** : an advocate of independence or autonomy for a part of a nation — **sep·a·rat·ism** \-rə-ˌtiz-əm\ *n* — **separatist** *adj, often cap* — **sep·a·ra·tis·tic** \ˌsep-rə-ˈtis-tik, -ə-rə-\ *adj*

sep·a·ra·tive \ˈsep-ə-ˌrāt-iv, ˈsep-rət-, ˈsep-ə-rət-\ *adj* : tending toward, causing, or expressing separation

sep·a·ra·tor \ˈsep-ə-ˌrāt-ər\ *n* : one that separates; *esp* : a device for separating liquids (as cream from milk) of different specific gravities or liquids from solids — compare CENTRIFUGE

Se·phar·di \sə-ˈfärd-ē\ *n, pl* **Se·phar·dim** \-ˈfärd-əm\ : a member of one of the two great divisions of Jews comprising the occidental branch of European Jews settling in Spain and Portugal — compare ASHKENAZI [Hebrew *sĕphāradhī*, from *Sĕphāradh* "Spain," from *sĕphāradh*, a region where Jews were once exiled (Obadiah 1:20)] — **Se·phar·dic** \-ˈfärd-ik\ *adj*

¹se·pia \ˈsē-pē-ə\ *n* **1** : a brown pigment from the ink of cuttlefishes **2** : a brownish gray to dark olive brown [Latin, "cuttlefish, ink," from Greek *sēpia*]

²sepia *adj* **1** : of the color sepia **2** : made of or done in sepia ⟨*sepia* print⟩

se·poy \ˈsē-ˌpȯi\ *n* : a native of India employed as a soldier by a European power [Portuguese *sipai*, from Hindi & Urdu *sipāhī*, from Persian, "cavalryman"]

sep·sis \ˈsep-səs\ *n, pl* **sep·ses** \ˈsep-ˌsēz\ : a poisoned condition resulting from the spread of bacteria or their poisonous products from a center of infection; *esp* : BLOOD POISONING [Greek *sēpsis* "decay," from *sēpein* "to make putrid"]

sep·tate \ˈsep-ˌtāt\ *adj* : divided by or having a septum

Sep·tem·ber \sep-ˈtem-bər, səp-\ *n* : the 9th month of the year according to the Gregorian calendar [Medieval French *septembre*, from Latin *September*, from *septem* "seven"; from its having been originally the 7th month of the Roman calendar]

sep·ten·ni·al \sep-ˈten-ē-əl\ *adj* **1** : consisting of or lasting for seven years **2** : occurring or being done every seven years [Late Latin *septennium* "period of 7 years," from Latin *septem* "seven" + *-ennium* (as in *biennium* "biennium")] — **sep·ten·ni·al·ly** \-ē-ə-lē\ *adv*

sep·tet *also* **sep·tette** \sep-ˈtet\ *n* **1** : a musical composition for seven instruments or voices **2** : a group or set of seven [German *Septet*, from Latin *septem* "seven"]

sep·tic \ˈsep-tik\ *adj* **1** : of, relating to, or causing putrefaction **2** : relating to, involving, caused by, or affected with sepsis ⟨*sep-*

tic patients⟩ **3 :** relating to or used for sewage treatment and disposal ⟨a *septic* system⟩ [Latin *septicus,* from Greek *sēptikos,* from *sēpein* "to make putrid"]

sep·ti·ce·mia \ˌsep-tə-ˈsē-mē-ə\ *n* **:** BLOOD POISONING — **sep·ti·ce·mic** \-ˈsē-mik\ *adj*

septic sore throat *n* **:** STREP THROAT

septic tank *n* **:** a tank in which the solid matter of continuously flowing sewage is broken down by bacteria

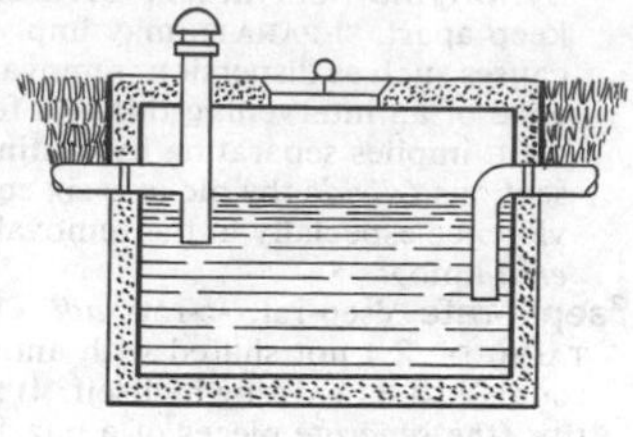

septic tank

sep·til·lion \sep-ˈtil-yən\ *n* — see NUMBER table [French, from Latin *septem* "seven" + French *-illion* (as in *million*)]

sep·tu·a·ge·nar·i·an \sep-ˌtü-ə-jə-ˈner-ē-ən, -ˌtyü-; ˌsep-tə-wə-jə-\ *n* **:** a person who is 70 or more but less than 80 years old [Late Latin *septuagenarius* "70 years old," derived from Latin *septuaginta* "seventy"] — **septuagenarian** *adj*

Sep·tu·a·ges·i·ma \ˌsep-tə-wə-ˈjes-ə-mə\ *n* **:** the 3rd Sunday before Lent [Late Latin, from Latin *septuagesimus* "70th," from *septuaginta* "seventy"]

Sep·tu·a·gint \sep-ˈtü-ə-jənt, -ˈtyü-; ˈsep-tə-wə-ˌjint\ *n* **:** a Greek version of the Jewish Scriptures put into writing in the third and second centuries B.C. by Jewish scholars and adopted by Greek-speaking Christians [Latin *septuaginta* "seventy"; from the approximate number of its translators]

sep·tum \ˈsep-təm\ *n, pl* **sep·ta** \-tə\ **:** a dividing wall or membrane especially between bodily spaces or masses of soft tissue [Latin *saeptum* "enclosure, wall," from *saepire* "to fence in," from *saepes* "fence"] — **sep·tal** \ˈsep-tl\ *adj*

¹sep·ul·cher *or* **sep·ul·chre** \ˈsep-əl-kər\ *n* **1 :** a place of burial **:** TOMB **2 :** a receptacle for religious relics especially in an altar [Medieval French *sepulcre,* from Latin *sepulcrum, sepulchrum,* from *sepelire* "to bury"]

²sepulcher *or* **sepulchre** *vt* **-chered** *or* **-chred; -cher·ing** *or* **-chring** \-kə-ring, -kring\ *archaic* **:** to place in or as if in a sepulcher **:** BURY

se·pul·chral \sə-ˈpəl-krəl\ *adj* **1 :** of or relating to burial, the grave, or monuments to the dead ⟨a *sepulchral* stone⟩ **2 :** DISMAL 1, GLOOMY — **se·pul·chral·ly** \-krə-lē\ *adv*

sep·ul·ture \ˈsep-əl-ˌchu̇r\ *n* **1 :** BURIAL **2 :** SEPULCHER [Medieval French, from Latin *sepultura,* from *sepelire* "to bury"]

se·qua·cious \si-ˈkwā-shəs\ *adj* **1** *archaic* **:** inclined to follow **:** TRACTABLE **2 :** intellectually servile [Latin *sequac-, sequax* "inclined to follow," from *sequi* "to follow"] — **se·qua·cious·ly** *adv* — **se·quac·i·ty** \-ˈkwas-ət-ē\ *n*

se·quel \ˈsē-kwəl\ *n* **1 :** an event that follows or comes afterward **:** RESULT **2 :** a work (as a novel or movie) that continues a story begun in another [Medieval French *sequele,* from Latin *sequela,* from *sequi* "to follow"]

se·que·la \si-ˈkwel-ə, -ˈkwē-lə\ *n, pl* **-que·lae** \-ˈkwel-ˌē, -ˌī; -ˈkwē-ˌlē\ **1 :** an aftereffect of disease or injury **2 :** a secondary result **:** CONSEQUENCE [Latin, "sequel"]

¹se·quence \ˈsē-kwəns, -ˌkwens\ *n* **1 :** a continuous or connected series: as **a :** an extended series of poems united by a single theme ⟨a sonnet *sequence*⟩ **b :** three or more playing cards usually of the same suit in consecutive order of rank **c :** a succession of repetitions of a melodic phrase each in a new position **d :** a set of mathematical elements (as numbers) having a definite order fixed by a rule ⟨the *sequence* 1, 1, 2, 3, 5, 8, . . .⟩ **e :** a succession of scenes developing a single subject or phase of a film story **f :** the exact order of bases in a nucleic acid or of amino acids in a protein **2 :** order of succession **3 a :** CONSEQUENCE 1, RESULT **b :** a subsequent development **4 :** continuity of progression [derived from Late Latin *sequentia* "sequel," from Latin *sequi* "to follow"] ***synonyms*** see SUCCESSION

²sequence *vt* **1 :** to arrange in a sequence **2 :** to determine the sequence of chemical constituents in ⟨*sequence* the bases in DNA⟩

se·quenc·er \ˈsē-kwən-sər, -ˌkwen-sər\ *n* **:** a device that determines a sequence

se·quen·cy \-kwən-sē\ *n, pl* **-cies** **1 :** SEQUENCE 2 **2 :** SEQUENCE 4

se·quent \ˈsē-kwənt\ *adj* **:** following in time or as an effect [Latin *sequens,* present participle of *sequi* "to follow"] — **sequent** *n*

se·quen·tial \si-ˈkwen-chəl\ *adj* **1 :** of, relating to, or arranged in a sequence **:** SERIAL 1 ⟨*sequential* file systems⟩ **2 :** following in sequence — **se·quen·tial·ly** \-chə-lē\ *adv*

se·ques·ter \si-ˈkwes-tər\ *vt* **-tered; -ter·ing** \-tə-ring, -tring\ **1 :** to set apart **:** SEGREGATE, WITHDRAW **2 :** to take custody of (as personal property) until a demand is satisfied [Medieval French *sequestrer,* from Late Latin *sequestrare* "to hand over to a trustee," from Latin *sequester* "third party to whom disputed property is entrusted, agent," from *secus* "beside, otherwise"]

se·ques·tra·tion \ˌsē-kwəs-ˈtrā-shən, si-ˌkwes-\ *n* **:** the act of sequestering **:** the state of being sequestered

se·quin \ˈsē-kwən\ *n* **1 :** an old gold coin of Italy and Turkey **2 :** a spangle used as an ornament on clothes [French, from Italian *zecchino,* from *zecca* "mint," from Arabic *(dar al-) sikka,* literally, "house of the minting die"]

se·quined *or* **se·quinned** \-kwənd\ *adj* **:** ornamented with or as if with sequins

se·quoia \si-ˈkwȯi-ə\ *n* **:** either of two huge cone-bearing California trees that are related the the bald cypresses and reach a height of over 300 feet (90 meters): **a :** GIANT SEQUOIA **b :** REDWOOD [*Sequoya* (George Guess), died 1843, American Indian credited with creation of the Cherokee syllabary]

sera *plural of* SERUM

se·rac \sə-ˈrak\ *n* **:** a pinnacle, sharp ridge, or block of ice among the crevasses of a glacier [French *sérac,* literally, a kind of white cheese, from Medieval Latin *seracium* "whey," from Latin *serum*]

se·ra·glio \sə-ˈral-yō\ *n, pl* **-glios** *also* **-gli** \-yē\ **:** HAREM 1a [Italian *serraglio* "enclosure, seraglio," partly from Medieval Latin *serraculum* "bar of a door, bolt," from Late Latin *serare* "to bolt"; partly from Turkish *saray* "palace"]

se·ra·pe *or* **sa·ra·pe** \sə-ˈräp-ē, -ˈrap-\ *n* **:** a colorful woolen shawl worn over the shoulder especially by Mexican men [Mexican Spanish *sarape*]

serape

ser·aph \ˈser-əf\ *n, pl* **ser·a·phim** \-ə-ˌfim\ *or* **seraphs :** an angel of the highest order [Late Latin *seraphim* "seraphs," from Hebrew *śĕrāphīm*]

Serb \ˈsərb\ *n* **1 :** a native or inhabitant of Serbia **2 :** SERBIAN 2 [Serbian *Srbin* (pl. *Srbi*)] — **Serb** *adj*

Ser·bi·an \ˈsər-bē-ən\ *n* **1 :** SERB 1 **2 :** a Slavic language spoken by the Serbian people and written in the Cyrillic alphabet — **Serbian** *adj*

Ser·bo–Cro·atian \ˌsər-bō-krō-ˈā-shən\ *n* **:** the Serbian and Croatian languages together with the Slavic speech of Bosnia, Herzegovina, and Montenegro taken as a single language with regional variants **2 :** one whose native language is Serbo-Croatian — **Serbo–Croatian** *adj*

sere \ˈsiər\ *adj* **:** being dried and withered ⟨*sere* leaves⟩ [Old English *sēar* "dry"]

¹ser·e·nade \ˌser-ə-ˈnād\ *n* **1 a :** a complimentary vocal or instrumental performance; *esp* **:** one given outdoors at night for a woman **b :** a work so performed **2 :** a work for chamber music orchestra resembling a suite [French *sérénade,* from Italian *serenata,* from *sereno* "clear, calm (of weather)," from Latin *serenus*]

²serenade *vb* **:** to entertain with or perform a serenade — **ser·e·nad·er** *n*

ser·en·dip·i·tous \ˌser-ən-ˈdip-ət-əs\ *adj* **:** obtained or characterized by serendipity ⟨*serendipitous* discoveries⟩

ser·en·dip·i·ty \ˌser-ən-ˈdip-ət-ē\ *n* **:** the gift of accidentally finding valuable or agreeable things [from its possession by the heroes of the Persian fairy tale *The Three Princes of Serendip*]

¹se·rene \sə-ˈrēn\ *adj* **1 a :** being clear and free of storms ⟨*serene* skies⟩ **b :** shining bright and steady **2 :** marked by utter calm **:** TRANQUIL **3 :** AUGUST — used as part of a title ⟨Your *Serene* Highness⟩ [Latin *serenus*] ***synonyms*** see CALM — **se·rene·ly** *adv* — **se·rene·ness** \-ˈrēn-nəs\ *n*

²serene *n* **1 :** a serene condition or expanse (as of sky, sea, or light) **2 :** SERENITY, TRANQUILLITY

se·ren·i·ty \sə-ˈren-ət-ē\ *n* **:** the quality or state of being serene

serf \ˈsərf\ *n* **:** a member of a servile feudal class bound to the soil [French, from Medieval French, from Latin *servus* "slave, servant"] — **serf·age** \'sər-fij\ *n* — **serf·dom** \'sərf-dəm\ *n* — **serf·hood** \-ˌhůd\ *n* — **serf·ish** \'sər-fish\ *adj* — **serf·ism** \-ˌfiz-əm\ *n*

serge \'sərj\ *n* : a durable twilled fabric having a smooth clear face and a diagonal rib on the front and the back [Medieval French *sarge,* derived from Latin *sericus* "of silk," from Greek *sērikos,* from *Sēres,* an eastern Asian people, probably the Chinese]

ser·gean·cy \'sär-jən-sē\ *n* : the function, office, or rank of a sergeant

ser·geant *also* **ser·jeant** \'sär-jənt\ *n* **1 :** an enlisted rank in the army and marine corps above corporal and below staff sergeant and in the air force above airman first class and below staff sergeant **2 :** a police officer ranking in the U.S. just below captain or sometimes lieutenant [Middle English, "servant, attendant, sergeant," from Medieval French *sergent,* from Latin *serviens,* present participle of *servire* "to serve"]

sergeant at arms *n* : an officer of an organization (as a court of law) appointed to keep order

sergeant first class *n* : an enlisted rank in the army above staff sergeant and below master sergeant

sergeant major *n, pl* **sergeants major** *or* **sergeant majors** **1 :** a noncommissioned officer (as in the army) serving as chief enlisted assistant in a headquarters **2 a :** an enlisted rank in the marine corps above master sergeant **b :** COMMAND SERGEANT MAJOR, STAFF SERGEANT MAJOR

[1]**se·ri·al** \'sir-ē-əl\ *adj* **1 :** of, consisting of, or arranged in a series, rank, or row ⟨*serial* order⟩ **2 :** appearing in parts or numbers that follow regularly ⟨a *serial* story⟩ **3 :** relating to or being a connection in a computer system in which the bits of a byte are transmitted in sequence over a single line — **se·ri·al·ly** \-ē-ə-lē\ *adv*

[2]**serial** *n* **1 :** a work appearing (as in a magazine or on television) in parts at intervals **2 :** one part of a serial work : INSTALLMENT — **se·ri·al·ist** \-ē-ə-ləst\ *n*

se·ri·al·ize \'sir-ē-ə-ˌlīz\ *vt* : to arrange or present in serial form — **se·ri·al·i·za·tion** \ˌsir-ē-ə-lə-'zā-shən\ *n*

se·ri·a·tim \ˌsir-ē-'āt-əm, -'at-\ *adv* : in a series : SERIALLY [Medieval Latin, from Latin *series* "series"]

seri·cul·ture \'ser-ə-ˌkəl-chər\ *n* : the raising of silkworms for silk production [Latin *sericum* "silk" + English *culture*] — **seri·cul·tur·al** \ˌser-ə-'kəlch-rəl, -ə-rəl\ *adj*

se·ries \'siər-ēz, -ˌēz\ *n, pl* **series** **1 a :** a number of things or events of the same class coming one after another **b :** a group with an order of arrangement exhibiting progression **2 :** the indicated sum of a usually infinite sequence of numbers ⟨the *series* 1 + ½ + ¼ + ⅓ + . . . ⟩ **3 :** a succession of volumes or issues published with related subjects or authors, similar format and price, or continuous numbering **4 :** a division of rock formations smaller than a system comprising rocks deposited during an epoch **5 :** an arrangement of the parts of or elements in an electric circuit whereby all the current passes through each part or element without branching **6 :** a group of chemical compounds related in composition and structure **7 :** a group of successive coordinate sentence elements joined together [Latin, from *serere* "to join, link together"] ***synonyms*** see SUCCESSION — **in series :** in a serial arrangement

ser·if \'ser-əf\ *n* : any of the short lines that cross the ends of the strokes of a printed letter [probably from Dutch *schreef* "stroke, line"]

seri·graph \'ser-ə-ˌgraf\ *n* : an original silk-screen color print made by an artist [Latin *sericum* "silk" + Greek *graphein* "to write, draw"] — **se·rig·ra·pher** \sə-'rig-rə-fər\ *n* — **se·rig·ra·phy** \-fē\ *n*

ser·ine \'seər-ˌēn\ *n* : a crystalline amino acid $C_3H_7NO_3$ that occurs as a structural part of many proteins [derived from Latin *sericum* "silk"]

se·rio·com·ic \ˌsir-ē-ō-'käm-ik\ *adj* : having a mixture of the serious and the comic — **se·rio·com·i·cal·ly** \-'käm-i-kə-lē, -klē\ *adv*

se·ri·ous \'sir-ē-əs\ *adj* **1 :** thoughtful or subdued in appearance or manner : SOBER **2 a :** requiring much thought or work ⟨*serious* study⟩ **b :** of or relating to a matter of importance ⟨a *serious* play⟩ **3 :** not joking or trifling : EARNEST **4 a :** not easily answered or solved ⟨*serious* objections⟩ **b :** having important or dangerous possible consequences ⟨a *serious* injury⟩ [Late Latin *seriosus,* alteration of Latin *serius* "weighty, serious"] — **se·ri·ous·ly** *adv* — **se·ri·ous·ness** *n*

synonyms SERIOUS, EARNEST, GRAVE, SOLEMN mean not funny or not playful. SERIOUS implies showing or having a concern for what really matters ⟨doctors are *serious* about finding a cure⟩. EARNEST adds an implication of sincerity or intensity of purpose ⟨an *earnest* reformer⟩. GRAVE implies both seriousness and dignity in expression or attitude ⟨read the proclamation in a *grave* voice⟩. SOLEMN suggests an impressive gravity free from levity ⟨a sad and *solemn* occasion⟩.

se·ri·ous–mind·ed \ˌsir-ē-ə-'smīn-dəd\ *adj* : having a serious disposition or trend of thought — **se·ri·ous–mind·ed·ly** *adv* — **se·ri·ous–mind·ed·ness** *n*

serjeant *variant of* SERGEANT

serjeant–at–law \ˌsär-jənt-ət-'lȯ\ *n, pl* **serjeants–at–law** : a barrister of the highest rank

ser·mon \'sər-mən\ *n* **1 :** a public speech usually by a member of the clergy giving religious instruction or exhortation **2 :** a lecture on conduct or duty [Medieval French *sermun,* from Medieval Latin *sermo,* from Latin, "speech, conversation," from *serere* "to join, link together"] — **ser·mon·ic** \ˌsər-'män-ik\ *adj*

ser·mon·ize \'sər-mə-ˌnīz\ *vb* **1 :** to compose or deliver a sermon : PREACH **2 :** to speak or write as if delivering a sermon : LECTURE — **ser·mon·iz·er** *n*

Sermon on the Mount : a talk by Jesus recorded in Matthew 5–7 and Luke 6:20–49

se·rol·o·gy \sə-'räl-ə-jē\ *n* : a science dealing blood serums and especially their antibody content — **se·ro·log·i·cal** \-'läj-i-kəl\ *or* **se·ro·log·ic** \ˌsir-ə-'läj-ik\ *adj* — **se·ro·log·i·cal·ly** \-i-kə-lē, -klē\ *adv* — **se·rol·o·gist** \sə-'räl-ə-jəst\ *n*

se·ro·sa \sə-'rō-zə\ *n* : a serous membrane that covers or encloses an internal body part (as the intestine) [New Latin, from *serosus* "serous," from Latin *serum* "serum"] — **se·ro·sal** \-'rō-zəl\ *adj*

se·ro·to·nin \ˌsir-ə-'tō-nən, ˌser-\ *n* : an amine neurotransmitter that causes narrowing of blood vessels and is found especially in the brain, blood serum, and gastric mucous membrane of mammals [*serum* + *tonic* + *-in*]

se·rous \'sir-əs\ *adj* : of, relating to, resembling, or producing serum; *esp* : thin and watery ⟨a *serous* fluid⟩

serous membrane *n* : a thin membrane (as the peritoneum) with cells that secrete a serous fluid; *esp* : SEROSA

ser·pent \'sər-pənt\ *n* **1 :** SNAKE 1; *esp* : a large snake **2 :** DEVIL 1 **3 :** a treacherous person [Medieval French, from Latin *serpens,* from *serpere* "to creep"]

[1]**ser·pen·tine** \'sər-pən-ˌtēn, -ˌtīn\ *adj* **1 :** of or resembling a serpent **2 :** subtly wily or tempting **3 :** winding or turning one way and another ⟨a *serpentine* path⟩ — **ser·pen·tine·ly** *adv*

[2]**serpentine** *n* : something that winds sinuously

[3]**ser·pen·tine** \-ˌtēn\ *n* : a mineral consisting essentially of a hydrous silicate of magnesium usually having a dull green color and often a mottled appearance

serpent star *n* : BRITTLE STAR

[1]**ser·rate** \'seər-ˌāt, sə-'rāt\ *or* **ser·rat·ed** \'ser-ˌāt-əd, sə-'rāt-\ *adj* : having a saw-toothed edge ⟨a *serrate* leaf⟩ [Latin *serratus,* from *serra* "saw"]

[2]**ser·rate** \sə-'rāt, 'seər-ˌāt\ *vt* : to mark with serrations : NOTCH [Late Latin *serrare* "to saw," from Latin *serra* "saw"]

ser·ra·tion \sə-'rā-shən, se-\ *n* **1 :** a serrate condition or formation **2 :** one of the teeth in a serrate margin

ser·ried \'ser-ēd\ *adj* : crowded together ⟨*serried* ranks of soldiers⟩ [from earlier *serry* "to crowd together," from Middle French *serrer* "to press, crowd," from Late Latin *serare* "to bolt, latch," from Latin *sera* "bar for fastening a door"] — **ser·ried·ness** *n* — **ser·ried·ly** *adv*

se·rum \'sir-əm\ *n, pl* **serums** *or* **se·ra** \-ə\ : the watery portion of a bodily fluid remaining after coagulation: as **a :** BLOOD SERUM **b :** ANTISERUM [Latin, "whey, wheylike fluid"]

serum albumin *n* : an albumin or mixture of albumins normally constituting more than half of the protein in blood serum and serving to maintain the osmotic pressure of the blood

serum globulin *n* : a globulin or mixture of globulins occurring in blood serum and containing most of the antibodies of the blood

\ə\ abut	\au̇\ out	\i\ tip	\ȯ\ saw	\u̇\ foot
\ər\ further	\ch\ chin	\ī\ life	\ȯi\ coin	\y\ yet
\a\ mat	\e\ pet	\j\ job	\th\ thin	\yü\ few
\ā\ take	\ē\ easy	\ng\ sing	\t͟h\ this	\yu̇\ cure
\ä\ cot, cart	\g\ go	\ō\ bone	\ü\ food	\zh\ vision

serum sickness *n* : an allergic reaction to the injection of foreign serum
ser·val \ˈsər-vəl, ˌsər-ˈval\ *n* : a tawny black-spotted African wildcat with large ears and long legs [French, from Portuguese *lobo serval* "lynx," from Medieval Latin *lupus cervalis,* literally, "deerlike wolf"]

serval

ser·vant \ˈsər-vənt\ *n* : one that serves others; *esp* : one that performs household or personal services [Medieval French, from *servir* "to serve"]
[1]serve \ˈsərv\ *vb* **1 a** : to be a servant **b** : to give the service and respect due to (a superior); *also* : WORSHIP ⟨*serve* God⟩ **c** : to comply with the commands or demands of : GRATIFY **d** (1) : to work through or perform a term of service especially in an army or navy (2) : to put in : SPEND ⟨*serve* 30 days in jail⟩ **2 a** : to officiate as a priest or member of the clergy **b** : to assist as server at mass **3 a** : to be of use : answer a purpose ⟨the tree *serves* as shelter⟩ **b** : to be favorable, opportune, or convenient ⟨when the time *serves*⟩ **c** : to be enough or satisfactory for ⟨a pie that will *serve* eight people⟩ **d** : to hold an office : discharge a duty or function ⟨*serve* on a jury⟩ **4 a** : to wait on (as at a table or counter) **b** : to set out or bring portions of (food or drink) **5 a** : to supply with something (as heat or light) needed or desired **b** : to furnish professional services to **6** : to make a serve (as in tennis) **7** : to treat or act toward in a specified way ⟨they *served* me ill⟩ **8 a** : to bring to notice, deliver, or execute as required by law **b** : to make legal service on (a person named in a writ) [Medieval French *servir,* from Latin *servire* "to be a slave, serve," from *servus* "slave, servant"]
[2]serve *n* : the act or privilege of putting the ball or shuttlecock in play (as in tennis or badminton); *also* : a stroke that begins a rally
serv·er \ˈsər-vər\ *n* **1** : one that serves food or drink **2** : the player who puts a ball or shuttlecock in play **3** : something (as a tray) used in serving food and drink **4** : the celebrant's assistant at low mass **5** : a computer in a network that is used to provide services (as access to files or the routing of e-mail) to other computers in the network
[1]ser·vice \ˈsər-vəs\ *n* **1** : the occupation or function of serving ⟨in active *service*⟩; *esp* : employment as a servant **2 a** : the work or action performed by one that serves ⟨gives good and quick *service*⟩ **b** : HELP, USE, BENEFIT ⟨be of *service* to them⟩ **c** : contribution to the welfare of others **d** : disposal for use ⟨at your *service*⟩ **3 a** : a form followed in worship or in a religious ceremony ⟨the burial *service*⟩ **b** : a meeting for worship ⟨held an evening *service*⟩ **4** : the act of serving: as **a** : a helpful act : good turn ⟨did us a *service*⟩ **b** : useful labor that does not produce a tangible commodity — usually used in plural ⟨charge for professional *services*⟩ **c** : [2]SERVE **5** : a set of articles for a particular use ⟨a coffee *service*⟩ **6 a** : an administrative division (as of a government) ⟨the consular *service*⟩ **b** : a nation's military forces or one of these forces ⟨called into the *service*⟩ **7** : a facility supplying some public demand ⟨bus *service*⟩ **8** : one providing maintenance and repair [Medieval French *servise,* from Latin *servitium* "condition of a slave," from *servus* "slave"]
[2]service *adj* **1 a** : of or relating to the armed services **b** : of, relating to, or constituting a branch of an army that provides service and supplies **2** : used in serving or supplying **3** : intended for everyday use : DURABLE **4** : providing services (as repairs or maintenance)
[3]service *vt* : to perform services for : repair or provide maintenance for
[4]service *n* : an Old World tree resembling the related mountain ashes but having larger flowers and larger edible fruit; *also* : a related Old World tree with small bitter fruits [Old English *syrfe,* derived from Latin *sorbus*]
ser·vice·able \ˈsər-və-sə-bəl\ *adj* **1** : HELPFUL, USEFUL **2** : wearing well in use — **ser·vice·abil·i·ty** \ˌsər-və-sə-ˈbil-ət-ē\ *n* — **ser·vice·ably** \-blē\ *adv*
ser·vice·ber·ry \ˈsər-vəs-ˌber-ē, *2 is also* ˈsär-\ *n* **1** : the edible purple or red fruit of any of various North American trees and shrubs related to the roses **2** : a tree or shrub that bears serviceberries — called also *Juneberry, shadblow, shadbush*
service book *n* : a book setting forth forms of worship used in religious services
service box *n* : the area of the court in which a player stands while serving in various wall and net games
service charge *n* : a fee charged for a particular service often in addition to a standard or basic fee
service club *n* **1** : a club of business or professional people organized for their common benefit and active in community service **2** : a recreation center for enlisted men provided by one of the armed services
service court *n* : a part of the court into which the ball or shuttlecock must be served (as in tennis or badminton)
ser·vice·man \ˈsər-vəs-ˌman, -mən\ *n* **1** : a man who is in the armed forces **2** : a man who repairs or maintains equipment
service mark *n* : a mark or device used to identify a service (as transportation or insurance) offered to customers
service medal *n* : a medal awarded to a person who does military service in a specified war or campaign
service module *n* : a space vehicle module that contains oxygen, water, propellant tanks, fuel cells, and the main rocket engine
service station *n* : GAS STATION
service stripe *n* : a stripe worn on the left sleeve of a military uniform to indicate three years of service in the Army or Air Force or four years in the Navy
ser·vice tree \ˈsər-vəs-\ *n* : [4]SERVICE
ser·vice·wom·an \ˈser-və-ˌswu̇m-ən\ *n* : a woman who is a member of the armed forces
ser·vi·ette \ˌsər-vē-ˈet\ *n, chiefly British* : a table napkin [French, from *servir* "to serve"]
ser·vile \ˈsər-vəl, -ˌvīl\ *adj* **1** : of or befitting a slave or an enslaved or menial class ⟨*servile* work⟩ ⟨*servile* flattery⟩ **2** : lacking spirit or independence : SUBMISSIVE ⟨*servile* to authority⟩ [Latin *servilis,* from *servus* "slave"] — **ser·vile·ly** \-vəl-lē, -ˌvīl-lē\ *adv* — **ser·vile·ness** \-vəl-nəs, -ˌvīl-\ *n* — **ser·vil·i·ty** \ˌsər-ˈvil-ət-ē\ *n*
serv·ing \ˈsər-ving\ *n* : a helping of food or drink
Ser·vite \ˈsər-ˌvīt\ *n* : a member of the mendicant Order of Servants of Mary founded at Florence in 1233 [Medieval Latin *Servitae* "Servites," from Latin *servus* "slave, servant"]
ser·vi·tor \ˈsər-vət-ər, -və-ˌtȯr\ *n* : a male servant [Medieval French *servitour,* from Late Latin *servitor,* from Latin *servire* "to serve"]
ser·vi·tude \ˈsər-və-ˌtüd, -ˌtyüd\ *n* : a state of subjection to another that constitutes or resembles slavery or serfdom [Medieval French *servitute,* from Latin *servitudo* "slavery," from *servus* "slave"]
ser·vo \ˈsər-vō\ *n, pl* **servos** **1** : SERVOMOTOR **2** : SERVOMECHANISM
ser·vo·mech·a·nism \ˈsər-vō-ˌmek-ə-ˌniz-əm\ *n* : a device for automatically correcting the performance of a mechanism [*servo-* (as in *servomotor*) + *mechanism*]
ser·vo·mo·tor \ˈsər-vō-ˌmōt-ər\ *n* : a motor in a servomechanism that supplements a primary control by correcting position or motion [French *servo-moteur,* from Latin *servus* "slave, servant" + French *moteur* "motor," from Latin *motor* "one that moves"]
ses·a·me \ˈses-ə-mē\ *n* **1** : an annual erect hairy herb of warm regions; *also* : its small somewhat flat seeds used as a source of oil and a flavoring agent **2** : OPEN SESAME [Latin *sesama,* from Greek *sēsamē,* of Semitic origin]
sesqui- *combining form* : one and a half times ⟨*sesqui*centennial⟩ [Latin, "one and a half," literally, "and a half," from *semis* "half of an as, one half" + *-que* "and"]
ses·qui·cen·ten·ni·al \ˌses-kwi-sen-ˈten-ē-əl\ *n* : a 150th anniversary or its celebration — **sesquicentennial** *adj*
ses·qui·pe·da·lian \ˌses-kwə-pə-ˈdāl-yən\ *adj* **1** : having many syllables : LONG **2** : given to or characterized by the use of long words

sesame 1

[Latin *sesquipedalis,* literally, "a foot and a half long," from *sesqui-* + *ped-, pes* "foot"]

ses•sile \'ses-ˌīl, -əl\ *adj* **1 :** attached directly by the base and not raised upon a stalk or peduncle ⟨a *sessile* leaf⟩ **2 :** permanently attached and not free to move about : SEDENTARY ⟨*sessile* coral polyps⟩ [Latin *sessilis* "of or fit for sitting, low," from *sessus,* past participle of *sedēre* "to sit"]

ses•sion \'sesh-ən\ *n* **1 :** a meeting or series of meetings of a body (as a court or legislature) to transact business **2 :** the period between the first and last of a series of meetings of a legislative or judicial body **3 :** the ruling body of a Presbyterian congregation **4 :** the period during the year or day in which a school conducts classes **5 :** a meeting or period devoted to an activity ⟨a recording *session*⟩ [Medieval French, from Latin *sessio,* literally, "act of sitting," from *sedēre* "to sit"] — **ses•sion•al** \'sesh-nəl, -ən-l\ *adj*

ses•terce \'ses-ˌtərs\ *n* **:** an ancient Roman coin equal to ¼ denarius [Latin *sestertius*]

ses•tet \se-'stet\ *n* **:** a stanza or poem of six lines; *esp* **:** the last six lines of an Italian sonnet — compare OCTAVE 2 [Italian *sestetto,* from *sesto* "sixth," from Latin *sextus,* from *sex* "six"]

¹set \'set\ *vb* **set; set•ting 1 :** to cause to sit : place in or on a seat **2 :** to give (a fowl) eggs to hatch or provide (eggs) with suitable conditions for hatching **3 a :** to put or fix in a place, condition, or position ⟨*set* a dish on the table⟩ ⟨*set* a trap⟩ **b :** to put (dough) aside to rise **4 :** to direct with fixed attention ⟨*set* your mind to it⟩ **5 :** to cause to assume a specified condition, relation, or occupation ⟨slaves were *set* free⟩ **6 :** to appoint or assign an office or duty ⟨*set* pickets around the camp⟩ **7 :** APPLY ⟨*set* a match to kindling⟩ **8 :** FIX, PRESCRIBE ⟨*set* a date⟩ **9 a :** to establish as the highest level or best performance ⟨*set* a speed record⟩ **b :** to furnish as a pattern or model ⟨*set* a good example⟩ **c :** to allot as a task ⟨I was *set* the job of dusting⟩ **10 a :** to arrange or put into a desired and especially a normal position ⟨*set* a broken bone⟩ ⟨*set* the sails⟩ **b :** to place in a specified literary or dramatic setting ⟨a story *set* in the distant past⟩ **11 a :** to put in order for use ⟨*set* the table⟩ **b :** to make scenically ready for a performance ⟨*set* the stage⟩ **c** (1) **:** to arrange (type) for printing (2) **:** to put into type or its equivalent **12 :** to dress (hair) especially by curling or waving **13 a :** to adorn with something attached or separate ⟨a sky *set* with stars⟩ **b :** to fix (as a jewel) in a setting **14 a :** to place in a relative rank or category ⟨*set* duty before pleasure⟩ **b :** VALUE, ESTIMATE ⟨*set* the loss at $2000⟩ **15 a :** to direct to action **b :** to incite to attack or antagonism ⟨war *sets* country against country⟩ **16 :** to put and fix in a direction ⟨*set* our faces toward home⟩ **17 a :** to fix firmly : make immobile ⟨*set* my jaw in determination⟩ **b :** to make unyielding or obstinate ⟨*set* your mind against all appeals⟩ **18 :** to become or cause to become firm or solid ⟨the jelly is *setting*⟩ **19 :** to form and bring (fruit or seed) to maturity ⟨the tree *sets* a good crop of apples⟩ **20** *chiefly dialect* **:** SIT 1a **21 :** to be becoming : be suitable : FIT ⟨your behavior doesn't *set* well with your years⟩ **22 :** to cover and warm eggs to hatch them ⟨*setting* hens⟩ **23 :** to become lodged or fixed ⟨the pudding *sets* heavily on the stomach⟩ **24 :** to pass below the horizon : go down ⟨the sun *sets*⟩ **25 :** to apply oneself ⟨*set* to work⟩ **26 :** to have a specified direction in motion : FLOW ⟨a current that *sets* to the north⟩ **27 :** to dance face-to-face with another in a square dance ⟨*set* to your partner and turn⟩ **28 :** to become permanent ⟨a dye that will not *set*⟩ **29 :** to become whole by knitting ⟨the bone has not *set*⟩ [Old English *settan*] — **set about :** to begin to do ⟨*set about* proving it could be done⟩ — **set aside 1 :** to put to one side : DISCARD **2 :** to save for future use **3 :** to reject from consideration **4 :** ANNUL, OVERRULE ⟨the verdict was *set aside* by the court⟩ — **set at :** ATTACK 1, ASSAIL — **set forth 1 :** to make known : PUBLISH **2 :** to start out on a journey : set out — **set forward 1 :** PROMOTE 2, FURTHER **2 :** to set out on a journey — **set in motion :** to give impetus to ⟨*set* the plan *in motion*⟩ — **set one's heart on :** RESOLVE 3a — **set store :** to consider valuable or worthwhile — used with *by* or *on* — **set to music :** to provide music for (lyrics) — **set upon :** to attack with violence ⟨*set upon* by a band of robbers⟩

²set *adj* **1 :** INTENT, DETERMINED ⟨were *set* on going⟩ **2 :** fixed by authority ⟨a *set* wage⟩ **3 :** INTENTIONAL, PREMEDITATED ⟨did it of *set* purpose⟩ **4 :** reluctant to change : OBSTINATE ⟨very *set* in your ways⟩ **5 a :** IMMOVABLE, RIGID ⟨a *set* frown⟩ **b :** BUILT-IN **6 :** remaining unchanged : PERSISTENT ⟨*set* defiance⟩ **7 a :** READY 1, PREPARED ⟨all *set* for an early start⟩ **b :** poised to start running or to dive in at the instant a signal is given ⟨ready, get *set,* go⟩

³set *n* **1 :** the act or action of setting : the condition of being set **2 :** mental inclination, tendency, or habit : BENT **3 :** a number of persons or things of the same kind that belong or are used together **4 :** direction of flow ⟨the *set* of the wind⟩ **5 :** form or carriage of the body or of its parts ⟨the *set* of your shoulders⟩ **6 :** the manner of fitting or of being placed or suspended ⟨the *set* of a coat⟩ **7 :** amount of deflection from a straight line **8 :** permanent change of form (as of metal) due to repeated or excessive stress **9 :** a young plant or a plant part (as a corm or a piece of tuber) suitable for planting or transplanting **10 :** an artificial setting for a scene of a play or movie **11 :** a division of a tennis match won usually by the player or side that first wins six games **12 :** SETTING 6 **13 :** the basic formation in a country-dance or square dance **14 :** a group of mathematical elements (as numbers or points) **15 :** an electronic apparatus ⟨a radio *set*⟩ ⟨a television *set*⟩

se•ta \'sēt-ə\ *n, pl* **se•tae** \'sē-ˌtē\ **:** a slender usually rigid or bristly and springy organ or part of an animal or plant [Latin *saeta, seta* "bristle"] — **se•tal** \'sēt-l\ *adj*

set•back \'set-ˌbak\ *n* **1 :** a checking of progress **2 :** an unexpected reverse or defeat

set down *vt* **1 :** to cause to sit down : SEAT **2 :** to cause or allow to get off a vehicle : DELIVER **3 :** to land (an aircraft) on the ground or water **4 :** to put in writing **5 a :** REGARD, CONSIDER ⟨*set* them *down* as crooks⟩ **b :** ATTRIBUTE ⟨*set down* their success to perseverance⟩

¹set–in \ˌset-ˌin\ *adj* **1 :** placed, located, or built as a part of another construction ⟨*set-in* bookcases⟩ **2 :** cut separately and stitched in ⟨*set-in* sleeves⟩

²set–in \'set-ˌin\ *n* **:** something that is set in : INSERT

set in *vb* **1 :** INSERT; *esp* **:** to stitch (a small part) within a larger article **2 :** to enter upon a particular state ⟨winter *set in* early⟩ **3 :** to begin to work

set•line \'set-ˌlīn\ *n* **:** a long heavy fishing line to which hooks are attached in a row

set•off \'set-ˌȯf\ *n* **1 :** something that is set off against another thing: **a :** DECORATION 2, ORNAMENT **b :** COUNTERBALANCE 2 **2 :** the discharge of a debt by setting against it a distinct claim in favor of the debtor; *also* **:** the claim itself

set off \set-'ȯf, 'set-\ *vb* **1 a :** to show up by contrast ⟨a pale face *set off* by dark eyes⟩ **b :** ADORN, EMBELLISH ⟨that pin *sets off* the dress⟩ **c :** to set apart : make distinct or outstanding ⟨commas *set off* words in a series⟩ **2 a :** OFFSET 1b, COMPENSATE **b :** to make a setoff of **3 a :** to set in motion : cause to begin ⟨that story *set* me *off* laughing⟩ **b :** to cause to explode **4 :** to measure off on a surface : lay off **5 :** to start out on a course or a journey ⟨*set off* for home⟩

set on *vb* **1 :** ATTACK 1 **2 a :** to urge (as a dog) to attack or pursue **b :** to incite to action : INSTIGATE ⟨*set* students *on* to riot⟩ **c :** to set to work **3 :** to go on : ADVANCE

set out *vb* **1 :** to state, describe, or recite at length **2 a :** to arrange and present graphically or systematically **b :** to mark out (as a design) : lay out the plan of **3 :** to begin with a definite purpose : INTEND ⟨*set out* to win⟩ **4 :** to start out on a course, a journey, or a career

set piece *n* **1 :** a realistic piece of stage scenery standing by itself **2 :** a composition (as in literature) executed in a fixed or ideal form often with great artistry and brilliant effect

set point *n* **:** a point that decides a tennis set if won by the side having an advantage in the score

set•screw \'set-ˌskrü\ *n* **1 :** a screw screwed through one part and tightly upon or into another part to prevent relative movement **2 :** a screw for regulating a valve opening or a spring tension

set•tee \se-'tē\ *n* **1 :** a long seat with a back **2 :** a medium-sized sofa with arms and a back [alteration of ¹*settle*]

set•ter \'set-ər\ *n* **1 :** one that sets **2 :** a large long-coated bird dog (as an Irish setter) of a type trained to point on finding game

set theory *n* **:** a branch of mathematics that deals with sets and the relations between them — **set–theoretic** *adj*

set·ting \'set-ing\ *n* **1 :** the way, position, or direction in which something is set **2 :** the frame or bed in which a gem is set **3 a :** the time, place, and circumstances in which something occurs or develops **b :** the time and place of the action of a story or dramatic work (as a play or movie) **c :** the scenery used in a play or a movie **4 :** the music composed for a text (as a poem) **5 :** the tableware required for arranging a place at a table **6 :** a batch of eggs for incubation

[1]set·tle \'set-l\ *n* **:** a wooden bench with arms, a high solid back, and an enclosed base [Old English *setl* "seat, chair"]

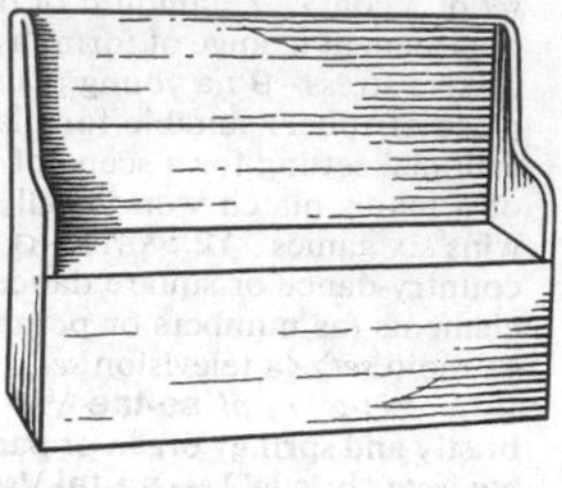
settle

[2]settle *vb* **set·tled; set·tling** \'set-ling, -l-ing\ **1 :** to place so as to stay **2 a :** to establish residence in **:** COLONIZE ⟨*settled* the West⟩ **b :** to make one's home ⟨*settle* in the country⟩ **3 a :** to cause to pack down or to become compact by sinking **:** sink gradually or to the bottom **b :** to clarify by causing dregs or impurities to sink **c :** to become clear by depositing sediment **4 a :** to make or become quiet or orderly ⟨reading *settles* my nerves⟩ **b :** to take up an ordered or stable life ⟨marry and *settle* down⟩ **5 a :** to fix or resolve conclusively ⟨*settle* the question⟩ **b :** to establish or secure permanently **6 :** to arrange in a desired position **7 a :** to make or arrange for final disposition of ⟨*settle* an estate⟩ **b :** to bestow or give possession of legally ⟨*settled* property on the child⟩ **c :** to pay in full ⟨*settle* a bill⟩ **8 :** to adjust differences or accounts [Old English *setlan* "to seat, place, settle," from *setl* "seat"]

set·tle·ment \'set-l-mənt\ *n* **1 :** the act or process of settling **2 :** final payment (as of a bill) **3 a :** a place or region newly settled **b :** a small village **4 :** SETTLEMENT HOUSE **5 :** an agreement composing differences

settlement house *n* **:** an institution providing various community services especially to people in a crowded part of a city

set·tler \'set-lər, -l-ər\ *n* **:** one that settles (as in a new region)

set·tling \'set-ling, -l-ing\ *n* **:** something that settles at the bottom of a liquid **:** SEDIMENT — usually used in plural

set·tlor \'set-ˌlȯr, -l-ˌȯr\ *n* **:** one that makes a settlement or creates a trust of property

set–to \'set-ˌtü\ *n, pl* **set–tos** \-ˌtüz\ **:** a usually brief and vigorous fight or argument

set to \set-'tü, 'set-\ *vi* **1 :** to begin actively and earnestly ⟨*set to* and ate with a will⟩ **2 :** to begin fighting

set·up \'set-ˌəp\ *n* **1 :** glass, ice, and mixer served to patrons who supply their own liquor **2 :** a task or contest intentionally made easy **3 :** the way in which something is set up **:** ARRANGEMENT

set up \set-'əp, 'set-\ *vb* **1 a :** to assemble the parts of and erect ⟨*set up* a printing press⟩ **b :** to put (a machine) in readiness or adjustment for a tooling operation **2 :** CAUSE, CREATE ⟨*set up* a clamor⟩ **3 a :** ELATE, GRATIFY ⟨*set up* by the victory⟩ **b :** to make proud or vain **4 a :** to put forward or extol as a model **b :** to claim (oneself) to be ⟨*set* yourself *up* as an authority⟩ **5 :** FOUND 3, INAUGURATE **6 :** to provide with a means of making a living ⟨*set* them *up* in a new shop⟩ **7 :** to make careful plans for ⟨*set up* a robbery⟩ **8 a :** to treat to (drinks) **b :** to treat (someone) to something **9 :** to make pretensions ⟨*setting up* to be a wise man⟩ — **set up housekeeping :** to establish one's living quarters — **set up shop :** to establish one's business

sev·en \'sev-ən\ *n* **1** — see NUMBER table **2 :** the seventh in a set or series **3 :** something having seven units or members [Old English *seofon*] — **seven** *adj or pron*

sev·en·teen \ˌsev-ən-'tēn, 'sev-ən-\ *n* — see NUMBER table [Old English *seofontēne*] — **seventeen** *adj or pron* — **sev·en·teenth** \-'tēnth, -'tēntth\ *adj or n*

seventeen–year locust *n* **:** a cicada of the U.S. with a life of 17 years in the North and 13 years in the South of which the greatest part is spent as a wingless underground nymph that feeds on roots and emerges from the soil to become a winged adult typically living only a few weeks

sev·enth \'sev-ənth, -ənth\ *n, pl* **sev·enths** \'sev-əns, -ənths, -ənths\ **1** — see NUMBER table **2 a :** the musical interval embracing seven diatonic degrees **b :** a tone at this interval **c :** the harmonic combination of two tones a seventh apart — **seventh** *adj or adv*

Seventh Day Adventist *n* **:** a member of an evangelical Protestant denomination organized in the U.S. in 1863 and marked by emphasis on preparation for Christ's Second Coming

seventh heaven *n* **:** a state of extreme joy [from the 7th being the highest of the 7 heavens of Muslim and cabalist doctrine]

sev·en·ty \'sev-ən-tē\ *n, pl* **-ties** — see NUMBER table [Old English *seofontig*] — **sev·en·ti·eth** \-tē-əth\ *adj or n* — **seventy** *adj or pron*

sev·en·ty–eight \ˌsev-ən-tē-'āt\ *n* **:** a phonograph record for play at 78 revolutions per minute

sev·er \'sev-ər\ *vb* **sev·ered; sev·er·ing** \'sev-ring, -e-ring\ **1 :** to put or keep apart **:** DIVIDE; *esp* **:** to remove (as a part) by or as if by cutting **2 :** to come or break apart [Medieval French *severer,* from Latin *separare*] ***synonyms*** see SEPARATE — **sev·er·abil·i·ty** \ˌsev-rə-'bil-ət-ē, -ə-rə-\ *n* — **sev·er·able** \'sev-rə-bəl, -ə-rə-\ *adj*

[1]sev·er·al \'sev-rəl, -ə-rəl\ *adj* **1 a :** separate or distinct from one another **:** DIFFERENT ⟨federal union of the *several* states⟩ **b :** PARTICULAR, RESPECTIVE ⟨specialists in their *several* fields⟩ **2 :** more than two but fewer than many ⟨moved *several* inches⟩ [Medieval French, from Medieval Latin *separalis,* derived from Latin *separare* "to separate"] — **sev·er·al·ly** \-ē\ *adv*

[2]several *pron, pl in constr* **:** an indefinite number more than two and fewer than many ⟨*several* of the guests⟩

sev·er·al·fold \ˌsev-rəl-'fōld, -ə-rəl-\ *adj* **1 :** having several parts or aspects **2 :** being several times as large, as great, or as many as some understood size, degree, or amount ⟨a *severalfold* increase⟩ — **severalfold** *adv*

sev·er·al·ty \'sev-rəl-tē, -ə-rəl-\ *n* **:** the quality or state of being several **:** DISTINCTNESS, SEPARATENESS

sev·er·ance \'sev-rəns, -ə-rəns\ *n* **:** the act or process of severing **:** the state of being severed

severance pay *n* **:** an allowance usually based on length of service that is payable to an employee on termination of employment

se·vere \sə-'viər\ *adj* **1 a :** strict in judgment, discipline, or government **b :** strict or stern in bearing or manner **:** AUSTERE **2 :** rigorous in restraint, punishment, or requirement **:** STRINGENT **3 :** strongly critical **4 :** sober or restrained in decoration or manner **:** PLAIN **5 a :** inflicting physical discomfort or hardship **:** HARSH ⟨*severe* winters⟩ **b :** inflicting pain or distress **:** GRIEVOUS ⟨a *severe* wound⟩ **6 :** requiring great effort **:** ARDUOUS ⟨a *severe* test⟩ **7 :** of a great degree **:** MARKED ⟨a *severe* economic depression⟩ [Latin *severus*] — **se·vere·ly** *adv* — **se·vere·ness** *n*

synonyms SEVERE, STERN, AUSTERE mean showing or requiring strict discipline or firm restraint. SEVERE implies enforcing standards without indulgence or laxity and may suggest harshness ⟨*severe* military discipline⟩. STERN stresses inflexibility and inexorability of temper or character ⟨a *stern* taskmaster in the classroom⟩. AUSTERE suggests absence of warmth, color, or feeling and may apply to rigorous simplicity or self-denial ⟨the *austere* furnishings of the cold little office⟩.

se·ver·i·ty \sə-'ver-ət-ē\ *n, pl* **-ties :** the quality or state of being severe

Sè·vres \'sev-rə, 'sev, 'sevr\ *n* **:** an often elaborately decorated French porcelain [*Sèvres,* France]

sew \'sō\ *vb* **sewed; sewn** \'sōn\ *or* **sewed; sew·ing 1 :** to join or fasten by stitches made with a flexible thread or filament ⟨*sew* on a button⟩ **2 :** to close or enclose by sewing ⟨*sew* the money in a bag⟩ **3 :** to practice or engage in sewing [Old English *sīwian*]

sew·age \'sü-ij\ *n* **:** refuse liquids or waste matter usually carried off by sewers [[3]*sewer*]

[1]sew·er \'sō-ər, 'sōr\ *n* **:** one that sews

[2]sew·er \'sü-ər, 'sù-ər, 'sùr\ *n* **:** a covered usually underground passage to carry off water and sewage [Medieval French, from *assewer, essiver* "to drain," derived from Latin *ex-* + *aqua* "water"]

sew·er·age \'sü-ə-rij, 'sù-ər-ij, 'sùr-ij\ *n* **1 :** SEWAGE **2 :** the removal and disposal of sewage and surface water by sewers **3 :** a system of sewers

sew·ing \'sō-ing\ *n* **1 :** the act, method, or occupation of one that sews **2 :** material that has been or is to be sewed

sew up *vt* **1 :** to get exclusive use or control of **2 :** to make certain of **:** ASSURE ⟨*sew up* a deal⟩

sex \ˈseks\ *n* **1 :** either of two major forms into which many organisms are divided especially on the basis of their reproductive organs and structures and which consist of males and females **2 :** the sum of the structural, functional, and behavioral characteristics of living things that are involved in reproduction and serve to distinguish males and females **3 :** sexual activity; *esp* **:** SEXUAL INTERCOURSE [Latin *sexus*]

sex- *or* **sexi-** *combining form* **:** six [Latin *sex*]

sex·a·ge·nar·i·an \ˌsek-sə-jə-ˈner-ē-ən, sek-ˌsaj-ə-\ *n* **:** a person who is 60 or more but less than 70 years old [Latin *sexagenarius* "60 years old, of 60," derived from *sexaginta* "sixty"] — **sexagenarian** *adj*

Sex·a·ges·i·ma \ˌsek-sə-ˈjes-ə-mə, -ˈjā-zə-mə\ *n* **:** the second Sunday before Lent [Late Latin, from Latin *sexagesimus* "sixtieth"]

sex·a·ges·i·mal \-ˈjes-ə-məl\ *adj* **:** of, relating to, or based on the number 60 ⟨*sexagesimal* measurement of angles⟩ [Latin *sexagesimus* "sixtieth," from *sexaginta* "sixty"]

sex appeal *n* **:** personal appeal or physical or sexual attractiveness

sex cell *n* **:** GAMETE

sex chromosome *n* **:** a chromosome that is inherited differently in the two sexes, that is concerned directly with the inheritance of sex, and that controls the inheritance of various sex-linked characters

sexed \ˈsekst\ *adj* **:** having sex or sexual instincts

sex gland *n* **:** GONAD

sex hormone *n* **:** a hormone (as estrogen or testosterone) that affects the growth or function of the reproductive organs or the development of secondary sex characteristics

sex·ism \ˈsek-ˌsiz-əm\ *n* **:** prejudice or discrimination based on sex — **sex·ist** \ˈsek-səst\ *adj or n*

sex·less \ˈsek-sləs\ *adj* **:** lacking sex **:** NEUTER — **sex·less·ness** *n*

sex–linked \ˈsek-ˌslingt, -ˌslingkt\ *adj* **1 :** located on one type of sex chromosome but not on the other ⟨a *sex-linked* gene⟩ **2 :** controlled by a sex-linked gene ⟨a *sex-linked* character⟩ — **sex–link·age** \-ˌsling-kij\ *n*

sext \ˈsekst\ *n, often cap* **:** the fourth of the canonical hours [Latin *sexta* "6th hour of the day," from *sextus* "sixth," from *sex* "six"]

sex·tant \ˈsek-stənt\ *n* **:** a navigational instrument for measuring the angle between the horizon and the sun or a star in order to determine the latitude (as of a ship) [New Latin *sextans* "6th part of a circle," from Latin, "6th part," from *sextus* "sixth"]

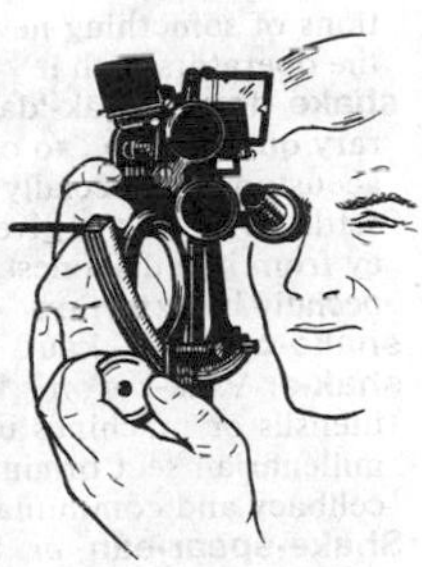

sextant

sex·tet \sek-ˈstet\ *n* **1 :** a musical composition for six instruments or voices **2 :** a group or set of six [alteration of *sestet*]

sex·til·lion \sek-ˈstil-yən\ *n* — see NUMBER table [French, from Latin *sex* "six" + French *-illion* (as in *million*)]

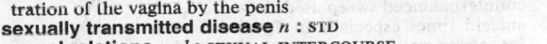

sex·ton \ˈsek-stən\ *n* **:** a church officer or employee who takes care of the church property and sometimes rings the bell for services and digs graves [Middle English *secresteyn, sexteyn,* from Medieval French *segrestein,* from Medieval Latin *sacristanus* "sacristan"]

[1]**sex·tu·ple** \sek-ˈstüp-əl, -ˈstyüp-, -ˈstəp-; ˈsek-stəp-\ *adj* **1 :** having six units or members **2 :** being six times as great or as many [probably from Medieval Latin *sextuplus,* from Latin *sextus* "sixth"] — **sextuple** *n*

[2]**sextuple** *vb* **sex·tu·pled; sex·tu·pling** \-ling, -ə-ling\ **:** to make or become six times as much or as many

sex·tup·let \sek-ˈstəp-lət, -ˈstüp-, -ˈstyüp-; ˈsek-stəp-\ *n* **1 :** a combination of six of a kind **2 :** one of six offspring born at one birth

sex·u·al \ˈseksh-wəl, -ə-wəl; ˈsek-shəl\ *adj* **1 :** of, relating to, or associated with sex or the sexes ⟨*sexual* differentiation⟩ ⟨*sexual* conflict⟩ **2 :** having or involving sex ⟨*sexual* reproduction⟩ — **sex·u·al·i·ty** \ˌsek-shə-ˈwal-ət-ē\ *n* — **sex·u·al·ly** \ˈseksh-wə-lē, -ə-wə-; ˈseksh-lē, -ə-lē\ *adv*

sexual harassment *n* **:** uninvited and unwelcome verbal or physical behavior of a sexual nature especially by a person in authority towards a subordinate (as an employee or student)

sexual intercourse *n* **:** sexual union especially involving penetration of the vagina by the penis

sexually transmitted disease *n* **:** STD

sexual relations *n pl* **:** SEXUAL INTERCOURSE

sexy \ˈsek-sē\ *adj* **sex·i·er; -est :** sexually suggestive or stimulating **:** EROTIC — **sex·i·ness** *n*

sfer·ics \ˈsfiər-iks, ˈsfer-\ *n pl* **:** ATMOSPHERICS [by shortening]

[1]**sfor·zan·do** \sfȯrt-ˈsän-dō, -ˈsan-\ *adj or adv* **:** played with prominent stress or accent — used of a single note or chord as a direction in music [Italian, literally, "forcing," from *sforzare* "to force"]

[2]**sforzando** *n, pl* **-dos** *or* **-di** \-dē\ **:** an accented tone or chord

sh \sh often prolonged\ *interj* — used often in prolonged or reduplicated form to urge or command silence or less noise [imitative]

shab·by \ˈshab-ē\ *adj* **shab·bi·er; -est 1 :** dressed in worn clothes **2 a :** threadbare and faded from wear **b :** ill kept **:** DILAPIDATED **3 a :** MEAN, UNFAIR ⟨*shabby* treatment⟩ **b :** inferior in quality [obsolete *shab* "scab, low fellow"] — **shab·bi·ly** \ˈshab-ə-lē\ *adv* — **shab·bi·ness** \ˈshab-ē-nəs\ *n*

Sha·bu·oth \shə-ˈvü-ˌōt, -ˌōth, -ˌōs, -əs\ *n* **:** a Jewish holiday celebrated in May or June to commemorate the revelation of the Ten Commandments at Mount Sinai and in biblical times as a harvest festival [Hebrew *shābhūʽōth,* literally, "weeks"]

shack \ˈshak\ *n* **1 :** HUT, SHANTY **2 :** a room or similar enclosed structure for a particular person or use ⟨a radio *shack*⟩ ⟨an ammunition *shack*⟩ [probably from English dialect *shackly* "rickety"]

[1]**shack·le** \ˈshak-əl\ *n* **1 :** something (as a manacle or fetter) that confines the legs or arms **2 :** something that checks or prevents free action as if by fetters — usually used in plural **3 :** a device (as a clevis) for making something fast [Old English *sceacul*]

[2]**shackle** *vt* **shack·led; shack·ling** \ˈshak-ling, -ə-ling\ **1 a :** to bind with shackles **b :** to make fast with a shackle **2 :** to deprive of freedom of action **:** HINDER ⟨*shackled* by poverty⟩ ***synonyms*** see HAMPER — **shack·ler** \ˈshak-lər, -ə-lər\ *n*

shad \ˈshad\ *n, pl* **shad :** any of several deep-bodied fishes that are closely related to the herrings but ascend rivers in the spring to lay or fertilize eggs and include important food fishes of Europe and North America [Old English *sceadd*]

shad·blow \ˈshad-ˌblō\ *n* **:** SERVICEBERRY 2

shad·bush \-ˌbu̇sh\ *n* **:** SERVICEBERRY 2

shad·dock \ˈshad-ək\ *n* **:** POMELO 2 [Captain *Shaddock,* 17th century English ship commander]

[1]**shade** \ˈshād\ *n* **1 a :** partial darkness caused by interception of the rays of light **b :** relative obscurity or retirement **2 :** space sheltered from the heat and glare of sunlight ⟨sit in the *shade* of a tree⟩ **3 :** a vaporous or unreal appearance **4** *pl* **a :** the shadows that gather as darkness comes on **b :** UNDERWORLD 1, HADES **5 :** a disembodied spirit **:** GHOST **6 :** something that intercepts or shelters from light, sun, or heat: as **a :** a device partially covering a lamp so as to reduce glare **b :** a screen usually on a roller for regulating the light or the view through a window **7 a :** the representation of the effect of shade in painting or drawing **b :** a subdued or somber feature **8 a :** a color produced by a pigment or dye mixture having some black in it **b :** a color slightly different from the one under consideration **9 :** a minute difference or variation ⟨*shades* of meaning⟩ **10 :** a facial expression of sadness or displeasure [Old English *sceadu*] ***synonyms*** see COLOR — **shade·less** \-ləs\ *adj*

[2]**shade** *vb* **1 a :** to shelter or screen by intercepting radiated light or heat **b :** to cover with a shade **2 :** to hide partly by or as if by a shadow **3 :** to darken with or as if with a shadow **4 :** to cast into the shade **:** OBSCURE **5 a :** to represent the effect of shade or shadow on **b :** to add shading to **c :** to color so that the shades pass gradually from one to another **6 :** to change by gradual transition or qualification **7 :** to reduce (as a price) slightly — **shad·er** *n*

shade tree *n* **:** a tree grown chiefly to produce shade

shad·ing \ˈshād-ing\ *n* **:** a filling up within outlines to suggest different degrees of light and dark in a picture or drawing

sha·doof \shə-ˈdüf, sha-\ *n* **:** a counterbalanced sweep used since ancient times especially in Egypt for raising water (as for irrigation) [Arabic *shādūf*]

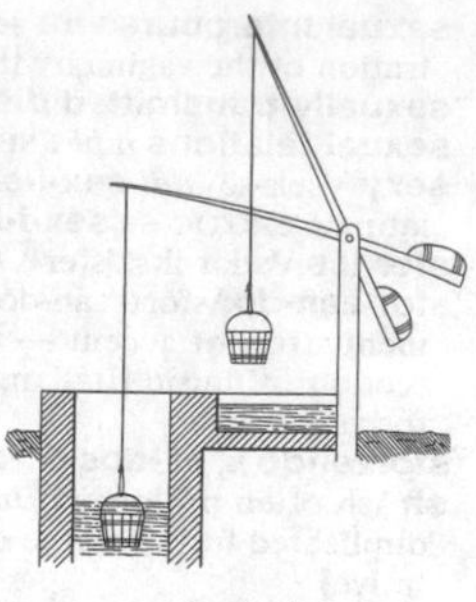
shadoof

¹shad·ow \ˈshad-ō\ *n* **1 :** shade within defined bounds **2 :** a reflected image **3 :** shelter from danger or observation **4 a :** an imperfect and faint representation **b :** IMITATION 2, COPY **5 :** the dark figure cast upon a surface by a body blocking rays from a light source **6 :** PHANTOM 1a **7 :** a shaded part of a picture **8 :** a form without substance **:** REMNANT, VESTIGE ⟨are only a *shadow* of your former self⟩ **9 a :** an inseparable companion or follower **b :** one that shadows as a spy or detective **10 :** a small degree or portion **:** TRACE ⟨not a *shadow* of a doubt⟩ **11 :** a gloomy influence [Old English *sceadu* "shade, shadow"] — **shad·ow·less** \-ləs\ *adj* — **shad·ow·like** \-ˌlīk\ *adj*

²shadow *vb* **1 a :** to cast a shadow on **b :** to cast a gloom over **:** CLOUD **2 :** to represent or indicate obscurely or faintly **3 :** to follow especially secretly **:** TRAIL **4 :** to pass gradually or by degrees **5 :** to become overcast with or as if with shadows — **shad·ow·er** \ˈshad-ə-wər\ *n*

³shadow *adj* **1 a :** set up in order to function if the opportunity arises ⟨a *shadow* government⟩ **b :** belonging to a shadow cabinet or shadow government ⟨*shadow* minister of foreign affairs⟩ **2 :** having an indistinct pattern ⟨a *shadow* plaid⟩

shad·ow·box \ˈshad-ō-ˌbäks, -ə-\ *vi* **:** to go through the motions of boxing as if with an imaginary opponent especially during training — **shad·ow·box·ing** *n*

shadow box *n* **:** a shallow enclosing case usually with a glass front in which something is displayed

shadow play *n* **:** a play in which the shadows of the actors are projected on a screen

shad·owy \ˈshad-ə-wē\ *adj* **1 a :** being or resembling a shadow **:** UNREAL **b :** faintly visible **:** INDISTINCT **2 :** being in or obscured by shadow **3 :** SHADY 1

shady \ˈshād-ē\ *adj* **shad·i·er; -est 1 :** producing or affording shade **2 :** sheltered from the sun **3 a :** of questionable merit **b :** DISREPUTABLE — **shad·i·ly** \ˈshād-l-ē\ *adv* — **shad·i·ness** \ˈshād-ē-nəs\ *n*

¹shaft \ˈshaft\ *n, pl* **shafts** \ˈshafs, ˈshafts, *in sense 3 also* ˈshavz\ **1 a :** the long handle of a weapon (as a spear) **b :** ¹SPEAR 1, LANCE **2 a :** the slender stem of an arrow **b :** ARROW 1 **3 :** POLE; *esp* **:** one of two poles between which a horse is hitched to pull a vehicle **4 :** a narrow beam of light **5 :** something resembling the shaft of an arrow or spear: as **a :** the handle of a tool **b :** a tall monument (as a column) **c :** a vertical opening or passage through the floors of a building ⟨an air *shaft*⟩ **d :** a commonly cylindrical bar used to support rotating pieces or to transmit power or motion by rotation **e :** a vertical or inclined opening of uniform and limited cross section made for finding or mining ore, raising water, or ventilating underground workings **f :** the midrib of a feather **g :** the cylindrical part of a long bone between the enlarged ends **h :** the part of a hair that is visible above the surface of the skin **6 a :** a projectile thrown like a spear or shot like an arrow **b :** a scornful or satirical remark **:** BARB **c :** harsh or unfair treatment [Old English *sceaft*]

²shaft *vt* **:** to fit with a shaft

¹shag \ˈshag\ *n* **1 a :** a shaggy tangled mass or covering **b :** long coarse or matted fiber or nap **2 :** CORMORANT 1 [Old English *sceacga*]

²shag *vb* **shagged; shag·ging 1 :** to fall or hang in shaggy masses **2 :** to make rough or shaggy

³shag *vt* **shagged; shag·ging 1 :** to chase after; *esp* **:** to run after and return (as a ball) **2 :** to chase away [origin unknown]

shag·bark hickory \ˈshag-ˌbärk-\ *n* **:** a hickory of eastern North America with a gray shaggy outer bark that peels off in long strips and sweet edible nuts — called also *shagbark*

shag·gy \ˈshag-ē\ *adj* **shag·gi·er; -est 1 a :** covered with or made up of long, coarse, or matted hair or thick, tangled, or unkempt vegetation **b :** having a rough or hairy surface **2 :** UNKEMPT, SHABBY — **shag·gi·ly** \ˈshag-ə-lē\ *adv* — **shag·gi·ness** \ˈshag-ē-nəs\ *n*

sha·green \sha-ˈgrēn, shə-\ *n* **1 :** an untanned leather covered with small round granulations and usually dyed green **2 :** the rough skin of various sharks and rays [French *chagrin,* from Turkish *sağri*] — **shagreen** *adj*

shah \ˈshä, ˈshȯ\ *n* **:** the sovereign of Iran [Persian *shāh* "king"] — **shah·dom** \ˈshäd-əm, ˈshȯd-\ *n*

¹shake \ˈshāk\ *vb* **shook** \ˈshu̇k\; **shak·en** \ˈshā-kən\; **shak·ing 1 :** to move irregularly to and fro **:** QUIVER, TREMBLE ⟨*shaking* with cold⟩ **2 :** to become unsteady **:** TOTTER **3 :** to brandish, wave, or flourish often in a threatening way **4 :** to cause to move in a quick jerky way **5 :** to free oneself from ⟨*shake* off a cold⟩ **6 :** to cause to waver **:** WEAKEN ⟨*shake* one's faith⟩ **7 :** to dislodge or eject by quick jerky movements ⟨*shake* the dust from a cloth⟩ **8 :** to clasp (hands) in greeting or as a sign of goodwill or agreement **9 :** to stir the feelings of **:** UPSET ⟨*shook* me up⟩ [Old English *sceacan*] — **shak·able** *or* **shake·able** \ˈshā-kə-bəl\ *adj* — **shake a leg 1 :** DANCE 1 **2 :** to hurry up

synonyms SHAKE, AGITATE, ROCK, CONVULSE mean to move up and down or back and forth with some violence. SHAKE applies to short, rapid movements often for a particular purpose ⟨*shake* well before using⟩. AGITATE suggests more violent and prolonged tossing or stirring ⟨the washer cleans by *agitating*⟩. ROCK implies a swinging or swaying motion resulting from violent impact or upheaval ⟨a city *rocked* by an earthquake⟩. CONVULSE suggests a violent wrenching as of a body in a fit ⟨*convulsed* with laughter⟩.

²shake *n* **1 :** an act of shaking: as **a :** an act of shaking hands **b :** an act of shaking oneself **2 a :** a blow or shock that upsets the equilibrium or disturbs the balance of something **b :** EARTHQUAKE **3** *pl* **:** a condition of trembling (as from chill) **4 :** something produced by shaking: as **a :** a fissure in strata **b :** MILK SHAKE **5 :** a wavering, quivering, or alternating motion caused by a blow or shock **6 :** TRILL 1a **7 :** a very brief period of time **:** INSTANT ⟨ready in two *shakes*⟩ **8** *pl* **:** one of importance or ability — usually used in the phrase *no great shakes* **9 :** a shingle split from a piece of log usually three to four feet (about one meter) long ⟨cedar *shakes*⟩ **10 :** ³DEAL 2 ⟨a fair *shake*⟩

shake·down \ˈshāk-ˌdau̇n\ *n* **1 :** an improvised bed (as one made up on the floor) **2 :** a boisterous dance **3 :** an act or instance of shaking someone down; *esp* **:** EXTORTION **4 :** a process or period of adjustment **5 :** a test under operating conditions of something new (as a ship) for defects or to familiarize the operators with it

shake down \shāk-ˈdau̇n, ˈshāk-\ *vb* **1 a :** to take up temporary quarters **b :** to occupy a makeshift bed **2 a :** to become accustomed especially to new surroundings or duties **b :** to settle down **c :** to give a shakedown test to **3 :** to obtain money from in a dishonest, contemptible, or illegal manner and especially by extortion **4 :** to bring about a reduction of

shake·out \ˈshā-ˌkau̇t\ *n* **:** a minor economic recession

shak·er \ˈshā-kər\ *n* **1 :** one that shakes; *esp* **:** any of various utensils or machines used in shaking **2** *cap* **:** a member of a millenarian sect originating in England in 1747 and practicing celibacy and communal living — **Shaker** *adj*

Shake·spear·ean *or* **Shake·spear·ian** \shāk-ˈspir-ē-ən\ *adj* **:** of, relating to, or characteristic of William Shakespeare or his writings

Shakespearean sonnet *n* **:** ENGLISH SONNET

shake–up \ˈshā-ˌkəp\ *n* **:** an act or instance of shaking up; *esp* **:** an extensive and often drastic reorganization ⟨lost my job in an office *shake-up*⟩

shake up \shā-ˈkəp, ˈshā-\ *vt* **1 :** to jar by or as if by a physical shock ⟨the collision *shook* both drivers *up*⟩ **2 :** to make an extensive often drastic reorganization of

sha·ko \ˈshā-kō, ˈshak-ō\ *n, pl* **sha·kos** *or* **sha·koes :** a stiff military cap with a high crown and plume [French, from Hungarian *csákó*]

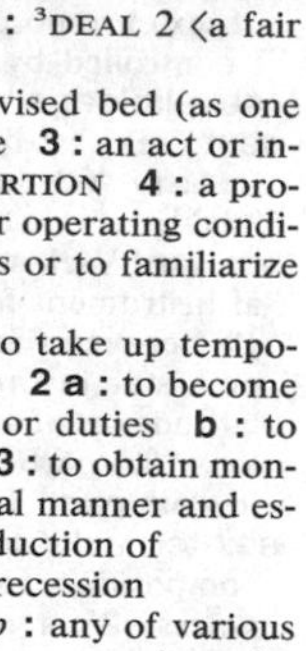
shako

shaky \ˈshā-kē\ *adj* **shak·i·er; -est 1 a :** lacking stability **b :** lacking in firmness (as of beliefs) **c :** lacking in authority or reliability **:** QUESTIONABLE ⟨*shaky* data⟩ **2 a :** somewhat unsound in health **b :** characterized by shaking **3 :** likely to give way or break down — **shak·i·ly** \-kə-lē\ *adv* — **shak·i·ness** \-kē-nəs\ *n*

shale \ˈshāl\ *n* **:** a rock that is formed by the consolidation of clay, mud, or silt, has a finely layered structure, and splits easily [Old English *scealu* "shell, scale"] — **shaley** \'shā-lē\ *adj*

shall \shəl, shal, 'shal\ *auxiliary verb, past* **should** \shəd, shu̇d, 'shu̇d\; *present sing & pl* **shall** **1 a** — used to express a command or exhortation ⟨you *shall* go⟩ **b** — used in laws, regulations, or directives to express what is mandatory ⟨it *shall* be unlawful to carry firearms⟩ **2 a** — used to express what is inevitable or what is likely to happen in the future ⟨we *shall* have to be ready⟩ ⟨we *shall* see⟩ **b** — used to express simple futurity ⟨when *shall* we expect you⟩ **3** — used to express determination ⟨they *shall* not pass⟩ [Old English *sceal* "owe, owes, ought to, must"]

shal·lop \'shal-əp\ *n* **:** a small open boat propelled by oars or sails [Middle French *chaloupe*]

shal·lot \shə-'lät\ *n* **:** a bulbous perennial onion that produces small clustered bulbs which resemble those of garlic and are used in seasoning; *also* **:** a bulb of the shallot [French *échalote*]

[1]**shal·low** \'shal-ō\ *adj* **1 :** having little depth ⟨*shallow* water⟩ ⟨a *shallow* pan⟩ **2 :** lacking in depth of knowledge, thought, or feeling [Middle English *schalowe*] ***synonyms*** see SUPERFICIAL — **shal·low·ly** *adv* — **shal·low·ness** *n*

[2]**shallow** *vb* **:** to make or become shallow

[3]**shallow** *n* **:** a shallow place or area in a body of water — usually used in plural

sha·lom \shä-'lōm, shə-\ *interj* — used as a Jewish greeting and farewell [Hebrew *shālōm* "peace"]

sha·lom alei·chem \ˌshȯ-lə-mə-'lā-kəm, ˌshō-, -k̲əm\ *interj* — used as a traditional Jewish greeting [Hebrew *shālōm 'alēkhem* "peace to you"]

shalt \shəlt, shalt, 'shalt\ *archaic present 2nd singular of* SHALL

[1]**sham** \'sham\ *n* **1 :** HOAX 1 **2 :** cheap falseness **:** HYPOCRISY **3 :** a decorative piece of cloth simulating an article of personal or household linen and used in place of or over it **4 :** an imitation or counterfeit intended to appear genuine **5 :** a person who shams [perhaps from English dialect *sham* "shame"]

[2]**sham** *vb* **shammed; sham·ming :** to act intentionally so as to give a false impression **:** FEIGN ***synonyms*** see ASSUME

[3]**sham** *adj* **1 :** not genuine **:** FALSE **2 :** having such poor quality as to seem false

sha·man \'shäm-ən, 'shā-mən\ *n, pl* **shamans :** a priest held to cure the sick, to discover the hidden, and to control events by magic [derived from Evenki (Tungusic language of Siberia) *šamān*]

sha·man·ism \-ˌiz-əm\ *n* **:** a religion practiced by indigenous peoples of far northern Europe and Siberia that is marked by belief in gods, demons, and ancestral spirits responsive only to the shamans; *also* **:** any similar religion — **sha·man·ist** \-əst\ *n or adj* — **sha·man·is·tic** \ˌshäm-ən-'is-tik, ˌshā-mən-\ *adj*

sham·ble \'sham-bəl\ *vi* **sham·bled; sham·bling** \-bə-liŋ, -bliŋ\ **:** to walk awkwardly with dragging feet **:** SHUFFLE [*shamble* "bowed, malformed"] — **shamble** *n*

sham·bles \'sham-bəlz\ *n sing or pl* **1 :** a place of mass slaughter **2 :** a scene or state of great confusion, disorder, or destruction [Middle English *shameles* "meat market," pl. of *schamel* "vendor's table, footstool," from Old English *sceamol* "stool," from Latin *scamillum,* from *scamnum* "stool, bench"]

sham·bling *adj* **:** marked by slow awkward movement

[1]**shame** \'shām\ *n* **1 a :** a painful emotion caused by consciousness of guilt, shortcoming, or impropriety **b :** the susceptibility to such emotion **2 :** a condition of humiliating disgrace or disrepute **3 a :** something that brings strong regret, censure, or reproach; *also* **:** something to be regretted **:** PITY **b :** a cause of feeling shame [Old English *scamu*]

[2]**shame** *vt* **1 :** to bring shame to **:** DISGRACE **2 :** to put to shame by outdoing **3 :** to cause to feel shame **4 :** to force by causing to feel guilty ⟨*shamed* into confessing⟩

shame·faced \'shām-'fāst\ *adj* **1 :** showing modesty **:** BASHFUL **2 :** ASHAMED 1 [alteration of earlier *shamefast,* from Old English *scamfæst,* from *scamu* "shame" + *fæst* "fixed, fast"] — **shame·faced·ly** \-'fā-səd-lē, -'fāst-lē\ *adv* — **shame·faced·ness** \-'fā-səd-nəs, -'fāst-nəs, -'fās-nəs\ *n*

Word History Some English words have been altered so as to give them an apparent relationship to other better-known or better-understood words. Such a process of alteration is called folk etymology. A common word formed by folk etymology is *shamefaced.* Old English *scamfæst* meant "bashful" or "modest" or, more literally, "held fast by shame." The second element of *shamefaced,* then, was originally the same as that of *steadfast.* The similarity of consonant sounds between *-fast* and *-faced* contributed to the alteration of *shamefast* to *shamefaced,* and the belief that modesty or bashfulness is reflected in a person's face probably had some influence too.

shame·ful \'shām-fəl\ *adj* **1 :** bringing shame **:** DISGRACEFUL ⟨*shameful* behavior⟩ **2 :** arousing the feeling of shame **:** INDECENT — **shame·ful·ly** \-fə-lē\ *adv* — **shame·ful·ness** *n*

shame·less \'shām-ləs\ *adj* **1 :** having no shame **:** BRAZEN **2 :** showing lack of shame **:** DISGRACEFUL — **shame·less·ly** *adv* — **shame·less·ness** *n*

sham·mer \'sham-ər\ *n* **:** one that shams

shammy *variant of* CHAMOIS

[1]**sham·poo** \sham-'pü\ *vt* **1** *archaic* **:** MASSAGE **2 a :** to wash (as the hair) with soap and water or with a special preparation **b :** to wash the hair of [Hindi & Urdu *cā̃po,* imperative of *cā̃pnā* "to press, shampoo"] — **sham·poo·er** *n*

[2]**shampoo** *n, pl* **shampoos** **1 :** an act or instance of shampooing **2 :** a preparation used in shampooing

sham·rock \'sham-ˌräk\ *n* **1 :** a plant of folk legend with leaves composed of three leaflets that is associated with St. Patrick and Ireland **2 :** any of several plants (as a clover or a wood sorrel) or their leaves that resemble, are worn to represent, or are held to be the shamrock of legend [Irish *seamróg,* from *seamar* "clover"]

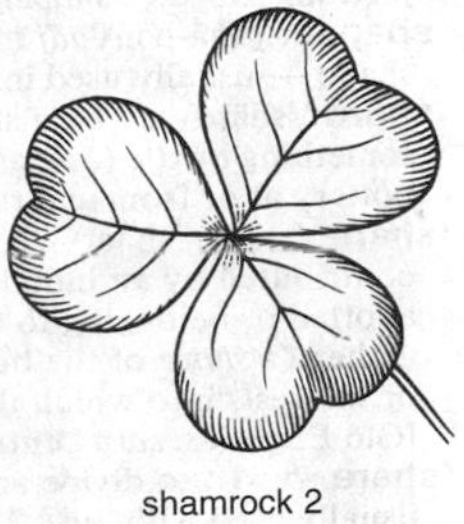
shamrock 2

sha·mus \'shäm-əs, 'shā-məs\ *n* **1** *slang* **:** POLICE OFFICER **2** *slang* **:** a private detective [perhaps from Yiddish *shames* "sexton of a synagogue"]

shang·hai \shaŋ-'hī, 'shaŋ-\ *vt* **shang·haied; shang·hai·ing** **1 a :** to put aboard a ship by force often with the help of liquor or drugs **b :** to put by force or threat of force into a place of detention **2 :** to put by trickery into an undesirable position [*Shanghai,* China; from the former use of this method to secure sailors for voyages to east Asia] — **shang·hai·er** \-'hī-ər, -'hīr\ *n*

Shan·gri–la \ˌshaŋ-gri-'lä\ *n* **1 :** a beautiful imaginary place where life approaches perfection **:** UTOPIA **2 :** a remote usually idyllic hideaway [*Shangri-La,* imaginary community depicted in the novel *Lost Horizon* by James Hilton]

shank \'shaŋk\ *n* **1 a :** the part of the leg between the knee and the ankle in humans or the corresponding part in various other vertebrates **b :** a cut of meat (as beef or lamb) from usually the upper part of a leg **2 :** a straight narrow usually essential part of an object: as **a :** a straight shaft (as of an anchor or fishhook) **b :** the stem of a tobacco pipe or the part between the stem and the bowl **c :** the narrow part of the sole of a shoe beneath the instep **3 :** a part of a tool that connects the acting part with a part (as a handle) by which it is held or moved ⟨the *shank* of a drill bit⟩ ⟨the *shank* of a key⟩ **4 a :** the latter part of a period of time **b :** the early or main part of a period of time [Old English *scanca*]

shan't \shant, 'shant, shȧnt, 'shȧnt\ **:** shall not

shan·tung \shan-'təŋ, 'shan-\ *n* **:** a fabric in plain weave having a slightly irregular surface [*Shantung* (Shandong), China]

[1]**shanty** *variant of* CHANTEY

[2]**shan·ty** \'shant-ē\ *n, pl* **shanties :** a small roughly built shelter or dwelling **:** HUT [probably from Canadian French *chantier* "lumber camp, hut," from French, "builders' yard, ways, support for barrels," from Medieval French, "support," from Latin *cantherius* "worn-out horse, rafter, trellis"]

shan·ty·town \-ˌtau̇n\ *n* **:** a town or section of a town consisting mostly of shanties

shap·able *or* **shape·able** \'shā-pə-bəl\ *adj* **1 :** capable of being shaped **2 :** SHAPELY

[1]**shape** \'shāp\ *vb* **1 :** FORM 1, CREATE; *esp* **:** to give a particular form or shape to **2 :** to adapt in shape so as to fit neatly and closely **3 :** DEVISE 1b, PLAN **4 :** to embody in definite form ⟨*shaping* a tradition into an epic⟩ **5 :** to make fit **:** ADAPT ⟨learn to *shape* your aims to your abilities⟩ **6 :** to determine or

\ə\ abut	\au̇\ out	\i\ tip	\ȯ\ saw	\u̇\ foot
\ər\ further	\ch\ chin	\ī\ life	\ȯi\ coin	\y\ yet
\a\ mat	\e\ pet	\j\ job	\th\ thin	\yü\ few
\ā\ take	\ē\ easy	\ŋ\ sing	\th̲\ this	\yu̇\ cure
\ä\ cot, cart	\g\ go	\ō\ bone	\ü\ food	\zh\ vision

direct the course of (as life) **7 :** to take on or approach a definite form : DEVELOP — often used with *up* [Old English *sceapen, gescapen,* past participle of *scieppan*]

[2]**shape** *n* **1 a :** the visible characteristic of a particular thing **b :** spatial form **c :** a standard or universally recognized spatial form ⟨in the *shape* of a circle⟩ **2 :** bodily contour especially of the trunk : FIGURE **3 a :** PHANTOM 1a, APPARITION **b :** assumed appearance : GUISE **4 :** form of embodiment (as in words) : a form (as of thought) that is definite and organized ⟨a plan took *shape*⟩ ⟨got the speech into *shape*⟩ **5 :** something having a particular form ⟨the *shape* of society now⟩ **6 :** the condition in which one exists at a particular time ⟨in good *shape* for your age⟩ ***synonyms*** see FORM — **shaped** *adj*

shape·less \'shā-pləs\ *adj* **1 :** having no definite shape **2 a :** deprived of usual or normal shape : MISSHAPEN **b :** not shapely — **shape·less·ly** *adv* — **shape·less·ness** *n*

shape·ly \'shā-plē\ *adj* **shape·li·er; -est :** having a regular or pleasing shape ⟨a *shapely* figure⟩ — **shape·li·ness** *n*

shap·en \'shā-pən\ *adj* **:** fashioned in or provided with a definite shape — usually used in combination ⟨an ill-*shapen* body⟩

shard \'shärd\ *n* **1 :** a small piece : SCRAP; *esp* **:** a fragment of something brittle (as glass) **2** *or* **sherd** \'shərd\ **:** a fragment of pottery at or from an archaeological site [Old English *sceard*]

[1]**share** \'sheər, 'shaər\ *n* **1 a :** a portion belonging to, due to, or contributed by an individual **b :** a fair portion **2 a :** the part allotted or belonging to one of a number owning something together ⟨a *share* of the business⟩ **b :** any of the equal portions or interests into which the property of a corporation is divided [Old English *scearu* "cutting, tonsure"]

[2]**share** *vb* **1 :** to divide and distribute in shares : APPORTION — usually used with *out* **2 :** to partake of, use, experience, or enjoy with others **3 a :** to give or be given a share in **b :** to have a share — used with *in* — **shar·er** *n*

[3]**share** *n* **:** PLOWSHARE [Old English *scear*]

share·crop \'sheər-ˌkräp, 'shaər-\ *vb* **:** to farm or produce as a sharecropper

share·crop·per \-ˌkräp-ər\ *n* **:** a farmer who works land for a landlord in return for a share of the crop

share·hold·er \-ˌhōl-dər\ *n* **:** one that owns a share in a property; *esp* **:** STOCKHOLDER

share·ware \-ˌwaər, -ˌweər\ *n* **:** software with usually only basic capability which is available for trial use at little or no cost but which can be upgraded for a fee

[1]**shark** \'shärk\ *n* **:** any of numerous usually rather large marine fishes that have rough grayish skin and a skeleton composed of cartilage, that typically prey on other animals and are somethimes dangerous to people, and that include some caught for the oil in their livers or for their hide from which a leather is made [origin unknown]

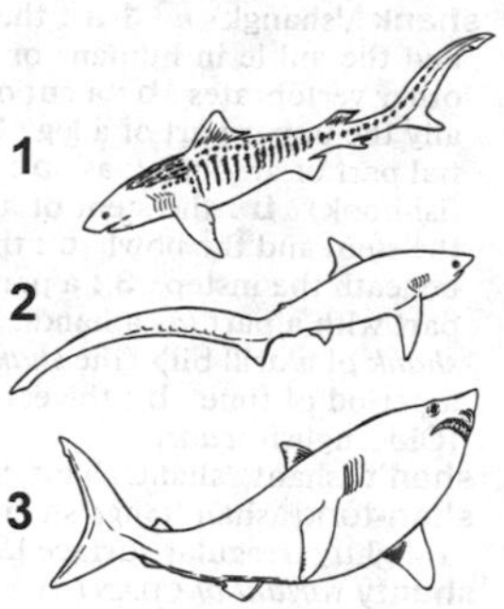

[1]shark: *1* tiger, *2* thresher, *3* great white

[2]**shark** *n* **1 :** a greedy crafty person who takes advantage of the needs of others ⟨a loan *shark*⟩ **2 :** a person who excels especially in a particular field ⟨a *shark* at math⟩ [probably from German *Schurke* "scoundrel"]

shark·skin \-ˌskin\ *n* **1 :** the hide of a shark or leather made from it **2 a :** a smooth durable woolen or worsted suiting in twill or basket weave with small woven designs **b :** a smooth crisp fabric with a dull finish made usually of rayon in basket weave

shark sucker *n* **:** REMORA

[1]**sharp** \'shärp\ *adj* **1 :** adapted to cutting or piercing: as **a :** having a thin keen edge or fine point **b :** briskly cold : CHILLY **2 a :** keen in intellect : QUICK-WITTED **b :** keen in perception : ACUTE, VIGILANT ⟨has *sharp* sight⟩ **c :** keen in attention to one's own interest sometimes to the point of being unethical **3 :** keen in spirit or action: as **a :** full of activity : BRISK **b :** capable of acting or reacting strongly; *esp* **:** CAUSTIC 1 **4 :** SEVERE, HARSH: as **a :** inclined to or marked by irritability or anger **b :** causing intense mental or physical distress ⟨a *sharp* pain⟩ **c :** cutting in language or import ⟨a *sharp* retort⟩ **5 a :** having a strong odor or flavor ⟨*sharp* cheese⟩ **b :** ACRID 1 **c :** having a strong piercing sound **6 a :** terminating in a point or edge ⟨*sharp* features⟩ **b :** involving an abrupt change in direction ⟨a *sharp* turn⟩ **c :** clear in outline or detail : DISTINCT **d :** set forth with clarity and distinctness ⟨*sharp* contrast⟩ **7 a :** higher by a half step ⟨tone of G *sharp*⟩ **b :** higher than the proper pitch **c :** having a sharp in the signature ⟨key of F *sharp*⟩ **8 :** STYLISH, DRESSY [Old English *scearp*] — **sharp·ly** *adv* — **sharp·ness** *n*

synonyms SHARP, KEEN, ACUTE mean having or showing alert competence and clear understanding. SHARP implies quick perception, clever resourcefulness, or sometimes questionable trickiness ⟨*sharp* traders⟩. KEEN suggests quickness, enthusiasm, and a penetrating mind ⟨a *keen* student of history⟩. ACUTE implies a power to penetrate and may suggest subtlety and sharpness of discrimination ⟨*acute* mathematical reasoning⟩.

[2]**sharp** *adv* **1 :** in a sharp manner : SHARPLY **2 :** EXACTLY 1, PRECISELY ⟨4 o'clock *sharp*⟩

[3]**sharp** *n* **1 :** a musical note or tone one half step higher than a specified note or tone; *also* **:** a character # on a line or space of the staff indicating such a note or tone **2 :** a real or self-styled expert; *also* **:** SHARPER

[4]**sharp** *vb* **1 :** to raise in pitch especially by a half step **2 :** to sing or play above the proper pitch

sharp·en \'shär-pən\ *vb* **sharp·ened; sharp·en·ing** \'shärp-ning, -ə-ning\ **:** to make or become sharp or sharper — **sharp·en·er** \'shärp-nər, -ə-nər\ *n*

sharp·er \'shär-pər\ *n* **:** CHEAT 2, SWINDLER

sharp–eyed \'shär-'pīd\ *adj* **:** having keen sight; *also* **:** keen in observing or penetrating

sharp·ie *or* **sharpy** \'shär-pē\ *n, pl* **sharp·ies** **1 :** SHARPER **2 :** an exceptionally keen or alert person

sharp–nosed \'shärp-'nōzd\ *adj* **:** keen in smelling

sharp practice *n* **:** unscrupulous seeking or taking of advantage (as in business)

sharp–set \'shärp-'set\ *adj* **1 :** set at a sharp angle or so as to present a sharp edge **2 :** eager in appetite or desire — **sharp–set·ness** *n*

sharp·shoot·er \'shärp-ˌshüt-ər\ *n* **:** a proficient marksman especially with a rifle — **sharp·shoot·ing** \-ˌshüt-ing\ *n*

sharp–sight·ed \-'sīt-əd\ *adj* **1 :** having acute sight **2 :** mentally keen or alert

sharp–tongued \-'təngd\ *adj* **:** harsh or bitter in speech

sharp–wit·ted \-'wit-əd\ *adj* **:** having or showing a keen mind

Shas·ta daisy \'shast-ə-\ *n* **:** a large-flowered garden daisy [Mount *Shasta,* northern California]

[1]**shat·ter** \'shat-ər\ *vb* **1 :** to cause to drop or be dispersed **2 :** to break at once into pieces **3 :** to damage badly : RUIN ⟨my health had been *shattered*⟩ **4 :** to drop or scatter parts (as leaves, petals, or fruit) [Middle English *schateren*]

[2]**shatter** *n* **:** FRAGMENT 1, SHRED ⟨the vase lay in *shatters*⟩

shat·ter·proof \ˌshat-ər-'prüf\ *adj* **:** made so as not to shatter ⟨*shatterproof* glass⟩

[1]**shave** \'shāv\ *vb* **shaved; shaved** *or* **shav·en** \'shā-vən\; **shav·ing** **1 a :** to cut off thin slices from (as a board with a plane) **b :** to cut off closely ⟨a lawn *shaven* close⟩ **2 :** to make bare or smooth by cutting the hair from ⟨had my head *shaved*⟩ **3 :** to cut or pare off by means of an edged instrument (as a razor); *esp* **:** to remove hair close to the skin with a razor **4 :** to come close to or touch lightly in passing [Old English *scafan*]

[2]**shave** *n* **1 :** any of various tools for shaving or cutting thin slices **2 :** a thin slice : SHAVING **3 :** an act or process of shaving **4 :** an act of coming very near to

shave·ling \'shāv-ling\ *n* **1** *usually disparaging* **:** a tonsured clergyman : PRIEST **2 :** STRIPLING

shav·er \'shā-vər\ *n* **1 :** a person who shaves **2 :** a tool or machine for shaving; *esp* **:** an electric razor **3 :** BOY 1, YOUNGSTER

shave·tail \'shāv-ˌtāl\ *n* **1 :** a pack mule especially when newly broken in **2** *usually disparaging* **:** SECOND LIEUTENANT [from the practice of shaving the tails of newly broken mules]

Sha·vi·an \'shā-vē-ən\ *n* **:** an admirer or devotee of G. B. Shaw, his writings, or his social and political theories [New Latin *Shavius,* latinized form of George Bernard *Shaw*] — **Shavian** *adj*

shav·ing \'shā-ving\ *n* **1 :** the act of one that shaves **2 :** something shaved off ⟨wood *shavings*⟩

shaw \'shȯ\ *n, dialect* **:** COPPICE, THICKET [Old English *sceaga*]

[1]**shawl** \'shȯl\ *n* **:** a square or oblong piece of fabric used especially as a covering for the head or shoulders [Persian *shāl*]
[2]**shawl** *vt* **:** to wrap in or as if in a shawl
shawm \'shȯm\ *n* **:** a medieval double-reed woodwind instrument [Middle French *chalemie,* derived from Latin *calamus* "reed," from Greek *kalamos*]
Shaw·nee \shȯ-'nē, shä-\ *n, pl* **Shawnee** *or* **Shawnees** **1 :** a member of an American Indian people originally of the central Ohio valley **2 :** the Algonquian language of the Shawnee people [derived from Shawnee *ša·wano·ki,* literally, "southerners"]
shay \'shā\ *n, chiefly dialect* **:** CHAISE 1 [back-formation from *chaise,* taken as pl.]
[1]**she** \shē, 'shē\ *pron* **1 :** that female one who is neither speaker nor hearer ⟨*she* is a doctor⟩ — compare HE, HER, HERS, IT, THEY **2 —** used to refer to one regarded as feminine (as by personification) ⟨*she* was a fine ship⟩ [Middle English]
[2]**she** \'shē\ *n* **:** a female person or animal — often used in combination ⟨*she*-cat⟩ ⟨*she*-cousin⟩
sheaf \'shēf\ *n, pl* **sheaves** \'shēvz\ **1 :** a bundle of stalks and ears of grain **2 :** something resembling or suggesting a sheaf of grain ⟨a *sheaf* of papers⟩ [Old English *scēaf*] — **sheaf·like** \'shē-,flīk\ *adj*

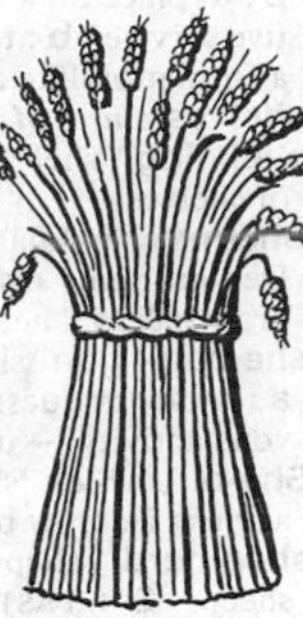
sheaf 1

[1]**shear** \'shiər\ *vb* **sheared; sheared** *or* **shorn** \'shōrn, 'shȯrn\; **shear·ing 1 :** to cut the hair or wool from ⟨*shearing* sheep⟩ **2 :** to deprive of by or as if by cutting ⟨*shorn* of their power⟩ **3 :** to cut or cut through with or as if with shears ⟨*shear* a metal sheet in two⟩ **4 :** to become divided or broken under the action of a shear ⟨bolts may *shear* off⟩ [Old English *scieran*] — **shear·er** *n*
[2]**shear** *n* **1 a :** a cutting implement similar or identical to a pair of scissors but typically larger — usually used in plural; *also* **:** one blade of a pair of shears **b :** any of various cutting machines operating by the action of opposed cutting edges of metal — usually used in plural **2 :** an action or force that causes or tends to cause two parts of a body to slide on each other in a direction parallel to their plane of contact
sheared \'shiərd\ *adj* **:** formed or finished by shearing; *esp* **:** having the pile cut to uniform length ⟨*sheared* beaver⟩
shear·wa·ter \'shiər-,wȯt-ər, -,wät-\ *n* **:** any of numerous oceanic birds related to the petrels and albatrosses that in flight usually skim close to the waves
sheath \'shēth\ *n, pl* **sheaths** \'shēt͟hz, 'shēths\ **1 :** a case for a blade (as of a knife) **2 :** a covering especially of an anatomical structure suggesting a sheath in form or use **3 :** a woman's close-fitting dress [Old English *scēath*]
sheathe \'shēt͟h\ *vt* **1 :** to put into or as if into a sheath **2 :** to encase or cover with something (as sheets of metal) that protects [Middle English *shethen,* from *shethe* "sheath"] — **sheath·er** *n*
sheath·ing \'shē-t͟hing, -thing\ *n* **:** material used to sheathe something; *esp* **:** the first covering of boards or of waterproof material on the outside wall of a frame house or on a timber roof
sheath knife *n* **:** a knife having a fixed blade and designed to be carried in a sheath
sheave \'shiv, 'shēv\ *n* **:** a grooved wheel **:** PULLEY [Middle English *sheve*]
she·bang \shi-'bang\ *n* **:** everything involved in what is under consideration — usually used in the phrase *the whole shebang* [origin unknown]
[1]**shed** \'shed\ *vb* **shed; shed·ding 1 :** to throw off **:** REPEL ⟨the duck's plumage *sheds* water⟩ **2 a :** to pour forth in drops ⟨*shed* tears⟩ **b :** to cause (blood) to flow by cutting or wounding **c :** to give off or out ⟨the sun *sheds* light⟩ **3 a :** to rid of **:** DISCARD ⟨*shed* excess weight⟩ **b :** to cast (as a natural covering) aside ⟨a snake *sheds* its skin⟩ ⟨the cat is *shedding* hair⟩ **c :** to let fall (as leaves) **d :** to eject or discharge from the body of a plant or animal ⟨molds *shed* spores⟩ [Old English *scēadan* "to divide, separate"] — **shed·der** *n*
[2]**shed** *n* **1 :** a slight structure built for shelter or storage ⟨tool *shed*⟩ **2 :** a single-storied building with one or more sides unenclosed ⟨customs *shed*⟩ [alteration of earlier *shadde,* probably from Middle English *shade* "shade"]
[3]**shed** *vt* **shed·ded; shed·ding :** to put or house in a shed
she'd \shēd, ,shēd\ **:** she had **:** she would
sheen \'shēn\ *n* **1 :** a bright or shining condition **2 :** subdued shininess of surface ⟨the *sheen* of satin⟩ [Old English *sciene*] — **sheeny** \'shē-nē\ *adj*
sheep \'shēp\ *n, pl* **sheep 1 :** any of various hollow-horned cud-chewing mammals related to the goats but stockier and lacking a beard in the male; *esp* **:** one long domesticated especially for its meat and wool **2 :** one that is like a sheep (as in being timid, defenseless, or easily led) **3 :** SHEEPSKIN 1a [Old English *scēap*] — **sheep** *adj*
sheep·cote \-,kōt, -,kät\ *n, chiefly British* **:** SHEEPFOLD
sheep·dog \-,dȯg\ *n* **:** a dog used to tend, drive, or guard sheep
sheep·fold \'shēp-,fōld\ *n* **:** a pen or shelter for sheep
sheep·herd·er \'shēp-,hərd-ər\ *n* **:** a worker in charge of a flock of sheep especially on open range — **sheep·herd·ing** \-,hərd-ing\ *n*
sheep·ish \'shē-pish\ *adj* **1 :** resembling a sheep in meekness, stupidity, or timidity **2 :** embarassed by consciousness of a fault ⟨a *sheepish* look⟩ — **sheep·ish·ly** *adv* — **sheep·ish·ness** *n*
sheep's eye *n* **:** a shy, longing, and usually amorous glance
sheeps·head \'shēps-,hed\ *n* **:** any of several fishes; *esp* **:** a food fish of the Atlantic and Gulf coasts of the U.S. with broad front teeth
sheep·shear·er \'shēp-,shir-ər\ *n* **:** one that shears sheep
sheep·shear·ing \-,shiər-ing\ *n* **1 :** the act of shearing sheep **2 :** the time or season for shearing sheep
sheep·skin \'shēp-,skin\ *n* **1 a :** the skin of a sheep or leather prepared from it **b :** PARCHMENT 1 **2 :** DIPLOMA
[1]**sheer** \'shiər\ *adj* **1 :** very thin or transparent ⟨*sheer* stockings⟩ **2 a :** UTTER ⟨*sheer* nonsense⟩ **b :** taken or acting apart from everything else ⟨by *sheer* force⟩ **3 :** marked by great and unbroken steepness [Middle English *schere* "free from guilt"] ***synonyms*** see STEEP — **sheer·ly** *adv* — **sheer·ness** *n*
[2]**sheer** *adv* **1 :** WHOLLY 1, ALTOGETHER **2 :** straight up or down
[3]**sheer** *vi* **:** to turn from a course **:** SWERVE [perhaps alteration of [1]*shear*]
[4]**sheer** *n* **:** a turning from or change in the course of a ship
[5]**sheer** *n* **:** the fore-and-aft curvature from bow to stern of a ship's deck as shown in side elevation [perhaps alteration of [2]*shear*]
[1]**sheet** \'shēt\ *n* **1 :** a broad piece of cloth; *esp* **:** an oblong of cloth used as an article of bedding next to the person **2 a :** a usually rectangular piece of paper **b** *pl* **:** the unbound pages of a book **c :** a newspaper, periodical, or occasional publication **d :** the unseparated postage stamps printed by one impression of a plate on a single piece of paper **3 :** a broad expanse or surface ⟨a *sheet* of ice⟩ **4 :** a portion of something that is thin in comparison to its length and breadth ⟨a *sheet* of plastic⟩ [Old English *scēte, sciete*]
[2]**sheet** *vt* **1 :** to cover with a sheet **:** SHROUD **2 :** to furnish with sheets
[3]**sheet** *n* **1 :** a rope or chain that regulates the angle at which a sail is set in relation to the wind **2** *pl* **:** the spaces at either end of an open boat not taken up by seats [Old English *scēata* "lower corner of a sail"]
sheet anchor *n* **1 :** an unusually large anchor especially for use in an emergency **2 :** something that constitutes a main support or dependence in danger
sheet·ing \'shēt-ing\ *n* **:** material in the form of sheets or suitable for forming into sheets
sheet lightning *n* **:** lightning in diffused or sheet form
sheet metal *n* **:** metal in the form of sheets
sheet music *n* **:** music printed on unbound sheets of paper
Sheet·rock \'shēt-,räk\ *trademark* — used for drywall
sheikh *or* **sheik** \'shēk, *for 1 also* 'shāk\ *n* **1 :** an Arab chief **2** *usually sheik* **:** a man held to be irresistibly attractive to romantic young women [Arabic *shaykh*] — **sheik·dom** \-dəm\ *n*
shek·el \'shek-əl\ *n* **1 :** an ancient unit of weight or value; *esp* **:** a Hebrew unit equal to about 252 grains troy (about 16.3

grams) **2** : a coin weighing one shekel **3 a** : the basic monetary unit of modern Israel **b** : a coin or note representing one shekel [Hebrew *sheqel*]

shel·drake \ˈshel-ˌdrāk\ *n* **1** : SHELDUCK **2** : MERGANSER [Middle English, from *sheld-* (akin to early Dutch *schillede* "parti-colored") + *drake* "drake"]

shel·duck \-ˌdək\ *n* : any of several Old World ducks; *esp* : a common mostly black-and-white European duck slightly larger than the mallard [*shel-* (as in *sheldrake*) + *duck*]

shelduck

shelf \ˈshelf\ *n, pl* **shelves** \ˈshelvz\ **1 a** : a thin flat usually long and narrow piece of firm material fastened horizontally (as on a wall) at a distance from the floor to hold objects **b** : the contents of a shelf **2** : something resembling a shelf: as **a** : a sandbank or ledge of rocks usually partially submerged **b** : a flat projecting layer of rock [Middle English] — **shelf·like** \ˈshel-ˌflīk\ *adj* — **on the shelf** : in a state of inactivity or uselessness

shelf fungus *n* : BRACKET FUNGUS

shelf life *n* : the period of time during which a material may be stored and remain suitable for use

[1]**shell** \ˈshel\ *n* **1 a** : a hard rigid outer covering of an animal (as a turtle, oyster, or beetle) **b** : the outer covering of an egg (as of a bird or reptile) **c** : the outer covering of a nut, fruit, or seed especially when hard or toughly fibrous **2** : shell material or shells especially of mollusks; *also* : a shell-bearing mollusk **3** : something that resembles a shell: as **a** : a framework or exterior structure **b** : a casing without substance ⟨the *shell* of my former self⟩ **c** : an edible case for holding a filling ⟨a pastry *shell*⟩ **d** : a reinforced concrete arched or domed roof used primarily over large undivided areas **4** : an impersonal manner that conceals the presence or absence of feeling **5** : a narrow light racing boat propelled by two, four, or eight persons pulling oars; *also* : SCULL **6** : any of the spheres defined by the orbits of a group of electrons of approximately equal energy surrounding the nucleus of an atom **7 a** : a hollow projectile for artillery containing an explosive bursting charge **b** : a metal or metal and plastic or paper case which holds the charge of powder and shot or a bullet used with breech-loading small arms **8** : a plain usually sleeveless blouse or sweater [Old English *sciell*] — **shell** *adj* — **shell·work** \ˈshel-ˌwərk\ *n* — **shelly** \ˈshel-ē\ *adj*

[2]**shell** *vb* **1 a** : to remove or fall from a natural enclosing cover (as a shell or husk) ⟨*shell* peas⟩ **b** : to remove the grains from (as an ear of corn) **2** : to shoot shells at, upon, or into : BOMBARD **3** : to collect shells (as from a beach)

she'll \shēl, shil, ˌshēl\ : she shall : she will

[1]**shel·lac** \shə-ˈlak\ *n* **1** : purified lac **2** : a preparation of lac dissolved in alcohol that is used in finishing wood [*shell* + *lac*]

[2]**shellac** *vt* **shel·lacked; shel·lack·ing** **1** : to coat with shellac **2** : to defeat decisively

shel·lack·ing \shə-ˈlak-ing\ *n* : a decisive defeat or sound drubbing ⟨took a *shellacking* in last year's election⟩

shell·back \ˈshel-ˌbak\ *n* : an old or veteran sailor

shell bean *n* **1** : a bean grown primarily for its edible seeds — compare SNAP BEAN **2** : the edible seed of a bean

shelled \ˈsheld\ *adj* **1 a** : having a shell ⟨a *shelled* creature⟩ **b** : having a shell especially of a specified kind — often used in combination ⟨hard-*shelled*⟩ **2 a** : having the shell removed ⟨*shelled* nuts⟩ **b** : removed from the cob ⟨*shelled* corn⟩

shell·fire \ˈshel-ˌfīr\ *n* : a firing or exploding of shells

shell·fish \-ˌfish\ *n* : an aquatic invertebrate animal with a shell; *esp* : an edible mollusk (as an oyster) or crustacean (as a crab)

shell out *vb* : PAY 1

shell pink *n* : a light yellowish pink

shell·proof \ˈshel-ˈprüf\ *adj* : capable of resisting shells or bombs

shell shock *n* : COMBAT FATIGUE

shell–shocked *adj* **1** : affected with combat fatigue **2** : mentally confused, upset, or exhausted as a result of excessive strain

[1]**shel·ter** \ˈshel-tər\ *n* **1 a** : something that covers or affords protection ⟨a fallout *shelter*⟩ **b** : a place that provides food and lodging (as to the homeless) **c** : a place that houses and feeds stray or unwanted animals **2** : the state of being covered and protected [origin unknown] — **shel·ter·less** \-ləs\ *adj*

[2]**shelter** *vb* **shel·tered; shel·ter·ing** \-tə-ring, -tring\ **1** : to constitute or provide a shelter for : PROTECT **2** : to place under shelter or protection **3** : to take shelter — **shel·ter·er** \-tər-ər\ *n*

shel·ter·belt \-tər-ˌbelt\ *n* : a barrier of trees and shrubs that protects (as soil and crops) from wind and storm and lessens erosion

shelter half *n* : one of the halves of a shelter tent

shelter tent *n* : a small tent for two persons usually consisting of two interchangeable pieces of waterproof cotton duck that fasten together at an overlap

shel·tie *or* **shel·ty** \ˈshel-tē\ *n, pl* **shelties** **1** : SHETLAND PONY **2** : SHETLAND SHEEPDOG [probably of Scandinavian origin]

shelve \ˈshelv\ *vb* **1** : to furnish with shelves ⟨*shelve* a closet⟩ **2** : to place on a shelf ⟨*shelve* books⟩ **3 a** : to remove from active service **b** : to put off or aside ⟨*shelve* a bill⟩ **4** : to slope in a formation like a shelf : INCLINE — **shelv·er** *n*

shelves *plural of* SHELF

shelv·ing \ˈshel-ving\ *n* **1** : material for shelves **2** : a number of shelves

She·ma \shə-ˈmä\ *n* : the central creed of Judaism comprising Deuteronomy 6:4–9 and 11:13–21 and Numbers 15:37–41 [Hebrew *shĕma*ʿ "hear," first word of Deuteronomy 6:4]

she·nan·i·gan \shə-ˈnan-i-gən\ *n* **1** : an underhanded trick **2 a** : tricky or questionable conduct **b** : high-spirited or mischievous activity — usually used in plural [origin unknown]

She·ol \shē-ˈōl, ˈshē-ˌ\ *n* **1** : the dwelling place of the dead in ancient Hebrew belief **2** : HELL 1 [Hebrew *Shĕʾōl*]

[1]**shep·herd** \ˈshep-ərd\ *n* **1** : a person who tends and guards sheep **2** : PASTOR **3** : GERMAN SHEPHERD [Old English *scēaphyrde,* from *scēap* "sheep" + *hierde* "herdsman"]

[2]**shepherd** *vt* **1** : to tend as a shepherd **2** : to guide or guard in the manner of a shepherd ⟨*shepherd* tourists through a museum⟩

shepherd dog *n* : SHEEPDOG

shep·herd·ess \-ˈshep-ərd-əs\ *n* : a woman or girl who tends and guards sheep

shepherd's check *n* : a pattern of small even black and white checks; *also* : a fabric woven in this pattern — called also *shepherd's plaid*

shepherd's pie *n* : a meat pie topped with mashed potatoes

Sher·a·ton \ˈsher-ət-n\ *adj* : of or relating to an early 19th century English furniture style characterized by delicate construction, graceful proportions, and the use of straight lines [Thomas *Sheraton,* died 1806, English cabinetmaker]

sher·bet \ˈshər-bət\ *also* **sher·bert** \-bərt\ *n* **1** : a cold drink of sweetened and diluted fruit juice **2** : an ice with milk, egg white, or gelatin added [Turkish *serbet,* from Persian *sharbat,* from Arabic *sharbah* "drink"]

sherd *variant of* SHARD

sher·got·tite \ˈshər-gə-ˌtīt\ *n* : any of a class of geologically young meteorites of feldspar and pyroxene [*Shergotty* (Sherghati), town in India]

sher·iff \ˈsher-əf\ *n* : a county official charged with keeping the peace and with judicial duties (as executing the processes and orders of courts) [Old English *scīrgerēfa,* from *scīr* "shire" + *gerēfa* "reeve"]

sher·lock \ˈshər-ˌläk\ *n, often cap* : DETECTIVE [*Sherlock* Holmes, detective in stories by Sir Arthur Conan Doyle]

Sher·pa \ˈsheər-pə, ˈshər-\ *n* : a member of a Tibetan people living on the high southern slopes of the Himalayas and known for providing support for foreign trekkers and mountain climbers

sher·ry \ˈsher-ē\ *n, pl* **sherries** : a fortified wine with a distinctive nutty flavor [*Xeres* (now *Jerez*), Spain]

Word History Wines and distilled spirits are often named after the places where they are made. The region around the town of Jerez (formerly Xeres) in southern Spain produced a type of fortified wine with a rather nutty flavor that was introduced into England in the 16th century. The name *Xeres* was rendered *Sherries* or *Sherris* in English—the initial *sh* was a good approximation of the then current pronunciation of the Spanish sound represented by *x* (which has since changed to a \k̲\ or \h\ sound). Consequently, the wine from Xeres was sold under the name *sherris.* Some English speakers, however, believing that *sherris* was a plural noun, created a singular form *sherry,* which has since become standard. Other English words created by this process of back-formation from a presumed plural form are *pea* from *pease* and *cherry* from *cherise,* a northern dialect form of Medieval French *cerise,* "cherry."

she's \shēz, ˌshēz\ : she is : she has

Shet·land \ˈshet-lənd\ *n* **1 a** : SHETLAND PONY **b** : SHETLAND SHEEPDOG **2** *often not cap* **a** : a lightweight loosely twisted yarn of Shetland wool used for knitting and weaving **b** : a fabric of Shetland wool

Shetland pony *n* : any of a breed of small stocky hardy ponies originating in the Shetland Islands and having a thick coat and long mane and tail

Shetland sheepdog *n* : any of a breed of small heavy-coated dogs developed in the Shetland Islands and resembling miniature collies

Shetland wool *n* : fine wool from sheep raised in the Shetland Islands; *also* : yarn spun from this wool

shew \ˈshō\ *British variant of* SHOW

Shia \ˈshē-ä\ *n* **1** : the Muslims of the branch of Islam comprising sects believing in Ali and the imams as the only rightful successors of Muhammad and in the concealment and messianic return of the last recognized imam **2** : SHIITE **3** : the branch of Islam formed by the Shia [Arabic *shīʿa* "followers, faction, sect"]

shi·at·su \shē-ˈät-sü\ *n* : ACUPRESSURE; *esp* : a form of acupressure that originated in Japan [short for Japanese *shiatsu-ryōhō,* literally, "finger-pressure therapy"]

shib·bo·leth \ˈshib-ə-ləth *also* -ˌleth\ *n* **1 a** : a word or saying used by members of a party or belief and usually regarded by others as empty of real meaning **b** : an idea or saying that is commonly believed **2** : a particular behavior or use of language that identifies a person as belonging to a group [Hebrew *shibbōleth* "stream"]

Word History In the 12th chapter of the book of Judges there is an account of a battle between the Gileadites and the Ephraimites. The Ephraimite army was routed, and the retreating Ephraimites tried to cross the Jordan River at a ford held by the Gileadites. Anyone wishing to pass was asked if he were an Ephraimite. If the reply was "no" he was asked to pronounce a Hebrew word meaning "stream, torrent." The spelling of the word that has come down in Hebrew is *shibbōleth* (in transliteration), but in the Hebrew dialect of the Gileadites the initial sound in this word was very likely \th\ rather than \sh\. (In the dialect of the Ephraimites and eventually in all dialects this \th\ came to be pronounced \sh\.) The Ephraimites had no \th\ sound in their speech, and when a man replied with "*sibbōleth,*" the Gileadites knew he was an Ephraimite and killed him.

[1]**shield** \ˈshēld\ *n* **1** : a broad piece of defensive armor carried on the arm **2** : one that protects or defends : DEFENSE **3** : ESCUTCHEON **4 a** : a device or part that serves as a protective cover or barrier **b** : a protective structure (as a carapace) of some animals **5** : the ancient mass of hard rock that forms the core of a continent **6** : something shaped like or resembling a shield: as **a** : a police officer's badge **b** : a decorative or identifying emblem [Old English *scield*]

[2]**shield** *vt* **1** : to protect with or as if with a shield **2** : to cut off from observation : HIDE ***synonyms*** see DEFEND

shield volcano *n* : a broad rounded volcano that is built up from many layers of lava

[1]**shift** \ˈshift\ *vb* **1** : to exchange for or replace by another : CHANGE **2 a** : to change the place, position, or direction of : MOVE **b** : to make a change in place, position, or direction **c** : to change the gear rotating the transmission shaft of an automobile **3** : to change phonetically **4** : to get along : MANAGE ⟨left the others to *shift* for themselves⟩ [Old English *sciftan* "to divide, arrange"]

[2]**shift** *n* **1 a** : a means or device for effecting an end **b** : a deceitful scheme : DODGE **c** : an effort or expedient exerted or tried in difficult circumstances : EXTREMITY **2** : SLIP 5a, CHEMISE **3** : a change in direction ⟨a *shift* in the wind⟩ **4** : a change in place or position **5** : a group of people who work together in turn with other groups; *also* : the period during which one such group works ⟨working the night *shift*⟩ **6** : a removal from one person or thing to another : TRANSFER ⟨a *shift* of responsibility⟩ **7** : GEARSHIFT

shift·er \ˈshif-tər\ *n* : one that shifts; *esp* : GEARSHIFT

shift key *n* : a key on a keyboard that when pressed enables an alternate character set to be produced by the other keys

shift·less \ˈshift-ləs, ˈshif-\ *adj* **1** : lacking in resourcefulness : INEFFICIENT **2** : lacking in ambition or incentive : LAZY — **shift·less·ly** *adv* — **shift·less·ness** *n*

shifty \ˈshif-tē\ *adj* **shift·i·er; -est** **1 a** : given to deception, evasion, or fraud : TRICKY **b** : capable of evasive movement : ELUSIVE **2** : indicative of a tricky nature ⟨*shifty* eyes⟩ — **shift·i·ly** \-tə-lē\ *adv* — **shift·i·ness** \-tē-nəs\ *n*

Shi·ite \ˈshē-ˌīt\ *n* : a member of the Shia branch of Islam — **Shiite** *adj*

shil·le·lagh *also* **shil·la·lah** \shə-ˈlā-lē\ *n* : CUDGEL, CLUB [*Shillelagh,* town in Ireland famed for its oak trees]

shil·ling \ˈshil-ing\ *n* **1 a** : a former monetary unit of the United Kingdom equal to 12 pence or 1/20 pound **b** : a former monetary unit equal to 1/20 pound of any of various countries in or formerly in the Commonwealth of Nations **2** : a coin representing one shilling **3** : any of several early American coins **4 a** : the basic monetary unit of Kenya, Somalia, Tanzania, and Uganda **b** : a coin representing this unit [Old English *scilling*]

[1]**shil·ly–shal·ly** \ˈshil-ē-ˌshal-ē\ *adj* : IRRESOLUTE [reduplication of *shall I*]

[2]**shilly–shally** *n* : INDECISION, IRRESOLUTION

[3]**shilly–shally** *vi* **shil·ly–shal·lied; shil·ly–shal·ly·ing** **1** : to show hesitation or lack of decisiveness : VACILLATE **2** : to waste time : DAWDLE

[1]**shim** \ˈshim\ *n* : a thin often tapered piece of wood, metal, or stone used to fill in space (as for support or leveling) [origin unknown]

[2]**shim** *vt* **shimmed; shim·ming** : to fill out or level up by the use of a shim

[1]**shim·mer** \ˈshim-ər\ *vi* **shim·mered; shim·mer·ing** \ˈshim-ring, -ə-ring\ **1** : to shine with a wavering light : GLIMMER ⟨leaves *shimmering* in the sunshine⟩ **2** : to appear in a constantly changing wavy form [Old English *scimerian*]

[2]**shimmer** *n* **1** : a wavering light : subdued sparkle or sheen **2** : a wavering image or effect especially when produced by heat waves — **shim·mery** \ˈshim-rē, -ə-rē\ *adj*

[1]**shim·my** \ˈshim-ē\ *n, pl* **shimmies** **1** : a jazz dance characterized by a shaking of the body from the shoulders down **2** : an abnormal vibration especially in the front wheels of an automobile [short for *shimmy-shake,* from *shimmy,* alteration of *chemise*]

[2]**shimmy** *vi* **shim·mied; shim·my·ing** **1** : to shake or quiver in or as if in dancing a shimmy **2** : to vibrate abnormally **3** : SHINNY

[1]**shin** \ˈshin\ *n* : the front part of the vertebrate leg below the knee [Old English *scinu*]

[2]**shin** *vb* **shinned; shin·ning** **1** : SHINNY **2** : to move forward rapidly on foot

shin·bone \ˈshin-ˈbōn, -ˌbōn\ *n* : TIBIA 1

shin·dig \ˈshin-ˌdig\ *n* : a festive occasion: as **a** : a social gathering with dancing **b** : a usually large or lavish party [probably alteration of *shindy*]

shin·dy \ˈshin-dē\ *n, pl* **shindys** *or* **shindies** **1** : SHINDIG a **2** : FRACAS, UPROAR [probably alteration of [1]*shinny*]

[1]**shine** \ˈshīn\ *vb* **shone** \ˈshōn\ *or* **shined; shin·ing** **1** : to send out rays of light **2** : to be bright by reflection of light : GLEAM **3** : to be eminent, noticeable, or distinguished ⟨*shines* in math⟩ **4** : to have a bright glowing appearance **5** : to be conspicuously evident or clear ⟨human sympathy *shone* through all their actions⟩ **6** : to throw or flash the light of **7** *past & past participle* *shined* : to make bright by polishing ⟨*shine* your shoes⟩ [Old English *scīnan*]

[2]**shine** *n* **1** : brightness caused by the emission or reflection of light **2** : a brilliance of quality or appearance **3** : fair weather : SUNSHINE ⟨we will go, rain or *shine*⟩ **4** : TRICK 1b, ANTIC — usually used in plural **5** : LIKING, FANCY ⟨took a *shine* to them⟩ **6** : a polish given to shoes

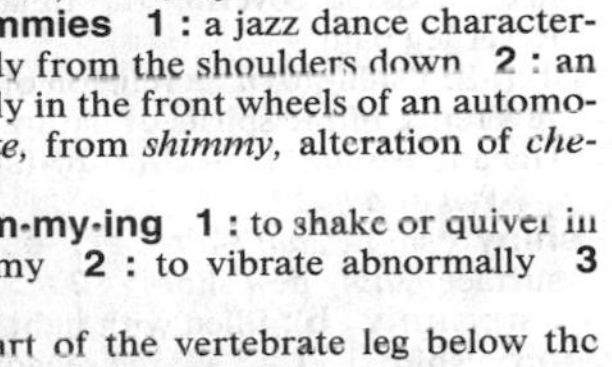
shiner 2

shin·er \ˈshī-nər\ *n* **1**

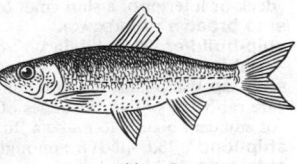

\ə\ **abut**	\au̇\ **out**	\i\ **tip**	\ȯ\ **saw**	\u̇\ **foot**
\ər\ **further**	\ch\ **chin**	\ī\ **life**	\ȯi\ **coin**	\y\ **yet**
\a\ **mat**	\e\ **pet**	\j\ **job**	\th\ **thin**	\yü\ **few**
\ā\ **take**	\ē\ **easy**	\ng\ **sing**	\th\ **this**	\yu̇\ **cure**
\ä\ **cot, cart**	\g\ **go**	\ō\ **bone**	\ü\ **food**	\zh\ **vision**

: one that shines **2** : a silvery fish; *esp* : any of numerous fresh-water American fishes related to the carp **3** : BLACK EYE

[1]**shin·gle** \'shing-gəl\ *n* **1** : a small thin piece of building material (as of wood or a composition of asphalt) for laying in overlapping rows as a covering for the roof or sides of a building **2** : a small signboard **3** : a woman's haircut with the hair trimmed short from the back of the head to the back of the neck [Middle English *schingel*]

[2]**shingle** *vt* **shin·gled; shin·gling** \-gə-ling, -gling\ **1** : to cover with or as if with shingles **2** : to bob and shape (the hair) in a shingle — **shin·gler** \'shing-glər\ *n*

[3]**shingle** *n* **1** : coarse pebbly gravel on the seashore **2** : a place (as a beach) strewn with shingle [Middle English *chyngell*]

shin·gles \'shing-gəlz\ *n* : a virus disease that is marked by inflammation of one or more ganglia accompanied by nerve pain and skin eruption and that is caused by reactivation of the virus causing chicken pox [Medieval Latin *cingulus,* from Latin *cingulum* "girdle," from *cingere* "to gird"]

shin·gly \'shing-gə-lē, -glē\ *adj* : composed of or abounding in shingle ‹a *shingly* beach›

shin·ing *adj* **1** : giving forth or reflecting light **2** : splendidly bright ‹*shining* newness› **3** : having a distinguished quality ‹*shining* prose›; *esp* : ILLUSTRIOUS ‹a *shining* example of integrity›

[1]**shin·ny** \'shin-ē\ *n* : the game of hockey played by children with a curved stick and a ball or block of wood [perhaps from [1]*shin*]

[2]**shinny** *vi* **shin·nied; shin·ny·ing** : to move oneself up or down something vertical (as a pole) especially by alternately hugging it with the arms or hands and the legs [[2]*shin*]

shin·plas·ter \'shin-ˌplas-tər\ *n* **1** : a piece of privately issued paper currency; *esp* : one poorly secured or depreciated in value **2** : a piece of paper currency in denominations of less than one dollar

shin splints *n sing or pl* : injury to and inflammation of the muscles at the point of attachment to the tibia and of the connective tissue covering the tibia that is marked especially by lower leg pain

Shin·to \'shin-ˌtō\ *n* : a religion of Japan consisting chiefly in the reverence of the spirits of natural forces, emperors, and heroes [Japanese *shintō*] — **Shin·to·ism** \-ˌiz-əm\ *n* — **Shin·to·ist** \-əst\ *n or adj*

shiny \'shī-nē\ *adj* **shin·i·er; -est** **1** : having a smooth glossy surface ‹*shiny* new shoes› **2 a** : bright with the rays of the sun : SUNSHINY **b** : filled with light — **shin·i·ness** *n*

[1]**ship** \'ship\ *n* **1 a** : a large seagoing vessel **b** : a square-rigged sailing vessel with three or more masts — compare [5]BARK, BRIG **2** : the crew of a ship **3 a** : AIRSHIP **b** : AIRPLANE **c** : SPACESHIP [Old English *scip*]

[2]**ship** *vb* **shipped; ship·ping** **1 a** : to place or receive on board a ship for transportation by water **b** : to cause to be transported ‹*ship* grain by rail› **2** : to put in place for use ‹*ship* the tiller› **3** : to take into a ship or boat ‹*ship* oars› **4** : to take (as water) over the side **5** : to engage to serve on shipboard **6** : to be sent for delivery (as to a customer) ‹the order will *ship* tomorrow›

-ship \ˌship\ *n suffix* **1** : state : condition : quality ‹friend*ship*› **2** : office : dignity : profession ‹author*ship*› ‹clerk*ship*› ‹lord*ship*› **3** : art : skill ‹seaman*ship*› **4** : something showing, exhibiting, or embodying a quality or state ‹town*ship*› **5** : one entitled to a (specified) rank, title, or appellation ‹your Lady*ship*› [Old English *-scipe*]

ship biscuit *n* : HARDTACK

ship·board \'ship-ˌbōrd, -ˌbȯrd\ *n* **1** : the side of a ship **2** : the deck or interior of a ship ‹met on *shipboard*›

ship bread *n* : HARDTACK

ship·build·er \'ship-ˌbil-dər\ *n* : one who designs or builds ships — **ship·build·ing** \-ding\ *n*

ship·lap \'ship-ˌlap\ *n* : wooden sheathing in which the boards are rabbeted so that the edges of each board lap over the edges of adjacent boards to make a flush joint

ship·load \-'lōd, -ˌlōd\ *n* : enough to fill a ship

ship·man \'ship-mən\ *n* **1** : SAILOR 1a **2** : SHIPMASTER

ship·mas·ter \-ˌmas-tər\ *n* : the master or commander of a ship other than a warship

ship·mate \-ˌmāt\ *n* : a fellow sailor

ship·ment \'ship-mənt\ *n* **1** : the act or process of shipping **2** : the goods shipped

ship of the line : a large warship; *esp* : a square-rigged warship having at least two gun decks and designed to be positioned for battle in a line with other such ships

ship·own·er \'ship-ˌō-nər\ *n* : the owner of a ship

ship·pa·ble \'ship-ə-bəl\ *adj* : suitable for shipping

ship·per \'ship-ər\ *n* : one that sends goods by any form of conveyance

ship·ping \'ship-ing\ *n* **1** : the body of ships in one place or belonging to one port or country **2** : the act or business of one that ships

shipping clerk *n* : one who is employed in a shipping room to assemble, pack, and send out or receive goods

ship·shape \'ship-'shāp\ *adj* : TRIM, TIDY

ship·side \-ˌsīd\ *n* : the area adjacent to a ship; *esp* : a dock at which a ship loads or unloads passengers and freight

ship's papers *n pl* : documents required on board a ship including certificates of ownership and registry, logbook, customs clearance, and crew, passenger, and cargo lists

ship·way \'ship-ˌwā\ *n* : the ways on which a ship is built

ship·worm \'ship-ˌwərm\ *n* : any of various marine clams that have a wormlike body and a shell used for burrowing in submerged wood and that cause damage to wharf piles and wooden ships

[1]**ship·wreck** \-ˌrek\ *n* **1** : a wrecked ship or its parts : WRECKAGE **2** : the destruction or loss of a ship **3** : total loss or failure : RUIN [Old English *scipwræc,* from *scip* "ship" + *wræc* "something driven by the sea"]

[2]**shipwreck** *vt* **1 a** : to cause to experience shipwreck **b** : RUIN **2** : to destroy (a ship) by grounding or foundering

ship·wright \'ship-ˌrīt\ *n* : a carpenter skilled in ship construction and repair

ship·yard \-ˌyärd\ *n* : a place where ships are built or repaired

shire \'shīr, *in place-name compounds* ˌshiər, shər\ *n* **1** : a territorial division of England usually identical with a county **2** : any of a British breed of tall draft horses [Old English *scīr* "office, shire"]

shirk \'shərk\ *vb* **1** : to evade the performance of an obligation **2** : AVOID [origin unknown] — **shirk·er** *n*

shirr \'shər\ *vt* **1** : to draw (as cloth) together in a shirring **2** : to bake (eggs removed from the shell) until set [origin unknown]

shirr·ing \'shər-ing\ *n* : a decorative gathering (as of cloth) made by drawing up the material along two or more parallel lines of stitching

shirring

shirt \'shərt\ *n* : a garment for the upper part of the body: as **a** : a loose cloth garment usually having a collar, sleeves, a front opening, and a tail long enough to be tucked inside trousers or a skirt **b** : UNDERSHIRT [Old English *scyrte*] — **shirted** *adj* — **shirt·less** \-ləs\ *adj*

shirt·front \-ˌfrənt\ *n* : the front of a shirt

shirt·ing \'shərt-ing\ *n* : fabric suitable for shirts

shirt·mak·er \'shərt-ˌmā-kər\ *n* : one that makes shirts

shirt·sleeve \-ˌslēv\ *n* : the sleeve of a shirt — **in one's shirtsleeves** *or* **in shirtsleeves** : wearing a shirt but no coat

shirt·tail \'shərt-ˌtāl\ *n* : the part of a shirt that reaches below the waist especially in the back

shirt·waist \'shərt-ˌwāst\ *n* : a woman's tailored garment (as a dress or blouse) with details copied from men's shirts

shirty \'shərt-ē\ *adj, chiefly British* : being annoyed : ANGRY

shish ke·bab \'shish-kə-ˌbäb\ *n* : kebab cooked on skewers [Turkish *şişkebabi,* from *şiş* "spit" + *kebap* "roasted meat"]

shiv·a·ree \ˌshiv-ə-'rē, 'shiv-ə-ˌrē\ *n* : a noisy mock serenade to a newly married couple [French *charivari*] — **shivaree** *vt*

[1]**shiv·er** \'shiv-ər\ *n* : one of the small pieces into which a brittle thing is broken by sudden violence [Middle English]

[2]**shiver** *vb* **shiv·ered; shiv·er·ing** \'shiv-ring, -ə-ring\ : to break into many small pieces : SHATTER

[3]**shiver** *vi* **shiv·ered; shiv·er·ing** \'shiv-ring, -ə-ring\ : to undergo trembling (as from cold or fear) : QUIVER [Middle English *chiveren*]

[4]**shiver** *n* **1** : an instance of shivering **2** : a thrill of emotion and especially fear — usually used in plural with *the* ‹horror movies give him the *shivers*›

shiv·ery \ˈshiv-rē, -ə-rē\ *adj* **1** : characterized by shivers **2** : causing shivers ⟨*shivery* ghost stories⟩
shlemiel *variant of* SCHLEMIEL
shlock *variant of* SCHLOCK
shm- — see SCHM-
shmooze *variant of* SCHMOOZE
[1]shoal \ˈshōl\ *adj* : SHALLOW ⟨*shoal* water⟩ [Old English *sceald*]
[2]shoal *n* **1** : a shallow place in a body of water (as the sea or a river) **2** : a sandbank or sandbar that makes the water shallow
[3]shoal *vi* : to become shallow
[4]shoal *n* : a large group (as of fish) : SCHOOL, CROWD [Old English *scolu* "multitude"]
[5]shoal *vi* : [4]SCHOOL, THRONG
shoat \ˈshōt\ *n* : a young hog and especially one that has been weaned [Middle English *shote*]
[1]shock \ˈshäk\ *n* : a pile of sheaves of grain or stalks of corn set up (as in a field) with the butt ends down [Middle English]
[2]shock *vt* : to collect into shocks
[3]shock *n* **1** : the impact or encounter of individuals or groups in combat **2** : a violent shake or jar : CONCUSSION **3 a** : a disturbance in the equilibrium or permanence of something **b** (1) : a sudden or violent mental or emotional disturbance (2) : something that causes such disturbance ⟨the loss came as a *shock*⟩ (3) : the state of being so disturbed ⟨were in *shock* at the news⟩ **4** : a state of bodily collapse associated with reduced blood volume and pressure and caused usually by severe especially crushing injuries, hemorrhage, or burns **5** : sudden stimulation of the nerves and convulsive contraction of the muscles caused by the discharge of electricity through the animal body **6 a** : STROKE 5 **b** : CORONARY THROMBOSIS [Middle French *choc,* from *choquer* "to strike against"]
[4]shock *vt* **1 a** : to strike with surprise, terror, horror, or disgust ⟨*shocked* by the city's slums⟩ **b** : to subject to the action of an electrical discharge **2** : to drive by or as if by a shock
[5]shock *n* : a thick bushy mass (as of hair) [perhaps from [1]*shock*]
shock absorber *n* : a device for absorbing the energy of sudden impulses or shocks in machinery or structures
shock·er \ˈshäk-ər\ *n* : one that shocks; *esp* : something horrifying or offensive (as a sensational film or work of fiction)
shock·ing *adj* : extremely startling, distressing, or offensive ⟨*shocking* news⟩ — **shock·ing·ly** \-ing-lē\ *adv*
shock therapy *n* : the treatment of mental disorder by causing coma or convulsions especially through use of electric currents — called also *shock treatment*
shock troops *n pl* : troops chosen for offensive work because of their high morale, training, and discipline
shock wave *n* : a wave formed by the sudden compression (as by an earthquake or supersonic aircraft) of the substance through which the wave travels
shod \ˈshäd\ *adj* **1** : wearing shoes **2** : furnished or equipped with a shoe
[1]shod·dy \ˈshäd-ē\ *n* **1** : a fabric manufactured wholly or partly from reclaimed wool **2** : inferior, imitation, or pretentious articles or matter [origin unknown]
[2]shoddy *adj* **shod·di·er; -est** **1** : made of shoddy **2 a** : cheaply imitative : vulgarly pretentious ⟨*shoddy* merchandise⟩ **b** : hastily or poorly done : INFERIOR ⟨*shoddy* workmanship⟩ **c** : SHABBY 2a — **shod·di·ly** \ˈshäd-l-ē\ *adv* — **shod·di·ness** \ˈshäd-ē-nəs\ *n*
[1]shoe \ˈshü\ *n* **1** : an outer covering for the human foot typically made of leather with a thick or stiff sole and an attached heel **2** : something that resembles a shoe in appearance or use: as **a** : HORSESHOE 1 **b** : the runner of a sled **c** : the part of a brake that presses on the wheel of a vehicle **3** : the outside casing of an automobile tire [Old English *scōh*]
[2]shoe *vt* **shod** \ˈshäd\ *also* **shoed** \ˈshüd\; **shoe·ing** **1** : to furnish with a shoe or shoes **2** : to cover for protection, strength, or ornament
shoe·black \ˈshü-ˌblak\ *n* : BOOTBLACK
shoe·box \-ˌbäks\ *n* : a box designed to hold a pair of shoes for retail sale
shoe·horn \-ˌhȯrn\ *n* : a curved piece (as of metal or plastic) to aid in slipping on a shoe

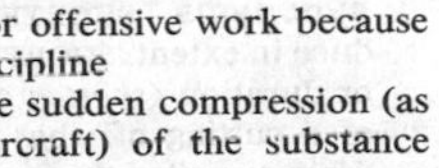
shoehorn

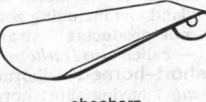

shoe·lace \-ˌlās\ *n* : a lace or string for fastening a shoe
shoe·mak·er \-ˌmā-kər\ *n* : a person whose business is making or repairing shoes
shoe·string \-ˌstring\ *n* **1** : SHOELACE **2** : a small or barely adequate amount of money or capital ⟨start a business on a *shoestring*⟩ [sense 2 from shoestrings being a typical item sold by itinerant vendors]
shoe tree *n* : a foot-shaped device for inserting in a shoe to preserve its shape
sho·far \ˈshō-ˌfär, -fər\ *n, pl* **sho·froth** \shō-ˈfrōt, -ˈfrōth, -ˈfrōs\ : a ram's-horn trumpet used in some synagogue observances [Hebrew *shōphār*]
sho·gun \ˈshō-gən\ *n* : one of a line of military governors ruling Japan until the revolution of 1867–68 [Japanese *shōgun*] — **sho·gun·ate** \ˈshō-gə-nət, -ˌnāt\ *n*
shone *past of* SHINE
[1]shoo \ˈshü\ *interj* — used especially in driving away an unwanted animal [Middle English *schowe*]
[2]shoo *vt* : to scare, drive, or send away by or as if by crying *shoo* ⟨*shooed* us out of the kitchen⟩
shoo·fly pie \ˈshü-ˌflī-\ *n* : a pie made of molasses or brown sugar with a crumbly topping
shoo–in \ˈshü-ˌin\ *n* : one that is a certain and easy winner
[1]shook *past or chiefly dialect past participle of* SHAKE
[2]shook \ˈshu̇k\ *n* **1** : a set of pieces of lumber for assembling one hogshead, cask, or barrel **2** : a bundle of parts (as of boxes) ready to be put together [origin unknown]
shook–up \ˌshu̇k-ˈəp\ *adj* : nervously upset : AGITATED
[1]shoot \ˈshüt\ *vb* **shot** \ˈshät\; **shoot·ing** **1 a** : to let fly or cause to be driven forward with force ⟨*shoot* an arrow⟩ **b** : to cause a missile to be driven forth from : DISCHARGE ⟨*shoot* off a gun⟩ **c** : to cause a weapon to discharge a missile ⟨*shoot* at a target⟩ **d** : to carry when discharged ⟨guns that *shoot* many miles⟩ **e** : to send forth with suddenness or intensity ⟨*shot* us a meaningful look⟩ **f** : to propel (as a ball or puck) toward a goal; *also* : to score by so doing ⟨*shoot* a basket⟩ **g** : to utter or emit rapidly, suddenly, or with force ⟨*shot* out the answer⟩ **2 a** : to strike with a missile especially from a bow or gun; *esp* : to wound or kill with a missile discharged from a firearm ⟨*shoot* deer⟩ **b** : to remove or destroy by use of firearms ⟨*shoot* off a lock⟩ **3** : to push or slide into or out of a fastening ⟨*shot* the door bolt⟩ **4 a** : PLAY ⟨*shoot* a round of golf⟩ ⟨*shoot* craps⟩ **b** : to achieve (a particular score) in a game that involves shooting ⟨*shoot* 80 in golf⟩ **5 a** : to push or thrust forward usually abruptly or swiftly ⟨lizards *shooting* out their tongues⟩ **b** : to sprout or grow rapidly ⟨children *shooting* up into adulthood⟩ **6 a** : to go or pass rapidly and precipitately ⟨*shot* out of the office⟩ ⟨the pain *shot* down my arm⟩ **b** : to pass swiftly along ⟨*shoot* the rapids in a canoe⟩ **c** : to stream out suddenly : SPURT **7** : SET OFF 3b, DETONATE ⟨*shoot* off fireworks⟩ **8** : to determine the altitude of ⟨*shoot* the sun with a sextant⟩ **9 a** : to take a picture of : PHOTOGRAPH **b** : to film a scene ⟨the director is ready to *shoot*⟩ **10 a** : to give an injection to **b** : to inject (an illicit drug) especially into the bloodstream [Old English *scēotan*] — **shoot·er** *n* — **shoot at** *or* **shoot for** : to aim at : strive for — **shoot oneself in the foot** : to act against one's own best interests — **shoot the breeze** : to converse idly — **shoot the works** : to put forth all one's efforts or available capital
[2]shoot *n* **1 a** : the aerial part of a plant : a stem with its leaves and appendages **b** : OFFSHOOT **2 a** : an act or the action of shooting **b** : a hunting trip or party **c** : a shooting match ⟨skeet *shoot*⟩
[3]shoot *interj* — used to express annoyance or surprise
shoot down *vt* **1** : to cause to fall by shooting ⟨*shot down* the helicopter⟩; *esp* : to kill in this way **2** : to put an end to : DEFEAT, REJECT ⟨*shot down* the proposal⟩ **3** : RIDICULE **4** : DISCREDIT 2 ⟨*shoot down* the theory⟩
shooting gallery *n* : a range usually covered and equipped with targets for practice with firearms
shooting iron *n* : FIREARM
shooting star *n* **1** : a meteor appearing as a temporary streak of light in the night sky **2** : a North American perennial herb related to the primroses and having oblong leaves and showy flowers **3** : one resembling a shooting star especially in sudden and temporary brilliance

\ə\ **abut**	\au̇\ **out**	\i\ **tip**	\ȯ\ **saw**	\u̇\ **foot**
\ər\ **further**	\ch\ **chin**	\ī\ **life**	\ȯi\ **coin**	\y\ **yet**
\a\ **mat**	\e\ **pet**	\j\ **job**	\th\ **thin**	\yü\ **few**
\ā\ **take**	\ē\ **easy**	\ng\ **sing**	\th\ **this**	\yu̇\ **cure**
\ä\ **cot, cart**	\g\ **go**	\ō\ **bone**	\ü\ **food**	\zh\ **vision**

shoot–out \'shüt-ˌau̇t\ *n* **1 :** a battle fought with handguns or rifles **2 :** something like a shoot-out **3 :** a shooting competition in overtime that is used to determine the winner of a game (as in soccer or hockey) tied at the end of regular play

[1]**shop** \'shäp\ *n* **1 :** a building or room stocked with merchandise for sale : STORE **2 :** FACTORY 2, MILL **3 a :** a school laboratory equipped for instruction in industrial arts education **b :** the art or science of working with tools and machinery **4 a :** a business establishment; *esp* : OFFICE **b :** SHOPTALK [Old English *sceoppa* "booth"]

[2]**shop** *vb* **shopped; shop•ping 1 :** to examine goods or services with intent to buy or in search of the best buy **2 :** to make a search : HUNT ⟨*shopped* around for the best-qualified person⟩ **3 :** to examine the stock or offerings of ⟨*shop* the stores for gift ideas⟩

shop•keep•er \'shäp-ˌkē-pər\ *n* : STOREKEEPER

shop•lift•er \'shäp-ˌlif-tər\ *n* : a thief who steals merchandise on display in stores — **shop•lift•ing** \-ting\ *n*

shop•per \'shäp-ər\ *n* **1 :** one who shops **2 :** one whose occupation is shopping as an agent for customers or for an employer

shopping center *n* : a group of retail and service stores usually with extensive parking space and usually designed to serve a community or neighborhood

shop steward *n* : a union member elected as the union representative of a shop or department in dealings with the management

shop•talk \'shäp-ˌtȯk\ *n* : the jargon or subject matter peculiar to an occupation or a special area of interest

shop•worn \-ˌwōrn, -ˌwȯrn\ *adj* **1 :** faded, soiled, or impaired by remaining too long in a store ⟨*shopworn* merchandise⟩ **2 :** stale from excessive use or familiarity ⟨a story on a *shopworn* theme⟩ ⟨full of clichés and *shopworn* anecdotes⟩

[1]**shore** \'shōr, 'shȯr\ *n* : the land bordering a usually large body of water; *esp* : COAST [Middle English]

[2]**shore** *n* : a prop or brace placed beneath or against something to support it [Middle English]

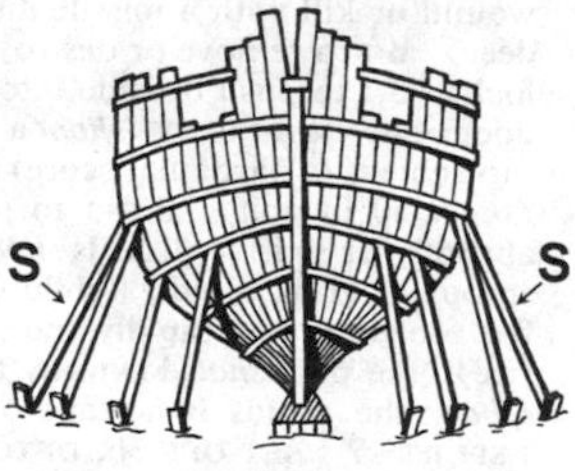

S [2]shore

[3]**shore** *vt* : to give support to : BRACE

shore•bird \-ˌbərd\ *n* : any of a group (Charadrii) of birds (as a plover or sandpiper) that frequent the seashore

shore leave *n* : a leave of absence to go on shore granted to a sailor or naval officer

shore•line \-ˌlīn\ *n* : the line where a body of water touches the shore; *also* : the strip of land along this line

shore patrol *n* : a branch of a navy that exercises guard and police functions

shore•ward \-wərd\ *or* **shore•wards** \-wərdz\ *adv* : toward the shore

shor•ing \'shōr-ing, 'shȯr-\ *n* : a system of group of shores ⟨the *shoring* for a wall⟩

shorn *past participle of* SHEAR

[1]**short** \'shȯrt\ *adj* **1 a :** having little length **b :** not tall : LOW **2 a :** not extended in time : BRIEF ⟨a *short* life⟩ **b :** not retentive ⟨a *short* memory⟩ **c :** QUICK, SPEEDY ⟨made *short* work of the job⟩ **d :** seeming to pass quickly ⟨a few *short* years later⟩ **3 a :** being a syllable or speech sound of relatively little duration **b :** being the member of a pair of similarly spelled vowel or vowel-containing sounds that is descended from a vowel short in duration ⟨*short* "a" in "fat"⟩ ⟨*short* "i" in "sin"⟩ **4 :** limited in distance ⟨a *short* walk⟩ **5 a :** not sufficient in quantity : INADEQUATE ⟨in *short* supply⟩ **b :** not reaching far enough **c :** not sufficiently supplied ⟨*short* of cash⟩ **6 a :** ABRUPT 1b, CURT ⟨I'm sorry I was *short* with you⟩ **b :** quickly provoked ⟨a *short* temper⟩ **7 :** containing or cooked with shortening; *also* : FLAKY 2 ⟨*short* pastry⟩ **8 a :** not lengthy or drawn out ⟨a *short* speech⟩ **b :** ABBREVIATED ⟨doc is *short* for doctor⟩ [Old English *sceort*] — **short•ish** \-ish\ *adj* — **short•ness** \-nəs\ *n* — **in short order :** with dispatch : QUICKLY

[2]**short** *adv* **1 :** in a curt manner **2 :** BRIEFLY ⟨*short*-lasting⟩ **3 :** at a disadvantage : UNAWARES ⟨caught *short*⟩ **4 :** so as to interrupt ⟨took us up *short*⟩ **5 :** ABRUPTLY, SUDDENLY ⟨stopped *short*⟩ **6 :** at some point before a goal or limit aimed at ⟨the arrow fell *short*⟩

[3]**short** *n* **1 :** the sum and substance : UPSHOT ⟨the *short* of it⟩ **2 a :** a short syllable **b :** a short sound or signal **3** *pl* **a :** a by-product of wheat milling that includes the germ, fine bran, and some flour **b :** refuse, clippings, or trimmings discarded in various manufacturing processes **4 :** something that is shorter than the usual or regular length **5** *pl* **a :** knee-length or less than knee-length trousers **b :** short underpants **6 :** SHORT CIRCUIT — **for short :** as an abbreviation ⟨named Katherine, or Kate for *short*⟩ — **in short :** by way of summary : BRIEFLY

[4]**short** *vt* : SHORT-CIRCUIT

short•age \'shȯrt-ij\ *n* : a lack in the amount needed : DEFICIT ⟨a *shortage* in the accounts⟩

short•bread \'shȯrt-ˌbred\ *n* : a thick cookie made of flour, sugar, and much shortening

short•cake \-ˌkāk\ *n* **1 :** a crisp and often unsweetened biscuit or cookie **2 :** a dessert made of usually very short baking-powder-biscuit dough topped with sweetened fruit

short•change \-'chānj\ *vt* **1 :** to give less than the correct amount of change to **2 :** to deprive of something due : CHEAT — **short•chang•er** *n*

short–cir•cuit \'shȯrt-'sər-kət\ *vb* **1 :** to make a short circuit in or have a short circuit **2 :** BYPASS

short circuit *n* : a connection of comparatively low resistance accidentally or intentionally made between points in an electric circuit between which the resistance is normally much greater

short•com•ing \'shȯrt-ˌkəm-ing, shȯrt-'kəm-, 'shȯrt-'kəm-\ *n* : an imperfection or lack that takes away from the whole; *also* : the quality or state of being flawed or lacking

[1]**short•cut** \'shȯrt-ˌkət, -'kət\ *n* **1 :** a route more direct than that usually taken **2 :** a quicker way of doing something

[2]**shortcut** *vb* **-cut; -cut•ting 1 :** to shorten (as a route or procedure) by use of a shortcut **2 :** to take or use a shortcut

short–day \'shȯrt-ˌdā\ *adj* : flowering or developing to maturity only in response to alternating short light and long dark periods — compare DAY-NEUTRAL, LONG-DAY

short division *n* : mathematical division in which the successive steps are performed without writing out the remainders

short•en \'shȯrt-n\ *vb* **short•ened; short•en•ing** \'shȯrt-ning, -n-ing\ : to make or become short or shorter — **short•en•er** \'shȯrt-nər, -n-ər\ *n*

synonyms SHORTEN, CURTAIL, ABBREVIATE mean to reduce in extent. SHORTEN may imply reduction either in extent or duration ⟨*shorten* a speech⟩. CURTAIL adds an implication of a cutting off that deprives of completeness or adequacy ⟨rain *curtailed* the ceremony⟩. ABBREVIATE implies a making shorter usually by omitting some part of a word or phrase ⟨Doctor can be *abbreviated* to Dr.⟩.

short•en•ing \'shȯrt-ning, -n-ing\ *n* **1 :** a making or becoming short or shorter **2 :** an edible fat (as butter or lard) used in baking especially to make pastry flaky

short fuse *n* : a tendency to get angry easily : a quick temper

short•hair \'shȯrt-ˌhaər, -ˌheər\ *n* : a domestic cat with a short thick coat

short–haired \'shȯrt-ˌhaərd, -ˌheərd\ *adj* : having short hair or fur ⟨a *short-haired* cat⟩

short•hand \'shȯrt-ˌhand\ *n* : a method of writing rapidly by substituting characters, abbreviations, or symbols for letters, words, or phrases : STENOGRAPHY — **shorthand** *adj*

short•hand•ed \-'han-dəd\ *adj* : having or working with fewer than the usual number of people

short–haul \-ˌhȯl\ *adj* : traveling or involving a short distance ⟨*short-haul* flights⟩

short•horn \'shȯrt-ˌhȯrn\ *n, often cap* : any of a breed of roan, red, white, or red and white short-horned beef cattle originating in northern England and including good milk-producing strains — called also *Durham*

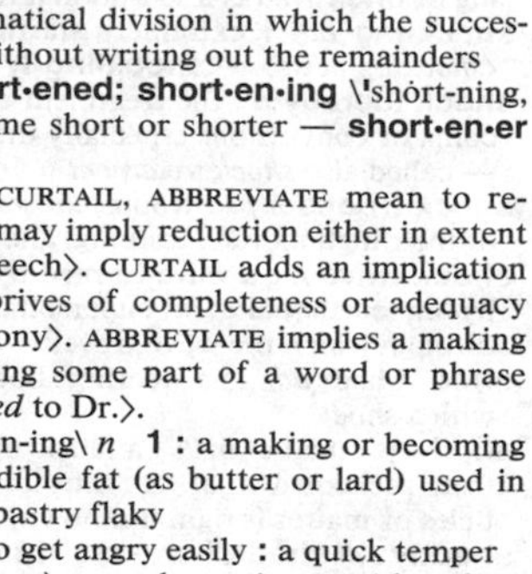
shorthorn

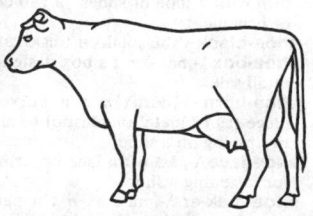

short–horned \-'hȯrnd\ *adj* : having short horns or antennae

short–horned grass-

hopper *n* : any of a family of grasshoppers with short antennae
short hundredweight *n* : HUNDREDWEIGHT 1
short–lived \ˈshȯrt-ˈlīvd, -ˈlivd\ *adj* : not living or lasting long
short•ly \ˈshȯrt-lē\ *adv* **1 a** : in a few words : BRIEFLY **b** : in an abrupt manner : CURTLY **2 a** : in a short time : SOON ⟨will arrive *shortly*⟩ **b** : at a short interval ⟨*shortly* after⟩
short of *prep* : EXCEPT, OTHER THAN; *esp* : of a lesser degree than ⟨few options *short of* replacing the motor⟩
short–or•der \-ˌȯrd-ər\ *adj* : preparing or serving food that can be cooked quickly when a customer orders it ⟨a *short-order* cook⟩
short–range \ˈshȯrt-ˈrānj\ *adj* **1** : involving or taking into account a short period of time ⟨*short-range* plans⟩ **2** : relating to or fit for short distances ⟨*short-range* radar⟩
short ribs *n pl* : a cut of beef consisting of rib ends between the rib roast and the plate
short shrift *n* **1** : barely adequate time for confession before execution **2 a** : little or no attention or consideration ⟨gave the problem *short shrift*⟩ **b** : quick work — usually used in the phrase *make short shrift of*
short•sight•ed \ˈshȯrt-ˈsīt-əd\ *adj* **1** : characterized by lack of foresight **2** : NEARSIGHTED — **short•sight•ed•ly** *adv* — **short•sight•ed•ness** *n*
short•stop \ˈshȯrt-ˌstäp\ *n* **1** : the position of the baseball player defending the area on the third-base side of second base **2** : the player stationed in the shortstop position
short story *n* : an invented prose narrative shorter than a novel usually dealing with a few characters and aiming at developing a single episode or creating a single mood
short–tem•pered \ˈshȯrt-ˈtem-pərd\ *adj* : having a quick temper : easily angered
short–term \-ˈtərm\ *adj* **1** : occurring over or involving a relatively short period of time **2** : of or relating to a financial transaction based on a term usually of less than a year
short ton *n* : a unit of weight — see MEASURE table
short•wave \-ˈwāv\ *n* : a radio wave having a wavelength between 10 and 100 meters
short–wind•ed \-ˈwin-dəd\ *adj* : affected with or characterized by shortness of breath
Sho•shone \shə-ˈshō-nē, -ˈshōn; ˈshō-ˌshōn\ *or* **Sho•sho•ni** \shə-ˈshō-nē\ *n, pl* **Shoshones** *or* **Shoshoni** *also* **Shoshone** *or* **Shoshonis** : a member of a group of American Indian peoples originally ranging through California, Idaho, Nevada, Utah, and Wyoming
[1]**shot** \ˈshät\ *n* **1 a** : an action of shooting **b** : a directed propelling of a missile (as an arrow, stone, or rocket); *esp* : a directed discharge of a gun or cannon **c** : a stroke or throw in a game; *esp* : an attempt at scoring **d** : a setting off of an explosive ⟨a nuclear *shot*⟩ **e** : an injection of something (as a medicine or antibody) into the body **2 a** *pl* **shot** : something propelled by shooting; *esp* : small lead or steel pellets fired from a shotgun **b** : a metal sphere of iron or brass that is heaved in the shot put **3 a** : the distance that a missile is or can be thrown **b** : RANGE, REACH ⟨not within rifle *shot*⟩ **4** : one that shoots : MARKSMAN **5 a** : ATTEMPT, TRY ⟨take another *shot* at the puzzle⟩ **b** : CHANCE ⟨the horse was a 10 to 1 *shot*⟩ **6** : a remark so directed as to have telling effect **7 a** : PHOTOGRAPH **b** : a single sequence of a motion picture or a television program shot by one camera without interruption **8 a** : a small measure or serving (as one ounce) of liquor or other beverage ⟨vodka *shots*⟩ ⟨a *shot* of espresso⟩ **b** : a small amount applied at one time : DOSE ⟨a *shot* of fertilizer⟩ ⟨a *shot* of humor⟩ [Old English *sceot, scot*] — **a shot** : for each one : APIECE ⟨50 dollars *a shot*⟩ — **like a shot** : very rapidly — **shot in the dark 1** : a wild guess **2** : an attempt that has little chance of success
[2]**shot** *past and past participle of* SHOOT
[3]**shot** *adj* **1 a** : having contrasting and changeable color effects : IRIDESCENT ⟨blue silk *shot* with silver⟩ **b** : suffused or streaked with a color ⟨hair *shot* with gray⟩ **c** : pervaded by a contrasting element ⟨satire *shot* with sympathy⟩ **2** : reduced to a ruined or useless state ⟨the business was *shot*⟩
shot•gun \ˈshät-ˌgən\ *n* **1** : a gun with a smooth bore used to fire shot at short range **2** : an offensive football formation in which the quarterback plays a few yards behind the line of scrimmage
shot hole *n* **1** : a drilled hole in which a charge of dynamite is exploded **2** : a hole made usually by a boring insect
shot put *n* : a field event in which the shot is heaved for distance — **shot–put•ter** \-ˌpu̇t-ər\ *n* — **shot–put•ting** \-ˌpu̇t-iŋ\ *n*
should \shəd, shu̇d, ˈshu̇d\ *past of* SHALL — used as an auxiliary verb to express (1) condition or possibility ⟨if you *should* see them, tell them this⟩, (2) obligation or propriety ⟨you *should* brush your teeth regularly⟩, (3) futurity from the point of view in the past ⟨thought I *should* soon be free⟩, (4) what is probable or expected ⟨they *should* be here soon⟩, and (5) politeness in softening a request or assertion ⟨I *should* like some coffee⟩ [Old English *sceolde* "owed, was obliged to"]
[1]**shoul•der** \ˈshōl-dər\ *n* **1 a** : the laterally projecting part of the human body formed of the bones and joints by which the arm is connected with the trunk together with the muscles covering these **b** : the corresponding but usually less projecting part of a nonhuman vertebrate **2** : a cut of meat including the upper joint of the foreleg and adjacent parts **3** : the part of a garment at the wearer's shoulder **4** : a part or projection resembling a human shoulder ⟨the *shoulder* of a hill⟩ **5** : either edge of a road; *esp* : the part of a road outside of the traveled way [Old English *sculdor*]
[2]**shoulder** *vb* **shoul•dered; shoul•der•ing** \-də-riŋ, -driŋ\ **1** : to push or thrust with the shoulder : JOSTLE ⟨*shouldered* my way through the crowd⟩ **2 a** : to place or bear on the shoulder ⟨*shouldered* the knapsack⟩ **b** : to assume the burden or responsibility of ⟨*shoulder* the blame⟩
shoulder blade *n* : a large triangular bone of the back part of the shoulder that is the principal bone of the corresponding half of the shoulder girdle and articulates with the corresponding clavicle or coracoid to form a socket for the humerus of the arm — called also *scapula*
shoulder girdle *n* : the arch of bone formed by the shoulder blade and clavicle
shoulder strap *n* : a strap that passes over the shoulder and holds up an article or garment
should•est \ˈshu̇d-əst\ *archaic past 2nd singular of* SHALL
shouldn't \ˈshu̇d-nt\ : should not
shouldst \shədst, shu̇dst, ˈshu̇dst\ *archaic past 2nd singular of* SHALL
[1]**shout** \ˈshau̇t\ *vb* **1** : to utter a sudden loud cry ⟨*shouted* with delight⟩ **2** : to utter in a loud voice ⟨*shouted* insults⟩ [Middle English] — **shout•er** *n*
[2]**shout** *n* : a loud cry or call
shouting distance *n* : a short distance : easy reach ⟨lived within *shouting distance* of their cousins⟩
[1]**shove** \ˈshəv\ *vb* **1** : to push with steady force **2** : to push carelessly or rudely ⟨*shove* a person out of the way⟩ [Old English *scūfan* "to thrust away"] ***synonyms*** see PUSH — **shov•er** *n*
[2]**shove** *n* : an act or instance of shoving : a forcible push
[1]**shov•el** \ˈshəv-əl\ *n* **1** : an implement consisting of a broad often curved blade attached to a long handle used for lifting and throwing loose material **2** : SHOVELFUL [Old English *scofl*]
[2]**shovel** *vb* **shov•eled** *or* **shov•elled; shov•el•ing** *or* **shov•el•ling** \ˈshəv-liŋ, -ə-liŋ\ **1** : to take up and throw with a shovel **2** : to dig or clean out with a shovel **3** : to throw or convey roughly or in a mass as if with a shovel ⟨*shovel* food into one's mouth⟩
shov•el•er *or* **shov•el•ler** \ˈshəv-lər, -ə-lər\ *n* **1** : one that shovels **2** : any of several freshwater ducks having a large and very broad bill
shov•el•ful \ˈshəv-əl-ˌfu̇l\ *n, pl* **shovelfuls** \-ˌfu̇lz\ *also* **shov•els•ful** \-əlz-ˌfu̇l\ : the amount held by a shovel
shov•el–nosed \ˌshəv-əl-ˈnōzd\ *adj* : having a broad flat head, nose, or beak
shovel pass *n* : a short underhand pass (as in football)
[1]**show** \ˈshō\ *vb* **showed; shown** \ˈshōn\ *or* **showed; showing** **1** : to place in sight : DISPLAY ⟨*showed* pictures of the baby⟩ **2** : to reveal by one's condition, nature, or behavior ⟨*showed* themselves to be cowards⟩ **3** : GRANT, BESTOW ⟨the king *showed* no mercy⟩ **4** : TEACH ⟨*showed* me how to knit⟩ **5 a** : to give an indication or record of ⟨his grades *showed* improvement⟩ **b** : PROVE ⟨the result *showed* that we were right⟩ **6** : DIRECT, GUIDE ⟨*show* a visitor to the door⟩ **7** : APPEAR ⟨anger *showed* in their faces⟩ **8** : to be noticeable ⟨the patch hardly *shows*⟩ **9** : to present (an animal) for judging in a show **10**

\ə\ abut	\au̇\ out	\i\ tip	\ȯ\ saw	\u̇\ foot
\ər\ further	\ch\ chin	\ī\ life	\ȯi\ coin	\y\ yet
\a\ mat	\e\ pet	\j\ job	\th\ thin	\yü\ few
\ā\ take	\ē\ easy	\ŋ\ sing	\th\ this	\yu̇\ cure
\ä\ cot, cart	\g\ go	\ō\ bone	\ü\ food	\zh\ vision

: to finish third or at least third in a horse race **11** : to be staged or presented ⟨now *showing* at the theater⟩ [Old English *scēawian* "to look, look at, see"] — **show one the door** : to tell someone to get out; *also* : FIRE 2

synonyms SHOW, EXHIBIT, DISPLAY mean to present so as to invite notice or attention. SHOW implies enabling another to see or examine ⟨*showed* me a picture of the lake⟩. EXHIBIT implies putting forward openly or publicly ⟨*exhibit* paintings at a gallery⟩. DISPLAY stresses putting in position where others may see to advantage ⟨*display* sale items⟩.

[2]**show** *n* **1** : a demonstrative display ⟨a *show* of strength⟩ **2 a** : a false semblance : PRETENSE ⟨made a *show* of friendship⟩ **b** : a more or less true appearance of something : SIGN ⟨a *show* of reason⟩ **c** : an impressive display **3** : something exhibited especially for wonder or ridicule : SPECTACLE **4** : a public presentation: as **a** : a competitive exhibition (as of animals) to demonstrate quality **b** : a theatrical presentation **c** : a radio or television program **d** : ENTERTAINMENT 2 **5** : ENTERPRISE, AFFAIR ⟨ran the whole *show*⟩ **6** : third place at the finish of a horse race

show–and–tell *n* **1** : a classroom exercise in which children display an item and talk about it **2** : a public display or demonstration

show·biz \ˈshō-ˌbiz\ *n* : SHOW BUSINESS

[1]**show·boat** \ˈshō-ˌbōt\ *n* **1** : a river steamboat containing a theater and carrying a troupe of actors to give plays at river communities **2** : one who tries to attract attention by conspicuous behavior

[2]**showboat** *vi* : SHOW OFF ⟨kids *showboating* for the camera⟩ — **show·boat·er** *n*

show business *n* : the arts, occupations, and businesses (as theater, motion pictures, and television) that make up the entertainment industry

[1]**show·case** \-ˌkās\ *n* **1** : a glass case or box to display and protect wares in a store or articles in a museum **2** : a setting, occasion, or medium for exhibiting something or someone especially in an attractive or favorable way ⟨a summer theater that is a *showcase* for young actors⟩

[2]**showcase** *vt* : to exhibit especially in an attractive or favorable way ⟨*showcase* new talent⟩

show·down \-ˌdau̇n\ *n* : the final settlement of a contested issue; *also* : the test of strength by which a contested issue is resolved

[1]**show·er** \ˈshau̇-ər, ˈshau̇r\ *n* **1 a** : a fall of rain of short duration **b** : a similar fall of sleet, hail, or snow; *esp* : a fall of meteors which belong to a single group **2** : something resembling a rain shower ⟨a *shower* of sparks⟩ ⟨a *shower* of tears⟩ **3** : a party given by friends who bring gifts often of a particular kind ⟨a bridal *shower*⟩ **4** : a bath in which water is showered on the body; *also* : the apparatus that provides a shower [Old English *scūr*] — **show·ery** \-ē\ *adj*

[2]**shower** *vb* **1** : to fall in or as if in a shower **2** : to bathe in a shower **3** : to wet copiously in a spray, fine stream, or drops **4** : to give in abundance ⟨*showered* them with gifts⟩

[3]**show·er** \ˈshō-ər, ˈshōr\ *n* : one that shows : EXHIBITOR

shower bath *n* : SHOWER 4

show·ing \ˈshō-iŋ\ *n* **1** : an act of putting something on view : EXHIBITION ⟨a *showing* of fall fashions⟩ ⟨a *showing* of a new feature film⟩ **2** : PERFORMANCE, RECORD ⟨made a good *showing* in the tournament⟩

show·man \ˈshō-mən\ *n* **1** : the producer of a theatrical show **2** : a notably spectacular, dramatic, or effective performer — **show·man·ship** \-ˌship\ *n*

show–off \ˈshō-ˌȯf\ *n* **1** : conspicuous behavior **2** : one that shows off

show off \shō-ˈȯf, ˈshō-\ *vb* **1** : to display proudly **2** : to seek to attract attention by conspicuous behavior

show·piece \-ˌpēs\ *n* : a prime or outstanding example used for exhibition

show·place \-ˌplās\ *n* : a place exhibited or regarded as an example of beauty or excellence

show·room \-ˌrüm, -ˌru̇m\ *n* : a room used for the display of merchandise or of samples ⟨a carpet *showroom*⟩

show·time \ˈshō-ˌtīm\ *n* : the scheduled or actual time at which a show or something likened to a show begins

show up *vb* **1** : to reveal the true nature of by uncovering faults : EXPOSE ⟨*showed up* their ignorance⟩ **2** : ARRIVE ⟨*showed up* late⟩ **3** : to be visible or evident ⟨the color *shows up* well in this light⟩

showy \ˈshō-ē\ *adj* **show·i·er; -est** **1** : making an attractive show ⟨*showy* blossoms⟩ **2** : GAUDY ⟨*showy* jewelry⟩ — **show·i·ly** \ˈshō-ə-lē\ *adv* — **show·i·ness** \ˈshō-ē-nəs\ *n*

shrap·nel \ˈshrap-nᵊl\ *n, pl* **shrapnel** **1** : a projectile that consists of a case provided with a powder charge and a large number of usually lead balls and is exploded in flight **2** : bomb, mine, or shell fragments [Henry *Shrapnel*, died 1842, English artillery officer]

[1]**shred** \ˈshred\ *n* **1 a** : a long narrow strip from a larger body of the same material ⟨*shreds* of cloth⟩ **b** *pl* : a shredded, damaged, or ruined condition ⟨a reputation torn to *shreds*⟩ **2** : PARTICLE, SCRAP ⟨hadn't a *shred* of evidence⟩ [Old English *scrēade*]

[2]**shred** *vb* **shred·ded; shred·ding** **1** : to cut or tear into shreds **2** : to break up into shreds — **shred·der** *n*

shrew \ˈshrü\ *n* **1** : any of numerous small chiefly nocturnal mammals that are related to the moles and have a long pointed snout, very small eyes, and short velvety fur **2** : a woman who scolds or quarrels constantly [Old English *scrēawa*] — **shrew·ish** *adj*

shrewd \ˈshrüd\ *adj* **1 a** : SEVERE, HARD ⟨a *shrewd* blow⟩ **b** : CUTTING 2 ⟨a *shrewd* wind⟩ **2** : marked by cleverness, discernment, or sagacity ⟨a *shrewd* observer⟩; *also* : given to wily ways or dealing ⟨a *shrewd* negotiator⟩ [Middle English *shrewed* "shrewish, evil, severe," from *shrewe* "shrew" + *-ed*] — **shrewd·ly** *adv* — **shrewd·ness** *n*

synonyms SHREWD, ASTUTE, SAGACIOUS mean acute in perception and sound in judgment. SHREWD stresses practical, hardheaded cleverness and judgment ⟨a *shrewd* judge of character⟩. ASTUTE stresses shrewdness in practical affairs and especially connotes an ability to act successfully in one's own interests ⟨an *astute* businessman when closing a deal⟩. SAGACIOUS suggests wisdom, penetration, and farsightedness ⟨*sagacious* investors⟩.

shrew·ish \ˈshrü-ish\ *adj* : QUARRELSOME, ILL-TEMPERED — **shrew·ish·ly** *adv* — **shrew·ish·ness** *n*

[1]**shriek** \ˈshrēk\ *vb* **1** : to utter a loud shrill cry or sound **2** : to utter with a shriek [probably from Middle English *shriken*]

[2]**shriek** *n* **1** : a shrill usually wild or involuntary cry **2** : a sound like a shriek ⟨a *shriek* of escaping steam⟩ ***synonyms*** see SCREAM

shrie·val \ˈshrē-vəl\ *adj* : of or relating to a sheriff [obsolete *shrieve* "sheriff," from Old English *scīrgerēfa*] — **shrie·val·ty** \-tē\ *n*

shrift \ˈshrift\ *n, archaic* : the confession of sins to a priest or the hearing of a confession by a priest [Old English *scrift*, from *scrīfan* "to shrive"]

shrike \ˈshrīk\ *n* : any of numerous usually largely gray or brownish singing birds that have a bill hooked at the tip, feed chiefly on insects, and often impale their prey on thorns [perhaps from Old English *scrīc* "thrush"]

[1]**shrill** \ˈshril\ *vb* : to utter or emit a sharp piercing sound : SCREAM [Middle English]

[2]**shrill** *adj* **1** : having, emitting, or being a sharp high-pitched tone or sound ⟨a *shrill* whistle⟩ **2** : accompanied by sharp high-pitched sounds or cries ⟨*shrill* gaiety⟩ **3** : having an intense or vivid effect on the senses ⟨*shrill* light⟩ — **shrill** *adv* — **shrill·ness** *n* — **shril·ly** \ˈshril-lē\ *adv*

[3]**shrill** *n* : a shrill sound

[1]**shrimp** \ˈshrimp\ *n, pl* **shrimp** *or* **shrimps** **1** : any of numerous small mostly marine crustaceans that are related to the lobsters, that have a long slender body, laterally compressed abdomen, and long legs and that include some commercially important as food; *also* : any small crustacean resembling a true shrimp **2** : a very small or puny person or thing [Middle English *shrimpe*] — **shrimp·like** \-ˌlīk\ *adj* — **shrimpy** \ˈshrim-pē\ *adj*

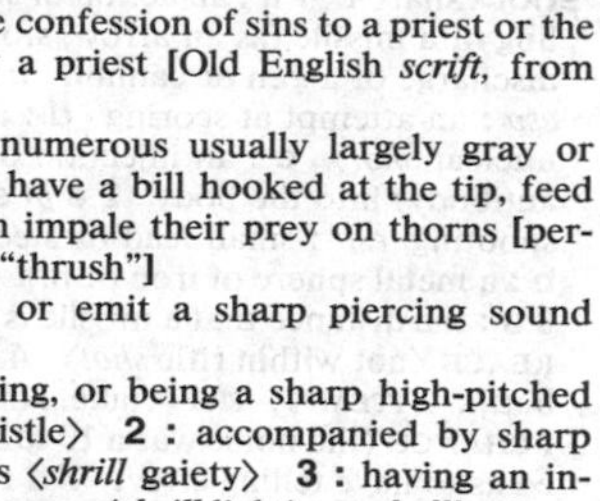

shrimp 1

[2]**shrimp** *vi* : to fish for or catch shrimp

[1]**shrine** \ˈshrīn\ *n* **1** : a case or box for sacred relics (as the bones of a saint) **2 a** : the tomb of a saint **b** : a place in which devotion is paid to a saint or deity **c** : a niche containing a religious image **3** : a place or object hallowed because of its associations

⟨Westminster Abbey is a *shrine* for tourists⟩ [Old English *scrīn*, from Latin *scrinium* "case, chest"]

[2]**shrine** *vt* **:** ENSHRINE

Shrin·er \ˈshrī-nər\ *n* **:** a member of a secret fraternal society that is not Masonic but admits only Knights Templars and 32nd-degree Masons to membership

[1]**shrink** \ˈshringk\ *vb* **shrank** \ˈshrangk\ *or* **shrunk** \ˈshrəngk\; **shrunk** *or* **shrunk·en** \ˈshrəng-kən\; **shrink·ing** **1 :** to contract or curl up the body or part of it **:** HUDDLE, COWER ⟨*shrink* in horror⟩ **2 a :** to become or cause to become smaller or more compacted ⟨the sweater *shrank* when it was washed⟩ **b :** to lose substance or weight ⟨meat *shrinks* in cooking⟩ **c :** to lessen in amount or value ⟨their fortune *shrank* during the depression⟩ **3 a :** to draw back ⟨*shrink* from a quarrel⟩ **b :** to hold oneself back **:** REFRAIN ⟨did not *shrink* from telling the truth⟩ [Old English *scrincan*] — **shrink·able** \ˈshring-kə-bəl\ *adj* — **shrink·er** *n*

[2]**shrink** *n* **1 :** the act of shrinking **2 :** PSYCHIATRIST

shrink·age \ˈshring-kij\ *n* **1 :** the act or process of shrinking **2 :** the amount lost by shrinkage

shrinking violet *n* **:** a bashful or retiring person

shrive \ˈshrīv\ *vb* **shrived** *or* **shrove** \ˈshrōv\; **shriv·en** \ˈshriv-ən\ *or* **shrived; shriv·ing** \ˈshrī-ving\ **1 a :** to administer the sacrament of reconciliation to **b :** to free from guilt **2** *archaic* **:** to confess one's sins especially to a priest [Old English *scrīfan* "to shrive, prescribe," from Latin *scribere* "to write"]

shriv·el \ˈshriv-əl\ *vb* **shriv·eled** *or* **shriv·elled; shriv·el·ing** *or* **shriv·el·ling** \ˈshriv-ling, -ə-ling\ **1 :** to draw into wrinkles especially with a loss of moisture **2 :** to reduce or become reduced to weakness, helplessness, or inefficiency [origin unknown]

Shrop·shire \ˈshräp-ˌshiər, -shər, *especially in the U.S.* -ˌshīr\ *n* **:** any of an English breed of dark-faced hornless sheep that are raised for both meat and wool [*Shropshire*, England]

[1]**shroud** \ˈshrau̇d\ *n* **1 :** burial garment **:** WINDING-SHEET **2 :** something that covers, screens, or guards ⟨a *shroud* of secrecy⟩ **3 a :** one of the lines leading usually in pairs from the top of a mast to provide lateral support to the mast **b :** one of the cords that suspend the harness of a parachute from the canopy [Old English *scrūd* "garment"]

[2]**shroud** *vt* **1 a :** to cut off from view **:** SCREEN ⟨trees *shrouded* in heavy mist⟩ **b :** to veil under another appearance ⟨*shrouded* in mystery⟩ **2 :** to dress for burial

Shrove·tide \ˈshrōv-ˌtīd\ *n* **:** the period usually of three days immediately preceding Ash Wednesday [Middle English *schroftide*]

Shrove Tuesday \ˈshrōv-\ *n* **:** the Tuesday before Ash Wednesday

[1]**shrub** \ˈshrəb\ *n* **:** a usually several-stemmed woody plant that is smaller than most trees [Old English *scrybb* "brushwood"]

[2]**shrub** *n* **1 :** a beverage that consists of an alcoholic liquor, fruit juice, fruit rind, and sugar **2 :** a beverage made by adding acidulated fruit juice to iced water [Arabic *sharāb* "beverage"]

shrub·bery \ˈshrəb-rē, -ə-rē\ *n, pl* **-ber·ies :** a planting or growth of shrubs

shrub·by \ˈshrəb-ē\ *adj* **shrub·bi·er; -est** **1 :** consisting of or covered with shrubs ⟨a *shrubby* hillside⟩ **2 :** resembling a shrub ⟨a *shrubby* plant⟩

[1]**shrug** \ˈshrəg\ *vb* **shrugged; shrug·ging :** to raise or draw in the shoulders especially to express lack of interest or dislike [Middle English *schruggen*]

[2]**shrug** *n* **1 :** an act of shrugging **2 :** a woman's small waist-length or shorter jacket

shrug off *vt* **1 :** to shake off ⟨*shrugging* off sleep⟩ **2 :** to brush aside **:** MINIMIZE ⟨*shrugs off* the problem⟩ **3 :** to remove (a garment) by wriggling out

[1]**shuck** \ˈshək\ *n* **1 :** SHELL, HUSK: as **a :** the outer covering of a nut or corn **b :** the shell of an oyster or clam **2 :** something of little value ⟨not worth *shucks*⟩ [origin unknown]

[2]**shuck** *vt* **1 :** to remove the shucks of **2 :** to peel off (as clothing) — often used with *off* ⟨*shucked* off his shirt⟩

shucks \ˈshəks\ *interj* — used especially to express mild disappointment or embarrassment ⟨*shucks,* it was nothing⟩

[1]**shud·der** \ˈshəd-ər\ *vi* **shud·dered; shud·der·ing** \ˈshəd-ring, -ə-ring\ **:** to tremble convulsively **:** SHIVER, QUIVER ⟨*shuddered* to think of the accident⟩ [Middle English *shoddren*]

[2]**shudder** *n* **:** an act of shuddering — **shud·dery** \-ə-rē\ *adj*

[1]**shuf·fle** \ˈshəf-əl\ *vb* **shuf·fled; shuf·fling** \ˈshəf-ling, -ə-ling\ **1 :** to mix in a mass confusedly **:** JUMBLE **2 :** to put or thrust aside or under cover **3 a :** to mix (as a pack of cards) so that cards will later appear in random order **b :** to move about, back and forth, or from one place to another **4 a :** to move (as the feet) by sliding along or dragging back and forth without lifting **b :** to move or walk in a sliding dragging manner without lifting the feet ⟨*shuffling* along⟩ **c :** to perform (as a dance) with a dragging sliding step **5 :** to get into or out of (a situation) especially by trickery **:** WORM ⟨*shuffle* out of a difficulty⟩ **6 :** to act or speak in an evasive manner [perhaps from [1]*shove*] — **shuf·fler** \-lər, -ə-lər\ *n*

[2]**shuffle** *n* **1 :** evasion of an issue **:** EQUIVOCATION **2 a :** an act of shuffling **b :** a right or turn to shuffle cards **c :** JUMBLE **3 a :** a dragging sliding movement; *esp* **:** a sliding or scraping step in dancing **b :** a dance characterized by such a step

shuf·fle·board \ˈshəf-əl-ˌbōrd, -ˌbȯrd\ *n* **1 :** a game in which players try to push disks into scoring areas of a diagram marked on a smooth surface **2 :** the diagram or court on which shuffleboard is played [alteration of obsolete *shove-board*]

shul \ˈshül\ *n* **:** SYNAGOGUE [Yiddish, school, synagogue]

shun \ˈshən\ *vt* **shunned; shun·ning :** to avoid deliberately and especially habitually [Old English *scunian*] — **shun·ner** *n*

[1]**shunt** \ˈshənt\ *vb* **1 a :** to turn off to one side **:** SHIFT ⟨was *shunted* aside⟩ **b :** to switch (as a train) from one track to another **2 :** to provide with or divert by means of an electrical shunt **3 :** to travel back and forth [Middle English, "to move suddenly, turn away, evade," perhaps from past participle of *shonen, shunnen* "to shun"] — **shunt·er** *n*

[2]**shunt** *n* **:** a means or mechanism for turning or thrusting aside: as **a** *chiefly British* **:** a railroad switch **b :** a conductor joining two points in an electrical circuit so as to form a parallel or alternative path through which a portion of the current may pass **c :** a passage created surgically to divert a bodily fluid (as blood) from one vessel or part to another; *also* **:** a device (as a narrow tube) used to establish a similar passage

shush \ˈshəsh, ˈshu̇sh\ *vt* **:** to urge to be quiet **:** HUSH [imitative] — **shush** *n*

shut \ˈshət\ *vb* **shut; shut·ting** **1 :** to close or become closed by bringing openings or covering parts together ⟨*shut* one's eyes⟩ **2 :** to prevent entrance to or passage to or from **3 :** to hold within limits by or as if by enclosure **:** IMPRISON ⟨*shut* up in a stalled elevator⟩ **4 :** to cease or cause to cease operation ⟨the epidemic *shut* down the school⟩ [Old English *scyttan*]

shut·down \ˈshət-ˌdau̇n\ *n* **:** a temporary or permanent ending of an activity (as work in a factory)

shut down *vb* **1 :** to settle so as to obscure vision **:** CLOSE IN ⟨the night *shut down* early⟩ **2 :** to make ineffective in competition ⟨*shut down* the opposition's offense⟩

shute *variant of* CHUTE

shut–eye \ˈshət-ˌī\ *n* **:** SLEEP

shut–in \ˌshət-ˌin\ *adj* **:** confined by illness or incapacity — **shut–in** \ˈshət-ˌin\ *n*

shut·off \ˈshət-ˌȯf\ *n* **1 :** something that shuts off **2 :** INTERRUPTION, STOPPAGE

shut off *vb* **1 :** to close off **:** SEPARATE ⟨*shut off* from the rest of the world⟩ **2 a :** to cut off (as flow or passage) **:** STOP ⟨*shuts off* the oxygen supply⟩ **b :** to stop the operation of ⟨*shut* the motor *off*⟩ **3 :** to stop operating ⟨*shuts off* automatically⟩

shut·out \ˈshət-ˌau̇t\ *n* **:** a game or contest in which one side is prevented from scoring

shut out \ˈshət-ˈau̇t, ˌshət-\ *vt* **1 :** to keep out **:** EXCLUDE **2 :** to prevent (an opponent) from scoring in a game or contest

[1]**shut·ter** \ˈshət-ər\ *n* **1 :** one that shuts **2 :** a usually movable cover or screen for a window or door **3 :** the part of a camera that opens and closes to allow light to enter

[2]**shutter** *vt* **:** to close with or by shutters

shut·ter·bug \-ˌbəg\ *n* **:** a photography enthusiast

[1]**shut·tle** \ˈshət-l\ *n* **1 a :** an instrument used in weaving to carry the thread back and forth from side to side through the threads that run lengthwise **b :** a spindle-shaped device holding the thread in tatting, knotting, or netting **c :** any of various thread holders for the lower thread of a sewing machine that carry the lower thread through a loop of the upper thread to make a stitch **2 a :** a going back and forth regularly over a specified

\ə\ **abut**	\au̇\ **out**	\i\ **tip**	\ȯ\ **saw**	\u̇\ **foot**
\ər\ **further**	\ch\ **chin**	\ī\ **life**	\ȯi\ **coin**	\y\ **yet**
\a\ **mat**	\e\ **pet**	\j\ **job**	\th\ **thin**	\yü\ **few**
\ā\ **take**	\ē\ **easy**	\ng\ **sing**	\t͟h\ **this**	\yu̇\ **cure**
\ä\ **cot, cart**	\g\ **go**	\ō\ **bone**	\ü\ **food**	\zh\ **vision**

and often short route by a vehicle **b :** a vehicle used in a shuttle ⟨a *shuttle* bus⟩ [Middle English *shittle, schootyl,* from Old English *scytel, scutel* "dart"]

[2]shuttle *vb* **shut·tled; shut·tling** \ˈshət-ling, -l-ing\ **1 :** to transport in, by, or as if by a shuttle ⟨*shuttled* them to school⟩ **2 :** to move or travel back and forth frequently **3 :** to move by or as if by a shuttle

[1]shut·tle·cock \ˈshət-l-ˌkäk\ *n* **:** a lightweight conical object with a rounded often rubber-covered nose used in badminton

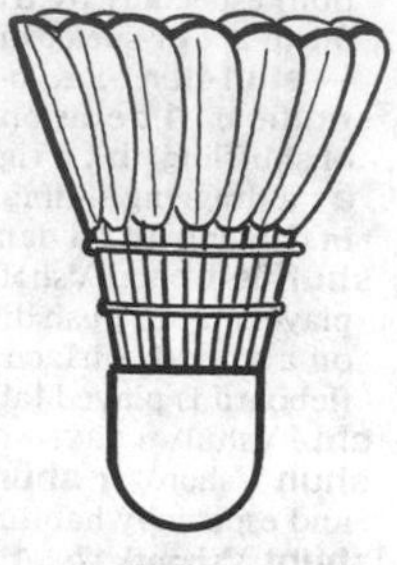
shuttlecock

[2]shuttlecock *vb* **:** to send, toss, or go to and fro **:** BANDY

shut up *vb* **1 :** to cause (a person) to stop talking **2 :** to stop writing or speaking

[1]shy \ˈshī\ *adj* **shi·er** *or* **shy·er** \ˈshī-ər, ˈshīr\; **shi·est** *or* **shy·est** \ˈshī-əst\ **1 :** easily frightened **:** TIMID **2 :** disposed to avoid a person or thing ⟨publicity *shy*⟩ **3 :** hesitant in committing oneself **:** CIRCUMSPECT **4 :** uncomfortable around people **:** reluctant to call attention to oneself; *also* **:** expressive of such a state or characteristic ⟨a *shy* smile⟩ **5 :** having less than the proper amount or number **:** SHORT ⟨just *shy* of six feet tall⟩ [Old English *scēoh*] — **shy·ly** *adv* — **shy·ness** *n*

synonyms SHY, BASHFUL, MODEST, COY mean not inclined to be forward. SHY implies a timid shrinking from contact or familiarity with others ⟨*shy* with strangers⟩. BASHFUL implies a frightened or hesitant shyness characteristic of childhood ⟨a *bashful* boy out on his first date⟩. MODEST suggests an absence of undue confidence or conceit ⟨*modest* about her success⟩. COY implies a pretended shyness ⟨put off by her *coy* manner⟩.

[2]shy *vi* **shied; shy·ing 1 :** to draw back in sudden dislike or distaste **:** RECOIL ⟨*shied* from publicity⟩ **2 :** to start suddenly aside through fright or alarm ⟨the horse *shied* at a blowing paper⟩

[3]shy *n, pl* **shies :** a sudden start aside (as of a horse)

[4]shy *vt* **shied; shy·ing :** to throw with a jerk **:** FLING [perhaps from [1]*shy*]

[5]shy *n, pl* **shies :** the act of shying **:** TOSS, THROW

shy·ster \ˈshī-stər\ *n* **:** an unscrupulous lawyer or politician [probably from German *Scheisser,* literally, "one who defecates"]

si \ˈsē\ *n* **:** the 7th note of the diatonic scale **:** TI [Italian]

[1]Si·a·mese \ˌsī-ə-ˈmēz, -ˈmēs\ *adj* **1 :** of, relating to, or characteristic of Thailand, the Thais, or their language **2 :** exhibiting great resemblance **:** very like [*Siam* (Thailand); sense 2 from *Siamese twin*]

[2]Siamese *n, pl* **Siamese 1 :** THAI 1 **2 :** THAI 2

Siamese cat *n* **:** any of a breed of slender blue-eyed domestic cats of Asian origin with short hair and a pale body and darker ears, paws, tail, and face

Siamese twin *n* **:** either of a pair of human or animal twins born joined together [from Chang, died 1874, and Eng, died 1874, congenitally united twins born in Siam]

sib \ˈsib\ *n* **1 :** KINDRED; *also* **:** a group of persons descended from the same real or supposed ancestor **2 :** one closely related to another **:** a blood relation **3 :** SIBLING [Old English *sibb* "related by blood," from *sibb* "kinship"] — **sib** *adj*

Si·be·ri·an husky \sī-ˌbir-ē-ən-\ *n* **:** any of a breed of medium-sized compact dogs developed as sled dogs in northeastern Siberia that have a thick coat, erect ears, and bushy tail

Siberian husky

[1]sib·i·lant \ˈsib-ə-lənt\ *adj* **:** having, containing, or producing the sound of or a sound resembling that of the *s* or the *sh* in *sash* [Latin *sibilare* "to hiss, whistle"]

[2]sibilant *n* **:** a sibilant speech sound (as English \s\, \z\, \sh\, \zh\, \ch (=tsh)\, or \j (=dzh)\)

sib·ling \ˈsib-ling\ *n* **:** a brother or sister without regard to sex; *also* **:** one of two or more individuals having one common parent

sib·yl \ˈsib-əl\ *n, often cap* **1 :** any of several ancient prophetesses **2 a :** PROPHETESS **b :** FORTUNE-TELLER [Latin *sibylla,* from Greek] — **si·byl·ic** *or* **si·byl·lic** \sə-ˈbil-ik\ *adj* — **sib·yl·line** \ˈsib-ə-ˌlīn\ *adj*

[1]sic *also* **sick** \ˈsik\ *vt* **sicced** *also* **sicked** \ˈsikt\; **sic·cing** *also* **sick·ing** \sik-ing\ **:** to attack or cause to attack or chase — usually used as a command to a dog ⟨*sic* 'em⟩ [alteration of *seek*]

[2]sic \ˈsik, ˈsēk\ *adv* **:** intentionally so written — used after a printed word or passage to indicate that it reproduces an original ⟨said they seed [*sic*] it all⟩ [Latin, "so, thus"]

sick \ˈsik\ *adj* **1 a** (1) **:** affected with disease or ill health (2) **:** of, relating to, or intended for use in sickness ⟨*sick* pay⟩ ⟨a *sick* ward⟩ **b :** NAUSEATED, QUEASY ⟨*sick* to one's stomach⟩ **2 :** spiritually or morally unsound or corrupt **3 a :** sickened by strong emotion ⟨*sick* with shame⟩ ⟨worried *sick*⟩ **b :** disgusted by some excess ⟨*sick* of their constant whining⟩ **c :** depressed and longing for something ⟨*sick* at heart⟩ **4 a :** mentally or emotionally unsound or disordered ⟨*sick* thoughts⟩ **b :** highly distasteful ⟨*sick* jokes⟩ **5 :** lacking or declining in vigor ⟨a *sick* market⟩ [Old English *sēoc*] — **sick·ly** *adv*

sick bay *n* **:** a compartment in a ship used as a dispensary and hospital

sick·bed \ˈsik-ˌbed\ *n* **:** the bed on which a sick person lies

sick call *n* **:** a scheduled time when persons (as soldiers) may report as sick to the medical officer

sick·en \ˈsik-ən\ *vb* **sick·ened; sick·en·ing** \ˈsik-ning, -ə-ning\ **1 :** to make or become sick **2 :** to cause revulsion in ⟨his selfishness *sickens* me⟩ — **sick·en·er** \ˈsik-nər, -ə-nər\ *n*

sick·en·ing *adj* **:** causing sickness or disgust ⟨a *sickening* sight⟩ — **sick·en·ing·ly** \ˈsik-ning-lē, -ə-ning-\ *adv*

sick headache *n* **:** MIGRAINE

sick·ish \ˈsik-ish\ *adj* **1 :** somewhat nauseated **:** QUEASY **2 :** somewhat sickening ⟨a *sickish* odor⟩ — **sick·ish·ly** *adv* — **sick·ish·ess** *n*

[1]sick·le \ˈsik-əl\ *n* **1 a :** a cutting tool consisting of a curved metal blade with a short handle **b :** a cutting mechanism (as of a combine) consisting of a bar with a series of cutting elements **2** *cap* **:** a group of six stars in the constellation Leo [Old English *sicol,* from Latin *secula*] — **sickle** *adj*

sickle 1a

[2]sickle *vb* **sick·led; sick·ling** \ˈsik-ling, -ə-ling\ **:** to change into a sickle cell ⟨the ability of red blood cells to *sickle*⟩

sick leave *n* **1 :** an absence from duty or work permitted because of illness **2 :** the number of days per year allowed an employee for sickness

sickle cell *n* **:** an abnormal red blood cell of crescent shape

sickle–cell anemia *n* **:** a chronic inherited anemia that occurs primarily in people of African, Mediterranean, or southwest Asian ancestry and is characterized especially by episodes in which small blood vessels become blocked with sickle cells

sickle–cell trait *n* **:** an inherited blood condition in which some red blood cells tend to sickle but not usually enough to produce anemia and which occurs primarily in people of African, Mediterranean, or southwest Asian ancestry

sick·ly \ˈsik-lē\ *adj* **sick·li·er; -est 1 :** somewhat unwell; *also* **:** often ailing **2 :** produced by or associated with sickness ⟨a *sickly* complexion⟩ ⟨a *sickly* appetite⟩ **3 :** producing or tending to sickness ⟨a *sickly* climate⟩ **4 :** appearing as if sick: as **a :** LANGUID, PALE ⟨a *sickly* flame⟩ **b :** WRETCHED, UNEASY ⟨a *sickly* smile⟩ **c :** lacking in vigor **:** WEAK ⟨a *sickly* plant⟩ **5 :** SICKENING ⟨a *sickly* odor⟩ — **sick·li·ness** \ˈsik-lē-nəs\ *n*

sick·ness \ˈsik-nəs\ *n* **1 :** ill health **:** ILLNESS **2 :** a specific disease **:** MALADY **3 :** NAUSEA 1

sick·room \ˈsik-ˌrüm, -ˌru̇m\ *n* **:** a room in which a person is confined by sickness

sid·dur \ˈsid-ər, -ˌu̇r\ *n, pl* **sid·du·rim** \sə-ˈdu̇r-əm\ **:** a Jewish prayer book containing liturgies for daily, Sabbath, and holiday observances [Late Hebrew *siddūr,* literally, "order, arrangement"]

[1]side \ˈsīd\ *n* **1 a :** the right or left part of the trunk or wall of the body ⟨a pain in the *side*⟩ **b :** the entire right or left half of an animal body ⟨a *side* of beef⟩ **2 :** a place, space, or direction with respect to a center line (as of an aisle, river, or street) **3 :** a surface forming a border or face of an object ⟨the *side* of the house⟩ **4 :** an outer portion of a thing considered as facing in a particular direction ⟨the upper *side*⟩ **5 :** a slope or declivity of a hill or ridge **6 a :** a line forming part of the boundary of a geometrical figure ⟨*side* of a square⟩ **b :** one of the surfaces that form the boundary of a solid; *esp* **:** one of the longer surfaces ⟨the *side* of the barn⟩ **c :** either surface of a thin object ⟨one *side* of a record⟩ **7 :** the space beside one ⟨stood by my *side*⟩ **8 :** the attitude or activity of one person or group with respect to another **:** PART ⟨no hard feelings on my *side*⟩ **9 :** a body of partisans or contestants ⟨victory for neither *side*⟩ **10 :** a line of descent traced through either parent ⟨a grandfather on his mother's *side*⟩ **11 :** an aspect or part of something held to be contrasted with some other aspect or part ⟨the better *side* of one's nature⟩ ⟨look on the bright *side*⟩ ⟨the sales *side* of the business⟩ **12 :** a recording of music **13 :** a side order or dish ⟨a *side* of fries⟩ [Old English *sīde*] — **on the side 1 :** in addition to but not part of the main portion ⟨a salad with dressing *on the side*⟩ **2 :** in addition to a principal occupation ⟨selling insurance *on the side*⟩ — **this side of :** short of **:** almost ⟨behavior just *this side of* reckless⟩

[2]**side** *adj* **1 :** of, relating to, or situated on the side ⟨a *side* window⟩ **2 a :** directed toward or from the side ⟨*side* thrust⟩ **b :** in addition to or secondary to something primary ⟨a *side* issue⟩ **c :** additional to the main portion ⟨a *side* order of salad⟩

[3]**side** *vb* **1 :** to take sides **:** join or form sides ⟨*sided* with the rebels⟩ **2 :** to furnish with sides or siding ⟨*side* a house⟩

[4]**side** *n* **:** swaggering or arrogant manner [obsolete *side* "proud, boastful," from Middle English, "wide"]

[1]**side·arm** \ˈsīd-ˌärm\ *n* **:** a weapon (as a sword or pistol) worn at the side or in the belt

[2]**sidearm** *adj* **:** of, relating to, using, or being a throw in which the arm is not raised above the shoulder and the ball is thrown with a sideways sweep of the arm between shoulder and hip ⟨a *sidearm* pitcher⟩ ⟨a *sidearm* pass⟩ — **sidearm** *adv*

side·board \ˈsīd-ˌbōrd, -ˌbȯrd\ *n* **:** a piece of dining-room furniture with drawers and compartments for dishes, silverware, and table linen

side·burns \ˈsīd-ˌbərnz\ *n pl* **1 :** short side-whiskers worn with a smooth chin **2 :** continuations of the hairline in front of the ears [anagram of *burnsides*]

Word History During the American Civil War, the Union general Ambrose Everett Burnside wore long bushy side-whiskers. His appearance struck the fancy of Washingtonians as he conducted parades and maneuvers with his regiment of Rhode Island volunteers in the early days of the war. This early popularity fostered the fashion for such whiskers, which came to be called *burnsides*. A later anagram of this word gives us *sideburns*.

side by side *adv* **1 :** beside one another ⟨walking *side by side*⟩ **2 :** in the same place, time, or circumstance ⟨lived peacefully *side by side* for many years⟩ — **side–by–side** *adj*

side·car \ˈsīd-ˌkär\ *n* **:** a car attached to the side of a motorcycle for a passenger

sid·ed \ˈsīd-əd\ *adj* **:** having sides often of a specified number or kind ⟨one-*sided*⟩ ⟨glass-*sided*⟩

side dish *n* **:** food served in addition to the main course ⟨served rice as a *side dish*⟩

side effect *n* **:** a secondary and usually unfavorable effect (as of a drug) — called also *side reaction*

side–glance \ˈsīd-ˌglans\ *n* **1 :** a glance directed to the side **2 :** an indirect or slight reference

side·kick \ˈsīd-ˌkik\ *n* **:** a person closely associated with another as subordinate or partner

side·light \-ˌlīt\ *n* **1 a :** light from the side **b :** incidental or additional information **2 :** the red light on the port side or the green light on the starboard side carried by ships or boats under way at night

[1]**side·line** \-ˌlīn\ *n* **1 :** a line at right angles to a goal line or end line and marking a side of a court or field of play **2 a :** a line of goods sold in addition to one's principal line **b :** a business or activity pursued in addition to one's regular occupation **3 a :** the space immediately outside the lines along either side of a playing area **b :** a sphere of little or no participation or activity — usually used in plural ⟨preferred to remain on the *sidelines* rather than get involved⟩

[2]**sideline** *vt* **:** to make unable to play in a game or sport ⟨*sidelined* by an injury⟩

side·lin·er \ˈsīd-ˌlī-nər\ *n* **:** one that remains on the sidelines during an activity **:** one that does not participate

[1]**side·ling** \ˈsīd-ling\ *adv, archaic* **:** in a sidelong direction **:** SIDEWAYS

[2]**sideling** *adj* **1** *archaic* **:** directed toward one side **2** *archaic* **:** SLOPING ⟨*sideling* ground⟩

[1]**side·long** \ˈsīd-ˌlȯng\ *adv* **1 :** SIDEWAYS ⟨glanced *sidelong* at them⟩ **2** *archaic* **:** on the side [alteration of [1]*sideling*]

[2]**sidelong** *adj* **1 :** lying or inclining to one side **:** SLANTING **2 a :** directed to one side ⟨*sidelong* looks⟩ **b :** indirect rather than straightforward

side·man \ˈsīd-ˌman\ *n* **:** a member of a band or orchestra and especially of a jazz or swing orchestra

side–out \ˈsīd-ˈau̇t\ *n* **:** the termination of a team's right to serve (as in volleyball)

side·piece \-ˌpēs\ *n* **:** a piece contained in or forming the side of something

si·de·re·al \sī-ˈdir-ē-əl\ *adj* **1 :** of or relating to the stars or constellations **2 :** measured by the apparent motion of fixed stars ⟨*sidereal* time⟩ [Latin *sidereus,* from *sider-, sidus* "star, constellation"]

sid·er·ite \ˈsid-ə-ˌrīt\ *n* **:** a natural carbonate of iron $FeCO_3$ that is a valuable iron ore [German *Siderit,* from Greek *sidēros* "iron"]

side·sad·dle \ˈsīd-ˌsad-l\ *n* **:** a saddle in which the rider sits with both legs on one side of the horse — **sidesaddle** *adv*

side·show \-ˌshō\ *n* **1 :** a minor show offered in addition to a main exhibition (as of a circus) **2 :** an incidental diversion or spectacle

side·slip \-ˌslip\ *vi* **1 :** to skid sideways — used especially of an automobile **2 :** to slide sideways through the air in a downward direction — **sideslip** *n*

side·spin \-ˌspin\ *n* **:** a rotary motion that causes a ball to spin around a vertical axis

side·split·ting \-ˌsplit-ing\ *adj* **:** extremely funny

side·step \ˈsīd-ˌstep\ *vb* **1 :** to take a side step **2 :** to avoid by a step to the side ⟨*sidestep* a blow⟩ **3 :** to avoid an issue or decision

side step *n* **1 :** a step to the side (as in boxing to avoid a blow) **2 :** a step taken sideways (as in climbing on skis)

side street *n* **:** a street joining and often terminated by a main thoroughfare

side·stroke \-ˌstrōk\ *n* **:** a swimming stroke performed while lying on the side in which the arms are swept in separate strokes towards the feet and downward and the legs do a scissors kick

[1]**side·swipe** \-ˌswīp\ *vt* **:** to strike with a glancing blow along the side ⟨*sideswiped* a parked car⟩

[2]**sideswipe** *n* **1 a :** the action of sideswiping **b :** an instance of sideswiping **:** a glancing blow **2 :** an incidental disapproving remark, allusion, or reference ⟨a *sideswipe* at the senator's voting record⟩

[1]**side·track** \-ˌtrak\ *n* **1 :** SIDING 1 **2 :** a position or state of secondary importance to which one may be diverted

[2]**sidetrack** *vt* **1 :** to transfer from a main railroad line to a siding ⟨*sidetrack* a train⟩ **2 :** to turn aside from a main purpose or use ⟨was *sidetracked* by phone calls⟩

side·walk \ˈsīd-ˌwȯk\ *n* **:** a usually paved walk for pedestrians at the side of a street

sidewalk superintendent *n* **:** a passerby who stops to watch construction or demolition work

side·wall \ˈsīd-ˌwȯl\ *n* **1 :** a wall forming the side of something **2 :** the side of an automotive tire between the tread shoulder and the bead

side·ward \-wərd\ *or* **side·wards** \-wərdz\ *adv or adj* **:** toward the side

side·way \-ˌwā\ *adv or adj* **:** SIDEWAYS

side·ways \-ˌwāz\ *adv or adj* **1 :** from one side ⟨viewing the building *sideways*⟩ **2 :** with one side forward ⟨turn *sideways*⟩ **3 :** toward one side ⟨hopped *sideways*⟩; *also* **:** ASKANCE ⟨look *sideways* at someone⟩

\ə\ **abut**	\au̇\ **out**	\i\ **tip**	\ȯ\ **saw**	\u̇\ **foot**
\ər\ **further**	\ch\ **chin**	\ī\ **life**	\ȯi\ **coin**	\y\ **yet**
\a\ **mat**	\e\ **pet**	\j\ **job**	\th\ **thin**	\yü\ **few**
\ā\ **take**	\ē\ **easy**	\ng\ **sing**	\t͟h\ **this**	\yu̇\ **cure**
\ä\ **cot, cart**	\g\ **go**	\ō\ **bone**	\ü\ **food**	\zh\ **vision**

side–wheel·er \ˈsīd-ˌhwē-lər, ˈsīd-ˌwē-\ *n* : a steamboat having a paddle wheel on each side

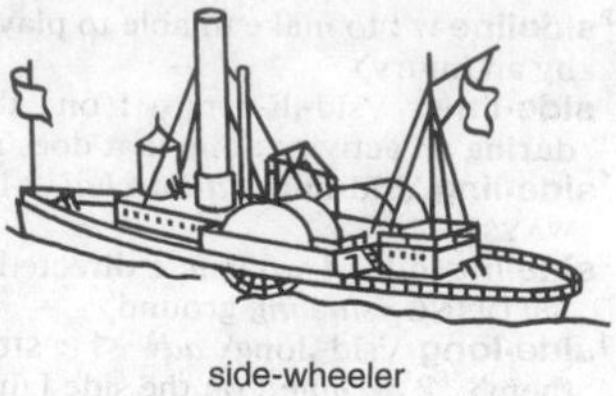

side-wheeler

side–whis·kers \ˈsīd-ˌhwis-kərz, ˈsīd-ˌwis-\ *n pl* : whiskers on the side of the face usually worn long with the chin shaven

side·wind·er \ˈsīd-ˌwīn-dər\ *n* **1** : a heavy swinging blow from the side **2** : a small rattlesnake of the southwestern U.S. that moves by thrusting its body diagonally forward in a series of flat S-shaped curves

side·wise \-ˌwīz\ *adv or adj* : SIDEWAYS

sid·ing \ˈsīd-ing\ *n* **1** : a short railroad track connected with the main track by switches at one or more places **2** : material (as boards or metal or plastic pieces) used to cover the outside walls of frame buildings

si·dle \ˈsīd-l\ *vb* **si·dled; si·dling** \ˈsīd-ling, -l-ing\ **1** : to advance obliquely usually in a furtive or unobtrusive way **2** : to cause to move or turn sideways [probably back-formation from [2]*sideling*] — **sidle** *n*

siege \ˈsēj\ *n* **1** : a military blockade of a fortified place **2** : a continued attempt to gain possession of something **3** : a persistent attack (as of illness) [Medieval French *sege* "seat, blockade," derived from Latin *sedēre* "to sit"]

si·en·na \sē-ˈen-ə\ *n* : an earthy substance containing oxides of iron and usually of manganese that is brownish yellow when raw and orange red or reddish brown when burnt and is used as a pigment [Italian *terra di Siena,* literally, "Siena earth," from *Siena,* Italy]

si·er·ra \sē-ˈer-ə\ *n* **1** : a range of mountains especially with jagged peaks **2** : the country about a sierra [Spanish, literally, "saw," from Latin *serra*]

si·es·ta \sē-ˈes-tə\ *n* : an afternoon nap or rest [Spanish, from Latin *sexta hora* "noon," literally, "sixth hour"]

sie·va bean \ˈsē-və-, ˈsiv-ē-\ *n* : a bean plant of tropical America that is closely related to and sometimes classed with the lima bean; *also* : its flat edible seed [origin unknown]

[1]sieve \ˈsiv\ *n* : a device with meshes or perforations through which finer particles of a mixture (as of ashes, flour, or sand) of various sizes are passed to separate them from coarser ones, through which the liquid is drained from liquid-containing material, or through which soft materials are forced for reduction to fine particles [Old English *sife*]

[2]sieve *vb* : to put through a sieve : SIFT

sieve plate *n* : an area in the end wall of a sieve tube pierced by fine pores

sieve tube *n* : a tube that consists of an end-to-end series of thin-walled living cells, is the characteristic element of the phloem, and is held to function chiefly in translocation of organic solutes

sift \ˈsift\ *vb* **1 a** : to put through a sieve ⟨*sift* flour⟩ **b** : to separate or separate out by or as if by putting through a sieve **2** : to go through especially to sort out what is useful or valuable ⟨*sifted* the evidence⟩ ⟨*sifted* through a pile of old letters⟩ **3** : to scatter by or as if by sifting ⟨*sift* sugar on a cake⟩ **4** : to pass through or as if through a sieve [Old English *siftan*] — **sift·er** *n*

sift·ing *n* **1** : the act or process of sifting **2** *pl* : sifted material

sigh \ˈsī\ *vb* **1** : to take or exhale a deep audible breath (as in weariness or grief) **2** : to make a sound like sighing **3** : GRIEVE, YEARN ⟨*sighing* for the past⟩ **4** : to express by sighs [Old English *sīcan*] — **sigh** *n* — **sigh·er** \ˈsī-ər, ˈsīr\ *n*

[1]sight \ˈsīt\ *n* **1** : something that is seen : SPECTACLE **2 a** : a thing that is worth seeing ⟨the *sights* of the city⟩ **b** : something ridiculous or disorderly in appearance ⟨you look a *sight*⟩ **3 a** : the process, power, or function of seeing; *esp* : the animal sense of which the eye is the sense organ and by which the position, shape, and color of objects are perceived **b** : mental or spiritual perception **c** : mental view; *esp* : JUDGMENT **4 a** : the act of looking at or beholding ⟨faints at the *sight* of blood⟩ **b** : INSPECTION ⟨this letter is for your *sight* only⟩ **c** : VIEW, GLIMPSE ⟨I caught *sight* of a friend⟩ **d** : an observation to determine direction or position (as by a navigator) **5 a** : perception of an object by or as if by the eye ⟨never lost *sight* of his goal⟩ **b** : the range of vision ⟨was nowhere in *sight*⟩ **6 a** : a device (as a small metal bead on a gun barrel) that aids the eye in aiming or in determining the direction of an object **b** *pl* : ASPIRATION 3a, GOAL 2 ⟨set her *sights* on a career in law⟩ [Old English *gesiht* "faculty or act of sight, thing seen"] — **in sight** : at or within a reasonable distance or time ⟨the end is *in sight*⟩ — **on sight** : as soon as seen ⟨a dog trained to attack *on sight*⟩ — **out of sight** : beyond comparison, expectation, or reason — **sight for sore eyes** : one whose appearance or arrival is an occasion for joy or relief

[2]sight *adj* **1** : based on recognition or comprehension without previous study ⟨*sight* translation⟩ **2** : payable on presentation ⟨a *sight* draft⟩

[3]sight *vb* **1** : to get or catch sight of ⟨several bears were *sighted*⟩ **2** : to look at through or as if through a sight **3** : to aim by means of sights **4** : to look carefully in a particular direction

sight·ed \ˈsīt-əd\ *adj* : having sight ⟨clear-*sighted*⟩

sight hound *n* : a hound (as a greyhound) that hunts and pursues game by sight rather than by scent

sight·less \ˈsīt-ləs\ *adj* : lacking sight : BLIND — **sight·less·ness** *n*

sight·ly \ˈsīt-lē\ *adj* **1** : pleasing to the sight : HANDSOME **2** : affording a good view — **sight·li·ness** *n*

sight–read \ˈsīt-ˌrēd\ *vb* **sight–read** \-ˌred\; **sight–read·ing** \-ˌrēd-ing\ : to read a foreign language or perform music without preparation or study — **sight reader** \-ˌrēd-ər\ *n*

sight·see \ˈsīt-ˌsē\ *vb* **-saw; -see·ing** : to go about seeing sights of interest — **sight·seer** \ˈsīt-ˌsē-ər, -ˌsiər\ *n*

sight·see·ing \ˈsīt-ˌsē-ing\ *adj* : devoted to or used for seeing sights — **sightseeing** *n*

sight unseen *adv* : without inspection or appraisal

sig·il \ˈsij-əl, ˈsig-ˌil\ *n* **1** : SEAL 1b, SIGNET **2** : a sign, word, or device of supposed occult power in astrology or magic [Latin *sigillum,* from *signum* "sign, seal"]

sig·ma \ˈsig-mə\ *n* : the 18th letter of the Greek alphabet — Σ or σ or ς

sig·moid \ˈsig-ˌmȯid\ *adj* **1 a** : curved like the letter C **b** : curved in two directions like the letter S **2** : of, relating to, or being the sigmoid colon [Greek *sigmoeidēs,* from *sigma* "sigma"; from a common form of sigma shaped like the Roman letter C] — **sig·moi·dal·ly** \sig-ˈmȯid-l-ē\ *adv*

sigmoid colon *n* : the S-shaped part of the colon immediately above the rectum

[1]sign \ˈsīn\ *n* **1 a** : a motion or gesture by which a thought is expressed or a command made known **b** : SIGNAL 1a **c** : SIGN LANGUAGE **2** : a mark having a conventional meaning and used in place of words or to represent a complex notion **3** : one of the 12 divisions of the zodiac **4 a** : a character (as a flat or sharp) used in musical notation **b** : a symbol (as $\div$ or $\surd$) indicating a mathematical operation; *also* : one of two symbols + and − characterizing a number as positive or negative **5 a** : a lettered board or other display used to identify or advertise a place of business **b** : a posted command, warning, or direction **c** : SIGNBOARD **6 a** : something that serves to indicate the presence or existence of something else ⟨*signs* of success⟩ **b** : PRESAGE 1, PORTENT ⟨*signs* of an early spring⟩ **c** : an objective evidence of plant or animal disease [Medieval French *signe,* from Latin *signum* "mark, sign, image, seal"]

synonyms SIGN, MARK, TOKEN, NOTE, SYMPTOM mean a discernible indication of what is not itself directly perceptible. SIGN applies to any indication to be perceived by the senses or the reason ⟨encouraging *signs* for the economy⟩. MARK suggests something impressed on or inherently characteristic of a thing often in contrast to general outward appearance ⟨a *mark* of a good upbringing⟩. TOKEN applies to something that serves as a proof of something intangible ⟨this gift is a *token* of my esteem⟩. NOTE suggests a distinguishing mark or characteristic ⟨a *note* of irony in her writing⟩. SYMPTOM suggests an outward indication of an internal change or condition ⟨rampant crime is a *symptom* of that city's decay⟩.

[2]sign *vb* **1 a** : to place a sign on or mark by signs ⟨*sign* a trail⟩ **b** : to represent or indicate by a sign **2 a** : to affix one's signature to ⟨*sign* a letter⟩ **b** : to assign or convey formally ⟨*signed* over his property to his brother⟩ **3 a** : to communicate by making a sign **b** : to use sign language **4** : to hire by securing the signature of — often used with *up* or *on* **5** : to write one's name to show agreement, responsibility, or obligation ⟨*signed* for the packages⟩ ⟨*signed* with the team for one season⟩ [Middle French *signer,* from Latin *signare,* from *signum* "sign"] — **sign·ee** \ˌsī-ˈnē\ *n* — **sign·er** *n*

[1]sig·nal \ˈsig-nᵊl\ *n* **1 a** : an act, event, or watchword that serves to start some action **b** : something that stirs to action **2** : a sound or gesture made to give warning or command **3 :** an object placed to give notice or warning **4 a :** the message, sound, or effect transmitted in electronic communication (as radio or television) **b :** a radio wave or electric current that transmits a message or effect (as in radio, television, or telephony) [Medieval Latin *signale,* derived from Latin *signum* "sign"]

[2]**signal** *vb* **-naled** *or* **-nalled; -nal·ing** *or* **-nal·ling 1 :** to notify by a signal **2 :** to communicate by or as if by signals **3 :** to make or send a signal — **sig·nal·er** *n*

[3]**signal** *adj* **1 :** distinguished from the ordinary **:** OUTSTANDING ⟨a *signal* achievement⟩ **2 :** used in signaling ⟨a *signal* beacon⟩ — **sig·nal·ly** \ˈsig-nᵊl-ē\ *adv*

sig·nal·ize \ˈsig-nᵊl-ˌīz\ *vt* **1 :** to make conspicuous **2 :** to point out carefully or distinctly **3 :** to make signals to **:** SIGNAL; *also* **:** INDICATE 1 — **sig·nal·i·za·tion** \ˌsig-nᵊl-ə-ˈzā-shən\ *n*

sig·nal·man \ˈsig-nᵊl-mən, -ˌman\ *n* **:** one who signals or works with signals

sig·nal·ment \-mənt\ *n* **:** description by peculiar, appropriate, or characteristic marks

sig·na·to·ry \ˈsig-nə-ˌtōr-ē, -ˌtȯr-\ *n, pl* **-ries :** a signer with another or others ⟨*signatories* to a petition⟩; *esp* **:** a government bound with others by a signed convention — **signatory** *adj*

sig·na·ture \ˈsig-nə-ˌchu̇r, -chər\ *n* **1 :** the name of a person written with his or her own hand **2 a :** a letter at the bottom of the first page of a sheet of printed pages (as of a book) to ensure placement in the right order in binding **b :** one unit of a book making up a group of printed sheets that are folded and stitched together **3 a :** KEY SIGNATURE **b :** TIME SIGNATURE **4 :** something (as a tune, style, or logo) that serves to set apart or identify; *also* **:** a characteristic mark [Medieval Latin *signatura,* derived from Latin *signare* "to sign, seal"]

sign·board \ˈsīn-ˌbōrd, -ˌbȯrd\ *n* **:** a board bearing a notice or sign

[1]**sig·net** \ˈsig-nət\ *n* **1 :** a seal used in place of a signature on a document **2 :** the impression made by or as if by a signet **3 :** a small intaglio seal [Medieval French, from *signe* "sign, seal"]

[2]**signet** *vt* **:** to stamp or authenticate with a signet

signet ring *n* **:** a finger ring engraved with a signet

sig·ni·fi·able \ˈsig-nə-ˌfī-ə-bəl\ *adj* **:** capable of being represented by a sign or symbol

sig·nif·i·cance \sig-ˈnif-i-kəns\ *n* **1 a :** something that is conveyed as a meaning often obscurely or indirectly **b :** the quality of communicating or implying **2 a :** IMPORTANCE **b :** the quality of being statistically significant ***synonyms*** see MEANING

sig·nif·i·cant \-kənt\ *adj* **1 :** having meaning **:** SUGGESTIVE, EXPRESSIVE ⟨a *significant* glance⟩ **2 :** having or likely to have influence or effect **:** IMPORTANT ⟨*significant* evidence⟩; *also* **:** of a noticeably or measurably large amount ⟨*significant* profits⟩ **3 :** probably caused by something other than chance ⟨a statistically *significant* correlation between vitamin deficiency and disease⟩ [Latin *significare* "to signify"] — **sig·nif·i·cant·ly** *adv*

significant digit *n* **:** any of the digits of a number beginning with the first digit on the left that is not zero and ending with the last digit on the right that is either not zero or that is a zero but is considered to be exact — called also *significant figure*

sig·ni·fi·ca·tion \ˌsig-nə-fə-ˈkā-shən\ *n* **1 :** a signifying by signs **2 :** IMPORT; *esp* **:** the meaning that a term, symbol, or character regularly conveys or is intended to convey ***synonyms*** see MEANING

sig·nif·i·ca·tive \sig-ˈnif-ə-ˌkāt-iv\ *adj* **1 :** INDICATIVE 2 **2 :** SIGNIFICANT 1, SUGGESTIVE — **sig·nif·i·ca·tive·ly** *adv* — **sig·nif·i·ca·tive·ness** *n*

sig·ni·fi·er \ˈsig-nə-ˌfī-ər, -ˌfīr\ *n* **:** one that signifies **:** SIGN

sig·ni·fy \ˈsig-nə-ˌfī\ *vb* **-fied; -fy·ing 1 :** MEAN 2, DENOTE **2 :** to show by a word, signal, or gesture **3 :** to have significance or importance [Medieval French *signifier,* from Latin *significare* "to indicate, signify," from *signum* "sign"]

sign in *vi* **:** to make a record of one's arrival or presence

sign language *n* **1 :** a formal language employing a system of hand gestures for communication (as by the deaf) **2 :** an unsystematic method of communicating chiefly by hand and arm gestures as used by people who do not speak the same language

sign off *vi* **1 :** to announce the end (as of a program or broadcast) **2 :** to approve or acknowledge something by or as if by a signature ⟨*sign off* on a memo⟩

sign of the cross : a gesture of the hand forming a cross especially on forehead, shoulders, and breast to profess Christian faith or ask for divine care and blessing

sign on *vi* **1 :** to engage oneself by or as if by a signature ⟨*signed on* to the new project⟩ **2 :** to announce the beginning of broadcasting

si·gnor \sēn-ˈyȯr, -ˈyōr\ *n, pl* **signors** *or* **si·gno·ri** \sēn-ˈyōr-ē, -ˈyȯr-\ — used by or to Italian-speaking people as a courtesy title equivalent to *Mr.* [Italian *signore, signor,* from Medieval Latin *senior* "superior, lord," from Latin, adj., "senior"]

si·gno·ra \sēn-ˈyōr-ə, -ˈyȯr-\ *n, pl* **-gnoras** *or* **-gno·re** \-ˈyōr-ā, -ˈyȯr-ā\ — used by or to Italian-speaking people as a courtesy title equivalent to *Mrs.* [Italian, feminine of *signore, signor*]

si·gno·ri·na \ˌsēn-yə-ˈrē-nə\ *n, pl* **-nas** *or* **-ne** \-nā\ — used by or to Italian-speaking people as a courtesy title equivalent to *Miss* [Italian, from *signora*]

sign out *vb* **1 :** to make a record of one's departure **2 :** to record or approve the release or departure of ⟨*signed out* the library books⟩

sign·post \ˈsīn-ˌpōst\ *n* **1 :** a post with a sign on it to direct travelers **2 :** something that points the way

sign up *vi* **:** to sign one's name (as to a contract) in order to obtain, do, or join something ⟨*sign up* for classes⟩ — **sign–up** \ˈsī-ˌnəp\ *n or adj*

Sikh \ˈsēk\ *n* **:** a believer in a monotheistic religion of India founded about 1500 and marked by rejection of idolatry and caste [Hindi, literally, "disciple"] — **Sikh** *adj* — **Sikh·ism** \-ˌiz-əm\ *n*

si·lage \ˈsī-lij\ *n* **:** fodder (as hay or corn) fermented (as in a silo) by bacteria under anaerobic conditions to produce a rich moist feed for livestock [short for *ensilage*]

[1]**si·lence** \ˈsī-ləns\ *n* **1 :** forbearance from speech or noise — often used interjectionally **2 :** absence of sound or noise **:** STILLNESS ⟨in the *silence* of the night⟩ **3 :** absence of mention: **a :** OBLIVION 2, OBSCURITY **b :** SECRECY 2 ⟨the investigation was conducted in *silence*⟩

[2]**silence** *vt* **1 :** to stop the noise or speech of **:** reduce to silence **2 :** to restrain from expression **3 :** to cause to cease hostile firing or criticism ⟨*silence* the opposition⟩

si·lenc·er \ˈsī-lən-sər\ *n* **:** one that silences; *esp* **:** a silencing device for small arms

si·lent \ˈsī-lənt\ *adj* **1 a :** not speaking **:** MUTE, SPEECHLESS **b :** unwilling to speak **2 :** free from sound or noise **:** STILL **3 :** UNSPOKEN ⟨*silent* disapproval⟩ **4 a :** making no mention ⟨history is *silent* about this person⟩ **b :** not widely or generally known ⟨the *silent* pressures of being a professional athlete⟩ **c :** making no protest or outcry ⟨the *silent* majority⟩ **5 :** not pronounced ⟨the *silent* "b" in "doubt"⟩ **6 a :** made without spoken dialogue ⟨*silent* movies⟩ **b :** of or relating to silent movies [Latin *silens,* from *silēre* "to be silent"] — **si·lent·ly** *adv* — **si·lent·ness** *n*

synonyms SILENT, TACITURN, RETICENT, RESERVED mean showing restraint in speaking. SILENT implies a habit of saying no more than is necessary and often less than expected ⟨a *silent* person who leads by example rather than words⟩. TACITURN suggests a temperamental disinclination to talk and a sullen avoidance of sociability ⟨a *taciturn* farmer who did not welcome visitors⟩. RETICENT implies a reluctance to speak out plainly especially about one's personal affairs ⟨were *reticent* about their plans⟩. RESERVED suggests the restraining influence of caution or formality in checking easy informal conversation ⟨greetings were brief, formal, and *reserved*⟩.

silent butler *n* **:** a container with hinged lid for collecting table crumbs and the contents of ashtrays

silent partner *n* **:** a partner who is known to the public but has no voice in the conduct of a firm's business

silent treatment *n* **:** an act of completely ignoring a person or thing by being silent especially as a means of expressing contempt or disapproval

si·lex \ˈsī-ˌleks\ *n* **:** SILICA [Latin, "flint, quartz"]

[1]**sil·hou·ette** \ˌsil-ə-ˈwet\ *n* **1 :** a drawing or cutout of the outline of an object filled in with black; *esp* **:** a profile portrait of this kind **2 :** the characteristic shape of an object (as an air-

plane) seen or as if seen against the light [French, from Étienne de *Silhouette,* died 1767, French controller general of finances]

2**silhouette** *vt* **-ett·ed; -ett·ing :** to represent by a silhouette; *also* **:** to project upon a background like a silhouette ⟨a flock of geese *silhouetted* against the evening sky⟩ — **sil·hou·et·tist** \-ˈwet-ist\ *n*

sil·i·ca \ˈsil-i-kə\ *n* **:** the dioxide of silicon SiO_2 occurring in crystalline, amorphous, and impure forms (as in quartz, opal, and sand) [New Latin, from Latin *silic-, silex* "flint, quartz"]

silica gel *n* **:** colloidal silica resembling coarse white sand in appearance but possessing many fine pores and therefore extremely adsorbent

sil·i·cate \ˈsil-i-kət, ˈsil-ə-ˌkāt\ *n* **:** a compound formed from silica and any of various oxides of metals

si·li·ceous *or* **si·li·cious** \sə-ˈlish-əs\ *adj* **:** of, relating to, or containing silica or a silicate ⟨*siliceous* limestone⟩

si·lic·ic \sə-ˈlis-ik\ *adj* **:** of, relating to, or derived from silica or silicon

silicic acid *n* **:** any of various weakly acid substances obtained as gelatinous masses by treating silicates with acids

silicified wood *n* **:** chalcedony in the form of petrified wood

si·lic·i·fy \sə-ˈlis-ə-ˌfī\ *vt* **-fied; -fy·ing :** to convert into or impregnate with silica — **si·lic·i·fi·ca·tion** \-ˌlis-ə-fə-ˈkā-shən\ *n*

sil·i·con \ˈsil-i-kən, ˈsil-ə-ˌkän\ *n* **:** a tetravalent nonmetallic element that occurs combined as the most abundant element next to oxygen in the earth's crust and is used especially in alloys and electronic devices — see ELEMENT table [*silica* + *-on* (as in *carbon*)]

silicon carbide *n* **:** a hard brittle crystalline compound SiC of silicon and carbon used as an abrasive

silicon dioxide *n* **:** SILICA

sil·i·cone \ˈsil-ə-ˌkōn\ *n* **:** any of various polymeric organic silicon compounds obtained as oils, greases, or plastics and used especially for water-resistant and heat-resistant lubricants, varnishes, binders, and electric insulators [from *silicon*]

sil·i·co·sis \ˌsil-ə-ˈkō-səs\ *n* **:** a disease of the lungs marked by formation of scar tissue and shortness of breath and caused by prolonged inhaling of silica dusts — **sil·i·cot·ic** \-ˈkät-ik\ *adj or n*

si·lique \sə-ˈlēk\ *n* **:** a long narrow 2-valved usually many-seeded capsule characteristic of the mustard family [French, from Latin *siliqua* "pod, husk"]

1**silk** \ˈsilk\ *n* **1 :** a fine continuous protein fiber produced by various insect larvae usually for cocoons; *esp* **:** a lustrous tough elastic fiber produced by silkworms and used for textiles **2 a :** thread, yarn, or fabric made from silk **b :** a garment of silk **3 a :** a filament resembling silk; *esp* **:** one produced by a spider **b :** silky material ⟨milkweed *silk*⟩; *esp* **:** the styles of an ear of corn [Old English *seolc*] — **silk** *adj*

2**silk** *vi* **:** to develop the silk ⟨the corn is *silking*⟩

silk cotton *n* **:** the silky or cottony covering of seeds of a silk-cotton tree; *esp* **:** KAPOK

silk–cotton tree *n* **:** any of various tropical trees with palmate leaves and large fruits with the seeds enveloped by silk cotton

silk·en \ˈsil-kən\ *adj* **1 :** made or consisting of silk **2 :** resembling silk especially in soft lustrous smoothness

silk hat *n* **:** a hat with a tall cylindrical crown and a silk-plush finish worn by men as a dress hat

silk moth *n* **:** the silkworm moth

Silk Road *n* **:** the ancient trade route that extended from China to the Mediterranean Sea

silk screen *n* **:** a stencil process in which coloring matter is forced onto the material to be printed through the meshes of a silk or organdy screen — called also *silk-screen process*

silk–stocking *adj* **1 :** fashionably dressed ⟨a *silk-stocking* audience⟩ **2 :** ARISTOCRATIC, WEALTHY ⟨the *silk-stocking* districts of a city⟩

silk·worm \ˈsil-ˌkwərm\ *n* **:** a moth larva that spins a large amount of strong silk in constructing its cocoon; *esp* **:** a rough wrinkled hairless yellowish caterpillar that is the larva of an Asian moth, feeds only on mulberry leaves, and has long been raised in captivity for the silk it produces

silky \ˈsil-kē\ *adj* **silk·i·er; -est 1 :** SILKEN 2 **2 :** having or covered with fine soft hairs, plumes, or scales — **silk·i·ly** \-kə-lē\ *adv* — **silk·i·ness** \-kē-nəs\ *n*

sill \ˈsil\ *n* **1 :** a horizontal piece (as a timber) that forms the lowest member of a framework or supporting structure (as of a house or bridge): as **a :** the horizontal member at the base of a window **b :** the timber or stone at the foot of a door **:** THRESHOLD **2 :** a flat mass of igneous rock injected while molten between other rocks [Old English *syll*]

sillabub *variant of* SYLLABUB

sil·li·man·ite \ˈsil-ə-mə-ˌnīt\ *n* **:** a brown, grayish, or pale green crystalline mineral that consists of an aluminum silicate [Benjamin *Silliman,* died 1864, American geologist]

sil·ly \ˈsil-ē\ *adj* **sil·li·er; -est 1 :** mentally feeble **:** FOOLISH **2 :** contrary to reason **:** ABSURD **3 :** lacking in seriousness **:** TRIFLING [Middle English *sely* "happy, innocent, pitiable, feeble," from Old English *sǣl* "happiness"] — **sil·li·ly** \ˈsil-ə-lē\ *adv* — **sil·li·ness** \ˈsil-ē-nəs\ *n* — **silly** *n or adv*

si·lo \ˈsī-lō\ *n, pl* **silos 1 :** a trench, pit, or especially a tall cylinder (as of wood or concrete) used for making and storing silage **2 a :** a deep bin for storing material (as coal) **b :** an underground structure for housing a guided missile [Spanish]

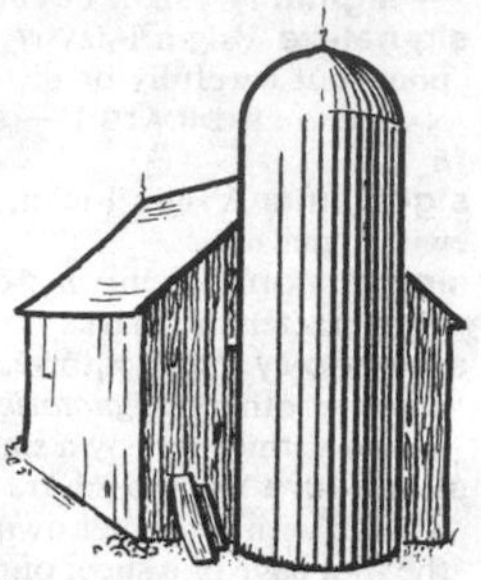
silo 1

1**silt** \ˈsilt\ *n* **1 :** loose sedimentary material with rock particles usually 1/20 millimeter or less in diameter; *also* **:** soil containing 80 percent or more of such silt and less than 12 percent of clay **2 :** a deposit of sediment (as by a river) [Middle English *cylte*] — **silty** \ˈsil-tē\ *adj*

2**silt** *vb* **:** to become or make choked, obstructed, or covered with silt ⟨the river channel *silted* up⟩ — **silt·a·tion** \sil-ˈtā-shən\ *n*

Si·lu·ri·an \sī-ˈlu̇r-ē-ən, sə-\ *n* **:** the period of the Paleozoic era between the Ordovician and Devonian marked by the appearance of very large crustaceans and of the first land plants; *also* **:** the corresponding system of rocks — see GEOLOGIC TIME table [Latin *Silures,* a people of ancient Britain] — **Silurian** *adj*

silvan *variant of* SYLVAN

1**sil·ver** \ˈsil-vər\ *n* **1 :** a white ductile and malleable metallic element that takes a high polish, is usually univalent in compounds, and has the highest thermal and electric conductivity — see ELEMENT table **2 a :** coin made of silver **b :** articles (as tableware) made of or plated with silver; *also* **:** similar articles and especially flatware made of other metals (as stainless steel) **3 :** a medium gray **4 :** a silver medal awarded as the second prize in a competition [Old English *seolfor*]

2**silver** *adj* **1 :** relating to, made of, or yielding silver ⟨*silver* jewelry⟩ ⟨*silver* ore⟩ **2 :** SILVERY

3**silver** *vt* **sil·vered; sil·ver·ing** \ˈsilv-ring, -ə-ring\ **1 a :** to cover with silver (as by electroplating) **b :** to coat with a substance (as a metal) resembling silver ⟨*silver* glass with an amalgam⟩ **2 :** to give a silvery appearance to — **sil·ver·er** \ˈsil-vər-ər\ *n*

silver bromide *n* **:** a compound AgBr extremely sensitive to light and much used for photographic materials

silver bullet *n* **:** something that acts as a magical weapon; *esp* **:** one that instantly solves a long-standing problem

silver chloride *n* **:** a compound AgCl sensitive to light and used especially for photographic emulsions

sil·ver·fish \ˈsil-vər-ˌfish\ *n* **1 :** any of various silvery fishes (as a tarpon) **2 :** any of various small wingless insects (order Thysanura); *esp* **:** one that is found in houses and feeds on starchy materials (as wallpaper paste and book bindings)

silver fox *n* **:** a genetically determined color phase of the common red fox in which the pelt is black tipped with white

silver iodide *n* **:** a compound AgI that is sensitive to light and is used in photography, rainmaking, and medicine

silver lining *n* **:** a consoling or hopeful prospect

silver maple *n* **:** a common maple of eastern North America with deeply cut 5-lobed leaves that are light green above and silvery white below; *also* **:** its hard close-grained but brittle light brown wood

sil·vern \ˈsil-vərn\ *adj* **1 :** made of silver **2 :** resembling or characteristic of silver **:** SILVERY

silver nitrate *n* **:** an irritant compound $AgNO_3$ that is used as a chemical reagent, in photography, and in medicine especially as an antiseptic

silver paper *n* **:** a metallic paper with a coating or lamination resembling silver

silver perch *n* **:** any of various somewhat silvery fishes that resemble perch

silver plate *n* **1 :** a plating of silver **2 :** domestic flatware and hollowware of silver or of a base metal plated with silver

silver protein *n* **:** a colloidal light-sensitive preparation of silver and protein used as an antiseptic

silver screen *n* **1 :** a motion-picture screen **2 :** SCREEN 3b

sil•ver•side \ˈsil-vər-ˌsīd\ *n* **:** any of a family of small chiefly marine fishes with a silvery stripe along each side of the body

sil•ver•sides \-ˌsīdz\ *n sing or pl* **:** SILVERSIDE

sil•ver•smith \-ˌsmith\ *n* **:** a person who makes articles of silver

silver spoon *n* **:** WEALTH; *esp* **:** inherited wealth [from the phrase *born with a silver spoon in one's mouth* "born wealthy"]

silver standard *n* **:** a monetary standard under which the currency unit is defined by a stated quantity of silver

sil•ver–tongued \ˌsil-vər-ˈtəngd\ *adj* **:** ELOQUENT ⟨a *silver-tongued* speaker⟩

sil•ver•ware \ˈsil-vər-ˌwaər, -ˌweər\ *n* **:** SILVER PLATE 2; *also* **:** FLATWARE

sil•very \ˈsilv-rē, -ə-rē\ *adj* **1 :** having a soft high clear ring ⟨a *silvery* voice⟩ **2 :** having the white lustrous sheen of silver — **sil•ver•i•ness** *n*

sil•vi•cul•ture \ˈsil-və-ˌkəl-chər\ *n* **:** a branch of forestry concerned with the development and growth of forest trees [French, from Latin *silva* "forest" + *cultura* "culture"] — **sil•vi•cul•tur•al** \ˌsil-və-ˈkəlch-rəl, -ə-rəl\ *adj* — **sil•vi•cul•tur•al•ly** \-ē\ *adv* — **sil•vi•cul•tur•ist** \-ˈkəlch-rəst, -ə-rəst\ *n*

Sim•chas To•rah \ˌsim-k̲äs-ˈtōr-ə, -ˈtȯr-\ *n* **:** a Jewish holiday observed in October or November in celebration of the completion of the annual reading of the Torah [Hebrew *śimḥath tōrāh* "rejoicing of the Torah"]

¹sim•i•an \ˈsim-ē-ən\ *adj* **:** of, relating to, or resembling monkeys or apes [Latin *simia* "ape," from *simus* "snub-nosed," from Greek *simos*]

²simian *n* **:** MONKEY 1, APE 1; *also* **:** any of a group (Anthropoidea) of primates that includes monkeys, apes, and humans

sim•i•lar \ˈsim-ə-lər\ *adj* **1 :** having characteristics in common **:** COMPARABLE **2 :** not differing in shape but only in size or position ⟨*similar* triangles⟩ [French *similaire,* from Latin *similis* "like, similar"] — **sim•i•lar•ly** *adv*

synonyms SIMILAR, ANALOGOUS, PARALLEL mean closely resembling each other. SIMILAR implies the possibility of being mistaken for each other ⟨all the houses in the neighborhood are *similar*⟩. ANALOGOUS applies to things belonging in essentially different categories but nevertheless having many similarities ⟨*analogous* political systems⟩. PARALLEL suggests a marked likeness in the development of two things ⟨the *parallel* careers of two movie stars⟩.

sim•i•lar•i•ty \ˌsim-ə-ˈlar-ət-ē\ *n, pl* **-ties 1 :** the quality or state of being similar **:** RESEMBLANCE **2 :** a point in which things are similar **:** CORRESPONDENCE ***synonyms*** see LIKENESS

sim•i•le \ˈsim-ə-lē, -ˌlē\ *n* **:** a figure of speech in which things different in kind or quality are compared by the use of the word *like* or *as* (as in "cheeks like roses") — compare METAPHOR [Latin, "comparison," from *similis* "like, similar"]

si•mil•i•tude \sə-ˈmil-ə-ˌtüd, -ˌtyüd\ *n* **1 :** a visible likeness **:** IMAGE **2 :** an imaginative comparison **:** SIMILE **3 a :** correspondence in kind or quality **b :** a point of comparison

sim•mer \ˈsim-ər\ *vb* **sim•mered; sim•mer•ing** \ˈsim-ring, -ə-ring\ **1 :** to stew gently below or just at the boiling point **2 a :** to be in a state of early development ⟨an idea *simmering* in the back of my mind⟩ **b :** to be in inward turmoil **:** SEETHE ⟨*simmered* with fury at the insult⟩ [Middle English *simperen*] — **simmer** *n*

simmer down *vi* **1 :** to become calm or peaceful ⟨*simmered down* after her outburst⟩ **2 :** to become reduced by or as if by simmering ⟨a sauce *simmered down* to half⟩

si•mo•ni•ac \sī-ˈmō-nē-ˌak, sə-\ *n* **:** one who practices simony — **simoniac** *or* **si•mo•ni•a•cal** \ˌsī-mə-ˈnī-ə-kəl, ˌsim-ə-\ *adj* — **si•mo•ni•a•cal•ly** \-ˈnī-ə-kə-lē, -klē\ *adv*

si•mo•nize \ˈsī-mə-ˌnīz\ *vt* **:** to polish with or as if with wax [from *Simoniz,* a trademark]

si•mon–pure \ˌsī-mən-ˈpyu̇r\ *adj* **:** of untainted purity or integrity; *also* **:** pretentiously or hypocritically pure [from *the real Simon Pure,* alluding to a character impersonated by another in the play *A Bold Stroke for a Wife* (1718) by Susanna Centlivre]

si•mo•ny \ˈsī-mə-nē, ˈsim-ə-\ *n* **:** the buying or selling of a church office [Late Latin *simonia,* from *Simon* Magus, Samaritan sorcerer in Acts 8:9–24]

si•moom \sə-ˈmüm, sī-\ *or* **si•moon** \-ˈmün\ *n* **:** a hot dry violent wind laden with dust from Asian and African deserts [Arabic *samūm*]

sim•pa•ti•co \sim-ˈpät-i-ˌkō, -ˈpat-\ *adj* **1 :** LIKABLE **2 :** on the same wavelength **:** CONGENIAL 2 ⟨were *simpatico* when it came to choosing vacation spots⟩ [Italian, from *simpatia* "sympathy, congeniality," from Latin *sympathia* "sympathy"]

¹sim•per \ˈsim-pər\ *vi* **sim•pered; sim•per•ing** \-pə-ring, -pring\ **1 :** to smile in a silly manner **2 :** to say with a simper ⟨*simpered* an apology⟩ [akin to early Dutch *zimperlijc* "elegant," Danish dialect *simper* "affected, coy"] — **sim•per•er** \-pər-ər\ *n*

²simper *n* **:** a silly smile **:** SMIRK

sim•ple \ˈsim-pəl\ *adj* **sim•pler** \-pə-lər, -plər\; **sim•plest** \-pə-ləst, -pləst\ **1 :** free from deceit or vanity **2 a :** of humble origin or modest position ⟨a *simple* farmer⟩ **b :** lacking in education, experience, or intelligence **3 a :** free from complexity or complications ⟨a *simple* melody⟩ **b :** consisting of only one main clause and no subordinate clauses ⟨a *simple* sentence⟩ **c :** not compound ⟨the *simple* noun "boat"⟩ **d** (1) **:** not subdivided into branches or leaflets ⟨a *simple* leaf⟩ (2) **:** developing from a single ovary ⟨*simple* fruits⟩ **4 a :** UTTER, ABSOLUTE ⟨the *simple* truth⟩ **b :** easily understood or performed ⟨a *simple* task⟩ [Medieval French, "plain, uncomplicated, artless," from Latin *simplus, simplex,* literally, "single"] — **sim•ple•ness** \-pəl-nəs\ *n*

synonyms SIMPLE, EASY mean not demanding great effort or involving difficulty. SIMPLE stresses lack of complexity or subtlety ⟨a *simple* case of theft⟩. EASY implies offering little resistance to being understood or accomplished or dealt with ⟨an *easy* problem⟩ ⟨an *easy* victory⟩.

simple eye *n* **:** an eye having a single lens — compare COMPOUND EYE

simple fraction *n* **:** a fraction having whole numbers for the numerator and denominator — compare COMPLEX FRACTION

simple fracture *n* **:** a breaking of a bone in such a way that the skin is not broken and bone fragments do not protrude — compare COMPOUND FRACTURE

simple interest *n* **:** interest paid or computed on the original principal only of a loan or on the amount of an account

simple machine *n* **:** any of various elementary mechanisms formerly considered as the elements of which all machines are composed and including the lever, the wheel and axle, the pulley, the inclined plane, the wedge, and the screw

sim•ple•mind•ed \ˌsim-pəl-ˈmīn-dəd\ *adj* **:** not subtle **:** UNSOPHISTICATED; *also* **:** FOOLISH — **sim•ple•mind•ed•ly** *adv* — **sim•ple•mind•ed•ness** *n*

simple sugar *n* **:** MONOSACCHARIDE

sim•ple•ton \ˈsim-pəl-tən\ *n* **:** a person lacking in common sense [*simple* + *-ton* (as in surnames such as *Washington*)]

sim•plex \ˈsim-ˌpleks\ *n, pl* **sim•pli•ces** \ˈsim-plə-ˌsēz\ *or* **sim•pli•cia** \sim-ˈplish-ə, -ē-ə\ **:** a word that is not a compound [Latin *simplic-, simplex* "simple, single"] — **sim•pli•cial** \sim-ˈplish-əl\ *adj*

sim•plic•i•ty \sim-ˈplis-ət-ē\ *n, pl* **-ties 1 :** the quality or state of being simple **2 :** freedom from pretense or guile **:** HONESTY **3 a :** directness or clarity of expression **b :** restraint in ornamentation **4 :** FOLLY 1, SILLINESS [Medieval French *simplicité,* from Latin *simplicitas,* from *simplic-, simplex* "simple"]

sim•pli•fy \ˈsim-plə-ˌfī\ *vt* **-fied; -fy•ing :** to make simple or simpler — **sim•pli•fi•ca•tion** \ˌsim-plə-fə-ˈkā-shən\ *n* — **sim•pli•fi•er** \ˈsim-plə-ˌfī-ər, -ˌfīr\ *n*

sim•plis•tic \sim-ˈplis-tik\ *adj* **1 :** SIMPLE 4b **2 :** characterized by too much simplicity **:** not involving or dealing with related complexities ⟨a *simplistic* solution⟩ ⟨a *simplistic* view of the situation⟩ — **sim•plis•ti•cal•ly** \-ti-kə-lē, -tik-lē\ *adv*

sim•ply \ˈsim-plē\ *adv* **1 a :** CLEARLY ⟨stated the directions *simply*⟩ **b :** PLAINLY ⟨*simply* dressed⟩ **c :** DIRECTLY, CANDIDLY ⟨told the story as *simply* as a child would⟩ **2 a :** MERELY, SOLELY ⟨eats *simply* to keep alive⟩ **b :** REALLY 1 ⟨*simply* marvelous⟩

sim•u•late \ˈsim-yə-ˌlāt\ *vt* **:** to give the appearance or effect of **:** IMITATE [Latin *simulare* "to copy, represent, feign," from *similis* "like, similar"] ***synonyms*** see ASSUME — **sim•u•la•tive** \-ˌlāt-iv\ *adj*

\ə\ **abut**	\au̇\ **out**	\i\ **tip**	\ȯ\ **saw**	\u̇\ **foot**
\ər\ **further**	\ch\ **chin**	\ī\ **life**	\ȯi\ **coin**	\y\ **yet**
\a\ **mat**	\e\ **pet**	\j\ **job**	\th\ **thin**	\yü\ **few**
\ā\ **take**	\ē\ **easy**	\ng\ **sing**	\t̲h̲\ **this**	\yu̇\ **cure**
\ä\ **cot, cart**	\g\ **go**	\ō\ **bone**	\ü\ **food**	\zh\ **vision**

sim·u·lat·ed \-ˌlāt-əd\ *adj* : made to look genuine : FAKE ⟨*simulated* pearls⟩
sim·u·la·tion \ˌsim-yə-ˈlā-shən\ *n* **1** : the act or process of simulating **2** : a sham object : COUNTERFEIT **3** : the imitation of the workings of one system or process using another ⟨a computer *simulation* of space flight⟩
sim·u·la·tor \ˈsim-yə-ˌlāt-ər\ *n* : one that simulates; *esp* : a device that enables the operator to reproduce or represent under test conditions phenomena likely to occur in actual performance
si·mul·cast \ˈsī-məl-ˌkast\ *vb* : to broadcast simultaneously by AM and FM radio or by radio and television [*simul*taneous broad*cast*] — **simulcast** *n*
si·mul·ta·neous \ˌsī-məl-ˈtā-nē-əs, -nyəs\ *adj* **1** : existing or occurring at the same time : COINCIDENT **2** : satisfied by the same values of the variables ⟨*simultaneous* equations⟩ [Latin *simul* "at the same time" + English *-taneous* (as in *instantaneous*)] ***synonyms*** see CONTEMPORARY — **si·mul·ta·ne·i·ty** \-tə-ˈnē-ət-ē, -ˈnā-\ *n* — **si·mul·ta·neous·ly** \-ˈtā-nē-ə-slē, -nyə-slē\ *adv* — **si·mul·ta·neous·ness** *n*
[1]**sin** \ˈsin\ *n* **1** : an offense against religious or moral law **2** : MISDEED, FAULT [Old English *synn*]
[2]**sin** *vi* **sinned; sin·ning** : to commit a sin
[1]**since** \sins, ˈsins\ *adv* **1** : from a definite past time until now ⟨has stayed there ever *since*⟩ **2** : before the present time : AGO ⟨long *since* dead⟩ **3** : after a time in the past : SUBSEQUENTLY ⟨has *since* become rich⟩ [Middle English *sithens, sins,* from *sithen,* from Old English *siththan,* from *sith tham* "after that"]
[2]**since** *prep* : from or after a specified time in the past ⟨has worked here *since* 1990⟩ ⟨happy *since* then⟩
[3]**since** *conj* **1** : at a time or times in the past after or later than ⟨have held two jobs *since* I graduated⟩ **2** : from the time in the past when ⟨ever *since* we were children⟩ **3** : in view of the fact that : BECAUSE ⟨*since* it was raining, I wore a hat⟩
sin·cere \sin-ˈsiər\ *adj* **1 a** : free from deceit : HONEST ⟨a *sincere* friend⟩ **b** : free from adulteration : PURE ⟨a *sincere* doctrine⟩ **2** : GENUINE 1, REAL ⟨a *sincere* work of art⟩ [Middle French, from Latin *sincerus*] — **sin·cere·ly** *adv* — **sin·cere·ness** *n* — **sin·cer·i·ty** \-ˈser-ət-ē, -ˈsir-\ *n*
sine \ˈsīn\ *n* **1** : a trigonometric function that for an acute angle in a right triangle is the ratio of the side opposite the angle to the hypotenuse — abbreviation *sin* **2** : a trigonometric function sin θ that for all real numbers θ is given by the sum of the alternating series

$$\sin\theta = \theta - \frac{\theta^3}{3!} + \frac{\theta^5}{5!} - \frac{\theta^7}{7!} + \frac{\theta^9}{9!} - \ldots$$

and that is exactly equal to the sine of an angle of measure θ in radians [Medieval Latin *sinus,* from Latin, "curve"]
si·ne·cure \ˈsī-ni-kyu̇r, ˈsin-i-\ *n* : an office or position that requires little or no work [Medieval Latin *sine cura* "without cure of souls"]
si·ne die \ˌsī-nē-ˈdī-ˌē, -ˈdī; sin-ē-ˈdē-ˌā\ *adv* : for an unspecified period of time : INDEFINITELY ⟨the meeting adjourned *sine die*⟩ [Latin, "without day"]
si·ne qua non \ˌsin-i-ˌkwä-ˈnän, -ˈnōn; *also* ˌsī-nē-ˌkwā-ˈnän\ *n* : something absolutely essential or indispensable ⟨reliability is a *sine qua non* for success⟩ [Late Latin, "without which not"]
sin·ew \ˈsin-yü, ˈsin-ü\ *n* **1** : TENDON; *esp* : one prepared for use as a cord or thread **2** : solid resilient strength : POWER [Old English *seono*]
sine wave *n* : a waveform that represents periodic oscillations in which the amplitude of displacement at each point is proportional to the sine of the angle of the displacement
sin·ewy \ˈsin-yə-wē, ˈsin-ə-wē\ *adj* **1** : full of sinews : TOUGH, STRINGY ⟨*sinewy* meat⟩ **2** : STRONG ⟨*sinewy* arms⟩
sin·fo·nia \ˌsin-fə-ˈnē-ə\ *n, pl* **-nie** \-ˈnē-ˌā\ **1** : an orchestral prelude to a vocal work (as an opera) especially in the 18th century **2** : SYMPHONY 2 [Italian, from Latin *symphonia* "symphony"]
sin·ful \ˈsin-fəl\ *adj* : marked by or full of sin : WICKED — **sin·ful·ly** \-fə-lē\ *adv* — **sin·ful·ness** *n*
[1]**sing** \ˈsing\ *vb* **sang** \ˈsang\ *or* **sung** \ˈsəng\; **sung; sing·ing** \ˈsing-ing\ **1 a** : to produce musical sounds by means of the voice **b** : to utter with musical sounds ⟨*sing* a song⟩ **c** : CHANT, INTONE ⟨*sing* mass⟩ **2** : to make pleasing musical sounds ⟨birds *singing* at dawn⟩ **3** : to make a slight shrill sound ⟨a kettle *singing* on the stove⟩ **4 a** : to tell a story in poetry : relate in verse **b** : to express vividly and enthusiastically ⟨*sing* their praises⟩ **5** : BUZZ, RING ⟨ears *singing* from the sudden descent⟩ **6** : to bring or accompany to a place or state by singing ⟨*sing* a baby to sleep⟩ **7 a** : to call aloud : cry out ⟨*sing* out when you find them⟩ **b** : to divulge information or give evidence [Old English *singan*] — **sing·able** \ˈsing-ə-bəl\ *adj*
[2]**sing** *n* : a singing especially in company
[1]**singe** \ˈsinj\ *vb* **singed** \ˈsinjd\; **singe·ing** \ˈsin-jing\ : to burn superficially or lightly : SCORCH; *esp* : to remove hair, down, or fuzz from usually by passing briefly over a flame [Old English *sæncgan, sengan*]
[2]**singe** *n* : a slight burn : SCORCH
[1]**sing·er** \ˈsing-ər\ *n* : one that sings
[2]**sing·er** \ˈsin-jər\ *n* : one that singes
[1]**sin·gle** \ˈsing-gəl\ *adj* **1** : not married **2** : unaccompanied by others : LONE, SOLE ⟨the *single* survivor ot the disaster⟩ **3 a** (1) : consisting of or having only one part or feature (2) : consisting of one as opposed to or in contrast with many : UNIFORM ⟨a *single* standard for men and women⟩ (3) : consisting of only one in number ⟨holds to a *single* ideal⟩ **b** : having but one whorl of petals or ray flowers ⟨a *single* rose⟩ **4 a** : consisting of a separate unique whole : INDIVIDUAL ⟨every *single* citizen⟩ **b** : of, relating to, or involving only one person **5** : FRANK, HONEST ⟨a *single* devotion⟩ **6** : being a whole ⟨a *single* world⟩ **7** : having no equal or like : SINGULAR **8** : designed for the use of one person only ⟨a *single* room⟩ ⟨a *single* bed⟩ [Medieval French *sengle,* from Latin *singulus* "one only"] — **sin·gle·ness** *n*
synonyms SINGLE, SOLITARY, SOLE, UNIQUE mean being the only one. SINGLE implies being unaccompanied or unassisted by any other ⟨operated by a *single* worker⟩ ⟨a *single* line of trees⟩. SOLITARY implies being both single and isolated ⟨a *solitary* oak in a field⟩. SOLE implies being the only one existing or acting ⟨the *sole* reason for refusing⟩ ⟨the *sole* survivor of the wreck⟩. UNIQUE implies being the only one of its kind or character in existence ⟨a *unique* mineral specimen⟩.
[2]**single** *n* **1 a** : a separate individual person or thing **b** : an unmarried person **c** (1) : a recording having one short tune on each side (2) : a music recording having two or more tracks that is shorter than a full-length album **2** : a base hit that permits the batter to reach first base **3** *pl* : a game (as of tennis or handball) between two players
[3]**single** *vb* **sin·gled; sin·gling** \ˈsing-gə-ling, -gling\ **1** : to select or distinguish (a person or thing) from a number or group — usually used with *out* **2** : to make a single in baseball
single bond *n* : a chemical bond in which one pair of electrons is shared by two atoms in a molecule especially when the atoms can share more than one pair of electrons — compare DOUBLE BOND, TRIPLE BOND
sin·gle–breast·ed \ˌsing-gəl-ˈbres-təd\ *adj* : having a center closing with one row of buttons and no overlapping lapel
single entry *n* : a method of bookkeeping that shows only one side of a business transaction and usually consists only of a record of accounts with debtors and creditors
single file *n* : a line of persons or things arranged one behind another — **single file** *adv*
[1]**sin·gle–foot** \ˈsing-gəl-ˌfu̇t\ *n, pl* **single–foots** : [4]RACK b
[2]**single–foot** *vi* : to go at a rack — **sin·gle–foot·er** *n*
sin·gle–hand·ed \ˌsing-gəl-ˈhan-dəd\ *adj* **1** : managed or done by one person **2** : working alone : lacking help — **single–handed** *adv* — **sin·gle–hand·ed·ly** *adv*
sin·gle–heart·ed \-ˈhärt-əd\ *adj* : characterized by sincerity and unity of purpose — **sin·gle–heart·ed·ly** *adv* — **sin·gle–heart·ed·ness** *n*
sin·gle–mind·ed \-ˈmīn-dəd\ *adj* : having one overriding purpose : DETERMINED — **sin·gle–mind·ed·ly** *adv* — **sin·gle–mind·ed·ness** *n*
sin·gle–space \-ˈspās\ *vt* : to type or print with no blank lines between lines of text
sin·gle·stick \ˈsing-gəl-ˌstik\ *n* : fighting or fencing with a wooden stick or sword held in one hand; *also* : the weapon used
sin·glet \ˈsing-glət\ *n, chiefly British* : an athletic jersey; *also* : UNDERSHIRT [from its having only one thickness of cloth]
single tax *n* : a tax levied on a single item (as real estate) as the sole source of public revenue
sin·gle·ton \ˈsing-gəl-tən\ *n* **1** : a playing card that is the only one of its suit originally held in a hand **2** : an individual distinct from others grouped with it [French, from English *single*]
sin·gle·tree \-ˌtrē\ *n* : WHIFFLETREE

sin·gly \'sing-gə-lē, -glē\ *adv* **1 :** by or with oneself **2 :** in a single-handed manner

1sing·song \'sing-ˌsȯng\ *n* **:** voice delivery marked by a regular rhythm, narrow range, or a monotonous rise and fall of pitch

2singsong *adj* **:** having a monotonous cadence or rhythm

1sin·gu·lar \'sing-gyə-lər\ *adj* **1 a :** of or relating to a separate person or thing **:** INDIVIDUAL **b :** of, relating to, or being a word form denoting one person, thing, or instance ⟨a *singular* noun⟩ **c :** of or relating to a single instance or to something considered by itself **2 :** EXCEPTIONAL 2 **3 :** being out of the ordinary **:** UNUSUAL **4 :** departing from general usage or expectation **:** PECULIAR [Medieval French *singuler,* from Latin *singularis,* from *singulus* "only one"] — **sin·gu·lar·ly** *adv*

2singular *n* **:** something that is singular; *esp* **:** the singular number, the inflectional form denoting it, or a word in that form

sin·gu·lar·i·ty \ˌsing-gyə-'lar-ət-ē\ *n, pl* **-ties 1 :** the quality or state of being singular **2 :** something that is peculiar **3 :** a point or region of infinite density which is held to be the final state of matter falling into a black hole

sin·gu·lar·ize \'sing-gyə-lə-ˌrīz\ *vt* **:** to make singular

Sin·ha·lese *or* **Sin·gha·lese** \ˌsing-gə-'lēz, ˌsin-ə-, ˌsin-hə-, -ˌlēs\ *n, pl* **Sinhalese** *or* **Singhalese 1 :** a member of a people forming a major part of the population of Sri Lanka **2 :** the Indo-Aryan language of the Sinhalese people [Sanskrit *Siṁhala* "Sri Lanka"] — **Sinhalese** *adj*

sin·is·ter \'sin-ə-stər\ *adj* **1 :** singularly evil or productive of evil **:** BAD **2 :** of, relating to, or situated to the left or on the left side of something **3 :** seriously threatening trouble or disaster **:** OMINOUS [Latin, "on the left side, unlucky"] — **sin·is·ter·ly** *adv* — **sin·is·ter·ness** *n*

sin·is·tral \'sin-ə-strəl\ *adj* **:** of, relating to, or inclined to the left; *esp* **:** LEFT-HANDED

1sink \'singk\ *vb* **sank** \'sangk\ *or* **sunk** \'səngk\; **sunk; sink·ing 1 :** to move or cause to move downward usually so as to be submerged or buried ⟨feet *sinking* into deep mud⟩ ⟨*sink* a ship⟩ **2 a :** to fall to a lower level ⟨the lake *sank* during the drought⟩ **b :** to make or become lower in pitch or volume ⟨my voice *sank* to a whisper⟩ **c :** to go downward in quality, state, amount, or worth ⟨*sink* into decay⟩ **d :** to disappear from view **:** SET ⟨the sun *sank* behind the hills⟩ **3 a :** to penetrate or cause to penetrate ⟨*sank* the ax into the tree⟩ **b :** to become absorbed ⟨water *sinking* into dry sand⟩; *also* **:** to be apprehended and retained ⟨the lesson *sank* in⟩ **4 :** to fail in strength, spirits, or health ⟨my heart *sank*⟩ ⟨the patient is *sinking* fast⟩ **5 :** to form by digging or boring usually in the earth ⟨*sink* a well⟩ **6 :** SUPPRESS ⟨*sinking* my pride, I apologized⟩ **7 :** 2INVEST 1 [Old English *sincan*] — **sink·able** \'sing-kə-bəl\ *adj* — **sink one's teeth into 1 :** to bite into **2 :** to eagerly devote one's attention to ⟨likes to *sink her teeth into* a good book⟩

2sink *n* **1 a :** CESSPOOL **b :** SEWER **c :** a stationary basin for washing (as in a kitchen) connected with a drain and usually a water supply **2 :** a place marked by vice, corruption, and filth **3 :** a depression in the land surface; *esp* **:** one having a saline lake with no outlet

sink·age \'sing-kij\ *n* **:** the act, process, or extent of sinking

sink·er \'sing-kər\ *n* **1 :** one that sinks; *esp* **:** a weight for sinking a line or net **2 :** DOUGHNUT

sink·hole \'singk-ˌhōl\ *n* **:** a hollow place in which drainage collects

sinking fund *n* **:** a fund set up and accumulated by usually regular deposits for paying off the principal of a debt

sin·less \'sin-ləs\ *adj* **:** free from sin — **sin·less·ly** *adv* — **sin·less·ness** *n*

sin·ner \'sin-ər\ *n* **:** one that sins

Sino- *combining form* **1 :** Chinese **2 :** Chinese and [Late Latin *Sinae,* pl., "Chinese," from Greek *Sinai,* probably of Indo-Aryan origin]

si·no·atri·al node \ˌsī-nō-ˌā-trē-əl-\ *n* **:** SINUS NODE [*sinus* + *atrium*]

sin·ter \'sint-ər\ *vt* **:** to cause to become a coherent mass by heating without melting [German *Sinter* "slag, cinder," from Old High German *sintar*] — **sinter** *n*

sin·u·os·i·ty \ˌsin-yə-'wäs-ət-ē\ *n, pl* **-ties 1 :** the quality or state of being sinuous **2 :** something that is sinuous

sin·u·ous \'sin-yə-wəs\ *adj* **1 a :** of a serpentine or wavy form **:** WINDING **b :** marked by strong lithe movements **2 :** INTRICATE, COMPLEX [Latin *sinuosus,* from *sinus* "curve"] — **sin·u·ous·ly** *adv* — **sin·u·ous·ness** *n*

si·nus \'sī-nəs\ *n* **:** CAVITY, HOLLOW: as **a :** a narrow passage by which pus is discharged **b :** any of several cavities in the skull that usually connect with the nostrils and contain air **c :** a dilatation in a bodily canal or vessel **d :** a cleft or indentation between adjoining lobes (as of a leaf) [Latin, "curve, fold, hollow"]

si·nus·itis \ˌsī-nə-'sīt-əs\ *n* **:** inflammation of a sinus of the skull

sinus node *n* **:** a small mass of tissue that is embedded in the musculature of the right atrium of higher vertebrates and that originates the impulses stimulating the heartbeat

si·nus ve·no·sus \ˌsī-nəs-vi-'nō-səs\ *n* **:** an enlarged pouch which adjoins the heart and through which venous blood enters the heart in lower vertebrates and embryos [New Latin, "venous sinus"]

Sion *variant of* ZION

Siou·an \'sü-ən\ *n* **1 :** a stock of American Indian languages spoken in central and southeastern North America **2 :** a member of any of the peoples speaking Siouan languages

Sioux \'sü\ *n, pl* **Sioux** \'sü, 'süz\ **1 :** DAKOTA **2 :** SIOUAN [French, from *Nadouessioux,* from Ojibwa *na·towe·ssiw-*]

1sip \'sip\ *vb* **sipped; sip·ping 1 :** to drink in small quantities or little by little **2 :** to take sips from **:** TASTE [Middle English *sippen*] — **sip·per** *n*

2sip *n* **1 :** the act of sipping **2 :** a small amount taken by sipping

1si·phon *also* **sy·phon** \'sī-fən\ *n* **1 a :** a tube bent to form two legs of unequal length by which a liquid can be transferred to a lower level over an intermediate elevation by the pressure of the atmosphere in forcing the liquid up the shorter branch of the tube immersed in it while the excess of weight of the liquid in the longer branch when once filled causes a continuous flow **b** *usually* **syphon :** a bottle for holding carbonated water that is driven out through a bent tube in its neck by the pressure of the gas when a valve in the tube is opened **2 :** any of various tubular organs in animals and especially mollusks or arthropods used for drawing in or ejecting fluids [French, from Latin *sipho* "tube, pipe, siphon," from Greek *siphōn*]

siphon 1a

2siphon *also* **syphon** *vb* **si·phoned** *also* **sy·phoned; si·phon·ing** *also* **sy·phon·ing** \'sīf-ning, -ə-ning\ **:** to draw off or pass off by or as if by a siphon ⟨*siphoned* off thousands of dollars⟩

si·pho·no·phore \sī-'fän-ə-ˌfōr, 'sī-fə-nə-, -ˌfȯr\ *n* **:** any of an order (Siphonophora) of mostly delicate, transparent, and colored colonial hydrozoans

sir \sər, 'sər\ *n* **1 :** a man entitled to be addressed as *sir* — used as a title before the name of a knight or baronet ⟨*Sir* Winston Churchill⟩ ⟨*Sir* Winston⟩ **2 a** — used as a usually respectful form of direct address ⟨yes, *sir*⟩ **b** *cap* — used sometimes as a salutation in a letter [Middle English, from *sire*]

Si·rach \'sī-rak *also* sə-'räk\ *n* **:** a didactic book of the Roman Catholic canon of the Old Testament — see BIBLE table

sir·dar *or* **sar·dar** \'sər-ˌdär\ *n* **:** a person of high rank or one holding a position of responsibility especially in India [Hindi and Urdu *sardār,* from Persian]

1sire \'sīr\ *n* **1 a :** FATHER 1a **b** *archaic* **:** a male ancestor **:** FOREFATHER **c :** AUTHOR 2, ORIGINATOR **2** *archaic* **:** a man of high station or great authority — used formerly as a form of address (as to a king) or as a title **3 :** the male parent of an animal and especially of a domestic animal [Medieval French "lord, feudal superior," from Latin *senior,* adj., "older"]

2sire *vt* **1 :** BEGET 1 — used especially of domestic animals **2 :** to bring into being **:** ORIGINATE

1si·ren \'sī-rən, *for 3 also* sī-'rēn\ *n* **1** *often cap* **:** one of a group of female and partly human creatures in Greek mythology that lured mariners to destruction by their singing **2 :** a woman held to be insidiously seductive **:** TEMPTRESS **3 a :** an apparatus producing musical tones by the rapid interruption of a current (as of air or steam) by a perforated rotating disk **b :** a device often electrically operated for producing a penetrating warning sound ⟨an ambulance *siren*⟩ ⟨an air-raid *siren*⟩ **4** : any of a genus of eel-shaped amphibians with small forelimbs but neither hind legs nor pelvis and with permanent external gills as well as lungs [Latin, from Greek *seirēn*]

2**si·ren** \'sī-rən\ *adj* : of, relating to, or resembling a siren : ENTICING

si·re·ni·an \sī-'rē-nē-ən\ *n* : any of an order (Sirenia) of aquatic plant-eating mammals having large paddlelike forelimbs, no hind limbs, and a flattened tail resembling a fin and including the manatee and dugong — called also *sea cow*

siren song *n* : an alluring utterance or appeal; *esp* : one that is seductive or deceptive

Sir·i·us \'sir-ē-əs\ *n* : a star of the constellation Canis Major constituting the brightest star in the heavens — called also *Dog Star* [Latin, from Greek *Seirios,* literally, "glowing"]

sir·loin \'sər-ˌlȯin\ *n* : a cut of meat and especially of beef from the part of the hindquarter just in front of the round [Middle French *surlonge,* from *sur* "over" (from Latin *super*) + *loigne, longe* "loin"]

si·roc·co \sə-'räk-ō\ *n, pl* **-cos** **1 a** : a hot dust-laden wind from the Libyan desert that blows on the northern Mediterranean coast chiefly in Italy, Malta, and Sicily **b** : a warm moist oppressive southeast wind in the same regions **2** : a hot or warm wind of cyclonic origin from an arid or heated region [Italian *scirocco, sirocco,* from Arabic *šlōq* "southeast wind," from Arabic *shalūq, shulūq*]

sir·rah *also* **sir·ra** \'sir-ə\ *n, obsolete* — used as a form of address implying inferiority in the person addressed [alteration of *sir*]

sir·ree *also* **sir·ee** \sər-'ē, ˌsər-'ē\ *n* : SIR 2a — used as an emphatic form usually after *yes* or *no*

sirup *variant of* SYRUP

si·sal \'sī-səl, -zəl\ *n* **1** : a strong durable white fiber used for cordage and twine **2** : a widely grown Mexican agave whose leaves yield sisal [*Sisal,* port in Yucatán, Mexico]

sis·kin \'sis-kən\ *n* : a small chiefly greenish and yellowish Old World finch related to the goldfinch [German dialect *Sisschen,* of Slavic origin]

sis·si·fied \'sis-i-ˌfīd\ *adj* : of, relating to, or having the characteristics of a sissy

sis·sy \'sis-ē\ *n, pl* **sissies** : an effeminate man or boy; *also* : a timid or cowardly person [*sis,* short for *sister*] — **sissy** *adj*

sis·ter \'sis-tər\ *n* **1** : a female who has one or both parents in common with another **2** *often cap* : a woman who is a member of a religious order — often used as a title ⟨*Sister* Mary Angelica⟩ **3 a** : a fellow female member of a group **b** : a girl or woman who shares a common national or racial origin with another **4** : one that is closely similar to or associated with another ⟨*sister* schools⟩ ⟨*sister* ships⟩ **5** *chiefly British* : NURSE 2 [Old English *sweoster*]

sis·ter·hood \-ˌhu̇d\ *n* **1 a** : the state of being a sister **b** : sisterly relationship **2** : a community or society of sisters; *esp* : a religious society of women

sis·ter–in–law \'sis-tə-rən-ˌlȯ, -trən-ˌlȯ, -tərn-ˌlȯ\ *n, pl* **sis·ters–in–law** \-tər-zən-\ **1** : the sister of one's spouse **2 a** : the wife of one's brother **b** : the wife of one's spouse's brother

sis·ter·ly \'sis-tər-lē\ *adj* : of, relating to, or typical of a sister — **sisterly** *adv*

Si·swa·ti *or* **Si·Swa·ti** \sē-'swät-ē\ *also* **Swa·zi** \'swä-zē\ *n* : the Bantu language of the Swazi people spoken in Swaziland and adjacent countries [Siswati]

1**sit** \'sit\ *vb* **sat** \'sat\; **sit·ting** **1 a** : to rest or cause to rest on the buttocks or haunches ⟨*sit* in a chair⟩ ⟨*sat* the baby down to eat⟩ **b** : PERCH 2, ROOST **c** : to keep one's seat upon ⟨*sit* a horse⟩ **d** : to provide seats or seating room for ⟨the car *sits* five people⟩ **2** : to occupy a place as a member of an official body ⟨*sit* in Congress⟩ **3** : to hold a session **4** : to cover eggs for hatching : BROOD **5 a** : to pose for a portrait or photograph **b** : to serve as a model **6** : to lie or hang relative to a wearer ⟨the collar *sits* awkwardly⟩ **7** : to lie or rest in any condition or location ⟨the vase *sits* on the table⟩ ⟨the house *sits* back from the road⟩ **8** : to remain inactive ⟨the car *sits* in the garage⟩ **9** : BABYSIT [Old English *sittan*] — **sit on** **1** : to hold deliberations about **2** : REPRESS 4, SQUELCH **3** : to delay action or decision concerning — **sit on one's hands** **1** : to withhold applause : fail to show approval or enthusiasm **2** : to fail to take action — **sit pretty** : to be in a very favorable position — **sit tight** : to maintain one's position without change

2**sit** *n* **1** : an act or period of sitting **2** : the way in which a garment fits

si·tar \si-'tär\ *n* : an Indian lute with a long neck and a varying number of strings [Hindi and Urdu *sitār*]

sitar

sit·com \'sit-ˌkäm\ *n* : SITUATION COMEDY

sit–down \'sit-ˌdau̇n\ *n* : a work stoppage in which protesting employees cease working but refuse to leave their place of employment — called also *sit-down strike*

1**site** \'sīt\ *n* **1** : the actual or planned location (as of a building or town) **2** : the place, scene, or point of an occurrence or event ⟨famous battle *sites*⟩ ⟨a picnic *site*⟩ **3** : WEB SITE [Latin *situs* "place, position," from *sinere* "to leave, allow"]

2**site** *vt* : to place on a site or in position : LOCATE

sith \sith, 'sith\ *or* **sith·ence** \'sith-əns\ *or* **sith·ens** \'sith-ənz\ *archaic variant of* SINCE

sit–in \'sit-ˌin\ *n* **1** : SIT-DOWN **2 a** : an act of occupying seats in a racially segregated establishment in organized protest against discrimination **b** : an act of sitting in the seats or on the floor of an establishment as a means of organized protest

Sit·ka spruce \'sit-kə-\ *n* : a tall spruce of the northern Pacific coast of North America with thin reddish brown bark and flat needles; *also* : its wood [*Sitka,* Alaska]

sit out *vt* : to refrain from participating in ⟨will *sit out* this dance⟩ ⟨*sat* the war *out*⟩

sit·ter \'sit-ər\ *n* : one that sits; *esp* : BABYSITTER

1**sit·ting** \'sit-ing\ *n* **1** : an act of one that sits; *esp* : a single occasion of continuous sitting **2 a** : a brooding over eggs for hatching **b** : SETTING 6 **3** : SESSION 1

2**sitting** *adj* **1** : that is setting ⟨a *sitting* hen⟩ **2** : easily hit ⟨a *sitting* target⟩ **3 a** : used in or for sitting ⟨a *sitting* position⟩ **b** : performed while sitting ⟨a *sitting* shot⟩

sitting duck *n* : an easy or defenseless target for attack, criticism, or unscrupulous dealings

sitting room *n* : LIVING ROOM

1**sit·u·ate** \'sich-ə-wət, -ˌwāt\ *adj* : SITUATED 1 [Late Latin *situatus,* from Latin *situs* "place, site"]

2**sit·u·ate** \'sich-ə-ˌwāt\ *vt* : to place in a site, context, category, or situation : LOCATE

sit·u·at·ed \-ˌwāt-əd\ *adj* **1** : having a site : LOCATED **2** : provided with money or possessions ⟨not rich but comfortably *situated*⟩

sit·u·a·tion \ˌsich-ə-'wā-shən\ *n* **1 a** : the way in which something is placed in relation to its surroundings **b** : SITE 1 **2 a** : position or place of employment : POST, JOB **b** : position in life : STATUS **3** : position with respect to conditions and circumstances ⟨the military *situation*⟩ **4 a** : relative position or combination of circumstances at a certain moment ⟨the *situation* at the beginning of the trial⟩ **b** : a particular or striking complex of affairs at a stage in the action of a narrative or drama — **sit·u·a·tion·al** \-shnəl, -shən-l\ *adj* — **sit·u·a·tion·al·ly** \-ē\ *adv*

situation comedy *n* : a radio or television comedy series that involves a continuing cast of characters in a succession of episodes

sit–up \'sit-ˌəp\ *n* : a conditioning exercise done by lying on the back and raising the trunk to a sitting position without lifting the feet and returning to the original position

sit up \sit-'əp\ *vi* **1 a** : to rise from a lying to a sitting position **b** : to sit with the back erect **2** : to show interest, alertness, or surprise **3** : to stay up beyond the usual bedtime

sitz bath \'sits-\ *n* : a tub in which one bathes in a sitting position; *also* : a bath so taken especially therapeutically [German *Sitzbad, from Sitz* "act of sitting" + *Bad* "bath"]

sitz·mark \'sit-ˌsmärk, 'zit-\ *n* : a depression left in the snow by a skier falling backward [probably from German *sitzen* "to sit" + *Marke* "mark"]

six \'siks\ *n* **1** — see NUMBER table **2** : the sixth in a set or series **3** : something having six units or members; *esp* : a 6-cylinder engine or automobile [Old English *siex*] — **six** *adj or pron* — **at sixes and sevens** : in disorder

six–gun \'siks-ˌgən\ *n* : a 6-chambered revolver

six–o–six *or* **606** \ˌsik-ˌsō-ˈsiks\ *n* : ARSPHENAMINE [from its having been the 606th compound tested and introduced by Paul Ehrlich, died 1915, German bacteriologist]
six–pack \ˈsik-ˌspak\ *n* **1** : a package of six bottles or cans **2** : the contents of a six-pack
six•pence \ˈsik-spəns, *in the U.S. also* -ˌspens\ *n* **1** : the sum of six pence **2** *pl* **sixpence** *or* **six•penc•es** : a British coin no longer issued worth six pence or half a shilling
six•pen•ny \-spə-nē, *in the U.S. also* -ˌspen-ē\ *adj* : costing or worth sixpence
six–shoot•er \ˈsik-ˈshüt-ər, ˈsiks-\ *n* : SIX-GUN
six•teen \sik-ˈstēn, ˈsik-\ *n* — see NUMBER table [Old English *sixtȳne*] — **sixteen** *adj or pron* — **six•teenth** \-ˈstēnth, -stēntth\ *adj or n*
sixteenth note *n* : a musical note with the time value of 1/16 of a whole note
sixteenth rest *n* : a musical rest equal in time value to a sixteenth note
sixth \ˈsiksth, ˈsikstth, ˈsikst\ *n, pl* **sixths** **1** — see NUMBER table **2 a** : the musical interval embracing six diatonic degrees **b** : a tone at this interval **c** : the harmonic combination of two tones a sixth apart — **sixth** *adj or adv* — **sixth•ly** \-lē\ *adv*
sixth sense *n* : a power of perception like but not one of the five senses : a keen intuitive power
six•ty \ˈsik-stē\ *n, pl* **sixties** — see NUMBER table [Old English *siextig*] — **six•ti•eth** \-stē-əth\ *adj or n* — **sixty** *adj or pron*
six•ty–fourth note \ˌsik-stē-ˈfōrth-, -ˈfȯrth-\ *n* : a musical note with the time value of 1/64 of a whole note
siz•able *or* **size•able** \ˈsī-zə-bəl\ *adj* : fairly large — **siz•able•ness** *n* — **siz•ably** \-blē\ *adv*
[1]**size** \ˈsīz\ *n* **1 a** : physical magnitude, extent, or bulk : relative or proportionate dimensions **b** : relative amount or number **c** : considerable proportions : BIGNESS **2** : one of a series of measurements especially of manufactured items (as of clothing) conventionally identified by numbers or letters ⟨a *size* 8 dress⟩ **3** : character or status of a person or thing especially with reference to importance, merit, or correspondence to needs ⟨try this idea on for *size*⟩ **4** : actual situation ⟨that's about the *size* of it⟩ [Medieval French *sise* "assize," short for *assise*]
[2]**size** *vt* **1** : to make a particular size : bring to proper or suitable size **2** : to arrange, grade, or classify as to size or bulk **3** : to form a judgment of — used with *up* ⟨*size* a job up⟩
[3]**size** *n* : a gluey material (as a preparation of glue, flour, varnish, or resins) used for filling the pores in a surface (as of plaster), as a stiffener (as of fabric), or as an adhesive for applying color or metal leaf to book edges or covers [Middle English *sise*]
[4]**size** *vt* : to apply size to
[5]**size** *adj* : SIZED 1 ⟨bite-*size* pieces⟩
sized \ˈsīzd\ *adj* **1** : having a specified size or bulk ⟨a small-*sized* house⟩ **2** : arranged or adjusted according to size
siz•ing \ˈsī-zing\ *n* : [3]SIZE
siz•zle \ˈsiz-əl\ *vb* **siz•zled; siz•zling** \ˈsiz-ling, -ə-ling\ **1** : to burn up or sear with or as if with a hissing sound **2** : to make a hissing sound in or as if in burning or frying **3** : SEETHE 4 [perhaps from earlier *siss* "to hiss"] — **sizzle** *n* — **siz•zler** \ˈsiz-lər, -ə-lər\ *n*
ska \ˈskä\ *n* : popular music of Jamaican origin that combines elements of traditional Caribbean rhythms and jazz [perhaps alteration of [2]*scat*]
skald *or* **scald** \ˈskȯld, ˈskäld\ *n* : an ancient Scandinavian poet [Old Norse *skāld*] — **skald•ic** \-ik\ *adj*
[1]**skate** \ˈskāt\ *n* : any of numerous rays with broadly winglike lateral fins [Old Norse *skata*]

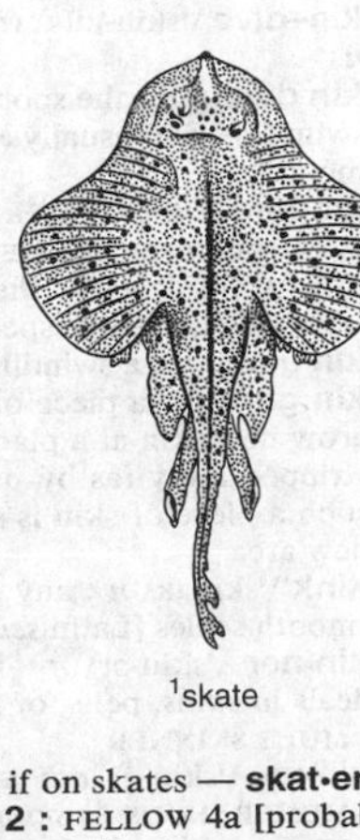

[1]skate

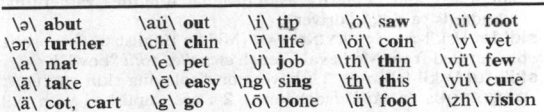

[2]**skate** *n* : a metal runner or a set of two pairs of wheels in tandem on a frame that may be attached to the bottom of a boot for use in gliding over ice or rolling over a hard flat surface; *also* : a boot with an attached runner or wheels [Dutch *schaats* "stilt, skate"]
[3]**skate** *vi* **1** : to glide on skates propelled by the alternate pushing action of the legs **2** : to slip or glide as if on skates — **skat•er** *n*
[4]**skate** *n* **1** : a decrepit horse : NAG **2** : FELLOW 4a [probably from English dialect *skite* "offensive person"]
[1]**skate•board** \ˈskāt-ˌbōrd, -ˌbȯrd\ *n* : a short board mounted on small wheels that is used for coasting and for performing athletic stunts
[2]**skateboard** *vi* : to ride or perform stunts on a skateboard — **skate•board•er** \-ˌbōrd-ər, -ˌbȯrd-\ *n*
skate park *n* : an outdoor area having structures and surfaces for roller-skating and skateboarding
skat•ing \ˈskāt-ing\ *n* : the sport, act, or art of gliding on skates
ske•dad•dle \ski-ˈdad-l\ *vi* **-dad•dled; -dad•dling** \-ˈdad-ling, -l-ing\ : RUN AWAY 1; *esp* : to flee in a panic [probably alteration of British dialect *scaddle* "to run off in a fright"]
skeet \ˈskēt\ *n* : clay pigeon shooting in which targets are thrown in such a way as to simulate the angles of flight of birds [Old Norse *skjōta* "to shoot"]
[1]**skein** \ˈskān\ *n* : a looped length of yarn or thread put up in a loose twist after it is taken from the reel [Medieval French *escagne*]
[2]**skein** *vt* : to wind into skeins ⟨*skein* yarn⟩
skel•e•tal \ˈskel-ət-l\ *adj* : of, relating or attached to, forming, or resembling a skeleton ⟨*skeletal* muscles⟩ ⟨the *skeletal* system⟩ — **skel•e•tal•ly** \-l-ē\ *adv*
[1]**skel•e•ton** \ˈskel-ət-n\ *n* **1** : a usually rigid supportive or protective structure or framework of an organism; *esp* : the framework of bone or sometimes cartilage that supports the soft tissues and protects the internal organs of a vertebrate (as a fish or human) **2** : something reduced to its minimum form or essential parts **3** : an emaciated person or animal **4 a** : something forming a structural framework **b** : the straight or branched chain or ring of atoms that forms the basic structure of an organic molecule **5** : something shameful and kept secret (as in a family) [Greek, neuter of *skeletos* "dried up"]
[2]**skeleton** *adj* : of, consisting of, or resembling a skeleton; *esp* : having the smallest possible number of people who can get a job done ⟨a *skeleton* crew⟩
skel•e•ton•ize \ˈskel-ət-n-ˌīz\ *vt* : to produce in or reduce to skeleton form
skel•e•ton•iz•er \-ˌī-zər\ *n* : a moth or butterfly larva that feeds on leaves reducing them to a skeleton of veins
skeleton key *n* : a key made to open many locks
skel•ter \ˈskel-tər\ *vi* : SCURRY [from *helter-skelter*]
skep \ˈskep\ *n* : a domed hive for housing honeybees made of twisted straw [Old English *sceppe* "basket," from Old Norse *skeppa* "bushel"]

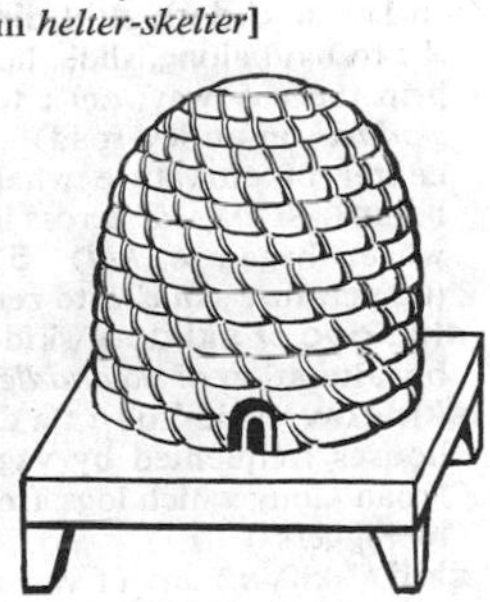

skep

skep•tic \ˈskep-tik\ *n* **1** : an adherent or advocate of skepticism **2** : a person slow to believe or ready to question : DOUBTER [Greek *skeptikos,* from *skeptikos* "thoughtful," from *skeptesthai* "to look, consider"]
skep•ti•cal \-ti-kəl\ *adj* : relating to, characteristic of, or marked by skepticism — **skep•ti•cal•ly** \-kə-lē, -klē\ *adv*
skep•ti•cism \ˈskep-tə-ˌsiz-əm\ *n* **1** : an attitude of doubt **2** : the philosophical doctrine that true and absolute knowledge is unattainable **3** : an attitude of doubt, suspicion, or uncertainty about religious matters
sker•ry \ˈsker-ē\ *n, pl* **skerries** : a rocky isle : REEF [of Scandinavian origin]
[1]**sketch** \ˈskech\ *n* **1 a** : a rough drawing representing the chief features of an object or scene and often made as a preliminary study **b** : a tentative draft (as for a literary work) **2** : a brief description or outline **3 a** : a short literary composition somewhat resembling the short story and the essay but intentionally casual in treatment and familiar in tone **b** : a short instrumental composition **c** : a theatrical piece having a single scene; *esp* : a brief comic skit [Dutch *schets,* from Italian *schizzo,* literally, "splash," from *schizzare* "to splash"]
[2]**sketch** *vb* **1** : to make a sketch, rough draft, or outline of **2** : to draw or paint a sketch — **sketch•er** *n*

sketch·book \'skech-ˌbu̇k\ *n* : a book of or for sketches

sketchy \'skech-ē\ *adj* **sketch·i·er; -est** **1** : of the nature of a sketch : roughly outlined **2** : lacking in completeness, clearness, or substance : SLIGHT, VAGUE ⟨the details are *sketchy*⟩ **3** : QUESTIONABLE, IFFY — **sketch·i·ly** \'skech-ə-lē\ *adv* — **sketch·i·ness** \'skech-ē-nəs\ *n*

¹skew \'skyü\ *vb* **1** : to take an oblique course : move or turn aside : TWIST, SWERVE **2** : to make, set, or cut on a slant **3** : to distort from a true value or symmetrical form ⟨*skewed* data⟩ [Medieval French *eschiver* "to escape, avoid"]

²skew *adj* : set, placed, or running obliquely to something else : SLANTING

³skew *n* : a deviation from a straight line : SLANT

skew·bald \'skyü-ˌbȯld\ *adj* : marked with spots and patches of white and any other color but black ⟨a *skewbald* horse⟩ [earlier *skewed* "skewbald" + *bald*]

¹skew·er \'skyü-ər, 'skyu̇-ər, 'skyu̇r\ *n* **1** : a pin for keeping meat in form while roasting or for holding small pieces of meat and vegetables for broiling **2** : something shaped or used like a meat skewer [Middle English *skeuier*]

²skewer *vt* : to fasten or pierce with or as if with a skewer

skew lines *n pl* : straight lines that do not intersect and are not in the same plane

skew·ness \'skyü-nəs\ *n* : lack of straightness or symmetry; *esp* : lack of symmetry in a frequency distribution

¹ski \'skē\ *n, pl* **skis** : one of a pair of narrow strips of wood, metal, or plastic curving upward in front that are worn by people for gliding over snow or water [Norwegian, from Old Norse *skīth* "stick, ski"]

²ski *vi* **skied; ski·ing** : to glide on skis — **ski·er** *n*

ski boot *n* : a boot or shoe used for skiing; *esp* : a heavy rigid boot that extends above the ankle

¹skid \'skid\ *n* **1** : a log or plank for supporting something (as above the ground) ⟨put a boat on *skids*⟩ **2** : one of the logs, planks, or rails along or on which something heavy is rolled or slid **3** : a device placed under a carriage wheel to prevent its turning : DRAG **4** : a runner used as part of the landing gear of an airplane or helicopter **5** : the act of skidding : SLIDE [perhaps of Scandinavian origin]

²skid *vb* **skid·ded; skid·ding** **1** : to slow or halt by use of a skid **2** : to haul along, slide, hoist, or store on skids **3 a** : to fail to grip the roadway; *esp* : to slip sideways on the road ⟨the car *skidded* on an icy road⟩ **b** : to slide sideways away from the center of curvature when turning ⟨a *skidding* airplane⟩ **c** : SLIDE, SLIP ⟨*skid* across ice⟩ **4** : to slide without rotating ⟨the wheels began to *skid*⟩ **5** : to fall rapidly, steeply, or far ⟨the temperature *skidded* to zero⟩

skid·doo *or* **ski·doo** \skid-'ü\ *vi* : to go away : DEPART [probably alteration of *skedaddle*]

skid row \'skid-'rō\ *n* : a district of cheap saloons and rooming houses frequented by vagrants and derelicts [from *skid road* "road along which logs are dragged, section of town frequented by loggers"]

skiff \'skif\ *n* : any of various small boats; *esp* : a flat-bottomed rowboat [Italian *schifo,* of Germanic origin]

ski·ing *n* : the art or sport of sliding and jumping on skis

ski jump *n* : a jump made by a person wearing skis; *also* : a course or track especially prepared for such jumping — **ski jump** *vi* — **ski jumper** *n*

ski lift *n* : a power-driven conveyor that consists of a series of bars or seats hanging from a moving cable and used for transporting skiers or sightseers up a long slope or mountainside

skill \'skil\ *n* **1** : ability or dexterity that comes from training or practice **2** : a developed or acquired ability : ACCOMPLISHMENT ⟨reading *skills*⟩ [Old Norse *skil* "distinction, knowledge"] ***synonyms*** see ART

skilled \'skild\ *adj* **1** : having acquired mastery of a skill : EXPERT ⟨a *skilled* mason⟩ **2** : requiring skill and training ⟨a *skilled* trade⟩

synonyms SKILLED, SKILLFUL mean having the knowledge and experience needed to succeed at what one does. SKILLED applies to one who has mastered the details and technique of a trade, art, or profession ⟨*skilled* craftsmen⟩. SKILLFUL stresses adeptness and dexterity as individual qualities rather than standards ⟨a *skillful* driver⟩.

skil·let \'skil-ət\ *n* : FRYING PAN [Middle English *skelet,* probably derived from Medieval French *escuelle, eskil* "bowl"]

skill·ful \'skil-fəl\ *adj* **1** : having or displaying skill : EXPERT, DEXTEROUS ⟨a *skillful* debater⟩ **2** : accomplished with skill ⟨*skillful* defense⟩ ***synonyms*** see PROFICIENT, SKILLED — **skill·ful·ly** \-fə-lē\ *adv* — **skill·ful·ness** *n*

skill–less *or* **skil·less** \'skil-ləs\ *adj* : having no skill — **skill–less·ness** *n*

¹skim \'skim\ *vb* **skimmed; skim·ming** **1 a** : to clear (a liquid) of scum or floating substance : remove (as film or scum) from the surface of a liquid **b** : to remove cream from by skimming **2** : to read, study, or examine superficially and rapidly; *esp* : to glance through (as a book) for the chief ideas or the plot **3** : to throw so as to ricochet along the surface of water **4** : to cover or become covered with or as if with a film or scum **5** : to pass swiftly or lightly over : glide above or near a surface [probably from Medieval French *escumer*, from *escume* "foam, scum," of Germanic origin]

²skim *n* **1** : a thin layer, coating, or film **2** : the act of skimming **3** : something skimmed; *esp* : SKIM MILK

³skim *adj* **1** : having the cream removed by skimming **2** : made of skim milk ⟨*skim* cheese⟩

skim·mer \'skim-ər\ *n* **1** : one that skims; *esp* : a flat perforated scoop or spoon used for skimming **2** : any of several long-winged seabirds related to the terns that fly low over the water and skim the surface with the lower bill in search of food **3** : a usually straw flat-crowned hat with a wide straight brim

skim milk *n* : milk from which the cream has been removed — called also *skimmed milk*

skim·ming \'skim-ing\ *n* : material skimmed from a liquid

ski·mo·bile \'skē-mō-ˌbēl\ *n* : SNOWMOBILE

skimp \'skimp\ *vb* **1** : to give insufficient or barely sufficient attention or effort to or funds for **2** : to save by or as if by skimping [perhaps alteration of *scrimp*]

skimpy \'skim-pē\ *adj* **skimp·i·er; -est** : deficient (as in supply) especially through skimping : SCANTY — **skimp·i·ly** \-pə-lē\ *adv* — **skimp·i·ness** \-pē-nəs\ *n*

¹skin \'skin\ *n* **1 a** : the outer layer of an animal separated from the body usually with its hair or feathers : HIDE, PELT **b** : a sheet of parchment or vellum made from a hide **c** : BOTTLE 1b **2 a** : the external limiting layer of an animal body; *esp* : the 2-layered covering of a vertebrate body consisting of an outer epidermis and an inner dermis **b** : an outer covering or surface layer ⟨a sausage *skin*⟩ ⟨apple *skins*⟩ **3** : the life or physical well-being of a person ⟨save one's *skin*⟩ **4** : a sheathing or casing forming the outside surface of a structure (as a ship or airplane) [Old Norse *skinn*] — **skin·less** \-ləs\ *adj* — **skinned** \'skind\ *adj* — **by the skin of one's teeth** : by a very narrow margin — **under one's skin** : beneath one's surface powers of resistance to the point of distressing or irritating

²skin *vb* **skinned; skin·ning** **1 a** : to strip, scrape, or rub off the skin of ⟨*skin* an animal⟩ ⟨*skin* one's knee⟩ **b** : to strip or peel off **2** : to cover or become covered with or as if with skin **3 a** : CHEAT 1, FLEECE **b** : to defeat badly **c** : CENSURE, REPRIMAND **4 a** : to climb up or down ⟨*skin* up and down a rope⟩ **b** : to pass or get by with scant room to spare

skin–deep \'skin-'dēp\ *adj* **1** : as deep as the skin **2** : not thorough or lasting in impression : SUPERFICIAL

skin–dive \'skin-ˌdīv\ *vi* : to engage in skin diving — **skin diver** *n*

skin diving *n* : the sport of swimming underwater with a mask, swim fins, and usually a snorkel especially without scuba equipment

skin·flint \'skin-ˌflint\ *n* : a person who would save or gain money by any means : MISER

skin·ful \-ˌfu̇l\ *n* **1** : the contents of a skin bottle **2** : a large or satisfying quantity especially of liquor

skin game *n* : a swindling game or trick

skin graft *n* : a piece of skin transferred from a donor area to grow new skin at a place where the skin has been destroyed or stripped away (as by burning); *also* : the procedure by which such a piece of skin is surgically removed and transferred to a new area

skink \'skingk\ *n* : any of a family of mostly small lizards with smooth scales [Latin *scincus*, from Greek *skinkos*]

skin·ner \'skin-ər\ *n* **1** : one that removes and processes or deals in skins, pelts, or hides **2** : a driver of draft animals; *esp* : MULE SKINNER

skin·ny \'skin-ē\ *adj* **skin·ni·er; -est** **1** : resembling skin : MEMBRANOUS ⟨a *skinny* layer⟩ **2** : very thin : LEAN, EMACIATED — **skin·ni·ness** *n*

skin·ny–dip *vi* : to swim in the nude — **skin·ny–dip·per** \ˌ-dip-ər\ *n*

skin test *n* : a test (as a scratch test) performed on the skin and used in detecting allergic hypersensitivity

skin·tight \ˈskin-ˈtīt\ *adj* : closely fitted to the figure

[1]**skip** \ˈskip\ *vb* **skipped; skip·ping 1 a** : to move or proceed with leaps and bounds or with a skip **b** : to bound or cause to bound off one point after another ⟨*skip* a stone across a pond⟩ **c** : to leap over lightly and nimbly **2** : to depart hurriedly or secretly ⟨*skip* town⟩ **3 a** : to pass over or omit (as an interval, item, or step) **b** : to omit or cause to omit a grade in school in advancing to the next **c** : to pass over without notice or mention **d** : to fail to attend ⟨*skipped* the meeting⟩ **e** : MISFIRE 1 [Middle English *skippen*]

[2]**skip** *n* **1 a** : a light bounding step **b** : a manner of moving by alternating hops and steps **2** : an act of omission or the thing omitted

[3]**skip** *n* : the captain of a side in some games (as curling or lawn bowling) [short for [2]*skipper*]

[4]**skip** *vt* **skipped; skip·ping** : to act as skipper of

skip·jack \ˈskip-ˌjak\ *n, pl* **skipjacks** *or* **skipjack** : any of various fishes (as a tuna or bluefish) that jump above or are active at the surface of the water

ski pole *n* : a pointed pole or stick used as an aid in skiing that is fitted with a strap for the hand at the top and an encircling disk set a little above the point

[1]**skip·per** \ˈskip-ər\ *n* **1** : one that skips **2** : any of various insects that differ from the related butterflies especially in having stout bodies, smaller wings, and usually hooked antennae

[2]**skipper** *n* : the master of a ship; *esp* : the master of a fishing, small trading, or pleasure boat [Dutch *schipper,* from *schip* "ship"]

[1]**skirl** \ˈskərl, ˈskirl\ *vb* : to sound the high shrill tone of the bagpipe [of Scandinavian origin]

[2]**skirl** *n* : the high shrill sound of a bagpipe

[1]**skir·mish** \ˈskər-mish\ *n* **1** : a minor fight in war **2 a** : a brisk preliminary verbal conflict **b** : a minor dispute or contest between opposing parties [Medieval French *escarmuche,* from Italian *scaramuccia,* of Germanic origin]

[2]**skirmish** *vi* **1** : to engage in a skirmish **2** : to search about (as for supplies) — **skir·mish·er** *n*

skirr \ˈskər\ *vb* **1** : to leave hurriedly : FLEE; *also* : to move rapidly **2** : to pass rapidly over especially in search of something [perhaps from [1]*scour*]

[1]**skirt** \ˈskərt\ *n* **1 a** : a free-hanging part of a garment extending from the waist down **b** : a separate free-hanging garment usually worn by women and girls covering the body from the waist down **c** : either of two flaps on a saddle covering the bars on which the stirrups are hung **2** *pl* : the outlying parts of a town or city : OUTSKIRTS **3** : a part or attachment serving as a rim, border, or edging **4** *slang* : GIRL 1b, WOMAN [Old Norse *skyrta* "shirt, kirtle"]

[2]**skirt** *vb* **1** : to form or run along the edge of : BORDER **2** : to provide a skirt or border for **3 a** : to go or pass around or about; *esp* : to go around or keep away from in order to avoid danger or discovery **b** : to avoid especially because of difficulty or fear of controversy ⟨*skirted* the issues⟩ **c** : to evade or miss by a narrow margin **4** : to be, lie, or move along an edge, border, or margin — **skirt·er** *n*

skirt·ing \ˈskərt-ing\ *n* **1** : something that skirts: as **a** : BORDER 1, MARGIN **b** *chiefly British* : BASEBOARD — called also *skirting board* **2** : fabric suitable for skirts

ski run *n* : a slope or trail suitable for skiing

skit \ˈskit\ *n* **1** : a satirical or humorous story or sketch; *esp* : a sketch included in a dramatic performance (as a revue) **2** : a short serious dramatic piece; *esp* : one done by amateurs [origin unknown]

ski tow *n* **1** : a power-driven conveyor for pulling skiers to the top of a slope that consists usually of an endless moving rope which the skier grasps **2** : SKILIFT

skit·ter \ˈskit-ər\ *vb* **1** : to glide or skip lightly or quickly : skim along a surface **2** : to move in or as if in a jittery or jerky way ⟨leaves *skittering* over the sidewalk⟩ [probably from English dialect *skite* "to move quickly"]

skit·tish \ˈskit-ish\ *adj* **1 a** : lively or frisky in action **b** : VARIABLE, FLUCTUATING **2** : easily frightened : RESTIVE ⟨a *skittish* horse⟩ **3 a** : tensely nervous or cautious : WARY **b** : inclined to be shy : COY [Middle English] — **skit·tish·ly** *adv* — **skit·tish·ness** *n*

skit·tle \ˈskit-l\ *n* **1** *pl* : an English version of ninepins played either with wooden disks or a ball **2** : one of the pins used in skittles [perhaps of Scandinavian origin]

skoal \ˈskōl\ *n* : TOAST 3, HEALTH — often used interjectionally [Danish *skaal,* literally, "cup"]

skua \ˈskyü-ə\ *n* : any of various seabirds related to the jaegers; *esp* : a large one that breeds chiefly along arctic and antarctic shores [New Latin, of Scandinavian origin]

skul·dug·gery *or* **skull·dug·gery** \ˌskəl-ˈdəg-rē, -ə-rē\ *n, pl* **-ger·ies** : underhanded or unscrupulous behavior [origin unknown]

[1]**skulk** \ˈskəlk\ *vi* **1** : to move in a stealthy or furtive manner : SNEAK **2** : to hide or conceal oneself from cowardice or fear or with treacherous intent [of Scandinavian origin] — **skulk·er** *n*

synonyms SKULK, SLINK, SNEAK mean to go or act so as to escape attention. SKULK may imply shyness or cowardice but often suggests an intent to spy or waylay ⟨*skulking* in the shadows⟩. SLINK stresses a moving so as to avoid notice rather than keeping actually out of sight ⟨*slunk* around the corner⟩. SNEAK may add an implication of furtively entering or leaving a place or of accomplishing a purpose by indirect and underhanded methods ⟨*sneaked* out early⟩.

[2]**skulk** *n* : one that skulks

skull \ˈskəl\ *n* **1** : the vertebrate head skeleton that forms a bony or cartilaginous case enclosing the brain and chief sense organs and supporting the jaws **2** : the seat of understanding or intelligence : MIND [of Scandinavian origin] — **skulled** \ˈskəld\ *adj*

skull and crossbones *n, pl* **skulls and crossbones** : a representation of a human skull over crossbones usually used as a warning of danger to life

skull·cap \ˈskəl-ˌkap\ *n* : a close-fitting cap; *esp* : a light cap without brim for indoor wear

skull session *n* : a strategy class for an athletic team — called also *skull practice*

[1]**skunk** \ˈskəngk\ *n, pl* **skunks** *also* **skunk 1** : any of various common black-and-white New World mammals related to the weasels and having glands near the anus from which a secretion of pungent and offensive odor is ejected when threatened **2** : an obnoxious or disliked person [earlier *squnncke,* from Massachusett (an Algonquian language of Massachusetts)]

skunk 1

[2]**skunk** *vt* : to defeat decisively; *esp* : to prevent entirely from scoring or succeeding : SHUT OUT

skunk cabbage *n* : either of two North American perennial herbs of the arum family that grow in wet to swampy areas, bloom in late winter or early spring, and have an odor suggestive of a skunk

skunky \ˈskəng-kē\ *adj* **skunk·i·er; -est** : having a rancid smell or taste suggestive of a skunk

sky \ˈskī\ *n, pl* **skies 1** : the expanse of space that appears to constitute a vault over the earth **2** : HEAVEN 2 **3** : WEATHER, CLIMATE ⟨the weatherman predicts sunny *skies*⟩ [Old Norse *ský* "cloud"]

sky blue *n* : a pale to light blue

sky·borne \ˈskī-ˌbōrn, -ˌbȯrn\ *adj* : AIRBORNE ⟨*skyborne* troops⟩

sky·box \ˈskī-ˌbäks\ *n* : a roofed enclosure of private seats situated high in a sports stadium and typically featuring luxurious conveniences

sky·cap \-ˌkap\ *n* : a person employed to carry hand luggage at an airport [*sky* + *-cap* (as in *redcap*)]

sky·div·ing \-ˌdī-ving\ *n* : the sport of jumping from an airplane with a parachute at a moderate altitude (as about 6000 feet or about 2000 meters) and performing various maneuvers before opening the parachute — **sky·dive** \-ˌdīv\ *vi* — **sky·div·er** \-ˌdī-vər\ *n*

sky·ey \ˈskī-ē\ *adj* : of or resembling the sky : ETHEREAL

[1]**sky–high** \ˈskī-ˈhī\ *adv* **1 a** : high into the air **b** : to a very high level or degree ⟨our spirits rose *sky-high*⟩ ⟨profits were *sky-high*⟩ **2** : in an enthusiastic manner **3** : to bits : APART ⟨blown *sky-high*⟩

[2]**sky–high** *adj* **1** : excessively expensive : EXORBITANT **2** : extremely or excessively high ⟨his blood pressure was *sky-high*⟩

sky·jack·er \-ˌjak-ər\ *n* : one who takes control of a flying airplane by threat of violence [*sky* + *-jacker* (as in *hijacker*)] — **sky·jack** \-ˌjak\ *vt* — **sky·jack·ing** \-ˌjak-iŋ\ *n*

[1]**sky·lark** \ˈskī-ˌlärk\ *n* : a common Old World lark noted for its continuous song uttered chiefly while in flight

skylark

[2]**skylark** *vi* : to play wild boisterous pranks : FROLIC — **sky·lark·er** *n*

sky·light \ˈskī-ˌlīt\ *n* : a window or group of windows in a roof or ceiling

sky·line \-ˌlīn\ *n* **1** : the line where earth and sky seem to meet : HORIZON **2** : an outline against the sky ⟨a *skyline* of tall buildings⟩

sky pilot *n* : CLERGYMAN; *esp* : CHAPLAIN

[1]**sky·rock·et** \ˈskī-ˌräk-ət\ *n* : ROCKET 1

[2]**skyrocket** *vb* : to rise or cause to rise abruptly and rapidly ⟨prices are *skyrocketing*⟩

sky·scrap·er \ˈskī-ˌskrā-pər\ *n* : a very tall building

sky·walk \-ˌwȯk\ *n* : a usually enclosed elevated walkway connecting two buildings

sky·ward \ˈskī-wərd\ *adv* **1** : toward the sky ⟨gaze *skyward*⟩ **2** : to a higher level

sky·way \ˈskī-ˌwā\ *n* **1** : an elevated highway **2** : SKYWALK

sky·writ·ing \ˈskī-ˌrīt-iŋ\ *n* : writing formed in the sky by means of a visible substance (as smoke) emitted from an airplane — **sky·writ·er** \-ˌrīt-ər\ *n*

slab \ˈslab\ *n* **1** : a thick slice or plate (as of stone, wood, or bread) **2** : the outside piece cut from a log in squaring it [Middle English *slabbe*]

slab–sid·ed \ˈslab-ˈsīd-əd\ *adj* : having flat sides; *also* : being tall or long and lank

[1]**slack** \ˈslak\ *adj* **1** : not properly diligent, careful, or prompt : NEGLIGENT **2** : marked by slowness or lack of energy ⟨a *slack* pace⟩ **3 a** : not tight or tightly drawn ⟨a *slack* rope⟩ **b** : lacking in firmness : WEAK ⟨*slack* control⟩ **4** : wanting in activity : DULL ⟨the *slack* season⟩ [Old English *sleac*] — **slack·ly** *adv* — **slack·ness** *n*

[2]**slack** *vb* **1 a** : to be or become slack or negligent in performing or doing ⟨*slack* one's vigilance⟩ **b** : MODERATE 1, LESSEN ⟨the wind *slacked* off⟩ **2** : to shirk or avoid work or duty **3** : LOOSEN 2 **4 a** : to cause to lessen **b** : SLAKE 4

[3]**slack** *n* **1** : cessation in movement or flow **2** : a part of something that hangs loose without strain ⟨take up the *slack* of a rope⟩ **3** *pl* : pants especially for casual wear **4** : a dull season or period : LULL **5** : additional leeway or relief from pressure ⟨cut me some *slack*⟩

[4]**slack** *n* : fine screenings of coal containing wastes that make it unusable as fuel unless cleaned [Middle English *sleck*]

slack·en \ˈslak-ən\ *vb* **slack·ened**; **slack·en·ing** \ˈslak-niŋ, -ə-niŋ\ **1** : to make or become less active : slow up ⟨*slacken* speed⟩ **2** : to make less taut : LOOSEN ⟨*slacken* sail⟩ **3** : to become slow or careless : SLACK 1a

slack·er \ˈslak-ər\ *n* **1** : a person who shirks work or evades an obligation especially for military service in time of war **2** : a person and especially a young person who is perceived to be lacking motivation or ambition

slack water *n* : the period at the turn of the tide when there is little or no horizontal motion of tidal water — called also *slack tide*

slag \ˈslag\ *n* : waste left after the smelting of ore [Low German *slagge*]

slain *past participle of* SLAY

slake \ˈslāk, *3 & 4 are also* ˈslak\ *vb* **1** *archaic* : to make or become less violent, intense, or severe : ABATE, MODERATE **2** : to relieve or satisfy especially with water or liquid : QUENCH ⟨*slake* one's thirst⟩ ⟨will *slake* your curiosity⟩ **3** : to become slaked ⟨lime may *slake* spontaneously in moist air⟩ **4** : to cause (lime) to heat and crumble by treatment with water : HYDRATE [Old English *slacian*, from *sleac* "slack"]

sla·lom \ˈsläl-əm\ *n* **1** : skiing in a zigzag or wavy course between upright obstacles (as flags) **2** : a timed race over a zigzag course [Norwegian *slalåm*, literally, "sloping track"]

[1]**slam** \ˈslam\ *n* : the winning of all or all but one of the tricks of a deal in bridge [origin unknown]

[2]**slam** *n* **1** : a heavy blow or impact **2 a** : a noisy violent closing **b** : a banging noise especially from the slamming of a door **3** : a cutting or violent criticism **4** : a poetry competition performed before a judge [perhaps of Scandinavian origin]

[3]**slam** *vb* **slammed**; **slam·ming** **1** : to strike or beat hard **2** : to shut forcibly and noisily : BANG ⟨*slam* the door⟩ **3 a** : to set or slap down violently or noisily ⟨*slammed* my fist on the table⟩ **b** : to put or set hard : JAM 2 ⟨*slammed* on the brakes⟩ **4** : to make a banging noise **5** : to criticize harshly

slam–bang \ˈslam-ˈbaŋ\ *adj* **1** : very noisy or violent **2** : having fast-paced often nonstop action

slam dunk *n* : DUNK SHOT — **slam–dunk** \ˈslam-ˈdəŋk\ *vb*

[1]**slan·der** \ˈslan-dər\ *n* **1** : the utterance of false charges or misrepresentations which defame and damage another's reputation **2** : a false and defamatory oral statement about a person — compare LIBEL [Medieval French *esclandre*, from Late Latin *scandalum* "stumbling block, offense," from Greek *skandalon*] — **slan·der·ous** \-də-rəs, -drəs\ *adj* — **slan·der·ous·ly** *adv* — **slan·der·ous·ness** *n*

[2]**slander** *vt* **slan·dered**; **slan·der·ing** \-də-riŋ, -driŋ\ : to utter slander against — **slan·der·er** \-dər-ər\ *n*

synonyms SLANDER, DEFAME, MALIGN mean to injure by speaking ill of. SLANDER stresses the suffering of the victim regardless of the intent of the slanderer ⟨*slandered* by thoughtless tongues⟩. DEFAME stresses the actual loss of or injury to one's good name and repute ⟨turning traitor forever *defamed* the family name⟩. MALIGN usually suggests the operation of hatred, prejudice, or bigotry often by subtle misrepresentation rather than direct accusation ⟨*maligned* and persecuted by evil forces⟩.

[1]**slang** \ˈslaŋ\ *n* **1** : language peculiar to a particular group, trade, or pursuit ⟨baseball *slang*⟩ **2** : an informal nonstandard vocabulary composed typically of coinages, arbitrarily changed words, and extravagant, forced, or facetious figures of speech [origin unknown] ***synonyms*** see DIALECT — **slang** *adj*

[2]**slang** *vb* **1** : to abuse with harsh or coarse language **2** : to use slang or vulgar abuse

slangy \ˈslaŋ-ē\ *adj* **slang·i·er**; **-est** **1** : of, relating to, or being slang : containing slang **2** : being in the habit of using slang — **slang·i·ly** \ˈslaŋ-ə-lē\ *adv* — **slang·i·ness** \ˈslaŋ-ē-nəs\ *n*

[1]**slant** \ˈslant\ *vb* **1** : to turn or incline from a straight line or a level : SLOPE **2** : to interpret or present in accordance with a special viewpoint ⟨stories *slanted* toward young adults⟩ [of Scandinavian origin]

[2]**slant** *n* **1** : a slanting direction, line, or plane : SLOPE **2 a** : something that slants **b** : [2]SLASH 4 **3** : a way of looking at something ⟨considered the problem from a new *slant*⟩ **4** : GLANCE 3, LOOK — **slant** *adj* — **slanty** \ˈslant-ē\ *adj*

slant height *n* **1** : the distance along the surface of a right circular cone from the edge of the base to the vertex **2** : the altitude of a side of a regular pyramid

slant·ways \ˈslant-ˌwāz\ *adv* : SLANTWISE

slant·wise \-ˌwīz\ *adv or adj* : so as to slant : at a slant : in a slanting direction or position

[1]**slap** \ˈslap\ *n* **1** : a quick sharp blow especially with the open hand; *also* : a noise suggesting that of a slap **2** : INSULT 1, SNUB [Low German *slapp*]

[2]**slap** *vt* **slapped**; **slap·ping** **1 a** : to strike with or as if with the open hand **b** : to make a sound like that of a slap **2** : to put, place, or throw with careless haste or force ⟨*slapped* down the paper⟩ **3** : to assail verbally : INSULT

[3]**slap** *adv* : DIRECTLY 1a, SMACK

slap·dash \ˈslap-ˌdash, -ˈdash\ *adj* : SLIPSHOD, HAPHAZARD

slap down *vt* **1** : to prohibit or restrain usually abruptly and with censure from acting in a specified way : SQUELCH **2** : to put an abrupt stop to : SUPPRESS

slap·jack \ˈslap-ˌjak\ *n* **1** : PANCAKE **2** : a card game in which each player tries to be first to slap a hand on any jack that appears faceup [[2]*slap* + *-jack* (as in *flapjack*)]

slap shot *n* : a shot in ice hockey made with a swinging stroke

slap·stick \'slap-ˌstik\ *n* **1 :** a device made of two flat sticks so fastened as to make a loud noise when used by an actor to strike a person **2 :** comedy stressing farce and horseplay — **slapstick** *adj* — **slap·sticky** \-ˌstik-ē\ *adj*

[1]**slash** \'slash\ *vb* **1 :** to cut with rough sweeping blows : GASH **2 :** to whip or strike with or as if with a cane **3 :** to criticize without mercy **4 :** to cut slits in (as a skirt) to reveal a color beneath **5 :** to reduce sharply : CUT ⟨*slash* prices⟩ [Middle English *slaschen*] — **slash·er** *n*

[2]**slash** *n* **1 :** an act or result of slashing; *esp* : a long cut or stroke made by slashing **2 :** an ornamental slit in a garment **3 :** an open tract in a forest scattered with debris (as from logging); *also* : the debris in such a tract **4 :** a mark / used typically to mean "or" (as in *and/or*), "and or" (as in *bottles/cans*), or "per" (as in *miles/hour*) — called also *diagonal, slant, virgule*

[3]**slash** *n* : a low swampy area often overgrown with brush [origin unknown]

slash–and–burn *adj* : characterized or developed by felling and burning trees to clear land especially for temporary agriculture ⟨*slash-and-burn* practices⟩

slash pine *n* : a pine of the southeastern U.S. important as a source of turpentine, lumber, and pulpwood

slash pocket *n* : a pocket suspended on the wrong side of a garment from a finished slit on the right side that serves as its opening

slat \'slat\ *n* : a thin narrow flat strip of wood, plastic, or metal ⟨the *slats* of a blind⟩ [Middle French *esclat* "splinter," from *esclater* "to burst, splinter"] — **slat·ted** \'slat-əd\ *adj*

[1]**slate** \'slāt\ *n* **1 :** a piece of construction material (as layered rock) prepared as a shingle for roofing and siding **2 :** a fine-grained rock that is formed by compression of shales or other rocks and that splits readily into thin layers or plates **3 :** a tablet of material (as slate) used for writing on **4 a :** a written or unwritten record (as of deeds) ⟨started with a clean *slate*⟩ **b :** a list of candidates for nomination or election **5 a :** a dark purplish gray **b :** a gray similar in color to common roofing slate [Medieval French *esclat* "splinter"] — **slate** *adj* — **slate·like** \-ˌlīk\ *adj*

[2]**slate** *vt* **1 :** to cover with slate or a slatelike substance ⟨*slate* a roof⟩ **2 :** to register or schedule for a special purpose or action ⟨*slate* a meeting⟩ — **slat·er** \'slāt-ər\ *n*

slath·er \'sla*th*-ər\ *vt* **slath·ered; slath·er·ing** \'sla*th*-ring, -ə-ring\ **1 :** to spread thickly or lavishly ⟨*slather* jam on bread⟩ **2 :** to cover thickly or lavishly ⟨*slather* bread with jam⟩ [from earlier *slather* "great quantity," of unknown origin]

slat·tern \'slat-ərn\ *n* : an untidy slovenly woman [probably from German *schlottern* "to hang loosely, slouch"]

slat·tern·ly \-lē\ *adj* : untidy and dirty through neglect; *also* : CARELESS, DISORDERLY — **slat·tern·li·ness** *n*

slaty \'slāt-ē\ *adj* : of, containing, or characteristic of slate; *also* : gray like slate

[1]**slaugh·ter** \'slȯt-ər\ *n* **1 :** the act of killing; *esp* : the butchering of livestock for market **2 :** killing of great numbers of human beings (as in battle or a massacre) : CARNAGE [of Scandinavian origin]

[2]**slaughter** *vt* **1 :** to kill (an animal) for food : BUTCHER **2 :** to kill ruthlessly or in large numbers : MASSACRE — **slaugh·ter·er** \'slȯt-ər-ər\ *n*

slaugh·ter·house \'slȯt-ər-ˌhau̇s\ *n* : an establishment where animals are butchered

slaugh·ter·ous \'slȯt-ə-rəs\ *adj* : of or relating to slaughter : MURDEROUS — **slaugh·ter·ous·ly** *adv*

Slav \'släv, 'slav\ *n* : a native speaker of a Slavic language [Medieval Latin *Sclavus,* from Late Greek *Sklabos,* from *Sklabēnoi* "Slavs," of Slavic origin]

[1]**slave** \'slāv\ *n* **1 :** a person held in servitude as the property of another **2 :** a person who has lost self-control and is dominated by something or someone ⟨a *slave* to drink⟩ **3 :** a device that is directly responsive to another **4 :** DRUDGE, TOILER [Medieval Latin *sclavus,* from *Sclavus* "Slav"] — **slave** *adj*

Word History In the Middle Ages the warring Germanic peoples subjugated a great part of the Slavic population of east-central Europe. Conquered Slavs were bought and sold as slaves throughout the West. The Slavs' own name for themselves became *Sclavus* in the Latin that served medieval Europe as a universal language. By the 9th or 10th century *sclavus* was used for any human chattel of no matter what origin. This *sclavus* is the ancestor of our English *slave.*

[2]**slave** *vi* : to work like a slave : DRUDGE

slave driver *n* **1 :** a supervisor of slaves at work **2 :** a harsh taskmaster

slave·hold·er \'slāv-ˌhōl-dər\ *n* : an owner of slaves — **slave·hold·ing** \-diŋ\ *adj or n*

[1]**sla·ver** \'slav-ər, 'släv-\ *vi* **sla·vered; sla·ver·ing** \'slav-ring, 'släv-, -ə-ring\ : DROOL 1b, SLOBBER [of Scandinavian origin]

[2]**slaver** *n* : saliva dribbling from the mouth

[3]**slav·er** \'slā-vər\ *n* : a person or ship engaged in the slave trade

slav·ery \'slāv-rē, -ə-rē\ *n* **1 :** DRUDGERY, TOIL **2 a :** the state of being a slave : SERVITUDE **b :** the practice of owning slaves

slave state *n* : a state of the U.S. in which slavery was legal until the American Civil War

slave trade *n* : traffic in slaves; *esp* : the buying and selling of blacks for profit prior to the American Civil War

slav·ey \'slā-vē\ *n, pl* **slaveys** : DRUDGE; *esp* : a servant who does general housework

[1]**Slav·ic** \'slav-ik, 'släv-\ *adj* : of, relating to, or characteristic of the Slavs or their languages

[2]**Slavic** *n* : a branch of the Indo-European language family including Belarusian, Bulgarian, Czech, Polish, Serbian and Croatian, Slovene, Russian, and Ukrainian

slav·ish \'slā-vish\ *adj* **1 :** of or characteristic of a slave : SERVILE **2 :** lacking in independence or originality ⟨*slavish* dependence on customary ways⟩ ⟨*slavish* imitators⟩ — **slav·ish·ly** *adv* — **slav·ish·ness** *n*

[1]**Sla·von·ic** \slə-'vän-ik\ *adj* : SLAVIC [Medieval Latin *Sclavonia, Slavonia* the Slavic-speaking countries, from *Sclavus* "Slav"]

[2]**Slavonic** *n* **1 :** SLAVIC **2 :** OLD CHURCH SLAVONIC

slaw \'slȯ\ *n* : COLESLAW

slay \'slā\ *vb* **slew** \'slü\; **slain** \'slān\; **slay·ing** : KILL; *esp* : to put to death violently or in great numbers [Old English *slēan* "to strike, slay"] ***synonyms*** see KILL — **slay·er** *n*

sleave \'slēv\ *n, archaic* : SKEIN [derived from Old English *-slǣfan* "to cut"]

slea·zy \'slē-zē, 'slā-\ *adj* **slea·zi·er; -est** **1 :** lacking firmness of texture : FLIMSY **2 :** made carelessly of inferior material : SHODDY **3 :** cheap in character or quality [origin unknown] — **slea·zi·ly** \-zə-lē\ *adv* — **slea·zi·ness** \-zē-nəs\ *n*

[1]**sled** \'sled\ *n* **1 :** a vehicle usually on runners for transportation especially over snow or ice **2 :** a sled used for coasting on snow-covered slopes [Dutch *sledde*]

[2]**sled** *vb* **sled·ded; sled·ding** : to ride or carry on a sled or sleigh — **sled·der** *n*

sled·ding *n* **1 :** the use of a sled; *also* : the conditions under which a sled is used **2 :** GOING 3 ⟨tough *sledding*⟩

sled dog *n* : a dog trained to draw a usually large sled especially in the Arctic regions — called also *sledge dog*

[1]**sledge** \'slej\ *n* : SLEDGEHAMMER [Old English *slecg*]

[2]**sledge** *n* : a strong heavy sled [Dutch dialect *sleedse*]

[3]**sledge** *vb* : to travel with or transport on a sledge

[1]**sledge·ham·mer** \'slej-ˌham-ər\ *n* : a large heavy hammer usually wielded with both hands [[1]*sledge*] — **sledgehammer** *vb*

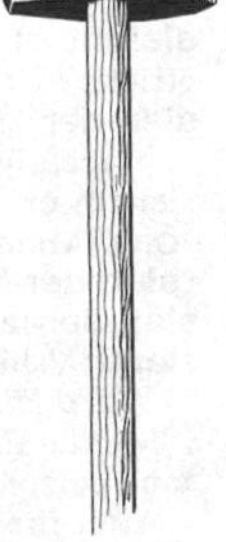

sledgehammer

[2]**sledgehammer** *adj* : marked by directness or strong force

[1]**sleek** \'slēk\ *vb* **1 :** to make or become sleek **2 :** to cover up : gloss over [Middle English *sliken*]

[2]**sleek** *adj* **1 a :** smooth and glossy as if polished ⟨*sleek* dark hair⟩ **b :** having a smooth healthy well-groomed look ⟨*sleek* cattle⟩ **2 :** having a prosperous air — **sleek·ly** *adv* — **sleek·ness** *n*

[1]**sleep** \'slēp\ *n* **1 :** the natural periodic suspension of consciousness during which the powers of the body are restored **2 :** a state resembling sleep: as **a :** a state of inactivity (as hibernation) likened to sleep **b :** DEATH 4 ⟨put a pet to *sleep*⟩; *also* : TRANCE, COMA **c :** a state marked by loss of feeling followed by tingling ⟨my foot's gone to *sleep*⟩ [Old English *slǣp*] — **sleep·like** \-ˌlīk\ *adj*

[2]**sleep** *vb* **slept** \'slept\; **sleep·ing** **1 :** to rest or be in a state of sleep **2 :** to have sexual intercourse — usually used with *with*

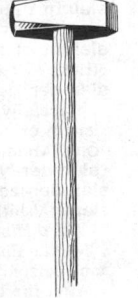

\ə\ **abut**	\au̇\ **out**	\i\ **tip**	\ȯ\ **saw**	\u̇\ **foot**
\ər\ **further**	\ch\ **chin**	\ī\ **life**	\ȯi\ **coin**	\y\ **yet**
\a\ **mat**	\e\ **pet**	\j\ **job**	\th\ **thin**	\yü\ **few**
\ā\ **take**	\ē\ **easy**	\ŋ\ **sing**	*th*\ **this**	\yu̇\ **cure**
\ä\ **cot, cart**	\g\ **go**	\ō\ **bone**	\ü\ **food**	\zh\ **vision**

3 : to get rid of or spend in or by sleep ⟨*slept* away my cares⟩ **4 :** to provide sleeping space for ⟨the boat *sleeps* six⟩

sleep·er \'slē-pər\ *n* **1 :** one that sleeps **2 :** a horizontal beam to support something at or near ground level **3 :** SLEEPING CAR **4 :** someone or something unpromising or unnoticed that suddenly attains prominence or value

sleeping bag *n* **:** a long fabric bag that is warmly lined or padded for sleeping outdoors or in a camp or tent

sleeping car *n* **:** a railroad passenger car having berths for sleeping

sleeping pill *n* **:** a drug and especially a barbiturate that is taken as a tablet or capsule to induce sleep

sleeping sickness *n* **1 :** a serious disease found in much of tropical Africa that is marked by fever, headache, drowsiness, and confusion and is caused by either of two trypanosomes transmitted by tsetse flies **2 :** any of various virus diseases of which lethargy or drowsiness is a prominent feature

sleep·less \'slē-pləs\ *adj* **1 :** not able to sleep **:** INSOMNIAC **2 :** affording no sleep **3 :** unceasingly alert or active — **sleep·less·ly** *adv* — **sleep·less·ness** *n*

sleep out *vi* **:** to sleep outdoors

sleep·over \'slēp-ō-vər\ *n* **1 :** an overnight stay (as at another's home) **2 :** an instance of hosting a sleepover in one's home

sleep·walk \'slēp-ˌwȯk\ *vi* **:** to walk while or as if while asleep — **sleep·walk·er** \-ˌwȯ-kər\ *n*

sleepy \'slē-pē\ *adj* **sleep·i·er; -est 1 :** ready to fall asleep **:** DROWSY **2 :** quietly inactive ⟨a *sleepy* village⟩ — **sleep·i·ly** \-pə-lē\ *adv* — **sleep·i·ness** \-pē-nəs\ *n*

sleepy·head \'slē-pē-ˌhed\ *n* **:** a sleepy person

[1]**sleet** \'slēt\ *n* **:** frozen or partly frozen rain [Middle English *slete*] — **sleety** \'slēt-ē\ *adj*

[2]**sleet** *vi* **:** to shower sleet

sleeve \'slēv\ *n* **1 :** the part of a garment covering the arm **2 :** a tubular part fitting over another part [Old English *slīefe*] — **sleeved** \'slēvd\ *adj* — **sleeve·less** \'slēv-ləs\ *adj* — **on one's sleeve :** in an honest and open manner ⟨wears his emotions *on his sleeve*⟩ — **up one's sleeve :** held secretly in reserve ⟨has a few tricks *up her sleeve*⟩

sleeve·let \'slēv-lət\ *n* **:** a covering for the forearm to protect clothing from wear or dirt

[1]**sleigh** \'slā\ *n* **:** an open usually horse-drawn vehicle with runners for use on snow or ice [Dutch *slee*, alteration of *slede*]

sleigh

[2]**sleigh** *vi* **:** to drive or travel in a sleigh

sleigh bell *n* **:** any of various bells commonly attached to a sleigh or to the harness of a horse drawing a sleigh

sleight \'slīt\ *n* **1 :** deceitful craftiness; *also* **:** STRATAGEM **2 :** DEXTERITY, SKILL [Old Norse *slægth*, from *slægr* "sly"]

sleight of hand 1 : skill and dexterity especially in magic tricks **2 :** a magic trick requiring skill in using the hands

slen·der \'slen-dər\ *adj* **1 a :** spare in frame or flesh; *esp* **:** gracefully slight **b :** small in circumference in proportion to length or height **2 :** limited or inadequate in amount **:** MEAGER [Middle English *sclendre, slendre*] ***synonyms*** see THIN — **slen·der·ly** *adv* — **slen·der·ness** *n*

slen·der·ize \-də-ˌrīz\ *vt* **:** to make slender

[1]**sleuth** \'slüth\ *n* **:** DETECTIVE [short for *sleuthhound*]

Word History A modern English *sleuth* is a detective, but in Middle English the word *sleuth* meant "the track of an animal or person." The word was a borrowing from Old Norse *slōth*. After the 15th century, *sleuth* was seldom used except in compounds like *sleuth-dog* and *sleuthhound*. These were terms for a dog trained to follow a track. The sleuthhound became a symbol of the eager and thorough pursuit of an object. In the U.S. during the 19th century, the metaphoric *sleuthhound* acquired a more specific meaning and became an epithet for a detective. This new term was soon shortened to *sleuth*.

[2]**sleuth** *vi* **:** to act as a detective

sleuth·hound \-ˌhau̇nd\ *n* **:** DETECTIVE [Middle English, from *sleuth* "track of an animal or person," from Old Norse *slōth*]

S level *n* **1 :** the highest of three levels of standardized British exams in a secondary school subject — called also *Scholarship level*; compare A LEVEL, O LEVEL **2 a :** the level of education required to pass an S-level exam **b :** a course leading to an S-level exam

[1]**slew** \'slü\ *past of* SLAY

[2]**slew** *variant of* [1]SLOUGH 1

[3]**slew** *also* **slue** *vb* **:** to turn, twist, or swing about especially out of a course **:** VEER

[4]**slew** *n* **:** a large number **:** LOT ⟨a whole *slew* of letters to write⟩ ⟨*slews* of work⟩ [perhaps from Irish *slua* "army, host, throng"]

[1]**slice** \'slīs\ *n* **1 a :** a thin flat piece cut from something ⟨a *slice* of bread⟩ **b :** a wedge-shaped piece (as of pie or cake) **2 :** a path of a ball that deviates from a straight course to the same side as the dominant hand of the player propelling it **3 a :** PORTION, SHARE ⟨a *slice* of the profits⟩ **b :** SEGMENT, SAMPLE ⟨a *slice* of society⟩ [Middle French *esclice* "splinter," from *esclicer* "to splinter," of Germanic origin]

[2]**slice** *vb* **1 a :** to cut with or as if with a knife **b :** to cut something into slices **2 :** to hit (a ball) so that a slice results — **slic·er** *n*

[1]**slick** \'slik\ *vt* **:** to make sleek or smooth [Middle English *sliken*]

[2]**slick** *adj* **1 a :** having a smooth surface **:** SLIPPERY **b :** having or showing style and appeal but no depth **:** GLOSSY ⟨*slick* advertising⟩ **2 a :** characterized by subtlety or nimble wit; *esp* **:** WILY **b :** DEFT, SKILLFUL — **slick·ly** *adv* — **slick·ness** *n*

[3]**slick** *n* **1 :** something that is smooth or slippery; *esp* **:** a smooth patch of water covered with a film of oil **2 :** a popular magazine printed on coated stock

slick·er \'slik-ər\ *n* **1 :** a long loose raincoat often of oilskin or plastic **2 a :** a clever crook **b :** a usually sophisticated or stylish person who lives in a city

slick·rock \'slik-ˌräk\ *n* **:** smooth wind-polished rock

[1]**slide** \'slīd\ *vb* **slid** \'slid\; **slid·ing** \'slīd-iŋ\ **1 a :** to move or cause to move smoothly along a surface **:** SLIP ⟨*slide* a paper under the door⟩ ⟨firefighters *slid* down the pole⟩ **b :** to coast on snow or ice **c :** to fall or dive feetfirst or headfirst when approaching a base in baseball **2 :** to slip and fall by a loss of footing, balance, or support ⟨the package *slid* from the heap⟩ **3 a :** to move or pass smoothly and easily ⟨*slid* into his sales pitch⟩ **b :** to move, pass, or put unobtrusively or stealthily ⟨*slid* quietly into the seat⟩ ⟨*slide* the note into my hand⟩ **c :** to pass unnoticed or unremarked ⟨let the criticism *slide*⟩ **4 :** to become worse gradually ⟨her grades started to *slide*⟩ [Old English *slīdan*]

[2]**slide** *n* **1 :** the act or motion of sliding **2 :** the descent of a mass (as of earth, rock, or snow) down a slope **3 a :** a surface down which a person or thing slides **b :** something (as a cover for an opening) that operates or adjusts by sliding **4 a :** a clear glass or plastic plate on which is placed an object to be examined under a microscope **b :** a photographic transparency arranged for projection

slide fastener *n* **:** ZIPPER

slid·er \'slīd-ər\ *n* **1 :** one that slides or operates a slide **2 :** a pitch in baseball that is thrown like a fastball but breaks slightly in the same direction as a curve **3 :** a very small meat sandwich typically served on a bun; *esp* **:** a small hamburger

slide rule *n* **:** an instrument used for calculation that consists in its simplest form of a ruler and a movable middle piece which are labeled with similar logarithmic scales

slide·way \'slīd-ˌwā\ *n* **:** a way along which something slides

slier *comparative of* SLY

sliest *superlative of* SLY

[1]**slight** \'slīt\ *adj* **1 a :** having a slim or delicate build **:** not stout or massive in body **b :** lacking in strength or substance **:** FLIMSY, FRAIL **c :** deficient in weight, solidity, or importance **:** TRIVIAL **2 :** small of its kind or in amount **:** SCANTY, MEAGER [Middle English, "smooth, slight"] ***synonyms*** see THIN — **slight·ly** *adv* — **slight·ness** *n*

[2]**slight** *vt* **1 :** to treat as slight or unimportant **:** make light of **2 :** to treat with disdain or discourteous indifference **3 :** to perform or attend to carelessly and inadequately ***synonyms*** see NEGLECT

[3]**slight** *n* **1 :** an act or an instance of slighting **2 :** a humiliating discourtesy

slight·ing *adj* **:** characterized by disregard or disrespect ⟨a *slighting* remark⟩ — **slight·ing·ly** \-iŋ-lē\ *adv*

sli·ly *variant of* SLYLY

[1]**slim** \'slim\ *adj* **slim·mer; slim·mest 1 :** of small diameter or thickness in proportion to the height or length **:** SLENDER **2 a :** inferior in quality or amount **:** SLIGHT **b :** SCANTY, SMALL ⟨a

slim chance⟩ [Dutch, "bad, inferior"] ***synonyms*** see THIN — **slim·ly** *adv* — **slim·ness** *n*

²**slim** *vb* **slimmed; slim·ming :** to make or become slender

slime \ˈslīm\ *n* **1 :** soft moist earth or clay; *esp* **:** sticky slippery mud **2 :** a slippery or sticky substance; *esp* **:** a skin secretion (as of a slug or catfish) [Old English *slīm*]

slime mold *n* **:** any of a group (Myxomycetes or Mycetozoa) of organisms that are usually held to be lower fungi or protists and that live vegetatively as single amoeboid cells or as plasmodia and reproduce by spores

slim–jim \ˈslim-ˈjim\ *adj* **:** notably slender [*slim* + *Jim,* nickname for *James*]

slimy \ˈslī-mē\ *adj* **slim·i·er; -est 1 :** of, relating to, or resembling slime **:** VISCOUS; *also* **:** covered with or yielding slime **2 :** VILE, OFFENSIVE ⟨a *slimy* traitor⟩ — **slim·i·ly** \-mə-lē\ *adv* — **slim·i·ness** \-mē-nəs\ *n*

¹**sling** \ˈsling\ *vt* **slung** \ˈsləng\; **sling·ing** \ˈsling-ing\ **1 :** to throw with a sudden sweeping motion ⟨*slung* the sack over my shoulder⟩ **2 :** to throw with a sling [Middle English *slingen*] — **sling·er** \ˈsling-ər\ *n*

²**sling** *n* **1 a :** a device for throwing something (as stones) that usually consists of a short strap with strings fastened to its ends and is whirled round to discharge its missile **b :** SLINGSHOT **2 a :** a usually looped line (as of rope) used to hoist, lower, support, or carry something; *esp* **:** a hanging bandage suspended from the neck to support an arm or hand **b :** a device (as a rope net) for enclosing material to be hoisted by a tackle or crane **3 :** a slinging or hurling of or as if of a missile

³**sling** *vt* **slung** \ˈsləng\; **sling·ing** \ˈsling-ing\ **1 :** to put in or move or support with a sling ⟨*sling* cargo from a ship's hold⟩ **2 :** to cause to become suspended ⟨*sling* a hammock⟩

sling·shot \ˈsling-ˌshät\ *n* **:** a forked stick with an elastic band attached for shooting small stones

slink \ˈslingk\ *vi* **slunk** \ˈsləngk\; **slink·ing :** to move or go stealthily (as in fear or shame) [Old English *slincan* "to creep"] ***synonyms*** see SKULK

slinky \ˈsling-kē\ *adj* **slink·i·er; -est 1 :** stealthily quiet ⟨*slinky* movements⟩ **2 :** sleek and sinuous in outline or movement; *esp* **:** following the lines of the figure in a gracefully flowing manner ⟨a *slinky* evening gown⟩

¹**slip** \ˈslip\ *vb* **slipped; slip·ping 1 a :** to move easily and smoothly **:** SLIDE ⟨the bolt *slipped* back⟩ ⟨*slip* the knife into its sheath⟩ **b :** to move or place quietly or stealthily **c :** to pass without being noted or used ⟨time *slipped* by⟩ ⟨let the opportunity *slip*⟩ **2 a :** to get away from **:** ELUDE ⟨*slipped* their pursuers⟩ **b :** to get free from ⟨the dog *slipped* its collar⟩ **c :** to escape the attention or memory of ⟨*slipped* my mind⟩ **d :** to utter or become uttered inadvertently or casually ⟨the secret *slipped* out⟩ **e :** to let loose from or let go of ⟨*slip* a dog from a leash⟩ **f :** to cause to slide open **:** RELEASE ⟨*slip* a bolt⟩ **3 :** to let (a knitting stitch) pass from one needle to another without working a new stitch **4 a :** to slide out of place, away from a support, or from one's grasp ⟨the dish *slipped* to the floor⟩ **b :** to slide so as to fall or lose balance ⟨*slip* on the ice⟩ **5 :** to slide or cause to slide especially in putting, passing, or inserting easily or quickly ⟨*slip* into a coat⟩ ⟨*slip* a dress on⟩ **6 :** DISLOCATE ⟨*slipped* my shoulder⟩ **7 :** to fall from some level or standard (as of conduct or activity) usually gradually or by degrees ⟨the market *slipped* from an earlier high⟩ [Middle English *slippen,* from Dutch or Low German]

²**slip** *n* **1 a :** a sloping ramp that extends out into the water and serves for landing or repairing ships **b :** a ship's berth between two piers **2 :** the act or an instance of departing secretly or hurriedly **3 a :** a mistake in judgment, policy, or procedure **b :** an unintentional and trivial mistake or fault **4 :** the act or an instance of slipping down or out of place ⟨a *slip* on the ice⟩ ⟨a *slip* in stock prices⟩; *also* **:** a sudden mishap **5 a :** an undergarment made in dress length with shoulder straps **b :** PILLOWCASE ***synonyms*** see ERROR

³**slip** *n* **1 :** a small shoot or twig cut for planting or grafting **:** CUTTING **2 a :** a long narrow strip of material **b :** a small piece of paper ⟨sales *slip*⟩ **3 :** a young and slender person [Middle English *slippe*]

⁴**slip** *vt* **slipped; slip·ping :** to take cuttings from (a plant)

⁵**slip** *n* **:** thin wet clay used in pottery for casting, for decoration, or as a cement [Old English *slypa* "slime, paste"]

slip·case \ˈslip-ˌkās\ *n* **:** a protective container for books or magazines with one open end

slip·cov·er \ˈslip-ˌkəv-ər\ *n* **:** a removable covering for an article of furniture

slip·knot \ˈslip-ˌnät\ *n* **:** a knot that slips along a line around which it is made; *esp* **:** one made by tying an overhand knot around a rope to form an adjustable loop — see KNOT illustration

slip noose *n* **:** a noose with a slipknot

slip–on \ˈslip-ˌȯn, -ˌän\ *n* **:** an article of clothing (as a glove, shoe, or girdle) that is easily slipped on or off

slip·page \ˈslip-ij\ *n* **1 :** an act, instance, or process of slipping **2 a :** a loss in transmission of power **b :** the difference between theoretical and actual output (as of power)

slipped disk *n* **:** a protrusion of one of the cartilage disks between vertebrae with pressure on spinal nerves resulting in lower back pain or sciatica

slip·per \ˈslip-ər\ *n* **:** a light low shoe without laces that is easily slipped on or off — **slip·pered** \-ərd\ *adj*

slip·pery \ˈslip-rē, -ə-rē\ *adj* **slip·per·i·er; -est 1 :** having a surface smooth enough to cause one to slide or lose one's hold ⟨a *slippery* floor⟩ **2 :** not worthy of trust **:** TRICKY, UNRELIABLE [Old English *slipor*] — **slip·per·i·ness** *n*

slippery elm *n* **:** a North American elm with hard wood and fragrant inner bark; *also* **:** its wood or bark

slippery slope *n* **:** a course of action that seems to lead inevitably from one action or result to another with unintended consequences

slip ring *n* **:** one of two or more continuous conducting rings from which the brushes take or to which they deliver current in a generator or motor

slip·shod \ˈslip-ˈshäd\ *adj* **:** very careless **:** SLOVENLY [earlier *slipshod* "wearing loose shoes, shabby," from ¹*slip* + *shod*]

slip stitch *n* **:** a concealed stitch for sewing folded edges (as hems) made by alternately running the needle inside the fold and picking up a thread or two from the body of the article

slip·stream \ˈslip-ˌstrēm\ *n* **:** the stream of air driven aft by the propeller of an aircraft

slip–up \ˈslip-ˌəp\ *n* **1 :** MISTAKE **2 :** MISCHANCE

slip up \slip-ˈəp, ˈslip-\ *vi* **:** to make a mistake **:** BLUNDER

¹**slit** \ˈslit\ *vt* **slit; slit·ting 1 a :** to make a slit in **:** SLASH **b :** to cut off or away **:** SEVER **2 :** to cut into long narrow strips [Middle English *slitten*] — **slit·ter** *n*

²**slit** *n* **:** a long narrow cut or opening — **slit** *adj* — **slit·less** \-ˌləs\ *adj*

slith·er \ˈsli*th*-ər\ *vb* **slith·ered; slith·er·ing** \ˈsli*th*-ring, -ə-ring\ **1 :** to slide or cause to slide on or as if on a loose gravelly surface **2 :** to slip or slide like a snake [Old English *slidrian,* from *slīdan* "to slide"]

slith·ery \ˈsli*th*-rē, -ə-rē\ *adj* **:** having a slippery surface, texture, or quality

¹**sliv·er** \ˈsliv-ər, *2 is usually* ˈslīv-\ *n* **1 a :** a long slender piece cut or torn off **:** SPLINTER **b :** a small and narrow portion ⟨a *sliver* of pie⟩ **2 :** an untwisted strand of textile fiber as it comes from a carding or combining machine [Middle English *slivere,* from *sliven* "to slice off," from Old English *-slīfan*]

²**sliv·er** \ˈsliv-ər\ *vb* **sliv·ered; sliv·er·ing** \ˈsliv-ring, -ə-ring\ **:** to cut or form into slivers **:** SPLINTER

slob \ˈsläb\ *n* **:** a slovenly or boorish person [Irish *slab* "mud, ooze, slovenly person"] — **slob·by** \ˈsläb-ē\ *adj*

¹**slob·ber** \ˈsläb-ər\ *vb* **slob·bered; slob·ber·ing** \ˈsläb-ring, -ə-ring\ **1 :** to let saliva or liquid dribble from the mouth **:** DROOL **2 :** to show feeling to excess **:** GUSH [Middle English *sloberen* "to eat in a slovenly manner"] — **slob·ber·er** \ˈsläb-ər-ər\ *n*

²**slobber** *n* **1 :** dripping saliva **2 :** silly excessive show of feeling — **slob·bery** \ˈsläb-rē, -ə-rē\ *adj*

sloe \ˈslō\ *n* **:** the tart bluish black globe-shaped fruit of the blackthorn; *also* **:** BLACKTHORN [Old English *slāh*]

sloe–eyed \ˈslō-ˈīd\ *adj* **1 :** having soft dark bluish or purplish black eyes **2 :** having slanted eyes

sloe gin *n* **:** a sweet reddish liqueur flavored chiefly with sloes

slog \ˈsläg\ *vb* **slogged; slog·ging 1 :** to hit hard **:** BEAT **2 :** to plod heavily ⟨*slogging* through the snow⟩ **3 :** to work hard and steadily ⟨*slogged* away at my homework⟩ [origin unknown] — **slog·ger** *n*

slo•gan \'slō-gən\ *n* **1** : a word or phrase that calls to battle **2** : a word or phrase used by a party, a group, or a business to attract attention [Scottish Gaelic *sluagh-ghairm* "army cry"]
slo•gan•eer \ˌslō-gə-'niər\ *n* : a coiner or user of slogans — **sloganeer** *vi*
slo–mo \'slō-ˌmō\ *n* : SLOW MOTION — **slo–mo** *adj*
sloop \'slüp\ *n* : a fore-and-aft rigged sailing boat with one mast and a single jib [Dutch *sloep*]
1**slop** \'släp\ *n* **1** : soft mud : SLUSH **2** : thin tasteless drink or liquid food — usually used in plural **3** : liquid spilled or splashed **4 a** : food waste (as garbage) or a thin gruel fed to animals : SWILL **b** : excreted body waste — usually used in plural [Middle English *sloppe*]
2**slop** *vb* **slopped; slop•ping 1** : to spill on or over ⟨*slop* milk from a glass⟩ ⟨*slopped* my shirt with gravy⟩ **2** : to feed slop to ⟨*slop* the hogs⟩
1**slope** \'slōp\ *adj* : being slanted or at an angle [Middle English *sloop,* probably from *aslope,* adv., "obliquely"]
2**slope** *vb* : to take a slanting direction : give a slant to : INCLINE — **slop•er** *n*
3**slope** *n* **1** : ground that forms a natural or artificial incline **2** : upward or downward slant or inclination or degree of slant **3** : the part of a continent draining to a particular ocean **4 a** : the tangent of the angle made by a straight line with the x-axis **b** : the slope of the line tangent to a plane curve at a point
slope–intercept form *n* : the equation of a straight line in the form $y = mx + b$ where m is the slope of the line and b is its y-intercept
slop•py \'släp-ē\ *adj* **slop•pi•er; -est 1 a** : wet so as to spatter easily : SLUSHY ⟨a *sloppy* racetrack⟩ **b** : wet with or as if with something slopped over **2** : SLOVENLY, CARELESS ⟨a *sloppy* dresser⟩ **3** : excessively sentimental — **slop•pi•ly** \'släp-ə-lē\ *adv* — **slop•pi•ness** \'släp-ē-nəs\ *n*
1**slosh** \'släsh\ *n* **1** : SLUSH 1 **2** : the slap or splash of liquid [probably blend of *slop* and *slush*]
2**slosh** *vb* **1** : to flounder through or splash about in or with water, mud, or slush **2** : to move with a splash
1**slot** \'slät\ *n* : a long narrow opening, groove, or passage : SLIT, NOTCH [Middle English, "hollow at the base of the throat above the breast-bone," from Medieval French *esclot* "hoofprint, track," of Germanic origin]
2**slot** *vt* **slot•ted; slot•ting** : to cut a slot in
3**slot** *n, pl* **slot** : the track of an animal (as a deer) [Middle French *esclot* "track"]
slot car *n* : a toy racing car that fits into a groove and is guided electrically by remote control
sloth \'slöth, 'slōth\ *n* **1** : INDOLENCE, LAZINESS **2** : any of several slow-moving mammals of the tropical forests of Central and South America that are related to the armadillos and live in trees where they hang back downward and feed on leaves, shoots, and fruits [Middle English *slouthe,* from *slow*]

sloth 2

sloth•ful \-fəl\ *adj* : LAZY 1, INDOLENT — **sloth•ful•ly** \-fə-lē\ *adv* — **sloth•ful•ness** *n*
slot machine *n* **1** : a machine whose operation is begun when a coin is dropped into a slot **2** : an originally coin-operated gambling machine that pays off for the matching of symbols on wheels spun by a handle
1**slouch** \'slau̇ch\ *n* **1** : an awkward, lazy, or incompetent person **2** : a gait or posture characterized by an awkward stooping of head and shoulders [origin unknown]
2**slouch** *vi* : to walk, stand, or sit with a slouch — **slouch•er** *n*
slouch hat *n* : a soft usually felt hat with a flexible brim
slouchy \'slau̇-chē\ *adj* **slouch•i•er; -est** : slouching or slovenly in appearance — **slouch•i•ly** \-chə-lē\ *adv* — **slouch•i•ness** \-chē-nəs\ *n*
1**slough** \'slü, 'slau̇; *in the U.S. (except New England)* 'slü *is usual for sense 1;* 'slau̇ *is more frequent for sense 2*\ *n* **1** *also* **slew** *or* **slue** \'slü\ : a wet and marshy or muddy place (as a swamp or backwater) **2** : a discouraged, degraded, or dejected state [Old English *slōh*]
2**slough** \'sləf\ *also* **sluff** *n* **1** : the cast-off skin of a snake **2** : a mass of dead tissue separating from an ulcer **3** : something that may be shed or cast off [Middle English *slughe*]
3**slough** \'sləf\ *also* **sluff** *vb* **1 a** : to cast off or become cast off **b** : to cast off one's skin or dead tissue from living tissue **c** : to get rid of or discard as irksome, objectionable, or disadvantageous **2** : to crumble slowly and fall away
slough of de•spond \ˌslau̇-əv-di-'spänd, ˌslü-\ : a state of extreme depression [from the *Slough of Despond,* deep bog into which Christian falls in the allegory *Pilgrim's Progress* (1678) by John Bunyan]
Slo•vak \'slō-ˌväk, -ˌvak\ *n* **1** : a member of a Slavic people of Slovakia **2** : the Slavic language of the Slovak people [Slovak *slovák*] — **Slovak** *adj* — **Slo•vak•i•an** \slō-'väk-ē-ən, -'vak-\ *adj or n*
slov•en \'sləv-ən\ *n* : one habitually negligent of neatness or cleanliness [Middle English *sloveyn* "rascal"]
Slo•vene \'slō-ˌvēn\ *n* **1** : a member of a Slavic people living largely in Slovenia **2** : the language of the Slovenes [German *Slowene,* from Slovene *Slovenec*] — **Slovene** *adj* — **Slo•ve•ni•an** \slō-'vē-nē-ən\ *adj or n*
slov•en•ly \'sləv-ən-lē\ *adj* **1 a** : untidy especially in dress or person **b** : lazily slipshod **2** : characteristic of a sloven — **slov•en•li•ness** *n* — **slovenly** *adv*
1**slow** \'slō\ *adj* **1 a** : not quick to understand ⟨a *slow* learner⟩ **b** : STUPID **c** : naturally inert or sluggish **2 a** : lacking in readiness, promptness, or willingness **b** : not hasty **3 a** : moving, flowing, or proceeding without speed or at less than usual speed ⟨*slow* traffic⟩ **b** : not vigorous or active ⟨a *slow* fire⟩ **c** : taking place at a low rate or over a considerable period of time ⟨*slow* growth⟩ **4** : having qualities that hinder or stop rapid progress or action ⟨a *slow* racetrack⟩ **5 a** : registering behind or below what is correct ⟨the clock is *slow*⟩ **b** : that is behind the time at a specified time or place **6** : lacking in activity or liveliness ⟨a *slow* market⟩ ⟨a *slow* party⟩ [Old English *slāw*] — **slow•ly** *adv* — **slow•ness** *n*
2**slow** *adv* : in a slow manner ⟨drive *slow*⟩
3**slow** *vb* : to make or go slow or slower — often used with *down* or *up*
slow•down \'slō-ˌdau̇n\ *n* : a slowing down
slow–foot•ed \'slō-'fu̇t-əd\ *adj* : moving at a very slow pace — **slow–foot•ed•ness** *n*
slow•ish \'slō-ish\ *adj* : somewhat slow ⟨a *slowish* reader⟩
slow match *n* : a match or fuse made so as to burn slowly and evenly and used for firing (as of blasting charges)
slow motion *n* : action in a projected motion picture or television program that proceeds at a rate slower than the action photographed or taped — **slow–motion** *adj*
slow•poke \'slō-ˌpōk\ *n* : a very slow person
slow–wit•ted \-'wit-əd\ *adj* : mentally slow
sludge \'sləj\ *n* **1** : MUD, MIRE **2** : a muddy or slushy mass, deposit, or sediment; *esp* : precipitated solid matter produced by water and sewage treatment processes [probably alteration of *slush*] — **sludgy** \'sləj-ē\ *adj*
1**slue** *variant of* 1SLOUGH 1
2**slue** *variant of* 3SLEW
1**slug** \'sləg\ *n* **1** : SLUGGARD **2** : a small piece of shaped metal: as **a** : a musket ball or bullet **b** : a metal disk for insertion in a slot machine in place of a coin **3** : any of numerous chiefly terrestrial mollusks that are closely related to the land snails but are long and wormlike and have only a rudimentary shell or none **4** : a smooth soft larva of a sawfly or moth that creeps like a snail **5** : a single drink of liquor : SHOT **6** : a line of type cast as one piece **7** : the gravitational unit of mass in the foot-pound-second system to which a pound force can impart an acceleration of one foot per second per second and which is equal to the mass of an object weighing 32 pounds (14.5 kilograms) [of Scandinavian origin]

1slug 3

2**slug** *vt* **slugged; slug•ging** : to strike heavily with or as if with the fist or a bat

[3]**slug** *n* : a heavy blow especially with the fist [perhaps from *slug* "to load with slugs"]

slug·abed \ˈsləg-ə-ˌbed\ *n* : one who stays in bed too long; *also* : SLUGGARD

slug·fest \ˈsləg-ˌfest\ *n* : a fight marked by exchange of heavy blows

slug·gard \ˈsləg-ərd\ *n* : an habitually lazy person [Middle English *sluggart*] — **sluggard** *adj* — **slug·gard·ly** *adj*

slug·ger \ˈsləg-ər\ *n* : one (as a batter or boxer) that strikes hard or with heavy blows

slug·gish \ˈsləg-ish\ *adj* : slow and inactive in movement or reaction by habit or condition — **slug·gish·ly** *adv* — **slug·gish·ness** *n*

[1]**sluice** \ˈslüs\ *n* **1** : an artificial passage for water with a gate for controlling its flow or changing its direction **2** : a body of water held back by a gate or a stream flowing through a gate **3** : a device (as a water gate) for controlling the flow of water **4** : a channel that carries off surplus water **5** : a long inclined trough (as for washing gold-bearing earth or for floating logs to a sawmill) [Middle French *escluse,* from Late Latin *exclusa,* from Latin *excludere* "to shut off, exclude"]

[2]**sluice** *vt* **1** : to draw off by or through a sluice **2 a** : to wash with or in water running through or from a sluice **b** : to drench with a sudden flow

sluice·way \ˈslü-ˌswā\ *n* : an artificial channel into which water is let by a sluice

[1]**slum** \ˈsləm\ *n* : a thickly populated usually urban area marked by crowding, run-down housing, poverty, and social disorganization [origin unknown]

[2]**slum** *vi* **slummed; slum·ming** : to visit slums especially out of curiosity or for pleasure — **slum·mer** *n*

[1]**slum·ber** \ˈsləm-bər\ *vi* **slum·bered; slum·ber·ing** \-bə-ring, -bring\ **1 a** : to sleep lightly : DOZE **b** : SLEEP **2** : to lie dormant ⟨a *slumbering* volcano⟩ [Middle English *slumberen,* from *slumen* "to doze"] — **slum·ber·er** \-bər-ər\ *n*

[2]**slumber** *n* : SLEEP

slum·ber·ous *or* **slum·brous** \ˈsləm-bə-rəs, -brəs\ *adj* **1** : SLEEPY 1 **2** : inviting slumber ⟨a *slumberous* sound⟩

slumber party *n* : an overnight gathering of teenage girls usually at one of their homes

slum·gul·lion \ˈsləm-ˌgəl-yən\ *n* : a meat stew [perhaps from earlier *slum* "slime" + English dialect *gullion* "mud, cesspool"]

slum·lord \ˈsləm-ˌlȯrd\ *n* : a landlord who receives unusually large profits from substandard properties [*slum* + land*lord*]

[1]**slump** \ˈsləmp\ *vi* **1** : to drop or slide down suddenly : COLLAPSE **2** : to assume a drooping or stooped posture or carriage : SLOUCH **3** : to fall sharply ⟨sales *slumped*⟩ [probably imitative]

[2]**slump** *n* : a large or prolonged decline especially in economic activity or prices

slung *past and past participle of* SLING

slunk *past and past participle of* SLINK

[1]**slur** \ˈslər\ *vb* **slurred; slur·ring 1 a** : to slide or slip over without due mention, consideration, or emphasis **b** : to perform hurriedly : SKIMP **2** : to perform (successive musical notes of different pitch) in a smooth or connected manner **3** : to speak indistinctly [probably from Low German *slurrn* "to shuffle"]

[2]**slur** *n* **1 a** : a curved line connecting notes to be sung or performed without a break **b** : the combination of two or more slurred tones **2** : a slurring manner of speech

[3]**slur** *vb* **slurred; slur·ring 1** : to make insulting remarks about : DISPARAGE **2** : to make indistinct : OBSCURE [Middle English *sloor* "thin mud"]

[4]**slur** *n* **1 a** : an insulting or disparaging remark **b** : a shaming or degrading effect **2** : a blurred spot in printed matter : SMUDGE

slurp \ˈslərp\ *vb* : to eat or drink noisily or with a sucking sound [Dutch *slurpen*] — **slurp** *n*

slur·ry \ˈslər-ē, ˈslə-rē\ *n, pl* **slurries** : a watery mixture of insoluble matter (as mud, lime, or pulverized ore) [Middle English *slory*]

slush \ˈsləsh\ *n* **1** : partly melted or watery snow **2** : soft mud : MIRE **3** : trashy and usually cheaply sentimental material [perhaps of Scandinavian origin]

slush fund *n* : a fund for carrying on corrupt activities (as bribing public officials)

slushy \ˈsləsh-ē\ *adj* **slush·i·er; -est** : full of or resembling slush ⟨a *slushy* road⟩ ⟨soft *slushy* ice⟩ — **slush·i·ness** *n*

slut \ˈslət\ *n* **1** : a slovenly woman **2** : a lewd woman; *esp* : PROSTITUTE [Middle English *slutte*] — **slut·tish** \ˈslət-ish\ *adj* — **slut·tish·ly** *adv* — **slut·tish·ness** *n*

sly \ˈslī\ *adj* **sli·er** *or* **sly·er** \ˈslī-ər, ˈslīr\; **sli·est** *or* **sly·est** \ˈslī-əst\ **1 a** : clever in concealing one's aims or ends ⟨too *sly* to be trusted⟩ **b** : lacking in straightforwardness and candor ⟨a *sly* explanation⟩ **2** : lightly mischievous : ROGUISH ⟨a *sly* smile⟩ [Old Norse *slœgr*] — **sly·ly** *also* **sli·ly** *adv* — **sly·ness** *n* — **on the sly** : in a manner intended to avoid notice

synonyms SLY, CRAFTY, ARTFUL, WILY mean apt to attain an end by devious means. SLY stresses furtiveness, lack of candor, and skill in concealing one's aims and methods ⟨a *sly* scheme⟩. CRAFTY suggests skill in deception acquired by experience ⟨a *crafty* trial lawyer⟩. ARTFUL suggests insinuating or ingratiating craftiness ⟨an *artful* matchmaker⟩. WILY stresses cleverness in setting or avoiding traps ⟨the *wily* fox⟩.

[1]**smack** \ˈsmak\ *n* **1** : characteristic or perceptible taste or flavor **2** : a small quantity [Old English *smæc*]

[2]**smack** *vi* : to have a flavor, trace, or suggestion ⟨the roast *smacks* of thyme⟩ ⟨such actions *smack* of treachery⟩

[3]**smack** *vb* **1** : to close and open (lips) noisily especially in eating **2** : to kiss usually loudly or boisterously **3 a** : to make a smack **b** : to hit so as to make a smack [related to Dutch *smacken* "to strike"]

[4]**smack** *n* **1** : a quick sharp noise made by rapidly compressing and opening the lips **2** : a loud kiss **3** : a sharp slap or blow

[5]**smack** *adv* : in a square and sharp manner : DIRECTLY ⟨it hit me *smack* in the face⟩

[6]**smack** *n* : a sailing ship (as a sloop or cutter) used chiefly in coasting and fishing [Dutch *smak* or Low German *smack*]

smack–dab \ˈsmak-ˈdab\ *adv* : SQUARELY, EXACTLY ⟨*smack-dab* in the middle⟩

smack·er \ˈsmak-ər\ *n* **1** : one that smacks **2** *slang* : DOLLAR 3

[1]**small** \ˈsmȯl\ *adj* **1** : little in size **2** : little in amount ⟨a *small* supply⟩ **3** : UNIMPORTANT ⟨a *small* matter⟩ **4 a** : minor in influence, power, or rank ⟨*small* success⟩ **b** : operating on a limited scale ⟨*small* dealers⟩ **5** : GENTLE, SOFT ⟨a *small* voice⟩ **6** : not generous : MEAN, PETTY ⟨a *small* nature⟩ **7** : made up of few or little units ⟨a *small* crowd⟩ **8** : HUMBLE, MODEST ⟨a *small* beginning⟩ **9** : HUMILIATED, HUMBLED ⟨felt very *small* to be caught cheating⟩ **10** : LOWERCASE [Old English *smæl*] — **small·ness** *n*

synonyms SMALL, LITTLE mean noticeably below average in size. SMALL and LITTLE are often interchangeable but SMALL, contrasting with large or great, applies more to relative size determined by capacity, value, number ⟨a *small* mouth⟩ ⟨a *small* quantity of salt⟩. LITTLE, contrasting with big or much, is more absolute in implication and may suggest pettiness, petiteness, insignificance, immaturity ⟨a *little* child⟩ ⟨had *little* hope of success⟩.

[2]**small** *adv* **1** : in or into small pieces ⟨cut the meat *small*⟩ **2** : without force or loudness ⟨speak *small*⟩ **3** : in a small manner ⟨most businesses begin *small*⟩

[3]**small** *n* **1** : a part smaller and especially narrower than the remainder ⟨the *small* of the back⟩ **2 a** *pl* : small-sized products **b** *pl, chiefly British* : SMALLCLOTHES 2

small arm *n* : a firearm fired while held in the hands — usually used in plural

small beer *n* **1** : a weak or inferior beer **2** : something of small importance : TRIVIA

small calorie *n* : CALORIE 1a

small capital *n* : a letter having the form of but smaller than a capital letter (as in THESE WORDS) — called also *small cap*

small change *n* **1** : money consisting of small coins **2** : something trifling or petty

small circle *n* : a circle on the surface of a sphere whose plane does not pass through the center of the sphere; *esp* : such a circle on the surface of the earth — compare GREAT CIRCLE

small–claims court *n* : a special court intended to quicken and simplify the settling of disputes over small debts

small·clothes \ˈsmȯl-ˌklōz, -ˌklōthz\ *n pl* **1** : close-fitting knee breeches worn especially in the 18th century **2** : small articles of clothing

\ə\ **abut**	\au̇\ **out**	\i\ **tip**	\ȯ\ **saw**	\u̇\ **foot**
\ər\ **further**	\ch\ **chin**	\ī\ **life**	\ȯi\ **coin**	\y\ **yet**
\a\ **mat**	\e\ **pet**	\j\ **job**	\th\ **thin**	\yü\ **few**
\ā\ **take**	\ē\ **easy**	\ng\ **sing**	\th\ **this**	\yu̇\ **cure**
\ä\ **cot, cart**	\g\ **go**	\ō\ **bone**	\ü\ **food**	\zh\ **vision**

small–fry \-ˌfrī\ *adj* **1** : MINOR, UNIMPORTANT ⟨a *small-fry* politician⟩ **2** : of or relating to children
small hours *n pl* : the early morning hours
small intestine *n* : the long narrow part of the intestine that lies between the stomach and colon, consists of the duodenum, jejunum, and ileum, secretes digestive enzymes, and is the chief site in which food is digested into small molecules and is absorbed into the body
small•ish \ˈsmȯ-lish\ *adj* : somewhat small
small–mind•ed \ˈsmȯl-ˈmīn-dəd\ *adj* **1** : having narrow interests, sympathies, or outlook **2** : marked by pettiness, narrowness, or meanness : typical of a small-minded person — **small–mind•ed•ly** *adv* — **small–mind•ed•ness** *n*
small•mouth bass \-ˌmau̇th-\ *n* : a black bass that lives in clear rivers and lakes and is bronze green above and lighter below — called also *smallmouth black bass*
small potatoes *n* : someone or something of trivial importance or worth
small•pox \ˈsmȯl-ˌpäks\ *n* : a contagious sometimes deadly virus disease that is marked by fever and skin eruption with pustules and scar formation and is believed to have been eradicated worldwide by widespread vaccination
small–scale \-ˈskāl\ *adj* **1** : small in scope; *esp* : small in output or operation **2** : having a scale (as one inch to 25 miles) that shows mainly large features ⟨a *small-scale* map⟩
small talk *n* : light or casual conversation
small–time \ˈsmȯl-ˈtīm\ *adj* : of insignificant standing : SMALL-SCALE, MINOR — **small–tim•er** \-ˈtī-mər\ *n*
smarmy \ˈsmär-mē\ *adj* **smarm•i•er; -est** : exhibiting or marked by smug, ingratiating, or false earnestness : UNCTUOUS [earlier *smarm* "to gush, slobber"]
[1]**smart** \ˈsmärt\ *vi* **1** : to cause or feel a sharp stinging pain **2** : to feel or endure distress, remorse, or embarrassment ⟨*smarts* under criticism⟩ [Old English *smeortan*]
[2]**smart** *adj* **1** : causing a sharp stinging sensation **2** : marked by forceful activity or vigorous strength **3** : BRISK 1, SPIRITED ⟨a *smart* pace⟩ **4 a** : mentally alert : BRIGHT **b** : sharp in scheming : SHREWD **5 a** : WITTY, CLEVER **b** : PERT, SAUCY ⟨don't get *smart* with me⟩ **6 a** : stylish or elegant in dress or appearance **b** : SOPHISTICATED 2 **c** : FASHIONABLE 1 **7 a** : being a guided missile ⟨a *smart* bomb⟩ **b** : operating by automation ⟨a *smart* machine tool⟩ [Old English *smeart*] ***synonyms*** see CLEVER — **smart•ly** *adv* — **smart•ness** *n*
[3]**smart** *adv* : in a smart manner : SMARTLY
[4]**smart** *n* **1** : a smarting pain; *esp* : a stinging pain in one small part of the body **2** : deep grief or remorse
smart al•eck \ˈsmärt-ˌal-ik, -ˌel-\ *n* : a person who says things that are clever or funny but that are also disrespectful or rude [*Aleck,* nickname for *Alexander*] — **smart–al•ecky** \-ˌal-ə-kē, -ˌel-\ *or* **smart–aleck** *adj*
smart card *n* : a small plastic card that has a built-in microprocessor to store and process data
smart•en \ˈsmärt-ⁿn\ *vb* **smart•ened; smart•en•ing** \ˈsmärt-ning, -ⁿn-ing\ **1** : to make smart or smarter : SPRUCE, FRESHEN ⟨*smarten* up the room for a party⟩ **2** : to make or become more alert or informed ⟨*smarten* up before you get into trouble⟩
smart•phone \ˈsmärt-ˌfōn\ *n* : a cell phone that includes additional software functions (as e-mail or an Internet browser)
smart•weed \ˈsmärt-ˌwēd\ *n* : any of various weedy plants with strong acrid juice that are related to the buckwheats
smarty *or* **smart•ie** \ˈsmärt-ē\ *n, pl* **smart•ies** : SMART ALECK
[1]**smash** \ˈsmash\ *vb* **1** : to break in pieces by force : SHATTER ⟨*smash* down a door⟩ ⟨the dish *smashed* on the floor⟩ **2** : to hit violently and very hard **3** : to destroy completely : WRECK **4** : to go to pieces suddenly : COLLAPSE [perhaps blend of *smack* and *mash*] — **smash•er** *n*
[2]**smash** *n* **1 a** : a smashing blow or attack **b** : a hard overhand stroke (as in tennis) **2 a** : the action or sound of smashing; *esp* : a wreck due to collision **b** : utter collapse : RUIN **3** : a striking success : HIT ⟨the new play is a *smash*⟩
smash•ing \ˈsmash-ing\ *adj* **1** : that smashes ⟨a *smashing* defeat⟩ **2** : extremely moving, effective, or attractive ⟨a *smashing* performance⟩
smash•up \ˈsmash-ˌəp\ *n* **1** : a complete collapse **2** : a destructive collision of motor vehicles
smat•ter \ˈsmat-ər\ *n* : SMATTERING 2 [Middle English *smatteren* "to chatter, talk ignorantly"]
smat•ter•ing \ˈsmat-ə-ring\ *n* **1** : superficial piecemeal knowledge **2** : a small scattered number
[1]**smear** \ˈsmiər\ *n* **1** : a spot made by or as if by an oily or sticky substance : SMUDGE **2** : material smeared on a surface; *esp* : material prepared for microscopic examination by smearing on a slide — compare PAP SMEAR **3** : a usually unproven charge or accusation [Old English *smeoru*]
[2]**smear** *vt* **1 a** : to spread or daub with something oily or sticky **b** : to spread over a surface **2 a** : to stain, smudge, or dirty by or as if by smearing **b** : to soil the reputation of **3** : to blot out or blur by or as if by smearing — **smear•er** *n*
smeary \ˈsmiər-ē\ *adj* **smear•i•er; -est** **1** : marked by smears **2** : likely to cause smears
[1]**smell** \ˈsmel\ *vb* **smelled** \ˈsmeld\ *or* **smelt** \ˈsmelt\; **smell•ing** **1** : to perceive the odor of through stimuli affecting the olfactory sense organs of the nose ⟨*smell* dinner cooking⟩ **2** : to detect or become aware of as if by the sense of smell ⟨could *smell* something amiss⟩ **3** : to use the sense of smell ⟨can't *smell* because of my cold⟩ **4 a** : to have or give off an odor ⟨the candles *smell* like roses⟩ **b** : to have an offensive odor : STINK ⟨the garbage *smells*⟩ **c** : to give off a suggestion of something ⟨the plan *smells* of trickery⟩ [Middle English *smellen*] — **smell•er** *n* — **smell a rat** : to have a suspicion of something wrong — **smell blood** : to sense an opponent's weakness or vulnerability — **smell the roses** : to enjoy or savor life
[2]**smell** *n* **1** : ODOR, SCENT **2** : the process or power of perceiving odor; *also* : the sense by which one perceives odor **3** : a pervading quality : AURA **4** : an act of smelling
synonyms SMELL, ODOR, SCENT, AROMA mean the quality that makes a thing perceptible to the nose. SMELL and ODOR may imply either a pleasant or unpleasant sensation though SMELL may cover a wider range of quality, intensity, or source ⟨an odd *smell* filled the room⟩ ⟨a cheese with a strong *odor*⟩. SCENT implies less strength and suggests a substance, an animal, or a plant giving off a characteristic smell ⟨the *scent* of pine⟩. AROMA suggests a pungent, pervasive, usually pleasant smell ⟨the *aroma* of fresh coffee⟩.
smelling salts *n pl* : a usually scented aromatic preparation of an ammonium salt and ammonia water used to relieve faintness
smelly \ˈsmel-ē\ *adj* **smell•i•er; -est** : having a smell and especially a bad smell ⟨*smelly* socks⟩
[1]**smelt** \ˈsmelt\ *n, pl* **smelts** *or* **smelt** : any of several very small food fishes of coastal or fresh waters that resemble and are related to the trout [Old English]
[2]**smelt** *vt* **1** : to melt or fuse (as ore) usually in order to separate the metal **2** : REFINE 1a [Dutch or Low German *smelten*]
smelt•er \ˈsmel-tər\ *n* : one that smelts: **a** : a worker in or an owner of a smeltery **b** *or* **smelt•ery** \-tə-rē, -trē\ : an establishment for smelting
smid•gen *also* **smid•geon** *or* **smid•gin** \ˈsmij-ən\ *or* **smidge** \ˈsmij\ *n* : a small amount : BIT [perhaps from English dialect *smitch* "soiling mark"]
smi•lax \ˈsmī-ˌlaks\ *n* **1** : GREENBRIER **2** : a delicate greenhouse twining plant related to the garden asparagus and having ovate bright green terminal branches in place of leaves [Latin, "bindweed, yew," from Greek]
[1]**smile** \ˈsmīl\ *vb* **1** : to have, produce, or exhibit a smile **2 a** : to look with amusement or ridicule **b** : to be propitious or agreeable ⟨weather *smiled* on our plans⟩ **3** : to express by a smile [Middle English *smilen*] — **smil•er** *n* — **smil•ing•ly** \ˈsmī-ling-lē\ *adv*
[2]**smile** *n* : a change of facial expression in which the eyes brighten and the corners of the mouth curve slightly upward especially in expression of amusement, pleasure, approval, or scorn — **smile•less** \ˈsmīl-ləs\ *adj*
[1]**smil•ey** \ˈsmī-lē\ *adj* : exhibiting a smile : frequently smiling
[2]**smiley** *n* : EMOTICON
smirch \ˈsmərch\ *vt* **1** : to make dirty, stained, or discolored especially by smearing with something that soils **2** : to bring discredit or disgrace on [Middle English *smorchen*] — **smirch** *n*
smirk \ˈsmərk\ *vi* : to smile in a smug or unpleasant way [Old English *smearcian* "to smile"] — **smirk** *n*
smirky \ˈsmər-kē\ *adj* **smirk•i•er; -est** : marked by or given to smirking
smite \ˈsmīt\ *vb* **smote** \ˈsmōt\; **smit•ten** \ˈsmit-ⁿn\ *or* **smote**; **smit•ing** \ˈsmīt-ing\ **1** : to strike sharply or heavily with the hand or a hand weapon **2 a** : to kill or injure by smiting **b** : to attack or afflict suddenly and injuriously ⟨*smitten* by disease⟩

3 : to affect like a sudden hard blow ⟨*smitten* with terror⟩ 4 : CAPTIVATE, TAKE ⟨*smitten* with the kitten⟩ [Old English *smītan*] — **smit·er** \ˈsmīt-ər\ *n*

smith \ˈsmith\ *n* 1 : a worker in metals 2 : MAKER — often used in combination ⟨gun*smith*⟩ ⟨tune*smith*⟩ [Old English]

smith·er·eens \ˌsmith-ə-ˈrēnz\ *n pl* : small pieces [perhaps from Irish *smidirīní*]

smith·ery \ˈsmith-ə-rē\ *n* 1 : the work, art, or trade of a smith 2 : SMITHY

smith·son·ite \ˈsmith-sə-ˌnīt\ *n* : a usually white or nearly white native zinc carbonate $ZnCO_3$ [James *Smithson,* died 1829, British chemist]

smithy \ˈsmith-ē, ˈsmith-\ *n, pl* **smith·ies** 1 : the workshop of a smith 2 : BLACKSMITH

[1]**smock** \ˈsmäk\ *n* 1 *archaic* : a woman's undergarment; *esp* : CHEMISE 2 : a light loose garment worn usually over regular clothing for protection from dirt [Old English *smoc*]

[2]**smock** *vt* : to embroider or shirr with smocking

smock·ing \ˈsmäk-ing\ *n* : a decorative embroidery or shirring made by gathering cloth in regularly spaced round tucks

smog \ˈsmäg, ˈsmȯg\ *n* : a thick haze caused by the action of sunlight on air polluted especially by smoke and automobile exhaust fumes [blend of *smoke* and *fog*] — **smog·gy** \-ē\ *adj*

smok·able *or* **smoke·able** \ˈsmō-kə-bəl\ *adj* : fit for smoking

[1]**smoke** \ˈsmōk\ *n* 1 a : the gas of burning organic materials (as coal, wood, or tobacco) made visible by small particles of carbon b : a suspension of solid or liquid particles in a gas 2 : a mass or column of smoke 3 : fume or vapor often resulting from the action of heat on moisture 4 : something of little substance, permanence, or value 5 : something that obscures 6 : something to smoke (as a cigarette); *also* : the smoking of this [Old English *smoca*] — **smoke·like** \ˈsmō-ˌklīk\ *adj*

[2]**smoke** *vb* 1 a : to emit or exhale smoke b : to emit excessive smoke 2 : to inhale and exhale the fumes of burning plant material and especially tobacco; *also* : to use in smoking ⟨*smoke* a cigar⟩ 3 : to act on with smoke: as a : to drive away by smoke b : to blacken or discolor with smoke c : to cure by exposure to smoke ⟨*smoked* meat⟩ d : to stun (as bees) by smoke

smoke and mirrors *n pl* : something intended to disguise or draw attention away especially from an embarrassing or unpleasant issue

smoke·chas·er \-ˌchā-sər\ *n* : one that fights forest fires

smoke detector *n* : an alarm that activates automatically when it detects smoke — called also *smoke alarm*

smoke–filled room \ˌsmōk-ˌfild-\ *n* : a room (as in a hotel) in which a small group of politicians carry on negotiations

smoke·house \ˈsmōk-ˌhau̇s\ *n* : a building where meat or fish is cured by means of dense smoke

smoke jumper *n* : a forest firefighter who parachutes to locations otherwise difficult to reach

smoke·less \ˈsmō-kləs\ *adj* : producing or containing little or no smoke ⟨*smokeless* fuel⟩ ⟨a *smokeless* sky⟩

smokeless tobacco *n* : pulverized or shredded tobacco chewed or placed between cheek and gum

smoke out *vt* 1 : to drive out by or as if by smoke 2 : to bring to public knowledge

smok·er \ˈsmō-kər\ *n* 1 : one that smokes 2 : a railroad car or compartment in which smoking is allowed 3 : an informal social gathering for men

smoke screen *n* : a screen of or as if of smoke to hinder observation or detection

smoke·stack \ˈsmōk-ˌstak\ *n* : a chimney or funnel through which smoke and gases are discharged (as from a ship or factory)

smoke tree *n* : either of two small shrubby trees related to the cashew and having large clusters of tiny flowers suggesting a cloud of smoke

smoking jacket *n* : a man's easy jacket for home wear

smoking lamp *n* : a lamp on a ship kept lighted during the hours when smoking is allowed

smoking room *n* : a room (as in a hotel or club) set apart for smokers

smoky \ˈsmō-kē\ *adj* **smok·i·er; -est** 1 : giving off smoke especially in large quantities ⟨*smoky* stoves⟩ 2 : resembling or suggestive of smoke ⟨a *smoky* flavor⟩ 3 : filled with or darkened by smoke ⟨a *smoky* room⟩ ⟨*smoky* ceilings⟩ — **smok·i·ly** \-kə-lē\ *adv* — **smok·i·ness** \-kē-nəs\ *n*

smoky quartz *n* : a yellow or smoky-brown often transparent crystalline quartz

[1]**smol·der** *or* **smoul·der** \ˈsmōl-dər\ *n* : a slow smoky fire [Middle English *smolder*]

[2]**smolder** *or* **smoulder** *vi* **smol·dered** *or* **smoul·dered; smol·der·ing** *or* **smoul·der·ing** \ˈsmōl-də-ring, -dring\ 1 : to burn sluggishly with smoke and usually without flame ⟨fire was *smoldering* in the grate⟩ 2 : to exist in a state of suppressed activity ⟨a *smoldering* rebellion⟩; *also* : to indicate a suppressed emotion ⟨eyes *smoldering* with anger⟩

smolt \ˈsmōlt\ *n* : a salmon or sea trout when it is about two years old and silvery and is ready to migrate to the sea from freshwater [Middle English]

smooch \ˈsmüch\ *vi* : KISS, PET [alteration of earlier *smouch* "to kiss loudly"] — **smooch** *n*

[1]**smooth** \ˈsmüth\ *adj* 1 a : having a continuous even curve or surface : not rough ⟨a *smooth* skin⟩ b : being without hairs or projections : GLABROUS ⟨a *smooth* leaf⟩ c : causing no resistance to sliding 2 : free from obstacles or difficulties ⟨a *smooth* path⟩ 3 : even and uninterrupted in flow or flight 4 : excessively and often artfully suave : INGRATIATING ⟨a *smooth* talker⟩ 5 a : calm or unruffled in manner or behavior : SERENE ⟨a *smooth* disposition⟩ b : AMIABLE, COURTEOUS 6 : not sharp or harsh ⟨a *smooth* sherry⟩ [Old English *smōth*] ***synonyms*** see SUAVE — **smooth·ly** *adv* — **smooth·ness** *n*

[2]**smooth** *vt* 1 : to make smooth ⟨*smooth* the edge of the board⟩ 2 a : to free from what is harsh or disagreeable : POLISH ⟨*smoothed* out my style⟩ b : to make calm : SOOTHE 3 : to minimize (as a fault) in order to allay ill will ⟨*smoothed* things over with apologies⟩ 4 : to free from obstruction or difficulty ⟨*smoothed* the way for a quick end to the dispute⟩ 5 : to press flat ⟨*smooth* down the folds of the tablecloth⟩ 6 : to cause to lie evenly and in order : PREEN ⟨a bird *smoothing* its feathers⟩ — **smooth·er** *n*

smooth·bore \ˈsmüth-ˈbōr, -ˈbȯr\ *adj* : having a smooth-surfaced bore — **smooth·bore** \ˈsmüth-ˌ\ *n*

smooth·en \ˈsmü-thən\ *vb* : to make or become smooth

smooth endoplasmic reticulum *n* : endoplasmic reticulum that lacks ribosomes

smooth muscle *n* : muscle that is made up of elongated cells with a single nucleus and no cross striations, is typical especially of hollow organs and structures (as the bladder and blood vessels), occurs chiefly in sheets and rings, and is not under voluntary control — called also *involuntary muscle*; compare STRIATED MUSCLE

smooth–tongued \ˈsmüth-ˈtəngd\ *adj* : ingratiating in speech

smoothy *or* **smooth·ie** \ˈsmü-thē\ *n, pl* **smooth·ies** 1 : a smooth-tongued person 2 a : a person with polished manners b : a man with an ingratiating manner toward women

smor·gas·bord \ˈsmȯr-gəs-ˌbȯrd, -ˌbōrd\ *n* : a buffet offering a large variety of foods and dishes [Swedish *smörgåsbord,* from *smörgås* "open sandwich" + *bord* "table"]

smote *past of* SMITE

[1]**smoth·er** \ˈsməth-ər\ *n* 1 : a dense cloud (as of fog, foam, or dust) 2 : a confused multitude of things [Middle English *smorther* "dense smoke," from *smoren* "to smother," from Old English *smorian* "to suffocate"]

[2]**smother** *vb* **smoth·ered; smoth·er·ing** \ˈsməth-ring, -ə-ring\ 1 : to be overcome or killed through or as if through lack of air 2 : to overcome or kill by depriving of air or exposing to smoke or fumes : SUFFOCATE 3 a : to prevent the development or activity of ⟨*smother* a child with too much care⟩; *also* : OVERWHELM b : to cover up : SUPPRESS ⟨*smother* a yawn⟩ c : to cover thickly : BLANKET ⟨broiled steak *smothered* with mushrooms⟩ d : to overcome or vanquish quickly or decisively

[1]**smudge** \ˈsməj\ *vb* 1 a : to make a smudge on b : to soil as if by smudging 2 : to smoke or protect by a smudge fire 3 : to make a smudge 4 : to become smudged [Middle English *smogen*]

[2]**smudge** *n* 1 a : a blurry spot or streak : SMEAR b : STAIN 2 2 : a fire made to smoke (as for driving away mosquitoes or protecting fruit from frost) — **smudg·i·ly** \ˈsməj-ə-lē\ *adv* — **smudg·i·ness** \ˈsməj-ē-nəs\ *n* — **smudgy** \ˈsməj-ē\ *adj*

smudge pot *n* : a container in which fuel (as oil) is burned to produce a smudge

smug \ˈsməg\ *adj* **smug·ger; smug·gest :** highly self-satisfied : COMPLACENT [probably from Low German *smuck* "neat"] — **smug·ly** *adv* — **smug·ness** *n*

smug·gle \ˈsməg-əl\ *vb* **smug·gled; smug·gling** \ˈsməg-ling, -ə-ling\ **1 :** to export or import secretly and unlawfully (as to avoid paying duty) ⟨*smuggle* jewels⟩ **2 :** to take, bring, or introduce secretly or stealthily [Low German *smuggeln* and Dutch *smokkelen*] — **smug·gler** \ˈsməg-lər\ *n*

[1]**smut** \ˈsmət\ *vb* **smut·ted; smut·ting 1 :** to stain, taint, or affect (a crop or plant) with smut **2 :** to become affected by smut [probably from Middle English *smotten* "to stain"]

[2]**smut** *n* **1 :** matter that soils or blackens; *esp* **:** a particle of soot **2 :** any of various destructive diseases of plants and especially of cereal grasses caused by parasitic fungi that transform plant structures (as seeds) into dark masses of spores; *also* **:** a fungus causing a smut **3 :** obscene or indecent language or matter

smutch \ˈsməch\ *n* **:** a dark stain : SMUDGE [related to Middle English *smogen* "to smudge"] — **smutch** *vt* — **smutchy** \-ē\ *adj*

smut·ty \ˈsmət-ē\ *adj* **smut·ti·er; -est 1 :** soiled with smut ⟨a *smutty* face⟩ **2 :** affected with smut fungus **3 :** OBSCENE 2, INDECENT ⟨*smutty* jokes⟩ — **smut·ti·ly** \ˈsmət-l-ē\ *adv* — **smut·ti·ness** \ˈsmət-ē-nəs\ *n*

snack \ˈsnak\ *n* **:** a light meal : LUNCH [Middle English *snak* "bite," from *snaken* "to bite"]

snack bar *n* **:** a public eating place where snacks are served usually at a counter

snaf·fle \ˈsnaf-əl\ *n* **:** a simple jointed bit for a bridle [origin unknown] — **snaffle** *vt*

sna·fu \sna-ˈfü\ *adj* **:** being in a state of confusion : AWRY [*s*ituation *n*ormal *a*ll *f*ouled *u*p] — **snafu** *n* — **snafu** *vt*

[1]**snag** \ˈsnag\ *n* **1 a :** a tree or branch embedded underwater and not visible from the surface **b :** a standing dead tree **2 :** an uneven or broken projection from a smooth or finished surface **3 :** a concealed or unexpected difficulty or hindrance [perhaps of Scandinavian origin] — **snag·gy** \ˈsnag-ē\ *adj*

[2]**snag** *vt* **snagged; snag·ging 1 a :** to catch and usually damage on or as if on a snag ⟨*snagged* my sleeve on a nail⟩ **b :** to halt or impede as if on a snag ⟨the bill was *snagged* in committee⟩ **2 :** to catch or obtain by quick action ⟨*snagged* two tickets for the big game⟩

snag·gle·tooth \ˈsnag-əl-ˈtüth\ *n* **:** an irregular, broken, or projecting tooth [English dialect *snaggle* "irregular tooth"] — **snag·gle·toothed** \ˌsnag-əl-ˈtütht\ *adj*

snail \ˈsnāl\ *n* **1 :** any of numerous typically small gastropod mollusks with an external spiral shell and including terrestrial and aquatic forms **2 :** a slow-moving person or thing [Old English *snægl*]

snail mail *n* **1 :** mail delivered by a postal system **2 :** MAIL 2

[1]**snake** \ˈsnāk\ *n* **1 :** any of numerous limbless scaled reptiles (suborder Serpentes or Ophidia) with a long tapering body and salivary glands often modified to produce venom which is injected through grooved or tubular fangs **2 :** a despicable or treacherous person [Old English *snaca*] — **snake·like** \ˈsnā-ˌklīk\ *adj*

[2]**snake** *vb* **1 :** to crawl or move sinuously, silently, or secretly **2 :** to move (as logs) by dragging

snake·bird \ˈsnāk-ˌbərd\ *n* **:** ANHINGA

snake·bite \-ˌbīt\ *n* **:** the bite of a snake and especially a venomous snake

snake charmer *n* **:** an entertainer who exhibits a professed power to charm or fascinate venomous snakes

snake dance *n* **:** a group of people moving single file in a wavy path (as in celebration of an athletic victory)

snake doctor *n* **:** DRAGONFLY

snake fence *n* **:** WORM FENCE

snake in the grass : a treacherous person pretending to be a friend

snake oil *n* **1 :** any of various substances or mixtures sold (as by a traveling medicine show) as medicine usually without regard to their medical worth or properties **2 :** NONSENSE 1

snake plant *n* **:** SANSEVIERIA

snake·root \ˈsnā-ˌkrüt, -ˌkru̇t\ *n* **:** any of various plants mostly with roots reputed to cure snakebites; *also* **:** the root of such a plant

snakeroot

snake·skin \ˈsnāk-ˌskin\ *n* **:** the skin of a snake or leather made from it

snaky \ˈsnā-kē\ *adj* **snak·i·er; -est 1 :** of or resembling a snake **2 :** abounding in snakes — **snak·i·ly** \-kə-lē\ *adv*

[1]**snap** \ˈsnap\ *vb* **snapped; snap·ping 1 a :** to close the jaws suddenly : seize something sharply with the mouth ⟨fish *snapping* at bait⟩ **b :** to grasp at something eagerly ⟨*snapped* at the chance to travel⟩ **c :** to take possession or advantage of suddenly or eagerly — usually used with *up* ⟨*snap* up a bargain⟩ **2 :** to speak or utter sharply or irritably ⟨*snap* at a friend⟩ ⟨*snapped* out an answer⟩ **3 a :** to break or break apart suddenly and especially with a sharp sound ⟨the twig *snapped*⟩ ⟨*snapped* the bone in two⟩ **b :** to give way or cause to give way suddenly under stress ⟨my nerves *snapped*⟩ ⟨the rope *snapped*⟩ **c :** to bring to a sudden end ⟨*snapped* the opposing team's winning streak⟩ **4 :** to make or cause to make a sharp or crackling sound ⟨*snap* a whip⟩ **5 a :** to close or fit in place with an abrupt movement ⟨the lid *snapped* shut⟩ **b :** to put into or remove from a position by a sudden movement or with a snapping sound ⟨*snap* off a switch⟩ **c :** to close by means of snaps or fasteners ⟨*snapped* up the back of the dress⟩ **6 :** FLASH ⟨eyes *snapping* in anger⟩ **7 a :** to move briskly or sharply ⟨*snapped* to attention⟩ **b :** to undergo a sudden and rapid change (as from one condition to another) ⟨*snapped* out of his bad mood⟩ **c :** to put (a football) in play especially by passing or handing backward between the legs **d :** to take a snapshot of [Dutch or Low German *snappen*]

[2]**snap** *n* **1 :** an abrupt closing (as of the mouth in biting or of scissors in cutting); *esp* **:** a biting or snatching with the teeth or jaws **2 :** CINCH 3a **3 :** a small amount : BIT ⟨don't care a *snap*⟩ **4 a :** a sudden snatching at something **b :** a quick short movement **c :** a sudden sharp breaking **5 :** a sound made by snapping something ⟨shut the book with a *snap*⟩ **6 :** a sudden interval of harsh weather ⟨a cold *snap*⟩ **7 :** a catch or fastening that closes or locks with a click ⟨the *snap* of a bracelet⟩ **8 :** a thin brittle cookie **9 :** SNAPSHOT **10 a :** ENERGY 2 **b :** a pleasing vigorous quality **11 :** an act or instance of snapping a football

[3]**snap** *adj* **1 :** made suddenly or without deliberation ⟨a *snap* judgment⟩ **2 :** shutting or fastening with a click or by means of a device that snaps ⟨a *snap* lock⟩ **3 :** unusually easy ⟨a *snap* course⟩

snap·back \ˈsnap-ˌbak\ *n* **:** a sudden rebound or recovery

snap back \snap-ˈbak, ˈsnap-\ *vi* **:** to make a quick or vigorous recovery ⟨*snap back* after an illness⟩

snap bean *n* **:** a bean grown primarily for its long pods cooked as a vegetable while young and tender and before the seeds have become enlarged — compare SHELL BEAN

snap·drag·on \ˈsnap-ˌdrag-ən\ *n* **:** any of a genus of herbs having showy 2-lipped flowers; *esp* **:** one of Mediterranean origin that is widely grown for its red, pink, yellow, or white flowers [from the fancied resemblance of the flowers to the face of a dragon]

snapdragon

snap·per \ˈsnap-ər\ *n, pl* **snappers 1 a :** one that snaps **b :** SNAPPING TURTLE **2** *pl also* **snapper a :** any of a large family of active flesh-eating fishes of warm seas important as food and sport fishes **b :** any of several immature fishes (as the young of the bluefish) that resemble a snapper

snapping turtle *n* **:** either of two large American freshwater turtles with powerful jaws, a long tail, and a strong musky odor

snap·pish \ˈsnap-ish\ *adj* **1 :** marked by or given to curt irritable speech : IRASCIBLE **2 :** inclined to bite ⟨a *snappish* dog⟩ — **snap·pish·ly** *adv* — **snap·pish·ness** *n*

snap·py \ˈsnap-ē\ *adj* **snap·pi·er; -est 1 :** SNAPPISH 1 **2 a :** LIVELY 4 **b :** briskly cold **c :** SMART 6a, STYLISH — **snap·pi·ly** \ˈsnap-ə-lē\ *adv* — **snap·pi·ness** \ˈsnap-ē-nəs\ *n*

snap·shot \ˈsnap-ˌshät\ *n* **:** a casual photograph made especially by an amateur with a small hand-held camera

[1]**snare** \ˈsnaər, ˈsneər\ *n* **1 :** a trap often consisting of a noose for catching small animals or birds **2 :** something by which one is entangled, trapped, or deceived **3 :** one of the catgut strings or metal spirals of a snare drum [Old English *sneare,* probably from Old Norse *snara*]

[2]**snare** *vt* **1 :** to capture or entangle by or as if by use of a snare

2 : to win or attain by skillful or deceptive maneuvers ***synonyms*** see CATCH — **snar·er** *n*

snare drum *n* : a small double-headed drum with one or more snares stretched across its lower head

[1]**snarl** \'snärl\ *n* **1** : a tangle especially of hairs or thread : KNOT **2** : a tangled situation ⟨a traffic *snarl*⟩ [Middle English *snarle* "snare, noose," probably from *snarlen,* verb]

[2]**snarl** *vb* : to become or cause to become tangled [Middle English, "to trap, entangle," probably from *snaren* "to snare"]

[3]**snarl** *vb* **1** : to growl with a snapping, gnashing, or display of teeth **2** : to express anger in a surly harsh way **3** : to utter with a snarl [obsolete *snar* "to growl"] — **snarl·er** *n*

[4]**snarl** *n* : a surly angry growl

[1]**snatch** \'snach\ *vb* **1** : to seize or try to seize something quickly or suddenly ⟨*snatched* at the rope⟩ **2** : to grasp or take suddenly without permission, ceremony, or right [Middle English *snacchen* "to snap, seize"] ***synonyms*** see TAKE — **snatch·er** *n*

[2]**snatch** *n* **1 a** : a short period ⟨slept in *snatches*⟩ **b** : something brief, fragmentary, or hurried ⟨*snatches* of old tunes⟩ **2 a** : a snatching at or of something **b** *slang* : an act or instance of kidnapping

snatchy \'snach-ē\ *adj* : marked by breaks in continuity

snaz·zy \'snaz-ē\ *adj* **snaz·zi·er; -est** : conspicuously or flashily attractive [origin unknown]

[1]**sneak** \'snēk\ *vb* **sneaked** \'snēkt\ *or* **snuck** \'snək\; **sneak·ing** **1** : to go stealthily or furtively : SLINK **2** : to put, bring, or take in a furtive or sly manner [related to Old English *snīcan* "to sneak along"] ***synonyms*** see SKULK

usage From its earliest appearance in print in the late19th century as a dialectal and probably uneducated form, the past and past participle *snuck* has risen to the status of standard and to approximate equality with *sneaked* ⟨*snuck* down the hall⟩ ⟨had quietly *snuck* in⟩, and it is continuing to grow in frequency. It is most common in the U.S. and Canada, but has also been spotted in British and Australian English.

[2]**sneak** *n* **1** : a person who acts in a stealthy, furtive, or sly manner **2** : the act or an instance of sneaking

[3]**sneak** *adj* **1** : carried on secretly : CLANDESTINE **2** : occurring without warning ⟨a *sneak* attack⟩

sneak·er \'snē-kər\ *n* **1** : one that sneaks **2** : a sports shoe with a pliable rubber sole

sneak·ing \'snē-king\ *adj* **1** : UNDERHANDED, FURTIVE **2 a** : not openly expressed or acknowledged ⟨a *sneaking* sympathy⟩ **b** : that is a persistent conjecture ⟨a *sneaking* suspicion⟩ — **sneak·ing·ly** \'snē-king-lē\ *adv*

sneak preview *n* : a special advance showing of a movie before its release for public viewing

sneak thief *n* : a thief who steals without using violence or forcibly breaking into buildings

sneaky \'snē-kē\ *adj* **sneak·i·er; -est** : UNDERHAND 1 — **sneak·i·ly** \-kə-lē\ *adv* — **sneak·i·ness** \-kē-nəs\ *n*

[1]**sneer** \'sniər\ *vb* **1** : to smile with facial contortions expressing scorn or contempt **2 a** : to speak or write in a scornfully jeering manner **b** : to express with a sneer [probably related to Middle High German *snerren* "to chatter, gossip"] ***synonyms*** see SCOFF — **sneer·er** *n*

[2]**sneer** *n* : a sneering expression or remark

[1]**sneeze** \'snēz\ *vi* : to expel the breath through the nose and mouth in a sudden violent audible spasm [Middle English *snesen,* alteration of *fnesen,* from Old English *fnēosan*] — **sneez·er** *n* — **sneeze at** : to treat as unimportant ⟨a cool million is nothing to *sneeze at*⟩

[2]**sneeze** *n* : an act or fact of sneezing

sneeze·weed \'snēz-ˌwēd\ *n* : a North American yellow-flowered perennial herb whose odor was formerly said to cause sneezing

sneezy \'snē-zē\ *adj* : given to or causing sneezing

snell \'snel\ *n* : a short line by which a fishhook is attached to a longer line [origin unknown]

[1]**snick** \'snik\ *vt* : to cut slightly : NICK [probably from obsolete *snick or snee* "to cut and thrust," from Dutch *steken of snijden* "to thrust or cut"]

[2]**snick** *n* : a slight often metallic sound : CLICK [imitative]

[1]**snick·er** \'snik-ər\ *vi* **snick·ered; snick·er·ing** \'snik-ring, -ə-ring\ : to laugh in a covert or partly suppressed way especially at the embarrassment of someone else [imitative]

[2]**snicker** *n* : an act or sound of snickering

snide \'snīd\ *adj* **1** : MEAN, LOW ⟨a *snide* trick⟩ **2** : slyly disparaging : INSINUATING ⟨*snide* remarks⟩ [origin unknown]

[1]**sniff** \'snif\ *vb* **1** : to draw air audibly up the nose especially for smelling ⟨*sniffed* at the cheese⟩ **2** : to show or express disdain or scorn ⟨*sniffed* at menial jobs⟩ **3** : to smell or take by inhalation through the nose : INHALE ⟨*sniff* perfume⟩ **4** : to detect by or as if by smelling ⟨*sniff* out trouble⟩ [Middle English *sniffen*] — **sniff·er** *n*

[2]**sniff** *n* **1** : an act or sound of sniffing **2** : an odor or amount sniffed

sniff·ish \'snif-ish\ *adj* : SNIFFY, HAUGHTY — **sniff·ish·ly** *adv* — **sniff·ish·ness** *n*

[1]**snif·fle** \'snif-əl\ *vi* **snif·fled; snif·fling** \'snif-ling, -ə-ling\ **1** : to sniff repeatedly : SNUFFLE **2** : to speak with or as if with sniffling [derived from *sniff*] — **snif·fler** \'snif-lər, -ə-lər\ *n*

[2]**sniffle** *n* **1** *pl* : a head cold marked by nasal discharge **2** : an act or sound of sniffling

sniffy \'snif-ē\ *adj* : inclined to sniff haughtily : SUPERCILIOUS — **sniff·i·ly** \'snif-ə-lē\ *adv* — **sniff·i·ness** \'snif-ē-nəs\ *n*

snif·ter \'snif-tər\ *n* : a short-stemmed goblet with a bowl narrowing toward the top [Middle English *snifteren* "to sniff, snort"]

snig·ger \'snig-ər\ *vi* **snig·gered; snig·ger·ing** \'snig-ring, -ə-ring\ : SNICKER [by alteration] — **snigger** *n*

[1]**snip** \'snip\ *n* **1** : a small piece that is snipped off; *also* : FRAGMENT **2** : an act or sound of snipping **3** : a presumptuous or impertinent person [Dutch or Low German]

[2]**snip** *vb* **snipped; snip·ping** : to cut or cut off with or as if with shears or scissors; *esp* : to clip suddenly or by bits

[1]**snipe** \'snīp\ *n, pl* **snipes** *or* **snipe** : any of several usually slender-billed birds especially of marshy areas that are related to the sandpipers [probably of Scandinavian origin]

[2]**snipe** *vi* **1** : to shoot at a person or persons from a usually concealed vantage point **2** : to aim a snide attack [earlier *snipe* "to shoot snipe"] — **snip·er** \'snī-pər\ *n*

snip·pet \'snip-ət\ *n* : a small part, piece, or thing

snip·py \'snip-ē\ *adj* **snip·pi·er; -est** **1** : SHORT-TEMPERED, SNAPPISH **2** : unduly brief or curt **3** : putting on airs — **snip·pi·ness** *n*

snips \'snips\ *n pl* : hand shears used especially for cutting sheet metal ⟨tin *snips*⟩

snit \'snit\ *n* : a state of irritated agitation [origin unknown]

[1]**snitch** \'snich\ *n* : a person who snitches : TATTLETALE, INFORMER

[2]**snitch** *vi* : INFORM, TATTLE ⟨always *snitching* on someone⟩ [origin unknown] — **snitch·er** *n*

[3]**snitch** *vt* : to take by stealth; *esp* : PILFER ⟨*snitched* a dime from me⟩ [probably alteration of *snatch*]

sniv·el \'sniv-əl\ *vi* **-eled** *or* **-elled; -el·ing** *or* **-el·ling** \'sniv-ling, -ə-ling\ **1** : to run at the nose **2** : to draw mucus up the nose audibly : SNUFFLE **3** : to cry or whine with snuffling **4** : to speak or act in a whining or weakly emotional way [Middle English *snivelen*] — **sniv·el·er** \'sniv-lər, -ə-lər\ *n*

snob \'snäb\ *n* **1** : one who obviously imitates, fawningly admires, or vulgarly seeks association with those in a superior position **2 a** : one who looks down on those in an inferior position **b** : one whose attitude is offensively superior (as in matters of taste) [obsolete *snob* "member of the lower classes," from English dialect, "shoemaker"]

snob appeal *n* : qualities in a product (as high price or foreign origin) that appeal to the snobbery in a purchaser

snob·bery \'snäb-rē, -ə-rē\ *n, pl* **-ber·ies** : snobbish conduct or outlook

snob·bish \'snäb-ish\ *adj* : being, characteristic of, or befitting a snob ⟨a *snobbish* attitude⟩ — **snob·bish·ly** *adv* — **snob·bish·ness** *n*

snob·bism \'snäb-ˌiz-əm\ *n* : SNOBBERY

snob·by \'snäb-ē\ *adj* : SNOBBISH

snood \'snüd\ *n* : a net or fabric bag pinned or tied on at the back of a woman's head for holding the hair [Old English *snōd* "hair band"]

snook \'snu̇k, 'snük\ *n, pl* **snook** *or* **snooks** : a large vigorous sport and food fish of coastal waters of the southern U.S. [Dutch *snoek*]

snook·er \'snu̇k-ər\ *n* : a variation of pool played with 15 red

\ə\ **about**	\au̇\ **out**	\i\ **tip**	\ȯ\ **saw**	\u̇\ **foot**
\ər\ **further**	\ch\ **chin**	\ī\ **life**	\ȯi\ **coin**	\y\ **yet**
\a\ **mat**	\e\ **pet**	\j\ **job**	\th\ **thin**	\yü\ **few**
\ā\ **take**	\ē\ **easy**	\ng\ **sing**	\t͟h\ **this**	\yu̇\ **cure**
\ä\ **cot, cart**	\g\ **go**	\ō\ **bone**	\ü\ **food**	\zh\ **vision**

object balls and 6 object balls of different colors [origin unknown]

¹snoop \'snüp\ *vi* : to look or pry especially in a sneaky or meddlesome way [Dutch *snoepen* "to buy or eat on the sly"] — **snoop·er** \'snü-pər\ *n*

²snoop *n* : one that snoops

snoopy \'snü-pē\ *adj* : given to snooping : PRYING

snoot \'snüt\ *n* **1** : SNOUT 1 **2** : NOSE 1a **3** : a snooty person : SNOB [Middle English *snute*]

snooty \'snüt-ē\ *adj* **snoot·i·er; -est** : haughtily contemptuous : SNOBBISH — **snoot·i·ly** \'snüt-l-ē\ *adv* — **snoot·i·ness** \'snüt-ē-nəs\ *n*

¹snooze \'snüz\ *vi* : NAP 1 [origin unknown] — **snooz·er** *n*

²snooze *n* : a short sleep : NAP

snooze button *n* : a button on an alarm clock that stops and resets the alarm for a short time later to allow for more rest — called also *snooze alarm*

snore \'snōr, 'snȯr\ *vi* : to breathe during sleep with a rough hoarse noise [Middle English *snoren*] — **snore** *n* — **snor·er** *n*

¹snor·kel \'snȯr-kəl\ *n* **1** : a tube or tubes that can be extended above the surface of the water to supply air to and remove exhaust from a submerged submarine **2** : a tube used by swimmers for breathing when the face is underwater [German *Schnorchel*]

snorkel 2

²snorkel *vi* **snor·keled; snor·kel·ing** \-kə-ling, -kling\ : to swim on the surface with the face in the water using a snorkel; *also* : to engage in skin diving

¹snort \'snȯrt\ *vb* **1 a** : to force air violently through the nose with a rough harsh sound **b** : to express scorn, anger, indignation, or surprise by a snort **2** : to express with a snort ⟨*snort* one's disgust⟩ **3** : to take in (a drug in powdered form) by inhaling through the nose [Middle English *snorten*] — **snort·er** *n*

²snort *n* **1** : an act or sound of snorting **2** : a drink of usually straight liquor taken in one draft

snot \'snät\ *n* **1** : nasal mucus **2** : a snotty person [Old English *gesnot*]

snot·ty \'snät-ē\ *adj* **snot·ti·er; -est** **1** : soiled with nasal mucus ⟨a *snotty* nose⟩ **2** : annoyingly or spitefully unpleasant; *esp* : SNOOTY ⟨a *snotty* remark⟩

snout \'snau̇t\ *n* **1 a** : a long projecting nose or muzzle (as of a pig) **b** : the projecting front of the head of various animals (as a weevil) **c** : the human nose especially when large or ugly **2** : something resembling an animal's snout [Middle English *snute*] — **snout·ed** \-əd\ *adj*

snout beetle *n* : WEEVIL

¹snow \'snō\ *n* **1 a** : small white crystals of frozen water formed directly from the water vapor of the air **b** : a fall of snow crystals : a mass of snow crystals fallen to earth **2** : something resembling snow: as **a** : a congealed or crystallized substance resembling snow in appearance ⟨carbon dioxide *snow*⟩ **b** *slang* : COCAINE **c** : small transient light or dark spots on a television or radar screen [Old English *snāw*]

²snow *vb* **1** : to fall or cause to fall in or as snow ⟨it had been *snowing* all day⟩ ⟨*snowed* messages on the senators⟩ **2 a** : to cover, shut in, or imprison with or as if with snow ⟨we were *snowed* in for two days⟩ **b** : to charm, persuade, or deceive glibly ⟨couldn't *snow* her with his compliments⟩

¹snow·ball \'snō-ˌbȯl\ *n* **1** : a round mass of snow pressed or rolled together **2** : a viburnum widely grown for its ball-shaped clusters of white flowers — called also *snowball bush*

²snowball *vb* **1** : to throw snowballs at **2** : to increase or expand at a rapidly accelerating rate

snow·bank \'snō-ˌbangk\ *n* : a mound or slope of snow

snow·ber·ry \-ˌber-ē\ *n* : a low-growing North American shrub related to the honeysuckles and having clusters of pinkish white flowers and white berries

snow·bird \-ˌbərd\ *n* : any of several small birds (as a junco) seen chiefly in winter

snow-blind \-ˌblīnd\ *or* **snow-blind·ed** \-'blīn-dəd\ *adj* : affected with snow blindness

snow blindness *n* : inflammation and inability to tolerate light caused by exposure of the eyes to ultraviolet rays reflected from snow or ice

snow·blow·er \'snō-ˌblō-ər\ *n* : a machine in which a rotating device picks up and throws snow aside

snow·board \'snō-ˌbōrd, -ˌbȯrd\ *n* : a board like a wide ski ridden in a surfing position over snow — **snowboard** *vi* — **snow·board·er** \-ˌbōrd-ər, -ˌbȯrd-ər\ *n* — **snow·board·ing** *n*

snow·bound \'snō-'bau̇nd\ *adj* : shut in or blockaded by snow

snow·cap \-ˌkap\ *n* : a covering cap of snow (as on a mountain peak) — **snow·capped** \-ˌkapt\ *adj*

snow·cat \'snō-ˌkat\ *n* : a vehicle with belted tracks for travel on snow

snow cone *n* : granular ice molded into a ball and flavored with a syrup

snow·drift \-ˌdrift\ *n* : a bank of drifted snow

snow·drop \-ˌdräp\ *n* : a European plant that is related to the amaryllises and bears nodding white flowers that often appear while snow is still on the ground

snow·fall \-ˌfȯl\ *n* **1** : a fall of snow **2** : the amount of snow that falls in a single storm or in a given period

snow fence *n* : a fence placed across the usual path of the wind to protect something (as a road) from snow drifts

snow·field \-ˌfēld\ *n* : a broad level expanse of snow; *esp* : a mass of perennial snow (as at the head of a glacier)

snow·flake \-ˌflāk\ *n* : a flake or crystal of snow

snow leopard *n* : a large cat of central Asia with long heavy grayish white fur marked with brownish black spots and rings

snow line *n* : the lower edge of an area of permanent snow (as on a mountain peak)

snow·man \'snō-ˌman\ *n* : snow shaped to resemble a person

snow·mo·bile \'snō-mō-ˌbēl\ *n* : any of various motor vehicles for travel on snow [*snow* + auto*mobile*] — **snow·mo·bil·er** \-ˌbē-lər\ *n* — **snow·mo·bil·ing** \-ˌbē-ling\ *n*

snow-on-the-mountain *n* : a spurge of the central and western U.S. with showy white-bracted flower clusters

snow pea *n* : a cultivated pea with flat edible pods; *also* : the pods

snow·plow \'snō-ˌplau̇\ *n* **1** : any of various devices used for clearing away snow **2** : a method of stopping in skiing in which the tails of the skis are pushed out to either side

¹snow·shoe \-ˌshü\ *n* : a light oval frame (as of wood or aluminum) strung with thongs that is attached to the foot to enable a person to walk on soft snow without sinking

snowshoe

²snowshoe *vi* **snow·shoed; snow·shoe·ing** : to travel on snowshoes

snowshoe hare *n* : a rather large hare of northern North America with heavy fur on the hind feet and a coat that is brown in the summer but usually white in winter — called also *snowshoe rabbit*

snow·slide \'snō-ˌslīd\ *n* : an avalanche of snow

snow·storm \-'stȯrm\ *n* : a storm of falling snow

snow·suit \-ˌsüt\ *n* : a one-piece or two-piece and usually lined garment for winter wear by children

snow thrower *n* : SNOWBLOWER

snow tire *n* : an automobile tire with a tread designed to give added traction on snow

snow under *vt* **1** : to overwhelm especially beyond capacity to absorb or deal with something **2** : to defeat by a large margin

snow-white \'snō-'hwīt, -'wīt\ *adj* : white as snow

snowy \'snō-ē\ *adj* **snow·i·er; -est** **1 a** : marked by snow ⟨a *snowy* day⟩ **b** : covered with snow ⟨*snowy* mountaintops⟩ **2** : whitened by or as if by snow ⟨an orchard *snowy* with apple blossoms⟩ **3** : SNOW-WHITE — **snow·i·ness** \'snō-ē-nəs\ *n*

snowy owl *n* : a large chiefly arctic ground-nesting owl that is white or white spotted with brown

¹snub \'snəb\ *vt* **snubbed; snub·bing** **1** : to check or stop with a cutting reply : REBUKE **2** : to check (as a line or cable that is running out) suddenly especially by turning around a fixed object (as a post) **3** : to treat with contempt or neglect **4** : to extinguish by stubbing [probably of Scandinavian origin]

²snub *n* : an act or an instance of snubbing : REBUFF

[3]snub *or* **snubbed** \ˈsnəbd\ *adj* **:** BLUNT, STUBBY ⟨a *snub* nose⟩ — **snub·ness** *n*

snub·ber \ˈsnəb-ər\ *n* **1 :** one that snubs **2 :** SHOCK ABSORBER

snub–nosed \ˈsnəb-ˈnōzd\ *adj* **:** having a stubby and usually slightly turned-up nose

snuck *past and past participle of* SNEAK ***usage*** see SNEAK

[1]snuff \ˈsnəf\ *n* **:** the charred part of the wick of a candle [Middle English *snoffe*]

[2]snuff *vt* **1 :** to cut or pinch off the snuff of (a candle) so as to brighten the light **2 :** EXTINGUISH ⟨*snuff* out a life⟩

[3]snuff *vb* **1 :** to draw forcibly through or into the nostrils **2 :** to sniff inquiringly [related to Dutch *snuffen* "to sniff, snuff"]

[4]snuff *n* **:** the act of snuffing **:** SNIFF

[5]snuff *n* **:** a preparation of finely ground or powdered tobacco to be chewed, placed against the gums, or inhaled through the nostrils [Dutch *snuf,* short for *snuftabak,* from *snuffen* "to sniff, snuff" + *tabak* "tobacco"] — **up to snuff :** meeting an acceptable standard

snuff·box \ˈsnəf-ˌbäks\ *n* **:** a small box for holding snuff

[1]snuff·er \ˈsnəf-ər\ *n* **1 :** a device somewhat like a pair of scissors for cutting and holding the snuff of a candle — usually used in plural **2 :** a device for extinguishing candles

[2]snuffer *n* **:** one that snuffs or sniffs

[1]snuf·fle \ˈsnəf-əl\ *vb* **snuf·fled; snuf·fling** \ˈsnəf-ling, -ə-ling\ **1 :** to snuff or sniff usually noisily and repeatedly **2 :** to breathe through a partly blocked nose with a sniffing sound **3 :** to speak in a nasal tone; *also* **:** WHIMPER, WHINE [related to Dutch *snuffelen* "to snuffle"] — **snuf·fler** \ˈsnəf-lər, -ə-lər\ *n*

[2]snuffle *n* **:** the sound made in snuffling

[1]snug \ˈsnəg\ *adj* **snug·ger; snug·gest 1 a :** SEAWORTHY **b :** fitting closely and comfortably ⟨a *snug* coat⟩ **2 :** enjoying or affording warm secure shelter and comfort **:** COZY ⟨a *snug* cottage⟩ **3 :** offering safe concealment ⟨a *snug* hideout⟩ [perhaps of Scandinavian origin] — **snug** *adv* — **snug·ly** *adv* — **snug·ness** *n*

[2]snug *vb* **snugged; snug·ging 1 :** to settle or lie down **:** NESTLE **2 :** to make snug

snug·gery \ˈsnəg-rē, -ə-rē\ *n, pl* **-ger·ies** *chiefly British* **:** a snug cozy place; *esp* **:** a small comfortable room

snug·gle \ˈsnəg-əl\ *vb* **snug·gled; snug·gling** \ˈsnəg-ling, -ə-ling\ **1 :** to curl up comfortably or cozily **2 :** to draw close especially for comfort or in affection [derived from *[2]snug*]

[1]so \sō, ˈsō, *especially before an adj or adv followed by "that"* sə\ *adv* **1 a :** in a manner or way that is indicated or suggested ⟨do you really think *so*⟩ ⟨it *so* happened that all were wrong⟩ — often used as a substitute for a preceding clause ⟨I didn't like it and I told her *so*⟩ **b :** in the same manner or way **:** ALSO ⟨you worked hard and *so* did we⟩ **c :** SUBSEQUENTLY, THEN ⟨and *so* home and to bed⟩ **2 a :** to an indicated or suggested extent or degree ⟨had never been *so* happy⟩ **b :** to a great extent or degree **:** VERY, EXTREMELY ⟨we loved her *so*⟩ **c :** to a definite but unspecified extent or degree ⟨can only do *so* much in a day⟩ **d :** most certainly **:** INDEED ⟨you did *so* do it⟩ **e :** most decidedly **:** SURELY ⟨I *so* don't believe you⟩ **3 :** THEREFORE, CONSEQUENTLY ⟨the witness was biased and *so* unreliable⟩ [Old English *swā*]

[2]so \sō, ˈsō\ *conj* **1 a :** with the result that ⟨your diction is good, *so* every word is clear⟩ **b :** in order that ⟨be quiet *so* that I can sleep⟩ **2** *archaic* **:** provided that **3 a :** for that reason **:** THEREFORE ⟨I want to go, *so* I will⟩ **b** (1) — used as an introductory particle ⟨*so* here we are⟩ often to belittle a point being discussed ⟨*so* what?⟩ (2) — used interjectionally to indicate awareness of a discovery ⟨*so,* that's who did it⟩ — **so as to :** in order to ⟨keep quiet *so as to* not attract attention⟩

[3]so \ˈsō\ *adj* **1 :** conforming with actual facts **:** TRUE ⟨said things that were not *so*⟩ **2 :** marked by a definite order ⟨your books are always just *so*⟩

[4]so \ˌsō, ˈsō\ *pron* **1 :** such as has been specified **:** the same ⟨if you have to sign up for the trip, do *so* as soon as possible⟩ **2 :** approximately that ⟨20 years or *so*⟩

[5]so *variant of* SOL

[1]soak \ˈsōk\ *vb* **1 a :** to remain steeping in liquid (as water) **b :** to place in a medium to wet or permeate thoroughly **2 a :** to enter or pass through something by or as if by pores **:** SATURATE **b :** to capture one's full attention ⟨let the remark *soak* in⟩ **3 :** to extract by or as if by steeping ⟨*soak* the dirt out⟩ **4 :** to draw in by or as if by suction or absorption ⟨*soaked* up the sunshine⟩ **5 :** to levy an exorbitant charge against ⟨*soaked* the taxpayers⟩ [Old English *socian*] — **soak·er** *n*

synonyms SOAK, SATURATE, DRENCH, STEEP, IMPREGNATE mean to permeate or be permeated with a liquid. SOAK implies usually prolonged immersion as for softening or cleansing ⟨*soak* the rags in soapy water⟩. SATURATE implies a resulting effect of complete absorption until no more liquid can be held ⟨the sponge is *saturated* with liquid⟩. DRENCH implies a thorough wetting by something that pours down or is poured ⟨clothes *drenched* by a heavy rain⟩. STEEP suggests either the extraction of an essence (as of tea leaves) by the liquid or the imparting of a quality (as a color) to the thing immersed ⟨*steep* the tea for five minutes⟩. IMPREGNATE implies a thorough penetration of one thing by another ⟨fabric *impregnated* with resin⟩

[2]soak *n* **1 :** the act or process of soaking **:** the state of being soaked **2 :** DRUNKARD

soak·age \ˈsō-kij\ *n* **1 :** liquid gained by absorption or lost by seepage **2 :** the act or process of soaking **:** the state of being soaked

so–and–so \ˈsō-ən-ˌsō\ *n, pl* **so–and–sos** *or* **so–and–so's** \-ən-ˌsōz\ **:** an unnamed or unspecified person or thing

[1]soap \ˈsōp\ *n* **1 :** a substance that is usually made by the action of alkali on fat, dissolves in water, and is used for washing **2 :** a salt of a fatty acid **3 :** SOAP OPERA [Old English *sāpe*]

[2]soap *vt* **:** to rub soap over or into

soap·ber·ry \ˈsōp-ˌber-ē\ *n* **:** any of a genus of chiefly tropical woody plants; *also* **:** the fruit of a soapberry and especially one used as a soap substitute

soap·box \-ˌbäks\ *n* **:** an improvised platform used by a self-appointed, spontaneous, or informal speaker — **soapbox** *adj*

Soap Box Derby *service mark* — used for a downhill race for youngsters' homemade racing cars without motors or pedals

soap bubble *n* **:** a hollow iridescent globe formed by blowing a film of soapsuds (as from a pipe)

soap opera *n* **:** a radio or television serial drama performed usually on a daytime commerical program [from its sponsorship by soap manufacturers]

soap plant *n* **:** a plant with a part (as leaves or root) that can be used as a soap substitute

soap·stone \ˈsōp-ˌstōn\ *n* **:** a soft stone having a soapy feel and composed essentially of talc, chlorite, and often some magnetite

soap·suds \-ˌsədz\ *n pl* **:** SUDS 1

soap·wort \-ˌwərt, -ˌwȯrt\ *n* **:** BOUNCING BET

soapy \ˈsō-pē\ *adj* **soap·i·er; -est 1 :** smeared with or full of soap ⟨a *soapy* face⟩ **2 :** containing or combined with soap ⟨*soapy* ammonia⟩ **3 :** resembling or having the qualities of soap — **soap·i·ly** \-pə-lē\ *adv* — **soap·i·ness** \-pē-nəs\ *n*

[1]soar \ˈsōr, ˈsȯr\ *vi* **1 a :** to fly aloft or about ⟨the plane *soared* into the sky⟩ **b :** to sail or hover in the air often at a great height **:** GLIDE ⟨vultures *soaring* over the plain⟩ **2 :** to rise or increase dramatically (as in position, value, or price) ⟨stocks *soared*⟩ **3 :** to ascend to a higher or more exalted level ⟨made my spirits *soar*⟩ **4 :** to rise majestically ⟨mountains *soar* towards the sky⟩ [Middle French *essorer* "to air, soar," derived from Latin *ex-* + *aura* "air"] — **soar·er** *n*

[2]soar *n* **:** the act of soaring **:** upward flight

[1]sob \ˈsäb\ *vb* **sobbed; sob·bing 1 :** to weep with convulsive catching of the breath **2 :** to make a sound like that of sobbing ⟨the wind *sobbed* through the trees⟩ **3 :** to bring to a specified state by sobbing ⟨*sobbed* myself to sleep⟩ **4 :** to utter with sobs ⟨*sobbed* out the story⟩ [Middle English *sobben*]

[2]sob *n* **1 :** an act of sobbing **2 :** a sound of or like that of sobbing

[1]so·ber \ˈsō-bər\ *adj* **so·ber·er** \-bər-ər\; **so·ber·est** \-bə-rəst, -brəst\ **1 a :** sparing or temperate in the use of food and drink **b :** not drunk **2 :** SERIOUS 1 **3 :** subdued in tone, color, or intensity **4 :** having or showing self-control **:** avoiding extremes of behavior [Medieval French *sobre,* from Latin *sobrius*] — **so·ber·ly** \-bər-lē\ *adv* — **so·ber·ness** *n*

[2]sober *vb* **so·bered; so·ber·ing** \-bə-ring, -bring\ **:** to make or become sober — often used with *up*

so·ber·sid·ed \ˌsō-bər-ˈsīd-əd\ *adj* **:** SERIOUS 1

so·ber·sides \ˈsō-bər-ˈsīdz\ *n sing or pl* **:** one who is sobersided

\ə\ abut	\au̇\ out	\i\ tip	\ȯ\ saw	\u̇\ foot
\ər\ further	\ch\ chin	\ī\ life	\ȯi\ coin	\y\ yet
\a\ mat	\e\ pet	\j\ job	\th\ thin	\yü\ few
\ā\ take	\ē\ easy	\ng\ sing	\t͟h\ this	\yu̇\ cure
\ä\ cot, cart	\g\ go	\ō\ bone	\ü\ food	\zh\ vision

so·bri·e·ty \sə-ˈbrī-ət-ē\ *n* **:** the state of being sober [Medieval French *sobreté,* from Latin *sobrietas,* from *sobrius* "sober"]

so·bri·quet \ˈsō-bri-ˌkā, -ˌket, ˌsō-bri-ˈ\ *also* **sou·bri·quet** \ˈsō-, ˌsō-, ˈsü-, ˌsü-\ *n* **:** a fanciful name or epithet [French]

sob story *n* **:** a sad story designed chiefly to evoke sympathy

so–called \ˈsō-ˈkȯld\ *adj* **1 :** commonly or popularly named ⟨the *so-called* pocket veto⟩ **2 :** falsely or inaccurately named ⟨your *so-called* friend⟩

soc·cer \ˈsäk-ər\ *n* **:** a game with two teams of 11 players in which a round ball is advanced by kicking or by propelling it with any part of the body except the hands and arms [by shortening and alteration from *association football*]

so·cia·bil·i·ty \ˌsō-shə-ˈbil-ət-ē\ *n, pl* **-ties :** the quality or state of being sociable **:** AFFABILITY; *also* **:** the act or an instance of being sociable

1so·cia·ble \ˈsō-shə-bəl\ *adj* **1 :** inclined to seek or enjoy companionship **:** AFFABLE, FRIENDLY ⟨*sociable* people⟩ **2 :** leading to friendliness or pleasant social relations [Latin *sociabilis,* from *sociare* "to join, associate," from *socius* "companion"] — **so·cia·ble·ness** *n* — **so·cia·bly** \-blē\ *adv*

2sociable *n* **:** SOCIAL

1so·cial \ˈsō-shəl\ *adj* **1 a :** marked by, devoted to, or engaged in for sociability ⟨*social* events⟩ ⟨my *social* life⟩ **b :** SOCIABLE 1 **2 :** of or relating to human society, the interaction of the group and its members, and the welfare of these members ⟨*social* institutions⟩ ⟨*social* legislation⟩ **3 a :** tending to form cooperative and interdependent relationships with one's fellows ⟨humans are *social* beings⟩ **b :** naturally living or growing in groups or communities ⟨bees are *social* insects⟩ **4 :** of, relating to, or based on status in a particular society ⟨different *social* circles⟩; *also* **:** of or relating to fashionable society ⟨a *social* leader⟩ [Latin *socialis,* from *socius* "companion, associate"]

2social *n* **:** an informal social gathering frequently involving a special activity or interest ⟨an ice cream *social*⟩

social climber *n* **:** one who attempts to gain a higher social position or acceptance in fashionable society

social democracy *n* **:** a political movement that uses principles of democracy to change a capitalist country to a socialist one — **social democrat** *n* — **social democratic** *adj*

social disease *n* **1 :** VENEREAL DISEASE **2 :** a disease (as tuberculosis) whose frequency is directly related to social and economic factors

so·cial·ism \ˈsō-shə-ˌliz-əm\ *n* **1 :** any of various economic and political theories or social systems based on collective or governmental ownership and administration of the means of production and distribution of goods **2 :** a stage of society in Marxist theory transitional between capitalism and communism and distinguished by unequal distribution of goods and pay according to work done — **so·cial·ist** \ˈsōsh-ləst, -ə-ləst\ *n* — **socialist** *or* **so·cial·is·tic** \ˌsō-shə-ˈlis-tik\ *adj* — **so·cial·is·ti·cal·ly** \-ti-kə-lē, -klē\ *adv*

so·cial·ite \ˈsō-shə-ˌlīt\ *n* **:** a socially prominent person

so·ci·al·i·ty \ˌsō-shē-ˈal-ət-ē\ *n, pl* **-ties 1 :** SOCIABILITY **2 :** the tendency to associate in or to form social groups

so·cial·ize \ˈsō-shə-ˌlīz\ *vb* **1 :** to make social; *esp* **:** to fit or train for a social environment **2 a :** to set up on a socialistic basis ⟨*socialize* industry⟩ **b :** to adapt to social needs and uses ⟨*socialize* science⟩ **3 :** to participate in social activities ⟨*socializing* with friends after work⟩ — **so·cial·iza·tion** \ˌsō-shə-lə-ˈzā-shən\ *n* — **so·cial·iz·er** \ˈsō-shə-ˌlī-zər\ *n*

socialized medicine *n* **:** medical and hospital services for the members of a class or population administered by an organized group (as a state agency) and paid for from funds obtained usually by assessments, philanthropy, or taxation

so·cial·ly \ˈsōsh-lē, -ə-lē\ *adv* **1 :** in a social manner ⟨birds living *socially* together⟩ **2 :** with respect to society ⟨*socially* disadvantaged⟩ **3 :** by or through society ⟨*socially* prescribed values⟩

social media *n pl but sing or pl in constr* **:** forms of electronic communication (as Web sites for social networking and microblogging) through which users create online communities to share information, ideas, personal messages, and other content (as videos)

so·cial–mind·ed \ˌsō-shəl-ˈmīn-dəd\ *adj* **:** having an interest in society; *esp* **:** actively interested in social welfare or the well-being of society as a whole

social networking *n* **:** the creation and maintenance of personal and business relationships especially online

social science *n* **1 :** a science (as psychology or sociology) that deals with the institutions and functioning of human society and with the interrelationships of individuals as members of society **2 :** a science (as economics) dealing with a particular phase or aspect of human society — **social scientist** *n*

social secretary *n* **:** a personal secretary employed to handle social correspondence and appointments

social security *n* **1 :** the principle or practice or a program of public provision for the economic security and social welfare of the individual and the family; *esp, cap both Ss* **:** a U.S. government program established in 1935 to include old-age and survivors insurance, contributions to state unemployment insurance, and old-age assistance **2 :** money paid out through a Social Security program ⟨began collecting *social security*⟩

social service *n* **:** an activity (as counseling, financial assistance, or job training) designed to promote social well-being (as of the economically, socially, or physically disadvantaged)

social studies *n pl* **:** studies (as history, civics, and geography) that deal with human relationships and the functions of society

social welfare *n* **:** organized public or private social services for the assistance of disadvantaged groups

social work *n* **:** any of various professional activities or methods concerned especially with providing social services — **social worker** *n*

1so·ci·ety \sə-ˈsī-ət-ē\ *n, pl* **-et·ies 1 :** companionship with one's associates **:** COMPANY **2 :** the social order or community life considered as a system within which the individual lives ⟨rural *society*⟩ **3 :** people in general ⟨the benefit of *society*⟩ **4 :** an association of persons for some purpose ⟨a mutual aid *society*⟩ **5 :** a part of a community regarded as a unit distinguished by common interests or standards; *esp* **:** the group or set of fashionable persons **6 :** a system of interdependent organisms or biological units; *also* **:** an assemblage of plants usually of a single species or habit within a larger ecological community [Middle French *societé,* from Latin *societas,* from *socius* "companion"] — **so·ci·etal** \-ət-l\ *adj*

2society *adj* **:** of, relating to, or typical of fashionable society

so·cio·eco·nom·ic \ˌsō-sē-ō-ˌek-ə-ˈnäm-ik, ˌsō-shē-, -ˌē-kə-\ *adj* **:** of, relating to, or involving a combination of social and economic factors

so·ci·ol·o·gy \ˌsō-sē-ˈäl-ə-jē, -shē-\ *n* **:** the science of society, social institutions, and social relationships [French *sociologie,* from Latin *socius* "companion"] — **so·cio·log·i·cal** \ˌsō-sē-ə-ˈläj-i-kəl, -shē-\ *also* **so·cio·log·ic** \-ə-ˈläj-ik\ *adj* — **so·cio·log·i·cal·ly** \-i-kə-lē, -klē\ *adv* — **so·ci·ol·o·gist** \-ˈäl-ə-jəst\ *n*

so·cio·path·ic \ˌsō-sē-ō-ˈpath-ik, ˌsō-shē-\ *adj* **:** of, relating to, or characterized by asocial or antisocial behavior — **so·cio·path** \ˈsō-sē-ə-ˌpath, ˈsō-shē-\ *n*

so·cio·po·lit·i·cal \ˌsō-sē-ō-pə-ˈlit-i-kəl, ˌsō-shē-\ *adj* **:** of, relating to, or involving both social and political factors

1sock \ˈsäk\ *n, pl* **socks** *also* **sox** \ˈsäks\ **:** a piece of clothing worn on the foot and usually extending above the ankle and sometimes to the knee [Old English *socc* "low shoe," from Latin *soccus*]

2sock *vb* **:** to hit hard **:** deliver a blow [origin unknown]

3sock *n* **:** a vigorous or violent blow **:** PUNCH

sock·et \ˈsäk-ət\ *n* **:** an opening or hollow that receives and holds something ⟨the eye *socket*⟩ ⟨screwed the lightbulb into the *socket*⟩ [Medieval French *soket* "small plowshare," from Medieval French *soc* "plowshare"]

socket wrench *n* **:** a wrench usually in the form of a bar and removable socket made to fit a bolt or nut

sock·eye salmon \ˈsäk-ˌī-\ *n* **:** a commercially important Pacific salmon that is red with a greenish head when mature — called also *red salmon, sockeye* [by folk etymology from Northern Straits (American Indian language of southern Vancouver Island and nearby islands) *sə́qəy̓*]

So·crat·ic \sə-ˈkrat-ik\ *adj* **:** of or relating to Socrates, his followers, or his philosophical method of systematic doubt and questioning of another

socket wrench

1sod \ˈsäd\ *n* **1 a :** TURF 1a **b :** the grass-and forb-covered surface of the ground **2 :** one's native land [Dutch or Low German *sode*]

2sod *vt* **sod·ded; sod·ding :** to cover with sod or turfs

so·da \ˈsōd-ə\ *n* **1 a :** SODIUM CARBONATE **b :** SODIUM BICAR-

BONATE **c** : SODIUM — used in combination ⟨*soda* alum⟩ **2 a** : SODA WATER **b** : SODA POP **c** : a sweet drink consisting of soda water, flavoring, and often ice cream [Italian, from Arabic *suwwād,* a plant from the ashes of which sodium carbonate is obtained]

soda ash *n* : commercial sodium carbonate

soda cracker *n* : a cracker leavened with bicarbonate of soda and cream of tartar

soda fountain *n* **1** : an apparatus for drawing soda water **2** : the equipment and counter for the preparation and serving of sodas, sundaes, and ice cream

soda jerk *n* : one who dispenses carbonated drinks and ice cream at a soda fountain

soda lime *n* : a mixture of sodium hydroxide and slaked lime used especially to absorb moisture and gases

so·da·list \ˈsōd-l-əst, sō-ˈdal-\ *n* : a sodality member

so·dal·i·ty \sō-ˈdal-ət-ē\ *n, pl* **-ties** : an organized society or fellowship; *esp* : a devotional or charitable association of Roman Catholic laity [Latin *sodalitas* "comradeship, club," from *sodalis* "comrade"]

soda pop *n* : a bottled soft drink consisting of soda water with added flavoring and a sweet syrup

soda water *n* : a beverage consisting of water highly charged with carbonic acid gas

sod·den \ˈsäd-n\ *adj* **1 a** : dull or lacking in expression ⟨*sodden* features⟩ **b** : SLUGGISH, UNIMAGINATIVE ⟨*sodden* minds⟩ **2** : heavy with moisture : SATURATED ⟨*sodden* ground⟩ [Middle English *soden,* from past participle of *sethen* "to seethe"] — **sod·den·ly** *adv* — **sod·den·ness** \-n-nəs, -n-əs\ *n*

so·di·um \ˈsōd-ē-əm\ *n* : a soft waxy silver-white metallic element that is chemically very active and is found abundantly in nature in combined form — see ELEMENT table [New Latin, from English *soda*]

sodium ben·zo·ate \-ˈben-zə-ˌwāt\ *n* : a crystalline or granular sodium salt $NaC_7H_5O_2$ used chiefly as a food preservative

sodium bicarbonate *n* : a white crystalline weakly alkaline salt $NaHCO_3$ used especially in baking powders and fire extinguishers and in medicine as an antacid — called also *baking soda, bicarbonate of soda*

sodium carbonate *n* : a sodium salt of carbonic acid; *esp* : a strongly alkaline compound Na_2CO_3 used in making soaps and chemicals, in water softening, in cleaning and bleaching, and in photography

sodium chloride *n* : an ionic chemical compound NaCl that consists of crystals having equal numbers of sodium and chlorine atoms : SALT 1a

sodium citrate *n* : a crystalline salt $Na_3C_6H_5O_7$ used chiefly to prevent stored blood from clotting

sodium cyanide *n* : a white poisonous salt NaCN used especially in electroplating, fumigating, and treating steel

sodium fluoride *n* : a poisonous crystalline salt NaF that is used as a pesticide and in trace amounts in the fluoridation of drinking water and toothpastes

sodium hydroxide *n* : a white brittle solid NaOH that is a strong caustic base used in making soap, rayon, and paper

sodium hypochlorite *n* : an unstable salt NaOCl used as a bleaching agent and disinfectant

sodium nitrate *n* : a deliquescent crystalline salt $NaNO_3$ used as a fertilizer, an oxidizing agent, and meat preservative

sodium nitrite *n* : a salt $NaNO_2$ used especially in dye manufacturing and as a meat preservative

sodium pump *n* : a molecular mechanism that uses the energy supplied by ATP to transport sodium ions out of a cell and potassium ions into a cell to create a difference in electrical charge on either side of the cell membrane which is necessary for various cell functions (as conduction of nerve impulses) — called also *sodium-potassium pump*

sodium silicate *n* : WATER GLASS 3

sodium sulfate *n* : a bitter salt Na_2SO_4 used especially in detergents, in the manufacture of wood pulp and rayon, and in dyeing and finishing textiles

sodium thiosulfate *n* : a hygroscopic crystalline salt $Na_2S_2O_3$ used especially as a photographic fixing agent and as a reducing or bleaching agent

sodium–vapor lamp *n* : an electric lamp that contains sodium vapor and electrodes between which a luminous discharge takes place

Sod·om \ˈsäd-əm\ *n* : a place notorious for vice or corruption [*Sodom,* city of ancient Palestine destroyed by God for its wickedness (Genesis 18:20, 21; 19:24–28)]

so·fa \ˈsō-fə\ *n* : a long upholstered seat usually with arms and a back and often convertible into a bed [Arabic *ṣuffah* "long bench"]

so far as *conj* : insofar as

sof·fit \ˈsäf-ət\ *n* : the underside of a part or member of a building and especially of an arch [French *soffite,* from Italian *soffitto,* derived from Latin *suffigere* "to fasten underneath"]

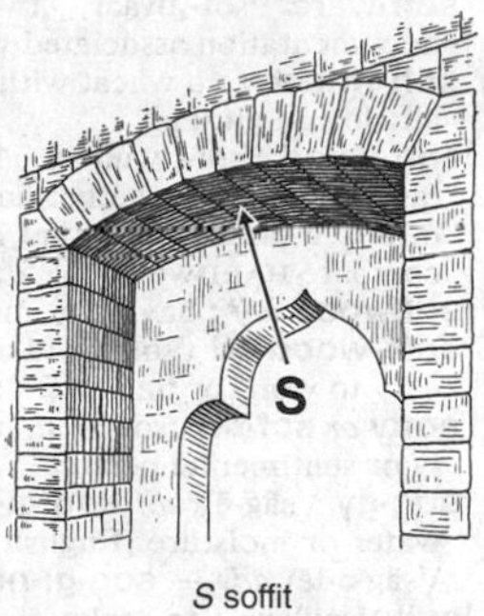

S soffit

soft \ˈsȯft\ *adj* **1 a** : having a pleasing, comfortable, or soothing quality or effect : GENTLE, MILD ⟨*soft* breezes⟩ **b** : quiet in pitch or volume ⟨*soft* voices⟩ **c** : not bright or glaring ⟨*soft* lighting⟩ **d** : demanding little effort : EASY ⟨a *soft* job⟩ **e** : smooth or delicate in appearance or texture ⟨*soft* cashmere⟩ **f** : pleasingly mild in taste or odor **2 a** : having a mild gentle nature : DOCILE **b** : lacking in strength or vigor : unfit for prolonged exertion or severe stress : FEEBLE ⟨*soft* from good living⟩ **c** : weak or deficient mentally **d** : advocating or being a moderate or conciliatory policy ⟨took a *soft* stand toward the rebels⟩ **3 a** : yielding to physical pressure ⟨a *soft* mattress⟩ **b** : relatively lacking in hardness ⟨*soft* wood⟩ **4** : gently or gradually curved or rounded : not harsh or jagged **5** : sounding as in *ace* and *gem* respectively — used of *c* and *g* **6** : deficient in or free from substances (as calcium and magnesium salts) that prevent lathering of soap ⟨*soft* water⟩ **7** : having relatively low penetrating power ⟨*soft* X-rays⟩ **8** : occurring at such a speed as to avoid destructive impact ⟨*soft* landing of a spacecraft on the moon⟩ [Old English *sēfte, sōfte*] — **soft·ly** \ˈsȯft-lē\ *or* **soft** *adv* — **soft·ness** \ˈsȯft-nəs, ˈsȯf-\ *n*

soft·ball \ˈsȯft-ˌbȯl, ˈsȯf-\ *n* : a variation of baseball played on a smaller diamond with a larger ball that is pitched underhanded; *also* : the ball used in this game

soft–boiled \-ˈbȯild\ *adj, of an egg* : boiled to a soft consistency

soft coal *n* : BITUMINOUS COAL

soft drink *n* : a sweet flavored often carbonated nonalcoholic beverage; *esp* : SODA POP

soft·en \ˈsȯ-fən\ *vb* **soft·ened; soft·en·ing** \ˈsȯf-ning, -ə-ning\ **1** : to make or become soft or softer **2** : to lessen the strength or resistance of — **soft·en·er** \ˈsȯf-nər, -ə-nər\ *n*

soft·head·ed \ˈsȯft-ˈhed-əd\ *adj* : having a weak, unrealistic, or uncritical mind : IMPRACTICAL — **soft·head·ed·ness** *n*

soft·heart·ed \-ˈhärt-əd\ *adj* : emotionally responsive : SYMPATHETIC — **soft·heart·ed·ly** *adv* — **soft·heart·ed·ness** *n*

soft–land \-ˈland\ *vb* : to make or cause to make a soft landing on a celestial body (as the moon) — **soft–land·er** *n*

soft palate *n* : a fold at the back of the hard palate that partially separates the mouth from the pharynx

soft–ped·al \ˈsȯft-ˈped-l, ˈsȯf-\ *vt* **1** : to use the soft pedal in playing **2** : PLAY DOWN ⟨*soft-pedal* the issue⟩

soft pedal *n* : a foot pedal on a piano that reduces the volume of sound

soft rot *n* : a mushy, watery, or slimy decay of a plant or plant part usually caused by bacteria or fungi

soft sell *n* : the use of suggestion or persuasion in selling rather than aggressive pressure

soft–serve \ˈsȯft-ˌsərv\ *n* : smooth semisolid ice cream made in and dispensed from a freezer in which it is aerated and continuously churned

soft–shell \ˈsȯft-ˌshel, ˈsȯf-\ *or* **soft–shelled** \-ˈsheld\ *adj* : having a soft or fragile shell especially as a result of recent shedding ⟨*soft-shell* crabs⟩

soft–shoe \ˈsȯft-ˈshü, ˈsȯf-\ *adj* : of or relating to tap dancing done in soft-soled shoes without metal taps

\ə\ **abut**	\au̇\ **out**	\i\ **tip**	\ȯi\ **saw**	\u̇\ **foot**
\ər\ **further**	\ch\ **chin**	\ī\ **life**	\ȯi\ **coin**	\y\ **yet**
\a\ **mat**	\e\ **pet**	\j\ **job**	\th\ **thin**	\yü\ **few**
\ā\ **take**	\ē\ **easy**	\ng\ **sing**	\t͟h\ **this**	\yu̇\ **cure**
\ä\ **cot, cart**	\g\ **go**	\ō\ **bone**	\ü\ **food**	\zh\ **vision**

soft–soap \-ˈsōp\ *vb* : to soothe or coax with flattery — **soft–soap·er** *n*

soft soap *n* **1** : a semifluid soap **2** : FLATTERY 2

soft–spo·ken \ˈsȯft-ˈspō-kən, ˈsȯf-\ *adj* : having a mild or gentle voice

soft·ware \ˈsȯf-ˌtwaər, -ˌtweər\ *n* : the programs and related documentation associated with a computer system

soft wheat *n* : a wheat with soft kernels high in starch but usually low in gluten

¹soft·wood \ˈsȯf-ˌtwu̇d\ *n* **1** : the wood of a cone-bearing tree (as a pine or fir) whether hard or soft as distinguished from that of a tree (as a maple) that is a broad-leaved flowering plant — compare HARDWOOD 1 **2** : a tree that yields softwood

²softwood *adj* : having or made of softwood

soft–wood·ed \ˈsȯf-ˈtwu̇d-əd\ *adj* **1** : having soft wood that is easy to work or finish **2** : SOFTWOOD

softy *or* **sof·tie** \ˈsȯf-tē\ *n, pl* **sof·ties** **1** : WEAKLING **2** : a silly or sentimental person

sog·gy \ˈsäg-ē\ *adj* **sog·gi·er; -est** : saturated or heavy with water or moisture [English dialect *sog* "to soak"] — **sog·gi·ly** \ˈsäg-ə-lē\ *adv* — **sog·gi·ness** \ˈsäg-ē-nəs\ *n*

¹soil \ˈsȯil\ *vb* : to make or become dirty or corrupt [Medieval French *soiller* "to wallow, soil," from *soil* "pigsty," from Latin *solium* "chair, bathtub"]

²soil *n* **1 a** : SOILAGE, STAIN **b** : moral defilement : CORRUPTION **2** : something that soils or pollutes

³soil *n* **1** : firm land : EARTH **2** : the loose surface material of the earth in which plants grow **3** : COUNTRY 2a, LAND ⟨our native *soil*⟩ **4** : the agricultural life or calling **5** : a medium in which something may take root and grow ⟨slums are fertile *soil* for crime⟩ [Medieval French, "soil, piece of land," from Latin *solea* "sandal, foundation timber"]

soil·age \ˈsȯi-lij\ *n* : the act of soiling : the condition of being soiled

soil·less \ˈsȯil-ləs\ *adj* : carried on without soil ⟨*soilless* agriculture⟩

soil science *n* : the science of soils — **soil scientist** *n*

soi·ree *or* **soi·rée** \swä-ˈrā\ *n* : an evening party or reception [French *soirée* "evening period, evening party," from *soir* "evening," from Latin *sero* "at a late hour," from *serus* "late"]

¹so·journ \ˈsō-ˌjərn, sō-ˈ\ *n* : a temporary stay [Medieval French *sujur, sujurn,* from *sujurner* "to sojourn," derived from Latin *sub* "under, during" + Late Latin *diurnum* "day"]

²sojourn *vi* : to stay as a temporary resident — **so·journ·er** *n*

¹sol \ˈsōl\ *also* **so** \ˈsō\ *n* : the 5th note of the diatonic scale [Medieval Latin]

²sol \ˈsäl, ˈsōl\ *n, pl* **so·les** \ˈsō-ˌlās\ **1** : the basic monetary unit of Peru **2** : a coin representing one sol [American Spanish, from Spanish, "sun," from Latin]

³sol \ˈsäl, ˈsȯl\ *n* : a fluid colloidal system [*solution*]

Sol \ˈsäl\ *n* : SUN 1a [Latin]

¹sol·ace \ˈsäl-əs\ *n* : a relieving of grief or anxiety or a source of this [Medieval French *solas,* from Latin *solacium,* from *solari* "to console"]

²solace *vt* **1** : to give solace to **2** : to make cheerful **3** : ALLAY, SOOTHE ⟨*solace* grief⟩ — **sol·ac·er** *n*

so·la·num \sə-ˈlā-nəm, -ˈlän-, -ˈlan-\ *n* : NIGHTSHADE 1 [Latin, "nightshade"]

so·lar \ˈsō-lər, -ˌlär\ *adj* **1** : of, derived from, relating to, or caused by the sun **2** : measured by the earth's course in relation to the sun ⟨*solar* time⟩ ⟨*solar* year⟩ **3 a** : produced or operated by the action of the sun's light or heat ⟨*solar* energy⟩ **b** : using the sun's rays especially to produce heat or electricity ⟨a *solar* house⟩ [Latin *solaris,* from *sol* "sun"]

solar cell *n* : a photoelectric cell that converts sunlight into electrical energy and is used as a power source

solar collector *n* : any of various devices for the absorption of solar radiation for the heating of water or buildings or the production of electricity

solar eclipse *n* : an eclipse of the sun by the moon

solar flare *n* : a sudden temporary outburst of gases from a small area of the sun's surface

so·lar·i·um \sō-ˈlar-ē-əm, sə-, -ˈler-\ *n, pl* **-ia** \-ē-ə\ *also* **-i·ums** : a room exposed to the sun [Latin, from *sol* "sun"]

solar mass *n* : the mass of the sun used as a unit for the expression of the masses of other celestial objects and equal to about 2 x 10^{30} kilograms

solar panel *n* : a group of solar cells forming a flat surface (as on a spacecraft)

so·lar plexus \ˈsō-lər-\ *n* **1** : a nerve plexus in the abdomen behind the stomach and in front of the aorta that contains ganglia distributing nerve fibers to the internal organs of the abdomen **2** : the pit of the stomach [from the radiating nerve fibers]

solar system *n* : a star with the group of heavenly bodies that revolve around it; *esp* : the sun with the planets, moons, asteroids, and comets that orbit it

solar wind *n* : plasma continuously ejected from the sun's surface into interplanetary space

sold *past of* SELL

¹sol·der \ˈsäd-ər, ˈsȯd-\ *n* : a metal or metallic alloy used when melted to join metallic surfaces; *esp* : an alloy of lead and tin so used [Medieval French *soudure,* from *souder* "to solder," from Latin *solidare* "to make solid," from *solidus* "solid"]

²solder *vb* **sol·dered; sol·der·ing** \ˈsäd-ring, ˈsȯd-, -ə-ring\ **1** : to unite or repair with solder **2** : to become joined or renewed by or as if by the use of solder — **sol·der·er** \-ər-ər\ *n*

soldering iron *n* : a metal device for applying heat in soldering

¹sol·dier \ˈsōl-jər\ *n* **1 a** : one engaged in military service and especially in the army **b** : an enlisted person **2** : a worker in a cause ⟨*soldiers* in the fight against hunger⟩ **3** : a termite or ant with a large head and jaws that is a member of a caste that protects the colony [Medieval French *soudeer, soudeour* "mercenary," from *soudee* "shilling's worth, pay," from *sou, soud* "shilling," from Late Latin *solidus,* a kind of coin, from Latin, "solid"] — **sol·dier·ly** \-lē\ *adj*

²soldier *vi* **sol·diered; sol·dier·ing** \ˈsōlj-ring, -ə-ring\ **1** : to serve as or act like a soldier **2** : to make a show of activity while really loafing

soldier of fortune : one who follows a military career wherever there is promise of profit, adventure, or pleasure

sol·diery \ˈsōlj-rē, -ə-rē\ *n, pl* **-dier·ies** : a body of soldiers

¹sole \ˈsōl\ *n* **1** : the undersurface of a foot **2** : the part of footwear on which the sole of the foot rests **3** : the bottom or lower part of something : the base on which something rests [Medieval French *sole, soele,* from Latin *solea* "sandal"] — **soled** \ˈsōld\ *adj*

²sole *vt* : to furnish with a sole ⟨*sole* shoes⟩

³sole *n* : any of a family of small-mouthed flatfishes having reduced fins and small closely set eyes and including important food fishes; *also* : any of several other market flatfishes [Medieval French, from Latin *solea* "sandal, a kind of flatfish"]

⁴sole *adj* **1** *archaic* : having no companion : ALONE **2 a** : having no sharer ⟨*sole* owner⟩ **b** : being the only one **3** : functioning independently and without assistance or interference ⟨the *sole* judge⟩ **4** : belonging exclusively to the one person, unit, or group named ⟨given *sole* authority⟩ [Medieval French *sul, soul, seul,* from Latin *solus*] ***synonyms*** see SINGLE — **sole·ness** *n*

so·le·cism \ˈsäl-ə-ˌsiz-əm, ˈsō-lə-\ *n* **1** : an ungrammatical combination of words in a sentence **2** : a breach of etiquette or decorum [Latin *soloecismus,* from Greek *soloikismos,* from *soloikos* "speaking incorrectly," literally, "inhabitant of Soloi," from *Soloi,* city in ancient Cilicia where a substandard form of Greek was spoken] — **so·le·cis·tic** \ˌsäl-lə-ˈsis-tik, ˌsō-lə-\ *adj*

sole·ly \ˈsōl-lē, ˈsō-lē\ *adv* **1** : without another : SINGLY, ALONE **2** : EXCLUSIVELY, ENTIRELY ⟨done *solely* for money⟩

sol·emn \ˈsäl-əm\ *adj* **1** : celebrated with religious rites or ceremony : SACRED **2** : FORMAL, STATELY ⟨a *solemn* procession⟩ **3** : done or made seriously and thoughtfully ⟨*solemn* promise⟩ **4** : gravely sober and serious ⟨at this *solemn* moment⟩ **5** : SOMBER ⟨robe of *solemn* black⟩ [Middle French *solempne,* from Latin *sollemnis* "regularly appointed, solemn"] ***synonyms*** see SERIOUS — **so·lem·ni·ty** \sə-ˈlem-nət-ē\ *n* — **sol·emn·ly** \ˈsäl-əm-lē\ *adv* — **sol·emn·ness** \-əm-nəs\ *n*

sol·em·nize \ˈsäl-əm-ˌnīz\ *vt* **1** : to observe or honor with solemnity **2** : to perform with pomp or ceremony; *esp* : to celebrate (a marriage) with religious rites **3** : to make solemn : DIGNIFY — **sol·em·ni·za·tion** \ˌsäl-əm-nə-ˈzā-shən\ *n*

so·le·noid \ˈsō-lə-ˌnȯid, ˈsäl-ə-\ *n* : a coil of wire commonly in the form of a cylinder that when carrying a current resembles a bar magnet so that a movable core is drawn into the coil when a current flows [French *solénoïde,* derived from Greek *sōlēn* "pipe"] — **so·le·noi·dal** \ˌsō-lə-ˈnȯid-l, ˌsäl-ə-\ *adj*

sole·plate \ˈsōl-ˌplāt\ *n* : the undersurface of a flatiron

sole·print \-ˌprint\ *n* : a print of the sole of the foot; *esp* : one made in the manner of a fingerprint and used for the identification of an infant

[1]**sol–fa** \sōl-ˈfä, ˈsōl-\ *vb* **1 :** to sing the sol-fa syllables **2 :** to sing (as a melody) to sol-fa syllables

[2]**sol–fa** *n* **1 :** SOL-FA SYLLABLES **2 :** SOLMIZATION; *also* **:** an exercise thus sung

sol–fa syllables *n pl* **:** the syllables *do, re, mi, fa, sol, la, ti* used in singing the tones of the scale

soli *plural of* SOLO

so·lic·it \sə-ˈlis-ət\ *vb* **1 :** BEG, ENTREAT; *esp* **:** to approach with a request or plea ⟨*soliciting* employers for jobs⟩ **2 :** to appeal for ⟨*solicit* funds⟩ **3 :** to accost a person for immoral purposes [Middle English, "to disturb, promote," from Medieval French *solliciter,* from Latin *sollicitare* "to disturb," from *sollicitus* "solicitous"] — **so·lic·i·ta·tion** \-ˌlis-ə-ˈtā-shən\ *n*

so·lic·i·tant \sə-ˈlis-ət-ənt\ *n* **:** one who solicits

so·lic·i·tor \sə-ˈlis-ət-ər\ *n* **1 :** one that solicits; *esp* **:** an agent that solicits (as contributions to charity) **2 :** a British lawyer who advises clients, represents them in the lower courts, and prepares cases for barristers to plead in the higher courts **3 :** the chief law officer of a municipality, county, or government department — **so·lic·i·tor·ship** *n*

so·lic·i·tous \sə-ˈlis-ət-əs\ *adj* **1 :** full of concern or fears **:** APPREHENSIVE **2 :** extremely careful **3 :** anxiously willing **:** EAGER [Latin *sollicitus,* from *sollus* "whole" + *citus,* past participle of *ciēre* "to move"] ***synonyms*** see THOUGHTFUL — **so·lic·i·tous·ly** *adv* — **so·lic·i·tous·ness** *n*

so·lic·i·tude \sə-ˈlis-ə-ˌtüd, -ˌtyüd\ *n* **1 :** the state of being solicitous **:** ANXIETY **2 :** excessive care or attention

[1]**sol·id** \ˈsäl-əd\ *adj* **1 a :** having an interior filled with matter **:** not hollow **b :** written as one word without a hyphen ⟨a *solid* compound⟩ **2 :** having, involving, or dealing with three dimensions or with solids ⟨a *solid* geometric shape⟩ **3 a :** not loose or spongy **:** COMPACT ⟨a *solid* mass of rock⟩ **b :** neither gaseous nor liquid **:** HARD, RIGID ⟨*solid* ice⟩ ⟨*solid* waste⟩ **4 :** of good substantial quality or kind ⟨*solid* comfort⟩ ⟨*solid* reasons⟩ **5 a :** not interrupted ⟨for three *solid* hours⟩ **b :** UNANIMOUS, UNITED ⟨we are *solid* for pay increases⟩ **6 a :** thoroughly dependable **:** RELIABLE ⟨a *solid* citizen⟩ **b :** serious in purpose or character ⟨*solid* reading⟩ **7 :** of one substance or character: as **a :** entirely of one metal or containing the minimum of alloy necessary to impart hardness ⟨*solid* gold⟩ **b :** of a single color or tone [Medieval French *solide,* from Latin *solidus*] — **solid** *adv* — **sol·id·ly** *adv* — **sol·id·ness** *n*

[2]**solid** *n* **1 :** a geometric figure or element (as a cube or sphere) having three dimensions **2 :** a solid substance **:** a substance that does not flow perceptibly under moderate stress **3 :** the part of a solution or suspension that when separated from the solvent or suspending medium has the qualities of a solid ⟨milk *solids* of protein and lactose⟩

sol·i·dar·i·ty \ˌsäl-ə-ˈdar-ət-ē\ *n, pl* **-ties :** unity based on community of interests, objectives, or standards [French *solidarité,* derived from Latin *solidus* "solid"] ***synonyms*** see UNITY

solid geometry *n* **:** a branch of geometry that deals with figures of three-dimensional space — compare PLANE GEOMETRY

so·lid·i·fy \sə-ˈlid-ə-ˌfī\ *vb* **-fied; -fy·ing :** to make or become solid, compact, or hard — **so·lid·i·fi·ca·tion** \sə-ˌlid-ə-fə-ˈkā-shən\ *n*

so·lid·i·ty \sə-ˈlid-ət-ē\ *n, pl* **-ties 1 :** the quality or state of being solid **2 :** moral, mental, or financial soundness

solid–state *adj* **1 :** relating to the properties, structure, or reactivity of solid material **2 :** utilizing the electric, magnetic, or optical properties of solid materials **:** not utilizing electron tubes

so·lil·o·quist \sə-ˈlil-ə-kwəst\ *n* **:** one who soliloquizes

so·lil·o·quize \sə-ˈlil-ə-ˌkwīz\ *vi* **:** to utter a soliloquy **:** talk to oneself — **so·lil·o·quiz·er** *n*

so·lil·o·quy \sə-ˈlil-ə-kwē\ *n, pl* **-quies 1 :** the act of talking to oneself **2 :** a dramatic monologue that represents a series of unspoken thoughts [Late Latin *soliloquium,* from Latin *solus* "alone" + *loqui* "to speak"]

sol·i·taire \ˈsäl-ə-ˌtaər, -ˌteər\ *n* **1 :** a single gem (as a diamond) set alone **2 :** a card game played by one person alone [French, from *solitaire,* adj., "solitary," from Latin *solitarius*]

[1]**sol·i·tary** \ˈsäl-ə-ˌter-ē\ *adj* **1 :** being or going alone ⟨a *solitary* traveler⟩ **2 :** seldom visited **:** UNFREQUENTED **3 :** being the only one **:** SOLE ⟨the *solitary* example⟩ **4 :** growing or living alone **:** not forming part of a group or cluster ⟨flowers terminal and *solitary*⟩ ⟨the *solitary* bees⟩ [Latin *solitarius,* from *solitas* "solitude," from *solus* "alone"] — **sol·i·tar·i·ly** \ˌsäl-ə-ˈter-ə-lē\ *adv* — **sol·i·tar·i·ness** \ˈsäl-ə-ˌter-ē-nəs\ *n*

synonyms SOLITARY, FORLORN, DESOLATE mean isolated from others. SOLITARY implies the absence of any others of the same kind ⟨a *solitary* stork wading in the marsh⟩. FORLORN stresses dejection and woe at separation from one held dear ⟨a *forlorn* lost child⟩. DESOLATE implies inconsolable grief at loss or bereavement ⟨*desolate* after his wife's death⟩. ***synonyms*** see in addition SINGLE

[2]**solitary** *n, pl* **-tar·ies 1 :** RECLUSE, HERMIT **2 :** solitary confinement in prison

sol·i·tude \ˈsäl-ə-ˌtüd, -ˌtyüd\ *n* **1 :** the quality or state of being alone or remote from society **2 :** a lonely place

sol·mi·za·tion \ˌsäl-mə-ˈzā-shən\ *n* **:** the act, practice, or system of using a set of syllables to denote the tones of a musical scale [French *solmisation,* from *solmiser* "to sing the syllables *do, re, mi, fa, sol, la, ti,*" from *sol* "sol" + *mi* "mi" + *-iser* "-ize"]

[1]**so·lo** \ˈsō-lō\ *n, pl* **solos 1** *or pl* **so·li** \ˈsō-lē\ **a :** a musical composition for a single voice or instrument with or without accompaniment **b :** the featured part of a concerto or similar work **2 :** an action in which there is only one performer [Italian, from *solo* "alone," from Latin *solus*]

[2]**solo** *adv or adj* **:** without a companion **:** ALONE

[3]**solo** *vi* **so·loed; so·lo·ing :** to perform by oneself; *esp* **:** to fly an airplane without one's instructor

so·lo·ist \ˈsō-lə-wəst, -ˌlō-əst\ *n* **:** one who performs a solo

Solomon's seal *n* **1 :** any of a genus of perennial herbs related to the lilies and having gnarled rhizomes **2 :** an emblem consisting of two triangles forming a 6-pointed star and formerly used as an amulet especially against fever

Solomon's seal 2

so·lon \ˈsō-lən, -ˌlän\ *n* **1 :** a wise and skillful lawgiver **2 :** a member of a legislative body [*Solon,* died about 559 B.C., Athenian lawgiver]

so long \sō-ˈlȯŋ\ *interj* — used to express farewell [origin unknown]

so long as *conj* **1 :** during and up to the end of the time that **:** WHILE ⟨*so long as* you are here, I feel safe⟩ **2 :** provided that ⟨you may go, *so long as* you return by dinnertime⟩

sol·stice \ˈsäl-stəs, ˈsōl-, ˈsȯl-\ *n* **1 :** the point in the path of the sun at which the sun is farthest from the equator either north or south **2 :** the time of the sun's passing a solstice which occurs on June 22nd to begin summer in the northern hemisphere and on December 22nd to begin winter in the northern hemisphere [Latin *solstitium,* from *sol* "sun" + *-stit-, -stes* "standing"] — **sol·sti·tial** \säl-ˈstish-əl, sōl-, sȯl-\ *adj*

sol·u·bil·i·ty \ˌsäl-yə-ˈbil-ət-ē\ *n, pl* **-ties 1 :** the quality or state of being soluble **2 :** the amount of a substance that will dissolve in a given amount of another substance

sol·u·ble \ˈsäl-yə-bəl\ *adj* **1 :** capable of being dissolved in a liquid ⟨sugar is *soluble* in water⟩ **2 :** capable of being solved or explained ⟨a *soluble* problem⟩ [Medieval French, "digestible, laxative," from Late Latin *solubilis,* from Latin *solvere* "to loosen, dissolve"] — **sol·u·ble·ness** *n* — **sol·u·bly** \-blē\ *adv*

sol·ute \ˈsäl-ˌyüt\ *n* **:** a dissolved substance [Latin *solutus,* past participle of *solvere* "to dissolve"]

so·lu·tion \sə-ˈlü-shən\ *n* **1 a :** an action or process of solving **b** (1) **:** an answer to a problem **:** EXPLANATION (2) **:** SOLUTION SET; *also* **:** a member of a solution set **2 a :** an act or the process by which a solid, liquid, or gaseous substance is uniformly mixed with a liquid or sometimes a gas or solid **b :** a typically liquid uniform mixture formed by the process of solution **c :** the condition of being dissolved **d :** a liquid containing a dissolved substance **3 :** a bringing or coming to an end or into a state of discontinuity [Medieval French, from Latin *solutio,* from *solvere* "to loosen, solve, dissolve"]

solution set *n* **:** a set of values that satisfy an equation or inequality; *also* **:** TRUTH SET

solv·able \ˈsäl-və-bəl, ˈsȯl-\ *adj* : capable of being solved ⟨a *solvable* problem⟩ — **solv·abil·i·ty** \ˌsäl-və-ˈbil-ət-ē, ˌsȯl-\ *n*

[1]**sol·vate** \ˈsäl-ˌvāt, ˈsȯl-\ *n* : a combination of a solute with a solvent or of a dispersed phase with a dispersion medium [*solvent* + *-ate*]

[2]**solvate** *vt* : to convert into a solvate — **sol·va·tion** \säl-ˈvā-shən, sȯl-\ *n*

Sol·vay process \ˈsäl-ˌvā-\ *n* : a process for making sodium carbonate Na_2CO_3 from common salt using carbon dioxide and ammonia [Ernest *Solvay,* died 1922, Belgian chemist]

solve \ˈsälv, ˈsȯlv\ *vt* : to find a solution for ⟨*solve* a puzzle⟩ [Latin *solvere* "to loosen, solve, dissolve," from *sed-, se-* "apart" + *luere* "to release"]

sol·ven·cy \ˈsäl-vən-sē, ˈsȯl-\ *n, pl* **-cies** : the quality or state of being solvent

[1]**sol·vent** \-vənt\ *adj* : able to pay all legal debts [Latin *solvens,* present participle of *solvere* "to dissolve, pay"] — **sol·vent·ly** *adv*

[2]**solvent** *n* **1** : a usually liquid substance capable of dissolving or dispersing one or more other substances **2** : something that provides a solution

So·ma·li \sō-ˈmäl-ē, sə-\ *n* : a member of a people of Somaliland [from or related to Somali (the language of the Somali) *Soomaali*] — **Somali** *adj*

so·mat·ic \sō-ˈmat-ik, sə-\ *adj* **1** : of, relating to, or affecting the body especially as distinguished from the germplasm or the mind ⟨*somatic* cells⟩ **2** : of or relating to the wall of the body : PARIETAL [Greek *sōmatikos,* from *sōmat-, sōma* "body"] — **so·mat·i·cal·ly** \-ˈmat-i-kə-lē, -klē\ *adv*

somatic cell *n* : any cell of an animal or plant other than a germ cell

somatic mutation *n* : a mutation occurring in a somatic cell and inducing a chimera

so·mato·tro·pin \sō-ˌmat-ə-ˈtrō-pən\ *or* **so·mato·tro·phin** \-fən\ *n* : GROWTH HORMONE 1

som·ber *or* **som·bre** \ˈsäm-bər\ *adj* **1** : so shaded as to be dark and gloomy **2** : GRAVE, MELANCHOLY ⟨a *somber* mood⟩ **3** : dull or dark colored [French *sombre*] — **som·ber·ly** *or* **som·bre·ly** *adv* — **som·ber·ness** *or* **som·bre·ness** *n*

som·bre·ro \səm-ˈbreər-ō, säm-\ *n, pl* **-ros** : a high-crowned hat of felt or straw with a very wide brim worn especially in the Southwest and Mexico [Spanish, from *sombra* "shade"]

sombrero

[1]**some** \ˈsəm, *sense 2* ˈsəm *or* səm\ *adj* **1** : being unknown, undetermined, or unspecified ⟨*some* stranger was looking for you⟩ **2 a** : being one, a part, or an unspecified number of something (as a class or group) named or implied ⟨*some* gems are hard⟩ **b** : being of an unspecified amount or number ⟨give me *some* water⟩ ⟨have *some* apples⟩ **3** : worthy of notice or consideration ⟨that was *some* party⟩ [Old English *sum*]

[2]**some** \ˈsəm\ *pron, sing or pl in constr* **1** : one indeterminate quantity, portion, or number as distinguished from the rest ⟨*some* of the milk⟩ ⟨*some* of the apples⟩ **2** : an indefinite additional amount ⟨ran a mile and then *some*⟩

[3]**some** \ˈsəm, ˌsəm\ *adv* **1** : ABOUT ⟨*some* eighty houses⟩ **2 a** : SOMEWHAT ⟨felt *some* better⟩ **b** : to some degree : a little ⟨the cut bled *some*⟩

usage When *some* is used to modify a number, it is almost always a round number ⟨a community of *some* 150,000 inhabitants⟩. Because *some* is slightly more emphatic than *about* or *approximately,* it is occasionally used with a more exact number as an intensifier ⟨has *some* 135 tackles to his credit⟩. When *some* is used without a number, *somewhat* is often recommended in its place. However, only when *some* modifies an adjective, usually a comparative, will *somewhat* always substitute smoothly ⟨with *some* [*somewhat*] higher temperatures expected⟩. When *some* modifies a verb or adverb, and especially when it follows a verb, substitution of *somewhat* may prove awkward ⟨the many hardships forced me to grow up *some*⟩ ⟨I've been around *some* in my day⟩.

[1]**-some** \səm\ *adj suffix* : characterized by a (specified) thing, quality, state, or action ⟨awe*some*⟩ ⟨burden*some*⟩ [Old English *-sum*]

[2]**-some** \səm\ *n suffix* : group of (so many) members and especially persons ⟨four*some*⟩ [Middle English *sum,* pron., "one, some"]

[3]**-some** \ˌsōm\ *n combining form* : body ⟨chromo*some*⟩ [Greek *sōma*]

[1]**some·body** \ˈsəm-ˌbäd-ē, -bəd-\ *pron* : one or some person of unspecified or indefinite identity ⟨*somebody* will come in⟩

[2]**somebody** *n* : a person of position or importance ⟨wanted to be *somebody*⟩

some·day \ˈsəm-ˌdā\ *adv* : at some future time ⟨may *someday* travel the world⟩

some·how \ˈsəm-ˌhau̇\ *adv* : in one way or another not known or designated : by some means ⟨we'll manage *somehow*⟩

some·one \-wən, -ˌwən\ *pron* : some person : SOMEBODY ⟨*someone* took my money⟩

some·place \-ˌplās\ *adv* : SOMEWHERE 1 ⟨fell *someplace* over there⟩

som·er·sault \ˈsəm-ər-ˌsȯlt\ *n* : a leap or roll in which a person turns forward or backward in a complete revolution with the feet moving up over the head [Middle French *sombresaut* "leap," derived from Latin *super* "over" + *saltus* "leap," from *salire* "to jump"] — **somersault** *vi*

som·er·set \-ˌset\ *n or vi* : SOMERSAULT [by alteration]

[1]**some·thing** \ˈsəm-thing, ˈsəmp-, *especially in rapid speech or for 2* ˈsəmp-m\ *pron* **1** : some undetermined or unspecified thing ⟨*something* must be done about it⟩ **2** : a person or thing of consequence ⟨decided to make *something* of myself⟩ — **something else** : something or someone special or extraordinary

[2]**something** *adv* **1** : in some degree : SOMEWHAT ⟨was *something* less than perfect⟩ **2** : EXTREMELY ⟨snores *something* awful⟩

[1]**some·time** \ˈsəm-ˌtīm\ *adv* **1** : at some time in the future ⟨I'll do it *sometime*⟩ **2** : at some not specified or definitely known point of time ⟨*sometime* last night⟩

[2]**sometime** *adj* : having been formerly : FORMER ⟨*sometime* mayor of the city⟩

some·times \ˈsəm-ˌtīmz; ˌsəm-ˈ, səm-ˈ\ *adv* : at times : now and then : OCCASIONALLY ⟨speaks *sometimes* very fast⟩

some·way \ˈsəm-ˌwā\ *also* **some·ways** \-ˌwāz\ *adv* : in some way : SOMEHOW ⟨tried to make him *someway* understand⟩

[1]**some·what** \-ˌhwät, -ˌhwət, -ˌwät, -ˌwət; ˌsəm-ˈ, səm-ˈ\ *pron* : SOMETHING 2 ⟨*somewhat* of what you say is true⟩

[2]**somewhat** *adv* : in some degree or measure : SLIGHTLY ⟨*somewhat* relieved⟩ ***usage*** see SOME

[1]**some·where** \ˈsəm-ˌhweər, -ˌhwaər, -hwər, -ˌwear, -ˌwaər, -wər\ *adv* **1** : in, at, or to a place unknown or unspecified ⟨mentions it *somewhere*⟩ **2** : to or into a stage or period of positive accomplishment ⟨now we're getting *somewhere*⟩ **3** : APPROXIMATELY ⟨*somewhere* about nine o'clock⟩

[2]**somewhere** *n* : an undetermined or unnamed place ⟨went to *somewhere* in France⟩

some·wheres \-ˌhweərz, -ˌhwaərz, -hwərz, -ˌweərz, -ˌwaərz, -wərz\ *adv, chiefly dialect* : SOMEWHERE 1

so·mite \ˈsō-ˌmīt\ *n* : one segment of the longitudinal series of segments into which the body of many animals is divided : METAMERE [Greek *sōma* "body"]

som·me·lier \ˌsəm-əl-ˈyā\ *n, pl* **sommeliers** \-ˈyā, -ˈyāz\ : an employee of a restaurant who has charge of wines and their serving [French, from Medieval French *soumelier* "court official charged with transportation of supplies," from Old Occitan *saumalier* "pack animal driver," probably from *somier* "pack animal," from Late Latin *sagma* "packsaddle," from Greek]

som·nam·bu·lant \säm-ˈnam-byə-lənt\ *adj* : walking or having the habit of walking while asleep

som·nam·bu·lism \säm-ˈnam-byə-ˌliz-əm\ *n* : a sleeping state in which motor acts (as walking) are performed; *also* : actions characteristic of this state [derived from Latin *somnus* "sleep" + *ambulare* "to walk"] — **som·nam·bu·list** \-ləst\ *n* — **som·nam·bu·lis·tic** \säm-ˌnam-byə-ˈlis-tik\ *adj*

som·nif·er·ous \säm-ˈnif-rəs, -ə-rəs\ *adj* : SOPORIFIC 1a [Latin *somnifer,* from *somnus* "sleep" + *-fer* "-ferous"]

som·no·lence \ˈsäm-nə-ləns\ *n* : the quality or state of being drowsy

som·no·lent \-lənt\ *adj* : inclined to or heavy with sleep : DROWSY ⟨a *somnolent* village⟩ [Medieval French *sompnolent,* from Latin *somnolentus,* from *somnus* "sleep"] — **som·no·lent·ly** *adv*

son \ˈsən\ *n* **1 a** : a male offspring especially of human beings **b** : a male adopted child **c** : a human male descendant **2** *cap* : the second person of the Trinity **3** : a person closely associated with or deriving from a formative agent (as a nation, school, or race) ⟨*sons* of modern technology⟩ [Old English *sunu*]

so·nant \ˈsō-nənt\ *adj* **1** : VOICED 2 **2** : SYLLABIC 2 [Latin *sonare* "to sound"] — **sonant** *n*

so·nar \ˈsō-ˌnär\ *n* : an apparatus that detects the presence and location of submerged objects (as submarines) by sound waves [*so*und *na*vigation *r*anging]

so·na·ta \sə-ˈnät-ə\ *n* : an instrumental musical composition typically of three or four movements in contrasting forms and keys [Italian, from *sonare* "to sound," from Latin]

sonata form *n* : a musical form consisting basically of an exposition, a development, and a recapitulation used especially for the first movement of a sonata

son·a·ti·na \ˌsän-ə-ˈtē-nə\ *n* : a short usually simplified sonata [Italian, from *sonata*]

song \ˈsȯŋ\ *n* **1** : the act or art of singing **2** : POETRY **3 a** : a short musical composition of words and music **b** : a collection of such compositions **4** : a distinctive or characteristic sound or series of sounds (as of a bird) **5 a** : a melody for a lyric poem or ballad **b** : a poem easily set to music **6** : a small amount ⟨can be bought for a *song*⟩ [Old English *sang*]

song·bird \-ˌbərd\ *n* **1** : a bird that utters a succession of musical tones **2** : any of various passerine birds (as larks, finches, and orioles) characterized by a vocal apparatus highly specialized for singing

song·fest \-ˌfest\ *n* : an informal session of group singing of popular or folk songs

song·ful \-fəl\ *adj* : given to singing : MELODIOUS — **song·ful·ly** \-fə-lē\ *adv* — **song·ful·ness** *n*

song·less \ˈsȯŋ-ləs\ *adj* : lacking in, incapable of, or not given to song — **song·less·ly** *adv*

Song of Sol·o·mon \-ˈsäl-ə-mən\ *n* : SONG OF SONGS — see BIBLE table

Song of Songs *n* : a collection of love poems forming a book that is found in the Jewish and Christian Scriptures as Song of Songs or Song of Solomon — see BIBLE table

song·smith \ˈsȯŋ-ˌsmith\ *n* : a composer of songs

song sparrow *n* : a common sparrow of North America that is brownish above and mostly white below and is noted for its sweet cheerful song

song·ster \ˈsȯŋ-stər\ *n* : one skilled in song : SINGER

song·stress \-strəs\ *n* : a female singer

song thrush *n* : a largely olive-brown Old World thrush noted for its song — called also *mavis, throstle*

song·writ·er \ˈsȯŋ-ˌrīt-ər\ *n* : a person who composes words or music or both especially for popular songs

son·ic \ˈsän-ik\ *adj* **1** : using, produced by, or relating to sound waves ⟨*sonic* altimeter⟩ **2** : having a frequency within the audibility range of the human ear — used of waves and vibrations [Latin *sonus* "sound"] — **son·i·cal·ly** \ˈsän-i-kə-lē, -klē\ *adv*

sonic boom *n* : a sound resembling an explosion produced when a pressure wave formed at the nose of an aircraft traveling at supersonic speed reaches the ground

son–in–law \ˈsən-ən-ˌlȯ\ *n, pl* **sons–in–law** \ˈsən-zən-\ : the husband of one's daughter

son·net \ˈsän-ət\ *n* : a poem of 14 lines usually in iambic pentameter rhyming according to a prescribed scheme — compare ENGLISH SONNET, ITALIAN SONNET [Italian *sonetto,* from Old Occitan *sonet* "little song," from *son* "sound, song," from Latin *sonus* "sound"]

son·ne·teer \ˌsän-ə-ˈtiər\ *n* : a writer of sonnets

sonnet sequence *n* : a series of sonnets often having a unifying theme

son·ny \ˈsən-ē\ *n* : a young boy — usually used in address

so·nor·i·ty \sə-ˈnȯr-ət-ē, -ˈnär-\ *n, pl* **-ties** **1** : the quality or state of being sonorous : RESONANCE **2** : a sonorous tone or speech

so·no·rous \sə-ˈnōr-əs, -ˈnȯr-; ˈsän-ə-rəs\ *adj* **1** : producing sound (as when struck) **2** : full or loud in sound : RESONANT **3** : imposing or impressive in effect or style [Latin *sonorus*] — **so·no·rous·ly** *adv* — **so·no·rous·ness** *n*

son·ship \ˈsən-ˌship\ *n* : the relationship of son to father

soon \ˈsün, *especially New England* ˈsůn\ *adv* **1** : before long : without undue time lapse ⟨*soon* after sunrise⟩ **2** : PROMPTLY, SPEEDILY ⟨as *soon* as possible⟩ **3** *archaic* : before the usual time **4** : by choice : WILLINGLY ⟨I'd *sooner* stay than go⟩ [Old English *sōna* "soon, immediately"]

soot \ˈsůt, ˈsət, ˈsüt\ *n* : a black substance that is formed by combustion, rises in fine particles, and adheres to the sides of the chimney or pipe conveying the smoke; *esp* : the fine powder consisting chiefly of carbon that colors smoke [Old English *sōt*]

[1]**sooth** \ˈsüth\ *adj, archaic* : agreeing with or telling the truth [Old English *sōth*]

[2]**sooth** *n, archaic* : the quality or state of being true

soothe \ˈsü*th*\ *vb* **1 a** : to please by or as if by attention or concern **b** : RELIEVE 1 ⟨the lotion *soothed* his sunburn⟩ **2** : to bring comfort, solace, or reassurance ⟨music *soothes* the soul⟩ [Old English *sōthian* "to prove the truth," from *sōth* "true"]

sooth·ing \ˈsü-*th*iŋ\ *adj* : tending to soothe or calm ⟨*soothing* sounds⟩ — **sooth·ing·ly** \-*th*iŋ-lē\ *adv* — **sooth·ing·ness** *n*

sooth·ly \ˈsüth-lē\ *adv, archaic* : in truth : TRULY

sooth·say·er \ˈsüth-ˌsā-ər\ *n* : a person who claims to foretell events — **sooth·say·ing** \-ˌsā-iŋ\ *n*

sooty \ˈsůt-ē, ˈsət-, ˈsüt-\ *adj* **soot·i·er; -est** **1 a** : of, relating to, or producing soot ⟨*sooty* fires⟩ **b** : soiled with soot ⟨*sooty* buildings⟩ **2** : of the color of soot ⟨*sooty* birds⟩ — **soot·i·ly** \-l-ē\ *adv* — **soot·i·ness** \-ē-nəs\ *n*

sooty mold *n* : a dark layer of fungus mycelium growing in insect honeydew on the leaves of plants; *also* : a fungus producing such growth

[1]**sop** \ˈsäp\ *n* **1** *chiefly dialect* : a piece of food dipped or steeped in a liquid (as bread dipped in milk or gravy) **2** : a bribe, gift, or gesture meant to pacify or win favor [Old English *sopp*]

[2]**sop** *vt* **sopped; sop·ping** **1 a** : to steep or dip in or as if in liquid **b** : to wet thoroughly : SOAK **2** : to mop up (as water) **3** : to give a bribe or conciliatory gift to

soph·ism \ˈsäf-ˌiz-əm\ *n* : an unsound misleading argument that on the surface seems reasonable

soph·ist \ˈsäf-əst\ *n* **1** *cap* : one of a class of ancient Greek teachers of rhetoric, philosophy, and the art of successful living noted for their subtle often specious reasoning **2** : one who argues by the use of sophisms [Latin *sophista,* from Greek *sophistēs,* literally, "expert, wise man," from *sophizesthai* "to become wise, deceive," from *sophos* "wise"]

so·phis·tic \sə-ˈfis-tik\ *or* **so·phis·ti·cal** \-ti-kəl\ *adj* : being clever and subtle but misleading — **so·phis·ti·cal·ly** \-ti-kə-lē, -klē\ *adv*

[1]**so·phis·ti·cate** \sə-ˈfis-tə-ˌkāt\ *vt* **1** : to alter deceptively; *esp* : ADULTERATE **2** : to deprive of genuineness, naturalness, or simplicity; *esp* : to deprive of naïveté and make worldly-wise — **so·phis·ti·ca·tion** \-ˌfis-tə-ˈkā-shən\ *n*

[2]**so·phis·ti·cate** \-ˈfis-ti-kət, -tə-ˌkāt\ *n* : a sophisticated person

so·phis·ti·cat·ed \-tə-ˌkāt-əd\ *adj* **1** : deprived of native or original simplicity: as **a** : highly complicated : COMPLEX ⟨*sophisticated* instruments⟩ **b** : WORLDLY-WISE, KNOWING **2** : devoid of grossness : SUBTLE: as **a** : finely experienced and aware ⟨a *sophisticated* columnist⟩ **b** : intellectually appealing ⟨*sophisticated* novels⟩ — **so·phis·ti·cat·ed·ly** *adv*

soph·ist·ry \ˈsäf-ə-strē\ *n, pl* **-ries** : subtle but deceptive reasoning or argumentation

soph·o·more \ˈsäf-ˌmōr, -ˌmȯr; ˈsäf-m-ˌōr, -ˌȯr\ *n* : a student in the second year at college or a 4-year secondary school [perhaps from Greek *sophos* "wise" + *mōros* "foolish"]

soph·o·mor·ic \ˌsäf-ə-ˈmōr-ik, -ˈmȯr-, -ˈmär-\ *adj* **1** : conceited and overconfident of knowledge but poorly informed and immature ⟨a *sophomoric* argument⟩ **2** : lacking in maturity, taste, or judgment ⟨*sophomoric* humor⟩

So·pho·ni·as \ˌsäf-ə-ˈnī-əs, ˌsō-fə-\ *n* : ZEPHANIAH

[1]**so·po·rif·ic** \ˌsäp-ə-ˈrif-ik, ˌsō-pə-\ *adj* **1 a** : causing or tending to cause sleep **b** : tending to dull awareness or alertness **2** : of, relating to, or characterized by sleepiness or lethargy [derived from Latin *sopor* "deep sleep"]

[2]**soporific** *n* : a soporific agent or drug

sop·ping \ˈsäp-iŋ\ *adj* : very wet : drenched through

sop·py \ˈsäp-ē\ *adj* **sop·pi·er; -est** **1** : soaked through **2** : very wet

[1]**so·prano** \sə-ˈpran-ō, -ˈprän-\ *n, pl* **-pran·os** **1** : the highest singing voice of women or boys; *also* : a singer having such a voice **2** : the highest voice part in a 4-part chorus — compare

\ə\ abut	\au̇\ out	\i\ tip	\ȯ\ saw	\u̇\ foot
\ər\ further	\ch\ chin	\ī\ life	\ȯi\ coin	\y\ yet
\a\ mat	\e\ pet	\j\ job	\th\ thin	\yü\ few
\ā\ take	\ē\ easy	\ŋ\ sing	*th*\ this	\yu̇\ cure
\ä\ cot, cart	\g\ go	\ō\ bone	\ü\ food	\zh\ vision

ALTO, BASS, TENOR [Italian, from *sopra* "above," from Latin *supra*]
[2]**soprano** *adj* **1** : relating to the soprano voice or part **2** : having a high range ⟨*soprano* sax⟩
so·ra \'sōr-ə, 'sȯr-\ *n* : a small short-billed North American rail common in marshes [origin unknown]
sorb \'sȯrb\ *vt* : to take up and hold by either adsorption or absorption [back-formation from *absorb* and *adsorb*]
sor·bet \sȯr-'bā\ *n* : a fruit-flavored ice served as a dessert or between courses to freshen the mouth
sor·cer·er \'sȯrs-rər, -ə-rər\ *n* : a person who practices sorcery : WIZARD
sor·cer·ess \'sȯrs-rəs, -ə-rəs\ *n* : a female sorcerer
sor·cer·ous \'sȯrs-rəs, -ə-rəs\ *adj* : of or relating to sorcery
sor·cery \'sȯrs-rē, -ə-rē\ *n* : the use of power gained from the assistance or control of evil spirits especially for divining : WITCHCRAFT [Medieval French *sorcerie,* derived from Latin *sors* "chance, lot"]
sor·did \'sȯrd-əd\ *adj* **1** : DIRTY, FILTHY ⟨*sordid* surroundings⟩ **2** : marked by baseness or grossness : VILE ⟨*sordid* motives⟩ **3** : meanly greedy : COVETOUS **4** : of a dull or muddy color [Latin *sordidus,* from *sordes* "dirt"] — **sor·did·ly** *adv* — **sor·did·ness** *n*
sor·di·no \sȯr-'dē-nō\ *n, pl* **-di·ni** \-nē\ : MUTE 2 [Italian, from *sordo* "silent," from Latin *surdus*]
[1]**sore** \'sōr, 'sȯr\ *adj* **1 a** : causing or tending to cause pain or distress ⟨a *sore* subject⟩ **b** : painfully sensitive : TENDER ⟨*sore* muscles⟩ **c**: hurt or inflamed so as to be or seem painful ⟨*sore* runny eyes⟩ **2** : attended by difficulties, hardship, or exertion ⟨in *sore* straits⟩ **3** : ANGRY 1a ⟨*sore* over a remark⟩ [Old English *sār*] — **sore·ness** *n*
[2]**sore** *n* **1** : a localized sore spot on the body; *esp* : one (as an ulcer) with the tissues broken and usually infected **2** : a source of pain or vexation : AFFLICTION
[3]**sore** *adv* : SORELY
sore·head \-ˌhed\ *n* : a person easily angered or disgruntled — **sorehead** *or* **sore·head·ed** \-'hed-əd\ *adj*
sore·ly \-lē\ *adv* : in a sore manner : VERY, EXTREMELY
sore throat *n* : pain in the throat due to inflammation of the fauces and pharynx
sor·ghum \'sȯr-gəm\ *n* **1** : any of an economically important genus of Old World tropical grasses similar to corn in habit but with the spikelets in pairs on a hairy axis; *esp* : one cultivated for grain, forage, or syrup — compare SORGO **2** : syrup from sorgo [New Latin, from Italian *sorgo*]
sor·go \'sȯr-gō\ *n, pl* **sorgos** : a sorghum grown primarily for its sweet juice from which syrup is made but also used for fodder and silage — called also *sweet sorghum* [Italian]
so·ro·ral \sə-'rōr-əl, -'rȯr-\ *adj* : of, relating to, or characteristic of a sister : SISTERLY [Latin *soror* "sister"]
so·ror·i·ty \sə-'rȯr-ət-ē, -'rär-\ *n, pl* **-ties** : a club of women especially at a college [Medieval Latin *sororitas* "sisterhood," from Latin *soror* "sister"]
sorp·tion \'sȯrp-shən\ *n* : the process of sorbing : the state of being sorbed [back-formation from *absorption* and *adsorption*]
[1]**sor·rel** \'sȯr-əl, 'sär-\ *n* **1** : a brownish orange to light brown **2** : a sorrel-colored animal; *esp* : a light chestnut horse often with cream mane and tail color [Medieval French *sorel,* from *sor* "reddish brown"]
[2]**sorrel** *n* : any of various plants (as dock or wood sorrel) with sour juice [Medieval French *surele,* from *sur* "sour," of Germanic origin]
[1]**sor·row** \'sär-ō, 'sȯr-\ *n* **1 a** : sadness or anguish due to loss (as of something loved) **b** : a cause of grief or sadness **2** : a display of grief or sadness [Old English *sorg*]
synonyms SORROW, GRIEF, ANGUISH, WOE mean distress of mind. SORROW implies a sense of loss often with feelings of guilt and remorse ⟨expressed *sorrow* for having caused the accident⟩. GRIEF implies a sharp feeling of distress for a definite and immediate cause ⟨their *grief* when their pet died⟩. ANGUISH implies a torturing grief or dread ⟨felt *anguish* over making the wrong decision⟩. WOE is deep or inconsolable grief or misery ⟨all my troubles left me in a state of *woe*⟩.
[2]**sorrow** *vi* : to feel or express sorrow : GRIEVE
sor·row·ful \-fəl\ *adj* **1** : full of or marked by sorrow ⟨a *sorrowful* good-bye⟩ **2** : expressive of or inducing sorrow ⟨*sorrowful* eyes⟩ — **sor·row·ful·ly** \-fə-lē\ *adv* — **sor·row·ful·ness** *n*
sor·ry \'sär-ē, 'sȯr-\ *adj* **sor·ri·er; -est** **1** : feeling sorrow, regret, or penitence **2** : MOURNFUL 2, SAD **3** : inspiring sorrow, pity, scorn, or ridicule : WRETCHED [Old English *sārig,* from *sār* "sore"] — **sor·ri·ly** \'sär-ə-lē, 'sȯr-\ *adv* — **sor·ri·ness** \'sär-ē-nəs, 'sȯr-\ *n*
[1]**sort** \'sȯrt\ *n* **1 a** : a group set up on the basis of any characteristic in common : CLASS, KIND **b** : PERSON, INDIVIDUAL ⟨you're not a bad *sort* at heart⟩ **2 a** *archaic* : method or manner of acting : WAY **b** : general character or disposition : NATURE ⟨people of an evil *sort*⟩ **3** : an instance of sorting ⟨a numeric *sort* of a data file⟩ [Medieval French *sort* "fate, lot, characteristic," from Latin *sors* "lot, share, category"] ***synonyms*** see KIND — **after a sort** : in a rough or haphazard way ⟨plays the piano, *after a sort*⟩ — **all sorts of** : many different : all kinds of ⟨knows *all sorts of* people⟩ — **of sorts** *or* **of a sort** : of an inconsequential or mediocre quality ⟨a poet *of sorts*⟩ — **out of sorts** **1** : easily angered : IRRITABLE **2** : not well
[2]**sort** *vb* **1 a** : to put in a certain place or rank according to kind, class, or nature ⟨*sort* mail⟩ **b** : to arrange according to characteristics : CLASSIFY ⟨*sort* out colors⟩ **2** : AGREE 6, SUIT ⟨our approach *sorts* poorly with theirs⟩ **3** : SEARCH ⟨*sort* through some old papers⟩ — **sort·able** \'sȯrt-ə-bəl\ *adj* — **sort·er** *n*
sor·tie \'sȯrt-ē, sȯr-'tē\ *n* **1** : a sudden issuing of troops from a defensive position against the enemy : SALLY **2** : one mission or attack by a single plane [French, from *sortir* "to go out"] — **sortie** *vi*
sort of \ˌsȯrt-əv, -ə, -ər\ *adv* : to a moderate degree : SOMEWHAT ⟨acted *sort of* wild⟩
so·rus \'sōr-əs, 'sȯr-\ *n, pl* **so·ri** \'sōr-ˌī, 'sȯr-, -ē\ : a cluster of plant reproductive bodies; *esp* : a cluster of sporangia on the underside of a fertile fern frond [New Latin, from Greek *sōros* "heap"]
SOS \ˌes-ō-'es, ˌes-ə-'wes\ *n* **1** : an internationally recognized signal of distress in radio code ··· ––– ··· used especially by ships calling for help **2** : a call or request for help or rescue
[1]**so–so** \'sō-'sō\ *adv* : moderately well : TOLERABLY ⟨played the violin only *so-so*⟩
[2]**so–so** *adj* : neither very good nor very bad ⟨a *so-so* performance⟩
so·ste·nu·to \ˌsō-stə-'nüt-ō, ˌsȯ-\ *adv or adj* : sustained to or beyond the note's full value — used as a direction in music [Italian, from *sostenere* "to sustain," from Latin *sustinēre*]
sot \'sät\ *n* : an habitual drunkard [Old English *sott* "fool"]
sot·ted \'sät-əd\ *adj* : become stupid or drunken : SOTTISH
sot·tish \'sät-ish\ *adj* : resembling a sot (as in folly or intemperance) — **sot·tish·ly** *adv* — **sot·tish·ness** *n*
sot·to vo·ce \ˌsät-ō-'vō-chē\ *adv or adj* **1** : under the breath : in an undertone; *also* : PRIVATELY **2** : very softly — used as a direction in music [Italian *sottovoce,* from *sotto* "under" + *voce* "voice"]
sou \'sü\ *n* : a French bronze coin of the period before 1914 worth 5 centimes or one twentieth of a franc [French, from Medieval French *sol,* from Late Latin *solidus,* a kind of coin, from Latin, "solid"]
sou·brette \sü-'bret\ *n* **1 a** : a coquettish maid or frivolous young woman in comedies **b** : an actress who plays such a part **2** : a soprano who sings supporting roles in comic opera [French]
soubriquet *variant of* SOBRIQUET
[1]**souf·flé** \sü-'flā, 'sü-ˌ\ *n* : a delicate spongy hot dish lightened in baking by stiffly beaten egg whites [French, from *souffler* "to puff up," from Latin *sufflare,* from *sub-* + *flare* "to blow"]
[2]**soufflé** *or* **souf·fléed** \-'flād, -ˌflād\ *adj* : puffed by or in cooking ⟨*soufflé* omelets⟩
sough \'sau̇, 'səf\ *vi* : to make a moaning or sighing sound [Old English *swōgan*] — **sough** *n*
sought *past of* SEEK
[1]**soul** \'sōl\ *n* **1** : the spiritual part of a person believed to give life to the body and in many religions regarded as immortal **2 a** : a person's moral and emotional nature ⟨my *soul* rebels against cruelty⟩ **b** : spiritual force : FERVOR **3** : the essential part of something **4** : the moving spirit : LEADER ⟨the *soul* of an enterprise⟩ **5** : PERSON ⟨a kind *soul*⟩ **6** : EMBODIMENT ⟨a friend who is the *soul* of honor⟩ **7** : a disembodied spirit **8 a** : a strong positive feeling (as of intense sensitivity and emotional fervor) conveyed especially by black American performers **b** : SOUL MUSIC [Old English *sāwol*]
synonyms SOUL, SPIRIT mean an immaterial entity distinguishable from and superior to the body. SOUL is preferred when the entity is considered as having functions, responsibilities, or a certain destiny ⟨to save one's *soul*⟩ ⟨sell one's *soul* to

the devil〉. SPIRIT is preferred when the quality, movement, or activity is stressed 〈their *spirits* were refreshed〉 or opposition to the material part is intended 〈the *spirit* is willing but the flesh is weak〉.

[2]**soul** *adj* **1 :** of, relating to, or characteristic of black Americans or their culture 〈*soul* food〉 **2 :** designed for or controlled by blacks 〈*soul* radio stations〉

soul·ful \-fəl\ *adj* **:** full of or expressing feeling or emotion 〈*soulful* music〉 — **soul·ful·ly** \-fə-lē\ *adv* — **soul·ful·ness** *n*

soul·less \ˈsōl-ləs\ *adj* **:** having no soul or no greatness or nobleness of mind or feeling — **soul·less·ly** *adv*

soul music *n* **:** music that originated in black American gospel singing, is closely related to rhythm and blues, and is characterized by intensity of feeling and earthiness

soul–search·ing \ˈsōl-ˌsər-ching\ *n* **:** examination of one's conscience especially with regard to motives and values

[1]**sound** \ˈsau̇nd\ *adj* **1 a :** free from injury or disease **:** HEALTHY 〈a *sound* mind in a *sound* body〉 **b :** free from flaw, defect, or decay **2 :** SOLID, FIRM 〈a building of *sound* construction〉 **3 a :** free from error or fallacy **:** VALID 〈a *sound* argument〉 **b :** showing good sense **:** WISE 〈*sound* advice〉 **c :** HONORABLE, HONEST 〈*sound* principles〉 **4 a :** THOROUGH 〈a *sound* revenge〉 **b :** not disturbed **:** DEEP 〈a *sound* sleep〉 **c :** SEVERE 〈a *sound* beating〉 [Old English *gesund*] ***synonyms*** see HEALTHY, VALID — **sound·ly** *adv* — **sound·ness** \ˈsau̇nd-nəs, ˈsau̇n-\ *n*

[2]**sound** *adv* **:** to the full extent **:** THOROUGHLY 〈*sound* asleep〉

[3]**sound** *n* **1 a :** the sensation perceived by the sense of hearing **b :** a particular auditory impression **:** NOISE, TONE **c :** mechanical energy that is transmitted by longitudinal pressure waves in a material medium (as air) and is the objective cause of hearing **2 a :** one of the noises that together make up human speech 〈the *sound* of *th* in *this*〉 **b :** a sequence of spoken noises 〈*-cher* of *teacher* and *-ture* of *creature* have the same *sound*〉 **3 a :** meaningless noise **b :** impression conveyed 〈the excuse has a suspicious *sound*〉 **4 :** hearing distance **:** EARSHOT [Medieval French *son,* from Latin *sonus,* from *sonare* "to sound"]

[4]**sound** *vb* **1 a :** to make or cause to make a sound **b :** RESOUND 1 〈the auditorium *sounded* with applause〉 **c :** RESOUND 2 〈cheers are *sounding* throughout the gymnasium〉 **d :** to give a summons by sound 〈the bugle *sounds* to battle〉 **2 a :** PRONOUNCE 3 **b :** to put into words **:** VOICE **3 a :** to make known **:** PROCLAIM **b :** to order, signal, or indicate by a sound 〈*sound* the alarm〉 **4 :** to make or convey an impression especially when heard 〈*sounds* incredible〉 **5 :** to examine by causing to emit sounds 〈*sound* the lungs〉 — **sound·able** \ˈsau̇n-də-bəl\ *adj*

[5]**sound** *n* **1 :** a long passage of water that is wider than a strait and often connects two larger bodies of water or forms a channel between the mainland and an island **2 :** the air bladder of a fish [Old English *sund* "sea" and Old Norse *sund* "strait"]

[6]**sound** *vb* **1 a :** to measure the depth of (as with a sounding line) **:** FATHOM **b :** to look into or investigate the possibility **2 :** to try to find out the views or intentions of **:** PROBE **3 :** to dive down suddenly 〈a *sounding* whale〉 [Medieval French *sonder,* from *sonde* "sounding line"]

sound barrier *n* **:** the sudden large increase in resistance that the air offers to an airplane nearing the speed of sound

sound·board \ˈsau̇nd-ˌbōrd, ˈsau̇n-, -ˌbȯrd\ *n* **1 :** a thin resonant board so placed in a musical instrument as to reinforce its tones by sympathetic vibration **2 :** SOUNDING BOARD 1a

sound box *n* **:** a hollow chamber in a musical instrument for increasing its sonority

sound card *n* **:** a circuit board in a computer system designed to produce or reproduce sound

sound effects *n pl* **:** variously produced effects that are imitative of sounds called for in a script (as of a play or movie)

sound·er \ˈsau̇n-dər\ *n* **:** one that sounds; *esp* **:** a device for making soundings

[1]**sound·ing** \ˈsau̇n-ding\ *adj* **1 :** SONOROUS 2, RESONANT **2 :** POMPOUS 1, HIGH-SOUNDING — **sound·ing·ly** \-ding-lē\ *adv*

[2]**sounding** *n* **1 a :** measurement by sounding **b :** the depth so ascertained **2 :** a probe, test, or sampling of opinion or intention

sounding board *n* **1 a :** a structure behind or over a pulpit, rostrum, or platform to give distinctness and sonority to sound **b :** a device or agency that helps spread opinions or utterances **2 :** SOUNDBOARD 1

sounding line *n* **:** a line, wire, or cord weighted at one end and often marked at intervals for sounding

[1]**sound·less** \ˈsau̇n-dləs\ *adj* **:** incapable of being sounded **:** UNFATHOMABLE 〈the *soundless* deep〉

[2]**soundless** *adj* **:** making no sound — **sound·less·ly** *adv*

sound off *vi* **1 :** to count cadence while marching **2 a :** to speak up in a loud voice **b :** to voice one's opinions freely and vigorously

sound pollution *n* **:** NOISE POLLUTION

[1]**sound·proof** \ˈsau̇nd-ˈprüf, ˈsau̇n-\ *adj* **:** impervious to sound

[2]**soundproof** *vt* **:** to insulate so as to obstruct the passage of sound

sound track *n* **1 :** the area on a motion-picture film that carries the sound record **2 :** a recording of the musical score of a motion picture

sound truck *n* **:** a truck equipped with a loudspeaker

sound waves *n pl* **:** longitudinal pressure waves in a material medium regardless of whether they constitute audible sound

soup \ˈsüp\ *n* **1 :** a liquid food with a meat, fish, or vegetable stock as a base and often containing pieces of solid food **2 :** something (as a heavy fog) having or suggesting the consistency of soup **3 :** an unfortunate predicament 〈in the *soup*〉 [French *soupe* "sop, soup," of Germanic origin]

soup·çon \süp-ˈsōⁿ, ˈsüp-ˌsän\ *n* **:** a little bit **:** TRACE 〈a *soupçon* of suspicion〉 [French, literally, "suspicion"]

souped–up \ˈsüpt-ˈəp\ *adj* **:** improved or increased in power, performance, or appeal 〈a *souped-up* car〉 [English slang *soup* "drug injected into a racehorse to improve its performance," from *soup*] — **soup up** *vt*

soup kitchen *n* **:** an establishment dispensing free food (as soup and bread) to the needy

soupy \ˈsü-pē\ *adj* **soup·i·er; -est 1 :** having the consistency of soup **2 :** densely foggy or cloudy

[1]**sour** \ˈsau̇r\ *adj* **1 :** being or inducing the one of the four basic taste sensations characterized by an acid or tart taste 〈*sour* as vinegar〉 **2 a :** having undergone a usually acid fermentation 〈*sour* milk〉 **b :** indicative of decay **:** PUTRID 〈a *sour* odor〉 **3 :** UNPLEASANT, DISAGREEABLE 〈a *sour* look〉 〈hit a *sour* note〉 **4 :** acid in reaction 〈*sour* soil〉 [Old English *sūr*] — **sour·ish** \-ish\ *adj* — **sour·ly** *adv* — **sour·ness** *n*

synonyms SOUR, ACID, TART mean having a taste devoid of sweetness. SOUR usually implies having lost sweetness or freshness through fermentation or spoiling 〈*sour* cream〉. ACID applies to things having naturally or normally a biting or stinging taste 〈*acid* fruits like lemons〉. TART suggests a sharp but agreeable acidity 〈*tart* applesauce〉.

[2]**sour** *n* **1 :** something sour **2 :** the primary taste sensation produced by sour stimuli

[3]**sour** *vb* **:** to become or make sour

sour ball *n* **:** a spherical piece of hard candy having a tart flavor

source \ˈsōrs, ˈsȯrs\ *n* **1 a :** a generative force **:** CAUSE **b** (1) **:** a point of origin (2) **:** one that initiates **:** AUTHOR; *also* **:** PROTOTYPE 2, MODEL (3) **:** one that supplies information **2 :** the point of origin of a stream of water **:** FOUNTAINHEAD **3 :** a firsthand document or primary reference work [Medieval French *surse* "spring, source," from *surdre* "to rise, spring forth," from Latin *surgere*] ***synonyms*** see ORIGIN

source book *n* **:** a fundamental document or record on which subsequent writings, beliefs, or practices are based

sour cherry *n* **:** a small cherry tree widely grown for its soft tart bright red to nearly black fruits; *also* **:** its fruit

sour cream *n* **:** a thick cream soured by the addition of bacteria that form lactic acid and used especially in cooking

sour·dough \ˈsau̇r-ˌdō\ *n* **1 :** a dough in which fermentation is active and which is used to start fermentation in other dough (as in making bread) **2 :** an old-time prospector in Alaska or northwestern Canada [sense 2 from the use of sourdough for making bread in prospectors' camps]

sour grapes *n pl* **:** the belittling of something that has proven unattainable [from the fable ascribed to Aesop of the fox who being unable to reach some grapes he had desired disparaged them as sour]

sour gum *n* **:** BLACK GUM

\ə\ **abut**	\au̇\ **out**	\i\ **tip**	\ȯ\ **saw**	\u̇\ **foot**
\ər\ **further**	\ch\ **chin**	\ī\ **life**	\ȯi\ **coin**	\y\ **yet**
\a\ **mat**	\e\ **pet**	\j\ **job**	\th\ **thin**	\yü\ **few**
\ā\ **take**	\ē\ **easy**	\ng\ **sing**	\th\ **this**	\yu̇\ **cure**
\ä\ **cot, cart**	\g\ **go**	\ō\ **bone**	\ü\ **food**	\zh\ **vision**

sour·sop \ˈsau̇r-ˌsäp\ *n* **:** a small tropical American tree related to the custard apple; *also* **:** its large edible fruit that has fleshy spines and slightly tart pulp

sou·sa·phone \ˈsü-zə-ˌfōn\ *n* **:** a large circular tuba with a flaring adjustable bell [John P. *Sousa*]

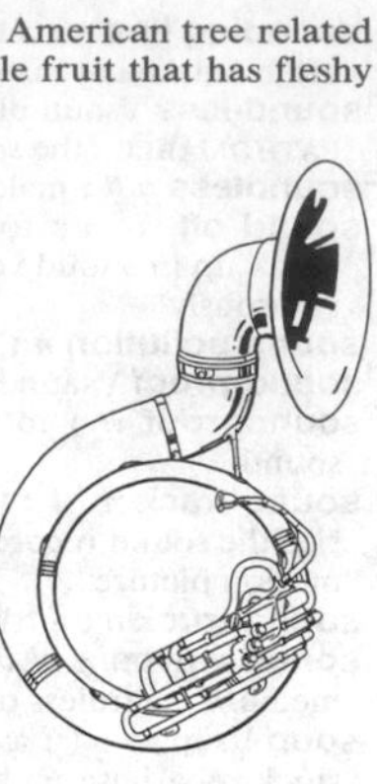
sousaphone

1**souse** \ˈsau̇s\ *vb* **1 :** PICKLE **2 a :** to plunge in liquid **:** IMMERSE **b :** DRENCH 2, SATURATE **3 :** to make or become drunk **:** INEBRIATE [Medieval French *souce* "pickling juice," of Germanic origin]

2**souse** *n* **1 :** something pickled; *esp* **:** seasoned and chopped pork trimmings, fish, or shellfish **2 :** an act or instance of drenching **3 :** an habitual drunkard

sou·tane \sü-ˈtän, -ˈtan\ *n* **:** CASSOCK [French, from Italian *sottana,* literally, "undergarment," derived from Latin *subtus* "underneath"]

1**south** \ˈsau̇th; *in compounds, as "south-west," also* sau̇ *or* ˈsau̇ *especially by seamen*\ *adv* **1 :** to, toward, or in the south ⟨houses facing *south*⟩ **2 :** into a state of decline or ruin ⟨the economy is going *south*⟩ [Old English *sūth*]

2**south** *adj* **1 :** situated toward or at the south ⟨the *south* entrance⟩ **2 :** coming from the south ⟨a *south* wind⟩

3**south** *n* **1 a :** the direction to the right of one facing east **b :** the compass point directly opposite to north **2** *cap* **:** regions or countries south of a specified or implied point

South African *n* **:** a native or inhabitant of the Republic of South Africa; *esp* **:** AFRIKANER — **South African** *adj*

south·bound \ˈsau̇th-ˌbau̇nd\ *adj* **:** headed south ⟨a *southbound* train⟩

1**south·east** \sau̇-ˈthēst, *nautical* sau̇-ˈēst\ *adv* **:** to, toward, or in the southeast

2**southeast** *n* **1 a :** the general direction between south and east **b :** the compass point midway between south and east **:** S 45° E **2** *cap* **:** regions or countries southeast of a specified or implied point

3**southeast** *adj* **1 :** coming from the southeast ⟨*southeast* winds⟩ **2 :** situated toward or at the southeast ⟨the *southeast* corner⟩

south·east·er \sau̇-ˈthē-stər, sau̇-ˈē-stər\ *n* **1 :** a strong southeast wind **2 :** a storm with southeast winds

south·east·er·ly \sau̇-ˈthē-stər-lē\ *adv or adj* **1 :** from the southeast **2 :** toward the southeast

south·east·ern \sau̇-ˈthē-stərn\ *adj* **1** *often cap* **:** of, relating to, or characteristic of a region conventionally designated Southeast **2 :** lying toward or coming from the southeast — **south·east·ern·most** \-stərn-ˌmōst\ *adj*

South·east·ern·er \-stər-nər, -stə-nər\ *n* **:** a native or inhabitant of a southeastern region (as of the U.S.)

1**south·east·ward** \sau̇-ˈthēs-twərd\ *adv or adj* **:** toward the southeast — **south·east·wards** \-twərdz\ *adv*

2**southeastward** *n* **:** SOUTHEAST

south·er \ˈsau̇-t͟hər\ *n* **:** a southerly wind

south·er·ly \ˈsət͟h-ər-lē\ *adv or adj* **1 :** from the south **2 :** toward the south

south·ern \ˈsət͟h-ərn\ *adj* **1** *often cap* **:** of, relating to, or characteristic of a region conventionally designated South **2 :** lying toward or coming from the south [Old English *sūtherne*] — **south·ern·most** \-ˌmōst\ *adj*

Southern *n* **:** the dialect of English spoken in most of the Chesapeake Bay area, the Coastal plain and the greater part of the upland plateau in Virginia, No. Carolina, So. Carolina, and Georgia, and the Gulf states at least as far west as the valley of the Brazos River in central Texas

Southern Cross *n* **:** four bright stars in the southern hemisphere situated as if at the extremities of a Latin cross; *also* **:** the constellation of which these four stars are the brightest

South·ern·er \ˈsət͟h-ər-nər, ˈsət͟h-ə-nər\ *n* **:** a native or inhabitant of the South (as of the U.S.)

southern hemisphere *n* **:** the half of the earth that lies south of the equator

southern lights *n pl* **:** AURORA AUSTRALIS

south·ing \ˈsau̇-thiŋ, -t͟hiŋ\ *n* **1 :** difference in latitude to the south from the last preceding point of reckoning **2 :** southerly progress

south·land \ˈsau̇th-ˌland, -lənd\ *n, often cap* **:** land in the south **:** the south of a country or region

south·paw \ˈsau̇th-ˌpȯ\ *n* **:** a left-handed person; *esp* **:** a left-handed baseball pitcher — **southpaw** *adj*

south pole *n* **1** *often cap S&P* **:** the southernmost point of the earth **:** the southern end of the earth's axis **2 :** the pole of a magnet that points toward the south

South·ron \ˈsət͟h-rən\ *n* **:** SOUTHERNER: as **a** *chiefly Scottish* **:** ENGLISHMAN **b** *chiefly Southern* **:** a native or inhabitant of the southern states of the U.S. [Middle English *southren* "southern," from Old English *sūtherne*]

south–seeking pole *n* **:** SOUTH POLE 2

south–southeast *n* **:** two points east of south **:** S 22° 30′ E

south–southwest *n* **:** two points west of south **:** S 22° 30′ W

1**south·ward** \ˈsau̇th-wərd\ *adv or adj* **:** toward the south — **south·wards** \-wərdz\ *adv*

2**southward** *n* **:** southward direction or part

1**south·west** \sau̇th-ˈwest, *nautical* sau̇-ˈwest\ *adv* **:** to, toward, or in the southwest

2**southwest** *n* **1 a :** the general direction between south and west **b :** the compass point midway between south and west **:** S 45° W **2** *cap* **:** regions or countries southwest of a specified or implied point

3**southwest** *adj* **1 :** coming from the southwest ⟨a *southwest* wind⟩ **2 :** situated toward or at the southwest ⟨the *southwest* corner⟩

south·west·er \sau̇th-ˈwes-tər, sau̇-ˈwes-\ *n* **1 :** a strong southwest wind **2 :** a storm with southwest winds

south·west·er·ly \-ˈwes-tər-lē\ *adv or adj* **1 :** from the southwest **2 :** toward the southwest

south·west·ern \sau̇th-ˈwes-tərn\ *adj* **1** *often cap* **:** of, relating to, or characteristic of a region conventionally designated Southwest **2 :** lying toward or coming from the southwest — **south·west·ern·most** \-stərn-ˌmōst\ *adj*

South·west·ern·er \-tər-nər, -tə-nər\ *n* **:** a native or inhabitant of a southwestern region (as of the U.S.)

1**south·west·ward** \sau̇th-ˈwes-twərd\ *adv or adj* **:** toward the southwest — **south·west·wards** \-twərdz\ *adv*

2**southwestward** *n* **:** SOUTHWEST

sou·ve·nir \ˈsü-və-ˌniər, ˌsü-və-ˈ\ *n* **:** something that serves as a reminder **:** MEMENTO [French, literally, "act of remembering," from (*se*) *souvenir* "to remember," from Latin *subvenire* "to come up, come to mind," from *sub-* "up" + *venire* "to come"]

sou'·west·er \sau̇-ˈwes-tər\ *n* **1 :** SOUTHWESTER **2 a :** a long oilskin coat worn especially at sea during stormy weather **b :** a waterproof hat with wide slanting brim longer in back than in front

sou'wester 2b

1**sov·er·eign** *also* **sov·ran** \ˈsäv-rən, -ərn, -ə-rən, ˈsəv-\ *n* **1 a :** one possessing or held to possess sovereignty; *esp* **:** a monarch exercising supreme authority **b :** one that exercises supreme authority within a limited sphere **:** CHIEF **c :** an acknowledged leader **:** ARBITER **2 :** a British gold coin no longer used worth one pound sterling

2**sovereign** *also* **sovran** *adj* **1 a :** superlative in quality **:** EXCELLENT ⟨their *sovereign* sense of style⟩ **b :** of the most exalted kind **:** SUPREME ⟨*sovereign* virtue⟩ **c :** having generalized curative powers ⟨a *sovereign* remedy for colds⟩ **2 a :** supreme in power or authority ⟨a *sovereign* ruler⟩ **b :** politically independent **:** AUTONOMOUS ⟨a *sovereign* state⟩ [Medieval French *soverain,* derived from Latin *super* "over, above"] ***synonyms*** see FREE — **sov·er·eign·ly** *adv*

sov·er·eign·ty \-tē\ *n, pl* **-ties 1 a :** supreme power especially over a political unit **b :** freedom from external control **2 :** one that is sovereign; *esp* **:** an autonomous state

so·vi·et \ˈsōv-ē-ˌet, ˈsäv-, -ē-ət\ *n* **1 :** an elected governmental council in a Communist country **2** *pl, cap* **a :** BOLSHEVIK 1 **b :** the people and especially the political and military leaders of the Union of Soviet Socialist Republics [Russian *sovet* "council, soviet"] — **soviet** *adj, often cap* — **so·vi·et·ism** \-ˌiz-əm\ *n, often cap*

so·vi·et·ize \-ˌīz\ *vt, often cap* **1 :** to bring under Soviet control **2 :** to force into conformity with Soviet cultural patterns or governmental policies — **so·vi·et·iza·tion** \ˌsōv-ē-ˌet-ə-ˈzā-shən, ˌsäv-ē-, -ē-ət-\ *n, often cap*

sov·khoz \säf-ˈkȯz\ *n, pl* **sov·kho·zy** \-ˈkȯ-zē\ *or* **sov·khoz·es** : a state-owned farm of the former Union of Soviet Socialist Republics paying wages to the workers — compare KOLKHOZ [Russian, from *sovetskoe khozyaĭstvo* "soviet farm"]

[1]**sow** \ˈsaù\ *n* : an adult female swine; *also* : the adult female of various other animals (as a bear) [Old English *sugu*]

[2]**sow** \ˈsō\ *vb* **sowed; sown** \ˈsōn\ *or* **sowed; sow·ing** **1 a** : to plant seed for growth especially by scattering **b** : PLANT 1a **c** : to strew with or as if with seed **d** : to introduce into a selected environment : DISTRIBUTE **2** : to set in motion : FOMENT ⟨*sow* suspicion⟩ **3** : to spread abroad : DISSEMINATE [Old English *sāwan*] — **sow·er** \ˈsō-ər, ˈsȯr\ *n*

sow·bel·ly \ˈsaù-ˌbel-ē\ *n* : fat salt pork or bacon

sow bug \ˈsaù-\ *n* : WOOD LOUSE; *esp* : a wood louse capable of curling itself into a ball

sow thistle \ˈsaù-\ *n* : any of a genus of spiny weedy Eurasian and African herbs related to the daisies and widely naturalized in North America

sox *plural of* SOCK

soy \ˈsȯi\ *n* **1** : SOY SAUCE **2** : SOYBEAN [Japanese *shōyu*]

soya \ˈsȯi-ə, ˈsȯi-yə\ *n* : SOYBEAN [Dutch *soja,* from Japanese *shōyu* "soy"]

soy·bean \ˈsȯi-ˈbēn, -ˌbēn\ *n* : a hairy annual Asian plant of the legume family widely grown for its oil-rich and protein-rich edible seeds and for forage and soil improvement; *also* : its seed

soybean

soy sauce *n* : a brown sauce made from soybeans fermented in brine and used especially in Chinese and Japanese cooking

spa \ˈspä, ˈspȯ\ *n* **1 a** : a mineral spring **b** : a resort with mineral springs **2** : a fashionable resort or hotel **3** : a commercial establishment (as a resort) providing facilities devoted especially to health, fitness, beauty, weight loss, or relaxation **4** : a hot tub with a whirlpool device [*Spa,* watering place in Belgium]

[1]**space** \ˈspās\ *n* **1** : a period of time; *also* : its duration **2 a** : a limited extent in one, two, or three dimensions **b** : an extent set apart or available ⟨parking *space*⟩ ⟨floor *space*⟩ **3** : one of the degrees between or above or below the lines of a musical staff **4** : a boundless three-dimensional extent in which objects and events occur and have relative position and direction **5** : the region beyond the earth's atmosphere **6 a** : a blank area separating words or lines **b** : something (as a piece of type) used to produce such a blank area **7** : a set of mathematical elements together with a set of geometric axioms ⟨a vector *space*⟩ **8 a** : LINAGE 1 **b** : broadcast time available especially to advertisers [Medieval French *espace,* from Latin *spatium* "area, room, interval of space or time"]

[2]**space** *vt* : to place at intervals or arrange with space between ⟨*space* out the chairs one foot apart⟩ — **spac·er** *n*

space–age \ˈspā-ˌsāj\ *adj* : of or relating to the age of space exploration; *esp* : MODERN ⟨*space-age* technology⟩

space cadet *n* : a person who is confused, forgetful, or markedly inattentive

space charge *n* : an electric charge (as the electrons in the region near the filament of a vacuum tube) distributed throughout a three-dimensional region

space·craft \ˈspā-ˌskraft\ *n, pl* **spacecraft** : a vehicle designed to operate outside the earth's atmosphere

spaced–out \ˈspā-ˈstaùt\ *adj* **1** *or* **spaced** : dazed or stupefied by or as if by a drug **2** : of very strange character : WEIRD ⟨a *spaced-out* fantasy⟩

space·flight \ˈspās-ˌflīt\ *n* : flight beyond the earth's atmosphere

space frame *n* : a usually open framework of struts and braces (as in buildings or vehicles) which defines a structure and distributes its weight evenly

space heater *n* : a usually portable device for heating a small area

space·less \ˈspā-sləs\ *adj* **1** : having no limits : BOUNDLESS **2** : occupying no space

space·man \-ˌsman, -smən\ *n* **1** : one who travels outside the earth's atmosphere **2** : a visitor to earth from outer space

space medicine *n* : a branch of medicine that deals with the effects of spaceflight on the human body

space out *vi* : to become inattentive or distracted ⟨*spaced out* halfway through the lecture⟩

space·port \ˈspā-ˌspōrt, -ˌspȯrt\ *n* : an installation for testing and launching rockets, missiles, and satellites

space·ship \ˈspās-ˌship, ˈspāsh-\ *n* : SPACECRAFT

space shuttle *n* : a spacecraft designed to transport people and cargo between earth and space that can be used repeatedly

space station *n* : an artificial satellite designed to stay in orbit permanently and be occupied by humans for long periods

space suit *n* : a suit equipped to make life in space possible for its wearer

space–time \ˈspā-ˈstīm\ *n* **1** : a system of one temporal and three spatial coordinates by which any physical object or event can be located **2** : the whole or a portion of physical reality determinable by a usually four-dimensional coordinate system

space walk *n* : a period of activity outside a spacecraft by an astronaut in space

spacial *variant of* SPATIAL

spac·ing \ˈspā-sing\ *n* **1** : an arrangement in space **2** : the distance between any two objects in a usually regular series

spa·cious \ˈspā-shəs\ *adj* **1** : vast or ample in extent : ROOMY ⟨a *spacious* hall⟩ **2** : large or magnificent in scale : EXPANSIVE — **spa·cious·ly** *adv* — **spa·cious·ness** *n*

[1]**spade** \ˈspād\ *n* **1** : a digging implement adapted for being pushed into the ground with the foot **2** : a spade-shaped instrument [Old English *spadu*] — **spade·ful** *n* — **call a spade a spade** **1** : to call a thing by its right name however coarse **2** : to speak frankly

[2]**spade** *vb* : to dig with or use a spade — **spad·er** *n*

[3]**spade** *n* : a black figure resembling an inverted heart with a short stem at the bottom used to distinguish a suit of playing cards; *also* : a card of the suit bearing spades [Italian *spada* or Spanish *espada* "broad sword"; both from Latin *spatha,* "blade," from Greek *spathē*]

spade·foot toad \ˈspād-ˌfùt\ *n* : any of several burrowing toads with the feet modified for digging — called also *spadefoot*

spade·work \ˈspād-ˌwərk\ *n* **1** : work done with a spade **2** : the preliminary hard work in an undertaking

spa·dix \ˈspād-iks\ *n, pl* **spa·di·ces** \ˈspād-ə-ˌsēz\ : a floral spike (as in the arums) with a fleshy or succulent axis usually enclosed in a spathe [Latin, "frond torn from a palm tree," from Greek, from *span* "to draw, pull"]

spa·ghet·ti \spə-ˈget-ē\ *n* : pasta made in thin solid strings [Italian, from pl. of *spaghetto* "little string," from *spago* "string"]

spaghetti squash *n* : an oval winter squash with flesh that once cooked is similar in appearance to spaghetti

spaghetti strap *n* : a very thin fabric shoulder strap

spake \ˈspāk\ *archaic past of* SPEAK

[1]**spam** \ˈspam\ *n* : unsolicited usually commercial e-mail sent to a large number of addresses [probably from a skit on the British television series *Monty Python's Flying Circus* in which chanting of the word *spam* overrides the other dialogue]

[2]**spam** *vt* : to send spam to — **spam·mer** *n*

[1]**span** \ˈspan\ *archaic past of* SPIN

[2]**span** *n* **1** : the distance from the end of the thumb to the end of the little finger of a spread hand; *also* : an English unit of length equal to 9 inches (about 22.9 centimeters) **2** : an extent, stretch, reach, or spread between two limits: as **a** : a limited space of time ⟨*span* of life⟩ **b** : the spread of an arch, beam, truss, or girder from one support to another; *also* : the portion thus extended [Old English *spann*]

[3]**span** *vt* **spanned; span·ning** **1 a** : to measure by or as if by the hand with fingers and thumb extended **b** : MEASURE 3 **2 a** : to reach or extend across ⟨a bridge *spans* the river⟩ **b** : to place or construct a span over

[4]**span** *n* : a pair of animals (as mules) driven together [Dutch, from *spannen* "to hitch up"]

\ə\ **abut**	\aù\ **out**	\i\ **tip**	\ȯ\ **saw**	\ù\ **foot**
\ər\ **further**	\ch\ **chin**	\ī\ **life**	\ȯi\ **coin**	\y\ **yet**
\a\ **mat**	\e\ **pet**	\j\ **job**	\th\ **thin**	\yü\ **few**
\ā\ **take**	\ē\ **easy**	\ng\ **sing**	\t͟h\ **this**	\yù\ **cure**
\ä\ **cot, cart**	\g\ **go**	\ō\ **bone**	\ü\ **food**	\zh\ **vision**

span·dex \ˈspan-ˌdeks\ *n* **:** any of various synthetic elastic textile fibers

span·drel *also* **span·dril** \ˈspan-drəl\ *n* **:** the sometimes ornamented space between the right or left exterior curve of an arch and an enclosing right angle [Medieval French *spaunder,* from *espandre* "to spread out, expand," from Latin *expandere*]

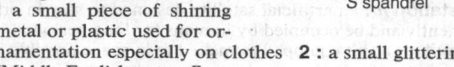

S spandrel

[1]**span·gle** \ˈspang-gəl\ *n* **1 :** a small piece of shining metal or plastic used for ornamentation especially on clothes **2 :** a small glittering object [Middle English *spangel*]

[2]**spangle** *vb* **span·gled; span·gling** \ˈspang-gə-ling, -gling\ **1 :** to set or sprinkle with or as if with spangles **2 :** to glitter as if covered with spangles **:** SPARKLE

Span·glish \ˈspang-glish, -lish\ *n* **:** Spanish marked by many borrowings from English; *also* **:** any of various combinations of Spanish and English

Span·iard \ˈspan-yərd\ *n* **:** a native or inhabitant of Spain [Medieval French *Espaignard,* from *Espaigne* "Spain," from Latin *Hispania*]

span·iel \ˈspan-yəl\ *n* **1 :** a member of any of several breeds of small or medium-sized mostly short-legged dogs usually having long wavy hair, feathered legs and tail, and large drooping ears **2 :** TOADY [Middle French *espaignol,* literally, "Spaniard," derived from Latin *Hispania* "Spain"]

spaniel 1

Span·ish \ˈspan-ish\ *n* **1 :** the Romance language of the largest part of Spain and of the countries colonized by Spaniards **2** *pl in constr* **:** the people of Spain [Middle English *Spainish,* from *Spain*] — **Spanish** *adj*

Spanish American *n* **1 :** a native or inhabitant of one of the countries of America in which Spanish is the national language **2 :** a resident of the U.S. whose native language is Spanish and whose culture is of Spanish origin — **Spanish–American** *adj*

Spanish fly *n* **:** a green blister beetle of southern Europe; *also* **:** a dried preparation of these formerly used in medicine and as an aphrodisiac

Spanish mackerel *n* **:** a large fish of the Atlantic coast of North America that is related to the common mackerel

Spanish moss *n* **:** an epiphytic plant related to the pineapple that forms hanging tufts of grayish green filaments on trees from the southern U.S. to Argentina

Spanish omelet *n* **:** an omelet made usually with chopped green pepper, onion, and tomato

Spanish rice *n* **:** rice cooked with onions, green pepper, and tomatoes

spank \ˈspangk\ *vt* **:** to strike especially on the buttocks with the open hand [imitative] — **spank** *n*

spank·er \ˈspang-kər\ *n* **:** the fore-and-aft sail on the mast nearest the stern of a square-rigged ship [origin unknown]

[1]**spank·ing** \ˈspang-king\ *adj* **1 :** remarkable of its kind **2 a :** moving or able to move briskly **b :** being fresh and strong ⟨a *spanking* wind⟩ [origin unknown]

[2]**spanking** *adv* **:** VERY 1 ⟨a *spanking* clean floor⟩ ⟨*spanking* new⟩

span·ner \ˈspan-ər\ *n* **1** *chiefly British* **:** WRENCH 2 **2 :** a wrench having a jaw or socket to fit a nut or head of a bolt, a pipe, or hose coupling; *esp* **:** one having a tooth or pin in its jaw to fit a hole or slot in an object [German, "instrument for winding springs," from *spannen* "to stretch"]

span–new \ˈspan-ˈnü, -ˈnyü\ *adj* **:** BRAND-NEW [Old Norse *spānnȳr,* from *spānn* "chip of wood" + *nȳr* "new"]

span·worm \ˈspan-ˌwərm\ *n* **:** LOOPER 1

[1]**spar** \ˈspär\ *n* **1 :** a stout pole **2 :** a stout rounded usually wood or metal piece (as a mast, boom, or yard) used to support sail rigging **3 :** one of the main longitudinal members of the wing of an airplane that carry the ribs [Middle English *sparre*]

S [1]spar 2

[2]**spar** *vi* **sparred; spar·ring 1 a :** BOX; *esp* **:** to gesture without landing a blow to draw one's opponent or create an opening **b :** to engage in a practice or exhibition bout of boxing **2 :** SKIRMISH 1, WRANGLE [Middle English *sparren* "to dart, spring"]

[3]**spar** *n* **:** a sparring match or session

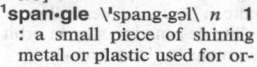

[1]**spare** \ˈspaər, ˈspeər\ *vb* **1 :** to refrain from destroying, punishing, or harming **:** be lenient ⟨*spare* a prisoner⟩ **2 :** to refrain from attacking or reprimanding ⟨the sermon *spared* no one⟩ **3 :** to free of the need to do or undergo something ⟨*spare* yourself the trouble⟩ **4 :** to refrain from **:** AVOID ⟨*spare* no cost⟩ **5 :** to use or give out frugally ⟨don't *spare* the syrup⟩ **6 a :** to give up as not strictly needed ⟨can you *spare* a dollar⟩ **b :** to have left over or as margin ⟨time to *spare*⟩ [Old English *sparian*] — **spare·able** \-ə-bəl\ *adj* — **spar·er** *n*

[2]**spare** *adj* **1 :** not being used; *esp* **:** held for emergency use ⟨a *spare* tire⟩ **2 :** being over and above what is needed **:** SUPERFLUOUS ⟨*spare* time⟩ **3 :** not liberal or profuse **:** MEAGER ⟨a *spare* diet⟩ **4 :** healthily lean ⟨a *spare* build⟩ **5 :** not abundant or plentiful **:** SCANTY [Old English *spær* "sparing, scant"] — **spare·ly** *adv* — **spare·ness** *n*

[3]**spare** *n* **1 :** a spare or duplicate piece or part (as an automobile tire) **2 a :** the knocking down of all 10 pins with 2 bowls in a frame in bowling **b :** the score made by this action

spare·ribs \ˈspaər-ˌribz, ˈspeər-, -ˌibz\ *n pl* **:** a cut of pork ribs separated from the bacon strip [by folk etymology from Low German *ribbesper* "pickled pork ribs roasted on a spit," from *ribbe* "rib" + *sper* "spear, spit"]

spar·ing \ˈspaər-ing, ˈspeər-\ *adj* **1 :** careful in the use of money or supplies **2 :** MEAGER 2, BARE ⟨the map is *sparing* of information⟩ — **spar·ing·ly** \-ing-lē\ *adv*

[1]**spark** \ˈspärk\ *n* **1 a :** a small particle of a burning substance **b :** a hot glowing particle struck from a larger mass; *esp* **:** one heated by friction **2 :** a luminous electrical discharge of very short duration between two conductors **3 :** SPARKLE 1, FLASH **4 :** something that sets off a sudden force ⟨the *spark* that set off the riot⟩ **5 :** SEED 4, GERM ⟨still has a *spark* of decency⟩ [Old English *spearca*]

[2]**spark** *vb* **1 a :** to throw out or produce sparks **b :** to flash or fall like sparks **2 :** to respond with enthusiasm **3 :** to set off in a burst of activity **:** ACTIVATE ⟨the question *sparked* a lively discussion⟩ **4 :** to stir to activity **:** INCITE ⟨the captain *sparked* the team to victory⟩ — **spark·er** *n*

[3]**spark** *n* **1 :** a foppish young man **:** GALLANT **2 :** SUITOR 3, SWAIN [perhaps from [1]*spark*] — **spark·ish** \ˈspär-kish\ *adj*

[4]**spark** *vb* **:** WOO 1a, COURT — **spark·er** *n*

sparking plug *n, British* **:** SPARK PLUG 1

[1]**spar·kle** \ˈspär-kəl\ *vi* **spar·kled; spar·kling** \-kə-ling, -kling\ **1 a :** SPARK 1a **b :** to give off or reflect bright moving points of light ⟨the diamond *sparkled*⟩ **2 :** to perform brilliantly ⟨*sparkled* at shortstop⟩ **3 :** EFFERVESCE ⟨wine that *sparkles*⟩ **4 :** to become lively or animated ⟨eyes *sparkling* with anger⟩ [from *spark*] ***synonyms*** see FLASH

[2]**sparkle** *n* **1 :** a little spark **:** SCINTILLATION ⟨the *sparkle* of a diamond⟩ **2 :** the quality of sparkling **3 a :** ANIMATION, LIVELINESS ⟨the *sparkle* of your wit⟩ **b :** EFFERVESCENCE

spar·kler \ˈspär-klər\ *n* **:** one that sparkles: as **a :** DIAMOND 1a **b :** a firework that throws off brilliant sparks on burning

sparkling wine *n* **:** an effervescent red or white wine

spark plug *n* **1 :** a part that fits into the cylinder head of an internal-combustion engine and produces the spark for combustion **2 :** one that activates or gives impetus to an undertaking — **spark·plug** \ˈspärk-ˌpləg\ *vt*

sparky \ˈspär-kē\ *adj* **spark·i·er; -est :** being lively and active ⟨*sparky* children⟩ — **spark·i·ly** \-kə-lē\ *adv*

spar·row \ˈspar-ō\ *n* **1 :** any of several small usually brownish or grayish songbirds related to the finches; *esp* : HOUSE SPARROW **2 :** any of numerous finches (as the song sparrow) resembling the true sparrows [Old English *spearwa*]

sparrow hawk *n* : any of various small hawks (as a kestrel)

sparse \ˈspärs\ *adj* : of few and scattered elements; *esp* : not thickly grown or settled [Latin *sparsus* "spread out," from *spargere* "to scatter"] ***synonyms*** see MEAGER — **sparse·ly** *adv* — **sparse·ness** *n* — **spar·si·ty** \ˈspär-sət-ē\ *n*

1**Spar·tan** \ˈspärt-n\ *n* **1 :** a native or inhabitant of ancient Sparta **2 :** a person of great courage and fortitude

2**Spartan** *adj* **1 :** of or relating to ancient Sparta **2 a** *often not cap* : marked by strict self-discipline or self-denial ⟨a *Spartan* athlete⟩ **b** *often not cap* : marked by simplicity and frugality ⟨*Spartan* living conditions⟩ **c :** LACONIC **d :** undaunted by pain or danger ⟨*Spartan* courage⟩ — **Spar·tan·ly** *adv*

spar varnish *n* : an exterior waterproof varnish [1*spar*]

spasm \ˈspaz-əm\ *n* **1 :** an involuntary and abnormal muscular contraction ⟨back *spasms*⟩ **2 :** a sudden violent and temporary effort, emotion, or sensation ⟨*spasms* of creativity⟩ ⟨*spasms* of pain⟩ [Medieval French *espasme,* from Latin *spasmus,* from Greek *spasmos,* from *span* "to draw, pull"] — **spasm** *vi*

spas·mod·ic \spaz-ˈmäd-ik\ *adj* **1 :** relating to or affected or characterized by spasm ⟨*spasmodic* movements⟩ **2 :** acting or proceeding fitfully : INTERMITTENT ⟨*spasmodic* interest⟩ **3 :** subject to outbursts of emotional excitement : EXCITABLE [Greek *spasmōdēs,* from *spasmos* "spasm"] — **spas·mod·i·cal·ly** \-ˈmäd-i-kə-lē, -klē\ *adv*

spas·tic \ˈspas-tik\ *adj* : of, relating to, characterized by, or affected with or as if with spasm ⟨a *spastic* colon⟩ [Latin *spasticus,* from Greek *spastikos* "drawing in," from *span* "to draw, pull"] — **spas·ti·cal·ly** \-ti-kə-lē, -klē\ *adv* — **spas·tic·i·ty** \spa-ˈstis-ət-ē\ *n*

spastic paralysis *n* : paralysis from rigidly contracted muscles and increased tendon reflexes

1**spat** \ˈspat\ *past of* SPIT

2**spat** *n, pl* **spat** *or* **spats :** a young bivalve mollusk (as an oyster) — usually used collectively [origin unknown]

3**spat** *n* : a cloth or leather gaiter covering the instep and ankle [short for *spatterdash,* a kind of legging worn as protection from water and mud]

3spat

4**spat** *n* **1** *chiefly dialect* : SLAP 1 **2 :** a brief petty quarrel : TIFF **3 :** a sound like that of rain falling in large drops ⟨the *spat* of bullets⟩ [origin unknown]

5**spat** *vb* **spat·ted; spat·ting 1** *chiefly dialect* : SLAP 1a **2 :** to quarrel pettily or briefly : TIFF **3 :** to strike with a sound like that of rain falling in large drops

spate \ˈspāt\ *n* **1 :** FLOOD 1a, FRESHET **2 a :** a large number or amount **b :** a sudden or strong outburst : RUSH ⟨a *spate* of anger⟩ [Middle English]

spathe \ˈspāth\ *n* : a sheathing bract or pair of bracts enclosing an inflorescence and especially a spadix [Latin *spatha* "blade, broad sword," from Greek *spathē* "blade"] — **spathed** \ˈspāthd\ *adj*

spa·tial *also* **spa·cial** \ˈspā-shəl\ *adj* **1 :** relating to, occupying, or having the character of space **2 :** of or relating to aptitude in perceiving relations (as of objects) in space ⟨tests of *spatial* ability⟩ [Latin *spatium* "space"] — **spa·ti·al·i·ty** \ˌspā-shē-ˈal-ət-ē\ *n* — **spa·tial·ly** \ˈspāsh-lē, -ə-lē\ *adv*

1**spat·ter** \ˈspat-ər\ *vb* **1 :** to splash with or as if with a liquid; *also* : to soil or spot in this way **2 :** to scatter by splashing ⟨*spatter* mud⟩ **3 :** to cast aspersions on : DEFAME ⟨*spatter* a good reputation⟩ **4 a :** to spurt out in scattered drops **b :** to drop with a sound like rain [related to Frisian *spatterje* "to spatter"]

2**spatter** *n* **1 :** the act or sound of spattering : the state of being spattered **2 a :** a drop or splash spattered on something **b :** a small amount or number : SPRINKLE ⟨a *spatter* of applause⟩

spat·ter·dock \ˈspat-ər-ˌdäk\ *n* : a common North American water lily with yellow flowers

spat·u·la \ˈspach-ə-lə\ *n* : a flat thin implement used especially for spreading or mixing soft substances, scooping, or lifting [Late Latin, "spoon, spatula," from Latin *spatha* "blade, sword," from Greek *spathē* "blade"]

spat·u·late \ˈspach-ə-lət\ *adj* : shaped like a spatula ⟨a *spatulate* leaf⟩ ⟨a *spatulate* tool⟩

spav·in \ˈspav-ən\ *n* : a bony enlargement of the hock of a horse associated with strain [Medieval French *espavin*]

spav·ined \-ənd\ *adj* **1 :** affected with spavin **2 :** old and decrepit

1**spawn** \ˈspȯn, ˈspän\ *vb* **1 a :** to deposit or fertilize eggs — used of an aquatic animal **b :** to induce (fish) to spawn **2 :** to bring forth : GENERATE ⟨*spawn* ideas⟩ **3 :** to produce young especially in large numbers [Medieval French *espandre* "to spread out, shed, scatter, spawn," from Latin *expandere* "to expand"] — **spawn·er** *n*

2**spawn** *n* **1 :** the eggs of aquatic animals (as fishes or oysters) that lay many small eggs **2 a :** PRODUCT 2 **b :** OFFSPRING; *also* : offspring produced in large quantities **3 :** the seed, germ, or source of something **4 :** mycelium especially prepared (as in bricks) for propagating mushrooms

spay \ˈspā\ *vt* : to remove the ovaries and uterus of (a female animal) [Medieval French *espeer* "to pierce, castrate," from *espee* "sword," from Latin *spatha,* from Greek *spathē* "blade"]

speak \ˈspēk\ *vb* **spoke** \ˈspōk\; **spo·ken** \ˈspō-kən\; **speak·ing 1 :** to utter words with the voice : TALK **2 :** to utter by means of words ⟨*speak* the truth⟩ **3 :** to address a gathering **4 :** to mention in speech or writing ⟨*spoke* of being ill⟩ **5 :** to serve as spokesperson ⟨*spoke* for the whole group⟩ **6 :** to express feelings in ways other than by words ⟨actions *speak* louder than words⟩ **7 :** to make a natural or characteristic sound ⟨the big gun *spoke*⟩ **8 :** to be indicative or suggestive ⟨wore clothes that *spoke* of poverty⟩ **9 :** to use or be able to use in speaking ⟨*speaks* French⟩ [Old English *sprecan, specan*] — **speak·able** \ˈspē-kə-bəl\ *adj* — **speak to :** REPROVE 2, REBUKE — **speak well for :** to be evidence in favor of — **to speak of :** worthy of mention or notice ⟨no help *to speak of*⟩

synonyms SPEAK, TALK mean to articulate words in order to express thoughts. SPEAK may apply to any articulated sounds ranging from the least to the most coherent ⟨is *speaking* gibberish⟩. TALK is less technical and less formal and implies a listener and connected discourse or exchange of thoughts ⟨likes to *talk* to me about his troubles⟩.

speak·easy \ˈspē-ˌkē-zē\ *n* : a place where alcoholic drinks are illegally sold

speak·er \ˈspē-kər\ *n* **1 a :** one that speaks **b :** a person who makes a public speech or acts as a spokesperson **2 :** the presiding officer of a deliberative assembly ⟨*Speaker* of the House of Representatives⟩ **3 :** LOUDSPEAKER

speak·er·ship \-ˌship\ *n* : the position of speaker especially of a legislative body

speak·ing \ˈspē-king\ *adj* **1 a :** that speaks : capable of speech **b :** having a population that speaks a specified language — usually used in combination ⟨English-*speaking* countries⟩ **c :** that involves talking or giving speeches ⟨a *speaking* role⟩ ⟨a *speaking* tour⟩ **2 :** highly significant or expressive : ELOQUENT ⟨*speaking* eyes⟩ **3 :** closely resembling a living being or a real object ⟨a *speaking* portrait of the child⟩

speaking tube *n* : a pipe through which conversation may be conducted (as between different parts of a building)

speak–out \ˈspēk-ˌau̇t\ *n* : an event in which people publicly share their experiences of or views on an issue

speak out *vi* **1 :** to speak loud enough to be heard **2 :** to speak boldly : express an opinion frankly ⟨*spoke out* on the issue⟩

speak up *vi* **1 :** to speak loudly and clearly **2 :** to express an opinion freely ⟨*speak up* for justice⟩

1**spear** \ˈspiər\ *n* **1 :** a thrusting or throwing weapon with a long shaft and sharp head or blade **2 :** a sharp-pointed instrument with barbs used in spearing fish **3 :** SPEARMAN [Old English *spere*]

2**spear** *adj* : PATERNAL 3 ⟨the *spear* side of the family⟩ [1*spear* — see *Word History* at DISTAFF]

3**spear** *vb* **1 :** to pierce or strike with or as if with a spear **2 :** to thrust with or as if with a spear — **spear·er** *n*

[4]**spear** *n* : a usually young blade, shoot, or sprout (as of grass) [alteration of [1]*spire*]

[1]**spear·fish** \ˈspiər-ˌfish\ *n* : any of several large sea fishes that have long slender jaws and are related to the marlins and sailfishes

[2]**spearfish** *vi* : to fish with a spear

spear·gun \ˈspiər-ˌgən\ *n* : a gun that shoots a spear and is used for spearfishing

[1]**spear·head** \ˈspiər-ˌhed\ *n* **1** : the sharp-pointed head of a spear **2** : a leading element, force, or influence in an undertaking or development

[2]**spearhead** *vt* : to serve as leader or leading element of

spear·man \ˈspiər-mən\ *n* : a person armed with a spear

spear·mint \-ˌmint, -mənt\ *n* : a common mint grown for flavoring and especially for its aromatic oil

spearmint

spec \ˈspek\ *n* : SPECIFICATION 2a(1) — usually used in plural

[1]**spe·cial** \ˈspesh-əl\ *adj* **1 a** : distinguished by some unusual quality ⟨a *special* occasion⟩; *esp* : being in some way superior ⟨a *special* blend of spices⟩ **b** : regarded with particular favor ⟨a *special* friend⟩ **2 a** : distinctive in character : PECULIAR ⟨a *special* case⟩ **b** : of, relating to, or constituting a species : SPECIFIC ⟨a *special* concept⟩ **3** : additional to what is usual ⟨a *special* edition⟩ **4** : designed for a particular purpose or occasion ⟨a *special* diet⟩ [Latin *specialis* "individual, particular," from *species* "species"] — **spe·cial·ly** \ˈspesh-lē, -ə-lē\ *adv*

[2]**special** *n* **1** : one that is used for a special service ⟨caught a commuter *special*⟩ **2** : something (as a television program) that is not part of a regular series **3** : a featured dish at a restaurant ⟨the *specials* of the day⟩

special delivery *n* : a messenger delivery of mail ahead of the regular carrier delivery for an extra fee

special education *n* : classes or instruction designed for students with special educational needs

special effects *n pl* : visual or sound effects introduced into a motion picture, video recording, or taped television production

spe·cial·ist \ˈspesh-ləst, -ə-ləst\ *n* **1** : one who specializes in a particular occupation, practice, or branch of learning ⟨an eye *specialist*⟩ **2** : an enlisted rank in the U.S. Army comparable to the grade of corporal; *also* : any of several former enlisted ranks comparable to sergeant through sergeant first class — **specialist** *or* **spe·cial·is·tic** \ˌspesh-ə-ˈlis-tik\ *adj*

spe·ci·al·i·ty \ˌspesh-ē-ˈal-ət-ē\ *n, pl* **-ties** **1** : a special mark or quality **2** : a special object or class of objects **3 a** : a special aptitude or skill **b** : SPECIALTY 3

spe·cial·i·za·tion \ˌspesh-lə-ˈzā-shən, -ə-lə-\ *n* **1** : a making or becoming specialized **2 a** : structural adaptation of a body part to a particular function or of an organism for life in a particular environment **b** : a body part or an organism adapted by specialization

spe·cial·ize \ˈspesh-ə-ˌlīz\ *vb* **1** : to make particular mention of : PARTICULARIZE **2** : to apply or direct to a specific end or use ⟨*specialized* study⟩ **3** : to concentrate one's efforts in a special activity or field ⟨*specialize* in French⟩ **4** : to undergo specialization; *esp* : to change adaptively

spe·cial·ized \-ˌlīzd\ *adj* **1** : characterized by or exhibiting biological specialization **2** : designed, trained, or fitted for one particular purpose or occupation

special relativity *n* : RELATIVITY 2a

spe·cial·ty \ˈspesh-əl-tē\ *n, pl* **-ties** **1** : a distinctive mark or quality **2 a** : a special object or class of objects; *esp* : a product of a special kind or of special excellence ⟨pancakes were the cook's *specialty*⟩ **b** : the state of being special, distinctive, or peculiar **3** : something in which one specializes or has special knowledge

spe·ci·a·tion \ˌspē-shē-ˈā-shən, ˌspē-sē-\ *n* : differentiation into new biological species — **spe·ci·ate** \ˈspē-shē-ˌāt, -sē-\ *vi*

spe·cie \ˈspē-shē, -sē\ *n* : money in coin [from in *specie* "in kind, in coin," from Latin, "in kind"] — **in specie** : in the same or like form or kind ⟨ready to return insult *in specie*⟩; *also* : in coin

[1]**spe·cies** \ˈspē-ˌshēz, -shēz, -ˌsēz, -sēz\ *n, pl* **species** **1 a** : a class of individuals with common qualities and a common name : KIND, SORT **b** (1) : a category of biological classification ranking below the genus, comprising related organisms or populations potentially capable of interbreeding, and being designated by a binomial that consists of the name of its genus followed by a Latin or latinized uncapitalized noun or adjective (2) : an individual or kind belonging to a biological species **2** : the consecrated eucharistic elements [Latin, "appearance, kind, species," from *specere* "to look at"]

[2]**species** *adj* : belonging to a biological species as distinguished from a horticultural variety ⟨a *species* rose⟩

[1]**spe·cif·ic** \spi-ˈsif-ik\ *adj* **1** : of, relating to, or being something that has been or can be specified ⟨a *specific* case⟩ ⟨do you have a *specific* question?⟩ ⟨a ban on *specific* pesticides⟩ **2 a** : restricted to a particular individual, situation, relation, effect, or reaction ⟨a disease *specific* to humans⟩ ⟨a *specific* enzyme⟩ **b** : exerting a distinctive and usually a causative or curative influence ⟨quinine is *specific* for malaria⟩ **3** : precisely and accurately formulated ⟨a *specific* statement of faith⟩ **4** : of, relating to, or constituting a species [Late Latin *specificus,* from Latin *species* "species"] ***synonyms*** see EXPLICIT — **spe·cif·i·cal·ly** \-ˈsif-i-kə-lē, -klē\ *adv*

[2]**specific** *n* **1 a** : something peculiarly adapted to a purpose or use **b** : a drug or remedy specific for a particular disease **2 a** : a characteristic quality or trait **b** : precise details or distinctions : PARTICULARS ⟨get down to *specifics*⟩ **c** *pl* : SPECIFICATION 2a

spec·i·fi·ca·tion \ˌspes-fə-ˈkā-shən, -ə-fə-\ *n* **1** : the act or process of specifying **2 a** (1) : a detailed precise presentation of something or of a plan or proposal for something — often used in plural ⟨the architect's *specifications* for a new building⟩ (2) : a written description of an invention for which a patent is sought **b** : a single item in such a detailed presentation

specific gravity *n* : the ratio of the density of a substance to the density of some other substance (as water) taken as a standard when both densities are obtained by weighing in air

specific heat *n* : the heat in calories required to raise the temperature of one gram of a substance one degree Celsius

spec·i·fic·i·ty \ˌspes-ə-ˈfis-ət-ē\ *n* : the quality or condition of being specific; *esp* : the condition of participating in or catalyzing only one or a few chemical reactions ⟨the *specificity* of an enzyme⟩

spec·i·fy \ˈspes-ə-ˌfī\ *vt* **-fied; -fy·ing** **1** : to name or state explicitly or in detail ⟨*specify* the reason for absence⟩ **2** : to include as an item in a specification ⟨*specify* oak flooring⟩ [Medieval French *specifier,* from Late Latin *specificare,* from *specificus* "specific"] — **spec·i·fi·able** \ˌspes-ə-ˈfī-ə-bəl\ *adj* — **spec·i·fi·er** \ˈspes-ə-ˌfī-ər, -ˌfīr\ *n*

spec·i·men \ˈspes-ə-mən\ *n* **1** : an item or part typical of a group or whole : SAMPLE **2** : a portion or quantity of material for use in testing, examination, or study ⟨a blood *specimen*⟩ **3** : PERSON, INDIVIDUAL ⟨a tough *specimen*⟩ **4** : a plant grown for exhibition or in the open for full display ⟨*specimen* trees⟩ [Latin, from *specere* "to look at"]

spe·cious \ˈspē-shəs\ *adj* : having a false look of truth, fairness, or genuineness ⟨a *specious* argument⟩ [Latin *speciosus* "beautiful, plausible," from *species* "appearance, species"] ***synonyms*** see PLAUSIBLE — **spe·cious·ly** *adv* — **spe·cious·ness** *n*

[1]**speck** \ˈspek\ *n* **1** : a small discoloration or spot especially from stain or decay **2** : PARTICLE 2a, BIT **3** : something marked or marred with specks [Old English *specca*]

[2]**speck** *vt* : to produce specks on or in

[1]**speck·le** \ˈspek-əl\ *n* : a little speck [Middle English]

[2]**speckle** *vt* **speck·led; speck·ling** \ˈspek-ling, -ə-ling\ **1** : to mark with speckles **2** : to be distributed in or on like speckles ⟨small lakes *speckled* the land⟩

specs \ˈspeks\ *n pl* : GLASS 2c [contraction of *spectacles*]

spec·ta·cle \ˈspek-ti-kəl\ *n* **1 a** : something exhibited to view as unusual, notable, or entertaining; *esp* : an eye-catching or dramatic public display **b** : an object of curiosity or contempt ⟨made a *spectacle* of herself at the party⟩ **2** *pl* : GLASS 2c [Medieval French, from Latin *spectaculum,* from *spectare* "to watch," from *specere* "to look at"]

spec·ta·cled \-kəld\ *adj* **1** : having or wearing spectacles **2** : having markings that look like a pair of spectacles ⟨a *spectacled* bear⟩

[1]**spec·tac·u·lar** \spek-ˈtak-yə-lər, spək-\ *adj* : of, relating to, or being a spectacle : STRIKING, SENSATIONAL ⟨a *spectacular* display of fireworks⟩ — **spec·tac·u·lar·ly** *adv*

[2]**spectacular** *n* : something that is spectacular; *esp* : an elaborate film, television, or theatrical production

spec·ta·tor \ˈspek-ˌtāt-ər, spek-ˈ\ *n* : one who watches without being involved or taking part [Latin, from *spectare* "to watch"] — **spectator** *adj*

spec·ter *or* **spec·tre** \ˈspek-tər\ *n* **1** : GHOST 2 **2** : something that haunts or perturbs the mind [French *spectre,* from Latin *spectrum* "appearance, specter," from *specere* "to look, look at"]

spec·tral \ˈspek-trəl\ *adj* **1** : of, relating to, or suggesting a specter : GHOSTLY **2** : of, relating to, or made by a spectrum ⟨*spectral* color⟩ — **spec·tral·ly** \-trə-lē\ *adv*

spec·tro·gram \ˈspek-trə-ˌgram\ *n* : a photograph or diagram of a spectrum

spec·tro·graph \ˈspek-trə-ˌgraf\ *n* : an instrument for spreading radiation into a spectrum and photographing or mapping the spectrum — **spec·tro·graph·ic** \ˌspek-trə-ˈgraf-ik\ *adj* — **spec·tro·graph·i·cal·ly** \-ˈgraf-i-kə-lē, -klē\ *adv*

spec·trom·e·ter \spek-ˈträm-ət-ər\ *n* **1** : an instrument used for measuring wavelengths of light spectra **2** : an instrument in which a quantity of particles or radiation is dispersed (as according to mass or energy) and measured — **spec·tro·met·ric** \ˌspek-trə-ˈme-trik\ *adj* — **spec·trom·e·try** \spek-ˈträm-ə-trē\ *n*

spec·tro·pho·tom·e·ter \ˌspek-trō-fə-ˈtäm-ət-ər\ *n* : an instrument for measuring the relative intensities of the light in different parts of a spectrum

spec·tro·scope \ˈspek-trə-ˌskōp\ *n* : an instrument that produces spectra from or by means of electromagnetic radiation — **spec·tro·scop·ic** \ˌspek-trə-ˈskäp-ik\ *adj* — **spec·tro·scop·i·cal·ly** \-ˈskäp-i-kə-lē, -klē\ *adv* — **spec·tros·co·pist** \spek-ˈträs-kə-pəst\ *n* — **spec·tros·co·py** \-pē\ *n*

spec·trum \ˈspek-trəm\ *n, pl* **spec·tra** \-trə\ *or* **spec·trums** **1 a** : a series of colors formed when a beam of white light is dispersed (as by passing through a prism) so that the component waves are arranged in the order of their wavelengths from red continuing through orange, yellow, green, blue, indigo, and violet **b** : a series of radiations arranged in regular order according to some varying characteristic especially wavelength; *esp* : ELECTROMAGNETIC SPECTRUM **2 a** : a continuous sequence or range ⟨a wide *spectrum* of political opinions⟩ **b** : a range of effectiveness against disease-causing organisms ⟨an antibiotic with a broad *spectrum*⟩ [Latin, "appearance, specter"]

spec·u·lar \ˈspek-yə-lər\ *adj* : of, relating to, or having the qualities of a mirror [Latin *specularis,* from *speculum* "mirror"] — **spec·u·lar·ly** *adv*

spec·u·late \ˈspek-yə-ˌlāt\ *vi* **1 a** : to meditate on or ponder a subject : REFLECT **b** : to think or theorize about something in which evidence is too slight for certainty to be reached **2** : to assume a business risk in hope of gain; *esp* : to buy or sell in expectation of profiting from market fluctuations [Latin *speculari* "to spy out, examine," from *specula* "lookout post," from *specere* "to look"] ***synonyms*** see THINK — **spec·u·la·tion** \ˌspek-yə-ˈlā-shən\ *n* — **spec·u·la·tor** \-ˌlāt-ər\ *n*

spec·u·la·tive \ˈspek-yə-lət-iv, -ˌlāt-\ *adj* **1** : involving, based on, or being intellectual speculation ⟨*speculative* knowledge⟩ **2** : marked by questioning curiosity ⟨gave him a *speculative* glance⟩ **3** : of, relating to, or being a financial speculation ⟨*speculative* stocks⟩ — **spec·u·la·tive·ly** *adv*

spec·u·lum \ˈspek-yə-ləm\ *n, pl* **-la** \-lə\ *also* **-lums** **1** : a tubular instrument inserted into a body passage especially to facilitate visual inspection or medication **2** : a reflector in an optical instrument [Latin, "mirror," from *specere* "to look"]

speech \ˈspēch\ *n* **1 a** : the communication or expression of thoughts in spoken words **b** : CONVERSATION **2 a** : something that is spoken **b** : a public discourse **3 a** : LANGUAGE 1a, DIALECT **b** : an individual manner or style of speaking **4** : the power of expressing or communicating thoughts by speaking [Old English *sprǣc, spǣc*]

speech community *n* : a group of people sharing characteristic patterns of vocabulary, grammar, and pronunciation

speech·ify \ˈspē-chə-ˌfī\ *vi* **-ified; -ify·ing** : to make a speech

speech·less \ˈspēch-ləs\ *adj* **1** : lacking or deprived of the power of speaking **2** : not speaking for a time : SILENT ⟨*speechless* with surprise⟩ — **speech·less·ly** *adv* — **speech·less·ness** *n*

[1]**speed** \ˈspēd\ *n* **1** *archaic* : prosperity in an undertaking : SUCCESS **2 a** : the act or state of moving swiftly : SWIFTNESS **b** : rate of motion : VELOCITY 1 **3** : swiftness or rate of performance or action : VELOCITY 3 **4 a** : the sensitivity of a photographic film, plate, or paper **b** : the light-gathering power of a lens expressed as relative aperture **5** : a transmission gear in automotive vehicles or bicycles ⟨a ten-*speed* bike⟩ **6** : METHAMPHETAMINE; *also* : a related stimulant drug and especially an amphetamine [Old English *spēd*] ***synonyms*** see HASTE — **up to speed** : operating at full effectiveness or potential

[2]**speed** *vb* **sped** \ˈsped\ *or* **speed·ed; speed·ing** **1 a** : to prosper in an undertaking **b** : to help to succeed : AID **2 a** : to make haste ⟨*sped* to her bedside⟩ **b** : to go or drive at excessive or illegal speed **3** : to move, work, or take place faster : ACCELERATE ⟨the heart *speeds* up⟩ **4 a** : to cause to move quickly : HASTEN **b** : to wish Godspeed to **c** : to increase the speed of : ACCELERATE — **speed·er** *n*

speed·ball \ˈspēd-ˌbȯl\ *n* : a game which resembles soccer but in which a ball caught in the air may be passed with the hands and in which a score is made by kicking or heading the ball between the goalposts or by a successful forward pass over the goal line

speed·boat \ˈspēd-ˌbōt\ *n* : a fast launch or motorboat — **speed·boat·ing** \-ˌbōt-ing\ *n*

speed bump *n* : a low raised ridge across a roadway (as in a parking lot) to limit vehicle speed

speed dial *n* : a telephone function by which a selected stored number can be dialed by pressing only one key — **speed–dial** *vb*

speed limit *n* : the highest or lowest speed allowed by law in a certain area

speed of light : a fundamental physical constant that is the speed at which electromagnetic radiation travels in a vacuum and that has a value of 299,792,458 meters per second

speed·om·e·ter \spi-ˈdäm-ət-ər\ *n* **1** : an instrument that measures speed **2** : an instrument that both measures speed and records distance traveled

speed–read·ing \ˈspēd-ˌrēd-ing\ *n* : a method of reading rapidly by skimming

speed·ster \ˈspēd-stər\ *n* : one that speeds or is capable of great speed

speed trap *n* : a stretch of road policed by concealed officers or devices (as radar) to catch speeders

speed·up \ˈspēd-ˌəp\ *n* **1** : ACCELERATION 2 **2** : an employer's demand for accelerated output without increased pay

speed·way \ˈspēd-ˌwā\ *n* : a racecourse for automobiles or motorcycles

speed·well \ˈspēd-ˌwel\ *n* : a creeping perennial European herb related to the snapdragons and having small bluish flowers; *also* : VERONICA

speedy \ˈspēd-ē\ *adj* **speed·i·er; -est** : rapid in motion or action ***synonyms*** see QUICK — **speed·i·ly** \ˈspēd-l-ē\ *adv* — **speed·i·ness** *n*

spe·le·ol·o·gy \ˌspē-lē-ˈäl-ə-jē, ˌspel-ē-\ *n* : the scientific study or exploration of caves [Latin *speleum* "cave" (from Greek *spēlaion*) + English *-logy*] — **spe·le·o·log·i·cal** \ˌspē-lē-ə-ˈläj-i-kəl, ˌspel-ē-\ *adj* — **spe·le·ol·o·gist** \-ˈäl-ə-jəst\ *n*

[1]**spell** \ˈspel\ *n* **1 a** : a spoken word or form of words believed to have magic power **b** : a state of enchantment **2** : a compelling influence or attraction [Old English, "talk, tale"]

[2]**spell** *vt* : to put under a spell : BEWITCH

[3]**spell** *vb* **spelled** \ˈspeld, ˈspelt\; **spell·ing** **1** : to read or discern slowly and with difficulty — often used with *out* **2 a** : to name, write, or print the letters of in order ⟨*spell* a word⟩ **b** : to constitute the letters of ⟨*c-a-t spells* "cat"⟩ **3** : MEAN, SIGNIFY ⟨another drought may *spell* famine⟩ **4** : to form words with letters [Medieval French *espeleir* "to mean, signify, read by spelling out letters," of Germanic origin]

[4]**spell** *vb* **spelled** \ˈspeld\; **spell·ing** **1** : to take the place of for a time : RELIEVE ⟨if we *spell* each other we won't get tired⟩ **2** : to allow an interval of rest to : REST [Old English *spelian*]

[5]**spell** *n* **1** : one's turn at work **2** : a period spent in a job or occupation **3 a** : a short period of time **b** : a stretch of a specified type of weather ⟨a dry *spell*⟩ **4** : a period of bodily or mental distress or disorder : ATTACK, FIT ⟨a *spell* of coughing⟩ [probably derived from Old English *spala*]

spell·bind \ˈspel-ˌbīnd\ *vt* **-bound** \-ˌbau̇nd\; **-bind·ing** : to hold by or as if by a spell : FASCINATE [back-formation from *spellbound*]

spell·bind·er \-ˌbīn-dər\ *n* : a speaker of compelling eloquence; *also* : one that compels attention

spell·bound \-ˈbau̇nd\ *adj* : held by or as if by a spell

spell–checker *n* : a computer program that identifies possible misspellings in a block of text by comparing the text with a database of accepted spellings — called also *spell-check, spelling checker* — **spell–check** \ˈspel-ˌchek\ *vb*

spell·er \ˈspel-ər\ *n* **1** : a person who spells words especially in a certain way ⟨a poor *speller*⟩ **2** : a book with exercises for teaching spelling

spell·ing \ˈspel-iŋ\ *n* : the forming of words from letters according to accepted usage; *also* : the letters of a word

spelling bee *n* : a spelling contest in which contestants are eliminated as soon as they misspell a word

spell out *vt* **1** : to make plain ⟨*spelled out* the orders in detail⟩ **2** : to write or print in letters and in full ⟨numbers are to be *spelled out*⟩

[1]**spelt** \ˈspelt\ *n* : an ancient wheat with light red grain; *also* : the grain of spelt [Old English, from Late Latin *spelta,* of Germanic origin]

[2]**spelt** *chiefly British past of* SPELL

spel·ter \ˈspel-tər\ *n* : ZINC; *esp* : zinc cast in slabs for commercial use [probably from early Dutch *speauter*]

spe·lunk·er \spi-ˈləŋ-kər, ˈspē-ˌ\ *n* : a person who makes a hobby of exploring and studying caves [Latin *spelunca* "cave," from Greek *spēlynx*] — **spe·lunk·ing** \-kiŋ\ *n*

spend \ˈspend\ *vt* **spent** \ˈspent\; **spend·ing** **1** : to use up or pay out : EXPEND **2 a** : to wear out : EXHAUST **b** : to consume wastefully : SQUANDER **3** : to cause or permit to elapse : PASS ⟨*spent* the evening reading⟩ [partly from Old English *spendan,* from Latin *expendere* "to expend"; partly from Medieval French *despendre,* from Latin *dispendere* "to weigh out," from *dis-* + *pendere* "to weigh"] — **spend·er** *n*

spend·able \ˈspen-də-bəl\ *adj* : available for spending

spending money *n* : money for small personal expenses

spend·thrift \ˈspend-ˌthrift, ˈspen-\ *n* : one who spends lavishly or wastefully — **spendthrift** *adj*

Spen·se·ri·an \spen-ˈsir-ē-ən\ *adj* : of, relating to, or characteristic of Edmund Spenser or his writings

Spenserian stanza *n* : a stanza consisting of eight lines of iambic pentameter and an alexandrine with a rhyme scheme *ababbcbcc*

spent \ˈspent\ *adj* **1** : used up **2** : drained of energy or effectiveness [past participle of *spend*]

sperm \ˈspərm\ *n, pl* **sperm** *or* **sperms** **1 a** : SEMEN **b** : a male gamete; *esp* : a motile male gamete of an animal usually with rounded or elongate head and a long posterior flagellum — called also *spermatozoon, sperm cell* **2** : a product (as oil) of the sperm whale [Medieval French *esperme,* from Late Latin *sperma,* from Greek, literally, "seed"]

sperm- *or* **spermo-** *or* **sperma-** *or* **spermi-** *combining form* : seed : germ : sperm ⟨*sperma*theca⟩ [Greek *sperma*]

sper·ma·ce·ti \ˌspər-mə-ˈsēt-ē, -ˈset-\ *n* : a waxy solid obtained from the oil of cetaceans and especially from a closed cavity in the heads of sperm whales and used mostly formerly in ointments, cosmetics, and candles [Medieval Latin *sperma ceti* "whale sperm"]

sper·ma·ry \ˈspərm-rē, -ə-rē\ *n, pl* **-ries** an organ in which male gametes are developed

spermat- *or* **spermato-** *combining form* : seed : spermatozoon ⟨*spermato*cyte⟩ [Greek *spermat-, sperma* "seed, sperm"]

sper·ma·the·ca \ˌspər-mə-ˈthē-kə\ *n* : a sac for sperm storage in the female reproductive tract of various lower animals and especially insects — **sper·ma·the·cal** \-kəl\ *adj*

sper·mat·ic \ˌspər-ˈmat-ik\ *adj* : of or relating to sperm or the male gonad

sper·ma·tid \ˈspər-mət-əd\ *n* : one of the haploid cells formed in meiosis of a spermatocyte and that differentiate into sperm cells

sper·ma·ti·um \ˌspər-ˈmā-shē-əm\ *n, pl* **-tia** \-shē-ə\ : a nonmotile cell functioning as a male gamete in some red algae, fungi, and lichens [New Latin, from Greek *spermation* "little seed," from *sperma* "seed, sperm"] — **sper·ma·tial** \-shē-əl, -shəl\ *adj*

sper·mato·cyte \ˌspər-ˈmat-ə-ˌsīt, ˈspər-mət-\ *n* : a cell giving rise to sperm cells

sper·mato·gen·e·sis \ˌspər-mət-ə-ˈjen-ə-səs, spər-ˌmat-\ *n, pl* **-e·ses** \-ə-ˌsēz\ : the process of male gamete formation including meiosis of a spermatocyte and transformation of the four resulting spermatids into sperm cells — **sper·mato·ge·net·ic** \spər-ˌmat-ə-jə-ˈnet-ik, ˌspər-mət-ō-\ *adj*

sper·mato·go·ni·um \ˌspər-mət-ə-ˈgō-nē-əm, spər-ˌmat-\ *n, pl* **-nia** \-nē-ə\ : a primitive male germ cell [New Latin, from *spermat-* + *gonium* "primitive germ cell," from Greek *gonos* "offspring, seed"] — **sper·mato·go·ni·al** \-nē-əl\ *adj*

sper·mato·phyte \ˌspər-ˈmat-ə-ˌfīt\ *n* : any of a group (Spermatophyta) of higher plants comprising those that produce seeds and including the gymnosperms and flowering plants — **sper·mato·phyt·ic** \spər-ˌmat-ə-ˈfit-ik, ˌspər-mət-\ *adj*

sper·mato·zo·on \spər-ˌmat-ə-ˈzō-ˌän, ˌspər-mət-, -ˈzō-ən\ *n, pl* **-zoa** \-ˈzō-ə\ : SPERM 1b [New Latin, from *spermat-* + Greek *zōion* "animal"] — **sper·mato·zo·al** \-ˈzō-əl\ *adj*

sperm cell *n* : SPERM 1b

sper·mi·cide \ˈspər-mə-ˌsīd\ *n* : a preparation or substance (as in a contraceptive) used to kill sperm

sperm nucleus *n* : either of two nuclei derived from the generative nucleus of a pollen grain that function in the double fertilization of a seed plant

sperm oil *n* : a pale yellow oil from the sperm whale used chiefly as a lubricant especially in the past

sperm whale \ˈspərm-\ *n* : a large toothed whale with a massive squarish head having a closed cavity containing a fluid mixture of spermaceti and oil [short for *spermaceti whale*]

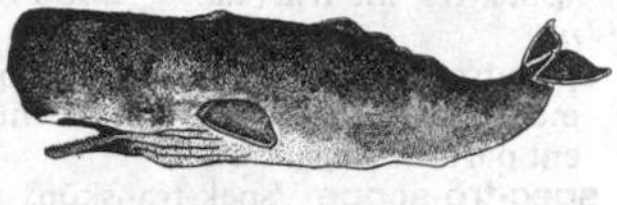
sperm whale

[1]**spew** \ˈspyü\ *vb* **1** : VOMIT **2** : to send or come out in a flood or gush [Old English *spīwan*] — **spew·er** *n*

[2]**spew** *n* : matter that is spewed

sphag·num \ˈsfag-nəm\ *n* **1** : any of a large genus of atypical mosses that grow only in wet acid areas (as bogs) where their remains become compacted with other plant debris to form peat **2** : a mass of sphagnum plants [New Latin, from Latin *sphagnos,* a kind of moss, from Greek] — **sphag·nous** \-nəs\ *adj*

sphal·er·ite \ˈsfal-ə-ˌrīt\ *n* : a mineral that is composed essentially of zinc sulfide and is the most important ore of zinc [German *Sphalerit,* from Greek *sphaleros* "deceitful"; from its often being mistaken for galena]

sphe·no·don \ˈsfē-nə-ˌdän, ˈsfen-ə-\ *n* : TUATARA [derived from Greek *sphēn* "wedge" + *odōn* "tooth"]

[1]**sphe·noid** \ˈsfē-ˌnȯid\ *or* **sphe·noi·dal** \sfi-ˈnȯid-l\ *adj* : of, relating to, or being a winged bone of the base of the cranium [Greek *sphēnoeidēs* "wedge-shaped," from *sphēn* "wedge"]

[2]**sphenoid** *n* : a sphenoid bone

sphe·nop·sid \sfi-ˈnäp-səd\ *n* : any of a major group (Sphenopsida) of primitive mostly extinct vascular plants having jointed ribbed stems and small leaves and including the horsetails [derived from Greek *sphēn* "wedge" + *opsis* "appearance, vision"]

sphere \ˈsfiər\ *n* **1 a** (1) : the apparent surface of the heavens of which half forms the dome of the visible sky (2) : one of the concentric and eccentric revolving spherical transparent shells in which according to ancient astronomy stars, sun, planets, and moon are set **b** : a globe representing the earth **2 a** : a globular body : BALL **b** : a solid geometric shape whose surface is made up of all the points that are an equal distance from the point that is the shape's center; *also* : the surface of a sphere **3** : natural, normal, or proper place; *esp* : social order or rank **4** : an area or range over or within which someone or something acts, exists, or has influence or significance ⟨the public *sphere*⟩ [Medieval French *espere* "globe, celestial sphere," from Latin *sphaera,* from Greek *sphaira,* literally, "ball"] — **spher·ic** \ˈsfiər-ik, ˈsfer-\ *adj, archaic* — **sphe·ric·i·ty** \sfir-ˈis-ət-ē\ *n*

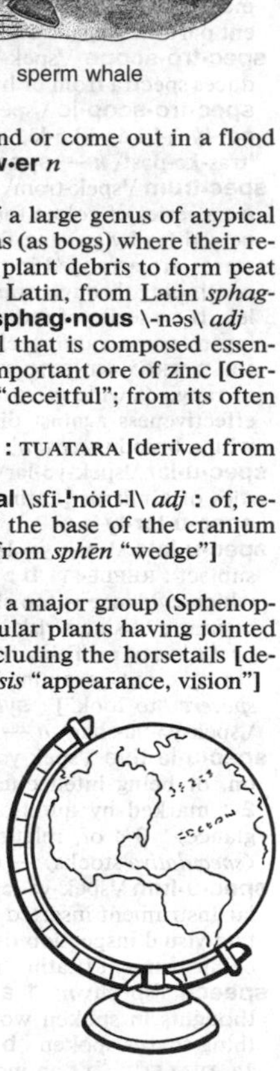
sphere 1b

sphere of influence : an area within which the political influence or interests of one nation are paramount

spher·i·cal \ˈsfir-i-kəl, ˈsfer-\ *adj* **1** : having the form of a sphere or of one of its segments **2** : relating to or dealing with a sphere or its properties — **spher·i·cal·ly** \-kə-lē, -klē\ *adv*

spherical aberration *n* : aberration caused by the spherical form of a lens or mirror that gives different foci for central and marginal rays

spherical angle *n* : the angle between two intersecting arcs of great circles of a sphere

spherical triangle *n* : a figure that looks similar to a triangle but that has sides which are three intersecting arcs of a sphere's great circles

sphe·roid \ˈsfiər-ˌȯid, ˈsfeər-\ *n* : a figure resembling a flattened sphere — **sphe·roi·dal** \sfir-ˈȯid-l\ *adj* — **sphe·roi·dal·ly** \-ˈȯid-l-ē\ *adv*

spher·ule \ˈsfiər-ül, ˈsfeər-, -yül\ *n* : a little sphere or spherical body

sphery \ˈsfiər-ē\ *adj* : suggestive of the heavenly spheres ⟨*sphery* eyes⟩ ⟨*sphery* music⟩

sphinc·ter \ˈsfing-tər, ˈsfingk-\ *n* : a ringlike muscle surrounding and able to contract or close a bodily opening [Late Latin, from Greek *sphinktēr,* literally, "band," from *sphingein* "to bind tight"]

sphinx \ˈsfings, ˈsfingks\ *n* **1 a** *cap* : a winged female monster in Greek mythology having a woman's head and a lion's body and noted for killing anyone unable to answer its riddle **b** : an enigmatic or mysterious person **2** : an ancient Egyptian image in the form of a recumbent lion having a man's head, a ram's head, or a hawk's head [Latin, from Greek]

sphinx 2

sphinx moth *n* : HAWK MOTH

sphyg·mo·ma·nom·e·ter \ˌsfig-mō-mə-ˈnäm-ət-ər\ *n* : an instrument for measuring blood pressure and especially arterial blood pressure [Greek *sphygmos* "pulse" + English *manometer*] — **sphyg·mo·ma·nom·e·try** \-mə-ˈnäm-ə-trē\ *n*

Spi·ca \ˈspī-kə\ *n* : a bright star in the constellation Virgo [Latin, literally, "spike of grain"]

spi·cate \ˈspī-ˌkāt\ *adj* : arranged in the form of a spike ⟨a *spicate* inflorescence⟩ [Latin *spicatus,* past participle of *spicare* "to arrange in the shape of heads of grain," from *spica* "ear of grain"]

[1]**spice** \ˈspīs\ *n* **1** : any of various aromatic plant products (as pepper or nutmeg) used to season or flavor foods **2** : something that gives zest or relish ⟨variety is the *spice* of life⟩ **3** : a pungent or fragrant odor : PERFUME [Medieval French *espece, espis,* from Late Latin *species* product, wares, drugs, spices, from Latin, appearance, species]

[2]**spice** *vt* : to season with or as if with spices

spice·bush \-ˌbu̇sh\ *n* : an aromatic shrub of the eastern U.S. and Canada that is related to the laurels and has clusters of small greenish flowers and usually red berries

spick–and–span \ˌspik-ən-ˈspan\ *or* **spic–and–span** *adj* **1** : BRAND-NEW, FRESH **2** : spotlessly clean and neat [derived from obsolete *spick* "spike" + *span-new*]

spic·ule \ˈspik-yül\ *n* : a minute slender pointed usually hard body; *esp* : one of the minute calcium- or silica-containing bodies that support the tissues of various invertebrates (as sponges) [Latin *spiculum* "head of a spear or arrow," from *spica* "ear of grain"]

spicy \ˈspī-sē\ *adj* **spic·i·er; -est** **1** : having the quality, flavor, or fragrance of spice **2** : producing or abounding in spices **3** : LIVELY, SPIRITED ⟨a *spicy* temper⟩ **4** : somewhat scandalous or lewd ⟨*spicy* gossip⟩ — **spic·i·ly** \-sə-lē\ *adv* — **spic·i·ness** \-sē-nəs\ *n*

spi·der \ˈspīd-ər\ *n* **1** : any of an order (Araneae) of arachnids having two or more pairs of abdominal organs for spinning threads of silk used in making cocoons for their eggs, nests for themselves, or webs for entangling their prey **2** : a cast-iron frying pan originally made with short feet to stand among coals on the hearth [Middle English *spithre*]

spider crab *n* : any of numerous crabs with extremely long legs and nearly triangular bodies

spider mite *n* : any of various small web-spinning mites that include destructive pests of plants — called also *red spider*

spider monkey *n* : any of a genus of New World monkeys with long slender limbs, the thumb absent or rudimentary, and a very long prehensile tail

spider plant *n* : any of several varieties of a southern African plant related to the lilies that have long narrow leaves and hanging stems often producing small plants at the end and that are widely grown as houseplants

spi·der·web \ˈspīd-ər-ˌweb\ *n* **1** : the silken web spun by most spiders and used as a resting place and a trap for small prey **2** : something like a spiderweb in appearance or function

spi·der·wort \-ˌwərt, -ˌwȯrt\ *n* : any of a genus of monocotyledonous plants with short-lived usually blue or violet flowers

spiderwort

spi·dery \ˈspīd-ə-rē\ *adj* **1** : resembling a spider; *also* : long and thin like the legs of a spider **2** : resembling a spiderweb **3** : full of spiders

spie·gel·ei·sen \ˈspē-gə-ˌlīz-n\ *also* **spie·gel** \ˈspē-gəl\ *n* : a pig iron containing 15 to 30 percent manganese and 4.5 to 6.5 percent carbon [German *Spiegeleisen,* from *Spiegel* "mirror" + *Eisen* "iron"]

[1]**spiel** \ˈspēl\ *vb* : to talk volubly or extravagantly [German *spielen* "to play"] — **spiel·er** *n*

[2]**spiel** *n* : a voluble line of often extravagant talk; *esp* : a sales pitch

spiffy \ˈspif-ē\ *adj* **spiff·i·er; -est** : fine looking : SMART ⟨a *spiffy* sports jacket⟩ [English dialect *spiff* "dandified"]

spig·ot \ˈspig-ət, ˈspik-ət\ *n* **1** : a pin or peg used to stop the vent in a cast **2** : FAUCET [Middle English]

[1]**spike** \ˈspīk\ *n* **1** : a very large nail **2 a** : one of a row of pointed irons placed (as on the top of a wall) to prevent passage **b** : one of several metal projections set in the sole and heel of a shoe to improve traction **c** *pl* : a pair of shoes having spikes attached **3** : an unbranched antler of a young deer **4** *pl* : SPIKE HEEL 2 **5** : the act or an instance of spiking (as in volleyball) **6** : a pointed element (as in a graph) **7** : a sudden sharp increase (as in prices or rates) [Middle English, probably of Scandinavian origin] — **spike·like** \ˈspī-ˌklīk\ *adj*

[2]**spike** *vt* **1** : to fasten or furnish with spikes **2 a** : to disable (a muzzle-loading cannon) temporarily by driving a spike into the vent **b** : to suppress or block completely : QUASH **3** : to pierce or impale with or on a spike **4** : to add alcohol or liquor to (a drink) **5** : to drive (a volleyball) down into the opponent's court with a hard blow **6** : to increase sharply ⟨battery sales *spiked* after the storm⟩ — **spik·er** *n*

[3]**spike** *n* **1** : an ear of grain **2** : a long usually rather narrow flower cluster in which the blossoms grow close to the central stem [Latin *spica*]

spiked \ˈspīkt\ *adj* **1** : borne on or having a floral spike ⟨*spiked* flowers⟩ **2** : having a sharp projecting point **3** : arranged in stiff clumps ⟨*spiked* hair⟩

spike heel *n* **1** : a very high tapering heel used on women's shoes **2** *pl* : shoes with spike heels

spike lavender *n* : a European mint related to and used like the true lavender

spike·let \ˈspī-klət\ *n* : a small or secondary spike; *esp* : one of the small few-flowered bracted spikes that make up the compound inflorescence of a grass or sedge

spike·nard \ˈspīk-ˌnärd\ *n* **1 a** : a fragrant ointment of the ancients **b** : a Himalayan aromatic plant related to the valerians and from which spikenard may have been derived **2** : a North American herb related to ginseng and having an aromatic root and clusters of small whitish flowers [Medieval Latin *spica nardi,* literally, "spike of nard"]

spiky *also* **spikey** \ˈspī-kē\ *adj* **spik·i·er; -est** **1** : of, relating to, or characterized by spikes **2** : sharp or biting in temper or manner — **spik·i·ly** \-kə-lē\ *adv* — **spik·i·ness** \-kē-nəs\ *n*

spile \ˈspīl\ *n* **1** : [1]PILE **2** : a small plug used to stop the vent of a cask : BUNG **3** : a spout inserted in a tree to draw off sap [probably from Dutch *spijl* "stake"] — **spile** *vt*

spil·ing \ˈspī-ling\ *n* : a set of piles : PILING

[1]**spill** \ˈspil\ *vb* **spilled** \ˈspild, ˈspilt\ *also* **spilt** \ˈspilt\; **spill·ing** **1** : to cause (blood) to flow **2 a** : to cause or allow uninten-

\ə\ **abut**	\au̇\ **out**	\i\ **tip**	\ȯ\ **saw**	\u̇\ **foot**
\ər\ **further**	\ch\ **chin**	\ī\ **life**	\ȯi\ **coin**	\y\ **yet**
\a\ **mat**	\e\ **pet**	\j\ **job**	\th\ **thin**	\yü\ **few**
\ā\ **take**	\ē\ **easy**	\ng\ **sing**	\th\ **this**	\yu̇\ **cure**
\ä\ **cot, cart**	\g\ **go**	\ō\ **bone**	\ü\ **food**	\zh\ **vision**

tionally to fall, flow, or run out **b :** to fall or run out so as to be lost or wasted **3 :** to relieve or lessen the pressure of (the wind) on sails by movement of the boat or adjustment of the sail **4 :** to fall or cause to fall from one's place ⟨the horse *spilled* its rider⟩ **5 :** to let out : DIVULGE ⟨*spilled* the secret⟩ **6 :** to spread beyond bounds ⟨crowds *spilled* into the street⟩ [Old English *spillan* "to kill, spill"] — **spill•able** \'spil-ə-bəl\ *adj* — **spill•er** *n* — **spill one's guts :** to make known especially personal information — **spill the beans :** to give away secret or hidden information by talking without thinking

[2]spill *n* **1 :** an act or instance of spilling; *esp* **:** a fall from a horse or vehicle **2 :** something spilled

spill•age \'spil-ij\ *n* **1 :** the act or process of spilling **2 :** the quantity that spills

spil•li•kin \'spil-i-kən\ *n* : JACKSTRAW [probably from Dutch *spelleken* "small peg"]

spill•way \'spil-ˌwā\ *n* **:** a passage for surplus water to run over or around a dam or similar obstruction

spilth \'spilth\ *n* **1 :** an act or instance of spilling **2 a :** something spilled **b :** TRASH 1a, RUBBISH

[1]spin \'spin\ *vb* **spun** \'spən\; **spin•ning** **1 :** to draw out and twist into yarn or thread ⟨*spin* flax⟩ **2 a :** to produce by drawing out and twisting fibers ⟨*spin* thread⟩ **b :** to form threads or a web or cocoon by extruding a sticky rapidly hardening fluid **3 a :** to revolve rapidly : GYRATE **b :** to be dizzy : feel as if turning rapidly ⟨my head is *spinning*⟩ **4 :** to cause to whirl : TWIRL ⟨*spin* a top⟩ **5 a :** to extend to great length : PROLONG **b :** to make up with the imagination ⟨*spun* a story⟩ **6 :** to move swiftly on or as if on wheels or in a vehicle **7 :** to shape into threadlike form in manufacture; *also* **:** to manufacture by a whirling process [Old English *spinnan*]

[2]spin *n* **1 a :** the act of spinning or twirling something **b :** whirling motion imparted by spinning : rapid rotation **c :** an excursion in a vehicle especially on wheels ⟨go for a *spin*⟩ **2 a :** an aerial maneuver or flight condition in which an airplane moves downward in a somewhat corkscrew path **b :** a plunging descent or downward spiral **c :** a state of mental confusion **3 a :** a usually ingenious twist ⟨puts an Asian *spin* on the pasta dish⟩ **b :** a special point of view, emphasis, or interpretation presented for the purpose of influencing opinion

spin•ach \'spin-ich\ *n* **:** an Asian herb related to the goosefoots and widely grown for its edible leaves; *also* **:** its leaves [Medieval French *espinaces,* from Medieval Latin *spinaachium,* derived from Arabic *isfānākh,* from Persian]

[1]spi•nal \'spīn-l\ *adj* **1 :** of, relating to, or situated near the spinal column **2 :** of, relating to, or affecting the spinal cord ⟨*spinal* neurons⟩ — **spi•nal•ly** \-l-ē\ *adv*

[2]spinal *n* **:** an anesthetic administered by way of the spinal cord

spinal column *n* **:** the axial skeleton of a vertebrate that consists of a jointed series of vertebrae which extend from the neck to the tail and protect the spinal cord — called also *backbone*

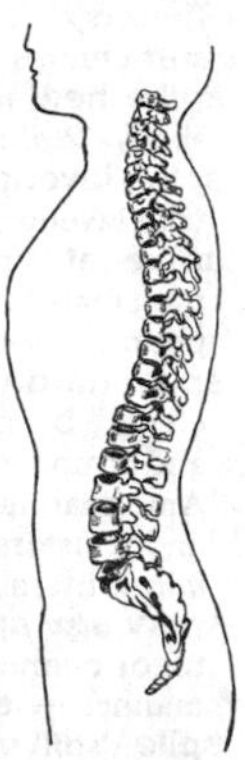

spinal column

spinal cord *n* **:** the cord of nervous tissue that extends from the brain along the back in the cavity of the spinal column, branches to form the spinal nerves, carries nerve impulses to and from the brain, and serves as a center for initiating and coordinating many reflex acts

spinal nerve *n* **:** any of the paired nerves which arise from the spinal cord and pass to various parts of the trunk and limbs and of which there are normally 31 pairs in humans

[1]spin•dle \'spin-dl\ *n* **1 a :** a round stick with tapered ends used to form and twist the yarn in hand spinning **b :** a rod holding a bobbin in a textile machine **c :** a device usually consisting of a long upright pin in a base on which papers can be stuck for filing — called also *spindle file* **2 :** something shaped like a spindle: as **a :** a network of fibers along which the chromosomes are distributed during mitosis and meiosis **b :** MUSCLE SPINDLE **3 a :** the bar that actuates the bolt of a lock **b** (1) **:** a turned often decorative piece of furniture or woodwork ⟨*spindles* of a chair⟩ (2) **:** NEWEL 2 **c :** a revolving piece usually smaller than a shaft **d :** the part of an axle on which a vehicle wheel turns [Old English *spinel*]

[2]spindle *vi* **spin•dled; spin•dling** \'spin-dling, -ling, -dl-ing\ **1 :** to form a long slender stalk usually without flower or fruit **2 :** to stick (as a piece of paper) on a spindle ⟨do not fold or *spindle*⟩

spin•dly \'spin-dlē, -lē, -dl-ē\ *adj* **spin•dli•er; -est :** of an excessively tall or long and thin appearance that often suggests physical weakness ⟨*spindly* legs⟩

spin doctor *n* **:** a person (as a political aide) responsible for ensuring that others interpret an event from a particular point of view — **spin–doctor** *vb*

spin•drift \'spin-ˌdrift\ *n* **:** spray blown from waves [Scots *speendrift,* from *speen* "to drive before a wind" + English *drift*]

spine \'spīn\ *n* **1 a :** SPINAL COLUMN **b :** something resembling a spinal column or constituting a central axis or chief support **c :** the part of a book to which the pages are attached and on the cover of which usually appear the title and the author's and publisher's names **2 :** a stiff pointed usually sharp process of a plant or animal ⟨protective *spines* cover the body of a porcupine fish⟩ ⟨cactus *spines* are highly modified leaves⟩ [Latin *spina* "thorn, spinal column"] — **spined** \'spīnd\ *adj*

spi•nel \spə-'nel\ *n* **1 :** a hard crystalline mineral consisting of an oxide of magnesium and aluminum that varies from colorless to ruby-red to black and is used as a gem **2 :** any of a group of minerals that are essentially oxides of magnesium, ferrous iron, zinc, or manganese [Italian *spinella,* from *spina* "thorn," from Latin]

spine•less \'spīn-ləs\ *adj* **1 :** free from spines, thorns, or prickles **2 :** having no spinal column : INVERTEBRATE **3 :** lacking courage or strength of character — **spine•less•ly** *adv* — **spine•less•ness** *n*

spin•et \'spin-ət\ *n* **1 :** a small early harpsichord having a single keyboard and only one string for each note **2 a :** a small upright piano **b :** a small electronic organ [Italian *spinetta*]

spin•na•ker \'spin-i-kər\ *n* **:** a large triangular sail set on a long light pole and used when running before the wind [origin unknown]

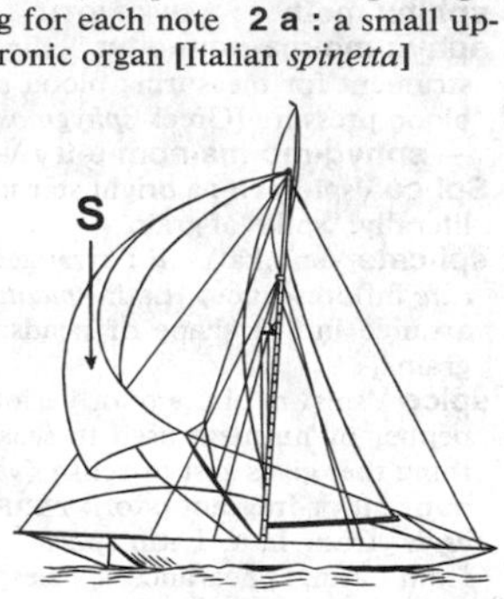

S spinnaker

spin•ner \'spin-ər\ *n* **1 :** one that spins **2 :** a fishing lure that revolves when drawn through the water

spin•ner•et \ˌspin-ə-'ret\ *n* **1 :** an organ especially of a spider or caterpillar for producing threads of silk from the secretion of silk glands **2** *or* **spin•ner•ette :** a small metal plate, thimble, or cap with fine holes through which a cellulose or chemical solution is forced in the spinning of man-made filaments (as rayon or nylon)

spin•ning \'spin-ing\ *n* **:** a method of fishing in which a lure is cast by means of a light flexible rod, a spinning reel, and a light line — called also *spin fishing*

spinning frame *n* **:** a machine that draws, twists, and winds yarn

spinning jen•ny \'spin-ing-ˌjen-ē\ *n* **:** an early multiple-spindle machine for spinning wool or cotton [*Jenny,* nickname for *Jane*]

spinning reel *n* **:** a fishing reel with a nonrevolving spool on which line is wound by a moving arm which is locked out of the way during casting to permit the line to spiral off the reel freely

spinning wheel *n* **:** a small domestic hand-driven or foot-driven machine for spinning yarn or thread in which a wheel drives a single spindle

spin–off \'spin-ˌȯf\ *n* **1 :** a secondary or derived product or effect : BY-PRODUCT ⟨medical devices and household products that are *spin-offs* from the space program⟩ **2 :** something that is imitative or derivative of an earlier work, product, or establishment ⟨a *spin-off* of a hit TV show⟩

spi•nous \'spī-nəs\ *adj* **1 a :** SPINY 2 ⟨a *spinous* plant⟩ **b :** SPINY 3 **2 :** difficult or unpleasant to handle or meet : THORNY

spin•ster \'spin-stər\ *n* **1 :** a woman whose occupation is to spin **2 a :** an unmarried woman and especially one past the common age for marrying **b :** a woman who seems unlikely to marry — **spin•ster•hood** \-ˌhu̇d\ *n* — **spin•ster•ish** \-stə-rish, -strish\ *adj* — **spin•ster•ly** *adv*

spin•thari•scope \spin-'thar-ə-ˌskōp\ *n* **:** an instrument consisting of a fluorescent screen and a magnifying lens system for visual detection of alpha rays [Greek *spintharis* "spark"]

spin the bottle *n* : a kissing game in which a bottle is spun to point to the one to be kissed

spi·nule \ˈspī-nyül\ *n* : a tiny spine — **spi·nu·lose** \-nyə-ˌlōs\ *adj*

spiny \ˈspī-nē\ *adj* **spin·i·er; -est** **1** : full of difficulties, obstacles, or annoyances : THORNY **2** : having spines, prickles, or thorns **3** : slender and pointed like a spine — **spin·i·ness** *n*

spiny anteater *n* : ECHIDNA

spiny–head·ed worm \ˌspī-nē-ˌhed-əd-\ *n* : any of a small phylum (Acanthocephala) of unsegmented parasitic worms with a proboscis bearing hooks used for attachment to the intestinal wall of the host

spiny lobster *n* : any of several edible crustaceans distinguished from the related true lobsters by the simple unenlarged first pair of legs and by the spiny carapace

spir·a·cle \ˈspir-i-kəl, ˈspī-ri-\ *n* : a breathing orifice: as **a** : BLOWHOLE 1 **b** : any of the external openings in the body of an arthropod and especially of an insect through which air enters a trachea [Latin *spiraculum,* from *spirare* "to breathe"]

1spi·ral \ˈspī-rəl\ *adj* **1** : winding around a center or pole and gradually receding from or approaching it **2** : HELICAL ⟨the *spiral* form of the thread of a screw⟩ **3** : of, relating to, or resembling a spiral ⟨a *spiral* staircase⟩ [Medieval Latin *spiralis,* from Latin *spira* "coil"] — **spi·ral·ly** \-rə-lē\ *adv*

2spiral *n* **1 a** : a curve in a plane that winds around a point while getting closer to or farther away from it **b** : a three-dimensional curve (as a helix) that winds around an axis **2** : a single turn or coil in a spiral object **3 a** : something having a spiral form **b** : SPIRAL GALAXY **4** : a continuously spreading and accelerating increase or decrease ⟨wage *spirals*⟩

3spiral *vb* **-raled** *or* **-ralled; -ral·ing** *or* **-ral·ling** **1** : to move in a spiral course **2** : to form into a spiral

spiral galaxy *n* : a galaxy with a central nucleus from which extend curved arms

spi·rant \ˈspī-rənt\ *n* : a consonant (as \f\, \s\, \sh\) uttered with friction of the breath against some part of the oral passage : FRICATIVE [Latin *spirans,* present participle of *spirare* "to breathe"] — **spirant** *adj*

1spire \ˈspīr\ *n* **1** : a slender tapering blade or stalk (as of grass) **2** : a sharp pointed tip (as of a tree or antler) **3 a** : a pointed roof especially of a tower **b** : STEEPLE [Old English *spīr*]

1spire 3a

2spire *vi* : to shoot up like a spire

3spire *n* : the upper part of a spiral mollusk shell [Latin *spira* "coil," from Greek *speira*]

4spire *vi* : to rise in or as if in a spiral

spi·rea *or* **spi·raea** \spī-ˈrē-ə\ *n* : any of a genus of shrubs related to the roses and having small usually white or pink flowers in dense clusters [Latin, a kind of plant, from Greek *speiraia*]

spired \ˈspīrd\ *adj* : having a spire ⟨a *spired* church⟩

spi·ril·lum \spī-ˈril-əm\ *n, pl* **-ril·la** \-ˈril-ə\ : any of a genus of long curved bacteria having tufts of flagella at both ends; *also* : any spiral filamentous bacterium (as a spirochete) [New Latin, from Latin *spira* "coil"]

1spir·it \ˈspir-ət\ *n* **1** : a life-giving force; *esp* : a force within a person held to endow the body with life, energy, and power : SOUL **2** : a supernatural being or essence: as **a** *cap* : HOLY SPIRIT **b** : an often evil being that is bodiless but can become visible : GHOST 2 **c** : a supernatural being that enters into and controls a person **3** : MOOD, DISPOSITION ⟨in good *spirits*⟩ **4** : a lively or brisk quality ⟨answered with *spirit*⟩ **5** : real meaning or intention ⟨the *spirit* of the law⟩ **6** : the feeling, quality, or disposition characterizing something ⟨said in a *spirit* of fun⟩ **7** : a person having a character or disposition of a specified nature ⟨a free *spirit*⟩ **8 a** : a distilled alcoholic liquor — usually used in plural **b** : an alcoholic solution of a volatile substance ⟨*spirit* of camphor⟩ — often used in plural [Latin *spiritus,* literally, "breath"] ***synonyms*** see SOUL

2spirit *vt* **1** : ANIMATE 2, ENCOURAGE **2** : to carry off or convey secretly or mysteriously

spir·it·ed \ˈspir-ət-əd\ *adj* : full of spirit, courage, or energy ⟨a *spirited* conversation⟩ — **spir·it·ed·ly** *adv* — **spir·it·ed·ness** *n*

spirit gum *n* : a solution (as of gum arabic in ether) used especially for attaching false hair to the skin

spir·it·ism \ˈspir-ət-ˌiz-əm\ *n* : SPIRITUALISM 2a — **spir·it·ist** \-ət-əst\ *n* — **spir·it·is·tic** \ˌspir-ət-ˈis-tik\ *adj*

spir·it·less \ˈspir-ət-ləs\ *adj* : lacking animation, cheer, or courage — **spir·it·less·ly** *adv* — **spir·it·less·ness** *n*

spirit level *n* : a level using the position of a bubble in a small tube of liquid (as alcohol) as an indicator

spirits of turpentine : TURPENTINE 2a

1spir·i·tu·al \ˈspir-ich-wəl, -ə-wəl, -ich-əl\ *adj* **1** : of, relating to, or consisting of spirit : not bodily or material **2 a** : of or relating to sacred matters ⟨*spiritual* songs⟩ **b** : ecclesiastical rather than lay or temporal ⟨*spiritual* authority⟩ **3** : related or joined in spirit : having a spiritual rather than physical relationship **4 a** : of or relating to supernatural beings **b** : of, relating to, or involving spiritualism : SPIRITUALISTIC — **spir·i·tu·al·ly** \-ē\ *adv* — **spir·i·tu·al·ness** *n*

2spiritual *n* : a religious song usually of a deeply emotional character that was developed especially among blacks in the southern U.S.

spir·i·tu·al·ism \ˈspir-ich-wə-ˌliz-əm, -ə-wə-, -ich-ə-ˌliz-\ *n* **1** : the belief that spirit is the principal aspect of reality **2 a** : a belief that the spirits of the dead communicate with the living **b** *cap* : a movement comprising religious organizations emphasizing spiritualism — **spir·i·tu·al·ist** \-ləst\ *n, often cap* — **spir·i·tu·al·is·tic** \ˌspir-ich-wə-ˈlis-tik, -ə-wə-, -ich-ə-ˈlis-\ *adj*

spir·i·tu·al·i·ty \ˌspir-ich-ə-ˈwal-ət-ē\ *n* **1** : concern with religious rather than material values **2** : the quality or state of being spiritual

spir·i·tu·al·ize \ˈspir-ich-wə-ˌlīz, -ə-wə-, -ich-ə-ˌlīz\ *vt* **1** : to make spiritual especially by freeing from worldly influences **2** : to give a spiritual meaning to or understand in a spiritual sense — **spir·i·tu·al·iza·tion** \ˌspir-ich-wə-lə-ˈzā-shən, -ə-wə-, -ich-ə-lə-\ *n*

spir·i·tu·ous \ˈspir-ich-wəs, -ə-wəs, -ich-əs, ˈspir-ət-əs\ *adj* : containing or being distilled alcohol ⟨*spirituous* liquors⟩ — **spir·i·tu·os·i·ty** \ˌspir-ich-ə-ˈwäs-ət-ē\ *n*

spi·ro·chete *also* **spi·ro·chaete** \ˈspī-rə-ˌkēt\ *n* : any of an order (Spirochaetales) of slender spirally undulating bacteria including those causing syphilis and Lyme disease [derived from Latin *spira* "coil" (from Greek *speira*) + Greek *chaitē* "long hair"] — **spi·ro·che·tal** \ˌspī-rə-ˈkēt-l\ *adj*

spi·ro·gy·ra \ˌspī-rə-ˈjī-rə\ *n* : any of a genus of freshwater green algae with spiral chloroplasts [New Latin, from Greek *speira* "coil" + *gyros* "ring, circle"]

spi·rom·e·ter \spī-ˈräm-ət-ər\ *n* : an instrument for measuring the air entering and leaving the lungs [Latin *spirare* "to breathe"] — **spi·ro·met·ric** \ˌspī-rə-ˈme-trik\ *adj* — **spi·rom·e·try** \spī-ˈräm-ə-trē\ *n*

spiry \ˈspīr-ē\ *adj* : resembling a spire; *esp* : tall, slender, and tapering ⟨*spiry* trees⟩

1spit \ˈspit\ *n* **1** : a slender pointed rod for holding meat over a fire **2** : a small point of land especially of sand or gravel running into a body or water [Old English *spitu*]

2spit *vt* **spit·ted; spit·ting** : to put on or as if on a spit

3spit *vb* **spit** *or* **spat** \ˈspat\; **spit·ting** **1 a** : to eject (as saliva) from the mouth : EXPECTORATE **b** : to express by or as if by spitting ⟨*spitting* a contemptuous reply⟩ **c** : to make a spitting sound ⟨the cat *spat* angrily⟩ **2 a** : to give off usually briskly or vigorously : EMIT ⟨the fire *spat* sparks⟩ **b** : to rain or snow in flurries [Old English *spittan*] — **spit·ter** *n*

4spit *n* **1 a** : SALIVA **b** : the act of spitting **2** : a frothy secretion produced by spittlebugs **3** : perfect likeness ⟨the *spit* and image of his father⟩

spit and polish *n* : extreme attention to cleanliness, orderliness, smartness of appearance, and ceremony often at the expense of operational efficiency [from the practice of polishing objects such as shoes by moistening them and then rubbing them with a cloth]

spit·ball \ˈspit-ˌbȯl\ *n* **1** : paper chewed and rolled into a ball to

\ə\ **abut**	\au̇\ **out**	\i\ **tip**	\ȯ\ **saw**	\u̇\ **foot**
\ər\ **further**	\ch\ **chin**	\ī\ **life**	\ȯi\ **coin**	\y\ **yet**
\a\ **mat**	\e\ **pet**	\j\ **job**	\th\ **thin**	\yü\ **few**
\ā\ **take**	\ē\ **easy**	\ng\ **sing**	\th\ **this**	\yu̇\ **cure**
\ä\ **cot, cart**	\g\ **go**	\ō\ **bone**	\ü\ **food**	\zh\ **vision**

be used as a missile **2 :** a baseball pitch delivered after the ball has been moistened with saliva or sweat
spit curl *n* **:** a small spiral curl that is usually pressed flat against the forehead, temple, or cheek
[1]**spite** \ˈspīt\ *n* **:** petty ill will or hatred with a desire to irritate, annoy, or thwart [Middle English, short for *despite*] — **in spite of :** in defiance or contempt of : without being prevented by ⟨succeeded *in spite of* opposition⟩
[2]**spite** *vt* **1 :** to treat maliciously (as by shaming or thwarting) **2 :** ANNOY, OFFEND ⟨did it to *spite* me⟩
spite·ful \ˈspīt-fəl\ *adj* **:** filled with or showing spite : MALICIOUS — **spite·ful·ly** \-fə-lē\ *adv* — **spite·ful·ness** *n*
spit·fire \ˈspit-ˌfīr\ *n* **:** a quick-tempered or highly emotional person
spit·ting image \ˌspit-n-, ˌspit-ing-\ *n* **:** perfect likeness
spit·tle \ˈspit-l\ *n* **1 :** SALIVA **2 :** [4]SPIT 2 [Old English *spǣtl*]
spit·tle·bug \-ˌbəg\ *n* **:** any of numerous leaping insects that are related to the cicadas and aphids and have larvae which produce a frothy secretion
spittle insect *n* **:** SPITTLEBUG
spit·toon \spi-ˈtün\ *n* **:** a receptacle for spit — called also *cuspidor* [[4]*spit* + *-oon* (as in *balloon*)]
spit up *vb* **:** REGURGITATE, VOMIT ⟨the baby *spit up* twice⟩ — **spit–up** *n*
spitz \ˈspits\ *n* **:** a member of any of several breeds of stocky heavy-coated dogs of northern origin with erect ears and a heavily furred tail tightly curled over the back [German, from *spitz* "pointed"]

spitz

splanch·nic \ˈsplangk-nik\ *adj* **:** of or relating to the internal organs : VISCERAL [Greek *splanchnikos,* from *splanchna* "viscera"]
[1]**splash** \ˈsplash\ *vb* **1 a :** to strike or move through a liquid or semifluid substance and cause it to spatter ⟨*splash* water⟩ ⟨*splash* through mud⟩ **b :** to wet or soil by dashing a liquid on : SPATTER ⟨*splashed* by a passing car⟩; *also* **:** to cause to soil or stain something by splashing ⟨*splashed* ink on the paper⟩ **2 :** to make a splashing sound (as in falling or moving) ⟨a brook *splashing* over rocks⟩ **3 a :** to spread or scatter like a splashed liquid ⟨sunbeams *splashed* through the curtain⟩ **b :** to display prominently ⟨a scandal *splashed* all over the newspaper⟩ [alteration of *plash*] — **splash·er** *n*
[2]**splash** *n* **1 :** splashed material; *also* **:** a spot or daub from or as if from splashed liquid **2 :** the sound or action of splashing **3 :** a vivid impression created especially by showy activity or appearance; *also* **:** a showy display
splash·down \ˈsplash-ˌdau̇n\ *n* **:** the controlled landing of a spacecraft in the ocean — **splash down** \splash-ˈdau̇n, ˈsplash-\ *vi*
splash guard *n* **:** a flap suspended behind a rear wheel to prevent tire splash from muddying windshields of following vehicles
splashy \ˈsplash-ē\ *adj* **splash·i·er; -est 1 :** moving or being moved with a splash or splashing sound **2 :** making a splash ⟨a *splashy* movie⟩ ⟨a *splashy* debut⟩ **3 :** consisting of, being, or covered with bright colored splashes ⟨a *splashy* shirt⟩ ⟨a *splashy* poster⟩ — **splash·i·ly** \-ə-lē\ *adv* — **splash·i·ness** \-ē-nəs\ *n*
[1]**splat** \ˈsplat\ *n* **:** a single flat thin usually vertical member of a back of a chair [obsolete *splat* "to spread flat," from Middle English *splatten*]
[2]**splat** *n* **:** a splattering or splashing sound [imitative]
splat·ter \ˈsplat-ər\ *vb* **1 :** SPATTER 1 **2 :** to scatter or fall in or as if in drops [probably blend of *splash* and *spatter*] — **splatter** *n*
[1]**splay** \ˈsplā\ *vb* **1 :** to spread out or apart **2 :** SLOPE, SLANT [Middle English *splayen,* short for *displayen* "to display"]

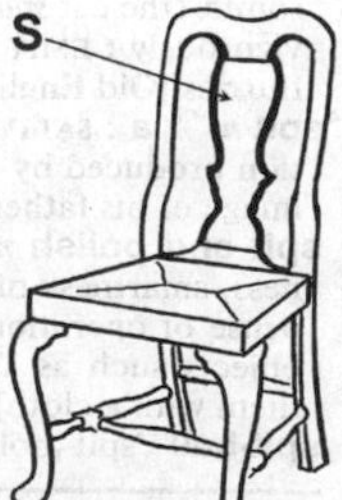

S [1]splat

[2]**splay** *n* **1 :** a slope or bevel especially of the sides of a door or window **2 :** degree of outward slope
[3]**splay** *adj* **1 :** turned outward ⟨*splay* knees⟩ **2 :** AWKWARD 2a, UNGAINLY
splay·foot \ˈsplā-ˌfu̇t, -ˈfu̇t\ *n* **:** a foot abnormally flattened and spread out : FLATFOOT — **splay·foot·ed** \-ˈfu̇t-əd\ *adj*
spleen \ˈsplēn\ *n* **1 :** a ductless organ near the stomach or intestine of most vertebrates that is supplied with many blood vessels and is concerned with final destruction of blood cells, filtration and storage of blood, and production of lymphocytes **2 :** feelings of anger or ill will often not expressed [Latin *splen,* from Greek *splēn*]
spleen·ful \-fəl\ *adj* **:** SPLENETIC
spleen·wort \-ˌwərt, -ˌwȯrt\ *n* **:** any of a genus of evergreen ferns having linear or oblong clusters of spores [from the belief in its power to cure disorders of the spleen]
spleeny \ˈsplē-nē\ *adj* **:** full of or displaying spleen
splen·dent \ˈsplen-dənt\ *adj* **1 :** SHINING 1, LUSTROUS **2 :** ILLUSTRIOUS, BRILLIANT [Late Latin *splendens,* from Latin *splendēre* "to shine"]
splen·did \ˈsplen-dəd\ *adj* **1 :** possessing or displaying splendor: as **a :** brilliantly shining : RADIANT **b :** SHOWY 1, MAGNIFICENT **2 :** ILLUSTRIOUS, GRAND **3 :** PRAISEWORTHY, EXCELLENT [Latin *splendidus,* from *splendēre* "to shine"] — **splen·did·ly** *adv* — **splen·did·ness** *n*
synonyms SPLENDID, GLORIOUS, GORGEOUS mean extraordinarily impressive. SPLENDID implies outshining the usual in brilliance or excellence ⟨the wedding was a *splendid* occasion⟩. GLORIOUS suggests beauty and distinction heightened by radiance ⟨a *glorious* sunset⟩. GORGEOUS implies a rich splendor especially in display of color ⟨a *gorgeous* red dress⟩.
splen·dif·er·ous \splen-ˈdif-rəs, -ə-rəs\ *adj* **1 :** SPLENDID 1, MAGNIFICENT **2 :** deceptively splendid [*splendor* + *-i-* + *-ferous*] — **splen·dif·er·ous·ly** *adv* — **splen·dif·er·ous·ness** *n*
splen·dor \ˈsplen-dər\ *n* **1 a :** great brightness or luster : BRILLIANCY ⟨the *splendor* of the sun⟩ **b :** MAGNIFICENCE, POMP ⟨an affair of great *splendor*⟩ **2 :** something splendid ⟨the *splendors* of the past⟩ [Latin *splendor,* from *splendēre* "to shine"] — **splen·dor·ous** *also* **splen·drous** \-də-rəs, -drəs\ *adj*
sple·net·ic \spli-ˈnet-ik\ *adj* **:** marked by bad temper, hatred, or spite [Late Latin *spleneticus,* from Latin *splen* "spleen"] — **sple·net·i·cal·ly** \spli-ˈnet-i-kə-lē, -klē\ *adv*
splen·ic \ˈsplen-ik\ *adj* **:** of, relating to, or located in the spleen
[1]**splice** \ˈsplīs\ *vt* **1 a :** to unite (as two ropes) by weaving the strands together **b :** to unite (as rails or timbers) by lapping the ends together and making them fast **2 :** to unite, link, or insert as if by splicing [obsolete Dutch *splissen*] — **splic·er** *n*
[2]**splice** *n* **:** a joining or joint made by splicing

splice

spline \ˈsplīn\ *n* **1 :** a thin wood or metal strip used in building construction **2 :** a key that is fixed to one of two connected mechanical parts and fits into a keyway in the other; *also* **:** a keyway for such a key [origin unknown]
[1]**splint** \ˈsplint\ *n* **1 a :** a thin strip of wood suitable for interweaving (as into baskets) **b :** SPLINTER 1 **c :** material or a device used to protect and immobilize a body part (as a broken arm) **2 :** a bony enlargement on the cannon bone of a horse [Low German *splinte, splente*]
[2]**splint** *vt* **:** to support and immobilize with or as if with a splint or splints
splint bone *n* **:** one of the slender rudimentary bones on each side of the cannon bone in the limb of a horse
[1]**splin·ter** \ˈsplint-ər\ *n* **1 a :** a thin piece split or torn off lengthwise : SLIVER **b :** a small jagged particle **2 :** a group or faction broken away from a parent body [early Dutch] — **splinter** *adj* — **splin·tery** \ˈsplint-ə-rē\ *adj*
[2]**splinter** *vb* **1 :** to split into long thin pieces **2 :** to split into fragments, parts, or factions
[1]**split** \ˈsplit\ *vb* **split; split·ting 1 a :** to divide lengthwise usually along a grain or seam or by layers : CLEAVE ⟨wood that *splits* easily⟩ ⟨*split* slate into shingles⟩ **b :** to divide or separate as if by forcing apart ⟨the river *split* the town⟩ **2 a :** to tear or break apart : BURST ⟨the pants *split* at the seams⟩ **b :** to subject (an atom or atomic nucleus) to artificial disintegration es-

pecially by fission **c** : to affect as if by breaking up or tearing apart : SHATTER ⟨a roar that *split* the air⟩ **3** : to divide into parts or portions: as **a** : to divide between individuals : SHARE ⟨the winning team *split* the prize⟩ **b** : to divide into factions, parties, or groups **c** : to mark (a ballot) or cast (a vote) for candidates of different parties **d** : to break down (a chemical compound) into constituents ⟨*split* a fat into glycerol and fatty acids⟩; *also* : to remove by such separation ⟨*split* off carbon dioxide⟩ **e** : to divide (stock) by issuing a larger number of shares to existing shareholders usually without increase in total face value **4** : LEAVE 4 **5** *British* : INFORM 2, TELL — usually used with *on* [Dutch *splitten*] — **split·ter** *n* — **split hairs** : to make trivial distinctions — **split one's sides** : to laugh heartily — **split the difference** : to arrive at a compromise

[2]**split** *n* **1** : a product or result of splitting: as **a** : a narrow break made by or as if by splitting : CRACK **b** : a part split off or made thin by splitting **c** : a group or faction formed by splitting **d** : a situation in bowling in which two or more pins are left standing after a delivery with one or more pins missing between them **2** : the act or process of splitting : DIVISION ⟨a stock *split*⟩; *esp* : a dividing into divergent or antagonistic elements **3** : the act of lowering oneself to the floor or leaping into the air with the legs extended in a straight line and in opposite directions

[3]**split** *adj* : divided by or as if by splitting ⟨a *split* lip⟩ ⟨*split* families⟩; *also* : prepared for use by splitting ⟨*split* hides⟩

split decision *n* : a decision in a boxing match reflecting a division of opinion among the referee and judges

split end *n* **1** : an offensive end in football who lines up several yards to the side of the formation **2** : a hair tip that has become frayed (as from dryness) — usually used in plural

split infinitive *n* : an infinitive with *to* having a modifier between the *to* and the verbal (as in "to really start")

split–lev·el \'split-'lev-əl\ *adj* : divided vertically so that the floor level of rooms in one part is about midway between the levels of two successive stories in an adjoining part ⟨*split-level* houses⟩ — **split–lev·el** \-ˌlev-əl\ *n*

split pea *n* : a dried hulled pea that is split into two parts

split personality *n* **1** : a mental and emotional disorder in which the personality becomes separated into two or more parts each of which controls behavior part of the time **2** : a double character or nature ⟨a city with a *split personality*⟩

split rail *n* : a fence rail split from a log

split–second *adj* **1** : occurring in a split second ⟨a *split-second* decision⟩ **2** : extremely precise ⟨*split-second* timing⟩

split second *n* : a very brief period : FLASH, INSTANT

split shift *n* : a shift of working hours divided into two or more working periods (as morning and evening)

split ticket *n* : a ballot cast by a voter who votes for candidates of more than one party

split·ting \'split-ing\ *adj* : very severe ⟨a *splitting* headache⟩

splotch \'spläch\ *n* : BLOTCH 2, SPOT [perhaps blend of *spot* and *blotch*] — **splotch** *vt* — **splotchy** \'spläch-ē\ *adj*

[1]**splurge** \'splərj\ *n* **1** : a showy display **2** : liberal indulgence [perhaps blend of *splash* and *surge*]

[2]**splurge** *vb* **1** : to make a showy display **2** : to indulge oneself or spend lavishly

[1]**splut·ter** \'splət-ər\ *n* **1** : a confused noise (as of hasty speaking) **2** : a splashing or sputtering sound [probably alteration of *sputter*] — **splut·tery** \'splət-ə-rē\ *adj*

[2]**splutter** *vb* **1** : to make a noise as if spitting **2** : to speak or utter hastily and confusedly — **splut·ter·er** \'splət-ər-ər\ *n*

[1]**spoil** \'spȯil\ *n* **1 a** : plunder taken from an enemy in war or from a victim in robbery : LOOT **b** : something won usually by effort or skill — usually used in plural **2** : earth and rock excavated or dredged **3** : an object damaged or flawed in the making [Medieval French *espuille,* from *espuiller,* "to despoil"]

[2]**spoil** *vb* **spoiled** \'spȯild, 'spȯilt\ *also* **spoilt** \'spȯilt\; **spoil·ing** **1** : PLUNDER, ROB **2 a** : to damage seriously : RUIN ⟨a crop *spoiled* by floods⟩ **b** : to impair the quality or effect of ⟨a quarrel *spoiled* the party⟩ **c** : to decay or lose freshness, value, or usefulness usually through being kept too long **3** : to damage the character or disposition of by pampering **4** : to have an eager desire ⟨*spoiling* for a fight⟩ [Medieval French *espuiller* "to despoil," from Latin *spoliare* "to strip of natural covering, despoil," from *spolium* "skin, hide"] ***synonyms*** see DECAY

spoil·age \'spȯi-lij\ *n* **1** : the act or process of spoiling **2** : something spoiled or wasted **3** : loss by spoilage

spoil·er \'spȯi-lər\ *n* **1 a** : one that spoils **b** : one (as a political candidate) having little or no chance of winning but capable of depriving a rival of success **2** : a device (as on an airplane or automobile) used to disrupt airflow and decrease lift **3** : information about the plot of a book, motion picture, or TV program that can spoil a reader's or viewer's sense of surprise or suspense; *also* : a person who discloses such information

spoils·man \'spȯilz-mən\ *n* : one who serves a political party in expectation of receiving a public office

spoil·sport \'spȯil-ˌspōrt, -ˌspȯrt\ *n* : one who spoils the sport or pleasure of others

spoils system *n* : the practice of distributing public offices and their privileges as plunder to members of the victorious political party

[1]**spoke** \'spōk\ *past & archaic past participle of* SPEAK

[2]**spoke** *n* **1** : one of the bars radiating from the hub of a wheel to support the rim **2** : something resembling the spoke of a wheel [Old English *spāca*]

spo·ken \'spō-kən\ *adj* **1 a** : expressed in speech rather than writing : ORAL ⟨a *spoken* message⟩ **b** : used in speaking ⟨*spoken* English⟩ **2** : speaking in (such) a manner — used in combination ⟨soft-*spoken*⟩ ⟨plain*spoken*⟩ [past participle of *speak*]

spoke·shave \'spōk-ˌshāv\ *n* : a two-handled tool that is used for planing curved pieces of wood [[2]*spoke*]

spokes·man \'spōk-smən\ *n* : a person who speaks as a representative of another person or of a group [probably from [1]*spoke*]

spokes·model \-ˌsmäd-l\ *n* : a model who is a spokesman or spokeswoman

spokes·per·son \'spōk-ˌspərs-n\ *n* : SPOKESMAN

spokes·wom·an \'spōk-ˌswu̇m-ən\ *n* : a woman who is a spokesperson

spo·li·a·tion \ˌspō-lē-'ā-shən\ *n* : the act of plundering : the state of being plundered especially in war [Latin *spoliatio,* from *spoliare* "to despoil," from *spolium* "skin, hide"]

spon·dee \'spän-ˌdē\ *n* : a metrical foot consisting of two accented syllables (as in *tom-tom*) [Medieval French, from Latin *spondeum* "foot of 2 long syllables," from Greek *spondeios,* from *spondē* "libation"; from its use in music accompanying libations] — **spon·da·ic** \spän-'dā-ik\ *adj*

[1]**sponge** \'spənj\ *n* **1 a** : an elastic porous mass of fibers and spicules that forms the internal skeleton of various marine animals (phylum Porifera) and is able when wetted to absorb water; *also* : a piece of this material or of a porous rubber or cellulose product of similar properties used especially for cleaning **b** : any of a phylum (Porifera) of aquatic chiefly marine invertebrate animals that have a double-walled body of loosely connected cells with a skeleton supported by spicules or spongin and are filter feeders that are permanently attached as adults **2** : a pad (as of folded gauze) used in surgery and medicine (as to remove discharges or apply medication) **3** : one who lives upon others : SPONGER **4 a** : raised dough **b** : a whipped dessert usually containing whites of eggs or gelatin **c** : a metal (as platinum) obtained in porous form usually by reduction without fusion [Old English, from Latin *spongia,* from Greek]

[2]**sponge** *vb* **1 a** : to cleanse, wipe, or moisten with or as if with a sponge **b** : to erase or destroy with or as if with a sponge **2** : to absorb with or as if with or like a sponge **3** : to get something from or live on another by imposing on hospitality or good nature ⟨lives by *sponging* off family⟩ **4** : to dive or dredge for sponges — **spong·er** *n*

sponge cake *n* : a light cake made without shortening

sponge rubber *n* : cellular rubber resembling a natural sponge in structure used especially for cushions and in weatherstripping

spon·gi·form en·ceph·a·lop·a·thy \'spən-ji-ˌfȯrm-in-ˌsef-ə-'läp-ə-thē\ *n* : any of a group of diseases in which brain tissue develops a structure like that of a porous sponge and functioning of the nervous system deteriorates [*spongiform* "resembling a sponge," from [1]*sponge* + *-iform*]

spon·gin \'spən-jən\ *n* : a fibrous protein that is the chief constituent of the flexible fibers in certain sponge skeletons [German, from Latin *spongia* "sponge"]

\ə\ **abut**	\au̇\ **out**	\i\ **tip**	\ȯ\ **saw**	\u̇\ **foot**
\ər\ **further**	\ch\ **chin**	\ī\ **life**	\ȯi\ **coin**	\y\ **yet**
\a\ **mat**	\e\ **pet**	\j\ **job**	\th\ **thin**	\yü\ **few**
\ā\ **take**	\ē\ **easy**	\ng\ **sing**	\th\ **this**	\yu̇\ **cure**
\ä\ **cot, cart**	\g\ **go**	\ō\ **bone**	\ü\ **food**	\zh\ **vision**

spongy \ˈspən-jē\ *adj* **spong·i·er; -est** **1** : resembling a sponge in appearance or absorbency **2** : soft and full of holes or moisture : not firm or solid — **spong·i·ness** *n*

spongy layer *n* : a spongy layer of irregular chlorophyll-bearing cells interspersed with air spaces that fills the part of a leaf between the palisade layer and the lower epidermis — called also *spongy parenchyma, spongy tissue*

spon·son \ˈspän-sən\ *n* **1** : a projection (as a gun platform) from the side of a ship or a tank **2** : an air chamber along a canoe or seaplane to increase stability and buoyancy on water [perhaps from *expansion*]

[1]**spon·sor** \ˈspän-sər\ *n* **1** : a person who takes the responsibility for some other person or thing ⟨agreed to be their *sponsor* at the club⟩ **2** : GODPARENT **3** : a person or an organization that pays for or plans and carries out a project or activity; *esp* : one that pays the cost of a radio or television program usually in return for limited advertising time [Latin, "guarantor, surety," from *spondēre* "to promise"] — **spon·sor·ship** \ˈspän-sər-ˌship\ *n*

[2]**sponsor** *vt* **spon·sored; spon·sor·ing** \ˈspäns-ring, -ə-ring\ : to be or act as sponsor for

spon·ta·ne·ity \ˌspänt-ən-ˈē-ət-ē, ˌspänt-n-, -ˈā-ət-\ *n* **1** : the quality or state of being spontaneous **2** : spontaneous action or movement

spon·ta·ne·ous \spän-ˈtā-nē-əs\ *adj* **1** : done, said, or produced freely and naturally ⟨*spontaneous* laughter⟩ **2** : acting or taking place without apparent external cause or influence ⟨*spontaneous* rebellion⟩ ⟨*spontaneous* recovery from illness⟩ [Late Latin *spontaneus,* from Latin *sponte* "of one's free will"] — **spon·ta·ne·ous·ly** *adv* — **spon·ta·ne·ous·ness** *n*

synonyms SPONTANEOUS, IMPULSIVE, INSTINCTIVE, AUTOMATIC mean acting or activated without deliberation. SPONTANEOUS implies lack of prompting and connotes genuineness ⟨*spontaneous* applause⟩. IMPULSIVE implies acting under immediate stress of emotion or spirit of the moment ⟨an *impulsive* act of generosity⟩. INSTINCTIVE stresses spontaneous action involving neither judgment nor conscious intention ⟨blinking is an *instinctive* reaction⟩. AUTOMATIC implies action engaging neither the mind nor the emotions and connotes a predictable response ⟨a soldier's *automatic* obedience to commands⟩.

spontaneous combustion *n* : a bursting into flame of combustible material through heat produced within itself by chemical action (as oxidation)

spontaneous generation *n* : spontaneous origination of living organisms directly from lifeless matter — called also *abiogenesis*

[1]**spoof** \ˈspüf\ *vt* **1** : to deceive by a hoax **2** : to make good-natured fun of [*Spoof,* a hoaxing game invented by Arthur Roberts, died 1933, English comedian]

[2]**spoof** *n* **1** : HOAX, DECEPTION **2** : a light good-natured parody

[1]**spook** \ˈspük\ *n* : GHOST 2 [Dutch] — **spook·ish** \ˈspü-kish\ *adj*

[2]**spook** *vb* : to make or become frightened or frantic

spooky \ˈspü-kē\ *adj* **spook·i·er; -est** **1** : relating to, resembling, or suggesting spooks ⟨a *spooky* movie⟩ **2** : NERVOUS, SKITTISH ⟨a *spooky* horse⟩ — **spook·i·ness** *n*

spool \ˈspül\ *n* **1** : a cylinder which has a rim at each end and usually a hollow center and on which material (as thread or tape) is wound **2** : material wound on a spool [early Dutch *spoele*] — **spool** *vb*

[1]**spoon** \ˈspün\ *n* **1** : an implement with a small shallow bowl and a handle that is used especially in eating and cooking **2** : something (as a tool or fishing lure) that resembles a spoon in shape [Old English *spōn* "splinter, chip"] — **spoon·like** \-ˌlīk\ *adj*

[2]**spoon** *vb* **1** : to take up and usually transfer in or as if in a spoon **2** : to make love by kissing and caressing [sense 2 probably from the Welsh custom of an engaged man's presenting his fiancée with an elaborately carved wooden spoon]

spoon·bill \ˈspün-ˌbil\ *n* **1** : any of several wading birds related to the ibises that have the bill broad, flat, and rounded at the tip **2** : any of several broad-billed ducks (as a shoveler)

spoon bread *n* : soft bread made of cornmeal mixed with milk, eggs, shortening, and leavening and served with a spoon

spoo·ner·ism \ˈspü-nə-ˌriz-əm\ *n* : a transposition of usually initial sounds of two or more words (as in tons of soil for sons of toil) [William A. *Spooner,* died 1930, English clergyman and educator]

spoon–feed \ˈspün-ˌfēd\ *vt* **-fed** \-ˌfed\; **-feed·ing** **1** : to feed by means of a spoon **2** : to present information to in so complete a manner as to prevent independent thought

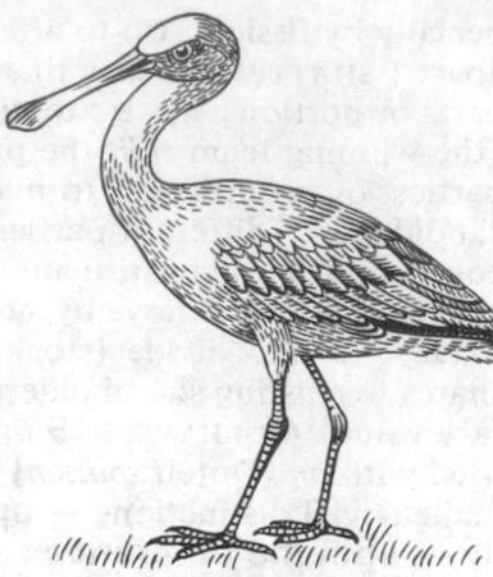

spoonbill 1

spoon·ful \ˈspün-ˌfu̇l\ *n, pl* **spoonfuls** \-ˌfu̇lz\ *also* **spoons·ful** \ˈspünz-ˌfu̇l\ : as much as a spoon can hold; *esp* : TEASPOONFUL 2

[1]**spoor** \ˈspu̇r, ˈspōr, ˈspȯr\ *n* : a track, a trail, a scent, or droppings especially of a wild animal [Afrikaans]

[2]**spoor** *vb* : to track something by its spoor

spor- *or* **sporo-** *combining form* : seed : spore ⟨*sporo*cyst⟩ [New Latin *spora*]

spo·rad·ic \spə-ˈrad-ik\ *adj* : occurring occasionally, singly, or in irregular or random instances ⟨*sporadic* outbreaks of disease⟩ [Medieval Latin *sporadicus,* from Greek *sporadikos,* from *sporadēn* "here and there," from *sporas* "scattered"] ***synonyms*** see INFREQUENT — **spo·rad·i·cal·ly** \-ˈrad-i-kə-lē, -klē\ *adv*

spo·ran·gi·o·phore \spə-ˈran-jē-ə-ˌfōr, -ˌfȯr\ *n* : a stalk (as a fungal hypha) that bears sporangia

spo·ran·gi·um \spə-ˈran-jē-əm\ *n, pl* **-gia** \-jē-ə\ : a sac or case within which spores are produced [New Latin, from *spor-* + Greek *angeion* "vessel"] — **spo·ran·gial** \-jē-əl, -jəl\ *adj*

[1]**spore** \ˈspōr, ˈspȯr\ *n* : a primitive usually one-celled reproductive body produced by fungi and by some plants and microorganisms (as ferns and bacteria) that is capable of developing either directly or after fusion with another spore into a new individual [New Latin *spora* "seed, spore," from Greek, "act of sowing, seed," from *speirein* "to sow"] — **spored** \ˈspōrd, ˈspȯrd\ *adj*

[2]**spore** *vi* : to produce spores or reproduce by spores

spore case *n* : SPORANGIUM

spo·ro·cyst \ˈspōr-ə-ˌsist, ˈspȯr-\ *n* **1** : a resting cell (as of a sporozoan) that may give rise to asexual spores **2** : a sac that is the first asexual reproductive form of some trematodes and buds off cells from its inner surface which develop into rediae

spo·ro·phore \ˈspōr-ə-ˌfōr, ˈspȯr-ə-ˌfȯr\ *n* : the part or organ of a sporophyte (as of a fungus) that produces spores

spo·ro·phyll \ˈspōr-ə-ˌfil, ˈspȯr-\ *n* : a usually greatly modified leaf that bears sporangia

spo·ro·phyte \-ˌfīt\ *n* : the diploid individual or generation of a plant having alternating sexual and asexual generations that produces asexual spores — compare GAMETOPHYTE — **spo·ro·phyt·ic** \ˌspōr-ə-ˈfit-ik, ˌspȯr-\ *adj*

spo·ro·zo·an \ˌspōr-ə-ˈzō-ən, ˌspȯr-\ *n* : any of a large class (Sporozoa) of strictly parasitic protozoans that have a complex life cycle usually involving both asexual and sexual generations often in different hosts and that include important pathogens (as the malaria parasites) [derived from *spor-* + Greek *zōion* "animal"] — **sporozoan** *adj*

spo·ro·zo·ite \-ˈzō-ˌīt\ *n* : a usually motile infective form of some sporozoans that is formed by division of a zygote and initiates an asexual cycle in the new host

spor·ran \ˈspȯr-ən, ˈspär-\ *n* : a pouch usually of skin with the hair or fur on that is worn in front of the kilt by Highlanders in full dress [Scottish Gaelic *sporan* "purse"]

S sporran

[1]**sport** \ˈspōrt, ˈspȯrt\ *vb* **1 a** : to amuse oneself : FROLIC **b** : to engage in a sport **2** : to speak or act in jest : TRIFLE **3** : to display or wear proudly : SHOW OFF ⟨*sport* a new hat⟩ **4** : to deviate or vary abruptly from type : MUTATE [Middle English *sporten,* short for *disporten* "to disport"]

[2]**sport** *n* **1 a** : a source of diversion : RECREATION **b** : physical activity engaged in for pleasure; *esp* : a particular activity (as hunting or an athletic game) so engaged in **2 a** : PLEASANTRY 2, JEST **b** : MOCKERY 1, DERISION **3 a** : some-

thing tossed or driven about in or as if in play ⟨the boat became the *sport* of wind and waves⟩ **b :** LAUGHINGSTOCK **4 a :** SPORTSMAN 1 **b :** one who lives up to the ideals of sportsmanship **5 :** a usually conspicuous mutant individual

[3]**sport** *or* **sports** \ˈspōrts, ˈspȯrts\ *adj* **:** of, relating to, or suitable for sports; *esp* **:** styled in a manner suitable for casual or informal wear ⟨*sport* coats⟩

sport fish *n* **:** a fish that is important to anglers

sport·ing \ˈspōrt-iŋ, ˈspȯrt-\ *adj* **1 a :** used or suitable for sport; *esp* **:** bred or trained for use in hunting ⟨a *sporting* dog⟩ **b :** marked by or calling for sportsmanship **c :** involving such risk as a sports contender may expect to take or encounter ⟨a *sporting* chance⟩ **2 :** of or relating to dissipation (as gambling)

sport·ive \ˈspōrt-iv, ˈspȯrt-\ *adj* **:** engaging in sport **:** FROLICSOME — **sport·ive·ly** *adv* — **sport·ive·ness** *n*

sports car *n* **:** a low small usually two-seat automobile that is especially fast and maneuverable

sports·cast \ˈspōrt-ˌskast, ˈspȯrt-\ *n* **:** a broadcast dealing with sports events [*sport* + broad*cast*] — **sports·cast·er** *n*

sports·man \ˈspōrt-smən, ˈspȯrt-\ *n* **1 :** a person who engages in or is interested in sports and especially outdoor sports **2 :** a person who shows sportsmanship — **sports·man·like** \-ˌlīk\ *adj* — **sports·man·ly** \-lē\ *adj*

sports·man·ship \-smən-ˌship\ *n* **:** conduct (as fairness, respect for one's opponent, and graciousness in winning or losing) appropriate for one participating in a sport

sports medicine *n* **:** a field of medicine concerned with the prevention and treatment of injuries and disorders that are related to participation in sports

sports·wear \-ˌswaər, -ˌsweər\ *n* **:** clothes suitable for sports or for casual or informal wear

sports·wom·an \ˈspōrt-ˌswu̇m-ən, ˈspȯrt-\ *n* **:** a woman who engages in sports and especially in outdoor sports

sports·writ·er \ˈspōrts-ˌrīt-ər, ˈspȯrts-\ *n* **:** a person who writes about sports especially for a newspaper

sport–util·i·ty vehicle \ˈspȯrt-yü-ˈtil-ət-ē-\ *n* **:** a rugged automotive vehicle similar to a station wagon but built on a light truck chassis — called also *SUV*

sporty \ˈspōrt-ē, ˈspȯrt-\ *adj* **sport·i·er; -est 1 :** of, relating to, or typical of sports, sportsmen, sportswomen, or sportswear **2 :** resembling a sports car in styling or performance ⟨a *sporty* sedan⟩ — **sport·i·ly** \ˈspōrt-l-ē, ˈspȯrt-\ *adv* — **sport·i·ness** \ˈspōrt-ē-nəs, ˈspȯrt-\ *n*

spor·u·la·tion \ˌspōr-yə-ˈlā-shən, ˌspȯr-\ *n* **:** formation of or division into spores [New Latin *sporula* "small spore," from *spora* "spore"] — **spor·u·late** \ˈspōr-yə-ˌlāt, ˈspȯr-\ *vi*

[1]**spot** \ˈspät\ *n* **1 :** a blemish or stain on character or reputation **:** FAULT **2 a :** a small area visibly different (as in color, finish, or material) from the surrounding area **b :** an area marred or marked (as by dirt); *also* **:** a small diseased or decayed area on the body surface of a plant or animal **3 :** a small quantity or amount **4 a :** a particular place, area, or part ⟨a good *spot* for a picnic⟩ **b :** a small extent of space **5 :** a particular position (as in an organization or on a program) ⟨have a *spot* open in sales⟩ **6 :** SPOTLIGHT 2 **7 :** a position usually of difficulty or embarrassment **:** FIX **8 :** a brief announcement or advertisement broadcast between scheduled radio or television programs [Middle English] — **on the spot 1 :** at once **:** IMMEDIATELY **2 :** at the place of action ⟨make an investigation *on the spot*⟩ **3 :** in a difficult or trying situation

[2]**spot** *vb* **spot·ted; spot·ting 1 :** to mark or become marked with or as if with spots **:** STAIN, BLEMISH ⟨a *spotted* reputation⟩ ⟨white *spots* so easily⟩ **2 :** to single out **:** IDENTIFY, DETECT ⟨*spot* an opportunity⟩; *also* **:** to locate precisely ⟨*spot* an enemy's position⟩ **3 a :** to lie at intervals in or over ⟨slopes *spotted* with plowed fields⟩ **b :** to place at intervals or in a desired spot ⟨*spot* a picture on the wall⟩ **4 :** to remove spots from **5 :** to allow a handicap or advantage ⟨was *spotted* 5 points⟩

[3]**spot** *adj* **1 :** being, originating, or done on the spot or in or for a particular spot ⟨*spot* coverage of the news⟩ **2 a :** paid out upon delivery ⟨*spot* cash⟩ **b :** involving immediate cash payment ⟨a *spot* transaction⟩ **c :** broadcast between scheduled programs ⟨*spot* announcements⟩ **3 :** made at random or restricted to a few places or instances ⟨a *spot* check⟩

spot–check \ˈspät-ˌchek\ *vb* **:** to sample or investigate quickly or at random **:** make a spot check

spot·less \ˈspät-ləs\ *adj* **:** free from spot or blemish **:** perfectly clean or pure — **spot·less·ly** *adv* — **spot·less·ness** *n*

[1]**spot·light** \ˈspät-ˌlīt\ *n* **1 a :** a projected spot of light used to illuminate something (as a person on a stage) brilliantly **b :** conspicuous public notice **2 :** a light designed to direct a narrow intense beam of light on a small area

[2]**spotlight** *vt* **1 :** to illuminate with a spotlight **2 :** to direct attention to **:** HIGHLIGHT

spot·ted \ˈspät-əd\ *adj* **1 a :** marked with spots **b :** being sullied **:** TARNISHED **2 :** accompanied by an eruption ⟨a *spotted* fever⟩ **3 :** SPOTTY 2

spotted fever *n* **:** any of various diseases (as Rocky Mountain spotted fever and typhus) that are characterized by fever and skin rash

spotted owl *n* **:** a rare large dark brown dark-eyed owl that has barred and spotted underparts and is found from British Columbia to Southern California and central Mexico

spotted turtle *n* **:** a small freshwater turtle of the eastern U.S. with a blackish shell covered with round yellow spots

spot·ter \ˈspät-ər\ *n* **1 :** one that makes, applies, or removes spots **2 :** one that keeps watch **:** OBSERVER; *esp* **:** a civilian who watches for approaching airplanes **3 :** a person who assists another during exercise (as to prevent injury)

spot·ty \ˈspät-ē\ *adj* **spot·ti·er; -est 1 :** SPOTTED 1a **2 :** lacking uniformity ⟨did a *spotty* job of cleaning up⟩ — **spot·ti·ly** \ˈspät-l-ē\ *adv* — **spot·ti·ness** \ˈspät-ē-nəs\ *n*

spou·sal \ˈspau̇-zəl, -səl\ *n* **:** WEDDING 1 — usually used in plural

spouse \ˈspau̇s *also* ˈspau̇z\ *n* **:** a married person **:** HUSBAND, WIFE [Medieval French *espus,* from Latin *sponsus* "betrothed, newly married," from *spondēre* "to promise, betroth"] — **spousal** *adj*

[1]**spout** \ˈspau̇t\ *vb* **1 :** to eject (as liquid) in a stream or jet ⟨wells *spouting* oil⟩ **2 :** to speak or utter readily, volubly, and at length **3 :** to issue with force or in a jet **:** SPURT ⟨blood *spouted* from the wound⟩ [Middle English] — **spout·er** *n*

[2]**spout** *n* **1 :** a tube, pipe, or hole through which something (as rainwater) spouts **2 :** a jet of liquid; *esp* **:** WATERSPOUT — **spout·ed** \ˈspau̇t-əd\ *n*

[1]**sprain** \ˈsprān\ *n* **1 :** a sudden or severe twisting of a joint with stretching or tearing of ligaments **2 :** a condition that results from a sprain and is usually marked by pain and swelling [origin unknown] ***synonyms*** see STRAIN

[2]**sprain** *vt* **:** to injure by a sudden or severe twist

sprat \ˈsprat\ *n* **1 :** a small European fish closely related to the herring **2 :** any of various small or young fish (as an anchovy) related to or resembling the herring [Old English *sprott*]

sprawl \ˈsprȯl\ *vb* **1 :** to creep or clamber awkwardly **2 :** to lie or sit with arms and legs spread out **3 :** to spread or cause to spread out irregularly or awkwardly ⟨a *sprawling* city⟩ [Old English *sprēawlian* "to thrash about"] — **sprawl** *n*

[1]**spray** \ˈsprā\ *n* **1 :** a usually flowering branch or shoot **2 :** a decorative flat arrangement of flowers and foliage **3 :** something (as an ornament) resembling a spray [Middle English]

[2]**spray** *n* **1 :** water flying in small drops or particles (as when blown from waves or thrown up by a waterfall) **2 a :** a jet of vapor or finely divided liquid (as from an atomizer) **b :** a device (as an atomizer or sprayer) by which a spray is dispersed or applied [obsolete *spray* "to sprinkle," from early Dutch *sprayen*]

[3]**spray** *vb* **1 :** to disperse or apply in a spray **2 :** to project spray on or into — **spray·er** *n*

spray gun *n* **:** a device for applying a substance (as paint or insecticide) as a spray

[1]**spread** \ˈspred\ *vb* **spread; spread·ing 1 a :** to open or expand over a larger area ⟨*spread* out a map⟩ **b :** to stretch out or apart **:** EXTEND ⟨*spread* your arms wide⟩ **2 a :** SCATTER, STREW ⟨*spread* fertilizer⟩ **b :** to distribute over a period or among a group ⟨*spread* the work to be done⟩ **c :** to apply on a surface ⟨*spread* butter on bread⟩ **d :** COVER, OVERLAY ⟨*spread* a floor with carpet⟩ **e** (1) **:** to prepare or furnish for dining **:** SET ⟨*spread* a table⟩ (2) **:** SERVE ⟨*spread* a banquet⟩ **3 a :** to become or cause to become widely known ⟨the news *spread* rapidly⟩ **b :** to extend the range or incidence of ⟨*spread* a disease⟩ **4 :** to stretch or move apart ⟨*spread* one's fingers⟩ [Old English *-sprǣdan*] — **spread·able** \ˈspred-ə-bəl\ *adj*

[2]**spread** *n* **1 a :** the act or process of spreading **b :** extent of spreading ⟨the *spread* of a bird's wings⟩ **2 :** something spread

\ə\ **abut**	\au̇\ **out**	\i\ **tip**	\ȯ\ **saw**	\u̇\ **foot**
\ər\ **further**	\ch\ **chin**	\ī\ **life**	\ȯi\ **coin**	\y\ **yet**
\a\ **mat**	\e\ **pet**	\j\ **job**	\th\ **thin**	\yü\ **few**
\ā\ **take**	\ē\ **easy**	\ŋ\ **sing**	\t͟h\ **this**	\yu̇\ **cure**
\ä\ **cot, cart**	\g\ **go**	\ō\ **bone**	\ü\ **food**	\zh\ **vision**

out: as **a** : EXPANSE **b** : a ranch or homestead especially in the western U.S. **c** : a prominent display in a periodical **3** : something spread on or over a surface: as **a** : a food to be spread (as on bread or crackers) **b** : FEAST 1a **c** : a cover for a table or bed **4** : distance between two points

spread–ea·gle \'spred-ˌē-gəl\ *vb* **spread–ea·gled; spread–ea·gling** \-gə-ling, -gling\ **1** : to stand or move with arms and legs stretched out **2** : to spread over : stretch across

spread eagle *n* **1** : a representation of an eagle with wings raised and legs extended **2** : something resembling or suggesting a spread eagle

spread·er \'spred-ər\ *n* : one that spreads: as **a** : an implement for scattering material **b** : a small knife used especially for spreading butter

spread·sheet \'spred-ˌshēt\ *n* : an accounting program for a computer; *also* : the ledger layout simulated by such a program

spree \'sprē\ *n* : an unrestrained indulgence in or outburst of an activity ⟨a buying *spree*⟩; *also* : BINGE 1 [origin unknown]

sprier *comparative of* SPRY

spriest *superlative of* SPRY

[1]**sprig** \'sprig\ *n* **1** : a small shoot or twig especially with leaves or flowers **2** : an ornament resembling a sprig, stemmed flower, or leaf **3** : a small headless nail : BRAD [Middle English *sprigge*]

[2]**sprig** *vt* **sprigged; sprig·ging** : to drive sprigs into

spright·ful \'sprīt-fəl\ *adj* : SPIRITED — **spright·ful·ly** \-fə-lē\ *adv* — **spright·ful·ness** *n*

spright·ly \'sprīt-lē\ *adj* **spright·li·er; -est** : SPIRITED ⟨a *sprightly* musical⟩ [obsolete *spright* "sprite," alteration of *sprite*] — **spright·li·ness** *n* — **sprightly** *adv*

[1]**spring** \'spring\ *vb* **sprang** \'sprang\ *or* **sprung** \'sprəng\; **sprung; spring·ing** \'spring-ing\ **1 a** (1) : DART 2, SHOOT ⟨sparks *sprang* out from the fire⟩ (2) : to be resilient or elastic; *also* : to move by elastic force ⟨the lid *sprang* shut⟩ **b** : to become warped **2** : to issue with speed and force or as a stream **3 a** : to grow as a plant **b** : to issue by birth or descent ⟨*sprang* from the upper class⟩ **c** : to come into being : ARISE **4 a** : to make a leap or series of leaps **b** : to jump up suddenly **5** : to stretch out in height : RISE **6** : PAY 1 — used with *for* ⟨I'll *spring* for the tickets⟩ **7** : to have (a leak) develop **8** : to cause to operate suddenly ⟨*spring* a trap⟩ **9** : to produce or disclose suddenly or unexpectedly ⟨*sprung* a surprise on us⟩ **10** : to release or cause to be released from custody or confinement [Old English *springan*] — **spring·er** \'spring-ər\ *n*

[2]**spring** *n* **1 a** : a source of supply; *esp* : a source of water issuing from the ground **b** : an ultimate source especially of action or motion **2 a** : the season between winter and summer comprising in the northern hemisphere usually the months of March, April, and May or as reckoned astronomically extending from the March equinox to the June solstice **b** : a time or season of growth or development **3** : an elastic body or device that recovers its original shape when released after being distorted **4 a** : the act or an instance of leaping up or forward : BOUND **b** : capacity for springing : RESILIENCE, BOUNCE

spring beauty *n* : a North American herb that sends up in early spring a 2-leaved stem bearing delicate pink flowers

spring·board \'spring-ˌbōrd, -ˌbȯrd\ *n* **1** : a flexible board usually secured at one end and used to gain height for gymnastic stunts or diving **2** : a point of departure

spring·bok \'spring-ˌbäk\ *n, pl* **springbok** *or* **springboks** : a swift and graceful southern African gazelle noted for its habit of leaping lightly and suddenly into the air [Afrikaans, from *spring* "to jump" + *bok* "male goat"]

spring–clean·ing \-'klē-ning\ *n* : the act or process of cleaning a place thoroughly

spring·er spaniel \ˌspring-ər-\ *n* : a medium-sized sporting dog of English or Welsh origin used chiefly for finding and flushing small game

spring fever *n* : a lazy or restless feeling often associated with the onset of spring

spring·house \'spring-ˌhau̇s\ *n* : a small building over a spring used for cool storage (as of dairy products or meat)

spring peeper *n* : a small brown tree frog of the eastern U.S. and Canada with a shrill piping call

spring roll *n* : EGG ROLL; *also* : any of various similar appetizers especially in Asian cuisine

spring·tail \'spring-ˌtāl\ *n* : any of an order (Collembola) of small primitive wingless insects that have a special appendage used for jumping

spring·tide \'spring-ˌtīd\ *n* : SPRINGTIME

spring tide *n* : a greater than usual tide occurring at each new moon and full moon

spring·time \'spring-ˌtīm\ *n* : the season of spring

spring wagon *n* : a light wagon equipped with springs

spring·wood \'spring-ˌwu̇d\ *n* : the softer, lighter, and more porous inner portion of an annual ring of wood that is made up of large thin-walled cells and develops early in the growing season — compare SUMMERWOOD

springy \'spring-ē\ *adj* **spring·i·er; -est** **1** : having an elastic quality : RESILIENT **2** : having or showing a lively and energetic movement ⟨walks with a *springy* step⟩ — **spring·i·ly** \'spring-ə-lē\ *adv* — **spring·i·ness** \'spring-ē-nəs\ *n*

[1]**sprin·kle** \'spring-kəl\ *vb* **sprin·kled; sprin·kling** \-kə-ling, -kling\ **1** : to scatter in drops or particles **2 a** : to scatter over **b** : to scatter at intervals in or among : DOT **c** : to wet lightly **3** : to rain lightly in scattered drops [Middle English *sprinclen*] — **sprin·kler** \-kə-lər, -klər\ *n*

[2]**sprinkle** *n* **1** : the act or an instance of sprinkling; *esp* : a light rain **2** : SPRINKLING

sprinkler system *n* : a system for protection against fire in which pipes are distributed for conveying an extinguishing fluid (as water) to outlets

sprin·kling \'spring-kling\ *n* : a limited quantity or amount; *esp* : SCATTERING

[1]**sprint** \'sprint\ *vi* : to run at top speed especially for a short distance [of Scandinavian origin] — **sprint·er** *n*

[2]**sprint** *n* **1** : the act or an instance of sprinting **2** : a race run at or near top speed the whole way : DASH

sprit \'sprit\ *n* : a spar attached to the mast that runs diagonally across a rectangular fore-and-aft sail to support it [Old English *sprēot* "pole, spear"]

sprite \'sprīt\ *n* **1** : GHOST 2 **2 a** : an often mischievous supernatural being **b** : an elfish person [Medieval French *espriz, espirit* "spirit, sprite," from Latin *spiritus* "spirit"]

sprit·sail \'sprit-ˌsāl, -səl\ *n* : a sail extended by a sprit

sprock·et \'spräk-ət\ *n* **1** : a projection on the rim of a wheel shaped so as to interlock with the links of a chain **2** : a wheel having sprockets [origin unknown]

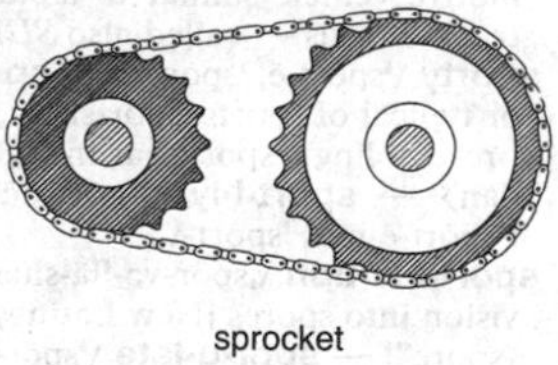

sprocket

[1]**sprout** \'sprau̇t\ *vb* **1** : to send out new growth **2** : to grow rapidly **3** : to cause to sprout ⟨*sprout* oats⟩ [Old English *-sprūtan*]

[2]**sprout** *n* **1** : SHOOT 1a; *esp* : a young shoot (as from a seed or root) **2** *pl* : edible young shoots especially from recently germinated seeds (as of alfalfa)

[1]**spruce** \'sprüs\ *n* : any of a genus of typically pyramid-shaped evergreen trees related to the pines and having flat or 4-sided needles, pendulous cones, and soft light wood; *also* : its wood [Middle English *Spruce* "Prussia," alteration of *Pruce,* from Medieval French]

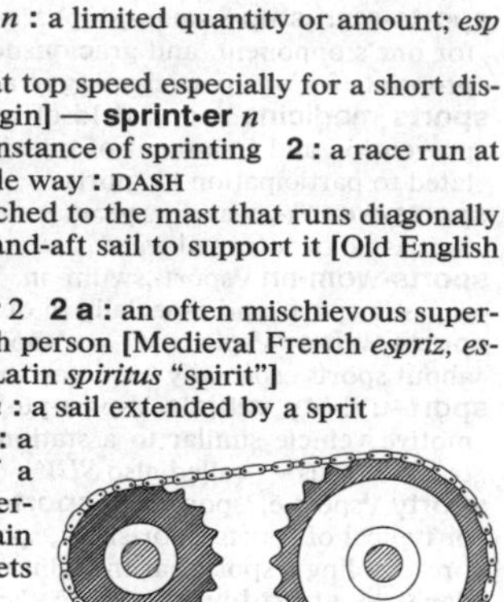

spruce

Word History Prussia was formerly called *Pruce* or *Spruce* in English. A number of goods imported from Prussia—*spruce* canvas, *spruce* iron, *spruce* leather—were all very well-thought-of. Perhaps the most important of these Prussian or *Spruce* products was the spruce tree, a tall, straight conifer that was especially desirable for use as the mast of a ship. About the middle of the 17th century, *Spruce* as the name for the country was largely supplanted by Prussia. But by this time *spruce* had become well established as the name of the tree.

[2]**spruce** *adj* : neat or smart in appearance : TRIM [perhaps from obsolete *spruce leather* "leather imported from Prussia"] — **spruce·ly** *adv* — **spruce·ness** *n*

[3]**spruce** *vb* : to make or make oneself spruce ⟨*spruce* up a room⟩ ⟨*spruce* up before dinner⟩

sprue \'sprü\ *n* : a chronic disease marked especially by fatty diarrhea and poor absorption of nutrients [Dutch *spruw*]

sprung *past of* SPRING
spry \ˈsprī\ *adj* **spri·er** *or* **spry·er** \ˈsprī-ər, ˈsprīr\; **spri·est** *or* **spry·est** \ˈsprī-əst\ : light and easy in motion : NIMBLE, SPRIGHTLY [origin unknown] — **spry·ly** *adv* — **spry·ness** *n*
¹**spud** \ˈspəd\ *n* **1** : a tool or device (as for digging, lifting, or cutting) combining the characteristics of spade and chisel **2** : POTATO 2b [Middle English *spudde* "dagger"]
²**spud** *vb* **spud·ded; spud·ding** : to dig with a spud
¹**spume** \ˈspyüm\ *n* : frothy matter on liquids : FOAM [Medieval French, from Latin *spuma*] — **spu·mous** \ˈspyü-məs\ *adj* — **spumy** \ˈspyü-mē\ *adj*
²**spume** *vi* : FROTH 3, FOAM
spu·mo·ni *also* **spu·mo·ne** \spu̇-ˈmō-nē\ *n* : ice cream in layers of different colors, flavors, and textures often with candied fruits and nuts [Italian *spumone,* from *spuma* "foam," from Latin]
spun *past of* SPIN
spun glass *n* : FIBERGLASS
spunk \ˈspəngk\ *n* **1** : METTLE 2a, PLUCK **2** : SPIRIT 4, LIVELINESS [earlier *spunk* "tinder," from Scottish Gaelic *spong* "sponge, tinder," from early Irish *sponge,* Latin *spongia* "sponge"]
spunky \ˈspəng-kē\ *adj* **spunk·i·er; -est** : full of spunk : SPIRITED — **spunk·i·ly** \-kə-lē\ *adv* — **spunk·i·ness** \-kē-nəs\ *n*
spun sugar *n* : sugar boiled to long threads and gathered up and shaped or heaped on a stick as a candy
¹**spur** \ˈspər\ *n* **1 a** : a pointed device secured to a rider's heel and used to urge on the horse **b** *pl* : recognition for achievement **2** : a goad to action : STIMULUS **3** : something projecting like or suggesting a spur: as **a** : a stiff sharp projecting part (as a broken branch of a tree or a horny process on a cock's leg) **b** : a hollow projecting appendage of a corolla or calyx (as in larkspur or columbine) **4** : a ridge that extends laterally from a mountain **5** : a railroad track diverging from a main line [Old English *spura*] — **on the spur of the moment** : on impulse : SUDDENLY
²**spur** *vb* **spurred; spur·ring 1** : to urge a horse on with spurs **2** : INCITE, STIMULATE ⟨*spur* the team to victory⟩
spurge \ˈspərj\ *n* : any of a family of mostly shrubby plants (as a poinsettia) often with a bitter milky juice [Medieval French *espurge,* from *espurger* "to clean out, purge," from Latin *expurgare*]
spur gear *n* : a gear with radial teeth parallel to its axis

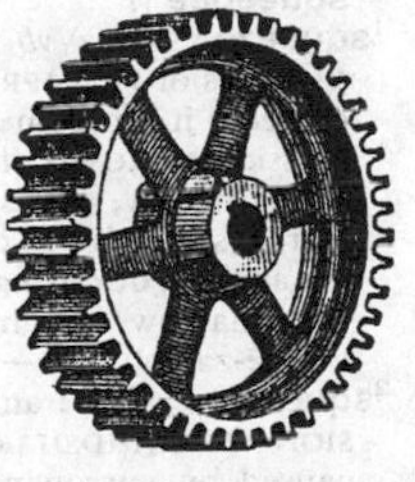
spur gear

spu·ri·ous \ˈspyu̇r-ē-əs\ *adj* : not genuine or authentic : FALSE, COUNTERFEIT [Late Latin *spurius,* from Latin, "bastard"] — **spu·ri·ous·ly** *adv* — **spu·ri·ous·ness** *n*
¹**spurn** \ˈspərn\ *vt* **1** : to kick aside **2** : to reject with disdain [Old English *spurnan*] ***synonyms*** see REJECT — **spurn·er** *n*
²**spurn** *n* **1** : KICK 1a(1) **2** : disdainful rejection
spur–of–the–moment *adj* : occurring or developing without prior planning ⟨a *spur-of-the-moment* decision⟩
spurred \ˈspərd\ *adj* **1** : wearing spurs **2** : having one or more spurs ⟨a *spurred* violet⟩
¹**spurt** \ˈspərt\ *n* **1** : a short period of time : MOMENT **2** : a sudden brief burst of effort, activity, or development ⟨a *spurt* of work⟩ ⟨a growth *spurt*⟩ [origin unknown]
²**spurt** *vi* : to make a spurt
³**spurt** *vb* **1** : SPOUT 3 **2** : SQUIRT [perhaps related to *sprout*]
⁴**spurt** *n* : a sudden gush : JET
Sput·nik \ˈspu̇t-nik, ˈspət-\ *n* : any of a series of satellites launched by the Soviet Union beginning in 1957 [Russian, literally, "traveling companion," from *s* "with" + *put'* "path"]
¹**sput·ter** \ˈspət-ər\ *vb* **1** : to spit or squirt particles of food or saliva noisily from the mouth **2** : to speak or utter hastily or explosively in confusion or excitement ⟨*sputtered* out their protests⟩ **3** : to make explosive popping sounds ⟨the motor *sputtered* and died⟩ [related to Dutch *sputteren* "to sputter"] — **sput·ter·er** \-ər-ər\ *n*
²**sputter** *n* : the act or sound of sputtering
spu·tum \ˈspyüt-əm, ˈspüt-\ *n, pl* **spu·ta** \-ə\ : a secretion primarily of mucous that is spit or coughed up from the lungs or bronchi [Latin, from *spuere* "to spit"]

¹**spy** \ˈspī\ *vb* **spied; spy·ing 1** : to watch, inspect, or examine secretly : act as a spy **2** : to catch sight of : SEE ⟨*spied* a friend in the crowd⟩ **3** : to search or search out usually by close study or examination [Medieval French *espier,* of Germanic origin]
²**spy** *n, pl* **spies 1** : one that secretly watches another so as to obtain information **2** : a person who tries secretly to obtain information for one country in the territory of another usually hostile country
spy·glass \ˈspī-ˌglas\ *n* : a small telescope

spyglass

squab \ˈskwäb\ *n, pl* **squabs** *or* **squab** : a fledgling bird; *esp* : a fledgling pigeon about four weeks old [probably of Scandinavian origin]
¹**squab·ble** \ˈskwäb-əl\ *n* : a noisy quarrel usually over petty matters [probably of Scandinavian origin]
²**squabble** *vi* **squab·bled; squab·bling** \ˈskwäb-ling, -ə-ling\ : to quarrel noisily and to no purpose : WRANGLE — **squab·bler** \-ler, -ə-lər\ *n*
squad \ˈskwäd\ *n* **1** : a small organized group of military personnel; *esp* : a tactical unit that can be easily directed in the field **2** : a small group engaged in a common effort or occupation ⟨a football *squad*⟩ [Middle French *esquade,* from Spanish *escuadra* and Italian *squadra,* both derived from Latin *quadrare* "to square"]
squad car *n* : a police automobile connected by a two-way radio with headquarters — called also *cruiser, prowl car*
squad·ron \ˈskwäd-rən\ *n* : any of several units of military organization [Italian *squadrone,* from *squadra* "squad"]
squad room *n* **1** : a room in a barracks used to billet soldiers **2** : a room in a police station where members of the force assemble
squal·id \ˈskwäl-əd\ *adj* **1** : marked by filthiness and degradation from neglect or poverty **2** : morally debased : SORDID [Latin *squalidus*] — **squal·id·ly** *adv* — **squal·id·ness** *n*
¹**squall** \ˈskwȯl\ *vb* : to utter a raucous cry [probably of Scandinavian origin] — **squall·er** *n*
²**squall** *n* : a raucous cry
³**squall** *n* **1** : a sudden violent wind often with rain or snow **2** : a short-lived commotion [probably of Scandinavian origin]
⁴**squall** *vi* : to blow a squall
squally \ˈskwȯl-lē\ *adj* **squall·i·er; -est** : marked by squalls : GUSTY, STORMY
squal·or \ˈskwäl-ər\ *n* : the quality or state of being squalid [Latin]
squa·mo·sal \skwə-ˈmō-səl, -zəl\ *adj* : of, relating to, or being a bone of the skull of many vertebrates corresponding to the squamous portion of the temporal bone of humans
squa·mous \ˈskwā-məs, ˈskwä-\ *adj* **1 a** : covered with or consisting of scales : SCALY **b** : of, relating to, or being an epithelium that consists at least in its outer layers of small flattened scalelike cells **2** : of, relating to, or being the anterior upper portion of the temporal bone of most mammals including human beings [Latin *squamosus,* from *squama* "scale"]
squan·der \ˈskwän-dər\ *vb* **squan·dered; squan·der·ing** \-də-ring, -dring\ : to spend extravagantly or wastefully [origin unknown] — **squan·der·er** \-dər-ər\ *n*
¹**square** \ˈskwaər, ˈskweər\ *n* **1** : an instrument having at least one right angle and two straight edges used to mark or test right angles **2** : a rectangle with all four sides equal **3** : any of the quadrilateral spaces marked out on a board for playing games **4** : the product of a number multiplied by itself ⟨36 is the *square* of 6⟩ **5 a** : an open place or area formed at the meeting of two or more streets **b** : BLOCK 5b, 5c **6** : a person who is

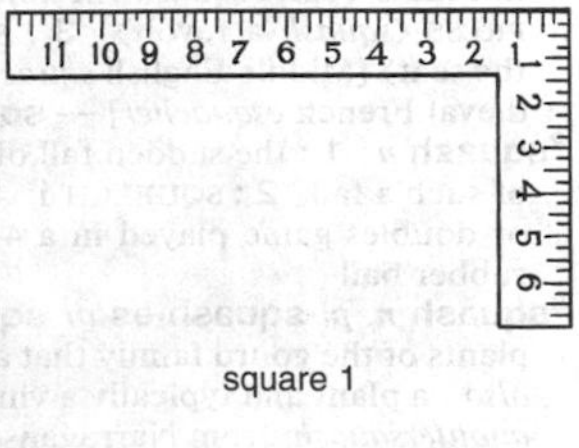

square 1

\ə\ abut	\au̇\ out	\i\ tip	\ȯ\ saw	\u̇\ foot
\ər\ further	\ch\ chin	\ī\ life	\ȯi\ coin	\y\ yet
\a\ mat	\e\ pet	\j\ job	\th\ thin	\yü\ few
\ā\ take	\ē\ easy	\ng\ sing	\th\ this	\yu̇\ cure
\ä\ cot, cart	\g\ go	\ō\ bone	\ü\ food	\zh\ vision

overly conventional or conservative [Medieval French *esquarre,* derived from Latin *ex-* + *quadrare* "to square"] — **on the square 1 :** at right angles **2 :** in a fair open manner : HONESTLY — **out of square :** not at an exact right angle

[2]**square** *adj* **1 a :** having four equal sides and four right angles ⟨a *square* piece of paper⟩ **b :** forming a right angle ⟨a *square* corner⟩ **c :** having a square base ⟨a *square* pyramid⟩ **2 a :** being approximately a cube ⟨a *square* cabinet⟩ **b :** of a shape suggesting strength and solidity ⟨a *square* jaw⟩ ⟨*square* shoulders⟩ **c :** having the shape of a square as its section ⟨a *square* tower⟩ **3 a :** being a unit of area that has the shape of a square and sides of a specified unit length ⟨a *square* meter⟩ **b :** being of a specified length in each of two equal dimensions ⟨10 meters *square*⟩ **4 a :** exactly adjusted or aligned **b :** FAIR 5a, JUST ⟨a *square* deal⟩ **c :** leaving no balance : SETTLED **d :** TIED ⟨the golfers were all *square* at the end of the 6th hole⟩ **e :** SUBSTANTIAL 2 ⟨a *square* meal⟩ **6 :** being unsophisticated, conservative, or conventional — **square·ness** *n*

[3]**square** *vb* **1 :** to make square or rectangular ⟨*square* a building stone⟩ **2 :** to bring approximately to a right angle ⟨*squared* my shoulders⟩ **3 a :** to multiply (a number) by itself : to raise (a number) to the second power **b :** to find a square equal in area to ⟨*square* a circle⟩ **4 :** to agree or make agree ⟨your story does not *square* with the facts⟩ **5 :** BALANCE, SETTLE ⟨*square* an account⟩ **6 :** to mark off into squares **7 :** to influence or settle by or as if by a bribe

square away *vb* **:** to put in order or readiness

square bracket *n* **:** BRACKET 3a

square dance *n* **:** a dance for four couples who form the sides of a square — **square–dance** *vb* — **square dancer** *n* — **square dancing** *n*

square knot *n* **:** a knot made of two reverse half-knots and typically used to join the ends of two cords — see KNOT illustration

square·ly \ˈskwaər-lē, ˈskweər-\ *adv* **1 :** in a plain or honest manner ⟨we must *squarely* face the issue⟩ **2 a :** EXACTLY 1a ⟨*squarely* in the middle⟩ **b :** so as to make solid contact ⟨hit the ball *squarely*⟩ **3 :** in a square form or manner : so as to be square ⟨a *squarely* cut dress⟩

square measure *n* **:** a unit or system of units for measuring area — see MEASURE table, METRIC SYSTEM table

square number *n* **:** a whole number (as 1, 4, or 9) that is the square of another whole number

square one *n* **:** the initial stage or starting point ⟨back to *square one*⟩

square–rigged \ˈskwaər-ˈrigd, ˈskweər-\ *adj* **:** having the principal sails extended on yards fastened to the masts horizontally and at their center

square–rig·ger \-ˈrig-ər\ *n* **:** a square-rigged vessel

square root *n* **:** a number that when squared equals a specified number ⟨the *square root* of 9 is ±3⟩

square sail \-ˌsāl, -səl\ *n* **:** a 4-sided sail used on a square-rigged vessel

square shooter *n* **:** a just or honest person

square–shoul·dered \-ˈshōl-dərd\ *adj* **:** having shoulders of a rectangular outline that are straight across the back

squar·ish \ˈskwaər-ish, ˈskweər-\ *adj* **:** somewhat square in form or appearance — **squar·ish·ly** *adv*

[1]**squash** \ˈskwäsh, ˈskwȯsh\ *vb* **1 :** to press or beat into a pulp or flat mass ⟨don't *squash* the tomatoes⟩ **2 :** to put down : SUPPRESS ⟨*squash* a revolt⟩ **3 :** SQUEEZE, PRESS ⟨*squashed* into the seat⟩ [Middle English *squachen* "to crush, annul," from Medieval French *esquacher*] — **squash·er** *n*

[2]**squash** *n* **1 :** the sudden fall of a heavy soft body or the sound of such a fall **2 :** SQUELCH 1 **3 :** a crushed mass **4 :** a singles or doubles game played in a 4-wall court with a racket and a rubber ball

[3]**squash** *n, pl* **squash·es** *or* **squash :** any of various fruits of plants of the gourd family that are used especially as vegetables; *also* **:** a plant and typically a vine that bears squashes [earlier *isquoutersquash,* from Narragansett *askútasquash*]

squash bug *n* **:** a large black American bug injurious to squash and other plants of the gourd family

squash racquets *n* **:** [2]SQUASH 4

squash tennis *n* **:** a game resembling squash played with an inflated ball the size of a tennis ball

squashy \ˈskwäsh-ē, ˈskwȯsh-\ *adj* **squash·i·er; -est :** easily squashed : SOFT ⟨*squashy* hats⟩ — **squash·i·ly** \ˈskwäsh-ə-lē, ˈskwȯsh-\ *adv* — **squash·i·ness** \ˈskwäsh-ē-nəs, ˈskwȯsh-\ *n*

[1]**squat** \ˈskwät\ *vb* **squat·ted; squat·ting 1 :** to sit or cause (oneself) to sit on one's haunches or heels **2 :** to occupy land as a squatter **3 :** CROUCH, COWER ⟨a *squatting* hare⟩ [Medieval French *esquatir,* from *es-* "ex-" + *quatir* "to hide," derived from Latin *cogere* "to drive together"]

[2]**squat** *n* **1 :** the act of squatting **2 :** a squatting posture

[3]**squat** *adj* **squat·ter; squat·test 1 :** sitting with the haunches close above the heels **2 a :** low to the ground **b :** being short and thick — **squat·ly** *adv* — **squat·ness** *n*

squat·ter \ˈskwät-ər\ *n* **1 :** one that squats **2 a :** one that settles on land without right or title or payment of rent **b :** one that settles on public land under government regulation with the purpose of acquiring title

squat·ty \ˈskwät-ē\ *adj* **squat·ti·er; -est :** SQUAT 2

squaw·fish \ˈskwȯ-ˌfish\ *n* **:** any of several mostly freshwater fishes of western North America

[1]**squawk** \ˈskwȯk\ *vi* **1 :** to utter a harsh abrupt scream **2 :** to complain or protest loudly or vehemently [probably blend of *squall* and *squeak*] — **squawk·er** *n*

[2]**squawk** *n* **1 :** a harsh abrupt scream **2 :** a noisy complaint

squawk box *n* **:** an intercom speaker

squaw·root \ˈskwȯ-ˌrüt, -ˌru̇t\ *n* **:** a North American herb that is parasitic especially on oak roots and has a thick stem with yellow fleshy scales

[1]**squeak** \ˈskwēk\ *vb* **1 :** to utter a sharp shrill cry or noise **2 :** to pass, succeed, or win by a narrow margin ⟨barely *squeaked* by⟩ **3 :** to utter in a shrill piping tone [Middle English *squeken*]

[2]**squeak** *n* **1 :** a sharp shrill cry or sound **2 :** ESCAPE 1 ⟨a close *squeak*⟩ — **squeaky** \ˈskwē-kē\ *adj*

[1]**squeal** \ˈskwēl\ *vb* **1 :** to utter a shrill cry or sound **2 a :** to turn informer ⟨*squealed* to the police⟩ **b :** COMPLAIN 1, PROTEST **3 :** to utter with or as if with a squeal **4 :** to cause to make a loud shrill noise ⟨*squealing* the tires⟩ [Middle English *squelen*] — **squeal·er** *n*

[2]**squeal** *n* **:** a shrill cry or sound

squea·mish \ˈskwē-mish\ *adj* **1 a :** easily nauseated : QUEASY **b :** affected with nausea **2 :** easily shocked or disgusted [Medieval French *escoymous*] — **squea·mish·ly** *adv* — **squea·mish·ness** *n*

squee·gee \ˈskwē-ˌjē\ *n* **:** a blade of leather or rubber set on a handle and used for spreading or wiping liquid material on, across, or off a surface (as a window) [perhaps imitative] — **squeegee** *vt*

[1]**squeeze** \ˈskwēz\ *vb* **1 a :** to exert pressure especially on opposite sides of : COMPRESS **b :** to extract or emit under pressure ⟨*squeeze* juice from a lemon⟩ **c :** to force or thrust by compression : CROWD ⟨two more *squeezed* into the car⟩ **2 a :** to extort money, goods, or services from ⟨*squeezed* their tenants mercilessly⟩ **b :** to cause hardship to : OPPRESS **c :** to reduce the amount of ⟨rising costs *squeezed* profits⟩ **3 :** to gain or win by a narrow margin [Old English *cwȳsan*] — **squeez·able** \ˈskwē-zə-bəl\ *adj* — **squeez·er** *n*

[2]**squeeze** *n* **1 a :** an act or instance of squeezing : COMPRESSION **b :** HANDSHAKE; *also* **:** EMBRACE **2 :** financial pressure caused by narrowing margins (as between costs and selling price) or by shortages **3 :** SQUEEZE PLAY **4** *slang* **:** a romantic partner ⟨she's my main *squeeze*⟩

squeeze bottle *n* **:** a bottle of flexible plastic that dispenses its contents by being pressed

squeeze play *n* **:** a baseball play in which a batter attempts to score a runner from third base by bunting

[1]**squelch** \ˈskwelch\ *n* **1 :** a sound of or as if of semiliquid matter under suction ⟨the *squelch* of mud⟩ **2 :** a retort that silences an opponent [imitative]

[2]**squelch** *vb* **1 a :** to fall or stamp on so as to crush **b :** to completely suppress : QUELL, SILENCE ⟨*squelch* resistance⟩ **2 :** to emit or cause to emit a sucking sound **3 :** to splash through water, slush, or mire — **squelch·er** *n*

sque·teague \skwi-ˈtēg\ *n, pl* **squeteague :** any of various weakfishes [of southeast New England Algonquian origin]

squib \ˈskwib\ *n* **1 a :** a small firecracker **b :** a broken firecracker that burns out with a fizz **2 :** a short humorous or satiric writing or speech [origin unknown]

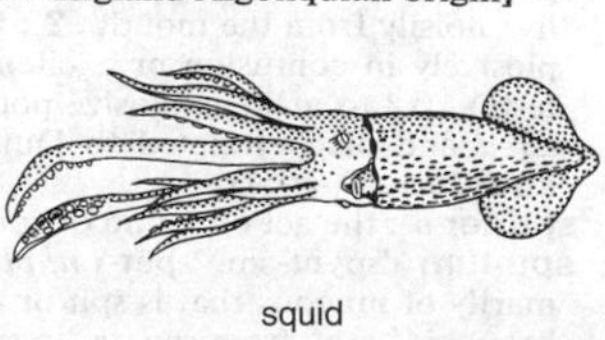
squid

squid \ˈskwid\ *n, pl* **squid** *or* **squids :** any of numerous cephalopod mollusks having eight short arms and two usually longer tentacles, a long tapered body with a fin on each side, and usually a slender internal chitinous support [origin unknown]

SQUID \ˈskwid\ *n* : an instrument for detecting and measuring very weak magnetic fields [*s*uperconducting *qu*antum *i*nterference *d*evice]

squig·gle \ˈskwig-əl\ *n* : a short wavy twist or line : CURLICUE [from earlier *squiggle* "to wriggle," blend of *squirm* and *wriggle*]

squill \ˈskwil\ *n* **1** : a Mediterranean bulbous herb related to the lilies and having narrow leaves and white flowers; *also* : its bulb used in medicine and in rat poisons **2** : SCILLA [Latin *squilla, scilla,* from Greek *skilla*]

[1]**squint** \ˈskwint\ *adj* : affected with cross-eye [Middle English *asquint*]

[2]**squint** *vi* **1 a** : to look with a side glance (as with envy or disdain) **b** : to be cross-eyed **2** : to look or peer with eyes partly closed — **squint·er** *n*

[3]**squint** *n* **1** : STRABISMUS **2** : an action or instance of squinting — **squinty** \ˈskwint-ē\ *adj*

squint–eyed \ˈskwint-ˈīd\ *adj* : having eyes affected with cross-eye

[1]**squire** \ˈskwīr\ *n* **1** : one who bears the shield or armor of a knight **2 a** : a male attendant on a great personage **b** : LADIES' MAN, ESCORT **3 a** : a member of the British gentry ranking below a knight and above a gentleman **b** : an owner of a country estate **c** : JUSTICE OF THE PEACE [Medieval French *esquier,* from Late Latin *scutarius* "guard armed with a shield," from Latin *scutum* "shield"]

[2]**squire** *vt* : to attend as a squire or escort

squire·archy *or* **squir·archy** \ˈskwīr-ˌär-kē\ *n* **1** : the gentry or landed-proprietor class **2** : government by a landed gentry

squirm \ˈskwərm\ *vi* **1** : to twist about like an eel or a worm **2** : to feel acutely embarrassed ⟨undeserved praise made us *squirm*⟩ [perhaps imitative] — **squirmy** \ˈskwər-mē\ *adj*

squir·rel \ˈskwər-əl, ˈskwə-rəl, ˈskwərl\ *n, pl* **squirrels** *also* **squirrel** **1** : any of various small or medium-sized rodents (family Sciuridae); *esp* : one with a long bushy tail and strong hind legs adapted to leaping from branch to branch **2** : the fur of a squirrel [Medieval French *escurel, esquirel,* derived from Latin *sciurus,* from Greek *skiouros,* probably from *skia* "shadow" + *oura* "tail"]

squirrel 1

squirrel monkey *n* : a small soft-haired South American monkey having a long tail not used for grasping and being colored chiefly yellowish gray with a white face and black nose

[1]**squirt** \ˈskwərt\ *vb* : to come forth, drive, or eject in a sudden rapid stream : SPURT [Middle English *squirten*]

[2]**squirt** *n* **1 a** : an instrument (as a syringe) for squirting a liquid **b** : a small quick stream : JET **c** : the action of squirting **2** : an impudent youngster

squirt gun *n* : WATER PISTOL

squishy \ˈskwish-ē\ *adj* : being soft, yielding, and damp [from earlier *squish* "to squash"]

SRO \ˌes-ˌär-ˈō\ *n* : a house, apartment building, or residential hotel in which low-income or welfare tenants live in single rooms [*s*ingle-*r*oom *o*ccupancy]

SS \es-ˌes, ˈes-\ *n* : a unit of Nazis created to serve as bodyguard to Hitler and later expanded to take charge of central security and extermination of undesirables [German, abbreviation for *Schutzstaffel,* literally, "protection echelon"]

SST \ˌes-ˌes-ˈtē\ *n* : an airplane used to transport people and goods at supersonic speeds [*s*uper*s*onic *t*ransport]

[1]**-st** — see -EST

[2]**-st** *symbol* — used after the figure 1 to indicate the ordinal number *first* ⟨1st⟩ ⟨71*st*⟩

[1]**stab** \ˈstab\ *n* **1** : a wound produced by a pointed object or weapon **2** : a thrust of a pointed weapon **3** : EFFORT 2, TRY ⟨I'll take a *stab* at it⟩ [Middle English *stabbe*]

[2]**stab** *vt* **stabbed; stab·bing** **1** : to wound or pierce by the thrust of a pointed object or weapon **2** : STICK 2 ⟨*stab* a needle into thick cloth⟩ — **stab·ber** *n*

sta·bil·i·ty \stə-ˈbil-ət-ē\ *n, pl* **-ties** : the quality, state, or degree of being stable: as **a** : the property of a body that causes it to return to its original condition when disturbed (as in balance) **b** : resistance to chemical change or to physical disintegration

sta·bi·lize \ˈstā-bə-ˌlīz\ *vb* : to make or become stable, steadfast, or firm; *also* : to hold steady (as by means of a stabilizer) — **sta·bi·li·za·tion** \ˌstā-bə-lə-ˈzā-shən\ *n*

sta·bi·liz·er \ˈstā-bə-ˌlī-zər\ *n* : one (as a chemical or a device) that stabilizes something; *esp* : a fixed surface for stabilizing the motion of an airplane

[1]**sta·ble** \ˈstā-bəl\ *n* **1** : a building in which domestic animals are sheltered and fed; *esp* : such a building having stalls or compartments ⟨a horse *stable*⟩ **2 a** : the racehorses of one owner **b** : a group of athletes (as boxers) under one management [Medieval French *estable, stable,* from Latin *stabulum,* from *stare* "to stand"] — **sta·ble·man** \-mən, -ˌman\ *n*

[2]**stable** *vb* **sta·bled; sta·bling** \-bə-ling, -bling\ : to put, keep, or live in or as if in a stable

[3]**stable** *adj* **sta·bler** \-bə-lər, -blər\; **sta·blest** \-bə-ləst, -bləst\ **1 a** : firmly established : FIXED ⟨a *stable* community⟩ **b** : not changing or fluctuating ⟨a *stable* income⟩ **c** : LASTING, PERMANENT ⟨*stable* institutions⟩ **2 a** : steady in purpose : CONSTANT **b** : not subject to insecurity or emotional illness : SANE ⟨*stable* personalities⟩ **3 a** : designed so as to develop forces that restore the original condition when disturbed from a condition of equilibrium or steady motion ⟨a *stable* airplane⟩ **b** : able to resist alteration in chemical, physical, or biological properties ⟨a *stable* compound⟩ ⟨*stable* emulsions⟩ [Medieval French *estable, stable,* from Latin *stabilis,* from *stare* "to stand"] — **sta·ble·ness** \-bəl-nəs\ *n* — **sta·bly** \-bə-lē, -blē\ *adv*

sta·bler \-bə-lər, -blər\ *n* : one that keeps a stable

sta·bling *n* : accommodation for animals in a building; *also* : the building for such accommodation ⟨*stabling* for six horses⟩

stac·ca·to \stə-ˈkät-ō\ *adj* **1 a** : cut short or apart in performing : DISCONNECTED ⟨*staccato* notes⟩ **b** : marked by short clear-cut playing or singing of tones or chords ⟨a *staccato* style⟩ **2** : ABRUPT, DISJOINTED ⟨the *staccato* noises of a skipping motor⟩ [Italian, from *staccare* "to detach," perhaps derived from Medieval French *estachier*] — **staccato** *adv* — **staccato** *n*

[1]**stack** \ˈstak\ *n* **1** : a large usually conical pile (as of hay, straw, or grain) **2** : an orderly pile of objects usually one on top of the other ⟨a *stack* of dishes⟩ **3** : a vertical pipe (as for carrying off smoke or vapor) **4 a** : a rack with shelves for storing books **b** *pl* : the part of a library in which books are stored in racks **5** : three or more rifles arranged together to stand in the form of a pyramid [Old Norse *stakkr*]

[2]**stack** *vb* : to arrange in or form a stack : PILE ⟨*stacked* the dishes on the table⟩ — **stack·er** *n*

stack up *vi* : to measure : COMPARE

sta·dia \ˈstād-ē-ə\ *n* : a surveying method for determination of distances and differences of elevation that uses a telescopic instrument having two horizontal lines through which the marks on a graduated rod are observed; *also* : the instrument or the rod used in this method [Italian, probably from Latin, pl. of *stadium*]

sta·di·um \ˈstād-ē-əm\ *n, pl* **-dia** \-ē-ə\ *or* **-di·ums** **1** : any of various ancient Greek or Roman units of length ranging from about 670 to 738 feet (185 to 225 meters) **2 a** : a course for footraces in ancient Greece with tiers of seats for spectators **b** *pl usually stadiums* : a large usually unroofed building with tiers of seats for spectators at modern sports events [Latin, from Greek *stadion*]

[1]**staff** \ˈstaf\ *n, pl* **staffs** \ˈstafs, ˈstavz\ *or* **staves** \ˈstavz, ˈstāvz\ **1 a** : a pole, stick, rod, or bar used as a support or as a sign of authority ⟨a flag hanging limp on its *staff*⟩ **b** : the long handle of a weapon (as

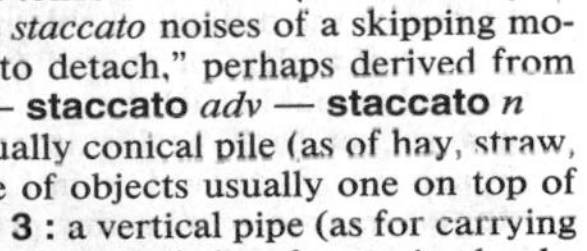

staff 3 with clef

\ə\ **abut**	\au̇\ **out**	\i\ **tip**	\ȯ\ **saw**	\u̇\ **foot**
\ər\ **further**	\ch\ **chin**	\ī\ **life**	\ȯi\ **coin**	\y\ **yet**
\a\ **mat**	\e\ **pet**	\j\ **job**	\th\ **thin**	\yü\ **few**
\ā\ **take**	\ē\ **easy**	\ng\ **sing**	\t͟h\ **this**	\yu̇\ **cure**
\ä\ **cot, cart**	\g\ **go**	\ō\ **bone**	\ü\ **food**	\zh\ **vision**

a lance or pike) **c** : CLUB 1a, CUDGEL **2** : something that props or sustains ⟨bread is the *staff* of life⟩ **3** : the five horizontal lines with their spaces on which music is written **4** *pl staffs* **a** : a group of persons serving as assistants to or employees under a chief ⟨a hospital *staff*⟩ **b** : a group of officers or aides appointed to assist a civil executive or commanding officer **c** : military officers not eligible for operational command but having administrative duties [Old English *stæf*] — **staff** *adj*

[2]staff *vt* : to supply with a staff (as of workers)

staff·er \ˈstaf-ər\ *n* : a member of a staff

staff sergeant *n* : an enlisted rank in the Army above sergeant and below sergeant first class, in the Marine Corps above sergeant and below gunnery sergeant, and in the Air Force above sergeant and below technical sergeant

staff sergeant major *n* : an enlisted rank in the Army above master sergeant

[1]stag \ˈstag\ *n, pl* **stags** **1** *or pl* **stag** : an adult male red deer; *also* : the male of various other deer **2** : a male animal castrated after sexual maturity **3 a** : a social gathering of men only **b** : a man who attends a dance or party unaccompanied by a woman [Old English *stagga*]

[2]stag *adj* **1** : intended or suitable for men only ⟨a *stag* party⟩ **2** : unaccompanied by someone of the opposite sex — **stag** *adv*

stag beetle *n* : any of numerous mostly large beetles whose males have long and often branched mandibles

[1]stage \ˈstāj\ *n* **1** : one of the horizontal levels into which a structure is divisible: as **a** : a floor of a building **b** : a shelf or layer especially as one of a series **c** : any of the levels attained by a river above an arbitrary zero point ⟨flood *stage*⟩ **2** : a raised platform (as a scaffold or landing stage): as **a** : a part of a theater including the acting area **b** : the small platform on which an object is placed for microscopic examination **3 a** : a center of attention : scene of action ⟨a key player on the world *stage*⟩ **b** : the theatrical profession or art **4 a** : a place of rest formerly provided for those traveling by stagecoach : STATION 3 **b** : the distance between stopping places in a journey **c** : STAGECOACH ⟨traveled by *stage*⟩ **5 a** : a period or step in a process, activity, or development ⟨an early *stage* of a disease⟩ **b** : one of the distinguishable periods of the growth and development of a plant or animal ⟨the larval *stage* of a beetle⟩; *also* : an individual in such a stage **6** : one of two or more sections of a rocket each having its own fuel and engine [Medieval French *estage,* derived from Latin *stare* "to stand"] — **on the stage** : in or into the acting profession

[2]stage *vt* : to produce or show publicly on or as if on the stage

stage·coach \ˈstāj-ˌkōch\ *n* : a horse-drawn passenger and mail coach running on a regular schedule

stage·craft \-ˌkraft\ *n* : the effective management of theatrical devices or techniques

stage direction *n* : a description or direction written or printed in a play

stage fright *n* : nervousness felt at appearing before an audience

stage·hand \ˈstāj-ˌhand\ *n* : a stage worker who handles scenery, properties, or lights

stage manager *n* : a person who is in charge of the stage and physical aspects of a theatrical production

stag·er \ˈstā-jər\ *n* : an experienced person ⟨an old *stager*⟩

stage·struck \ˈstāj-ˌstrək\ *adj* : fascinated by the stage; *esp* : having a strong desire to become an actor

stage whisper *n* : a loud whisper by an actor that is audible to the spectators but is supposed not to be heard by persons on the stage

[1]stag·ger \ˈstag-ər\ *vb* **stag·gered; stag·ger·ing** \ˈstag-ring, -ə-ring\ **1 a** : to move unsteadily from side to side as if about to fall : REEL **b** : to cause to reel or totter **2 a** : to begin to doubt and waver : become less confident **b** : to cause to doubt, waver, or hesitate **3** : to place or arrange in a zigzag or alternate but regular way [Old Norse *stakra,* from *staka* "to push"] — **stag·ger·er** \ˈstag-ər-ər\ *n*

[2]stagger *n* **1** *pl* : an abnormal condition of domestic animals associated with damage to the central nervous system and marked by incoordination and a reeling unsteady gait **2** : a reeling or unsteady gait or stance

stag·ger·ing *adj* : serving to stagger : ASTONISHING, OVERWHELMING — **stag·ger·ing·ly** \ˈstag-ring-lē, -ə-ring-\ *adv*

stag·ing \ˈstā-jing\ *n* **1** : SCAFFOLDING **2** : the putting of a play on the stage **3** : the assembling of troops or supplies in a particular place

stag·nant \ˈstag-nənt\ *adj* **1 a** : not flowing in a current or stream **b** : STALE ⟨*stagnant* air⟩ **2** : DULL, INACTIVE ⟨*stagnant* business⟩ — **stag·nan·cy** \-nən-sē\ *n* — **stag·nant·ly** *adv*

stag·nate \ˈstag-ˌnāt\ *vi* : to be or become stagnant [Latin *stagnare,* from *stagnum* "body of standing water"] — **stag·na·tion** \stag-ˈnā-shən\ *n*

stagy \ˈstā-jē\ *adj* **stag·i·er; -est** : of or resembling the stage; *esp* : theatrical or artificial in manner — **stag·i·ly** \-jə-lē\ *adv* — **stag·i·ness** \-jē-nəs\ *n*

[1]staid \ˈstād\ *adj* : marked by sedateness and often prim self-restraint : SOBER, GRAVE [from past participle of [3]*stay*] — **staid·ly** *adv* — **staid·ness** *n*

[2]staid *past of* STAY

[1]stain \ˈstān\ *vb* **1** : to soil or discolor especially in spots **2** : to give color to (as by dyeing) **3** : to taint with guilt, vice, or corruption [partly from Medieval French *desteindre* "to discolor," from *des-* "dis-" + *teindre* "to dye," from Latin *tingere;* partly of Scandinavian origin] — **stain·abil·i·ty** \ˌstā-nə-ˈbil-ət-ē\ *n* — **stain·able** \ˈstā-nə-bəl\ *adj* — **stain·er** *n*

[2]stain *n* **1** : a soiled or discolored spot **2** : a taint of guilt : STIGMA **3** : a preparation (as of dye or pigment) used in staining: as **a** : one capable of penetrating the pores of wood **b** : a dye or mixture of dyes used in microscopy to make very small and transparent structures visible, to color tissue elements so that they can be told apart, and to produce specific chemical reactions — **stain·less** \ˈstān-ləs\ *adj* — **stain·less·ly** *adv*

stained glass *n* : glass colored or stained (as for windows)

stainless steel *n* : steel alloyed with chromium and highly resistant to stain, rust, and corrosion

stair \ˈstaər, ˈsteər\ *n* **1** : a series of steps or flights of steps for passing from one level to another — often used in plural ⟨ran down the *stairs*⟩ **2** : one step of a stairway [Old English *stǣger*]

stair·case \-ˌkās\ *n* : a flight of stairs with the supporting framework, casing, and balusters

stair·way \-ˌwā\ *n* : one or more flights of stairs usually with landings to pass from one level to another

stair·well \-ˌwel\ *n* : a vertical shaft in which stairs are located

[1]stake \ˈstāk\ *n* **1** : a pointed piece (as of wood) driven or to be driven into the ground especially as a marker or support **2 a** : a post to which a person is bound for execution by burning **b** : execution by burning at a stake **3 a** : something that is staked for gain or loss **b** : the prize in a contest **c** : an interest or share in a commercial venture **4** : a Mormon territorial unit comprising a number of wards **5** : GRUBSTAKE [Old English *staca*] — **at stake** : at issue : in jeopardy ⟨there's more *at stake* than just the money⟩

[2]stake *vt* **1 a** : to mark the limits of by or as if by stakes ⟨*stake* out a mining claim⟩ **b** : to tether to a stake **c** : to fasten up or support (as plants) with stakes **2 a** : BET 1, HAZARD **b** : to back financially; *esp* : GRUBSTAKE

sta·lac·tite \stə-ˈlak-ˌtīt\ *n* : a deposit of calcium carbonate resembling an icicle hanging from the roof or sides of a cavern [Greek *stalaktos* "dripping," from *stalassein* "to let drip"] — **stal·ac·tit·ic** \ˌstal-ˌak-ˈtit-ik\ *adj*

sta·lag·mite \stə-ˈlag-ˌmīt\ *n* : a deposit of calcium carbonate like an inverted stalactite found on the floor of a cave [Greek *stalagma* "drop" or *stalagmos* "dripping"] — **stal·ag·mit·ic** \ˌstal-ˌag-ˈmit-ik\ *adj*

1 stalactite, *2* stalagmite

[1]stale \ˈstāl\ *adj* **1** : tasteless, unpleasant, or unwholesome from age ⟨*stale* food⟩ **2** : tedious from familiarity ⟨*stale* news⟩ **3** : WEAK, INEFFECTIVE ⟨felt *stale* and listless after a long illness⟩ [Middle English, "settled, clear (of ale), not fresh," from Medieval French *estale,* probably from Dutch *stel* "old" (of beer)] — **stale·ly** \ˈstāl-lē\ *adv* — **stale·ness** *n*

[2]stale *vb* : to make or become stale

[1]stale·mate \ˈstāl-ˌmāt\ *n* **1** : a drawing position in chess in which only the king can move and although not in check can move only into check **2** : a drawn contest : DEADLOCK [obsolete *stale* "stalemate" (derived from Medieval French *estal* "position, stall") + *mate*]

[2]**stalemate** *vt* : to bring into a stalemate

Sta·lin·ism \ˈstäl-ə-ˌniz-əm, ˈstal-\ *n* : the theory and practice of communism developed by Stalin from Marxism-Leninism and characterized especially by rigid authoritarianism, widespread use of terror, and often by Russian nationalism — **Sta·lin·ist** \-nəst\ *n or adj*

[1]**stalk** \ˈstȯk\ *n* **1** : a slender supporting or connecting structure; *esp* : PEDUNCLE **2** : a plant stem; *esp* : the main stem of an herbaceous plant [Middle English *stalke*] — **stalked** \ˈstȯkt\ *adj* — **stalk·less** \ˈstȯk-ləs\ *adj* — **stalky** \ˈstȯ-kē\ *adj*

[2]**stalk** *vb* **1** : to hunt stealthily ⟨a *stalking* cat⟩ ⟨*stalk* a deer⟩; *also* : to go through (an area) in stalking prey ⟨*stalk* the woods for deer⟩ **2** : to walk with haughty or pompous bearing **3** : to move through or follow usually in a persistent or furtive way ⟨famine *stalked* the land⟩ ⟨*stalk* a criminal⟩ **4** : to pursue obsessively and to the point of harassment [Old English *bestealcian*] — **stalk·er** *n*

[3]**stalk** *n* **1** : the act of stalking **2** : a stalking gait

stalk·ing horse \ˈstȯ-king-ˌhȯrs\ *n* **1** : a horse or a figure like a horse behind which a hunter stalks game **2** : something used to mask a purpose

[1]**stall** \ˈstȯl\ *n* **1 a** : a compartment for a domestic animal in a stable or barn **b** : a space set off (as for parking a motor vehicle) **2 a** : a seat in the chancel of a church with back and sides wholly or partly enclosed **b** *chiefly British* : a front orchestra seat in a theater — usually used in plural **3** : a booth, stand, or counter at which articles are displayed for sale **4** : a protective sheath for a finger or toe **5** : a small compartment ⟨a shower *stall*⟩; *esp* : one with a toilet or urinal [Old English *steall*]

[2]**stall** *vb* **1** : to put into or keep in a stall **2** : to bring or come to a standstill: as **a** : MIRE **b** (1) : to stop running ⟨the car *stalled*⟩ (2) : to cause (an engine) to stop usually unintentionally **c** : to experience or cause (as an airplane) to experience a stall in flying

[3]**stall** *n* : the condition of an aircraft or a wing of an aircraft in which lift is lost and the aircraft or wing tends to drop

[4]**stall** *n* : a ruse to deceive or delay [English dialect *stale* "lure, decoy"]

[5]**stall** *vb* : to hold off, divert, or delay by evasion or deception

stal·lion \ˈstal-yən\ *n* : a male horse; *esp* : one kept primarily for breeding [Medieval French *estalon*, of Germanic origin]

[1]**stal·wart** \ˈstȯl-wərt\ *adj* : marked by outstanding strength and vigor of mind, body, or spirit ⟨*stalwart* common sense⟩ [Old English *stælwierthe* "serviceable"] ***synonyms*** see STRONG — **stal·wart·ly** *adv* — **stal·wart·ness** *n*

[2]**stalwart** *n* **1** : a stalwart person **2** : an unwavering partisan (as in politics)

sta·men \ˈstā-mən\ *n, pl* **stamens** *also* **sta·mi·na** \ˈstā-mə-nə, ˈstam-ə-\ : an organ of a flower that produces pollen, consists of an anther and a filament, and is morphologically a sporophyll [Latin, "warp, thread"]

stam·i·na \ˈstam-ə-nə\ *n* : the capacity or ability to endure or perform a lot or for a long time [Latin, pl. of *stamen* "warp, thread, thread of life"]

sta·mi·nate \ˈstā-mə-nət, ˈstam-ə-, -ˌnāt\ *adj* : having stamens; *esp* : having stamens but no pistils ⟨*staminate* flowers⟩

[1]**stam·mer** \ˈstam-ər\ *vb* **stam·mered; stam·mer·ing** \ˈstam-ring, -ə-ring\ : to utter with or make involuntary stops and repetitions in speaking [Old English *stamerian*] — **stam·mer·er** \ˈstam-ər-ər\ *n*

synonyms STAMMER, STUTTER mean to speak haltingly or stumblingly. STAMMER often suggests a temporary inhibition through fear, embarrassment, or shock ⟨breathlessly *stammered* out thanks⟩. STUTTER suggests an habitual defect of speech although it may imply merely the effect of haste or excitement ⟨*stuttered* an unplanned invitation⟩.

[2]**stammer** *n* : an act or instance of stammering

[1]**stamp** \ˈstamp; *1b & 2 are also* ˈstämp *or* ˈstȯmp\ *vb* **1 a** : to pound or crush with a heavy instrument **b** : to strike or beat forcibly with the bottom of the foot **c** : to bring down forcibly or noisily ⟨*stamp* one's feet⟩ **d** : to extinguish or destroy by or as if by stamping with the foot ⟨*stamp* out cancer⟩ **2** : to walk heavily or noisily **3 a** : IMPRESS, IMPRINT ⟨*stamp* "paid" on the bill⟩ **b** : to attach a stamp to ⟨*stamp* a letter⟩ **4** : to form with a stamp or die **5** : CHARACTERIZE 1 ⟨*stamped* as a reliable player⟩ [Middle English *stampen*] — **stamp·er** *n*

[2]**stamp** \ˈstamp\ *n* **1** : a device or instrument for stamping **2** : the impression or mark made by stamping **3** : a distinctive character, indication, or mark **4** : the act of stamping **5** : a stamped or printed paper affixed in evidence that a tax has been paid; *also* : POSTAGE STAMP

[1]**stam·pede** \stam-ˈpēd\ *n* **1** : a wild headlong rush or flight of frightened animals **2** : a mass movement of people at a common impulse [American Spanish *estampida*, from Spanish, "crash," from *estampar* "to stamp," of Germanic origin]

[2]**stampede** *vb* **1** : to run away or cause (as cattle) to run away in panic **2** : to act together or cause to act together suddenly and without thought (as in panic)

stamp·ing ground \ˈstamp-, ˈstämp-, ˈstȯmp-\ *n* : STOMPING GROUND

stance \ˈstans\ *n* **1** : way of standing or being placed : POSTURE ⟨an erect *stance*⟩ **2** : intellectual or emotional attitude ⟨an antiwar *stance*⟩ [Middle French *estance* "position, posture, stay," derived from Latin *stare* "to stand"]

[1]**stanch** *also* **staunch** \ˈstȯnch, ˈstänch\ *vt* **1** : to stop the flowing of ⟨*stanch* tears⟩; *also* : to stop the flow of blood from (a wound) **2** : to stop in its course ⟨trying to *stanch* the crime wave⟩ [Medieval French *estancher*] — **stanch·er** *n*

[2]**stanch** *variant of* STAUNCH

stan·chion \ˈstan-chən\ *n* **1** : an upright bar, post, or support **2** : a device that fits loosely around an animal's neck and limits forward and backward motion (as in a stall) [Medieval French *estançon*, from *estance* "stance, stay, prop"] — **stan·chioned** \-chənd\ *adj*

stanchion 2

[1]**stand** \ˈstand\ *vb* **stood** \ˈstu̇d\; **stand·ing** **1 a** : to support oneself on the feet in an erect position **b** : to be a specified height when fully erect ⟨*stands* six feet tall⟩ **c** : to rise to one's feet **2 a** : to take up or maintain a specified position or posture ⟨*stand* aside⟩ ⟨can you *stand* on your head⟩ ⟨where do we *stand* on this question⟩ **b** : to maintain one's position ⟨*stand* firm⟩ **3** : to be in a particular state or situation ⟨*stands* accused⟩ **4** : to hold a course at sea ⟨*standing* away from the shore⟩ **5** *chiefly British* : to be a candidate : RUN **6 a** : to have or maintain a relative position in or as if in a scale ⟨*stands* first in the class⟩ **b** : to be in a position to gain or lose ⟨*stands* to make quite a profit⟩ **7 a** : to rest, remain, or set upright on a base or lower end ⟨the clock *stood* on the mantle⟩ **b** : to occupy a place or location ⟨a house *standing* on a knoll⟩ **8 a** : to remain stationary or inactive ⟨the car *stood* in the garage⟩ ⟨rainwater *standing* in pools⟩ **b** : to remain in effect ⟨the order *stands*⟩ **9** : AGREE — used chiefly in the expression *it stands to reason* **10** : to exist in a definite form ⟨you must take or leave the offer as it *stands*⟩ **11 a** : to endure or undergo successfully : BEAR, WITHSTAND ⟨*stand* pain⟩ ⟨this book will *stand* the test of time⟩ **b** : to derive benefit or enjoyment from ⟨you look like you could *stand* some sleep⟩ **12** : to submit to ⟨*stand* trial⟩ **13** : to perform the duty of ⟨*stand* guard⟩ **14** : to pay for ⟨I'll *stand* you dinner⟩ **15** : to set upright [Old English *standan*] — **stand·er** *n* — **stand for** **1** : to be a symbol for : REPRESENT **2** : to put up with : PERMIT ⟨doesn't *stand for* any nonsense⟩ — **stand on** **1** : to depend upon **2** : to insist on ⟨never *stands on* ceremony⟩ — **stand one's ground** : to maintain one's position — **stand on one's own** : to think or act independently — **stand pat** : to oppose or resist change

[2]**stand** *n* **1** : an act or instance of stopping or staying in one place: as **a** : a halt for defense or resistance ⟨a goal-line *stand*⟩ **b** : a stop made to give a performance ⟨booked for a three-night *stand*⟩ **2 a** : a place or post where one stands **b** : a position with respect to an issue ⟨took a *stand* against more taxes⟩ **3 a** : the place occupied by a witness testifying in court **b** *pl* : a tier of seats for spectators of an outdoor sport or spectacle **c** : a raised platform (as for a speaker) **4 a** : a small often open-air structure for a small retail business ⟨a vegetable *stand*⟩ **b** : a place where a passenger vehicle stops or parks ⟨a taxi *stand*⟩ **5** : a support (as a rack or table) on or in which something may be

\ə\ **abut**	\au̇\ **out**	\i\ **tip**	\ȯ\ **saw**	\u̇\ **foot**
\ər\ **further**	\ch\ **chin**	\ī\ **life**	\ȯi\ **coin**	\y\ **yet**
\a\ **mat**	\e\ **pet**	\j\ **job**	\th\ **thin**	\yü\ **few**
\ā\ **take**	\ē\ **easy**	\ng\ **sing**	\t͟h\ **this**	\yu̇\ **cure**
\ä\ **cot, cart**	\g\ **go**	\ō\ **bone**	\ü\ **food**	\zh\ **vision**

placed ⟨umbrella *stands*⟩ **6 :** a group of plants growing in a continuous area ⟨a good *stand* of wheat⟩

[1]**stan·dard** \'stan-dərd\ *n* **1 :** a conspicuous object (as a banner) formerly carried at the top of a pole and used to mark a rallying point especially in battle or to serve as an emblem **2 a :** the personal flag of the head of a state or of a member of a royal family **b :** an organization flag carried by a mounted or motorized military unit ⟨the regimental *standard*⟩ **3 a :** something set up by authority or by general consent as a model or example ⟨*standards* of good manners⟩ **b :** something set up and established by authority as a rule for the measure of quantity, weight, extent, value, or quality **c :** the basis of value in a monetary system ⟨the gold *standard*⟩ **4 :** a structure that serves as a support ⟨a lamp *standard*⟩ **5 :** an enlarged upper petal of a flower; *esp* **:** one of the three inner usually erect and incurved petals of an iris [Medieval French *estandard* "banner, standard," of Germanic origin]

synonyms STANDARD, GAUGE, CRITERION denote a means of determining what a thing should be. STANDARD applies to any definite rule, principle, or measure established by authority or custom ⟨*standards* of education⟩. GAUGE applies to a means of testing a particular dimension (as thickness, depth, or diameter) or a particular quality or aspect ⟨viewed awards as a *gauge* of quality in books⟩. CRITERION may apply to anything used as a test of quality whether or not it is formulated as a rule or principle ⟨the sole *criterion* for passing⟩.

[2]**standard** *adj* **1 a :** constituting or conforming to a standard established by law or custom ⟨*standard* weight⟩ **b :** being sound and usable but not of special or the highest quality ⟨*standard* beef⟩ **2 :** regularly and widely used, available, or supplied ⟨*standard* practice in the trade⟩ ⟨*standard* automobile parts⟩ **3 :** having recognized and permanent value ⟨a *standard* reference work⟩ **4 :** substantially uniform and well established by usage in the speech and writing of the educated and widely recognized as acceptable ⟨*standard* pronunciation in the region⟩

stan·dard–bear·er \-ˌbar-ər, -ˌber-\ *n* **1 :** one who bears a standard or banner **2 :** the leader of an organization or movement

stan·dard·bred \-ˌbred\ *n* **:** any of a breed of trotting and pacing horses developed in the U.S. and noted for speed and endurance

standard deviation *n* **:** the square root of the arithmetic mean of the squares of differences between the arithmetic mean of a frequency distribution and the values of the variable

Standard English *n* **:** the English that with respect to spelling, grammar, pronunciation, and vocabulary is substantially uniform though not devoid of regional differences, that is well established by usage in the formal and informal speech and writing of educated people, and that is widely recognized as acceptable wherever English is spoken and understood

stan·dard·ize \'stan-dər-ˌdīz\ *vt* **:** to compare with or bring into conformity with a standard — **stan·dard·i·za·tion** \ˌstan-dərd-ə-'zā-shən\ *n*

standard of living : the necessities, comforts, and luxuries that a person or group is accustomed to

standard time *n* **:** the time established by law or by general usage over a region or country

[1]**stand·by** \'stand-ˌbī, 'stan-\ *n, pl* **stand·bys 1 a :** one available or to be relied upon especially in emergencies **b :** a favorite or reliable choice or resource **2 :** one that is held in reserve ready for use as a substitute — **on standby :** ready or available for immediate action or use

[2]**standby** *adj* **1 :** held near at hand and ready for use ⟨*standby* equipment⟩ **2 :** relating to the act or condition of standing by ⟨a *standby* period⟩ **3 :** of, relating to, or traveling by a mode of transportation (as airline service) in which the passenger must wait for an available unreserved spot ⟨*standby* passengers⟩

[3]**standby** *adv* **:** on a standby basis ⟨fly *standby*⟩

stand by *vi* **1 :** to be present; *also* **:** to remain aloof **2 :** to be waiting in a state of readiness ⟨please *stand by*⟩ **3 :** to remain loyal or faithful to ⟨*stood by* us to the end⟩ ⟨*stood by* his decision⟩

stand down *vb* **1 :** to leave the witness stand **2 :** to remove (as a military unit) from active duty

stand·ee \stan-'dē\ *n* **:** one who occupies standing room

stand–in \'stan-ˌdin\ *n* **1 :** someone employed to occupy a performer's place while lights and camera are readied **2 :** SUBSTITUTE

STANDARD TIME

IN PLACES THROUGHOUT THE WORLD WHEN IT IS 12:00 NOON IN NEW YORK CITY

CITY	TIME	CITY	TIME
Amsterdam, Netherlands[1]	6:00 P.M.	Montevideo, Uruguay[2]	2:00 P.M.
Anchorage, Alaska	8:00 A.M.	Montreal, Quebec	12:00 NOON
Athens, Greece	7:00 P.M.	Moscow, Russia[1]	8:00 P.M.
Bangkok, Thailand	12:00 MIDNIGHT	Nairobi, Kenya	8:00 P.M.
Beijing, China	1:00 A.M. (next day)	Ottawa, Ontario	12:00 NOON
Berlin, Germany	6:00 P.M.	Paris, France[1]	6:00 P.M.
Bombay, India	10:30 P.M.	Perth, Australia	1:00 A.M. (next day)
Brussels, Belgium[1]	6:00 P.M.	Reykjavik, Iceland	5:00 P.M.
Buenos Aires, Argentina[2]	2:00 P.M.	Rio de Janeiro, Brazil	2:00 P.M.
Cairo, Egypt	7:00 P.M.	Riyadh, Saudi Arabia	8:00 P.M.
Calcutta, India	10:30 P.M.	Rome, Italy	6:00 P.M.
Cape Town, South Africa	7:00 P.M.	Saint John's, Newfoundland	1:30 P.M.
Casablanca, Morocco	5:00 P.M.	Salt Lake City, Utah	10:00 A.M.
Chicago, Illinois	11:00 A.M.	San Francisco, California	9:00 A.M.
Delhi, India	10:30 P.M.	San Juan, Puerto Rico	1:00 P.M.
Denver, Colorado	10:00 A.M.	Santiago, Chile	1:00 P.M.
Halifax, Nova Scotia	1:00 P.M.	Shanghai, China	1:00 A.M. (next day)
Hong Kong	1:00 A.M. (next day)	Singapore	1:00 A.M. (next day)
Honolulu, Hawaii	7:00 A.M.	Stockholm, Sweden	6:00 P.M.
Istanbul, Turkey	7:00 P.M.	Sydney, Australia	3:00 A.M. (next day)
Jakarta, Indonesia	12:00 MIDNIGHT	Tehran, Iran	8:30 P.M.
Juneau, Alaska	8:00 A.M.	Tokyo, Japan	2:00 A.M. (next day)
Karachi, Pakistan	10:00 P.M.	Toronto, Ontario	12:00 NOON
Lima, Peru	12:00 NOON	Vancouver, British Columbia	9:00 A.M.
London, England	5:00 P.M.	Vladivostok, Russia[1]	3:00 A.M. (next day)
Los Angeles, California	9:00 A.M.	Warsaw, Poland	6:00 P.M.
Madrid, Spain[1]	6:00 P.M.	Washington, D.C.	12:00 NOON
Manilla, Philippines	1:00 A.M. (next day)	Wellington, New Zealand	5:00 A.M. (next day)
Mexico City, Mexico	11:00 A.M.	Winnipeg, Manitoba	11:00 A.M.

[1]Time in France, Spain, Netherlands, Belgium, and Russia is one hour in advance of the standard meridians.
[2]Time in Argentina and Uruguay is one hour in advance of the standard meridian.

stand in \stan-ˈdin, ˈstan-\ *vi* : to act as a stand-in — **stand in with** : to be in a specially favored position with

[1]**stand·ing** \ˈstan-diŋ\ *adj* **1 a** : not yet cut or harvested ‹*standing* timber› **b** : upright on the feet or base : ERECT ‹a *standing* audience› **2 a** : not flowing : STAGNANT ‹*standing* water› **b** : remaining the same for an indeterminate period ‹a *standing* offer› **c** : continuing in existence or use indefinitely : PERMANENT ‹a *standing* army› ‹*standing* committees› **3** : done from a standing position ‹*standing* jump›

[2]**standing** *n* **1** : the action or position of one that stands **2** : DURATION ‹a quarrel of long *standing*›; *esp* : length of service or experience especially as determining status ‹postgraduate *standing*› **3** : position or comparative rank (as in society, a profession, or a competitive activity) ‹had the highest *standing* on the test›; *also* : good reputation ‹people of *standing* in the community›

standing room *n* : space for standing; *esp* : accommodation available for spectators or passengers after all seats are filled

standing wave *n* : a vibration of a body or physical system in which the amplitude varies from place to place, is constantly zero at fixed points, and has maxima at other points

stand·off \ˈstan-ˌdȯf\ *n* **1** : the act of standing off **2 a** : a counterbalancing effect **b** : TIE 4b, DRAW

stand off \stan-ˈdȯf, ˈstan-\ *vb* **1 a** : to keep or hold at a distance : REPEL **b** : PUT OFF, STALL **2** : to stay at a distance from something

stand·off·ish \stan-ˈdȯ-fish\ *adj* : somewhat cold and reserved : not friendly

stand·out \ˈstan-ˌdau̇t\ *n* : one that is prominent or conspicuous especially because of excellence

stand out \stan-ˈdau̇t, ˈstan-\ *vi* **1 a** : to appear as if in relief : PROJECT **b** : to be prominent or conspicuous **2** : to be stubborn in resolution or resistance

stand·pat \ˈstand-ˌpat, ˈstan-\ *adj* : stubbornly conservative — **stand·pat·ter** \-ˌpat-ər\ *n*

stand·pipe \ˈstand-ˌpīp, ˈstan-\ *n* : a high vertical pipe or reservoir used to deliver water at uniform pressure

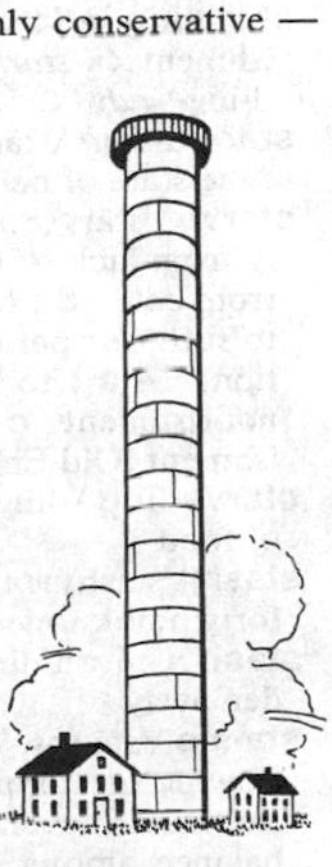

standpipe

stand·point \-ˌpȯint\ *n* : a position from which objects or principles are viewed and according to which they are compared and judged

stand·still \-ˌstil\ *n* : a complete stop

stand–up \-ˌəp\ *adj* **1** : UPRIGHT **2** : performed in or requiring a standing position; *esp* : of, relating to, performing, or being a monologue of jokes or humor delivered usually while standing alone on a stage or in front of a camera ‹*stand-up* comedy› ‹a *stand-up* comedian› **3** : marked by a high degree of integrity or loyalty ‹a real *stand-up* guy› — **stand–up** *n*

stand up *vb* **1** : to remain sound and intact **2** : to fail to keep an appointment with — **stand up for** : DEFEND ‹*stand up for* one's beliefs› — **stand up to** **1** : to meet fairly and fully **2** : to face boldly

stank *past of* STINK

stan·nic \ˈstan-ik\ *adj* : of, relating to, or containing tin especially with a valence of four [derived from Late Latin *stannum* "tin"]

stan·nous \ˈstan-əs\ *adj* : of, relating to, or containing tin especially when bivalent

stan·za \ˈstan-zə\ *n* : a division of a poem consisting of a series of lines arranged together in a usually recurring pattern of meter and rhyme [Italian, "stay, abode, room, stanza," derived from Latin *stare* "to stand"] — **stan·za·ic** \stan-ˈzā-ik\ *adj*

sta·pes \ˈstā-ˌpēz\ *n, pl* **stapes** *or* **sta·pe·des** \ˈstā-pə-ˌdēz\ : the innermost ossicle of the middle ear of a mammal — compare INCUS, MALLEUS [Medieval Latin, "stirrup"] — **sta·pe·di·al** \stā-ˈpēd-ē-əl, stə-\ *adj*

staph \ˈstaf\ *n* : STAPHYLOCOCCUS; *also* : an infection with staphylococci

staph·y·lo·coc·cus \ˌstaf-ə-lō-ˈkäk-əs\ *n, pl* **-coc·ci** \-ˈkäk-ˌsī, -ˌī, -ˌsē, -ˌē\ : any of a genus of nonmotile spherical bacteria that occur especially in irregular clusters and include causative agents of various diseases (as food poisoning and skin infections) [derived from Greek *staphylē* "bunch of grapes" + *kokkos* "grain, seed"] — **staph·y·lo·coc·cal** \-ˈkäk-əl\ *also* **staph·y·lo·coc·cic** \-ˈkäk-sik, -ik\ *adj*

[1]**sta·ple** \ˈstā-pəl\ *n* : a usually U-shaped fastener: as **a** : a piece of metal usually with sharp points to be driven into a surface to hold something (as fence wire) in place **b** : a piece of thin wire to be driven through layers of thin material (as paper) and bent over at the ends to fasten them together **c** : a usually metal surgical fastener used to hold layers of tissue together (as in the closing of a wound) [Old English *stapol* "post"]

[2]**staple** *vt* **sta·pled; sta·pling** \-pə-liŋ, -pliŋ\ : to fasten with staples

[3]**staple** *n* **1** : a town established formerly as a center for the sale or exportation of commodities in bulk **2** : a place of supply : SOURCE **3** : a chief commodity or product of a place **4 a** : something in widespread and constant use or demand **b** : the sustaining or principal element : SUBSTANCE **5** : RAW MATERIAL **6** : textile fiber (as wool or rayon) of relatively short length that when spun and twisted forms a yarn rather than a filament [Medieval French *estaple*, from Dutch *stapel* "emporium"]

[4]**staple** *adj* **1** : used, needed, or enjoyed constantly usually by many individuals **2** : produced regularly or in large quantities ‹*staple* crops such as wheat and rice› **3** : PRINCIPAL, CHIEF ‹bamboo is the *staple* diet of the panda›

sta·pler \ˈstā-plər\ *n* : a device that staples

[1]**star** \ˈstär\ *n* **1** : a natural luminous body visible in the sky especially at night **2** : a self-luminous gaseous spheroidal celestial body (as the sun) of great mass which produces energy by means of nuclear fusion **3 a** : a planet or a configuration of the planets that is held in astrology to influence one's destiny or fortune — usually used in plural **b** : FORTUNE 2, FAME **c** *obsolete* : DESTINY 2 **4 a** : a conventional figure with five or more points that represents or resembles a star; *esp* : ASTERISK **b** : an often star-shaped ornament or medal worn as a badge of honor, authority, or rank or as the insignia of an order **5 a** : the principal member of a theatrical or operatic company **b** : an outstandingly talented performer **c** : one who stands out among one's peers ‹one of the brightest *stars* in the legal profession› [Old English *steorra*] — **star·less** \-ləs\ *adj* — **star·like** \-ˌlīk\ *adj*

[2]**star** *vb* **starred; star·ring** **1** : to sprinkle or adorn with stars **2 a** : to mark with a star as being superior **b** : to mark with an asterisk **3** : to present in the role of a star **4** : to play the most prominent or important role ‹will *star* in a new play› **5** : to perform outstandingly ‹*starred* at shortstop›

[3]**star** *adj* **1** : of, relating to, or being a star **2** : being of outstanding excellence ‹a *star* athlete›

[1]**star·board** \ˈstär-bərd\ *n* : the right side of a ship or aircraft looking forward — compare [3]PORT [Old English *stēorbord*, from *stēor-* "steering oar" + *bord* "ship's side"]

[2]**starboard** *adj* : of, relating to, or situated to starboard

[1]**starch** \ˈstärch\ *vt* : to stiffen with or as if with starch [Middle English *sterchen*]

[2]**starch** *n* **1** : a white odorless tasteless granular or powdery complex carbohydrate $(C_6H_{10}O_5)_x$ that is the chief storage form of carbohydrate in plants, is an important foodstuff, and is used also in adhesives and sizes, in laundering, and in pharmacy and medicine **2** : a stiff formal manner : FORMALITY **3** : resolute vigor : ENERGY

Star Chamber *n* : a court existing in England from the 15th century until 1641 with wide civil and criminal jurisdiction and marked by secret often arbitrary and oppressive procedures

starchy \ˈstär-chē\ *adj* **starch·i·er; -est** **1** : containing, consisting of, or resembling starch ‹*starchy* foods› **2** : consisting of or marked by formality or stiffness — **starch·i·ness** *n*

star–crossed \ˈstär-ˌkrȯst\ *adj* : not favored by the stars : ILL-FATED

star·dom \ˈstärd-əm\ *n* : the status or position of a star ‹rose to *stardom* in Hollywood›

star·dust \ˈstär-ˌdəst\ *n* : a feeling or impression of romance, magic, or ethereality

[1]**stare** \ˈstaər, ˈsteər\ *vb* **1** : to look fixedly often with wide-open eyes ‹*stare* at a stranger› **2** : to show up conspicuously **3** : to

\ə\ **abut**	\au̇\ **out**	\i\ **tip**	\ȯ\ **saw**	\u̇\ **foot**
\ər\ **further**	\ch\ **chin**	\ī\ **life**	\ȯi\ **coin**	\y\ **yet**
\a\ **mat**	\e\ **pet**	\j\ **job**	\th\ **thin**	\yü\ **few**
\ā\ **take**	\ē\ **easy**	\ŋ\ **sing**	\t͟h\ **this**	\yu̇\ **cure**
\ä\ **cot, cart**	\g\ **go**	\ō\ **bone**	\ü\ **food**	\zh\ **vision**

have an effect upon by looking fixedly [Old English *starian*] — **star·er** *n*

[2]**stare** *n* : the act or an instance of staring

stare down *vt* : to cause to waver or submit by or as if by staring ⟨*stare down* a dog⟩

star·fish \'stär-ˌfish\ *n* : any of a class (Asteroidea) of echinoderms that have a body of usually five arms radially arranged about a central disk and feed largely on mollusks (as oysters)

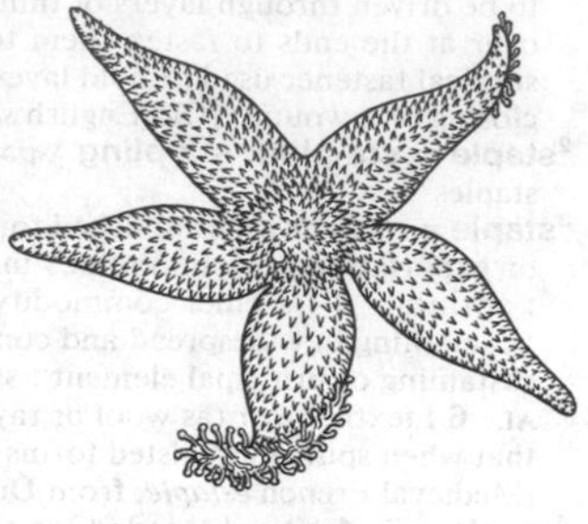

starfish

star·flow·er \-ˌflaů-ər, -ˌflaůr\ *n* : any of several plants having star-shaped 5-petaled flowers

star fruit *n* : a green to yellow tropical Asian fruit that has the shape of a 5-pointed star when cut across the middle — called also *carambola*

star·gaze \-ˌgāz\ *vi* **1** : to gaze at stars **2** : to stare absentmindedly : DAYDREAM [back-formation from *stargazer*]

star·gaz·er \-ˌgā-zər\ *n* : one that gazes at the stars: as **a** : ASTROLOGER **b** : ASTRONOMER

[1]**stark** \'stärk\ *adj* **1** : STRONG 1, ROBUST **2 a** : rigid in or as if in death **b** : INFLEXIBLE 3, STRICT ⟨*stark* discipline⟩ **3** : SHEER, UTTER ⟨*stark* nonsense⟩ **4 a** : BARREN, DESOLATE ⟨a *stark* landscape⟩ **b** (1) : having few or no ornaments : BARE (2) : HARSH, UNADORNED ⟨*stark* realism⟩ **5** : sharply delineated [Old English *stearc* "stiff, strong"] — **stark·ly** *adv* — **stark·ness** *n*

[2]**stark** *adv* **1** : in a stark manner **2** : WHOLLY 1 ⟨*stark* mad⟩

star·let \'stär-lət\ *n* : a young movie actress being coached and publicized for starring roles

star·light \-ˌlīt\ *n* : the light given by the stars

star·ling \'stär-ling\ *n* : any of a family of usually dark birds that tend to flock together; *esp* : a dark brown or in summer glossy greenish black European bird naturalized nearly worldwide and often considered a pest [Old English *stærlinc,* from *stær* "starling" + *-ling, -linc* "-ling"]

star·lit \'stär-ˌlit\ *adj* : lighted by the stars

star–nosed mole \'stär-ˌnōzd-\ *n* : a black long-tailed semiaquatic mole of the northeastern U.S. and adjacent Canada that has a series of pink fleshy projections surrounding the nostrils which are used as feelers in searching for food

star–of–Beth·le·hem \-'beth-li-ˌhem, -lē-həm, -lē-əm\ *n* : an Old World herb related to the lilies that has white star-shaped flowers and is naturalized in the eastern U.S.

star of Bethlehem : a star held to have guided the three wise men to the infant Jesus in Bethlehem

Star of Da·vid \-'dā-vəd\ : a hexagram used as a symbol of Judaism

star·ry \'stär-ē\ *adj* **star·ri·er; -est** **1** : adorned with stars ⟨*starry* heavens⟩ **2** : of, relating to, or consisting of the stars : STELLAR ⟨*starry* light⟩ **3** : shining like stars : SPARKLING ⟨*starry* eyes⟩

star·ry–eyed \ˌstär-ē-'īd\ *adj* : regarding an object or a prospect in an overly favorable light ⟨grew *starry-eyed* when thinking about restoration of the old house⟩

Stars and Bars *n sing or pl* : the first flag of the Confederate States of America having three bars of red, white, and red respectively and a blue union with white stars in a circle representing the seceded states

Stars and Stripes *n sing or pl* : the flag of the U.S. having 13 alternately red and white horizontal stripes and a blue union with one white star for each state — called also *Star-Spangled Banner*

star·ship \'stär-ˌship\ *n* : a vehicle designed for interstellar travel

star–span·gled \'stär-ˌspang-gəld\ *adj* : studded with stars

[1]**start** \'stärt\ *vb* **1** : to move suddenly and sharply : react with a quick involuntary movement **2 a** : to issue with sudden force ⟨blood *starting* from the wound⟩ **b** : to come into being, activity, or operation : BEGIN **3** : BULGE ⟨eyes *starting* from their sockets⟩ **4** : to become or cause to become loosened or forced out of place **5 a** : to begin a course or journey **b** : to range from a specified initial point ⟨the rates *start* at ten dollars⟩ **6** : to be or cause to be a participant in a game or contest; *esp* : to be or cause to be in the lineup at the beginning of a game **7** : to cause to leave a place of concealment : FLUSH ⟨*start* a rabbit⟩ **8** *archaic* : STARTLE 2, ALARM **9** : to bring up for consideration or discussion **10** : to bring into being ⟨*start* a rumor⟩ **11** : to begin the use or employment of ⟨*start* a new box of cereal⟩ **12 a** : to cause to move, act, or operate ⟨*start* the motor⟩ **b** : to care for during early stages ⟨*start* seedlings indoors⟩ **13** : to perform the first stages or action of ⟨*started* studying music⟩ [Middle English *sterten*]

[2]**start** *n* **1 a** : a quick involuntary bodily reaction **b** : a brief and sudden action or movement **c** : a sudden impulse or outburst **2** : a beginning of movement, activity, or development **3** : a lead or advantage at the beginning of a race or competition : HEAD START **4** : a place of beginning **5** : the act or an instance of being a competitor in a race or a member of a lineup at the beginning of a game

start·er \'stärt-ər\ *n* **1** : one that initiates or sets going: as **a** : an official who gives the signal to begin a race **b** : one who dispatches vehicles **2 a** : one that enters a competition or that regularly appears in a lineup at the beginning of games **b** : one that begins to engage in an activity or process **3** : one that causes something to begin operating: as **a** : SELF-STARTER **b** : material containing microorganisms (as yeast) used to induce a desired fermentation **4** : something that is the beginning of a process, activity, or series

[1]**star·tle** \'stärt-l\ *vb* **star·tled; star·tling** \'stärt-ling, -l-ing\ **1** : to move or jump suddenly (as in surprise or alarm) ⟨the kitten *startles* easily⟩ **2** : to frighten or surprise suddenly and usually not seriously ⟨the loud noise *startled* the baby⟩ [Middle English *stertlen,* from *sterten* "to start"]

[2]**startle** *n* : a sudden mild shock (as of surprise or alarm)

star·tling *adj* : causing a momentary fright, surprise, or astonishment ⟨a *startling* discovery⟩ — **star·tling·ly** \'stärt-ling-lē, -l-ing-\ *adv*

star·va·tion \stär-'vā-shən\ *n* : the act or an instance of starving : the state of being starved

starve \'stärv\ *vb* **starved; starv·ing** **1** : to die or suffer greatly from lack of food **2** *archaic* **a** : to die of or suffer greatly from cold **b** : to kill with cold **3** : to suffer or perish or cause to suffer or perish from deprivation ⟨a child *starving* for affection⟩ **4 a** : to kill or subdue with hunger **b** : to deprive of nourishment **c** : to cause to submit as if by depriving of nourishment [Old English *steorfan* "to die"]

starve·ling \-ling\ *n* : one thin and weakened by or as if by lack of food

[1]**stash** \'stash\ *vt* : to store in a usually secret place for future use [origin unknown]

[2]**stash** *n* **1** : hiding place : CACHE **2** : something stored or hidden away

sta·sis \'stā-səs, 'stas-əs\ *n, pl* **sta·ses** \'stā-ˌsēz, 'stas-ˌēz\ **1** : a slowing or stoppage of a normal bodily flow (as of blood) or rhythmic movement (as of the intestine) **2** : a state of static balance among opposing tendencies or forces : STAGNATION [Greek, "act or condition of standing, stopping," from *histasthai* "to stand"]

stat·able *or* **state·able** \'stāt-ə-bəl\ *adj* : capable of being stated

[1]**state** \'stāt\ *n* **1 a** : mode or condition of being ⟨a *state* of readiness⟩ **b** (1) : condition of mind or temperament ⟨in a highly nervous *state*⟩ (2) : a condition of abnormal tension or excitement **2 a** : a condition or stage of the physical makeup of something ⟨water in the gaseous *state*⟩ **b** : a stage in the growth or development of a plant or animal ⟨the larval *state*⟩ **3 a** : social position; *esp* : high rank **b** (1) : elaborate or luxurious style of living (2) : formal dignity ⟨travel in *state*⟩ **4 a** : ESTATE 3 **b** *obsolete* : a person of high rank : NOBLE **5 a** : a politically organized body of people usually occupying a definite territory; *esp* : one that is sovereign **b** : the political organization of such a body of people **c** : a government or politically organized society having a particular character ⟨a police *state*⟩ ⟨the welfare *state*⟩ **6** : the operations or concerns of the government of a country **7** : one of the units which make up a nation having a federal government ⟨the United *States* of America⟩ **8** : the territory of a state [Latin *status,* from *stare* "to stand"] — **state·less** \-ləs\ *adj* — **state·less·ness** *n*

[2]**state** *adj* **1** : suitable or used for ceremonial or formal occasions ⟨*state* robes⟩ **2** : of or relating to a national state or to one of the units which make up a federal government ⟨a *state*

church⟩ ⟨a *state* legislature⟩ **3** : GOVERNMENTAL ⟨*state* secrets⟩

[3]**state** *vt* **1** : to set by regulation or authority **2** : to express the particulars of especially in words; *also* : to express in words ⟨*state* an opinion⟩

state bank *n* : a bank chartered by and operating under the laws of a state especially of the U.S.

state bird *n* : a bird selected (as by the legislature) as an emblem of a state of the U.S.

state capitalism *n* : an economic system in which capital is largely under government ownership and control while other economic relations are little changed from capitalism

state college *n* : a college that is financially supported by a state government and often specializes in a branch of technical or professional education

state·craft \'stāt-ˌkraft\ *n* : the art of conducting government affairs

stat·ed \'stāt-əd\ *adj* **1** : FIXED, REGULAR ⟨at *stated* times⟩ **2** : set down definitely — **stat·ed·ly** *adv*

stated clerk *n* : an executive officer of a Presbyterian governing body (as a synod) ranking below the moderator

state flower *n* : a flowering plant selected (as by the legislature) as an emblem of a state of the U.S.

state·hood \'stāt-ˌhu̇d\ *n* : the condition of being a state; *esp* : the condition or status of one of the states of the U.S.

state·house \-ˌhau̇s\ *n* : the building in which a state legislature sits

state·ly \'stāt-lē\ *adj* **state·li·er; -est** **1 a** : HAUGHTY, UNAPPROACHABLE **b** : marked by lofty or imposing dignity **2** : impressive in size or proportions — **state·li·ness** *n* — **stately** *adv*

state·ment \'stāt-mənt\ *n* **1** : the act or process of stating or presenting orally or on paper **2** : something stated: as **a** : a report of facts or opinions **b** : a single declaration or remark : ASSERTION **3** : PROPOSITION 2 **4** : a brief summarized record of activity in a financial account over a particular period of time ⟨a monthly bank *statement*⟩ **5** : an instruction in a computer program

state·room \'stāt-ˌrüm, -ˌru̇m\ *n* : a private room on a boat or ship or on a railroad car

state's evidence *n, often cap S* : one who gives evidence for the prosecution in U.S. state or federal criminal proceedings; *also* : evidence for the prosecution in a criminal proceeding — used chiefly in the phrase *turn state's evidence*

States General *n pl* : the assembly of the three orders of clergy, nobility, and third estate in France before the Revolution

[1]**state·side** \'stāt-ˌsīd\ *adj* : being in, going to, coming from, or characteristic of the 48 coterminous states of the U.S. ⟨transferred from Europe to *stateside* duty⟩ [*(United) States* + *side*]

[2]**stateside** *adv* : in or to the continental states of the U.S. ⟨traveling *stateside*⟩

states·man \'stāt-smən\ *n* : a person engaged in fixing the policies and conducting the affairs of a government; *esp* : one having unusual wisdom in such matters — **states·man·like** \-ˌlīk\ *adj* — **states·man·ly** \-lē\ *adj* — **states·man·ship** \-ˌship\ *n*

state socialism *n* : an economic system with limited socialist characteristics introduced by usually gradual political action

states' rights *n pl* : all rights not vested by the Constitution of the U.S. in the federal government nor forbidden by it to the separate states

state·wide \'stāt-'wīd\ *adj* : including all parts of a state

[1]**stat·ic** \'stat-ik\ *adj* **1** : exerting force by reason of weight alone without motion ⟨*static* load⟩ **2** : of or relating to bodies at rest or forces in equilibrium **3** : showing little change **4 a** : marked by a lack of movement, animation, or progress **b** : producing an effect of rest or interruption **5** : standing or fixed in one place : STATIONARY **6** : of, relating to, producing, or being stationary charges of electricity (as those produced by friction or induction) **7** : of, relating to, or caused by radio static [Greek *statikos* "causing to stand," from *histanai* "to cause to stand, weigh"] — **stat·i·cal·ly** \'stat-i-kə-lē, -klē\ *adv*

[2]**static** *n* : noise produced in a radio or television receiver by atmospheric or electrical disturbances; *also* : the electrical disturbances producing this noise [*static electricity*]

static electricity *n* : electricity that consists of isolated stationary charges

static line *n* : a cord attached to a parachute pack and to an airplane to open the parachute after a jumper clears the plane

stat·ics \'stat-iks\ *n* : a branch of mechanics dealing with the relations of forces that produce equilibrium among material bodies

[1]**sta·tion** \'stā-shən\ *n* **1** : the place or position in which something or someone stands or is assigned to stand or remain **2** : the act or manner of standing : POSTURE **3** : a stopping place: as **a** : a regular stopping place in a transportation route **b** : a building at such a stopping place : DEPOT **4 a** : a post or sphere of duty or occupation **b** : a stock farm of Australia or New Zealand **5** : social standing : RANK **6** : a place for specialized observation and study of scientific phenomena ⟨a weather *station*⟩ **7 a** : a place established to provide a public service ⟨police *station*⟩ ⟨power *station*⟩ ⟨gas *station*⟩ **b** : a branch post office **8 a** : a complete assemblage of radio or television equipment for transmitting or receiving **b** : the place in which such a station is located [Medieval French *estation, statiun*, from Latin *statio*, from *stare* "to stand"]

[2]**station** *vt* **sta·tioned; sta·tion·ing** \'stā-shə-ning, -shning\ : to assign or set in a station or position : POST

sta·tion·ary \'stā-shə-ˌner-ē\ *adj* **1** : fixed in a station, course, or mode : IMMOBILE **2** : unchanging in condition : STABLE

station break *n* : a pause in a radio or television broadcast for announcement of the identity of the network or station

sta·tio·ner \'stā-shə-nər, -shnər\ *n* **1** *archaic* **a** : BOOKSELLER **b** : PUBLISHER **2** : one that sells stationery [Medieval Latin *stationarius*, from *statio* "market stall," from Latin, "station"]

sta·tio·nery \'stā-shə-ˌner-ē\ *n* **1** : materials (as paper, pens, and ink) for writing or typing **2** : letter paper usually with matching envelopes [*stationer*]

station house *n* : a police station

sta·tion·mas·ter \'stā-shən-ˌmas-tər\ *n* : an official in charge of the operation of a railroad station

stations of the cross *often cap S&C* **1** : a series of usually 14 images or pictures especially in a church that represent the stages of Christ's passion **2** : a devotion involving commemorative meditation before the stations of the cross

station wagon *n* : an automobile that has a passenger compartment which extends to the back of the vehicle, that has no trunk, that has one or more rear seats readily folded to make space for light cargo, and that has a tailgate or liftgate

stat·ism \'stāt-ˌiz-əm\ *n* : a concentration of economic controls and planning in the hands of a highly centralized government

sta·tis·tic \stə-'tis-tik\ *n* : a single term or datum in a statistical collection [back-formation from *statistics*]

stat·is·ti·cian \ˌstat-ə-'stish-ən\ *n* : a person who specializes in statistics

sta·tis·tics \stə-'tis-tiks\ *n sing or pl* : a branch of mathematics dealing with the collection, analysis, interpretation, and presentation of masses of numerical data; *also* : a collection of such numerical data [German *Statistik* "study of political data," derived from Latin *status* "state"] — **sta·tis·ti·cal** \-'tis-ti-kəl\ *adj* — **sta·tis·ti·cal·ly** \-ti-kə-lē, -klē\ *adv*

stato- *combining form* **1** : resting **2** : equilibrium ⟨*stato*cyst⟩ [Greek *statos* "stationary," from *histasthai* "to stand"]

stat·o·cyst \'stat-ə-ˌsist\ *n* : an organ of equilibrium occurring especially in invertebrate animals and consisting usually of a fluid-filled vesicle lined with specialized hairs that detect the position of suspended statoliths

stat·o·lith \'stat-l-ˌith\ *n* : a calcium-containing body suspended in the fluid of a statocyst

sta·tor \'stāt-ər\ *n* : a stationary part in a machine in or about which a rotor revolves [Latin, "one that stands," from *stare* "to stand"]

stat·u·ary \'stach-ə-ˌwer-ē\ *n, pl* **-ar·ies** **1 a** : the art of making statues **b** : a collection of statues **2** : SCULPTOR — **statuary** *adj*

stat·ue \'stach-ü\ *n* : a likeness (as of a person or animal) sculptured, modeled, or cast in a solid substance [Medieval French *estatue, statue*, from Latin *statua*, from *statuere* "to set up," from *status* "position, state"]

stat·u·esque \ˌstach-ə-'wesk\ *adj* : resembling a statue especially in well-proportioned or massive dignity ⟨a *statuesque* actress⟩ — **stat·u·esque·ly** *adv* — **stat·u·esque·ness** *n*

stat·u·ette \ˌstach-ə-'wet\ *n* : a small statue

\ə\ abut	\au̇\ out	\i\ tip	\ȯ\ saw	\u̇\ foot
\ər\ further	\ch\ chin	\ī\ life	\ȯi\ coin	\y\ yet
\a\ mat	\e\ pet	\j\ job	\th\ thin	\yü\ few
\ā\ take	\ē\ easy	\ng\ sing	\t͟h\ this	\yu̇\ cure
\ä\ cot, cart	\g\ go	\ō\ bone	\ü\ food	\zh\ vision

stat·ure \ˈstach-ər\ *n* **1 :** natural height (as of a person) in an upright position **2 :** quality or status gained by growth, development, or achievement ⟨reached adult *stature*⟩ [Medieval French *estature, stature,* from Latin *statura,* from *stare* "to stand"]

sta·tus \ˈstāt-əs, ˈstat-\ *n* **1 :** position or rank in relation to others **:** STANDING **2 :** CONDITION, SITUATION ⟨the economic *status* of a country⟩ [Latin]

sta·tus quo \ˌstāt-əs-ˈkwō, ˌstat-\ *n* **:** the existing state of affairs ⟨maintaining the *status quo* rather than changing⟩ [Latin, "state in which"]

stat·ute \ˈstach-üt, -ət\ *n* **:** a law enacted by the legislative branch of a government [Medieval French *estatut,* from Late Latin *statutum* "law, regulation," from Latin *statuere* "to set up," from *status* "position, state"] ***synonyms*** see LAW

statute mile *n* **:** MILE 1

statute of limitations : a statute assigning a certain time after which rights cannot be enforced by legal action

stat·u·to·ry \ˈstach-ə-ˌtōr-ē, -ˌtȯr-\ *adj* **1 :** of, relating to, or of the nature of a statute **2 :** enacted, created, or regulated by statute

[1]**staunch** *variant of* STANCH

[2]**staunch** *or* **stanch** \ˈstȯnch, ˈstänch\ *adj* **1 a :** WATERTIGHT, SOUND ⟨a *staunch* ship⟩ **b :** strongly built **:** SUBSTANTIAL ⟨*staunch* foundations⟩ **2 :** steadfast in loyalty or principle ⟨a *staunch* friend⟩ [Medieval French *estanche,* from *estancher* "to stanch"] — **staunch·ly** *adv* — **staunch·ness** *n*

[1]**stave** \ˈstāv\ *n* **1 :** a wooden stick **2 :** one of the narrow strips of wood or narrow iron plates placed edge to edge to form the sides, covering, or lining of a vessel (as a barrel) or structure **3 :** STANZA **4 :** STAFF 3 [back-formation from *staves*]

S stave 2

[2]**stave** *vb* **staved** *or* **stove** \ˈstōv\; **stav·ing 1 :** to break in the stave of (a cask) **2 :** to smash a hole in ⟨*stave* in a boat⟩; *also* **:** to crush or break inward ⟨*staved* in several ribs⟩ **3 :** to drive or thrust away **4 :** to become staved in — used of a boat or ship

stave off *vt* **:** to ward or fend off ⟨*stave off* trouble⟩

staves *plural of* STAFF

[1]**stay** \ˈstā\ *n* **:** a strong rope or wire used to steady or brace something (as a mast) [Old English *stæg*]

[2]**stay** *vb* **1 :** to fasten (as a smokestack) with stays **2 :** to go about **:** TACK

[3]**stay** *vb* **stayed** \ˈstād\ *or* **staid** \ˈstād\; **stay·ing 1 :** to stop going forward **:** PAUSE **2 :** to continue in a place or condition **:** REMAIN **3 :** to stand firm **4 :** to take up residence **:** LODGE ⟨*staying* with friends⟩ **5 :** WAIT 1 **6 :** to last out (as a race) **7 :** CHECK, HALT ⟨*stay* an execution⟩ **8 :** ALLAY ⟨*stayed* the unrest⟩ [Medieval French *ester* "to stand, stay," from Latin *stare*]

synonyms STAY, REMAIN, ABIDE, LINGER mean to continue in a place. STAY often implies the status of a guest or visitor ⟨*stayed* at a posh resort⟩. REMAIN suggests a continuing after others have gone ⟨only two competitors *remain*⟩. ABIDE may imply either continuing indefinitely in a residence or waiting patiently for an outcome ⟨*abiding* his beloved's return⟩. LINGER implies failing to depart when it is time to do so ⟨*lingered* at the beach past sunset⟩.

[4]**stay** *n* **1 :** the action of halting **:** the state of being stopped **2 :** a residence or visit in a place

[5]**stay** *n* **1 a :** something that serves as a prop **:** SUPPORT **b :** a thin firm strip (as of steel or plastic) used for stiffening a garment (as a corset) or part (as a shirt collar) **2 :** a corset stiffened with stays — usually used in plural [Middle French *estaie,* of Germanic origin]

[6]**stay** *vt* **1 :** to provide physical or moral support for **:** SUSTAIN **2 :** to fix on something as a foundation **:** REST

stay–at–home \ˈstā-ət-ˌhōm\ *n* **:** one that seldom travels or wanders from home **:** HOMEBODY

staying power *n* **:** capacity for endurance

stay·sail \ˈstā-ˌsāl, -səl\ *n* **:** a fore-and-aft sail hoisted on a stay

STD \ˌes-ˌtē-ˈdē\ *n* **:** any of various diseases or infections (as gonorrhea or chlamydia) that are usually transmitted by direct sexual contact and that include some (as hepatitis and AIDS) that may be contracted by other than sexual means [*s*exually *t*ransmitted *d*isease]

stead \ˈsted\ *n* **1 :** ADVANTAGE, SERVICE ⟨my knowledge of French stood me in good *stead*⟩ **2 :** the office, place, or function ordinarily occupied or carried out by someone or something else ⟨acted in the mayor's *stead*⟩ [Old English *stede* "place, position"]

stead·fast \ˈsted-ˌfast\ *adj* **1 a :** firmly fixed in place **b :** not subject to change ⟨a *steadfast* purpose⟩ **2 :** firm in belief, determination, or adherence **:** LOYAL ⟨*steadfast* friends⟩ [Old English *stedefæst,* from *stede* "place" + *fæst* "fixed, fast"] ***synonyms*** see FAITHFUL — **stead·fast·ly** *adv* — **stead·fast·ness** \-ˌfast-nəs, -ˌfas-\ *n*

stead·ing \ˈsted-iŋ\ *n* **:** a small farm or homestead [Middle English *steding,* from *stede* "place, farm"]

[1]**steady** \ˈsted-ē\ *adj* **stead·i·er; -est 1 a :** firm in position **:** FIXED **b :** direct or sure in movement **:** UNFALTERING **2 a :** REGULAR, UNIFORM ⟨a *steady* pace⟩ **b :** not changing constantly or varying widely **3 a :** not easily moved or upset **b :** constant in feeling, principle, purpose, or attachment **:** DEPENDABLE **c :** not given to dissipation or disorderly behavior [Middle English *stedy,* from *stede*] — **stead·i·ly** \ˈsted-l-ē\ *adv* — **steadi·ness** \ˈsted-ē-nəs\ *n*

synonyms STEADY, EVEN, UNIFORM mean not varying throughout a course or extent. STEADY implies lack of fluctuation or interruption of movement ⟨the *steady* beating of the waves⟩. EVEN suggests an absence of variation in quality or character ⟨spoke in an *even* tone⟩. UNIFORM stresses the sameness or alikeness of all the elements of an aggregate, a series, or a set ⟨following *uniform* procedures⟩.

[2]**steady** *vb* **stead·ied; steady·ing :** to make, keep, or become steady

[3]**steady** *adv* **1 :** in a steady manner **:** STEADILY **2 :** on the course set — used as a direction to the helmsman of a ship

[4]**steady** *n, pl* **stead·ies :** one that is steady; *esp* **:** a boyfriend or girlfriend with whom one goes steady

steady state *n* **:** a state or condition of a system or process that does not change or changes only slightly over time

steady state theory *n* **:** a theory in astronomy: the universe has always existed and has always been expanding with hydrogen being created continuously — compare BIG BANG THEORY

steak \ˈstāk\ *n* **1 a :** a slice of meat cut from a fleshy part of a beef carcass **b :** a similar slice of a specified meat other than beef ⟨ham *steak*⟩ **2 :** a cross-sectional slice of a large fish (as salmon) [Old Norse *steik*]

steak knife *n* **:** a table knife having a blade with a sharp often serrated edge

[1]**steal** \ˈstēl\ *vb* **stole** \ˈstōl\; **sto·len** \ˈstō-lən\; **steal·ing 1 :** to come or go secretly, quietly, gradually, or unexpectedly ⟨*stole* out of the room⟩ **2 a :** to take and carry away without right and with intent to keep the property of another **b :** to take surreptitiously and without permission ⟨*steal* a kiss⟩ **c :** to take entirely to oneself or beyond one's proper share ⟨*steal* the show⟩ **3 a :** to move, transfer, or introduce secretly **:** SMUGGLE **b :** to accomplish or get in a concealed or unobserved manner ⟨*steal* a nap⟩ **4 a :** to seize, gain, or win by trickery, skill, or daring ⟨a basketball player good at *stealing* the ball⟩ **b :** to reach a base in baseball by running without the aid of a hit or an error [Old English *stelan*] — **steal·er** *n* — **steal one's thunder :** to grab attention from another especially by anticipating an idea, plan, or presentation; *also* **:** to claim credit for another's idea

[2]**steal** *n* **1 :** the act or an instance of stealing **2 :** something offered or purchased at a low price **:** BARGAIN

[1]**stealth** \ˈstelth\ *n* **1 :** furtive or secret action ⟨entered the building by *stealth*⟩ **2 :** an aircraft-design style intended to make an aircraft difficult to detect by radar [Middle English *stelthe*]

[2]**stealth** *adj* **:** intended not to attract attention **:** STEALTHY ⟨a *stealth* campaign⟩

stealthy \ˈstel-thē\ *adj* **stealth·i·er; -est 1 :** slow and secret in action or character **2 :** intended to escape observation ⟨*stealthy* glances⟩ — **stealth·i·ly** \-thə-lē\ *adv* — **stealth·i·ness** \-thē-nəs\ *n*

[1]**steam** \ˈstēm\ *n* **1 a :** the invisible vapor into which water is converted when heated to the boiling point **b :** the mist formed by the condensation on cooling of water vapor **2 a :** water vapor kept under pressure so as to supply energy for heating, cooking, or mechanical work; *also* **:** the power so gen-

erated **b :** driving force : POWER ⟨arrived under their own *steam*⟩ **c :** emotional tension ⟨needed to let off a little *steam* after exams⟩ **3 a :** STEAMER 2a **b :** travel by or a trip in a steamer [Old English *stēam*]

[2]**steam** *vb* **1 :** to rise or pass off as vapor **2 :** to give off steam or vapor **3 :** to move or travel by or as if by the agency of steam **4 :** to be angry : BOIL **5 :** to expose to the action of steam (as for softening or cooking)

steam·boat \-ˌbōt\ *n* **:** a boat propelled by steam power

steam engine *n* **:** an engine driven by steam; *esp* **:** a reciprocating engine having a piston driven in a closed cylinder by steam

steam·er \ˈstē-mər\ *n* **1 :** a vessel in which something is steamed **2 a :** a ship propelled by steam **b :** an engine, machine, or vehicle operated by steam **3 :** a thin-shelled clam eaten especially when steamed

steamer rug *n* **:** a warm covering for the lap and feet especially of a person sitting on a ship's deck

steamer trunk *n* **:** a trunk suitable for use in a stateroom of a steamer

steam fitter *n* **:** one that installs or repairs equipment (as steam pipes) for heating, ventilating, or refrigerating systems — **steam fitting** *n*

steam iron *n* **:** a pressing iron with a compartment holding water that is converted to steam by the iron's heat and emitted through the bottom onto the fabric being pressed

[1]**steam·roll·er** \ˈstēm-ˈrō-lər\ *n* **1 :** a machine formerly driven by steam that is equipped with heavy wide rollers for compacting roads and pavements **2 :** a power or force that crushes opposition

[2]**steamroller** *also* **steam·roll** \-ˈrōl\ *vb* **1 :** to crush with a steamroller **2 a :** to overcome by greatly superior force **b :** to exert crushing force or pressure with respect to **3 :** to move or proceed with irresistible force

steam·ship \ˈstēm-ˌship\ *n* **:** STEAMER 2a

steam shovel *n* **:** a power shovel formerly operated by steam

steam table *n* **:** a table having openings to hold containers of cooked food over steam or hot water circulating beneath them

steam turbine *n* **:** a turbine that is driven by the pressure of steam discharged at high velocity against the turbine vanes

steamy \ˈstē-mē\ *adj* **steam·i·er; -est 1 :** consisting of, characterized by, or full of steam **2 :** EROTIC — **steam·i·ly** \-mə-lē\ *adv* — **steam·i·ness** \-mē-nəs\ *n*

stea·rate \ˈstē-ə-ˌrāt, ˈsti-ər-ˌāt, ˈstir-ˌāt\ *n* **:** a salt or ester of stearic acid

stea·ric acid \stē-ˌar-ik-, ˌstiər-ik-\ *n* **:** a white crystalline fatty acid obtained by saponifying tallow or other hard fats containing stearin [derived from Greek *stear* "hard fat"]

stea·rin \ˈstē-ə-rən, ˈsti-ər-ən, ˈstir-ən\ *n* **1 :** an ester of glycerol and stearic acid **2** *also* **stea·rine** *same or* -ˌrēn, -ˌēn\ **:** the solid portion of a fat

ste·atite \ˈstē-ə-ˌtīt\ *n* **:** a massive talc having a grayish green or brown color : SOAPSTONE [Latin *steatitis,* a precious stone, from Greek, from *steat-, stear* "fat"]

steed \ˈstēd\ *n* **:** HORSE 1a(1); *esp* **:** a spirited horse [Old English *stēda* "stallion"]

[1]**steel** \ˈstēl\ *n* **1 :** commercial iron that contains carbon in any amount up to about 1.7 percent as an essential alloying constituent and is distinguished from cast iron by its malleability and lower carbon content **2 :** an instrument or implement of or characteristically of steel: as **a :** a thrusting or cutting weapon **b :** an instrument (as a fluted round rod with a handle) for sharpening knives **c :** a piece of steel for striking sparks from flint **3 :** a hard cold quality suggestive of steel ⟨nerves of *steel*⟩ [Old English *stȳle, stēle*]

[2]**steel** *vt* **1 :** to overlay, point, or edge with steel **2 :** to make hard or unbending ⟨*steel* one's heart⟩

[3]**steel** *adj* **1 :** made of or resembling steel **2 :** of or relating to the production of steel

steel guitar *n* **1 :** HAWAIIAN GUITAR **2 :** PEDAL STEEL

steel·head \ˈstēl-ˌhed\ *n, pl* **steelhead** *also* **steelheads :** a rainbow trout that migrates to the sea to mature and returns to rivers to breed — called also *steelhead trout*

steel·ie *also* **steely** \ˈstē-lē\ *n, pl* **steelies :** a small steel ball used in playing marbles

steel wool *n* **:** an abrasive material composed of long fine steel shavings and used especially for scouring and burnishing

steel·work \ˈstēl-ˌwərk\ *n* **1 :** work in steel **2** *pl* **:** an establishment where steel is made — **steel·work·er** \-ˌwər-kər\ *n*

steely \ˈstē-lē\ *adj* **steel·i·er; -est 1 :** made of steel **2 :** resembling steel ⟨*steely* determination⟩ — **steel·i·ness** *n*

steel·yard \ˈstēl-ˌyärd\ *n* **:** a balance on which something to be weighed is hung from the shorter arm of a lever and is balanced by a weight that slides along the longer arm which is marked with a scale

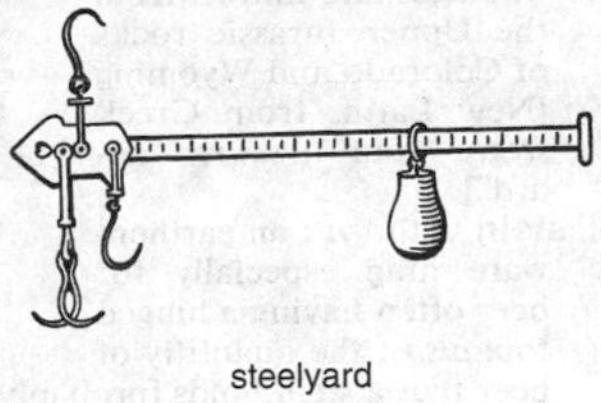
steelyard

[1]**steep** \ˈstēp\ *adj* **1 :** making a large angle with the plane of the horizon : almost straight up and down **2 :** being or characterized by a very rapid decline or increase ⟨a *steep* rise in costs⟩ **3 :** difficult to accept, meet, or perform : STIFF ⟨*steep* prices⟩ [Old English *stēap* "high, deep"] — **steep·ly** *adv* — **steepness** *n*

synonyms STEEP, PRECIPITOUS, SHEER mean having an incline approaching the perpendicular. STEEP implies such sharpness of pitch that ascent or descent is very difficult ⟨*steep* hills⟩ ⟨a *steep* roof⟩. PRECIPITOUS suggests an incline closely approaching the vertical ⟨*precipitous* canyon walls⟩. SHEER implies an unbroken perpendicular expanse ⟨a *sheer* cliff⟩.

[2]**steep** *n* **:** a place with steep sides or slope

[3]**steep** *vb* **1 a :** to soak in a liquid (as for softening, bleaching, or extracting a flavor) at a temperature under the boiling point ⟨*steep* tea⟩ **b :** to undergo the process of soaking in a liquid **2 :** BATHE, WET **3 :** to saturate with or subject thoroughly to (some strong or pervading influence) ⟨*steeped* in learning⟩ [Middle English *stepen*] ***synonyms*** see SOAK — **steep·er** *n*

steep·en \ˈstē-pən\ *vb* **steep·ened; steep·en·ing** \ˈstēp-ning, -ə-ning\ **:** to make or become steeper ⟨the trail *steepened*⟩

stee·ple \ˈstē-pəl\ *n* **:** a tall structure that tops a church tower and usually bears a small spire at the top; *also* **:** a church tower [Old English *stēpel* "tower"] — **stee·pled** \-pəld\ *adj*

stee·ple·chase \ˈstē-pəl-ˌchās\ *n* **1 a :** a cross-country race on horseback **b :** a race on a closed course over obstacles (as hedges, walls, and a water jump) **2 :** a footrace of usually 3000 meters run over hurdles and a water jump [from the use of church steeples as landmarks to guide the riders] — **stee·ple·chas·er** \-ˌchā-sər\ *n*

stee·ple·jack \-ˌjak\ *n* **:** one whose work is building smokestacks, towers, or steeples or climbing up the outside of such structures to paint and make repairs

[1]**steer** \ˈstiər\ *n* **1 :** a domestic ox castrated before sexual maturity and especially one raised for beef **2 :** an ox less than four years old [Old English *stēor* "young ox"]

[2]**steer** *vb* **1 a :** to direct the course or the course of ⟨*steer* by the stars⟩ ⟨*steer* a conversation⟩ **b :** to take or maintain a course ⟨*steer* for home⟩ **c :** to set and hold to (a course) ⟨*steer* a course for home⟩ **2 :** to pursue a course of action **3 :** to respond to steering ⟨a car that *steers* well⟩ [Old English *stīeran*] ***synonyms*** see GUIDE — **steer·able** \ˈstir-ə-bəl\ *adj* — **steer·er** \ˈstir-ər\ *n* — **steer clear :** to keep entirely away ⟨*steer clear* of arguments⟩

[3]**steer** *n* **:** a hint as to procedure : TIP ⟨gave us a bum *steer*⟩

steer·age \ˈstiər-ij\ *n* **1 :** the act or practice of steering; *also* **:** DIRECTION 1 **2 :** a section in a passenger ship for passengers paying the lowest fares [sense 2 from its originally being located near the rudder]

steer·age·way \-ˌwā\ *n* **:** sufficient forward motion of a boat or ship for it to be able to respond to steering

steering column *n* **:** the column that encloses the connections to the steering gear of a vehicle (as an automobile)

steering committee *n* **:** a managing or directing committee

steering gear *n* **:** a mechanism by which something is steered

steering wheel *n* **:** a hand-operated wheel by means of which one steers something

steers·man \ˈstiərz-mən\ *n* **:** one who steers : HELMSMAN

stego·saur \ˈsteg-ə-ˌsȯr\ *n* **:** any of a suborder of four-footed plant-eating dinosaurs with bony plates and spikes on the back and tail [derived from New Latin *stegosaurus*]

\ə\ **abut**	\au̇\ **out**	\i\ **tip**	\ȯ\ **saw**	\u̇\ **foot**
\ər\ **further**	\ch\ **chin**	\ī\ **life**	\ȯi\ **coin**	\y\ **yet**
\a\ **mat**	\e\ **pet**	\j\ **job**	\th\ **thin**	\yü\ **few**
\ā\ **take**	\ē\ **easy**	\ng\ **sing**	\t͟h\ **this**	\yu̇\ **cure**
\ä\ **cot, cart**	\g\ **go**	\ō\ **bone**	\ü\ **food**	\zh\ **vision**

stego·sau·rus \ˌsteg-ə-ˈsȯr-əs\ *n* : any of a genus of stegosaurs known from the Upper Jurassic rocks of Colorado and Wyoming [New Latin, from Greek *stegos* "roof" + *sauros* "lizard"]

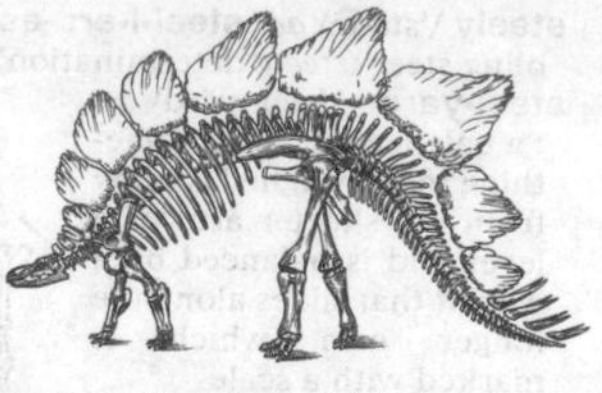

stegosaurus skeleton

stein \ˈstīn\ *n* : an earthenware mug especially for beer often having a hinged top; *also* : the quantitiy of beer that a stein holds [probably from German *Steingut* "stoneware," from *Stein* "stone" + *Gut* "goods"]

stele \ˈstēl, ˈstē-lē\ *n* : the usually cylindrical central vascular portion of the axis of a vascular plant [Greek *stēlē* "pillar"] — **ste·lar** \ˈstē-lər\ *adj*

stel·lar \ˈstel-ər\ *adj* **1 a** : of or relating to the stars : ASTRAL ⟨*stellar* light⟩ **b** : composed of stars **2** : of or relating to a theatrical or film star **3** : OUTSTANDING 3 ⟨a *stellar* production⟩ ⟨a *stellar* performance⟩ [Late Latin *stellaris*, from Latin *stella* "star"]

[1]**stem** \ˈstem\ *n* **1 a** : the main axis of a plant that develops buds and shoots instead of roots **b** : a plant part (as a petiole or stipe) that supports some other part (as a leaf or fruit) **2** : the bow of a ship **3** : a line of ancestry : STOCK; *esp* : a fundamental line from which others have arisen **4** : the part of an inflected word that remains unchanged throughout an inflection **5** : something felt to resemble a plant stem: as **a** : a main or heavy stroke of a letter **b** : the short perpendicular line extending from the head of a musical note **c** : the part of a tobacco pipe from the bowl outward **d** : the slender support of a piece of stemware (as a goblet) **e** : a shaft of a watch [Old English *stefn, stemn*] — **stem·less** \-ləs\ *adj* — **stemmed** \ˈstemd\ *adj* — **from stem to stern** : THROUGHOUT, THOROUGHLY

[2]**stem** *vt* **stemmed; stem·ming** **1** : to make headway against (as an adverse tide, current, or wind) **2** : to go counter to (something adverse) ⟨*stem* an angry crowd⟩

[3]**stem** *vb* **stemmed; stem·ming** **1** : to remove the stem from **2** : to have or trace an origin or development : DERIVE ⟨illness that *stems* from unsanitary conditions⟩ — **stem·mer** *n*

[4]**stem** *vb* **stemmed; stem·ming** **1** : to stop, check, or restrain by or as if by damming ⟨*stem* the flow of blood from the wound⟩; *also* : to become checked **2 a** : to push (a ski) out to the side in preparation for turning or to slow down **b** : to restrain oneself by forcing the heels of both skis outward from the line of progress [Old Norse *stemma* "to dam up"]

[5]**stem** *n* : an act or instance of stemming on skis

stem cell *n* : an unspecialized cell that can give rise by differentiation to a cell (as a blood cell or skin cell) with a specialized function

stem·my \ˈstem-ē\ *adj* **stem·mi·er; -est** : abounding in stems ⟨*stemmy* hay⟩

stem·ware \ˈstem-ˌwaər, -ˌweər\ *n* : stemmed glass hollowware

stem–wind·er \-ˌwīn-dər\ *n* **1** : a stem-winding watch **2** : one that is first-rate of its kind; *esp* : a stirring speech

stem–wind·ing \-ˌwīn-diŋ\ *adj* : wound by an inside mechanism turned by the knurled knob at the outside end of the stem ⟨a *stem-winding* watch⟩

stench \ˈstench\ *n* : an extremely disagreeable smell : STINK [Old English *stenc*]

[1]**sten·cil** \ˈsten-səl\ *n* **1** : impervious material (as paper or metal) perforated with lettering or a design through which a substance (as ink) is forced onto a surface to be printed **2** : a pattern, design, or print produced by means of a stencil **3** : a printing process that uses a stencil [Middle French *estanceler* "to ornament with sparkling colors," from *estancele* "spark," derived from Latin *scintilla*]

[2]**stencil** *vt* **-ciled** *or* **-cilled; -cil·ing** *or* **-cil·ling** \-sə-liŋ, -sliŋ\ **1** : to mark or paint with a stencil **2** : to produce by stencil

stencil paper *n* : strong tissue paper impregnated or coated (as with paraffin) for stencils

steno \ˈsten-ō\ *n, pl* **sten·os** : STENOGRAPHER

ste·nog·ra·pher \stə-ˈnäg-rə-fər\ *n* **1** : a writer of shorthand **2** : one employed chiefly to take and transcribe dictation

ste·nog·ra·phy \-fē\ *n* **1** : the art or process of writing in shorthand **2** : shorthand especially written from dictation or oral discourse **3** : the making of shorthand notes and subsequent transcription of them [Greek *stenos* "narrow"] — **sten·o·graph·ic** \ˌsten-ə-ˈgraf-ik\ *adj* — **sten·o·graph·i·cal·ly** \-ˈgraf-i-kə-lē, -klē\ *adv*

ste·no·sis \stə-ˈnō-səs\ *n, pl* **-no·ses** \-ˈnō-ˌsēz\ : a narrowing or constriction of a bodily passage or orifice [Greek *stenōsis* "act of narrowing," from *stenoun* "to narrow," from *stenos* "narrow"] — **ste·nosed** \-ˈnōzd, -ˈnōst\ *adj* — **ste·not·ic** \-ˈnät-ik\ *adj*

sten·tor \ˈsten-ˌtȯr, ˈstent-ər\ *n* **1** : a person having a loud voice **2** : any of a genus of large trumpet-shaped ciliated protozoans living in fresh water [Latin, from Greek *Stentōr*, a Greek herald in the Trojan War noted for his loud voice]

sten·to·ri·an \sten-ˈtōr-ē-ən, -ˈtȯr-\ *adj* : extremely loud ⟨a *stentorian* voice⟩

[1]**step** \ˈstep\ *n* **1** : a rest for the foot in ascending or descending: as **a** : STAIR 2 **b** : a ladder rung **2 a** (1) : an advance or movement made by raising the foot and bringing it down elsewhere (2) : a combination of foot or foot and body movements constituting a unit or a repeated pattern (as in a dance) (3) : manner of walking : STRIDE ⟨know you by your *step*⟩ **b** : FOOTPRINT **c** : the sound of a footstep **3 a** : the space passed over in one step **b** : a short distance ⟨only a *step* away⟩ **c** : the height of one stair **4** *pl* : COURSE, WAY ⟨directed their *steps* for home⟩ **5 a** : a degree, grade, or rank in a scale ⟨one *step* nearer graduation⟩ **b** : a stage in a process ⟨was guided through every *step* in my career⟩ **6** : a block supporting the heel of a mast **7** : an action, proceeding, or measure often occurring as one in a series ⟨taking *steps* to correct the situation⟩ **8** : a steplike offset or part usually occurring in a series **9** : a musical scale degree [Old English *stæpe*] — **step·like** \-ˌlīk\ *adj* — **stepped** \ˈstept\ *adj*

[2]**step** *vb* **stepped; step·ping** **1 a** : to move or take by raising the foot and bringing it down elsewhere or by moving each foot in succession ⟨*stepped* off the curb⟩ ⟨*step* a pace forward⟩ **b** : DANCE 1 **2 a** : to go on foot : WALK ⟨*step* outside⟩ **b** : to move briskly ⟨kept us *stepping*⟩ **3 a** : to press down with the foot ⟨*step* on a nail⟩ **b** : to move (the foot) in any direction : SET ⟨first man to *step* foot on the moon⟩ **4** : to come as if at a single step ⟨*step* into a good job⟩ **5** : to erect (a mast) by fixing the lower end in a step **6** : to measure by steps ⟨*step* off 50 meters⟩ **7** : to make steps in **8** : to construct or arrange in or as if in steps — **step on it** : to hurry up

step- *combining form* : related by virtue of a remarriage (as of a parent) and not by blood ⟨*step*parent⟩ ⟨*step*sister⟩ [Old English *stēop-*]

step·broth·er \ˈstep-ˌbrəth-ər\ *n* : a son of one's stepparent by a former partner

step–by–step \ˌstep-bə-ˈstep\ *adj* : marked by successive degrees usually of limited extent : GRADUAL

step·child \ˈstep-ˌchīld\ *n* : a child of one's spouse by a former partner

step·daugh·ter \-ˌdȯt-ər\ *n* : a daughter of one's spouse by a former partner

step down \step-ˈdau̇n, ˈstep-\ *vb* **1** : to give up a position ⟨will *step down* as chairman at the end of the year⟩ **2** : to lower the voltage of (a current) by means of a transformer **3** : to decrease or reduce especially by one or more steps — **step–down** \ˈstep-ˌdau̇n\ *adj*

step·fa·ther \ˈstep-ˌfäth-ər\ *n* : the husband of one's mother when distinct from one's natural or legal father

step–in \ˈstep-ˌin\ *n* : an article of clothing that is put on by being stepped into: as **a** : a shoe resembling a pump but usually having a higher ramp **b** : a woman's brief panties — usually used in plural

step·lad·der \ˈstep-ˌlad-ər\ *n* : a ladder that has broad flat steps and two pairs of legs connected by a hinge at the top and that opens at the bottom to become freestanding

step·moth·er \-ˌməth-ər\ *n* : the wife of one's father when distinct from one's natural or legal mother

step out *vi* **1** : to go away from a place usually for a short distance and for a short time **2** : to go or march at a vigorous or increased pace **3** : to engage in social activity away from home

step·par·ent \ˈstep-ˌpar-ənt, -ˌper-\ *n* : a person who is a stepmother or stepfather

steppe \ˈstep\ *n* : dry usually level largely grass-covered land in regions of wide temperature range (as in southeastern Europe and parts of Asia) [Russian *step'*]

stepped–up \ˈstep-ˈtəp\ *adj* : made more vigorous and intensive ⟨a *stepped-up* advertising program⟩

step·per \'step-ər\ *n* **:** one that steps lively (as a fast horse or a dancer)
stepper motor *n* **:** a motor whose driveshaft rotates in small steps rather than continuously — called also *stepping motor*
step·ping–off place \ˌstep-ing-'ȯf-\ *n* **1 :** the outbound end of a transportation line **2 :** a place from which one leaves
step·ping–stone \'step-ing-ˌstōn\ *n* **1 :** a stone to step on (as in crossing a stream) **2 :** a means of progress or advancement ⟨a *stepping-stone* to success⟩
step·sis·ter \'step-ˌsis-tər\ *n* **:** a daughter of one's stepparent by a former partner
step·son \-ˌsən\ *n* **:** a son of one's spouse by a former partner
step stool *n* **:** a stool with one or two steps that often fold away beneath the seat
step–up \'step-ˌəp\ *n* **:** an increase in size or amount
step up \step-'əp, 'step-\ *vb* **1 :** to increase the voltage of (a current) by means of a transformer **2 :** to increase, augment, or advance ⟨*step up* production⟩ **3 a :** to come forward ⟨*stepped up* to claim responsibility⟩ **b :** to succeed in meeting a challenge (as by increased effort or improved performance) — **step–up** \'step-ˌəp\ *adj*
step·wise \'step-ˌwīz\ *adj* **:** marked by steps **:** GRADUAL
-ster \stər\ *n combining form* **1 :** one that does or handles or operates ⟨spin*ster*⟩ ⟨tap*ster*⟩ ⟨team*ster*⟩ **2 :** one that makes or uses ⟨pun*ster*⟩ ⟨song*ster*⟩ **3 :** one that is associated with or participates in ⟨game*ster*⟩ ⟨gang*ster*⟩ **4 :** one that is ⟨old*ster*⟩ ⟨young*ster*⟩ [Old English *-estre* "female agent"]
stere- *or* **stereo-** *combining form* **1 :** solid ⟨*stereo*scope⟩ **2 :** stereoscopic ⟨*stereo*microscope⟩ [Greek *stereos*]
ste·reo \'ster-ē-ˌō, 'stir-\ *n* **1 :** STEREOTYPE 1 **2 a :** a stereoscopic method, system, or effect **b :** a stereoscopic photograph **3 a :** stereophonic reproduction **b :** a stereophonic sound system — **stereo** *adj*
ste·re·og·ra·phy \ˌster-ē-'äg-rə-fē, ˌstir-\ *n* **:** stereoscopic photography — **ste·reo·graph·ic** \-ē-ə-'graf-ik\ *adj*
ste·reo·isom·er·ism \ˌster-ē-ō-ī-'säm-ə-ˌriz-əm, ˌstir-\ *n* **:** isomerism in which atoms are linked in the same order but differ in their spatial arrangement — **ste·reo·iso·mer** \-'ī-sə-mər\ *n* — **ste·reo·iso·mer·ic** \-ˌī-sə-'mer-ik\ *adj*
ste·reo·mi·cro·scope \-'mī-krə-ˌskōp\ *n* **:** a microscope having a set of lenses for each eye to make an object appear in three dimensions
ste·reo·phon·ic \ˌster-ē-ə-'fän-ik, ˌstir-\ *adj* **:** giving, relating to, or constituting a three-dimensional effect of reproduced sound — compare MONOPHONIC
ste·re·op·ti·con \ˌster-ē-'äp-ti-kən, ˌstir-\ *n* **:** a projector for transparent slides [*stere-* + Greek *optikon,* neuter of *optikos* "optic"]
ste·reo·scope \'ster-ē-ə-ˌskōp, 'stir-\ *n* **:** an optical instrument with two eyepieces for helping the observer to combine the images of two pictures taken from points of view a little way apart and thus to get the effect of solidity or depth
ste·reo·scop·ic \ˌster-ē-ə-'skäp-ik, ˌstir-\ *adj* **1 :** of or relating to the stereoscope **2 :** characterized by stereoscopy ⟨*stereoscopic* vision⟩ — **ste·reo·scop·i·cal·ly** \-i-kə-lē, -klē\ *adv*
ste·re·os·co·py \ˌster-ē-'äs-kə-pē, ˌstir-\ *n* **:** the seeing of objects in three dimensions
ste·reo·tac·tic \ˌster-ē-ə-'tak-tik, ˌstir-\ *adj* **:** involving, being, utilizing, or used in a surgical technique for precisely directing the tip of a delicate instrument (as a needle) or beam of radiation in three planes in order to reach a specific point in the body and especially in the brain — **ste·reo·tac·ti·cal·ly** \-ti-kə-lē, -klē\ *adv*
ste·reo·tax·ic \ˌster-ē-ə-'tak-sik, ˌstir-\ *adj* **:** STEREOTACTIC [derived from *stere-* + *taxis*] — **ste·reo·tax·i·cal·ly** \-si-kə-lē, -klē\ *adv*
[1]**ste·reo·type** \'ster-ē-ə-ˌtīp, 'stir-\ *n* **1 :** a plate made by molding a matrix of a printing surface and making from this a cast in type metal **2 :** something conforming to a general pattern and lacking individual distinguishing marks or qualities; *esp* **:** a standardized mental picture that is held in common by members of a group and that represents an oversimplified opinion, emotional attitude, or uncritical judgment
[2]**stereotype** *vt* **1 :** to make a stereotype from **2 a :** to repeat without variation **b :** to develop a mental stereotype about ⟨unfairly *stereotyped* salesmen as dishonest⟩ — **ste·reo·typ·er** *n*
ste·reo·typed \-ˌtīpt\ *adj* **:** lacking originality or individuality ⟨a cast of *stereotyped* characters⟩ ***synonyms*** see TRITE

ste·rig·ma \stə-'rig-mə\ *n, pl* **-ma·ta** \-mət-ə\ **:** a slender stalk at the top of the basidium of some fungi that forms basidiospores [Greek *stērigma* "support," from *stērizein* "to prop"]
ster·ile \'ster-əl\ *adj* **1 :** not able to bear fruit, crops, or offspring **:** not fertile **:** BARREN ⟨*sterile* soil⟩ ⟨*sterile* seeds⟩ **2 :** free from microorganisms and especially germs (as bacteria and viruses) ⟨*sterile* dressing for a wound⟩ **3 :** lacking in ideas or originality [Latin *sterilis*] — **ste·ril·i·ty** \stə-'ril-ət-ē\ *n*
ster·il·ize \'ster-ə-ˌlīz\ *vt* **:** to make sterile: as **a :** to deprive of the power of reproducing or germinating ⟨had their cat *sterilized*⟩ **b :** to make powerless or useless **c :** to free from living microorganisms and especially germs (as bacteria) ⟨*sterilize* the dental instruments⟩ — **ster·il·i·za·tion** \ˌster-ə-lə-'zā-shən\ *n* — **ster·il·iz·er** \'ster-ə-ˌlī-zər\ *n*
[1]**ster·ling** \'stər-ling\ *n* **1 :** British money **2 :** sterling silver or articles of it [Middle English, "silver penny"]
[2]**sterling** *adj* **1 :** of, relating to, or calculated in terms of British sterling **2 a :** a fixed standard of purity usually defined legally as represented by an alloy of 925 parts of silver with 75 parts of copper ⟨*sterling* silver⟩ **b :** made of sterling silver **3 :** conforming to the highest standard ⟨a person of *sterling* quality⟩ — **ster·ling·ly** \-ling-lē\ *adv* — **ster·ling·ness** *n*
[1]**stern** \'stərn\ *adj* **1 a :** hard and severe in nature or manner ⟨a *stern* judge⟩ **b :** showing severity **:** HARSH **2 :** not inviting or attractive **:** FORBIDDING **3 :** FIRM, RESOLUTE ⟨a *stern* resolve to win⟩ [Old English *styrne*] ***synonyms*** see SEVERE — **stern·ly** *adv* — **stern·ness** \'stərn-nəs\ *n*
[2]**stern** *n* **1 :** the rear end of a boat or ship **2 :** a rear part [Middle English "rudder"]
stern·most \'stərn-ˌmōst\ *adj* **:** farthest astern
stern·post \-ˌpōst\ *n* **:** the principal member at the stern of a ship extending from keel to deck
ster·num \'stər-nəm\ *n, pl* **sternums** *or* **ster·na** \-nə\ **:** a compound often flattened bone or cartilage in the thorax of most vertebrates other than fishes connecting the ribs or the shoulder girdle or both and in humans consisting of the manubrium, gladiolus, and xiphoid process — called also *breastbone* [New Latin, from Greek *sternon* "chest, breastbone"] — **ster·nal** \'stərn-l\ *adj*
stern–wheel·er \-'hwē-lər, -'wē-lər\ *n* **:** a steamboat having a single paddle wheel at the stern instead of on the sides
ste·roid \'stiər-ˌȯid *also* 'steər-\ *n* **:** any of numerous compounds with four rings of carbon atoms that include sterols and various hormones (as estrogen and testosterone) and glycosides — compare ANABOLIC STEROID
ste·rol \'stiər-ˌȯl, 'steər-, -ˌōl\ *n* **:** any of various solid alcohols (as cholesterol) widely distributed in animal and plant lipids [*cholesterol*]
ster·to·rous \'stərt-ə-rəs\ *adj* **:** characterized by a harsh snoring or gasping sound ⟨*stertorous* breathing⟩ [derived from Latin *stertere* "to snore"] — **ster·to·rous·ly** *adv*
stet \'stet\ *vt* **stet·ted; stet·ting :** to annotate (a word or passage) with or as if with the word *stet* in order to nullify a previous order to delete or omit from a manuscript or printer's proof [Latin, "let it stand," from *stare* "to stand"]
Stet·son \'stet-sən\ *trademark* — used for a broad-brimmed high-crowned felt hat
stetho·scope \'steth-ə-ˌskōp *also* 'steth-\ *n* **:** a medical instrument used for listening to sounds produced in the body and especially those of the heart and lungs [French *stéthoscope,* from Greek *stēthos* "chest"] — **stetho·scop·ic** \ˌsteth-ə-'skäp-ik *also* ˌsteth-\ *adj*

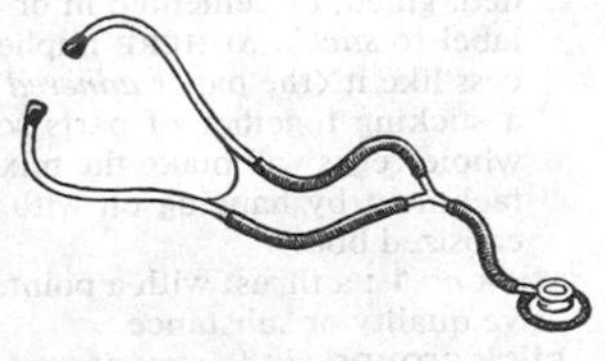
stethoscope

ste·ve·dore \'stē-və-ˌdōr, -ˌdȯr\ *n* **:** a person whose work is to load and unload ships or boats in port [Spanish *estibador,* from *estibar* "to pack," from Latin *stipare* "to press together"] — **stevedore** *vb*
[1]**stew** \'stü, 'styü\ *n* **1 :** food (as meat with vegetables) prepared

\ə\ **about**	\au̇\ **out**	\i\ **tip**	\ȯ\ **saw**	\u̇\ **foot**
\ər\ **further**	\ch\ **chin**	\ī\ **life**	\ȯi\ **coin**	\y\ **yet**
\a\ **mat**	\e\ **pet**	\j\ **job**	\th\ **thin**	\yü\ **few**
\ā\ **take**	\ē\ **easy**	\ng\ **sing**	\th\ **this**	\yu̇\ **cure**
\ä\ **cot, cart**	\g\ **go**	\ō\ **bone**	\ü\ **food**	\zh\ **vision**

by slow boiling **2** : a state of excitement, worry, or confusion [Middle English *stewe* "heated room for a steam bath," from Medieval French *estuve*]

[2]**stew** *vb* **1** : to cook in liquid over a low heat **2** : to become agitated or worried : FRET

stew•ard \ˈstü-ərd, ˈstu̇-, ˈstyü-, ˈstyu̇-, ˈstu̇rd, ˈstyu̇rd\ *n* **1** : a manager of a large household, estate, or organization **2** : a person employed to supervise the provision and distribution of food and attend the needs of passengers (as on a ship, airplane, or train) [Old English *stīweard,* from *stī, stig* "hall, sty" + *weard* "ward"]

stew•ard•ess \-əs\ *n* : a woman who performs the duties of a steward; *esp* : one who attends passengers on an airplane

stew•ard•ship \-ˌship\ *n* **1** : the office, duties, and obligations of a steward **2** : the careful and responsible management of something entrusted to one's care ⟨*stewardship* of our natural resources⟩

stib•nite \ˈstib-ˌnīt\ *n* : a mineral Sb_2S_3 consisting of a sulfide of antimony occurring in lead-gray crystals of metallic luster [French *stibine,* from Latin *stibium* "antimony," from Greek *stibi,* from Egyptian *stm*]

[1]**stick** \ˈstik\ *n* **1** : a cut or broken branch or twig especially when dry and dead **2** : a long slender piece of wood or metal: as **a** : a club or staff used as a weapon **b** : WALKING STICK 1 **c** : an implement used for striking or propelling an object in a game **3** : something like a stick in shape, origin, or use ⟨a *stick* of dynamite⟩; *esp* : an airplane lever operating the elevators and ailerons **4** : something prepared in a long and slender form ⟨a *stick* of butter⟩ **5** : a person who is dull, stiff, and lifeless **6** *pl* : remote usually rural districts ⟨way out in the *sticks*⟩ [Old English *sticca*]

[2]**stick** *vb* **stuck** \ˈstək\; **stick•ing** **1 a** : PIERCE 1, STAB **b** : to kill by piercing **2** : to cause (as a pointed instrument) to penetrate ⟨*stuck* a needle in my finger⟩ **3 a** : to fasten by thrusting in ⟨*stuck* a flower in my buttonhole⟩ **b** : IMPALE ⟨*stuck* an apple on a fork⟩ **c** : to push out, up, or under ⟨*stuck* out my hand⟩ **4** : to put or set in a specified place or position ⟨*stick* a roast in the oven⟩ **5** : to attach by or as if by causing to adhere to a surface ⟨*stick* a stamp on a letter⟩ **6** : to bring to a halt : prevent the movement or action of ⟨the car got *stuck* in traffic⟩ **7** : BAFFLE 1, STUMP ⟨got *stuck* on the first problem⟩ **8 a** : CHEAT 1, DEFRAUD **b** : to saddle with something disadvantageous or disagreeable ⟨*stuck* with the job of cleaning up⟩ **9** : to hold to something firmly by or as if by adhesion ⟨the glue *stuck* to my fingers⟩; *esp* : to become fixed in place by or as if by gluing ⟨his foot *stuck* in the mud⟩ **10 a** : to remain in a place, situation, or environment ⟨decided to *stick* where he was⟩ **b** : to hold fast or adhere resolutely : CLING ⟨she *stuck* to her story⟩ **11 a** : to become blocked, wedged, or jammed ⟨the desk drawer always *sticks*⟩ **b** : to be unable to proceed (as through fear or conscience) **12** : PROJECT 3, PROTRUDE [Old English *stician*] — **stick one's neck out** : to make oneself vulnerable (as to criticism or punishment) by taking a risk — **stick to one's guns** : to maintain one's position especially in the face of opposition — **stuck on** : infatuated with

synonyms STICK, ADHERE, COHERE, CLING mean to become or remain closely attached. STICK implies being embedded, glued, or cemented in or on something ⟨couldn't get the label to *stick*⟩. ADHERE implies a growing together or a process like it ⟨the paper *adhered* to the shelf⟩. COHERE suggests a sticking together of parts so as to form a unified mass or whole ⟨eggs will make the mixture *cohere*⟩. CLING implies attachment by hanging on with arms or tendrils ⟨*clinging* to a capsized boat⟩.

[3]**stick** *n* **1** : a thrust with a pointed instrument : STAB **2** : adhesive quality or substance

stick around *vi* : to stay or wait about : LINGER

stick•ball \ˈstik-ˌbȯl\ *n* : baseball adapted for play in small areas using a broomstick and a lightweight ball

stick•er \ˈstik-ər\ *n* **1** : one (as a bramble or knife) that pierces with a point **2 a** : something that adheres (as a bur) or causes adhesion (as glue) **b** : a slip of paper with gummed back that can be fastened to a surface

stick figure *n* : a drawing showing the head of a human being or animal as a circle and all other parts as straight lines

stick•han•dle \ˈstik-ˌhan-dl\ *vi* : to maneuver a puck (as in hockey) or a ball (as in lacrosse) with a stick — **stick•han•dler** \-ˌhan-dlər, -lər, -dl-ər\ *n*

stick insect *n* : any of various usually wingless insects that have a long round body resembling a stick — called also *walking stick*

stick–in–the–mud \ˈstik-ən-t͟hə-ˌməd\ *n* : one who is slow, old-fashioned, or unprogressive; *esp* : an old fogy

stick•le \ˈstik-əl\ *vi* **stick•led; stick•ling** \ˈstik-ling, -ə-ling\ **1** : to contend especially stubbornly and usually on insufficient grounds **2** : to feel often excessive scruples [Middle English *stightlen,* from *stighten* "to arrange," from Old English *stihtan*]

stick•le•back \ˈstik-əl-ˌbak\ *n* : any of numerous small scaleless fishes having two or more free spines in front of the dorsal fin [Old English *sticel* "goad"]

stickleback

stick•ler \ˈstik-lər, -ə-lər\ *n* **1** : a person who insists on exactness or completeness in the observation of something ⟨a *stickler* for the rules⟩ **2** : something that baffles or puzzles

stick•man \ˈstik-ˌman, -mən\ *n* : one who handles a stick: as **a** : one who supervises the play at a dice table, calls the decisions, and retrieves the dice **b** : a player in any of various games (as lacrosse) played with a stick

stick out *vb* **1 a** : to jut out : PROJECT **b** : to be conspicuous ⟨you will certainly *stick out* with that red hat and coat⟩ **2** : to be persistent (as in a demand or an opinion) ⟨*stuck out* for higher wages⟩ **3** : to put up with : ENDURE ⟨*stuck* it *out* to the end⟩

stick•pin \ˈstik-ˌpin\ *n* : an ornamental pin worn in a necktie

stick shift *n* : a manually operated gearshift usually mounted on the floor of an automobile vehicle

stick•tight \ˈstik-ˌtīt\ *n* : BUR MARIGOLD

stick–to–it•ive•ness \stik-tü-ət-iv-nəs\ *n* : determined perseverance : TENACITY

stick•up \ˈstik-ˌəp\ *n* : a robbery at gunpoint : HOLDUP

stick up \stik-ˈəp, ˈstik-\ *vb* **1** : to stand upright or on end : PROTRUDE **2** : to rob at gunpoint — **stick up for** : to speak or act in defense of : SUPPORT

stick•work \ˈstik-ˌwərk\ *n* : the use (as in lacrosse) of one's stick in offensive and defensive techniques

sticky \ˈstik-ē\ *adj* **stick•i•er; -est** **1 a** : ADHESIVE, GLUEY ⟨*sticky* syrup⟩ **b** : coated with a sticky substance ⟨the tabletop was *sticky*⟩ **2** : HUMID, MUGGY ⟨a hot, *sticky* day⟩ **3** : tending to stick ⟨a *sticky* valve⟩ **4 a** : DISAGREEABLE 1, PAINFUL ⟨came to a *sticky* end⟩ **b** : DIFFICULT, TROUBLESOME ⟨a *sticky* situation⟩ — **stick•i•ly** \ˈstik-ə-lē\ *adv* — **stick•i•ness** \ˈstik-ē-nəs\ *n*

[1]**stiff** \ˈstif\ *adj* **1 a** : not easily bent : RIGID **b** : lacking in normal or usual suppleness, mobility, or flexibility ⟨*stiff* muscles⟩ **2 a** : marked by moral courage **b** : STUBBORN 2, UNYIELDING **c** : formally reserved in manner; *also* : lacking in ease or grace **3** : hard fought ⟨drives a *stiff* bargain⟩ **4 a** : exerting great force : STRONG ⟨a *stiff* wind⟩ **b** : POTENT ⟨a *stiff* dose⟩ **5** : not flowing easily : THICK ⟨beat egg whites until *stiff*⟩ **6 a** : HARSH, SEVERE ⟨a *stiff* penalty⟩ **b** : RUGGED ⟨*stiff* terrain⟩ **7** : EXPENSIVE 1, STEEP ⟨paid a *stiff* price⟩ [Old English *stīf*] — **stiff•ly** *adv* — **stiff•ness** *n*

[2]**stiff** *adv* **1** : in a stiff manner ⟨frozen *stiff*⟩ **2** : to an extreme degree ⟨bored *stiff*⟩

[3]**stiff** *n* **1** : CORPSE **2** : PERSON, FELLOW ⟨you lucky *stiff*⟩

stiff–arm \ˈstif-ˌärm\ *vb* : STRAIGHT-ARM — **stiff–arm** *n*

stiff•en \ˈstif-ən\ *vb* **stiff•ened; stiff•en•ing** \ˈstif-ning, -ə-ning\ : to make or become stiff or stiffer — **stiff•en•er** \-nər, -ə-nər\ *n*

stiff–necked \ˈstif-ˈnekt\ *adj* : arrogantly stubborn

[1]**sti•fle** \ˈstī-fəl\ *n* : the joint next above the hock in the hind leg of a four-footed animal (as a horse or dog) corresponding to the knee in humans [Middle English]

[2]**stifle** *vb* **sti•fled; sti•fling** \-fə-ling, -fling\ **1 a** : to kill by depriving of or die from lack of oxygen or air **b** : to smother by or as if by depriving of air ⟨*stifle* a fire⟩ **2** : to check or keep in check by deliberate effort : REPRESS ⟨*stifled* my anger⟩ [Middle English *stuflen*] — **sti•fling•ly** \-fə-ling-lē, -fling-\ *adv*

stig•ma \ˈstig-mə\ *n, pl* **stig•ma•ta** \stig-ˈmät-ə, ˈstig-mət-ə\ *or* **stigmas** **1 a** : a mark of shame or discredit : STAIN **b** : an identifying mark or characteristic; *esp* : a specific diagnostic sign of a disease **2** *stigmata pl* : bodily marks or pains resembling the wounds of the crucified Jesus **3 a** : a small spot, scar, or opening on a plant or animal **b** : the usually upper part of the pistil of a flower which receives the pollen grains and on which they germinate [Latin *stigmat-, stigma* "mark, brand," from Greek, from *stizein* "to tattoo"] — **stig·mal** \'stig-məl\ *adj* — **stig·mat·ic** \stig-'mat-ik\ *adj* — **stig·mat·i·cal·ly** \-'mat-i-klē, -kə-lē\ *adv*

stig·ma·tize \'stig-mə-ˌtīz\ *vt* **:** to mark with a stigma; *esp* **:** to characterize or identify as disgraceful or shameful — **stig·ma·ti·za·tion** \ˌstig-mət-ə-'zā-shən\ *n*

¹stile \'stīl\ *n* **:** a step or set of steps for passing over a fence or wall; *also* **:** TURNSTILE [Old English *stigel*]

²stile *n* **:** one of the vertical members in a frame or panel (as of a window or door) into which the secondary members are fitted [probably from Dutch *stijl* "post"]

sti·let·to \stə-'let-ō\ *n, pl* **-tos** *or* **-toes 1 :** a slender dagger with a blade thick in proportion to its width **2 :** a pointed instrument for piercing holes for eyelets or embroidery [Italian, from *stilo* "stylus, dagger," from Latin *stilus* "stylus"]

¹still \'stil\ *adj* **1 a :** not moving ⟨lying quiet and *still*⟩ **b :** not carbonated ⟨*still* wine⟩ **c :** of, relating to, or being an ordinary photograph as distinguished from a motion picture **2 :** uttering no sound **:** QUIET ⟨be *still* and listen⟩ **3 a :** CALM, TRANQUIL ⟨a *still* lake⟩ **b :** free from noise or turbulence **:** PEACEFUL [Old English *stille*] — **still·ness** *n*

²still *vb* **1 a :** ALLAY 2, CALM ⟨*still* their fears⟩ **b :** to put an end to **:** SETTLE **2 :** to make or become motionless or silent

³still *adv* **1 :** without motion ⟨sit *still*⟩ **2** *archaic* **:** ALWAYS, CONTINUALLY **3** — used as a function word to indicate the continuance of an action or condition ⟨*still* lives there⟩ ⟨it's *still* hot⟩ **4 :** in spite of that **:** NEVERTHELESS ⟨those who take the greatest care *still* make mistakes⟩ **5 a :** EVEN ⟨a *still* more difficult problem⟩ **b :** IN ADDITION, YET ⟨won *still* another game⟩

⁴still *n* **1 :** QUIET, SILENCE **2 :** a still photograph; *esp* **:** one of actors or scenes of a motion picture for publicity or documentary purposes

⁵still *n* **1 :** DISTILLERY **2 :** apparatus used in distillation [Middle English *stillen* "to distill," short for *distillen*]

still alarm *n* **:** a fire alarm transmitted (as by telephone call) without sounding the signal apparatus

still·birth \'stil-ˌbərth\ *n* **:** the birth of a dead fetus

still·born \-'bȯrn\ *adj* **1 :** dead at birth **2 :** failing from the start **:** ABORTIVE — **still·born** \-ˌbȯrn\ *n*

still hunt *n* **:** a quiet pursuing or ambushing of game — **still–hunt** \'stil-ˌhənt\ *vb*

still life *n, pl* **still lifes** \-ˌlīfs, -ˌlīvz\ **:** a picture consisting predominantly of inanimate objects

still·man \'stil-mən\ *n* **:** a person who runs or operates a still

stilly \'stil-ē\ *adj* **:** showing stillness **:** CALM, QUIET

¹stilt \'stilt\ *n* **1 a :** one of two poles each with a rest or strap for the foot used to elevate the wearer above the ground in walking **b :** a pile or post serving as one of the supports of a structure above ground or water level **2** *pl also* **stilt :** any of several very long-legged three-toed birds related to the avocets that frequent inland ponds and marshes and nest in small colonies [Middle English *stilte*]

²stilt *vt* **:** to raise on or as if on stilts

stilt·ed \'stil-təd\ *adj* **1 :** stiffly formal **:** not easy and natural ⟨*stilted* speech⟩ **2 :** raised on or as if on stilts ⟨a *stilted* arch⟩ — **stilt·ed·ly** *adv* — **stilt·ed·ness** *n*

stim·u·lant \'stim-yə-lənt\ *n* **1 :** an agent (as a drug) that temporarily increases the activity or efficiency of the body or one of its parts ⟨a heart *stimulant*⟩ **2 :** STIMULUS ⟨a *stimulant* to trade⟩ **3 :** an alcoholic beverage — **stimulant** *adj*

stim·u·late \-ˌlāt\ *vt* **1 :** to make active or more active **:** ANIMATE, AROUSE ⟨*stimulate* industry⟩ **2 :** to act on as a physiological stimulus or stimulant [Latin *stimulare,* from *stimulus* "goad, stimulus"] ***synonyms*** see PROVOKE — **stim·u·la·tion** \ˌstim-yə-'lā-shən\ *n* — **stim·u·la·tive** \'stim-yə-ˌlāt-iv\ *adj* — **stim·u·la·tor** \-ˌlāt-ər\ *n* — **stim·u·la·to·ry** \-lə-ˌtōr-ē, -ˌtȯr-\ *adj*

stim·u·lus \'stim-yə-ləs\ *n, pl* **-li** \-ˌlī, -ˌlē\ **1 :** something that rouses or incites to activity **:** INCENTIVE ⟨new *stimuli* to business⟩ **2 :** an agent (as an environmental change) that directly influences the activity of a living organism or one of its parts (as by exciting a sensory organ) [Latin]

¹sting \'sting\ *vb* **stung** \'stəng\; **sting·ing** \'sting-ing\ **1 a :** to prick painfully especially with a sharp or poisonous process ⟨*stung* by a bee⟩ **b :** to affect with or feel sharp, quick, and usually burning pain or smart ⟨hail *stung* their faces⟩ ⟨faces *stinging* from the cold⟩ **2 :** to cause to suffer severely ⟨*stung* with remorse⟩ **3 :** OVER-CHARGE, CHEAT ⟨some people always get *stung*⟩ **4 :** to use a stinger ⟨bees *sting*⟩ [Old English *stingan*]

²sting *n* **1 a :** the act of stinging **b :** a wound or pain caused by or as if by stinging **2 :** STINGER 2 **3 :** a stinging element, force, or quality — **sting·less** \'sting-ləs\ *adj*

sting·a·ree \'sting-ə-rē\ *n* **:** STINGRAY [by alteration]

sting·er \'sting-ər\ *n* **1 :** one that stings; *esp* **:** a sharp blow or remark **2 :** a sharp organ (as of a bee or scorpion) usually adapted to wound, paralyze, or kill prey or an enemy by piercing and injecting a poisonous secretion

stinging cell *n* **:** NEMATOCYST

sting·ray \'sting-ˌrā\ *n* **:** any of numerous rays with one or more large sharp barbed spines near the base of the whiplike tail capable of inflicting severe wounds

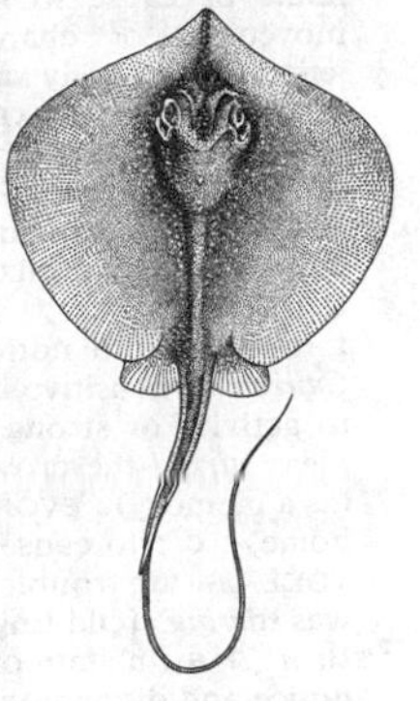

stingray

stin·gy \'stin-jē\ *adj* **stin·gi·er; -est 1 :** not generous or liberal **:** sparing or scant in giving, using, or spending **2 :** SCANTY, MEAGER ⟨*stingy* portions⟩ [probably related to *sting*] — **stin·gily** \-jə-lē\ *adv* — **stin·gi·ness** \-jē-nəs\ *n*

synonyms STINGY, CLOSE, PENURIOUS, MISERLY mean being unwilling or showing unwillingness to share with others. STINGY implies an unwillingness to spend, give, or share freely and a marked lack of generosity ⟨a *stingy* child, not given to sharing⟩. CLOSE suggests keeping a tight grip on one's money and possessions ⟨folks who are very *close* when charity calls⟩. PENURIOUS implies a frugality that gives an appearance of actual poverty ⟨inherited a fortune from the *penurious* eccentric⟩. MISERLY suggests a sordid avariciousness and a morbid pleasure in hoarding ⟨a *miserly* couple lacking a social conscience⟩.

¹stink \'stingk\ *vb* **stank** \'stangk\ *or* **stunk** \'stəngk\; **stunk; stink·ing 1 :** to give forth or cause to have a strong and offensive smell ⟨the garbage pail *stinks*⟩ ⟨*stink* up a room⟩ **2 :** to be offensive or have something to an offensive degree ⟨the election *stank* of corruption⟩ **3 :** to be extremely bad or unpleasant ⟨that news really *stinks*⟩ [Old English *stincan*]

²stink *n* **1 :** a strong offensive odor **:** STENCH **2 :** a public outcry against something **:** FUSS ⟨made a big *stink* about his remarks⟩ — **stinky** \'sting-kē\ *adj*

stink·bug \'stingk-ˌbəg\ *n* **:** any of various true bugs that emit a disagreeable odor

stink·er \'sting-kər\ *n* **1 :** one that stinks **2 :** an offensive or contemptible person

stink·pot \'stingk-ˌpät\ *n* **:** a musk turtle of the U.S. and Canada

¹stint \'stint\ *vb* **1 :** to limit in share or portion **:** cut short in amount ⟨*stint* the children's allowance⟩ **2 :** to be sparing or frugal ⟨not *stinting* with their praise⟩ [Old English *styntan* "to blunt, dull"] — **stint·er** *n*

²stint *n* **1 a :** a definite quantity of work assigned **b :** a period of time spent at a particular activity ⟨served a brief *stint* as a waiter⟩ **2 :** RESTRICTION 1, LIMITATION

stipe \'stīp\ *n* **:** a usually short stalk of a plant or fungus; *esp* **:** one supporting a fern frond or the cap of a mushroom [Latin *stipes* "tree trunk"] — **stiped** \'stīpt\ *adj*

sti·pend \'stī-ˌpend, -pənd\ *n* **:** a fixed sum of money paid periodically for services or to defray expenses [Latin *stipendium,* from *stips* "gift" + *pendere* "to weigh, pay"]

stip·ple \'stip-əl\ *vt* **stip·pled; stip·pling** \'stip-ling, -ə-ling\ **1 :** to engrave by means of dots and flicks **2 a :** to make (as in paint or ink) by small short touches that together produce an even or softly graded shadow **b :** to apply (as paint) by repeated small touches **3 :** SPECKLE 1, FLECK [Dutch *stippelen* "to spot, dot"] — **stipple** *n* — **stip·pler** \-lər, -ə-lər\ *n*

stip·u·late \'stip-yə-ˌlāt\ *vb* **1 :** to make an agreement or arrange as part of an agreement **2 :** to demand or insist on as a condition in an agreement [Latin *stipulari*] — **stip·u·la·tor** \-ˌlāt-ər\ *n* — **stip·u·la·to·ry** \-lə-ˌtōr-ē, -ˌtȯr-\ *adj*

stip·u·la·tion \ˌstip-yə-ˈlā-shən\ *n* **1** : an act of stipulating **2** : something stipulated; *esp* : a condition required as part of an agreement

stip·ule \ˈstip-yül\ *n* : either of a pair of small leaflike appendages at the base of the petiole in many plants [Latin *stipula* "stalk"] — **stip·u·lar** \-yə-lər\ *adj* — **stip·u·late** \-yə-lət\ *adj*

S stipule

[1]**stir** \ˈstər\ *vb* **stirred; stir·ring** **1 a** : to make or cause to make a usually slight movement or change of position ⟨the leaves were barely *stirring*⟩ **b** : to disturb the quiet of : AGITATE ⟨the bear *stirred* up the bees⟩ **2 a** : to alter the relative position of the particles or parts of especially by a continued circular movement ⟨*stir* the pudding⟩ **b** : to mix by or as if by stirring ⟨*stir* in the spices⟩ **3** : BESTIR, EXERT **4** : to bring into notice or debate : RAISE ⟨*stirred* up sensitive issues⟩ **5 a** : to rouse to activity or strong feeling : INCITE ⟨his pleas *stirred* the crowd⟩ **b** : to call forth (as a memory) : EVOKE ⟨*stirred* thoughts of home⟩ **c** : to cause to take place : PROVOKE ⟨*stir* up trouble⟩ **6** : to be active or busy ⟨not a creature was *stirring*⟩ [Old English *styrian*] — **stir·rer** *n*

[2]**stir** *n* **1 a** : a state of disturbance or activity **b** : widespread notice and discussion : IMPRESSION **2** : a slight movement **3** : a stirring movement

[1]**stir–fry** \ˈstər-ˈfrī\ *vb* : to fry quickly over high heat while stirring continuously

[2]**stir–fry** \ˈstər-ˌfrī\ *n* : a dish of something stir-fried

stir·ring \ˈstər-iŋ\ *adj* **1** : ACTIVE 4, BUSTLING **2** : MOVING 3, INSPIRING ⟨a *stirring* speech⟩

stir·rup \ˈstər-əp *also* ˈstir-əp *or* ˈstə-rəp\ *n* **1** : either of a pair of small light frames often of metal hung by straps from a saddle and used as a support for the foot of a horseback rider **2 a** : something (as a support or clamp) resembling or functioning like a stirrup **b** : STAPES [Old English *stigrāp,* literally, "mounting rope"]

stirrup cup *n* **1** : a small cup of drink (as wine) taken by a rider about to depart **2** : a farewell cup

[1]**stitch** \ˈstich\ *n* **1** : a local sharp and sudden pain especially in the side **2 a** : one in-and-out movement of a threaded needle in sewing, embroidering, or suturing **b** : a portion of thread left in the material after one stitch **3** : a least bit especially of clothing ⟨didn't have a *stitch* on⟩ **4** : a single loop of thread or yarn around an implement (as a knitting needle or crochet hook) **5** : a stitch or series of stitches formed in a particular way ⟨basting *stitch*⟩ [Old English *stice*] — **in stitches** : in a state of uncontrollable laughter

[2]**stitch** *vb* **1 a** : to join with or as if with stitches ⟨*stitched* a seam⟩ **b** : to make, mend, or decorate with or as if with stitches **2** : to unite by means of staples **3** : to do needlework : SEW — **stitch·er** *n*

stithy \ˈstith-ē, ˈstith-\ *n, pl* **stith·ies** **1** *archaic* : ANVIL 1 **2** *archaic* : SMITHY 1 [Old Norse *stethi*]

sti·ver \ˈstī-vər\ *n* **1 a** : a former monetary unit of the Netherlands equal to ¹⁄₂₀ gulden **b** : a coin representing one stiver **2** : something of little value [Dutch *stuiver*]

stoat \ˈstōt\ *n* : a common ermine of northern regions especially in its brown summer coat [Middle English *stote*]

stob \ˈstäb\ *n, chiefly dialect* : STAKE 1, POST [Middle English, "stump"]

[1]**stock** \ˈstäk\ *n* **1 a** *archaic* : STUMP 1b **b** *archaic* : a log or block of wood **c** (1) *archaic* : something without life or consciousness (2) : a dull, stupid, or lifeless person **2** : a supporting framework or part: as **a** *pl* : a timber frame with holes to contain the feet or feet and hands of an offender undergoing public punishment **b** : the wooden part by which a rifle, shotgun, or crossbow is held during firing **c** : the butt of an implement **3 a** : the main stem of a plant : TRUNK **b** : a plant or plant part joined to a scion in grafting and supplying the lower or underground parts to a graft **4** : the crosspiece of an anchor **5 a** : the original (as a person, race, or language) from which others derive : SOURCE **b** : the descendants of one individual : FAMILY, LINEAGE **6 a** (1) : the equipment of an establishment (2) : farm animals : LIVESTOCK **b** : a store or supply accumulated or available; *esp* : the inventory of goods of a merchant or manufacturer **7 a** : the ownership element in a corporation divided into shares giving to the owners an interest in its assets and earnings and usually voting power **b** : a portion of such stock **8** : any of a genus of herbaceous or shrubby plants related to the mustards and having clusters of usually sweet-scented flowers **9** : a wide band or scarf worn about the neck especially by some members of the clergy **10 a** : liquid in which meat, fish, or vegetables have been simmered that is used as a basis for soup, gravy, or sauce **b** : RAW MATERIAL **11 a** : the estimation in which someone or something is held **b** : confidence placed in one **12** : the production and presentation of plays by a stock company [Old English *stocc*] — **in stock** : in the store and ready for delivery

[2]**stock** *vb* **1** : to fit to or with a stock **2** : to provide with or acquire stock or a stock ⟨*stock* a family with linens⟩ ⟨*stock* up on sundries⟩ **3** : to procure or keep a stock of ⟨a store that *stocks* only the finest goods⟩ **4** : to graze (livestock) on land

[3]**stock** *adj* **1 a** : kept regularly in stock ⟨comes in *stock* sizes⟩ ⟨a *stock* model⟩ **b** : commonly used or brought forward : STANDARD ⟨the *stock* answer⟩ **2 a** : kept for breeding purposes ⟨a *stock* mare⟩ **b** : devoted to or used or intended for livestock ⟨*stock* train⟩ ⟨*stock* farm⟩ **3** : employed in taking care of the stock of merchandise on hand ⟨a *stock* clerk⟩

[1]**stock·ade** \stä-ˈkād\ *n* **1** : a line of stout posts set firmly to form a defense **2 a** : an enclosure or pen made with posts and stakes **b** : an enclosure in which prisoners are kept [Spanish *estacada,* from *estaca* "stake," of Germanic origin]

[2]**stockade** *vt* : to fortify or surround with a stockade

stock·bro·ker \ˈstäk-ˌbrō-kər\ *n* : one that carries out orders to buy and sell securities — **stock·brok·ing** \-ˌbrō-kiŋ\ *or* **stock·bro·ker·age** \-kə-rij, -krij\ *n*

stock car *n* : a racing car having the basic structure of a commercially produced assembly-line model

stock certificate *n* : a formal legal document showing evidence of ownership of one of more shares of the stock of a corporation

stock company *n* **1** : a corporation or joint-stock company whose capital is represented by stock **2** : a theatrical company attached to a repertory theater; *esp* : one without outstanding stars

stock exchange *n* **1** : a place where organized trading in securities is conducted **2** : an association of people organized to provide a market among themselves for the purchase and sale of securities

stock·fish \ˈstäk-ˌfish\ *n* : fish (as cod, haddock, or hake) dried hard in the open air without salt [early Dutch *stocvisch,* from *stoc* "stick" + *visch* "fish"]

stock·hold·er \-ˌhōl-dər\ *n* : an owner of stocks

stock·i·nette *or* **stock·i·net** \ˌstäk-ə-ˈnet\ *n* : a soft elastic usually cotton fabric used especially for bandages and infants' wear [alteration of earlier *stocking net*]

stock·ing \ˈstäk-iŋ\ *n* **1 a** : a usually knit close-fitting covering for the foot and leg **b** : SOCK **2** : something resembling a stocking; *esp* : a ring of distinctive color on the lower part of the leg of an animal [obsolete *stock* "to cover with a stocking," from English dialect *stock* "stocking"] — **stock·inged** \-iŋd\ *adj*

stocking cap *n* : a long knitted cone-shaped cap usually with a tassel or pom-pom worn especially for winter sports or play

stock–in–trade \ˌstäk-ən-ˈtrād, ˈstäk-ən-ˌ\ *n* **1** : the equipment, merchandise, or materials necessary to or used in a trade or business **2** : something held to resemble the standard equipment of a business or person with a trade

stock·man \ˈstäk-mən, -ˌman\ *n* : one occupied as an owner or worker in the raising of livestock

stock market *n* **1** : STOCK EXCHANGE 1 **2** : a market for stocks or for a particular stock

stock·pile \ˈstäk-ˌpīl\ *n* : a reserve supply especially of something essential accumulated within a country for use during a shortage — **stockpile** *vt*

stock·pot \-ˌpät\ *n* : a pot in which soup stock is prepared

stock·room \-ˌrüm, -ˌru̇m\ *n* : a storage place for supplies or goods used in a business

stock–still \-ˈstil\ *adj* : very still : MOTIONLESS ⟨stood *stock-still*⟩

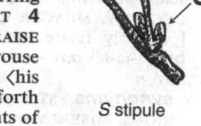

stocky \ˈstäk-ē\ *adj* **stock·i·er; -est** : compact, sturdy, and relatively thick in build : THICKSET — **stock·i·ly** \ˈstäk-ə-lē\ *adv* — **stock·i·ness** \ˈstäk-ē-nəs\ *n*

stock·yard \'stäk-ˌyärd\ *n* **:** a yard for stock; *esp* **:** one in which livestock are kept temporarily for slaughter, market, or shipping

stodgy \'stäj-ē\ *adj* **stodg·i·er; -est** **1 :** having a rich filling quality **:** HEAVY ⟨*stodgy* bread⟩ **2 :** moving in a slow plodding way especially as a result of physical bulkiness **3 :** having no excitement **:** DULL ⟨a *stodgy* day⟩ **4 :** extremely old-fashioned in attitude or outlook **5 a :** DRAB 2 **b :** DOWDY ⟨*stodgy* clothes⟩ [earlier *stodge* "to stuff with food"] — **stodg·i·ly** \'stäj-ə-lē\ *adv* — **stodg·i·ness** \'stäj-ē-nəs\ *n*

sto·gie *or* **sto·gy** \'stō-gē\ *n, pl* **stogies :** a slender cylindrical cigar; *also* **:** CIGAR [*Conestoga,* Pennsylvania]

[1]**sto·ic** \'stō-ik\ *n* **1** *cap* **:** a member of an ancient Greek school of philosophy holding that the wise person should be free from passion, unmoved by joy or grief, and submissive to natural law **2 :** one who appears or claims to be indifferent to pleasure or pain [Latin *stoicus,* from Greek *stōïkos,* from *Stoa Poikilē* "the Painted Portico (portico at Athens where Zeno taught)"]

[2]**stoic** *or* **sto·i·cal** \'stō-i-kəl\ *adj* **1** *cap* **:** of or relating to the Stoics or their doctrines **2 :** indifferent to pleasure or pain — **sto·i·cal·ly** \-i-kə-lē, -klē\ *adv*

sto·i·cism \'stō-ə-ˌsiz-əm\ *n* **1** *cap* **:** the philosophy of the Stoics **2 :** indifference to pleasure or pain **:** IMPASSIVENESS

stoke \'stōk\ *vb* **1 :** to stir up or tend (as a fire) **:** supply (as a furnace) with fuel **2 :** to stir up a fire **:** tend the fires of furnaces **3 :** to feed (as oneself) abundantly [Dutch *stoken*]

stoke·hold \-ˌhōld\ *n* **:** a room containing a ship's boilers

stok·er \'stō-kər\ *n* **1 :** one that tends a furnace and supplies it with fuel; *esp* **:** one that tends a ship's steam boiler **2 :** a machine for feeding a fire

[1]**stole** *past of* STEAL

[2]**stole** \'stōl\ *n* **1 :** a long loose garment **:** ROBE **2 :** a long narrow band worn around the neck by bishops and priests and over the left shoulder by deacons in ceremonies **3 :** a long wide scarf or similar covering worn usually across the shoulders [Old English, from Latin *stola,* from Greek *stolē*]

stolen *past participle of* STEAL

stol·id \'stäl-əd\ *adj* **:** having or expressing little or no sensibility **:** not easily aroused or excited **:** UNEMOTIONAL ⟨a *stolid* person⟩ ⟨waited in *stolid* silence⟩ [Latin *stolidus* "dull, stupid"] ***synonyms*** see IMPASSIVE — **sto·lid·i·ty** \stä-'lid-ət-ē, stə-\ *n* — **stol·id·ly** \'stäl-əd-lē\ *adv*

sto·lon \'stō-lən, -ˌlän\ *n* **1 :** a horizontal branch from the base of a plant that produces new plants from buds at its tip or nodes (as in the strawberry) — called also *runner* **2 :** a branch of fungus mycelium spreading over the surface of the medium on which it is growing [Latin *stolon-, stolo* "branch, sucker"] — **sto·lon·if·er·ous** \ˌstō-lə-'nif-rəs, -ə-rəs\ *adj*

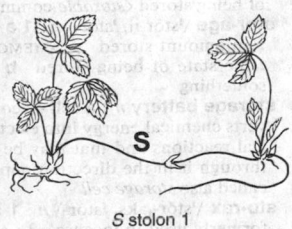

S stolon 1

sto·ma \'stō-mə\ *n* **1** *pl* **stomas :** any of various small simple bodily openings especially in a lower animal **2** *pl* **sto·ma·ta** \-mət-ə\ **:** any of the minute openings surrounded by two guard cells in the epidermis of a leaf through which moisture and gases pass [Greek *stomat-, stoma* "mouth"]

[1]**stom·ach** \'stəm-ək, -ik\ *n* **1 a :** a pouch of the vertebrate alimentary canal into which food passes from the esophagus for mixing and digestion before passing to the duodenum **b :** a cavity with a similar function in an invertebrate animal **c :** the part of the body that contains the stomach **:** BELLY, ABDOMEN **2 a :** desire for food caused by hunger **:** APPETITE **b :** INCLINATION, DESIRE ⟨had no *stomach* for an argument⟩ **3** *obsolete* **a :** VALOR, SPIRIT **b :** PRIDE 1a **c :** RESENTMENT [Medieval French *estomac,* from Latin *stomachus* "gullet, esophagus, stomach," from Greek *stomachos,* from *stoma* "mouth"] — **stomach** *adj*

[2]**stomach** *vt* **1** *archaic* **:** to take offense at **2 :** to bear without open reaction or resentment **:** TOLERATE ⟨could not *stomach* the hypocrisy⟩

stom·ach·ache \-ˌāk\ *n* **:** pain in or in the region of the stomach

stom·ach·er \'stəm-i-kər, -i-chər\ *n* **:** the center front section of a bodice appearing between the laces of an outer garment or an embroidered or jeweled ornament for the front of a bodice (as in 16th century costume)

[1]**sto·mach·ic** \stə-'mak-ik\ *adj* **:** of or relating to the stomach ⟨*stomachic* vessels⟩

[2]**stomachic** *n* **:** a stimulant or tonic for the stomach

sto·ma·tal \'stō-mət-l\ *adj* **:** of, relating to, or constituting stomata ⟨*stomatal* openings⟩

sto·mate \'stō-ˌmāt\ *n* **:** STOMA 2 [derived from *stoma*]

[1]**stomp** \'stämp, 'stȯmp\ *vb* **:** STAMP 2 ⟨*stomped* on the brakes⟩ [alteration of *stamp*] — **stomp·er** *n*

[2]**stomp** *n* **1 :** STAMP 4 **2 :** a jazz dance characterized by heavy stamping

stomping ground *n* **:** a favorite or frequently sought out place ⟨the museum became my new *stomping ground*⟩; *also* **:** familiar territory ⟨returned to the *stomping grounds* of my youth⟩

[1]**stone** \'stōn\ *n* **1 :** earth or mineral matter hardened in a mass **2 :** a piece of rock not as fine as gravel ⟨throw *stones*⟩ **3 :** rock used as a material especially for building **4 :** a piece of rock used for some special purpose (as for a monument at a grave) **5 :** JEWEL, GEM ⟨precious *stones*⟩ **6 :** CALCULUS 2 **7 :** a hard stony seed or one (as of a plum) enclosed in a stony cover **8** *pl usually* **stone :** any of various units of weight; *esp* **:** an official British unit equal to 14 pounds (6.3 kilograms) [Old English *stān*]

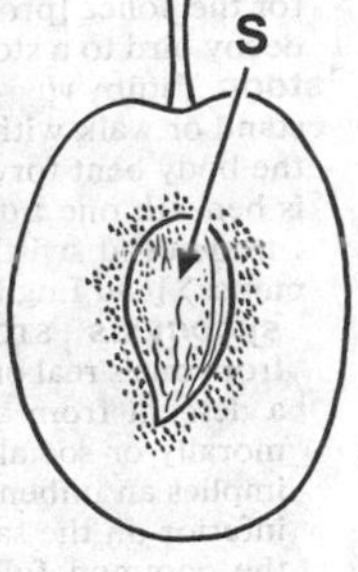

S stone 7

[2]**stone** *adj* **:** of, relating to, or made of stone

[3]**stone** *vt* **1 :** to hurl stones at; *esp* **:** to kill by hitting with stones **2 :** to remove the stones or seeds of (a fruit) **3 a :** to rub, scour, or polish (as leather or machined metal) with a stone **b :** to sharpen with a whetstone — **ston·er** *n*

[4]**stone** *adv* **:** in a complete manner **:** ENTIRELY, UTTERLY — used as an intensive ⟨the soup is *stone* cold⟩; often used in combination ⟨*stone*-broke⟩

Stone Age *n* **1 :** the first known period of prehistoric human culture characterized by the use of stone tools **2 :** a stage in a human institution or field of endeavor regarded as primitive, outmoded, or obsolete ⟨the *Stone Age* of computers⟩

stone–blind \'stōn-'blīnd\ *adj* **:** totally blind

stone cell *n* **:** SCLEREID

stone·crop \'stōn-ˌkräp\ *n* **:** SEDUM; *esp* **:** an Old World creeping evergreen sedum with pungent leaves and yellow flowers

stone·cut·ter \-ˌkət-ər\ *n* **1 :** one that cuts, carves, or dresses stone **2 :** a machine for dressing stone — **stone·cut·ting** \-ˌkət-ing\ *n*

stoned \'stōnd\ *adj* **1 :** DRUNK 1 **2 :** being under the influence of a drug

stone–deaf \'stōn-'def\ *adj* **:** totally deaf

stone fly *n* **:** any of an order (Plecoptera) of 4-winged insects that have aquatic gilled nymphs and are used by anglers for bait when immature or fully developed

stone fruit *n* **:** DRUPE

stone–ground \'stōn-'grau̇nd\ *adj* **:** ground by the use of millstones ⟨*stone-ground* flour⟩

stone·ma·son \'stōn-ˌmās-n\ *n* **:** a mason who builds with stone — **stone·ma·son·ry** \-rē\ *n*

stone's throw *n* **:** a short distance ⟨lives within a *stone's throw* of the school⟩

stone wall *n* **1 :** a fence made of stones; *esp* **:** one built of rough stones without mortar to enclose a field **2 :** an immovable block or obstruction (as in public affairs)

stone·ware \'stōn-ˌwaər, -ˌweər\ *n* **:** a strong opaque ceramic ware that is high-fired, well vitrified, and nonporous

stone·washed \-ˌwȯsht, -ˌwäsht\ *adj* **:** subjected to a washing process during manufacture that includes the use of abrasive stones especially to create a softer fabric ⟨*stonewashed* jeans⟩

stone·work \-ˌwərk\ *n* **1 :** a structure or part built of stone **:** MASONRY **2 :** the shaping, preparation, or setting of stone

stone·wort \-ˌwərt, -ˌwȯrt\ *n* : any of a family of freshwater green algae often encrusted with calcium-containing deposits

stony *also* **ston·ey** \'stō-nē\ *adj* **ston·i·er; -est** **1 a** : abounding in or having the nature of stone : ROCKY ⟨*stony* soils⟩ **b** : resembling stone in hardness ⟨a *stony* seed⟩ **2 a** : insensitive to human feeling : PITILESS, HARDHEARTED **b** : showing no movement or reaction : EXPRESSIONLESS ⟨a *stony* face⟩ — **ston·i·ly** \'stōn-l-ē\ *adv* — **ston·i·ness** \'stō-nē-nəs\ *n*

stood *past and past participle of* STAND

stooge \'stüj\ *n* **1** : one who slavishly follows or serves another **2** : STRAIGHT MAN [origin unknown] — **stooge** *vi*

stool \'stül\ *n* **1 a** : a seat usually without back or arms supported by three or four legs or by a central pedestal **b** : FOOTSTOOL **2 a** : a seat used while defecating or urinating **b** : a discharge of fecal matter [Old English *stōl*]

stool pigeon *n* **1** : a pigeon used as a decoy to draw others within a net **2** : a person acting as a spy or informer especially for the police [probably from the early practice of fastening the decoy bird to a stool]

[1]stoop \'stüp\ *vb* **1** : to bend forward and downward **2** : to stand or walk with the head and shoulders or the upper part of the body bent forward **3** : to descend to doing something that is beneath one : degrade or debase oneself ⟨*stoop* to lying⟩ **4** : to descend swiftly on prey : SWOOP ⟨a hawk *stooping* after a mouse⟩ [Old English *stūpian*]

synonyms STOOP, CONDESCEND, DEIGN mean to descend from one's real or pretended level of dignity. STOOP may imply a descent from a relatively high plane to a much lower one morally or socially ⟨don't *stoop* to their level⟩. CONDESCEND implies an unbending by one of high position to meet a social inferior on the same level ⟨royalty *condescended* to dine with the common folk⟩. DEIGN suggests a haughty or reluctant condescension ⟨would not even *deign* to talk to him⟩.

[2]stoop *n* **1 a** : an act of bending the body forward **b** : a temporary or habitual forward bend of the back and shoulders **2** : the descent of a bird especially on its prey **3** : a lowering of oneself either in condescension or in submission

[3]stoop *n* : a porch, platform, or entrance stairway at a house door [Dutch *stoep*]

[3]stoop

[1]stop \'stäp\ *vb* **stopped; stop·ping** **1** : to close an opening by filling or blocking it : PLUG ⟨nose *stopped* up by a cold⟩ ⟨*stopped* their ears with cotton⟩ **2** : RESTRAIN 1a, PREVENT ⟨*stop* a person from going⟩ **3** : to interrupt or prevent from continuing or occurring : CHECK ⟨couldn't *stop* the noise⟩ **4** : to halt the movement or progress of ⟨*stop* the car⟩ **5** : to instruct one's bank not to honor or pay ⟨*stop* payment on a check⟩ **6** : to change the pitch of (as a violin string) by pressing with the finger **7 a** : to cease activity or operation ⟨the motor *stopped*⟩ ⟨his heart *stopped*⟩ **b** : to come to an end ⟨sit down when the music *stops*⟩ **8** : to break one's journey ⟨*stopping* with friends for the weekend⟩ [Old English *-stoppian*, derived from Latin *stuppa* "oakum, tow"]

synonyms STOP, CEASE, DESIST, QUIT mean to suspend or cause to suspend activity. STOP applies to action or progress or to what is operating or progressing and may imply suddenness or definiteness ⟨*stopped* at the red light⟩. CEASE applies to states, conditions, or existence and may add a suggestion of gradualness and a degree of finality ⟨*ceased* raining during the night⟩. DESIST implies forbearance or restraint as a motive for stopping or ceasing ⟨*desisted* from further efforts to persuade them⟩. QUIT may stress either finality or abruptness in stopping or ceasing ⟨the engine faltered, sputtered, then *quit*⟩.

[2]stop *n* **1 a** : CESSATION, END ⟨his father put a *stop* to the arguing⟩ **b** : a pause or breaking off in speech **2 a** : a graduated set of organ pipes of like kind and tone quality **b** : STOP KNOB — often used figuratively in phrases like *pull out all the stops* to suggest holding nothing back **3 a** : something that impedes, obstructs, or brings to a halt : IMPEDIMENT, OBSTACLE **b** : the aperture of a camera lens **c** : a drain plug : STOPPER **4** : a device for arresting or limiting motion **5** : the act of stopping : the state of being stopped : CHECK ⟨the train was brought to a sudden *stop*⟩ **6 a** : a halt in a journey : STAY ⟨made a brief *stop* to refuel⟩ **b** : a stopping place ⟨a bus *stop*⟩ **7 a** *chiefly British* : any of several punctuation marks **b** — used in telegrams and cables to indicate a period **8** : a consonant in the articulation of which there is a stage (as in the *p* of *apt* or the *g* of *tiger*) when the breath passage is completely closed **9** : a function of an electronic device that stops a recording

[3]stop *adj* : serving to stop : designed to stop ⟨*stop* line⟩ ⟨*stop* signal⟩ ⟨*stop* valve⟩

stop–ac·tion \'stäp-'ak-shən\ *n* : STOP-MOTION

stop bath *n* : an acid bath used to stop the development of a photographic negative or print

stop·cock \'stäp-ˌkäk\ *n* : a device for stopping or regulating flow (as through a pipe)

stop down *vt* : to reduce the aperture of (a lens) by means of a diaphragm

stope \'stōp\ *n* : a usually steplike excavation underground for the removal of ore [probably from Low German *stope*, literally, "step"]

stop·gap \'stäp-ˌgap\ *n* : something that serves as a temporary substitute : MAKESHIFT ***synonyms*** see RESOURCE

stop knob *n* : one of the handles by which an organist draws or shuts off a particular stop

stop·light \'stäp-ˌlīt\ *n* : TRAFFIC SIGNAL

stop–mo·tion \-'mō-shən\ *n* : a filming technique in which successive positions of objects (as clay models) are photographed to produce the appearance of movement — called also *stop-action*

stop·over \'stäp-ˌō-vər\ *n* **1** : a stop at an intermediate point in one's journey **2** : a stopping place on a journey

stop·page \'stäp-ij\ *n* : the act of stopping : the state of being stopped : HALT, OBSTRUCTION

[1]stop·per \'stäp-ər\ *n* **1** : one that brings to a halt : CHECK **2** : one that closes, shuts, or fills up; *esp* : something (as a bung or cork) used to plug an opening

[2]stopper *vt* : to close or secure with or as if with a stopper

stop·ple \'stäp-əl\ *n* : something that closes an aperture : STOPPER, PLUG [Middle English *stoppell*, from *stoppen* "to stop"] — **stopple** *vt*

stop·watch \'stäp-ˌwäch\ *n* : a watch having a hand or a digital display that can be started and stopped at will for exact timing (as of a race)

stor·able \'stōr-ə-bəl, 'stȯr-\ *adj* : suitable for storage : capable of being stored ⟨*storable* commodities⟩

stor·age \'stōr-ij, 'stȯr-\ *n* **1 a** : space or a place for storing **b** : an amount stored **c** : MEMORY 4a **2 a** : the act of storing : the state of being stored **b** : the price charged for storing something

storage battery *n* : a cell or connected group of cells that converts chemical energy into electrical energy by reversible chemical reactions and that may be recharged by passing a current through it in the direction opposite to that of its discharge — called also *storage cell*

sto·rax \'stōr-ˌaks, 'stȯr-\ *n* **1** : a resin related to benzoin and formerly used in incense **2** : a fragrant balsam from either of two trees related to the witch hazels that is sometimes used in perfumery [Late Latin, from Latin *styrax*, from Greek]

[1]store \'stōr, 'stȯr\ *vt* **1** : to lay away : ACCUMULATE ⟨*store* vegetables for winter use⟩ **2** : FURNISH, SUPPLY ⟨*store* a ship with provisions⟩ **3 a** : to deposit in a place (as a warehouse) for safekeeping or disposal ⟨*stored* my furniture until I found a new apartment⟩ **b** : to place (as data) in a computer for later use **4** : to provide storage room for : HOLD ⟨elevators for *storing* surplus wheat⟩ [Medieval French *estorer* "to establish, restore, supply," from Latin *instaurare* "to resume, restore"]

[2]store *n* **1** *pl* : accumulated supplies (as of food) ⟨a ship's *stores*⟩ **2** : something stored : STOCK ⟨a *store* of good jokes⟩ **3** : VALUE 3, IMPORTANCE ⟨a family that set great *store* by tradition⟩ **4** : a place where goods are sold : SHOP — **in store** : in readiness : WAITING ⟨there's trouble *in store* for you⟩

[3]store *adj* : purchased from a store : READY-MADE ⟨*store* clothes⟩ ⟨*store* bread⟩

store cheese *n* : CHEDDAR

store·front \'stōr-ˌfrənt, 'stȯr-\ *n* **1** : the front side of a store or store building facing a street **2** : a building, room, or group of rooms having a storefront — **storefront** *adj*

storefront church *n* : a city church that uses storefront facilities as a meeting place

store·house \'stōr-ˌhau̇s, 'stȯr-\ *n* **1** : a building for storing

goods : WAREHOUSE **2 :** an abundant supply or source : REPOSITORY ⟨a *storehouse* of knowledge⟩
store•keep•er \-ˌkē-pər\ *n* **1 :** one that is in charge of supplies **2 :** one who manages a retail store
store•room \-ˌrüm, -ˌru̇m\ *n* **:** a room in which goods are stored
store•wide \-ˈwīd\ *adj* **:** including all or most merchandise in a store ⟨a *storewide* sale⟩
¹sto•ried \ˈstōr-ēd, ˈstȯr-\ *adj* **1 :** decorated with designs representing scenes from story or history ⟨a *storied* tapestry⟩ **2 :** having an interesting history : celebrated in story or history ⟨a *storied* castle⟩
²storied *or* **sto•reyed** *adj* **:** having stories ⟨a two-*storied* house⟩
stork \ˈstȯrk\ *n* **:** any of various large mostly African and Asian wading birds that have a long stout bill and are related to the herons and ibises [Old English *storc*]

stork

storks•bill \ˈstȯrks-ˌbil\ *n* **:** any of several plants related to the geraniums and having long beaked fruits
¹storm \ˈstȯrm\ *n* **1 a :** a disturbance of the atmosphere accompanied by wind and usually by rain, snow, hail, sleet, or thunder and lightning **b :** a heavy fall of rain, snow, or hail **c :** wind having a speed of 64 to 72 miles (about 103 to 116 kilometers) per hour **d :** a serious disturbance of any element of nature — compare MAGNETIC STORM **2 :** a disturbed or agitated state : a sudden or violent commotion **3 :** a sudden heavy influx or onset **4 :** a heavy discharge of objects (as missiles) **5 :** a tumultuous outburst ⟨a *storm* of protests⟩ **6 :** a violent assault on a defended position [Old English] — **by storm :** by or as if by employing a bold swift frontal movement especially with the intent of defeating or winning over quickly ⟨took the fashion world *by storm*⟩ — **up a storm :** in a remarkable or energetic fashion — used as an intensifier ⟨dancing *up a storm*⟩
²storm *vb* **1 a :** to blow with violence **b :** to rain, hail, snow, or sleet heavily **2 :** to attack by storm ⟨*stormed* ashore at zero hour⟩ ⟨*storm* the fort⟩ **3 :** to show violent emotion : RAGE ⟨*storming* at the delay⟩ **4 :** to rush about violently ⟨the mob *stormed* through the streets⟩ ***synonyms*** see ATTACK
storm•bound \-ˌbau̇nd\ *adj* **:** cut off from outside communication by a storm or its effects : stopped or delayed by storms
storm door *n* **:** an additional door placed outside an ordinary outside door for protection against severe weather
storm petrel *n* **:** any of various small dark petrels that typically return to land only to nest usually in burrows — called also *Mother Carey's chicken*
storm trooper *n* **:** a member of a private Nazi army noted for aggressiveness, violence, and brutality
storm window *n* **:** a framed glass window placed outside an ordinary window as a protection against severe weather — called also *storm sash*
stormy \ˈstȯr-mē\ *adj* **storm•i•er; -est 1 :** relating to, characterized by, or indicative of a storm ⟨a *stormy* day⟩ ⟨*stormy* skies⟩ **2 :** marked by turmoil or fury : PASSIONATE, TURBULENT ⟨a *stormy* life⟩ — **storm•i•ly** \-mə-lē\ *adv* — **storm•i•ness** \-mē-nəs\ *n*
stormy petrel *n* **1 :** STORM PETREL **2 :** a person who is fond of conflict or disagreement
¹sto•ry \ˈstōr-ē, ˈstȯr-\ *n, pl* **stories 1 a :** an account of incidents or events **b :** ANECDOTE **2 a :** a fictional narrative shorter than a novel; *esp* **:** SHORT STORY **b :** the plot of a narrative or dramatic work **3 :** a widely circulated rumor **4 :** FALSEHOOD 1, LIE **5 :** LEGEND 1a, ROMANCE **6 :** a news article or broadcast [Medieval French *estoire, estorie* "story, history," from Latin *historia*]
²story *vt* **sto•ried; sto•ry•ing 1** *archaic* **:** to narrate or describe in story **2 :** to adorn with a story or a scene from history
³story *also* **sto•rey** *n, pl* **stories** *also* **storeys 1 :** a set of rooms on one floor level of a building **2 :** a horizontal division of a building's exterior not necessarily corresponding exactly with the stories within [Medieval Latin *historia* "narrative, illustration, story of a building," from Latin, "tale, history"; probably from narrative friezes on the window level of medieval buildings]
sto•ry•book \ˈstōr-ē-ˌbu̇k, ˈstȯr-\ *n* **:** a book of stories (as for children)
sto•ry•tell•er \-ˌtel-ər\ *n* **:** a teller of stories: as **a :** a relator of anecdotes **b :** a reciter of tales (as in a children's library) **c :** one that tells lies : FIBBER **d :** a writer of stories — **sto•ry•tell•ing** \-ˌtel-iŋ\ *n*
stoup \ˈstüp\ *n* **1 :** a container (as a large glass or a tankard) for beverages **2 :** a basin for holy water at the entrance of a church [Middle English *stowp,* probably of Scandinavian origin]
¹stout \ˈstau̇t\ *adj* **1 :** strong of character: as **a :** BOLD 1a, BRAVE **b :** firmly resolute : DETERMINED **2 a :** physically strong : POWERFUL **b :** STURDY 2a, VIGOROUS **c :** sturdily constructed : SOLID ⟨*stout* boots⟩ **3 :** full of energy : FORCEFUL ⟨a *stout* attack⟩ **4 :** bulky in body : OVERWEIGHT [Medieval French *estout,* of Germanic origin] ***synonyms*** see STRONG — **stout•ish** \ˈstau̇t-ish\ *adj* — **stout•ly** *adv* — **stout•ness** *n*
²stout *n* **1 :** a heavy-bodied dark brew made with a malty flavor **2 a :** an overweight person **b :** a clothing size for the large figure
stout•en \ˈstau̇t-n\ *vb* **stout•ened; stout•en•ing** \ˈstau̇t-niŋ, -n-iŋ\ **:** to make or become stout
stout•heart•ed \stau̇t-ˈhärt-əd\ *adj* **:** COURAGEOUS, BOLD — **stout•heart•ed•ly** *adv* — **stout•heart•ed•ness** *n*
¹stove \ˈstōv\ *n* **1 :** an apparatus that burns fuel or uses electricity to provide heat (as for cooking or heating) **2 :** KILN [early Dutch or Low German, "heated room"]
²stove *past and past participle of* STAVE
stove•pipe \ˈstōv-ˌpīp\ *n* **1 :** a metal pipe for carrying off smoke from a stove **2 :** a tall silk hat
sto•ver \ˈstō-vər\ *n* **:** dried stalks of corn with the ears removed that are used as feed for livestock [Medieval French *estovers* "necessary supplies," from *estove* "to be necessary," derived from Latin *est opus* "there is need"]
stow \ˈstō\ *vt* **1 :** HOUSE 1a, LODGE **2 :** to put away : STORE ⟨*stowed* their belongings in the closet⟩ **3 a :** to dispose in an orderly fashion : ARRANGE, PACK ⟨quickly *stowed* the cargo⟩ **b :** to fill with cargo : LOAD ⟨*stowed* the ships to capacity⟩ **4** *slang* **:** to put aside : STOP — usually used in the phrase *stow it* **5 :** to eat or drink up — usually used with *away* ⟨*stowed* away a large dinner⟩ [Middle English *stowen* "to place," from *stowe* "place," from Old English *stōw*]
stow•age \ˈstō-ij\ *n* **1 a :** an act or process of stowing **b :** goods stowed or to be stowed **2 a :** storage capacity **b :** a place for storage **3 :** STORAGE 2a
stow•away \ˈstō-ə-ˌwā\ *n* **:** one that stows away
stow away \ˌstō-ə-ˈwā, ˈstō-ə-ˌ\ *vi* **:** to conceal oneself aboard a vehicle as a way to obtain transportation
STP \ˌes-ˌtē-ˈpē\ *n* **:** a powerful hallucinogenic drug that is chemically related to amphetamine [from *STP,* a trademark for a motor fuel additive]
stra•bis•mus \strə-ˈbiz-məs\ *n* **:** an eye disorder in which the two eyes cannot be directed to the same point because of an imbalance of the muscles of the eyeball [Greek *strabismos* "condition of squinting," from *strabizein* "to squint," from *strabos* "squint-eyed"] — **stra•bis•mic** \-mik\ *adj*
¹strad•dle \ˈstrad-l\ *vb* **strad•dled; strad•dling** \ˈstrad-liŋ, -l-iŋ\ **1 :** to part the legs wide : stand, sit, or walk with the legs wide apart **2 :** to stand, sit, or be astride of ⟨*straddle* a horse⟩ **3 :** to spread out irregularly : SPRAWL ⟨branches *straddled* in every direction⟩ **4 :** to be noncommittal : favor or seem to favor two apparently opposite sides ⟨*straddle* an issue⟩ [akin to *stride*] — **strad•dler** \ˈstrad-lər, -l-ər\ *n*
²straddle *n* **1 :** the act or position of one that straddles **2 :** a noncommittal or uncertain position
strafe \ˈstrāf\ *vt* **:** to fire on (as troops) at close range and especially with machine guns from low-flying airplanes [German

\ə\ **abut**	\au̇\ **out**	\i\ **tip**	\ȯ\ **saw**	\u̇\ **foot**
\ər\ **further**	\ch\ **chin**	\ī\ **life**	\ȯi\ **coin**	\y\ **yet**
\a\ **mat**	\e\ **pet**	\j\ **job**	\th\ **thin**	\yü\ **few**
\ā\ **take**	\ē\ **easy**	\ng\ **sing**	\t͟h\ **this**	\yu̇\ **cure**
\ä\ **cot, cart**	\g\ **go**	\ō\ **bone**	\ü\ **food**	\zh\ **vision**

Gott strafe England "God punish England," propaganda slogan during World War I] — **straf·er** *n*

strag·gle \ˈstrag-əl\ *vi* **strag·gled; strag·gling** \ˈstrag-ling, -ə-ling\ **1 :** to wander from a direct course or way : ROVE, STRAY **2 :** to trail off from others of its kind : spread out irregularly ⟨little cabins *straggling* off into the woods⟩ [Middle English *straglen*] — **strag·gler** \-lər, -ə-lər\ *n*

strag·gly \ˈstrag-lē, -ə-lē\ *adj* **strag·gli·er; -est :** spread out or scattered irregularly ⟨a *straggly* beard⟩

¹straight \ˈstrāt\ *adj* **1 a :** free from curves, bends, angles, or irregularities ⟨*straight* hair⟩ ⟨*straight* timber⟩ **b :** generated by a point moving continuously in the same direction ⟨a *straight* line⟩ **2 a :** lying along or holding to a direct or proper course or method ⟨a *straight* thinker⟩ **b :** CANDID, FRANK ⟨a *straight* answer⟩ **c :** coming directly from a trustworthy source ⟨a *straight* tip on the horses⟩ **d :** made up of elements arranged in a logical order; *also* **:** CONSECUTIVE ⟨five *straight* hours⟩ **e :** VERTICAL 2, UPRIGHT ⟨the picture isn't quite *straight*⟩ **3 a :** JUST, FAIR ⟨*straight* dealings⟩ **b :** properly ordered or arranged ⟨set the kitchen *straight*⟩; *also* **:** CORRECT ⟨get the facts *straight*⟩ **c :** free from extraneous matter ⟨*straight* whiskey⟩ **d :** making no exceptions in one's support of a party ⟨vote a *straight* ticket⟩ **e :** not deviating from the general norm or prescribed pattern ⟨a *straight* dramatic part⟩ **f :** CONVENTIONAL 1; *also* **:** SQUARE 6 **g :** not using or under the influence of drugs **h :** HETEROSEXUAL **4 :** being the only form of financial compensation ⟨salespeople on *straight* commission⟩ [Middle English, from past participle of *strecchen* "to stretch"] — **straight·ness** *n*

²straight *adv* **:** in a straight manner, course, or line ⟨came *straight* home from school⟩

³straight *n* **1 :** something that is straight: as **a :** a straight line or arrangement **b :** STRAIGHTAWAY; *esp* **:** HOMESTRETCH **c :** a true or honest report or course **2 a :** a sequence (as of shots, strokes, or moves) resulting in a perfect score in a game or contest **b :** first place at the finish of a horse race : WIN **3 :** a combination of five cards in sequence but not of the same suit in a poker hand **4 :** a conventional person

straight angle *n* **:** an angle whose sides lie in opposite directions from the vertex in the same straight line and that equals two right angles

straight–arm \ˈstrāt-ˌärm\ *vb* **:** to ward off a person or thing by pushing with the palm of the hand with the arm held straight — **straight–arm** *n*

¹straight·away \ˈstrāt-ə-ˌwā\ *adj* **1 :** proceeding in a straight line : continuous in direction : STRAIGHTFORWARD **2 :** IMMEDIATE ⟨made a *straightaway* reply⟩

²straightaway *n* **:** a straight course: as **a :** the straight part of a closed racecourse : STRETCH **b :** a straight and unimpeded stretch of road or way

³straight·away \ˌstrāt-ə-ˈwā\ *adv* **:** without hesitation or delay : IMMEDIATELY ⟨found an answer *straightaway*⟩

straight·edge \ˈstrāt-ˌej\ *n* **:** a bar of wood, metal, or plastic with a straight edge for testing straight lines and surfaces or for cutting along or drawing straight lines

straight·en \ˈstrāt-n\ *vb* **straight·ened; straight·en·ing** \ˈstrāt-ning, -n-ing\ **:** to make or become straight — usually used with *up* or *out* ⟨*straighten* up a room⟩ ⟨*straightened* out my accounts⟩ — **straight·en·er** \ˈstrāt-nər, -n-ər\ *n*

straight face *n* **:** a face showing no emotion and especially no merriment — **straight–faced** \ˈstrāt-ˈfāst\ *adj*

straight flush *n* **:** a combination of five cards of the same suit in sequence in a poker hand

¹straight·for·ward \strāt-ˈfȯr-wərd, ˈstrāt-\ *adj* **1 a :** OUTSPOKEN, CANDID ⟨a *straightforward* reply⟩ **b :** CLEAR-CUT 2, UNMISTAKABLE ⟨a *straightforward* responsibility⟩ **2 :** proceeding in a straight course or manner : DIRECT, UNDEVIATING — **straight·for·ward·ly** *adv* — **straight·for·ward·ness** *n*

²straight·for·ward *also* **straight·for·wards** \-wərdz\ *adv* **:** in a straightforward way

straight man *n* **:** an entertainer who feeds lines to a comedian

straight off *adv* **:** at once : IMMEDIATELY

straight razor *n* **:** a razor with a rigid cutting blade hinged to a case that forms a handle when the razor is open for use

straight·way \ˈstrāt-ˌwā, -ˈwā\ *adv* **1 :** in a direct course : DIRECTLY ⟨fell *straightway* down the stairs⟩ **2 :** RIGHT AWAY, IMMEDIATELY ⟨*straightway* the clouds began to part⟩

¹strain \ˈstrān\ *n* **1 a :** LINEAGE, ANCESTRY **b :** a group of plants or animals that look alike but have characteristics (as the ability to resist disease) that make them slightly different **c :** VARIETY 3b ⟨a high-yielding *strain* of winter wheat⟩ **c :** SORT 1, KIND ⟨discussions of a lofty *strain*⟩ **2 a :** inherited or inherent character, quality, or disposition ⟨a *strain* of genius in the family⟩ **b :** TRACE, STREAK ⟨a *strain* of sadness in the story⟩ **3 a :** TUNE 1b, MELODY **b :** a passage of verbal or musical expression **4 a :** the general tone of an utterance or of a course of action or conduct **b :** TEMPER 4c, MOOD [Middle English *streen* "progeny, lineage," from Old English *strēon* "gain, acquisition"]

²strain *vb* **1 a :** to draw tight : cause to clasp firmly **b :** to stretch to maximum extension and tautness **2 a :** to exert oneself to the utmost : STRIVE **b :** to injure or undergo injury by overuse, misuse, or excessive pressure ⟨*strain* one's back by lifting⟩ **c :** to cause a change of form or size in (a body) by application of external force **3 :** to squeeze or clasp tightly: as **a :** HUG 1 **b :** to compress painfully : CONSTRICT **4 a :** to pass or cause to pass through or as if through a strainer : FILTER **b :** to remove by straining ⟨*strain* lumps out of the gravy⟩ **5 :** to stretch beyond a proper limit ⟨*strain* the truth⟩ **6 :** to make great difficulty or resistance : BALK ⟨a horse *straining* at the lead⟩ [Medieval French *estreindre,* from Latin *stringere*]

³strain *n* **:** an act of straining or the condition of being strained: as **a :** excessive physical or mental tension; *also* **:** a force, influence, or factor causing such tension ⟨a *strain* on the friendship⟩ **b :** bodily injury from excessive tension, effort, or use ⟨heart *strain*⟩; *esp* **:** one resulting from a wrench or twist and involving undue stretching of muscles or ligaments ⟨back *strain*⟩ **c :** deformation of a material body under the action of applied forces

synonyms STRAIN, SPRAIN mean damage to muscles or tendons through overstretching or overexertion. STRAIN may apply to any part of the body ⟨*strained* my back and arms moving the piano⟩. SPRAIN applies chiefly to the tearing of ligaments at a joint by sharp wrenching or twisting ⟨*sprained* my ankle⟩.

strained \ˈstrānd\ *adj* **1 :** FORCED ⟨a *strained* smile⟩ **2 :** pushed by antagonism near to open conflict ⟨*strained* relations between countries⟩

strain·er \ˈstrā-nər\ *n* **:** one that strains; *esp* **:** a device (as a screen, sieve, or filter) to retain solid pieces while a liquid passes through

¹strait \ˈstrāt\ *adj* **1** *archaic* **a :** NARROW 1 **b :** limited in space or time **c :** closely fitting : TIGHT **2** *archaic* **:** RIGOROUS, EXACTING **3 a :** causing distress : DIFFICULT **b :** limited as to means or resources [Medieval French *estreit,* from Latin *strictus* "strait, strict"] — **strait·ly** *adv* — **strait·ness** *n*

²strait *n* **1 a** *archaic* **:** a narrow space or passage **b :** a comparatively narrow passageway connecting two large bodies of water — often used in plural **c :** ISTHMUS **2 :** a situation of perplexity or distress — often used in plural ⟨in dire *straits*⟩

strait·en \ˈstrāt-n\ *vt* **strait·ened; strait·en·ing** \ˈstrāt-ning, -n-ing\ **1 a :** to make strait or narrow **b :** to hem in : CONFINE **2** *archaic* **:** to restrict in freedom or scope : HAMPER **3 :** to subject to distress, privation, or deficiency ⟨in *straitened* circumstances⟩

strait·jack·et *also* **straight·jack·et** \ˈstrāt-ˌjak-ət\ *n* **:** a cover or overgarment of strong material (as canvas) used to bind the body and especially the arms closely in restraining a violent prisoner or patient

strait·laced *or* **straight·laced** \ˈstrāt-ˈlāst\ *adj* **:** excessively strict in manners, morals, or opinion — **strait·laced·ly** \-ˈlā-səd-lē, -lās-tlē\ *adv* — **strait·laced·ness** \-ˈlāst-nəs, -ˈlās-; -ˈlā-səd-nəs\ *n*

strake \ˈstrāk\ *n* **:** a continuous band of hull planking or plates on a ship; *also* **:** the width of such a band [Middle English]

stra·mo·ni·um \strə-ˈmō-nē-əm\ *n* **:** the dried leaves of the jimsonweed that contain poisonous substances (as atropine) used in medicine (as to treat asthma) [New Latin, "jimsonweed"]

¹strand \ˈstrand\ *n* **:** the land bordering a body of water : SHORE, BEACH [Old English]

²strand *vb* **1 :** to run, drive, or cause to drift onto a strand : run aground : BEACH ⟨boats *stranded* by the storm⟩ **2 :** to leave in a strange or an unfavorable place especially without funds or means to depart ⟨*stranded* in a strange city⟩

³strand *n* **1 :** one of the threads, strings, or wires twisted to make a cord, rope, or cable **2 :** an elongated or twisted and plaited body resembling a rope ⟨a *strand* of pearls⟩ **3 :** something (as a chain of molecules) resembling a strand ⟨a *strand* of DNA⟩ **4 :** one of the elements of a complex whole ⟨the *strands* of a legal argument⟩ [Middle English *strond*]

[4]**strand** *vt* **1** : to form (as a rope) from strands **2** : to play out, twist, or arrange in a strand

strand·ed \'stran-dəd\ *adj* : having a strand or strands especially of a specified kind or number — usually used in combination ⟨double-*stranded* DNA⟩

strange \'strānj\ *adj* **1 a** *archaic* : FOREIGN 2 **b** : not native to or naturally belonging in a place : of external origin, kind, or character **2 a** : not known, heard, or seen before ⟨*strange* surroundings⟩ **b** : causing surprise or wonder : UNUSUAL, BIZARRE ⟨*strange* clothes⟩ **3** : ill at ease ⟨feel *strange* on your first day in school⟩ [Medieval French *estrange,* from Latin *extraneus,* literally, "external," from *extra* "outside"] — **strange·ly** *adv* — **strange·ness** *n*

synonyms STRANGE, PECULIAR, ODD, OUTLANDISH mean departing from what is ordinary, usual, or to be expected. STRANGE emphasizes unfamiliarity and may apply to what is foreign or unnatural or unaccountable ⟨*strange* behavior⟩. PECULIAR implies a marked distinctiveness ⟨a *peculiar* taste⟩. ODD applies to a departure from the regular or expected ⟨an *odd* sense of humor⟩. OUTLANDISH implies a strangeness that is strikingly out of the ordinary ⟨*outlandish* clothes⟩.

strang·er \'strān-jər\ *n* **1** : one who is strange: as **a** : FOREIGNER **b** : one in the house of another as a guest, visitor, or intruder **c** : a person or thing that is unknown or with whom one is unacquainted **d** : one who does not belong to or is kept from the activities of a group **2** : one ignorant of or unacquainted with someone or something ⟨a *stranger* to good manners⟩

stran·gle \'strang-gəl\ *vb* **stran·gled; stran·gling** \-gə-ling, -gling\ **1 a** : to choke to death by squeezing the throat **b** : to obstruct seriously or fatally the normal breathing of **2** : to suppress or hinder the rise, expression, or growth of ⟨the rules were *strangling* my creativity⟩ **3** : to become strangled **4** : to die by or as if by interference with breathing [Medieval French *estrangler,* from Latin *strangulare,* from Greek *strangalan,* from *strangalē* "halter"] — **stran·gler** \-gə-lər, -glər\ *n*

stran·gle·hold \'strang-gəl-ˌhōld\ *n* **1** : an illegal wrestling hold by which one's opponent is choked **2** : a force or influence that chokes or suppresses freedom of movement or expression

stran·gu·late \'strang-gyə-ˌlāt\ *vb* **1** : STRANGLE 1 **2** : to become constricted so as to stop circulation ⟨a hernia may *strangulate*⟩ [Latin *strangulare*]

stran·gu·la·tion \ˌstrang-gyə-'lā-shən\ *n* **1** : an act or process of strangling or strangulating **2** : the state of being strangled or strangulated

[1]**strap** \'strap\ *n* **1** : a band, plate, or loop of metal for binding objects together or for clamping an object in position **2 a** : a narrow usually flat strip or thong of a flexible material and especially leather used variously (as for securing, holding together, or wrapping) **b** : something made of a strap forming a loop ⟨a boot *strap*⟩ **c** : a strip of leather used for flogging **d** : STROP [alteration of *strop*] — **strap·py** \'strap-ē\ *adj*

[2]**strap** *vt* **strapped; strap·ping** **1 a** : to secure with or attach by means of a strap **b** : BIND, CONSTRICT **c** : to support (as a sprained joint) with strips of adhesive plaster **2** : to beat or punish with a strap **3** : STROP **4** : to cause to suffer from an extreme scarcity ⟨I'm *strapped* for cash⟩

strap·hang·er \'strap-ˌhang-ər\ *n* : a standing passenger in a subway, streetcar, bus, or train who clings for support to one of the devices (as short straps) placed along the aisle

strap·less \-ləs\ *adj* : having no strap; *esp* : made or worn without shoulder straps ⟨a *strapless* gown⟩

strap·per \'strap-ər\ *n* : one that is unusually large or robust

strap·ping \'strap-ing\ *adj* : having a vigorously sturdy constitution : ROBUST ⟨a *strapping* young man⟩

strat·a·gem \'strat-ə-jəm\ *n* **1 a** : a trick in war for deceiving and outwitting the enemy **b** : a cleverly contrived trick or scheme for gaining an end **2** : skill in ruses or trickery [Italian *stratagemma,* from Latin *strategema,* from Greek *stratēgēma,* from *stratēgein* "to be a general, maneuver," from *stratēgos* "general"] ***synonyms*** see TRICK

stra·te·gic \strə-'tē-jik\ *adj* **1** : of, relating to, or marked by strategy ⟨a *strategic* retreat⟩ **2 a** : required for the conduct of war ⟨*strategic* materials⟩ **b** : of great importance within an integrated whole or to a planned effect ⟨emphasized the *strategic* points of the argument⟩ **3** : designed or trained to strike at the sources of an enemy's power ⟨*strategic* bombers⟩ — **stra·te·gi·cal** \-ji-kəl\ *adj* — **stra·te·gi·cal·ly** \-ji-kə-lē, -klē\ *adv*

strat·e·gist \'strat-ə-jəst\ *n* : one skilled in strategy

strat·e·gize \-ˌjīz\ *vi* : to devise a strategy or course of action ⟨*strategized* with her teammates⟩

strat·e·gy \'strat-ə-jē\ *n, pl* **-gies** **1 a (1)** : the science and art of using the political, economic, psychological, and military forces of a country so as to support adopted policies in peace or war **(2)** : the science and art of military command exercised to meet the enemy in combat under advantageous conditions **b** : a variety of or instance of the use of strategy **2 a** : a careful plan or method : STRATAGEM **b** : the art of devising or employing plans or stratagems to achieve a goal **3** : an adaptation or group of adaptations (as of behavior or structure) that serves or appears to serve an important function in achieving evolutionary success ⟨foraging *strategies* of insects⟩ [Greek *stratēgia* "generalship," from *stratēgos* "general," from *stratos* "army" + *agein* "to lead"]

synonyms STRATEGY, TACTICS mean a planned out method or action to reach one's goals. STRATEGY applies to the devising of a general plan of attack, defense, or action so as to achieve an end with the forces or means available ⟨attempting to trade blows at close range with a stronger hitter is a mistake in *strategy*⟩. TACTICS applies to the technique of utilizing forces properly or skillfully in action or combat ⟨failing to protect the jaw is poor boxing *tactics*⟩.

strath \'strath\ *n* : a flat wide river valley or the low-lying grassland along it [Scottish Gaelic *srath*]

strat·i·fy \'strat-ə-ˌfī\ *vb* **-fied; -fy·ing** **1** : to form, deposit, or arrange in strata ⟨*stratified* rock⟩ **2** : to divide or arrange into classes, castes, or social strata ⟨a society *stratified* by custom⟩ **3** : to become arranged in strata — **strat·i·fi·ca·tion** \ˌstrat-ə-fə-'kā-shən\ *n*

stra·tig·ra·phy \strə-'tig-rə-fē\ *n* **1** : geology that deals with the origin, composition, distribution, and succession of strata **2** : the arrangement of strata — **strat·i·graph·ic** \ˌstrat-ə-'graf-ik\ *adj*

stra·to·cu·mu·lus \ˌstrāt-ō-'kyü-myə-ləs, ˌstrat-\ *n* : stratified cumulus consisting of large balls or rolls of dark cloud which often cover the whole sky especially in winter

strato·sphere \'strat-ə-ˌsfiər\ *n* : the upper portion of the earth's atmosphere extending from the top of the troposphere to about 30 miles (50 kilometers) above the surface and in which temperature changes but little with altitude and clouds of water are rare [French *stratosphère,* from New Latin *stratum* "stratum" + French *sphère* "sphere"] — **strato·spher·ic** \ˌstrat-ə-'sfiər-ik, -'sfer-\ *adj*

stra·to·vol·ca·no \-väl-'kā-nō, -vȯl-\ *n* : a volcano composed of explosively erupted cinders and ash with occasional lava flows

stra·tum \'strāt-əm, 'strat-\ *n, pl* **stra·ta** \-ə\ **1** : a layer of a substance; *esp* : one having parallel layers of other kinds lying above or below or both above and below it ⟨a rock *stratum*⟩ ⟨a cold *stratum* in a lake⟩ ⟨the deep *stratum* of the skin⟩ **2 a** : a stage of historical or cultural development **b** : a level of society made up of persons with the same or similar social, economic, or cultural status [Latin, "spread, bed," from *sternere* "to spread out"]

stra·tus \'strāt-əs, 'strat-\ *n, pl* **stra·ti** \'strāt-ˌī, 'strat-\ : a cloud form extending horizontally over a relatively large area at altitudes of usually 2000 to 7000 feet (600 to 2100 meters) [Latin, past participle of *sternere* "to spread out"]

[1]**straw** \'strȯ\ *n* **1 a** : stalks of grain after threshing; *also* : any dry stalky plant part used like grain straw (as for bedding or in packing) ⟨pine *straw*⟩ **b** : a natural or artificial heavy fiber used for weaving, plaiting, or braiding **2** : a dry coarse stem especially of a cereal grass **3 a (1)** : something of little value or significance ⟨not worth a *straw*⟩ **(2)** : something too insubstantial to give support or help in a desperate situation ⟨clutch at *straws*⟩ **b** : CHAFF 2 **4** : a tube (as of paper, plastic, or glass) for sucking up a beverage [Old English *strēaw*] — **strawy** \'strȯ-i, 'strȯi\ *adj*

[2]**straw** *adj* **1 a** : made of straw ⟨a *straw* hat⟩ **b** : of, relating to, or used for straw ⟨a *straw* barn⟩ **2** : of the color of straw **3** : of little or no value : WORTHLESS

\ə\ abut	\au̇\ out	\i\ tip	\ȯ\ saw	\u̇\ foot
\ər\ further	\ch\ chin	\ī\ life	\ȯi\ coin	\y\ yet
\a\ mat	\e\ pet	\j\ job	\th\ thin	\yü\ few
\ā\ take	\ē\ easy	\ng\ sing	\th\ this	\yu̇\ cure
\ä\ cot, cart	\g\ go	\ō\ bone	\ü\ food	\zh\ vision

straw·ber·ry \ˈstrȯ-ˌber-ē, -bə-rē, -brē\ *n* **:** an edible juicy red fruit of a low-growing white-flowered herb related to the roses and having long slender runners; *also* **:** a plant that bears strawberries — **strawberry** *adj*

strawberry

strawberry mark *n* **:** a usually red and elevated birthmark that is a small tumor of a blood vessel

strawberry roan *n* **:** a roan horse with a light red base color

straw boss *n* **:** a foreman of a small group of workers

straw·flow·er \ˈstrȯ-ˌflau̇-ər, -ˌflau̇r\ *n* **:** any of several plants having everlasting flowers

straw·hat \ˌstrȯ-ˌhat\ *adj* **:** of, relating to, or being a summer theater [from the former fashion of wearing straw hats in summer]

straw man *n* **1 :** a weak or imaginary argument or adversary set up only to be easily refuted **2 :** a person set up to serve as a cover for a usually questionable transaction

straw vote *n* **:** an unofficial vote to test the relative strength of opposing candidates or issues — called also *straw poll*

[1]**stray** \ˈstrā\ *n* **1 :** a domestic animal wandering at large or lost **2 :** a person or thing that strays **:** STRAGGLER, WAIF

[2]**stray** *vi* **1 :** to wander from company, restraint, or proper limits ⟨the dog *strayed* from the yard⟩ **2 a :** to wander from a fixed or chosen route or at random **b :** to become distracted from an argument or train of thought ⟨*strayed* from the point⟩ **c :** ERR 2 [Medieval French *estraier,* derived from Latin *extra-* "outside" + *vagari* "to wander"] — **stray·er** *n*

[3]**stray** *adj* **1 :** having strayed or escaped from a proper or intended place ⟨a *stray* dog⟩ ⟨fixed a few *stray* hairs⟩ **2 :** occurring at random or as detached individuals ⟨*stray* remarks⟩

[1]**streak** \ˈstrēk\ *n* **1 :** a line or mark that is not the same color or texture as its background **2 a :** the color of the fine powder of a mineral obtained by scratching or rubbing against a hard white surface **b :** microorganisms implanted in a line on a solid culture medium **3 a :** a narrow band of light **b :** a lightning bolt **4 a :** QUALITY 4 ⟨a mean *streak*⟩ **b :** a brief run (as of luck) **c :** a consecutive series ⟨a winning *streak*⟩ **5 :** a narrow layer ⟨a *streak* of fat in bacon⟩ [Old English *strica*]

[2]**streak** *vb* **1 :** to make streaks on or in **2 :** to move swiftly **:** RUSH ⟨a jet *streaking* across the sky⟩

streak camera *n* **:** a camera for recording very fast or short-lived phenomena (as fluorescence or shock waves)

streaked \ˈstrēkt, ˈstrē-kəd\ *adj* **:** marked with stripes or linear discolorations

streaky \ˈstrē-kē\ *adj* **streak·i·er; -est 1 :** marked with streaks **2 :** likely to vary **:** CHANGEABLE ⟨a *streaky* hitter in baseball⟩ — **streak·i·ness** *n*

[1]**stream** \ˈstrēm\ *n* **1 :** a body of running water (as a river or brook) flowing on the earth; *also* **:** a body of flowing fluid (as water or gas) **2 a :** a steady succession ⟨an endless *stream* of chatter⟩ **b :** a constantly renewed supply ⟨a *stream* of revenue⟩ **c :** a continuous moving procession ⟨a *stream* of traffic⟩ **3 :** an unbroken flow (as of gas or particles of matter) **4 :** a ray or beam of light **5 :** a dominant attitude, group, or line of development ⟨going against the *stream*⟩ [Old English *strēam*]

[2]**stream** *vb* **1 a :** to flow or cause to flow in or as if in a stream **b :** to leave a bright trail **2 a :** to give off a bodily fluid in large amounts ⟨her eyes were *streaming*⟩ **b :** to become wet with a discharge of bodily fluid ⟨*streaming* with perspiration⟩ **3 :** to trail out at full length ⟨hair *streaming* behind her⟩ **4 :** to pour in large numbers ⟨complaints came *streaming* in⟩ **5 :** to display fully extended **6 :** to transfer (digital data, such as audio or video material) in a continuous stream especially for immediate processing or playback

stream·er \ˈstrē-mər\ *n* **1 a :** a flag that streams in the wind; *esp* **:** PENNANT **b :** a long narrow wavy strip like or suggesting a banner floating in the wind **c :** BANNER 2 **2** *pl* **:** AURORA BOREALIS

stream·ing \-miŋ\ *adj* **:** relating to or being the transfer of data (as audio or video material) in a continuous stream especially for immediate processing or playback

stream·let \ˈstrēm-lət\ *n* **:** a small stream

stream·line \ˈstrēm-ˌlīn\ *vt* **1 :** to design or construct with a contour for decreasing resistance to motion through water or air or as if for this purpose **2 :** to bring up to date **:** MODERNIZE **3 :** to make simpler or more efficient

stream·lined \-ˌlīnd\ *adj* **1 a :** contoured to reduce resistance to motion through water or air or as if for this purpose **b :** stripped of nonessentials **2 :** brought up to date

[1]**street** \ˈstrēt\ *n* **1 a :** a thoroughfare especially in a city, town, or village usually including sidewalks and being wider than an alley or lane **b :** the part of a street reserved for vehicles **c :** a thoroughfare and the property along it ⟨lived on Maple *Street*⟩ **2 :** the people occupying property on a street ⟨the whole *street* was excited⟩ [Old English *strǣt,* from Late Latin *strata* "paved road," from Latin *stratus,* past participle of *sternere* "to spread out"]

[2]**street** *adj* **1 :** of or relating to the street or streets ⟨a *street* door⟩ ⟨a *street* map⟩ ⟨*street* clothes⟩ **2 :** of or relating to the environment of the streets ⟨*street* people⟩

street·car \ˈstrēt-ˌkär\ *n* **:** a vehicle on rails used primarily for transporting passengers and typically operating on city streets

streetcar

street hockey *n* **:** a game similar to ice hockey played on a hard surface by players wearing shoes or roller skates and using hockey sticks and a small ball

street·light \-ˌlīt\ *n* **:** a light usually mounted on a pole that forms one in a series spaced at intervals along a public road

street railway *n* **:** a company operating streetcars or buses

street–smart \ˈstrēt-ˌsmärt\ *adj* **:** STREETWISE

street smarts *n pl* **:** the quality of being streetwise

street·wise \ˈstrēt-ˌwīz\ *adj* **:** having the knowledge needed to survive in difficult or dangerous places or situations in a city

strength \ˈstreŋth, ˈstreŋkth\ *n* **1 :** the quality or state of being strong **:** inherent power **2 :** power to resist force **:** SOLIDITY, TOUGHNESS **3 :** power of resisting attack **:** INVULNERABILITY **4 a :** legal, logical, or moral force **b :** a strong attribute or inherent asset ⟨list the *strengths* and weaknesses of the book⟩ **5 a :** degree of potency of effect or of concentration ⟨liquid cleaners in varying *strengths*⟩ **b :** intensity of light, color, sound, or odor **6 :** force as measured in numbers ⟨an army at full *strength*⟩ **7 :** SUPPORT ⟨has enough *strength* in the senate to pass the bill⟩ [Old English *strengthu*] ***synonyms*** see POWER

strength·en \ˈstreŋ-thən, ˈstreŋk-\ *vb* **strength·ened; strength·en·ing** \ˈstreŋth-niŋ, ˈstreŋkth-, -ə-niŋ\ **:** to make or become stronger — **strength·en·er** \ˈstreŋth-nər, ˈstreŋkth-, -ə-nər\ *n*

stren·u·os·i·ty \ˌstren-yə-ˈwäs-ət-ē\ *n* **:** the quality or state of being strenuous

stren·u·ous \ˈstren-yə-wəs\ *adj* **1 a :** vigorously active **:** ENERGETIC ⟨leads a *strenuous* life⟩ **b :** FERVENT, ZEALOUS ⟨*strenuous* protest⟩ **2 :** marked by or calling for energy or stamina **:** ARDUOUS ⟨*strenuous* work⟩ [Latin *strenuus*] ***synonyms*** see VIGOROUS — **stren·u·ous·ly** *adv* — **stren·u·ous·ness** *n*

strep \ˈstrep\ *n* **:** STREPTOCOCCUS

strep throat *n* **:** a sore throat that is marked by inflammation of the throat and pharynx and by fever and weakness and is cause by infection with streptococci

strep·to·ba·cil·lus \ˌstrep-tō-ba-ˈsil-əs\ *n* **:** any of various bacilli in which the individual cells are joined in a chain [New Latin, from Greek *streptos* "twisted, pliant" (from *strephein* "to twist, turn") + New Latin *bacillus*]

strep·to·coc·cus \ˌstrep-tə-ˈkäk-əs\ *n, pl* **-coc·ci** \-ˈkäk-ˌsī, -ˌī, -ˌsē, -ˌē\ **:** any of a genus of nonmotile mostly parasitic spherical bacteria that occur in pairs or chains and include important pathogens of humans and domestic animals [New Latin, from Greek *streptos* "twisted" + *kokkos* "grain, seed"] — **strep·to·coc·cal** \-ˈkäk-əl\ *adj*

strep·to·my·ces \ˌstrep-tə-ˈmī-ˌsēz\ *n, pl* **streptomyces :** any of a genus of mostly soil actinomycetes including some that form antibiotics as by-products of their metabolism [New Latin, from Greek *streptos* "twisted" + *mykēs* "fungus"]

strep·to·my·cin \ˌstrep-tə-ˈmīs-n\ *n* : an antibiotic produced by a soil streptomyces and used especially in the treatment of bacterial infections (as tuberculosis)

[1]**stress** \ˈstres\ *n* **1** : constraining force or influence: as **a** : a force that acts when one body or part of a body presses on, pulls on, pushes against, or tends to squeeze or twist another body or part of a body **b** : the change in shape caused in a body by such a force **c** : a physical, chemical, or emotional factor that induces bodily or mental tension and may be a factor in the causing of disease; *also* : a state of tension resulting from a stress **2** : EMPHASIS, WEIGHT ⟨lay *stress* on a point⟩ **3** : intensity of utterance given to a speech sound, syllable, or word **4** : relative force or prominence of sound in verse; *also* : a syllable having this stress **5** : ACCENT 6 [Middle English *stresse* "stress, distress," from *destresse,* from Medieval French] — **stress·less** \-ləs\ *adj* — **stress·less·ness** *n*

[2]**stress** *vb* **1** : to subject to physical or psychological stress ⟨*stressing* the equipment⟩ ⟨*stressed* by the traffic⟩ **2** : ACCENT ⟨*stress* the first syllable⟩ **3** : to lay stress on : EMPHASIZE ⟨*stressed* the importance of teamwork⟩ **4** : to feel stress ⟨*stressing* out about the big test⟩

stressed–out \ˈstrest-ˈau̇t\ *adj* : suffering from high levels of physical or especially psychological stress

stress fracture *n* : a usually hairline fracture of a bone that has been subjected to repeated stress

stress·ful \-fəl\ *adj* : full of or tending to induce stress — **stress·ful·ly** \-fə-lē\ *adv*

stress mark *n* : a mark used with (as before, after, or over) a written syllable in the respelling of a word to show that this syllable is to be stressed when spoken : ACCENT MARK

stress·or \ˈstres-ər, -ˌȯr\ *n* : a stimulus that causes stress

[1]**stretch** \ˈstrech\ *vb* **1** : to extend (as one's limbs or body) in a reclining position ⟨*stretch* oneself out on the bed⟩ **2** : to reach out : EXTEND ⟨*stretched* out her arm⟩ **3 a** : to extend or become extended in length or breadth or both : SPREAD ⟨*stretched* his neck to see what was going on⟩ **b** : to extend over a continuous period ⟨the dynasty *stretches* back several centuries⟩ **4** : to draw up (one's body) from a cramped, stooping, or relaxed position ⟨awoke and *stretched* myself⟩ **5** : to pull taut ⟨*stretch* the canvas on the frame⟩ **6 a** : to enlarge or distend especially by force **b** : to extend or expand as if by physical force ⟨*stretch* one's mind with a good book⟩ **c** : to make excessive demands on : STRAIN ⟨*stretched* her already thin patience⟩ **7** : to cause to reach or continue ⟨*stretch* a wire between two posts⟩ **8** : to extend often unduly the scope or meaning of ⟨*stretch* the truth⟩ **9** : to become extended without breaking **10** : to extend one's body or limbs ⟨*stretched* before jogging⟩ [Middle English *strechen,* from Old English *streccan*] — **stretch·abil·i·ty** \ˌstrech-ə-ˈbil-ət-ē\ *n* — **stretch·able** \ˈstrech-ə-bəl\ *adj* — **stretch one's legs** : to take a walk in order to relieve stiffness caused by prolonged sitting

[2]**stretch** *n* **1 a** : an exercise of something (as the imagination or understanding) beyond ordinary or normal limits **b** : an extension of the scope or application of something **2** : the extent to which something may be stretched **3** : the act of stretching : the state of being stretched **4 a** : an extent in length or area **b** : a continuous period of time ⟨silent for a *stretch*⟩ **5** : a walk to relieve fatigue **6** : a term of imprisonment **7 a** : either of the straight sides of a racecourse; *esp* : HOMESTRETCH **b** : a final stage **8** : the capacity for being stretched : ELASTICITY

[3]**stretch** *adj* **1** : easily stretched : ELASTIC ⟨*stretch* socks⟩ **2** : longer than the standard size ⟨a *stretch* limousine⟩

stretch·er \ˈstrech-ər\ *n* **1** : one that stretches; *esp* : a device or machine for stretching or expanding something (as curtains) **2** : a device resembling a cot for carrying a sick, injured, or dead person **3** : a rod or bar extending between two legs of a chair or table

stretch receptor *n* : MUSCLE SPINDLE

strew \ˈstrü\ *vt* **strewed; strewed** *or* **strewn** \ˈstrün\; **strew·ing** **1** : to spread (as seeds or flowers) by scattering **2** : to cover by or as if by scattering something over or on ⟨*strewing* the highways with litter⟩ **3** : to become dispersed over **4** : to spread abroad : DISSEMINATE [Old English *strewian*]

stria \ˈstrī-ə\ *n, pl* **stri·ae** \ˈstrī-ˌē\ **1** : STRIATION 2 **2** : a stripe of line (as in the skin) distinguished from the surrounding area by color, texture, or elevation [Latin, "furrow, channel"]

stri·at·ed \ˈstrī-ˌāt-əd\ *adj* : marked with lines, bands, or grooves

striated muscle *n* : muscle tissue that is made up of usually elongated cells with many nuclei and with alternate light and dark cross striations, that is typical of the muscles which move the vertebrate skeleton, and that is mostly under voluntary control — compare SMOOTH MUSCLE, VOLUNTARY MUSCLE

stri·a·tion \strī-ˈā-shən\ *n* **1** : the fact or state of being striated **2** : a minute groove, scratch, or channel especially when one of a parallel series **3** : any of the alternate dark and light cross bands of a myofibril of striated muscle

strick·en \ˈstrik-ən\ *adj* **1** : afflicted with disease, misfortune, or sorrow **2** : hit or wounded by or as if by a missile [from past participle of *strike*]

strict \ˈstrikt\ *adj* **1 a** : stringent in requirement or control ⟨under *strict* orders⟩ **b** : severe in discipline **2 a** : inflexibly maintained or adhered to : COMPLETE, ABSOLUTE ⟨*strict* secrecy⟩ **b** : rigorously conforming to principle or to a norm ⟨a *strict* vegetarian⟩ **3** : EXACT, PRECISE ⟨in the *strict* meaning of the word⟩ [Latin *strictus,* from *stringere* "to bind tight"] ***synonyms*** see RIGID — **strict·ly** *adv* — **strict·ness** \ˈstrikt-nəs, ˈstrik-\ *n*

stric·ture \ˈstrik-chər\ *n* **1** : an abnormal narrowing of a bodily passage; *also* : the narrowed part **2** : something that closely restrains or limits : RESTRICTION **3** : an adverse criticism : CENSURE [Late Latin *strictura,* from Latin *stringere* "to bind tight"]

[1]**stride** \ˈstrīd\ *vb* **strode** \ˈstrōd\; **strid·den** \ˈstrid-n\; **strid·ing** \ˈstrīd-ing\ **1** : BESTRIDE, STRADDLE **2** : to step over **3** : to move with or as if with long measured steps ⟨*strode* across the room⟩ **4** : to take a very long step [Old English *strīdan*] — **strid·er** \ˈstrīd-ər\ *n*

[2]**stride** *n* **1 a** : a cycle of locomotor movements (as of a horse) completed when the feet regain their initial relative positions; *also* : the distance covered by this **b** : the most effective natural pace : the maximum competence or capability — often used in the phrase *hit one's stride* **2** : a long step **3** : an act of striding **4** : a stage of progress : ADVANCE ⟨made great *strides* toward their goal⟩ **5** : a manner of striding ⟨a purposeful *stride*⟩ — **in stride** : with little or no emotional reaction ⟨took the news in *stride*⟩

stri·dent \ˈstrīd-nt\ *adj* **1** : sounding harsh, grating, or shrill ⟨a *strident* voice⟩ **2** : unpleasantly discordant ⟨*strident* colors⟩ [Latin *stridens,* past participle of *stridere, stridēre* "to make a harsh noise"] — **stri·den·cy** \-n-sē\ *n* — **stri·dent·ly** *adv*

stri·dor \ˈstrīd-ər, ˈstrī-ˌdȯr\ *n* : a strident noise [Latin, from *stridere, stridēre* "to make a harsh noise"]

strid·u·late \ˈstrij-ə-ˌlāt\ *vi* : to make a shrill creaking noise by rubbing together special bodily structures — used especially of male insects (as crickets or grasshoppers) [derived from Latin *stridulus* "shrill," from *stridere, stridēre* "to make a harsh noise"] — **strid·u·la·tion** \ˌstrij-ə-ˈlā-shən\ *n*

strid·u·lous \ˈstrij-ə-ləs\ *adj* : making a shrill creaking sound [Latin *stridulus*] — **strid·u·lous·ly** *adv*

strife \ˈstrīf\ *n* **1** : bitter sometimes violent conflict or dissension ⟨political *strife*⟩ **2** : an act of contention : FIGHT, STRUGGLE [Medieval French *estrif*]

strife·less \-ləs\ *adj* : free from strife

[1]**strike** \ˈstrīk\ *vb* **struck** \ˈstrək\; **struck** *also* **strick·en** \ˈstrik-ən\; **strik·ing** \ˈstrī-king\ **1** : to take a course : GO ⟨*strike* across the field⟩ **2 a** : to deliver a stroke, blow, or thrust : HIT **b** : to drive or remove by or as if by a blow ⟨*struck* the knife from my hand⟩ **c** : to attack or seize especially with fangs or claws ⟨*struck* by a snake⟩ **3** : to remove or cancel with or as if with a stroke of the pen ⟨*struck* out a word in the text⟩ **4** : to lower, take down, or take apart ⟨*strike* a flag⟩ ⟨*strike* the tents⟩ **5 a** : to indicate or become indicated by a clock, bell, or chime ⟨the hour had just *struck*⟩ **b** : to indicate by sounding ⟨the clock *struck* one⟩ **6** : to pierce or penetrate or to cause to pierce or penetrate ⟨the wind seemed to *strike* through our clothes⟩ **7** : to make a military attack : FIGHT ⟨*strike* for freedom⟩ **8** : to seize the bait ⟨a fish *struck*⟩ **9** : to begin or cause to grow : take root or cause to take root ⟨some plant cuttings *strike* quickly⟩ **10** : to stop work in order to force an employer to comply with demands **11** : to make a beginning : LAUNCH ⟨the orchestra *struck* into another waltz⟩ **12** : to afflict suddenly : lay low ⟨*struck* down at the height of one's career⟩ **13 a** : to bring into forceful contact ⟨*struck* my knee against the

dash⟩ **b** : to come into contact or collision with ⟨the car *struck* the tree⟩ **c** : to thrust oneself forward ⟨he *struck* into the midst of the argument⟩ **d** : to fall on ⟨sunlight *struck* the glass⟩ **e** : to become audible to ⟨a loud sound *strikes* the ear⟩ **14 a** : to affect with a mental or emotional state or a strong emotion ⟨*struck* with horror⟩ **b** : to bring about : INDUCE, CAUSE ⟨the words *struck* fear in them⟩ **c** : to cause to become by or as if by a sudden blow ⟨*struck* them dead⟩ **15 a** : to produce by stamping ⟨*strike* a coin⟩ **b** : to produce (as fire) by or as if by striking or rubbing **c** : to cause to ignite by friction ⟨*strike* a match⟩ **16** : to agree on the terms of ⟨*strike* a bargain⟩ **17 a** : to play by strokes on the keys or strings ⟨*struck* a chord on the piano⟩ **b** : to produce as if by playing a musical instrument ⟨his voice *struck* a note of concern⟩ **18 a** : to occur to ⟨the answer *struck* me suddenly⟩ **b** : to appear remarkable or make a strong impression on : IMPRESS ⟨I was *struck* by its beauty⟩ **19** : to arrive at by or as if by computation ⟨*strike* a balance⟩ **20 a** : to come to ⟨*strike* the main road⟩ **b** : to run across : DISCOVER ⟨the best story I ever *struck*⟩ **21** : to take on : ASSUME ⟨*strike* a pose⟩ [Old English *strīcan* "to stroke, go"]

[2]**strike** *n* **1** : an act or instance of striking **2 a** : a work stoppage by a body of workers to force an employer to comply with demands **b** : a temporary stoppage of activities in protest against an act or condition **3** : the direction of the line of intersection of a horizontal plane with an uptilted geological stratum **4** : a pull on a line by a fish in striking **5** : a stroke of good luck; *esp* : a discovery of a valuable mineral deposit **6** : a pitched baseball that passes through the strike zone or that is swung at and is not hit fair **7** : DISADVANTAGE 2, HANDICAP ⟨his poor attendance was a *strike* against him⟩ **8** : an act or instance of knocking down all the bowling pins with the first bowl **9 a** : a military attack; *esp* : an air attack on a single objective **b** : a group of airplanes taking part in such an attack

strike•bound \ˈstrīk-ˌbau̇nd\ *adj* : subjected to or shut down by a strike ⟨a *strikebound* factory⟩

strike•break•er \ˈstrīk-ˌbrā-kər\ *n* : a person hired to replace a striking worker

strike•break•ing \-king\ *n* : action designed to break up a strike

strike down *vt* : ANNUL, NULLIFY ⟨*struck down* the proposal⟩; *esp* : to declare (a law) illegal and unenforceable ⟨the court *struck down* the law⟩

strike off *vt* **1** : to produce with ease ⟨*strike off* a poem for the occasion⟩ **2** : to depict clearly and exactly

strike•out \ˈstrī-ˌkau̇t\ *n* : an out in baseball resulting from a batter's being charged with three strikes

strike out \strī-ˈkau̇t, ˈstrī-\ *vb* **1** : to enter upon a course of action ⟨*strike out* on one's own⟩ **2** : to set out vigorously ⟨*struck out* for home immediately⟩ **3** : to retire or be retired by a strikeout ⟨the shortstop *struck out*⟩ ⟨the pitcher *struck* him *out* with a curve⟩

strike•over \ˈstrī-ˌkō-vər\ *n* : an act or instance of striking a typewriter character on a spot already occupied by another character

strik•er \ˈstrī-kər\ *n* : one that strikes: as **a** : a player in any of several games who strikes the ball **b** : the hammer of the striking mechanism of a clock or watch **c** : a worker on strike

strike–slip \ˈstrīk-ˌslip\ *n* **1** : a geological fault around which movement is predominantly horizontal **2** : a slipping movement along the strike of a fault ⟨*strike-slip* earthquakes⟩

strike up *vb* **1** : to begin or cause to begin to sing or play ⟨the band *struck up*⟩ ⟨a waltz *struck up*⟩ **2** : to cause to begin ⟨*strike up* a conversation⟩

strike zone *n* : the area (as between the knees and armpits of a batter) over home plate through which a pitched baseball must pass to be called a strike

strik•ing \ˈstrī-king\ *adj* : REMARKABLE, IMPRESSIVE ⟨a *striking* costume⟩ ⟨a *striking* resemblance⟩ ***synonyms*** see NOTICEABLE — **strik•ing•ly** \-king-lē\ *adv*

[1]**string** \ˈstring\ *n* **1** : a cord usually used to bind, fasten, or tie **2** : a thin tough plant structure (as the fiber connecting the halves of a bean pod) **3 a** : the gut, wire, or nylon cord of a musical instrument **b** *pl* (1) : the stringed instruments of an orchestra (2) : the players of such instruments **4** : the gut, wire, or cord of a racket or shooting bow **5 a** : a group of objects threaded on a string ⟨a *string* of pearls⟩ **b** (1) : a series of things arranged in or as if in a line ⟨a *string* of cars⟩ (2) : a sequence of like items (as words, characters, or computer bits) **c** : the animals and especially horses belonging to or used by one individual **6** : LINE 14 **7** : a group of players ranked according to skill ⟨the second *string* of the football team⟩ **8** : a series in time : SUCCESSION ⟨a *string* of victories⟩ **9** *pl* **a** : contingent conditions or obligations ⟨an agreement with no *strings* attached⟩ **b** : CONTROL 1, DOMINATION [Old English *streng*] — **string•less** \ˈstring-ləs\ *adj* — **on the string** : subject to one's pleasure or influence

[2]**string** *vb* **strung** \ˈstrəng\; **string•ing** \ˈstring-ing\ **1** : to equip (as a tennis racket) with strings **2** : to make tense **3 a** : to thread on or as if on a string ⟨*string* beads⟩ **b** : to thread with objects **c** : to tie, hang, or fasten with string **4** : to hang by the neck ⟨*strung* up from a high tree⟩ **5** : to remove the strings of ⟨*string* beans⟩ **6 a** : to extend or stretch like a string ⟨*string* wires from tree to tree⟩ **b** : to set out in a line or series **c** : to move, progress, or lie in a string **d** : to form into strings

[3]**string** *adj* : of or relating to stringed musical instruments ⟨the *string* section of an orchestra⟩

string along *vb* **1** : to go along : AGREE ⟨*string along* with the majority⟩ **2** : to keep waiting ⟨*strung* him *along* until the boss returned from lunch⟩ **3** : FOOL 3, DECEIVE ⟨*stringing* customers *along* with false promises⟩

string bass *n* : DOUBLE BASS

string bean *n* **1** : a bean of one of the older varieties of kidney bean that have stringy fibers on the lines of separation of the pods; *also* : SNAP BEAN **2** : a very tall thin person

string•course \ˈstring-ˌkōrs, -ˌkȯrs\ *n* : a horizontal band (as of bricks) in a building forming a part of the design

stringed instrument \ˈstringd-\ *n* : a musical instrument (as a violin, harp, or piano) sounded by plucking or striking or by drawing a bow across tense strings

strin•gent \ˈstrin-jənt\ *adj* **1** : binding, drawing, or pressing tight **2** : marked by rigor, strictness, or severity especially with regard to rule or standard ⟨*stringent* procedures⟩ [Latin *stringens,* present participle of *stringere* "to bind tight"] ***synonyms*** see RIGID — **strin•gen•cy** \-jən-sē\ *n* — **strin•gent•ly** *adv*

string•er \ˈstring-ər\ *n* **1** : one that strings **2 a** : a long horizontal member in a framed structure or under a floor **b** : one of the inclined sides of a stair supporting the treads and risers **3** : a longitudinal member (as in an airplane fuselage or wing) to reinforce the skin **4** : one estimated to be of specified excellence or quality or efficiency — usually used in combination ⟨first-*stringer*⟩ ⟨second-*stringer*⟩

string•halt \ˈstring-ˌhȯlt\ *n* : lameness of the hind legs of a horse due to muscular spasm — **string•halt•ed** \-ˌhȯl-təd\ *adj*

string•ing \ˈstring-ing\ *n* : the gut, silk, or nylon with which a racket is strung

string tie *n* : a narrow necktie

stringy \ˈstring-ē\ *adj* **string•i•er; -est** **1 a** : containing, consisting of, or resembling fibrous matter or a string ⟨*stringy* meat⟩ ⟨*stringy* hair⟩ **b** : lean and sinewy in build : WIRY **2** : capable of being drawn out to form a string : ROPY ⟨a *stringy* precipitate⟩ — **string•i•ness** *n*

[1]**strip** \ˈstrip\ *vb* **stripped** *also* **stript** \ˈstript\; **strip•ping** **1 a** : to remove clothing, covering, or surface matter from ⟨*stripped* the baby for a bath⟩ **b** : to remove (as clothing) from a person ⟨*stripped* the gloves from my hands⟩ **c** : UNDRESS ⟨*stripped* and showered⟩ **d** : to remove a layer that covers : SKIN, PEEL ⟨*strip* bark from a tree⟩ **2** : to divest of honors, privileges, or functions **3 a** : to remove unnecessary or superficial matter from ⟨a prose style *stripped* to the bones⟩ **b** : to remove furniture, equipment, or accessories from **4** : PLUNDER, SPOIL ⟨troops *stripped* the captured town⟩ **5** : to make bare or clear (as by cutting or grazing) **6** : to tear or damage the screw thread of (as a bolt or nut) [Old English *-strīepan*] — **strip•per** *n*

[2]**strip** *n* **1** : a long narrow piece or area ⟨*strips* of bacon⟩ ⟨a *strip* of land⟩ **2** : AIRSTRIP [perhaps from [3]*stripe*]

strip cropping *n* : the growing of a cultivated crop (as corn) in strips alternating with strips of a sod-forming crop (as hay) arranged to follow land contours and minimize erosion — **strip–crop** \-ˌkräp\ *vb*

[1]**stripe** \ˈstrīp\ *n* : a stroke or blow with a rod or lash [Middle English]

[2]**stripe** *vt* : to make stripes on [Middle English, "to place bands or edging on (a garment)," from early Dutch *stripan,* from *stripe, strepe* "stripe"]

[3]**stripe** *n* **1** : a line or long narrow section differing in color or texture from parts adjoining **2** : a piece of braid (as on the sleeve) to indicate military rank or length of service **3** : a dis-

tinct variety or sort : TYPE ⟨persons of the same political *stripe*⟩ — **stripe·less** \ˈstrī-pləs\ *adj*

striped \ˈstrīpt, ˈstrī-pəd\ *adj* : having stripes or streaks

striped bass *n* : a large silvery marine food and sport fish that has black horizontal stripes on the sides, occurs along the Atlantic coast of the U.S., and has been introduced into inland waters (as lakes) along the Pacific coast

strip·ling \ˈstrip-liŋ\ *n* : a youth just passing from boyhood to manhood [Middle English]

strip mine *n* : a mine that is worked from the earth's surface by the stripping away of overlying material — **strip–mine** *vb* — **strip miner** *n*

strive \ˈstrīv\ *vi* **strove** \ˈstrōv\ *also* **strived** \ˈstrīvd\; **striv·en** \ˈstriv-ən\ *or* **strived; striv·ing** \ˈstrī-viŋ\ **1** : to devote serious effort or energy : ENDEAVOR ⟨*strive* to win⟩ **2** : to struggle in opposition : CONTEND [Middle English, "to quarrel, contend, fight, endeavor," from Medieval French *estriver* "to quarrel," from *estrif* "strife"] ***synonyms*** see TRY — **striv·er** \ˈstrī-vər\ *n*

strobe \ˈstrōb\ *n* **1** : STROBOSCOPE **2** : a device that uses a flashtube for high-speed illumination (as in photography) — called also *strobe light*

stro·bi·lus \strō-ˈbī-ləs, ˈstrō-bə-\ *n, pl* **-li** \-ˌlī\ **1** : an aggregation of sporophylls resembling a cone (as in a club moss or horsetail) **2** : the cone of a gymnosperm [Late Latin, "pinecone," from Greek *strobilos* "top, pinecone," from *strobos* "whirl"]

stro·bo·scope \ˈstrō-bə-ˌskōp\ *n* : an instrument for determining speeds of rotation or frequencies of vibration especially by means of a rapidly flashing light that illuminates an object intermittently [Greek *strobos* "whirl"] — **stro·bo·scop·ic** \ˌstrō-bə-ˈskäp-ik\ *adj* — **stro·bo·scop·i·cal·ly** \-ˈskäp-i-kə-lē, -klē\ *adv*

strode *past of* STRIDE

[1]**stroke** \ˈstrōk\ *vt* **1** : to rub gently in one direction; *also* : to pass the hand over gently in kindness or tenderness **2** : to flatter or pay attention to in a manner designed to reassure or persuade [Old English *strācian*] — **strok·er** *n*

[2]**stroke** *n* **1** : the act of striking; *esp* : a blow with a weapon or implement **2** : a single unbroken movement; *esp* : one of a series of repeated or to-and-fro movements **3** : a striking of the ball in a game; *esp* : a striking or attempt to strike the ball that constitutes the scoring unit in golf **4 a** : a sudden action or process producing an impact ⟨a *stroke* of lightning⟩ **b** : an unexpected result ⟨a *stroke* of luck⟩ **5** : sudden weakening or loss of consciousness, sensation, and voluntary motion caused by rupture or obstruction (as by a clot) of a blood vessel of the brain — called also *apoplexy* **6** : one of a series of propelling movements against a resisting medium ⟨*strokes* of an oar⟩ **7 a** : a vigorous or energetic effort by which something is done, produced, or accomplished ⟨a *stroke* of genius⟩ **b** : a delicate or clever touch in a narrative, description, or construction **8** : HEARTBEAT 1 **9** : the movement or the distance of the movement in either direction of a mechanical part (as a piston rod) having a reciprocating motion **10** : the sound of a bell being struck ⟨at the *stroke* of twelve⟩ **11 a** : a mark made by a single movement of a tool **b** : one of the lines of a letter of the alphabet [Middle English] ***synonyms*** see [5]BLOW

[3]**stroke** *vt* **1** : to mark or cancel with a line ⟨*stroked* out my name⟩ **2** : HIT 1a ⟨gently *stroked* the ball toward the hole⟩

stroll \ˈstrōl\ *vb* : to walk in a leisurely or idle manner : RAMBLE [probably from German dialect *strollen*] — **stroll** *n*

stroll·er \ˈstrō-lər\ *n* **1** : one that strolls **2** : a small carriage in which a baby sits and may be pushed

stro·ma \ˈstrō-mə\ *n, pl* **stro·ma·ta** \-mət-ə\ : a supporting framework in or of an organism: as **a** : the network of connective tissue that supports an animal organ **b** : an irregular mass of fungal hyphae supporting and enclosing spore-bearing structures [Latin, "bed covering," from Greek *strōma,* from *stornynai* "to spread out"]

strong \ˈstrȯŋ\ *adj* **strong·er** \ˈstrȯŋ-gər\; **strong·est** \ˈstrȯŋ-gəst\ **1** : having or marked by great physical power : ROBUST **2** : having moral or intellectual power **3** : having great resources (as of wealth) **4** : of a specified number ⟨an army ten thousand *strong*⟩ **5** : being great or striking ⟨bears a *strong* resemblance to me⟩ **6** : FORCEFUL, COGENT ⟨*strong* arguments⟩ **7** : not mild or weak : INTENSE: as **a** : rich in some active agent (as a flavor or extract) ⟨*strong* coffee⟩ **b** : high in saturation and medium in lightness ⟨a *strong* red⟩ **c** : ionizing freely in solution ⟨*strong* acids and bases⟩ **d** : magnifying by refracting greatly ⟨a *strong* lens⟩ **8** : moving with rapidity or force ⟨*strong* wind⟩ **9** : ENTHUSIASTIC, ZEALOUS ⟨*strong* advocates of peace⟩ **10 a** : able to withstand stress : not easily injured : SOLID **b** : not easily subdued or taken ⟨a *strong* fort⟩ **11** : well established : FIRM ⟨*strong* beliefs⟩ **12** : having or being an offensive or intense odor or flavor : RANK **13** : of, relating to, or constituting a verb or verb conjugation that forms the past tense by a change in the root vowel and the past participle usually by the addition of *-en* with or without change of the root vowel (as *strive, strove, striven* or *drink, drank, drunk*) [Old English *strang*] — **strong** *adv* — **strong·ly** \ˈstrȯŋ-lē\ *adv*

synonyms STRONG, STOUT, STURDY, STALWART, TOUGH, TENACIOUS mean showing power to resist or to endure. STRONG may imply power derived from muscular vigor, large size, structural soundness, intellectual or spiritual resources ⟨*strong* arms⟩ ⟨made a *strong* case for his innocence⟩. STOUT suggests an ability to endure stress, pain, or hard use without giving way ⟨*stout* hiking boots⟩. STURDY implies strength derived from vigorous growth, determination of spirit, or solidity of construction ⟨a *sturdy* table⟩ ⟨people of *sturdy* independence⟩. STALWART suggests an unshakable dependability ⟨a *stalwart* fan⟩. TOUGH implies great firmness and resiliency ⟨a *tough* political opponent⟩. TENACIOUS suggests strength in seizing, retaining, clinging to, or holding together ⟨a *tenacious* drive to succeed⟩.

[1]**strong–arm** \ˈstrȯŋ-ˈärm\ *adj* : having, using, or involving undue force : VIOLENT ⟨*strong-arm* methods⟩

[2]**strong–arm** *vt* **1** : to use force on : ASSAULT **2** : to rob by force

strong·box \ˈstrȯŋ-ˌbäks\ *n* : a strongly made container for money or valuables

strong force *n* : a fundamental force of nature that acts between the particles of an atomic nucleus, holds the nucleus together, and is the strongest known force

strong·hold \-ˌhōld\ *n* **1** : a fortified place : FORTRESS **2** : a place dominated by a particular group or marked by a particular characteristic ⟨campaigned in her rival party's *stronghold*⟩

strong–mind·ed \-ˈmīn-dəd\ *adj* : markedly independent in thought and judgment — **strong–mind·ed·ly** *adv* — **strong–mind·ed·ness** *n*

strong suit *n* **1** : a long suit containing high cards **2** : something in which one excels : FORTE

stron·tium \ˈsträn-chē-əm, -chəm; ˈstränt-ē-əm\ *n* : a soft malleable ductile metallic element occurring only in combined form that is used especially in color TV picture tubes and red fireworks — see ELEMENT table [New Latin, from *strontia* "strontium monoxide," from *Strontian,* village in Scotland]

strontium 90 *n* : a heavy radioactive isotope of strontium having the mass number 90 that is present in nuclear waste and fallout

[1]**strop** \ˈsträp\ *n* : STRAP; *esp* : a usually leather band for sharpening a razor [Old English, "thong for securing an oar," from Latin *struppus* "band, strap," from Greek *strophos*]

[2]**strop** *vt* **stropped; strop·ping** : to sharpen (a razor) on a strop

stro·phe \ˈstrō-fē\ *n* : a division of a poem : STANZA [Greek *strophē,* literally, "turn," from *strephein* "to turn, twist"] — **stro·phic** \ˈstrō-fik, ˈsträf-ik\ *adj*

strove *past & chiefly dialect past participle of* STRIVE

[1]**struck** *past and past participle of* STRIKE

[2]**struck** \ˈstrək\ *adj* : closed or affected by a labor strike ⟨a *struck* factory⟩

struc·tur·al \ˈstrək-chə-rəl, ˈstrək-shrəl\ *adj* **1** : of, relating to, or affecting structure ⟨*structural* defects⟩ ⟨*structural* principles⟩ **2** : used or formed for use in construction ⟨*structural* steel⟩ — **struc·tur·al·ly** \-ē\ *adv*

structural formula *n* : an expanded molecular formula showing the arrangement within the molecule of atoms and of bonds

structural gene *n* : a gene that codes for the amino acid sequence of a protein or for a ribosomal RNA or transfer RNA

[1]**struc·ture** \ˈstrək-chər\ *n* **1** : the action of building : CONSTRUCTION **2 a** : something constructed **b** : something made up of interdependent parts in a definite pattern of organization **3** : manner of construction : MAKEUP **4** : the arrangement or relationship of elements (as particles, parts, or organs) in a sub-

stance, body, or system ⟨soil *structure*⟩ ⟨the *structure* of a language⟩ **5** : regular order or consistent organization ⟨tried to give some *structure* to the children's lives⟩ [Latin *structura,* from *structus,* past participle of *struere* "to heap up, build"] — **struc·ture·less** \-ləs\ *adj*

²**structure** *vt* **struc·tured; struc·tur·ing** \'strək-chə-ring, 'strək-shring\ : to form into a structure : ORGANIZE

stru·del \'strüd-l, 'shtrüd-l\ *n* : a pastry made from a sheet of thin dough rolled up with filling and baked [German, literally, "whirlpool"]

¹**strug·gle** \'strəg-əl\ *vi* **strug·gled; strug·gling** \'strəg-ling, -ə-ling\ **1** : to make violent or strenuous efforts in the face of difficulties or opposition ⟨*struggling* with the problem⟩ **2** : to proceed with difficulty or with great effort ⟨*struggle* through deep snow⟩ [Middle English *struglen*] — **strug·gler** \-lər, -ə-lər\ *n*

²**struggle** *n* **1** : CONTEST, STRIFE ⟨a power *struggle*⟩ **2** : a violent or strenuous effort or exertion ⟨a *struggle* to make ends meet⟩

struggle for existence : the competition (as for food, space, or light) between members of a natural population that tends to eliminate weaker or less efficient individuals and thereby to increase the chance that the stronger or more efficient will pass on their traits

strum \'strəm\ *vb* **strummed; strum·ming** : to play on a stringed instrument by brushing the strings with the fingers [imitative] — **strum·mer** *n*

strum·pet \'strəm-pət\ *n* : PROSTITUTE, HARLOT [Middle English]

strung *past and past participle of* STRING

¹**strut** \'strət\ *vb* **strut·ted; strut·ting** **1** : to walk with a stiff proud gait **2** : to parade (as clothes) with a show of pride [Old English *strūtian* "to stand out stiffly, struggle"] — **strut·ter** *n*

synonyms STRUT, SWAGGER mean to assume an air of importance. STRUT emphasizes pompous dignity and vanity as expressed by one's gait or bearing ⟨a movie star *strutting* into the restaurant⟩. SWAGGER suggests conspicuous arrogance or boastfulness especially in one's manners and movements ⟨the victors *swaggered* down the street⟩.

²**strut** *n* **1** : a bar or brace that resists pressure in the direction of its length **2** : a pompous step or walk

strych·nine \'strik-ˌnīn, -nən, -ˌnēn\ *n* : a bitter poisonous alkaloid that is obtained from nux vomica and related plants, acts as a stimulant to the central nervous system, and is used especially as a rat poison [French, from Latin *strychnos* "nightshade," from Greek]

¹**stub** \'stəb\ *n* **1** : STUMP 1b **2** : something having or worn to a short or blunt shape; *esp* : a pen with a short blunt nib **3** : a short part left after a larger part has been broken off or used up ⟨a pencil *stub*⟩ **4 a** : a small part of a check kept as a record of the contents of the check **b** : the part of a ticket returned to the user [Old English *stybb*]

²**stub** *vt* **stubbed; stub·bing** **1** : to extinguish (as a cigarette) by crushing **2** : to strike (as one's toe) against an object

stub·ble \'stəb-əl\ *n* **1** : the stem ends of herbaceous plants and especially cereal grasses remaining attached to the soil after harvest **2** : a rough surface or growth resembling stubble; *esp* : a short growth of beard [Medieval French *estuble,* from Latin *stipula, stupula,* "stalk, straw"] — **stub·bly** \'stəb-lē, -ə-lē\ *adj*

stub·born \'stəb-ərn\ *adj* **1 a** : hard to convince, persuade, or move to action : OBSTINATE ⟨*stubborn* as a mule⟩ **b** : having or characterized by a firm idea or purpose : DETERMINED ⟨*stubborn* courage⟩ **2** : done or continued in an obstinate or persistent manner ⟨*stubborn* refusal⟩ **3** : difficult to handle, manage, or treat ⟨*stubborn* hair⟩ [Middle English *stibourne, stuborn*] ***synonyms*** see OBSTINATE — **stub·born·ly** *adv* — **stub·born·ness** \-ərn-nəs\ *n*

stub·by \'stəb-ē\ *adj* **stub·bi·er; -est** **1** : abounding with stubs : BRISTLY **2** : resembling a stub especially in shortness and broadness ⟨*stubby* fingers⟩ — **stub·bi·ness** *n*

stuc·co \'stək-ō\ *n, pl* **stuccos** *or* **stuccoes** : a plaster (as of portland cement, sand, and lime) used to cover exterior walls or ornament interior walls [Italian, of Germanic origin] — **stuc·coed** \-ōd\ *adj*

stuc·co·work \'stək-ō-ˌwərk\ *n* : work done in stucco

stuck *past and past participle of* STICK

stuck–up \'stək-'əp\ *adj* : CONCEITED, SELF-IMPORTANT

¹**stud** \'stəd\ *n* **1** : a group of animals and especially horses kept primarily for breeding; *also* : the place where they are kept **2** : a male animal (as a stallion) kept for breeding [Old English *stōd*] — **at stud** : for breeding as a stud

²**stud** *n* **1** : one of the smaller upright supports in the framing of the walls of a building to which sheathing, paneling, or laths are fastened : SCANTLING **2 a** : a boss, rivet, or nail with a large head used (as on a shield or belt) for ornament or protection **b** : a solid button with a shank or eye on the back inserted through an eyelet in a garment as a fastener or ornament **3 a** : a piece (as a rod or pin) projecting from a machine and serving chiefly as a support or axis **b** : one of the metal or rubber cleats projecting from a snow tire to increase traction [Old English *studu* "post"]

³**stud** *vt* **stud·ded; stud·ding** **1** : to furnish (as a building or wall) with studs **2** : to adorn, cover, or protect with studs **3** : to mark, decorate, or dot at random ⟨a sky *studded* with stars⟩

stud·book \'stəd-ˌbu̇k\ *n* : an official record of the pedigree of purebred animals (as horses or dogs)

stud·ding \'stəd-ing\ *n* : the studs of a building or wall

stud·ding sail \'stəd-ing-ˌsāl, 'stən-səl\ *n* : a light sail set at the side of a principal square sail of a ship [origin unknown]

stu·dent \'stüd-nt, 'styüd-, *especially South* -ənt\ *n* **1** : LEARNER, SCHOLAR; *esp* : one who attends a school or college **2** : one who studies : an attentive and systematic observer ⟨a *student* of life⟩ [Latin *studens,* from *studēre* "to study"]

student council *n* : a group elected from a body of students to serve as representatives in student government

student government *n* : the organization and management of student life, activities, or discipline by various student organizations in a school or college

student teacher *n* : a student engaged in practice teaching

stud·horse \'stəd-ˌhȯrs\ *n* : a stallion kept especially for breeding

stud·ied \'stəd-ēd\ *adj* **1** : KNOWLEDGEABLE, LEARNED ⟨well *studied* in math⟩ **2** : carefully considered or prepared : THOUGHTFUL ⟨a *studied* response⟩ **3** : produced or marked by conscious design ⟨*studied* indifference⟩ — **stud·ied·ly** *adv* — **stud·ied·ness** *n*

stu·dio \'stüd-ē-ˌō, 'styüd-\ *n, pl* **-di·os** **1 a** : the working place of an artist **b** : a place for the study of an art ⟨a dance *studio*⟩ **2** : a place where motion pictures are made **3** : a place maintained and equipped for the transmission of radio or television programs [Italian, literally, "study," from Latin *studium,* from *studēre* "to devote oneself, study"]

studio couch *n* : an upholstered usually backless couch that can be made to serve as a double bed by sliding from underneath it the frame of a single cot

stu·di·ous \'stüd-ē-əs, 'styüd-\ *adj* **1** : given to, concerned with, or tending to promote study ⟨*studious* habits⟩ **2** : marked by purposefulness or diligence : EARNEST ⟨made a *studious* effort⟩ — **stu·di·ous·ly** *adv* — **stu·di·ous·ness** *n*

¹**study** \'stəd-ē\ *n, pl* **stud·ies** **1** : a state of contemplation : REVERIE **2 a** : application of the mind to the acquisition of knowledge often about a particular field or topic ⟨years of *study*⟩ ⟨the *study* of Latin⟩ **b** : careful or extended consideration ⟨the proposal is under *study*⟩ **c** : a careful examination or analysis of something; *also* : a report or publication on such a study **3** : a building or room devoted to study or literary pursuits **4 a** : a branch or department of learning : SUBJECT ⟨American *studies*⟩ **b** : the activity or work of a student ⟨returned to her *studies* after vacation⟩ **5** : a person who learns or memorizes something (as a part in a play) — usually used with a qualifying adjective ⟨he's a quick *study*⟩ **6** : a usually preliminary or elementary artistic production concerned especially with problems of technique ⟨a series of *studies* of classic heads⟩ [Medieval French *estudie,* from Latin *studium*]

²**study** *vb* **stud·ied; study·ing** **1** : to engage in study or the study of ⟨*studied* hard⟩ ⟨like to *study* history⟩ **2** : ENDEAVOR, TRY ⟨*studied* to appear disinterested⟩ **3** : to consider attentively or in detail ⟨*studied* the question carefully⟩

study hall *n* **1** : a room in a school set aside for study **2** : a period in a student's day set aside for study and homework

¹**stuff** \'stəf\ *n* **1** : materials, supplies, or equipment used in some activity; *esp* : PERSONAL PROPERTY **2** : material to be manufactured, wrought, or used in construction **3** : a finished textile suitable for clothing; *esp* : wool or worsted material **4 a** : writing, discourse, or ideas often of little or temporary worth **b** : actions or talk of a particular and often objectionable kind ⟨how do they get away with such *stuff*⟩ **5 a** : an unspecified substance or aggregate of matter ⟨volcanic rock is curious

stuff⟩ **b** : a matter to be considered ⟨the truth was heady *stuff*⟩ **c** : a group or scattering of unspecified objects or articles ⟨sold tons of the *stuff*⟩ **6 a** : fundamental material : SUBSTANCE ⟨the *stuff* of greatness⟩ **b** : subject matter ⟨teachers who know their *stuff*⟩ **7** : special knowledge or capability ⟨has the *stuff* to do well here⟩ [Medieval French *estuffes* "goods," from *estuffer* "to fill in (with rubble), furnish, equip," of Germanic origin]

2**stuff** *vt* **1 a** : to fill by or as if by packing things in : CRAM ⟨was *stuffing* her pockets with candy⟩ **b** : to eat too much ⟨don't *stuff* yourself with pizza⟩ **c** : to fill with a stuffing ⟨*stuffed* the pillow⟩ **2** : to fill with ideas or information ⟨*stuffed* their heads with facts⟩ **3** : to fill or block up ⟨a sore throat and *stuffed* nose⟩ **4** : to cause to enter or fill : THRUST ⟨*stuffed* the clothes into the drawer⟩ — **stuff·er** *n*

stuffed shirt *n* : a smug, conceited, and usually pompous person often with an inflexibly conservative attitude

stuff·ing \ˈstəf-iŋ\ *n* : material used to stuff something; *esp* : a seasoned mixture used to stuff meat, vegetables, eggs, or poultry

stuffy \ˈstəf-ē\ *adj* **stuff·i·er; -est** **1** : SULLEN 1, ILL-HUMORED **2 a** : oppressive to the breathing : CLOSE ⟨a *stuffy* room⟩ **b** : stuffed or choked up ⟨a *stuffy* feeling in my head⟩ **3** : lacking in vitality or interest : DULL **4** : narrowly inflexible in standards of conduct : SELF-RIGHTEOUS — **stuff·i·ly** \ˈstəf-ə-lē\ *adv* — **stuff·i·ness** \ˈstəf-ē-nəs\ *n*

stul·ti·fy \ˈstəl-tə-ˌfī\ *vt* **-fied; -fy·ing** **1** : to cause to appear or be stupid, foolish, or absurdly illogical **2** : to make futile or useless especially through weakening or repressive influences ⟨*stultify* initiative⟩ [Late Latin *stultificare* "to make foolish," from Latin *stultus* "foolish"] — **stul·ti·fi·ca·tion** \ˌstəl-tə-fə-ˈkā-shən\ *n*

stum·ble \ˈstəm-bəl\ *vi* **stum·bled; stum·bling** \-bə-liŋ, -bliŋ\ **1** : to blunder morally **2** : to trip in walking or running **3 a** : to walk unsteadily **b** : to speak or act in a hesitant or clumsy manner **4** : to come or happen unexpectedly or by chance ⟨*stumbled* on a discovery⟩ [Middle English, probably of Scandinavian origin] — **stumble** *n* — **stum·bler** \-bə-lər, -blər\ *n* — **stum·bling·ly** \-bə-liŋ-lē, -bliŋ-\ *adv*

stum·bling block \ˈstəm-bliŋ-\ *n* **1** : an impediment to belief or understanding **2** : an obstacle to progress

1**stump** \ˈstəmp\ *n* **1 a** : the base of a bodily part (as an arm or leg) remaining after the rest is removed **b** : the part of a plant and especially a tree remaining attached to the root after the top is cut off **2** : a part (as of a pencil) remaining after the rest is worn away or lost : STUB **3** : a place or occasion for political public speaking [Middle English *stumpe*]

2**stump** *vb* **1 a** : CHALLENGE 4, DARE **b** : BEWILDER 2, CONFOUND **2** : to clear (land) of stumps **3 a** : to walk or walk over heavily or clumsily **b** : STUB 2 **4** : to go about making political speeches or supporting a cause ⟨*stump* the state for the reform candidate⟩ — **stump·er** *n*

stump·age \ˈstəm-pij\ *n* **1** : the value of standing timber **2** : uncut timber; *also* : the right to cut it

stumpy \ˈstəm-pē\ *adj* **stump·i·er; -est** **1** : short and thick : SQUAT **2** : full of stumps

stun \ˈstən\ *vt* **stunned; stun·ning** **1** : to make senseless or dizzy by or as if by a blow **2** : to overcome with astonishment or disbelief : SHOCK ⟨*stunned* by the news⟩ [Medieval French *estoner* "to astonish," derived from Latin *ex-* + *tonare* "to thunder"] — **stun** *n*

stung *past and past participle of* STING

stunk *past and past participle of* STINK

stun·ner \ˈstən-ər\ *n* : one that stuns or is stunning

stun·ning \ˈstən-iŋ\ *adj* **1** : causing astonishment or disbelief ⟨*stunning* news⟩ **2** : strikingly impressive especially in beauty or excellence ⟨a *stunning* view⟩ ⟨a *stunning* effort⟩ — **stun·ning·ly** \-iŋ-lē\ *adv*

1**stunt** \ˈstənt\ *vt* : to hinder the normal growth, development, or progress of [English dialect *stunt* "stunted, abrupt"]

2**stunt** *n* : a plant disease in which dwarfing occurs

3**stunt** *n* : an unusual or difficult feat performed or undertaken usually to gain attention or publicity [origin unknown]

4**stunt** *vi* : to perform stunts

stupe \ˈstüp, ˈstyüp\ *n* : a hot wet often medicated cloth applied externally (as to stimulate circulation) [Medieval French, literally, "tow," from Latin *stuppa* "coarse part of flax, tow," from Greek *styppē*]

stu·pe·fy \ˈstü-pə-ˌfī, ˈstyü-\ *vt* **-fied; -fy·ing** **1** : to make stupid, groggy, or insensible ⟨*stupefied* by the heat and humidity⟩ **2** : ASTONISH, BEWILDER ⟨the strange sight *stupefied* the crowd⟩ [Latin *stupefacere,* from *stupēre* "to be astonished" + *facere* "to make, do"] — **stu·pe·fac·tion** \ˌstü-pə-ˈfak-shən, ˌstyü-\ *n*

stu·pen·dous \stü-ˈpen-dəs, styü-\ *adj* : stupefying or amazing especially because of size, complexity, or greatness [Latin *stupendus* "to be wondered at," from *stupēre* "to be astonished"] ***synonyms*** see MONSTROUS — **stu·pen·dous·ly** *adv* — **stu·pen·dous·ness** *n*

stu·pid \ˈstü-pəd, ˈstyü-\ *adj* **1 a** : slow of mind : OBTUSE **b** : given to unwise decisions or actions **2** : dulled in feeling or sensation **3** : marked by or resulting from foolish thinking or acting : SENSELESS ⟨a *stupid* mistake⟩ **4** : lacking interest or point : BORING ⟨a *stupid* plot⟩ [Middle French *stupide,* from Latin *stupidus,* from *stupēre* "to be numb, be astonished"] — **stu·pid·ly** *adv* — **stu·pid·ness** *n*

synonyms STUPID, DULL, DENSE mean lacking in power to take in ideas or impressions. STUPID implies a slow-witted or dazed state of mind that may be either congenital or temporary ⟨was *stupid* to turn down the offer⟩. DULL suggests a slow or sluggish mind such as results from disease, depression, or shock ⟨repetitive work that leaves the mind *dull*⟩. DENSE implies a relative imperviousness to new or complex ideas ⟨too *dense* to take a hint⟩.

stu·pid·i·ty \stü-ˈpid-ət-ē, styu-\ *n, pl* **-ties** **1** : the quality or state of being stupid **2** : something (as an idea or act) that is stupid

stu·por \ˈstü-pər, ˈstyü-\ *n* **1** : a condition characterized by great dulling or suspension of sense or feeling ⟨a drunken *stupor*⟩ **2** : a state of extreme apathy or torpor resulting often from stress or shock [Latin, from *stupēre* "to be numb, be astonished"] ***synonyms*** see LETHARGY — **stu·por·ous** \-pə-rəs, -prəs\ *adj*

stur·dy \ˈstərd-ē\ *adj* **stur·di·er; -est** **1 a** : firmly built or made ⟨*sturdy* boxes⟩ **b** : HARDY 3 ⟨a *sturdy* plant⟩ **2 a** : marked by or reflecting physical strength or vigor : ROBUST **b** : FIRM 3, RESOLUTE ⟨*sturdy* self-reliance⟩ [Middle English, "brave, stubborn," from Medieval French *esturdi* "stunned," from *esturdir* "to stun," derived from Latin *ex-* + *turdus* "thrush"] ***synonyms*** see STRONG — **stur·di·ly** \ˈstərd-l-ē\ *adv* — **stur·di·ness** \ˈstərd-ē-nəs\ *n*

stur·geon \ˈstər-jən\ *n* : any of various usually large long-bodied fishes that have a thick skin with rows of bony plates and are valued especially for their roe which is made into caviar [Medieval French *estourgeon,* of Germanic origin]

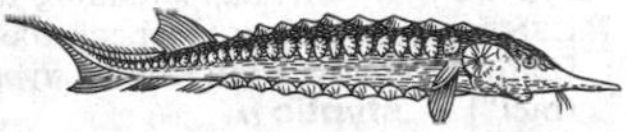

sturgeon

1**stut·ter** \ˈstət-ər\ *vb* : to speak with involuntary repetition, disruption, or blocking of vocal sounds [Middle English *stutten*] ***synonyms*** see STAMMER — **stut·ter·er** \ˈstət-ər-ər\ *n*

2**stutter** *n* **1** : an act or instance of stuttering **2** : a speech disorder involving stuttering

1**sty** \ˈstī\ *n, pl* **sties** *also* **styes** \ˈstīz\ : PIGPEN [Old English *stig*]

2**sty** *or* **stye** \ˈstī\ *n, pl* **sties** *or* **styes** \ˈstīz\ : an inflamed swelling of a skin gland on the edge of an eyelid [from obsolete *styan,* from Old English *stīgend,* from *stīgan* "ro rise"]

sty·gian \ˈstij-ən, ˈstij-ē-ən\ *adj, often cap* : INFERNAL, GLOOMY ⟨*stygian* darkness⟩ [Latin *stygius,* from Greek *stygios,* from *Styg-, Styx* "Styx"]

1**style** \ˈstīl\ *n* **1** : mode of address : TITLE 2 **2 a** : a distinctive manner of expression (as in writing or speech) **b** : a distinctive manner or custom of behaving or conducting oneself ⟨his *style* is abrasive⟩ **c** : a particular manner or technique by which something is done, created, or performed ⟨a unique *style* of horseback riding⟩ **3 a** : STYLUS **b** : a column built so that its shadow indicates the time of day **c** : the usually long slender part of the pistil of a flower that bears a stigma at its apex **d** : a slender bodily process (as a bristle) of an animal **4** : a distinctive quality, form, or type of something ⟨the Greek *style* of architecture⟩ **5 a** : the state of being popular : FASHION ⟨clothes

\ə\ **abut**	\au̇\ **out**	\i\ **tip**	\ȯ\ **saw**	\u̇\ **foot**
\ər\ **further**	\ch\ **chin**	\ī\ **life**	\ȯi\ **coin**	\y\ **yet**
\a\ **mat**	\e\ **pet**	\j\ **job**	\th\ **thin**	\yü\ **few**
\ā\ **take**	\ē\ **easy**	\ŋ\ **sing**	\t͟h\ **this**	\yu̇\ **cure**
\ä\ **cot, cart**	\g\ **go**	\ō\ **bone**	\ü\ **food**	\zh\ **vision**

that are always in *style*⟩ **b** : fashionable elegance **c** : beauty, grace, or ease of doing something ⟨handled the awkward moment with *style*⟩ **6** : the custom or plan followed in spelling, capitalization, punctuation, and typographic arrangement and display [Latin *stilus* "spike, stem, stylus, style of writing"] ***synonyms*** see DICTION, FASHION — **style·less** \ˈstīl-ləs\ *adj*

[2]**style** *vt* **1** : NAME, CALL ⟨*style* themselves scientists⟩ **2 a** : to give a particular style to ⟨cuts and *styles* hair⟩ **b** : to design or make in accord with the current fashion — **styl·er** *n*

style·book \ˈstīl-ˌbu̇k\ *n* : a book explaining, describing, or illustrating the prevailing, accepted, or authorized style ⟨a *stylebook* for printers⟩

sty·let \ˈstī-lət\ *n* **1** : a slender surgical probe **2** : a relatively rigid elongated organ or appendage (as a piercing mouth part) of an animal [French, from Middle French *stilet* "stiletto," from Italian *stiletto*]

stylet 1

styl·ish \ˈstī-lish\ *adj* : having style; *esp* : conforming to current fashion — **styl·ish·ly** *adv* — **styl·ish·ness** *n*

styl·ist \ˈstī-ləst\ *n* **1** : a master or model of style; *esp* : a writer or speaker eminent in matters of style **2** : one who develops, designs, or advises on styles ⟨a hair *stylist*⟩ — **sty·lis·tic** \stī-ˈlis-tik\ *adj* — **sty·lis·ti·cal·ly** \-ti-kə-lē, -klē\ *adv*

styl·ize \ˈstīl-ˌīz\ *vt* : to conform to a style; *esp* : to represent or design according to a style or stylistic pattern rather than according to nature or tradition — **styl·iza·tion** \ˌstī-lə-ˈzā-shən\ *n*

sty·lo·bate \ˈstī-lə-ˌbāt\ *n* : a continuous flat coping or pavement on which a row of architectural columns is supported [Latin *stylobates,* from Greek *stylobatēs,* from *stylos* "pillar" + *bainein* "to walk, go"]

sty·loid \ˈstīl-ˌȯid\ *adj* : resembling a style ⟨the slender pointed *styloid* process of the ulna⟩

sty·lus \ˈstī-ləs\ *n, pl* **sty·li** \ˈstīl-ˌī\ *also* **sty·lus·es** \ˈstī-lə-səz\ : an instrument for writing or marking: as **a** : an instrument used by the ancients for writing on wax or clay tablets **b** : NEEDLE 3d [Latin *stilus* "spike, stylus"]

stymie *vt* **sty·mied; sty·mie·ing** : to present an obstacle to : stand in the way of ⟨an unexpected snowstorm *stymied* travelers' plans⟩ [Scots, to obstruct a golf shot]

styp·tic \ˈstip-tik\ *adj* : tending to contract or bind : ASTRINGENT; *esp* : tending to check bleeding ⟨*styptic* effect of cold⟩ [Latin *stypticus,* from Greek *styptikos,* from *styphein* "to contract"] — **styptic** *n*

styptic pencil *n* : a stick of a medicated styptic substance used especially in shaving to stop the bleeding from small cuts

sty·rax \ˈstī-ˌraks\ *n* : STORAX

sty·rene \ˈstī-ˌrēn\ *n* : a fragrant liquid hydrocarbon used chiefly in making synthetic rubber, resins, and plastics; *also* : any of various plastics made from styrene [derived from Latin *styrax* "storax"]

Sty·ro·foam \ˈstī-rə-ˌfōm\ *trademark* — used for an expanded rigid polystyrene plastic

sua·sion \ˈswā-zhən\ *n* : the act of influencing or persuading ⟨moral *suasion*⟩ [Latin *suasio,* from *suadēre* "to urge, persuade"] — **sua·sive** \ˈswā-siv, -ziv\ *adj* — **sua·sive·ly** *adv* — **sua·sive·ness** *n*

suave \ˈswäv\ *adj* **suav·er; -est** : smoothly but often superficially polite and agreeable [French, from Middle French, "pleasant, sweet," from Latin *suavis*] — **suave·ly** *adv* — **suave·ness** *n* — **sua·vi·ty** \ˈswäv-ət-ē\ *n*

synonyms SUAVE, URBANE, BLAND, SMOOTH mean pleasingly tactful and well-mannered. SUAVE implies a specific ability to deal with others easily and without friction ⟨a *suave* headwaiter⟩. URBANE suggests courtesy and poise developed by wide social experience ⟨an *urbane* outlook on life⟩. BLAND emphasizes mildness of manner and absence of irritating qualities ⟨a *bland,* kindly old soul⟩. SMOOTH usually suggests a deliberately assumed suavity ⟨a *smooth* liar⟩.

[1]**sub** \ˈsəb\ *n* : SUBSTITUTE

[2]**sub** *vi* **subbed; sub·bing** : to act as a substitute ⟨the rookie *subbed* for the injured linebacker⟩

[3]**sub** *n* : SUBMARINE

sub- *prefix* **1** : under : beneath : below ⟨*sub*aqueous⟩ ⟨*sub*soil⟩ **2 a** : subordinate : secondary ⟨*sub*station⟩ **b** : subdivision of ⟨*sub*committee⟩ ⟨*sub*species⟩ **c** : with repetition (as of a process) so as to form, stress, or deal with subordinate parts or relations ⟨*sub*let⟩ **3** : less than completely, perfectly, or normally : somewhat ⟨*sub*dominant⟩ **4** : falling nearly in the category of and often adjoining : bordering upon ⟨*sub*arctic⟩ [Latin, "under, below, secretly, from below, up, near," from *sub* "under, close to"]

subadolescent
subagency
subagent
suballocation
subaverage
subbasement
subbranch
subcaste
subcategorization
subcategorize
subcategory
subcluster
subcollege
subcollegiate
subcolony
subcommission
subcomponent
subcult
subdepartment
subdevelopment
subdialect
subdirector
subdiscipline
subdistrict
subfield
subfile
subframe
subgenre
subgoal
subhumid
subindustry
sublevel
sublot
submarket
submaximal
subminimal
subminimum
subnational
subnetwork
subniche
suboptimal
suboptimization
suboptimize
suboptimum
suborganization
subpar
subparagraph
subpart
subprocess
subproduct
subproject
subsea
subsite
subsociety
subspecialist
subspecialize
subspecialty
subsystem
subtask
subtest
subtheme
subtreasury
subtribe
subtype
subunit
subvisible
subzone

sub·acute \ˌsəb-ə-ˈkyüt\ *adj* **1** : having a tapered but not sharply pointed form ⟨leaves *subacute* at tip⟩ **2** : falling between acute and chronic in character ⟨*subacute* eczema⟩

sub·aer·i·al \ˌsəb-ˈar-ē-əl, ˈsəb-, -ˈer-; ˌsəb-ā-ˈir-ē-əl\ *adj* : situated or occurring on or close to the surface of the earth ⟨*subaerial* habitat⟩ ⟨*subaerial* roots⟩ — **sub·aer·i·al·ly** \-ē-ə-lē\ *adv*

sub·al·pine \ˌsəb-ˈal-ˌpīn, ˈsəb-\ *adj* **1** : of or relating to the region about the foot and lower slopes of the Alps **2** : of, relating to, or growing on upland slopes near the timberline

[1]**sub·al·tern** \sə-ˈbȯl-tərn, *especially British* ˈsəb-əl-tərn\ *adj* : of low or lower rank : SUBORDINATE [Late Latin *subalternus,* from Latin *sub-* + *alternus* "alternate"]

[2]**subaltern** *n* : SUBORDINATE; *esp* : a commissioned officer in the British army below the rank of captain

sub·ant·arc·tic \ˌsəb-ant-ˈärk-tik, -ˈant-, -ˈärt-ik\ *adj* : of, relating to, or being a region just outside the antarctic circle ⟨*subantarctic* islands⟩ ⟨*subantarctic* seals⟩

sub·aque·ous \ˌsəb-ˈā-kwē-əs, ˈsəb-, -ˈak-wē-\ *adj* : formed, occurring, or existing in or under water ⟨a *subaqueous* tunnel⟩

sub·arc·tic \-ˈärk-tik, -ˈärt-ik\ *adj* : of, relating to, or being regions immediately outside of the arctic circle or regions similar to these in climate or conditions of life ⟨*subarctic* waters⟩ ⟨*subarctic* plants⟩

sub·as·sem·bly \ˌsəb-ə-ˈsem-blē\ *n* : an assembled unit designed to be incorporated with other units in a finished product

sub·atom·ic \ˌsəb-ə-ˈtäm-ik\ *adj* : of or relating to the inside of the atom or particles smaller than atoms

sub·cab·i·net \-ˈkab-ə-nət, -ˈkab-nət\ *adj* : of, relating to, or being a high administrative position in the U.S. government that ranks below the cabinet level

sub·cel·lu·lar \ˌsəb-ˈsel-yə-lər, ˈsəb-\ *adj* : of less than cellular scope or level of organization ⟨*subcellular* organelles⟩

sub·class \ˈsəb-ˌklas\ *n* : a primary division of a class: as **a** : a category in biological classification ranking below a class and above an order **b** : SUBSET

sub·clas·si·fi·ca·tion \ˌsəb-ˌklas-ə-fə-ˈkā-shən, -ˌklas-fə-\ *n* **1** : a primary division of a classification **2** : arrangement into or assignment to subclassifications — **sub·clas·si·fy** \-ˈklas-ə-ˌfī\ *vt*

[1]**sub·cla·vi·an** \ˌsəb-ˈklā-vē-ən\ *adj* : of, relating to, being, or inserted into a part (as an artery) located under the clavicle

[2]**subclavian** *n* : a subclavian part (as an artery or vein)

sub·clin·i·cal \ˌsəb-ˈklin-i-kəl, ˈsəb-\ *adj* : not severe enough to be detectable by the usual clinical tests ⟨a *subclinical* infection⟩ — **sub·clin·i·cal·ly** \-kə-lē, -klē\ *adv*

sub·com·mit·tee \ˈsəb-kə-ˌmit-ē, ˌsəb-kə-ˈ\ *n* : a subdivision of a committee usually organized for a specific purpose

sub·com·mu·ni·ty \ˌsəb-kə-ˈmyü-nət-ē\ *n* : a distinct grouping within a community

sub·com·pact \'səb-'käm-ˌpakt\ *n* : an automobile smaller than a compact

[1]**sub·con·scious** \ˌsəb-'kän-chəs, 'səb-\ *adj* : existing in the mind but not immediately available to consciousness ⟨a *subconscious* motive⟩ — **sub·con·scious·ly** *adv* — **sub·con·scious·ness** *n*

[2]**subconscious** *n* : the mental activities just below the threshold of consciousness

sub·con·ti·nent \'səb-'känt-n-ənt, -'känt-nənt\ *n* : a large landmass smaller than a continent; *esp* : a major subdivision of a continent ⟨the Indian *subcontinent*⟩ — **sub·con·ti·nen·tal** \ˌsəb-ˌkänt-n-'ent-l\ *adj*

[1]**sub·con·tract** \ˌsəb-'kän-ˌtrakt, 'səb-; ˌsəb-kən-'\ *vb* **1** : to engage a third party to perform (work included in an original contract) under a subcontract **2** : to let out or undertake work under a subcontract — **sub·con·trac·tor** \-ˌtrak-tər\ *n*

[2]**sub·con·tract** \'səb-'kän-ˌtrakt, -ˌkän-\ *n* : a contract between a party to an original contract and a third party who usually agrees to supply work or materials required in the original

sub·crit·i·cal \ˌsəb-'krit-i-kəl, 'səb-\ *adj* **1** : less or lower than critical **2** : of insufficient size to sustain a chain reaction ⟨*subcritical* mass of fissionable material⟩

sub·cul·ture \'səb-ˌkəl-chər\ *n* **1** : a culture (as of bacteria) derived from another culture; *also* : an act or instance of producing a subculture **2** : a distinguishable subdivision of a culture ⟨a criminal *subculture*⟩ — **sub·cul·tur·al** \-'kəlch-rəl, -ə-rəl\ *adj*

sub·cu·ta·ne·ous \ˌsəb-kyü-'tā-nē-əs\ *adj* : being, living, occurring, or administered under the skin ⟨*subcutaneous* fat⟩ ⟨a *subcutaneous* injection⟩ — **sub·cu·ta·ne·ous·ly** *adv*

sub·dea·con \ˌsəb-'dē-kən, 'səb-\ *n* : a cleric ranking below a deacon; *esp* : a cleric in the lowest of the former major orders of the Roman Catholic Church

sub·deb \'səb-ˌdeb\ *n* : SUBDEBUTANTE

sub·deb·u·tante \ˌsəb-'deb-yu-ˌtänt, 'səb-\ *n* : a young girl who is about to become a debutante; *also* : a girl in her middle teens

sub·di·vide \ˌsəb-də-'vīd\ *vb* **1** : to divide the parts of into more parts **2** : to divide into several parts; *esp* : to divide (a tract of land) into building lots — **sub·di·vid·able** \-də-'vīd-ə-bəl\ *adj*

sub·di·vi·sion \ˌsəb-də-'vizh-ən, 'səb-də-ˌ\ *n* **1** : the act or process of subdividing **2** : one of the parts into which something is subdivided

sub·dom·i·nant \ˌsəb-'däm-ə-nənt, 'səb-\ *n* **1** : the 4th tone of a major or minor scale (as F in the scale of C) **2** : something partly but incompletely dominant; *esp* : an ecologically important life form subordinate in influence to the dominants of a community — **subdominant** *adj*

sub·duc·tion \səb-'dək-shən\ *n* : the action or process in plate tectonics of the edge of one crustal plate descending below the edge of another [French, from Late Latin *subductio* "withdrawal," from Latin *subducere* "to withdraw"] — **sub·duct** \-'dəkt\ *vb*

sub·due \səb-'dü, -'dyü\ *vt* **1** : to conquer and bring into subjection : VANQUISH ⟨*subdued* the enemy⟩ **2** : to bring under control especially by willpower ⟨*subdued* his fear⟩ **3** : to reduce the intensity or degree of ⟨tried to *subdue* the light⟩ [Middle English *sodewen, subduen,* from Medieval French *soduire, subdure* "to lead astray, overcome, arrest" (influenced in form and meaning by Latin *subduere* "to subject"), from Latin *subducere* "to withdraw, remove stealthily," from *sub-* + *ducere* "to lead, draw"] ***synonyms*** see CONQUER — **sub·du·er** *n*

sub·dued \-'düd, -'dyüd\ *adj* : lacking in vitality, intensity, or strength ⟨*subdued* colors⟩

sub·en·try \'səb-ˌen-trē\ *n* : an entry (as in a catalog or an account) made under a more general entry

su·ber·in \'sü-bə-rən\ *n* : a complex fatty substance found especially in the walls of cells comprising cork [French *subérine,* from Latin *suber* "cork"]

sub·fam·i·ly \'səb-ˌfam-lē, -ə-lē\ *n* : a category in biological classification ranking below a family and above a genus

sub·floor \-ˌflōr, flȯr\ *n* : a rough floor laid as a base for a finished floor

sub·freez·ing \'səb-'frē-zing\ *adj* : being or marked by temperature below the freezing point (as of water) ⟨*subfreezing* weather⟩

sub·ge·nus \'səb-ˌjē-nəs\ *n* : a category in biological classification ranking below a genus and above a species

sub·gla·cial \ˌsəb-'glā-shəl\ *adj* : of or relating to the bottom of a glacier or the area immediately underlying a glacier — **sub·gla·cial·ly** \-shə-lē\ *adv*

sub·grade \'səb-ˌgrād\ *n* : a surface of earth or rock leveled off to receive a foundation (as of a road)

sub·group \'səb-ˌgrüp\ *n* : a group whose members usually share some common quality that makes them different from the other members of a larger group to which they belong

sub·head \'səb-ˌhed\ *n* **1** : a heading of a subdivision (as in an outline) **2** : a subordinate caption, title, or headline

sub·head·ing \-ing\ *n* : SUBHEAD

sub·hu·man \ˌsəb-'hyü-mən, 'səb-, -'yü-\ *adj* : less than human: as **a** : failing to reach the level (as of intelligence) associated with normal human beings **b** : unsuitable to or unfit for human beings ⟨*subhuman* living conditions⟩

sub·ja·cent \ˌsəb-'jās-nt\ *adj* : lying under or below; *also* : lower than but not directly below ⟨hills and *subjacent* valleys⟩ [Latin *subjacens,* present participle of *subjacēre* "to lie under," from *sub-* + *jacēre* "to lie"] — **sub·ja·cen·cy** \-n-sē\ *n* — **sub·ja·cent·ly** *adv*

[1]**sub·ject** \'səb-jikt\ *n* **1** : one that is placed under authority or control: as **a** : one subject to a monarch and governed by the monarch's law **b** : one who lives in the territory of, enjoys the protection of, and owes allegiance to a sovereign power or state **2** : the thing or person of which a quality, attribute, or relation is affirmed **3 a** : a department of knowledge or learning **b** (1) : an individual (as a person or a mouse) that is studied or experimented on (2) : a dead body for anatomical dissection **c** (1) : something about which something is said or done ⟨the *subject* of an essay⟩ (2) : something (as a scene or figure) that is represented or dealt with in a work of art **4** : a noun or noun equivalent (as a pronoun, gerund, or phrase) about which something is stated by the predicate **5** : the principal melodic phrase on which a musical composition or movement is based [Middle English *suget, subget,* from Medieval French, from Latin *subjectus* "one under authority" and *subjectum* "subject of a proposition," both from *subicere* "to throw under, subject," from *sub-* + *jacere* "to throw"] ***synonyms*** see CITIZEN

[2]**subject** *adj* **1** : owing obedience or allegiance to another (as a parent or ruler) **2 a** : LIABLE 2b, INCLINED ⟨*subject* to temptation⟩ **b** : SUSCEPTIBLE, PRONE ⟨*subject* to colds⟩ **3** : CONDITIONAL, CONTINGENT ⟨*subject* to approval⟩

[3]**sub·ject** \səb-'jekt\ *vt* **1 a** : to bring under control or dominion : SUBJUGATE **b** : to make responsive to the discipline and control of a superior **2** : to make liable : PREDISPOSE ⟨his conduct *subjected* him to intense scrutiny⟩ **3** : to cause to undergo or endure (something unpleasant, inconvenient, or trying) ⟨*subject* one to ridicule⟩ — **sub·jec·tion** \səb-'jek-shən\ *n*

sub·jec·tive \səb-'jek-tiv\ *adj* **1** : of, relating to, or being a subject **2** : of, relating to, or arising within one's self or mind in contrast to what is outside : PERSONAL ⟨*subjective* experience⟩ ⟨*subjective* symptoms of disease⟩ — **sub·jec·tive·ly** *adv* — **sub·jec·tiv·i·ty** \səb-ˌjek-'tiv-ət-ē, ˌsəb-\ *n*

subjective complement *n* : a grammatical complement relating to the subject of an intransitive verb ⟨in "I had fallen sick" *sick* is a *subjective complement*⟩

subject matter *n* : matter presented for consideration in discussion, thought, or study ⟨the poem's *subject matter*⟩

sub·join \səb-'jȯin, ˌsəb-\ *vt* : APPEND, ANNEX ⟨*subjoined* a statement of expenses to her report⟩

sub·ju·gate \'səb-jə-ˌgāt\ *vt* **1** : to force to submit to control : CONQUER **2** : to bring into servitude : SUBDUE [Latin *subjugare,* literally, "to bring under the yoke," from *sub-* + *jugum* "yoke"] ***synonyms*** see CONQUER — **sub·ju·ga·tion** \ˌsəb-jə-'gā-shən\ *n* — **sub·ju·ga·tor** \'səb-jə-ˌgāt-ər\ *n*

[1]**sub·junc·tive** \səb-'jəng-tiv, -'jəngk-\ *adj* : of, relating to, or being a verb form that represents a denoted act or state not as fact but as conditional or possible or viewed emotionally (as with doubt or desire) ⟨the verb "were" is in the *subjunctive* mood in "if I were you, I wouldn't go"⟩ [Late Latin *subjunctivus,* from Latin *subjungere* "to subordinate," from *sub-* + *jungere* "to join"]

[2]**subjunctive** *n* : the subjunctive mood of a language; *also* : a verb in the subjunctive mood

\ə\ **abut**	\au̇\ **out**	\i\ **tip**	\ȯ\ **saw**	\u̇\ **foot**
\ər\ **further**	\ch\ **chin**	\ī\ **life**	\ȯi\ **coin**	\y\ **yet**
\a\ **mat**	\e\ **pet**	\j\ **job**	\th\ **thin**	\yü\ **few**
\ā\ **take**	\ē\ **easy**	\ng\ **sing**	\t͟h\ **this**	\yu̇\ **cure**
\ä\ **cot, cart**	\g\ **go**	\ō\ **bone**	\ü\ **food**	\zh\ **vision**

sub·king·dom \'səb-ˌking-dəm\ *n* : a category in biological classification ranking below a kingdom and above a phylum

sub·lease \'səb-'lēs, -ˌlēs\ *n* : a lease by a tenant of part or all of leased premises to another person — **sublease** *vt*

sub·let \'səb-'let\ *vb* **sub·let; sub·let·ting** **1** : to lease or rent all or part of a leased or rented property **2** : SUBCONTRACT 1

sub·le·thal \ˌsəb-'lē-thəl\ *adj* : less than but usually only slightly less than lethal ⟨a *sublethal* dose⟩

sub·li·mate \'səb-lə-ˌmāt\ *vt* **1** : SUBLIME 1 **2** : to direct the expression of (instinctive desires and impulses) from an unacceptable form to one that is considered more socially or culturally acceptable — **sub·li·ma·tion** \ˌsəb-lə-'mā-shən\ *n*

[1]**sub·lime** \sə-'blīm\ *vb* **1** : to pass or cause to pass from a solid to a gaseous state on heating and sometimes back to solid form on cooling without passing through a liquid state; *also* : to release or purify by such action ⟨*sublime* sulfur from a mixture⟩ **2** : to make finer or more worthy : convert (something inferior) into something of higher worth [Medieval French *sublimer,* from Medieval Latin *sublimare* "to refine, sublime," from Latin, "to elevate," from *sublimis* "high, elevated"] — **sub·lim·er** *n*

[2]**sublime** *adj* **sub·lim·er; -est** **1 a** : lofty, grand, or exalted in thought, expression, or manner ⟨a *sublime* prose style⟩ **b** : of outstanding spiritual, intellectual, or moral worth ⟨*sublime* devotion to duty⟩ **2** : tending to inspire awe usually because of impressive quality ⟨*sublime* beauty⟩ [Latin *sublimis,* "high, elevated," from *sub* "under, up to" + *limen* "threshold, lintel"] — **sub·lime·ly** *adv* — **sub·lime·ness** *n*

sub·lim·i·nal \ˌsəb-'lim-ən-l, 'səb-\ *adj* **1** : inadequate to produce a sensation or a perception ⟨*subliminal* stimuli⟩ **2** : existing or functioning below the threshold of conscious awareness ⟨the *subliminal* mind⟩ ⟨*subliminal* techniques in advertising⟩ [*sub-* + Latin *limin-, limen* "threshold"] — **sub·lim·i·nal·ly** \-l-ē\ *adv*

sub·lim·i·ty \sə-'blim-ət-ē\ *n, pl* **-ties** **1** : the quality or state of being sublime **2** : something sublime

sub·lin·gual \ˌsəb-'ling-gyə-wəl, 'səb-, -'ling-wəl\ *adj* : situated or administered under the tongue ⟨*sublingual* salivary glands⟩

sub·lux·a·tion \ˌsəb-ˌlək-'sā-shən\ *n* : a partial dislocation of a bone or joint [*sub-* + Late Latin *luxatio* "dislocation," from Latin *luxare* "to dislocate," from *luxus* "dislocated"]

sub·ma·chine gun \ˌsəb-mə-'shēn-ˌgən\ *n* : a lightweight automatic or semiautomatic portable firearm fired from the shoulder or hip

sub·man·dib·u·lar \-man-'dib-yə-lər\ *adj* : of, relating to, or situated below the lower jaw

sub·mar·gin·al \ˌsəb-'märj-nəl, 'səb-, -ən-l\ *adj* **1** : located near or beneath a margin or a marginal part **2** : inadequate for some end or use ⟨farming *submarginal* land⟩

[1]**sub·ma·rine** \'səb-mə-ˌrēn, ˌsəb-mə-'\ *adj* : UNDERWATER; *esp* : UNDERSEA ⟨*submarine* plants⟩

[2]**submarine** *n* **1** : something that functions or operates underwater; *esp* : a naval combat vessel designed for on-the-surface or underwater operations **2** : a large sandwich made from a long roll filled usually with cold cuts, cheese, onion, lettuce, and tomato

sub·ma·rin·er \'səb-mə-ˌrē-nər, ˌsəb-mə-'; ˌsəb-'mar-ə-\ *n* : a member of a submarine crew

sub·max·il·lary \ˌsəb-'mak-sə-ˌler-ē, 'səb-\ *adj* : SUBMANDIBULAR

sub·me·di·ant \ˌsəb-'mēd-ē-ənt, 'səb-\ *n* : the 6th tone of a minor or major scale

sub·merge \səb-'mərj\ *vb* **1** : to put or go underwater ⟨the whale *submerged*⟩ **2** : to cover or become covered with or as if with water ⟨floodwaters *submerged* the town⟩ ⟨memories *submerged* by time⟩ [Latin *submergere,* from *sub-* + *mergere* "to plunge"] — **sub·mer·gence** \-'mər-jəns\ *n* — **sub·merg·ible** \-'mər-jə-bəl\ *adj*

sub·merse \səb-'mərs\ *vt* **sub·mersed; sub·mers·ing** : SUBMERGE [Latin *submersus,* past participle of *submergere* "to submerge"]

submersed *adj* **1** : covered with water **2** : growing or adapted to grow underwater ⟨*submersed* plants⟩

[1]**sub·mers·ible** \səb-'mər-sə-bəl\ *adj* : capable of being submerged ⟨*submersible* pumps⟩

[2]**submersible** *n* : a boat that is capable of submerging; *esp* : SUBMARINE 1

sub·mer·sion \səb-'mər-zhən, -shən\ *n* : the action of submerging : the state of being submerged

sub·mi·cro·scop·ic \ˌsəb-ˌmī-krə-'skäp-ik\ *adj* : too small to be seen in an ordinary light microscope

sub·min·i·a·ture \ˌsəb-'min-ē-ə-ˌchůr, 'səb-, -'min-i-ˌchůr, -chər\ *adj* : very small ⟨*subminiature* electronic equipment⟩

sub·mis·sion \səb-'mish-ən\ *n* **1** : an act of submitting something (as for consideration, inspection, or comment); *also* : something submitted (as a manuscript) **2** : the condition of being submissive, humble, or compliant **3** : an act of submitting to the authority or control of another [Medieval French, from Latin *submissio* "act of lowering," from *submittere* "to lower, submit"]

sub·mis·sive \-'mis-iv\ *adj* : inclined or willing to submit to others : YIELDING, MEEK — **sub·mis·sive·ly** *adv* — **sub·mis·sive·ness** *n*

sub·mit \səb-'mit\ *vb* **sub·mit·ted; sub·mit·ting** **1** : to subject to a process or practice ⟨the metal was *submitted* to analysis⟩ **2 a** : to present or propose to another for review, consideration or decision ⟨*submit* a bid on a contract⟩ ⟨*submit* a report⟩ **b** : to deliver formally ⟨*submitted* my resignation⟩ **3** : to put forward as an opinion or contention ⟨we *submit* that the charge is not proved⟩ **4** : to yield to the power or will of another [Latin *submittere* "to lower, submit," from *sub-* + *mittere* "to send"] ***synonyms*** see YIELD

sub·mu·co·sa \ˌsəb-myü-'kō-zə\ *n* : a supporting layer of loose connective tissue just under a mucous membrane — **sub·mu·co·sal** \-zəl\ *adj*

sub·mu·ni·tion \səb-myů-'nish-ən\ *n* : any of a group of smaller weapons carried as a warhead by a missile or projectile and expelled as the carrier approaches its target

sub·nor·mal \ˌsəb-'nȯr-məl, 'səb-\ *adj* : being lower, smaller, or less than what is considered normal ⟨*subnormal* temperatures⟩ — **sub·nor·mal·i·ty** \ˌsəb-nȯr-'mal-ət-ē\ *n* — **sub·nor·mal·ly** \ˌsəb-'nȯr-mə-lē, 'səb-\ *adv*

sub·note·book \'səb-'nōt-ˌbůk\ *n* : a portable computer similar to but smaller and lighter than a notebook computer

sub·oce·an·ic \ˌsəb-ˌō-shē-'an-ik\ *adj* : situated, taking place, or formed beneath the ocean or its bottom ⟨*suboceanic* oil resources⟩

sub·or·bit·al \ˌsəb-'ȯr-bət-l, 'səb-\ *adj* **1** : situated beneath the eye or its orbit **2** : being or involving less than one orbit ⟨a spacecraft's *suborbital* flight⟩

sub·or·der \'səb-ˌȯrd-ər\ *n* : a subdivision of an order; *esp* : a category in biological classification ranking below an order and above a family

[1]**sub·or·di·nate** \sə-'bȯrd-n-ət, -'bȯrd-nət\ *adj* **1** : placed in or occupying a lower class or rank : INFERIOR ⟨a *subordinate* officer⟩ **2** : submissive to or controlled by authority **3 a** : of, relating to, or being a clause that functions as a noun, adjective, or adverb **b** : SUBORDINATING [Medieval Latin *subordinatus,* past participle of *subordinare* "to subordinate," from Latin *sub-* + *ordinare* "to order"] — **sub·or·di·nate·ly** *adv* — **sub·or·di·nate·ness** *n*

[2]**subordinate** *n* : one that is subordinate

[3]**sub·or·di·nate** \sə-'bȯrd-n-ˌāt\ *vt* : to make subordinate or subservient — **sub·or·di·na·tion** \-ˌbȯrd-n-'ā-shən\ *n* — **sub·or·di·na·tive** \-'bȯrd-n-ˌāt-iv\ *adj*

sub·or·di·nat·ing \sə-'bȯrd-n-ˌat-ing\ *adj* : introducing and linking a subordinate clause to a main clause ⟨a *subordinating* conjunction⟩

sub·orn \sə-'bȯrn\ *vt* : to induce secretly to do an unlawful thing and especially to commit perjury ⟨*suborn* a witness⟩ [Middle French *suborner,* from Latin *subornare,* from *sub-* "secretly" + *ornare* "to furnish, equip"] — **sub·or·na·tion** \ˌsəb-ˌȯr-'nā-shən\ *n* — **sub·orn·er** \sə-'bȯr-nər\ *n*

sub·phy·lum \'səb-ˌfī-ləm\ *n* : a category in biological classification ranking below a phylum and above a class

sub·plot \-ˌplät\ *n* : a subordinate plot in fiction or drama

[1]**sub·poe·na** \sə-'pē-nə\ *n* : a writ commanding a person designated in it to appear in court under a penalty for failure to appear [Latin *sub poena* "under penalty"]

[2]**subpoena** *vt* **-naed; -na·ing** : to serve or summon with a writ of subpoena

sub·po·lar \ˌsəb-'pō-lər, 'səb-\ *adj* **1** : SUBARCTIC **2** : SUBANTARCTIC

sub·pop·u·la·tion \'səb-ˌpäp-yə-ˌlā-shən\ *n* : an identifiable part of a population

sub·prob·lem \'səb-ˌpräb-ləm\ *n* : a problem that is contingent on or forms a part of another more inclusive problem

sub·pro·gram \'səb-ˌprō-ˌgram, -grəm\ *n* **:** a partially independent self-contained portion of a program (as for a computer)

sub·re·gion \'səb-ˌrē-jən\ *n* **1 :** a subdivision of a region **2 :** one of the primary divisions of a biogeographic region — **sub·re·gion·al** \'səb-ˌrēj-nəl, -ən-l\ *adj*

sub ro·sa \ˌsəb-'rō-zə\ *adv* **:** in confidence **:** SECRETLY [New Latin, literally, "under the rose"; from the ancient association of the rose with secrecy]

sub·rou·tine \ˌsəb-rü-'tēn, -ˌrü-\ *n* **:** a sequence of computer instructions for performing a specified task that can be used repeatedly

sub–Sa·ha·ran \ˌsəb-sə-'har-ən, 'səb-, -'her-, -'här-\ *adj* **:** of, relating to, or being the part of Africa south of the Sahara

sub·scribe \səb-'skrīb\ *vb* **1 a :** to write (one's name) underneath **:** SIGN **b :** to give consent or approval by or as if by signing one's name ⟨unwilling to *subscribe* to the agreement⟩ **2 a :** to pledge (a gift or contribution) by writing one's name with the amount ⟨*subscribed* $100 to the fund⟩ **b :** to agree to contribute something; *also* **:** to make an agreed contribution **3 a :** to enter one's name for a publication or service; *also* **:** to receive a periodical or service regularly on order ⟨*subscribe* to a newspaper⟩ **b :** to agree to buy and pay for securities especially of a new offering ⟨*subscribed* for 1000 shares⟩ **4 :** to feel favorably inclined ⟨I *subscribe* to your sentiments⟩ [Latin *subscribere,* literally, "to write below," from *sub-* + *scribere* "to write"] — **sub·scrib·er** *n*

sub·script \'səb-ˌskript\ *n* **:** a distinguishing symbol (as a letter or number) written immediately below or below and to the right or left of another character [Latin *subscriptus,* past participle of *subscribere* "to write below"] — **subscript** *adj*

sub·scrip·tion \səb-'skrip-shən\ *n* **1 :** an act or instance of subscribing **2 :** something (as a document containing a signature) that is subscribed **3 :** an arrangement for providing, receiving, or making use of something of a continuing or periodic nature on a prepayment plan; *esp* **:** a purchase by prepayment for a certain number of future issues (as of a periodical) [Latin *subscriptio* "act of writing below, signature," from *subscribere* "to write below"]

sub·sense \'səb-ˌsen(t)s\ *n* **:** a subordinate division of a sense (as in a dictionary)

sub·se·quent \'səb-si-kwənt, -sə-ˌkwent\ *adj* **:** following in time, order, or place **:** SUCCEEDING ⟨*subsequent* events⟩ [Latin *subsequens,* present participle of *subsequi* "to follow close," from *sub-* "near" + *sequi* "to follow"] — **sub·se·quence** \-sə-ˌkwens, -si-kwəns\ *n* — **subsequent** *n* — **sub·se·quent·ly** \-ˌkwent-lē, -kwənt-\ *adv*

sub·serve \səb-'sərv\ *vt* **1 :** to serve as a means in carrying on or out or in aiding **2 :** to promote the welfare or purposes of [Latin *subservire,* from *sub-* + *servire* "to serve"]

sub·ser·vi·ence \səb-'sər-vē-əns\ *n* **1 :** a subservient or subordinate place or function **2 :** obedience befitting one of a menial position

sub·ser·vi·en·cy \-ən-sē\ *n* **:** SUBSERVIENCE

sub·ser·vi·ent \-ənt\ *adj* **1 :** useful in an inferior capacity **:** SUBORDINATE **2 :** submissively obedient **:** OBSEQUIOUS [Latin *subserviens,* present participle of *subservire* "to subserve"] — **sub·ser·vi·ent·ly** *adv*

sub·set \'səb-ˌset\ *n* **:** a mathematical set that is a part of another mathematical set ⟨the set of even numbers is a *subset* of the set of all numbers⟩

sub·side \səb-'sīd\ *vi* **1 :** to sink or fall to the bottom **:** SETTLE **2 :** to tend downward **:** DESCEND ⟨the flood *subsided* slowly⟩ **3 :** to let oneself settle down ⟨*subside* into a chair⟩ **4 :** to become quiet or less **:** ABATE ⟨as the fever *subsides*⟩ ⟨my anger *subsided*⟩ [Latin *subsidere,* from *sub-* + *sidere* "to sit down, sink"] — **sub·sid·ence** \səb-'sīd-ns, 'səb-səd-əns\ *n*

¹sub·sid·i·ary \səb-'sid-ē-ˌer-ē, -'sid-ə-rē\ *adj* **1 a :** furnishing aid or support **:** AUXILIARY ⟨*subsidiary* details⟩ **b :** of secondary importance **:** TRIBUTARY ⟨*subsidiary* streams⟩ **2 :** of, relating to, affected by, or being a subsidy ⟨*subsidiary* payments⟩ [Latin *subsidiarius,* from *subsidium* "reserve troops"] — **sub·sid·i·ar·i·ly** \-ˌsid-ē-'er-ə-lē\ *adv*

²subsidiary *n, pl* **-ar·ies :** one that is subsidiary; *esp* **:** a company wholly controlled by another

sub·si·dize \'səb-sə-ˌdīz, -zə-\ *vt* **:** to aid or furnish with a subsidy — **sub·si·di·za·tion** \ˌsəb-səd-ə-'zā-shən, ˌsəb-zəd-\ *n* — **sub·si·diz·er** *n*

sub·si·dy \'səb-səd-ē, -zəd-\ *n, pl* **-dies :** a grant or gift of money; *esp* **:** a grant by a government to a private individual, a company, or another government to aid an enterprise beneficial to the public [Latin *subsidium* "reserve troops, support, assistance," from *sub-* "near" + *sedēre* "to sit"]

sub·sist \səb-'sist\ *vi* **1 :** to have or continue to have existence **:** BE, PERSIST **2 :** to have or acquire the necessities of life (as food and clothing); *esp* **:** to nourish oneself ⟨*subsisting* on roots and berries⟩ [Late Latin *subsistere,* from Latin, "to halt, remain," from *sub-* + *sistere* "to take a standing position"]

sub·sist·ence \səb-'sis-təns\ *n* **1 a :** real being **:** EXISTENCE **b :** the condition of remaining in existence **:** CONTINUATION, PERSISTENCE **2 :** means of subsisting: as **a :** the minimum (as of food and shelter) necessary to support life **b :** a source or means of obtaining the necessities of life **:** LIVELIHOOD [Late Latin *subsistentia,* from *subsistere* "to subsist"] — **sub·sist·ent** \-tənt\ *adj*

¹sub·soil \'səb-ˌsȯil\ *n* **:** a layer of weathered material that lies just under the surface soil

²subsoil *vt* **:** to turn, break, or stir the subsoil of

sub·son·ic \ˌsəb-'sän-ik, 'səb-\ *adj* **1 :** of, relating to, or being a speed less than that of sound in air **2 :** moving, capable of moving, or utilizing air currents moving at a subsonic speed **3 :** INFRASONIC 1

sub·spe·cies \'səb-ˌspē-shēz, -sēz\ *n* **:** a subdivision of a species: as **a :** a category in biological classification that ranks immediately below a species and designates a physically distinguishable and geographically isolated group whose members interbreed with those of other subspecies of the same species where their ranges overlap **b :** a named subdivision (as a race or variety) of a taxonomic species — **sub·spe·cif·ic** \ˌsəb-spi-'sif-ik\ *adj*

sub·stage \'səb-ˌstāj\ *n* **:** an attachment to a microscope by means of which accessories (as a mirror or lamp) are held in place beneath the stage of the instrument

sub·stance \'səb-stəns\ *n* **1 a :** essential nature **:** ESSENCE ⟨divine *substance*⟩ **b :** a fundamental or characteristic part or quality ⟨the *substance* of the speech⟩ **2 a :** physical material from which something is made or which has discrete existence **b :** matter of particular or definite chemical constitution **c :** something (as drugs or alcoholic beverages) deemed harmful and usually subject to legal restriction ⟨*substance* abuse⟩ **3 :** material possessions **:** PROPERTY ⟨a person of *substance*⟩ [Medieval French, from Latin *substantia,* from *substare* "to stand under," from *sub-* + *stare* "to stand"]

sub·stan·dard \ˌsəb-'stan-dərd, 'səb-\ *adj* **1 :** deviating from or falling short of a standard or norm ⟨*substandard* housing⟩ **2 :** conforming to a pattern of linguistic usage existing within a speech community but not that of the prestige group in that community ⟨*substandard* English⟩

sub·stan·tial \səb-'stan-chəl\ *adj* **1 a :** existing as or in substance **:** MATERIAL **b :** not imaginary or illusory **:** REAL ⟨the *substantial* world⟩ **c :** IMPORTANT 1, ESSENTIAL ⟨a *substantial* difference in the stories⟩ **2 :** ample to satisfy and nourish ⟨a *substantial* diet⟩ **3 a :** having means **:** WELL-TO-DO ⟨a *substantial* farmer⟩ **b :** considerable in quantity **:** significantly large ⟨a *substantial* increase⟩ ⟨a *substantial* wage⟩ **4 :** well and sturdily built ⟨*substantial* buildings⟩ **5 :** being largely but not wholly what is specified ⟨a *substantial* lie⟩ — **sub·stan·ti·al·i·ty** \-ˌstan-chē-'al-ət-ē\ *n* — **sub·stan·tial·ly** \-'stanch-lē-, -ə-lē\ *adv*

sub·stan·ti·ate \səb-'stan-chē-ˌāt\ *vt* **1 :** to give substance or body to **:** EMBODY **2 :** to provide evidence for **:** PROVE ⟨*substantiate* claims in court⟩ — **sub·stan·ti·a·tion** \-ˌstan-chē-'ā-shən\ *n*

¹sub·stan·tive \'səb-stən-tiv\ *n* **:** a word or word group functioning syntactically as a noun [Medieval French *sustentif,* from *sustentif* "having or expressing substance," from Late Latin *substantivus*] — **sub·stan·ti·val** \ˌsəb-stən-'tī-vəl\ *adj* — **sub·stan·ti·val·ly** \-və-lē\ *adv*

²substantive *adj* **1 :** of, relating to, or being something totally independent **2 a :** real rather than apparent ⟨*substantive* evidence⟩ **b :** belonging to the substance of a thing **:** ESSENTIAL ⟨*substantive* rights⟩ **c :** expressing existence ⟨the *substantive* verb is the verb *to be*⟩ **3 :** functioning as a grammatical substantive ⟨a *substantive* phrase⟩ **4 :** considerable in amount or

\ə\ **abut**	\au̇\ **out**	\i\ **tip**	\ȯ\ **saw**	\u̇\ **foot**
\ər\ **further**	\ch\ **chin**	\ī\ **life**	\ȯi\ **coin**	\y\ **yet**
\a\ **mat**	\e\ **pet**	\j\ **job**	\th\ **thin**	\yü\ **few**
\ā\ **take**	\ē\ **easy**	\ng\ **sing**	\th\ **this**	\yu̇\ **cure**
\ä\ **cot, cart**	\g\ **go**	\ō\ **bone**	\ü\ **food**	\zh\ **vision**

numbers : SUBSTANTIAL ⟨made *substantive* progress⟩ **5** : creating and defining rights and duties ⟨*substantive* law⟩ **6** : having substance : involving matters of major or practical importance to all concerned ⟨*substantive* discussions among world leaders⟩ [Late Latin *substantivus* "having substance," from Latin *substantia* "substance"] — **sub·stan·tive·ly** *adv* — **sub·stan·tive·ness** *n*

sub·sta·tion \ˈsəb-ˌstā-shən\ *n* **1** : a branch post office **2** : a subsidiary station in which electric current is transformed

¹sub·sti·tute \ˈsəb-stə-ˌtüt, -ˌtyüt\ *n* : a person or thing that takes the place of another [Latin *substitutus,* past participle of *substituere* "to put in place of," from *sub-* + *statuere* "to set up, place"] — **substitute** *adj*

²substitute *vb* **1** : to put in the place of another : EXCHANGE **2** : to serve as a substitute : REPLACE — **sub·sti·tu·tion** \ˌsəb-stə-ˈtü-shən, -ˈtyü-\ *n* — **sub·sti·tu·tion·al** \-shnəl, shən-l\ *adj* — **sub·sti·tu·tion·al·ly** \-ē\ *adv* — **sub·sti·tu·tion·ary** \-shə-ˌner-ē\ *adj*

sub·strate \ˈsəb-ˌstrāt\ *n* **1** : an underlying layer: as **a** : SUBSTRATUM a **b** : the base on which an organism lives or over which it moves ⟨the soil is the *substrate* of most plants⟩ **2** : a substance acted upon (as by an enzyme)

sub·stra·tum \ˈsəb-ˌstrāt-əm, -ˌstrat-\ *n* : an underlying support or layer : FOUNDATION: as **a** : the material of which something is made and from which it derives its special qualities **b** : a layer beneath the surface soil : SUBSOIL **c** : SUBSTRATE b [Medieval Latin, from Latin *substernere* "to spread under," from *sub-* + *sternere* "to spread"]

sub·struc·ture \ˈsəb-ˌstrək-chər\ *n* : an underlying or supporting part of a structure : FOUNDATION

sub·sume \səb-ˈsüm\ *vt* : to include or place within something larger or more general ⟨red, yellow, and green are *subsumed* under the term "color"⟩ [Latin *sub-* + *sumere* "to take up"] — **sub·sump·tion** \səb-ˈsəm-shən, -ˈsəmp-\ *n*

¹sub·sur·face \ˈsəb-ˌsər-fəs\ *n* : earth material (as rock) near but not exposed at the surface of the ground

²sub·sur·face \ˌsəb-ˈsər-fəs\ *adj* : of, relating to, or involving an area or material beneath a surface (as of the earth) ⟨*subsurface* water⟩

sub·teen \ˈsəb-ˈtēn\ *n* : a child approaching adolescence

sub·ten·ant \ˌsəb-ˈten-ənt, ˈsəb-\ *n* : one who rents from a tenant — **sub·ten·an·cy** \-ˈten-ən-sē\ *n*

sub·tend \səb-ˈtend\ *vt* **1 a** : to be opposite to and extend from one side to the other of ⟨a hypotenuse *subtends* a right angle⟩ **b** : to have the angular measure of when using a fixed point or object as the vertex ⟨the moon *subtends* at your eye an angle of about .5 degrees⟩ **c** : to bound or establish the limits of by marking off the endpoints of ⟨a chord *subtends* an arc⟩ **2 a** : to underlie so as to include **b** : to occupy an adjacent and usually lower position to and often so as to enclose ⟨a bract that *subtends* a flower⟩ [Latin *subtendere* "to stretch beneath," from *sub-* + *tendere* "to stretch"]

sub·ter·fuge \ˈsəb-tər-ˌfyüj\ *n* **1** : deception by skill or plan in order to conceal, escape, or evade **2** : a deceptive device or plan [Late Latin *subterfugium,* from Latin *subterfugere* "to evade," from *subter-* "beneath, secretly" + *fugere* "to flee"]

sub·ter·ra·nean \ˌsəb-tə-ˈrā-nē-ən, -nyən\ *also* **sub·ter·ra·neous** \-nē-əs, -nyəs\ *adj* **1** : being, living, or operating under the surface of the earth **2** : existing or working in secret : HIDDEN [Latin *subterraneus,* from *sub* "under" + *terra* "earth"] — **sub·ter·ra·ne·an·ly** *adv*

sub·tile \ˈsət-l, ˈsəb-tl\ *adj* **sub·til·er** \ˈsət-lər, -l-ər, ˈsəb-tə-lər\; **sub·til·est** \ˈsət-ləst, -l-əst, ˈsəb-tə-ləst\ **1** : SUBTLE 1a, ELUSIVE ⟨a *subtile* aroma⟩ **2** : ARTFUL 3b, CRAFTY [Latin *subtilis*] — **sub·tile·ly** \ˈsət-lē, -l-lē, -l-ē; ˈsəb-tə-lē\ *adv* — **sub·tile·ness** \ˈsət-l-nəs, ˈsəb-tl-\ *n*

sub·til·ty \ˈsət-l-tē, ˈsəb-tl-\ *n, pl* **-ties** : SUBTLETY

sub·ti·tle \ˈsəb-ˌtīt-l\ *n* **1** : a secondary or explanatory title **2** : a printed statement or fragment of dialogue appearing on the screen between the scenes of a silent motion picture or appearing as a translation at the bottom of the screen during the scenes especially of a foreign-language movie — **subtitle** *vt*

sub·tle \ˈsət-l\ *adj* **sub·tler** \ˈsət-lər, -l-ər\; **sub·tlest** \ˈsət-ləst, -l-əst\ **1 a** : DELICATE 1a, ELUSIVE ⟨a *subtle* fragrance⟩ **b** : difficult to understand or distinguish : OBSCURE ⟨*subtle* differences in vowel sounds⟩ **2** : marked by insight and sensitivity : PERCEPTIVE ⟨a *subtle* mind⟩ **3 a** : SKILLFUL, EXPERT ⟨*subtle* workmanship⟩ **b** : cleverly made or contrived : INGENIOUS ⟨a *subtle* mechanism⟩ **4** : ARTFUL 3b, CRAFTY **5** : working slowly but effectively : INSIDIOUS ⟨a *subtle* poison⟩ [Medieval French *sotil, subtile,* from Latin *subtilis,* literally, "fine in texture," from *sub-* + *tela* "cloth on a loom"] — **sub·tle·ness** \ˈsət-l-nəs\ *n* — **sub·tly** \ˈsət-lē, -l-lē, -l-ē\ *adv*

sub·tle·ty \ˈsət-l-tē\ *n, pl* **-ties** **1** : the quality or state of being subtle **2** : something subtle; *esp* : a fine distinction

sub·ton·ic \ˌsəb-ˈtän-ik, ˈsəb-\ *n* : LEADING TONE [from its being a half tone below the upper tonic]

sub·top·ic \ˈsəb-ˌtäp-ik\ *n* : a secondary topic : one of the subdivisions into which a topic may be divided

sub·to·tal \ˈsəb-ˌtōt-l\ *n* : the sum of part of a series of figures

sub·tract \səb-ˈtrakt\ *vb* **1** : to take away by deducting ⟨*subtract* 5 from 9⟩ **2** : to perform a subtraction [Latin *subtractus,* past participle of *subtrahere* "to draw from beneath, withdraw," from *sub-* + *trahere* "to draw"] — **sub·tract·er** *n*

sub·trac·tion \səb-ˈtrak-shən\ *n* **1** : an act or instance of subtracting **2** : the operation of deducting one number from another

sub·trac·tive \-ˈtrak-tiv\ *adj* **1** : tending to subtract **2** : constituting or involving subtraction ⟨a *subtractive* correction⟩

sub·tra·hend \ˈsəb-trə-ˌhend\ *n* : a number that is to be subtracted from a minuend [Latin *subtrahendus* "to be withdrawn," from *subtrahere* "to withdraw"]

sub·trop·i·cal \ˌsəb-ˈträp-i-kəl, ˈsəb-\ *also* **sub·trop·ic** \-ˈträp-ik\ *adj* : of, relating to, or being the regions bordering on the tropical zone ⟨*subtropical* forests⟩ ⟨*subtropical* waters⟩

sub·trop·ics \-ˈträp-iks\ *n pl* : subtropical regions

sub·urb \ˈsəb-ˌərb\ *n* **1 a** : an outlying part of a city or town **b** : a smaller community adjacent to or within commuting distance of a city **c** *pl* : the residential area adjacent to a city or large town **2** *pl* : the near vicinity : ENVIRONS [Latin *suburbium,* from *sub-* "near" + *urbs* "city"] — **sub·ur·ban** \se-ˈbər-bən\ *adj or n*

sub·ur·ban·ite \sə-ˈbər-bə-ˌnīt\ *n* : a person who lives in the suburbs

sub·ur·bia \sə-ˈbər-bē-ə\ *n* **1** : the suburbs of a city **2** : people who live in the suburbs **3** : the manners, styles, and customs typical of suburban life

sub·ven·tion \səb-ˈven-chən\ *n* : financial support especially in the form of an endowment or a subsidy [Medieval French *subvencion,* from Late Latin *subventio* "assistance," from Latin *subvenire* "to come up, come to the rescue," from *sub-* "up" + *venire* "to come"]

sub·ver·sion \səb-ˈvər-zhən\ *n* : the act of subverting : the state of being subverted; *esp* : a systematic attempt to overthrow or undermine a government or political system by persons working secretly within the country involved [Medieval French, from Late Latin *subversio,* from Latin *subvertere* "to subvert"] — **sub·ver·sive** \-ˈvər-siv, -ziv\ *adj or n* — **sub·ver·sive·ly** *adv*

sub·vert \səb-ˈvərt\ *vt* **1** : to overturn or overthrow from the foundation : RUIN **2** : to corrupt by undermining the morals, allegiance, or faith of [Medieval French *subvertir,* from Latin *subvertere,* literally, "to turn from below," from *sub-* + *vertere* "to turn"] — **sub·vert·er** *n*

sub·way \ˈsəb-ˌwā\ *n* **1** : an underground passage **2** : a usually electric underground railway

sub·woof·er \ˈsəb-ˈwu̇f-ər\ *n* : a loudspeaker responsive only to the lowest acoustic frequencies

sub·ze·ro \ˌsəb-ˈzē-rō, -ˈziər-ō\ *adj* : being or marked by temperature below zero

suc·ceed \sək-ˈsēd\ *vb* **1 a** : to come next after another in possession of an office or estate; *esp* : to inherit sovereignty, rank, or title **b** : to follow after another in order **2 a** : to turn out well **b** : to attain a desired object or end : be successful ⟨students who *succeed* in school⟩ [Medieval French *succeeder,* from Latin *succedere,* from *sub-* "near" + *cedere* "to go"] ***synonyms*** see FOLLOW — **suc·ceed·er** *n*

suc·cess \sək-ˈses\ *n* **1 a** : degree or measure of succeeding **b** : a favorable completion of something **c** : the gaining of wealth, favor, or prestige **2** : one that succeeds [Latin *successus,* from *succedere* "to succeed"]

suc·cess·ful \-fəl\ *adj* **1** : resulting or terminating in success **2** : gaining or having gained success — **suc·cess·ful·ly** \-fə-lē\ *adv* — **suc·cess·ful·ness** *n*

suc·ces·sion \sək-ˈsesh-ən\ *n* **1** : the order, action, or right of succeeding to a throne, title, or property **2 a** : a repeated following of one person or thing after another **b** : a process of one-way ecological change in a biological community in which one group of plants or animals is replaced by a different group [Latin *successio,* from *succedere* "to succeed"] — **suc·ces·sion·al** \-'sesh-nəl, -ən-l\ *adj* — **suc·ces·sion·al·ly** \-ē\ *adv*

synonyms SUCCESSION, SEQUENCE, SERIES mean an order of things or people following one another. SUCCESSION may apply to things of any sort that follow in order of time or place and usually without interruption ⟨walked through a *succession* of rooms⟩. SEQUENCE suggests a uniform, logical, or regular succession ⟨the *sequence* of events⟩. SERIES implies that the objects are of a similar nature or stand in similar relation to each other ⟨a *series* of monthly payments⟩.

suc·ces·sive \sək-'ses-iv\ *adj* **:** following in succession or serial order **:** following each other without interruption ⟨failed in three *successive* tries⟩ ***synonyms*** see CONSECUTIVE — **suc·ces·sive·ly** *adv* — **suc·ces·sive·ness** *n*

suc·ces·sor \sək-'ses-ər\ *n* **:** one that follows; *esp* **:** a person who succeeds to a throne, title, estate, or office

suc·cinct \sək-'singt, ˌsek-, ˌsə-, -'singkt\ *adj* **1** *archaic* **a :** being girded **b :** close-fitting **2 :** marked by briefness and compactness of expression **:** CONCISE [Latin *succinctus* "having one's clothes gathered up by a belt, tightly wrapped, concise," from *sub-* + *cinctus,* past participle of *cingere* "to gird"] — **suc·cinct·ly** *adv* — **suc·cinct·ness** *n*

[1]suc·cor \'sək-ər\ *n* **:** RELIEF 1a; *also* **:** AID, HELP [Medieval French *sucors,* from Medieval Latin *succursus,* from Latin *succurrere* "to run to the rescue, bring aid," from *sub-* + *currere* "to run"]

[2]succor *vt* **suc·cored; suc·cor·ing :** to go to the aid of (one in need or distress) **:** RELIEVE — **suc·cor·er** *n*

suc·co·ry \'sək-rē, -ə-rē\ *n, pl* **-ries :** CHICORY [Middle English *cicoree*]

suc·co·tash \'sək-ə-ˌtash\ *n* **:** lima or shell beans and kernels of green corn cooked together [Narragansett *msíckquatash* "boiled corn kernels"]

suc·cu·bus \'sək-yə-bəs\ *n, pl* **suc·cu·bi** \-ˌbī, -ˌbē\ **:** a demon assuming female form to have sexual intercourse with men in their sleep [Medieval Latin, from Latin *succuba* "prostitute," from Latin *succubare* "to lie under," from *sub-* + *cubare* "to lie, recline"]

[1]suc·cu·lent \'sək-yə-lənt\ *adj* **1 a :** full of juice **:** JUICY ⟨*succulent* cherries⟩ **b :** moist and tasty ⟨a *succulent* meal⟩ **c :** having fleshy tissues that conserve moisture ⟨*succulent* plants⟩ **2 :** full of vitality, freshness, or richness ⟨a *succulent* book⟩ [Latin *suculentus,* from *sucus* "juice"] — **suc·cu·lence** \-ləns\ *n* — **suc·cu·lent·ly** *adv*

[2]succulent *n* **:** a succulent plant (as a cactus or an aloe)

suc·cumb \sə-'kəm\ *vi* **1 :** to yield to superior strength or force or overpowering appeal or desire ⟨*succumb* to temptation⟩ **2 :** to cease to exist **:** DIE ⟨many of the early settlers *succumbed* during the winter⟩ [Latin *succumbere,* from *sub-* + *-cumbere* "to lie down"] ***synonyms*** see YIELD

[1]such \səch, 'səch, sich, ˌsich\ *adj* **1 a :** of a kind or character to be stated or suggested ⟨a coat *such* as a doctor wears⟩ **b :** having a quality to a degree to be indicated ⟨our excitement was *such* that we shouted⟩ **2 :** having a quality already specified ⟨deeply moved by *such* acts of kindness⟩ **3 :** of so extreme a degree or quality ⟨has *such* courage⟩ ⟨*such* a storm⟩ **4 :** of the same class, type, or sort ⟨other *such* stores throughout the state⟩ [Old English *swilc*]

[2]such *pron* **1 :** such a person or thing ⟨had a plan if it may be called *such*⟩ **2 :** someone or something stated, implied, or exemplified ⟨*such* were the Romans⟩ ⟨*such* was the result⟩ **3 :** someone or something similar ⟨ships and planes and *such*⟩ — **as such :** in itself ⟨*as such* the gift was worth little⟩

[3]such *adv* **1 :** to such a degree **:** SO ⟨*such* tall buildings⟩ ⟨*such* a fine person⟩ **2 :** VERY, ESPECIALLY ⟨hasn't been in *such* good spirits lately⟩ **3 :** in such a way ⟨spoke *such* that we listened attentively⟩

[1]such and such *pron* **:** something not specified ⟨it's easy to say we want the system to produce *such and such*⟩

[2]such and such *adj* **:** not named or specified ⟨wait until *such and such* a date⟩

[1]such·like \'səch-ˌlīk\ *adj* **:** of like kind **:** SIMILAR ⟨the third *suchlike* event⟩

[2]suchlike *pron* **:** someone or something of the same sort **:** a similar person or thing ⟨rumors and *suchlike*⟩

[1]suck \'sək\ *vb* **1 a :** to draw in (liquid) or draw liquid from through suction created by movements of the mouth ⟨*suck* venom from a snakebite⟩ **b :** to draw milk from a breast or udder with the mouth ⟨young pigs *sucking* well⟩ **c** (1) **:** to consume by applying the lips or tongue to ⟨*suck* a lollipop⟩ (2) **:** to apply the mouth to in order to or as if to suck out liquid ⟨*suck* a bruised finger⟩ **2 :** to take something in or up or remove something from by or as if by suction ⟨plants *sucking* moisture from the soil⟩ ⟨a well *sucked* dry by constant pumping⟩ **3 :** to make or cause to make a sound or motion like that of sucking ⟨*suck* in your stomach⟩ **4 :** to act in an overly flattering or servile manner ⟨*sucking* up to the boss⟩ [Old English *sūcan*]

[2]suck *n* **1 :** the act of sucking **2 :** a sucking movement or force

[1]suck·er \'sək-ər\ *n* **1 :** one that sucks **2 :** a part of an animal's body used for sucking or for clinging by suction **3 :** a secondary shoot from the roots or lower part of a plant **4 :** any of numerous chiefly North American freshwater fishes related to the carps but having usually thick soft lips for sucking in food **5 :** LOLLIPOP **6 a :** a person easily cheated or deceived **b :** a person irresistibly attracted to something ⟨a *sucker* for new cars⟩

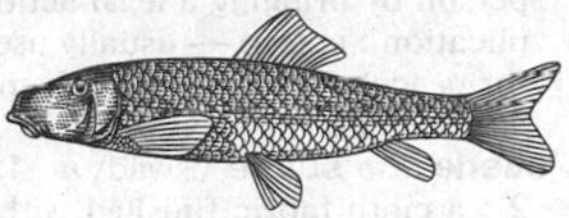
sucker 4

[2]sucker *vb* **suck·ered; suck·er·ing** \'sək-ring, -ə-ring\ **1 :** to remove suckers from **2 :** to send out suckers

sucker punch *vt* **:** to punch (a person) suddenly without warning and often for no apparent reason — **sucker punch** *n*

sucking louse *n* **:** any of an order (Anoplura) of wingless insects comprising the true lice with mouthparts adapted to sucking body fluids

suck·le \'sək-əl\ *vb* **suck·led; suck·ling** \'sək-ling, -ə-ling\ **1 a :** to give milk to from the breast or udder ⟨a mother *suckling* her child⟩ **b :** to bring up **:** NOURISH ⟨was *suckled* on cartoons⟩ **2 :** to draw milk from the breast or udder ⟨the lambs are *suckling*⟩ [probably back-formation from *suckling*]

suck·ling \'sək-ling\ *n* **:** a young unweaned animal

su·crase \'sü-ˌkrās\ *n* **:** INVERTASE [French *sucre* "sugar"]

su·crose \'sü-ˌkrōs\ *n* **:** a sweet crystalline disaccharide sugar $C_{12}H_{22}O_{11}$ that occurs naturally in most plants and is the sugar obtained from sugarcane or sugar beets [French *sucre* "sugar"]

[1]suc·tion \'sək-shən\ *n* **1 :** the act or process of sucking **2 a :** the action of exerting a force upon something by means of reduced air pressure over part of its surface so that the normal air pressure on another part of its surface pushes or tends to push it toward the region of reduced pressure **b :** force so exerted [Late Latin *suctio,* from Latin *sugere* "to suck"] — **suc·tion·al** \-shən-l, -shnəl\ *adj*

[2]suction *vt* **:** to remove by suction ⟨*suctioned* fluid from the lungs⟩

suction cup *n* **:** a cup-shaped device in which a partial vacuum can be produced when applied to a surface

Su·dan grass \sü-'dan-, -'dän-\ *n* **:** a vigorous tall-growing annual sorghum widely grown for hay and fodder

[1]sud·den \'səd-n\ *adj* **1 a :** happening quickly and unexpectedly ⟨a *sudden* shower⟩ **b :** changing angle or character all at once ⟨a *sudden* turn in the road⟩ ⟨a *sudden* drop in the ocean bottom⟩ **2 :** marked by or showing hastiness **:** RASH ⟨a *sudden* decision⟩ **3 :** made or brought about in a short time **:** PROMPT ⟨a *sudden* cure⟩ [Medieval French *sudain,* from Latin *subitaneus,* from *subitus* "sudden," from *subire* "to come up," from *sub-* "up" + *ire* "to go"] — **sud·den·ly** *adv* — **sud·den·ness** \'səd-n-nəs, 'səd-n-əs\ *n*

[2]sudden *n, obsolete* **:** an unexpected occurrence **:** EMERGENCY — **all of a sudden** *also* **on a sudden :** sooner than was expected **:** SUDDENLY

sudden death *n* **:** extra play to break a tie in a sports contest in which the first to score or gain the lead wins

sudden infant death syndrome *n* **:** death of an apparently healthy infant usually before one year of age that is of unknown cause and occurs usually during sleep — abbreviation *SIDS*

su·do·ku \sü-'dō-kü\ *n* **:** a puzzle in which several numbers are to be filled into a 9x9 grid of squares so that every row, every

\ə\ **abut**	\au̇\ **out**	\i\ **tip**	\ȯ\ **saw**	\u̇\ **foot**
\ər\ **further**	\ch\ **chin**	\ī\ **life**	\ȯi\ **coin**	\y\ **yet**
\a\ **mat**	\e\ **pet**	\j\ **job**	\th\ **thin**	\yü\ **few**
\ā\ **take**	\ē\ **easy**	\ng\ **sing**	\t͟h\ **this**	\yu̇\ **cure**
\ä\ **cot, cart**	\g\ **go**	\ō\ **bone**	\ü\ **food**	\zh\ **vision**

column, and every 3x3 box contains the numbers 1 through 9 [Japanese *sūdoku*]

su·do·rif·ic \-ˈrif-ik\ *adj* : causing or inducing sweat ⟨*sudorific* herbs⟩ [Latin *sudor* "sweat"] — **sudorific** *n*

[1]**suds** \ˈsədz\ *n pl* **1** : water mixed with soap or detergent especially when frothy; *also* : the froth on such water **2** : BEER 1 [probably from Dutch *sudse* "marsh"]

[2]**suds** *vb* **1** : to wash in suds **2** : to form suds

sudsy \ˈsəd-zē\ *adj* **suds·i·er; -est** : full of suds : FROTHY

sue \ˈsü\ *vb* **1** : to pay court to : WOO **2** : to seek justice from a person by bringing a legal action **3** : to make a request or application : PLEAD — usually used with *for* or *to* ⟨the nation *sued* for peace⟩ [Medieval French *sivre, siure,* derived from Latin *sequi* "to follow"] — **su·er** *n*

suede *also* **suède** \ˈswād\ *n* **1** : leather with a napped surface **2** : a cloth fabric finished with a short nap to resemble suede [French *gants de Suède* "Swedish gloves"]

su·et \ˈsü-ət\ *n* : the hard fat about the kidneys and loins in beef and mutton from which tallow is made [Medieval French *suet, siuet,* from *seu, su* "hard animal fat," from Latin *sebum*]

suf·fer \ˈsəf-ər\ *vb* **suf·fered; suf·fer·ing** \ˈsəf-ring, -ə-ring\ **1** : to feel or endure pain **2** : EXPERIENCE, UNDERGO ⟨*suffer* a defeat⟩ **3** : to bear loss or damage ⟨the business *suffered* during your illness⟩ **4** : to allow especially because of indifference [Medieval French *souffrir,* from Latin *suffere,* from *sub-* "up" + *ferre* "to bear"] — **suf·fer·able** \ˈsəf-rə-bəl, -ə-rə-\ *adj* — **suf·fer·ably** \-blē\ *adv* — **suf·fer·er** \ˈsəf-ər-ər\ *n*

suf·fer·ance \ˈsəf-rəns, -ə-rəns\ *n* **1** : consent or approval implied by a lack of interference or failure to enforce a prohibition **2** : power or ability to withstand ⟨pain beyond *sufferance*⟩

suf·fer·ing *n* **1** : the state or experience of one that suffers **2** : mental or physical pain ***synonyms*** see DISTRESS

suf·fice \sə-ˈfīs\ *vb* **1** : to meet or satisfy a need : be sufficient **2** : to be competent or capable **3** : to be enough for [Medieval French *suffis-,* stem of *suffire* "to suffice," from Latin *sufficere* "to provide, be adequate," from *sub-* + *facere* "to make, do"]

suf·fi·cien·cy \sə-ˈfish-ən-sē\ *n, pl* **-cies** **1** : sufficient means to meet one's needs : COMPETENCY **2** : the quality or state of being sufficient : ADEQUACY

suf·fi·cient \sə-ˈfish-ənt\ *adj* **1** : enough to meet the needs of a situation or a proposed end **2** : being a proposition whose truth is adequate to insure the truth of another proposition ⟨*p* is necessary and *sufficient* for *q*⟩ [Latin *sufficiens,* from *sufficere* "to suffice"] — **suf·fi·cient·ly** *adv*

synonyms SUFFICIENT, ENOUGH, ADEQUATE mean being what is necessary or desirable. SUFFICIENT suggests a fairly exact meeting of a need ⟨*sufficient* savings⟩. ENOUGH is less exact or less formal than SUFFICIENT ⟨do you have *enough* food?⟩. ADEQUATE may imply barely meeting a requirement or a moderate standard ⟨the service was *adequate*⟩.

[1]**suf·fix** \ˈsəf-ˌiks\ *n* : an affix occurring at the end of a word [Latin *suffixus,* past participle of *suffigere* "to fasten underneath," from *sub-* + *figere* "to fasten"] — **suf·fix·al** \-ˌik-səl\ *adj*

[2]**suf·fix** \ˈsəf-ˌiks, sə-ˈfiks\ *vt* : to attach as a suffix — **suf·fix·a·tion** \ˌsəf-ˌik-ˈsā-shən\ *n*

suf·fo·cate \ˈsəf-ə-ˌkāt\ *vb* **1 a** (1) : to stop the breath of (as by strangling or asphyxiation) (2) : to deprive of oxygen **b** : to make uncomfortable by want of fresh air **2** : to hinder or stop the development of **3** : to be or become suffocated; *esp* : to die or suffer from lack of oxygen or being unable to breathe [Latin *suffocare,* from *sub-* + *fauces* "throat"] — **suf·fo·ca·tion** \ˌsəf-ə-ˈkā-shən\ *n* — **suf·fo·ca·tive** \ˈsəf-ə-ˌkāt-iv\ *adj*

suf·fo·cat·ing \-ˌkāt-ing\ *adj* : tending or serving to suffocate or overpower : OVERWHELMING — **suf·fo·cat·ing·ly** *adv*

[1]**suf·fra·gan** \ˈsəf-ri-gən\ *n* **1** : a diocesan bishop (as in the Roman Catholic Church and the Church of England) of lower rank than a metropolitan **2** : an Anglican Episcopal bishop assisting a diocesan bishop and not having the right of succession [Medieval French, from Medieval Latin *suffraganeus,* from *suffragium* "support"]

[2]**suffragan** *adj* **1** : of or being a suffragan **2** : of lower rank than a metropolitan or archiepiscopal see

suf·frage \ˈsəf-rij\ *n* **1** : an intercessory prayer **2** : a vote given in deciding a disputed question or in electing a person to office **3** : the right of voting : FRANCHISE; *also* : the exercise of such right [Latin *suffragium* "vote, political support"]

suf·frag·ette \ˌsəf-ri-ˈjet\ *n* : a woman who supports suffrage for her sex

suf·frag·ist \ˈsəf-ri-jəst\ *n* : one who supports extension of suffrage especially to women

suf·fuse \sə-ˈfyüz\ *vt* : to spread over or through in the manner of fluid or light : FLUSH, FILL [Latin *suffusus,* past participle of *suffundere* "to pour beneath, suffuse," from *sub-* + *fundere* "to pour"] ***synonyms*** see INFUSE — **suf·fu·sion** \-ˈfyü-zhən\ *n* — **suf·fu·sive** \-ˈfyü-siv, -ziv\ *adj*

Su·fi \ˈsü-fē\ *n* : a Muslim mystic [Arabic *ṣūfī,* perhaps from *ṣuf* "wool"] — **Sufi** *adj* — **Su·fic** \-fik\ *adj* — **Su·fism** \-ˌfiz-əm\ *n*

[1]**sug·ar** \ˈshu̇g-ər\ *n* **1** : a sweet crystallizable material that consists wholly or essentially of sucrose, is colorless or white when pure, is obtained commercially from sugarcane or sugar beet and less extensively from sorghum, maples, and palms, and is nutritionally important as a source of dietary carbohydrate and as a sweetener and preservative of other foods **2** : any of various water-soluble compounds that vary widely in sweetness and comprise the simpler carbohydrates [Medieval French *sucre,* from Medieval Latin *zuccarum,* from Italian *zucchero,* from Arabic *sukkar,* from Persian *shakar,* ultimately from Sanskrit *śarkarā*]

[2]**sugar** *vb* **sug·ared; sug·ar·ing** \ˈshu̇g-ring, -ə-ring\ **1** : to mix, cover, or sprinkle with sugar **2** : to make something less hard to take or bear **3** : to change to crystals of sugar

sugar beet *n* : a white-rooted beet grown for the sugar in its roots

sugar bush *n* : woods in which sugar maples predominate

sug·ar·cane \ˈshu̇g-ər-ˌkān\ *n* : a tall perennial grass native to tropical southeastern Asia that has a thick jointed stem and is widely grown in warm regions as a source of sugar

sug·ar·coat \ˌshu̇g-ər-ˈkōt\ *vt* **1** : to coat with sugar **2** : to make attractive or agreeable on the surface

sug·ar·house \ˈshu̇g-ər-ˌhau̇s\ *n* : a building where sugar is made or refined; *esp* : one where maple sap is boiled in the making of maple syrup and maple sugar

sug·ar·less \ˈshu̇g-ər-ləs\ *adj* : containing no sugar ⟨*sugarless* gum⟩

sug·ar·loaf \-ˌlōf\ *n* **1** : refined sugar molded into a cone **2** : a hill or mountain shaped like a sugarloaf — **sugarloaf** *adj*

sugar maple *n* : a maple of eastern North America with 3-lobed to 5-lobed leaves, hard close-grained wood much used for cabinetwork, and sap that is the chief source of maple syrup and maple sugar

sugar maple

sugar pine *n* : a very tall pine of California and Oregon that has large cones up to 18 inches (46 centimeters) long and a soft reddish brown wood

sug·ar·plum \ˈshu̇g-ər-ˌpləm\ *n* : a round piece of candy

sug·ary \ˈshu̇g-rē, -ə-rē\ *adj* **1** : containing, resembling, or tasting of sugar **2** : affectedly or over sweet

sug·gest \səg-ˈjest, sə-ˈjest\ *vt* **1 a** : to put (as a thought, plan, or desire) into a person's mind **b** : to propose as an idea or possibility ⟨*suggest* going for a walk⟩ **2** : to call to mind through close connection or association [Latin *suggestus,* past participle of *suggerere* "to pile up, furnish, suggest," from *sub-* + *gerere* "to carry"] — **sug·gest·er** *n*

synonyms SUGGEST, HINT, INTIMATE mean to convey an idea indirectly. SUGGEST stresses putting into the mind by association of ideas ⟨a book title that *suggests* its subject matter⟩. HINT implies the use of slight or remote suggestion with a minimum of overt statement ⟨*hinted* that she might get the job⟩. INTIMATE stresses delicacy of suggestion without connoting any lack of candor ⟨*intimates* that there is more to the situation than meets the eye⟩.

sug·gest·ible \səg-ˈjes-tə-bəl, sə-ˈjes-\ *adj* : easily influenced by suggestion — **sug·gest·ibil·i·ty** \-ˌjes-tə-ˈbil-ət-ē\ *n*

sug·ges·tion \səg-ˈjes-chən, sə-ˈjes-, -ˈjesh-\ *n* **1 a** : the act or process of suggesting **b** : something suggested **2 a** : the process by which a physical or mental state is influenced by a thought or idea ⟨the power of *suggestion*⟩ **b** : the process by which one thought leads to another especially through association of ideas **c** : a way of influencing attitudes and behavior hypnotically **3** : a slight indication : TRACE

sug·ges·tive \səg-ˈjes-tiv, sə-ˈjes-\ *adj* **1 a** : giving a suggestion : INDICATIVE **b** : full of suggestions : PROVOCATIVE **c** : stirring mental associations **2** : suggesting or tending to suggest something indelicate : RISQUÉ — **sug·ges·tive·ly** *adv* — **sug·ges·tive·ness** *n*

sui·cid·al \ˌsü-ə-ˈsīd-l\ *adj* **1 a** : very dangerous to life ⟨*suicidal* risks⟩ **b** : destructive of one's own interests **2** : relating to or of the nature of suicide **3** : marked by an impulse to kill oneself — **sui·cid·al·ly** \-l-ē\ *adv*

[1]**sui·cide** \ˈsü-ə-ˌsīd\ *n* **1 a** : the act of taking one's own life voluntarily **b** : ruin of one's own interests ⟨political *suicide*⟩ **2** : one that commits or attempts suicide [Latin *sui* "of oneself" + English *-cide*]

[2]**suicide** *adj* : of or relating to suicide; *esp* : being or performing an act resulting in the voluntary death of the person who does it ⟨a *suicide* bomber⟩

sui ge·ner·is \ˌsü-ˌī-ˈjen-ə-rəs, ˌsü-ē-ˈjen-, -ˈgen-\ *adj* : forming a class alone : PECULIAR [Latin, "of its own kind"]

[1]**suit** \ˈsüt\ *n* **1** : an action or process in a court for enforcing a right or claim **2** : an act or instance of suing or seeking by entreaty; *esp* : COURTSHIP **3** : a number of things used together : SET **4** : a set of garments: as **a** : an outer costume of two or more pieces **b** : a costume to be worn for a special purpose or under particular conditions ⟨a gym *suit*⟩ **5 a** : all the playing cards of one kind (as spades or hearts) in a pack; *also* : all the cards of the same suit held by a player ⟨a 5-card *suit*⟩ **b** : all the dominoes bearing the same number on one half of the face [Medieval French *siute, suite* "act of following, suite," derived from Latin *sequi* "to follow"]

[2]**suit** *vb* **1** : to be in accordance : AGREE ⟨the job *suits* with your abilities⟩ **2** : to be appropriate or acceptable ⟨these prices don't *suit*⟩ **3** : to outfit with clothes : DRESS **4** : ADAPT ⟨*suit* the action to the word⟩ **5 a** : to be proper for : BEFIT ⟨a mood that *suits* the occasion⟩ **b** : to be becoming to ⟨that dress *suits* you⟩ **6** : to meet the needs or desires of : PLEASE ⟨*suits* me fine⟩

suit·able \ˈsüt-ə-bəl\ *adj* **1** : adapted to a use or purpose **2** : satisfying propriety : PROPER ⟨clothes *suitable* to the occasion⟩ **3** : QUALIFIED 1 ⟨*suitable* candidates⟩ ***synonyms*** see FIT — **suit·abil·i·ty** \ˌsüt-ə-ˈbil-ət-ē\ *n* — **suit·able·ness** \ˈsüt-ə-bəl-nəs\ *n* — **suit·ably** \-blē\ *adv*

suit·case \ˈsüt-ˌkās\ *n* : a portable case designed to hold a traveler's clothing and personal articles

suite \ˈswēt, *2c is also* ˈsüt\ *n* **1** : RETINUE; *esp* : the personal staff accompanying a ruler, diplomat, or dignitary on official business **2** : a group of things forming a unit or making up a collection : SET: as **a** : a group of rooms occupied as a unit : APARTMENT **b** (1) : a 17th and 18th century instrumental musical form consisting of a series of dances in the same or related keys (2) : a modern instrumental composition in several movements of different character (3) : an orchestral concert arrangement in suite form of material drawn from a longer work (as a ballet) **c** : a set of matched furniture for a room **d** : a set of computer programs designed to work together and usually sold as a single unit [French, from Medieval French *siute, suite*]

suit·ing \ˈsüt-ing\ *n* : fabric for suits of clothes

suit·or \ˈsüt-ər\ *n* **1** : one that petitions or pleads **2** : a party to a suit at law **3** : a man who courts a woman or seeks to marry her

su·ki·ya·ki \skē-ˈäk-ē, ˌsu̇k-ē-ˈäk-ē\ *n* : a dish prepared from meat, tofu, and vegetables (as onions, celery, bamboo sprouts, and mushrooms) cooked in soy sauce, sake, and sugar [Japanese, from *suki-* "slice" + *yaki* "broil"]

Suk·koth *or* **Suk·kot** \ˈsu̇k-ˌōt, -ˌōth, -ˌōs\ *n* : a Jewish holiday celebrated in September or October as a harvest festival of thanksgiving that commemorates the temporary shelters used by the Jews during their wanderings in the wilderness [Hebrew *sukkōth,* plural of *sukkāh*]

sul·cus \ˈsəl-kəs\ *n, pl* **sul·ci** \-ˌkī, -ˌkē\ : an anatomical furrow or groove; *esp* : a shallow furrow on the surface of the brain separating adjacent convolutions [Latin] — **sul·cate** \-ˌkāt\ *adj*

sulf- *combining form* : sulfur : containing sulfur ⟨*sulf*ide⟩

sul·fa \ˈsəl-fə\ *adj* **1** : related chemically to sulfanilamide **2** : of, relating to, or containing sulfa drugs [short for *sulfanilamide*]

sulfa drug *n* : any of various synthetic bacteria-inhibiting drugs that are sulfonamides derived especially from sulfanilamide

sul·fa·nil·a·mide \ˌsəl-fə-ˈnil-ə-ˌmīd, -məd\ *n* : a crystalline compound that is the parent compound of most of the sulfa drugs [*sulfanil*ic + *amide*]

sul·fate \ˈsəl-ˌfāt\ *n* : a salt or ester of sulfuric acid

sul·fide \ˈsəl-ˌfīd\ *n* : a compound of sulfur with one or more other elements : a salt of hydrogen sulfide

sul·fite \ˈsəl-ˌfīt\ *n* : a salt or ester of sulfurous acid — **sul·fit·ic** \ˌsəl-ˈfit-ik\ *adj*

sul·fon·amide \ˌsəl-ˈfän-ə-ˌmīd, -ˈfō-nə-, -məd\ *n* : the amide (as sulfanilamide) of a sulfonic acid; *also* : SULFA DRUG

sul·fon·ic acid \ˌsəl-ˌfän-ik-, -ˈfōn-\ *n* : any of numerous acids that may be derived from sulfuric acid by replacement of a hydroxyl group by either an inorganic anion or a univalent organic radical [derived from *sulf-*]

sul·fur *also* **sul·phur** \ˈsəl-fər\ *n* : a nonmetallic element that occurs either free or in combined form, is a constituent of proteins, exists in several forms including yellow crystals, and is used especially in the chemical and paper industries, in rubber vulcanization, and in medicine for treating skin diseases — see ELEMENT table [Latin]

sulfur dioxide *n* : a heavy strong-smelling gas SO_2 that is used especially in making sulfuric acid, in bleaching, as a preservative, and as a refrigerant and is a major air pollutant especially in industrial areas

sul·fu·ric \ˌsəl-ˈfyu̇r-ik\ *adj* : of, relating to, or containing sulfur especially in a higher valence

sulfuric acid *n* : a heavy corrosive oily strong acid H_2SO_4 that is colorless when pure and is a vigorous oxidizing and dehydrating agent

sul·fu·rous *also* **sul·phu·rous** \ˈsəl-fyə-rəs, -fə-, *also esp for 1* ˌsəl-ˈfyu̇r-əs\ *adj* **1** : of, relating to, or containing sulfur especially in a lower valence **2 a** : of, relating to, or dealing with the fire of hell : INFERNAL **b** : FIERY, INFLAMED ⟨*sulfurous* sermons⟩ **c** : PROFANE, BLASPHEMOUS ⟨*sulfurous* language⟩ — **sul·fu·rous·ly** *adv* — **sul·fu·rous·ness** *n*

sulfurous acid *n* : a weak unstable acid H_2SO_3 known in solution and through its salts and used as a reducing and bleaching agent

[1]**sulk** \ˈsəlk\ *vi* : to be moodily silent or ill-humored [back-formation from *sulky*]

[2]**sulk** *n* **1** : the state of one sulking — often used in plural ⟨had a case of the *sulks*⟩ **2** : a sulky mood or spell ⟨was in a *sulk*⟩

[1]**sulky** \ˈsəl-kē\ *adj* **sulk·i·er; -est** **1** : inclined to sulk : given to fits of sulking **2** : MALCONTENT, GLOOMY [probably from obsolete *sulke* "sluggish"] ***synonyms*** see SULLEN — **sulk·i·ly** \-kə-lē\ *adv* — **sulk·i·ness** \-kē-nəs\ *n*

[2]**sulky** *n, pl* **sulk·ies** : a light 2-wheeled vehicle having a seat for the driver only and usually no body [probably from [1]*sulky*]

sul·len \ˈsəl-ən\ *adj* **1 a** : gloomily or resentfully silent or repressed **b** : suggesting a sullen state ⟨a *sullen* refusal⟩ **2** : dull or somber in sound or color **3** : DISMAL 1, GLOOMY ⟨a *sullen* morning⟩ [Middle English *solein* "solitary," from Medieval French *sulein, solain,* perhaps from *sol, soul* "single, sole" + *-ain* after Medieval French *soltain* "solitary, private," from Late Latin *solitaneus,* ultimately from Latin *solus* "alone"] — **sul·len·ly** *adv* — **sul·len·ness** \ˈsəl-ən-nəs, -ən-əs\ *n*

synonyms SULLEN, SURLY, SULKY mean showing a forbidding or disagreeable mood. SULLEN implies a gloomy silent bad humor and a refusal to be sociable ⟨remained *sullen* at the party⟩. SURLY implies rudeness and gruffness especially in response to requests or questions ⟨a *surly* and selfish child⟩. SULKY suggests childish resentment expressed in fits of peevish sullenness ⟨grew *sulky* after losing the game⟩.

sul·ly \ˈsəl-ē\ *vb* **sul·lied; sul·ly·ing** : to make soiled or tarnished [probably from Middle English *sulen* "to soil," from Old English *sylian*]

sul·phur butterfly \ˌsəl-fər-\ *n* : any of numerous rather small butterflies having usually yellow or orange wings with a black border

\ə\ **abut**	\au̇\ **out**	\i\ **tip**	\ȯ\ **saw**	\u̇\ **foot**
\ər\ **further**	\ch\ **chin**	\ī\ **life**	\ȯi\ **coin**	\y\ **yet**
\a\ **mat**	\e\ **pet**	\j\ **job**	\th\ **thin**	\yü\ **few**
\ā\ **take**	\ē\ **easy**	\ng\ **sing**	\t͟h\ **this**	\yu̇\ **cure**
\ä\ **cot, cart**	\g\ **go**	\ō\ **bone**	\ü\ **food**	\zh\ **vision**

sulphur yellow *n* : a brilliant greenish yellow

sul·tan \ˈsəlt-ⁿn\ *n* : a king or sovereign especially of a Muslim state [Middle French, from Arabic *sulṭān*]

sul·tana \ˌsəl-ˈtan-ə\ *n* **1** : a woman who is a member of a sultan's family; *esp* : a sultan's wife **2** : a pale yellow seedless grape grown for raisins and wine; *also* : the raisin of this grape [Italian, from *sultano* "sultan," from Arabic *sulṭān*]

sul·tan·ate \ˈsəlt-ⁿn-ˌāt\ *n* **1** : the office, dignity, or power of a sultan **2** : a state or country governed by a sultan

sul·try \ˈsəl-trē\ *adj* **sul·tri·er; -est** **1** : very hot and humid ⟨a *sultry* day⟩ **2** : burning hot ⟨the *sultry* sun⟩ **3** : exciting or capable of exciting strong sexual desire ⟨*sultry* glances⟩ [derived from *swelter*] — **sul·tri·ly** \-trə-lē\ *adv* — **sul·tri·ness** \-trē-nəs\ *n*

[1]**sum** \ˈsəm\ *n* **1** : an indefinite or specified amount of money **2** : the whole amount **3 a** : a summary of the chief points or thoughts **b** : GIST ⟨the *sum* and substance of an argument⟩ **4 a** : the result of adding numbers ⟨the *sum* of 5 and 7 is 12⟩ **b** : the limit of the sum of the first *n* terms of an infinite series as *n* increases indefinitely ⟨the *sum* of $1 + \frac{1}{2} + \frac{1}{4} + \frac{1}{8} + \frac{1}{16} + \ldots$ is 2⟩ **c** : a problem in arithmetic [Medieval French *sume, somme,* from Latin *summa,* from *summus* "highest"] — **in sum** : in short : BRIEFLY

synonyms SUM, AMOUNT, AGGREGATE, TOTAL mean the entire quantity or number obtained by taking or putting together all in a given group or mass. SUM indicates the result of simple addition of numbers or particulars ⟨four is the *sum* of two and two⟩. AMOUNT implies the result of accumulating or successive additions ⟨measured the *amount* of rainfall⟩. AGGREGATE stresses the notion of the grouping or massing together of distinct individuals ⟨an *aggregate* of states that form a nation⟩. TOTAL stresses the completeness or inclusiveness of the addition ⟨invited a *total* of 20 guests⟩.

[2]**sum** *vb* **summed; sum·ming** **1** : to calculate the sum of : TOTAL **2** : to reach a sum : AMOUNT — usually used with *to* **3** : SUMMARIZE

su·mac *also* **su·mach** \ˈsü-ˌmak, ˈshü-\ *n* **1** : any of a genus of trees, shrubs, and woody vines related to the cashew and having compound leaves turning to brilliant colors in autumn and spikes or loose clusters of red or whitish berries — compare POISON IVY, POISON OAK, POISON SUMAC **2** : a material used in tanning and dyeing made of the leaves and flowers of sumac [Medieval French *sumac,* from Arabic *summāq*]

sumac 1

Su·mer·i·an \sü-ˈmer-ē-ən, -ˈmir-\ *n* **1** : a native of Sumer **2** : the language of the Sumerians that has no known relationships to other languages — **Sumerian** *adj*

sum·ma cum lau·de \ˌsüm-ə-ˌküm-ˈlaüd-ə, -ˈlaüd-ē; ˌsəm-ə-ˌkəm-ˈlòd-ē\ *adv or adj* : with highest academic distinction ⟨graduated *summa cum laude*⟩ [Latin, "with highest praise"]

sum·mand \ˈsəm-ˌand, ˌsə-ˈmand\ *n* : a term in a summation : ADDEND [Medieval Latin *summandus,* from *summare* "to sum," from Latin *summa* "sum"]

sum·ma·rize \ˈsəm-ə-ˌrīz\ *vb* **1** : to tell in or reduce to a summary **2** : to make a summary — **sum·ma·ri·za·tion** \ˌsəm-rə-ˈzā-shən, -ə-rə-\ *n* — **sum·ma·riz·er** \ˈsəm-ə-ˌrī-zər\ *n*

[1]**sum·ma·ry** \ˈsəm-ə-rē\ *adj* **1** : expressing or covering the main points briefly ⟨a *summary* account⟩ **2** : done without delay or formality : quickly carried out ⟨a *summary* dismissal⟩ [Medieval Latin *summarius,* from Latin *summa* "sum"] — **sum·mar·i·ly** \ˌsə-ˈmer-ə-lē, ˈsəm-ə-rə-lē\ *adv*

[2]**summary** *n, pl* **-ries** : a concise statement of the main ideas (as of a book or report)

sum·ma·tion \ˌsə-ˈmā-shən\ *n* **1** : the act or process of forming a sum : ADDITION **2** : SUM 2, TOTAL **3** : a final part of an argument reviewing points made and expressing conclusions — **sum·ma·tion·al** \-shnəl, -shən-l\ *adj*

[1]**sum·mer** \ˈsəm-ər\ *n* **1 a** : the season between spring and autumn comprising usually the months of June, July, and August or as determined astronomically extending from the June solstice to the September equinox **b** : the warmer half of the year **2** : YEAR ⟨a youth of 16 *summers*⟩ **3** : a time or season of fulfillment [Old English *sumor*]

[2]**summer** *adj* : of, relating to, or suitable for summer ⟨*summer* vacation⟩ ⟨a *summer* house⟩

[3]**summer** *vb* **sum·mered; sum·mer·ing** \ˈsəm-ring, -ə-ring\ **1** : to pass the summer **2** : to keep or carry through the summer; *esp* : to provide (as cattle) with pasture during the summer

sum·mer·house \ˈsəm-ər-ˌhaüs\ *n* **1** : a house for summer residence **2** : a covered structure in a garden or park designed to provide a shady resting place in summer

summer kitchen *n* : a small building or shed built adjacent to a house and used as a kitchen in warm weather

summersault *variant of* SOMERSAULT

summer school *n* : a school or school session conducted in summer enabling students to accelerate progress toward a diploma or degree, to make up credits lost through absence or failure, or to round out professional education

summer squash *n* : any of various garden squashes closely related to the typical pumpkins and used as a vegetable while immature and before hardening of the seeds and rind

sum·mer·time \ˈsəm-ər-ˌtīm\ *n* : the summer season or a period like summer

summer time *n, chiefly British* : DAYLIGHT SAVING TIME

sum·mer·wood \ˈsəm-ər-ˌwüd\ *n* : the harder and heavier less porous outer portion of an annual ring of wood that is made up of small thick-walled cells and develops late in the growing season — compare SPRINGWOOD

sum·mery \ˈsəm-rē, -ə-rē\ *adj* : of, resembling, or fit for summer

sum·mit \ˈsəm-ət\ *n* **1** : TOP, APEX; *esp* : the highest point (as of a mountain) **2** : the highest level attainable : PINNACLE **3** : the highest level (as of officials) [Middle French *sumet,* from *sum* "top," from Latin *summus* "highest"]

synonyms SUMMIT, PEAK, PINNACLE, APEX mean the highest point attained or attainable. SUMMIT implies the topmost level attainable ⟨a view from the *summit*⟩. PEAK suggests the highest among other high points ⟨*peak* of excitement⟩. PINNACLE suggests a dizzying often insecure height ⟨reach a *pinnacle* of success on the stage⟩. APEX implies the point at which all ascending lines converge and contrasts with *base* ⟨*apex* of cultural achievement⟩.

sum·mon \ˈsəm-ən\ *vt* **1** : to issue a call to convene **2** : to command by service of a summons to appear in court **3** : to send for : CALL ⟨*summon* a physician⟩ **4** : to call forth or arouse ⟨*summon* up enough courage to act⟩ [Medieval French *somondre,* from Latin *summonēre* "to remind secretly," from *sub-* "secretly" + *monēre* "to warn"] — **sum·mon·er** *n*

[1]**sum·mons** \ˈsəm-ənz\ *n, pl* **sum·mons·es** **1** : the act of summoning; *esp* : a call by authority to appear at a place named or to attend to some duty **2** : a warning or notice to appear in court **3** : a call, signal, or knock that summons

[2]**summons** *vt* : SUMMON 2

sum·mum bo·num \ˌsüm-əm-ˈbō-nəm, ˌsəm-\ *n* : the supreme or greatest good [Latin]

su·mo \ˈsü-mō\ *n* : a Japanese form of wrestling in which each competitor seeks to force the opponent out of the ring or make the opponent touch the ground with any part of the body other than the soles of the feet [Japanese *sumō*]

sump \ˈsəmp\ *n* : a pit or reservoir serving as a receptacle or as a drain for fluids [Middle English *sompe* "swamp"]

sump·ter \ˈsəm-tər, ˈsəmp-\ *n* : a pack animal [Medieval French *sumeter* "driver of a packhorse," derived from Late Latin *sagma* "packsaddle," from Greek]

sump·tu·ary \ˈsəm-chə-ˌwer-ē, ˈsəmp-\ *adj* **1** : designed to regulate personal expenses and especially to prevent luxury **2** : designed to regulate habits on moral or religious grounds [Latin *sumptuarius,* from *sumptus* "expense"]

sump·tu·ous \ˈsəm-chə-wəs, ˈsəmp-, -chəs\ *adj* : involving large expense : LUXURIOUS ⟨a *sumptuous* feast⟩ [Latin *sumptuosus,* from *sumptus* "expense," from *sumere* "to take, spend"] — **sump·tu·ous·ly** *adv* — **sump·tu·ous·ness** *n*

sum total *n* **1** : a total arrived at through the counting of sums **2** : total result : TOTALITY ⟨the *sum total* of weeks of discussion was a deadlock⟩

sum up *vb* **1** : to be the sum of : bring to a total ⟨10 victories *summed up* his record⟩ **2** : to present or show concisely ⟨*sum up* the evidence presented⟩ **3** : to present a summary

1**sun** \'sən\ *n* **1 a** : the luminous celestial body around which the planets revolve, from which they receive heat and light, and which has a mean distance from the earth of about 93,000,000 miles (150,000,000 kilometers), a diameter of 864,000 miles (1,390,000 kilometers), and a mass 332,000 times greater than earth **b** : a celestial body like the sun **2** : the heat or light radiated from the sun : SUNSHINE **3** : one resembling the sun usually in brilliance **4** : the rising or setting of the sun ⟨from *sun* to *sun*⟩ [Old English *sunne*] — **in the sun** : in the public eye — **under the sun** : in the world : on earth

2**sun** *vb* **sunned; sun·ning 1** : to expose to or as if to the rays of the sun **2** : to sun oneself

sun·baked \'sən-ˌbākt\ *adj* **1** : baked by exposure to sunlight ⟨*sunbaked* bricks⟩ **2** : heated, parched, or compacted especially by excessive sunlight

sun·bath \'sən-ˌbath, -ˌbȧth\ *n* : exposure to sunlight or a sunlamp

sun·bathe \-ˌbāth\ *vi* : to take a sunbath — **sun·bath·er** \-ˌbā-thər\ *n*

sun·beam \-ˌbēm\ *n* : a ray of sunlight

sun·bird \-ˌbərd\ *n* : any of a family of brightly colored Old World birds resembling hummingbirds

sun·block \-ˌbläk\ *n* : a preparation (as a lotion) applied to the skin to prevent sunburn (as by physically blocking out ultraviolet radiation from the sun); *also* : its active ingredient (as titanium dioxide)

sun·bon·net \-ˌbän-ət\ *n* : a woman's bonnet with a wide brim framing the face and usually a ruffle at the back to protect the neck from the sun

1**sun·burn** \-ˌbərn\ *vb* **1** : to burn or discolor by the sun **2** : to become sunburned

2**sunburn** *n* : a skin inflammation caused by excessive exposure to sunlight

sun·burst \'sən-ˌbərst\ *n* **1** : a burst of sunlight especially through a break in the clouds **2 a** : a jeweled brooch representing a sun surrounded by rays **b** : a design in the form of rays spreading from a central point

sun·dae \'sən-dē\ *n* : a portion of ice cream served with topping (as crushed fruit, syrup, or nuts) [probably alteration of *Sunday*]

1**Sun·day** \'sən-dē\ *n* : the 1st day of the week : the Christian Sabbath [Old English *sunnandæg,* literally, "day of the sun"]

2**Sunday** *adj* **1** : of, relating to, or associated with Sunday **2** : BEST 1 ⟨*Sunday* suit⟩ **3** : AMATEUR ⟨*Sunday* painters⟩

Sunday punch *n* : a blow in boxing capable of knocking out an opponent; *also* : a devastating blow

Sunday School *n* : a school held on Sunday for religious education

sun·deck \'sən-ˌdek\ *n* : a deck of a ship or a roof or terrace used for sunbathing

sun·der \'sən-dər\ *vb* **sun·dered; sun·der·ing** \-də-ring, -dring\ : to break, force, or come apart or in two : sever especially with violence [Old English *gesundrian, syndrian*]

sun·dew \'sən-ˌdü, -ˌdyü\ *n* : any of a genus of wetland herbs that trap and digest insects with the sticky glandular hairs on their leaves

sun·di·al \-ˌdī-əl, -ˌdīl\ *n* : a device to show the time of day by the position of the shadow cast on a plate or disk typically by an upright indicator

sun dog *n* : PARHELION

sun·down \'sən-ˌdaun\ *n* : SUNSET 2

sun·dries \'sən-drēz\ *n pl* : miscellaneous small articles or items (as pins, needles, or thread)

sun·drops \'sən-ˌdräps\ *n sing or pl* : a day-flowering herb similar to the related evening primrose

1**sun·dry** \'sən-drē\ *adj* : VARIOUS 3 ⟨for *sundry* reasons⟩ [Old English *syndrig* "different for each"]

2**sundry** *pron, pl in constr* : various ones — usually used in the phrase *all and sundry*

sun·fish \'sən-ˌfish\ *n* **1** : a very large saltwater fish that is flattened from side to side and has long fins and a small mouth **2** : any of numerous North American freshwater fishes that are related to the perches and usually have a body that is flattened from side to side and a metallic luster

sun·flow·er \-ˌflau̇-ər, -ˌflau̇r\ *n* : any of a genus of tall herbs related to the daisies that are often grown for their large showy yellow-rayed flower heads and for their oil-rich seeds

sung *past of* SING

Sung \'su̇ng\ *n* : a Chinese dynasty dated A.D. 960–1279 and marked by cultural refinement and achievements in philosophy, literature, and art [Chinese (Pekingese dialect) *Sòng*] — **Sung** *adj*

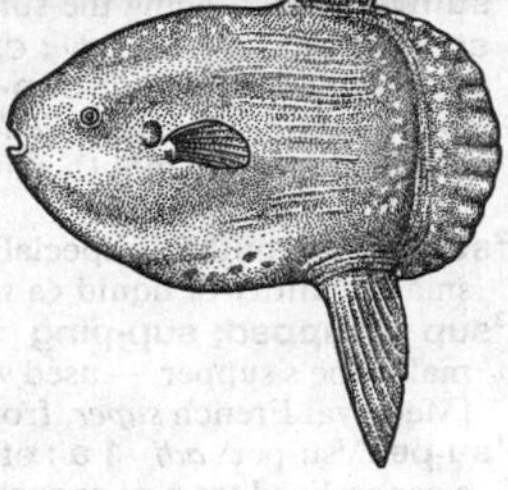

sunfish 1

sun·glass·es \'sən-ˌglas-əz\ *n pl* : tinted glasses that protect the eyes from sunlight

sun god *n, often cap S&G* : a god that represents or personifies the sun in various religions

sun goddess *n, often cap S&G* : a goddess that represents or personifies the sun in various religions

sunk *past of* SINK

sunk·en \'səng-kən\ *adj* **1** : submerged especially in the depths of a body of water ⟨*sunken* ships⟩ **2** : fallen in : HOLLOW ⟨*sunken* cheeks⟩ **3 a** : lying in a depression ⟨a *sunken* garden⟩ **b** : constructed below the general floor level ⟨a *sunken* living room⟩

sun·lamp \'sən-ˌlamp\ *n* : an electric lamp designed to emit radiation of wavelengths from ultraviolet to infrared

sun·less \'sən-ləs\ *adj* : lacking sunlight : GLOOMY

sun·light \-ˌlīt\ *n* : the light of the sun : SUNSHINE

sun·lit \-ˌlit\ *adj* : lighted by or as if by the sun

Sun·ni \'su̇n-nē\ *n* **1** : the Muslims of the branch of Islam that adheres to the orthodox tradition and acknowledges the first four caliphs as rightful successors of Muhammad **2** : a Sunni Muslim [Arabic *sunnī,* from *sunna* "body of Islamic custom and practice based on the words and deeds of Muhammad"] — **Sunni** *adj*

sun·ny \'sən-ē\ *adj* **sun·ni·er; -est 1** : bright with or warmed by sunshine ⟨a *sunny* day⟩ ⟨*sunny* rooms⟩ **2** : MERRY 1, CHEERFUL ⟨*sunny* dispositions⟩ — **sun·ni·ly** \'sən-l-ē\ *adv* — **sun·ni·ness** \'sən-ē-nəs\ *n*

sun·ny–side up \ˌsən-ē-ˌsīd-'əp\ *adj, of an egg* : fried on one side only

sun·porch \'sən-ˌpōrch-, -ˌpȯrch\ *n* : a screened-in or glassed-in porch with a sunny exposure

sun·rise \'sən-ˌrīz\ *n* **1** : the apparent rising of the sun above the horizon; *also* : the accompanying atmospheric effects **2** : the time at which the sun rises

sun·roof \'sən-ˌrüf, -ˌru̇f\ *n* : a panel in the roof of an automobile that can be opened

sun·room \'sən-ˌrüm, -ˌru̇m\ *n* : a glass-enclosed porch or living room with a sunny exposure — called also *sun parlor*

sun·screen \-ˌskrēn\ *n* : a preparation (as a lotion) applied to the skin to prevent sunburn (as by chemically absorbing ultraviolet radiation from the sun); *also* : its active ingredient (as para-aminobenzoic acid)

sun·set \-ˌset\ *n* **1** : the apparent descent of the sun below the horizon; *also* : the accompanying atmospheric effects **2** : the time at which the sun sets **3** : a period of decline; *esp* : old age

sun·shade \-ˌshād\ *n* : something used as a protection from the sun's rays: as **a** : PARASOL **b** : AWNING

sun·shine \-ˌshīn\ *n* **1 a** : the sun's light or direct rays **b** : the warmth and light given by the sun's rays **c** : a spot or surface on which the sun's light shines **2** : something that radiates warmth, cheer, or happiness — **sun·shiny** \-ˌshī-nē\ *adj*

sun·spot \-ˌspät\ *n* : one of the dark spots that appear from time to time on the sun's surface and are usually visible only with the telescope

sun·stroke \-ˌstrōk\ *n* : heatstroke caused by direct exposure to the sun

sun·struck \-ˌstrək\ *adj* : affected or touched by the sun

sun·suit \-ˌsüt\ *n* : an outfit (as of halter and shorts) worn usually for sunbathing and play

sun·tan \-ˌtan\ *n* **1** : a browning of the skin from exposure to

\ə\ **abut**	\au̇\ **out**	\i\ **tip**	\ȯ\ **saw**	\u̇\ **foot**
\ər\ **further**	\ch\ **chin**	\ī\ **life**	\ȯi\ **coin**	\y\ **yet**
\a\ **mat**	\e\ **pet**	\j\ **job**	\th\ **thin**	\yü\ **few**
\ā\ **take**	\ē\ **easy**	\ng\ **sing**	\th\ **this**	\yu̇\ **cure**
\ä\ **cot, cart**	\g\ **go**	\ō\ **bone**	\ü\ **food**	\zh\ **vision**

the rays of the sun **2** *pl* **:** a tan-colored summer uniform — **sun·tanned** \-ˌtand\ *adj*

sun·up \ˈsən-ˌəp\ *n* **:** SUNRISE

[1]sun·ward \-wərd\ *or* **sun·wards** \-wərdz\ *adv* **:** toward the sun

[2]sunward *adj* **:** facing the sun

sun·wise \ˈsən-ˌwīz\ *adv* **:** CLOCKWISE

[1]sup \ˈsəp\ *vb* **supped; sup·ping 1 :** to take or drink in swallows or gulps **2** *chiefly dialect* **:** to take food and especially liquid food into the mouth a little at a time (as from a spoon) [Old English *sūpan, suppan*]

[2]sup *n* **:** a mouthful especially of liquor or broth **:** SIP; *also* **:** a small quantity of liquid ⟨a *sup* of tea⟩

[3]sup *vi* **supped; sup·ping 1 :** to eat the evening meal **2 :** to make one's supper — used with *on* or *off* ⟨*supped* on roast beef⟩ [Medieval French *super,* from *supe* "sop, soup"]

[1]su·per \ˈsü-pər\ *adj* **1 a :** of high grade or quality **b** — used as a generalized term of approval ⟨a *super* cook⟩ **2 :** very large or powerful ⟨a *super* atomic bomb⟩ **3 :** showing the characteristics of its type to an extreme or excessive degree ⟨*super* secrecy⟩ [*super-*]

[2]super *n* **1 a :** SUPERNUMERARY 2 **b :** SUPERINTENDENT, SUPERVISOR **2 :** a removable upper story of a beehive **3 :** a superfine grade or extra large size

[3]super *adv* **1 :** VERY 1, EXTREMELY ⟨a *super* fast car⟩ **2 :** to an excessive degree ⟨*super* critical⟩

super- *prefix* **1 a :** over and above **:** higher in quantity, quality, or degree than **:** more than ⟨*super*human⟩ **b :** in addition **:** extra ⟨*super*tax⟩ **c :** exceeding or so as to exceed a norm ⟨*super*heat⟩ **2 a :** situated or placed above, on, or at the top of ⟨*super*structure⟩ **b :** next above or higher ⟨*super*tonic⟩ **3 :** constituting a more inclusive category than that specified ⟨*super*family⟩ **4 :** superior in status, title, or position ⟨*super*power⟩ [Latin, "over, above, in addition to," from *super* "over, above, on top of"]

superadministrator	**superhit**	**supersize**
superambitious	**superintellectual**	**supersized**
superathlete	**superintelligence**	**supersleuth**
superbad	**superintelligent**	**superslick**
superbomb	**superintensity**	**supersmart**
superbomber	**superluxurious**	**supersmooth**
superbright	**superluxury**	**supersoft**
superbureaucrat	**supermasculine**	**supersophisticated**
supercautious	**supermassive**	**superspecial**
superchic	**supermodern**	**superspecialist**
superclean	**supernation**	**superspecialization**
supercolossal	**supernational**	**superspecialized**
supercomfortable	**superpatriot**	**superspectacle**
supercompetitive	**superpatriotic**	**superspectacular**
superconfident	**superpatriotism**	**superspy**
superconservative	**superperson**	**superstate**
superconvenient	**superpersonal**	**superstrong**
supercop	**superplane**	**supersubtle**
supercorporation	**superplayer**	**supersubtlety**
supercriminal	**superpolite**	**supersurgeon**
superdiplomat	**superport**	**supersweet**
supereffective	**superpowerful**	**supertanker**
superefficiency	**superrich**	**superthick**
superefficient	**superromantic**	**superthin**
supereminence	**supersafe**	**superthriller**
supereminent	**supersale**	**supertight**
supereminently	**supersalesman**	**supervirtuoso**
superexpensive	**superscout**	**superwave**
superfast	**supersecrecy**	**superweapon**
supergood	**supersecret**	**superwide**
supergovernment	**supersensitive**	
superheroine	**supersensitivity**	

su·per·a·ble \ˈsü-pə-rə-bəl, -prə-bəl\ *adj* **:** capable of being overcome or conquered ⟨*superable* odds⟩ [Latin *superabilis,* from *superare* "to surmount," from *super* "over"] — **su·per·a·ble·ness** *n* — **su·per·a·bly** \-blē\ *adv*

su·per·abound \ˌsü-pə-rə-ˈbau̇nd\ *vi* **:** to abound or prevail greatly or to excess

su·per·abun·dant \-ˈbən-dənt\ *adj* **:** more than ample **:** EXCESSIVE — **su·per·abun·dance** \-dəns\ *n* — **su·per·abun·dant·ly** *adv*

su·per·add \ˌsü-pə-ˈrad\ *vt* **:** to add over and above something or in extra or superfluous amount — **su·per·ad·di·tion** \ˈpə-rə-ˈdish-ən\ *n*

su·per·an·nu·ate \ˌsü-pə-ˈran-yə-ˌwāt\ *vb* **1 a :** to make or declare obsolete or out-of-date **b :** to retire and pension because of age or infirmity **2 :** to become retired or antiquated [back-formation from *superannuated*] — **su·per·an·nu·a·tion** \-ˌran-yə-ˈwā-shən\ *n*

su·per·an·nu·at·ed *adj* **1 :** too old or outmoded for work or use **2 a :** incapacitated or disqualified for active duty by advanced age **b :** older than the typical member of a specified group ⟨a *superannuated* graduate student⟩ [Medieval Latin *superannuatus,* past participle of *superannuari* "to be too old," from Latin *super-* + *annus* "year"]

su·perb \su̇-ˈpərb\ *adj* **:** extremely fine, brilliant, or splendid ⟨a *superb* craftsman⟩ ⟨*superb* palaces⟩ [Latin *superbus* "excellent, proud," from *super* "above"] — **su·perb·ly** *adv* — **su·perb·ness** *n*

su·per·car·go \ˌsü-pər-ˈkär-gō\ *n* **:** an officer on a merchant ship in charge of the commercial concerns of the voyage [Spanish *sobrecargo,* from *sobre-* "over" (from Latin *super-*) + *cargo* "cargo"]

su·per·charge \ˈsü-pər-ˌchärj\ *vt* **1 :** to supply a charge to the intake of (as an engine) at a pressure higher than that of the surrounding atmosphere **2 :** PRESSURIZE 1

su·per·char·ger \-ˌchär-jər\ *n* **:** a device (as a blower or compressor) for increasing the volume air charge of an internal-combustion engine or for pressurizing the cabin of an airplane

su·per·cil·i·ous \ˌsü-pər-ˈsil-ē-əs\ *adj* **:** haughtily scornful [Latin *superciliosus,* from *supercilium* "eyebrow, haughtiness"] — **su·per·cil·i·ous·ly** *adv* — **su·per·cil·i·ous·ness** *n*

su·per·com·put·er \ˈsü-pər-kəm-ˌpyüt-ər\ *n* **:** a large very fast mainframe used especially for scientific computations

su·per·con·duct \ˌsü-pər-kən-ˈdəkt\ *vi* **:** to exhibit superconductivity

su·per·con·duc·tiv·i·ty \ˌsü-pər-ˌkän-ˌdək-ˈtiv-ət-ē\ *n* **:** a complete disappearance of electrical resistance in various metals at temperatures near absolute zero — **su·per·con·duc·tive** \-kən-ˈdək-tiv\ *adj* — **su·per·con·duc·tor** \-kən-ˈdək-tər\ *n*

su·per·con·ti·nent \ˈsü-pər-ˌkänt-n-ənt, -ˌkänt-nənt\ *n* **:** a former large continent which is assumed to have existed and from which other continents broke off and drifted away

[1]su·per·cool \ˌsü-pər-ˈkül\ *vt* **:** to cool below the freezing point without solidification or crystallization

[2]supercool *adj* **:** extremely cool: as **a :** showing extraordinary reserve and self-control **b :** being the latest style or fashion ⟨*supercool* sunglasses⟩

su·per·ego \ˌsü-pə-ˈrē-gō\ *n* **:** the one of the three divisions of the mind in psychoanalytic theory that is only partly conscious, represents the incorporation of parental conscience and the rules of society, and functions to reward and punish through a system of moral attitudes, conscience, and a sense of guilt — compare EGO 3, ID

su·per·er·o·ga·tion \ˌsü-pə-ˌrer-ə-ˈgā-shən\ *n* **:** the act of performing more than is required by duty, obligation, or need [Medieval Latin *supererogatio,* from *supererogare* "to perform beyond the call of duty," derived from Latin *super-* + *e-* + *rogare* "to ask"]

su·per·erog·a·to·ry \ˌsü-pə-ri-ˈräg-ə-ˌtōr-ē, -ˌtȯr-\ *adj* **1 :** observed or performed to an extent not demanded or needed **2 :** SUPERFLUOUS, NONESSENTIAL

su·per·fam·i·ly \ˈsü-pər-ˌfam-lē, -ə-lē\ *n* **1 :** a category of biological classification ranking below an order and above a family **2 :** a large group of closely related molecules or chemical compounds

su·per·fi·cial \ˌsü-pər-ˈfish-əl\ *adj* **1 a :** of or relating to a surface **b :** situated on or near or affecting only the surface ⟨a *superficial* wound⟩ **2 :** concerned only with the obvious or apparent **:** not profound or thorough **:** SHALLOW [Late Latin *superficialis,* from Latin *superficies* "surface," from *super-* + *facies* "face"] — **su·per·fi·ci·al·i·ty** \-ˌfish-ē-ˈal-ət-ē\ *n* — **su·per·fi·cial·ly** \-ˌfish-lē, -ə-lē\ *adv* — **su·per·fi·cial·ness** \-ˈfish-əl-nəs\ *n*

synonyms SUPERFICIAL, CURSORY, SHALLOW mean lacking in depth, solidity, or completeness. SUPERFICIAL implies a concern only with what appears at the surface or at first glance ⟨a *superficial* analysis of the problem⟩. CURSORY suggests a neglect of details through haste or indifference ⟨gave the letter only a *cursory* reading⟩. SHALLOW is usually derogatory and implies lack of depth in knowledge, reasoning, emotions, or character ⟨a light, *shallow,* and frivolous review⟩.

su·per·fi·cies \-'fish-ēz, -ē-ˌēz\ *n, pl* **superficies** **1** : the surface of a body or the boundary of a region of space **2** : the external aspects or appearance of a thing [Latin, "surface"]

su·per·fine \ˌsü-pər-'fīn\ *adj* **1** : very refined : FINICKY **2** : very finely divided **3** : of high quality or grade

su·per·flu·i·ty \ˌsü-pər-'flü-ət-ē\ *n, pl* **-ties** **1** : EXCESS 1a, OVERSUPPLY **2** : something unnecessary or more than enough

su·per·flu·ous \su̇-'pər-flə-wəs\ *adj* : exceeding what is sufficient or necessary : EXTRA [Latin *superfluus,* from *superfluere* "to overflow," from *super-* + *fluere* "to flow"] — **su·per·flu·ous·ly** *adv* — **su·per·flu·ous·ness** *n*

su·per·gi·ant \'sü-pər-ˌjī-ənt\ *n* : a star of very great luminosity and enormous size

su·per·glue \-ˌglü\ *n* : a very strong glue; *esp* : a glue whose chief ingredient is a substance that becomes adhesive by polymerization rather than evaporation of a solvent — **superglue** *vb*

su·per·group \'sü-pər-ˌgrüp\ *n* : a rock group made up of prominent former members of other rock groups; *also* : an extremely successful rock group

su·per·heat \ˌsü-pər-'hēt\ *vt* **1 a** : to heat (steam) to a higher temperature than the normal boiling point of water **b** : to heat (a liquid) above the boiling point without converting to vapor **2** : to heat very much or excessively — **su·per·heat·er** *n*

su·per·hero \'sü-per-ˌhē-rō, -ˌhiər-ō\ *n* : a fictional hero having extraordinary or superhuman powers; *also* : a very successful person

su·per·het·er·o·dyne \ˌsü-pər-'het-ə-rə-ˌdīn\ *adj* : of or relating to a form of radio reception in which beats are produced of a frequency above audibility but below that of the received signals and the current of the beat frequency is then rectified, amplified, and finally rectified again so as to reproduce the sound [*super*sonic + *heterodyne*] — **superheterodyne** *n*

su·per·high frequency \'sü-pər-ˌhī-\ *n* : a radio frequency in the range between 3000 and 30,000 megacycles — abbreviation *SHF*

su·per·high·way \ˌsü-pər-'hī-ˌwā\ *n* **1** : a broad highway designed for high-speed traffic **2** : INTERNET

su·per·hu·man \-'hyü-mən, -'yü-\ *adj* **1** : being above the human : DIVINE **2** : exceeding normal human power, size, or capability : HERCULEAN ⟨*superhuman* effort⟩ — **su·per·hu·man·ly** *adv* — **su·per·hu·man·ness** *n*

su·per·im·pose \ˌsü-pə-rim-'pōz\ *vt* : to place or lay over or above something — **su·per·im·pos·able** \-'pō-zə-bəl\ *adj* — **su·per·im·po·si·tion** \-ˌrim-pə-'zish-ən\ *n*

su·per·in·duce \-rin-'düs, -'dyüs\ *vt* : to introduce as an addition over or above something already existing [Latin *superinducere,* from *super-* + *inducere* "to lead in"] — **su·per·in·duc·tion** \-'dək-shən\ *n*

su·per·in·tend \ˌsü-pə-rin-'tend, ˌsü-prin-, ˌsü-pərn-\ *vt* : to have or exercise the charge and oversight of : DIRECT [Late Latin *superintendere,* from Latin *super-* + *intendere* "to stretch out, direct"]

su·per·in·tend·ence \-'ten-dəns\ *n* : the act, duty, or office of superintending or overseeing : SUPERVISION

su·per·in·tend·en·cy \-dən-sē\ *n, pl* **-cies** : the office, post, or jurisdiction of a superintendent; *also* : SUPERINTENDENCE

su·per·in·tend·ent \-'ten-dənt\ *n* : a person who oversees, manages, or maintains something ⟨a building *superintendent*⟩ ⟨*superintendent* of schools⟩ [Medieval Latin *superintendens,* from Late Latin *superintendere* "to superintend"]

¹su·pe·ri·or \su̇-'pir-ē-ər\ *adj* **1** : situated higher up : UPPER: as **a** : situated above or anterior or dorsal to another and especially a corresponding part ⟨a *superior* artery⟩ **b** : attached to and arising from a plant ovary ⟨a *superior* calyx⟩ **c** : free from the calyx or other floral envelope ⟨a *superior* plant ovary⟩ **2 a** : of higher rank, quality, or importance **b** : greater in quantity or numbers **3** : courageously or serenely indifferent (as to something painful or disheartening) **4 a** : excellent of its kind **b** : affecting or assuming an air of superiority : SUPERCILIOUS **5** : more comprehensive ⟨a genus is *superior* to a species⟩ [Medieval French, from Latin, comparative of *superus* "upper," from *super* "over, above"] — **su·pe·ri·or·i·ty** \-ˌpir-ē-'ȯr-ət-ē, -'är-\ *n* — **su·pe·ri·or·ly** \-'pir-ē-ər-lē\ *adv*

²superior *n* **1** : one who is above another in rank, station, or office; *esp* : the head of a religious house or order **2** : one that surpasses another in quality or merit

superior court *n* **1** : a court intermediate between inferior courts and higher appellate courts **2** : a court with juries having original jurisdiction

superiority complex *n* : an exaggerated opinion of oneself

superior planet *n* : a planet (as Jupiter) whose orbit lies outside that of Earth

superior vena cava *n* : the branch of the vena cava that returns blood from the head and forelimbs to the heart

su·per·jet \'sü-pər-ˌjet\ *n* : a supersonic jet airplane

¹su·per·la·tive \su̇-'pər-lət-iv\ *adj* **1** : of, relating to, or constituting the degree of grammatical comparison that denotes an extreme or unsurpassed level or extent **2** : surpassing all others : SUPREME **3** : EXCESSIVE, EXAGGERATED [Medieval French *superlatif,* from Late Latin *superlativus,* from Latin *superlatus,* past participle of *superferre* "to carry over, raise high," from *super-* + *ferre* "to carry"] — **su·per·la·tive·ly** *adv* — **su·per·la·tive·ness** *n*

²superlative *n* **1** : the superlative degree or a superlative form in a language **2** : the superlative or utmost degree of something : ACME; *also* : something that is superlative

su·per·ma·jor·i·ty \'sü-pər-mə-'jȯr-ət-ē, -'jär-\ *n* : a majority (as two-thirds or three-fifths) greater than a simple majority

su·per·man \'sü-pər-ˌman\ *n* : a person with exceptional powers [translation of German *Übermensch*]

su·per·mar·ket \-ˌmär-kət\ *n* : a self-service retail market selling foods and household merchandise

su·per·mi·cro \-ˌmī-ˌkrō\ *n* : a very fast and powerful microcomputer

su·per·mini \-ˌmin-ē\ *n* : SUPERMINICOMPUTER

su·per·mini·com·put·er \-'min-ē-kəm-ˌpyüt-ər\ *n* : a very fast and powerful minicomputer

su·per·mod·el \'sü-pər-ˌmäd-l\ *n* : a famous and successful fashion model

su·per·mom \'sü-pər-ˌmäm\ *n* : exemplary mother; *also* : a woman who performs the traditional duties of housekeeping and childrearing while also having a full-time job

su·per·nal \su̇-'pərn-l\ *adj* **1 a** : being or coming from on high **b** : being or seeming more than earthly ⟨*supernal* beauty⟩ ⟨*supernal* joy⟩ **2** : located or originating in the sky [Medieval French *supernel,* from Latin *supernus,* from *super* "over, above"] — **su·per·nal·ly** \-l-ē\ *adv*

su·per·na·tant \ˌsü-pər-'nāt-nt\ *adj* : floating on the surface [Latin *supernatare* "to float," from *super-* + *natare* "to swim"] — **supernatant** *n*

su·per·nat·u·ral \ˌsü-pər-'nach-rəl, -ə-rəl\ *adj* **1** : of or relating to an order of existence beyond the visible observable universe; *esp* : of or relating to God or a god, demigod, spirit, or demon **2 a** : departing from what is usual or normal especially so as to appear to transcend the laws of nature **b** : attributed to an invisible agent (as a ghost or spirit) — **supernatural** *n* — **su·per·nat·u·ral·ly** \-'nach-rə-lē, -ə-rə-; -'nach-ər-lē\ *adv* — **su·per·nat·u·ral·ness** \-'nach-rəl-nəs, -ə-rəl-\ *n*

su·per·nat·u·ral·ism \-'nach-rə-ˌliz-əm, -ə-rə-\ *n* **1** : the quality or state of being supernatural **2** : belief in a supernatural power and order of existence — **su·per·nat·u·ral·ist** \-ləst\ *n or adj* — **su·per·nat·u·ral·is·tic** \-ˌnach-rə-'lis-tik, -ə-rə-\ *adj*

su·per·nor·mal \-'nȯr-məl\ *adj* **1** : exceeding the normal or average **2** : being beyond natural human powers — **su·per·nor·mal·ly** \-mə-lē\ *adv*

su·per·no·va \-'nō-və\ *n* : the explosion of a very large star in which the star temporarily radiates up to one billion times more energy than the sun

¹su·per·nu·mer·ary \ˌsü-pər-'nü-mə-ˌrer-ē, -'nyü-\ *adj* **1** : exceeding the usual, stated, or prescribed number ⟨*supernumerary* teeth⟩ **2** : exceeding what is necessary, required, or desired [Late Latin *supernumerarius,* from Latin *super-* + *numerus* "number"]

²supernumerary *n, pl* **-ar·ies** **1** : a supernumerary person or thing **2** : an actor employed to play a small usually nonspeaking part

su·per·phos·phate \ˌsü-pər-'fäs-ˌfāt\ *n* : a soluble mixture of phosphates used as fertilizer

su·per·po·si·tion \ˌsü-pər-pə-'zish-ən\ *n* : the act or process of laying one thing over or above another especially so that they coincide [French, from Late Latin *superpositio,* from Latin *superponere* "to superpose," from *super-* + *ponere* "to place"] — **su·per·pose** \ˌsü-pər-ˈpōz\ *vt*

su·per·pow·er \ˈsü-pər-ˌpau̇-ər, -ˌpau̇r\ *n* : an extremely powerful nation

su·per·sat·u·rate \ˌsü-pər-ˈsach-ə-ˌrāt\ *vt* : to add something to beyond saturation

su·per·sat·u·rat·ed \-ˈsach-ə-ˌrāt-əd\ *adj* : containing an amount of something greater than the amount required for saturation by having been cooled from a higher temperature to a temperature below that at which saturation occurs ⟨a *supersaturated* solution⟩ ⟨air *supersaturated* with water vapor⟩

su·per·sat·u·ra·tion \-ˌsach-ə-ˈrā-shən\ *n* : the state of being supersaturated

su·per·scribe \ˈsü-pər-ˌskrīb\ *vt* : to write or engrave on the top or outside; *esp* : to write (as a name or address) on the outside or cover of [Latin *superscribere,* from *super-* + *scribere* "to write"]

su·per·script \ˈsü-pər-ˌskript\ *n* : a distinguishing symbol or letter written immediately above or above and to the right or left of another character [Latin *superscriptus,* past participle of *superscribere* "to superscribe"] — **superscript** *adj*

su·per·scrip·tion \ˌsü-pər-ˈskrip-shən\ *n* **1** : the act of superscribing **2** : something superscribed on something else : INSCRIPTION; *esp* : ADDRESS

su·per·sede \ˌsü-pər-ˈsēd\ *vt* **1** : to force out of use as inferior **2** : to take the place, room, or position of **3** : to displace in favor of another : SUPPLANT [Middle French *superceder* "to defer," from Latin *supersedēre* "to sit on top, refrain from," from *super-* + *sedēre* "to sit"] ***synonyms*** see REPLACE — **su·per·sed·er** *n* — **su·per·se·dure** \-ˈsē-jər\ *n*

su·per·ses·sion \ˌsü-pər-ˈsesh-ən\ *n* : the act of superseding : the state of being superseded [Medieval Latin *supersessio,* from Latin *supersedēre* "to sit on top, refrain from"]

su·per·son·ic \-ˈsän-ik\ *adj* **1** : ULTRASONIC **2** : of, being, or relating to speeds from one to five times the speed of sound in air **3** : moving, capable of moving, or utilizing air currents moving at supersonic speed ⟨a *supersonic* airplane⟩ — **su·per·son·i·cal·ly** \-ˈsän-i-kə-lē, -klē\ *adv*

su·per·son·ics \-ˈsän-iks\ *n* : the science of supersonic phenomena

su·per·star \ˈsü-pər-ˌstär\ *n* : a star (as in sports or the movies) who is considered extremely talented, has great public appeal, and can usually command a high salary — **su·per·star·dom** \-dəm\ *n*

su·per·sti·tion \ˌsü-pər-ˈstish-ən\ *n* **1** : beliefs or practices resulting from ignorance, fear of the unknown, or belief in fate, omens, magic, or chance as governing principles **2** : an attitude of resignation toward or fear of nature, the unknown, or God resulting from superstition [Medieval French *supersticion,* from Latin *superstitio,* from *superstes* "standing over (as witness or survivor)," from *super-* + *stare* "to stand"] — **su·per·sti·tious** \-ˈstish-əs\ *adj* — **su·per·sti·tious·ly** *adv* — **su·per·sti·tious·ness** *n*

su·per·store \ˈsü-pər-ˌstōr, -ˌstȯr\ *n* : a very large store often offering a wide variety of merchandise for sale

su·per·struc·ture \ˈsü-pər-ˌstrək-chər\ *n* : a structure built upon something else: as **a** : all of a building above the basement **b** : the structural part of a ship above the main deck — **su·per·struc·tur·al** \-ˌstrək-chə-rəl, -ˌstrək-shrəl\ *adj*

su·per·sys·tem \ˈsü-pər-ˌsis-təm\ *n* : a system that is made up of systems

su·per·tax \ˈsü-pər-ˌtaks\ *n* : SURTAX

su·per·ton·ic \ˌsü-pər-ˈtän-ik\ *n* : the second tone of a major or minor scale

su·per·vene \ˌsü-pər-ˈvēn\ *vi* **-vened; -ven·ing** : to take place as an additional or unexpected development [Latin *supervenire,* from *super-* + *venire* "to come"] — **su·per·ven·tion** \-ˈven-chən\ *n*

su·per·ve·nient \ˌsü-pər-ˈvē-nyənt\ *adj* : coming or occurring as something additional or unexpected [Latin *superveniens,* from *supervenire* "to take place as an additional or unexpected development"]

su·per·vise \ˈsü-pər-ˌvīz\ *vt* : to be in charge of : SUPERINTEND [Medieval Latin *supervisus,* past participle of *supervidēre* "to supervise," from Latin *super-* + *vidēre* "to see"]

su·per·vi·sion \ˌsü-pər-ˈvizh-ən\ *n* : the action, process, or occupation of supervising; *esp* : a critical watching and directing (as of activities or a course of action)

su·per·vi·sor \ˈsü-pər-ˌvī-zər\ *n* : one that supervises; *esp* : an administrative officer in charge of a business, government, or school unit or operation — **su·per·vi·so·ry** \ˌsü-pər-ˈvīz-rē, -ə-rē\ *adj*

su·per·wom·an \ˈsü-pər-ˌwu̇m-ən\ *n* : an exceptional woman; *esp* : a woman who succeeds in having a career and raising a family

su·pi·na·tion \ˌsü-pə-ˈnā-shən\ *n* : rotation of the hand or forearm so as to bring the palm facing upward or forward; *also* : a corresponding movement of the foot and leg in which the foot rolls outward with an elevated arch [Latin *supinare* "to lay on the back," from *supinus* "supine"] — **su·pi·nate** \ˈsü-pə-ˌnāt\ *vb*

su·pi·na·tor \ˈsü-pə-ˌnāt-ər\ *n* : a muscle that produces the motion of supination

[1]**su·pine** \su̇-ˈpīn\ *adj* **1** : lying on the back or with the face upward **2** : showing mental or moral slackness : APATHETIC [Latin *supinus*] ***synonyms*** see PRONE — **su·pine·ly** *adv* — **su·pine·ness** \-ˈpīn-nəs\ *n*

[2]**su·pine** \ˈsü-ˌpīn\ *n* **1** : a Latin verbal noun having an accusative of purpose in *-um* and an ablative of specification in *-u* **2** : an English infinitive with *to*

sup·per \ˈsəp-ər\ *n* **1 a** : the evening meal especially when dinner is taken at midday **b** : a social affair featuring a supper; *esp* : an evening social especially for raising funds ⟨a church *supper*⟩ **2** : the food served as a supper ⟨eat your *supper*⟩ **3** : a light meal served late in the evening [Medieval French *super,* from *super* "to sup"]

sup·plant \sə-ˈplant\ *vt* **1** : to take the place of (another) especially by force or treachery **2 a** : to remove and supply a substitute for ⟨efforts to *supplant* the vernacular⟩ **b** : to gain the place of especially by reason of superiority [Medieval French *supplanter,* from Latin *supplantare* "to trip up, to cause to stumble," from *sub-* + *planta* "sole of the foot"] ***synonyms*** see REPLACE — **sup·plan·ta·tion** \sə-ˌplan-ˈtā-shən\ *n* — **sup·plant·er** \sə-ˈplant-ər\ *n*

[1]**sup·ple** \ˈsəp-əl\ *adj* **sup·pler** \ˈsəp-lər, -ə-lər\; **sup·plest** \ˈsəp-ləst, -ə-ləst\ **1 a** : yielding easily and often submissively to the wishes of others **b** : readily adaptable to new situations **2 a** : capable of being bent or folded without creases or breaks : PLIANT ⟨*supple* leather⟩ **b** : able to bend or twist with ease : LIMBER ⟨*supple* legs of a dancer⟩ [Medieval French *suple,* from Latin *supplex* "submissive, suppliant," literally, "bending under"] — **sup·ple·ness** \-əl-nəs\ *n*

[2]**supple** *vt* **sup·pled; sup·pling** \ˈsəp-ling, -ə-ling\ : to make supple

[1]**sup·ple·ment** \ˈsəp-lə-mənt\ *n* **1** : something that completes or makes an addition ⟨vitamin pills used as dietary *supplements*⟩ ⟨the *supplement* at the back of the book⟩ **2** : an angle or arc that when added to a given angle or arc equals 180 degrees [Latin *supplementum,* from *supplēre* "to fill up, complete, supply"] — **sup·ple·men·tal** \ˌsəp-lə-ˈment-l\ *adj* — **sup·ple·men·ta·tion** \ˌsəp-lə-ˌmen-ˈtā-shən\ *n*

[2]**sup·ple·ment** \ˈsəp-lə-ˌmənt\ *vt* : to add to : fill a deficiency of

sup·ple·men·ta·ry \ˌsəp-lə-ˈment-ə-rē, -ˈmen-trē\ *adj* **1** : added as a supplement : ADDITIONAL **2** : being or relating to a supplement or a supplementary angle

supplementary angle *n* : one of two angles or arcs whose sum is 180 degrees — usually used in plural

[1]**sup·pli·ant** \ˈsəp-lē-ənt\ *n* : one who supplicates [Medieval French, from *supplier* "to supplicate," from Latin *supplicare*]

[2]**suppliant** *adj* : earnestly and humbly imploring — **sup·pli·ant·ly** *adv*

sup·pli·cant \ˈsəp-li-kənt\ *n* : one who supplicates — **supplicant** *adj* — **sup·pli·cant·ly** *adv*

sup·pli·cate \ˈsəp-lə-ˌkāt\ *vb* **1** : to make a humble appeal; *esp* : to pray to God **2** : to ask for or of earnestly and humbly : BESEECH [Latin *supplicare,* from *supplex* "submissive, supplicant"] — **sup·pli·ca·tion** \ˌsep-lə-ˈkā-shən\ *n* — **sup·pli·ca·to·ry** \ˈsəp-li-kə-ˌtōr-ē, -ˌtȯr-\ *adj*

[1]**sup·ply** \sə-ˈplī\ *vt* **sup·plied; sup·ply·ing 1** : to add as a supplement **2** : to provide for : SATISFY ⟨to *supply* their wants⟩ **3** : to provide or furnish with ⟨*supply* provisions⟩ **4** : to satisfy the needs or wishes of ⟨*supply* them with fuel⟩ [Medieval French *souppller,* from Latin *supplēre* "to fill up, complete," from *sub-* "up" + *plēre* "to fill"] — **sup·pli·er** \-ˈplī-ər, -ˈplīr\ *n*

[2]**supply** *n, pl* **supplies 1 a** : the quantity or amount (as of a

commodity) needed or available **b** : PROVISION 2, STORE — usually used in plural **2** : the act or process of filling a want or need : PROVISION **3** : the quantities of goods or services offered for sale at a particular time or at one price

[1]**sup·port** \sə-ˈpōrt, -ˈpȯrt\ *vt* **1** : to endure bravely or quietly : BEAR **2 a** (1) : to promote the interests or cause of (2) : to uphold or defend as valid or right : ADVOCATE ⟨*supports* fair play⟩ (3) : to argue or vote for ⟨*supported* the motion to lower taxes⟩ **b** : ASSIST, HELP ⟨bombers *supported* the ground troops⟩ **c** : to act in a lesser role with (a star actor) **d** : SUBSTANTIATE 2, VERIFY ⟨*support* an alibi⟩ **3** : to pay the costs of : MAINTAIN ⟨*support* a family⟩ **4 a** : to hold up or in position or serve as a foundation or prop for **b** : to maintain (the price of a commodity) at a high level by purchases or loans **5** : to keep (something) going : SUSTAIN [Medieval French *supporter,* from Late Latin *supportare* "to carry," from *sub-* + *portare* "to carry"] — **sup·port·able** \-ə-bəl\ *adj* — **sup·port·ive** \-iv\ *adj* — **sup·port·ive·ness** *n*

[2]**support** *n* **1 a** : the act or process of supporting : the condition of being supported **b** : assistance provided by a company to users of its products ⟨customer *support*⟩ **2** : one that supports

sup·port·er \sə-ˈpōrt-ər, -ˈpȯrt-\ *n* : one that supports; *esp* : ADVOCATE 2

support group *n* : a group of people with common experiences and concerns who provide emotional and moral support for one another

support system *n* : a network of people who provide an individual with practical or emotional support

sup·pose \sə-ˈpōz\ *vb* **1** : to take as true or as a fact for the sake of argument : lay down as a hypothesis ⟨*suppose* a fire should break out⟩ **2** : to hold as an opinion : BELIEVE ⟨they *supposed* they were on the right bus⟩ **3** : THINK, GUESS ⟨who do you *suppose* will win⟩ ⟨I *suppose* so⟩ [Medieval French *supposer,* derived from Latin *supponere* "to put under, substitute," from *sub-* + *ponere* "to put, place"]

sup·posed \sə-ˈpōzd, *in the phrase "supposed to" often* -ˈpōz, -ˈpōs, -ˈpōst\ *adj* **1 a** : believed to be true or real ⟨a *supposed* cure⟩ **b** : considered probable or certain : EXPECTED ⟨they are *supposed* to be here tomorrow⟩ **2** : made or fashioned by intent or design ⟨what's the button *supposed* to do⟩ **3 a** : required by or as if by authority ⟨she was *supposed* to practice two hours daily⟩ **b** : given permission ⟨you're not *supposed* to do that⟩ — **sup·pos·ed·ly** \-ˈpō-zəd-lē\ *adv*

sup·po·si·tion \ˌsəp-ə-ˈzish-ən\ *n* **1** : something that is supposed : HYPOTHESIS **2** : the act of supposing [Late Latin *suppositio,* derived from Latin *supponere* "to put under"] — **sup·po·si·tion·al** \-ˈzish-nəl, -ən-l\ *adj* — **sup·po·si·tion·al·ly** \-ē\ *adv*

sup·po·si·tious \-ˈzish-əs\ *adj* : SUPPOSITITIOUS

sup·pos·i·ti·tious \sə-ˌpäz-ə-ˈtish-əs\ *adj* **1** : fraudulently substituted : SPURIOUS **2** : of the nature of a supposition : HYPOTHETICAL [Latin *suppositicius,* from *supponere* "to put under, substitute"] — **sup·pos·i·ti·tious·ly** *adv* — **sup·pos·i·ti·tious·ness** *n*

sup·pos·i·to·ry \sə-ˈpäz-ə-ˌtōr-ē, -ˌtȯr-\ *n, pl* **-ries** : a solid but readily meltable cone or cylinder of usually medicated material for insertion into a bodily passage or cavity (as the rectum) [Medieval Latin *suppositorium,* derived from Latin *supponere* "to put under"]

sup·press \sə-ˈpres\ *vt* **1** : to put down by authority or force : SUBDUE ⟨*suppress* a riot⟩ **2 a** : to keep from being made known **b** : to stop the publication or circulation of ⟨*suppressed* the test results⟩ **3 a** : to exclude from consciousness **b** : to hold back : RESTRAIN ⟨*suppress* a cough⟩ **4** : to inhibit the growth or development of : STUNT [Latin *suppressus,* past participle of *supprimere* "to suppress," from *sub-* + *premere* "to press"] — **sup·press·ible** \-ə-bəl\ *adj* — **sup·pres·sion** \-ˈpresh-ən\ *n* — **sup·pres·sive** \-ˈpres-iv\ *adj* — **sup·pres·sor** \-ˈpres-ər\ *n*

sup·pres·sant \sə-ˈpres-nt\ *n* : an agent (as a drug) that tends to suppress or reduce in intensity rather than eliminate something ⟨a cough *suppressant*⟩

sup·pres·sor T cell \sə-ˌpres-ər-ˈtē-\ *n* : a T cell that suppresses the immune response of B cells and other T cells to an antigen — called also *suppressor cell*

sup·pu·rate \ˈsəp-yə-ˌrāt\ *vi* : to form or give off pus [Latin *suppurare,* from *sub-* + *pur-, pus* "pus"] — **sup·pu·ra·tion** \ˌsəp-yə-ˈrā-shən\ *n* — **sup·pu·ra·tive** \ˈsəp-yə-ˌrāt-iv\ *adj*

supra- *prefix* **1** : SUPER- 2a ⟨*supra*orbital⟩ **2** : transcending ⟨*supra*national⟩ [Latin, from *supra* "above, beyond"]

su·pra·na·tion·al \ˌsü-prə-ˈnash-nəl, -ˈnash-ən-l\ *adj* : transcending national boundaries or authority

su·pra·or·bit·al \ˈȯr bət l\ *adj* : situated or occurring above the orbit of the eye

[1]**su·pra·re·nal** \-ˈrēn-l\ *adj* : situated above or in front of the kidneys; *esp* : ADRENAL

[2]**suprarenal** *n* : a suprarenal part; *esp* : ADRENAL GLAND

su·prem·a·cist \su̇-ˈprem-ə-səst\ *n* : an advocate of supremacy of a particular group (as a race)

su·prem·a·cy \su̇-ˈprem-ə-sē\ *n, pl* **-cies** : the quality or state of being supreme; *also* : supreme authority or power [*supreme* + *-acy* (as in *primacy*)]

synonyms SUPREMACY, ASCENDANCY mean a being first in rank, power, or influence. SUPREMACY implies definite superiority over all others ⟨*supremacy* in steel production⟩. ASCENDANCY implies domination of one by another which may or may not involve supremacy ⟨seeking to keep one's *ascendancy* over an old rival⟩.

su·preme \su̇-ˈprēm\ *adj* **1** : highest in rank or authority **2** : highest in degree or quality **3** : ULTIMATE, FINAL ⟨the *supreme* sacrifice⟩ [Latin *supremus,* superlative of *superus* "upper," from *super* "over, above"] — **su·preme·ly** *adv* — **supreme·ness** *n*

Supreme Being *n* : GOD 1

supreme court *n* : the highest court in a political unit (as a nation or state)

sur- *prefix* : over : above ⟨*sur*tax⟩ [Medieval French, from Latin *super-*]

sur·cease \ˈsər-ˌsēs, ˌsər-ˈ\ *n* : CESSATION; *esp* : a temporary respite or end [Medieval French *surceser,* alteration of *surseoir,* from Latin *supersedēre* "to sit on top, refrain from," from *super-* + *sedēre* "to sit"]

[1]**sur·charge** \ˈsər-ˌchärj\ *vt* **1 a** : OVERCHARGE 1 **b** : to charge an extra fee usually for a special service **2** : to fill or load to excess **3** : to mark (as a stamp) with a surcharge

[2]**surcharge** *n* **1** : an additional tax or charge **2** : an excessive load **3 a** : an overprint on a stamp; *esp* : one that alters the denomination **b** : a stamp bearing such an overprint

sur·cin·gle \ˈsər-ˌsing-gəl\ *n* : a belt, band, or girth passing around the body of a horse to bind a saddle or pack fast to the horse's back [Medieval French *surcengle,* from *sur-* + *cengle* "girdle," from Latin *cingulum*]

sur·coat \ˈsər-ˌkōt\ *n* : an outer coat or cloak; *esp* : a tunic worn over armor

[1]**surd** \ˈsərd\ *adj* : VOICELESS — used of speech sounds [Latin *surdus* "deaf, silent, stupid"]

[2]**surd** *n* **1** : an irrational root (as $\sqrt{3}$) **2** : a surd speech sound

[1]**sure** \ˈshu̇r, *especially South* ˈshōr\ *adj* **1** : firmly established : STEADFAST ⟨a *sure* foundation⟩ **2** : RELIABLE, TRUSTWORTHY ⟨a *sure* friend⟩ **3 a** : marked by or given to feelings of confident certainty ⟨I'm *sure* I'm right⟩ **b** : characterized by a lack of wavering or hesitation ⟨*sure* brush strokes⟩ ⟨a *sure* hand⟩ **4** : admitting of no doubt : CERTAIN ⟨spoke from *sure* knowledge⟩ **5 a** : bound to happen : INEVITABLE ⟨*sure* disaster⟩ **b** : destined as if by fate ⟨*sure* to win⟩ [Medieval French *seur,* from Latin *securus* "secure"] — **sure·ness** *n* — **for sure** : without doubt or question : CERTAINLY — **to be sure** : it must be acknowledged : ADMITTEDLY

S surcoat

synonyms SURE, CERTAIN, POSITIVE mean having no doubt of one's opinion or conclusion. SURE usually stresses the subjective or intuitive feeling of assurance ⟨I am *sure* I have seen that face before⟩. CERTAIN implies basing a conclusion on definite grounds or indubitable evidence ⟨police are *certain* about the cause of the fire⟩. POSITIVE intensifies sureness and may imply opinionated conviction or forceful expression of it ⟨I'm *positive* that's the person I saw⟩.

[2]**sure** *adv* : SURELY

sure•fire \-ˈfīr\ *adj* : certain to get results : DEPENDABLE

sure–foot•ed \-ˈfu̇t-əd\ *adj* : not liable to stumble or fall — **sure–foot•ed•ly** *adv* — **sure–foot•ed•ness** *n*

sure•ly \ˈshu̇r-lē\ *adv* **1 a** : with assurance : CONFIDENTLY ⟨answered quickly and *surely*⟩ **b** : without doubt : CERTAINLY ⟨will *surely* be there⟩ **2** : INDEED 1, REALLY — often used as an intensive ⟨I *surely* am tired this afternoon⟩

sure•ty \ˈshu̇r-ət-ē, ˈshu̇rt-ē\ *n, pl* **sureties 1** : sure knowledge : CERTAINTY **2** : a pledge for the fulfillment of an undertaking : GUARANTEE **3** : one who assumes legal liability for another's debt, default, or failure to do a duty — **sure•ty•ship** \-ē-ˌship\ *n*

[1]**surf** \ˈsərf\ *n* **1** : the swell of the sea that breaks upon the shore **2** : the foam, splash, and sound of breaking waves [origin unknown]

[2]**surf** *vb* **1** : to ride the surf (as on a surfboard) **2** : to scan the offerings of (as television or the Internet) for something of interest — **surf•er** *n*

[1]**sur•face** \ˈsər-fəs\ *n* **1** : the outside or upper boundary of an object or body ⟨on the *surface* of the water⟩ ⟨the earth's *surface*⟩ **2** : a flat or curved two-dimensional area in space ⟨the *surface* of a sphere⟩ **3** : the external or superficial aspect of something ⟨the *surface* of society⟩ **4** : an external part or layer ⟨sanded the rough *surfaces*⟩ [French, from *sur-* + *face* "face"] — **on the surface** : to all outward appearances

[2]**surface** *adj* **1 a** : of, located on, or designed for use at the surface of something **b** : situated, transported, or employed on the surface of the earth ⟨*surface* vehicles⟩ **2** : appearing to be such on the surface only : SUPERFICIAL ⟨*surface* friendships⟩

[3]**surface** *vb* **1** : to give a surface to: as **a** : to plane or make smooth **b** : to apply a surface layer to ⟨*surface* a road⟩ **2** : to bring or come to the surface ⟨the submarine *surfaced*⟩ — **sur•fac•er** *n*

surface tension *n* : the attractive force felt by surface molecules of a liquid from the molecules beneath that tends to draw the surface molecules into the mass of the liquid and makes the liquid assume the shape having the least surface area

surface–to–air *adj* : launched from the ground against a target in the air

sur•fac•ing \ˈsər-fə-sing\ *n* : material forming or used to form a surface (as on a road)

surf•board \ˈsərf-ˌbōrd, -ˌbȯrd\ *n* : a buoyant board used in the sport of surfing — **surf•board•er** *n* — **surf•board•ing** \-ing\ *n*

surf•boat \-ˌbōt\ *n* : a boat for use in heavy surf

surf casting *n* : a method of fishing in which artificial or natural bait is cast into the open ocean or in a bay where waves break on a beach — **surf caster** *n*

[1]**sur•feit** \ˈsər-fət\ *n* **1** : an overabundant supply : EXCESS **2** : an intemperate indulgence in something (as food or drink) **3** : disgust caused by excess : SATIETY [Medieval French *surfet,* from *surfaire* "to overdo," from *sur-* + *faire* "to do," from Latin *facere*]

[2]**surfeit** *vb* : to feed, supply, or indulge to the point of surfeit : CLOY

surfing \ˈsər-fing\ *n* : the sport of riding the surf especially on a surfboard

[1]**surge** \ˈsərj\ *vi* **1** : to rise and fall actively **2** : to rise and move in or as if in waves or billows ⟨the sea *surged*⟩ ⟨a crowd *surged* toward the door⟩ **3** : to rise or increase suddenly or forcefully ⟨the stock market *surged*⟩ [earlier, to ride (at anchor), probably in part from Middle French *sourgir* "to cast anchor, land"; in part from Latin *surgere* "to go straight up, rise," from *sub-* "up" + *regere* "to lead straight"]

[2]**surge** *n* **1** : a swelling, rolling, or sweeping forward like that of a wave **2** : a large wave or billow : SWELL **3** : a transient sudden rise of current or voltage in an electrical circuit

sur•geon \ˈsər-jən\ *n* : a physician who specializes in surgery [Medieval French *surgien, cirurgien,* from *cirurgerie* "surgery"]

surgeon general *n, pl* **surgeons general** : the chief medical officer of a branch of the armed services or of a public health service

sur•gery \ˈsərj-rē, -ə-rē\ *n, pl* **-ger•ies 1** : a branch of medicine concerned with the correction of physical defects, the repair and healing of injuries, and the treatment of diseased conditions especially by operations **2 a** : work done by a surgeon **b** : OPERATION 3 **3 a** *British* : a physician's or dentist's office **b** : a room or area where surgery is performed [Medieval French *cirurgerie, surgerie,* from Latin *chirurgia,* from Greek *cheirourgia,* derived from *cheir* "hand" + *ergon* "work"]

sur•gi•cal \ˈsər-ji-kəl\ *adj* : of, relating to, or associated with surgeons or surgery ⟨*surgical* skills⟩ ⟨*surgical* implements⟩ ⟨*surgical* fevers⟩ — **sur•gi•cal•ly** \-kə-lē, -klē\ *adv*

sur•ly \ˈsər-lē\ *adj* **sur•li•er; -est** : irritably sullen and churlish in mood or manner [Middle English *serreli* "lordly, imperious," probably from *sire, ser* "sire"] ***synonyms*** see SULLEN — **sur•li•ness** *n*

[1]**sur•mise** \sər-ˈmīz\ *vb* : to form an idea of from very little evidence : GUESS [Medieval French *surmis,* past participle of *surmettre* "to place on, suppose, accuse," from Latin *supermittere* "to throw on," from *super-* + *mittere* "to send"] ***synonyms*** see CONJECTURE

[2]**sur•mise** \sər-ˈmīz, ˈsər-ˌ\ *n* : a thought or idea based on scanty evidence : CONJECTURE

sur•mount \sər-ˈmau̇nt\ *vt* **1** : to rise above or prevail over : OVERCOME ⟨*surmount* an obstacle⟩ **2** : to get to the top of : CLIMB **3** : to stand or lie at the top of : CROWN ⟨a cross *surmounts* the church steeple⟩ — **sur•mount•able** \-ə-bəl\ *adj*

[1]**sur•name** \ˈsər-ˌnām\ *n* **1** : an added name derived from occupation or other circumstance : NICKNAME 1 **2** : the name borne in common by members of a family [earlier *surname* "added name, nickname"]

[2]**surname** *vt* : to give a surname to

sur•pass \sər-ˈpas\ *vt* **1** : to be greater, better, or stronger than : EXCEED **2** : to go beyond the reach, powers, or capacity of ***synonyms*** see EXCEED — **sur•pass•able** \-ə-bəl\ *adj*

sur•plice \ˈsər-pləs\ *n* : a loose white tunic worn at service by a member of the clergy or choir [Medieval French *surplis,* from Medieval Latin *superpellicium,* from *super-* + *pellicium* "coat of skins," derived from Latin *pellis* "skin"]

sur•plus \ˈsər-ˌpləs, -pləs\ *n* **1** : the amount that remains when use or need is satisfied : EXCESS **2** : an excess of income over spending [Medieval French, from Medieval Latin *superplus,* from Latin *super-* + *plus* "more"] — **surplus** *adj*

sur•plus•age \-ij\ *n* **1** : SURPLUS **2** : excessive or nonessential matter

surplus value *n* : the difference in Marxist theory between the value of work done or the commodities produced by labor and the wages paid by the employer

[1]**sur•prise** \sər-ˈprīz, sə-ˈprīz\ *n* **1 a** : an attack made without warning **b** : a taking unawares ⟨we were taken by *surprise*⟩ **2** : something that surprises **3** : the state of being surprised : ASTONISHMENT [Medieval French *sousprise, supprise,* from *surprendre & susprendre* "to capture, take by surprise," from *sur-* + *prendre* "to take"]

[2]**surprise** *also* **sur•prize** *vb* **sur•prised** *also* **sur•prized; sur•pris•ing** *also* **sur•priz•ing 1** : to attack unexpectedly; *also* : to capture by an unexpected attack **2** : to take unawares : come upon unexpectedly **3** : to strike with wonder or amazement because unexpected — **sur•pris•er** *n*

synonyms SURPRISE, ASTONISH, ASTOUND mean to impress strongly through unexpectedness. SURPRISE stresses causing an effect through being unexpected but not necessarily unusual or novel ⟨*surprised* to find them at home⟩. ASTONISH implies surprising so greatly as to seem incredible ⟨a discovery that *astonished* the world⟩. ASTOUND stresses the shock of astonishment ⟨too *astounded* to reply⟩.

sur•pris•ing *adj* : of a kind to cause surprise

sur•pris•ing•ly \-ˈprī-zing-lē\ *adv* **1** : in a surprising manner : to a surprising degree ⟨a *surprisingly* fast runner⟩ **2** : it is surprising that ⟨*surprisingly,* voter turnout was high⟩

sur•re•al•ism \sə-ˈrē-ə-ˌliz-əm\ *n* : the principles, ideals, or practice of producing fantastic or incongruous imagery in art, literature, film, or theater by means of unnatural or irrational juxtapositions and combinations — **sur•re•al•ist** \-ləst\ *n or adj* — **sur•re•al•is•tic** \-ˌrē-ə-ˈlis-tik\ *adj* — **sur•re•al•is•ti•cal•ly** \-ti-kə-lē, -klē\ *adv*

[1]**sur•ren•der** \sə-ˈren-dər\ *vb* **sur•ren•dered; sur•ren•der•ing** \-də-ring, -dring\ **1** : to give over to the power, control, or possession of another especially under compulsion ⟨*surrendered* the fort⟩ **2** : to give oneself up into the power of another especially as a prisoner **3** : to give oneself over to something (as an influence or course of action) [Medieval French *surrendre, susrendre* "to relinquish," from *sur- & sus-, suz* "under" + *rendre* "to give back"] ***synonyms*** see RELINQUISH

[2]**surrender** *n* : the giving of oneself or something into the power of another person or thing

sur·rep·ti·tious \ˌsər-əp-ˈtish-əs, ˌsə-rəp-\ *adj* : done, made, or acquired by stealth : CLANDESTINE, STEALTHY [Latin *surrepticius,* from *surripere* "to snatch secretly," from *sub-* + *rapere* "to seize"] ***synonyms*** see SECRET — **sur·rep·ti·tious·ly** *adv* — **sur·rep·ti·tious·ness** *n*

sur·rey \ˈsər-ē, ˈsə-rē\ *n, pl* **surreys** : a four-wheel two-seated horse-drawn pleasure carriage [*Surrey,* England]

surrey

sur·ro·gate \ˈsər-ə-ˌgāt, ˈsə-rə-, -gət\ *n* **1** : DEPUTY 1, SUBSTITUTE **2** : a local judicial officer in some states having jurisdiction over the settling of estates [Latin *surrogatus,* past participle of *surrogare* "to substitute," from *sub-* + *rogare* "to ask"] — **surrogate** *adj*

[1]**sur·round** \sə-ˈrau̇nd\ *vt* : to enclose on all sides : ENCIRCLE, ENCOMPASS [Medieval French *surunder* "to overflow," from Late Latin *superundare* "to overflow," from Latin *super-* + *unda* "wave"]

[2]**surround** *n* : something (as a border or edging) that surrounds

sur·round·ings \-ˈrau̇n-dingz\ *n pl* : ENVIRONMENT 1

surround sound *n* : sound reproduction that often uses three or more transmission channels to enhance the illusion of a live hearing

sur·sum cor·da \ˌsu̇r-səm-ˈkȯrd-ə\ *n* **1** *often cap S&C* : a versicle exhorting thanksgiving to God **2** : something inspiriting [Late Latin, "(lift) up (your) hearts"]

sur·tax \ˈsər-ˌtaks\ *n* : an additional tax over and above a general tax

sur·tout \sər-ˈtü, ˌsər-\ *n* : a man's long close-fitting overcoat [French, from *sur* "over" + *tout* "all"]

sur·veil·lance \sər-ˈvā-ləns *also* -ˈvāl-yəns *or* -ˈvā-əns\ *n* : close watch [French, from *surveiller* "to watch over," from *sur-* + *veiller* "to watch," from Latin *vigilare,* from *vigil* "watchful"]

sur·veil·lant \-ˈvā-lənt *also* -ˈvāl-yənt *or* -ˈvā-ənt\ *n* : one that keeps another under surveillance

[1]**sur·vey** \sər-ˈvā, ˈsər-ˌ\ *vb* **sur·veyed; sur·vey·ing** **1** : to look over and examine closely **2** : to determine the form, boundaries, and position of (as a piece of land) **3** : to view or study as a whole **4** : to make a survey [Medieval French *surveer,* from *sur-* + *veer* "to see," from Latin *vidēre*]

[2]**sur·vey** \ˈsər-ˌvā, sər-ˈ\ *n, pl* **surveys** **1** : the act or an instance of surveying: as **a** : a broad treatment of a subject **b** : POLL 4a **2** : something that is surveyed

sur·vey·ing \sər-ˈvā-ing\ *n* : a branch of mathematics concerned with finding the area of any part of the earth's surface, the lengths and directions of the boundary lines, and the contour of the surface and with accurately depicting the whole on paper

sur·vey·or \sər-ˈvā-ər\ *n* : one that surveys; *esp* : one whose occupation is surveying land

sur·viv·al \sər-ˈvī-vəl\ *n* **1** : the act or fact of living or continuing longer than another person or thing **2** : the continuation of life despite difficult conditions ⟨techniques for *survival* in the desert⟩ **3** : one that survives

survival of the fittest : NATURAL SELECTION

sur·vive \sər-ˈvīv\ *vb* **1** : to remain alive or in existence : live on **2** : to remain alive after the death of ⟨he is *survived* by his wife⟩ **3** : to continue to exist or live after ⟨*survived* the flood⟩ [Medieval French *survivre* "to outlive," from Latin *supervivere,* from *super-* + *vivere* "to live"] — **sur·vi·vor** \-ˈvī-vər\ *n*

sus·cep·ti·bil·i·ty \sə-ˌsep-tə-ˈbil-ət-ē\ *n, pl* **-ties** **1** : the quality or state of being susceptible; *esp* : lack of ability to resist some outside agent (as a pathogen or drug) : SENSITIVITY **2 a** : a susceptible temperament or constitution **b** *pl* : FEELING 2b, SENSIBILITIES

sus·cep·ti·ble \sə-ˈsep-tə-bəl\ *adj* **1** : capable of submitting to an action, process, or operation ⟨a theory *susceptible* to proof⟩ **2** : open, subject, or unresistant to some stimulus, influence, or agency ⟨persons *susceptible* to colds⟩ **3** : easily influenced or affected [Late Latin *susceptibilis,* from Latin *suscipere* "to take up," from *sub-, sus-* "up" + *capere* "to take"] — **sus·cep·ti·ble·ness** *n* — **sus·cep·ti·bly** \-blē\ *adv*

su·shi \ˈsü-shē\ *n* : cold rice formed into any of various shapes and topped or wrapped with bits of raw seafood or vegetables [Japanese]

[1]**sus·pect** \ˈsəs-ˌpekt, sə-ˈspekt\ *adj* **1** : regarded with or deserving suspicion **2** : DOUBTFUL 2, QUESTIONABLE [Medieval French, from Latin *suspectus,* from *suspicere* "to suspect"]

[2]**sus·pect** \ˈsəs-ˌpekt\ *n* : one that is suspected; *esp* : a person suspected of a crime

[3]**sus·pect** \sə-ˈspekt\ *vb* **1** : to have doubts of : DISTRUST ⟨*suspects* her motives⟩ **2** : to believe to be guilty on slight evidence or without proof ⟨*suspected* him of theft⟩ **3** : to imagine to exist or be true, likely, or probable : SURMISE ⟨I *suspect* he's right⟩ [Latin *suspectare,* from *suspicere* "to look up at, regard with awe, suspect," from *sub-, sus-* "up, secretly" + *specere* "to look at"]

sus·pend \sə-ˈspend\ *vb* **1** : to bar temporarily especially from any privilege or office ⟨*suspend* a student from school⟩ **2 a** : to stop or do away with (as an activity) for a time ⟨*suspend* publication⟩ **b** : to defer on specified conditions ⟨*suspend* sentence on an offender⟩ ⟨*suspend* judgment⟩ **3** : to cease for a time from operation or activity **4 a** : HANG; *esp* : to hang so as to be free on all sides except at the point of support ⟨*suspend* a ball by a thread⟩ **b** : to keep from falling or sinking by some invisible support (as buoyancy) ⟨dust *suspended* in the air⟩ **c** : to put or hold in suspension ⟨*suspended* sediment⟩ [Medieval French *suspendre,* from Latin *suspendere,* from *sub-, sus-* "up" + *pendere* "to cause to hang, weigh"]

suspended animation *n* : temporary suspension of the vital functions (as in persons nearly drowned)

sus·pend·er \sə-ˈspen-dər\ *n* **1** : one that suspends **2** : a device by which something may be suspended; *esp* : either of two supporting bands worn across the shoulders to support pants, skirt, or belt — usually used in plural ⟨a pair of *suspenders*⟩

sus·pense \sə-ˈspens\ *n* **1** : the state of being suspended : SUSPENSION **2 a** : mental uncertainty : ANXIETY 1a **b** : pleasant excitement as to a decision or outcome ⟨a novel of *suspense*⟩ **3** : the state of being undecided or doubtful ⟨our next move was still in *suspense*⟩ [Medieval French, from *suspendre* "to suspend"] — **sus·pense·ful** \-fəl\ *adj*

sus·pen·sion \sə-ˈspen-chən\ *n* **1** : the act of suspending or the state or period of being suspended: as **a** : temporary removal (as from office or privileges) **b** : temporary withholding (as of belief or decision) **c** : temporary setting aside of a law or rule **2** : the act of hanging : the state of being hung **3 a** : the state of a substance when its particles are mixed with but undissolved in a fluid or solid; *also* : a substance in this state **b** : a system consisting of a solid dispersed in a solid, liquid, or gas usually in particles of larger than colloidal size **4** : something suspended **5 a** : a device by which something is suspended **b** : the system of devices (as springs) supporting the upper part of a vehicle on the axles [Late Latin *suspensio,* from Latin *suspendere* "to suspend"]

suspension bridge *n* : a bridge that has its roadway suspended from two or more cables usually passing over towers and securely anchored at the ends

suspension points *n pl, chiefly British* : usually three spaced periods used to show the omission of a word or word group

sus·pen·sive \sə-ˈspen-siv\ *adj* **1** : stopping temporarily **2** : characterized by suspense, suspended judgment, or indecisiveness — **sus·pen·sive·ly** *adv*

sus·pen·sor \sə-ˈspen-sər\ *n* : a suspending part or structure; *esp* : a group of cells that pushes the developing embryo of a seed plant into the endosperm

sus·pen·so·ry \sə-ˈspens-rē, -ə-rē\ *adj* : fitted or serving to suspend something **2** : temporarily leaving something undetermined

suspensory ligament *n* : a fibrous membrane holding the iris of the eye in place

[1]**sus·pi·cion** \sə-ˈspish-ən\ *n* **1** : the act or an instance of suspecting or being suspected **2** : a state of mental uneasiness and uncertainty : DOUBT **3** : a slight touch or trace : SUGGESTION

\ə\ **abut**	\au̇\ **out**	\i\ **tip**	\ȯ\ **saw**	\u̇\ **foot**
\ər\ **further**	\ch\ **chin**	\ī\ **life**	\ȯi\ **coin**	\y\ **yet**
\a\ **mat**	\e\ **pet**	\j\ **job**	\th\ **thin**	\yü\ **few**
\ā\ **take**	\ē\ **easy**	\ng\ **sing**	\t͟h\ **this**	\yu̇\ **cure**
\ä\ **cot, cart**	\g\ **go**	\ō\ **bone**	\ü\ **food**	\zh\ **vision**

⟨just a *suspicion* of garlic⟩ [Medieval French, from Latin *suspicio,* from *suspicere* "to suspect"] ***synonyms*** see DOUBT

[2]**suspicion** *vt* **sus·pi·cioned; sus·pi·cion·ing** \-ˈspish-ning, -ə-ning\ *chiefly substandard* : SUSPECT

sus·pi·cious \sə-ˈspish-əs\ *adj* **1** : arousing or tending to arouse suspicion ⟨*suspicious* characters⟩ **2** : disposed to suspect : DISTRUSTFUL ⟨*suspicious* of strangers⟩ **3** : indicative of suspicion ⟨a *suspicious* glance⟩ — **sus·pi·cious·ly** *adv* — **sus·pi·cious·ness** *n*

sus·pire \sə-ˈspīr\ *vi* : to draw a long deep breath : SIGH [Latin *suspirare,* from *sub-* + *spirare* "to breathe"] — **sus·pi·ra·tion** \ˌsəs-pə-ˈrā-shən\ *n*

sus·tain \sə-ˈstān\ *vt* **1** : to give support or relief to **2** : to supply with sustenance : NOURISH **3** : to keep up : PROLONG ⟨a book that will *sustain* your interest⟩ **4** : to support the weight of : CARRY **5** : to keep up the spirits or courage of ⟨hope *sustained* the people⟩ **6 a** : to bear up under : ENDURE **b** : UNDERGO 1 ⟨*sustained* a serious wound⟩ **7** : to support as true, legal, valid, or just ⟨the court *sustained* the earlier verdict⟩ **8** : PROVE 2a, CONFIRM [Medieval French *sustenir,* from Latin *sustinēre* "to hold up, sustain," from *sub-, sus-* "up" + *tenēre* "to hold"] — **sus·tain·able** \-ˈstā-nə-bəl\ *adj* — **sus·tain·er** *n*

sus·te·nance \ˈsəs-tə-nəns\ *n* **1 a** : means of support, maintenance, or subsistence **b** : FOOD; *also* : NOURISHMENT **2 a** : the act of sustaining : the state of being sustained **b** : a supplying with the necessaries of life **3** : something that gives support, endurance, or strength [Medieval French, from *sustenir* "to sustain"]

su·sur·ra·tion \ˌsü-sə-ˈrā-shən\ *n* : a rustling or whispering sound [Late Latin *susurratio,* from Latin *susurrare* "to whisper"]

sut·ler \ˈsət-lər\ *n* : a civilian provisioner to an army post often with a shop on the post [Dutch *soeteler,* from Low German *suteler* "sloppy worker, camp cook"]

su·tra \ˈsü-trə\ *n* **1** : a precept summarizing Vedic teaching; *also* : a collection of these precepts **2** : one of the discourses of the Buddha that constitute the basic text of Buddhist scripture [Sanskrit *sūtra* "precept," literally, "thread"]

sut·tee \sə-ˈtē, ˌsə-ˈtē\ *n* : the act or custom of a Hindu widow willingly being cremated on the funeral pyre of her husband; *also* : a woman so cremated [Hindi *satī* "wife who performs suttee," from Sanskrit "devoted woman," from *sat* "true, good"]

[1]**su·ture** \ˈsü-chər\ *n* **1 a** : a strand or fiber used to sew parts of the living body; *also* : a stitch made with this **b** : the act or process of sewing with sutures **2 a** : the line of union in an immovable joint (as between the bones of the skull); *also* : such a joint **b** : a furrow at the junction of adjacent bodily parts; *esp* : a line along which a fruit dehisces [Latin *sutura* "seam, suture," from *suere* "to sew"] — **su·tur·al** \ˈsüch-rəl, -ə-rəl\ *adj* — **su·tur·al·ly** \-ē\ *adv*

[2]**suture** *vt* **su·tured; su·tur·ing** \ˈsüch-ring, -ə-ring\ : to unite, close, or secure with sutures ⟨*suture* a wound⟩

SUV \ˌes-ˌyü-ˈvē\ *n* : SPORT-UTILITY VEHICLE

su·zer·ain \ˈsüz-rən, -ə-rən, ˈsüz-ə-ˌrān\ *n* **1** : a superior feudal lord : OVERLORD **2** : a state controlling the foreign relations of another but allowing it internal sovereignty [French, from Medieval French *sus* "up" + *-erain* (as in *soverain* "sovereign")] — **su·zer·ain·ty** \-tē\ *n*

svelte \ˈsfelt\ *adj* **1** : slender and graceful in form **2** : URBANE, SUAVE [French, from Italian *svelto,* from *svellere* "to pluck out," from Latin *evellere,* from *e-* + *vellere* "to pluck"] — **svelte·ly** *adv* — **svelte·ness** *n*

Sven·ga·li \sfen-ˈgäl-ē\ *n* : a person who manipulates or exerts excessive control over another [*Svengali,* evil hypnotist in the novel *Trilby* by George du Maurier, died 1896, British artist and novelist]

[1]**swab** \ˈswäb\ *n* **1 a** : MOP; *esp* : a yarn mop **b** : a wad of absorbent material usually wound around one end of a small stick and used especially for applying medication or for removing material (as from a wound); *also* : a specimen taken with a swab **2** : SAILOR 1a [probably from Dutch *swabbe*]

[2]**swab** *vt* **swabbed; swab·bing** : to use a swab on

swad·dle \ˈswäd-l\ *vt* **swad·dled; swad·dling** \ˈswäd-ling, -l-ing\ **1** : to wrap (an infant) with swaddling clothes **2** : to wrap closely : SWATHE [Middle English *swadelen*]

swaddling clothes *n pl* **1** : narrow strips of cloth wrapped around an infant to restrict movement **2** : limitations or restrictions imposed upon the immature or inexperienced

swag \ˈswag\ *n* **1 a** : something hanging in a curve between two points : FESTOON **b** : a suspended cluster (as of evergreen branches) **2** : goods acquired by unlawful means : LOOT [earlier *swag* "to sway," perhaps of Scandinavian origin]

[1]**swag·ger** \ˈswag-ər\ *vi* **swag·gered; swag·ger·ing** \ˈswag-ring, -ə-ring\ **1** : to conduct oneself in an arrogant or overbearing manner; *esp* : to walk with an air of superiority **2** : BOAST, BRAG [probably from *swag* "to sway"] ***synonyms*** see STRUT — **swag·ger·er** \ˈswag-ər-ər\ *n* — **swag·ger·ing·ly** \-ring-lē, -ə-ring-\ *adv*

[2]**swagger** *n* : an act or instance of swaggering

swagger stick *n* : a short light stick usually covered with leather or tipped with metal at each end and intended for carrying in the hand (as by military officers)

Swa·hi·li \swä-ˈhē-lē\ *n* **1** : a member of a Bantu-speaking people of Zanzibar and the adjacent coast of Africa **2** : a Bantu language that is a trade and governmental language over much of East Africa and in the Congo region [Arabic *sawāḥil,* pl. of *sāḥil* "coast"]

swain \ˈswān\ *n* **1** : RUSTIC, PEASANT; *esp* : SHEPHERD **2** : a male admirer or suitor [Old Norse *sveinn* "boy, servant"]

swale \ˈswāl\ *n* : a small, low-lying and usually wet stretch of land [origin unknown]

[1]**swal·low** \ˈswäl-ō\ *n* **1** : any of a family of small birds that have long pointed wings and usually a deeply forked tail and that feed on insects caught while in flight **2** : any of several birds that superficially resemble swallows [Old English *swealwe*]

[2]**swallow** *vb* **1 a** : to take into the stomach through the mouth and throat **b** : to perform the actions used in swallowing something **2** : to envelop or take in as if by swallowing ⟨was *swallowed* up by the crowd⟩ **3** : to accept without question, protest, or resentment ⟨a hard story to *swallow*⟩ **4** : to take back : RETRACT ⟨had to *swallow* those words⟩ **5** : to keep from expressing or showing : REPRESS ⟨*swallow* one's anger⟩ **6** : to utter (as words) indistinctly [Old English *swelgan*] — **swal·low·er** \ˈswäl-ə-wər\ *n*

[3]**swallow** *n* **1** : an act of swallowing **2** : an amount that can be swallowed at one time

swal·low·tail \ˈswäl-ō-ˌtāl\ *n* **1** : a deeply forked and tapering tail (as of a swallow) **2** : any of various usually large brightly marked butterflies with each hind wing having an elongated process resembling a tail — **swal·low-tailed** \ˌswäl-ō-ˈtāld\ *adj*

swallowtail 2

swam *past of* SWIM

swa·mi \ˈswäm-ē\ *n* **1** : a Hindu mystic or religious teacher — used as a title **2** : SEER 2 [Hindi *svāmī,* from Sanskrit *svāmin* "owner, lord," from *sva* "one's own"]

[1]**swamp** \ˈswämp, ˈswȯmp\ *n* : wet spongy land or a tract of this often partially or intermittently covered with water and usually overgrown with shrubs and trees — compare MARSH [Middle English *sompe,* from Dutch *somp* "morass"] — **swamp·i·ness** \-pē-nəs\ *n* — **swampy** \ˈswäm-pē, ˈswȯm-\ *adj*

[2]**swamp** *vb* **1 a** : to cause to capsize in water or fill with water and sink **b** : to fill with or as if with water : SUBMERGE **2** : to overwhelm by an excess of something ⟨*swamped* with work⟩

swamp buggy *n* : a vehicle designed to travel over swampy terrain; *esp* : a four-wheeled motor vehicle with oversize tires

swamp·land \ˈswäm-ˌpland, ˈswȯm-\ *n* : SWAMP

swampy \ˈswäm-pē, ˈswȯm-\ *adj* **swamp·i·er; -est** : consisting of or resembling swamp : MARSHY — **swamp·i·ness** *n*

swan \ˈswän\ *n, pl* **swans** *also* **swan** : any of various large heavy-bodied long-necked mostly pure white aquatic birds with webbed feet that are related to but larger than the geese [Old English]

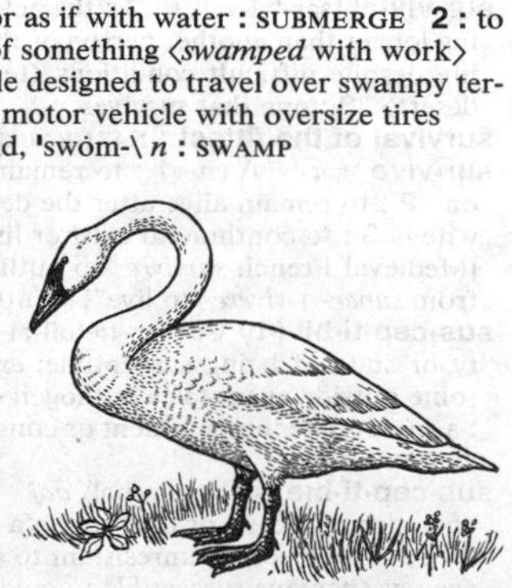

swan

swan dive *n* : a headfirst

forward dive made with the back arched, the head back, the arms out to either side, and the legs together

[1]**swank** \'swaŋk\ *vi* : SHOW OFF 2, SWAGGER [perhaps from Middle High German *swanken* "to sway"]

[2]**swank** *n* : a sometimes flashy show of elegance or pretense

[3]**swank** *or* **swanky** \'swaŋ-kē\ *adj* **swank·er** *or* **swank·i·er; -est** **1** : characterized by showy display : OSTENTATIOUS ⟨a *swank* limousine⟩ **2** : fashionably elegant : SMART ⟨a *swank* restaurant⟩ — **swank·i·ly** \'swaŋ-kə-lē\ *adv* — **swank·i·ness** \-kē-nəs\ *n*

swans·down \'swänz-ˌdau̇n\ *n* **1** : the very soft fluffy white feathers of the swan **2** : a heavy cotton flannel with a thick nap on the face

swan song *n* **1** : a song of unusual beauty formerly thought to be sung by a dying swan **2** : a farewell appearance or final act or pronouncement

[1]**swap** \'swäp\ *vb* **swapped; swap·ping** : to give in exchange : make an exchange : BARTER [Middle English *swappen* "to strike"; from the practice of striking hands in closing a business deal]

[2]**swap** *n* : EXCHANGE 1, TRADE

sward \'swȯrd\ *n* : the grassy surface of land : TURF [Old English *sweard* "skin, rind"]

[1]**swarm** \'swȯrm\ *n* **1** : a great number of honeybees emigrating together from a hive in company with a queen to start a new colony elsewhere; *also* : a colony of honeybees settled in a hive **2** : an extremely large number massed together and usually in motion ⟨*swarms* of shoppers⟩ [Old English *swearm*]

[2]**swarm** *vb* **1** : to form and depart from a hive in a swarm **2** : to migrate, move, or gather in a crowd : THRONG **3** : to contain or fill with a swarm : TEEM — **swarm·er** *n*

[3]**swarm** *vb* : to climb with the hands and feet; *esp* : SHIN ⟨*swarm* up a pole⟩ [origin unknown]

swarm spore *n* : ZOOSPORE

swart \'swȯrt\ *adj* : SWARTHY [Old English *sweart*] — **swart·ness** *n*

swar·thy \'swȯr-thē, -thē\ *adj* **swar·thi·er; -est** : of a dark color, complexion, or cast : DUSKY [derived from *swart*] — **swar·thi·ness** *n*

[1]**swash** \'swäsh\ *vb* **1** : BLUSTER 2, SWAGGER **2** : to make violent noisy movements **3** : to move or cause to move with a splashing sound [probably imitative]

[2]**swash** *n* **1** : SWAGGER **2** : a dashing of water against or upon something

swash·buck·ler \-ˌbək-lər\ *n* : a swaggering or daring soldier or adventurer [[1]*swash* + *buckler*] — **swash·buck·le** \-ˌbək-əl\ *vi*

swash·buck·ling \-ˌbək-liŋ\ *adj* **1** : acting in the manner of a swashbucker **2** : characteristic of, marked by, or done by swashbucklers [*swashbuckler*]

swas·ti·ka \'swäs-ti-kə *also* swä-'stē-kə\ *n* : a symbol or ornament in the form of a Greek cross with the ends of the arms extended at right angles all in the same rotary direction [Sanskrit *svastika,* from *svasti* "well-being," from *su-* "well" + *as-* "to be"; from its being regarded as a good luck symbol]

swat \'swät\ *vb* **swat·ted; swat·ting** : to hit with a quick hard blow [English dialect *swat* "to squat," alteration of *squat*] — **swat** *n* — **swat·ter** *n*

SWAT \'swät\ *n* : a police or military unit specially trained and equipped to handle unusually hazardous situations or missions ⟨the *SWAT* team⟩

swatch \'swäch\ *n* **1 a** : a sample piece (as of fabric) or a collection of samples **b** : a typical sample **2** : PATCH ⟨a *swatch* of color⟩ [origin unknown]

swath \'swäth, 'swȯth\ *or* **swathe** \'swäth, 'swȯth, 'swāth\ *n* **1 a** : the sweep of a scythe or machine in mowing or the path cut in one course **b** : a row of cut grain or grass **2** : a long broad strip or belt ⟨a long *swath* of land⟩ **3** : a space devastated as if by a scythe [Old English *swæth* "footstep, trace"]

[1]**swathe** \'swäth, 'swȯth, 'swāth\ *vt* **1** : to bind, wrap, or swaddle with or as if with a bandage **2** : ENVELOP [Old English *swathian*]

[2]**swathe** \'swäth, 'swȯth, 'swāth\ *or* **swath** \'swäth, 'swäth, 'swȯth, 'swȯth\ *n* **1** : a band used in swathing **2** : an enveloping medium

[1]**sway** \'swā\ *vb* **1 a** : to swing or cause to swing slowly back and forth from a base or pivot **b** : to move gently from an upright to a leaning position **2** : to hold sway : act as ruler or governor **3** : to fluctuate or veer between one point, position, or opinion and another **4** : to cause to turn aside (as from a thought or course of action) **5** : to exert a guiding or controlling influence upon [Middle English *sweyen* "to fall, swoon"] ***synonyms*** see INFLUENCE — **sway·er** *n*

synonyms SWAY, OSCILLATE, VIBRATE, WAVER mean to move back and forth. SWAY implies a slow swinging or teetering movement as of something large and heavy ⟨trees *swaying* in the breeze⟩. OSCILLATE suggests a usually regular alternation of direction ⟨the fan *oscillates*⟩. VIBRATE suggests the rapid oscillation of an elastic body under stress or impact ⟨the *vibrating* strings of a piano⟩. WAVER stresses irregular movement suggestive of reeling or tottering ⟨the exhausted runner *wavered* before collapsing⟩. ***synonyms*** see in addition INFLUENCE

[2]**sway** *n* **1** : the action or an instance of swaying or of being swayed : an oscillating, fluctuating, or sweeping motion **2** : an inclination or deflection caused by or as if by swaying **3 a** : a controlling force or influence **b** : sovereign power : DOMINION

sway·backed \'swā-ˌbakt\ *also* **sway·back** \'swā-'bak\ *adj* : having an unusually hollow or sagging back ⟨a *swaybacked* mare⟩ — **sway·back** *n*

Swazi *variant of* SISWATI

swear \'swaər, 'sweər\ *vb* **swore** \'swōər, 'swȯər\; **sworn** \'swōrn, 'swȯrn\; **swear·ing** **1** : to utter or take solemnly (an oath) **2 a** : to assert as true or promise under oath ⟨*swore* to uphold the Constitution⟩ **b** : to assert or promise emphatically or earnestly ⟨*swore* he'd study harder next time⟩ **3 a** : to administer an oath to ⟨*swear* the witness⟩ **b** : to bind by an oath ⟨*swore* them to secrecy⟩ **4** : to bring into a specified state by swearing ⟨*swear* your life away⟩ **5** : to take an oath **6** : to use profane or obscene language : CURSE [Old English *swerian*] — **swear·er** *n* — **swear by** : to place great confidence in — **swear off** : to vow to abstain from ⟨*swear off* smoking⟩

swear in *vt* : to induct into office by administration of an oath

swear out *vt* : to procure (a warrant for arrest) by making a sworn accusation

swear·word \'swaər-ˌwərd, 'sweər-\ *n* : a profane or dirty word

[1]**sweat** \'swet\ *vb* **sweat** *or* **sweat·ed; sweat·ing** **1** : to give off perceptible salty moisture through the openings of the sweat glands : PERSPIRE **2** : to give off or cause to give off moisture **3** : to collect drops of moisture ⟨stones *sweat* at night⟩ **4 a** : to work so hard that one perspires : TOIL ⟨*sweat* over a lesson⟩ **b** : to undergo anxiety or mental distress ⟨*sweated* through the test⟩ **5** : to soak with sweat ⟨*sweat* a collar⟩ **6** : to get rid of or lose by perspiring ⟨*sweat* off weight⟩ ⟨*sweat* out a fever⟩ **7** : to drive hard : OVERWORK; *esp* : to force to work hard at low wages and under bad conditions ⟨a factory that *sweats* its employees⟩ **8** : to heat (as solder) so as to melt and cause to run especially between surfaces to unite them; *also* : to unite by such means ⟨*sweat* a pipe joint⟩ **9** *slang* : to worry about [Old English *swǣtan,* from *swāt* "sweat"] — **sweat blood** : to work or worry intensely

[2]**sweat** *n* **1** : hard work : DRUDGERY **2** : fluid excreted from the sweat glands of the skin : PERSPIRATION **3** : moisture issuing from or gathering in drops on a surface **4** : the condition of one sweating or sweated **5** : a state of anxiety or impatience

sweat·band \'swet-ˌband\ *n* **1** : a band lining the inner edge of a hat or cap to prevent sweat damage **2** : a band of material worn around the head or wrist to absorb sweat

sweat·er \'swet-ər\ *n* **1** : one that sweats or causes sweating **2** : a knitted or crocheted jacket or pullover

sweat gland *n* : a gland of the skin that excretes perspiration and opens by a minute pore in the skin

sweat lodge *n* : a hut, lodge, or cavern heated by steam from water poured on hot stones and used especially by American Indians for ritual or therapeutic sweating

sweat out *vt* **1** : to endure or wait through the course of **2** : to work one's way painfully through or to

sweat pants *n pl* : pants having a drawstring waist and elastic cuffs at the ankle that are worn especially for exercise

sweat shirt *n* : a loose collarless usually long-sleeved pullover or jacket of heavy cotton jersey

sweat·shop \'swet-ˌshäp\ *n* : a shop or factory in which em-

\ə\ abut	\au̇\ out	\i\ tip	\ȯ\ saw	\u̇\ foot
\ər\ further	\ch\ chin	\ī\ life	\ȯi\ coin	\y\ yet
\a\ mat	\e\ pet	\j\ job	\th\ thin	\yü\ few
\ā\ take	\ē\ easy	\ŋ\ sing	\th\ this	\yu̇\ cure
\ä\ cot, cart	\g\ go	\ō\ bone	\ü\ food	\zh\ vision

ployees work for long hours at low wages and under unhealthy conditions

sweaty \ˈswet-ē\ *adj* **sweat·i·er; -est** **1 :** causing sweat ⟨*sweaty* work⟩ **2 :** wet or stained with or smelling of sweat ⟨*sweaty* socks⟩ — **sweat·i·ly** \ˈswet-l-ē\ *adv* — **sweat·i·ness** \ˈswet-ē-nəs\ *n*

swede \ˈswēd\ *n* **1** *cap* **a :** a native or inhabitant of Sweden **b :** a person of Swedish descent **2** *chiefly British* **:** RUTABAGA

Swed·ish \ˈswēd-ish\ *n* **1 :** the Germanic language spoken in Sweden **2** *pl in constr* **:** the people of Sweden — **Swedish** *adj*

[1]**sweep** \ˈswēp\ *vb* **swept** \ˈswept\; **sweep·ing** **1 a :** to remove from a surface with or as if with a broom or brush ⟨*swept* the crumbs from the table⟩ **b :** to remove or take with a single continuous forceful action ⟨*swept* the books off the desk⟩ **c :** to drive or carry along with irresistible force **2 a :** to clean with or as if with a broom or brush **b :** to move across or along swiftly, violently, or overwhelmingly ⟨a storm *swept* across the plains⟩ **c :** to win an overwhelming victory in or on ⟨*sweep* the elections⟩ **d :** to win all the games or contests of **3 :** to touch in passing with a swift continuous movement **4 :** to go with stately or sweeping movements ⟨proudly *swept* into the room⟩ **5 :** to trace the outline of (as a curve or angle) **6 :** to cover the entire range of ⟨his eyes *swept* the horizon⟩ **7 :** to move or extend in a wide curve or range [Middle English *swepen*] — **sweep·er** *n*

[2]**sweep** *n* **1 :** something that sweeps or works with a sweeping motion: as **a :** a long pole pivoted on a post and used to raise and lower a bucket (as in a well) **b :** a long oar **c :** a windmill sail **2 a :** an act or instance of sweeping; *esp* **:** a clearing out or away with or as if with a broom **b :** an overwhelming victory (as the winning of all the contests or prizes in a competition) **3 a :** a movement of great range and force **b :** a curving or circular course or line **c :** the compass of a sweeping movement **:** SCOPE **d :** a broad extent **4 :** CHIMNEY SWEEP **5 :** SWEEPSTAKES

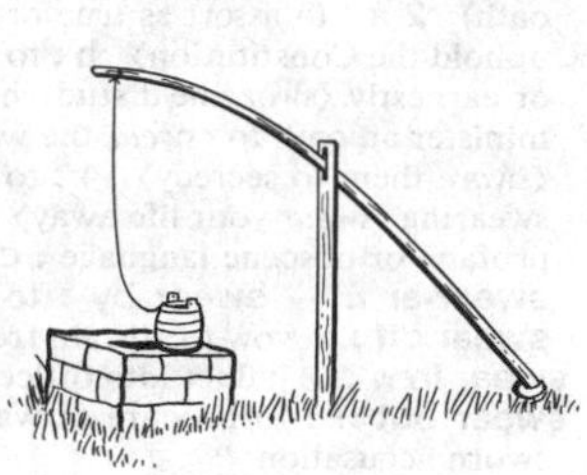

sweep 1a

sweep·back \ˈswēp-ˌbak\ *n* **:** the backward slant of an airplane wing in which the outer portion of the wing is downstream from the inner portion

sweep hand *n* **:** SWEEP-SECOND HAND

[1]**sweep·ing** *n* **1 :** the act or action of one that sweeps ⟨gave the room a good *sweeping*⟩ **2** *pl* **:** things collected by sweeping **:** REFUSE

[2]**sweeping** *adj* **1 a :** moving or extending in a wide curve or over a wide area **b :** having a curving line or form **2 a :** EXTENSIVE ⟨*sweeping* reforms⟩ **b :** broadly and indiscriminately inclusive ⟨*sweeping* generalizations⟩ — **sweep·ing·ly** \ˈswē-ping-lē\ *adv*

sweep net *n* **:** a bag-shaped net with a handle used by entomologists for catching insects by sweeping it over vegetation

sweep–sec·ond hand \ˈswēp-ˌsek-ənd-, -ənt-\ *n* **:** a hand marking seconds on a timepiece mounted concentrically with the other hands and read on the same dial

sweep·stakes \-ˌstāks\ *n sing or pl, also* **sweep–stake** \-ˌstāk\ **1 a :** a race or contest in which the entire prize may be awarded to the winner **b :** a horse race in which the stake awarded to the winner or distributed among the top finishers is made up at least in part of the entry fees or money contributed by the owners of the horses **2 :** CONTEST, COMPETITION **3 :** any of various lotteries [Middle English *swepestake* "one who wins all the stakes in a game," from *swepen* "to sweep" + *stake*]

[1]**sweet** \ˈswēt\ *adj* **1 a :** pleasing to the taste **b :** being or inducing the one of the four basic taste sensations that is typically induced by table sugar and is identified especially by the taste buds at the front of the tongue **c :** having a relatively large sugar content **2 a :** pleasing to the mind or feelings **:** AGREEABLE ⟨victory is *sweet*⟩ **b :** marked by gentle good humor or kindliness ⟨a *sweet* elderly couple⟩ **c :** FRAGRANT ⟨a *sweet* aroma⟩ **d :** delicately pleasing to the ear or eye ⟨a *sweet* melody⟩ **e :** SACCHARINE 2, CLOYING **f :** very good or appealing ⟨a *sweet* job offer⟩ **3 :** much loved **:** DEAR ⟨my *sweet* child⟩ **4 a :** not sour, rancid, decaying, or stale **:** WHOLESOME ⟨*sweet* milk⟩ **b :** not salt or salted **:** FRESH ⟨*sweet* butter⟩ **c :** free from excessive acidity ⟨*sweet* soil⟩ **d :** free from noxious gases and odors **5 —** used as an intensive ⟨take your own *sweet* time⟩ [Old English *swēte*] — **sweet·ly** *adv* — **sweet·ness** *n* — **sweet on :** in love with

[2]**sweet** *adv* **:** in a sweet way

[3]**sweet** *n* **1 :** something that is sweet to the taste: as **a :** a food (as a candy or preserve) having a high sugar content **b** *British* **:** DESSERT **c** *British* **:** CANDY 2 **2 :** a sweet taste sensation **3 :** a pleasant or gratifying experience, possession, or state **4 :** DARLING

sweet alyssum *n* **:** a European herb related to the mustards and widely grown for its clusters of small fragrant usually white or pink flowers

sweet basil *n* **:** a common basil that has whitish or purple flowers and leaves used especially as a seasoning

sweet·bread \ˈswēt-ˌbred\ *n* **:** the thymus or pancreas especially of a young animal (as a calf) used as food

sweet·bri·ar *also* **sweet·bri·er** \-ˌbrī-ər, -ˌbrīr\ *n* **:** an Old World rose with stout recurved prickles and white to deep rosy pink single flowers — called also *eglantine*

sweet cherry *n* **:** a white-flowered Eurasian cherry widely grown for its large sweet-flavored fruits; *also* **:** its fruit

sweet cic·e·ly \-ˈsis-lē, -ə-lē\ *n, pl* **-lies :** any of several herbs related to the carrot and having white flowers and an aromatic root [*cicely* from Latin *seselis,* from Greek]

sweet clover *n* **:** any of a genus of Old World herbs of the legume family widely grown for soil improvement or hay

sweet corn *n* **:** corn with kernels containing much sugar

sweet·en \ˈswēt-n\ *vb* **sweetened; sweet·en·ing** \ˈswēt-ning, -n-ing\ **:** to make or become sweet — **sweeten·er** \ˈswēt-nər, -n-ər\ *n*

sweet·en·ing *n* **1 :** the act or process of making sweet **2 :** something that sweetens

sweet fern *n* **:** a small North American shrub related to the wax myrtle and having sweet-scented or aromatic leaves

sweet flag *n* **:** a perennial marsh herb of the arum family with long narrow leaves and an aromatic rhizome

sweet gum *n* **:** a North American tree related to the witch hazels and having palmately lobed leaves, hard reddish brown wood, and a long-stemmed round woody fruit cluster; *also* **:** its wood

sweet·heart \ˈswēt-ˌhärt\ *n* **1 :** DARLING **2 :** the person one is in love with **:** LOVER

sweet·ing \ˈswēt-ing\ *n* **1** *archaic* **:** SWEETHEART **2 :** a sweet apple

sweet·ish \ˈswēt-ish\ *adj* **:** somewhat and often unpleasantly sweet — **sweet·ish·ly** *adv*

sweet marjoram *n* **:** an aromatic European herb with dense spikelike flower clusters

sweet·meat \ˈswēt-ˌmēt\ *n* **:** a food rich in sugar: as **a :** a candied or crystallized fruit **b :** CANDY 2

sweet pea *n* **:** a widely grown Italian herb of the legume family having slender climbing stems and large fragrant flowers; *also* **:** its flower

sweet pepper *n* **:** a large mild-flavored thick-walled capsicum fruit; *also* **:** a pepper plant bearing sweet peppers

sweet potato *n* **1 :** a tropical vine related to the morning glories and having variously shaped leaves and purplish flowers; *also* **:** its large sweet starchy tuberous root that is cooked and eaten as a vegetable **2 :** OCARINA

sweet·shop \ˈswēt-ˌshäp\ *n, chiefly British* **:** a candy store

sweet sorghum *n* **:** SORGO

sweet tooth *n* **:** a craving or fondness for sweet food

sweet wil·liam \swēt-ˈwil-yəm\ *n, often cap W* **:** a widely grown Eurasian pink with small white to deep red or purple flowers often showily spotted, banded, or mottled and borne in flat clusters on erect stalks [from the name *William*]

[1]**swell** \ˈswel\ *vb* **swelled; swelled** *or* **swol·len** \ˈswō-lən\; **swell·ing** **1 a :** to expand (as in size, volume, or numbers) gradually beyond a normal or original limit ⟨the population *swelled*⟩ **b :** to be distended

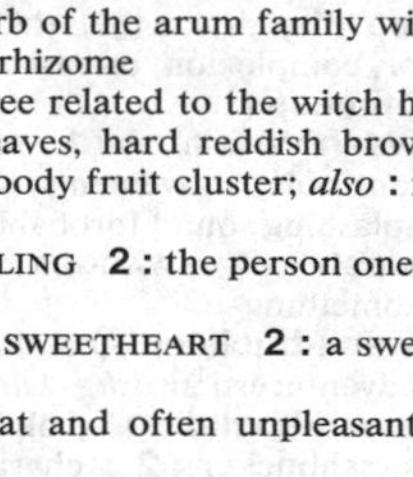

sweet william

or puffed up ⟨the ankle is badly *swollen*⟩ **c :** to form a bulge or rounded elevation **2 :** to fill or become filled with pride and arrogance **3 :** to fill or become filled with emotion [Old English *swellan*]

2swell *n* **1 a :** a rounded elevation **b :** the condition of being protuberant **2 :** a long often massive crestless wave or succession of waves **3 a :** a gradual increase and decrease of the loudness of a musical sound; *also* **:** a sign < > indicating a swell **b :** a device used in an organ for governing loudness **4 a :** a person dressed in the height of fashion **b :** a person of high social position or outstanding competence

3swell *adj* **1 :** STYLISH, FASHIONABLE **2 :** EXCELLENT, FIRST-RATE

swelled head *n* **:** an exaggerated opinion of oneself **:** SELF-CONCEIT — **swelled–head·ed** \ˈsweld-ˈhed-əd\ *adj* — **swelled–head·ed·ness** *n*

swell·ing \ˈswel-iŋ\ *n* **1 :** something that is swollen; *esp* **:** an abnormal bodily protuberance or localized enlargement **2 :** the condition of being swollen

1swel·ter \ˈswel-tər\ *vb* **swel·tered; swel·ter·ing** \ˈswel-triŋ, -tə-riŋ\ **1 :** to suffer, sweat, or be faint from heat **2 :** to oppress with heat [Middle English *sweltren,* from *swelten* "to die, be overcome by heat," from Old English *sweltan* "to die"]

2swelter *n* **1 :** a state of oppressive heat **2 :** an excited or overwrought state of mind ⟨in a *swelter*⟩

swel·ter·ing *adj* **:** oppressively hot ⟨*sweltering* summer days⟩ — **swel·ter·ing·ly** \-tə-riŋ-lē, -triŋ-\ *adv*

swept *past of* SWEEP

swept–back \ˈswept-ˈbak, ˈswep-\ *adj* **:** possessing sweepback

swerve \ˈswərv\ *vb* **swerved; swerv·ing :** to turn aside suddenly from a straight line or course ⟨*swerved* to avoid an oncoming car⟩ [Old English *sweorfan* "to wipe, grind away"] — **swerve** *n*

synonyms SWERVE, VEER mean to turn aside from a straight course. SWERVE may suggest a physical, mental, or moral turning that may be small in degree but is usually sudden or sharp ⟨*swerved* to avoid hitting the dog⟩. VEER implies a sharp change in course or direction ⟨at the point the path *veers* to the right⟩.

1swift \ˈswift\ *adj* **1 :** moving or capable of moving with great speed **2 :** occurring suddenly or within a very short time ⟨*swift* changes⟩ **3 :** quick to act or respond ⟨*swift* in thought and deed⟩ [Old English] ***synonyms*** see FAST — **swift·ly** *adv* — **swift·ness** \ˈswift-nəs, ˈswif-\ *n*

2swift *adv* **:** SWIFTLY ⟨*swift*-flowing⟩

3swift *n* **1 :** any of several lizards that run swiftly **2 :** any of numerous small and usually mostly black birds that are related to the hummingbirds but superficially resemble swallows

swift 2

swift fox *n* **:** a small fox of the central and western U.S. and Canada with large ears — compare KIT FOX

1swig \ˈswig\ *n* **:** a quantity drunk at one time **:** DRAFT [origin unknown]

2swig *vb* **swigged; swig·ging :** to drink in gulps ⟨*swig* cider⟩ — **swig·ger** *n*

1swill \ˈswil\ *vb* **1 :** WASH 2, DRENCH **2 :** to drink great drafts of **:** consume freely, greedily, or to excess **3 :** to feed (as a pig) with swill [Old English *swillan*] — **swill·er** *n*

2swill *n* **1 :** food for animals (as swine) composed of edible refuse mixed with water or skimmed or sour milk **2 :** GARBAGE, REFUSE **3 :** a draft of liquor

1swim \ˈswim\ *vb* **swam** \ˈswam\; **swum** \ˈswəm\; **swim·ming 1 a :** to move through water by natural means (as the action of limbs, fins, or tail) **b :** to move quietly and smoothly **:** GLIDE **2 a :** to float on or in or be covered with or as if with a liquid ⟨toy boats *swimming* in the tub⟩ ⟨potatoes *swimming* in gravy⟩ **b :** to experience or suffer from or as if from vertigo ⟨my head *swam* in the stuffy room⟩ **3 :** to surmount difficulties ⟨sink or *swim*⟩ **4 :** to cross by propelling oneself through water ⟨*swim* a stream⟩ [Old English *swimman*] — **swim·ma·ble** \ˈswim-ə-bəl\ *adj* — **swim·mer** *n*

2swim *n* **1 :** an act or period of swimming **2 :** a temporary dizziness or unconsciousness **3 :** the main current of activity ⟨in the *swim* of things⟩

swim bladder *n* **:** the air bladder of a fish

swim fin *n* **:** a rubber shoe with the front expanded into a paddle for use in skin diving or scuba diving

swim·mer·et \ˌswim-ə-ˈret\ *n* **:** one of a series of small appendages under the abdomen of many crustaceans that are used especially for swimming or for carrying eggs

swimmer's ear *n* **:** redness, swelling, and pain of the ear canal that typically occurs when water trapped in the ear canal during swimming becomes infected usually with bacteria

swimmer's itch *n* **:** an itchy skin inflammation caused by superficial invasion of the skin by larval trematode worms that are not normally parasites of human beings

swim·ming *adj* **:** marked by, adapted to, or used in or for swimming

swim·ming·ly \-iŋ-lē\ *adv* **:** very well **:** SPLENDIDLY

swimming pool *n* **:** a tank (as of concrete or plastic) made for swimming

swim·my \ˈswim-ē\ *adj* **:** verging on, causing, or affected by dizziness — **swim·mi·ly** \ˈswim-ə-lē\ *adv* — **swim·mi·ness** \ˈswim-ē-nəs\ *n*

swim·suit \ˈswim-ˌsüt\ *n* **:** a suit for swimming or bathing

1swin·dle \ˈswin-dl\ *vb* **swin·dled; swin·dling** \-dliŋ, -dl-iŋ\ **:** to deprive of something by deception or fraud [back-formation from *swindler,* from German *Schwindler* "giddy person," from *schwindeln* "to be dizzy"] ***synonyms*** see CHEAT — **swin·dler** \-dlər, -dl-ər\ *n*

2swindle *n* **:** an act or instance of swindling **:** FRAUD

swine \ˈswīn\ *n, pl* **swine 1 :** any of a family of stout-bodied short-legged hoofed mammals with a thick bristly skin and a long flexible snout; *esp* **:** a domesticated one descended from the European wild boar and widely raised for meat **2 :** a contemptible person [Old English *swīn*]

swine·herd \-ˌhərd\ *n* **:** a person who tends swine

1swing \ˈswiŋ\ *vb* **swung** \ˈswəŋ\; **swing·ing** \ˈswiŋ-iŋ\ **1 a :** to move or cause to move quickly through a wide arc or circle ⟨*swing* an axe⟩ **b :** to cause to sway to and fro or turn on an axis; *also* **:** to face or move in another direction ⟨*swing* the car into a side road⟩ **2 a :** to hang or be hung so as to permit swaying or turning ⟨*swing* a hammock⟩ **b :** to die by hanging **c :** to move freely to and fro from or rotate about a point of suspension ⟨the door *swung* open⟩ **d :** to hang freely from a support **e :** to shift or fluctuate between extremes ⟨the market *swung* sharply downward⟩ **3 :** to handle successfully **:** MANAGE ⟨learning to *swing* a new job⟩ **4 :** to play or sing (as a melody) in the style of swing music **:** perform swing music **5 a :** to move along rhythmically **b :** to start up in a smooth vigorous manner ⟨*swing* into action⟩ **6 :** to hit at something with a sweeping movement **7 :** to be lively, exciting, and up-to-date [Old English *swingan* "to beat, fling oneself, rush"] — **swing·able** \ˈswiŋ-ə-bəl\ *adj* — **swing·ably** \-blē\ *adv* — **swing·er** \ˈswiŋ-ər\ *n*

2swing *n* **1 :** an act of swinging **2 :** a swinging movement, blow, or rhythm: as **a :** a regular to-and-fro movement of or as if of a suspended body **b :** a steady pulsing rhythm (as in poetry or music); *also* **:** dancing to swing music **c :** a repeated shifting from one condition, form, or position to another **3 :** the distance through which something swings ⟨a pendulum with a 25-centimeter *swing*⟩ **4 :** a swinging seat usually hung by overhead ropes **5 a :** a curving course or outline **b :** a course beginning and ending at the same point ⟨took a *swing* through the hills⟩ **6 :** a style of jazz in which the melody is freely interpreted and improvised on by the individual players within a steadily maintained rhythm — **swing** *adj*

swin·gle·tree \ˈswiŋ-gəl-ˌtrē\ *n* **:** WHIFFLETREE [Middle English *swyngyll* "rod for beating flax"]

swing shift *n* **:** the work shift between the day and night shifts (as from 4 p.m. to midnight)

swin·ish \ˈswī-nish\ *adj* **:** of, suggesting, or characteristic of swine **:** BEASTLY — **swin·ish·ly** *adv* — **swin·ish·ness** *n*

1swipe \ˈswīp\ *n* **:** a strong sweeping blow [probably alteration of *sweep*]

\ə\ **abut**	\au̇\ **out**	\i\ **tip**	\ȯ\ **saw**	\u̇\ **foot**
\ər\ **further**	\ch\ **chin**	\ī\ **life**	\ȯi\ **coin**	\y\ **yet**
\a\ **mat**	\e\ **pet**	\j\ **job**	\th\ **thin**	\yü\ **few**
\ā\ **take**	\ē\ **easy**	\ŋ\ **sing**	\t͟h\ **this**	\yu̇\ **cure**
\ä\ **cot, cart**	\g\ **go**	\ō\ **bone**	\ü\ **food**	\zh\ **vision**

[2]**swipe** *vb* **1 :** to strike or wipe with a sweeping motion **2 :** STEAL 2a, PILFER **3 :** to slide (a card with a magnetic strip or bar code) through a slot in a reading device so that information stored on the strip can be processed (as in making a purchase)

[1]**swirl** \ˈswərl\ *n* **1 :** a whirling mass or motion **:** EDDY **2 :** whirling confusion **3 :** a twisting shape or mark [Middle English]

[2]**swirl** *vb* **1 :** to move with or pass in a swirl **2 :** to be marked with or arranged in swirls **3 :** to cause to swirl — **swirl·ing·ly** \ˈswər-ling-lē\ *adv*

[1]**swish** \ˈswish\ *vb* **:** to make, move, or strike with a rustling or hissing sound [imitative] — **swish·ing·ly** \-ing-lē\ *adv*

[2]**swish** *n* **1 a :** a prolonged hissing sound (as of a whip cutting the air) **b :** a light sweeping or brushing sound ⟨heard the *swish* of the horse's tail⟩ **2 :** a swishing movement — **swishy** \-ē\ *adj*

Swiss \ˈswis\ *n* **1** *pl* **Swiss a :** a native or inhabitant of Switzerland **b :** a person of Swiss descent **2** *often not cap* **:** a fine sheer cotton fabric often with raised dots originally made in Switzerland **3 :** a hard cheese characterized by elastic texture, mild nutlike flavor, and large holes that form during ripening [Middle French *Suisse,* from Middle High German *Swīzer,* from *Swīz* "Switzerland"] — **Swiss** *adj*

Swiss chard *n* **:** a beet of a variety lacking an enlarged root and having large leaves and juicy stalks often cooked as a vegetable; *also* **:** the stalks

[1]**switch** \ˈswich\ *n* **1 :** a slender flexible whip, rod, or twig **2 :** an act of switching: as **a :** a blow with a switch **b :** a shift from one to another ⟨a *switch* of political parties⟩ **3 :** a tuft of long hairs at the end of the tail of an animal (as a cow) **4 :** a device made usually of two movable rails and necessary connections and designed to turn a locomotive or train from one track to another **5 :** a device for making, breaking, or changing the connections in an electrical circuit **6 :** a strand of added or artificial hair used in some coiffures [perhaps from Dutch *swijch* "twig"]

[2]**switch** *vb* **1 :** to strike or whip with or as if with a switch **2 :** to lash from side to side **:** WHISK ⟨a cat *switching* its tail⟩ **3 :** to turn, shift, or change by or as if by operating a switch ⟨*switched* to a different channel⟩ ⟨*switch* off the light⟩ **4 :** to change one for another **:** EXCHANGE ⟨*switched* seats⟩ ⟨*switched* to a different brand⟩ — **switch·er** *n*

switch·back \ˈswich-ˌbak\ *n* **:** a zigzag road, trail, or section of railroad tracks for climbing a steep hill

switch·blade \ˌswich-ˌblād-\ *n* **:** a pocketknife having the blade spring-operated so that pressure on a release catch causes it to fly open

switch·board \ˈswich-ˌbōrd, -ˌbȯrd\ *n* **:** a device (as in a telephone exchange) consisting of a panel on which are mounted electric switches so arranged that a number of circuits may be connected, combined, and controlled

switch–hit·ter \ˈswich-ˈhit-ər\ *n* **:** a baseball player who can bat either left-handed or right-handed

switch·man \ˈswich-mən\ *n* **:** one who attends a railroad switch

switch·yard \-ˌyärd\ *n* **:** a place where railroad cars are switched from one track to another and trains are made up

Swit·zer \ˈswit-sər\ *n* **:** SWISS 1 [Middle High German *Swīzer*]

[1]**swiv·el** \ˈswiv-əl\ *n* **:** a device joining two parts so that one or both can pivot freely (as on a bolt or pin) [Middle English]

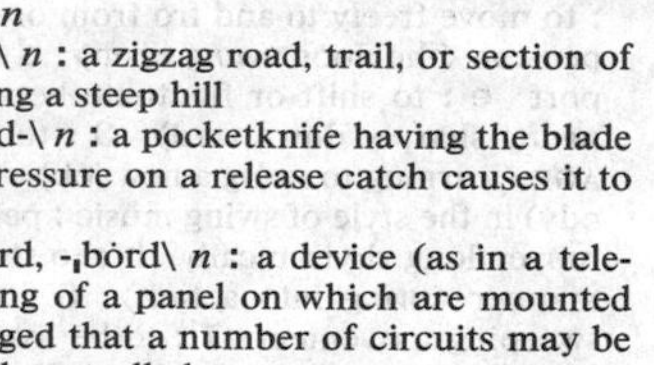

swivel

[2]**swivel** *vb* **swiv·eled** *or* **swiv·elled; swiv·el·ing** *or* **swiv·el·ling** \ˈswiv-ling, -ə-ling\ **:** to turn on or as if on a swivel

swivel chair *n* **:** a chair that swivels on its base

swiv·et \ˈswiv-ət\ *n* **:** a state of extreme agitation ⟨in a *swivet*⟩ [origin unknown]

swiz·zle stick \ˈswiz-əl-\ *n* **:** a stick used to stir mixed drinks [*swizzle,* a kind of cocktail]

swob *archaic variant of* SWAB

swollen *past participle of* SWELL

[1]**swoon** \ˈswün\ *vi* **1 :** FAINT 2 **2 :** to drift or fade gradually [Middle English *swounen*] — **swoon·er** *n* — **swoon·ing·ly** \ˈswü-ning-lē\ *adv*

[2]**swoon** *n* **1 :** a partial or total loss of consciousness; *also* **:** a dazed enraptured state **2 :** a dreamy flow (as of music)

[1]**swoop** \ˈswüp\ *vb* **1 :** to descend or pounce suddenly ⟨the eagle *swooped* down on its prey⟩ **2 :** to carry off abruptly [Old English *swāpan* "to sweep"]

[2]**swoop** *n* **1 :** an act or instance of swooping **2 :** a single concentrated and quickly effective effort — often used with *fell* ⟨solved everything at one fell *swoop*⟩

swoosh \ˈswüsh, ˈswu̇sh\ *vb* **:** to make, move, or discharge with a rushing sound [imitative] — **swoosh** *n*

swop *chiefly British variant of* SWAP

sword \ˈsōrd, ˈsȯrd\ *n* **1 :** a weapon having a long usually sharp-pointed and sharp-edged blade **2 a :** a means or instrument of destruction or combat **b :** the use of force **3 :** coercive power **4 :** something that resembles a sword [Old English *sweord*] — **sword·like** \-ˌlīk\ *adj* — **at swords' points :** mutually antagonistic

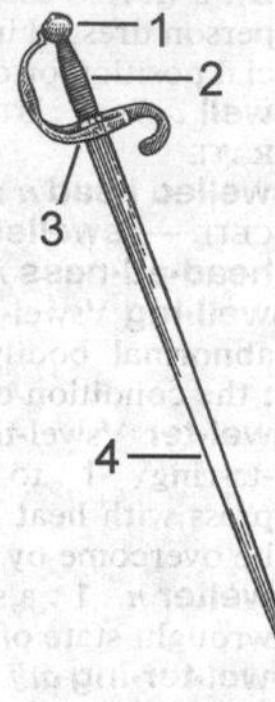

sword 1: *1* pommel, *2* hilt, *3* guard, *4* blade

sword cane *n* **:** a cane in which a sword blade is contained

sword dance *n* **:** any of several folk dances in which performers hold, swing, or dance around swords — **sword dancer** *n*

sword·fish \ˈsōrd-ˌfish, ˈsȯrd-\ *n* **:** a very large oceanic food fish that has a long swordlike beak formed by the bones of the upper jaw and is an important food and game fish

sword grass *n* **:** a grass or sedge having leaves with a sharp or toothed edge

sword knot *n* **:** an ornamental cord or tassel tied to the hilt of a sword

sword·play \-ˌplā\ *n* **:** the art or skill of using a sword especially in fencing

swords·man \ˈsōrdz-mən, ˈsȯrdz-\ *n* **1 :** one who fights with a sword **2 :** one skilled in the use of the sword **:** FENCER

swords·man·ship \-ˌship\ *n* **:** SWORDPLAY

sword·tail \ˈsōrd-ˌtāl, ˈsȯrd-\ *n* **:** a small brightly marked Central American topminnow with many color varieties that is often kept in tropical aquariums

swore *past of* SWEAR

sworn *past participle of* SWEAR

swum *past participle of* SWIM

swung *past of* SWING

syc·a·more \ˈsik-ə-ˌmōr, -ˌmȯr\ *n* **1 :** a common fig tree of Africa and the Middle East **2 :** a Eurasian maple with yellowish green flowers in long clusters **3 :** a large spreading plane tree of the eastern and central U.S. with light-brown bark that peels off in thin flakes and small round brown fruits hanging on long stalks [Medieval French *sicamour,* from Latin *sycomorus,* from Greek *sykomoros*]

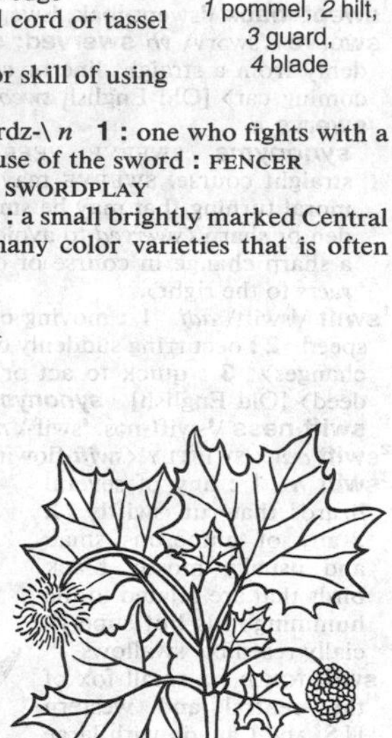

sycamore 3

syc·o·phant \ˈsik-ə-fənt\ *n* **:** a servile self-seeking flatterer **:** PARASITE [Latin *sycophanta* "slanderer, swindler," from Greek *sykophantēs* "slanderer"] — **syc·o·phan·cy** \-fən-sē\ *n* — **syc·o·phan·tic** \ˌsik-ə-ˈfant-ik\ *adj* — **syc·o·phan·ti·cal·ly** \-ˈfant-i-kə-lē, -klē\ *adv*

sy·enite \ˈsī-ə-ˌnīt\ *n* **:** an igneous rock composed chiefly of feldspar [Latin *Syenites lapis* "stone of Syene," from *Syene,* ancient city in Egypt] — **sy·enit·ic** \ˌsī-ə-ˈnit-ik\ *adj*

syl·la·bary \ˈsil-ə-ˌber-ē\ *n, pl* **-bar·ies :** a series or set of written characters each one of which is used to represent a syllable

syl·lab·ic \sə-ˈlab-ik\ *adj* **1 :** of, relating to, or denoting syllables ⟨*syllabic* accent⟩ **2** *of a consonant* **:** not accompanied in the same syllable by a vowel ⟨\n\ is *syllabic* in \ˈbät-n-ē\ botany but is nonsyllabic in \ˈbät-nē\⟩ **3 :** characterized by distinct enunciation or separation of syllables — **syl·lab·i·cal·ly** \-ˈlab-i-kə-lē, -klē\ *adv*

syl·lab·i·ca·tion \sə-ˌlab-ə-ˈkā-shən\ *n* **:** the forming of syllables **:** the division of words into syllables — **syl·lab·i·cate** \-ˈlab-ə-ˌkāt\ *vb*

syl·lab·i·fi·ca·tion \sə-ˌlab-ə-fə-ˈkā-shən\ *n* **:** SYLLABICATION

syl·lab·i·fy \sə-ˈlab-ə-ˌfī\ *vt* **-fied; -fy·ing** : to form or divide into syllables

[1]**syl·la·ble** \ˈsil-ə-bəl\ *n* **1** : a unit of spoken language that consists of one or more vowel sounds alone or of a syllabic consonant alone or of either with one or more consonant sounds preceding or following **2** : one or more letters (as *syl, la,* and *ble*) in a word (as *syl·la·ble*) usually set off from the rest of the word by a centered dot or a hyphen and treated as guides to dividing a word at the end of a line **3** : the smallest conceivable expression or unit of something ⟨not the least *syllable* of wit⟩ [Medieval French *sillabe, silable,* from Latin *syllaba,* from Greek *syllabē,* from *syllambanein* "to combine," from *syn-* + *lambanein* "to take"]

[2]**syllable** *vt* **syl·la·bled; syl·la·bling** \-bə-ling, -bling\ : to express or utter in syllables

syl·la·bub *also* **sil·la·bub** \ˈsil-ə-ˌbəb\ *n* : milk or cream that is curdled with an acid beverage (as wine or cider) and often sweetened and served as a drink or topping or thickened with gelatin and served as a dessert [origin unknown]

syl·la·bus \-bəs\ *n, pl* **-bi** \-ˌbī, -ˌbē\ *or* **-bus·es** : a summary outline (as of a course of study) [Latin *sillybus* "label for a book," from Greek *sillybos*]

syl·lo·gism \ˈsil-ə-ˌjiz-əm\ *n* **1** : a brief form for stating an argument from the general to the particular that consists of two statements and a conclusion that must be true if these two statements are true ⟨"all lawbreakers deserve punishment; this person is a lawbreaker; therefore this person deserves punishment" is a *syllogism*⟩ **2** : deductive reasoning [Medieval French *sillogisme,* from Latin *syllogismus,* from Greek *syllogismos,* from *syllogizesthai* "to reason deductively," derived from *syn-* + *logos* "reckoning, word"] — **syl·lo·gis·tic** \ˌsil-ə-ˈjis-tik\ *adj* — **syl·lo·gis·ti·cal·ly** \-ti-kə-lē, -klē\ *adv*

sylph \ˈsilf\ *n* **1** : an imaginary aerial spirit **2** : a slender graceful woman [New Latin *sylphus*] — **sylph·like** \ˈsil-ˌflīk\ *adj*

syl·van *also* **sil·van** \ˈsil-vən\ *adj* **1 a** : living or located in the woods or forest **b** : of, relating to, or characteristic of the woods or forest **2** : abounding in woods or trees : WOODED [Medieval Latin *silvanus, sylvanus,* from Latin *silva, sylva* "woods"]

syl·vat·ic \sil-ˈvat-ik\ *adj* : occurring in or affecting wild animals ⟨a *sylvatic* plague⟩ [Latin *silvaticus* "of the woods, wild," from *silva* "woods"]

sym- — see SYN-

sym·bi·ont \ˈsim-ˌbī-ˌänt, -bē-\ *n* : an organism living in symbiosis; *esp* : the smaller member of a symbiotic pair [derived from Greek *symbioun* "to live together"] — **sym·bi·on·tic** \ˌsim-ˌbī-ˈänt-ik, -bē-\ *adj*

sym·bi·o·sis \ˌsim-ˌbī-ˈō-səs, -bē-\ *n, pl* **-o·ses** \-ˈō-ˌsēz\ **1** : the living together in close association of two different kinds of organisms (as a fungus and an alga making up a lichen) especially when such an association is of benefit to both **2** : a cooperative relationship (as between two persons or groups) [German *Symbiose,* from Greek *symbiōsis* "state of living together," from *symbioun* "to live together," derived from *syn-* + *bios* "life"] — **sym·bi·ot·ic** \-ˈät-ik\ *adj* — **sym·bi·ot·i·cal·ly** \-i-kə-lē, -klē\ *adv*

sym·bol \ˈsim-bəl\ *n* **1** : something that stands for something else; *esp* : something concrete that represents or suggests another thing that cannot in itself be represented or visualized ⟨the lion is a *symbol* of courage⟩ **2** : a letter, character, or sign used (as to represent a quantity, position, relationship, direction, or something to be done) instead of a word or group of words ⟨the sign + is the *symbol* for addition⟩ [derived from Greek *symbolon* "token of identity to be verified by matching it with its other half, symbol," from *symballein* "to throw together, compare," from *syn-* + *ballein* "to throw"]

sym·bol·ic \sim-ˈbäl-ik\ *also* **sym·bol·i·cal** \-ˈbäl-i-kəl\ *adj* **1** : of, relating to, or using symbols or symbolism ⟨a *symbolic* meaning⟩ **2** : having the function or significance of a symbol — **sym·bol·i·cal·ly** \-i-kə-lē, -klē\ *adv*

sym·bol·ism \ˈsim-bə-ˌliz-əm\ *n* **1** : the art or practice of using symbols or indicating symbolically (as in art or literature) **2** : a system of symbols or representations

sym·bol·ist \-ləst\ *n* **1** : a user of symbols or symbolism (as in artistic expression) **2** : an expert in the interpretation or explanation of symbols — **symbolist** *adj*

sym·bol·is·tic \ˌsim-bə-ˈlis-tik\ *adj* : SYMBOLIC

sym·bol·ize \ˈsim-bə-ˌlīz\ *vb* **1** : to serve as a symbol of ⟨a pineapple *symbolizes* hospitality⟩ **2** : to use symbols : represent by a symbol or set of symbols — **sym·bol·i·za·tion** \ˌsim-bə-lə-ˈzā-shən\ *n* — **sym·bol·iz·er** \ˈsim-bə-ˌlī-zər\ *n*

sym·met·ri·cal \sə-ˈme-tri-kəl\ *or* **sym·met·ric** \-trik\ *adj* **1** : having, involving, or exhibiting symmetry **2** : having corresponding points that can be connected by lines in such a way that each line is cut exactly in half by one specified point, line, or plane ⟨*symmetrical* curves⟩ **3** *symmetric* : being a relation or expression for which the terms may be interchanged without altering the value, character, or truth ⟨*R* is a *symmetric* relation if *aRb* implies *bRa*⟩ **4 a** : capable of division by a longitudinal plane into similar halves ⟨a *symmetrical* leaf⟩ **b** : having the same number of members in each whorl of floral leaves ⟨*symmetrical* flowers⟩ — **sym·met·ri·cal·ly** \-tri-kə-lē, -klē\ *adv* — **sym·met·ri·cal·ness** \-kəl-nəs\ *n*

sym·me·try \ˈsim-ə-trē\ *n, pl* **-tries** **1** : balanced proportions; *also* : beauty of form arising from balanced proportions **2** : correspondence in size, shape, and relative position of parts on opposite sides of a dividing line or plane or about a center or axis — compare BILATERAL SYMMETRY, RADIAL SYMMETRY [Latin *symmetria,* from Greek, derived from *syn-* + *metron* "measure"]

sym·pa·thet·ic \ˌsim-pə-ˈthet-ik\ *adj* **1 a** : appropriate to one's mood or disposition : CONGENIAL ⟨a *sympathetic* environment⟩ **b** : marked by kindly or pleased appreciation ⟨the biographer's approach was *sympathetic*⟩ **2** : given to or arising from sympathy, compassion, friendliness, and sensitivity to others ⟨a *sympathetic* person⟩ ⟨a *sympathetic* remark⟩ **3 a** : of or relating to the sympathetic nervous system **b** : mediated by or acting on the sympathetic nerves — **sym·pa·thet·i·cal·ly** \-ˈthet-i-kə-lē, -klē\ *adv*

sympathetic nervous system *n* : the part of the autonomic nervous system that prepares the body to react to situations of stress or emergency, that controls dilation of the pupil and air passages, increases the heart rate, slows digestion, and narrows most blood vessels, and that is composed of nerve fibers that trigger the release of norepinephrine — compare PARASYMPATHETIC NERVOUS SYSTEM

sympathetic vibration *n* : a vibration produced in one body by vibrations of exactly the same period in a neighboring body

sym·pa·thize \ˈsim-pə-ˌthīz\ *vi* **1** : to react or respond in sympathy **2** : to be in accord or harmony **3** : to share in some distress, suffering, or grief ⟨*sympathize* with a friend in trouble⟩; *also* : to express such sympathy **4** : to be in sympathy intellectually ⟨*sympathize* with a proposal⟩ — **sym·pa·thiz·er** *n*

sym·pa·tho·mi·met·ic \ˌsim-pə-thō-mə-ˈmet-ik, -mī-\ *adj* : resembling the action of the sympathetic nervous system in physiological effect ⟨*sympathomimetic* drugs⟩

sym·pa·thy \ˈsim-pə-thē\ *n, pl* **-thies** **1** : a relationship between persons or things wherein whatever affects one similarly affects the other **2 a** : inclination to think or feel alike : emotional or intellectual accord forming a bond of goodwill ⟨in *sympathy* with their goals⟩ **b** : tendency to favor or support ⟨republican *sympathies*⟩ **3 a** : the act of or capacity for entering into or sharing the feelings or interests of another **b** : the feeling or mental state brought about by such sensitivity ⟨have *sympathy* for the poor⟩ [Latin *sympathia,* from Greek *sympatheia,* derived from *syn-* + *pathos* "feelings, experience"]

sym·pat·ric \sim-ˈpa-trik\ *adj* : occurring in the same geographical area ⟨*sympatric* species of birds⟩; *also* : occurring between populations that are not geographically separated ⟨*sympatric* speciation⟩ — compare ALLOPATRIC [*syn-* + Greek *patra* "fatherland," from *patēr* "father"]

sym·phon·ic \sim-ˈfän-ik\ *adj* **1** : HARMONIOUS 1 **2** : of, relating to, or suggesting a symphony or symphony orchestra — **sym·phon·i·cal·ly** \-ˈfän-i-kə-lē, -klē\ *adv*

sym·pho·ny \ˈsim-fə-nē, ˈsimp-\ *n, pl* **-nies** **1** : harmonious arrangement (as of sound or color) **2 a** : a usually long and complex sonata for symphony orchestra **b** : something resembling a symphony in complexity or variety **3 a** : SYMPHONY ORCHESTRA **b** : a symphony orchestra concert [Medieval French *symphonie* "harmony of sounds," from Latin *symphonia,* from Greek *symphōnia,* derived from *syn-* + *phōnē* "voice, sound"]

\ə\ **abut**	\au̇\ **out**	\i\ **tip**	\ȯ\ **saw**	\u̇\ **foot**
\ər\ **further**	\ch\ **chin**	\ī\ **life**	\ȯi\ **coin**	\y\ **yet**
\a\ **mat**	\e\ **pet**	\j\ **job**	\th\ **thin**	\yü\ **few**
\ā\ **take**	\ē\ **easy**	\ng\ **sing**	\t͟h\ **this**	\yu̇\ **cure**
\ä\ **cot, cart**	\g\ **go**	\ō\ **bone**	\ü\ **food**	\zh\ **vision**

symphony orchestra *n* : a large orchestra of wind, string, and percussion instruments that plays symphonic works

sym·phy·sis \ˈsim-fə-səs, ˈsimp-\ *n, pl* **-phy·ses** \-fə-ˌsēz\ : a largely or completely immovable joint between bones (as the two bones comprising the pubis) especially with the surfaces connected by pads of cartilage [Greek, "state of growing together," from *symphyesthai* "to grow together," from *syn-* + *phyein* "to make grow, bring forth"] — **sym·phy·se·al** \ˌsim-fə-ˈsē-əl, ˌsimp-\ *adj*

sym·po·si·um \sim-ˈpō-zē-əm *also* -zhē-əm, -zhəm\ *n, pl* **-sia** \-zē-ə, -zhē-ə, -zhə\ *or* **-si·ums** **1** : a formal meeting at which several speakers deliver short addresses on a topic or on related topics **2 a** : a collection of opinions on a subject **b** : DISCUSSION 2 [Latin, "drinking party after a banquet," from Greek *symposion,* from *sympinein* "to drink together," from *syn-* + *pinein* "to drink"]

symp·tom \ˈsim-təm, ˈsimp-\ *n* **1** : a change in an organism indicative of disease or physical abnormality; *esp* : one (as headache) that is directly perceptible only to the individual affected **2 a** : something that indicates the existence of something else ⟨the revolt was a *symptom* of social oppression⟩ **b** : a slight indication : TRACE [Late Latin *symptomat-, symptoma,* from Greek *symptōma* "occurrence, attribute, symptom," from *sympiptein* "to occur," from *syn-* + *piptein* "to fall"] ***synonyms*** see SIGN — **symp·tom·less** \-ləs\ *adj*

symp·tom·at·ic \ˌsim-tə-ˈmat-ik, ˌsimp-\ *adj* **1 a** : being a symptom (as of disease) ⟨an itchy skin rash is *symptomatic* of poison ivy⟩ **b** : concerned with, affecting, or having symptoms ⟨a *symptomatic* patient⟩ **2** : CHARACTERISTIC, INDICATIVE ⟨his behavior was *symptomatic* of his character⟩ — **symp·tom·at·i·cal·ly** \-ˈmat-i-kə-lē, -klē\ *adv*

syn- *or* **sym-** *prefix* : with : along with : together ⟨*sym*patric⟩ ⟨*syn*gamy⟩ [Greek, from *syn* "with, together with"]

syn·a·gogue *also* **syn·a·gog** \ˈsin-ə-ˌgäg\ *n* **1** : a Jewish congregation **2** : the house of worship and communal center of a Jewish congregation [Medieval French *synagoge,* from Late Latin *synagoga,* from Greek *synagōgē* "assembly, synagogue," from *synagein* "to bring together," from *syn-* + *agein* "to lead"] — **syn·a·gog·al** \ˌsin-ə-ˈgäg-əl\ *adj*

¹**syn·apse** \ˈsin-ˌaps, sə-ˈnaps\ *n* : the point at which a nerve impulse passes from one neuron to another [Greek *synapsis* "juncture," from *synaptein* "to fasten together," from *syn-* + *haptein* "to fasten"]

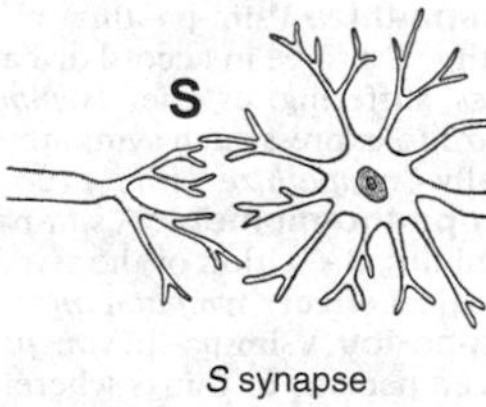

S synapse

²**synapse** *vi* : to form a synapse or come together in synapsis

syn·ap·sis \sə-ˈnap-səs\ *n, pl* **-ap·ses** \-ˌsēz\ : the pairing of homologous chromosomes that occurs in the first meiotic prophase and during which crossing over may occur [Greek, "juncture"]

syn·ap·tic \sə-ˈnap-tik\ *adj* : of or relating to a synapse or synapsis

¹**sync** \ˈsingk\ *n* : SYNCHRONIZATION, SYNCHRONISM ⟨moving in *sync*⟩ ⟨out of *sync* with the world⟩ — **sync** *adj*

²**sync** *vb* **synced** \ˈsingt, ˈsingkt\; **sync·ing** \ˈsing-king\ : SYNCHRONIZE

synchro- *combining form* : synchronized : synchronous ⟨*synchro*flash⟩ ⟨*synchro*mesh⟩

syn·chro–cy·clo·tron \ˌsing-krō-ˈsī-klə-ˌträn, ˌsin-\ *n* : a modified cyclotron that achieves greater energies for the charged particles

syn·chro·mesh \-ˌmesh\ *adj* : designed for effecting synchronized shifting of gears — **synchromesh** *n*

syn·chro·nism \ˈsing-krə-ˌniz-əm, ˈsin-\ *n* **1** : the quality or state of being synchronous **2** : chronological arrangement of historical events and personages so as to indicate coincidence or coexistence — **syn·chro·nis·tic** \ˌsing-krə-ˈnis-tik, ˌsin-\ *adj*

syn·chro·ni·za·tion \ˌsing-krə-nə-ˈzā-shən, ˌsin-\ *n* **1** : the act or result of synchronizing **2** : the state of being synchronous

syn·chro·nize \ˈsing-krə-ˌnīz, ˈsin-\ *vb* **1** : to happen at the same time : agree in time **2 a** : to cause to agree in time ⟨*synchronize* your watches⟩ **b** : to represent, arrange, or tabulate according to dates or time ⟨*synchronize* the events of European history⟩ **3** : to make (as two gears) synchronous in operation — **syn·chro·niz·er** \ˈsing-krə-ˌnī-zər, ˈsin-\ *n*

synchronized swimming *n* : swimming in which the movements of one or more swimmers are synchronized with a musical accompaniment so as to form changing patterns — **synchronized swimmer** *n*

syn·chro·nous \ˈsing-krə-nəs, ˈsin-\ *adj* **1** : happening or existing at the same time : SIMULTANEOUS ⟨*synchronous* meetings⟩ **2** : working, moving, or occurring together at the same rate and at the proper time with respect to each other ⟨the *synchronous* beat of a bird's wings⟩; *esp* : having the same period and phase ⟨*synchronous* vibration⟩ **3** : of, used in, or being digital communication (as between computers) in which a common timing signal is established which allows for very high rates of data transfer [Late Latin *synchronos,* from Greek, from *syn-* + *chronos* "time"] — **syn·chro·nous·ly** *adv* — **syn·chro·nous·ness** *n*

synchronous motor *n* : an electric motor having a speed strictly proportional to the frequency of the operating current

syn·chro·tron \ˈsing-krə-ˌträn, ˈsin-\ *n* : an apparatus for imparting very high speeds to charged particles

syn·cline \ˈsin-ˌklīn\ *n* : a place in the earth's crust where the rock layers form a trough — compare ANTICLINE [back-formation from *synclinal,* from Greek *syn-* + *klinein* "to lean"] — **syn·cli·nal** \sin-ˈklīn-l\ *adj*

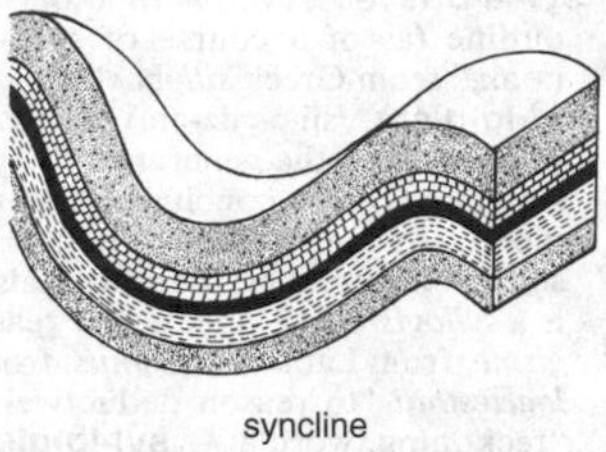
syncline

syn·co·pate \ˈsing-kə-ˌpāt, ˈsin-\ *vt* **1 a** : to shorten or produce by syncope **b** : to cut short **2** : to modify or affect (musical rhythm) by syncopation — **syn·co·pa·tor** \-ˌpāt-ər\ *n*

syn·co·pa·tion \ˌsing-kə-ˈpā-shən, ˌsin-\ *n* **1** : a shifting of the regular metrical accent in music caused typically by stressing the weak beat **2** : a syncopated rhythm, passage, or dance step — **syn·co·pa·tive** \ˈsing-kə-ˌpāt-iv, ˈsin-\ *adj*

syn·co·pe \ˈsing-kə-pē, ˈsin-\ *n* **1** : FAINT 2, SWOON **2** : the loss of one or more sounds or letters in the interior of a word (as *fo'c'sle* for *forecastle*) [Late Latin, from Greek *synkopē,* literally, "cutting short," from *synkoptein* "to cut short," from *syn-* + *koptein* "to cut"]

syn·cy·tium \sin-ˈsish-əm, -ˈsish-ē-əm\ *n, pl* **-tia** \-ə\ : a multinucleate mass of cytoplasm resulting from fusion of cells [New Latin, from *syn-* + *cyt-*] — **syn·cy·tial** \-ˈsish-əl\ *adj*

syn·di·cal·ism \ˈsin-di-kə-ˌliz-əm\ *n* **1** : a revolutionary doctrine by which workers seize control of the economy and the government by direct means (as a general strike) **2** : a system of economic organization in which industries are owned and managed by the workers [French *syndicalisme,* from *chambre syndicale* "trade union"] — **syn·di·cal** \ˈsin-di-kəl\ *adj* — **syn·di·cal·ist** \-ləst\ *adj or n*

¹**syn·di·cate** \ˈsin-di-kət\ *n* **1** : an association of persons officially authorized to undertake some duty or negotiate some business **2 a** : a group of persons or concerns who combine to carry out a particular transaction or project **b** : a loose association of racketeers in control of organized crime **c** : a European labor union **3** : a business concern that sells materials for publication in a number of newspapers or periodicals simultaneously **4** : a group of newspapers under one management [French *syndicat,* from *syndic* "municipal magistrate," from Late Latin *syndicus* "representative of a corporation," from Greek *syndikos* "advocate, representative of a state," from *syn-* + *dikē* "judgment, case at law"]

²**syn·di·cate** \ˈsin-də-ˌkāt\ *vb* **1** : to subject to or manage as a syndicate **2** : to sell (as a cartoon) to a publication syndicate; *also* : to sell the work of (as a writer) in this way ⟨a *syndicated* columnist⟩ **3** : to unite to form a syndicate — **syn·di·ca·tion** \ˌsin-də-ˈkā-shən\ *n* — **syn·di·ca·tor** \ˈsin-də-ˌkāt-ər\ *n*

syn·drome \ˈsin-ˌdrōm\ *n* : a group of signs and symptoms that occur together and characterize a particular abnormality or condition [Greek *syndromē,* from *syn-* + *dramein* "to run"]

syn·er·gid \sə-ˈnər-jəd, ˈsin-ər-\ *n* : either of two small cells of the embryo sac of a flowering plant lying near the micropyle of the ovule [derived from Greek *synergos* "working together"]

syn·er·gism \ˈsin-ər-ˌjiz-əm\ *n* : interaction of discrete parts or forces such that the total effect is greater than the sum of the effects taken independently [derived from Greek *synergos* "working together," from *syn-* + *ergon* "work"] — **syn•er•gist** \-jəst\ *n*

syn•er•gis•tic \ˌsin-ər-ˈjis-tik\ *adj* : of, relating to, or able to act in synergism ⟨a *synergistic* reaction⟩ ⟨*synergistic* drugs⟩ — **syn•er•gis•ti•cal•ly** \-ti-kə-lē, -klē\ *adv*

syn•ga•my \ˈsing-gə-mē\ *n* : FERTILIZATION b

syn•od \ˈsin-əd\ *n* **1** : an ecclesiastical assembly or council: as **a** : an assembly of bishops in the Roman Catholic Church **b** : the governing assembly of an Episcopal province **c** : a Presbyterian governing body ranking between the presbytery and the general assembly **d** : a regional or national organization of Lutheran congregations **2** : a group assembled (as for consultation) : MEETING, CONVENTION ⟨a *synod* of cooks⟩ [Late Latin *synodus,* from Greek *synodos* "meeting, assembly," from *syn-* + *hodos* "way, journey"] — **syn•od•al** \-əd-l\ *adj*

syn•od•ic \sə-ˈnäd-ik\ *or* **syn•od•i•cal** \-ˈnäd-i-kəl\ *adj* **1** : of or relating to a synod : SYNODAL **2** : relating to conjunction; *esp* : relating to the period between two successive conjunctions of the same celestial bodies

syn•o•nym \ˈsin-ə-ˌnim\ *n* **1** : one of two or more words of the same language that have the same or nearly the same meaning in some or all senses **2** : a word or phrase that by association is held to represent something (as a concept or quality) ⟨a tyrant whose name has become a *synonym* for oppression⟩ **3** : one of two or more scientific names used in biological classification to designate the same group [Latin *synonymum,* from Greek *synōnymon,* derived from *syn-* + *onyma* "name"] — **syn•o•nym•i•ty** \ˌsin-ə-ˈnim-ət-ē\ *n*

syn•on•y•mize \sə-ˈnän-ə-ˌmīz\ *vt* **-mized; -miz•ing** : to give or analyze the synonyms of (a word)

syn•on•y•mous \sə-ˈnän-ə-məs\ *adj* : having the character of a synonym; *also* : alike in meaning or significance — **syn•on•y•mous•ly** *adv*

syn•on•y•my \sə-ˈnän-ə-mē\ *n, pl* **-mies** **1 a** : the study or discrimination of synonyms **b** : a list or collection of synonyms often defined and discriminated from each other **2** : the quality or state of being synonymous

syn•op•sis \sə-ˈnäp-səs\ *n, pl* **-op•ses** \-ˈäp-ˌsēz\ : a condensed statement or outline (as of a narrative or treatise) : SUMMARY, ABSTRACT [Late Latin, from Greek, literally, "comprehensive view," from *synopsesthai* "to be going to see together," from *syn-* + *opsesthai* "to be going to see"]

syn•op•tic \sə-ˈnäp-tik\ *adj* **1** : affording a general view of a whole **2** : showing or characterized by comprehensiveness or breadth of view ⟨a *synoptic* genius⟩ **3 a** : presenting or sharing the same or a common view **b** *often cap* : of or relating to the first three Gospels of the New Testament **4** : relating to or displaying conditions (as of the atmosphere or weather) as they exist simultaneously over a broad area [Greek *synoptikos,* from *synopsesthai* "to be going to see together"] — **syn•op•ti•cal** \-ti-kəl\ *adj* — **syn•op•ti•cal•ly** \-ti-kə-lē, -klē\ *adv*

syn•o•vi•al \sə-ˈnō-vē-əl\ *adj* : of, relating to, or secreting synovial fluid ⟨*synovial* membranes⟩; *also* : lined with synovial membrane ⟨the knee and other *synovial* joints are freely moving⟩ [New Latin *synovia* "fluid secreted by synovial membranes"]

synovial fluid *n* : a transparent lubricating fluid secreted by a membrane (as of a joint)

syn•tac•tic \sin-ˈtak-tik\ *adj* : of, relating to, or according to the rules of syntax [Greek *syntaktikos* "arranging together," from *syntassein* "to arrange together"] — **syn•tac•ti•cal** \-ti-kəl\ *adj* — **syn•tac•ti•cal•ly** \-ti-kə-lē, -klē\ *adv*

syn•tax \ˈsin-ˌtaks\ *n* **1** : a connected or orderly system or arrangement **2 a** : the way in which words are put together to form phrases, clauses, or sentences **b** : the part of grammar dealing with this [Late Latin *syntaxis,* from Greek, from *syntassein* "to arrange together," from *syn-* + *tassein* "to arrange"]

syn•the•sis \ˈsin-thə-səs, ˈsint-\ *n, pl* **-the•ses** \-thə-ˌsēz\ **1 a** : the composition or combination of parts or elements so as to form a whole **b** : the production of a substance by union of chemically simpler substances **c** : the combining of often diverse conceptions into a coherent whole; *also* : the complex so formed **2 a** : deductive reasoning from general principles or causes to particular effects **b** : the final stage of a dialectic process combining thesis and antithesis into a higher stage of truth [Greek, from *syntithenai* "to put together," from *syn-* + *tithenai* "to put, place"] — **syn•the•sist** \-səst\ *n*

syn•the•size \-ˌsīz\ *vt* : to combine or produce by synthesis

syn•the•siz•er \-ˌsī-zər\ *n* **1** : one that synthesizes **2** : a computer-controlled device that creates and modifies sound (as for producing music)

[1]**syn•thet•ic** \sin-ˈthet-ik\ *adj* **1** : relating to or involving synthesis **2** : of, relating to, or produced by chemical synthesis; *esp* : produced artificially ⟨*synthetic* drugs⟩ ⟨*synthetic* fibers⟩ [Greek *synthetikos* "of composition," from *syntithenai* "to put together"] ***synonyms*** see ARTIFICIAL — **syn•thet•i•cal•ly** \-ˈthet-i-kə-lē, -klē\ *adv*

[2]**synthetic** *n* : a product of chemical synthesis

synthetic division *n* : a simplified method for dividing a polynomial by another polynomial of the first degree by writing down only the coefficients of the several powers of the variable and changing the sign of the constant term in the divisor in order to replace the usual subtractions by additions

syph•i•lis \ˈsif-ləs, -ə-ləs\ *n* : a chronic contagious usually venereal disease that is caused by a spirochete and if left untreated is marked by a series of three stages extending over many years [New Latin, from *Syphilus,* hero of the poem *Syphilis sive Morbus Gallicus* (*Syphilis or the French disease*) (1530) by Girolamo Fracastoro] — **syph•i•lit•ic** \ˌsif-ə-ˈlit-ik\ *adj or n*

syphon *variant of* SIPHON

Syr•i•ac \ˈsir-ē-ˌak\ *n* **1** : a literary language based on an eastern Aramaic dialect and used as the literary and liturgical language by several Eastern Christian churches **2** : Aramaic spoken by Christian communities [Latin *syriacus* "Syrian," from Greek *syriakos,* from *Syria,* ancient country in Asia] — **Syriac** *adj*

sy•rin•ga \sə-ˈring-gə\ *n* : MOCK ORANGE [New Latin, "saxifrage," from Greek *syring-, syrinx* "panpipe"]

[1]**sy•ringe** \sə-ˈrinj *also* ˈsir-inj\ *n* : a device used to inject fluids into or withdraw them from the body or its cavities [Medieval Latin *syringa,* from Greek *syring-, syrinx* "panpipe, tube"]

syringe

[2]**syringe** *vt* : to flush or cleanse with or as if with a syringe

syr•inx \ˈsir-ings, -ingks\ *n, pl* **sy•rin•ges** \sə-ˈring-ˌgēz, -ˈrin-ˌjēz\ *or* **syr•inx•es** \ˈsir-ing-səz, -ingk-\ **1** : PANPIPE **2** : the vocal organ of birds that is a special modification of the lower part of the trachea or of the bronchi or of both [Greek] — **sy•rin•ge•al** \sə-ˈring-gē-əl, -ˈrin-jē-\ *adj*

syr•up *also* **sir•up** \ˈsər-əp, ˈsir-əp, ˈsə-rəp\ *n* **1** : a thick sticky solution of sugar and water often flavored or medicated **2** : the concentrated juice of a fruit or plant [Medieval French *sirop,* from Medieval Latin *syrupus,* from Arabic *sharāb*] — **syr•upy** *adj*

sys•op \ˈsis-ˌäp\ *n* : the administrator of a computer bulletin board [*sys*tem *op*erator]

sys•tem \ˈsis-təm\ *n* **1 a** : a group of objects or units so combined as to form a whole and work, function, or move interdependently and harmoniously ⟨a railroad *system*⟩ ⟨steam heating *systems*⟩ ⟨a park *system*⟩ **b** (1) : a group of bodily organs that together carry on one or more vital functions ⟨the digestive *system*⟩ (2) : the body considered as a functional unit ⟨a *system* weakened by disease⟩ **c** : a particular form of societal organization ⟨the capitalist *system*⟩ **d** : a major division of rocks usually greater than a series **2 a** : an organized set of doctrines or principles usually designed to explain the ordering or functioning of some whole **b** : a method of classifying, symbolizing, or schematizing ⟨a decimal *system* of numbers⟩ ⟨taxonomic *systems*⟩ **3** : harmonious arrangement or pattern [Late Latin *systemat-, systema,* from Greek *systēmat-, systēma,* from *synistanai* "to combine," from *syn* + *histanai* "to cause to stand"] — **sys•tem•less** \-ləs\ *adj*

sys•tem•at•ic \ˌsis-tə-ˈmat-ik\ *adj* **1** : relating to or forming a system ⟨*systematic* thought⟩ **2** : presented or formulated as a system **3 a** : methodical in procedure or plan ⟨*systematic* investigation⟩ **b** : marked by thoroughness or regularity ⟨*systematic* efforts⟩ **4** : of, relating to, or concerned with classification : TAXONOMIC — **sys•tem•at•i•cal•ly** \-i-kə-lē, -klē\ *adv* — **sys•tem•at•ic•ness** *n*

\ə\ **a**but	\au̇\ **ou**t	\i\ t**i**p	\ȯ\ s**aw**	\u̇\ f**oo**t
\ər\ f**ur**ther	\ch\ **ch**in	\ī\ l**i**fe	\ȯi\ c**oi**n	\y\ **y**et
\a\ m**a**t	\e\ p**e**t	\j\ **j**ob	\th\ **th**in	\yü\ f**ew**
\ā\ t**a**ke	\ē\ **ea**sy	\ng\ si**ng**	\t͟h\ **th**is	\yu̇\ c**ure**
\ä\ c**o**t, c**ar**t	\g\ **g**o	\ō\ b**o**ne	\ü\ f**oo**d	\zh\ vi**s**ion

systematic error *n* : an error in data that is due to the method of measurement or observation and not due to chance

sys·tem·at·ics \-ˈmat-iks\ *n sing or pl* **1** : the science of classification **2 a** : a system of classification **b** : the classification and study of organisms with regard to their natural relationships : TAXONOMY

sys·tem·a·tist \ˈsis-tə-mət-əst, sis-ˈtem-ət-\ *n* **1** : a maker or follower of a system **2** : TAXONOMIST

sys·tem·a·tize \ˈsis-tə-mə-ˌtīz\ *vt* : to make into or arrange according to a system — **sys·tem·a·ti·za·tion** \ˌsis-tə-mət-ə-ˈzā-shən\ *n* — **sys·tem·a·tiz·er** \ˈsis-tə-mə-ˌtī-zər\ *n*

sys·tem·ic \sis-ˈtem-ik\ *adj* : of, relating to, or common to a system: as **a** : affecting the body generally ⟨a *systemic* disease⟩ **b** : relating to or being part of the systemic circulation ⟨*systemic* arteries⟩ **c** : acting by being taken into bodily systems of plants or animals and making the organism toxic to a pest (as a fungus or insect) — **sys·tem·i·cal·ly** \-ˈtem-i-kə-lē, -klē\ *adv*

systemic circulation *n* : the passage of oxygen-rich blood from the left side of the heart through arteries to all organs and tissues of the body and the return of oxygen-poor blood through veins to the right side of the heart

sys·tem·ize \ˈsis-tə-ˌmīz\ *vt* : SYSTEMATIZE — **sys·tem·i·za·tion** \ˌsis-tə-mə-ˈzā-shən\ *n*

systems analyst *n* : a person who studies an activity (as a procedure or business) to find out its goals and to discover the most efficient ways to accomplish them

sys·to·le \ˈsis-tə-lē\ *n* : the contraction of the heart by which the blood is forced onward and the circulation kept up — compare DIASTOLE [Greek *systolē,* from *systellein* "to contract," from *syn-* + *stellein* "to send"]

sys·tol·ic \sis-ˈtäl-ik\ *adj* : of, relating to, caused by, or occurring during systole ⟨*systolic* blood pressure⟩

T

t \ˈtē\ *n, pl* **t's** *or* **ts** \ˈtēz\ *often cap* : the 20th letter of the English alphabet — **to a T** : to perfection [short for *to a tittle*]

't \t\ *pron* : IT ⟨*'twill* do⟩

¹tab \ˈtab\ *n* **1 a** : a short projection used as an aid for filing, pulling, or hanging **b** : a small insert, addition, or remnant **c** : an appendage or extension of something; *esp* : one of a series of small pendants forming a decorative border or edge of a garment **d** : a small auxiliary airfoil hinged to a control surface (as a trailing edge) to help stabilize an airplane in flight **2 a** : SURVEILLANCE, WATCH ⟨keep *tab* on the situation⟩ **b** : a creditor's statement : BILL, CHECK **3** : a key on a keyboard especially for arranging data in columns [origin unknown]

²tab *vt* **tabbed; tab·bing** **1** : to furnish or ornament with tabs **2** : to single out **3** : to hit the tab key on a keyboard

tab·ard \ˈtab-ərd\ *n* **1** : a tunic worn by a knight over his armor and emblazoned with his arms **2** : a herald's official cape or coat displaying his lord's arms [Medieval French]

tabard 2

¹tab·by \ˈtab-ē\ *n, pl* **tabbies** **1** : a domestic cat with a striped and mottled coat **2** : a female cat [French *tabis* "silk taffeta with moiré finish," from Medieval Latin *attabi,* from Arabic *ʽattābī*]

²tabby *adj* : striped and mottled with darker color ⟨*tabby* fur⟩

tab·er·na·cle \ˈtab-ər-ˌnak-əl\ *n* **1 a** *often cap* : a tent sanctuary used by the Israelites during the Exodus **b** *archaic* : a dwelling place **2** : an ornamental locked box fixed to the middle of the altar and used for reserving bread consecrated at Mass **3** : a house of worship; *esp* : a building or shelter used for evangelistic services [Medieval French, from Latin *tabernaculum* "tent," from *taberna* "hut, tavern"]

¹ta·ble \ˈtā-bəl\ *n* **1** : TABLET 1a **2 a** : a piece of furniture consisting of a smooth flat slab fixed on legs **b** : FOOD, FARE ⟨sets a good *table*⟩ **c** : an act or instance of assembling to eat ⟨sit down to *table*⟩ **d** : a group of people assembled at or as if at a table **3 a** : a systematic arrangement of data in rows or columns for ready reference ⟨a *table* of weights⟩ **b** : LIST ⟨the *table* of contents⟩ **4 a** : TABLELAND **b** : a horizontal stratum [Medieval English *tabule* and Medieval French *table,* both from Latin *tabula* "board, tablet, list"] — **on the table** : up for consideration or negotiation ⟨the subject is not *on the table*⟩

²table *vt* **ta·bled; ta·bling** \-bə-ling, -bling\ **1** : TABULATE **2** : to remove (a parliamentary motion) from consideration indefinitely **3** : to put on a table

tab·leau \ˈtab-ˌlō, ta-ˈblō\ *n, pl* **tab·leaux** \-ˌlōz, -ˈblōz\ *also* **tableaus** : a lifelike representation of a scene or event by a costumed grouping of persons who remain silent and motionless [French, derived from Medieval French *table* "table"]

ta·ble·cloth \ˈtā-bəl-ˌklȯth\ *n* : a covering spread over a dining table before the places are set

ta·ble d'hôte \ˌtäb-əl-ˈdōt, ˌtab-\ *n* **1** : a meal served to all guests of a hotel at a stated hour and fixed price **2** : a complete meal of several courses offered at a fixed price — compare À LA CARTE [French, literally, "host's table"]

ta·ble·land \ˈtā-bəl-ˌland, -ˌand\ *n* : a broad level elevated area : PLATEAU

table linen *n* : linen (as tablecloths and napkins) for the table

table salt *n* : salt for use on food and in cooking

table soccer *n* : FOOSBALL

ta·ble·spoon \ˈtā-bəl-ˌspün\ *n* **1** : a large spoon used especially for serving rather than eating **2** : a unit of measure used especially in cookery equal to ½ fluid ounce (about 15 milliliters)

ta·ble·spoon·ful \ˌtā-bəl-ˈspün-ˌfu̇l, ˈtā-bəl-ˌ\ *n, pl* **-spoonfuls** \-ˌfu̇lz\ *also* **-spoons·ful** \-ˈspünz-ˌfu̇l, -ˌspünz-\ **1** : as much as a tablespoon can hold **2** : TABLESPOON 2

table sugar *n* : SUGAR 1; *esp* : granulated white sugar

tab·let \ˈtab-lət\ *n* **1 a** : a flat slab or plaque suited for or bearing an inscription **b** : a collection of sheets of writing paper glued together at one edge **2 a** : a compressed or molded block of a solid material **b** : a small piece of medicine usually in the shape of a disk **3 a** : GRAPHICS TABLET **b** *or* **tablet computer** : a mobile computing device that has a flat rectangular form, is usually controlled by means of a touch screen, and is typically used for accessing the Internet, watching videos, and reading e-books [Medieval French *tablet,* from *table* "tablet, table"]

table talk *n* : informal conversation at or as if at a dining table

table tennis *n* : a game resembling tennis that is played on a tabletop with wooden paddles and a small hollow plastic ball

ta·ble·top \ˈtā-bəl-ˌtäp\ *n* : the top of a table — **tabletop** *adj*

ta·ble·ware \ˈtā-bəl-ˌwaər, -ˌweər\ *n* : utensils (as of china, glass, or silver) for table use

table wine *n* : an inexpensive wine drunk at ordinary meals

¹tab·loid \ˈtab-ˌlȯid\ *adj* **1** : compressed or condensed into small scope ⟨*tabloid* information⟩ **2** : of, relating to, or resembling tabloids; *esp* : featuring stories presented in a sensational manner ⟨*tabloid* television⟩ [from *Tabloid,* a trademark applied to a concentrated form of drugs and chemicals]

²tabloid *n* : a newspaper that contains short often sensational news stories and much photographic matter

¹ta·boo *also* **ta·bu** \tə-ˈbü, ta-\ *adj* : prohibited by a taboo [Tongan (a Polynesian language of the Tonga islands) *tabu*]

²taboo *also* **tabu** *n, pl* **taboos** *also* **tabus** **1** : a prohibition against touching, saying, or doing something for fear of immediate harm from a mysterious superhuman force **2** : a prohibition imposed by social custom

³taboo *also* **tabu** *vt* : to place under a taboo

ta·bor \ˈtā-bər\ *n* : a small drum with one head used to accompany a pipe played by the same person [Medieval French] — **ta·bor·er** \-bər-ər\ *n*

tab·o·ret *or* **tab·ou·ret** \ˌtab-ə-ˈret, -ˈrā\ *n* **1 :** a low stool without arms or back **2 :** a small ornamental stand (as for a plant) [French *tabouret,* literally, "small drum," from Medieval French *tabor, tabour* "drum"]

tab·u·lar \ˈtab-yə-lər\ *adj* **1 :** having a flat surface **2 a :** arranged or entered in a table **b :** computed by means of a table [Latin *tabularis* "of boards," from *tabula* "board, tablet"] — **tab·u·lar·ly** *adv*

ta·bu·la ra·sa \ˌtab-yə-lə-ˈräz-ə, -ˈräs-\ *n, pl* **ta·bu·lae ra·sae** \-ˌlī-ˈräz-ˌī, -ˈräs-\ **:** the mind in its hypothetical primary blank or empty state before receiving outside impressions [Latin, "smoothed or erased tablet"]

tab·u·late \ˈtab-yə-ˌlāt\ *vt* **:** to put into tabular form — **tab·u·la·tion** \ˌtab-yə-ˈlā-shən\ *n* — **tab·u·la·tor** \ˈtab-yə-ˌlāt-ər\ *n*

tac·a·ma·hac \ˈtak-ə-mə-ˌhak\ *n* **:** BALSAM POPLAR [Spanish *tacamahaca,* from Nahuatl *tecamac* "medicinal resin"]

tach \ˈtak\ *n* **:** TACHOMETER

ta·chis·to·scope \tə-ˈkis-tə-ˌskōp\ *n* **:** an apparatus that presents visual stimuli for very brief periods [Greek *tachistos,* superlative of *tachys* "swift"]

ta·chom·e·ter \ta-ˈkäm-ət-ər, tə-\ *n* **:** a device for indicating speed of rotation (as of the crankshaft of an automobile engine) [Greek *tachos* "speed"]

tachy·car·dia \ˌtak-i-ˈkärd-ē-ə\ *n* **:** rapid heart action [Greek *tachys* "swift" + *kardia* "heart"]

tac·it \ˈtas-ət\ *adj* **1 :** expressed or carried on without words or speech **2 :** implied or indicated (as by an act or by silence) but not actually expressed ⟨*tacit* consent⟩ [Latin *tacitus* "silent," from *tacēre* "to be silent"] — **tac·it·ly** *adv* — **tac·it·ness** *n*

tac·i·turn \ˈtas-ə-ˌtərn\ *adj* **:** habitually or temperamentally disinclined to talk [Latin *taciturnus,* from *tacitus* "silent"] ***synonyms*** see SILENT — **tac·i·tur·ni·ty** \ˌtas-ə-ˈtər-nət-ē\ *n* — **tac·i·turn·ly** \ˈtas-ə-ˌtərn-lē\ *adv*

[1]**tack** \ˈtak\ *vb* **1 :** ATTACH; *esp* **:** to fasten or affix with tacks **2 :** to join in a slight or hasty manner **3 :** to add as a supplement **4 :** to change the direction of a sailing vessel when sailing close-hauled by putting the helm alee and shifting the sails **5 a :** to sail in a different direction by a tack **b :** to follow a zigzag course **c :** to modify one's policy or an attitude abruptly [Middle English *takken*] — **tack·er** *n*

[2]**tack** *n* **1 :** a small short sharp-pointed nail usually with a broad flat head for fastening some light object or material to a solid surface **2 a :** the direction a vessel is sailing as shown by the way the sails are trimmed; *also* **:** the movement of a vessel with respect to the direction of the wind ⟨on the port *tack*⟩ **b :** a change of course from one tack to another **3 :** a zigzag movement on land **4 :** a course or method of action ⟨on the wrong *tack*⟩ **5 :** a slight or temporary sewing or fastening [Middle English *tak* "fastener"]

[3]**tack** *n* **:** HARDTACK [origin unknown]

[4]**tack** *n* **:** stable gear; *esp* **:** equipment (as a saddle and bridle) for use on a saddle horse [perhaps short for *tackle*]

tack·i·ness \ˈtak-ē-nəs\ *n* **:** the quality or state of being tacky

[1]**tack·le** \ˈtak-əl, *nautical often* ˈtāk-\ *n* **1 :** a set of the equipment used in a particular activity **:** GEAR ⟨fishing *tackle*⟩ **2 a :** a ship's rigging **b :** an assemblage of ropes and pulleys arranged to gain mechanical advantage for hoisting and pulling **3 a :** the act or an instance of tackling **b :** either of two football linemen who line up inside the ends [Middle English *takel*]

tackle 2b

[2]**tackle** *vt* **tack·led; tack·ling** \ˈtak-ling, -ə-ling\ **1 a :** to seize, take hold of, or grapple with especially in order to stop or subdue **b :** to seize and stop or throw down (a player) in football **2 :** to set about dealing with ⟨*tackle* the problem⟩ — **tack·ler** \-lər, -ə-lər\ *n*

[1]**tacky** \ˈtak-ē\ *adj* **tack·i·er; -est :** somewhat sticky to the touch **:** ADHESIVE ⟨*tacky* varnish⟩

[2]**tacky** *adj* **tack·i·er; -est 1 a :** characterized by lack of good breeding **b :** SHABBY 2b, SEEDY **2 a :** marked by lack of style or good taste **:** DOWDY **b :** marked by cheap showiness **:** GAUDY ⟨a *tacky* outfit⟩ [from earlier *tacky* "low-class person"]

ta·co \ˈtäk-ō\ *n, pl* **tacos** \-ōz\ **:** a usually fried tortilla that is folded or rolled and stuffed with a mixture (as of seasoned meat, cheese, and lettuce) [Mexican Spanish]

tac·o·nite \ˈtak-ə-ˌnīt\ *n* **:** a flinty rock high enough in iron content to be used as a low-grade iron ore [*Taconic* mountain range, U.S.]

tact \ˈtakt\ *n* **:** a keen understanding of how to act in getting along with others; *esp* **:** the ability to deal with others without offending them [French, "sense of touch," from Latin *tactus,* from *tangere* "to touch"]

tact·ful \ˈtakt-fəl\ *adj* **:** having or showing tact — **tact·ful·ly** \-fə-lē\ *adv* — **tact·ful·ness** *n*

tactic *n* **1 :** a method of employing forces in combat **2 :** a planned action or maneuver for accomplishing an end

tac·ti·cal \ˈtak-ti-kəl\ *adj* **1 a :** of or relating to combat tactics **b :** of, relating to, or designed for air attack in close support of friendly ground forces ⟨*tactical* air force⟩ **2 a :** of or relating to small-scale actions serving a larger purpose **b :** skillful in planning or maneuvering — **tac·ti·cal·ly** \-kə-lē, -klē\ *adv*

tac·ti·cian \tak-ˈtish-ən\ *n* **:** one skilled in tactics

tac·tics \ˈtak-tiks\ *n sing or pl* **1 a :** the science and art of disposing and maneuvering forces in combat **b :** the art or skill of employing available means to accomplish an end **2 :** a system or mode of procedure [Greek *taktika,* from *taktikos* "of order, of tactics," from *tassein* "to arrange, place in battle formation"] ***synonyms*** see STRATEGY

tac·tile \ˈtak-tl, -ˌtīl\ *adj* **1 :** perceptible by touch **2 :** of, relating to, or used in the sense of touch [Latin *tactilis,* from *tangere* "to touch"] — **tac·til·i·ty** \tak-ˈtil-ət-ē\ *n*

tact·less \ˈtak-tləs\ *adj* **:** having or showing no tact — **tact·less·ly** *adv* — **tact·less·ness** *n*

tac·tu·al \ˈtak-chə-wəl, -chəl\ *adj* **:** TACTILE [Latin *tactus* "sense of touch," from *tangere* "to touch"] — **tac·tu·al·ly** \-ē\ *adv*

tad \ˈtad\ *n* **1 :** BOY 1 **2 :** [3]BIT 1 [probably from Old English *tāde* "toad"] — **a tad :** SOMEWHAT ⟨was *a tad* rude⟩

tad·pole \ˈtad-ˌpōl\ *n* **:** an aquatic frog or toad larva that has a rounded body with a long tail and breathes with gills [Middle English *taddepol,* from *tode* "toad" + *polle* "head, poll"]

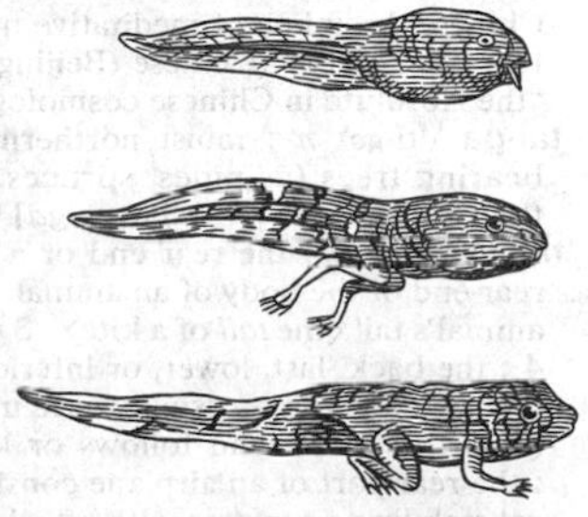
tadpole in stages

tae kwon do \ˈtī-ˈkwän-ˈdō\ *n, often cap T&K&D* **:** a Korean art of self-defense resembling karate [Korean *t'aekwŏndo*]

tael \ˈtāl\ *n* **1 :** any of various units of weight of eastern Asia **2 :** any of various Chinese units of value based on the value of a tael weight of silver [Portuguese, from Malay *tahil*]

tae·nia *also* **te·nia** \ˈtē-nē-ə\ *n, pl* **-ni·ae** \-nē-ˌē\ *or* **-ni·as 1 :** a band on a Doric order separating the frieze from the architrave **2 :** TAPEWORM **3 :** an ancient Greek fillet [Latin, "ribbon," from Greek *tainia*]

taf·fe·ta \ˈtaf-ət-ə\ *n* **:** a crisp plain-woven lustrous fabric of various fibers used especially for women's clothing [Middle French *taffata,* from Italian *taffettà,* from Turkish *tafta,* from Persian *tāftah* "woven"]

taff·rail \ˈtaf-ˌrāl, -rəl\ *n* **:** the rail around the stern of a ship [Dutch *tafereel*]

taf·fy \ˈtaf-ē\ *n, pl* **taffies :** a candy usually of molasses or brown sugar boiled and pulled until porous and light-colored [origin unknown]

[1]**tag** \ˈtag\ *n* **1 :** a loose hanging piece of cloth **:** TATTER **2 :** a metal or plastic binding on an end of a shoelace **3 :** a piece of hanging or attached material **4 a :** a brief quotation used for emphasis or effect **b :** TAG LINE **5 :** something (as a marker) used for identification or classification ⟨a price *tag*⟩ **6 :** LABEL 3 **7 :** an element of code in a computer document used especially to control format and layout or to establish a hyperlink

\ə\ **abut**	\au̇\ **out**	\i\ **tip**	\ȯ\ **saw**	\u̇\ **foot**
\ər\ **further**	\ch\ **chin**	\ī\ **life**	\ȯi\ **coin**	\y\ **yet**
\a\ **mat**	\e\ **pet**	\j\ **job**	\th\ **thin**	\yü\ **few**
\ā\ **take**	\ē\ **easy**	\ng\ **sing**	\t͟h\ **this**	\yu̇\ **cure**
\ä\ **cot, cart**	\g\ **go**	\ō\ **bone**	\ü\ **food**	\zh\ **vision**

8 : an identifying name or symbol made on a wall ⟨graffiti *tags*⟩ [Middle English *tagge*]

[2]**tag** *vb* **tagged; tag·ging** **1 :** to provide or mark with or as if with a tag **2 :** to attach as an addition : APPEND **3 :** to follow closely and persistently **4 :** LABEL 2a

[3]**tag** *n* **1 :** a children's game in which one player is it and chases the others and tries to tag one of them to make that player it **2 :** an act or instance of tagging a runner in baseball [origin unknown]

[4]**tag** *vt* **tagged; tag·ging** **1 a :** to touch in or as if in a game of tag **b :** to put out (a runner in baseball) by a touch with the ball or the gloved hand containing the ball **2 :** to hit solidly : catch with a blow

Ta·ga·log \tə-ˈgäl-əg, -ˌȯg\ *n* **1 :** a member of a people of central Luzon **2 :** an Austronesian language of the Tagalog people [Tagalog]

tag·along \ˈtag-ə-ˌlȯŋ\ *n* **:** one that persistently and often annoyingly follows the lead of another

tag along *vi* **:** to follow another's lead especially in going from one place to another

tag end *n* **1 :** the last part **2 :** a miscellaneous or random bit

tag·ger \ˈtag-ər\ *n* **:** one that tags; *esp* **:** a person who marks surfaces with graffiti

tag line *n* **1 :** a final line (as in a play or joke); *esp* **:** one that serves to clarify a point or create a dramatic effect **2 :** a phrase identified with an individual, group, or product : SLOGAN

tag up *vi* **:** to touch a base before running in baseball after a fly ball is caught

Ta·hi·tian \tə-ˈhē-shən\ *n* **1 :** a native or inhabitant of Tahiti **2 :** the Polynesian language of the Tahitians — **Tahitian** *adj*

Tai \ˈtī\ *n, pl* **Tai** **1 :** a member of a group of peoples of southeast Asia **2 :** a family of languages including Tai that is spoken in southeast Asia and China

tai chi *also* **t'ai chi** \ˈtī-ˈjē, -ˈchē\ *n, often cap T&C* **:** an ancient Chinese discipline of meditative movements practiced as a system of exercises [Chinese (Beijing dialect) *tàijíquán,* from *tàijí* "the Absolute in Chinese cosmology" + *quán* "fist, boxing"]

tai·ga \ˈtī-gə\ *n* **:** moist northern forest dominated by cone-bearing trees (as pines, spruces, and firs) beginning where the tundra ends [Russian *taĭga*]

[1]**tail** \ˈtāl\ *n* **1 :** the rear end or a lengthened growth from the rear end of the body of an animal **2 :** something resembling an animal's tail ⟨the *tail* of a kite⟩ **3** *pl* **:** full evening dress for men **4 :** the back, last, lower, or inferior part of something **5 :** the reverse of a coin — usually used in plural ⟨*tails,* I win⟩ **6 :** one (as a detective) who follows or keeps watch on someone **7 :** the rear part of an airplane consisting of horizontal and vertical stabilizing surfaces with attached control surfaces **8 :** a location immediately or not far behind ⟨had a posse on his *tail*⟩ [Old English *tægel*] — **tailed** \ˈtāld\ *adj* — **tail·less** \ˈtāl-ləs\ *adj* — **tail·like** \ˈtāl-ˌlīk\ *adj*

[2]**tail** *adj* **1 :** being at the rear ⟨*tail* gunner⟩ **2 :** coming from the rear ⟨*tail* wind⟩

[3]**tail** *vb* **1 a :** to make or furnish with a tail **b :** to follow or be drawn behind like a tail **2 :** to place the end of (as a rafter) in a wall or other support **3 :** to follow closely for purposes of observation : SHADOW **4 :** to grow progressively smaller, fainter, or more scattered — usually used with *off*

tail·back \ˈtāl-ˌbak\ *n* **:** the offensive football back who lines up farthest from the line of scrimmage

tail·board \-ˌbōrd, -ˌbȯrd\ *n* **:** TAILGATE

tail·bone \-ˈbōn, -ˌbōn\ *n* **1 :** a hind or lower vertebra **2 :** COCCYX

tail end *n* **1 :** the hindmost end ⟨the *tail end* of the line⟩ **2 :** the concluding period ⟨the *tail end* of the season⟩

[1]**tail·gate** \ˈtāl-ˌgāt\ *n* **:** a gate at the back end of a vehicle (as a station wagon) that can be let down for loading and unloading

[2]**tailgate** *vb* **:** to drive dangerously close behind

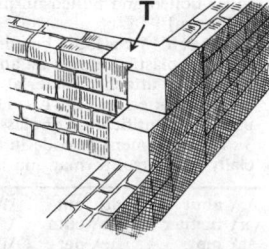

tail·ing \ˈtā-liŋ\ *n* **1** *pl* **:** refuse material separated as residue in the preparation of various products (as grain or ores) **2 :** the part of a projecting stone or brick inserted in a wall

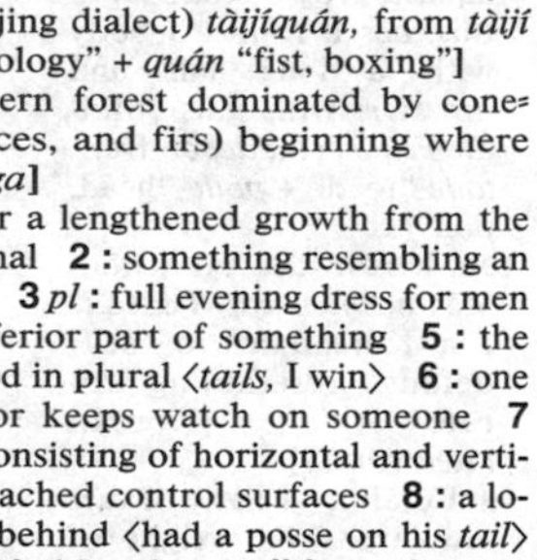

T tailing 2

tail lamp *n* **:** TAILLIGHT

tail·light \ˈtāl-ˌlīt\ *n* **:** a red warning light mounted at the rear of a vehicle

[1]**tai·lor** \ˈtā-lər\ *n* **:** a person whose occupation is making or altering outer garments [Medieval French *taillur,* from *tailler, taillier* "to cut," from Late Latin *taliare,* from Latin *talea* "plant, cutting, thin piece of wood"]

[2]**tailor** *vt* **1 a :** to make or fashion as the work of a tailor **b :** to make or adapt to suit a special need or purpose **2 :** to fit with clothes **3 :** to style with trim straight lines and details completed by hand

tail·or·bird \ˈtā-lər-ˌbərd\ *n* **:** any of a genus of chiefly Asian warblers that stitch leaves together to support and hide their nests

tai·lored \-lərd\ *adj* **1 :** made by a tailor **2 :** fashioned or fitted to resemble a tailor's work **3 :** CUSTOM-MADE

tai·lor·ing *n* **1 a :** the business or occupation of a tailor **b :** the work or workmanship of a tailor **2 :** the making or adapting of something to suit a particular purpose

tai·lor–made \ˌtā-lər-ˈmād\ *adj* **1 :** made by or as if by a tailor; *esp* **:** characterized by precise fit and simplicity of style **2 :** made or as if made to suit a particular need

tail·piece \ˈtāl-ˌpēs\ *n* **1 :** a piece added at the end **2 :** a device from which the strings of a stringed instrument are stretched to the pegs **3 :** an ornament placed below the text matter of a page (as at the end of a chapter) **4 :** a beam tailed in a wall and supported by a header

tail pipe *n* **:** an outlet by which engine exhaust gases are expelled from a vehicle (as an automobile or jet aircraft)

tailplane *n* **:** the horizontal tail surfaces of an airplane

tail·race \ˈtāl-ˌrās\ *n* **:** the part of a millrace below the waterwheel or turbine

tail·spin \-ˌspin\ *n* **1 :** SPIN 2a **2 :** a collapse into depression or confusion

tail wind *n* **:** a wind having the same general direction as the course of a moving object (as an aircraft)

Tai·no \ˈtī-nō\ *n* **:** a member of an American Indian people of the Greater Antilles and the Bahamas; *also* **:** the language of the Taino people [Taino *nitaino, tayno* "noble, lesser chief"]

[1]**taint** \ˈtānt\ *vt* **1 :** to touch or affect slightly with something bad **2 :** SPOIL 2c **3 :** to contaminate morally : CORRUPT [Middle English *teynten* "to color" & *taynten* "to affect by attainder"; Middle English *teynten,* derived from Medieval French *teindre,* from Latin *tingere*; Middle English *taynten,* from Middle French *ataint,* past participle of *ataindre* "to affect by attainder, attain"]

[2]**taint** *n* **1 :** a trace of decay : STAIN, BLEMISH **2 :** a contaminating influence — **taint·less** \-ləs\ *adj*

[1]**take** \ˈtāk\ *vb* **took** \ˈtu̇k\; **tak·en** \ˈtā-kən\; **tak·ing** **1 :** to get into one's hands or into one's possession, power, or control **2 :** to seize or capture physically ⟨*took* them as prisoners⟩ **3 :** WIN 3a ⟨*took* first prize⟩ **4 :** to get possession of (as by buying or capturing) ⟨decided to *take* the house⟩ ⟨*took* several trout with hook and line⟩ **5 :** to seize and affect suddenly ⟨*taken* with a fever⟩ **6 :** CHARM 1, DELIGHT ⟨were much *taken* with our new acquaintance⟩ **7 :** EXTRACT 1c ⟨*take* material from an encyclopedia⟩ **8 a :** REMOVE, SUBTRACT ⟨*take* 78 from 112⟩ **b :** to put an end to (as life) **9 :** to find out by testing or examining ⟨*take* a patient's temperature⟩ **10 :** to pick out : CHOOSE, SELECT ⟨*take* your choice⟩ **11 a :** ASSUME 1 ⟨its government *took* the form of a democratic republic⟩ **b :** to enter into or undertake the duties of ⟨*take* a job⟩ **c :** to move onto or into ⟨*take* the witness stand⟩ **12 :** to become soaked with or make part of itself : ABSORB ⟨this cloth *takes* dye well⟩ **13 a :** to be affected by : CONTRACT ⟨*took* cold⟩ **b :** to be seized or attacked in a specified way : BECOME ⟨*took* sick⟩ **14 :** ACCEPT 2a, FOLLOW ⟨*take* my advice⟩ **15 :** to introduce into the body ⟨*take* your medicine⟩ **16 a :** to submit to ⟨*took* the punishment without complaint⟩ **b :** WITHSTAND ⟨*takes* a punch well⟩ **17 :** to subscribe to ⟨*takes* two newspapers⟩ **18 a :** UNDERSTAND 1 ⟨*take* a nod to mean yes⟩ **b :** CONSIDER 3 ⟨wanted to be *taken* for a genius⟩ **19 :** EXPERIENCE 1, FEEL ⟨*take* pride in one's work⟩ ⟨*take* offense⟩ **20 :** to be formed or used with ⟨a noun that *takes* an *s* in the plural⟩ ⟨this verb *takes* an object⟩ **21 :** to convey, lead, carry, or cause to come along with one **22 a :** to avail oneself of ⟨*take* shelter⟩ **b :** to pro-

ceed to occupy ⟨*take* a chair⟩ **23 :** NEED 1, REQUIRE ⟨this job *takes* a lot of time⟩ **24 :** to obtain an image or copy of ⟨*take* a photograph⟩ ⟨*take* fingerprints⟩ **25 :** to set out to make, do, or perform ⟨*take* a walk⟩ — often used with *on* ⟨*took* on a new assignment⟩ **26 :** to let in and hold : ADMIT, ACCOMMODATE ⟨the boat was *taking* in water fast⟩ ⟨the suitcase wouldn't *take* another thing⟩ **27 :** to keep from hitting at (a pitched ball) ⟨*take* a strike⟩ **28 :** to go or get away ⟨*take* to the hills⟩ [Old English *tacan,* from Old Norse *taka*] — **take a back seat :** to have or assume a secondary position ⟨everything else *takes a back seat* to survival⟩ — **take a bath :** to suffer a heavy financial loss — **take advantage of 1 :** to use to advantage : profit by **2 :** to impose upon : EXPLOIT — **take after 1 :** to take as an example : FOLLOW **2 :** to look like : RESEMBLE — **take a hike** *also* **take a walk :** to go away : LEAVE — **take aim at :** TARGET 1 ⟨new legislation that *takes aim at* crime⟩ — **take care :** to be careful : exercise caution or prudence — **take care of :** to attend to or provide for the needs, operation, or treatment of — **take charge :** to assume care or control — **take effect 1 :** to become operative **2 :** to produce a result as expected or intended : be effective — **take five** *or* **take ten :** to take a break especially from work — **take for :** to suppose to be; *esp* : to suppose mistakenly to be — **take for a ride :** TRICK 1, CHEAT — **take for granted 1 :** to assume as true, real, or expected **2 :** to value too lightly — **take hold :** to become attached or established : take effect — **take into account :** to make allowance for — **take in vain :** to use (a name) profanely or without proper respect — **take issue :** to take up the opposite side — **take no prisoners :** to be merciless or relentless (as in exploiting an advantage) — **take one's time :** to be slow or unhurried about doing something — **take part :** PARTICIPATE — **take place :** to come about or occur : HAPPEN — **take ship :** to set out on a voyage by ship — **take the cake :** to carry off the prize : rank first — **take the count 1 :** to be knocked out in a boxing match **2 :** to go down in defeat — **take the floor :** to rise (as in a meeting) to make an address — **take the plunge :** to do or undertake something decisively especially after a period of hesitation or uncertainty — **take to 1 :** to go to or into ⟨*take to* the streets⟩ **2 :** to apply or devote oneself to (as a practice, habit, or occupation) ⟨*take to* begging⟩ **3 :** to adapt oneself to : respond to ⟨*takes to* water like a duck⟩ **4 :** to conceive a liking for — **take to court :** to bring before a judicial body; *esp* : SUE 2 — **take to task :** to call to account for a shortcoming : REPROVE — **take turns :** ALTERNATE 1

synonyms TAKE, SEIZE, GRASP, SNATCH mean to get hold of by or as if by catching up with the hand. TAKE applies to any manner of getting something into one's possession or control ⟨*take* some salad from the bowl⟩. SEIZE suggests a sudden forcible taking of something tangible ⟨*seized* the suspect⟩. GRASP stresses a laying hold so as to have firmly in possession ⟨*grasped* the handrail⟩. SNATCH suggests more suddenness but less force than SEIZE ⟨*snatched* a doughnut and ran out⟩. ***synonyms*** see in addition BRING

²take *n* **1 :** an act or the action of taking (as by seizing, accepting, or coming into possession) **2 :** something that is taken: **a :** money taken in **b :** SHARE, CUT ⟨wanted a bigger *take*⟩ **c :** the quantity (as of game) taken at one time : CATCH **d** (1) : a scene recorded (as on film or videotape) at one time without stopping the camera (2) : a sound recording made during a single recording period (3) : a trial recording **3 a :** a bodily reaction that indicates a successful immunization (as against smallpox) **b :** a successful union of a graft **4 :** mental response or reaction ⟨a delayed *take*⟩

take·away \ˈtā-kə-ˌwā\ *n* **1** *chiefly British* : TAKEOUT 3 **2 :** an act or instance of taking possession of the ball or puck from an opposing team

take back *vt* : RETRACT, WITHDRAW ⟨*take back* what you said⟩

¹take·down \ˈtāk-ˌdau̇n\ *adj* : constructed so as to be readily taken apart ⟨a *takedown* rifle⟩

²takedown *n* : the action or an act of taking down: as **a :** the action of humiliating **b :** the action of taking apart **c :** the act of bringing one's wrestling opponent to the mat from a standing position

take down \tāk-ˈdau̇n, ˈtāk-\ *vb* **1 a :** to pull to pieces **b :** DISASSEMBLE **2 :** to lower the spirit or vanity of **3 a :** to write down **b :** to record by mechanical means **4 :** to become seized or attacked especially by illness ⟨*took down* with the mumps⟩

take–home pay \ˈtāk-ˌhōm-\ *n* : the money left in one's pay after all deductions (as taxes) have been made : the money one actually gets on payday

take in *vt* **1 :** to draw into a smaller compass ⟨*take in* a slack line⟩: **a :** FURL ⟨*take in* the sail⟩ **b :** to make (a garment) smaller by enlarging seams or tucks **2 a :** to receive as a guest or lodger **b :** to give shelter to **c :** to take to a police station as a prisoner **3 a :** to receive in payment or as a return **b :** to receive (work) into one's house to be done for pay ⟨*take in* washing⟩ **4 :** to encompass within fixed limits : COMPRISE, INCLUDE **5 :** ATTEND ⟨*take in* a movie⟩ **6 :** to receive into the mind : PERCEIVE ⟨paused to *take* the situation *in*⟩ **7 :** CHEAT, DECEIVE ⟨*taken in* by a hard luck story⟩

taken *past participle of* TAKE

take–no–prisoners *adj* : having a fierce, relentless, or merciless character ⟨*take-no-prisoners* politics⟩

take·off \ˈtā-ˌkȯf\ *n* **1 :** an imitation especially in the form of caricature **2 a :** a rise or leap from a surface in making a jump or flight or an ascent in an airplane **b :** an action of starting out or setting out **3 :** a spot at which one takes off **4 :** a mechanism for transmission of the power of an engine or vehicle to operate some other mechanism

take off \tā-ˈkȯf, ˈtā-\ *vb* **1 :** REMOVE ⟨*take* your hat *off*⟩ **2 :** RELEASE ⟨*take* the brake *off*⟩ **3 :** to spend (time) away from work or duty ⟨*took* two weeks *off* in August⟩ **4 :** to take away : DEDUCT, DETRACT **5 a :** to start off or away often suddenly : SET OUT ⟨*took off* without delay⟩ **b :** to branch off (as from a main stream or stem) **c :** to begin a leap or spring **d :** to leave the surface : begin flight **e :** to embark on rapid activity, development, or growth **f :** to spring into wide use or popularity

take on *vb* **1 :** to contend with or face as an opponent **2 :** ENGAGE, HIRE ⟨*took* me *on* for the summer⟩ **3 :** to assume or acquire (as an appearance or quality) as or as if one's own **4 :** to show one's feelings especially of grief or anger in a demonstrative way

take·out \ˈtā-ˌkau̇t\ *n* **1 :** the action or an act of taking out **2 :** something taken out or prepared to be taken out **3 :** prepared food packaged to be eaten away from its place of sale

take out \tā-ˈkau̇t, ˈtā-\ *vb* **1 a :** to take away : DEDUCT **b :** to get rid of **2 :** to find release for : EXPEND ⟨*took* their frustration *out* on us⟩ **3 :** to escort and usually pay the way especially on a social occasion **4 :** to take as an equivalent in another form ⟨*took* the debt *out* in goods⟩ **5 :** to obtain from the proper authority ⟨*take out* a charter⟩ **6 :** to start on a course : SET OUT — **take it out on :** to expend anger, vexation, or frustration in harassment of

takeover \ˈtā-ˌkō-vər\ *n* : the action or an act of taking over

take over \tā-ˈkō-vər, ˈtā-\ *vb* : to assume control or possession of or responsibility for something ⟨*took over* the government⟩

take–up \ˈtā-ˌkəp\ *n* : the action of taking up

take up \tā-ˈkəp, ˈtā-\ *vb* **1 :** to remove by lifting or pulling up **2 :** to accept or adopt for the purpose of assisting **3 :** to take or accept (as a belief, idea, or practice) as one's own **4 :** to absorb or incorporate into itself ⟨plants *taking up* water and minerals⟩ **5 :** to establish oneself in ⟨*took up* residence in town⟩ **6 :** to occupy entirely or exclusively : fill up ⟨the meeting was *taken up* with old business⟩ **7 :** to make tighter or shorter ⟨*take up* the slack⟩ **8 :** to respond favorably to (as a bet, challenge, or proposal) **9 :** to make a beginning where another has left off — **take up with 1 :** to become interested or absorbed in **2 :** to begin to associate with

tak·ings \ˈtā-kiŋz\ *n pl, chiefly British* : receipts especially of money

talc \ˈtalk\ *n* : a very soft mineral consisting of a basic silicate of magnesium that has a soapy feel and is used especially in making talcum powder [Medieval French, *talk,* from Medieval Latin *talc, talcum* from Arabic *ṭalq*]

tal·cum powder \ˈtal-kəm-\ *n* : a powder composed of perfumed talc or talc and a mild antiseptic for sprinkling or rubbing over the skin [Medieval Latin *talcum* "talc"]

tale \ˈtāl\ *n* **1 :** a series of events or facts told or presented : ACCOUNT ⟨a *tale* of woe⟩ **2 :** a story about an imaginary event ⟨a fairy *tale*⟩ **3 :** a false story : LIE **4 :** a piece of harmful gossip ⟨all sorts of *tales* were going around about them⟩ **5 a :** COUNT

\ə\ **abut**	\au̇\ **out**	\i\ **tip**	\ȯ\ **saw**	\u̇\ **foot**
\ər\ **further**	\ch\ **chin**	\ī\ **life**	\ȯi\ **coin**	\y\ **yet**
\a\ **mat**	\e\ **pet**	\j\ **job**	\th\ **thin**	\yü\ **few**
\ā\ **take**	\ē\ **easy**	\ng\ **sing**	\t͟h\ **this**	\yu̇\ **cure**
\ä\ **cot, cart**	\g\ **go**	\ō\ **bone**	\ü\ **food**	\zh\ **vision**

1, TALLY **b** : a number of things taken together : TOTAL [Old English *talu*]

tale·bear·er \-ˌbar-ər, -ˌber-\ *n* : one that spreads gossip, scandal, or idle rumors : GOSSIP — **tale·bear·ing** \-iŋ\ *adj or n*

tal·ent \ˈtal-ənt\ *n* **1** : any of several ancient units of weight and money value **2** : the abilities, power, and gifts a person is born with **3 a** : a special often athletic, creative, or artistic aptitude **b** : general intelligence or mental power : ABILITY **4** : persons of talent in a field or activity [Old English *talente,* from Latin *talentum,* from Greek *talanton* "pan of a scale, weight"; senses 2–4 from the parable of the talents in Matthew 25:14–30] — **tal·ent·ed** \-ən-təd\ *adj*

synonyms TALENT, GENIUS, KNACK mean a special ability for doing something. TALENT suggests a marked special ability without implying a mind of extraordinary power ⟨a *talent* for singing⟩. GENIUS may also imply marked talent but more often suggests an inborn creative intelligence far above ordinary ⟨true *genius* usually appears very early in life⟩. KNACK implies a comparatively minor but special ability making for easy performance ⟨has a *knack* for writing poetry⟩.

talent scout *n* : a person engaged in discovering and recruiting people of talent (as in music or a sport)

talent show *n* : a show consisting of a series of individual performances (as singing) by amateurs who may be selected for special recognition as performing talent

ta·ler *also* **tha·ler** \ˈtäl-ər\ *n* : any of numerous silver coins issued by various German states from the 15th to the 19th centuries [German *thaler, taler,* short for *joachimsthaler,* from Sankt *Joachimsthal,* Bohemia, where the first talers were made]

tales·man \ˈtālz-mən, ˈtā-lēz-\ *n* : a person added to a jury usually from among bystanders to make up a deficiency in the available number of jurors [Middle English *tales* "talesmen," from Medieval Latin *tales de circumstantibus* "such (persons) of the bystanders"; from the wording of the writ summoning them]

tale–tell·er \ˈtāl-ˌtel-ər\ *n* **1** : one who tells tales or stories **2** : TALEBEARER — **tale–tell·ing** \-iŋ\ *adj or n*

tal·is·man \ˈtal-ə-smən, -əz-mən\ *n, pl* **talismans** : a ring or stone carved with symbols and believed to have magical powers : CHARM [French *talisman* or Spanish *talismán* or Italian *talismano*; all from Arabic *ṭilsam,* from Middle Greek *telesma,* from Greek, "consecration"] — **tal·is·man·ic** \ˌtal-ə-ˈsman-ik, -əzˈman-\ *adj* — **tal·is·man·i·cal·ly** \-i-kə-lē, -klē\ *adv*

[1]**talk** \ˈtȯk\ *vb* **1** : to deliver or express in speech : UTTER ⟨*talk* sense⟩ **2** : to make the subject of conversation or discourse : DISCUSS ⟨*talk* business⟩ **3** : to persuade, affect, or cause by talking ⟨*talked* them into agreeing⟩ **4** : to use (a language) for conversing or communicating : SPEAK ⟨can *talk* Italian⟩ **5 a** : to express or exchange ideas by means of spoken words : CONVERSE **b** : to convey information or communicate in any way (as with signs or sounds) **c** : to use speech : SPEAK ⟨babies can't *talk*⟩ **6 a** : to speak idly : PRATE **b** : GOSSIP **c** : to reveal secret or confidential information **7** : to give a talk : LECTURE [Middle English *talken*] ***synonyms*** see SPEAK — **talk·er** *n* — **talk back** : to answer impertinently — **talk turkey** : to speak frankly or bluntly

[2]**talk** *n* **1** : the act or an instance of talking : SPEECH **2** : a way of speaking : LANGUAGE **3** : pointless or fruitless discussion : VERBIAGE **4** : a formal discussion, negotiation, or exchange of views **5** : RUMOR, GOSSIP **6** : the topic of interested comment, conversation, or gossip ⟨it's the *talk* of the village⟩ **7** : an analysis or discussion presented in an informal manner

talk·ative \ˈtȯ-kət-iv\ *adj* : fond of talking — **talk·ative·ness** *n*

synonyms TALKATIVE, GARRULOUS, VOLUBLE mean fond of talking. TALKATIVE implies a readiness to talk and engage in conversation ⟨a good group discussion needs a few *talkative* people⟩. GARRULOUS suggests wordy, rambling, or tedious talkativeness ⟨a *garrulous* old politician⟩. VOLUBLE suggests keeping up an uninterrupted seemingly endless flow of talk ⟨a *voluble* salesclerk who wouldn't quit⟩.

talk down *vb* **1** : to overcome or silence by argument or by loud talking **2** : to speak in a condescending or superior way

talk·ie \ˈtȯ-kē\ *n* : a motion picture with a synchronized sound track

talking book *n* : a recording of a reading of a book or magazine

talking machine *n* : an early phonograph

talk·ing–to \ˈtȯ-kiŋ-ˌtü\ *n* : REPRIMAND, LECTURE ⟨father gave them a severe *talking-to*⟩

talk out *vt* : to clarify or settle by oral discussion ⟨*talk out* their differences⟩

talk over *vt* : to have a talk about : DISCUSS

talk up *vt* **1** : to discuss favorably : ADVOCATE **2** : to speak clearly or directly

talky \ˈtȯ-kē\ *adj* **talk·i·er; -est** **1** : fond of talking : TALKATIVE **2** : containing too much talk

tall \ˈtȯl\ *adj* **1 a** : great in stature or height **b** : of a specified height ⟨five feet *tall*⟩ **2 a** : large or formidable in amount, extent, or degree ⟨a *tall* order to fill⟩ **b** : FLOWERY 2, GRANDILOQUENT ⟨*tall* talk⟩ **c** : INCREDIBLE, IMPROBABLE ⟨a *tall* story⟩ [Middle English *tal* "brave," probably from Old English *getæl* "quick, ready"] — **tall** *adv* — **tall·ish** \ˈtȯ-lish\ *adj* — **tall·ness** *n*

tall·boy \ˈtȯl-ˌbȯi\ *n* **1** : HIGHBOY **2** : a double chest of drawers

tal·lith \ˈtäl-əs, -ət, -əth\ *or* **tal·lis** \-əs\ *n* : a shawl with fringed corners worn over the head or shoulders by Jewish men especially during morning prayers [Hebrew *ṭallīth* "cover, cloak"]

tall oil \ˈtäl-, ˈtȯl-\ *n* : a resinous by-product from the manufacture of chemical wood pulp used especially in making soaps, coatings, and oils [German *Tallöl,* from Swedish *tallolja,* from *tall* "pine" + *olja* "oil"]

tal·low \ˈtal-ō\ *n* : the white nearly tasteless solid rendered fat of cattle and sheep used chiefly in soap, candles, and lubricants [Middle English *talgh, talow*] — **tal·lowy** \ˈtal-ə-wē\ *adj*

tall ship *n* : a sailing vessel with at least two masts; *esp* : SQUARE-RIGGER

[1]**tal·ly** \ˈtal-ē\ *n, pl* **tallies** **1** : a device for recording business transactions; *esp* : a rod notched with marks representing numbers and serving as a record of a transaction and of the amount due or paid **2 a** : a reckoning or recorded account; *also* : a total recorded **b** : a score or point made (as in a game) **3 a** : a part that corresponds to an opposite or companion member : COMPLEMENT **b** : CORRESPONDENCE 1a [Medieval French *talie, taille,* in part from *tailler* "to cut, measure, count"; in part from Medieval Latin *tallia,* from Latin *talea* "twig, cutting," thin piece of wood]

[2]**tally** *vb* **tal·lied; tal·ly·ing** **1** : to keep a reckoning of : COUNT **2** : to make a tally : SCORE **3** : MATCH 4, AGREE

tal·ly·ho \ˌtal-ē-ˈhō\ *n, pl* **tallyhos** : a call of a huntsman at the sight of the fox [probably from French *taïaut,* a cry used to excite hounds in deer hunting]

tal·ly·man \ˈtal-ē-mən\ *n* **1** *British* : one who sells goods on the installment plan **2** : one who tallies, checks, or keeps an account or record (as of a receipt of goods)

Tal·mud \ˈtäl-ˌmu̇d, ˈtal-məd\ *n* : the authoritative body of Jewish tradition [Hebrew *talmūdh,* literally, "instruction"] — **Tal·mu·dic** \tal-ˈmüd-ik, -ˈmyüd-, -ˈməd-, täl-ˈmu̇d-\ *adj* — **tal·mud·ism** \ˈtäl-ˌmu̇d-ˌiz-əm, ˈtal-məd-\ *n, often cap* — **Tal·mud·ist** \-əst\ *n*

tal·on \ˈtal-ən\ *n* **1** : the claw of an animal and especially of a bird of prey **2** : a part or object shaped like or suggestive of a claw [Medieval French *talun* "heel, hind claw of a bird of prey," derived from Latin *talus* "ankle, anklebone"] — **taloned** \-ənd\ *adj*

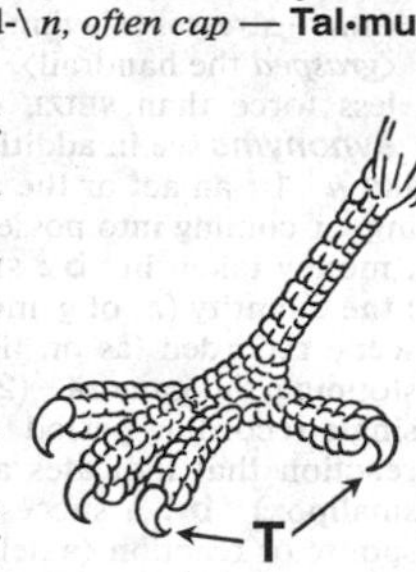
T talon 1

[1]**ta·lus** \ˈtā-ləs\ *n* : rock debris at the base of a cliff [French]

[2]**talus** *n, pl* **ta·li** \ˈtā-ˌlī\ **1** : the bone that in humans bears the weight of the body and with the tibia and fibula forms the ankle joint — called also *anklebone* **2** : the entire ankle [Latin]

tam \ˈtam\ *n* : TAM-O'-SHANTER

tam·able *or* **tame·able** \ˈtā-mə-bəl\ *adj* : capable of being tamed

ta·ma·le \tə-ˈmäl-ē\ *n* : ground meat seasoned with chili, rolled in cornmeal dough, wrapped in corn husks, and steamed [Mexican Spanish *tamales,* pl. of *tamal* "tamale," from Nahuatl *tamalli* "steamed cornmeal dough"]

tam·a·rack \ˈtam-ə-ˌrak\ *n* **1** : any of several American larches; *esp* : one of the northern U.S. and Canada **2** : the wood of a tamarack [origin unknown]

tam·a·rind \ˈtam-ə-rənd, -ˌrind\ *n* : a tropical tree of the legume family with hard yellowish wood, feathery leaves, and red=

striped yellow flowers; *also* : its pod which has an acid pulp used especially for preserves or as a seasoning in cooking [Spanish and Portuguese *tamarindo,* from Arabic *tamr hindī,* literally, "Indian date"]

tam·a·risk \ˈtam-ə-ˌrisk\ *n* : any of a genus of chiefly desert shrubs of Eurasia and Africa having tiny narrow leaves and masses of minute flowers [Late Latin *tamariscus,* from Latin *tamarix*]

1tam·bour \ˈtam-ˌbu̇r, tam-ˈ\ *n* **1** : 1DRUM 1 **2 a** : an embroidery frame; *esp* : a set of two interlocking hoops between which cloth is stretched before stitching **b** : embroidery made on a tambour frame **3** : a rolling top or front (as of a desk) of narrow strips of wood glued on canvas [Medieval French "drum," from Arabic *ṭanbūr,* from Persian *tabīr*]

2tambour *vb* **1** : to embroider (cloth) with tambour **2** : to work at a tambour frame — **tam·bour·er** *n*

tam·bou·rine \ˌtam-bə-ˈrēn\ *n* : a small drum; *esp* : a shallow one-headed drum with loose metallic disks at the sides that is played especially by shaking or striking with the hand

tambourine

1tame \ˈtām\ *adj* **1** : changed from a state of native wildness especially so as to become useful and obedient to humans : DOMESTICATED ⟨a *tame* elephant⟩ **2** : made docile and submissive : SUBDUED **3** : lacking spirit, zest, or interest : INSIPID [Old English *tam*] — **tame·ly** *adv* — **tame·ness** *n*

2tame *vb* **1 a** : to make or become tame ⟨*tame* a lion⟩ **b** : to subject to cultivation ⟨wilderness *tamed* by farmers⟩ **2** : to deprive of spirit : HUMBLE, SUBDUE **3** : to tone down : SOFTEN — **tam·er** *n*

tame·less \ˈtām-ləs\ *adj* : not tamed or capable of being tamed

Ta·mil \ˈtam-əl, ˈtäm-\ *n* **1** : a Dravidian language of Tamil Nadu state, India, and of northern and eastern Sri Lanka **2** : a Tamil-speaking person or a descendant of Tamil-speaking ancestors

tam–o'–shan·ter \ˈtam-ə-ˌshant-ər\ *n* : a cap of Scottish origin with a tight headband, wide flat circular crown, and often a pompon in the center [*Tam o' Shanter,* hero of the poem *Tam o' Shanter* by Robert Burns]

tamp \ˈtamp\ *vt* **1** : to drive in or down by a succession of light or medium blows : COMPACT ⟨*tamp* wet concrete⟩ **2** : to put a check on : LESSEN ⟨*tamp* down rumors⟩ [probably from Middle English *tampion* "plug," from Middle French *tapon, tampon,* of Germanic origin] — **tamp·er** *n*

tam·per \ˈtam-pər\ *vi* **tam·pered; tam·per·ing** \-pə-ring, -pring\ **1** : to use underhanded or improper methods (as bribery) **2 a** : to interfere so as to cause a weakening or change for the worse **b** : to try foolish or dangerous experiments : MEDDLE [probably from Middle French *temprer* "to temper, mix, meddle"] — **tam·per·er** \-pər-ər\ *n*

tam·pi·on \ˈtam-pē-ən, ˈtäm-\ *n* : a wooden plug or a metal or canvas cover for the muzzle of a gun [Middle English, "plug"]

1tam·pon \ˈtam-ˌpän\ *n* : a wad of absorbent material (as of cotton) introduced into a body cavity or canal usually to absorb secretions (as from menstruation) or stop heavy or uncontrollable bleeding [French, literally, "plug"]

2tampon *vt* : to place or insert a tampon into

tam–tam \ˈtam-ˌtam, ˈtäm-ˌtäm\ *n* **1** : TOM-TOM **2** : GONG 1 [Hindi & Urdu *ṭamṭam*]

1tan \ˈtan\ *vb* **tanned; tan·ning 1** : to convert (hide) into leather by treatment with a solution (as of tannin) **2** : to make or become tan or brown by exposure to the sun **3** : THRASH 2a, WHIP [Medieval French *tanner,* from Medieval Latin *tannare,* from *tannum* "tanbark"]

2tan *n* **1** : TANBARK 1 **2** : a tanning material or its active agent (as tannin) **3** : a brown color imparted to the skin especially by exposure to the sun **4** : a light yellowish brown [French, from Medieval Latin *tannum*]

3tan *adj* **tan·ner; tan·nest** : of the color tan

tanager

tan·a·ger \ˈtan-i-jər\ *n* : any of numerous small mostly tropical American woodland birds that are often brightly colored — compare SCARLET TANAGER [Portuguese *tangará,* from Tupi]

tan·bark \ˈtan-ˌbärk\ *n* **1** : bark rich in tannin that is used in tanning **2** : a surface (as a circus ring) covered with spent tanbark

1tan·dem \ˈtan-dəm\ *n* **1 a** : a 2-seated carriage drawn by horses harnessed one before the other; *also* : a team so harnessed **b** : TANDEM BICYCLE **2** : a group of two or more arranged one behind the other or used or acting in conjunction [Latin, "at last, at length" (taken to mean "lengthwise")]

Word History When a pair of horses pulls a carriage, the two are usually harnessed side by side. But there is a type of carriage that is drawn by two horses harnessed one before the other. This carriage owes its name, *tandem,* to a rather contorted Latin-English pun. The Latin word *tandem* means "at length, at last, finally." We do not know who the punster was who first suggested that a carriage pulled by horses arranged lengthwise, "at length," should be called a *tandem,* but he or she need not have been a scholar. The Latin word is not a rare one and would be known to any student, however shallow, of the language. In English *tandem* came eventually to be used for any arrangement of things or of people one behind another.

2tandem *adv or adj* : one after or behind another

tandem bicycle *n* : a bicycle for two or more persons sitting tandem

tandem bicycle

1tang \ˈtang\ *n* **1** : a projecting part (as on a knife, file, or sword) to connect with the handle **2 a** : a sharp distinctive often lingering flavor **b** : a pungent odor **3 a** : a faint suggestion : TRACE **b** : a distinguishing characteristic that sets apart or gives a special individuality [of Scandinavian origin] — **tanged** \ˈtangd\ *adj*

2tang *vb* : CLANG, RING [imitative]

3tang *n* : a sharp twanging sound

Tang *or* **T'ang** \ˈtäng\ *n* : a Chinese dynasty dated A.D. 618–907 and marked by wide contacts with other cultures and by the development of printing and the flourishing of poetry and art [Chinese (Beijing dialect) *Táng*]

tan·ge·lo \ˈtan-jə-ˌlō\ *n, pl* **-los** : the fruit of a tree that is a hybrid between a tangerine and a grapefruit; *also* : the tree [blend of *tangerine* and *pomelo* "grapefruit" (from Dutch *pompelmoes*)]

tan·gen·cy \ˈtan-jən-sē\ *n, pl* **-cies** : the quality or state of being tangent

1tan·gent \-jənt\ *adj* **1 a** : touching a curve or surface at only one point in the given location ⟨straight line *tangent* to a curve⟩ **b (1)** : having a common tangent line at a point ⟨*tangent* curves⟩ **(2)** : having a common tangent plane at a point ⟨*tangent* surfaces⟩ **2** : diverging from an original purpose or course : IRRELEVANT ⟨*tangent* remarks⟩ [Latin *tangens,* from *linea tangens* "tangent line"]

2tangent *n* **1 a** : the trigonometric function that for an acute angle in a right triangle is the ratio of the side opposite the angle to the side adjacent — abbreviation *tan* **b** : a trigonometric function that is equal to the sine divided by the cosine for all real numbers θ for which the cosine is not equal to zero and that is exactly equal to the tangent of an angle of measure θ in radians **2** : a line that is tangent **3** : an abrupt change of course : DIGRESSION ⟨went off on a *tangent* and never got to the point⟩

tan·gen·tial \tan-ˈjen-chəl\ *adj* **1** : of, relating to, or of the nature of a tangent **2** : acting along or lying in a tangent ⟨*tangential* forces⟩ **3** : DIVERGENT, DIGRESSIVE ⟨*tangential* comment⟩ — **tan·gen·tial·ly** \-ˈjench-lē, -ə-lē\ *adv*

tan·ger·ine \ˈtan-jə-ˌrēn, ˌtan-jə-ˈ\ *n* **1** : any of various mandarin oranges having a usually deep orange skin and pulp **2** : a tree producing tangerines [French *Tanger* "Tangier, Morocco"]

1tan·gi·ble \ˈtan-jə-bəl\ *adj* **1 a** : capable of being perceived especially by the sense of touch : PALPABLE **b** : having substance or reality ⟨a *tangible* advantage⟩: MATERIAL **2** : capable of being appraised at an actual or approximate value ⟨*tangible* assets⟩ [Late Latin *tangibilis,* from Latin *tangere* "to touch"] — **tan·gi·bil·i·ty** \ˌtan-jə-ˈbil-ət-ē\ *n* — **tan·gi·ble·ness** \ˈtan-jə-bəl-nəs\ *n* — **tan·gi·bly** \-blē\ *adv*

[2]**tangible** *n* : something tangible; *esp* : a tangible asset

[1]**tan·gle** \ˈtang-gəl\ *vb* **tan·gled; tan·gling** \-gə-ling, -gling\ **1** : to make or become involved so as to hamper or embarrass : be or become entangled ⟨hopelessly *tangled* in argument⟩ **2** : to twist or become twisted together into a mass hard to straighten out again [Middle English *tanglen, tagilen,* probably from Medieval French *entagler, entangler* "to prosecute (for), implicate"]

[2]**tangle** *n* **1** : a tangled twisted mass (as of vines or hairs) confusedly interwoven **2** : a complicated or confused state or condition **3** : DISPUTE, ARGUMENT ⟨had a *tangle* with their neighbor⟩

tan·gle·ment \ˈtang-gəl-mənt\ *n* : ENTANGLEMENT

tan·gly \ˈtang-gə-lē, -glē\ *adj* **tan·gli·er; -est** : full of tangles

[1]**tan·go** \ˈtang-gō\ *n, pl* **tangos** : a ballroom dance of Latin-American origin marked by pauses between steps and a variety of body postures; *also* : music for this dance [American Spanish]

[2]**tango** *vi* : to dance the tango

tan·gram \ˈtang-grəm, ˈtan-\ *n* : a Chinese puzzle made by cutting a square of thin material into a number of pieces which can be recombined into many different figures [perhaps from Chinese (Beijing dialect) *táng* "Chinese" + English *-gram*]

tangy \ˈtang-ē\ *adj* **tang·i·er; -est** : having or suggestive of a tang ⟨a *tangy* smell⟩ — **tang·i·ness** *n*

[1]**tank** \ˈtangk\ *n* **1** : a usually large receptacle for holding, transporting, or storing liquids **2** : an enclosed heavily armed and armored combat vehicle that moves on tracks [Portuguese *tanque,* alteration of *estanque,* from *estancar* "to stanch"]

[2]**tank** *vt* : to place, store, or treat in a tank

tank·age \ˈtang-kij\ *n* **1** : the capacity or contents of a tank **2** : dried animal residues usually freed from the fat and gelatin and used as fertilizer and in feeds

tan·kard \ˈtang-kərd\ *n* : a tall one-handled drinking vessel; *esp* : a silver or pewter mug with a lid [Middle English]

tankard

tank car *n* : a railroad car for transporting liquids or gases in bulk

tank·er \ˈtang-kər\ *n* : a vehicle (as a ship, truck, or aircraft) designed for the transportation of liquids

tank·i·ni \tang-ˈkē-nē\ *n* : a woman's two-piece swimsuit consisting of bikini briefs and a tank top [blend of *tank (top)* and *bikini*]

tank top *n* : a sleeveless collarless shirt with usually wide shoulder straps and no front opening

tank town *n* : a small town [from the fact that formerly trains stopped at such towns only to take on water]

tan·nage \ˈtan-ij\ *n* : the act, process, or result of tanning

tan·ner \ˈtan-ər\ *n* : a person who tans hides

tan·nery \ˈtan-rē, -ə-rē\ *n, pl* **tan·ner·ies** : a place where hides are tanned

tan·nic acid \ˌtan-ik-\ *n* : TANNIN

tan·nin \ˈtan-ən\ *n* : any of various substances of plant origin used in tanning leather, dyeing textiles, manufacturing inks, and as an astringent [French, from *tanner* "to tan"]

tan·ning *n* **1** : the art or process by which an animal skin is tanned **2** : a browning of the skin especially by exposure to sunlight **3** : WHIPPING

tan·nish \ˈtan-ish\ *adj* : somewhat tan

tan·sy \ˈtan-zē\ *n, pl* **tansies** : any of a genus of mostly weedy herbs related to the daisies; *esp* : one with finely cut aromatic bitter-tasting leaves [Medieval French *tanesie,* from Late Latin *tanacita*]

tan·ta·lite \ˈtant-l-ˌīt\ *n* : a mineral consisting of a dark shiny oxide of tantalum and usually other metals (as iron)

tan·ta·lize \ˈtant-l-ˌīz\ *vt* : to tease or torment by or as if by presenting something desirable to the view but continually keeping it out of reach [*Tantalus*] — **tan·ta·liz·er** *n*

tan·ta·liz·ing *adj* : possessing a quality that arouses or stimulates desire or interest; *also* : mockingly or teasingly out of reach — **tan·ta·liz·ing·ly** \-ˌī-zing-lē\ *adv*

tan·ta·lum \ˈtant-l-əm\ *n* : a gray-white ductile acid-resisting metallic element found combined in rare minerals and used especially in electronic components — see ELEMENT table [New Latin, from Latin *Tantalus* "Tantalus"; from its inability to absorb acid]

tan·ta·mount \ˈtant-ə-ˌmau̇nt\ *adj* : equal in value, meaning, or effect [obsolete *tantamount,* n., "equivalent," from Anglo-French *tant amunter* "to amount to as much"]

tan·tara \tan-ˈtar-ə, -ˈtär-\ *n* : the blare of a trumpet or horn [Latin *taratantara,* of imitative origin]

[1]**tan·tivy** \tan-ˈtiv-ē\ *adv or adj* : at a gallop [origin unknown]

[2]**tantivy** *n* : a rapid gallop or ride : a headlong rush

tan·trum \ˈtan-trəm\ *n* : a fit of bad temper [origin unknown]

tan·yard \ˈtan-ˌyärd\ *n* : the section or part of a tannery housing tanning vats

Tao \ˈdau̇, ˈtau̇\ *n* **1 a** : the unknowable source and guiding principle of all reality according to Taoism **b** : the process of nature by which all things change and which is followed for a life of harmony **2** *often not cap* : the path of virtuous conduct according to Confucians [Chinese (Beijing dialect) *dào,* literally, "way"]

Tao·ism \-ˌiz-əm\ *n* **1** : a Chinese mystical philosophy traditionally founded by Lao-tzu in the 6th century B.C. that teaches conformity to the Tao by unassertive action and simplicity **2** : a religion developed from Taoist philosophy and Buddhist and folk religion and concerned with obtaining long life and good fortune often by magical means [*Tao*] — **Tao·ist** \-əst\ *adj or n* — **Tao·is·tic** \dau̇-ˈis-tik, tau̇-\ *adj*

[1]**tap** \ˈtap\ *n* **1 a** : FAUCET, SPIGOT **b** : liquor drawn through a tap **2** : the procedure of removing fluid from a container or cavity by tapping **3** : a tool for forming an internal screw thread **4** : an intermediate point in an electric circuit where a connection may be made **5** : WIRETAP [Old English *tæppa*] — **on tap 1** : ready to be drawn ⟨ale *on tap*⟩ **2** : on hand : AVAILABLE

[2]**tap** *vt* **tapped; tap·ping 1** : to release or cause to flow by piercing or by drawing a plug from the containing vessel or cavity ⟨*tap* wine from a cask⟩ **2 a** : to pierce so as to let out or draw off a fluid ⟨*tap* maple trees⟩ **b** : to draw from or upon ⟨*tap* the nation's resources⟩ **c** : to connect into (as a telephone or radio signal) to get information **3** : to form a female screw in by means of a tap — **tap·per** *n* — **tap into** : to make a strong or advantageous connection with ⟨trying to *tap into* a new market⟩

[3]**tap** *vb* **tapped; tap·ping 1** : to strike or rap lightly especially with a slight sound ⟨*tap* the desk with a pencil⟩ ⟨*tap* on the window⟩ **2** : to make or produce by repeated light blows ⟨a woodpecker *tapped* a hole in the tree⟩ **3** : to repair (a shoe) by putting a half sole on **4** : SELECT; *esp* : to elect to membership (as in a fraternity or sorority) [Middle French *taper* "to strike with the flat of the hand," of Germanic origin] — **tap·per** *n*

[4]**tap** *n* **1** : a light usually audible blow; *also* : its sound **2** : HALF SOLE **3** : a small metal plate for the sole or heel of a shoe (as for tap dancing)

ta·pa \ˈtäp-ə, ˈtap-\ *n* : the bark of a tree pounded to make a coarse cloth usually decorated with geometric patterns; *also* : this cloth [Tahitian]

tap dance *n* : a dance tapped out audibly with the feet — **tap-dance** \ˈtap-ˌdans\ *vi* — **tap dancer** *n* — **tap dancing** *n*

[1]**tape** \ˈtāp\ *n* **1** : a narrow band of woven fabric **2** : a string stretched breast-high above the finishing line of a race **3 a** : a narrow flexible strip or band; *esp* : MAGNETIC TAPE **b** : CASSETTE 2 **4** : a recording on magnetic tape [Old English *tæppe*]

[2]**tape** *vt* **1** : to fasten, tie, bind, cover, or support with tape **2** : to measure with a tape measure **3** : to record on magnetic tape

tape deck *n* : a device used to play back and often to record on magnetic tapes that usually has to be connected to a separate audio system

tape measure *n* : a tape marked off in units (as inches or centimeters) and used for measuring

[1]**ta·per** \ˈtā-pər\ *n* **1 a** : a long waxed wick used especially for lighting lamps, pipes, or fires; *also* : a slender candle **b** : a feeble light **2 a** : a tapering form or figure **b** : gradual lessening of thickness, diameter, or width in an elongated object **c** : a gradual decrease [Old English]

[2]**taper** *vb* **ta·pered; ta·per·ing** \-pə-ring, -pring\ **1** : to make or become gradually smaller toward one end **2** : to diminish gradually

tape–re·cord \ˌtā-pri-ˈkȯrd\ *vt* : to make a recording of on magnetic tape — **tape recording** *n*
tape recorder *n* : a device for recording on and playing back magnetic tapes
taper off *vb* : to stop or decrease gradually
tap·es·try \ˈtap-ə-strē\ *n, pl* **-tries** : a heavy textile used especially as a wall hanging or furniture covering [Medieval French *tapicerie,* from *tapit, tapis* "carpet, hanging," from Greek *tapēs* "carpet"] — **tap·es·tried** \-strēd\ *adj*
tapestry carpet *n* : a carpet in which the designs are printed in colors on the threads before the fabric is woven
tape·worm \ˈtāp-ˌwərm\ *n* : any of a class (Cestoda) of flatworms that are parasitic when adult in the intestine of vertebrates and consist of a scolex and an often long series of proglottids generated by a neck region — called also *cestode*
tap·hole \ˈtap-ˌhōl\ *n* : a hole for a tap; *esp* : a hole at or near the bottom of a furnace or ladle through which molten metal or slag can be tapped
tap·i·o·ca \ˌtap-ē-ˈō-kə\ *n* : a usually granular preparation of cassava starch used especially in puddings and as a thickening in liquid foods; *also* : a food (as pudding) containing tapioca [Portuguese, from Tupi *tipiˀóka*]
ta·pir \ˈtā-pər\ *n, pl* **tapirs** *also* **tapir** : any of several plant-eating chiefly nocturnal hoofed mammals of tropical America, and southeastern Asia that have long flexible snouts and very short tails and are related to the horses and rhinoceroses [Portuguese *tapir, tapira,* from Tupi *tapiˀira*]

tapir

tap·pet \ˈtap-ət\ *n* : a lever or projection moved by some other piece (as a cam) or intended to tap or touch something else to cause a particular motion [[3]*tap*]
tap·room \ˈtap-ˌrüm, -ˌrům\ *n* : BARROOM
tap·root \-ˌrüt, -ˌrůt\ *n* : a large main root that grows vertically downward and gives off smaller lateral roots — compare FIBROUS ROOT [[1]*tap*]
taps \ˈtaps\ *n sing or pl* : the last bugle call at night blown as a signal that lights are to be put out; *also* : a similar call blown at military funerals and memorial services [probably from earlier *taptoo* "tattoo"]
tap·ster \ˈtap-stər\ *n* : BARTENDER
tap water *n* : water as it comes from a tap (as in a home)
[1]**tar** \ˈtär\ *n* **1** : a dark usually odorous viscous liquid obtained by destructive distillation of organic material (as wood, coal, or peat) **2** : a substance that resembles tar; *esp* : a residue present in tobacco smoke that contains combustion by-products (as resins, acids, and phenols) **3** : SAILOR 1 [Old English *teoru*]
[2]**tar** *vt* **tarred; tar·ring** : to treat or smear with or as if with tar
tar·an·tel·la \ˌtar-ən-ˈtel-ə\ *n* : a lively folk dance of southern Italy in 6/8 time [Italian, from *Taranto,* Italy]
ta·ran·tu·la \tə-ˈranch-lə, -ə-lə; -ˈrant-l-ə\ *n* **1** : a large European spider whose bite was once thought to cause an uncontrollable desire to dance **2** : any of a family of large hairy American spiders that are mostly rather sluggish and have a sharp bite but are not very poisonous to humans [Medieval Latin, from Italian *tarantola,* from *Taranto,* Italy]

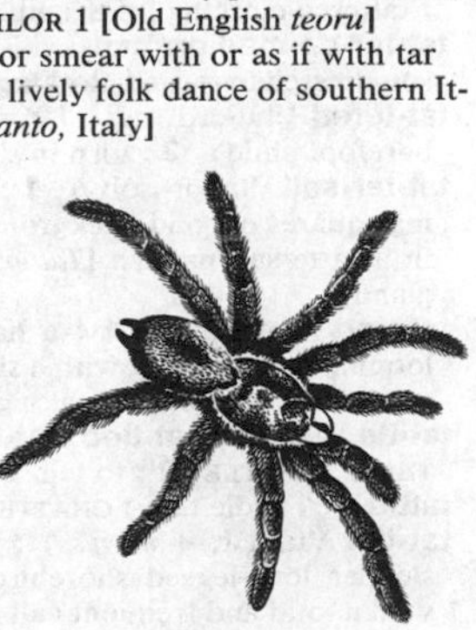
tarantula 2

tar·boosh *also* **tar·bush** \tär-ˈbüsh, ˈtär-ˌ\ *n* : a red hat similar to the fez worn especially by Muslim men [Arabic *ṭarbūsh*]
tar·dy \ˈtärd-ē\ *adj* **tar·di·er; -est** **1** : moving slowly : SLUGGISH **2** : being late or delayed [Medieval French *tardif,* derived from Latin *tardus*] — **tar·di·ly** \ˈtärd-l-ē\ *adv* — **tar·di·ness** \ˈtärd-ē-nəs\ *n*
[1]**tare** \ˈtaər, ˈteər\ *n* **1 a** : any of several vetches; *also* : the seed of a vetch **b** : a weed of grain fields mentioned in the Bible **2** *pl* : an undesirable element [Middle English]
[2]**tare** *n* : a deduction of weight made to allow for the weight of a container [Medieval French, from Italian *tara,* from Arabic *ṭarḥa*] — **tare** *vt*
targe \ˈtärj\ *n* : a light shield used especially by the Scots [Medieval French]
[1]**tar·get** \ˈtär-gət\ *n* **1 a** : a mark to shoot at **b** : a goal to be achieved : OBJECTIVE **2 a** : an object of ridicule or criticism **b** : something or someone to be affected by an action or development **3** : the surface usually of platinum or tungsten upon which the cathode rays within an X-ray tube are focused and from which the X-rays are emitted [Medieval French *targette, targuete* "small shield," from *targe* "light shield," of Germanic origin] — **off target** : not valid : INACCURATE — **on target** : precisely correct or valid especially in interpreting or addressing a problem or important issue
[2]**target** *vt* **1** : to make a target of ⟨*targeted* her for promotion⟩; *esp* : to set as a goal **2** : to direct or use toward a target
target date *n* : the date set for an event or for the completion of a project, goal, or quota
tar·iff \ˈtar-əf\ *n* **1 a** : a schedule of duties imposed by a government on imported or in some countries exported goods **b** : a duty or rate of duty imposed in such a schedule **2** : a schedule of rates or charges of a business or public utility [Italian *tariffa,* from Arabic *taʿrīf* "notification"]
tar·la·tan \ˈtär-lət-n\ *n* : a thin stiff transparent muslin [French *tarlatane*]
tar·mac \ˈtär-ˌmak\ *n* : a tarmacadam road, apron, or runway [from *Tarmac,* a trademark]
tar·mac \ˈtär-ˌmak\ *n* : a road, apron, or runway paved with layers of crushed stone covered with tar
tar·mac·ad·am \ˌtär-mə-ˈkad-əm\ *n* **1** : a pavement made by putting tar over courses of crushed stone and then rolling **2** : a material of tar and aggregates mixed in a plant and shaped on the roadway [*tar* + *macadam*]
tarn \ˈtärn\ *n* : a small mountain lake or pool usually of glacial origin [of Scandinavian origin]
[1]**tar·nish** \ˈtär-nish\ *vb* **1** : to make or become dull, dim, or discolored ⟨silver *tarnishes*⟩ **2** : to lessen the prestige or quality of ⟨a *tarnished* reputation⟩ [Medieval French *terniss-,* stem of *ternir* "to tarnish"] — **tar·nish·able** \-ə-bəl\ *adj*
[2]**tarnish** *n* : something that tarnishes; *esp* : a film of chemically altered material on the surface of a metal (as silver)
ta·ro \ˈtär-ō, ˈtar-, ˈter-\ *n, pl* **taros** : a large-leaved tropical Asian plant of the arum family grown throughout the tropics for its edible starchy rounded underground stem; *also* : the underground stem typically cooked as a vegetable or ground into flour [Tahitian and Maori]
tarp \ˈtärp\ *n* : TARPAULIN
tar paper *n* : a heavy paper coated or saturated with tar for use especially in building
tar·pau·lin \tär-ˈpȯ-lən, ˈtär-pə-\ *n* : a piece of material (as waterproof canvas) used for protecting exposed objects [probably derived from *tar* + *pall*]
tar·pon \ˈtär-pən\ *n, pl* **tarpon** *or* **tarpons** : a large silvery sport fish found in the Gulf of Mexico and warm coastal waters of the Atlantic Ocean [origin unknown]
tar·ra·gon \ˈtar-ə-ˌgän, -gən\ *n* : an herb grown for its aromatic narrow leaves; *also* : its leaves used as a seasoning [Middle French *targon,* from Medieval Latin *tarchon,* from Arabic *ṭarkhūn*]
[1]**tar·ry** \ˈtar-ē\ *vi* **tar·ried; tar·ry·ing** **1** : to be tardy : DELAY, LINGER **2** : to stay in or at a place [Middle English *tarien*]
[2]**tar·ry** \ˈtär-ē\ *adj* : of, resembling, or covered with tar
[1]**tar·sal** \ˈtär-səl\ *adj* : of or relating to the tarsus
[2]**tarsal** *n* : a tarsal part (as a bone or cartilage)
tar sand *n* : a natural saturation of sand or sandstone with heavy sticky portions of petroleum
tar·si·er \ˈtär-sē-ər, -sē-ˌā\ *n* : any of several small nocturnal arboreal primates of the Malay Archipelago related to the lemurs and having large round eyes, long legs, and a long nearly hair-

\ə\ abut	\au̇\ **out**	\i\ **tip**	\ȯ\ **saw**	\u̇\ **foot**
\ər\ **further**	\ch\ **chin**	\ī\ **life**	\ȯi\ **coin**	\y\ **yet**
\a\ mat	\e\ **pet**	\j\ **job**	\th\ **thin**	\yü\ **few**
\ā\ take	\ē\ **easy**	\ng\ **sing**	\t͟h\ **this**	\yu̇\ **cure**
\ä\ cot, cart	\g\ **go**	\ō\ **bone**	\ü\ **food**	\zh\ **vision**

less tail [French, from *tarse* "tarsus"] — **tar·si·oid** \-sē-ˌȯid\ *adj or n*

tar·so·meta·tar·sus \ˈtär-sō-ˈmet-ə-ˌtär-səs\ *n* : the large compound bone of the tarsus of a bird; *also* : the segment of the limb it supports

tar·sus \ˈtär-səs\ *n, pl* **tar·si** \-ˌsī, -ˌsē\ **1** : the part of the vertebrate foot between the metatarsus and the leg; *also* : the small bones that support this part of the foot and include bones of the ankle, heel, and arch **2** : the lower and longest part of a bird's leg **3** : the part of the limb of an arthropod (as an insect) most distant from the body [New Latin, from Greek *tarsos* "wickerwork mat, flat of the foot, ankle"]

1**tart** \ˈtärt\ *adj* **1** : agreeably sharp or acid to the taste **2** : sharp and unkind ⟨a *tart* reply⟩ [Old English *teart* "sharp, severe"] ***synonyms*** see SOUR — **tart·ly** *adv* — **tart·ness** *n*

2**tart** *n* **1** : a small pie or pastry shell containing jelly, custard, or fruit **2** : PROSTITUTE [Medieval French *tarte*]

tar·tan \ˈtärt-n\ *n* **1** : a plaid textile design of Scottish origin usually distinctively patterned to designate a clan **2** : a fabric or garment with tartan design [perhaps from Middle French *tiretaine* "linsey-woolsey"]

1**tar·tar** \ˈtärt-ər\ *n* **1** : a substance consisting essentially of cream of tartar found in the juice of grapes and deposited in wine casks as a reddish crust or sediment **2** : a hard crust that forms on the teeth and consists of plaque that has become hardened by the deposition of mineral salts (as calcium carbonate) [Medieval Latin *tartarum*]

2**tartar** *n* **1** *cap* : a native or inhabitant of Tatary **2** : a bad-tempered or unexpectedly formidable person [Middle French *Tartare,* probably from Medieval Latin *Tartarus,* from Persian *Tātār*] — **Tartar** *adj* — **Tar·tar·i·an** \tär-ˈtar-ē-ən, -ˈter-\ *adj*

tartar emetic *n* : a poisonous salt of sweetish metallic taste that is used in dyeing and especially formerly in medicine

tar·tar·ic acid \tär-ˌtar-ik-\ *n* : a strong organic acid $C_4H_6O_6$ that occurs in four forms, is usually obtained from grape tartar, and is used especially in food and medicines and in photography

tar·tar sauce *or* **tar·tare sauce** \ˌtärt-ər-\ *n* : a sauce made chiefly of mayonnaise and chopped pickles [French *sauce tartare*]

tart·ish \ˈtärt-ish\ *adj* : somewhat tart — **tart·ish·ly** *adv*

tart·let \ˈtärt-lət\ *n* : a small tart

tar·trate \ˈtär-ˌtrāt\ *n* : a salt or ester of tartaric acid

tase \ˈtāz\ *vb, often cap* **tased; tas·ing** : to shoot with a Taser gun

Tas·er \ˈtā-zər\ *trademark* — used for a gun that fires electrified darts to stun and immobilize a person

task \ˈtask\ *n* : a piece of work usually as assigned by another : DUTY, FUNCTION [Medieval French *tasque,* from Medieval Latin *tasca* "tax or service imposed by a feudal superior," from *taxare* "to tax"]

synonyms TASK, DUTY, ASSIGNMENT, JOB mean a piece of work to be done. TASK implies work imposed by one in authority or by circumstance ⟨every child had a daily *task* to perform⟩. DUTY implies an obligation to perform or responsibility for performance ⟨the limits of their *duties* as guardians⟩. ASSIGNMENT implies a definite limited task assigned by one in authority ⟨the student's *assignment*⟩. JOB applies to a piece of work one is asked to do or agrees to do voluntarily ⟨a helper to do *jobs* around the house⟩ and often stresses quality or difficulty of performance ⟨did a good *job* on the project⟩.

task force *n* : a temporary grouping especially of military units to accomplish a particular objective

task·mas·ter \ˈtask-ˌmas-tər\ *n* : one who imposes a task or burdens another with labor

task·mis·tress \-ˌmis-trəs\ *n* : a woman who is a taskmaster

Tas·ma·ni·an devil \taz-ˌmā-nē-ən-\ *n* : a heavily built burrowing flesh-eating marsupial of Tasmania that is about the size of a small dog and has powerful jaws and a mostly black coat

Tasmanian tiger *n* : a somewhat doglike flesh-eating marsupial formerly found in Tasmania but now considered extinct — called also *Tasmanian wolf*

1**tas·sel** \ˈtas-əl, *usually of corn* ˈtäs-, ˈtȯs-\ *n* **1** : a hanging ornament made of a bunch of cords of even length fastened at one end **2** : something resembling a tassel; *esp* : the terminal male inflorescence of some plants and especially corn [Medieval French, "clasp, tassel," from Latin *taxillus* "small die"]

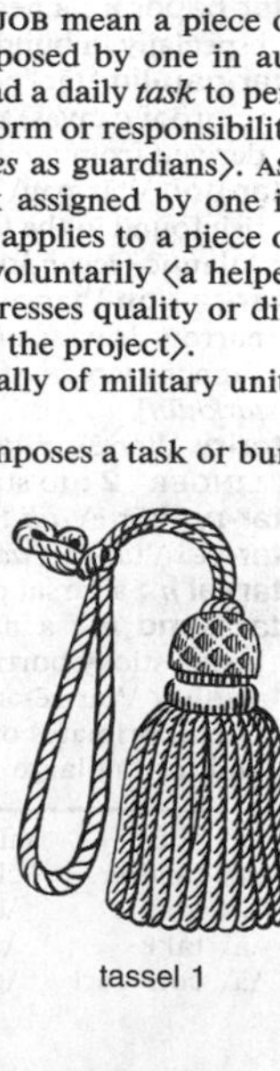

tassel 1

2**tassel** *vb* **-seled** *or* **-selled; -sel·ing** *or* **-sel·ling** \-ə-ling, -ling\ : to adorn with or put forth tassels

1**taste** \ˈtāst\ *vb* **1** : EXPERIENCE ⟨*taste* freedom⟩ **2** : to find out the flavor of by taking a little into the mouth **3** : to eat or drink especially in small quantities **4** : to perceive or recognize by or as if by the sense of taste ⟨can *taste* the garlic⟩ **5** : to have a specific flavor ⟨the food *tastes* sour⟩ [Medieval French *taster* "to touch, taste," derived from Latin *taxare* "to touch"]

2**taste** *n* **1 a** : a small amount tasted **b** : a small sample of experience ⟨their first *taste* of battle⟩ **2** : the special sense that perceives and distinguishes the sweet, sour, bitter, or salty quality of a dissolved substance and is mediated by taste buds on the tongue **3 a** : the objective quality of a dissolved substance perceptible to the sense of taste **b** : a complex sensation resulting from usually combined stimulation of the senses of taste, smell, and touch : FLAVOR **4** : the distinctive quality of an experience ⟨that gruesome scene left a bad *taste* in my mouth⟩ **5** : individual preference : INCLINATION ⟨has expensive *tastes*⟩ **6 a** : critical judgment, discernment, or appreciation ⟨a person of *taste*⟩ **b** : manner or aesthetic quality indicative of discernment or appreciation ⟨in bad *taste*⟩

synonyms TASTE, RELISH, GUSTO, ZEST mean a liking for something that gives pleasure. TASTE may imply a natural or acquired specific liking or interest ⟨a *taste* for classical music⟩. RELISH suggests a capability for keen gratification of appetite or other senses ⟨has little *relish* for sports⟩. GUSTO implies a heartiness in relishing that goes with vitality or high spirits ⟨a *gusto* for winning⟩. ZEST implies an eagerness for and keen perception of a thing's peculiar pleasure ⟨has a *zest* for living⟩.

taste bud *n* : any of the sensory organs by means of which taste is perceived and which are usually on the surface of the tongue

taste·ful \ˈtāst-fəl\ *adj* : having, showing, or conforming to good taste — **taste·ful·ly** \-fə-lē\ *adv* — **taste·ful·ness** *n*

taste·less \ˈtāst-ləs\ *adj* **1** : lacking flavor : FLAT, INSIPID ⟨*tasteless* soup⟩ **2** : not having or showing good taste ⟨*tasteless* decorations⟩ — **taste·less·ly** *adv* — **taste·less·ness** *n*

tast·er \ˈtā-stər\ *n* : one that tastes: as **a** : a person who samples food or drink prepared for another usually to test for poison **b** : a person able to taste the chemical phenylthiocarbamide

tasty \ˈtā-stē\ *adj* **tast·i·er; -est** **1** : pleasing to the taste : SAVORY **2** : very appealing or interesting ⟨a *tasty* bit of gossip⟩ — **tast·i·ly** \-stə-lē\ *adv* — **tast·i·ness** \-stē-nəs\ *n*

tat \ˈtat\ *vb* **tat·ted; tat·ting** : to work at or make by tatting [back-formation from *tatting*]

Ta·tar \ˈtät-ər\ *n* : a member of any of a group of Turkic peoples found mainly in the Tatar Republic of Russia and parts of Siberia and central Asia [Persian *Tātār,* of Turkic origin]

tat·ter \ˈtat-ər\ *n* **1** : a part torn and left hanging : SHRED **2** *pl* : tattered clothing [of Scandinavian origin] — **tatter** *vb*

tat·ter·de·ma·lion \ˌtat-ərd-i-ˈmāl-yən, -ˈmal-, -ē-ən\ *n* : a person dressed in ragged clothing : RAGAMUFFIN [origin unknown]

tat·tered \ˈtat-ərd\ *adj* **1** : wearing ragged clothes ⟨a *tattered* barefoot child⟩ **2** : torn in shreds : RAGGED ⟨a *tattered* flag⟩

tat·ter·sall \ˈtat-ər-ˌsȯl\ *n* **1** : a pattern of colored lines enclosing squares of solid background **2** : a fabric woven or printed in a tattersall pattern [*Tattersall's* horse market, London, England]

tat·ting \ˈtat-ing\ *n* **1** : a handmade lace formed usually by looping and knotting with a single thread and a small shuttle **2** : the act or process of making tatting [origin unknown]

1**tat·tle** \ˈtat-l\ *vb* **tat·tled; tat·tling** \ˈtat-ling, -l-ing\ **1** : CHATTER 2, PRATTLE **2** : to tell secrets [Dutch *tatelen*]

2**tattle** *n* **1** : idle talk : CHATTER **2** : GOSSIP 2, TALEBEARING

tat·tler \ˈtat-lər, -l-ər\ *n* **1** : TATTLETALE **2** : any of various slender long-legged shorebirds (as the willet and yellowlegs) with a loud and frequent call

tat·tle·tale \ˈtat-l-ˌtāl\ *n* : one that tattles : INFORMER

1**tat·too** \ta-ˈtü\ *n, pl* **tattoos** **1 a** : a call sounded shortly before taps as notice to go to quarters **b** : an outdoor military exercise given by troops as evening entertainment **2** : a rapid rhythmic rapping ⟨hoofs beating a *tattoo* on the road⟩ [Dutch *taptoe,* from the phrase *tap toe!* "taps shut!"]

2**tattoo** *n* : an indelible mark or figure fixed on the body by insertion of pigment under the skin or by production of scars [Tahitian *tatau*]

[3]tattoo *vt* **1 :** to mark or color (the skin) with a tattoo **2 :** to mark the skin with (a tattoo) — **tat·too·er** *n*

tau \ˈtaů, ˈtȯ\ *n* **:** the 19th letter of the Greek alphabet — T or τ

taught *past of* TEACH

taunt \ˈtȯnt, ˈtänt\ *vt* **:** to reproach or challenge in a mocking or insulting way **:** jeer at [perhaps from Middle French *tenter* "to try, tempt"] ***synonyms*** see RIDICULE — **taunt** *n* — **taunt·er** *n* — **taunt·ing·ly** \-ing-lē\ *adv*

taupe \ˈtōp\ *n* **:** a brownish gray [French, literally, "mole," from Latin *talpa*]

[1]tau·rine \ˈtȯr-ˌīn\ *adj* **:** of or relating to a bull; *also* **:** BOVINE [Latin *taurinus,* from *taurus* "bull"]

[2]tau·rine \ˈtȯr-ˌēn\ *n* **:** a crystalline acid formed in the body from cysteine and methionine that is similar to amino acids but is not a component of proteins [Latin *taurus* "bull"]

Tau·rus \ˈtȯr-əs\ *n* **1 :** a zodiacal constellation that contains the Pleiades and Hyades **2 :** the 2nd sign of the zodiac; *also* **:** one born under this sign [Latin, literally, "bull"]

taut \ˈtȯt\ *adj* **1 a :** tightly drawn **:** not slack ⟨a *taut* rope⟩ **b :** HIGH-STRUNG, TENSE ⟨*taut* nerves⟩ **2 a :** kept in proper order or condition ⟨a *taut* ship⟩ **b :** not loose or flabby **:** FIRM ⟨*taut* muscles⟩ [Middle English *tought*] ***synonyms*** see TIGHT — **taut·ly** *adv* — **taut·ness** *n*

taut·en \ˈtȯt-n\ *vb* **taut·ened; taut·en·ing** \ˈtȯt-ning, -n-ing\ **:** to make or become taut

tau·tog \ˈtȯ-ˌtȯg\ *n* **:** an edible fish related to the wrasses and found along the Atlantic coast of the U.S. and Canada — called also *blackfish* [Narragansett (Algonquian language of Rhode Island) *tautaŭog,* pl.]

tau·tol·o·gy \tȯ-ˈtäl-ə-jē\ *n, pl* **-gies :** needless repetition of an idea, statement, or word; *also* **:** an instance of such repetition ⟨"a beginner who has just started" is a *tautology*⟩ [Late Latin *tautologia,* from Greek, from *tautologos* "tautologous," from *tauto* "the same" (contraction of *to auto*) + *legein* "to say"] — **tau·to·log·i·cal** \ˌtȯt-l-ˈäj-i-kəl\ *adj* — **tau·to·log·i·cal·ly** \-kə-lē, -klē\ *adv* — **tau·tol·o·gous** \tȯ-ˈtäl-ə-gəs\ *adj* — **tau·tol·o·gous·ly** *adv*

tav·ern \ˈtav-ərn\ *n* **1 :** an establishment where alcoholic beverages are sold to be drunk on the premises **2 :** INN 1 [Medieval French *taverne,* from Latin *taberna,* literally, "shed, hut, shop"]

tav·ern·er \ˈtav-ər-nər, ˈtav-ə-nər\ *n* **:** one who keeps a tavern

taw \ˈtȯ\ *n* **1 :** a playing marble used as a shooter **2 :** the line from which players shoot at marbles [origin unknown]

taw·dry \ˈtȯd-rē, ˈtäd-\ *adj* **taw·dri·er; -est :** cheap and gaudy in appearance and quality [*tawdry lace* "tie of lace for the neck," from *Saint Audrey* (Etheldreda), died 679, queen of Northumbria] ***synonyms*** see GAUDY — **taw·dri·ly** \-rə-lē\ *adv* — **taw·dri·ness** \-rē-nəs\ *n*

Word History When Etheldreda, queen of Northumbria, renounced her husband and her royal position and became a nun, she was soon appointed abbess of a monastery in the Isle of Ely. She was renowned for her saintliness and is said to have died of a swelling in her throat, which she took as a judgment upon her fondness for wearing necklaces in her youth. An annual fair was held in Saint Etheldreda's honor on 17 October, and her name became simplified to *Saint Audrey.* At these fairs cheap knickknacks were sold, among them a type of necklace called "Saint Audrey's lace," which was eventually altered to "tawdry lace." *Tawdry* came to be used for other cheap finery and is now an adjective meaning "cheap and gaudy."

[1]taw·ny \ˈtȯ-nē, ˈtän-ē\ *adj* **taw·ni·er; -est :** of the color tawny [Medieval French *tané, tauné,* past participle of *tanner* "to tan"] — **taw·ni·ness** *n*

[2]tawny *n, pl* **tawnies :** a brownish orange to light brown color

[1]tax \ˈtaks\ *vt* **1 :** to levy a tax on **2 :** to call to account **:** ACCUSE ⟨*taxed* him with neglect of duty⟩; *also* **:** CENSURE **3 :** to make heavy and rigorous demands on **:** subject to excessive stress ⟨the job *taxed* my strength⟩ [Medieval French *taxer,* from Medieval Latin *taxare,* from Latin, "to feel, estimate, censure," from *tangere* "to touch"] — **tax·abil·i·ty** \ˌtak-sə-ˈbil-ət-ē\ *n* — **tax·able** \ˈtak-sə-bəl\ *adj* — **tax·er** *n*

[2]tax *n* **1 a :** a charge usually of money imposed by authority upon persons or property for public purposes **b :** a sum levied on members of an organization to defray expenses **2 :** a heavy demand ⟨the trip would be too great a *tax* on your health⟩

tax·a·tion \tak-ˈsā-shən\ *n* **1 :** the action of taxing; *esp* **:** the imposition of taxes **2 :** income obtained from taxes

tax evasion *n* **:** deliberate failure to pay taxes usually by false reports of taxable income or property

tax–ex·empt \ˌtak-sig-ˈzemt, -ˈzempt\ *adj* **1 :** exempted from a tax **2 :** bearing interest free from federal or state income tax ⟨*tax-exempt* securities⟩

[1]taxi \ˈtak-sē\ *n, pl* **tax·is** \-sēz\ *also* **tax·ies :** TAXICAB; *also* **:** a similarly operated boat or airplane

[2]taxi *vb* **tax·ied; taxi·ing; tax·is** *or* **tax·ies 1 :** to operate or move at low speed along the surface of the ground ⟨the plane *taxied* to the hangar⟩ **2 a :** to ride in a taxicab **b :** to transport by taxi

taxi·cab \ˈtak-sē-ˌkab\ *n* **:** an automobile that carries passengers for a fare usually determined by the distance traveled and often shown by a meter [earlier *taxi*meter *cab*]

taxi dancer *n* **:** a woman employed by a dance hall, café, or cabaret to dance with patrons who pay a certain amount for each dance

taxi·der·my \ˈtak-sə-ˌdər-mē\ *n* **:** the skill or occupation of preparing, stuffing, and mounting skins of animals [derived from Greek *taxis* "arrangement" + *derma* "skin"] — **taxi·der·mic** \ˌtak-sə-ˈdər-mik\ *adj* — **taxi·der·mist** \ˈtak-sə-ˌdər-məst\ *n*

taxi·me·ter \ˈtak-sē-ˌmēt-ər\ *n* **:** an instrument for use in a hired vehicle (as a taxicab) for automatically showing the fare due [French *taximètre,* from German *Taxameter,* from Medieval Latin *taxa* "tax, charge" (from *taxare* "to tax") + German *-meter* "-meter"]

tax·is \ˈtak-səs\ *n, pl* **tax·es** \ˈtak-ˌsēz\ **:** reflex movement by a freely moving organism in relation to a source of stimulation (as a light or a temperature or chemical gradient); *also* **:** a reflex reaction involving such movement — compare TROPISM [Greek, "arrangement," from *tassein* "to arrange"]

taxi stand *n* **:** a place where taxis may park awaiting hire

tax·on \ˈtak-ˌsän\ *n, pl* **taxa** \-sə\ *also* **tax·ons :** a taxonomic group or entity; *also* **:** its name in a formal system of nomenclature [back-formation from *taxonomy*]

tax·on·o·my \tak-ˈsän-ə-mē\ *n* **1 :** the study of scientific classification **:** SYSTEMATICS **2 a :** CLASSIFICATION 2a(1) **b :** orderly classification of plants and animals according to their presumed natural relationships [French *taxonomie,* from Greek *taxis* "arrangement" + *nomos* "system of laws"] — **tax·o·nom·ic** \ˌtak-sə-ˈnäm-ik\ *adj* — **tax·o·nom·i·cal·ly** \-ˈnäm-i-kə-lē, -klē\ *adv* — **tax·on·o·mist** \tak-ˈsän-ə-məst\ *n*

tax·pay·er \ˈtak-ˌspā-ər\ *n* **:** one that pays or is subject to a tax

tax·us \ˈtak-səs\ *n, pl* **tax·us** \-səs\ **:** YEW 1a [Latin]

Tay–Sachs disease \ˈtā-ˈsaks-\ *n* **:** a hereditary disease that is caused by an enzyme deficiency, is marked by a build-up of lipids especially in nerve tissues, occurs especially in individuals of eastern European Jewish ancestry, and causes death in early childhood — called also *Tay-Sachs* [Warren Tay, died 1927, British physician, and Bernard P. Sachs, died 1944, American neurologist]

TB \tē-ˈbē, ˈtē-\ *n* **:** TUBERCULOSIS [*TB* (abbreviation for *tubercle bacillus*)]

T–ball \ˈtē-ˌbȯl\ *n* **:** baseball for youngsters in which the ball is batted from a tee rather than being pitched [[2]*tee*]

T–bone \ˈtē-ˌbōn\ *n* **:** a small beefsteak from behind the ribs containing a T-shaped bone and a small piece of tenderloin

T cell \ˈte-ˌsel\ *n* **:** any of several lymphocytes (as a helper T cell) that differentiate in the thymus and include some that exert control over immune functions and others that destroy antigen-bearing cells — called also *T lymphocyte*; compare B CELL [*t*hymus-derived *cell*]

TCP/IP \ˌtē-ˌsē-ˈpē-ˌī-ˈpē\ *n* **:** a set of communications protocols used for the exchange of information over networks (as the Internet) [*t*ransmission-*c*ontrol *p*rotocol/*I*nternet *p*rotocol]

tea \ˈtē\ *n* **1 a :** a shrub related to the camellia that has fragrant white flowers and is grown mainly in China, Japan, India, and Sri Lanka **b :** the leaves and leaf buds of this plant prepared for use in beverages usually by immediate curing by heat or by such curing following a period of fermentation **2 :** an aromatic beverage prepared from tea leaves by soaking them in boiling water **3 :** any of various plants used like tea; *also* **:** a drink prepared by soaking their parts (as leaves or roots) and used medicinally or as a beverage ⟨mint *tea*⟩ **4 a :** a late afternoon serving of tea and a light meal **b :** a reception, snack, or meal at which tea is served **5** *slang* **:** MARIJUANA 2 [Chinese (Xiamen dialect) *dê*]

tea bag *n* **:** a bag usually of filter paper holding enough tea for an individual serving

tea ball *n* **:** a perforated metal ball that holds tea leaves and is used in brewing tea in a pot or cup

tea ball

tea·ber·ry \ˈtē-ˌber-ē\ *n* **:** CHECKERBERRY [from the use of its leaves as a substitute for tea]

teach \ˈtēch\ *vb* **taught** \ˈtȯt\; **teach·ing 1 a :** to cause to know or understand ⟨*taught* us German⟩ **b :** to assist in learning how to do something **:** show how ⟨*teach* a child to read⟩ **2 :** to guide the studies of **:** INSTRUCT ⟨*teach* a class⟩ **3 :** to give lessons in **:** instruct pupils in ⟨*teach* music⟩ **4 :** to be or work as a teacher ⟨was *teaching* in Chicago⟩ **5 :** to cause to learn **:** cause to know the consequences of an action ⟨*taught* by experience⟩ [Old English *tǣcan*] ***usage*** see LEARN

synonyms TEACH, INSTRUCT, EDUCATE, TRAIN mean to cause to acquire knowledge or skill. TEACH applies to any manner of imparting information or skill so that others may learn ⟨*taught* us a lot about our planet⟩. INSTRUCT suggests methodical or formal teaching ⟨*instructed* them in swimming⟩. EDUCATE implies development of the mind ⟨more things than formal schooling serve to *educate* a person⟩. TRAIN stresses the end in view and usually implies practice and drill as the means to that end ⟨*train* an apprentice in a trade⟩ ⟨toilet-*train* a young child⟩.

teach·able \ˈtē-chə-bəl\ *adj* **1 :** capable of being taught; *esp* **:** apt and willing to learn **2 :** well adapted for use in teaching ⟨a *teachable* textbook⟩ — **teach·abil·i·ty** \ˌtē-chə-ˈbil-ət-ē\ *n*

teach·er \ˈtē-chər\ *n* **:** one that teaches; *esp* **:** one whose occupation is to instruct

teachers college *n* **:** a college for the training of teachers usually offering a full 4-year course and granting a bachelor's degree

teach–in \ˈtē-ˌchin\ *n* **:** a get-together especially of college students and faculty for discussion especially of a controversial public issue

[1]**teach·ing** *n* **1 :** the act, practice, or profession of a teacher **2 :** something taught; *esp* **:** DOCTRINE

[2]**teaching** *adj* **:** of, relating to, used for, or engaged in teaching ⟨a *teaching* aid⟩ ⟨the *teaching* profession⟩

tea·cup \ˈtē-ˌkəp\ *n* **:** a small cup used with a saucer for hot beverages — **tea·cup·ful** \ˈtē-ˌkəp-ˌfu̇l\ *n*

tea dance *n* **:** a dance held in the late afternoon

tea·house \ˈtē-ˌhau̇s\ *n* **:** a public house or restaurant where tea and light refreshments are sold

teak \ˈtēk\ *n* **1 :** a tall tropical Asian timber tree related to the vervains **2 :** the hard durable yellowish brown wood of teak [Portuguese *teca,* from Malayalam (the Dravidian language of Kerala, southwest India) *tēkka*]

tea·ket·tle \ˈtē-ˌket-l\ *n* **:** a covered kettle that is used for boiling water and that has a handle and spout

teak·wood \ˈtē-ˌkwu̇d\ *n* **:** TEAK 2

teal \ˈtēl\ *n, pl* **teal** *or* **teals :** any of various widely distributed small short-necked ducks [Middle English *tele*]

[1]**team** \ˈtēm\ *n* **1 :** a group of animals: as **a :** two or more draft animals harnessed to the same vehicle or implement; *also* **:** one or more animals with harness and attached vehicle **b :** a brood especially of young pigs or ducks **c :** a matched group of animals for exhibition **2 :** a number of persons associated together in work or activity: as **a :** a group on one side (as in football or a debate) **b :** CREW 2a, GANG [Old English *tēam* "group of draft animals"]

[2]**team** *vb* **1 :** to yoke or join in a team **2 :** to haul with or drive a team **3 :** to form a team ⟨*team* up together⟩

team handball *n* **:** a game developed from soccer which is played between two teams of seven players and in which the ball is thrown, caught, and dribbled with the hands

team·mate \ˈtēm-ˌmāt\ *n* **:** a fellow member of a team

team·ster \ˈtēm-stər, ˈtēmp-\ *n* **:** one who drives a team or truck especially as an occupation

team·work \ˈtēm-ˌwərk\ *n* **:** the work or activity of a number of persons acting in close association as members of a unit ⟨*teamwork* won the game⟩

tea·pot \ˈtē-ˌpät\ *n* **:** a vessel that is used for brewing and serving tea and that has a spout

[1]**tear** \ˈtiər\ *n* **1 :** a drop of the salty liquid that keeps the eye and the inner eyelids moist **2 :** a transparent drop of fluid or hardened fluid matter (as resin) **3** *pl* **:** an act of crying or grieving ⟨burst into *tears*⟩ [Old English *tæhher, tēar*] — **teary** \ˈtiər-ē\ *adj*

[2]**tear** *vi* **:** to shed tears

[3]**tear** \ˈtaər, ˈteər\ *vb* **tore** \ˈtōər, ˈtȯər\; **torn** \ˈtōrn, ˈtȯrn\; **tear·ing 1 a :** to separate or pull apart by force **:** REND **b :** to wound by or as if by tearing **:** LACERATE ⟨*tear* the skin⟩ **2 :** to divide or disrupt by the pull of contrary forces ⟨a mind *torn* by doubts⟩ **3 :** to remove by force ⟨children *torn* from their families⟩ **4 :** to cause or make by force or violent means ⟨*tore* a hole in the wall⟩ **5 :** to move or act with violence, haste, or force ⟨*tore* down the street⟩ [Old English *teran*] — **tear·er** *n*

[4]**tear** \ˈtaər, ˈteər\ *n* **1 a :** the act of tearing **b :** damage from being torn; *esp* **:** a torn place **2 a :** a hurried pace **:** HURRY **b :** SPREE ⟨got paid and went on a *tear*⟩

tear down *vt* **1 a :** to cause to decompose or disintegrate **:** DESTROY **b :** VILIFY 2, DENIGRATE **2 :** to take apart

tear·drop \ˈtiər-ˌdräp\ *n* **1 :** [1]TEAR 1 **2 :** something (as a pendent gem) shaped like a dropping tear

tear·ful \ˈtiər-fəl\ *adj* **:** flowing with, accompanied by, or causing tears — **tear·ful·ly** \-fə-lē\ *adv* — **tear·ful·ness** *n*

tear gas *n* **:** a solid, liquid, or gaseous substance that causes eye irritation and blinds the eyes with tears when released into the air and that is used mostly to scatter mobs — **tear·gas** \ˈtiər-ˌgas\ *vt*

tear·jerk·er \ˈtiər-ˌjər-kər\ *n* **:** a story, song, play, film, or broadcast that moves or is intended to move its audience to tears — **tear·jerk·ing** \-king\ *adj*

tea·room \ˈtē-ˌrüm, -ˌru̇m\ *n* **:** a small restaurant serving light meals

tea rose *n* **:** a garden bush rose of Chinese origin having abundant large usually tea-scented blossoms

tear·stain \ˈtiər-ˌstān\ *n* **:** a spot or streak left by tears — **tear·stained** \-ˌstānd\ *adj*

tear up *vt* **1 :** to damage, remove, or bring about an opening in ⟨*tore up* the street to lay new water pipes⟩ **2 :** to perform or compete with great success on, in, or against ⟨couples *tearing up* the dance floor⟩

[1]**tease** \ˈtēz\ *vt* **1 a :** to disentangle and lay parallel by combing or carding ⟨*tease* wool⟩ **b :** TEASEL **2 a :** to annoy persistently **:** PESTER **b :** TANTALIZE **c :** to make fun of [Old English *tǣsan*] — **teas·er** *n*

[2]**tease** *n* **1 :** the act of teasing **:** the state of being teased **2 :** one that teases

[1]**tea·sel** \ˈtē-zəl\ *n* **1 :** an Old World prickly herb with flower heads that are covered with stiff hooked bracts — called also *fuller's teasel* **2 :** a dried flower head of the teasel used to raise a nap on woolen cloth; *also* **:** a wire substitute for this **3 :** a plant related to the teasel [Old English *tǣsel*]

teasel 1

[2]**teasel** *vt* **-seled** *or* **-selled; -sel·ing** *or* **-sel·ling** \ˈtēz-ling, -ə-ling\ **:** to raise a nap on (cloth) with teasels

tea·spoon \ˈtē-ˌspün, -ˈspün\ *n* **1 :** a small spoon used especially for eating soft foods and stirring beverages **2 :** a unit of measure used especially in cookery equal to 1/6 fluid ounce or 1/3 tablespoon (about 5 mililiters)

tea·spoon·ful \-ˌfu̇l\ *n, pl* **-spoonfuls** \-ˌfu̇lz\ *also* **-spoons·ful** \-ˌspünz-ˌfu̇l, -ˈspünz-\ **1 :** as much as a teaspoon can hold **2 :** TEASPOON 2

teat \ˈtit, ˈtēt\ *n* **1 :** the protuberance through which milk is drawn from an udder or breast **:** NIPPLE **2 :** a small projection (as on a mechanical part) [Medieval French *tete,* of Germanic origin] — **teat·ed** \-əd\ *adj*

teatime \ˈtē-ˌtīm\ *n* **:** the customary time for tea **:** late afternoon or early evening

tea wagon *n* **:** a small table on wheels used in serving tea and light refreshments

[1]**tech** \ˈtek\ *n* : TECHNICIAN ⟨lab *techs*⟩ ⟨a computer *tech*⟩
[2]**tech** *n* : TECHNOLOGY
tech·ne·tium \tek-ˈnē-shē-əm, -shəm\ *n* : a radioactive metallic element obtained especially from nuclear fuel as a product of uranium fission — see ELEMENT table [New Latin, from Greek *technētos*, "artificial," derived from *technē* "art"]
tech·nic \ˈtek-nik, *for 1 also* tek-ˈnēk\ *n* **1** : TECHNIQUE 1 **2** *pl* : TECHNOLOGY 1a
tech·ni·cal \ˈtek-ni-kəl\ *adj* **1 a** : having special usually practical knowledge especially of a mechanical or scientific subject ⟨*technical* experts⟩ **b** : marked by or characteristic of specialization ⟨a *technical* language⟩ **2** : of or relating to a particular subject; *esp* : of or relating to a practical subject organized on scientific principles ⟨*technical* training⟩ **3** : existing by application of laws or rules **4** : of or relating to technique **5** : of, relating to, or produced by commercial processes ⟨*technical* sulfuric acid⟩ [Greek *technikos* "of art, skillful," from *technē* "art, skill"] — **tech·ni·cal·ly** \-kə-lē, -klē\ *adv*
technical foul *n* : a foul that is less serious than a personal foul or that involves unsportsmanlike conduct
tech·ni·cal·i·ty \ˌtek-nə-ˈkal-ət-ē\ *n, pl* **-ties** **1** : the quality or state of being technical **2** : something technical; *esp* : a detail meaningful only to a specialist
technical knockout *n* : the termination of a boxing match when one boxer is unable or is declared by the referee to be unable to continue — called also *TKO*
technical sergeant *n* : an enlisted rank in the Air Force above staff sergeant and below master sergeant
tech·ni·cian \tek-ˈnish-ən\ *n* : a specialist in the technical details or in the technique of a subject, art, or occupation
tech·nique \tek-ˈnēk\ *n* **1** : the way in which technical details are treated (as by a writer) or basic physical movements are used (as by a dancer); *also* : ability to treat such details or use such movements ⟨good piano *technique*⟩ **2 a** : technical methods (as in scientific research) ⟨laboratory *technique*⟩ **b** : a method of accomplishing a desired aim [French, from *technique* "technical," from Greek *technikos*]
tech·noc·ra·cy \tek-ˈnäk-rə-sē\ *n, pl* **-cies** : management of society by technical experts — **tech·no·crat** \ˈtek-nə-ˌkrat\ *n*
tech·no·log·i·cal \ˌtek-nə-ˈläj-i-kəl\ *also* **tech·no·log·ic** \-ˈläj-ik\ *adj* : of, relating to, or characterized or caused by technology — **tech·no·log·i·cal·ly** \-ˈläj-i-kə-lē, -klē\ *adv*
tech·nol·o·gy \tek-ˈnäl-ə-jē\ *n, pl* **-gies** **1 a** : the application of knowledge especially in a particular area : ENGINEERING 2 ⟨medical *technology*⟩ **b** : a technical method of achieving a practical purpose **2** : a manner of accomplishing a task especially using technical processes, methods, or knowledge ⟨new *technologies* for information storage⟩ [Greek *technologia* "systematic treatment of an art," from *technē* "art" + *-logia* "-logy"] — **tech·nol·o·gist** \-jəst\ *n*
tech·no–pop \ˈtek-nō-ˌpäp\ *n* : popular music featuring extensive use of synthesizers
tec·ton·ic \tek-ˈtän-ik\ *adj* : of or relating to tectonics [Greek *tektonikos* "of a builder," from *tektōn* "builder"]
tec·ton·ics \-iks\ *n sing or pl* **1** : a branch of geology concerned with the structure of the crust of a planet (as earth) or moon and especially with the formation of folds and faults in it **2** : TECTONISM
tec·to·nism \ˈtek-tə-ˌniz-əm\ *n* : the process of deformation that produces the earth's continents, ocean basins, mountains, folds, and faults
ted·dy bear \ˈted-ē-\ *n* : a stuffed toy bear [*Teddy*, nickname of President Theodore Roosevelt; from a cartoon showing him sparing the life of a bear cub while hunting]
Te Deum \tā-ˈdā-əm, tē-ˈdē-\ *n, pl* **Te Deums** : a hymn of praise to God [Late Latin *Te Deum laudamus* "Thee, God, we praise"]
te·dious \ˈtēd-ē-əs, ˈtē-jəs\ *adj* : tiresome because of length or dullness : BORING — **te·dious·ly** *adv* — **te·dious·ness** *n*
te·di·um \ˈtēd-ē-əm\ *n* : the quality or state of being tedious : TEDIOUSNESS, BOREDOM [Latin *taedium* "disgust, irksomeness," from *taedēre* "to disgust, weary"]
[1]**tee** \ˈtē\ *n* **1** : the letter *t* **2** : something shaped like a capital *T* [Middle English] — **to a tee** : in a perfect manner : EXACTLY
[2]**tee** \ˈtē\ *n* **1 a** : a small mound or a peg on which a golf ball is placed before being struck at the beginning of play on a hole **b** : a device for holding a football in position for kicking **c** : an adjustable post on which a ball is placed for batting (as in T-ball) **2** : the area from which a golf ball is struck in starting play on a hole [origin unknown]
[3]**tee** *vt* **teed tee·ing** : to place (a ball) on a tee — often used with *up*
teem \ˈtēm\ *vi* **1** : to become filled to overflowing : ABOUND ⟨lakes *teeming* with fish⟩ **2** : to be present in large quantity [Old English *tīman, tǣman* "to bring forth, give birth to"]
teen \ˈtēn\ *adj* : TEENAGER — **teen** *adj*
teen·age \ˈtē-ˌnāj\ *or* **teen·aged** \ˈtē-ˌnājd\ *adj* : of, being, or relating to people in their teens
teen·ag·er \-ˌnā-jər\ *n* : a teenage person
teens \ˈtēnz\ *n pl* **1** : the numbers 13 through 19; *esp* : the years 13 through 19 in a lifetime or century **2** : teenage people [*-teen* (as in *thirteen*)]
tee·ny \ˈtē-nē\ *adj* **tee·ni·er; -est** : TINY [by alteration]
teeny·bop·per \-ˌbäp-ər\ *n* : a young teenager who is enthusiastically devoted to popular music and to current fads [*teeny* "teenager" + *bopper*, perhaps from *bop* "to go quickly or unceremoniously"]
tee off *vi* **1** : to drive a golf ball from a tee at the beginning of play on a hole **2** : BEGIN 1, START
teepee *variant of* TEPEE
tee shirt *variant of* T-SHIRT
tee·ter \ˈtēt-ər\ *vi* **1 a** : to move unsteadily **b** : WAVER 1, VACILLATE **2** : SEESAW 1b [Middle English *titeren* "to totter, reel"] — **teeter** *n*
tee·ter·board \-ˌbōrd, -ˌbȯrd\ *n* **1** : SEESAW 2b **2** : a board placed on a raised support in such a way that a person standing on one end of the board is thrown into the air if another person jumps on the opposite end
tee·ter–tot·ter \ˈtēt-ər-ˌtät-ər\ *n* : SEESAW 2b
teeth *plural of* TOOTH
teethe \ˈtēth\ *vi* **teethed; teeth·ing** : to experience the emergence of one's teeth through the gums : grow teeth
teeth·ridge \ˈtē-ˌthrij\ *n* : the inner surface of the gums of the upper front teeth
tee·to·tal·er *or* **tee·to·tal·ler** \ˈtē-ˈtōt-l-ər\ *n* : a person who practices or advocates teetotalism [*t*otal + *total* (abstinence)]
tee·to·tal·ism \-l-ˌiz-əm\ *n* : the principle or practice of complete abstinence from drinking alcoholic beverages
Tef·lon \ˈtef-ˌlän\ *trademark* — used for synthetic fluorine-containing resins used especially for nonstick coatings
tek·tite \ˈtek-ˌtīt\ *n* : a glassy body of probably meteoric origin and of rounded but indefinite shape [Greek *tēktos* "molten," from *tēkein* "to melt"]
tel·co \ˈtel-kō\ *n* : a telecommunications company [*tel*ephone *co*mpany]
tele- *or* **tel-** *combining form* **1** : over or at a distance ⟨*tele*communication⟩ ⟨*tele*pathy⟩ **2 a** : telegraph ⟨*tele*typewriter⟩ **b** : television ⟨*tele*cast⟩ [Greek *tēle* "far off"]
tele·cast \ˈtel-i-ˌkast\ *vb* **telecast** *also* **tele·cast·ed; tele·cast·ing** : to broadcast by television [*tele-* + broad*cast*] — **telecast** *n* — **tele·cast·er** *n*
tel·e·com \ˈtel-i-ˌkäm\ *n* **1** : TELECOMMUNICATION **2** : the telecommunications industry
tele·com·mu·ni·ca·tion \ˌtel-i-kə-ˌmyü-nə-ˈkā-shən\ *n* **1** : communication at a distance (as by cable, radio, telephone, or television) **2** : technology that deals with telecommunication — usually used in plural
tele·com·mute \ˈtel-i-kə-ˌmyüt\ *vi* : to work at home using an electronic link (as the Internet) with a central office — **tele·com·mut·er** *n*
tele·course \ˈtel-i-ˌkōrs, -ˌkȯrs\ *n* : a course of study conducted over television
tele·ge·nic \ˌtel-ə-ˈjen-ik, -ˈjēn-\ *adj* : suitable for television broadcast; *esp* : having an appearance and manner that are markedly attractive to television viewers — **tele·ge·ni·cal·ly** \-i-kə-lē, -klē\ *adv*
tele·gram \ˈtel-ə-ˌgram, *Southern also* -grəm\ *n* : a message sent by telegraph
[1]**tele·graph** \-ˌgraf\ *n* : an apparatus for communication at a distance by coded signals; *esp* : an apparatus, system, or process for communication at a distance by electric transmission of such signals over wire — **tele·graph·ic** \ˌtel-ə-ˈgraf-ik\ *adj* — **tele·graph·i·cal·ly** \-ˈgraf-i-kə-lē, -klē\ *adv*

\ə\ **abut**	\au̇\ **out**	\i\ **tip**	\ȯ\ **saw**	\u̇\ **foot**
\ər\ **further**	\ch\ **chin**	\ī\ **life**	\ȯi\ **coin**	\y\ **yet**
\a\ **mat**	\e\ **pet**	\j\ **job**	\th\ **thin**	\yü\ **few**
\ā\ **take**	\ē\ **easy**	\ng\ **sing**	\th\ **this**	\yu̇\ **cure**
\ä\ **cot, cart**	\g\ **go**	\ō\ **bone**	\ü\ **food**	\zh\ **vision**

[2]**telegraph** *vt* **1 a :** to send by or as if by telegraph **b :** to send a telegram to **c :** to send (as flowers or money) by means of a telegraphic order **2 :** to make known by signs especially unknowingly and in advance ⟨*telegraph* a punch⟩ — **te·leg·ra·pher** \tə-ˈleg-rə-fər\ *n* — **te·leg·ra·phist** \-fəst\ *n*

te·leg·ra·phy \tə-ˈleg-rə-fē\ *n* **:** the use or operation of a telegraph apparatus or system

tele·ki·ne·sis \ˌtel-i-kə-ˈnē-səs, -kī-\ *n* **:** the apparent production of motion in objects (as by a spiritualistic medium) without physical contact or other explainable means [*tele-* + Greek *kinēsis* "motion," from *kinein* "to move"]

tele·mar·ket·ing \ˌtel-ə-ˈmär-kət-ing\ *n* **:** the marketing of goods or services by telephone — **tele·mar·ket·er** \-kət-ər\ *n*

tele·me·ter \ˈtel-ə-ˌmēt-ər\ *n* **:** an electrical apparatus for measuring something (as pressure, speed, or temperature) and transmitting the result especially by radio to a distant station where the result is indicated or recorded — **telemeter** *vb*

te·lem·e·try \tə-ˈlem-ə-trē\ *n* **1 :** the science or process of transmitting data by telemeter **2 :** data transmitted by telemetry — **tele·met·ric** \ˌtel-ə-ˈme-trik\ *adj* — **tele·met·ri·cal·ly** \-tri-kə-lē, -klē\ *adv*

te·le·ol·o·gist \ˌtel-ē-ˈäl-ə-jəst, ˌtē-lē-\ *n* **:** a specialist or believer in teleology

te·le·ol·o·gy \ˌtel-ē-ˈäl-ə-jē, ˌtē-lē-\ *n* **:** a doctrine that attributes a purpose to nature or that explains natural phenomena as directed toward a goal [Greek *telos* "end, purpose"] — **te·le·o·log·i·cal** \ˌtel-ē-ə-ˈläj-i-kəl, ˌtē-lē-\ *adj*

te·le·ost \ˈtel-ē-ˌäst, ˈtē-lē-\ *n* **:** BONY FISH [derived from Greek *teleios* "complete, perfect" (from *telos* "end") + *osteon* "bone"] — **teleost** *adj*

tele·path \ˈtel-ə-ˌpath\ *n* **:** a person who is able to communicate by telepathy

te·lep·a·thy \tə-ˈlep-ə-thē\ *n* **:** apparent communication from one mind to another by means other than the known physical senses — **tele·path·ic** \ˌtel-ə-ˈpath-ik\ *adj* — **tele·path·i·cal·ly** \-ˈpath-i-kə-lē, -klē\ *adv*

[1]**tele·phone** \ˈtel-ə-ˌfōn\ *n* **:** an instrument for transmitting and receiving sounds over long distances by electricity

[2]**telephone** *vb* **1 :** to communicate by telephone **2 :** to send by telephone **3 :** to speak to by telephone — **tele·phon·er** *n*

telephone booth *n* **:** an enclosure within which one may stand or sit while making a telephone call

tele·phon·ic \ˌtel-ə-ˈfän-ik\ *adj* **1 :** conveying sound to a distance **2 :** of, relating to, or conveyed by telephone

[1]**tele·pho·to** \ˌtel-ə-ˈfōt-ō\ *adj* **:** being a camera lens system designed to give a large image of a distant object; *also* **:** relating to or being photography done with a telephoto lens

[2]**telephoto** *n* **:** a telephoto lens

Telephoto *trademark* — used for an apparatus for transmitting photographs electrically or for a photograph so transmitted

tele·play \ˈtel-ə-ˌplā\ *n* **:** a story prepared for television production

tele·print·er \ˈtel-ə-ˌprint-ər\ *n* **:** a device capable of producing hard copy from signals received over a communications circuit; *esp* **:** TELETYPEWRITER

tele·prompt·er \ˈtel-ə-ˌpräm-tər, -ˌprämp-\ *n* **:** a device for displaying prepared text to a speaker or performer [from a trademark]

[1]**tele·scope** \ˈtel-ə-ˌskōp\ *n* **1 :** a usually tubular optical instrument for viewing distant objects by means of the refraction of light rays through a lens or the reflection of light rays by a concave mirror — compare REFLECTOR, REFRACTOR **2 :** any of various tubular magnifying optical instruments **3 :** RADIO TELESCOPE

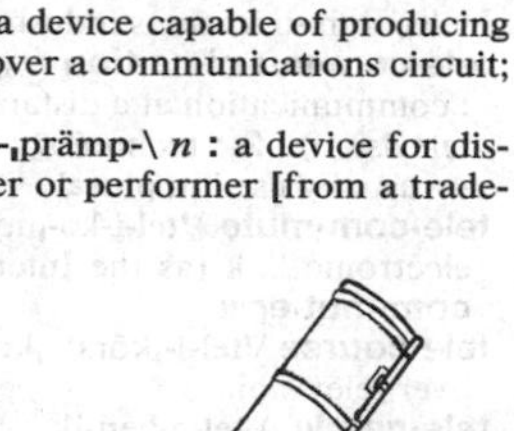

telescope 1

[2]**telescope** *vb* **1 :** to slide or pass or cause to slide or pass one within another like the cylindrical sections of a hand telescope **2 :** CONDENSE 1, COMPRESS

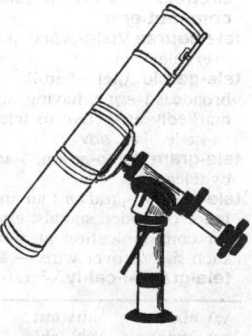

tele·scop·ic \ˌtel-ə-ˈskäp-ik\ *adj* **1 a :** of, with, or relating to a telescope **b :** suitable for seeing or magnifying distant objects **2 :** seen or discoverable only by a telescope ⟨*telescopic* stars⟩ **3 :** able to discern objects at a distance **4 :** having parts that telescope — **tele·scop·i·cal·ly** \-ˈskäp-i-kə-lē, -klē\ *adv*

tele·thon \ˈtel-ə-ˌthän\ *n* **:** a long television program usually to solicit funds (as for a charity) [*tele-* + *-thon* (as in *marathon*)]

Tele·type \ˈtel-ə-ˌtīp\ *trademark* — used for a teletypewriter

tele·type·writ·er \ˌtel-ə-ˈtīp-ˌrīt-ər\ *n* **:** a printing device resembling a typewriter that is used to send and receive telephonic signals

tel·evan·ge·list \ˌtel-i-ˈvan-jə-ləst\ *n* **:** an evangelist who conducts regularly televised religious programs — **tel·evan·ge·lism** \-ˌliz-əm\ *n*

tele·view \ˈtel-ə-ˌvyü\ *vi* **:** to observe or watch by means of a television receiver — **tele·view·er** *n*

tele·vise \ˈtel-ə-ˌvīz\ *vt* **:** to broadcast (as a sports event) by television [back-formation from *television*]

tele·vi·sion \ˈtel-ə-ˌvizh-ən\ *n* **1 :** an electronic system of transmitting images of fixed or moving objects together with sound over a wire or through space by apparatus that converts light and sound into electrical waves and reconverts them into visible light rays and audible sound **2 :** a television receiving set **3 a :** the television broadcasting industry **b :** television as a medium of communication

[1]**tel·ex** \ˈtel-ˌeks\ *n* **1 :** a communication service involving teletypewriters connected by wire through automatic exchanges **2 :** a message sent by telex [*tele*printer + *ex*change]

[2]**telex** *vt* **1 :** to send (as a message) by telex **2 :** to communicate with by telex

te·lio·spore \ˈtē-lē-ə-ˌspōr, -ˌspȯr\ *n* **:** a thick-walled spore forming the final stage in the life cycle of a rust fungus and giving rise to a basidium [Greek *teleios* "complete" (from *telos* "end") + English *spore*]

tell \ˈtel\ *vb* **told** \ˈtōld\; **tell·ing 1 :** COUNT, ENUMERATE **2 a :** to relate in detail **:** NARRATE ⟨*tell* a story⟩ **b :** to give an account ⟨an article *telling* of her experience⟩ **c :** SAY, UTTER ⟨*tell* a lie⟩ **3 a :** to make known **:** REVEAL ⟨*tell* a secret⟩ **b :** to express in words ⟨can't *tell* you how pleased we are⟩ **4 :** to give information to **:** INFORM ⟨*tell* us about your job⟩ **5 :** ORDER, DIRECT ⟨*told* me to wait⟩ **6 :** to ascertain by observing **:** FIND OUT ⟨I can *tell* you're honest⟩ **7 :** to act as an informer ⟨*tell* on a cheater⟩ **8 :** to have a marked effect ⟨the pressure *told* on them⟩ **9 :** to serve as evidence or indication ⟨smiles *telling* of success⟩ [Old English *tellan*]

tell·er \ˈtel-ər\ *n* **1 :** one that relates or communicates ⟨a *teller* of tales⟩ **2 :** a person appointed to count votes **3 :** a bank employee who receives and pays out money

tell·ing \ˈtel-ing\ *adj* **:** producing a marked effect ⟨a *telling* argument⟩ ⟨a *telling* blow⟩ — **tell·ing·ly** \-ing-lē\ *adv*

tell off *vt* **1 :** to number and set apart; *esp* **:** to assign to a special duty **2 :** SCOLD 2, REPRIMAND ⟨*told* him *off* for spreading rumors⟩

[1]**tell·tale** \ˈtel-ˌtāl\ *n* **1 a :** TALEBEARER, INFORMANT **b :** an outward sign **:** INDICATION **2 :** a device for indicating or recording something

[2]**telltale** *adj* **:** indicating or giving evidence of something ⟨*telltale* fingerprints⟩

tel·lu·ride \ˈtel-yə-ˌrīd\ *n* **:** a binary compound of tellurium with another element or a radical

tel·lu·ri·um \tə-ˈlu̇r-ē-əm, te-\ *n* **:** an element that occurs in crystalline form, in a dark amorphous form, or combined with metals and is used especially in alloys and catalysts — see ELEMENT table [New Latin, from Latin *tellur-*, *tellus* "earth"]

tel·ly \ˈtel-ē\ *n, pl* **tellys** *also* **tellies** *chiefly British* **:** TELEVISION

telo·phase \ˈtē-lə-ˌfāz, ˈtel-ə-\ *n* **1 :** the final stage of mitosis and of the second division of meiosis in which the spindle disappears and two new nuclei appear each with a set of chromosomes **2 :** the final stage in the first division of meiosis in which half of the original number of chromosomes including one from each homologous pair gather at opposite poles of the cell [Greek *telos* "end"]

tel·son \ˈtel-sən\ *n* **:** the terminal segment of the body of an arthropod or segmented worm; *esp* **:** that of a crustacean forming the middle lobe of the tail [Greek, "end of a plowed field"]

tem·blor \ˈtem-blər, -ˌblȯr, -ˌblōr\ *n* **:** EARTHQUAKE [Spanish, literally, "trembling," from *temblar* "to tremble," from Medieval Latin *tremulare*]

tem·er·ar·i·ous \ˌtem-ə-ˈrer-ē-əs, -ˈrar-\ *adj* **:** marked by temerity **:** rashly or presumptuously daring ⟨a *temerarious* comment⟩

[Latin *temerarius,* from *temere* "at random, rashly"] — **tem·er·ar·i·ous·ly** *adv*

te·mer·i·ty \tə-'mer-ət-ē\ *n, pl* **-ties** : unreasonable or foolhardy contempt of danger or opposition : RECKLESSNESS [Latin *temeritas,* from *temere* "at random, rashly"]

synonyms TEMERITY, AUDACITY mean conspicuous or flagrant boldness. TEMERITY suggests boldness arising from reckless or heedless contempt of danger ⟨had the *temerity* to challenge the dictatorial order⟩. AUDACITY implies a disregard of restraints commonly imposed by prudence or convention ⟨had the *audacity* to come to the party uninvited⟩.

temp \'temp\ *n* : TEMPERATURE

¹tem·per \'tem-pər\ *vb* **tem·pered; tem·per·ing** \'tem-pə-ring, -pring\ **1** : MODERATE, SOFTEN ⟨*temper* justice with mercy⟩ **2** : to control by reducing : SUBDUE ⟨*temper* one's anger⟩ **3** : to bring to the desired consistency or texture ⟨*temper* modeling clay⟩ **4** : to bring (as steel or glass) to the desired hardness or strength by heating and cooling **5** : to be or become tempered [Old English *temprian* and Medieval French *temprer,* both from Latin *temperare* "to moderate, mix, temper"] — **tem·per·able** \-pə-rə-bəl, -prə-bəl\ *adj*

²temper *n* **1** : characteristic tone : TREND, TENDENCY ⟨the *temper* of the times⟩ **2** : high quality of mind or spirit : COURAGE, METTLE **3** : the state of a substance with respect to certain desired qualities (as hardness, elasticity, or workability) ⟨the *temper* of a knife blade⟩ **4 a** : a characteristic cast of mind or state of feeling : DISPOSITION **b** : calmness of mind : COMPOSURE ⟨lost my *temper*⟩ **c** : state of feeling or frame of mind at a particular time usually dominated by a single strong emotion **d** : a state of anger ⟨left in a *temper*⟩ **e** : a tendency to anger ⟨has a hot *temper*⟩ ***synonyms*** see MOOD

tem·pera \'tem-pə-rə\ *n* : a process of painting in which the colors are mixed with substances (as egg, glue, or gum) other than oil [Italian, literally, "temper"]

tem·per·a·ment \'tem-pə-rə-mənt, -prə-mənt\ *n* **1** : characteristic mode of emotional response ⟨is of a nervous *temperament*⟩ **2** : excessive sensitiveness or irritability [Latin *temperamentum* "mixture, makeup, constitution," from *temperare* "to mix, temper"]

tem·per·a·men·tal \ˌtem-pə-rə-'ment-l, -prə-'ment-\ *adj* **1** : of, relating to, or arising from temperament ⟨*temperamental* peculiarities⟩ **2 a** : marked by extreme sensitivity and impulsive changes of mood ⟨a *temperamental* singer⟩ **b** : unpredictable in behavior or performance ⟨a *temperamental* car⟩ — **tem·per·a·men·tal·ly** \-l-ē\ *adv*

tem·per·ance \'tem-pə-rəns, -prəns, -pərns\ *n* **1** : moderation in action, thought, or feeling : RESTRAINT **2** : habitual moderation in the indulgence of the appetites or passions; *esp* : moderation in or abstinence from the use of alcoholic beverages

tem·per·ate \'tem-pə-rət, -prət\ *adj* **1** : marked by moderation: as **a** : not excessive or extreme **b** : moderate in satisfying one's needs or desires **c** : moderate in the use of alcoholic beverages **d** : marked by self-control : RESTRAINED ⟨*temperate* speech⟩ **2** : having, found in, or associated with a moderate climate which typically lacks extremes of temperature ⟨*temperate* heat⟩ **3** : existing as a prophage in infected cells and rarely causing lysis ⟨*temperate* bacteriophages⟩ ***synonyms*** see MODERATE — **tem·per·ate·ly** *adv* — **tem·per·ate·ness** *n*

temperate rain forest *n* : woodland that has a temperate climate with heavy rainfall and that usually includes numerous kinds of trees but differs from a tropical rain forest especially in having one or two dominant trees

temperate zone *n, often cap T&Z* : the area or region between the Tropic of Cancer and the arctic circle or between the Tropic of Capricorn and the antarctic circle

tem·per·a·ture \'tem-pər-ˌchůr, -pə-ˌchůr, -pə-rə-ˌchůr, -prə-ˌchůr, -chər\ *n* **1** : the degree of hotness or coldness of something (as air, water, or the body) as shown by a thermometer **2** : FEVER 1 ⟨has a *temperature*⟩

temperature inversion *n* : INVERSION 3

tem·pered \'tem-pərd\ *adj* **1 a** : having the elements mixed in satisfying proportions **b** : qualified, lessened, or diluted by the mixture or influence of an additional ingredient : made moderate ⟨stylishness *tempered* with good taste⟩ **2** : brought to the desired state (as of hardness, toughness, or flexibility) ⟨*tempered* steel⟩ ⟨*tempered* glass⟩ **3** : having a particular kind of temper — used in combination ⟨short-*tempered*⟩

tem·pest \'tem-pəst\ *n* **1** : an extensive violent wind; *esp* : one accompanied by rain, hail, or snow **2** : TUMULT 1, UPROAR ⟨a political *tempest*⟩ [Medieval French *tempeste,* from Latin *tempestas* "season, weather, storm," from *tempus* "time"]

tem·pes·tu·ous \tem-'pes-chə-wəs, -'pesh-\ *adj* : STORMY 2 ⟨*tempestuous* weather⟩ ⟨a *tempestuous* relationship⟩ — **tem·pes·tu·ous·ly** *adv* — **tem·pes·tu·ous·ness** *n*

Tem·plar \'tem-plər\ *n* **1** : a knight of a religious military order established early in the 12th century in Jerusalem to protect pilgrims and Christ's burial place **2** : KNIGHT TEMPLAR 2 [Medieval French *templer,* from Medieval Latin *templarius,* from Latin *templum* "temple"]

tem·plate \'tem-plət\ *n* **1** : a gauge, pattern, or mold (as a thin plate or board) used as a guide to the form of a piece being made **2** : a molecule (as of DNA) that serves as a pattern for the generation of another molecule **3** : something that establishes or serves as a pattern [probably derived from French *temple,* a part of a loom]

¹tem·ple \'tem-pəl\ *n* **1** : a building for worship: as **a** *often cap* : either of two successive national sanctuaries in ancient Jerusalem **b** : a building for Mormon sacred ordinances **c** : the house of worship of Reform and some Conservative Jewish congregations **2** : a local lodge of a fraternal order [Old English *tempel* and Medieval French *temple,* both from Latin *templum*] — **tem·pled** \-pəld\ *adj*

²temple *n* : the flattened space on each side of the forehead of some mammals including humans [Medieval French, derived from Latin *tempora,* pl., "temples"]

tem·po \'tem-pō\ *n, pl* **tem·pi** \-pē\ *or* **tempos** **1** : the rate of speed of a musical piece or passage indicated by one of a series of directions (as largo, presto, or allegro) and often by an exact metronome marking **2** : rate of motion or activity : PACE [Italian, literally, "time," from Latin *tempus*]

¹tem·po·ral \'tem-pə-rəl, -prəl\ *adj* **1** : of or relating to time as opposed to eternity : TEMPORARY **2 a** : of or relating to earthly life **b** : of or relating to nonreligious matters [Latin *temporalis,* from *tempor-, tempus* "time"] — **tem·po·ral·ly** \-ē\ *adv*

²temporal *adj* : of or relating to the temples or to the sides of the skull behind the orbits [Middle French, derived from Latin *tempora* "temples"] — **tem·po·ral·ly** \-ē\ *adv*

temporal bone *n* : a compound bone of the side of the skull of some mammals including humans that is composed of four major parts

tem·po·ral·i·ty \ˌtem-pə-'ral-ət-ē\ *n, pl* **-ties** **1 a** : civil or political as distinguished from spiritual or church power or authority **b** : church property or income — often used in plural **2** : the quality or state of being temporal

tem·po·rary \'tem-pə-ˌrer-ē\ *adj* : lasting for a limited time ⟨a *temporary* shortage⟩ [Latin *temporarius,* from *tempor-, tempus* "time"] — **tem·po·rar·i·ly** \ˌtem-pə-'rer-ə-lē\ *adv* — **tem·po·rar·i·ness** \'tem-pə-ˌrer-ē-nəs\ *n*

temporary duty *n* : temporary military service away from one's regular unit

tem·po·rize \'tem-pə-ˌrīz\ *vi* **1** : to act to suit the time or occasion : yield to current or dominant opinion **2** : to draw out negotiations so as to gain time [Middle French *temporiser,* from Medieval Latin *temporizare* "to pass the time," from Latin *tempor-, tempus* "time"] — **tem·po·ri·za·tion** \ˌtem-pə-rə-'zā-shən\ *n* — **tem·po·riz·er** \'tem-pə-ˌrī-zər\ *n*

tempt \'temt, 'tempt\ *vt* **1** : to entice to do wrong by promising pleasure or gain **2 a** *obsolete* : to make trial of : TEST **b** : to try presumptuously : PROVOKE ⟨*tempted* fate by speeding⟩ **c** : to risk the dangers of **3 a** : to induce to do something : INCITE ⟨*tempted* her to taste the cake⟩ **b** : to cause to be strongly inclined : almost move or persuade ⟨was *tempted* to call it quits⟩ [Medieval French *tempter, tenter,* from Latin *temptare, tentare* "to feel, try"] ***synonyms*** see LURE — **tempt·able** \'tem-tə-bəl, 'temp-\ *adj*

temp·ta·tion \tem-'tā-shən, temp-\ *n* **1** : the act of tempting : the state of being tempted especially to evil : ENTICEMENT **2** : something tempting

tempt·er \'tem-tər, 'temp-\ *n* : one that tempts

tempt·ing *adj* : that attracts strongly ⟨a *tempting* offer⟩ — **tempt·ing·ly** \'tem-ting-lē, 'temp-\ *adv*

tempt·ress \'tem-trəs, 'temp-\ *n* : a woman who tempts

ten \ˈten\ *n* **1** — see NUMBER table **2** : the tenth in a set or series **3** : something having ten units or members **4** : a 10-dollar bill [Old English *tīene*] — **ten** *adj or pron*

ten·a·ble \ˈten-ə-bəl\ *adj* : capable of being held, maintained, or defended ⟨a *tenable* argument⟩ ⟨retreated since the position was not *tenable*⟩ [Middle French, from *tenir* "to hold," from Latin *tenēre*] — **ten·a·bil·i·ty** \ˌten-ə-ˈbil-ət-ē\ *n* — **ten·a·ble·ness** \ˈten-ə-bəl-nəs\ *n* — **ten·a·bly** \-blē\ *adv*

te·na·cious \tə-ˈnā-shəs\ *adj* **1 a** : not easily pulled apart : COHESIVE, TOUGH ⟨a *tenacious* metal⟩ **b** : tending to adhere to another substance : STICKY ⟨*tenacious* burs⟩ **2 a** : holding fast or tending to hold fast : PERSISTENT, STUBBORN ⟨*tenacious* of their rights⟩ **b** : RETENTIVE ⟨a *tenacious* memory⟩ [Latin *tenac-, tenax* "tending to hold fast," from *tenēre* "to hold"] ***synonyms*** see STRONG — **te·na·cious·ly** *adv* — **te·na·cious·ness** *n*

te·nac·i·ty \tə-ˈnas-ət-ē\ *n* : the quality or state of being tenacious

ten·an·cy \ˈten-ən-sē\ *n, pl* **-cies** **1** : the temporary possession or occupancy of another's property; *also* : the period of such occupancy or possession **2** : the ownership of property

[1]**ten·ant** \ˈten-ənt\ *n* **1 a** : the owner or possessor of real estate or sometimes personal property **b** : one who occupies or temporarily possesses property of another; *esp* : one who rents or leases (as a house) from a landlord **2** : OCCUPANT, DWELLER [Medieval French, from *tenir* "to hold"]

[2]**tenant** *vt* : to hold or occupy as or as if as a tenant : INHABIT — **ten·ant·able** \-ən-tə-bəl\ *adj*

tenant farmer *n* : a farmer who works land owned by another and pays rent either in cash or in shares of produce

ten·ant·less \ˈten-ənt-ləs\ *adj* : having no tenants

ten·ant·ry \ˈten-ən-trē\ *n, pl* **-ries** **1** : the condition of being a tenant **2** : a group of tenants

tench \ˈtench\ *n, pl* **tench** *or* **tench·es** : a Eurasian freshwater fish related to the carp and noted for its ability to survive in poorly oxygenated water [Medieval French *tenche,* from Late Latin *tinca*]

Ten Commandments *n pl* : the commandments of God given to Moses on Mount Sinai

[1]**tend** \ˈtend\ *vb* **1** : to pay attention ⟨*tend* to business⟩ **2 a** : to take care of ⟨*tended* her sick father⟩ **b** : to help the growth or development of ⟨*tend* a garden⟩ **3** : to have charge of as caretaker or overseer ⟨*tended* the sheep⟩ **4** : to manage the operation of or do the necessary work connected with ⟨*tend* the store⟩ ⟨*tend* the fire⟩ [Middle English *tenden,* short for *attenden* "to attend"]

[2]**tend** *vi* **1** : to move or turn in a certain direction : LEAD ⟨the road *tends* to the right⟩ **2** : to have a tendency : to be likely ⟨people who *tend* to slouch⟩ [Medieval French *tendre* "to stretch, direct oneself," from Latin *tendere*]

ten·dance \ˈten-dəns\ *n* : watchful care : ATTENDANCE

ten·den·cy \ˈten-dən-sē\ *n, pl* **-cies** **1 a** : direction or approach toward a place, object, effect, or limit **b** : a proneness to a particular kind of thought or action : PROPENSITY **2** : the purposeful trend of something written or said : AIM [Medieval Latin *tendentia,* from Latin *tendere* "to stretch, tend"]

synonyms TENDENCY, TREND, DRIFT, TENOR mean movement in a particular direction. TENDENCY implies an ever-present inclination or force ⟨had a *tendency* to exaggerate⟩ ⟨counteracts the *tendency* of engines to knock⟩. TREND implies a general direction maintained in spite of irregularities and more often subject to change than TENDENCY ⟨*trends* in current fiction⟩. DRIFT suggests a tendency determined by external influences ⟨the present *drift* of the population away from large cities⟩ or it may apply to an underlying trend of a discourse ⟨lost the *drift* of the conversation⟩. TENOR stresses a clearly perceptible direction and a continuous, undeviating course ⟨the *tenor* of the times⟩.

ten·den·tious \ten-ˈden-chəs\ *adj* : marked by a tendency in favor of a particular point of view : BIASED — **ten·den·tious·ly** *adv* — **ten·den·tious·ness** *n*

[1]**ten·der** \ˈten-dər\ *adj* **1 a** : having a soft or yielding texture : easily broken, cut, or damaged : FRAGILE ⟨*tender* feet⟩ **b** : easily chewed : SUCCULENT ⟨*tender* meat⟩ **2 a** : physically weak : DELICATE **b** : IMMATURE, YOUNG ⟨children of *tender* years⟩ **c** : incapable of resisting cold ⟨*tender* plants⟩ **3** : FOND, LOVING ⟨a *tender* look⟩ **4 a** : showing care : CONSIDERATE ⟨*tender* regard⟩ **b** : highly susceptible to impressions or emotions : IMPRESSIONABLE ⟨a *tender* conscience⟩ **5 a** : appropriate or conducive to a delicate or sensitive constitution or character : GENTLE, MILD ⟨*tender* irony⟩ **b** : delicate or soft in quality or tone **6 a** : sensitive to touch : easily hurt ⟨a *tender* bruise⟩ **b** : sensitive to injury or insult : TOUCHY ⟨*tender* pride⟩ **c** : demanding careful and sensitive handling : TICKLISH ⟨a *tender* situation⟩ [Medieval French *tendre,* from Latin *tener*] — **ten·der·ly** *adv* — **ten·der·ness** *n*

[2]**tender** *vt* **ten·dered; ten·der·ing** \-də-ring, -dring\ **1** : to make a tender of ⟨*tender* the amount of rent⟩ **2** : to present for acceptance : PROFFER ⟨*tendered* my resignation⟩

[3]**tender** *n* **1** : an offer of money in payment of a debt **2** : an offer or proposal made for acceptance; *esp* : an offer of a bid for a contract **3** : something that may by law be offered in payment; *esp* : MONEY [Middle French *tendre* "to stretch, hold out, offer, direct"]

[4]**tend·er** \ˈten-dər\ *n* : one that tends or takes care: as **a** : a ship employed to serve other ships (as by supplying provisions) **b** : a boat that carries passengers or freight between shore and a larger ship **c** : a vehicle attached to a locomotive for carrying a supply of fuel and water

[5]**tender** *n* : an often breaded strip of usually breast meat ⟨chicken *tenders*⟩ [probably short for *tenderloin*]

ten·der·foot \ˈten-dər-ˌfu̇t\ *n, pl* **-feet** \-ˌfēt\ *also* **-foots** **1** : a person who is not hardened to a rough outdoor life; *esp* : a newcomer in a recent settlement (as on a frontier) **2** : an inexperienced beginner : NOVICE

ten·der·heart·ed \ˌten-dər-ˈhärt-əd\ *adj* : easily moved to love, pity, or sorrow : COMPASSIONATE — **ten·der·heart·ed·ly** *adv* — **ten·der·heart·ed·ness** *n*

ten·der·ize \ˈten-də-ˌrīz\ *vt* : to make (meat or meat products) tender by using a process or substance that breaks down connective tissue — **ten·der·iza·tion** \ˌten-də-rə-ˈzā-shən\ *n* — **ten·der·iz·er** \ˈten-də-ˌrī-zər\ *n*

ten·der·loin \ˈten-dər-ˌlȯin\ *n* **1** : a strip of tender meat (as beef or pork) on each side of the backbone **2** : a district of a city largely devoted to vice [sense 2 from such a district's making possible a luxurious diet for a corrupt police officer]

ten·di·nous \ˈten-də-nəs\ *adj* **1** : consisting of tendons : SINEWY ⟨*tendinous* tissue⟩ **2** : of, relating to, or resembling a tendon [New Latin *tendinosus,* from *tendin-, tendo* "tendon," from Medieval Latin *tendon-, tendo*]

ten·don \ˈten-dən\ *n* : a tough cord or band of fibrous connective tissue that unites a muscle with some other part (as a bone) and transmits the force exerted by the muscle [Medieval Latin *tendon-, tendo,* from Latin *tendere* "to stretch"]

tendon of Achilles \-ə-ˈkil-ēz\ : ACHILLES TENDON

ten·dril \ˈten-drəl\ *n* **1** : a leaf, stipule, or stem modified into a slender spirally coiling sensitive organ serving to attach a plant to its support **2** : something (as a ringlet of hair) that curls like a tendril [probably from Middle French *tendron* "bud, cartilage," alteration of *tenrun,* from Latin *tener* "tender"] — **ten·driled** *or* **ten·drilled** \-drəld\ *adj* — **ten·dril·ous** \-drə-ləs\ *adj*

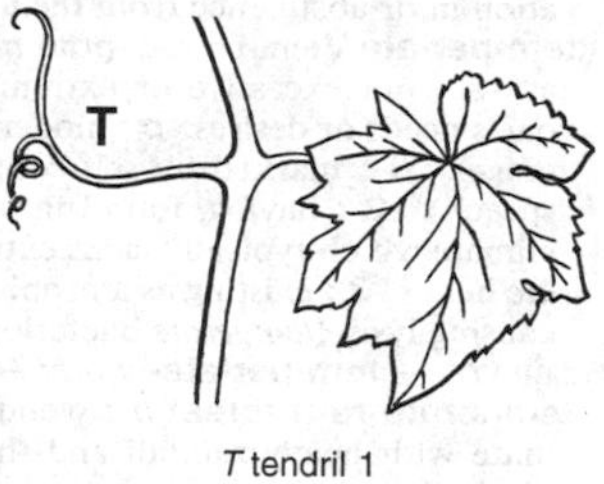

T tendril 1

Ten·e·brae \ˈten-ə-ˌbrā, -ˌbrī, -ˌbrē\ *n sing or pl* : a church service observed during the final part of Holy Week commemorating the sufferings and death of Christ [Medieval Latin, from Latin, "darkness"]

1080 *also* **ten–eighty** \te-ˈnāt-ē\ *n* : a poisonous substance used to kill rodents [from its laboratory serial number]

ten·e·ment \ˈten-ə-mənt\ *n* **1 a** : a house used as a dwelling **b** : APARTMENT 1, FLAT **c** : TENEMENT HOUSE **2** : a dwelling place [Medieval French, "land or buildings held by one person from another," from Medieval Latin *tenementum,* from Latin *tenēre* "to hold"]

tenement house *n* : APARTMENT BUILDING; *esp* : one barely meeting minimum standards of sanitation, safety, and comfort and housing poorer families

ten·et \ˈten-ət\ *n* : a principle, belief, or doctrine generally held to be true; *esp* : one held in common by members of an organization, group, or profession [Latin, "he holds," from *tenēre* "to hold"] ***synonyms*** see DOCTRINE

ten·fold \ˈten-ˌfōld, -ˈfōld\ *adj* **1 :** having 10 units or members **2 :** being 10 times as great or as many — **tenfold** *adv*

tenia *variant of* TAENIA

ten·nis \ˈten-əs\ *n* **:** a game that is played with rackets and a light elastic ball by two players or pairs of players on a level court divided by a low net [Middle English *tenetz, tenys,* probably from Medieval French *tenez,* second person plural imperative of *tenir* "to hold," from Latin *tenēre*]

tennis elbow *n* **:** inflammation and pain over the outer side of the elbow usually resulting from excessive strain on and twisting of the forearm

tennis shoe *n* **:** a lightweight usually low-cut sneaker

[1]**ten·on** \ˈten-ən\ *n* **:** a projecting part in a piece of material (as wood) for insertion into a mortise to make a joint [Medieval French, from *tenir* "to hold," from Latin *tenēre*]

[2]**tenon** *vt* **1 :** to unite by a tenon **2 :** to cut or fit for insertion in a mortise

[1]**ten·or** \ˈten-ər\ *n* **1 :** the general drift of something spoken or written ⟨the *tenor* of the book⟩ **2 a :** the voice part next to the lowest in a 4-part chorus — compare ALTO, BASS, SOPRANO **b :** the highest natural adult male singing voice; *also* **:** a singer having such a voice **c :** an instrument playing a part between that of an alto and a bass **3 :** a continuance in a course, movement, or activity **:** TREND ⟨the *tenor* of my life⟩ [Medieval French, from Latin *tenor* "uninterrupted course," from *tenēre* "to hold"] ***synonyms*** see TENDENCY

[2]**tenor** *adj* **:** relating to or having the range or part of a tenor

ten·pen·ny \ˌten-ˌpen-ē\ *adj* **:** equal to, worth, or costing ten pennies

tenpenny nail *n* **:** a nail 3 inches (7.6 centimeters) long [from its original price per hundred]

ten·pin \ˈten-ˌpin\ *n* **1 :** a bottle-shaped bowling pin 15 inches (about 38 centimeters) high **2** *pl* **:** a bowling game using 10 tenpins and a large ball with each player allowed to bowl 2 balls in each of 10 frames

ten·pound·er \ˈten-ˈpau̇n-dər\ *n* **:** LADYFISH

tens digit *n* **:** the numeral (as 5 in 456) occupying the tens place in a number expressed in the Arabic system of writing numbers

[1]**tense** \ˈtens\ *n* **1 :** a distinction of form in a verb to express past, present, or future time or duration of the action or state it denotes **2 :** a particular inflectional form or set of inflectional forms of a verb expressing a specific time distinction ⟨used the wrong *tense* of the verb⟩ [Middle French *tens* "time, tense," from Latin *tempus*]

[2]**tense** *adj* **1 :** stretched tight **:** made taut **:** RIGID ⟨*tense* muscles⟩ **2 a :** feeling or showing nervous tension **:** HIGH-STRUNG ⟨a *tense* smile⟩ **b :** marked by strain or suspense ⟨a *tense* thriller⟩ **3 :** produced with the speech muscles in a relatively tense state ⟨the *tense* vowels \ē\ and \ü\⟩ — compare LAX [Latin *tensus,* from *tendere* "to stretch"] ***synonyms*** see TIGHT — **tense·ly** *adv* — **tense·ness** *n*

[3]**tense** *vb* **:** to make or become tense

ten·sile \ˈten-səl *also* ˈten-ˌsīl\ *adj* **1 :** capable of stretching or being stretched **:** DUCTILE **2 :** of or relating to tension

tensile strength *n* **:** the greatest longitudinal stress a substance can bear without tearing apart

[1]**ten·sion** \ˈten-chən\ *n* **1 a :** the act or action of stretching or the condition or degree of being stretched to stiffness **:** TAUTNESS ⟨*tension* of a muscle⟩ **b :** STRESS 1c **2 a :** either of two balancing forces causing or tending to cause extension of a body **b :** the condition in an elastic body resulting from elongation **c :** PRESSURE ⟨oxygen *tension* in lake water⟩ **3 a :** a state of mental unrest often accompanied by physical signs (as perspiring) of emotion **b :** a state of latent hostility or opposition between individuals or groups **4 :** a device to produce a desired tension [Latin *tensio,* from *tendere* "to stretch"] — **ten·sion·al** \ˈtench-nəl, -ən-l\ *adj* — **ten·sion·less** \ˈten-chən-ləs\ *adj*

[2]**tension** *vt* **:** to subject to tension

ten·si·ty \ˈten-sət-ē\ *n, pl* **-ties :** the quality or state of being tense

ten·sor \ˈten-sər, ˈten-ˌsȯr\ *n* **:** a muscle that stretches a part

ten–speed \ˈten-ˌspēd\ *n* **:** a bicycle with ten possible combinations of gears

tens place *n* **:** the place two to the left of the decimal point in a number expressed in the Arabic system of writing numbers ⟨2 is in the *tens place* in the number 124.6⟩

ten–strike \ˈten-ˌstrīk\ *n* **:** a strike in bowling

[1]**tent** \ˈtent\ *n* **1 :** a collapsible shelter (as of canvas or nylon) stretched and held in place by poles and used especially as temporary housing (as by campers) **2 :** something that resembles a tent or that serves as a shelter; *esp* **:** a canopy or enclosure placed over the head and shoulders to retain vapors or oxygen administered medically **3 :** the web of a tent caterpillar [Medieval French *tente,* derived from Latin *tendere* "to stretch"]

[2]**tent** *vb* **1 :** to live or lodge in a tent **2 :** to cover with or as if with a tent

ten·ta·cle \ˈtent-i-kəl\ *n* **1 :** any of various long flexible processes usually about the head or mouth of an animal (as a jellyfish or sea anemone) used especially for feeling, grasping, or handling **2 a :** something resembling a tentacle especially in or as if in grasping or feeling out **b :** a sensitive hair on a plant (as a sundew) [New Latin *tentaculum,* from Latin *tentare* "to feel, touch"] — **ten·ta·cled** \-kəld\ *adj* — **ten·tac·u·lar** \ten-ˈtak-yə-lər\ *adj*

ten·ta·tive \ˈtent-ət-iv\ *adj* **1 :** not fully worked out or developed **:** not final ⟨*tentative* plans⟩ **2 :** HESITANT, UNCERTAIN ⟨a *tentative* smile⟩ [Medieval Latin *tentativus,* from Latin *tentare, temptare* "to feel, try"] — **ten·ta·tive·ly** *adv* — **ten·ta·tive·ness** *n*

tent caterpillar *n* **:** any of several destructive caterpillars that live in groups and construct large silken webs on trees

ten·ter \ˈtent-ər\ *n* **:** a frame or endless track with hooks or clips along two sides that is used for drying and stretching cloth [Middle English *teyntur*]

ten·ter·hook \ˈtent-ər-ˌhu̇k\ *n* **:** a sharp hooked nail used especially for fastening cloth on a tenter — **on tenterhooks :** in a state of uneasiness, strain, or suspense

tenth \ˈtenth, ˈtentth\ *n* **1 :** number 10 in a countable series — see NUMBER table **2 :** one of 10 equal parts — **tenth** *adj or adv*

tenths digit *n* **:** the numeral (as 5 in 4.56) in the tenths place in a number expressed in the Arabic system of writing numbers

tenths place *n* **:** the first place to the right of the decimal point in a number expressed in the Arabic system of writing numbers ⟨4 is in the *tenths place* in the number 12.46⟩

tent stitch *n* **:** a short stitch slanting to the right that is used (as in embroidery) to form even lines of solid background

ten·u·ous \ˈten-yə-wəs\ *adj* **:** having little substance or strength **:** FLIMSY, WEAK ⟨a *tenuous* hold on reality⟩ [Latin *tenuis* "thin, slight"] — **te·nu·i·ty** \te-ˈnü-ət-ē, tə-, -ˈnyü-\ *n* — **ten·u·ous·ly** \ˈten-yə-wəs-lē\ *adv* — **ten·u·ous·ness** *n*

ten·ure \ˈten-yər\ *n* **1 :** the act, right, manner, or term of holding something (as real property, a position, or an office); *esp* **:** a status granted after a trial period to a teacher that gives protection from dismissal except for cause determined by formal proceedings **2 :** GRASP 3b, HOLD [Medieval French, derived from Latin *tenēre* "to hold"] — **ten·ur·i·al** \te-ˈnyu̇r-ē-əl\ *adj* — **ten·ur·i·al·ly** \-ē-ə-lē\ *adv*

ten·ured \ˈten-yərd\ *adj* **:** having tenure ⟨*tenured* faculty⟩

te·o·sin·te \ˌtā-ō-ˈsint-ē\ *n* **:** a tall annual grass chiefly of Mexico that is closely related to and possibly ancestral to corn [Mexican Spanish, from Nahuatl *teōcintli,* from *teōtl* "god" + *cintli* "dried ears of maize"]

te·pee *or* **tee·pee** *also* **ti·pi** \ˈtē-ˌpē\ *n* **:** a conical tent usually of skins used especially by American Indians of the Great Plains [Dakota (a Siouan language of the Dakota Indians) *tʰípi,* from *tʰi-* "to dwell"]

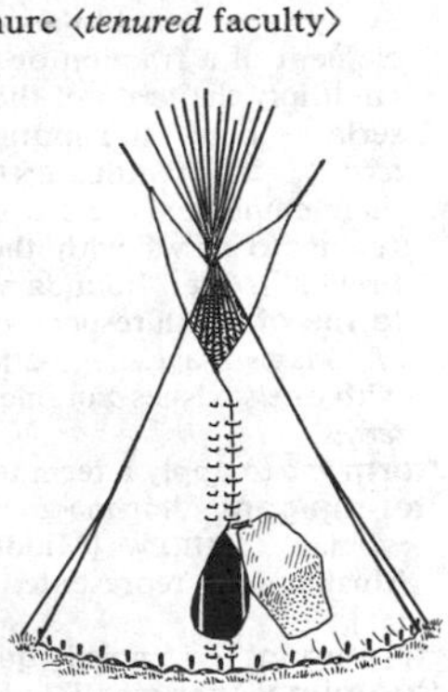

tepee

tep·id \ˈtep-əd\ *adj* **1 :** moderately warm **:** LUKEWARM ⟨a *tepid* bath⟩ **2 :** lacking enthusiasm or conviction **:** HALFHEARTED ⟨a *tepid* response⟩ [Latin *tepidus,* from *tepēre* "to be moderately

\ə\ **abut**	\au̇\ **out**	\i\ **tip**	\ȯ\ **saw**	\u̇\ **foot**
\ər\ **further**	\ch\ **chin**	\ī\ **life**	\ȯi\ **coin**	\y\ **yet**
\a\ **mat**	\e\ **pet**	\j\ **job**	\th\ **thin**	\yü\ **few**
\ā\ **take**	\ē\ **easy**	\ng\ **sing**	\t͟h\ **this**	\yu̇\ **cure**
\ä\ **cot, cart**	\g\ **go**	\ō\ **bone**	\ü\ **food**	\zh\ **vision**

warm"] — **te·pid·i·ty** \tə-ˈpid-ət-ē, te-\ *n* — **tep·id·ly** \ˈtep-əd-lē\ *adv* — **tep·id·ness** *n*

tep·pan·ya·ki \ˌtep-än-ˈyäk-ē\ *n* : a Japanese dish of meat, fish, or vegetables cooked on a large griddle usually built into the diner's table; *also* : this style of cooking [Japanese, from *teppan* "griddle" + *yaki* "broiling"]

te·qui·la \tə-ˈkē-lə\ *n* : a Mexican liquor distilled from the fermented sap of an agave [Spanish, from *Tequila,* town in Jalisco state, Mexico]

tera- \ˈter-ə\ *combining form* : trillion ⟨*tera*byte⟩ [Greek *teras* "monster"]

tera·byte \ˈter-ə-ˌbīt\ *n* : 1024 gigabytes or 1,099,511,627,776 bytes; *also* : one trillion bytes

ter·a·to·gen·ic \ˌter-ət-ə-ˈjen-ik\ *adj* : of, relating to, or causing abnormalities in growth or structure during the process of development ⟨*teratogenic* drugs⟩

tera·watt \ˈter-ə-ˌwät\ *n* : a unit of power equal to one trillion watts

ter·bi·um \ˈtər-bē-əm\ *n* : a rare metallic element — see ELEMENT table [New Latin, from *Ytterby,* Sweden]

terce \ˈtərs\ *also* **tierce** \ˈtiərs\ *n, often cap* : the third of the canonical hours [Medieval French *terce, tierce,* from *terz* "third," from Latin *tertius*]

tercel *variant of* TIERCEL

ter·cen·ten·a·ry \ˌtər-ˌsen-ˈten-ə-rē; tər-ˈsent-n-ˌer-ē, ˈtər-\ *n, pl* **-ries** : a 300th anniversary or its celebration [Latin *ter* "three times"] — **tercentenary** *adj*

ter·cen·ten·ni·al \ˌtər-ˌsen-ˈten-ē-əl\ *adj or n* : TERCENTENARY

ter·cet \ˈtər-sət\ *n* : a unit or group of three lines of verse [Italian *terzetto,* from *terzo* "third," from Latin *tertius*]

ter·e·binth \ˈter-ə-ˌbinth, -ˌbintth\ *n* : a small European tree related to the cashew and yielding turpentine [Medieval French *terebinte,* from Latin *terebinthus,* from Greek *terebinthos*]

te·re·do \tə-ˈrēd-ō, -ˈrād-\ *n, pl* **-dos** : SHIPWORM [Latin, from Greek *terēdōn*]

ter·gi·ver·sate \ˈtər-ji-vər-ˌsāt\ *vi* : to desert one's party or position; *esp* : EQUIVOCATE 1 [Latin *tergiversari* "to show reluctance," from *tergum* "back" + *versare* "to turn," from *versus,* past participle of *vertere* "to turn"] — **ter·gi·ver·sa·tion** \ˌtər-ji-vər-ˈsā-shən\ *n* — **ter·gi·ver·sa·tor** \ˈtər-ji-vər-ˌsāt-ər\ *n*

ter·gum \ˈtər-gəm\ *n, pl* **ter·ga** \-gə\ : the dorsal part or plate of a segment of an arthropod [Latin, "back"]

[1]**term** \ˈtərm\ *n* **1** : END, TERMINATION; *also* : a point in time assigned to something (as payment of rent or interest) **2** : a fixed extent of time; *esp* : the time for which something lasts : DURATION ⟨the governor served two *terms*⟩ ⟨ready for the new school *term*⟩ **3** *pl* : provisions determining the nature and scope of something and especially of an agreement ⟨*terms* of sale⟩ **4 a** : a word or expression that has a precise meaning in some uses or is peculiar to a particular field ⟨legal *terms*⟩ **b** *pl* : an expression of a specified kind ⟨spoke in glowing *terms* of their prospects⟩ **5 a** : a mathematical expression (as $3x$ in $x^2 + 3x - y$) connected to another by a plus or a minus sign **b** : an element of a fraction or proportion or of a series or sequence ⟨multiply the *terms* of the proportion⟩ ⟨the seventh *term* in the series⟩ **6** *pl* **a** : mutual relationship : FOOTING ⟨on good *terms*⟩ **b** : AGREEMENT 1b, CONCORD ⟨came to *terms* with their employer⟩ **c** : a state of acceptance or understanding ⟨came to *terms* with the failure of his business⟩ [Medieval French *terme* "boundary, end," from Latin *terminus*] — **in terms of** : with respect to or in relation to ⟨considered *in terms of* today's wages⟩ — **on one's own terms** : in accordance with one's wishes : in one's own way ⟨prefers to live *on his own terms*⟩

[2]**term** *vt* : to apply a term to : CALL, NAME

[1]**ter·ma·gant** \ˈtər-mə-gənt\ *n* : an overbearing quarrelsome woman : SHREW [Middle English *Termagant,* an imaginary Muslim deity represented in medieval plays as a violent character]

[2]**termagant** *adj* : noisily quarrelsome

[1]**ter·mi·nal** \ˈtər-mən-l\ *adj* **1 a** : of or relating to an end, extremity, boundary, or terminus ⟨*terminal* pillar⟩ **b** : growing at the end of a branch or stem ⟨a *terminal* bud⟩ **2 a** : of, relating to, or occurring in a term or each term ⟨*terminal* payments⟩ **b** : leading ultimately to death : FATAL ⟨a *terminal* illness⟩ **3** : occurring at or constituting the end of a period or series — **ter·mi·nal·ly** \-l-ē\ *adv*

[2]**terminal** *n* **1** : a part that forms the end **2** : a device attached to the end (as of a wire) for convenience in making electrical connections **3 a** : either end of a carrier line (as a railroad or shipping line) with its handling and storage facilities, offices, and stations **b** : a freight or passenger station that serves a large area or acts as a junction between lines ⟨a bus *terminal*⟩ **c** : a town at the end of a carrier line : TERMINUS **4** : a device (as in a computer system) used for data entry and display

terminal side *n* : a straight line that has been rotated around a point on another line to form an angle — compare INITIAL SIDE

ter·mi·nate \ˈtər-mə-ˌnāt\ *vb* **1 a** : to bring to or come to an end : CLOSE ⟨*terminate* a meeting⟩ **b** : to form the conclusion of : form an ending ⟨review questions *terminate* each chapter⟩ **c** : to discontinue the employment of ⟨workers *terminated* because of slow business⟩ **2** : to serve as a limit or boundary of : BOUND ⟨a fence *terminated* the yard⟩ **3** : to extend only to a limit (as a point or line); *esp* : to reach a terminus ⟨a railroad line *terminating* at a seaport⟩ **4** : ASSASSINATE 1, KILL [Latin *terminare,* from *terminus* "end"] ***synonyms*** see CLOSE — **ter·mi·na·ble** \-mə-nə-bəl\ *adj* — **ter·mi·na·tive** \-ˌnāt-iv\ *adj*

terminating decimal *n* : a decimal that can be written as a finite sequence of digits (as 3.25) or for which all the digits to the right of some place are zero (as 1.40000 . . .) — compare REPEATING DECIMAL

ter·mi·na·tion \ˌtər-mə-ˈnā-shən\ *n* **1** : end in time or existence : CONCLUSION ⟨*termination* of life⟩ **2** : a limit in space or extent : BOUND **3** : the last part of a word : SUFFIX; *esp* : an inflectional ending **4** : the act of terminating ***synonyms*** see END — **ter·mi·na·tion·al** \-shnəl, -shən-l\ *adj*

ter·mi·na·tor \ˈtər-mə-ˌnāt-ər\ *n* **1** : one that terminates **2** : the dividing line between the illuminated and the unilluminated part of the moon's or a planet's disk

ter·mi·nol·o·gy \ˌtər-mə-ˈnäl-ə-jē\ *n, pl* **-gies** : the technical or special terms used in a business, art, science, or special subject ⟨the *terminology* of law⟩ [Medieval Latin *terminus* "term, expression," from Latin, "boundary, end"] — **ter·mi·no·log·i·cal** \ˌtərm-nə-ˈläj-i-kəl, ˌtərm-ən-l-ˈäj-\ *adj*

term insurance *n* : insurance for a specified period that pays only for losses suffered during this period

ter·mi·nus \ˈtər-mə-nəs\ *n, pl* **-ni** \-ˌnī, -ˌnē\ *or* **-nus·es** **1** : final goal : finishing point **2** : a post or stone marking a boundary **3 a** : either end of a transportation line or travel route **b** : the station or the town or city at such a place **4** : EXTREMITY, TIP ⟨the *terminus* of a glacier⟩ [Latin, "boundary, marker, limit"]

ter·mite \ˈtər-ˌmīt\ *n* : any of an order (Isoptera) of pale-colored soft-bodied social insects that live in colonies consisting of usually winged sexual forms, wingless sterile workers, and often soldiers, feed on wood, and include some very destructive to wooden structures and trees — called also *white ant* [Late Latin *termit-, termes,* a worm that eats wood]

term paper *n* : a major written assignment in a school or college course involving a student's individual research and study in a subject area

tern \ˈtərn\ *n* : any of numerous seabirds that often have a forked tail, black cap, and white or gray body and that in comparison to the related gulls have a smaller and more slender body and bill and narrower wings [of Scandinavian origin]

tern

ter·na·ry \ˈtər-nə-rē\ *adj* **1** : of, relating to, or proceeding by threes **2** : having three elements or parts [Latin *ternarius,* from *terni* "three each"]

ter·pene \ˈtər-ˌpēn\ *n* : any of various hydrocarbons $(C_5H_8)_n$ found especially in essential oils, resins, and balsams and used mostly as solvents and in organic synthesis [German *Terpentin* "turpentine"]

terp·si·cho·re·an \ˌtərp-sik-ə-ˈrē-ən\ *adj* : of or relating to dancing [*Terpsichore,* Greek muse of dancing]

[1]**ter·race** \ˈter-əs\ *n* **1 a** : a flat roof or open platform : BALCONY, DECK **b** : a relatively level paved or planted area adjoining a building **2 a** : a raised embankment with the top leveled **b** : one of a series of horizontal ridges made in a hillside to conserve moisture and prevent loss of soil for agriculture **3 a** (1) : a row of houses on raised ground or a sloping site (2) : a group of such houses **b** : a strip of park in the middle of a

street **c** : STREET [Middle French, "platform, terrace," from Old Occitan *terrassa,* from *terra* "earth," from Latin]

[2]**terrace** *vt* : to make into a terrace or supply with terraces ⟨the front yard had been *terraced* down to the road⟩

ter·ra–cot·ta \ˌter-ə-ˈkät-ə\ *n, pl* **terra–cottas** **1** : glazed or unglazed fired earthenware; *also* : something made of this material **2** : a brownish orange [Italian *terra cotta,* literally, "baked earth"]

ter·ra firma \-ˈfər-mə\ *n* : dry land : solid ground [New Latin, literally, "solid land"]

ter·rain \tə-ˈrān, te-\ *n* : the surface features of a tract of land ⟨a rough *terrain*⟩ [French, "land, ground," from Latin *terrenum,* derived from *terra* "earth, land"]

ter·ra·pin \ˈter-ə-pən, ˈtar-\ *n* : any of various North American turtles living in fresh or brackish water — compare DIAMONDBACK TERRAPIN [from Virginia Algonquian **to·rape·w*]

ter·rar·i·um \tə-ˈrar-ē-əm, -ˈrer-\ *n, pl* **-ia** \-ē-ə\ *or* **-i·ums** : a usually transparent enclosure for keeping or raising plants or usually small animals (as turtles) indoors [Latin *terra* "earth" + *-arium* (as in *vivarium*)]

ter·raz·zo \tə-ˈraz-ō, -ˈrät-sō\ *n* : a mosaic flooring made by embedding small pieces of marble or granite in mortar and given a high polish [Italian, literally, "terrace"]

ter·res·tri·al \tə-ˈres-trē-əl, -ˈres-chəl, -ˈresh-chəl\ *adj* **1 a** : of or relating to the earth or its inhabitants ⟨*terrestrial* magnetism⟩ **b** : PROSAIC 2, COMMONPLACE **2** : of or relating to land as distinct from air or water ⟨*terrestrial* transportation⟩ **3 a** : living on or in or growing from land ⟨*terrestrial* plants⟩ ⟨*terrestrial* birds⟩ **b** : of or relating to terrestrial organisms ⟨*terrestrial* habits⟩ [Latin *terrestris,* from *terra* "earth"] — **terrestrial** *n* — **ter·res·tri·al·ly** \-ē\ *adv*

ter·ri·ble \ˈter-ə-bəl\ *adj* **1 a** : causing terror or awe : FEARFUL, DREADFUL ⟨a *terrible* disaster⟩ **b** : hard to bear ⟨a *terrible* responsibility⟩ **2** : EXTREME 1a, GREAT ⟨a *terrible* disappointment⟩ **3 a** : very bad or extremely unpleasant ⟨had a *terrible* time⟩ **b** : of notably inferior quality ⟨a *terrible* movie⟩ [Medieval French, from Latin *terribilis,* from *terrēre* "to frighten"] — **ter·ri·bly** \-blē\ *adv*

ter·ri·er \ˈter-ē-ər\ *n* : any of various usually small energetic dogs originally used by hunters to dig for small game and attack the quarry underground or drive it out [French *chen terrer,* literally, "earth dog"]

ter·rif·ic \tə-ˈrif-ik\ *adj* **1** : TERRIBLE 1a, FRIGHTFUL ⟨*terrific* destruction⟩ **2** : EXTRAORDINARY, ASTOUNDING ⟨*terrific* speed⟩; *esp* : TREMENDOUS ⟨a *terrific* explosion⟩ **3** : unusually fine : MAGNIFICENT ⟨the party was *terrific*⟩ — **ter·rif·i·cal·ly** \-ˈrif-i-kə-lē, -klē\ *adv*

ter·ri·fy \ˈter-ə-ˌfī\ *vt* **-fied; -fy·ing** : to fill with or move to some action by terror

ter·ri·fy·ing \-ˌfī-ing\ *adj* : causing terror or great apprehension — **ter·ri·fy·ing·ly** *adv*

[1]**ter·ri·to·ri·al** \ˌter-ə-ˈtōr-ē-əl, -ˈtȯr-\ *adj* **1 a** : of or relating to territory or a territory ⟨a *territorial* government⟩ **b** : of or relating to or organized chiefly for home defense ⟨a *territorial* army⟩ **2** : exhibiting or involving territoriality ⟨*territorial* birds⟩ — **ter·ri·to·ri·al·ly** \-ē-ə-lē\ *adv*

[2]**territorial** *n* : a member of a territorial military unit

ter·ri·to·ri·al·ism \ˌter-ə-ˈtōr-ē-ə-ˌliz-əm, -ˈtȯr-\ *n* : TERRITORIALITY

ter·ri·to·ri·al·i·ty \ˌter-ə-ˌtōr-ē-ˈal-ət-ē, -ˌtȯr-\ *n* : the pattern of behavior associated with the defense of an animal's territory

ter·ri·to·ri·al·ize \-ˈtōr-ē-ə-ˌlīz, -ˈtȯr-\ *vt* : to organize on a territorial basis — **ter·ri·to·ri·al·i·za·tion** \-ˌtōr-ē-ə-lə-ˈzā-shən, -ˌtȯr-\ *n*

territorial waters *n pl* : the waters under the sovereign jurisdiction of a nation or state including both marginal sea and inland waters

ter·ri·to·ry \ˈter-ə-ˌtōr-ē, -ˌtȯr-\ *n, pl* **-ries** **1** : a geographic area belonging to or under the jurisdiction of a government **b** : an administrative subdivision of a country **c** : a part of the U.S. not included within any state but organized with a separate legislature **d** : a geographic area (as a colonial possession) dependent upon an external government but having some degree of autonomy **2 a** : an indeterminate geographic area **b** : a field of knowledge or interest **3 a** : an assigned area ⟨a salesman's *territory*⟩ **b** : an area that is occupied and defended by an animal or group of animals [Latin *territorium,* from *terra* "land"]

ter·ror \ˈter-ər\ *n* **1** : a state of intense fear **2 a** : a cause of fear or anxiety **b** : a dreadful person or thing; *esp* : an unruly child **3** : REIGN OF TERROR **4** : violent or destructive acts (as bombing) committed by groups for the purpose of intimidating a population or government into granting their demands [Medieval French *terrour,* from Latin *terror,* from *terrēre* "to frighten"]

ter·ror·ism \ˈter-ər-ˌiz-əm\ *n* : systematic use of terror especially as a means of gaining some political end — **ter·ror·ist** \-ər-əst\ *adj or n* — **ter·ror·is·tic** \ˌter-ər-ˈis-tik\ *adj*

ter·ror·ize \ˈter-ər-ˌīz\ *vt* **1** : to fill with terror or anxiety **2** : to coerce by threat or violence — **ter·ror·i·za·tion** \ˌter-ər-ə-ˈzā-shən\ *n*

ter·ry \ˈter-ē\ *n, pl* **terries** : an absorbent fabric with a loose pile of uncut loops — called also *terry cloth* [perhaps from French *tiré,* past participle of *tirer* "to draw"]

terse \ˈtərs\ *adj* **ters·er; ters·est** : using as few words as possible without loss of force or clearness : CONCISE ⟨a *terse* summary⟩; *also* : BRUSQUE, CURT ⟨dismissed me with a *terse* "no"⟩ [Latin *tersus* "clean, neat," from *tergēre* "to wipe off"] — **terse·ly** *adv* — **terse·ness** *n*

ter·tian \ˈtər-shən\ *adj* : recurring at approximately 48-hour intervals ⟨the *tertian* fever of malaria⟩ [Latin *tertianus,* from *tertius* "third"]

[1]**ter·ti·ary** \ˈtər-shē-ˌer-ē\ *n, pl* **-ar·ies** **1** : a member of a monastic third order especially of lay people **2** *cap* : the Tertiary period or system of rocks

[2]**tertiary** *adj* **1 a** : of third rank, importance, or value **b** : of, relating to, or constituting the third strongest of three or four degrees of stress ⟨the third syllable of *basketball team* carries *tertiary* stress⟩ **2** *cap* : of, relating to, or being the first period of the Cenozoic era or the corresponding system of rocks marked by the formation of high mountains (as the Alps and Himalayas) and the dominance of mammals on land — see GEOLOGIC TIME table **3** : formed by the substitution of three atoms or groups ⟨a *tertiary* salt⟩ **4** : occurring in or being a third stage [Latin *tertiarius* "of or containing a third," from *tertius* "third"]

ter·za rima \ˌtert-sə-ˈrē-mə\ *n* : a verse form consisting of tercets usually in iambic pentameter with an interlaced rhyme scheme (as *aba, bcb, cdc*) [Italian, literally, "third rhyme"]

tes·la \ˈtes-lə\ *n* : a unit of magnetic flux density that is used to express the magnitude of a magnetic field [Nikola *Tesla,* died 1943, American electrical engineer and inventor]

tes·sel·late \ˈtes-ə-ˌlāt\ *vt* : to form into or adorn with mosaic [Late Latin *tessellare* "to pave with tesserae," from Latin *tessella* "small tessera," from *tessera*] — **tes·sel·la·tion** \ˌtes-ə-ˈlā-shən\ *n*

tes·sel·lat·ed \ˈtes-ə-ˌlāt-əd\ *adj* : made of or resembling mosaic; *esp* : having a checkered appearance

tes·sera \ˈtes-ə-rə\ *n, pl* **-ser·ae** \-ˌrē, -ˌrī\ **1** : a small tablet (as of wood, bone, or ivory) used by the ancient Romans as a ticket, tally, voucher, or means of identification **2** : a small piece (as of marble, glass, or tile) used in mosaic work [Latin]

[1]**test** \ˈtest\ *n* **1 a** : a critical examination, observation, or evaluation : TRIAL ⟨put their courage to the *test*⟩ **b** : something that tries quality or resistance ⟨ideas that can only be judged by the *test* of time⟩ **2** : a means of testing: as **a** : a procedure, reaction, or reagent used to identify or characterize something ⟨a *test* for starch⟩ ⟨a series of allergy *tests*⟩ **b** : something (as a series of questions or exercises) for measuring the skill, knowledge, intelligence, capacities, or aptitudes of an individual or group **3** : a result of or rating based on a test ⟨uses 80-pound *test* fishing line⟩ [Medieval French, "vessel in which metals were assayed, cupel," from Latin *testum* "earthen vessel"]

Word History Latin *testum* was a general word for an earthen vessel. In the Middle Ages its French descendant, *test,* was the word for a specific type of vessel used in the assaying of precious metals, a cupel. A cupel is a shallow porous cup. When impure silver or gold is heated in it, the impurities are absorbed in the porous material, leaving a relatively pure button of silver or gold. As the name for a cupel, *test* was borrowed into English in the 14th century. It was later used figuratively. To "put something to the test" was to make trial of it, to determine its quality or genuineness, as a precious metal might be tried in a cupel.

\ə\ **abut**	\au̇\ **out**	\i\ **tip**	\ȯ\ **saw**	\u̇\ **foot**
\ər\ **further**	\ch\ **chin**	\ī\ **life**	\ȯi\ **coin**	\y\ **yet**
\a\ **mat**	\e\ **pet**	\j\ **job**	\th\ **thin**	\yü\ **few**
\ā\ **take**	\ē\ **easy**	\ng\ **sing**	\th\ **this**	\yu̇\ **cure**
\ä\ **cot, cart**	\g\ **go**	\ō\ **bone**	\ü\ **food**	\zh\ **vision**

²test *vb* **1 :** to put to test or proof : TRY — often used with *out* ⟨*test* out the new car⟩ **2 a :** to undergo a test **b :** to achieve or be assigned a rating on the basis of tests ⟨the class *tested* high in math⟩ **3 :** to use tests as a means of analysis or diagnosis — used with *for* ⟨*test* for copper⟩ ⟨*test* for allergens⟩ — **test·able** \ˈtes-tə-bəl\ *adj*

³test *n* **:** a firm or rigid outer covering (as a shell) of many invertebrates [Latin *testa* "shell"]

tes·ta \ˈtes-tə\ *n, pl* **tes·tae** \-ˌtē, -tī\ **:** the hard outer coat of a seed [Latin, "shell"]

tes·ta·cy \ˈtes-tə-sē\ *n, pl* **-cies :** the state of being testate

tes·ta·ment \ˈtes-tə-mənt\ *n* **1 a** *archaic* **:** a covenant between God and the human race **b** *cap* **:** either of two chief divisions of the Bible **2 a :** tangible proof or tribute : EVIDENCE ⟨the result is *testament* to her determination and hard work⟩ **b :** an expression of conviction : CREED **3 :** a legal instrument by which a person determines the disposition of his or her property after death [Late Latin *testamentum* "covenant, holy scripture," from Latin, "last will," from *testari* "to call to witness, make a will," from *testis* "witness"] — **tes·ta·men·ta·ry** \ˌtes-tə-ˈment-ə-rē, -ˈmen-trē\ *adj*

tes·tate \ˈtes-ˌtāt, -tət\ *adj* **:** having left a valid will ⟨he died *testate*⟩ [Latin *testatus,* past participle of *testari* "to make a will"]

tes·ta·tor \ˈtes-ˌtāt-ər, tes-ˈ\ *n* **:** a person who leaves a will in force at death

tes·ta·trix \tes-ˈtā-triks\ *n* **:** a woman who is a testator

test ban *n* **:** a self-imposed ban on the atmospheric testing of nuclear weapons by countries having such weapons

test bed *n* **:** a vehicle (as an airplane) used for testing new equipment; *also* **:** any device, facility, or means for testing something in development

test case *n* **1 :** a representative case whose outcome is likely to serve as a precedent **2 :** a proceeding brought by agreement or on an understanding of the parties to obtain a decision as to the constitutionality of a statute

test·cross \ˈtest-ˌkrȯs, ˈtes-\ *n* **:** a cross between an individual expressing a recessive trait and one expressing a dominant trait to determine whether or not the latter is heterozygous

test·ed \ˈtes-təd\ *adj* **:** subjected to or qualified through testing ⟨time-*tested* principles⟩ ⟨tuberculin-*tested* cattle⟩

¹tes·ter \ˈtē-stər, ˈtes-\ *n* **:** a canopy over a bed, pulpit, or altar [Middle French *tester* "headboard of a bed, canopy," from *teste* "head," from Late Latin *testa* "skull," from Latin, "shell"]

²test·er \ˈtes-tər\ *n* **:** one that tests

testes *plural of* TESTIS

tes·ti·cle \ˈtes-ti-kəl\ *n* **:** TESTIS [Latin *testiculus,* from *testis*] — **tes·tic·u·lar** \tes-ˈtik-yə-lər\ *adj*

tes·ti·fy \ˈtes-tə-ˌfī\ *vb* **-fied; -fy·ing 1 a :** to make a statement based on personal knowledge or belief ⟨could *testify* to the student's devotion to her studies⟩ **b :** to declare solemnly (as under oath) ⟨*testified* that the signature was genuine⟩ **2 :** to serve as a sign ⟨smiles *testifying* to contentment⟩ [Latin *testificari,* from *testis* "witness"] — **tes·ti·fi·er** \-ˌfī-ər, -ˌfīr\ *n*

¹tes·ti·mo·ni·al \ˌtes-tə-ˈmō-nē-əl\ *adj* **1 :** of, relating to, or being testimony **2 :** expressive of appreciation or esteem ⟨a *testimonial* dinner⟩

²testimonial *n* **1 :** an indication of worth or quality: as **a :** an endorsement of a product or service ⟨an athlete's *testimonial* for a tennis racket⟩ **b :** a character reference : letter of recommendation **2 :** an expression of appreciation : TRIBUTE

tes·ti·mo·ny \ˈtes-tə-ˌmō-nē\ *n, pl* **-nies 1 a :** the tablets inscribed with the Mosaic law or the ark containing them **b :** a divine decree attested in the Scriptures **2 a :** evidence based on observation or knowledge : authoritative evidence **b :** a solemn declaration usually made orally by a witness under oath in response to interrogation by a lawyer or authorized public official **3 :** a public acknowledgement or profession (as of religious experience) [Latin *testimonium* "evidence, witness," from *testis* "witness"]

tes·tis \ˈtes-təs\ *n, pl* **tes·tes** \ˈtes-ˌtēz\ **:** a typically paired male reproductive gland that produces sperm and secretes testosterone and in most mammals is contained within the scrotum [Latin, "witness, testis"]

tes·tos·ter·one \te-ˈstäs-tə-ˌrōn\ *n* **:** a male hormone produced by the testis or made synthetically that causes the development of the male reproductive system and secondary sex characteristics [derived from *testis* + *-o-* + *-sterone*]

test paper *n* **:** paper saturated with a reagent that changes color in testing for various substances

test pilot *n* **:** a pilot employed to put new airplanes through severe tests

test tube *n* **:** a tube of thin glass closed at one end and used especially in chemistry and biology

tes·tu·do \tes-ˈtüd-ō, -ˈtyüd-\ *n, pl* **-dos :** a cover of overlapping shields or a shed wheeled up to a wall used by the ancient Romans to protect an attacking force [Latin, literally, "tortoise, tortoise shell"]

tes·ty \ˈtes-tē\ *adj* **tes·ti·er; -est 1 :** easily annoyed : IRRITABLE **2 :** marked by impatience or ill humor ⟨*testy* remarks⟩ [Medieval French *testif* "headstrong," from *teste* "head"] ***synonyms*** see IRASCIBLE — **tes·ti·ly** \-tə-lē\ *adv* — **tes·ti·ness** \-tē-nəs\ *n*

te·tan·ic \te-ˈtan-ik\ *adj* **:** of, relating to, being, or tending to produce tetanus or tetany

tet·a·nus \ˈtet-n-əs, ˈtet-nəs\ *n* **1 :** an acute infectious disease characterized by contraction of voluntary muscles especially of the jaw and caused by the toxin of a bacterium which usually enters a wound and multiplies in damaged tissue — compare LOCKJAW **2 :** prolonged contraction of a muscle resulting from rapidly repeated motor impulses [Latin, from Greek *tetanos,* from *tetanos* "stretched, rigid"]

tet·a·ny \ˈtet-n-ē, ˈtet-nē\ *n* **:** a condition marked by contraction of muscles and caused by deficient calcium in the blood

tetchy \ˈtech-ē\ *adj* **tetchi·er; -est :** irritably or peevishly sensitive : TOUCHY [perhaps from obsolete *tetch* "habit"]

¹tête–à–tête \ˌtāt-ə-ˈtāt\ *adv* **:** in private [French, literally, "head to head"]

²tête–à–tête \ˈtāt-ə-ˌtāt, *2 is also* ˈtēt-ə-ˌtēt\ *n* **1 :** a private conversation between two persons **2 :** a seat for two persons facing each other

³tête–à–tête \ˌtāt-ə-ˌtāt\ *adj* **:** being face-to-face : PRIVATE

¹teth·er \ˈteth-ər\ *n* **1 :** a line (as of rope or chain) by which something (as an animal or balloon) is fastened so as to restrict its range **2 :** the limit of one's strength or resources : SCOPE ⟨at the end of my *tether*⟩ [Middle English *tethir*]

²tether *vt* **teth·ered; teth·er·ing** \ˈteth-ring, -ə-ring\ **:** to fasten or restrain by or as if by a tether ⟨felt *tethered* to her desk until the work was done⟩

teth·er·ball \ˈteth-ər-ˌbȯl\ *n* **:** a game played with a ball suspended by a string from an upright pole in which the object is to wrap the string around the pole by striking the ball in a direction opposite to that of one's opponent

tet·ra \ˈte-trə\ *n* **:** any of various small brightly colored South American fishes often kept in tropical aquariums [New Latin *Tetragonopterus,* former genus name, from Late Latin *tetragonum* "quadrangle" + Greek *pteron* "wing"]

tetra- *or* **tetr-** *combining form* **:** four : having four : having four parts ⟨*tetra*valent⟩ [Greek]

tet·ra·chlo·ride \ˌte-trə-ˈklōr-ˌīd, -ˈklȯr-\ *n* **:** a chloride containing four atoms of chlorine

tet·ra·chord \ˈte-trə-ˌkȯrd\ *n* **:** a diatonic series of four tones : half an octave

tet·ra·cy·cline \ˌte-trə-ˈsī-ˌklēn\ *n* **:** a yellow crystalline broad-spectrum antibiotic produced by a streptomyces or made synthetically

tet·rad \ˈte-ˌtrad\ *n* **:** a group or arrangement of four: as **a :** a group of four cells produced by the successive divisions of a mother cell ⟨a *tetrad* of spores⟩ **b :** a group of four chromatids that come together when replicated homologous chromosomes pair during synapsis in the first meiotic prophase [Greek *tetrad-, tetras,* from *tetra-*] — **te·trad·ic** \te-ˈtrad-ik\ *adj*

tet·ra·eth·yl lead \ˌte-trə-ˌeth-əl-\ *n* **:** a heavy oily poisonous liquid $Pb(C_2H_5)_4$ used as an antiknock agent

tet·ra·he·dron \ˌte-trə-ˈhē-drən\ *n, pl* **-drons** *or* **-dra** \-drə\ **:** a polyhedron that has four faces — **tet·ra·he·dral** \-drəl\ *adj*

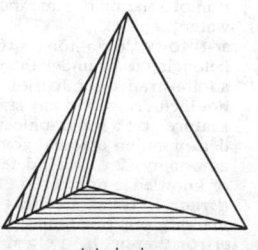

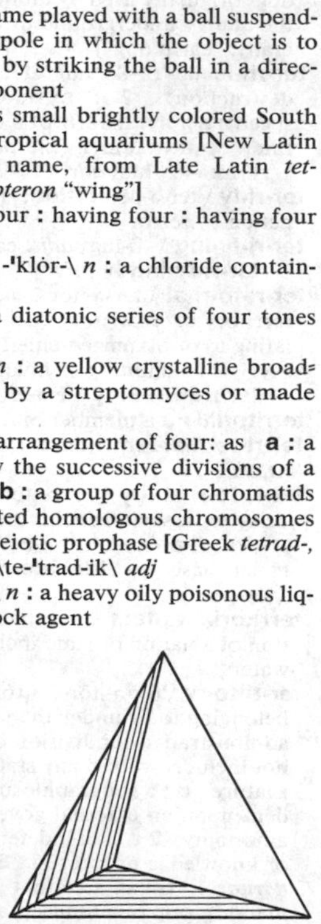
tetrahedron

te·tra·hy·dro·can·nab·i·nol \-ˌhi-drə-kə-ˈnab-ə-ˌnȯl, -ˌnōl\ *n* **:** THC [*tetra-* + *hydr-* "hydrogen" + *cannabis* + *-in* + *-ol*]

te·tral·o·gy \te-ˈträl-ə-jē, -ˈtral-\ *n, pl* **-gies :** a series of four connected works (as operas or novels)

te·tram·e·ter \te-ˈtram-ət-ər\ *n* **:** a line of verse consisting of four metrical feet [Greek *tetrametron,* derived from *tetra-* + *metron* "measure"]

tet•ra•ploid \'te-trə-ˌplȯid\ *adj* **:** having or being a chromosome number four times the monoploid number ⟨a *tetraploid* cell⟩ — **tetraploid** *n* — **tet•ra•ploi•dy** \-ˌplȯid-ē\ *n*

tet•ra•pod \'te-trə-ˌpäd\ *n* **:** a vertebrate (as an amphibian, a bird, or a mammal) with two pairs of limbs

tet•rarch \'te-ˌträrk, 'tē-\ *n* **:** a governor of the fourth part of a province (as of ancient Rome) [Latin *tetrarcha,* from Greek *tetrarchēs,* from *tetra-* + *archein* "to rule"]

te•trar•chy \'te-ˌträr-kē, 'tē-\ *n, pl* **-chies :** government by four persons ruling jointly

tet•ra•va•lent \ˌte-trə-'vā-lənt\ *adj* **:** having a valence of four

tet•rode \'te-ˌtrōd\ *n* **:** a vacuum tube with four electrodes

te•trox•ide \te-'träk-ˌsīd\ *n* **:** a compound of an element or radical with four atoms of oxygen

Teu•ton \'tüt-n, 'tyüt-n\ *n* **1 :** a member of an ancient probably Germanic or Celtic people **2 :** a member of a people speaking a language of the Germanic branch of the Indo-European language family; *esp* **:** GERMAN 1 [Latin *Teutoni* "Teutons"]

1**Teu•ton•ic** \tü-'tän-ik, tyü-\ *adj* **:** of, relating to, or characteristic of the Teutons — **Teu•ton•i•cal•ly** \-'tän-i-kə-lē, -klē\ *adv*

2**Teutonic** *n* **:** GERMANIC

tex•as \'tek-səs, -siz\ *n* **:** a structure on an upper deck of a steamer containing the officers' cabins and having the pilothouse in front or on top [*Texas,* state of the U.S.; from the fact that cabins on Mississippi steamboats were once named after states and the officers' cabins were the largest]

Texas fever *n* **:** an infectious disease of cattle transmitted by a tick and caused by a protozoan that multiplies in the blood and destroys the red blood cells

Texas leaguer *n* **:** a fly that falls between the infielders and the outfielders [*Texas League,* a baseball minor league]

Texas Ranger *n* **:** a member of a mounted police force in Texas

Tex–Mex \'teks-'meks\ *adj* **:** of, relating to, or being the Mexican-American culture or cuisine existing or originating in especially southern Texas [*Texas* + *Mexico*] — **Tex–Mex** *n*

1**text** \'tekst\ *n* **1 a :** the original written or printed words and form of a literary work **b :** an edited or emended copy of an original work ⟨several *texts* of the play are in print⟩ **2 a :** the main body of printed or written matter on a page **b :** the principal part of a book exclusive of front and back matter **3 a :** a passage of Scripture chosen for the subject of a sermon; *also* **:** a passage providing a basis (as for a speech) **b :** a source of information or authority **4 :** a subject on which one writes or speaks **:** TOPIC **5 :** matter handled with a computer that is chiefly in the form of words **6 :** TEXTBOOK **7 :** TEXT MESSAGE [Medieval French *texte,* from Latin *textus* "texture, context," from *texere* "to weave"]

2**text** *vb* **:** to send a text message from one cell phone to another

text•book \'tekst-ˌbu̇k, 'teks-\ *n* **:** a book used in the study of a subject; *esp* **:** one that presents the principles of a subject

tex•tile \'tek-ˌstīl, 'teks-tl\ *n* **1 :** CLOTH 1; *esp* **:** a woven or knit cloth **2 :** a fiber, filament, or yarn used in making cloth [Latin, from *textilis* "woven," from *texere* "to weave"] — **textile** *adj*

text message *n* **:** a short message sent electronically usually from one cell phone to another

text messaging *n* **:** the sending of short text messages electronically from one cell phone to another

tex•tu•al \'teks-chə-wəl, -chəl\ *adj* **:** of, relating to, or based on a text — **tex•tu•al•i•ty** \ˌteks-chə-'wal-ət-ē\ *n* — **tex•tu•al•ly** \'teks-chə-wəl-ē, -chəl-\ *adv*

textual criticism *n* **1 :** the study of a literary work that aims to establish the original text **2 :** a critical study of literature emphasizing a close reading and analysis of the text — **textual critic** *n*

1**tex•ture** \'teks-chər\ *n* **1 :** something (as cloth) formed by or as if by weaving **2 a :** the structure, feel, and appearance of a textile that result from the kind and arrangement of its threads ⟨the harsh *texture* of burlap⟩ **b :** similar qualities dependent on the nature and arrangement of the constituent particles of a substance ⟨a gritty *texture*⟩ ⟨a fine *texture*⟩ **3 :** an essential or identifying part or quality ⟨the truly American *texture* of the experience⟩ [Latin *textura,* from *texere* "to weave"] — **tex•tur•al** \-chə-rəl\ *adj* — **tex•tured** \-chərd\ *adj*

2**texture** *vt* **:** to give a particular and especially a rough texture to ⟨*texture* a ceiling⟩

tex•tur•ize \'teks-chə-ˌrīz\ *vt* **:** TEXTURE

T formation *n* **:** an offensive football formation in which the fullback lines up behind the quarterback and one halfback lines up on either side of the fullback

1**-th** — see -ETH

2**-th** *or* **-eth** *adj suffix* — used in forming ordinal numbers ⟨hundred*th*⟩ ⟨fort*ieth*⟩ [Old English *-tha*]

3**-th** *n suffix* **1 :** act or process ⟨spil*th*⟩ **2 :** state or condition ⟨dear*th*⟩ [Old English]

4**-th** *symbol* — used with the figures 4, 5, 6, 7, 8, 9, and 0 to indicate an ordinal number ⟨*25th*⟩ ⟨*50th* anniversary⟩ [2*-th*]

Thai \'tī\ *n* **1 :** a native or inhabitant of Thailand **2 :** the official language of Thailand — **Thai** *adj*

thal•a•mus \'thal-ə-məs\ *n, pl* **-mi** \-ˌmī, -ˌmē\ **:** the largest subdivision of the diencephalon that serves chiefly to relay nerve impulses and especially sensory nerve impulses to and from the cerebral cortex [New Latin, from Greek *thalamos* "chamber"] — **tha•lam•ic** \thə-'lam-ik\ *adj*

tha•las•sic \thə-'las-ik\ *adj* **:** of, relating to, or situated or developed about the inland seas ⟨*thalassic* civilizations of the Aegean⟩ [French *thalassique,* from Greek *thalassa* "sea"]

thaler *variant of* TALER

tha•lid•o•mide \thə-'lid-ə-ˌmīd, -məd\ *n* **:** a drug that was formerly used as a sedative and that was found to cause malformations of infants born to mothers using it during pregnancy [derived from *naphthalene* + *amide*]

thal•li•um \'thal-ē-əm\ *n* **:** a soft poisonous metallic element resembling lead in physical properties and used especially in light-sensitive devices — see ELEMENT table [New Latin, from Greek *thallos* "green shoot"; from the green line in its spectrum]

thal•lo•phyte \'thal-ə-ˌfīt\ *n* **:** any of a group of plants or plantlike organisms (as fungi and algae) that lack true stems, leaves, and roots and were formerly classified together as a division of the plant kingdom [derived from Greek *thallos* "green shoot" + *phyton* "plant"]

thal•lus \'thal-əs\ *n, pl* **thal•li** \'thal-ˌī, -ˌē\ *or* **thal•lus•es :** a plant body that lacks distinct parts (as stem, leaves, or roots), does not grow from an apical point, and is characteristic of organisms (as fungi and algae) formerly classified as thallophytes [New Latin, from Greek *thallos* "green shoot," from *thallein* "to sprout"] — **thal•loid** \'thal-ˌȯid\ *adj*

1**than** \thən, than, 'than\ *conj* **1 —** used as a function word after a comparative adjective or adverb to introduce the second part of a comparison expressing inequality ⟨older *than* I am⟩ ⟨easier said *than* done⟩ **2 —** used as a function word to indicate difference of kind, manner, or identity; used especially with some adjectives and adverbs that express diversity ⟨anywhere else *than* at home⟩ [Old English *thonne, thænne* "then, than"]

2**than** *prep* **:** in comparison with ⟨you are taller *than* me⟩

usage After about 200 years of occasional use, the preposition *than* was called into question by 18th century grammarians. Usage experts today tend to agree with their conclusions: *than whom* is standard but clumsy ⟨the president, *than* whom no one holds higher office⟩; *than me* may be acceptable in speech ⟨they were both stronger *than* me⟩; *than* followed by a third-person objective pronoun (*her, him, them*) is usually frowned upon. Our evidence shows that the conjunction *than* ⟨he is older *than* I am⟩ is more common than the preposition, that *than whom* is chiefly limited to writing, and that *me* is more common after the preposition than the third-person objective pronouns. In short, you can use *than* either as a conjunction or as a preposition.

thane \'thān\ *n* **1 :** a free retainer of an Anglo-Saxon lord; *esp* **:** one holding lands of the king and performing military service **2 :** a Scottish feudal lord [Old English *thegn*]

thank \'thangk\ *vt* **1 :** to express gratitude to ⟨*thanked* them for the present⟩ **2 :** to hold responsible ⟨had only themselves to *thank* for their loss⟩ [Old English *thancian*]

thank•ful \'thangk-fəl\ *adj* **1 :** conscious of benefit received **2 :** expressive of thanks **3 :** well pleased **:** GLAD ***synonyms*** see GRATEFUL — **thank•ful•ly** \-fə-lē\ *adv* — **thank•ful•ness** *n*

thank•less \'thang-kləs\ *adj* **1 :** not likely to obtain thanks ⟨a *thankless* task⟩ **2 :** not expressing or feeling gratitude **:** UNGRATEFUL — **thank•less•ly** *adv* — **thank•less•ness** *n*

\ə\ **abut**	\au̇\ **out**	\i\ **tip**	\ȯ\ **saw**	\u̇\ **foot**
\ər\ **further**	\ch\ **chin**	\ī\ **life**	\ȯi\ **coin**	\y\ **yet**
\a\ **mat**	\e\ **pet**	\j\ **job**	\th\ **thin**	\yü\ **few**
\ā\ **take**	\ē\ **easy**	\ng\ **sing**	\th\ **this**	\yu̇\ **cure**
\ä\ **cot, cart**	\g\ **go**	\ō\ **bone**	\ü\ **food**	\zh\ **vision**

thanks \ˈthangks\ *n pl* **1 :** kindly or grateful thoughts **:** GRATITUDE ⟨express my *thanks* for their kindness⟩ **2 :** an expression of gratitude ⟨return *thanks* before the meal⟩ — often used in an utterance containing no verb and serving as a courteous and somewhat informal expression of gratitude ⟨many *thanks*⟩ [Old English *thanc* "gratitude"]

thanks·giv·ing \thangs-ˈgiv-ing, thangks-\ *n* **1 :** the act of giving thanks **2 :** a prayer expressing gratitude **3** *cap* **:** THANKSGIVING DAY

Thanksgiving Day *n* **:** a day appointed for giving thanks for divine goodness: as **a :** the fourth Thursday in November observed as a legal holiday in the U.S. **b :** the second Monday in October observed as a legal holiday in Canada

thanks to *prep* **:** with the help of **:** BECAUSE OF ⟨arrived early, *thanks to* good weather⟩ — **no thanks to :** not as a result of any help from ⟨he feels better now, *no thanks to* you⟩

thank·wor·thy \ˈthang-ˌkwər-thē\ *adj* **:** worthy of thanks or gratitude **:** MERITORIOUS

thank–you \ˈthangk-ˌyü\ *n* **:** a polite expression of one's gratitude

thank–you–ma'am \ˈthangk-yu̇-ˌmam, -yē, -ē-\ *n* **:** a bump or depression in a road [probably from its causing a nodding of the head]

[1]**that** \ˈthat, ˈthat\ *pron, pl* **those** \thōz, ˈthōz\ **1 a :** the person, thing, or idea indicated, mentioned, or understood from the situation ⟨*that* is my father⟩ **b :** the time, action, or event specified ⟨after *that* I went to bed⟩ **c :** the kind or thing specified as follows ⟨the purest water is *that* produced by distillation⟩ **2 a :** the one farther away or less immediately under observation or discussion ⟨*those* are elms and these are maples⟩ **b :** the former one **3 a :** the one **:** the thing **:** the kind **:** SOMETHING, ANYTHING ⟨what's *that* you say⟩ **b** *pl* **:** some persons ⟨*those* who think the time has come⟩ [Old English *thæt,* neuter demonstrative pron. and definite article] — **all that :** everything of the kind indicated ⟨tact, discretion, and *all that*⟩ — **at that 1 :** in spite of what has been said or implied ⟨we might be worse off *at that*⟩ **2 :** in addition **:** [2]BESIDES ⟨told a lie, and a bad lie *at that*⟩

[2]**that** \thət, that, ˌthat\ *conj* **1 a** (1) — used to introduce a noun clause that is usually the subject or object of a verb or a predicate nominative ⟨said *that* they were afraid⟩ (2) — used to introduce a subordinate clause that is joined as complement to a noun or adjective ⟨certain *that* this is true⟩ ⟨the certainty *that* this is true⟩ ⟨the fact *that* you are here⟩ (3) — used to introduce a subordinate clause modifying an adverb or adverbial expression ⟨will go anywhere *that* he is invited⟩ **b** — used to introduce an exclamatory clause expressing surprise, sorrow, or indignation ⟨*that* it should come to this!⟩ **2 a** — used to introduce a subordinate clause expressing purpose or desired result ⟨saved money so *that* they could buy bicycles⟩ **b** — used to introduce an exclamatory clause expressing a wish ⟨oh, *that* they were here⟩ **3** — used to introduce a subordinate clause expressing a reason or cause ⟨delighted *that* you could come⟩ **4** — used to introduce a subordinate clause expressing result, consequence, or effect ⟨worked so hard *that* they became exhausted⟩

[3]**that** *adj, pl* **those 1 :** being the person, thing, or idea specified, mentioned, or understood ⟨*that* child did it⟩ **2 :** the farther away or less immediately under observation or discussion ⟨this chair or *that* one⟩

[4]**that** \thət, that, ˌthat\ *pron* **1** — used as a function word to introduce a relative clause and to serve as a substitute within that clause for the substantive modified by that clause ⟨the house *that* Jack built⟩ **2 a :** at which **:** in which **:** on which **:** by which **:** with which **:** to which ⟨each year *that* the lectures are given⟩ **b :** according to what **:** to the extent of what — used after a negative ⟨has never been there *that* I know of⟩ [Old English *thæt,* neuter relative pronoun from *thæt,* neuter demonstrative pronoun]

usage *That, which, who*: In current usage *that* refers to persons, animals, or things ⟨the person *that* I saw⟩ ⟨the book *that* she wrote⟩, *which* chiefly to things ⟨the vase *which* holds the flowers⟩, *who* chiefly to persons and sometimes to animals ⟨the child *who* had everything⟩ ⟨the dog *who* ran across the street⟩. The notion that *that* should not be used to refer to persons is without foundation; such use is entirely standard. Because *that* has no form in the genitive—the grammatical case marking typically a relationship of possessor or source—*of which* or *whose* must be used in contexts that call for the genitive.

usage *That, which*: Although some grammar books say otherwise, *that* and *which* are both regularly used to introduce restrictive clauses—clauses essential to the description of the word they refer to ⟨the book *that* [*which*] you ordered is in⟩. *Which* is also used to introduce nonrestrictive clauses—clauses that are not essential to the meaning of the preceding word ⟨the street, *which* is on the left, leads to the park⟩. *That* was formerly used to introduce nonrestrictive clauses; such use is virtually nonexistent in present-day edited prose, though it may occasionally be found in poetry.

[5]**that** \ˈthat\ *adv* **1 :** to such an extent ⟨a nail about *that* long⟩ **2 :** VERY 1, EXTREMELY ⟨it's not *that* important⟩

[1]**thatch** \ˈthach\ *vt* **:** to cover with or as if with thatch [Old English *theccan* "to cover"] — **thatch·er** *n*

[2]**thatch** *n* **1 :** a plant material (as straw) for use as roofing **2 :** a cover (as a roof) of thatch or as if of thatch ⟨a *thatch* of unruly hair⟩ **3 :** a mat of plant matter (as grass clippings) that has not undergone decomposition and has accumulated on the soil surface of a grassy area (as a lawn)

[1]**thaw** \ˈthȯ\ *vb* **1 :** to melt or cause to melt **:** reverse the effect of freezing ⟨ice on the pond is *thawing*⟩ **2 a :** to become so warm or mild as to melt ice or snow **b :** to become free of the effects (as numbness or hardness) of cold as a result of exposure to warmth ⟨the skiers *thawed* out in front of the fire⟩ ⟨frozen foods *thawing* before cooking⟩ **3 :** to grow less cold or reserved in manner **:** become more friendly [Old English *thawian*]

[2]**thaw** *n* **1 :** the action, fact, or process of thawing **2 :** a warmth of weather sufficient to thaw ice

THC \ˌtē-ˌāch-ˈsē\ *n* **:** a physiologically active liquid from hemp plant resin that is the chief intoxicant in marijuana — called also *tetrahydrocannabinol* [*t*etra*h*ydro*c*annabinol]

[1]**the** *before consonant and especially South sometimes vowel sounds* thə; *before vowel sounds* thē; *1g is often* ˈthē\ *definite article* **1 a** — used as a function word to indicate that a following noun or noun equivalent is definite or has been previously specified by context or by circumstance ⟨put *the* cat out⟩ **b** — used as a function word to indicate that a following noun or noun equivalent is a unique or a particular member of its class ⟨*the* President⟩ ⟨*the* sun⟩ **c** — used as a function word before nouns that designate natural phenomena or points of the compass ⟨*the* night is cold⟩ ⟨wind came from *the* east⟩ **d** — used as a function word before a noun denoting time to indicate reference to what is present or immediate or is under consideration ⟨in *the* future⟩ **e** — used as a function word before names of some parts of the body or of the clothing as an equivalent of a possessive adjective ⟨how's *the* arm today⟩ ⟨grabbed me by *the* collar⟩ **f** — used as a function word before the name of a branch of human endeavor or proficiency ⟨*the* law⟩ **g** — used as a function word in prepositional phrases to indicate that the noun in the phrase serves as a basis for computation ⟨sold by *the* dozen⟩ **h** — used as a function word before a proper name (as of a ship or a well-known building) ⟨*the* Mayflower⟩ **i** — used as a function word before a proper name to indicate the distinctive characteristics of a person or thing ⟨*the* John Doe that we know wouldn't lie⟩ **j** — used as a function word before the plural form of a surname to indicate all the members of a family ⟨*the* Johnsons⟩ **k** — used as a function word before the plural form of a numeral that is a multiple of ten to denote a particular decade of a century or of a person's life ⟨life in *the* twenties⟩ **l** — used as a function word before the name of something used in daily life to indicate reference to the individual thing, part, or supply thought of as at hand ⟨talked on *the* telephone⟩ **m** — used as a function word to designate one of a class as the best, most typical, best known, or most worth singling out ⟨this is *the* life⟩ ⟨was *the* player in today's game⟩ **2 a** (1) — used as a function word with a noun modified by an adjective or by an attributive noun to limit the application of the modified noun to that specified by the adjective or by the attributive noun ⟨*the* right answer⟩ ⟨Peter *the* Great⟩ (2) — used as a function word before an absolute adjective or an ordinal number ⟨nothing but *the* best⟩ ⟨payment is due on *the* first⟩ **b** (1) — used as a function word before a noun to limit its application to that specified by a succeeding element in the sentence ⟨*the* poet Wordsworth⟩ ⟨didn't have *the* time to write⟩ (2) — used as a function word after a person's name to indicate a characteristic trait or notorious activity specified by the succeeding noun ⟨Jack *the* Ripper⟩ **3 a** — used as a function

word before a singular noun to indicate that the noun is to be understood as representative of a whole class ⟨good advice for *the* beginner⟩ **b** — used as a function word before an adjective functioning as a noun to indicate an abstract idea ⟨an essay on *the* sublime⟩ **4** — used as a function word before a noun or an adjective functioning as a noun to indicate reference to a group as a whole ⟨*the* elite⟩ ⟨*the* homeless⟩ [Old English *thē,* masculine demonstrative pron. and definite article, alteration of *sē*]

²the *adv* **1 :** than before : than otherwise — used before a comparative ⟨none *the* wiser for attending⟩ **2 a :** to what extent ⟨*the* sooner the better⟩ **b :** to that extent ⟨the sooner *the* better⟩ **3 :** beyond all others ⟨likes this *the* best⟩ [Old English *thȳ* "by that," from *thæt* "that"]

the- *or* **theo-** *combining form* **:** god : God ⟨*the*ism⟩ [Greek *theos*]

the·ater *or* **the·atre** \ˈthē-ət-ər, *sometimes* ˈthē-ˌāt-ər\ *n* **1 :** a building or area for dramatic performances or for showing movies **2 :** a place resembling a theater in form or use; *esp* **:** a room often with rising tiers of seats for assemblies (as for a lecture) **3 :** a place of enactment of significant events or action ⟨a *theater* of war⟩ **4 :** dramatic literature or performance [Medieval French *theatre,* from Latin *theatrum,* from Greek *theatron,* from *theasthai* "to view," from *thea* "act of seeing"]

the·a·ter·go·er \-ˌgō-ər, -ˌgōr\ *n* **:** a person who frequently goes to the theater — **the·a·ter·go·ing** \-ˌgō-iŋ\ *n*

theater–in–the–round *n* **:** ARENA THEATER

the·at·ri·cal \thē-ˈa-tri-kəl\ *adj* **1 :** of or relating to the theater or the presentation of plays ⟨a *theatrical* costume⟩ **2 :** marked by pretense or artificiality of emotion : not natural and simple ⟨a *theatrical* acceptance speech⟩ ***synonyms*** see DRAMATIC — **the·at·ri·cal·ism** \-kə-ˌliz-əm\ *n* — **the·at·ri·cal·i·ty** \-ˌa-trə-ˈkal-ət-ē\ *n* — **the·at·ri·cal·ly** \-ˈa-tri-kə-lē, -klē\ *adv*

the·at·ri·cals \thē-ˈa-tri-kəlz\ *n pl* **1 :** the performance of plays ⟨amateur *theatricals*⟩ **2 :** the arts of acting and stagecraft

the·at·rics \-triks\ *n pl* **1 :** THEATRICALS 1 **2 :** staged or contrived effects

the·ca \ˈthē-kə\ *n, pl* **the·cae** \ˈthē-ˌsē, -ˌkē\ **:** an envelope or sheath enclosing an organism or one of its parts : CAPSULE, TEST [New Latin, from Greek *thēkē* "case"] — **the·cal** \ˈthē-kəl\ *adj*

the·co·dont \ˈthē-kə-ˌdänt\ *n* **:** any of an order (Thecodontia) of Triassic reptiles believed to be ancestral to the dinosaurs, crocodiles, and birds [derived from Greek *thēkē* "case" + *odont-, odous* "tooth"] — **thecodont** *adj*

thee \thē, ˈthē\ *pron, objective case of* THOU

theft \ˈtheft\ *n* **:** the act of stealing: as **a :** LARCENY **b :** unlawful taking (as by embezzlement or burglary) of property [Old English *thīefth*]

thegn \ˈthān\ *n* **:** THANE 1 [Old English]

their \thər, theər, thaər, ˌtheər, ˌthaər\ *adj* **1 :** of or relating to them or themselves especially as possessors, agents, or objects of an action ⟨*their* clothes⟩ ⟨*their* deeds⟩ ⟨*their* being seen⟩ **2 :** his or her : HIS, HER, ITS — used with an indefinite third person singular antecedent ⟨anyone in *their* right mind⟩ [Old Norse *theirra,* pron.] ***usage*** see THEY

theirs \ˈtheərz, ˈthaərz\ *pron, sing or pl in constr* **1 :** that which belongs to them : those which belong to them — used without a following noun as an equivalent in meaning to the adjective *their* ⟨*theirs* are on the table⟩ **2 :** his or hers : HIS, HERS — used with an indefinite third person singular antecedent ⟨I will do my part if everybody else will do *theirs*⟩

the·ism \ˈthē-ˌiz-əm\ *n* **:** belief in the existence of a god or gods; *esp* **:** belief in the existence of God as creator and ruler of the universe — **the·ist** \ˈthē-əst\ *n* — **the·is·tic** \thē-ˈis-tik\ *adj* — **the·is·ti·cal** \-ˈis-ti-kəl\ *adj* — **the·is·ti·cal·ly** \-ti-kə-lē, -klē\ *adv*

them \thəm, əm, them, ˈthem, *after* p, b, v, f *also* ᵊm\ *pron, objective case of* THEY

theme \ˈthēm\ *n* **1 a :** a subject of discourse, artistic representation, or musical composition ⟨guilt and punishment is the *theme* of the story⟩ **b :** a specific and distinctive quality, characteristic, or concern ⟨the house was decorated in a country *theme*⟩ **2 :** a written exercise : COMPOSITION [Latin *themat-, thema,* from Greek, literally, "something laid down," from *tithenai* "to place"] — **the·mat·ic** \thi-ˈmat-ik\ *adj* — **the·mat·i·cal·ly** \-ˈmat-i-kə-lē, -klē\ *adv*

theme park *n* **:** an amusement park in which the structures and settings are based on a central theme

theme song *n* **1 :** a melody recurring so often in a production (as a movie or a musical) that it characterizes the production or one of its characters **2 :** a song used as a signature

them·selves \thəm ˈselvz, them-\ *pron pl* **1 a :** those identical ones that are they — used reflexively or for emphasis ⟨nations that govern *themselves*⟩ ⟨they *themselves* were present⟩ **b :** himself or herself : HIMSELF, HERSELF — used with an indefinite third person singular antecedent ⟨nobody can call *themselves* worthy⟩ **2 :** their normal, healthy, or sane condition or selves ⟨were *themselves* again after a night's rest⟩ ***usage*** see THEY

¹then \then, ˈthen\ *adv* **1 :** at that time ⟨it was *then* believed the world was flat⟩ **2 a :** soon after that ⟨walked to the door, *then* turned⟩ **b :** following next after in order ⟨first came the clowns, *then* came the elephants⟩ **c :** in addition : BESIDES ⟨*then* there is the interest to be paid⟩ **3 a :** in that case ⟨take it, *then,* if you want it so much⟩ **b** — used after *but* to qualify a preceding statement ⟨she lost the race, but *then* she never really expected to win⟩ **c :** according to that ⟨your mind is made up, *then*⟩ **d :** as it appears ⟨the cause of the accident, *then,* is established⟩ **e :** as a necessary consequence ⟨if you were there, *then* you saw them⟩ [Old English *thonne, thænne*]

²then \ˈthen\ *n* **:** that time ⟨wait until *then*⟩

³then \ˈthen\ *adj* **:** existing or acting at or belonging to the time mentioned ⟨the *then* king⟩

thence \ˈthens, ˈthens\ *adv* **1 :** from that place ⟨proceeding *thence* directly to class⟩ **2** *archaic* **:** from that time : THENCEFORTH **3 :** from that fact or circumstance : THEREFROM ⟨a natural conclusion follows *thence*⟩ [Middle English *thannes,* from Old English *thanne,* from *thanon*]

thence·forth \-ˌfōrth, -ˌfȯrth\ *adv* **:** from that time forward : THEREAFTER ⟨the park was *thenceforth* open to residents only⟩

thence·for·ward \thens-ˈfȯr-wərd, thens-\ *also* **thence·for·wards** \-wərdz\ *adv* **:** onward from that place or time : THENCEFORTH

theo- — see THE-

the·oc·ra·cy \thē-ˈäk-rə-sē\ *n, pl* **-cies 1 :** government of a country by officials regarded as divinely guided **2 :** a country governed by a theocracy — **theo·crat** \ˈthē-ə-ˌkrat\ *n* — **theo·crat·ic** \ˌthē-ə-ˈkrat-ik\ *adj* — **theo·crat·i·cal·ly** \-ˈkrat-i-kə-lē, -klē\ *adv*

the·od·o·lite \thē-ˈäd-l-ˌīt\ *n* **:** a surveyor's instrument for measuring horizontal and usually also vertical angles [New Latin *theodelitus*]

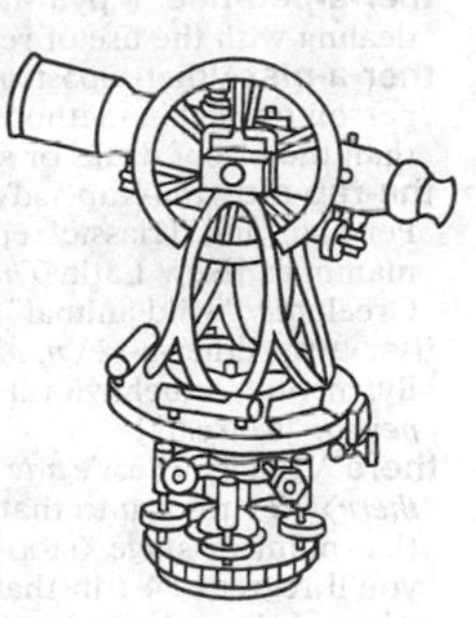

theodolite

theo·lo·gian \ˌthē-ə-ˈlō-jən\ *n* **:** a specialist in theology

theo·log·i·cal \ˌthē-ə-ˈläj-i-kəl\ *adj* **:** of or relating to theology — **theo·log·i·cal·ly** \-kə-lē, -klē\ *adv*

theological virtue *n* **:** a spiritual grace (as faith, hope, or charity) held to perfect the natural virtues

the·ol·o·gy \thē-ˈäl-ə-jē\ *n, pl* **-gies 1 :** the study of religious faith, practice, and experience; *esp* **:** the study of God and of God's relation to the world **2 :** a set of religious beliefs ⟨Catholic *theology*⟩ **3 :** a course of specialized religious training in a Roman Catholic seminary

the·o·rem \ˈthē-ə-rəm, ˈthi-ər-əm, ˈthir-əm\ *n* **1 :** a formula, proposition, or statement in mathematics or logic that has been or is to be proved from other formulas or propositions **2 :** an idea accepted or proposed as a demonstrable truth [Late Latin *theorema,* from Greek *theōrēma,* from *theōrein* "to look at," derived from *thea* "act of seeing"]

the·o·ret·i·cal \ˌthē-ə-ˈret-i-kəl\ *also* **the·o·ret·ic** \-ˈret-ik\ *adj* **1 a :** relating to or having the character of theory : ABSTRACT **b :** confined to theory or speculation : SPECULATIVE ⟨*theoretical* physics⟩ **2 :** given to or skilled in theorizing ⟨a *theoretical* physicist⟩ **3 :** existing only in theory : HYPOTHETICAL ⟨a *theo-*

retical situation⟩ [Late Latin *theoreticus,* from Greek *theōrētikos,* from *theōrein* "to look at"] — **the·o·ret·i·cal·ly** \-i-kə-lē, -klē\ *adv*

the·o·re·ti·cian \ˌthē-ə-rə-ˈtish-ən\ *n* : THEORIST

the·o·rist \ˈthē-ə-rəst, ˈthi-ər-əst, ˈthir-əst\ *n* : a person who theorizes

the·o·rize \ˈthē-ə-ˌrīz\ *vb* **-rized; -riz·ing** : to form a theory : SPECULATE — **the·o·ri·za·tion** \ˌthē-ə-rə-ˈzā-shən\ *n* — **the·o·riz·er** \ˈthē-ə-ˌrī-zər\ *n*

the·o·ry \ˈthē-ə-rē, ˈthi-ər-ē, ˈthir-ē\ *n, pl* **-ries** **1** : abstract thought : SPECULATION **2** : the general or abstract principles of a body of fact, a science, or an art ⟨music *theory*⟩ — compare PRACTICE **3 a** : a belief, policy, or procedure proposed or followed as the basis of action ⟨her method is based on the *theory* that all dogs can be trained⟩ **b** : an ideal or hypothetical set of facts, principles, or circumstances — often used in the phrase *in theory* ⟨in *theory,* we have always advocated freedom for all⟩ **4** : a plausible or scientifically acceptable general principle or body of principles offered to explain phenomena ⟨the wave *theory* of light⟩ **5 a** : a hypothesis assumed for the sake of argument or investigation ⟨the *theory* of relativity⟩ **b** : an unproved assumption : CONJECTURE ⟨had a *theory* that the house was once occupied by spies⟩ [Late Latin *theoria,* from Greek *theōria,* from *theōrein* "to look at"] ***synonyms*** see HYPOTHESIS

the·os·o·phy \thē-ˈäs-ə-fē\ *n* **1** : belief about God and the world held to be based on mystical insight **2** *often cap* : the teachings of a modern movement originating in the U.S. in 1875 and following chiefly Buddhist and Hindu theories especially of pantheistic evolution and reincarnation [Medieval Latin *theosophia,* from Late Greek, from Greek *theos* "god" + *sophia* "wisdom"] — **the·o·soph·i·cal** \ˌthē-ə-ˈsäf-i-kəl\ *adj* — **the·o·soph·i·cal·ly** \-ˈsäf-i-kə-lē, -klē\ *adv* — **the·os·o·phist** \thē-ˈäs-ə-fəst\ *n*

ther·a·peu·tic \ˌther-ə-ˈpyüt-ik\ *adj* : of or relating to the treatment of diseases or disorders by using healing agents or methods ⟨*therapeutic* studies⟩; *also* : CURATIVE, MEDICINAL ⟨*therapeutic* diets⟩ [Greek *therapeutikos,* from *therapeuein* "to attend, treat," from *theraps* "attendant"] — **ther·a·peu·ti·cal·ly** \-ˈpyüt-i-kə-lē, -klē\ *adv*

ther·a·peu·tics \-ˈpyüt-iks\ *n* : a branch of medical science dealing with the use of remedies

ther·a·pist \ˈther-ə-pəst\ *n* : one specializing in therapy; *esp* : a person trained in methods of treatment and rehabilitation other than the use of drugs or surgery ⟨a speech *therapist*⟩

the·rap·sid \thə-ˈrap-səd\ *n* : any of an order (Therapsida) of Permian and Triassic reptiles believed to be ancestors of the mammals [New Latin *Therapsida,* from *ther-* "mammal" (from Greek *thēr* "wild animal") + *apsis* "arch, vault"]

ther·a·py \ˈther-ə-pē\ *n, pl* **-pies** : therapeutic treatment of bodily, mental, or behavioral disorder [Greek *therapeia,* from *therapeuein* "to treat"]

[1]there \ˈthaər, ˈtheər\ *adv* **1** : in or at that place ⟨stand over *there*⟩ **2** : to or into that place ⟨went *there* after work⟩ **3** : at that point or stage ⟨stop right *there* before you say something you'll regret⟩ **4** : in that matter, respect, or relation ⟨*there* is where I disagree with you⟩ **5** — used interjectionally to express satisfaction, approval, soothing, or defiance ⟨*there,* I'm through⟩ ⟨so *there*⟩ [Old English *thǣr*]

[2]there \thaər, theər, ˌthaər, ˌtheər, *1 is also* thər\ *pron* **1** — used as a function word to introduce a sentence or clause ⟨*there* shall come a time⟩ **2** — used as an indefinite substitute for a name ⟨hi *there*⟩

[3]there *like* [1]\ *n* **1** : that place or position ⟨get away from *there*⟩ **2** : that point ⟨you take it from *there*⟩

[4]there *like* [1]\ *adj* **1** — used for emphasis especially after a demonstrative pronoun or a noun modified by a demonstrative adjective ⟨those people *there* can tell you⟩ **2** : capable of being relied on for support or aid ⟨she is always *there* for him⟩ **3** : fully conscious, rational, or aware ⟨not all *there*⟩

there·abouts *also* **there·about** \ˌthar-ə-ˈbau̇ts, ˌther-, -ə-ˈbau̇t\ *adv* **1** : near that place or time ⟨came from that town or *thereabouts*⟩ **2** : near that number, degree, or quantity ⟨fifty people or *thereabouts*⟩

there·af·ter \tha-ˈraf-tər, the-\ *adv* : after that ⟨it was returned shortly *thereafter*⟩

there·at \-ˈrat\ *adv* **1** : at that place **2** : at that occurrence : on that account

there·by \thaər-ˈbī, theər-\ *adv* **1** : by that : by that means ⟨*thereby* lost her chance to win⟩ **2** : connected with or with reference to that ⟨*thereby* hangs a tale⟩

there'd \ˈtherd, ˈther-əd\ : there had : there would

there·for \-ˈfȯr\ *adv* : for or in return for that ⟨ordered a change and gave his reasons *therefor*⟩

there·fore \ˈthaər-ˌfōr, ˈtheər-, -ˌfȯr\ *adv* **1** : for that reason : because of that : on that ground : CONSEQUENTLY ⟨he lost the bet, *therefore* he must pay⟩ **2** : to that end ⟨the water must be sterilized, *therefore* it was boiled for 15 minutes⟩

there·from \thaər-ˈfrəm, theər-, -ˈfräm\ *adv* : from that or it ⟨learned much *therefrom*⟩

there·in \tha-ˈrin, the-\ *adv* **1** : in or into that place, time, or thing ⟨the world and all *therein*⟩ **2** : in that particular or respect ⟨*therein* they disagreed⟩

there·in·af·ter \ˌthar-in-ˈaf-tər, ˌther-\ *adv* : in the following part of that matter (as writing, document, or speech)

there'll \ˈtherl, ˈther-əl\ : there will : there shall

there·of \tha-ˈrəv, the-, -ˈräv\ *adv* **1** : of that or it ⟨the problem and solution *thereof*⟩ **2** : from that cause or particular : THEREFROM

there·on \-ˈrȯn, -ˈrän\ *adv* : on that ⟨text and commentary *thereon*⟩

there's \ˈtherz, thərz\ : there is : there has

there·to \thaər-ˈtü, theər-\ *adv* : to that ⟨voiced no objections *thereto*⟩

there·to·fore \ˈthart-ə-ˌfōr, ˈthert-, -ˌfȯr\ *adv* : up to that time ⟨noticed the *theretofore* undetected mistake⟩

there·up·on \ˈthar-ə-ˌpȯn, ˈther-, -ˌpän\ *adv* **1** : on that matter : THEREON ⟨they disagreed *thereupon*⟩ **2** : THEREFORE **3** : immediately after that : at once ⟨saw his bad grades and *thereupon* cut off his allowance⟩

there've \ˈtherv, thərv\ : there have

there·with \thaər-ˈwith, theər-, -ˈwith\ *adv* : with that ⟨led a simple life and was happy *therewith*⟩

there·with·al \ˈthaər-with-ˌȯl, ˈtheər-, -with-\ *adv* **1** *archaic* : BESIDES **2** : THEREWITH

therm- *or* **thermo-** *combining form* : heat ⟨*therm*ion⟩ ⟨*thermo*stat⟩ [Greek *thermē*]

[1]ther·mal \ˈthər-məl\ *adj* **1** : of or relating to a hot spring ⟨*thermal* springs⟩ **2** : of, relating to, or caused by heat : WARM, HOT — **ther·mal·ly** \-mə-lē\ *adv*

[2]thermal *n* : a rising body of warm air

thermal pollution *n* : the discharge of heated liquid (as water) into a natural body of water at a temperature harmful to the environment

thermal printer *n* : a dot matrix printer (as for a computer) in which heat is applied to the pins of the matrix to form dots on usually heat-sensitive paper

therm·ion \ˈthər-ˌmī-ən, -ˌmī-ˌän\ *n* : an electrically charged particle emitted by an incandescent substance — **therm·ion·ic** \ˌthər-mī-ˈän-ik\ *adj*

therm·is·tor \ˈthər-ˌmis-tər\ *n* : an electrical resistor made of a material whose resistance varies sharply in a known manner with the temperature [*therm*al res*istor*]

ther·mo·cline \ˈthər-mə-ˌklīn\ *n* : a layer in a body of water (as a lake) which separates warmer surface water from cold deep water

ther·mo·cou·ple \ˈthər-mə-ˌkəp-əl\ *n* : a device for measuring temperature in which a pair of wires of dissimilar metals (as copper and iron) are joined and the free ends of the wires are connected to an instrument (as a voltmeter) that measures the difference in potential created at the junction of the two metals

ther·mo·dy·nam·ics \ˌthər-mō-dī-ˈnam-iks, -də-\ *n* : physics that deals with the mechanical action or relations of heat — **ther·mo·dy·nam·ic** \-ik\ *adj* — **ther·mo·dy·nam·i·cal·ly** \-ˈnam-i-kə-lē, -klē\ *adv*

ther·mo·elec·tric \ˌthər-mō-i-ˈlek-trik\ *adj* : of or relating to phenomena involving relations between the temperature and the electrical condition in a metal or in contacting metals

ther·mo·elec·tric·i·ty \ˌthər-mō-i-ˌlek-ˈtris-ət-ē, -ˈtris-tē\ *n* : electricity produced by the direct action of heat (as by the unequal heating of a circuit composed of two dissimilar metals)

ther·mo·gram \ˈthər-mə-ˌgram\ *n* : a photograph that shows differences in temperature between different parts of an object (as the body or a building)

ther·mo·graph \ˈ-ˌgraf\ *n* : a self-recording thermometer

ther·mo·la·bile \ˌthər-mō-ˈlā-ˌbīl, -bəl\ *adj* : unstable when heated ⟨many enzymes and vitamins are *thermolabile*⟩ — compare THERMOSTABLE — **ther·mo·la·bil·i·ty** \-lā-ˈbil-ət-ē\ *n*

ther·mom·e·ter \thər-ˈmäm-ət-ər, thə-ˈmäm-\ *n* : an instrument for measuring temperature; *esp* : one consisting of a glass bulb attached to a fine glass tube with a numbered scale and containing a liquid (as mercury or colored alcohol) that is sealed in and rises and falls with changes of temperature — **ther·mo·met·ric** \ˌthər-mə-ˈme-trik\ *adj* — **ther·mo·met·ri·cal·ly** \-tri-kə-lē, -klē\ *adv*

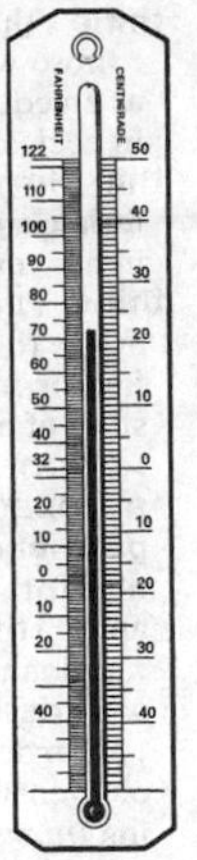

thermometer

ther·mom·e·try \thər-ˈmäm-ə-trē, thə-ˈmäm-\ *n* : the measurement of temperature

ther·mo·nu·cle·ar \ˌthər-mō-ˈnü-klē-ər, -ˈnyü-\ *adj* **1** : of or relating to the transformations in the nucleus of atoms of low atomic weight (as hydrogen) that require a very high temperature (as in the hydrogen bomb or in the sun) ⟨a *thermonuclear* reaction⟩ ⟨a *thermonuclear* weapon⟩ **2** : of, utilizing, or relating to a thermonuclear bomb ⟨*thermonuclear* war⟩

ther·mo·phile \ˈthər-mə-ˌfīl\ *n* : an organism living at a high temperature — **ther·mo·phil·ic** \ˌthər-mə-ˈfil-ik\ *adj*

ther·mo·pile \ˈthər-mə-ˌpīl\ *n* : an apparatus consisting of a number of thermoelectric couples combined so as to multiply the effect and used for generating electric currents or for determining intensities of radiation

ther·mo·plas·tic \ˌthər-mə-ˈplas-tik\ *adj* : having the property of softening or fusing when heated and of hardening again when cooled ⟨*thermoplastic* synthetic resins⟩ — **thermoplastic** *n*

ther·mo·reg·u·la·tor \ˌthər-mō-ˈreg-yə-ˌlāt-ər\ *n* : a device (as a thermostat) for the regulation of temperature

ther·mos \ˈthər-məs\ *n* : a container (as a bottle) with a vacuum between an inner and an outer wall used to keep material (as liquids) hot or cold [from *Thermos,* a former trademark]

ther·mo·set·ting \ˈthər-mō-ˌset-ing\ *adj* : having the property of becoming permanently rigid when heated or cured ⟨a *thermosetting* synthetic resin⟩

ther·mo·sphere \ˈthər-mə-ˌsfiər\ *n* : the part of the earth's atmosphere that begins at about 50 miles (80 kilometers) above the earth's surface and is characterized by a steady increase in temperature with height

ther·mo·sta·ble \ˌthər-mō-ˈstā-bəl\ *adj* : stable when heated ⟨*thermostable* enzymes⟩ — compare THERMOLABILE

ther·mo·stat \ˈthər-mə-ˌstat\ *n* : an automatic device for regulating temperature (as of a heating system); *also* : a device for actuating fire alarms or for controlling automatic sprinklers [*therm-* + Greek *-statēs* "one that stops or steadies," from *histanai* "to cause to stand"] — **ther·mo·stat·ic** \ˌthər-mə-ˈstat-ik\ *adj* — **ther·mo·stat·i·cal·ly** \-ˈstat-i-kə-lē, -klē\ *adv*

ther·mo·tax·is \ˌthər-mə-ˈtak-səs\ *n* : a taxis in which temperature is the directive factor

ther·mot·ro·pism \ˌthər-ˈmä-trə-ˌpiz-əm\ *n* : a tropism in which a temperature gradient determines the orientation — **ther·mo·trop·ic** \ˌthər-mə-ˈträp-ik\ *adj*

the·ro·pod \ˈthir-ə-ˌpäd\ *n* : any of a group (Theropoda) of flesh-eating saurischian dinosaurs (as a tyrannosaur or velociraptor) that walked on two legs and usually had small forelimbs [New Latin *Theropoda,* from Greek *thēr* "wild animal" + *pod-, pous* "foot"]

the·sau·rus \thi-ˈsȯr-əs\ *n, pl* **-sau·ri** \-ˈsȯr-ˌī, -ˌē\ *or* **-sau·rus·es** \-ˈsȯr-ə-səz\ **1** : a book of words or of information about a particular field; *esp* : a book of words and their synonyms **2** : TREASURY 3, STOREHOUSE [Latin, "treasure, collection," from Greek *thēsauros*]

these *plural of* THIS

the·sis \ˈthē-səs\ *n, pl* **the·ses** \ˈthē-ˌsēz\ **1** : a proposition to be proved or one advanced without proof : HYPOTHESIS **2** : an essay bringing together the results of original research; *esp* : one written by a candidate for an academic degree [Latin, from Greek, literally, "act of laying down," from *tithenai* "to put"]

[1]thes·pi·an \ˈthes-pē-ən\ *adj, often cap* : relating to the drama : DRAMATIC [from the tradition that Thespis was the originator of the actor's role]

[2]thespian *n* : ACTOR 1b

Thes·sa·lo·nians \ˌthes-ə-ˈlō-nyənz, -nē-ənz\ *n* : either of two letters written by Saint Paul to the Christians of Thessalonica and included as books in the New Testament — see BIBLE table

the·ta \ˈthāt-ə\ *n* : the 8th letter of the Greek alphabet — Θ or θ

they \t͟hā, ˈt͟hā\ *pron, pl in constr* **1 a** : those ones — used as third person pronoun serving as the plural of *he, she,* or *it* or referring to a group of two or more individuals not all of the same sex ⟨*they* dance well⟩ **b** : [1]HE 2 — often used with an indefinite third person singular antecedent ⟨anyone can leave if *they* like⟩ **2** : PEOPLE 1 — used in a generic sense ⟨as lazy as *they* come⟩ ⟨*they* say it will rain⟩ [Old Norse *their*]

usage *They* used as an indefinite subject (sense 2) ⟨*they* are tearing down the building tomorrow⟩ is sometimes objected to on the grounds that it does not have an antecedent. Not every pronoun requires an antecedent, however. The indefinite *they* is used in all varieties of contexts and is standard.

usage *They, their, them, themselves*: English lacks a common-gender third person singular pronoun that can be used to refer to indefinite pronouns (as *everyone, anyone, someone*). Writers and speakers have supplied this lack by using the plural pronouns ⟨everyone should try it once in *their* life⟩ ⟨anyone who knows *their* facts would agree⟩. The plural pronouns have also been put to use as pronouns of indefinite number to refer to singular nouns that stand for many persons ⟨no player plans on getting hurt, but *they* sometimes do get hurt⟩. The use of *they, their, them,* and *themselves* as pronouns of indefinite gender and indefinite number is well established in speech and writing, even in literary and formal contexts. This gives you the option of using the plural pronouns where you think they sound best, and of using the singular pronouns (as *he, she, he or she,* and their inflected forms) where you think they sound best.

they'd \t͟hād, ˌt͟hād\ : they had : they would

they'll \t͟hāl, ˌt͟hāl, t͟hel\ : they shall : they will

they're \t͟hər, t͟heər, ˌt͟heər, ˌt͟hā-ər\ : they are

they've \t͟hāv, ˌt͟hāv\ : they have

thi- *or* **thio-** *combining form* : containing sulfur ⟨*thio*urea⟩ [Greek *theion* "sulfur"]

thi·a·mine \ˈthī-ə-mən, -ˌmēn\ *also* **thi·a·min** \-mən\ *n* : a vitamin of the vitamin B complex essential to normal metabolism and nerve function and widely distributed in plants and animals — called also *vitamin* B_1 [*thiamine* alteration of *thiamin,* from *thi-* + *-amin* (as in *vitamin*)]

[1]thick \ˈthik\ *adj* **1 a** : having or being of relatively great depth or extent from one surface to its opposite ⟨a *thick* plank⟩ **b** : heavily built : THICKSET **2 a** : close-packed : DENSE ⟨a *thick* forest⟩ **b** : occurring in large numbers : NUMEROUS ⟨flies were *thick* in the barn⟩ **c** : viscous in consistency ⟨*thick* syrup⟩ **d** : STUFFY ⟨air *thick* with smoke⟩ **e** : marked by haze, fog, or mist ⟨*thick* weather⟩ **f** : impenetrable to the eye ⟨*thick* fog⟩ **g** : extremely intense ⟨*thick* silence⟩ **3** : measuring in thickness ⟨12 inches *thick*⟩ **4 a** : imperfectly articulated : INDISTINCT ⟨*thick* speech⟩ **b** : plainly apparent : PRONOUNCED ⟨a *thick* French accent⟩ **c** : producing inarticulate speech ⟨a *thick* tongue⟩ **5** : OBTUSE 3a, STUPID ⟨too *thick* to understand⟩ **6** : associated on close terms : INTIMATE ⟨those two are really *thick*⟩ **7** : going beyond what is proper or enough ⟨the flattery was a bit *thick*⟩ [Old English *thicce*] — **thick·ish** \-ish\ *adj* — **thick·ly** *adv*

[2]thick *n* **1** : the most crowded or active part ⟨in the *thick* of battle⟩ **2** : the part of greatest thickness ⟨the *thick* of the thumb⟩

[3]thick *adv* : in a thick manner ⟨misfortunes came *thick* and fast⟩

thick and thin *n* : every difficulty and obstacle ⟨stood by their friend through *thick and thin*⟩

thick·en \ˈthik-ən\ *vb* **thick·ened; thick·en·ing** \ˈthik-ning, -ə-ning\ **1** : to make or become thick, dense, or viscous ⟨*thicken* gravy with flour⟩ **2** : to increase the thickness of : add to the depth or diameter of **3 a** : to make inarticulate ⟨alcohol *thickened* his speech⟩ **b** : to grow blurred, obscure, or dark ⟨the weather *thickened*⟩ **4** : to grow broader or bulkier **5** : to grow complicated or keen ⟨the plot *thickens*⟩ — **thick·en·er** \ˈthik-nər, -ə-nər\ *n*

thick·en·ing *n* **1** : the act of making or becoming thick ⟨underwent a gradual *thickening*⟩ **2** : something used to thicken (as flour in a gravy) **3** : a thickened part or place

thick·et \ˈthik-ət\ *n* **1** : a dense usually small patch of shrubbery, small trees, or underbrush **2** : something resembling a thicket in density or impenetrability ⟨a *thicket* of reporters⟩ [Old English *thiccet,* from *thicce* "thick"] — **thick·et·ed** \-ət-əd\ *adj*

thick·head·ed \'thik-'hed-əd\ *adj* **1 :** mentally dull : STUPID **2 :** having a thick head

thick·ness \'thik-nəs\ *n* **1 :** the quality or state of being thick **2 :** the smallest of the three dimensions of something ⟨length, width, and *thickness* of a board⟩ **3 :** viscous consistency ⟨the *thickness* of honey⟩ **4 :** the thick part of something **5 :** CONCENTRATION 3, DENSITY **6 :** dullness of mind : STUPIDITY **7 :** LAYER, PLY, SHEET ⟨a single *thickness* of canvas⟩

thick·set \'thik-'set\ *adj* **1 :** closely placed or planted **2 :** of short stout build : STOCKY

thick–skinned \-'skind\ *adj* **1 :** having a thick skin **2 a :** CALLOUS 2, INSENSITIVE **b :** not easily bothered by criticism

thick–wit·ted \-'wit-əd\ *adj* : dull or slow of mind : STUPID

thief \'thēf\ *n, pl* **thieves** \'thēvz\ : one that steals [Old English *thēof*] — **thiev·ish** \'thē-vish\ *adj* — **thiev·ish·ly** *adv* — **thiev·ish·ness** *n*

thieve \'thēv\ *vb* **thieved; thiev·ing :** STEAL 2a, ROB

thiev·ery \'thēv-rē, -ə-rē\ *n, pl* **-er·ies :** the action of stealing : THEFT

thigh \'thī\ *n* **1 a :** the segment of the vertebrate hind or lower limb extending from the hip to the knee; *also* : the next outer segment in a bird or in a four-footed animal in which the true thigh is obscured **b :** the femur of an insect **2 :** something resembling or covering a thigh [Old English *thēoh*]

thigh·bone \-'bōn, -ˌbōn\ *n* : FEMUR 1

thig·mo·tax·is \ˌthig-mə-'tak-səs\ *n* : a taxis in which contact especially with a solid or rigid surface is the directive factor [Greek *thigma* "contact," from *thinganein* "to touch"]

thig·mot·ro·pism \thig-'mä-trə-ˌpiz-əm\ *n* : a tropism in which contact especially with a solid or rigid surface is the orienting factor [Greek *thigma* "contact," from *thinganein* "to touch"]

thim·ble \'thim-bəl\ *n* **1 :** a cap or cover used in sewing to protect the finger that pushes the needle **2 :** a grooved ring of thin metal used to fit in a loop in a wire or rope **3 :** a lining (as of metal) for an opening (as in a roof or wall) through which a stovepipe or chimney passes [Middle English *thymbyl,* probably from Old English *thȳmel* "covering for the thumb," from *thūma* "thumb"]

thim·ble·ber·ry \-ˌber-ē\ *n* : any of several American raspberries or blackberries with thimble-shaped fruit

thim·ble·ful \-ˌfu̇l\ *n* **1 :** as much as a thimble will hold **2 :** a very small quantity

[1]**thim·ble·rig** \'thim-bəl-ˌrig\ *n* : a swindling trick in which a small ball or pea is quickly shifted from under one to another of three small cups to fool a spectator guessing its location

[2]**thimblerig** *vt* **-rigged; -rig·ging 1 :** to swindle by thimblerig **2 :** to cheat by trickery — **thim·ble·rig·ger** *n*

[1]**thin** \'thin\ *adj* **thin·ner; thin·nest 1 a :** having little extent from one surface to its opposite ⟨*thin* paper⟩ **b :** measuring little in cross section or diameter ⟨*thin* rope⟩ **2 :** not dense in arrangement or distribution ⟨*thin* hair⟩ **3 :** not plump or fat : LEAN ⟨a tall *thin* boy⟩ **4 a :** more fluid or rarefied than normal ⟨*thin* air⟩ **b :** not well filled or supplied : SCANTY ⟨a *thin* market⟩ **5 :** lacking substance or strength ⟨*thin* broth⟩ ⟨a *thin* excuse⟩ **6 :** somewhat feeble, shrill, and lacking in resonance ⟨a *thin* voice⟩ [Old English *thynne*] — **thin·ly** *adv* — **thin·ness** \'thin-nəs\ *n* — **thin·nish** \'thin-ish\ *adj* — **on thin ice :** in a precarious or risky situation

synonyms THIN, SLENDER, SLIM, SLIGHT mean not thick, broad, abundant, or dense. THIN implies comparatively little extension between surfaces or in diameter ⟨a *thin* layer of ice⟩ ⟨*thin* wire⟩ or it may imply lack of substance, richness, or abundance ⟨*thin* soup⟩ ⟨a *thin* hedge⟩. SLENDER implies leanness often with graceful proportions ⟨*slender* columns⟩. SLIM suggests scantiness or fragile slenderness ⟨a *slim* paycheck⟩. SLIGHT implies thinness and smallness ⟨a person of *slight* build⟩.

[2]**thin** *adv* **thin·ner; thin·nest :** THINLY ⟨*thin*-clad⟩

[3]**thin** *vb* **thinned; thin·ning :** to make or become thin or thinner: **a :** to reduce in thickness or depth **b :** to make less dense or viscous ⟨*thinned* the glue with alcohol⟩ **c :** DILUTE 2, WEAKEN **d :** to cause to lose flesh ⟨*thinned* by months of hardship⟩ **e :** to reduce in number or bulk ⟨*thin* young carrots in the garden to prevent crowding⟩

[1]**thine** \thīn, 'thīn\ *adj, archaic* : THY — used especially before a word beginning with a vowel [Old English *thīn*]

[2]**thine** \'thīn\ *pron, sing or pl in constr* : that which belongs to thee : those which belong to thee — used without a following noun as an equivalent in meaning to the adjective *thy;* used especially in ecclesiastical or literary language

thin film *n* : a very thin layer of a substance on a supporting material; *esp* : a coating (as of a semiconductor) that is deposited in a layer one atom or one molecule thick

thing \'thing\ *n* **1 a :** a matter of concern : AFFAIR ⟨many *things* to do⟩ **b** *pl* : state of affairs in general or within a specified or implied sphere ⟨*things* are improving⟩ **c :** a particular state of affairs : SITUATION ⟨look at this *thing* another way⟩ **d :** EVENT 1a, CIRCUMSTANCE ⟨that flood was a terrible *thing*⟩ **2 a :** DEED 1, ACT, ACCOMPLISHMENT ⟨do great *things*⟩ **b :** a product of work or activity ⟨likes to build *things*⟩ **c :** the aim of effort or activity ⟨the *thing* is to get well⟩ **3 a :** a separate and distinct item or object : ENTITY; *esp* : a physical object **b :** an inanimate object as distinguished from a living being **4 a** *pl* : POSSESSIONS, PERSONAL PROPERTY ⟨pack your *things*⟩ **b :** an article of clothing ⟨not a *thing* to wear⟩ **c** *pl* : equipment or utensils especially for a particular purpose ⟨bring the cooking *things*⟩ **5 :** an object or entity not precisely designated or capable of being designated ⟨how do you use this *thing*⟩ **6 a :** DETAIL 1b, POINT ⟨checks every little *thing*⟩ **b :** a material or substance of a specified kind ⟨avoid starchy *things*⟩ **7 a :** a spoken or written observation or point **b :** IDEA 2, NOTION ⟨say the first *thing* you think of⟩ **c :** a piece of news or information ⟨couldn't get a *thing* out of him⟩ **8 :** INDIVIDUAL 1; *esp* : PERSON 1 ⟨you poor *thing*⟩ **9 :** the proper or fashionable way of behaving, talking, or dressing — used with *the* ⟨it is the *thing* to wear⟩ **10 a :** a usually mild fear or obsession ⟨has a *thing* about snakes⟩ **b :** something (as an activity) that makes a strong appeal to the individual ⟨allowed to do their own *thing*⟩ [Old English, "thing, assembly"]

thing·am·a·bob \'thing-ə-mə-ˌbäb\ *n* : THINGAMAJIG

thing·am·a·jig *or* **thing·um·a·jig** \'thing-ə-mə-ˌjig\ *n* : something that is hard to classify or whose name is unknown or forgotten [derived from *thing*]

thing·um·my \'thing-ə-mē\ *n, pl* **-mies :** THINGAMAJIG [derived from *thing*]

[1]**think** \'thingk\ *vb* **thought** \'thȯt\; **think·ing 1 :** to form or have in the mind ⟨afraid to *think* what might happen⟩ **2 :** INTEND, PLAN ⟨*thought* to return early⟩ **3 a :** to have as an opinion : BELIEVE ⟨*think* it's so⟩ **b :** to regard as : CONSIDER ⟨*think* the rule unfair⟩ **4 :** to reflect on : PONDER ⟨*think* the matter over⟩ **5 :** to call to mind : REMEMBER ⟨couldn't *think* of the name⟩ **6 :** to create or devise by thinking — usually used with *up* ⟨*think* up a caption for the picture⟩ **7 :** to subject to the processes of logical thought ⟨*think* things out⟩ **8 :** to exercise the powers of judgment, conception, or inference : REASON ⟨*think* before you write your answer⟩ **9 a :** to have the mind engaged in reflection : MEDITATE ⟨*thinking* sadly of the past⟩ **b :** to consider the suitability ⟨*thought* of you for captain⟩ **10 :** to have a view or opinion ⟨*think* of myself as a good skier⟩ **11 :** to have concern ⟨*think* of just yourself⟩ **12 :** EXPECT 4a ⟨*thought* to find them at home⟩ [Old English *thencan*] — **think·able** \'thing-kə-bəl\ *adj* — **think·er** *n* — **think better of :** to reconsider and make a wiser decision — **think much of :** to view with satisfaction — usually used in negative constructions ⟨didn't *think much of* the idea⟩

synonyms THINK, REFLECT, REASON, SPECULATE mean to use one's powers of conception, judgment, or inference. THINK may apply to any mental activity but often suggests attainment of clear ideas or conclusions ⟨the exercise teaches students how to *think*⟩. REFLECT suggests unhurried consideration of something recalled to mind ⟨*reflecting* on my life⟩. REASON stresses orderly logical thinking especially in reaching a conclusion ⟨able to *reason* brilliantly in debate⟩. SPECULATE implies reasoning but stresses the uncertain, theoretical, or problematic character of the conclusions ⟨*speculated* on the fate of the lost explorers⟩.

[2]**think** *n* : an act of thinking ⟨has another *think* coming⟩

[1]**think·ing** *n* **1 :** the action of using one's mind to produce thoughts **2 a :** OPINION 1a, JUDGMENT ⟨it is, to my *thinking,* utter nonsense⟩ **b :** THOUGHT 3b ⟨the current *thinking* on censorship⟩

[2]**thinking** *adj* : marked by use of the intellect : RATIONAL ⟨*thinking* citizens⟩ — **think·ing·ly** \'thing-king-lē\ *adv* — **think·ing·ness** *n*

thinking cap *n* : a state or mood in which one thinks ⟨put on your *thinking cap*⟩
think piece *n* : a piece of writing meant to be thought-provoking that consists chiefly of background material and personal opinion and analysis
think tank *n* : an institute, corporation, or group organized to think up new solutions especially for social and scientific problems — called also *think factory*
thin·ner \ˈthin-ər\ *n* : one that thins; *esp* : a volatile liquid (as turpentine) used to thin paint
thin–skinned \ˈthin-ˈskind\ *adj* **1** : having a thin skin ⟨*thin-skinned* oranges⟩ **2** : unduly sensitive to criticism or insult : TOUCHY
thio- — see THI-
thio·urea \ˌthī-ō-yu̇-ˈrē-ə\ *n* : a colorless crystalline bitter compound $CS(NH_2)_2$ analogous to and resembling urea that is used especially as a photographic and organic chemical reagent
thi·ram \ˈthī-ˌram\ *n* : a sulfur-containing fungicide and seed disinfectant [derived from Greek *theion* "sulfur"]
[1]**third** \ˈthərd\ *adj* **1 a** : being number three in a countable series **b** : being next after the second (as in order, time, or importance) ⟨the *third* taxi in line⟩ **2** : being one of three equal parts into which something is divisible ⟨a *third* share of the money⟩ [Old English *thridda, thirdda*] — **third** *adv* — **third·ly** *adv*
[2]**third** *n* **1 a** : number three in a countable series — see NUMBER table **b** : one next after a second (as in time, order, or importance) ⟨the *third* in line⟩ **2** : one of three equal parts of something ⟨a *third* of the pie⟩ **3 a** : a musical interval embracing three diatonic degrees; *also* : a tone at this interval **b** : the harmonic combination of two tones a third apart **4** : THIRD BASE **5** : the third forward gear or speed of an automotive vehicle
third base *n* **1** : the base that must be touched third by a base runner in baseball **2** : the position of the player defending the area around third base
third base·man \-ˈbā-smən\ *n* : the player defending the area around third base
third class *n* : the class next below second class in a classification ⟨travel by *third class* to Europe⟩; *esp* : a class of U.S. mail including various printed matter and merchandise that weighs less than 16 ounces and is open to inspection — **third–class** *adj or adv*
third degree *n* : severe or brutal treatment of a prisoner (as by police) in order to get information or a confession
third–degree burn *n* : a burn in which there is destruction of the whole thickness of the skin and sometimes of underlying tissues with loss of fluid and often shock
third dimension *n* : thickness, depth, or apparent thickness or depth that confers solidity on an object — **third–di·men·sion·al** *adj*
third estate *n* : the third of the traditional political orders : COMMON 3a; *also* : MIDDLE CLASS
third force *n* : a grouping (as of political parties or international powers) intermediate between two opposing political forces
third order *n, often cap T&O* **1** : an organization composed of lay people living in secular society under a religious rule and directed by a religious order **2** : a congregation especially of teaching or nursing sisters affiliated with a religious order
third party *n* **1** : a person other than the principals ⟨a *third party* to a divorce proceeding⟩ **2 a** : a political party operating usually for a limited time in addition to the two major parties in a 2-party system **b** : MINOR PARTY
third person *n* **1** : a set of words or forms (as verb forms or pronouns) referring to someone or something that is neither the speaker or writer of the utterance in which they occur nor the one to whom that utterance is addressed; *also* : a word or form belonging to such a set **2** : a writing style marked by general use of verbs and pronouns of the third person
third rail *n* **1** : a metal rail which is parallel to the tracks and through which electric current is led to the motors of an electric locomotive **2** : a controversial issue usually avoided by politicians
third–rate \ˈthər-ˈdrāt\ *adj* : of third quality or value; *esp* : worse than second-rate — **third–rat·er** \-ˈdrāt-ər\ *n*
third world *n, often cap T&W* **1** : a group of nations especially of Africa and Asia not aligned with either the communist or the noncommunist blocs **2** : the underdeveloped nations of the world — **third world·er** \-ˈwərl-dər\ *n, often cap T&W*
[1]**thirst** \ˈthərst\ *n* **1 a** : a feeling of dryness in the mouth and throat associated with a desire for liquids; *also* : the bodily condition (as of dehydration) that induces this feeling **b** : a desire or need to drink **2** : an ardent desire : CRAVING ⟨a *thirst* for knowledge⟩ [Old English *thurst*]
[2]**thirst** *vi* **1** : to suffer thirst **2** : to have a strong desire : CRAVE
thirsty \ˈthər-stē\ *adj* **thirst·i·er; -est** **1 a** : feeling thirst **b** : lacking moisture : PARCHED ⟨*thirsty* land⟩ **c** : highly absorbent ⟨*thirsty* towels⟩ **2** : having a strong desire : AVID ⟨*thirsty* for knowledge⟩ — **thirst·i·ly** \-stə-lē\ *adv* — **thirst·i·ness** \-stē-nəs\ *n*
thir·teen \ˌthər-ˈtēn, ˌthərt-, ˈthər-, ˈthərt-\ *n* — see NUMBER table [Old English *thrēotīne*] — **thirteen** *adj or pron* — **thir·teenth** \-ˈtēnth, -ˈtēntth\ *adj or n*
thir·ty \ˈthərt-ē\ *n, pl* **thirties** **1** — see NUMBER table **2** *pl* : the numbers 30 to 39; *esp* : the years 30 to 39 in a lifetime or century **3** : a mark or sign of completion — usually written 30 **4** : the 2nd point scored by a side in a game of tennis [Old English *thrītig*] — **thir·ti·eth** \-ē-əth\ *n or adj* — **thirty** *adj or pron*
thir·ty–eight \ˌthərt-ē-ˈāt\ *n* : a .38 caliber pistol — usually written .38
thirty–second note *n* : a musical note having the time value of one thirty-second of a whole note
thir·ty–thir·ty \ˌthərt-ē-ˈthərt-ē\ *n* : a rifle that fires a .30 caliber cartridge having a 30 grain powder charge — usually written .30-30
thir·ty–three \-ˈthrē\ *n* : a phonograph record for play at 33⅓ revolutions per minute — usually written 33
thir·ty–two \-ˈtü\ *n* : a .32 caliber pistol — usually written .32
[1]**this** \this, ˈthis, t͟həs\ *pron, pl* **these** \t͟hēz, ˈt͟hēz\ **1 a (1)** : the person, thing, or idea that is present or near in place, time, or thought or that has just been mentioned ⟨*these* are my hands⟩ **(2)** : what is stated in the following phrase, clause, or discourse ⟨I can only say *this*: they aren't here⟩ **b** : this time or place ⟨hoped to return before *this*⟩ **2 a** : the one nearer or more immediately under observation ⟨*this* is iron and that is tin⟩ **b** : the one more recently referred to [Old English *thes* (masculine), *this* (neuter)]
[2]**this** *adj, pl* **these** **1 a** : being the one that is present or near in place, time, or thought or that has just been mentioned ⟨*this* book is mine⟩ ⟨early *this* morning⟩ ⟨all *these* years⟩ **b** : being one not previously mentioned — used especially in narrative to give a sense of immediacy or vividness ⟨I had on *this* bright red shirt⟩ **2** : being the nearer at hand or more immediately under observation or discussion ⟨*this* car or that one⟩
[3]**this** \ˈt͟his\ *adv* : to the degree or extent indicated by something immediately present ⟨didn't expect to wait *this* long⟩
this·tle \ˈthis-əl\ *n* : any of various prickly plants related to the daisies and having often showy heads of mostly tubular flowers [Old English *thistel*] — **this·tly** \ˈthis-lē, -ə-lē\ *adj*
this·tle·down \-əl-ˌdau̇n\ *n* : the mass of seed-carrying fluffy bristles from the ripe flower head of a thistle
thistle tube *n* : a funnel tube usually of glass with a bulging top and flaring mouth

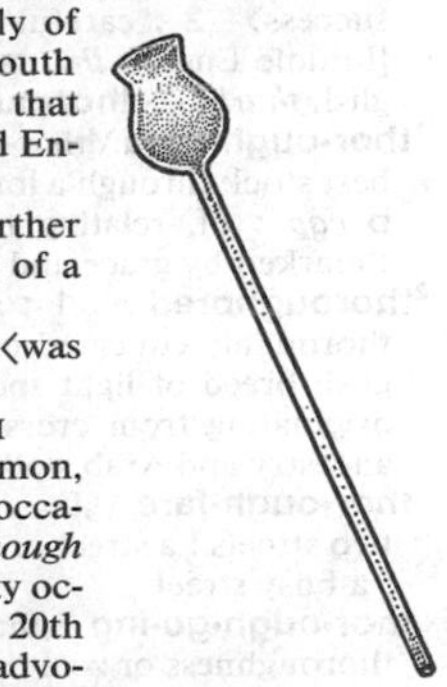
thistle tube

[1]**thith·er** \ˈthith-ər *also* ˈt͟hith-\ *adv* : to that place : THERE ⟨I shall go *thither*⟩ [Old English *thider*]
[2]**thither** *adj* : being on the other and farther side : more remote ⟨the *thither* bank of a river⟩
thith·er·to \-ˌtü\ *adv* : until that time ⟨was *thitherto* unknown to me⟩
tho \ˈt͟hō, t͟hō, ˌt͟hō\ *variant of* THOUGH

usage While never extremely common, *tho* and *thru* have a long history of occasional use as spelling variants of *though* and *through*. Their greatest popularity occurred in the late 19th and early 20th centuries, when their adoption was advocated by spelling reformers. Their current use occurs chiefly in informal writing (as in personal letters) and in some technical journals.

thole \ˈthōl\ *also* **thole·pin** \-ˌpin\ *n* : a pin set in the gunwale of a boat as a pivot for an oar [Old English *thol*]

\ə\ **abut**	\au̇\ **out**	\i\ **tip**	\ȯ\ **saw**	\u̇\ **foot**
\ər\ **further**	\ch\ **chin**	\ī\ **life**	\ȯi\ **coin**	\y\ **yet**
\a\ **mat**	\e\ **pet**	\j\ **job**	\th\ **thin**	\yü\ **few**
\ā\ **take**	\ē\ **easy**	\ng\ **sing**	\t͟h\ **this**	\yu̇\ **cure**
\ä\ **cot, cart**	\g\ **go**	\ō\ **bone**	\ü\ **food**	\zh\ **vision**

Tho·mism \'tō-ˌmiz-əm\ *n* : the scholastic philosophical and theological system of Saint Thomas Aquinas — **Tho·mist** \-məst\ *n or adj* — **Tho·mis·tic** \tō-'mis-tik\ *adj*

Thomp·son submachine gun \'täm-sən-, 'tämp-\ *n* : a submachine gun with a pistol grip and stock for firing from the shoulder — called also *tommy gun* [John T. *Thompson,* died 1940, American army officer]

thong \'thȯng\ *n* **1** : a strip of leather used especially for fastening something **2** : a sandal held on the foot by a thong fitting between the toes and connected to a strap across the top or around the sides of the foot [Old English *thwong*]

tho·rac·ic \thə-'ras-ik\ *adj* : of, relating to, located within, or involving the thorax ⟨the *thoracic* cavity⟩ ⟨*thoracic* surgery⟩

thoracic duct *n* : the chief lymphatic vessel lying along the front of the spinal column and opening into the left subclavian vein

tho·rax \'thōr-ˌaks, 'thȯr-\ *n, pl* **tho·rax·es** *or* **tho·ra·ces** \'thōr-ə-ˌsēz, 'thȯr-\ **1** : the part of the body of a mammal between the neck and the abdomen; *also* : its cavity in which the heart and lungs lie **2** : the middle of the three chief divisions of the body of an insect [Latin *thorac-, thorax* "breastplate, thorax," from Greek *thōrak-, thōrax*]

Tho·ra·zine \'thōr-ə-ˌzēn, 'thȯr-\ *trademark* — used for chlorpromazine

tho·ria \'thōr-ē-ə, 'thȯr-\ *n* : a powdery white oxide of thorium used especially in crucibles and optical glass [New Latin, from *thorium*]

tho·ri·um \'thōr-ē-əm, 'thȯr-\ *n* : a radioactive metallic element — see ELEMENT table [New Latin, from Old Norse *Thōrr* "Thor"]

thorn \'thȯrn\ *n* **1** : a woody plant bearing sharp processes (as prickles or spines); *esp* : HAWTHORN **2 a** : a sharp rigid process on a plant; *esp* : one that is a short, rigid, sharp-pointed, and leafless modified stem **b** : a sharp rigid process on an animal **3** : something that causes distress or irritation — often used in the phrase *thorn in one's side* [Old English] — **thorned** \'thȯrnd\ *adj* — **thorn·less** \'thȯrn-ləs\ *adj* — **thorn·like** \-ˌlīk\ *adj*

thorn apple *n* **1** : JIMSONWEED **2** : the fruit of a hawthorn; *also* : HAWTHORN

thorn·bush \'thȯrn-ˌbu̇sh\ *n* **1** : any of various spiny or thorny shrubs or small trees **2** : a low growth of thorny shrubs especially of dry tropical regions

thorny \'thȯr-nē\ *adj* **thorn·i·er; -est** **1** : full of or covered with thorns : SPINY ⟨*thorny* rose bushes⟩ **2** : full of difficulties or controversial points : TICKLISH ⟨a *thorny* problem⟩ — **thorn·i·ness** *n*

thoro \'thər-ō, 'thə-rō\ *nonstandard variant of* THOROUGH

thor·ough \'thər-ō, 'thə-rō\ *adj* **1** : being such to the fullest degree : EXHAUSTIVE, COMPLETE ⟨a *thorough* search⟩ ⟨*thorough* success⟩ **2** : careful about detail ⟨a very *thorough* worker⟩ [Middle English *thorow,* from *thorow* "through," from Old English *thurh*] — **thor·ough·ly** *adv* — **thor·ough·ness** *n*

[1]**thor·ough·bred** \'thər-ə-ˌbred, 'thə-rə-\ *adj* **1 a** : bred from the best stock through a long line : PUREBRED ⟨*thoroughbred* dogs⟩ **b** *cap* : of, relating to, or being a Thoroughbred horse **2** : marked by grace and elegance

[2]**thoroughbred** *n* **1** : a purebred or pedigreed animal **2** : a thoroughly educated or skilled person **3** *cap* : any of an English breed of light speedy horses kept chiefly for racing and originating from crosses between English mares of uncertain ancestry and Arab stallions

thor·ough·fare \-ˌfaər, -ˌfeər\ *n* **1** : a public way connecting two streets : a street or road open at both ends **2** : a main road : a busy street

thor·ough·go·ing \ˌthər-ə-'gō-ing, ˌthə-rə-\ *adj* : marked by thoroughness or zeal : COMPLETE ⟨*thoroughgoing* cooperation⟩

thorp \'thȯrp\ *n, archaic* : VILLAGE 1, HAMLET [Old English]

those *plural of* THAT

[1]**thou** \t̲h̲au̇, 't̲h̲au̇\ *pron* : the one spoken to — used especially in ecclesiastical or literary language; compare THEE, THINE, THY, YE, YOU [Old English *thū*]

[2]**thou** \'thau̇\ *n, pl* **thou** : a thousand of something (as dollars) ⟨paid 15 *thou* for the car⟩

[1]**though** \ˌt̲h̲ō\ *conj* **1** : in spite of the fact that ⟨*though* it was raining, we went for a walk⟩ **2** : even if : even supposing ⟨*though* I may fail, I will try⟩

[2]**though** *adv* : HOWEVER 2, NEVERTHELESS ⟨not for long, *though*⟩ [of Scandinavian origin]

[1]**thought** *past and past participle of* THINK

[2]**thought** \'thȯt\ *n* **1 a** : the act or process of thinking **b** : serious consideration : careful attention ⟨give *thought* to the future⟩ **2 a** : power of thinking and especially of reasoning and judging **b** : power of imagining or comprehending ⟨beauty beyond *thought*⟩ **3 a** : a product of thinking (as an idea, fancy, or invention) ⟨idle *thoughts*⟩ ⟨a pleasing *thought*⟩ **b** : the intellectual product or the organized views and principles of a period, place, group, or individual ⟨modern scientific *thought*⟩ [Old English *thōht*] — **a thought** : a slight amount : BIT ⟨add just *a thought* more salt to the stew⟩

thought·ful \'thȯt-fəl\ *adj* **1 a** : absorbed in thought : MEDITATIVE **b** : characterized by careful reasoned thinking ⟨a *thoughtful* essay⟩ **2 a** : having thought : HEEDFUL ⟨became *thoughtful* about her future plans⟩ **b** : given to heedful anticipation of the needs of others ⟨a kind and *thoughtful* friend⟩ — **thought·ful·ly** \-fə-lē\ *adv* — **thought·ful·ness** *n*

synonyms THOUGHTFUL, CONSIDERATE, SOLICITOUS mean mindful of others. THOUGHTFUL implies unselfish concern and ability to anticipate another's needs ⟨the thank-you note was a *thoughtful* gesture⟩. CONSIDERATE implies kind concern for the feelings of others ⟨the *considerate* boy offered to help⟩. SOLICITOUS implies deep concern and suggests anxiety for the welfare of another ⟨*solicitous* about our family⟩.

thought·less \'thȯt-ləs\ *adj* **1 a** : insufficiently alert : CARELESS **b** : RECKLESS 1, RASH ⟨*thoughtless* actions⟩ **2** : devoid of thought : INSENSATE **3** : lacking concern for others : INCONSIDERATE ⟨a *thoughtless* remark⟩ — **thought·less·ly** *adv* — **thought·less·ness** *n*

thought–out \-'au̇t\ *adj* : produced or arrived at through careful and thorough consideration ⟨a well *thought-out* plan⟩

thou·sand \'thau̇z-nd, 'thau̇z-n\ *n, pl* **thousands** *or* **thousand** **1** : ten times 100; *also* : a symbol representing this — see NUMBER table **2** : a very large or indefinitely great number ⟨*thousands* of ants⟩ [Old English *thūsend*] — **thousand** *adj*

thou·sand–leg·ger \ˌthau̇z-n-'leg-ər, -'dleg-ər\ *n* : MILLIPEDE

thousands digit *n* : the numeral (as 1 in 1456) occupying the thousands place in a number expressed in the Arabic system of writing numbers

thousands place *n* : the place four to the left of the decimal point in a number expressed in the Arabic system of writing numbers

thou·sandth \'thau̇z-nth, -ntth\ *n* **1** : one of 1000 equal parts **2** : number 1000 in a countable series — see NUMBER table — **thousandth** *adj*

thrall \'thrȯl\ *n* **1** : SLAVE 1; *also* : SERF **2 a** : a state of servitude or submission ⟨in *thrall* to his emotions⟩ **b** : a state of complete absorption ⟨the book held me in *thrall*⟩ [Old English *thræl,* from Old Norse *thræll*] — **thrall·dom** *or* **thral·dom** \-dəm\ *n*

[1]**thrash** \'thrash\ *vb* **1** : THRESH 1 **2 a** : to beat soundly or strike about with or as if with a stick or whip : FLOG **b** : to defeat decisively or severely ⟨*thrashed* the visiting team⟩ **3** : to swing, beat, or stir about in the manner of a rapidly moving flail ⟨*thrash* one's arms⟩ **4 a** : to go over again and again ⟨*thrash* the matter over in your mind⟩ **b** : HAMMER OUT, FORGE ⟨*thrash* out a plan⟩ [alteration of *thresh*]

[2]**thrash** *n* : an act of thrashing

[1]**thrash·er** \'thrash-ər\ *n* : one that thrashes or threshes

[2]**thrasher** *n* : any of various long-tailed American songbirds that have a usually long curved bill and are related to the mockingbird [probably alteration of *thrush*]

[1]**thread** \'thred\ *n* **1** : a thin continuous filament ⟨the spider's sticky *thread*⟩; *esp* : a textile cord made by twisting together strands of spun fiber (as cotton, flax, or silk) **2 a** : something (as a streak or slender stream) suggesting a filament ⟨a *thread* of light⟩ **b** : SCREW THREAD **3** : a line of reasoning or train of thought that connects the parts in a sequence (as of ideas or events) ⟨lost the *thread* of the story⟩ [Old English *thrǣd*] — **thread·like** \-ˌlīk\ *adj*

[2]**thread** *vb* **1** : to put a thread in working position in ⟨*thread* a needle⟩ **2 a** : to pass something through in the manner of a thread ⟨*thread* a pipe with wire⟩ **b** : to make one's way through or between ⟨*threading* narrow alleys⟩; *also* : to make (one's way) usually cautiously through a hazardous situation **3** : to put together on or as if on a thread : STRING ⟨*thread* beads⟩ **4** : to interweave with or as if with threads : INTERSPERSE ⟨dark hair *threaded* with silver⟩ **5** : to form a screw thread on or in **6** : to form a thread — **thread·er** *n*

thread·bare \ˈthred-ˌbaər, -ˌbeər\ *adj* **1 a :** having the nap worn off so that the thread shows : SHABBY ⟨*threadbare* clothes⟩ **b :** wearing threadbare clothing : very poor ⟨*threadbare* neighbors⟩ **c :** barely adequate ⟨a *threadbare* store with few items⟩ ⟨a *threadbare* event lacking excitement⟩ **2 :** having lost freshness and interest from overuse ⟨*threadbare* jokes⟩ ***synonyms*** see TRITE — **thread·bare·ness** *n*

thread·worm \-ˌwərm\ *n* **:** a slender nematode worm (as a pinworm)

thready \ˈthred-ē\ *adj* **1 :** consisting of or bearing fibers or filaments ⟨a *thready* bark⟩ **2 :** having the form or appearance of a thread **3 :** lacking in fullness, body, or vigor ⟨a *thready* voice⟩ ⟨a *thready* pulse⟩ — **thread·i·ness** *n*

threat \ˈthret\ *n* **1 :** an expression of an intent to do harm or something wrong or foolish ⟨stop making *threats*⟩ **2 :** something that threatens ⟨the crumbling cliff was a *threat* to the village below⟩ **3 :** an indication of something impending ⟨the sky held a *threat* of rain⟩ [Old English *thrēat* "coercion"]

threat·en \ˈthret-n\ *vb* **threat·ened; threat·en·ing** \ˈthret-ning, -n-ing\ **1 :** to utter threats : make threats against ⟨*threaten* trespassers with arrest⟩ **2 a :** to give signs or warning of : PORTEND ⟨clouds *threatening* rain⟩ **b :** to be an imminent danger to : MENACE ⟨famine *threatens* the city⟩ **3 :** to announce as intended or possible ⟨the workers *threatened* a strike⟩ ⟨*threatened* to buy a car⟩ **4 :** to cause to feel insecure or anxious ⟨felt *threatened* by his brother's success⟩ — **threat·en·er** \ˈthret-nər, -n-ər\ *n* — **threat·en·ing·ly** \ˈthret-ning-lē, -n-ing-lē\ *adv*

synonyms THREATEN, MENACE mean to announce or forecast impending danger or evil. THREATEN applies to a probable occurrence of evil or affliction or to an impersonal warning of trouble, punishment, or retribution ⟨the drought *threatened* starvation⟩. MENACE implies alarming by a hostile or fearful aspect or character ⟨nuclear arms that *menace* humanity⟩.

threatened *adj* **:** having an uncertain chance of continued survival ⟨a *threatened* species⟩

three \ˈthrē\ *n* **1** — see NUMBER table **2 :** the third in a set or series ⟨the *three* of hearts⟩ **3 a :** something having three units or members **b :** THREE-POINTER [Old English *thrīe* (masculine), *thrēo* (feminine and neuter)] — **three** *adj or pron*

3–D \ˈthrē-ˈdē\ *n* **:** the three-dimensional form or a picture produced in it

three–deck·er \ˈthrē-ˈdek-ər\ *n* **1 :** a wooden warship carrying guns on three decks **2 :** something having three floors, tiers, or layers; *esp* **:** a sandwich with three slices of bread and two layers of filling

three–dimensional *adj* **1 :** of, relating to, or having three dimensions (as length, width, and height) **2 :** giving the illusion of depth or varying distances — used of a pictorial representation or a sound system

three·fold \ˈthrē-ˌfōld, -ˈfōld\ *adj* **1 :** having three parts or members **2 :** being three times as great or as many — **three·fold** *adv*

three–gait·ed \-ˈgāt-əd\ *adj* **:** trained to use the walk, trot, and canter ⟨*three-gaited* saddle horses⟩

three–hand·ed \-ˈhan-dəd\ *adj* **:** played or to be played by three players ⟨*three-handed* bridge⟩

Three Hours *n* **:** a service of devotion between noon and three o'clock on Good Friday

three–legged \ˈthrē-ˈleg-əd, -ˈlegd\ *adj* **:** having three legs ⟨a *three-legged* stool⟩

three–legged race *n* **:** a race between pairs of competitors with each pair having their adjoining legs bound together

three–mile limit *n* **:** an area of the sea extending three miles (about five kilometers) out from shore included in the territorial jurisdiction of a state

three·pence \ˈthrep-əns, ˈthrip-, ˈthrəp-, *U.S. also* ˈthrē-ˌpens\ *n* **1** *pl* **threepence** *or* **three·penc·es :** a coin worth threepence **2 :** the sum of three British pennies

three·pen·ny \ˈthrep-nē, ˈthrip-, ˈthrəp-, -ə-nē, *U.S. also* ˈthrē-ˌpen-ē\ *adj* **1 :** costing or worth threepence **2 :** of little value : POOR

three–pointer *n* **:** a basketball shot or field goal from beyond the three-point line

three–point landing *n* **:** an airplane landing in which the two main wheels of the landing gear and the tail wheel or skid or the nose wheel touch the ground simultaneously

three–point line *n* **:** a line on a basketball court forming an arc at a set distance (as 22 feet) from the basket beyond which a field goal counts for three points

three–ring circus *n* **1 :** a circus with simultaneous performances in three rings **2 a :** something wild, confusing, or chaotic ⟨five activities at one time turned the classroom into a *three-ring circus*⟩ **b :** something made into a spectacle ⟨the actor's court appearance became a *three-ring circus*⟩

three R's *n pl* **:** the fundamentals taught in elementary school; *esp* **:** reading, writing, and arithmetic [from the phrase *reading, 'riting, and 'rithmetic*]

three·score \ˈthrē-ˈskōr, -ˈskȯr\ *adj* **:** SIXTY

three·some \ˈthrē-səm\ *n* **:** a group of three persons or things

three–spined stickleback \ˌthrē-ˌspīnd-, -ˌspīn-\ *n* **:** a stickleback of fresh and brackish waters that typically has three dorsal spines

three–toed sloth *n* **:** any of a genus of sloths having three claws on each foot and eight or nine vertebrae in the neck — compare TWO-TOED SLOTH

three–wheeler \ˈthrē-ˌhwē-lər, -ˌwē-\ *n* **:** any of various vehicles having three wheels

thren·o·dy \ˈthren-əd-ē\ *n, pl* **-dies :** a song of lamentation or sorrow : DIRGE [Greek *thrēnōidia,* from *thrēnos* "dirge" + *aeidein* "to sing"]

thre·o·nine \ˈthrē-ə-ˌnēn\ *n* **:** an amino acid that is essential to normal nutrition [probably derived from *threose,* a sugar]

thresh \ˈthrash, ˈthresh\ *vb* **1 a :** to separate seed from (a harvested plant) especially by using a machine or tool **b :** to separate (grain) from straw **2 :** THRASH 4 ⟨*thresh* over a problem⟩ **3 :** THRASH 3 ⟨*threshed* about in bed⟩ [Old English *threscan*]

thresh·er \-ər\ *n* **1 :** one that threshes; *esp* **:** THRESHING MACHINE **2 :** THRESHER SHARK

thresher shark *n* **:** a large shark that has a very long curved upper lobe on its tail which it often uses to round up and stun fish to feed on — called also *thresher*

threshing machine *n* **:** a machine for separating grain or seeds from straw

thresh·old \ˈthresh-ˌhōld, -ˌōld\ *n* **1 :** the sill of a door **2 a :** GATE 1, DOOR **b :** a place or point of entering or beginning : OUTSET ⟨at the *threshold* of an adventure⟩ **3 :** the point or level at which a physiological or psychological effect begins to be produced ⟨has a high *threshold* for pain⟩ [Old English *threscwald*] — **threshold** *adj*

threw *past of* THROW

thrice \ˈthrīs\ *adv* **1 :** three times **2 :** to a high degree [Middle English *thrie, thries,* from Old English *thriga*]

thrift \ˈthrift\ *n* **1 :** careful management especially of money **2 :** a stemless herb having heads of pink or white flowers and clumps of grasslike leaves growing on mountains and seacoasts [Old Norse, "prosperity," from *thrīfask* "to thrive"]

thrift·less \ˈthrift-ləs\ *adj* **:** wasteful of money or resources — **thrift·less·ness** *n*

thrifty \ˈthrif-tē\ *adj* **thrift·i·er; -est 1 :** thriving by industry and frugality : PROSPEROUS **2 :** thriving in health and growth ⟨*thrifty* cattle⟩ **3 :** given to or marked by economy and good management — **thrift·i·ly** \-tə-lē\ *adv* — **thrift·i·ness** \-tē-nəs\ *n*

¹thrill \ˈthril\ *vb* **1 a :** to experience or cause to experience a sudden intense feeling of excitement ⟨the news *thrilled* him⟩ **b :** to have or cause to have a shivering or tingling sensation **2 :** VIBRATE 3, TREMBLE ⟨a voice *thrilling* with emotion⟩ [Old English *thyrlian* "to pierce," from *thyrel* "hole," from *thurh* "through"]

²thrill *n* **1 a :** a sudden sharp emotion often accompanied by a tingling sensation ⟨gets a *thrill* from finding a bargain⟩ ⟨felt a *thrill* of fear⟩ **b :** something that thrills ⟨seeing my picture in the newspaper was a *thrill*⟩ **2 :** VIBRATION 1b

thrill·er \-ər\ *n* **:** one that produces thrills; *esp* **:** a work of fiction or drama designed to hold the interest by the use of a high degree of action, intrigue, adventure, or suspense

thrips \ˈthrips\ *n, pl* **thrips :** any of an order (Thysanoptera) of small to tiny sucking insects many of which feed often destructively on plant juices [Latin, "worm that bores in wood," from Greek]

thrive \ˈthrīv\ *vi* **thrived** *or* **throve** \ˈthrōv\; **thrived** *also* **thriv-**

\ə\ **abut**	\au̇\ **out**	\i\ **tip**	\ȯ\ **saw**	\u̇\ **foot**
\ər\ **further**	\ch\ **chin**	\ī\ **life**	\ȯi\ **coin**	\y\ **yet**
\a\ **mat**	\e\ **pet**	\j\ **job**	\th\ **thin**	\yü\ **few**
\ā\ **take**	\ē\ **easy**	\ng\ **sing**	\t͟h\ **this**	\yu̇\ **cure**
\ä\ **cot, cart**	\g\ **go**	\ō\ **bone**	\ü\ **food**	\zh\ **vision**

en \'thriv-ən\; **thriv·ing** \'thrī-viŋg\ **1** : to grow vigorously : FLOURISH **2** : to gain in wealth or possessions : PROSPER [Old Norse *thrīfask*] — **thriv·er** \'thrī-vər\ *n* — **thriv·ing·ly** \-viŋg-lē\ *adv*

throat \'thrōt\ *n* **1** : the part of the neck in front of the spinal column; *also* : the passage through the neck to the stomach and lungs **2** : something resembling the throat especially in being an entrance, a passageway, a constriction, or a narrowed part [Old English *throte*] — **throat·ed** \-əd\ *adj*

throat·latch \-ˌlach\ *n* : a strap of a bridle or halter passing under a horse's throat

throaty \'thrōt-ē\ *adj* **throat·i·er; -est** : uttered or produced from or as if from low in the throat ⟨a *throaty* voice⟩ — **throat·i·ly** \'thrōt-l-ē\ *adv* — **throat·i·ness** \'thrōt-ē-nəs\ *n*

[1]**throb** \'thräb\ *vi* **throbbed; throb·bing** **1** : to pulsate or pound with abnormal force or rapidity (as from fright or pain) ⟨her injured ankle was *throbbing*⟩ **2** : to beat or vibrate rhythmically [Middle English *throbben*]

[2]**throb** *n* : a single beat of a pulsating movement or sensation

throe \'thrō\ *n* **1** : PANG, SPASM ⟨death *throes*⟩ ⟨*throes* of childbirth⟩ **2** *pl* : a hard or painful struggle ⟨a state in the *throes* of revolution⟩ [Old English *thrawu, thrēa* "threat, pang"]

thromb- *or* **thrombo-** *combining form* : blood clot : clotting of blood ⟨*thromb*in⟩ ⟨*thrombo*plastic⟩ [Greek *thrombos* "clot"]

throm·bin \'thräm-bən\ *n* : a proteolytic enzyme that is formed from prothrombin and assists the clotting of blood by promoting conversion of fibrinogen to fibrin

throm·bo·cyte \-bə-ˌsīt\ *n* : PLATELET — **throm·bo·cyt·ic** \ˌthräm-bə-'sit-ik\ *adj*

throm·bo·em·bo·lism \ˌthräm-bō-'em-bə-ˌliz-əm\ *n* : the blocking of a blood vessel by a particle that has broken away from a blood clot and become lodged elsewhere

throm·bo·plas·tin \-'plas-tən\ *n* : a complex enzyme found especially in platelets that functions in the conversion of prothrombin into thrombin in the clotting of blood

throm·bo·sis \thräm-'bō-səs\ *n, pl* **-bo·ses** \-'bō-ˌsēz\ : the formation or presence of a blood clot within a blood vessel — **throm·bot·ic** \-'bät-ik\ *adj*

throm·bus \'thräm-bəs\ *n, pl* **throm·bi** \-ˌbī, -ˌbē\ : a clot of blood formed within a blood vessel and remaining attached to its place of origin — compare EMBOLUS [New Latin, from Greek *thrombos* "clot"]

[1]**throne** \'thrōn\ *n* **1 a** : the chair of state of a sovereign or high dignitary (as a bishop) **b** : the seat of a deity **2** : royal power and dignity : SOVEREIGNTY [Medieval French *trone,* from Latin *thronus,* from Greek *thronos*]

[2]**throne** *vt* : to seat on a throne : ENTHRONE

throne room *n* : a formal audience room containing the throne of a sovereign

[1]**throng** \'thrȯŋ\ *n* **1 a** : a multitude of assembled persons ⟨a *throng* of over 3000⟩ **b** : a large number : CROWD ⟨a *throng* of fans⟩ ⟨a *throng* of vehicles⟩ **2** : a crowding together of many individuals [Old English *thrang*] ***synonyms*** see MULTITUDE

[2]**throng** *vb* **thronged; throng·ing** \'thrȯŋ-iŋ\ **1** : to crowd upon or into ⟨a celebrity *thronged* by fans⟩⟨shoppers *thronged* the store⟩ **2** : to move, pass, advance, or crowd together in great numbers ⟨the commuters *thronged* towards the station⟩

thros·tle \'thräs-əl\ *n* : [1]THRUSH; *esp* : SONG THRUSH [Old English]

[1]**throt·tle** \'thrät-l\ *vb* **throt·tled; throt·tling** \'thrät-liŋ, -l-iŋ\ **1 a** : to impede or check the breathing of : CHOKE, STRANGLE **b** : to prevent or check expression or activity of : SUPPRESS ⟨rules that *throttle* creativity⟩ **2 a** : to decrease the flow of (as fuel to an engine) by closing a valve **b** : to reduce the speed of (an engine) by such means [Middle English *throtlen,* from *throte* "throat"] — **throt·tler** \'thrät-lər, -l-ər\ *n*

[2]**throttle** *n* : a valve controlling the volume of steam or of fuel (as gasoline) delivered to the cylinders of an engine; *also* : a lever controlling this valve [perhaps derived from Middle English *throte* "throat"] — **at full throttle** : at maximum speed or capacity ⟨jet engines operating *at full throttle*⟩ ⟨an economy *at full throttle*⟩

throt·tle·hold \'thrät-l-ˌhōld\ *n* : a vicious, strangling, or repressive control

[1]**through** \thrü, 'thrü\ *prep* **1 a** : in at one side and out at the opposite side of ⟨drove *through* the town⟩ **b** : by way of ⟨left *through* the window⟩ **c** : in the midst of : AMONG ⟨a trail *through* the trees⟩ **d** : without stopping for ⟨drove *through* a red light⟩ **2 a** : by means of ⟨succeeded *through* perseverance⟩ **b** : because of ⟨failed *through* lack of planning⟩ **3** : over the whole surface or extent of ⟨all *through* the country⟩ **4 a** : from the beginning to the end of : DURING ⟨*through* the summer⟩ **b** : to and including ⟨Monday *through* Friday⟩ **5 a** : to a point of completion or exhaustion in ⟨got *through* the book⟩ **b** : to a state of especially official acceptance or approval ⟨got the bill *through* the legislature⟩ [Old English *thurh, thruh*] ***synonyms*** see BY

[2]**through** \'thrü\ *adv* **1 a** : from one end or side to the other ⟨the shield was pierced *through*⟩ **b** : over the whole distance ⟨shipped *through* to Boston⟩ **2 a** : from beginning to end ⟨read the book *through* at one sitting⟩ **b** : to completion, conclusion, or accomplishment ⟨see it *through*⟩ **3** : to the core : COMPLETELY ⟨soaked *through*⟩ **4** : into the open : OUT ⟨break *through*⟩

[3]**through** \'thrü\ *adj* **1 a** : extending from one surface to another ⟨a *through* mortise⟩ **b** : admitting free or continuous passage : DIRECT ⟨a *through* street⟩ **2 a** (1) : going from point of origin to destination without change or reshipment ⟨a *through* train⟩ (2) : of or relating to such movement ⟨a *through* ticket⟩ **b** : initiated at and destined for points outside a local zone ⟨*through* traffic⟩ **3 a** : arrived at completion or accomplishment ⟨*through* with the job⟩ **b** : having no further strength or resources; *also* : no longer needed or wanted ⟨you're *through*—that was your last chance⟩

[1]**through·out** \thrü-'au̇t\ *adv* **1** : in or to every part : EVERYWHERE ⟨of one color *throughout*⟩ **2** : during the whole time or action : from beginning to end ⟨remained loyal *throughout*⟩

[2]**throughout** *prep* **1** : in or to every part of ⟨*throughout* the house⟩ **2** : during the whole time of ⟨*throughout* the evening⟩

throve *past of* THRIVE

[1]**throw** \'thrō\ *vb* **threw** \'thrü\; **thrown** \'thrōn\; **throw·ing** **1 a** : to propel through the air by a forward motion of the hand and arm **b** : PITCH 6b ⟨*threw* a no-hitter⟩ **2** : to propel through the air in any way ⟨a fire engine *throwing* a stream of water⟩ **3 a** : to cause to fall or fall off ⟨the wrestler *threw* the opponent⟩ ⟨a horse shied and *threw* the rider⟩ **b** : to cast (oneself) heavily or forcefully ⟨*threw* herself on the sofa⟩ **c** : to get the better of : OVERCOME ⟨the problem didn't *throw* her⟩ **4 a** : to put suddenly in a certain condition or position ⟨*threw* her arms around him⟩ ⟨*thrown* into chaos⟩ ⟨*threw* him into prison⟩ **b** : to form or shape on a potter's wheel **c** : to bring to bear : EXERT ⟨*threw* all their efforts into repairing the damage⟩ **5** : to put on or take off hastily ⟨*throw* on a coat⟩ **6** : to twist two or more fibers of (as silk) to form one thread **7** : to make a cast of or at dice **8** : SHED ⟨*throw* some light on the matter⟩ **9** : to commit (oneself) for help, support, or protection ⟨*threw* himself on the mercy of the court⟩ **10** : to move quickly ⟨*throw* in reinforcements⟩ **11** : to indulge in : give way to ⟨*threw* a temper tantrum⟩ **12** : to lose (a game or contest) intentionally ⟨was paid to *throw* the fight⟩ **13 a** : to move (as a switch or a lever) to an open or closed position **b** : to put (an automobile) in a different gear especially quickly or suddenly ⟨*threw* the car into reverse⟩ **14** : to give by way of entertainment ⟨*throw* a party⟩ [Old English *thrāwan* "to cause to twist or turn"] — **throw·er** \'thrō-ər, 'thrōr\ *n* — **throw one's weight around** *or* **throw one's weight about** : to exercise influence or authority especially to an excessive degree or in an objectionable manner

synonyms THROW, FLING, HURL, TOSS mean to cause to move swiftly through space by a propulsive movement or a propelling force. THROW is interchangeable with the other terms but basically implies a movement of the arm propelling an object through the air ⟨*throw* the ball⟩. FLING stresses less control and more force in throwing and may suggest an emotional basis for the action ⟨madly rushed to the window and *flung* it open⟩. HURL implies power as in throwing a massive weight ⟨ocean waves *hurling* their weight upon the shore⟩. TOSS suggests a light or aimless throwing ⟨leaves *tossed* by the wind⟩.

[2]**throw** *n* **1 a** : an act of throwing, hurling, or flinging **b** (1) : one's turn to throw something (as dice) (2) : the number thrown with a cast of dice **c** : a method of throwing an opponent in wrestling or judo **2** : the distance that something is or may be thrown or projected **3 a** : a light coverlet (as for a bed) **b** : a woman's scarf or light wrap

[1]**throw·away** \'thrō-ə-ˌwā\ *n* **1** : one that is or is designed to be thrown away **2** : a handbill or circular distributed free

[2]**throwaway** *adj* : designed to be thrown away : DISPOSABLE ⟨*throwaway* containers⟩

throw away \ˌthrō-ə-ˈwā\ *vt* **1 :** to get rid of : DISCARD ‹*threw* the old ones *away*› **2 :** SQUANDER, WASTE ‹careful not to *throw* money *away*›

throw·back \ˈthrō-ˌbak\ *n* **:** reversion to an earlier type or phase; *also* **:** an instance or product of such reversion

throw back \thrō-ˈbak, ˈthrō-\ *vt* **1 :** to cause to rely : make dependent **2 :** REFLECT 1

throw in *vt* **:** to add as a supplement or bonus ‹offered to *throw in* new tires if I bought his car›

throw off *vt* **1 a :** to free oneself from ‹*threw off* his inhibitions› **b :** to cast off often in a hurried or vigorous manner ‹*threw off* all restraint› **c :** DIVERT 1 ‹was *thrown off* the scent› **2 :** to give off : EMIT ‹stacks *throwing off* plumes of smoke› **3 :** to produce in an offhand manner ‹*threw off* a catchy tune› **4 :** to cause to make a mistake : MISLEAD ‹was *thrown off* in my calculations›

throw out *vt* **1 a :** to remove from a place, office, or employment usually in a sudden or unexpected manner **b :** to reject or get rid of as worthless or unnecessary **2 :** to give expression to : UTTER ‹*threw out* some thoughts for consideration› **3 :** to give forth from within : EMIT ‹the flowers *threw out* a nice fragrance› **4 :** to cause to project : EXTEND **5 :** to make a throw that enables a teammate in baseball to put out (a base runner) **6 :** DISENGAGE ‹*throw out* the clutch›

throw over *vt* **:** to forsake despite bonds of attachment or duty

throw rug *n* **:** a rug of such a size that several can be used (as to fill vacant places) in a room

throw up *vb* **1 :** to raise quickly ‹*throw up* the window› **2 :** to give up : QUIT ‹just want to *throw* the whole thing *up*› **3 :** to build hurriedly ‹new houses *thrown up* almost overnight› **4 :** VOMIT 1 **5 :** to mention repeatedly by way of reproach ‹*throw up* a past mistake›

thru \ˈthrü\ *variant of* THROUGH ***usage*** see THO

[1]thrum \ˈthrəm\ *vb* **thrummed; thrum·ming 1 :** to play or pluck a stringed instrument idly : STRUM **2 :** to sound with a monotonous hum : recite tiresomely or monotonously [imitative]

[2]thrum *n* **:** the monotonous sound of thrumming

[1]thrush \ˈthrəsh\ *n* **:** any of a large family of small or medium-sized songbirds that are mostly of a plain color often with spotted underparts [Old English *thrysce*]

[2]thrush *n* **:** a fungal disease especially of infants marked by white patches in the mouth [probably of Scandinavian origin]

[1]thrust \ˈthrəst\ *vb* **thrust; thrust·ing 1 :** to push or drive with force : SHOVE **2 :** to cause to enter or pierce something by or as if by pushing ‹*thrust* a knife into the bread› **3 :** to push forth : EXTEND ‹*thrust* out roots› **4 :** to introduce often improperly into a position : INTERPOLATE **5 :** to press or force the acceptance of upon someone ‹*thrust* new responsibilities upon her› **6 :** to make a thrust, stab, or lunge with or as if with a pointed weapon [Old Norse *thrȳsta*] ***synonyms*** see PUSH

[2]thrust *n* **1 a :** a push or lunge with a pointed weapon **b :** a verbal attack **c :** a military assault **2 a :** a strong continued pressure **b :** the sideways pressure of one part of a structure against another part (as of an arch against an abutment) **c :** the force produced by a propeller or jet or rocket engine that drives an aircraft or rocket forward **3 a :** a forward or upward push **b :** a movement in a specified direction

thrust·er \ˈthrəs-tər\ *n* **:** one that thrusts; *esp* **:** an engine that produces thrust by discharging a jet of fluid or a stream of particles

thru·way \ˈthrü-ˌwā\ *n* **:** EXPRESSWAY

[1]thud \ˈthəd\ *vi* **thud·ded; thud·ding :** to move or strike so as to make a thud [imitative]

[2]thud *n* **1 :** [5]BLOW 1 **2 :** a dull sound : THUMP

thug \ˈthəg\ *n* **:** a brutal ruffian or assassin : GANGSTER, TOUGH [Hindi & Urdu *ṭhag*] — **thug·gery** \ˈthəg-ə-rē\ *n*

Word History *Thug* was used in English in the early 19th century as a transliteration of Hindi *ṭhag,* which literally means "thief," but which was applied specifically by the British to robbers and murderers active in India in the early 19th century who assaulted travelers. The word caught on in English, especially in the U.S., and is now used to label any brutal ruffian, gangster, or killer.

thu·li·um \ˈthü-lē-əm, ˈthyü-\ *n* **:** a soft rare metallic element — see ELEMENT table [New Latin, from Latin *Thule* "Thule"]

[1]thumb \ˈthəm\ *n* **1 :** the short thick first digit of the human hand opposable to the other fingers; *also* **:** the corresponding digit in lower animals **2 :** the part of a glove or mitten that covers the thumb [Old English *thūma*]

[2]thumb *vt* **1 a :** to leaf through with the thumb : TURN ‹*thumb* the pages of a book› **b :** to soil or wear by or as if by repeated thumbing ‹a well-*thumbed* book› **2 :** to request or obtain (a ride) in a passing automobile by signaling with the thumb

thumb drive *n* **:** FLASH DRIVE

[1]thumb·nail \ˈthəm-ˌnāl, -ˈnāl\ *n* **1 :** the nail of the thumb **2 :** a miniature computer graphic sometimes connected by a hyperlink to a larger version

[2]thumb·nail \ˌthəm-ˌnāl\ *adj* **:** very short or brief

thumb·print \ˈthəm-ˌprint\ *n* **:** a print or impression made by the thumb

thumb·screw \ˈthəm-ˌskrü\ *n* **1 :** a screw having a flat-sided or knurled head so that it may be turned by the thumb and index finger **2 :** an instrument of torture for squeezing the thumb by a screw

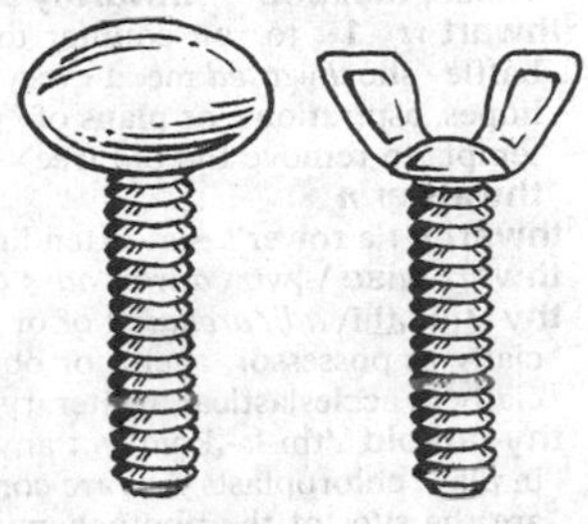

thumbscrew 1

thumb·tack \-ˌtak\ *n* **:** a tack with a broad flat head for pressing into a board or wall with the thumb

[1]thump \ˈthəmp\ *vb* **1 :** to strike or beat with or as if with something thick or heavy so as to cause a dull sound **2 :** to beat heavily : POUND ‹my heart *thumped* at the sight› **3 :** to inflict or emit a thump [imitative]

[2]thump *n* **:** a blow or knock with or as if with something blunt or heavy; *also* **:** the sound made by such a blow

[1]thump·ing *adj* **:** impressively large, great, or excellent ‹a *thumping* majority› — **thump·ing·ly** *adv*

[2]thumping *adv* **:** VERY 1, EXTREMELY ‹a *thumping* good time›

[1]thun·der \ˈthən-dər\ *n* **1 :** the loud sound that follows a flash of lightning and is caused by sudden expansion of the air in the path of the electrical discharge **2 :** a loud utterance or threat **3 :** BANG, RUMBLE ‹the *thunder* of guns› [Old English *thunor*]

[2]thunder *vb* **thun·dered; thun·der·ing** \-də-riŋ, driŋ\ **1 :** to produce thunder ‹it *thundered*› **2 :** to produce a sound like thunder ‹horses *thundered* down the road› **3 :** ROAR ‹the crowd *thundered* its approval› — **thun·der·er** \-dər-ər\ *n*

thun·der·bolt \ˈthən-dər-ˌbōlt\ *n* **1 :** a single discharge of lightning with the accompanying thunder **2 a :** a person or thing likened to lightning in suddenness, effectiveness, or destructive power **b :** a vehement threat or censure

thun·der·clap \-ˌklap\ *n* **1 :** a crash of thunder **2 :** something sharp, loud, or sudden like a clap of thunder

thun·der·cloud \-ˌklau̇d\ *n* **:** a dark storm cloud that produces lightning and thunder

thun·der·head \-ˌhed\ *n* **:** a rounded mass of cumulus cloud often appearing before a thunderstorm

thun·der·ing *adj* **:** awesomely great, intense, or unusual ‹a *thundering* success› — **thun·der·ing·ly** \-də-riŋ-lē, -driŋ-\ *adv*

thunder lizard *n* **:** BRONTOSAURUS

thun·der·ous \ˈthən-də-rəs, -drəs\ *adj* **1 :** producing thunder **2 :** as loud as thunder : very loud ‹*thunderous* applause› — **thun·der·ous·ly** *adv*

thun·der·show·er \ˈthən-dər-ˌshau̇-ər, -ˌshau̇r\ *n* **:** a shower accompanied by lightning and thunder

thun·der·storm \-ˌstȯrm\ *n* **:** a storm accompanied by lightning and thunder

thun·der·struck \-ˌstrək\ *adj* **:** stunned or astonished as if struck by a thunderbolt ‹*thunderstruck* at the news›

thunk \ˈthəŋk\ *vi* **:** to make a flat hollow sound [imitative] — **thunk** *n*

thu·ri·ble \ˈthu̇r-ə-bəl, ˈthyu̇r-, ˈthər-\ *n* **:** CENSER [Latin *thuribulum,* from *thur-, thus* "incense," from Greek *thyos,* from *thyein* "to sacrifice"]

\ə\ abut	\au̇\ out	\i\ tip	\ȯ\ saw	\u̇\ foot
\ər\ further	\ch\ chin	\ī\ life	\ȯi\ coin	\y\ yet
\a\ mat	\e\ pet	\j\ job	\th\ thin	\yü\ few
\ā\ take	\ē\ easy	\ŋ\ sing	\t͟h\ this	\yu̇\ cure
\ä\ cot, cart	\g\ go	\ō\ bone	\ü\ food	\zh\ vision

thu·ri·fer \-ə-fər\ *n* : one who carries a censer [Latin, "incense-bearing," from *thur-, thus* "incense" + *ferre* "to carry"]

Thurs·day \'thərz-dē\ *n* : the 5th day of the week [Old English *thursdæg,* from Old Norse *thōrsdagr,* literally, "day of Thor"]

thus \'thəs\ *adv* **1** : in this or that manner or way ⟨described it *thus*⟩ **2** : to this degree or extent : SO ⟨a mild winter *thus* far⟩ **3** : because of this or that : HENCE ⟨attendance was poor, *thus* the meeting was canceled⟩ **4** : as an example [Old English]

thwack \'thwak\ *vt* : to strike with or as if with something flat or heavy : WHACK [imitative] — **thwack** *n*

[1]**thwart** \'thwȯrt, *nautical often* 'thȯrt\ *adv* : ATHWART [Old Norse *thvert,* from *thverr* "transverse, oblique"]

[2]**thwart** *adj* : situated or placed across something else : TRANSVERSE, OBLIQUE — **thwart·ly** *adv*

[3]**thwart** *vt* **1** : to run counter to so as to effectively oppose or baffle ⟨she *thwarted* me at every opportunity⟩ **2** : to defeat the hopes, aspirations, or plans of ⟨public outcry *thwarted* their attempts to remove the old tree⟩ ***synonyms*** see FRUSTRATE — **thwart·er** *n*

[4]**thwart** *n* : a rower's seat extending across a boat

thwart·wise \-ˌwīz\ *adv or adj* : CROSSWISE 2

thy \thī, ˌthī\ *adj, archaic* : of or relating to thee or thyself especially as possessor, agent, or object of an action — used especially in ecclesiastical or literary language [Old English *thīn*]

thy·la·koid \'thī-lə-ˌkȯid\ *n* : any of the thin membranous disks in plant chloroplasts that are composed of protein and lipid and are the sites of the photochemical reactions of photosynthesis [Greek *thylakos* "sack"]

thyme \'tīm *also* 'thīm\ *n* **1** : any of a genus of Eurasian mints with small pungent aromatic leaves; *esp* : one grown for use in seasoning food **2** : thyme leaves used as a seasoning [Medieval French *time, thime,* from Latin *thymum,* from Greek *thymon,* probably from *thyein* "to make a burnt offering, sacrifice"]

thy·mine \'thī-ˌmēn\ *n* : a pyrimidine base $C_5H_6N_2O_2$ that is one of the four bases coding genetic information in the polynucleotide chain of DNA — compare ADENINE, CYTOSINE, GUANINE, URACIL [New Latin *thymus*]

thy·mol \'thī-ˌmȯl, -ˌmōl\ *n* : a crystalline compound $C_{10}H_{14}O$ of aromatic odor and antiseptic properties used as a fungicide and preservative [Latin *thymum* "thyme"]

thy·mus \'thī-məs\ *n, pl* **thy·mus·es** *also* **thy·mi** \-ˌmī\ : a glandular structure of mostly lymphoid tissue that is present in the young of most vertebrates typically in the upper chest near the heart, that before and for a time after birth has very important effects on the production and development of T cells, and that becomes less active and gradually shrinks or disappears with age [New Latin, from Greek *thymos* "warty growth, thymus"] — **thy·mic** \-mik\ *adj*

thymy *or* **thym·ey** \'tī-mē *also* 'thī-\ *adj* : abounding in or fragrant with thyme

thy·ro·cal·ci·to·nin \ˌthī-rō-ˌkal-sə-'tō-nən\ *n* : CALCITONIN

[1]**thy·roid** \'thī-ˌrȯid\ *adj* **1** : of, relating to, or being the thyroid gland **2** : of, relating to, or being the chief cartilage of the larynx [Greek *thyreoeidēs* "shield-shaped, thyroid," from *thyreos* "shield shaped like a door," from *thyra* "door"]

[2]**thyroid** *n* **1** : a large endocrine gland at the base of the neck of most vertebrates that produces iodine-containing hormones (as thyroxine) that affect growth, development, and metabolism **2** : a preparation of the thyroid gland of various domestic animals used in treating thyroid disorders

thyroid–stimulating hormone *n* : a hormone secreted by the pituitary gland that regulates the formation and secretion of the thyroid hormones

thy·ro·tro·pin \ˌthī-rə-'trō-pən\ *n* : THYROID-STIMULATING HORMONE [*thyr*oid + *-tropin* "hormone"]

thy·rox·ine *or* **thy·rox·in** \thī-'räk-ˌsēn, -sən\ *n* : an iodine-containing hormone of the thyroid gland used to treat thyroid disorders

thy·self \thī-'self\ *pron, archaic* : YOURSELF — used especially in ecclesiastical or literary language

ti \'tē\ *n* : the 7th note of the diatonic scale [alteration of *si*]

ti·ara \tē-'ar-ə, -'er-, -'är-\ *n* **1** : a 3-tiered crown worn by the pope **2** : a decorative band or semicircular ornament for the head for formal wear by women [Latin, "royal Persian headdress," from Greek]

Ti·bet·an \tə-'bet-n\ *n* **1** : a member of the predominant people of Tibet and adjacent areas of Asia **2** : the language of the Tibetan people — **Tibetan** *adj*

Tibetan Buddhism *n* : a form of Buddhism that evolved in Tibet and is dominated by the sect of the Dalai Lama

tib·ia \'tib-ē-ə\ *n, pl* **-i·ae** \-ē-ˌē, -ē-ˌī\ *also* **-i·as** **1** : the inner and usually larger of the two bones of the vertebrate hind or lower limb between the knee and ankle — called also *shinbone* **2** : the fourth joint of the leg of an insect between the femur and tarsus [Latin] — **tib·i·al** \-ē-əl\ *adj*

tib·io·fib·u·la \ˌtib-ē-ō-'fib-yə-lə\ *n* : a bone especially in frogs and toads that is formed by fusion of the tibia and fibula

tic \'tik\ *n* **1** : a regularly repeating twitching movement of a particular muscle and especially one of the face **2** : a particular form of behavior or speech that is often repeated ⟨"you know" is a verbal *tic*⟩ [French]

[1]**tick** \'tik\ *n* : any of numerous bloodsucking arachnids that are larger than the related mites, attach themselves to warm-blooded vertebrates to feed, and include important vectors of infectious diseases [Middle English *tyke*]

[2]**tick** *n* **1** : a light rhythmic audible tap or beat (as of a clock); *also* : a series of such ticks **2** : a small spot or mark; *esp* : one used to direct attention to something, to check an item on a list, or to represent a point on a scale [Middle English *tek*]

[3]**tick** *vb* **1 a** : to make the sound of a tick or a series of ticks **b** : to mark, count, or announce by or as if by ticking beats ⟨a meter *ticking* off the cab fare⟩ **2** : to operate as or in the manner of a functioning mechanism : RUN ⟨tried to understand what made them *tick*⟩ **3** : to mark with a written tick : CHECK ⟨*ticking* off names on a list⟩

[4]**tick** *n* **1** : the fabric case of a mattress, pillow, or bolster; *also* : a mattress consisting of a tick and its filling **2** : TICKING [Middle English *tike,* probably derived from Latin *theca* "cover," from Greek *thēkē* "case"]

[5]**tick** *n, chiefly British* : CREDIT, TRUST; *also* : a credit account ⟨bought on *tick*⟩ [short for *ticket*]

ticked \'tikt\ *adj* **1** : marked with small spots **2** : banded with two or more colors ⟨*ticked* hairs in the coat of a rabbit⟩

tick·er \'tik-ər\ *n* : something that ticks or produces a ticking sound: as **a** : WATCH 6 **b** : a telegraphic receiving instrument that automatically prints off stock quotations or news on a paper ribbon **c** : a graphic strip of information that moves across the top or bottom of a television or computer screen **d** *slang* : HEART 1a

ticker tape *n* : the paper ribbon on which a telegraphic ticker prints off its information

[1]**tick·et** \'tik-ət\ *n* **1 a** : a document that serves as a certificate, license, or permit; *esp* : a mariner's or airman's certificate **b** : TAG, LABEL ⟨price *ticket*⟩ **2** : a summons or warning issued to a traffic offender **3** : a document or token showing that a fare or admission fee has been paid **4** : a list of candidates for nomination or election **5** : a slip or card recording a transaction or undertaking or giving instructions ⟨sales *ticket*⟩ ⟨a driver's trip *ticket*⟩ ⟨repair *ticket*⟩ [Middle French *etiquet* (now *étiquette*) "label," from *estiquier* "to attach," from Dutch *steken* "to stick"]

[2]**ticket** *vt* **1** : to attach a ticket to : LABEL; *also* : DESIGNATE **2** : to serve with a traffic ticket

ticket agent *n* **1** : one who acts as an agent of a transportation company to sell tickets for travel **2** : one who sells theater and entertainment tickets — **ticket agency** *n*

ticket–of–leave *n, pl* **tickets–of–leave** : a license or permit formerly given in the United Kingdom and the Commonwealth of Nations to a convict to go free subject to certain conditions

tick·ing \'tik-ing\ *n* : a strong fabric used in upholstering and as a covering for mattresses and pillows

[1]**tick·le** \'tik-əl\ *vb* **tick·led; tick·ling** \'tik-ling, -ə-ling\ **1** : to have a tingling or prickling sensation ⟨my back *tickles*⟩ **2 a** : to excite or stir up agreeably : PLEASE ⟨food that *tickles* the palate⟩ **b** : to provoke to laughter or merriment : AMUSE ⟨*tickled* by the clown's antics⟩ **3** : to touch a body part lightly so as to excite the surface nerves and cause uneasiness, laughter, or spasmodic movements [Middle English *tikelen*] — **tick·ler** \'tik-lər, -ə-lər\ *n*

[2]**tickle** *n* **1** : the act of tickling **2** : a tickling sensation **3** : something that tickles

tick·lish \'tik-lish, -ə-lish\ *adj* **1 a** : TOUCHY, OVERSENSITIVE ⟨*ticklish* about being bald⟩ **b** : easily overturned : UNSTABLE ⟨a canoe is a *ticklish* craft⟩ **2** : requiring delicate handling : CRITICAL ⟨a *ticklish* subject⟩ ⟨a *ticklish* situation⟩ **3** : sensitive to tickling — **tick·lish·ly** *adv* — **tick·lish·ness** *n*

tick·tock \'tik-'täk, -ˌtäk\ *n* : the ticking sound of a large clock [imitative]

tick trefoil *n* : any of various plants of the legume family having leaves with three leaflets and rough sticky fruits [[1]*tick*]

tic–tac–toe *or* **tick–tack–toe** \ˌtik-ˌtak-'tō\ *n* : a game in which two players alternately put Xs and Os in compartments of a figure formed by two vertical lines crossing two horizontal lines with each player trying to get a row of three Xs or three Os before the opponent does [*tic-tac-toe,* a former game in which players with eyes shut brought down a pencil on a slate marked with numbers and scored the number hit]

tid·al \'tīd-l\ *adj* **1** : of or relating to tides : periodically rising and falling or flowing and ebbing ⟨*tidal* waters⟩ **2** : dependent (as to the time of arrival or departure) on the state of the tide ⟨a *tidal* steamer⟩ — **tid·al·ly** \-l-ē\ *adv*

tidal wave *n* **1** : something overwhelming especially in quantity or volume ⟨a *tidal wave* of tourists⟩ **2 a** : an unusually high sea wave that is triggered especially by an earthquake **b** : an unusual rise of water alongshore due to strong winds

tid·bit \'tid-ˌbit\ *also* **tit·bit** \'tit-ˌbit\ *n* **1** : a choice morsel of food **2** : a choice or pleasing bit (as of news) [perhaps from *tit-* (as in *titmouse*) + *bit*]

tid·dle·dy·winks *or* **tid·dly·winks** \'tid-l-ē-ˌwiŋks, 'tid-l-dē-, 'tid-lē-, -ˌwiŋks\ *n* : a game in which players try to snap small disks from a flat surface into a small container [probably from English dialect *tiddly* "little"]

[1]tide \'tīd\ *n* **1 a** *obsolete* : a space of time : PERIOD **b** : a fit or opportune time : OPPORTUNITY **c** : an ecclesiastical anniversary or festival; *also* : its season **2 a** (1) : the alternate rising and falling of the surface of the ocean that occurs twice a day and is caused by the gravitational attraction of the sun and moon occurring unequally on different parts of the earth (2) : a less marked rising and falling of an inland body of water **b** : FLOOD TIDE 1 **3** : something that fluctuates like the tides of the sea : VICISSITUDE ⟨the *tides* of fortune⟩ **4** : a flowing stream : CURRENT [Old English *tīd* "time"]

[2]tide *vb* **1** : to drift or cause to drift with the tide **2** : to enable to surmount or endure a difficulty ⟨the money *tided* us over⟩

tide·land \-ˌland, -lənd\ *n* **1** : land overflowed during flood tide **2** : land underlying the ocean beyond the low-water limit of the tide but within a nation's territorial waters — often used in plural

tide·mark \'tīd-ˌmärk\ *n* **1 a** : a high-water or sometimes low-water mark left by tidal water or a flood **b** : a mark placed to indicate this point **2** : the point to which something has risen or below which it has fallen

tide pool *n* : a pool of saltwater left (as in a rock basin) by an ebbing tide

tide·wa·ter \'tīd-ˌwot-ər, -ˌwät-\ *n* **1** : water overflowing land at flood tide **2** : low-lying coastal land

tid·ing \'tīd-iŋ\ *n* : a piece of news — usually used in plural ⟨good *tidings*⟩ [Old English *tīdung,* from *tīdan* "to happen"]

[1]ti·dy \'tīd-ē\ *adj* **ti·di·er; -est** **1** : properly filled out : PLUMP **2** : ADEQUATE 1, SATISFACTORY ⟨a *tidy* arrangement⟩ **3 a** : neat and orderly in appearance or habits : well ordered and cared for ⟨a *tidy* house⟩ **b** : METHODICAL, PRECISE ⟨a *tidy* mind⟩ **4** : LARGE, SUBSTANTIAL ⟨a *tidy* sum⟩ [Middle English, "timely, in good condition," from *tide* "time"] — **ti·di·ly** \'tīd-l-ē\ *adv* — **ti·di·ness** \'tīd-ē-nəs\ *n*

[2]tidy *vb* **ti·died; ti·dy·ing** **1** : to put in order ⟨*tidy* up a room⟩ **2** : to make things tidy ⟨*tidying* up after supper⟩

[3]tidy *n, pl* **tidies** : a piece of fancywork used to protect the back, arms, or headrest of a chair or sofa from wear or soiling

[1]tie \'tī\ *n* **1 a** : a line, ribbon, or cord used for fastening, uniting, or drawing something closed; *esp* : SHOELACE **b** (1) : a structural element (as a beam) holding two pieces together : a tension member in a construction (2) : one of the transverse supports to which railroad rails are fastened **2** : something that serves as a connecting link: as **a** : a moral or legal obligation to someone or something **b** : a bond of kinship or affection **3** : a curved line that joins two musical notes indicating the same pitch used to denote a single tone sustained through the time value of the two **4 a** : an equality in number (as of votes or scores) **b** : equality in a contest; *also* : a contest that ends in a draw **5** : a method or style of tying or knotting **6** : something that is knotted or is to be knotted when worn: as **a** : NECKTIE **b** : a low laced shoe : OXFORD [Old English *tēag*]

[2]tie *vb* **tied; ty·ing** \'tī-iŋ\ *or* **tie·ing** **1 a** : to fasten, attach, or close by means of a tie **b** : to form a knot or bow in ⟨*tie* your scarf⟩ **c** : to make by tying separate parts together ⟨*tied* a wreath⟩ ⟨*tie* a fishing fly⟩ **2 a** : to unite in marriage **b** : to unite (musical notes) by a tie **3** : to restrain or constrain the acts of **4 a** (1) : to make or have an equal score with in a contest (2) : to cause to be a tie ⟨*tied* the score⟩ **b** : to provide or offer something equal to : EQUAL **5** : to make a tie: as **a** : to make a bond or connection **b** : to make an equal score **c** : to be connected : fit in — **tie the knot** : to perform a marriage ceremony; *also* : to get married

tie–down \'tī-ˌdau̇n\ *n* : a fitting or a system of lines and fittings used to secure something (as an aircraft or cargo)

tie–dye·ing \'tī-ˌdī-iŋ\ *n* : a hand method of producing patterns in textiles by tying portions of the fabric or yarn so that they will not absorb the dye — **tie–dye** \-ˌdī\ *n* — **tie–dyed** *adj*

tie–in \'tī-ˌin\ *n* : something that ties in, relates, or connects

tie in \tī-'in, 'tī-\ *vb* **1** : to bring into connection with something relevant **2** : to make the final connection of ⟨the pipeline *ties in* here⟩ **3** : to become connected

tie·pin \-ˌpin\ *n* : an ornamental pin used to hold the ends of a necktie in place

[1]tier \'tiər\ *n* : a row, rank, or layer of articles; *esp* : one of two or more rows, levels, or ranks arranged one above another [Middle French *tire* "rank," of Germanic origin]

[2]tier *vb* **1** : to place or arrange in tiers **2** : to rise in tiers

[3]ti·er *or* **ty·er** \'tī-ər, 'tīr\ *n* : one that ties

tierce *variant of* TERCE

tier·cel \'tiər-səl\ *or* **ter·cel** \'tər-\ *n* : a male hawk; *esp* : a male peregrine falcon — compare FALCON [Middle French *tercel,* derived from Latin *tertius* "third"]

tiered \'tiərd\ *adj* : having or arranged in tiers, rows, or layers

tie–up \'tī-ˌəp\ *n* **1** : a suspension of traffic or business (as by a strike or lockout or a mechanical breakdown) **2** : CONNECTION 4b, ASSOCIATION ⟨looking for a helpful financial *tie-up*⟩

tie up \tī-'əp, 'tī-\ *vt* **1** : to attach, fasten, or bind securely; *also* : to wrap up and fasten **2 a** : to use in such a manner as to make unavailable for other purposes **b** : to restrain from operation or progress ⟨traffic was *tied up* for miles⟩ **3** : DOCK ⟨the ferry *ties up* at the south slip⟩ **4** : to place in or assume a relationship with something else ⟨this *ties up* with what was said before⟩

[1]tiff \'tif\ *n* : a petty quarrel [origin unknown]

[2]tiff *vi* : to have a minor quarrel

tif·fin \'tif-ən\ *n, chiefly British* : a midday meal : LUNCHEON [probably derived from obsolete English *tiff* "to eat between meals"]

ti·ger \'tī-gər\ *n, pl* **tigers** **1** *pl also* **tiger** **a** : a large Asian flesh-eating mammal of the same family as the domestic cat with a coat that is typically light brown to orange with mostly vertical black stripes **b** : any of several large wildcats (as the jaguar or cougar) **c** : TIGER CAT 2 **2** : a fierce, daring, or aggressive person or quality [Old English *tiger* and Medieval French *tigre,* both from Latin *tigris,* from Greek, probably of Iranian origin] — **ti·ger·like** \-gər-ˌlīk\ *adj*

tiger 1a

tiger beetle *n* : any of numerous active strong-jawed beetles that feed on other insects, have larvae that tunnel in the soil, and include some capable of giving a painful bite

tiger cat *n* **1** : any of various wildcats (as the serval, ocelot, or margay) of moderate size and variegated coloration **2** : a striped or sometimes blotched tabby cat

ti·ger·ish \'tī-gə-rish, -grish\ *adj* : suggesting a tiger (as in grace, fierceness, or vigor) — **ti·ger·ish·ly** *adv* — **ti·ger·ish·ness** *n*

tiger lily *n* : a common Asian lily widely grown for its nodding usually orange-colored flowers spotted with black

tiger moth *n* : any of a family of stout-bodied moths usually with broad striped or spotted wings

\ə\ abut	\au̇\ **out**	\i\ tip	\ȯ\ saw	\u̇\ foot
\ər\ further	\ch\ **chin**	\ī\ life	\ȯi\ coin	\y\ yet
\a\ mat	\e\ pet	\j\ **job**	\th\ **thin**	\yü\ few
\ā\ take	\ē\ **easy**	\ŋ\ sing	\t͟h\ **this**	\yu̇\ cure
\ä\ cot, cart	\g\ go	\ō\ **bone**	\ü\ **food**	\zh\ vision

tiger salamander *n* : a large North American salamander that is variably colored with black blotches, bars, or spots

tiger shark *n* : a large brown or gray shark of warm seas that sometimes attacks humans

1**tight** \ˈtīt\ *adj* **1 a** : so close in structure as not to permit passage of a fluid or light ⟨a *tight* roof⟩ **b** : fitting close to the body; *also* : too snug ⟨*tight* shoes⟩ **c** (1) : closely packed : very full ⟨a *tight* bale of hay⟩ (2) : barely allowing time for completion ⟨a *tight* schedule⟩ **2 a** : strongly fixed or held : SECURE ⟨a *tight* jar lid⟩ ⟨a *tight* grip⟩ **b** : not slack or loose : TAUT ⟨kept the rope *tight*⟩ ⟨a *tight* knot⟩ **3** : difficult to get through or out of : TRYING ⟨in a *tight* situation⟩ **4 a** : firm in control ⟨kept a *tight* hand on the business⟩ **b** : STINGY 1, MISERLY **5** : characterized by little difference in the relative positions of contestants with respect to final outcome : CLOSE ⟨a *tight* race for mayor⟩ **6** : DRUNK 1 **7** : low in supply : SCARCE ⟨money is *tight* right now⟩ **8** : having a close personal or working relationship ⟨in *tight* with the boss⟩ [of Scandinavian origin] — **tight·ly** *adv* — **tight·ness** *n*

synonyms TIGHT, TAUT, TENSE mean drawn or stretched to the limit. TIGHT may suggest that one thing is drawn around another as closely as possible ⟨the dog's collar was snug but not too *tight*⟩. TAUT suggests the pulling of a rope or fabric until there is no give or slack ⟨the rope was *taut* and firm⟩. TENSE often adds to TAUT the suggestion of strain impairing normal functioning ⟨*tense* muscles⟩.

2**tight** *adv* **1** : in a tight manner ⟨the door was shut *tight*⟩ **2** : SOUND ⟨sleep *tight*⟩

tight·en \ˈtīt-ᵊn\ *vb* **tight·ened; tight·en·ing** \ˈtīt-niŋ, -ᵊn-iŋ\ : to make or become tight or tighter — **tight·en·er** \ˈtīt-nər, -ᵊn-ər\ *n*

tight end *n* : an offensive football end who lines up close to the tackle and can act as a lineman or receiver

tight·fist·ed \ˈtīt-ˈfis-təd\ *adj* : MISERLY, STINGY

tight–lipped \-ˈlipt\ *adj* **1** : having the lips closed tight (as in determination) **2** : reluctant to speak

tight·rope \ˈtīt-ˌrōp\ *n* : a rope or wire stretched taut for acrobats to perform on

tights \ˈtīts\ *n pl* : a skintight garment covering the body from the neck down or from the waist down

tight·wad \ˈtīt-ˌwäd\ *n* : a stingy person

tight·wire \-ˌwīr\ *n* : a tightrope made of wire

ti·gress \ˈtī-grəs\ *n* : a female tiger

tike *variant of* TYKE

tik·ka \ˈtik-ə\ *n* : an Indian dish of marinated meat cooked on a skewer [Hindi & Urdu *tikkā* "small piece of meat," from Persian *tikka*]

til·de \ˈtil-də\ *n* : a mark ˜ placed especially over the letter *n* (as in Spanish *señor* sir) to denote the sound \n^{y}\ or over vowels (as in Portuguese *profissão* profession) to indicate nasality [Spanish, from Medieval Latin *titulus* "tittle"]

1**tile** \ˈtīl\ *n* **1** *pl* **tiles** *or* **tile a** : a flat or curved piece of fired clay, stone, or concrete used especially for roofs, floors, or walls **b** : a hollow or concave piece of fired clay or concrete used for a drain **2** : TILING 2b **3** : a thin piece of resilient material (as linoleum or rubber) for covering floors or walls [Old English *tigele,* from Latin *tegula*]

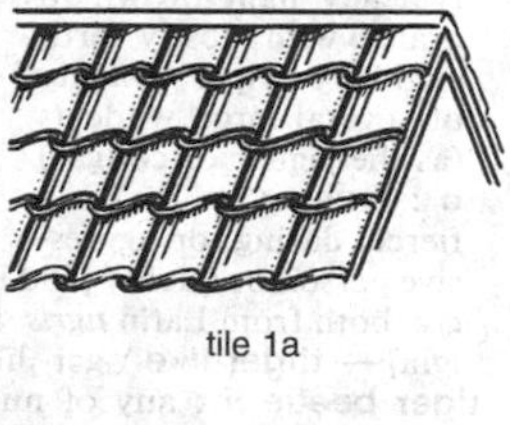

tile 1a

2**tile** *vt* **1** : to cover with tiles **2** : to install drainage tile in — **til·er** *n*

til·ing \ˈtī-liŋ\ *n* **1** : the act of one who tiles **2 a** : TILES **b** : a surface of tiles

1**till** *or* **'til** *also* **til** \tl, təl, til, ˌtil\ *prep or conj* : UNTIL [Old English *til*]

2**till** \ˈtil\ *vt* : to work by plowing, sowing, and raising crops on or in ⟨*tilled* the land⟩ ⟨help *till* the soil⟩ [Old English *tilian*] — **till·able** \-ə-bəl\ *adj*

3**till** \ˈtil\ *n* : a receptacle (as a drawer) for money [Middle English *tille* "locker, chest"]

4**till** \ˈtil\ *n* : unstratified glacial drift consisting of clay, sand, gravel, and boulders intermingled [origin unknown]

till·age \ˈtil-ij\ *n* **1** : the process of tilling land **2** : cultivated land

1**till·er** \ˈtil-ər\ *n* : a person who tills; *also* : CULTIVATOR

2**til·ler** \ˈtil-ər\ *n* **1** : a lever used to turn the rudder of a boat from side to side **2** : a steering wheel for the rear wheels or trailer section of a vehicle (as a fire truck) — called also *tiller wheel* [Middle French *teiler* "stock of a crossbow," literally, "beam of a loom," from Medieval Latin *telarium,* from Latin *tela* "web"]

3**til·ler** *n* : SPROUT 1, STALK; *esp* : one from the base of a cereal grass [Old English *telgor, telgra* "twig, shoot"]

4**til·ler** *vi* : to put forth tillers ⟨the oats are *tillering*⟩

til·ler·man \ˈtil-ər-mən\ *n* : STEERSMAN

1**tilt** \ˈtilt\ *vb* **1** : to cause to slope : INCLINE **2** : to move or shift so as to lean or incline : SLANT **3** : to engage in a combat with lances : JOUST [Middle English *tilten* "to fall over, cause to fall"] — **tilt·er** *n*

2**tilt** *n* **1** : a contest on horseback in which two combatants charging with lances try to unhorse each other : JOUST **2 a** : a verbal encounter involving sharp exchanges : ALTERCATION **b** : SPEED 2a — used in the phrase *at full tilt* **3 a** : the act of tilting : the state or position of being tilted **b** : a sloping surface

tilth \ˈtilth\ *n* **1** : cultivated land : TILLAGE **2** : the state of a soil with respect to the suitability of its particle size and structure for growing crops [Old English, from *tilian* "to till"]

tilt·me·ter \ˈtilt-ˌmēt-ər\ *n* : an instrument to measure the tilting of the earth's surface

tim·bale *also* **tim·bal** \ˈtim-bəl\ *n* : one of a set of single-headed cylindrical drums played with sticks — usually used in plural [French "kettledrum"]

1**tim·ber** \ˈtim-bər\ *n* **1 a** : growing trees or their wood **b** — used interjectionally to warn of a falling tree **2** : wood for use in making something **3** : a usually large piece of wood squared or finished for use **4** : a curving frame branching outward from the keel of a ship that is usually composed of several pieces united : RIB [Old English, "building, wood"] — **timber** *adj*

2**timber** *vt* **tim·bered; tim·ber·ing** \-bə-riŋ, -briŋ\ : to frame, cover, or support with timbers

tim·bered \ˈtim-bərd\ *adj* **1** : furnished with, made of, or covered with timber **2** : having walls framed by exposed timbers

timber hitch *n* : a knot used to secure a line to a log or spar

tim·ber·ing \ˈtim-bə-riŋ, -briŋ\ *n* : a set of timbers : timber construction

tim·ber·land \ˈtim-bər-ˌland\ *n* : wooded land especially with marketable timber

tim·ber·line \-ˌlīn\ *n* : the upper limit of tree growth in mountains or high latitudes — called also *tree line*

timber wolf *n* : GRAY WOLF

tim·ber·work \ˈtim-bər-ˌwərk\ *n* : a timber construction

tim·bre \ˈtam-bər, ˈtim-\ *n* : the quality given to a sound by its overtones: as **a** : the resonance by which the ear recognizes and identifies a voiced speech sound **b** : the tone distinctive of a singing voice or a musical instrument [French, from Medieval French, "bell struck by a hammer, drum," derived from Greek *tympanon* "kettledrum"]

tim·brel \ˈtim-brəl\ *n* : a small hand drum or tambourine [obsolete English *timbre* "small drum, tambourine," from Medieval French, "drum"] — **tim·brelled** \-brəld\ *adj*

1**time** \ˈtīm\ *n* **1 a** : the measured or measurable period during which an action, process, or condition exists or continues : DURATION **b** : LEISURE ⟨*time* for reading⟩ **2** : the point or period when something occurs : OCCASION ⟨remember the *time* we went camping⟩ **3** : an appointed, fixed, or customary moment or hour for something to happen, begin, or end ⟨arrived ahead of *time*⟩ **4 a** : a historical period : AGE **b** : a division of geologic chronology **c** : conditions at present or at some specified period — usually used in plural ⟨*times* are hard⟩ ⟨move with the *times*⟩ **d** : the present time ⟨issues of the *time*⟩ **5 a** : LIFETIME **b** : a period or term especially of military service **c** : a prison sentence **6** : SEASON 2 **7 a** : rate of speed : TEMPO **b** : the rhythmic grouping of beats in music shown in the time signature as a fraction (as 3/4, 4/4, or 6/8) with the top number showing the number of beats in a measure and the bottom number showing the kind of note (as quarter note or eighth note) for each beat ⟨a song in 3/4 *time*⟩ **8 a** : a moment, hour, day, or year as indicated by a clock or calendar ⟨what *time* is it⟩ **b** : any of various systems (as sidereal or solar) of reckoning time **9 a** : one of a series of recurring instances or repeated actions ⟨told you many *times*⟩ **b** *pl* (1) : added or accumulated quantities or instances ⟨five *times* greater⟩ (2) : equal fractional parts of which an indicated number equals a comparatively greater quantity ⟨seven *times* smaller⟩ **c** : TURN 4b ⟨three *times* at bat〉 **10 :** finite as contrasted with infinite duration **11 :** a person's experience during a specified period or on a particular occasion 〈had a good *time*〉 **12 a :** the period of one's work 〈make up *time*〉 **b :** an hourly pay rate **13 a :** the playing time of a game **b :** TIME-OUT 1 〈called *time* to make a substitution〉 [Old English *tīma*] — **at the same time :** HOWEVER 2, NEVERTHELESS — **at times :** now and then — **from time to time :** once in a while : OCCASIONALLY — **in no time :** in the shortest possible time — **in time 1 :** early enough **2 :** in the course of time : EVENTUALLY **3 :** in correct rhythm or tempo — **on time 1 :** at the time set : PUNCTUALLY **2 :** on an installment payment plan

^{2}**time** *vt* **1 a :** to arrange or set the time of : SCHEDULE **b :** to regulate (a watch) to keep correct time **2 :** to set the tempo, speed, or duration of **3 :** to cause to keep time with something **4 :** to determine or record the time, duration, or rate of **5 :** to adjust (as a mechanical part) so that an action occurs at a desired instant

^{3}**time** *adj* **1 a :** of or relating to time **b :** recording time **2 :** timed to ignite or explode at a specific moment 〈a *time* bomb〉 **3 :** payable on a specified future day or a certain length of time after presentation for acceptance 〈*time* deposits〉

time and a half *n* **:** payment of a worker (as for overtime) at one and a half times the regular wage rate

time capsule *n* **:** a container holding historical records or objects representative of current culture that is deposited (as in a cornerstone) for preservation until discovery in the future

time card *n* **:** a card used with a time clock to record an employee's starting and quitting times each day or on each job

time clock *n* **:** a clock that stamps an employee's starting and quitting times on a time card

timed \'tīmd\ *adj* **1 :** done or taking place at a time of a specified sort 〈an ill-*timed* arrival〉 **2 :** made to occur at or in a set time 〈a *timed* explosion〉

time exposure *n* **:** exposure of a photographic film for a definite time usually of more than one half second; *also* **:** a photograph taken by such exposure

time–hon·ored \'tī-ˌmän-ərd\ *adj* **:** honored or respected because of age or long-established usage

time·keep·er \'tīm-ˌkē-pər\ *n* **1 :** TIMEPIECE **2 :** a clerk who keeps records of the time worked by employees **3 :** an official who keeps track of the time in an athletic game or contest — **time·keep·ing** \-piŋ\ *n*

time lag *n* **:** an interval of time between two related phenomena (as a cause and its effect)

time·less \'tīm-ləs\ *adj* **1 a :** having no beginning or end : UNENDING **b :** not restricted to a particular time or date **2 :** not affected by time — **time·less·ly** *adv* — **time·less·ness** *n*

time lock *n* **:** a lock controlled by clockwork to prevent its being opened before a set time

time·ly \'tīm-lē\ *adj* **time·li·er; -est 1 :** coming early or at the right time : OPPORTUNE **2 :** appropriate or adapted to the times or the occasion 〈a *timely* book〉 — **time·li·ness** *n*

time machine *n* **:** a hypothetical device that permits travel into the past or future

time–out \'tī-'maůt\ *n* **1 :** a suspension of play in an athletic game **2 :** a quiet period used especially as a way to discipline children

time·piece \'tīm-ˌpēs\ *n* **:** a device (as a clock or watch) to measure the passage of time

tim·er \'tī-mər\ *n* **:** one that times: as **a :** TIMEPIECE; *esp* **:** a stopwatch for timing races **b :** TIMEKEEPER **c :** a device (as a clock) that indicates by an audible signal the end of an interval of time or that automatically starts or stops a device

times \ˌtīmz\ *prep* **:** multiplied by 〈two *times* two is four〉

time–sav·ing \'tīm-ˌsā-viŋ\ *adj* **:** intended or serving to lessen the amount of time needed to do something 〈a *time-saving* device〉 — **time–sav·er** \-ˌsā-vər\ *n*

time·scale \-ˌskāl\ *n* **:** an arrangement of events used as a measure of the duration or age of a period of history or geologic or cosmic time

time·serv·er \-ˌsər-vər\ *n* **:** a person who only does what everyone else does or what pleases a supervisor — **time·serv·ing** \-viŋ\ *adj or n*

time–sharing \'tīm-ˌsheər-iŋ, -ˌshaər-\ *n* **:** use of a computer system by many users at the same time

time signature *n* **:** a sign used to indicate musical meter and usually written with one number above another with the bottom number indicating the kind of note used as a unit of measurement and the top number indicating the number of these units in each bar

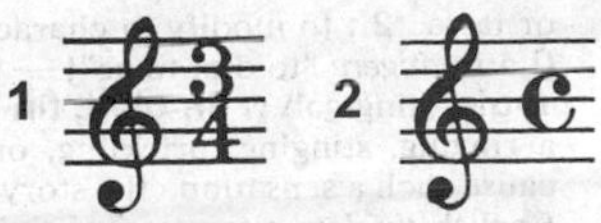
time signature: *1* 3/4 time, *2* common time

times sign *n* **:** the symbol × used to indicate multiplication

time·ta·ble \'tīm-ˌtā-bəl\ *n* **1 :** a table of departure and arrival times (as of trains, buses, or airplanes) **2 :** a schedule showing a planned order or sequence

time·worn \-ˌwōrn, -ˌwȯrn\ *adj* **1 :** worn or impaired by time **2 a :** AGE-OLD, ANCIENT 〈*timeworn* procedures〉 **b :** HACKNEYED, STALE 〈a *timeworn* joke〉

time zone *n* **:** a geographic region within which the same standard time is used

tim·id \'tim-əd\ *adj* **:** lacking in courage or self-confidence : FEARFUL, SHY [Latin *timidus,* from *timēre* "to fear"] — **ti·mid·i·ty** \tə-'mid-ət-ē\ *n* — **tim·id·ly** \'tim-əd-lē\ *adv* — **tim·id·ness** *n*

tim·ing *n* **1 :** selection for maximum effect of the precise moment for beginning or doing something **2 :** observation and recording (as by a stopwatch) of the elapsed time of an act, action, or process

tim·o·rous \'tim-rəs, -ə-rəs\ *adj* **1 :** FEARFUL 2 **2 :** expressing or suggesting timidity [Middle French *timoureus,* from Medieval Latin *timorosus,* from Latin *timor* "fear," from *timēre* "to fear"] — **tim·o·rous·ly** *adv* — **tim·o·rous·ness** *n*

tim·o·thy \'tim-ə-thē\ *n* **:** a European grass having long cylindrical spikes and widely grown for hay in the U.S. [probably after *Timothy* Hanson, 18th century American farmer said to have introduced it from New England to the southern states]

Tim·o·thy \'tim-ə-thē\ *n* **:** either of two letters written with regard to pastoral care in the early church and included as books in the New Testament — see BIBLE table

tim·pa·ni *also* **tym·pa·ni** \'tim-pə-nē\ *n pl* **:** a set of two or three kettledrums played by one performer [Italian *timpani,* pl. of *timpano* "kettledrum," from Latin *tympanum* "drum"] — **tim·pa·nist** \-nəst\ *n*

^{1}**tin** \'tin\ *n* **1 :** a soft bluish white lustrous crystalline metallic chemical element that is malleable and ductile at ordinary temperatures and that is used as a protective coating in tinfoil and in soft solders and alloys — see ELEMENT table **2 a :** a box, can, pan, vessel, or a sheet made of tinplate **b :** a scaled can holding food [Old English] — **tin** *adj*

^{2}**tin** *vt* **tinned; tin·ning 1 :** to cover or plate with tin or an alloy of tin **2 :** to put up or pack in tins : CAN

tin can *n* **:** a can made of tinplate; *also* **:** ^{2}CAN 1c

tinct \'tiŋt, 'tiŋkt\ *n* **:** TINCTURE 1 — **tinct** *adj*

^{1}**tinc·ture** \'tiŋ-chər, 'tiŋk-\ *n* **1 :** a substance that colors, dyes, or stains **2 :** a slight admixture : TRACE **3 :** a solution that contains a medicinal substance (as a drug) mixed with alcohol [Latin *tinctura* "act of dyeing," from *tingere* "to tinge"]

^{2}**tincture** *vt* **1 :** to tint or stain with a color : TINGE **2 :** to infuse or instill with a property or quality : IMPREGNATE

tin·der \'tin-dər\ *n* **:** a very flammable substance that can be used as kindling [Old English *tynder*] — **tin·dery** \-də-rē\ *adj*

tin·der·box \-ˌbäks\ *n* **1 a :** a metal box for holding tinder and usually a flint and steel for striking a spark **b :** a highly flammable object or place **2 :** a place or situation likely to erupt in or produce hostile reaction or violence

tine \'tīn\ *n* **:** a slender pointed projecting part : PRONG 〈the *tines* of a fork〉 [Old English *tind*]

tin·ea \'tin-ē-ə\ *n* **:** any of several fungal infections of the skin; *esp* **:** RINGWORM [Latin, "worm, moth"] — **tin·e·al** \-ē-əl\ *adj*

tin·foil \'tin-ˌfȯil\ *n* **1 :** a thin metal sheeting usually of aluminum or tin-lead alloy **2 :** SILVER PAPER

ting \'tiŋ\ *n* **:** a high-pitched sound (as from a light stroke on a glass) [Middle English *tingen* "to ting," of imitative origin] — **ting** *vb*

tinge \'tinj\ *vt* **tinged; tinge·ing** *or* **ting·ing** \'tin-jiŋ\ **1 a :** to color slightly : TINT **b :** to affect or modify with a slight odor or taste **2 :** to modify in character ⟨respect *tinged* with envy⟩ [Latin *tingere* "to dip, tinge"] — **tinge** *n*

tin·gle \'ting-gəl\ *vi* **tin·gled; tin·gling** \-gə-ling, -gling\ **:** to feel a ringing, stinging, prickling, or thrilling sensation; *also* **:** to cause such a sensation ⟨the story *tingles* with suspense⟩ [Middle English *tinglen,* alteration of *tinklen* "to tinkle, tingle"] — **tin·gle** *n* — **tin·gly** \-gə-lē, -glē\ *adj*

tin hat *n* **:** a metal helmet

tin·horn \'tin-ˌhȯrn\ *n* **:** a pretentious or boastful person (as a gambler) with little money, power, or ability

¹tin·ker \'ting-kər\ *n* **1 :** a mender of household utensils (as pots and pans) who usually travels from place to place **2 :** an unskilled mender **:** BUNGLER [Middle English *tinkere*]

²tinker *vi* **tin·kered; tin·ker·ing** \-kə-ring, -kring\ **:** to work in the manner of a tinker; *esp* **:** to repair or adjust something in an unskilled or experimental manner — **tin·ker·er** \-kər-ər\ *n*

tinker's damn *also* **tinker's dam** *n* **:** something absolutely worthless [probably from the tinkers' reputation for blasphemy]

¹tin·kle \'ting-kəl\ *vb* **tin·kled; tin·kling** \-kə-ling, -kling\ **1 :** to make or emit a tinkle **2 a :** to cause to make a tinkle **b :** to produce by tinkling ⟨*tinkle* a tune on the piano⟩ [Middle English *tinklen,* from *tinken* "to tinkle"]

²tinkle *n* **:** a series of short high ringing or clinking sounds — **tinkly** \-kə-lē, -klē\ *adj*

tin liz·zie \-'liz-ē\ *n* **:** a small cheap early automobile [from *Tin Lizzie,* nickname for the Model T Ford automobile]

tin·man \'tin-mən\ *n* **:** TINSMITH

tin·ni·tus \'tin-ə-təs\ *n* **:** a sensation of noise (as a ringing or roaring) that is caused by a bodily condition (as a disorder of the auditory nerve) [Latin, "ringing, tinnitus," from *tinnire* "to ring"]

tin·ny \'tin-ē\ *adj* **tin·ni·er; -est 1 :** of, abounding in, or yielding tin **2 a :** resembling tin **b :** LIGHT 1c, CHEAP ⟨a *tinny* watch⟩ **c :** lacking depth or substance ⟨*tinny* arguments⟩ **3 :** thin in tone ⟨a *tinny* voice⟩ — **tin·ni·ly** \'tin-l-ē\ *adv* — **tin·ni·ness** \'tin-ē-nəs\ *n*

Tin Pan Alley *n* **:** a district occupied chiefly by composers or publishers of popular music; *also* **:** the body of such composers or publishers

tin·plate \'tin-'plāt\ *n* **:** thin sheet iron or steel coated with tin — **tin–plate** *vt*

¹tin·sel \'tin-səl\ *n* **1 :** a thread, strip, or sheet of metal, paper, or plastic used to produce a glittering and sparkling appearance (as in fabrics, yarns, or decorations) **2 :** something superficially attractive or glamorous but of little real worth [probably from Middle French *tencelé,* past participle of *tenceler, estenceler* "to sparkle," from *etincelle* "spark," from Latin *scintilla*]

²tinsel *adj* **1 :** made of or covered with tinsel **2 :** cheaply gaudy **:** TAWDRY

³tinsel *vt* **-seled** *or* **-selled; -sel·ing** *or* **-sel·ling** \-sə-ling, -sling\ **1 :** to adorn with or as if with tinsel **2 :** to give a superficial brightness to

tin·sel·ly \'tin-sə-lē, -slē\ *adj* **:** TINSEL

tin·smith \'tin-ˌsmith\ *n* **:** a worker who makes or repairs things of metal (as tin)

¹tint \'tint\ *n* **1 :** a slight or pale coloring **:** TINGE ⟨white with a *tint* of yellow⟩ **2 :** a color produced by a pigment or dye mixture having some white in it **3 :** a usually slight modifying quality or characteristic **4 :** dye for the hair [Latin *tinctus* "act of dyeing," from *tingere* "to tinge"] ***synonyms*** see COLOR

²tint *vt* **:** to impart or apply a tint to **:** COLOR — **tint·er** *n*

tin·tin·nab·u·la·tion \ˌtin-tə-ˌnab-yə-'lā-shən\ *n* **1 :** the ringing or sounding of bells **2 :** a jingling or tinkling sound as if of bells [Latin *tintinnabulum* "bell," from *tintinnare* "to ring, jingle"]

tin·type \'tin-ˌtīp\ *n* **:** an early photograph consisting of a positive image taken directly on a thin iron plate having a darkened surface

tin·ware \-ˌwaər, -ˌweər\ *n* **:** articles made of tinplate

tin·work \-ˌwərk\ *n* **1 :** work in tin **2** *pl* **:** an establishment where tin is smelted, rolled, or otherwise worked

ti·ny \'tī-nē\ *adj* **ti·ni·er; -est :** very small or diminutive **:** MINUTE [Middle English *tine*] — **ti·ni·ness** *n*

¹tip \'tip\ *vb* **tipped; tip·ping 1 :** OVERTURN, UPSET ⟨*tipped* over a glass⟩ **2 :** TILT 2 ⟨the bench *tipped* on the uneven floor⟩ **3 :** to raise and tilt forward in salute ⟨*tipped* my hat⟩ [Middle English *tipen*] — **tip the scales 1 :** to register weight **2 :** to shift the balance of power or influence

²tip *n* **:** the act or an instance of tipping **:** TILT

³tip *vt* **tipped; tip·ping 1 a :** to furnish with a tip **b :** to cover or decorate the tip of **2 :** to affix (an insert) in a book — often used with *in* **3 :** to remove the ends of (as plant shoots) [from ⁴*tip*]

⁴tip *n* **1 :** the pointed or rounded end of something **:** END **2 :** a small piece or part serving as an end, cap, or point [Middle English] — **tipped** \'tipt\ *adj* — **on the tip of one's tongue 1 :** about to be uttered **2 :** just escaping memory ⟨his name was *on the tip of my tongue*⟩

⁵tip *n* **:** a light touch or blow **:** TAP [Middle English *tippe*]

⁶tip *vt* **tipped; tip·ping 1 :** to strike lightly **:** TAP **2 :** to give (a baseball) a glancing blow

⁷tip *n* **:** a piece of useful or confidential information ⟨a *tip* on a sure winner in a horse race⟩ [origin unknown]

⁸tip *vt* **tipped; tip·ping :** to give information or advice often in a secret or confidential manner ⟨was *tipped* off as to what would happen⟩

⁹tip *vb* **tipped; tip·ping 1 :** to give a gratuity to ⟨*tip* a waitress⟩ **2 :** to give gratuities ⟨was miserly about *tipping*⟩ [perhaps from ⁶*tip*]

¹⁰tip *n* **:** a gift or small sum of money tendered for a service **:** GRATUITY

tip·cart \'tip-ˌkärt\ *n* **:** a cart whose body can be tipped on the frame to empty its contents

tip·cat \-ˌkat\ *n* **:** a game in which one player lightly bats a wooden peg and as it flies up strikes it again to drive it as far as possible while fielders try to recover it; *also* **:** the peg used in this game

tipi *variant of* TEPEE

tip–off \'tip-ˌȯf\ *n* **:** ⁷TIP, WARNING

tip·per \'tip-ər\ *n* **:** one that tips

tip·pet \'tip-ət\ *n* **1 :** a long hanging part of a garment (as on a sleeve or cape) **2 :** a shoulder cape usually with hanging ends **3 :** a long black scarf worn over the robe by members of the Anglican clergy [Middle English *tipet*]

¹tip·ple \'tip-əl\ *vi* **tip·pled; tip·pling** \'tip-ling, -ə-ling\ **:** to drink liquor especially continuously in small amounts [back-formation from obsolete *tippler* "barkeep," from Middle English *tipeler*] — **tip·pler** \'tip-lər, -ə-lər\ *n*

²tipple *n* **:** an intoxicating beverage **:** DRINK

³tipple *n* **1 :** an apparatus by which loaded cars are emptied by tipping **2 :** the place where tipping is done; *esp* **:** a coal-screening plant [derived from ¹*tip*]

tip·staff \'tip-ˌstaf\ *n, pl* **tip·staves** \-ˌstavz, -ˌstāvz\ **:** a court officer whose duties include assisting the judge and acting as crier [obsolete *tipstaff* "staff tipped with metal"]

tip·ster \'tip-stər\ *n* **:** one who gives or sells tips especially for gambling or speculation

tip·sy \'tip-sē\ *adj* **tip·si·er; -est 1 :** unsteady, staggering, or foolish from the effects of alcohol **:** somewhat drunk **2 :** UNSTEADY, ASKEW ⟨a *tipsy* angle⟩ [¹*tip* + *-sy* (as in *tricksy*)] — **tip·si·ly** \-sə-lē\ *adv* — **tip·si·ness** \-sē-nəs\ *n*

¹tip·toe \'tip-ˌtō, -'tō\ *n* **:** the tip of a toe; *also* **:** the ends of the toes — **on tiptoe :** ALERT 1, EXPECTANT

²tiptoe *adv* **:** on or as if on tiptoe ⟨walk *tiptoe*⟩

³tiptoe *adj* **1 :** marked by standing or walking on tiptoe **2 :** CAUTIOUS ⟨a *tiptoe* approach⟩

⁴tiptoe *vi* **:** to stand, raise oneself, or walk on or as if on tiptoe

¹tip–top \'tip-'täp, -ˌtäp\ *n* **:** the highest point **:** SUMMIT

²tip–top *adj* **:** EXCELLENT, FIRST-RATE — **tip–top** *adv*

ti·rade \tī-'rād, 'tī-ˌ\ *n* **:** a long furious usually abusive speech [French, "shot, tirade," from Italian *tirata,* from *tirare* "to draw, shoot"]

¹tire \'tīr\ *vb* **1 :** to become weary **2 :** to exhaust or greatly decrease the physical strength of **:** FATIGUE ⟨the long ride *tired* us out⟩ **3 :** to wear out the patience or attention of **:** bore completely [Old English *tēorian, tȳrian*]

²tire *n* **1 :** a metal hoop forming the tread of a wheel **2 a :** a rubber cushion that encircles a wheel and usually consists of a rubber-and-fabric covering containing a cavity or a separate inner tube that is filled with compressed air **b :** the external rubber-and-fabric covering of a pneumatic tire that uses an inner tube [probably from earlier *tire* "headband," from Middle English *attire* "attire"]

tired \'tīrd\ *adj* **1 :** drained of strength and energy **:** fatigued often to the point of exhaustion **2 :** obviously worn by hard use

: RUN-DOWN 3 **3 a** : FED UP ⟨I'm *tired* of all this nonsense⟩ **b** : HACKNEYED ⟨*tired* old jokes⟩ — **tired·ly** *adv* — **tired·ness** *n*

tire·less \'tīr-ləs\ *adj* : not easily tired ⟨a *tireless* worker⟩ — **tire·less·ly** *adv* — **tire·less·ness** *n*

tire·some \'tīr-səm\ *adj* : WEARISOME, TEDIOUS — **tire·some·ly** *adv* — **tire·some·ness** *n*

tir·ing–room \'tī-ring-ˌrüm, -ˌru̇m\ *n* : a dressing room especially in a theater [derived from *attire*]

'tis \tiz, 'tiz\ : it is

tis·sue \'tish-ü\ *n* **1 a** : a fine lightweight often sheer fabric **b** : MESH, NETWORK, WEB ⟨a *tissue* of lies⟩ **2** : a piece of soft absorbent paper used especially as a handkerchief or for removing cosmetics **3** : a mass or layer of cells usually of one kind that together with their intercellular substance form one of the structural materials of a plant or an animal — compare CONNECTIVE TISSUE [Medieval French *tissue,* a rich fabric, from *tistre* "to weave," from Latin *texere*]

tissue paper *n* : a thin gauzy paper often used to wrap delicate articles

[1]tit \'tit\ *n* : TEAT [Old English]

[2]tit *n* : any of various small plump often long-tailed birds of Eurasia and Africa that are related to the chickadees and titmice

ti·tan \'tīt-n\ *n* **1** *cap* : one of a family of giants ruling the universe until overthrown by the Olympian gods **2** : one of gigantic size, power, or achievement [Greek]

ti·ta·nate \'tīt-n-ˌāt\ *n* **1** : any of various oxides of titanium and another metal **2** : a titanium ester

ti·tan·ess \'tīt-n-əs\ *n, often cap* : a female titan

ti·tan·ic \tī-'tan-ik\ *adj* : vast in size, force, or power : COLOSSAL ⟨a *titanic* struggle⟩

ti·ta·ni·um \tī-'tā-nē-əm, tə-\ *n* : a silvery gray light strong metallic element found combined in various minerals and used especially in alloys (as steel) — see ELEMENT table [New Latin, from Greek *Titan* "Titan"]

titanium dioxide *n* : an oxide TiO_2 of titanium used especially as a white pigment

titanium white *n* : titanium dioxide used as a pigment

ti·tan·o·there \tī-'tan-ə-ˌthiər\ *n* : any of various large often horned extinct mammals distantly related to the horses [derived from Greek *Titan* "Titan" + *thērion* "wild animal"]

titbit *variant of* TIDBIT

tit for tat \ˌtit-fər-'tat\ : an equivalent given in return (as for an injury) : RETALIATION [alteration of earlier *tip for tap*]

[1]tithe \'tīt͟h\ *vb* **1** : to pay or give a tithe **2** : to levy a tithe on [Old English *teogothian,* from *teogotha* "tenth"] — **tith·er** *n*

[2]tithe *n* **1** : a tenth part paid in kind or money as a voluntary contribution or as a tax especially for the support of a religious establishment **2 a** : TENTH 2 **b** : a small part

ti·tian \'tish-ən\ *adj, often cap* : of a brownish orange color [*Titian,* Italian painter]

tit·il·late \'tit-l-ˌāt\ *vt* **1** : TICKLE 2 **2** : to excite pleasurably [Latin *titillare*] — **tit·il·la·tion** \ˌtit-l-'ā-shən\ *n*

tit·i·vate *or* **tit·ti·vate** \'tit-ə-ˌvāt\ *vb* : to dress up : spruce up : SMARTEN [perhaps from *tidy* + *-vate* (as in *renovate*)] — **tit·i·va·tion** \ˌtit-ə-'vā-shən\ *n*

[1]ti·tle \'tīt-l\ *n* **1 a** : the elements constituting legal ownership **b** : a legal document (as a deed) that is evidence of a right **2 a** : something that justifies or substantiates a claim **b** : an alleged or recognized right **3 a** : a descriptive or general heading (as of a chapter in a book) **b** : the heading of an act or statute or of a legal action or proceeding **4** : the distinguishing name of a written, printed, or filmed production or of a musical composition or a work of art **5** : a division of a legal document or a book or bill; *esp* : one larger than a section or article **6** : an appellation of dignity or honor attached to a person or family (as by hereditary right) ⟨a *title* of nobility⟩ **7** : CHAMPIONSHIP 2a [Medieval French, from Latin *titulus* "inscription, title"]

[2]title *vt* **ti·tled; ti·tling** \'tīt-ling, -l-ing\ : to call by a title : TERM

ti·tled \'tīt-ld\ *adj* : having a title especially of nobility

title deed *n* : the deed constituting the evidence of a person's legal ownership

ti·tle·hold·er \'tīt-l-ˌhōl-dər\ *n* : one that holds a title; *esp* : CHAMPION 3

title page *n* : a page of a book bearing the title and usually the names of the author and publisher and the place of publication

title role *n* : a part or character that gives a play or movie its name

ti·tlist \'tīt-l-əst, 'tīt-ləst\ *n* : TITLEHOLDER

tit·mouse \'tit-ˌmau̇s\ *n, pl* **tit·mice** \-ˌmīs\ : any of several small North American insect-eating songbirds usually having small bills and long tails and related to the chickadees [Middle English *titmose*]

Ti·to·ism \'tēt-ō-ˌiz-əm\ *n* : nationalistic policies and practices followed by a Communist state or group independently of and often in opposition to the U.S.S.R. and especially as practiced in Yugoslavia by Marshal Tito

ti·trate \'tī-ˌtrāt\ *vt* : to subject to titration [French *titre* "title, proportion of gold or silver in a coin," from Medieval French *title* "inscription, title"]

ti·tra·tion \tī-'trā-shən\ *n* : the process of determining the strength of a solution or the concentration of a substance in solution by finding the smallest amount of a reagent required to cause a given effect (as color change) in reaction with a known volume of the test solution

ti·tri·met·ric \ˌtī-trə-'me-trik\ *adj* : determined by titration

tit·ter \'tit-ər\ *vi* : to laugh in a nervous or partly suppressed manner [imitative] — **titter** *n*

tit·tle \'tit-l\ *n* **1** : a point or small sign used as a diacritical mark in writing or printing **2** : a very small part or amount [Medieval Latin *titulus,* from Latin "inscription, title"]

tit·tle–tat·tle \'tit-l-ˌtat-l\ *n* : GOSSIP 2 [reduplication of *tattle*] — **tittle–tattle** *vi*

tit·u·lar \'tich-lər, -ə-lər\ *adj* **1 a** : existing in title only **b** : having the title belonging to an office or dignity without its duties or responsibilities ⟨the *titular* head of a nation⟩ **2** : bearing a title **3** : of, relating to, or being a title [Latin *titulus* "title"] — **tit·u·lar·ly** *adv*

Ti·Vo \'tē-ˌvō\ *vb* **Ti·Voed; Ti·Vo·ing** : to record (as a television program) with a DVR [*TiVo,* trademark for a brand of DVR and software]

tiz·zy \'tiz-ē\ *n, pl* **tizzies** : a highly excited and distracted state of mind [origin unknown]

TKO \ˌtē-ˌkā-'ō\ *n* : TECHNICAL KNOCKOUT

T lymphocyte *n* : T CELL

tme·sis \'mē-səs, tə-'mē-səs\ *n* : separation of parts of a compound word by the intervention of one or more words (as *what place soever* for *whatsoever place*) [Late Latin, from Greek *tmēsis* "act of cutting," from *temnein* "to cut"]

TNT \'tē-ˌen-'tē\ *n* : a flammable toxic compound $C_7H_5N_3O_6$ used especially as a high explosive [*tri*nitro*t*oluene]

[1]to \tə, tu̇, tü, 'tü; *before vowels usually* tə; *after* -t *(as in "want") often* ə\ *prep* **1 a** — used as a function word to indicate movement or an action or condition suggestive of movement toward a place, person, or thing reached ⟨walked *to* school⟩ ⟨went back *to* my first idea⟩ **b** — used as a function word to indicate direction ⟨a mile *to* the south⟩ ⟨turned her back *to* the window⟩ **c** : close against : ON ⟨applied polish *to* the table⟩ **d** : as far as ⟨stripped *to* the waist⟩ **2** — used as a function word to indicate purpose, intention, tendency, result, or end ⟨came *to* our aid⟩ ⟨a toast *to* the winner⟩ ⟨broken *to* pieces⟩ **3 a** : BEFORE ⟨ten minutes *to* five⟩ **b** : UNTIL 1 ⟨from eight *to* five⟩ **4** — used as a function word to indicate addition, attachment, connection, belonging, possession, accompaniment, or response ⟨a key *to* the door⟩ ⟨sang *to* the music⟩ ⟨comes *to* her call⟩ **5 a** : in an indicated relation with ⟨similar *to* that one⟩ **b (1)** : in accordance with ⟨add salt *to* taste⟩ **(2)** : within the range of ⟨*to* my knowledge⟩ **c** : contained, occurring, or included in ⟨400 *to* the box⟩ **6 a** — used as a function word to indicate the relation of adjective to noun ⟨agreeable *to* all of us⟩ or verb to complement ⟨sticks *to* business⟩ **b** — used as a function word to indicate the receiver of an action or the one for which something is done or exists ⟨spoke *to* his mother⟩ ⟨gave it *to* me⟩ **c** : for no one except ⟨had a room *to* myself⟩ **7** — used as a function word to indicate that the following verb is an infinitive ⟨wants *to* go⟩ and often used by itself at the end of a clause to stand for an infinitive ⟨don't want *to*⟩ [Old English *tō*]

[2]to \'tü\ *adv* **1** — used as a function word to indicate direction toward ⟨run *to* and fro⟩ **2** : into contact, position, or attachment especially with a frame (as of a door) ⟨wind blew the door *to*⟩ **3** : to the matter or business at hand ⟨the boxers set *to* with

\ə\ **abut**	\au̇\ **out**	\i\ **tip**	\ȯ\ **saw**	\u̇\ **foot**
\ər\ **further**	\ch\ **chin**	\ī\ **life**	\ȯi\ **coin**	\y\ **yet**
\a\ **mat**	\e\ **pet**	\j\ **job**	\th\ **thin**	\yü\ **few**
\ā\ **take**	\ē\ **easy**	\ng\ **sing**	\t͟h\ **this**	\yu̇\ **cure**
\ä\ **cot, cart**	\g\ **go**	\ō\ **bone**	\ü\ **food**	\zh\ **vision**

a flurry of blows⟩ **4 :** to a state of consciousness or awareness ⟨came *to*⟩ **5 :** at hand : BY ⟨saw the moose close *to*⟩

toad \ˈtōd\ *n* **:** any of numerous tailless leaping amphibians that lay their eggs in water and are distinguished from the related frogs by being more terrestrial in habit, by having a build that is squatter and shorter with weaker and shorter hind limbs, and by having skin that is rough, dry, and warty rather than smooth and moist [Old English *tāde*]

toad·fish \-ˌfish\ *n* **:** any of various marine fishes having a broad flat head, a wide mouth, and scaleless slimy skin and producing sounds (as grunts) by means of a swim bladder

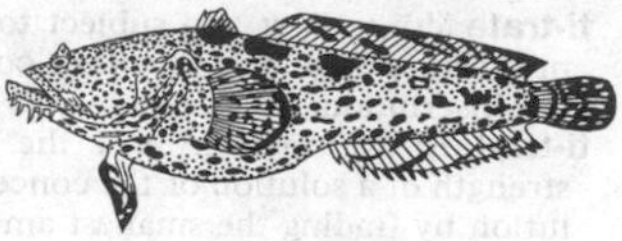

toadfish

toad·flax \-ˌflaks\ *n* **:** BUTTER-AND-EGGS

toad·stone \ˈtōd-ˌstōn\ *n* **:** a stone or similar object held to have formed in the head or body of a toad and formerly often worn as a charm or an antidote to poison

toad·stool \ˈtōd-ˌstül\ *n* **:** a fungus having an umbrella-shaped cap : MUSHROOM; *esp* **:** one that is poisonous or inedible

[1]**toady** \ˈtōd-ē\ *n, pl* **toad·ies :** a person who flatters or fawns upon another in the hope of receiving favors

[2]**toady** *vi* **toad·ied; toady·ing :** to behave as a toady — **toady·ism** \-ē-ˌiz-əm\ *n*

to–and–fro \ˌtü-ən-ˈfrō\ *adj* **:** forward and backward

[1]**toast** \ˈtōst\ *vb* **1 :** to make (as bread) crisp, hot, and brown by heat **2 :** to warm thoroughly; *also* **:** to become toasted [Medieval French *toster,* from Late Latin *tostare* "to roast," from Latin *torrēre* "to dry, parch"]

[2]**toast** *n* **1 :** sliced toasted bread browned on both sides by heat **2 a :** a person whose health is drunk or something in honor of which persons drink **b :** a highly admired person ⟨she's the *toast* of society⟩ **3 :** an act of proposing or of drinking in honor of a toast [sense 2 from the use of pieces of spiced toast to flavor drinks]

[3]**toast** *vt* **:** to propose or drink to as a toast

toast·er \ˈtō-stər\ *n* **:** one that toasts; *esp* **:** an electrical appliance for toasting

toaster oven *n* **:** an electric kitchen appliance that bakes, broils, and toasts and that fits on a counter top

toast·mas·ter \ˈtōst-ˌmas-tər, ˈtōs-\ *n* **:** a person who presides at a banquet and introduces the after-dinner speakers

toast·mis·tress \-ˌmis-trəs\ *n* **:** a girl or woman who presides as toastmaster

to·bac·co \tə-ˈbak-ō\ *n, pl* **-cos 1 :** any of a genus of chiefly American plants of the nightshade family with sticky foliage and tubular flowers; *esp* **:** a tall erect annual tropical American herb with pink or white flowers that is grown for its leaves **2 :** the leaves of cultivated tobacco prepared for use in smoking or chewing or as snuff **3 :** manufactured products of tobacco (as cigars or cigarettes); *also* **:** smoking as a practice [Spanish *tabaco,* probably from Taino (aboriginal language of the Greater Antilles and the Bahamas) "roll of tobacco leaves"]

tobacco mosaic *n* **:** any of a group of virus diseases of tobacco and related plants

to·bac·co·nist \tə-ˈbak-ə-nəst\ *n* **:** a dealer in tobacco especially at retail

to–be \tə-ˈbē\ *adj* **:** that is to be : FUTURE — usually used in combination ⟨a bride-*to-be*⟩

Tobias \tə-ˈbī-əs\ *n* **:** TOBIT

To·bit \ˈtō-bət\ *n* **:** a book of Scripture included in the Roman Catholic canon of the Old Testament and in the Protestant Apocrypha — see BIBLE table

[1]**to·bog·gan** \tə-ˈbäg-ən\ *n* **1 :** a long flat-bottomed light sled made without runners and curved up at the front **2 :** a downward course or a sharp decline [Canadian French *tobogan,* of Algonquian origin]

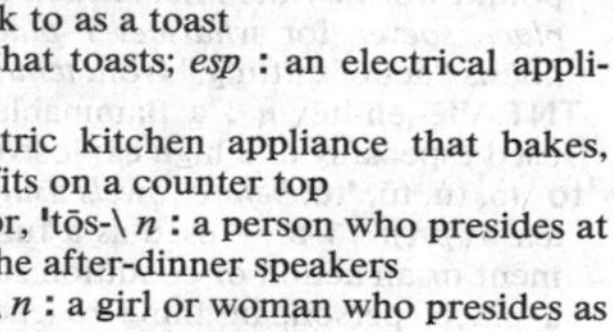

toboggan 1

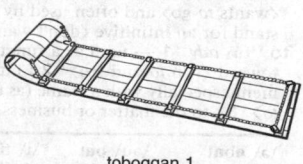

[2]**toboggan** *vi* **1 :** to coast on a toboggan **2 :** to decline suddenly and sharply (as in value) — **to·bog·gan·er** *n* — **to·bog·gan·ist** \tə-ˈbäg-ə-nəst\ *n*

to·by jug \ˈtō-bē-\ *n, often cap* **:** a small jug, pitcher, or mug modeled in the form of a stout man with a cocked hat for the brim [*Toby,* nickname from the name *Tobias*]

toc·ca·ta \tə-ˈkät-ə\ *n* **:** a musical composition usually for organ or harpsichord in a free style [Italian, from *toccare* "to touch"]

to·coph·er·ol \tō-ˈkäf-ə-ˌrȯl, -ˌrōl\ *n* **:** any of several fat-soluble oily phenolic compounds; *esp* **:** VITAMIN E [derived from Greek *tokos* "childbirth, offspring" + *pherein* "to carry, bear"]

toc·sin \ˈtäk-sən\ *n* **1 :** an alarm bell or the ringing of it **2 :** a warning signal [Middle French *toquassen,* from Old Occitan *tocasenh,* from *tocar* "to touch, ring" + *senh* "sign, bell," from Latin *signum* "sign"]

[1]**to·day** \tə-ˈdā\ *adv* **1 :** on or for this day **2 :** at the present time : NOWADAYS

[2]**today** *n* **:** the present day, time, or age

tod·dle \ˈtäd-l\ *vi* **tod·dled; tod·dling** \ˈtäd-ling, -l-ing\ **:** to walk with short tottering steps in the manner of a young child [origin unknown] — **toddle** *n* — **tod·dler** \ˈtäd-lər, -l-ər\ *n*

tod·dy \ˈtäd-ē\ *n, pl* **toddies 1 :** the sap of various mostly Asian palms often fermented to form an alcoholic liquor **2 :** a hot drink consisting of an alcoholic liquor, water, sugar, and spices [Hindi and Urdu *tāṛī* "juice of the palmyra palm," from *tār* "palmyra palm," from Sanskrit *tāla*]

to–do \tə-ˈdü\ *n, pl* **to–dos** \-ˈdüz\ **:** BUSTLE, STIR

[1]**toe** \ˈtō\ *n* **1 a :** one of the jointed members that make up the front end of a vertebrate foot **b :** the front end or part of a foot or hoof **c :** the forepart of something (as a shoe) worn on the foot **2 :** something that resembles the toe of a foot especially in form or position ⟨the *toe* of Italy⟩ [Old English *tā*] — **toe·less** \-ləs\ *adj*

[2]**toe** *vb* **toed; toe·ing 1 :** to furnish with a toe ⟨*toe* off a sock in knitting⟩ **2 :** to touch, reach, or drive with the toe ⟨*toe* a football⟩ **3 :** to drive (as a nail) slantwise; *also* **:** to fasten by nails so driven **4 :** to stand or walk so that the toes assume an indicated position or direction ⟨*toe* in⟩ — **toe the line :** to conform rigorously to a rule or standard

toed \ˈtōd\ *adj* **1 :** having a toe or such or so many toes — used especially in combination ⟨5-*toed*⟩ ⟨round-*toed* shoes⟩ **2 :** driven obliquely ⟨a *toed* nail⟩; *also* **:** secured by toed nails

toe dance *n* **:** a dance executed on the tips of the toes — **toe–dance** \ˈtō-ˌdans\ *vi* — **toe dancer** *n* — **toe dancing** *n*

toe·hold \ˈtō-ˌhōld\ *n* **1 :** a small foothold : a means of progressing **2 :** a hold in which the offensive wrestler bends or twists the opponent's foot

[1]**toe·nail** \ˈtō-ˌnāl, -ˈnāl\ *n* **:** a nail of a toe

[2]**toenail** *vt* **:** to fasten by toed nails : TOE

tof·fee *also* **tof·fy** \ˈtȯ-fē, ˈtäf-ē\ *n, pl* **toffees** *also* **toffies :** brittle but tender candy made by boiling sugar and butter together [alteration of *taffy*]

to·fu \ˈtō-fü\ *n* **:** a soft food product prepared by coagulating soybean milk — called also *bean curd* [Japanese *tōfu*]

tog \ˈtäg, ˈtȯg\ *vt* **togged; tog·ging :** to dress especially in fine clothing — usually used with *up* or *out*

to·ga \ˈtō-gə\ *n* **:** the loose outer garment worn in public by citizens of ancient Rome; *also* **:** a similar loose wrap or a professional, official, or academic gown [Latin] — **to·gaed** \-gəd\ *adj*

to·geth·er \tə-ˈgeth-ər\ *adv* **1 :** in or into one group, body, or place ⟨gathered *together*⟩ **2 :** in or into association, union, or contact with each other ⟨in business *together*⟩ ⟨mix all *together*⟩ **3 a :** at one time ⟨cheered *together*⟩ **b :** in succession ⟨work for hours *together*⟩ **4 a :** in or by combined effort ⟨worked *together*⟩ **b :** in or into agreement ⟨get *together* on a plan⟩ **c :** so as to form an integrated or coherent whole ⟨put words *together* in sentences⟩ **5 :** considered as a whole ⟨more than all the others *together*⟩ [Old English *togædere,* from *tō* "to" + *gædere* "together"] — **to·geth·er·ness** *n*

tog·gery \ˈtäg-rē, ˈtȯg-, -ə-rē\ *n, pl* **-ger·ies :** CLOTHING

[1]**tog·gle** \ˈtäg-əl\ *n* **1 :** a crosspiece attached to the end of or to a loop in a rope, chain, or belt to prevent slipping or to serve as a fastening or as a grip for tightening **2 :** a device consisting of two bars jointed together end to end but not in line so that when a force is applied to the joint tending to straighten it pressure will be exerted on the parts fixed at the ends of the bars [origin unknown]

[2]**toggle** *vb* **tog·gled; tog·gling** \ˈtäg-ling, -ə-ling\ **1 :** to fasten with or as if with a toggle **2 :** to furnish with a toggle **3 :** to switch between two options especially of an electronic device usually by pressing a single button or a simple key combination

toggle bolt *n* **:** a bolt that has a nut with wings that close for passage through a small hole and spring open after passing through the hole to keep the bolt from slipping back through

toggle switch *n* : an electric switch operated by pushing a lever through a small arc

togs \ˈtägz, ˈtȯgz\ *n pl* : CLOTHING; *esp* : a set of clothes and accessories for a specified use ⟨riding *togs*⟩ [English slang *tog* "coat," short for obsolete English argot *togeman, togman*]

[1]**toil** \ˈtȯil\ *n* : long hard tiring labor : DRUDGERY [Medieval French *toyl* "struggle, battle," from *toiller* "to make dirty, fight, wrangle," from Latin *tudiculare* "to crush, grind," derived from *tudes* "hammer"] — **toil·ful** \-fəl\ *adj* — **toil·ful·ly** \-fə-lē\ *adv*

[2]**toil** *vi* **1** : to work hard and long : LABOR **2** : PLOD 1, TRUDGE ⟨*toiling* up a steep hill⟩ — **toil·er** *n*

[3]**toil** *n* : something that involves or holds one fast : SNARE, TRAP — usually used in plural [Middle French *toile* "cloth, net," from Latin *tela* "cloth on a loom," from *texere* "to weave"]

[1]**toi·let** \ˈtȯi-lət\ *n* **1** : the act or process of dressing and grooming oneself **2 a** : BATHROOM **b** : a fixture for defecation and urination that consists essentially of a water-flushed bowl and seat [Middle French *toilette* "cloth on which items used for grooming are placed," from *toile* "cloth," from Latin *tela* "web"]

[2]**toilet** *vb* **1** : to dress and groom oneself **2** : to help (as a child) use the toilet

toilet paper *n* : a thin sanitary absorbent paper usually in a roll for bathroom use chiefly for drying or cleaning oneself after defecation or urination

toi·let·ry \ˈtȯi-lə-trē\ *n, pl* **-ries** : an article or preparation (as a soap, lotion, toothpaste, or cologne) used in grooming oneself — usually used in plural

toilet soap *n* : a mild often perfumed and colored soap

toi·lette \twä-ˈlet\ *n* **1** : TOILET 1 **2 a** : formal or fashionable attire or style of dressing **b** : a particular costume or outfit [French]

toilet training *n* : the process of training a child to control bladder and bowel movements and to use the toilet — **toilet train** *vt*

toilet water *n* : a perfumed liquid containing a high percentage of alcohol for use in or after a bath or as a skin freshener

toil·some \ˈtȯil-səm\ *adj* : marked by or full of toil or fatigue : LABORIOUS — **toil·some·ly** *adv* — **toil·some·ness** *n*

toil·worn \-ˌwōrn, -ˌwȯrn\ *adj* : showing the effects of or worn out by long hard work

[1]**to·ken** \ˈtō-kən\ *n* **1** : an outward sign or expression ⟨*tokens* of grief⟩ **2** : SYMBOL 1, EMBLEM ⟨the white flag is a *token* of surrender⟩ **3 a** : SOUVENIR, KEEPSAKE **b** : a small part representing the whole : INDICATION ⟨a mere *token* of future benefits⟩ **4 a** : something given or shown as a guarantee (as of identity, right, or authority) **b** : a piece resembling a coin issued for use (as for fare on a bus) [Old English *tācen*] ***synonyms*** see SIGN — **by the same token** : for the same reason

[2]**token** *adj* **1** : done or given in partial fulfillment of an obligation or undertaking ⟨a *token* payment⟩ **2** : MINIMAL, PERFUNCTORY ⟨*token* resistance⟩

to·ken·ism \ˈtō-kə-ˌniz-əm\ *n* : the policy or practice of making only a token effort (as to desegregate)

token money *n* : money of regular government issue having a greater face value than intrinsic value

tol·booth \ˈtōl-ˌbüth, ˈtō-, ˈtäl-, ˈtȯl-\ *n* **1** *Scottish* : a town or market hall **2** *Scottish* : JAIL, PRISON [Middle English *tolbothe* "tollbooth, town hall, jail"]

tol·bu·ta·mide \täl-ˈbyüt-ə-ˌmīd\ *n* : a sulfonamide that lowers blood sugar level and is used in the treatment of diabetes [*tol*uene + *but*yric + *amide*]

told *past and past participle of* TELL

tole \ˈtōl\ *n* : usually japanned or painted sheet metal (as tinplate) used mostly for decorative objects (as trays or boxes) and finished in various colors often with stenciled designs [French *tôle* "sheet metal," from French dialect *taule,* from Latin *tabula* "board, tablet"]

To·le·do \tə-ˈlēd-ō\ *n, pl* **-dos** : a finely tempered sword of a kind made in Toledo, Spain

tol·er·a·ble \ˈtäl-rə-bəl, -ə-rə-; ˈtäl-ər-bəl\ *adj* **1** : capable of being borne or endured ⟨*tolerable* pain⟩ **2** : moderately good or agreeable : PASSABLE ⟨a *tolerable* singing voice⟩ — **tol·er·a·bil·i·ty** \ˌtäl-rə-ˈbil-ət-ē, -ə-rə-\ *n* — **tol·er·a·bly** \ˈtäl-rə-blē, -ə-rə-; ˈtäl-ər-blē\ *adv*

tol·er·ance \ˈtäl-rəns, -ə-rəns\ *n* **1** : ability to endure pain or hardship **2 a** : sympathy or indulgence for beliefs or practices differing from one's own **b** : the act of allowing something : TOLERATION **3** : allowable deviation from a standard **4 a** : the capacity of the body to endure or become less responsive to a substance (as a drug) especially with repeated use or exposure **b** : the capacity of an organism to grow or thrive when subjected to an unfavorable environmental factor (as shade) — **tol·er·ant** \-rənt\ *adj* — **tol·er·ant·ly** *adv*

tol·er·ate \ˈtäl-ə-ˌrāt\ *vt* **1** : to allow to be done or to exist : put up with : ENDURE **2** : to show tolerance toward ⟨plants that *tolerate* drought⟩ ⟨*tolerate* a drug⟩ [Latin *tolerare*] — **tol·er·a·tion** \ˌtäl-ə-ˈrā-shən\ *n* — **tol·er·a·tor** \ˈtäl-ə-ˌrāt-ər\ *n*

[1]**toll** \ˈtōl\ *n* **1** : a tax paid for a privilege (as the use of a highway or bridge) **2** : a charge paid for a service (as placing a long-distance telephone call) **3** : a ruinous price; *esp* : cost in life or health ⟨the death *toll* from the hurricane⟩ [Old English]

[2]**toll** *vt* : to take as toll; *also* : to take a toll from

[3]**toll** *vb* **1** : to sound (a bell) by pulling the rope **2 a** : to give signal or announcement of ⟨the clock *tolled* the hour⟩ **b** : to announce by tolling **c** : to call to or from a place or occasion ⟨bells *tolled* the congregation to church⟩ **3** : to sound with slow measured strokes ⟨the bell *tolls* solemnly⟩ [Middle English *tollen,* perhaps alteration of *toilen* "to struggle"]

[4]**toll** *n* : the sound of a tolling bell

toll·booth \ˈtōl-ˌbüth\ *n* : a booth where tolls are paid

toll call *n* : a long-distance telephone call at charges above a local rate

toll–free \ˈtōl-ˈfrē\ *adj or adv* : having or using a direct telephone line or number (as an 800 number) for a long-distance call that is not charged to the caller ⟨a *toll-free* number⟩ ⟨called *toll-free*⟩

toll·gate \ˈtōl-ˌgāt\ *n* : a point where vehicles stop to pay a toll

toll·house \-ˌhau̇s\ *n* : a house or booth where tolls are collected

Tol·tec \ˈtōl-ˌtek, ˈtäl-\ *n* : a member of a people that dominated central and southern Mexico prior to the Aztecs [Spanish *tolteca,* of Nahuatl origin] — **Tol·tec·an** \-ən\ *adj*

tol·u·ene \ˈtäl-yə-ˌwēn\ *n* : a hydrocarbon similar to benzene but less volatile, less flammable, and less toxic that is used especially as a solvent and in organic synthesis [Spanish *tolu,* a balsam from which toluene was distilled, from Santiago de *Tolú,* Colombia]

tom \ˈtäm\ *n* : the male of various animals: as **a** : TOMCAT **b** : GOBBLER [*Tom,* nickname for *Thomas*]

[1]**tom·a·hawk** \ˈtäm-i-ˌhȯk\ *n* : a light ax used as a weapon especially by North American Indians [Virginia Algonquian *tomahak*]

[2]**tomahawk** *vt* : to cut, strike, or kill with a tomahawk

to·ma·to \tə-ˈmāt-ō, -ˈmät-\ *n, pl* **-toes** **1** : the usually large rounded red or sometimes yellow pulpy berry that is eaten as a vegetable **2** : a widely grown South American plant of the nightshade family that produces tomatoes [Spanish *tomate,* from Nahuatl *tomatl*]

tomb \ˈtüm\ *n* **1 a** : GRAVE **b** : a place of burial **2** : a house, chamber, or vault for the dead **3** : a building or structure resembling a tomb [Anglo-French *tumbe,* from Late Latin *tumba* "sepulchral mound," from Greek *tymbos*]

tom·boy \ˈtäm-ˌbȯi\ *n* : a girl of boyish behavior — **tom·boy·ish** \-ish\ *adj* — **tom·boy·ish·ness** *n*

tomb·stone \ˈtüm-ˌstōn\ *n* : GRAVESTONE

tom·cat \ˈtäm-ˌkat\ *n* : a male domestic cat

tom·cod \-ˌkäd\ *n* : either of two small fishes resembling the related cod

Tom, Dick, and Harry \ˌtäm-ˌdik-ən-ˈhar-ē\ *n* : the ordinary person : ANYONE — often used with *every* ⟨helps every *Tom, Dick, and Harry* in need⟩

tome \ˈtōm\ *n* : BOOK 1a; *esp* : a large or scholarly book [Latin *tomus,* from Greek *tomos* "section, tome," from *temnein* "to cut"]

to·men·tose \tō-ˈmen-ˌtōs, ˈtō-mən-\ *adj* : covered with densely matted woolly hairs ⟨a *tomentose* leaf⟩ [Latin *tomentum* "cushion stuffing"]

tom·fool \ˈtäm-ˈfül\ *n* : a great fool : BLOCKHEAD — **tomfool** *adj* — **tom·fool·ery** \täm-ˈfül-rē, -ə-rē\ *n*

Tom·my \ˈtäm-ē\ *n, pl* **Tommies** : a British soldier [*Thomas* Atkins, name used as model in official army forms]

tom·my gun \ˈtäm-ē-ˌgən\ *n* : SUBMACHINE GUN [*Thompson* submachine gun]

tom·my·rot \ˈtäm-ē-ˌrät\ *n* : NONSENSE 1 [English dialect *tommy* "fool" + *rot*]

to·mo·gram \ˈtō-mə-ˌgram\ *n* : an image generated by tomography [Greek *tomos* "section"]

to·mog·ra·phy \tō-ˈmäg-rə-fē\ *n* : a method of producing a three-dimensional image of the internal structures of an object (as the human body or the earth) by recording differences in the ways that waves of energy pass through those structures [Greek *tomos* "section" + *-graphy*] — **to·mo·graph·ic** \ˌtō-mə-ˈgraf-ik\ *adj*

[1]**to·mor·row** \tə-ˈmär-ō, -ˈmȯr-\ *adv* : on or for the day after today [Old English *tō morgen,* from *tō* "to" + *morgen* "morrow, morning"]

[2]**tomorrow** *n* **1** : the day after today **2** : FUTURE 1a

Tom Thumb \ˈtäm-ˈthəm\ *n* : a very small individual [*Tom Thumb,* legendary English dwarf]

tom–tom \ˈtäm-ˌtäm, ˈtəm-ˌtəm\ *n* : a usually long narrow small-headed drum commonly beaten with the hands [Hindi and Urdu *ṭamṭam*]

-t·o·my \t-ə-mē\ *n combining form, pl* **-tomies** : cutting : incision ⟨tracheo*tomy*⟩ [Greek *-tomos* "that cuts," from *temnein* "to cut"]

ton \ˈtən\ *n, pl* **tons** *also* **ton** **1** : any of various units of weight: **a** — see MEASURE table **b** : METRIC TON **2 a** : a unit of internal capacity for ships equal to 100 cubic feet (about 2.83 cubic meters) **b** : a unit approximately equal to the volume of a long ton weight of seawater used in reckoning the displacement of ships and equal to 35 cubic feet (about 0.99 cubic meters) **c** : a unit of volume for cargo freight usually reckoned at 40 cubic feet (about 1.13 cubic meters) **3** : a great quantity : LOT — often used in plural ⟨*tons* of money⟩ [Middle English *tunne,* a unit of weight or capacity, from Old English *tunne* "tun"]

ton·al \ˈtōn-l\ *adj* **1** : of, relating to, or having tonality **2** : of or relating to tone or tonicity — **ton·al·ly** \-l-ē\ *adv*

to·nal·i·ty \tō-ˈnal-ət-ē\ *n, pl* **-ties** : tonal quality: as **a** : the character of a musical composition dependent on its key or on the relation of its tones and chords to a keynote **b** : the arrangement or interrelation of color tones of a picture

[1]**tone** \ˈtōn\ *n* **1 a** : quality of vocal or musical sound **b** : a sound of definite pitch or vibration **c** : pitch, inflection, or modulation of voice especially as an individual characteristic, a mode of emotional expression, or a linguistic device ⟨a shrill *tone*⟩ ⟨in angry *tones*⟩ **2** : a style or way of speaking or writing ⟨a scholarly *tone*⟩ **3** : general character, quality, or trend ⟨the depressing *tone* of your thoughts⟩ **4 a** : color quality or value : a tint or shade of color ⟨decorated in soft *tones*⟩ **b** : a color that modifies another ⟨gray with a blue *tone*⟩ **5 a** : a healthy state of the body or any of its parts **b** : normal tension or responsiveness to stimulation; *esp* : the state of normal tension of a muscle in which it is partly contracted **6** : healthy elasticity : RESILIENCY [Latin *tonus* "tension, tone," from Greek *tonos,* literally, "act of stretching"] — **toned** \ˈtōnd\ *adj*

[2]**tone** *vb* **1** : to give a particular intonation or inflection to **2** : to impart tone to : STRENGTHEN **3** : to soften or reduce in intensity, color, appearance, or sound — often used with *down* — **ton·er** *n*

tone arm *n* : the movable part of a phonograph that carries the pickup and permits the needle to follow the record groove

tone–deaf \ˈtōn-ˌdef\ *adj* : relatively insensitive to differences in musical pitch

tone language *n* : a language (as Chinese) in which variations in tone distinguish words of different meaning that otherwise would sound alike

tong \ˈtäng, ˈtȯng\ *vb* **1** : to take, hold, or handle with tongs **2** : to use tongs especially in taking or handling something — **tong·er** \ˈtäng-ər, ˈtȯng-\ *n*

tongs \ˈtängz, ˈtȯngz\ *n pl* : any of numerous grasping devices commonly having two pieces joined at one end by a pivot or hinged like scissors [Old English *tang*]

[1]**tongue** \ˈtəng\ *n* **1 a** : a fleshy movable muscular process of the floor of the mouth in most vertebrates that bears sensory organs (as taste buds) and small glands and functions especially in taking and swallowing food and in human beings as a speech organ **b** : a part of various invertebrate animals that is analogous to the tongue **2** : the flesh of a tongue (as of the ox or sheep) used as food **3** : the power of communication through speech **4 a** : LANGUAGE; *esp* : a spoken language **b** : manner or quality of utterance with respect to tone or sound, meaning, or the intention of the speaker ⟨a clever *tongue*⟩ ⟨a sharp *tongue*⟩ **c** : ecstatic usually unintelligible utterance usually accompanying religious excitation — usually used in plural **5** : something resembling an animal's tongue in being elongated and fastened at one end only: as **a** : a movable pin in a buckle **b** : a metal piece suspended inside a bell so as to strike against the sides as the bell is swung **c** : the flap under the lacing of a shoe **6** : a projecting ridge or rib (as on one edge of a board) [Old English *tunge*] — **tongue·less** \-ləs\ *adj* — **tongue·like** \-ˌlīk\ *adj*

[2]**tongue** *vb* **tongued; tongu·ing** \ˈtəng-ing\ **1** : to touch or lick with or as if with the tongue **2** : to cut a tongue on **3** : to articulate notes on a wind instrument by interrupting the stream of wind with the action of the tongue

tongue and groove *n* : a joint made by a tongue on one edge of a board fitting into a corresponding groove on the edge of another board

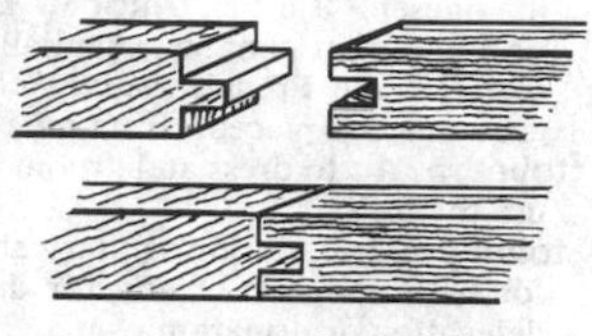

tongue and groove

tongue in cheek *adv* : with insincerity, irony, or whimsical exaggeration — **tongue–in–cheek** *adj*

tongue–lash \ˈtəng-ˌlash\ *vb* : SCOLD 2, BERATE — **tongue–lash·ing** *n*

tongue–tied \-ˌtīd\ *adj* : unable to speak clearly or freely (as from shyness)

tongue twister *n* : a word, phrase, or sentence difficult to articulate because of a succession of similar consonant sounds (as in "she sells seashells")

[1]**ton·ic** \ˈtän-ik\ *adj* **1** : of, relating to, or marked by tension and especially muscular tension : exhibiting tonus **b** : producing or tending to produce healthy muscular condition and reaction **c** : being or marked by excessive and prolonged muscular contraction ⟨*tonic* convulsions⟩ **2 a** : improving physical or mental tone : INVIGORATING **b** : yielding a tonic substance **3** : relating to or based on the first tone of a scale ⟨*tonic* harmony⟩ **4** : bearing a principal stress or accent ⟨a *tonic* syllable⟩ [Greek *tonikos,* from *tonos* "tension, tone"] — **ton·i·cal·ly** \ˈtän-i-kə-lē, -klē\ *adv*

[2]**tonic** *n* **1** : the first degree of a major or minor musical scale **2 a** : an agent (as a drug) that increases body tone **b** : one that invigorates, restores, refreshes, or stimulates ⟨a day in the country was a *tonic* for him⟩ **c** : a liquid preparation for the scalp or hair **d** *chiefly New England* : a carbonated flavored beverage **e** : TONIC WATER **3** : a voiced sound

to·nic·i·ty \tō-ˈnis-ət-ē\ *n* : the quality of having tone and especially healthy vigor of body or mind

tonic water *n* : a carbonated beverage flavored with a small amount of quinine, lemon, and lime

[1]**to·night** \tə-ˈnīt\ *adv* : on this present night or the night following this present day

[2]**tonight** *n* : the night that ends the present day

ton·nage \ˈtən-ij\ *n* **1 a** : a duty on ships based on cargo capacity **b** : a duty on goods per ton transported **2** : ships in terms of the total number of tons registered or carried or of their carrying capacity **3 a** : the cubical content of a merchant ship in units of 100 cubic feet (about 2.83 cubic meters) **b** : the displacement of a warship **4** : total weight in tons shipped, carried, or mined [Middle English, "duty levied on every tun of imported wine," from Medieval French *tonne* "tun," from Medieval Latin *tunna*]

ton·neau \tə-ˈnō\ *n, pl* **tonneaus** : the rear seating compartment of an automobile; *also* : the entire seating compartment [French, literally, "tun," derived from Medieval French *tonel,* from *tone*]

ton·sil \ˈtän-səl\ *n* : either of a pair of masses of lymphoid tissue that lie one on each side of the throat at the back of the mouth [Latin *tonsillae* "tonsils"] — **ton·sil·lar** \-sə-lər\ *adj*

ton·sil·lec·to·my \ˌtän-sə-ˈlek-tə-mē\ *n, pl* **-mies** : the surgical removal of the tonsils

ton·sil·li·tis \-ˈlīt-əs\ *n* : inflammation of the tonsils

ton·so·ri·al \tän-ˈsōr-ē-əl, -ˈsȯr-\ *adj* : of or relating to a barber or a barber's work [Latin *tonsorius,* from *tondēre* "to shear"]

ton·sure \ˈtän-chər\ *n* **1** : the Roman Catholic or Eastern rite of admission to the clergy by the clipping or shaving of the head **2 :** the shaven crown or patch worn by monks and many clerics [Latin *tonsura* "act of shearing," from *tondēre* "to shear"] — **ton•sured** \-chərd\ *adj*

to•nus \'tō-nəs\ *n* **:** TONE 5; *esp* **:** the state of partial contraction characteristic of normal muscle [Latin, "tension, tone"]

too \tü, 'tü\ *adv* **1 :** ALSO 2, BESIDES ⟨sell the house and furniture *too*⟩ **2 a :** OVER 2a, EXCESSIVELY ⟨it's *too* late⟩ **b :** to such a degree as to be regrettable ⟨this has gone *too* far⟩ **c :** VERY 1 ⟨only *too* glad to help⟩ **3 :** SO 2d, INDEED ⟨I didn't! You did *too*!⟩ [Old English *tō* "to, too"]

took *past of* TAKE

[1]**tool** \'tül\ *n* **1 :** an instrument (as a hammer, saw, or wrench) used or worked by hand or by a machine; *also* **:** a machine for shaping metal **2 a :** an instrument or apparatus used in performing an operation or necessary in the practice of a vocation or profession ⟨a scholar's books are *tools*⟩ **b :** an element of a computer program (as a graphics application) that activates and controls a particular function ⟨a drawing *tool*⟩ **c :** a means to an end ⟨a book's cover can be a marketing *tool*⟩ **3 :** a person used or manipulated by another **:** DUPE [Old English *tōl*] ***synonyms*** see IMPLEMENT

[2]**tool** *vb* **1 :** DRIVE ⟨*tooled* along the road⟩ **2 :** to shape, form, or finish with a tool; *esp* **:** to letter or ornament (as leather or gold) by means of hand tools **3 :** to equip a plant or industry with machines and tools for production — often used with *up*

tool•box \'tül-ˌbäks\ *n* **:** a chest for tools

tool•hold•er \-ˌhōl-dər\ *n* **:** a short steel bar having a shank at one end by which it is clamped to a machine and a clamp at the other end to hold small interchangeable cutting bits

tool•house \-ˌhau̇s\ *n* **:** a building (as in a garden) for storing tools

tool•mak•er \'tül-ˌmā-kər\ *n* **1 :** one (as a human or animal) that makes tools **2 :** a machinist who specializes in the construction, repair, maintenance, and calibration of the tools, jigs, fixtures, and instruments of a machine shop

tool•mak•ing \-ˌmā-king\ *n* **:** the act, process, or art of making tools

tool•room \-ˌrüm, -ˌru̇m\ *n* **:** a room where tools are kept; *esp* **:** a room in a machine shop in which tools are made, stored, or loaned out to the workers

tool•shed \-ˌshed\ *n* **:** TOOLHOUSE

[1]**toot** \'tüt\ *vb* **1 :** to sound a short blast ⟨a horn *tooted*⟩ **2 :** to blow or sound (an instrument) especially so as to produce short blasts ⟨*toot* a whistle⟩ [probably imitative] — **toot•er** *n*

[2]**toot** *n* **:** a short blast (as on a horn); *also* **:** a sound resembling such a blast

[3]**toot** *n* **:** a drinking bout **:** SPREE ⟨went on a *toot*⟩ [Scottish *toot* "to drink heavily"]

tooth \'tüth\ *n, pl* **teeth** \'tēth\ **1 a :** one of the hard bony structures borne especially on the jaws of vertebrates and used for seizing and chewing food and as weapons **b :** any of various usually hard and sharp processes especially about the mouth of an invertebrate **2 :** TASTE, LIKING ⟨a *tooth* for sweets⟩ **3 :** a projection resembling or suggesting the tooth of an animal in shape, arrangement, or action ⟨the *tooth* of a saw⟩ **4 :** one of the projections on the rim of a cogwheel **:** COG **5 a :** something that injures, tortures, devours, or destroys ⟨sailed into the *teeth* of the hurricane⟩ **b** *pl* **:** effective means of enforcement ⟨drug laws with *teeth*⟩ **6 :** a roughness of surface produced by mechanical or artificial means [Old English *tōth*] — **toothed** \'tütht\ *adj* — **tooth•less** \'tüth-ləs\ *adj* — **tooth-like** \-ˌlīk\ *adj* — **to the teeth :** FULLY, COMPLETELY ⟨armed *to the teeth*⟩

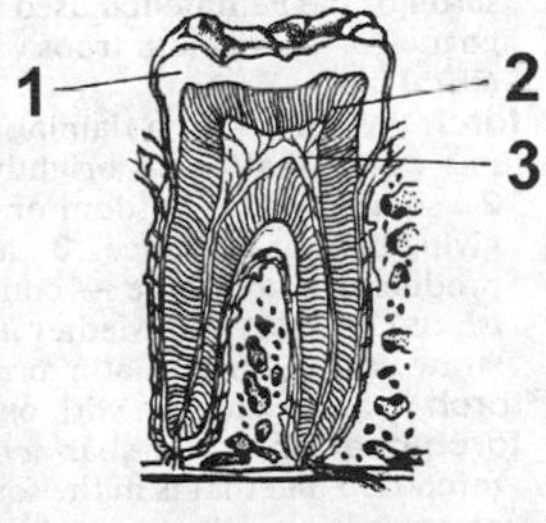

tooth 1a: *1* enamel, *2* dentine, *3* pulp

tooth•ache \'tü-ˌthāk\ *n* **:** pain in or about a tooth

tooth and nail *adv* **:** with every available means **:** ALL OUT ⟨fight *tooth and nail*⟩

tooth•brush \'tüth-ˌbrəsh\ *n* **:** a brush for cleaning the teeth

toothed whale *n* **:** any of a group (Odontoceti) of cetaceans (as a dolphin or killer whale) having usually numerous simple conical teeth — compare BALEEN WHALE

tooth•paste \'tüth-ˌpāst\ *n* **:** a paste for cleaning the teeth

tooth•pick \-ˌpik\ *n* **:** a pointed instrument (as a small tapering piece of wood) used for removing food particles lodged between the teeth

tooth powder *n* **:** a powder for cleaning the teeth

tooth shell *n* **:** any of a class (Scaphopoda) of burrowing marine mollusks with a tapering tubular shell; *also* **:** this shell

tooth•some \'tüth-səm\ *adj* **1 :** pleasing to the taste **:** DELICIOUS ⟨a *toothsome* dessert⟩ **2 :** physically attractive **:** LOVELY — **tooth•some•ly** *adv* — **tooth•some•ness** *n*

toothy \'tü-thē\ *adj* **tooth•i•er; -est :** having or showing prominent teeth ⟨a *toothy* grin⟩ — **tooth•i•ly** \-thə-lē\ *adv*

[1]**top** \'täp\ *n* **1 a :** the highest point, level, or part ⟨the *top* of the hill⟩ **b :** the upper end, edge, or surface ⟨the *top* of the page⟩ ⟨filled the glass to the *top*⟩ **2 :** the stalk and leaves of a plant and especially of one with edible roots ⟨beet *tops*⟩ **3 :** a part serving as an upper piece, lid, or covering ⟨a pajama *top*⟩ ⟨put the *top* on the jar⟩ **4 :** the highest position or rank **:** ACME ⟨reached the *top* of the profession⟩; *also* **:** one in such a position ⟨secrets known only to the *top*⟩ [Old English] — **topped** \'täpt\ *adj* — **off the top of one's head :** in an impromptu way — **on top of 1 a :** in control of ⟨was *on top of* the job⟩ **b :** informed about ⟨tried to keep *on top of* new developments⟩ **2 :** in sudden unexpected nearness to ⟨the motorboat was *on top of* us⟩ **3 :** in addition to — **on top of the world :** in a position of great success, happiness, or fame

[2]**top** *vt* **topped; top•ping 1 :** to remove or cut the top of ⟨*top* a tree⟩ **2 a :** to cover with a top **:** provide, form, or serve as a top for **b :** to supply with a decorative or protective finish or a final touch ⟨*topped* the sundae with nuts⟩ ⟨a meal *topped* off with coffee⟩ **c :** to resupply or refill to capacity ⟨*topped* off the gas tank⟩ **3 a :** to be or become higher than **b :** to be superior to **:** EXCEL, SURPASS ⟨*topped* the record⟩ **c :** to gain ascendancy over **:** DOMINATE **4 a :** to rise to, reach, or be at the top of **b :** to go over the top of **:** CLEAR, SURMOUNT **5 :** to strike (a ball) above the center creating topspin

[3]**top** *adj* **1 :** of, relating to, or being at the top **2 :** LEADING 1, CHIEF **3 :** of the highest quality, amount, or degree ⟨*top* value⟩

[4]**top** *n* **:** a commonly cylindrical or cone-shaped toy that has a point on which it is made to spin [Old English]

to•paz \'tō-ˌpaz\ *n* **1 :** a hard mineral consisting of a silicate of aluminum and occurring in crystals of various colors with the yellow variety being the one usually cut and prized as a gem **2 :** a gem (as a yellow sapphire) resembling the true topaz [Medieval French *topace,* from Latin *topazus,* from Greek *topazos*]

top billing *n* **1 :** the position at the top of a theatrical bill usually featuring the star's name **2 :** prominent emphasis, featuring, or advertising

top boot *n* **:** a high boot with light-colored leather bands around the upper part

top•coat \'täp-ˌkōt\ *n* **:** a lightweight overcoat

top•cross \-ˌkrȯs\ *n* **:** a cross between a superior or purebred male and inferior female stock to improve the average quality of the progeny; *also* **:** an offspring from such a cross

top dog *n* **:** one that is in a position of authority especially by winning in a hard-fought competition

top dollar *n* **:** the highest amount being paid for a commodity or service ⟨paid *top dollar* for the tickets⟩

top drawer *n* **:** the highest level of society, authority, or excellence

tope \'tōp\ *n* **:** a widely distributed small shark with a liver rich in vitamin A [origin unknown]

to•pee *or* **to•pi** \tō-'pē, 'tō-pē\ *n* **:** a lightweight helmet-shaped hat made of pith or cork [Hindi and Urdu *ṭopī*]

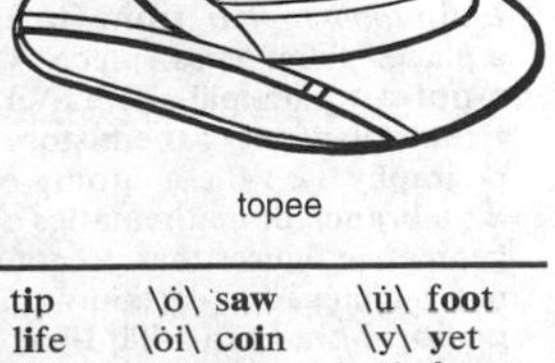
topee

top–end \'täp-'end\ *adj* **:** TOP-FLIGHT ⟨*top-end* equipment⟩

top•er \'tō-pər\ *n* **:** a heavy

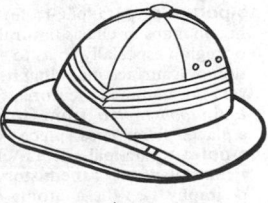

\ə\ **abut**	\au̇\ **out**	\i\ **tip**	\ȯ\ **saw**	\u̇\ **foot**
\ər\ **further**	\ch\ **chin**	\ī\ **life**	\ȯi\ **coin**	\y\ **yet**
\a\ **mat**	\e\ **pet**	\j\ **job**	\th\ **thin**	\yü\ **few**
\ā\ **take**	\ē\ **easy**	\ng\ **sing**	\t͟h\ **this**	\yu̇\ **cure**
\ä\ **cot, cart**	\g\ **go**	\ō\ **bone**	\ü\ **food**	\zh\ **vision**

drinker; *esp* : DRUNKARD [obsolete *tope,* interjection used to wish good health before drinking]

top·flight \'täp-'flīt\ *adj* : of, relating to, or being the highest level of achievement, excellence, or eminence — **top flight** *n*

Top 40 *n pl* : the 40 best-selling audio recordings for a given period

top·gal·lant \täp-'gal-ənt, 'täp-, tə-'gal-\ *n* **1** *archaic* : the topmost point **2** : the sail just above a topsail and below the royal on a square-rigged ship

top hat *n* : a tall-crowned hat usually of beaver or silk

top–heavy \'täp-ˌhev-ē\ *adj* : having the top part too heavy for the lower part

To·phet \'tō-fət\ *n* : HELL 2 [Hebrew *tōpheth,* shrine south of ancient Jerusalem where human sacrifices were performed to Moloch (Jeremiah 7:31)]

1**to·pi·ary** \'tō-pē-ˌer-ē\ *adj* **1 a** : relating to or being the art or practice of topiary **b** : shaped or created by topiary ⟨a *topiary* elephant⟩ **2** : characterized by or containing topiary ⟨a *topiary* garden⟩

2**topiary** *n, pl* **-ar·ies** **1** : the art or practice of training and trimming trees or shrubs into odd or ornamental shapes **2** : a garden or park containing plants shaped by topiary; *also* : a plant or plants shaped by topiary [Latin *topiarius,* from *topia* "ornamental gardening," from Greek *topos* "place"]

top·ic \'täp-ik\ *n* **1** : a heading in an outlined argument or exposition **2** : the subject of a discourse or a section of it : THEME [Latin *Topica,* a work by Aristotle on forms of argument, from Greek *Topika,* derived from *topos* "place, commonplace"]

top·i·cal \'täp-i-kəl\ *adj* **1 a** : of, relating to, or arranged by topics ⟨a *topical* outline⟩ **b** : referring to the topics of the day or place : of local or temporary interest ⟨a *topical* novel⟩ **2** : designed for or involving local application and action (as on the body) ⟨a *topical* remedy⟩ ⟨a *topical* anesthetic⟩ [Greek *topikos* "of a place," from *topos* "place"] — **top·i·cal·i·ty** \ˌtäp-ə-'kal-ət-ē\ *n* — **top·i·cal·ly** \'täp-i-kə-lē, -klē\ *adv*

topic sentence *n* : a sentence that states the main thought of a paragraph or of a larger unit of discourse

top·knot \'täp-ˌnät\ *n* **1** : an ornament (as a bow) forming a headdress or worn as part of a hairstyle **2** : a crest of feathers or hair on the top of the head

top·less \'täp-ləs\ *adj* **1** : being without a top **2** : wearing no clothing on the upper body

top·lofty \'täp-ˌlȯf-tē\ *also* **top·loft·i·cal** \täp-'lȯf-ti-kəl\ *adj* : very superior in air or attitude : HAUGHTY — **top·loft·i·ness** \'täp-ˌlȯf-tē-nəs\ *n*

top·mast \-ˌmast, -məst\ *n* : the mast that is next above the lower mast and topmost in a fore-and-aft rig

top·min·now \'täp-ˌmin-ō\ *n* : any of several small surface-feeding fishes

top·most \-ˌmōst\ *adj* : highest of all : UPPERMOST

top–notch \-'näch\ *adj* : of the highest quality : FIRST-RATE — **top·notch·er** \-'näch-ər\ *n*

top–of–the–line *adj* : TOP-NOTCH ⟨a *top-of-the-line* stereo system⟩

to·po·graph·ic \ˌtäp-ə-'graf-ik, ˌtō-pə-\ *adj* : of, relating to, or concerned with topography ⟨a *topographic* map⟩

to·po·graph·i·cal \-'graf-i-kəl\ *adj* **1** : TOPOGRAPHIC **2** : of, relating to, or concerned with the artistic representation of a particular locality ⟨*topographical* paintings⟩ — **to·po·graph·i·cal·ly** \-kə-lē, -klē\ *adv*

to·pog·ra·phy \tə-'päg-rə-fē\ *n* **1** : the art or practice of detailing on maps or charts natural and man-made features of a place or region especially so as to show elevations **2** : the configuration of a surface including its relief and the position of its natural and man-made features ⟨a map showing *topography*⟩ [Late Latin *topographia,* from Greek, from *topographein* "to describe a place," from *topos* "place" + *graphein* "to write"]

to·pol·o·gy \tə-'päl-ə-jē, tä-\ *n* **1** : topographical study of a particular place; *esp* : the history of a region as indicated by its topography **2** : the anatomy of a particular region of the body **3** : a branch of mathematics concerned with those properties of geometric figures that do not change when the shape of the figure is changed in certain ways (as twisting or stretching) — **to·po·log·i·cal** \ˌtäp-ə-'läj-i-kəl, ˌtō-pə-\ *adj* — **to·pol·o·gist** \tə-'päl-ə-jəst, tä-\ *n*

top·per \'täp-ər\ *n* **1** : one that is at or on the top **2 a** : SILK HAT **b** : OPERA HAT **3** : something (as a joke) that caps everything preceding **4** : a woman's usually short and loose-fitting lightweight outer coat

1**top·ping** \'täp-ing\ *n* **1** : something that forms a top; *esp* : a garnish (as a sauce, bread crumbs, or whipped cream) placed on top of a food **2** : the action of one that tops

2**topping** *adj* **1** : highest in rank or eminence **2** *chiefly British* : SUPERIOR 4a, EXCELLENT

top·ple \'täp-əl\ *vb* **top·pled; top·pling** \'täp-ling, -ə-ling\ **1** : to fall or cause to fall from or as if from being top-heavy **2** : to be or seem unsteady : TOTTER **3** : OVERTHROW ⟨*topple* a government⟩ [derived from 2*top*]

tops \'täps\ *adj* : topmost in quality, ability, popularity, or eminence ⟨*tops* in your profession⟩

top·sail \'täp-ˌsāl, -səl\ *also* **top·s'l** \-səl\ *n* **1** : the sail next above the lowermost sail on a mast in a square-rigged ship **2** : the sail set above and sometimes on the gaff in a fore-and-aft rigged ship

top secret *adj* **1** : protected by a high degree of secrecy ⟨a *top secret* meeting⟩ **2** : containing information that is very important to the safety and defense of a nation ⟨*top secret* messages⟩

top sergeant *n* : FIRST SERGEANT 1

top·side \'täp-'sīd\ *adv or adj* **1** : on deck **2** : to or on the top or surface

top·soil \-ˌsȯil\ *n* : surface soil usually including the organic layer in which plants have most of their roots and which the farmer turns over in plowing

top·spin \'täp-ˌspin\ *n* : rotary motion imparted to a ball causing it to rotate forward in the direction of movement [1*top*]

top·sy–tur·vi·ness \ˌtäp-sē-'tər-vē-nəs\ *n* : the quality or state of being topsy-turvy

1**top·sy–tur·vy** \ˌtäp-sē-'tər-vē\ *adv* **1** : UPSIDE DOWN 1 **2** : in utter confusion or disorder [probably derived from 1*top* + obsolete *terve* "to turn upside down"]

2**topsy–turvy** *adj* : turned topsy-turvy : totally disordered — **top·sy–tur·vi·ly** \-'tər-və-lē\ *adv* — **top·sy–tur·vy·dom** \-'tər-vēd-əm\ *n*

3**topsy–turvy** *n* : TOPSY-TURVINESS

toque \'tōk\ *n* : a woman's small hat without a brim made in any of various soft close-fitting shapes [Middle French, "soft hat with a narrow brim," from Spanish *toca* "headdress"]

toque

tor \'tȯr\ *n* : a high craggy hill [Old English *torr*]

To·rah \'tōr-ə, 'tȯr-; 'tȯi-rə\ *n* **1** : the body of wisdom and law found in the Jewish Scripture and other sacred writings and oral tradition **2** : the five books of Moses constituting the Pentateuch **3** : a leather or parchment scroll of the Pentateuch used in a synagogue for liturgical purposes [Hebrew *tōrāh*]

1**torch** \'tȯrch\ *n* **1** : a flaming light made of something (as resinous wood) that burns brightly and usually carried in the hand **2** : something (as wisdom or knowledge) likened to a torch as giving light or guidance **3** : any of various portable devices for producing a hot flame — compare BLOWTORCH **4** *chiefly British* : FLASHLIGHT 3 [Medieval French *torche* "bundle of twisted straw or tow," from Latin *torqua* "something twisted"]

2**torch** *vt* : to set on fire with or as if with a torch

torch·bear·er \'tȯrch-ˌbar-ər, -ˌber-\ *n* **1** : one that carries a torch **2** : one that is in the forefront of a movement, campaign, or crusade

torch·light \'tȯrch-ˌlīt\ *n* : light given by torches

torch singer *n* : a singer of torch songs

torch song *n* : a popular sentimental song of unrequited love

tore *past of* TEAR

to·re·ador \'tȯr-ē-ə-ˌdȯr, 'tōr-, 'tär-\ *n* : BULLFIGHTER [Spanish, from *torear* "to fight bulls," from *toro* "bull," from Latin *taurus*]

to·re·ro \tə-'reər-ō\ *n, pl* **-ros** : BULLFIGHTER [Spanish, from Latin *taurarius,* from *taurus* "bull"]

tori *plural of* TORUS

to·rii \'tōr-ē-ˌē, 'tȯr-\ *n, pl* **torii** : a Japanese gateway of light construction built at the approach to a Shinto temple [Japanese]

1**tor·ment** \'tȯr-ˌment\ *n* **1** : the infliction of torture (as by rack or wheel) **2** : extreme physical or mental pain or anguish : AGONY **3** : a source of irritation or pain [Medieval French, from Latin *tormentum* "torture"]

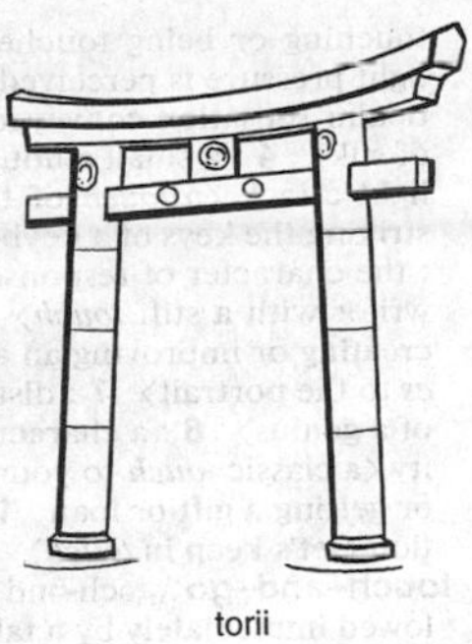

torii

²tor·ment \tȯr-ˈment, ˈtȯr-ˌ\ *vt* **1 a :** to cause severe suffering of body or mind to **b :** to cause worry or vexation to : TROUBLE ⟨a mystery that has *tormented* us for years⟩ **2 :** DISTORT 1, TWIST *synonyms* see AFFLICT — **tor·men·tor** \-ər\ *n*

torn *past participle of* TEAR

tor·na·dic \tȯr-ˈnād-ik, -ˈnad-\ *adj* **:** relating to, characteristic of, or being a tornado ⟨*tornadic* winds⟩

tor·na·do \tȯr-ˈnād-ō\ *n, pl* **-does** *or* **-dos :** a violent destructive whirling wind accompanied by a funnel-shaped cloud that progresses in a narrow path over the land [Spanish *tronada* "thunderstorm," from *tronar* "to thunder," from Latin *tonare*]

¹tor·pe·do \tȯr-ˈpēd-ō\ *n, pl* **-does 1 :** ELECTRIC RAY **2 :** a weapon for destroying ships by rupturing their hulls below the waterline: as **a :** a submarine mine **b :** a thin cylindrical self-propelled submarine projectile **3 :** a small firework that explodes when thrown against a hard object [Latin, literally, "numbness," from *torpēre* "to be numb"]

²torpedo *vt* **1 :** to hit or sink (a ship) with a naval torpedo **2 :** to destroy or nullify altogether : WRECK ⟨*torpedo* a plan⟩

torpedo boat *n* **:** a small fast boat for firing torpedoes

tor·pid \ˈtȯr-pəd\ *adj* **1 a :** having lost motion or the power of exertion or feeling **b :** exhibiting or characterized by topor : DORMANT ⟨a bear *torpid* in its winter sleep⟩ **c :** sluggish in functioning or acting ⟨a *torpid* mind⟩ **2 :** lacking in energy or vigor : APATHETIC, DULL [Latin *torpidus,* from *torpēre* "to be numb"] — **tor·pid·i·ty** \tȯr-ˈpid-ət-ē\ *n* — **tor·pid·ly** \ˈtȯr-pəd-lē\ *adv*

tor·por \ˈtȯr-pər\ *n* **1 a :** temporary loss or suspension of motion or feeling **b :** a state of lowered bodily activity that is typically characterized by reduced or slowed metabolism, heart rate, and body temperature, that may occur on a daily basis or over a longer period (as during hibernation), and that is a response to an adverse environmental condition (as drought or cold) **2 :** APATHY 2, DULLNESS [Latin, from *torpēre* "to be sluggish or numb"] *synonyms* see LETHARGY

torque \ˈtȯrk\ *n* **:** a force which produces or tends to produce rotation or twisting [Latin *torquēre* "to twist"]

tor·rent \ˈtȯr-ənt, ˈtär-\ *n* **1 :** a violent or rushing stream of a liquid (as water or lava) **2 :** a large, rapid, or violent flow (as of orders, activity, or abuse) : SURGE [Middle French, from Latin *torrens,* from *torrens,* adj., "burning, seething, rushing," from *torrēre* "to parch, burn"]

tor·ren·tial \tȯ-ˈren-chəl, tə-\ *adj* **1 a :** relating to or having the character of a torrent ⟨*torrential* rains⟩ **b :** caused by or resulting from action of rapid streams ⟨*torrential* gravel⟩ **2 :** resembling a torrent in violence or rapidity of flow — **tor·ren·tial·ly** \-ˈrench-lē, -ə-lē\ *adv*

tor·rid \ˈtȯr-əd, ˈtär-\ *adj* **1 a :** parched with heat especially of the sun ⟨*torrid* sands⟩ **b :** giving off intense heat **2 :** ARDENT, PASSIONATE ⟨*torrid* love letters⟩ [Latin *torridus,* from *torrēre* "to parch"] — **tor·rid·i·ty** \tȯ-ˈrid-ət-ē\ *n* — **tor·rid·ly** \ˈtȯr-əd-lē, ˈtär-\ *adv* — **tor·rid·ness** *n*

torrid zone *n* **:** the area or region between the Tropic of Cancer and the Tropic of Capricorn

tor·sion \ˈtȯr-shən\ *n* **1 :** the act or process of turning or twisting **2 :** the state of being twisted [Late Latin *torsio* "torment," derived from Latin *torquēre* "to twist"] — **tor·sion·al** \-shnəl, -shən-l\ *adj*

torsion bar *n* **:** a long metal piece in an automobile suspension that has one end firmly attached to the frame and the other end twisted and connected to the axle and that acts like a spring

tor·so \ˈtȯr-sō\ *n, pl* **torsos** *or* **tor·si** \-ˌsē\ **1 :** the trunk of a sculptured representation of a human body; *esp* **:** the trunk of a statue whose head and limbs are mutilated **2 :** something (as a piece of writing) that is mutilated or left unfinished **3 :** the human trunk [Italian, literally, "stalk," from Latin *thyrsus,* from Greek *thyrsos*]

tort \ˈtȯrt\ *n* **:** a wrongful act which does not involve a breach of contract and for which the injured party can recover damages in a civil action [Middle English, "injury," from Middle French, from Medieval Latin *tortum,* from Latin *tortus* "twisted," from *torquēre* "to twist"]

torte \ˈtȯrt-ə, ˈtȯrt\ *n, pl* **tor·ten** \ˈtȯrt-n\ *or* **tortes :** a cake made of many eggs and often grated nuts or dry bread crumbs and usually covered with a rich frosting [German]

tor·tel·li·ni \ˌtȯrt-ə-ˈlē-nē\ *n, pl* **tortellini** *also* **tortellinis :** pasta in the form of little ring-shaped cases containing a filling (as of meat or cheese) [Italian, plural of *tortellino* "pasta round," from *torta* "cake"]

tor·ti·lla \tȯr-ˈtē-ə, -ˈtē-yə\ *n* **:** a thin round of cornmeal or wheat flour bread [American Spanish, from Spanish *torta* "cake," from Late Latin, "round loaf of bread"]

tor·toise \ˈtȯrt-əs\ *n* **:** ²TURTLE; *esp* **:** any of a family of land-dwelling turtles [Medieval French *tortue*]

¹tor·toise·shell \ˈtȯrt-əs-ˌshel, -əsh-ˌshel\ *n* **:** the mottled horny substance of the hawksbill turtle used especially formerly in inlaying and in making various ornamental articles

²tortoiseshell *adj* **1 :** made of or resembling tortoiseshell especially in spotted brown and yellow coloring **2 :** of, relating to, or being a color pattern of the domestic cat consisting of patches of black, orange, and cream

tor·to·ni \tȯr-ˈtō-nē\ *n* **:** ice cream made of heavy cream often with minced almonds and chopped maraschino cherries and often flavored with rum [probably from *Tortoni,* 19th century Italian restaurateur in Paris]

tor·tu·ous \ˈtȯrch-wəs, -ə-wəs\ *adj* **1 :** marked by repeated twists, bends, or turns : WINDING ⟨a *tortuous* stream⟩ **2 a :** marked by devious or indirect tactics : CROOKED, TRICKY ⟨a *tortuous* conspiracy⟩ **b :** confusingly roundabout ⟨the *tortuous* workings of the law⟩ [Medieval French *tortueux,* from Latin *tortuosus,* from *tortus* "twist," from *torquēre* "to twist"] — **tor·tu·ous·ly** *adv* — **tor·tu·ous·ness** *n*

¹tor·ture \ˈtȯr-chər\ *n* **1 a :** physical or mental anguish : AGONY **b :** something that causes agony **2 :** the infliction of intense pain especially to punish or obtain a confession [Medieval French, from Late Latin *tortura,* from Latin *torquēre* "to twist"]

²torture *vt* **tor·tured; tor·tur·ing** \ˈtȯrch-ring, -ə-ring\ **1 :** to cause intense suffering to : TORMENT **2 :** to punish or coerce by inflicting excruciating pain **3 :** to twist or wrench out of shape : DISTORT *synonyms* see AFFLICT — **tor·tur·er** \ˈtȯr-chər-ər\ *n*

tor·tur·ous \ˈtȯrch-rəs, -ə-rəs\ *adj* **:** causing torture : cruelly painful — **tor·tur·ous·ly** *adv*

to·rus \ˈtōr-əs, ˈtȯr-\ *n, pl* **to·ri** \ˈtōr-ˌī, ˈtȯr-, -ˌē\ **1 :** a large molding of convex profile commonly occurring as the lowest molding in the base of a column **2 :** a doughnut-shaped surface generated by a circle rotated about an axis in its plane that does not intersect the circle [Latin, "protuberance, bulge, torus molding"]

To·ry \ˈtōr-ē, ˈtȯr-\ *n, pl* **Tories 1 a :** a member of a British political group of the 18th and early 19th centuries favoring royal authority and the established church and seeking to preserve the traditional political structure — compare WHIG **b :** CONSERVATIVE 1b **2 :** an American supporting the cause of the British Crown during the American Revolution : LOYALIST **3** *often not cap* **:** an extreme conservative especially in politics and economics [Irish *tōraidhe* "pursued man, robber," from *tóir* "pursuit"; from Irish royalists outlawed in the 17th century] — **Tory** *adj*

¹toss \ˈtȯs, ˈtäs\ *vb* **1 :** to keep throwing here and there or backward and forward : cause to pitch or roll ⟨waves *tossed* the ship about⟩ **2 :** to throw with a quick light motion ⟨*toss* a ball into the air⟩ **3 :** to lift with a sudden motion ⟨*toss* the head⟩ **4 :** to pitch or bob about rapidly ⟨a canoe *tossing* on the waves⟩ **5 :** to accomplish, provide, or dispose of easily ⟨*tossed* off a few verses⟩ **6 :** to be restless : fling oneself about ⟨*toss* in one's sleep⟩ **7 :** to stir or mix lightly ⟨*toss* a salad⟩ **8 :** to decide an issue by flipping a coin [Middle English *tossen*] *synonyms* see THROW

²toss *n* **1 :** the state or fact of being tossed **2 a :** an act or instance of tossing **b :** a deciding by chance and especially by flipping a coin

toss–up \-ˌəp\ *n* **1 :** TOSS 2b **2 :** an even chance

\ə\ **abut**	\au̇\ **out**	\i\ **tip**	\ȯ\ **saw**	\u̇\ **foot**
\ər\ **further**	\ch\ **chin**	\ī\ **life**	\ȯi\ **coin**	\y\ **yet**
\a\ **mat**	\e\ **pet**	\j\ **job**	\th\ **thin**	\yü\ **few**
\ā\ **take**	\ē\ **easy**	\ng\ **sing**	\t͟h\ **this**	\yu̇\ **cure**
\ä\ **cot, cart**	\g\ **go**	\ō\ **bone**	\ü\ **food**	\zh\ **vision**

[1]tot \ˈtät\ *n* **1** : a small child : TODDLER **2** : SHOT 8a [origin unknown]

[2]tot *vb* **tot·ted; tot·ting** : to add together : TOTAL — usually used with *up* [*tot.,* abbreviation of *total*]

[1]to·tal \ˈtōt-l\ *adj* **1** : making up or being the whole : ENTIRE ⟨the *total* amount⟩ **2** : ABSOLUTE 4, UTTER ⟨*total* ruin⟩ **3** : making use of every available means to accomplish a single objective ⟨*total* war⟩ [Medieval French, from Medieval Latin *totalis,* from Latin *totus* "whole, entire"]

[2]total *n* **1** : a product of addition : SUM **2** : an entire quantity : AMOUNT ***synonyms*** see SUM

[3]total *vt* **to·taled** *or* **to·talled; to·tal·ing** *or* **to·tal·ling** **1** : to add up : COMPUTE **2** : to amount to : NUMBER **3** : to make a total wreck of ⟨*totaled* the car⟩

total eclipse *n* : an eclipse in which one celestial body is completely obscured by the shadow or body of another

to·tal·i·tar·i·an \tō-ˌtal-ə-ˈter-ē-ən\ *adj* **1** : of, relating to, or being a political regime based on subordination of the individual to the state and strict control of all aspects of life especially by use of force **2** : advocating or characteristic of such a regime [Italian *totalitario,* from *totalità* "totality"] — **totalitarian** *n* — **to·tal·i·tar·i·an·ism** \-ē-ə-ˌniz-əm\ *n*

to·tal·i·ty \tō-ˈtal-ət-ē\ *n, pl* **-ties** **1** : an aggregate amount : SUM, WHOLE **2** : the quality or state of being total : ENTIRETY

to·tal·ize \ˈtōt-l-ˌīz\ *vt* **1** : to add up : TOTAL **2** : to express as a whole

to·tal·ly \ˈtōt-l-ē\ *adv* : in a total manner : to a total or complete degree : WHOLLY, ENTIRELY

[1]tote \ˈtōt\ *vt* **1** : to carry by hand : LUG **2** : HAUL 1c, CONVEY [probably from an English-based creole] — **tot·er** *n*

[2]tote *n* : a large handbag — called also *tote bag*

to·tem \ˈtōt-əm\ *n* : an object (as an animal or plant) or a representation of an object serving as the emblem of a family or clan and often as a reminder of its ancestry [Ojibwa *oto·te·man* "his totem"] — **to·tem·ic** \tō-ˈtem-ik\ *adj*

totem pole *n* : a pole carved and painted with totemic symbols that is erected by Indian tribes of the northwest coast of North America

to·ti·po·tent \tō-ˈtip-ət-ənt, ˌtōt-ə-ˈpōt-nt\ *adj* : capable of developing into a complete organism or differentiating into any of its cells or tissues ⟨*totipotent* stem cells⟩ [Latin *totus* "whole, entire" + English *potent*]

[1]tot·ter \ˈtät-ər\ *vi* **1 a** : to tremble or rock as if about to fall : SWAY **b** : to become unstable : threaten to collapse **2** : to move unsteadily : STAGGER, WOBBLE [Middle English *toteren*] — **tot·ter·ing·ly** \ˈtät-ə-ring-lē\ *adv*

[2]totter *n* : an unsteady gait : WOBBLE

tot·tery \ˈtät-ə-rē\ *adj* : of an infirm or precarious nature

tou·can \ˈtü-ˌkan, tü-ˈ\ *n* : any of a family of chiefly fruit-eating birds of tropical America with brilliant coloring and a very large but light and thin-walled bill [French, from Portuguese *tucano,* from Tupi *tukána*]

totem pole

[1]touch \ˈtəch\ *vb* **1** : to feel or handle (as with fingers or hands) especially so as to be aware of by the sense of touch ⟨loved to *touch* soft velvet⟩ **2** : to come close : VERGE ⟨actions *touching* on treason⟩ **3 a** : to take into the hands or mouth ⟨never *touches* meat⟩ **b** : to put hands on in any way or degree ⟨don't *touch* the exhibits⟩ ⟨wouldn't *touch* your money⟩; *esp* : HARM ⟨swore they hadn't *touched* the child⟩ **4** : to persuade to give or lend ⟨*touched* me for $10⟩ **5** : to cause to be briefly in contact with something ⟨*touched* spurs to the horse⟩ ⟨*touch* a match to kindling⟩ **6 a** : to meet without overlapping or penetrating : ADJOIN **b** : to rival in quality or value ⟨this car doesn't *touch* my old one⟩ **7** : to speak or tell of especially in passing ⟨barely *touched* on domestic politics⟩ **8** : to affect the interest of : CONCERN ⟨a problem *touching* everyone⟩ **9 a** : to affect physically; *esp* : to harm slightly by or as if by contact ⟨fruit *touched* by frost⟩ **b** : to give a delicate tint, line, or expression to ⟨a smile *touched* her lips⟩ **10** : to move emotionally ⟨*touched* by your loyalty⟩ **11** : to make a brief or incidental stop on shore during a trip by water ⟨*touched* at several ports⟩ [Medieval French *tuchier*] — **touch·able** \-ə-bəl\ *adj* — **touch·er** *n*

[2]touch *n* **1** : a light stroke, tap, or blow **2** : the act or fact of touching or being touched **3 a** : the special sense by which light pressure is perceived ⟨fabric soft to the *touch*⟩ **b** : a particular sensation conveyed by this sense : FEEL ⟨the soft *touch* of silk⟩ **4** : a small amount : TRACE ⟨a *touch* of garlic⟩; *esp* : a light attack ⟨a *touch* of fever⟩ **5** : a manner of touching or striking the keys of a keyboard ⟨a firm *touch* on the piano⟩; *also* : the character of response of the keys to being struck ⟨a typewriter with a stiff *touch*⟩ **6** : an effective and subtle detail in creating or improving an artistic work ⟨applied finishing *touches* to the portrait⟩ **7** : distinctive manner or method ⟨the *touch* of a genius⟩ **8** : a characteristic or distinguishing trait or quality ⟨a classic *touch* to your writing⟩ **9** *slang* : an act of seeking or getting a gift or loan **10** : a state of contact or communication ⟨let's keep in *touch*⟩

touch–and–go \ˌtəch-ənd-ˈgō\ *n* : a landing of an airplane followed immediately by a takeoff of the same airplane usually executed as a series for practice

touch and go *adj* : unpredictable as to outcome : UNCERTAIN ⟨it was *touch and go* there for a while⟩

touch·back \ˈtəch-ˌbak\ *n* : a situation in football in which the defending team downs the ball behind its own goal line after receiving a kick or intercepting a pass

touch·down \-ˌdau̇n\ *n* **1 a** : the act of touching a football to the ground behind an opponent's goal **b** : a score of six points in American football made by carrying the ball over the opponent's goal line **2** : the act or moment of touching down (as with an airplane or spacecraft)

touch down \təch-ˈdau̇n, ˈtəch-\ *vi* : to reach the ground : LAND

tou·ché \tü-ˈshā\ *interj* — used to acknowledge a hit in fencing or the success of an argument [French, from *toucher* "to touch," from Medieval French *tuchier*]

touched \ˈtəcht\ *adj* **1** : emotionally stirred (as with gratitude) **2** : slightly unbalanced mentally

touch football *n* : football chiefly characterized by the substitution of touching for tackling

touch·hole \ˈtəch-ˌhōl\ *n* : the vent in old-time cannons or firearms through which the charge was ignited

[1]touch·ing *prep* : in reference to : CONCERNING

[2]touching *adj* : arousing tenderness or compassion ⟨a *touching* story⟩ — **touch·ing·ly** \-ing-lē\ *adv*

touch–me–not \ˈtəch-mē-ˌnät\ *n* : either of two North American impatiens that grow in moist areas [from the bursting of the ripe pods and scattering of their seeds when touched]

touch off *vt* **1** : to describe or characterize with precision **2 a** : to cause to explode by or as if by touching with fire **b** : to release or start with sudden violence ⟨*touched off* a riot⟩

touch pad *n* : a keypad for an electronic device (as a microwave oven) that consists of a flat surface divided into several differently marked areas which are touched to choose options

touch screen *n* : a display screen (as for a computer) on which the user selects options by touching the screen

touch·stone \ˈtəch-ˌstōn\ *n* **1** : a black stone formerly used to test the purity of gold and silver by the streak left on the stone when rubbed by the metal **2** : a test or standard for judging something

touch system *n* : a method of typewriting that assigns a particular finger to each key and makes it possible to type without looking at the keyboard

touch–tone \ˈtəch-ˈtōn, -ˌtōn\ *adj* : of, relating to, or being a telephone having push buttons that produce tones corresponding to numbers [from *Touch-Tone,* a former trademark]

touch–type \ˈtəch-ˌtīp\ *vi* : to type by the touch system

touch up *vt* **1** : to improve or perfect by small additional strokes or alterations **2** : to stimulate by or as if by a flick of a whip

touch·wood \ˈtəch-ˌwu̇d\ *n* : [3]PUNK

touchy \ˈtəch-ē\ *adj* **touch·i·er; -est** **1** : marked by readiness to take offense on slight provocation **2** : calling for tact, care, or caution in treatment ⟨a *touchy* subject⟩ ***synonyms*** see IRASCIBLE — **touch·i·ly** \ˈtəch-ə-lē\ *adv* — **touch·i·ness** \ˈtəch-ē-nəs\ *n*

touchy–feely \ˌtəch-ē-ˈfē-lē\ *adj* : characterized by or encouraging interpersonal touching especially in the free expression of emotions ⟨*touchy-feely* therapy⟩; *also* : openly or excessively emotional and personal ⟨*touchy-feely* management⟩

[1]tough \ˈtəf\ *adj* **1** : able to undergo great strain : flexible and not brittle ⟨*tough* fibers⟩ **2** : not easily chewed ⟨*tough* meat⟩ **3** : able to stand hard work and hardship ⟨*tough* soldiers⟩ **4 a** : hard to influence : STUBBORN ⟨a *tough* bargainer⟩ **b** : very difficult ⟨a *tough* problem⟩ **5 :** ROWDY, LAWLESS ⟨a *tough* neighborhood⟩ **6 :** free from softness or sentimentality ⟨a *tough* critic⟩; *esp* **:** marked by firm uncompromising determination ⟨a *tough* foreign policy⟩ [Old English *tōh*] ***synonyms*** see STRONG — **tough·ly** *adv* — **tough·ness** *n*

[2]**tough** *n* **:** a vicious and unruly person; *also* **:** ROWDY

tough·en \ˈtəf-ən\ *vb* **tough·ened; tough·en·ing** \ˈtəf-ning, -ə-ning\ **:** to make or become tough

tough·ie *also* **toughy** \ˈtəf-ē\ *n, pl* **toughies :** one that is tough: as **a :** a loud rough rowdy person **b :** a difficult problem or question

tough–mind·ed \ˈtəf-ˈmīn-dəd\ *adj* **:** realistic or unsentimental in temper or point of view — **tough–mind·ed·ness** *n*

tou·pee \tü-ˈpā\ *n* **:** a usually small wig or hairpiece for a man [French *toupet* "forelock," of Germanic origin]

[1]**tour** \ˈtu̇r, *1 is also* ˈtau̇r\ *n* **1 a :** one's turn in an orderly schedule **b :** a period of work or duty ⟨a long *tour* abroad⟩ **2 :** a trip or excursion usually ending at the point of beginning ⟨a *tour* of the city⟩ **3 :** a series of professional tournaments (as in golf or tennis) [Medieval French, from *tur, tourn* "turning, circuit, journey," from Latin *tornus* "lathe"]

[2]**tour** *vb* **:** to make a tour of **:** travel as a tourist

tour de force \ˌtu̇rd-ə-ˈfōrs, -ˈfȯrs\ *n, pl* **tours de force** *same*\ **:** a feat or display of strength, skill, or ingenuity [French]

touring car *n* **:** an old-fashioned open automobile with two cross seats, usually four doors, and a folding top

tour·ism \ˈtu̇r-ˌiz-əm\ *n* **:** the practice of traveling for recreation or the business of encouraging and serving such traveling

tour·ist \ˈtu̇r-əst\ *n* **:** one who travels for pleasure — **tourist** *adj*

tourist class *n* **:** economy accommodations (as on a ship)

tourist court *n* **:** MOTEL

tourist trap *n* **:** a place that attracts and exploits tourists

tour·ma·line \ˈtu̇r-mə-lən, -ˌlēn\ *n* **:** a mineral of variable color that is a complex silicate and when transparent is cut for use as a gemstone [Sinhalese *toramalli* "carnelian"]

tour·na·ment \ˈtu̇r-nə-mənt *also* ˈtər- *or* ˈtȯr-\ *n* **1 a :** a contest of skill and courage between armored knights fighting with blunted lances or swords **b :** a series of knightly contests occurring at one time and place **2 :** a series of athletic contests, sports events, or games for a championship ⟨a tennis *tournament*⟩ [Medieval French *turneiement*]

tour·ney \ˈtu̇r-nē *also* ˈtər- *or* ˈtȯr-\ *n, pl* **tourneys :** TOURNAMENT [Medieval French *tornei,* from *torneier* "to twist, whirl around, fight, tourney"]

tour·ni·quet \ˈtu̇r-ni-kət, ˈtər-\ *n* **:** a device (as a band of rubber) that stops or slows bleeding or blood flow by compressing blood vessels [French, from *tourner* "to turn"]

[1]**tou·sle** \ˈtau̇-zəl, -səl\ *vt* **tou·sled; tou·sling** \ˈtau̇z-ling, ˈtau̇s-, -ə-ling\ **:** DISHEVEL, RUMPLE ⟨*tousled* hair⟩ [Middle English *touselen*]

[2]**tousle** *n* **:** a tangled mass (as of hair)

[1]**tout** \ˈtau̇t\ *vb* **1 :** to solicit for patronage, trade, votes, or support **2 a** *chiefly British* **:** to spy about at racing stables and tracks to get information to be used in betting **b :** to give a tip or solicit bets on a racehorse **3 :** to make much of **:** PROMOTE ⟨the college's much *touted* women's studies program⟩ [Middle English *tuten* "to peer"]

[2]**tout** *n* **:** one who touts: as **a :** one who solicits patronage **b :** one who gives tips or solicits bets on a horse race

tout·er \ˈtau̇t-ər\ *n* **:** one that touts

[1]**tow** \ˈtō\ *vt* **:** to draw or pull along behind **:** HAUL [Old English *togian*]

[2]**tow** *n* **1 :** an act or instance of towing or the fact or condition of being towed **2 :** a line or rope for towing **3 :** something (as a tugboat or barge) that tows or is towed — **in tow 1 :** under guidance or protection ⟨taken *in tow* by a friendly guide⟩ **2 :** accompanying or following usually as an attending or dependent party ⟨not easy shopping with toddlers *in tow*⟩

[3]**tow** *n* **1 :** short broken fiber from flax, hemp, or jute used for yarn, twine, or stuffing **2 :** yarn or cloth made of tow [Old English *tow-* "spinning"]

tow·age \ˈtō-ij\ *n* **1 :** the act of towing **2 :** the price paid for towing

[1]**to·ward** \ˈtō-ərd, ˈtȯ-ərd, ˈtōrd, ˈtȯrd\ *adj* **1** *also* **to·wards** \ˈtō-ərdz, ˈtȯ-ərdz, ˈtōrdz, ˈtȯrdz\ **a :** coming soon **:** IMMINENT ⟨could move fast enough if a meal was *toward*⟩ **b :** happening at the moment **:** AFOOT **2 a** *obsolete* **:** quick to learn **:** APT **b :** PROPITIOUS 3 ⟨a *toward* breeze⟩ [Old English *tōweard* "facing, imminent," from *tō* "to" + *-weard* "-ward"]

[2]**to·ward** \tō-ərd, ˈtō-, twō-, ˈtwō-; tōrd, ˈtōrd, twōrd, ˈtwōrd; tə-ˈwȯrd\ *or* **to·wards** *same followed by* z\ *prep* **1 :** in the direction of ⟨driving *toward* town⟩ **2 a :** along a course leading to ⟨efforts *toward* reconciliation⟩ **b :** in relation to ⟨attitude *toward* life⟩ **3 :** so as to face ⟨her back was *toward* me⟩ **4 :** not long before ⟨*toward* noon⟩ **5 :** in order to provide part of the payment for ⟨save *toward* a college education⟩

tow·boat \ˈtō-ˌbōt\ *n* **1 :** TUGBOAT **2 :** a compact shallow-draft boat for pushing barges on inland waterways

[1]**tow·el** \ˈtau̇-əl, ˈtau̇l\ *n* **:** a cloth or piece of absorbent paper for wiping or drying [Medieval French *tuaille,* of Germanic origin]

[2]**towel** *vb* **-eled** *or* **-elled; -el·ing** *or* **-el·ling 1 :** to rub or dry with a towel **2 :** to use a towel

tow·el·ing *or* **tow·el·ling** \ˈtau̇-ling, -ə-ling\ *n* **:** material for towels

[1]**tow·er** \ˈtau̇-ər, ˈtau̇r\ *n* **1 :** a building or structure typically higher than it is wide and high relative to its surroundings that may stand apart (as a campanile) or be attached (as a church belfry) to a larger structure and that may be of skeleton framework (as an observation or transmission tower) **2 :** a towering citadel **:** FORTRESS [Old English *torr* and Medieval French *tur, tour,* both from Latin *turris,* from Greek *tyrris, tyrsis*] — **tow·ered** \ˈtau̇-ərd, ˈtau̇rd\ *adj*

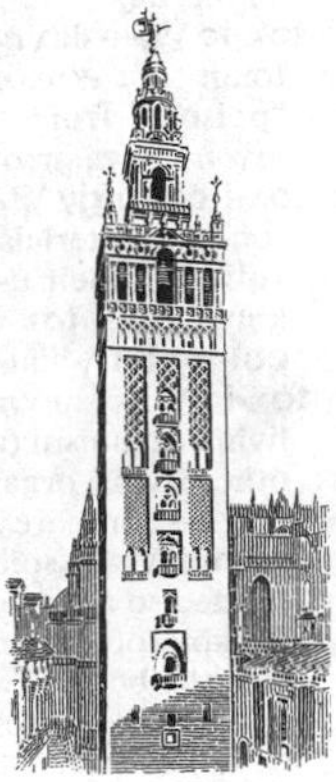
tower 1

[2]**tower** *vi* **1 :** to reach or rise to a great height **2 :** to exhibit superior qualities ⟨her intellect *towered* over the others'⟩

tow·er·ing *adj* **1 :** impressively high or great **:** IMPOSING **2 :** reaching a high point of intensity ⟨a *towering* rage⟩ **3 :** going beyond proper bounds **:** EXCESSIVE ⟨*towering* ambition⟩

tower wagon *n* **:** a wagon or motortruck with a high adjustable platform on which workers can stand

tow·head \ˈtō-ˌhed\ *n* **:** a person having flaxen hair — **tow·head·ed** \-ˈhed-əd\ *adj*

to·whee \ˈtō-ˌhē, ˈtō-ē, tō-ˈhē\ *n* **:** a finch of eastern North America of which the male has a black back, a white belly, and reddish sides; *also* **:** any of various related birds chiefly of the western U.S. and Mexico [imitative]

to wit \tə-ˈwit\ *adv* **:** that is to say **:** NAMELY [Middle English *to witen,* literally, "to know"]

tow·line \ˈtō-ˌlīn\ *n* **:** a line used in towing

town \ˈtau̇n\ *n* **1 a :** a heavily populated area as distinguished from surrounding rural territory; *esp* **:** one larger than a village but smaller than a city **b :** CITY 1a **c :** an English village having a periodic fair or market **2 a :** the city or urban life as contrasted with the country **b :** TOWNSPEOPLE 1 **3 :** a New England territorial and political unit usually containing both rural and urban areas under a single town government — called also *township* [Old English *tūn* "enclosure, village, town"] — **town** *adj*

town clerk *n* **:** an official who keeps the town records

town crier *n* **:** a town officer who makes public proclamations

town hall *n* **:** a public building used for town-government offices and meetings

town house *n* **1 :** the city residence of one having a country-seat or a chief residence elsewhere **2 :** a house connected to another by a common sidewall

town meeting *n* **:** a meeting of inhabitants or taxpayers of a town to transact public business

towns·folk \ˈtau̇nz-ˌfōk\ *n pl* **:** TOWNSPEOPLE

town·ship \ˈtau̇n-ˌship\ *n* **1 a :** TOWN 3 **b :** a unit of local government in some northeastern and north central states **c :** a subdivision of the county especially in the southern U.S. **2 :** a division of territory in surveys of U.S. public land containing 36 sections or 36 square miles (about 93.2 square kilometers)

towns·man \ˈtau̇nz-mən\ *n* **1 :** a native or resident of a town or city **2 :** a fellow citizen of a town

\ə\ **about**	\au̇\ **out**	\i\ **tip**	\ȯ\ **saw**	\u̇\ **foot**
\ər\ **further**	\ch\ **chin**	\ī\ **life**	\ȯi\ **coin**	\y\ **yet**
\a\ **mat**	\e\ **pet**	\j\ **job**	\th\ **thin**	\yü\ **few**
\ā\ **take**	\ē\ **easy**	\ng\ **sing**	\th\ **this**	\yu̇\ **cure**
\ä\ **cot, cart**	\g\ **go**	\ō\ **bone**	\ü\ **food**	\zh\ **vision**

towns·peo·ple \-ˌpē-pəl\ *n pl* **1 :** the inhabitants of a town or city **2 :** town-dwelling or town-bred persons

towns·wom·an \-ˌwu̇m-ən\ *n* **1 :** a woman native or resident of a town or city **2 :** a woman who is a fellow citizen of a town

tow·path \ˈtō-ˌpath, -ˌpȧth\ *n* **:** a path (as along a canal) traveled especially by draft animals (as horses or mules) towing boats — called also *towing path*

tow·plane \ˈtō-ˌplān\ *n* **:** an airplane that tows gliders

tow·rope \ˈtō-ˌrōp\ *n* **:** a line used in towing

tow truck *n* **:** a truck equipped to tow wrecked or disabled vehicles

tox- *or* **toxi-** *or* **toxo-** *combining form* **:** poisonous **:** poison ⟨*tox*emia⟩ [Latin *toxicum* "poison"]

tox·emia \täk-ˈsē-mē-ə\ *n* **:** an abnormal condition associated with the presence of toxic substances in the blood — **tox·emic** \-mik\ *adj*

tox·ic \ˈtäk-sik\ *adj* **1 :** of, relating to, or caused by a poison or toxin **2 :** POISONOUS [Late Latin *toxicus,* from Latin *toxicum* "poison," from Greek *toxikon* "arrow poison," derived from *toxon* "bow, arrow"] — **tox·ic·i·ty** \täk-ˈsis-ət-ē\ *n*

tox·i·col·o·gy \ˌtäk-si-ˈkäl-ə-jē\ *n* **:** a science that deals with poisonous materials and their effect and with the problems involved in their use and control — **tox·i·co·log·i·cal** \-kə-ˈläj-i-kəl\ *adj* — **tox·i·co·log·i·cal·ly** \-i-kə-lē, -klē\ *adv* — **tox·i·col·o·gist** \-ˈkäl-ə-jəst\ *n*

tox·in \ˈtäk-sən\ *n* **:** a substance that is a metabolic product of a living organism (as a bacterium or fungus), is very poisonous to other living organisms, and typically induces antibody formation — compare ANTITOXIN

tox·oid \ˈtäk-ˌsȯid\ *n* **:** a toxin of a disease-causing organism treated so as to destroy its poisonous effects while leaving it still capable of causing the formation of antibodies when injected into the body

1toy \ˈtȯi\ *n* **1 :** something (as a trinket) of small or no real value or importance **:** TRIFLE **2 :** something for a child to play with **3 :** something tiny; *esp* **:** an animal of a breed or variety characterized by exceptionally small size [Middle English *toye* "dalliance"] — **toy** *adj* — **toy·like** \-ˌlīk\ *adj*

2toy *vi* **1 :** to act or deal with something lightly or without purpose ⟨*toyed* with the idea⟩ **2 :** to amuse oneself as if with a toy **:** PLAY ⟨they're just *toying* with him⟩ — **toy·er** *n*

toy·on \ˈtȯi-ˌän\ *n* **:** a chiefly Californian ornamental evergreen shrub related to the roses and having white flowers and bright red berries [American Spanish *tollon*]

tra·bec·u·la \trə-ˈbek-yə-lə\ *n, pl* **-lae** \-ˌlē, -ˌlī\ *also* **-las :** a small anatomical bar, rod, strand, or septum often bridging a gap or forming part of the framework of an organ or part (as a bone) ⟨spleen *trabeculae*⟩ [Latin, "little beam," from *trabs, trabes* "beam"] **tra·bec·u·lar** \-lər\ *adj*

1trace \ˈtrās\ *n* **1 :** a mark or line left by something that has passed **:** TRAIL, TRACK; *also* **:** FOOTPRINT **2 :** a sign or evidence of some past thing **:** VESTIGE ⟨*traces* of an earlier civilization⟩ **3 :** something (as a line) traced or drawn; *esp* **:** the marking made by a recording instrument (as a seismograph or kymograph) **4 :** the intersection of a line or plane with a plane **5 a :** a minute amount or indication ⟨a *trace* of red⟩ **b :** an amount of a chemical constituent not quantitatively determined because of minuteness [Medieval French, from *tracer* "to trace"]

synonyms TRACE, VESTIGE, TRACK mean a sign left by something that has passed. TRACE may suggest any line or mark or discernible effect ⟨*traces* of a deer in the snow⟩ ⟨*traces* of their native dialect in their speech⟩. VESTIGE applies to tangible remains, as a fragment, remnant, or relic ⟨*vestiges* of a primitive society⟩. TRACK suggests a continuous line that can be followed ⟨hounds on the *track* of a fox⟩.

2trace *vb* **1 a :** DELINEATE 1, SKETCH **b :** to form (as letters or figures) carefully or painstakingly **c :** to copy (as a drawing) by following lines or letters seen through a transparent superimposed sheet **d :** to make a graphic instrumental record of ⟨*trace* the heart action⟩ **e :** to adorn with linear ornamentation (as tracery) **2 a :** to follow the footprints, track, or trail of **b :** to study out or follow the development and progress of in detail or step by step **3 :** to be traceable historically ⟨a family that *traces* to the Norman conquest⟩ [Medieval French *tracer,* derived from Latin *trahere* "to pull, draw"]

3trace *n* **1 :** either of two straps, chains, or lines of a harness for attaching a horse to something (as a vehicle) to be drawn **2 :** one or more vascular bundles supplying a leaf or twig [Middle French *tres,* pl. of *trait* "pull, draft, trace," from Latin *tractus* "act of drawing," from *trahere* "to pull, draw"]

trace·able \ˈtrā-sə-bəl\ *adj* **1 :** capable of being traced **2 :** that can be attributed ⟨a failure *traceable* to laziness⟩ — **trace·ably** \-blē\ *adv*

trace element *n* **:** a chemical element present in minute amounts; *esp* **:** one used by organisms and considered essential to the functions necessary for life

trace fossil *n* **:** a fossil (as of a dinosaur footprint) that shows the activity of an animal or plant but is not formed from the organism itself

trace·less \ˈtrās-ləs\ *adj* **:** having or leaving no trace — **trace·less·ly** *adv*

trac·er \ˈtrā-sər\ *n* **1 a :** a person who traces missing persons or property **b :** an inquiry sent out in tracing something lost in transit **2 :** a draftsman who traces designs, patterns, or markings **3 :** a device (as a stylus) used in tracing **4 a :** ammunition containing a chemical composition to mark the flight of projectiles by a trail of smoke or fire **b :** a substance and especially a labeled element or atom used to trace the course of a chemical or biological process **:** LABEL 3

trac·ery \ˈtrās-rē, -ə-rē\ *n, pl* **-er·ies 1 :** architectural ornamental work with branching lines; *esp* **:** decorative openwork in the upper part of a Gothic window **2 :** a decorative interlacing of lines suggestive of Gothic tracery — **trac·er·ied** \-rēd\ *adj*

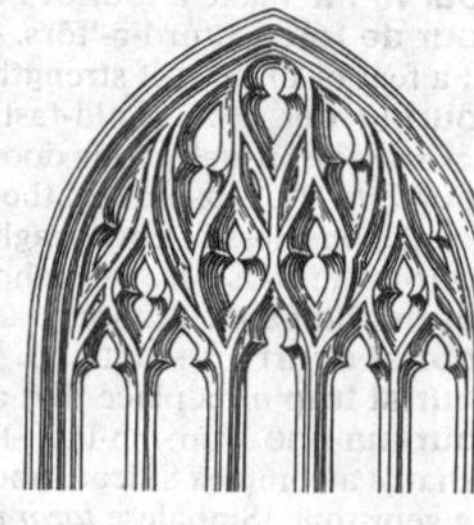

tracery 1

tra·chea \ˈtrā-kē-ə\ *n, pl* **-che·ae** \-kē-ˌē, -kē-ˌī\ *also* **-che·as** *or* **-chea 1 :** the main trunk of the system of tubes by which air passes to and from the lungs in vertebrates — called also *windpipe* **2 :** one of the air-conveying tubules forming the respiratory system of most insects and many other terrestrial arthropods [Medieval Latin, from Late Latin *trachia,* from Greek *tracheia artēria* "rough artery," from *trachys* "rough"] — **tra·che·al** \-kē-əl\ *adj* — **tra·che·ate** \-kē-ˌāt, -ət\ *adj*

tra·cheid \ˈtrā-kē-əd, -ˌkēd\ *n* **:** a long tubular xylem cell that functions in conduction and support and has tapering closed ends and thickened lignified walls [derived from *trachea*]

tra·cheo·phyte \ˈtrā-kē-ə-ˌfīt\ *n* **:** any of a division (Tracheophyta) comprising green plants (as ferns and seed plants) with a vascular system that contains tracheids

tra·che·ot·o·my \ˌtrā-kē-ˈät-ə-mē\ *n, pl* **-mies :** the surgical operation of cutting into the trachea especially through the skin

tra·cho·ma \trə-ˈkō-mə\ *n* **:** a chronic contagious eye disease that is marked by inflammation of the conjunctiva, is caused by a bacterium, and often results in blindness if left untreated [Greek *trachōma,* from *trachys* "rough"]

trac·ing \ˈtrā-siŋ\ *n* **1 :** the act of one that traces **2 :** something that is traced

tracing wheel *n* **:** a usually toothed wheel with a handle that is used on tracing paper to trace a pattern

1track \ˈtrak\ *n* **1 a :** detectable evidence (as the wake of a ship, a line of footprints, or a wheel rut) that something has passed **b :** a path made by or as if by repeated footfalls **:** TRAIL **c** (1) **:** a course laid out especially for racing (2) **:** the parallel rails of a railroad **d :** a path along which something (as music or data) is recorded (as on magnetic tape or a CD); *also* **:** the material recorded **2 :** the course along which something moves or progresses **3 a :** a sequence of events or a train of ideas **:** SUCCESSION **b :** awareness of a fact or progression ⟨lose *track* of the time⟩ **4 a :** the width of a wheeled vehicle from wheel to wheel **b :** either of two endless metal belts on which a track-laying vehicle (as a tank) travels **5 :** track-and-field sports; *esp* **:** those performed on a racing track [Middle French *trac*]

synonyms see TRACE — **in one's tracks :** where one is at the moment **:** on the spot **:** INSTANTLY ⟨dropped the deer *in its tracks*⟩ — **on track :** achieving or doing what is necessary or expected ⟨he was *on track* to break the record⟩

2track *vb* **1 a :** to follow the tracks or traces of **:** TRAIL ⟨*track* an animal⟩ **b :** to search for by following evidence until found ⟨*track* down the source⟩ **2 :** to observe or plot the moving path of (as a spacecraft or missile) with instruments **3 :** to pass over

: TRAVERSE ⟨*track* a desert⟩ **4** : to make tracks upon or with ⟨*track* up the floor⟩ ⟨*track* mud on the floor⟩ — **track·er** *n*

track·age \ˈtrak-ij\ *n* **1** : lines of railway track **2 a** : a right to use the tracks of another railroad **b** : the charge for such right

track–and–field \ˌtrak-ən-ˈfēld\ *adj* : of, relating to, or being any of various competitive athletic events (as running, jumping, and weight throwing) performed on a running track or on the adjacent field

track·ball \ˈtrak-ˌbȯl\ *n* : a ball that is mounted usually in a computer console so as to be only partially exposed and is rotated to control the movement of a cursor on a display

track·lay·ing \ˈtrak-ˌlā-iŋ\ *adj* : of, relating to, or being a vehicle that travels on two endless metal belts

track·less \ˈtrak-ləs\ *adj* : having no track : PATHLESS — **track·less·ly** *adv* — **track·less·ness** *n*

[1]**tract** \ˈtrakt\ *n, often cap* : verses of Scripture (as from the Psalms) used between the gradual and the Gospel at some masses [Medieval Latin *tractus,* from Latin, "action of drawing, extension"; perhaps from its being sung without a break by one voice]

[2]**tract** *n* : a small publication that usually states a group's political or religious ideas [Medieval Latin *tractus,* perhaps from Latin *tractatus* "treatise," from *tractare* "to draw out, handle, treat"]

[3]**tract** *n* **1 a** : an indefinite stretch especially of land ⟨broad *tracts* of prairie⟩ **b** : a defined area especially of land ⟨a garden *tract*⟩ **2** : a system of body parts or organs that act together to perform some function ⟨the digestive *tract*⟩ [Latin *tractus* "action of drawing, extension," from *trahere* "to pull, draw"]

trac·ta·ble \ˈtrak-tə-bəl\ *adj* **1** : easily led, taught, or controlled : DOCILE ⟨a *tractable* horse⟩ **2** : easily handled, managed, or wrought : MALLEABLE [Latin *tractabilis,* from *tractare* "to handle, treat"] — **trac·ta·bil·i·ty** \ˌtrak-tə-ˈbil-ət-ē\ *n* — **trac·ta·ble·ness** \ˈtrak-tə-bəl-nəs\ *n* — **trac·ta·bly** \-blē\ *adv*

trac·tion \ˈtrak-shən\ *n* **1** : the act of drawing : the state of being drawn; *also* : the force exerted in drawing **2** : the drawing of a vehicle by motive power; *also* : the motive power employed **3** : the adhesive friction of a body on a surface on which it moves ⟨the *traction* of a wheel on a rail⟩ **4** : a pulling force exerted on a skeletal structure (as in a fracture) by means of a special device; *also* : a state of tension caused by such a pulling force ⟨a leg in *traction*⟩ [Medieval Latin *tractio,* from Latin *trahere* "to draw"] — **trac·tion·al** \-shnəl, -shən-l\ *adj*

trac·tive \ˈtrak-tiv\ *adj* : serving to pull : used in pulling

trac·tor \ˈtrak-tər\ *n* **1** : a 4-wheeled or tracklaying rider-controlled automotive vehicle used especially for drawing implements (as agricultural) or for bearing and propelling such implements **2** : a smaller 2-wheeled apparatus controlled usually through handlebars by a walking operator **3** : a truck with short chassis and no body used in combination with a trailer for the highway hauling of freight [Latin *trahere* "to pull, draw"]

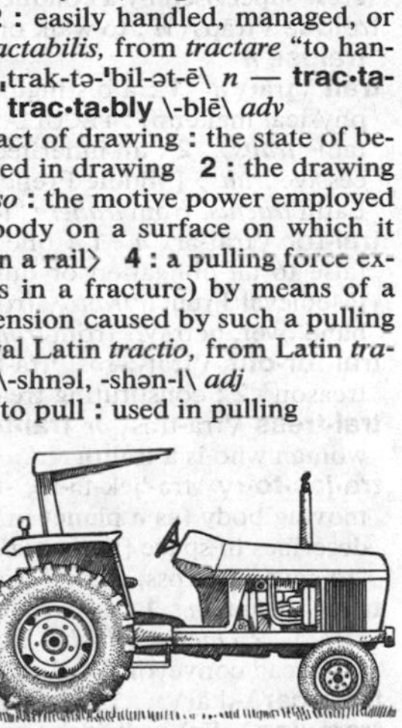

tractor 1

[1]**trade** \ˈtrād\ *n* **1** : a customary course of action : PRACTICE **2 a** : the business or work in which one engages regularly : OCCUPATION **b** : an occupation requiring manual or mechanical skill : CRAFT **c** : the persons engaged in an occupation, business, or industry **3 a** : the business of buying and selling or bartering commodities : COMMERCE **b** : BUSINESS 1b ⟨was in the novelty *trade*⟩ **4 a** : an act or instance of trading : TRANSACTION; *also* : an exchange of property without use of money **b** : a firm's customers : CLIENTELE **c** : the concerns engaged in a business or industry **5** : TRADE WIND — usually used in plural [Middle English, "path, track, course of action," from Low German, "path"] ***synonyms*** see BUSINESS

[2]**trade** *vb* **1 a** : to give in exchange for another commodity : BARTER; *also* : to make an exchange of **b** : to buy and sell (as stock) regularly **2 a** : to engage in the exchange, purchase, or sale of goods **b** : to make one's purchases : SHOP

[3]**trade** *adj* **1** : of, relating to, or used in trade **2** : intended for persons in a business or industry ⟨a *trade* journal⟩ **3** : of, composed of, or representing the trades or trade unions **4** : of or associated with a trade wind ⟨the *trade* belts⟩

trade acceptance *n* : a time draft or bill of exchange for the amount of a purchase drawn by the seller on the buyer and bearing the buyer's acceptance

trade dollar *n* : a U.S. silver dollar issued from 1873 to 1885 for use in east Asian trade

trade–in \ˈtrād-ˌin\ *n* : something given in trade usually as part payment of the price of another

trade in \trād-ˈin, ˈtrād-\ *vt* : to turn in as usually part payment for a purchase ⟨*trade* an old car *in* on a new one⟩

[1]**trade·mark** \-ˌmärk\ *n* : a device (as a word) pointing distinctly to the origin or ownership of merchandise to which it is applied and legally reserved to the exclusive use of the owner as maker or seller

[2]**trademark** *vt* : to secure trademark rights for : register the trademark of

trade name *n* **1** : the name by which an article is called in its own trade **2** : BRAND NAME **3** : the name under which a firm does business

trad·er \ˈtrād-ər\ *n* **1** : a person who trades **2** : a ship engaged in trade

trade school *n* : a secondary school teaching the skilled trades

trades·man \ˈtrādz-mən\ *n* **1** : one who runs a retail store : SHOPKEEPER **2** : a worker in a skilled trade : CRAFTSMAN

trades·peo·ple \-ˌpē-pəl\ *n pl* : people (as shopkeepers) engaged in trade

trade route *n* **1** : one of the sea-lanes used by merchant ships **2** : a route followed by traders (as in caravans)

trade union *n* : LABOR UNION; *esp* : CRAFT UNION — compare INDUSTRIAL UNION — **trade unionism** *n* — **trade unionist** *n*

trade wind *n* : a wind blowing almost continually in the same course, from northeast to southwest in a belt north of the equator and from southeast to northwest in one south of the equator [[1]*trade* ("habitual course")]

trading card *n* : a card that usually has pictures and information about someone or something and is part of a set that is collected by trading with other people

trading post *n* : a station or store of a trader or trading company established in a sparsely settled region

trading stamp *n* : a printed stamp given as a premium to a retail customer to be accumulated and redeemed in merchandise

tra·di·tion \trə-ˈdish-ən\ *n* : the handing down of information, beliefs, or customs from one generation to another; *also* : something thus handed down [Latin *traditio* "action of handing over, tradition," from *tradere* "to hand over, hand down," from *trans-* + *dare* "to give"] — **tra·di·tion·al** \-ˈdish-nəl, -ən-l\ *adj* — **tra·di·tion·al·ly** \-ē\ *adv*

tra·di·tion·al·ism \-ˈdish-nə-ˌliz-əm, -ən-l-ˌiz-\ *n* : the doctrines or practices of those who follow or accept tradition — **tra·di·tion·al·ist** \-nə-ləst, -ən-l-əst\ *n or adj* — **tra·di·tion·al·is·tic** \-ˌdish-nə-ˈlis-tik, -ən-l-ˈis-\ *adj*

tra·duce \trə-ˈdüs, -ˈdyüs\ *vt* : to injure the reputation of by falsehood or misrepresentation : DEFAME [Latin *traducere* "to lead across, transfer, degrade," from *trans-* + *ducere* "to lead"] — **tra·duce·ment** \-mənt\ *n* — **tra·duc·er** *n*

[1]**traf·fic** \ˈtraf-ik\ *n* **1 a** : import and export trade **b** : the business of buying and selling **2** : communication or dealings between individuals or groups **3 a** : the movement (as of vehicles or pedestrians) through an area or along a route **b** : the vehicles, pedestrians, ships, or airplanes moving along a route **c** : a crowded mass of vehicles **4 a** : the passengers or cargo carried by a transportation system **b** : the business of transporting passengers or freight [Middle French *trafique,* from Italian *traffico,* from *trafficare* "to trade in coastal waters"]

[2]**traffic** *vb* **traf·ficked; traf·fick·ing** : to carry on traffic : TRADE, DEAL — **traf·fick·er** *n*

traffic circle *n* : ROTARY 2

traffic island *n* : a paved or planted island in a roadway designed to guide the flow of traffic

traffic light *n* : a visual signal (as a system of colored lights) for controlling traffic

traffic signal *n* : a signal (as a traffic light) for controlling traffic

trag·a·canth \ˈtraj-ə-ˌkanth, ˈtrag-, -ˌkantth\ *n* : a gum from various Old World plants of the legume family that swells in water and is used chiefly as an emulsifying, suspending, or thickening agent — called also *gum tragacanth* [Middle French *tragacanthe,* from Latin *tragacantha,* from Greek *tragakantha,* from *tragos* "goat" + *akantha* "thorn"]

tra·ge·di·an \trə-ˈjēd-ē-ən\ *n* **1 :** a writer of tragedies **2 :** an actor of tragic roles

tra·ge·di·enne \trə-ˌjēd-ē-ˈen\ *n* **:** an actress who plays tragic roles [French *tragédienne,* from *tragédie* "tragedy"]

trag·e·dy \ˈtraj-əd-ē\ *n, pl* **-dies** **1 :** a serious drama having a sorrowful or disastrous conclusion **2 a :** a disastrous event **:** CALAMITY **b :** MISFORTUNE 2 **3 :** tragic quality or element [Middle French *tragedie,* from Latin *tragoedia,* from Greek *tragōidia,* from *tragos* "goat" + *aeidein* "to sing"]

Word History Our word *tragedy* is derived from Greek *tragōidia,* a compound of *tragos,* "goat," and *aeidein,* "to sing." The Greeks' reasons for calling this dramatic form "goat song" are obscure. Tragedy developed in the 6th and 5th centuries B.C. out of the performance of originally lyric recitations. Prizes were sometimes given for dramatic performances, and it may be that competition for the prize of a goat accounts for the word *tragōidia.* Another possibility is that a goat was sacrificed in earlier religious rituals out of which tragedy may have developed. A third theory is that tragedy developed out of the performance of lyric hymns to the god Dionysus in which the chorus was dressed as satyrs, mythical beings with some of the attributes of goats.

trag·ic \ˈtraj-ik\ *adj* **1 :** of, marked by, or expressive of tragedy **2 a :** dealing with or treated in tragedy ⟨the *tragic* hero⟩ **b :** appropriate to or typical of tragedy **3 a :** regrettably serious or unpleasant ⟨a *tragic* mistake⟩ **b :** marked by a sense of tragedy — **trag·i·cal** \-i-kəl\ *adj* — **trag·i·cal·ly** \-i-kə-lē, -klē\ *adv*

tragi·com·e·dy \ˌtraj-i-ˈkäm-əd-ē\ *n* **:** a drama or a situation blending tragic and comic elements — **tragi·com·ic** \-ˈkäm-ik\ *also* **tragi·com·i·cal** \-ˈkäm-i-kəl\ *adj*

[1]**trail** \ˈtrāl\ *vb* **1 a :** to drag or draw along behind ⟨the horse *trailed* its reins⟩ **b :** to hang down or rest on or creep over the ground ⟨*trailing* vines⟩ **2 :** to lag behind **:** do poorly in relation to others **3 :** to carry or bring along as a burden or bother **4 a :** to follow upon the scent or trace of **:** TRACK ⟨dogs *trailing* a fox⟩ **b :** to follow in the tracks of **:** PURSUE ⟨photographers *trailed* the actor⟩ **5 :** to hang or let hang so as to touch the ground ⟨a *trailing* skirt⟩ **6 :** to form a trail **:** STRAGGLE ⟨smoke *trailed* from the chimney⟩ **7 :** DWINDLE ⟨the sound *trailed* off⟩ [perhaps from Medieval French *trainer* "to drag, trail on the ground"] ***synonyms*** see CHASE

[2]**trail** *n* **1 :** something that trails or is trailed: as **a :** the train of a gown **b :** the part of a gun carriage that rests on the ground when the piece is ready for action **2 a :** something that follows or moves along as if being drawn along **:** TRAIN **b** (1) **:** the streak produced by a meteor (2) **:** a line produced photographically by the moving image of a celestial body ⟨star *trails*⟩ **3 a :** a trace or mark left by something that has passed or been drawn along ⟨a *trail* of blood⟩ **b :** a track made by passage (as through a wilderness) **:** a beaten path **c :** a path marked to show a route (as through a forest) ⟨hiking *trails*⟩

trail·blaz·er \-ˌblā-zər\ *n* **1 :** one that marks or points out a trail to guide others **:** PATHFINDER **2 :** PIONEER 1 — **trail·blaz·ing** \-zing\ *adj*

trail·er \ˈtrā-lər\ *n* **1 :** one that trails **2 a :** a vehicle designed to be hauled (as by a tractor) **b :** a vehicle designed to serve wherever parked as a dwelling or as a place of business **3 :** PREVIEW 2

trailer park *n* **:** an area equipped to provide space for house trailers — called also *trailer camp, trailer court*

trailing arbutus *n* **:** ARBUTUS 2

trailing edge *n* **:** the rearmost edge of an airfoil

trail mix *n* **:** a mixture of seeds, nuts, and dried fruits eaten as a snack [*trail* from its use by hikers]

[1]**train** \ˈtrān\ *n* **1 :** a part of a gown that trails behind the wearer **2 :** RETINUE **3 :** a moving file of persons, vehicles, or animals **4 a :** order designed to lead to some result **b :** an orderly succession or sequence ⟨a *train* of thought⟩ **c :** accompanying circumstances **d :** SEQUEL 1, AFTERMATH **5 :** a line of combustible material (as gunpowder) laid to lead fire to a charge **6 :** a series of moving machine parts (as gears) for transmitting and modifying motion **7 a :** a connected line of railroad cars with or without a locomotive **b :** an automotive tractor with one or more trailer units [Medieval French, from *trainer* "to draw, drag"]

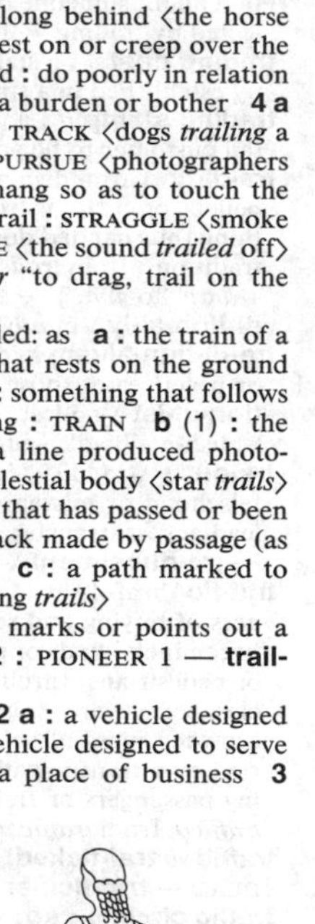

train 1

[2]**train** *vb* **1 :** to direct the growth of (a plant) usually by bending, pruning, and tying **2 a :** to teach something (as a skill, profession, or trade) to ⟨was *trained* in the law⟩ **b :** to teach (an animal) to obey **3 :** to make ready (as by exercise) for a test of skill **4 :** to aim at an object or objective **:** DIRECT ⟨*trained* his camera on the deer⟩ ⟨*training* every effort toward success⟩ **5 :** to undergo instruction, discipline, or drill [Medieval French *trainer* "to draw, drag"] ***synonyms*** see TEACH — **train·able** \ˈtrā-nə-bəl\ *adj* — **train·ee** \trā-ˈnē\ *n*

train·er \ˈtrā-nər\ *n* **1 :** one that trains **2 :** a person who treats the minor ailments and injuries of the members of an athletic team

train·ing \ˈtrā-ning\ *n* **1 :** the course followed by one who trains or is being trained ⟨take nursing *training*⟩ **2 :** the condition of one who has trained for a test or contest ***synonyms*** see EDUCATION

training wheels *n pl* **:** a pair of small wheels connected to the rear axle of a bicycle to help a beginning bicyclist maintain balance

train·load \ˈtrān-ˈlōd\ *n* **:** the full freight or passenger capacity of a railroad train

train·man \ˈtrān-mən, -ˌman\ *n* **:** a member of a railroad train crew supervised by a conductor

traipse \ˈtrāps\ *vi* **:** to walk or tramp about [origin unknown] — **traipse** *n*

trait \ˈtrāt\ *n* **1 :** a distinguishing quality (as of personality or physical makeup) **:** PECULIARITY 2 ⟨curiosity is one of her notable *traits*⟩ **2 :** an inherited characteristic ⟨dominant and recessive *traits*⟩ [Middle French, literally, "act of drawing," from Latin *tractus,* from *trahere* "to draw, drag"]

trai·tor \ˈtrāt-ər\ *n* **1 :** one who betrays another's trust or is false to an obligation or duty **2 :** one who commits treason [Medieval French *traitre,* from Latin *traditor,* from *tradere* "to hand over, betray," from *trans-* + *dare* "to give"]

trai·tor·ous \ˈtrāt-ə-rəs, ˈtrā-trəs\ *adj* **1 :** guilty or capable of treason **2 :** constituting treason — **trai·tor·ous·ly** *adv*

trai·tress \ˈtrā-trəs\ *or* **trai·tor·ess** \ˈtrāt-ə-rəs, ˈtrā-trəs\ *n* **:** a woman who is a traitor

tra·jec·to·ry \trə-ˈjek-tə-rē, -trē\ *n, pl* **-ries** **:** the curve that a moving body (as a planet in its orbit, a projectile, or a rocket) describes in space [Latin *traiectorius* "of passing," from *traicere* "to cause to cross, cross," from *trans-* + *jacere* "to throw"]

tram \ˈtram\ *n* **1 :** a cart or wagon running on rails (as in a mine) **2** *chiefly British* **:** STREETCAR **3 :** the carriage of an overhead conveyor [English dialect, "shaft of a wheelbarrow"]

tram·car \-ˌkär\ *n* **1** *chiefly British* **:** STREETCAR **2 :** TRAM 1

tram·line \-ˌlīn\ *n, British* **:** a streetcar line

[1]**tram·mel** \ˈtram-əl\ *n* **1 :** a net for catching birds or fish **2 :** something hindering activity, progress, or freedom **:** RESTRAINT — usually used in plural **3 :** an adjustable pothook for a fireplace crane **4 :** a compass for drawing large circles that consists of a beam with two sliding parts — usually used in plural [Medieval French *tramail,* from Late Latin *tremaculum,* from Latin *tres* "three" + *macula* "mesh, spot"]

[2]**trammel** *vt* **-meled** *or* **-melled; -mel·ing** *or* **-mel·ling** \ˈtram-ling, -ə-ling\ **1 :** to catch or hold in or as if in a net **:** ENMESH **2 :** to prevent or hinder the free play of **:** CONFINE

[1]**tramp** \ˈtramp, *1 & 2 are also* ˈträmp, ˈtrȯmp\ *vb* **1 :** to walk heavily **2 :** to tread on forcibly and repeatedly **:** TRAMPLE **3 a :** to wander through or travel on foot **b :** to journey as a tramp [Middle English *trampen*] — **tramp·er** *n*

[2]**tramp** \ˈtramp, *3 is also* ˈträmp, ˈtrȯmp\ *n* **1 :** a begging or thieving vagrant **2 :** a walking trip **:** HIKE **3 :** the succession of sounds made by the beating of marching feet **4 :** a ship not making regular trips but taking cargo to any port when and where it offers — called also *tramp steamer*

tram·ple \ˈtram-pəl\ *vb* **tram·pled; tram·pling** \-pə-ling, -pling\ **1 a :** to tramp or tread heavily so as to bruise, crush, or injure ⟨the cattle *trampled* on the young wheat⟩ **b :** to crush, injure, or destroy by or as if by treading ⟨*trampled* the flowers⟩ **2 :** to inflict pain, injury, or loss by ruthless or heartless treatment ⟨*trample* on the rights of others⟩ [Middle English *tramplen,* from *trampen* "to tramp"] — **trample** *n* — **tram·pler** \-pə-lər, -plər\ *n*

tram·po·line \ˌtram-pə-ˈlēn, ˈtram-pə-ˌ\ *n* : a resilient canvas sheet or web supported by springs in a metal frame used as a springboard and landing area for performing jumps and flips [Italian *trampolino* "springboard," from *trampoli* "stilts," of Germanic origin] — **tram·po·lin·er** \-ˈlē-nər, -ˌlē-\ *n* — **tram·po·lin·ist** \-nəst\ *n*

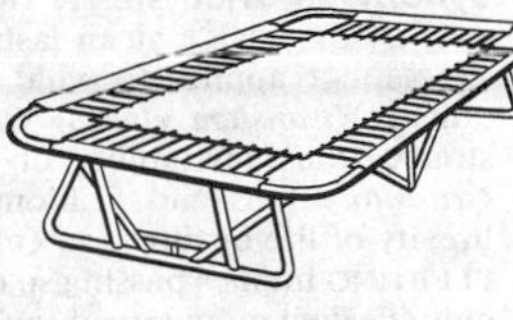
trampoline

tram·po·lin·ing \-ˈlē-ning, -ˌlē-\ *n* : the sport of jumping and performing acrobatic feats on a trampoline

tram·way \ˈtram-ˌwā\ *n* **1** : a road or way for trams **2** *British* : a streetcar line

trance \ˈtrans\ *n* **1** : STUPOR 1 **2** : a sleeplike state (as of deep hypnosis) usually characterized by diminished or absent sensory and motor activity **3** : a state of profound abstraction or absorption [Middle French *transe,* from *transir* "to pass away, swoon," from Latin *transire* "to cross over, pass away," from *trans-* + *ire* "to go"] — **trance·like** \-ˌlīk\ *adj*

tran·ny \ˈtran-ē\ *n, pl* **trannies** : TRANSMISSION 3

tran·quil \ˈtrang-kwəl, ˈtran-\ *adj* **1** : free from agitation, disturbance, or turmoil : SERENE **2** : STABLE 1b [Latin *tranquillus*] ***synonyms*** see CALM — **tran·quil·ly** \-kwə-lē\ *adv* — **tran·quil·ness** *n*

tran·quil·ize *also* **tran·quil·lize** \-kwə-ˌlīz\ *vb* : to make or become tranquil or relaxed; *esp* : to relieve of mental tension and anxiety usually by means of drugs

tran·quil·iz·er *also* **tran·quil·liz·er** \-ˌlī-zər\ *n* : one that tranquilizes; *esp* : a drug used to reduce anxiety and nervous tension

tran·quil·li·ty *or* **tran·quil·i·ty** \tran-ˈkwil-ət-ē, trang-\ *n* : the quality or state of being tranquil

trans \ˈtrans, ˈtranz\ *adj* : having certain atoms or groups of atoms attached on opposite sides and opposite ends of a double bond

trans- *prefix* **1** : on or to the other side of : across : beyond ⟨*trans*atlantic⟩ **2** : through ⟨*trans*lucent⟩ **3** : so or such as to change or transfer ⟨*trans*location⟩ ⟨*trans*ship⟩ [Latin *trans-, tra-,* from *trans* "across, beyond"]

trans·act \trans-ˈakt, tranz-\ *vt* **1** : to carry through : bring about : NEGOTIATE ⟨*transact* a sale⟩ **2** : to carry on : CONDUCT ⟨*transact* business⟩ [Latin *transactus,* past participle of *transigere* "to drive through, transact," from *trans-* + *agere* "to drive"] — **trans·ac·tor** \-ˈak-tər\ *n*

trans·ac·tion \-ˈak-shən\ *n* **1 a** : an act, process, or instance of transacting **b** : an action or activity involving two parties or things that influence or affect each other **2 a** : something transacted; *esp* : a business deal **b** *pl* : the record of the meeting of a society — **trans·ac·tion·al** \-shnəl, -shən-l\ *adj*

trans·at·lan·tic \ˌtrans-ət-ˈlant-ik, ˌtranz-\ *adj* **1** : extending across or crossing the Atlantic Ocean **2** : located or coming from beyond the Atlantic Ocean

trans·bor·der \ˌtrans-ˈbȯrd-ər\ *adj* : crossing or extending across a border

trans·ceiv·er \trans-ˈē-vər, tranz-\ *n* : a radio transmitter-receiver that uses many of the same components for transmission and reception [*trans*mitter + re*ceiver*]

tran·scend \tran-ˈsend\ *vt* **1** : to rise above or go beyond the limits of : EXCEED **2** : to outdo in some attribute, quality, or power : SURPASS ⟨a poem *transcending* all others⟩ [Latin *transcendere* "to climb across, transcend," from *trans-* + *scandere* "to climb"] ***synonyms*** see EXCEED

tran·scend·ence \-ˈsen-dəns\ *also* **tran·scend·en·cy** \-dən-sē\ *n* : the quality or state of being transcendent

tran·scend·ent \-dənt\ *adj* **1** : exceeding usual limits **2** : extending or lying beyond the limits of ordinary experience [Latin *transcendens,* present participle of *transcendere* "to transcend"] — **tran·scend·ent·ly** *adv*

tran·scen·den·tal \ˌtran-ˌsen-ˈdent-l, ˌtran-sən-\ *adj* **1** : TRANSCENDENT 2 **2** : incapable of being the root of an algebraic equation with rational coefficients ⟨π is a *transcendental* number⟩ **3** : of or relating to transcendentalism **4** : TRANSCENDENT 1 — **tran·scen·den·tal·ly** \-l-ē\ *adv*

tran·scen·den·tal·ism \-l-ˌiz-əm\ *n* **1** : a philosophy that emphasizes the construction of knowledge from sense impressions of independently existing realities and the unknowable character of ultimate reality **2** : a philosophy that values the spiritual and intuitive over the material and empirical and that asserts the essential unity of all creation — **tran·scen·den·tal·ist** \-l-əst\ *adj or n*

trans·con·ti·nen·tal \ˌtrans-ˌkänt-n-ˈent-l\ *adj* : extending or going across a continent ⟨*transcontinental* flight⟩

tran·scribe \tran-ˈskrīb\ *vt* **1 a** : to make a written copy of **b** : to make a copy of (dictated or recorded matter) in longhand or on a machine (as a typewriter) **2 a** : to represent (speech sounds) by means of phonetic symbols **b** : to transfer (data) from one recording form to another **c** : to record (as on magnetic tape) for later broadcast **3** : to make a musical transcription of **4** : to cause (as DNA) to undergo genetic transcription [Latin *transcribere,* from *trans-* + *scribere* "to write"] — **tran·scrib·er** *n*

tran·script \ˈtran-ˌskript\ *n* **1** : a written, printed, or typed copy **2** : an official copy (as of a student's educational record) [Medieval Latin *transcriptum,* from Latin *transcribere* "to transcribe"]

tran·scrip·tion \tran-ˈskrip-shən\ *n* **1** : an act, process, or instance of transcribing **2 a** : COPY 1, TRANSCRIPT **b** : an arrangement of a musical composition for some instrument or voice other than the original **3** : the process of constructing a messenger RNA molecule using a DNA molecule as a template with resulting transfer of genetic information to the messenger RNA — compare TRANSLATION 4 — **tran·scrip·tion·al** \-shnəl, -shən-l\ *adj* — **tran·scrip·tion·al·ly** \-ē\ *adv*

trans·cul·tur·al \trans-ˈkəlch-rəl, -ə-rəl, tranz-\ *adj* : involving, encompassing, or extending across two or more cultures

trans·duc·er \trans-ˈdü-sər, tranz-, -ˈdyü-\ *n* : a device that is actuated by power from one system and supplies power in any other form to a second system [Latin *transducere* "to lead across," from *trans-* + *ducere* "to lead"]

[1]**tran·sect** \tran-ˈsekt\ *vt* : to cut transversely [*trans-* + inter*sect*] — **tran·sec·tion** \-ˈsek-shən\ *n*

[2]**tran·sect** \ˈtran-ˌsekt\ *n* : a sample area (as of vegetation) usually in the form of a long continuous strip

tran·sept \ˈtran-ˌsept\ *n* : the part forming the short arm of a cross-shaped church; *also* : either of the projecting ends of a transept [Latin *trans-* + *saeptum* "enclosure, wall," from *saepire* "to fence in," from *saepes* "fence"]

trans fat *n* : a fat containing trans-fatty acids

trans–fat·ty acid \ˈtrns-ˈfat-ē-, ˈtranz-\ *n* : an unsaturated fatty acid characterized by a trans arrangement of alkyl chains that is formed especially during the hydrogenation of vegetable oils and has been linked to an increase in blood cholesterol

[1]**trans·fer** \trans-ˈfər, ˈtrans-ˌ\ *vb* **trans·ferred; trans·fer·ring** **1 a** : to convey from one person, place, or situation to another : MOVE **b** : to cause to pass from one to another : TRANSMIT **2** : to make over the possession or ownership of : CONVEY **3** : to print or otherwise copy from one surface to another by contact **4** : to move to a different place, region, or situation; *esp* : to withdraw from one educational institution to enroll at another **5** : to change from one vehicle or transportation line to another [Latin *transferre,* from *trans-* + *ferre* "to carry"] — **trans·fer·abil·i·ty** \ˌtrans-ˌfər-ə-ˈbil-ət-ē\ *n* — **trans·fer·able** \trans-ˈfər-ə-bəl\ *adj* — **trans·fer·al** \-ˈfər-əl\ *n* — **trans·fer·rer** \-ˈfər-ər\ *n*

[2]**trans·fer** \ˈtrans-ˌfər\ *n* **1** : conveyance of right, title, or interest in real or personal property from one person to another **2** : an act, process, or instance of transferring : TRANSFERENCE **3** : one that transfers or is transferred; *esp* : a graphic image transferred by contact from one surface to another **4** : a place where a transfer is made (as of trains to ferries) **5** : a ticket entitling a passenger on a public conveyance to continue the journey on another route

trans·fer·ee \ˌtrans-fər-ˈē\ *n* **1** : a person to whom a conveyance is made **2** : a person who is transferred

trans·fer·ence \trans-ˈfər-əns\ *n* : an act, process, or instance of transferring : TRANSFER

\ə\ **abut**	\au̇\ **out**	\i\ **tip**	\ȯ\ **saw**	\u̇\ **foot**
\ər\ **further**	\ch\ **chin**	\ī\ **life**	\ȯi\ **coin**	\y\ **yet**
\a\ **mat**	\e\ **pet**	\j\ **job**	\th\ **thin**	\yü\ **few**
\ā\ **take**	\ē\ **easy**	\ng\ **sing**	\t͟h\ **this**	\yu̇\ **cure**
\ä\ **cot, cart**	\g\ **go**	\ō\ **bone**	\ü\ **food**	\zh\ **vision**

trans·fer·or \ˌtrans-fər-ˈȯr\ *n* : one that transfers a title, right, or property

trans·fer RNA \ˈtrans-ˌfər-\ *n* : a relatively small RNA that transfers a particular amino acid to a growing protein at the ribosomal site of protein synthesis during genetic translation — compare MESSENGER RNA

transfer station *n* : a site where recyclable materials and garbage are collected and sorted in preparation for processing or landfill

trans·fig·u·ra·tion \ˌtrans-ˌfig-yə-ˈrā-shən, -ˌfig-ə-ˈrā-\ *n* **1** : a change of form or appearance; *esp* : a glorifying, spiritual, or exalting change **2** *cap* **a** : a Christian festival that commemorates the transfiguration of Jesus on a mountaintop as witnessed by three disciples

trans·fig·ure \trans-ˈfig-yər, *especially British* -ˈfig-ər\ *vt* : to give a new and typically exalted or spiritual appearance to ***synonyms*** see TRANSFORM

trans·fix \trans-ˈfiks\ *vt* **1** : to pierce through with or as if with a pointed weapon : IMPALE **2** : to hold motionless by or as if by piercing ⟨stood *transfixed* by her gaze⟩ — **trans·fix·ion** \-ˈfik-shən\ *n*

trans·form \trans-ˈfȯrm\ *vb* **1 a** : to change in composition, structure, or character : CONVERT **b** : to change in outward appearance **2** : to subject to mathematical transformation — **trans·form·able** \-ˈfȯr-mə-bəl\ *adj* — **trans·for·ma·tive** \-ˈfȯr-mət-iv\ *adj*

synonyms TRANSFORM, METAMORPHOSE, TRANSMUTE, TRANSFIGURE mean to change something into a different thing. TRANSFORM implies a change in form, nature, or function ⟨*transform* a desert into a fertile plain⟩. METAMORPHOSE suggests an abrupt or striking alteration induced as if supernaturally or by natural (as chemical) agencies ⟨the ugly duckling *metamorphosed* into a swan⟩. TRANSMUTE implies a change from a lower to a higher element or thing ⟨the artist *transmutes* ordinary scenes into extraordinary ones⟩. TRANSFIGURE implies a change that exalts and glorifies ⟨joy *tranfigured* her face⟩.

trans·for·ma·tion \ˌtrans-fər-ˈmā-shən\ *n* **1** : an act, process, or instance of transforming or being transformed **2** : the operation of changing (as by rotation or mapping) one mathematical configuration or expression into another in accordance with a mathematical rule **3** : genetic modification of a cell and especially of a bacterium by introduction of DNA from a genetically different source — **trans·for·ma·tion·al** \-shnəl, -shə-nl\ *adj*

trans·form·er \trans-ˈfȯr-mər\ *n* : one that transforms; *esp* : a device without moving parts for changing an electric current into one of different voltage by electromagnetic induction

trans·fuse \trans-ˈfyüz\ *vt* **1 a** : to cause to pass from one to another : TRANSMIT **b** : to spread into or through : PERMEATE **2 a** : to transfer (as blood) into a vein or an artery of a person or animal **b** : to subject (a patient) to transfusion [Latin *transfusus,* past participle of *transfundere* "to transfuse," from *trans-* + *fundere* "to pour"] — **tran·fus·ible** *or* **trans·fus·able** \-ˈfyü-zə-bəl\ *adj*

trans·fu·sion \trans-ˈfyü-zhən\ *n* **1** : an act, process, or instance of transfusing; *esp* : the process of transfusing a fluid and especially blood into a vein or an artery **2** : something transfused

trans·gen·der \trans-ˈjendər\ *or* **trans·gen·dered** \-dərd\ *adj* : having personal characteristics that differ from traditional gender boundaries and expectations

trans·gen·ic \trans-ˈjen-ik\ *adj* : being or used to produce an organism or cell of one species into which one or more genes of another species have been incorporated ⟨a *transgenic* mouse⟩ ⟨*transgenic* plants⟩; *also* : produced by or consisting of transgenic plants or animals ⟨*transgenic* fruits⟩

trans·gress \trans-ˈgres, tranz-\ *vb* **1** : to go beyond limits set by : VIOLATE ⟨*transgress* divine law⟩ **2** : to pass beyond or go over a limit or boundary **3** : to violate a command or law : SIN [Medieval French *transgresser,* from Latin *transgressus,* past participle of *transgredi* "to step beyond or across," from *trans-* + *gradi* "to step"] — **trans·gres·sive** \-ˈgres-iv\ *adj* — **trans·gres·sor** \-ˈgres-ər\ *n*

trans·gres·sion \-ˈgresh-ən\ *n* : an act, process, or instance of trangressing; *esp* : violation of a law, command, or duty

tran·sience \ˈtran-chəns\ *n* : the quality or state of being transient

[1]**tran·sient** \-chənt\ *adj* : not lasting or staying long ⟨a *transient* population⟩ ⟨a *transient* scene⟩ [Latin *transiens,* present participle of *transire* "to cross, pass," from *trans-* + *ire* "to go"] — **transient·ly** *adv*

synonyms TRANSIENT, TRANSITORY, EPHEMERAL, FLEETING, EVANESCENT mean lasting or staying only a short time. TRANSIENT applies to what is short in duration and passes quickly ⟨*transient* guests⟩ ⟨*transient* as music⟩. TRANSITORY stresses the inevitability of changing, ending, or dying out ⟨*transitory* fads and fashions⟩. EPHEMERAL implies notable brevity of life or duration ⟨many slang words are *ephemeral*⟩. FLEETING implies passing so quickly as to make catching difficult ⟨*fleeting* moments of joy⟩. EVANESCENT suggests a quickly vanishing and airy or fragile quality ⟨the *evanescent* beauty of bubbles blown by the breeze⟩.

[2]**transient** *n* : one that is transient: as **a** : a transient guest **b** : a person traveling about usually in search of work

tran·sis·tor \tran-ˈzis-tər, -ˈsis-\ *n* **1** : an electronic device that is used to control the flow of electricity in electronic equipment and usually consists of a small block of a semiconductor (as germanium) with at least three electrodes **2** : a radio having transistors — called also *transistor radio* [[1]*trans*fer + re*sistor;* from its transferring an electrical signal across a resistor]

tran·sis·tor·ized \-tə-ˌrīzd\ *adj* : equipped with transistors ⟨a *transistorized* amplifier⟩

[1]**tran·sit** \ˈtrans-ət, ˈtranz-\ *n* **1 a** : an act, process, or instance of passing through or over : PASSAGE **b** : transporting of persons or things from one place to another ⟨goods lost in *transit*⟩ **c** : local transportation of people by public conveyance; *also* : the vehicles or system used in such transportation **2 a** : passage of a celestial body over the meridian of a place or through the field of a telescope **b** : passage of a smaller body (as Venus) across the disk of a larger (as the sun) **3** : a theodolite with the telescope mounted so that it can be transited [Latin *transitus,* from *transire* "to cross, pass," from *trans-* + *ire* "to go"]

[2]**transit** *vb* **1** : to make a transit **2** : to pass or cause to pass over, across, or through **3** : to turn (a telescope) about the horizontal transverse axis in surveying

[1]**tran·si·tion** \trans-ˈish-ən, tranz-\ *n* **1** : a passing from one state, stage, place, or subject to another **2** : a musical passage leading from one section of a piece to another — **tran·si·tion·al** \-ˈish-nəl, -ən-l\ *adj* — **tran·si·tion·al·ly** \-ē\ *adv*

[2]**transition** *vi* : to make a transition ⟨*transitioning* to a new job⟩

transition element *n* : any of various metallic elements (as chromium, iron, and nickel) that can form bonds using electrons from two energy levels instead of only one

tran·si·tive \ˈtrans-ət-iv, ˈtranz-\ *adj* **1** : characterized by having or containing a direct object ⟨a *transitive* verb⟩ **2** : relating to or being a mathematical relation with the property that if the relation holds between a first element and a second and between the second element and a third then it holds between the first and third elements ⟨if $a = b$ and $b = c$ then $a = c$ because equality is a *transitive* relation⟩ **3** : of, relating to, or involving transition — **tran·si·tive·ly** *adv* — **tran·si·tive·ness** *n* — **tran·si·tiv·i·ty** \ˌtrans-ə-ˈtiv-ət-ē, ˌtranz-\ *n*

tran·si·to·ry \ˈtrans-ə-ˌtōr-ē, ˈtranz-, -ˌtȯr-\ *adj* : lasting only a short time : SHORT-LIVED, TEMPORARY ⟨the *transitory* pleasures of the world⟩ ***synonyms*** see TRANSIENT — **tran·si·to·ri·ly** \ˌtrans-ə-ˈtōr-ə-lē, ˌtranz-, -ˈtȯr-\ *adv* — **tran·si·to·ri·ness** \ˈtrans-ə-ˌtōr-ē-nəs, ˈtranz-, -ˌtȯr-\ *n*

trans·late \trans-ˈlāt, tranz-\ *vb* **1 a** : to bear or change from one place, state, form, or appearance to another : TRANSFER, TRANSFORM ⟨*translate* plans into action⟩ **b** : to transport to heaven without death **2 a** : to turn from one language into another **b** : to transfer or turn from one set of symbols into another : TRANSCRIBE **c** : to express in different words : PARAPHRASE **d** : to explain in a clearer way : INTERPRET ⟨needed a lawyer to *translate* the contract⟩ **3** : to subject (as genetic information) to translation in protein synthesis **4** : to undergo translation **5** : to have as a result — usually used with *into* ⟨believed that more homework would *translate* into better grades⟩ [Latin *translatus,* past participle of *transferre* "to transfer, translate"] — **trans·lat·abil·i·ty** \-ˌlāt-ə-ˈbil-ət-ē\ *n* — **trans·lat·able** \-ˈlāt-ə-bəl\ *adj* — **trans·la·tor** \-ˈlāt-ər\ *n*

trans·la·tion \trans-ˈlā-shən, tranz-\ *n* **1** : an act, process, or instance of translating **2** : the product of translating ⟨a German *translation* of the novel⟩ **3** : a mathematical transformation of coordinates in which the new axes are parallel to the old ones **4** : the process of forming a protein molecule at a ribosomal site of protein synthesis from information contained in messenger

RNA — compare TRANSCRIPTION 3 — **trans·la·tion·al** \-shnəl, -shən-l\ *adj*

trans·lit·er·ate \trans-ˈlit-ə-ˌrāt, tranz-\ *vt* : to represent or spell in the characters of another alphabet [*trans-* + Latin *littera* "letter"] — **trans·lit·er·a·tion** \-ˌlit-ə-ˈrā-shən\ *n*

trans·lo·cate \ˈtrans-lō-ˌkāt, ˈtranz-, trans-ˈ, tranz-ˈ\ *vt* : to transfer by translocation

trans·lo·ca·tion \ˌtrans-lō-ˈkā-shən, ˌtranz-\ *n* : a changing of location : DISPLACEMENT: as **a** : the conducting of soluble material from one part of a plant to another **b** : exchange of parts between nonhomologous chromosomes

trans·lu·cence \trans-ˈlüs-ns, tranz-\ *n* : the quality or state of being translucent

trans·lu·cen·cy \-n-sē\ *n* **1** : TRANSLUCENCE **2** : something that is translucent

trans·lu·cent \-nt\ *adj* **1** : shining or glowing through ⟨a *translucent* lake⟩ **2** : admitting and diffusing light so that objects beyond cannot be clearly distinguished ⟨a *translucent* window⟩ **3** : free from disguise or falseness ⟨his *translucent* affection⟩ [Latin *translucens,* present participle of *translucēre* "to shine through," from *trans-* + *lucēre* "to shine"] ***synonyms*** see CLEAR — **trans·lu·cent·ly** *adv*

trans·ma·rine \ˌtrans-mə-ˈrēn, ˌtranz-\ *adj* : being or coming from beyond or across the sea

transmigrate \trans-ˈmī-ˌgrāt, tranz-\ *vb* **1** : to change one's home from one country to another : MIGRATE 1 **2** *of the soul* : to pass at death from one body or being to another — **trans·mi·gra·tion** \ˌtrans-ˌmī-ˈgrā-shən, ˌtranz-\ *n* — **trans·mi·gra·to·ry** \-ˈmī-grə-ˌtōr-ē, -ˌtȯr-\ *adj*

trans·mis·si·ble \trans-ˈmis-ə-bəl, tranz-\ *adj* : capable of being transmitted ⟨*transmissible* diseases⟩ — **trans·mis·si·bil·i·ty** \-ˌmis-ə-ˈbil-ət-ē\ *n*

trans·mis·sion \-ˈmish-ən\ *n* **1** : an act, process, or instance of transmitting something **2** : the passage of radio waves in the space between transmitting and receiving stations; *also* : the act or process of transmitting by radio or television **3** : an assembly of parts including the speed-changing gears and a rotating shaft by which power is transmitted from an engine to a live axle **4** : something transmitted [Latin *transmissio,* from *transmittere* "to transmit"] — **trans·mis·sive** \-ˈmis-iv\ *adj* — **trans·mis·siv·i·ty** \ˌtrans-mis-ˈiv-ət-ē, ˌtranz-\ *n*

transmission electron microscope *n* : an electron microscope which produces an image of a cross-sectional slice of a specimen all points of which are illuminated by the electron beam at the same time — **transmission electron microscopy** *n*

trans·mit \trans-ˈmit, tranz-\ *vb* **trans·mit·ted; trans·mit·ting** **1 a** : to send or transfer from one person or place to another : FORWARD **b** : to transfer by or as if by inheritance **c** : to convey (infection) abroad or to another **2 a** (1) : to cause (as light or force) to pass or be passed through space or a medium (2) : to admit the passage of ⟨glass *transmits* light⟩ **b** : to send out a signal either by radio waves or over a wire [Latin *transmittere,* from *trans-* + *mittere* "to send"] — **trans·mit·ta·ble** \-ˈmit-ə-bəl\ *adj* — **trans·mit·tal** \-ˈmit-l\ *n*

trans·mit·ter \-ˈmit-ər\ *n* : one that transmits; *esp* : an apparatus that sends out radio or television signals

trans·mog·ri·fy \trans-ˈmäg-rə-ˌfī, tranz-\ *vt* **-fied; -fy·ing** : to change or alter often with grotesque or humorous effect [origin unknown] — **trans·mog·ri·fi·ca·tion** \-ˌmäg-rə-fə-ˈkā-shən\ *n*

trans·mu·ta·tion \ˌtrans-myü-ˈtā-shən, ˌtranz-\ *n* : an act or instance of transmuting or being transmuted: as **a** : the hypothetical changing of base metals into gold or silver **b** : the changing of one element or nuclide into another either naturally or artificially — **trans·mut·a·tive** \trans-ˈmyüt-ət-iv, tranz-\ *adj*

trans·mute \trans-ˈmyüt, tranz-\ *vb* **1** : to change in form, appearance, or nature especially to a higher form **2** : to subject to transmutation **3** : to undergo transmutation [Latin *transmutare,* from *trans-* + *mutare* "to change"] ***synonyms*** see TRANSFORM — **trans·mut·able** \-ˈmyüt-ə-bəl\ *adj*

trans·na·tion·al \trans-ˈnash-nəl, ˈtrans-, tranz-, ˈtranz-, -ən-l\ *adj* : extending beyond national boundaries

trans·oce·an·ic \ˌtrans-ˌō-shē-ˈan-ik, ˌtranz-\ *adj* **1** : being or living beyond the ocean **2** : crossing or extending across the ocean ⟨*transoceanic* cables⟩

tran·som \ˈtran-səm\ *n* **1** : a transverse piece in a structure : CROSSPIECE: as **a** : LINTEL **b** : a horizontal crossbar in a window, over a door, or between a door and a window or fanlight above it **2** : a window above a door or above another window built on and commonly hinged to a transom [Middle English *transyn, traunsom*]

T transom 1b

tran·son·ic *also* **trans·son·ic** \trans-ˈsän-ik, tran-ˈsän-\ *adj* **1** : being or relating to a speed approximating the speed of sound in air or about 741 miles (1185 kilometers) per hour at sea level **2** : moving, capable of moving, or utilizing air currents moving at a transonic speed ⟨*transonic* bomber⟩ [*trans-* + *-sonic* (as in *supersonic*)]

trans·pa·cif·ic \ˌtrans-pə-ˈsif-ik\ *adj* **1** : crossing or extending across the Pacific Ocean **2** : located or occurring beyond the Pacific Ocean

trans·par·ence \trans-ˈpar-əns, -ˈper-\ *n* : TRANSPARENCY 1

trans·par·en·cy \-ən-sē\ *n, pl* **-cies** **1** : the quality or state of being transparent **2** : a picture or design on glass, thin cloth, paper, or film viewed by light shining through it or by projection

trans·par·ent \-ənt\ *adj* **1 a** (1) : having the property of transmitting light so that bodies lying beyond are entirely visible (2) : allowing the passage of a specified form of radiation (as X-rays or ultraviolet light) **b** : fine or sheer enough to be seen through **2 a** : FRANK 1, GUILELESS **b** : easily detected, seen through, or understood : OBVIOUS [Medieval Latin *transparens,* present participle of *transparēre* "to show through," from Latin *trans-* + *parēre* "to show oneself, appear"] ***synonyms*** see CLEAR — **trans·par·ent·ly** *adv* — **trans·par·ent·ness** *n*

tran·spi·ra·tion \ˌtrans-pə-ˈrā-shən\ *n* : the act or process or an instance of transpiring; *esp* : the process by which plants give off water vapor through the stomata in their leaves

tran·spire \trans-ˈpīr\ *vb* **1** : to pass off or give passage to (a fluid) through small openings; *esp* : to excrete (as water) in the form of vapor through a living membrane (as the skin) **2** : to give off vaporous material (as watery vapor from the surfaces of leaves); *esp* : to give off watery vapor through the stomata in leaves ⟨a plant *transpires* more freely on a hot dry day⟩ **3** : to pass in the form of a vapor from a living body ⟨water *transpires* through the skin⟩ **4** : to become known or apparent ⟨it *transpired* that the wrong name was called⟩ **5** : to come to pass : OCCUR ⟨a great deal *transpired* in your absence⟩ [Middle French *transpirer,* from Medieval Latin *transpirare,* from Latin *trans-* + *spirare* "to breathe"] ***synonyms*** see HAPPEN

usage The use of *transpire* to mean "to come to pass" or "occur" ⟨the events that *transpired* last night⟩ is often criticized as incorrect by those who suppose "to become known" or "turn out" to be the only meaning of the word. However, the disputed use is firmly established in both informal and formal prose.

[1]**trans·plant** \trans-ˈplant\ *vb* **1** : to lift and reset (a plant) in another soil or situation ⟨*transplant* seedlings⟩ **2** : to remove from one place and settle elsewhere ⟨*transplanted* beavers to other parts of the state⟩ ⟨a New Yorker *transplanted* to the west coast⟩ **3** : to transfer (an organ or tissue) from one part or individual to another **4** : to tolerate being transplanted ⟨does not *transplant* as well as other plant varieties⟩ — **trans·plant·able** \-ə-bəl\ *adj* — **trans·plan·ta·tion** \ˌtrans-ˌplan-ˈtā-shən\ *n* — **trans·plant·er** \trans-ˈplant-ər\ *n*

[2]**trans·plant** \ˈtrans-ˌplant\ *n* **1** : something or someone transplanted **2** : the act or process of transplanting

trans·po·lar \trans-ˈpō-lər, ˈtrans-\ *adj* : going or extending across either of the polar regions

[1]**trans·port** \trans-ˈpōrt, -ˈpȯrt\ *vt* **1** : to transfer or convey from one place to another : CARRY **2** : to carry away with strong and often intensely pleasant emotion ⟨*transported* by the beauty of the music⟩ ⟨*transported* with delight⟩ **3** : to send to a penal colony overseas [Latin *transportare,* from *trans-* + *portare* "to carry"] — **trans·port·abil·i·ty** \-ˌpōrt-ə-ˈbil-ət-ē -ˌpȯrt-\ *n* — **trans·port·able** \-ˈpōrt-ə-bəl, -ˈpȯrt-\ *adj* — **trans·port·er** *n*

\ə\ **abut**	\au̇\ **out**	\i\ **tip**	\ȯ\ **saw**	\u̇\ **foot**
\ər\ **further**	\ch\ **chin**	\ī\ **life**	\ȯi\ **coin**	\y\ **yet**
\a\ **mat**	\e\ **pet**	\j\ **job**	\th\ **thin**	\yü\ **few**
\ā\ **take**	\ē\ **easy**	\ng\ **sing**	\th\ **this**	\yu̇\ **cure**
\ä\ **cot, cart**	\g\ **go**	\ō\ **bone**	\ü\ **food**	\zh\ **vision**

[2]trans·port \ˈtrans-ˌpōrt, -ˌpȯrt\ *n* **1** : the act of transporting : TRANSPORTATION **2** : strong or intensely pleasurable emotion : ECSTASY, RAPTURE ⟨*transports* of joy⟩ **3 a** : a ship for carrying soldiers or military equipment **b** : a vehicle used to transport persons or goods **c** : a system of public transportation

trans·por·ta·tion \ˌtrans-pər-ˈtā-shən\ *n* **1** : an act, process, or instance of transporting or being transported **2** : banishment to a penal colony **3 a** : means of conveyance or travel from one place to another **b** : public conveyance of passengers or goods especially as a commercial enterprise

trans·pose \trans-ˈpōz\ *vt* **1** : TRANSFORM 1a **2** : TRANSLATE 2 **3** : to transfer from one place or period to another : SHIFT **4** : to change the relative place or normal order of **5** : to write or perform (a musical composition) in a different key **6** : to bring (a term) from one side of an algebraic equation to the other with change of sign ⟨given the equation $y = 3-2x$, *transpose* the $2x$ to get $y + 2x = 3$⟩ [Medieval French *transposer,* from Latin *transponere* "to change the position of," from *trans-* + *ponere* "to put, place"] ***synonyms*** see REVERSE — **trans·pos·able** \-ˈpō-zə-bəl\ *adj* — **trans·po·si·tion** \ˌtrans-pə-ˈzish-ən\ *n*

trans·sex·u·al \trans-ˈseksh-wəl, ˈtrans-, -ə-wəl, -ˈsek-shəl\ *n* : a person whose sex at birth differs from that with which he or she identifies and who may therefore seek to change sex especially by undergoing therapy with hormones and surgery to obtain the necessary physical appearance (as by changing the sex organs) — **transsexual** *adj* — **trans·sex·u·al·ism** \-wə-ˌliz-əm, -shə-ˌliz-\ *n* — **trans·sex·u·al·i·ty** \-ˌsek-shə-ˈwal-ət-ē\ *n*

trans·ship \tran-ˈship, trans-\ *vb* : to transfer for further transportation from one means of transport to another — **trans·ship·ment** \-mənt\ *n*

tran·sub·stan·ti·ate \ˌtran-səb-ˈstan-chē-ˌāt\ *vb* : to change into another substance [Medieval Latin *transubstantiare,* from Latin *trans-* + *substantia* "substance"]

tran·sub·stan·ti·a·tion \-ˌstan-chē-ˈā-shən\ *n* **1** : an act or instance of transubstantiating or being transubstantiated **2** : the miraculous change by which according to Roman Catholic and Eastern Orthodox belief the consecrated bread and wine at Mass become the body and blood of Christ while maintaining their appearances

trans·ura·ni·um \ˌtran-shə-ˈrā-nē-əm, ˌtran-zhə-\ *or* **trans·ura·nic** \-ˈran-ik, -ˈrā-nik\ *adj* : having an atomic number greater than that of uranium

trans·ver·sal \trans-ˈvər-səl, tranz-\ *n* : a line that intersects a system of lines

[1]trans·verse \trans-ˈvərs, tranz-ˈ, ˈtrans-ˌ, ˈtranz-\ *adj* : lying or being across : set crosswise [Latin *transversus,* from *transvertere* "to turn across," from *trans-* + *vertere* "to turn"] — **trans·verse·ly** *adv*

[2]trans·verse \ˈtrans-ˌvərs, ˈtranz-\ *n* : something that is transverse

transverse wave *n* : a wave in which the vibrating element moves in a direction perpendicular to the direction of advance of the wave

trans·ves·tite \trans-ˈves-ˌtīt, tranz-\ *n* : a person and especially a male who adopts the dress and often the behavior typical of the opposite sex [German *Transvestit,* from Latin *trans-* + *vestire* "to clothe"] — **trans·ves·tism** \-ˌtiz-əm\ *n* — **transvestite** *adj*

[1]trap \ˈtrap\ *n* **1** : a device (as a snare or pitfall) for catching animals; *esp* : one that holds by springing shut suddenly **2** : something by which one is caught or stopped unawares **3 a** : a device for hurling clay pigeons into the air **b** : SAND TRAP **4** : a light usually one-horse carriage with springs **5** : any of various devices for preventing passage of something often while allowing other matter to proceed; *esp* : a device for drains or sewers consisting of a bend or partitioned chamber in which the liquid forms a seal to prevent the passage of sewer gas **6** *pl* : a group of percussion instruments (as in a dance band) [Old English *treppe* and Medieval French *trape*]

[2]trap *vb* **trapped; trap·ping** **1 a** : to catch in or as if in a trap **b** : to place in a restricted position : CONFINE **2** : to provide with a trap **3** : to separate out (as water from steam) **4** : to engage in trapping animals (as for fur) ***synonyms*** see CATCH — **trap·per** *n*

[3]trap *vt* **trapped; trap·ping** : to decorate with or as if with trappings [Middle English *trappen,* from *trappe* "caparison," from Medieval French *trape*]

[4]trap *n* : TRAPROCK [Swedish *trapp,* from *trappa* "stair," from Low German *trappe*]

trap·door \ˈtrap-ˈdōr, -ˈdȯr\ *n* : a lifting or sliding door covering an opening in a roof, ceiling, or floor

trap–door spider *n* : any of various often large spiders that build silk-lined underground nests topped with a hinged lid

tra·peze \tra-ˈpēz\ *n* : an acrobatic apparatus consisting of a short horizontal bar suspended at a height by two parallel ropes [French *trapèze,* from New Latin *trapezium* "trapezium"]

tra·pez·ist \-ˈpē-zəst\ *n* : a performer on the trapeze

tra·pe·zi·um \trə-ˈpē-zē-əm\ *n, pl* **-zi·ums** *or* **-zia** \-ze-ə\ **1** : a quadrilateral with no parallel sides **2** *British* : TRAPEZOID 2 [New Latin, from Greek *trapezion,* literally, "small table," from *trapeza* "table," from *tra-* "four" + *peza* "foot"]

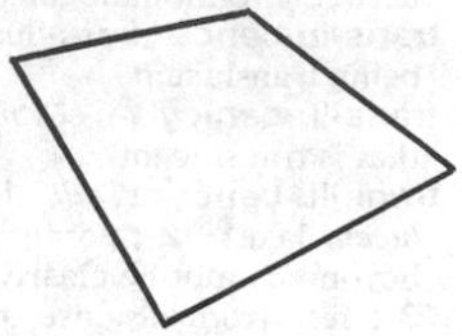
trapezium 1

tra·pe·zi·us \-zē-əs\ *n* : a large flat triangular superficial muscle of each side of the back [New Latin, from *trapezium;* from the figure formed by the two muscles]

trap·e·zoid \ˈtrap-ə-ˌzȯid\ *n* **1** *British* : TRAPEZIUM 1 **2** : a quadrilateral having only two sides parallel — **trap·e·zoi·dal** \ˌtrap-ə-ˈzȯid-l\ *adj*

trap·line \ˈtrap-ˌlīn\ *n* : a line or series of traps especially for fur-bearing animals; *also* : the route along which such traps are set

trap·ping \ˈtrap-ing\ *n* **1** : CAPARISON 1 — usually used in plural **2** *pl* : outward decoration or dress **3** *pl* : outward signs ⟨the *trappings* of success⟩

Trap·pist \ˈtrap-əst\ *n* : a monk of an austere branch of the Roman Catholic Cistercian Order [French *trappiste,* from La *Trappe,* France, where the branch was established] — **Trappist** *adj*

trap·rock \ˈtrap-ˈräk\ *n* : any of various fine-grained igneous rocks used especially in road making [[4]*trap*]

traps \ˈtraps\ *n pl* : personal belongings : LUGGAGE [Middle English *trappe* "caparison"]

trap·shoot·ing \ˈtrap-ˌshüt-ing\ *n* : shooting at clay pigeons thrown from a trap into the air away from the shooters — **trap·shoot·er** \-ˌshüt-ər\ *n*

tra·pun·to \trə-ˈpün-tō, -ˈpu̇n-\ *n, pl* **-tos** : a type of quilting in which a design outlined in a single row of stitches is padded from behind to produce a decorative raised effect [Italian, from *trapungere* "to embroider," from *tra-* "across" (from Latin *trans-*) + *pungere* "to prick," from Latin]

trash \ˈtrash\ *n* **1** : something worth little or nothing: as **a** : [1]JUNK 2a, RUBBISH **b** : empty talk : NONSENSE **c** : low-grade or worthless artistic matter **2** : something in a crumbled or broken condition or mass; *esp* : debris from pruning or processing plant material **3** : a worthless person; *also* : such persons as a group : RIFFRAFF [Middle English *trasch* "fall leaves and twigs," perhaps of Scandinavian origin]

trashy \ˈtrash-ē\ *adj* **trash·i·er; -est** : resembling trash : WORTHLESS — **trash·i·ness** *n*

trat·to·ria \ˌträt-ə-ˈrē-ə\ *n, pl* **-ri·as** *or* **-rie** \-ˈrē-ˌā\ : an eating house : RESTAURANT [Italian]

trau·ma \ˈtrau̇-mə, ˈtrȯ-\ *n, pl* **traumas** *also* **trau·ma·ta** \-mət-ə\ **1 a** : a serious bodily injury (as that caused by an accident or violent act) ⟨head *trauma*⟩ **b** : a disordered psychological or behavioral state resulting from severe mental or emotional stress or injury **2** : a cause of trauma [Greek *traumat-, trauma* "wound"] — **trau·mat·ic** \trə-ˈmat-ik, trȯ-, trau̇-\ *adj* — **trau·mat·i·cal·ly** \-ˈmat-i-kə-lē, -klē\ *adv*

trau·ma·tize \ˈtrau̇-mə-ˌtīz, ˈtrȯ-\ *vt* : to inflict trauma upon ⟨was *traumatized* by the accident⟩

[1]tra·vail \trə-ˈvāl, ˈtrav-ˌāl\ *n* **1 a** : work especially of a painful or laborious nature : TOIL **b** : a piece of work : TASK **c** : AGONY 1a, TORMENT **2** : LABOR 1c, CHILDBIRTH [Medieval French, from *travailler* "to torment, labor," derived from Late Latin *trepalium* "instrument of torture," Latin *tripalis* "having 3 stakes," from *tri-* + *palus* "stake"]

[2]travail *vi* : to work hard : TOIL

[1]trav·el \ˈtrav-əl\ *vb* **-eled** *or* **-elled; -el·ing** *or* **-el·ling** \ˈtrav-ling, -ə-ling\ **1** : to journey from place to place or to a distant place **2** : to journey from place to place as a sales representative or business agent ⟨*travels* frequently for work⟩ **3 a** : to move or advance from one place to another ⟨goods *traveling* by plane⟩ ⟨the news *traveled* fast⟩ **b** : to undergo transportation ⟨a pasta dish that *travels* well⟩ **c** : to walk or run with a basketball in violation of the rules **4** : to journey through or over : TRAVERSE ⟨this trail can be *traveled* only on horseback⟩ [Middle English *travelen, travailen* "to torment, labor, strive, journey," from Medieval French *travailler*]

Word History For many of us in the U.S. travel is usually for pleasure and work is not very taxing physically, so that we are unlikely to associate travel with hard labor, and labor with torture. However, travel, labor, and torture are all bound up in the history of the word *travel*. The ultimate source of both *travel* and *travail* is an unattested spoken Latin verb *trepaliare,* "to torture," a derivative of Late Latin *trepalium,* a name for an instrument of torture. *Trepaliare* developed into Medieval French *travailler,* which meant "to torture, torment" and intransitively "to suffer, labor." Middle English borrowed the French verb as well as its noun derivative *travail,* and Modern English *travail* preserves the original sense "torment." But the difficulties in getting from place to place in the Middle Ages—when any journey was a wearisome, dangerous effort and a pilgrimage to a distant religious shrine a real act of devotion—led medieval Englishmen to apply *travailen,* "to labor," to the act of making a trip. Shift in sense and weakening of the vowel in the second syllable eventually led to a distinction between *travail* and *travel*.

2travel *n* **1 a** : the act of traveling : PASSAGE **b** : JOURNEY, TRIP — often used in plural **2** *pl* : an account of one's travels **3** : the number traveling : TRAFFIC **4 a** : MOVEMENT ⟨the *travel* of satellites around the earth⟩ **b** : the motion of a piece of machinery; *esp* : reciprocating motion

travel agency *n* : an agency engaged in selling and arranging transportation, accommodations, tours, and trips for travelers — called also *travel bureau* — **travel agent** *n*

trav·eled *or* **trav·elled** \ˈtrav-əld\ *adj* **1** : experienced in travel ⟨a widely *traveled* journalist⟩ **2** : used by travelers ⟨a heavily *traveled* road⟩

trav·el·er *or* **trav·el·ler** \ˈtrav-lər, -ə-lər\ *n* : one that travels

traveler's check *n* : a draft purchased from a bank or express company and signed by the purchaser at the time of purchase and again at the time of cashing

traveling *or* **travelling** *adj* **1** : that travels ⟨a *traveling* opera company⟩ **2** : carried, used, or accompanying a traveler ⟨a *traveling* alarm clock⟩ ⟨a *traveling* companion⟩

traveling bag *n* : SUITCASE

traveling salesman *n* : a traveling representative of a business concern who solicits orders

trav·el·ogue *or* **trav·el·og** \ˈtrav-ə-ˌlȯg, -ˌläg\ *n* **1** : a usually illustrated lecture or film on travel **2** : a piece of writing about travel [*travel* + *-logue*]

tra·vers·al \trə-ˈvər-səl\ *n* : the act or an instance of traversing

1trav·erse \ˈtrav-ərs, *especially for 5 also* trə-ˈvərs\ *n* **1** : something that crosses or lies across **2** : OBSTACLE, ADVERSITY **3** : a gallery providing access from one side to another in a large building **4** : a route or way across or over; *esp* : a curve or zigzag path along the face of a steep slope **5** : the act or an instance of traversing : CROSSING **6** : a protective projecting wall or bank of earth in a trench **7** : a line surveyed across a plot of ground [Medieval French *travers* (as in *a travers, de travers* "across"), from Latin *transversum* (as in *in transversum* "set crosswise"), neuter of *transversus* "lying across," from *trans-* + *-versum* (as in *adversum* "adverse")]

2tra·verse \trə-ˈvərs\ *vb* **1** : to go against or act in oppostion to : OPPOSE **2** : to pass through, across, or over **3** : to make a study of : EXAMINE **4** : to ascend, descend, or cross (a slope or gap) at an angle **5** : to move back and forth or from side to side **6** : to move or turn laterally : SWIVEL **7** : to climb or ski at an angle or in a zigzag course [Medieval French *traverser,* from Late Latin *transversare,* from Latin *transversus*] — **tra·vers·able** \-ˈvər-sə-bəl\ *adj* — **tra·vers·er** *n*

3trav·erse \ˈtrav-ərs, -ˌərs; trə-ˈvərs\ *adj* : lying across : TRANSVERSE

trav·er·tine \ˈtrav-ər-ˌtēn, -tən\ *n* : a mineral consisting of a massive usually layered calcium carbonate formed by deposition from spring waters or especially from hot springs [French *travertin,* from Italian *trevertino, travertino,* from Latin *tiburtinus* "of Tivoli," from *Tibur* "Tivoli"]

1trav·es·ty \ˈtrav-ə-stē\ *n, pl* **-ties** **1** : a burlesque and usually grotesque translation or imitation **2** : a grossly inferior imitation or likeness ⟨a *travesty* of justice⟩ [obsolete *travesty* "disguised, parodied," from French *travestir* "to disguise," from Italian *travestire,* from *tra-* "trans-" + *vestire* "to dress," from Latin, from *vestis* "garment"] ***synonyms*** see CARICATURE

2travesty *vt* **-tied; -ty·ing** : to make a travesty of : PARODY

tra·vois \trə-ˈvȯi, ˈtrav-ˌȯi\ *n, pl* **tra·vois** \-ˈvȯiz, -ˌȯiz\ *also* **tra·vois·es** \-ˈvȯi-zəz, -ˌȯi-zəz\ : a vehicle used by Plains Indians consisting of two trailing poles serving as shafts and bearing a platform or net for the load [American French *travail,* from Canadian French, "shaft of a cart," from Middle French *traveil* "catafalque, prop," from Late Lain *trepalium* "instrument of torture"]

1trawl \ˈtrȯl\ *vb* : to fish or catch with a trawl [probably from obsolete Dutch *tragelen*]

2trawl *n* **1** : a large conical net dragged along the sea bottom in gathering fish or other marine life **2** : SETLINE

trawl·er \ˈtrȯ-lər\ *n* : a person or vessel that fishes by trawling

tray \ˈtrā\ *n* : an open receptacle with flat bottom and low rim for holding, carrying, or exhibiting articles ⟨a serving *tray*⟩ ⟨the *trays* of a trunk⟩ [Old English *trīg, trēg*]

treach·er·ous \ˈtrech-rəs, -ə-rəs\ *adj* **1** : guilty of or inclined to treachery **2 a** : not reliable ⟨a *treacherous* memory⟩ **b** : giving a false appearance of safety ⟨*treacherous* quicksand⟩ — **treach·er·ous·ly** *adv* — **treach·er·ous·ness** *n*

treach·ery \ˈtrech-rē, -ə-rē\ *n, pl* **-er·ies** **1** : violation of allegiance or of faith and confidence : TREASON **2** : an act of treason [Medieval French *trecherie,* from *trecher* "to deceive"]

trea·cle \ˈtrē-kəl\ *n* **1** *chiefly British* : MOLASSES **2** : something (as a tone of voice) heavily sweet and cloying [Medieval French *triacle,* an antidote against poison, from Latin *theriaca,* from Greek *thēriakē* "antidote against a poisonous bite," derived from *thēr* "wild animal"] — **trea·cly** \-kə-lē, -klē\ *adj*

1tread \ˈtred\ *vb* **trod** \ˈträd\; **trod·den** \ˈträd-n\ *or* **trod; tread·ing** **1 a** : to step or walk on or over **b** : to walk or proceed along : FOLLOW **2 a** : to beat or press with the feet : TRAMPLE **b** : to bring under control or put down by force **3 a** : to form by treading ⟨*tread* a path⟩ **b** : to execute by stepping or dancing ⟨*tread* a measure⟩ **4 a** : to set foot **b** : to put one's foot : STEP [Old English *tredan*] — **tread·er** *n* — **tread water** : to keep the body nearly upright in the water and the head above water by a treading motion of the feet usually aided by the hands

2tread *n* **1** : a mark made by or as if by treading **2** : the action, manner, or sound of treading **3 a** : the part of a sole that touches the ground **b** : the part of a wheel that bears on a road or rail; *esp* : the ridges or grooves on the surface of a tire **4** : the distance between the points of contact with the ground of the two front wheels or the two rear wheels of a vehicle **5** : the horizontal part of a step

1trea·dle \ˈtred-l\ *n* : a lever or other device pressed by the foot to drive a machine [Old English *tredel* "step of a stair," from *tredan* "to tread"]

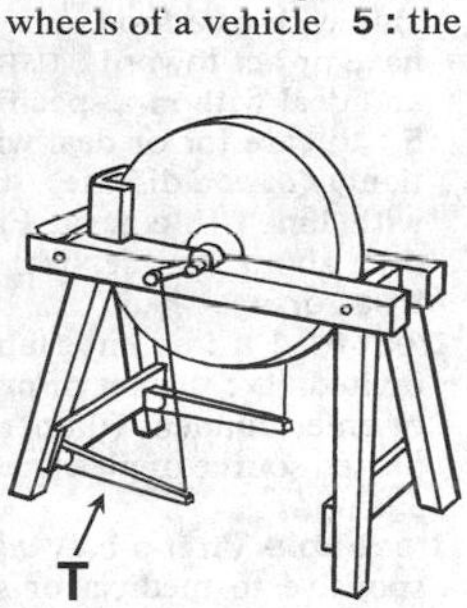

T treadle

2treadle *vb* **trea·dled; trea·dling** \ˈtred-ling, -l-ing\ : to operate a treadle or operate the treadle of

tread·mill \ˈtred-ˌmil\ *n* **1 a** : a device moved by persons treading on steps set around the rim of a wide wheel or by animals walking on an endless belt **b** : a device having an endless belt on which an individual walks or runs in place for exercise or physiological testing **2** : a wearisome or monotonous routine

trea·son \ˈtrēz-n\ *n* **1** : the betrayal of a trust : TREACHERY **2** : the offense of attempting by overt acts to overthrow the government of the state to which one owes allegiance or to kill or personally injure the ruler or the ruler's family [Medieval French *traisun,* from Latin *traditio* "act of handing over, teaching, tradition"]

Word History *Treason* and *tradition* are derived from the same Latin source. Latin *traditio* means "teaching" or "tradi-

\ə\ **abut**	\au̇\ **out**	\i\ **tip**	\ȯ\ **saw**	\u̇\ **foot**
\ər\ **further**	\ch\ **chin**	\ī\ **life**	\ȯi\ **coin**	\y\ **yet**
\a\ **mat**	\e\ **pet**	\j\ **job**	\th\ **thin**	\yü\ **few**
\ā\ **take**	\ē\ **easy**	\ng\ **sing**	\t͟h\ **this**	\yu̇\ **cure**
\ä\ **cot, cart**	\g\ **go**	\ō\ **bone**	\ü\ **food**	\zh\ **vision**

tion," but these senses are developed from its literal sense, "the act of handing over something." Tradition is maintained by passing information from one generation to another, whereas treason is committed when someone who has been entrusted with information passes it on to someone else. The difference in form between the two words can be accounted for by the fact that *treason* came to us through Medieval French, where *traditio* underwent sound change, while *tradition* was later borrowed directly from Latin.

trea·son·able \ˈtrēz-nə-bəl, -n-ə-bəl\ *adj* : relating to, consisting of, or involving treason — **trea·son·ably** \-blē\ *adv*

trea·son·ous \ˈtrēz-nəs, -n-əs\ *adj* : TREASONABLE

¹trea·sure \ˈtrezh-ər, ˈtrāzh-\ *n* **1 a** (1) : wealth (as money, jewels, or precious metals) stored up or hoarded ⟨buried *treasure*⟩ (2) : RICHES **b** : a store of money in reserve **2** : something of great worth or value; *also* : a person esteemed as rare or precious [Medieval French *tresor,* from Latin *thesaurus,* from Greek *thēsauros*]

²treasure *vt* **trea·sured; trea·sur·ing** \ˈtrezh-ring, ˈtrāzh-, -ə-ring\ **1** : to collect and store up (something of value) for future use **2** : to hold or keep as precious : CHERISH — **trea·sur·able** \ˈtrezh-rə-bəl, ˈtrāzh-, -ə-rə-\ *adj*

trea·sur·er \ˈtrezh-rər, ˈtrezh-ər-ər, ˈtrāzh-\ *n* : a person trusted with charge of a treasure or a treasury; *esp* : an officer of a club, business, or government who has charge of money taken in and paid out — **trea·sur·er·ship** \-ˌship\ *n*

treasure trove \ˈtrezh-ər-ˌtrōv, ˈtrāzh-\ *n* **1** : treasure found buried in the ground or hidden away and of unknown ownership **2** : a valuable discovery, resource, or collection [Medieval French *tresor trové,* literally, "found treasure"]

trea·sury \ˈtrezh-rē, ˈtrāzh-, -ə-rē\ *n, pl* **trea·sur·ies** **1 a** : a place in which stores of wealth are kept **b** : the place of deposit and disbursement of collected funds; *esp* : one where public revenues are deposited, kept, and disbursed **c** : funds kept in a place of deposit **2** *cap* : a governmental department in charge of finances **3** : a repository for treasures ⟨a *treasury* of poems⟩

treasury note *n* **1** : a currency note issued by the U.S. Treasury in payment for silver bullion purchased under the Sherman Silver Purchase Act of 1890 **2** : a U.S. government bond usually with a maturity of not less than one year or more than seven years

¹treat \ˈtrēt\ *vb* **1** : to discuss terms of accommodation or settlement : NEGOTIATE ⟨*treat* with the enemy⟩ **2 a** : to deal with a matter especially in writing : DISCOURSE ⟨books *treating* of crime⟩ **b** : to present or represent artistically **c** : to deal with : HANDLE **3 a** : to pay for another's entertainment **b** : to provide with free food, entertainment, or enjoyment **4 a** : to behave or act toward : USE ⟨*treat* a horse cruelly⟩ **b** : to regard and deal with in a specified manner ⟨*treat* this as confidential⟩ **5** : to care for or deal with medically or surgically ⟨*treat* a patient⟩ ⟨*treat* a disease⟩ **6** : to subject to some action ⟨*treat* soil with lime⟩ [Medieval French *traiter,* from Latin *tractare* "to drag about, handle, deal with," from *trahere* "to drag, pull"] — **treat·er** *n*

²treat *n* **1 a** : an entertainment given without expense to those invited **b** : the act of providing another with free food, drink, or entertainment ⟨dinner was my *treat*⟩ **2** : an especially unexpected source of pleasure or amusement ⟨the *treat* of seeing you again⟩

treat·able \ˈtrēt-ə-bəl\ *adj* : capable of being treated; *esp* : responsive to medical or surgical treatment ⟨a *treatable* condition⟩ — **treat·abil·i·ty** \ˌtrēt-ə-ˈbil-ət-ē\ *n*

trea·tise \ˈtrēt-əs\ *n* : a book or an article treating a subject systematically ⟨a *treatise* on war⟩ [Medieval French *tretiz, tretez, traitet,* from Medieval Latin *tractatus,* from Latin *tractare* "to handle, deal with"]

treat·ment \ˈtrēt-mənt\ *n* **1** : the act or manner or an instance of treating someone or something **2** : a substance or technique used in treating ⟨a beauty *treatment*⟩

trea·ty \ˈtrēt-ē\ *n, pl* **treaties** : an agreement or arrangement made by negotiation; *esp* : a contract between two or more states or sovereigns [Medieval French *treté,* from *treter, traiter* "to deal with, discuss"]

treaty port *n* : a port or inland city of China, Japan, and Korea formerly open by treaty to foreign commerce

¹tre·ble \ˈtreb-əl\ *n* **1 a** : the highest of the four voice parts in vocal music : SOPRANO **b** : a singer or instrument having the highest range **c** : a high-pitched voice, tone, or sound **d** : the upper half of the musical pitch range — compare BASS **2** : something triple in construction, uses, amount, number, or value [Middle English, "the highest part in a three-part composition," from *treble,* adj.]

²treble *adj* **1 a** : having three parts **b** : triple in number or amount **2 a** : relating to or having the range of a musical treble ⟨*treble* voices⟩ **b** : HIGH-PITCHED, SHRILL [Medieval French, from Latin *triplus* "triple"] — **tre·bly** \ˈtreb-lē, -ə-lē\ *adv*

³treble *vb* **tre·bled; tre·bling** \ˈtreb-ling, -ə-ling\ **1** : to make or become three times the size, amount, or number ⟨*treble* its weight⟩ **2** : to sing treble

treble clef *n* **1** : a clef that places G above middle C on the second line of the staff **2** : TREBLE STAFF [from its use for the notation of treble parts]

treble staff *n* : the musical staff carrying the treble clef

¹tree \ˈtrē\ *n* **1 a** : a woody perennial plant having a single usually tall main stem with few or no branches on its lower part **b** : a shrub or herb that looks like a tree ⟨rose *trees*⟩ ⟨a banana *tree*⟩ **2** : a piece of wood (as a post or pole) usually adapted to a particular use or forming part of a structure or implement **3** : something in the form of or resembling a tree: as **a** : a diagram that depicts a branching from an original stem ⟨genealogical *tree*⟩ **b** : a much-branched system of channels especially in an animal body ⟨the bronchi together with their branches make up the bronchial *tree*⟩ **4** : a structure typically or originally of wood: as **a** : SHOE TREE **b** *archaic* : GALLOWS [Old English *trēow*] — **tree·less** \-ləs\ *adj* — **tree·like** \-ˌlīk\ *adj*

²tree *vt* **treed; tree·ing** **1 a** : to drive to or up a tree ⟨*treed* by a bull⟩ **b** : to put into a position of extreme disadvantage : CORNER; *esp* : to bring to bay **2** : to plant or cover with trees **3** : to furnish or fit (as a shoe) with a tree

treed \ˈtrēd\ *adj* **1** : driven up a tree **2** : planted or grown with trees : WOODED

tree farm *n* : an area of forest land managed to ensure continuous commercial production — **tree farmer** *n* — **tree farming** *n*

tree fern *n* : a tropical fern with a woody stalk and a crown of large often feathery fronds

tree frog *n* : any of numerous often tree-dwelling tailless amphibians (as the spring peeper) that typically have adhesive disks on the toes

tree·hop·per \ˈtrē-ˌhäp-ər\ *n* : any of several small leaping insects that are related to the leafhoppers and feed on sap from branches and twigs

tree house *n* : a structure (as a playhouse) built among the branches of a tree

tree line *n* : TIMBERLINE

tree of heaven : a Chinese tree that is widely planted as a shade and ornamental tree and has leaves divided into many leaflets and ill-smelling male flowers

tree ring *n* : ANNUAL RING

tree shrew *n* : any of a family of southeast Asian mammals that resemble squirrels, often frequent trees, feed chiefly on insects and fruit, and are sometimes classified as true insectivores and sometimes as primitive primates

tree shrew

tree toad *n* : TREE FROG

tree·top \ˈtrē-ˌtäp\ *n* **1** : the topmost part of a tree **2** *pl* : the height or line marked by the tops of a group of trees

tre·foil \ˈtrē-ˌfȯil, ˈtref-ˌȯil\ *n* **1 a** : CLOVER **b** : any of several herbs of the legume family with leaves that have or appear to have three leaflets **2** : an ornament or symbol in the form of a 3-parted leaf [Medieval French, from Latin *trifolium,* from *tri-* + *folium* "leaf"]

trek \ˈtrek\ *vi* **trekked; trek·king** **1** *chiefly South African* : to migrate by ox wagon or in a train of such wagons **2** : to make one's way arduously [Afrikaans, from Dutch *trecken* "to pull, haul, migrate"] — **trek** *n* — **trek·ker** *n*

¹trel·lis \ˈtrel-əs\ *n* : a frame of latticework used especially as a screen or a support for climbing plants [Medieval French *treleis,* from *treille* "arbor," from Latin *trichila* "summerhouse"] — **trel·lised** \-əst\ *adj*

[2]trellis *vt* **1 :** to provide with or train on a trellis ‹*trellis* a vine› **2 :** to cross or interlace on or through : INTERWEAVE

trel·lis·work \ˈtrel-ə-ˌswərk\ *n* : LATTICEWORK

trem·a·tode \ˈtrem-ə-ˌtōd\ *n* : any of a class (Trematoda) of parasitic flatworms including the flukes [derived from Greek *trēmatōdēs* "pierced with holes," from *trēma* "hole," from *tetrainein* "to bore"] — **trematode** *adj*

[1]trem·ble \ˈtrem-bəl\ *vi* **trem·bled; trem·bling** \-bə-ling, -bling\ **1 :** to shake involuntarily (as with fear or cold) : SHIVER **2 :** to move, sound, or occur as if shaken or tremulous ‹his voice *trembled*› **3 :** to be affected with great fear or anxiety ‹*tremble* for the safety of a friend› [Medieval French *trembler,* from Medieval Latin *tremulare,* from Latin *tremulus* "tremulous"] — **trem·bler** \-bə-lər, -blər\ *n*

[2]tremble *n* **1 :** a fit or spell of involuntary shaking or quivering **2 :** a tremor or series of tremors

trem·bly \ˈtrem-bə-lē, -blē\ *adj* : marked by trembling

tre·men·dous \tri-ˈmen-dəs\ *adj* **1 :** such as may excite trembling or arouse dread, awe, or terror **2 :** astonishing by reason of extreme size, power, greatness, or excellence ‹*tremendous* problems› ‹a writer of *tremendous* talent› [Latin *tremendus,* from *tremere* "to tremble"] ***synonyms*** see MONSTROUS — **tre·men·dous·ly** *adv* — **tre·men·dous·ness** *n*

trem·o·lo \ˈtrem-ə-ˌlō\ *n, pl* **-los** **1 a :** the rapid reiteration of a musical tone or of alternating tones to produce a tremulous effect **b :** a perceptible rapid variation of pitch in singing similar to the vibrato of a stringed instrument **2 :** a mechanical device in an organ for causing a tremulous effect [Italian, from *tremolo* "tremulous," from Latin *tremulus*]

trem·or \ˈtrem-ər\ *n* **1 :** a trembling or shaking usually from weakness or disease **2 :** a quivering or vibratory motion; *esp* **:** a small movement of the earth before or after an earthquake **3 :** a feeling of uncertainty or insecurity ‹a *tremor* of hesitation› [Medieval French *tremour,* from Latin *tremor,* from *tremere* "to tremble"]

trem·u·lous \ˈtrem-yə-ləs\ *adj* **1 :** characterized by or affected with trembling or tremors ‹*tremulous* hands› **2 :** affected with timidity : TIMOROUS ‹a shy *tremulous* child› **3 :** such as is caused by nervousness or shakiness ‹a *tremulous* smile› **4 :** exceedingly sensitive : easily shaken or disturbed [Latin *tremulus,* from *tremere* "to tremble"] — **trem·u·lous·ly** *adv* — **trem·u·lous·ness** *n*

[1]trench \ˈtrench\ *n* **1 a :** a long narrow cut in land : DITCH **b :** a long ditch protected by a bank of earth thrown before it that is used to shelter soldiers **2 :** a long narrow steep-sided depression in the ocean floor [Medieval French *trenche* "act of cutting, ditch," from *trencher* "to cut"]

[2]trench *vb* **1 :** to protect with or as if with a trench **2 :** to cut a trench in : DITCH **3 :** to come close : VERGE ‹the answer *trenched* on rudeness›

tren·chan·cy \ˈtren-chən-sē\ *n* : the quality of being trenchant

tren·chant \ˈtren-chənt\ *adj* **1 :** having a sharp edge or point : CUTTING ‹a *trenchant* blade› ‹*trenchant* sarcasm› **2 :** vigorously effective and articulate ‹a *trenchant* analysis› **3 :** sharply clear : PENETRATING ‹a *trenchant* view of the situation› [Medieval French, present participle of *trencher* "to cut"] ***synonyms*** see INCISIVE — **tren·chant·ly** *adv*

trench coat *n* **1 :** a waterproof overcoat with a removable lining designed for wear in trenches **2 :** a loose double-breasted raincoat with deep pockets, a belt, and straps on the shoulders

[1]tren·cher \ˈtren-chər\ *n* : a wooden platter for serving food [Medieval French *trenchour* "knife, serving platter," from *trencher*]

[2]trench·er \ˈtren-chər\ *n* : one that digs trenches; *esp* **:** a usually self-propelled excavating machine typically employing a bucket conveyor and used to dig trenches especially for pipelines and cables

tren·cher·man \-mən\ *n* **1 :** a hearty eater **2** *archaic* **:** HANGER-ON, SPONGER

trench fever *n* : a disease that is marked by fever and pain (as in joints) and is caused by a bacterium transmitted by the body louse

trench foot *n* : a painful foot disorder resembling frostbite and resulting from prolonged exposure to cold and wet

trench mouth *n* **1 :** VINCENT'S ANGINA **2 :** VINCENT'S INFECTION

[1]trend \ˈtrend\ *vi* **1 a :** to extend in a general direction **b :** to veer in a new direction : BEND **2 a :** to show a tendency : INCLINE **b :** SHIFT ‹opinions *trending* toward conservatism› [Old English *trendan* "to turn, revolve"]

[2]trend *n* **1 :** general direction taken ‹easterly *trend* of the shoreline› **2 a :** a prevailing tendency or inclination ‹economic *trends*› **b :** a general movement : SWING ‹the *trend* toward suburban living› **c :** a current style or preference ‹new fashion *trends*› **d :** a line of development ‹new *trends* in research› ***synonyms*** see TENDENCY

trendy \ˈtren-dē\ *adj* **trend·i·er; -est** **1 :** very fashionable : UP-TO-DATE **2 :** marked by passing or superficial appeal or taste

tre·pan \tri-ˈpan\ *vt* **tre·panned; tre·pan·ning :** to remove a disk from (the skull) [Medieval Latin *trepanum* "trephine," from Greek *trypanon* "auger," from *trypan* "to bore," from *trypa* "hole"] — **trep·a·na·tion** \ˌtrep-ə-ˈnā-shən\ *n*

tre·pang \tri-ˈpang\ *n* : any of several large Pacific sea cucumbers that are boiled, dried, and used especially in Asian cooking — called also *bêche-de-mer* [Malay *tĕripang*]

tre·phine \ˈtrē-ˌfīn\ *n* : a surgical instrument for cutting out circular sections (as of bone or corneal tissue) [French *tréphine,* from obsolete English *trafine,* from Latin *tres fines* "three ends"]

trep·i·da·tion \ˌtrep-ə-ˈdā-shən\ *n* **1** *archaic* **:** a tremulous motion **2 :** a state of alarm or nervousness : FEAR [Latin *trepidatio,* from *trepidare* "to tremble," from *trepidus* "agitated"]

trepo·ne·ma \ˌtrep-ə-ˈnē-mə\ *n, pl* **-ma·ta** \-mət-ə\ *or* **-mas** : any of a genus of spirochetes that parasitize warm-blooded animals and include the causative agents of syphilis and yaws [New Latin, from Greek *trepein* "to turn" + *nēma* "thread"] — **trepo·ne·mal** \-məl\ *adj*

[1]tres·pass \ˈtres-pəs, -ˌpas\ *n* **1 a :** a violation of morals : TRANSGRESSION; *esp* **:** SIN **b :** an unwarranted infringement **2 a :** an unlawful act committed on the person, property, or rights of another; *esp* **:** a wrongful entry on real property **b :** the legal action for injuries resulting from a trespass [Medieval French *trespas* "passage, overstepping, misdeed," from *trespasser* "overtake, exceed, wrong," from *tres* "to a high degree," (from Latin *trans* "beyond") + *passer* "to pass"]

[2]trespass *vi* **1 :** ERR 1, SIN **2 :** to commit a trespass; *esp* **:** to enter unlawfully upon the land of another — **tres·pass·er** *n*

tress \ˈtres\ *n* **1** *archaic* **:** a plait of hair : BRAID **2 a :** a long lock of hair **b :** long unbound hair — usually used in plural [Medieval French *trece*]

tres·tle \ˈtres-əl\ *n* **1 :** a braced frame that consists usually of a horizontal piece with spreading legs at each end and that supports something (as a tabletop or drawing board) **2 :** a braced framework of timbers or steel for carrying a road or railroad over a depression [Medieval French *trestel,* derived from Latin *transtillum* "small beam," from *transtrum* "traverse beam"]

tres·tle·work \-ˌwərk\ *n* : a system of connected trestles supporting a structure (as a bridge)

trews \ˈtrüz\ *n pl* **:** close-cut tartan shorts worn under the kilt in Highland dress [Scottish Gaelic *triubhas*]

trey \ˈtrā\ *n, pl* **treys :** a card or the side of a domino or die with three spots [Medieval French *treis, treie* "three," from Latin *tres*]

T. rex \ˈtē-ˈreks\ *n* : TYRANNOSAUR

tri- *combining form* **1 :** three : having three elements or parts ‹*tri*axial› ‹*tri*graph› **2 :** into three ‹*tri*sect› **3 a :** thrice ‹*tri*weekly› **b :** every third ‹*tri*monthly› [Latin (from *tri-, tres*) and Greek, from *tri-, treis*]

tri·able \ˈtrī-ə-bəl\ *adj* : liable or subject to judicial or quasi-judicial examination or trial ‹a case *triable* without a jury›

tri·ac·e·tate \trī-ˈas-ə-ˌtāt, ˈtrī-\ *n* : a textile fiber or fabric made by the chemical addition of acetate groups to cellulose

tri·ad \ˈtrī-ˌad *also* -əd\ *n* **1 :** a union or group of three usually closely related persons or things **2 :** a chord of three tones usually consisting of the first, third, and fifth notes of a scale and constituting the harmonic basis of tonal music [Latin *triad-, trias,* from Greek, from *treis* "three"] — **tri·ad·ic** \trī-ˈad-ik\ *adj* — **tri·ad·i·cal·ly** \-ˈad-i-kə-lē, -klē\ *adv*

tri·age \trē-ˈäzh\ *n* : the sorting of patients (as in an emergency room) according to the urgency of their need for care [French, literally, "sorting, sifting," from *trier* "to sort," from Medieval French]

[1]tri·al \ˈtrī-əl, ˈtrīl\ *n* **1 a :** the action or process of testing some-

\ə\ abut	\au̇\ out	\i\ tip	\ȯ\ saw	\u̇\ foot
\ər\ further	\ch\ chin	\ī\ life	\ȯi\ coin	\y\ yet
\a\ mat	\e\ pet	\j\ job	\th\ thin	\yü\ few
\ā\ take	\ē\ easy	\ng\ sing	\t͟h\ this	\yu̇\ cure
\ä\ cot, cart	\g\ go	\ō\ bone	\ü\ food	\zh\ vision

thing (as by use or examination) **b** : a preliminary contest (as in a sport) **2** : formal examination before a court of justice of the matter in issue in a civil or criminal case **3** : a test of faith, patience, or stamina **4** : a tryout or experiment to test quality, value, or usefulness **5** : ATTEMPT, EFFORT [Medieval French, from *trier* "to sort, examine, try"]

[2]**trial** *adj* **1** : of, relating to, or used in a trial **2** : made or done as a test or experiment **3** : used or tried out in a test or experiment

trial and error *n* : the trying of one thing or another until something succeeds

trial balance *n* : a list of the debit and credit balances of accounts in a ledger made primarily to verify their equality

trial balloon *n* : a project or scheme tentatively announced in order to test public opinion

trial run *n* : a testing exercise

tri·an·gle \ˈtrī-ˌang-gəl\ *n* **1** : a polygon that has three sides **2 a** : a musical percussion instrument made of a rod of steel bent into the form of a triangle open at one angle and sounded by striking with a small metal rod **b** : a drafting instrument consisting of a thin flat right-angled triangle with acute angles of 45 degrees or of 30 degrees and 60 degrees [derived from Latin *triangulus* "triangular," from *tri-* + *angulus* "angle"]

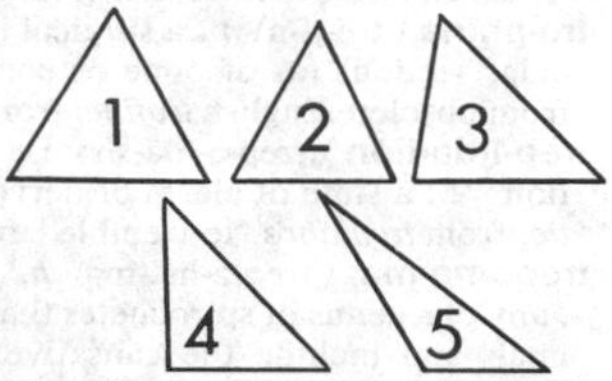

triangle 1: *1* equilateral, *2* isosceles, *3* scalene, *4* right, *5* obtuse

tri·an·gu·lar \trī-ˈang-gyə-lər\ *adj* **1 a** : of, relating to, or having the form of a triangle **b** : having a triangular base or principal surface ‹a *triangular* pyramid› **2** : of, relating to, or involving three parts or persons ‹a *triangular* love affair› — **tri·an·gu·lar·i·ty** \trī-ang-gyə-ˈlar-ət-ē\ *n* — **tri·an·gu·lar·ly** \trī-ˈang-gyə-lər-lē\ *adv*

triangular number *n* : a number (as 3, 6, 10, or 15) that can be represented by that many dots arranged in rows that form a triangle and that for some positive whole number *n* equals the sum of all the whole numbers from 1 to *n* or

$$\frac{n(n+1)}{2}$$

[1]**tri·an·gu·late** \trī-ˈang-gyə-lət\ *adj* : consisting of or marked with triangles

[2]**tri·an·gu·late** \-ˌlāt\ *vt* **1 a** : to divide into triangles **b** : to give triangular form to **2** : to survey, map, or determine by triangulation

tri·an·gu·la·tion \trī-ˌang-gyə-ˈlā-shən\ *n* : the measurement of the elements necessary to determine the network of triangles into which any part of the earth's surface is divided in surveying

Tri·as·sic \trī-ˈas-ik\ *n* : the earliest period of the Mesozoic era marked by the first appearance of the dinosaurs; *also* : the corresponding system of rocks — see GEOLOGIC TIME table [Latin *trias* "triad"; from the 3 subdivisions of the European Triassic] — **Triassic** *adj*

tri·ath·lete \ˌtrī-ˈath-ˌlēt\ *n* : an athlete who competes in a triathlon

tri·ath·lon \-ˈath-ˌlän\ *n* : an athletic contest that is a long-distance race consisting of three phases (as swimming, bicycling, and running) [*tri-* + *-athlon* (as in *decathlon*)]

tri·atom·ic \ˌtrī-ə-ˈtäm-ik\ *adj* : having three atoms in the molecule ‹ozone is *triatomic* oxygen›

tri·ax·i·al \trī-ˈak-sē-əl, ˈtrī-\ *adj* : having or involving three axes

trib·al \ˈtrī-bəl\ *adj* : of, relating to, or characteristic of a tribe ‹*tribal* customs› — **trib·al·ly** \-bə-lē\ *adv*

trib·al·ism \-bə-ˌliz-əm\ *n* **1** : tribal consciousness and loyalty; *esp* : exaltation of the tribe above other groups **2** : strong loyalty within a social group

tribe \ˈtrīb\ *n* **1** : a social group comprising numerous families, clans, or generations **2** : a group of persons having a common character, occupation, or interest **3** : a category of biological classification ranking below a subfamily and above a genus; *also* : a natural group irrespective of taxonomic rank ‹the cat *tribe*› [Latin *tribus* "a division of the Roman people, tribe"]

tribes·man \ˈtrībz-mən\ *n* : a member of a tribe

trib·u·la·tion \ˌtrib-yə-ˈlā-shən\ *n* : distress or suffering resulting from oppression, persecution, or affliction; *also* : a trying experience ‹the trials and *tribulations* of raising young children› [Medieval French *tribulacion,* from Latin *tribulatio,* from *tribulare* "to press, oppress," from *tribulum* "drag used in threshing," from *terere* "to rub"]

tri·bu·nal \trī-ˈbyün-l, trib-ˈyün-\ *n* **1** : the seat of a judge : [2]TRIBUNE **2** : a court or other forum of justice **3** : something that decides or determines ‹the *tribunal* of public opinion› [Latin, "platform for magistrates," from *tribunus* "tribune"]

trib·u·nate \ˈtrib-yə-ˌnāt, trib-ˈyü-nət\ *n* : the office, function, or term of office of a tribune

[1]**trib·une** \ˈtrib-ˌyün, trib-ˈyün\ *n* **1** : a Roman official under the monarchy and the republic with the function of protecting the plebeian citizen from arbitrary action by patrician magistrates **2** : a defender of the people especially against arbitrary abuse of authority [Latin *tribunus,* from *tribus* "tribe"] — **trib·une·ship** \-ˌship\ *n*

[2]**tribune** *n* : a platform from which an assembly is addressed [French, from Italian *tribuna,* from Latin *tribunal*]

[1]**trib·u·tary** \ˈtrib-yə-ˌter-ē\ *adj* **1** : paying tribute to another : SUBJECT **2** : paid or owed as tribute **3** : contributing to something larger or more important **4** : flowing into a larger stream or lake

[2]**tributary** *n, pl* **-tar·ies** **1** : a ruler or state that pays tribute to a conqueror **2** : a stream feeding a larger stream or a lake

trib·ute \ˈtrib-ˌyüt, -yət\ *n* **1 a** : a payment made by one ruler or nation to another to show submission or to secure peace or protection **b** : a tax to raise money for this payment **c** : the obligation to pay tribute ‹nations under *tribute*› **2** : something given or contributed voluntarily as due or deserved; *esp* : a gift or service showing respect, gratitude, or affection ‹a floral *tribute*› [Latin *tributum,* from *tribuere* "to allot, pay," from *tribus* "tribe"]

trice \ˈtrīs\ *n* : a brief space of time : INSTANT — used chiefly in the phrase *in a trice* [Middle English *trise,* literally, "pull," from *trisen* "to pull," from early Dutch, "to hoist"]

tri·ceps \ˈtrī-ˌseps\ *n, pl* **triceps** : a muscle that arises from three heads; *esp* : the large extensor muscle along the back of the upper arm that acts to extend the forearm [Latin, "three-headed," from *tri-* + *caput* "head"]

tri·cer·a·tops \trī-ˈser-ə-ˌtäps\ *n* : a large plant-eating four-footed Cretaceous dinosaur with three horns, a bony hood or crest on the neck, and hoofed toes [New Latin, from Greek *tri-* + *kerat-, keras* "horn" + *ōps* "face"]

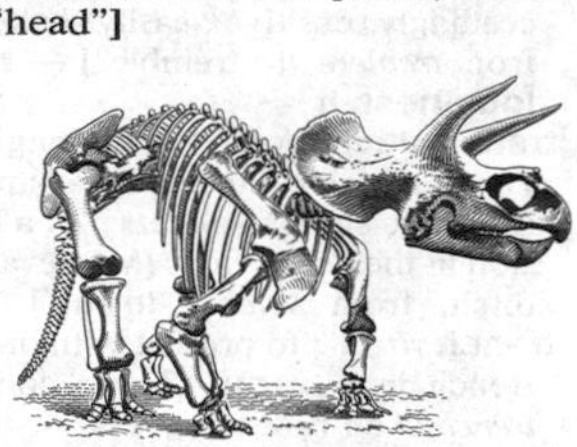
triceratops skeleton

-trices *plural of* -TRIX

tri·chi·na \trə-ˈkī-nə\ *n, pl* **-nae** : a small slender nematode worm which enters the body of flesh-eating mammals (as hogs and human beings) when infected meat is eaten and whose larvae migrate to and form cysts in striated muscles causing trichinosis [New Latin, from Greek *trichinos* "made of hair," from *trich-, thrix* "hair"] — **tri·chi·nal** \trə-ˈkīn-l\ *adj* — **tri·chi·nous** \ˈtrik-ə-nəs, trə-ˈkī-nəs\ *adj*

trich·i·no·sis \ˌtrik-ə-ˈnō-səs\ *n, pl* **-no·ses** \-ˈnō-ˌsēz\ : a disease caused by trichinae and marked especially by muscular pain, difficulty in breathing, fever, and edema

tricho·cyst \ˈtrik-ə-ˌsist\ *n* : any of the minute lassoing or stinging organs of a protozoan [Greek *trich-, thrix* "hair"]

tri·chome \ˈtrik-ˌōm, ˈtrī-ˌkōm\ *n* : a threadlike outgrowth; *esp* : an epidermal filament on a plant [German *Trichom,* from Greek *trichōma* "growth of hair," from *trich-, thrix* "hair"]

tricho·mo·nad \ˌtrik-ə-ˈmō-ˌnad, -ˈmō-nəd\ *n* : any of a genus of flagellated protozoans parasitic in various animals including humans [derived from Greek *trich-, thrix* "hair" + Late Latin *monad-, monas* "monad"]

tricho·mo·ni·a·sis \ˌtrik-ə-mə-ˈnī-ə-səs\ *n, pl* **-a·ses** \-ə-ˌsēz\ : infection with or disease caused by trichomonads; *esp* : a human vaginal inflammation with a persistent discharge

tri·chot·o·mous \trī-ˈkät-ə-məs\ *adj* : divided or dividing into three parts or into threes : THREEFOLD ‹*trichotomous* branching› [Late Greek *trichotomein* "to trisect," from Greek *tricha* "in three" (related to *treis* "three") + *temnein* "to cut"] — **tri·chot·o·mous·ly** *adv* — **tri·chot·o·my** \-mē\ *n*

1**trick** \ˈtrik\ *n* **1 a :** a crafty procedure or practice meant to deceive or defraud **b :** a mischievous act : PRANK **c :** an indiscreet or childish action **d :** a dexterous or ingenious feat designed to puzzle or amuse ⟨a juggler's *tricks*⟩ **2 a :** habitual peculiarity of behavior or manner **b :** a characteristic and identifying feature ⟨a *trick* of speech⟩ **c :** an optical illusion ⟨a mere *trick* of the light⟩ **3 a** (1) **:** a quick or artful way of getting a result : KNACK ⟨the *trick* is to do it quickly⟩ (2) **:** an instance of getting a desired result ⟨that should do the *trick*⟩ **b :** a technical device (as of an art or craft) ⟨the *tricks* of stage technique⟩ **4 :** the cards played in one round of a card game often used as a scoring unit **5 :** a working shift [derived from Medieval French *trikier* "to deceive, cheat"]

synonyms TRICK, RUSE, STRATAGEM, WILE mean an indirect means to gain an end. TRICK may imply deception, roguishness, or illusion and either an evil or harmless end ⟨ten *tricks* to make you look younger⟩. RUSE stresses an attempt to mislead by a false impression ⟨the *ruse* of smugglers⟩. STRATAGEM implies a ruse to entrap or outwit and suggests a more or less carefully laid-out plan ⟨the *strategem*-filled game⟩. WILE suggests an attempt to entrap or deceive with false allurements ⟨used all his *wiles* to win the teacher's favor⟩.

2**trick** *adj* **1 a :** of, relating to, or involving tricks or trickery ⟨*trick* photography⟩ **b :** skilled in or used for tricks ⟨a *trick* horse⟩ **2 a :** somewhat defective and unreliable ⟨a *trick* lock⟩ **b :** inclined to give way unexpectedly ⟨a *trick* knee⟩

3**trick** *vt* **1 :** to deceive by cunning or artifice : CHEAT **2 :** to dress or adorn especially fancifully or ornately ⟨*tricked* out in a gaudy uniform⟩

trick·ery \ˈtrik-rē, -ə-rē\ *n, pl* **-er·ies :** the use of tricks to deceive or defraud ***synonyms*** see DECEPTION

1**trick·le** \ˈtrik-əl\ *vi* **trick·led; trick·ling** \ˈtrik-ling, -ə-ling\ **1 a :** to flow or fall in drops **b :** to flow in a thin gentle stream **2 a :** to move or go one by one or little by little ⟨customers began to *trickle* in⟩ **b :** to dissipate slowly ⟨his enthusiasm *trickled* away⟩ [Middle English *triklen*]

2**trickle** *n* **:** a trickling stream ⟨a *trickle* of syrup⟩

trick or treat *n* **:** a children's Halloween practice of asking for treats from door to door under threat of playing tricks on those who refuse — **trick–or–treat** *vi* — **trick–or–treater** *n*

trick·ster \ˈtrik-stər\ *n* **:** one who tricks: as **a :** a dishonest person who cheats others by trickery **b :** a person (as a stage magician) skilled in the use of tricks and illusion

tricky \ˈtrik-ē\ *adj* **trick·i·er; -est 1 :** of or characteristic of a trickster : SLY **2 :** requiring skill, aptitude, or caution : DELICATE **3 :** TRICK 2 — **trick·i·ly** \ˈtrik-ə-lē\ *adv* — **trick·i·ness** \ˈtrik-ē-nəs\ *n*

tri·clin·ic \trī-ˈklin-ik, ˈtrī-\ *adj* **:** having three unequal axes intersecting at oblique angles — used especially of a crystal [*tri-* + *-clinic*]

1**tri·col·or** \ˈtrī-ˌkəl-ər\ *n* **:** a flag of stripes of three colors ⟨the French *tricolor*⟩

2**tricolor** *or* **tri·col·ored** \ˈtrī-ˌkəl-ərd\ *adj* **:** having, using, or marked with three colors

tri·corn \ˈtrī-ˌkȯrn\ *adj* **:** having three horns or corners [Latin *tricornis,* from *tri-* + *cornu* "horn"]

tri·corne *or* **tri·corn** \ˈtrī-ˌkȯrn\ *n* **:** COCKED HAT

tri·cor·nered \ˈtrī-ˈkȯr-nərd\ *adj* **:** having three corners

tri·cot \ˈtrē-kō, ˈtrī-kət\ *n* **1 :** a plain run-resistant knitted fabric (as for underwear) **2 :** a twilled clothing fabric of wool or wool and cotton [French, from *tricoter* "to move the legs rapidly, knit"]

1**tri·cus·pid** \trī-ˈkəs-pəd, ˈtrī-\ *adj* **:** having three cusps

2**tricuspid** *n* **:** a tooth having three cusps

tri·cus·pid valve \trī-ˌkəs-pəd-\ *n* **:** a valve of three flaps that prevents backward flow of blood from the right ventricle to the right atrium [Latin *tricuspid-, tricuspis* "having three points," from *tri-* + *cuspis* "point"]

tri·cy·cle \ˈtrī-ˌsik-əl\ *n* **:** a 3-wheeled vehicle propelled by pedals or a motor [French from Greek *tri-* + *kyklos* "wheel"]

tri·dent \ˈtrīd-nt\ *n* **:** a 3-pronged spear [Latin *trident-, tridens,* from *tri-* + *dent-, dens* "tooth"] — **trident** *adj*

tri·di·men·sion·al \ˌtrīd-ə-ˈmench-nəl, -ən-l\ *adj* **:** of or relating to three dimensions

trid·u·um \ˈtrij-ə-wəm, ˈtrid-yə-\ *n* **:** a period of three days of prayer usually preceding a Roman Catholic feast [Latin, "period of three days"]

tried \ˈtrīd\ *adj* **:** found good, faithful, or trustworthy through experience or testing ⟨a *tried* recipe⟩ [from past participle of *try*]

tried–and–true *adj* **:** shown or known to be reliable ⟨a *tried-and-true* friend⟩ ⟨a *tried-and-true* remedy⟩

tri·en·ni·al \trī-ˈen-ē-əl, ˈtrī-\ *adj* **1 :** consisting of or lasting for three years **2 :** occurring or being done every three years — **triennial** *n* — **tri·en·ni·al·ly** \-ē-ə-lē\ *adv*

tri·en·ni·um \trī-ˈen-ē-əm\ *n, pl* **-ni·ums** *or* **-nia** \-ē-ə\ **:** a period of three years [Latin, from *tri-* + *annus* "year"]

tri·er \ˈtrī-ər, ˈtrīr\ *n* **:** one that tries

1**tri·fle** \ˈtrī-fəl\ *n* **1 :** something of little value or importance **2 :** a dessert of sponge cake spread with jam or jelly covered with custard and whipped cream [Medieval French *trufle, triffle* "fraud, trick, nonsense"] — **a trifle :** to a small degree : SLIGHTLY ⟨*a trifle* annoyed⟩

2**trifle** *vb* **tri·fled; tri·fling** \-fə-ling, -fling\ **1 a :** to talk in a jesting or mocking manner with intent to mislead **b :** to treat someone or something as unimportant **2 :** to spend or waste in trifling or on trifles ⟨*trifle* away money⟩ **3 :** to handle something idly : TOY — **tri·fler** \-fə-lər, -flər\ *n*

tri·fling \ˈtrī-fling\ *adj* **:** lacking in significance or solid worth: as **a :** FRIVOLOUS ⟨*trifling* talk⟩ **b :** TRIVIAL ⟨a *trifling* gift⟩

tri·fo·li·ate \trī-ˈfō-lē-ət, ˈtrī-\ *adj* **:** having three leaves ⟨a *trifoliate* plant⟩ **2 :** TRIFOLIOLATE [*tri-* + Latin *folium* "leaf"]

tri·fo·li·o·late \trī-ˈfō-lē-ə-ˌlāt, ˈtrī-\ *adj* **:** having three leaflets ⟨a *trifoliolate* leaf⟩ [*tri-* + Late Latin *foliolum* "leaflet"]

tri·fur·cate \trī-ˈfər-kət, ˈtrī-, -ˌkāt; ˈtrī-fər-ˌkāt\ *adj* **:** TRICHOTOMOUS [Latin *trifurcus* "having three branches," from *tri-* + *furca* "fork"] — **tri·fur·cate** \ˈtrī-fər-ˌkāt, trī-ˈfər-\ *vi* — **tri·fur·ca·tion** \ˌtrī-fər-ˈkā-shən\ *n*

1**trig** \ˈtrig\ *adj* **:** stylishly trim : SMART, NEAT [Middle English, "trusty, nimble," of Scandinavian origin]

2**trig** *n* **:** TRIGONOMETRY

tri·gem·i·nal nerve \trī-ˌjem-ən-l-\ *n* **:** either of the 5th pair of cranial nerves that supply motor and sensory fibers mostly to the face — called also *trigeminal* [Latin *trigeminus* "threefold," from *tri-* + *geminus* "twin"]

1**trig·ger** \ˈtrig-ər\ *n* **1 a :** a movable lever attached to a catch that when released by pressure allows a mechanism to go into action; *esp* **:** the part of the lock of a firearm that releases the hammer and so fires the gun **b :** a similar movable part by which a mechanism is activated ⟨*trigger* of a spray gun⟩ **2 :** something that acts like a mechanical trigger initiating a process or reaction ⟨the *trigger* that caused the fight⟩ [Dutch *trekker,* from *trekken* "to pull, draw"] — **trigger** *adj* — **trig·gered** \-ərd\ *adj*

2**trigger** *vb* **trig·gered; trig·ger·ing** \ˈtrig-ring, -ə-ring\ **1 :** to fire by pulling a mechanical trigger ⟨*trigger* a rifle⟩; *also* **:** to cause the explosion of (as a missile) **2 :** to initiate or set in motion as if by pulling a trigger ⟨*triggered* the laughter⟩

trig·ger–hap·py \ˈtrig-ər-ˌhap-ē\ *adj* **:** irresponsible in the use of firearms; *esp* **:** inclined to shoot before clearly identifying the target

tri·glyc·er·ide \trī-ˈglis-ə-ˌrīd\ *n* **:** any of a group of lipids that are composed of one molecule of glycerol and three molecules of one or more fatty acids, are widespread in adipose tissue, and circulate in the blood in the form of lipoproteins

tri·glyph \ˈtrī-ˌglif\ *n* **:** a slightly projecting rectangular tablet in a Doric frieze with two vertical channels and two corresponding half channels on the vertical sides [Latin *triglyphus,* from Greek *triglyphos,* from *tri-* + *glyphein* "to carve"]

trig·o·no·met·ric \ˌtrig-ə-nə-ˈme-trik\ *also* **trig·o·no·met·ri·cal** \-tri-kəl\ *adj* **:** of, relating to, or in accordance with trigonometry — **trig·o·no·met·ri·cal·ly** \-tri-kə-lē, -klē\ *adv*

trigonometric function *n* **:** a function (as the sine, cosine, tangent, cotangent, secant, or cosecant) of an arc or angle most simply expressed in terms of the ratios of pairs of sides of a right triangle — called also *circular function*

trig·o·nom·e·try \ˌtrig-ə-ˈnäm-ə-trē\ *n* **:** the study of the properties of triangles and trigonometric functions and of their applications [Greek *trigōnon* "triangle," from *tri-* + *gōnia* "angle"]

\ə\ **abut**	\au̇\ **out**	\i\ **tip**	\ȯ\ **saw**	\u̇\ **foot**
\ər\ **further**	\ch\ **chin**	\ī\ **life**	\ȯi\ **coin**	\y\ **yet**
\a\ **mat**	\e\ **pet**	\j\ **job**	\th\ **thin**	\yü\ **few**
\ā\ **take**	\ē\ **easy**	\ng\ **sing**	\t͟h\ **this**	\yu̇\ **cure**
\ä\ **cot, cart**	\g\ **go**	\ō\ **bone**	\ü\ **food**	\zh\ **vision**

tri·graph \ˈtrī-ˌgraf\ *n* : three letters spelling a single consonant, vowel, or diphthong — **tri·graph·ic** \trī-ˈgraf-ik\ *adj*

tri·he·dral \trī-ˈhē-drəl, ˈtrī-\ *adj* **1** : having three faces ⟨a *trihedral* angle⟩ **2** : of or relating to a trihedral angle [*tri-* + *-hedral*] — **trihedral** *n*

tri·lat·er·al \trī-ˈlat-ə-rəl, ˈtrī-, -ˈla-trəl\ *adj* : having three sides

tri·lin·gual \trī-ˈling-gwəl, -gyə-wəl\ *adj* **1** : of, containing, or expressed in three languages **2** : using or able to use three languages — **tri·lin·gual·ly** \-gwə-lē\ *adv*

1trill \ˈtril\ *n* **1 a** : the alternation of two musical tones a scale degree apart — called also *shake* **b** : VIBRATO 1 **2** : a sound resembling a musical trill : WARBLE **3** : the rapid vibration of one speech organ against another (as of the tip of the tongue against the teethridge); *also* : a speech sound so made [Italian *trillo*]

2trill *vb* **1** : to utter as or with a trill ⟨*trills* the letter "r"⟩ **2** : to play or sing with a trill : QUAVER — **trill·er** *n*

tril·lion \ˈtril-yən\ *n* **1** — see NUMBER table **2** : a very large number ⟨a *trillion* mosquitoes out tonight⟩ [French, from *tri-* "tri-" + *-illion* (as in *million*)] — **trillion** *adj* — **tril·lionth** \-yənth, -yəntth\ *adj or n*

tril·li·um \ˈtril-ē-əm\ *n* : any of a genus of herbs related to the lilies and having an erect stem bearing a whorl of three leaves and a solitary three-petaled flower — called also *wake-robin* [New Latin, from Swedish *trilling* "triplet"; from its three leaves]

tri·lo·bite \ˈtrī-lə-ˌbīt\ *n* : any of a group (Trilobita) of extinct Paleozoic marine arthropods having a segmented body divided lengthwise by furrows on the back into three parts [derived from Greek *trilobos* "three-lobed," from *tri-* + *lobos* "lobe"]

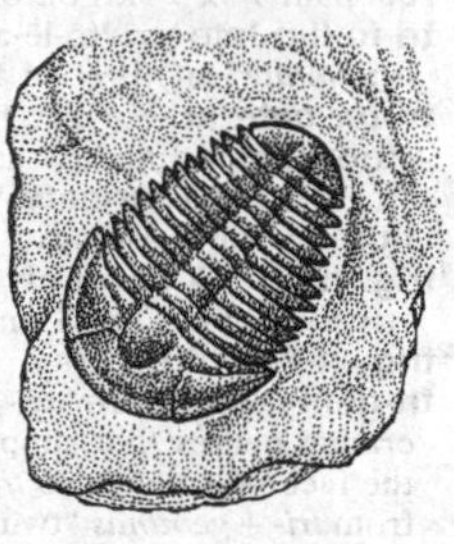

trilobite fossil

tril·o·gy \ˈtril-ə-jē\ *n, pl* **-gies** : a series of three literary, dramatic, or musical compositions that are closely related and develop a single theme

1trim \ˈtrim\ *vb* **trimmed; trim·ming** **1** : to decorate with something (as ribbons or ornaments) : ADORN ⟨*trim* the Christmas tree⟩ ⟨a jacket *trimmed* with leather⟩ **2 a** : to administer a beating to **b** : to defeat in a game or contest **3 a** : to make trim and neat especially by cutting or clipping ⟨*trim* the bushes⟩ **b** : to free of excess or unnecessary matter by or as if by cutting ⟨*trim* a budget⟩ **4 a** (1) : to cause (a ship or boat) to assume a desirable position in the water by arrangement of ballast, cargo, or passengers (2) : to adjust (as an airplane or submarine) for horizontal movement or for motion upward or downward **b** : to adjust (as a sail) to a desired position **5** : to maintain neutrality between opposing parties [Old English *trymian* "to strengthen, arrange," from *trum* "strong, firm"]

2trim *adj* **trim·mer; trim·mest** **1** : ready for service or use **2** : slim and physically fit ⟨keeps *trim* by jogging⟩ **3** : neat, orderly, and compact in line or structure ⟨a *trim* house⟩ — **trim·ly** *adv* — **trim·ness** *n*

3trim *adv* : in a trim manner : TRIMLY

4trim *n* **1** : suitable or excellent condition : FITNESS **2 a** : material used for ornament or trimming **b** : the woodwork in the finish of a building especially around openings **c** : the interior furnishings of an automobile **3 a** : the position of a ship or boat especially with reference to the horizontal **b** : the relation between the plane of a sail and the direction of the ship **c** : the position of an airplane at which it will continue in level flight with no adjustments to the controls **4** : something that is cut out or trimmed off **5** : a haircut that neatens a previous haircut

tri·ma·ran \ˈtrī-mə-ˌran, ˌtrī-mə-ˈ\ *n* : a sailboat consisting of three hulls side by side [*tri-* + *-maran* (as in *catamaran*)]

tri·mes·ter \trī-ˈmes-tər, ˈtrī-ˌ\ *n* **1** : a period of three or about three months; *esp* : any of the three periods of approximately three months each into which a human pregnancy is divided **2** : one of three terms into which an academic year is sometimes divided [French *trimestre,* from Latin *trimestris* "of three months," from *tri-* + *mensis* "month"]

trim·e·ter \ˈtrim-ət-ər\ *n* : a line consisting of three metrical feet [Latin *trimetrus,* from Greek *trimetros* "having three measures," from *tri-* + *metron* "measure"]

trim·mer \ˈtrim-ər\ *n* **1 a** : one that trims articles **b** : something with which trimming is done **2** : a beam that holds the end of a header in floor framing **3** : a person who modifies a policy, position, or opinion especially as a means to accomplish an end

trim·ming \ˈtrim-ing\ *n* **1** : the action of one that trims **2** : a severe defeat or beating **3** : something that trims, ornaments, or completes ⟨the *trimming* on a hat⟩ ⟨roast turkey and all the *trimmings*⟩ **4** *pl* : parts removed by trimming

tri·month·ly \trī-ˈmənth-lē, ˈtrī-, -ˈmənth-\ *adj* : occurring every three months

tri·mo·tor \ˈtrī-ˌmōt-ər\ *n* : an airplane with three engines

trine \ˈtrīn\ *adj* : THREEFOLD, TRIPLE [Medieval French *trin,* from Latin *trinus,* from *trini* "three each"]

trin·i·tar·i·an \ˌtrin-ə-ˈter-ē-ən\ *adj* **1** *cap* : of or relating to the Trinity, the doctrine of the Trinity, or adherents to that doctrine **2** : having three parts or aspects

Trinitarian *n* : one who subscribes to the doctrine of the Trinity — **Trin·i·tar·i·an·ism** \-ē-ə-ˌniz-əm\ *n*

tri·ni·tro·tol·u·ene \ˌtrī-nī-trō-ˈtäl-yə-ˌwēn\ *n* : TNT

Trin·i·ty \ˈtrin-ət-ē\ *n, pl* **-ties** **1** : the unity of Father, Son, and Holy Spirit as three persons in one Godhead according to some Christian doctrines **2** *not cap* : TRIAD 1 **3** : TRINITY SUNDAY [Medieval French *trinité,* from Late Latin *trinitas* "state of being threefold," from Latin *trinus* "threefold"]

Trinity Sunday *n* : the 8th Sunday after Easter

trin·ket \ˈtring-kət\ *n* **1** : a small ornament (as a jewel or ring) **2** : a thing of little value : TRIFLE [origin unknown]

trin·ket·ry \ˈtring-kə-trē\ *n* : small items of personal ornament

1tri·no·mi·al \trī-ˈnō-mē-əl\ *n* **1** : a polynomial that has three terms **2** : a biological taxonomic name consisting of three terms of which the first designates the genus, the second the species, and the third the variety or subspecies [*tri-* + *-nomial* (as in *binomial*)]

2trinomial *adj* **1** : consisting of three mathematical terms **2** : of or relating to trinomials

trio \ˈtrē-ō\ *n, pl* **tri·os** **1 a** : a musical composition for three voice parts or three instruments **b** : a dance by three people **c** : the performers of a musical or dance trio **2** : a group or set of three [French, from Italian, from Latin *tri-, tres* "three"]

tri·ode \ˈtrī-ˌōd\ *n* : a vacuum tube with three electrodes

tri·o·let \ˈtrī-ə-lət, ˈtrē-\ *n* : a poem or stanza of eight lines in which the first line is repeated as the fourth and seventh and the second line as the eighth and which has a rhyme scheme of ABaAabAB [French]

tri·ose \ˈtrī-ˌōs\ *n* : either of two monosaccharides containing three carbon atoms

tri·ox·ide \trī-ˈäk-ˌsīd, ˈtrī-\ *n* : an oxide containing three atoms of oxygen

1trip \ˈtrip\ *vb* **tripped; trip·ping** **1** : to move (as in dancing or walking) with light quick steps **2 a** : to catch one's foot against something so as to stumble ⟨don't *trip* over the rock⟩ **b** : to cause to stumble ⟨someone must have *tripped* him⟩ **3 a** : to make or cause to make a mistake **b** : to catch making a false statement, error, or blunder ⟨questions designed to *trip* her up⟩ **4** : to put (as a mechanism) into operation usually by release of a catch or detent ⟨*tripped* the fire alarm⟩; *also* : to become operative [Medieval French *treper, triper,* of Germanic origin]

2trip *n* **1** : a stroke or catch by which a wrestler is made to lose footing **2 a** : VOYAGE, JOURNEY ⟨a *trip* to Europe⟩ **b** : a single visit or round having a specific aim or recurring regularly ⟨a *trip* to the dentist's⟩ **3** : ERROR 4, MISSTEP **4** : a quick light step **5** : a faltering step : STUMBLE **6 a** : the action of tripping mechanically **b** : a device (as a catch) for tripping a mechanism **7** : the experience of a person under the influence of a psychedelic drug (as LSD)

tri·par·tite \trī-ˈpär-ˌtīt, ˈtrī-\ *adj* **1** : having three parts **2** : having three corresponding parts or copies **3** : made between or involving three parties — **tri·par·tite·ly** *adv*

tripe \ˈtrīp\ *n* **1** : stomach tissue of a ruminant animal (as a cow) used as food **2** : something poor, worthless, or offensive [Medieval French]

trip–ham·mer \ˈtrip-ˌham-ər\ *n* : a massive hammer raised by machinery and then tripped to fall on the work below

triph·thong \ˈtrif-ˌthȯng, ˈtrip-\ *n* **1** : a 3-element speech sound **2** : TRIGRAPH [*tri-* + *-phthong* (as in *diphthong*)]

1tri·ple \ˈtrip-əl\ *vb* **tri·pled; tri·pling** \ˈtrip-ling, -ə-ling\ **1** : to make or become three times as great or as many : multiply by three ⟨their profits *tripled* last year⟩ **2 :** to make a triple in baseball

^{2}**triple** *n* **1 a :** a triple sum, quantity, or number **b :** a combination, group, or series of three **2 :** a base hit that enables the batter to reach third base

^{3}**triple** *adj* **1 :** being three times as great or as many **2 :** having three units or members **3 a :** three times repeated **b :** having three full revolutions ⟨a *triple* somersault⟩ [Latin *triplus,* from *tri-* + *-plus* "-fold"]

triple bond *n* **:** a chemical bond in which three pairs of electrons are shared by two atoms in a molecule — compare DOUBLE BOND, SINGLE BOND

triple jump *n* **:** a track-and-field event in which competitors jump for distance from a running start combining in succession a hop, a stride, and a jump

triple play *n* **:** a play in baseball by which three players are put out

triple point *n* **:** the condition of temperature and pressure under which the gaseous, liquid, and solid phases of a substance can exist in equilibrium

tri·ple–space \ˌtrip-əl-ˈspās\ *vb* **1 :** to type (copy) leaving two blank lines between lines of copy **2 :** to type on every third line

tri·plet \ˈtrip-lət\ *n* **1 :** a unit of three lines of verse **2 :** a combination, set, or group of three **3 :** one of three children or offspring born at one birth **4 :** a group of three notes played in the time of two of the same value **5 :** CODON

^{1}**tri·plex** \ˈtrip-ˌleks, ˈtrī-ˌpleks\ *adj* **:** TRIPLE 2 [Latin, from *tri-* + *-plex* "-fold"]

^{2}**triplex** *n* **:** something that is triplex (as an apartment with three floors)

^{1}**trip·li·cate** \ˈtrip-li-kət\ *adj* **:** having or being three corresponding or identical parts or examples [Latin *triplicatus,* past participle of *triplicare* "to triple," from *triplic-, triplex* "triplex"]

^{2}**triplicate** *n* **:** three copies all alike — used with *in* ⟨typed in *triplicate*⟩

^{3}**trip·li·cate** \-lə-ˌkāt\ *vt* **1 :** to make triple **2 :** to prepare in triplicate ⟨*triplicate* the forms⟩ — **trip·li·ca·tion** \ˌtrip-lə-ˈkā-shən\ *n*

trip·lo·blas·tic \ˌtrip-lō-ˈblas-tik\ *adj* **:** having three primary germ layers

trip·loid \ˈtrip-ˌlȯid\ *adj* **:** having or being a chromosome number three times the monoploid number — **triploid** *n* — **trip·loi·dy** \-ˌlȯid-ē\ *n*

tri·ply \ˈtrip-lē, -ə-lē\ *adv* **:** in a triple degree, amount, or manner

tri·pod \ˈtrī-ˌpäd\ *n* **1 :** something (as a container or stool) resting on three legs **2 :** a three-legged stand (as for a camera) [Latin *tripod-, tripus,* from Greek *tripod-, tripous,* from *tri-* + *pod-, pous* "foot"] — **tripod** *or* **trip·o·dal** \ˈtrip-əd-l, ˈtrī-ˌpäd-\ *adj*

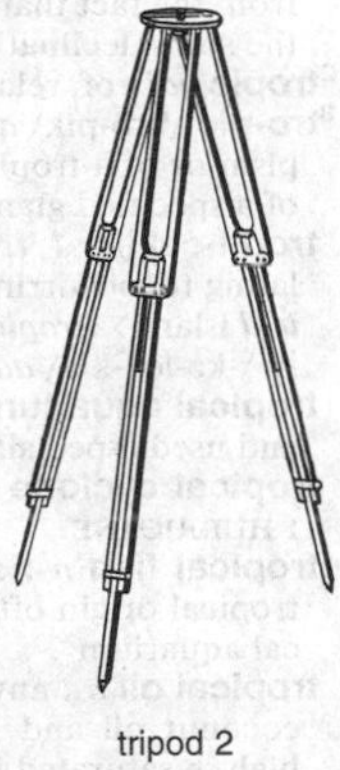

tripod 2

trip·per \ˈtrip-ər\ *n* **1** *chiefly British* **:** one that takes a trip **:** TOURIST **2 :** a tripping device (as for operating a railroad signal)

trip·ping·ly \ˈtrip-ing-lē\ *adv* **:** in a nimble or lively manner

trip·tych \ˈtrip-tik, -ˌtik\ *n* **1 :** an ancient Roman writing tablet with three waxed leaves hinged together **2 :** a picture or carving in three panels side by side [Greek *triptychos* "having three folds," from *tri-* + *ptychē* "fold"]

tri·reme \ˈtrī-ˌrēm\ *n* **:** an ancient galley having three banks of oars [Latin *triremis,* from *tri-* + *remus* "oar"]

tri·sac·cha·ride \trī-ˈsak-ə-ˌrīd, ˈtrī-\ *n* **:** any sugar that yields on complete hydrolysis three monosaccharide molecules

tri·sect \ˈtrī-ˌsekt, trī-ˈ\ *vt* **:** to divide into three usually equal parts [*tri-* + *-sect* (as in *intersect*)] — **tri·sec·tion** \ˈtrī-ˌsek-shən, trī-ˈ\ *n* — **tri·sec·tor** \ˈtrī-ˌsek-tər, trī-ˈ\ *n*

tri·so·di·um \ˌtrī-ˌsōd-ē-əm\ *adj* **:** containing three atoms of sodium in the molecule

tri·so·my \ˈtrī-ˌsō-mē\ *n* **:** the condition (as in Down syndrome) of having one or a few chromosomes triploid in an otherwise diploid set [*tri-* + ^{3}*-some* + ^{2}*-y*] — **trisomic** \trī-ˈsō-mik, ˈtrī-\ *adj or n*

triste \ˈtrēst\ *adj* **:** SAD, MOURNFUL; *also* **:** WISTFUL [French, from Latin *tristis*]

tri·syl·lab·ic \ˌtrī-sə-ˈlab-ik\ *adj* **:** having three syllables — **tri·syl·la·ble** \ˈtrī-ˌsil-ə-bəl, trī-ˈ, ˈtrī-ˈ\ *n*

trite \ˈtrīt\ *adj* **trit·er; trit·est :** so common that the novelty has worn off **:** STALE, HACKNEYED ⟨a *trite* remark⟩ [Latin *tritus,* from *terere* "to rub, wear away"] — **trite·ly** *adv* — **trite·ness** *n*

synonyms TRITE, HACKNEYED, STEREOTYPED, THREADBARE mean lacking freshness and power to interest or compel attention. TRITE applies to a once effective phrase or idea spoiled by long familiarity ⟨"you win some, you lose some" is a *trite* expression⟩. HACKNEYED stresses being worn out by overuse so as to become dull and meaningless ⟨all of the metaphors in the poem are *hackneyed*⟩. STEREOTYPED implies falling invariably into the same pattern or form ⟨views that are *stereotyped* and out-of-date⟩. THREADBARE applies to something that has been used so often it no longer can be interesting ⟨a mystery novel with a *threadbare* plot⟩.

tri·ti·um \ˈtrit-ē-əm, ˈtrish-ē-\ *n* **:** a radioactive isotope of hydrogen with atoms of about three times the mass of ordinary hydrogen atoms [New Latin, from Greek *tritos* "third"]

trit·o·ma \ˈtrit-ə-mə\ *n* **:** any of a genus of African herbs related to the lilies and often grown for their spikes of showy red or yellow flowers [New Latin, from Greek *tritomos* "cut thrice," from *tri-* + *temnein* "to cut"]

tri·ton \ˈtrīt-n\ *n* **:** any of various large sea snails with a heavy cone-shaped shell; *also* **:** the shell [*Triton,* son of Poseidon]

trit·u·rate \ˈtrich-ə-ˌrāt\ *vt* **1 :** CRUSH 3, GRIND **2 :** to reduce to a fine powder by rubbing or grinding [Late Latin *triturare* "to thresh," from Latin *tritura* "act of rubbing, threshing," from *tritus,* past participle of *terere* "to rub"] — **trit·u·ra·ble** \-rə-bəl\ *adj* — **trit·u·rate** \-rət\ *n* — **trit·u·ra·tion** \ˌtrich-ə-ˈrā-shən\ *n* — **trit·u·ra·tor** \ˈtrich-ə-ˌrāt-ər\ *n*

^{1}**tri·umph** \ˈtrī-əmf, -əmpf\ *n, pl* **triumphs** **1 :** an ancient Roman ceremonial honoring a victorious general **2 :** joy or exultation over victory or success **3 a :** a military victory or conquest **b :** a notable success ⟨a *scientific* triumph⟩ [Medieval French *triumphe,* from Latin *triumphus*] ***synonyms*** see VICTORY

^{2}**triumph** *vi* **1 :** to celebrate victory or success boastfully or rejoicingly **2 :** to obtain victory **:** PREVAIL, WIN

tri·um·phal \trī-ˈəm-fəl, -ˈəmp-\ *adj* **:** of, relating to, or used in a triumph ⟨a *triumphal* march⟩

tri·um·phant \trī-ˈəm-fənt, -ˈəmp-\ *adj* **1 :** VICTORIOUS, CONQUERING ⟨*triumphant* armies⟩ **2 :** rejoicing for or celebrating victory **:** EXULTANT ⟨a *triumphant* shout⟩ **3 :** notably successful ⟨a *triumphant* performance⟩ — **tri·um·phant·ly** *adv*

tri·um·vir \trī-ˈəm-vər\ *n* **:** one of a commission or ruling body of three especially in ancient Rome [Latin, back-formation from *triumviri,* pl., "commission of three men," from *trium virum* "of three men"]

tri·um·vi·rate \-və-rət\ *n* **1 :** the office or government of triumvirs **2 :** a group of three persons who share power or office **3 :** a group or association of three

tri·une \ˈtrī-ˌün, -ˌyün\ *adj* **:** three in one; *esp* **:** of or relating to the Trinity ⟨the *triune* God⟩ [Latin *tri-* + *unus* "one"]

tri·va·lent \trī-ˈvā-lənt, ˈtrī-\ *adj* **:** having a chemical valence of three — **tri·va·lence** \-ləns\ *or* **tri·va·len·cy** \-lən-sē\ *n*

triv·et \ˈtriv-ət\ *n* **1 :** a three-legged stand or support **:** TRIPOD **2 :** a usually metal plate on very short legs used under a hot dish to protect the table [Old English *trefet*]

triv·ia \ˈtriv-ē-ə\ *n sing or pl* **:** unimportant matters or facts [New Latin, back-formation from Latin *trivialis* "trivial"]

triv·i·al \ˈtriv-ē-əl\ *adj* **1 :** ORDINARY 2a, COMMONPLACE **2 :** of little worth or importance **:** INSIGNIFICANT ⟨*trivial* problems⟩ [Latin *trivialis* "found everywhere, commonplace, trivial," from *trivium* "crossroads," from *tri-* + *via* "way"] — **triv·i·al·ly** \-ē-ə-lē\ *adv*

triv·i·al·i·ty \ˌtriv-ē-ˈal-ət-ē\ *n, pl* **-ties** **1 :** the quality or state of being trivial **2 :** something trivial **:** TRIFLE

trivial name *n* **1 :** the second term of a taxonomic binomial **2 :** a common or vernacular name of an organism or chemical

^{1}**tri·week·ly** \trī-ˈwē-klē, ˈtrī-\ *adj* **1 :** occurring, appearing, or done three times a week **2 :** occurring, appearing, or done every three weeks — **triweekly** *adv*

\ə\ **abut**	\au̇\ **out**	\i\ **tip**	\ȯ\ **saw**	\u̇\ **foot**
\ər\ **further**	\ch\ **chin**	\ī\ **life**	\ȯi\ **coin**	\y\ **yet**
\a\ **mat**	\e\ **pet**	\j\ **job**	\th\ **thin**	\yü\ **few**
\ā\ **take**	\ē\ **easy**	\ng\ **sing**	\t͟h\ **this**	\yu̇\ **cure**
\ä\ **cot, cart**	\g\ **go**	\ō\ **bone**	\ü\ **food**	\zh\ **vision**

[2]triweekly *n* : a triweekly publication

-trix \triks, ˌtriks\ *n suffix, pl* **-tri·ces** \trə-ˌsēz, ˈtrī-sēz\ *or* **-trix·es** \trik-səz, ˌtrik-\ **1** : female that does or is associated with a (specified) thing ⟨avia*trix*⟩ **2** : geometric line, point, or surface ⟨genera*trix*⟩ [Latin, feminine of *-tor,* suffix denoting an agent]

tRNA \ˌtē-ˌär-ˌen-ˈā, ˈtē-ˌär-ˌen-ˌā\ *n* : TRANSFER RNA

tro·chan·ter \trō-ˈkant-ər\ *n* : the second segment of an insect's leg adjacent to the coxa [Greek *trochantēr* "rough process at the upper part of the femur"]

tro·che \ˈtrō-kē, *British also* ˈtrōsh\ *n* : LOZENGE 2 [earlier *trochisk,* from Late Latin *trochiscus,* from Greek *trochiskos,* from *trochos* "wheel," from *trechein* "to run"]

tro·chee \ˈtrō-ˌkē\ *n* : a metrical foot consisting of one accented syllable followed by one unaccented syllable (as in *hungry*) [French *trochée,* from Latin *trochaeus,* from Greek *trochaios,* from *trochaios* "running," from *trochē* "run, course," from *trechein* "to run"] — **tro·cha·ic** \trō-ˈkā-ik\ *adj*

troch·le·ar nerve \ˌträk-lē-ər-\ *n* : either of the fourth pair of cranial nerves which control movements of some of the eye muscles — called also *trochlear* [*trochlea* "anatomical structure resembling a pulley," from Latin "block of pulleys," from Greek *trochileia*]

trocho·phore \ˈträk-ə-ˌfōr, -ˌfȯr\ *n* : a free-swimming ciliated larva occurring in several invertebrate groups (as mollusks and marine annelid worms) [derived from Greek *trochos* "wheel" + *pherein* "to carry"]

trod *past and past participle of* TREAD

trodden *past participle of* TREAD

trog·lo·dyte \ˈträg-lə-ˌdīt\ *n* **1** : a member of any of various peoples (as in antiquity) who lived or were reputed to live chiefly in caves **2** : a person characterized by solitary habits or outdated attitudes [Latin *troglodytae,* pl., from Greek *trōglodytai,* from *trōglē* "hole, cave" + *dyein* "to enter"] — **trog·lo·dyt·ic** \ˌträg-lə-ˈdit-ik\ *adj*

troi·ka \ˈtrȯi-kə\ *n* **1** : a Russian vehicle drawn by three horses abreast; *also* : a team for such a vehicle **2** : a group of three [Russian *troĭka,* from *troe* "three"]

Tro·jan \ˈtrō-jən\ *n* **1** : a native or inhabitant of ancient Troy **2** : one who shows pluck, endurance, or determined energy [Latin *trojanus* "of Troy," from *Troia, Troja* "Troy," from Greek *Trōïa*] — **Trojan** *adj*

Trojan horse *n* **1** : one intended to undermine or subvert from within **2** : a seemingly useful computer program that contains concealed instructions which when activated perform an illicit or malicious action — compare VIRUS 3, WORM 5 [from the large hollow wooden horse filled with Greek soldiers and introduced within the walls of Troy by a stratagem during the Trojan War]

Trojan War *n* : a 10-year war between the ancient Greeks and Trojans brought on by the abduction of Helen by Paris and ended with the destruction of Troy

[1]troll \ˈtrōl\ *vb* **1 a** : to sing the parts of (as a round or catch) in succession **b** : to sing loudly or in a jovial way **2** : to speak rapidly **3** : to fish or fish for with a hook and line drawn through the water (as behind a slowly moving boat) [Middle English *trollen* "to roll"] — **troll·er** *n*

[2]troll *n* : a lure or a line with its lure and hook used in trolling

[3]troll *n* : a dwarf or giant in Scandinavian folklore inhabiting caves or hills [Norwegian *troll* and Danish *trold,* from Old Norse *troll* "giant, demon"]

trol·ley *also* **trol·ly** \ˈträl-ē\ *n, pl* **trolleys** *also* **trollies** **1 a** : a device for carrying current from a wire to an electrically driven vehicle **b** : a streetcar that runs on tracks and gets its electric power through a trolley — called also *trolley car* **2** : a wheeled carriage running on an overhead rail or track [probably from earlier *troll* "to roll," from Middle English *trollen*]

trol·ley·bus \ˈträl-ē-ˌbəs\ *n* : a bus powered by electric power from two overhead wires

trol·lop \ˈträl-əp\ *n* : a disreputable woman; *esp* : one who engages in lewd behavior [related to *trull*]

trom·bone \träm-ˈbōn, trəm-, ˌtram-\ *n* : a brass wind instrument that has a cupped mouthpiece, that consists of a long cylindrical metal tube bent twice upon itself and ending in a bell, and that has a movable slide with which to vary the pitch [Italian, from *tromba* "trumpet," of Germanic origin] — **trom·bon·ist** \-ˈbō-nəst\ *n*

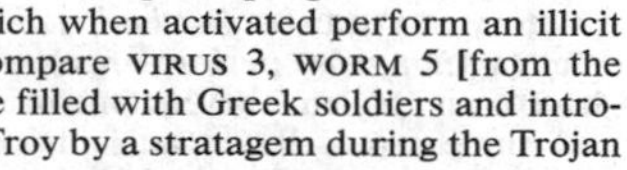

trombone

tromp \ˈträmp, ˈtrȯmp\ *vb* : TRAMP 1 ⟨*tromped* from room to room⟩ [alteration of *tramp*]

-tron \ˌträn\ *n suffix* : device for the manipulation of subatomic particles ⟨cyclo*tron*⟩ [Greek, suffix denoting an instrument]

[1]troop \ˈtrüp\ *n* **1 a** : a group of soldiers **b** : a cavalry unit corresponding to an infantry company **c** *pl* : ARMED FORCES **2** : a collection of people or things : COMPANY **3** : a flock of mammals or birds **4** : a unit of Boy Scouts or Girl Scouts under an adult leader [Middle French *troupe* "company, herd," of Germanic origin]

[2]troop *vi* **1** : to move or gather in crowds **2** : to spend time together : ASSOCIATE ⟨a dove *trooping* with crows⟩

troop·er \ˈtrü-pər\ *n* **1** : an enlisted member of a cavalry unit **2 a** : a mounted police officer **b** : a state police officer

troop·ship \ˈtrüp-ˌship\ *n* : a ship or aircraft for carrying troops

trop- *or* **tropo-** *combining form* : turn : turning : change ⟨*tropism*⟩ ⟨*tropo*sphere⟩ [Greek *tropos,* from *trepein* "to turn"]

trope \ˈtrōp\ *n* : the use of a word or expression in a figurative sense : FIGURE OF SPEECH [Latin *tropus,* from Greek *tropos* "turn, way, trope"]

tro·phic \ˈtrō-fik\ *adj* **1** : of or relating to nutrition : NUTRITIONAL ⟨*trophic* disorders⟩ **2** : [3]TROPIC [French *trophique,* from Greek *trophikos,* from *trophē* "nourishment," from *trephein* "to nourish"] — **tro·phi·cal·ly** \-fi-kə-lē, -klē\ *adv*

trophic level *n* : the position an organism occupies in a food chain based on its method of obtaining food ⟨plant-eating animals were assigned to the second *trophic level*⟩

[1]tro·phy \ˈtrō-fē\ *n, pl* **trophies** **1 a** : a memorial of an ancient Greek or Roman victory raised on the field of battle **b** : a representation of such a memorial (as on a medal) **2** : something won or given in victory or conquest especially when preserved or mounted as a memorial ⟨took the enemy's flags as *trophies*⟩ ⟨a tennis *trophy*⟩ [Medieval French *trophee,* from Latin *tropaeum, trophaeum,* from Greek *trepaion,* derived from *tropē* "turn, rout," from *trepein* "to turn"] — **tro·phied** \-fēd\ *adj*

[2]trophy *vt* **tro·phied; tro·phy·ing** : to win a trophy ⟨the racer *trophied* in two events⟩

-tro·phy \trə-fē\ *n combining form, pl* **-trophies** : nutrition : nurture : growth ⟨hyper*trophy*⟩ [Greek *-trophia,* from *trephein* "to nourish"]

[1]trop·ic \ˈträp-ik\ *n* **1** : either of the two parallels of the earth's latitude that are approximately 23½ degrees north of the equator and approximately 23½ degrees south of the equator **2** *pl, often cap* : the region lying between the two tropics [Latin *tropicus* "of the solstice," from Greek *tropikos,* from *tropē* "turn"; from the fact that their projections on the celestial sphere mark the sun's declination at the solstices]

[2]tropic *adj* : of, relating to, or occurring in the tropics : TROPICAL

[3]tro·pic \ˈtrō-pik\ *adj* **1** : of, relating to, or characteristic of tropism or of a tropism **2** *of a hormone* : influencing the activity of a specified gland

trop·i·cal *for 1* ˈträp-i-kəl, *for 2* ˈtrōp- *also* ˈträp-\ *adj* **1** : of, relating to, occurring in, or suitable for use in the tropics ⟨a *tropical* island⟩ ⟨*tropical* diseases⟩ **2** : FIGURATIVE 2 — **trop·i·cal·ly** \-kə-lē, -klē\ *adv*

tropical aquarium *n* : an aquarium kept at a uniform warmth and used especially for tropical fish

tropical cyclone *n* : a cyclone originating in the tropics; *esp* : HURRICANE

tropical fish *n* : any of various small usually showy fishes of tropical origin often kept in a tropical aquarium

tropical oil *n* : any of several oils (as coconut oil and palm oil) that are high in saturated fatty acids

tropical rain forest *n* : RAIN FOREST 1

tropical storm *n* : a tropical cyclone with strong winds of less than hurricane intensity

tropic bird *n* : any of several web-footed oceanic birds related to the pelicans that are mostly white with a little black and a very long central pair of tail feathers

Tropic of Cancer : the parallel of latitude that is approximately 23½ degrees north of the equator and is the northernmost latitude reached

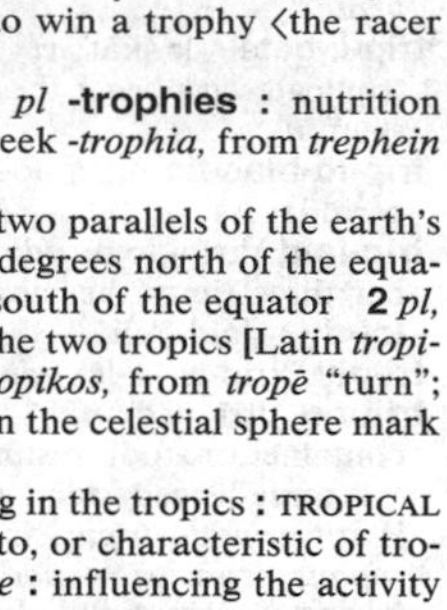

tropic bird

by the overhead sun [from the sign of the zodiac which its celestial projection intersects]

Tropic of Capricorn : the parallel of latitude that is approximately 23½ degrees south of the equator and is the southernmost latitude reached by the overhead sun [from the sign of the zodiac which its celestial projection intersects]

tro•pism \ˈtrō-ˌpiz-əm\ *n* : orientation by a plant or sessile animal or one of its parts that involves turning or growing toward or away from a stimulus (as light or moisture); *also* : a reflex reaction involving such movement — compare TAXIS [Greek *tropos* "turn," from *trepein* "to turn"] — **tro•pis•tic** \trō-ˈpis-tic\ *adj*

tro•po•pause \ˈtrōp-ə-ˌpȯz, ˈträp-\ *n* : the region at the top of the troposphere

tro•po•sphere \ˈtrōp-ə-ˌsfiər, ˈträp-\ *n* : the lowest part of the earth's atmosphere in which most weather changes occur and temperature decreases rapidly with altitude and which extends from the surface to the bottom of the stratosphere [Greek *tropos* "turn"] — **tro•po•spher•ic** \ˌtrōp-ə-ˈsfiər-ik, ˌträp-, -ˈsfer-\ *adj*

[1]**trot** \ˈträt\ *n* **1 a** (1) : a moderately fast gait of a four-footed animal (as a horse) in which a front foot and the opposite hind foot move at the same time (2) : a jogging gait of humans that falls between a walk and a run **b** : a ride on horseback **2** : a literal translation of a foreign text [Medieval French, from *troter* "to trot," of Germanic origin]

[2]**trot** *vb* **trot•ted; trot•ting** **1 a** : to ride, drive, or go at a trot **b** : to cause to go at a trot **2** : to proceed briskly : HURRY

[1]**troth** \ˈträth, ˈtrȯth, ˈtrōth *or with* t͟h\ *n* **1** : loyal or pledged faithfulness : FIDELITY **2** : one's pledged word; *also* : BETROTHAL [Old English *trēowth*]

[2]**troth** *vt* : BETROTH, PLEDGE

trot out *vt* : to bring forward for display or use ⟨*trotted* out a new excuse⟩

Trots•ky•ism \ˈträt-skē-ˌiz-əm, ˈtrȯt-\ *n* : the Communist principles developed by or associated with Leon Trotsky and usually including adherence to the concept of worldwide revolution — **Trots•ky•ist** \-skē-əst\ *n or adj* — **Trots•ky•ite** \-skē-ˌīt\ *n or adj*

trot•ter \ˈträt-ər\ *n* : one that trots; *esp* : a standardbred horse trained for harness racing

trou•ba•dour \ˈtrü-bə-ˌdōr, -ˌdȯr, -ˌdu̇r\ *n* : a poet-musician of medieval France and Italy [French, from Occitan *trobador,* from *trobar* "to compose"]

[1]**trou•ble** \ˈtrəb-əl\ *vb* **trou•bled; trou•bling** \ˈtrəb-ling, -ə-ling\ **1 a** : to agitate or become agitated mentally or spiritually : WORRY, DISTURB ⟨her continued absence *troubled* him⟩ **b** : to produce physical disorder in : AFFLICT ⟨*troubled* with weak knees⟩ **c** : to put to exertion or inconvenience ⟨may I *trouble* you for the salt⟩ **2** : to put into confused motion ⟨wind *troubled* the sea⟩ **3** : to make an effort : take pains ⟨do not *trouble* to come⟩ [Medieval French *trubler,* derived from Latin *turbulentus* "turbulent"]

[2]**trouble** *n* **1 a** : the quality or state of being troubled : MISFORTUNE ⟨help people in *trouble*⟩ **b** : an instance of distress or annoyance ⟨made light of her *troubles*⟩ **2** : civil disorder or agitation ⟨labor *trouble*⟩ **3** : an effort made : PAIN 4 ⟨took the *trouble* to call⟩ **4** : a state or condition of distress, annoyance, or difficulty ⟨in big financial *trouble*⟩: as **a** : a condition of physical distress : AILMENT ⟨having back *trouble*⟩ **b** : failure to work properly : MALFUNCTION ⟨engine *trouble*⟩ ⟨*trouble* with the plumbing⟩ **c** : a condition of doing something badly or only with great difficulty ⟨has *trouble* breathing⟩ ⟨had *trouble* reading⟩ **5 a** : a cause of distress, annoyance, or inconvenience ⟨don't mean to be any *trouble*⟩ **b** : a negative feature : DRAWBACK ⟨laziness is your biggest *trouble*⟩ **c** : the unhappy or sad fact ⟨the *trouble* is, I'm broke⟩ ***synonyms*** see EFFORT

troubled *adj* **1 a** : showing concern : ANXIOUS ⟨*troubled* feelings⟩ **b** : exhibiting emotional or behavioral problems ⟨a program for *troubled* youth⟩ **2** : characterized by or indicative of trouble ⟨our *troubled* cities⟩

trou•ble•mak•er \ˈtrəb-əl-ˌmā-kər\ *n* : a person who causes problems or disagreements

trou•ble•shoot \-ˌshüt\ *vb* **-shot** \-ˌshät\; **-shoot•ing** **1** : to operate or serve as a troubleshooter ⟨is *troubleshooting* for an electronics firm⟩ **2** : to investigate or deal with in the role of a troubleshooter ⟨*troubleshoot* a problem⟩

trou•ble•shoot•er \-ˌshüt-ər\ *n* **1** : a skilled worker employed to locate trouble and make repairs in machinery and technical equipment **2** : one that is expert in resolving disputes or problems

trou•ble•some \ˈtrəb-əl-səm\ *adj* **1** : requiring or involving continued or tiring effort, attention, or study : DIFFICULT, BURDENSOME ⟨a *troublesome* task⟩ **2** : giving trouble or anxiety : VEXATIOUS ⟨*troublesome* news⟩ — **trou•ble•some•ly** *adv* — **trou•ble•some•ness** *n*

trou•blous \ˈtrəb-ləs, -ə-ləs\ *adj* **1** : full of trouble ⟨*troublous* times⟩ **2** : causing troubles : TROUBLESOME ⟨*troublous* dreams⟩ — **trou•blous•ly** *adv* — **trou•blous•ness** *n*

trough \ˈtrȯf, ˈtrȯth\ *n, pl* **troughs** \ˈtrȯfs, ˈtrȯvz, ˈtrȯths, ˈtrȯt͟hz, ˈtrȯz\ **1 a** : a long shallow often V-shaped receptacle for the drinking water or feed of domestic animals **b** : any of various domestic or industrial containers **2 a** : a conduit, drain, or channel for water; *esp* : a gutter along the eaves of a building **b** : a long and narrow or shallow depression (as between waves or hills) **3** : the low point in a cycle; *esp* : an elongated area of low barometric pressure [Old English *trog*]

trounce \ˈtrau̇ns\ *vt* : to thrash or punish severely; *esp* : to defeat decisively [origin unknown]

[1]**troupe** \ˈtrüp\ *n* : COMPANY, TROOP; *esp* : a group of stage performers [French, of Germanic origin]

[2]**troupe** *vi* : to travel in a troupe; *also* : to perform as a member of a stage troupe — **troup•er** *n*

trou•ser \ˈtrau̇-zər\ *adj* : of, relating to, or designed for trousers ⟨*trouser* pockets⟩

trou•sers \ˈtrau̇-zərz\ *n pl* : PANTS 1 [earlier *trouse,* from Scottish Gaelic *triubhas*]

trous•seau \ˈtrü-ˌsō\ *n, pl* **trous•seaux** \-ˌsōz\ *or* **trous•seaus** : the personal possessions (as clothes and household linens) of a bride [French, from *trousse* "bundle," from *trousser* "to truss"]

trout \ˈtrau̇t\ *n, pl* **trout** *also* **trouts** **1** : any of various food and sport fishes that are mostly smaller than the related salmons and are restricted to cool clear fresh water or are anadromous **2** : any of various fishes that resemble the true trouts [Old English *trūht,* from Late Latin *trocta, tructa,* a kind of fish with sharp teeth, from Greek *trōktēs,* literally, "gnawer," from *trōgein* "to gnaw"]

trout lily *n* : DOGTOOTH VIOLET [probably from its speckled leaves]

trove \ˈtrōv\ *n* **1** : DISCOVERY 2, FIND **2** : a valuable collection : TREASURE; *also* : HAUL 1a [short for *treasure trove*]

trow \ˈtrō\ *vb* **1** *obsolete* : BELIEVE 3, TRUST **2** *archaic* : THINK 3, SUPPOSE [Old English *trēowan*]

[1]**trow•el** \ˈtrau̇-əl, ˈtrau̇l\ *n* **1** : a small hand tool consisting of a flat blade with a handle used for spreading and smoothing mortar or plaster **2** : a small hand tool with a curved blade used by gardeners [Medieval French *truelle,* from Late Latin *truella,* from Latin *trulla* "ladle"]

[2]**trowel** *vt* **-eled** *or* **-elled; -el•ing** *or* **-el•ling** : to smooth, mix, or apply with a trowel

troy \ˈtrȯi\ *adj* : expressed in troy weight [Middle English *troye,* probably from *Troyes,* France]

troy weight *n* : a series of units of weight based on a pound of 12 ounces and the ounce of 20 pennyweights or 480 grains — see MEASURE table

tru•ant \ˈtrü-ənt\ *n* : one who shirks duty; *esp* : one who stays out of school without permission [Medieval French, "vagabond, idler," of Celtic origin] — **tru•an•cy** \-ən-sē\ *n* — **truant** *adj*

truant officer *n* : a person employed by a public-school system to investigate the continued absences of pupils

truce \ˈtrüs\ *n* **1** : a temporary interruption of fighting by mutual agreement of the combatants : ARMISTICE **2** : a temporary rest especially from a disagreeable state or activity [Middle English *trewes,* pl. of *trewe* "agreement," from Old English *trēow* "fidelity"]

[1]**truck** \ˈtrək\ *vb* : to exchange goods : BARTER [Medieval French *troquer*]

[2]**truck** *n* **1** : BARTER **2** : goods for barter or for small trade **3** : close association or connection ⟨will have no *truck* with liars⟩ **4** : payment of wages in goods instead of cash **5** : vegetables grown for market **6** : small articles of little value; *also* : RUBBISH

\ə\ **abut**	\au̇\ **out**	\i\ **tip**	\ȯ\ **saw**	\u̇\ **foot**
\ər\ **further**	\ch\ **chin**	\ī\ **life**	\ȯi\ **coin**	\y\ **yet**
\a\ **mat**	\e\ **pet**	\j\ **job**	\th\ **thin**	\yü\ **few**
\ā\ **take**	\ē\ **easy**	\ng\ **sing**	\t͟h\ **this**	\yu̇\ **cure**
\ä\ **cot, cart**	\g\ **go**	\ō\ **bone**	\ü\ **food**	\zh\ **vision**

[3]**truck** *n* **1** : a small wooden cap at the top of a flagpole or mast **2** : a vehicle (as a small flat-topped car on wheels, a two-wheeled barrow with long handles, or a strong heavy wagon or automobile) for carrying heavy articles **3 a** : a swiveling carriage with springs and one or more pairs of wheels used to carry one end of a railroad car or a locomotive **b** : a short heavy-duty automotive vehicle equipped with a swiveling device for hauling a trailer; *also* : a truck with attached trailer [probably back-formation from *truckle*]

[4]**truck** *vb* **1** : to transport on or by truck **2** : to be employed as a truck driver

truck·er \ˈtrək-ər\ *n* **1** : a person whose business is transporting goods by truck **2** : a truck driver

truck farm *n* : a farm growing vegetables for market — **truck farmer** *n*

truck garden *n* : a garden where vegetables are raised for market

truck·ing \ˈtrək-iŋ\ *n* : the process or business of transporting goods on trucks

truck·le \ˈtrək-əl\ *vi* **truck·led; truck·ling** \ˈtrək-liŋ, -ə-liŋ\ : to act in a servile way : yield to the will of another : SUBMIT ⟨*truckle* to a conqueror⟩ [from the lower position of the truckle bed] — **truck·ler** \-lər, -ə-lər\ *n*

truckle bed *n* : TRUNDLE BED [*truckle* "small wheel," from Middle English *trokell* "small wheel, pulley," from Latin *trochlea* "block of pulleys"]

truck·line \ˈtrək-ˌlīn\ *n* : a transportation line using trucks

truck·load \ˈtrək-ˈlōd, -ˌlōd\ *n* : a load or amount that fills or could fill a truck

truck·man \ˈtrək-mən\ *n* **1** : TRUCKER **2** : a member of a fire department unit that operates a ladder truck

truck system *n* : the system of paying wages in goods instead of cash

truc·u·lent \ˈtrək-yə-lənt *also* ˈtrük-\ *adj* **1** : feeling or displaying ferocity : CRUEL, SAVAGE ⟨*truculent* warriors⟩ **2** : DESTRUCTIVE, DEADLY **3** : very bitter and harsh ⟨*truculent* criticism⟩ **4** : AGGRESSIVE, BELLIGERENT ⟨a *truculent* child⟩ [Latin *truculentus,* from *truc-, trux* "fierce"] — **truc·u·lence** \-ləns\ *also* **truc·u·len·cy** \-lən-sē\ *n* — **truc·u·lent·ly** *adv*

[1]**trudge** \ˈtrəj\ *vb* **1** : to walk or march steadily and usually laboriously ⟨*trudged* through deep snow⟩ **2** : to walk or march along or over ⟨*trudged* the trail⟩ [origin unknown] — **trudg·er** *n*

[2]**trudge** *n* : a long tiring walk : TRAMP

trud·gen stroke \ˈtrəj-ən-\ *n* : a swimming stroke in which a double overarm motion is combined with a scissors kick [John *Trudgen,* died 1902, English swimmer]

[1]**true** \ˈtrü\ *adj* **tru·er; tru·est** **1** : STEADFAST 2, LOYAL **2** *archaic* : TRUTHFUL **3 a** : corresponding to fact or actuality : ACCURATE, CORRECT ⟨a *true* description⟩ **b** : logically necessary **c** : CONSISTENT 2 ⟨*true* to character⟩ **4** : fully realized or fulfilled ⟨dreams come *true*⟩ **5** : properly so called : GENUINE ⟨the abomasum or *true* stomach of a ruminant animal⟩ ⟨*true* love⟩; *also* : TYPICAL ⟨the *true* cats⟩ **6** : that is fitted or formed or that functions accurately **7** : RIGHTFUL, LEGITIMATE ⟨the *true* owner⟩ ⟨our *true* ruler⟩ **8** : determined with reference to the earth's axis rather than the magnetic poles ⟨*true* north⟩ **9** : NARROW 2, STRICT ⟨in the *truest* sense⟩ [Old English *trēowe*] ***synonyms*** see REAL — **true·ness** *n*

[2]**true** *n* **1** : TRUTH 2a(1), REALITY — usually used with *the* **2** : the quality or state of being accurate (as in alignment or adjustment) — used in the phrases *in true* and *out of true*

[3]**true** *vt* **trued; true·ing** *also* **tru·ing** : to make level, square, balanced, or concentric : bring to desired mechanical accuracy or form ⟨*true* up a board⟩ ⟨*true* up an engine cylinder⟩

[4]**true** *adv* **1** : in agreement with fact or reality **2 a** : without deviation : ACCURATELY ⟨the arrow flew straight and *true*⟩ **b** : without variation from type ⟨breed *true*⟩

true bill *n* : a bill of indictment endorsed by a grand jury as justifying prosecution of the accused

true–blue \ˈtrü-ˈblü\ *adj* **1** : marked by unswerving loyalty (as to a political party) **2** : GENUINE 1 ⟨a *true-blue* romantic⟩

true·born \-ˌbȯrn\ *adj* : genuinely such by birth ⟨a *trueborn* American⟩

true bug *n* : BUG 1b

true–false test *n* : a test consisting of a series of statements to be marked as true or false

true·heart·ed \ˈtrü-ˈhärt-əd\ *adj* : STEADFAST 2, LOYAL

true–life \ˌtrü-ˌlīf\ *adj* : true to life ⟨a *true-life* story⟩

true·love \ˈtrü-ˌləv\ *n* : one truly beloved or loving : SWEETHEART

true lover's knot *n* : a complicated ornamental knot not easily untied and symbolic of mutual love — called also *truelove knot*

true rib *n* : one of the ribs connected directly with the sternum by cartilage and in humans constituting the first seven pairs

true seal *n* : HAIR SEAL

truf·fle \ˈtrəf-əl, ˈtrüf-\ *n* : the dark or light wrinkled edible subterranean fruiting body of any of several European fungi; *also* : a fungus that produces truffles [Middle French *truffe,* from Occitan *trufa*]

tru·ism \ˈtrü-ˌiz-əm\ *n* : an obvious truth — **tru·is·tic** \trü-ˈis-tik\ *adj*

trull \ˈtrəl\ *n* : PROSTITUTE, STRUMPET [probably from Middle English *trollen* (in *trollen forth* "to travel about, wander"), derived from Medieval French *troller, treiller* "to hunt for game without a scent or path"]

tru·ly \ˈtrü-lē\ *adv* **1** : SINCERELY — often used in a letter as a complimentary close after *yours* **2** : in agreement with fact : TRUTHFULLY **3** : with exactness of construction or operation : ACCURATELY **4 a** : INDEED — often used as an intensive ⟨*truly,* you are nice⟩ or interjectionally to express astonishment or doubt **b** : without pretense : GENUINELY **5** : as it ought to be

[1]**trump** \ˈtrəmp\ *n* **1** : TRUMPET 1 **2** : a sound of or as if of trumpeting [Medieval French *trumpe*]

[2]**trump** *n* **1 a** : a card of a suit whose cards will win over any card of any other suit **b** : the suit whose cards are trumps for a particular hand — often used in plural **2** : TRUMP CARD **3** : a dependable and exemplary person [alteration of [1]*triumph*]

[3]**trump** *vb* **1** : to take with a trump ⟨*trump* a trick⟩ **2** : to play a trump **3** : to get the better of : OUTDO ⟨*trumped* her competitors⟩

trump card *n* : a decisive overriding factor or final resource ⟨knew his *trump card* was the allegiance of his followers⟩

trumped–up \ˈtrəm-ˈtəp, ˈtrəmp-\ *adj* : MADE-UP 2, SPURIOUS ⟨*trumped-up* charges⟩

trum·pery \ˈtrəm-pə-rē, -prē\ *n, pl* **-per·ies** **1 a** : trivial or useless articles : JUNK **b** : worthless nonsense **2** *archaic* : tawdry finery [Medieval French *tromperie* "deceit," from *tromper* "to deceive"] — **trumpery** *adj*

[1]**trum·pet** \ˈtrəm-pət\ *n* **1** : a wind instrument consisting of a long cylindrical metal tube commonly once or twice curved and ending in a bell **2** : a trumpet player **3** : something that resembles a trumpet or its tonal quality: as **a** : a funnel-shaped instrument (as a megaphone) for collecting, directing, or intensifying sound ⟨an ear *trumpet*⟩ **b** (1) : a very loud voice (2) : a penetrating cry (as of an elephant) [Medieval French *trompette,* from *trumpe*] — **trum·pet·like** \-ˌlīk\ *adj*

[2]**trumpet** *vb* **1** : to blow a trumpet **2** : to sound or proclaim on or as if on a trumpet ⟨*trumpeted* the news⟩ **3** : to make a sound similar to that of a trumpet

trum·pet·er \ˈtrəm-pət-ər\ *n* **1** : a trumpet player; *esp* : one that gives signals with a trumpet **2 a** : TRUMPETER SWAN **b** : any of an Asian breed of pigeons with a rounded crest and heavily feathered feet

trumpeter swan *n* : a rare pure white swan of western North America noted for its loud low-pitched call

trumpet vine *n* : a North American woody vine with pinnate leaves and large typically red trumpet-shaped flowers — called also *trumpet creeper*

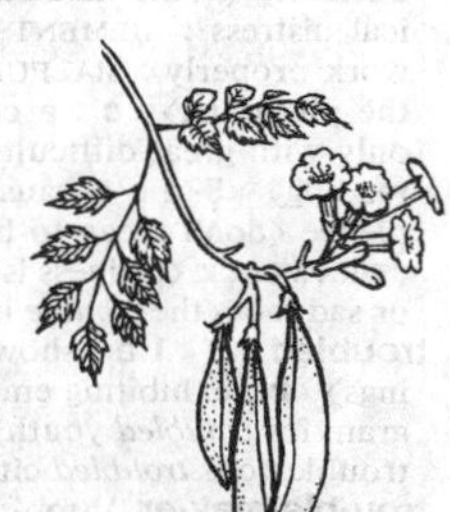
trumpet vine

trump up *vt* **1** : to concoct especially with intent to deceive : FABRICATE, INVENT ⟨*trump up* false charges⟩ **2** *archaic* : to cite as support for an action or claim : ALLEGE

[1]**trun·cate** \ˈtrəŋ-ˌkāt, ˈtrən-\ *adj* : having the end square or blunt ⟨a *truncate* leaf⟩

[2]**truncate** *vt* : to shorten by or as if by cutting off [Latin *truncare,* from *truncus* "trunk"] — **trun·ca·tion** \ˌtrəŋ-ˈkā-shən, ˌtrən-\ *n*

trun·cat·ed \-ˌkāt-əd\ *adj* **1** : having the top replaced by a plane section and especially by one parallel to the base ⟨a *truncated* cone⟩ **2 a** : cut short : CURTAILED

⟨a *truncated* schedule⟩ **b** : lacking an expected or normal element (as a syllable) at beginning or end
¹trun·cheon \ˈtrən-chən\ *n* **1** : a shattered spear or lance **2 a** *obsolete* : CLUB 1a **b** : BATON 1 **c** : a police officer's club [Medieval French *trunchun,* derived from Latin *truncus* "trunk"]
²truncheon *vt, archaic* : to beat with a truncheon
trun·dle \ˈtrən-dᵊl\ *vb* **trun·dled; trun·dling** \ˈtrən-dling, -dᵊl-ing\ **1 a** : to propel by causing to rotate : ROLL ⟨*trundled* a tire down the street⟩ **b** : to progress by revolving **2** : to transport in or as if in a wheeled vehicle : HAUL ⟨*trundled* her off to school⟩ **3** : to move on or as if on wheels ⟨buses *trundling* through the city⟩ [*trundle, trendle* "small wheel," from Old English *trendel* "circle, ring, wheel"] — **trun·dler** \-dlər, -dᵊl-ər\ *n*
trundle bed *n* : a low bed usually on small wheels that can be slid under a higher bed — called also *truckle bed*
trunk \ˈtrəngk\ *n* **1 a** : the main stem of a tree apart from branches or roots **b** : the body of a person or animal apart from the head and limbs : TORSO **c** : the main or central part of something ⟨the *trunk* of an artery⟩ **2 a** : a box or chest for holding clothes or other goods especially for traveling **b** : the enclosed space usually in the rear of an automobile for carrying articles (as luggage) **3** : the long flexible muscular nose of an elephant or a related mammal (as a woolly mammoth) **4** *pl* : men's shorts worn chiefly for sports ⟨swimming *trunks*⟩ **5** : TRUNK LINE [Medieval French *trunc,* from Latin *truncus* "tree trunk, torso"]
trunk hose *n pl* : short full breeches reaching about halfway down the thigh worn chiefly in the late 16th and early 17th centuries
trunk line *n* **1** : a transportation system (as a railroad) handling long-distance through traffic **2** : a main supply channel
trun·nion \ˈtrən-yən\ *n* : PIVOT 1, PIN; *esp* : either of two opposite projections on which a cannon is supported and elevated [French *trognon* "core, stump"]
¹truss \ˈtrəs\ *vt* **1 a** : to secure tightly : BIND ⟨they *trussed* up their captive⟩ **b** : to arrange for cooking by binding close the wings or legs of ⟨*truss* a turkey⟩ **2** : to support, strengthen, or stiffen by a truss [Middle English "to pack, load, bind," from Medieval French *trousser*] — **truss·er** *n*
²truss *n* **1** : a rigid framework of beams, bars, or rods ⟨a *truss* for a roof⟩ **2** : a device worn to hold a hernia in place
truss bridge *n* : a bridge supported mainly by trusses
¹trust \ˈtrəst\ *n* **1 a** : assured reliance on the character, ability, strength, or truth of someone or something **b** : one in which confidence is placed **2 a** : dependence on something future or contingent : HOPE **b** : reliance on future payment for goods delivered : CREDIT ⟨bought furniture on *trust*⟩ **3 a** : a property interest held by one person or concern (as a bank or trust company) for the benefit of another **b** : a combination of firms or corporations formed by a legal agreement; *esp* : one that reduces or threatens to reduce competition **4 a** : something (as a public office) committed to one to be used or cared for in the interest of another **b** : responsible charge or office **c** : CUSTODY, CARE [Middle English, probably of Scandinavian origin] — **in trust** : in the care or possession of a trustee
²trust *vb* **1 a** : to place confidence : DEPEND ⟨*trust* in God⟩ ⟨*trust* to luck⟩ **b** : to be confident : HOPE **2** : to commit or place in one's care or keeping : ENTRUST ⟨*trusted* him with my car⟩ **3 a** : to rely on the truthfulness or accuracy of : BELIEVE ⟨never *trust* a rumor⟩ **b** : to place confidence in : rely on ⟨a friend you can *trust*⟩ **c** : to hope or expect confidently ⟨*trusts* that a solution will be found soon⟩ **4 a** : to sell or deliver on credit **b** : to extend credit to — **trust·er** *n*
trust·bust·er \ˈtrəst-ˌbəs-tər\ *n* : one that seeks to break up business trusts; *esp* : a federal official who prosecutes trusts under the antitrust laws — **trust–bust·ing** \-ting\ *n*
trust company *n* : a corporation (as a bank) organized to act as a trustee
trust·ee \ˌtrəs-ˈtē\ *n* **1** : a person to whom property is legally committed to be administered for the benefit of a beneficiary (as a person or charitable organization) **2** : a country charged with the supervision of a trust territory
trust·ee·ship \-ˌship\ *n* **1** : the office or function of a trustee **2** : supervisory control by one or more countries over a trust territory
trust·ful \ˈtrəst-fəl\ *adj* : full of trust : CONFIDING — **trust·ful·ly** \-fə-lē\ *adv* — **trust·ful·ness** *n*
trust fund *n* : property (as money or securities) settled or held in trust
trust·ing \ˈtrəs-ting\ *adj* : having trust, faith, or confidence : TRUSTFUL — **trust·ing·ly** \-ting-lē\ *adv*
trust territory *n* : a non-self-governing territory placed under an administrative authority by the Trusteeship Council of the United Nations
trust·wor·thy \ˈtrəst-ˌwər-t͟hē\ *adj* : worthy of confidence : DEPENDABLE ⟨*trustworthy* information⟩ ⟨a *trustworthy* babysitter⟩ — **trust·wor·thi·ly** \-t͟hə-lē\ *adv* — **trust·wor·thi·ness** \-t͟hē-nəs\ *n*
¹trusty \ˈtrəs-tē\ *adj* **trust·i·er; -est** : TRUSTWORTHY, DEPENDABLE ⟨a Boy Scout's *trusty* pocketknife⟩
²trusty \ˈtrəs-tē, ˌtrəs-ˈtē\ *n, pl* **trust·ies** : a trusty or trusted person; *esp* : a convict considered trustworthy and allowed special privileges
truth \ˈtrüth\ *n, pl* **truths** \ˈtrüt͟hz, ˈtrüths\ **1 a** *archaic* : FIDELITY 1a, CONSTANCY **b** : sincerity in action, character, and utterance **2 a** (1) : the real state of things : FACT (2) : the body of real things, events, and facts : ACTUALITY **b** (1) : a judgment, proposition, idea, or statement that is true or accepted as true ⟨the *truths* of science⟩ (2) : the body of such truths **3** : the property of being in accord with fact or reality [Old English *trēowth* "fidelity"] — **in truth** : in fact : ACTUALLY
truth·ful \ˈtrüth-fəl\ *adj* : telling or inclined to tell the truth — **truth·ful·ly** \-fə-lē\ *adv* — **truth·ful·ness** *n*
truth serum *n* : a drug (as thiopental) used to induce a subject under questioning to talk freely
truth set *n* : a mathematical or logical set containing all the elements that make a given statement of relationships true when substituted in it ⟨the equation $x + 7 = 10$ has as its *truth set* the single number 3⟩
¹try \ˈtrī\ *vb* **tried; try·ing** **1 a** : to examine or investigate judicially ⟨*try* a case⟩ **b** : to conduct the trial of **2 a** : to put to test or trial ⟨*try* your luck⟩ ⟨*try* out something new⟩ **b** : to test to the limit or breaking point : STRAIN ⟨*try* one's patience⟩ **3** : to melt down and obtain in a pure state : RENDER ⟨*try* lard from fat pork⟩ **4** : to make an attempt : ENDEAVOR ⟨*tried* to fix the car⟩ [Medieval French *trier* "to select, sort, examine, determine," probably from Late Latin *tritare* "to grind," from Latin *terere* "to rub, thresh"] — **try one's hand** : to attempt something for the first time

synonyms TRY, ATTEMPT, STRIVE mean to make an effort to accomplish an end. TRY suggests effort or experiment made in the hope of determining facts or of testing or proving something ⟨*tried* to determine her guilt or innocence⟩. ATTEMPT suggests a beginning of or venturing upon something and often implies failure ⟨*attempted* to break the world record in the long jump⟩. STRIVE implies great exertion against great difficulty and suggests persistent effort ⟨*strive* to achieve lasting peace⟩.

²try *n, pl* **tries** : an experimental trial : ATTEMPT
try for point : an attempt made after scoring a touchdown in football to kick a goal or to again carry the ball across into the opponents' end zone so as to score one or two additional points
try·ing \ˈtrī-ing\ *adj* : hard to bear or put up with ⟨a *trying* experience⟩
try on \trī-ˈȯn, ˈtrī-, -ˈän\ *vt* : to put on (a garment) in order to test the fit — **try–on** \ˈtrī-ˌȯn, -ˌän\ *n*
try·out \ˈtrī-ˌau̇t\ *n* : an experimental performance or demonstration: as **a** : a testing of one's ability to perform especially as an athlete or actor **b** : a test performance of a play before its formal opening
try out \trī-ˈau̇t, ˈtrī-\ *vi* : to compete for a position especially on an athletic team or for a part in a play
try·pano·so·ma \trip-ˌan-ə-ˈsō-mə\ *n* : TRYPANOSOME
try·pano·some \trip-ˈan-ə-ˌsōm\ *n* : any of a genus of parasitic flagellate protozoans that infect the blood of various vertebrates including humans, are usually transmitted by the bite of an insect, and include some that cause serious diseases (as sleeping sickness) [New Latin *Trypanosoma,* genus name, from Greek *trypanon* "auger" + *sōma* "body"]
try·pano·so·mi·a·sis \trip-ˌan-ə-sə-ˈmī-ə-səs\ *n, pl* **-a·ses** \-ə-ˌsēz\ : infection with or disease caused by trypanosomes
tryp·sin \ˈtrip-sən\ *n* : an enzyme that is secreted in the pancre-

atic juice in the form of trypsinogen, that is activated in the duodenum, and that breaks down protein [perhaps from Greek *tryein* "to wear down" + English *-psin* (as in *pepsin*)] — **tryp·tic** \ˈtrip-tik\ *adj*

tryp·sin·o·gen \trip-ˈsin-ə-jən\ *n* **:** an inactive substance released by the pancreas into the duodenum to form trypsin

tryp·to·phan \ˈtrip-tə-ˌfan\ *also* **tryp·to·phane** \-ˌfān\ *n* **:** a crystalline essential amino acid that is widely distributed in proteins [derived from *trypsin* + Greek *phanēs* "appearing," from *phainein* "to show"]

try square *n* **:** an instrument used for laying off right angles and testing whether work is square

[1]tryst \ˈtrist, *especially British* ˈtrīst\ *n* **1 :** an agreement (as between lovers) to meet **2 :** an appointed meeting or meeting place [Middle English *triste* "appointed station for hunters," probably from *trist, trust* "confidence, trust"]

[2]tryst *vi* **:** to make or keep a tryst

try·works \ˈtrī-ˌwərks\ *n* **:** a brick furnace (as on a whaling ship) for melting down blubber to produce whale oil

tsar, tsarevitch, tsarina, tsarism *variant of* CZAR, CZAREVITCH, CZARINA, CZARISM

tset·se fly \ˈset-sē-, ˈtset-, ˈsēt-, ˈtsēt-, ˈtēt-\ *n* **:** any of a genus of two-winged flies found mostly in Africa south of the Sahara Desert that include vectors of human and animal trypanosomes — called also *tsetse* [Tswana (Bantu language of southern Africa) *tsètsè* "fly"]

T–shirt *also* **tee shirt** \ˈtē-ˌshərt\ *n* **:** a collarless short-sleeved or sleeveless usually cotton undershirt; *also* **:** a jersey outer shirt of similar design [from its being shaped like a T]

tsk *a t-sound made by suction rather than explosion; often read as* ˈtisk\ *interj* — used to express disapproval

T square *n* **:** a ruler with a crosspiece or head at one end used in making parallel lines

tsu·na·mi \sü-ˈnäm-ē, tsü-\ *n* **:** TIDAL WAVE 2a [Japanese, from *tsu* "harbor" + *nami* "wave"] — **tsu·na·mic** \-ˈnäm-ik\ *adj*

tsu·tsu·ga·mu·shi disease \ˌsüt-sə-gə-ˈmü-shē-, ˌtsüt-, ˌtüt-, -ˈgäm-ü-shē-\ *n* **:** SCRUB TYPHUS [Japanese *tsutsugamushi* "scrub typhus mite," from *tsutsuga* "sickness" + *mushi* "insect"]

Tua·reg \ˈtwä-ˌreg\ *n, pl* **Tuareg** *or* **Tuaregs :** a member of a nomadic people of the central and western Sahara and the middle Niger from Timbuktu to Nigeria [Arabic *Tawāriq*]

tu·a·ta·ra \ˌtü-ə-ˈtär-ə\ *n, pl* **-tara** *or* **-taras :** a large spiny four-footed reptile of islands off the coast of New Zealand that has a vestigial third eye in the middle of the forehead and is the only living member of a once widely distributed order [Maori *tuatàra*]

tuatara

[1]tub \ˈtəb\ *n* **1 :** a wide low vessel originally formed with wooden staves, round bottom, and hoops **2 :** an old or slow boat **3 :** BATHTUB; *also* **:** BATH 2a **4 :** the amount that a tub will hold [Dutch *tubbe*]

[2]tub *vb* **tubbed; tub·bing :** to wash or bathe in a tub — **tub·ba·ble** \ˈtəb-ə-bəl\ *adj*

tu·ba \ˈtü-bə, ˈtyü-\ *n* **:** low-pitched brass instrument usually oval in shape and having a conical tube and a cup-shaped mouthpiece [Italian, from Latin, "trumpet"]

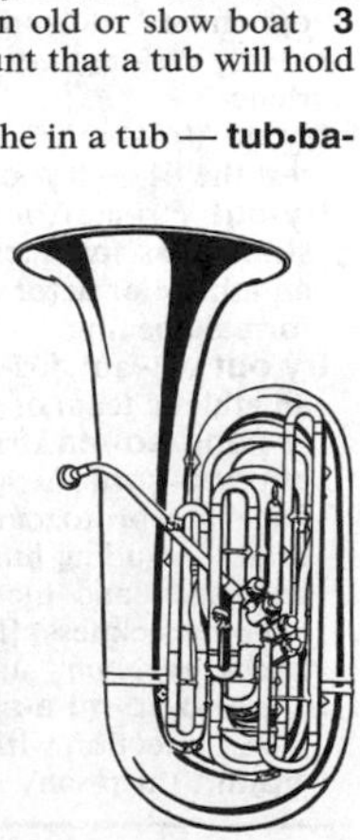

tuba

tub·al \ˈtü-bəl, ˈtyü-\ *adj* **:** of, relating to, or involving a tube

tub·by \ˈtəb-ē\ *adj* **tub·bi·er; -est :** PUDGY, CHUBBY

tube \ˈtüb, ˈtyüb\ *n* **1 a :** a hollow elongated cylinder; *esp* **:** one to convey fluids **b :** a slender channel within a plant or animal body **:** DUCT **2 :** any of various usually cylindrical structures or devices: as **a :** a round container from which a paste is dispensed by squeezing **b** (1) **:** TUNNEL (2) *British* **:** SUBWAY 2 **c :** the basically cylindrical part connecting the mouthpiece and bell of a wind instrument **d :** INNER TUBE **e :** ELECTRON TUBE **f :** TELEVISION ⟨watching the *tube*⟩ **3 :** an article of clothing shaped like a tube ⟨a *tube* top⟩ ⟨*tube* socks⟩ [French, from Latin *tubus*] — **tubed** \ˈtübd, ˈtyübd\ *adj* — **tube·like** \ˈtü-ˌblīk, ˈtyü-\ *adj*

tube foot *n* **:** one of the small flexible tubular processes of most echinoderms (as a starfish or sea urchin) that are extensions of the water-vascular system used especially in locomotion and grasping

tube·less \ˈtü-bləs, ˈtyü-\ *adj* **:** lacking a tube; *esp* **:** being a pneumatic tire that does not depend on an inner tube for airtightness

tube nucleus *n* **:** a nucleus of a pollen grain that is held to control growth of the pollen tube — compare GENERATIVE NUCLEUS

tu·ber \ˈtü-bər, ˈtyü-\ *n* **:** a short fleshy usually underground stem (as of a potato plant) bearing minute scale leaves each with a bud in its axil potentially able to produce a new plant — compare BULB, CORM **2 :** a fleshy root or rhizome resembling a tuber [Latin, "lump, tuber, truffle"]

tu·ber·cle \ˈtü-bər-kəl, ˈtyü-\ *n* **1 :** a small knobby prominence or outgrowth especially on a plant or animal **2 :** a small abnormal lump in the substance of an organ or in the skin; *esp* **:** one caused by tuberculosis [Latin *tuberculum,* from *tuber* "lump, tuber"] — **tu·ber·cled** \-kəld\ *adj*

tubercle bacillus *n* **:** the bacterium that causes tuberculosis

tu·ber·cu·lar \tu̇-ˈbər-kyə-lər, tyu̇-\ *adj* **1 :** of, relating to, or affected with tuberculosis **:** TUBERCULOUS ⟨a *tubercular* patient⟩ **2 :** characterized by tubercular lesions ⟨*tubercular* leprosy⟩ **3 :** relating to, resembling, or constituting a tubercle ⟨a *tubercular* lump⟩ — **tu·ber·cu·lar·ly** *adv*

tu·ber·cu·lin \tu̇-ˈbər-kyə-lən, tyu̇-\ *n* **:** a sterile liquid containing substances from the tubercle bacillus that is used in the diagnosis of tuberculosis

tuberculin test *n* **:** a test for sensitivity to tuberculin as a sign of past or present infection with the tubercle bacillus

tu·ber·cu·lo·sis \tu̇-ˌbər-kyə-ˈlō-səs, tyu̇-\ *n* **:** a communicable disease humans and some other vertebrates that is caused by a bacterium and is typically marked by wasting, fever, and formation of cheesy tubercles that in human beings occur mostly in the lungs

tu·ber·cu·lous \tu̇-ˈbər-kyə-ləs, tyu̇-\ *adj* **1 :** constituting or affected with tuberculosis **2 :** caused by or resulting from the tubercle bacillus ⟨*tuberculous* arthritis⟩

tube·rose \ˈtü-ˌbrōz, ˈtyü- (by folk etymology); *also* ˈtü-bə-ˌrōz, ˈtyü-, -bə-ˌrōs\ *n* **:** a Mexican bulbous herb related to the agaves and grown for its spike of fragrant white flowers [Latin *tuberosus* "tuberous," from *tuber* "tuber"]

tu·ber·os·i·ty \ˌtü-bə-ˈräs-ət-ē, ˌtyü-\ *n, pl* **-ties :** a rounded prominence; *esp* **:** one on a bone usually serving for the attachment of muscles or ligaments

tu·ber·ous \ˈtü-bə-rəs, ˈtyü-, -brəs\ *adj* **1 :** consisting of, resembling, or producing a tuber **2 :** of, relating to, or being a plant tuber or tuberous root

tube worm *n* **:** a worm that lives in a tube (as one made of sand grains or calcium carbonate): as **a :** any of various terrestrial or aquatic annelid worms **b :** any of a group of worms that may grow to 9 feet (3 meters) in length, are found especially near deep-sea hydrothermal vents, and are related to the annelids

tu·bi·fex worm \ˈtü-bə-ˌfeks-, ˈtyü-\ *n* **:** any of a genus of slender reddish oligochaete worms that live in tubes in fresh or brackish water and are widely used as food for aquarium fish [New Latin *Tubifex,* genus name, from Latin *tubus* "tube" + *facere* "to make"]

tub·ing \ˈtü-bing, ˈtyü-\ *n* **1 :** material in the form of a tube; *also* **:** a length or piece of tube **2 :** a series or system of tubes **3 :** the sport or activity of riding an inner tube (as down a river or snowy slope)

tu·bu·lar \ˈtü-byə-lər, ˈtyü-\ *adj* **1 :** having the form of or consisting of a tube **2 :** made or provided with tubes — **tu·bu·lar·i·ty** \ˌtü-byə-ˈlar-ət-ē, ˌtyü-\ *n*

tu·bule \ˈtü-byül, ˈtyü-\ *n* **:** a small tube; *esp* **:** a long slender anatomical channel

[1]tuck \ˈtək\ *vb* **1 a :** to pull up or draw together into folds **b :** to make a tuck in **2 :** to put or fit into a snug or safe place ⟨a cottage *tucked* away in the hill⟩ ⟨*tucked* their money away in the bank⟩ **3 a :** to push in the loose end of so as to hold tightly ⟨*tuck* in your shirt⟩ **b :** to cover by tucking in bedclothes ⟨a child *tucked* in for the night⟩ [Middle English "to finish (cloth) by stretching and beating, tuck," from Old English *tūcian* "to mistreat"]

[2]**tuck** *n* **1 :** a fold stitched into cloth to shorten, decorate, or control fullness **2 :** an act or instance of tucking

[3]**tuck** *n* **:** VIGOR 1, ENERGY [probably from [2]*tuck*]

[1]**tuck·er** \ˈtək-ər\ *n* **1 :** one that tucks **2 :** a piece of lace or cloth in the neckline of a dress

[2]**tucker** *vt* **tuck·ered; tuck·er·ing** \ˈtək-ring, -ə-ring\ **:** EXHAUST 2b — often used with *out* ⟨*tuckered* out by the hard work⟩ [obsolete English *tuck* "to reproach" + *-er* (as in [1]*batter*)]

Tu·dor \ˈtüd-ər, ˈtyüd-\ *adj* **1 :** of or relating to the English royal family that ruled from 1485 to 1603 **2 :** of, relating to, or characteristic of the Tudor period [Henry *Tudor* (Henry VII of England)] — **Tudor** *n*

Tues·day \ˈtüz-dē, ˈtyüz-\ *n* **:** the 3rd day of the week [Old English *tīwesdæg,* literally, "day of Tiu (god of war)"]

tu·fa \ˈtü-fə, ˈtyü-\ *n* **1 :** TUFF **2 :** a porous rock formed as a deposit from springs or streams; *esp* **:** TRAVERTINE [Italian *tufo,* from Latin *tophus*] — **tu·fa·ceous** \tü-ˈfā-shəs, tyü-\ *adj*

tuff \ˈtəf\ *n* **:** a rock composed of the finer kinds of volcanic detritus [Middle French *tuf,* from Italian *tufo*] — **tuff·a·ceous** \ˌtə-ˈfā-shəs\ *adj*

tuf·fet \ˈtəf-ət\ *n* **1 :** TUFT 1a **2 :** a low seat [Medieval French *tuffete*]

[1]**tuft** \ˈtəft\ *n* **1 a :** a small cluster of long flexible outgrowths (as hairs, feathers, or blades of grass) attached or close together at the base and free at the opposite end **b :** a bunch of soft fluffy threads cut off short and used as ornament **2 :** CLUMP 1, CLUSTER **3 :** one of the projections of yarns drawn through a fabric or otherwise making up a fabric so as to produce a surface of raised loops or cut pile [Medieval French *touffe*] — **tuft·ed** \ˈtəf-təd\ *adj* — **tufty** \ˈtəf-tē\ *adj*

[2]**tuft** *vt* **1 :** to provide or adorn with a tuft **2 :** to make (as a mattress) firm by stitching at intervals and sewing on tufts **3 :** to make (a fabric) of or with tufts

[1]**tug** \ˈtəg\ *vb* **tugged; tug·ging 1 a :** to pull hard **b :** to move by pulling hard **:** DRAG, HAUL **2 :** to struggle in opposition **3 :** to tow with a tugboat [Middle English *tuggen*] — **tug·ger** *n*

[2]**tug** *n* **1 a :** a harness trace **b :** a rope or chain used for pulling **2 a :** an act or instance of tugging **:** PULL **b :** a strong pulling force **3 a :** a straining effort **b :** a struggle between opposing individuals or opposite forces **4 :** TUGBOAT

tug·boat \ˈtəg-ˌbōt\ *n* **:** a strongly built powerful boat used for towing and pushing (as ships in harbors)

tug–of–war \ˌtəg-əv-ˈwȯr, ˌtəg-ə-\ *n, pl* **tugs–of–war 1 :** a struggle for supremacy or control **2 :** a contest in which two teams pull against each other at opposite ends of a rope

tu·i·tion \tu̇-ˈish-ən, tyu̇-\ *n* **1 :** the act or profession of teaching **:** INSTRUCTION **2 :** the price of or payment for instruction [Medieval French *tuicioun* "protection," from Latin *tuitio,* from *tueri* "to look at, look after"] — **tu·i·tion·al** \-ˈish-nəl, -ən-l\ *adj*

tu·la·re·mia \ˌtü-lə-ˈrē-mē-ə, ˌtyü-\ *n* **:** an infectious bacterial disease of rodents, wild rabbits, humans, and some domestic animals that is transmitted especially by the bites of insects or ticks and in humans is marked by variable symptoms (as fever, swollen glands, or diarrhea) — called also *rabbit fever* [New Latin, from *Tulare* county, California] — **tu·la·re·mic** \-mik\ *adj*

tu·le \ˈtü-lē\ *n* **:** either of two large sedges growing on wet land especially of the southwestern U.S. [Spanish, from Nahuatl *tōllin*]

tu·lip \ˈtü-ləp, ˈtyü-\ *n* **:** any of a genus of Eurasian bulbous herbs that are related to the lilies, have linear or broadly lance-shaped leaves, and are widely grown for their showy flowers; *also* **:** the flower or bulb of a tulip [New Latin *tulipa,* from Turkish *tülbent* "turban"]

tulip

tulip tree *n* **:** a tall North American timber tree related to the magnolias and having large greenish yellow tulip-shaped flowers and soft white wood used especially for cabinetwork and woodenware

tulle \ˈtül\ *n* **:** a sheer often stiffened silk, rayon, or nylon net used chiefly for veils, evening dresses, or ballet costumes [French, from *Tulle,* France]

tul·li·bee \ˈtəl-ə-bē\ *n* **:** any of several American whitefishes; *esp* **:** a common cisco that is a commercially important food fish [Canadian French *toulibi*]

[1]**tum·ble** \ˈtəm-bəl\ *vb* **tum·bled; tum·bling** \-bə-ling, -bling\ **1 a :** to perform gymnastic feats of rolling and turning **b :** to turn end over end in falling or flight **2 a :** to fall suddenly and helplessly **b :** to suffer a sudden decline, downfall, or defeat **:** COLLAPSE **3 :** to move or go hurriedly and confusedly **4 :** to come to understand ⟨didn't *tumble* to the seriousness of the problem⟩ **5 :** to cause to tumble (as by pushing) **6 a :** to toss together into a confused mass **b :** RUMPLE [Middle English *tumblen,* from *tumben* "to dance," from Old English *tumbian*]

[2]**tumble** *n* **1 a :** a disordered mass of objects or material **b :** a disorderly state **2 :** an act or instance of tumbling

tum·ble·bug \ˈtəm-bəl-ˌbəg\ *n* **:** a large stout-bodied beetle that rolls dung into small balls, buries them in the ground, and lays eggs in them

tum·ble·down \ˌtəm-bəl-ˌdau̇n\ *adj* **:** DILAPIDATED

tumble dry *vt* **:** to dry (as clothes) in a dryer

tum·bler \ˈtəm-blər\ *n* **1 :** one that tumbles: as **a :** GYMNAST, ACROBAT **b :** a domestic pigeon that often tumbles backward in flight **2 :** a drinking glass without foot or stem and originally with pointed or convex base **3 :** a movable part in a lock that must be adjusted (as by a key) before the bolt can be thrown **4 :** a device or mechanism for tumbling (as a revolving cage in which clothes are dried)

tum·ble·weed \ˈtəm-bəl-ˌwēd\ *n* **:** a plant (as Russian thistle) that breaks away from its roots in autumn and is blown about by the wind

tum·bling \ˈtəm-bə-ling, -bling\ *n* **:** the skill, practice, or sport of executing acrobatic feats (as somersaults, rolls, and handsprings) on a mat usually without apparatus

tum·brel *or* **tum·bril** \ˈtəm-brəl\ *n* **:** a farmer's cart used during the French Revolution to carry condemned persons to the guillotine [Medieval French *tomberel* "tipcart," from *tomber* "to tumble," perhaps of Germanic origin]

tu·mes·cence \tü-ˈmes-ns, tyü-\ *n* **:** a swelling or becoming swollen or the resulting state [Latin *tumescens,* present participle of *tumescere* "to swell up," from *tumēre* "to swell"] — **tu·mes·cent** \-nt\ *adj*

tu·mid \ˈtü-məd, ˈtyü-\ *adj* **1 :** marked by swelling ⟨a *tumid* leg⟩ **2 :** TURGID 2, BOMBASTIC ⟨*tumid* speech⟩ [Latin *tumidus,* from *tumēre* "to swell"]

tum·my \ˈtəm-ē\ *n, pl* **tummies :** STOMACH 1c [baby-talk for *stomach*]

tu·mor \ˈtü-mər, ˈtyü-\ *n* **1 :** a swollen or distended part **2 :** an abnormal mass of tissue that possesses no physiological function and arises from uncontrolled usually rapid proliferation of cells — called also *neoplasm* [Latin, from *tumēre* "to swell"] — **tu·mor·like** \-ˌlīk\ *adj* — **tu·mor·ous** \ˈtüm-rəs, ˈtyüm-, -ə-rəs\ *adj*

tump·line \ˈtəm-ˌplīn\ *n* **:** a sling formed by a strap slung over the forehead or chest used for carrying a pack on the back or in hauling loads [*tump* of Algonquian origin]

tu·mult \ˈtü-ˌməlt, ˈtyü-\ *n* **1 :** violent and disorderly commotion or disturbance (as of a crowd) with uproar and confusion **2 :** violent agitation of mind or feelings [Medieval French *tumulte,* from Latin *tumultus*]

tu·mul·tu·ous \tu̇-ˈməl-chə-wəs, tyu̇-, -chəs\ *adj* **:** marked by tumult and especially by violent turbulence or upheaval — **tu·mul·tu·ous·ly** *adv* — **tu·mul·tu·ous·ness** *n*

tu·mu·lus \ˈtü-myə-ləs, ˈtyü-\ *n, pl* **-li** \-ˌlī, -ˌlē\ **:** an artificial hillock or mound usually over an ancient grave [Latin]

tun \ˈtən\ *n* **1 :** a large cask for liquids and especially wine **2 :** any of various units of liquid measure; *esp* **:** a measure of 252 gallons (about 954 liters) [Old English *tunne* and Medieval French *tone,* both from Medieval Latin *tunna*]

[1]**tu·na** \ˈtü-nə\ *n* **:** any of several flat-jointed prickly pears; *also* **:** the edible fruit of a tuna [Spanish, from Taino (aboriginal langugae of the Greater Antilles and the Bahamas)]

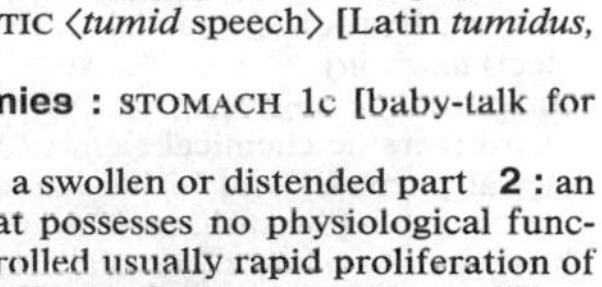
[2]tuna

[2]**tu·na** \ˈtü-nə, ˈtyü-\ *n, pl* **tuna** *or* **tunas 1 :** any of various mostly large active

\ə\ **abut**	\au̇\ **out**	\i\ **tip**	\ȯ\ **saw**	\u̇\ **foot**
\ər\ **further**	\ch\ **chin**	\ī\ **life**	\ȯi\ **coin**	\y\ **yet**
\a\ **mat**	\e\ **pet**	\j\ **job**	\th\ **thin**	\yü\ **few**
\ā\ **take**	\ē\ **easy**	\ng\ **sing**	\th\ **this**	\yu̇\ **cure**
\ä\ **cot, cart**	\g\ **go**	\ō\ **bone**	\ü\ **food**	\zh\ **vision**

sea fishes (as an albacore or bluefin tuna) related to the mackerels and valued for food and sport **2** : the flesh of a tuna especially when canned for use as food — called also *tuna fish* [American Spanish, from Spanish *atún,* from Arabic *tūn,* from Latin *thunnus,* from Greek *thynnos*]

tun·able \ˈtü-nə-bəl, ˈtyü-\ *adj* : capable of being tuned — **tun·able·ness** *n* — **tun·ably** \-blē\ *adv*

tun·dra \ˈtən-drə *also* ˈtün-\ *n* : a treeless plain of arctic and subarctic regions having permanently frozen subsoil and vegetation consisting chiefly of mosses, lichens, herbs, and very small shrubs [Russian, of Finno-Ugric origin]

[1]**tune** \ˈtün, ˈtyün\ *n* **1 a** : a musical composition or air **b** : a dominant theme **2** : correct musical pitch or consonance ⟨the piano was not in *tune*⟩ **3 a** : AGREEMENT 1b, HARMONY ⟨in *tune* with the times⟩ **b** : general attitude ⟨you'll change your *tune* after you read this⟩ **4** : AMOUNT 1, EXTENT ⟨a subsidy to the *tune* of $5,000,000⟩ [Middle English, "quality of sound, tone," from Medieval French *tun, tuen*]

[2]**tune** *vb* **1** : to come or bring into harmony : ATTUNE **2** : to adjust a radio or television receiver to either receive or reject a broadcast **3** : to adjust in musical pitch ⟨*tune* my guitar⟩ **4** : to adjust for precise functioning ⟨*tune* a motor⟩

tune·ful \ˈtün-fəl, ˈtyün-\ *adj* : MELODIOUS 1, MUSICAL — **tune·ful·ly** \-fə-lē\ *adv* — **tune·ful·ness** *n*

tune in *vb* **1** : to listen to or view a broadcast ⟨*tune in* next week for the conclusion⟩ **2** : to pay attention to what is happening or to one's surroundings

tune out *vb* : to stop paying attention to what is happening or to one's surroundings

tun·er \ˈtü-nər, ˈtyü-\ *n* **1** : one that tunes ⟨piano *tuner*⟩ **2** : something used for tuning; *esp* : the part of a receiving set that selects radio signals for conversion into audio or visual signals

tune–up \ˈtü-ˌnəp, ˈtyü-\ *n* **1** : a general adjustment to ensure efficient functioning ⟨a motor *tune-up*⟩ **2** : a preliminary trial : WARM-UP

tung \ˈtəŋ\ *n* : TUNG TREE

tung oil *n* : a pale yellow oil obtained from the seeds of tung trees and used chiefly in quick-drying varnishes and paints and for waterproofing [partial translation of Chinese (Beijing dialect) *tóngyóu*]

tung·sten \ˈtəŋ-stən, ˈtəŋk-\ *n* : a gray-white heavy ductile hard metallic chemical element that is used especially for electrical purposes and in hardening alloys (as steel) — see ELEMENT table [Swedish, from *tung* "heavy" + *sten* "stone"]

tung tree *n* : any of several trees of the spurge family whose seeds yield tung oil; *esp* : an Asian tree widely grown in warm regions [Chinese (Beijing dialect) *tóng*]

Tun·gu·sic \tu̇ŋ-ˈgü-zik, tən-\ *n* : a family of Altaic languages spoken in Manchuria and northward [*Tungus,* an indigenous people of central and southeastern Siberia, from Russian] — **Tungusic** *adj*

tu·nic \ˈtü-nik, ˈtyü-\ *n* **1** : a simple belted knee-length or longer slip-on garment worn by ancient Greeks and Romans **2** : a long usually plain and close-fitting jacket with high collar worn especially as part of a uniform **3** : a blouse or jacket reaching to or just below the hips [Latin *tunica,* of Semitic origin]

tu·ni·ca \ˈtü-ni-kə, ˈtyü-\ *n, pl* **-cae** \-nə-ˌkē, -ˌkī\ : an enveloping membrane or layer of animal or plant tissue [Latin, "tunic, membrane"]

tu·ni·cate \ˈtü-ni-kət, ˈtyü-, -nə-ˌkāt\ *n* : any of a major group (Tunicata) of marine chordate animals (as ascidians) that are filter feeders having a reduced nervous system, a thick secreted outer covering, and only in the larval stage a notochord — **tunicate** *adj*

tuning fork *n* : a 2-pronged metal instrument that gives a fixed tone when struck and is useful for tuning musical instruments and ascertaining standard pitch

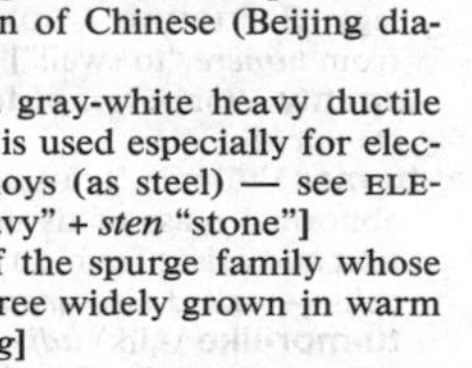
tuning fork

[1]**tun·nel** \ˈtən-ᵊl\ *n* : an enclosed passage (as a tube or conduit); *esp* : one underground (as under an obstruction or in a mine [Middle French *tonel* "tun," from Medieval French *tonne,* from Medieval Latin *tunna*] — **tun·nel·like** \-ᵊl-ˌlīk, -ᵊl-ˌīk\ *adj*

[2]**tunnel** *vb* **-neled** *or* **-nelled; -nel·ing** *or* **-nel·ling** \ˈtən-liŋ, -ᵊl-iŋ\ : to make or use a tunnel or form a tunnel in — **tun·nel·er** \ˈtən-lər, -ᵊl-ər\ *n*

tunnel vision *n* **1** : narrowing of the field of vision resulting in loss of peripheral vision **2** : extreme narrowness of viewpoint : NARROW-MINDEDNESS — **tun·nel–vi·sioned** \-ˈvizh-ənd\ *adj*

tun·ny \ˈtən-ē\ *n, pl* **tunnies** *also* **tunny** : [2]TUNA 1 [derived from Latin *thunnus*]

tu·pe·lo \ˈtü-pə-ˌlō, ˈtyü-\ *n, pl* **-los** **1** : any of a genus of mostly North American trees having usually small greenish white flowers; *esp* : BLACK GUM **2** : the pale soft wood of a tupelo [perhaps from Creek *etó* "tree" + *piló:(fa), opiló:(fa)* "swamp"]

Tu·pi \tü-ˈpē, ˈtü-ˌ\ *n, pl* **Tupi** *or* **Tupis** **1** : a member of a group of American Indian peoples of the Amazon valley **2** : the language of the Tupi people

tuppence *variant of* TWOPENCE

tuque \ˈtük, ˈtyük\ *n* : a warm knitted usually pointed stocking cap [Canadian French, from French *toque*]

tur·ban \ˈtər-bən\ *n* **1** : a headdress worn chiefly in countries of the eastern Mediterranean and southern Asia especially by Muslims and made of a cap around which is wound a long cloth **2** : a headdress resembling a turban; *esp* : a woman's close-fitting hat without a brim [Middle French *turbant,* from Italian *turbante,* from Turkish *tülbent,* from Persian *dulband*] — **tur·baned** *or* **tur·banned** \-bənd\ *adj*

tur·bel·lar·i·an \ˌtər-bə-ˈler-ē-ən, -ˈlar-\ *n* : any of a class (Turbellaria) of mostly aquatic and free-living flatworms (as a planarian) [derived from Latin *turbellae* "bustle, stir," from *turba* "confusion, crowd"] — **turbellarian** *adj*

tur·bid \ˈtər-bəd\ *adj* **1 a** : thick or opaque with matter in suspension ⟨a *turbid* stream⟩ **b** : heavy with smoke or mist : DENSE **2** : confused in thought or feeling [Latin *turbidus* "confused, turbid," from *turba* "confusion, crowd"] — **tur·bid·i·ty** \ˌtər-ˈbid-ət-ē\ *n* — **tur·bid·ly** \ˈtər-bəd-lē\ *adv* — **tur·bid·ness** *n*

tur·bi·nate \ˈtər-bə-nət\ *n* : one of the thin bony or cartilaginous plates on the walls of the nasal passages [Latin *turbinatus* "shaped like a top," from *turbo* "top"] — **turbinate** *adj*

tur·bine \ˈtər-bən, -ˌbīn\ *n* : an engine whose central driving shaft is fitted with vanes whirled around by the pressure of water or hot gases (as steam or exhaust gases) [French, from Latin *turbo* "top, whirlwind"]

tur·bo \ˈtər-bō\ *n, pl* **turbos** **1** : TURBINE **2** : TURBOSUPERCHARGER

tur·bo- *combining form* **1** : coupled directly to a driving turbine **2** : consisting of or incorporating a turbine ⟨*turbo*jet engine⟩

tur·bo·charg·er \ˈtər-bō-ˌchär-jər\ *n* : a blower driven by exhaust gas turbines and used to supercharge an engine

tur·bo·jet \ˈtər-bō-ˌjet\ *n* : an airplane powered by turbojet engines

turbojet engine *n* : a jet engine in which a turbine drives a compressor that supplies air to a burner and hot gases from the burner drive the turbine before being discharged rearward

tur·bo·prop \ˈtər-bō-ˌpräp\ *n* **1** : TURBOPROP ENGINE **2** : an airplane powered by turboprop engines

turboprop engine *n* : a jet engine designed to produce thrust principally by means of a propeller driven by a turbine with additional thrust usually obtained by the rearward discharge of hot exhaust gases

tur·bo·su·per·charg·er \-ˈsü-pər-ˌchär-jər\ *n* : a turbine compressor driven by hot exhaust gases of an airplane engine for feeding rarefied air at high altitudes into the carburetor of the engine at sea-level pressure so as to increase engine power

tur·bot \ˈtər-bət\ *n, pl* **turbot** *also* **turbots** : a large brownish European flatfish that is a popular food fish; *also* : any of various flatfishes resembling the turbot [Medieval French *turbut*]

tur·bu·lence \ˈtər-byə-ləns\ *n* : the quality or state of being turbulent: as **a** : a great commotion or agitation ⟨emotional *turbulence*⟩ **b** : irregular atmospheric motion especially when characterized by up and down currents **c** : departure in a fluid from a smooth flow

tur·bu·len·cy \-lən-sē\ *n, pl* **-cies** *archaic* : TURBULENCE

tur·bu·lent \-lənt\ *adj* **1** : causing unrest, violence, or disturbance **2** : characterized by agitation or tumult : TEMPESTUOUS ⟨a *turbulent* relationship⟩ [Latin *turbulentus,* from *turba* "confusion, crowd"] — **tur·bu·lent·ly** *adv*

turbulent flow *n* : a fluid flow in which the velocity at a given point varies erratically in magnitude and direction

Tur·co- *or* **Tur·ko-** *combining form* : Turkish : Turkish and

tu•reen \tə-ˈrēn, tyu̇-\ *n* **:** a deep bowl from which food (as soup) is served [French *terrine,* from *terrin* "earthen," derived from Latin *terra* "earth"]

turf \ˈtərf\ *n, pl* **turfs** \ˈtərfs\ *also* **turves** \ˈtərvz\ **1 a :** the upper layer of soil bound by grass and plant roots into a thick mat; *also* **:** a piece of this **b :** an artificial substitute for turf (as on a playing field) **c :** GRASS 3 **2 a :** PEAT 2 **b :** a piece of peat dried for fuel **3 a :** a track or course for horse racing **b :** the sport or business of horse racing **4 :** an area or a place that is or is felt to be under one's control [Old English] — **turfy** \ˈtər-fē\ *adj*

turf•man \ˈtərf-mən\ *n* **:** a devotee of horse racing; *esp* **:** one who owns and races horses

tur•ges•cent \ˌtər-ˈjes-nt\ *adj* **:** becoming turgid, distended, or inflated [Latin *turgescens,* present participle of *turgescere* "to swell," from *turgēre* "to be swollen"] — **tur•ges•cence** \-ns\ *n*

tur•gid \ˈtər-jəd\ *adj* **1 a :** affected with swelling ⟨*turgid* limbs⟩ **b :** exhibiting turgor ⟨*turgid* plant cells⟩ **2 :** excessively embellished in style or language **:** BOMBASTIC, POMPOUS [Latin *turgidus,* from *turgēre* "to be swollen"] — **tur•gid•i•ty** \ˌtər-ˈjid-ət-ē\ *n* — **tur•gid•ly** \ˈtər-jəd-lē\ *adv* — **tur•gid•ness** *n*

tur•gor \ˈtər-gər, -ˌgȯr\ *n* **:** the normal state of firmness and tension typical of living cells [Late Latin, "turgidity," from Latin *turgēre* "to be swollen"]

Turk \ˈtərk\ *n* **1 :** a member of any of numerous Asian peoples speaking Turkic languages who live in a region ranging from the Balkans to eastern Siberia and western China **2 :** a native or inhabitant of Turkey [Medieval French *Turc,* from Medieval Latin *Turcus,* from Turkish *Türk*]

tur•key \ˈtər-kē\ *n, pl* **turkeys** **1** *pl also* **turkey :** a large North American bird which is related to the domestic chicken and is domesticated in most parts of the world **2 :** FLOP 2, FAILURE **3 :** a stupid, foolish, or inept person [*Turkey*; from confusion with the guinea fowl, supposed to be imported from Turkish territory]

tur•key–cock \ˈtər-kē-ˌkäk\ *n* **1 :** GOBBLER **2 :** a strutting pompous person

turkey shoot *n* **:** a contest of marksmanship with a gun at a moving target with a turkey offered as a prize

turkey vulture *n* **:** an American vulture with a red head and whitish hooked bill — called also *turkey buzzard*

Turk•ic \ˈtər-kik\ *n* **:** a family of Altaic languages including Turkish — **Turkic** *adj*

¹Turk•ish \ˈtər-kish\ *adj* **1 :** of, relating to, or characteristic of Turkey, the Turks, or Turkish **2 :** TURKIC

²Turkish *n* **:** the Turkic language of Turkey

Turkish bath *n* **:** a bath in which the bather passes through a series of steam rooms of increasing temperature and then receives a rubdown, massage, and cold shower

Turkish coffee *n* **:** a drink made by boiling powdered coffee in a thin sugar syrup

Turkish delight *n* **:** a jellylike or gummy confection usually cut in cubes and dusted with sugar — called also *Turkish paste*

Turkish towel *n* **:** a towel made of cotton terry cloth

Tur•ko•man *or* **Tur•co•man** \ˈtər-kə-mən\ *n, pl* **Turkomans** *or* **Turcomans :** a member of a Turkic-speaking traditionally nomadic people living chiefly in Turkmenistan, Afghanistan, and Iran [Medieval Latin *Turcomannus,* from Persian *Turkmān,* from *turkmān* "resembling a Turk," from *Turk* "Turk," from Turkish *Türk*]

tur•mer•ic \ˈtər-mə-rik *also* ˈtü-mə-, ˈtyü-\ *n* **1 :** an Indian herb related to ginger and having a large yellow rhizome **2 :** the boiled, dried, and usually ground rhizome of turmeric used especially as a flavoring or coloring agent; *also* **:** a yellow to reddish brown dye obtained from the rhizome [Middle English *turmeryte*]

tur•moil \ˈtər-ˌmȯil\ *n* **:** an utterly confused or extremely agitated state or condition [origin unknown]

¹turn \ˈtərn\ *vb* **1 a :** to move or cause to move around an axis or center **:** ROTATE, REVOLVE ⟨wheels *turning* slowly⟩ ⟨*turn* a crank⟩; *also* **:** to operate or cause to operate by so turning ⟨*turn* a key in a lock⟩ **b :** to whirl giddily **:** become dizzy ⟨heights always made his head *turn*⟩ **c :** to have as a center (as of interest) or a decisive factor ⟨their decision must *turn* on circumstances⟩ ⟨the story *turns* about the fate of a family⟩ **d :** to think over **:** PONDER **e :** to execute by rotating or revolving ⟨*turn* handsprings⟩ **2 a :** to alter or reverse in position usually by moving through an arc ⟨*turn* toward your partner⟩: as (1) **:** to dig or plow so as to bring the lower soil to the surface ⟨*turn* the soil⟩ (2) **:** to make over by reversing the material and resewing ⟨*turn* a collar⟩ **b :** to disturb or upset the order or state or balance of ⟨everything was *turned* topsy-turvy⟩ **c :** to injure by a sudden twist **:** WRENCH ⟨*turned* my ankle⟩ **3 :** to change or cause to change ⟨water *turned* to ice⟩: as **a** (1) **:** TRANSFORM 1 ⟨*turn* wildland into fruitful farms⟩ (2) **:** BECOME ⟨the weather *turned* bad⟩ ⟨she just *turned* fifteen⟩ **b :** TRANSLATE 2a, PARAPHRASE **c :** to exchange for something else ⟨*turn* property into cash⟩ **d :** to cause to spoil **:** SOUR ⟨*turned* milk⟩ **e :** to change in color ⟨leaves *turning* in the fall⟩ **f :** to cause to be **:** MAKE ⟨hair *turned* white by sorrow⟩ **g :** to be inconstant **:** VARY **4 a :** to take or cause to take or move in another, an opposite, or a particular direction ⟨*turned* the overflow into an old stream bed⟩ ⟨the road *turns* to the left⟩ ⟨*turned* the car around⟩ ⟨when the tide *turns*⟩; *also* **:** to go around ⟨*turn* a corner⟩ **b :** to alter from a previous or anticipated course ⟨these few votes *turned* the election⟩ **c :** to change one's behavior or attitude to opposition or hostility ⟨felt the world had *turned* against them⟩ **d :** to go over to another side or party **:** DEFECT **e :** to attack suddenly and usually unexpectedly and violently ⟨the dog *turned* on a neighbor⟩ **f :** to bring to bear (as by aiming, pointing, or focusing) **:** TRAIN ⟨*turned* the light into the dark doorway⟩ ⟨*turned* a questioning eye toward her⟩; *also* **:** to direct or point usually toward or away from something ⟨*turned* their thoughts homeward⟩ **g :** to influence toward a change (as in one's way of life) **h :** DEVOTE 1, APPLY ⟨*turned* their skills to the service of the poor⟩ **i :** to cause to recoil ⟨*turns* their own argument against them⟩ **j :** to drive or send from or to a specified place or condition ⟨*turn* cattle into a field⟩ ⟨*turn* mutineers adrift⟩ **k :** to seek out as a source ⟨*turn* to a friend for help⟩ **5 a :** to give a rounded form to by means of a lathe and cutting tool **b :** to give a well-rounded or graceful shape or form to ⟨*turn* the heel of a sock⟩ ⟨*turned* a phrase⟩ **c :** to become or cause to become bent or curved ⟨the edge of the knife had *turned*⟩ **6 :** to gain in the course of business ⟨*turning* a quick profit⟩ [Old English *tyrnan, turnian* and Medieval French *turner, tourner,* both from Latin *tornare* "to turn on a lathe," from *tornus* "lathe," from Greek *tornos*] — **turn a deaf ear :** to refuse to listen — **turn a hair :** to be or become upset or frightened — **turn heads :** to attract favorable attention — **turn one's back on 1 :** REJECT 1 **2 :** ABANDON 3 — **turn one's hand** *or* **turn a hand :** to set to work **:** apply oneself usefully — **turn one's head :** to cause to have great notions of pride or conceit — **turn one's stomach :** to disgust completely **:** SICKEN ⟨the foul smell *turned his stomach*⟩ — **turn tail :** to run away **:** FLEE — **turn the other cheek :** to respond to injury or unkindness with patience — **turn the tables :** to bring about a switch in the positions or fortunes of two opposing people or sides — **turn the trick :** to bring about the desired result or effect — **turn turtle :** CAPSIZE, OVERTURN

²turn *n* **1 :** the action or an act of turning about a center or axis ⟨each *turn* of the wheel⟩ **2 a :** a change or changing of direction, course, or position **b :** a place where something turns **:** BEND, CURVE ⟨at the *turn* of the road⟩ **c :** a change or changing of condition or trend ⟨took a *turn* for the better⟩ ⟨a *turn* in the weather⟩ **d :** the beginning of a new period of time **:** the time when one period changes to the next ⟨the *turn* of the century⟩ **3 :** a short walk or ride ⟨took a *turn* through the park⟩ **4 :** an act affecting another ⟨did me a very bad *turn*⟩ **5 a :** a period of action or activity **:** SPELL ⟨each took a *turn* at the job⟩ **b :** place or appointed time in a succession or scheduled order ⟨wait your *turn*⟩ **6 :** a musical ornament consisting of a group of notes including the one next above and next below the principal note **7 :** special purpose or need ⟨it served my *turn*⟩ **8 a :** distinctive quality or character ⟨a neat *turn* of phrase⟩ **b :** the form in accord with which something is fashioned **:** CAST ⟨a peculiar *turn* of mind⟩ **c :** the state or manner of being coiled or twisted; *also* **:** a single round (as of a rope) ⟨took a *turn* around a post to hold the horse⟩ **d :** a special twist or interpretation ⟨gave the old tale a new *turn*⟩ **9 :** particular or special aptitude or skill **:** BENT ⟨a *turn* for languages⟩ **10 :** a usually sudden and brief attack or spell of nerves or faintness

⟨gave me a *turn*⟩ — **at every turn :** CONSTANTLY, CONTINUOUSLY — **by turns :** one after another — **out of turn 1 :** not in order ⟨play *out of turn*⟩ **2 :** at a wrong time or place ⟨talking *out of turn*⟩ — **to a turn :** to perfection

turn·about \ˈtər-nə-ˌbau̇t\ *n* **:** a change or reversal of direction, trend, policy, or role

turn·around \-ˌrau̇nd\ *n* **1 a :** the process of readying a vehicle for departure after its arrival; *also* **:** the time spent in this process ⟨a quick *turnaround* between flights⟩ **b :** the action of receiving, processing, and returning something ⟨24-hour *turnaround* time on most orders⟩ **2 :** a space permitting the turning around of a vehicle **3 :** TURNABOUT

turn around *vb* **1 :** to act in a sudden, different, or surprising manner ⟨he *turned around* and changed his mind at the last minute⟩ **2 :** to change for the better ⟨*turned* her life *around*⟩

turn away *vb* **1 :** DEFLECT, AVERT **2 a :** to send away **:** REJECT, DISMISS **b :** to refuse admittance or acceptance to **3 :** to start to go away **:** DEPART

turn back *vb* **1 :** to refer to an earlier time or place **2 :** to drive back or away **3 :** to stop the advance of **:** CHECK

turn·buck·le \ˈtərn-ˌbək-əl\ *n* **:** a link with a screw thread at one or both ends used for tightening a rod or stay by pulling together the ends that it connects

turn·coat \ˈtərn-ˌkōt\ *n* **:** one who forsakes his or her party or principles; *esp* **:** TRAITOR

turn down \ˌtərn-ˈdau̇n, ˈtərn-\ *vt* **1 :** to turn upside down **:** INVERT **2 :** to reduce in intensity by turning a control ⟨*turn down* the volume⟩ **3 :** REJECT 1 ⟨*turned down* the offer⟩ — **turn-down** \ˌtərn-ˌdau̇n\ *adj or n*

turn·er \ˈtər-nər\ *n* **:** one that turns or is used for turning ⟨a pancake *turner*⟩; *esp* **:** a person who forms articles with a lathe

Tur·ner's syndrome \ˈtər-nərz-\ *n* **:** a genetically determined condition associated with the presence of one X chromosome and no Y chromosome and characterized by an outwardly female bodily type with incomplete and infertile sex organs [Henry Hubert *Turner,* died 1970, American physician]

turn·ery \ˈtər-nə-rē\ *n, pl* **-er·ies :** the work, products, or shop of a turner

turn in *vb* **1 :** to give up or hand over ⟨*turn in* extra supplies⟩ **2 :** to inform on **:** BETRAY **3 :** PRODUCE 5, DO ⟨*turn in* good work⟩ **4 :** to turn from a road or path so as to enter ⟨*turn in* at the gate⟩ **5 :** to go to bed

turning point *n* **:** a point at which a significant change occurs

tur·nip \ˈtər-nəp\ *n* **1 :** either of two biennial herbs related to cabbage and having thick roots eaten as a vegetable or fed to livestock: **a :** one with usually white roundish roots and leaves that are cooked as a vegetable when young and tender **b :** RUTABAGA **2 :** the root of a turnip [probably from ^{1}*turn* + English dialect *neep* "turnip," from the rounded root]

turn·key \ˈtərn-ˌkē\ *n, pl* **turnkeys :** one who has charge of a prison's keys **:** JAILER

turn·off \ˈtər-ˌnȯf\ *n* **1 :** a turning off **2 :** a place where one turns off **3 :** one that causes loss of interest or enjoyment ⟨the music was a *turnoff*⟩

turn off \ˌtər-ˈnȯf, ˈtər-\ *vt* **1 :** DISMISS, DISCHARGE ⟨*turn off* employees⟩ **2 :** to turn aside or aside from something ⟨*turn off* a puzzling question⟩ ⟨*turned off* into a side road⟩ **3 :** to stop the functioning or flow of by or as if by turning a control ⟨*turn* the light *off*⟩ **4 :** to cause to lose interest or responsiveness

turn on *vt* **1 :** to cause to function or flow by or as if by turning a control ⟨*turn* the water *on* full⟩ ⟨*turn on* the lights⟩ ⟨*turned on* all my charm⟩ **2 :** to excite or become excited pleasurably ⟨rock music *turns* me *on*⟩ — **turn–on** \ˈtər-ˌnȯn, -ˌnän\ *n*

turn·out \ˈtər-ˌnau̇t\ *n* **1 :** an act of turning out **2 :** the number of people who participate in or attend an event ⟨a heavy voter *turnout*⟩ **3 :** a widened space (as in a highway) for vehicles to pass or park **4 :** a clearing out and cleaning **5 a :** a carriage with its team and equipment **b :** an outfit of clothes **:** COSTUME **6 :** YIELD, OUTPUT

turn out \ˌtər-ˈnau̇t, ˈtər-\ *vb* **1 :** to put out of some shelter **:** EVICT **2 :** to empty of contents; *also* **:** CLEAN **3 :** to produce often rapidly or regularly by or as if by machine ⟨a writer *turning out* stories⟩ **4 :** to equip, dress, or finish in a careful or elaborate way **5 :** to turn off (as a light) **6 :** to call (as a guard) from rest or shelter **7 a :** to come or go out from home in or as if in answer to a summons ⟨*turn out* for practice⟩ **b :** to get out of bed **8 a :** to prove to be in the result or end ⟨*turned out* to be a spy⟩ **b :** END 2 ⟨how did the game *turn out*⟩

^{1}**turn·over** \ˈtər-ˌnō-vər\ *n* **1 :** an act or result of turning over **:** UPSET **2 :** a shifting usually in position or opinion **3 :** a reorganization especially of personnel **4 :** a filled pastry with one half of the crust turned over the other **5 :** the amount of business done or work accomplished; *also* **:** the rate at which material is processed **6 :** the buying, selling, and replacing of goods considered as one complete process ⟨the annual *turnover* in shoes⟩ **7 :** the number of employees hired in a given time to replace those leaving or discharged **8 :** the continuous process of loss and replacement of a constituent (as a cell or tissue) of a living organism

^{2}**turn·over** \ˌtər-ˌnō-vər\ *adj* **:** capable of being turned over

turn over \ˌtər-ˈno-vər, ˈtər-\ *vb* **1 :** to turn from an upright position **:** OVERTURN **2 :** to search (as clothes or papers) by lifting or moving one by one **3 :** to think over **:** meditate on ⟨*turn over* a problem in search of a solution⟩ **4 a :** to hand over **:** TRANSFER **b :** to lose possession of ⟨*turned* the ball *over* three times⟩ **5 a :** to receive and dispose of (as a stock of merchandise) usually in the course of business **b :** to do business to the amount of ⟨expected to *turn over* $1000 a week⟩ **6 :** to heave with nausea ⟨your stomach will *turn over* with shock⟩ **7 :** to begin or cause to begin to run ⟨*turned over* the engine⟩ — **turn over a new leaf :** to make a change for the better

turn·pike \ˈtərn-ˌpīk\ *n* **1 :** TOLLGATE **2 a :** a road (as an expressway) for the use of which tolls are collected **b :** a main road [Middle English *turnepike* "revolving frame bearing spikes and serving as a barrier," from *turnen* "to turn" + *pike*]

turn·spit \-ˌspit\ *n* **1 :** one that turns a spit **2 :** a rotatable spit

turn·stile \-ˌstīl\ *n* **:** a post with arms pivoted on the top set in a passageway so that persons can pass through only on foot one by one

turn·stone \-ˌstōn\ *n* **:** either of two shorebirds resembling the related plovers and sandpipers

turnstone

turn·ta·ble \-ˌtā-bəl\ *n* **:** a revolvable platform: as **a :** a platform with a track for turning wheeled vehicles (as locomotives) **b :** LAZY SUSAN **c :** a rotating platform that carries a phonograph record

turn to \ˈtərn-ˈtü\ *vi* **:** to apply oneself to work **:** act vigorously

turn·up \ˌtər-ˌnəp\ *adj* **1 :** turned up ⟨a *turnup* nose⟩ **2 :** made or fitted to be turned up ⟨a *turnup* collar⟩

turn up \ˌtər-ˈnəp, ˈtər-\ *vb* **1 :** to bring or come to light unexpectedly or after being lost ⟨the papers will *turn up*⟩ **2 :** to raise or increase by or as if by adjusting a control ⟨*turn up* the heat⟩ **3 a :** to turn out to be ⟨*turned up* missing⟩ **b :** to become evident **:** APPEAR ⟨that name is always *turning up*⟩ **c :** to arrive or show up at an expected time or place ⟨*turned up* half an hour late⟩ **4 :** to happen unexpectedly — **turn up one's nose :** to show scorn or disdain

tur·pen·tine \ˈtər-pən-ˌtīn\ *n* **1 :** an oleoresin obtained from various conifers (as some pines and firs) **2 a :** an essential oil obtained from turpentines by distillation and used especially as a solvent and thinner — called also *gum turpentine* **b :** a similar oil obtained by distillation or carbonization of pinewood — called also *wood turpentine* [Medieval Latin *terbentina* "oleoresin obtained from the terebinth," derived from Latin *terebinthus* "terebinth"]

tur·pi·tude \ˈtər-pə-ˌtüd, -ˌtyüd\ *n* **:** inherent baseness **:** DEPRAVITY ⟨moral *turpitude*⟩ [Medieval French, from Latin *turpitudo,* from *turpis* "vile, base"]

turps \ˈtərps\ *n* **:** TURPENTINE

tur·quoise \ˈtər-ˌkwȯiz, -ˌkȯiz\ *n* **1 :** a mineral that is a blue, bluish green, or greenish gray hydrous basic copper aluminum phosphate, takes a high polish, and sometimes is valued as a gem **2 :** a light greenish blue [Medieval French *turkeise,* from *turqueis* "Turkish," from *Turc* "Turk"]

tur·ret \ˈtər-ət, ˈtə-rət, ˈtu̇r-ət\ *n* **1 :** a little tower often at a corner of a building **2 a :** a pivoted and revolvable holder in a machine tool **b :** a

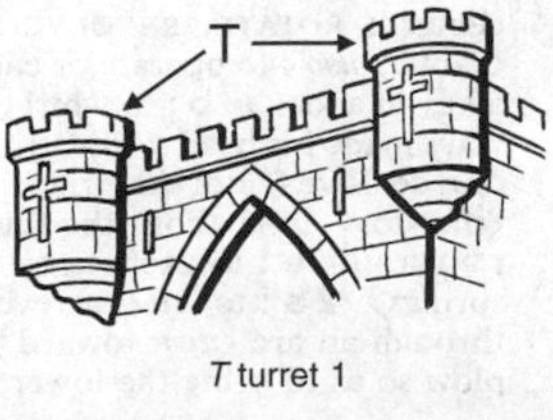

T turret 1

device (as on a microscope or television camera) for holding several lenses **3** : a gunner's fixed or movable enclosure in an airplane **b** : a revolving structure on a warship or on a tank in which guns are mounted [Medieval French *turette, tourette,* from *tour, tur* "tower"] — **tur•ret•ed** \-əd\ *adj*

¹tur•tle \ˈtərt-l\ *n, archaic* : TURTLEDOVE [Old English *turtla,* from Latin *turtur*]

²turtle *n, pl* **turtles** *also* **turtle** : any of an order (Testudines) of land, freshwater, and marine reptiles with a toothless horny beak and a bony shell which encloses the trunk and into which the head, limbs, and tail usually may be withdrawn — compare TERRAPIN, TORTOISE [French *tortue,* from Late Latin *(bestia) tartarucha* "beast from Tartarus," derived from Greek *Tartaros* "Tartarus"; from the former association of the turtle with infernal forces]

tur•tle•back \ˈtərt-l-ˌbak\ *n* : a raised convex surface — **turtle-back** *or* **tur•tle–backed** \ˌtərt-l-ˈbakt\ *adj*

tur•tle•dove \ˈtərt-l-ˌdəv\ *n* : any of several small wild African and Eurasian pigeons noted for cooing [¹*turtle*]

tur•tle•neck \-ˌnek\ *n* : a high close-fitting turnover collar used especially for sweaters; *also* : a garment (as a sweater) with a turtleneck

tur•tling \ˈtərt-ling, -l-ing\ *n* : the action of catching turtles

turves *plural of* TURF

¹Tus•can \ˈtəs-kən\ *n* **1** : a native or inhabitant of Tuscany **2 a** : the Italian language spoken in Tuscany **b** : the standard literary dialect of Italian [Latin *tuscanus,* adj., "Etruscan," from *Tusci* "Etruscans"]

²Tuscan *adj* : of, relating to, or characteristic of Tuscany, the Tuscans, or Tuscan

Tus•ca•ro•ra \ˌtəs-kə-ˈrōr-ə, -ˈrȯr-\ *n, pl* **Tuscarora** *or* **Tuscaroras** : a member of an American Indian people originally of North Carolina and later of New York and Ontario [Tuscarora *Ska-ru-rĕⁿ,* literally, "Indian hemp gatherers"]

¹tush \ˈtəsh\ *n* : a long pointed tooth (as of a horse) [Old English *tūsc*]

²tush *interj* — used to express disdain or reproach [Middle English *tussch*]

¹tusk \ˈtəsk\ *n* **1** : a long greatly enlarged tooth (as of an elephant, walrus, or boar) that projects when the mouth is closed and is used especially for digging food or as a weapon **2** : a tooth-shaped part [Old English *tūx*] — **tusked** \ˈtəskt\ *adj*

²tusk *vt* : to dig up or gash with a tusk

tusk•er \ˈtəs-kər\ *n* : an animal with tusks; *esp* : a male elephant with two normally developed tusks

¹tus•sle \ˈtəs-əl\ *vi* **tus•sled; tus•sling** \ˈtəs-ling, -ə-ling\ : to struggle roughly : SCUFFLE [Middle English *tussillen*]

²tussle *n* **1** : a physical contest or struggle : SCUFFLE **2** : an intense argument, controversy, or struggle

tus•sock \ˈtəs-ək\ *n* : a compact tuft especially of grass or sedge; *also* : an area of raised solid ground in a marsh or bog that is bound together by plant roots [origin unknown] — **tus•socky** \ˈtəs-ə-kē\ *adj*

tussock moth *n* : any of numerous dull-colored moths that usually have wingless females and larvae with long tufts of hair

tut *a t-sound made by suction rather than explosion; often read as* ˈtət\ *or* **tut–tut** *interj* — used to express disapproval or disbelief [origin unknown]

tu•tee \tü-ˈtē, tyü-\ *n* : one who is being tutored

tu•te•lage \ˈtüt-l-ij, ˈtyüt-\ *n* **1** : an act of guarding or protecting : GUARDIANSHIP **2** : the state of being under a guardian or tutor; *also* : the right, power, or influence of a tutor over a pupil **3** : INSTRUCTION [Latin *tutela* "protection, guardian," from *tueri* "to look at, guard"]

tu•te•lar \ˈtüt-l-ər, ˈtyüt-\ *adj* : TUTELARY

tu•te•lary \ˈtüt-l-ˌer-ē, ˈtyüt-\ *adj* **1** : having the guardianship of a person or a thing **2** : of or relating to a guardian

¹tu•tor \ˈtüt-ər, ˈtyüt-\ *n* : a person charged with the instruction and guidance of another: as **a** : a private teacher **b** : a college teacher especially in a British university who guides the individual studies of undergraduates in a particular field [Latin, "guardian, tutor," from *tueri* "to look at, guard"] — **tu•tor•ship** \-ˌship\ *n*

²tutor *vb* : to teach usually individually

¹tu•to•ri•al \tü-ˈtōr-ē-əl, tyü-, -ˈtȯr-\ *adj* : of, relating to, or involving a tutor or a tutorial

²tutorial *n* **1** : a class conducted by a tutor for one student or a small number of students **2** : a paper, book, film, or computer program that provides practical information about a subject

Tut•si \ˈtü-sē, ˈtüt-\ *n, pl* **Tutsi** *or* **Tutsis** : a member of a people of Rwanda and Burundi probably of Nilotic origin

tut•ti–frui•ti \ˌtüt-ē-ˈfrüt-ē\ *n* : a confection or ice cream containing chopped usually candied fruits [Italian *tutti frutti,* literally, "all fruits"]

tu•tu \ˈtü-tü\ *n* : a very short projecting skirt worn by a ballerina [French, from baby talk *cucu, tutu* "backside," alteration of *cul*]

tux \ˈtəks\ *n* : TUXEDO

tux•e•do \ˌtək-ˈsēd-ō\ *n, pl* **-dos** *or* **-does** : a semiformal suit for men [*Tuxedo* Park, New York]

Word History *Tuxedo* can be traced back to the name of a village in southeastern New York. In the 1880's a large tract of land called Tuxedo Park, near the village and on the shore of Tuxedo Lake, became a fashionable resort community. It was here, near the turn of the century, that some young men began to wear dress jackets without tails. The new style which they made popular was soon called *tuxedo.*

tu•yere \twē-ˈeər\ *n* : a nozzle through which an air blast is delivered to a forge or blast furnace [French *tuyère,* from *tuyau* "pipe"]

TV \ˈtē-ˈvē\ *n* : TELEVISION [*television*]

twa \ˈtwȧ\ *or* **twae** \ˈtwȧ, ˈtwē\ *Scottish variant of* TWO

twad•dle \ˈtwäd-l\ *n* **1** : silly idle talk : DRIVEL **2** : something insignificant or worthless : NONSENSE [probably alteration of English dialect *twattle*]

twain \ˈtwān\ *n* **1** : TWO **2** : COUPLE, PAIR [Old English *twēgen,* adj. and pron., "two"]

¹twang \ˈtwang\ *n* **1** : a harsh quick ringing sound like that of a plucked bowstring **2 a** : nasal speech or resonance **b** : the characteristic speech of a region, locality, or group of people [imitative]

²twang *vb* **twanged; twang•ing** \ˈtwang-ing\ **1** : to sound or cause to sound with a twang **2** : to speak with a nasal intonation

'twas \ˈtwəz, ˈtwäz\ : it was

¹tweak \ˈtwēk\ *vt* **1** : to pinch and pull with a sudden jerk and twist **2** : to make small adjustments in or to ⟨*tweak* the controls⟩ **3** : to injure slightly ⟨*tweaked* my knee⟩ [Old English *twiccian* "to pluck"]

²tweak *n* : an act of tweaking : PINCH

tweed \ˈtwēd\ *n* **1** : a rough woolen fabric made usually in twill weaves **2** *pl* : tweed clothing; *esp* : a tweed suit [Scottish *tweel* "twill," from Middle English *twyll*]

tweedy \ˈtwēd-ē\ *adj* **tweed•i•er; -est 1** : of or resembling tweed **2 a** : given to wearing tweeds **b** : informal or suggestive of the outdoors in taste or habits

tween \ˈtwēn\ *n* : PRETEEN [blend of *between* and *teen*]

¹tweet \ˈtwēt\ *n* **1** : CHIRP **2** : a post made on the Twitter online message service [imitative]

²tweet *vb* **1** : to make a chirping sound **2** : to post a message to the Twitter online message service

tweet•er \ˈtwēt-ər\ *n* : a small loudspeaker responsive only to the higher acoustic frequencies and reproducing sounds of high pitch — compare WOOFER

tweeze \ˈtwēz\ *vt* : to pluck or remove with tweezers [back-formation from *tweezers*]

tweez•ers \ˈtwē-zərz\ *n pl* : any of various small metal instruments that are used for plucking, holding, or manipulating, and consist of two legs joined at one end [obsolete *tweeze* "case for small implements," from French *étui*]

Twelfth Day *n* : EPIPHANY 1

Twelfth Night *n* : the evening or sometimes the eve of Epiphany

twelve \ˈtwelv\ *n* **1** — see NUMBER table **2** *cap* : the twelve original disciples of Jesus **3** : the 12th in a set or series **4** : something having 12 units or members [Old English *twelf*] — **twelve** *adj or pron* — **twelfth** \ˈtwelfth, ˈtwelftth\ *n* — **twelfth** *adj or adv*

twelve•month \-ˌmənth, -ˌməntth\ *n* : YEAR

twen•ty \ˈtwent-ē\ *n, pl* **twenties** — see NUMBER table [Old English *twēntig*] — **twenty** *adj or pron* — **twen•ti•eth** \-ē-əth\ *adj or n*

twen•ty–one \ˌtwent-ē-ˈwən\ *n* : BLACKJACK 3

twen•ty–twen•ty *or* **20/20** \ˌtwent-ē-ˈtwent-ē\ *adj* : of normal acuity ⟨*twenty-twenty* vision⟩ [from the custom of testing vision chiefly at a distance of 20 feet]

twen·ty–two \ˌtwent-ē-ˈtü\ *n* : a .22-caliber rifle or pistol — usually written .22

twerp \ˈtwərp\ *n* : a silly, insignificant, or contemptible person [origin unknown]

twice \ˈtwīs\ *adv* : two times ⟨*twice* absent⟩ ⟨*twice* two is four⟩ [Middle English *twiges, twies,* from Old English *twiga*]

twice–born \-ˈbȯrn\ *adj* : having undergone a spiritual rebirth or regeneration through religious conversion or renewal or by an initiation ceremony

twice–laid \-ˈlād\ *adj* : made from the ends of rope and strands of used rope ⟨*twice-laid* rope⟩

twice–told \ˌtwīs-ˌtōld\ *adj* **1** : narrated twice **2** : HACKNEYED, TRITE — used chiefly in the phrase *a twice-told tale*

[1]**twid·dle** \ˈtwid-l\ *vb* **twid·dled; twid·dling** \ˈtwid-ling, -l-ing\ **1** : to be busy with trifles : FIDDLE **2** : to rotate lightly or idly ⟨*twiddle* one's thumbs⟩ [origin unknown]

[2]**twiddle** *n* : an act of twiddling : TURN, TWIST

[1]**twig** \ˈtwig\ *n* : a small shoot or branch usually without its leaves [Old English *twigge*] — **twigged** \ˈtwigd\ *adj* — **twig·gy** \ˈtwig-ē\ *adj*

[2]**twig** *vb* **twigged; twig·ging** : to catch on : NOTICE, UNDERSTAND [perhaps from Irish and Scottish Gaelic *tuig-* "understand"]

twi·light \ˈtwī-ˌlīt\ *n* **1 a** : the light from the sky between full night and sunrise or between sunset and full night **b** : the time of twilight **2 a** : a state of indistinctness **b** : a period of decline [Middle English, from *twi-* "two" + *light*] — **twilight** *adj*

twilight sleep *n* : a state produced by injection of morphine and scopolamine in which awareness and memory of pain is dulled or effaced

[1]**twill** \ˈtwil\ *n* **1** : a fabric with a twill weave **2** : a textile weave that produces a pattern of diagonal lines or ribs [Middle English *twyll,* from Old English *twilic* "having a double thread," from Latin *bilic-, bilix,* from *bi-* + *licium* "thread"]

twill 2

[2]**twill** *vt* : to make (cloth) with a twill weave

[1]**twin** \ˈtwin\ *adj* **1** : born with one other or as a pair at one birth ⟨my *twin* brother⟩ ⟨*twin* girls⟩ **2 a** : made up of two similar, related, or connected members or parts **b** : paired in a close or necessary relationship **c** : having or consisting of two identical units **d** : being one of a pair ⟨a *twin* city⟩ [Old English *twinn* "twofold"]

[2]**twin** *n* **1** : either of two offspring produced at a birth — compare FRATERNAL TWIN, IDENTICAL TWIN **2** : one of two persons or things closely related to or resembling each other

[3]**twin** *vb* **twinned; twin·ning** **1** : to bring together in close association : COUPLE **2** : MATCH 4 **3** : to produce or give birth to twins

twin bill *n* : DOUBLEHEADER

[1]**twine** \ˈtwīn\ *n* **1** : a strong string of two or more strands twisted together **2** *archaic* : a twined or interlaced part or object **3** *archaic* : an act of twining, interlacing, or embracing [Old English *twīn*]

[2]**twine** *vb* **1 a** : to twist together **b** : to form by twining **2 a** : to coil or cause to coil about a support **b** : WRAP ⟨*twined* their arms about each other⟩ **3** : MEANDER 1, WIND

[1]**twinge** \ˈtwinj\ *vb* **twinged; twing·ing** *or* **twinge·ing** : to affect with or feel a sudden sharp pain [Old English *twengan* "to pinch"]

[2]**twinge** *n* **1** : a sudden sharp stab of pain **2** : a moral or emotional pang ⟨a *twinge* of regret⟩

[1]**twin·kle** \ˈtwing-kəl\ *vb* **twin·kled; twin·kling** \ˈtwing-kə-ling, -kling\ **1** : to shine or cause to shine with a flickering or sparkling light : SCINTILLATE **2** : to appear bright with merriment ⟨his eyes *twinkled*⟩ **3** : to move or flutter rapidly : FLIT [Old English *twinclian*] — **twin·kler** \-kə-lər, -klər\ *n*

[2]**twinkle** *n* **1** : a wink of the eyelids **2** : a very brief period : TWINKLING **3** : SPARKLE, FLICKER ⟨that *twinkle* in your eye⟩ — **twin·kly** \-kə-lē, -klē\ *adj*

twin·kling \ˈtwing-kə-ling, -kling\ *n* : the time required for a wink : INSTANT ⟨in a *twinkling*⟩

twin primes *n pl* : a pair of prime numbers (as 3 and 5 or 11 and 13) whose difference is two

twin–screw \ˈtwin-ˈskrü\ *adj* : having a right-handed and a left-handed propeller parallel to each other on each side of the plane of the keel

twin–size \ˈtwin-ˈsīz\ *adj* : having a size of 39 inches by 75 inches (about 1.0 by 1.9 meters) ⟨a *twin-size* bed⟩

[1]**twirl** \ˈtwərl\ *vb* **1** : to revolve or cause to revolve rapidly : SPIN, WHIRL ⟨*twirl* a baton⟩ **2** : to pitch in a baseball game **3** : CURL, TWIST ⟨*twirl* one's hair⟩ [perhaps of Scandinavian origin] — **twirl·er** *n*

[2]**twirl** *n* **1** : an act of twirling **2** : COIL, WHORL

[1]**twist** \ˈtwist\ *vb* **1** : to unite by winding one thread, strand, or wire around another **2** : TWINE 2a, COIL **3 a** : to turn so as to sprain or hurt ⟨*twisted* my ankle⟩ **b** : to alter the meaning of ⟨*twisted* the facts⟩ **c** : CONTORT ⟨*twist* one's face into a grin⟩ **d** : to pull off, rotate, or break by a turning force **4** : to follow a winding course **5 a** : to turn or change shape under a turning force **b** : SQUIRM ⟨*twisting* in their seats⟩ **6** : to turn around [Middle English *twisten,* from *twist* "twine, discord, quarrel"]

[2]**twist** *n* **1** : something formed by twisting or winding: as **a** : a thread, yarn, or cord formed by twisting two or more strands together **b** : a baked piece of twisted dough **c** : tobacco leaves twisted into a thick roll **2 a** : an act of twisting : the state of being twisted **b** : a lively dance in which the hips are turned from side to side **c** : a spiral turn or curve **3 a** : a turning off a straight course **b** : ECCENTRICITY **c** : a distortion of meaning ⟨gave the facts a *twist*⟩ **4 a** : an unexpected turn or development **b** : a different approach or method ⟨a new *twist* on an old recipe⟩

twist·er \ˈtwis-tər\ *n* **1** : one that twists **2** : a tornado, waterspout, or dust devil in which the rotatory ascending movement of a column of air is visible

twist tie *n* : a tie used for closing or securing (as a plastic bag) by twisting the ends together

[1]**twit** \ˈtwit\ *n* **1** : an act of twitting **2** : a silly annoying person

[2]**twit** *vt* **twit·ted; twit·ting** : to poke fun at gently [Old English *ætwītan* "to reproach," from *æt* "at" + *wītan* "to reproach"]

[1]**twitch** \ˈtwich\ *vb* **1** : to move or pull with a sudden motion **2** : PLUCK ⟨*twitched* at my sleeve⟩ **3** : to move jerkily **4** : to undergo a brief muscular contraction ⟨his hand *twitched*⟩ [Middle English *twicchen*]

[2]**twitch** *n* **1** : an act of twitching **2 a** : a brief contraction of muscle fibers **b** : a slight jerk of a body part

[1]**twit·ter** \ˈtwit-ər\ *vb* **1** : to utter successive chirping sounds **2 a** : to talk in a chattering fashion **b** : GIGGLE, TITTER **3** : to shake with agitation : FLUTTER [Middle English *twiteren*]

[2]**twitter** *n* **1** : a trembling agitation **2** : a succession of chirping sounds (as of birds) **3** : a light chattering — **twit·tery** \-ə-rē\ *adj*

twixt \twikst, ˈtwikst\ *prep* : BETWEEN [Middle English *twix,* short for *betwix, betwixt*]

two \ˈtü\ *n* **1** — see NUMBER table **2** : the second in a set or series **3** : something having two units or members [Old English *twā,* adj. and pron. (feminine and neuter)] — **two** *adj or pron*

two–base hit *n* : DOUBLE 1b

two–bit \ˌtü-ˌbit\ *adj* **1** : of the value of two bits **2** : being cheap, petty, or small-time

two bits *n sing or pl* **1** : QUARTER 3d **2** : something of small worth or importance

[1]**two–by–four** \ˌtü-bə-ˈfōr, -ˈfȯr\ *n* : a piece of lumber approximately 2 by 4 inches (5 by 10 centimeters) as sawed and usually 1⅝ by 3⅝ inches (about 4 by 9 centimeters) when dressed

[2]**two–by–four** *adj* **1** : measuring two units (as inches) by four **2** : very small or petty

2–D \ˈtü-ˈdē\ *n* : a two-dimensional form ⟨displayed in *2-D*⟩ [*D,* abbreviation of *dimensional*] — **2–D** *adj*

two–dimensional *adj* **1** : of, relating to, or having two dimensions **2** : lacking depth of characterization ⟨*two-dimensional* fiction⟩

two–faced \ˈtü-ˈfāst\ *adj* **1** : having two faces **2** : deceptively false — **two–faced·ly** \-ˈfā-səd-lē, -ˈfāst-lē\ *adv*

two–fist·ed \ˈtü-ˈfis-təd\ *adj* : VIRILE, VIGOROUS

two·fold \ˈtü-ˌfōld, -ˈfōld\ *adj* **1** : having two units or members **2** : being twice as great or as many — **twofold** *adv*

2, 4–D \ˌtü-ˌfōr-ˈdē, -ˌfȯr-\ *n* : a white crystalline irritant compound $C_8H_5Cl_3O_3$ used as a weed killer

two–hand·ed \ˈtü-ˈhan-dəd\ *adj* **1** : used with both hands ⟨a *two-handed* sword⟩ **2 :** requiring two persons ⟨a *two-handed* saw⟩ **3 :** having or efficient with two hands

two·pence \ˈtə-pəns, *U.S. also* ˈtü-ˌpens\ *or* **tup·pence** \ˈtə-pəns\ *n* **:** the sum of two pence

two·pen·ny \ˈtə-pnē, -ə-nē, *U.S. also* ˈtü-ˌpen-ē\ *adj* **:** of the value of or costing twopence

two–piece \ˈtü-ˈpēs\ *adj* **:** consisting of matching top and bottom parts ⟨a *two-piece* swimsuit⟩ — **two–piece** \-ˌpēs\ *n*

two–ply \ˈtü-ˈplī\ *adj* **:** consisting of two strands or thicknesses

two·some \ˈtü-səm\ *n* **:** a group of two persons or things

two–step \ˈtü-ˌstep\ *n* **1 :** a ballroom dance in 2/4 or 4/4 time having a basic pattern of step-close-step **2 :** a piece of music for the two-step — **two–step** *vi*

two–time \ˈtü-ˌtīm\ *vt* **:** to be unfaithful or treacherous to; *esp* **:** to be sexually unfaithful to (a spouse or lover)

two–toed sloth *n* **:** any of a genus of sloths having two claws on each front foot, three claws on each back foot, and six or seven vertebrae in the neck — compare THREE-TOED SLOTH

two–way *adj* **1 :** moving or allowing movement in either direction ⟨a *two-way* bridge⟩ **2 a :** involving two persons or groups ⟨communication is a *two-way* process⟩ **b :** made to send and receive messages ⟨*two-way* radio⟩

two–wheel·er \ˈtü-ˈhwē-lər, -ˈwē-\ *n* **:** a 2-wheeled vehicle (as a bicycle)

two–winged fly \ˌtü-ˌwingd-\ *n* **:** any of a large order (Diptera) of winged or rarely wingless insects (as a housefly, mosquito, or gnat) that have the anterior wings functional and the posterior wings reduced to halteres and that have segmented often headless, eyeless, and legless larvae

-ty *n suffix* **:** -ITY [Medieval French *-té,* from Latin *-tat-, -tas*]

ty·coon \tī-ˈkün\ *n* **1 :** SHOGUN **2 :** a business executive of exceptional wealth and power [Japanese *taikun*]

tying *present participle of* TIE

tyke *also* **tike** \ˈtīk\ *n* **1 :** DOG 1a; *esp* **:** an inferior or mongrel dog **2 :** a small child [Old Norse *tīk* "bitch"]

tympani *variant of* TIMPANI

tym·pan·ic \tim-ˈpan-ik\ *adj* **:** of, relating to, or being a tympanum

tympanic membrane *n* **:** EARDRUM

tym·pa·num \ˈtim-pə-nəm\ *n, pl* **-na** \-nə\ *also* **-nums 1 a** (1) **:** EARDRUM (2) **:** MIDDLE EAR **b :** a thin membrane of an insect covering an organ of hearing and transmitting vibrations produced by sound waves to it **2 a :** the recessed usually triangular face of a pediment within the frame made by the upper and lower cornices **b :** the space within an arch and above a lintel or a subordinate arch [Latin, "drum, architectural panel," from Greek *tympanon* "drum"]

^{1}**type** \ˈtīp\ *n* **1 a :** a person or thing believed to foreshadow or symbolize another **b** (1) **:** one having qualities of a higher category **:** MODEL (2) **:** a specimen or series of specimens on which a taxonomic species or subspecies is actually based **2 a :** a rectangular block typically of metal or wood bearing a relief character from which an inked print is made **b :** a collection of such blocks or the letters printed by them **c :** characters (as numbers, letters, or punctuation marks) for printing ⟨the *type* for this book has been photocomposed⟩ **3 a :** general form or character common to a number of individuals that distinguishes them as an identifiable class ⟨horses of draft *type*⟩ **b :** a particular kind, class, or group **:** SORT ⟨a seedless *type* of orange⟩ [Latin *typus* "image," from Greek *typos* "blow, impression, model," from *typtein* "to strike, beat"] ***synonyms*** see KIND

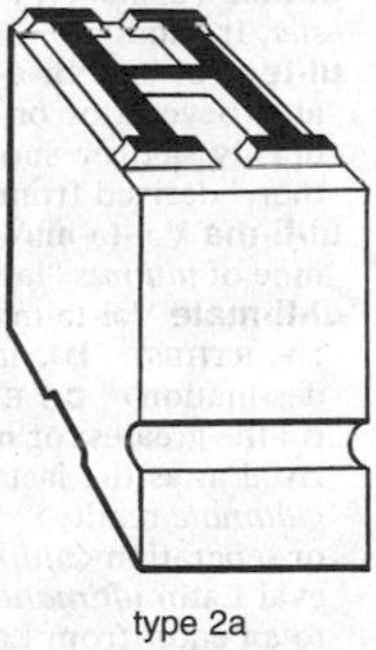

type 2a

^{2}**type** *vb* **1 :** TYPIFY **2 :** to write or produce (as a document) using a keyboard (as on a typewriter or computer) **3 :** to identify as belonging to a type: as **a :** to determine the natural type of (as a blood sample) **b :** TYPECAST — **type·able** \ˈtī-pə-bəl\ *adj*

type·cast \ˈtīp-ˌkast\ *vt* **1 :** to cast (an actor or actress) in a part calling for the same characteristics as those he or she possesses **2 :** to cast (an actor or actress) repeatedly in the same type of role

type·face \ˈtīp-ˌfās\ *n* **:** all type of a single design

type·found·er \-ˌfau̇n-dər\ *n* **:** one engaged in the design and production of metal printing type for hand composition — **type·found·ing** \-diŋ\ *n* — **type·found·ry** \-drē\ *n*

type metal *n* **:** an alloy that consists essentially of lead, antimony, and tin and is used in making printing type

type 1 diabetes *n* **:** a form of diabetes mellitus that usually develops during childhood or adolescence and results from a severe deficiency in insulin production

type·script \-ˌskript\ *n* **:** something that is typewritten [*type* + manu*script*]

type·set \ˈtīp-ˌset\ *vt* **-set; -set·ting :** to set in type **:** COMPOSE

type·set·ter \-ˌset-ər\ *n* **:** one that sets type for printing — **type·set·ting** \-ˌset-iŋ\ *n*

type 2 diabetes *n* **:** a form of diabetes mellitus that develops especially in adults and results from impaired insulin utilization coupled with the body's inability to compensate with increased insulin production

type·write \ˈtī-ˌprīt\ *vb* **:** TYPE 2

type·writ·er \ˈtī-ˌprīt-ər\ *n* **1 :** a machine for writing in characters similar to those produced by printer's type by means of keyboard-operated types striking through an inked ribbon **2 :** TYPIST

type·writ·ing \-ˌprīt-iŋ\ *n* **1 :** the act or study of or skill in using a typewriter **2 :** the printing done with a typewriter

typ·ey *also* **typy** \ˈtī-pē\ *adj* **typ·i·er; -est :** of superior bodily conformation ⟨a *typey* steer⟩

^{1}**ty·phoid** \ˈtī-ˌfȯid, tī-ˈ, ˈtī-ˈ\ *adj* **:** of, relating to, or being typhoid fever

^{2}**typhoid** *n* **:** TYPHOID FEVER

typhoid fever *n* **:** a bacterial disease that is marked especially by fever, diarrhea, weakness, headache, and intestinal inflammation and is transmitted from one person to another in contaminated food or water [derived from New Latin *typhus*]

ty·phoon \tī-ˈfün\ *n* **:** a hurricane occurring in the region of the Philippines or the China sea [earlier *touffon,* from Arabic *ṭūfān* "hurricane," from Greek *typhōn* "violent storm"]

ty·phus \ˈtī-fəs\ *n* **:** any of various bacterial diseases caused by rickettsias: as **a :** a severe disease marked by high fever, muscle and joint pain, cough, intense headache, delirium, and a red rash and transmitted especially by body lice **b :** MURINE TYPHUS **c :** SCRUB TYPHUS [New Latin, from Greek *typhos* "fever"]

typhus fever *n* **:** TYPHUS

typ·i·cal \ˈtip-i-kəl\ *adj* **1 :** being or having the nature of a type ⟨*typical* species⟩ **2 :** combining or exhibiting the essential characteristics of a group ⟨a *typical* suburban house⟩ ***synonyms*** see REGULAR — **typ·i·cal·i·ty** \ˌtip-ə-ˈkal-ət-ē\ *n* — **typ·i·cal·ly** \ˈtip-i-kə-lē, -klē\ *adv* — **typ·i·cal·ness** \-kəl-nəs\ *n*

typ·i·fy \ˈtip-ə-ˌfī\ *vt* **-fied; -fy·ing 1 :** PREFIGURE 1, REPRESENT **2 :** to have or embody the essential or main characteristics of

typ·ist \ˈtī-pəst\ *n* **:** a person who types especially as a job

ty·po \ˈtī-pō\ *n, pl* **typos :** a typographical error

ty·pog·ra·pher \tī-ˈpäg-rə-fər\ *n* **:** a person (as a compositor, printer, or designer) who specializes in the design, choice, or arrangement of type matter

ty·pog·ra·phy \-fē\ *n* **:** the style, arrangement, or appearance of typeset matter — **ty·po·graph·ic** \ˌtī-pə-ˈgraf-ik\ *adj* — **ty·po·graph·i·cal** \-ˈgraf-i-kəl\ *adj* — **ty·po·graph·i·cal·ly** \-i-kə-lē, -klē\ *adv*

ty·ran·ni·cal \tə-ˈran-i-kəl, tī-\ *also* **ty·ran·nic** \-ˈran-ik\ *adj* **:** of, relating to, or characteristic of a tyrant or tyranny **:** DESPOTIC — **ty·ran·ni·cal·ly** \-ˈran-i-kə-lē, -klē\ *adv*

tyr·an·nize \ˈtir-ə-ˌnīz\ *vb* **1 :** to act like a tyrant **2 :** to treat tyrannically — **tyr·an·niz·er** *n*

ty·ran·no·saur \tə-ˈran-ə-ˌsȯr, tī-\ *n* **:** a very large North American flesh-eating dinosaur of the Cretaceous period having small forelegs and walking on its hind legs [derived from Greek *tyrannos* "tyrant" + *sauros* "lizard"]

ty·ran·no·sau·rus \tə-ˌran-ə-ˈsȯr-əs, tī-\ *n* **:** TYRANNOSAUR

tyr·an·nous \ˈtir-ə-nəs\ *adj* **:** marked by tyranny; *esp* **:** unjustly severe — **tyr·an·nous·ly** *adv*

tyr·an·ny \ˈtir-ə-nē\ *n, pl* **-nies 1 a :** a government in which ab-

\ə\ **abut**	\au̇\ **out**	\i\ **tip**	\ȯ\ **saw**	\u̇\ **foot**
\ər\ **further**	\ch\ **chin**	\ī\ **life**	\ȯi\ **coin**	\y\ **yet**
\a\ **mat**	\e\ **pet**	\j\ **job**	\th\ **thin**	\yü\ **few**
\ā\ **take**	\ē\ **easy**	\ŋ\ **sing**	\t͟h\ **this**	\yu̇\ **cure**
\ä\ **cot, cart**	\g\ **go**	\ō\ **bone**	\ü\ **food**	\zh\ **vision**

solute power is held by a single ruler **b :** the office, authority, and administration of such a ruler **2 :** arbitrary and despotic government; *esp* **:** rigorous, cruel, and oppressive government **3 :** SEVERITY, RIGOR ⟨the *tyranny* of the alarm clock⟩ **4 :** a tyrannical act [Medieval French *tyrannie,* from Medieval Latin *tyrannia,* from Latin *tyrannus* "tyrant"]

ty·rant \ˈtī-rənt\ *n* **1 :** an absolute ruler unrestrained by law or constitution **2 a :** a ruler who exercises absolute power in an oppressive or brutal manner **b :** one resembling such a tyrant in the harsh use of authority or power [Medieval French *tyran, tyrant,* from Latin *tyrannus,* from Greek *tyrannos*]

tyrant flycatcher *n* **:** any of a family of American flycatchers with a flattened bill usually hooked at the tip

tyre *chiefly British variant of* TIRE

Tyr·i·an purple \ˌtir-ē-ən-\ *n* **:** a synthetic crimson or purple dye formerly obtained by the ancient Greeks and Romans from gastropod mollusks [*Tyre,* city of ancient Phoenicia]

ty·ro \ˈtī-rō\ *n, pl* **tyros :** a beginner in learning [Latin *tiro* "young soldier, tyro"]

ty·ro·sine \ˈtī-rə-ˌsēn\ *n* **:** an amino acid that is a precursor of several important substances (as epinephrine) [derived from Greek *tyros* "cheese"]

tzar, tzarevitch, tzarina, tzarism *variant of* CZAR, CZAREVITCH, CZARINA, CZARISM

U

u \ˈyü\ *n, pl* **u's** *or* **us** \ˈyüz\ *often cap* **:** the 21st letter of the English alphabet

ubiq·ui·tous \yu̇-ˈbik-wət-əs\ *adj* **:** existing or being everywhere at the same time **:** widely or generally present [from *ubiquity,* from Latin *ubique* "everywhere"] — **ubiq·ui·tous·ly** *adv* — **ubiq·ui·tous·ness** *n* — **ubiq·ui·ty** \-wət-ē\ *n*

U–boat \ˈyü-ˈbōt\ *n* **:** a German submarine [German *U-boot,* short for *Unterseeboot,* literally, "undersea boat"]

ud·der \ˈəd-ər\ *n* **1 :** a large bag-shaped organ (as of a cow) consisting of two or more mammary glands enclosed in a common pouch but each having a separate nipple **2 :** a mammary gland [Old English *ūder*]

UFO \ˌyü-ef-ˈō\ *n, pl* **UFO's** *or* **UFOs** \-ˈōz\ **:** an unidentified flying object; *esp* **:** FLYING SAUCER [*u*nidentified *f*lying *o*bject]

ugh *often read as* ˈəg *or* ˈək *or* ˈə\ *interj* — used to indicate the sound of a cough or grunt or to express disgust or horror

ug·li·fy \ˈəg-li-ˌfī\ *vt* **-fied; -fy·ing :** to make ugly

ug·ly \ˈəg-lē\ *adj* **ug·li·er; -est 1 :** FRIGHTFUL ⟨an *ugly* wound⟩ **2 a :** unpleasant to look at **b :** offensive or unpleasing to any sense ⟨an *ugly* sound⟩ **3 :** morally offensive or objectionable ⟨*ugly* habits⟩ **4 a :** likely to cause inconvenience or discomfort **:** TROUBLESOME ⟨an *ugly* situation⟩ **b :** SURLY ⟨an *ugly* disposition⟩ [Old Norse *uggligr,* from *uggr* "fear"] — **ug·li·ness** *n*

ugly duckling *n* **:** a person or thing that seems unpromising but later develops great beauty, talent, or worth [*The Ugly Duckling,* story by Hans Christian Andersen in which a supposed ugly duckling develops into a swan]

Ugri·an \ˈü-grē-ən, ˈyü-\ *n* **:** a member of a division of the Finno-Ugric peoples that includes the Hungarians and two peoples of western Siberia [Old Russian *Ugre* "Hungarians"] — **Ugrian** *adj*

uh–huh *two m's separated by the voiceless sound* h, ə^{n}-hə^{n}, ˈə^{n}-ˌhə^{n}\ *interj* — used to indicate affirmation, agreement, or gratification

uh·lan \ˈü-ˌlän, ˈü-lən, ˈyü-lən\ *n* **:** any of a body of Prussian light cavalry originally modeled on Tatar lancers [German, from Polish *ulan,* from Turkish *oğlan* "boy, servant"]

uh–uh \ˈə^{n}-ˌə^{n}; ˈm-ˌm, ˈn-ˌn\ *interj* — used to indicate negation

ukase \yü-ˈkās, -ˈkāz, ˈyü-ˌ; ˈü-ˌkäz\ *n* **:** an edict especially of a Russian emperor or government [French, from Russian *ukaz*]

uke \ˈyük\ *n* **:** UKULELE

Ukrai·ni·an \yü-ˈkrā-nē-ən\ *n* **1 :** a native or inhabitant of Ukraine **2 :** the Slavic language of the Ukrainian people — **Ukrainian** *adj*

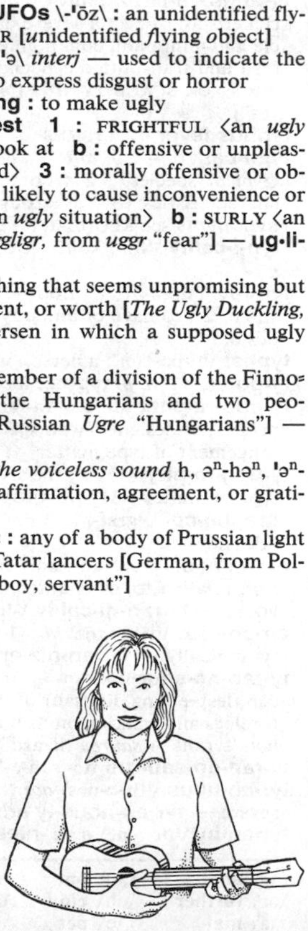
ukulele

uku·le·le \ˌyü-kə-ˈlā-lē, ˌü-kə-\ *n* **:** a small guitar popularized in Hawaii that is strung usually with four strings and is played with the fingers or a pick [Hawaiian *'ukulele,* from *'uku* "flea" + *lele* "jumping"]

-u·lar \yə-lər, ə-lər\ *adj suffix* **:** of, relating to, or resembling ⟨val*vular*⟩ [Latin *-ularis,* from *-ulus, -ula, -ulum* "-ule" + *-aris* "-ar"]

ul·cer \ˈəl-sər\ *n* **1 :** a slow-healing open sore that often discharges pus **2 :** something that festers and corrupts like an open sore [Latin *ulcer-, ulcus*]

ul·cer·ate \ˈəl-sə-ˌrāt\ *vb* **:** to cause or become affected with an ulcer ⟨an *ulcerated* wound⟩

ul·cer·a·tion \ˌəl-sə-ˈrā-shən\ *n* **1 :** the process of forming or state of having an ulcer **2 :** ULCER 1

ul·cer·ous \ˈəls-rəs, -ə-rəs\ *adj* **1 :** characterized or caused by ulceration ⟨*ulcerous* lesions⟩ **2 :** affected with an ulcer

-ule \ˌül, ˌyül\ *n suffix* **:** little one ⟨lob*ule*⟩ [Latin *-ulus, -ula, -ulum*]

ul·lage \ˈəl-ij\ *n* **:** the amount that a container (as a cask) is short of being full [Medieval French *ulliage* "act of filling a cask," from Medieval French *oel* "eye, bunghole," from Latin *oculus* "eye"]

ul·na \ˈəl-nə\ *n, pl* **ul·nae** \-ˌnē, -ˌnī\ *or* **ulnas :** the bone on the little-finger side of the human forearm; *also* **:** a corresponding part of the forelimb of vertebrates [Latin, "elbow"] — **ul·nar** \-nər\ *adj*

ul·ster \ˈəl-stər\ *n* **:** a long loose overcoat of heavy material [*Ulster,* Ireland]

ul·te·ri·or \ˌəl-ˈtir-ē-ər\ *adj* **1 a :** lying farther away **b :** situated beyond or on the farther side **2 :** going beyond what is openly said or shown ⟨*ulterior* motives⟩ [Latin, "farther, further," derived from *uls* "beyond"] — **ul·te·ri·or·ly** *adv*

ul·ti·ma \ˈəl-tə-mə\ *n* **:** the last syllable of a word [Latin, feminine of *ultimus* "last"]

[1]**ul·ti·mate** \ˈəl-tə-mət\ *adj* **1 a :** most remote in space or time **:** FARTHEST **b :** last in a progression **:** FINAL ⟨their *ultimate* destination⟩ **c :** EVENTUAL ⟨they hoped for *ultimate* success⟩ **d :** the greatest or most extreme ⟨the *ultimate* sacrifice⟩ **2 :** arrived at as the last result ⟨the *ultimate* question⟩ **3 a :** BASIC ⟨*ultimate* reality⟩ **b :** not capable of further analysis, division, or separation ⟨*ultimate* particles⟩ **4 :** being the greatest [Medieval Latin *ultimatus* "last," from Late Latin *ultimare* "to come to an end," from Latin *ultimus* "last, farthest," derived from *uls* "beyond"] ***synonyms*** see LAST — **ul·ti·mate·ly** *adv*

[2]**ultimate** *n* **1 :** something ultimate **2** *cap* **:** ULTIMATE FRISBEE

Ultimate Frisbee *n, often not cap* **:** a game played on a field between two seven-player teams in which a team scores by throwing a plastic disc from player to player until it is caught in the opponent's end zone — called also *Ultimate*

ul·ti·ma·tum \ˌəl-tə-ˈmāt-əm, -ˈmät-\ *n, pl* **-tums** *or* **-ta** \-ə\ **:** a final proposition, condition, or demand; *esp* **:** one whose rejection will bring about an end of negotiations and a resort to direct action (as by force) [New Latin, from Medieval Latin *ultimatus* "last"]

ul·ti·mo \ˈəl-tə-ˌmō\ *adj* **:** of or occurring the month preceding the present [Latin *ultimo mense* "in the last month"]

[1]**ul·tra** \ˈəl-trə\ *adj* **:** greater than usual **:** EXTREME [*ultra-*]

[2]**ultra** *n* **:** EXTREMIST

ultra- *prefix* **1 :** beyond in space : on the other side of ⟨*ultra*violet⟩ **2 :** beyond the range or limits of : transcending ⟨*ultra*microscopic⟩ ⟨*ultra*sonic⟩ **3 :** beyond what is ordinary, proper, or moderate : excessively ⟨*ultra*modern⟩ [Latin, from *ultra* "beyond," derived from *uls* "beyond"]

ultracareful
ultracasual
ultracautious
ultrachic
ultracivilized
ultraclean
ultracommercial
ultraconservatism
ultraconservative
ultraconvenient
ultracritical
ultrafast
ultrafastidious
ultrafeminine
ultraglamorous
ultrahazardous
ultrahigh
ultraleft
ultraleftism
ultraleftist
ultraliberal
ultraliberalism
ultralow
ultramasculine
ultramilitant
ultramodern
ultramodernist
ultranationalism
ultranationalist
ultranationalistic
ultraorthodox
ultrapatriotic
ultrapowerful
ultrapractical
ultraprecise
ultraprecision
ultrapure
ultraradical
ultrarapid
ultrarare
ultrarational
ultrarealism
ultrarealist
ultrarealistic
ultrarefined
ultrareligious
ultrarespectable
ultrarevolutionary
ultrarich
ultrarightist
ultraromantic
ultrasafe
ultrasecret
ultrasensitive
ultraserious
ultrasharp
ultrasmall
ultrasophisticated
ultrathin
ultratraditional
ultrawide

ul·tra·cen·tri·fuge \ˌəl-trə-ˈsen-trə-ˌfyüj\ *n* : a high-speed centrifuge able to separate small (as colloidal) particles — **ul·tra·cen·trif·u·gal** \-ˌsen-ˈtrif-yə-gəl, -ˈtrif-i-gəl\ *adj*

ul·tra·high frequency \ˌəl-trə-ˌhī-\ *n* : any radio frequency in the range between 300 and 3000 megahertz — abbreviation *UHF*

[1]**ul·tra·light** \ˌəl-trə-ˈlīt\ *adj* : extremely light in mass or weight ⟨an *ultralight* alloy⟩

[2]**ultralight** *n* : a very light gasoline-powered recreational aircraft typically for one person

[1]**ul·tra·ma·rine** \ˌəl-trə-mə-ˈrēn\ *n* **1 :** a deep blue pigment **2 :** a vivid blue

[2]**ultramarine** *adj* : situated beyond the sea

ul·tra·mi·cro \ˌəl-trə-ˈmī-krō\ *adj* : being or dealing with something smaller than micro

ul·tra·mi·cro·scope \ˌəl-trə-ˈmī-krə-ˌskōp\ *n* : an apparatus that uses scattered light to view particles too small to be seen with an ordinary microscope

ul·tra·mi·cro·scop·ic \-ˌmī-krə-ˈskäp-ik\ *adj* **1 :** too small to be seen with an ordinary microscope **2 :** of or relating to an ultramicroscope — **ul·tra·mi·cro·scop·i·cal·ly** \-ˈskäp-i-kə-lē, -klē\ *adv*

ul·tra·short \-ˈshȯrt\ *adj* : very short

[1]**ul·tra·son·ic** \-ˈsän-ik\ *adj* **1 :** having a frequency above the human ear's ability to hear **2 :** using, produced by, or relating to ultrasonic waves or vibrations — **ul·tra·son·i·cal·ly** \-ˈsän-i-kə-lē, -klē\ *adv*

[2]**ultrasonic** *n* : an ultrasonic wave or frequency

ul·tra·son·ics \-ˈsän-iks\ *n* : the science or technology of ultrasonic phenomena

ul·tra·so·nog·ra·phy \-sə-ˈnäg-rə-fē\ *n* : ULTRASOUND 2 — **ultrasonographer** *n*

ul·tra·sound \ˌəl-trə-ˈsau̇nd\ *n* **1 :** vibrations of the same physical nature as sound but with frequencies above the range of human hearing **2 :** the use of ultrasound for medical diagnosis and treatment and especially a technique involving the formation of a two-dimensional image used for the examination and measurement of internal body structures and the detection of bodily abnormalities **3 :** a diagnostic examination using ultrasound

ul·tra·vi·o·let \-ˈvī-ə-lət\ *adj* **1 :** situated beyond the visible spectrum at its violet end and having a wavelength shorter than those of visible light but longer than those of X-rays **2 :** relating to, producing, or using ultraviolet radiation — **ultraviolet** *n*

ultraviolet light *n* : ultraviolet radiation

ul·u·late \ˈəl-yə-ˌlāt\ *vi* : to utter a howl or wail [Latin *ululare,* of imitative origin] — **ul·u·lant** \-lənt\ *adj* — **ul·u·la·tion** \ˌəl-yə-ˈlā-shən\ *n*

ul·va \ˈəl-və\ *n* : SEA LETTUCE [Latin, "sedge"]

um *a prolonged* m *sound,* əm\ *interj* — used to express hesitation ⟨well, *um,* I don't know⟩

uma·mi \ü-ˈmäm-ē\ *n* : a taste sensation that is meaty or savory and is produced by several amino acids and nucleotides [Japanese, "savoriness, flavor"]

um·bel \ˈəm-bəl\ *n* : an inflorescence typical of the carrot in which the flower stalks arise from about the same point to form a flat or rounded flower cluster [Latin *umbella* "umbrella"] — **um·bel·late** \ˈəm-bə-ˌlāt, ˌəm-ˈbel-ət\ *adj*

um·ber \ˈəm-bər\ *n* **1 :** a brown earth valued as a pigment **2 a :** a moderate to dark yellowish brown **b :** a moderate brown [probably from obsolete *umber* "shade, color," from Medieval French *umbre* "shade, shadow," from Latin *umbra*] — **umber** *adj*

um·bil·i·cal \ˌəm-ˈbil-i-kəl\ *adj* : of, relating to, or adjacent to the navel

umbilical cord *n* : a cord arising from the navel that connects the fetus with the placenta and through which respiratory gases, nutrients, and wastes pass

um·bil·i·cate \ˌəm-ˈbil-i-kət\ *or* **um·bil·i·cat·ed** \-ˈbil-ə-ˌkāt-əd\ *adj* : having or suggesting an umbilicus — **um·bil·i·ca·tion** \ˌəm-ˌbil-ə-ˈkā-shən\ *n*

um·bil·i·cus \ˌəm-ˈbil-i-kəs\ *n, pl* **-bil·i·ci** \-ˈbil-ə-ˌkī, -ˌkē, -ˌsī\ *or* **-bil·i·cus·es** **1 a :** NAVEL 1 **b :** any of various depressions of a plant or animal; *esp* : HILUM 1 **2 :** a central point [Latin]

um·bles \ˈəm-bəlz\ *n pl* : the internal organs of an animal and especially of a deer used as food [Middle English *noumbles,* from Medieval French *nombles* "loins," from Latin *lumbulus* "little loin," from *lumbus* "loin"]

um·bo \ˈəm-bō\ *n, pl* **um·bo·nes** \ˌəm-ˈbō-nēz\ *or* **umbos** **1 :** the boss of a shield **2 :** a rounded anatomical elevation; *esp* : one of the lateral prominences just above the hinge of a bivalve shell [Latin] — **um·bo·nate** \ˈəm-bə-ˌnāt\ *adj*

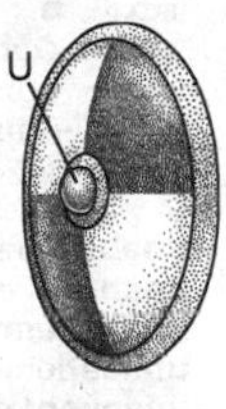

U umbo 1

um·bra \ˈəm-brə\ *n, pl* **umbras** *or* **um·brae** \-brē, -ˌbrī\ **1 :** a shaded area **2 :** the conical part of the shadow of a celestial body excluding all light from the primary source [Latin, "shade, shadow"]

um·brage \ˈəm-brij\ *n* **1 a :** SHADE 1a **b :** a growth (as of tangled branches) that gives shade **2 :** RESENTMENT, OFFENSE ⟨take *umbrage* at a remark⟩ [Medieval French, derived from Latin *umbra*] — **um·bra·geous** \ˌəm-ˈbrā-jəs\ *adj*

Word History English *umbrage* originally meant "shade, shadow." This is also the meaning of its ultimate Latin source, *umbra. Umbrage* was often used figuratively, and in the 17th century the word took on the pejorative sense "a shadow of suspicion cast on someone." From this usage it was but a short semantic leap to "resentment, offense," which is the sense used in the common phrases "give umbrage" and "take umbrage."

um·brel·la \ˌəm-ˈbrel-ə\ *n* **1 :** a collapsible shade for protection against weather consisting of fabric stretched over hinged ribs radiating from a center pole; *esp* : a small one for carrying in the hand **2 :** the bell-shaped or saucer-shaped largely jellylike structure that forms the main part of most jellyfishes [Italian *ombrella,* from Latin *umbella,* from *umbra* "shade"]

umbrella plant *n* : a sedge of Madagascar that has large terminal whorls of slender leaves and is often grown as a houseplant

umbrella tree *n* : any of various trees or shrubs resembling an umbrella especially in the arrangement of leaves or the shape of the crown

Um·bri·an \ˈəm-brē-ən\ *n* **1 a :** a member of a people of ancient Italy occupying Umbria **b :** a native or inhabitant of the Italian province of Umbria **2 :** the Italic language of ancient Umbria — **Umbrian** *adj*

umi·ak \ˈü-mē-ˌak\ *n* : an open Eskimo boat made of a wooden frame covered with hide [Inuit *umiaq*]

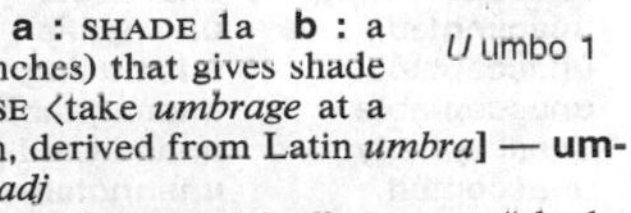
umiak

[1]**um·laut** \ˈu̇m-ˌlau̇t, ˈüm-\ *n* **1 a :** the change of a

\ə\ **abut**	\au̇\ **out**	\i\ **tip**	\ȯ\ **saw**	\u̇\ **foot**
\ər\ **further**	\ch\ **chin**	\ī\ **life**	\ȯi\ **coin**	\y\ **yet**
\a\ **mat**	\e\ **pet**	\j\ **job**	\th\ **thin**	\yü\ **few**
\ā\ **take**	\ē\ **easy**	\ng\ **sing**	\t͟h\ **this**	\yu̇\ **cure**
\ä\ **cot, cart**	\g\ **go**	\ō\ **bone**	\ü\ **food**	\zh\ **vision**

vowel caused by partial assimilation to a succeeding sound **b** : a vowel resulting from such partial assimilation **2** : a diacritical mark ¨ placed especially over a German vowel to indicate umlaut [German, from *um-* "around, transforming," + *Laut* "sound"]

²umlaut *vt* **1** : to produce by umlaut **2** : to write or print an umlaut over

¹um•pire \ˈəm-ˌpīr\ *n* **1** : one having authority to decide finally a controversy or question between parties **2** : an official in a sport who conducts the game and rules on plays [Middle English *oumpere,* from *noumpere* (the phrase *a noumpere* being understood as *an oumpere*), from Medieval French *nounpier* "single, odd, without equal," from *non-* + *per* "equal," from Latin *par*]

²umpire *vb* : to supervise or act as umpire ⟨*umpire* a baseball game⟩

ump•teen \ˈəm-ˈtēn, ˈəmp-, ˌəm-, ˌəmp-\ *adj* : very many : indefinitely numerous [blend of earlier *umpty* "such and such" and *-teen* (as in *thirteen*)] — **ump•teenth** \-ˈtēnth, -ˈtēntth\ *adj*

¹un- \ˌən, ˈən\ *prefix* **1** : not : IN-, NON- — in adjectives formed from adjectives ⟨*un*certain⟩ ⟨*un*skilled⟩ or participles ⟨*un*dressed⟩ and in nouns formed from nouns ⟨*un*concern⟩ **2** : opposite of : contrary to — in adjectives formed from adjectives ⟨*un*constitutional⟩ or participles ⟨*un*believing⟩ and in nouns formed from nouns ⟨*un*reason⟩ [Old English]

²un- *prefix* **1** : do the opposite of : reverse (a specified action) : DE- 1a, DIS- 1a — in verbs formed from verbs ⟨*un*bend⟩ ⟨*un*dress⟩ ⟨*un*fold⟩ **2 a** : deprive of : remove (a specified thing) from : remove — in verbs formed from nouns ⟨*un*frock⟩ ⟨*un*sex⟩ **b** : release from : free from — in verbs formed from nouns ⟨*un*hand⟩ **c** : remove from : extract from : bring out of — in verbs formed from nouns ⟨*un*bosom⟩ **d** : cause to cease to be — in verbs formed from nouns ⟨*un*man⟩ **3** : completely ⟨*un*loose⟩ [Old English *on-, un-,* alteration of *and-* "against"]

unabsorbed
unabsorbent
unacademic
unacademically
unaccented
unacceptability
unacceptable
unacceptably
unaccepted
unacclimated
unacclimatized
unaccommodated
unaccommodating
unaccredited
unachieved
unacknowledged
unacquainted
unactable
unacted
unadaptable
unadapted
unaddressed
unadjusted
unadmitted
unadoptable
unadventurous
unadvertised
unaesthetic
unaffectionate
unaffectionately
unaffiliated
unaffluent
unaffordable
unafraid
unaggressive
unaided
unair–conditioned
unalienated
unalike
unalleviated
unallocated
unaltered
unambiguous
unambiguously
unambitious
unamenable
unamended
unamiable
unamplified
unamusing
unanalyzable
unanalyzed
unannotated
unannounced
unanticipated
unapologetic
unapologetically
unapparent
unappeased
unappreciated
unappreciative
unapproachability
unapproachable
unapproachably
unappropriated
unapproved
unarguable
unarguably
unarmored
unarrogant
unartistic
unashamed
unashamedly
unaspirated
unassailed
unassembled
unassigned
unassimilable
unassimilated
unassisted
unassociated
unassuaged
unathletic
unattainable
unattended
unattested
unattributable
unattributed
unaudited
unauthentic
unauthorized
unavailability
unavailable
unavowed
unawakened
unawarded
unbaptized
unbelligerent
unbeloved
unbemused
unbitter
unbleached
unblemished
unblended
unbookish
unbowdlerized
unbracketed
unbranded
unbreakable
unbridgeable
unbridged
unbrilliant
unbruised
unbrushed
unbudgeted
unburied
unburnable
unburned
unburnt
unbusinesslike
unbusy
uncalcified
uncalled
uncanceled
uncanonical
uncap
uncapitalized
uncared–for
uncaring
uncarpeted
uncastrated
uncataloged
uncatchable
uncaught
uncelebrated
uncensored
uncensured
uncertified
unchallenged
unchallenging
unchanged
unchaperoned
uncharacteristic
uncharacteristically
uncharismatic
uncharming
unchecked
unchic
unchivalrous
unchivalrously
unchristened
unchronicled
unchronological
unciliated
unclad
unclaimed
unclassifiable
unclear
unclimbable
unclouded
uncluttered
uncoated
uncoerced
uncoercive
uncoercively
uncollected
uncollectible
uncolored
uncombed
uncombined
uncomely
uncomic
uncommercialized
uncompassionate
uncompelling
uncompensated
uncompleted
uncomplicated
uncompounded
uncomprehended
uncomprehending
unconcealed
unconfessed
unconfined
unconfirmed
unconfuse
unconnected
unconquered
unconsecrated
unconsolidated
unconstrained
unconsumed
uncontainable
uncontaminated
uncontemporary
uncontested
uncontradicted
uncontrived
uncontrolled
uncontroversial
uncontroversially
unconverted
unconvinced
unconvincing
unconvincingly
uncooked
uncooperative
uncoordinated
uncorrectable
uncorrected
uncorroborated
uncorrupt
uncountable
uncourageous
uncreative
uncredited
uncrippled
uncropped
uncrossable
uncrowded
uncrystallized
uncultivable
uncultivated
uncultured
uncured
uncurious
uncurtained
uncustomarily
uncustomary
uncynical
uncynically
undamaged
undamped
undated
undecidable
undecided
undecipherable
undeciphered
undeclared
undecorated
undedicated
undefeated
undefended
undefiled
undefinable
undefined
undeformed
undeliverable
undelivered
undemanding
undemocratic
undemocratically
undenominational
undependable
undescribable
undeserved
undeserving
undesired
undetectable
undetected
undeterminable
undetermined
undeterred
undeveloped
undiagnosable
undiagnosed
undialectical
undifferentiated
undigested
undigestible
undignified
undiluted
undiminished
undimmed
undiplomatic
undiplomatically
undischarged
undisciplined
undisclosed
undiscouraged
undiscoverable
undiscovered
undiscriminating
undiscussed
undismayed
undisputable
undisputed
undissolved
undistinguished
undistorted
undistracted
undistributed
undisturbed
undivided
undoable
undoctored
undoctrinaire
undocumented
undogmatic
undomestic
undomesticated
undoubtable
undoubting
undrained
undramatic
undrinkable
undutiful
undutifully
undutifulness
undyed
undynamic
uneager
uneatable
uneaten
unedifying
unedited
uneducable
uneducated
unelected
unembarrassed
unembellished
unemotional
unemotionally
unemphatic
unemphatically
unenclosed
unencouraging
unencumbered
unendurable
unendurably
unenforceable
unenforced
unenlarged
unenlightened
unenlightening
unenterprising
unenthusiastic
unenthusiastically
unenviable
unenvious
unescapable
unessential
unethical
unevaluated
unexamined
unexcelled
unexcitable
unexcited
unexciting
unexotic
unexpended
unexpired
unexplainable
unexplained
unexploded
unexplored
unexposed
unexpressed
unexpurgated
unextraordinary
unfaltering
unfalteringly
unfashionable
unfashionably
unfastidious
unfazed
unfeasible
unfelt

unfeminine
unfenced
unfermented
unfertile
unfertilized
unfilled
unfiltered
unfired
unflamboyant
unflattering
unflyable
unfocused
unfond
unforced
unforeseeable
unforeseen
unforgivable
unforgiving
unformulated
unfortified
unfossiliferous
unframed
unfree
unfrozen
unfulfilled
unfunny
unfurnished
unfused
unfussy
ungallant
ungallantly
ungarnished
ungenial
ungenteel
ungentle
ungentlemanly
ungerminated
ungifted
unglamorized
unglamorous
unglazed
ungraceful
ungracefully
ungraded
ungrammatical
ungrammatically
ungraspable
unguessable
unguided
unhackneyed
unhampered
unharmed
unharvested
unhatched
unhealed
unheated
unheeded
unheeding
unhelpful
unheralded
unheroic
unhesitating
unhesitatingly
unhindered
unhip
unhistorical
unhonored
unhopeful
unhoused
unhumorous
unhurt
unhygienic
unhysterical
unidentifiable
unidentified
unideological
unidiomatic
unilluminating
unimaginable
unimaginably
unimaginative
unimaginatively
unimpaired
unimpassioned
unimpeded
unimportant
unimposing
unimpressed
unimpressive
unincorporated
unindexed
unindicted
unindustrialized
uninfected
uninflected
uninfluenced
uninformative
uninformatively
uninformed
uninhabitable
uninhabited
uninitiated
uninjured
uninoculated
uninspected
uninspired
uninspiring
uninstructed
uninstructive
uninsulated
uninsurable
uninsured
unintegrated
unintellectual
unintelligible
unintelligibly
unintended
unintentional
unintentionally
uninteresting
uninterrupted
unintimidated
uninventive
uninvited
uninviting
uninvolved
unirradiated
unirrigated
unissued
unjoined
unjointed
unjustifiable
unjustifiably
unjustified
unkept
unknowing
unknowingly
unknowledgeable
unkosher
unlabeled
unladylike
unlamented
unleavened
unliberated
unlicensed
unlikable
unlined
unlit
unliterary
unlivable
unlovable
unloved
unloving
unmalicious
unmaliciously
unmanageable
unmapped
unmarked
unmarketable
unmarred
unmasculine
unmatchable
unmatched
unmeasurable
unmeasured
unmechanized
unmediated
unmelodious
unmemorable
unmentioned
unmerited
unmet
unmetabolized
unmilitary
unmilled
unmindful
unmixed
unmodernized
unmodified
unmolested
unmonitored
unmotivated
unmounted
unmovable
unmoved
unmusical
unnameable
unnamed
unneeded
unnewsworthy
unnoticeable
unnoticed
unnourishing
unobjectionable
unobservable
unobserved
unobstructed
unobtainable
unofficial
unofficially
unopenable
unopened
unopposed
unordered
unoriginal
unorthodox
unorthodoxly
unostentatious
unostentatiously
unowned
unoxygenated
unpainted
unpalatable
unparasitized
unpardonable
unpassable
unpasteurized
unpatentable
unpatriotic
unpaved
unpedantic
unpeeled
unperceived
unperceptive
unperformable
unperformed
unpersuaded
unpersuasive
unperturbed
unpicturesque
unplanned
unplausible
unplayable
unpleased
unpleasing
unplowed
unpoetic
unpoliced
unpolished
unpolluted
unposed
unpractical
unpredictability
unpredictable
unpredictably
unpremeditated
unprepared
unpreparedness
unprepossessing
unpressed
unpressured
unpressurized
unpretty
unprivileged
unprocessed
unproductive
unprogrammed
unprogressive
unprompted
unpronounceable
unpronounced
unpropitious
unprosperous
unprovable
unproved
unproven
unprovoked
unpruned
unpublicized
unpublished
unpunctual
unpunctuality
unpunished
unquenchable
unquestioned
unraised
unranked
unravished
unreachable
unreached
unrealizable
unrealized
unreceptive
unreclaimable
unrecognizable
unrecognizably
unrecognized
unreconcilable
unreconciled
unrecorded
unrecoverable
unrecovered
unrecyclable
unredeemed
unredressed
unrefined
unreflective
unreformed
unregistered
unregulated
unrehearsed
unreinforced
unrelated
unrelaxed
unreliability
unreliable
unrelieved
unreluctant
unremarkable
unremarkably
unremembered
unreminiscent
unremovable
unrepeatable
unrepentant
unrepentantly
unreported
unrepresentative
unrepresented
unrepressed
unrequited
unresistant
unresolvable
unresolved
unrespectable
unrestful
unrestricted
unretouched
unreturnable
unrevealed
unreviewed
unrevised
unrevolutionary
unrewarded
unrewarding
unrhymed
unrhythmic
unridable
unripened
unromantic
unromantically
unromanticized
unroofed
unrushed
unsafe
unsaid
unsalable
unsalaried
unsalted
unsalvageable
unsanctioned
unsanitary
unsatisfactorily
unsatisfactoriness
unsatisfactory
unsatisfied
unscalable
unscarred
unscented
unscheduled
unscholarly
unscreened
unscriptural
unseasoned
unseaworthy
unsecured
unseeded
unsegmented
unself–conscious
unself–consciously
unself–consciousness
unsensational
unsensitized
unsent
unsentimental
unseparated
unserious
unserved
unserviceable
unsexual
unsexy
unshaded
unshakable
unshaken
unshapely
unshared
unsharp
unshaven
unshorn
unsigned
unsinkable
unslaked
unsmiling
unsoiled
unsold
unsoldierly
unsolicited
unsolvable
unsolved
unsorted
unsown
unspecialized
unspecifiable
unspecific
unspecified
unspectacular
unspent
unspiritual
unsplit
unspoiled
unspoilt
unspoken
unsportsmanlike
unsprayed
unstained
unstandardized
unsterile
unsterilized
unstinted
unstratified
unstructured
unstylish
unsubdued
unsubsidized
unsubstantiated
unsubtle
unsuited
unsullied
unsupervised
unsupported
unsure
unsurpassable
unsurpassed
unsurprised
unsurprising
unsurprisingly
unsusceptible
unsuspected
unsuspecting
unsuspicious
unsustainable
unsweetened
unsympathetic
unsympathetically
unsynchronized
unsystematic
unsystematically
unsystematized
untactful
untagged
untainted
untalented
untamable
untamed
untarnished

\ə\ abut	\au̇\ out	\i\ tip	\ȯ\ saw	\u̇\ foot
\ər\ further	\ch\ chin	\ī\ life	\ȯi\ coin	\y\ yet
\a\ mat	\e\ pet	\j\ job	\th\ thin	\yü\ few
\ā\ take	\ē\ easy	\ŋ\ sing	\t͟h\ this	\yu̇\ cure
\ä\ cot, cart	\g\ go	\ō\ bone	\ü\ food	\zh\ vision

untaxed
unteachable
untechnical
untempered
untenanted
untended
untestable
untested
unthreatening
unthrifty
untillable
untilled
untiring
untraceable
untraditional
untrained
untrammeled
untranslatable
untranslated
untraveled
untraversed
untreated
untrimmed
untroubled
untrusting
untrustworthy
untucked
untufted
untypical
untypically
ununderstandable
unusable
unutilized
unvaccinated
unvaried
unvarying
unventilated
unverifiable
unversed
unviable
unvisited
unwanted
unwarlike
unwarranted
unwavering
unwaveringly
unwaxed
unweaned
unwearable
unweathered
unwed
unwelcome
unwinnable
unwomanly
unwon
unworkable
unworked
unworried
unwounded
unwoven
unwrinkled

un·abashed \ˌən-ə-ˈbasht\ *adj* : not abashed — **un·abash·ed·ly** \-ˈbash-əd-lē\ *adv*
un·abat·ed \ˌən-ə-ˈbāt-əd\ *adj* : not abated : at full strength or force — **un·abat·ed·ly** *adv*
un·able \ˌən-ˈā-bəl, ˈən-\ *adj* : not able : INCAPABLE
un·abridged \ˌən-ə-ˈbrijd\ *adj* **1** : not abridged : COMPLETE ⟨an *unabridged* reprint of a novel⟩ **2** : complete of its class : not based on one larger ⟨an *unabridged* dictionary⟩
un·ac·cept·able \ˌən-ik-ˈsep-tə-bəl, -ak-\ *adj* : not acceptable : not pleasing or welcome — **un·ac·cept·abil·i·ty** \-ˌsep-tə-ˈbil-ət-ē\ *n* — **un·ac·cept·ably** \-blē\ *adv*
un·ac·com·pa·nied \ˌən-ə-ˈkəmp-nēd, -ə-nēd\ *adj* : not accompanied; *esp* : being without instrumental accompaniment
un·ac·count·able \ˌən-ə-ˈkau̇nt-ə-bəl\ *adj* **1** : not to be accounted for : INEXPLICABLE **2** : not to be called to account : not responsible — **un·ac·count·abil·i·ty** \-ˌkau̇nt-ə-ˈbil-ət-ē\ *n* — **un·ac·count·ably** \ˌən-ə-ˈkau̇nt-ə-blē\ *adv*
un·ac·count·ed \-ˈkau̇nt-əd\ *adj* : not accounted or made clear — often used with *for*
un·ac·cus·tomed \ˌən-ə-ˈkəs-təmd\ *adj* **1** : UNUSUAL, UNFAMILIAR ⟨*unaccustomed* scenes⟩ **2** : not used : not habituated ⟨*unaccustomed* to travel⟩
una cor·da \ˌü-nə-ˈkȯrd-ə\ *adv or adj* : with soft pedal depressed — used as a direction in piano music [Italian, literally, "one string"]
una corda pedal *n* : SOFT PEDAL 1
un·adorned \ˌən-ə-ˈdȯrnd\ *adj* : not adorned : lacking embellishment or decoration
un·adul·ter·at·ed \ˌən-ə-ˈdəl-tə-ˌrāt-əd\ *adj* : free from adulterants : PURE ⟨*unadulterated* food⟩ ⟨*unadulterated* beauty⟩ — **un·adul·ter·at·ed·ly** *adv*
un·ad·vised \ˌən-əd-ˈvīzd\ *adj* **1** : done without due consideration : RASH **2** : not prudent ⟨done with *unadvised* haste⟩ — **un·ad·vis·ed·ly** \-ˈvī-zəd-lē\ *adv*
un·af·fect·ed \ˌən-ə-ˈfek-təd\ *adj* **1** : not influenced or changed mentally, physically, or chemically **2** : free from affectation : GENUINE — **un·af·fect·ed·ly** *adv* — **un·af·fect·ed·ness** *n*
un·ag·ing *or* **un·age·ing** \ˌən-ˈā-jing\ *adj* : AGELESS
un·alien·able \ˌən-ˈāl-yə-nə-bəl, ˈən-, -ˈā-lē-ə-nə-\ *adj* : INALIENABLE
un·aligned \ˌən-l-ˈīnd\ *adj* : NONALIGNED
un·al·loyed \ˌən-l-ˈȯid\ *adj* : free from all admixture : PURE ⟨*unalloyed* metal⟩ ⟨*unalloyed* bliss⟩
un·al·ter·able \ˌən-ˈȯl-trə-bəl, -tə-rə-, ˈən-\ *adj* : not capable of being changed ⟨*unalterable* hatred⟩ — **un·al·ter·ably** \-blē\ *adv*
un–Amer·i·can \ˌən-ə-ˈmer-ə-kən\ *adj* : not American : not characteristic of or consistent with American customs or principles
un·aneled \ˌən-ə-ˈnēld\ *adj, archaic* : not having received extreme unction [earlier *anele* "to anoint," from Old English *an* "on" + *ele* "oil," from Latin *oleum*]
una·nim·i·ty \ˌyü-nə-ˈnim-ət-ē\ *n* : the quality or state of being unanimous
unan·i·mous \yu̇-ˈnan-ə-məs\ *adj* **1** : being of one mind : agreeing completely **2** : having the agreement and consent of all ⟨an *unanimous* vote⟩ [Latin *unanimus,* from *unus* "one" + *animus* "mind"] — **unan·i·mous·ly** *adv*
un·an·swer·able \ˌən-ˈans-rə-bəl, -ə-rə-, ˈən-\ *adj* : not answerable; *esp* : IRREFUTABLE ⟨the arguments were *unanswerable*⟩
un·an·swered \ˌən-ˈan-sərd\ *adj* **1** : not answered ⟨*unanswered* letters⟩ **2** : scored in succession during a period in which an opponent fails to score ⟨scored 20 *unanswered* points in the second half⟩
un·ap·peal·able \ˌən-ə-ˈpē-lə-bəl\ *adj* : not appealable : not subject to appeal
un·ap·peal·ing \ˌən-ə-ˈpē-ling\ *adj* : lacking appeal
un·ap·peas·able \ˌən-ə-ˈpē-zə-bəl\ *adj* : not to be appeased : IMPLACABLE — **un·ap·peas·ably** \-blē\ *adv*
un·ap·pe·tiz·ing \ˌən-ˈap-ə-ˌtī-zing\ *adj* : not appetizing : INSIPID, UNATTRACTIVE — **un·ap·pe·ti·zing·ly** *adv*
un·apt \ˌən-ˈapt, ˈən-\ *adj* **1** : UNSUITABLE, INAPPROPRIATE ⟨an *unapt* quote⟩ **2** : not accustomed and not likely ⟨a teacher *unapt* to tolerate carelessness⟩ **3** : DULL, BACKWARD ⟨*unapt* students⟩ — **un·apt·ly** \-ˈap-tlē, -lē\ *adv* — **un·apt·ness** \-ˈap-nəs, -ˈapt-\ *n*
un·arm \ˌən-ˈärm, ˈən-\ *vt* : DISARM 1
un·armed \-ˈärmd\ *adj* **1** : not armed or armored ⟨*unarmed* civilians⟩; *also* : not using or involving a weapon ⟨*unarmed* robbery⟩ **2** : having no hard and sharp projections (as spines or claws)
un·ar·tic·u·lat·ed \ˌən-är-ˈtik-yə-ˌlāt-əd\ *adj* : not articulated; *esp* : not carefully reasoned or analyzed
un·asked \ˌən-ˈaskt, -ˈast, -ˈȧskt, -ˈȧst, ˈən-\ *adj* : not asked or asked for ⟨*unasked* questions⟩ ⟨*unasked* advice⟩
un·as·sail·able \ˌən-ə-ˈsā-lə-bəl\ *adj* : not assailable : not liable to doubt, attack, or question — **un·as·sail·ably** \-blē\ *adv*
un·as·ser·tive \ˌən-ə-ˈsərt-iv\ *adj* : not assertive : MODEST, SHY
un·as·sum·ing \ˌən-ə-ˈsü-ming\ *adj* : not assuming : MODEST ⟨an *unassuming* librarian⟩ ⟨an *unassuming* manner⟩ ⟨an *unassuming* neighborhood⟩ — **un·as·sum·ing·ly** \-ming-lē\ *adv* — **un·as·sum·ing·ness** *n*
un·at·tached \ˌən-ə-ˈtacht\ *adj* **1** : not attached **2** : not married or engaged
un·at·trac·tive \ˌən-ə-ˈtrak-tiv\ *adj* : not attractive : PLAIN, DULL — **un·at·trac·tive·ly** *adv* — **un·at·trac·tive·ness** *n*
un·avail·ing \ˌən-ə-ˈvā-ling\ *adj* : of no avail : not successful : VAIN — **un·avail·ing·ly** \-ling-lē\ *adv*
un·avoid·able \ˌən-ə-ˈvȯid-ə-bəl\ *adj* : not avoidable ⟨the accident was *unavoidable*⟩ — **un·avoid·ably** \-blē\ *adv*
[1]**un·aware** \ˌən-ə-ˈwaər, -ˈweər\ *adv* : UNAWARES
[2]**unaware** *adj* : not aware : IGNORANT — **un·aware·ness** *n*
un·awares \-ˈwaərz, -ˈweərz\ *adv* **1** : without knowing **2** : without warning : by surprise ⟨taken *unawares*⟩
un·backed \ˌən-ˈbakt, ˈən-\ *adj* : not supported or encouraged
un·bal·ance \ˌən-ˈbal-əns, ˈən-\ *vt* : to put out of balance
un·bal·anced \-ənst\ *adj* **1** : not in equilibrium **2** : not completely sane **3** : not adjusted so as to make credits equal to debits ⟨an *unbalanced* account⟩
un·bal·last·ed \ˌən-ˈbal-ə-stəd, ˈən-\ *adj* : not furnished with or steadied by ballast : UNSTEADY
un·bar \ˌən-ˈbär, ˈən-\ *vt* : to remove a bar from : UNBOLT, OPEN
un·barred \-ˈbärd\ *adj* **1** : not secured by a bar : UNLOCKED **2** : not marked with bars
un·bear·able \ˌən-ˈbar-ə-bəl, ˈən-, -ˈber-\ *adj* : greater than can be borne ⟨*unbearable* pain⟩ — **un·bear·ably** \-blē\ *adv*
un·beat·able \-ˈbēt-ə-bəl\ *adj* : not capable of being defeated
un·beat·en \-ˈbēt-n\ *adj* **1** : not pounded or beaten **2** : not traveled ⟨an *unbeaten* path⟩ **3** : not defeated
un·beau·ti·ful \ˌən-ˈbyüt-i-fəl\ *adj* : not beautiful : UNATTRACTIVE — **un·beau·ti·ful·ly** \-fə-lē, -flē\ *adv*
un·be·com·ing \ˌən-bi-ˈkəm-ing\ *adj* : not becoming : UNSUITABLE ***synonyms*** see INDECOROUS — **un·be·com·ing·ly** \-ing-lē\ *adv* — **un·be·com·ing·ness** *n*
un·be·knownst \ˌən-bi-ˈnōnst\ *also* **un·be·known** \-ˈnōn\ *adj* : happening without one's knowledge : UNKNOWN — usually used with *to*
un·be·lief \ˌən-bə-ˈlēf\ *n* : the withholding or absence of belief : DOUBT
synonyms UNBELIEF, DISBELIEF, INCREDULITY mean the attitude or state of mind of one who does not believe. UNBELIEF suggests withholding of belief especially in religious matters ⟨warned against skepticism and *unbelief*⟩. DISBELIEF stresses rejection of what is asserted or stated ⟨a firm *disbelief* in ghosts⟩. INCREDULITY suggests rejection on general

grounds rather than immediate evidence ⟨received the news with *incredulity*⟩.

un·be·liev·able \-ˈlē-və-bəl\ *adj* **1** : too improbable for belief ⟨an *unbelievable* story⟩ **2** : very significant or impressive ⟨made an *unbelievable* catch in center field⟩ — **un·be·liev·ably** \-blē\ *adv*

un·be·liev·er \-ˈlē-vər\ *n* **1** : one who does not believe in a particular religious faith **2** : one who does not believe : DOUBTER

un·be·liev·ing \-ˈlē-ving\ *adj* : marked by unbelief — **un·be·liev·ing·ly** \-ving-lē\ *adv*

un·bend \ˌən-ˈbend, ˈən-\ *vb* **-bent** \-ˈbent\; **-bend·ing** **1** : to free from being bent : make or become straight **2** : to make or become less stiff or more affable : RELAX

un·bend·ing \ˌən-ˈben-ding, ˈən-\ *adj* : formal and distant in manner

un·be·seem·ing \ˌən-bi-ˈsē-ming\ *adj* : not befitting : UNBECOMING

un·bi·ased \ˌən-ˈbī-əst, ˈən-\ *adj* : free from bias ⟨an *unbiased* opinion⟩; *esp* : UNPREJUDICED ***synonyms*** see FAIR

un·bid·den \-ˈbid-n\ *also* **un·bid** \-ˈbid\ *adj* : not bidden : UNASKED ⟨barged in *unbidden*⟩

un·bind \-ˈbīnd\ *vt* **-bound** \-ˈbau̇nd\; **-bind·ing** **1** : to remove a band from : free from fastenings **2** : to set free : RELEASE

un·bit·ted \-ˈbit-əd\ *adj, archaic* : UNRESTRAINED 1, UNBRIDLED

un·blenched \-ˈblencht\ *adj* : not disconcerted : UNDAUNTED

un·blessed *also* **un·blest** \-ˈblest\ *adj* **1** : not blessed ⟨an *unblessed* marriage⟩ **2** : EVIL 2a

un·blush·ing \-ˈbləsh-ing\ *adj* **1** : not blushing **2** : SHAMELESS, UNABASHED ⟨*unblushing* greed⟩ — **un·blush·ing·ly** \-ing-lē\ *adv*

un·bod·ied \-ˈbäd-ēd\ *adj* **1** : having no body; *also* : freed from the body ⟨*unbodied* soul⟩ **2** : FORMLESS

un·bolt \ˌən-ˈbōlt, ˈən-\ *vt* : to open or unfasten by withdrawing a bolt

un·bolt·ed \-ˈbōl-təd\ *adj* : not sifted ⟨*unbolted* flour⟩

un·born \-ˈbȯrn\ *adj* **1** : not born : not brought into life **2** : still to appear : FUTURE ⟨*unborn* generations⟩

un·bos·om \-ˈbu̇z-əm\ *vb* **1** : to give expression to : DISCLOSE, REVEAL **2** : to disclose one's thoughts or feelings

un·bound \-ˈbau̇nd\ *adj* : not bound: as **a (1)** : not fastened or tied up **(2)** : not confined ⟨an *unbound* spirit⟩ **b** : not having the leaves fastened together ⟨an *unbound* book⟩

un·bound·ed \-ˈbau̇n-dəd\ *adj* : having no limits ⟨*unbounded* space⟩ ⟨*unbounded* enthusiasm⟩

un·bowed \ˌən-ˈbau̇d, ˈən-\ *adj* **1** : not bowed down **2** : not subdued

un·brace \-ˈbrās\ *vt* **1** : to free or detach by or as if by untying or removing a brace or bond **2** : to make feeble : WEAKEN

un·braid \-ˈbrād\ *vt* : to separate the strands of

un·branched \ˌən-ˈbrancht, ˈən-\ *adj* : free from or not divided into branches ⟨a straight *unbranched* trunk⟩ ⟨a leaf with *unbranched* veins⟩

un·bred \-ˈbred\ *adj* : not bred : never having been bred ⟨an *unbred* heifer⟩

un·bri·dled \-ˈbrīd-ld\ *adj* **1** : UNRESTRAINED ⟨greeted the star's appearance with *unbridled* enthusiasm⟩ **2** : not confined by a bridle

un·bro·ken \-ˈbrō-kən\ *adj* **1** : not damaged : WHOLE **2** : not subdued or tamed; *esp* : not trained for service or use ⟨an *unbroken* colt⟩ **3** : not interrupted : CONTINUOUS ⟨an *unbroken* row of trees⟩

un·buck·le \ˌən-ˈbək-əl, ˈən-\ *vt* : to unfasten the buckle of

un·budg·ing \ˌən-ˈbəj-ing\ *adj* : not budging : resisting movement or change — **un·budg·ing·ly** *adv*

un·build \-ˈbild\ *vt* : to pull down : DEMOLISH, RAZE

un·built \-ˈbilt\ *adj* **1** : not built : not yet constructed **2** : not built on ⟨an *unbuilt* plot⟩

un·bur·den \-ˈbərd-n\ *vt* **1** : to free from a burden **2** : to relieve oneself of (as cares, fears, or worries) : cast off

un·but·ton \-ˈbət-n\ *vt* : to unfasten the buttons of (as a garment)

un·but·toned \-nd\ *adj* **1 a** : not buttoned **b** : not provided with buttons **2** : not under constraint : free and unrestricted in action and expression ⟨the musician's *unbuttoned* energy⟩

un·cage \ˌən-ˈkāj, ˈən-\ *vt* : to release from or as if from a cage

un·called–for \-ˈkȯld-ˌfȯr\ *adj* : not called for : not needed or wanted : not proper ⟨an *uncalled-for* remark⟩

un·can·ny \-ˈkan-ē\ *adj* **1** : seeming to have a supernatural character or origin : MYSTERIOUS **2** : being beyond what is normal or expected : suggesting superhuman or supernatural powers ⟨an *uncanny* sense of direction⟩ ***synonyms*** see WEIRD — **un·can·ni·ly** \-ˈkan-l-ē\ *adv*

un·ceas·ing \-ˈsē-sing\ *adj* : never ceasing : CONTINUOUS, INCESSANT — **un·ceas·ing·ly** \-ˈsē-sing-lē\ *adv*

un·cer·e·mo·ni·ous \ˌən-ˌser-ə-ˈmō-nē-əs\ *adj* : acting without or lacking ordinary courtesy : ABRUPT ⟨an *unceremonious* departure⟩ — **un·cer·e·mo·ni·ous·ly** *adv* — **un·cer·e·mo·ni·ous·ness** *n*

un·cer·tain \ˌən-ˈsərt-n, ˈən-\ *adj* **1** : not determined or fixed ⟨an *uncertain* quantity⟩ **2** : subject to chance or change : not dependable ⟨an *uncertain* temper⟩ **3 a** : not definitely known ⟨an *uncertain* claim⟩ **b** : not sure ⟨*uncertain* of the truth⟩ — **un·cer·tain·ly** *adv* — **un·cer·tain·ness** \-n-nəs, -n-əs\ *n*

un·cer·tain·ty \-n-tē\ *n* **1** : lack of certainty **2** : something that is uncertain ***synonyms*** see DOUBT

un·chain \ˌən-ˈchān, ˈən-\ *vt* : to free by or as if by removing a chain : set loose

un·chancy \-ˈchan-sē\ *adj* **1** *chiefly Scottish* : ILL-FATED **2** *chiefly Scottish* : DANGEROUS

un·change·able \-ˈchān-jə-bəl\ *adj* : not changing or to be changed : IMMUTABLE ⟨*unchangeable* facts⟩ — **un·change·able·ness** *n* — **un·change·ably** \-blē\ *adv*

un·chang·ing \ˌən-ˈchān-jing\ *adj* : not changing or capable of change : CONSTANT ⟨*unchanging* beliefs⟩

un·charged \-ˈchärjd\ *adj* : having no electric charge

un·char·i·ta·ble \-ˈchar-ət-ə-bəl\ *adj* : lacking in charity; *esp* : severe in judging others ⟨*uncharitable* comments⟩ — **un·char·i·ta·ble·ness** *n* — **un·char·i·ta·bly** \-blē\ *adv*

un·chart·ed \-ˈchärt-əd\ *adj* : not recorded or plotted on a map, chart, or plan : UNKNOWN ⟨a vast *uncharted* wilderness⟩

un·chaste \-ˈchāst\ *adj* : not chaste : lacking in chastity — **un·chaste·ly** *adv* — **un·chaste·ness** \-ˈchāst-nəs, -ˈchās-\ *n* — **un·chas·ti·ty** \-ˈchas-tət-ē\ *n*

un·chris·tian \-ˈkris-chən\ *adj* **1** : not of the Christian faith **2 a** : contrary to the Christian spirit or character **b** : BARBAROUS 2, UNCIVILIZED

un·cir·cum·cised \ˌən-ˈsər-kəm-ˌsīzd, ˈən-\ *adj* **1** : not circumcised **2** : spiritually impure : HEATHEN — **un·cir·cum·ci·sion** \ˌən-ˌsər-kəm-ˈsizh-ən\ *n*

un·civ·il \ˌən-ˈsiv-əl, ˈən-\ *adj* **1** : not civilized : BARBAROUS **2** : lacking in courtesy : ILL-MANNERED ⟨*uncivil* remarks⟩

un·civ·i·lized \-ˈsiv-ə-ˌlīzd\ *adj* **1** : not civilized : BARBAROUS **2** : remote from civilization : WILD

un·clar·i·ty \ˌən-ˈklar-ət-ē\ *n, pl* **-ties** : lack of clarity : AMBIGUITY, OBSCURITY

un·clasp \-ˈklasp\ *vb* **1** : to open the clasp of **2** : to loosen a hold or grip or the hold or grip of

un·clas·si·fied \-ˈklas-ə-ˌfīd\ *adj* : not classified; *esp* : not subject to a security classification

un·cle \ˈəng-kəl\ *n* **1** : the brother of one's father or mother **2** : the husband of one's aunt **3** — used as a cry of surrender ⟨was forced to cry *uncle*⟩ [Medieval French, from Latin *avunculus* "mother's brother"]

un·clean \ˌən-ˈklēn, ˈən-\ *adj* **1** : morally or spiritually impure **2** : prohibited by ritual law for use or contact **3** : DIRTY 1, FILTHY — **un·clean·ness** \-ˈklēn-nəs\ *n*

¹un·clean·ly \-ˈklen-lē\ *adj* : morally or physically unclean — **un·clean·li·ness** *n*

²un·clean·ly \-ˈklēn-lē\ *adv* : in an unclean manner

un·clench \-ˈklench\ *vb* : to open from a clenched position : RELAX

Un·cle Sam \ˌəng-kəl-ˈsam\ *n* **1** : the U.S. government personified **2** : the American nation or people [expansion of *U.S.*, abbreviation of *United States*]

Uncle Tom \-ˈtäm\ *n* : a black eager to win the approval of whites and willing to cooperate with them [*Uncle Tom*, pious and faithful slave in the novel *Uncle Tom's Cabin* by Harriet Beecher Stowe]

un·cloak \ˌən-ˈklōk, ˈən-\ *vb* **1** : to remove a cloak or cover from **2** : REVEAL 1, UNMASK **3** : to take off a cloak

un·clog \ˌən-ˈkläg\ *vt* : to free from a difficulty or obstruction

un·close \-ˈklōz\ *vb* : OPEN
un·closed \-ˈklōzd\ *adj* : not closed or settled : not concluded
un·clothe \-ˈklōth\ *vt* : to strip of clothes or a covering
un·clothed \-ˈklōthd\ *adj* : not clothed
un·coil \ˌən-ˈkȯil, ˈən-\ *vb* : to release or become released from a coiled state : UNWIND
un·coined \-ˈkȯind\ *adj* **1** : not minted ⟨*uncoined* metal⟩ **2** : not fabricated : NATURAL
un·com·fort·able \-ˈkəm-fərt-ə-bəl, -ˈkəmp-; -ˈkəmf-tə-bəl, -ˈkəmp-, -ˈkəmpf-, -ˈkəm-, -tər-\ *adj* **1** : causing discomfort ⟨an *uncomfortable* chair⟩ **2** : feeling discomfort : UNEASY — **un·com·fort·ably** \-blē\ *adv*
un·com·mer·cial \ˌən-kə-ˈmər-shəl\ *adj* **1** : not engaged in or related to commerce **2** : not based on commercial principles **3** : not likely to result in financial success ⟨an *uncommercial* book⟩
un·com·mit·ted \ˌən-kə-ˈmit-əd\ *adj* : not committed; *esp* : not pledged to a particular belief, allegiance, or program ⟨*uncommitted* voters⟩
un·com·mon \ˌən-ˈkäm-ən, ˈən-\ *adj* **1** : not ordinarily encountered : UNUSUAL ⟨when airplanes were *uncommon*⟩ **2** : EXTRAORDINARY 1, EXCEPTIONAL ⟨a run of *uncommon* luck⟩ — **un·com·mon·ly** *adv* — **un·com·mon·ness** \-ən-nəs\ *n*
un·com·mu·ni·ca·tive \ˌən-kə-ˈmyü-nə-ˌkāt-iv, -ni-kət-\ *adj* : not inclined to talk or give out information : RESERVED
un·com·pet·i·tive \ˌən-kəm-ˈpet-ət-iv\ *adj* : not competitive : unable to compete — **un·com·pet·i·tive·ness** *n*
un·com·plain·ing \ˌən-kəm-ˈplā-ning\ *adj* : not complaining : PATIENT ⟨*uncomplaining* acceptance⟩ — **un·com·plain·ing·ly** *adv*
un·com·pli·men·ta·ry \ˌən-ˌkäm-plə-ˈment-ə-rē, -ˈmen-trē\ *adj* : not complimentary : DEROGATORY
un·com·pro·mis·ing \ˌən-ˈkäm-prə-ˌmī-zing, ˈən-\ *adj* : not making or accepting a compromise : making no concessions — **un·com·pro·mis·ing·ly** \-zing-lē\ *adv*
un·con·cern \ˌən-kən-ˈsərn\ *n* **1** : lack of care or interest : INDIFFERENCE **2** : freedom from excessive concern or anxiety ***synonyms*** see INDIFFERENCE
un·con·cerned \-ˈsərnd\ *adj* **1** : not involved : having no part or interest **2** : not anxious or upset : free of worry — **un·con·cern·ed·ly** \-ˈsər-nəd-lē\ *adv* — **un·con·cern·ed·ness** \-nəd-nəs\ *n*
un·con·di·tion·al \ˌən-kən-ˈdish-nəl, -ˈdish-ən-l\ *adj* : not limited : ABSOLUTE, UNQUALIFIED ⟨*unconditional* surrender⟩ — **un·con·di·tion·al·ly** \-ē\ *adv*
un·con·di·tioned \-ˈdish-ənd\ *adj* **1** : not subject to conditions **2** : not dependent on or subjected to conditioning or learning : INHERENT ⟨*unconditioned* responses⟩
un·con·form·able \ˌən-kən-ˈfȯr-mə-bəl\ *adj* **1** : not conforming **2** : exhibiting geological unconformity — **un·con·form·ably** \-blē\ *adv*
un·con·for·mi·ty \ˌən-kən-ˈfȯr-mət-ē\ *n* **1** : lack of continuity in deposition between rock strata in contact due especially to weathering **2** : the surface of contact between strata exhibiting unconformity
un·con·ge·nial \ˌən-kən-ˈjē-nyəl\ *adj* **1** : not sympathetic or compatible ⟨*uncongenial* roommates⟩ **2 a** : not fitted : UNSUITABLE ⟨a soil *uncongenial* to most crops⟩ **b** : not to one's taste : DISAGREEABLE ⟨an *uncongenial* task⟩ — **un·con·ge·nial·i·ty** \-ˌjē-nē-ˈal-ət-ē, -ˌjēn-ˈyal-\ *n*
un·con·quer·able \ˌən-ˈkäng-krə-bəl, -kə-rə-, ˈən-\ *adj* : incapable of being conquered or overcome ⟨*unconquerable* difficulties⟩ — **un·con·quer·ably** \-blē\ *adv*
un·con·scio·na·ble \-ˈkänch-nə-bəl, -ə-nə-\ *adj* **1** : not guided or controlled by conscience ⟨an *unconscionable* villain⟩ **2** : EXCESSIVE, UNREASONABLE ⟨paid an *unconscionable* price⟩ **3** : shockingly unfair or unjust ⟨*unconscionable* sales practices⟩ [earlier *conscionable* "conscientious," derived from *conscience*] — **un·con·scio·na·bly** \-blē\ *adv*
[1]**un·con·scious** \-ˈkän-chəs\ *adj* **1** : not aware ⟨*unconscious* of the risk⟩ **2 a** : of or relating to the unconscious **b** : having lost consciousness ⟨knocked *unconscious* by a fall⟩ **3** : not realized by oneself : not consciously done ⟨an *unconscious* mistake⟩ — **un·con·scious·ly** *adv* — **un·con·scious·ness** *n*
[2]**unconscious** *n* : the part of mental life that does not ordinarily enter the individual's awareness yet may influence behavior and perception or be revealed (as in slips of the tongue or in dreams)
un·con·sid·ered \ˌən-kən-ˈsid-ərd\ *adj* **1** : not considered or worth consideration **2** : not resulting from consideration or study ⟨*unconsidered* remarks⟩
un·con·sti·tu·tion·al \ˌən-ˌkän-stə-ˈtüsh-nəl, -ˈtyüsh-, -ən-l\ *adj* : not according to or consistent with the constitution of a state or society — **un·con·sti·tu·tion·al·i·ty** \-ˌtü-shə-ˈnal-ət-ē, -ˌtyü-\ *n* — **un·con·sti·tu·tion·al·ly** \-ˈtüsh-nə-lē, -ˈtyüsh-, -ən-l-ē\ *adv*
un·con·trol·la·ble \ˌən-kən-ˈtrō-lə-bəl\ *adj* : incapable of being controlled : UNGOVERNABLE — **un·con·trol·la·bly** \-blē\ *adv*
un·con·ven·tion·al \ˌən-kən-ˈvench-nəl, -ən-l\ *adj* : not conventional: as **a** : not bound by or in accordance with convention **b** : being out of the ordinary — **un·con·ven·tion·al·i·ty** \-ˌven-chə-ˈnal-ət-ē\ *n* — **un·con·ven·tion·al·ly** \-ˈvench-nə-lē, -ən-l-ē\ *adv*
un·cork \ˌən-ˈkȯrk, ˈən-\ *vt* **1** : to draw a cork from **2 a** : to release from a sealed or pent-up state ⟨*uncork* a surprise⟩ **b** : to let go : RELEASE ⟨*uncork* a wild pitch⟩
un·count·ed \-ˈkau̇nt-əd\ *adj* **1** : not counted **2** : INNUMERABLE
un·cou·ple \-ˈkəp-əl\ *vt* **-cou·pled; -cou·pling** \-ˈkəp-ling, -ə-ling\ **1** : to release (hunting dogs) to seek game **2** : DISCONNECT ⟨*uncouple* railroad cars⟩
un·couth \-ˈküth\ *adj* **1** : strange, awkward, and clumsy in shape or appearance **2** : vulgar in conduct or speech : RUDE [Old English *uncūth* "strange, unfamiliar," from [1]*un-* + *cūth* "known"]
un·cov·er \-ˈkəv-ər\ *vb* **1** : to make known : bring to light : DISCLOSE, REVEAL **2** : to expose to view by removing some covering **3 a** : to take the cover from **b** : to remove the hat from; *also* : to take off the hat as a token of respect
un·cov·ered \-ˈkəv-ərd\ *adj* : not covered or supplied with a covering
un·cre·at·ed \ˌən-krē-ˈāt-əd\ *adj* **1** : not existing by creation : ETERNAL **2** : not yet created
un·crit·i·cal \ˌən-ˈkrit-i-kəl, ˈən-\ *adj* **1** : not critical : lacking in discrimination **2** : showing lack or improper use of critical standards or procedures — **un·crit·i·cal·ly** \-kə-lē, -klē\ *adv*
un·cross \-ˈkrȯs\ *vb* : to change from a crossed position
un·crown \-ˈkrau̇n\ *vt* : to take the crown from : DEPOSE
unc·tion \ˈəng-shən, ˈəngk-\ *n* **1** : the act of anointing as a rite of consecration or healing **2** : exaggerated, assumed, or superficial earnestness of language or manner [Latin *unctio*, from *unguere* "to anoint"]
unc·tu·ous \ˈəng-chə-wəs, -chəs, ˈəngk-; ˈəngsh-wəs, ˈəngksh-\ *adj* **1** : smooth and greasy in texture or appearance : OILY **2** : full of unction in speech and manner; *esp* : insincerely smooth [Medieval Latin *unctuosus*, from Latin *unctus* "act of anointing," from *unguere* "to anoint"] — **unc·tu·ous·ly** *adv* — **unc·tu·ous·ness** *n*
un·curl \ˌən-ˈkərl, ˈən-\ *vb* : to make or become straightened out from a curled or coiled position
un·cut \ˌən-ˈkət, ˈən-\ *adj* **1** : not cut down or cut into **2** : not shaped by cutting ⟨an *uncut* diamond⟩ **3** *of a book* : not having the folds of the leaves slit **4** : not abridged or curtailed ⟨the movie's *uncut* version⟩
un·daunt·ed \ˌən-ˈdȯnt-əd, -ˈdänt-\ *adj* : not daunted : not discouraged or dismayed : FEARLESS — **un·daunt·ed·ly** *adv*
un·dead \ˌən-ˈded\ *n, pl* **undead** **1** : VAMPIRE 1 **2** : ZOMBIE
un·de·ceive \ˌən-di-ˈsēv\ *vt* : to free from deception, illusion, or error
un·de·mon·stra·tive \ˌən-di-ˈmän-strət-iv\ *adj* : restrained or reserved in expression of feeling — **un·de·mon·stra·tive·ly** *adv* — **un·de·mon·stra·tive·ness** *n*
un·de·ni·able \ˌən-di-ˈnī-ə-bəl\ *adj* **1** : plainly true : INCONTESTABLE ⟨an *undeniable* fact⟩ **2** : unquestionably excellent or genuine ⟨an applicant with *undeniable* references⟩ — **un·de·ni·able·ness** *n* — **un·de·ni·ably** \-blē\ *adv*
[1]**un·der** \ˈən-dər\ *adv* **1** : in or into a position below or beneath something ⟨the duck surfaced, then went *under* again⟩ **2** : below some quantity, level, or norm ⟨10 dollars or *under*⟩ — often used in combination ⟨*under*played the part⟩ **3** : in or into a condition of subjection, subordination, or unconsciousness ⟨put the patient *under* for surgery⟩ **4** : down to defeat, ruin, or death ⟨forced competing businesses *under*⟩ **5** : so as to be covered or hidden ⟨turned *under* by the plow⟩ [Old English]
[2]**un·der** \ˌən-dər, ˈən-\ *prep* **1** : below or beneath so as to be overhung, surmounted, covered, protected, or concealed by ⟨*under* a tree⟩ ⟨*under* sunny skies⟩ ⟨*under* cover of darkness⟩ **2 a** : subject to the authority or guidance of ⟨served *under* the

general⟩ **b :** subject to the action, operation, or effect of ⟨*under* pressure⟩ ⟨*under* an anesthetic⟩ **3 :** within the group or designation of ⟨*under* this heading⟩ **4 a :** less or lower than (as in size, amount, or rank) ⟨all weights *under* 12 ounces⟩ ⟨nobody *under* a colonel⟩ **b :** below the standard or required degree of ⟨*under* legal age⟩

³under \'ən-dər\ *adj* **1 a :** lying or placed below, beneath, or on the ventral side — often used in combination ⟨the sea's *under*currents⟩ ⟨the *under*side of a car⟩ **b :** facing or protruding downward — often used in combination ⟨the *under*surface of a leaf⟩ **2 :** lower in rank or authority : SUBORDINATE — often used in combination ⟨the *under*secretary of defense⟩ **3 :** lower than usual, proper, or desired in amount, quality, or degree — often used in combination ⟨*under*nourished children⟩

un•der•achiev•er \ˌən-də-rə-'chē-vər\ *n* **:** one (as a student) that fails to do as well as expected

un•der•act \ˌən-də-'rakt\ *vb* **:** to perform feebly or with restraint: as **a :** to perform (a dramatic part) with less than the necessary skill or vigor **b :** to perform with restraint for greater dramatic impact or personal force

un•der•ac•tive \ˌən-də-'rak-tiv\ *adj* **:** having an abnormally low degree of activity ⟨an *underactive* thyroid gland⟩ — **un•der•ac•tiv•i•ty** \-rak-'tiv-ət-ē\ *n*

un•der•age \ˌən-də-'rāj\ *adj* **:** of less than mature or legal age

¹un•der•arm \ˌən-də-ˌrärm\ *adj* **1 :** UNDERHAND 2 ⟨an *underarm* toss⟩ **2 :** placed under or on the underside of the arm ⟨*underarm* seams⟩

²un•der•arm \ˌən-də-'rärm\ *adv* **:** with an underarm motion

³un•der•arm \'ən-də-ˌrärm\ *n* **1 :** ARMPIT **2 :** the part of a garment that covers the underside of the arm

un•der•bel•ly \'ən-dər-ˌbel-ē\ *n* **:** the under surface of a body or mass; *also* **:** a vulnerable area

un•der•bid \ˌən-dər-'bid\ *vb* **-bid; -bid•ding 1 :** to bid less than (a competing bidder) **2 :** to bid too low (as in cards) — **un•der•bid•der** *n*

un•der•body \'ən-dər-ˌbäd-ē\ *n* **:** the lower part or underside of something (as an animal or car)

un•der•bred \ˌən-dər-'bred\ *adj* **:** marked by lack of good breeding **:** ILL-BRED

un•der•brush \'ən-dər-ˌbrəsh\ *n* **:** shrubs and small trees growing among large trees **:** UNDERGROWTH

un•der•car•riage \-ˌkar-ij\ *n* **1 :** a supporting framework or underside (as of an automobile) **2 :** the landing gear of an airplane

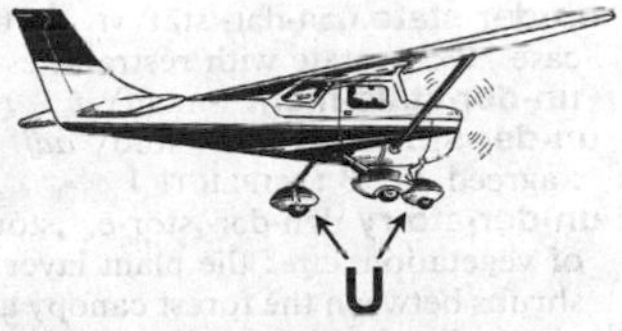

U undercarriage 2

un•der•charge \ˌən-dər-'chärj\ *vt* **:** to charge (as a person) too little — **un•der•charge** \'ən-dər-ˌ\ *n*

un•der•class \'ən-dər-ˌklas\ *n* **:** the lowest social class usually made up of disadvantaged minority groups

un•der•class•man \ˌən-dər-'klas-mən\ *n* **:** a member of the freshman or sophomore class in a school or college

un•der•clothes \'ən-dər-ˌklōz, -ˌklōthz\ *n pl* **:** UNDERWEAR

un•der•cloth•ing \-ˌklō-thing\ *n* **:** UNDERWEAR

un•der•coat \-ˌkōt\ *n* **1 :** a coat or jacket worn under another **2 :** a growth of short hair or fur partly concealed by a longer growth of usually coarser guard hairs ⟨a dog's *undercoat*⟩ **3 :** a coat (as of paint) applied as a base for another coat **4 :** UNDERCOATING — **undercoat** *vt*

un•der•coat•ing \-ˌkōt-ing\ *n* **:** a special waterproof coating applied to the undersurfaces of a vehicle

un•der•cov•er \-'kəv-ər\ *adj* **:** acting or done in secret; *esp* **:** employed or engaged in spying or secret investigation ⟨an *undercover* agent⟩ — **undercover** *adv*

un•der•croft \'ən-dər-ˌkrȯft\ *n* **:** a subterranean room; *esp* **:** a vaulted chamber under a church [Middle English, from *under* + *crofte* "crypt," from Dutch, from Latin *crypta*]

un•der•cur•rent \'ən-dər-ˌkər-ənt, -ˌkə-rənt\ *n* **1 :** a current below the upper currents or surface **2 :** a hidden tendency of opinion or feeling often contrary to the one publicly shown

¹un•der•cut \ˌən-dər-'kət\ *vb* **-cut; -cut•ting 1 a :** to cut away the under part of ⟨*undercut* a vein of ore⟩ **b :** to cut away a base or material below a surface **2 :** to cut away material from the underside of (an object) so as to leave an overhanging portion in relief **3 :** to offer to sell at lower prices than or to work for lower wages than (a competitor) **4 :** to strike (a ball) with a downward glancing blow so as to give a backspin or height to the shot

²un•der•cut \'ən-dər-ˌkət\ *n* **:** the action or result of cutting away from the underside of something

un•der•de•vel•oped \ˌən-dər-di-'vel-əpt\ *adj* **1 :** not normally or adequately developed ⟨*underdeveloped* muscles⟩ **2 :** having a low economic level of industrial production and standard of living (as from lack of capital) ⟨the *underdeveloped* nations⟩

un•der•dog \'ən-dər-ˌdȯg\ *n* **1 :** the loser or predicted loser in a struggle **2 :** a victim of injustice or persecution

un•der•done \ˌən-dər-'dən\ *adj* **:** not thoroughly cooked **:** RARE ⟨*underdone* steak⟩

un•der•draw•ers \'ən-dər-ˌdrȯ-ərz, -ˌdrȯrz\ *n pl* **:** UNDERPANTS

un•der•dress \ˌən-dər-'dres\ *vb* **:** to dress more simply or informally than is appropriate for an occasion

un•der•es•ti•mate \ˌən-də-'res-tə-ˌmāt\ *vt* **1 :** to estimate as being less than the actual size, quantity, or number **2 :** to place too low a value on **:** UNDERRATE — **un•der•es•ti•mate** \-mət\ *n* — **un•der•es•ti•ma•tion** \-ˌres-tə-'mā-shən\ *n*

un•der•ex•pose \ˌən-də-rik-'spōz\ *vt* **:** to expose (a photographic plate or film) for less time than is needed — **un•der•ex•po•sure** \-'spō-zhər\ *n*

un•der•feed \ˌən-dər-'fēd\ *vt* **-fed** \-'fed\; **-feed•ing :** to feed with too little food

un•der•foot \ˌən-dər-'fu̇t\ *adv* **1 :** under the feet **2 :** in the way ⟨a puppy always *underfoot*⟩

un•der•fur \'ən-dər-ˌfər\ *n* **:** an undercoat of fur especially when thick and soft

un•der•gar•ment \-ˌgär-mənt\ *n* **:** a garment to be worn under another

un•der•gird \ˌən-dər-'gərd\ *vt* **1 :** to make secure underneath **2 :** to brace up **:** STRENGTHEN

un•der•go \ˌən-dər-'gō\ *vt* **-went** \-'went\; **-gone** \-'gȯn, -'gän\; **-go•ing** \-'gō-ing\ **1 :** to submit or be subjected to **:** ENDURE ⟨*undergo* an operation⟩ **2 :** to pass through **:** EXPERIENCE ⟨*undergo* a change⟩

un•der•grad•u•ate \-'graj-wət, -ə-wət, -ə-ˌwāt\ *n* **:** a student at a college or university who has not received a first degree

¹un•der•ground \ˌən-dər-'grau̇nd\ *adv* **1 :** beneath the surface of the earth **2 :** in or into hiding or secret operation ⟨the political party went *underground*⟩

²un•der•ground \'ən-dər-ˌgrau̇nd\ *n* **1 :** a space under the surface of the ground; *esp* **:** an underground railway **2 a :** a secret political movement or group **b :** an organized body working in secret to overthrow a government or an occupying power **c :** a usually avant-garde group or movement that functions outside the establishment

³un•der•ground \'ən-dər-ˌgrau̇nd\ *adj* **1 :** being, growing, operating, or situated below the surface of the ground ⟨an *underground* stream⟩ **2 :** conducted by secret means ⟨an *underground* resistance movement⟩ **3 :** produced or published outside the establishment ⟨*underground* newspapers⟩; *also* **:** of or relating to the avant-garde underground ⟨an *underground* theater⟩

Underground Railroad *n* **:** a system of cooperation among active antislavery people in the U.S. before 1863 by which fugitive slaves were secretly helped to reach the North or Canada

un•der•growth \'ən-dər-ˌgrōth\ *n* **:** low growth on the floor of a forest including seedlings and saplings, shrubs, and herbs

¹un•der•hand \'ən-dər-ˌhand\ *adv* **1 :** in an underhanded or secret way **2 :** with an underhand motion ⟨pitch *underhand*⟩

²underhand *adj* **1 :** UNDERHANDED **2 :** performed with the hand brought forward and up from below the level of the shoulder ⟨an *underhand* pitch⟩

¹un•der•hand•ed \ˌən-dər-'han-dəd\ *adv* **:** UNDERHAND

²underhanded *adj* **:** marked by secrecy, chicanery, and deception **:** SLY ⟨an *underhanded* attempt to gain power⟩ — **un•der•hand•ed•ly** *adv* — **un•der•hand•ed•ness** *n*

¹un•der•lay \ˌən-dər-'lā\ *vt* **-laid** \-'lād\; **-lay•ing 1 :** to provide a layer of something beneath often as a support or backing ⟨*underlay* shingles with tar paper⟩ **2 :** to raise or support by something laid under

\ə\ **abut**	\au̇\ **out**	\i\ **tip**	\ȯ\ **saw**	\u̇\ **foot**
\ər\ **further**	\ch\ **chin**	\ī\ **life**	\ȯi\ **coin**	\y\ **yet**
\a\ **mat**	\e\ **pet**	\j\ **job**	\th\ **thin**	\yü\ **few**
\ā\ **take**	\ē\ **easy**	\ng\ **sing**	\th\ **this**	\yu̇\ **cure**
\ä\ **cot, cart**	\g\ **go**	\ō\ **bone**	\ü\ **food**	\zh\ **vision**

[2]**un·der·lay** \ˈən-dər-ˌlā\ *n* : something that is laid under
un·der·lie \ˌən-dər-ˈlī\ *vt* **-lay** \-ˈlā\; **-lain** \-ˈlān\; **-ly·ing** \-ˈlī-ing\ **1** : to be situated under **2** : to form the foundation of : SUPPORT ⟨ideas *underlying* the revolution⟩
un·der·line \ˈən-dər-ˌlīn, ˌən-dər-ˈ\ *vt* **1** : to draw a line under **2** : STRESS 3 — **un·der·line** \ˈən-dər-ˌlīn\ *n*
un·der·ling \ˈən-dər-ling\ *n* : one who is under the orders of another : SUBORDINATE, INFERIOR
un·der·lip \ˌən-dər-ˈlip\ *n* : the lower lip
un·der·ly·ing \ˌən-dər-ˌlī-ing\ *adj* **1** : lying under or below ⟨the *underlying* rock is shale⟩ **2** : FUNDAMENTAL 1b, BASIC ⟨*underlying* principles⟩
un·der·mine \ˌən-dər-ˈmīn\ *vt* **1** : to dig out or wear away the supporting earth beneath ⟨*undermine* a wall⟩ **2** : to weaken or wear away secretly or gradually ⟨*undermine* a government⟩
un·der·most \ˈən-dər-ˌmōst\ *adj* : lowest in relative position — **undermost** *adv*
[1]**un·der·neath** \ˌən-dər-ˈnēth\ *prep* **1** : directly under **2** : under subjection to [Old English *underneothan,* from *under* + *neothan* "below"]
[2]**underneath** *adv* **1** : under or below an object or a surface : BENEATH **2** : on the lower side
un·der·nour·ished \ˌən-dər-ˈnər-isht, -ˈnə-risht\ *adj* : supplied with insufficient nourishment and especially foods for sound health and growth — **un·der·nour·ish·ment** \-ˈnər-ish-mənt, -ˈnə-rish-\ *n*
un·der·pants \ˈən-dər-ˌpans\ *n pl* : short or long pants worn under an outer garment
un·der·part \-ˌpärt\ *n* **1** : a part lying on the lower side (as of a bird or mammal) **2** : a subordinate or auxiliary part or role
un·der·pass \-ˌpas\ *n* : a passage underneath something (as for a road passing under a railroad or another road)

underpass

un·der·pay \ˌən-dər-ˈpā\ *vt* **-paid** \-ˈpād\; **-pay·ing** : to pay too little
un·der·pin \-ˈpin\ *vt* **1** : SUBSTANTIATE 2, VERIFY ⟨*underpin* a thesis with evidence⟩ **2** : to form part of, strengthen, or replace the foundation of ⟨*underpin* a structure⟩
un·der·pin·ning \ˈən-dər-ˌpin-ing\ *n* **1** : the material and construction (as a foundation) used for support of a structure **2** : PROP, SUPPORT **3** : a person's legs — usually used in plural
un·der·play \ˌən-dər-ˈplā\ *vb* : to handle without exaggeration; *esp* : to play down ⟨*underplay* a dramatic role⟩
un·der·plot \ˈən-dər-ˌplät\ *n* : a dramatic plot that is subordinate to the main action
un·der·priv·i·leged \ˌən-dər-ˈpriv-lijd, -ə-lijd\ *adj* **1** : deprived of some of the basic economic and social rights that others enjoy **2** : of or relating to underprivileged people
un·der·pro·duc·tion \ˌən-dər-prə-ˈdək-shən\ *n* : production of less than enough to satisfy demand or of less than the usual amount
un·der·rate \ˌən-dər-ˈrāt, -də-ˈrāt\ *vt* : to rate too low : UNDERVALUE
un·der·run \-ˈrən\ *n* : the amount by which something produced falls below an estimate
un·der·score \ˈən-dər-ˌskōr, -ˌskȯr\ *vt* **1** : to draw a line under : UNDERLINE **2** : STRESS 3 — **underscore** *n*
[1]**un·der·sea** \ˈən-dər-ˈsē\ *adj* **1** : being or carried on under the sea or under the surface of the sea ⟨*undersea* oil deposits⟩ **2** : designed for use under the surface of the sea ⟨an *undersea* fleet⟩
[2]**un·der·sea** \ˌən-dər-ˈsē\ *or* **un·der·seas** \-ˈsēz\ *adv* : under the sea : beneath the surface of the sea
un·der·sec·re·tary \ˌən-dər-ˈsek-rə-ˌter-ē\ *n* : a secretary immediately subordinate to a principal secretary ⟨*undersecretary* of state⟩
un·der·sell \ˌən-dər-ˈsel\ *vt* **-sold** \-ˈsōld\; **-sell·ing** : to sell articles cheaper than ⟨*undersell* a competitor⟩
un·der·shirt \ˈən-dər-ˌshərt\ *n* : a collarless undergarment with or without sleeves
un·der·shoot \ˌən-dər-ˈshüt\ *vt* **-shot** \-ˈshät\; **-shoot·ing** : to shoot or fall short of or below (a target) ⟨an airplane *undershooting* the runway⟩
un·der·shorts \ˈən-dər-ˌshȯrts\ *n pl* : underpants for men or boys
un·der·shot \ˌən-dər-ˌshät\ *adj* : having the lower incisor teeth or lower jaw projecting beyond the upper when the mouth is closed
un·der·side \ˈən-dər-ˌsīd, ˌən-dər-ˈ\ *n* : the side or surface lying underneath
un·der·signed \ˈən-dər-ˌsīnd\ *n, pl* **undersigned** : one who signs his or her name at the end of a document
un·der·sized \ˌən-dər-ˈsīzd\ *adj* : smaller than is usual or standard ⟨*undersized* trout⟩
un·der·skirt \ˈən-dər-ˌskərt\ *n* : a skirt worn under an outer skirt; *esp* : PETTICOAT
un·der·slung \ˌən-dər-ˈsləng\ *adj* **1** : suspended so as to extend below the axles ⟨an *underslung* automobile frame⟩ **2** : having a low center of gravity
un·der·spin \ˈən-dər-ˌspin\ *n* : BACKSPIN
un·der·stand \ˌən-dər-ˈstand\ *vb* **-stood** \-ˈstu̇d\; **-stand·ing** **1** : to grasp the meaning of : COMPREHEND **2** : to have thorough knowledge of ⟨*understand* the arts⟩ **3** : to accept as a settled fact or truth ⟨it is *understood* that I will pay⟩ **4** : to have reason to believe : GATHER, INFER ⟨we *understand* that you're leaving today⟩ **5** : to take as meaning something not openly made known : INTERPRET, EXPLAIN ⟨I *understand* the letter to be a refusal⟩ **6** : to supply in thought as if expressed ⟨"to be married" is commonly *understood* after the word *engaged*⟩ **7** : to have a sympathetic attitude ⟨you just don't *understand* about these things⟩ [Old English *understandan,* from *under* + *standan* "to stand"] — **un·der·stand·abil·i·ty** \-ˌstan-də-ˈbil-ət-ē\ *n* — **un·der·stand·able** \-ˈstan-də-bəl\ *adj* — **un·der·stand·ably** \-blē\ *adv*
[1]**un·der·stand·ing** \ˌən-dər-ˈstan-ding\ *n* **1** : mental grasp : COMPREHENSION **2** : the ability to understand and judge ⟨a person of *understanding*⟩ **3 a** : agreement of opinion and feeling **b** : a mutual agreement not formally entered into but in some degree binding on each side ⟨an economic *understanding* between two nations⟩ **4** : EXPLANATION 1, INTERPRETATION **5** : SYMPATHY 3
[2]**understanding** *adj* : endowed with understanding : TOLERANT, SYMPATHETIC ⟨an *understanding* teacher⟩ — **un·der·stand·ing·ly** \-ˈstan-ding-lē\ *adv*
un·der·state \ˌən-dər-ˈstāt\ *vt* **1** : to represent as less than is the case **2** : to state with restraint especially for greater effect — **un·der·state·ment** \-mənt\ *n*
un·der·stood \ˌən-dər-ˈstu̇d\ *adj* **1** : fully apprehended **2** : agreed on **3** : IMPLICIT 1
un·der·sto·ry \ˈən-dər-ˌstōr-ē, -ˌstȯr-\ *n* **1** : an underlying layer of vegetation; *esp* : the plant layer and especially the trees and shrubs between the forest canopy and the ground cover **2** : the plants that form the understory
[1]**un·der·study** \ˈən-dər-ˌstəd-ē, ˌən-dər-ˈ\ *vb* **1** : to study an actor's part in order to substitute in an emergency **2** : to prepare as understudy to (as an actor)
[2]**un·der·study** \ˈən-dər-ˌstəd-ē\ *n* : one who is prepared to act another's part or take over another's duties
un·der·sur·face \-ˌsər-fəs\ *n* : UNDERSIDE
un·der·take \ˌən-dər-ˈtāk\ *vt* **-took** \-ˈtu̇k\; **-tak·en** \-ˈtā-kən\; **-tak·ing** **1** : to take in hand : set about ⟨*undertake* a task⟩ **2** : to put oneself under obligation to perform : AGREE ⟨*undertake* to deliver a package⟩ **3** : GUARANTEE 2, PROMISE
un·der·tak·er \ˈən-dər-ˌtā-kər\ *n* : one whose business is to prepare the dead for burial and to take charge of funerals
un·der·tak·ing \ˈən-dər-ˌtā-king, ˌən-dər-ˈ; *2 is* ˈən-dər-ˌ *only*\ *n* **1** : the act of one that undertakes something (as a project) **2** : the business of an undertaker **3** : something undertaken : ENTERPRISE **4** : PROMISE 1, GUARANTEE
un·der·ten·ant \ˈən-dər-ˌten-ənt\ *n* : SUBTENANT
un·der–the–count·er *adj* : covert and usually unlawful ⟨*under-the-counter* liquor sales⟩ [from the hiding of illicit wares under the counters of stores where they are sold]
un·der·throw \ˈən-dər-ˌthrō\ *vt* : to throw (a ball or pass) short of the intended receiver in football
un·der·tone \ˈən-dər-ˌtōn\ *n* **1** : a low or subdued tone ⟨spoke in an *undertone*⟩ **2** : a subdued color
un·der·tow \-ˌtō\ *n* : a current beneath the surface of the water that moves away from or along the shore while the surface water above it moves toward the shore
un·der·val·ue \ˌən-dər-ˈval-yü\ *vt* **1** : to value below the real

worth **2 :** to set little value on — **un·der·val·u·a·tion** \ˌ-ˌval-yə-ˈwā-shən\ *n*

un·der·wa·ter \ˈən-dər-ˈwȯt-ər, -ˈwät-\ *adj* **:** lying, growing, worn, performed, or operating below the surface of the water ⟨*underwater* plants⟩ ⟨an *underwater* cave⟩ — **un·der·wa·ter** \-ˈwȯt-, -ˈwät-\ *adv*

un·der·way \ˌən-dər-ˌwā\ *adj* **:** occurring, performed, or used while traveling or in motion ⟨*underway* refueling⟩

under way \-ˈwā\ *adv* **1 :** in motion; *esp* **:** not at anchor or aground **2 :** into motion from a standstill **3 :** in progress **:** AFOOT ⟨preparations were *under way*⟩ [probably from Dutch *onderweg,* from earlier *onderwegen,* literally, "under or among the ways"]

un·der·wear \ˈən-dər-ˌwaər, -ˌweər\ *n* **:** clothing worn next to the skin and under other clothing

[1]**un·der·weight** \ˌən-dər-ˈwāt\ *n* **:** weight below what is normal, average, or necessary

[2]**underweight** *adj* **:** weighing less than the normal or requisite amount

[1]**un·der·wing** \ˈən-dər-ˌwing\ *n* **1 :** either of the posterior pair of wings of an insect **2 :** the underside of a bird's wing

[2]**underwing** *adj* **:** located or growing beneath or on the under surface of a wing ⟨*underwing* coverts⟩

un·der·wood \ˈən-dər-ˌwu̇d\ *n* **:** UNDERBRUSH, UNDERGROWTH

un·der·wool \-ˌwu̇l\ *n* **:** short woolly underfur

un·der·world \-ˌwərld\ *n* **1 :** the place of departed souls **:** HADES **2** *archaic* **:** EARTH **3 :** the side of the earth opposite to one **:** ANTIPODES **4 :** a social level regarded as below the level of ordinary life; *esp* **:** the world of organized crime

un·der·write \ˈən-dər-ˌrīt, -də-; ˌən-dər-ˈ, -də-\ *vt* **-wrote** \-ˌrōt, -ˈrōt\; **-writ·ten** \-ˌrit-n, -ˈrit-n\; **-writ·ing** \-ˌrīt-ing, -ˈrīt-\ **1 :** to write under or at the end of something else **2 a :** to put one's name to (an insurance policy) and thereby become answerable for a designated loss or damage **b :** to insure life or property **3 :** to subscribe to **:** agree to ⟨refused to *underwrite* the government's foreign policy⟩ **4 a :** to agree to purchase (a security issue) usually on a fixed date at a fixed price with a view to public resale **b :** to guarantee financial support of ⟨*underwrite* an expedition⟩ — **un·der·writ·er** \ˈən-dər-ˌrīt-ər, ˈən-də-\ *n*

[1]**un·de·sir·able** \-ˈzī-rə-bəl\ *adj* **:** not desirable **:** OBJECTIONABLE — **un·de·sir·abil·i·ty** \ˌzī-rə-ˈbil-ət-ē\ *n* — **un·de·sir·able·ness** \-ˈzī-rə-bəl-nəs\ *n* — **un·de·sir·ably** \-blē\ *adv*

[2]**undesirable** *n* **:** one that is undesirable

un·de·vi·at·ing \ˌən-ˈdē-vē-ˌāt-ing, ˈən-\ *adj* **:** keeping a true course **:** UNSWERVING — **un·de·vi·at·ing·ly** \-ing-lē\ *adv*

un·dies \ˈən-dēz\ *n pl* **:** UNDERWEAR; *esp* **:** women's underwear

un·dine \ˌən-ˈdēn, ˈən-ˌ\ *n* **:** WATER NYMPH [New Latin *undina,* from Latin *unda* "wave"]

un·di·rect·ed \ˌən-də-ˈrek-təd, -dī-\ *adj* **:** not directed, planned, or guided ⟨*undirected* efforts⟩

un·dis·guised \ˌən-dis-ˈgīzd\ *adj* **:** not disguised or concealed ⟨*undisguised* impatience⟩ — **un·dis·guis·ed·ly** \-ˈgī-zəd-lē\ *adv*

un·do \ˌən-ˈdü, ˈən-\ *vb* **-did** \-ˈdid\; **-done** \-ˈdən\; **-do·ing** \-ˈdü-ing\ **1 :** to make or become unfastened or loosened **2 :** to make of no effect or as if not done **:** NULLIFY **3 a :** to ruin the worldly means, reputation, or hopes of ⟨*undone* by greed⟩ **b :** UPSET 3a ⟨she's come *undone*⟩ — **un·do·er** *n*

un·do·ing \ˌən-ˈdü-ing\ *n* **1 :** the act of loosening or unfastening **2 :** RUIN; *also* **:** a cause of ruin ⟨greed was to prove his *undoing*⟩ **3 :** ANNULMENT, REVERSAL

un·done \ˌən-ˈdən, ˈən-\ *adj* **:** not done or finished

un·doubt·ed \-ˈdau̇t-əd\ *adj* **:** not doubted or doubtful **:** CERTAIN ⟨*undoubted* proof of guilt⟩ — **un·doubt·ed·ly** *adv*

un·drape \-ˈdrāp\ *vt* **:** to strip of drapery **:** UNVEIL

un·draw \-ˈdrȯ\ *vt* **-drew** \-ˈdrü\; **-drawn** \-ˈdrȯn\; **-draw·ing** **:** to draw (as a curtain) aside **:** OPEN

un·dreamed \ˌən-ˈdremt, -ˈdrempt, -ˈdrēmd, ˈən-\ *also* **un·dreamt** \-ˈdremt, -ˈdrempt\ *adj* **:** not dreamed or thought of ⟨technical advances *undreamed* of a few years ago⟩

[1]**un·dress** \ˌən-ˈdres, ˈən-\ *vb* **1 :** to remove the clothes of **2 :** to take off one's clothes

[2]**undress** *n* **1 :** informal dress: as **a :** a loose robe or dressing gown **b :** ordinary dress **2 :** a state of nudity

un·dressed \-ˈdrest\ *adj* **:** not dressed: as **a :** partially, improperly, or informally clothed **b :** not fully processed or finished ⟨*undressed* hides⟩ **c :** not cared for or tended ⟨an *undressed* wound⟩ ⟨*undressed* fields⟩

un·due \-ˈdü, -ˈdyü\ *adj* **1 :** not due **:** not yet payable **2 :** going beyond what is proper or fit ⟨*undue* force⟩

un·du·lant \ˈən-jə-lənt, ˈən-dyə-, -də-\ *adj* **:** rising and falling in waves

undulant fever *n* **:** a human brucellosis marked by fluctuating fever, weakness, chills, and weight loss and contracted by contact with infected domestic animals

un·du·late \ˈən-jə-ˌlāt, ˈən-dyə-, -də-\ *vb* **1 :** to form or move in waves **:** FLUCTUATE **2 :** to rise and fall in volume, pitch, or cadence **3 :** to present a wavy appearance [Late Latin *undula* "small wave," from Latin *unda* "wave"]

un·du·la·tion \ˌən-jə-ˈlā-shən, ˌən-dyə-, -də-\ *n* **1 a :** the action of undulating **b :** a wavelike motion to and fro in a fluid or elastic medium **:** VIBRATION **2 :** a wavy appearance or form

un·du·la·to·ry \ˈən-jə-lə-ˌtōr-ē, ˈən-dyə-, -də-, -ˌtȯr-\ *adj* **:** of or relating to undulation; *also* **:** UNDULANT

un·du·ly \ˌən-ˈdü-lē, -ˈdyü-, ˈən-\ *adv* **:** in an undue manner **:** EXCESSIVELY ⟨an *unduly* harsh punishment⟩

un·dy·ing \-ˈdī-ing\ *adj* **:** not dying **:** IMMORTAL

un·earned \-ˈərnd\ *adj* **1 :** not gained by labor, service, or skill ⟨*unearned* income⟩ **2 :** scored as a result of an error by the opposing team ⟨an *unearned* run⟩

un·earth \ˌən-ˈərth, ˈən-\ *vt* **1 :** to dig up out of or as if out of the earth ⟨*unearth* a forgotten photo⟩ **2 :** to make known **:** bring to light ⟨*unearth* a plot⟩ ***synonyms*** see DISCOVER

un·earth·ly \-lē\ *adj* **:** not earthly: as **a :** SUPERNATURAL 2 ⟨*unearthly* beings⟩ **b :** STRANGE 2b, EERIE ⟨*unearthly* howls⟩ **c :** not usual or reasonable ⟨an *unearthly* hour to get up⟩ — **un·earth·li·ness** *n*

un·easy \ˌən-ˈē-zē, ˈən-\ *adj* **1 :** not easy in manner **:** AWKWARD ⟨gave an *uneasy* laugh⟩ **2 :** disturbed by pain or worry **:** RESTLESS ⟨an *uneasy* night⟩ **3 :** UNSTABLE ⟨an *uneasy* truce⟩ — **un·eas·i·ly** \-ˈē-zə-lē\ *adv* — **un·eas·i·ness** \-ˈē-zē-nəs\ *n*

un·em·ploy·able \ˌən-im-ˈplȯi-ə-bəl\ *adj* **:** not acceptable for employment — **unemployable** *n*

un·em·ployed \-ˈplȯid\ *adj* **:** not employed: **a :** not being used **b :** not engaged in a gainful occupation — **unemployed** *n*

un·em·ploy·ment \ˌən-im-ˈplȯi-mənt\ *n* **:** the state of being out of work **:** involuntary idleness of workers

unemployment compensation *n* **:** money paid at regular intervals to an unemployed worker (as by an employer or a government agency) — called also *unemployment benefit*

un·end·ing \ˌən-ˈen-ding, ˈən-\ *adj* **:** being without ending **:** ENDLESS — **un·end·ing·ly** \-ding-lē\ *adv*

[1]**un·equal** \-ˈē-kwəl\ *adj* **1 a :** not of the same measurement, quantity, or number as another **b :** not like or not the same as another in degree, worth, or status **2 :** not uniform **:** VARIABLE, UNEVEN **3 :** badly balanced or matched ⟨an *unequal* fight⟩ **4 :** INADEQUATE, INSUFFICIENT ⟨timber *unequal* to the strain⟩ — **un·equal·ly** \-kwə-lē\ *adv*

[2]**unequal** *n* **:** one that is not equal to another

un·equaled *or* **un·equalled** \-ˈē-kwəld\ *adj* **:** not equaled **:** UNPARALLELED ⟨an artist of *unequaled* talent⟩

un·equiv·o·cal \ˌən-i-ˈkwiv-ə-kəl\ *adj* **:** leaving no doubt **:** CLEAR — **un·equiv·o·cal·ly** \-kə-lē, -klē\ *adv*

un·err·ing \ˌən-ˈeər-ing, -ˈər-ing, ˈən-\ *adj* **:** making no errors **:** UNFAILING — **un·err·ing·ly** \-ing-lē\ *adv*

un·even \ˌən-ˈē-vən, ˈən-\ *adj* **1 :** ODD 3a **2 a :** not even **:** not level or smooth **:** RUGGED ⟨large *uneven* teeth⟩ ⟨*uneven* handwriting⟩ **b :** varying from the straight or parallel **c :** not uniform **:** IRREGULAR ⟨*uneven* combustion⟩ **d :** varying in quality ⟨an *uneven* performance⟩ **3 :** UNEQUAL 3 ⟨an *uneven* confrontation⟩ — **un·even·ly** *adv* — **un·even·ness** \-vən-nəs\ *n*

un·event·ful \ˌən-i-ˈvent-fəl\ *adj* **:** not eventful **:** lacking interesting or noteworthy happenings ⟨an *uneventful* trip⟩ — **un·event·ful·ly** \-fə-lē\ *adv*

un·ex·am·pled \ˌən-ig-ˈzam-pəld\ *adj* **:** having no example or parallel **:** UNPRECEDENTED

un·ex·cep·tion·able \ˌən-ik-ˈsep-shnə-bəl, -shə-nə-\ *adj* **:** not open to objection or criticism **:** beyond reproach **:** UNIMPEACHABLE [[1]*un-* + obsolete *exception* "to take exception, object" + *-able*] — **un·ex·cep·tion·able·ness** *n* — **un·ex·cep·tion·ably** \-blē\ *adv*

un·ex·cep·tion·al \-ˈsep-shnəl, -shən-l\ *adj* : ORDINARY 1
un·ex·pect·ed \ˌən-ik-ˈspek-təd\ *adj* : not expected or foreseen — **un·ex·pect·ed·ly** *adv* — **un·ex·pect·ed·ness** *n*
un·ex·ploit·ed \ˌən-ik-ˈsplȯit-əd\ *adj* : not exploited or developed : not taken advantage of ⟨*unexploited* resources⟩
un·ex·pres·sive \ˌən-ik-ˈspres-iv\ *adj* : INEXPRESSIVE
un·fad·ing \ˌən-ˈfād-ing\ *adj* **1** : not losing color or freshness **2** : not diminishing ⟨*unfading* loyalty⟩ — **un·fad·ing·ly** *adv*
un·fail·ing \-ˈfā-ling\ *adj* **1** : CONSTANT 1 ⟨*unfailing* courtesy⟩ **2** : EVERLASTING, INEXHAUSTIBLE ⟨an *unfailing* topic of interest⟩ **3** : INFALLIBLE 2, SURE ⟨an *unfailing* judge of character⟩ — **un·fail·ing·ly** *adv*
un·fair \-ˈfaər, -ˈfeər\ *adj* **1** : marked by injustice, partiality, or deception : UNJUST, DISHONEST ⟨an *unfair* trial⟩ **2** : not equitable in business dealings ⟨*unfair* to workers⟩ — **un·fair·ly** *adv* — **un·fair·ness** *n*
un·faith \ˌən-ˈfāth, ˈən-ˈ, ˈən-ˌ\ *n* : absence of faith : DISBELIEF
un·faith·ful \ˌən-ˈfāth-fəl, ˈən-\ *adj* : not faithful: **a** : not adhering to vows, allegiance, or duty : DISLOYAL **b** : not faithful to marriage vows **c** : INACCURATE ⟨an *unfaithful* translation⟩ — **un·faith·ful·ly** \-fə-lē\ *adv* — **un·faith·ful·ness** *n*
un·fa·mil·iar \ˌən-fə-ˈmil-yər\ *adj* **1** : not well known : STRANGE ⟨an *unfamiliar* place⟩ **2** : not well acquainted ⟨*unfamiliar* with the subject⟩ — **un·fa·mil·iar·i·ty** \-ˌmil-ˈyar-ət-ē, -ˌmil-ē-ˈar-\ *n* — **un·fa·mil·iar·ly** \-ˈmil-yər-lē\ *adv*
un·fas·ten \ˌən-ˈfas-n, ˈən-\ *vb* : to make loose: as **a** : UNPIN, UNBUCKLE **b** : UNDO 1 ⟨*unfasten* a button⟩ **c** : DETACH 1 ⟨*unfasten* a boat from its moorings⟩
un·fath·om·able \ˌən-ˈfa<u>th</u>-ə-mə-bəl\ *adj* : not capable of being fathomed: **a** : IMMEASURABLE **b** : impossible to comprehend
un·fa·vor·able \-ˈfāv-rə-bəl, -ə-rə-; -ˈfā-vər-bəl\ *adj* **1 a** : not disposed to favor **b** : expressing disapproval ⟨*unfavorable* reviews⟩ **2** : likely to cause difficulties ⟨*unfavorable* weather⟩ **3** : not pleasing ⟨an *unfavorable* feature of the plan⟩ — **un·fa·vor·able·ness** *n* — **un·fa·vor·ably** \-blē\ *adv*
un·feel·ing \-ˈfē-ling\ *adj* **1** : lacking feeling : INSENSATE **2** : lacking kindness or sympathy : HARDHEARTED — **un·feel·ing·ly** \-ling-lē\ *adv* — **un·feel·ing·ness** *n*
un·feigned \ˌən-ˈfānd, ˈən-\ *adj* : not feigned or hypocritical : GENUINE — **un·feigned·ly** \-ˈfā-nəd-lē, -ˈfān-dlē\ *adv*
un·fet·ter \ˌən-ˈfet-ər, ˈən-\ *vt* : LIBERATE 1, EMANCIPATE
un·fil·ial \-ˈfil-ē-əl, -ˈfil-yəl\ *adj* : not observing the obligations of a child to a parent : UNDUTIFUL — **un·fil·ial·ly** *adv*
un·fin·ished \-ˈfin-isht\ *adj* : not finished; *esp* : not brought to the final desired state
[1]un·fit \-ˈfit\ *adj* : not fit: **a** : not adapted to a purpose : UNSUITABLE **b** : not qualified : INCOMPETENT **c** : physically or mentally unsound — **un·fit·ly** *adv* — **un·fit·ness** *n*
[2]unfit *vt* : to make unfit : DISABLE, DISQUALIFY
un·fix \ˌən-ˈfiks, ˈən-\ *vt* **1** : to loosen from a fastening : DETACH, DISENGAGE **2** : to make unstable : UNSETTLE
un·flag·ging \-ˈflag-ing\ *adj* : CONSTANT ⟨*unflagging* enthusiasm⟩ — **un·flag·ging·ly** *adv*
un·flap·pa·ble \-ˈflap-ə-bəl\ *adj* : not easily upset or panicked : COOL [[1]*un-* + [1]*flap* "state of excitement" + *-able*]
un·fledged \-ˈflejd\ *adj* **1** : not feathered or ready for flight **2** : not fully developed : IMMATURE ⟨an *unfledged* writer⟩
un·flinch·ing \-ˈflin-ching\ *adj* : not flinching or shrinking : STEADFAST, UNCOMPROMISING ⟨*unflinching* determination⟩ — **un·flinch·ing·ly** \-ching-lē\ *adv*
un·fold \-ˈfōld\ *vb* **1 a** : to spread or cause to spread or straighten out from a folded position or arrangement ⟨*unfolded* the map⟩ **b** : UNWRAP **2** : BLOOM 1 **3** : to become clear gradually or in detail ⟨as the story *unfolds*⟩ **4** : to open out or cause to open out gradually to view or understanding ⟨the mountainous view *unfolded* before their eyes⟩
un·for·get·ta·ble \ˌən-fər-ˈget-ə-bəl\ *adj* : incapable of being forgotten : lasting in memory — **un·for·get·ta·bly** \-blē\ *adv*
un·formed \ˌən-ˈfȯrmd\ *adj* : not arranged in regular shape, order, or relations; *esp* : IMMATURE
[1]un·for·tu·nate \-ˈfȯrch-nət, -ə-nət\ *adj* **1 a** : UNLUCKY **b** : coming or happening by bad luck **2 a** : INAPPROPRIATE ⟨an *unfortunate* choice of words⟩ **b** : DEPLORABLE ⟨an *unfortunate* lack of taste⟩ — **un·for·tu·nate·ly** *adv*
[2]unfortunate *n* : an unfortunate person
un·found·ed \ˌən-ˈfau̇n-dəd, ˈən-\ *adj* : lacking a sound basis : GROUNDLESS ⟨an *unfounded* accusation⟩
un·fre·quent·ed \ˌən-frē-ˈkwent-əd; ˌən-ˈfrē-kwənt-, ˈən-\ *adj* : not often visited or traveled over
un·friend \ˌən-ˈfrend\ *vb* : to remove (someone) from a list of designated friends on a person's social networking Web site
un·friend·ed \ˌən-ˈfren-dəd, ˈən-\ *adj* : having no friends
un·friend·ly \ˌən-ˈfren-dlē, -lē, ˈən-\ *adj* **1 a** : not friendly or social **b** : not kind : HOSTILE ⟨an *unfriendly* greeting⟩ **2** : not favorable ⟨an *unfriendly* environment⟩ — **un·friend·li·ness** *n*
un·frock \-ˈfräk\ *vt* : to deprive (as a priest) of the right to exercise the functions of office
un·fruit·ful \-ˈfrüt-fəl\ *adj* **1** : not bearing fruit or offspring **2** : not producing a desired result ⟨*unfruitful* efforts⟩ — **un·fruit·ful·ly** \-fə-lē\ *adv* — **un·fruit·ful·ness** *n*
un·fund·ed \ˌən-ˈfən-dəd, ˈən-\ *adj* **1** : not funded : FLOATING ⟨an *unfunded* debt⟩ **2** : not provided with funds ⟨*unfunded* schools⟩
un·furl \-ˈfərl\ *vb* : to loose from a furled state : UNFOLD ⟨*unfurl* a flag⟩
un·gain·ly \-ˈgān-lē\ *adj* **1** : AWKWARD 1, CLUMSY **2** : AWKWARD 2b [earlier *gainly* "graceful," from Old English *gēn* "direct, straight," from Old Norse *gegn*] — **un·gain·li·ness** *n*
un·gen·er·ous \-ˈjen-rəs, -ə-rəs\ *adj* **1** : PETTY 3, MEAN **2** : STINGY 1 — **un·gen·er·ous·ly** *adv*
un·gird \ˌən-ˈgərd, ˈən-\ *vt* : to free from a restraining band or girdle : UNBIND
un·glue \-ˈglü\ *vt* : to separate by or as if by dissolving an adhesive
un·glued \-ˈglüd\ *adj* **1** : emotionally upset : DISTRAUGHT **2** : in a state of complete failure
un·god·ly \-ˈgäd-lē, *also* -ˈgȯd-\ *adj* **1** : not godly: as **a** : IRRELIGIOUS **b** : WICKED 1, EVIL **2** : UNREASONABLE 2, OUTRAGEOUS ⟨got up at an *ungodly* hour⟩ ⟨an *ungodly* racket⟩ — **un·god·li·ness** *n*
un·gov·ern·able \-ˈgəv-ər-nə-bəl\ *adj* : not capable of being governed, guided, or restrained ***synonyms*** see UNRULY
un·gra·cious \-ˈgrā-shəs\ *adj* **1** : not courteous : RUDE ⟨*ungracious* treatment⟩ **2** : not pleasing : DISAGREEABLE ⟨an *ungracious* task⟩ — **un·gra·cious·ly** *adv* — **un·gra·cious·ness** *n*
un·grate·ful \ˌən-ˈgrāt-fəl, ˈən-\ *adj* **1** : not thankful for favors ⟨an *ungrateful* child⟩ **2** : not pleasing : DISAGREEABLE ⟨an *ungrateful* task⟩ — **un·grate·ful·ly** \-fə-lē\ *adv* — **un·grate·ful·ness** *n*
un·ground·ed \-ˈgrau̇n-dəd\ *adj* **1** : GROUNDLESS, UNFOUNDED **2** : not instructed or informed
un·grudg·ing \-ˈgrəj-ing\ *adj* : free from envy or unwillingness — **un·grudg·ing·ly** *adv*
un·guard·ed \-ˈgärd-əd\ *adj* **1** : vulnerable to attack **2** : free from guile or wariness : INCAUTIOUS ⟨*unguarded* remarks⟩ — **un·guard·ed·ly** *adv*
un·guent \ˈəng-gwənt, ˈən-; ˈən-jənt\ *n* : a soothing or healing salve : OINTMENT [Latin *unguentum,* from *unguere* "to anoint"]
[1]un·gu·late \ˈəng-gyə-lət, ˈən-, -ˌlāt\ *adj* **1** : having hooves **2** : of or relating to the ungulates [Late Latin *ungulatus,* from Latin *ungula* "hoof," from *unguis* "nail, hoof"]
[2]ungulate *n* : a hoofed typically plant-eating four-footed mammal (as a cow, sheep, pig, horse, camel, or rhinoceros) of a group formerly considered a major mammalian taxon (Ungulata)
un·hal·lowed \ˌən-ˈhal-ōd, ˈən-\ *adj* **1** : not blessed or holy ⟨*unhallowed* ground⟩ **2** : IMPIOUS a, PROFANE
un·hand \ˌən-ˈhand, ˈən-\ *vt* : to remove the hand from : let go
un·hand·some \-ˈhan-səm\ *adj* : not handsome: as **a** : not beautiful : HOMELY **b** : UNBECOMING ⟨an *unhandsome* habit⟩ **c** : lacking in courtesy or taste — **un·hand·some·ly** *adv*
un·handy \-ˈhan-dē\ *adj* **1** : hard to handle : INCONVENIENT ⟨a thick *unhandy* book⟩ **2** : lacking in skill or dexterity : AWKWARD — **un·hand·i·ly** \-də-lē\ *adv* — **un·handi·ness** *n*
un·hap·py \-ˈhap-ē\ *adj* **1** : not fortunate : UNLUCKY ⟨an *unhappy* mistake⟩ **2** : not cheerful : SAD, MISERABLE **3** : INAPPROPRIATE ⟨an *unhappy* choice⟩ — **un·hap·pi·ly** \-ˈhap-ə-lē\ *adv* — **un·hap·pi·ness** \-ˈhap-i-nəs\ *n*
un·har·ness \-ˈhär-nəs\ *vt* : to remove a harness from
un·health·ful \-ˈhelth-fəl\ *adj* : UNHEALTHY 1
un·healthy \-ˈhel-thē\ *adj* **1** : not conducive to good health : not healthful ⟨an *unhealthy* climate⟩ **2** : not in good health : SICKLY **3 a** : DANGEROUS 1, RISKY **b** : causing harm : INJURIOUS **c** : CORRUPT 1, DEPRAVED ⟨an *unhealthy* imagination⟩ — **un·health·i·ly** \-thə-lē\ *adv* — **un·health·i·ness** \-thē-nəs\ *n*
un·heard \ˌən-ˈhərd, ˈən-\ *adj* **1** : not perceived by the ear **2** : not given a hearing ⟨*unheard* protests⟩

un·heard–of \-ˌəv, -ˌäv\ *adj* : previously unknown : UNPRECEDENTED ⟨moving at *unheard-of* speeds⟩

un·hinge \ˌən-ˈhinj, ˈən-\ *vt* **1** : to make unstable : UNSETTLE, DISRUPT ⟨a mind *unhinged* by grief⟩ **2** : to remove (as a door) from the hinges

un·hitch \-ˈhich\ *vt* : to free from or as if from being hitched

un·ho·ly \-ˈhō-lē\ *adj* **1** : not holy : PROFANE, WICKED **2** : deserving of censure ⟨an *unholy* alliance⟩ **3** : very unpleasant ⟨an *unholy* noise⟩ — **un·ho·li·ness** *n*

un·ho·mog·e·nized \-hə-ˈmäj-ə-ˌnīzd, -hō-\ *adj* : that has not been homogenized

un·hood \-ˈhu̇d\ *vt* : to remove a hood or covering from

un·hook \-ˈhu̇k\ *vt* **1** : to remove from a hook **2** : to unfasten by releasing a hook

un·horse \-ˈhȯrs\ *vt* : to dislodge from or as if from a horse : UNSEAT

un·hou·seled \-ˈhau̇-zəld\ *adj, archaic* : not having received the Eucharist especially just before death [derived from earlier *housel* "Eucharist," from Old English *hūsel* "sacrifice, Eucharist"]

un·hur·ried \-ˈhər-ēd, -ˈhə-rēd\ *adj* : not hurried : LEISURELY ⟨an *unhurried* pace⟩ — **un·hur·ried·ly** *adv*

uni- *prefix* : one : single ⟨*uni*cellular⟩ [Latin, from *unus* "one"]

Uni·ate *or* **Uni·at** \ˈü-nē-ˌat, ˈyü-\ *n* : a Christian belonging to a church adhering to an Eastern rite but accepting papal authority [Ukrainian *uniat, uniyat* "one in favor of the union of the Greek and Roman Catholic churches," from *uniya* "union," from Polish *unija,* from Late Latin *unio*] — **Uniate** *adj*

uni·ax·i·al \ˌyü-nē-ˈak-se-əl\ *adj* **1** : having only one axis **2** : of or relating to only one axis — **uni·ax·i·al·ly** \-sē-ə-lē\ *adv*

uni·cam·er·al \ˌyü-ni-ˈkam-rəl, -ə-rəl\ *adj* : having or consisting of a single legislative chamber [Late Latin *camera* "chamber"] — **uni·cam·er·al·ly** \-rə-lē\ *adv*

uni·cel·lu·lar \-ˈsel-yə-lər\ *adj* : having or consisting of a single cell ⟨*unicellular* microorganisms⟩

uni·corn \ˈyü-nə-ˌkȯrn\ *n* : a mythical animal generally depicted with the body and head of a horse, the hind legs of a stag, the tail of a lion, and a single horn on its forehead [Medieval French *unicorne,* from Late Latin *unicornis,* from Latin *uni-* + *cornu* "horn"]

uni·cy·cle \ˈyü-ni-ˌsī-kəl\ *n* : a vehicle that has a single wheel and is usually propelled by pedals [*uni-* + *-cycle* (as in *tricycle*)]

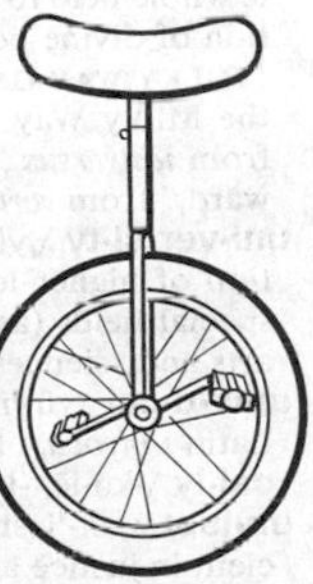

unicycle

uni·di·rec·tion·al \ˌyü-ni-də-ˈrek-shnəl, -dī-, -shən-l\ *adj* : having, moving in, or responsive in a single direction ⟨a *unidirectional* antenna⟩

[1]**uni·form** \ˈyü-nə-ˌfȯrm\ *adj* **1** : having always the same form, manner, or degree : not varying or variable **2** : of the same form with others : conforming to one rule ***synonyms*** see STEADY — **uni·for·mi·ty** \ˌyü-nə-ˈfȯr-mət-ē\ *n* — **uni·form·ly** \ˈyü-nə-ˌfȯrm-lē, ˌyü-nə-ˈ\ *adv* — **uni·form·ness** *n*

[2]**uniform** *vt* : to clothe with a uniform

[3]**uniform** *n* : distinctive dress worn by members of a particular group (as an army or a police force)

uni·for·mi·tar·i·an·ism \ˌyü-nə-ˌfȯr-mə-ˈter-ē-ə-ˌniz-əm\ *n* : a geological doctrine that existing processes acting in the same manner as at present are sufficient to account for all geological changes

uniform resource locator *n* : URL

uni·fy \ˈyü-nə-ˌfī\ *vt* **-fied; -fy·ing** : to make into a unit or a coherent whole : UNITE — **uni·fi·able** \-ˌfī-ə-bəl\ *adj* — **uni·fi·ca·tion** \ˌyü-nə-fə-ˈkā-shən\ *n* — **uni·fi·er** \ˈyü-nə-ˌfī-ər, -ˌfīr\ *n*

uni·lat·er·al \ˌyü-ni-ˈlat-ə-rəl, -ˈla-trəl\ *adj* : of, relating to, affecting, or done by one side only ⟨*unilateral* paralysis⟩ ⟨*unilateral* disarmament⟩ — **uni·lat·er·al·ly** \-ē\ *adv*

un·im·peach·able \ˌən-im-ˈpē-chə-bəl\ *adj* : not impeachable: as **a** : reliable beyond a doubt ⟨*unimpeachable* evidence⟩ **b** : not liable to accusation : IRREPROACHABLE ⟨an *unimpeachable* reputation⟩ — **un·im·peach·ably** \-blē\ *adv*

un·im·proved \-ˈprüvd\ *adj* : not improved: as **a** : not tilled, built upon, or otherwise prepared for use ⟨*unimproved* land⟩ **b** : not used or employed advantageously **c** : not selectively bred for better quality or productiveness

un·in·hib·it·ed \ˌən-in-ˈhib-ət-əd\ *adj* : free from inhibition; *esp* : unrestrainedly informal ⟨a festive *uninhibited* party⟩ — **un·in·hib·it·ed·ly** *adv* — **un·in·hib·it·ed·ness** *n*

un·in·stall \ˌən-in-ˈstȯl\ *vt* : to remove (software) from a computer system especially by using a specially designed program

un·in·tel·li·gent \ˌən-in-ˈtel-ə-jənt\ *adj* : lacking intelligence : UNWISE, IGNORANT — **un·in·tel·li·gent·ly** *adv*

un·in·ter·est·ed \ˌən-ˈint-ə-ˌres-təd, ˈən-; -ˈin-trəs-, -ˌtres-; -ˈint-ərs-, -ˈint-ə-rəs-\ *adj* : not interested : not having the mind or feelings engaged

usage DISINTERESTED and UNINTERESTED mean marked by a lack of interest or concern. UNINTERESTED in discriminating use means having no interest and implies being indifferent through lack of sympathy for or curiosity toward something ⟨*uninterested* in the outcome of the game⟩. DISINTERESTED in comparable use suggests a freedom from concern for personal or financial advantage that enables one to judge, advise, or act without bias ⟨*disinterested* referees⟩.

union \ˈyün-yən\ *n* **1 a** : an act or instance of uniting two or more things into one: as (1) : the formation of a single political unit from two or more separate and independent units (2) : a uniting in marriage (3) : the growing together of severed parts **b** : a unified condition : COMBINATION, JUNCTION **2** : something formed by a combining of parts or members: as **a** : a confederation of independent individuals (as nations or persons) for a common purpose **b** : a political unit constituting an organized whole formed usually from units which were previously governed separately **c** : LABOR UNION **d** *cap* : an organization on a college or university campus providing recreational, social, cultural, and sometimes dining facilities; *also* : the building housing it **e** : the mathematical set that contains all of the elements which are included in at least one of two or more sets ⟨the *union* of the set {1, 2, 3} and the set {3, 4, 5} is the set {1, 2, 3, 4, 5}⟩ **3 a** : a device symbolizing national unity that is borne on a flag **b** : the upper inner corner of a flag **4 a** : a device for connecting parts (as of a machine) **b** : a coupling for pipes [Medieval French, from Late Latin *unio* "oneness," from Latin *unus* "one"] ***synonyms*** see UNITY

Union *adj* : of, relating to, or being the side favoring the federal union in the American Civil War

union card *n* : a card certifying personal membership in good standing in a labor union

union·ism \ˈyün-yə-ˌniz-əm\ *n* **1** : the principle or policy of forming or adhering to a union **2** *cap* : adherence to the policy of a firm federal union prior to or during the American Civil War **3** : the principles, theory, or system of trade unions — **union·ist** \-yə-nəst\ *n, often cap*

union·ize \ˈyün-yə-ˌnīz\ *vt* : to cause to become a member of or subject to the rules of a labor union : form into a labor union — **union·iza·tion** \ˌyün-yə-nə-ˈzā-shən\ *n*

union jack *n* **1** : a jack consisting of the part of a national flag that signifies union **2** *cap U&J* : the state flag of the United Kingdom

union shop *n* : an establishment in which the employer is free to hire nonunion workers but retains them on the payroll only on condition of their becoming members of the union within a specified time

union suit *n* : an undergarment with shirt and pants in one piece

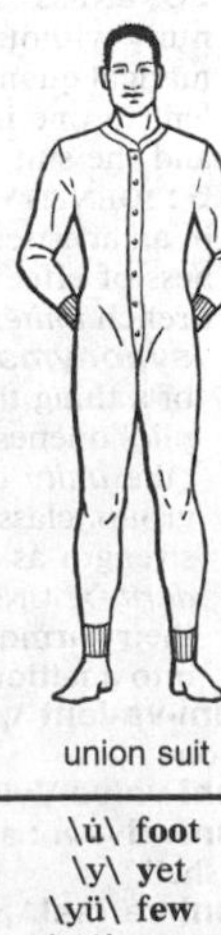

union suit

uni·pa·ren·tal \ˌyü-ni-pə-ˈrent-l\ *adj* : having, involving, or derived from a single parent; *also* : PARTHENOGENETIC — **uni·pa·ren·tal·ly** \-l-ē\ *adv*

unique \yu̇-ˈnēk\ *adj* **1 a** : being the only one ⟨the *unique* factorization of a number into prime factors⟩ **b** : PECULIAR 1 ⟨a custom *unique* to Mexico⟩ **2** : very unusual : NOTABLE ⟨*unique* talent⟩ [French, from Latin *unicus,* from *unus* "one"] ***synonyms*** see SINGLE — **unique·ly** *adv* — **unique·ness** *n*

uni·sex \ˈyü-nə-ˌseks\ *adj* : suitable or designed for both males and females ⟨*unisex* clothing⟩

uni·sex·u·al \ˌyü-ni-ˈsek-shəl, -shwəl, -shə-wəl\ *adj* **1** : of, relating to, or restricted to one sex:

a : male or female but not hermaphroditic **b** : DICLINOUS ⟨a *unisexual* flower⟩ **2** : UNISEX — **uni·sex·u·al·i·ty** \-ˌsek-shə-ˈwal-ət-ē\ *n*

uni·son \ˈyü-nə-sən, -zən\ *n* **1 a** : identity in musical pitch **b** : the condition of being tuned or sounded at the same pitch or at an octave **2** : harmonious agreement : CONCORD [Medieval French *unisson*, from Medieval Latin *unisonus* "having the same sound," from Latin *uni-* + *sonus* "sound"] — **in unison 1** : in perfect agreement : so as to harmonize exactly ⟨a class reciting *in unison*⟩ **2** : at the same time

unit \ˈyü-nət\ *n* **1 a** : the first and least natural number : ONE **b** : a single quantity regarded as a whole in calculation **2** : a definite quantity (as of length, time, or value) adopted as a standard of measurement; *esp* : an amount of work used in calculating student credits **3 a** : a single thing, person, or group that is a constituent of a whole **b** : a part of a military establishment that has a prescribed organization **c** : a piece or complex of apparatus serving to perform one particular function **d** : a part of a school course focusing on a central theme **e** : an area in a medical facility and especially a hospital that is specially staffed and equipped to provide a particular type of care ⟨an intensive care *unit*⟩ [back-formation from *unity*]

uni·tard \ˈyü-nə-ˌtärd\ *n* : a close-fitting one-piece garment for the torso and legs and often the arms and feet [*uni-* + leo*tard*]

uni·tar·i·an \ˌyü-nə-ˈter-ē-ən\ *n* **1 a** *often cap* : one who believes that the deity exists only in one person **b** *cap* : a member of a Christian denomination that stresses individual freedom of belief, the free use of reason in religion, a united world community, and liberal social action **2** : an advocate of unity or a unitary system [Latin *unitas* "unity"] — **unitarian** *adj, often cap* — **uni·tar·i·an·ism** \-ē-ə-ˌniz-əm\ *n, often cap*

uni·tary \ˈyü-nə-ˌter-ē\ *adj* **1 a** : of or relating to a unit **b** : based on or characterized by unity or units **2** : having the character of a unit : WHOLE — **uni·tar·i·ly** \ˌyü-nə-ˈter-ə-lē\ *adv*

unit circle *n* : a circle with a radius of 1

unite \yu̇-ˈnīt\ *vb* **1 a** : to put or come together to form a single unit **b** : to cause to adhere **c** : to link by a legal or moral bond **2** : to become one or as if one **3** : to join in action : act in concert [Medieval French *uniter*, from Latin *unitus*, past participle of *unire* "to unite," from *unus* "one"] ***synonyms*** see JOIN — **unit·er** *n*

unit·ed \yu̇-ˈnīt-əd\ *adj* **1** : made one or as if one **2** : relating to or produced by joint action ⟨a *united* effort⟩ **3** : being in agreement : HARMONIOUS ⟨a *united* family⟩ — **unit·ed·ly** *adv*

unit·ize \ˈyü-nət-ˌīz\ *vt* : to form or convert into a unit

units digit \ˈyü-nəts-\ *n* : the numeral (as 6 in 456) occupying the units place in a number expressed in the Arabic system of writing numbers

units place *n* : the place immediately to the left of the decimal point in a number expressed in the Arabic system of writing numbers

uni·ty \ˈyü-nət-ē\ *n, pl* **-ties 1** : the quality or state of being one : ONENESS **2** : a condition of harmony : CONCORD **3** : continuity without change (as in purpose or action) **4 a** : a mathematical quantity or combination of quantities treated as equivalent to one in a calculation ⟨called the distance between earth and the sun *unity* and calculated other distances as multiples⟩ **b** : IDENTITY ELEMENT **5** : a combination or ordering of parts in an artistic or literary work that produces a total effect : oneness of effect or style **6** : a totality of related parts [Medieval French *unité*, from Latin *unitas*, from *unus* "one"]

synonyms UNITY, SOLIDARITY, UNION mean the character of a thing that is a whole composed of many parts. UNITY implies oneness gained by the interdependence of its varied parts ⟨the *unity* of a family⟩. SOLIDARITY implies such unity in a group, class, or community that enables it to show undivided strength as through opinion or influence ⟨working-class *solidarity*⟩. UNION implies a thorough integration of parts and their harmonious cooperation ⟨the *union* of the thirteen states into a nation⟩.

uni·va·lent \ˌyü-ni-ˈvā-lənt\ *adj* : having a chemical valence of one

¹uni·valve \ˈyü-ni-ˌvalv\ *adj* : having or consisting of one valve

²univalve *n* : a univalve mollusk shell or a mollusk having such a shell

uni·ver·sal \ˌyü-nə-ˈvər-səl\ *adj* **1** : including or covering all or a whole without limit or exception **2** : present or occurring everywhere or under all conditions ⟨*universal* cultural patterns⟩ **3 a** : embracing a major part or the greatest portion ⟨*universal* practices⟩ **b** : comprehensively broad and versatile ⟨a *universal* genius⟩ **4** : adapted or adjustable to meet varied requirements (as of use, shape, or size) ⟨a *universal* wrench⟩ — **uni·ver·sal·i·ty** \-ˌvər-ˈsal-ət-ē\ *n* — **uni·ver·sal·ly** \-ˈvər-sə-lē, -slē\ *adv* — **uni·ver·sal·ness** \-səl-nəs\ *n*

synonyms UNIVERSAL, GENERAL mean of all or of the whole. UNIVERSAL implies reference to each individual without exception in the category considered ⟨a *universal* franchise⟩. GENERAL implies reference to all or nearly all ⟨the theory has *general* but not *universal* acceptance⟩.

universal donor *n* : a person with blood group O blood which can be donated to any recipient

uni·ver·sal·ism \ˌyü-nə-ˈvər-sə-ˌliz-əm\ *n, often cap* **1** : a theological doctrine that all people will eventually be saved **2** : the principles and practices of a liberal Christian denomination founded in the 18th century to uphold belief in universal salvation and now united with Unitarianism — **uni·ver·sal·ist** \-sə-ləst, -sləst\ *n or adj, often cap*

uni·ver·sal·ize \-ˈvər-sə-ˌlīz\ *vt* : to make universal — **uni·ver·sal·iza·tion** \-ˌvər-sə-lə-ˈzā-shən\ *n*

universal joint *n* : a shaft coupling capable of transmitting rotation from one shaft to another not in a straight line with it

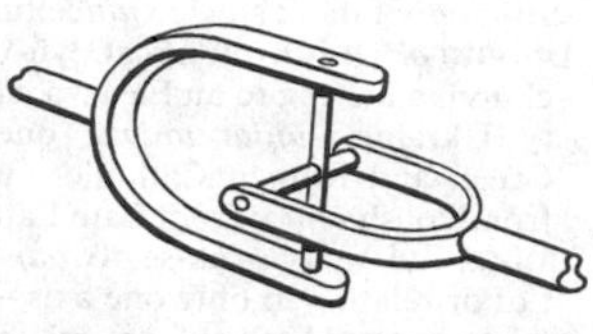

universal joint

Universal Product Code *n* : a combination of a bar code and numbers by which a scanner can identify a product and usually assign a price

universal recipient *n* : a person with blood group AB blood who can receive blood from any donor

universal resource locator *n* : URL

universal set *n* : a set that contains all the elements relating to a particular discussion or problem

uni·verse \ˈyü-nə-ˌvərs\ *n* **1** : the whole body of things and phenomena observed or postulated : COSMOS **2 a** : a systematic whole held to arise by and persist through the direct intervention of divine power **b** : the world of human experience **3 a** : MILKY WAY GALAXY **b** : an aggregate of stars comparable to the Milky Way galaxy **4** : UNIVERSAL SET [Latin *universum*, from *universus* "entire, whole," from *uni-* + *versus* "turned toward," from *vertere* "to turn"] ***synonyms*** see EARTH

uni·ver·si·ty \ˌyü-nə-ˈvər-sət-ē, -ˈvər-stē\ *n, pl* **-ties** : an institution of higher learning authorized to grant degrees in various special fields (as law, medicine, and theology) as well as in the arts and sciences

univ·o·cal \yü-ˈniv-ə-kəl\ *adj* : having one meaning only [Late Latin *univocus*, from Latin *uni-* + *voc-*, *vox* "voice"] — **univ·o·cal·ly** \-kə-lē, -klē\ *adv*

un·just \ˌən-ˈjəst, ˈən-\ *adj* : characterized by injustice : deficient in justice and fairness : WRONGFUL ⟨complained of *unjust* treatment by the court⟩ — **un·just·ly** *adv* — **un·just·ness** \-ˈjəst-nəs, -ˈjəs-\ *n*

un·kempt \-ˈkemt, -ˈkempt\ *adj* **1** : not combed ⟨*unkempt* hair⟩ **2** : being messy and untidy : DISHEVELED [*un-* + Middle English *kempt* "neat, combed," from *kemben* "to comb," from Old English *cemban*]

un·ken·nel \-ˈken-l\ *vt* **1 a** : to drive (as a fox) from a hiding place or den **b** : to free (dogs) from a kennel **2** : to bring into the open : DISCLOSE

un·kind \-ˈkīnd\ *adj* : lacking in kindness or sympathy : HARSH, CRUEL — **un·kind·ly** *adv* — **un·kind·ness** \-ˈkīnd-nəs, -ˈkīn-\ *n*

un·kind·ly \-ˈkīn-dlē\ *adj* : UNKIND — **un·kind·li·ness** *n*

un·know·able \ˌən-ˈnō-ə-bəl\ *adj* : not knowable; *esp* : lying beyond the limits of human experience or understanding

¹un·known \ˌən-ˈnōn, ˈən-\ *adj* : not known; *also* : having an unknown value ⟨find the *unknown* parts of the triangle⟩

²unknown *n* **1** : something that is unknown **2** : a symbol (as *x*, *y*, or *z*) representing a quantity whose value is not known ⟨an equation with two *unknowns*⟩

Unknown Soldier *n* : an unidentified soldier whose body is selected to receive national honors as a representative of all of the same nation who died in a war

un·lace \ˌən-ˈlās, ˈən-\ *vt* : to loose by undoing a lacing

un·lade \-ˈlād\ *vb* **1** : to take the load or cargo from **2** : to discharge cargo

un·lash \-ˈlash\ *vt* : to untie the lashing of : LOOSE, UNDO

un·latch \-ˈlach\ *vb* **1** : to open or loose by lifting the latch **2** : to become loosed or opened

un·law·ful \-ˈlȯ-fəl\ *adj* **1** : not lawful : contrary to law : ILLEGAL **2** : not morally right or conventional — **un·law·ful·ly** \-fə-lē, -flē\ *adv* — **un·law·ful·ness** \-fəl-nəs\ *n*

un·lay \-ˈlā\ *vb* **-laid** \-ˈlād\; **-lay·ing** **1** : to untwist the strands of (as a rope) **2** : UNTWIST 2

un·lead·ed \-ˈled-əd\ *adj* **1** : stripped of lead **2** : not mixed with lead or lead compounds ⟨*unleaded* fuel⟩

un·learn \-ˈlərn\ *vt* : to put out of one's knowledge or memory

un·learned \-ˈlər-nəd *for 1,* -ˈlərnd *for 2, 3*\ *adj* **1** : having little formal learning or education **2** : not learned by study : not known ⟨lessons *unlearned* by many⟩ **3** : not learned by previous experience ⟨breathing is *unlearned* behavior⟩ ***synonyms*** see IGNORANT

un·leash \-ˈlēsh\ *vt* : to free from or as if from a leash : let loose ⟨*unleash* a dog⟩ ⟨the storm *unleashed* its fury⟩

un·less \ən-ˈles, ˌən-, *in some contexts* ᵊn-, ᵊm-, ᵊng-\ *conj* : except on the condition that ⟨we will fail *unless* we work harder⟩ [Middle English *onlesse,* from *on + lesse* "less"]

un·let·tered \ˌən-ˈlet-ərd, ˈən-\ *adj* **1** : not educated **2** : ILLITERATE ***synonyms*** see IGNORANT

[1]**un·like** \ˌən-ˈlīk, ˈən-\ *adj* : not like: as **a** : marked by dissimilarity : DIFFERENT ⟨the children are quite *unlike*⟩ **b** : UNEQUAL ⟨*unlike* amounts⟩ — **un·like·ness** *n*

[2]**unlike** *prep* **1** : different from ⟨feeling completely *unlike* a hero⟩ **2** : not characteristic of ⟨it was *unlike* him to be late⟩ **3** : differently from ⟨behaving *unlike* your associates⟩

[3]**unlike** *conj* : in a manner that is different : not as

un·like·li·hood \ˌən-ˈlī-klē-ˌhu̇d, ˈən-\ *n* **1** : the quality or state of being unlikely **2** : something unlikely

un·like·ly \-ˈlī-klē\ *adj* **1** : not likely : IMPROBABLE **2** : likely to fail : UNPROMISING — **un·like·li·ness** *n*

un·lim·ber \ˌən-ˈlim-bər, ˈən-\ *vb* : to prepare for action [earlier *unlimber* "to ready a gun for use by removing it from the vehicle to which it is attached," from *limber* "2-wheeled vehicle to which a gun may be attached," from Middle English *lymour*]

un·lim·it·ed \-ˈlim-ət-əd\ *adj* **1** : lacking any controls : UNRESTRICTED ⟨*unlimited* access⟩ **2** : BOUNDLESS, INFINITE ⟨*unlimited* possibilities⟩ **3** : not restricted by exceptions ⟨*unlimited* and unconditional surrender⟩

un·link \-ˈlingk\ *vt* **1** : to unfasten the links of **2** : to separate by or as if by unlinking a chain

un·list·ed \-ˈlis-təd\ *adj* : not appearing upon a list: as **a** : not listed on an organized securities exchange ⟨*unlisted* stocks⟩ **b** : not in the telephone book ⟨an *unlisted* number⟩

un·live \-ˈliv\ *vt* : LIVE DOWN, ANNUL, REVERSE

un·load \-ˈlōd\ *vb* **1 a** : to take away or off : REMOVE ⟨*unload* cargo⟩ **b** : to take a load from ⟨*unload* a ship⟩; *also* : UNBURDEN ⟨*unload* your mind of worries⟩ **2** : to get rid of a load or burden ⟨the ship is *unloading* now⟩ **3** : to sell in volume : DUMP ⟨*unload* surplus goods⟩

un·lock \-ˈläk\ *vb* **1** : to open or unfasten through release of a lock ⟨*unlock* the door⟩ ⟨the chest won't *unlock*⟩ **2** : to free from restraints or restrictions : RELEASE ⟨*unlock* a flood of emotions⟩ **3** : DISCLOSE, REVEAL ⟨*unlock* the secrets of nature⟩

un·looked–for \-ˈlu̇kt-ˌfȯr\ *adj* : not foreseen : UNEXPECTED

un·loose \ˌən-ˈlüs, ˈən-\ *vt* **1** : to relax the strain of ⟨*unloose* a grip⟩ **2** : to release from or as if from restraints : set free **3** : to loosen the ties of : UNDO

un·loos·en \-ˈlüs-n\ *vt* : UNLOOSE

un·love·ly \-ˈləv-lē\ *adj* : not likable : DISAGREEABLE, UNPLEASANT — **un·love·li·ness** *n*

un·lucky \-ˈlək-ē\ *adj* **1** : marked by bad luck or failure ⟨an *unlucky* day⟩ **2** : likely to bring misfortune ⟨an *unlucky* number⟩ **3** : having or meeting with misfortune ⟨*unlucky* people⟩ **4** : producing dissatisfaction : REGRETTABLE — **un·luck·i·ly** \-ˈlək-ə-lē\ *adv* — **un·luck·i·ness** \-ˈlək-ē-nəs\ *n*

un·make \-ˈmāk\ *vt* **-made** \-ˈmād\; **-mak·ing** **1** : to cause to disappear : DESTROY **2** : to deprive of rank or office : DEPOSE **3** : to change the nature of

un·man \-ˈman\ *vt* : to deprive of courage, strength, or vigor

un·man·ly \ˌən-ˈman-lē\ *adj* : not manly: as **a** : being of weak character : COWARDLY **b** : EFFEMINATE 1 — **un·man·li·ness** \-nəs\ *n*

un·manned \ˌən-ˈmand, ˈən-\ *adj* : having no crew aboard

un·man·nered \-ˈman-ərd\ *adj* **1** : lacking good manners : RUDE **2** : UNAFFECTED 2 — **un·man·nered·ly** *adv*

[1]**un·man·ner·ly** \-ˈman-ər-lē\ *adv* : in an unmannerly fashion

[2]**unmannerly** *adj* : RUDE 3, IMPOLITE — **un·man·ner·li·ness** *n*

un·mar·ried \ˌən-ˈmar-ēd\ *adj* : not married: **a** : not now or previously married **b** : being divorced or widowed

un·mask \ˌən-ˈmask, ˈən-\ *vb* **1** : to strip of a mask or disguise : EXPOSE ⟨*unmask* a traitor⟩ **2** : to take off one's own disguise

un·mean·ing \-ˈmē-ning\ *adj* : having no meaning

un·meant \-ˈment\ *adj* : not meant : UNINTENTIONAL

un·meet \-ˈmēt\ *adj* : not meet : UNSUITABLE, IMPROPER

un·men·tion·able \-ˈmench-nə-bəl, -ə-nə-\ *adj* : not fit or proper to be talked about — **unmentionable** *n*

un·mer·ci·ful \ˌən-ˈmər-si-fəl, ˈən-\ *adj* : not merciful : MERCILESS, CRUEL — **un·mer·ci·ful·ly** \-fə-lē, -flē\ *adv*

un·mis·tak·able \ˌən-mə-ˈstā-kə-bəl\ *adj* : not capable of being mistaken or misunderstood : CLEAR, OBVIOUS — **un·mis·tak·ably** \-blē\ *adv*

un·mit·i·gat·ed \ˌən-ˈmit-ə-ˌgāt-əd, ˈən-\ *adj* **1** : not softened or lessened **2** : THOROUGH, UTTER ⟨an *unmitigated* liar⟩ ⟨*unmitigated* impudence⟩ — **un·mit·i·gat·ed·ly** *adv*

un·moor \-ˈmu̇r\ *vb* **1** : to loose from or as if from moorings **2** : to cast off moorings

un·mor·al \-ˈmȯr-əl, -ˈmär-\ *adj* : having no moral quality or relation : AMORAL — **un·mor·al·ly** \-ə-lē\ *adv*

un·muf·fle \-ˈməf-əl\ *vt* : to free from something that muffles

un·muz·zle \-ˈməz-əl\ *vt* : to remove a muzzle from

un·my·elin·at·ed \-ˈmī-ə-lə-ˌnāt-əd\ *adj* : lacking a myelin sheath ⟨*unmyelinated* axons⟩

un·nail \ˌən-ˈnāl, ˈən-\ *vt* : to unfasten by removing nails

un·nat·u·ral \ˌən-ˈnach-rəl, ˈən-, -ə-rəl\ *adj* **1** : not being in accordance with nature or consistent with a normal course of events **2 a** : not according with normal feelings or behavior : PERVERSE, ABNORMAL **b** : ARTIFICIAL ⟨their heartiness was forced and *unnatural*⟩ **c** : STRANGE, IRREGULAR ⟨an *unnatural* alliance⟩ — **un·nat·u·ral·ly** \-ˈnach-rə-lē, -ə-rə-, -ˈnach-ər-lē\ *adv* — **un·nat·u·ral·ness** \-ˈnach-rəl-nəs, -ə-rəl-\ *n*

un·nec·es·sar·i·ly \ˌən-ˌnes-ə-ˈser-ə-lē\ *adv* **1** : not by necessity ⟨spent money *unnecessarily*⟩ **2** : to an unnecessary degree ⟨*unnecessarily* harsh⟩

un·nec·es·sary \ˌən-ˈnes-ə-ˌser-ē, ˈən-\ *adj* : not necessary

un·nerve \ˌən-ˈnərv, ˈən-\ *vt* : to deprive of nerve, courage, or self-control

un·nil·hex·i·um \ˌyün-l-ˈhek-sē-əm\ *n* : SEABORGIUM

un·nil·pen·ti·um \-ˌpent-ē-əm\ *n* : DUBNIUM

un·nil·qua·di·um \-ˌkwäd-ē-əm\ *n* : RUTHERFORDIUM

un·num·bered \ˌən-ˈnəm-bərd, ˈən-\ *adj* **1** : INNUMERABLE ⟨*unnumbered* stars⟩ **2** : not having an identifying number ⟨*unnumbered* pages⟩

un·ob·tru·sive \ˌən-əb-ˈtrü-siv, -ziv\ *adj* : not obtrusive : not blatant or aggressive : INCONSPICUOUS — **un·ob·tru·sive·ly** *adv* — **un·ob·tru·sive·ness** *n*

un·oc·cu·pied \ˌən-ˈäk-yə-ˌpīd, ˈən-\ *adj* **1** : not busy : UNEMPLOYED **2** : not occupied : EMPTY

un·or·ga·nized \ˌən-ˈȯr-gə-ˌnīzd, ˈən-\ *adj* : not subjected to organization: as **a** : not formed or brought into an integrated or ordered whole **b** : not organized into unions

un·pack \ˌən-ˈpak, ˈən-\ *vb* **1** : to separate and remove things packed **2** : to open and remove the contents of

un·paid \ˌən-ˈpād\ *adj* **1** : not paid ⟨an *unpaid* volunteer⟩ **2** : not paying a salary ⟨an *unpaid* position⟩

un·paired \-ˈpaərd, -ˈpeərd\ *adj* **1** : not paired; *esp* : not matched or mated **2** : situated in the median plane of the body ⟨an *unpaired* fin⟩

un·par·al·leled \-ˈpar-ə-ˌleld\ *adj* : having no parallel; *esp* : having no equal or match ⟨an *unparalleled* talent for golf⟩

un·par·lia·men·ta·ry \ˌən-ˌpär-lə-ˈment-ə-rē, -ˌpärl-yə-, -ˈmen-trē\ *adj* : contrary to parliamentary practice or rules

un·peg \ˌən-ˈpeg, ˈən-\ *vt* : to open by or as if by removing a peg

un·peo·ple \ˌən-ˈpē-pəl, ˈən-\ *vt* : DEPOPULATE

un·pile \-ˈpīl\ *vb* : to separate or become separated from a pile

un·pin \-ˈpin\ *vt* : to undo by or as if by removing a pin

\ə\ **abut**	\au̇\ **out**	\i\ **tip**	\ȯ\ **saw**	\u̇\ **foot**
\ər\ **further**	\ch\ **chin**	\ī\ **life**	\ȯi\ **coin**	\y\ **yet**
\a\ **mat**	\e\ **pet**	\j\ **job**	\th\ **thin**	\yü\ **few**
\ā\ **take**	\ē\ **easy**	\ng\ **sing**	\t͟h\ **this**	\yu̇\ **cure**
\ä\ **cot, cart**	\g\ **go**	\ō\ **bone**	\ü\ **food**	\zh\ **vision**

un·pleas·ant \ˌən-ˈplez-ᵊnt\ *adj* : not pleasant : not amiable or agreeable — **un·pleas·ant·ly** *adv*

un·pleas·ant·ness \-ˈplez-ᵊnt-nəs\ *n* **1** : the quality or state of being unpleasant **2** : an unpleasant situation, experience, or event

un·plug \ˌən-ˈpləg\ *vt* **1 a** : to take a plug out of **b** : to remove an obstruction from **2 a** : to remove (as an electric plug) from a socket or receptacle **b** : to disconnect from an electric circuit by removing a plug ⟨*unplug* the refrigerator⟩

un·plugged \ˌən-ˈpləgd\ *adj* : ACOUSTIC 2 ⟨an *unplugged* performance⟩

un·plumbed \ˌən-ˈpləmd, ˈən-\ *adj* **1** : not tested or measured with a plumb line **2** : not thoroughly explored ⟨*unplumbed* possibilities⟩

un·po·lit·i·cal \ˌən-pə-ˈlit-i-kəl\ *adj* : not interested or engaged in politics

un·pop·u·lar \ˌən-ˈpäp-yə-lər, ˈən-\ *adj* : not popular : viewed or received unfavorably : disliked by many people — **un·pop·u·lar·i·ty** \ˌən-ˌpäp-yə-ˈlar-ət-ē\ *n*

un·prec·e·dent·ed \ˌən-ˈpres-ə-ˌdent-əd, ˈən-\ *adj* : having no precedent : NOVEL — **un·prec·e·dent·ed·ly** *adv*

un·prej·u·diced \ˌən-ˈprej-əd-əst, ˈən-\ *adj* : not prejudiced : IMPARTIAL

un·pre·ten·tious \ˌən-pri-ˈten-chəs\ *adj* : not pretentious : not showy or pompous : SIMPLE, MODEST — **un·pre·ten·tious·ly** *adv* — **un·pre·ten·tious·ness** *n*

un·prin·ci·pled \ˌən-ˈprin-sə-pəld, ˈən-, -sə-bəld, -spəld\ *adj* : lacking moral principles : UNSCRUPULOUS

un·print·able \-ˈprint-ə-bəl\ *adj* : unfit to be printed

un·pro·fes·sion·al \ˌən-prə-ˈfesh-nəl, ˈən-, -ən-l\ *adj* : not professional; *esp* : not conforming to the standards of a profession — **un·pro·fes·sion·al·ly** \-ē\ *adv*

un·prof·it·able \ˌən-ˈpräf-ət-ə-bəl, ˈən-, -ˈpräf-tə-bəl\ *adj* : producing no profit, gain, or result — **un·prof·it·able·ness** *n* — **un·prof·it·ably** \-blē\ *adv*

un·prom·is·ing \-ˈpräm-ə-sing\ *adj* : appearing unlikely to prove worthwhile or result favorably ⟨won despite their *unpromising* start⟩ — **un·prom·is·ing·ly** \-sing-lē\ *adv*

un·pro·tect·ed \ˌən-prə-ˈtek-təd\ *adj* **1** : lacking protection or defense ⟨*unprotected* troops⟩ ⟨skin *unprotected* from the sun's rays⟩ **2** : performed without the use of birth control to prevent pregnancy; *also* : performed without the use of a condom to prevent the spread of a sexually transmitted disease ⟨*unprotected* sex⟩

un·pub·lish·able \ˌən-ˈpə-blish-ə-bəl\ *adj* : UNPRINTABLE

un·qual·i·fied \-ˈkwäl-ə-ˌfīd\ *adj* **1** : not fit : lacking necessary qualifications **2** : not modified or restricted by reservations : COMPLETE ⟨an *unqualified* denial⟩ — **un·qual·i·fied·ly** \-ˌfī-əd-lē, -ˌfīd-\ *adv*

un·ques·tion·able \-ˈkwes-chə-nə-bəl, -ˈkwesh-, *rapid* -ˈkwesh-nə-\ *adj* **1** : acknowledged as beyond question or doubt ⟨*unquestionable* authority⟩ **2** : not questionable : INDISPUTABLE ⟨*unquestionable* evidence⟩ — **un·ques·tion·ably** \-blē\ *adv*

un·ques·tion·ing \-ˈkwes-chə-ning, -ˈkwesh-\ *adj* : not questioning : not expressing or marked by doubt or hesitation ⟨*unquestioning* loyalty⟩ — **un·ques·tion·ing·ly** \-ning-lē\ *adv*

un·qui·et \-ˈkwī-ət\ *adj* **1** : not quiet : TURBULENT **2** : physically, emotionally, or mentally restless : UNEASY — **un·qui·et·ly** *adv* — **un·qui·et·ness** *n*

un·quote \ˈən-ˌkwōt\ *n* — used orally to indicate the end of a direct quotation

un·rav·el \ˌən-ˈrav-əl, ˈən-\ *vb* **1** : to separate the threads of : DISENTANGLE ⟨*unravel* a snarl⟩ **2** : SOLVE ⟨*unravel* a mystery⟩ **3** : to become unraveled

un·read \-ˈred\ *adj* **1** : not read ⟨an *unread* book⟩ **2** : not well informed through reading ⟨*unread* in political science⟩

un·read·able \-ˈrēd-ə-bəl\ *adj* **1** : too dull or unattractive to read ⟨an *unreadable* dissertation⟩ **2** : not legible or decipherable : ILLEGIBLE — **un·read·abil·i·ty** \ˌən-ˌrēd-ə-ˈbil-ət-ē\ *n*

synonyms UNREADABLE, ILLEGIBLE mean difficult or impossible to read. ILLEGIBLE usually implies a physical impossibility of making out letters or signs ⟨*illegible* handwriting⟩. UNREADABLE more often implies a psychological impossibility of continuing to read with interest or pleasure ⟨a novel now thought *unreadable*⟩.

un·ready \ˌən-ˈred-ē, ˈən-\ *adj* : not ready or qualified ⟨*unready* to deal with a crisis⟩ — **un·read·i·ness** *n*

un·re·al \-ˈri-əl, -ˈril, -ˈrē-əl, -ˈrēl\ *adj* : lacking in reality, substance, or genuineness : ILLUSORY; *also* : FANTASTIC 2

un·re·al·is·tic \ˈən-ˌri-ə-ˈlis-tik, -ˌrē-ə-\ *adj* : not realistic : inappropriate to reality or fact — **un·re·al·is·ti·cal·ly** \-ti-kə-lē, -klē\ *adv*

un·re·al·i·ty \ˌən-rē-ˈal-ət-ē\ *n* **1 a** : the quality or state of being unreal **b** : something unreal, insubstantial, or visionary **2** : inability to deal with reality

un·rea·son \ˌən-ˈrēz-ᵊn, ˈən-\ *n* : the absence of reason or sanity

un·rea·son·able \-ˈrēz-nə-bəl, -ᵊn-ə-bəl\ *adj* **1 a** : not governed by or acting according to reason ⟨*unreasonable* people⟩ **b** : not conformable to reason : ABSURD ⟨*unreasonable* arguments⟩ **2** : exceeding the bounds of reason or moderation ⟨*unreasonable* suspicion⟩ ***synonyms*** see IRRATIONAL — **un·rea·son·able·ness** *n* — **un·rea·son·ably** \-blē\ *adv*

un·rea·soned \ˌən-ˈrēz-ᵊnd\ *adj* : not founded on reason or reasoning ⟨*unreasoned* fears⟩ ⟨an *unreasoned* decision⟩

un·rea·son·ing \-ˈrēz-ning, -ᵊn-ing\ *adj* : not reasoning; *esp* : not using or showing the use of reason as a guide or control ⟨*unreasoning* fear⟩ ⟨*unreasoning* beasts⟩ — **un·rea·son·ing·ly** *adv*

un·re·con·struct·ed \ˌən-ˌrē-kən-ˈstrək-təd\ *adj* : not reconciled to some political, economic, or social change; *esp* : holding stubbornly to principles, beliefs, or views that are held to be outmoded

un·reel \ˌən-ˈrēl, ˈən-\ *vb* : to unwind from or as if from a reel

un·re·gen·er·ate \ˌən-ri-ˈjen-rət, -ə-rət\ *adj* **1** : not spiritually regenerate ⟨*unregenerate* people⟩ **2 a** : not reformed : UNRECONSTRUCTED ⟨*unregenerate* opponents⟩ **b** : OBSTINATE 1, STUBBORN — **un·re·gen·er·ate·ly** *adv*

un·re·lent·ing \ˌən-ri-ˈlent-ing\ *adj* **1** : not softening or yielding in determination : HARD, STERN **2** : not letting up or weakening in vigor or pace — **un·re·lent·ing·ly** \-ing-lē\ *adv*

un·re·mit·ting \ˌən-ri-ˈmit-ing\ *adj* : not stopping : UNCEASING ⟨hard *unremitting* labor⟩ **un·re·mit·ting·ly** \-ing-lē\ *adv*

un·re·serve \ˌən-ri-ˈzərv\ *n* : absence of reserve : FRANKNESS

un·re·served \ˌən-ri-ˈzərvd\ *adj* **1** : not held in reserve : not kept back **2** : having or showing no reserve in manner or speech — **un·re·serv·ed·ly** \-ˈzər-vəd-lē\ *adv* — **un·re·served·ness** \-ˈzər-vəd-nəs, -ˈzərvd-nəs, -ˈzərv-nəs\ *n*

un·re·spon·sive \ˌən-ri-ˈspän-siv\ *adj* : not responsive — **un·re·spon·sive·ly** *adv* — **un·re·spon·sive·ness** *n*

un·rest \ˌən-ˈrest, ˈən-\ *n* : a disturbed or uneasy state

un·re·strained \ˌən-ri-ˈstrānd\ *adj* **1** : not restrained : IMMODERATE **2** : free of constraint : SPONTANEOUS — **un·re·strain·ed·ly** \-ˈstrā-nəd-lē\ *adv*

un·re·straint \-ˈstrānt\ *n* : lack of restraint

un·rid·dle \ˌən-ˈrid-ᵊl, ˈən-\ *vt* : to find the explanation of : SOLVE

un·righ·teous \-ˈrī-chəs\ *adj* **1** : not righteous : SINFUL, WICKED **2** : UNJUST, UNCALLED-FOR ⟨*unrighteous* interference⟩ — **un·righ·teous·ly** *adv* — **un·righ·teous·ness** *n*

un·ripe \-ˈrīp\ *adj* **1** : not ripe : IMMATURE ⟨*unripe* fruit⟩ **2** : not ready : UNPREPARED ⟨*unripe* plans⟩ — **un·ripe·ness** *n*

un·ri·valed *or* **un·ri·valled** \-ˈrī-vəld\ *adj* : having no rival : INCOMPARABLE, UNEQUALED ⟨*unrivaled* greatness⟩

un·robe \ˌən-ˈrōb, ˈən-\ *vb* : DISROBE, UNDRESS

un·roll \-ˈrōl\ *vb* **1** : to unwind a roll of : open out ⟨*unroll* a carpet⟩ **2** : to spread out like a scroll for reading or inspection : UNFOLD, REVEAL ⟨snowcapped mountains *unrolled* before their eyes⟩

un·roof \-ˈrüf, -ˈrůf\ *vt* : to strip off the roof or covering of

un·round \-ˈraůnd\ *vt* : to pronounce (a sound) without or with decreased rounding of the lips — **un·round·ed** \-ˈraůn-dəd\ *adj*

un·ruf·fled \-ˈrəf-əld\ *adj* **1** : not upset or agitated **2** : not ruffled : SMOOTH ⟨*unruffled* water⟩

un·ruly \ˌən-ˈrü-lē, ˈən-\ *adj* **un·rul·i·er; -est** : not yielding readily to rule or restraint : hard to handle or manage ⟨an *unruly* temper⟩ ⟨an *unruly* horse⟩ — **un·rul·i·ness** *n*

synonyms UNRULY, UNGOVERNABLE, REFRACTORY, RECALCITRANT mean not submissive to control. UNRULY implies lack of discipline or incapacity for discipline and often connotes waywardness or turbulence of behavior ⟨*unruly* children⟩. UNGOVERNABLE implies either an escape from control or guidance or a state of being unsubdued and incapable of controlling the self or being controlled by others ⟨*ungovernable* rage⟩. REFRACTORY stresses resistance to attempts to manage or to mold ⟨special schools for *refractory* children⟩. RECALCITRANT suggests determined resistance to or defiance of authority ⟨sabotage by a *recalcitrant* populace⟩.

un·sad·dle \ˌən-ˈsad-ᵊl, ˈən-\ *vb* **1 a** : to remove the saddle from a horse **b** : to remove a saddle from **2** : UNHORSE

un•sat•u•rate \-'sach-rət, -ə-rət\ *n* **:** an unsaturated chemical compound

un•sat•u•rat•ed \-'sach-ə-ˌrāt-əd\ *adj* **1 :** capable of absorbing or dissolving more of something ⟨an *unsaturated* salt solution⟩ **2 :** able to form a new product by direct chemical combination with another substance; *esp* **:** containing double or triple bonds between carbon atoms ⟨an *unsaturated* fat⟩ — **un•sat•u•ra•tion** \ˌən-ˌsach-ə-'rā-shən\ *n*

un•saved \ˌən-'sāvd, 'ən-\ *adj* **:** not saved; *esp* **:** not rescued from eternal punishment

un•sa•vory \-'sāv-rē, -ə-rē\ *adj* **1 :** having little or no taste **2 :** having a bad taste or smell **3 :** morally offensive ⟨an *unsavory* character⟩ — **un•sa•vor•i•ly** \-'sāv-rə-lē, -ə-rə-\ *adv*

un•say \-'sā\ *vt* **-said** \-'sed\; **-say•ing** \-'sā-ing\ **:** to take back (something said) **:** RETRACT, WITHDRAW

un•scathed \ˌən-'skāthd, 'ən-\ *adj* **:** wholly unharmed **:** not injured

un•schooled \-'sküld\ *adj* **:** not schooled **:** UNTAUGHT

un•sci•en•tif•ic \ˌən-ˌsī-ən-'tif-ik\ *adj* **:** not scientific: as **a :** not according with the principles and methods of science ⟨an *unscientific* poll⟩ **b :** not showing scientific knowledge or familiarity with scientific methods ⟨an *unscientific* explanation⟩ — **un•sci•en•tif•i•cal•ly** \-'tif-i-kə-lē, -klē\ *adv*

un•scram•ble \ˌən-'skram-bəl, 'ən-\ *vt* **1 :** to separate into original components **:** RESOLVE, CLARIFY **2 :** to restore (as a radio message) to intelligible form

un•screw \-'skrü\ *vb* **1 :** to remove the screws from **2 :** to loosen or withdraw by turning

un•scru•pu•lous \-'skrü-pyə-ləs\ *adj* **:** UNPRINCIPLED — **un•scru•pu•lous•ly** *adv* — **un•scru•pu•lous•ness** *n*

un•seal \-'sēl\ *vt* **:** to break or remove the seal of **:** OPEN

un•seam \-'sēm\ *vt* **:** to open the seams of

un•search•able \-'sər-chə-bəl\ *adj* **:** impossible to explore or examine — **un•search•ably** \-blē\ *adv*

un•sea•son•able \-'sēz-nə-bəl, -'sēz-n-ə-\ *adj* **1 :** happening or coming at the wrong time **:** UNTIMELY ⟨an *unseasonable* visit⟩ **2 :** not normal for the season of the year ⟨*unseasonable* weather⟩ — **un•sea•son•able•ness** *n* — **un•sea•son•ably** \-blē\ *adv*

un•seat \ˌən-'sēt, 'ən-\ *vt* **1 :** to dislodge from a seat especially on horseback **2 :** to dislodge from a place or position; *esp* **:** to remove from political office

[1]**un•seem•ly** \-'sēm-lē\ *adj* **:** not suitable or proper **:** UNBECOMING ⟨*unseemly* bickering in public⟩ ***synonyms*** see INDECOROUS

[2]**unseemly** *adv* **:** in an unseemly manner

un•seen \-'sēn\ *adj* **:** not seen or perceived **:** INVISIBLE

un•seg•re•gat•ed \-'seg-ri-ˌgāt-əd\ *adj* **:** not segregated; *esp* **:** free from racial segregation

un•self•ish \-'sel-fish\ *adj* **:** not selfish **:** GENEROUS — **un•self•ish•ly** *adv* — **un•self•ish•ness** *n*

un•set•tle \ˌən-'set-l, 'ən-\ *vb* **1 :** to move or loosen from a settled state **2 :** to disturb or trouble mentally or emotionally ⟨new situations *unsettle* some people⟩

un•set•tled \-'set-ld\ *adj* **1 :** VARIABLE 1a ⟨*unsettled* weather⟩ **2 :** not calm or tranquil ⟨*unsettled* waters⟩ ⟨an *unsettled* economy⟩ **3 :** not decided in mind ⟨*unsettled* about what to do⟩ **4 :** not paid ⟨an *unsettled* account⟩; *also* **:** not disposed of according to law ⟨an *unsettled* estate⟩ **5 :** not occupied by settlers ⟨an *unsettled* region⟩

un•sew \ˌən-'sō, 'ən-\ *vt* **-sewed; -sewn** \-'sōn\ *or* **-sewed; -sew•ing :** to undo the sewing of

un•sex \-'seks\ *vt* **:** to deprive of sex or of qualities typical of one's sex

un•shack•le \-'shak-əl\ *vt* **:** to free from shackles

un•shaped \-'shāpt\ *adj* **:** not shaped: as **a :** not dressed or finished to final form ⟨an *unshaped* timber⟩ **b :** imperfect in form or formulation ⟨*unshaped* ideas⟩

un•shap•en \-'shā-pən\ *adj* **:** UNSHAPED [Middle English, from [1]*un-* + *shapen,* past participle of *shapen* "to shape"]

un•sheathe \-'shēth\ *vt* **:** to draw from or as if from a sheath or scabbard ⟨*unsheathe* a sword⟩

un•ship \ˌən-'ship, 'ən-\ *vb* **1 :** to remove from a ship **2 :** to remove or become removed from position ⟨*unship* an oar⟩

un•shod \-'shäd\ *adj* **:** lacking shoes

un•sight•ly \-'sīt-lē\ *adj* **:** unpleasant to the sight **:** UGLY ⟨an *unsightly* scar⟩ — **un•sight•li•ness** *n*

un•skilled \-'skild\ *adj* **1 :** not skilled; *esp* **:** not skilled in a specified branch of work **:** lacking technical training ⟨*unskilled* workers⟩ **2 :** not requiring skill ⟨*unskilled* jobs⟩ **3 :** marked by lack of skill ⟨*unskilled* writing⟩

un•skill•ful \-'skil-fəl\ *adj* **:** lacking in skill or proficiency — **un•skill•ful•ly** \-fə-lē\ *adv* — **un•skill•ful•ness** *n*

un•sling \-'sling\ *vt* **-slung** \-'sləng\; **-sling•ing** \-'sling-ing\ **:** to remove from being slung

un•snap \-'snap\ *vt* **:** to loosen or free by or as if by undoing a snap

un•snarl \-'snärl\ *vt* **:** to straighten out a snarl in

un•so•cia•bil•i•ty \ˌən-ˌsō-shə-'bil-ət-ē\ *n* **:** the quality or state of being unsociable

un•so•cia•ble \ˌən-'sō-shə-bəl, 'ən-\ *adj* **1 :** having or showing a preference for avoiding society or conversation **:** SOLITARY, RESERVED **2 :** not conducive to sociability — **un•so•cia•ble•ness** *n* — **un•so•cia•bly** \-blē\ *adv*

un•so•cial \-'sō-shəl\ *adj* **:** having or showing a lack of desire for society or close association — **un•so•cial•ly** \-'sōsh-lē, -ə-lē\ *adv*

un•so•phis•ti•cat•ed \ˌən-sə-'fis-tə-ˌkāt-əd\ *adj* **:** not sophisticated: as **a :** not changed or corrupted **:** GENUINE **b (1) :** not worldly-wise **:** lacking sophistication **(2) :** lacking adornment or complexity of structure **:** PLAIN, SIMPLE

un•so•phis•ti•ca•tion \-ˌfis-tə-'kā-shən\ *n* **:** lack of sophistication

un•sought \ˌən-'sȯt, 'ən-\ *adj* **:** not sought **:** not searched for or asked for ⟨*unsought* honors⟩

un•sound \-'sau̇nd\ *adj* **:** not sound: as **a :** not healthy or whole ⟨an *unsound* horse⟩ **b :** not mentally normal **:** not wholly sane ⟨of *unsound* mind⟩ **c :** not firmly made, placed, or fixed ⟨structurally *unsound*⟩ **d :** not valid or true ⟨*unsound* beliefs⟩ — **un•sound•ly** *adv* — **un•sound•ness** \-'sau̇nd-nəs, -'sau̇n-\ *n*

un•spar•ing \-'spaər-ing, -'speər-\ *adj* **1 :** not merciful **:** HARD, RUTHLESS ⟨an *unsparing* satire⟩ **2 :** not frugal **:** LIBERAL ⟨*unsparing* generosity⟩ — **un•spar•ing•ly** \-ing-lē\ *adv*

un•speak•able \-'spē-kə-bəl\ *adj* **1 :** impossible to express in words ⟨*unspeakable* beauty⟩ **2 :** extremely bad ⟨*unspeakable* conduct⟩ — **un•speak•ably** \-blē\ *adv*

un•spot•ted \ˌən-'spät-əd, 'ən-\ *adj* **1 :** not spotted **:** free from spot or stain **2 :** free from moral stain ⟨an *unspotted* reputation⟩

un•sprung \-'sprəng\ *adj* **:** not sprung; *esp* **:** not equipped with springs

un•sta•ble \-'stā-bəl\ *adj* **:** not stable **:** not firm or fixed **:** not constant: as **a :** not steady in action or movement **:** IRREGULAR ⟨an *unstable* pulse⟩ **b :** wavering in purpose or intent ⟨*unstable* beliefs⟩ **c :** lacking steadiness **:** apt to move, sway, or fall ⟨an *unstable* tower⟩ **d (1) :** likely to change ⟨*unstable* weather⟩ **(2) :** readily changing in chemical composition or physical state or properties ⟨an *unstable* emulsion⟩; *esp* **:** tending to decompose spontaneously ⟨an *unstable* atomic nucleus⟩ **e :** characterized by lack of emotional control ⟨an *unstable* person⟩ — **un•sta•ble•ness** *n* — **un•sta•bly** \-bə-lē, -blē\ *adv*

un•steady \-'sted-ē\ *adj* **:** lacking in stability or regularity **:** UNSTABLE — **un•stead•i•ly** \-'sted-l-ē\ *adv* — **un•stead•i•ness** \-'sted-ē-nəs\ *n*

un•stick \-'stik\ *vt* **-stuck** \-'stək\; **-stick•ing :** to release from being stuck or bound

un•stint•ing \ˌən-'stint-ing\ *adj* **:** not restricting or holding back **:** giving or being given freely or generously ⟨*unstinting* praise⟩ — **un•stint•ing•ly** *adv*

un•stop \-'stäp\ *vt* **1 :** to free from an obstruction **:** OPEN ⟨*unstop* a drain⟩ **2 :** to remove a stopper from

un•strap \-'strap\ *vt* **:** to remove or loose a strap from

un•stressed \-'strest\ *adj* **1 :** not bearing a stress or accent ⟨*unstressed* syllables⟩ **2 :** not stressed

un•string \-'string\ *vt* **-strung** \-'strəng\; **-string•ing** \-'string-ing\ **1 :** to loosen or remove the strings of **2 :** to remove from a string **3 :** to make weak, disordered, or unstable

un•stud•ied \-'stəd-ēd\ *adj* **1 :** not acquired by study **2 :** not planned with a certain effect in mind **:** NATURAL ⟨moves with *unstudied* grace⟩

un•sub•stan•tial \ˌən-səb-'stan-chəl\ *adj* **:** lacking substance,

\ə\ abut	\au̇\ out	\i\ tip	\ȯ\ saw	\u̇\ foot
\ər\ further	\ch\ chin	\ī\ life	\ȯi\ coin	\y\ yet
\a\ mat	\e\ pet	\j\ job	\th\ thin	\yü\ few
\ā\ take	\ē\ easy	\ng\ sing	\th\ this	\yu̇\ cure
\ä\ cot, cart	\g\ go	\ō\ bone	\ü\ food	\zh\ vision

firmness, or strength — **un·sub·stan·ti·al·i·ty** \-ˌstan-chē-ˈal-ət-ē\ *n* — **un·sub·stan·tial·ly** \-ˈstanch-lē, -ə-lē\ *adv*
un·suc·cess·ful \ˌən-sək-ˈses-fəl\ *adj* : not meeting with or producing success — **un·suc·cess·ful·ly** \-fə-lē\ *adv*
un·suit·able \ˌən-ˈsüt-ə-bəl, ˈən-\ *adj* : not fitting : UNBECOMING, INAPPROPRIATE — **un·suit·abil·i·ty** \-ˌsüt-ə-ˈbil-ət-ē\ *n* — **un·suit·ably** \-ˈsüt-ə-blē\ *adv*
un·sung \-ˈsəng\ *adj* **1** : not sung **2** : not celebrated or praised (as in song or verse) ⟨*unsung* heroes⟩
un·swathe \-ˈswāth, -ˈswȯth, -ˈswāth\ *vt* : to free from something that swathes
un·swear \-ˈswaər, -ˈsweər\ *vb* **-swore** \-ˈswōər, -ˈswȯər\; **-sworn** \-ˈswōrn -ˈswȯrn\; **-swear·ing** *archaic* : RECANT, RETRACT
un·swerv·ing \-ˈswər-ving\ *adj* **1** : not swerving or turning aside **2** : STEADY ⟨*unswerving* loyalty⟩
un·sym·met·ri·cal \ˌən-sə-ˈme-tri-kəl\ *adj* : not symmetrical : ASYMMETRIC — **un·sym·met·ri·cal·ly** \-tri-kə-lē, -klē\ *adv*
un·tan·gle \ˌən-ˈtang-gəl, ˈən-\ *vt* **1** : to remove a tangle from ⟨*untangle* a knot⟩ **2** : to straighten (as something complex or confused) out : RESOLVE ⟨*untangle* a mystery⟩ ***synonyms*** see EXTRICATE
un·tapped \ˌən-ˈtapt\ *adj* **1** : not subjected to tapping ⟨an *untapped* keg⟩ **2** : not drawn upon or used ⟨as yet *untapped* markets⟩
un·taught \-ˈtȯt\ *adj* **1** : not instructed or trained : IGNORANT **2** : NATURAL, SPONTANEOUS ⟨*untaught* kindness⟩
un·teth·er \-ˈteth-ər\ *vt* : to free from a tether
un·think·able \-ˈthing-kə-bəl\ *adj* : not to be thought of or considered as possible ⟨*unthinkable* cruelty⟩ — **un·think·ably** \-blē\ *adv*
un·think·ing \-ˈthing-king\ *adj* **1** : not taking thought : HEEDLESS, UNMINDFUL ⟨*unthinking* onlookers⟩ **2** : not indicating thought or reflection ⟨an *unthinking* decision⟩ **3** : not having the power of thought — **un·think·ing·ly** \-king-lē\ *adv*
un·thought–of \-ˈthȯt-ˌəv, -ˌäv\ *adj* : not thought of : not considered : not imagined
un·thread \-ˈthred\ *vt* **1** : to draw or take out a thread from **2** : to loosen the threads or connections of **3** : to make one's way through ⟨*unthread* a maze⟩
un·throne \-ˈthrōn\ *vt* : to remove from or as if from a throne
un·ti·dy \-ˈtīd-ē\ *adj* **1** : not neat : CARELESS, SLOVENLY **2 a** : not neatly organized or carried out **b** : tending to cause a lack of neatness — **un·ti·di·ly** \-ˈtīd-l-ē\ *adv* — **un·ti·di·ness** \-ˈtīd-ē-nəs\ *n*
un·tie \-ˈtī\ *vb* **-tied; -ty·ing** *or* **-tie·ing** **1** : to free from something that ties, fastens, or restrains : UNBIND ⟨*untie* a horse⟩ **2 a** : to disengage the knotted parts of ⟨*untied* her shoe⟩ **b** : DISENTANGLE, RESOLVE ⟨*untie* a traffic jam⟩ **3** : to become loosened or unbound ⟨the strings *untied* easily⟩
[1]**un·til** \ən-ˌtil, -tl, -ˌtel, ˌən-, in some contexts ᵊn-, ᵊm-, ᵊng-\ *prep* **1** : up to the time of ⟨stayed *until* morning⟩ **2** : BEFORE 2 ⟨doesn't open *until* ten⟩ [Middle English, from *un-* "to, until" + *til* "till"]
[2]**until** *conj* : up to the time that ⟨played *until* it got dark⟩ ⟨ran *until* I was breathless⟩
[1]**un·time·ly** \ˌən-ˈtīm-lē, ˈən-\ *adv* **1** : at an inopportune time : UNSEASONABLY **2** : too soon
[2]**untimely** *adj* **1** : occurring or done before the due, natural, or proper time : too early : PREMATURE ⟨*untimely* death⟩ **2** : UNSEASONABLE 1 ⟨an *untimely* joke⟩ ⟨*untimely* frost⟩ — **un·time·li·ness** *n*
un·ti·tled \-ˈtīt-ld\ *adj* **1** : having no title especially of nobility **2** : not named ⟨an *untitled* painting⟩
un·to \ˈən-tə, -tü\ *prep* : TO [Middle English, from *un-* "to, until" + *to*]
un·told \ˌən-ˈtōld, ˈən-\ *adj* **1** : not told : not revealed ⟨*untold* secrets⟩ ⟨a story yet *untold*⟩ **2** : not counted : VAST, NUMBERLESS ⟨*untold* resources⟩
[1]**un·touch·able** \-ˈtəch-ə-bəl\ *adj* **1 a** : forbidden to the touch **b** : exempt from criticism or control **2** : being out of reach **3** : disagreeable or defiling to the touch — **un·touch·abil·i·ty** \-ˌtəch-ə-ˈbil-ət-ē\ *n*
[2]**untouchable** *n* : one that is untouchable; *esp* : a member of a large formerly segregated hereditary group in India having in traditional Hindu belief the quality of defiling by contact a member of a higher caste
un·touched \ˌən-ˈtəcht\ *adj* **1** : not subjected to touching : not handled **2** : not described or dealt with **3 a** : not tasted **b** : being in the first or a primeval state or condition ⟨an *untouched* wilderness⟩ **4** : not influenced : UNAFFECTED
un·to·ward \ˌən-ˈtō-ərd, -ˈtȯ-ərd, -ˈtōrd, -ˈtȯrd, ˈən-\ *adj* **1** : difficult to manage : STUBBORN, WILLFUL ⟨an *untoward* child⟩ **2** : causing trouble or unhappiness : UNLUCKY ⟨an *untoward* encounter⟩ — **un·to·ward·ly** *adv* — **un·to·ward·ness** *n*
un·tread \ˌən-ˈtred, ˈən-\ *vt* **-trod** \-ˈträd\; **-trod·den** \-ˈträd-n\; **-tread·ing** *archaic* : to tread back : RETRACE
un·tried \-ˈtrīd\ *adj* **1** : not tested or proved by experience or trial ⟨*untried* soldiers⟩ **2** : not tried in court ⟨a backlog of *untried* cases⟩
un·trod·den \ˌən-ˈträd-n\ *also* **un·trod** \-ˈträd\ *adj* : not trod : UNTRAVERSED
un·true \-ˈtrü\ *adj* **1** : not faithful : DISLOYAL **2** : not according with a standard of correctness : not level or exact **3** : not according with the facts : FALSE — **un·tru·ly** \-ˈtrü-lē\ *adv*
un·truth \-ˈtrüth\ *n* **1** : lack of truthfulness : FALSITY **2** : something that is untrue : FALSEHOOD
un·truth·ful \-ˈtrüth-fəl\ *adj* : not containing or telling the truth : FALSE, INACCURATE ⟨*untruthful* report⟩ — **un·truth·ful·ly** \-fə-lē\ *adv* — **un·truth·ful·ness** *n*
un·tune \-ˈtün, -ˈtyün\ *vt* **1** : to put out of tune **2** : DISARRANGE, DISCOMPOSE
un·tu·tored \ˌən-ˈtüt-ərd, -ˈtyüt-, ˈən-\ *adj* **1** : lacking schooling **2** : not gained from instruction : NATIVE ⟨*untutored* shrewdness⟩ ***synonyms*** see IGNORANT
un·twine \-ˈtwīn\ *vb* **1** : to unwind the twisted or tangled parts of **2** : to remove by unwinding **3** : to become disentangled or unwound
un·twist \-ˈtwist\ *vb* **1** : to separate the twisted parts of : UNTWINE **2** : to become untwined
un·used \-ˈyüzd, *in the phrase "unused to" usually* -ˈyüs, -ˈyüst\ *adj* **1** : not habituated : UNACCUSTOMED 2 ⟨*unused* to crowds⟩ **2** : not used: as **a** : never yet used : NEW **b** : not now being used **c** : not used up ⟨*unused* vacation time⟩
un·usu·al \-ˈyüzh-wəl, -ə-wəl, -ˈyüzh-əl\ *adj* : not usual : UNCOMMON, RARE — **un·usu·al·ly** \-ˈyüzh-wə-lē, -ə-wə-, -ˈyüzh-lē, -ˈyüzh-ə-lē\ *adv* — **un·usu·al·ness** \-ˈyüzh-wəl-nəs, -ə-wəl-, -ˈyüzh-əl-\ *n*
un·ut·ter·able \-ˈət-ə-rə-bəl\ *adj* : not capable of being put into words : INEXPRESSIBLE — **un·ut·ter·ably** \-blē\ *adv*
un·val·ued \ˌən-ˈval-yüd, ˈən-\ *adj* **1** : not important or prized **2** : not having an estimated value
un·var·nished \-ˈvär-nisht\ *adj* **1** : not embellished or glossed over : PLAIN, STRAIGHTFORWARD ⟨the *unvarnished* truth⟩ **2** : not covered with or as if with varnish
un·veil \-ˈvāl\ *vb* **1 a** : to remove a veil or covering from ⟨*unveil* a statue⟩ **b** : to throw off a veil or protective cloak **2** : to make public : REVEAL ⟨*unveiled* their plans⟩
un·ver·bal·ized \-ˈvər-bə-ˌlīzd\ *adj* : not put into words or given conscious expression
un·vo·cal \-ˈvō-kəl\ *adj* : not eloquent or outspoken
un·voiced \-ˈvȯist\ *adj* **1** : not verbally expressed ⟨an *unvoiced* agreement⟩ **2** : VOICELESS 2
un·war·rant·able \-ˈwȯr-ənt-ə-bəl, -ˈwär-\ *adj* : not justifiable : INEXCUSABLE — **un·war·rant·ably** \-blē\ *adv*
un·wary \-ˈwaər-ē, -ˈweər-\ *adj* : easily fooled or surprised : HEEDLESS, GULLIBLE — **un·war·i·ly** \-ˈwar-ə-lē, -ˈwer-\ *adv* — **un·war·i·ness** \-ˈwar-ē-nəs, -ˈwer-\ *n*
un·wea·ried \-ˈwiər-ēd\ *adj* : not tired or bored : FRESH
un·weave \ˌən-ˈwēv, ˈən-\ *vt* **-wove** \-ˈwōv\; **-wo·ven** \-ˈwō-vən\; **-weav·ing** : DISENTANGLE, RAVEL
un·well \-ˈwel\ *adj* : being in poor health : AILING, SICK
un·whole·some \-ˈhōl-səm\ *adj* : detrimental to physical, mental, or moral well-being : UNHEALTHY ⟨*unwholesome* food⟩ ⟨*unwholesome* influences⟩
un·wieldy \-ˈwēl-dē\ *adj* : not easily handled or managed because of size or weight : AWKWARD, CLUMSY, CUMBERSOME ⟨an *unwieldy* tool⟩ — **un·wield·i·ness** *n*
un·willed \-ˈwild\ *adj* : not willed : INVOLUNTARY
un·will·ing \ˌən-ˈwil-ing\ *adj* : not willing: as **a** : LOATH, RELUCTANT ⟨was *unwilling* to learn⟩ **b** : done or given reluctantly ⟨*unwilling* approval⟩ **c** : offering opposition : OBSTINATE ⟨an *unwilling* debater⟩ — **un·will·ing·ly** *adv* — **un·will·ing·ness** *n*
un·wind \-ˈwīnd\ *vb* **-wound** \-ˈwau̇nd\; **-wind·ing** **1 a** : to cause to uncoil : wind off **b** : to become uncoiled or untangled **c** : to free from or as if from a binding or wrapping **2** : to make or become free of tension : RELAX

un·wise \-ˈwīz\ *adj* : not wise : FOOLISH — **un·wise·ly** *adv*
un·wit·ting \-ˈwit-iŋ\ *adj* **1** : not intended : INADVERTENT ⟨an *unwitting* mistake⟩ **2** : not knowing : UNAWARE ⟨tricked his *unwitting* friends⟩ — **un·wit·ting·ly** \-iŋ-lē\ *adv*
un·wont·ed \-ˈwȯnt-əd, -ˈwōnt-\ *adj* **1** : being out of the ordinary : RARE, UNUSUAL **2** : not accustomed by experience — **un·wont·ed·ly** *adv* — **un·wont·ed·ness** *n*
un·world·ly \-ˈwərl-dlē\ *adj* **1** : not of this world; *esp* : SPIRITUAL **2 a** : not wise in the ways of the world : NAIVE **b** : not moved by worldly considerations — **un·world·li·ness** *n*
un·worn \-ˈwōrn, -ˈwȯrn\ *adj* **1** : not damaged by use or wear **2** : not worn : NEW
un·wor·thy \ˌən-ˈwər-t͟hē, ˈən-\ *adj* **1** : BASE, DISHONORABLE ⟨*unworthy* duties⟩ **2** : of insufficient merit or worth ⟨*unworthy* to be trusted⟩ — **un·wor·thi·ly** \-t͟hə-lē\ *adv* — **un·wor·thi·ness** \-t͟hē-nəs\ *n*
un·wrap \-ˈrap\ *vt* : to remove the wrapping from
un·writ·ten \-ˈrit-n\ *adj* **1** : not put in writing : ORAL, TRADITIONAL **2** : containing no writing : BLANK
unwritten law *n* : law based chiefly on custom rather than legislative enactments
un·yield·ing \ˌən-ˈyēl-diŋ, ˈən-\ *adj* **1** : marked by lack of softness or flexibility **2** : marked by firmness or stubbornness
un·yoke \-ˈyōk\ *vt* **1** : to free (as oxen) from a yoke **2** : SEPARATE 1a, DISCONNECT
un·zip \-ˈzip\ *vb* : to open by means of a zipper
[1]**up** \ˈəp\ *adv* **1 a** : in or to a higher position or level; *esp* : away from the center of the earth **b** : from beneath a surface (as ground or water) **c** : from below the horizon **d** : in or into an upright position ⟨sit *up*⟩ **e** : out of bed ⟨stayed *up* late⟩ **2** : with greater strength, force, or energy ⟨speak *up*⟩ **3 a** : in or into a better or more advanced state **b** : at an end ⟨your time is *up*⟩ **c** : in or into a state of greater intensity or activity ⟨stir *up* a fire⟩ **d** : to or at a greater speed, rate, or amount ⟨prices went *up*⟩ **e** : in a continual sequence ⟨priced $10 and *up*⟩ ⟨*up* until now⟩ **4 a** : into existence, evidence, or knowledge ⟨the missing ring turned *up*⟩ **b** : into consideration ⟨brought the matter *up*⟩ **5** : into possession or custody **6 a** : WHOLLY 1, COMPLETELY ⟨eat it *up*⟩ **b** — used for emphasis ⟨clean *up* a room⟩ **7** : in or into storage : ASIDE, BY ⟨lay *up* supplies⟩ ⟨put my car *up* for the winter⟩ **8 a** : so as to arrive or approach ⟨came *up* the drive⟩ **b** : in a direction conventionally opposite to down **9** : in or into parts ⟨tear *up* paper⟩ **10** : to a stop ⟨pull *up*⟩ ⟨drew *up* at the curb⟩ **11** : for each side ⟨score was 15 *up*⟩ [Old English *ūp*]
[2]**up** *adj* **1 a** : risen above the horizon **b** : being out of bed **c** : relatively high ⟨the river is *up*⟩ ⟨prices are *up*⟩ **d** : raised so as to be open ⟨windows are *up*⟩ **e** : put together ⟨the house is *up*⟩ **f** : grown above a surface ⟨the corn is *up*⟩ **g** : moving, inclining, or directed upward or in a direction regarded as up ⟨the *up* escalator⟩ **2 a** : marked by agitation, excitement, or activity ⟨was eager to be *up* and doing⟩ **b** : well prepared ⟨the team was *up* for the game⟩ **c** : going on : taking place ⟨find out what is *up*⟩ **3** : well informed ⟨always *up* on the news⟩ **4** : being ahead or in advance of an opponent ⟨was three games *up* in the series⟩ **5 a** : presented for or under consideration ⟨*up* for reelection⟩ **b** : charged before a court ⟨was *up* for robbery⟩ **c** : being the one whose turn it is ⟨you're *up* next⟩ — **up to 1** : capable of performing or dealing with ⟨was fully *up to* the job⟩ **2** : engaged in ⟨what are you *up to*⟩ **3** : being the responsibility of ⟨it's *up to* me⟩
[3]**up** \ˌəp, ˈəp\ *prep* **1** : to, toward, or at a higher point of ⟨*up* the hill⟩ **2 a** : toward the source of ⟨going *up* the river⟩ **b** : toward the northern or upper end or part of ⟨sailing *up* the coast⟩ **3** : along the course of ⟨walking *up* the street⟩
[4]**up** \ˈəp\ *n* **1** : an upward course or slope **2** : a period or state of prosperity or success ⟨have my *ups* and downs⟩
[5]**up** *vb* **upped** *or in 1* **up; upped; up·ping; ups** *or in 1* **up 1** : to act abruptly or surprisingly — usually followed by *and* and another verb ⟨they *up* and left⟩ **2** : to rise from a lying or sitting position **3** : to move or cause to move upward : ASCEND, RAISE
up–and–coming \ˌəp-ən-ˈkəm-iŋ, ˌəp-m-\ *adj* : gaining prominence and likely to advance or succeed
up–and–down \ˌəp-m-ˈdau̇n, ˌəp-ən-\ *adj* **1** : marked by alternate upward and downward movement, action, or surface **2** : very steep : PERPENDICULAR
Upa·ni·shad \ü-ˈpän-ə-ˌshäd, yü-ˈpan-ə-ˌshad\ *n* : one of a class of Vedic philosophical treatises [Sanskrit *upaniṣad*]
[1]**up·beat** \ˈəp-ˌbēt\ *n* : an unaccented beat in a musical measure; *esp* : the last beat of the measure
[2]**upbeat** *adj* : marked by optimism : OPTIMISTIC, CHEERFUL
up·braid \ˌəp-ˈbrād\ *vt* : to criticize or scold severely or vehemently [Old English *ūpbregdan*] — **up·braid·er** *n*
up·bring·ing \ˈəp-ˌbriŋ-iŋ\ *n* : early training; *esp* : a particular way of bringing up a child
up·chuck \ˈəp-ˌchək\ *vb* : VOMIT 1
up·com·ing \ˌəp-ˌkəm-iŋ\ *adj* : being in the near future : FORTHCOMING
up–coun·try \ˌəp-ˌkən-trē\ *adj* : of or relating to the interior of a country or a region — **up–coun·try** \ˈəp-\ *n* — **up–coun·try** \ˈəp-ˈkən-\ *adv*
[1]**up·date** \ˌəp-ˈdāt\ *vt* : to bring up to date
[2]**up·date** \ˈəp-ˌdāt\ *n* **1** : an act or instance of updating **2** : current information for updating something **3** : an up-to-date version, account, or report
up·draft \ˈəp-ˌdraft, -ˌdráft\ *n* : an upward movement of gas (as air)
up·end \ˌə-ˈpend\ *vb* : to set, stand, or rise on end
[1]**up·grade** \ˈəp-ˌgrād\ *n* **1** : an upward grade or slope **2** : INCREASE 1 ⟨crime is on the *upgrade*⟩ **3** : IMPROVEMENT 2b
[2]**up·grade** \-ˌgrād\ *vb* **1** : to raise to a higher grade or position **2** : to improve or replace especially software or a device for increased usefulness — **up·grad·abil·i·ty** *or* **up·grade·abil·i·ty** \ˌəp-ˌgrād-ə-ˈbil-ət-ē\ *n* — **up·grad·able** *or* **up·grade·able** \-ˈgrād-ə-bəl\ *adj*
up·growth \ˈəp-ˌgrōth\ *n* : the process of increasing (as in height or complexity) : DEVELOPMENT; *also* : a product or result of this
up·heav·al \ˌəp-ˈhē-vəl, ə-ˈpē-\ *n* **1** : the action or an instance of upheaving especially of part of the earth's crust **2** : an instance of violent agitation or change
up·heave \ˌəp-ˈhēv, ə-ˈpēv\ *vb* **-heaved; -heav·ing** : to heave or lift up from beneath — **up·heav·er** *n*
[1]**up·hill** \ˈəp-ˈhil\ *adv* **1** : upward on a hill or incline **2** : against difficulties
[2]**up·hill** \ˈəp-ˌhil\ *adj* **1 a** : situated on elevated ground **b** : going or directed toward higher ground **2** : requiring much effort
up·hold \ˌəp-ˈhōld\ *vt* **-held** \-ˈheld\; **-hold·ing 1 a** : to give support to **b** : to support against an opponent **2 a** : to keep elevated **b** : to lift up — **up·hold·er** *n*
up·hol·ster \ˌəp-ˈhōl-stər, əp-ˈhōl-; ə-ˈpōl-\ *vt* **-stered; -ster·ing** \-stə-riŋ, -striŋ\ : to furnish with or as if with upholstery [back-formation from *upholstery*] — **up·hol·ster·er** \-stər-ər, -strər\ *n*
up·hol·stery \-stə-rē, -strē\ *n, pl* **-ster·ies** : materials (as fabric, padding, and springs) used to make a soft covering especially for a seat [Middle English *upholdester* "upholsterer," from *upholden* "to uphold, maintain"]
up·keep \ˈəp-ˌkēp\ *n* **1** : the act of maintaining in good condition : the state of being maintained **2** : the cost of maintaining in good condition
up·land \ˈəp-lənd, -ˌland\ *n* : high land especially at some distance from the sea — **upland** *adj*
upland cotton *n* : any of various usually short-staple cottons cultivated especially in the U.S.
[1]**up·lift** \əp-ˈlift, ˌəp-\ *vb* **1** : to lift up : ELEVATE **2** : to improve the condition of especially spiritually, socially, or intellectually — **up·lift·er** *n*
[2]**up·lift** \ˈəp-ˌlift\ *n* : an act, process, or result of uplifting: as **a** : the uplifting of a part of the earth's surface **b** : moral or social improvement; *also* : a movement to make such improvement **c** : influences intended to uplift
up·link \ˈəp-ˌliŋk\ *n* **1** : a communications channel for transmissions to a spacecraft or satellite; *also* : the transmissions themselves **2** : a facility on earth for transmitting to a spacecraft or satellite — **uplink** *vb*
up·load \ˌəp-ˈlōd, ˈəp-ˌ\ *vt* : to transfer (information) from a computer to another device (as a remote computer)
up·most \ˈəp-ˌmōst\ *adj* : being in the highest or most important position : UPPERMOST

\ə\ **abut**	\au̇\ **out**	\i\ **tip**	\ȯ\ **saw**	\u̇\ **foot**
\ər\ **further**	\ch\ **chin**	\ī\ **life**	\ȯi\ **coin**	\y\ **yet**
\a\ **mat**	\e\ **pet**	\j\ **job**	\th\ **thin**	\yü\ **few**
\ā\ **take**	\ē\ **easy**	\ŋ\ **sing**	\t͟h\ **this**	\yu̇\ **cure**
\ä\ **cot, cart**	\g\ **go**	\ō\ **bone**	\ü\ **food**	\zh\ **vision**

up·on \ə-ˈpȯn, -ˈpän, -ˌpən, -pən\ *prep* : ON

[1]**up·per** \ˈə-pər\ *adj* **1** : higher in physical position, rank, or order ⟨the *upper* lip⟩ **2** : constituting the smaller and senior branch of a bicameral legislature **3** *cap* : of, relating to, or being a later geologic period or formation ⟨the *Upper* Cretaceous period⟩ **4** : being toward the interior : further inland ⟨the *upper* Amazon⟩ **5** : NORTHERN ⟨*upper* New York state⟩

[2]**upper** *n* : one that is upper: as **a** : the parts of a shoe or boot above the sole **b** : an upper tooth or denture **c** : an upper berth

[3]**upper** *n* : a stimulant drug; *esp* : AMPHETAMINE

up·per·case \ˌə-pər-ˈkās\ *adj* : CAPITAL 2 [from the printer's practice of keeping capitals in the upper of two typecases] — **uppercase** *n*

upper class *n* : a social class occupying a position above the middle class and having the highest status in a society — **upper–class** *adj*

up·per·class·man \ˌə-pər-ˈklas-mən\ *n* : a junior or senior in a college or high school

upper crust *n* : the highest social class or group

up·per·cut \ˈə-pər-ˌkət\ *n* : a swinging blow (as in boxing) directed upward with a bent arm — **uppercut** *vb*

upper hand *n* : ADVANTAGE 1, CONTROL

up·per·most \ˈə-pər-ˌmōst\ *adv* : in or into the highest or most prominent position — **uppermost** *adj*

up·per·part \-ˌpärt\ *n* : a part lying on the upper side (as of a bird)

up·pish \ˈə-pish\ *adj* : UPPITY — **up·pish·ness** *n*

up·pi·ty \ˈə-pə-tē\ *adj* : putting on airs of superiority : ARROGANT [probably from *up* + *-ity* (as in *persnickity,* variant of *persnickety*)] — **up·pi·ti·ness** *n*

up·raise \ˌə-ˈprāz, ə-\ *vt* : to raise or lift up : ELEVATE

up·rate \ˈəp-ˌrāt\ *vt* : UPGRADE; *esp* : to improve the power output of (as an engine)

[1]**up·right** \ˈəp-ˌrīt\ *adj* **1 a** : PERPENDICULAR 2, VERTICAL **b** : erect in carriage or posture **c** : having the main axis or a main part perpendicular **2** : morally correct : HONEST, HONORABLE — **up·right·ly** *adv* — **up·right·ness** *n*

[2]**upright** *n* **1** : the state of being upright : PERPENDICULAR ⟨a pillar out of *upright*⟩ **2** : something upright **3** : UPRIGHT PIANO

upright piano *n* : a piano with vertical frame and strings

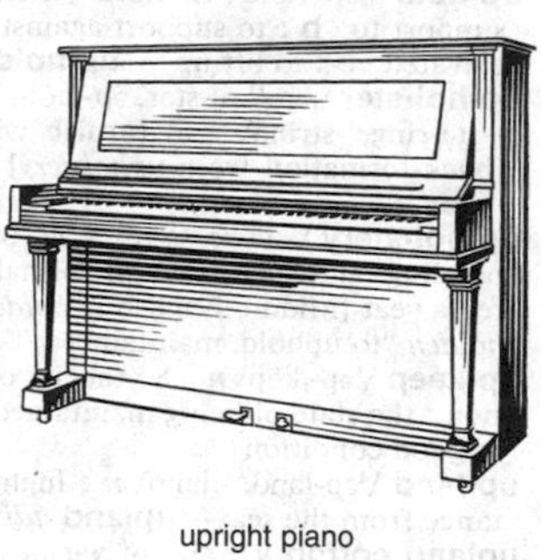

upright piano

[1]**up·rise** \ˌə-ˈprīz\ *vi* **up·rose** \-ˈprōz\; **up·ris·en** \-ˈpriz-ᵊn\; **up·ris·ing** \-ˈprī-ziŋ\ **1** : to rise to a higher positon **2** : to get up (as from sleep or a sitting position) — **up·ris·er** *n*

[2]**up·rise** \ˈəp-ˌrīz\ *n* **1** : an act or instance of uprising **2** : an upward slope

up·ris·ing \ˈəp-ˌrī-ziŋ\ *n* : an act or instance of rising up; *esp* : a usually localized revolt against an established government ***synonyms*** see REBELLION

up·riv·er \ˈəp-ˈriv-ər\ *adv or adj* : toward or at a point nearer the source of a river

up·roar \ˈəp-ˌrōr, -ˌrȯr\ *n* : a state of commotion, excitement, or violent disturbance [by folk etymology from Dutch *oproer,* from *op* "up" + *roer* "motion"]

up·roar·i·ous \ˌəp-ˈrōr-ē-əs, -ˈrȯr-\ *adj* **1** : marked by uproar **2** : extremely funny — **up·roar·i·ous·ly** *adv* — **up·roar·i·ous·ness** *n*

up·root \ˌəˈprüt, -ˈpru̇t\ *vt* **1** : to remove by or as if by pulling up by the roots **2** : to displace from a country or traditional habitat — **up·root·er** *n*

[1]**up·set** \ˌəp-ˈset, əp-\ *vb* **-set; -set·ting** **1** : to thicken and shorten (as a heated bar of iron) by hammering on the end : SWAGE **2** : to force or be forced out of the usual upright, level, or proper position : OVERTURN, CAPSIZE **3 a** : to trouble emotionally ⟨the news *upset* me⟩ **b** : to make somewhat ill ⟨spicy food *upsets* my stomach⟩ **4 a** : to throw into disorder : DISARRANGE **b** : INVALIDATE ⟨*upset* a will⟩ **c** : to defeat unexpectedly ⟨was *upset* in the primary⟩ — **up·set·ter** *n*

[2]**up·set** \ˈəp-ˌset\ *n* **1** : an act or result of upsetting : a state of being upset **2 a** : a minor physical disorder ⟨a stomach *upset*⟩ **b** : an emotional disturbance **3** : a part of a rod (as the head on a bolt) that is upset

[3]**up·set** \əp-ˈset\ *adj* : emotionally disturbed or agitated ⟨was too *upset* to speak⟩

up·shot \ˈəp-ˌshät\ *n* : final result : OUTCOME

up·side down \ˌəp-ˌsīd-ˈdau̇n\ *adv* **1** : with the upper and the lower parts reversed in position **2** : in or into great disorder [Middle English *up so doun,* from *up* + *so* + *doun* "down"] — **upside–down** *adj*

upside–down cake *n* : a cake baked with a layer of fruit (as pineapple) on the bottom and served with the fruit side up

up·si·lon \ˈyüp-sə-ˌlän, ˈəp-, -lən\ *n* : the 20th letter of the Greek alphabet — Υ or υ

[1]**up·stage** \ˈəp-ˈstāj\ *adv* **1** : toward or at the rear of a stage **2** : away from a motion-picture or television camera

[2]**upstage** *adj* **1** : of or relating to the rear of a stage **2** : HAUGHTY

[3]**up·stage** \ˌəp-ˈstāj\ *vt* : to steal attention away from [earlier *upstage* "to force (an actor) to face away from the audience by staying upstage"]

[1]**up·stairs** \ˈəp-ˈstaərz, -ˈsteərz\ *adv* **1** : up the stairs : to or on a higher floor **2** : to or at a high altitude or higher position

[2]**up·stairs** \-ˈstaərz, -ˈsteərz\ *adj* : situated above the stairs especially on an upper floor ⟨an *upstairs* bedroom⟩

[3]**up·stairs** \ˈəp-ˈ, ˈəp-ˌ\ *n* : the part of a building above the ground floor

up·stand·ing \ˌəp-ˈstan-diŋ, ˈəp-ˌ\ *adj* **1** : ERECT 1a **2** : marked by integrity : HONEST — **up·stand·ing·ness** *n*

[1]**up·start** \ˌəp-ˈstärt\ *vi* : to jump up suddenly

[2]**up·start** \ˈəp-ˌstärt\ *n* : one that has risen suddenly (as from a low position to wealth or power) : PARVENU; *esp* : one that claims more personal importance than is warranted — **up·start** \ˌəp-ˌ\ *adj*

up·state \ˈəp-ˌstāt\ *n* : the chiefly northerly sections of a state; *esp* : the chiefly rural part of a state when the major urban area is in the south — **up·state** \-ˈstāt\ *adv or adj* — **up·stat·er** \-ˈstāt-ər\ *n*

up·stream \ˈəp-ˈstrēm\ *adv* : at or toward the source of a stream : against the current — **upstream** *adj*

up·stroke \ˈəp-ˌstrōk\ *n* : an upward stroke (as of a pen)

up·surge \ˈəp-ˌsərj\ *n* : a rapid or sudden rise

up·sweep \ˈəp-ˌswēp\ *vi* **-swept** \-ˌswept\; **-sweep·ing** : to sweep upward : curve or slope upward — **upsweep** *n*

up·swept \ˈəp-ˌswept\ *adj* : swept upward; *esp* : brushed up to the top of the head ⟨*upswept* hair⟩

up·swing \ˈəp-ˌswiŋ\ *n* **1** : an upward swing **2** : a marked increase or improvement (as in activity)

up·take \ˈəp-ˌtāk\ *n* **1** : UNDERSTANDING, COMPREHENSION ⟨quick on the *uptake*⟩ **2** : a flue leading upward **3** : an act or instance of absorbing and incorporating especially into a living organism, tissue, or cell ⟨oxygen *uptake*⟩ [Scottish *uptake* "to understand"]

up·throw \ˈəp-ˌthrō\ *n* : an upward displacement (as of a rock stratum) : UPHEAVAL

up·thrust \ˈəp-ˌthrəst\ *n* : an upward thrust; *esp* : an uplift of part of the earth's crust

up·tight \ˈəp-ˈtīt, ˌəp-ˈ, əp-ˈ; ˌəp-ˌ\ *adj* **1** : TENSE, UNEASY **2** : ANGRY, INDIGNANT **3** : rigidly conventional

up·tilt \ˌəp-ˈtilt\ *vt* : to tilt upward

up to *prep* **1** : as far as a designated part or place ⟨sank *up to* my hips⟩ **2** — used as a function word to indicate a limit or boundary ⟨save *up to* 15 percent⟩

up–to–date *adj* **1** : extending up to the present time : including the latest information **2** : abreast of the times (as in style or technique) : MODERN — **up–to–date·ness** *n*

up·town \ˈəp-ˈtau̇n\ *adv* : toward, to, or in the upper part of a town — **up·town** \ˌəp-ˌtau̇n\ *adj*

up·trend \ˈəp-ˌtrend\ *n* : an upturn especially in business or economic activity

[1]**up·turn** \ˈəp-ˌtərn, ˌəp-ˈ\ *vb* **1** : to turn up or over ⟨an *upturned* boat⟩ **2** : to turn or direct upward ⟨*upturned* faces⟩

[2]**up·turn** \ˈəp-ˌtərn\ *n* : an upward turn (as toward better conditions or higher prices)

[1]**up·ward** \ˈəp-wərd\ *or* **up·wards** \-wərdz\ *adv* **1** : in a direction from lower to higher **2** : toward a higher or better condition **3** : toward a greater amount or higher number, degree, or rate

[2]**upward** *adj* **:** directed toward or situated in a higher place or level — **up·ward·ly** *adv* — **up·ward·ness** *n*
upwards of *also* **upward of** *adv* **:** more than **:** in excess of
up·well·ing \ˌəp-ˈwel-iŋ\ *n* **:** the proces or an instance of rising or appearing to rise to the surface and flowing outward; *esp* **:** the movement of deeper, cooler, and often nutrient-rich layers of ocean water to the surface
up·wind \ˈəp-ˈwind\ *adv or adj* **:** in the direction from which the wind is blowing
ur- *or* **uro-** *combining form* **1 :** urine ⟨*ur*ic⟩ **2 :** urinary tract ⟨*uro*logy⟩ **3 :** urinary and ⟨*uro*genital⟩ **4 :** urea ⟨*ur*acil⟩ [Greek *ouron*]
ura·cil \ˈyu̇r-ə-ˌsil, -səl\ *n* **:** a pyrimidine base $C_4H_4N_2O_2$ that is one of the four bases coding genetic information in the polynucleotide chain of RNA — compare ADENINE, CYTOSINE, GUANINE, THYMINE [derived from *ur-* + *acetic*]
Ural–Al·ta·ic \ˌyu̇r-ə-lal-ˈtā-ik\ *n* **:** a hypothesized language family comprising the Uralic and Altaic languages [*Ural* mountains + *Altai* mountains] — **Ural–Altaic** *adj*
Ural·ic \yu̇-ˈral-ik\ *n* **:** a language family comprising the Finno-Ugric languages and some languages of northwest Siberia
ura·ni·nite \yu̇-ˈrā-nə-ˌnīt\ *n* **:** a mineral that is a black oxide of uranium, contains also various metals (as thorium and lead), and is the chief ore of uranium [German *Uranin,* from New Latin *uranium*]
ura·ni·um \yu̇-ˈrā-nē-əm\ *n* **:** a silvery heavy radioactive metallic element that is found especially in uraninite and exists naturally as a mixture of mostly nonfissionable isotopes — see ELEMENT table [New Latin, from *Uranus*]
uranium hexafluoride *n* **:** a compound of uranium and fluorine that is used in one major process for the separation of uranium 235 from ordinary uranium
uranium 238 *n* **:** an isotope of uranium of mass number 238 that is the most stable uranium isotope, that constitutes over 99 percent of natural uranium, that can be used to produce an isotope of plutonium, and that has a half-life of 4.5 billion years
uranium 235 *n* **:** a light isotope of uranium of mass number 235 that when bombarded with low-energy neutrons undergoes rapid fission into smaller atoms with the release of neutrons and atomic energy and that is used in nuclear reactors and atomic bombs
Ura·nus \ˈyu̇r-ə-nəs, yu̇-ˈrā-\ *n* **:** the planet 7th in order from the sun — see PLANET table [*Uranus,* a Greek god]
urate \ˈyu̇r-ˌāt\ *n* **:** a salt of uric acid
ur·ban \ˈər-bən\ *adj* **:** of, relating to, characteristic of, or constituting a city [Latin *urbanus,* from *urbs* "city"]
ur·bane \ˌər-ˈbān\ *adj* **:** notably polite or finished in manner **:** SUAVE [Latin *urbanus* "urban, urbane"] ***synonyms*** see SUAVE — **ur·bane·ly** *adv*

Word History The advantages of city over country life (and vice versa) have been debated for many years, and this debate is reflected in our vocabulary. Alongside of *urban,* "relating to or characteristic of a city," we have *urbane,* which developed the sense of "smoothly courteous or polite" from the belief (encouraged by city dwellers especially) that the social life of the city is more suave and polished than life in the country. Both *urban* and *urbane* come from the Latin *urbanus,* from *urbs,* "city."

ur·ban·ite \ˈər-bə-ˌnīt\ *n* **:** one living in a city
ur·ban·i·ty \ˌər-ˈban-ət-ē\ *n, pl* **-ties 1 :** the quality or state of being urbane **2** *pl* **:** urbane acts or conduct
ur·ban·ize \ˈər-bə-ˌnīz\ *vt* **1 :** to cause to take on urban characteristics ⟨*urbanized* areas⟩ **2 :** to impart an urban way of life to — **ur·ban·i·za·tion** \ˌər-bə-nə-ˈzā-shən\ *n*
urban renewal *n* **:** a construction program to replace or restore substandard buildings in an urban area
urban sprawl *n* **:** the spreading of urban developments (as houses and shopping centers) on undeveloped land near a city
ur·chin \ˈər-chən\ *n* **1** *archaic* **:** HEDGEHOG 1 **2 :** a mischievous and often poor and raggedly clothed youngster **3 :** SEA URCHIN [Medieval French *heriçun, hirechoun,* from Latin *ericius*]
Ur·du \ˈu̇r-dü, ˈər-\ *n* **:** an Indo-Aryan language that is an official language of Pakistan and is widely used by Muslims in India [Hindi and Urdu *urdū,* from Persian *zabān -e- urdū -e- muallā* "language of the Exalted Camp" (the imperial bazaar in Delhi)]
-ure *n suffix* **1 :** act **:** process ⟨expos*ure*⟩ **2 a :** office **:** function **b :** body performing (such) a function ⟨legislat*ure*⟩ [Latin *-ura*]
urea \yu̇-ˈrē-ə\ *n* **:** a soluble nitrogen-containing compound that is the chief solid substance in mammalian urine and is an end product of protein breakdown [New Latin, from French *urée,* from *urine* "urine"] — **ure·ic** \-ˈrē-ik\ *adj*
ure·ase \ˈyu̇r-ē-ˌās, -ˌāz\ *n* **:** an enzyme that promotes the hydrolysis of urea
ure·mia \yu̇-ˈrē-mē-ə\ *n* **:** accumulation in the blood usually in severe kidney disease of constituents normally eliminated in the urine resulting in a severe toxic condition — **ure·mic** \-mik\ *adj*
ure·ter \ˈyu̇r-ət-ər\ *n* **:** a duct that carries urine from a kidney to the bladder or cloaca [Greek *ourētēr,* from *ourein* "to urinate"] — **ure·ter·al** \yu̇-ˈrēt-ə-rəl\ *also* **ure·ter·ic** \ˌyu̇r-ə-ˈter-ik\ *adj*
ure·thra \yu̇-ˈrē-thrə\ *n, pl* **-thras** *or* **-thrae** \-thrē\ **:** the canal that in most mammals carries off the urine from the bladder and in the male serves also as a genital duct [Late Latin, from Greek *ourēthra,* from *ourein* "to urinate"] — **ure·thral** \-thrəl\ *adj*
[1]**urge** \ˈərj\ *vt* **1 :** to present, advocate, or demand earnestly ⟨continually *urging* reform⟩ **2 a :** to try to persuade or sway ⟨*urge* a guest to stay longer⟩ **b :** to serve as a motive or reason for **3 :** to press or move to some course or activity (as greater speed) ⟨*urge* on a runner⟩ [Latin *urgēre* "to press, push, entreat"] — **urg·er** *n*
[2]**urge** *n* **1 :** the act or process of urging **2 :** a force or impulse that urges; *esp* **:** a continuing impulse toward an activity or goal
ur·gent \ˈər-jənt\ *adj* **1 a :** calling for immediate attention **:** PRESSING ⟨*urgent* appeals⟩ **b :** conveying a sense of urgency ⟨an *urgent* manner⟩ **2 :** urging insistently [Medieval French, from Latin *urgens,* present participle of *urgēre* "to urge"] — **ur·gen·cy** \-jən-sē\ *n* — **ur·gent·ly** *adv*
uric \ˈyu̇r-ik\ *adj* **:** of, relating to, or found in urine
uric acid *n* **:** a white odorless nearly insoluble nitrogen-containing acid that is present in small quantity in mammalian urine and is the chief nitrogen-containing waste especially of birds, reptiles, and insects
uri·nal \ˈyu̇r-ən-l\ *n* **1 :** a receptacle for urine **2 :** a place for urinating
uri·nal·y·sis \ˌyu̇r-ə-ˈnal-ə-səs\ *n, pl* **uri·nal·y·ses** \-ə-ˌsēz\ **:** the chemical analysis of urine
uri·nary \ˈyu̇r-ə-ˌner-ē\ *adj* **1 :** relating to, occurring in, affecting, or constituting the organs of the urinary tract ⟨the *urinary* bladder⟩ **2 :** of, relating to, or used for urine **3 :** excreted as or in urine ⟨*urinary* sugar⟩
urinary tract *n* **:** the body organs and passages through which urine passes and which consists of the tubules and pelvis of the kidney, the ureters, the bladder, and the urethra
uri·nate \ˈyu̇r-ə-ˌnāt\ *vi* **:** to discharge urine — **uri·na·tion** \ˌyu̇r-ə-ˈnā-shən\ *n*
urine \ˈyu̇r-ən\ *n* **:** waste material that is secreted by the kidney, is rich in end products of protein metabolism together with salts and pigments, and is usually a yellowish liquid in mammals but semisolid in birds and reptiles [Medieval French, from Latin *urina*]
URL \ˌyü-ˌär-ˈel, ˈərl\ *n* **:** an address (as of a document or Web site) on the Internet that consists of a communications protocol, an address on the network, and often additional information (as a computer directory or file name) [*u*niform *r*esource *l*ocator or *u*niversal *r*esource *l*ocator]
urn \ˈərn\ *n* **1 :** a vessel that typically has the form of a vase on a pedestal and often is used for preserving the ashes of the dead **2 :** a closed vessel usually with a spigot for serving a hot beverage ⟨a coffee *urn*⟩ [Latin *urna*]

urn 2

uro- — see UR-
uro·dele \ˈyu̇r-ə-ˌdēl\ *n* **:** any of an order (Caudata) of amphibians (as newts and salamanders) with a tail throughout life [French *urodèle,* de-

\ə\ **abut**	\au̇\ **out**	\i\ **tip**	\ȯ\ **saw**	\u̇\ **foot**
\ər\ **further**	\ch\ **chin**	\ī\ **life**	\ȯi\ **coin**	\y\ **yet**
\a\ **mat**	\e\ **pet**	\j\ **job**	\th\ **thin**	\yü\ **few**
\ā\ **take**	\ē\ **easy**	\ŋ\ **sing**	\t͟h\ **this**	\yu̇\ **cure**
\ä\ **cot, cart**	\g\ **go**	\ō\ **bone**	\ü\ **food**	\zh\ **vision**

rived from Greek *oura* "tail" + *dēlos* "evident, showing"] — **urodele** *adj*

uro·gen·i·tal \ˌyu̇r-ō-ˈjen-ə-tl\ *adj* : of, relating to, or being the organs or functions of excretion and reproduction

urol·o·gy \yu̇-ˈräl-ə-jē\ *n* : a branch of medical science dealing with the urinary or urogenital tract and its disorders — **uro·log·i·cal** \-ˈläj-i-kəl\ *also* **uro·log·ic** *adj* — **urol·o·gist** \yu̇-ˈräl-ə-jəst\ *n*

uro·pod \ˈyu̇r-ə-ˌpäd\ *n* : either of the flat lateral appendages of the last abdominal segment of a crustacean [derived from Greek *oura* "tail" + *pod-, pous* "foot"]

uro·style \ˈyu̇r-ə-ˌstīl\ *n* : a bony rod made of fused vertebrae that forms the end of the spinal column of a frog or toad [derived from Greek *oura* "tail" + *stylos* "pillar"]

Ur·sa Ma·jor \ˌər-sə-ˈmā-jər\ *n* : the most conspicuous of the northern constellations that is situated near the north pole of the heavens and contains the stars forming the Big Dipper two of which are in a line indicating the direction of the North Star — called also *Great Bear* [Latin, literally, "greater bear"]

Ursa Mi·nor \-ˈmī-nər\ *n* : the constellation including the north pole of the heavens and the stars that form the Little Dipper with the North Star at the tip of the handle — called also *Little Bear* [Latin, literally, "lesser bear"]

Ur·su·line \ˈər-sə-lən, -ˌlīn, -ˌlēn\ *n* : a member of a Roman Catholic teaching order of nuns founded in Italy in 1535 [Saint *Ursula,* legendary Christian martyr] — **Ursuline** *adj*

ur·ti·car·ia \ˌərt-ə-ˈkar-ē-ə, -ˈker-\ *n* : HIVES [New Latin, from Latin *urtica* "nettle"] — **ur·ti·car·i·al** \-ē-əl\ *adj*

urus \ˈyu̇r-əs\ *n* : AUROCHS [Latin, of Germanic origin]

us \əs, ˈəs\ *pron, objective case of* WE [Old English *ūs*]

us·able *also* **use·able** \ˈyü-zə-bəl\ *adj* : suitable or fit for use ⟨*usable* waste⟩ — **us·abil·i·ty** \ˌyü-zə-ˈbil-ət-ē\ *n* — **us·ably** \ˈyü-zə-blē\ *adv*

us·age \ˈyü-sij, -zij\ *n* **1 a** : firmly established and generally accepted practice or procedure **b** : the way in which words and phrases are actually used in a language community **2 a** : the action or mode of using : USE ⟨a decreased *usage* of electricity⟩ **b** : way of treating : TREATMENT ⟨rough *usage*⟩ ***synonyms*** see HABIT

USB \ˌyü-ˌes-ˈbē\ *n* : a system for connecting a computer to another device (as a printer, keyboard, or mouse) by using a special kind of cord [*U*niversal *S*erial *B*us]

[1]**use** \ˈyüs\ *n* **1 a** : the act or practice of using something ⟨put knowledge to *use*⟩ **b** : the fact or state of being used ⟨a dish in daily use⟩ **c** : way of using ⟨the proper *use* of tools⟩ **2 a** : the privilege or benefit of using something ⟨had the *use* of a car⟩ **b** : the ability or power to use something (as a limb) ⟨regained the *use* of her arm⟩ **3 a** : FUNCTION 2 ⟨what's the *use* of this dial⟩ **b** : the quality of being suitable for employment : USEFULNESS ⟨old clothes that are still of some *use*⟩ **c** : the occasion or need to employ ⟨took only what I had *use* for⟩ **4** : a favorable attitude : LIKING ⟨had no *use* for modern art⟩ [Medieval French *us,* from Latin *usus,* from *uti* "to use"]

[2]**use** \ˈyüz\ *vb* **used** \ˈyüzd, *in the phrase "used to" usually* ˈyüs, ˈyüst\; **us·ing** \ˈyü-zing\ **1** : to put into action or service : EMPLOY **2** : to consume or take (as liquor or drugs) regularly **3** : to carry out a purpose or action by means of : UTILIZE ⟨*use* tact⟩ **4** : to expend or consume by putting to use ⟨the car *uses* a lot of gas⟩ **5** : to behave toward : TREAT ⟨*used* the prisoners cruelly⟩ **6** — used in the past with *to* to indicate a former practice, fact, or state ⟨claims winters *used* to be harder⟩ — **us·er** \ˈyü-zər\ *n*

synonyms USE, EMPLOY, UTILIZE mean to put into service especially to attain an end. USE implies availing oneself of something as a means or instrument to an end ⟨willing to *use* any means to win⟩. EMPLOY suggests the use of a person or thing that is available because idle, inactive, or disengaged ⟨looking for better ways to *employ* their skills⟩. UTILIZE suggests the discovery of a new, profitable, or practical use for something ⟨how to *utilize* scrap metal⟩.

used \ˈyüzd, *in the phrase "used to" usually* ˈyüs, ˈyüst\ *adj* **1** : employed in accomplishing something **2** : that has endured use; *esp* : SECONDHAND ⟨a *used* car⟩ **3** : made familiar by experience : ACCUSTOMED ⟨is *used* to working hard⟩

use·ful \ˈyüs-fəl\ *adj* : capable of being put to use : USABLE ⟨*useful* scraps of material⟩; *also* : of a kind to be valuable or productive ⟨a *useful* invention⟩ — **use·ful·ly** \-fə-lē\ *adv* — **use·ful·ness** *n*

use·less \ˈyü-sləs\ *adj* : having or being of no use : WORTHLESS — **use·less·ly** *adv* — **use·less·ness** *n*

Use·net \ˈyüz-ˌnet\ *n* : the aggregation of all the newsgroups on the Internet [probably from *Use*nix, an association of computer programmers using the operating system Unix (from *use*rs of *U*nix) + *net* "network"]

user name *n* : a sequence of characters that identifies a user when logging onto a computer or Web site — called also *user ID*

use up *vt* : to take (all of something) from a supply

[1]**ush·er** \ˈəsh-ər\ *n* **1** : an officer who walks before a person of rank **2** : one who escorts persons to seats (as in a theater) [Medieval French *ussier, usscher,* literally, "doorkeeper," derived from Latin *ostium, ustium* "door"]

[2]**usher** *vt* **ush·ered; ush·er·ing** \ˈəsh-ring, -ə-ring\ **1** : to conduct to a place **2** : to cause to enter ⟨*usher* in a new era⟩

usu·al \ˈyüzh-wəl, -ə-wəl, ˈyüzh-əl\ *adj* **1** : accordant with usage, custom, or habit : NORMAL **2** : commonly or ordinarily used **3** : found in ordinary practice or in the ordinary course of events [Late Latin *usualis,* from Latin *usus* "use"] — **usu·al·ly** \ˈyüzh-wə-lē, -ə-wə-, ˈyüzh-lē, ˈyüzh-ə-lē, *rapid* ˈyüz-lē\ *adv* — **usu·al·ness** \ˈyüzh-wəl-nəs, -ə-wəl-, ˈyüzh-əl-\ *n*

synonyms USUAL, CUSTOMARY, HABITUAL, ACCUSTOMED mean familiar through frequent or regular repetition. USUAL stresses the absence of strangeness or unexpectedness ⟨my *usual* order⟩. CUSTOMARY applies to what accords with the practices, conventions, or usages of an individual or community ⟨their *customary* dress⟩. HABITUAL suggests a practice established by much repetition ⟨a *habitual* routine⟩. ACCUSTOMED is less emphatic than HABITUAL and suggests something that is noticed or expected by others ⟨*accustomed* graciousness⟩.

usu·fruct \ˈyü-zə-ˌfrəkt\ *n* : the legal right of using and enjoying the fruits or profits of something belonging to another [Latin *usufructus,* from *usus et fructus* "use and enjoyment"]

usu·rer \ˈyü-zhər-ər, ˈyüzh-rər\ *n* : one that lends money especially at an excessively high rate of interest

usu·ri·ous \yu̇-ˈzhu̇r-ē-əs, -ˈzu̇r-\ *adj* : practicing, involving, or constituting usury ⟨*usurious* interest⟩ — **usu·ri·ous·ly** *adv* — **usu·ri·ous·ness** *n*

usurp \yu̇-ˈsərp *also* -ˈzərp\ *vt* : to seize and hold by force or without right ⟨*usurp* a throne⟩ [Medieval French *usorper,* from Latin *usurpare,* from *usu* "by use" + *rapere* "to seize"] — **usur·pa·tion** \ˌyü-sər-ˈpā-shən *also* ˌyü-zər-\ *n* — **usurp·er** \yu̇-ˈsər-pər *also* -ˈzər-\ *n*

usu·ry \ˈyüzh-rē, -ə-rē\ *n, pl* **usuries** **1** : the lending of money with an interest charge for its use **2** : an excessive rate or amount of interest charged; *esp* : interest above an established legal rate [Medieval Latin *usuria* "interest," from Latin *usura,* from *usus,* past participle of *uti* "to use"]

Ute \ˈyüt\ *n, pl* **Ute** *or* **Utes** : a member of an American Indian people of what is now Colorado, New Mexico, Arizona, and Utah having a Nahuatl-related language [short for earlier *Utah, Utaw,* from American Spanish *Yuta*]

uten·sil \yu̇-ˈten-səl\ *n* **1** : an instrument or vessel used in a household and especially a kitchen **2** : an article serving a useful purpose ⟨a writing *utensil*⟩ [Middle French *utensile* "vessels for domestic use," from Latin *utensilia,* from *utensilis* "useful," from *uti* "to use"] ***synonyms*** see IMPLEMENT

uter·ine \ˈyüt-ə-ˌrīn, -rən\ *adj* : of, relating to, or affecting the uterus ⟨the *uterine* lining⟩ ⟨*uterine* cancer⟩

uter·us \ˈyüt-ə-rəs\ *n, pl* **uter·us·es** *or* **uteri** \-ˌrī\ **1** : a muscular organ of the female mammal for containing and usually for nourishing the young during development prior to birth — called also *womb* **2** : a structure in some lower animals analogous to the uterus of mammals in which eggs or young develop [Latin]

utile \ˈyüt-l, ˈyü-ˌtīl\ *adj* : USEFUL [Middle French, from Latin *utilis*]

[1]**util·i·tar·i·an** \yü-ˌtil-ə-ˈter-ē-ən\ *n* : an advocate or adherent of utilitarianism

[2]**utilitarian** *adj* **1** : of or relating to utilitarianism **2 a** : of or relating to utility **b** : aiming at usefulness rather than beauty ⟨*utilitarian* furnishings⟩

util·i·tar·i·an·ism \-ē-ə-ˌniz-əm\ *n* : a doctrine that one's conduct should be determined by the usefulness of its consequences; *esp* : a theory that the aim of action should be the greatest happiness of the greatest number

[1]**util·i·ty** \yü-ˈtil-ət-ē\ *n, pl* **-ties** **1** : fitness for some purpose or worth to some end **2** : something useful or designed for use **3 a** : PUBLIC UTILITY **b** (1) : a public service or a commodity (as power or water) provided by a public utility (2) : equipment

or a piece of equipment (as plumbing in a house) to provide such or a similar service **4 :** a program designed to perform or facilitate especially routine operations (as copying files or editing text) on a computer [Middle French *utilité,* from Latin *utilitas,* from *utilis* "useful," from *uti* "to use"]

[2]**utility** *adj* **1 :** capable of serving as a substitute in various roles or positions ⟨*utility* infielder⟩ **2 :** being of a usable but inferior grade ⟨*utility* beef⟩ **3 :** serving primarily for usefulness rather than beauty : UTILITARIAN ⟨*utility* furniture⟩ **4 :** designed for general use ⟨a *utility* tool⟩

utility knife *n* **:** a knife designed for general use ⟨a chef's *utility knife*⟩; *esp* **:** a cutting tool having a sharp replaceable blade that can be retracted into a usually metal handle

uti·lize \ˈyüt-l-ˌīz\ *vt* **:** to make use of : convert to use ***synonyms*** see USE — **uti·liz·able** \-ˌī-zə-bəl\ *adj* — **uti·li·za·tion** \ˌyüt-l-ə-ˈzā-shən\ *n* — **uti·liz·er** *n*

ut·most \ˈət-ˌmōst, *especially South* -məst\ *adj* **1 :** situated at the farthest or most distant point : EXTREME **2 :** of the greatest or highest degree, quantity, number, or amount [Old English *ūtmest,* superlative adj., from *ūt,* adv., "out"] — **utmost** *n*

uto·pia \yu̇-ˈtō-pē-ə\ *n* **1** *often cap* **:** a place of ideal perfection especially in laws, government, and social conditions **2 :** an impractical scheme for social improvement [*Utopia,* imaginary ideal country in *Utopia* by Sir Thomas More, from Greek *ou* "not, no" + *topos* "place"] — **uto·pi·an** \-pē-ən\ *adj or n, often cap*

Word History In 1516 Sir Thomas More published his book *Utopia,* in which the social and economic conditions of Europe, outlined in Book I, are compared with those of an ideal society described in Book II, a society established on an imaginary island off the shore of the New World. That such an ideal state is unattainable in reality is implied by the name More gave to this island, *Utopia,* which literally means "no place." In modern English *utopia* has become a generic term for any place of ideal perfection. Less optimistically *utopia* has also come to mean an impractical scheme for social improvement.

utri·cle \ˈyü-tri-kəl\ *n* **:** the larger chamber of the membranous labyrinth of the inner ear into which the semicircular canals open — compare SACCULE [Latin *utriculus* "small leather bag," from *uter* "leather bag"] — **utric·u·lar** \yu̇-ˈtrik-yə-lər\ *adj*

utric·u·lus \yu̇-ˈtrik-yə-ləs\ *n* **:** UTRICLE [Latin, "small bag"]

[1]**ut·ter** \ˈət-ər\ *adj* **:** ABSOLUTE, TOTAL ⟨an *utter* impossibility⟩ ⟨*utter* strangers⟩ [Old English *ūtera* "outer," comparative adj., from *ūt,* adv., "out"] — **ut·ter·ly** *adv*

[2]**utter** *vt* **1 :** to send forth as a sound **2 :** to express in usually spoken words **3 :** PASS 16a [Middle English *uttren* "to put forth, offer for sale," from *utter,* adv., "outside," from Old English *ūtor,* comparative of *ūt* "out"] — **ut·ter·able** \ˈət-ə-rə-bəl\ *adj* — **ut·ter·er** \ˈət-ər-ər\ *n*

ut·ter·ance \ˈət-ə-rəns\ *n* **1 :** something uttered; *esp* **:** an oral or written statement **2 :** the action of uttering with the voice : SPEECH **3 :** power, style, or manner of speaking

ut·ter·most \ˈət-ər-ˌmōst\ *adj* **:** EXTREME 3, UTMOST — **uttermost** *n*

uvu·la \ˈyü-vyə-lə\ *n, pl* **-las** *or* **-lae** \-ˌlē, -ˌlī\ **:** the fleshy lobe hanging down from the back part of the soft palate [Medieval Latin, from Latin *uva* "cluster of grapes, uvula"]

uvu·lar \-lər\ *adj* **1 :** of or relating to the uvula ⟨*uvular* glands⟩ **2 :** produced with the aid of the uvula ⟨a *uvular* sound⟩

ux·o·ri·ous \ˌək-ˈsōr-ē-əs, -ˈsȯr-; ˌəg-ˈzōr-, -ˈzȯr-\ *adj* **:** excessively fond of or submissive to a wife [Latin *uxorius,* from *uxor* "wife"] — **ux·o·ri·ous·ly** *adv* — **ux·o·ri·ous·ness** *n*

Uz·bek \ˈu̇z-ˌbek, ˈəz-\ *or* **Uz·beg** \-ˌbeg\ *n* **1 :** a member of a people of Central Asia and especially of Uzbekistan **2 :** the Turkic language of the Uzbek people

V

v \ˈvē\ *n, pl* **v's** *or* **vs** \ˈvēz\ *often cap* **1 :** the 22nd letter of the English alphabet **2 :** five in Roman numerals

va·can·cy \ˈvā-kən-sē\ *n, pl* **-cies** **1 a :** a vacating of an office, post, or property **b :** the time such office or property is vacant **2 :** a vacant office, post, or tenancy ⟨two *vacancies* in a building⟩ **3 :** empty space ⟨stare into *vacancy*⟩ **4 :** the state of being vacant

va·cant \ˈvā-kənt\ *adj* **1 :** having no occupant : not being used or filled ⟨a *vacant* room⟩ ⟨*vacant* chairs⟩ ⟨a *vacant* office⟩ **2 :** free from business or care : LEISURE ⟨a few *vacant* hours⟩ **3 :** showing lack of thought or expression ⟨a *vacant* smile⟩ [Medieval French, from Latin *vacans,* present participle of *vacare* "to be empty, be free"] ***synonyms*** see EMPTY — **va·cant·ly** *adv* — **va·cant·ness** *n*

va·cate \ˈvā-ˌkāt, vā-ˈ\ *vt* **1 :** to make void : ANNUL ⟨*vacate* an agreement⟩ **2 :** to make vacant : leave empty ⟨*vacate* a building⟩ ⟨*vacate* a position⟩ [Latin *vacare* "to be empty, be free"]

[1]**va·ca·tion** \vā-ˈkā-shən, və-\ *n* **1 :** a respite or a time of respite from something : INTERMISSION **2 a :** a period during which activity (as of a school) is suspended **b :** a period of freedom from work granted to an employee **3 :** a period spent away from home or business in travel or recreation ⟨had a restful *vacation* at the beach⟩ **4 :** an act or an instance of vacating

[2]**vacation** *vi* **-tioned; -tion·ing** \-shə-niŋ, -shniŋ\ **:** to take or spend a vacation ⟨*vacation* in July⟩

va·ca·tion·er \-shə-nər, -shnər\ *n* **:** a person taking a vacation

va·ca·tion·ist \-shə-nəst, -shnəst\ *n* **:** VACATIONER

va·ca·tion·land \-shən-ˌland\ *n* **:** an area with recreational attractions and facilities for vacationers

vac·ci·nate \ˈvak-sə-ˌnāt\ *vt* **:** to administer a vaccine to usually by injection — **vac·ci·na·tor** \-ˌnāt-ər\ *n*

vac·ci·na·tion \ˌvak-sə-ˈnā-shən\ *n* **1 :** the act of vaccinating **2 :** the scar left by vaccinating

vac·cine \vak-ˈsēn, ˈvak-ˌ\ *n* **:** a preparation of killed, weakened, or fully infectious microbes (as viruses) that is given (as by injection) to produce or increase immunity to a particular disease [French *vaccine* "cowpox," from Latin *vaccinus* "of cows," from *vacca* "cow"] — **vaccine** *adj*

Word History Our word *vaccine* was derived from Latin *vacca,* "cow." The Latin adjective *vaccinus,* "of or from cows," was used by scientists in the name of a disease called *variolae vaccinae,* or "cowpox." The Latin word *vaccinae* from that phrase was then borrowed into French and respelled as *vaccine,* which was originally used as an adjective with the same meaning as the Latin. A substance derived from a cow infected with cowpox would be called a *vaccine* substance. In the late 18th century the English physician Edward Jenner discovered that inoculation with a form of cowpox was an effective preventive of smallpox. The substance used in such inoculation came to be called a *vaccine.*

vac·cin·ia \vak-ˈsin-ē-ə\ *n* **:** a virus that is closely related to the viruses causing smallpox and cowpox and that includes a strain used in making vaccines against smallpox [New Latin, from Latin *vaccinus* "of cows"] — **vac·cin·i·al** \-ē-əl\ *adj*

vac·il·late \ˈvas-ə-ˌlāt\ *vi* **1 :** FLUCTUATE ⟨a *vacillating* stock market⟩ **2 :** to incline first to one course or opinion and then to another : WAVER [Latin *vacillare* "to sway, waver"] ***synonyms*** see HESITATE — **vac·il·lat·ing·ly** \-iŋ-lē\ *adv* — **vac·il·la·tion** \ˌvas-ə-ˈlā-shən\ *n* — **vac·il·la·tor** \ˈvas-ə-ˌlāt-ər\ *n*

va·cu·i·ty \va-ˈkyü-ət-ē, və-\ *n, pl* **-ties** **1 :** an empty space **2**

\ə\ **abut**	\au̇\ **out**	\i\ **tip**	\ȯ\ **saw**	\u̇\ **foot**
\ər\ **further**	\ch\ **chin**	\ī\ **life**	\ȯi\ **coin**	\y\ **yet**
\a\ **mat**	\e\ **pet**	\j\ **job**	\th\ **thin**	\yü\ **few**
\ā\ **take**	\ē\ **easy**	\ng\ **sing**	\t͟h\ **this**	\yu̇\ **cure**
\ä\ **cot, cart**	\g\ **go**	\ō\ **bone**	\ü\ **food**	\zh\ **vision**

: the state, fact, or quality of being vacuous **3** : something (as a remark or idea) that is vacuous or inane

vac·u·ole \'vak-yə-ˌwōl\ *n* : a usually fluid-filled cavity in tissues or in the cytoplasm of a cell [French, literally, "small vacuum," from Latin *vacuum*] — **vac·u·o·lar** \ˌvak-yə-'wō-lər, -lär\ *adj*

vac·u·ous \'vak-yə-wəs\ *adj* **1** : EMPTY 1 **2** : marked by lack of ideas or intelligence : STUPID ⟨a *vacuous* expression⟩ **3** : having no serious occupation : IDLE [Latin *vacuus*] — **vac·u·ous·ly** *adv* — **vac·u·ous·ness** *n*

1vac·u·um \'vak-ˌyüm, -yəm, -yu̇-əm\ *n, pl* **-u·ums** *or* **-ua** \-yə-wə\ **1 a** : a space absolutely devoid of matter **b** : a space partially exhausted (as to the highest degree possible) by artificial means (as an air pump) **2 a** : a state or condition resembling a vacuum : VOID **b** : a state of isolation from outside influences **3** : a device creating or utilizing a partial vacuum; *esp* : VACUUM CLEANER [Latin, from *vacuus* "empty"]

2vacuum *adj* : of, containing, producing, or making use of a partial vacuum

3vacuum *vt* **1** : to use a vacuum device (as a vacuum cleaner) upon ⟨*vacuum* the living room⟩ **2** : to draw or take in by or as if by suction ⟨*vacuumed* the crumbs⟩

vacuum bottle *n* : THERMOS

vacuum cleaner *n* : an electrical appliance for cleaning (as floors or carpets) by suction

vac·u·um–packed \ˌvak-yu̇-əm-'pakt, -yüm-, -yəm-\ *adj* : having much of the air removed before being sealed ⟨a *vacuum-packed* can of coffee⟩

vacuum pump *n* : a pump for exhausting gas from an enclosed space

vacuum tube *n* : an electron tube evacuated to a high degree of vacuum

va·de me·cum \ˌvād-ē-'mē-kəm, ˌväd-ē-'mā-\ *n, pl* **vade mecums** **1** : a book for ready reference : MANUAL **2** : something regularly carried about by a person [Latin, "go with me"]

1vag·a·bond \'vag-ə-ˌbänd\ *adj* **1** : moving from place to place without a fixed home ⟨*vagabond* minstrels⟩ **2 a** : of, relating to, or characteristic of a wanderer **b** : leading an unsettled, irresponsible, or disreputable life [Medieval French *vacabund,* from Late Latin *vagabundus,* from Latin *vagari* "to wander"]

2vagabond *n* : one who leads a vagabond life; *esp* : VAGRANT 1a, TRAMP — **vag·a·bond·age** \-ˌbän-dij\ *n* — **vag·a·bond·ism** \-ˌbän-ˌdiz-əm\ *n*

vag·a·bond·ish \-ˌbän-dish\ *adj* : of, relating to, or characteristic of a vagabond

va·gal \'vā-gəl\ *adj* : of, relating to, mediated by, or being the vagus nerve

va·ga·ry \'vā-gə-rē; və-'geər-ē, -'gaər-, vā-\ *n, pl* **-ries** : an eccentric or unpredictable manifestation, action, or notion [probably from Latin *vagari* "to wander"] ***synonyms*** see CAPRICE

va·gi·na \və-'jī-nə\ *n, pl* **-nas** *also* **-nae** \-nē\ **1** : a canal in a female mammal that leads from the uterus to the external opening of the genital canal **2** : a canal that is similar in function to the vagina and occurs in various animals other than mammals [Latin, literally, "sheath"] — **vag·i·nal** \'vaj-ən-l\ *adj*

va·gran·cy \'vā-grən-sē\ *n, pl* **-cies** **1** : VAGARY **2** : the state, action, or offense of being vagrant or a vagrant

1va·grant \'vā-grənt\ *n* **1 a** : one who wanders idly from place to place without a home or apparent means of support **b** : a person (as a drunkard or prostitute) classed as a vagrant by statute **2** : one that leads a wandering life [probably from Medieval French *vageraunt* "wandering," from *vagrer, wacrer* "to wander about," of Germanic origin]

2vagrant *adj* **1** : wandering about from place to place usually with no means of support **2 a** : having a fleeting, wayward, or inconstant quality **b** : having no fixed course : RANDOM ⟨*vagrant* thoughts⟩

va·grom \'vā-grəm\ *adj* : VAGRANT ⟨a *vagrom* impulse⟩

vague \'vāg\ *adj* **vagu·er; vagu·est** **1 a** : not clearly expressed : stated in indefinite terms ⟨*vague* accusations⟩ **b** : not having a precise meaning **2** : not clearly felt, grasped, or understood : INDISTINCT ⟨*vague* ideas⟩ ⟨a *vague* longing⟩ **3** : not thinking or expressing one's thoughts clearly or precisely ⟨*vague* about dates and places⟩ **4** : not sharply outlined : HAZY, SHADOWY [Middle French, from Latin *vagus,* literally, "wandering"] ***synonyms*** see OBSCURE — **vague·ly** *adv* — **vague·ness** *n*

vagus nerve *n* : either of the 10th pair of cranial nerves that arise from the medulla and supply autonomic sensory and motor fibers mostly to the internal organs — called also *vagus* [New Latin *vagus nervus,* literally, "wandering nerve"]

vail \'vāl\ *vt* : to lower especially as a sign of respect or submission [Medieval French *valer,* short for *avaler* "to let fall," from *aval* "downward," from *a* "to" + *val* "valley"]

vain \'vān\ *adj* **1** : WORTHLESS ⟨*vain* promises⟩ **2** : not succeeding : FUTILE ⟨a *vain* attempt⟩ **3** : proud of one's looks or abilities : CONCEITED [Medieval French, from Latin *vanus* "empty, futile"] — **vain·ly** *adv* — **vain·ness** \'vān-nəs\ *n* — **in vain** **1** : to no purpose : without success ⟨her efforts were *in vain*⟩ **2** : in an irreverent or blasphemous manner

synonyms VAIN, FUTILE mean producing no result. VAIN usually implies simple failure to achieve a purpose or succeed in an attempt ⟨made a *vain* attempt at finishing⟩. FUTILE may suggest completeness of failure or folly of undertaking ⟨a *futile* effort to escape⟩.

vain·glo·ri·ous \vān-'glōr-ē-əs, 'vān-, -'glȯr-\ *adj* : marked by vainglory : BOASTFUL — **vain·glo·ri·ous·ly** *adv* — **vain·glo·ri·ous·ness** *n*

vain·glo·ry \'vān-ˌglōr-ē, -ˌglȯr-\ *n* **1** : excessive or showy pride in oneself and one's achievements **2** : vain display or show : VANITY

vair \'vaər, 'veər\ *n* : the bluish gray and white fur of a squirrel prized for ornament during the Middle Ages [Medieval French, from *vair* "variegated," from Latin *varius* "variegated, various"]

val·ance \'val-əns, 'vāl-\ *n* **1** : a drapery hung along the edge of a bed, table, altar, canopy, or shelf **2** : a short drapery or wood or metal frame used as a decorative heading to conceal the top of curtains and fixtures [Medieval French *valence,* probably from *valer* "to lower," from *avaler* "to let fall," from *aval* "downward," from *a* "to" + *val* "valley"]

V valance 2

vale \'vāl\ *n* : VALLEY 1, DALE [Medieval French *val,* from Latin *valles, vallis*]

val·e·dic·tion \ˌval-ə-'dik-shən\ *n* : an act or utterance of leave-taking : FAREWELL [Latin *valedicere* "to say farewell," from *vale* "farewell" + *dicere* "to say"]

vale·dic·to·ri·an \ˌval-ə-ˌdik-'tōr-ē-ən, -'tȯr-\ *n* : the student usually of the highest rank in a graduating class who delivers the valedictory oration at commencement exercises

1vale·dic·to·ry \-'dik-tə-rē, -trē\ *adj* : of or relating to leave-taking : expressing a farewell ⟨a *valedictory* address⟩

2valedictory *n, pl* **-ries** : a valedictory oration or statement

va·lence \'vā-ləns\ *n* **1** : the degree of combining power of an element as shown by the number of atomic weights of a univalent element (as hydrogen) with which the atomic weight of the element will combine or for which it can be substituted **2** : relative capacity to unite, react, or interact (as with antigens or a biological substrate) [Late Latin *valentia* "power, capacity," from Latin *valēre* "to be strong"]

valence electron *n* : an electron in the outer shell of an atom that is responsible for the chemical properties of the atom

Va·len·ci·ennes \və-ˌlen-sē-'en, ˌval-ən-sē-, -'enz\ *n* : a fine handmade lace [*Valenciennes,* France]

-va·lent \'vā-lənt\ *adj combining form* : having a (specified) valence or valences ⟨poly*valent*⟩ ⟨uni*valent*⟩

val·en·tine \'val-ən-ˌtīn\ *n* **1** : a sweetheart chosen or honored (as by a gift) on Valentine's Day **2** : a gift or greeting sent or given on Valentine's Day

Valentine's Day *also* **Valentine Day** *n* : February 14 observed in honor of St. Valentine and as a time for sending valentines

va·le·ri·an \və-'lir-ē-ən\ *n* **1** : any of a genus of perennial herbs mostly with flat-topped clusters of flowers and with roots and rhizomes having medicinal properties **2** : a medicinal preparation consisting of the dried roots and rhizomes of the garden heliotrope [Medieval Latin *valeriana*]

va·let \'val-ət, 'val-ˌā, va-'lā\ *n* **1** : a male servant who takes care of a man's clothes and performs personal services **2** : an employee (as of a hotel) who performs personal services for customers [Medieval French *vadlet, valet* "page, domestic servant," from Medieval Latin *vassus* "servant, vassal"]

val·e·tu·di·nar·i·an \ˌval-ə-ˌtüd-n-'er-ē-ən, -ˌtyüd-\ *n* : a person of a weak or sickly constitution; *esp* : one whose chief concern is his or her health [Latin *valetudinarius* "sickly, infirm," from *valetudo* "state of health, sickness," from *valēre* "to be strong, be well"] — **valetudinarian** *adj* — **val·e·tu·di·nar·i·an·ism** \-ˌiz-əm\ *n*

Val·hal·la \val-ˈhal-ə\ *n* **1** : the great hall in Norse mythology where heroes slain in battle are received **2** : a place of honor or happiness ⟨an actor's *Valhalla*⟩ [German *Walhalla,* from Old Norse *Valhǫll,* literally, "hall of the slain"]

val·iance \ˈval-yəns\ *n* : VALOR

val·ian·cy \-yən-sē\ *n* : VALOR

[1]val·iant \ˈval-yənt\ *adj* **1** : boldly brave : COURAGEOUS ⟨a *valiant* leader⟩ **2** : HEROIC ⟨*valiant* fighting⟩ ⟨a *valiant* effort⟩ [Medieval French *vaillant* "worthy, strong, courageous," from *valer* "to be of worth," from Latin *valēre* "to be strong"] — **val·iant·ly** *adv* — **val·iant·ness** *n*

[2]valiant *n* : a valiant person

val·id \ˈval-əd\ *adj* **1** : having legal strength or force; *esp* : binding in law : SOUND ⟨a *valid* contract⟩ **2 a** : founded on truth or fact : WELL-GROUNDED ⟨*valid* excuse⟩ **b** : logically correct ⟨a *valid* argument⟩ [Medieval Latin *validus,* from Latin, "strong," from *valēre* "to be strong"] — **va·lid·i·ty** \və-ˈlid-ət-ē, va-\ *n* — **val·id·ly** \ˈval-əd-lē\ *adv*

synonyms VALID, SOUND, COGENT mean having such force as to compel consideration and usually acceptance. VALID implies being supported by objective truth or generally accepted authority ⟨a *valid* reason for being late⟩. SOUND implies being based on solid fact and reasoning ⟨a *sound* plan⟩. COGENT stresses soundness or lucidness that makes argument or evidence conclusive ⟨a *cogent* summation of the facts⟩.

val·i·date \ˈval-ə-ˌdāt\ *vt* **1** : to make valid **2** : to support or confirm on a sound or authoritative basis ⟨experiments designed to *validate* the hypothesis⟩ — **val·i·da·tion** \ˌval-ə-ˈdā-shən\ *n*

va·line \ˈval-ˌēn, ˈvā-ˌlēn\ *n* : a crystalline essential amino acid $C_5H_{11}NO_2$ that is one of the building blocks of plant and animal proteins [derived from *valeric acid,* an acid that occurs in the roots of valerian, from *valerian*]

va·lise \və-ˈlēs\ *n* : SUITCASE [French, from Italian *valigia*]

Val·i·um \ˈval-ē-əm\ *trademark* — used for diazepam

Val·kyr·ie \val-ˈkir-ē\ *n* : any of the maidens of Odin who in Norse mythology choose the heroes to be slain in battle and conduct them to Valhalla [Old Norse *valkyrja,* literally, "chooser of the slain"]

val·ley \ˈval-ē\ *n, pl* **valleys** **1** : an elongate depression of the earth's surface usually between ranges of hills or mountains **2 a** : DEPRESSION 2, HOLLOW **b** : the place of meeting of two slopes of a roof forming a drainage channel [Medieval French *valee,* from *val* "valley, vale"]

val·or \ˈval-ər\ *n* : personal bravery in the face of danger [Medieval French *valour,* from Medieval Latin *valor* "value, valor," from Latin *valēre* "to be strong"] ***synonyms*** see COURAGE

val·or·ous \ˈval-ə-rəs\ *adj* **1** : possessing or showing valor : BRAVE ⟨*valorous* soldiers⟩ **2** : marked by or performed with valor ⟨*valorous* feats⟩ — **val·or·ous·ly** *adv*

valse \vȧls\ *n* : WALTZ; *esp* : a concert waltz [French, from German *Walzer*]

[1]valu·able \ˈval-yə-bəl, -yə-wə-bəl\ *adj* **1 a** : having monetary value **b** : worth a great deal of money ⟨*valuable* jewelery⟩ **2** : having value : of great use or service ⟨*valuable* information⟩ ***synonyms*** see COSTLY — **valu·able·ness** *n* — **valu·ably** \-blē\ *adv*

[2]valuable *n* : a personal possession (as a jewel) of relatively great monetary value ⟨stored *valuables* in the safe⟩

val·u·ate \ˈval-yə-ˌwāt\ *vt* : to place a value on : APPRAISE — **val·u·a·tor** \-ˌwāt-ər\ *n*

val·u·a·tion \ˌval-yə-ˈwā-shən\ *n* **1** : the act or process of valuing; *esp* : appraisal of property **2** : the estimated or determined value of a thing **3** : judgment or appreciation of worth or character — **val·u·a·tion·al** \-shnəl, -shən-l\ *adj* — **val·u·a·tion·al·ly** \-ē\ *adv*

[1]val·ue \ˈval-yü\ *n* **1** : a fair return in goods, services, or money for something exchanged **2** : the amount of money that something is worth **3** : relative worth, utility, or importance ⟨had nothing of *value* to say⟩ **4** : a numerical quantity that is assigned or is determined by calculation or measurement ⟨find the *value* of *x*⟩ **5** : the relative duration of a musical note **6 a** : relative lightness or darkness of a color : LUMINOSITY **b** : the relation of one part in a picture to another with respect to lightness and darkness **7** : something (as a principle or quality) having or held to have real worth or merit ⟨the *values* of the old and young are often very different⟩ **8** : DENOMINATION 4 [Medieval French, derived from Latin *valēre* "to be worth, be strong"] ***synonyms*** see WORTH

[2]value *vt* **val·ued; val·u·ing** **1 a** : to estimate or assign the monetary worth of : APPRAISE ⟨*value* a necklace⟩ **b** : to rate or scale in usefulness, importance, or general worth **2** : to consider or rate highly : PRIZE, ESTEEM ⟨*valued* their friendship⟩ — **valu·er** \-yə-wər\ *n*

value judgment *n* : a judgment assigning a value (as good or bad) to something

val·ue·less \ˈval-yü-ləs, -yə-\ *adj* : of no value : WORTHLESS

valve \ˈvalv\ *n* **1** : a bodily structure (as in a vein or the heart) that closes temporarily to prevent passage of material or permits movement of a fluid in one direction only — compare MITRAL VALVE, SEMILUNAR VALVE, TRICUSPID VALVE **2 a** : a mechanical device by which the flow of liquid, gas, or loose material in bulk may be started, stopped, or regulated by a movable part; *also* : the movable part of such a device **b** : a device in a brass wind instrument for quickly varying the tube length in order to change the tone by some definite interval **c** *chiefly British* : ELECTRON TUBE **3** : one of the pair of pieces comprising the hinged shell of some shell-bearing animals and especially of bivalve mollusks **4** : one of the segments or pieces into which a ripe seed capsule or pod separates [Latin *valva* "leaf of a double door"] — **valved** \ˈvalvd\ *adj*

val·vu·lar \ˈval-vyə-lər\ *adj* **1** : resembling or functioning as a valve; *also* : opening by valves **2** : of, relating to, or affecting a valve especially of the heart

va·moose \və-ˈmüs, va-\ *vi* : to depart quickly : SCRAM [Spanish *vamos* "let us go"]

[1]vamp \ˈvamp\ *n* : the part of a shoe upper or boot upper covering especially the forepart of the foot and sometimes also extending forward over the toe or backward to the back seam of the upper [Medieval French *avantpié* "part of a hose leg or shoe covering the forefoot," from *avant-* "fore-" + *pié* "foot," from Latin *pes*]

[2]vamp *vt* **1 a** : to provide (a shoe) with a new vamp **b** : to piece (something old) with a new part : PATCH ⟨*vamp* up old sermons⟩ **2** : INVENT ⟨*vamp* up an excuse⟩

[3]vamp *n* : a woman who uses her charm or wiles to seduce and exploit men [short for *vampire*]

[4]vamp *vt* : to practice seductive wiles on

vam·pire \ˈvam-ˌpīr\ *n* **1** : the body of a dead person believed to come from the grave at night and suck the blood of persons asleep **2 a** : one who lives by preying on others **b** : a woman who exploits and ruins her lover **3** : VAMPIRE BAT [French, from German *Vampir,* from Serbian *vampir*] — **vam·pir·ism** \-ˌpīr-ˌiz-əm\ *n*

vampire bat *n* : any of three bats of Mexico and South and Central America that feed on blood especially of domestic animals and are sometimes vectors of disease (as rabies); *also* : any of several other bats that do not feed on blood but are sometimes said to do so

vampire bat

[1]van \ˈvan\ *n* : VANGUARD

[2]van *n* **1 a** : a usually enclosed wagon or motortruck used for transportation of goods or animals **b** : a multipurpose enclosed motor vehicle having a boxlike shape, rear or side doors, and side panels often with windows **2** *chiefly British* : an enclosed railroad freight or baggage car [short for *caravan*]

va·na·di·um \və-ˈnād-ē-əm\ *n* : a grayish malleable metallic element found combined in minerals and used especially to form alloys and in catalysts — see ELEMENT table [New Latin, from Old Norse *Vanadīs* "Freya (goddess of love and beauty)"]

Van Al·len belt \va-ˈnal-ən-, və-\ *n* : a belt of intense ionizing ra-

\ə\ **abut**	\au̇\ **out**	\i\ **tip**	\ȯ\ **saw**	\u̇\ **foot**
\ər\ **further**	\ch\ **chin**	\ī\ **life**	\ȯi\ **coin**	\y\ **yet**
\a\ **mat**	\e\ **pet**	\j\ **job**	\th\ **thin**	\yü\ **few**
\ā\ **take**	\ē\ **easy**	\ng\ **sing**	\t͟h\ **this**	\yu̇\ **cure**
\ä\ **cot, cart**	\g\ **go**	\ō\ **bone**	\ü\ **food**	\zh\ **vision**

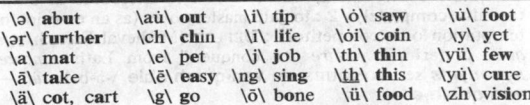

diation that surrounds the earth in the magnetosphere [James A. *Van Allen,* born 1914, American physicist]

van·dal \'van-dl\ *n* **1** *cap* : one of a Germanic people overrunning Gaul, Spain, and northern Africa in the 4th and 5th centuries A.D. and in 455 sacking Rome **2** : one who willfully destroys, damages, or defaces public or private property [Latin *Vandalii* "Vandals," of Germanic origin] — **vandal** *adj, often cap*

van·dal·ism \'van-dl-ˌiz-əm\ *n* : willful or malicious destruction or defacement of public or private property

van·dal·is·tic \ˌvan-dl-'is-tik\ *adj* : of or relating to vandalism

van·dal·ize \'van-dl-ˌīz\ *vt* : to subject to vandalism : DAMAGE

Van de Graaff generator \ˌvan-də-ˌgraf-\ *n* : a device for producing high-voltage electrical discharges commonly consisting of an insulated hollow conducting sphere that builds up the charge in its interior [Robert J. *Van de Graaff,* died 1967, American physicist]

Van·dyke \van-'dīk\ *n* : a trim pointed beard [Sir Anthony *Vandyke*]

Vandyke

vane \'vān\ *n* **1** : a movable device attached to an elevated object (as a spire) for showing the direction of the wind **2** : a flat or curved object that is rotated about an axis by a flow of fluid (as air or water) or that rotates to cause a fluid to flow or that changes the direction of a flow of fluid **3 a** : the flat expanded part of a feather — called also *web* **b** : a feather fastened to the shaft near the nock of an arrow [Old English *fana* "banner"] — **vaned** \'vānd\ *adj*

van·guard \'van-ˌgärd\ *n* **1** : the troops moving at the head of an army **2** : the forefront of an action or movement or those in the forefront [Medieval French *vantgarde, avantgarde,* from *avant-* "fore-" + *garde* "guard"]

va·nil·la \və-'nil-ə, -'nel-\ *n* **1** : any of a genus of tropical American climbing orchids **2 a** : VANILLA BEAN **b** : the flavoring extract from the vanilla bean [Spanish *vainilla,* from *vaina* "sheath," from Latin *vagina*]

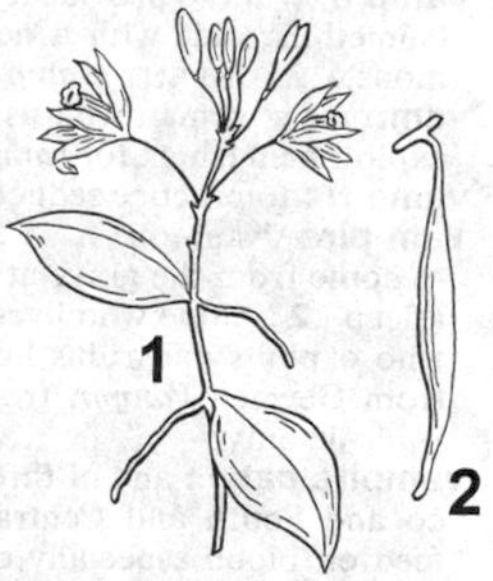

1 vanilla 1, *2* vanilla bean

vanilla bean *n* : the long pod of a vanilla that is an important article of commerce for the flavoring extract that it yields

va·nil·lin \'van-l-ən\ *n* : a compound that is the chief fragrant component of vanilla

van·ish \'van-ish\ *vi* **1** : to pass quickly from sight : DISAPPEAR **2** : to pass completely from existence [Medieval French *vaniss-,* stem of *vanir, envanir, esvanir* "to vanish," from Latin *evanescere,* from *e-* + *vanescere* "to vanish," from *vanus* "empty, vain"] — **van·ish·er** *n*

vanishing cream *n* : a cosmetic preparation that is less oily than cold cream and is used chiefly as a foundation for face powder

vanishing point *n* **1** : a point at which receding parallel lines seem to meet **2** : a point at which something disappears or ceases to exist

van·i·ty \'van-ət-ē\ *n, pl* **-ties** **1** : something that is vain **2** : the quality or fact of being vain **3** : inflated pride in oneself or one's appearance : CONCEIT **4** : a fashionable article or knickknack **5 a** : ^{3}COMPACT 1 **b** : DRESSING TABLE [Medieval French *vanité,* from Latin *vanitas,* from *vanus* "empty, vain"]

vanity fair *n, often cap V&F* : a scene or place marked by frivolity and pointless show [*Vanity-Fair,* a fair held in the frivolous town of Vanity in John Bunyan's *Pilgrim's Progress*]

van·quish \'vang-kwish, 'van-\ *vt* **1** : to overcome in battle : subdue completely **2** : to gain mastery over (as an emotion or temptation or a competitor) : DEFEAT [Medieval French *venquis,* preterit of *veintre* "to conquer," from Latin *vincere*] ***synonyms*** see CONQUER — **van·quish·able** \-ə-bəl\ *adj* — **van·quish·er** *n*

van·tage \'vant-ij\ *n* **1** : superiority in a contest **2** : a position giving a strategic advantage, commanding perspective, or comprehensive view **3** : ADVANTAGE 4 [Medieval French *vantage, avantage* "benefit, gain"]

vantage point *n* : a position or standpoint from which something is viewed or considered; *esp* : POINT OF VIEW

van·ward \'van-wərd\ *adj* : located in the vanguard : ADVANCED — **vanward** *adv*

vap·id \'vap-əd\ *adj* : lacking liveliness, tang, briskness, or force : FLAT, UNINTERESTING ⟨a *vapid* remark⟩ ⟨a *vapid* smile⟩ [Latin *vapidus* "flat tasting"] ***synonyms*** see INSIPID — **va·pid·i·ty** \va-'pid-ət-ē\ *n* — **vap·id·ly** \'vap-əd-lē\ *adv* — **vap·id·ness** *n*

^{1}**va·por** \'vā-pər\ *n* **1** : fine particles of matter (as fog or smoke) floating in the air and clouding it **2** : a substance in a gaseous state; *esp* : such a substance that is liquid under ordinary conditions **3** : something insubstantial or fleeting [Medieval French *vapor,* from Latin, "steam, vapor"]

^{2}**vapor** *vi* **va·pored; va·por·ing** \-pə-ring, -pring\ **1 a** : to rise or pass off in vapor **b** : to emit vapor **2** : to indulge in bragging, blustering, or idle talk — **va·por·er** \-pər-ər\ *n*

va·por·ing \'vā-pə-ring, -pring\ *n* : the act or speech of one that vapors; *esp* : an idle, extravagant, or high-flown expression or speech — usually used in plural

va·por·ish \'vā-pə-rish, -prish\ *adj* **1** : resembling or suggestive of vapor **2** : given to fits of depression or hysteria

va·por·ize \'vā-pə-ˌrīz\ *vb* : to turn from a liquid or solid into vapor — **va·por·iz·able** \-ˌrī-zə-bəl\ *adj* — **va·por·i·za·tion** \ˌvā-pə-rə-'zā-shən\ *n*

va·por·iz·er \'vā-pə-ˌrī-zər\ *n* : a device that vaporizes something (as a fuel oil, water, or a medicated liquid)

vapor lock *n* : a partial or complete interruption of fuel flow in an internal-combustion engine caused by the formation of bubbles of vapor in the fuel-feeding system

va·por·ous \'vā-pə-rəs, -prəs\ *adj* **1** : consisting or characteristic of vapor **2** : containing or obscured by vapors : MISTY **3** : UNSUBSTANTIAL, VAGUE — **va·por·ous·ly** *adv* — **va·por·ous·ness** *n*

vapor pressure *n* : the pressure exerted by a vapor that is in equilibrium with its solid or liquid form — called also *vapor tension*

vapor trail *n* : CONTRAIL

va·por·ware \'vā-pər-ˌwaər, -ˌweər\ *n* : a new computer-related product that has been widely advertised but has not and may never become available

va·pory \'vā-pə-rē, -prē\ *adj* : VAPOROUS, MISTY

vapour *chiefly British variant of* VAPOR

va·que·ro \vä-'keər-ō\ *n, pl* **-ros** : a ranch hand : COWBOY [Spanish, from *vaca* "cow," from Latin *vacca*]

var·ia \'ver-ē-ə, 'var-\ *n pl* : MISCELLANY; *esp* : a literary miscellany [Latin, neuter pl. of *varius* "various"]

^{1}**vari·able** \'ver-ē-ə-bəl, 'var-\ *adj* **1 a** : able or apt to vary : CHANGEABLE ⟨*variable* winds⟩ **b** : FICKLE, INCONSTANT **2 a** : characterized by variations **b** : not true to type : ABERRANT ⟨a *variable* species⟩ **3** : having the characteristics of a variable — **vari·abil·i·ty** \ˌver-ē-ə-'bil-ət-ē, ˌvar-\ *n* — **vari·able·ness** \'ver-ē-ə-bəl-nəs, 'var-\ *n* — **vari·ably** \-blē\ *adv*

^{2}**variable** *n* **1 a** : a quantity that may assume any one of a set of values **b** : a mathematical symbol representing a variable **2** : something that is variable **3** : a factor in a scientific experiment that may be subject to change ⟨controlling all *variables* except temperature⟩

variable star *n* : a star whose brightness changes usually in more or less regular periods

vari·ance \'ver-ē-əns, 'var-\ *n* **1** : the fact, quality, or state of being variable or variant : DIFFERENCE ⟨yearly *variance* in crops⟩ **2** : the fact or state of being in disagreement : DISSENSION, DISPUTE **3** : the square of the standard deviation — **at variance** : not in harmony or agreement

^{1}**vari·ant** \'ver-ē-ənt, 'var-\ *adj* **1** : differing from others of its kind or class **2** : varying usually slightly from the standard form ⟨a *variant* spelling⟩

^{2}**variant** *n* : one of two or more persons or things exhibiting usually slight differences: as **a** : one that exhibits variation from a type or norm **b** : one of two or more different spellings or pronunciations of the same word

vari·a·tion \ˌver-ē-'ā-shən, ˌvar-\ *n* **1 a** : the act or process of varying : the state or fact of being varied **b** : an instance of varying **c** : the extent to which or range in which a thing varies **2** : DECLINATION 5 **3** : the repetition of a musical theme with modifications in rhythm, tune, harmony, or key **4 a :** divergence in the characteristics that are typical or usual for a species or group **b :** an individual or group exhibiting variation — **vari·a·tion·al** \-shnəl, -shən-ᵊl\ *adj* — **vari·a·tion·al·ly** \-ē\ *adv*

vari·col·ored \ˈver-i-ˌkəl-ərd, ˈvar-\ *adj* **:** having various colors **:** VARIEGATED ⟨*varicolored* marble⟩

var·i·cose \ˈvar-ə-ˌkōs\ *adj* **:** abnormally swollen or dilated ⟨*varicose* veins⟩ [Latin *varicosus* "full of dilated veins," from *varic-, varix* "dilated vein"]

var·i·cos·i·ty \ˌvar-ə-ˈkäs-ət-ē\ *n, pl* **-ties** **1 :** the quality or state of being varicose **2 :** a varicose part (as of a vein)

var·ied \ˈveər-ēd, ˈvaər-\ *adj* **1 :** having numerous forms or types **:** DIVERSE **2 :** VARIEGATED 1 — **var·ied·ly** *adv*

var·ie·gate \ˈver-ē-ə-ˌgāt, ˈver-i-ˌgāt, ˈvar-\ *vt* **1 :** to diversify in external appearance especially with different colors **2 :** to make interesting by variety [Latin *variegare,* from *varius* "various"] — **var·ie·ga·tion** \ˌver-ē-ə-ˈgā-shən, ˌver-i-ˈgā-, ˌvar-\ *n* — **var·ie·ga·tor** \ˈver-ē-ə-ˌgāt-ər, ˈver-i-ˌgāt-, ˈvar-\ *n*

var·ie·gat·ed \ˈver-ē-ə-ˌgāt-əd, ˈver-i-ˌgāt-, ˈvar-\ *adj* **1 :** having patches, stripes, or marks of different colors ⟨*variegated* flowers⟩ **2 :** VARIED 1

va·ri·ety \və-ˈrī-ət-ē\ *n, pl* **-eties** **1 :** the quality or state of having different forms or types **2 :** a number or collection of different things **:** ASSORTMENT ⟨the store stocks a large *variety* of goods⟩ **3 a :** something differing from others of the same general kind **b :** any of various groups of plants or animals within a species that are distinguished from other groups by characteristics not constant enough or too trivial to distinguish species **4 :** VARIETY SHOW [Latin *varietas,* from *varius* "various"] — **va·ri·etal** \-ət-ᵊl\ *adj* — **va·ri·etal·ly** \-ᵊl-ē\ *adv*

variety meat *n* **:** an edible part (as the liver) of a slaughter animal other than skeletal muscle

variety show *n* **:** a theatrical entertainment of performances (as of songs, dances, and skits) that follow one another and are not related

variety store *n* **:** a retail store that carries a large variety of usually inexpensive merchandise

va·ri·o·la \ˌver-ē-ˈō-lə, ˌvar-; və-ˈrī-ə-lə\ *n* **:** COWPOX; *also* **:** the virus causing smallpox [Late Latin, "pustule"]

var·i·o·rum \ˌver-ē-ˈōr-əm, ˌvar-, -ˈór-\ *n* **:** an edition or text especially of a classical author with notes by different persons and often with variant readings of the text [Latin *cum notis variorum* "with the notes of various persons"]

var·i·ous \ˈver-ē-əs, ˈvar-\ *adj* **1 :** marked by variation or variety (as in appearance or properties) **:** of differing kinds ⟨*various* enterprises use metals⟩ ⟨my *various* responsibilities⟩ **2 :** differing one from another **:** UNLIKE ⟨animals as *various* as cat and mouse⟩ **3 :** consisting of an indefinite number greater than one ⟨*various* schemes⟩ ⟨stop at *various* towns⟩ [Latin *varius*] — **var·i·ous·ly** *adv* — **var·i·ous·ness** *n*

vari·sized \ˈver-i-ˌsīzd, ˈvar-\ *adj* **:** of various sizes

va·ris·tor \va-ˈris-tər, ve-\ *n* **:** an electrical resistor whose resistance depends on the applied voltage [*vari-* "varied" (from Latin *varius*) + *resistor*]

var·let \ˈvär-lət\ *n* **1 :** [2]RETAINER 1, ATTENDANT **2 :** an unprincipled person [Medieval French, "young nobleman, page," from Medieval Latin *vassus* "servant, vassal"]

var·mint \ˈvär-mənt\ *n* **1 :** an animal considered a pest **2 :** a contemptible person **:** RASCAL [alteration of *vermin*]

[1]**var·nish** \ˈvär-nish\ *n* **1 a :** a liquid preparation that is spread like paint and dries to a hard lustrous typically transparent coating **b :** the covering or glaze given by the application of varnish **2 :** deceptive outer appearance [Medieval French *vernis*] — **var·nishy** \-ē\ *adj*

[2]**varnish** *vt* **:** to cover with or as if with varnish — **var·nish·er** *n*

var·si·ty \ˈvär-sət-ē, -stē\ *n, pl* **-ties** **:** a principal squad representing a university, college, school, or club especially in a sport [from *university*]

varve \ˈvärv\ *n* **:** a pair of layers of alternately finer and coarser silt or clay believed to comprise an annual cycle of deposition in a body of still water [Swedish *varv* "turn, layer"]

vary \ˈveər-ē, ˈvaər-\ *vb* **var·ied; vary·ing** **1 a :** to make a usually minor or partial change in ⟨the rule must not be *varied*⟩ **b :** to give variety to **:** DIVERSIFY ⟨*vary* a diet⟩ ⟨a program *varied* to avoid monotony⟩ **2 a :** to exhibit or undergo change ⟨*varying* skies⟩ ⟨the accuracy of the several chapters *varies* greatly⟩ **b :** to be different ⟨laws *vary* from state to state⟩ **3 :** to take on successive values ⟨*y varies* inversely with *x*⟩ **4 :** to diverge structurally or physiologically from typical members of a group [Latin *variare,* from *varius* "various"] ***synonyms*** see CHANGE — **vary·ing·ly** \-iŋ-lē\ *adv*

varying hare *n* **:** SNOWSHOE HARE

vas·cu·lar \ˈvas-kyə-lər\ *adj* **:** of, relating to, or being a tube or channel for carrying a body fluid (as blood of an animal or sap of a plant) or to a system of such tubes or channels; *also* **:** supplied with or made up of such tubes or channels and especially blood vessels ⟨a *vascular* tumor⟩ ⟨a *vascular* system⟩ [Latin *vasculum* "small vessel," from *vas* "vessel"] — **vas·cu·lar·i·ty** \ˌvas-kyə-ˈlar-ət-ē\ *n*

vascular bundle *n* **:** a unit of the vascular system of a higher plant (as a fern or conifer) consisting usually of xylem and phloem together with parenchyma cells and fibers

vascular cambium *n* **:** a ring of meristem between the phloem and xylem of a vascular plant which gives rise to phloem on its outer side and xylem on its inner side

vascular cylinder *n* **:** STELE

vas·cu·lar·i·za·tion \ˌvas-kyə-lə-rə-ˈzā-shən\ *n* **:** the development of vessels in tissue

vascular plant *n* **:** a plant having a specialized conducting system that includes xylem and phloem **:** TRACHEOPHYTE

vascular ray *n* **:** a band of tissue partly in the phloem and partly in the xylem of a plant root or stem that looks in cross section like a spoke of a wheel and that carries fluids along a radius away from the center of the root or stem

vascular tissue *n* **:** a specialized conducting tissue of higher plants that consists essentially of phloem and xylem and forms a continuous system throughout the plant body

vas·cu·lum \ˈvas-kyə-ləm\ *n, pl* **-la** \-lə\ **:** a usually metal and commonly cylindrical covered box used in collecting botanical specimens [Latin, "small vessel"]

vas de·fer·ens \ˈvas-ˈdef-ə-rənz, -ˌrenz\ *n, pl* **va·sa de·fer·en·tia** \ˌvas-ə-ˌdef-ə-ˈren-chē-ə, -chə\ **:** a duct conveying sperm especially in a higher vertebrate that in the human male arises from the epididymis and eventually joins the duct of the seminal vesicle to form the duct through which semen is discharged from the body [New Latin, literally, "vessel that brings down"]

vase *U.S.* ˈvās *also* ˈvāz, *Canadian* ˈvāz *also* ˈväz, *British* ˈväz\ *n* **:** a usually round vessel of greater depth than width used chiefly for ornament or for flowers

va·sec·to·my \və-ˈsek-tə-mē, va-ˈzek-\ *n, pl* **-mies** **:** surgical removal of part of the vas deferens especially to induce sterility

Vas·e·line \ˈvas-ə-ˌlēn, ˌvas-ə-ˈ\ *trademark* — used for petroleum jelly

va·so·con·stric·tion \ˌvā-zō-kən-ˈstrik-shən\ *n* **:** narrowing of the diameter of blood vessels [Latin *vas* "vessel"] — **vaso·con·stric·tive** \-ˈstrik-tiv\ *adj*

va·so·con·stric·tor \-ˈstrik-tər\ *n* **:** an agent (as a sympathetic nerve fiber or a drug) that induces or initiates vasoconstriction

va·so·di·la·tion \ˌvā-zō-dī-ˈlā-shən\ *or* **va·so·di·la·ta·tion** \-ˌdil-ə-ˈtā-shən, -ˌdī-lə-\ *n* **:** widening of the diameter of blood vessels

va·so·di·la·tor \-dī-ˈlāt-ər, -ˈdī-ˌ\ *n* **:** an agent (as a parasympathetic nerve fiber or a drug) that induces or initiates vasodilation

va·so·mo·tor \ˌvā-zə-ˈmōt-ər\ *adj* **:** of, relating to, or being nerves or centers controlling the diameter of blood vessels

va·so·pres·sin \ˌvā-zō-ˈpres-ᵊn\ *n* **:** a protein hormone secreted by the pituitary gland that increases blood pressure and decreases urine flow [from *Vasopressin,* a former trademark]

vas·sal \ˈvas-əl\ *n* **1 :** a person under the protection of a feudal lord to whom homage and fealty are vowed **:** a feudal tenant **2 :** one in a subservient or subordinate position [Medieval French, from Medieval Latin *vassallus,* from *vassus* "servant, vassal," of Celtic origin] — **vassal** *adj*

vas·sal·age \ˈvas-ə-lij\ *n* **1 :** the condition of being a vassal **2 :** homage and loyalty due a lord from his vassal **3 :** a position of subordination or submission (as to a political power)

[1]**vast** \ˈvast\ *adj* **:** very great in size, amount, degree, intensity, or especially in extent or range ⟨*vast* knowledge⟩ ⟨a *vast* expanse of desert⟩ [Latin *vastus*] ***synonyms*** see ENORMOUS — **vast·ly** *adv* — **vast·ness** \ˈvast-nəs, ˈvas-\ *n*

[2]**vast** *n* **:** a boundless space **:** IMMENSITY

vasty \ˈvas-tē\ *adj* **vast·i·er; -est** **:** VAST, IMMENSE

\ə\ **abut**	\aù\ **out**	\i\ **tip**	\ó\ **saw**	\ù\ **foot**
\ər\ **further**	\ch\ **chin**	\ī\ **life**	\ói\ **coin**	\y\ **yet**
\a\ **mat**	\e\ **pet**	\j\ **job**	\th\ **thin**	\yü\ **few**
\ā\ **take**	\ē\ **easy**	\ŋ\ **sing**	\t͟h\ **this**	\yù\ **cure**
\ä\ **cot, cart**	\g\ **go**	\ō\ **bone**	\ü\ **food**	\zh\ **vision**

vat \ˈvat\ *n* : a large vessel (as a cistern, tub, or barrel) especially for liquids [Old English *fæt*]

vat dye *n* : a textile dye in a colorless reduced solution in which material to be dyed is steeped and which on exposure to air is oxidized and deposited in the fibers of the material — **vat–dyed** \ˈvat-ˈdīd\ *adj*

vat·ic \ˈvat-ik\ *adj* : PROPHETIC 1, ORACULAR [Latin *vates* "seer, prophet"]

Vat·i·can \ˈvat-i-kən\ *n* : the headquarters or the government of the Roman Catholic Church [Latin *Vaticanus* "Vatican Hill (in Rome)"]

vau·de·ville \ˈvȯd-vəl, ˈväd-, ˈvōd-, -ə-vəl, -ˌvil\ *n* : light theatrical entertainment featuring usually unrelated variety acts (as songs, dances, and sketches) [French, from Middle French *vaudevire, vaudeville* "satirical song," from *vau-de-Vire* "valley of Vire (town in France where such songs were composed)"] — **vau·de·vil·lian** \ˌvȯd-ˈvil-yən, ˌväd-, ˌvōd-, -ə-ˈvil\ *adj or n*

[1]**vault** \ˈvȯlt\ *n* **1 a** : an arched structure of masonry usually forming a ceiling or roof **b** : something suggesting a vault especially in arched or domed structure ⟨the blue *vault* of the sky⟩ **2 a** : a space covered by an arched structure; *esp* : an underground passage or room **b** : an underground storage compartment **c** : a room or compartment for the safekeeping of valuables **3 a** : a burial chamber **b** : a case usually of metal or concrete in which a casket is enclosed at burial [Middle French *voute*]

[1]vault 1a

[2]**vault** *vt* : to form or cover with or as if with a vault : ARCH

[3]**vault** *vb* : to execute a leap using the hands or a pole to lift and support the body; *also* : to leap over [Middle French *volter,* from Italian *voltare,* derived from Latin *volvere* "to roll"] — **vault·er** \ˈvȯl-tər\ *n*

[4]**vault** *n* : an act of vaulting; *also* : LEAP

vault·ed \ˈvȯl-təd\ *adj* **1** : built in the form of a vault **2** : covered with a vault

vault·ing \-tiŋ\ *adj* **1** : reaching or stretching for the heights ⟨a *vaulting* ambition⟩ ⟨a *vaulting* imagination⟩ **2** : designed for use in vaulting or in gymnastic exercises ⟨a *vaulting* block⟩ — **vault·ing·ly** *adv*

vaulting horse *n* : a padded rectangular or cylindrical form supported off the floor over which gymnasts vault

[1]**vaunt** \ˈvȯnt, ˈvänt\ *vb* : BRAG, BOAST [Medieval French *vanter,* from Late Latin *vanitare,* from Latin *vanus* "vain"] — **vaunt·er** *n* — **vaunt·ing·ly** \-iŋ-lē\ *adv*

[2]**vaunt** *n* **1** : a boastful display (as of worth or accomplishment) **2** : a bragging assertive speech

vaunt·ed \ˈvȯn-təd\ *adj* : highly or widely praised or boasted about ⟨the team's *vaunted* offense⟩

vaunt·ful \-fəl\ *adj* : BOASTFUL, VAINGLORIOUS

V–chip \ˈvē-ˌchip\ *n* : a computer chip in a television set that can prevent the viewing of certain programs or channels especially on the basis of content [*v*iolence]

VCR \ˌvē-ˌsē-ˈär\ *n* : a videotape recorder that uses videocassettes [*v*ideo*c*assette *r*ecorder]

've \v, əv\ *vb* : HAVE ⟨we've been there⟩

veal \ˈvēl\ *n* **1** : the flesh of a young calf **2** : CALF 1a; *esp* : VEALER [Medieval French *veel,* from Latin *vitellus* "small calf," from *vitulus* "calf"]

veal·er \ˈvē-lər\ *n* : a calf grown for or suitable for veal

vec·tor \ˈvek-tər\ *n* **1** : a quantity that has magnitude and direction and that is commonly represented by a line segment oriented in the given direction and with a length representing the magnitude **2** : an organism (as an insect) that transmits a pathogen [Latin, "carrier," from *vectus,* past participle of *vehere* "to carry"] — **vec·to·ri·al** \vek-ˈtōr-ē-əl, -ˈtȯr-\ *adj* — **vec·to·ri·al·ly** \-ē-ə-lē\ *adv*

Ve·da \ˈväd-ə\ *n* : any of four canonical collections of hymns, prayers, and liturgical formulas that make up the earliest Hindu sacred writings [Sanskrit, literally, "knowledge"]

Ve·dan·ta \vā-ˈdänt-ə, və-, -ˈdant-\ *n* : an orthodox system of Hindu philosophy [Sanskrit *Vedānta,* literally, "end of the Veda"] — **Ve·dan·tic** \-ik\ *adj*

ve·dette *or* **vi·dette** \vi-ˈdet\ *n* : a mounted sentinel stationed in advance of pickets [French, from Italian *veletta, vedetta*]

Ve·dic \ˈväd-ik\ *adj* : of or relating to the Vedas, the language in which they are written, or Hindu history and culture between 1500 B.C. and 500 B.C.

vee·jay \ˈvē-ˌjā\ *n* : an announcer of a program (as on television) that features music videos [*v*ideo *j*ockey]

veep \ˈvēp\ *n* : VICE PRESIDENT [from *v.p.,* abbreviation for *vice president*]

[1]**veer** \ˈviər\ *vb* **1** : to change direction or course : TURN ⟨the economy *veered* sharply downward⟩ **2** : to shift in a clockwise direction ⟨the wind *veered* from northwest to northeast⟩ [Medieval French *virer* "to veer, throw with a twisting motion," derived from Latin *vibrare* "to wave, propel suddenly"] ***synonyms*** see SWERVE — **veer·ing·ly** \-iŋ-lē\ *adv*

[2]**veer** *n* : a change in course or direction ⟨a *veer* to the right⟩

vee·ry \ˈviər-ē\ *n, pl* **veeries** : a reddish brown thrush common in woodlands of the eastern U.S. [probably imitative]

Ve·ga \ˈvē-gə, ˈvā-\ *n* : a bright star in the constellation Lyra [New Latin, from Arabic (al-Nasr) *al-Wāqi'*, literally, "the falling (vulture)"]

veg·an \ˈvē-gən\ *n* : a strict vegetarian who consumes no animals or dairy products for food [contraction of *vegetarian*] — **vegan** *adj* — **veg·an·ism** \ˈvē-gə-ˌniz-əm\ *n*

[1]**veg·e·ta·ble** \ˈvej-tə-bəl, ˈvej-ət-ə-bəl\ *adj* **1** : of, relating to, consisting of, or growing like plants ⟨the *vegetable* kingdom⟩ ⟨*vegetable* growth⟩ **2** : made from, obtained from, or containing plants or plant products ⟨*vegetable* soup⟩ **3** : suggesting that of a plant (as in monotony or inertness) ⟨a *vegetable* existence⟩ [Medieval Latin *vegetabilis* "vegetative," from *vegetare* "to grow," from Latin, "to animate," from *vegetus* "lively," from *vegēre* "to liven"] — **veg·e·ta·bly** \-blē\ *adv*

[2]**vegetable** *n* **1 a** : PLANT 1 **b** : a usually herbaceous plant (as the cabbage, bean, or potato) grown for an edible part that is usually eaten as part of a meal; *also* : such an edible part **2 a** : a person having a dull or merely physical existence **b** : a person whose mental and physical functioning is severely impaired (as from brain injury or disease) — not used technically

vegetable oil *n* : an oil obtained from plant parts and especially from seeds or fruits

[1]**veg·e·tar·i·an** \ˌvej-ə-ˈter-ē-ən\ *n* **1** : a person who excludes meat from the diet; *esp* : one who believes in or practices living solely on vegetables, fruits, grains, nuts, and sometimes eggs or dairy products **2** : HERBIVORE — **veg·e·tar·i·an·ism** \-ē-ə-ˌniz-əm\ *n*

[2]**vegetarian** *adj* : of, relating to, or suitable for vegetarians ⟨a *vegetarian* diet⟩

veg·e·tate \ˈvej-ə-ˌtāt\ *vb* **1** : to live or grow in the manner of a plant **2** : to lead a passive effortless existence **3** : to establish vegetation in or on ⟨richly *vegetated* slopes⟩ [Medieval Latin *vegetare* "to grow"]

veg·e·ta·tion \ˌvej-ə-ˈtā-shən\ *n* **1** : the act or process of vegetating **2** : inert existence : dull or inactive living ⟨a life of tranquil *vegetation*⟩ **3** : plant life or cover (as of an area) — **veg·e·ta·tion·al** \-shnəl, -shən-l\ *adj*

veg·e·ta·tive \ˈvej-ə-ˌtāt-iv\ *adj* **1 a** : of, relating to, or functioning in nutrition and growth as contrasted with reproduction ⟨the stem and leaf are *vegetative* organs⟩ **b** : of, relating to, or involving propagation by other than sexual means **2** : relating to, composed of, or suggesting vegetation ⟨*vegetative* cover⟩ **3** : affecting, arising from, or relating to involuntary bodily functions : AUTONOMIC ⟨*vegetative* nerves⟩ **4** : VEGETABLE 3 — **veg·e·ta·tive·ly** *adv* — **veg·e·ta·tive·ness** *n*

veg·gie *also* **veg·ie** \ˈvej-ē\ *n* : VEGETABLE

veggie burger *n* : a patty chiefly of vegetable-derived protein used as a meat substitute; *also* : a sandwich containing such a patty

veg out \ˌvej-ˈau̇t, ˈvej-\ *vi* **vegged out; veg·ging out** : to spend time idly or passively [short for *vegetate*]

ve·he·ment \ˈvē-ə-mənt\ *adj* : marked by forceful energy : POWERFUL ⟨a *vehement* wind⟩: as **a** : intensely emotional : IMPASSIONED, FERVID ⟨*vehement* patriotism⟩ ⟨*vehement* denunciations⟩ **b** : deeply felt ⟨*vehement* suspicion⟩ **c** : forcibly expressed ⟨*vehement* denials⟩ [Medieval French, from Latin *vehemens*] — **ve·he·mence** \-məns\ *n* — **ve·he·ment·ly** *adv*

ve·hi·cle \ˈvē-ˌik-əl, -ˌhik-, ˈvē-ə-kəl\ *n* **1 a** : a medium through which something is administered, transmitted, expressed, achieved, or displayed ⟨movies are *vehicles* of ideas⟩ **b** : a substance that acts as a solvent, carrier, or binder for an active ingredient or pigment ⟨turpentine is a common *vehicle* for paint⟩ **2** : something used to transport persons or goods : CONVEYANCE [French *véhicule,* from Latin *vehiculum* "carriage, conveyance," from *vehere* "to carry"]

ve·hic·u·lar \vē-ˈhik-yə-lər\ *adj* : of, relating to, or designed for vehicles and especially motor vehicles

V–8 \ˈvē-ˈāt\ *n* : an internal-combustion engine having two banks of four cylinders each with the banks at an angle to each other; *also* : an automobile having such an engine [from the resemblance of the angle formed by the two banks to the letter V]

[1]**veil** \ˈvāl\ *n* **1 a** : a length of cloth worn by women as a covering for the head and shoulders and often especially in Eastern countries for the face **b** : a length of veiling or netting worn over the head or face or attached to a hat or headdress **2** : the life of a nun ⟨take the *veil*⟩ **3** : a concealing curtain or cover of cloth **4** : something that covers or obscures like a veil ⟨a *veil* of secrecy⟩ [Medieval French *veil, veile,* from Latin *vela,* pl. of *velum* "sail, awning, curtain"]

[2]**veil** *vt* : to cover, provide, obscure, or conceal with or as if with a veil

veil·ing \ˈvā-liŋ\ *n* **1** : VEIL 1a **2** : a light sheer fabric (as net or chiffon) suitable for veils

[1]**vein** \ˈvān\ *n* **1** : LODE **2 a** : one of the blood vessels that carry blood from the capillaries toward the heart **b** : one of the vascular bundles forming the framework of a leaf **c** : one of the thickened ribs that stiffen the wings of an insect **3** : something like a vein usually in irregular linear form or in forming a channel ⟨underground water *veins*⟩; *esp* : a wavy band or streak (as of a different color or texture) ⟨marble with greenish *veins*⟩ **4 a** : a distinctive mode of expression : STYLE ⟨writing in a humorous *vein*⟩ **b** : a pervasive element or quality : STRAIN ⟨a *vein* of mysticism in one's character⟩ **c** : [1]MOOD [Medieval French *veine,* from Latin *vena*] — **vein·al** \ˈvān-l\ *adj* — **veiny** \ˈvā-nē\ *adj*

[2]**vein** *vt* : to form veins in or mark with veins

veined \ˈvānd\ *adj* : marked with or as if with veins : having venation ⟨a *veined* leaf⟩

vein·ing \ˈvā-niŋ\ *n* : a pattern of veins : VENATION

vein·let \ˈvān-lət\ *n* : a small vein especially of a leaf

[1]**ve·lar** \ˈvē-lər\ *adj* **1** : formed with the back of the tongue touching or near the soft palate ⟨the *velar* \k\ of \ˈkül\ *cool*⟩ **2** : of, relating to, or forming a velum and especially the soft palate

[2]**velar** *n* : a velar sound

Vel·cro \ˈvel-krō\ *trademark* — used for a closure consisting of a piece of fabric of small hooks that sticks to a corresponding fabric of small loops

veld *or* **veldt** \ˈvelt, ˈfelt\ *n* : a grassland especially of southern Africa usually with scattered shrubs or trees [Afrikaans *veld,* from Dutch, "field"]

vel·le·ity \ve-ˈlē-ət-ē\ *n, pl* **-ities** **1** : the lowest degree of volition **2** : a slight wish or tendency : INCLINATION [Latin *velle* "to wish, will"]

vel·lum \ˈvel-əm\ *n* **1** : a fine-grained lambskin, kidskin, or calfskin prepared especially for writing on or for binding books **2** : a strong cream-colored paper resembling vellum [Medieval French *velim, veeslin,* from *veel* "calf"] — **vellum** *adj*

ve·loc·i·pede \və-ˈläs-ə-ˌpēd\ *n* : a lightweight wheeled vehicle propelled by the rider; *esp* : TRICYCLE [French *vélocipède,* from Latin *veloc-, velox* "quick" + *ped-, pes* "foot"]

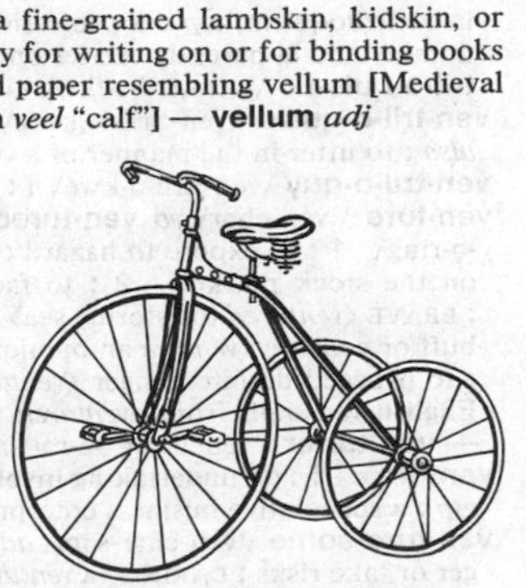

velocipede

ve·loc·i·rap·tor \və-ˈläs-ə-ˌrap-tər\ *n* : a dinosaur of the Cretaceous period having a long head with a flat snout and a large hooked claw on the second toe of each foot [New Latin, from Latin *veloc-, velox* "quick" + *raptor* "plunderer, predator"]

ve·loc·i·ty \və-ˈläs-ət-ē, -ˈläs-tē\ *n, pl* **-ties** **1** : quickness of motion : SPEED ⟨the *velocity* of sound⟩ **2** : the rate of change of position along a straight line with respect to time **3** : rate of occurrence or action : RAPIDITY ⟨the *velocity* of political change⟩ [Middle French *velocité,* from Latin *velocitas,* from *veloc-, velox* "quick"]

ve·lour *or* **ve·lours** \və-ˈlu̇r\ *n, pl* **velours** \-ˈlu̇rz\ : a usually heavy fabric with a pile or napped surface resembling velvet [French *velours,* from Medieval French *velous,* from Latin *villosus* "shaggy," from *villus* "shaggy hair"]

ve·lum \ˈvē-ləm\ *n* : a membrane or membranous anatomical partition resembling a veil or curtain; *esp* : SOFT PALATE [Latin, "curtain, veil"]

[1]**vel·vet** \ˈvel-vət\ *n* **1** : a usually silk or synthetic fabric with a thick soft short pile **2** : something suggesting velvet (as in softness); *esp* : the soft vascular skin covering the developing antlers of a deer **3** : an unanticipated gain or profit [Middle English *veluet, velvet,* from Middle French *velu* "shaggy," derived from Latin *villus* "shaggy hair"]

[2]**velvet** *adj* **1** : made of or covered with velvet **2** : resembling or suggesting velvet : VELVETY ⟨a *velvet* voice⟩

velvet ant *n* : any of various solitary burrowing usually brightly colored wasps with the females wingless

vel·ve·teen \ˌvel-və-ˈtēn\ *n* : a cotton fabric made in imitation of velvet

vel·vety \ˈvel-vət-ē\ *adj* **1** : soft, smooth, or thick like velvet ⟨*velvety* leaves⟩ **2** : smooth to the taste ⟨*velvety* sauce⟩

ven- *or* **veni-** *combining form* : vein ⟨*venation*⟩ ⟨*veni*puncture⟩ [Latin *vena*]

ve·na ca·va \ˌvē-nə-ˈkā-və\ *n, pl* **ve·nae ca·vae** \ˌvē-ni-ˈkā-vē\ : one of the large veins by which the blood is returned to the right atrium of the heart in an air-breathing vertebrate [New Latin, literally, "hollow vein"]

ve·nal \ˈvēn-l\ *adj* **1** : willing to take bribes : open to corrupt influences ⟨*venal* officials⟩ **2** : influenced by bribery : CORRUPT ⟨*venal* conduct⟩ [Latin *venalis* "for sale," from *venum* "sale"] — **ve·nal·i·ty** \vi-ˈnal-ət-ē\ *n* — **ve·nal·ly** \ˈvēn-l-ē\ *adv*

ve·na·tion \ve-ˈnā-shən, vē-\ *n* : an arrangement or system of veins ⟨the *venation* of the hand⟩ ⟨the *venation* of a leaf⟩ — **ve·na·tion·al** \-shnəl, -shən-l\ *adj*

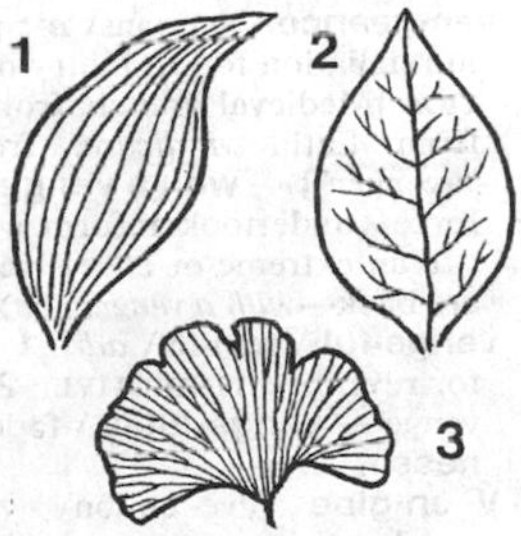

venation: *1* parallel-veined, *2* net-veined, *3* dichotomously veined

vend \ˈvend\ *vb* : to sell or offer for sale especially as a hawker or peddler ⟨*vend* fruit⟩ [Latin *vendere* "to sell," from *venum dare* "to give for sale"] — **ven·dor** \ˈven-dər, ven-ˈdȯr\ *also* **vend·er** \ˈven-dər\ *n* — **vend·ible** *also* **vend·able** \ˈven-də-bəl\ *adj*

vend·ee \ven-ˈdē\ *n* : one to whom a thing is sold : BUYER

ven·det·ta \ven-ˈdet-ə\ *n* **1** : BLOOD FEUD **2** : a series of acts marked by bitter hostility and motivated by a desire for revenge ⟨waged a personal *vendetta* against those who opposed his candidacy⟩ [Italian, literally, "revenge," from Latin *vindicta*]

vending machine *n* : a coin-operated machine for selling merchandise

ven·di·tion \ven-ˈdish-ən\ *n* : the act of selling : SALE

ven·due \ven-ˈdü, vän-, -ˈdyü\ *n* : AUCTION [obsolete French, from *vendre* "to sell," from Latin *vendere*]

[1]**ve·neer** \və-ˈniər\ *n* **1** : a thin sheet of a material: as **a** : a layer of a valuable or beautiful wood to be glued to an inferior wood **b** : any of the thin layers bonded together to form plywood **2** : a protective or ornamental facing (as of brick or stone) **3** : a superficial or deceptively attractive appearance : GLOSS ⟨a *veneer* of courtesy⟩ [German *Furnier,* from *furnieren* "to veneer," from French *fournir* "to furnish"]

[2]**veneer** *vt* : to overlay with a veneer — **ve·neer·er** *n*

ven·er·a·ble \ˈven-ər-bəl, -ər-ə-bəl, ˈven-rə-bəl\ *adj* **1** *often cap* : deserving to be venerated — used as a title usually preceded by *the* before the name of an Anglican archdeacon or a Roman Catholic in the first stage of canonization **2 :** made sacred especially by religious or historical association **3 a :** calling forth respect through age, character, and attainments ⟨a *venerable* jazz musician⟩ **b :** impressive by reason of age ⟨*venerable* pines⟩ — **ven·er·a·bil·i·ty** \ˌven-rə-ˈbil-ət-ē, -ə-rə-\ *n* — **ven·er·a·ble·ness** \ˈven-ər-bəl-nəs, -ər-ə-bəl-, ˈven-rə-bəl-\ *n* — **ven·er·a·bly** \-blē\ *adv*

ven·er·ate \ˈven-ə-ˌrāt\ *vt* **:** to regard with reverential respect or with admiration and deference ⟨*venerated* their ancestors⟩ [Latin *venerari,* from *vener-, venus* "love, charm"] ***synonyms*** see REVERE — **ven·er·a·tor** \-ˌrāt-ər\ *n*

ven·er·a·tion \ˌven-ə-ˈrā-shən\ *n* **1 :** a feeling of reverence or deep respect **:** DEVOTION **2 :** the act of venerating **:** the state of being venerated ⟨the *veneration* of saints⟩

ve·ne·re·al \və-ˈnir-ē-əl\ *adj* **:** resulting from or contracted during sexual intercourse ⟨a *venereal* infection⟩ [Latin *venereus,* from *vener-, venus* "love, sexual desire"]

venereal disease *n* **:** a contagious disease (as gonorrhea or syphilis) that is usually transmitted by sexual intercourse with an infected person

[1]**ven·ery** \ˈven-ə-rē\ *n* **1 :** the art, act, or practice of hunting **2 :** animals that are hunted **:** GAME [Medieval French *venerie,* from *vener* "to hunt," from Latin *venari*]

[2]**venery** *n* **:** the pursuit of or indulgence in sexual pleasure; *also* **:** SEXUAL INTERCOURSE [Medieval Latin *veneria,* from Latin *vener-, venus* "love, sexual desire"]

vene·sec·tion *also* **veni·sec·tion** \ˈven-ə-ˌsek-shən, ˈvēn-\ *n* **:** PHLEBOTOMY [New Latin *venae sectio,* literally, "cutting of a vein"]

ve·ne·tian blind \və-ˌnē-shən-\ *n* **:** a blind having thin horizontal slats that can be set at different angles to vary the amount of light admitted [*Venetian* "of Venice, Italy"]

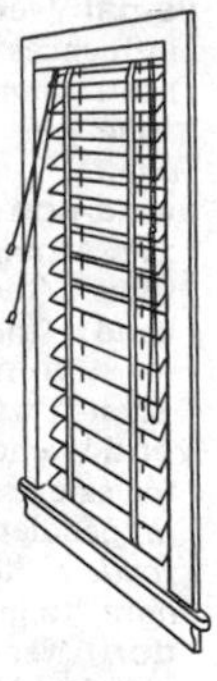

venetian blind

Venetian red *n* **:** an earthy hematite used as a pigment; *also* **:** a synthetic iron oxide pigment

ven·geance \ˈven-jəns\ *n* **:** punishment inflicted in retaliation for an injury or offense **:** RETRIBUTION [Medieval French, from *venger* "to avenge," from Latin *vindicare,* from *vindic-, vindex* "avenger"] — **with a vengeance 1 :** with great force ⟨undertook reform *with a vengeance*⟩ **2 :** to an extreme or excessive degree ⟨the tourists are back—*with a vengeance*⟩

venge·ful \ˈvenj-fəl\ *adj* **1 :** filled with a desire for revenge **:** VINDICTIVE **2 :** serving to gain revenge — **venge·ful·ly** \-fə-lē\ *adv* — **venge·ful·ness** *n*

V–en·gine \ˈvē-ˈen-jən\ *n* **:** an internal-combustion engine whose cylinders are arranged in two banks forming an acute angle

veni- — see VEN-

ve·nial \ˈvē-nē-əl, -nyəl\ *adj* **:** of a kind that can be pardoned **:** FORGIVABLE, EXCUSABLE ⟨*venial* faults⟩ [Medieval French *veniel,* from Late Latin *venialis,* from Latin *venia* "indulgence, pardon"] — **ve·ni·al·ly** \-ē\ *adv* — **ve·ni·al·ness** *n*

ve·ni·punc·ture \ˈvēn-ə-ˌpəng-chər, ˈven-, -ˌpəngk-\ *n* **:** a puncturing of a vein usually to withdraw blood or to introduce medication

ve·ni·re \və-ˈnī-rē\ *n* **:** a panel from which a jury is drawn

ve·ni·re fa·ci·as \və-ˌnī-rē-ˈfā-shē-əs\ *n* **:** a writ summoning persons to appear in court to serve as jurors [Medieval Latin, "you should cause to come"]

ven·i·son \ˈven-ə-sən *also* -ə-zən\ *n, pl* **venisons** *also* **venison** **:** the edible flesh of a game animal and especially a deer [Medieval French *veneisun* "game, venison," from Latin *venatio* "hunting," from *venari* "to hunt"]

Venn diagram \ˈven-\ *n* **:** a diagram that uses overlapping circles to represent mathematical sets and the elements they have in common [John *Venn,* died 1923, English logician]

ven·om \ˈven-əm\ *n* **1 :** poisonous matter normally secreted by some animals (as a snake, scorpion, or bee) and transmitted to prey or an enemy chiefly by biting or stinging **2 a :** a spiteful malicious state of mind **:** MALEVOLENCE **b :** a venomous utterance [Medieval French *venim,* derived from Latin *venenum* "magic charm, drug, poison"]

ven·om·ous \ˈven-ə-məs\ *adj* **1 :** filled with venom: as **a :** POISONOUS **b :** SPITEFUL, MALIGNANT ⟨*venomous* words⟩ **2 :** secreting and using venom ⟨*venomous* snakes⟩ — **ven·om·ous·ly** *adv* — **ven·om·ous·ness** *n*

ve·nous \ˈvē-nəs\ *adj* **1 :** of, relating to, or full of veins ⟨a *venous* rock⟩ ⟨a *venous* system⟩ **2 :** being blood which has passed through the capillaries, given up oxygen to the tissues, and become loaded with carbon dioxide — **ve·nous·ly** *adv*

[1]**vent** \ˈvent\ *vt* **1 a :** to provide with an outlet **b :** to serve as an outlet for ⟨chimneys *vent* smoke⟩ **2 :** to give often forceful or emotional expression to ⟨*vented* her frustration on her sister⟩ **3 :** to relieve by venting [Middle English *venten*]

[2]**vent** *n* **1 :** an opening for the escape or passage of something: as **a :** the external opening of the cloaca **b :** FUMAROLE **c :** HYDROTHERMAL VENT **2 :** an opportunity or means of release **:** OUTLET ⟨his writing gives *vent* to his pent-up emotions⟩

[3]**vent** *n* **:** a slit in a garment and especially in the lower part of a seam [Medieval French *fente* "slit, fissure," from *fendre* "to split," from Latin *findere*]

ven·ter \ˈvent-ər\ *n* **:** a protuberant and often hollow anatomical structure [Latin, "belly, womb"]

ven·ti·fact \ˈvent-ə-ˌfakt\ *n* **:** a stone worn, polished, or faceted by windblown sand [Latin *ventus* "wind" + English *-ifact* (as in *artifact*)]

ven·ti·late \ˈvent-l-ˌāt\ *vt* **1 :** to discuss freely and openly **:** make public ⟨*ventilate* a complaint⟩ **2 a :** to expose to air and especially to a current of fresh air ⟨*ventilate* stored grain⟩ **b :** to provide with ventilation ⟨*ventilate* a room by fans⟩ [Late Latin *ventilare,* from Latin, "to fan, winnow," derived from *ventus* "wind"] — **ven·ti·la·tive** \-ˌāt-iv\ *adj*

ven·ti·la·tion \ˌvent-l-ˈā-shən\ *n* **1 :** the act or process of ventilating **2 :** circulation of air ⟨a room with good *ventilation*⟩ **3 :** a system or means of providing fresh air

ven·ti·la·tor \ˈvent-l-ˌāt-ər\ *n* **1 :** one that ventilates; *esp* **:** a contrivance for introducing fresh air or expelling foul or stagnant air **2 :** RESPIRATOR 2

ven·tral \ˈven-trəl\ *adj* **1 :** of or relating to the belly **:** ABDOMINAL **2 :** being or located on or near the surface of the body that in humans is the front but in most other animals is the lower surface ⟨a fish's *ventral* fins⟩ [French, from Latin *ventralis,* from *venter* "belly"] — **ven·tral·ly** \-trə-lē\ *adv*

ven·tri·cle \ˈven-tri-kəl\ *n* **:** a cavity of a bodily part or organ: as **a :** a chamber of the heart which receives blood from a corresponding atrium and from which blood is forced into the arteries **b :** one of the communicating cavities in the brain that are continuous with the central canal of the spinal cord [Latin *ventriculus,* from *venter* "belly"]

ven·tric·u·lar \ven-ˈtrik-yə-lər, vən-\ *adj* **:** of, relating to, or being a ventricle

ven·tril·o·quism \ven-ˈtril-ə-ˌkwiz-əm\ *n* **:** the production of the voice in such a manner that the sound appears to come from a source other than the vocal organs of the speaker [Late Latin *ventriloquus* "ventriloquist," from Latin *venter* "belly" + *loqui* "to speak"; from the belief that the voice is produced from the ventriloquist's stomach] — **ven·tri·lo·qui·al** \ˌven-trə-ˈlō-kwē-əl\ *adj* — **ven·tri·lo·qui·al·ly** \-kwē-ə-lē\ *adv*

ven·tril·o·quist \ven-ˈtril-ə-kwəst\ *n* **:** one who uses or is skilled in ventriloquism; *esp* **:** a professional entertainer who holds a dummy and apparently carries on conversation with it — **ven·tril·o·quis·tic** \ˌven-ˌtril-ə-ˈkwis-tik\ *adj*

ven·tril·o·quize \ven-ˈtril-ə-ˌkwīz\ *vb* **:** to use ventriloquism; *also* **:** to utter in the manner of a ventriloquist

ven·tril·o·quy \ven-ˈtril-ə-kwē\ *n* **:** VENTRILOQUISM

[1]**ven·ture** \ˈven-chər\ *vb* **ven·tured; ven·tur·ing** \ˈvench-ring, -ə-ring\ **1 :** to expose to hazard **:** RISK ⟨*ventured* their savings on the stock market⟩ **2 :** to face the risks and dangers of **:** BRAVE ⟨*ventured* the stormy sea⟩ **3 :** to offer at the risk of rebuff or censure ⟨*venture* an opinion⟩ ⟨I *venture* to disagree⟩ **4 :** to proceed despite danger ⟨*ventured* down the cliff⟩ [Middle English *venteren,* from *aventuren,* from *aventure* "adventure"] — **ven·tur·er** \ˈvench-rər, -ə-rər\ *n*

[2]**venture** *n* **1 :** an undertaking involving chance, risk, or danger; *esp* **:** a speculative business enterprise **2 :** a venturesome act

ven·ture·some \ˈven-chər-səm\ *adj* **1 :** inclined to court danger or take risks **:** DARING ⟨a *venturesome* investor⟩ **2 :** involving risk **:** HAZARDOUS ⟨a *venturesome* journey⟩ ***synonyms*** see ADVENTUROUS — **ven·ture·some·ly** *adv* — **ven·ture·some·ness** *n*

ven·tur·ous \ˈvench-rəs, -ə-rəs\ *adj* **1 :** VENTURESOME 1 ⟨*venturous* spirit⟩ **2 :** HAZARDOUS ⟨*venturous* enterprises⟩ — **ven·tur·ous·ly** *adv* — **ven·tur·ous·ness** *n*

ven•ue \ˈven-ˌyü\ *n* **1 a :** the place from which a jury is drawn and in which trial is held **b :** the place in which events from which a legal action arises are claimed to take place **2 :** LOCALE 1; *also* **:** a place where events of a specific type are held ⟨music *venues*⟩ [Medieval French, alteration of *vinné, visné* "neighborhood, neighbors," derived from Latin *vicinitas* "vicinity"]

ven•ule \ˈvēn-yül, ˈven-\ *n* **:** a small vein; *esp* **:** one of the minute veins connecting blood capillaries with larger veins

Ve•nus \ˈvē-nəs\ *n* **:** the planet 2nd in order from the sun — see PLANET table [*Venus,* Roman goddess]

Venus fly•trap \-ˈflī-ˌtrap\ *or* **Venus's–flytrap** *n* **:** an insect-eating plant that is related to the sundews, grows along the Carolina coast, and has the leaf tip modified into an insect trap

Ve•nu•sian \vi-ˈnü-zhən, -ˈnyü-\ *adj* **:** of or relating to the planet Venus — **Venusian** *n*

Venus's flower–basket *or* **Venus flower basket** *n* **:** a usually cylindrical or funnel-shaped glass sponge of the Indian and western Pacific oceans

ve•ra•cious \və-ˈrā-shəs\ *adj* **1 :** TRUTHFUL, HONEST **2 :** marked by truth **:** ACCURATE, TRUE ⟨a *veracious* account of the events⟩ [Latin *verac-, verax,* from *verus* "true"] — **ve•ra•cious•ly** *adv* — **ve•ra•cious•ness** *n*

ve•rac•i•ty \və-ˈras-ət-ē\ *n, pl* **-ties 1 :** devotion to the truth **:** TRUTHFULNESS ⟨questioned the *veracity* of the witness⟩ **2 :** conformity with truth or fact ⟨described it with *veracity*⟩ **3 :** something true ⟨makes lies sound like *veracities*⟩

ve•ran•da *or* **ve•ran•dah** \və-ˈran-də\ *n* **:** a long roofed gallery or portico extending along one or more sides of a building [Hindi and Urdu *varaṇḍā*]

veranda

verb \ˈvərb\ *n* **:** a word that characteristically is the grammatical center of a predicate and expresses an act, occurrence, or mode of being and that in various languages is inflected (as for agreement with the subject or for tense) — compare ²AUXILIARY 2, COPULA [Medieval French *verbe,* from Latin *verbum* "word, verb"]

¹**ver•bal** \ˈvər-bəl\ *adj* **1 a :** of, relating to, or consisting of words ⟨*verbal* instructions⟩ **b :** consisting of or using words only and not involving action ⟨*verbal* abuse⟩ **2 :** of, relating to, or formed from a verb ⟨*verbal* adjectives⟩ **3 :** spoken rather than written ⟨a *verbal* contract⟩ **4 :** VERBATIM ⟨a *verbal* translation⟩ [Late Latin *verbalis,* from Latin *verbum* "word"] — **ver•bal•ly** \-bə-lē\ *adv*

²**verbal** *n* **:** a word that combines characteristics of a verb with those of a noun or adjective

ver•bal•ism \ˈvər-bə-ˌliz-əm\ *n* **1 :** a verbal expression **:** TERM **2 :** words used as if they were more important than the realities they represent **3 a :** a wordy expression of little meaning **b :** the quality or state of being wordy

ver•bal•ist \ˈvər-bə-ləst\ *n* **1 :** one who stresses words above substance or reality **2 :** a person who uses words skillfully — **ver•bal•is•tic** \ˌvər-bə-ˈlis-tik\ *adj*

ver•bal•ize \ˈvər-bə-ˌlīz\ *vb* **1 :** to speak or write in wordy or empty fashion **2 :** to express or express something in words **:** describe verbally ⟨found it difficult to *verbalize* her feelings⟩ **3 :** to convert into a verb ⟨nouns are often *verbalized*⟩ — **ver•bal•i•za•tion** \ˌvər-bə-lə-ˈzā-shən\ *n* — **ver•bal•iz•er** \ˈvər-bə-ˌlī-zər\ *n*

verbal noun *n* **:** a noun derived directly from a verb or verb stem and in some uses having the sense and constructions of a verb

ver•ba•tim \ˌvər-ˈbāt-əm\ *adv or adj* **:** word for word **:** in the same words **:** LITERAL ⟨a *verbatim* translation⟩ ⟨wrote down the speech *verbatim*⟩ [Medieval Latin, from Latin *verbum* "word"]

ver•be•na \ˌvər-ˈbē-nə\ *n* **:** VERVAIN; *esp* **:** any of various garden vervains of hybrid origin widely grown for their showy spikes of white, pink, red, or blue flowers which are borne in profusion over a long season [New Latin, genus of plants, from Latin, leafy branch used in ceremonies or as medicine]

ver•bi•age \ˈvər-bē-ij\ *n* **1 :** an excess of words used to say very little **2 :** DICTION 1, WORDING ⟨concise *verbiage*⟩

ver•bo•ten \vər-ˈbōt-n, fər-\ *adj* **:** forbidden especially by authority [German, "forbidden"]

ver•bose \ˌvər-ˈbōs\ *adj* **1 :** containing more words than necessary **:** WORDY ⟨a *verbose* reply⟩ **2 :** given to wordiness ⟨a *verbose* speaker⟩ — **ver•bose•ly** *adv* — **ver•bose•ness** *n* — **ver•bos•i•ty** \-ˈbäs-ət-ē\ *n*

ver•dant \ˈvərd-nt\ *adj* **1 a :** green in color ⟨*verdant* grass⟩ **b :** green with growing plants ⟨*verdant* fields⟩ **2 :** lacking experience or judgment [Middle French *verdoyant,* from *verdoyer* "to be green," from Medieval French *verd, vert* "green," from Latin *viridis,* from *virēre* "to be green"] — **ver•dan•cy** \-n-sē\ *n* — **ver•dant•ly** *adv*

ver•dict \ˈvər-dikt\ *n* **1 :** the decision of a jury on the matter submitted to them in trial **2 :** an opinion held or expressed **:** JUDGMENT [Medieval French *veirdit,* from *veir dit* "true dictum"]

ver•di•gris \ˈvərd-ə-ˌgrēs, -ˌgris\ *n* **1 :** a green or greenish blue poisonous pigment produced by the action of acetic acid on copper **2 :** a green or bluish carbonate of copper formed on copper, bronze, or brass surfaces [Medieval French *vert de Grece,* literally, "green of Greece"]

ver•dure \ˈvər-jər\ *n* **:** the greenness of growing vegetation; *also* **:** such vegetation itself [Medieval French, from *verd* "green"] — **ver•dured** \-jərd\ *adj* — **ver•dur•ous** \ˈvərj-rəs, -ə-rəs\ *adj*

¹**verge** \ˈvərj\ *n* **1 :** a staff carried as an emblem of authority or office **2 a :** something that borders, limits, or bounds **:** EDGE, BOUNDARY ⟨the *verge* of the sea⟩ **b :** BRINK, THRESHOLD ⟨on the *verge* of bankruptcy⟩ [Medieval French "rod, area of jurisdiction," from Latin *virga* "twig, rod, line"]

²**verge** *vi* **1 :** to be contiguous ⟨Canada *verges* on the U.S.⟩ **2 :** to be on the verge ⟨courage that *verged* on recklessness⟩

³**verge** *vi* **1 :** to move or extend in some direction or toward some condition **:** INCLINE **2 :** to be in transition or change [Latin *vergere* "to bend, incline"]

verg•er \ˈvər-jər\ *n* **1** *chiefly British* **:** an attendant who carries a verge (as before a bishop or justice) **2 :** a church official who keeps order during services or serves as an usher or a sacristan

ver•i•fi•able \ˈver-ə-ˌfī-ə-bəl\ *adj* **:** capable of being verified — **ver•i•fi•able•ness** *n* — **ver•i•fi•ably** \-blē\ *adv*

ver•i•fy \ˈver-ə-ˌfī\ *vt* **-fied; -fy•ing :** to prove or check the truth, accuracy, or reality of ⟨*verify* the claim⟩ [Medieval French *verifier,* from Medieval Latin *verificare,* from Latin *verus* "true"] ***synonyms*** see CONFIRM — **ver•i•fi•ca•tion** \ˌver-ə-fə-ˈkā-shən\ *n* — **ver•i•fi•er** \ˈver-ə-ˌfī-ər, -ˌfīr\ *n*

ver•i•ly \ˈver-ə-lē\ *adv* **:** in fact **:** CERTAINLY [Middle English *verraily,* from *verray* "very"]

veri•sim•i•lar \ˌver-ə-ˈsim-lər, -ə-lər\ *adj* **:** having the appearance of truth **:** PROBABLE [Latin *verisimilis,* from *veri similis* "like the truth"] — **veri•sim•i•lar•ly** *adv*

veri•si•mil•i•tude \-sə-ˈmil-ə-ˌtüd, -ˌtyüd\ *n* **1 :** the quality or state of being verisimilar **2 :** something verisimilar

ver•i•ta•ble \ˈver-ət-ə-bəl\ *adj* **:** ACTUAL, TRUE — often used to stress the aptness of a metaphor ⟨a *veritable* mountain of papers⟩ — **ver•i•ta•ble•ness** *n* — **ver•i•ta•bly** \-blē\ *adv*

ver•i•ty \ˈver-ət-ē\ *n, pl* **-ties 1 :** the quality or state of being true or real **2 :** something (as a statement) that is true **3 :** the quality or state of being truthful or honest **:** VERACITY [Medieval French *verité,* from Latin *veritas,* from *verus* "true"]

ver•juice \ˈvər-ˌjüs\ *n* **1 :** the sour juice of crab apples or unripe fruit (as grapes) or an acid liquor made from this **2 :** sourness of disposition or manner [Medieval French *vertjous,* literally, "green juice"]

ver•meil *n* **1** \ˈvər-məl, -ˌmāl\ **:** VERMILION **2** \veər-ˈmā\ **:** gilded silver, bronze, or copper [Middle French, from *vermeil,* adj.] — **vermeil** *adj*

vermi- *combining form* **:** worm ⟨*vermi*fuge⟩ [Latin *vermis*]

ver•mi•cel•li \ˌvər-mə-ˈchel-ē, -ˈsel-\ *n* **:** pasta that is thinner than spaghetti [Italian, from pl. of *vermicello* "little worm," from *verme* "worm," from Latin *vermis*]

ver•mic•u•late \ˌvər-ˈmik-yə-lət\ *or* **ver•mic•u•lat•ed** \-ˌlāt-əd\ *adj* **:** TORTUOUS 2b, INVOLUTE [Latin *vermiculatus,* from *vermiculus* "little worm," from *vermis* "worm"] — **ver•mic•u•la•tion** \-ˌmik-yə-ˈlā-shən\ *n*

\ə\ **abut**	\au̇\ **out**	\i\ **tip**	\ȯ\ **saw**	\u̇\ **foot**
\ər\ **further**	\ch\ **chin**	\ī\ **life**	\ȯi\ **coin**	\y\ **yet**
\a\ **mat**	\e\ **pet**	\j\ **job**	\th\ **thin**	\yü\ **few**
\ā\ **take**	\ē\ **easy**	\ng\ **sing**	\t͟h\ **this**	\yu̇\ **cure**
\ä\ **cot, cart**	\g\ **go**	\ō\ **bone**	\ü\ **food**	\zh\ **vision**

ver·mic·u·lite \ˌvər-ˈmik-yə-ˌlīt\ *n* **:** any of numerous minerals that are usually altered micas whose granules expand greatly at high temperatures to give a lightweight absorbent heat-resistant material used especially in seedbeds and as insulation [Latin *vermiculus* "little worm," from *vermis* "worm"]

vermiform appendix *n* **:** APPENDIX 2a

ver·mi·fuge \ˈvər-mə-ˌfyüj\ *n* **:** an agent that expels or destroys parasitic worms [*vermi* + Latin *fugare* "to put to flight"]

ver·mil·ion *also* **ver·mil·lion** \vər-ˈmil-yən\ *n* **1 :** a bright red pigment; *esp* **:** one consisting of a sulfide of mercury **2 :** a vivid reddish orange color [Medieval French *vermeilloun,* from *vermeil,* adj., "bright red, vermilion," from Late Latin *vermiculus* "kermes," from Latin, "little worm," from *vermis* "worm"]

ver·min \ˈvər-mən\ *n, pl* **vermin 1 :** small common harmful or objectionable animals (as fleas or mice) that are difficult to control **2 :** an offensive person [Medieval French, from Latin *vermis* "worm"]

ver·min·ous \ˈvər-mə-nəs\ *adj* **1 :** consisting of or full of vermin ⟨*verminous* houses⟩ **2 :** caused by vermin ⟨*verminous* disease⟩

ver·mouth \vər-ˈmüth\ *n* **:** a wine flavored with aromatic herbs and used as an aperitif or in mixed drinks [French *vermout,* from German *Wermut* "wormwood"]

[1]**ver·nac·u·lar** \vər-ˈnak-yə-lər, və-ˈnak-\ *adj* **1 :** using a language or dialect native to a region or country rather than a literary, cultured, or foreign language **2 :** of, relating to, or used in the normal spoken form of a language [Latin *vernaculus* "native," from *verna* "slave born in his master's house, native"] — **ver·nac·u·lar·ly** *adv*

[2]**vernacular** *n* **1 :** a vernacular language **2 :** the mode of expression of a group or class **3 :** a common name of a plant or animal as distinguished from the latinized taxonomic name

ver·nal \ˈvərn-l\ *adj* **1 :** of, relating to, or occurring in the spring ⟨the *vernal* equinox⟩ ⟨*vernal* sunshine⟩ **2 :** fresh or new like the spring; *also* **:** YOUTHFUL [Latin *vernalis,* from *vernus* "vernal," from *ver* "spring"] — **ver·nal·ly** \-l-ē\ *adv*

ver·nal·ize \ˈvərn-l-ˌīz\ *vt* **:** to hasten the flowering and fruiting of (plants) by treating seeds, bulbs, or seedlings so as to shorten the vegetative period — **ver·nal·i·za·tion** \ˌvərn-l-ə-ˈzā-shən\ *n*

ver·na·tion \vər-ˈnā-shən\ *n* **:** the arrangement of foliage leaves within the bud [derived from Latin *vernare* "to behave as in spring," from *vernus* "vernal"]

ver·ni·er \ˈvər-nē-ər\ *n* **1 :** a short scale made to slide along the divisions of a graduated instrument for indicating parts of divisions **2 :** a small auxiliary device used with a main device to obtain fine adjustment [Pierre *Vernier,* died 1637, French mathematician]

vernier caliper *n* **:** a caliper gauge with a graduated beam and a sliding jaw having a vernier

ve·ron·i·ca \və-ˈrän-i-kə\ *n* **:** any of a genus of herbs (as the speedwell) related to the snapdragons and having small pink, white, blue, or purple flowers [New Latin]

ver·ru·cose \və-ˈrü-ˌkōs\ *adj* **:** covered with warty elevations [Latin *verrucosus,* from *verruca* "wart"]

ver·sa·tile \ˈvər-sət-l\ *adj* **1 :** changing or fluctuating readily **:** VARIABLE ⟨a *versatile* disposition⟩ **2 a :** taking in a variety of subjects, fields, or skills ⟨*versatile* knowledge⟩ **b :** turning with ease from one thing or position to another **:** having a wide range of skills, aptitudes, or interests ⟨a *versatile* performer⟩ **3 :** having many uses or applications ⟨a *versatile* building material⟩ [Latin *versatilis* "turning easily," from *versare* "to turn," from *versus,* past participle of *vertere* "to turn"] — **ver·sa·tile·ly** \-sət-l-lē, -sət-l-ē\ *adv* — **ver·sa·tile·ness** \-l-nəs\ *n* — **ver·sa·til·i·ty** \ˌvər-sə-ˈtil-ət-ē\ *n*

[1]**verse** \ˈvərs\ *n* **1 :** a line of metrical writing **2 a :** metrical writing distinguished from poetry especially by its lower level of intensity **b :** POETRY ⟨Elizabethan *verse*⟩ **c :** POEM ⟨read the group some *verses*⟩ **3 :** STANZA **4 :** one of the short divisions into which a chapter of the Bible is traditionally divided [Medieval French *vers,* from Latin *versus,* literally, "turning," from *vertere* "to turn"]

[2]**verse** *vb* **:** VERSIFY

[3]**verse** *vt* **:** to familiarize by study or experience ⟨well *versed* in history⟩ [back-formation from *versed,* from Latin *versatus,* past participle of *versari* "to be active, be occupied (in)," passive of *versare* "to turn"]

ver·si·cle \ˈvər-si-kəl\ *n* **1 :** a short verse or sentence said or sung in public worship by a leader and followed by a response from the people **2 :** a little verse [Latin *versiculus* "small verse," from *versus* "verse"]

ver·si·fi·ca·tion \ˌvər-sə-fə-ˈkā-shən\ *n* **1 :** the making of verses **2 :** metrical arrangement of poetry

ver·si·fy \ˈvər-sə-ˌfī\ *vb* **-fied; -fy·ing 1 :** to compose or turn into verse **2 :** to relate or describe in verse — **ver·si·fi·er** \-ˌfī-ər, -ˌfīr\ *n*

ver·sion \ˈvər-zhən\ *n* **1 :** a translation from another language; *esp* **:** a translation of the Bible or a part of it **2 a :** an account or description from one point of view especially as contrasted with another **b :** an adaptation of a literary or musical work ⟨a stage *version* of the novel⟩ **3 :** a form or variation of an original ⟨an experimental *version* of the airplane⟩ [Middle French, from Medieval Latin *versio* "act of turning," from *vertere* "to turn"] — **ver·sion·al** \ˈvərzh-nəl, -ən-l\ *adj*

ver·so \ˈvər-sō\ *n, pl* **versos :** a left-hand page — compare RECTO [New Latin *verso folio* "the page being turned"]

verst \ˈvərst\ *n* **:** a Russian unit of distance equal to 0.6629 mile (1.067 kilometers) [French *verste* and German *Werst,* both from Russian *versta*]

ver·sus \ˈvər-səs, -səz\ *prep* **1 :** AGAINST 1a ⟨the champion *versus* the challenger⟩ **2 :** in contrast to or as the alternative of ⟨free trade *versus* protection⟩ [Medieval Latin, "towards, against," derived from Latin *vertere* "to turn"]

vert \ˈvərt\ *n* **:** the heraldic color green [Medieval French *vert* "green"]

ver·te·bra \ˈvərt-ə-brə\ *n, pl* **-brae** \-ˌbrē, -ˌbrā\ *or* **-bras :** one of the bony or cartilaginous segments composing the spinal column that in higher vertebrates have a short nearly cylindrical body with ends articulating with adjacent vertebrae and a bony arch enclosing the spinal cord [Latin, "joint, vertebra," from *vertere* "to turn"]

ver·te·bral \vər-ˈtē-brəl\ *adj* **:** of, relating to, or made up of vertebrae **:** SPINAL — **ver·te·bral·ly** \-ē\ *adv*

vertebral column *n* **:** SPINAL COLUMN

[1]**ver·te·brate** \ˈvərt-ə-brət, -ˌbrāt\ *adj* **1 a :** having a spinal column **b :** of or relating to the vertebrates **2 :** organized or constructed in orderly or developed form ⟨a *vertebrate* essay⟩

[2]**vertebrate** *n* **:** any of a large group (Vertebrata) of chordates comprising animals (as mammals, birds, reptiles, amphibians, and fishes) typically having a bony or cartilaginous spinal column which replaces the notochord, a distinct head containing a brain which arises as an enlarged part of the nerve cord, and an internal usually bony skeleton and including some primitive forms (as lampreys) in which the spinal column is absent and the notochord persists throughout life

ver·tex \ˈvər-ˌteks\ *n, pl* **ver·ti·ces** \ˈvərt-ə-ˌsēz\ *also* **ver·tex·es 1 a :** the point opposite to and farthest from a base of a figure ⟨the *vertex* of the triangle⟩ **b :** the endpoint of a line or curve or the point where two or more sides or edges (as of an angle, polygon, or polyhedron) meet **c :** a point where an axis of an ellipse, parabola, or hyperbola intersects the curve itself **2 :** the top of the head **3 :** the highest point **:** SUMMIT, APEX [Latin *vertic-, vertex* "whirlpool, top of the head, summit," from *vertere* "to turn"]

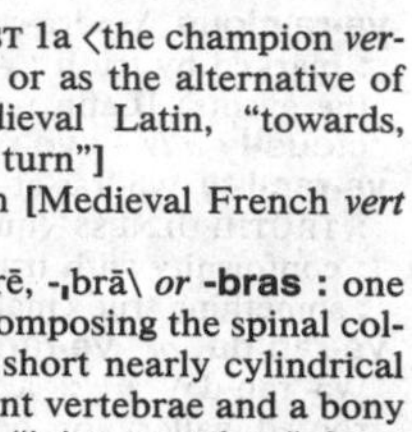
vertex 1b

[1]**ver·ti·cal** \ˈvərt-i-kəl\ *adj* **1 :** situated at the highest point **:** directly overhead or in the zenith **2 :** perpendicular to the plane of the horizon or to a primary axis **:** UPRIGHT **3 :** of, relating to, or composed of persons of different status ⟨the *vertical* arrangement of society⟩ — **ver·ti·cal·i·ty** \ˌvərt-ə-ˈkal-ət-ē\ *n* — **ver·ti·cal·ly** \ˈvərt-i-kə-lē, -klē\ *adv* — **ver·ti·cal·ness** \-kəl-nəs\ *n*

synonyms VERTICAL, PERPENDICULAR, PLUMB mean being at right angles to a baseline. VERTICAL suggests a line or direction rising straight upward toward a zenith ⟨the side of the cliff is almost *vertical*⟩. PERPENDICULAR may stress the straightness of a line making a right angle with any other line, not necessarily a horizontal one ⟨the tabletop is *perpendicular* to the table's legs⟩. PLUMB stresses an exact verticality determined (as with a plumb line) by earth's gravity ⟨make sure that the wall is *plumb*⟩.

[2]**vertical** *n* **1 :** something (as a line or plane) that is vertical **2 :** a vertical direction

vertical angle *n* **:** either of two angles that have the same vertex and are on opposite sides of two intersecting straight lines

vertical circle *n* **:** a great circle of the celestial sphere whose plane is perpendicular to that of the horizon

vertical file *n* **:** a collection especially of pamphlets and clippings maintained (as in a library) to answer brief questions or to provide information not easily located elsewhere

ver·ti·go \ˈvərt-i-ˌgō\ *n, pl* **-goes** *or* **-gos** **1 :** a sensation in which a person or a person's surroundings seem to whirl dizzily **2 :** a confused or bewildered state of mind [Latin, from *vertere* "to turn"]

ver·vain \ˈvər-ˌvān\ *n* **:** any of a genus of mostly American herbaceous or shrubby plants with often showy heads or spikes of flowers — called also *verbena* [Medieval French *verveine,* from Latin *verbena* "leafy branch"]

verve \ˈvərv\ *n* **1 :** the spirit and enthusiasm that animate artistic composition or performance **:** VIVACITY **2 :** ENERGY 1, VITALITY [French, from Middle French, "caprice," from Medieval French, "word, gossip," from Latin *verba,* pl. of *verbum* "word"]

¹very \ˈver-ē\ *adj* **ver·i·er; -est** **1 a :** properly entitled to the name or designation **:** TRUE **b :** ACTUAL 1, REAL **2 a :** EXACT 1, PRECISE ⟨the *very* heart of the city⟩ **b :** exactly suitable or necessary ⟨the *very* thing for the purpose⟩ **3 :** ABSOLUTE, UTTER ⟨the *veriest* fool alive⟩ **4** — used as an intensive especially to emphasize identity ⟨before my *very* eyes⟩ **5 :** MERE, BARE ⟨the *very* thought terrified me⟩ **6 :** being the same one **:** SELFSAME ⟨the *very* person I saw⟩ [Medieval French *verai,* derived from Latin *verax* "truthful," from *verus* "true"]

²very *adv* **1 :** in actual fact **:** TRULY ⟨the *very* best store in town⟩ ⟨told the *very* same story⟩ **2 :** to a high degree **:** EXTREMELY ⟨a *very* hot day⟩ ⟨*very* much better⟩

very high frequency *n* **:** a radio frequency in the range between 30 and 300 megahertz — abbreviation *VHF*

Very light \ˌver-ē-, ˌviər-ē-\ *n* **:** a pyrotechnic signal in a system of signaling using white or colored balls of fire shot from a special pistol [Edward W. *Very,* died 1910, American naval officer]

very low frequency *n* **:** a radio frequency in the range between 3 and 30 kilohertz — abbreviation *VLF*

Very Reverend — used as a title for various religious officials (as cathedral deans and canons and rectors of Roman Catholic seminaries and colleges)

ves·i·cant \ˈves-i-kənt\ *n* **:** an agent (as a chemical weapon) that causes blistering [Latin *vesica* "bladder, blister"] — **vesicant** *adj*

ves·i·cle \ˈves-i-kəl\ *n* **1 :** a membranous and usually fluid-filled pouch (as a cyst or vacuole) in a plant or animal **2 :** a small abnormal elevation of the outer layer of skin enclosing a watery liquid **:** BLISTER [Middle French *vesicule,* from Latin *vesicula* "small bladder," from *vesica* "bladder"] — **ve·sic·u·lar** \və-ˈsik-yə-lər\ *adj*

ves·per \ˈves-pər\ *adj* **:** of or relating to vespers or the evening

ves·pers \ˈves-pərz\ *n pl, often cap* **1 :** the sixth of the canonical hours **2 :** a late afternoon or evening worship service [derived from Latin *vesper* "evening"]

ves·per·tine \ˈves-pər-ˌtīn\ *adj* **:** of, relating to, or occurring in the evening ⟨*vespertine* shadows⟩ [Latin *vespertinus,* from *vesper* "evening"]

ves·sel \ˈves-əl\ *n* **1 a :** a hollow or concave utensil (as a cask, bottle, kettle, cup, or bowl) for holding something **b :** a person held to be the recipient of a quality (as grace) **2 :** a structure built for transportation on water **:** BOAT, SHIP; *esp* **:** one larger than a rowboat **3 a :** a tube or canal (as an artery) in which a body fluid is contained and conveyed or circulated **b :** a chiefly water-conducting tube in the xylem of a vascular plant [Medieval French *vaissel,* from Late Latin *vascellum,* from Latin *vas* "vase, vessel"]

¹vest \ˈvest\ *vb* **1 a :** to place or give (as a right, authority, or title) into the possession or discretion of some person or body ⟨powers *vested* in the presidency⟩ **b :** to become legally vested ⟨the title *vests* in the purchaser⟩ **2 a :** to clothe with or as if with a garment; *esp* **:** to garb in clerical vestments **b :** to put on garments and especially clerical vestments [Medieval French *vestir* "to clothe, invest," from Latin *vestire* "to clothe," from *vestis* "clothing, garment"]

²vest *n* **1 a :** a sleeveless garment typically worn under a suit coat **b :** a protective usually sleeveless garment (as a life preserver) that extends to the waist **2 :** a knitted undershirt for women **3 :** a plain or decorative piece used to fill in the front neckline of a woman's outer garment (as a blouse or dress) [French *veste* "robe, jacket," from Italian, from Latin *vestis* "garment"]

ves·tal \ˈves-tl\ *n* **1 :** a virgin consecrated to the Roman goddess Vesta and to the service of watching the sacred fire perpetually kept burning on her altar — called also *vestal virgin* **2 :** a chaste woman — **vestal** *adj*

vested interest *n* **1 :** a special concern or interest in maintaining or influencing a condition, arrangement, or action especially for selfish ends **2 :** one having a vested interest in something

vest·ee \ve-ˈstē\ *n* **1 :** DICKEY; *esp* **:** one made to resemble a vest **2 :** VEST 3

ves·ti·ary \ˈves-tē-ˌer-ē, ˈves-chē-\ *n, pl* **-ar·ies** **1 :** a room where clothing is kept **2 :** CLOTHING; *esp* **:** clerical vestments [Latin *vestiarium* "cupboard for storing clothes"]

ves·tib·u·lar \ve-ˈstib-yə-lər\ *adj* **:** of, relating to, or functioning as a vestibule

ves·ti·bule \ˈves-tə-ˌbyül\ *n* **1 a :** a passage or room between the outer door and the interior of a building **:** LOBBY **b :** an enclosed entrance at the end of a railway passenger car **2 :** any of various bodily cavities mostly serving as or resembling an entrance to some other cavity or space; *esp* **:** the central cavity of the bony labyrinth of the inner ear [Latin *vestibulum* "an open court in front of a building"]

ves·tib·u·lo·co·chle·ar nerve \ve-ˌstib-yə-lō-ˈkō-klē-ər-, -ˈkäk-lē-\ *n* **:** AUDITORY NERVE

ves·tige \ˈves-tij\ *n* **1 a :** a visible sign left by something vanished or lost ⟨searching for *vestiges* of lost civilizations⟩ **b :** the smallest amount or trace ⟨not a *vestige* of sorrow in her eyes⟩ **2 :** a small and imperfectly developed bodily part or organ that remains from one more fully developed in an earlier stage of the individual, in a past generation, or in closely related forms [Medieval French, from Latin *vestigium* "footprint, track, vestige"] ***synonyms*** see TRACE — **ves·ti·gial** \ve-ˈstij-əl, -ˈstij-ē-əl\ *adj* — **ves·ti·gial·ly** \-ē\ *adv*

vest·ment \ˈvest-mənt, ˈves-\ *n* **1 a :** an outer garment; *esp* **:** a ceremonial or official robe **b** *pl* **:** CLOTHING, GARB **2 :** a covering resembling a garment **3 :** a ceremonial garment worn by a person officiating at a religious service — **vest·ment·al** \vest-ˈment-l, ves-\ *adj*

vestment 3

vest–pock·et \ˌvest-ˌpäk-ət\ *adj* **1 :** adapted to fit into the vest pocket **2 :** of very small size or scope

ves·try \ˈves-trē\ *n, pl* **vestries** **1 a :** SACRISTY **b :** a room used for church meetings and classes **2 a :** the business meeting of an English parish; *also* **:** the parishioners assembled for it **b :** an elective body administering the business affairs of an Episcopal parish [probably from Medieval French *vestiarie,* from Medieval Latin *vestiarium,* from Latin, "cupboard for storing clothes," from *vestis* "garment"; from its use as a robing room for the clergy]

ves·try·man \-mən\ *n* **:** a member of a vestry

ves·ture \ˈves-chər\ *n* **1 a :** a covering garment (as a robe or vestment) **b :** CLOTHING, APPAREL **2 :** something that covers like a garment

¹vet \ˈvet\ *n* **:** VETERINARIAN, VETERINARY

²vet *vt* **vet·ted; vet·ting** **1** *chiefly British* **:** to provide veterinary care for (an animal) or medical care for (a person) **2 a :** to subject to expert appraisal or correction ⟨*vet* a manuscript⟩ **b :** to evaluate for possible approval or acceptance ⟨*vet* the college applicants⟩

³vet *adj or n* **:** VETERAN

vetch \ˈvech\ *n* **:** any of a genus of twining herbs of the legume family

vetch

\ə\ **abut**	\au̇\ **out**	\i\ **tip**	\ȯ\ **saw**	\u̇\ **foot**
\ər\ **further**	\ch\ **chin**	\ī\ **life**	\ȯi\ **coin**	\y\ **yet**
\a\ **mat**	\e\ **pet**	\j\ **job**	\th\ **thin**	\yü\ **few**
\ā\ **take**	\ē\ **easy**	\ng\ **sing**	\t͟h\ **this**	\yu̇\ **cure**
\ä\ **cot, cart**	\g\ **go**	\ō\ **bone**	\ü\ **food**	\zh\ **vision**

that include valuable fodder and soil-enriching plants [Medieval French *veche,* from Latin *vicia*]

vet·er·an \ˈvet-ə-rən, ˈve-trən\ *n* **1** : a person who has had long experience especially in some occupation or skill (as politics or the arts) **2** : a former member of the armed forces especially during wartime [Latin *veteranus* "soldier of long experience," derived from *veter-, vetus* "old"]

Veterans Day *n* : November 11 set aside in commemoration of the end of hostilities in 1918 and 1945 and observed as a legal holiday in the U.S. to honor the veterans of the armed forces

vet·er·i·nar·i·an \ˌvet-ə-rən-ˈer-ē-ən, ˌve-trən-, ˌvet-n-\ *n* : a person qualified and authorized to treat diseases and injuries of animals

[1]**vet·er·i·nary** \ˈvet-ə-rən-ˌer-ē, ˈve-trən-ˌ ˈvet-n-\ *adj* : of, relating to, or being the medical care of animals and especially domestic animals ⟨*veterinary* medicine⟩ [derived from Latin *veterinus* "of beasts of burden"]

[2]**veterinary** *n, pl* **-nar·ies** : VETERINARIAN

[1]**veto** \ˈvēt-ō\ *n, pl* **vetoes** **1** : an authoritative rejection or prohibition **2 a** : a power of one branch of a government to forbid or prohibit the carrying out of projects attempted by another department; *esp* : the power of a chief executive to prevent a measure passed by a legislature from becoming law **b** : the exercise of such authority [Latin, "I forbid," from *vetare* "to forbid"]

[2]**veto** *vt* : to refuse to admit or approve : PROHIBIT; *esp* : to refuse assent to (a legislative bill) so as to prevent enactment or cause reconsideration — **ve·to·er** \ˈvēt-ˌō-ər, -ˌōr\ *n*

vex \ˈveks\ *vt* **vexed** *also* **vext; vex·ing** **1 a** : to bring trouble, distress, or agitation to ⟨*vexed* by thoughts of what might have been⟩ **b** : to irritate or annoy by petty provocations : HARASS ⟨*vexed* by the children⟩ **c** : PUZZLE 1, BAFFLE ⟨a puzzle to *vex* a clever mind⟩ **2** : to shake or toss about [Medieval French *vexer,* from Latin *vexare* "to agitate, harry"] ***synonyms*** see ANNOY

vex·a·tion \vek-ˈsā-shən\ *n* **1** : the quality or state of being vexed : IRRITATION **2** : the act of vexing : ANNOYANCE **3** : a cause of trouble or worry

vex·a·tious \-shəs\ *adj* **1 a** : causing vexation ⟨a *vexatious* child⟩ **b** : intended to harass ⟨a *vexatious* lawsuit⟩ **2** : full of disorder or stress ⟨a *vexatious* period in her life⟩ — **vex·a·tious·ly** *adv* — **vex·a·tious·ness** *n*

vexed \ˈvekst\ *adj* : debated or discussed at length ⟨a *vexed* question⟩

vexed·ly \ˈvek-səd-lē, ˈvekst-\ *adv* : with vexation

vexing *adj* : causing or likely to cause vexation : VEXATIOUS ⟨a *vexing* problem⟩ — **vex·ing·ly** *adv*

via \ˌvī-ə, ˌvē-ə\ *prep* **1** : by way of ⟨entered *via* the back door⟩ **2** : through the medium of : by means of ⟨expressed herself *via* poetry⟩ [Latin, ablative of *via* "way"]

vi·a·ble \ˈvī-ə-bəl\ *adj* **1** : capable of living; *esp* : having attained such form and development of organs as to be normally capable of surviving outside the mother's womb ⟨a *viable* fetus⟩ **2** : capable of growing or developing ⟨*viable* seeds⟩ ⟨*viable* eggs⟩ **3 a** : capable of being put into practice : WORKABLE ⟨a *viable* plan⟩ **b** : having a reasonable chance of succeeding ⟨a *viable* contestant⟩ [French, from *vie* "life," from Latin *vita*] — **vi·a·bil·i·ty** \ˌvī-ə-ˈbil-ət-ē\ *n* — **vi·a·bly** \ˈvī-ə-blē\ *adv*

vi·a·duct \ˈvī-ə-ˌdəkt\ *n* : a bridge with high supporting towers or piers for carrying a road or railroad over something (as a gorge or a highway) [Latin *via* "way, road" + English *-duct* (as in *aqueduct*)]

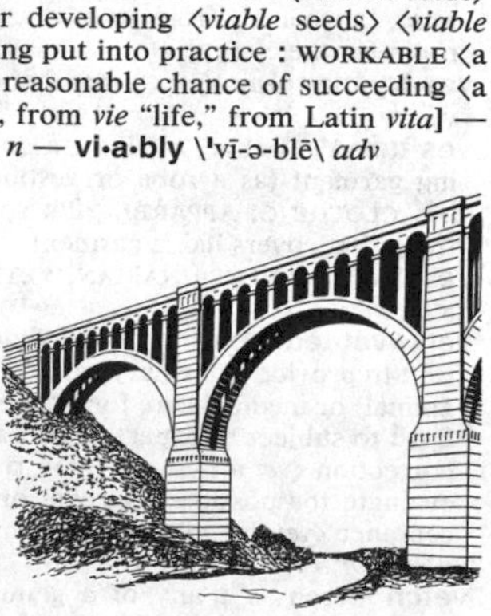

viaduct

vi·al \ˈvī-əl, ˈvīl\ *n* : a small vessel for liquids (as medicines or chemicals) [Medieval French *fiole, viole,* from Latin *phiala,* from Greek *phialē*]

vi·and \ˈvī-ənd\ *n* **1** : an item of food **2** *pl* : PROVISION 2, FOOD [Medieval French *viaunde,* from Medieval Latin *vivanda* "food," derived from Latin *vivere* "to live"]

vi·at·i·cum \vī-ˈat-i-kəm, vē-\ *n, pl* **-cums** *or* **-ca** \-kə\ **1** : the Christian Eucharist given to a person in danger of death **2** : money or provisions for a journey [Latin, "traveling money," from *viaticus* "of a journey," from *via* "way"]

vibe \ˈvīb\ *n* : VIBRATION 3 — usually used in plural ⟨got bad *vibes* from him⟩

vibes \ˈvībz\ *n pl* : VIBRAPHONE — **vib·ist** \ˈvī-bist\ *n*

vi·brant \ˈvī-brənt\ *adj* **1 a** (1) : oscillating or pulsating rapidly (2) : pulsating with life, vigor, or activity ⟨a *vibrant* personality⟩ **b** (1) : readily set in vibration (2) : RESPONSIVE 2, SENSITIVE **2** : sounding as a result of vibration : RESONANT ⟨a *vibrant* voice⟩ **3** : BRIGHT 2 ⟨a *vibrant* orange⟩ — **vi·bran·cy** \-brən-sē\ *n* — **vi·brant·ly** \-brənt-lē\ *adv*

vi·bra·phone \ˈvī-brə-ˌfōn\ *n* : a percussion musical instrument resembling the xylophone but having metal bars and motor-driven resonators for sustaining the tone and producing a vibrato — **vi·bra·phon·ist** \-ˌfō-nəst\ *n*

vi·brate \ˈvī-ˌbrāt\ *vb* **1** : to swing or move back and forth ⟨a *vibrating* pendulum⟩ **2** : to set in vibration **3** : to oscillate very rapidly so as to produce a quivering effect or sound : SHAKE, QUIVER ⟨guitar strings *vibrate* when plucked⟩ **4** : to respond sympathetically : THRILL ⟨*vibrate* to the idea⟩ **5** : WAVER 1, FLUCTUATE ⟨*vibrate* between two choices⟩ [Latin *vibrare* "to brandish, wave, rock"] ***synonyms*** see SWAY

vi·bra·tile \ˈvī-brət-l, -brə-ˌtīl\ *adj* **1** : characterized by vibration **2** : adapted to, used in, or capable of vibratory motion ⟨*vibratile* cilia⟩

vi·bra·tion \vī-ˈbrā-shən\ *n* **1 a** : a periodic motion of the particles of an elastic body or medium rapidly to and fro (as when a stretched cord is pulled or struck and produces a musical tone or when molecules in the air transmit sounds to the ear) **b** : the action of vibrating : the state of being vibrated **c** : motion or a movement to and fro : OSCILLATION ⟨the *vibration* of a pendulum⟩ **d** : a quivering or trembling motion ⟨*vibration* of a house caused by a passing truck⟩ **2** : vacillation in opinion or action : WAVERING **3** : a feeling or impression that someone or something gives off — usually used in plural ⟨good *vibrations*⟩ — **vi·bra·tion·al** \-shnəl, -shən-l\ *adj* — **vi·bra·tion·less** \-shən-ləs\ *adj*

vi·bra·to \vi-ˈbrät-ō, vī-\ *n, pl* **-tos** **1** : a slightly trembling effect given to vocal or instrumental tone by slight and rapid variations in pitch **2** : TREMOLO 1b [Italian, from *vibrare* "to vibrate," from Latin]

vi·bra·tor \ˈvī-ˌbrāt-ər\ *n* **1** : one that vibrates or causes vibration **2** : an electromagnetic device that converts low direct current to pulsating direct current or alternating current

vi·bra·to·ry \ˈvī-brə-ˌtōr-ē, -ˌtȯr-\ *adj* **1** : consisting of, capable of, or causing vibration **2** : characterized by vibration

vib·rio \ˈvib-rē-ˌō\ *n, pl* **-ri·os** : any of a genus of short rigid motile bacteria that are straight or curved rods and include pathogens especially of gastrointestinal diseases (as cholera) [New Latin, from Latin *vibrare* "to wave"] — **vib·ri·on·ic** \ˌvib-rē-ˈän-ik\ *adj*

vi·bris·sa \vī-ˈbris-ə, və-\ *n, pl* **vi·bris·sae** \vī-ˈbris-ē; və-ˈbris-ē, -ˌī\ : any of the stiff mostly tactile hairs especially about the nostrils or on other parts of the face in many mammals [Medieval Latin, from Latin *vibrare* "to wave"] — **vi·bris·sal** \-ˈbris-əl\ *adj*

vi·bur·num \vī-ˈbər-nəm\ *n* : any of a genus of widely distributed shrubs or small trees related to the honeysuckles and having white or sometimes pink flowers in broad clusters [Latin]

vic·ar \ˈvik-ər\ *n* **1** : one serving as a substitute or agent; *esp* : an administrative deputy **2** : an Anglican parish priest who does not hold the right to the tithes **3** : a member of the Episcopal clergy in charge of a mission or a dependent parish [Latin *vicarius,* from *vicarius* "vicarious"] — **vic·ar·ship** \-ˌship\ *n*

vic·ar·age \ˈvik-rij, -ə-rij\ *n* : the benefice or house of a vicar

vicar apostolic *n, pl* **vicars apostolic** : a Roman Catholic titular bishop who administers an ecclesiastical territory not organized as a diocese

vicar–general *n, pl* **vicars–general** : an administrative deputy of a Roman Catholic or Anglican bishop or of the head of a religious order

vi·car·i·al \vī-ˈker-ē-əl, və-, -ˈkar-\ *adj* **1** : VICARIOUS 1 **2** : of or relating to a vicar

vi·car·i·ate \-ē-ət\ *n* : the office, jurisdiction, or tenure of a vicar

vi·car·i·ous \vī-ˈker-ē-əs, və-, -ˈkar-\ *adj* **1** : serving instead of someone or something else **2** : performed or suffered by one person as a substitute for another or to the benefit of another ⟨a *vicarious* sacrifice⟩ **3** : experienced or realized through imaginative or sympathetic participation in the experience of another ⟨*vicarious* joy⟩ [Latin *vicarius,* from *vicis* "change, alternation, stead"] — **vi·car·i·ous·ly** *adv* — **vi·car·i·ous·ness** *n*

Vicar of Christ : the Roman Catholic pope

1**vice** \ˈvīs\ *n* **1 a :** moral depravity or corruption : WICKEDNESS **b :** a moral fault or failing ⟨deceitfulness was his *vice*⟩ **c :** a minor fault : FOIBLE ⟨eating too much candy is my *vice*⟩ **2 :** BLEMISH, DEFECT **3 :** an undesirable behavior pattern in a domestic animal (as pulling out feathers by a bird) **4 :** sexual immorality; *esp* : PROSTITUTION [Medieval French, from Latin *vitium* "fault, vice"]

2**vice** *chiefly British variant of* VISE

3**vi·ce** \ˈvī-sē\ *prep* : in the place of ⟨I will preside, *vice* the absent chairperson⟩ [Latin, ablative of *vicis* "change, alternation, stead"]

vice- \vīs, ˈvīs, ˌvīs\ *prefix* : one that takes the place of ⟨*vice*-chancellor⟩

vice admiral *n* : an officer rank in the navy and coast guard above rear admiral and below admiral

vice–chan·cel·lor \vīs-ˈchan-sə-lər, ˈvīs-, -slər\ *n* **1 :** an officer ranking next below a chancellor and serving as deputy to the chancellor **2 :** a judge appointed to act for or to assist a chancellor

vice–con·sul \-ˈkän-səl\ *n* : a consular officer subordinate to a consul general or to a consul

vi·cen·ni·al \vī-ˈsen-ē-əl\ *adj* : occurring once every 20 years [Late Latin *vicennium* "period of 20 years," from Latin *vicies* "20 times" + *annus* "year"]

vice presidency *n* : the office of vice president

vice president *n* : an official whose rank is next below that of the president and who takes the place of the president when necessary — **vice presidential** *adj*

vice·re·gal \-ˈrē-gəl\ *adj* : of or relating to a viceroy or viceroyalty — **vice·re·gal·ly** \-gə-lē\ *adv*

vice–re·gent \-ˈrē-jənt\ *n* : a regent's deputy

vice·reine \ˈvīs-ˌrān\ *n* **1 :** the wife of a viceroy **2 :** a woman who is a viceroy [French, from *vice-* "vice-" + *reine* "queen," from Latin *regina,* from *reg-, rex* "king"]

vice·roy \ˈvīs-ˌrȯi\ *n* **1 :** the governor of a country or province who represents a sovereign **2 :** a black and orange North American butterfly resembling but smaller than the monarch butterfly [Middle French *vice-roi,* from *vice-* "vice-" + *roi* "king," from Latin *reg-, rex*] — **vice·roy·ship** \-ˌship\ *n*

vice·roy·al·ty \ˈvīs-ˌrȯi-əl-tē, -ˌrȯil-tē\ *n* : the office, authority, or term of service of a viceroy; *also* : the territory or jurisdiction of a viceroy

vice ver·sa \ˌvī-si-ˈvər-sə, vīs-ˈvər-, ˈvīs-ˈvər-\ *adv* : with the order changed : CONVERSELY ⟨the disease is transmitted from animals to humans, but not *vice versa*⟩ [Latin]

vi·chys·soise \ˌvish-ē-ˈswäz, ˌvē-shē-\ *n* : a soup typically made of pureed leeks or onions and potatoes, cream, and chicken stock and usually served cold [French, from *vichyssois* "of Vichy," from *Vichy,* France]

Vi·chy water \ˈvish-ē-\ *n* : a natural sparkling mineral water from Vichy, France; *also* : an imitation of or substitute for this

vic·i·nage \ˈvis-n-ij, ˈvis-nij\ *n* : VICINITY 2

vic·i·nal \ˈvis-n-əl, ˈvis-nəl\ *adj* : of or relating to a limited district : LOCAL

vi·cin·i·ty \və-ˈsin-ət-ē\ *n, pl* **-ties 1 :** the quality or state of being near : PROXIMITY **2 :** a surrounding area or district ⟨in the *vicinity* of her home⟩ **3 :** NEIGHBORHOOD 2b ⟨walks in the *vicinity* of 20 miles a week⟩ [Middle French *vicinité,* from Latin *vicinitas,* from *vicinus* "neighboring," from *vicus* "row of houses, village"]

vi·cious \ˈvish-əs\ *adj* **1 a :** given to vice : WICKED **b :** constituting vice : IMMORAL **2 a :** DEFECTIVE 1, FAULTY **b :** INVALID **3 :** IMPURE b, NOXIOUS **4 a :** dangerously aggressive ⟨a *vicious* dog⟩ **b :** extreme in degree, power, or effect : FIERCE ⟨a *vicious* storm⟩ **5 :** MALICIOUS, SPITEFUL ⟨*vicious* gossip⟩ — **vi·cious·ly** *adv* — **vi·cious·ness** *n*

vicious circle *n* **1 :** an argument or definition that assumes as true something that is to be proved or defined **2 :** a chain of events in which the solution of one difficulty creates a new problem that makes the original difficulty worse — called also *vicious cycle*

vi·cis·si·tude \və-ˈsis-ə-ˌtüd, vī-, -ˌtyüd\ *n* : a change or succession from one thing to another; *esp* : an often unfavorable event or situation that occurs by chance ⟨the *vicissitudes* of the weather⟩ [Middle French, from Latin *vicissitudo,* from *vicissim* "in turn," from *vicis* "change, alternation"] — **vi·cis·si·tu·di·nous** \-ˌsis-ə-ˈtüd-n-əs, -ˈtyüd-\ *adj*

vic·tim \ˈvik-təm\ *n* **1 :** a living being offered as a sacrifice in a religious rite **2 :** an individual injured or killed (as by disease or accident) **3 :** a person cheated, fooled, or harmed by someone else or by an impersonal force ⟨a mugger's *victim*⟩ ⟨a *victim* of circumstance⟩ [Latin *victima*]

vic·tim·ize \ˈvik-tə-ˌmīz\ *vt* : to make a victim of especially by deception : CHEAT — **vic·tim·i·za·tion** \ˌvik-tə-mə-ˈzā-shən\ *n* — **vic·tim·iz·er** \ˈvik-tə-ˌmī-zər\ *n*

vic·tor \ˈvik-tər\ *n* : one that defeats an enemy or opponent : WINNER [Latin, from *vincere* "to conquer, win"] — **victor** *adj*

vic·to·ria \vik-ˈtōr-ē-ə, -ˈtȯr-\ *n* : a low four-wheeled pleasure carriage for two with a folding top and a raised seat in front for the driver [*Victoria,* queen of England]

victoria

1**Vic·to·ri·an** \vik-ˈtōr-ē-ən, -ˈtȯr-\ *adj* **1 :** of or relating to the reign of Queen Victoria of England or the art, literature, or taste of her time **2 :** typical of the moral standards or conduct of the age of Victoria especially when regarded as stuffy, prudish, or hypocritical — **Vic·to·ri·an·ism** \-ē-ə-ˌniz-əm\ *n*

2**Victorian** *n* : a person living during Queen Victoria's reign; *esp* : a typical figure of that time

vic·to·ri·ous \vik-ˈtōr-ē-əs, -ˈtȯr-\ *adj* : having won a victory ⟨a *victorious* army⟩ ⟨a *victorious* strategy⟩ — **vic·to·ri·ous·ly** *adv* — **vic·to·ri·ous·ness** *n*

vic·to·ry \ˈvik-tə-rē, -trē\ *n, pl* **-ries 1 :** the overcoming of an enemy or opponent **2 :** achievement of success in a struggle against odds or difficulties [Medieval French *victorie,* from Latin *victoria,* derived from *vincere* "to conquer, win"]

synonyms VICTORY, CONQUEST, TRIUMPH mean a successful outcome in a contest or struggle. VICTORY stresses the fact of winning against an opponent or against odds ⟨the *victory* of good over evil⟩. CONQUEST implies the subjugation of a defeated opponent ⟨the Roman *conquest* of the Greeks⟩. TRIUMPH suggests praise and personal satisfaction to the victor following a brilliant victory or achievement ⟨the *triumphs* of the space flights⟩.

1**vict·ual** \ˈvit-l\ *n* **1 :** food usable by humans **2** *pl* **a :** supplies of food **b :** PROVISIONS [Middle French *vitaille,* from Late Latin *victualia* "victuals," derived from Latin *victus* "nourishment," from *vivere* "to live"]

2**victual** *vb* **-ualed** *or* **-ualled; -ual·ing** *or* **-ual·ling 1 :** to supply with food **2 :** EAT 1 **3 :** to store provisions

vict·ual·ler *or* **vict·ual·er** \ˈvit-l-ər\ *n* **1 :** one that furnishes provisions (as to an army or a ship) **2 :** the keeper of a restaurant or tavern

vi·cu·ña *or* **vi·cu·na** \vi-ˈkün-yə, vī-; vī-ˈkü-nə, və-, -ˈkyü-\ *n* **1 :** a wild ruminant of the Andes that is related to the llama and alpaca **2 a :** the wool from the vicuña's fine lustrous undercoat **b :** a fabric made of vicuña wool; *also* : a sheep's wool imitation of this [Spanish *vicuña,* from Quechua *wikúña*]

vicuña 1

vi·de \ˈvīd-ē, ˈvē-ˌdā\ *vb imperative* : SEE — used to direct a reader to another item [Latin, from *vidēre* "to see"]

vi·de·li·cet \və-ˈdel-ə-ˌset, vī-; vi-ˈdā-li-ˌket\ *adv*

\ə\ abut	\au̇\ out	\i\ tip	\ȯ\ saw	\u̇\ foot
\ər\ further	\ch\ chin	\ī\ life	\ȯi\ coin	\y\ yet
\a\ mat	\e\ pet	\j\ job	\th\ thin	\yü\ few
\ā\ take	\ē\ easy	\ng\ sing	\t͟h\ this	\yu̇\ cure
\ä\ cot, cart	\g\ go	\ō\ bone	\ü\ food	\zh\ vision

: that is to say : NAMELY — abbreviation *viz.* [Latin, from *vidēre* "to see" + *licet* "it is permitted"]

¹vid·eo \ˈvid-ē-ˌō\ *n* **1** : TELEVISION **2** : VIDEOTAPE: as **a** : a recording of a motion picture or television program for playing through a television set **b** : a videotaped performance of a song often featuring an interpretation of the lyrics through visual images **3** : a recording similar to a videotape but stored in digital form (as on an optical disk or a computer's hard drive)

²video *adj* **1** : relating to or used in the transmission or reception of the television image ⟨a *video* channel⟩ — compare AUDIO **2** : being, relating to, or involving images on a television screen or computer display ⟨*video* terminal⟩ [Latin *vidēre* "to see" + English *-o* (as in *audio*)]

video camera *n* : a camera that records video and usually audio; *esp* : CAMCORDER

video card *n* : a circuit board in a computer system designed to generate output for the system's video display screen

vid·eo·cas·sette \ˌvid-ē-ō-kə-ˈset\ *n* **1** : a case containing videotape for use with a VCR **2** : a recording (as of a movie) on a videocassette

videocassette recorder *n* : VCR

vid·eo·disc *or* **vid·eo·disk** \ˈvid-ē-ō-ˌdisk\ *n* **1** : a disc similar to a phonograph record on which programs have been recorded for playback on a television set; *also* : OPTICAL DISK **2** : a recording (as of a movie) on a videodisc

video game *n* : a game played with images on a video screen

vid·e·og·ra·phy \ˌvid-ē-ˈäg-rə-fē\ *n* : the practice or art of recording images with a video camera — **vid·e·og·ra·pher** \-fər\ *n*

vid·eo·phile \ˈvid-ē-ō-ˌfīl\ *n* : a person fond of video; *esp* : one interested in video equipment or in producing videos

vid·eo·phone \ˈvid-ē-ə-ˌfōn\ *n* : a telephone equipped for transmission of a picture as well as sound so that users can see each other

¹vid·eo·tape \ˈvid-ē-ō-ˌtāp\ *n* **1** : a recording of visual images and sound (as of a television production) made on magnetic tape **2** : the magnetic tape used for a videotape

²videotape *vt* : to make a videotape of ⟨*videotape* a show⟩

videotape recorder *n* : a device for recording on videotape — called also *video recorder*

vidette *variant of* VEDETTE

vie \ˈvī\ *vi* **vied; vy·ing** \ˈvī-ing\ : to strive for superiority : CONTEND ⟨candidates *vying* with each other for the electorate's votes⟩ [Middle French *envier* "to invite, challenge, wager," from Latin *invitare* "to invite"] — **vi·er** \ˈvī-ər, ˈvīr\ *n*

Vi·en·na sausage \vē-ˌen-ə-\ *n* : a short slender frankfurter [*Vienna,* Austria]

Viet·cong \vē-ˈet-ˈkäng, -ˈkȯng\ *n, pl* **Vietcong** : a guerrilla member of the Vietnamese Communist movement from the late 1950s to 1975 [Vietnamese *Việt-cộng*]

Viet·nam·ese \vē-ˌet-nə-ˈmēz, ˌvyet-, ˌvē-ət-, ˌvēt-, -na-, -nä-, -ˈmēs\ *n, pl* **Vietnamese** **1** : a native or inhabitant of Vietnam **2** : the language of the largest group in Vietnam and the official language of the country — **Vietnamese** *adj*

¹view \ˈvyü\ *n* **1** : the act of seeing or examining : INSPECTION; *also* : SURVEY ⟨a *view* of English literature⟩ **2** : manner of looking at or regarding something : OPINION, JUDGMENT ⟨state one's *views*⟩ **3** : SCENE, PROSPECT ⟨the *view* from my window⟩ **4** : extent or range of vision : SIGHT ⟨the planes passed out of *view*⟩ **5** : something that is looked toward or kept in sight : OBJECT ⟨studied hard with a *view* to getting an A⟩ **6** : the foreseeable future ⟨no hope in *view*⟩ **7** : a pictorial representation [Middle French *veu, viewe,* past participle of *veer* "to see," from Latin *vidēre*] — **in view of** : in regard to : in consideration of — **on view** : open to public inspection : on exhibition

²view *vt* **1** : to look at attentively : SCRUTINIZE, OBSERVE ⟨*view* an exhibit⟩ **2 a** : SEE 1a, WATCH ⟨*view* a film⟩ **b** : to look on in a particular light : REGARD ⟨doesn't *view* himself as a troublemaker⟩ **3** : to survey or examine mentally : CONSIDER ⟨*view* all sides of a question⟩ — **view·able** \-ə-bəl\ *adj*

view·er \ˈvyü-ər\ *n* **1** : one that views; *esp* : a person who watches television **2** : an optical device used in viewing

view·find·er \ˈvyü-ˌfīn-dər\ *n* : a device on a camera for showing the area of the subject to be included in the picture

view·less \ˈvyü-ləs\ *adj* **1** : INVISIBLE, UNSEEN **2** : affording no view ⟨a *viewless* room⟩ **3** : expressing no views — **view·less·ly** *adv*

view·point \ˈvyü-ˌpȯint\ *n* : POINT OF VIEW, STANDPOINT

vi·ges·i·mal \vī-ˈjes-ə-məl\ *adj* : based on the number 20 [Latin *vicesimus, vigesimus* "twentieth"]

vig·il \ˈvij-əl\ *n* **1 a** : a watch formerly kept on the night before a religious feast with devotions **b** : the day before a religious feast **c** : prayers or devotional services held in the evening or at night — usually used in plural **2** : the act of keeping awake at times when sleep is customary; *also* : a period of wakefulness ⟨an all-night *vigil* spent awaiting her return⟩ **3** : an act or period of watchful observation : WATCH ⟨kept *vigil* at the bedside of his ill son⟩ [Medieval French *vigile,* from Latin *vigilia* "wakefulness, watch," from *vigil* "awake, watchful"]

vig·i·lant \ˈvij-ə-lənt\ *adj* : alertly watchful especially to avoid danger ***synonyms*** see WATCHFUL — **vig·i·lance** \-ləns\ *n* — **vig·i·lant·ly** \-lənt-lē\ *adv*

vig·i·lan·te \ˌvij-ə-ˈlant-ē\ *n* : a member of a local volunteer group organized to suppress and punish crime especially where official law enforcement seems inadequate [Spanish, "watchman, guard," from *vigilante* "vigilant"]

¹vi·gnette \vin-ˈyet, vēn-\ *n* **1** : a small decorative design or picture put on or just before a title page or at the beginning or end of a chapter **2** : a picture that shades off gradually into the surrounding ground **3** : a brief description in words : SKETCH [French, from *vigne* "vine"] — **vi·gnett·ist** \-ˈyet-əst\ *n*

²vignette *vt* **1** : to finish (as a photograph) like a vignette **2** : to describe briefly — **vi·gnett·er** *n*

vig·or \ˈvig-ər\ *n* **1** : active physical or mental strength or energy ⟨the full *vigor* of youth⟩ **2** : active healthy growth especially of plants **3** : intensity of action or effort : FORCE ⟨the *vigor* of their quarrel⟩ [Medieval French *vigour,* from Latin *vigor,* from *vigēre* "to be vigorous"]

vi·go·ro·so \ˌvig-ə-ˈrō-sō\ *adj or adv* : energetic in style — used as a direction in music [Italian, literally, "vigorous"]

vig·or·ous \ˈvig-rəs, -ə-rəs\ *adj* **1** : having vigor : ROBUST ⟨*vigorous* youth⟩ ⟨a *vigorous* plant⟩ **2** : done with force and energy ⟨a *vigorous* protest⟩ ⟨*vigorous* exercise⟩ — **vig·or·ous·ly** *adv* — **vig·or·ous·ness** *n*

synonyms VIGOROUS, ENERGETIC, STRENUOUS mean having or showing great vitality and force. VIGOROUS further implies showing no signs of depletion or diminishing of freshness or robustness ⟨still *vigorous* in their old age⟩. ENERGETIC suggests a capacity for intense activity ⟨*energetic* travelers always going places⟩. STRENUOUS suggests the making or meeting of arduous and challenging demands ⟨the *strenuous* life of a lumberjack⟩.

vig·our \ˈvig-ər\ *chiefly British variant of* VIGOR

Vi·king \ˈvī-king\ *n* : one of the pirate Norsemen plundering the European coasts in the 8th to 10th centuries [Old Norse *vikingr*]

vile \ˈvīl\ *adj* **1 a** : morally base : WICKED ⟨*vile* deeds⟩ **b** : physically repulsive : FOUL ⟨*vile* living quarters⟩ **2** : of little worth or account **3** : tending to degrade ⟨*vile* tasks⟩ **4** : CONTEMPTIBLE, DESPICABLE ⟨a *vile* temper⟩ ⟨*vile* weather⟩ [Medieval French *vil,* from Latin *vilis*] — **vile·ly** \ˈvīl-lē\ *adv* — **vile·ness** *n*

vil·i·fy \ˈvil-ə-ˌfī\ *vt* **-fied; -fy·ing** **1** : to lower in estimation or importance : DEGRADE **2** : to utter slanderous and abusive statements against : DEFAME — **vil·i·fi·ca·tion** \ˌvil-ə-fə-ˈkā-shən\ *n* — **vil·i·fi·er** \ˈvil-ə-ˌfī-ər, -ˌfīr\ *n*

vil·la \ˈvil-ə\ *n* **1** : a country estate **2** : the rural or suburban residence of a wealthy person [Italian, from Latin]

vil·lage \ˈvil-ij\ *n* **1** : a settlement usually larger than a hamlet and smaller than a town **2** : the residents of a village ⟨the whole *village* knows about it⟩ [Medieval French *vilage,* from *vil* "manorial estate, farmstead," from Latin *villa* "country estate"]

vil·lag·er \ˈvil-ij-ər\ *n* : an inhabitant of a village

vil·lain \ˈvil-ən\ *n* **1** : VILLEIN **2** : an uncouth ill-mannered person : BOOR **3** : a deliberate scoundrel or criminal **4** : a character in a story or play who opposes the hero **5** : one blamed for an evil or difficulty [Middle English *vilain, vilein* "villein"]

Word History In the feudal society of medieval Europe a *villein* was a member of one of the lower classes, at some times and places a free man and at others fully bound in service to a lord. Because the higher classes often look on the lower as inferior, Middle English *vilein* or *vilain* developed the depreciatory sense of "a person of uncouth mind and manners." This disparaging tendency gained in strength and currency through the common equation of manners and morals, so that the modern *villain* is a scoundrel or criminal or a person or thing blamed for a particular evil or difficulty.

vil·lain·ess \ˈvil-ə-nəs\ *n* : a woman who is a villain

vil·lain·ous \ˈvil-ə-nəs\ *adj* **1** : befitting a villain ⟨*villainous* attacks⟩; *also* : DEPRAVED ⟨a *villainous* foe⟩ **2** : highly objectionable : WRETCHED ⟨*villainous* living conditions⟩ — **vil·lain·ous·ly** *adv* — **vil·lain·ous·ness** *n*

vil·lainy \ˈvil-ə-nē\ *n, pl* **-lain·ies** **1 a** : villainous conduct **b** : a villainous act **2** : villainous character : WICKEDNESS

vil·la·nelle \ˌvil-ə-ˈnel\ *n* : a verse form running on two rhymes and consisting typically of five tercets and a quatrain in which the first and third lines of the opening tercet recur alternately at the end of the other tercets and together as the last two lines of the quatrain [French, from Italian *villanella*]

vil·lein \ˈvil-ən, ˈvil-ˌān, vil-ˈān\ *n* **1** : a free peasant of any of various feudal classes **2** : an unfree peasant ranking as a slave of a feudal lord but free in legal relations with others [Middle English *vilain, vilein,* from Medieval French, from Medieval Latin *villanus,* from Latin *villa* "country estate"]

vil·len·age \ˈvil-ə-nij\ *n* **1** : tenure of land given by a feudal lord to a villein **2** : the status of a villein

vil·lous \ˈvil-əs\ *adj* : having soft long hairs ⟨leaves *villous* underneath⟩ [Latin *villosus* "hairy, shaggy," from *villus* "shaggy hair"] — **vil·los·i·ty** \vil-ˈäs-ət-ē\ *n*

vil·lus \ˈvil-əs\ *n, pl* **vil·li** \ˈvil-ˌī, -ē\ : a small slender usually vascular process; *esp* : one of the tiny finger-shaped processes of the mucous membrane of the small intestine that function in the absorption of nutrients [Latin, "shaggy hair"]

vim \ˈvim\ *n* : robust energy and enthusiasm : VITALITY [Latin, accusative of *vis* "strength"]

vin·ai·grette \ˌvin-i-ˈgret\ *n* **1** : a small ornamental box or bottle with perforated top used for holding an aromatic preparation (as smelling salts) **2** : a sauce made of oil, vinegar, and seasonings and used especially on salad, cold meats, or fish — called also *vinaigrette dressing* [French, from *vinaigre* "vinegar"]

vin·ca \ˈving-kə\ *n* : [1]PERIWINKLE [New Latin, from Latin *vincapervinca*]

Vin·cen·tian \vin-ˈsen-chən\ *n* : a member of the Roman Catholic Congregation of the Mission founded in 1625 by St. Vincent de Paul and devoted to missions and seminaries — **Vincentian** *adj*

Vin·cent's angina \ˌvin-səns-, vaⁿ-ˌsäⁿz-\ *n* : Vincent's infection in which the ulceration has spread to surrounding tissues (as of the pharynx) [Jean Hyacinthe *Vincent,* died 1950, French bacteriologist]

Vincent's infection *n* : a bacterial infection of the mouth marked by ulceration especially of the mucous membranes and bleeding of the gums

vin·ci·ble \ˈvin-sə-bəl\ *adj* : capable of being overcome or subdued : SURMOUNTABLE ⟨*vincible* obstacles⟩ [Latin *vincibilis,* from *vincere* "to conquer"]

vin·cu·lum \ˈving-kyə-ləm\ *n, pl* **-lums** *or* **-la** \-lə\ **1** : a unifying bond : LINK, TIE **2** : a straight horizontal mark that is placed over two or more members of a mathematical expression and is equivalent to parentheses or brackets around them (as in $a\text{-}\overline{b\text{-}c}=a\text{-}[b\text{-}c]$) [Latin, from *vincire* "to bind"]

vin·di·cate \ˈvin-də-ˌkāt\ *vt* **1 a** : to free from blame or guilt ⟨evidence that will *vindicate* me⟩ **b** (1) : CONFIRM 2, SUBSTANTIATE ⟨later discoveries *vindicated* the claim⟩ (2) : to provide defense for : JUSTIFY ⟨circumstances *vindicated* his actions⟩ **c** : to protect from attack or encroachment : DEFEND **2** : to maintain a right to : ASSERT [Latin *vindicare* "to lay claim to, avenge," from *vindic-, vindex* "claimant, avenger"] ***synonyms*** see MAINTAIN — **vin·di·ca·tor** \-ˌkāt-ər\ *n* — **vin·di·ca·to·ry** \-kə-ˌtōr-ē, -ˌtȯr-\ *adj*

vin·di·ca·tion \ˌvin-də-ˈkā-shən\ *n* : the act of vindicating : the state of being vindicated; *esp* : justification against denial or censure

vin·dic·tive \vin-ˈdik-tiv\ *adj* **1 a** : inclined to seek revenge : VENGEFUL ⟨a *vindictive* person⟩ **b** : intended for or involving revenge ⟨a *vindictive* punishment⟩ **2** : intended to cause pain or anguish : SPITEFUL ⟨*vindictive* remarks⟩ [Latin *vindicta* "revenge," from *vindicare* "to avenge"] — **vin·dic·tive·ly** *adv* — **vin·dic·tive·ness** *n*

[1]**vine** \ˈvīn\ *n* **1** : GRAPE 2 **2 a** : a plant whose stem requires support and which climbs by tendrils or twining or creeps along the ground; *also* : the stem of such a plant **b** : any of various sprawling herbaceous plants (as a tomato) that resemble vines but lack a specialized means for climbing [Medieval French *vigne,* from Latin *vinea* "vine, vineyard," derived from *vinum* "wine"]

[2]**vine** *vi* : to form or grow in the manner of a vine

vine·dress·er \ˈvīn-ˌdres-ər\ *n* : a person who cultivates and prunes grapevines

vin·e·gar \ˈvin-i-gər\ *n* **1** : a sour liquid obtained by fermentation of cider, wine, or malt and used to flavor or preserve foods **2** : ill humor **3** : VIM [Medieval French *vinegre,* from *vin* "wine" (from Latin *vinum*) + *aigre* "keen, sour," from Latin *acer* "sharp"]

vinegar eel *n* : a tiny nematode worm often found in unpasteurized vinegar or other acidic fermenting vegetable or vegetable-derived matter

vinegar fly *n* : DROSOPHILA

vin·e·gar·ish \ˈvin-i-gə-rish, -grish\ *adj* : VINEGARY 2

vin·e·gary \-gə-rē, -grē\ *adj* **1** : resembling vinegar : SOUR **2** : disagreeable or bitter in character or manner : CRABBED ⟨a *vinegary* fellow⟩

vin·ery \ˈvīn-rē, -ə-rē\ *n, pl* **-er·ies** : an area or building in which vines are grown

vine·yard \ˈvin-yərd\ *n* : a field or planting of grapevines — **vine·yard·ist** \-əst\ *n*

vingt–et–un \ˌvan-ˌtā-ˈən\ *n* : BLACKJACK 3 [French, literally, "twenty-one"]

vi·ni·cul·ture \ˈvin-ə-ˌkəl-chər, ˈvī-nə-\ *n* : VITICULTURE

vi·nos·i·ty \vī-ˈnäs-ət-ē\ *n* : the characteristic body, flavor, and color of a wine

vi·nous \ˈvī-nəs\ *adj* **1** : of, relating to, or made with wine ⟨*vinous* flavors⟩ **2** : showing the effects of the use of wine [Latin *vinosus,* from *vinum* "wine"]

vin·tage \ˈvint-ij\ *n* **1 a** (1) : the grapes or wine produced during one season (2) : WINE; *esp* : a wine of a particular type, region, and year and usually of superior quality **b** : a collection or category of comparable persons or things **2** : the act or time of gathering grapes or making wine **3 a** : a period of origin or manufacture ⟨a piano of 1845 *vintage*⟩ **b** : length of existence : AGE [probably from Medieval French *vendage, vendenge,* from Latin *vindemia* "grape-gathering, vintage," from *vinum* "wine, grapes" + *demere* "to take off"] — **vintage** *adj*

vint·ner \ˈvint-nər\ *n* : a person who makes or sells wine [Medieval French *vineter,* derived from Latin *vinum* "wine"]

viny \ˈvī-nē\ *adj* **vin·i·er; -est** **1** : of, relating to, or resembling vines ⟨*viny* plants⟩ **2** : covered with or abounding in vines

vi·nyl \ˈvīn-l\ *n* **1** : a univalent radical $CH_2{=}CH$ derived from ethylene by removal of one hydrogen atom **2** : a polymer of a vinyl compound or a product made from such a polymer ⟨*vinyl* upholstery⟩ [Latin *vinum* "wine"]

vinyl resin *n* : any of a group of elastic resins that are resistant to chemical agents and are used for protective coatings and molded articles — called also *vinyl plastic*

vi·ol \ˈvī-əl, ˈvīl\ *n* : an old bowed stringed instrument like the violin but weaker in tone and simpler in construction and playing technique [Medieval French *viele, viole,* from Old Occitan *viola*]

[1]**vi·o·la** \vē-ˈō-lə\ *n* : a stringed musical instrument similar to a violin but slightly larger and lower in pitch [Italian and Spanish, "viol, viola," from Old Occitan, "viol"]

[2]**vi·ola** \vī-ˈō-lə, vē-\ *n* : VIOLET 1a; *esp* : any of various garden hybrids with solitary white, yellow, or purple often variegated flowers resembling but smaller than typical pansies [Latin]

vi·o·la·ble \ˈvī-ə-lə-bəl\ *adj* : capable of being or likely to be violated ⟨*violable* rules⟩ — **vi·o·la·bil·i·ty** \ˌvī-ə-lə-ˈbil-ət-ē\ *n* — **vi·o·la·ble·ness** \ˈvi-ə-lə-bəl-nəs\ *n* — **vi·o·la·bly** \-blē\ *adv*

vi·o·late \ˈvī-ə-ˌlāt\ *vt* **1** : to fail to keep or observe ⟨*violate* the law⟩ **2** : to do harm to the person or the chastity of; *esp* : RAPE 2 **3** : PROFANE, DESECRATE ⟨vandals *violated* the church⟩ **4** : INTERRUPT 1, DISTURB ⟨*violated* their privacy⟩ [Latin *violare*] — **vi·o·la·tor** \-ˌlāt-ər\ *n*

vi·o·la·tion \ˌvī-ə-ˈlā-shən\ *n* : the act of violating : the state of being violated: as **a** : TRANSGRESSION **b** : an act of irreverence or desecration **c** : DISTURBANCE 1 **d** : [3]RAPE 2

vi·o·lence \ˈvī-ə-ləns\ *n* **1** : the use of physical force in a way that harms a person or a person's property **2** : injury especially to something that deserves respect or reverence ⟨does *violence* to our principles⟩ **3 a** : intense, furious, and often destructive action or force ⟨the *violence* of the storm⟩ **b** : vehement feel-

\ə\ **abut**	\au̇\ **out**	\i\ **tip**	\ȯ\ **saw**	\u̇\ **foot**
\ər\ **further**	\ch\ **chin**	\ī\ **life**	\ȯi\ **coin**	\y\ **yet**
\a\ **mat**	\e\ **pet**	\j\ **job**	\th\ **thin**	\yü\ **few**
\ā\ **take**	\ē\ **easy**	\ng\ **sing**	\t͟h\ **this**	\yu̇\ **cure**
\ä\ **cot, cart**	\g\ **go**	\ō\ **bone**	\ü\ **food**	\zh\ **vision**

ing or expression : FERVOR **4 :** improper or damaging alteration (as of the wording or the meaning of a text)

vi•o•lent \-lənt\ *adj* **1 :** marked by extreme force or sudden intense activity ⟨a *violent* attack of coughing⟩ ⟨*violent* storms⟩ **2 a :** notably furious or vehement ⟨a *violent* denunciation⟩ **b :** EXTREME, INTENSE ⟨*violent* pain⟩ **3 :** caused by force ⟨a *violent* death⟩ **4 a :** acting with or characterized by harmful physical force : exercising or marked by violence ⟨a *violent* individual⟩ ⟨*violent* actions⟩ **b :** prone to commit acts of violence ⟨*violent* prison inmates⟩ [Medieval French, from Latin *violentus*] — **vi•o•lent•ly** *adv*

vi•o•let \ˈvī-ə-lət\ *n* **1 a :** any of a genus of mostly herbs that often produce showy fragrant flowers in the spring and small closed inconspicuous flowers without petals in the summer; *esp* **:** one with small usually solid-colored flowers as distinguished from the usually larger-flowered violas and pansies **b :** any of several plants of other genera — compare DOGTOOTH VIOLET **2 :** a reddish blue [Medieval French *violete,* from *viole* "violet," from Latin *viola*]

vi•o•lin \ˌvī-ə-ˈlin\ *n* **1 :** a bowed stringed instrument with four strings that has a shallower body and a more curved bridge than the viol **2 :** VIOLINIST [Italian *violino,* from *viola* "viola"]

violin 1

vi•o•lin•ist \-ˈlin-əst\ *n* **:** one who plays the violin

vi•o•list \vē-ˈō-ləst\ *n* **:** one who plays the viola

vi•o•lon•cel•list \ˌvī-ə-lən-ˈchel-əst, ˌvē-\ *n* **:** CELLIST

vi•o•lon•cel•lo \ˌvī-ə-lən-ˈchel-ō, ˌvē-\ *n* **:** CELLO [Italian, from *violone,* from *viola* "viola, viol"]

VIP \ˌvē-ˌī-ˈpē\ *n, pl* **VIPs** \-ˈpēz\ **:** a person of great influence or prestige [*v*ery *i*mportant *p*erson]

vi•per \ˈvī-pər\ *n* **1 a :** any of a family of heavy-bodied broad-headed venomous snakes having hollow tubular fangs and including Old World snakes and the pit vipers **b :** a venomous or reputedly venomous snake **2 :** a malicious or treacherous person [Latin *vipera*]

vi•per•ine \ˈvī-pə-ˌrīn\ *adj* **:** of, relating to, or resembling a viper

vi•per•ish \ˈvī-pə-rish, -prish\ *adj* **:** given to spiteful abusive speech : VENOMOUS

vi•per•ous \ˈvī-pə-rəs, -prəs\ *adj* **1 :** VIPERINE **2 :** having the qualities attributed to a viper : SPITEFUL, VENOMOUS ⟨a *viperous* treachery⟩ — **vi•per•ous•ly** *adv*

vi•ra•go \və-ˈräg-ō, -ˈrāg-; ˈvir-ə-ˌgō\ *n, pl* **-goes** *or* **-gos 1 :** a woman of great stature, strength, and courage **2 :** a loud overbearing woman [Latin *viragin-, virago,* from *vir* "man"] — **vi•rag•i•nous** \və-ˈraj-ə-nəs\ *adj*

vi•ral \ˈvī-rəl\ *adj* **1 :** of, relating to, or caused by a virus ⟨a *viral* infection⟩ **2 :** quickly and widely spread or popularized especially by person-to-person electronic communication ⟨a *viral* video⟩

vir•eo \ˈvir-ē-ˌō\ *n, pl* **-e•os :** any of various small insect-eating American songbirds that are chiefly olive-green or grayish in color [Latin, a small bird, from *virēre* "to be green"]

vir•ga \ˈvər-gə\ *n* **:** wisps of precipitation evaporating before reaching the ground [Latin, "branch, streak in the sky suggesting rain"]

[1]**vir•gin** \ˈvər-jən\ *n* **1 :** an unmarried woman devoted to religion **2 :** a person who has not had sexual intercourse [Medieval French *virgine,* from Latin *virgin-, virgo* "young woman, virgin"]

[2]**virgin** *adj* **1 :** being, characteristic of, or befitting a virgin : MODEST **2 :** not soiled or marred ⟨*virgin* snow⟩; *esp* **:** not altered by human activity ⟨*virgin* soil⟩ **3 :** being used or worked for the first time or produced by a simple extractive process ⟨*virgin* wool⟩ ⟨*virgin* oil⟩

[1]**vir•gin•al** \ˈvər-jən-l\ *adj* **:** of, relating to, characteristic of, or suitable for a virgin or virginity; *esp* **:** CHASTE — **vir•gin•al•ly** \-l-ē\ *adv*

[2]**virginal** *n* **:** a small rectangular spinet having no legs and only one wire to a note

virgin birth *n* **1 :** birth from a virgin **2** *often cap V&B* **:** the theological doctrine that Jesus was miraculously begotten of God and born of a virgin mother

Vir•gin•ia creeper \vər-ˌjin-yə-, -ˌjin-ē-ə-\ *n* **:** a common North American tendril-climbing vine related to the grape and having leaves with five leaflets and bluish black berries — called also *woodbine* [*Virginia,* U.S.]

Virginia creeper

Virginia deer *n* **:** WHITE-TAILED DEER

Virginia reel *n* **:** an American dance in which two lines of couples face each other and all couples in turn participate in a series of figures

vir•gin•i•ty \vər-ˈjin-ət-ē\ *n, pl* **-ties :** the quality or state of being virgin; *esp* **:** MAIDENHOOD

virgin's bower *n* **:** any of several usually small-flowered and climbing clematises

Vir•go \ˈvər-gō, ˈviər-\ *n* **1 :** a zodiacal constellation due south of the handle of the Big Dipper **2 :** the 6th sign of the zodiac; *also* **:** one born under this sign [Latin, literally, "virgin"]

vir•gule \ˈvər-gyül\ *n* **:** [2]SLASH 4 [French, from Latin *virgula* "little rod," from *virga* "branch, rod"]

vir•i•des•cent \ˌvir-ə-ˈdes-nt\ *adj* **:** slightly green : GREENISH [Latin *viridis* "green"]

vir•ile \ˈvir-əl, ˈviər-ˌīl\ *adj* **1 a :** having the nature, powers, or qualities of an adult male : MASCULINE **b :** having traditionally masculine traits especially to a marked degree **2 a :** ENERGETIC, VIGOROUS **b :** MASTERFUL 1, FORCEFUL [Latin *virilis,* from *vir* "man, male"]

vi•ril•i•ty \və-ˈril-ət-ē\ *n* **:** the quality or state of being virile: **a :** MANHOOD 2 **b :** manly vigor : MASCULINITY

vi•ri•on \ˈvī-rē-ˌän, ˈvir-ē-\ *n* **:** a complete extracellular virus particle consisting of an RNA or DNA core with a protein coat sometimes with an external envelope [French, from *virien* "viral" (from *virus* "virus") + *-on* "-on"]

vi•roid \ˈvī-ˌrȯid\ *n* **:** any of several infectious agents that consist of a single-stranded RNA arranged in a closed loop without a covering of protein and that are capable of causing diseases in plants

vi•rol•o•gy \vī-ˈräl-ə-jē\ *n* **:** a branch of science that deals with viruses and viral diseases — **vi•ro•log•i•cal** \ˌvī-rə-ˈläj-i-kəl\ *adj* — **vi•rol•o•gist** \vī-ˈräl-ə-jəst\ *n*

vir•tu•al \ˈvərch-wəl, -ə-wəl; ˈvər-chəl\ *adj* **1 :** being in essence or effect but not in fact or name ⟨a *virtual* dictator⟩ **2 a :** occurring or existing primarily online ⟨a *virtual* library⟩ **b :** of, relating to, or existing within a virtual reality ⟨a *virtual* world⟩ [Medieval Latin *virtualis* "efficacious, potential," from Latin *virtus* "strength, virtue"] — **vir•tu•al•i•ty** \ˌvər-chə-ˈwal-ət-ē\ *n* — **vir•tu•al•ly** \ˈverch-wə-lē, -ə-wə-; ˈvərch-lē, -ə-lē\ *adv*

virtual image *n* **:** an image (as seen in a plane mirror) formed of points from which divergent rays (as of light) seem to emanate without actually doing so

virtual reality *n* **:** an artificial environment which is experienced through sights and sounds provided by a computer and in which one's actions partially determine what happens in the environment

vir•tue \ˈvər-chü\ *n* **1 :** conformity to a standard of right : MORALITY **2 :** a particular moral excellence ⟨justice and charity are *virtues*⟩ **3 a :** an active beneficial power ⟨quinine has *virtue* in the treatment of malaria⟩ **b :** a desirable or commendable quality or trait : MERIT ⟨the *virtues* of country life⟩ **4 :** chastity especially in a woman [Medieval French *virtu, vertu,* from Latin *virtus* "manliness, courage, virtue," from *vir* "man"] — **by virtue of** *or* **in virtue of :** through the force of : by authority of

Word History From *vir,* meaning "man," the Romans derived the word *virtus* to denote the sum of the excellent qualities of men, including physical strength, valorous conduct, and moral rectitude. The Christian church stressed the moral virtues, and French *virtu* or *vertu,* developed from Latin *virtus,* was used specifically to mean "morality." The French word was borrowed into English in the 13th century. In the 14th century *virtue* came to be applied to any quality, moral or otherwise, felt to be excellent. During the 16th century the sense "chastity, purity" appeared, especially in reference to women.

vir•tu•os•i•ty \ˌvər-chə-ˈwäs-ət-ē\ *n, pl* **-ties :** great technical skill in the practice of the fine arts

vir•tu•o•so \ˌvər-chə-ˈwō-sō, -zō\ *n, pl* **-sos** *or* **-si** \-sē, -zē\ **1 :** one skilled in or having a taste for the fine arts **2 :** one who excels in the technique of an art; *esp* **:** a highly skilled musical performer (as on the violin) [Italian, from *virtuoso* "virtuous, skilled"] — **virtuoso** *adj*

vir·tu·ous \ˈvər-chə-wəs\ *adj* **1 a :** having or exhibiting virtue **b :** morally excellent ⟨a *virtuous* decision⟩ **2 :** CHASTE 1 — **vir·tu·ous·ly** *adv* — **vir·tu·ous·ness** *n*

vir·u·lent \ˈvir-ə-lənt, -yə-\ *adj* **1 a :** marked by a rapid, severe, and often deadly course ⟨a *virulent* infection⟩ **b :** able to overcome bodily defensive mechanisms **:** markedly pathogenic ⟨*virulent* bacteria⟩ **2 :** extremely poisonous or venomous **:** NOXIOUS **3 :** full of malice ⟨*virulent* hostility⟩ [Latin *virulentus,* from *virus* "poison"] — **vir·u·lence** \-ləns\ *or* **vir·u·len·cy** \-lən-sē\ *n* — **vir·u·lent·ly** *adv*

vi·rus \ˈvī-rəs\ *n, pl* **vi·rus·es** **1 a :** any of a large group of submicroscopic infective agents that are considered by some to be living simple microorganisms and by others to be complex molecules, that typically contain a protein coat surrounding an RNA or DNA core of genetic material but no semipermeable membrane, that are capable of growth and replication only in living cells, and that cause various important diseases in plants and animals including humans — compare BACTERIOPHAGE, FILTERABLE VIRUS **b :** a disease or illness caused by a virus **2 :** something that poisons the mind or spirit **3 :** a computer program that is usually hidden within another seemingly harmless program and that produces copies of itself and inserts them into other programs and usually performs a malicious action (as destroying data) — compare TROJAN HORSE 2, WORM 5 [Latin, "venom, poisonous emanation"]

1**vi·sa** \ˈvē-zə *also* -sə\ *n* **:** an endorsement made on a passport by the proper authorities denoting that it has been examined and that the bearer may proceed [French, from Latin *visus,* past participle of *vidēre* "to see"]

2**visa** *vt* **vi·saed** \-zəd, -səd\; **vi·sa·ing** \-zə-ing, -sə-ing\ **:** to give a visa to

vis·age \ˈviz-ij\ *n* **1 :** the face or countenance of a person or sometimes an animal **2 :** ASPECT 2, APPEARANCE ⟨the grimy *visage* of a mining town⟩ [Medieval French, from *vis* "face," from Latin *visus* "sight," from *vidēre* "to see"]

vis·aged \-ijd\ *adj* **:** having a visage of a specified kind — usually used in combination ⟨grim–*visaged*⟩

1**vis–à–vis** \ˌvēz-ə-ˈvē, ˌvēs- *also* -ä-ˈvē\ *prep* **1 :** face-to-face with **:** OPPOSITE **2 :** in relation to **3 :** as compared with

2**vis–à–vis** *n, pl* **vis–à–vis** \-ˈvē, -ˈvēz\ **1 :** one that is face-to-face with another **2 a :** ESCORT 1b, DATE **b :** COUNTERPART **3 :** TÊTE-À-TÊTE 1 [French, literally, "face to face"]

3**vis–à–vis** *adv* **:** in company **:** TOGETHER ⟨found themselves *vis-à-vis* for the first time⟩

viscera *plural of* VISCUS

vis·cer·al \ˈvis-ə-rəl\ *adj* **1 a :** felt in or as if in the viscera ⟨a *visceral* conviction⟩ **b :** of, relating to, or being the viscera **:** SPLANCHNIC ⟨*visceral* organs⟩ **2 :** not intellectual **:** INSTINCTIVE ⟨a *visceral* reaction⟩ — **vis·cer·al·ly** \-rə-lē\ *adv*

vis·cid \ˈvis-əd\ *adj* **1 :** VISCOUS **2 :** covered with a sticky layer [Late Latin *viscidus,* from Latin *viscum* "birdlime"] — **vis·cid·i·ty** \vis-ˈid-ət-ē\ *n* — **vis·cid·ly** \ˈvis-əd-lē\ *adv*

vis·co·elas·tic \ˌvis-kō-i-ˈlas-tik\ *adj* **:** having both viscous and elastic properties in appreciable degree ⟨*viscoelastic* asphalt⟩

vis·com·e·ter \vis-ˈkäm-ət-ər\ *n* **:** an instrument with which to measure viscosity — **vis·co·met·ric** \ˌvis-kə-ˈme-trik\ *adj*

1**vis·cose** \ˈvis-ˌkōs, -ˌkōz\ *n* **1 :** a viscous golden-brown solution made by treating cellulose with caustic alkali solution and carbon disulfide and used in making rayon **2 :** viscose rayon

2**viscose** *adj* **:** of, relating to, or made from viscose

vis·cos·i·ty \vis-ˈkäs-ət-ē\ *n, pl* **-ties** **:** the quality of being viscous; *esp* **:** a tendency of a liquid to flow slowly resulting from friction of its molecules ⟨an oil of high *viscosity*⟩

vis·count \ˈvī-ˌkau̇nt\ *n* **:** a member of the British peerage ranking below an earl and above a baron [Medieval French *visquens, visconte,* from Medieval Latin *vicecomes,* from Late Latin *vice-* "vice-" + *comes* "count"] — **vis·count·cy** \-sē\ *n* — **vis·county** \-ˌkau̇nt-ē\ *n*

vis·count·ess \-ˌkau̇nt-əs\ *n* **1 :** the wife or widow of a viscount **2 :** a woman who holds the rank of viscount in her own right

vis·cous \ˈvis-kəs\ *adj* **1 :** somewhat sticky or glutinous **:** ADHESIVE **2 :** having or characterized by viscosity [Late Latin *viscosus,* from Latin *viscum* "birdlime"] — **vis·cous·ly** *adv* — **vis·cous·ness** *n*

vis·cus \ˈvis-kəs\ *n, pl* **vis·cera** \ˈvis-ə-rə\ **:** an internal organ of the body; *esp* **:** one (as the heart, liver, or intestine) located in the great cavity of the trunk [Latin]

vise \ˈvīs\ *n* **:** any of various tools having two jaws for holding work that operate usually by a screw, lever, or cam [Middle French *vyz,* from Latin *vitis* "vine"]

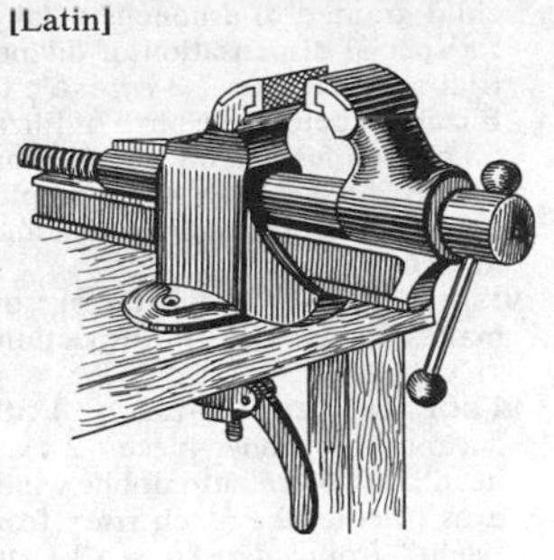

vise

vis·i·bil·i·ty \ˌviz-ə-ˈbil-ət-ē\ *n* **1 :** the quality or state of being visible **2 :** the degree of clearness of the atmosphere especially as affording clear vision toward the horizon

vis·i·ble \ˈviz-ə-bəl\ *adj* **1 :** capable of being seen **:** apparent to the eye ⟨stars *visible* to the naked eye⟩ **2 :** CONSPICUOUS 1 ⟨has played a highly *visible* role in building the new park⟩ **3 :** capable of being discovered, perceived, or recognized ⟨has no *visible* means of support⟩ **4 :** WELL-KNOWN ⟨a highly *visible* politician⟩ [Latin *visibilis,* from *vidēre* "to see"] — **vis·i·ble·ness** *n* — **vis·i·bly** \-blē\ *adv*

Visi·goth \ˈviz-ə-ˌgäth\ *n* **:** a member of the western division of the Goths [Late Latin *Visigothi* "Visigoths"] — **Visi·goth·ic** \ˌviz-ə-ˈgäth-ik\ *adj*

1**vi·sion** \ˈvizh-ən\ *n* **1 a :** something seen in a dream, trance, or ecstasy **b :** a thought, concept, or object formed by the imagination **c :** GHOST 2, APPARITION **2 a :** the act or power of imagination **b :** unusual discernment or foresight ⟨a person of *vision*⟩ **3 a :** the act or power of seeing **:** SIGHT **b :** the special sense by which the qualities of an object (as color, luminosity, or shape) constituting its appearance are perceived through a process in which light rays entering the eye are transformed by the retina into electrical signals that are transmitted to the brain via the optic nerve **4 :** something seen; *esp* **:** a lovely or charming sight [Medieval French, from Latin *visio,* from *vidēre* "to see"] — **vi·sion·al** \ˈvizh-nəl, -ən-l\ *adj* — **vi·sion·al·ly** \-ē\ *adv*

2**vision** *vt* **vi·sioned; vi·sion·ing** \ˈvizh-ning, -ə-ning\ **:** IMAGINE 1, ENVISION ⟨couldn't *vision* it happening⟩

1**vi·sion·ary** \ˈvizh-ə-ˌner-ē\ *adj* **1 :** given to dreaming or imagining **2 :** resembling a vision especially in fanciful or impractical quality ⟨*visionary* schemes⟩ — **vi·sion·ar·i·ness** *n*

2**visionary** *n, pl* **-ar·ies** **1 :** one whose ideas or projects are impractical **:** DREAMER **2 :** one who sees visions **:** SEER **3 :** one having unusual foresight and imagination ⟨a *visionary* in the computer industry⟩

vi·sion·less \ˈvizh-ən-ləs\ *adj* **1 :** SIGHTLESS, BLIND ⟨*visionless* eyes⟩ **2 :** lacking vision or inspiration ⟨a *visionless* leader⟩

1**vis·it** \ˈviz-ət\ *vb* **vis·it·ed** \ˈviz-ət-əd, ˈviz-təd\; **vis·it·ing** \ˈviz-ət-ing, ˈviz-ting\ **1 a :** to come to or upon as a reward, affliction, or punishment **b :** to present itself to or come over momentarily ⟨was *visited* by a strange notion⟩ **2 :** to go to see in order to comfort or help **3 a :** to pay a call upon as an act of friendship or courtesy **b :** to go or come to see in an official or professional capacity **c :** to dwell with temporarily as a guest **d :** to go to see or stay at (a place) for a particular purpose (as business or sightseeing) **4 :** to make a visit or frequent or regular visits **5 :** CHAT 2, CONVERSE ⟨enjoys *visiting* with the neighbors⟩ [Medieval French *visiter,* from Latin *visitare,* from *visere* "to go to see," from *vidēre* "to see"]

2**visit** *n* **1 :** a brief stay **:** CALL ⟨a *visit* with friends⟩ **2 :** a stay as a guest or nonresident ⟨a weekend *visit*⟩ **3 :** a journey to and brief stay at a place especially for a particular purpose ⟨a *visit* to the museum⟩ **4 :** an official or professional call (as of a doctor to treat a patient)

vis·it·able \ˈviz-ət-ə-bəl, ˈviz-tə-\ *adj* **1 :** subject to or allowing visitation or inspection **2 :** socially eligible to receive visits

vis·i·tant \ˈviz-ət-ənt, ˈviz-tənt\ *n* **:** VISITOR; *esp* **:** one thought to come from a spirit world — **visitant** *adj*

vis·i·ta·tion \ˌviz-ə-ˈtā-shən\ *n* **1 a :** an instance of visiting; *esp*

\ə\ **abut**	\au̇\ **out**	\i\ **tip**	\ȯ\ **saw**	\u̇\ **foot**
\ər\ **further**	\ch\ **chin**	\ī\ **life**	\ȯi\ **coin**	\y\ **yet**
\a\ **mat**	\e\ **pet**	\j\ **job**	\th\ **thin**	\yü\ **few**
\ā\ **take**	\ē\ **easy**	\ng\ **sing**	\t͟h\ **this**	\yu̇\ **cure**
\ä\ **cot, cart**	\g\ **go**	\ō\ **bone**	\ü\ **food**	\zh\ **vision**

: an official visit (as for inspection) **b** : temporary custody of a child granted to a noncustodial parent ⟨*visitation* rights⟩ **2 a** : a special dispensation of divine favor or wrath **b** : a severe trial : AFFLICTION **3** *cap* **a** : the visit of the Virgin Mary to Elizabeth before the birth of Elizabeth's son John the Baptist **b** : a church festival on July 2 commemorating this visit

visiting nurse *n* : a nurse employed to perform public health services and especially to visit and provide care for sick persons in a community

vis·i·tor \ˈviz-ət-ər, ˈviz-tər\ *n* : one that visits: as **a** : one that makes formal visits of inspection **b** : GUEST 1a **c** : TOURIST, TRAVELER

vi·sor *also* **vizor** \ˈvī-zər\ *n* **1** : the front piece of a helmet; *esp* : a movable upper piece **2** : a projecting part (as on a cap, headband, or an automobile windshield) to protect or shade the eyes [Medieval French *viser,* from *vis* "face," from Latin *visus* "sight," from *vidēre* "to see"] — **vi·sored** \-zərd\ *adj* — **vi·sor·less** \-zər-ləs\ *adj*

vis·ta \ˈvis-tə\ *n* **1** : a distant view through or along an avenue or opening : PROSPECT **2** : an extensive mental view (as over a stretch of time or a series of events) [Italian, "sight," from *vedere* "to see," from Latin *vidēre*]

[1]**vi·su·al** \ˈvizh-wəl, -ə-wəl; ˈvizh-əl\ *adj* **1** : of, relating to, or used in vision ⟨*visual* organs⟩ **2** : attained or maintained by sight ⟨*visual* impressions⟩ **3** : VISIBLE 1 ⟨*visual* objects⟩ **4** : producing mental images : VIVID ⟨*visual* descriptions⟩ **5** : of, relating to, or employing visual aids ⟨a *visual* presentation⟩ [Late Latin *visualis,* from Latin *visus* "sight," from *vidēre* "to see"] — **vi·su·al·ly** \-ē\ *adv*

[2]**visual** *n* : something (as a picture, chart, or film) that appeals to the sight and is used for effect or illustration — usually used in plural

visual acuity *n* : the relative capacity of the visual organ to resolve detail

visual aid *n* : an instructional device (as a chart, map, or model) that appeals chiefly to vision; *esp* : an educational movie or filmstrip

visual field *n* : the entire space visible at a given instant without moving the eyes — called also *field of vision*

vi·su·al·i·za·tion \ˌvizh-wə-lə-ˈzā-shən, -ə-wə-; ˌvizh-ə-lə-\ *n* **1** : formation of mental visual images **2** : the act or process of interpreting in visual terms or of putting into visible form

vi·su·al·ize \ˈvizh-wə-ˌlīz, -ə-wə-; ˈvizh-ə-ˌlīz\ *vb* : to make visible; *esp* : to see or form a mental image of : ENVISAGE — **vi·su·al·iz·er** \ˈvizh-wə-ˌlī-zər, -ə-wə-, ˈvizh-ə-ˌlī-\ *n*

visual purple *n* : a photosensitive red or purple pigment in the retinal rods of various vertebrates; *esp* : RHODOPSIN

vi·ta \ˈvēt-ə, ˈvīt-ə\ *n, pl* **vi·tae** \ˈvē-ˌtī, ˈvīt-ē\ : a brief autobiographical sketch [Latin, literally, "life"]

vi·tal \ˈvīt-l\ *adj* **1** : concerned with or necessary to the maintenance of life ⟨the heart and lungs are *vital* organs⟩ **2** : full of vitality : ANIMATED **3** : of, relating to, or characteristic of life : showing the qualities of living things ⟨*vital* activites⟩ **4** : destructive of life : MORTAL ⟨a *vital* wound⟩ **5** : of first importance ⟨a *vital* clue⟩ ⟨*vital* resources⟩ [Middle French, from Latin *vitalis* "of life," from *vita* "life"] ***synonyms*** see ESSENTIAL — **vi·tal·ly** \-l-ē\ *adv*

vital capacity *n* : the breathing capacity of the lungs expressed as the number of cubic inches or cubic centimeters of air that can be forcibly exhaled after a full inspiration

vi·tal·ism \ˈvīt-l-ˌiz-əm\ *n* : the doctrine that the life processes are not wholly explainable by the laws of physics and chemistry and that life is in some part self-determining — compare MECHANISM — **vi·tal·ist** \-l-əst\ *n or adj* — **vi·tal·is·tic** \ˌvīt-l-ˈis-tik\ *adj*

vi·tal·i·ty \vī-ˈtal-ət-ē\ *n, pl* **-ties** **1 a** : the property by which the living can be distinguished from the nonliving **b** : capacity to live and develop; *also* : physical or mental vigor especially when highly developed **2 a** : power of enduring or continuing ⟨the *vitality* of bad habits⟩ **b** : lively and animated character : VIGOR

vi·tal·ize \ˈvīt-l-ˌīz\ *vt* : to give vitality to : ANIMATE ⟨the good news *vitalized* his supporters⟩ — **vi·tal·i·za·tion** \ˌvīt-l-ə-ˈzā-shən\ *n*

vi·tals \ˈvīt-lz\ *n pl* **1** : vital organs (as the heart and liver) **2** : essential parts

vital signs *n pl* : the pulse rate, number of breaths taken per minute, body temperature, and often blood pressure of a person

vital statistics *n pl* **1** : statistics relating to births, deaths, marriages, health, and disease **2** : facts (as physical dimensions or quantities) considered to be interesting or important

vi·ta·min \ˈvīt-ə-mən\ *n* : any of various organic substances that are essential in minute quantities to the nutrition of most animals and some plants, act as coenzymes or precursors of coenzymes in the regulation of metabolic processes but do not provide energy, and are present naturally in many foods or sometimes produced within the body [Latin *vita* "life" + English *amine*]

vitamin A *n* : a fat-soluble vitamin or vitamin mixture found especially in green and orange vegetables (as spinach or carrots) and animal products (as egg yolk, butter, or liver) whose lack causes injury to epithelial tissues (as in the eye with resulting visual defects)

vitamin B *n* **1** : VITAMIN B COMPLEX **2** *or* **vitamin B_1** : THIAMINE

vitamin B complex *n* : a group of water-soluble vitamins found widely in foods that include essential coenzymes and growth factors — called also *B complex*; compare BIOTIN, NIACIN, PANTOTHENIC ACID, RIBOFLAVIN, THIAMINE

vitamin B_6 \-ˈbē-ˈsiks\ *n* : PYRIDOXINE; *also* : a closely related compound

vitamin B_{12} \-ˈbē-ˈtwelv\ *n* : a complex cobalt-containing member of the vitamin B complex that occurs especially in liver, is essential to normal blood formation, nerve function, and growth, and is used especially in treating pernicious anemia; *also* : any of several compounds with similar activity

vitamin B_2 \-ˈbē-ˈtü\ *n* : RIBOFLAVIN

vitamin C *n* : a water-soluble vitamin $C_6H_8O_6$ that is present especially in citrus fruits, tomatoes, and green leafy vegetables and is used in the prevention and treatment of scurvy and as an antioxidant in foods — called also *ascorbic acid*

vitamin D *n* : any of several fat-soluble vitamins that are chemically related to steroids, are essential for normal bone and tooth structure, and are found especially in fish-liver oils, egg yolk, and milk or produced by activation (as by ultraviolet irradiation) of sterols

vitamin E *n* : any of several fat-soluble vitamins that are chemically tocopherols, occur especially in green leafy vegetables and seed-germ oils, and are necessary in the body to prevent infertility and muscular degeneration

vitamin H *n* : BIOTIN

vitamin K *n* : any of several fat-soluble vitamins essential for the clotting of blood because of their role in the production of prothrombin [Danish and Swedish *k*oagulation "coagulation"]

vi·tel·line membrane \vī-ˈtel-ən-, və-\ *n* : a membrane that encloses an egg and that in mammals is a thick transparent noncellular layer [Medieval Latin *vitellinus* "resembling the yolk of an egg," from *vitellus* "egg yolk"]

vi·ti·ate \ˈvish-ē-ˌāt\ *vt* **1** : to impair the quality of : SPOIL ⟨grammatical errors *vitiated* the impact of her writing⟩ **2** : to destroy the validity of : make ineffective ⟨fraud *vitiates* a contract⟩ [Latin *vitiare,* from *vitium* "fault, vice"] — **vi·ti·a·tion** \ˌvish-ē-ˈā-shən\ *n* — **vi·ti·a·tor** \ˈvish-ē-ˌāt-ər\ *n*

vi·ti·cul·ture \ˈvit-ə-ˌkəl-chər, ˈvīt-ə-\ *n* : the growing of grapes especially for the making of wine [Latin *vitis* "vine"] — **vi·ti·cul·tur·al** \ˌvit-ə-ˈkəlch-rəl, -ə-rəl, ˌvīt-\ *adj* — **vi·ti·cul·tur·ist** \-ˈkəlch-rəst, -ə-rəst\ *n*

vit·i·li·go \ˌvit-l-ˈī-gō, -ˈē-gō\ *n* : a skin disorder in which smooth white spots appear on the body [Latin, a skin disease]

vit·re·ous \ˈvi-trē-əs\ *adj* **1** : of, relating to, derived from, or resembling glass : GLASSY ⟨*vitreous* rocks⟩ ⟨a *vitreous* luster⟩ **2** : of, relating to, or being the vitreous humor [Latin *vitreus,* from *vitrum* "glass"] — **vit·re·ous·ness** *n*

vitreous humor *n* : the clear colorless transparent jelly that fills the eyeball posterior to the lens

vit·ri·fy \ˈvi-trə-ˌfī\ *vb* **-fied; -fy·ing** : to change into glass or a glassy substance by heat and fusion [French *vitrifier,* from Latin *vitrum* "glass"] — **vit·ri·fi·able** \-ˌfī-ə-bəl\ *adj* — **vit·ri·fi·ca·tion** \ˌvi-trə-fə-ˈkā-shən\ *n*

vit·ri·ol \ˈvi-trē-əl\ *n* **1 a** : a sulfate of any of various metals (as copper, iron, or zinc) **b** : OIL OF VITRIOL **2** : bitter feelings or harsh speech [Medieval French, from Medieval Latin *vitriolum,* derived from Latin *vitreus* "vitreous"] — **vit·ri·ol·ic** \ˌvi-trē-ˈäl-ik\ *adj*

vit·tles \ˈvit-lz\ *n pl* : VICTUALS

vi·tu·per·ate \vī-ˈtü-pə-ˌrāt, və-, -ˈtyü-\ *vb* : to abuse or censure severely : use harsh condemning language [Latin *vituperare,* from *vitium* "fault" + *parare* "to make"] — **vi·tu·per·a·tive**

\-ˈtü-pə-rət-iv, -pə-ˌrāt-, -prət-iv, -ˈtyü-\ *adj* — **vi·tu·per·a·tive·ly** *adv* — **vi·tu·per·a·tor** \-pə-ˌrāt-ər\ *n* — **vi·tu·per·a·to·ry** \-rə-ˌtōr-ē, -ˌtȯr-\ *adj*

vi·tu·per·a·tion \-ˌtü-pə-ˈrā-shən, -ˌtyü-\ *n* : sustained and bitter railing and condemnation ***synonyms*** see ABUSE

vi·va \ˈvē-və, -ˌvä\ *interj* — used to express approval or goodwill [Italian and Spanish, "long live," from *vivere* "to live," from Latin]

vi·va·ce \vē-ˈväch-ā, vi-, -ē\ *adv or adj* : in a brisk spirited manner — used as a direction in music [Italian, "vivacious"]

vi·va·cious \və-ˈvā-shəs *also* vī-\ *adj* : lively in temper or conduct : SPRIGHTLY [Latin *vivac-, vivax,* literally, "long-lived," from *vivere* "to live"] ***synonyms*** see LIVELY — **vi·va·cious·ly** *adv* — **vi·va·cious·ness** *n*

vi·vac·i·ty \-ˈvas-ət-ē\ *n* : the quality or state of being vivacious

vi·var·i·um \vī-ˈvar-ē-əm, -ˈver-\ *n, pl* **-ia** \-ē-ə\ *or* **-i·ums** : a terrarium used especially for small animals [Latin, "park, preserve," from *vivus* "alive"]

[1]**vi·va vo·ce** \ˌvī-və-ˈvō-sē, ˌvē-və-ˈvō-chā\ *adv* : by word of mouth : ORALLY ⟨gave an account *viva voce*⟩ [Medieval Latin, "with the living voice"]

[2]**viva voce** *adj* : expressed or conducted by word of mouth : ORAL ⟨*viva voce* voting⟩

viv·id \ˈviv-əd\ *adj* **1** : very strong or intense : of very high saturation ⟨a *vivid* red⟩ **2** : having the appearance of vigorous life or freshness : very lively ⟨a *vivid* personality⟩ **3** : producing a strong or clear impression on the senses : SHARP; *esp* : producing distinct mental images ⟨a *vivid* description⟩ **4** : acting clearly and vigorously ⟨a *vivid* imagination⟩ [Latin *vividus,* from *vivere* "to live"] ***synonyms*** see GRAPHIC — **viv·id·ly** *adv* — **viv·id·ness** *n*

viv·i·fy \ˈviv-ə-ˌfī\ *vt* **-fied; -fy·ing** **1** : to provide with the quality or appearance of life : ANIMATE ⟨rains that *vivified* the barren hills⟩ **2** : to make vivid [Middle French *vivifier,* from Late Latin *vivificare,* derived from Latin *vivus* "alive"] — **viv·i·fi·ca·tion** \ˌviv-ə-fə-ˈkā-shən\ *n* — **viv·i·fi·er** \ˈviv-ə-ˌfī-ər, -ˌfīr\ *n*

vi·vip·a·rous \vī-ˈvip-rəs, -ə-rəs\ *adj* : giving birth to living young from within the body rather than laying eggs ⟨nearly all mammals and some reptiles are *viviparous* animals⟩ [Latin *viviparus,* from *vivus* "alive" + *parere* "to produce"] — **vi·vi·par·i·ty** \ˌvī-və-ˈpar-ət-ē\ *n* — **vi·vip·a·rous·ly** \vī-ˈvip-rəs-lē, -ə-rəs-\ *adv*

vivi·sec·tion \ˌviv-ə-ˈsek-shən\ *n* : the cutting of or operation on a living animal usually for scientific or medical investigation; *also* : animal experimentation especially if considered to cause distress to the subject [Latin *vivus* "alive" + English *section*] — **vivi·sect** \ˈviv-ə-ˌsekt\ *vb* — **vivi·sec·tion·al** \ˌviv-ə-ˈsek-shnəl, -shən-l\ *adj* — **vivi·sec·tion·ist** \-ˈsek-shə-nəst, -shnəst\ *n* — **vivi·sec·tor** \ˈviv-ə-ˌsek-tər\ *n*

vix·en \ˈvik-sən\ *n* **1** : a female fox **2** : a quick-tempered argumentative woman [Middle English *fixen,* from Old English *fyxe,* feminine of *fox*] — **vix·en·ish** \-sə-nish, -snish\ *adj*

viz·ard \ˈviz-ərd, -ˌärd\ *n* : a mask for disguise or protection [Middle English *viser* "mask, visor"]

vi·zier \və-ˈziər\ *n* : a high executive officer of various Muslim countries and especially of the Ottoman Empire [Turkish *vezir,* from Arabic *wazīr*] — **vi·zier·ial** \-ˈzir-ē-əl\ *adj*

vi·zier·ate \və-ˈziər-ət, -ˌāt\ *n* **1** : the office or authority of a vizier **2** : the term of office of a vizier

vizor *variant of* VISOR

VJ \ˈvē-ˌjā\ *n* : VEEJAY

vlog \ˈvlȯg, ˈvläg\ *n* : a blog that contains recorded video [*v*ideo + b*log*]

vo·cab \ˈvō-ˌkab\ *n* : VOCABULARY

vo·ca·ble \ˈvō-kə-bəl\ *n* : a word composed of various sounds or letters without regard to its meaning [Middle French, from Latin *vocabulum,* from *vocare* "to call"]

vo·cab·u·lary \vō-ˈkab-yə-ˌler-ē\ *n, pl* **-lar·ies** **1** : a list or collection of words or of words and phrases usually alphabetically arranged and explained or defined **2** : a sum or stock of words employed by a language, group, individual, or work or in a field of knowledge [Middle French *vocabulaire,* probably from Medieval Latin *vocabularium,* derived from Latin *vocabulum* "name, term," from *vocare* "to call"]

vocabulary entry *n* : a word (as the noun *book*), hyphenated or open compound (as the adjective *light-headed* or the noun *book review*), word element (as the affix *pro-*), abbreviation (as *agt*), verbalized symbol (as *Na*), or term (as *point of view*) entered alphabetically in a dictionary for the purpose of definition or identification or expressly included as an inflectional form (as the noun *mice* or the verb *saw*) or as a derived form (as the noun *godlessness* or the adverb *globally*) or related phrase (as *one for the book*) run on at its base word and usually set in a type (as boldface) readily distinguishable from that of the lightface text which defines, explains, or identifies the entry

[1]**vo·cal** \ˈvō-kəl\ *adj* **1 a** : uttered by the voice : ORAL **b** : VOICED 2 **2** : relating to, composed or arranged for, or sung by the human voice ⟨*vocal* music⟩ **3** : VOCALIC **4** : given to expressing oneself freely or insistently : OUTSPOKEN ⟨a *vocal* critic⟩ **5** : of, relating to, or resembling the voice [Latin *vocalis,* from *voc-, vox* "voice"] — **vo·cal·ly** \-kə-lē\ *adv*

[2]**vocal** *n* **1** : a vocal sound **2** : a usually accompanied musical composition for the human voice : SONG; *also* : a performance of such a composition

vocal cords *n pl* : either of two pairs of elastic folds of mucous membrane that project into the cavity of the larynx of which the lower pair produce sound when air exhaled from the lungs causes them to vibrate — called also *vocal folds*

vo·cal·ic \vō-ˈkal-ik\ *adj* **1** : marked by or consisting of vowels **2** : of, relating to, or functioning as a vowel [Latin *vocalis* "vowel," from *vocalis* "vocal"] — **vo·cal·i·cal·ly** \-i-kə-lē, -klē\ *adv*

vo·cal·ist \ˈvō-kə-ləst\ *n* : [1]SINGER

vo·cal·i·za·tion \ˌvō-kə-lə-ˈzā-shən\ *n* : an act, process, or instance of vocalizing

vo·cal·ize \ˈvō-kə-ˌlīz\ *vb* **1 a** : to give vocal expression to **b** : SING; *esp* : to sing without words (as in practicing) **2 a** : VOICE 2 **b** : to convert to a vowel — **vo·cal·iz·er** *n*

vo·ca·tion \vō-ˈkā-shən\ *n* **1** : a summons or strong inclination to a particular state or course of action; *esp* : a divine call to the religious life **2 a** : the work in which a person is regularly employed : OCCUPATION **b** : the persons engaged in a particular occupation **3** : the special function of an individual or group : ROLE [Latin *vocatio* "summons," from *vocare* "to call"]

vo·ca·tion·al \-shnəl, -shən-l\ *adj* **1** : of, relating to, or concerned with a vocation **2** : of, relating to, or undergoing training in a skill or trade to be pursued as a career ⟨*vocational* guidance⟩ ⟨a *vocational* school⟩ — **vo·ca·tion·al·ly** \-ē\ *adv*

vo·ca·tion·al·ism \-ˌiz-əm\ *n* : emphasis on vocational training in education

voc·a·tive \ˈväk-ət-iv\ *adj* : of, relating to, or being a grammatical case marking the one addressed [Medieval French *vocatif,* from Latin *vocativus,* from *vocare* "to call"] — **vocative** *n* — **voc·a·tive·ly** *adv*

vo·cif·er·ant \vō-ˈsif-ə-rənt\ *adj* : VOCIFEROUS — **vo·cif·er·ance** \-rəns\ *n*

vo·cif·er·ate \vō-ˈsif-ə-ˌrāt\ *vb* : to cry out or utter loudly : CLAMOR, SHOUT [Latin *vociferari,* from *voc-, vox* "voice" + *ferre* "to carry"] — **vo·cif·er·a·tion** \-ˌsif-ə-ˈrā-shən\ *n* — **vo·cif·er·a·tor** \-ˈsif-ə-ˌrāt-ər\ *n*

vo·cif·er·ous \vō-ˈsif-rəs, -ə-rəs\ *adj* : making a loud outcry : NOISY, CLAMOROUS — **vo·cif·er·ous·ly** *adv* — **vo·cif·er·ous·ness** *n*

vod·ka \ˈväd-kə\ *n* : a colorless alcoholic liquor distilled from a mash (as of rye or wheat) [Russian, from *voda* "water"]

vogue \ˈvōg\ *n* **1 a** : popular approval or favor : POPULARITY **b** : a period of popularity **2** : something or someone in fashion at a particular time [Middle French, "action of rowing, course, fashion," from *voguer* "to sail," from Medieval French, from Italian *vogare* "to row"] ***synonyms*** see FASHION — **vogue** *adj*

vogu·ish \ˈvō-gish\ *adj* **1** : FASHIONABLE 1 ⟨*voguish* outfits⟩ **2** : suddenly or temporarily popular ⟨a *voguish* phrase⟩

[1]**voice** \ˈvȯis\ *n* **1** : sound produced by vertebrates in the larynx or syrinx; *esp* : sound so produced by human beings (as in speaking) **2 a** : musical sound produced by the vocal cords and resonated by the cavities of the head and throat **b** : the power or ability to produce musical tones **c** : [1]SINGER **d** : one of the melodic parts of a vocal or instrumental composition **e** : the quality of the vocal mechanism with respect to the production of musical tones ⟨in good *voice* today⟩ **f** : the use of the voice in speaking, acting, or singing **3** : expiration of air with the vocal cords drawn close so as to vibrate audibly (as in

\ə\ **abut**	\au̇\ **out**	\i\ **tip**	\ȯ\ **saw**	\u̇\ **foot**
\ər\ **further**	\ch\ **chin**	\ī\ **life**	\ȯi\ **coin**	\y\ **yet**
\a\ **mat**	\e\ **pet**	\j\ **job**	\th\ **thin**	\yü\ **few**
\ā\ **take**	\ē\ **easy**	\ng\ **sing**	\t͟h\ **this**	\yu̇\ **cure**
\ä\ **cot, cart**	\g\ **go**	\ō\ **bone**	\ü\ **food**	\zh\ **vision**

uttering vowels and consonants as \v\ or \z\) **4 :** the power of speaking ⟨lost my *voice*⟩ **5 :** something resembling or likened to a vocal utterance ⟨the *voice* of conscience⟩ **6 :** a medium of expression ⟨the newspaper was the *voice* of conservatism⟩ **7 a :** wish, choice, or opinion openly or formally expressed ⟨the law was passed despite many dissenting *voices*⟩ **b :** right of expression; *also* **:** influential power **8 :** distinction of form or a system of inflections of a verb to indicate the relation of the subject of the verb to the action which the verb expresses ⟨active and passive *voices*⟩ [Medieval French *vois,* from Latin *voc-, vox*] — **with one voice :** without dissent **:** UNANIMOUSLY

[2]**voice** *vt* **1 :** to express in words **:** UTTER ⟨*voiced* serious objections to our proposal⟩ **2 :** to pronounce (as a consonant) with voice

voice box *n* **:** LARYNX

voiced \ˈvȯist\ *adj* **1 :** having or furnished with a voice especially of a specified kind — often used in combination ⟨soft-*voiced*⟩ **2 :** uttered with vocal cord vibration ⟨a *voiced* consonant like \v\⟩

voice·less \ˈvȯi-sləs\ *adj* **1 :** having no voice **2 :** not voiced ⟨a *voiceless* consonant like \f\⟩ — **voice·less·ly** *adv* — **voice·less·ness** *n*

voice mail *n* **:** an electronic communication system in which spoken messages are recorded or digitized for later playback to the intended recipient; *also* **:** such a message

voice–over \ˈvois-ˌō-vər\ *n* **1 :** the voice of an unseen narrator speaking (as in a television commercial) **2 :** the voice of a visible character (as in a movie) expressing unspoken thoughts

voice part *n* **:** VOICE 2d

voice·print \ˈvoi-ˌsprint\ *n* **:** an individually distinctive pattern of certain voice characteristics that is spectrographically produced [*voice* + *-print* (as in *fingerprint*)]

[1]**void** \ˈvȯid\ *adj* **1 a :** not occupied **:** VACANT **b :** not inhabited **:** DESERTED **2 :** containing nothing ⟨*void* space⟩ **3 :** being without something specified **:** DEVOID ⟨hearts *void* of mercy⟩ **4 :** of no legal force or effect ⟨a *void* contract⟩

[2]**void** *n* **1 a :** empty space **b :** an unfilled opening **2 :** LACK 1, DEFICIENCY **3 :** a feeling of want or hollowness **4 :** absence of cards of a particular suit in a hand as dealt

[3]**void** *vt* **1 :** to make empty or vacant **:** CLEAR **2 :** DISCHARGE, EMIT ⟨*void* urine⟩ **3 :** NULLIFY, ANNUL ⟨*void* a contract⟩ — **void·er** *n*

void·able \ˈvȯid-ə-bəl\ *adj* **:** capable of being voided

voile \ˈvȯil\ *n* **:** a soft sheer fabric of silk, cotton, rayon, or wool used especially for curtains or women's summer clothing [French, "veil," from Latin *velum*]

vo·lan·te \vō-ˈlän-tā\ *adj* **:** moving with light rapidity — used as a direction in music [Italian, literally, "flying," from Latin *volare* "to fly"]

vo·lar \ˈvō-lər, -ˌlär\ *adj* **:** relating to the palm of the hand or the sole of the foot [Latin *vola* "palm, sole"]

[1]**vol·a·tile** \ˈväl-ət-l\ *adj* **1 :** readily becoming a vapor at a relatively low temperature ⟨a *volatile* solvent⟩ **2 a :** LIGHTHEARTED, LIVELY ⟨a *volatile* mind⟩ **b :** easily aroused ⟨a *volatile* temper⟩ **3 a :** tending or likely to erupt into violent action ⟨a *volatile* situation⟩ **b :** subject to often sudden change ⟨a *volatile* stock market⟩ [French, "flying, volatile," from Latin *volatilis* "flying," from *volare* "to fly"] — **vol·a·tile·ness** *n* — **vol·a·til·i·ty** \ˌväl-ə-ˈtil-ət-ē\ *n*

[2]**volatile** *n* **:** a volatile substance

vol·a·til·ize \ˈväl-ət-l-ˌīz\ *vb* **:** to pass off or cause to pass off in vapor — **vol·a·til·i·za·tion** \ˌväl-ət-l-ə-ˈzā-shən\ *n*

[1]**vol·ca·nic** \väl-ˈkan-ik, vȯl- *also* -ˈkān-\ *adj* **1 a :** of or relating to a volcano ⟨a *volcanic* eruption⟩ **b :** having volcanoes ⟨a *volcanic* region⟩ **c :** made of materials from volcanoes ⟨*volcanic* dust⟩ **2 :** explosively violent **:** VOLATILE ⟨*volcanic* passions⟩ — **vol·ca·ni·cal·ly** \-i-kə-lē, -klē\ *adv*

[2]**volcanic** *n* **:** a volcanic rock

volcanic glass *n* **:** natural glass produced by the cooling of molten lava too rapidly to permit crystallization

vol·ca·nism \ˈväl-kə-ˌniz-əm, ˈvȯl-\ *n* **:** volcanic activity

vol·ca·no \väl-ˈkā-nō, vȯl-\ *n, pl* **-noes** *or* **-nos :** a vent in the earth's crust from which molten or hot rock and steam issue; *also* **:** a hill or mountain composed wholly or in part of ejected volcanic material [Italian *vulcano,* from Spanish *volcán,* derived from Latin *Volcanus* "Vulcan"]

vol·ca·nol·o·gy \ˌväl-kə-ˈnäl-ə-jē, ˌvȯl-\ *n* **:** a branch of science that deals with volcanic phenomena — **vol·ca·no·log·i·cal** \-kən-l-ˈäj-i-kəl\ *adj* — **vol·ca·nol·o·gist** \-kə-ˈnäl-ə-jəst\ *n*

vole \ˈvōl\ *n* **:** any of various small rodents that are closely related to the lemmings and muskrats but in general resemble stocky mice or rats and that sometimes do much damage to crops [of Scandinavian origin]

vole

vo·li·tion \vō-ˈlish-ən, və-\ *n* **1 :** the act or power of making one's choices or decisions **:** WILL ⟨they do not do this of their own *volition*⟩ **2 :** a choice or decision made [French, from Medieval Latin *volitio,* from Latin *velle* "to will, wish"] — **vo·li·tion·al** \-ˈlish-nəl, -ən-l\ *adj*

[1]**vol·ley** \ˈväl-ē\ *n, pl* **volleys 1 a :** a flight of missiles (as arrows or bullets) **b :** simultaneous discharge of a number of missile weapons (as rifles) **2 a :** a return of the ball before it touches the ground (as in tennis or volleyball) **b :** a kick of the ball in soccer before it rebounds **c :** the exchange of the shuttlecock in badminton following the serve **3 :** a bursting forth of many things at once ⟨a *volley* of bubbles⟩ ⟨a *volley* of praise⟩ [Middle French *volee* "flight," from *voler* "to fly," from Medieval French, from Latin *volare*]

[2]**volley** *vb* **vol·leyed; vol·ley·ing 1 :** to discharge in a volley **2 :** to propel an object (as a ball) while it is in the air before it touches the ground

vol·ley·ball \ˈväl-ē-ˌbȯl\ *n* **:** a game played by volleying a large inflated ball over a net; *also* **:** the ball used in this game

vol·plane \ˈväl-ˌplān, ˈvȯl-\ *vi* **:** to glide in or as if in an airplane [French *vol plané* "gliding flight"]

volt \ˈvōlt\ *n* **:** a unit of electrical potential difference and electromotive force equal to the difference of potential between two points in a conducting wire carrying a constant current of one ampere when the power dissipated between these two points is equal to one watt [Alessandro *Volta,* died 1827, Italian physicist]

volt·age \ˈvōl-tij\ *n* **:** potential difference expressed in volts

voltage divider *n* **:** a resistor or series of resistors provided with taps at certain points and used to provide various potential differences from a single power source

vol·ta·ic \väl-ˈtā-ik, vōl-, vȯl-\ *adj* **:** of, relating to, or producing direct electric current by chemical action (as in a battery) ⟨*voltaic* cell⟩ [Alessandro *Volta,* died 1827, Italian physicist]

volt–am·pere \ˈvōl-ˈtam-ˌpiər\ *n* **:** a unit of electric measurement equal to the product of a volt and an ampere that for direct current constitutes a measure of power equivalent to a watt

volte–face \ˌvȯlt-ˈfäs, ˌvȯlt-ə-\ *n* **:** reversal of attitude especially in policy **:** ABOUT-FACE [French, from Italian *voltafaccia,* from *voltare* "to turn" + *faccia* "face"]

volt·me·ter \ˈvōlt-ˌmēt-ər\ *n* **:** an instrument for measuring in volts the differences of potential between different points of an electrical circuit

vol·u·ble \ˈväl-yə-bəl\ *adj* **:** characterized by ready or rapid speech **:** GLIB, FLUENT [Latin *volubilis,* from *volvere* "to roll"] ***synonyms*** see TALKATIVE — **vol·u·bil·i·ty** \ˌväl-yə-ˈbil-ət-ē\ *n* — **vol·u·ble·ness** \ˈväl-yə-bəl-nəs\ *n* — **vol·u·bly** \ˈväl-yə-blē\ *adv*

vol·ume \ˈväl-yəm, -yüm\ *n* **1 :** a series of printed sheets bound together between a front and back cover **:** BOOK ⟨a dozen *volumes* on the shelf⟩ **2 :** any of a series of books forming a complete work or collection ⟨the fifth *volume* of an encyclopedia⟩ **3 :** an amount of space as measured in cubic units ⟨find the *volume* of the container⟩ **4 a :** AMOUNT 1 ⟨produced a considerable *volume* of paintings⟩ **b :** a considerable quantity ⟨*volumes* of smoke⟩ ⟨a *volume* of criticism poured in⟩ **5 :** intensity or quantity of sound ⟨turn up the *volume* on the radio⟩ [Medieval French, from Latin *volumen* "roll, book," from *volvere* "to roll"] ***synonyms*** see BULK

Word History The earliest books were rolls of papyrus. The Romans took their name for such a roll, *volumen,* from the verb *volvere,* "to roll." Later, books were made of parchment, which, unlike papyrus, could be folded and bound. This eliminated the need for rolls. French *volume,* from Latin *volumen,* originally referred to papyrus rolls but was later used for bound books as well. The French word was borrowed into English in the 14th century. By the 16th century *volume* had acquired the additional sense "the size (of a book)," which led to the development of a generalized sense, "quantity, amount, or mass (of anything)." In the 19th century *volume* acquired the meaning "strength" or "intensity" in reference to sound.

vol·u·meter \ˈväl-yu̇-ˌmēt-ər\ *n* : an instrument for measuring volumes (as of gases or liquids) directly or (as of solids) by displacement of a liquid

vol·u·met·ric \ˌväl-yə-ˈme-trik\ *adj* : of or relating to the measurement of volume — **vol·u·met·ri·cal·ly** \-tri-kə-lē, -klē\ *adv*

vo·lu·mi·nous \və-ˈlü-mə-nəs\ *adj* **1** : having many folds, coils, or convolutions **2 a** : having or marked by great volume or bulk : LARGE ⟨a *voluminous* discharge of lava⟩; *also* : FULL 3b ⟨*voluminous* curtains⟩ **b** : NUMEROUS ⟨*voluminous* slips of paper⟩ **3 a** : filling or capable of filling a large volume or several volumes ⟨a *voluminous* correspondence⟩ **b** : writing or speaking much or at great length ⟨a *voluminous* writer⟩ [Late Latin *voluminosus* "full of folds," from Latin *volumen* "roll, book"] — **vo·lu·mi·nous·ly** *adv* — **vo·lu·mi·nous·ness** *n*

vol·un·tar·i·ly \ˌväl-ən-ˈter-ə-lē\ *adv* : of one's own free will ⟨admitted *voluntarily* that he was guilty⟩

[1]**vol·un·tary** \ˈväl-ən-ˌter-ē\ *adj* **1** : done, given, or made in accordance with one's own free will or choice ⟨*voluntary* assistance⟩ **2** : not accidental : INTENTIONAL ⟨*voluntary* manslaughter⟩ **3** : of or relating to the will : controlled by the will ⟨*voluntary* behavior⟩ [Latin *voluntarius,* from *voluntas* "will," from *velle* "to will, wish"]

synonyms VOLUNTARY, INTENTIONAL, DELIBERATE, WILLING mean done or brought about of one's own accord. VOLUNTARY implies spontaneousness and freedom from compulsion ⟨a *voluntary* confession⟩ or stresses control of the will ⟨*voluntary* eye movements⟩. INTENTIONAL stresses an awareness of an end to be achieved ⟨an *intentional* oversight⟩. DELIBERATE implies full consciousness of the nature of an intended action and its consequences ⟨a *deliberate* insult⟩. WILLING implies a readiness and eagerness to go along with or anticipate the wishes of another ⟨*willing* obedience⟩.

[2]**voluntary** *n, pl* **-tar·ies** : an organ piece often improvised and played before, during, or after a religious service

voluntary muscle *n* : muscle (as most striated muscle) under voluntary control

[1]**vol·un·teer** \ˌväl-ən-ˈtiər\ *n* **1** : one who enters into a service or offers to serve of his or her own free will **2** : a volunteer plant [French *volontaire,* from *volontaire* "voluntary," from Latin *voluntarius*]

[2]**volunteer** *adj* **1** : being, consisting of, or engaged in by volunteers ⟨a *volunteer* army⟩ ⟨*volunteer* activities⟩ **2** : growing spontaneously without direct human care especially from seeds lost from a previous crop ⟨*volunteer* corn plants⟩

[3]**volunteer** *vb* **1** : to offer or bestow voluntarily ⟨*volunteered* one's services⟩ **2** : to offer oneself as a volunteer ⟨*volunteered* to do the job⟩

vo·lup·tu·ary \və-ˈləp-chə-ˌwer-ē\ *n, pl* **-ar·ies** : one whose chief interest is luxury and the gratification of sensual appetites — **voluptuary** *adj*

vo·lup·tu·ous \-chə-wəs, -chəs\ *adj* **1 a** : giving pleasure to the senses : providing sensual or sensuous gratification ⟨*voluptuous* furnishings⟩ **b** : suggesting sensual pleasure by fullness and beauty of form ⟨a *voluptuous* figure⟩ **2** : given to or spent in the enjoyment of pleasure and luxury ⟨a *voluptuous* holiday⟩ [Latin *voluptuosus,* from *voluptas* "pleasure"]

vo·lute \və-ˈlüt\ *n* **1** : a spiral or scroll-shaped form **2** : a spiral scroll-shaped ornament forming the chief feature of the Ionic capital [Latin *voluta,* from *volvere* "to roll"] — **vo·lute** *or* **vo·lut·ed** \-ˈlüt-əd\ *adj*

vol·va \ˈväl-və, ˈvȯl-\ *n* : a membraneous sac or cup about the base of the stem in many mushrooms [Latin *volva, vulva* "integument"] — **vol·vate** \-ˌvāt\ *adj*

vol·vox \-ˌväks\ *n* : any of a genus of flagellated unicellular green algae that form spherical colonies [New Latin, from Latin *volvere* "to roll"]

vo·mer \ˈvō-mər\ *n* : a bone of the lower skull of most vertebrates that in humans forms part of the nasal septum [Latin, "plowshare"] — **vo·mer·ine** \-mə-ˌrīn\ *adj*

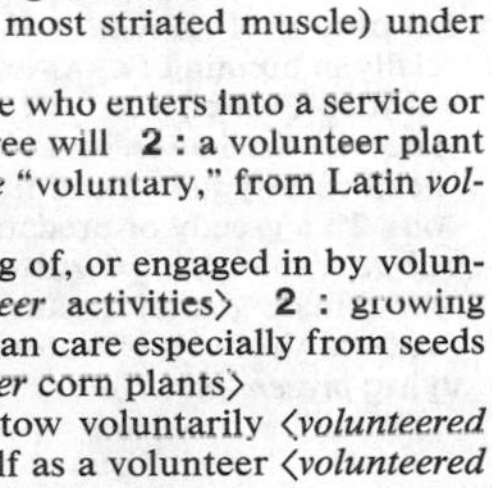

V volva

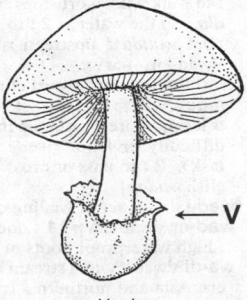

vom·ero·na·sal organ \ˌväm-ə-rō-ˈnā-zəl-, ˌvō-mə-\ *n* : either of a pair of specialized sense organs in many vertebrates that are small tubes located in the nasal cavity or roof of the mouth, are reduced to small pits in humans, and function as chemoreceptors in reptiles, amphibians, and some mammals (as cats, mice, dogs, and elephants)

[1]**vom·it** \ˈväm-ət\ *n* : an act or instance of ejecting the contents of the stomach through the mouth; *also* : the matter ejected [Medieval French *vomite,* from Latin *vomitus,* from *vomere* "to vomit"]

[2]**vomit** *vb* **1** : to eject the contents of the stomach through the mouth **2** : DISGORGE 2 ⟨lava *vomited* from the volcano⟩ — **vom·it·er** *n*

vom·i·tus \ˈväm-ət-əs\ *n* : material discharged by vomiting [Latin]

[1]**voo·doo** \ˈvüd-ü\ *n, pl* **voodoos** **1** : a religion that is derived from African ancestor worship and is practiced chiefly in Haiti **2 a** : a person who deals in spells and necromancy **b** (1) : a sorcerer's spell (2) : a hexed object [Louisiana Creole *voudou,* of African origin] — **voodoo** *adj*

[2]**voodoo** *vt* : to bewitch by or as if by means of voodoo : HEX

voo·doo·ism \ˈvüd-ü-ˌiz-əm\ *n* **1** : VOODOO 1 **2** : the practice of witchcraft — **voo·doo·ist** \ˈvüd-ˌü-əst\ *n* — **voo·doo·is·tic** \ˌvüd-ü-ˈis-tik\ *adj*

vo·ra·cious \vȯ-ˈrā-shəs, və-\ *adj* **1** : having a huge appetite : RAVENOUS ⟨*voracious* fish⟩ **2** : excessively eager : INSATIABLE ⟨a *voracious* reader⟩ [Latin *vorac-, vorax,* from *vorare* "to devour"] — **vo·ra·cious·ly** *adv* — **vo·ra·cious·ness** *n* — **vo·rac·i·ty** \-ˈras-ət-ē\ *n*

vor·tex \ˈvȯr-ˌteks\ *n, pl* **vor·ti·ces** \ˈvȯrt-ə-ˌsēz\ *also* **vor·tex·es** \ˈvȯr-ˌtek-səz\ **1** : something that resembles a whirlpool ⟨sucked into a *vortex* of controversy⟩ **2** : a mass of fluid and especially of a liquid having a whirling motion that tends to form a cavity in the center and to draw things toward this cavity; *esp* : WHIRLPOOL, EDDY [Latin *vortex* "whirlpool," from *vertere* "to turn"]

vor·ti·cal \ˈvȯrt-i-kəl\ *adj* : of, relating to, or resembling a vortex

vor·ti·cel·la \ˌvȯrt-ə-ˈsel-ə\ *n, pl* **-cel·lae** \-ˈsel-ē\ *or* **-cellas** : any of a genus of stalked bell-shaped ciliates [New Latin, from Latin *vortex* "whirlpool"]

vor·tic·i·ty \vȯr-ˈtis-ət-ē\ *n* : the state of a fluid in vortical motion

vo·ta·rist \ˈvōt-ə-rəst\ *n* : VOTARY

vo·ta·ry \ˈvōt-ə-rē\ *n, pl* **-ries** **1 a** : ENTHUSIAST, DEVOTEE **b** : a devoted adherent or admirer **2** : a devout or zealous worshipper [Latin *votum* "vow"]

[1]**vote** \ˈvōt\ *n* **1 a** : a formal expression of opinion or will; *esp* : one given as an indication of approval or disapproval of a proposal or a candidate for office **b** : the total number of such expressions of opinion made known at a single time (as at an election) **c** : BALLOT 1 **2** : the collective opinion of a body of persons expressed by voting **3** : the right to cast a vote : SUFFRAGE **4 a** : the act or process of voting ⟨bring the issue to a *vote*⟩ **b** : a method of voting **5 a** : VOTER **b** : a group of voters with common characteristics ⟨the farm *vote*⟩ [Latin *votum* "vow, wish," from *vovēre* "to vow"]

[2]**vote** *vb* **1** : to express one's wish or choice by a vote : cast a vote **2** : to choose, endorse, decide, defeat, or authorize by vote ⟨he was *voted* out of office⟩ **3** : to declare by common agreement **4** : PROPOSE 1, SUGGEST ⟨I *vote* we all go home⟩

vote·less \ˈvōt-ləs\ *adj* : having no vote; *esp* : denied the political franchise

vot·er \ˈvōt-ər\ *n* : one that votes or has the legal right to vote

voting machine *n* : a mechanical device for recording and counting votes cast on it in an election

vo·tive \ˈvōt-iv\ *adj* **1** : offered or performed in fulfillment of a vow or in gratitude or devotion **2** : consisting of or expressing a vow, wish, or desire ⟨a *votive* prayer⟩ [Latin *votivus,* from *votum* "vow"]

votive candle *n* **1** : a candle lit in devotion or gratitude **2** : a small squat candle — called also *votive*

votive mass *n* : a mass celebrated for a special intention (as for a wedding or funeral) in place of the mass of the day

vouch \'vau̇ch\ *vb* **1** *archaic* **a** : ASSERT 1, AFFIRM **b** : ATTEST **2** : to give a guarantee : become surety ⟨I'll *vouch* for your honesty⟩ **3 a** : to supply supporting evidence or testimony **b** : to give personal assurance ⟨*vouch* for the truth of a story⟩ [Medieval French *voucher* "to call, vouch," from Latin *vocare* "to call, summon," from *vox* "voice"]

vouch·er \'vau̇-chər\ *n* **1** : a person who vouches for another **2** : a document that serves to establish the truth of something; *esp* : a paper (as a receipt) showing payment of a bill or debt

vouch·safe \vau̇ch-'sāf, 'vau̇ch-,\ *vt* : to grant in the manner of one doing a favor : condescend to give or grant [Middle English *vouchen sauf* "to grant, consent, deign," from Medieval French *voucher salf*]

vous·soir \vü-'swär\ *n* : one of the wedge-shaped pieces forming an arch or vault [French, derived from Latin *volvere* "to roll"]

¹vow \'vau̇\ *n* : a solemn promise or assertion; *esp* : one by which one binds oneself to an act, service, or condition [Medieval French *vou,* from Latin *votum,* from *vovēre* "to vow"]

²vow *vb* **1** : to make a vow : promise solemnly **2** : to bind or consecrate by a vow

³vow *vt* : AVOW, DECLARE [short for *avow*]

vow·el \'vau̇-əl, 'vau̇l\ *n* **1** : a speech sound in the articulation of which the oral part of the breath channel is not blocked and is not constricted enough to cause audible friction **2** : a letter representing a vowel; *esp* : any of the letters *a, e, i, o, u,* and sometimes *y* in English [Medieval French *vowele,* from Latin *vocalis,* from *vocalis* "vocal"]

vox po·pu·li \'väk-'späp-yə-,lī, -yə-lē\ *n* : popular sentiment [Latin, "voice of the people"]

¹voy·age \'vȯi-ij, 'vȯ-ij, 'voij\ *n* **1** : a journey by water : CRUISE **2** : a journey through air or space [Medieval French *veiage* "journey," derived from Latin *viaticum* "traveling money," from *viaticus* "of a journey," from *via* "way"]

²voyage *vb* **1** : to take a trip : TRAVEL **2** : SAIL 1b, TRAVERSE — **voy·ag·er** *n*

voya·geur \,vȯi-ə-'zhər, ,vwä-yä-\ *n* : a person employed by a fur company to transport goods and people to and from remote stations in the Canadian Northwest [Canadian French, from French, "traveler"]

Vul·ca·ni·an \,vəl-'kā-nē-ən\ *adj* : of or relating to Vulcan or to working in metals (as iron)

vul·can·ism \'vəl-kə-,niz-əm\ *n* : VOLCANISM

vul·can·ize \'vəl-kə-,nīz\ *vt* : to treat (rubber or similar plastic material) chemically in order to give useful properties (as elasticity, strength, or stability) [Latin *Vulcanus* "Vulcan, fire"] — **vul·can·i·za·tion** \,vəl-kə-nə-'zā-shən\ *n*

vul·gar \'vəl-gər\ *adj* **1** : generally used, applied, or accepted **2** : VERNACULAR ⟨the *vulgar* name of a plant⟩ **3 a** : of or relating to the common people : PLEBEIAN ⟨the *vulgar* opinion of the time⟩ **b** : of the usual, typical, or ordinary kind **4 a** : lacking in cultivation, perception, or taste : COARSE ⟨a loud *vulgar* belch⟩ **b** : morally crude **c** : ostentatious or excessive in expenditure or display : PRETENTIOUS **5** : offensive in language : OBSCENE, PROFANE ⟨a *vulgar* joke⟩ [Latin *vulgaris* "of the mob, vulgar," from *vulgus* "mob, common people"] ***synonyms*** see COARSE — **vul·gar·ly** *adv*

vul·gar·i·an \,vəl-'gar-ē-ən, -'ger-\ *n* : a vulgar person

vul·gar·ism \'vəl-gə-,riz-əm\ *n* **1 a** : a word or expression originated or used chiefly by illiterate persons **b** : a coarse word or phrase **2** : VULGARITY 1

vul·gar·i·ty \,vəl-'gar-ət-ē\ *n, pl* **-ties** **1** : the quality or state of being vulgar **2** : something vulgar

vul·gar·ize \'vəl-gə-,rīz\ *vt* **1** : to make generally known or liked : POPULARIZE **2** : to make vulgar : COARSEN — **vul·gar·i·za·tion** \,vəl-gə-rə-'zā-shən\ *n* — **vul·gar·iz·er** \'vəl-gə-,rī-zər\ *n*

Vulgar Latin *n* : the nonclassical Latin of ancient Rome including the speech of plebeians and the informal speech of the educated established by comparative evidence as the chief source of the Romance languages

Vul·gate \'vəl-,gāt\ *n* : a Latin version of the Bible authorized and used by the Roman Catholic Church [Late Latin *vulgata editio* "edition in general circulation"]

vul·ner·a·ble \'vəln-rə-bəl, -ə-rə-; 'vəl-nər-bəl\ *adj* **1** : capable of being physically or emotionally wounded **2** : open to attack or damage ⟨a *vulnerable* fort⟩ **3** : liable to increased penalties but entitled to increased bonuses in a game of contract bridge [Late Latin *vulnerabilis,* from Latin *vulnerare* "to wound," from *vulner-, vulnus* "wound"] — **vul·ner·a·bil·i·ty** \,vəln-rə-'bil-ət-ē, -ə-rə-\ *n* — **vul·ner·a·bly** \'vəln-rə-blē, -ə-rə-; 'vəl-nər-blē\ *adv*

vul·pine \'vəl-,pīn\ *adj* : of, relating to, or resembling a fox especially in cunning : CRAFTY [Latin *vulpinus,* from *vulpes* "fox"]

vul·ture \'vəl-chər\ *n* **1** : any of various large birds that are related to the hawks and eagles but have weaker claws and the head usually naked and that subsist chiefly or entirely on carrion **2** : a greedy or predatory person [Latin *vultur*]

vul·va \'vəl-və\ *n, pl* **vul·vae** \-,vē, -,vī\ : the external parts of the female genital organs [Latin, "womb, female genitals"] — **vul·val** \'vəl-vəl\ *or* **vul·var** \-vər, -,vär\ *adj*

vying *present participle of* VIE

W

w \'dəb-əl-,yü, -yə, *rapid* 'dəb-ə-yə, 'dəb-yə\ *n, pl* **w's** *or* **ws** \-,yüz, -yəz\ *often cap* : the 23rd letter of the English alphabet

wabble *variant of* WOBBLE

Wac \'wak\ *n* : a member of a U.S. Army unit created for women during World War II and discontinued in the 1970s [*W*omen's *A*rmy *C*orps]

wacky \'wak-ē\ *adj* **wack·i·er; -est** : absurdly or amusingly eccentric or irrational : CRAZY [perhaps from English dialect *whacky* "fool"] — **wack·i·ly** \'wak-ə-lē\ *adv* — **wack·i·ness** \'wak-ē-nəs\ *n*

¹wad \'wäd\ *n* **1** : a small mass, bundle, or tuft ⟨a *wad* of chewing gum⟩: as **a** : a soft mass of usually light fibrous material ⟨a cotton *wad*⟩ **b** : a pliable pad or plug (as of felt) used to retain a powder charge in a gun or cartridge **2 a** : a considerable amount (as of money) **b** : a roll of paper money [origin unknown]

²wad *vt* **wad·ded; wad·ding** **1** : to form into a wad ⟨*wad* up a handkerchief⟩ **2** : to push a wad into ⟨*wad* a gun⟩ **3** : to hold in by a wad ⟨*wad* a bullet in a gun⟩ **4** : to stuff or line with soft material

wad·ding \'wäd-ing\ *n* **1** : wads or material for making wads **2** : a soft mass or sheet of short loose fibers used for stuffing or padding

¹wad·dle \'wäd-l\ *vi* **wad·dled; wad·dling** \'wäd-ling, -l-ing\ **1** : to walk with short steps swaying from side to side ⟨ducks *waddling* to the water⟩ **2** : to move slowly and awkwardly ⟨the big boat *waddled* upstream⟩ [derived from *wade*] — **wad·dler** \'wäd-lər, -l-ər\ *n*

²waddle *n* : an awkward clumsy swaying gait

¹wade \'wād\ *vb* **1** : to step in or through a medium (as water) offering more resistance than air **2** : to move or proceed with difficulty or labor ⟨*wade* through a dull book⟩ ⟨*wade* into a task⟩ **3** : to pass or cross by wading ⟨*wade* a stream⟩ [Old English *wadan*]

²wade *n* : an act of wading ⟨a *wade* in the brook⟩

wad·er \'wād-ər\ *n* **1** : one that wades **2** : WADING BIRD **3** *pl* : high waterproof boots or trousers for wading

wa·di \'wäd-ē\ *n* : a stream bed or valley especially of southwestern Asia and northern Africa that is usually dry except during the rainy season [Arabic *wādi*]

wading bird *n* : any of various long-legged birds (as herons, storks, and ibises) that wade in water in search of food

wading pool *n* : a shallow pool of portable or permanent construction used by children for wading

Waf \'waf\ *n* : a member of the women's component of the U.S. Air Force formed after World War II and discontinued in the 1970s [*W*omen in the *A*ir *F*orce]

wa·fer \'wā-fər\ *n* **1 a** : a thin crisp cake or cracker **b** : a round thin piece of unleavened bread used in the sacrament of Communion **2** : something (as a piece of candy or an adhesive seal) resembling a wafer especially in thin round form [Medieval French *wafer, walfe,* of Germanic origin]

wader 3

waf·fle \'wäf-əl\ *n* : a crisp cake of batter baked in a waffle iron [Dutch *wafel*]

waffle iron *n* : a cooking utensil with two hinged metal parts that shut upon each other and impress surface projections on waffles being cooked

1**waft** \'wäft, 'waft\ *vb* : to move or cause to move or go lightly by or as if by the impulse of wind or waves [perhaps from past participle of Middle English dialect *waffen,* a form of Middle English *waven* "to wave"] — **waft·er** *n*

2**waft** *n* **1** : WHIFF 1a **2** : a slight movement (as of air) : PUFF

1**wag** \'wag\ *vb* **wagged; wag·ging 1** : to move or swing to and fro or from side to side especially with quick jerky movements ⟨the dog *wagged* its tail⟩ ⟨*wagged* his finger as he scolded⟩ **2** : to move in chatter or gossip ⟨scandal caused tongues to *wag*⟩ [Middle English *waggen*] — **wag·ger** *n*

2**wag** *n* : an act of wagging : SHAKE

3**wag** *n* : WIT 3b, JOKER [probably from obsolete *waghalter* "person who deserves hanging"]

1**wage** \'wāj\ *vb* **1** : to engage in or carry on ⟨*wage* war⟩ ⟨*wage* a campaign⟩ **2** : to be waged ⟨the fight *waged* wildly⟩ [Medieval French *wagier* "to pledge, give as security," from *wage* "pledge"]

2**wage** *n* **1** : a payment for labor or services usually according to contract and on an hourly, daily, or piecework basis — often used in plural **2** *pl* : RECOMPENSE, REWARD [Medieval French *wage* "pledge, wage," of Germanic origin]

waged \'wājd\ *adj* : compensated by wages ⟨*waged* labor⟩

wage earner *n* : a person who works for wages or salary

1**wa·ger** \'wā-jər\ *n* **1** : something (as a sum of money) risked on an uncertain event : BET **2** : something (as the outcome of a game or race) on which a bet is made : GAMBLE [Medieval French *wageour* "pledge, bet," from Medieval French *wagier* "to pledge"]

2**wager** *vb* **wa·gered; wa·ger·ing** \'wāj-ring, -ə-ring\ : to risk on an outcome : VENTURE; *esp* : GAMBLE — **wa·ger·er** \'wā-jər-ər\ *n*

wag·gery \'wag-ə-rē\ *n, pl* **-ger·ies 1** : mischievous fun : PLEASANTRY **2** : JEST 1a; *esp* : PRACTICAL JOKE

wag·gish \'wag-ish\ *adj* **1** : resembling or characteristic of a wag : FROLICSOME **2** : done or made in or for sport ⟨a *waggish* trick⟩ — **wag·gish·ly** *adv* — **wag·gish·ness** *n*

wag·gle \'wag-əl\ *vb* **wag·gled; wag·gling** \'wag-ling, -ə-ling\ : to move backward and forward or from side to side : WAG 1 [derived from 1*wag*] — **waggle** *n* — **wag·gly** \'wag-lē, -ə-lē\ *adj*

wag·on \'wag-ən\ *n* **1** : a usually four-wheeled vehicle for transporting goods and passengers; *esp* : one drawn by animals **2** : a low four-wheeled vehicle with an open rectangular body for the play or use of a child **3** : STATION WAGON **4** : PATROL WAGON [Dutch *wagen*] — **wag·on·er** \'wag-ə-nər\ *n* — **on the wagon** : abstaining from alcoholic liquors

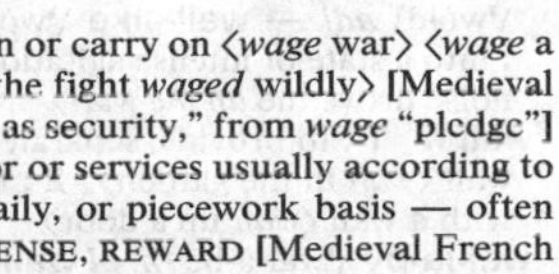
wagon 1

wag·on·ette \ˌwag-ə-'net\ *n* : a light wagon with two facing seats along the sides in back of a transverse front seat

wa·gon–lit \vȧ-gō^{n}-lē\ *n, pl* **wagons–lits** *or* **wagon–lits** \-gō^{n}-lē\ : a railroad sleeping car [French, from *wagon* "railroad car" + *lit* "bed"]

wag·on·load \'wag-ən-ˌlōd\ *n* **1** : a load that fills or could fill a wagon ⟨a *wagonload* of apples⟩ **2** : a very large amount ⟨a *wagonload* of choices⟩

wagon master *n* : a person in charge of one or more wagons especially for transporting freight

wagon train *n* : a group of wagons (as of pioneers) traveling overland

wag·tail \'wag-ˌtāl\ *n* : any of various mostly Old World birds related to the pipits and having a long tail that is frequently jerked up and down

1**wa·hoo** \'wä-ˌhü, 'wȯ-\ *n, pl* **wahoos** : a shrubby North American tree having bright autumn foliage and fruit with purple capsules which open to expose scarlet seeds [origin unknown]

2**wahoo** *n, pl* **wahoos** : a large vigorous fish related to the mackerel that is a common food and sport fish in warm seas [origin unknown]

waif \'wāf\ *n* **1** : something found without an owner and especially by chance **2** : a stray person or animal; *esp* : a homeless child [Medieval French, "lost, unclaimed"]

1**wail** \'wāl\ *vb* **1** : to express sorrow audibly : LAMENT **2** : to make a sound suggestive of a mournful cry **3** : to express dissatisfaction plaintively : COMPLAIN [perhaps of Scandinavian origin] — **wail·er** *n*

2**wail** *n* **1 a** : a usually prolonged cry or sound expressing grief or pain **b** : a sound suggestive of this ⟨the *wail* of a siren⟩ **2** : an irritable expressing of grievance : COMPLAINT

wail·ful \'wāl-fəl\ *adj* : SORROWFUL, MOURNFUL ⟨the *wailful* sound of distant bagpipes⟩ — **wail·ful·ly** \-fə-lē\ *adv*

wain \'wān\ *n* : a usually large and heavy vehicle for farm use [Old English *wægn*]

1**wain·scot** \'wān-skət, -ˌskōt, -ˌskät\ *n* **1** : a usually paneled and wooden lining of an interior wall **2** : the lower three or four feet (about one meter) of an interior wall when finished differently from the remainder of the wall [Dutch *wagenschot*]

2**wainscot** *vt* **-scot·ed** *or* **-scot·ted; -scot·ing** *or* **-scot·ting** : to line with or as if with boards or paneling

wain·scot·ing \-ˌskōt-ing, -ˌskät-, -skət-\ *or* **wain·scot·ting** \-ˌskät-, -skət-\ *n* : material for wainscot; *also* : WAINSCOT

wain·wright \'wān-ˌrīt\ *n* : a maker and repairer of wagons

waist \'wāst\ *n* **1 a** : the usually narrowed part of the body between the chest and hips **b** : the greatly constricted front part of the abdomen of some insects (as a wasp) **2** : a part resembling the human waist especially in narrowness or central position ⟨the *waist* of a ship⟩ ⟨the *waist* of a violin⟩ **3** : a garment or the part of a garment that covers the body from the neck to the waist [Middle English *wast*]

waist·band \'wāst-ˌband, 'wās-\ *n* : a band (as of trousers or a skirt) fitting around the waist

waist·coat \'wāst-ˌkōt, 'wās-; 'wes-kət\ *n, chiefly British* : VEST 1a — **waist·coat·ed** \-əd\ *adj*

waist·line \'wāst-ˌlīn\ *n* **1 a** : WAIST 1a **b** : the circumference of the waist at its narrowest point **2** : the part of a garment surrounding the waist

1**wait** \'wāt\ *vb* **1** : to remain inactive in readiness (as for action) or expectation (as of a coming event) : AWAIT ⟨*wait* for sunrise⟩ ⟨*wait* your turn⟩ ⟨*wait* for orders⟩ **2** : POSTPONE, DELAY ⟨*wait* dinner for a guest⟩ **3** : to attend as a waiter or waitress : SERVE ⟨*wait* tables⟩ ⟨*wait* at a luncheon⟩ [Medieval French *waiter, guaiter* "to watch over, await," of Germanic origin] — **wait on** *also* **wait upon 1 a** : to attend as a servant **b** : to supply the wants of : SERVE ⟨*wait on* a customer⟩ **2** : to make a formal call on — **wait up** : to delay going to bed : stay up

2**wait** *n* **1 a** : a hidden or concealed position — used chiefly in the expression *lie in wait* **b** : a state or attitude of watchfulness and expectancy **2** : an act or period of waiting

wait·er \'wāt-ər\ *n* **1** : one that waits upon another; *esp* : a person who waits tables (as in a restaurant) **2** : a tray on which something is carried

waiting game *n* : a strategy in which one or more participants withhold action temporarily in the hope of having a favorable opportunity for more effective action later

\ə\ abut	\au̇\ out	\i\ tip	\ȯ\ saw	\u̇\ foot
\ər\ further	\ch\ chin	\ī\ life	\ȯi\ coin	\y\ yet
\a\ mat	\e\ pet	\j\ job	\th\ thin	\yü\ few
\ā\ take	\ē\ easy	\ng\ sing	\t͟h\ this	\yu̇\ cure
\ä\ cot, cart	\g\ go	\ō\ bone	\ü\ food	\zh\ vision

waiting list *n* : a list or roster of those waiting (as for admission to an organization or institution)

waiting room *n* : a room (as in a doctor's office) for the use of persons (as patients) who are waiting

wait–list \ˈwāt-ˌlist\ *vt* : to put on a waiting list

wait·per·son \ˈwāt-ˌpərs-n\ *n* : a waiter or waitress

wait·ress \ˈwā-trəs\ *n* : a woman who waits tables (as in a restaurant) — **waitress** *vi*

wait·staff \ˈwāt-ˌstaf\ *n* : a staff of servers at a restaurant

waive \ˈwāv\ *vt* **waived; waiv·ing** **1** : to give up claim to ⟨*waive* the right to answer⟩ **2** : to let pass ⟨*waive* the fee⟩ **3** : to put off the consideration of : POSTPONE **4** : to dismiss with or as if with a wave of the hand ⟨*waived* the problem aside⟩ [Medieval French *waiver, gaiver,* from *waif* "lost, unclaimed"]

waiv·er \ˈwā-vər\ *n* **1** : the act of waiving a right, claim, or privilege **2** : a document containing the declaration of a waiver [Medieval French *weyver,* from Medieval French *waiver* "to waive"]

¹wake \ˈwāk\ *vb* **woke** \ˈwōk\ *also* **waked; wo·ken** \ˈwō-kən\ *or* **waked** *also* **woke; wak·ing** **1** : to be or remain awake **2** : to stand watch over (as a dead body); *esp* : to hold a wake over **3** : to rouse from or as if from sleep : AWAKE — often used with *up* [Old English *wacan* "to awake" and *wacian* "to be awake"] — **wak·er** *n*

²wake *n* : a watch held over the body of a dead person prior to burial and sometimes accompanied by festivity

³wake *n* : the track left by a moving body (as a ship) in the water; *also* : a track or path left [of Germanic origin] — **in the wake of** **1** : close behind and on the same course **2** : as a result of

wake·ful \ˈwāk-fəl\ *adj* : not sleeping or able to sleep — **wake·ful·ly** \-fə-lē\ *adv* — **wake·ful·ness** *n*

wak·en \ˈwā-kən\ *vb* **wak·ened; wak·en·ing** \ˈwāk-ning, -ə-ning\ : AROUSE 1 — often used with *up* — **wak·en·er** \ˈwāk-nər, -ə-nər\ *n*

wake–rob·in \ˈwā-ˌkräb-ən\ *n* : TRILLIUM

wake–up call *n* **1** : something (as a telephone call from a hotel employee to a guest) that serves to wake up a sleeper **2** : something that serves to alert a person to a problem, danger, or need

Wal·den·ses \wȯl-ˈden-ˌsēz\ *n pl* : a Christian sect arising in southern France in the 12th century, adopting Calvinist doctrines in the 16th century, and later living chiefly in Piedmont [Medieval Latin, from Peter *Waldo,* 12th century French heretic] — **Wal·den·sian** \-ˈden-chən\ *adj or n*

Wal·dorf salad \ˌwȯl-ˌdȯrf-\ *n* : a salad made typically of diced apples, celery, and nuts and dressed with mayonnaise [*Waldorf*=Astoria Hotel, New York City]

wale \ˈwāl\ *n* **1 a** : a streak or ridge made on the skin usually by a rod or whip **b** : a narrow raised surface or ridge (as on corduroy) **2** : one of the extra–strong strakes on the sides of a wooden ship just above the waterline [Old English *walu*]

¹walk \ˈwȯk\ *vb* **1 a** : to move or cause to move along on foot usually at a natural unhurried gait ⟨*walk* to town⟩ ⟨*walk* a horse up a hill⟩ **b** : to pass over, through, or along by walking ⟨*walk* the streets⟩ **c** : to perform or accomplish by walking ⟨*walk* guard⟩ **2** : to follow a course of action or way of life : BEHAVE **3** : to take or cause to take first base with a base on balls **4** : to move or cause to move in a manner suggestive of walking ⟨*walked* my fingers across the table⟩ [Old English *wealcan* "to roll, toss"] — **walk away from** **1** : to outrun or get the better of without difficulty **2** : to survive (an accident) with little or no injury **3** : to give up or leave behing willingly : ABANDON — **walk off with** **1** : STEAL 2 **2** : to win or gain especially by outdoing one's competitors without difficulty — **walk over** : to disregard the wishes or feelings of — **walk through** **1** : to go through (as a theatrical role or familiar activity) perfunctorily (as in an early stage of rehearsal) **2** : to guide (as a beginner) through an unfamiliar or difficult procedure step-by-step

²walk *n* **1** : a going on foot ⟨go for a *walk*⟩ **2** : a place, path, or course for walking **3** : distance to be walked **4 a** : manner of living : CONDUCT, BEHAVIOR **b** : social or economic status ⟨various *walks* of life⟩ **5 a** : manner of walking **b** : a gait of a four-footed animal in which there are always at least two feet on the ground; *esp* : a slow 4-beat gait of a horse in which the feet strike the ground in the sequence left hind foot, left front foot, right hind foot, right front foot **6** : BASE ON BALLS — **walk in the park** : an easy or pleasurable experience : PICNIC

walk·able \ˈwȯ-kə-bəl\ *adj* : capable of or suitable for being walked ⟨a very *walkable* city⟩ ⟨a *walkable* distance⟩

walk·a·thon \ˈwȯ-kə-ˌthän\ *n* : a walk covering a considerable distance organized especially to raise money for a cause

walk·er \ˈwȯ-kər\ *n* **1** : one that walks **2** : something used in walking; *esp* : a framework designed to support one who walks with difficulty

walk·ie–talk·ie \ˌwȯ-kē-ˈtȯ-kē\ *n* : a small portable radio set for receiving and sending messages

¹walk–in \ˈwȯ-ˌkin\ *adj* **1** : large enough to be walked into ⟨a *walk-in* refrigerator⟩ **2** : of, relating to, or intended for people who walk in without an appointment ⟨a *walk-in* medical clinic⟩

²walk–in *n* **1** : a walk-in refrigerator or cold storage room **2** : a person who walks in without an appointment

walking papers *n pl* : DISMISSAL, DISCHARGE

walking pneumonia *n* : a usually mild pneumonia marked by cough, tiredness, headache, and fever

walking stick *n* **1** : a stick used in walking **2** : STICK INSECT

Walk·man \ˈwȯk-mən, -ˌman\ *trademark* — used for a small portable audio player listened to by means of headphones or earphones

walk–on \ˈwȯ-ˌkȯn, -ˌkän\ *n* : a small usually nonspeaking part in a dramatic production

walk·out \ˈwȯ-ˌkau̇t\ *n* **1** : STRIKE 2a **2** : the leaving of a meeting or organization as an expression of disapproval

walk out \wȯ-ˈkau̇t, ˈwȯ-\ *vi* **1** : to go on strike **2** : to leave suddenly often as an expression of disapproval — **walk out on** : ABANDON 3, DESERT

walk·over \ˈwȯ-ˌkō-vər\ *n* : a one-sided contest or an easy or uncontested victory

walk–up \ˈwȯ-ˌkəp\ *n* : an apartment or office building without an elevator — **walk–up** \ˌwȯ-ˌkəp\ *adj*

walk·way \ˈwȯ-ˌkwā\ *n* : a passage for walking : WALK

¹wall \ˈwȯl\ *n* **1** : a structure (as of brick or stone) raised to some height and meant to enclose or shut off a space; *esp* : a side of a room or building **2** : a material layer enclosing space ⟨the heart *wall*⟩ ⟨the *walls* of a boiler⟩ **3** : something like a wall; *esp* : something that acts as a barrier or defense ⟨a *wall* of reserve⟩ [Old English *weall,* from Latin *vallum* "rampart"] — **walled** \ˈwȯld\ *adj* — **wall–like** \ˈwȯl-ˌlīk\ *adj* — **up the wall** *slang* : into a state of intense agitation, annoyance, or frustration ⟨the noise drove me *up the wall*⟩

²wall *vt* **1** : to provide, separate, or surround with or as if with a wall ⟨*wall* in the garden⟩ **2** : to close (an opening) with or as if with a wall ⟨*wall* up a door⟩

wal·la·by \ˈwäl-ə-bē\ *n, pl* **wallabies** *also* **wallaby** : any of various small or medium–sized kangaroos [Dharuk (Australian aboriginal language of the Port Jackson area) *walabi, waliba*]

wall·board \ˈwȯl-ˌbōrd, -ˌbȯrd\ *n* : a structural material (as of wood pulp, gypsum, or plastic) made in large rigid sheets and used especially for sheathing interior walls and ceilings

wal·let \ˈwäl-ət\ *n* **1** : a bag or sack for carrying things on a journey **2** : a folding pocketbook with compartments for personal papers and usually unfolded money; *also* : BILLFOLD [Middle English *walet*]

wall·eye \ˈwȯ-ˌlī\ *n* **1 a** : an eye with a whitish iris or an opaque white cornea **b** : an eye that turns outward away from the nose; *also* : the condition of having such eyes **2** : a large vigorous North American freshwater food and sport fish that has prominent eyes and is related to the perches but resembles the true pike — called also *walleyed pike* [back-formation from *walleyed* "having walleyes," from Old Norse *vagl-eygr,* from *vagl* "beam, roost" + *eygr* "eyed"] — **wall·eyed** \-ˈlīd\ *adj*

wall·flow·er \ˈwȯl-ˌflau̇-ər, -ˌflau̇r\ *n* **1** : any of several Old World perennial herbs related to the mustards; *esp* : one widely grown for its showy fragrant flowers **2 a** : a person who from shyness or unpopularity remains on the sidelines of a social activity (as a dance) **b** : a shy or reserved person

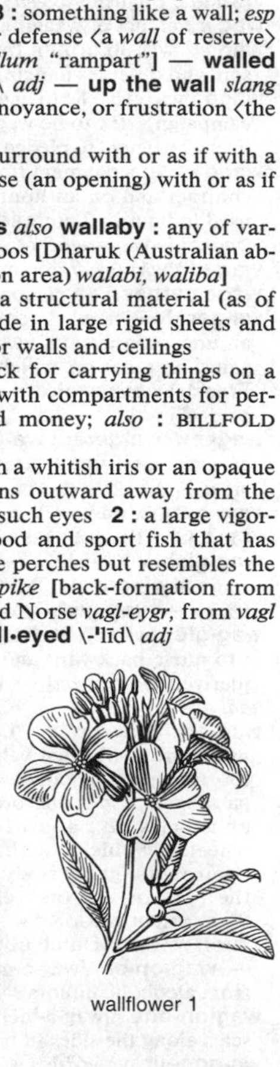
wallflower 1

Wal·loon \wä-ˈlün\ *n* : a member of a people of southern and southeastern Belgium and adjacent parts of France [Middle French *Wallon,* of Germanic origin] — **Walloon** *adj*

¹wal·lop \ˈwäl-əp\ *vt* **1** : to beat soundly : TROUNCE **2** : to hit with force : SOCK [Medieval French *waloper* "to gallop"] — **wal·lop·er** *n*

[2]**wallop** *n* **1 :** a powerful blow or impact **2 :** the ability (as of a boxer) to hit hard

wal•lop•ing \ˈwäl-ə-piŋ\ *adj* **1 :** very large **2 :** exceptionally fine or impressive

[1]**wal•low** \ˈwäl-ō\ *vi* **1 :** to roll about in or as if in deep mud ⟨elephants *wallowing* in the river⟩ **2 a :** to enjoy or indulge oneself in something without restraint **b :** to become abundantly supplied ⟨*wallow* in luxury⟩ **3 :** to become or remain helpless ⟨allowed to *wallow* in ignorance⟩ [Old English *wealwian* "to roll"]

[2]**wallow** *n* **1 :** an act or instance of wallowing **2 :** a muddy or dust–filled area used by animals for wallowing

wall•pa•per \ˈwȯl-ˌpā-pər\ *n* **:** decorative paper for the walls of a room — **wallpaper** *vb*

wall plug *n* **:** an electric receptacle in a wall

Wall Street \ˈwȯl-\ *n* **:** the influential financial interests of the U.S. economy [*Wall Street,* New York City, on which the New York Stock Exchange is located]

wal•nut \ˈwȯl-ˌnət, -nət\ *n* **1 a :** an edible furrowed nut of any of a genus of trees related to the hickories; *esp* **:** the large nut of an English walnut **b :** a tree that produces walnuts — compare BLACK WALNUT, ENGLISH WALNUT **c :** the usually reddish to dark brown wood of a walnut widely used for cabinetwork and veneers **2 :** a moderate reddish brown [Old English *wealh-hnutu,* literally, "foreign nut," from *wealh* "Welshman, foreigner" + *hnutu* "nut"]

Word History Walnut trees have been cultivated in so many countries for so many centuries that the early distribution and origin of the walnut cannot now be clearly discerned. It would appear, however, that the walnut was known to southern Europe for some time before it was introduced into England. The walnut's Old English name, *wealhhnutu,* means literally "foreign nut." It was apparently so called to distinguish the walnut of southern Europe from the nut native to more northern countries, the hazelnut.

Wal•pur•gis Night \väl-ˈpu̇r-gəs-\ *n* **:** the eve of May Day on which witches are held to ride to an appointed rendezvous [German *Walpurgis* "Saint Walburga (died A.D. 779, English saint whose feast day falls on May Day)"]

wal•rus \ˈwȯl-rəs, ˈwäl-\ *n, pl* **walrus** *or* **wal•rus•es :** a large mammal of arctic seas that is related to the seals and has long ivory tusks, a tough wrinkled hide with a thick layer of blubber below, stiff whiskers, and limbs modified into flippers [Dutch, of Scandinavian origin]

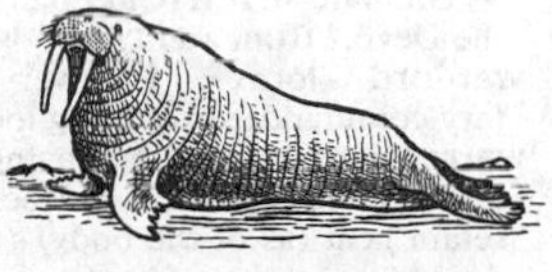
walrus

[1]**waltz** \ˈwȯls, ˈwȯlts\ *n* **1 :** a ballroom dance in ¾ time with strong accent on the first beat **2 :** music for or suitable for waltzing [German *Walzer,* from *walzen* "to roll, dance"]

[2]**waltz** *vb* **1 a :** to dance a waltz **b :** to dance a waltz with **2 a :** to advance easily or successfully ⟨*waltzed* through the test⟩ **b :** to approach boldly ⟨can't just *waltz* up and introduce ourselves⟩ — **waltz•er** *n*

wam•pum \ˈwäm-pəm\ *n* **1 :** beads of shells strung in strands, belts, or sashes and used by North American Indians as money and ornaments **2 :** MONEY 1 [short for Massachusett (Algonquian language of Massachusetts) *wampompeag,* from *wampan* "white" + *api* "string"]

wan \ˈwän\ *adj* **1 a :** SICKLY, PALLID ⟨a *wan* complexion⟩ **b :** lacking vitality **:** FEEBLE **2 :** DIM 1, FAINT **3 :** LANGUID ⟨a *wan* smile⟩ [Old English, "dark, livid"] — **wan•ly** *adv* — **wan•ness** \ˈwän-nəs\ *n*

wand \ˈwänd\ *n* **1 :** a slender rod used by conjurers or magicians **2 :** the rigid tube between nozzle and hose of a vacuum cleaner **3 :** a handheld device used to enter information (as from a bar code) into a computer [Old Norse *vǫndr* "slender stick"]

wan•der \ˈwän-dər\ *vb* **wan•dered; wan•der•ing** \-də-riŋ, -driŋ\ **1 :** to move about aimlessly or without a fixed course or goal **:** RAMBLE **2 a :** to deviate (as from a course) **:** STRAY **b :** to go astray morally **:** ERR **c :** to lose normal mental concentration **:** stray in thought ⟨her mind *wandered*⟩ [Old English *wandrian*] — **wander** *n* — **wan•der•er** \-dər-ər\ *n*

synonyms WANDER, ROAM, RAMBLE, MEANDER mean to go about from place to place usually without a plan or definite purpose. WANDER implies a lack of or an indifference to a fixed course ⟨*wandered* around the square just watching the people⟩. ROAM suggests wandering about freely and often over a large area ⟨liked to *roam* through the woods⟩. RAMBLE stresses carelessness and indifference to one's course or objective ⟨tourists *rambled* through the park⟩. MEANDER implies a winding or intricate course suggestive of aimless or listless wandering ⟨the river *meanders* for miles through rich farmland⟩.

wandering Jew *n* **:** any of several mostly creeping plants related to the spiderworts and often grown for their showy leaves [the *Wandering Jew,* legendary person condemned to wander the earth until Christ's 2nd coming for having mocked Him on the day of the crucifixion]

wan•der•lust \ˈwän-dər-ˌləst\ *n* **:** strong longing to travel [German, from *wandern* "to wander" + *Lust* "desire, pleasure"]

[1]**wane** \ˈwān\ *vi* **1 :** to grow smaller or less: as **a :** to diminish in phase or intensity — used chiefly of the moon **b :** to become less brilliant or powerful **:** DIM **2 :** to fall gradually from power, prosperity, or influence **:** DECLINE [Old English *wanian*]

[2]**wane** *n* **1 :** the act or process of waning **2 :** a period or time of waning; *esp* **:** the period from full phase of the moon to the new moon

wan•gle \ˈwaŋ-gəl\ *vb* **wan•gled; wan•gling** \-gə-liŋ, -gliŋ\ **1 :** to use trickery or devious means to achieve an end **2 a :** to adjust or manipulate for personal ends **b :** to make or get by devious means **:** FINAGLE [perhaps alteration of *waggle*] — **wan•gler** \-gə-lər, -glər\ *n*

Wan•kel engine \ˌväŋ-kəl-, ˌwaŋ-\ *n* **:** an internal-combustion rotary engine that has a rounded triangular rotor functioning as a piston and rotating in a space in the engine and that has only two major moving parts [Felix *Wankel,* died 1988, German engineer]

wan•na•be \ˈwän-ə-ˌbē\ *n* **:** a person who wants or tries to be someone or something else or who tries to look and act like someone else [from the phrase *want to be*]

[1]**want** \ˈwȯnt *also* ˈwänt, ˈwənt\ *vb* **1 :** to be without **:** LACK ⟨this coat is *wanting* a button⟩ **2 :** to have or feel need ⟨never *wants* for friends⟩ **3 a :** to have need of **:** REQUIRE ⟨the house *wants* painting⟩ **b :** to suffer from the lack of ⟨thousands still *want* food and shelter⟩ **4 :** to desire, wish, or long for something **5 :** OUGHT ⟨you *want* to be very careful⟩ **6 :** to hunt or seek in order to arrest ⟨*wanted* for murder⟩ [Old Norse *vanta*] ***synonyms*** see DESIRE

[2]**want** *n* **1 a :** a lack of a required or usual amount **b :** great need **:** DESTITUTION **2 :** something wanted **:** NEED, DESIRE

want ad *n* **:** an advertisement stating that something (as an employee or a specified item) is wanted

[1]**want•ing** *adj* **1 :** not present or in evidence **:** ABSENT **2 a :** falling below standards or expectations **b :** lacking in ability or capacity **:** DEFICIENT

[2]**wanting** *prep* **1 :** WITHOUT ⟨a book *wanting* a cover⟩ **2 :** LESS, MINUS ⟨a month *wanting* two days⟩

[1]**wan•ton** \ˈwȯnt-n, ˈwänt-\ *adj* **1 :** playfully mean or cruel **:** MISCHIEVOUS **2 :** LEWD 1, BAWDY; *also* **:** SENSUAL **3 a :** MERCILESS, INHUMANE ⟨*wanton* cruelty⟩ **b :** having no just cause **:** MALICIOUS ⟨a *wanton* attack⟩ **4 :** UNRESTRAINED 1, EXTRAVAGANT ⟨*wanton* luxury⟩ [Middle English, "unruly"] — **wan•ton•ly** *adv* — **wan•ton•ness** \-n-nəs\ *n*

[2]**wanton** *n* **1 :** a wanton individual; *esp* **:** a lewd or lascivious person **2 :** a pampered person or animal **:** PET; *esp* **:** a spoiled child

[3]**wanton** *vb* **1 :** to be wanton or act wantonly **2 :** to pass or waste wantonly

wa•pi•ti \ˈwäp-ət-ē\ *n, pl* **wapiti** *or* **wapitis :** ELK 1b [Shawnee (Algonquian language of the Shawnees) *wa·piti,* literally, "white rump"]

[1]**war** \ˈwȯr\ *n* **1 a :** a state or period of armed hostile conflict between states or nations **b :** the science of warfare **2 a :** a state of hostility, conflict, or antagonism **b :** a struggle between opposing forces or for a particular end ⟨a *war* against disease⟩ [Medieval French *werre, guerre,* of Germanic origin]

[2]**war** *vi* **warred; war•ring 1 :** to engage in warfare **2 :** to be in conflict

\ə\ **abut**	\au̇\ **out**	\i\ **tip**	\ȯ\ **saw**	\u̇\ **foot**
\ər\ **further**	\ch\ **chin**	\ī\ **life**	\ȯi\ **coin**	\y\ **yet**
\a\ **mat**	\e\ **pet**	\j\ **job**	\th\ **thin**	\yü\ **few**
\ā\ **take**	\ē\ **easy**	\ŋ\ **sing**	\t͟h\ **this**	\yu̇\ **cure**
\ä\ **cot, cart**	\g\ **go**	\ō\ **bone**	\ü\ **food**	\zh\ **vision**

¹**war·ble** \ˈwȯr-bəl\ *n* **1** : a melodious succession of low pleasing sounds **2** : a musical trill **3** : the action of warbling [Medieval French *werble* "tune," of Germanic origin]

²**warble** *vb* **war·bled; war·bling** \-bə-liŋ, -bliŋ\ **1** : to sing in a trilling manner or with many turns and variations **2** : to express by or as if by warbling

³**warble** *n* : a swelling under the skin (as of the back of cattle) caused by infestation with maggots of a warble fly or botfly; *also* : such a maggot [perhaps of Scandinavian origin] — **war·bled** \-bəld\ *adj*

warble fly *n* : any of various two-winged flies whose larvae cause warbles

war·bler \ˈwȯr-blər\ *n* **1** : one that warbles : SINGER **2 a** : any of numerous small mostly Old World songbirds many of which are noted for their melodious song and are closely related to the thrushes **b** : any of numerous small brightly colored American songbirds with a usually weak and unmusical song — called also *wood warbler*

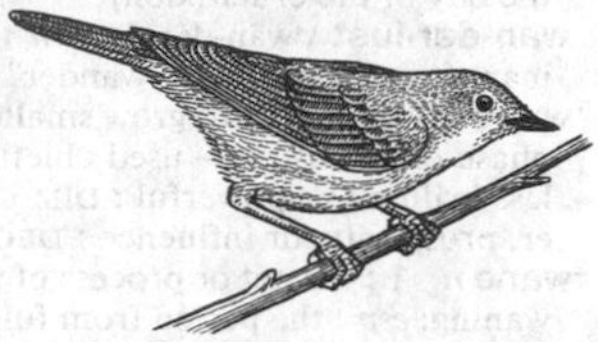

warbler 2a

war·bon·net \ˈwȯr-ˌbän-ət\ *n* : an American Indian ceremonial headdress often with a feathered extension down the back

war chest *n* : a fund accumulated for a specific purpose, action, or campaign

war crime *n* : a crime (as genocide or maltreatment of prisoners) committed during or in connection with war — usually used in plural — **war criminal** *n*

war cry *n* **1** : a cry used by a body of fighters in war **2** : a slogan used especially to rally people to a cause

¹**ward** \ˈwȯrd\ *n* **1** : a guarding or being under guard; *esp* : CUSTODY **2 a** : a division (as a cell or block) of a prison **b** : a division in a hospital; *esp* : a large room in a hospital where a number of patients often requiring similar treatment stay **3 a** : an electoral or administrative division of a city **b** : a local Mormon congregation **4** : a projecting ridge of metal in a lock casing or keyhole permitting only the insertion of a key with a corresponding notch; *also* : a corresponding notch in a key **5 a** : a person (as a child) who is under the care of a court or a guardian **b** : a person, group, or territory under the protection or tutelage of a government [Old English *weard*] — **ward·ed** \-əd\ *adj*

²**ward** *vt* **1** : to keep watch over : GUARD **2** : to turn aside : DEFLECT — usually used with *off* ⟨*ward* off a cold⟩ [Old English *weardian*]

¹**-ward** \wərd\ *also* **-wards** \wərdz\ *adj suffix* **1** : that moves, tends, faces, or is directed toward ⟨wind*ward*⟩ **2** : that occurs or is situated in the direction of ⟨left*ward*⟩ [Old English *-weard*]

²**-ward** *or* **-wards** *adv suffix* **1** : in a (specified) spatial or temporal direction ⟨after*ward*⟩ ⟨up*wards*⟩ **2** : toward a (specified) point, position, or area ⟨coast*ward*⟩ ⟨heaven*wards*⟩

war dance *n* : a dance performed (as by American Indians) in preparation for battle or in celebration of victory

war·den \ˈwȯrd-n\ *n* **1** : one having care or charge of something : GUARDIAN **2** : the governor of a town, district, or fortress **3 a** : an official charged with special duties or with the enforcement of specified laws ⟨game *wardens*⟩ ⟨air raid *wardens*⟩ **b** : an official in charge of a prison **4 a** : a lay officer of an Episcopal parish **b** : any of various British college officials [Medieval French *wardein,* from *warder* "to guard," of Germanic origin] — **war·den·ship** \-ˌship\ *n*

ward·er \ˈwȯrd-ər\ *n* : a person who keeps guard [Medieval French *wardere,* from *warde* "act of guarding," of Germanic origin]

ward heeler *n* : a local worker for a political boss [from his following at the heels of a political boss]

ward·ress \ˈwȯr-drəs\ *n* : a woman supervising female prisoners (as in a jail)

ward·robe \ˈwȯr-ˌdrōb\ *n* **1** : a room, closet, or chest where clothes are kept **2** : a collection of wearing apparel (as of one person or for one activity) [Medieval French *warderobe,* from *warder* "to guard" + *robe* "robe"]

ward·room \ˈwȯr-ˌdrüm, -ˌdrům\ *n* : the space in a warship allotted for living quarters to the officers excepting the captain; *esp* : the mess assigned to them

ward·ship \ˈwȯrd-ˌship\ *n* **1** : care and protection of a ward **2** : the state of being under a guardian

¹**ware** \ˈwaər, ˈweər\ *adj* : AWARE, CONSCIOUS [Old English *wær* "careful, aware"]

²**ware** *vt* : to beware of — used chiefly as a command to hunting animals [Old English *warian*]

³**ware** *n* **1 a** : manufactured articles or products of art or craft : GOODS ⟨*ware* whittled from wood⟩ — often used in combination ⟨tin*ware*⟩ **b** : an article of merchandise ⟨peddlers hawking their *wares*⟩ **2** : items (as dishes) of fired clay : POTTERY ⟨earthen*ware*⟩ [Old English *waru*]

¹**ware·house** \ˈwaər-ˌhaůs, ˈweər-\ *n* : a place for storing merchandise or commodities

²**ware·house** \-ˌhaůz, -ˌhaůs\ *vt* : to deposit, store, or stock in or as if in a warehouse

ware·house·man \ˈwaər-ˌhaůs-mən, ˈweər-\ *n* : a person who manages or works in a warehouse

ware·room \-ˌrüm, -ˌrům\ *n* : a room in which goods are exhibited for sale

war·fare \ˈwȯr-ˌfaər, -ˌfeər\ *n* **1 a** : military operations between enemies : WAR **b** : an activity undertaken by one country to weaken or destroy another ⟨economic *warfare*⟩ **2** : a struggle between competitors ⟨industrial *warfare*⟩

war·fa·rin \ˈwȯr-fə-rən\ *n* : a crystalline compound that deters blood clotting and is used as a rodent poison and in medicine [*W*isconsin *A*lumni *R*esearch *F*oundation (its patentee) + cou*marin,* a chemical]

war footing *n* : the condition of being prepared to undertake or maintain war

war·head \ˈwȯr-ˌhed\ *n* : the section of a missile containing the explosive, chemical, or incendiary charge

war·horse \-ˌhȯrs\ *n* **1** : a horse used in war : CHARGER **2** : a veteran soldier or public person (as a politician)

war·less \ˈwȯr-ləs\ *adj* : free from war

war·like \-ˌlīk\ *adj* **1** : fit for, disposed to, or fond of war ⟨a *warlike* people⟩ **2** : of, relating to, or useful in war ⟨*warlike* supplies⟩ **3** : befitting or characteristic of war or of soldiers ⟨*warlike* cries⟩ ***synonyms*** see MARTIAL

war·lock \-ˌläk\ *n* : a man practicing the black arts : SORCERER — compare WITCH [Old English *wǣrloga* "one that breaks faith, the Devil," from *wǣr* "faith" + *lēogan* "to lie"]

war·lord \-ˌlȯrd\ *n* **1** : a very high military leader **2** : a military commander exercising local civil power by force

¹**warm** \ˈwȯrm\ *adj* **1 a** : having or giving out heat to a moderate or adequate degree ⟨*warm* food⟩ ⟨a *warm* stove⟩ **b** : serving to retain heat (as of the body) ⟨*warm* clothes⟩ **c** : feeling or inducing sensations of heat ⟨*warm* from exertion⟩ ⟨a *warm* walk⟩ **2 a** : showing or marked by strong feeling : ARDENT ⟨a *warm* supporter⟩ ⟨a *warm* temperament⟩ **b** : marked by tense excitement or hot anger ⟨a *warm* debate⟩ **3** : marked by or tending toward injury, distress, or pain ⟨gave the enemy a *warm* reception⟩ **4** : newly made : FRESH ⟨a *warm* scent⟩ **5 a** : giving a pleasant impression of warmth or friendliness ⟨a *warm* greeting⟩ **b** : of a color in the range yellow through orange to red **6** : near to a goal, object, or answer sought ⟨not there yet but getting *warm*⟩ [Old English *wearm*] — **warm·ness** *n*

²**warm** *vb* **1** : to make or become warm **2 a** : to give a feeling of warmth or vitality to ⟨it *warms* my heart to see you⟩ **b** : to experience feelings of affection or pleasure ⟨*warmed* to the young guests⟩ **3** : to reheat (cooked food) for eating **4 a** : to make or become ready by some preliminary action ⟨*warm* up the car⟩ **b** : to become ardent or interested ⟨a speaker *warming* to the topic⟩

³**warm** *adv* : WARMLY — usually used in combination ⟨*warm*-clad⟩

warm–blood·ed \ˈwȯrm-ˈbləd-əd\ *adj* **1** : able to maintain a relatively high and constant internally regulated body temperature that is essentially independent of the environment ⟨birds and mammals are *warm-blooded*⟩ **2** : warm in feeling : ARDENT — **warm–blood·ed·ness** *n*

warmed–over \ˈwȯrm-ˈdō-vər\ *adj* **1** : heated again ⟨*warmed-over* beans⟩ **2** : not fresh or new : STALE

warm·er \ˈwȯr-mər\ *n* : one that warms; *esp* : a device for keeping something warm ⟨a hand *warmer*⟩

warm front *n* : an advancing edge of a warm air mass

warm·heart·ed \ˈwȯrm-ˈhärt-əd\ *adj* : marked by warmth of feeling — **warm·heart·ed·ness** *n*

warming pan *n* : a long-handled covered pan filled with live coals and formerly used to warm a bed

warm·ish \ˈwȯr-mish\ *adj* : somewhat warm

warm·ly \ˈwȯrm-lē\ *adv* **1** : in a manner showing or characterized by warmth of emotion ⟨greeted us *warmly*⟩ **2** : in a manner that causes or maintains warmth ⟨dressed *warmly*⟩

war·mon·ger \ˈwȯr-ˌməŋ-gər, -ˌmäŋ-\ *n* : one who urges or attempts to stir up war — **war·mon·ger·ing** \-gə-riŋ, -griŋ\ *n*

warmth \ˈwȯrmth, ˈwȯrmpth\ *n* : the quality or state of being warm: as **a** : emotional intensity (as of enthusiasm, anger, or love) **b** : a glowing effect produced by or as if by the use of warm colors

warm–up \ˈwȯr-ˌməp\ *n* : the act or an instance of warming up; *also* : a procedure (as a set of exercises) used in warming up

warm up \wȯr-ˈməp, ˈwȯr-\ *vi* : to engage in exercise or practice especially before entering a game or contest; *also* : to get ready

warn \ˈwȯrn\ *vt* **1 a** : to give notice to beforehand especially of danger or evil **b** : ADMONISH 1 **c** : to call to one's attention : INFORM **2** : to order to go or stay away ⟨*warned* us off their land⟩ [Old English *warnian*] — **warn·er** *n*

synonyms WARN, CAUTION mean to let one know of approaching danger or risk. WARN may range from simple notification of something to be watched for to threats of violence or reprisal ⟨*warned* travelers of bad road conditions⟩. CAUTION stresses giving advice that suggests the need of taking care or watching out ⟨*cautioned* about cooking meat thoroughly⟩.

[1]warn·ing \ˈwȯr-niŋ\ *n* **1** : the act of warning : the state of being warned **2** : something that warns or serves to warn

[2]warning *adj* : serving as an alarm, signal, summons, or admonition ⟨a *warning* bell⟩ — **warn·ing·ly** \-niŋ-lē\ *adv*

warning coloration *n* : bright color patterns on the body of an organism (as on the wings of a monarch butterfly) that serve to warn potential predators that the organism is undesirable as prey (as by being poisonous or bad-tasting)

war of nerves : a conflict characterized by psychological tactics (as bluff, threats, and intimidation) designed primarily to create confusion, indecision, or breakdown of morale

[1]warp \ˈwȯrp\ *n* **1 a** : a series of yarns extended lengthwise in a loom and crossed by the woof **b** : FOUNDATION 2, BASE **2 a** : a twist or curve that has developed in something originally flat or straight ⟨a *warp* in a door panel⟩ **b** : a mental aberration [Old English *wearp*]

[2]warp *vb* **1 a** : to turn or twist out of shape; *also* : to become so turned or twisted **b** : to cause to judge, choose, or act wrongly : PERVERT **c** : DISTORT 1, FALSIFY **2** : to arrange (yarns) so as to form a warp **3** : to move (as a ship) by hauling on a line attached to a fixed object — **warp·er** *n*

war paint *n* **1** : paint put on parts of the body (as the face) by American Indians on going to war **2** : MAKEUP 2

war·path \ˈwȯr-ˌpath, -ˌpȧth\ *n* **1** : the route taken by a party of American Indians going on a warlike expedition or to a war **2** : a hostile or combative course of action or frame of mind

warp knit *n* : a knit fabric produced by a machine in which the knitting is done with the yarns running in a lengthwise direction — compare WEFT KNIT — **warp knitting** *n*

war·plane \-ˌplān\ *n* : a military airplane; *esp* : one armed for combat

warp speed *n* : the highest possible speed [from the use in science fiction of space-time warps to allow faster-than-light travel] — **warp–speed** *adj*

[1]war·rant \ˈwȯr-ənt, ˈwär-\ *n* **1 a** : SANCTION 2, AUTHORIZATION **b** : GROUND 2, JUSTIFICATION **2** : evidence of authority or authorization: as **a** : a legal writ authorizing an officer to make an arrest, seizure, or search **b** : a certificate of appointment issued to a warrant officer [Medieval French *warant* "protector, warrant," of Germanic origin]

[2]warrant *vt* **1 a** : to declare or maintain positively : be sure that **b** : to assure (a person) that what is said is true **2** : to guarantee (something) to be as it appears or as it is represented **3** : to guarantee security or immunity to : SECURE **4** : to give sanction to ⟨the law *warrants* this procedure⟩ **5 a** : to give proof of : ATTEST **b** : GUARANTEE 1 **6** : to serve as adequate reason for : JUSTIFY — **war·rant·able** \ˈwȯr-ənt-ə-bəl, ˈwär-\ *adj* — **war·rant·able·ness** *n* — **war·rant·ably** \-blē\ *adv* — **warran·tor** \ˌwȯr-ən-ˈtȯr, ˌwär-; ˈwȯr-ənt-ər, ˈwär-\ *also* **war·rant·er** \ˈwȯr-ənt-ər, ˈwär-\ *n*

war·ran·tee \ˌwȯr-ən-ˈtē, ˌwär-\ *n* : the person to whom a warranty is made

warrant officer *n* : an officer in the armed forces holding rank by virtue of a warrant and ranking below a commissioned officer and above a noncommissioned officer

war·ran·ty \ˈwȯr-ənt-ē, ˈwär-\ *n, pl* **-ties** : an explicit or implied statement that a situation or thing is as it appears or is represented to be; *esp* : a usually written guarantee of a product's integrity and of the maker's responsiblity for the repair or replacement of defective parts [Medieval French *warantie,* from *warentir* "to guarantee, warrant," from *warant* "warrant"]

war·ren \ˈwȯr-ən, ˈwär-\ *n* **1** : a place where rabbits breed **2** : a crowded tenement or district [Medieval French *warenne*]

war·rior \ˈwȯr-yər; ˈwȯr-ē-ər, ˈwär-ē-\ *n* : a person engaged or experienced in warfare [Medieval French *werreieur,* from *warreier* "to make war," from *werre* "war"]

war·ship \ˈwȯr-ˌship\ *n* : a ship armed for combat

wart \ˈwȯrt\ *n* **1** : an irregular growth on the skin often caused by a virus **2** : a protuberance (as on a plant) resembling a wart [Old English *wearte*] — **wart·ed** \ˈwȯrt-əd\ *adj* — **warty** \-ē\ *adj*

wart·hog \ˈwȯrt-ˌhȯg, -ˌhäg\ *n* : a wild African hog with large curved tusks and in the male two pairs of rough warty growths on the face

warthog

war·time \ˈwȯr-ˌtīm\ *n* : a period of war

war whoop *n* : a war cry especially of American Indians

wary \ˈwaər-ē, ˈweər-\ *adj* **war·i·er; -est** : marked by keen caution, cunning, and watchfulness especially in detecting and escaping danger [Old English *wær* "careful, aware, wary"] — **war·i·ly** \ˈwar-ə-lē, ˈwer-\ *adv* — **war·i·ness** \ˈwar-ē-nəs, ˈwer-\ *n*

was *past 1st & 3rd singular of* BE [Old English *wæs,* 1st and 3rd singular past indicative of *wesan* "to be"]

[1]wash \ˈwȯsh, ˈwäsh\ *vb* **1** : to clean with or as if with water and usually a cleaning substance (as soap or detergent) ⟨*wash* clothes⟩ ⟨*wash* your hands⟩ **2** : to wet thoroughly with liquid **3** : to flow along the border of ⟨waves *wash* the shore⟩ **4** : to pour or flow in a stream or current ⟨the river *washes* against its banks⟩ **5** : to move or carry by the action of water ⟨a passenger *washed* overboard⟩ **6** : to cover or daub lightly with a liquid (as whitewash or varnish) **7** : to run water over in order to separate valuable matter from refuse ⟨*wash* sand for gold⟩ **8** : to undergo laundering ⟨a shirt that *washes* well⟩ **9** : to stand a test for truthfulness ⟨that story won't *wash*⟩ **10** : to wear or be worn by water ⟨heavy rain *washed* away the road⟩ [Old English *wascan*] — **wash one's hands of** : to deny interest in, responsibility for, or further connection with

[2]wash *n* **1 a** : the act or process or an instance of washing or being washed **b** : articles to be or being washed **2** : the surging action of waves or its sound **3 a** : a piece of ground washed by the sea or river **b** : BOG, MARSH **c** : a shallow body of water or creek **d** *West* : the dry bed of a stream — called also *dry wash* **4** : worthless especially liquid waste : REFUSE **5 a** : a sweep or splash especially of color made by or as if by a long stroke of a brush **b** : a thin coat of paint (as watercolor) **c** : a thin liquid used for coating a surface (as a wall) **6** : LOTION **7** : loose or eroded surface material of the earth (as rock debris) transported and deposited by running water **8 a** : BACKWASH 1 **b** : a disturbance in the air produced by the passage of an airfoil or propeller

[3]wash *adj* : WASHABLE ⟨*wash* fabric⟩

wash·able \ˈwȯsh-ə-bəl, ˈwäsh-\ *adj* : capable of being washed without damage ⟨a *washable* silk⟩ — **wash·abil·i·ty** \ˌwȯsh-ə-ˈbil-ət-ē, ˌwäsh-\ *n*

wash–and–wear *adj* : of, relating to, or being a fabric or garment that needs little or no ironing after washing

wash·ba·sin \ˈwȯsh-ˌbās-n, ˈwäsh-\ *n* : WASHBOWL

wash·board \-ˌbōrd, -ˌbȯrd\ *n* : a corrugated rectangular surface to scrub clothes on

\ə\ **abut**	\au̇\ **out**	\i\ **tip**	\ȯ\ **saw**	\u̇\ **foot**
\ər\ **further**	\ch\ **chin**	\ī\ **life**	\ȯi\ **coin**	\y\ **yet**
\a\ **mat**	\e\ **pet**	\j\ **job**	\th\ **thin**	\yü\ **few**
\ā\ **take**	\ē\ **easy**	\ŋ\ **sing**	\t͟h\ **this**	\yu̇\ **cure**
\ä\ **cot, cart**	\g\ **go**	\ō\ **bone**	\ü\ **food**	\zh\ **vision**

wash•bowl \-ˌbōl\ *n* : a large bowl or sink for water especially to wash one's hands and face
wash•cloth \-ˌklȯth\ *n* : a cloth for washing one's face and body — called also *washrag*
wash drawing *n* : watercolor painting in or chiefly in washes
washed–out \ˈwȯsh-ˈtau̇t, ˈwäsh-\ *adj* **1** : faded in color **2** : depleted of vigor or animation
washed–up \-ˈtəp\ *adj* : no longer successful, skillful, popular, or needed
wash•er \ˈwȯsh-ər, ˈwäsh-\ *n* **1** : a ring (as of metal or rubber) used to make something fit tightly or to prevent rubbing **2** : one that washes; *esp* : WASHING MACHINE

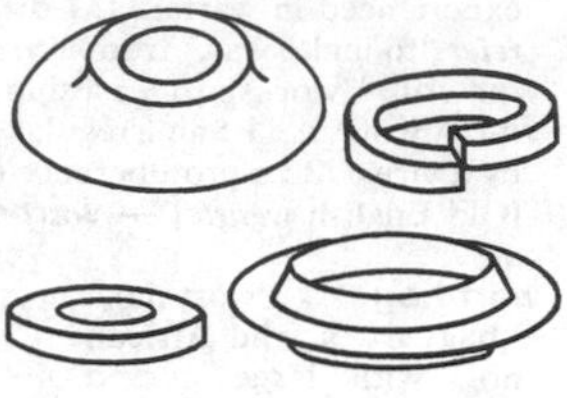
washer 1

wash•er•man \-mən\ *n* : LAUNDRYMAN; *also* : a man operating any of various industrial washing machines
wash•er•wom•an \-ˌwu̇m-ən\ *n* : LAUNDRESS; *esp* : one who takes in washing
wash•house \ˈwȯsh-ˌhau̇s, ˈwäsh-\ *n* : a building used or equipped for washing; *esp* : one for washing clothes
wash•ing \ˈwȯsh-ing, ˈwäsh-\ *n* **1** : material obtained by washing **2** : a thin covering or coat ⟨a *washing* of silver⟩ **3** : articles washed or to be washed
washing machine *n* : a machine for washing; *esp* : one for washing clothes and household linen
washing soda *n* : a transparent crystalline hydrated sodium carbonate
Wash•ing•ton pie \ˌwȯsh-ing-tən-, ˌwäsh-\ *n* : cake layers put together with a jam or jelly filling [George *Washington*]
Washington's Birthday *n* **1** : February 22 formerly observed as a legal holiday in most of the U.S. **2** : the third Monday in February observed as a legal holiday in most of the U.S — called also *Presidents' Day* [George *Washington*]
wash•out \ˈwȯsh-ˌau̇t, ˈwäsh-\ *n* **1** : the washing out or away of earth especially in a roadbed by a freshet; *also* : a place where earth is washed away **2** : one that fails to measure up : FAILURE; *esp* : one who fails in a course of training or study
wash out \wȯsh-ˈau̇t, ˈwȯsh-, wäsh-, ˈwäsh-\ *vb* **1 a** : to cause to fade by laundering **b** : to deplete the strength or vitality of **c** : to eliminate as useless or unsatisfactory : REJECT **2** : to become depleted of color or vitality : FADE **3** : to fail to measure up (as to a standard)
wash•rag \ˈwȯsh-ˌrag, ˈwäsh-\ *n* : WASHCLOTH
wash•room \-ˌrüm, -ˌru̇m\ *n* : a room equipped with washing and toilet facilities : LAVATORY
wash•stand \-ˌstand\ *n* **1** : a stand holding articles needed for washing one's face and hands **2** : a washbowl permanently set in place and attached to water pipes and drainpipes
wash•tub \-ˌtəb\ *n* : a tub for washing (as clothes)
wash up *vb* **1** : to wash one's face and hands **2** : FINISH 1 ⟨the scandal *washed* them *up*⟩ **3** : to be deposited by or as if by waves ⟨seaweed *washed up* on the shore⟩
wash•wom•an \ˈwȯsh-ˌwu̇m-ən, ˈwäsh-\ *n* : WASHERWOMAN
washy \ˈwȯsh-ē, ˈwäsh-\ *adj* **wash•i•er; -est** **1** : WEAK, WATERY ⟨*washy* tea⟩ **2** : lacking in color : PALLID **3** : lacking in vigor, individuality, or definiteness
wasn't \ˈwəz-ⁿt, ˈwäz-\ : was not
wasp \ˈwäsp, ˈwȯsp\ *n* : any of numerous social or solitary winged insects related to the bees and ants that have a slender smooth body with the abdomen attached by a narrow stalk and in females and workers a powerful sting [Old English *wæps, wæsp*]

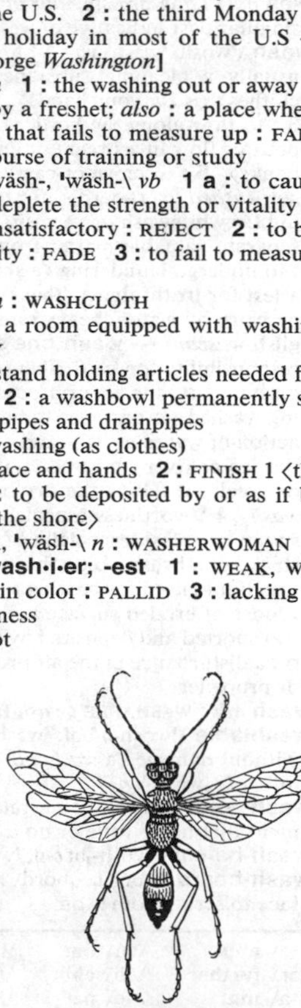
wasp

WASP *or* **Wasp** \ˈwäsp, ˈwȯsp\ *n, sometimes disparaging* : an American of North European and especially English Protestant ancestry and background [*w*hite *A*nglo-*S*axon *P*rotestant]
wasp•ish \ˈwäs-pish, ˈwȯs-\ *adj* **1** : SNAPPISH, IRRITABLE ⟨a *waspish* retort⟩ **2** : resembling a wasp in form; *esp* : slightly built — **wasp•ish•ly** *adv* — **wasp•ish•ness** *n*
wasp waist *n* : a very slender waist — **wasp–waist•ed** \ˈwäsp-ˌwā-stəd, ˈwȯsp-\ *adj*
[1]**was•sail** \ˈwäs-əl *also* wä-ˈsāl\ *n* **1** : an early English toast to someone's health **2** : a hot drink that is made with wine, beer, or cider, spices, sugar, and usually baked apples and is served in a large bowl usually at Christmas **3** : riotous drinking : REVELRY [Old Norse *ves heill* "be well"]
[2]**wassail** *vb* **1** : to indulge in wassail : CAROUSE **2** : to drink to the health of
was•sail•er \ˈwäs-ə-lər *also* wä-ˈsā-lər\ *n* **1** : one that carouses : REVELER **2** *archaic* : one who goes about singing carols
wast \wəst, wäst, ˈwäst\ *archaic past 2nd singular of* BE
wast•age \ˈwā-stij\ *n* : loss by use, decay, erosion, or leakage or through wastefulness; *esp* : wasteful or avoidable loss of something valuable
[1]**waste** \ˈwāst\ *n* **1 a** : a sparsely settled or barren region : DESERT **b** : uncultivated land **c** : a broad and empty expanse (as of water) **2** : the act or an instance of wasting : the state of being wasted **3** : gradual loss or decrease by use, wear, or decay **4 a** : damaged, defective, or superfluous material produced by a manufacturing process: as (1) : material rejected during a textile manufacturing process (2) : fluid (as steam) allowed to escape without being utilized **b** (1) : refuse (as garbage, sewage, or rubbish) that accumulates about places of human or animal habitations ⟨collection of city *wastes*⟩ (2) : material (as carbon dioxide or feces) that is produced by a living body and is of no value to the organism that produces it [Medieval French *wast,* from *wast,* adj., "desolate, waste," from Latin *vastus*]
[2]**waste** *vb* **1** : to lay waste usually by violence : DEVASTATE ⟨lands *wasted* by war⟩ **2** : to wear away or impair gradually : CONSUME ⟨fields *wasted* by erosion⟩ **3** : to spend or use carelessly : SQUANDER **4** : to lose or cause to lose weight, strength, or vitality — often used with *away* ⟨was *wasting* away from illness⟩ **5 a** : to become diminished in bulk or substance **b** : to become consumed ***synonyms*** see RAVAGE
[3]**waste** *adj* **1** : being wild and uninhabited : DESOLATE **2** : being ruined or devastated **3** : discarded as worthless, defective, or useless **4** : excreted from or stored in inert form in a living body as a byproduct of biological activity ⟨*waste* products⟩
waste•bas•ket \ˈwāst-ˌbas-kət, ˈwās-\ *n* : an open receptacle for trash and especially for wastepaper
waste•ful \ˈwāst-fəl\ *adj* : given to or marked by waste — **waste•ful•ly** \-fə-lē\ *adv* — **waste•ful•ness** *n*
waste•land \ˈwāst-ˌland\ *n* **1** : barren or uncultivated land **2** : an ugly often devastated or barely inhabitable place or area
waste•pa•per \ˈwāst-ˈpā-pər, ˈwās-\ *n* : paper discarded as used, superfluous, or not fit for use
waste pipe *n* : a pipe for carrying off waste fluid
waste product *n* : material resulting from a process (as of metabolism or manufacture) that is of no further use to the system producing it
wast•er \ˈwā-stər\ *n* : one that wastes or squanders
wast•rel \ˈwā-strəl\ *n* : WASTER, SPENDTHRIFT [derived from [2]*waste*]
[1]**watch** \ˈwäch, ˈwȯch\ *vb* **1** : to stay awake intentionally (as at the bedside of a sick person) **2 a** : to be on the alert or on the lookout **b** : to keep guard ⟨*watch* outside the door⟩ **3** : to keep one's eyes on : keep in view ⟨*watch* a game⟩ **4** : to observe so as to prevent harm or danger ⟨*watch* a brush fire carefully⟩ **5** : to keep oneself informed about ⟨*watch* a competitor's plans⟩ **6** : to be on the alert for the chance to make use of ⟨*watched* my opportunity⟩ [Old English *wæccan*] — **watch•er** *n* — **watch it** : to look out : be careful — **watch one's step** : to proceed with great care — **watch over** : to have charge of
[2]**watch** *n* **1 a** : the act of keeping awake to guard, protect, or attend **b** : a state of alert and continuous attention ⟨a winter storm *watch*⟩ **c** : close observation : SURVEILLANCE ⟨kept a close *watch* over the baby⟩ **2** : one of the indeterminate wakeful intervals marking the passage of night — usually used in plural ⟨the silent *watches* of the night⟩ **3** : one that watches : LOOKOUT **4 a** : a body of soldiers or sentinels making up a guard **b** : a watchman or body of watchmen formerly assigned to patrol the streets **5 a** : a portion of time during which a part of a ship's company is on duty **b** : the part of a ship's company on duty during a particular watch **c** : a period of duty : SHIFT

6 : a portable timepiece designed to be worn (as on the wrist) or carried in the pocket
watch•band \-ˌband\ *n* : the bracelet or strap of a wristwatch
watch•case \-ˌkās\ *n* : the outside covering of a watch
watch•dog \-ˌdȯg\ *n* **1** : a dog kept to guard property **2** : one that guards against loss, waste, theft, or undesirable practices
watch•ful \-fəl\ *adj* : steadily attentive and alert especially to danger — **watch•ful•ly** \-fə-lē\ *adv* — **watch•ful•ness** *n*
synonyms WATCHFUL, VIGILANT, ALERT mean being on the lookout especially for opportunity or danger. WATCHFUL is the general and least explicit term ⟨the *watchful* eye of the principal⟩. VIGILANT suggests maintaining a keen, unremitting watchfulness ⟨*vigilant* in protecting our freedom⟩. ALERT stresses readiness or promptness in meeting danger or seizing opportunity ⟨an *alert* reader noticed the error⟩.
watch glass *n* **1** : a glass that is usually convex outwardly and used for covering a watch dial **2** : a small circular glass dish used especially in laboratory work
watch•mak•er \ˈwäch-ˌmā-kər\ *n* : one that makes or repairs watches or clocks — **watch•mak•ing** \-kiŋ\ *n*
watch•man \-mən\ *n* : a person who keeps watch : GUARD
watch night *n* : a devotional service lasting until after midnight especially on New Year's Eve
watch out *vi* : to be vigilant or alert : be on the lookout ⟨*watch out* for cars⟩
watch•tow•er \ˈwäch-ˌtau̇-ər, -ˌtau̇r\ *n* : a tower for a lookout
watch•word \-ˌwərd\ *n* **1** : a secret word used as a signal or sign of recognition **2** : a motto used as a slogan or rallying cry
[1]**wa•ter** \ˈwȯt-ər, ˈwät-\ *n* **1 a** : the liquid that descends from the clouds as rain, forms streams, lakes, and seas, and is a major constituent of all living matter and that is an odorless, tasteless, very slightly compressible oxide of hydrogen H_2O **b** : a natural mineral water — usually used in plural **2** *pl* : a band of seawater bordering on and under the control of a country ⟨sailing Canadian *waters*⟩ **3** : travel or transportation on water ⟨came by *water*⟩ **4** : the level of water at a particular state of the tide : TIDE **5** : liquid containing or resembling water: as **a** : a pharmaceutical or cosmetic preparation made with water **b** : a watery fluid (as tears, urine, or sap) formed or circulating in a living body **6** : the transparency and luster of a precious stone and especially a diamond ⟨a perfectly clear diamond of the first *water*⟩ [Old English *wæter*] — **above water** : out of difficulty — **in deep water** : in serious difficulties
[2]**water** *vb* **1** : to moisten or soak with water ⟨*water* the lawn⟩ **2 a** : to supply with water ⟨*water* horses⟩ **b** : to get or take water **3** : to treat with or as if with water; *esp* : to impart a lustrous appearance and wavy pattern to (cloth) by calendering ⟨*watered* silk⟩ **4 a** : to dilute by or as if by adding water ⟨someone *watered* down the punch⟩ **b** : to increase the total stated value of (stock) without a corresponding addition to capital **5** : to form or secrete water or watery matter (as tears or saliva) ⟨smog makes my eyes *water*⟩
water ballet *n* : a synchronized sequence of movements performed by a group of swimmers
water bed *n* : a bed whose mattress is a plastic bag filled with water
water beetle *n* : any of numerous oval flattened aquatic beetles (as a whirligig beetle) that swim by means of their fringed hind legs which act together as oars
wa•ter•bird \ˈwȯt-ər-ˌbərd, ˈwät-\ *n* : a swimming or wading bird
water blister *n* : a blister with a clear watery content
water bloom *n* : BLOOM 1d
water boatman *n* : any of various oval flattened aquatic bugs with fringed hind legs modified into paddles
wa•ter•borne \ˈwȯt-ər-ˌbōrn, ˈwät-, -ˌbȯrn\ *adj* : supported, carried, or transmitted by water ⟨*waterborne* diseases⟩
water boy *n* : one who keeps a group (as of football players) supplied with drinking water
wa•ter•buck \ˈwȯt-ər-ˌbək, ˈwät-\ *n, pl* **waterbuck** *or* **waterbucks** : a stocky antelope of sub-Saharan Africa that commonly frequents streams or wet areas
water buffalo *n* : an often domesticated Asian buffalo somewhat resembling a large ox
water bug *n* : any of various insects (as a German cockroach or various true bugs) that live in or near water or in damp places
water chestnut *n* : a whitish crunchy vegetable used especially in Chinese cooking that is the peeled tuber of an Asian sedge; *also* : the tuber or the sedge itself
water clock *n* : an instrument designed to measure time by the fall or flow of water
water closet *n* **1** : a compartment or room with a toilet bowl **2** : a toilet bowl along with its accessories

water buffalo

wa•ter•col•or \ˈwȯt-ər-ˌkəl-ər, ˈwät-\ *n* **1** : a paint whose liquid part is water **2** : the art of painting with watercolor **3** : a picture or design painted with watercolor — **wa•ter•col•or•ist** \-ˌkəl-ə-rəst\ *n*
wa•ter•cool•er \ˈwȯt-ər-ˌkü-lər, ˈwät-\ *n* : a device for dispensing refrigerated drinking water
wa•ter•course \ˈwȯt-ər-ˌkōrs, ˈwät-, -ˌkȯrs\ *n* **1** : a bed over which or channel through which water flows **2** : a stream of water (as a river, brook, or underground stream)
wa•ter•craft \-ˌkraft\ *n* **1** : skill in water activities (as managing boats) **2** : craft (as boats) for water transport
wa•ter•cress \-ˌkres\ *n* **1** : any of several cresses growing in or near water; *esp* : a perennial Eurasian cress that is naturalized in the U.S., grows mostly in clear running water, and has peppery-testing leaves used especially in salads or as a potherb **2** : the leaves of a watercress
water cycle *n* : HYDROLOGIC CYCLE
water dog *n* : a large salamander; *esp* : MUD PUPPY
wa•ter•er \ˈwȯt-ər-ər, ˈwät-\ *n* : one that waters ⟨an automatic plant *waterer*⟩
wa•ter•fall \ˈwȯt-ər-ˌfȯl, ˈwät-\ *n* : a perpendicular or very steep descent of the water of a stream
water flea *n* : any of various small active dark or brightly colored freshwater crustaceans (as a cyclops or daphnia)
wa•ter•fowl \ˈwȯt-ər-ˌfau̇l, ˈwät-\ *n, pl* **-fowl** *also* **-fowls** : a bird that frequents water; *esp* : a swimming game bird (as a duck or goose) as distinguished from an upland game bird or shorebird
wa•ter•front \-ˌfrənt\ *n* : land or a section of an urban area bordering on a body of water
water gap *n* : a pass in a mountain ridge through which a stream runs
water gas *n* : a poisonous flammable gaseous mixture that consists chiefly of carbon monoxide and hydrogen, is usually made by blowing air and then steam over red-hot coke or coal, and is used as a fuel
water gate *n* **1** : a gate (as of a building) giving access to a body of water **2** : FLOODGATE 1
water glass *n* **1** : a glass vessel (as a drinking glass) for holding water **2** : an instrument consisting of an open box or tube with a glass bottom used for examining objects in or under water **3** : a water-soluble substance that consists usually of sodium silicate in the form of a glassy mass, a stony powder, or dissolved in water as a syrupy liquid and is used as a protective coating and in preserving eggs
water hemlock *n* : any of a genus of poisonous plants related to the carrot; *esp* : a tall Eurasian perennial herb
water hole *n* **1** : a natural hole or hollow containing water **2** : a hole in a surface of ice
water hyacinth *n* : a showy South American floating aquatic plant that is related to pickerelweed and often clogs waterways in the southern U.S.
water ice *n* : a frozen dessert of water, sugar, and flavoring
watering can *n* : a vessel usually with a perforated spout used to sprinkle water especially on plants
watering place *n* **1** : a place where water may be obtained; *esp* : one where animals and especially livestock come to drink **2** : a health or recreational resort featuring mineral springs or water activities
wa•ter•ish \ˈwȯt-ə-rish, ˈwät-\ *adj* : somewhat watery — **wa•ter•ish•ness** *n*

\ə\ **abut**	\au̇\ **out**	\i\ **tip**	\ȯ\ **saw**	\u̇\ **foot**
\ər\ **further**	\ch\ **chin**	\ī\ **life**	\ȯi\ **coin**	\y\ **yet**
\a\ **mat**	\e\ **pet**	\j\ **job**	\th\ **thin**	\yü\ **few**
\ā\ **take**	\ē\ **easy**	\ŋ\ **sing**	\t͟h\ **this**	\yu̇\ **cure**
\ä\ **cot, cart**	\g\ **go**	\ō\ **bone**	\ü\ **food**	\zh\ **vision**

water jacket *n* : an outer casing which holds water or through which water circulates for cooling something
water jump *n* : an obstacle (as in a steeplechase) consisting of a pool, stream, or ditch of water
wa·ter·less \ˈwȯt-ər-ləs, ˈwät-\ *adj* **1** : lacking water : DRY **2** : not requiring water (as for cooling or cooking) — **wa·ter·less·ly** *adj* — **wa·ter·less·ness** *n*
water lily *n* : any of a family of aquatic plants with rounded floating leaves and usually showy flowers

water lily

wa·ter·line \ˈwȯt-ər-ˌlīn, ˈwät-\ *n* : a line marked upon the outside of a ship that corresponds with the surface of the water when the ship is afloat on an even keel
wa·ter·logged \-ˌlȯgd, -ˌlägd\ *adj* : so filled or soaked with water as to be heavy or hard to manage ⟨a *waterlogged* boat⟩ [*water* + *log* "to accumulate in the hold"]
wa·ter·loo \ˌwȯt-ər-ˈlü, ˌwät-\ *n, pl* **-loos** *often cap* : a decisive or final defeat or setback ⟨a political *waterloo*⟩ [*Waterloo*, Belgium, scene of Napoléon's defeat in 1815]
water main *n* : a pipe or conduit for conveying water (as from a reservoir)
¹wa·ter·mark \-ˌmärk\ *n* **1** : a mark that shows the height to which water has risen **2** : a mark (as the maker's name or trademark) made in paper during manufacture and visible when the paper is held up to the light
²watermark *vt* : to mark (paper) with a watermark
wa·ter·mel·on \ˈwȯt-ər-ˌmel-ən, ˈwät-\ *n* **1** : a large oblong or rounded fruit with a hard green or white rind often striped or variegated, a sweet watery pink, yellowish, or red pulp, and usually many seeds **2** : a widely grown African vine of the gourd family that bears watermelons
water meter *n* : an instrument for recording the quantity of water passing through a particular outlet
water milfoil *n* : any of a genus of aquatic herbs with feathery submersed leaves
water moccasin *n* : a venomous semiaquatic pit viper of the southern U.S. closely related to the copperhead — called also *cottonmouth*

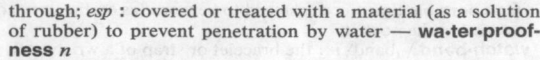

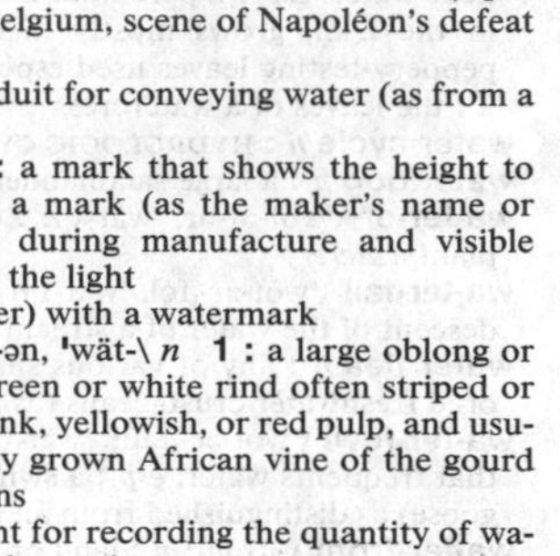
water moccasin

water mold *n* : any of various fungi of water or moist soils
water nymph *n* : a nymph (as a naiad) of classical mythology associated with a body of water
water oak *n* : any of several American oaks that thrive in wet soil
water of crystallization : water of hydration present in many crystallized substances
water of hydration : water chemically combined with a substance to form a hydrate that can be expelled (as by heating) without essentially altering the composition of the substance
water ouzel *n* : DIPPER 2
water park *n* : an amusement park with pools and wetted slides for entertainment
water pipe *n* **1** : a pipe for conveying water **2** : a tobacco-smoking device so arranged that the smoke is drawn through water
water pistol *n* : a toy pistol designed to throw a jet of liquid — called also *squirt gun, water gun*
water plantain *n* : any of a genus of marsh or aquatic herbs with 3-petaled flowers
water polo *n* : a goal game similar to soccer that is played in water by teams of swimmers using a ball resembling a soccer ball
wa·ter·pow·er \ˈwȯt-ər-ˌpau̇-ər, ˈwät-, -ˌpau̇r\ *n* : the power of moving water used to run machinery (as for generating electricity)
¹wa·ter·proof \ˌwȯt-ər-ˈprüf, ˌwät-\ *adj* : not letting water through; *esp* : covered or treated with a material (as a solution of rubber) to prevent penetration by water — **wa·ter·proof·ness** *n*
²wa·ter·proof \ˈwȯt-ər-ˌ, ˈwät-\ *n* **1** : a waterproof fabric **2** *chiefly British* : RAINCOAT
³wa·ter·proof \ˌwȯt-ər-ˈ, ˌwät-\ *vt* : to make waterproof — **wa·ter·proof·er** *n*
wa·ter·proof·ing \-ˈprü-fiŋ\ *n* **1 a** : the act or process of making something waterproof **b** : the condition of being made waterproof **2** : something (as a coating) capable of imparting waterproofness
water rat *n* **1** : a rodent that frequents water **2** : a waterfront loafer or petty thief
wa·ter–re·pel·lent \ˌwȯt-ər-ri-ˈpel-ənt, ˌwȯt-ə-ri-, ˌwät-\ *adj* : treated with a finish that is resistant to penetration by water but not waterproof
wa·ter–re·sis·tant \-ri-ˈzis-tənt\ *adj* : WATER-REPELLENT
water scorpion *n* : any of various large aquatic true bugs with the end of the abdomen prolonged by a long breathing tube
wa·ter·shed \ˈwȯt-ər-ˌshed, ˈwät-\ *n* **1** : a dividing ridge (as a mountain range) separating one drainage area from others **2** : the whole area that drains into a particular river or lake **3** : a crucial or dividing point, line, or factor
wa·ter·side \-ˌsīd\ *n* : the land bordering a body of water
water–ski *vi* : to ski on water while towed by a speedboat — **wa·ter–ski·er** \ˈwȯt-ər-ˌskē-ər, ˈwät-\ *n*
water ski *n* : a ski used on water
water·ski·ing \ˈwȯt-ər-ˌskē-iŋ, ˈwät-\ *n* : the sport of planing and jumping on water skis when towed by a motorboat
wa·ter·slide \-ˌslīd\ *n* : a continuously wetted chute (as at an amusement park) down which people slide into a pool
water snake *n* : any of various snakes frequenting or inhabiting fresh waters and feeding largely on aquatic animals
wa·ter–soak \ˈwȯt-ər-ˌsōk, ˈwät-\ *vt* : to soak in water
water spaniel *n* : a rather large spaniel of either of two breeds with heavy curly coats
wa·ter·spout \ˈwȯt-ər-ˌspau̇t, ˈwät-\ *n* **1** : a pipe for carrying off water from a roof **2** : a column of rotating wind extending from a cloud down to a cloud of spray torn up from the surface of a body of water by the winds
water sprite *n* : a sprite inhabiting or haunting water : WATER NYMPH
water strider *n* : any of various long-legged true bugs that move about on the surface of the water

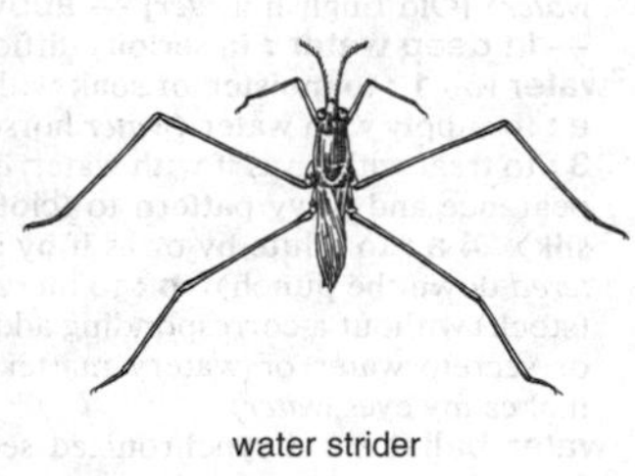
water strider

water table *n* : the upper limit of the ground wholly saturated with water
wa·ter·tight \ˌwȯt-ər-ˈtīt, ˌwät-\ *adj* **1** : of such tight construction or fit as to be waterproof **2** : leaving no possibility of misunderstanding or evasion ⟨a *watertight* case against the defendant⟩ — **wa·ter·tight·ness** *n*
water tower *n* : a tower or standpipe serving as a reservoir to deliver water
water vapor *n* : the vapor of water especially when below the boiling temperature and in diffused form (as in the atmosphere)
water–vascular system *n* : a system of vessels in echinoderms containing a circulating watery fluid that is used for the movement of tentacles and tube feet
wa·ter·way \ˈwȯt-ər-ˌwā, ˈwät-\ *n* : a channel or a body of water by which ships can travel
wa·ter·weed \-ˌwēd\ *n* : any of various floating or submerged plants (as elodea) usually with inconspicuous flowers
wa·ter·wheel \-ˌhwēl, -ˌwēl\ *n* : a wheel made to turn by a flow of water against it
water wings *n pl* : an air-filled device to give support to a person learning to swim
wa·ter·works \ˈwȯt-ər-ˌwərks, ˈwät-\ *n pl* : the system of reservoirs, channels, mains, and pumping and purifying equipment by which a water supply is obtained and distributed (as to a city)
wa·ter·worn \-ˌwōrn, -ˌwȯrn\ *adj* : worn, smoothed, or polished by the action of water
wa·tery \ˈwȯt-ə-rē, ˈwät-\ *adj* **1 a** : consisting of, filled with, or

surrounded by water **b :** containing, full of, or giving out water or a thin liquid ⟨a *watery* mixture⟩ ⟨*watery* eyes⟩ **2 :** resembling water or watery matter especially in thinness, sogginess, paleness, or lack of taste ⟨*watery* lemonade⟩ ⟨*watery* soup⟩ — **wa·ter·i·ness** *n*

Wat·son–Crick model \ˌwät-sən-ˈkrik-\ *n* **:** a model of DNA structure in which the molecule is a double-stranded helix cross-linked by pairs of purine and pyrimidine bases joined by hydrogen bonds with adenine paired with thymine and cytosine paired with guanine — compare *double helix* [J. D. *Watson,* born 1928, American biologist and F. H. C. *Crick,* born 1916, English biologist]

watt \ˈwät\ *n* **:** a unit of power equal to the work done at the rate of one joule per second [James *Watt,* died 1819, Scottish engineer]

watt·age \-ij\ *n* **:** amount of power expressed in watts

watt–hour \ˈwät-ˈau̇r\ *n* **:** a unit of work or energy equivalent to the power of one watt operating for one hour

1wat·tle \ˈwät-l\ *n* **1 a :** a structure of poles interwoven with slender branches, withes, or reeds and used especially formerly in building **b :** material for such construction **c** *pl* **:** poles laid on a roof to support thatch **2** *Australian* **:** ACACIA 2 [Old English *watel*] — **wat·tled** \-ld\ *adj*

2wattle *vt* **wat·tled; wat·tling** \ˈwät-ling, -l-ing\ **1 :** to form or build of or with wattle **2 a :** to form into wattle **:** interlace to form wattle **b :** to unite or make solid by interweaving light flexible material

3wattle *n* **:** a fleshy process hanging usually about the head or neck (as of a bird) [origin unknown]

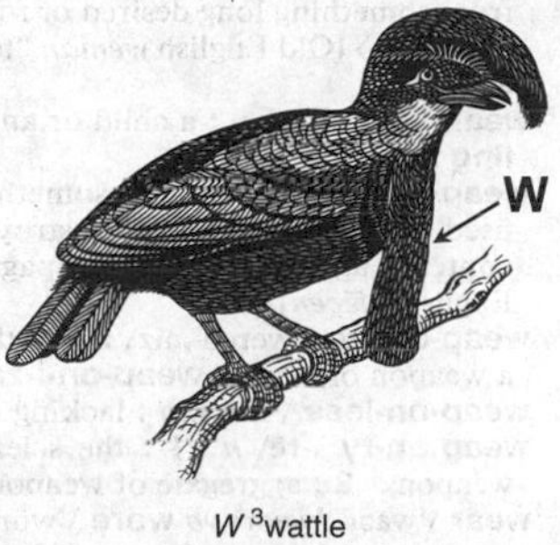

W 3wattle

watt·me·ter \ˈwät-ˌmēt-ər\ *n* **:** an instrument for measuring electric power in watts

1wave \ˈwāv\ *vb* **1 :** to float, play, or shake in an air current **:** move or cause to move loosely to and fro **:** FLUTTER **2 :** to motion with the hands or with something held in them in signal or salute **3 a :** to become moved or brandished to and fro ⟨signs *waved* in the crowd⟩ **b :** BRANDISH, FLOURISH ⟨*waved* a pistol menacingly⟩ **4 :** to move before the wind with a wavelike motion **5 :** to follow or cause to follow a curving line or take a wavy form ⟨*waved* her hair⟩ [Old English *wafian* "to wave with the hands"]

2wave *n* **1 :** a moving swell or crest on the surface of water **2 :** a wavelike formation or shape ⟨a *wave* in the hair⟩ **3 :** a waving motion (as of the hand or a flag) **4 :** FLOW, GUSH ⟨a *wave* of color swept the child's face⟩ **5 :** a surge or rapid increase ⟨a *wave* of buying⟩ ⟨a heat *wave*⟩ **6 :** a display of people in a large crowd (as at a sports event) successively rising, lifting their arms overhead, and quickly sitting so as to form a swell moving through the crowd **7 :** a disturbance that transfers energy progressively from point to point and that may take the form of an elastic deformation or of a variation of pressure, electric or magnetic intensity, electric potential, or temperature ⟨a light *wave*⟩ — **wave·less** \-ləs\ *adj* — **wave·less·ly** *adv* — **wave·like** \-ˌlīk\ *adj*

Wave \ˈwāv\ *n* **:** a woman serving in the U.S. Navy [*W*omen *A*ccepted for *V*olunteer *E*mergency Service]

waved \ˈwāvd\ *adj* **:** having a wavelike form or outline: as **a :** marked by undulations ⟨the *waved* cutting edge of a bread knife⟩ **b :** having wavy lines of color ⟨*waved* cloth⟩

wave·form \ˈwāv-ˌfȯrm\ *n* **:** a usually graphic representation of the shape of a wave that indicates its characteristics (as frequency and amplitude)

wave·length \ˈwāv-ˌlength, -ˌlengkth\ *n* **1 :** the distance (as from crest to crest) in the line of advance of a wave from any one point to the next corresponding point **2 :** a particular course or line of thought especially as related to a common understanding ⟨teammates on the same *wavelength*⟩

wave·let \-lət\ *n* **:** a little wave **:** RIPPLE

wave mechanics *n* **:** a branch of physics dealing with the wave nature of elementary particles

wave pool *n* **:** a large swimming pool equipped with a machine for producing waves

1wa·ver \ˈwā-vər\ *vi* **wa·vered; wa·ver·ing** \ˈwāv-ring, -ə-ring\ **1 :** to swing back and forth uncertainly between choices **:** fluctuate in opinion, allegiance, or direction **2 a :** to weave or sway unsteadily to and fro **:** REEL, TOTTER **b :** QUIVER, FLICKER ⟨*wavering* flames⟩ **c :** FALTER 3 **3 :** to give an unsteady sound **:** QUAVER [Middle English *waveren*] ***synonyms*** see HESITATE, SWAY — **wa·ver·er** \ˈwā-vər-ər\ *n* — **wa·ver·ing·ly** \ˈwāv-ring-lē, -ə-ring-\ *adv*

2waver *n* **:** an act of wavering, quivering, or fluttering

wavy \ˈwā-vē\ *adj* **wav·i·er; wav·i·est :** having waves **:** moving in waves ⟨*wavy* hair⟩ ⟨a *wavy* surface⟩ — **wav·i·ly** \-və-lē\ *adv* — **wav·i·ness** \-vē-nəs\ *n*

1wax \ˈwaks\ *n* **1 :** a yellowish moldable substance secreted by bees and used by them for constructing the honeycomb — called also *beeswax* **2 :** any of various substances resembling the wax of bees in physical or chemical properties: as **a :** a plant or animal product that is harder and less greasy than a typical fat **b :** a solid mixture of higher hydrocarbons **c :** EARWAX **3 :** something likened to wax as soft, impressionable, or readily molded [Old English *weax*] — **wax·like** \-ˌlīk\ *adj*

2wax *vt* **:** to treat or rub with wax

3wax *vi* **1 :** to grow larger or greater: as **a :** to grow in volume or duration ⟨a stream *waxing* with melting snows⟩ **b :** to increase in apparent size and brightness ⟨the moon *waxes*⟩ **2 :** to pass from one state to another **:** BECOME ⟨the party *waxed* merry⟩ [Old English *weaxan*]

4wax *n* **1 :** INCREASE 1, GROWTH **2 :** the period from the new moon to the full phase of the moon

wax bean *n* **:** a kidney bean with pods that are yellow when mature enough for use as snap beans

waxed paper *or* **wax paper** *n* **:** paper treated with wax to make it impervious to water and grease

wax·en \ˈwak-sən\ *adj* **1 :** made of wax **2 :** resembling wax (as in pliability, pallor, or lustrous smoothness)

wax museum *n* **:** a place where wax effigies (as of famous historical persons) are exhibited

wax myrtle *n* **:** any of a genus of trees or shrubs with aromatic foliage; *esp* **:** a shrub or small tree of the eastern U.S. having small hard berries with a thick coating of bluish white wax used for candles — compare BAYBERRY 1

wax·wing \ˈwak-ˌswing\ *n* **:** any of a genus of American and Eurasian birds that are mostly brown or gray with a showy crest, velvety plumage, and sometimes red waxy material on the tip of the lower wing feathers

wax·work \ˈwak-ˌswərk\ *n* **1 :** an effigy in wax usually of a person **2** *pl* **:** WAX MUSEUM

waxy \ˈwak-sē\ *adj* **wax·i·er; -est 1 :** covered with wax ⟨a *waxy* surface⟩ ⟨*waxy* berries⟩ **2 :** resembling wax **:** WAXEN ⟨a *waxy* complexion⟩ — **wax·i·ness** *n*

1way \ˈwā\ *n* **1 a :** a track or passage for travel or transportation from place to place **b :** an opening for passage (as through a crowd or a gate) ⟨no *way* out⟩ **2 :** the course traveled from one place to another **:** ROUTE ⟨knew the *way* home⟩ **3 a :** a course of action ⟨chose the easy *way*⟩ **b :** opportunity, capability, or fact of doing as one pleases ⟨determined to have our *way*⟩ **c :** POSSIBILITY 1 ⟨no two *ways* about it⟩ **4 a :** method in which something is done or happens ⟨a new *way* of painting⟩ ⟨the *way* the mind works⟩ **b :** FEATURE 2, RESPECT ⟨a good worker in many *ways*⟩ **c :** the usual or characteristic state of affairs ⟨as is the *way* with dreams⟩ **d :** STATE, CONDITION ⟨that's the *way* things are⟩ ⟨was in a bad *way* with rheumatism⟩ **5 :** a particular or characteristic manner or behavior ⟨it's just my *way*⟩ ⟨has a nice *way* with animals⟩ ⟨championing the American *way*⟩ **6 a :** the length of a course **:** DISTANCE ⟨still have a *way* to go⟩ **b :** progress or movement along a course ⟨earning my *way* through school⟩ **7 :** DIRECTION 3 ⟨come this *way*⟩ ⟨visit when you are out our *way*⟩ ⟨stroking the fur the wrong *way*⟩ **8** *pl* **a :** an inclined support on which a ship is built and from which it is launched **b :** the guiding surfaces on the bed of a machine along which a table or carriage moves **9 :** CATEGORY 2, KIND

\ə\ **abut**	\au̇\ **out**	\i\ **tip**	\ȯ\ **saw**	\u̇\ **foot**
\ər\ **further**	\ch\ **chin**	\ī\ **life**	\ȯi\ **coin**	\y\ **yet**
\a\ **mat**	\e\ **pet**	\j\ **job**	\th\ **thin**	\yü\ **few**
\ā\ **take**	\ē\ **easy**	\ng\ **sing**	\t͟h\ **this**	\yu̇\ **cure**
\ä\ **cot, cart**	\g\ **go**	\ō\ **bone**	\ü\ **food**	\zh\ **vision**

⟨get what you need in the *way* of supplies⟩ **10 :** motion or speed of a boat through the water ⟨making slow *way* down the harbor⟩ [Old English *weg*] — **by the way :** aside or apart from that : INCIDENTALLY — **by way of 1 :** for the purpose of ⟨*by way of* illustration⟩ **2 :** by the route through : VIA — **in one's way** *also* **in the way 1 :** in or along one's course **2 :** in a position to hinder or obstruct — **on the way** *or* **on one's way :** moving along a course : in progress ⟨*on our way* home⟩ — **out of the way 1 :** WRONG 2, IMPROPER ⟨didn't know I'd said anything *out of the way*⟩ **2 :** in or to a secluded place **3 :** brought to an end : DONE, COMPLETED ⟨got his homework *out of the way*⟩

[2]way *adj* **:** of, connected with, or constituting an intermediate point on a route ⟨*way* station⟩

[3]way *adv* **1 a :** AWAY ⟨is *way* ahead of the class⟩ **b :** by far : MUCH ⟨ate *way* too much⟩ **c :** VERY 1 ⟨*way* cool⟩ **2 :** all the way ⟨pull the switch *way* back⟩

way·bill \ˈwā-ˌbil\ *n* **:** a document prepared by the carrier of a shipment of goods and containing details of the shipment, route, and charges

way·far·er \-ˌfar-ər, -ˌfer-\ *n* **:** a traveler especially on foot — **way·far·ing** \-ˌfar-iŋ, -ˌfer-\ *adj*

way·lay \ˈwā-ˌlā\ *vt* **-laid** \-ˌlād\; **-lay·ing :** to wait for and attack or intercept

Way of the Cross : STATIONS OF THE CROSS

-ways \ˌwāz\ *adv suffix* **:** in (such) a way, course, direction, or manner ⟨side*ways*⟩ [Middle English, from *ways,* genitive of *way*]

ways and means *n pl* **:** methods and resources for accomplishing something and especially for raising money needed by a nation or state; *also* **:** a legislative committee concerned with this function

way·side \ˈwā-ˌsīd\ *n* **:** the side of or land adjacent to a road or path — **wayside** *adj*

way·ward \ˈwā-wərd\ *adj* **1 :** tending to do as one pleases : DISOBEDIENT ⟨*wayward* children⟩ **2 :** following no clear principle : UNPREDICTABLE **3 :** opposite to what is desired or expected ⟨*wayward* fate⟩ [Middle English, from *awayward* "turned away"] — **way·ward·ly** *adv* — **way·ward·ness** *n*

way·worn \-ˌwōrn, -ˌwȯrn\ *adj* **:** wearied by traveling

we \wē, ˈwē\ *pron, pl in constr* **1 :** I and one or more others — used as pronoun of the 1st person plural; compare I, OUR, OURS, US **2 :** I — used by sovereigns; used by writers to keep an impersonal character [Old English *wē*]

weak \ˈwēk\ *adj* **1 :** lacking strength: as **a :** deficient in physical vigor : FEEBLE ⟨*weak* as a kitten⟩ **b :** not able to sustain or resist much weight, pressure, or strain ⟨a *weak* rope⟩ **c :** deficient in vigor of mind or character; *also* **:** resulting from or indicative of such deficiency ⟨a *weak* policy⟩ **d :** easily upset or nauseated ⟨a *weak* stomach⟩ **e :** DILUTE ⟨*weak* tea⟩ **2 :** not factually grounded or logically presented ⟨a *weak* argument⟩ **3 a :** not able to function properly ⟨*weak* eyes⟩ **b :** lacking skill or proficiency; *also* **:** indicative of such a lack ⟨math's my *weakest* subject⟩ **c :** wanting in vigor of expression or effect ⟨a *weak* translation of the poem⟩ **4 a :** not having or exerting authority ⟨a *weak* government⟩ **b :** INEFFECTIVE, IMPOTENT ⟨*weak* measures to control crime⟩ **5 :** of, relating to, or constituting an English verb or verb conjugation that forms the past tense and past participle by adding the suffix *-ed* or *-d* or *-t* **6 :** bearing the minimal degree of stress occurring in the language ⟨a *weak* syllable⟩ **7 :** ionizing only slightly in solution ⟨*weak* acids⟩ [Old Norse *veikr*] — **weak·ly** *adv*

weak·en \ˈwē-kən\ *vb* **weak·ened; weak·en·ing** \ˈwēk-niŋ, -ə-niŋ\ **:** to make or become weak or weaker ⟨disease *weakens* the body⟩ ⟨a steadily *weakening* storm⟩

weak·fish \ˈwēk-ˌfish\ *n* **:** a common fish of the eastern coast of the U.S. that is related to the drums and is an important food and sport fish; *also* **:** any of several related fishes used for food [Dutch *weekvis,* from *week* "soft" + *vis* "fish"; from its tender flesh]

weak force *n* **:** a fundamental force experienced by elementary particles that causes some forms of radioactivity and also causes some types of particles to break down into other particles

weak·heart·ed \-ˈhärt-əd\ *adj* **:** lacking courage : FAINTHEARTED

weak–kneed \ˈwēk-ˈnēd\ *adj* **:** lacking willpower or determination : IRRESOLUTE

weak·ling \ˈwē-kliŋ\ *n* **:** one that is weak in body or character — **weakling** *adj*

weak·ly \ˈwē-klē\ *adj* **weak·li·er; -est :** FEEBLE 1, WEAK — **weak·li·ness** *n*

weak–mind·ed \ˈwēk-ˈmīn-dəd\ *adj* **1 :** lacking in judgment or good sense : FOOLISH **2 :** FEEBLEMINDED — **weak–mind·ed·ness** *n*

weak·ness \ˈwēk-nəs\ *n* **1 :** the quality or state of being weak; *also* **:** an instance or period of being weak ⟨backed down in a moment of *weakness*⟩ **2 :** DEFECT, FAULT **3 a :** a special desire or fondness ⟨has a *weakness* for chocolate⟩ **b :** an object of special desire or fondness ⟨pizza is my *weakness*⟩

[1]weal \ˈwēl\ *n* **:** WELL-BEING, PROSPERITY [Middle English *wele,* from Old English *wela*]

[2]weal *n* **:** WELT 2a [alteration of *wale*]

weald \ˈwēld\ *n* **1 :** a heavily wooded area : FOREST **2 :** a wild or uncultivated usually upland region [the *Weald,* wooded district in southeastern England]

wealth \ˈwelth\ *n* **1 :** abundance of possessions or resources : AFFLUENCE **2 :** abundant supply : PROFUSION ⟨a *wealth* of detail⟩ **3 a :** all property that has a money or an exchange value **b :** all material objects that have economic utility; *esp* **:** the stock of useful goods having economic value in existence at any one time ⟨national *wealth*⟩ [Middle English *welthe,* from *wele* "weal"]

wealthy \ˈwel-thē\ *adj* **wealth·i·er; -est 1 :** having wealth : AFFLUENT **2 :** characterized by abundance — **wealth·i·ly** \-thə-lē\ *adv* — **wealth·i·ness** \-thē-nəs\ *n*

wean \ˈwēn\ *vt* **1 :** to accustom (as a young child or animal) to take food otherwise than by nursing **2 :** to turn (one) away from something long desired or followed ⟨*wean* a person from a bad habit⟩ [Old English *wenian* "to accustom, wean"] — **wean·er** *n*

wean·ling \-liŋ\ *n* **:** a child or animal newly weaned — **weanling** *adj*

weap·on \ˈwep-ən\ *n* **1 :** something (as a gun, knife, or club) used to injure, defeat, or destroy **2 :** a means by which one contends against another ⟨propaganda is a *weapon* of war⟩ [Old English *wǣpen*]

weap·on·ize \ˈwep-ə-ˌnīz\ *vt* **-ized; -iz·ing :** to adopt for use as a weapon of war — **weap·on·i·za·tion** \ˌwep-ən-ə-ˈzā-shən\ *n*

weap·on·less \-ləs\ *adj* **:** lacking weapons : UNARMED

weap·on·ry \-rē\ *n* **1 :** the science of designing and making weapons **2 :** aggregate of weapons

[1]wear \ˈwaər, ˈweər\ *vb* **wore** \ˈwōr, ˈwȯr\; **worn** \ˈwōrn, ˈwȯrn\; **wear·ing 1 a :** to bear on the person or use habitually for clothing, adornment, or assistance ⟨*wore* a jacket⟩ ⟨*wears* glasses⟩ **b :** to carry on the person ⟨*wear* a watch⟩ **2 :** to have or show an appearance of ⟨*wore* a happy smile⟩ **3 a :** to impair, diminish, or decay by use or attrition ⟨the towel finally *wore* to bits⟩ ⟨letters on the stone *worn* away by weathering⟩ **b :** to produce gradually by attrition ⟨*wear* a hole in the rug⟩ **c :** to exhaust or lessen the strength of : WEARY, FATIGUE ⟨soldiers *worn* by the strain of war⟩ **4 :** to stand up under use or the passage of time ⟨a coat that has *worn* well⟩ **5 :** to lessen or fail with the passage of time ⟨nagging *wore* my patience away⟩ ⟨the day *wore* on⟩ ⟨the effect of the medicine *wore* off⟩ **6 :** to go or cause to go about by turning the stern to the wind [Old English *werian*] — **wear·able** \ˈwar-ə-bəl, ˈwer-\ *adj* — **wear·er** \-ər\ *n* — **wear on :** IRRITATE 1, FRAY

[2]wear *n* **1 :** the act of wearing : the state of being worn : USE ⟨clothes for everyday *wear*⟩ **2 :** clothing or an article of clothing usually of a particular kind or for a special occasion or use ⟨casual *wear*⟩ **3 :** wearing quality : durability under use **4 :** the result of wearing or use : diminution or impairment due to use ⟨*wear*-resistant surface⟩

wear and tear *n* **:** the loss or injury to which something is subjected by or in the course of use; *esp* **:** normal depreciation

wear down *vt* **:** to weary and overcome by persistent effort or pressure

wea·ri·less \ˈwir-ē-ləs\ *adj* **:** not subject to fatigue : TIRELESS — **wea·ri·less·ly** *adv*

wear·ing \ˈwaər-iŋ, ˈweər-\ *adj* **:** subjecting to or inflicting wear; *esp* **:** that fatigues ⟨a *wearing* journey⟩ — **wear·ing·ly** \-iŋ-lē\ *adv*

wea·ri·some \ˈwir-ē-səm\ *adj* **:** causing weariness : TIRESOME — **wea·ri·some·ly** *adv* — **wea·ri·some·ness** *n*

wear out *vb* **1 :** to make or become useless by wear **2 :** to weary especially to exhaustion

[1]wea·ry \ˈwiər-ē\ *adj* **wea·ri·er; -est 1 :** worn out in strength, endurance, vigor, or freshness **2 :** expressing or characteristic of weariness ⟨a *weary* sigh⟩ **3 :** having one's patience, tolerance, or pleasure exhausted — used with *of* ⟨grew *weary* of their complaining⟩ **4 :** WEARISOME [Old English *wērig*] — **wea·ri·ly** \ˈwir-ə-lē\ *adv* — **wea·ri·ness** \ˈwir-ē-nəs\ *n*

[2]**weary** *vb* **wea·ried; wea·ry·ing :** to become or make weary

wea·sand \ˈwēz-nd\ *n* : THROAT 1, GULLET; *also* : TRACHEA [Middle English *wesand*]

[1]**wea·sel** \ˈwē-zəl\ *n, pl* **weasels 1** *or pl* **weasel :** any of various small slender active mammals that are related to the minks, feed on small animals (as mice, voles, and birds), are mostly brown with white or yellowish underparts, and in northern forms turn white in winter — compare ERMINE 1a **2 :** a sneaky, untrustworthy, or dishonest person [Old English *weosule*]

weasel 1

[2]**weasel** *vi* **wea·seled; wea·sel·ing** \ˈwēz-ling, -ə-ling\ **1 :** to speak evasively : EQUIVOCATE **2 :** to escape from or evade a situation or obligation — often used with *out* [*weasel word*]

weasel word *n* : a word used in order to avoid being clear or direct [from the weasel's reputed habit of sucking the contents from an egg while leaving the shell superficially intact]

[1]**weath·er** \ˈwe<u>th</u>-ər\ *n* **1 :** state of the atmosphere with respect to heat or cold, wetness or dryness, calm or storm, clearness or cloudiness **2 :** a particular and especially a disagreeable atmospheric state ⟨stormy *weather*⟩ [Old English *weder*] — **under the weather :** somewhat ill or drunk

[2]**weather** *adj* : WINDWARD — compare LEE

[3]**weather** *vb* **weath·ered; weath·er·ing** \ˈwe<u>th</u>-ring, -ə-ring\ **1 :** to change by exposure to the weather ⟨shingles *weathered* to a silvery gray⟩ **2 :** to bear up against and come safely through ⟨*weather* a storm⟩

weath·er·abil·i·ty \ˌwe<u>th</u>-rə-ˈbil-ət-ē, -ə-rə-\ *n* : capability of withstanding weather ⟨*weatherability* of a plastic⟩

weath·er–beat·en \ˈwe<u>th</u>-ər-ˌbēt-n\ *adj* **1 :** toughened or colored by the weather ⟨a *weather-beaten* face⟩ **2 :** worn or damaged by exposure to the weather ⟨a *weather-beaten* old barn⟩

weath·er·board \-ˌbōrd, -ˌbȯrd\ *n* : CLAPBOARD, SIDING

weath·er·board·ing \-ˌbōrd-ing, -ˌbȯrd-\ *n* : SIDING 2

weath·er–bound \-ˌbau̇nd\ *adj* : restrained or forced to be inactive by bad weather

weather bureau *n* : a government organization that collects weather reports, formulates weather predictions and storm warnings, and compiles weather statistics

weath·er·cock \-ˌkäk\ *n* **1 :** a vane often in the figure of a rooster that turns with the wind to show the wind's direction **2 :** one that changes readily or often

weath·er·glass \-ˌglas\ *n* : a simple instrument for showing changes in atmospheric pressure by the changing level of liquid in a spout connected with a closed reservoir

weatherglass

weath·er·ing *n* : alteration of exposed objects by action of the elements; *esp* : physical disintegration and chemical decomposition of earth materials at or near the earth's surface

weath·er·ize \ˈwe<u>th</u>-ə-ˌrīz\ *vt* : to make (as a house) better protected against winter weather

weath·er·man \ˈwe<u>th</u>-ər-ˌman\ *n* : one who reports and forecasts the weather : METEOROLOGIST

weather map *n* : a chart showing the principal meteorological features at a given hour over an extended region

weath·er·per·son \ˈweth-ər-ˌpərs-n\ *n* : a person who reports and forecasts the weather : METEOROLOGIST

weath·er·proof \ˌwe<u>th</u>-ər-ˈprüf\ *adj* : able to withstand exposure to weather without damage or loss of function ⟨a *weatherproof* coat⟩ ⟨*weatherproof* cameras⟩ — **weatherproof** *vt*

weather station *n* : a station for taking, recording, and reporting meteorological observations

weather strip *n* : a strip of material used to make a seal where a door or window joins the sill or casing — called also *weather stripping* — **weather–strip** *vt*

weather vane *n* : VANE 1

weath·er·worn \-ˌwōrn, -ˌwȯrn\ *adj* : worn by exposure to the weather

[1]**weave** \ˈwēv\ *vb* **wove** \ˈwōv\ *or* **weaved; wo·ven** \ˈwō-vən\ *or* **weaved; weav·ing 1 a :** to form by interlacing strands of material; *esp* : to make (cloth) on a loom by interlacing warp and filling threads **b :** to interlace (as threads) into a fabric and especially cloth **2 :** SPIN 2b ⟨a caterpillar *weaves* a cocoon⟩ **3 a :** to produce by elaborately combining elements ⟨*weave* a plot⟩ **b :** to unite in a coherent whole **c :** to introduce as an appropriate element : work in ⟨*wove* the episodes into a story⟩ ⟨*weave* a moral into a tale⟩ **4 :** to direct or move in a winding or zigzag course especially to avoid obstacles ⟨*weaving* through traffic⟩ [Old English *wefan*]

[2]**weave** *n* : a pattern or method of weaving ⟨a loose *weave*⟩

[3]**weave** *vi* : to move in a wavering manner from side to side : SWAY [Middle English *weven* "to move to and fro, wave"]

weav·er \ˈwē-vər\ *n* **1 :** one that weaves especially as an occupation **2 :** WEAVER BIRD

weaver bird *n* : any of a family of Old World birds that resemble finches and typically construct elaborate nests of interlaced vegetation

weaver bird

[1]**web** \ˈweb\ *n* **1 :** a fabric on a loom or in process of being removed from a loom **2 a :** COBWEB 1, SPIDERWEB **b :** a network of silken threads spun especially by the larvae of various insects (as a tent caterpillar) and usually serving as a nest or shelter **c :** SNARE 2, ENTANGLEMENT ⟨caught in a *web* of fear⟩ **3 :** a membrane of an animal or plant; *esp* : one uniting toes (as of many waterbirds) **4 :** the plate connecting the upper and lower flanges of a girder or rail **5 :** an intricate pattern or structure suggestive of something woven : NETWORK ⟨a *web* of little roads⟩ ⟨a complex *web* of relationships⟩ **6 :** VANE 3a **7 :** a continuous sheet of paper manufactured or undergoing manufacture or a reel of this for use in a rotary printing press **8** *cap* : WORLD WIDE WEB [Old English] — **web·by** \ˈweb-ē\ *adj* — **web·like** \ˈweb-ˌlīk\ *adj*

[2]**web** *vb* **webbed; web·bing 1 :** to cover or provide with webs or a network **2 :** to form a web

webbed \ˈwebd\ *adj* : having or joined by a web ⟨*webbed* feet⟩

web·bing \ˈweb-ing\ *n* : a strong closely woven tape used especially for straps, harness, or upholstery

web·cam \ˈweb-ˌkam\ *n, often cap* : a camera used in transmitting live images over the World Wide Web

web·foot \ˈweb-ˈfu̇t\ *n* : a foot having webbed toes — **web–foot·ed** \-əd\ *adj*

web·i·sode \ˈweb-ə-ˌsōd\ *n* : an episode (as of a television series) that is shown over the Internet instead of being broadcast [blend of *Web* and *episode*]

web·mas·ter \ˈweb-ˌmas-tər\ *n* : a person whose job is to create and maintain a Web site

Web site *n* : a group of World Wide Web pages usually containing hyperlinks to each other and made available online by an individual, company, or organization

web·worm \ˈweb-ˌwərm\ *n* : any of various caterpillars that spin large webs

wed \ˈwed\ *vb* **wed·ded** *also* **wed; wed·ding 1 :** to marry or get married **2 :** to unite firmly [Old English *weddian*]

we'd \wēd, ˌwēd\ : we had : we should : we would

wed·ding \ˈwed-ing\ *n* **1 :** a marriage ceremony usually with accompanying festivities **2 :** a joining in close association

[1]wedge \ˈwej\ *n* **1 :** a piece of wood or metal tapered to a thin edge and used especially to split wood or rocks and in lifting heavy weights — compare SIMPLE MACHINE **2 :** something (as a piece of pie or land or a formation of wild geese) shaped like a wedge **3 a :** something (as a policy or action) that serves to cause a separation or break ⟨the decision drove a *wedge* between them⟩ **b :** something that serves to open the way for an action or development [Old English *wecg*]

wedge 1

[2]wedge *vt* **1 :** to fasten or tighten by or as if by driving in a wedge **2 a :** to press or force (something) into a narrow space ⟨*wedged* paper under the table leg⟩ **b :** to force (one's way) into or through ⟨*wedged* his way into the crowd⟩ **3 :** to separate or split with or as if with a wedge ⟨he *wedged* open the log to split smaller pieces⟩

Wedg·wood \ˈwej-ˌwu̇d\ *trademark* — used for ceramic wares

wed·lock \ˈwed-ˌläk\ *n* **:** the state of being married **:** MARRIAGE [Old English *wedlāc* "marriage bond," from *wedd* "pledge" + *-lāc,* suffix denoting activity] — **out of wedlock :** with the natural parents not legally married to each other ⟨born *out of wedlock*⟩

Wednes·day \ˈwenz-dē\ *n* **:** the 4th day of the week [Old English *wōdnesdæg,* literally, "day of Odin"]

wee \ˈwē\ *adj* **1 :** very small **:** TINY **2 :** very early ⟨*wee* hours of the morning⟩ [Middle English *we,* from *we* "little bit," from Old English *wǣge* "weight"]

[1]weed \ˈwēd\ *n* **1 :** a plant not valued where it is growing and usually of vigorous growth; *esp* **:** one tending to overgrow or choke out more desirable plants **2 :** something like a weed in harmfulness [Old English *wēod*] — **weed·less** \-ləs\ *adj*

[2]weed *vb* **1 a :** to free from or remove weeds ⟨*weed* a garden⟩ **b :** to free from something harmful, inferior, or superfluous ⟨*weeded* his stamp collection⟩ **2 :** to get rid of ⟨*weed* out the troublemakers⟩ — **weed·er** *n*

[3]weed *n* **1 :** GARMENT — often used in plural **2 :** dress worn (as by a widow) as a sign of mourning — usually used in plural [Old English *wǣd*]

weedy \ˈwēd-ē\ *adj* **weed·i·er; -est 1 :** abounding with or consisting of weeds ⟨a *weedy* field⟩ **2 :** resembling a weed especially in strong rapid growth **3 :** noticeably lean and scrawny **:** LANKY ⟨*weedy* cattle⟩

week \ˈwēk\ *n* **1 :** a calendar period of seven days beginning with Sunday and ending with Saturday **2 a :** seven successive days ⟨was sick for a *week*⟩ **b :** the working or school days of the calendar week ⟨had a hard *week*⟩ [Old English *wicu*]

week·day \-ˌdā\ *n* **:** a day of the week except Sunday or sometimes except Saturday and Sunday

week·days \-ˌdāz\ *adv* **:** on weekdays repeatedly **:** on any weekday ⟨takes a bus *weekdays*⟩

[1]week·end \ˈwē-ˌkend\ *n* **:** the end of the week; *esp* **:** the period between the close of one working or school week and the beginning of the next

[2]weekend *vi* **:** to spend the weekend ⟨likes to *weekend* with friends at the beach⟩

week·ends \-ˌendz, -ˌenz\ *adv* **:** on weekends repeatedly **:** on any weekend ⟨travels *weekends*⟩

[1]week·ly \ˈwē-klē\ *adj* **1 :** occurring, done, produced, or issued every week ⟨*weekly* meetings⟩ **2 :** computed in terms of one week ⟨*weekly* wages⟩ — **weekly** *adv*

[2]weekly *n, pl* **week·lies :** a weekly publication

wee·ny \ˈwē-nē\ *adj* **:** exceptionally small [alteration of *wee*]

weep \ˈwēp\ *vb* **wept** \ˈwept\; **weep·ing 1 a :** to express emotion and especially sorrow by shedding tears **:** CRY **b :** to pour forth (tears) from the eyes **2 :** to give off (liquid) slowly or in drops **:** OOZE ⟨a tree *weeping* sap⟩ [Old English *wēpan*] — **weep·er** \ˈwē-pər\ *n*

weep·ing \ˈwē-ping\ *adj* **1 :** TEARFUL **2** *archaic* **:** RAINY **3 :** having slender pendent branches ⟨a *weeping* cherry⟩

weeping willow *n* **:** an Asian willow naturalized in North America that has slender drooping branches

weepy \ˈwē-pē\ *adj* **weep·i·er; -est :** inclined to weep ⟨friends growing *weepy* as graduation drew near⟩

wee·vil \ˈwē-vəl\ *n* **:** any of a family of mostly small beetles that have the head long and usually curved downward to form a snout bearing the jaws at the tip and that include many that feed on and are destructive to plants or plant products (as nuts, fruit, or grain) especially as larvae — compare BOLL WEEVIL [Old English *wifel*] — **wee·vily** *or* **wee·vil·ly** \ˈwēv-lē, -ə-lē\ *adj*

weft \ˈweft\ *n* **1 a :** WOOF 1 **b :** yarn used for the woof **2 :** material made by spinning or weaving [Old English]

weft knit *n* **:** a knit fabric in which the knitting is done with the yarns running in a crosswise or circular direction (as in hand knitting) — compare WARP KNIT — **weft knitting** *n*

wei·ge·la \wī-ˈjē-lə\ *n* **:** any of a genus of showy East Asian shrubs related to the honeysuckles; *esp* **:** one widely grown for its usually pink or red flowers [Christian E. *Weigel,* died 1831, German physician]

weigh \ˈwā\ *vb* **1 a :** to ascertain the heaviness of by or as if by a balance ⟨*weighed* the bag of onions on a scale⟩ **b :** to have weight or a specified weight ⟨he *weighs* 200 pounds⟩ **2 a :** to consider carefully **:** PONDER ⟨*weigh* the pros and cons⟩ **b :** to merit consideration as important **:** COUNT ⟨fears the new evidence will *weigh* against them⟩ **3 :** to heave up (an anchor) preparatory to sailing **4 :** to measure or apportion (a definite quantity) on or as if on a scale ⟨*weigh* out one gram of tin⟩ **5 a :** to press down with or as if with a heavy weight ⟨the helmet was *weighing* on my head⟩ **b :** to have a saddening or disheartening effect ⟨guilt *weighed* on my mind⟩ [Old English *wegan* "to move, carry, weigh"] — **weigh·able** \ˈwā-ə-bəl\ *adj* — **weigh·er** *n*

weigh down *vt* **1 :** OVERBURDEN ⟨branches *weighed down* by fruit⟩ **2 :** OPPRESS 1, DEPRESS ⟨financial difficulties *weighed* the family *down*⟩

weigh in *vi* **:** to have oneself or one's possessions weighed; *esp* **:** to have oneself weighed prior to a sports event

[1]weight \ˈwāt\ *n* **1 a :** the amount that something weighs ⟨worth its *weight* in gold⟩ **b :** the standard or established amount that something should weigh ⟨a coin of full *weight*⟩ **2 a :** a quantity or portion weighing a usually specific amount ⟨add the necessary *weight* of sand⟩ **b :** a heavy object (as a metal ball) thrown, put, or lifted as an athletic exercise or contest **3 a :** a unit (as a pound or kilogram) of weight or mass — see MEASURE table; see METRIC SYSTEM table **b :** an object (as a piece of metal) of known specified weight for balancing a scale in weighing other objects **c :** a system of related units of weight **4 a :** something heavy **:** LOAD **b :** a heavy object used to hold or press something down or to counterbalance **5 :** a mental or emotional burden ⟨had a *weight* on my conscience⟩ **6 a :** relative heaviness **:** MASS **b :** the force with which a body is attracted toward the earth or a celestial body by gravitation and which is equal to the product of the mass and the local gravitational acceleration **7 a :** the relative importance or authority accorded something **:** NOTE ⟨opinions that carry *weight*⟩ **b :** measurable influence especially on others ⟨throw one's *weight* behind a candidate⟩ **8 :** overpowering force ⟨the *weight* of the evidence favors this view⟩ [Old English *wiht*]

[2]weight *vt* **1 :** to load or make heavy with or as if with a weight **2 :** to oppress with a burden ⟨*weighted* down with cares⟩ **3 :** to assign a relative importance to (as in a statistical study)

weight·less \ˈwāt-ləs\ *adj* **:** having little weight **:** lacking apparent gravitational pull — **weight·less·ly** *adv* — **weight·less·ness** *n*

weight lifter *n* **:** one who lifts barbells in competition or as an exercise — **weight lifting** *n*

weighty \ˈwāt-ē\ *adj* **weight·i·er; -est 1 :** having much weight **:** HEAVY **2 a :** of much importance or consequence **:** SERIOUS ⟨*weighty* problems⟩ **b :** expressing seriousness **:** SOLEMN ⟨a *weighty* manner⟩ **3 :** exerting authority or influence ⟨*weighty* arguments in favor of change⟩ — **weight·i·ly** \ˈwāt-l-ē\ *adv* — **weight·i·ness** \ˈwāt-ē-nəs\ *n*

wei·ma·ra·ner \ˌvī-mə-ˈrän-ər, ˈwī-mə-ˌ\ *n* **:** any of a German breed of large gray short-haired pointers [German, from *Weimar,* Germany]

weir \ˈwaər, ˈweər, ˈwiər\ *n* **1 :** a fence set in a stream to catch fish **2 :** a dam in a stream to raise the water level or divert its flow [Old English *wer*]

weird \ˈwiərd\ *adj* **1 :** of, relating to, or caused by witchcraft or the supernatural **:** MAGICAL **2 :** of strange or extraordinary character **:** ODD, FANTASTIC ⟨cold temperatures that were *weird* for June⟩ [Middle English *werd* "fate," from Old English *wyrd*] — **weird·ly** *adv* — **weird·ness** *n*

Word History *Weird* is derived from an Old English noun *wyrd,* meaning "fate." The Middle English form *werd* is found primarily as a noun in Scottish and northern contexts. Not until the 15th century is this word recorded in an attributive or adjectival position, and then only in the combination *weird sister.* The Weird Sisters were the three Fates. Finally in the 18th century *weird* began to appear in other contexts as an adjective meaning "magical," "odd," or "fantastic."

synonyms WEIRD, EERIE, UNCANNY mean mysteriously strange or fantastic. WEIRD may imply an unearthly or supernatural strangeness or it may stress queerness or oddness ⟨*weird* creatures from another world⟩. EERIE suggests an uneasy or fearful consciousness of the presence of mysterious and malign powers ⟨an *eerie* calm preceded the storm⟩. UNCANNY implies unsettling strangeness or mysteriousness ⟨an *uncanny* resemblance between the two strangers⟩.

Weird Sisters *n pl* : the three Fates

Welch *variant of* WELSH

[1]**wel•come** \'wel-kəm\ *interj* — used to express a greeting to a guest or newcomer upon arrival [Old English *wilcume,* from *wilcuma* "desirable guest"]

[2]**welcome** *vt* **1** : to greet hospitably and with courtesy **2** : to meet or face with pleasure ⟨*welcomes* a challenge⟩ — **wel•com•er** *n*

[3]**welcome** *adj* **1** : received gladly into one's presence or companionship ⟨a *welcome* visitor⟩ **2** : giving pleasure ⟨*welcome* news⟩ **3** : willingly permitted to do, have, or enjoy something ⟨anyone is *welcome* to join⟩ **4** — used in the phrase "You're welcome" as a reply to an expression of thanks

[4]**welcome** *n* : a cordial greeting or reception

[1]**weld** \'weld\ *vb* **1** : to join (pieces of metal or plastic) by heating and allowing the edges to flow together or by hammering or pressing together **2** : to join as if by welding ⟨*welded* together in friendship⟩ **3** : to become or be capable of being welded ⟨not all metals *weld* well⟩ [Middle English *wellen* "to boil, well, weld"] — **weld•er** *n*

[2]**weld** *n* **1** : a welded joint **2** : union by welding

weld•ment \'weld-mənt\ *n* : a unit formed by welding together an assembly of pieces

wel•fare \'wel-ˌfaər, -ˌfeər\ *n* **1** : the state of doing well especially in respect to happiness, well-being, or prosperity ⟨must look out for your own *welfare*⟩ **2 a** : aid in the form of money or necessities for those in need **b** : an agency or program through which such aid is distributed [Middle English, from *wel faren* "to fare well"] — **welfare** *adj*

welfare state *n* : a social system in which the government takes on much of the responsibility for the individual and social welfare of its citizens

wel•kin \'wel-kən\ *n* **1** : SKY 1 **2** : AIR 1a [Old English *wolcen* "cloud"]

[1]**well** \'wel\ *n* **1 a** : an issue of water from the earth : a pool fed by a spring **b** : a source of supply : WELLSPRING ⟨was a *well* of information⟩ **2** : a hole sunk into the earth to reach a natural deposit (as of water, oil, or gas) **3** : an enclosure in the middle of a ship's hold around the pumps **4** : an open space extending vertically through floors of a structure (as for a staircase) **5** : something suggesting a well (as in being damp, cool, deep, or dark) [Old English *welle*]

[2]**well** *vi* : to rise to the surface and flow forth ⟨tears *welled* from their eyes⟩ [Middle English *wellen,* from Old English *wellan* "to cause to well"]

[3]**well** *adv* **bet•ter** \'bet-ər\; **best** \'best\ **1 a** : in a pleasing or desirable manner ⟨the party turned out *well*⟩ **b** : in a good or proper manner ⟨did the work *well*⟩ **2** : in a full or generous manner ⟨eat *well*⟩ ⟨the orchard bore *well*⟩ **3** : with reason or courtesy : PROPERLY ⟨we could not very *well* refuse⟩ **4** : in all respects ⟨a *well* deserved ovation⟩ **5** : in an intimate way ⟨know a person *well*⟩ **6** : MUCH 1a, FAR ⟨*well* ahead⟩ ⟨*well* over the quota⟩ **7** : without trouble or difficulty ⟨I could *well* have gone⟩ **8** : EXACTLY 1a ⟨remember it *well*⟩ [Old English *wel*] — **as well 1** : in addition : ALSO ⟨other features *as well*⟩ **2** : with the same result ⟨might *as well* stop here⟩

[4]**well** *interj* **1** — used to express surprise or expostulation **2** — used to begin a discourse or to resume one that was interrupted

[5]**well** *adj* **1** : SATISFACTORY, PLEASING ⟨all's *well* that ends well⟩ **2 a** : PROSPEROUS 2, WELL-OFF **b** : being in satisfactory condition or circumstances **3** : ADVISABLE, DESIRABLE ⟨not *well* to anger them⟩ **4 a** : free or recovered from illness or disease : HEALTHY ⟨he's not a *well* man⟩ **b** : completely cured or healed ⟨the wound is nearly *well*⟩ **5** : being a cause for thankfulness : FORTUNATE ⟨it is *well* that this has happened⟩

synonyms see HEALTHY

we'll \wēl, ˌwēl\ : we shall : we will

well–ad•vised \ˌwel-əd-'vīzd\ *adj* : acting wisely or properly : based on wise counsel ⟨was *well-advised* to follow orders⟩

wel•la•way \ˌwel-ə-'wā\ *interj* — used to express sorrow or lamentation [Old English *weilāwei,* from *wā lā wā* "woe! lo! woe!"]

well–be•ing \'wel-'bē-ing\ *n* : the state of being happy, healthy, or prosperous : WELFARE

well–be•loved \ˌwel-bi-'ləvd\ *adj* **1** : sincerely and deeply loved **2** : sincerely respected — used in various ceremonial forms of address

well•born \'wel-'bòrn\ *adj* : born of noble or wealthy lineage

well–bred \-'bred\ *adj* : having or displaying good breeding : REFINED

well–con•di•tioned \ˌwel-kən-'dish-ənd\ *adj* **1** : characterized by proper disposition, morals, or behavior **2** : having a good physical condition : SOUND ⟨a *well-conditioned* animal⟩

well–de•fined \ˌwel-di-'fīnd\ *adj* **1** : having clearly distinguishable limits or boundaries ⟨a *well-defined* scar⟩ **2** : clearly stated or described ⟨*well-defined* policies⟩

well–dis•posed \-dis-'pōzd\ *adj* : disposed to be friendly, favorable, or sympathetic ⟨*well-disposed* to our plan⟩

well–done \'wel-'dən\ *adj* **1** : rightly or properly performed **2** : cooked thoroughly ⟨a *well-done* steak⟩

well–en•dowed \'wel-in-'daůd\ *adj* : WELL-FIXED

well–fa•vored \'wel-'fā-vərd\ *adj* : good-looking : HANDSOME

well–fixed \-'fikst\ *adj* : well-off financially

well–found \-'faůnd\ *adj* : fully furnished : properly equipped ⟨a *well-found* ship⟩

well–found•ed \-'faůn-dəd\ *adj* : based on sound reasoning, information, judgment, or grounds ⟨*well-founded* suspicions⟩

well–groomed \-'grümd, -'grůmd\ *adj* **1** : well dressed and extremely neat **2** : made neat, tidy, and attractive down to the smallest details ⟨a *well-groomed* lawn⟩

well–ground•ed \-'graůn-dəd\ *adj* : having a firm foundation : WELL-FOUNDED

well•head \'wel-ˌhed\ *n* **1 a** : the source of a spring or a stream **b** : principal source **2** : the top of or a structure over a well

well–heeled \'wel-'hēld\ *adj* : WELL-FIXED

well–known \-'nōn\ *adj* : fully or widely known

well–mean•ing \-'mē-ning\ *adj* : having or based on good intentions

well•ness \'wel-nəs\ *n* : the quality or state of being in good health especially as an actively sought goal

well–nigh \-'nī\ *adv* : ALMOST, NEARLY

well–off \'wel-'òf\ *adj* : being in good condition or circumstances; *esp* : well supplied with material possessions

well–or•dered \-'òrd-ərd\ *adj* : having an orderly procedure or arrangement ⟨a *well-ordered* household⟩

well–read \-'red\ *adj* : well informed or deeply versed through reading ⟨*well-read* in history⟩

well–spo•ken \-'spō-kən\ *adj* **1** : having a good command of language : speaking well and especially courteously **2** : spoken with propriety ⟨*well-spoken* words⟩

well•spring \'wel-ˌspring\ *n* **1** : FOUNTAINHEAD 1 **2** : a source of continual supply

well–timed \'wel-'tīmd\ *adj* : occurring opportunely : TIMELY

well–to–do \ˌwel-tə-'dü\ *adj* : having more than adequate material resources : PROSPEROUS

well–turned \'wel-'tərnd\ *adj* **1** : pleasingly shaped : SHAPELY **2** : pleasingly and appropriately expressed ⟨a *well-turned* phrase⟩

well–wish•er \'wel-ˌwish-ər\ *n* : one that wishes well to another — **well–wish•ing** \-ˌwish-ing\ *adj or n*

well–worn \-'wōrn, -'wòrn\ *adj* **1 a** : worn by much use ⟨*well-worn* shoes⟩ **b** : made stale by overuse : TRITE ⟨a *well-worn* quotation⟩ **2** : worn well or properly ⟨*well-worn* honors⟩

welsh *also* **welch** \'welsh, 'welch\ *vi* **1** *sometimes offensive* : to avoid payment — used with *on* **2** *sometimes offensive* : to break one's work : RENEGE 2 [probably from *Welsh,* adj.] — **welsh•er** *n, sometimes offensive*

Welsh *also* **Welch** \'welsh *also* 'welch\ *n* **1** *pl in constr* : the natives or inhabitants of Wales **2** : the Celtic language of the Welsh people [Old English *wǣlisc* "Celtic, Welsh, foreign," from *Wealh* "Celt, Welshman, foreigner," of Celtic origin] — **Welsh**

\ə\ **a**bout	\aů\ **ou**t	\i\ t**i**p	\ò\ s**aw**	\ů\ f**oo**t
\ər\ f**ur**ther	\ch\ **ch**in	\ī\ l**i**fe	\òi\ c**oi**n	\y\ **y**et
\a\ m**a**t	\e\ p**e**t	\j\ **j**ob	\th\ **th**in	\yü\ f**ew**
\ā\ t**a**ke	\ē\ **ea**sy	\ng\ si**ng**	\t͟h\ **th**is	\yů\ c**ur**e
\ä\ c**o**t, c**a**rt	\g\ **g**o	\ō\ b**o**ne	\ü\ f**oo**d	\zh\ vi**si**on

also **Welch** *adj* — **Welsh•man** \-mən\ *n* — **Welsh•wom•an** \-ˌwu̇m-ən\ *n*

Welsh cor•gi \-ˈkȯr-gē\ *n* : a Welsh dog that has a foxy head, short legs, and long body and occurs in two breeds: **a** : CARDIGAN WELSH CORGI **b** : PEMBROKE WELSH CORGI [Welsh *corgi,* from *cor* "dwarf" + *ci* "dog"]

Welsh•man \ˈwelsh-mən *also* ˈwelch-\ *n* : a native or inhabitant of Wales

Welsh rabbit *n* : melted often seasoned cheese poured over toast or crackers

Welsh rare•bit \-ˈraər-bət, -ˈreər-\ *n* : WELSH RABBIT [by alteration]

[1]welt \ˈwelt\ *n* **1** : the narrow strip of leather between a shoe upper and sole to which other parts are stitched **2 a** : a ridge or lump raised on the skin (as by a blow or allergic reaction) **b** : a heavy blow [Middle English *welte*]

[2]welt *vt* **1** : to furnish with a welt **2 a** : to raise a welt on ⟨mosquitoes *welted* my arms⟩ **b** : to hit hard

[1]wel•ter \ˈwel-tər\ *vi* **1 a** : to twist or roll one's body about : WALLOW **b** : to rise and fall or toss about in or with waves **2** : to become deeply sunk, soaked, or involved ⟨*weltered* in misery⟩ **3** : to be in turmoil [Middle English *welteren*]

[2]welter *n* **1** : a state of wild disorder : TURMOIL **2** : a chaotic mass or jumble ⟨a *welter* of conflicting regulations⟩

[3]welter *n* : WELTERWEIGHT

wel•ter•weight \-ˌwāt\ *n* : a boxer in a weight division having an upper limit of 147 pounds [*welter* (probably from [1]*welt*) + *weight*]

wen \ˈwen\ *n* : a cyst formed by obstruction of a skin gland and filled with fatty material [Old English *wenn*]

wench \ˈwench\ *n* **1** : a young woman : GIRL **2** : a female servant [Middle English *wenchel, wenche* "child," from Old English *wencel*]

wend \ˈwend\ *vb* : to direct one's course : proceed on (one's way) ⟨*wending* their way home⟩ [Old English *wendan*]

went *past of* GO [Middle English, past of *wenden* "to wend"]

wen•tle•trap \ˈwent-l-ˌtrap\ *n* : any of a family of marine snails with usually spirally coiled white shells; *also* : one of the shells [Dutch *wenteltrap* "winding stair"]

wept *past and past participle of* WEEP

were *past 2nd sing, past pl, or past subjunctive of* BE [Old English *wǣron,* past pl., *wǣre,* past subjunctive sing., *wǣren,* past subjunctive pl. of *wesan* "to be"]

we're \wiər, ˌwiər, wər, ˌwər\ : we are

weren't \wərnt, ˈwərnt, ˈwər-ənt\ : were not

were•wolf \ˈwiər-ˌwu̇lf, ˈwər-, ˈweər-\ *n, pl* **were•wolves** \-ˌwu̇lvz\ : a person held to be transformed or able to transform into a wolf [Old English *werwulf,* from *wer* "man" + *wulf* "wolf"]

wert \wərt, ˈwərt\ *archaic past 2nd singular of* BE

wes•kit \ˈwes-kət\ *n* : VEST 1a [alteration of *waistcoat*]

Wes•ley•an \ˈwes-lē-ən, ˈwez-\ *adj* **1** : of or relating to John or Charles Wesley **2** : of or relating to the Methodism taught by John Wesley

[1]west \ˈwest\ *adv* : to, toward, or in the west [Old English]

[2]west *adj* **1** : situated toward or at the west ⟨the *west* entrance⟩ **2** : coming from the west ⟨a *west* wind⟩

[3]west *n* **1 a** : the general direction of sunset **b** : the compass point directly opposite to east **2** *cap* **a** : regions or countries west of a specified or implied point **b** : the noncommunist countries of Europe and America **3** : the end of a church opposite the chancel

west•bound \ˈwest-ˌbau̇nd, ˈwes-\ *adj* : headed west ⟨a *westbound* train⟩

west•er \ˈwes-tər\ *vi* **wes•tered; wes•ter•ing** \-tə-ring, -tring\ : to turn or move westward

[1]west•er•ly \ˈwes-tər-lē\ *adv or adj* **1** : from the west ⟨the wind blew *westerly*⟩ ⟨a *westerly* breeze⟩ **2** : toward the west ⟨the *westerly* side of the house⟩ ⟨the ship sailed *westerly*⟩

[2]westerly *n, pl* **-lies** : a wind from the west

[1]west•ern \ˈwes-tərn\ *adj* **1** *cap* : of, relating to, or characteristic of a region conventionally designated West **2** : lying toward or coming from the west ⟨a *western* storm⟩ **3** *cap* : of or relating to the Roman Catholic or Protestant segment of Christianity ⟨*Western* liturgies⟩ [Old English *westerne*] — **west•ern•most** \-ˌmōst\ *adj*

[2]western *n* **1** : one that is produced in or characteristic of a western region and especially the western U.S. **2** *often cap* : a novel, story, motion picture, or broadcast dealing with life in the western U.S. during the latter half of the 19th century

West•ern•er \ˈwes-tər-nər, -tə-nər\ *n* : a native or inhabitant of the West (as of the U.S.)

western hemisphere *n, often cap W&H* : the half of the earth comprising North and South America and surrounding waters

western hemlock *n* : a hemlock ranging from Alaska to California that is commercially important as a timber tree; *also* : its light strong wood

west•ern•ize \ˈwes-tər-ˌnīz\ *vt, often cap* : to give western characteristics to — **west•ern•i•za•tion** \ˌwes-tər-nə-ˈzā-shən\ *n, often cap*

western larch *n* : an important timber tree of western North America related to the pines and having deciduous needles; *also* : its strong hard wood

western omelet *n* : an omelet made usually with diced ham, green pepper, and onion

western saddle *n, often cap W* : a large saddle having a deep broad seat and a high front and back

West Germanic *n* : a subdivision of the Germanic languages including English, Frisian, Dutch, and German

West Highland white terrier *n* : any of a breed of small white long-haired terriers developed in Scotland

West Highland white terrier

west•ing \ˈwes-ting\ *n* : westerly progress : a going west

West Nile virus \-ˈnīl-\ *n* **1** : a virus that causes an illness marked by fever, headache, muscle ache, skin rash, and sometimes encephalitis or meningitis and that is spread especially from birds to humans by mosquitos **2** : the illness caused by West Nile virus [from *West Nile* province of Uganda]

west–northwest *n* : a compass point that is two points north of due west : N67°30′W

west–southwest *n* : a compass point that is two points south of due west : S67°30′W

[1]west•ward \ˈwes-twərd\ *adv or adj* : toward the west ⟨moved *westward*⟩ ⟨a *westward* voyage⟩ — **west•wards** \-twərdz\ *adv*

[2]westward *n* : westward direction or part

[1]wet \ˈwet\ *adj* **wet•ter; wet•test** **1 a** : consisting of, containing, covered with, or soaked with liquid (as water) **b** : RAINY ⟨*wet* weather⟩ **2** : still moist enough to smudge or smear ⟨*wet* paint⟩ **3** : permitting or openly supporting the manufacture and sale of alcoholic liquor **4** : involving the use or presence of liquid ⟨*wet* processes⟩ [Old English *wǣt*] — **wet•ly** *adv* — **wet•ness** *n* — **all wet** : completely wrong : in error — **wet behind the ears** : lacking experience : IMMATURE

[2]wet *n* **1** : WATER; *also* : MOISTURE **2** : rainy weather : RAIN **3** : a supporter of a wet liquor policy

[3]wet *vb* **wet** *or* **wet•ted; wet•ting** **1** : to make or become wet **2** : to urinate or urinate in or on ⟨*wet* his pants⟩ — **wet one's whistle** : to take a drink especially of liquor

wet blanket *n* : one that quenches or dampens enthusiasm or pleasure

wet down *vt* : to dampen by sprinkling with water

weth•er \ˈwet͟h-ər\ *n* : a male sheep castrated before sexual maturity [Old English]

wet•land \ˈwet-ˌland\ *n* : land or areas (as marshes or swamps) having much soil moisture — usually used in plural

wet–nurse \ˈwet-ˈnərs\ *vt* **1** : to act as a wet nurse to **2** : to give constant and often excessive care to

wet nurse *n* : a woman who cares for and breast-feeds children not her own

wet suit *n* : a close-fitting rubber suit that traps a thin layer of water against the body to hold body heat and that is worn (as by a skin diver) especially in cold water

wet•ta•ble \ˈwet-ə-bəl\ *adj* : capable of being wetted — **wet•ta•bil•i•ty** \ˌwet-ə-ˈbil-ət-ē\ *n*

wetting agent *n* : a substance that when adsorbed on a surface reduces its tendency to repel a liquid

wet•tish \ˈwet-ish\ *adj* : somewhat wet : MOIST

wet wash *n* : laundry returned damp and not ironed
we've \wēv, ˌwēv\ : we have
[1]**whack** \ˈhwak, ˈwak\ *vb* **1** : to strike with a smart or resounding blow ⟨*whacked* the ball into left field⟩ **2** : to cut with or as if with a whack : CHOP [probably imitative] — **whack·er** *n*
[2]**whack** *n* **1** : a smart or resounding blow; *also* : the sound of or as if of such a blow **2** : PORTION, SHARE ⟨we must each pay our *whack*⟩ **3** : CONDITION, STATE **4 a** : an opportunity or attempt to do something : CHANCE ⟨took a *whack* at it⟩ **b** : a single action or occasion ⟨solved several problems with one *whack*⟩ — **out of whack** : not in good working order or shape
[1]**whack·ing** \ˈhwak-ing, ˈwak-\ *adj* : very large : WHOPPING
[2]**whacking** *adv* : VERY ⟨a *whacking* good story⟩
whack up *vt* : to divide into shares
[1]**whale** \ˈhwāl, ˈwāl\ *n, pl* **whales** **1** *or pl* **whale** : an aquatic mammal (as a humpback whale or a killer whale) that is a cetacean of usually very large size with a torpedo-shaped body, front limbs modified into flippers but no hind limbs, and a tail flattened and extended to the sides as flukes and that usually breathes through an opening on the top of the head; *also* : CETACEAN — compare BALEEN WHALE, TOOTHED WHALE **2** : a person or thing impressive in size or qualities ⟨a *whale* of a story⟩ ⟨it made a *whale* of a difference⟩ [Old English *hwæl*]
[2]**whale** *vi* **whaled; whal·ing** : to hunt whales
[3]**whale** *vt* **1** : THRASH 2 **2** : to strike or hit hard ⟨*whale* the ball⟩ [origin unknown]
whale·boat \-ˌbōt\ *n* **1** : a long narrow rowboat made with both ends sharp and raking, often steered with an oar, and formerly used by whalers for hunting whales **2** : a long narrow rowboat or motorboat resembling the original whaleboats that is often carried by warships and merchant ships
whale·bone \-ˌbōn\ *n* : BALEEN
whalebone whale *n* : BALEEN WHALE
whale oil *n* : an oil obtained from the blubber of whales and formerly used especially in lamps
whal·er \ˈhwā-lər, ˈwā-\ *n* **1** : a person or ship engaged in hunting for whales **2** : WHALEBOAT 2
whale shark *n* : a harmless shark of warm waters that feeds on plankton, may sometimes reach a length of up to 60 feet (18.3 meters), and is the largest known fish

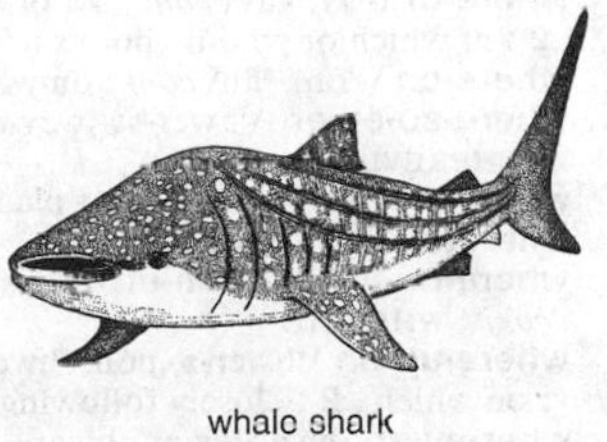

whale shark

whal·ing \ˈhwā-ling, ˈwā-\ *n* : the occupation of catching whales and extracting commercial products from them
[1]**wham** \ˈhwam, ˈwam\ *n* **1** : the loud sound of a hard impact **2** : a solid blow [imitative]
[2]**wham** *vb* **whammed; wham·ming** : to propel, strike, or beat so as to produce a loud impact
wham·my \ˈhwam-ē, ˈwam-\ *n, pl* **whammies** **1** : a supernatural power held to bring bad luck **2** : a magic curse or spell [probably from [1]*wham*]
[1]**whang** \ˈhwang, ˈwang\ *vb* **1** : to propel or strike with force **2** : to beat or work with force or violence [Middle English *thong, thwang* "thong"]
[2]**whang** *n* : a loud sharp vibrant or resonant sound [imitative]
whap *variant of* WHOP
wharf \ˈhwȯrf, ˈwȯrf\ *n, pl* **wharves** \ˈhwȯrvz, ˈwȯrvz\ *also* **wharfs** : a structure built along or out from the shore of navigable waters so that ships may lie alongside to receive and discharge cargo and passengers [Old English *hwearf*]
wharf·age \ˈhwȯr-fij, ˈwȯr-\ *n* **1** : the provision or the use of a wharf **2** : the charge for the use of a wharf
wharf·in·ger \-fən-jər\ *n* : the operator or manager of a commercial wharf [derived from *wharfage*]
wharf·mas·ter \ˈhwȯrf-ˌmas-tər, ˈwȯrf-\ *n* : WHARFINGER
[1]**what** \hwät, ˈhwät, hwət, ˈhwət, wät, ˈwät, wət, ˈwət\ *pron* **1 a** (1) — used as an interrogative in asking about the identity, nature, or value of an object or matter ⟨*what* is this⟩ ⟨*what* do they earn⟩ ⟨*what* is wealth without friends⟩ (2) — used to ask for repetition of an utterance or part of an utterance not properly heard or understood ⟨you said *what*⟩ **b** — used as an interrogative in asking about the character, occupation, or position of a person ⟨*what* do you think I am, a fool⟩ **c** — used as an exclamation expressing surprise or excitement and frequently introducing a question ⟨*what*, no breakfast⟩ **d** — used in expressions directing attention to a statement that the speaker is about to make ⟨you know *what*⟩ **e** (1) — used at the end of a question to express inquiry about additional possibilities ⟨is it raining, or snowing, or *what*⟩ (2) — used with *or* at the end of a question in expectation of agreement ⟨is this exciting, or *what*⟩ **2 a** : that which : the one or ones that ⟨no income but *what* I get from my writings⟩ **b** : the thing or things that ⟨*what* you need is a vacation⟩ **3** : WHATEVER 1a ⟨say *what* you will⟩ [Old English *hwæt,* neuter of *hwā* "who"] — **what for** : for what purpose or reason : WHY — **what have you** : [1]WHATNOT — **what if** **1** : what would happen if ⟨*what if* they find out⟩ **2** : what does it matter if ⟨so *what if* he doesn't like it⟩
[2]**what** *adv* **1** : in what respect : HOW ⟨*what* do you care⟩ **2** — used with *with* to introduce a prepositional phrase that expresses cause ⟨kept busy *what* with studies and athletics⟩
[3]**what** *adj* **1 a** — used as an interrogative expressing inquiry about the identity or nature of a person, object, or matter ⟨*what* minerals do we export⟩ **b** : how remarkable or surprising ⟨*what* a suggestion⟩ ⟨*what* a charming view⟩ **2** : WHATEVER 1a
[1]**what·ev·er** \hwät-ˈev-ər, wät-, hwət-, ˌhwət-, wət-, ˌwət-\ *pron* **1 a** : anything or everything that ⟨take *whatever* is needed⟩ **b** : no matter what ⟨obey orders, *whatever* happens⟩ **2** : [1]WHAT 1a(1) — used to express astonishment or perplexity ⟨*whatever* do you mean by that⟩
[2]**whatever** *adj* **1 a** : any . . . that : all . . . that ⟨take *whatever* action is needed⟩ **b** : no matter what ⟨*whatever* book she reads, she enjoys it⟩ **2** : of any kind at all ⟨no food *whatever*⟩
[1]**what·not** \ˈhwät-ˌnät, ˈhwət-, ˈwät-, ˈwət-\ *pron* : any of various other things that might also be mentioned ⟨pencils and paper and *whatnot*⟩
[2]**whatnot** *n* : a light open set of shelves for bric-a-brac
what·so·ev·er \ˌhwät-sə-ˈwev-ər, ˌhwət-, ˌwät-, ˌwət-\ *pron or adj* : WHATEVER
wheal \ˈhwēl, ˈwēl\ *n* : a suddenly formed elevation of the skin surface : WELT; *esp* : a flat burning or itching eminence on the skin [alteration of *wale*]
wheat \ˈhwēt, ˈwēt\ *n* **1** : a cereal grain that yields a fine white flour used mostly in breads, baked goods (as cakes and crackers), and pastas (as macaroni or spaghetti) and that is important in animal feeds **2** : any of a genus of Old World grasses grown in most temperate areas for the wheat they yield; *esp* : an annual cereal grass with long dense flower spikes and white to dark red grains that is the chief source of wheat and is known only in cultivation [Old English *hwǣte*] — **wheat·en** \-n\ *adj*
wheat cake *n* : a pancake made of wheat flour
wheat·ear \ˈhwēt-ˌiər, ˈwēt-\ *n* : a small white-rumped northern thrush [earlier *wheatears,* probably derived from *white* + Old English *ears* "backside"]
wheat germ *n* : the embryo of the wheat kernel separated in milling and used especially as a source of vitamins and protein
wheat rust *n* : a destructive disease of wheat caused by rust fungi; *also* : a fungus causing a wheat rust
whee \ˈhwē, ˈwē\ *interj* — used to express delight or high spirits
whee·dle \ˈhwēd-l, ˈwēd-\ *vt* **whee·dled; whee·dling** \ˈhwēd-ling, ˈwēd-, -l-ing\ **1** : to coax or entice by soft words or flattery ⟨*wheedled* them into agreeing⟩ **2** : to gain or get by wheedling ⟨*wheedle* one's way into favor⟩ [origin unknown]
[1]**wheel** \ˈhwēl, ˈwēl\ *n* **1** : a disk or circular frame capable of turning on a central axis **2** : something that is like a wheel (as in being round) ⟨a *wheel* of cheese⟩ **3** : a device having as its principal part a wheel: as **a** : BICYCLE **b** : POTTER'S WHEEL **c** : STEERING WHEEL **4 a** : a curving or circular movement **b** : a turning movement of troops or ships in line in which the units preserve alignment and relative positions as they change direction **5 a** : a moving or essential part of something compared to a machine ⟨the *wheels* of government⟩ **b** : a person of importance especially in an organization ⟨he was a big *wheel* in town⟩ **6** *pl, slang* : a wheeled vehicle; *esp* : AUTOMOBILE [Old English *hwēol*] — **wheeled** \ˈhwēld, ˈwēld\ *adj* — **wheel·less** \ˈhwēl-ləs, ˈwēl-\ *adj*
[2]**wheel** *vb* **1** : to carry or move on wheels or in a vehicle with wheels ⟨*wheel* a load into the barn⟩ **2** : to turn or cause to turn

on an axis : REVOLVE ⟨the earth *wheels* about the sun⟩ **3** : to change direction as if revolving on an axis ⟨*wheeled* about⟩ **4** : to move or extend in a circle or curve ⟨birds in *wheeling* flight⟩ — **wheel and deal** : to make deals or do business especially in a shrewd or brisk manner

wheel and axle *n* : a simple machine consisting of a grooved wheel turned by a cord or chain with a rigidly attached axle (as for winding up a weight) together with supports

wheel animal *n* : ROTIFER

wheel·bar·row \ˈhwēl-ˌbar-ō, ˈwēl-\ *n* : a small usually one-wheeled vehicle that is used for carrying small loads and is fitted with handles at the rear by which it can be pushed and guided

wheel·base \-ˌbās\ *n* : the distance between the front and rear axles of an automotive vehicle

wheel·chair \-ˌcheər, -ˌchaər\ *n* : a chair on wheels used especially by sick, injured, or disabled people to get about

wheel·er \ˈhwē-lər, ˈwē-\ *n* **1** : one that wheels **2** : one of a team of horses that pulls from the position nearest the front wheels of a wagon **3** : something (as a vehicle or ship) that has wheels — used especially in combination ⟨side-*wheeler*⟩

wheel·er–deal·er \ˌhwē-lər-ˈdē-lər, ˌwē-\ *n* : a shrewd operator especially in business or politics [from the phrase *wheel* and *deal*]

wheel·horse \ˈhwēl-ˌhȯrs, ˈwēl-\ *n* **1** : WHEELER 2 **2** : a steady and effective worker especially in a political body

wheel·house \-ˌhau̇s\ *n* : PILOTHOUSE

wheels·man \ˈhwēlz-mən, ˈwēlz-\ *n* : one who steers with a wheel; *esp* : HELMSMAN

wheel·wright \ˈhwēl-ˌrīt, ˈwēl-\ *n* : a person whose occupation is to make or repair wheels and wheeled vehicles

[1]wheeze \ˈhwēz, ˈwēz\ *vi* **1** : to breathe with difficulty usually with a whistling sound **2** : to make a sound resembling that of wheezing [Middle English *whesen*]

[2]wheeze *n* **1** : a sound of wheezing **2 a** : an old joke **b** : a trite saying

wheezy \ˈhwē-zē, ˈwē-\ *adj* **wheez·i·er; -est** **1** : tending to wheeze ⟨a *wheezy* infant⟩ **2** : making or having the sound of wheezing ⟨a *wheezy* cough⟩ ⟨*wheezy* old cars⟩ — **wheez·i·ly** \-zə-lē\ *adv* — **wheez·i·ness** \-zē-nəs\ *n*

whelk \ˈhwelk, ˈwelk, ˈwilk\ *n* : any of numerous large marine snails; *esp* : one used as food in Europe [Old English *weoloc*]

whelm \ˈhwelm, ˈwelm\ *vt* : to overcome or engulf completely : OVERWHELM [Middle English *whelmen*]

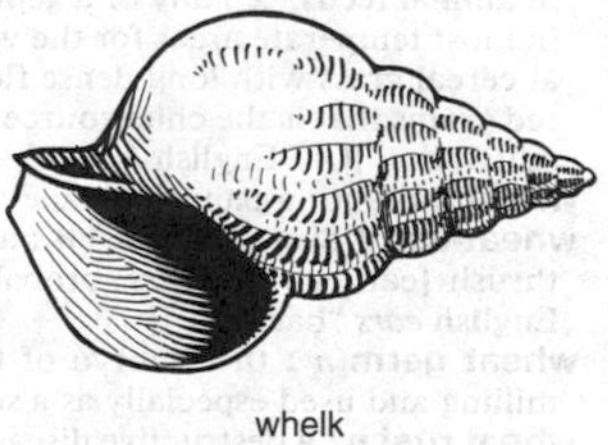

whelk

[1]whelp \ˈhwelp, ˈwelp\ *n* **1** : one of the young of various flesh-eating mammals and especially of the dog **2** : a young person [Old English *hwelp*]

[2]whelp *vb* **1** : to give birth to (whelps) **2** : to bring forth whelps

[1]when \hwen, ˈhwen, wen, ˈwen, hwən, wən\ *adv* **1** : at what time ⟨asked us *when* it happened⟩ **2** : at or during which time ⟨an era *when* the arts decayed⟩ [Old English *hwanne, hwenne*]

[2]when *conj* **1 a** : at or during the time that : WHILE ⟨we go *when* we can⟩ **b** : just at the moment that ⟨left *when* the bell rang⟩ **c** : at any or every time that ⟨my mouth waters *when* I see food⟩ **2** : in the event that : IF ⟨a team is disqualified *when* it disobeys the rules⟩ **3** : in spite of the fact that : ALTHOUGH ⟨gave up politics *when* I might have made a great career in it⟩ **4** : the time or occasion at or in which ⟨tomorrow is *when* we must decide⟩

[3]when \ˌhwen, ˌwen\ *pron* : what or which time ⟨since *when* have you known that⟩

[1]whence \hwens, ˈhwens, wens, ˈwens\ *adv* : from what place, source, or cause ⟨*whence* come all these doubts⟩ [Middle English *whenne, whennes,* from Old English *hwanon*]

[2]whence *conj* : from or out of which place, source, or cause ⟨the land *whence* they came⟩

[1]when·ev·er \hwe-ˈnev-ər, we-, hwə-, wə-\ *conj* : at any or every time that ⟨stop *whenever* you wish⟩

[2]whenever *adv* : at whatever time ⟨available *whenever* needed⟩

when·so·ev·er \ˈhwen-sə-ˌwev-ər, ˈwen-\ *conj* : WHENEVER

[1]where \ˈhweər, ˈhwaər, ˈweər, ˈwaər, ˌhwər, ˌwər; or without stress\ *adv* **1** : at, in, or to what place ⟨*where* are we going⟩ **2** : at, in, or to what situation, position, direction, or circumstances ⟨*where* am I wrong⟩ [Old English *hwǣr*]

[2]where *conj* **1 a** : at, in, or to what place ⟨knows *where* the house is⟩ **b** : at, in, or to what situation, position, direction, or circumstances ⟨see *where* the plan leads⟩ **2** : WHEREVER ⟨sit *where* you please⟩ **3 a** : at, in, or to which place ⟨the town *where* we live⟩ **b** : at or in which ⟨has reached the size *where* maneuverability is a problem⟩ **4 a** : at, in, or to the place at, in, or to which ⟨stay *where* you are⟩ **b** : in a case, situation, or respect in which ⟨outstanding *where* endurance is called for⟩

[3]where \ˈhweər, ˈhwaər, ˈweər, ˈwaər\ *n* **1** : PLACE, LOCATION ⟨the *where* and the how of the accident⟩ **2** : what place, source, or cause ⟨*where* are you from⟩

[1]where·abouts \-ə-ˌbau̇ts\ *also* **where·about** \-ˌbau̇t\ *adv* : about where : near what place ⟨*whereabouts* is the house⟩

[2]whereabouts *n sing or pl* : the place or general locality where a person or thing is ⟨do you know their *whereabouts*⟩

where·as \hwer-ˈaz, hwar-, wer-, war-, hwər-, wər-\ *conj* **1** : in view of the fact that : SINCE — used especially to introduce a preamble (as to a law or contract) **2** : while on the contrary ⟨water puts out fire, *whereas* gasoline feeds it⟩

where·at \-ˈat\ *conj* **1** : at or toward which **2** : as a result of which : WHEREUPON

where·by \hweər-ˈbī, hwaər-, weər-, waər-, hwər-, wər-\ *conj* : by, through, or in accordance with which

[1]where·fore \ˈhweər-ˌfōr, ˈhwaər-, ˈweər-, ˈwaər-, -ˌfȯr\ *adv* **1** : for what reason or purpose : WHY **2** : THEREFORE 1 [Middle English *wherfor, wherfore,* from *where, wher* "where" + *for, fore* "for"]

[2]wherefore *n* : an answer or statement giving an explanation : REASON ⟨wants to know the whys and *wherefores*⟩

where·from \-ˌfrəm, -ˌfräm\ *conj* : from which

[1]where·in \hwer-ˈin, hwar-, wer-, war-, hwər-, wər-\ *adv* : in what : in what particular or respect ⟨*wherein* was I wrong⟩

[2]wherein *conj* **1** : in which : WHERE ⟨the city *wherein* they live⟩ **2** : during which ⟨the epoch *wherein* feudalism arose⟩ **3** : in what way : HOW ⟨showed me *wherein* I was wrong⟩

where·of \-ˈəv, -ˈäv\ *conj* **1** : of what ⟨I know *whereof* I speak⟩ **2** : of which or whom ⟨books *whereof* the best are lost⟩

where·on \-ˈȯn, -ˈän\ *conj* : on which ⟨the base *whereon* it rests⟩

where·so·ev·er \ˈhwer-sə-ˌwev-ər, ˈhwar-, ˈwer-, ˈwar-\ *conj* : WHEREVER 1

[1]where·to \-ˌtü\ *adv* : to what place or purpose

[2]whereto *conj* : to which

where·un·to \hwer-ˈən-tü, hwar-, wer-, war-, hwər-, wər-\ *adv or conj* : WHERETO

where·up·on \ˈhwer-ə-ˌpȯn, ˈhwar-, ˈwer-, ˈwar-, -ˌpän\ *conj* **1** : on which **2** : closely following and as a result of which

[1]wher·ev·er \hwer-ˈev-ər, hwar-, wer-, war-, hwər-, wər-\ *adv* : WHERE 1 — used in questions expressing astonishment or bewilderment ⟨*wherever* did you get that hat⟩

[2]wherever *conj* **1** : at, in, or to whatever place ⟨thrive *wherever* they go⟩ **2** : in any circumstance in which ⟨*wherever* it is possible, I try to help⟩

[1]where·with \ˈhweər-ˌwith, ˈhwaər-, ˈweər-, ˈwaər-, -ˌwith\ *conj* : with or by means of which ⟨we lack tools *wherewith* to repair the damage⟩

[2]wherewith *adv, obsolete* : with what

where·with·al \ˈhweər-with-ˌȯl, ˈhwaər-, ˈweər-, ˈwaər-, -with-\ *n* : MEANS, RESOURCES; *esp* : MONEY ⟨didn't have the *wherewithal* for an expensive trip⟩

wher·ry \ˈhwer-ē, ˈwer-\ *n, pl* **wherries** : any of various light boats; *esp* : a long light rowboat pointed at both ends [Middle English *whery*]

[1]whet \ˈhwet, ˈwet\ *vt* **whet·ted; whet·ting** **1** : to sharpen by rubbing on or with something (as a stone) ⟨*whet* a knife⟩ **2** : to make keen : STIMULATE ⟨*whet* the appetite⟩ [Old English *hwettan*]

[2]whet *n* **1** : GOAD 2 **2** : APPETIZER 1; *also* : a drink of liquor

wheth·er \ˈhweth-ər, ˈweth-, ˌhwəth-ər, ˌwəth-, hwəth-, wəth-\ *conj* **1 a** : if it is or was true that ⟨ask *whether* they are going⟩ **b** : if it is or was better ⟨uncertain *whether* to go or stay⟩ **2** — used to introduce alternative conditions or possibilities ⟨*whether* we succeed or fail, we must try⟩ ⟨seated us together *whether* by accident or design⟩ [Old English *hwæther, hwether,* from *hwæther, hwether,* pron., "which of two"]

whet·stone \ˈhwet-ˌstōn, ˈwet-\ *n* : a stone for whetting sharp-edged tools

whew *often read as* ˈhwü, ˈwü, ˈhyü; *the interjection is a whistle* *ending with a voiceless* ü\ *n* : a whistling sound or a sound like a half-formed whistle uttered as an exclamation — used interjectionally chiefly to express amazement, discomfort, or relief [imitative]

whey \'hwā, 'wā\ *n* : the watery part of milk that separates after the milk sours and thickens especially in the process of making cheese — compare CURD [Old English *hwæg*] — **whey·like** \-ˌlīk\ *adj*

[1]**which** \hwich, wich, 'hwich, 'wich\ *adj* **1** : being what one or ones out of a group — used as an interrogative ⟨*which* coat should I wear⟩ ⟨knew *which* one would win⟩ **2** : WHICHEVER ⟨it will not fit, turn it *which* way you like⟩ [Old English *hwilc* "of what kind, which"]

[2]**which** *pron* **1** : what one or ones out of a group — used as an interrogative ⟨*which* of those houses do you live in⟩ ⟨*which* of you want tea and *which* want lemonade⟩ ⟨they are swimming or canoeing, I don't know *which*⟩ **2** : WHICHEVER ⟨take *which* you like⟩ **3** — used to introduce a relative clause; used in any grammatical relation except that of a possessive; used especially in reference to animals, inanimate objects, groups, or ideas ⟨the books *which* I bought⟩ ***usage*** see THAT

[1]**which·ev·er** \hwich-'ev-ər, wich-\ *pron* : whatever one or ones out of a group ⟨take two of the four elective subjects, *whichever* you prefer⟩

[2]**whichever** *adj* : being whatever one or ones out of a group : no matter which ⟨*whichever* way you go⟩

which·so·ev·er \ˌhwich-sə-'wev-ər, ˌwich-\ *pron or adj, archaic* : WHICHEVER

whicker \'hwik-ər, 'wik-\ *vi* : WHINNY [imitative] — **whicker** *n*

[1]**whiff** \'hwif, 'wif\ *n* **1 a** : a quick puff or slight gust especially of air, odor, gas, smoke, or spray **b** : an inhalation of odor, gas, or smoke **2** : a slight trace : HINT ⟨a *whiff* of deception⟩ [imitative]

[2]**whiff** *vb* **1 a** : to expel, puff out, or blow away in or as if in whiffs **b** : SMOKE 2 **2** : to inhale an odor

whif·fle·tree \'hwif-əl-ˌtrē, 'wif-\ *n* : the pivoted swinging bar to which the traces of a harness are fastened and by which a vehicle or implement is drawn [alteration of *whippletree*]

Whig \'hwig, 'wig\ *n* **1** : a member or supporter of a British political group of the late 17th through early 19th centuries seeking to limit royal authority and increase parliamentary power — compare TORY **2** : an American favoring independence from Great Britain during the American Revolution **3** : a member or supporter of a 19th century American political party formed in opposition to the Jacksonian Democrats [*Whiggamore* "member of a Scottish group that marched to Edinburgh in 1648 to oppose the court party"] — **Whig** *adj* — **Whig·gish** \-ish\ *adj*

[1]**while** \'hwīl, 'wīl\ *n* **1** : a period of time ⟨stay here for a *while*⟩ **2** : the time and effort used (as in the performance of an action) : TROUBLE ⟨worth your *while*⟩ [Old English *hwīl*]

[2]**while** *conj* **1 a** : during the time that ⟨take a nap *while* I'm out⟩ **b** : as long as ⟨*while* there's life there's hope⟩ **2 a** : when on the other hand : WHEREAS ⟨easy for an expert, *while* it is dangerous for a novice⟩ **b** : in spite of the fact that : ALTHOUGH ⟨*while* respected, he is not liked⟩

[3]**while** *vt* : to cause to pass especially without boredom or in a pleasant manner — usually used with *away* ⟨*while* away the time⟩

[1]**whi·lom** \'hwī-ləm, 'wī-\ *adv, archaic* : FORMERLY [Middle English, literally, "at times," from Old English *hwīlum,* from *hwīl* "time, while"]

[2]**whilom** *adj* : FORMER ⟨our *whilom* friends⟩

whilst \'hwīlst, 'wīlst\ *conj, chiefly British* : WHILE

whim \'hwim, 'wim\ *n* : a sudden wish, desire, or change of mind : a sudden notion or fancy [earlier *whim-wham,* of unknown origin] ***synonyms*** see CAPRICE

whim·brel \'hwim-brəl, 'wim-\ *n* : a curlew of northern coastal regions of North America and Eurasia [origin unknown]

[1]**whim·per** \'hwim-pər, 'wim-\ *vi* **whim·pered; whim·per·ing** \-pə-ring, -pring\ **1** : to make a low whining or broken sound ⟨*whimpered* in pain⟩ **2** : to complain with or as if with a whimper [imitative]

[2]**whimper** *n* : a low whining or broken sound or cry

whim·si·cal \'hwim-zi-kəl, 'wim-\ *adj* **1** : full of whims : CAPRICIOUS ⟨a *whimsical* person⟩ **2 a** : resulting from or characterized by whim or caprice; *esp* : lightly fanciful ⟨*whimsical* decorations⟩ **b** : ERRATIC ⟨*whimsical* behavior⟩ — **whim·si·cal·i·ty** \ˌhwim-zə-'kal-ət-ē, ˌwim-\ *n* — **whim·si·cal·ly** \'hwim-zi-kə-lē, 'wim-, -klē\ *adv* — **whim·si·cal·ness** \-kəl-nəs\ *n*

whim·sy *also* **whim·sey** \'hwim-zē, 'wim-\ *n, pl* **whimsies** *also* **whimseys** **1** : WHIM, CAPRICE **2** : the quality or state of being whimsical or fanciful ⟨the designer's new line of swimwear showed a touch of *whimsy*⟩ **3** : a fanciful or fantastic device, object, or creation especially in writing or art [derived from *whim-wham* "whim"]

whin \'hwin, 'win\ *n* : GORSE [of Scandinavian origin]

whin·chat \'hwin-ˌchat, 'win-\ *n* : a small brown and buff European singing bird of grassy meadows

[1]**whine** \'hwīn, 'wīn\ *vi* **1** : to utter a whine or similar sound ⟨the child *whined*⟩ ⟨wind *whined* in the chimney⟩ **2** : to complain with or as if with a whine ⟨always *whining* about his chores⟩ [Old English *hwīnan* "to whiz"] — **whin·er** *n* — **whin·ing·ly** \'hwī-ning-lē, 'wī-\ *adv*

[2]**whine** *n* **1** : a prolonged usually high-pitched sad or distressed cry or a similar sound **2** : a complaint uttered with or as if with a whine — **whiny** *also* **whin·ey** \'hwī-nē, 'wī-\ *adj*

[1]**whin·ny** \'hwin-ē, 'win-\ *vi* **whin·nied; whin·ny·ing** : to neigh especially in a low or gentle way [probably imitative]

[2]**whinny** *n, pl* **whinnies** **1** : the neigh of a horse especially when low or gentle **2** : a sound resembling a neigh

[1]**whip** \'hwip, 'wip\ *vb* **whipped; whip·ping** **1** : to move, snatch, or jerk very quickly and forcefully ⟨*whip* out a camera⟩ **2 a** : to strike (as with a lash or rod) especially as a punishment; *also* : SPANK **b** : to drive or urge on by or as if by using a whip **3 a** : to bind or wrap (as a rope) with cord in order to protect, strengthen, or prevent unraveling **b** : to wind or wrap around something **4** : to defeat utterly : TROUNCE **5** : to stir up : INCITE ⟨*whip* up enthusiasm⟩ **6** : to produce in a hurry ⟨*whip* up a short article⟩ **7** : to beat (as eggs or cream) into a froth **8** : to gather or hold together for united action ⟨*whipped* the doubtful members into line⟩ **9 a** : to move nimbly or briskly ⟨*whipped* through her work⟩ **b** : to thrash about flexibly like a whiplash ⟨a flag *whipping* in the wind⟩ [Middle English *whippen*] — **whip·per** *n*

[2]**whip** *n* **1** : an instrument consisting usually of a handle and lash forming a flexible rod that is used for whipping **2** : a stroke or cut with or as if with a whip **3 a** : a dessert containing one or more whipped ingredients **b** : a kitchen utensil used in whipping **4** : one that handles a whip; *esp* : a driver of horses **5** : a member of a legislative body appointed by a party to enforce discipline and to secure the attendance of party members at important sessions **6** : a whipping or thrashing motion **7** : a flexible radio antenna — called also *whip antenna* — **whip·like** \'hwip-ˌlīk, 'wip-\ *adj*

whip·cord \'hwip-ˌkȯrd, 'wip-\ *n* **1** : a thin tough cord made of braided or twisted hemp or catgut **2** : a cloth of hard-twisted yarns that has fine diagonal cords or ribs

whip hand *n* : positive control : ADVANTAGE

whip·lash \'hwip-ˌlash, 'wip-\ *n* **1** : the lash of a whip **2** : injury resulting from a sudden sharp jerking movement of the head and neck (as of a person in a vehicle that is struck from the rear by another vehicle)

whip·per·snap·per \'hwip-ər-ˌsnap-ər, 'wip-\ *n* : a small, insignificant, or overly confident person [alteration of earlier *snippersnapper,* of unknown origin]

whip·pet \'hwip-ət, 'wip-\ *n* : any of a breed of small swift slender dogs often used for hunting small game or racing [probably from [1]*whip*]

whipping boy *n* : SCAPEGOAT 2 [from the former practice of maintaining a boy to share the education of a prince and be punished in the prince's stead]

whipping post *n* : a post to which offenders are tied to be legally whipped

whip·ple·tree \'hwip-əl-ˌtrē, 'wip-\ *n* : WHIFFLETREE

whip–poor–will \ˌhwip-

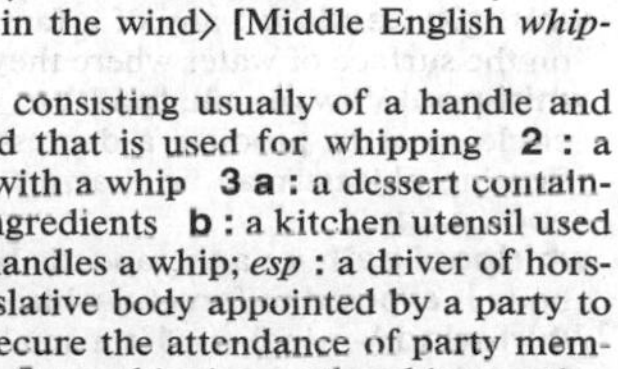

whip-poor-will

ər-ˈwil, ˌwip-; ˈhwip-ər-ˌ, ˈwip-\ *n* : an insect-eating bird of the eastern U.S. and Canada that is active at night and has a loud repeated call suggestive of its name

[1]**whip·saw** \ˈhwip-ˌsȯ, ˈwip-\ *n* : a narrow saw operated by two people

[2]**whipsaw** *vt* **whip·sawed; whip·saw·ing** **1** : to saw with a whipsaw **2** : to victimize in two opposite ways at once, by a two-phase operation, or by the combined action of two opponents

whip scorpion *n* : any of an order (Uropygi) of chiefly tropical arachnids somewhat resembling true scorpions but having a long slender tail process and no sting

whip·worm \ˈhwip-ˌwərm, ˈwip-\ *n* : a parasitic nematode worm with a body thickened behind and very long and slender in front; *esp* : one of the human intestine

[1]**whir** *also* **whirr** \ˈhwər, ˈwər\ *vb* **whirred; whir·ring** : to fly, revolve, or move rapidly with a whir ⟨ceiling fans *whirred* overhead⟩ [Middle English *quirren*]

[2]**whir** *also* **whirr** *n* : a continuous fluttering or vibrating sound made by something in rapid motion ⟨the *whir* of machinery⟩

[1]**whirl** \ˈhwərl, ˈwərl\ *vb* **1** : to move or drive in a circle or curve especially with force or speed ⟨cars *whirling* around the track⟩ **2 a** : to turn or cause to turn on or around an axis : SPIN **b** : to turn about abruptly : WHEEL ⟨*whirled* around in surprise⟩ **3** : to pass, move, or go quickly ⟨*whirled* down the street⟩ **4** : to become giddy or dizzy : REEL ⟨my head is *whirling*⟩ [Middle English *whirlen*] — **whirl·er** \ˈhwər-lər, ˈwər-\ *n*

[2]**whirl** *n* **1 a** : a rapid whirling movement **b** : something whirling ⟨a *whirl* of dust⟩ **2 a** : COMMOTION 2, BUSTLE ⟨a *whirl* of activity⟩ **b** : a confused or giddy mental state **3** : an experimental attempt : TRY ⟨give it a *whirl*⟩

whirl·i·gig \ˈhwər-li-ˌgig, ˈwər-\ *n* **1** : a toy that has a whirling motion **2** : one that continuously whirls or changes; *also* : a whirling course (as of events) [Middle English *whirlegigg,* from *whirlen* "to whirl" + *gigg* "top"]

whirligig beetle *n* : any of a family of beetles that live mostly on the surface of water where they swim swiftly about in circles

whirl·pool \ˈhwərl-ˌpül, ˈwərl-\ *n* **1** : water moving rapidly in a circle so as to produce a depression in the center into which floating objects may be drawn : EDDY, VORTEX **2** : WHIRLPOOL BATH

whirlpool bath *n* : a therapeutic bath in which all or part of the body is exposed to forceful whirling currents of hot water

[1]**whirl·wind** \-ˌwind\ *n* **1** : a small rotating windstorm marked by an inward and upward spiral motion of the lower air **2** : a confused rush : WHIRL ⟨a *whirlwind* of meetings⟩

[2]**whirlwind** *adj* : resembling a whirlwind especially in speed or force ⟨a *whirlwind* campaign⟩ ⟨a *whirlwind* romance⟩

whirly·bird \ˈhwər-lē-ˌbərd, ˈwər-\ *n* : HELICOPTER

[1]**whish** \ˈhwish, ˈwish\ *vb* **1** : to urge on or cause to move with a whish **2** : to make a whizzing or swishing sound **3** : to move with a whish especially at high speed : WHIZ [imitative]

[2]**whish** *n* : a rushing sound : SWISH

[1]**whisk** \ˈhwisk, ˈwisk\ *n* **1** : a quick light brushing or sweeping motion ⟨a *whisk* of the hand⟩ **2 a** : a usually wire kitchen implement for beating food **b** : WHISK BROOM [Middle English *wisk*]

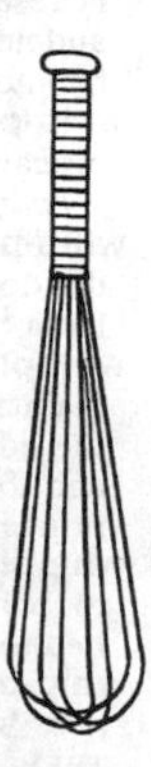
whisk 2a

[2]**whisk** *vb* **1** : to move nimbly and quickly ⟨squirrels *whisked* up the trees⟩ **2** : to move or convey briskly ⟨*whisked* the children off to bed⟩ **3** : to mix or fluff up by or as if by beating with a whisk ⟨*whisk* eggs⟩ **4** : to brush or wipe off lightly ⟨*whisk* crumbs from a table⟩

whisk broom *n* : a small broom with a short handle

whis·ker \ˈhwis-kər, ˈwis-\ *n* **1 a** : a hair of the beard **b** *pl* : the part of the beard growing on the sides of the face or on the chin **c** : HAIRBREADTH ⟨lost the race by a *whisker*⟩ **2** : one of the long projecting hairs or bristles growing near the mouth of an animal (as a cat or mouse) [derived from [2]*whisk*] — **whis·kered** \-kərd\ *adj*

whis·key *or* **whis·ky** \ˈhwis-kē, ˈwis-\ *n, pl* **whiskeys** *or* **whiskies** : a distilled alcoholic liquor made from fermented wort (as that obtained from rye, corn, or barley mash) [Irish and Scottish Gaelic *uisce beatha,* literally, "water of life"]

[1]**whis·per** \ˈhwis-pər, ˈwis-\ *vb* **whis·pered; whis·per·ing** \-pə-ring, -pring\ **1** : to speak very low or under the breath **2** : to tell or utter by whispering ⟨*whisper* a secret⟩ **3** : to make a low rustling sound ⟨*whispering* leaves⟩ [Old English *hwisperian*] — **whis·per·er** \-pər-ər\ *n*

[2]**whisper** *n* **1** : something communicated by or as if by whispering; *esp* : RUMOR ⟨*whispers* of a scandal⟩ **2 a** : an act or instance of whispering; *esp* : speech without vibration of the vocal cords **b** : a sibilant sound that resembles whispered speech **3** : HINT 2a, TRACE ⟨showed barely a *whisper* of concern⟩

whispering campaign *n* : the systematic spreading of derogatory rumors or charges especially against a candidate for public office

whis·pery \ˈhwis-pə-rē, -prē, ˈwis-\ *adj* : resembling a whisper ⟨a *whispery* voice⟩

whist \ˈhwist, ˈwist\ *n* : a card game for four players from which bridge developed [earlier *whisk,* probably from [2]*whisk;* from whisking up the tricks]

[1]**whis·tle** \ˈhwis-əl, ˈwis-\ *n* **1** : a device by which a shrill sound is produced ⟨a tin *whistle*⟩ ⟨a steam *whistle*⟩ **2 a** : a shrill clear sound produced by forcing breath out or air in through puckered lips **b** : the sound or signal produced by a whistle or as if by whistling **3** : the shrill clear note of a bird or other animal [Old English *hwistle*]

[2]**whistle** *vb* **whis·tled; whis·tling** \ˈhwis-ling, ˈwis-, -ə-ling\ **1 a** : to make a whistle through the puckered lips **b** : to utter a shrill note or call resembling a whistle **c** : to make a shrill clear sound especially by rapid movement ⟨the wind *whistled*⟩ **d** : to blow or sound a whistle **2** : to signal, order, or summon someone or something by or as if by whistling ⟨*whistle* to a dog⟩ **3** : to send, bring, signal, or call by or as if by whistling ⟨*whistle* the dog back⟩ **4** : to produce, utter, or express by whistling ⟨*whistle* a tune⟩ — **whis·tler** \ˈhwis-lər, ˈwis-, -ə-lər\ *n*

[1]**whis·tle–stop** \ˈhwis-əl-ˌstäp, ˈwis-\ *n* **1 a** : a small station at which trains stop only on signal **b** : a small community **2** : a brief personal appearance by a political candidate usually on the rear platform of a touring train

[2]**whistle–stop** *vi* : to tour especially in a political campaign with many brief personal appearances in small communities

whit \ˈhwit, ˈwit\ *n* : the smallest part imaginable : BIT ⟨cared not a *whit*⟩ [Old English *wiht* "creature, thing"]

[1]**white** \ˈhwīt, ˈwīt\ *adj* **1 a** : free from color **b** : of the color of new snow or milk; *esp* : of the color white **c** : light or pale in color ⟨*white* hair⟩ ⟨lips *white* with fear⟩ **d** : lustrous pale gray : SILVERY; *also* : made of silver **2 a** : of, relating to, or being a member of a group or race characterized by relatively light pigmentation of the skin **b** : FAIR 5a, HONEST **3** : free from spot or blemish: as **a** : free from moral impurity : INNOCENT **b** : unmarked by writing or printing **c** : not intended to cause harm ⟨a *white* lie⟩ ⟨*white* magic⟩ **d** : FAVORABLE, FORTUNATE ⟨a *white* day in my life⟩ **4 a** : wearing or clothed in white **b** : marked by the presence of snow : SNOWY ⟨a *white* Christmas⟩ **5** : very ardent : PASSIONATE ⟨in a *white* fury⟩ **6** : conservative or reactionary in political outlook and action **7** : consisting of a wide range of frequencies ⟨*white* light⟩ [Old English *hwīt*] — **white·ly** *adv* — **white·ness** *n*

[2]**white** *n* **1** : the color of fresh snow **2** : a white or light-colored thing or part: as **a** : a mass of albuminous material surrounding the yolk of an egg **b** : the white part of the eyeball **c** : the light-colored pieces in a 2-player board game (as chess); *also* : the player by whom these are played **3** : one that is or approaches the color white: as **a** : white clothing ⟨washed a load of *whites*⟩ **b** *pl* : TEETH — used in the phrase *pearly whites* **4** : a person belonging to a light-skinned race **5** *often cap* : a member of a conservative or reactionary political group

white ant *n* : TERMITE

white bass *n* : a North American freshwater food fish

white·beard \ˈhwīt-ˌbiərd, ˈwīt-\ *n* : an old man : GRAYBEARD

white blood cell *n* : any of the blood cells (as lymphocytes, monocytes, or neutrophils) that are colorless, lack hemoglobin, and contain a nucleus — called also *leukocyte, white blood corpuscle, white cell, white corpuscle*

white·board \-ˌbōrd, -ˌbȯrd\ *n* : a hard smooth white surface used for writing or drawing on with markers

white·cap \ˈhwīt-ˌkap, ˈwīt-\ *n* : a wave crest breaking into white foam — usually used in plural

white cedar *n* **1** : either of two trees related to the cypresses: **a** : a strong-scented evergreen swamp tree occurring along the eastern coast of the U.S. **b** : a common arborvitae especially of eastern Canada and the northeastern U.S. **2** : the wood of a white cedar

white cell *n* : WHITE BLOOD CELL

white chocolate *n* : a confection of cocoa butter, sugar, milk, lecithin, and flavorings
white clover *n* : a Eurasian clover with round heads of white flowers that is widely used in grass-seed mixtures and is an important source of nectar for honeybees — called also *Dutch clover, white Dutch clover*
white–col·lar \ˈhwīt-ˈkäl-ər, ˈwīt-\ *adj* : of, relating to, or being the group of salaried employees whose duties do not require the wearing of work clothes or protective clothing
white corpuscle *n* : WHITE BLOOD CELL
white crappie *n* : an edible silvery North American sunfish often stocked in small ponds
white dwarf *n* : a small very dense whitish star of high surface temperature and low luminosity
white elephant *n* **1** : something requiring much care and expense and yielding little profit **2** : an object no longer wanted by its owner though not without value to others [from the fact that in parts of India pale-colored elephants are considered sacred and are maintained without being required to work]
white–faced \ˈhwīt-ˈfāst, ˈwīt-\ *adj* **1** : having the face white in whole or in part ⟨a *white-faced* steer⟩ **2** : having a wan pale face
white feather *n* : a mark or symbol of cowardice — used chiefly in the phrase *show the white feather* [from the superstition that a white feather in the plumage of a gamecock is a mark of a poor fighter]
white·fish \ˈhwīt-ˌfish, ˈwīt-\ *n* : any of various freshwater food fishes usually of cold northern waters that are related to the salmons and trouts and are mostly greenish above and silvery white below
white flag *n* : a flag of plain white used as a sign of truce or of surrender
white·fly \ˈhwīt-ˌflī, ˈwīt-\ *n* : any of various small white winged insects that are related to the aphids and are injurious plant pests
white friar *n, often cap W&F* : CARMELITE [from the white habit]
white gold *n* : a pale alloy of gold especially with nickel or palladium that resembles platinum in appearance
white goods *n pl* **1** : cotton or linen fabrics or articles (as sheets or towels) originally or typically white-colored **2** : major household appliances (as stoves and refrigerators) that are typically finished in white enamel
white grub *n* : a grub that is a destructive pest of grass roots and is the larva of various beetles and especially june bugs
White·hall \ˈhwīt-ˌhȯl, ˈwīt-\ *n* : the British government [*Whitehall,* street of London in which are located the chief offices of the British government]
white·head \ˈhwīt-ˌhed, ˈwīt-\ *n* : a small whitish lump in the skin caused by accumulation of oil gland secretions when the duct of the gland is blocked by dried oil gland secretions and dead skin cells
white heat *n* **1** : a temperature at which a body (as of metallic or ceramic material) becomes brightly incandescent so as to appear white **2** : a state of intense mental or physical strain, emotion, or activity
white–hot \ˈhwīt-ˈhät, ˈwīt-\ *adj* : being at or radiating white heat
White House *n* : the executive department of the U.S. government [the *White House,* mansion in Washington, D.C. assigned to the use of the president of the U.S.]
white lead *n* : a heavy white poisonous carbonate of lead formerly used as a pigment
white–liv·ered \ˈhwīt-ˈliv-ərd, ˈwīt-\ *adj* : COWARDLY 1, LILY-LIVERED
white matter *n* : whitish nerve tissue especially of the brain and spinal cord that consists largely of nerve fibers sheathed in a fatty material and underlies the gray matter
whit·en \ˈhwīt-n, ˈwīt-\ *vb* **whit·ened; whit·en·ing** \ˈhwīt-ning, ˈwīt-, -n-ing\ : to make or become white or whiter
synonyms WHITEN, BLANCH, BLEACH mean to make or grow white or whiter. WHITEN implies making white often by the application or addition of an agent that causes or provides whiteness ⟨a toothpaste guaranteed to *whiten* teeth⟩. BLANCH implies the removal or withdrawal of color especially from living tissue ⟨*blanch* plants by growing them in darkness⟩. BLEACH implies the action of sunlight or chemicals in removing color ⟨hair *bleached* by the summer sun⟩.
whit·en·er \ˈhwīt-nər, ˈwīt-, -n-ər\ *n* : one that whitens; *esp* : an agent (as a bleach) used to impart whiteness to something
white noise *n* **1** : a heterogeneous mixture of sound waves extending over a wide frequency range **2** : a constant background noise; *esp* : one that drowns out other sounds
white oak *n* : any of various oaks with acorns that mature in one year and leaf veins that never extend beyond the margin of the leaf; *also* : the hard, strong, durable, and moisture-resistant wood of a white oak
white pages *n pl* : the section of a telephone directory that lists individuals and businesses alphabetically
white paper *n* : a government report on a subject
white pepper *n* : a pungent seasoning that consists of the fruit of the Indian pepper ground after the black outer husk has been removed
white perch *n* : a small silvery bass of the coast and coastal streams of the eastern U.S.
white pine *n* : a tall-growing pine of eastern North America with long needles in clusters of five; *also* : its wood which is much used in building construction
white–pine blister rust *n* : a destructive disease of white pine caused by a rust fungus that passes part of its life on currant or gooseberry bushes; *also* : this fungus
white potato *n* : POTATO 2b
white rice *n* : rice from which the hull and bran have been removed by processing
white rust *n* : any of various plant diseases caused by fungi and marked by production of masses of white spores that escape through ruptures in the host tissue; *also* : a fungus causing a white rust
white sale *n* : a sale of white goods
white sauce *n* : a sauce consisting essentially of milk, cream, or stock with flour and seasoning
white sea bass *n* : a large croaker of the Pacific coast of North America that is an important sport and food fish
white shark *n* : GREAT WHITE SHARK
white·tail \ˈhwīt-ˌtāl, ˈwīt-\ *n* : WHITE-TAILED DEER
white–tailed deer *n* : a North American deer with a rather long tail that is white on the underside and antlers which arch forward — called also *whitetail deer*

white-tailed deer

white–throat·ed sparrow \ˈhwīt-ˌthrōt-əd-, ˈwīt-\ *n* : a common brown sparrow chiefly of eastern North America with black and white stripes on the top of its head and a white patch on its throat — called also *whitethroat*
white–tie *adj* : characterized by or requiring the wearing of formal evening clothes consisting of white bow tie and tailcoat for men and a formal gown for women ⟨a *white-tie* dinner⟩
white tie *n* : formal evening dress for men
white·wall \ˈhwīt-ˌwȯl, ˈwīt-\ *n* : an automobile tire having a white band on the sidewall
white walnut *n* : a tree that bears butternuts; *also* : its light-colored wood
[1]**white·wash** \ˈhwīt-ˌwȯsh, ˈwīt-, -ˌwäsh\ *vt* **1** : to whiten with whitewash **2 a** : to gloss over or cover up (as vices or crimes) ⟨refused to *whitewash* the scandal⟩ **b** : to clear of a charge of wrongdoing by offering excuses, hiding facts, or conducting a superficial investigation **3** : to prevent (an opponent) from scoring in a game or contest — **white·wash·er** *n*
[2]**whitewash** *n* **1** : a composition (as of lime and water) for whitening structural surfaces **2** : a covering up, glossing over, or clearing of wrongdoing

\ə\ abut	\au̇\ out	\i\ tip	\ȯ\ saw	\u̇\ foot
\ər\ further	\ch\ chin	\ī\ life	\ȯi\ coin	\y\ yet
\a\ mat	\e\ pet	\j\ job	\th\ thin	\yü\ few
\ā\ take	\ē\ easy	\ng\ sing	\t͟h\ this	\yu̇\ cure
\ä\ cot, cart	\g\ go	\ō\ bone	\ü\ food	\zh\ vision

white water *n* : rough foamy water (as in rapids or waterfalls) — **white–water** *adj*

white·wood \ˈhwīt-ˌwu̇d, ˈwīt-\ *n* **1** : any of various trees with pale or white wood: as **a** : COTTONWOOD **b** : TULIP TREE **2** : the wood of a whitewood and especially of the tulip tree

[1]**whith·er** \ˈhwith-ər, ˈwith-\ *adv* **1** : to what place ⟨*whither* will they go⟩ **2** : to what situation, position, degree, or end ⟨*whither* will this success drive me⟩ [Old English *hwider*]

[2]**whither** *conj* **1 a** : to the place at, in, or to which **b** : to which place **2** : to whatever place

whith·er·so·ev·er \ˌhwith-ər-sə-ˈwev-ər, ˌwith-\ *conj* : WHITHER 2

whith·er·ward \ˈhwith-ər-wərd, ˈwith-\ *adv, archaic* : toward what or which place

[1]**whit·ing** \ˈhwīt-ing, ˈwīt-\ *n, pl* **whiting** *also* **whitings** : any of several edible fishes (as the hake) found mostly near seacoasts [Dutch *witinc,* from *wit* "white"]

[2]**whiting** *n* : calcium carbonate prepared as fine powder and used especially as a pigment and extender, in putty, and in rubber compounding

whit·ish \ˈhwīt-ish, ˈwīt-\ *adj* : somewhat white

whit·low \ˈhwit-ˌlō, ˈwit-\ *n* : a deep inflammation of a finger or toe usually with pus and located especially near the end or around the nail [Middle English *whitflawe, whitflowe, whitlowe*]

Whit·sun \ˈhwit-sən, ˈwit-\ *adj* : of, relating to, or observed on Whitsunday or at Whitsuntide

Whit·sun·day \-sən-dē, -sən-ˌdā\ *n* : PENTECOST 2 [Old English *hwīta sunnandæg,* literally, "white Sunday"]

Whit·sun·tide \-sən-ˌtīd\ *n* : the week beginning with Whitsunday; *esp* : the first three days of this week

whit·tle *vb* **whit·tled; whit·tling** \ˈhwit-ling, ˈwit-, -l-ing\ **1 a** : to pare or cut off chips from the surface of (wood) with a knife **b** : to shape or form by paring or cutting **c** : to cut or shape something by or as if by whittling it **2** : to reduce gradually : PARE ⟨*whittle* down expenses⟩ [Middle English *thwitel, whittel* "large knife," from *thwiten* "to whittle," from Old English *thwītan*] — **whit·tler** \ˈhwit-lər, ˈwit-, -l-ər\ *n*

[1]**whiz** *or* **whizz** \ˈhwiz, ˈwiz\ *vb* **whizzed; whiz·zing 1** : to buzz, whir, or hiss like a speeding object (as an arrow or ball) passing through air **2** : to fly or move swiftly with a whiz ⟨cars *whizzing* by⟩ **3** : to rotate very rapidly [imitative] — **whiz·zer** *n*

[2]**whiz** *or* **whizz** *n, pl* **whiz·zes 1** : a hissing, buzzing, or whirring sound **2** : a movement or passage of something accompanied by a whizzing sound

[3]**whiz** *n, pl* **whiz·zes** : WIZARD 2 ⟨a math *whiz*⟩ [probably from *wizard*]

whiz·bang *also* **whizz·bang** \ˈhwiz-ˌbang, ˈwiz-\ *n* : one that is conspicuous for noise, speed, or startling effect

whiz–bang *adj* : EXCELLENT, FIRST-CLASS ⟨a *whiz-bang* mechanic⟩

who \hü, ˈhü, ü\ *pron* **1** : what or which person or persons — used as an interrogative ⟨*who* was elected president⟩ ⟨find out *who* they are⟩; used by speakers on all educational levels and by many reputable writers, though disapproved by some grammarians, as the object of a verb or a following preposition ⟨*who* did you meet⟩ ⟨*who* is it for⟩ **2** : the person or persons that : WHOEVER **3** — used as a function word to introduce a relative clause; used especially in reference to persons but also in reference to groups, to animals, or to inanimate objects ⟨my friend, *who* was a lawyer⟩ ⟨a generation *who* has grown up⟩ ⟨dogs *who* bark too much⟩ ⟨earlier sources *who* disagree⟩; used by speakers on all educational levels and by many reputable writers though disapproved by some grammarians, as the object of a verb or a following preposition ⟨a person *who* you all know well⟩ [Old English *hwā*] ***usage*** see [4]THAT, WHOM

whoa \ˈwō, ˈhō, ˈhwō\ *imperative verb* **1** — a command (as to a draft animal) to stand still **2** : cease or slow a course of action or a line of thought : pause to consider or reconsider — often used to express a strong reaction (as alarm or astonishment) [Middle English *whoo*]

who·dun·it \hü-ˈdən-ət\ *n* : a detective story or mystery story presented as a novel, play, or motion picture [*who done it?*]

who·ev·er \hü-ˈev-ər\ *pron* : whatever person : no matter who — used in any grammatical relation except that of a possessive ⟨sells to *whoever* has the money to buy⟩

[1]**whole** \ˈhōl\ *adj* **1** : being in healthy or sound condition : free from defect or damage : WELL ⟨careful nursing made me *whole* again⟩ **2** : having all its proper parts or elements : COMPLETE ⟨*whole* milk⟩ ⟨*whole* grain⟩ **3 a** : constituting the total sum of : ENTIRE ⟨owns the *whole* island⟩ **b** : each or all of the ⟨the *whole* 10 days⟩ **4 a** : constituting an undivided unit : UNCUT ⟨a *whole* pie⟩ **b** : directed to one end : CONCENTRATED ⟨give it your *whole* attention⟩ **5 a** : seemingly complete or total ⟨the *whole* sky was red⟩ **b** : very great in quantity, extent, or scope ⟨feels a *whole* lot better⟩ [Old English *hāl*] — **whole·ness** *n*

synonyms WHOLE, ENTIRE, PERFECT mean not lacking or faulty in any particular. WHOLE suggests a completeness or perfection that is normal and can be sought, gained, or regained ⟨education makes a person *whole*⟩. ENTIRE implies wholeness deriving from integrity, soundness, or completeness with nothing omitted or taken away ⟨had *entire* freedom of choice⟩. PERFECT implies the soundness and excellence of every part or element often as an unattainable or theoretical state ⟨a *perfect* set of teeth⟩.

[2]**whole** *n* **1** : a complete amount or sum : a number, aggregate, or totality lacking no part, member, or element **2** : something constituting a complex unity : an orderly system or organization of parts fitting or working together as one — **in whole** : to the full or entire extent : WHOLLY — usually used in the phrase *in whole or in part* — **on the whole 1** : in view of all the circumstances or conditions : all things considered ⟨*on the whole* you did a good job⟩ **2** : in general : in most instances : TYPICALLY ⟨children *on the whole* are more energetic than adults⟩

whole·heart·ed \ˈhōl-ˈhärt-əd\ *adj* : undivided in purpose, enthusiasm, or will : HEARTY ⟨*wholehearted* support⟩ — **whole·heart·ed·ly** *adv* — **whole·heart·ed·ness** *n*

[1]**whole hog** *n* : the whole way or farthest limit : ALL ⟨go the *whole hog* and invite all your friends⟩

[2]**whole hog** *adv* : to the fullest extent : without reservation : COMPLETELY ⟨accepted *whole hog* their explanation of events⟩ — **whole–hog** \ˈhōl-ˈhȯg, -ˈhäg\ *adj*

whole language *n* : a method of teaching reading and writing that emphasizes learning whole words and phrases by encountering them in meaningful contexts rather than by phonics exercises

whole note *n* : a musical note equal in value to four quarter notes or two half notes to one measure

whole number *n* : any of the set of nonnegative integers; *also* : INTEGER

whole rest *n* : a musical rest equal in time value to a whole note

[1]**whole·sale** \ˈhōl-ˌsāl\ *n* : the sale of goods in large quantities usually for resale (as by a retail merchant)

[2]**wholesale** *adj* **1** : of, relating to, or engaged in the sale of goods in quantity for resale ⟨a *wholesale* grocer⟩ ⟨*wholesale* prices⟩ **2** : done on a large scale ⟨*wholesale* destruction of historical artifacts⟩ — **wholesale** *adv*

[3]**wholesale** *vb* : to sell in quantity usually for resale — **whole·sal·er** *n*

whole·some \ˈhōl-səm\ *adj* **1** : promoting mental, spiritual, or bodily health or well-being ⟨*wholesome* advice⟩ ⟨a *wholesome* environment⟩ **2** : sound in body, mind, or morals ⟨a *wholesome* family movie⟩ **3** : based on well-grounded fear : PRUDENT ⟨*wholesome* respect for the law⟩ ***synonyms*** see HEALTHFUL — **whole·some·ly** *adv* — **whole·some·ness** *n*

whole–souled \-ˈsōld\ *adj* : WHOLEHEARTED

whole step *n* : a musical interval comprising two half steps — called also *whole tone*

whole wheat *adj* : made of or containing ground entire wheat kernels ⟨*whole wheat* bread⟩

whol·ly \ˈhōl-lē, ˈhō-lē\ *adv* **1** : to the full or entire extent : COMPLETELY ⟨*wholly* incompetent⟩ **2** : to the exclusion of other things : SOLELY ⟨a book devoted *wholly* to modern art⟩

whom \hüm, ˈhüm, üm\ *pron, objective case of* WHO — used as an interrogative or relative; used as object of a verb or a preceding preposition ⟨to *whom* was it given⟩ or less frequently as the object of a following preposition ⟨the person *whom* you spoke to⟩ though now often considered stilted especially as an interrogative and especially in oral use [Old English *hwām,* dative of *hwā* "who"]

usage *Whom* continues to flourish, though many observers of the English language have been predicting its demise for over a hundred years. To many English speakers, *whom* seems stilted or dated. It is used as the object of a verb ⟨not sure *whom* he should hire⟩ or a preceding preposition ⟨for *whom* she has little regard⟩, and sometimes as the object of a preposition that follows it ⟨the man *whom* you wrote to⟩. In speech and speechlike writing, *who* is commonly used in place of *whom* when the preposition or verb follows ⟨*who* did you write to?〉 〈*who* did you see?〉 〈the man *who* you spoke to〉. Uncertainty about whether to use *whom* or *who* has led to incorrect usage in the form of hypercorrection 〈*whom* shall I say is calling?〉, and to constructions that reveal confusion 〈I couldn't remember *who* or *whom* arrived first〉.

whom·ev·er \hü-ˈmev-ər\ *pron, objective case of* WHOEVER

whom·so \ˈhüm-ˌsō\ *pron, objective case of* WHOSO

whom·so·ev·er \ˌhüm-sə-ˈwev-ər\ *pron, objective case of* WHOSOEVER

[1]**whoop** \ˈhüp, ˈhwüp, ˈhu̇p, ˈhwu̇p, ˈwüp\ *vb* **1 :** to shout or call loudly and vigorously especially in eagerness, enthusiasm, or enjoyment 〈the children *whooped* with joy〉 **2 :** to make the sound that follows an attack of coughing in whooping cough **3 :** to go or pass with a loud noise **4 a :** to utter or express with a whoop 〈*whooped* a welcome〉 **b :** to urge, drive, or cheer on with a whoop [Middle French *huper*] — **whoop it up 1 :** to celebrate riotously : CAROUSE **2 :** to stir up enthusiasm

[2]**whoop** *n* **1 a :** a loud yell expressive of eagerness, exuberance, or jubilation **b :** a shout of hunters or of persons in battle or pursuit **c :** a loud booming cry of a bird (as an owl or crane) **d :** a crowing sound accompanying the intake of breath after a coughing attack in whooping cough **2 :** a minimum amount or degree : the least bit 〈not worth a *whoop*〉

[1]**whoop·ee** \ˈhwu̇p-ˌē, ˈwu̇p-; ˈhwü-ˌpē, ˈhü-, ˈwü-\ *interj* — used to express delight or high spirits [derived from [2]*whoop*]

[2]**whoopee** *n* **:** boisterous lively fun — usually used with *make*

whooping cough *n* **:** an infectious bacterial disease especially of children marked by a convulsive spasmodic cough sometimes followed by a high-pitched gasping intake of breath — called also *pertussis*

whooping crane *n* **:** a large white nearly extinct North American crane noted for its loud trumpeting call

whooping crane

whoop·la \ˈhüp-ˌlä, ˈhwüp-, ˈhu̇p-, ˈhwu̇p-\ *n* **1 :** a noisy commotion **2 :** boisterous merrymaking [alteration of *hoopla*]

whoops *variant of* OOPS

[1]**whoosh** \ˈhwüsh, ˈwüsh, ˈhwu̇sh, ˈwu̇sh\ *n* **:** a swift or explosive rush; *also* **:** the sound created by such a rush [imitative]

[2]**whoosh** *vb* **:** to move or pass along with an explosive or hissing rush 〈cars *whooshing* along the highway〉

whop *or* **whap** \ˈhwäp, ˈwäp\ *vt* **whopped** *or* **whapped; whop·ping** *or* **whap·ping 1 :** BEAT, HIT 〈*whopped* me with a bat〉 **2 :** to defeat totally : WHIP 4 [Middle English *wappen, whappen* "to throw violently"]

whop·per \ˈhwäp-ər, ˈwäp-\ *n* **1 :** an unusually large thing **2 :** a big lie

whop·ping \ˈhwäp-ing, ˈwäp-\ *adj* **:** very large or great 〈got a *whopping* increase in salary〉; *also* **:** INCREDIBLE 〈a *whopping* success〉

whore \ˈhōr, ˈhȯr, ˈhu̇r\ *n* **:** PROSTITUTE [Old English *hōre*]

whorl \ˈhwȯrl, ˈwȯrl, ˈhwərl, ˈwərl\ *n* **1 :** an arrangement of similar parts (as leaves or petals) encircling an axis and especially a stem **2 :** something that whirls, coils, or spirals or whose form suggests such movement 〈a *whorl* of smoke〉 **3 :** one of the turns of a univalve shell **4 :** a fingerprint in which the central ridges on the skin turn through at least one complete circle [Middle English *wharle, whorle*] — **whorled** \ˈhwȯrld, ˈhwərld\ *adj*

whor·tle·ber·ry \ˈhwərt-l-ˌber-ē, ˈwərt-\ *n* **1 :** BILBERRY **2 :** BLUEBERRY [Middle English *hurtilberye*, from Old English *horte* "whortleberry"]

[1]**whose** \hüz, ˈhüz, üz\ *adj* **:** of or relating to whom or which especially as possessor or possessors, agent or agents, or object or objects of an action 〈asked *whose* cars they were〉 〈*whose* plays are greater than Shakespeare's?〉 〈the book *whose* publication was announced〉 [Middle English *whos*, genitive of *who, what*]

[2]**whose** \hüz, ˈhüz\ *pron, sing or pl in constr* **:** that which belongs to whom — used without a following noun as a pronoun equivalent in meaning to the adjective whose 〈*whose* is it?〉 〈*whose* were they?〉

whose·so·ev·er \ˌhüz-sə-ˈwev-ər\ *adj* **:** of or relating to whomsoever

whoso \ˈhü-ˌsō\ *pron* **:** WHOEVER

who·so·ev·er \ˌhü-sə-ˈwev-ər\ *pron* **:** WHOEVER

[1]**why** \hwī, ˈhwī, wī, ˈwī\ *adv* **:** for what cause, reason, or purpose 〈*why* did you do it〉 [Old English *hwȳ*, from *hwæt* "what"]

[2]**why** *conj* **1 :** the cause, reason, or purpose for which 〈know *why* you did it〉 〈that is *why* you did it〉 **2 :** for which : on account of which 〈know the reason *why* you did it〉

[3]**why** \ˈhwī, ˈwī\ *n, pl* **whys :** REASON, CAUSE 〈explained the *whys* and wherefores〉

[4]**why** \wī, ˌwī, hwī, ˌhwī\ *interj* — used to express mild surprise, hesitation, approval, disapproval, or impatience 〈*why*, here's what I was looking for〉

whyd·ah \ˈhwid-ə, ˈwid-\ *n* **:** any of various mostly brownish African birds often kept as cage birds and distinguished in the male by black-and-white plumage and very long tail feathers during the breeding season [from earlier *widow (bird);* from its long black tail feathers resembling a widow's veil]

Wic·ca \ˈwik-ə\ *n* **:** a religion influenced by pre-Christian beliefs and practices of western Europe that emphasizes powers in nature [Old English *wicca* "wizard"] — **Wic·can** \-ən\ *adj*

[1]**wick** \ˈwik\ *n* **:** a cord, strip, or ring of loosely woven material through which a liquid (as melted tallow, wax, or oil) is drawn by capillary action to the top in a candle, lamp, or oil stove for burning [Old English *wēoce*]

[2]**wick** *vt* **:** to absorb or drain (as a fluid or moisture) like a wick 〈a fabric that *wicks* away perspiration〉

wick·ed \ˈwik-əd\ *adj* **1 :** morally bad : EVIL **2 a :** FIERCE, VICIOUS 〈a *wicked* dog〉 **b :** inclined to mischief : ROGUISH 〈a *wicked* glance〉 **3 a :** REPUGNANT, VILE 〈a *wicked* odor〉 **b :** causing or likely to cause harm or trouble 〈a *wicked* storm〉 [Middle English *wicke*] — **wick·ed·ly** *adv* — **wick·ed·ness** *n*

wick·er \ˈwik-ər\ *n* **1 :** a flexible twig or branch (as of osier) : WITHE **2 :** WICKERWORK [of Scandinavian origin] — **wicker** *adj*

wick·er·work \-ˌwərk\ *n* **:** something (as a basket or chair) made of interlaced flexible twigs or branches

wick·et \ˈwik-ət\ *n* **1 :** a small gate or door; *esp* **:** one in or near a larger one **2 :** a small window with a grille or grate (as at a ticket office) **3 :** either of the two sets of three rods topped by two crosspieces at which the ball is bowled in cricket **4 :** an arch or hoop (as of wire) through which a ball is hit in croquet [Medieval French *wiket*, of Germanic origin]

wick·et·keep·er \-ˌkē-pər\ *n* **:** the player who plays immediately behind the wicket in cricket

wick·ing \ˈwik-ing\ *n* **:** material for wicks

wick·i·up \ˈwik-ē-ˌəp\ *n* **:** a cone-shaped hut used by the nomadic American Indians of the western and southwestern U.S. and consisting of a rough frame covered with reed mats, grass, or brushwood [Fox (an Algonquian language) *wi·kiya·pi* "house"]

wickiup

[1]**wide** \ˈwīd\ *adj* **1 a :** having or covering great extent : VAST 〈the whole *wide* world〉 **b :** extending over, reaching, or affecting a vast area : EXTENSIVE 〈*wide* publicity〉 **c :** extending throughout a specified area or scope — usually used in combination 〈nation*wide*〉 〈industry-*wide*〉 **d :** not limited : COMPREHENSIVE 〈a *wide* assortment〉 〈*wide* experience〉 **2 a :** having a specified extent from side to side 〈cloth 40 feet *wide*〉 **b :** having a generous measure across : BROAD 〈the road isn't very *wide*〉 **c :** opened as far as possible 〈eyes *wide* with wonder〉 **3 a :** extending or fluctuating considerably between limits 〈a *wide* variation〉 **b :** straying or deviating from something specified 〈a charge *wide* of the truth〉 [Old English *wīd*] ***synonyms*** see BROAD — **wide·ly** *adv* — **wide·ness** *n*

[2]**wide** *adv* **1 a :** over a great distance or extent : WIDELY

\ə\ **abut**	\au̇\ **out**	\i\ **tip**	\ȯ\ **saw**	\u̇\ **foot**
\ər\ **further**	\ch\ **chin**	\ī\ **life**	\ȯi\ **coin**	\y\ **yet**
\a\ **mat**	\e\ **pet**	\j\ **job**	\th\ **thin**	\yü\ **few**
\ā\ **take**	\ē\ **easy**	\ng\ **sing**	\th\ **this**	\yu̇\ **cure**
\ä\ **cot, cart**	\g\ **go**	\ō\ **bone**	\ü\ **food**	\zh\ **vision**

⟨searched far and *wide*⟩ **b** : over a specified distance, area, or extent — usually used in combination ⟨expanded the business country-*wide*⟩ **2 a** : so as to leave much space or distance between ⟨placed *wide* apart⟩ **b** : so as to pass at or clear by a considerable distance ⟨ran *wide* around left end⟩ **3** : to the fullest extent : COMPLETELY ⟨opened my eyes *wide*⟩

wide–awake \ˌwīd-ə-ˈwāk\ *adj* **1** : fully awake **2** : knowingly watchful especially for advantages or opportunities : ALERT

wide–body \ˈwīd-ˌbäd-ē\ *n* : a large jet aircraft characterized by a wide cabin

wide–eyed \ˈwīd-ˈīd\ *adj* **1** : having the eyes wide open especially with wonder or astonishment **2** : marked by unsophisticated or uncritical acceptance or admiration : NAIVE ⟨*wide-eyed* innocence⟩

wide·mouthed \-ˈmau̇thd, -ˈmau̇tht\ *adj* **1** : having a wide mouth ⟨*widemouthed* jars⟩ **2** : having one's mouth opened wide (as in awe)

wid·en \ˈwīd-n\ *vb* **wid·ened; wid·en·ing** \ˈwīd-ning, -n-ing\ : to make or become wide or wider : BROADEN — **wid·en·er** *n*

wide receiver *n* : an offensive football player principally used to catch passes who lines up several yards wide of the formation

wide·spread \ˈwīd-ˈspred\ *adj* **1** : widely extended ⟨*widespread* wings⟩ **2** : widely distributed or prevalent ⟨*widespread* hostility⟩

wid·ish \ˈwīd-ish\ *adj* : somewhat wide

[1]**wid·ow** \ˈwid-ō\ *n* : a woman who has lost her husband by death and usually has not remarried [Old English *widuwe*] — **wid·ow·hood** \-ˌhu̇d\ *n*

[2]**widow** *vt* : to cause to become a widow or widower

wid·ow·er \ˈwid-ə-wər\ *n* : a man who has lost his wife by death and usually has not remarried — **wid·ow·er·hood** \-ˌhu̇d\ *n*

widow's peak *n* : a point formed by the hairline on the forehead

widow's walk *n* : a railed observation platform atop a usually coastal house

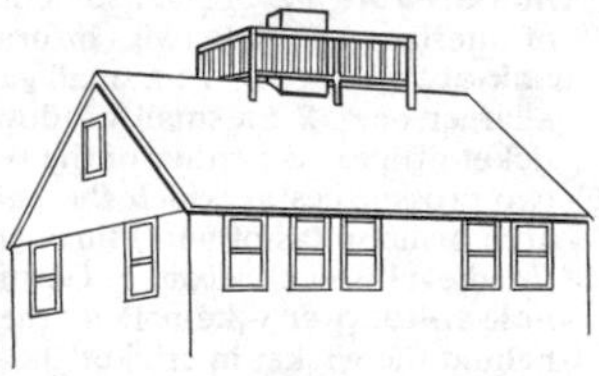
widow's walk

width \ˈwidth, ˈwitth\ *n* **1** : a distance from side to side : the measurement taken at right angles to the length : BREADTH **2** : largeness of extent or scope **3** : a measured and cut piece of material ⟨a *width* of cloth⟩ ⟨a *width* of lumber⟩ [[1]*wide*]

wield \ˈwēld\ *vt* **1** : to handle effectively ⟨*wield* a broom⟩ **2** : to exert one's authority by means of ⟨*wield* influence⟩ [Old English *wieldan*] — **wield·er** *n*

wieldy \ˈwēl-dē\ *adj* : capable of being wielded easily

wie·ner \ˈwē-nər, -nē, ˈwin-ē\ *n* : FRANKFURTER [German *Wienerwurst* "Vienna sausage"]

Wie·ner schnit·zel \ˈvē-nər-ˌshnit-səl, ˌsnit-; ˈwē-nər-ˌsnit-\ *n* : a thin breaded veal cutlet [German, literally, "Vienna cutlet"]

wife \ˈwīf\ *n, pl* **wives** \ˈwīvz\ **1 a** *dialect* : WOMAN 1 **b** : a woman acting in a specified capacity — used in combination ⟨house*wife*⟩ **2** : a married woman [Old English *wīf*] — **wife·hood** \ˈwīf-ˌhu̇d, ˈwī-ˌfu̇d\ *n* — **wife·less** \ˈwī-fləs\ *adj*

wife·ly \ˈwī-flē\ *adj* : of, relating to, or befitting a wife — **wife·li·ness** *n*

Wi–Fi \ˈwī-ˈfī\ *certification mark* — used to certify the ability of wireless computer networking devices to interoperate

wig \ˈwig\ *n* : a manufactured covering of natural or artificial hair for the head; *also* : TOUPEE [short for *periwig*]

wi·geon *or* **wid·geon** \ˈwij-ən\ *n, pl* **wigeon** *or* **wigeons** *or* **widgeon** *or* **widgeons** : any of several freshwater ducks with a large white patch on each wing [origin unknown]

wig·gle \ˈwig-əl\ *vb* **wig·gled; wig·gling** \ˈwig-ling, -ə-ling\ **1** : to move to and fro with quick jerky or shaking motions : JIGGLE ⟨*wiggled* my toes⟩ **2** : to proceed with twisting and turning movements : WRIGGLE [Middle English *wiglen*] — **wiggle** *n*

wig·gler \ˈwig-lər, -ə-lər\ *n* **1** : a larval or pupal mosquito — called also *wriggler* **2** : one that wiggles

wig·gly \ˈwig-lē, -ə-lē\ *adj* **wig·gli·er; -est** **1** : tending to wiggle ⟨a *wiggly* worm⟩ **2** : WAVY ⟨*wiggly* lines⟩

wight \ˈwīt\ *n* : a living being : CREATURE; *esp* : HUMAN [Old English *wiht* "creature, thing"]

[1]**wig·wag** \ˈwig-ˌwag\ *vb* **wig·wagged; -wag·ging** **1** : to signal by or as if by a flag or light waved according to a code **2** : to make or cause to make a signal (as with the hand or arm) [English dialect *wig* "to move" + English *wag*]

[2]**wigwag** *n* : the art or practice of wigwagging

wig·wam \ˈwig-ˌwäm\ *n* : a hut used by the American Indians of the Great Lakes region and eastward having typically an arched framework of poles overlaid with bark, rush mats, or hides [Eastern Abenaki (an Algonquian language) *wikəwəm* "house"]

wigwam

wil·co \ˈwil-kō\ *interj* — used especially in radio and signaling to indicate that a message received will be complied with [*wil*l *co*mply]

[1]**wild** \ˈwīld\ *adj* **1 a** : living in a state of nature and not ordinarily tame or domesticated ⟨*wild* ducks⟩ **b** : growing or produced without the aid and care of humans ⟨*wild* honey⟩; *also* : related to or resembling a corresponding cultivated or domesticated organism ⟨*wild* plums⟩ **c** : of or relating to wild organisms ⟨the *wild* state⟩ **2** : not inhabited or cultivated ⟨*wild* land⟩ **3 a** : UNRULY ⟨a *wild* rage⟩ ⟨*wild* mobs⟩ **b** : TURBULENT, STORMY ⟨a *wild* night⟩ **c** : EXTRAVAGANT, FANTASTIC ⟨*wild* colors⟩ ⟨*wild* ideas⟩ **d** : indicative of strong passion, desire, or emotion ⟨a *wild* stare⟩ **4** : UNCIVILIZED 1, SAVAGE **5 a** : deviating from the natural or expected course ⟨a *wild* price increase⟩ ⟨a *wild* throw⟩ **b** : having no basis in fact ⟨a *wild* guess⟩ **6** : able to represent any card designated by the holder ⟨poker with deuces *wild*⟩ [Old English *wilde*] — **wild·ly** *adv* — **wild·ness** \ˈwīld-nəs, ˈwīl-\ *n*

[2]**wild** *n* **1** : WILDERNESS **2** : a natural uncultivated or undomesticated state or existence

[3]**wild** *adv* **1** : in a wild manner **2** : without regulation or control ⟨running *wild*⟩

wild boar *n* : an Old World wild hog from which most domestic swine have been developed

wild boar

wild·card \ˈwīld-ˌkärd\ *n* : a symbol (as ? or *) used in a database search to represent the presence of zero, one, or more than one unspecified characters

wild carrot *n* : QUEEN ANNE'S LACE

[1]**wild·cat** \ˈwīld-ˌkat, ˈwīl-\ *n, pl* **wildcats** **1** *or pl* **wildcat** : any of various small or medium-sized cats (as the lynx or ocelot) **2** : a savage quick-tempered person

[2]**wildcat** *adj* **1 a** : financially irresponsible or unreliable ⟨*wildcat* banks⟩ **b** : issued by a wildcat bank ⟨*wildcat* currency⟩ **2** : operating, produced, or carried on outside the bounds of standard or legitimate business practices **3** : of, relating to, or being an oil or gas well drilled in territory not known to be productive **4** : begun by a group of workers without union approval or in violation of a contract ⟨a *wildcat* strike⟩

[3]**wildcat** *vi* **-cat·ted; -cat·ting** : to prospect and drill an experimental oil or gas well or mine shaft in territory not known to be productive — **wild·cat·ter** *n*

wil·de·beest \ˈwil-də-ˌbēst\ *n, pl* **wildebeests** *also* **wildebeest** : either of two large African antelopes with a head like that of an ox, short mane, a long tail, and horns that curve downward and outward — called also *gnu* [Afrikaans *wildebees*, from *wilde* "wild" + *bees* "beast, ox"]

wil·der·ness \ˈwil-dər-nəs\ *n* : a tract of land or region uncultivated and uninhabited by human beings and more or less in its natural state [Middle English, from *wildern* "wild," from Old English *wilddēoren* "of wild beasts"]

wilderness area *n, often cap W&A* : an often large tract of public land maintained essentially in its natural state

wild–eyed \ˈwīl-ˈdīd\ *adj* **1** : having a wild expression in the eyes **2** : consisting of or favoring extreme measures ⟨*wild-eyed* schemes⟩

wild·fire \ˈwīld-ˌfīr, ˈwīl-\ *n* **1** : a sweeping and destructive fire **2** : GREEK FIRE

wild·flow·er \-ˌflau̇-ər, -ˌflau̇r\ *n* : the flower of a wild or uncultivated plant or the plant bearing it

wild·fowl \ˈwīld-ˌfau̇l, ˈwīl-\ *n* : a game bird; *esp* : a game waterfowl (as a wild duck or goose) — **wild·fowl·er** \-ˌfau̇-lər\ *n* — **wild·fowl·ing** \-liŋ\ *n*
wild geranium *n* : a geranium of the eastern U.S. and Canada with rosy purple flowers
wild ginger *n* : a North American perennial woodland herb with an aromatic rhizome and usually heart-shaped leaves
wild–goose chase *n* : a complicated or lengthy and usually unsuccessful pursuit or search
wild·ing \ˈwīl-diŋ\ *n* : a plant or animal growing or living in the wild — **wilding** *adj*
wild·land \ˈwīld-ˌland\ *n* : land that is uncultivated or unfit for cultivation
wild·life \ˈwīl-ˌdlīf, -ˌlīf\ *n* : nonhuman living things and especially wild animals living in their natural state — **wildlife** *adj*
wild·ling \ˈwīl-dliŋ, -liŋ\ *n* : WILDING
wild marjoram *n* : OREGANO
wild oat *n* **1** : any of several wild grasses closely related to the cultivated oat **2** *pl* : offenses and indiscretions blamed on youthful high spirits — usually used in the phrase *sow one's wild oats*
wild pansy *n* : a common and long-cultivated European viola which has small short-spurred flowers usually blue or purple mixed with white and yellow and from which most of the garden pansies are derived — called also *heartsease, Johnny-jump-up*
wild pitch *n* : a pitched ball that cannot be stopped by the catcher and that allows a base runner to advance
wild rice *n* : a tall aquatic North American perennial grass yielding an edible grain; *also* : the grain
wild type *n* : the typical form of an organism as ordinarily encountered in nature as contrasted with mutant individuals
Wild West *n* : the western U.S. in its frontier period characterized by roughness and lawlessness
wild·wood \ˈwīl-ˌdwu̇d, -ˌwu̇d\ *n* : a woodland unaltered or unfrequented by humans
[1]**wile** \ˈwīl\ *n* **1** : a trick or stratagem intended to tempt or deceive **2** : TRICKERY, GUILE [Middle English *wil*] ***synonyms*** see TRICK
[2]**wile** *vt* : to lure by or as if by a magic spell : ENTICE ⟨the balmy weather *wiled* them from their work⟩
[1]**will** \wəl, l, əl, əl, wil, ˈwil\ *vb, past* **would** \wəd, d, əd, wu̇d, ˈwu̇d\; *present sing & pl* **will 1** : DESIRE, WISH ⟨call it what you *will*⟩ **2** — used as an auxiliary verb (1) to express desire, willingness, or in negative constructions refusal ⟨*will* you have another helping⟩ ⟨no one *would* do it⟩ ⟨they *won't* stop pestering me⟩, (2) to express frequent, customary, or habitual action or natural tendency ⟨*will* get angry over nothing⟩, (3) to express future action ⟨tomorrow we *will* go⟩ (4) to express capability or sufficiency ⟨the back seat *will* hold three⟩, (5) to express probability or recognition and often to serve as the equivalent to the simple verb ⟨that *will* be the mail carrier ringing the doorbell⟩, (6) to express determination or willfulness ⟨I *will* go despite them⟩, (7) to express inevitability ⟨accidents *will* happen⟩, and (8) to express a command ⟨you *will* do as I say⟩ [Old English *wille*]
[2]**will** \ˈwil\ *n* **1** : wish or desire often combined with determination ⟨the *will* to win⟩ **2** : something desired; *esp* : a choice or determination of one having authority or power ⟨the king's *will*⟩ **3** : the act, process, or experience of willing : VOLITION **4** : the process or power of wishing, choosing, desiring, or intending **5** : the power of control over one's actions or emotions ⟨a person of iron *will*⟩ **6** : a legal declaration in which a person states how his or her property is to be disposed of after death [Old English *willa* "will, desire"] — **at will** : as or whenever one wishes
[3]**will** \ˈwil\ *vb* **1** : to dispose of by or as if by a will : BEQUEATH ⟨*willed* her entire estate to her husband⟩ **2 a** : to determine by an act of choice ⟨*willed* myself to sleep⟩ **b** : DECREE, ORDAIN ⟨Providence *wills* it⟩ **c** : INTEND, PURPOSE ⟨I *willed* it so⟩ **d** : to cause or change by an act of will ⟨willed himself to succeed⟩ **3** : to exercise the will **4** : CHOOSE 3 ⟨do as you *will*⟩
willed \ˈwild\ *adj* : having a will especially of a specified kind — usually used in combination ⟨strong-*willed*⟩
wil·lem·ite \ˈwil-ə-ˌmīt\ *n* : a mineral Zn_2SiO_4 of variable color that consists of zinc silicate occurring especially in massive or granular forms [German *Willemit*, from *Willem* (William) I, died 1843, king of the Netherlands]
wil·let \ˈwil-ət\ *n, pl* **willets** *also* **willet** : a large North American shorebird with gray legs [imitative]
will·ful *or* **wil·ful** \ˈwil-fəl\ *adj* **1** : stubbornly wanting one's own way : OBSTINATE ⟨a *willful* child⟩ **2** : done deliberately : INTENTIONAL ⟨*willful* actions⟩ — **will·ful·ly** \-fə-lē\ *adv* — **will·ful·ness** *n*
wil·lies \ˈwil-ēz\ *n pl* : a fit of nervousness : JITTERS ⟨gives me the *willies*⟩ [origin unknown]
will·ing \ˈwil-iŋ\ *adj* **1** : being agreeable and ready ⟨*willing* to go⟩ **2** : prompt to act or respond ⟨*willing* workers⟩ **3** : done, borne, or accepted by choice or without reluctance ⟨a *willing* sacrifice⟩ ***synonyms*** see VOLUNTARY — **will·ing·ly** \-iŋ-lē\ *adv* — **will·ing·ness** *n*
wil·li·waw \ˈwil-i-ˌwȯ\ *n* **1** : a sudden violent gust of cold land air common along mountainous coasts of high latitudes **2** : a violent commotion or agitation [origin unknown]
will–less \ˈwil-ləs\ *adj* **1** : involving no exercise of the will ⟨*will-less* obedience⟩ **2** : not exercising the will
will–o'–the–wisp \ˌwil-ə-t͟hə-ˈwisp\ *n* **1** : IGNIS FATUUS 1 **2** : a delusive or unreachable goal [*Will* (nickname for *William*) + *of* + *the* + *wisp*]
wil·low \ˈwil-ō\ *n* **1** : any of a genus of trees and shrubs bearing catkins of flowers without petals and including forms of value for wood, osiers, or tanbark and a few ornamentals **2** : an object made of willow wood; *esp* : a cricket bat [Old English *welig*] — **wil·low·like** \-ˌlīk\ *adj*
willow herb *n* : any of a genus of herbs related to the evening primrose; *esp* : FIREWEED 1
willow oak *n* : an oak with lance-shaped leaves
wil·low·ware \ˈwil-ə-ˌwaər, ˈwil-ō-, -ˌweər\ *n* : china that is usually blue and white and that is decorated with a design featuring a large willow tree by a little bridge
wil·lowy \ˈwil-ə-wē\ *adj* **1** : full of willows ⟨a *willowy* valley⟩ **2** : resembling a willow; *esp* : gracefully tall and slender ⟨a *willowy* young dancer⟩
will·pow·er \ˈwil-ˌpau̇-ər, -ˌpau̇r\ *n* : energetic determination ⟨the temptation tested her *willpower*⟩
wil·ly–nil·ly \ˌwil-ē-ˈnil-ē\ *adv or adj* **1** : by compulsion : without choice ⟨rushed us along *willy-nilly*⟩ **2** : in a haphazard or spontaneous manner ⟨children running about *willy-nilly*⟩ [alteration of *will I nill* (archaic negative of *will*) *I* or *will ye nill ye* or *will he nill he*]
[1]**wilt** \wəlt, wilt, ˈwilt\ *archaic present 2nd singular of* WILL
[2]**wilt** \ˈwilt\ *vb* **1** : to lose or cause to lose freshness and become limp : DROOP ⟨*wilting* roses⟩ **2** : to grow weak or faint : LANGUISH ⟨was *wilting* after hours of dancing⟩ [Middle English *welken*]
[3]**wilt** \ˈwilt\ *n* **1** : an act or instance of wilting : the state of being wilted **2** : a plant disease (as one caused by a fungus)
wily \ˈwī-lē\ *adj* **wil·i·er; -est** : full of deceit : TRICKY ⟨a *wily* negotiator⟩ ***synonyms*** see SLY — **wil·i·ness** *n*
wim·ble \ˈwim-bəl\ *n* : any of various instruments for boring holes [Medieval French, from Dutch *wimmel* "auger"]
wimp \ˈwimp\ *n* : a weak, cowardly, or ineffectual person [origin unknown] — **wimp·i·ness** \ˈwim-pē-nəs\ *n* — **wimpy** \ˈwim-pē\ *adj*
[1]**wim·ple** \ˈwim-pəl\ *n* : a cloth covering worn over the head and around the neck and chin by women especially in the late medieval period and by some nuns [Old English *wimpel*]

wimple

[2]**wimple** *vb* **wim·pled; wim·pling** \-pə-liŋ, -pliŋ\ **1** : to cover with or as if with a wimple **2** : to cause to ripple : RIPPLE **3** *archaic* : to fall or lie in folds
[1]**win** \ˈwin\ *vb* **won** \ˈwən\; **win·ning 1** : to be first or best in or as if in a contest : SUCCEED ⟨I always dream of *winning*⟩ **2 a** : to get possession of by effort or fortune ⟨*won* praise for my hard work⟩

\ə\ **abut**	\au̇\ **out**	\i\ **tip**	\ȯ\ **saw**	\u̇\ **foot**
\ər\ **further**	\ch\ **chin**	\ī\ **life**	\ȯi\ **coin**	\y\ **yet**
\a\ **mat**	\e\ **pet**	\j\ **job**	\th\ **thin**	\yü\ **few**
\ā\ **take**	\ē\ **easy**	\ŋ\ **sing**	\t͟h\ **this**	\yu̇\ **cure**
\ä\ **cot, cart**	\g\ **go**	\ō\ **bone**	\ü\ **food**	\zh\ **vision**

⟨*win* money in a raffle⟩ **b** : to obtain by work : EARN ⟨strove to *win* a living from the soil⟩ **3 a** : to gain in or as if in battle or contest ⟨*win* the championship⟩ **b** : to be the victor in ⟨*won* the war⟩ **4 a** : to seek and gain the favor or support of ⟨*won* them over with a convincing argument⟩ **b** : to gain a promise of marriage from [Old English *winnan* "to struggle"]

[2]**win** *n* : VICTORY; *esp* : first place at the finish of a horse race

wince \ˈwins\ *vi* : to shrink back involuntarily (as from pain) : FLINCH ⟨the cut on my leg caused me to *wince*⟩ ⟨the crowd *winced* when the skater fell on the ice⟩ [Middle English *wynsen* "to kick out, start," from Medieval French *guenchir* "to shift direction, dodge," probably of Germanic origin] — **wince** *n*

winch \ˈwinch\ *n* : a machine that has a roller on which a rope, cable, or chain is coiled for hauling or hoisting [Old English *wince*]

[1]**wind** \ˈwind\ *n* **1** : a movement of the air of any velocity **2** : a force or agency that carries along or influences ⟨the *winds* of change⟩ **3 a** : BREATH 2a ⟨the fall knocked the *wind* out of me⟩ **b** : the pit of the stomach : SOLAR PLEXUS **4** : gas generated in the stomach or the intestines **5** : something insubstantial; *esp* : idle words **6 a** : air carrying a scent (as of a hunter or game) **b** : slight information especially about something secret ⟨got *wind* of our plans⟩ **7 a** *pl* : the wind instruments of an orchestra or band **b** *pl* : the players of wind instruments **8 a** : a point of the compass; *esp* : one of the cardinal points **b** : the direction from which the wind is blowing [Old English] — **have the wind of 1** : to be to windward of **2** : to be on the scent of **3** : to have a superior position to — **in the wind** : about to happen : ASTIR, AFOOT ⟨change is *in the wind*⟩ — **near the wind 1** : close to the wind : CLOSE-HAULED **2** : close to a point of danger : near the permissible limit — **off the wind** : away from the direction from which the wind is blowing — **to the wind** *or* **to the winds** : [1]AWAY 4, ASIDE ⟨threw caution *to the wind*⟩ — **under the wind 1** : to leeward **2** : in a place protected from the wind : under the lee

[2]**wind** *vt* **1** : to get a scent of ⟨the dogs *winded* game⟩ **2** : to cause to be out of breath ⟨the long climb *winded* us⟩ **3** : to allow (as a horse) to rest so as to catch the breath

[3]**wind** \ˈwīnd, ˈwind\ *vt* **wind•ed** \ˈwīn-dəd, ˈwin-\ *or* **wound** \ˈwau̇nd\; **wind•ing** : to sound by blowing ⟨*wind* a horn⟩ [[1]*wind*]

[4]**wind** \ˈwīnd\ *vb* **wound** \ˈwau̇nd\ *also* **wind•ed; wind•ing 1** : WARP 1a, BEND **2** : to have a curving course or shape ⟨a river *winding* through the valley⟩ **3** : to move or lie so as to encircle something ⟨vines *winding* around a tree⟩ **4** : to turn when lying at anchor **5 a** : ENTANGLE 2 **b** : to introduce sinuously or stealthily : INSINUATE **6 a** : to encircle or cover with something pliable **b** : to turn completely or repeatedly about an object : COIL, TWINE ⟨*wind* thread on a spool⟩ **c** : to hoist or haul by means of a rope or chain and a windlass ⟨*wind* up a pail⟩ **d** (1) : to tighten the spring of ⟨*wind* a clock⟩ ⟨*wind* up a toy train⟩ (2) : CRANK 3 ⟨*wound* down the car window⟩ **e** : to raise to a high level (as of excitement or tension) ⟨sugar gets him *wound* up⟩ **7 a** : to cause to move in a curving line or path **b** : to traverse on a curving course ⟨the river *winds* the valley⟩ [Old English *windan* "to twist, brandish"] — **wind•er** *n*

[5]**wind** \ˈwīnd\ *n* : TURN 8c, TWIST ⟨took a *wind* around the post⟩

[6]**wind** \ˈwind\ *adj* : of or relating to wind instruments ⟨the *wind* section of an orchestra⟩

wind•age \ˈwin-dij\ *n* **1** : the influence of the wind in turning the course of a projectile (as a bullet) **2** : the amount of deflection caused by the wind

wind•bag \ˈwind-ˌbag, ˈwin-\ *n* : a person who talks a lot without saying anything important

wind•blown \-ˌblōn\ *adj* : blown or looking as if blown by the wind ⟨*windblown* seeds⟩ ⟨*windblown* streets⟩

wind•break \-ˌbrāk\ *n* : something (as a growth of trees or shrubs) serving to break the force of wind

Wind•break•er \-ˌbrā-kər\ *trademark* — used for a wind-resistant jacket

wind–bro•ken \-ˌbrō-kən\ *adj* : having an impaired ability to breathe because of disease ⟨*wind-broken* horses⟩

wind•burn \-ˌbərn\ *n* : skin irritation caused by wind — **wind-burned** \-ˌbərnd\ *adj*

wind•chill \ˈwind-ˌchil, ˈwin-\ *n* : a still-air temperature that would have the same cooling effect on exposed human flesh as a given combination of temperature and wind speed — called also *windchill factor, windchill index*

wind•fall \ˈwind-ˌfȯl, ˈwin-\ *n* **1** : something (as a tree or fruit) blown down by the wind **2** : an unexpected or sudden gift, gain, or advantage

wind•flow•er \-ˌflau̇-ər, -ˌflau̇r\ *n* : ANEMONE 1

wind gap *n* : a notch in the crest of a mountain ridge

[1]**wind•ing** \ˈwīn-ding\ *n* : material (as wire) wound or coiled about an object (as an armature); *also* : a single turn of the wound material

[2]**winding** *adj* : marked by winding: as **a** : having a pronounced curved or spiral form ⟨a *winding* staircase⟩ **b** : having a course that winds ⟨a *winding* road⟩

wind•ing–sheet \-ˌshēt\ *n* : a sheet used to wrap a corpse for burial : SHROUD

wind instrument *n* : a musical instrument (as a flute or horn) sounded by the vibration of a stream of air and especially by the player's breath

wind•jam•mer \ˈwind-ˌjam-ər, ˈwin-\ *n* : a sailing ship or one of its crew

wind•lass \ˈwin-dləs\ *n* : a winch used especially on ships for hauling and hoisting [Middle English *wyneles, wyndlas,* from Old Norse *vindāss,* from *vinda* "to wind" + *āss* "pole"]

[1]**wind•mill** \ˈwind-ˌmil, ˈwin-\ *n* : a mill or a machine (as for pumping water) worked by the wind turning sails or vanes at the top of a tower

[2]**windmill** *vb* : to move or cause to move like the vanes of a windmill

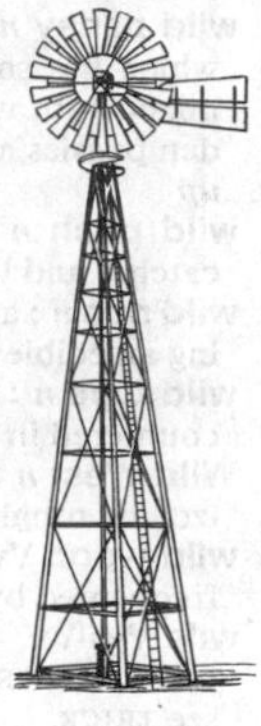

windmill

win•dow \ˈwin-dō\ *n* **1 a** : an opening especially in the wall of a building for admission of light and air usually closed by casements or sashes containing glass **b** : WINDOWPANE **c** : an opening in a partition or wall through which business is conducted ⟨a bank teller's *window*⟩ **2** : a means of access or of obtaining information ⟨a *window* on history⟩ **3** : an opening suggestive of or functioning like a window **4** : an interval of time during which a certain condition exists ⟨a *window* of opportunity⟩ **5** : any of the areas into which a computer display may be divided and on which distinctly different types of information are displayed [Old Norse *vindauga,* from *vindr* "wind" + *auga* "eye"] — **win•dow•less** *adj*

window box *n* : a box designed to hold growing plants on a windowsill

window dressing *n* **1** : display of merchandise in a store window **2** : a showing made to create a good but sometimes false impression

window envelope *n* : an envelope having a transparent panel through which the address on the enclosure is visible

win•dow•pane \-ˌpān\ *n* : a pane in a window

window seat *n* : a seat built into a window recess

window shade *n* : a shade or curtain for a window

win•dow–shop \-ˌshäp\ *vi* : to look at the displays in store windows without going inside the stores to make purchases — **win-dow–shop•per** *n*

win•dow•sill \-ˌsil\ *n* : the horizontal member at the bottom of a window opening

wind•pipe \ˈwind-ˌpīp, ˈwin-\ *n* : TRACHEA 1

wind–pollinated *adj* : pollinated by pollen borne by the wind

wind•proof \ˈwind-ˈprüf, ˈwin-\ *adj* : resistant to the passage of wind ⟨a *windproof* jacket⟩

[1]**wind•row** \ˈwin-ˌdrō, -ˌrō\ *n* **1** : hay raked up into a row to dry **2** : a row of something (as sand or dry leaves) heaped up by or as if by the wind

[2]**windrow** *vt* : to put into windrows

wind•screen \ˈwind-ˌskrēn, ˈwin-\ *n, chiefly British* : an automobile windshield

wind shear *n* : a radical shift in wind speed and direction that occurs over a very short distance

wind•shield \-ˌshēld\ *n* : a transparent screen (as of glass) in front of the occupants of a vehicle

wind sock *n* : a truncated cloth cone open at both ends and mounted in an elevated position to indicate the direction of the wind

Wind•sor chair \ˈwin-zər-\ *n* : a wooden chair with spindle back and raking legs [*Windsor,* England]

Windsor knot *n* : a symmetrical knot used for tying neckties

wind sprint *n* : a sprint performed as a training exercise to develop the breathing capacity especially during exertion

wind·storm \ˈwind-ˌstȯrm, ˈwin-\ *n* **:** a storm marked by high wind with little or no precipitation

wind·surf·ing \-ˌsər-fiŋ\ *n* **:** the sport or activity of riding a modified surfboard mounted with a sail — **wind·surf** \-ˌsərf\ *vi* — **wind·surf·er** \-ˌsər-fər\ *n*

Windsor chair

wind·swept \-ˌswept\ *adj* **:** disturbed by or as if by wind ⟨*windswept* plains⟩

wind tunnel *n* **:** a tunnellike passage through which air is blown at a known speed to investigate airflow around an object (as an airplane part) placed in the passage

[1]**wind·up** \ˈwīn-ˌdəp\ *n* **1 a :** the act of bringing to an end **b :** a concluding act or part **:** FINISH **2 :** a series of regular and distinctive motions (as swinging the arms over the head) made by a pitcher preparatory to releasing a pitch

[2]**windup** *adj* **:** operated by a spring wound by hand ⟨*windup* toys⟩

wind up \wīn-ˈdəp, ˈwīn-\ *vb* **1 :** to bring or come to a conclusion **:** END ⟨the concert *wound up* with a nostalgic song⟩ **2 :** to put in order for the purpose of bringing to an end ⟨*wind up* the meeting⟩ **3 :** to arrive in a place, situation, or condition at the end or as a result of a course of action ⟨and that's how we happened to *wind up* in Baltimore⟩ ⟨*wound up* as millionaires⟩ **4 :** to make a windup in pitching a baseball

[1]**wind·ward** \ˈwin-dwərd, -wərd\ *adj* **:** moving or situated toward the direction from which the wind is blowing — compare LEEWARD

[2]**windward** *n* **:** the side or direction from which the wind is blowing ⟨sail to *windward*⟩

windy \ˈwin-dē\ *adj* **wind·i·er; -est 1 :** having or exposed to wind ⟨a *windy* day⟩ ⟨a *windy* prairie⟩ **2 :** given to or marked by useless talk ⟨a *windy* speaker⟩ — **wind·i·ly** \-də-lē\ *adv* — **wind·i·ness** \-dē-nəs\ *n*

[1]**wine** \ˈwīn\ *n* **1 a :** an alcoholic beverage made from fermented grape juice **b :** an alcoholic beverage made from the usually fermented juice of other fruits (as peaches or berries) **2 :** something that invigorates or intoxicates **3 :** a dark red [Old English *wīn*]

[2]**wine** *vb* **1 :** to drink wine **2 :** to provide with wine ⟨*wined* and dined their friends⟩

wine cellar *n* **:** a room for storing wines; *also* **:** a stock of wines

wine·grower \ˈwīn-ˌgrō-ər, -ˌgrōr\ *n* **:** a person who cultivates a vineyard and makes wine

wine·press \-ˌpres\ *n* **:** a vat in which juice is squeezed from grapes

win·ery \ˈwīn-rē, -ə-rē\ *n, pl* **-er·ies :** a wine-making establishment

wine·shop \ˈwīn-ˌshäp\ *n* **:** a tavern that specializes in serving wine

wine·skin \-ˌskin\ *n* **:** a bag made from the skin of an animal (as a goat) and used for holding wine

win·ey *or* **winy** \ˈwī-nē\ *adv* **win·i·er; -est 1 :** having the taste or qualities of wine **2 :** crisply fresh ⟨*winy* autumn breezes⟩

[1]**wing** \ˈwiŋ\ *n* **1 :** one of the movable feathered or membranous paired appendages by means of which a bird, bat, or insect is able to fly **2 :** an appendage or part resembling a wing in shape, appearance, or position: as **a** (1) **:** a flat or broadly expanded plant or animal part **:** ALA ⟨the *wings* of the nose⟩ ⟨a stem with woody *wings*⟩ (2) **:** either lateral petal of a pealike flower **b :** a sidepiece at the top of an armchair **c :** one of the airfoils that develop a major part of the lift which supports a heavier-than-air aircraft **3 :** a means of flight or rapid progress **4 :** the act or manner of flying **:** FLIGHT **5 :** a side or outlying region or district **6 :** a part or feature of a building projecting from and subordinate to the main or central part ⟨the rear *wing* of the house⟩ **7** *pl* **:** the area at the side of the stage out of sight **8 a :** a left or right section of an army or fleet **b :** one of the offensive positions or players on each side of a center position in various team sports **9 a :** either of two opposing groups in an organization or society **:** FACTION **b :** a section of a legislative chamber representing a distinct group or faction **10 :** a unit of the U.S. Air Force **11** *pl* **:** insignia consisting of a stylized pair of outspread bird's wings which are awarded to a qualified pilot or aircrew member [of Scandinavian origin] — **wing·like** \-ˌlīk\ *adj* — **on the wing :** in flight **:** FLYING — **under one's wing :** under one's protection **:** in one's charge or care

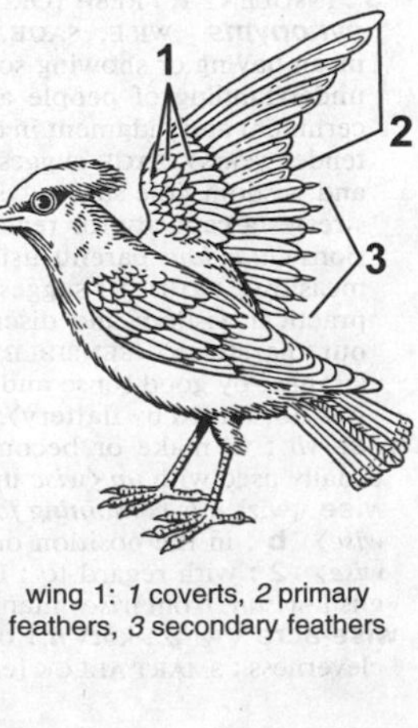

wing 1: *1* coverts, *2* primary feathers, *3* secondary feathers

[2]**wing** *vb* **1 :** to pass through in flight **2 :** to go with or as if with wings **:** FLY **3 :** to wound in the wing ⟨*wing* a duck⟩; *also* **:** to wound without killing ⟨*wing* a deer⟩ **4 :** to do or perform without preparation or guidelines ⟨*winging* it⟩

wing case *n* **:** ELYTRON

wing chair *n* **:** an upholstered armchair with high solid back and sides that provide a rest for the head and protection from drafts

wing·ding \ˈwiŋ-ˌdiŋ\ *n* **:** a wild or lively or lavish party [origin unknown]

winged \ˈwiŋd *also except for 1b* ˈwiŋ-əd\ *adj* **1 a :** having wings ⟨*winged* seeds⟩ ⟨a *winged* statue⟩ **b :** having wings of a specified character — used in combination ⟨white-*winged*⟩ **2 a :** soaring with or as if with wings **:** ELEVATED ⟨*winged* ideas⟩ **b :** SWIFT 1, RAPID ⟨a *winged* victory⟩

wing·less \ˈwiŋ-ləs\ *adj* **:** having no wings or very rudimentary wings ⟨*wingless* insects⟩ — **wing·less·ness** *n*

wing·man \-mən\ *n* **:** a pilot who flies somewhat behind and to the side of the leader of a flying formation

wing nut *n* **:** a nut with wings affording a grip for the thumb and finger

wing·span \ˈwiŋ-ˌspan\ *n* **:** the distance between the tips of a pair of wings (as of a bird or airplane)

wing·spread \-ˌspred\ *n* **:** the spread of the wings **:** WINGSPAN; *esp* **:** the distance between the tips of the fully extended wings of a winged animal

[1]**wink** \ˈwiŋk\ *vb* **1 :** to close and open one eye quickly as a signal or hint ⟨saw her friend *wink* and knew it was time to go⟩ **2 :** to close and open the eyes quickly **:** BLINK **3 :** to avoid seeing or noting something **:** pay no attention ⟨*wink* at a violation of the law⟩ **4 :** to gleam or flash intermittently **:** TWINKLE, FLICKER [Old English *wincian*] — **wink·er** \ˈwiŋ-kər\ *n*

[2]**wink** *n* **1 :** a brief period of sleep **:** NAP ⟨catching a *wink*⟩ **2 a :** a hint or sign given by winking the eye **b :** an act of winking **3 :** the time of a wink **:** INSTANT ⟨quick as a *wink*⟩

win·kle \ˈwiŋ-kəl\ *n* **:** [2]PERIWINKLE

win·na·ble \ˈwin-ə-bəl\ *adj* **:** able to be won

win·ner \ˈwin-ər\ *n* **:** one that wins

winner's circle *n* **:** an enclosure near the finish line of a racetrack where the winning horse and jockey are brought for photographs and awards

[1]**win·ning** \ˈwin-iŋ\ *n* **1 :** the act of one that wins **:** VICTORY **2 :** something won; *esp* **:** money won at gambling — often used in plural

[2]**winning** *adj* **1 a :** of or relating to winning **:** that wins ⟨the *winning* ticket⟩ **b :** successful especially in competition ⟨a *winning* team⟩ **2 :** tending to please or delight ⟨a *winning* personality⟩ — **win·ning·ly** \-iŋ-lē\ *adv*

win·now \ˈwin-ō\ *vt* **1 a :** to remove (as chaff from grain) by a current of air **b :** to subject (as grain) to a current of air to remove waste **2 :** to get rid of (something unwanted) or to sort or separate (something) as if by winnowing ⟨*winnowed* the group of contestants down to five finalists⟩ [Old English *windwian*] — **win·now·er** \ˈwin-ə-wər\ *n*

wino \ˈwī-nō\ *n, pl* **win·os :** one who is habitually drunk especially on wine

win·some \ˈwin-səm\ *adj* **1 :** having a charming or pleasing quality ⟨a *winsome* smile⟩ **2 :** CHEERFUL 1a, LIGHTHEARTED

\ə\ **abut**	\au̇\ **out**	\i\ **tip**	\ȯ\ **saw**	\u̇\ **foot**
\ər\ **further**	\ch\ **chin**	\ī\ **life**	\ȯi\ **coin**	\y\ **yet**
\a\ **mat**	\e\ **pet**	\j\ **job**	\th\ **thin**	\yü\ **few**
\ā\ **take**	\ē\ **easy**	\ŋ\ **sing**	\t͟h\ **this**	\yu̇\ **cure**
\ä\ **cot, cart**	\g\ **go**	\ō\ **bone**	\ü\ **food**	\zh\ **vision**

⟨a *winsome* disposition⟩ [Old English *wynsum,* from *wynn* "joy"] — **win·some·ly** *adv* — **win·some·ness** *n*

[1]**win·ter** \ˈwint-ər\ *n* **1 a :** the season between autumn and spring comprising in the northern hemisphere usually the months of December, January, and February or as determined astronomically extending from the December solstice to the March equinox **b :** the colder half of the year **2 :** YEAR ⟨many *winters* ago⟩ **3 :** a time or season of inactivity or decay [Old English]

[2]**winter** *vb* **win·tered; win·ter·ing** \ˈwint-ə-ring, ˈwin-tring\ **1 :** to pass or live through the winter ⟨the cattle *wintered* on the range⟩ **2 :** to keep, feed, or manage during the winter ⟨*winter* livestock⟩

[3]**winter** *adj* **1 :** of, relating to, or suitable for winter ⟨a *winter* vacation⟩ ⟨*winter* clothes⟩ **2 :** sown in autumn for harvesting in the following spring or summer ⟨*winter* wheat⟩ ⟨*winter* rye⟩

win·ter·ber·ry \ˈwint-ər-ˌber-ē\ *n* **:** any of various American hollies with bright red berries persistent through the winter

win·ter·green \ˈwint-ər-ˌgrēn\ *n* **1 a :** a low-growing North American evergreen shrub of the heath family with white bell-shaped flowers and spicy red berries — called also *checkerberry* **b :** an essential oil from the wintergreen or its flavor **2 :** any of several plants related to the wintergreen

win·ter·ize \ˈwint-ə-ˌrīz\ *vt* **:** to make ready for winter ⟨*winterize* a car⟩ — **win·ter·iza·tion** \ˌwint-ə-rə-ˈzā-shən\ *n*

win·ter–kill \ˈwint-ər-ˌkil\ *vb* **:** to kill (as a plant) by exposure to winter conditions; *also* **:** to die as a result of such exposure — **winterkill** *n*

winter melon *n* **:** any of several muskmelons (as a casaba or honeydew melon) with smooth rind and sweet white or greenish flesh that keeps well

winter quarters *n pl* **:** a winter residence or station (as of a military unit or a circus)

winter squash *n* **:** any of various hard-shelled squashes (as an acorn squash or butternut squash) that keep well in storage

win·ter·tide \ˈwint-ər-ˌtīd\ *n* **:** WINTERTIME

win·ter·time \-ˌtīm\ *n* **:** the winter season

win through *vi* **:** to survive difficulties and reach a desired or satisfactory end

win·try \ˈwin-trē\ *adj* **win·tri·er; -est** **1 :** of, relating to, or characteristic of winter ⟨*wintry* weather⟩ **2 :** not warm and friendly **:** CHEERLESS ⟨a *wintry* welcome⟩ — **win·tri·ly** \-trə-lē\ *adv* — **win·tri·ness** \-trē-nəs\ *n*

winy *variant of* WINEY

[1]**wipe** \ˈwīp\ *vt* **1 :** to clean or dry by rubbing ⟨*wipe* dishes⟩ **2 :** to remove by or as if by rubbing ⟨*wipe* away tears⟩ ⟨*wipe* up spilled milk⟩ **3 :** to pass or draw over a surface ⟨*wiped* a hand across my face⟩ [Old English *wīpian*]

[2]**wipe** *n* **1 :** an act or instance of wiping **2 :** something used for wiping

wipe·out \ˈwī-ˌpau̇t\ *n* **1 :** the act or an instance of wiping out **:** complete or utter destruction **2 :** a fall or crash caused usually by losing control ⟨*wipeouts* on the downhill ski course are common⟩ **3 :** total or final defeat ⟨couldn't bear to watch the team's *wipeout*⟩

wipe out \wī-ˈpau̇t, ˈwī-\ *vt* **1 :** to destroy completely ⟨crops *wiped out* by flooding⟩ **2 :** to fall or crash usually as a result of losing control ⟨the surfer *wiped out*⟩

wip·er \ˈwīp-ər\ *n* **:** one that wipes; *esp* **:** a device in the form of a rubber squeegee attached to an oscillating arm for wiping a windshield

[1]**wire** \ˈwīr\ *n* **1 a :** metal in the form of a usually very flexible thread or slender rod **b :** a thread or rod of metal **2** *usually pl* **a :** a system of wires used to operate the puppets in a puppet show **b :** hidden or secret influences on a person or organization **3 a :** a line of wire for conducting electrical current — compare CORD 3b **b :** a telephone or telegraph wire or system **c :** TELEGRAM, CABLEGRAM **4 a :** the finish line of a race **b :** the final decisive moment ⟨the game came down to the *wire*⟩ [Old English *wīr*] — **wire·like** \-ˌlīk\ *adj* — **under the wire :** at the last moment — **wire to wire** *or* **from wire to wire :** from start to finish

[2]**wire** *vb* **1 :** to provide or equip with wire or electricity ⟨*wire* a house⟩ **2 :** to bind, string, or mount with wire **3 a :** to send or send word to by telegraph ⟨*wire* me the news⟩ **b :** to send a telegraphic message ⟨*wire* home for money⟩ — **wir·able** \ˈwī-rə-bəl\ *adj*

wired \ˈwīrd\ *adj* **1 :** reinforced or bound with wire ⟨a *wired* container⟩ **2 :** having a netting or fence of wire ⟨a *wired* enclosure for chickens⟩ **3 a :** furnished with wires (as for electric connections) **b :** connected to a telecommunications network and especially to the Internet **4 :** feverishly excited ⟨were *wired* after their victory⟩

wire gauge *n* **:** a gauge especially for measuring the diameter of wire or thickness of sheet metal

wire grass *n* **:** any of various grasses or rushes having wiry stems or leaves

wire·haired \ˈwīr-ˈhaərd, -ˈheərd\ *adj* **:** having a stiff wiry outer coat of hair ⟨a *wirehaired* dog⟩

[1]**wire·less** \ˈwīər-ləs\ *adj* **1 :** having no wire **2 :** of or relating to radio communications ⟨a *wireless* phone⟩

[2]**wireless** *n* **1 :** communication at a distance involving signals transmitted by radio waves rather than over wires **2** *chiefly British* **:** RADIO — **wireless** *vb*

wireless telegraphy *n* **:** telegraphy carried on by radio waves and without connecting wires — called also *radiotelegraph, radiotelegraphy, wireless telegraph*

wire·man \ˈwīr-mən\ *n* **:** a maker of or worker with wire; *esp* **:** LINEMAN 1

Wire·pho·to \ˈwīr-ˈfōt-ō\ *trademark* — used for a photograph transmitted by electrical signals over telephone wires

wire–pull·er \-ˌpu̇l-ər\ *n* **:** one who uses secret or underhanded means to influence the acts of a person or organization — **wire–pull·ing** \-ˌpu̇l-ing\ *n*

wire recorder *n* **:** a magnetic recorder using magnetic wire — **wire–re·cord·ing** *n*

wire rope *n* **:** a rope formed wholly or chiefly of wires

wire service *n* **:** a news agency that sends out syndicated news copy by wire to subscribers

[1]**wire·tap** \ˈwīr-ˌtap\ *vi* **:** to tap a telephone or telegraph wire to get information — **wire·tap·per** *n*

[2]**wiretap** *n* **1 :** an act or instance of wiretapping **2 :** an electrical connection for wiretapping

wire·worm \-ˌwərm\ *n* **:** the slender hard-coated larva of various click beetles that is often destructive to plant roots

wir·ing \ˈwīr-ing\ *n* **1 :** the act of providing or using wire **2 :** a system of wires; *esp* **:** an arrangement of wires used for electric distribution

wiry \ˈwīr-ē\ *adj* **wir·i·er; wir·i·est** **1 :** resembling wire in form and flexibility ⟨*wiry* stems⟩ **2 :** being slender yet strong and sinewy ⟨a *wiry* physique⟩ — **wir·i·ness** \ˈwī-rē-nəs\ *n*

wis·dom \ˈwiz-dəm\ *n* **1 a :** accumulated learning **:** KNOWLEDGE **b :** ability to discern inner qualities and relationships **:** INSIGHT **c :** good sense **:** JUDGMENT **2 :** a wise attitude, belief, or course of action **3 :** the teachings of the ancient sages **4** *cap* — see BIBLE table [Old English *wīsdōm,* from *wīs* "wise"]

Wisdom of Sol·o·mon \-ˈsäl-ə-mən\ — see BIBLE table

wisdom tooth *n* **:** the last tooth of the full set on each side of the upper and lower jaws in humans [from its being cut usually in the late teens when children were formerly believed to be approaching wisdom]

[1]**wise** \ˈwīz\ *n* **:** WAY 4a, MANNER — used in such phrases as *in any wise, in no wise, in this wise* [Old English *wīse*]

[2]**wise** *adj* **1 :** having or showing wisdom, good sense, or good judgment **:** SENSIBLE ⟨a *wise* person⟩ ⟨a *wise* investment⟩ **2 :** aware of what is going on **:** INFORMED ⟨was *wise* to our plans⟩ **3 :** INSOLENT 1, FRESH [Old English *wīs*] — **wise·ly** *adv*

synonyms WISE, SAGE, JUDICIOUS, PRUDENT, SENSIBLE mean having or showing sound judgment. WISE suggests great understanding of people and of situations and unusual discernment and judgment in dealing with them ⟨*wise* beyond her tender years⟩. SAGE suggests wide experience, great learning, and wisdom ⟨the *sage* advice of my grandfather⟩. JUDICIOUS stresses a capacity for reaching wise decisions or just conclusions ⟨*judicious* parents using kindness and discipline in equal measure⟩. PRUDENT suggests exercise of the restraint of sound practical wisdom and discretion ⟨a *prudent* decision to wait out the storm⟩. SENSIBLE applies to action guided and restrained by good sense and rationality ⟨a *sensible* person who was not fooled by flattery⟩.

[3]**wise** *vb* **:** to make or become informed or knowledgeable — usually used with *up* ⟨*wise* up if you want to get ahead⟩

-wise \ˌwīz\ *adv combining form* **1 a :** in the manner of ⟨crab*wise*⟩ **b :** in the position or direction of ⟨clock*wise*⟩ ⟨length*wise*⟩ **2 :** with regard to **:** in respect of ⟨dollar*wise*⟩ [Old English *-wīsan,* from *wīse* "manner"]

wise·acre \ˈwī-ˌzā-kər\ *n* **:** one who pretends to knowledge or cleverness **:** SMART ALECK [early Dutch *wijssegger* "soothsayer"]

[1]**wise·crack** \ˈwīz-ˌkrak\ *n* : a clever or sarcastic remark : QUIP *synonyms* see JEST

[2]**wisecrack** *vb* : to make a wisecrack — **wise·crack·er** *n*

wise guy \ˈwīz-ˌgī\ *n* : SMART ALECK

wi·sen·hei·mer *also* **wei·sen·hei·mer** \ˈwīz-n-ˌhī-mər\ *n* : SMART ALECK [[2]*wise* + *-enheimer* (as in family names such as *Guggenheimer, Oppenheimer*)]

wi·sent \ˈvē-ˌzent\ *n* : a nearly extinct European bison that is sometimes considered to belong to the same species as the North American buffalo [German]

wisent

[1]**wish** \ˈwish\ *vb* **1** : to have a desire : long for : WANT ⟨*wish* you were here⟩ ⟨*wish* for a puppy⟩ **2** : to form or express a desire concerning ⟨*wish* them good night⟩ **3** : to request by expressing a desire ⟨I *wish* you to go now⟩ [Old English *wȳscan*] *synonyms* see DESIRE — **wish·er** *n*

[2]**wish** *n* **1 a** : an act or instance of wishing : WANT, DESIRE ⟨a *wish* to travel⟩ **b** : an object of desire : GOAL ⟨I got my *wish*—a good score on the test⟩ **2 a** : an expressed will or desire **b** : a request or order expressed as a wish **3** : an invocation of usually good fortune on someone ⟨sends her best *wishes*⟩

wish·bone \ˈwish-ˌbōn\ *n* : a forked bone in front of the breastbone of a bird consisting chiefly of two fused clavicles [from the superstition that when two people pull it apart the one getting the longer fragment will be granted a wish]

wish·ful \ˈwish-fəl\ *adj* **1** : having a wish : DESIROUS **2** : based on wishes rather than fact ⟨*wishful* thinking⟩ — **wish·ful·ly** \-fə-lē\ *adv* — **wish·ful·ness** *n*

wish list *n* : a list of desired but often realistically unobtainable items ⟨a *wish list* of equipment for the school's gymnasium⟩

wishy–washy \ˈwish-ē-ˌwȯsh-ē, -ˌwäsh-\ *adj* **1** : lacking in character or determination : INEFFECTUAL ⟨*wishy-washy* leadership⟩ **2** : lacking in strength or flavor : WEAK [reduplication of *washy*]

wisp \ˈwisp\ *n* **1** : a small bunch of hay or straw **2 a** : a thin strip or fragment **b** : a thready streak ⟨a *wisp* of smoke⟩ **c** : something frail, slight, or fleeting ⟨a *wisp* of a smile⟩ [Middle English] — **wispy** \ˈwis-pē\ *adj*

wist \ˈwist\ *vt, archaic* : KNOW [earlier *wis,* from *iwis* "certainly," from Old English *gewis* "certain"]

wis·te·ria \wis-ˈtir-ē-ə\ *also* **wis·tar·ia** \wis-ˈtir-ē-ə *also* -ˈter-\ *n* : any of a genus of mostly woody vines of China, Japan, and the southeastern U.S. that belong to the legume family and have compound leaves and showy blue, white, purple, or rose pealike flowers in long hanging clusters [Caspar *Wistar,* died 1818, American physician]

wist·ful \ˈwist-fəl\ *adj* : full of unfulfilled longing or desire : YEARNING ⟨a *wistful* gaze⟩ [blend of *wishful* and obsolete *wistly* "intently"] — **wist·ful·ly** \-fə-lē\ *adv* — **wist·ful·ness** *n*

[1]**wit** \ˈwit\ *vb* **wist** \ˈwist\; **wit·ting**; *present 1st & 3rd sing* **wot** \ˈwät\ *archaic* : KNOW, LEARN [Old English *witan*]

[2]**wit** *n* **1** : reasoning power : INTELLIGENCE **2 a** : mental soundness : SANITY — usually used in plural ⟨scared out of my *wits*⟩ **b** : mental capability and resourcefulness ⟨had the *wit* to leave quickly⟩ **3 a** : the ability to relate seemingly unlike things so as to illuminate or amuse **b** : clever or apt humor **c** : a cleverly amusing remark; *also* : one noted for making such remarks [Old English] — **at one's wit's end** *or* **at one's wits' end** : at a loss for a means of solving a problem

synonyms WIT, HUMOR mean a mode of expression intended to arouse amusement. WIT is more purely intellectual than HUMOR and depends for its effect chiefly on verbal ingenuity or swift perception, especially of the incongruous ⟨a speech noted for insight and *wit*⟩. HUMOR implies an ability to perceive the ludicrous, the comical, and the absurd in human life and to express these sympathetically and without bitterness ⟨a man of great *humor,* full of jokes and laughter⟩.

wi·tan \ˈwi-ˌtän\ *n pl* : members of the witenagemot [Old English, pl. of *wita* "sage, adviser"]

[1]**witch** \ˈwich\ *n* **1** : a person believed to have magic powers **2** : an ugly old woman : HAG [Old English *wicca* (masculine) and *wicce* (feminine)]

[2]**witch** *vb* **1** : BEWITCH **2** : DOWSE

witch·craft \ˈwich-ˌkraft\ *n* **1** : the use of sorcery or magic **2** : WICCA

witch doctor *n* : a person usually in a primitive society who uses magic to treat sickness and to fight off evil spirits

witch·ery \ˈwich-rē, -ə-rē\ *n, pl* **-er·ies** **1 a** : the practice of witchcraft : SORCERY **b** : an act of witchcraft **2** : an irresistible fascination : CHARM

witch·es'–broom \ˈwich-əz-ˌbrüm, -ˌbru̇m\ *n* : an abnormal tufted growth of small branches on a tree or shrub caused especially by parasitic organisms (as fungi, viruses, or aphids)

[1]**witch·grass** \ˈwich-ˌgras\ *n* : QUACK GRASS [probably alteration of *quitch* (*grass*), from Old English *cwice*]

[2]**witchgrass** *n* : a North American grass with slender brushy panicles that is often a weed on cultivated land [[1]*witch*]

witch ha·zel \ˈwich-ˌhā-zəl\ *n* **1** : any of a genus of shrubs or small trees with slender-petaled usually yellow flowers borne in late fall or early spring; *esp* : one of eastern North America that blooms in the fall **2** : an alcoholic solution of material from the bark of the common witch hazel used as a soothing and mildly astringent lotion [Old English *wice,* a tree with pliant branches]

witch–hunt \-ˌhənt\ *n* **1** : a searching out and persecution of persons accused of witchcraft **2** : the searching out and deliberate harassment of those (as political opponents) with unpopular views — **witch–hunt·er** *n* — **witch–hunt·ing** *n or adj*

witch·ing \ˈwich-ing\ *adj* : of, relating to, or suitable for sorcery or supernatural occurrences ⟨the *witching* hour⟩

wi·te·na·ge·mot *or* **wi·te·na·ge·mote** \ˈwit-n-ə-gə-ˌmōt\ *n* : an Anglo-Saxon council of nobles, prelates, and officials convened to advise the king on administrative and judicial matters [Old English *witena gemōt,* from *wita* "sage, adviser" + *gemōt* "assembly"]

with \wit͟h, ˈwit͟h, with, ˈwith\ *prep* **1 a** : in opposition to : AGAINST ⟨fought *with* his brother⟩ **b** : so as to be separated from ⟨parting *with* friends⟩ **2** : in mutual relation to ⟨talking *with* a friend⟩ ⟨trade *with* other countries⟩ **3** : in regard to : TOWARD ⟨angry *with* me⟩ **4 a** : compared to : equal to ⟨on equal terms *with* the others⟩ **b** : on the side of ⟨voted *with* the majority⟩ **c** : as well as ⟨can sing *with* the best of them⟩ **5 a** : in the judgment or estimation of ⟨in good standing *with* our classmates⟩ **b** : in the experience or practice of ⟨*with* them a promise is a real obligation⟩ **6 a** : by means of ⟨write *with* a pen⟩ **b** : because of ⟨danced *with* joy⟩ **7** : having or showing as manner of action or attendant circumstance ⟨spoke *with* ease⟩ ⟨stood there *with* hat in hand⟩ **8 a** : in possession of : HAVING ⟨animals *with* horns⟩ ⟨arrived *with* the news⟩ **b** : characterized or distinguished by ⟨a person *with* a hot temper⟩ **9 a** : in the company of ⟨went to the movies *with* me⟩; *also* : in addition to ⟨your money, *with* ours, will be enough⟩ **b** : inclusive of ⟨costs five dollars *with* the tax⟩ **c** : that contains ⟨tea *with* sugar⟩ **10 a** : at the time of ⟨*with* the outbreak of war they went home⟩; *also* : at the same time as ⟨rose *with* the sun⟩ **b** : in proportion to ⟨the pressure varies *with* the depth⟩ **11** : in the possession or care of ⟨left the money *with* your cousin⟩ **12** : in spite of ⟨even *with* all the obstacles, you managed to succeed⟩ **13** : in the direction of ⟨drift *with* the current⟩ ⟨easier to run *with* the wind than against it⟩ [Old English, "against, from, with"] *synonyms* see BY

[1]**with·al** \wit͟h-ˈȯl, with-\ *adv* **1** : together with this : BESIDES **2** : on the other hand : NEVERTHELESS [Middle English, from *with* + *all, al* "all"]

[2]**withal** *prep, archaic* : WITH — used with a preceding relative or interrogative pronoun as its object

with·draw \wit͟h-ˈdrȯ, with-\ *vb* **-drew** \-ˈdrü\; **-drawn** \-ˈdrȯn\; **-draw·ing** **1** : to take back or away usually from a holder, a place, or a condition : REMOVE ⟨*withdraw* money from the bank⟩ ⟨the troops were *withdrawn* from combat⟩ **2** : to call back (as from consideration or circulation) : RECALL, RESCIND ⟨*withdrew* the nomination⟩ ⟨*withdraw* the product⟩; *also* : RETRACT, RECANT ⟨*withdrew* the remarks and apologized⟩ **3 a**

\ə\ **abut**	\au̇\ **out**	\i\ **tip**	\ȯ\ **saw**	\u̇\ **foot**
\ər\ **further**	\ch\ **chin**	\ī\ **life**	\ȯi\ **coin**	\y\ **yet**
\a\ **mat**	\e\ **pet**	\j\ **job**	\th\ **thin**	\yü\ **few**
\ā\ **take**	\ē\ **easy**	\ng\ **sing**	\t͟h\ **this**	\yu̇\ **cure**
\ä\ **cot, cart**	\g\ **go**	\ō\ **bone**	\ü\ **food**	\zh\ **vision**

: to go away : RETREAT, LEAVE ⟨*withdrew* to the country⟩ **b** : to end one's participation or involvement in something ⟨ready to *withdraw* from the firm⟩ **c** : to be socially or emotionally detached [Middle English *withdrawen,* from *with* "from" + *drawen* "to draw"] — **with·draw·able** \-ˈdrȯ-ə-bəl\ *adj*

with·draw·al \-ˈdrȯ-əl, -ˈdrȯl\ *n* **1** : an act or instance of withdrawing (as a removal, a retreat, or a retraction) **2 a** : the discontinuance of administration or use of a drug **b** : the syndrome of often painful physical and psychological symptoms that follows the discontinuance of an addicting drug ⟨a heroin addict going through *withdrawal*⟩ **3** : social or emotional detachment

with·drawn \-ˈdrȯn\ *adj* **1** : removed from immediate contact or easy approach : ISOLATED, SECLUDED ⟨*withdrawn* mountain communities⟩ **2** : socially detached and unresponsive : INTROVERTED ⟨a shy and *withdrawn* child⟩ — **with·drawn·ness** \-ˈdrȯn-nəs\ *n*

withe \ˈwith, ˈwith, ˈwīth\ *n* : a slender flexible branch or twig; *esp* : one used for tying or binding [Old English *withthe*]

with·er \ˈwith-ər\ *vb* **with·ered; with·er·ing** \ˈwith-ring, -ə-ring\ **1** : to shrivel from or as if from loss of bodily moisture and especially sap ⟨the crops *withered* during the drought⟩ **2** : to lose vitality, force, or freshness ⟨support for the candidate *withered*⟩ **3** : to cause to wither **4** : to make speechless or incapable of action : STUN ⟨*withered* them with a glance⟩ [Middle English *widren*]

with·er·ing *adj* : acting or serving to destroy ⟨a *withering* fire from the enemy⟩ ⟨*withering* criticism⟩

with·er·ite \ˈwith-ə-ˌrīt\ *n* : a translucent white or gray mineral $BaCO_3$ consisting of a carbonate of barium [German *Witherit,* from William *Withering,* died 1799, English physician]

with·ers \ˈwith-ərz\ *n pl* : the ridge between the shoulder bones of a horse; *also* : a corresponding part in other four-footed animals (as dogs) [probably from obsolete English *wither-* "against," from Old English, from *wither* "against"; from the withers being the parts which resist the pull in drawing a load]

with·hold \with-ˈhōld, with-\ *vt* **-held** \-ˈheld\; **-hold·ing** **1** : to hold back : RESTRAIN ⟨*withhold* an angry answer⟩ **2** : to refrain from granting, giving, or allowing ⟨*withhold* permission⟩ **3** : to deduct (withholding tax) from income [Middle English *withholden,* from *with* "from" + *holden* "to hold"] — **with·hold·er** *n*

withholding tax *n* : a deduction (as from wages, fees, or dividends) taken at a source of income as advance payment on income tax

¹with·in \with-ˈin, with-\ *adv* **1** : in or into the interior : INSIDE **2** : inside oneself : INWARDLY ⟨look *within* for creative inspiration⟩ [Old English *withinnan,* from *with* + *innan* "inwardly, within," from *in*]

²within *prep* **1** — used to indicate enclosure or containment ⟨*within* the house⟩ ⟨*within* each mind⟩ **2** : falling inside expressed or implied limits: as **a** : before the end of ⟨left *within* a week⟩ **b** : inside the limitations of ⟨live *within* one's means⟩ **c** : in or into the scope, sphere, or range of ⟨*within* reach⟩ ⟨*within* sight⟩

³within *n* : an inner place or area ⟨revolt from *within*⟩

with–it \ˈwith-ət, ˈwith-\ *adj* : socially or culturally up-to-date

¹with·out \with-ˈau̇t, with-\ *prep* **1 a** : OUTSIDE 1 ⟨they stood *without* the castle gates⟩ **b** : out of the range or limits of ⟨not *without* our capabilities⟩ **2 a** : not having : LACKING ⟨*without* food⟩ **b** : with absence or omission of ⟨listened *without* answering⟩ [Old English *withūtan,* from *with* + *ūtan* "outside," from *ūt* "out"]

²without *adv* **1** : on the outside **2** : with something lacking or absent ⟨has learned to do *without*⟩

³without *n* : an outer place or area ⟨came from *without*⟩

with·stand \with-ˈstand, with-\ *vt* **-stood** \-ˈstu̇d\; **-stand·ing** : to stand against : RESIST; *esp* : to oppose (as an attack or bad influence) successfully [Old English *withstandan,* from *with* "against" + *standan* "to stand"] ***synonyms*** see OPPOSE

withy \ˈwith-ē\ *n, pl* **with·ies** : OSIER 1 [Old English *wīthig*]

wit·less \ˈwit-ləs\ *adj* : lacking wit or understanding : FOOLISH — **wit·less·ly** *adv* — **wit·less·ness** *n*

wit·loof \ˈwit-ˌlōf\ *n* : CHICORY; *also* : ENDIVE 2 [Dutch dialect *witloof* "chicory," from Dutch *wit* "white" + *loof* "foliage"]

¹wit·ness \ˈwit-nəs\ *n* **1 a** : an attesting of a fact or event : TESTIMONY ⟨bear false *witness*⟩ **b** : public testimony to a religious faith **2** : one that gives evidence; *esp* : one who testifies in a cause or before a court **3 a** : one present at a transaction so as to be able to testify to its having taken place **b** : one who has personal knowledge or experience of something **4** : something serving as evidence or proof : SIGN **5** *cap* : JEHOVAH'S WITNESS [Old English *witnes* "knowledge, testimony, witness," from ²*wit*]

²witness *vb* **1** : to testify to : ATTEST **2** : to act as legal witness of ⟨*witness* the making of a will⟩ **3** : to give or constitute evidence or furnish proof of ⟨your actions *witness* your guilt⟩ **4** : to be a witness of ⟨thousands *witnessed* the parade⟩

witness stand *n* : an area from which a witness gives evidence in a court

wit·ted \ˈwit-əd\ *adj* : having wit or understanding — usually used in combination ⟨quick-*witted*⟩

wit·ti·cism \ˈwit-ə-ˌsiz-əm\ *n* : a witty saying [*witty* + *-cism* (as in *criticism*)]

wit·ting \ˈwit-ing\ *adj* **1** : aware of something : CONSCIOUS ⟨a *witting* participant⟩ **2** : done deliberately : INTENTIONAL ⟨a *witting* violation⟩

wit·ting·ly \ˈwit-ing-lē\ *adv* : with knowledge or awareness of what one is doing : CONSCIOUSLY ⟨had *wittingly* misled them⟩

wit·ty \ˈwit-ē\ *adj* **wit·ti·er; -est** : marked by or full of wit ⟨a *witty* writer⟩ ⟨a *witty* remark⟩ — **wit·ti·ly** \ˈwit-l-ē\ *adv* — **wit·ti·ness** \ˈwit-ē-nəs\ *n*

synonyms WITTY, HUMOROUS, FACETIOUS mean provoking or intended to provoke laughter. WITTY suggests cleverness and quickness of mind ⟨a *witty* speech⟩. HUMOROUS applies broadly to anything that evokes usually genial laughter and may contrast with *witty* in suggesting whimsicality or eccentricity ⟨*humorous* anecdotes⟩. FACETIOUS stresses a desire to produce laughter and may be derogatory in implying dubious or ill-timed attempts at wit or humor ⟨*facetious* remarks⟩.

wive \ˈwīv\ *vb* **1** : to marry a woman **2** : to take for a wife [Old English *wīfian,* from *wīf* "woman, wife"]

wives *plural of* WIFE

wiz \ˈwiz\ *n* : WIZARD 2

wiz·ard \ˈwiz-ərd\ *n* **1** : one skilled in magic : SORCERER **2** : a very clever or skillful person ⟨a *wizard* at chess⟩ [Middle English *wysard,* from *wis, wys* "wise"]

wiz·ard·ry \ˈwiz-ər-drē\ *n, pl* **-ries** **1** : the art or practices of a wizard : SORCERY **2 a** : seeming magical power or influence ⟨electronic *wizardry*⟩ **b** : extraordinary skill or ability ⟨athletic *wizardry*⟩

wiz·en \ˈwiz-n\ *vb* **wiz·ened; wiz·en·ing** : to become or cause to become dry, shriveled, and wrinkled especially with age [Old English *wisnian*]

woad \ˈwōd\ *n* : a European herb related to the mustards and formerly grown for a blue dye yielded by its leaves; *also* : this dye [Old English *wād*]

¹wob·ble *also* **wab·ble** \ˈwäb-əl\ *vb* **wob·bled** *also* **wab·bled; wob·bling** *also* **wab·bling** \ˈwäb-ling, -ə-ling\ **1 a** : to move or cause to move with an irregular rocking or side-to-side motion ⟨the baby's head *wobbled* from side-to-side⟩ **b** : TREMBLE, QUAVER ⟨a voice that *wobbles*⟩ **2** : WAVER 1 ⟨his opinion *wobbled*⟩ [probably from Low German *wabbeln*] — **wob·bler** *also* **wab·bler** \ˈwäb-lər, -ə-lər\ *n* — **wob·bly** *also* **wab·bly** \ˈwäb-lē, -ə-lē\ *adj*

²wobble *also* **wabble** *n* : a wobbling action or movement ⟨the wheel had a bad *wobble*⟩

¹woe \ˈwō\ *interj* — used to express grief, regret, or distress [Old English *wā*]

²woe *n* **1** : a condition of deep suffering from misfortune, affliction, or grief **2** : CALAMITY, MISFORTUNE ⟨economic *woes*⟩ ***synonyms*** see SORROW

woe·be·gone \ˈwō-bi-ˌgȯn, -ˌgän\ *adj* **1** : exhibiting great woe, sorrow, or misery ⟨*woebegone* faces⟩ **2** : being in a sorry state ⟨*woebegone* clothes⟩ [Middle English *wo begon,* from *wo* "woe" + *begon,* past participle of *begon* "to go about, beset," from Old English *begān,* from *be-* + *gān* "to go"]

woe·ful *also* **wo·ful** \ˈwō-fəl\ *adj* **1** : full of woe : WRETCHED ⟨a *woeful* tale⟩ **2** : involving or bringing woe ⟨a *woeful* occurrence⟩ **3** : pitifully bad or serious : DEPLORABLE ⟨a *woeful* lack of knowledge⟩ — **woe·ful·ly** \-fə-lē, -flē\ *adv* — **woe·ful·ness** \-fəl-nəs\ *n*

wok \ˈwäk\ *n* : a large bowl-shaped cooking utensil used especially in stir-frying [Chinese (dialect of Guangzhou and Hong Kong) *wohk*]

woke *past and past participle of* WAKE

woken *past participle of* WAKE

wold \ˈwōld\ *n* : a high plain or hilly area usually without woods [Old English *weald, wald* "forest"]

¹wolf \ˈwu̇lf\ *n, pl* **wolves** \ˈwu̇lvz\ **1** *pl also* **wolf** : any of several large erect-eared bushy-tailed predatory mammals that resemble the related dogs and tend to live and hunt in packs; *esp* : GRAY WOLF — compare COYOTE, JACKAL **2 a** (1) : a person resembling a wolf (as in ferocity or guile) (2) : a man forward and zealous in attentions to women **b** : dire poverty ⟨trying to keep the *wolf* from the door⟩ [Old English *wulf*] — **wolf·ish** \ˈwu̇l-fish\ *adj* — **wolf·like** \ˈwu̇l-ˌflīk\ *adj* — **wolf in sheep's clothing** : one who hides a hostile intention behind a friendly manner

wolf 1

²wolf *vt* : to eat greedily : DEVOUR ⟨*wolfed* down the sandwich⟩

wolf dog *n* **1** : any of various large dogs formerly kept for hunting wolves **2** : a hybrid offspring of a wolf and a domestic dog

wolf·hound \ˈwu̇lf-ˌhau̇nd\ *n* : any of several large dogs used especially formerly in hunting large animals (as wolves)

wol·fram \ˈwu̇l-frəm\ *n* : TUNGSTEN [German]

wol·fram·ite \ˈwu̇l-frə-ˌmīt\ *n* : a brownish or grayish mineral that consists of an iron manganese tungstate and is a source of tungsten

wolf spider *n* : any of various active wandering ground-dwelling spiders of which most do not build a web but chase and catch their prey

wol·ver·ine \ˌwu̇l-və-ˈrēn\ *n* : a mostly dark brown shaggy-furred flesh-eating mammal of northern forests that is related to the weasels, martens, and sables and is noted for its strength [probably from *wolv-* (as in *wolves*)]

wom·an \ˈwu̇m-ən\ *n, pl* **wom·en** \ˈwim-ən\ **1** : an adult female person **2** : WOMANKIND **3** : a feminine nature : womanly character **4** : a woman who is a servant or attendant [Old English *wīfman,* from *wīf* "woman, wife" + *man* "human being, man"] — **woman** *adj*

wom·an·hood \ˈwu̇m-ən-ˌhu̇d\ *n* **1** : the state of being a woman **2** : the distinguishing character or qualities of a woman or of womankind **3** : WOMANKIND

wom·an·ish \ˈwu̇m-ə-nish\ *adj* **1** : associated with or characteristic of a woman **2** : UNMANLY a — **wom·an·ish·ly** *adv* — **wom·an·ish·ness** *n*

wom·an·kind \ˈwu̇m-ən-ˌkīnd\ *n* : female human beings : women especially as distinguished from men

wom·an·like \-ˌlīk\ *adj* : resembling or characteristic of a woman : WOMANLY

wom·an·ly \-lē\ *adj* : having qualities appropriate to or associated with a woman — **wom·an·li·ness** *n*

woman's rights *n pl* : legal, political, and social rights for women equal to those of men

woman suffrage *n* : the possession and exercise of the suffrage by women

womb \ˈwüm\ *n* **1** : UTERUS 1 **2** : a place where something is generated or developed [Old English] — **wombed** \ˈwümd\ *adj*

wom·bat \ˈwäm-ˌbat\ *n* : any of several stocky burrowing Australian marsupials resembling small bears [Dharuk (native Australian language of the Sydney area) *wambad*]

wom·en·folk \ˈwim-ən-ˌfōk\ *also* **wom·en·folks** \-ˌfōks\ *n pl* : WOMANKIND

¹won \ˈwən\ *past and past participle of* WIN

²won \ˈwo̐n\ *n* **1** : the basic monetary unit of North Korea and South Korea **2** : a coin or note representing one won [Korean *wŏn*]

¹won·der \ˈwən-dər\ *n* **1 a** : a cause of astonishment or surprise : MARVEL ⟨it's a *wonder* you weren't hurt⟩ ⟨the pyramid is a *wonder* of ancient Egypt⟩ **b** : MIRACLE **2 a** : a feeling (as of awed astonishment or of uncertainty) aroused by something extraordinary, mysterious, or new to one's experience **b** : the quality of exciting wonder ⟨the charm and *wonder* of the scene⟩ [Old English *wundor*]

²wonder *vb* **won·dered; won·der·ing** \-də-ring, -dring\ **1** : to feel surprise or amazement **2** : to feel curiosity or doubt ⟨*wondered* about the cost⟩ — **won·der·er** \-dər-ər\ *n*

wonder drug *n* : a usually newly discovered drug capable of producing a marked and favorable change in a patient's condition — called also *miracle drug*

won·der·ful \ˈwən-dər-fəl\ *adj* **1** : exciting wonder : MARVELOUS ⟨a sight *wonderful* to behold⟩ **2** : unusually good : ADMIRABLE ⟨having a *wonderful* time⟩ — **won·der·ful·ly** \-fə-lē, -flē\ *adv* — **won·der·ful·ness** \-fəl-nəs\ *n*

won·der·land \ˈwən-dər-ˌland, -lənd\ *n* **1** : an imaginary place of delicate beauty or magical charm **2** : a place that excites admiration or wonder ⟨a scenic *wonderland*⟩

won·der·ment \-mənt\ *n* **1** : a state or feeling of wonder : ASTONISHMENT, SURPRISE **2** : curiosity about something

won·der–work·er \-ˌwər-kər\ *n* : one that performs wonders

won·drous \ˈwən-drəs\ *adj* : WONDERFUL 1, MARVELOUS ⟨a *wondrous* place⟩ — **wondrous** *adv, archaic* — **won·drous·ly** *adv* — **won·drous·ness** *n*

¹wont \ˈwo̐nt, ˈwōnt\ *adj* : ACCUSTOMED 3, USED ⟨as they are *wont* to do⟩ [Middle English, from past participle of *wonen* "to dwell, be used to," from Old English *wunian*]

²wont *n* : usual custom : HABIT ⟨according to our *wont*⟩

won't \wōnt, ˈwōnt, ˈwənt\ : will not

wont·ed \ˈwo̐nt-əd, ˈwōnt-\ *adj* : CUSTOMARY 2, USUAL ⟨took my *wonted* rest⟩ — **wont·ed·ly** *adv* — **wont·ed·ness** *n*

won·ton \ˈwän-ˌtän\ *n* : filled pockets of noodle dough served boiled in soup or fried

woo \ˈwü\ *vb* **1 a** : to try to gain the love of : make love : COURT **b** : to try to win over ⟨a young author trying to *woo* the reader⟩ **2** : to seek usually urgently to gain or bring about ⟨a clever auctioneer *wooing* dollars from the audience⟩ [Old English *wōgian*]

¹wood \ˈwu̇d\ *n* **1 a** : a dense growth of trees usually greater in extent than a grove and smaller than a forest — often used in plural ⟨a thick *woods* runs along the ridge⟩ **b** : WOODLAND **2** : a hard fibrous substance that is basically xylem and makes up the greater part of the stems, branches, and roots of trees or shrubs beneath the bark; *also* : this material suitable or prepared for some use (as burning or building) **3** : something made of wood; *esp* : a golf club having a wooden head [Old English *widu, wudu*] — **out of the woods** : clear of danger or difficulty

²wood *adj* **1** : WOODEN 1 **2** : suitable for cutting or working wood ⟨*wood* chisels⟩ **3** *or* **woods** \ˈwu̇dz\ : living, growing, or existing in woods

wood alcohol *n* : METHANOL

wood anemone *n* : any of several anemones that grow in open woodlands

wood·bine \ˈwu̇d-ˌbīn\ *n* **1** : any of several honeysuckles; *esp* : a climbing Eurasian shrub **2** : VIRGINIA CREEPER [Old English *wudubinde,* from *wudu* "wood" + *bindan* "to tie, bind"; from its winding around trees]

wood block *n* : WOODCUT

wood–carv·er \ˈwu̇d-ˌkär-vər\ *n* : a person who carves usually ornamental objects of wood — **wood carv·ing** \-ving\ *n*

wood·chop·per \-ˌchäp-ər\ *n* : one engaged in chopping wood and especially in chopping down trees

wood·chuck \-ˌchək\ *n* : a grizzled thickset marmot chiefly of Alaska, Canada, and the northeastern U.S. — called also *groundhog* [by folk etymology from Narragansett *ockqutchaun* "woodchuck" or a related word in another Algonquian language]

woodchuck

wood·cock \-ˌkäk\ *n, pl* **woodcocks** *or* **woodcock** : a long-billed mottled and usually brownish woodland game bird chiefly of the eastern and central U.S. that is related to the snipes; *also* : a related and similar bird of Eurasia

wood·craft \-ˌkraft\ *n* **1** : knowledge about the woods and how to take care of oneself in them **2** : skill in working with or making things of wood

\ə\ abut	\au̇\ out	\i\ tip	\o̐\ saw	\u̇\ foot
\ər\ further	\ch\ chin	\ī\ life	\o̐i\ coin	\y\ yet
\a\ mat	\e\ pet	\j\ job	\th\ thin	\yü\ few
\ā\ take	\ē\ easy	\ng\ sing	\t͟h\ this	\yu̇\ cure
\ä\ cot, cart	\g\ go	\ō\ bone	\ü\ food	\zh\ vision

wood·cut \-ˌkət\ *n* **1 :** a printing surface consisting of a wooden block with a usually pictorial design cut with the grain **2 :** a print from a woodcut

wood·cut·ter \-ˌkət-ər\ *n* **:** one that cuts wood especially as an occupation

wood duck *n* **:** a showy American duck that nests in tree cavities and the male of which has a large crest and plumage colored with green, purple, black, white, and chestnut

wood duck

wood·ed \ˈwu̇d-əd\ *adj* **:** covered with trees

wood·en \ˈwu̇d-ⁿn\ *adj* **1 :** made of wood ⟨a *wooden* box⟩ **2 a :** lacking flexibility **:** STIFF ⟨a *wooden* expression⟩ **b :** lacking ease, interest, or zest ⟨written in a *wooden* style⟩ — **wood·en·ly** *adv* — **wood·en·ness** \-ⁿn-nəs\ *n*

wood engraving *n* **1 :** the art or process of cutting a design upon wood and especially upon the end grain of wood for use as a printing surface; *also* **:** such a printing surface **2 :** a design printed from a wood engraving

wood·en·ware \ˈwu̇d-ⁿn-ˌwaər, -ˌweər\ *n* **:** articles made of wood for domestic use

wood frog *n* **:** a common North American frog that is found mostly in moist woodlands and is dark brown, yellowish brown, or pink with a black stripe on each side of the head

[1]**wood·land** \ˈwu̇d-lənd, -ˌland\ *n* **:** land covered with woody vegetation **:** FOREST — **wood·land·er** \-ər\ *n*

[2]**woodland** *adj* **1 :** growing, living, or occurring in woodland ⟨a *woodland* bird⟩ **2 :** of, relating to, or made up of woodland ⟨*woodland* areas⟩

wood·lot \ˈwu̇d-ˌlät\ *n* **:** an area of trees usually privately maintained as a source of fuel and lumber needs

wood louse *n* **:** a small flat grayish crustacean that is an isopod, lives in damp places (as under stones, fallen leaves, and rotting logs), and is often capable of rolling its body into a ball — called also *pill bug, sow bug*

wood·man \ˈwu̇d-mən\ *n* **:** WOODSMAN

wood·note \-ˌnōt\ *n* **:** verbal expression that is natural and artless

wood nymph *n* **:** a nymph in classical mythology that lives in the woods — called also *dryad*

wood·peck·er \ˈwu̇d-ˌpek-ər\ *n* **:** any of numerous usually brightly marked birds with specialized feet, strong claws, and stiff spiny tail feathers used in climbing or resting on tree trunks, a long flexible tongue, and a very hard bill used to drill into trees for insect food or to excavate nesting cavities

wood·pile \-ˌpīl\ *n* **:** a pile of wood and especially firewood

wood pulp *n* **:** pulp from wood used in making cellulose derivatives (as paper or rayon)

wood pussy *n* **:** SKUNK 1

wood rat *n* **:** any of numerous soft-furred rodents of North and Central America that have well-furred tails, large ears, and a tendency to hoard food and debris — compare PACK RAT

wood ray *n* **:** XYLEM RAY

woods *variant of* WOOD

wood·shed \ˈwu̇d-ˌshed\ *n* **:** a shed for storing wood and especially firewood

woods·man \ˈwu̇dz-mən\ *n* **:** a person who frequents or works in the woods; *esp* **:** one skilled in woodcraft

wood sorrel *n* **:** any of a genus of herbs with acid sap, compound leaves, and 5-petaled flowers; *esp* **:** a stemless herb having leaves with three leaflets that is sometimes considered to be the original shamrock

woodsy \ˈwu̇d-zē\ *adj* **woods·i·er; -est :** relating to or suggestive of woods ⟨a *woodsy* smell⟩

wood thrush *n* **:** a large thrush of eastern North America noted for its loud clear song

wood turning *n* **:** the art or process of fashioning useful articles from wooden pieces or blocks by means of a lathe

wood turpentine *n* **:** TURPENTINE 2b

wood warbler *n* **:** WARBLER 2b

wood·wind \ˈwu̇d-ˌwind\ *n* **1 :** one of a group of wind instruments including flutes, clarinets, oboes, bassoons, and sometimes saxophones **2** *pl* **a :** the woodwind instruments of a band or orchestra **b :** the players of woodwind instruments — **woodwind** *adj*

wood·work \-ˌwərk\ *n* **:** work made of wood; *esp* **:** interior fittings (as moldings or stairways) of wood

wood·work·ing \-ˌwər-king\ *n* **:** the act, process, or occupation of working with wood — **wood·work·er** \-kər\ *n* — **woodworking** *adj*

woody \ˈwu̇d-ē\ *adj* **wood·i·er; -est 1 :** abounding or overgrown with trees ⟨*woody* land⟩ **2 :** of or containing wood or wood fibers **:** LIGNEOUS ⟨*woody* plant tissue⟩ **3 :** characteristic of or resembling wood ⟨a *woody* texture⟩ — **wood·i·ness** *n*

woo·er \ˈwü-ər\ *n* **:** one that woos **:** SUITOR

[1]**woof** \ˈwu̇f, ˈwüf\ *n* **1 :** the threads that cross the warp in a woven fabric **2 :** a woven fabric or its texture [Old English *ōwef,* from *on* + *wefan* "to weave"]

[2]**woof** \ˈwu̇f\ *vi* **:** to make the sound of a woof

[3]**woof** *n* **:** a deep harsh sound typically produced by a dog

woof·er \ˈwu̇f-ər\ *n* **:** a loudspeaker that is usually larger than a tweeter, is responsive only to the lower acoustic frequencies, and is used for reproducing sounds of low pitch — compare TWEETER

wool \ˈwu̇l\ *n* **1 :** the soft wavy or curly usually thick undercoat of various mammals and especially the sheep **2 :** a product of wool; *esp* **:** a woven fabric or garment of such fabric **3 a :** dense hair especially on a plant **b :** material (as of glass or metal) drawn or formed into a thready mass [Old English *wull*] — **wooled** \ˈwu̇ld\ *adj*

[1]**wool·en** *or* **wool·len** \ˈwu̇l-ən\ *adj* **1 :** made of wool — compare WORSTED **2 :** of or relating to the manufacture or sale of woolen products ⟨a *woolen* mill⟩

[2]**woolen** *or* **woollen** *n* **1 :** a fabric made of wool **2 :** garments of woolen fabric — usually used in plural

wool·gath·er·ing \ˈwu̇l-ˌgath-ring, -ə-ring\ *n* **:** idle daydreaming

[1]**wool·ly** *also* **wooly** \ˈwu̇l-ē\ *adj* **wool·li·er; -est 1 a :** of, relating to, or bearing wool ⟨*woolly* animals⟩ **b :** resembling wool **2 :** lacking in clearness **:** BLURRY ⟨*woolly* thinking⟩ **3 :** marked by roughness or lack of order or restraint ⟨the wild and *woolly* West⟩ — **wool·li·ness** *n*

[2]**wool·ly** *also* **wooly** *or* **wool·ie** \ˈwu̇l-ē\ *n, pl* **wool·lies :** a garment made from wool; *esp* **:** underclothing of knitted wool — usually used in plural

woolly aphid *n* **:** any of several aphids that secrete a dense coating of woolly white filaments

woolly bear *n* **:** any of various rather large very hairy moth caterpillars; *esp* **:** one that is the larva of a tiger moth

woolly mammoth *n* **:** a heavy-coated mammoth formerly of cold northern regions that is known from fossil remains, from Paleolithic drawings, and from entire frozen bodies unearthed in Siberia

woolly mammoth

wool·sack \ˈwu̇l-ˌsak\ *n* **1 :** a sack for wool **2 :** the official seat of the Lord Chancellor or his deputy in the House of Lords

woo·zy \ˈwü-zē\ *adj* **woo·zi·er; -est 1 :** having the senses dulled **2 :** affected with dizziness, mild nausea, or weakness [origin unknown] — **woo·zi·ly** \-zə-lē\ *adv* — **woo·zi·ness** \-zē-nəs\ *n*

Worces·ter·shire sauce \ˌwu̇s-tər-ˌshiər-, ˌwu̇s-tə-, -shər\ *n* **:** a pungent sauce whose ingredients include soy sauce, vinegar, and garlic — called also *Worcestershire* [from *Worcestershire,* England, where it was first made]

[1]**word** \ˈwərd\ *n* **1 a :** something that is said **b** *pl* **:** TALK, DISCOURSE ⟨putting one's feelings into *words*⟩ **c :** a brief remark or conversation ⟨would like to have a *word* with you⟩ **2 a :** a speech sound or series of speech sounds that symbolizes and communicates a meaning without being divisible into smaller units capable of independent use **b :** a written or printed character or combination of characters representing a spoken word **c :** a combination of electrical or magnetic impulses conveying a unit of information in communication and computer work **3 :** ORDER 5c, COMMAND ⟨don't advance until you get the *word*⟩ **4** *often cap* **a :** LOGOS **b :** GOSPEL 1a **c :** the expressed or

manifested mind and will of God **5 :** NEWS, INFORMATION ⟨got *word* of the accident⟩ **6 :** PROMISE, DECLARATION ⟨kept her *word*⟩ **7 :** a quarrelsome utterance or conversation — usually used in plural ⟨they had *words* and parted in anger⟩ **8 :** a verbal signal **:** PASSWORD [Old English] — **good word 1 :** a favorable statement ⟨put in a *good word* for me⟩ **2 :** good news ⟨what's the *good word*⟩ — **in a word :** in short — **in so many words 1 :** in exactly those words ⟨implied that such behavior was unacceptable but didn't say so *in so many words*⟩ **2 :** in plain straightforward language ⟨told him *in so many words* that he wasn't welcome⟩ — **of few words :** not saying more than is necessary ⟨a man *of few words*⟩ — **of one's word :** that can be relied on to keep a promise ⟨a woman *of her word*⟩ — **upon my word :** with my assurance **:** INDEED ⟨*upon my word,* I've never heard of such a thing⟩

[2]**word** *vt* **:** to express in words **:** PHRASE ⟨*worded* their request with great care⟩

word•age \ˈwərd-ij\ *n* **:** a quantity or number of words

word•book \ˈwərd-ˌbu̇k\ *n* **:** VOCABULARY 1, DICTIONARY

word class *n* **:** a linguistic form class whose members are words; *esp* **:** PART OF SPEECH

word–for–word *adj* **:** being in or following the exact words **:** VERBATIM ⟨a *word-for-word* translation⟩

word for word *adv* **:** in the exact words **:** VERBATIM ⟨repeated the message *word for word*⟩

word•ing \ˈwərd-iŋ\ *n* **1 :** expression in words **2 :** the manner or style of expressing in words **:** PHRASING

word•less \ˈwərd-ləs\ *adj* **1 :** not expressed in or accompanied by words ⟨a *wordless* picture book⟩ **2 :** SILENT 1a, SPEECHLESS ⟨sat *wordless* throughout the meeting⟩ — **word•less•ly** *adv* — **word•less•ness** *n*

word of mouth : spoken communication

word order *n* **:** the order of arrangement of words in a phrase, clause, or sentence

word•play \ˈwərd-ˌplā\ *n* **:** playful use of words **:** verbal wit

word processing *n* **:** the production of typewritten documents (as business letters) with automated and usually computerized equipment for preparing text

word processor *n* **:** a keyboard-operated terminal usually with a video display and a magnetic storage device for use in word processing; *also* **:** software (as for a computer system) to perform word processing

word stress *n* **:** the manner in which stresses are distributed on the syllables of a word — called also *word accent*

wordy \ˈwərd-ē\ *adj* **word•i•er; -est :** using or containing many or too many words **:** VERBOSE — **word•i•ly** \ˈwərd-l-ē\ *adv* — **word•i•ness** \ˈwərd-ē-nəs\ *n*

wore *past of* WEAR

[1]**work** \ˈwərk\ *n* **1 a :** the use of strength or ability to get something done **b :** the activity engaged in as a means of livelihood **:** OCCUPATION; *also* **:** the place of one's employment ⟨didn't go to *work* today⟩ **c :** something that needs to be done **:** TASK ⟨there is *work* to do⟩ **2 :** the energy expended by a force acting over a given distance **3 a :** something that results from a particular method or manner of working ⟨careful police *work*⟩ **b :** something that results from the use or fashioning of a particular material ⟨porcelain *work*⟩ **4 :** a fortified structure (as a fort or trench) **5** *pl* **:** a place where industrial labor is carried on **:** PLANT, FACTORY ⟨chemical *works*⟩ **6** *pl* **:** the working or moving parts of a mechanical device ⟨the *works* of a watch⟩ **7 :** a product of effort, exertion, or skill; *esp* **:** an artistic production ⟨a writer's first *work*⟩ **8** *pl* **:** performance of moral or religious acts ⟨salvation by *works*⟩ **9 a :** effective operation **:** EFFECT ⟨wait for time to do its healing *work*⟩ **b :** the manner or quality of working **:** WORKMANSHIP ⟨careless *work*⟩ **10 :** the material that is operated on at some stage in a process ⟨place the *work* to the right of the machine⟩ **11 a** *pl* **:** everything possessed, available, or appropriate ⟨ordered a hot dog with the *works*⟩ **b :** the harshest treatment possible ⟨gave him the *works*⟩ [Old English *werc, weorc*] — **at work 1 :** engaged in working **:** BUSY; *esp* **:** engaged in one's regular occupation **2 :** having effect **:** OPERATING, FUNCTIONING ⟨medicine *at work* in the body⟩ — **in the works :** in process of preparation, development, or completion ⟨a plan for change is now *in the works*⟩ — **out of work :** without regular employment **:** JOBLESS

[2]**work** *adj* **1 :** used for work ⟨a *work* elephant⟩ **2 :** suitable or styled for wear while working ⟨*work* clothes⟩

[3]**work** *vb* **worked** \ˈwərkt\ *or* **wrought** \ˈrȯt\; **work•ing 1 :** to bring to pass **:** EFFECT ⟨*work* miracles⟩ **2 :** to fashion or create by expending labor or exertion upon ⟨*work* flint into tools⟩ **3 a :** to prepare for use by stirring or kneading ⟨*work* dough⟩ **b :** to bring into a desired form by a gradual process of cutting, hammering, scraping, pressing, or stretching ⟨*work* cold steel⟩ **4 :** to set or keep in motion or operation ⟨a pump *worked* by hand⟩ **5 :** to solve (a problem) by reasoning or calculation **6 a :** to cause to toil or labor **:** get work out of ⟨*work* horses in the field⟩ **b :** to make use of **:** EXPLOIT ⟨*work* a mine⟩ **c :** to control or guide the operation of ⟨switches are *worked* from a central tower⟩ **7 a :** to carry on an operation through or in or along ⟨the salespeople *worked* both sides of the street⟩ **b :** to greet and talk with in a friendly way in order to gain acceptance or achieve a purpose ⟨politicians *working* the crowd⟩ **8 :** to pay for or achieve with labor or service ⟨*worked* my way through college⟩ ⟨*worked* my way up in the company⟩ **9 a :** to get (as oneself or an object) into or out of a condition or position by stages ⟨*work* the nut loose⟩ **b :** CONTRIVE 1, ARRANGE ⟨if we can *work* it⟩ **10 a :** to practice trickery or deception on for some end ⟨*worked* the management for a free ticket⟩ **b :** EXCITE 1b, PROVOKE ⟨*work* myself into a rage⟩ **11 a :** to exert oneself physically or mentally especially in sustained effort for a purpose or under compulsion or necessity **b :** to perform a task requiring sustained effort or repeated operations **c :** to perform work regularly for wages ⟨*works* in publishing⟩ **12 :** to function or operate according to plan or design ⟨hinges *work* better with oil⟩ **13 :** to produce the desired effect **:** SUCCEED ⟨the plan *worked* well⟩ **14 :** to make way slowly and with difficulty ⟨*worked* up to president⟩ **15 :** to react in a specified way to being worked ⟨this wood *works* easily⟩ **16 a :** to be in agitation or restless motion **b :** FERMENT 1 **c :** to move slightly in relation to another part **d :** to get into a specific condition by slow or imperceptible movements ⟨the knot *worked* loose⟩ [Old English *wyrcan*] — **work on 1 :** AFFECT ⟨*worked on* our sympathies⟩ **2 :** to strive to influence or persuade

work•able \ˈwər-kə-bəl\ *adj* **1 :** capable of being worked **2 :** FEASIBLE 1, PRACTICABLE ⟨a *workable* solution to the problem⟩ — **work•abil•i•ty** \ˌwər-kə-ˈbil-ət-ē\ *n* — **work•able•ness** \ˈwər-kə-bəl-nəs\ *n*

work•a•day \ˈwər-kə-ˌdā\ *adj* **1 :** of, relating to, or suited for working days ⟨*workaday* clothes⟩ **2 :** ORDINARY 1 ⟨a *workaday* life⟩ [obsolete *workyday* "workday"]

work•bag \ˈwərk-ˌbag\ *n* **:** a bag for implements or materials for work; *esp* **:** a bag for needlework

work•bas•ket \-ˌbas-kət\ *n* **:** a basket for needlework

work•bench \-ˌbench\ *n* **:** a bench on which work especially of mechanics, machinists, and carpenters is performed

work•book \-ˌbu̇k\ *n* **1 :** a booklet outlining a course of study **2 :** a worker's manual **3 :** a record of work done **4 :** a student's book of problems to be solved directly on the pages

work•box \-ˌbäks\ *n* **:** a box for work instruments and materials

work•day \-ˌdā\ *n* **1 :** a day on which work is performed as distinguished from a day off **2 :** the period of time in a day during which work is performed — **workday** *adj*

worked \ˈwərkt\ *adj* **:** that has been subjected to some process of development, treatment, or manufacture ⟨a newly *worked* field⟩

worked up *adj* **:** emotionally aroused **:** EXCITED ⟨all *worked up* over the football game⟩

work•er \ˈwər-kər\ *n* **1 a :** one that works **b :** a member of the working class **2 :** one of the members of a colony of social ants, bees, wasps, or termites that are incompletely developed sexually and usually sterile and that perform most of the labor and protective duties of the colony

workers' compensation *n* **:** a system of insurance that reimburses an employer for damages that must be paid to an employee for injury occurring in the course of employment — called also *workers' comp* \-ˈkämp\

work farm *n* **:** a farm on which persons convicted of minor law violations are confined and put to work

workforce \ˈwərk-ˌfōrs, -ˌfȯrs\ *n* **1 :** the workers engaged in a specific activity or business ⟨the factory's *workforce*⟩ **2 :** the

number of workers potentially assignable for any purpose ⟨the nation's *workforce*⟩
work·horse \ˈwərk-ˌhȯrs\ *n* **1** : a horse used chiefly for labor **2 a** : a person who performs most of the work of a group task **b** : something that is markedly useful, durable, or dependable
work·house \-ˌhau̇s\ *n* **1** *British* : POORHOUSE **2** : an institution where persons who have committed minor law violations are confined
¹**work·ing** \ˈwər-king\ *n* **1** : the manner of functioning or operating : OPERATION — usually used in plural ⟨the inner *workings* of the government⟩ **2** : an excavation or group of excavations made in mining, quarrying, or tunneling — usually used in plural
²**working** *adj* **1 a** : doing work especially for a living ⟨*working* people⟩ **b** : being in a state that allows for further work or activity ⟨a *working* model⟩ **2** : good enough to allow work to be done ⟨a *working* majority⟩ ⟨had a *working* knowledge of French⟩ **3 a** : of, relating to, or occupied with work ⟨*working* hours⟩ **b** : used or fit for use in work ⟨*working* clothes⟩ **4** : being in use or operation ⟨a *working* farm⟩
working class *n* : the class of people who are employed for wages usually in manual labor — **working–class** *adj*
work·ing·man \ˈwər-king-ˌman\ *n* : one who works for wages usually at manual labor or in industry
working papers *n pl* : official documents legalizing the employment of a minor
work·ing·wom·an \ˈwər-king-ˌwu̇m-ən\ *n* : WORKWOMAN
work·less \ˈwər-kləs\ *adj* : being without work : UNEMPLOYED — **work·less·ness** *n*
work·load \ˈwərk-ˌlōd\ *n* **1** : the amount of work or of working time expected or assigned ⟨students with a heavy *workload*⟩ **2** : the amount of work performed or capable of being performed usually within a specific period ⟨a machine's *workload*⟩
work·man \ˈwərk-mən\ *n* **1** : WORKINGMAN **2** : ARTISAN, CRAFTSMAN
work·man·like \-ˌlīk\ *or* **work·man·ly** \-lē\ *adj* : exhibiting good workmanship : SKILLFUL ⟨a *workmanlike* job⟩
work·man·ship \ˈwərk-mən-ˌship\ *n* **1** : the art or skill of an artisan : CRAFTSMANSHIP **2** : the quality or character of a piece of work ⟨the excellent *workmanship* of the desk⟩
workmen's compensation insurance *n* : WORKERS' COMPENSATION
work of art : a product of one of the fine arts; *esp* : a painting or sculpture of high artistic quality
work off *vt* : to get rid of by work or activity ⟨*work off* a debt⟩
work·out \ˈwərk-ˌau̇t\ *n* : a practice or period of exercise to test or improve one's fitness especially for athletic competition, ability, or performance
work out *vb* **1** : to bring about by labor and exertion **2 a** : SOLVE ⟨*work out* a problem⟩ **b** : to bring about especially by resolving difficulties ⟨*work out* a compromise⟩ **c** : DEVELOP, ELABORATE ⟨*work out* a plan⟩ **3** : to discharge (as a debt) by labor **4** : to exhaust (as a mine) by working **5 a** : to prove effective, practicable, or suitable ⟨don't know if your idea will *work out*⟩ **b** : to amount to a total or calculated figure — usually used with *at* or *to* **6** : to engage in a workout ⟨*works out* daily at the gym⟩
work over *vt* **1** : to do over : REWORK **2** : to beat up ⟨was *worked over* in a dark alley⟩
work·room \ˈwərk-ˌrüm, -ˌru̇m\ *n* : a room used especially for manual work
work·shop \ˈwərk-ˌshäp\ *n* **1** : a small establishment where manufacturing or the production of handicrafts is carried on **2** : WORKROOM **3** : a usually brief intensive educational program for a small group of people that focuses especially on techniques and skills in a particular field
work·sta·tion \ˈwərk-ˌstā-shən\ *n* **1** : a terminal or personal computer usually connected to a computer network **2** : a powerful microcomputer used especially for scientific or engineering work
work·ta·ble \-ˌtā-bəl\ *n* : a table for holding working materials and implements (as for needlework)
work·up \ˈwərk-ˌəp\ *n* : a thorough examination usually conducted to diagnose a medical condition ⟨a blood *workup*⟩
work up *vt* **1** : to stir up : ROUSE ⟨*worked up* voter support⟩ **2** : to produce by mental or physical work ⟨*worked up* a sweat while exercising⟩
work·week \ˈwərk-ˌwēk\ *n* : the hours or days of work in a calendar week ⟨a 40-hour *workweek*⟩ ⟨a 5-day *workweek*⟩
work·wom·an \-ˌwu̇m-ən\ *n* : a woman who works
world \ˈwərld\ *n* **1** : the earth with its inhabitants and all things upon it **2** : people in general : HUMANITY **3** : the concerns of the earth and its affairs as distinguished from heaven and the life to come **4** : the system of created things : UNIVERSE **5** : a part or section of the earth or its inhabitants by itself **6** : the scene of one's life and action ⟨living in your own little *world*⟩ **7** : a great number or quantity ⟨a *world* of troubles⟩ **8** : human society ⟨withdraw from the *world*⟩ **9** : a distinctive class of persons or their sphere of interest or activity ⟨the musical *world*⟩ **10** : a heavenly body (as a planet) especially if inhabited [Old English *woruld* "human existence, this world, age"] ***synonyms*** see EARTH — **in the world** : among innumerable possibilities : EVER — used as an intensive ⟨what *in the world* is it⟩ — **out of this world** : of extraordinary excellence : SUPERB
world beat *n* : WORLD MUSIC — **world–beat** *adj*
world–beat·er \ˈwərld-ˌbēt-ər\ *n* : one that excels all others of its kind : CHAMPION
world–class *adj* : being of the highest degree of excellence in the world ⟨a *world-class* athlete⟩
world·ling \ˈwərld-ˌling\ *n* : a person engrossed in the concerns of this present world
world·ly \ˈwərld-lē\ *adj* **world·li·er; -est** **1** : of, relating to, or devoted to this world and its pursuits rather than to spiritual affairs **2** : WORLDLY-WISE ***synonyms*** see EARTHLY — **world·li·ness** *n*
world·ly–mind·ed \ˈwərld-lē-ˌmīn-dəd\ *adj* : devoted to or engrossed in worldly interests — **world·ly–mind·ed·ness** *n*
world·ly–wise \ˈwərld-lē-ˌwīz\ *adj* : having a practical and often shrewd understanding of human affairs
world music *n* : popular music originating from or influenced by non-Western musical traditions and often having a danceable rhythm — **world–music** *adj*
world power *n* : a political unit (as a nation) powerful enough to affect the entire world by its influence or actions
World Series *n* : a contest or event that is the most important or prestigious of its kind ⟨the *World Series* of dog shows⟩
world war *n* : a war involving all or most of the chief nations of the world; *esp, cap both Ws* : either of two such wars of the 20th century
world–wea·ry \ˈwərld-ˌwiər-ē\ *adj* : feeling or showing fatigue from or boredom with the life of the world and especially with material pleasures — **world–wea·ri·ness** \-ˌwir-ē-nəs\ *n*
world·wide \ˈwərld-ˈwīd\ *adj* : extended throughout or involving the entire world
World Wide Web *n* : a part of the Internet designed to allow easier navigation of the network through the use of text and graphics that link to other documents
¹**worm** \ˈwərm\ *n* **1 a** : EARTHWORM; *also* : any annelid worm **b** : any of various relatively small long usually soft-bodied creeping animals (as a grub or tapeworm) **2 a** : a human being who is an object of contempt, loathing, or pity : WRETCH **b** : something that inwardly torments or devours **3** *pl* : infestation with or disease caused by parasitic worms **4** : something (as a mechanical device) spiral in form or appearance: as **a** : the thread of a screw **b** : a short revolving screw whose threads gear with the teeth of a worm wheel or rack **5** : a usually small self-contained and self-replicating computer program that invades computers on a network and usually performs a destructive action — compare TROJAN HORSE 2, VIRUS 3 [Old English *wyrm* "serpent, worm"] — **worm** *adj* — **worm·like** \-ˌlīk\ *adj*
²**worm** *vb* **1** : to move or cause to move or proceed sinuously or deceptively ⟨spies *worm* into important positions⟩ ⟨*wormed* out of the crowd⟩ **2** : to insinuate or introduce (oneself) by devious or subtle means ⟨seeks to *worm* himself into an important position⟩ **3** : to rid (as a dog) of parasitic worms **4** : to obtain or extract by artful or insidious questioning or by pleading, asking, or persuading ⟨*wormed* the truth out of me⟩
worm–eat·en \ˈwər-ˌmēt-n\ *adj* **1 a** : eaten or burrowed by worms ⟨*worm-eaten* timber⟩ **b** : marked with pits **2** : WORN-OUT, ANTIQUATED ⟨*worm-eaten* methods⟩
worm·er \ˈwərm-ər\ *n* : a drug used to destroy parasitic worms in an animal
worm fence *n* : a zigzag fence consisting of interlocking rails supported by crossed poles — called also *snake fence*

worm gear *n* **1** : WORM WHEEL **2** : a gear of a worm and a worm wheel working together

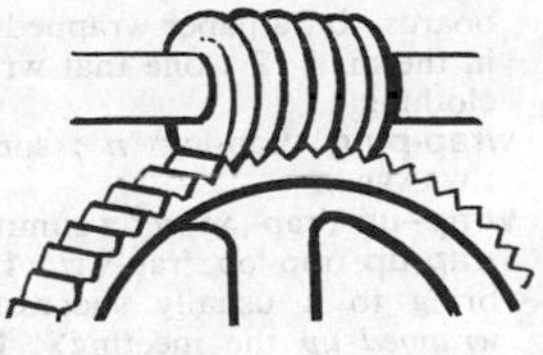

worm gear 2

worm·hole \ˈwərm-ˌhōl\ *n* **1** : a hole or passage burrowed by a worm **2** : a hypothetical structure of space-time envisioned as a tunnel connecting points that are separated in space and time

worm·seed \-ˌsēd\ *n* : any of various plants (as a goosefoot) whose seeds contain substances destructive to parasitic worms

worm wheel *n* : a toothed wheel that meshes with the thread of a worm

worm·wood \ˈwərm-ˌwu̇d\ *n* **1** : any of a genus of aromatic herbs and shrubs (as sagebrush) related to the daisies; *esp* : a European plant yielding a bitter dark green oil used in absinthe **2** : something bitter or grievous ⟨it was *wormwood* for him to accept charity⟩ [Middle English *wormwode,* from Old English *wermōd*]

wormy \ˈwər-mē\ *adj* **worm·i·er; -est** **1** : containing, infested with, or damaged by worms ⟨*wormy* flour⟩ ⟨*wormy* timbers⟩ **2** : resembling or suggestive of a worm

worn *past participle of* WEAR

worn–out \ˈwōr-ˈnau̇t, ˈwȯr-\ *adj* **1** : useless from long or hard wear ⟨*worn-out* skates⟩ **2** : very weary ⟨*worn-out* shoppers⟩

wor·ried *adj* : having worries : marked by or showing worry ⟨very *worried* about the test⟩ ⟨a *worried* look⟩ — **wor·ried·ly** *adv*

wor·ri·ment \ˈwər-ē-mənt, ˈwə-rē-\ *n* : an act or instance of worrying; *also* : TROUBLE, WORRY

wor·ri·some \-səm\ *adj* **1** : causing distress or worry ⟨*worrisome* news⟩ **2** : inclined to worry or fret ⟨*worrisome* parents⟩ — **wor·ri·some·ly** *adv*

1**wor·ry** \ˈwər-ē, ˈwə-rē\ *vb* **wor·ried; wor·ry·ing** **1 a** : to shake and tear or mangle with the teeth ⟨a puppy *worrying* an old shoe⟩ **b** : to torment with persistent attacks **2** : to cause to be anxious ⟨his absence *worried* his friends⟩ **3** : to feel or express great anxiety : FRET ⟨*worrying* about her health⟩ [Old English *wyrgan* "to strangle"] — **wor·ri·er** *n*

2**worry** *n, pl* **worries** **1** : ANXIETY 1a **2** : a cause of anxiety : TROUBLE

wor·ry·wart \-ˌwȯrt\ *n* : a person who worries without reasonable cause

1**worse** \ˈwərs\ *adj, comparative of* BAD *or of* ILL **1** : of more inferior quality, value, or condition ⟨that car is in *worse* shape than the one you sold⟩ **2 a** : more unfavorable, unpleasant, or painful ⟨a *worse* punishment⟩ **b** : more faulty, unsuitable, or incorrect ⟨can't imagine *worse* ideas⟩ **c** : less skillful or efficient ⟨*worse* than any mechanic I know⟩ **3** : bad, evil, or corrupt in a greater degree : more reprehensible ⟨is stealing *worse* than cheating?⟩ **4** : being in poorer health : SICKER ⟨I was *worse* the next day⟩ [Old English *wiersa, wyrsa*]

2**worse** *n* **1** : one that is worse ⟨threatened detention and *worse*⟩ **2** : a greater degree of ill or badness ⟨a turn for the *worse*⟩

3**worse** *adv, comparative of* BAD *or* BADLY *or of* ILL : in a worse manner : to a worse extent or degree ⟨slept *worse* than ever⟩

wors·en \ˈwərs-n\ *vb* **wors·ened; wors·en·ing** \ˈwərs-ning, -ning\ : to make or become worse ⟨the weather *worsened*⟩

1**wor·ship** \ˈwər-shəp\ *n* **1** *chiefly British* : a person of importance — used as a title for various officials (as magistrates and some mayors) **2** : reverence offered a divine being or supernatural power; *also* : the expression of such reverence **3** : extravagant respect or admiration for or devotion to an object of esteem ⟨*worship* of the dollar⟩ [Old English *weorthscipe* "worthiness, respect, reverence," from *weorth* "worthy, worth" + *-scipe* "-ship"]

2**worship** *vb* **-shipped** *also* **-shiped; -ship·ping** *also* **-ship·ing** **1** : to honor or reverence as a divine being or supernatural power **2** : to regard with extravagant respect, honor, or devotion : IDOLIZE **3** : to perform or take part in worship or an act of worship ***synonyms*** see REVERE — **wor·ship·per** *or* **wor·ship·er** *n*

wor·ship·ful \-fəl\ *adj* **1** *archaic* : EMINENT, NOTABLE **2** : giving worship or veneration — **wor·ship·ful·ly** \-fə-lē\ *adv* — **wor·ship·ful·ness** *n*

1**worst** \ˈwərst\ *adj, superlative of* BAD *or of* ILL **1** : most bad, evil, ill, or corrupt ⟨his *worst* fault⟩ **2 a** : most unfavorable, unpleasant, or painful ⟨your *worst* enemy⟩ **b** : most unsuitable, faulty, unattractive, or ill-conceived ⟨has the *worst* table manners⟩ **c** : least skillful or efficient ⟨the *worst* plumber you can hire⟩ **3** : most wanting in quality, value, or condition ⟨the *worst* results⟩ [Old English *wierresta, wyrsta*] — **the worst way** : very much ⟨wanted a car in *the worst way*⟩

2**worst** *n* **1** : one that is worst ⟨always chooses the *worst*⟩ **2** : the greatest degree of ill or badness ⟨if worse comes to *worst*⟩

3**worst** *adv, superlative of* BAD *or* BADLY *or of* ILL **1** : to the extreme degree of badness or inferiority ⟨sings *worst*⟩ **2** : to the greatest degree ⟨needed help *worst*⟩

4**worst** *vt* : to get the better of : DEFEAT ⟨*worsted* his opponents⟩

wor·sted \ˈwu̇s-təd, ˈwərs-\ *n* **1** : a smooth compact yarn from long wool fibers used especially for firm napless fabrics, carpeting, or knitting **2** : a fabric made from worsted yarns [*Worstead,* England] — **worsted** *adj*

1**wort** \ˈwərt, ˈwȯrt\ *n* : PLANT 1; *esp* : an herbaceous plant — usually used in combination ⟨figwort⟩ [Old English *wyrt* "root, herb, plant"]

2**wort** *n* : a sweet liquid that is drained from mash made from crushed malt or grain meal and that is fermented to make beer and whiskey [Old English *wyrt*]

1**worth** \ˈwərth\ *prep* **1 a** : equal in value to ⟨the painting is *worth* $1000⟩ **b** : having possessions or income equal to ⟨an actor *worth* millions⟩ **2** : deserving of ⟨well *worth* the effort⟩ **3** : capable of ⟨ran for all I was *worth*⟩ [Old English *weorth* "having value, worthy"]

2**worth** *n* **1 a** : monetary value ⟨possessions of little *worth*⟩ **b** : the equivalent of a specified amount or figure ⟨a dollar's *worth* of cheese⟩ **2** : the value of something measured by its qualities or by the esteem in which it is held ⟨an experience of great *worth*⟩ **3 a** : moral or personal value **b** : EXCELLENCE 1, MERIT **4** : the value of one's property

synonyms WORTH, VALUE, PRICE mean an equivalence in quality or amount. WORTH applies to what is intrinsically excellent, admirable, useful, or desirable ⟨the *worth* of such a man to the community⟩. VALUE may imply the immediate estimation of the worth of something to an individual or at a particular time or place ⟨information of great *value*⟩. PRICE applies to what is actually exchanged for something else and may or may not imply an equivalent intrinsic worth ⟨peace at the *price* of war⟩.

worth·ful \ˈwərth-fəl\ *adj* **1** : full of merit : HONORABLE **2** : having value : VALUABLE — **worth·ful·ness** *n*

worth·less \ˈwərth-ləs\ *adj* **1 a** : lacking worth : VALUELESS **b** : USELESS ⟨*worthless* to continue searching⟩ **2** : DESPICABLE, LOW ⟨a *worthless* coward⟩ — **worth·less·ly** *adv* — **worth·less·ness** *n*

worth·while \ˈwərth-ˈhwīl, -ˈwīl\ *adj* **1** : being worth the time or effort spent ⟨*worthwhile* preparations⟩ **2** : WORTHY 1a — **worth·while·ness** *n*

1**wor·thy** \ˈwər-t͟hē\ *adj* **wor·thi·er; -est** **1 a** : having worth or value : ESTIMABLE ⟨a *worthy* cause⟩ **b** : MERITORIOUS, HONORABLE ⟨*worthy* candidates⟩ **2** : having sufficient worth ⟨you are *worthy* of the honor⟩ — **wor·thi·ly** \-t͟hə-lē\ *adv* — **wor·thi·ness** \-t͟hē-nəs\ *n*

2**worthy** *n, pl* **worthies** : a worthy person

wot *present 1st & 3rd singular of* WIT

would \wəd, əd, d, wu̇d, ˈwu̇d\ *vb, past of* WILL **1 a** *archaic* : WISHED, DESIRED **b** *archaic* : wish for : WANT **c** : strongly desire : WISH ⟨I *would* I were young again⟩ **2** — used as an auxiliary verb (1) with *rather* or *sooner* to express preference between alternatives ⟨*would* sooner die than face them⟩, (2) to express wish, desire, or intent ⟨those who *would* forbid gambling⟩, (3) to express willingness or preference, (4) to express plan or intention ⟨said they *would* come⟩, (5) to express custom or habitual action ⟨we *would* meet often for lunch⟩, (6) to express consent or choice ⟨*would* put it off if they could⟩, (7) to express contingency or possibility ⟨if they were coming, they *would* be here now⟩, (8) to express completion of a statement of desire, request, or advice ⟨we wish that you *would* go⟩, and (9) to express probability or presumption in past or present time ⟨*would* have won if I had not tripped⟩ **3** : COULD ⟨the barrel

\ə\ **abut**	\au̇\ **out**	\i\ **tip**	\ȯ\ **saw**	\u̇\ **foot**
\ər\ **further**	\ch\ **chin**	\ī\ **life**	\ȯi\ **coin**	\y\ **yet**
\a\ **mat**	\e\ **pet**	\j\ **job**	\th\ **thin**	\yü\ **few**
\ā\ **take**	\ē\ **easy**	\ng\ **sing**	\t͟h\ **this**	\yu̇\ **cure**
\ä\ **cot, cart**	\g\ **go**	\ō\ **bone**	\ü\ **food**	\zh\ **vision**

would hold 20 gallons⟩ **4** — used as an auxiliary verb (1) to express a request with which voluntary compliance is expected ⟨*would* you please help us⟩ and (2) to express doubt or uncertainty ⟨the explanation *would* seem satisfactory⟩ **5 :** SHOULD ⟨knew I *would* enjoy the trip⟩ ⟨*would* be glad to know the answer⟩ [Old English *wolde*]

would–be \ˌwu̇d-ˌbē\ *adj* **:** desiring, intending, or professing to be ⟨a *would-be* poet⟩

wouldn't \ˈwu̇d-nt\ **:** would not

wouldst \wədst, wu̇dst, ˈwu̇dst, wətst\ *or* **would·est** \ˈwu̇d-əst\ *archaic past 2nd singular of* WILL

[1]**wound** \ˈwünd\ *n* **1 :** an injury typically involving cutting or breaking of bodily tissue (as by violence, accident, or surgery) **2 :** a mental or emotional hurt or blow [Old English *wund*]

[2]**wound** *vb* **1 :** to cause a wound to or in ⟨the broken glass *wounded* several people⟩ **2 :** to inflict a wound ⟨a *wounding* remark⟩

[3]**wound** \ˈwau̇nd\ *past and past participle of* WIND

[1]**wound·ed** \ˈwün-dəd\ *n pl* **:** persons that have been wounded

[2]**wounded** *adj* **:** injured, hurt by, or suffering from a wound ⟨a *wounded* leg⟩ ⟨*wounded* feelings⟩

wove *past of* WEAVE

woven *past participle of* WEAVE

[1]**wow** \ˈwau̇\ *interj* — used to express strong feeling (as pleasure or surprise)

[2]**wow** *n* **:** a distortion in reproduced sound consisting of a slow rise and fall in pitch caused by speed variation in the reproducing system [imitative]

[1]**wrack** \ˈrak\ *n* **1 :** RUIN 1, DESTRUCTION **2 :** a remnant of something destroyed [Old English *wræc* "misery, punishment, something driven by the sea"]

[2]**wrack** *n* **1 :** a wrecked ship **2 :** a piece of wreckage [early Dutch or Low German *wrak*]

[3]**wrack** *vt* **:** to utterly ruin **:** WRECK

[4]**wrack** *vt* **1 :** [2]RACK 2 **2 :** [2]RACK 3

[5]**wrack** *n* **:** [1]RACK 2

wraith \ˈrāth\ *n, pl* **wraiths** \ˈrāths *also* ˈrathz\ **1 a :** an apparition of a living person seen usually as an exact likeness and just before death **b :** GHOST 2 **2 :** an insubstantial appearance of something **:** SHADOW [origin unknown]

[1]**wran·gle** \ˈrang-gəl\ *vb* **wran·gled; wran·gling** \-gə-ling, -gling\ **1 :** to dispute angrily or peevishly **:** BICKER **2 :** ARGUE **2 3 :** to obtain by persistent arguing **4 :** to herd and care for (livestock and especially horses) on the range [Middle English *wranglen*]

[2]**wrangle** *n* **1 :** an angry, noisy, or prolonged dispute or quarrel **2 :** the action or process of wrangling

wran·gler \-gə-lər, -glər\ *n* **1 :** one that wrangles or bickers **2 :** a ranch hand who takes care of the saddle horses [short for *horse-wrangler,* probably partial translation of Mexican Spanish *caballerango* "groom"]

[1]**wrap** \ˈrap\ *vb* **wrapped; wrap·ping 1 a :** to cover especially by winding or folding ⟨*wrap* a baby in a blanket⟩ **b :** to envelop and secure (as for transportation or storage) ⟨*wrap* a gift⟩ **c :** to enclose by grasping or embracing ⟨*wrapped* her in my arms⟩ **d :** to coil, fold, draw, or twine about something ⟨*wrap* a rubber band around the sticks⟩ **2 a :** to envelop closely or completely **:** SURROUND ⟨mist *wrapped* the houses⟩ **b :** to involve completely **:** ENGROSS ⟨they were *wrapped* up in studying for exams⟩ **3 :** to conceal or obscure as if by enveloping ⟨a city *wrapped* in darkness⟩ **4 :** to put on clothing **:** DRESS ⟨*wrapped* up warmly⟩ **5 :** to be subject to covering, enclosing, or packaging ⟨*wraps* up into a small package⟩ **6 :** to come to completion in filming or recording ⟨the movie *wrapped*⟩ [Middle English *wrappen*]

[2]**wrap** *n* **1 a** (1) **:** a covering that encloses something **:** WRAPPER (2) **:** material used for wrapping ⟨plastic *wrap*⟩ **b :** an article of clothing that may be wrapped around a person; *esp* **:** an outer garment (as a coat or shawl) **2 :** a single turn or convolution of something wound around an object **3** *pl* **a :** RESTRAINT 2a **b :** SECRECY 2 ⟨a plan kept under *wraps*⟩ **4 :** the completion of a schedule or session for filming or recording

[1]**wrap·around** \ˌrap-ə-ˌrau̇nd\ *adj* **1 :** made to be wrapped around the body ⟨a *wraparound* skirt⟩ **2 :** shaped to follow a contour; *esp* **:** made to curve from the front around to the side ⟨*wraparound* sunglasses⟩

[2]**wraparound** \ˈrap-ə-ˌrau̇nd\ *n* **:** a wraparound garment

wrap·per \ˈrap-ər\ *n* **1 :** that in which something is wrapped: as **a** (1) **:** JACKET 2c (2) **:** the paper cover of a book not bound in boards **b :** a paper wrapped around a newspaper or magazine in the mail **2 :** one that wraps **3 :** a wraparound article of clothing

wrap·ping \ˈrap-ing\ *n* **:** something used to wrap an object **:** WRAPPER

wrap–up \ˈrap-ˌəp\ *n* **:** a summarizing report

wrap up \rap-ˈəp, ˈrap-\ *vt* **1 :** SUMMARIZE, SUM UP **2 a :** to bring to a usually successful conclusion **:** END ⟨quickly *wrapped up* the meeting⟩ **b :** to guarantee the success of **:** CINCH ⟨*wrapped up* the nomination⟩

wrasse \ˈras\ *n* **:** any of various usually brilliantly colored marine fishes especially of warm waters that include some important food fishes and popular aquarium fishes [Cornish *gwragh, wragh* "hag, wrasse"]

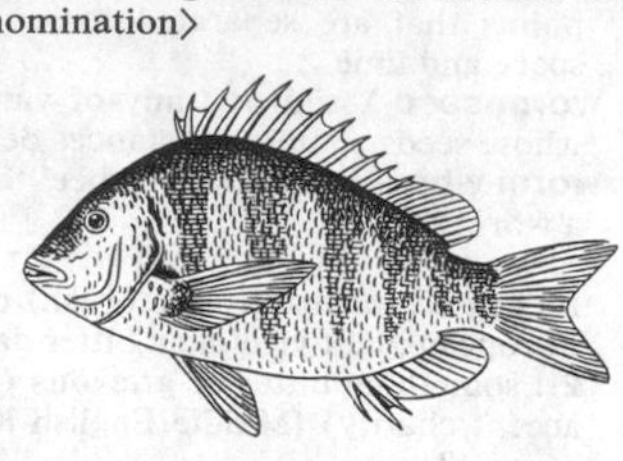

wrasse

wrath \ˈrath\ *n* **1 :** strong vengeful anger **2 :** retributory punishment for sin or crime [Old English *wrǣththo,* from *wrāth* "wroth"] ***synonyms*** see ANGER — **wrathy** \-ē\ *adj*

wrath·ful \ˈrath-fəl\ *adj* **1 :** filled with wrath **:** IRATE **2 :** arising from, marked by, or indicative of wrath ⟨a *wrathful* expression⟩ — **wrath·ful·ly** \-fə-lē\ *adv* — **wrath·ful·ness** *n*

wreak \ˈrēk\ *vt* **1 :** to exact as a punishment **:** INFLICT ⟨*wreak* vengeance⟩ **2 :** to give free scope or rein to ⟨*wreaked* their wrath⟩ **3 :** BRING ABOUT, CAUSE ⟨*wreak* havoc⟩ [Old English *wrecan* "to drive, punish, avenge"]

wreath \ˈrēth\ *n, pl* **wreaths** \ˈrēthz, ˈrēths\ **1 :** something (as a garland or chaplet) intertwined or arranged into a circular shape ⟨a *wreath* of flowers⟩ **2 :** something having a circular or coiling form ⟨a *wreath* of smoke⟩ [Old English *writha*]

wreathe \ˈrēth\ *vb* **1 :** to twist or contort so as to show folds or creases ⟨a face *wreathed* in smiles⟩ **2 a :** to shape into a wreath **b :** to take on the shape of a wreath **:** move or extend in circles or spirals ⟨smoke *wreathed* upward⟩ **c :** to cause to coil about something **3 :** to encircle or adorn with or as if with a wreath ⟨ivy *wreathed* the pole⟩

[1]**wreck** \ˈrek\ *n* **1 :** goods cast upon the land by the sea after a shipwreck **2 a :** SHIPWRECK 2 **b :** the action of wrecking or fact or state of being wrecked **:** DESTRUCTION **c :** a violent and destructive crash ⟨was injured in a car *wreck*⟩ **3 :** the broken remains of something wrecked or otherwise ruined **4 :** something disabled or in a state of ruin or dilapidation ⟨the old house was a *wreck*⟩; *also* **:** an individual broken in health or spirits [Medieval French *wrek,* of Scandinavian origin]

[2]**wreck** *vt* **1 a :** to reduce to a ruinous state by or as if by violence ⟨a country *wrecked* by war⟩ ⟨jealousy *wrecked* their friendship⟩ **b :** SHIPWRECK 2 **2 :** to ruin, damage, or imperil by a wreck ⟨*wrecked* the car⟩ **3 :** BRING ABOUT, WREAK ⟨*wreck* havoc⟩

wreck·age \ˈrek-ij\ *n* **1 :** the act of wrecking **:** the state of being wrecked **2 :** the remains of a wreck

wreck·er \ˈrek-ər\ *n* **1 :** one that wrecks **2 :** a person who searches for or works on wrecks of ships **3 :** a ship used in salvaging wrecks **4 :** TOW TRUCK

wrecking bar *n* **:** a small crowbar with a claw for pulling nails at one end and a slight bend for prying at the other end

wren \ˈren\ *n* **1 :** any of a family of small mostly brown singing birds with short rounded wings and short erect tail **2 :** any of various small singing birds resembling the true wrens in size and habits [Old English *wrenna*]

[1]**wrench** \ˈrench\ *vb* **1 :** to move with a violent twist **2 :** to pull, strain, or tighten with violent twisting **3 :** to injure or disable by a violent twisting or straining ⟨*wrenched* her back⟩ **4 :** DISTORT 1, PERVERT **5 :** to snatch forcibly **:** WREST **6 :** to cause to suffer anguish **:** RACK [Old English *wrencan*]

[2]**wrench** *n* **1 a :** a violent twisting or a pull with or as if with twisting **b :** a sharp twist or sudden jerk straining muscles or ligaments; *also* **:** the resultant injury (as of a joint) **c :** a distorting or perverting alteration **d :** acute emotional distress **:** sudden violent mental change **2 :** a hand or power tool for holding, twisting, or turning an object (as a bolt or nut)

[1]**wrest** \ˈrest\ *vt* **1 :** to pull, force, or move by violent wringing or twisting movements **2 :** to gain with difficulty by or as if by

force or violence ⟨*wrest* a living⟩ ⟨*wrest* the power from the king⟩ [Old English *wrǣstan*] — **wrest·er** *n*

[2]**wrest** *n* : a forcible twist : WRENCH

[1]**wres·tle** \'res-əl\ *vb* **wres·tled; wres·tling** \'res-ling, -ə-ling\ **1** : to grapple with an opponent in an attempt to trip or throw the opponent down **2** : to contend against in wrestling **3** : to combat an opposing tendency or force ⟨*wrestling* with his conscience⟩ **4** : to engage in deep thought, consideration, or debate ⟨*wrestled* with the problem⟩ **5** : to engage in or as if in a violent or determined struggle ⟨*wrestling* with the heavy luggage⟩ [Old English *wrǣstlian,* from *wrǣstan* "to wrest"] — **wres·tler** \'res-lər\ *n*

[2]**wrestle** *n* : the action or an instance of wrestling : STRUGGLE

wres·tling \'res-ling\ *n* : a sport or contest in which two unarmed individuals struggle hand to hand with each attempting to subdue or unbalance the other

wretch \'rech\ *n* **1** : a miserable unhappy person **2** : a base, despicable, or vile person [Old English *wrecca* "outcast"]

wretch·ed \'rech-əd\ *adj* **1** : deeply afflicted, dejected, or distressed : MISERABLE **2** : very or annoyingly bad ⟨a *wretched* accident⟩ **3 a** : being or appearing mean or contemptible ⟨a *wretched* trick⟩ **b** : very poor in quality or ability ⟨*wretched* workmanship⟩ — **wretch·ed·ly** *adv* — **wretch·ed·ness** *n*

[1]**wrig·gle** \'rig-əl\ *vb* **wrig·gled; wrig·gling** \'rig-ling, -ə-ling\ **1** : to move to and fro with short writhing motions like a worm : SQUIRM ⟨*wriggled* in the chair⟩ ⟨*wriggled* my toes⟩ **2** : to move or progress by twisting and turning ⟨the eel *wriggled* its way upstream⟩ **3** : to extricate or insinuate oneself or reach a goal as if by wriggling ⟨*wriggle* out of a difficulty⟩ [Middle English *wrigglen*] — **wrig·gly** \'rig-lē, -ə-lē\ *adj*

[2]**wriggle** *n* **1** : a short or quick twisting motion **2** : a formation or marking having a winding or twisting course or appearance

wrig·gler \'rig-lər, -ə-lər\ *n* : one that wriggles; *esp* : WIGGLER 1

wright \'rīt\ *n* : a workman in wood : CARPENTER — usually used in combination ⟨ship*wright*⟩ ⟨wheel*wright*⟩ [Old English *wyrhta, wryhta* "worker, maker"]

wring \'ring\ *vt* **wrung** \'rəng\; **wring·ing** \'ring-ing\ **1** : to squeeze or twist especially so as to make dry or to extract moisture or liquid ⟨*wring* wet clothes⟩ **2** : to get by or as if by twisting or pressing ⟨*wring* the truth out of you⟩ **3 a** : to twist into a distorted shape with a forcible or violent motion ⟨*wring* a chicken's neck⟩ **b** : to twist together (clasped hands) as a sign of anguish **4** : to affect painfully as if by wringing : TORMENT ⟨a tragedy that *wrung* our hearts⟩ [Old English *wringan*] — **wring** *n*

wring·er \'ring-ər\ *n* : one that wrings; *esp* : a machine or device for pressing out liquid or moisture ⟨clothes *wringer*⟩

[1]**wrin·kle** \'ring-kəl\ *n* **1** : a crease or small fold on a surface (as of the skin or a piece of cloth) **2 a** : METHOD 1, TECHNIQUE **b** : a change in usual procedure or method **c** : something new or different : INNOVATION **3** : IMPERFECTION, IRREGULARITY [Middle English back-formation from *wrinkled* "twisted, winding," probably from Old English *gewrinclod,* past participle of *gewrinclian* "to wind"] — **wrin·kly** \-kə-lē, -klē\ *adj*

[2]**wrinkle** *vb* **wrin·kled; wrin·kling** \-kə-ling, -kling\ : to develop or cause to develop wrinkles

wrist \'rist\ *n* : the joint or the region of the joint between the human hand and the arm; *also* : a corresponding part of a lower animal [Old English]

wrist·band \'rist-ˌband, 'ris-\ *n* **1** : the part of a sleeve covering the wrist **2** : a band encircling the wrist

wrist·let \'rist-lət, 'ris-\ *n* : a band encircling the wrist; *esp* : a close-fitting knitted band worn for warmth

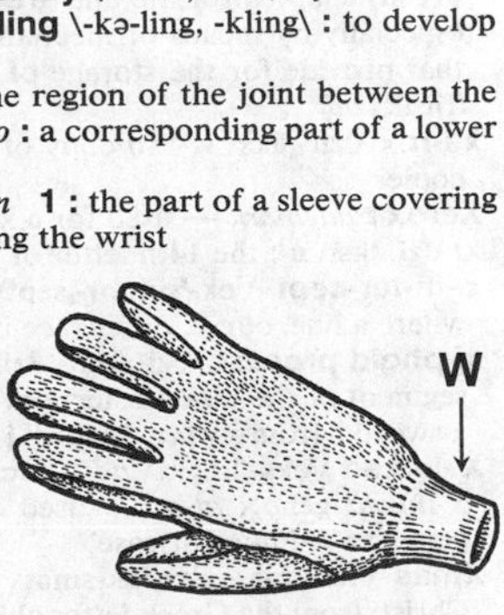

W wristlet

wrist pin *n* : a pin by which a connecting rod (as a piston rod) is fastened to another moving part (as of an engine)

wrist·watch \'ris-ˌtwäch\ *n* : a small watch attached to a bracelet or strap to fasten about the wrist

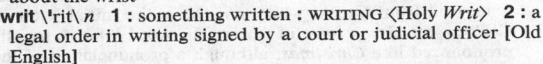

writ \'rit\ *n* **1** : something written : WRITING ⟨Holy *Writ*⟩ **2** : a legal order in writing signed by a court or judicial officer [Old English]

writ·able \'rīt-ə-bəl\ *adj* **1** : capable of being put in writing **2** : being an electronic storage medium that is capable of having new data written on it ⟨a *writable* DVD⟩

write \'rīt\ *vb* **wrote** \'rōt\; **writ·ten** \'rit-n\ *also* **writ** \'rit\; **writ·ing** \'rīt-ing\ **1** : to form letters or words with pen or pencil ⟨learn to read and *write*⟩ **2 a** : to form the letters or the words of (as on paper) : INSCRIBE ⟨*write* one's name⟩ **b** : to cover, fill, or fill in by writing ⟨*write* a check⟩ **c** : to spell in writing ⟨words *written* alike but pronounced differently⟩ **3** : to put down on paper : give expression to in writing ⟨*write* an account of the festivities⟩ **4** : to make up and set down for others to read : COMPOSE ⟨*write* a book⟩ ⟨*wrote* music⟩ **5** : to communicate with in writing ⟨*write* the president⟩ **6** : to communicate by letter ⟨*writes* that they are coming⟩ **7** : to be fitted for writing ⟨this pen *writes* easily⟩ **8** : to transfer (as data) from the memory of a computer to an output device ⟨*write* data onto magnetic tape⟩ [Old English *wrītan* "to scratch, draw, inscribe"]

write down *vb* **1** : to record in written form **2 a** : to reduce in status, rank, or value **b** : to play down in writing **3** : to write so as to appeal to a less sophisticated audience ⟨*write down* to meet the needs of children⟩

write–in \'rīt-ˌin\ *n* **1** : a vote cast by writing in the name of a candidate **2** : a candidate whose name is written in

write in *vt* : to insert (a name not listed on a ballot or voting machine) in an appropriate space

write–off \'rīt-ˌȯf\ *n* **1** : an elimination of an item from the books of account **2 a** : a reduction in book value of an item (as by way of depreciation) **b** : a tax deduction of an amount of depreciation, expense, or loss

write off *vt* **1** : to eliminate (an asset) from the books : enter as a loss or expense ⟨*write off* a bad debt⟩ **2** : to consider to be lost ⟨the candidate has already *written off* the southern states⟩; *also* : DISMISS 3 ⟨*wrote off* my losing as bad luck⟩

write out *vt* : to put in writing; *esp* : to put into a full and complete written form

writ·er \'rīt-ər\ *n* **1** : AUTHOR 1 **2** : one that can write

writer's block *n* : a usually temporary psychological condition in which a writer is unable to proceed with a piece of writing

writer's cramp *n* : a painful spasmodic contraction of muscles of the hand or fingers brought on by excessive writing

write–up \'rīt-ˌəp\ *n* : a written account (as in a newspaper); *esp* : a flattering article

write up \rīt-'əp, 'rīt-\ *vt* **1** : to write an account of : DESCRIBE **2** : to increase the book value of **3** : to report (a person) especially for some violation of law or rules

writhe \'rīth\ *vb* **1** : to twist and turn this way and that ⟨*writhe* in pain⟩ **2** : to suffer with shame or confusion : SQUIRM [Old English *wrīthan*]

writ·ing \'rīt-ing\ *n* **1** : the act or process of one that writes: as **a** : the formation of letters : HANDWRITING 1 **b** : the art or practice of literary or musical composition **2 a** : something (as a letter, book, or document) that is written or printed **b** : INSCRIPTION 1 **3** : a style or form of composition **4** : the occupation of a writer

writing desk *n* : a desk often with a sloping top for writing on

writing paper *n* : paper that has a smooth surface so that it can be written on with ink

writ·ings \'rīt-ingz\ *n pl* : the third part of the Jewish scriptures — compare LAW 3b, PROPHETS; see BIBLE table

writ of assistance : a writ issued (as by British authorities in the American colonies) to an officer (as a sheriff) to aid in the search for smuggled or illegal goods

[1]**wrong** \'rȯng\ *n* **1 a** : an injurious, unfair, or unjust act **b** : a violation of the legal rights of another; *esp* : TORT **2** : principles, practices, or conduct contrary to justice, goodness, equity, or law ⟨know right from *wrong*⟩ **3 a** : the state, position, or fact of being or doing wrong ⟨in the *wrong*⟩ **b** : the state of being guilty [Old English *wrang,* of Scandinavian origin]

[2]**wrong** *adj* **wrong·er** \'rȯng-ər\; **wrong·est** \'rȯng-əst\ **1** : not according to the moral standard : SINFUL, IMMORAL **2** : not right or proper according to a code, standard, or convention : IMPROPER ⟨it was *wrong* not to thank the host⟩ **3** : not according to truth or facts : INCORRECT ⟨the *wrong* answer⟩ **4** : not satisfactory (as in condition, results, health, or temper) **5**

\ə\ **abut**	\au̇\ **out**	\i\ **tip**	\ȯ\ **saw**	\u̇\ **foot**
\ər\ **further**	\ch\ **chin**	\ī\ **life**	\ȯi\ **coin**	\y\ **yet**
\a\ **mat**	\e\ **pet**	\j\ **job**	\th\ **thin**	\yü\ **few**
\ā\ **take**	\ē\ **easy**	\ng\ **sing**	\th\ **this**	\yu̇\ **cure**
\ä\ **cot, cart**	\g\ **go**	\ō\ **bone**	\ü\ **food**	\zh\ **vision**

: not in accordance with one's needs or intent ⟨took the *wrong* bus⟩ **6** : being the side of something that is opposite to the principal one, that is the one naturally turned down, inward, or away, or that is the least finished or polished ⟨the *wrong* side of a fabric⟩ — **wrong** *adv* — **wrong·ly** \ˈrȯng-lē\ *adv* — **wrong·ness** *n*

[3]**wrong** *vt* **wronged; wrong·ing** \ˈrȯng-iŋ\ **1** : to do wrong to : INJURE, HARM **2** : to make unjust remarks about : DISHONOR, MALIGN — **wrong·er** \ˈrȯng-ər\ *n*

wrong·do·er \ˈrȯng-ˈdü-ər\ *n* : a person who does wrong and especially moral wrong — **wrong·do·ing** \-ˈdü-iŋ\ *n*

wrong·ful \ˈrȯng-fəl\ *adj* **1** : WRONG 2, UNJUST ⟨a *wrongful* act⟩ **2** : UNLAWFUL 1 ⟨*wrongful* possession of another's property⟩ — **wrong·ful·ly** \-fə-lē\ *adv* — **wrong·ful·ness** *n*

wrong·head·ed \ˈrȯng-ˈhed-əd\ *adj* **1** : stubborn in adherence to wrong opinion or principles **2** : contrary to sound judgment ⟨*wrongheaded* advice⟩ — **wrong·head·ed·ly** *adv* — **wrong·head·ed·ness** *n*

wrote *past of* WRITE

wroth \ˈrȯth *also* ˈrōth\ *adj* : filled with wrath : ANGRY [Old English *wrāth*]

[1]**wrought** *past and past participle of* WORK

[2]**wrought** \ˈrȯt\ *adj* **1** : worked into shape by artistry or effort ⟨a carefully *wrought* essay⟩ **2** : elaborately decorated **3** : processed for use ⟨*wrought* silk⟩ **4** : beaten into shape by tools ⟨*wrought* metals⟩ **5** : deeply stirred : EXCITED ⟨gets easily *wrought* up⟩

wrought iron *n* : a commercial form of iron that is tough, malleable, and relatively soft

wrung *past and past participle of* WRING

wry \ˈrī\ *adj* **wry·er** \ˈrī-ər, ˈrīr\; **wry·est** \ˈrī-əst\ **1** : bent, twisted, or turned usually abnormally to one side ⟨a *wry* nose⟩ **2 a** : expressive of irony ⟨a *wry* smile⟩ **b** : cleverly and often ironically or grimly humorous ⟨a *wry* reply⟩ [earlier *wry* "to twist," from Old English *wrigian* "to turn"] — **wry·ly** *adv* — **wry·ness** *n*

wry·neck \ˈrī-ˌnek\ *n* : a disorder marked by a twisting of the neck to one side that results in an unnatural position of the head

wurst \ˈwərst, ˈwu̇rst, ˈwu̇st, ˈwu̇sht\ *n* : SAUSAGE [German]

wy·an·dotte \ˈwī-ən-ˌdät\ *n* : any of a U.S. breed of medium-sized domestic chickens raised for meat and eggs [probably from *Wyandot,* member of a group of American Indians]

WYS·I·WYG \ˈwiz-ē-ˌwig\ *n* : a computer display generated by word-processing software that shows exactly how a printout of the document will appear [*w*hat *y*ou *s*ee *i*s *w*hat *y*ou *g*et]

X

[1]**x** \ˈeks\ *n, pl* **x's** *or* **xs** \ˈek-səz\ *often cap* **1** : the 24th letter of the English alphabet **2** : ten in Roman numerals **3** : an unknown quantity

Word History The standard use of the letter *x* to designate an unknown quantity goes back to the practice of René Descartes, 17th century French mathematician and philosopher. Descartes, in his book *La géométrie* ("Geometry"), used the first letters of the alphabet for known quantities and the final letters, *x, y, z* (and most commonly *x*), for unknowns. Later mathematicians have simply followed Descartes's example.

[2]**x** *vt* **x–ed** *also* **x'd** *or* **xed** \ˈekst\; **x–ing** *or* **x'ing** \ˈek-siŋ\ **1** : to mark with an x **2** : to cancel or cover over with a series of x's — usually used with *out* ⟨*x-ed* out the mistake⟩

X \ˈeks\ *adj, of a motion picture* : of such a nature that admission is denied to persons under a specified age (as 17) — used before the adoption of *NC-17*

xan·tho·phyll \ˈzan-thə-ˌfil\ *n* : any of several yellow to orange carotenoid pigments that are usually oxygen derivatives of carotenes [French *xanthophylle,* from Greek *xanthos* "yellow" + *phyllon* "leaf"]

x–ax·is \ˈek-ˌsak-səs\ *n* : the axis in a plane Cartesian coordinate system parallel to which abscissas are measured

X chromosome *n* : a sex chromosome that is associated with femaleness and usually occurs paired in each female cell and single in each male cell in organisms (as humans and most mammals) in which the male typically has two unlike sex chromosomes — compare Y CHROMOSOME

x–co·or·di·nate \ˌek-skō-ˈȯrd-nət, -n-ət, -n-ˌāt\ *n* : ABSCISSA

xe·bec \ˈzē-ˌbek, zi-ˈ\ *n* : a usually 3-masted Mediterranean sailing ship with long overhanging bow and stern [probably from French *chebec,* from Arabic *shabbāk*]

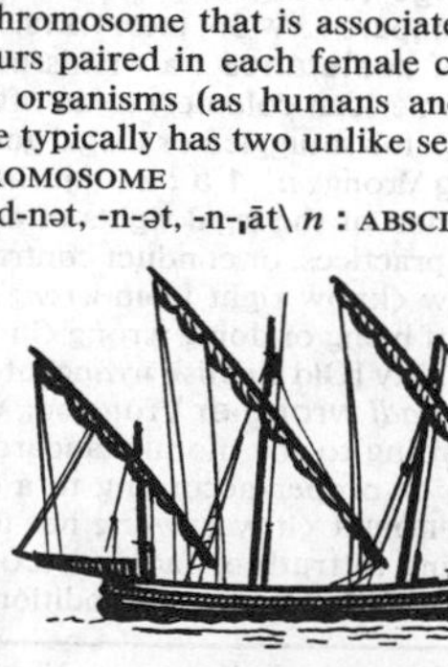

xebec

xe·non \ˈzē-ˌnän, ˈzen-ˌän\ *n* : a heavy gaseous chemical element occurring in air in minute quantities and used especially in specialized electric lamps — see ELEMENT table [Greek, neuter of *xenos* "strange"]

xe·no·phobe \ˈzen-ə-ˌfōb, ˈzēn-\ *n* : a person who is unreasonably fearful of what is foreign and especially of people of foreign origin — **xe·no·pho·bic** \ˌzen-ə-ˈfō-bik, ˌzēn-\ *adj*

xe·no·pho·bia \ˌzen-ə-ˈfō-bē-ə, ˌzēn-\ *n* : fear and hatred of strangers or foreigners or of anything that is strange or foreign [Greek *xenos* "strange, stranger"]

xer- *or* **xero-** *combining form* : dry ⟨*xeric*⟩ ⟨*xero*phyte⟩ [Greek *xēros*]

xe·ric \ˈzir-ik, ˈzer-\ *adj* : characterized by, relating to, or requiring only a small amount of moisture ⟨*xeric* woodlands⟩ ⟨a *xeric* plant⟩

xe·rog·ra·phy \zə-ˈräg-rə-fē, zir-ˈäg-\ *n* : the formation of pictures or copies of graphic matter by the action of light on an electrically charged surface in which the latent image is developed with powders — **xe·ro·graph·ic** \ˌzir-ə-ˈgraf-ik\ *adj*

xe·roph·thal·mia \ˌzir-ˌäf-ˈthal-mē-ə, -ˌäp-ˈthal-\ *n* : a dry thickened lusterless condition of the eyeball resulting especially from a severe systemic deficiency of vitamin A — **xe·roph·thal·mic** \-mik\ *adj*

xe·ro·phyte \ˈzir-ə-ˌfīt\ *n* : a plant (as a cactus, yucca, or sagebrush) adapted for life and growth with a limited water supply especially by means of mechanisms that limit transpiration or that provide for the storage of water — **xe·ro·phyt·ic** \ˌzir-ə-ˈfit-ik\ *adj*

xe·rox \ˈzir-ˌäks\ *vt* : to copy or make a copy on a xerographic copier

Xerox *trademark* — used for a xerographic copier

xi \ˈzī, ˈksī\ *n* : the 14th letter of the Greek alphabet — Ξ or ξ

x–in·ter·cept \ˈek-ˈsint-ər-ˌsept\ *n* : the abscissa of a point where a line, curve, or surface intersects the x-axis

xi·phoid process \ˈzī-ˌfȯid-, ˈzif-ˌȯid-\ *n* : the third and lowest segment of the human sternum [Greek *xiphoeidēs* "shaped like a sword," from *xiphos* "sword"]

X–linked \ˈeks-ˌliŋkt\ *adj* : located on an X chromosome ⟨an *X-linked* gene⟩; *also* : caused or transmitted by an X-linked gene ⟨an *X-linked* disease⟩

Xmas \ˈkris-məs *also* ˈek-sməs\ *n* : CHRISTMAS [*X,* symbol for Christ, from the Greek letter chi (X), initial of *Christos* "Christ"]

Word History Since the 16th century *Xmas* has been used in English as a short form of *Christmas. X* as a symbol for Christ is derived from Greek, where *chi* (X) is the initial letter of *Christos,* the Greek form of *Christ.* The word *Xmas* is usually pronounced like *Christmas,* although a pronunciation of the letter *x* plus *-mas* as in *Christmas* is also heard.

x–ra·di·a·tion \ˌeks-ˌrād-ē-ˈā-shən\ *n, often cap X* **1** : exposure to X-rays **2** : radiation consisting of X-rays

x–ray \ˈeks-ˌrā\ *vt, often cap X* : to examine, treat, or photograph with X-rays

X–ray \ˈeks-ˌrā\ *n* **1** : any of the electromagnetic radiations that have very short wavelengths, that are able to penetrate various thicknesses of solids, and that act on photographic film like light **2** : a photograph especially of conditions inside the surface of a body taken by the use of X-rays [translation of German *X-Strahl*] — **X–ray** *adj*

Word History In 1895 Wilhelm Conrad Röntgen was conducting experiments on the properties of cathode rays. He noticed that a fluorescent surface in the neighborhood of a cathode-ray tube would become luminous even if shielded. A thick metal object placed before the tube would cast a dark shadow on the fluorescent surface, but an object made of a less dense substance like wood would cast only a weak shadow. Röntgen's explanation was that the tube produced some kind of invisible radiation that could pass through substances not transparent to ordinary light. Because he did not know the nature of this radiation he had discovered, he named it *X-Strahl,* which was translated into English as *X-ray.*

X–ray therapy *n* : medical treatment (as of a cancer) by controlled application of X-rays

X–ray tube *n* : a vacuum tube in which a concentrated stream of electrons strikes a metal target and produces X-rays

xyl- *or* **xylo-** *combining form* : wood ⟨*xylo*phone⟩ [Greek *xylon*]

xy·lem \ˈzī-ləm, -ˌlem\ *n* : a complex tissue in the vascular system of higher plants that transports water and dissolved materials upward, functions also in support and storage, lies internal to the phloem, and typically constitutes the woody part (as of a plant stem) — compare PHLOEM [German, from Greek *xylon* "wood"]

xylem ray *n* : a vascular ray or portion of a vascular ray located in xylem — compare PHLOEM RAY

xy·lene \ˈzī-ˌlēn\ *n* : a colorless flammable liquid obtained from wood tar, coal tar, coke-oven gas, or petroleum and used chiefly as a solvent

xy·lol \ˈzī-ˌlȯl, -ˌlōl\ *n* : XYLENE

xy·lo·phone \ˈzī-lə-ˌfōn\ *n* : a musical instrument consisting of a series of wooden bars graduated in length to sound the musical scale and played by striking with two wooden hammers — **xy·lo·phon·ist** \-ˌfō-nəst\ *n*

Y

y \ˈwī\ *n, pl* **y's** *or* **ys** \ˈwīz\ *often cap* : the 25th letter of the English alphabet

Y \ˈwī\ *n* **1** : YMCA **2** : YWCA

[1]**-y** *also* **-ey** \ē\ *adj suffix* **-ier; -iest** **1 a** : characterized by : full of ⟨clay*ey*⟩ ⟨dirt*y*⟩ ⟨mudd*y*⟩ **b** : having the character of : composed of ⟨ic*y*⟩ ⟨wax*y*⟩ **c** : like : like that of ⟨home*y*⟩ ⟨stag*y*⟩ ⟨wintr*y*⟩ **2 a** : tending or inclined to ⟨chatt*y*⟩ ⟨sleep*y*⟩ **b** : giving occasion for (specified) action ⟨chew*y*⟩ **c** : performing (specified) action ⟨curl*y*⟩ [Old English *-ig*]

[2]**-y** \ē\ *n suffix, pl* **-ies** **1** : state : condition : quality ⟨beggar*y*⟩ **2** : activity, place of business, or goods dealt with ⟨laundr*y*⟩ **3** : whole body or group ⟨soldier*y*⟩ [Medieval French *-ie,* from Latin *-ia,* from Greek *-ia, -eia*]

[3]**-y** *n suffix, pl* **-ies** : instance of a (specified) action ⟨entreat*y*⟩ ⟨inquir*y*⟩ [Anglo-French *-ie,* from Latin *-ium*]

[4]**-y** — see -IE

[1]**yacht** \ˈyät\ *n* : any of various sailing or motor-driven vessels that are used especially for pleasure cruising or racing [obsolete Dutch *jaght,* from Low German *jacht,* short for *jachtschip,* literally, "hunting ship"]

Word History In the 16th century the Dutch began building light, fast ships designed to chase the ships of pirates and smugglers from the Dutch coast. The Dutch appropriately called this type of vessel *jaght,* which is a derivative of a Low German word for a fast, light sailing vessel, *jachtschip,* meaning literally "hunting ship." The ship was introduced into England in 1660 when the Dutch East India Company presented one to King Charles II, who used it as a pleasure boat. The ship's design was copied by British shipbuilders for those wealthy gentlemen who desired and could afford such pleasure craft.

[2]**yacht** *vi* : to race or cruise in a yacht

yacht·ing *n* : the action, fact, or sport of racing or cruising in a yacht

yachts·man \ˈyät-smən\ *n* : a person who owns or sails a yacht

[1]**ya·hoo** \ˈyā-hü, ˈyä-\ *n, pl* **yahoos** : a crude, stupid, or rowdy person [*Yahoo,* member of a race of brutes in Swift's *Gulliver's Travels* who have the form and the vices of people]

[2]**ya·hoo** \yä-ˈhü\ *interj* : YIPPEE [perhaps alteration of *yo-ho,* interjection used to attract attention]

Yah·weh \ˈyä-ˌwā, -ˌvā\ *also* **Jah·veh** *or* **Yah·veh** \-ˌvā\ *n* : GOD 1 — used especially by the ancient Hebrews [Hebrew *Yahweh*]

[1]**yak** \ˈyak\ *n, pl* **yaks** *also* **yak** : a large long-haired wild or domesticated ox of Tibet and adjacent elevated parts of central Asia [Tibetan (Lhasa dialect) *yaʔ*]

[1]yak

[2]**yak** *also* **yack** *n* : persistant or rapid talk [probably imitative] — **yak** *vi*

y'all *variant of* YOU-ALL

yam \ˈyam\ *n* **1** : an edible starchy tuberous root that is a staple food in tropical areas; *also* : a plant producing yams **2** : a moist-fleshed and usually orange-fleshed sweet potato [Portuguese *inhame* and Spanish *ñame,* of African origin]

yam·mer \ˈyam-ər\ *vi* **yam·mered; yam·mer·ing** \ˈyam-ring, -ə-ring\ **1** : to utter repeated cries of distress or sorrow **2** : to complain persistently **3** : CHATTER 2 [Old English *geōmrian* "to murmur, be sad"] — **yammer** *n*

yang \ˈyäng\ *n* : the masculine active principle (as of light, heat, or dryness) in nature that in Chinese cosmic philosophy combines with yin to produce all that comes to be [Chinese (Beijing dialect) yáng]

yank \ˈyangk\ *n* : a strong sudden pull : JERK [origin unknown] — **yank** *vb*

Yank \ˈyangk\ *n* : YANKEE

Yan·kee \ˈyang-kē\ *n* **1 a** : a native or inhabitant of New England **b** : a native or inhabitant of the northern U.S. **2** : a native or inhabitant of the U.S. [origin unknown]

Ya·no·ma·mi \ˌyän-ō-ˈmäm-ē\ *also* **Ya·no·ma·mo** \-ō\ *or* **Ya·no·ma·ma** \-ə\ *n, pl* **Yanomami** *also* **Yanomamis** *or* **Yanomamo** *or* **Yanomama** **1** : an indigenous people living in the rain forests of southern Venezuela and northern Brazil; *also* : a member of the Yanomami people **2** : the family of four closely related languages spoken by the Yanomami [Yanomami (language of the western Yanomami) *yanomami*]

yan·qui \ˈyäng-kē\ *n, often cap* : a citizen of the U.S. as distinguished from a Latin American [Spanish, from English *Yankee*]

[1]**yap** \ˈyap\ *vi* **yapped; yap·ping** **1** : to bark in yaps : YELP **2** : to talk with shrill insistence : CHATTER [imitative]

\ə\ abut	\au̇\ out	\i\ tip	\ȯ\ saw	\u̇\ foot
\ər\ further	\ch\ chin	\ī\ life	\ȯi\ coin	\y\ yet
\a\ mat	\e\ pet	\j\ job	\th\ thin	\yü\ few
\ā\ take	\ē\ easy	\ng\ sing	\th\ this	\yu̇\ cure
\ä\ cot, cart	\g\ go	\ō\ bone	\ü\ food	\zh\ vision

²yap *n* **1 :** a quick sharp bark **:** YELP **2 :** shrill insistent talk **:** CHATTER **3** *slang* **:** MOUTH

¹yard \ˈyärd\ *n* **1 :** any of various units of measure; *esp* **:** a unit of length equal in the U.S. to 0.9144 meter — see MEASURE table **2 :** a long spar that supports and spreads the head of a square sail, lateen, or lugsail [Old English *gierd* "twig, measure, yard"]

²yard *n* **1 a :** a small usually enclosed area open to the sky and adjacent to a building **b :** the grounds of a building or group of buildings (as the grassy area around a house) **2 a :** an enclosure for livestock **b :** an area with its buildings and facilities set aside for a particular business or activity ⟨navy *yard*⟩ **c :** a system of railroad tracks for storage and maintenance of cars and making up trains **3 :** a locality in a forest where deer herd in winter [Old English *geard* "enclosure, yard"]

³yard *vb* **:** to drive into, gather, or confine in or as if in a yard

yard·age \ˈyärd-ij\ *n* **:** a total number of yards; *also* **:** the length, extent, or volume of something as measured in yards

yard·arm \ˈyärd-ˌärm\ *n* **:** either end of the yard of a square-rigged ship

yard goods *n pl* **:** fabrics sold by the yard

yard·man \ˈyärd-mən, -ˌman\ *n* **1 :** one who is employed to do outdoor work (as mowing lawns) **2 :** one who works in or about a yard (as a lumberyard or a railroad yard)

yard·mas·ter \-ˌmas-tər\ *n* **:** a person in charge of operations in a railroad yard

yard sale *n* **:** GARAGE SALE

yard·stick \-ˌstik\ *n* **1 :** a measuring stick a yard long **2 :** a rule or standard by which something is measured or judged **:** CRITERION ⟨was a success by any *yardstick*⟩

yar·mul·ke \ˈyäm-ə-kə, ˈyär-məl-\ *n* **:** a skullcap worn especially by Jewish males [Yiddish *yarmlke*]

¹yarn \ˈyärn\ *n* **1 a :** a continuous strand of natural or manufactured fibers (as of wool, cotton, or rayon) that is used in knitting or weaving **b :** a similar strand of another material (as metal, glass, or plastic) **2 :** an interesting or exciting often made-up story [Old English *gearn*]

²yarn *vi* **:** to tell a yarn

yarn–dye \-ˈdī\ *vt* **:** to dye before weaving or knitting

yar·row \ˈyar-ō\ *n* **:** a strong-scented Eurasian herb related to the daisies that has finely divided leaves and small usually white flowers in flat clusters [Old English *gearwe*]

yat·a·ghan \ˈyat-ə-ˌgan\ *n* **:** a long knife or short saber that is made without a guard for the hand and usually with a double curve to the edge [Turkish *yatağan*]

yataghan

yau·pon \ˈyü-ˌpän *also* ˈyō-, ˈyȯ-\ *n* **:** a holly of the southern U.S. with smooth leaves containing substances that can cause vomiting [Catawpa (American Indian language of North and South Carolina) *yą́pą*, from *yą-* "tree" + *pą* "leaf"]

yaw \ˈyȯ\ *vi* **:** to turn abruptly from a straight course **:** SWERVE, VEER ⟨a heavy sea made the ship *yaw*⟩ [origin unknown] — **yaw** *n*

yawl \ˈyȯl\ *n* **:** a 2-masted fore-and-aft rigged sailing vessel with one mast behind the rudder — compare KETCH [Low German *jolle*]

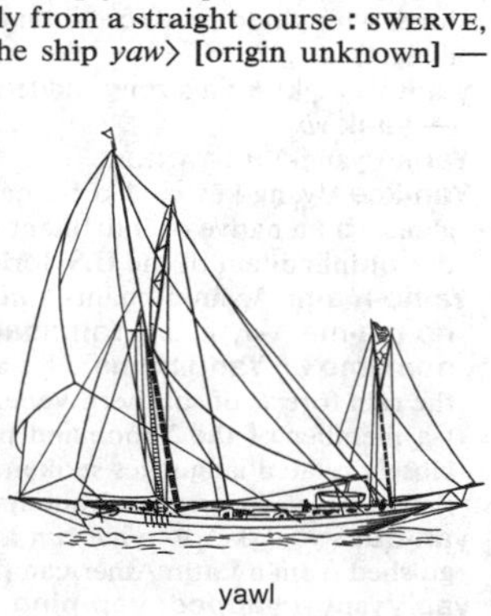

yawl

¹yawn \ˈyȯn, ˈyän\ *vb* **1 :** to open wide **:** GAPE **2 :** to open the mouth wide and take a deep breath usually as an involuntary reaction to fatigue or boredom **3 :** to utter with a yawn [Old English *ginian*] — **yawn·er** *n*

²yawn *n* **:** an opening of the mouth wide while taking a deep breath often as an involuntary reaction

yawn·ing *adj* **1 :** wide open **:** CAVERNOUS ⟨a *yawning* hole⟩ **2 :** showing fatigue or boredom by yawns ⟨a *yawning* audience⟩

¹yawp *or* **yaup** \ˈyȯp\ *vi* **1 :** to make a raucous noise **:** SQUAWK **2 :** CLAMOR 2, COMPLAIN [Middle English *yolpen*] — **yawp·er** *n*

²yawp *also* **yaup** *n* **:** a raucous noise **:** SQUAWK

yaws \ˈyȯz\ *n sing or pl* **:** a contagious tropical disease especially of children that is caused by a spirochete, is marked by skin lesions, and if untreated results in deformed bones and joints [probably from an English-based creole of the Caribbean]

y–ax·is \ˈwī-ˌak-səs\ *n* **:** the axis in a plane Cartesian coordinate system parallel to which ordinates are measured

Y chromosome *n* **:** a sex chromosome that is associated with maleness and occurs only in male cells paired with an X chromosome in organisms (as humans and most mammals) in which the male typically has two unlike sex chromosomes — compare X CHROMOSOME

yclept \i-ˈklept\ *or* **ycleped** \-ˈklēpt, -ˈklept\ *adj, archaic* **:** known as **:** CALLED [Middle English, from Old English *geclipod,* past participle of *clipian* to cry out, name]

y–co·or·di·nate \ˌwī-kō-ˈȯrd-nət, -n-ət, -n-ˌāt\ *n* **:** ORDINATE

¹ye \yē, ˈyē\ *pron* **:** YOU 1 — used originally only as a plural pronoun of the 2nd person in the subjective case and now used especially in ecclesiastical or literary language and in various English dialects [Old English *gē*]

²ye \yē, yə, *or like* THE\ *definite article, archaic* **:** THE ⟨*Ye* Olde Gifte Shoppe⟩ [Middle English *þe* "the"; from the similarity of the handwritten forms of þ (th) and *y*]

Word History The use of *ye* instead of *the* to suggest an earlier time is the result of changes in handwriting styles which took place before the introduction of printing in England. The alphabet used by the Anglo-Saxons included several letters not found in the Latin alphabet but borrowed from the runic alphabet used by several early Germanic peoples. One of these letters was þ, called *thorn,* which represented the sounds now most often indicated by *th* in English. This letter was used in the Middle English period as well, but by the end of the 14th century the written form of the thorn was often indistinguishable from that of *y*. After 1400, the thorn fell into disuse except in a few words such as *the* and *that.* As the thorn was forgotten, the archaic form of *the* came to be written *ye.*

¹yea \ˈyā\ *adv* **1 :** YES — used in oral voting **2 :** more than this **:** not only but — used to introduce a more explicit or emphatic phrase ⟨most people, *yea* everyone, would agree with that⟩ [Old English *gēa*]

²yea *n* **1 :** ASSENT, AFFIRMATION **2 a :** an affirmative vote **b :** a person casting a yea vote

yeah \ˈye-ə, ˈyeů, ˈya-ə\ *adv* **:** YES

year \ˈyiər\ *n* **1 :** the period of one apparent revolution of the sun around the ecliptic or of the earth's revolution around the sun amounting to approximately 365¼ days **2 a :** a period of 365 days or in leap year 366 days beginning January 1 **b :** a period of time equal to this but beginning at a different time ⟨a fiscal *year*⟩ **3 :** a calendar year specified usually by a number ⟨was born in the *year* 1960⟩ **4** *pl* **:** AGE ⟨wise beyond her *years*⟩ **5 :** a continuous period of time that constitutes the period of some event (as revolution of a planet about its sun) or activity whether greater or less than the calendar year ⟨a school *year* of nine months⟩ [Old English *gēar*]

year·book \-ˌbůk\ *n* **1 :** a book published yearly especially as a factual report **2 :** a school publication recording the history and activities of a graduating class

year·ling \-ling\ *n* **:** one that is a year old: as **a :** an animal one year old or in the second year after birth **b :** a racehorse between January 1st of the year after the year in which it was born and the next January 1st — **yearling** *adj*

year·long \-ˈlȯng\ *adj* **:** lasting through a year

year·ly \-lē\ *adj* **1 :** computed in terms of one year **2 :** occurring, done, produced, or acted upon every year **:** ANNUAL — **yearly** *adv*

yearn \ˈyərn\ *vb* **1 :** to feel a longing or craving **2 :** to feel tenderness or compassion [Old English *giernan*] ***synonyms*** see LONG — **yearn·er** *n*

yearn·ing *n* **:** a tender or urgent longing

year of grace : a year of the Christian era ⟨the *year of grace* 1979⟩

year–round \ˈyiər-ˈraůnd, ˈyiə-ˈraůnd\ *adj* **:** effective, employed, or operating for the full year **:** not seasonal ⟨a *year-round* resort⟩ — **year–round** *adv*

yeast \ˈyēst, ˈēst\ *n* **1 a :** a one-celled fungus that reproduces by budding and produces alcohol during the process of fermentation; *also* **:** any of various similar fungi **b :** a yellowish froth that may occur on the surface of sweet liquids (as fruit juices) undergoing fermentation and that consists chiefly of yeast cells and carbon dioxide **c :** a commercial product containing living yeast cells mixed with an inactive material that is typically used in the making of alcoholic beverages and as a leaven especially in baking bread **2** *archaic* **:** the foam or froth especially of waves **3 :** something that causes ferment or activity [Old English *gist*] — **yeasty** \ˈyē-stē, ˈē-stē\ *adj*

yegg \ˈyeg, ˈyāg\ *n* **:** SAFECRACKER; *also* **:** ROBBER [origin unknown]

[1]**yell** \ˈyel\ *vb* **1 :** to utter a loud cry, scream, or shout **2 :** to give a cheer usually in unison **3 :** to utter or declare with or as if with a yell **:** SHOUT [Old English *giellan*] — **yell·er** *n*

[2]**yell** *n* **1 :** SCREAM 1, SHOUT **2 :** a usually rhythmic cheer used especially in schools to encourage athletic teams

[1]**yel·low** \ˈyel-ō\ *adj* **1 a :** of the color yellow **b :** yellowish from age, disease, or discoloration **2 a :** featuring sensational or scandalous items or ordinary news sensationally distorted ⟨*yellow* journalism⟩ **b :** COWARDLY 1 [Old English *geolu*] — **yel·low·ish** \ˈyel-ə-wish\ *adj* — **yel·low·ness** *n*

[2]**yellow** *vb* **:** to make or turn yellow

[3]**yellow** *n* **1 a :** a color whose hue resembles that of ripe lemons or sunflowers or is that of the portion of the spectrum lying between green and orange **b :** a pigment or dye that colors yellow **2 :** something yellow or marked by a yellow color; *esp* **:** the yolk of an egg **3** *pl* **a :** JAUNDICE **b :** any of several plant diseases caused especially by bacteria and marked by yellowing of the foliage and stunting

yellow–dog contract *n* **:** an employment contract under which a worker agrees not to join a labor union during the period of his or her employment

yellow fever *n* **:** an infectious disease of warm regions (as sub-Saharan Africa) that is marked by sudden onset, fever, headache, muscle aches, vomiting, jaundice, and sometimes death and that is caused by a virus transmitted by a mosquito

yellow–fever mosquito *n* **:** a small dark-colored mosquito that is the usual vector of yellow fever

yellow–green alga *n* **:** any of a class (Xanthophyceae) of mostly freshwater algae with the chlorophyll masked by brown or yellow pigment

yel·low·ham·mer \ˈyel-ō-ˌham-ər, ˈyel-ə-\ *n* **1 :** a common European finch having the male largely yellow and chestnut **2 :** YELLOW-SHAFTED FLICKER [Old English *amore* "yellowhammer"]

yellowhammer 1

yellow jack *n* **:** YELLOW FEVER

yellow jacket *n* **:** any of various small yellow-marked social wasps that commonly nest in the ground and can sting repeatedly and painfully

yellow jessamine *n* **:** a twining evergreen shrub related to the nux vomica and grown in warm regions for its fragrant yellow flowers — called also *yellow jasmine*

yel·low·legs \ˈyel-ō-ˌlegz, ˈyel-ə-, -ˌlāgz\ *n sing or pl* **:** either of two American shorebirds related to the sandpipers and having long yellow legs

yellow ocher *n* **1 :** a yellow mixture of limonite usually with clay and silica used as a pigment **2 :** a moderate orange yellow

yellow pages *n pl, often cap Y&P* **:** the section of a telephone directory that lists businesses and professional firms by category and includes advertising

yellow perch *n* **:** a common North American freshwater fish that is related to the European perch, has yellowish sides with broad green vertical stripes, and that is a popular food and sport fish

yellow pine *n* **:** the yellowish resinous wood of any of several American pines; *also* **:** a pine (as the longleaf pine or ponderosa pine) that yields such wood

yel·low–shaft·ed flicker \ˌyel-ō-ˌshaf-təd-, ˌyel-ə-\ *n* **:** a flicker of the form found in the more eastern parts of North America that is golden yellow on the underside of the tail and wings, has a red mark on the back of the neck, and in the male has a black streak on each side of the base of the bill — called also *yellowhammer*

yellow spot *n* **:** MACULA LUTEA

yel·low·tail \ˈyel-ō-ˌtāl, ˈyel-ə-\ *n, pl* **yellowtail** *or* **yellowtails** **:** any of various fishes having a yellow or yellowish tail and including several food and sport fishes

yel·low·throat \-ˌthrōt\ *n* **:** a largely olive American warbler with yellow breast and throat

yel·low·wood \-ˌwu̇d\ *n* **1 :** any of various trees having yellowish wood or yielding a yellow extract; *esp* **:** one of the southern U.S. that belongs to the legume family and has showy white fragrant flowers **2 :** the wood of a yellowwood tree

[1]**yelp** \ˈyelp\ *n* **:** a sharp quick shrill bark or cry ⟨the *yelps* of turkeys⟩

[2]**yelp** *vi* **:** to utter a yelp or a similar sound ⟨he *yelped* in pain⟩ ⟨heard the dog *yelping* again⟩ [Old English *gielpan* "to boast, exult"] — **yelper** *n*

[1]**yen** \ˈyen\ *n, pl* **yen** **1 :** the basic monetary unit of Japan **2 :** a coin representing one yen [Japanese *en*]

[2]**yen** *n* **:** an intense desire **:** URGE, LONGING ⟨have a *yen* to travel⟩ [Chinese (Guangdong dialect) *yīn-yáhn* "craving for opium," from *yīn* "opium" + *yáhn* "craving"]

Word History During the 18th and 19th centuries China suffered under the encouragement, which amounted to virtual enforcement, of widespread opium addiction by foreign nations whose traders found the drug profitable. In the mid-19th century many Chinese immigrated to the U.S., and the word *yin-yahn,* "craving for opium," came with them. In English the Chinese syllables became assimilated to *yen-yen.* Eventually the word was shortened to *yen* and generalized from a craving for opium to any strong desire.

yeo·man \ˈyō-mən\ *n* **1 a :** an attendant or officer in a royal or noble household **b :** a naval petty officer who performs clerical duties **2 :** a small farmer who cultivates his or her own land; *esp* **:** one of a class of English freeholders below the gentry [Middle English *yoman, yeman*]

yeo·man·ly \-lē\ *adj* **:** becoming to a yeoman **:** STURDY, SELF-RELIANT, LOYAL

yeoman of the guard : a member of a military corps of the British royal household serving as ceremonial attendants of the sovereign

yeo·man·ry \ˈyō-mən-rē\ *n* **1 :** the body of yeomen and especially of small landed proprietors **2 :** a British volunteer cavalry force created from yeomen in 1761 and incorporated in 1907 into the territorial force

-yer — see [2]-ER

yer·ba ma·té \ˌyer-bə-ˈmä-ˌtā, ˌyər-\ *n* **:** MATÉ [American Spanish *yerba mate,* from *yerba* "herb" + *mate* "maté"]

[1]**yes** \ˈyes\ *adv* **1** — used to express assent, agreement, or affirmation ⟨are you ready? *Yes,* I am⟩ **2** — used to introduce correction or contradiction of a negative assertion, direction, or request ⟨don't say that! *Yes,* I will⟩ **3** — used to introduce a more emphatic or explicit phrase ⟨we are glad, *yes,* very glad to see you⟩ **4** — used to indicate interest or attentiveness ⟨*yes,* what is it you want⟩ [Old English *gēse*]

[2]**yes** *n* **:** an affirmative reply

ye·shi·va *or* **ye·shi·vah** \yə-ˈshē-və\ *n, pl* **yeshivas** *or* **ye·shi·vot** \-ˌshē-ˈvōt, -ˈvōth\ **1 :** a school for talmudic study **2 :** an Orthodox Jewish rabbinical seminary **3 :** a Jewish day school providing secular and religious instruction [Hebrew *yĕshībhāh*]

yes–man \ˈyes-ˌman\ *n* **:** a person who agrees with everything that is said especially by the boss

[1]**yes·ter·day** \ˈyes-tərd-ē, -tər-ˌdā\ *adv* **1 :** on the day before today **2 :** only a short time ago [Old English *giestran dæg,* from *giestran* "yesterday" + *dæg* "day"]

[2]**yesterday** *n* **1 :** the day before today **2 :** time not long past ⟨*yesterday's* fashions⟩ **3 :** past time — usually used in plural

yes·ter·year \ˈyes-tər-ˌyiər\ *n* **1 :** last year **2 :** the recent past [*yesterday* + *year*]

[1]**yet** \yet, ˈyet\ *adv* **1 a :** in addition **:** BESIDES ⟨gives *yet* another reason⟩ **b :** EVEN 2b ⟨a *yet* higher speed⟩ **2 a (1) :** up to now **:** so far ⟨hasn't done much *yet*⟩ **(2) :** at this or that time ⟨not time to go *yet*⟩ **b :** continuously up to the present or a specified time **:** STILL ⟨is *yet* a new country⟩ **c :** at a future time ⟨may *yet* see the light⟩ **3 :** NEVERTHELESS, HOWEVER ⟨led a quiet, *yet* happy life⟩ [Old English *gīet*]

\ə\ **about**	\au̇\ **out**	\i\ **tip**	\ȯ\ **saw**	\u̇\ **foot**
\ər\ **further**	\ch\ **chin**	\ī\ **life**	\ȯi\ **coin**	\y\ **yet**
\a\ **mat**	\e\ **pet**	\j\ **job**	\th\ **thin**	\yü\ **few**
\ā\ **take**	\ē\ **easy**	\ng\ **sing**	\t͟h\ **this**	\yu̇\ **cure**
\ä\ **cot, cart**	\g\ **go**	\ō\ **bone**	\ü\ **food**	\zh\ **vision**

[2]**yet** *conj* : despite that fact : BUT ⟨bought more milk *yet* it was not enough for everyone⟩

ye·ti \ˈyet-ē, ˈyāt-\ *n* : ABOMINABLE SNOWMAN [Sherpa (Tibetan dialect of the Sherpas)]

yew \ˈyü\ *n* **1 a** : any of a genus of evergreen trees and shrubs that are gymnosperms with short stiff flattened needlelike leaves and seeds surrounded by a fleshy red aril **b** : the wood of a yew; *esp* : the heavy fine-grained wood of an Old World yew that is used especially for bows and small articles **2** *archaic* : an achery bow made of yew [Old English *īw*]

yew 1a

Yid·dish \ˈyid-ish\ *n* : a High German language spoken by Jews and descendants of Jews of central and eastern European origin and written in Hebrew characters [Yiddish *yidish,* short for *yidish daytsh,* literally, "Jewish German"] — **Yiddish** *adj*

[1]**yield** \ˈyēld\ *vb* **1** : to give up possession of on claim or demand : hand over possession of **2** : to give (oneself) up to an inclination, temptation, or habit **3 a** : to bear or bring forth as a natural product especially as a result of cultivation ⟨the tree always *yields* good fruit⟩ **b** : to produce as a result of expended effort ⟨this soil should *yield* good crops⟩ **c** : to produce as return from an expenditure or investment : furnish as profit or interest ⟨a bond that *yields* 12 percent⟩ **d** : to produce as revenue : bring in ⟨the tax will *yield* millions⟩ **4** : to be fruitful or productive **5** : to give up and cease resistance or contention ⟨would not *yield* to their enemies⟩ ⟨*yielded* to temptation⟩ **6** : to give way to pressure or influence : submit to urging, persuasion, or entreaty **7** : to give way under physical force so as to bend, stretch, or break **8 a** : to give place or precedence : acknowledge the superiority of someone else **b** : to give way to or become succeeded by someone or something else [Old English *gieldan*] — **yield·er** *n*

synonyms YIELD, SUBMIT, SUCCUMB mean to give way to someone or something that one can no longer resist. YIELD may apply to any sort or degree of giving way before force, argument, persuasion, or entreaty ⟨*yields* too easily in an argument⟩. SUBMIT suggests full surrendering after resistance or conflict to the will or control of another ⟨*submitted* to the plan but under protest⟩. SUCCUMB suggests weakness and helplessness on the part of the one giving way or the overwhelming power of the opposing force ⟨*succumbed* to pressure from the opposition⟩. ***synonyms*** see in addition RELINQUISH

[2]**yield** *n* : something yielded : PRODUCT; *esp* : the amount or quantity produced or returned ⟨a high *yield* of wheat per acre⟩

yield·ing *adj* **1** : lacking rigidity or stiffness : FLEXIBLE ⟨a *yielding* mass⟩ **2** : disposed to submit or comply ⟨a cheerful *yielding* nature⟩

yin \ˈyin\ *n* : the feminine passive principle (as of darkness, cold, or wetness) in nature that in Chinese cosmic philosophy combines with yang to produce all that comes to be [Chinese (Beijing dialect) *yīn*]

y–in·ter·cept \ˌwī-ˈint-ər-ˌsept\ *n* : the ordinate of a point where a line, curve, or surface intersects the y-axis

yip \ˈyip\ *vi* : to bark sharply, quickly, and often continuously ⟨the poodle ran around *yipping*⟩; *also* : to utter a short sharp cry ⟨*yipped* with joy⟩ [imitative] — **yip** *n*

yip·pee \ˈyip-ē\ *interj* — used to express exuberant delight or triumph

-yl \əl, ᵊl, il, ˌil\ *n combining form* : chemical and usually univalent group or radical ⟨eth*yl*⟩ ⟨hydrox*yl*⟩ [Greek *hylē* "matter, material," literally, "wood"]

YMCA \ˌwī-ˌem-ˌsē-ˈā\ *n* : an international organization that promotes the spiritual, intellectual, social, and physical welfare originally of young Christian men [*Y*oung *M*en's *C*hristian *A*ssociation]

YMHA \ˌwī-ˌem-ˌā-ˈchā\ *n* : an international organization that promotes the spiritual, intellectual, social, and physical welfare originally of young Jewish men [*Y*oung *M*en's *H*ebrew *A*ssociation]

[1]**yo·del** \ˈyōd-l\ *vb* **-deled** *or* **-delled; -del·ing** *or* **-del·ling** \ˈyōd-ling, -l-ing\ : to sing by suddenly changing from the natural voice to falsetto and the reverse; *also* : to shout or call in this manner [German *jodeln*] — **yo·del·er** \ˈyōd-lər, -l-ər\ *n*

[2]**yodel** *n* : a song or refrain sung by yodeling; *also* : a yodeled shout

yo·ga \ˈyō-gə\ *n* **1** *cap* : a Hindu theistic philosophy teaching that by suppressing the activity of body, mind, and will one can know one's true self and be free **2** : a system of exercises for attaining bodily or mental control and well-being [Sanskrit, literally, "yoking"] — **yo·gic** \-gik\ *adj, often cap*

yo·gi \ˈyō-gē\ *also* **yo·gin** \-gən, -ˌgin\ *n* **1** : a person who practices yoga **2** *cap* : an adherent of Yoga philosophy [Sanskrit *yogin,* from *yoga*]

yo·gurt *also* **yo·ghurt** \ˈyō-gərt\ *n* : a slightly acidic semisolid food that is often flavored and sweetened and is made of milk that has been soured by the addition of fermenting bacteria [Turkish *yoğurt*]

[1]**yoke** \ˈyōk\ *n, pl* **yokes 1 a** : a wooden bar or frame by which two draft animals (as oxen) are joined at the heads or necks for working together (as in pulling a plow) **b** : a frame fitted to a person's shoulders to carry a load in two equal portions **c** : a clamp or similar piece that embraces two parts to hold or unite them in position **2** *pl usually* **yoke** : two animals yoked together **3 a** : an oppressive agency ⟨freed from the tyrant's *yoke*⟩ **b** : SERVITUDE, BONDAGE **c** : TIE, LINK ⟨the *yoke* of matrimony⟩ **4** : a fitted or shaped piece at the top of a skirt or at the shoulder of various garments [Old English *geoc*]

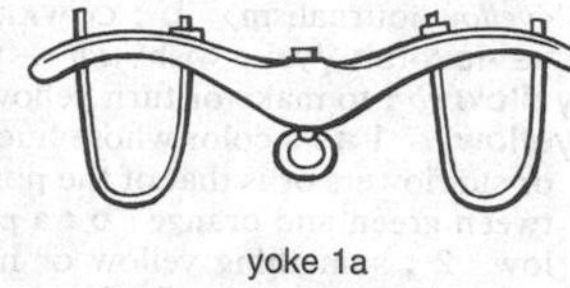
yoke 1a

[2]**yoke** *vb* **1 a** : to put a yoke on or join with a yoke **b** : to attach (a draft animal) to something ⟨*yoke* a horse to a cart⟩ **2** : to join as if by a yoke **3** : to put to work

yoke·fellow \ˈyōk-ˌfel-ō\ *n* : a close companion : MATE

yo·kel \ˈyō-kəl\ *n* : RUSTIC, BUMPKIN [perhaps from English dialect *yokel,* a kind of woodpecker]

yolk \ˈyōk, ˈyelk also ˈyōlk\ *n* **1 a** : the yellow inner mass of stored food in the egg of a bird or reptile **b** : the material stored in an animal ovum that supplies food material to the developing embryo **2** : oily material in unprocessed sheep wool [Old English *geoloca,* from *geolu* "yellow"] — **yolk** *adj* — **yolked** *adj* — **yolky** *adj*

yolk sac *n* : a membranous sac of most vertebrates that encloses the yolk, is usually attached through the yolk stalk with the intestinal cavity of the embryo, and transports nutritive yolk products to the developing embryo

yolk stalk *n* : a narrow tubular stalk connecting the yolk sac with the embryo

Yom Kip·pur \ˌyōm-ki-ˈpu̇r, ˌyȯm-, ˌyäm-, -ˈkip-ər\ *n* : a Jewish holiday observed in September or October with fasting and prayer as a day of atonement [Hebrew *yōm kippūr,* from *yōm* "day" + *kippūr* "atonement"]

[1]**yon** \ˈyän\ *adj* : YONDER [Old English *geon*]

[2]**yon** *adv* **1** : YONDER **2** : THITHER ⟨ran hither and *yon*⟩

[1]**yond** \ˈyänd\ *adv, archaic* : YONDER [Old English *geond*]

[2]**yond** *adj, dialect* : YONDER

[1]**yon·der** \ˈyän-dər\ *adv* : at or to that place : over there [Middle English, from *yond* + *-er* (as in *hither*)]

[2]**yonder** *adj* **1** : farther removed : more distant ⟨the *yonder* side of the river⟩ **2** : being at a distance within view ⟨*yonder* hills⟩

yore \ˈyōr, ˈyȯr\ *n* : time long past — usually used in the phrase *of yore* [Old English *gēara* "long ago," from *gēar* "year"]

York·ist \ˈyȯr-kəst\ *adj* : of or relating to the English royal house that ruled from 1461 to 1485 — compare LANCASTRIAN [Edward, Duke of *York* (Edward IV of England)] — **Yorkist** *n*

York·shire \ˈyȯrk-ˌshiər, -shər\ *n* : a white swine of any of several breeds or strains originated in Yorkshire, England

York·shire pudding \ˌyȯrk-ˌshiər, -shər-\ *n* : a batter of eggs, flour, and milk baked in meat drippings

Yorkshire terrier *n* : any of a breed of small toy terriers with long straight silky hair that is mostly bluish gray but tan on the head and chest

you \yü, ˈyü, yə, yē\ *pron* **1** : the one or ones spoken to — used as the pronoun of the 2nd person singular or plural in any grammatical relation except that of a possessive ⟨*you* are my friends⟩ ⟨can I pour *you* a cup of tea⟩; used formerly only as a plural pronoun of the 2nd person in the dative or accusative case as direct or indirect object of a verb or as object of a preposition; compare THEE, THOU, YE, YOUR, YOURS **2 :** [3]ONE 1b ⟨*you* never know what will happen⟩ [Old English *ēow,* dative and accusative of *gē* "you"]

you–all \yü-ˈȯl, ˈyü-ˌȯl, ˈyȯl\ *or* **y'all** \ˈyȯl\ *pron, chiefly Southern* **:** YOU — usually used in addressing two or more persons

you'd \yüd, ˌyüd, yu̇d, ˌyu̇d, yəd\ **:** you had **:** you would

you'll \yül, ˌyül, yu̇l, ˌyu̇l, yəl\ **:** you shall **:** you will

[1]**young** \ˈyəng\ *adj* **youn·ger** \ˈyəng-gər\; **youn·gest** \ˈyəng-gəst\ **1 a :** being in the first or an early stage of life, growth, or development **b :** JUNIOR 1a **2 :** having little experience **3 a :** recently come into being **:** NEW ⟨the *young* democracies⟩ **b :** YOUTHFUL 4 ⟨*young* mountains⟩ **4 :** of, relating to, or having the characteristics of youth or a young person ⟨*young* at heart⟩ [Old English *geong*] — **young·ness** \ˈyəng-nəs\ *n*

[2]**young** *n, pl* **young 1** *pl* **a :** young persons **:** YOUTH **b :** immature or recently born offspring ⟨a bear and her *young*⟩ **2 :** a single recently born or hatched animal ⟨produces one *young* each year⟩ — **with young :** PREGNANT — used of animals

young·ber·ry \ˈyəng-ˌber-ē\ *n* **:** the large sweet reddish black fruit of a cultivated bramble closely related to the boysenberry and loganberry and grown in the western and southern U.S.; *also* **:** the bramble that bears youngberries [B. M. *Young,* 20th century American fruit grower]

youn·ger \ˈyəng-gər\ *n* **:** an inferior in age **:** JUNIOR — usually used with a possessive pronoun ⟨is several years my *younger*⟩

youn·gest \ˈyəng-gəst\ *n* **:** one that is the least old; *esp* **:** the youngest child or member of a family

young·ish \ˈyəng-ish\ *adj* **:** somewhat young

young·ling \ˈyəng-ling\ *n* **:** one that is young; *esp* **:** a young person or animal — **youngling** *adj*

young·ster \ˈyəng-stər\ *n* **1 :** a young person **:** YOUTH **2 :** CHILD 2a

young Turk *n, often cap Y* **:** an insurgent or a member of an insurgent group in a political party [*Young Turks,* a 20th century revolutionary party in Turkey]

youn·ker \ˈyəng-kər\ *n* **1 :** a young man **2 :** CHILD 2a, YOUNGSTER [Dutch *jonker* "young nobleman"]

your \yər, yu̇r, ˈyu̇r, yōr, ˈyōr, yȯr, ˈyȯr\ *adj* **1 :** of or relating to you or yourself or yourselves especially as possessor or possessors, agent or agents, or object or objects of an action ⟨*your* house⟩ ⟨*your* contributions⟩ ⟨*your* discharge⟩ **2 :** of or relating to one or oneself ⟨when you face the north, east is at *your* right⟩ **3** — used before a title of honor in address ⟨*your* Honor⟩ [Old English *ēower*]

you're \yər, yu̇r, ˌyu̇r, yōr, ˌyōr, yȯr, ˌyȯr\ **:** you are

yours \yu̇rz, ˈyōrz, ˈyȯrz\ *pron, sing or pl in construction* **:** that which belongs to you **:** those which belong to you — used without a following noun as an equivalent in meaning to the adjective *your*; often used especially with an adverbial modifier in the complimentary close of a letter ⟨*yours* truly⟩

your·self \yər-ˈself\ *pron* **1 a :** that identical one that is you — used reflexively or for emphasis ⟨don't hurt *yourself*⟩ ⟨do it *yourself*⟩ **b :** your normal, healthy, or sane condition or self ⟨you're not *yourself* today⟩ **2 :** ONESELF

your·selves \-ˈselvz\ *pron pl* **1 :** those identical ones that are you — used reflexively or for emphasis ⟨get *yourselves* a treat⟩ ⟨carry them *yourselves*⟩ **2 :** your normal, healthy, or sane conditions or selves

youth \ˈyüth\ *n, pl* **youths** \ˈyüt͟hz, ˈyüths\ **1 :** the time of life when one is young; *esp* **:** the period between childhood and maturity **2 a :** a young man **b :** young persons — usually pl. in construction ⟨the *youth* of the nation are a fine lot⟩ **3 :** YOUTHFULNESS [Old English *geoguth*]

youth·ful \ˈyüth-fəl\ *adj* **1 :** of, relating to, or appropriate to youth **2 :** being young and not yet mature **3 :** having the freshness and energy of youth **:** VIGOROUS ⟨*youthful* grandparents⟩ **4 :** having accomplished or undergone little erosion ⟨a *youthful* valley⟩ ⟨*youthful* streams⟩ — **youth·ful·ly** \-fə-lē\ *adv* — **youth·ful·ness** *n*

youth hostel *n* **:** HOSTEL 2

you've \yüv, ˌyüv, yəv\ **:** you have

yowl \ˈyau̇l\ *vi* **:** to utter a loud long often mournful cry or howl ⟨the cats were *yowling* all night⟩ [Middle English *yowlen*] — **yowl** *n*

yo–yo \ˈyō-ˌyō\ *n, pl* **yo–yos 1 :** a thick divided disk that is made to fall and rise to the hand by unwinding and rewinding on a string **2 :** a stupid or foolish person [probably from Ilocano (Austronesian language of the Philippines) *yóyo*]

yt·ter·bi·um \i-ˈtər-bē-əm, ə-\ *n* **:** a metallic element that occurs in several minerals — see ELEMENT table [New Latin, from *Ytterby,* Sweden]

yt·tri·um \ˈi-trē-əm\ *n* **:** a metallic element usually included among the rare earth elements with which it occurs in minerals — see ELEMENT table [New Latin, from *yttria* "yttrium oxide," from *Ytterby,* Sweden]

yu·an \ˈyü-ən, yu̇-ˈän\ *n, pl* **yuan 1 :** the basic monetary unit of China **2 :** a coin or note representing one yuan [Chinese (Beijing dialect) *yuán*]

yuc·ca \ˈyək-ə\ *n* **:** any of a genus of plants that are related to the agaves, grow in dry warm regions chiefly of western North America, have long sword-shaped often stiff leaves mostly in a rosette at the base, and produce a tall stalk with clusters of whitish flowers [Spanish *yuca*]

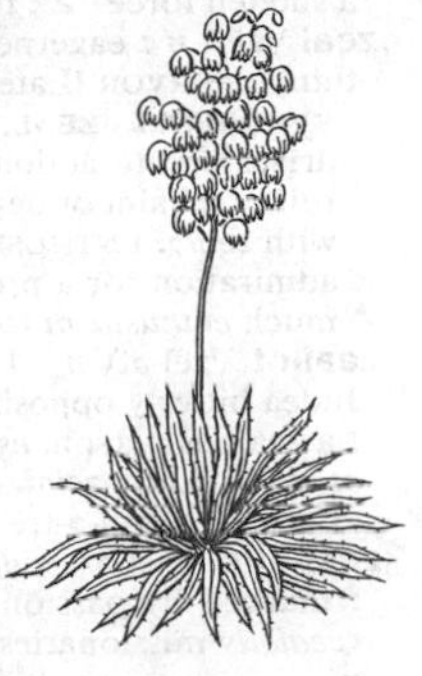
yucca

yucky \ˈyək-ē\ *adj* **yuck·i·er; -est :** DISGUSTING, DISTASTEFUL; *also* **:** UNPLEASANT, DISAGREEABLE

yule \ˈyül\ *n, often cap* **:** the feast of the nativity of Jesus Christ **:** CHRISTMAS [Old English *geōl*]

Yule log *n* **:** a large log formerly put on the hearth on Christmas Eve as the foundation of the fire

yule·tide \ˈyül-ˌtīd\ *n, often cap* **:** the Christmas season **:** CHRISTMASTIDE

yum·my \ˈyəm-ē\ *adj* **yum·mi·er; -est :** highly attractive or pleasing **:** DELICIOUS, DELECTABLE [*yum-yum,* interj. expressing pleasure in the taste of food]

yurt \ˈyu̇rt\ *n* **:** a light round tent of skins or felt stretched over a lattice framework used by various nomadic tribes in Central Asia [Russian *yurta,* of Turkic origin]

YWCA \ˌwī-ˌdəb-əl-yu̇-ˌsē-ˈā\ *n* **:** an international organization that promotes the spiritual, intellectual, social, and physical welfare originally of young Christian women [*Y*oung *W*omen's *C*hristian *A*ssociation]

YWHA \ˌwī-ˌdəb-əl-yu̇-ˌā-ˈchā\ *n* **:** an international organization that promotes the spiritual, intellectual, social, and physical welfare originally of young Jewish women [*Y*oung *W*omen's *H*ebrew *A*ssociation]

Z

z \zē, *British & Canadian* ˈzed\ *n, pl* **z's** *or* **zs** *often cap* **1 :** the 26th and last letter of the English alphabet **2 :** a brief nap ⟨catch some *z's* before dinner⟩

¹za•ny \ˈzā-nē\ *n, pl* **zanies** **1 :** CLOWN 2a **2 :** a silly or foolish person [Italian *zanni,* from *Zanni,* nickname for *Giovanni* "John"]

Word History In the 16th century the Italian theater developed a form of comedy improvised from standard situations and stock characters. One of these characters is a subordinate fool, clown, acrobat, or mountebank who mimics ludicrously the tricks of his principal. In Italian the stock name for such a character is *Zanni,* a nickname (in the dialect of Lombardy) for the name *Giovanni,* the Italian form of *John.* Italian *zanni* was soon borrowed into English, and by the early 17th century English *zany* was used for anyone who makes a laughingstock of himself, a buffoon.

²zany *adj* **za•ni•er; -est** **1 :** being or having the characteristics of a zany **2 :** fantastically or irrationally ludicrous **:** CRAZY — **za•ni•ly** \ˈzān-l-ē\ *adv* — **za•ni•ness** \ˈzā-nē-nəs\ *n*

¹zap \ˈzap\ *interj* — used to indicate a sudden or instantaneous occurrence [imitative]

²zap *vt* **zapped; zap•ping** **1 :** to destroy or kill with or as if with a sudden force **2 :** to hit suddenly and forcefully

zeal \ˈzēl\ *n* **:** eagerness and ardent interest in pursuit of something **:** FERVOR [Late Latin *zelus,* from Greek *zēlos*]

synonyms ZEAL, ENTHUSIASM mean intense emotion that drives one to action. ZEAL implies energetic and tireless pursuit of an aim or devotion to a cause ⟨supported the politician with *zeal*⟩. ENTHUSIASM suggests lively or eager interest in or admiration for a proposal or cause or activity ⟨never showed much *enthusiasm* for sports⟩.

zeal•ot \ˈzel-ət\ *n* **1** *cap* **:** one of a fanatical sect of ancient Judea bitterly opposing the Roman domination of Palestine **2 :** a zealous person; *esp* **:** a fanatical supporter ⟨a religious *zealot*⟩ [Late Latin *zelotes,* from Greek *zēlōtēs,* from *zēlos* "zeal"] — **zeal•ot•ry** \ˈzel-ə-trē\ *n*

zeal•ous \ˈzel-əs\ *adj* **:** filled with or characterized by zeal **:** marked by passionate support for a person, cause, or ideal ⟨*zealous* missionaries⟩ — **zeal•ous•ly** *adv* — **zeal•ous•ness** *n*

ze•bra \ˈzē-brə\ *n, pl* **zebras** *also* **zebra :** any of several hoofed plant-eating African mammals that are related to the horse, are distinctively patterned in stripes of black or dark brown and white or buff, and are swift runners [Portuguese *zebra, zebro* "wild ass"]

zebra

ze•bu \ˈzē-bü, -byü\ *n* **:** any of various breeds of domestic oxen developed in India that have a large fleshy hump over the shoulders and loose skin prolonged into dewlap and folds and that are able to withstand the injurious effects of heat and insect attack [French *zébu*]

Zech•a•ri•ah \ˌzek-ə-ˈrī-ə\ *n* **:** a prophetic book of canonical Jewish and Christian Scriptures — see BIBLE table

zed \ˈzed\ *n, chiefly British* **:** the letter z [Middle French *zede,* from Late Latin *zeta* "zeta," from Greek *zēta*]

ze•in \ˈzē-ən\ *n* **:** a protein from corn used especially in making textile fibers, plastics, and adhesives [New Latin *Zea,* genus that includes corn, from Greek *zea* "wheat"]

zeit•geist \ˈtsīt-ˌgīst, ˈzīt-\ *n, often cap* **:** the general intellectual, moral, and cultural state of an era [German, from *Zeit* "time" + *Geist* "spirit"]

zemst•vo \ˈzemst-vō, ˈzempst-, -və\ *n, pl* **zemstvos :** one of the district and provincial assemblies established in Russia in 1864 [Russian]

Zen \ˈzen\ *n* **:** a Japanese Buddhist sect that stresses the attainment of enlightenment by direct intuition through meditation rather than through intellectual concepts [Japanese, "religious meditation"]

ze•nith \ˈzē-nəth\ *n* **1 :** the point in the heavens directly overhead **2 :** the highest point **:** PEAK ⟨the *zenith* of our civilization⟩ [Medieval French *cenit,* from Medieval Latin, from Spanish *zenit,* from Arabic *samt* (*al-ra's*) "way (over one's head)"]

ze•nith•al \-əl\ *adj* **:** of, relating to, or located at or near the zenith

ze•o•lite \ˈzē-ə-ˌlīt\ *n* **:** any of various silicates chemically related to the feldspars that are used especially in water softening [Swedish *zeolit,* from Greek *zein* "to boil"] — **ze•o•lit•ic** \ˌzē-ə-ˈlit-ik\ *adj*

Zeph•a•ni•ah \ˌzef-ə-ˈnī-ə\ *n* **:** a book of canonical Jewish and Christian Scriptures about the end of the world — see BIBLE table

zeph•yr \ˈzef-ər\ *n* **1 a :** a breeze from the west **b :** a gentle breeze **2 :** any of various lightweight fabrics and articles of clothing [Latin *Zephyrus,* god of the west wind, west wind, from Greek *Zephyros*]

zep•pe•lin \ˈzep-lən, -ə-lən\ *n* **:** a rigid airship consisting of a cylindrical covered frame supported by internal gas cells [Count Ferdinand von *Zeppelin,* died 1917, German airship manufacturer]

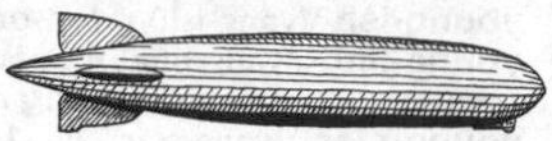

zeppelin

zerk \ˈzərk\ *n* **:** a grease fitting [Oscar U. *Zerk,* died 1968, American (Austrian-born) inventor]

¹ze•ro \ˈzē-rō, ˈziər-ō\ *n, pl* **zeros** *also* **zeroes** **1 :** the numerical symbol 0 indicating the absence of all magnitude or quantity — see NUMBER table **2 a :** the point of departure in reckoning; *also* **:** the point from which the graduation of a scale (as of a speedometer) commences **b :** a value or reading of zero; *esp* **:** the temperature represented by the zero mark on a thermometer **3 :** a person or thing having no importance or significance **:** NONENTITY **4 a :** a state of total absence or neutrality **:** NOTHING **b :** the lowest point **:** NADIR [Italian, from Medieval Latin *zephirum,* from Arabic *ṣifr*]

²zero *adj* **1 a :** of, relating to, or being a zero **b :** having no magnitude or quantity ⟨*zero* growth⟩ **c :** having no modified inflectional form ⟨*zero* plurals⟩ **2 a :** limiting vision to 50 feet (15 meters) or less ⟨*zero* cloud ceiling⟩ **b :** limited in a horizontal direction to 165 feet (about 50 meters) or less ⟨*zero* visibility⟩

³zero *vb* **1 :** to determine or adjust the zero of ⟨*zero* a scale⟩ **2 a :** to concentrate firepower (as of artillery) on the exact range of — usually used with *in* **b :** to adjust fire on a specific target — usually used with *in* **3 :** to close in on or focus attention on an objective — usually used with *in* ⟨*zeroing* in on the problem⟩

zero gravity *n* **:** the state or condition of lacking apparent gravitational pull **:** WEIGHTLESSNESS

zero hour *n* **1 :** the hour at which a planned military movement is scheduled to start **2 :** the moment at which something significant, vital, or crucial is to begin or take place [from its being marked by the count of zero in a countdown]

zero–zero *adj* **:** characterized by or being atmospheric conditions that reduce ceiling and visibility to zero

zest \ˈzest\ *n* **1 :** a piece of the peel of a citrus fruit (as an orange or lemon) used as flavoring **2 :** a quality of enhancing enjoyment **:** PIQUANCY ⟨adds *zest* to the performance⟩ **3 :** keen enjoyment **:** RELISH, GUSTO ⟨has a *zest* for living⟩ [French, "orange or lemon peel used as flavoring"] ***synonyms*** see TASTE — **zest•ful** \-fəl\ *adj* — **zest•ful•ly** \-fə-lē\ *adv* — **zest•ful•ness** *n* — **zesty** \ˈzes-tē\ *adj*

Word History *Zest* was borrowed into English in the 17th century from the French *zest* (now spelled *zeste*), meaning "orange or lemon peel." Where the French got the word we do not know. The peels of citrus fruits are still used to add flavoring to food and drinks, and the earliest citations for *zest* in English refer to the peel of such fruit used in this way. By the early 18th century, however, the sense was extended beyond the culinary domain, and *zest* was used to refer to a quality that adds enjoyment or piquancy to something.

ze•ta \'zāt-ə\ *n* : the 6th letter of the Greek alphabet — Z or ζ

zi•do•vu•dine \zi-'dō-vyü-ˌdēn\ *n* : AZT

[1]**zig** \'zig\ *n* : one of the sharp turns or changes or a straight section of a zigzag course [*zigzag*]

[2]**zig** *vi* **zigged; zig•ging** : to execute a turn or follow a section of a zigzag course

zig•gu•rat \'zig-ə-ˌrat\ *n* : an ancient Mesopotamian temple tower consisting of a lofty pyramidal structure built in successive stages with outside staircases and a shrine at the top [Akkadian *ziqqurratu* "pinnacle"]

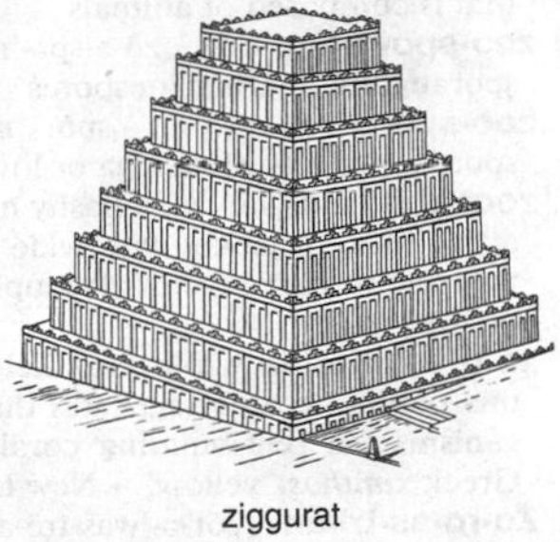
ziggurat

[1]**zig•zag** \'zig-ˌzag\ *n* : one of a series of sharp turns, angles, or changes in a course; *also* : something having the form or character of such a series ⟨a shirt with green *zigzags*⟩ ⟨*zigzags* in pricing⟩ [French]

[2]**zigzag** *adv* : in or by a zigzag path or course

[3]**zigzag** *adj* : having short sharp turns or angles ⟨a *zigzag* road⟩

[4]**zigzag** *vb* **zig•zagged; zig•zag•ging** : to lie in, proceed along, consist of, or form a zigzag course

zilch \'zilch\ *adj or n* : ZERO [origin unknown]

zil•lion \'zil-yən\ *n* : an indeterminately large number ⟨*zillions* of bugs⟩ [*z* + *-illion* (as in *million*)] — **zil•lionth** \-yənth\ *adj*

zinc \'zingk\ *n* : a bluish white metallic element that occurs abundantly in minerals and is used especially in alloys and as a protective coating for iron and steel — see ELEMENT table [German *Zink*]

zinc blende *n* : SPHALERITE [German *Blende* "sphalerite," from *blenden* "to deceive," literally, "to blind"]

zinc chloride *n* : a poisonous caustic deliquescent salt $ZnCl_2$ used especially as a wood preservative and catalyst

zinc oxide *n* : a white solid ZnO used especially as a pigment, in compounding rubber, and in pharmaceutical and cosmetic preparations (as ointments and sunblocks)

zinc sulfide *n* : a fluorescent white to yellowish compound ZnS used as a white pigment and a phosphor

zinc white *n* : a white pigment used especially in house paints and glazes that consists of zinc oxide

zine \'zēn\ *n* : MAGAZINE 3; *esp* : a homemade or online publication often devoted to specialized and unconventional subject matter ⟨a punk *zine*⟩ [*-zine* (as in *fanzine*)]

[1]**zing** \'zing\ *n* **1** : a shrill humming noise **2** : an enjoyably exciting or stimulating quality [imitative]

[2]**zing** *vi* : to move with or make a high-pitched hum ⟨tires *zinging* on wet pavement⟩

zing•er \'zing-ər\ *n* **1** : something causing or meant to cause interest or surprise **2** : a pointed witty remark

zin•nia \'zin-ē-ə, 'zin-yə, 'zēn-\ *n* : any of a genus of tropical American herbs related to the daisies and having showy flower heads with long-lasting ray flowers [Johann G. *Zinn*, died 1759, German botanist]

Zi•on \'zī-ən\ *also* **Si•on** \'sī-ən\ *n* **1 a** : the Jewish people : ISRAEL **b** : the Jewish homeland as a symbol of Judaism or of Jewish national aspiration **c** : the ideal nation or society envisioned by Judaism **2** : HEAVEN 2a **3** : UTOPIA 1 [*Zion*, citadel in Palestine which was the nucleus of Jerusalem, derived from Hebrew *Ṣīyōn*]

Zi•on•ism \'zī-ə-ˌniz-əm\ *n* : an international movement originally for the establishment of a Jewish homeland in Palestine and later for the support of modern Israel — **Zi•on•ist** \-nəst\ *adj or n* — **Zi•on•is•tic** \ˌzī-ə-'nis-tik\ *adj*

[1]**zip** \'zip\ *vb* **zipped; zip•ping** **1** : to move or act with speed and vigor **2** : to travel with a sharp hissing or humming sound **3** : to add zest, interest, or life to — often used with *up* [imitative of the sound of a speeding object]

[2]**zip** *n* **1** : a sudden sharp hissing or sibilant sound **2** : ENERGY 2, VIM

[3]**zip** *n* : NOTHING, ZERO ⟨the final score was 27 to *zip*⟩

[4]**zip** *vb* **zipped; zip•ping** : to close or open or attach by means of a zipper [back-formation from *zipper*]

[5]**zip** *n, often all cap* : ZIP CODE

zip code *n, often cap Z&I&P* : a number that identifies each postal delivery area in the U.S.

zip gun *n* : a crude homemade single-shot pistol

zip line *n* : a cable suspended above a slope to which a pulley and harness are attached for a rider

zip•per \'zip-ər\ *n* : a fastener consisting of two rows of metal or plastic teeth and a sliding piece that closes an opening by drawing the teeth together [from *Zipper*, a former trademark]

zip•pered \-ərd\ *adj* : equipped with a zipper

zip•py \'zip-ē\ *adj* **zip•pi•er; -est** : full of zip : BRISK, SNAPPY

zi•ram \'zī-ˌram\ *n* : an organic zinc salt used especially as an agricultural fungicide [*zi*nc + dithiocarb*am*ate]

zir•con \'zər-ˌkän, -kən\ *n* : a crystalline mineral $ZrSiO_4$ which is a silicate of zirconium and of which several transparent varieties are used as gemstones [German]

zir•co•nia \ˌzər-'kō-nē-ə\ *n* : a white crystalline compound ZrO_2 used especially in refractories, in thermal and electric insulation, in abrasives, and in enamels and glazes — called also *zirconium oxide*

zir•co•ni•um \ˌzər-'kō-nē-əm\ *n* : a steel-gray strong ductile metallic element with a high melting point that is highly resistant to corrosion and is used especially in alloys — see ELEMENT table [New Latin, from English *zircon*]

zit \'zit\ *n, slang* : PIMPLE [origin unknown]

zith•er \'zith-ər, 'zith-\ *n* : a stringed musical instrument having usually 30 to 40 strings over a flat soundboard played with the tips of the fingers and a pick [German, from Latin *cithara* "lyre," from Greek *kithara*] — **zith•er•ist** \-ə-rəst\ *n*

zither

zi•ti \'zēt-ē\ *n, pl* **ziti** : medium-sized tubular pasta [Italian, plural of *zito*, from *zita* "piece of tubular pasta," probably short for *maccheroni di zita*, literally, "bride's macaroni"]

zlo•ty \'zlot-ē, zə-'lȯt-\ *n, pl* **zlo•tys** \-ēz\ *or* **zloty** **1** : the basic monetary unit of Poland **2** : a coin representing one zloty [Polish *złoty*]

zo- *or* **zoo-** *combining form* : animal : animal kingdom or kind ⟨*zo*oid⟩ ⟨*zo*ology⟩ [Greek *zōion* "animal"]

zo•di•ac \'zōd-ē-ˌak\ *n* **1** : a zone in the heavens that encompasses the apparent paths of all the planets, that has as its central line the apparent path of the sun, and that is divided into 12 constellations or signs each taken for astrological purposes to extend 30 degrees of longitude **2** : a figure representing the signs of the zodiac and their symbols [Medieval French *zodiaque*, from Latin *zodiacus*, from Greek *zōidiakos*, derived from *zōidion* "carved figure, sign of the zodiac," from *zōion* "animal, figure"] — **zo•di•a•cal** \zō-'dī-ə-kəl, zə-\ *adj*

SIGNS OF THE ZODIAC

NO.	NAME	SYMBOL	SUN ENTERS[1]
1	Aries the Ram	♈	March 21
2	Taurus the Bull	♉	April 20
3	Gemini the Twins	♊	May 21
4	Cancer the Crab	♋	June 22
5	Leo the Lion	♌	July 23
6	Virgo the Virgin	♍	August 23
7	Libra the Balance	♎	September 23
8	Scorpio the Scorpion	♏	October 24
9	Sagittarius the Archer	♐	November 22
10	Capricorn the Goat	♑	December 22
11	Aquarius the Water Bearer	♒	January 20
12	Pisces the Fishes	♓	February 19

[1] Though no longer astronomically accurate, these traditional dates continue to be used in astrology.

-zoic \'zō-ik\ *adj combining form* : of, relating to, or being a (specified) geological era ⟨Archeo*zoic*⟩ [Greek *zōē* "life"]

\ə\ **abut**	\au̇\ **out**	\i\ **tip**	\ȯ\ **saw**	\u̇\ **foot**
\ər\ **further**	\ch\ **chin**	\ī\ **life**	\ȯi\ **coin**	\y\ **yet**
\a\ **mat**	\e\ **pet**	\j\ **job**	\th\ **thin**	\yü\ **few**
\ā\ **take**	\ē\ **easy**	\ng\ **sing**	\th\ **this**	\yu̇\ **cure**
\ä\ **cot, cart**	\g\ **go**	\ō\ **bone**	\ü\ **food**	\zh\ **vision**

zom·bie *also* **zom·bi** \ˈzäm-bē\ *n* **:** a person that according to voodoo belief especially in Haiti has died and been brought back to life without a will or the power of speech and capable only of automatic movement [Louisiana Creole or Haitian Creole *zonbi,* of Bantu origin]

zon·al \ˈzō-nᵊl\ *adj* **1 :** of, relating to, or having the form of a zone ⟨a *zonal* boundary⟩ **2 :** of, relating to, or being a soil or major soil group marked by well-developed characteristics that are determined primarily by the action of climate and organisms (as plants) — compare AZONAL, INTRAZONAL

zo·na pel·lu·ci·da \ˌzō-nə-pə-ˈlü-səd-ə\ *n, pl* **zo·nae pel·lu·ci·dae** \ˌzō-nē-pə-ˈlü-səd-ē\ **:** the transparent noncellular outer layer or envelope of a mammalian ovum [New Latin, "transparent zone"]

zo·na·tion \zō-ˈnā-shən\ *n* **:** distribution or arrangement in zones ⟨altitudinal *zonation* of plant species⟩

[1]**zone** \ˈzōn\ *n* **1 :** any of five great divisions of the earth's surface with respect to latitude and temperature — compare FRIGID ZONE, TEMPERATE ZONE, TORRID ZONE **2** *archaic* **:** GIRDLE, BELT **3 a :** an encircling anatomical structure **b :** an area (as a moist cool treed mountain slope) that supports a similar flora and fauna throughout its extent **c :** a distinctive belt, layer, or series of layers of earth materials (as rock) **4 :** a region or area set off as distinct from surrounding or adjoining parts or created for a particular purpose: as **a :** a zoned section (as of a city) **b :** any of the eight concentric bands of territory centered on a given U.S. parcel-post shipment point to which mail is charged at a single rate **5 :** a temporary state of heightened concentration experienced by a performing athlete that enables peak performance ⟨a player in the *zone*⟩ [Latin *zona* "belt, zone," from Greek *zōnē*]

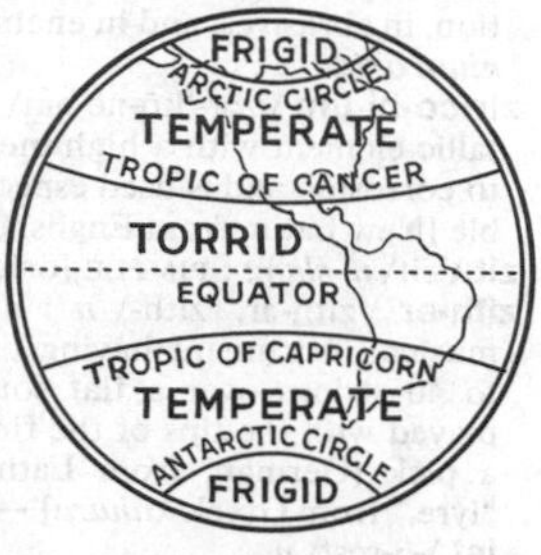

zone 1

[2]**zone** *vt* **1 :** to surround with a zone **:** ENCIRCLE **2 :** to arrange in or mark off into zones; *esp* **:** to divide (as a city) into sections reserved for different purposes

zone defense *n* **:** a system of defense (as in basketball or football) in which each player guards an assigned area rather than a specific opponent

zone out *vi* **:** to become oblivious to one's surroundings especially in order to relax ⟨*zone out* in front of the television⟩

zoo \ˈzü\ *n, pl* **zoos :** a garden or park where living usually wild animals are kept for exhibition [short for *zoological garden*]

zoo- — see ZO-

zoo·ge·og·ra·phy \ˌzō-ə-jē-ˈäg-rə-fē\ *n* **:** a branch of biogeography concerned with the geographic distribution of animals — **zoo·geo·graph·ic** \-ˌjē-ə-ˈgraf-ik\ *or* **zoo·geo·graph·i·cal** \-ˈgraf-i-kəl\ *adj* — **zoo·geo·graph·i·cal·ly** \-i-kə-lē, -klē\ *adv*

zo·oid \ˈzō-ˌȯid\ *n* **:** one of the asexually produced individuals of a compound organism (as a coral colony)

zoo·keep·er \ˈzü-ˌkē-pər\ *n* **:** one who maintains or cares for animals in a zoo

zo·o·log·i·cal \ˌzō-ə-ˈläj-i-kəl\ *adj* **1 :** of, relating to, or concerned with zoology **2 :** of, relating to, or affecting lower animals often as distinguished from humans ⟨*zoological* infections⟩ — **zo·o·log·i·cal·ly** \-i-kə-lē, -klē\ *adv*

zoological garden *n* **:** ZOO

zoological park *n* **:** ZOO

zo·ol·o·gy \zō-ˈäl-ə-jē, zə-ˈwäl-\ *n* **1 :** a branch of biology concerned with the animal kingdom and animal life **2 a :** animal life (as of a region) **:** FAUNA **b :** the properties or characteristics exhibited by an animal, animal type, or group — **zo·ol·o·gist** \-jəst\ *n*

[1]**zoom** \ˈzüm\ *vb* **1 :** to move with a loud low hum or buzz ⟨cars *zoomed* down the highway⟩ **2 :** to climb for a short time at an angle greater than that which can be maintained in steady flight ⟨the airplane *zoomed* and vanished in the distance⟩ **3 :** to focus a camera or microscope using a special lens that permits the apparent distance of the object to be varied — often used with *in* or *out* **4 :** to cause to zoom [imitative]

[2]**zoom** *n* **1 :** an act or process of zooming **2 :** a zooming sound

zoom lens *n* **:** a camera lens in which the image size can be varied continuously so that the image remains in focus at all times

zoo·no·sis \zō-ˈän-ə-səs, ˌzō-ə-ˈnō-\ *n, pl* **-no·ses** \-ˌsēz\ **:** a disease capable of being transmitted from animals to humans under natural conditions [New Latin, from *zo-* + Greek *nosos* "disease"] — **zoo·not·ic** \ˌzō-ə-ˈnät-ik\ *adj*

zoo·plank·ton \ˌzō-ə-ˈplang-tən, -ˈplangk-, -ˌtän\ *n* **:** plankton that is composed of animals

zoo·spo·ran·gi·um \ˌzō-ə-spə-ˈran-jē-əm\ *n* **:** a spore case or sporangium bearing zoospores

zoo·spore \ˈzō-ə-ˌspōr, -ˌspȯr\ *n* **:** a flagellated motile asexual spore especially of an alga or lower fungus

zoot suit \ˈzüt-ˌsüt\ *n* **:** a flashy man's suit typically consisting of a thigh-length jacket with wide padded shoulders and trousers tapering to narrow cuffs [reduplication of [1]*suit*] — **zoot-suit·er** \-ər\ *n*

zo·o·xan·thel·la \ˌzō-ə-zan-ˈthel-ə\ *n, pl* **-lae** \-ē\ **:** any of various symbiotic dinoflagellates that live within cells of other organisms (as reef-building coral polyps) [derived from *zo-* + Greek *xanthos* "yellow" + New Latin *-ella, a diminutive suffix*]

Zo·ro·as·tri·an \ˌzōr-ə-ˈwas-trē-ən, ˌzȯr-\ *adj* **:** of or relating to the Persian prophet Zoroaster or the religion founded by him and marked by belief in a cosmic war between good and evil — **Zoroastrian** *n* — **Zo·ro·as·tri·an·ism** \-trē-ə-ˌniz-əm\ *n*

Zou·ave \zü-ˈäv\ *n* **1 :** a member of a French infantry unit originally composed of Algerians wearing a colorful uniform and conducting a quick spirited drill **2 :** a member of a military unit modeled on the Algerian Zouaves [French, from Arabic dialect *Zwāwa,* Berber tribal confederation of Kabylia]

zounds \ˈzau̇nz, ˈzwau̇nz, ˈzünz, ˈzwünz\ *interj* — used as a mild oath [euphemism for *God's wounds*]

zow·ie \ˈzau̇-ē\ *interj* — used to express astonishment or admiration especially in response to something sudden or speedy

zoy·sia \ˈzȯi-shə, -zhə, -sē-ə, -zē-ə\ *n* **:** any of a genus of creeping perennial grasses of southeastern Asia and New Zealand having fine wiry leaves and including some used as lawn grasses especially in warm regions [Karl von *Zois,* died 1799, Slovenian botanist]

Z particle *n* **:** a neutral elementary particle about 90 times heavier than a proton

zuc·chet·to \zü-ˈket-ō, tsü-\ *n, pl* **-tos :** a small round skullcap worn by Roman Catholic ecclesiastics in colors that vary according to the rank of the wearer [Italian, from *zucca* "gourd, head," from Late Latin *cucutia* "gourd"]

zuc·chi·ni \zu̇-ˈkē-nē\ *n, pl* **-ni** *or* **-nis :** a smooth cylindrical usually dark green summer squash; *also* **:** a plant that bears zucchini [Italian, pl. of *zucchino,* from *zucca* "gourd," from Late Latin *cucutia*]

Zu·lu \ˈzü-lü\ *n* **1 :** a member of a Bantu-speaking people of Natal **2 :** a Bantu language of the Zulus — **Zulu** *adj*

Zu·ni \ˈzü-nē\ *also* **Zu·ñi** \ˈzün-yē\ *n, pl* **Zuni** *or* **Zunis** *also* **Zuñi** *or* **Zuñis :** a member of an American Indian people of western New Mexico [American Spanish *Zuñi*]

zwie·back \ˈswē-ˌbak, ˈswī-, ˈzwē-, ˈzwī-, -ˌbäk\ *n* **:** a usually sweet bread enriched with eggs that is baked and then sliced and toasted until dry and crisp [German, literally, "twice baked"]

Zwing·li·an \ˈzwing-lē-ən, ˈswing-, -glē-; ˈtsfing-lē-ən\ *adj* **:** of or relating to Ulrich Zwingli or his doctrine that in the Eucharist the true body of Jesus Christ is present symbolically and not literally — **Zwinglian** *n*

zy·de·co \ˈzīd-ə-ˌkō\ *n* **:** popular music of southern Louisiana that combines tunes of French origin with elements of Caribbean music and blues [perhaps modification of French *les haricots* "beans," from the Cajun dance tune *Les Haricots Sont Pas Salés*]

zyg- *or* **zygo-** *combining form* **1 :** yoke ⟨*zygo*morphic⟩ **2 :** pair ⟨*zygo*dactyl⟩ **3 :** concerned with or produced in sexual reproduction ⟨*zygo*spore⟩ [Greek *zygon*]

zy·go·dac·tyl \ˌzī-gə-ˈdak-tᵊl\ *adj* **:** having the toes arranged two in front and two behind — used of a bird [derived from *zyg-* + Greek *daktylos* "finger, digit"]

zy·go·mat·ic \ˌzī-gə-ˈmat-ik\ *adj* **:** of, relating to, being, or situated in the region of the cheekbone [Greek *zygōmat-, zygōma* "zygomatic arch," from *zygoun* "to yoke," from *zygon* "yoke"]

zygomatic bone *n* **:** CHEEKBONE

zy·go·mor·phic \-ˈmȯr-fik\ *adj* : bilaterally symmetrical in respect to but one longitudinal axis ⟨*zygomorphic* flowers⟩

zy·go·spore \ˈzī-gə-ˌspōr, -ˌspȯr\ *n* : a thick-walled spore of some algae and fungi that is formed by union of two similar sexual cells, usually serves as a resting spore, and ultimately produces the sporophyte

zy·gote \ˈzī-ˌgōt\ *n* : a cell formed by the union of two gametes; *also* : the developing individual produced from such a cell [Greek *zygōtos* "yoked," from *zygoun* "to yoke," from *zygon* "yoke"] — **zy·got·ic** \zī-ˈgät-ik\ *adj* — **zy·got·i·cal·ly** \-ˈgät-i-kə-lē, -klē\ *adv*

-zy·gous \ˈzī-gəs\ *adj combining form* : having (such) a zygotic constitution ⟨hetero*zygous*⟩

zym- *or* **zymo-** *combining form* **1** : fermentation ⟨*zym*ase⟩ **2** : enzyme ⟨*zymo*gen⟩ [Greek *zymē* "leaven"]

zy·mase \ˈzī-ˌmās, -ˌmāz\ *n* : an enzyme or enzyme complex of yeast that promotes fermentation of sugar

-zyme \ˌzīm\ *n combining form* : enzyme ⟨lyso*zyme*⟩

zy·mo·gen \ˈzī-mə-jən\ *n* : an inactive precursor of an enzyme secreted by living cells and converted (as by an acid) into an active form — called also *proenzyme* — **zy·mo·gen·ic** \ˌzī-mə-ˈjen-ik\ *adj*

ABBREVIATIONS

AND SYMBOLS FOR CHEMICAL ELEMENTS

For a list of special abbreviations used in this dictionary see page 21a preceding the vocabulary.

Most of these abbreviations have been normalized to one form. Variation in use of periods, in typeface, and in capitalization is frequent and widespread (as *mph, MPH, m.p.h., Mph*).

a absent, acre, answer, are, area, atto-

A ace, ampere, argon

Å angstrom unit

AA administrative assistant, Alcoholics Anonymous, associate in arts, author's alterations

AAA American Automobile Association

A and M agricultural and mechanical

AAR against all risks

AB able-bodied seaman, Alberta, bachelor of arts [New Latin *artium baccalaureus*]

abbr abbreviation

ABC American Broadcasting Companies

abl ablative

abp archbishop

abs absolute, abstract

ABS antilock braking system

abstr abstract

ac account, acre

Ac actinium, altocumulus

AC air-conditioning, alternating current, before Christ [Latin *ante Christum*], area code

acad academic, academy

acc, accus accusative

accel accelerando

acct account, accountant

ack acknowledge, acknowledgment

ACLU American Civil Liberties Union

act active, actor, actual

ACT American College Test, Australian Capital Territory

actg acting

AD after date, Alzheimer's disease, anno Domini, athletic director

ADC aide-de-camp, Aid to Dependent Children

addn addition

ad int ad interim

adj adjective, adjunct, adjustment, adjutant

ad loc to or at the place [Latin *ad locum*]

ADM admiral

admin administration, administrative

adv adverb, advertisement, advertising

ad val ad valorem

advt advertisement

AEC Atomic Energy Commission

AEF American Expeditionary Force

aero aerodynamic

aet, aetat of age, aged [Latin *aetatis*]

AF air force, audio frequency

AFB air force base

AFDC Aid to Families with Dependent Children

afft affidavit

AFL–CIO American Federation of Labor and Congress of Industrial Organizations

Afr Africa, African

Ag silver [Latin *argentum*]

agcy agency

agr, agric agricultural, agriculture

agt agent

AI artificial intelligence

AK Alaska

aka also known as

Al aluminum

AL Alabama, American League, American Legion

Ala Alabama

Alas Alaska

Alb Albania, Albanian

alc alcohol

ald alderman

alg algebra

alk alkaline

alt alternate, altitude

Alta Alberta

a.m., AM ante meridiem

Am America, American, americium

AM master of arts [New Latin *artium magister*]

amb ambassador

amdt amendment

Amer America, American

AmerInd American Indian

Amn airman

amt amount

amu atomic mass unit

anal analogy, analysis, analytic

anat anatomical, anatomy

anc ancient

ANC African National Congress

ann annals, annual

anon anonymous, anonymously

ans answer

ant antenna, antonym

Ant Antarctica

anthrop anthropology

AO account of, and others

ap apostle, apothecaries'

AP additional premium, American plan, arithmetic progression, Associated Press

APB all points bulletin

APO army post office

app apparatus, appendix

appl applied

approx approximate, approximately

appt appointment

Apr April

apt apartment, aptitude

aq aqua, aqueous

ar arrival, arrive

Ar Arabic, argon

AR accounts receivable, Arkansas

Arab Arabian, Arabic

arch architect, architectural, architecture

archeol archeology

arith arithmetic

Ariz Arizona

Ark Arkansas

arr arranged, arrival, arrive

art article, artificial

ARV American Revised Version

As altostratus, arsenic

AS American Samoa, Anglo-Saxon

ASAP as soon as possible

ASL American Sign Language

ASPCA American Society for the Prevention of Cruelty to Animals

assn association

assoc associate, associated, association

asst assistant

astrol astrologer, astrology

astron astronomer, astronomy

ASV American Standard Version

At astatine

ATC air traffic control

Atl Atlantic

atm atmosphere, atmospheric

at no atomic number

att attached, attention, attorney

attn attention

attrib attributive, attributively

atty attorney

at wt atomic weight

Au gold [Latin *aurum*]

AU astronomical unit

Aug August

AUS Army of the United States

Austral Australian

auth authentic, author, authorized

aux auxiliary verb

av avenue, average, avoirdupois

AV ad valorem, audiovisual, Authorized Version

avdp avoirdupois

ave avenue

avg average

awd all-wheel drive

AZ Arizona

b bachelor, back, bass, basso, bat, before, billion, bishop, book, born

B Bible, boron

Ba barium

BA bachelor of arts, batting average

bal balance

bar barometer, barometric, barrel

Bart baronet

BBC British Broadcasting Corporation

bbl barrel, barrels

BBQ barbeque

BBS bulletin board system

BC before Christ, British Columbia

BCE before the Christian Era, before the Common Era

bd board, bound

BD bachelor of divinity, bank draft, bills discounted, brought down

bd ft board foot

bdl, bdle bundle

Be beryllium

BE bill of exchange

Belg Belgian, Belgium

bet between

BeV billion electron volts

bf boldface

BF board foot, brought forward
bg background, bag
Bh bohrium
Bi bismuth
bib Bible, biblical
bid twice a day [Latin *bis in die*]
biog biographer, biographical, biography
biol biologic, biological, biologist, biology
bk bank, book, break
Bk berkelium
bkg banking, bookkeeping
bkt basket, bracket
bl bale, barrel, black, blue
bldg building
blk black, block
blvd boulevard
BM basal metabolism, board measure, bowel movement
BMI body mass index
BMR basal metabolic rate
BO back order, best offer, body odor, box office, branch office, buyer's option
BOQ bachelor officers' quarters
bor borough
bot botanical, botanist, botany, bottle, bottom, bought
bp baptized, birthplace, bishop
BP batting practice, before the present, bills payable, blood pressure, blueprint, boiling point
bpl birthplace
BPW Board of Public Works
br branch, brown
Br Britain, British, bromine
Braz Brazil, Brazilian
brb be right back
brig brigade, brigadier
Brit Britain, British
BS bachelor of science, balance sheet, bill of sale
BSA Boy Scouts of America
BSc bachelor of science
bskt basket
Bt baronet
btry battery
BTW by the way
bu bureau, bushel
Bu butyl
bull bulletin
bur bureau
bus business
BVM Blessed Virgin Mary
BWI British West Indies
bx box
BX base exchange
c calorie, carat, cent, centi-, centimeter, century, chapter, circa, circumference, contralto, copyright, cubic, cup, curie
C capacitance, carbon, Celsius, centigrade
ca circa
Ca calcium
CA California, chartered accountant, chief accountant, chronological age
CAD computer-aided design
CAF, C and F cost and freight
cal calorie (small)
Cal California, calorie (large)
Calif California
Can, Canad Canada, Canadian
canc canceled
C & W country and western
cap capacity, capital, capitalize, capitalized
CAP Civil Air Patrol
caps capitals, capsule
Capt captain
card cardinal
cat catalog
CATV cable television, community antenna television
Cb columbium, cumulonimbus
CBC Canadian Broadcasting Corporation
CBD cash before delivery
CBS Columbia Broadcasting System
cc cubic centimeter
CC carbon copy, common carrier, community college
CCTV closed-circuit television
CCU cardiac care unit, coronary care unit, critical care unit
cd candela, candle, cord
Cd cadmium
CD carried down, civil defense
CDR commander
CDT central daylight time
Ce cerium
CE chemical engineer, Christian Era, civil engineer, Common Era
cent centigrade, central, century
cert certificate, certification, certified, certify
cf compare [Latin *confer*]
Cf californium
CF carried forward, cystic fibrosis
CFC chlorofluorocarbon
CFI cost, freight, and insurance
cg centigram
CG coast guard
cgs centimeter-gram-second
ch chain, champion, chapter, church
CH clearinghouse, courthouse, customhouse
chap chapter
chem chemical, chemist, chemistry
chg change, charge
Chin Chinese
chm chairman, checkmate
Chmn chairman
chron chronicle, chronology
CIA Central Intelligence Agency
CIF cost, insurance, and freight
C in C commander in chief
cir circle, circuit, circular, circumference
circ circular
CIS Commonwealth of Independent States
cit citation, cited, citizen
civ civil, civilian, civilization
CJ chief justice
ck cask, check
cl centiliter, class, clause
Cl chlorine
CL carload
clk clerk
clo clothing
cm centimeter
Cm curium
Cmdr commander
cml commercial
Cn copernicium
CN credit note
CNA certified nurse's aid
CNMI Commonwealth of the Northern Mariana Islands
CNN Cable News Network
CNO chief of naval operations
CNS central nervous system
co company, county
Co cobalt
CO cash order, Colorado, commanding officer, conscientious objector
c/o care of
COD cash on delivery, collect on delivery
C of C Chamber of Commerce
C of S chief of staff
cog cognate
col colonial, colony, color, colored, column, counsel
Col colonel, Colorado
collat collateral
colloq colloquial
Colo Colorado
colog cologarithm
com comedy, comic, comma, commercial organization
comb combination, combined, combining
comdg commanding
comdr commander
comdt commandant
coml commercial
comm commander, commission, committee, commonwealth, community
comp comparative, compensation, compiled, compiler, composition, compound, comprehensive, comptroller
comr commissioner
con consolidated, consul
conc concentrated
cond condition, conductivity
conf conference, confidential
Confed Confederate
cong congress, congressional
conj conjunction
Conn Connecticut
cons conservative, consonant
consol consolidated
const constant, constitution, constitutional, construction
constr construction
cont containing, contents, continent, continental, continued, control
contd continued
contg containing
contr contract, contraction, contralto
contrib contribution, contributor
CORE Congress of Racial Equality
corp corporal, corporation
corr correct, corrected, correction, correspondence, corresponding
cos companies, cosine, counties
COS cash on shipment, chief of staff
cosec cosecant
cot cotangent
cp compare, coupon
CP candlepower, chemically pure, Communist party
CPA certified public accountant
cpd compound
Cpl corporal
CPO chief petty officer
CPR cardiopulmonary resuscitation
CPS cycles per second
CQ charge of quarters
cr credit, creditor
Cr chromium
cresc crescendo
crit critical, criticism, criticized
cryst crystalline, crystallized
cs case, cases
Cs cesium, cirrostratus
CS civil service
CSA Confederate States of America
csc cosecant
CSF cerebrospinal fluid
C–Span cable-satellite public affairs network
CST central standard time
ct carat, cent, count, court
CT central time, certified teacher, computed tomography, computerized tomography, Connecticut
ctn carton, cotangent
ctr center, counter
cu cubic
Cu copper [Latin *cuprum*], cumulus
cur currency, current
CV cardiovascular
CWO cash with order, chief warrant officer
cwt hundredweight
cyl cylinder
CZ Canal Zone
d date, daughter, day, dead, deceased, deci-, degree, diameter, penny, pence [Latin *denarius, denarii*]
D Democrat, deuterium, doctor
da deka-
DA days after acceptance, deposit account, district attorney
dag dekagram
dal, daL dekaliter
dam dekameter
Dan Danish
DAR Daughters of the American Revolution
dat dative

dB decibel
Db dubnium
d/b/a doing business as
DBH diameter at breast height
dbl, dble double
DC da capo, direct current, District of Columbia, doctor of chiropractic, double crochet
DD days after date, doctor of divinity
DDS doctor of dental surgery
DE Delaware
deb debenture
dec deceased, decrease, decrescendo
Dec December
def defendant, definite, definition
deg degree
del delegate, delegation
Del Delaware
dely delivery
Den Denmark
dent dental, dentist, dentistry
dep depart, departure, deposit, deputy
dept department
der, deriv derivation, derivative
det detached, detachment, detail, determine
DEW distant early warning
DF damage free
DFC Distinguished Flying Cross
dg decigram
DG by the grace of God [Late Latin *Dei gratia*], director general
dia, diam diameter
diag diagonal, diagram
dial dialect, dialectical
dict dictionary
dig digest
dil dilute
dim dimension, diminished, diminuendo, diminutive
dir direction, director
disc discount
dist distance, district
distr distribute, distribution
div divided, dividend, division, divorced
dk dark, deck, dock
dl deciliter
DL disabled list
DLitt, DLit doctor of letters, doctor of literature [Latin *doctor litterarum*]
DLO dead letter office
dm decimeter
DMD doctor of dental medicine [Latin *dentariae medicinae*]
DMV Department of Motor Vehicles
DMZ demilitarized zone
dn down
DO doctor of osteopathy
DOA dead on arrival
DOB date of birth
doc document
DOD Department of Defense
dom domestic, dominion
DOS disk operating system
doz dozen
DP data processing, dew point
dpi dots per inch
dpt department
dr debtor, dram, drive, drum
Dr doctor
Ds darmstadtium
DS dal segno
DSC Distinguished Service Cross
DSL digital subscriber line
DSM Distinguished Service Medal
DSO Distinguished Service Order
DSP died without issue [Latin *decessit sine prole*]
DST daylight saving time
DTP diphtheria, tetanus, pertussis
Du Dutch
dup duplex, duplicate
DV Deo volente, Douay Version
DVM doctor of veterinary medicine
DVR digital video recorder
dwt pennyweight
DX distance
Dy dysprosium
dz dozen
e east, eastern, excellent
E energy, English, error
ea each
E and OE errors and omissions excepted
EB eastbound
EC European Community
eccl ecclesiastical
ECG electrocardiogram
ecol ecological, ecology
econ economics, economist, economy
Ecua Ecuador
ed edited, edition, editor
EDT eastern daylight time
edu educational institution
educ education, educational
EEG electroencephalogram, electroencephalograph
EEO equal employment opportunity
e.g. for example [Latin *exempli gratia*]
Eg Egypt, Egyptian
EHF extremely high frequency
EKG electrocardiogram, electrocardiograph [German *elektrokardiogramm*]
el, elev elevation
elec electric, electrical, electricity
elem elementary
ELF extremely low-frequency
EM electromagnetic, electron microscope
emer emeritus
emp emperor, empress
EMS emergency medical service
emu electromagnetic unit
enc, encl enclosure
ency, encyc encyclopedia
ENE east-northeast
eng engine, engineer, engineering
Eng England, English
engr engineer, engraved, engraver, engraving
enl enlarged, enlisted
ENS ensign
entom, entomol entomological, entomology
env envelope
EOE equal opportunity employer
EOM end of month
EP European plan, extended play
EPA Environmental Protection Agency
EPO erythropoietin
eq equal, equation
equip equipment
equiv equivalency, equivalent
Er erbium
ER earned run, emergency room
ERA earned run average
Es einsteinium
ESE east-southeast
Esk Eskimo
ESL English as a second language
esp especially
ESPN Entertainment and Sports Programming Network
Esq, Esqr esquire
est established, estimate, estimated
EST eastern standard time
ET eastern time
ETA estimated time of arrival
et al and others [Latin *et alii*]
etc et cetera
ETD estimated time of departure
et seq and the following one [Latin *et sequens*], and the following ones [Latin *et sequentes* or *et sequentia*]
Eu europium
EU European Union
Eur Europe, European
eV electron volt
evap evaporate
ex example, exchange, executive, express, extra
exc excellent, except
exch exchange, exchanged
exp expense, experiment, experimental, export, express
expt experiment
exptl experimental
ext extension, exterior, external, externally, extra, extract
f and the following one [*following*], failure, false, faraday, female, feminine, femto-, focal length, folio, force, forte, frequency, from
F Fahrenheit, farad, fluorine, French, Friday
FAA Federal Aviation Administration
fac facsimile, faculty
FADM fleet admiral
Fah, Fahr Fahrenheit
FAO Food and Agricultural Organization of the United Nations
FAQ frequently asked question
FAS free alongside ship
fath fathom
FB freight bill
FBI Federal Bureau of Investigation
FCC Federal Communications Commission
fcp foolscap
FD fire department
FDA Food and Drug Administration
FDIC Federal Deposit Insurance Corporation
Fe iron [Latin *ferrum*]
Feb February
fed federal, federation
fem female, feminine
FEPC Fair Employment Practices Commission
ff and the following ones [*following*], folios, fortissimo
FHA Federal Housing Administration
FICA Federal Insurance Contributions Act
FIFO first in, first out
fig figurative, figuratively, figure
fin finance, financial, finish
Finn Finnish
fl flanker, floor, flourished [Latin *floruit*], fluid
FL, Fla Florida
fl dr fluid dram
Flem Flemish
fl oz fluid ounce
fm fathom
Fm fermium
fn footnote
fo, fol folio
FOB free on board
FOC free of charge
for foreign, forestry
FOR free on rail
4WD four-wheel drive
fp freezing point
fpm feet per minute
FPO fleet post office
fps feet per second, foot-pound-second
fr father, franc, friar, from
Fr France, francium, French, Friday
freq frequency, frequent, frequently
FRG Federal Republic of Germany
Fri Friday
front frontispiece
FRS Federal Reserve System
frt freight
frwy freeway
FSH follicle-stimulating hormone
ft feet, foot, fort
ft lb foot-pound
F2F face-to-face
fur furlong
fut future
fwd foreword, forward
FWD front-wheel drive
FYI for your information

g acceleration of gravity, gauge, good, gram, gravity
G German, giga-
ga gauge
Ga gallium, Georgia
GA general agent, general assembly, general average, Georgia
gal gallery, gallon
gar garage
gaz gazette
GB gigabyte, Great Britain
GCA ground-controlled approach
GCD greatest common divisor
GCF greatest common factor
Gd gadolinium
Ge germanium
GED general equivalency diploma
gen general, genitive, genus
genl general
geog geographic, geographical, geography
geol geologic, geological, geology
geom geometric, geometrical, geometry
ger gerund
Ger German, Germany
GH growth hormone
GHQ general headquarters
GHz gigahertz
gi gill
GI gastrointestinal, general issue, government issue
Gib, Gibr Gibraltar
Gk Greek
gm gram
GM general manager, genetically modified, grand master, guided missile
GMT Greenwich mean time
GNP gross national product
GOP Grand Old Party (Republican)
Goth Gothic
gov government, governmental organization, governor
govt government
gp group
GP general practice, general practitioner, geometric progression
GPA grade point average
GPO general post office, Government Printing Office
GQ general quarters
gr grade, grain, gram, gravity, gross
Gr Greece, Greek
gram grammar, grammatical
GRAS generally recognized as safe
gro gross
GSA Girl Scouts of America
GSUSA Girl Scouts of the United States of America
gt great
Gt Brit Great Britain
GU genitourinary, Guam
GUI graphical user interface
GUT grand unified theory
Gy gray
h hard, hardness, hect-, hecto-, height, high, hit, hour, husband
H heroin, hydrogen
ha hectare
HAST Hawaii-Aleutian standard time
Hb hemoglobin
HBM Her Britannic Majesty, His Britannic Majesty
HC House of Commons
HCF highest common factor
HCFC hydrochlorofluorocarbon
hd head
HD heavy-duty
HDTV high-definition television
He helium
HE Her Excellency, high explosive, His Eminence, His Excellency
Heb Hebrew
HEW Department of Health, Education, and Welfare
hf half
Hf hafnium
HF high frequency
hg hectogram, hemoglobin
Hg mercury [Latin *hydrargyrum*, literally, water silver]
hgt height
hgwy highway
HH Her Highness, His Highness, His Holiness
HI Hawaii, high intensity
hist historian, historical, history
hl hectoliter
HL House of Lords
hm hectometer
HM Her Majesty, Her Majesty's, His Majesty, His Majesty's
HMS Her Majesty's ship, His Majesty's ship
Ho holmium
hon honor, honorable, honorary
hor horizontal
hort horticultural, horticulture
hosp hospital
HOV high-occupancy vehicle
hp horsepower
HP high pressure
HQ headquarters
hr here, hour
HR home run, House of Representatives
HRH Her Royal Highness, His Royal Highness
Hs hassium
HS high school
HST Hawaiian standard time
ht height
HT Hawaii time, high-tension
http hypertext transfer protocol
Hung Hungarian, Hungary
HVAC heating, ventilating, and air-conditioning; heating, ventilation, and air-conditioning
hwy highway
hyp hypothesis, hypothetical
Hz hertz
i initial, intransitive, island, isle
I electric current, Indian, interstate, iodine, Israeli
Ia, IA Iowa
IAA indoleacetic acid
ibid ibidem
ICC Interstate Commerce Commission
ICJ International Court of Justice
ICU intensive care unit
id idem
ID Idaho, identification
i.e. that is [Latin *id est*]
IL Illinois
ill, illus, illust illustrated, illustration
Ill Illinois
ILS instrument landing system
IM instant message
IMHO in my humble opinion
imit imitative
imp imperative, imperfect, imperial, import, imported
imperf imperfect
in inch, inlet
In indium
IN Indiana
inc incomplete, incorporated, increase
incl include, included, including, inclusive
incog incognito
ind independent, index, industrial, industry
Ind Indian, Indiana
indef indefinite
indic indicative
inf infantry, infinitive
infl influenced
INP International News Photo
INRI Jesus of Nazareth, King of the Jews [Latin *Iesus Nazarenus Rex Iudaeorum*]
ins inches, insurance
INS Immigration and Naturalization Service
insol insoluble
inst instant, institute, institution, institutional
instr instructor, instrument, instrumental
int interest, interior, intermediate, internal, international, intransitive
interj interjection
interrog interrogative
intl, intnl international
intrans intransitive
introd introduction
inv inventor, invoice
I/O input/output
IOC International Olympic Committee
IP innings pitched, Internet protocol
iq the same as [Latin *idem quod*]
Ir iridium, Irish
IR infrared
IRA Irish Republican Army
IRBM intermediate range ballistic missile
Ire Ireland
irreg irregular
IRS Internal Revenue Service
is island, isle
ISBN International Standard Book Number
ISP Internet service provider
Isr Israel, Israeli
ISV International Scientific Vocabulary
It Italian, Italy
IT information technology
ital italic, italicized
Ital Italian
IU international unit
IV intravenous, intravenously
IWW Industrial Workers of the World
j jack
J joule
Jam Jamaica
Jan January
JC junior college
JCS joint chiefs of staff
jct junction
JD justice department, juvenile delinquent
jg junior grade
jour journal, journeyman
JP jet propulsion, justice of the peace
Jpn Japan, Japanese
Jr junior
jt, jnt joint
jun junior
junc junction
juv juvenile
JV junior varsity
k karat, kindergarten, king, knit, knot, kosher — often enclosed in a circle
K Kelvin, kilometer, potassium [Latin *kalium*]
Kan, Kans Kansas
KB kilobyte
Kbps kilobytes per second
kc kilocycle
KC Kansas City, King's Counsel
kcal kilocalorie
kc/s kilocycles per second
KD knocked down
kg kilogram, king
KG knight of the Order of the Garter
kHz kilohertz
KIA killed in action
kJ kilojoule
KJV King James Version
KKK Ku Klux Klan
kl kiloliter
km kilometer
kn knot
kPa kilopascal
kph kilometers per hour
Kr krypton
KS Kansas
kt karat, knight, knot
kV kilovolt
kW kilowatt
kWh kilowatt-hour
Ky, KY Kentucky
l lake, large, late, left, line, liter, pound [Latin *libra*]
L Latin, long, loss, losses
La lanthanum, Louisiana

LA law agent, Los Angeles, Louisiana
Lab Labrador
lang language
lat latitude
Lat Latin
lb pound [Latin *libra*]
lc lowercase
LC landing craft, Library of Congress
LCD least common denominator, lowest common denominator
LCM least common multiple
ld load, lord
LD learning disabled, learning disability, lethal dose
ldg landing, loading
leg legal, legato, legislative, legislature
legis legislation, legislative, legislature
LEM lunar excursion module, lunar module
lf lightface
LF low frequency
lg large, long
LGBT lesbian, gay, bisexual, and transgender
LH left hand, luteinizing hormone
Li lithium
LI Long Island
lib liberal, librarian, library
lieut lieutenant
lin lineal, linear
liq liquid, liquor
lit liter, literal, literally, literary
lith, litho lithographic, lithography
Litt D, Lit D doctor of letters, doctor of literature [Latin *litterarum doctor*]
ll lines
LLD doctor of laws [Latin *legum doctor*]
LM lunar module
ln lane
LNG liquefied natural gas
loc cit in the place cited [Latin *loco citato*]
log logic
Lond London
long longitude
loq he speaks, she speaks [Latin *loquitur*]
LP low pressure
Lr lawrencium
LS left side, letter signed, place of the seal [Latin *locus sigilli*]
LSI large-scale integrated circuit, large-scale integration
lt light
Lt lieutenant
LT long ton
LTC, Lt Col lieutenant colonel
ltd limited
ltr letter, lighter
Lu lutetium
lv leave
m male, married, masculine, mass, meridian, meter, mile, milli-, minute, molal, molality, month, moon, noon [Latin *meridies*], thousand [Latin *mille*]
M Mach, medium, mega-, million, molar, molarity, monsieur
mA milliampere
MA Massachusetts, master of arts [Latin *magister artium*], mental age, Middle Ages
mach machine, machining, machinist
mag magazine, magnesium, magnetism, magneto, magnitude
Maj major
man manual
Man Manitoba
manuf manufacturer
mar maritime
Mar March
masc masculine
Mass Massachusetts
MAT master of arts in teaching
math mathematical, mathematician
mb millibar
Mb megabit
MB megabyte
Mbps megabits per second
mc megacycle
MC member of Congress
Md Maryland, mendelevium
MD doctor of medicine [Latin *medicinae doctor*], Maryland, months after date, muscular dystrophy
mdse merchandise
MDT mountain daylight time
Me Maine, methyl
ME Maine, mechanical engineer, medical examiner, Middle English
meas measure
mech mechanical, mechanics
med medical, medicine, medieval, medium
meg megohm
mem member, memoir, memorial
mer meridian
met meteorological, meteorology, metropolitan
MeV million electron volts
Mex Mexican, Mexico
mf mezzo forte
MF medium frequency, microfiche
mfd manufactured
mfg manufacturing
mfr manufacture, manufacturer
mg milligram
Mg magnesium
mgmt, mgt management
mgr manager, monseigneur, monsignor
MHz megahertz
mi mile, miles, mill
MI, Mich Michigan
MIA missing in action
mil military, million
min minim, minimum, mining, minor, minute, minutes
Minn Minnesota
misc miscellaneous
Miss Mississippi
MKS meter-kilogram-second
ml milliliter
MLB Major League Baseball
MLD minimum lethal dose
Mlle mademoiselle [French]
Mlles mesdemoiselles [French]
mm millimeter
MM messieurs [French]
Mme madame [French]
MMes mesdames [French]
Mn manganese
MN magnetic north, Minnesota
mo month
Mo Missouri, molybdenum, Monday
MO mail order, medical officer, Missouri, money order
mod moderate, modification, modified, modulo, modulus
modif modification
mol molecular, molecule
mol wt molecular weight
MOM middle of month
Mon Monday
Mont Montana
mos months
MP melting point, metropolitan police
mpg miles per gallon
mph miles per hour
MRE meals ready to eat
mRNA messenger RNA
ms millisecond
MS manuscript, master of science, Mississippi, motor ship, multiple sclerosis
MSc master of science
msec millisecond
MSG master sergeant, monosodium glutamate
msgr monsignor
MSgt master sergeant
MSS manuscripts
MST mountain standard time
mt mount, mountain
Mt meitnerium
MT metric ton, Montana, mountain time
mtg meeting, mortgage
mtge mortgage
mtn mountain
mun municipal
mus museum, music, musical, musician
mV millivolt
MVP most valuable player
MW megawatt
mya million years ago
n nano-, net, neuter, neutron, noon, north, northern, normal, note, noun, number
N newton, nitrogen
Na sodium [Latin *natrium*]
NA no account, North America, not applicable, not available
NAACP National Association for the Advancement of Colored People
NAS naval air station
NASA National Aeronautics and Space Administration
nat national, native, natural
natl, nat'l national
NATO North Atlantic Treaty Organization
naut nautical
nav naval, navigable, navigation
Nb niobium
NB New Brunswick, northbound, nota bene
NBC National Broadcasting Company
NBS National Bureau of Standards
NC no charge, North Carolina
nd no date
Nd neodymium
ND North Dakota
N Dak North Dakota
Ne neon
NE Nebraska, New England, northeast
NEA National Education Association, National Endowment for the Arts
Neb, Nebr Nebraska
NEB New English Bible
NED New English Dictionary
neg negative
Neth Netherlands
neurol neurological, neurology
neut neuter
Nev Nevada
NF Newfoundland, no funds
Nfld Newfoundland
NG National Guard, no good
NH New Hampshire
Ni nickel
NIST National Institute of Standards and Technology
NJ New Jersey
NL National League, Newfoundland and Labrador
nm nanometer, nautical mile
NM, N Mex New Mexico
NNE north-northeast
NNW north-northwest
no north, northern, number [Latin *numero*]
No nobelium
nom nominative
Nor, Norw Norway, Norwegian
nos numbers
NOS not otherwise specified
Nov November
NOW National Organization for Women
NO_x nitrogen oxide
Np neptunium
NP no protest, notary public, noun phrase
NPN nonprotein nitrogen
ns nanosecond
NS New Style, not specified, Nova Scotia
NSF not sufficient funds
NT New Testament, Northwest Territories
NTP normal temperature and pressure
NV Nevada
NW northwest
NWT Northwest Territories
NY New York
NYC New York City

NZ New Zealand
o ocean, ohm
O Ohio, oxygen
o/a on or about
OAS Organization of American States
ob he died, she died [Latin *obit*]
OB obstetric, obstetrician, obstetrics
obj object, objective
obl oblique, oblong
OBO or best offer
obs obsolete
obv obverse
OC officer candidate
occas occasionally
OCS officer candidate school, Old Church Slavic, Old Church Slavonic
Oct October
OD doctor of optometry, officer of the day, olive drab, on demand, overdraft, overdrawn
OE Old English
OED Oxford English Dictionary
OF outfield
off office, officer, official
OH Ohio
OJ orange juice
OK, Okla Oklahoma
ON, Ont Ontario
op operation, operative, operator, opportunity, opus
OP out of print
op cit in the work cited [Latin *opere citato*]
opp opposite
opt optical, optician, optics, optional
OR operating room, Oregon, owner's risk
ord order, ordnance
Ore, Oreg Oregon
org organic, organization, organized
orig original, originally
Os osmium
OS Old Style, operating system, out of stock
OSHA Occupational Safety and Health Administration
OT occupational therapy, Old Testament, overtime
OTS officers' training school
oz ounce, ounces [obsolete Italian *onza* (now *oncia*)]
p page, pages, participle, past, pawn, pence, penny, per, piano, pico-, pint, proton, purl
P phosphorus, pressure
Pa pascal, Pennsylvania, protactinium
PA Pennsylvania, personal assistant, power of attorney, press agent, public address, purchasing agent
Pac Pacific
PAC political action committee
Pan Panama
P & L profit and loss
para paragraph
part participial, participle, particular
pass passenger, passive
pat patent
path, pathol pathological, pathology
payt payment
pb paperback
Pb lead [Latin *plumbum*]
PB personal best
PB&J peanut butter and jelly
PBS Public Broadcasting Service
PC Peace Corps, percent, percentage, political correctness, politically correct, postcard
PCR polymerase chain reaction
pct percent, percentage
pd paid
Pd palladium
PD per diem, police department, potential difference, public defender
PDT Pacific daylight time
PE physical education, printer's error
PEI Prince Edward Island
pen peninsula
Penn, Penna Pennsylvania
per period, person
perf perfect, perforated, performance
perh perhaps
perp perpendicular
pers person, personal, personnel
Pers Persia, Persian
pf preferred
PFC, Pfc private first class
pg page
PG postgraduate
pharm pharmaceutical, pharmacist, pharmacy
PhD doctor of philosophy [Latin *philosophiae doctor*]
philos philosophy
photog photography
phr phrase
phys physical, physics
physiol physiologist, physiology
PI Philippine Islands, private investigator, programmed instruction
PIN personal identification number
pizz pizzicato
pk park, peak, peck, pike
pkg package
pkt packet
PKU phenylketonuria
pkwy parkway
pl place, plate, plural
PLO Palestine Liberation Organization
pls please
pm premium
p.m., PM post meridiem
Pm promethium
PM paymaster, postmaster, postmortem, prime minister, provost marshal
pmk postmark
pmt payment
PN promissory note
PnP plug and play
Po polonium
PO petty officer, post office
POB post office box
POD pay on delivery
POE port of embarkation, port of entry
Pol Poland, Polish
polit political, politician
pop population
Port Portugal, Portuguese
pos position, positive
poss possessive, possible
pp pages, past participle, pianissimo
PP parcel post, postpaid, prepaid
ppd postpaid, prepaid
PPS an additional postscript [Latin *post postscriptum*]
ppt precipitate
PPV pay-per-view
PQ Province of Quebec
pr pair, price, printed
Pr praseodymium
PR payroll, Puerto Rico
prec preceding
pred predicate
pref preface, preference, preferred, prefix
prep preparatory, preposition
pres present, president
prev previous, previously
prf proof
prim primary, primitive
prin principal, principle
PRO public relations officer
prob probable, probably, problem
proc proceedings
prod product, production
prof professional
prom promontory
pron pronoun, pronunciation
prop property, proposition, proprietor
Prot Protestant
prov province, provincial, provisional
PS postscript [Latin *postscriptum*], public school
PSA public service announcement
pseud pseudonym, pseudonymous
psf pounds per square foot
psi pounds per square inch
PST Pacific standard time
psych psychology
psychol psychological, psychologist
pt part, payment, pint, point, port
Pt platinum
PT Pacific time, part-time, physical therapy, physical training
PTA Parent-Teacher Association
pte private (British)
ptg printing
PTO Parent-Teacher Organization, please turn over
PTV public television
Pu plutonium
pub public, publication, publicity, published, publisher, publishing
publ publication, published, publisher
PVC polyvinyl chloride
pvt private
PW prisoner of war
pwt pennyweight
PX post exchange
q quart, quartile, quarto, queen, query, question, quetzal, quire
QC Queen's Counsel
QED which was to be demonstrated [Latin *quod erat demonstrandum*]
qid four times a day [Latin *quater in die*]
QM quartermaster
QMC quartermaster corps
QMG quartermaster general
qq v which see [Latin pl. *quae vide*]
qr quarter
qt quantity, quart
qty quantity
qu, ques question
Que Quebec
quot quotation
qv which see [Latin *quod vide*]
qy query
r radius, rare, resistance, right, roentgen, rook, run
R rabbi, radical — used especially of a univalent hydrocarbon radical, radius, regular, Republican, river
Ra radium
RA regular army, royal academy
rad radian, radical, radius
RADM rear admiral
RAF Royal Air Force
R & B rhythm and blues
R & D research and development
R & R rest and recreation, rest and recuperation, rest and relaxation
Rb rubidium
RBC red blood cells
RC Red Cross, Roman Catholic
RCAF Royal Canadian Air Force
RCMP Royal Canadian Mounted Police
rd road, rod, round
RD rural delivery
RDA recommended daily allowance, recommended dietary allowance
Re rhenium
rec receipt, record, recording, recreation, recreational
rec'd received
ref reference, refunding
refl reflex, reflexive
refrig refrigerator
reg region, register, registered, registration, regular
regt regiment
rel relative, released, religion, religious
relig religion
rep report, reporter, republic, representative
Rep Republican
repl replace, replacement, replacing

rept report
req request, require, required, requisition
res research, reservation, reserve, reservoir, residence, resident, resolution
resp respectively
ret retired
retd retired, returned
rev revenue, reverse, review, reviewed, revised, revision, revolution
Rev reverend
Rf rutherfordium
RF radio frequency
RFD rural free delivery
RFID radio-frequency identification
Rg roentgenium
Rh rhodium
RH right hand, right-hander
RI Rhode Island
RIP may he [she] rest in peace [Latin *requiescat in pace*]
rit ritardando
riv river
rm room
Rn radon
RN Royal Navy
rnd round
Rom Roman, Romania, Romanian
ROTC Reserve Officers' Training Corps
RP relief pitcher, Republic of the Philippines
rpm revolutions per minute
rps revolutions per second
RQ respiratory quotient
RR railroad, rural route
RS recording secretary, revised statutes, right side, Royal Society
RSV Revised Standard Version
RSVP please reply [French *répondez s'il vous plaît*]
rt right, route
rte route
Ru ruthenium
Russ Russia, Russian
RV Revised Version
RW right worthy
rwy, ry railway
s saint, scruple, second, secondary, section, senate, series, shilling, signor, sine, singular, small, son, south, southern
S satisfactory, short, sulfur
SA Salvation Army, sex appeal, South Africa, South America, subject to approval, without year [Latin *sine anno*]
SAC Strategic Air Command
SASE self-addressed stamped envelope
Sask Saskatchewan
sat satellite, saturated
Sat Saturday
sb substantive
Sb antimony [Latin *stibium*]
SB bachelor of science [Latin *scientiae baccalaureus*], southbound
SBN Standard Book Number
sc scene, science, scilicet
Sc scandium, Scots, Scottish
SC small capitals, South Carolina, supreme court
Scand Scandinavia, Scandinavian
SCAT School and College Ability Test
sch school
sci science, scientific
Scot Scotland, Scottish
sd sine die
SD South Dakota, special delivery
S Dak South Dakota
Se selenium
SE self-explanatory, southeast, Standard English
SEATO Southeast Asia Treaty Organization
sec secant, second, secondary, secretary, section
sect section, sectional
secy secretary
sel select, selected, selection
sem seminar, seminary
SEM scanning electron microscope
sen senate, senator, senior
sep separate, separated
Sept, Sep September
ser serial, series, service
sergt sergeant
serv service
sf, sfz sforzando
SF sacrifice fly, science fiction, sinking fund, square feet, square foot
SFC sergeant first class
sg specific gravity
Sg seaborgium
SG sergeant, solicitor general, surgeon general
Sgt sergeant
sh share
Shak Shakespeare
SHF superhigh frequency
Si silicon
SI International System of Units [French *Système International d'Unités*]
SIDS sudden infant death syndrome
sig signature
sin sine
sing singular
SJ Society of Jesus
Skt Sanskrit
SL sea level
sm small
Sm samarium
SM master of science [Latin *scientiae magister*], sergeant major
Sn tin [Latin *stannum*]
so south, southern
SO seller's option, strikeout
soc social, society
sociol sociologist, sociology
sol soluble
soln solution
SOP standard operating procedure, standing operating procedure
soph sophomore
sp special, species, spelling
Sp Spain, Spanish
SP shore patrol, shore patrolman, shore police, specialist
Span Spanish
SPCA Society for the Prevention of Cruelty to Animals
SPCC Society for the Prevention of Cruelty to Children
spec special, specifically
specif specific, specifically
SpED, SPED special education
SPF sun protection factor
sp gr specific gravity
spp species (*pl*)
sq squadron, square
Sr senior, senor, señor, sister, strontium
SR seaman recruit
Sra senora, señora
SRO standing room only
Srta senorita, señorita
SS saints, Social Security, steamship
SSE south-southeast
SSG, SSgt staff sergeant
SSN Social Security number
ssp subspecies
SSR Soviet Socialist Republic
SSS Selective Service System
SSW south-southwest
st stanza, state, stitch, stone
St saint, street
ST standard time
sta station
stat immediately [Latin *statim*], statute
std standard
STD doctor of sacred theology [Latin *sacrae theologiae doctor*]
Ste saint (female) [French *sainte*]
STEM science, technology, engineering, and mathematics
ster, stg sterling
STP standard temperature and pressure
stud student
sub subscription, suburb
subj subject, subjunctive
suff sufficient, suffix
Sun Sunday
sup superior, supra
supp supplement
supt superintendent
surg surgeon, surgery, surgical
surv survey
sv under the word [Latin *sub verbo* or *sub voce*]
Sw, Swed Sweden, Swedish
SW shortwave, southwest
Switz Switzerland
sym symmetrical
syn synonym, synonymy
syst system
t metric ton, tablespoon, teaspoon, temperature, ton, transitive, troy, true
T tritium, T-shirt
Ta tantalum
tan tangent
tb tablespoon, tablespoonful
Tb terbium
TBA to be announced
tbs, tbsp tablespoon, tablespoonful
Tc technetium
TD touchdown
TDD telecommunications device for the deaf
TDN total digestible nutrients
Te tellurium
tech technical, technically, technological
TEFL teaching English as a foreign language
tel telephone
temp in the time of [Latin *tempore*] temporary
Tenn Tennessee
ter terrace, territory
terr territory
Tex Texas
TGIF thank God it's Friday
Th thorium, Thursday
ThD doctor of theology [Latin *theologiae doctor*]
theol theological, theology
Thurs, Thur, Thu Thursday
Ti titanium
tid three times a day [Latin *ter in die*]
Tl thallium
TLC tender loving care
Tm thulium
TM trademark
tn ton, town
TN Tennessee
tnpk turnpike
TO turn over
topo topographic, topographical
tot total
tp title page, township
tpk, tpke turnpike
tr translated, translation, translator, transpose
trans transaction, transitive, translated, translation, translator, transmission, transportation
transl translated, translation, translator
transp transportation
treas treasury
trib tributary
TSgt technical sergeant
TSH thyroid-stimulating hormone
tsp teaspoon, teaspoonful
TTY teletypewriter
Tues, Tue, Tu Tuesday
Turk Turkey, Turkish
TVA Tennessee Valley Authority
TX Texas
u unit
U university, unsatisfactory, uranium
UAE United Arab Emirates
UAR United Arab Republic
UC uppercase
UHF ultrahigh frequency
UK United Kingdom
ult ultimo
ultim ultimately
UN United Nations
UNCF United Negro College Fund

UNESCO United Nations Educational, Scientific, and Cultural Organization
UNICEF United Nations Children's Fund [*United Nations International Children's Emergency Fund,* its former name]
univ university
UNRWA United Nations Relief and Works Agency
UPC Universal Product Code
UPI United Press International
US United States
USA United States Army, United States of America
USAF United States Air Force
USCG United States Coast Guard
USDA United States Department of Agriculture
USMC United States Marine Corps
USN United States Navy
USO United Service Organizations
USP United States Pharmacopeia
USPS United States Postal Service
USS United States ship
USSR Union of Soviet Socialist Republics
usu usual, usually
USVI United States Virgin Islands
UT Utah
UV ultraviolet
UW underwriter
v vector, velocity, verb, verse, versus, vice, victory, vide, voice, voltage, volume, vowel
V vanadium, violence, violent, volt
Va Virginia
VA Veterans Administration, vice admiral, Virginia, visual aid
VADM vice admiral
val value, valued
var variable, variant, variation, variety, various
vb verb, verbal
VC Victoria Cross, Vietcong
VD venereal disease
vel velocity
Ven venerable
vert vertical
VFW Veterans of Foreign Wars
VG very good
VHF very high frequency
vi verb intransitive
VI Virgin Islands
vic vicinity
Vic Victoria
VIN vehicle identification number
vis visibility, visible, visual
VISTA Volunteers in Service to America
viz videlicet
VLF very low frequency
VNA Visiting Nurse Association
voc vocational, vocative
vol volcano, volume, volunteer
VOR very-high-frequency omnidirectional radio (range)
VP verb phrase, vice president
VR virtual reality
vs verse, versus
vt verb transitive
Vt, VT Vermont
VTR videotape recorder
vv verses
w water, week, weight, white, wide, width, wife, with
W tungsten [German *wolfram*], watt, west, western
WA Washington
Wash Washington
WB waybill, westbound
WBC white blood cell
WC water closet
WCTU Women's Christian Temperance Union
wd wood, word, would
We, Wed Wednesday
wh white
WH watt-hour
WHO World Health Organization
WI, Wis, Wisc Wisconsin
WIA wounded in action
wk week, work
WMD weapons of mass destruction
WNW west-northwest
w/o without
WO warrant officer
WPM words per minute
wrnt warrant
WSW west-southwest
wt weight
WTO World Trade Organization
WV, W Va West Virginia
WW world war
www World Wide Web
WY, Wyo Wyoming
x cross, ex, experimental, extra
Xe xenon
XL extra large, extra long
XS extra small
y yard, year
Y yttrium
YA young adult
Yb ytterbium
YBP years before present
yd yard
YK Yukon (Territory)
YOB year of birth
yr year, your
yrbk yearbook
YT Yukon (Territory)
Yug Yugoslavia
z zero, zone
Zn zinc
zool zoological, zoology
ZPG zero population growth
Zr zirconium

Biographical, Biblical, and Mythological Names

This section constitutes a pronouncing dictionary of the names of important figures from contemporary life, history, biblical tradition, legend, and myth likely to be of interest to the student. In cases where figures have alternate names, they are entered under the name by which they are best known. Names containing connectives like *d', de, di, van,* or *von* are alphabetized generally under the part of the name following the connective. Parts of names that are not commonly used are often given in parentheses. When two sets of dates are given, the first set indicates the dates of the person's birth and death, and the second pertains only to the particular office, honor, or achievement which it immediately follows. Italicized names within an entry refer to a person's nickname, original name, title, or other name.

Aar·on \ˈar-ən, ˈer-\ brother of Moses and high priest of the Hebrews in the Bible

Aaron Hank 1934– *Henry Louis Aaron* American baseball player

Abel \ˈā-bəl\ son of Adam and Eve and brother of Cain in the Bible

Ab·er·nathy \ˈab-ər-ˌnath-ē\ Ralph David 1926–1990 American clergyman and civil rights leader

Abra·ham \ˈā-brə-ˌham\ patriarch and founder of the Hebrew people in the Bible; also revered by Muslims

Achil·les \ə-ˈkil-ēz\ hero of the Trojan War in Greek mythology

Ad·am \ˈad-əm\ the first man in biblical tradition

Ad·ams \ˈad-əmz\ Abigail 1744–1818 née *Smith* American writer; wife of John Adams

Adams Ansel Easton 1902–1984 American photographer

Adams John 1735–1826 2nd president of the U.S. (1797–1801)

Adams John Quin·cy \ˈkwin-zē, -sē\ 1767–1848 6th president of the U.S. (1825–29); son of John and Abigail Adams

Adams Samuel 1722–1803 American Revolutionary patriot

Ad·dams \ˈad-əmz\ Jane 1860–1935 American social worker; Nobel Prize winner (1931)

Ad·di·son \ˈad-ə-sən\ Joseph 1672–1719 English essayist

Ado·nis \ə-ˈdän-əs, -ˈdō-nəs\ beautiful youth in Greek mythology who is loved by Aphrodite

Ae·ne·as \i-ˈnē-əs\ Trojan hero in classical mythology

Ae·o·lus \ˈē-ə-ləs\ god of the winds in Greek mythology

Aes·chy·lus \ˈes-kə-ləs, ˈēs-\ 525–456 B.C. Greek playwright

Aes·cu·la·pi·us \ˌes-kyə-ˈlā-pē-əs\ god of medicine in Roman mythology — compare ASCLEPIUS

Ae·sop \ˈē-ˌsäp, -səp\ Greek writer of fables; probably legendary

Ag·a·mem·non \ˌag-ə-ˈmem-ˌnän, -nən\ leader of the Greeks during the Trojan War in Greek mythology

Aggeus — see HAGGAI

Ag·nes \ˈag-nəs\ Saint *died* 304 A.D. Christian martyr

Ag·rip·pi·na \ˌag-rə-ˈpī-nə, -ˈpē-\ *about* 14 B.C.–33 A.D. mother of Caligula

Ahab \ˈā-ˌhab\ king of Israel in the 9th century B.C. and husband of Jezebel

Ajax \ˈā-ˌjaks\ hero in Greek mythology who kills himself during the Trojan War because the armor of Achilles is awarded to Odysseus

Alad·din \ə-ˈlad-n\ youth in the *Arabian Nights' Entertainments* who comes into possession of a magic lamp

Al·a·ric \ˈal-ə-rik\ *about* 370–410 A.D. king of the Visigoths; conqueror of Rome

Al·ber·tus Mag·nus \al-ˈbərt-ə-ˈsmag-nəs\ Saint *about* 1200–1280 German philosopher and theologian

Al·bright \ˈȯl-ˌbrīt\ Madeleine 1937– née *Korbel* American (Czech-born) diplomat; U.S. secretary of state (1997–2001)

Al·ci·bi·a·des \ˌal-sə-ˈbī-ə-ˌdēz\ *about* 450–404 B.C. Athenian general and politician

Al·cott \ˈȯl-kət\ Louisa May 1832–1888 American author

Al·ex·an·der \ˌal-ig-ˈzan-der, ˌel-\ name of 8 popes: especially **VI** (*Rodrigo Borgia*) 1431–1503 (pope 1492–1503)

Alexander name of 3 emperors of Russia: **I** 1777–1825 (reigned 1801–25); **II** 1818–1881 (reigned 1855–81); **III** 1845–1894 (reigned 1881–94)

Alexander the Great 356–323 B.C. *Alexander III* king of Macedonia (336–323)

Al·fred \ˈal-frəd, -fərd\ 849–899 *Alfred the Great* king of Wessex (871–899)

Ali \ä-ˈlē\ Muhammad 1942– originally *Cassius Marcellus Clay* American boxer

Al·len \ˈal-ən\ Ethan 1738–1789 American Revolutionary soldier

Am·brose \ˈam-ˌbrōz\ Saint 339–397 A.D. bishop of Milan

Amerigo Vespucci — see VESPUCCI

Am·herst \ˈam-ərst, -ˌərst\ Jeffery 1717–1797 Baron *Amherst* British general in America

Amos \ˈā-məs\ Hebrew prophet of the 8th century B.C.

Amund·sen \ˈäm-ən-sən\ Roald 1872–1928 Norwegian explorer; discoverer of the South Pole (1911)

An·a·ni·as \ˌan-ə-ˈnī-əs\ early Christian who in the Bible is struck dead for lying

An·chi·ses \an-ˈkī-sēz, ang-\ father of Aeneas in classical mythology

An·der·sen \ˈan-dər-sən\ Hans Christian 1805–1875 Danish writer of fairy tales

An·der·son \ˈan-dər-sən\ Marian 1897–1993 American contralto

An·drea del Sar·to \än-ˌdrā-ə-ˌdel-ˈsärt-ō\ 1486–1530 Florentine painter

An·dro·cles \ˈan-drə-ˌklēz\ legendary Roman slave spared in the arena by a lion from whose foot he had once taken a thorn

An·drom·a·che \an-ˈdräm-ə-kē\ wife of Hector in Greek mythology

An·drom·e·da \an-ˈdräm-ə-də\ Ethiopian princess rescued from a monster by Perseus in Greek mythology

An·ge·li·co \än-ˈjā-lē-kō\ Fra *about* 1400–1455 originally *Guido di Pietro* Florentine painter and Dominican friar

An·ge·lou \ˈan-jə-ˌlō\ Maya 1928–2014 originally *Marguerite Johnson* American author

\ə\ **abut**	\au̇\ **out**	\i\ **tip**	\ȯ\ **saw**	\u̇\ **foot**
\ər\ **further**	\ch\ **chin**	\ī\ **life**	\ȯi\ **coin**	\y\ **yet**
\a\ **mat**	\e\ **pet**	\j\ **job**	\th\ **thin**	\yü\ **few**
\ā\ **take**	\ē\ **easy**	\ng\ **sing**	\th\ **this**	\yu̇\ **cure**
\ä\ **cot, cart**	\g\ **go**	\ō\ **bone**	\ü\ **food**	\zh\ **vision**

An·nan \ä-ˈnän\ Kofi 1938– Ghanaian United Nations official; secretary-general (1997–2006)
Anne \ˈan\ 1665–1714 queen of Great Britain (1702–14); daughter of James II
An·tho·ny \ˈan-thə-nē, *chiefly British* ˈan-tə-nē\ Saint *about* 250–355 A.D. Egyptian monk
Anthony Mark — see ANTONY
Anthony Susan Brownell 1820–1906 American suffragist
Anthony of Padua Saint 1195–1231 Franciscan friar
An·tig·o·ne \an-ˈtig-ə-nē\ daughter of Oedipus and Jocasta in Greek mythology
An·to·ni·nus Marcus Au·re·lius — see MARCUS AURELIUS
An·to·ny \ˈan-tə-nē\ Mark *about* 82–30 B.C. *Marc Anthony; Marcus An·to·ni·us* \an-ˈtō-nē-əs\ Roman general and triumvir (43–30)
Aph·ro·di·te \ˌaf-rə-ˈdīt-ē\ goddess of love and beauty in Greek mythology — compare VENUS
Apol·lo \ə-ˈpäl-ō\ *or* **Phoe·bus** \ˈfē-bəs\ god of sunlight, prophecy, music, and poetry in classical mythology
Ap·ple·seed \ˈap-əl-ˌsēd\ Johnny 1774–1845 *John Chapman* American pioneer
Aqui·nas \ə-ˈkwī-nəs\ Saint Thomas 1224 (or 1225)–1274 Italian theologian
Arach·ne \ə-ˈrak-nē\ girl in Greek mythology who is changed into a spider for challenging Athena to a contest in weaving
Ar·chi·me·des \ˌär-kə-ˈmēd-ēz\ *about* 287–212 B.C. Greek mathematician and inventor
Ares \ˈaər-ēz, ˈeər-; ˈā-ˌrēz\ god of war in Greek mythology — compare MARS
Ar·gus \ˈär-gəs\ hundred-eyed monster in Greek mythology
Ar·i·ad·ne \ˌar-ē-ˈad-nē\ daughter of Minos who helps Theseus escape from a labyrinth in Greek mythology
Ar·is·ti·des \ˌar-ə-ˈstīd-ēz\ *about* 530–*about* 468 B.C. *Aristides the Just* Athenian statesman and general
Ar·is·toph·a·nes \ˌar-ə-ˈstäf-ə-ˌnēz\ *about* 450–*about* 388 B.C. Greek playwright
Ar·is·tot·le \ˈar-ə-ˌstät-l\ 384–322 B.C. Greek philosopher
Ari·us \ə-ˈrī-əs; ˈar-ē-əs, ˈer-\ *about* 250–336 A.D. Greek theologian
Arm·strong \ˈärm-ˌstrȯŋ\ Lance 1971– American cyclist
Armstrong Louis 1901–1971 *Satch·mo* \ˈsach-ˌmō\ American jazz musician
Armstrong Neil Alden 1930–2012 American astronaut; first man on the moon (1969)
Ar·nold \ˈärn-ld\ Benedict 1741–1801 American Revolutionary general and traitor
Arnold Matthew 1822–1888 English poet and critic
Ar·te·mis \ˈärt-ə-məs\ goddess of the moon, wild animals, and hunting in Greek mythology — compare DIANA
Ar·thur \ˈär-thər\ legendary king of the Britons whose story is based on traditions of a 6th-century military leader — **Ar·thu·ri·an** \är-ˈthu̇r-ē-ən, -ˈthyu̇r-\ *adj*
Arthur Chester Alan 1829–1886 21st president of the U.S. (1881–85)
As·cle·pi·us \ə-ˈsklē-pē-əs\ god of medicine in Greek mythology — compare AESCULAPIUS
Ashe \ˈash\ Arthur Robert 1943–1993 American tennis player
As·tar·te \ə-ˈstärt-ē\ Phoenician goddess of love and fertility
As·tor \ˈas-tər\ John Jacob 1763–1848 American (German-born) fur trader and capitalist
At·a·lan·ta \ˌat-l-ˈant-ə\ beautiful fleet-footed heroine in Greek mythology who challenges her suitors to a race and is defeated when she stops to pick up three golden apples
Ath·el·stan \ˈath-əl-ˌstan\ *died* 939 Anglo-Saxon ruler
Athe·na \ə-ˈthē-nə\ *or* **Athe·ne** \-nē\ goddess of wisdom in Greek mythology — compare MINERVA
At·las \ˈat-ləs\ Titan in Greek mythology forced to bear the heavens on his shoulders
Atreus \ˈā-ˌtrüs, -trē-əs\ king of Mycenae and father of Agamemnon and Menelaus in Greek mythology
At·ti·la \ˈat-l-ə, ə-ˈtil-ə\ 406?–453 A.D. king of the Huns
At·tucks \ˈat-əks\ Crispus 1723?–1770 American patriot
Au·du·bon \ˈȯd-ə-bən, -ˌbän\ John James 1785–1851 American (Haitian-born) artist and ornithologist
Au·gus·tine \ˈȯ-gə-ˌstēn; ȯ-ˈgəs-tən, ə-\ Saint 354–430 A.D. church father; bishop of Hippo (396–430)
Augustine of Canterbury Saint *died about* 604 A.D. *Apostle of the English* 1st archbishop of Canterbury (601–604)
Au·gus·tus \ȯ-ˈgəs-təs, ə-\ *or* **Caesar Augustus** *or* **Oc·ta·vi·an** \äk-ˈtā-vē-ən\ 63 B.C.–14 A.D. originally *Gaius Octavius* 1st Roman emperor 27 B.C.–14 A.D.
Au·ro·ra \ə-ˈrōr-ə, ȯ-, -ˈrȯr-\ goddess of the dawn in Roman mythology — compare EOS
Aus·ten \ˈȯs-tən, ˈäs-\ Jane 1775–1817 English author
Bab·bage \ˈbab-ij\ Charles 1791–1871 British inventor
Bac·chus \ˈbak-əs\ — see DIONYSUS
Bach \ˈbäḵ, ˈbäk\ Johann Sebastian 1685–1750 German composer and organist
Ba·con \ˈbā-kən\ Francis 1561–1626 English philosopher
Bacon Roger *about* 1220–1292 English philosopher and scientist
Ba·den–Pow·ell \ˌbād-n-ˈpō-əl\ Robert Stephenson Smyth 1857–1941 Baron *Baden-Powell* British general and founder of Boy Scout movement
Bal·boa \bal-ˈbō-ə\ Vasco Núñez de 1475–1519 Spanish explorer and discoverer of the Pacific Ocean (1513)
Bald·win \ˈbȯld-wən\ James 1924–1987 American author
Baltimore Lord — see CALVERT
Bal·zac \ˈbȯl-ˌzak, ˈbal-, *French* bȧl-zȧk\ Honoré de 1799–1850 French author
Ban Ki–moon \ˈbän-ˈgē-ˈmün\ 1944– South Korean United Nations official; secretary-general (2007–)
Ba·rab·bas \bə-ˈrab-əs\ prisoner in the Bible released in preference to Jesus at the demand of the multitude
Barbarossa — see FREDERICK I
Bar·num \ˈbär-nəm\ P. T. 1810–1891 *Phineas Taylor Barnum* American showman
Bar·rie \ˈbar-ē\ Sir James Matthew 1860–1937 Scottish author
Bar·ry·more \ˈbar-i-ˌmōr, -ˌmȯr\ family of American actors: Maurice (originally *Herbert Blythe*) 1847–1905; his wife Georgiana Emma (née *Drew*) 1854–1893; their children Lionel 1878–1954, Ethel 1879–1959, and John Blythe 1882–1942
Bar·thol·di \bär-ˈtäl-dē, -ˈtȯl-, -ˈthäl-, -ˈthȯl-\ Frédéric-Auguste 1834–1904 French sculptor of the Statue of Liberty
Bar·tók \ˈbar-ˌtäk, -ˌtȯk\ Bé·la \ˈbā-lə\ 1881–1945 Hungarian composer
Bar·ton \ˈbärt-n\ Clara 1821–1912 founder of American Red Cross Society
Ba·rysh·ni·kov \bə-ˈrish-nə-ˌkȯf\ Mikhail 1948– American (Russian-born) dancer
Ba·sie \ˈbā-sē\ William 1904–1984 *Count Basie* American bandleader and pianist
Ba·sil \ˈbaz-əl, ˈbās-, ˈbas-, ˈbāz-\ Saint *about* 329–379 A.D. *Basil the Great* church father; bishop of Caesarea
Bau·de·laire \bōd-ˈlaər, -ˈleər\ Charles (-Pierre) 1821–1867 French poet
Beau·re·gard \ˈbōr-ə-ˌgärd, ˈbȯr-\ Pierre Gustave Toutant 1818–1893 American Confederate general
Beck·et \ˈbek-ət\ Saint Thomas *about* 1118–1170 *Thomas à Becket* archbishop of Canterbury (1162–70)
Bede \ˈbēd\ Saint *about* 672–735 A.D. *the Venerable Bede* Anglo-Saxon historian and theologian
Beel·ze·bub \bē-ˈel-zi-ˌbəb, ˈbēl-zi-, ˈbel-\ prince of the demons identified with Satan in the New Testament
Bee·tho·ven \ˈbā-ˌtō-vən\ Ludwig van 1770–1827 German composer
Bell \ˈbel\ Alexander Graham 1847–1922 American (Scottish-born) inventor of the telephone
Bel·ler·o·phon \bə-ˈler-ə-fən, -ˌfän\ hero in Greek mythology who slays the monster Chimera with the help of his horse Pegasus
Bel·li·ni \bə-ˈlē-nē\ Vincenzo 1801–1835 Italian composer
Bel·low \ˈbel-ō\ Saul 1915–2005 American (Canadian-born) author; Nobel Prize winner (1976)
Ben·e·dict \ˈben-ə-dikt\ name of 16 popes: especially **XIV** (*Prospero Lambertini*) 1675–1758 (pope 1740–58); **XV** (*Giacomo della Chiesa*) 1854–1922 (pope 1914–22); **XVI** (*Joseph Alois Ratz·ing·er* \ˈrät-siŋ-ər\) 1927– (pope 2005–13)
Benedict of Nur·sia \ˈnər-shə, -shē-ə\ Saint *about* 480–*about* 547 A.D. Italian founder of Benedictine order
Be·nét \bə-ˈnā\ Stephen Vincent 1898–1943 American author
Ben·ja·min \ˈbenj-mən, -ə-mən\ Jacob's youngest son and ancestor of one of the 12 tribes of Israel in the Bible
Ben·tham \ˈben-thəm\ Jeremy 1748–1832 English philosopher
Ben·ton \ˈbent-n\ Thomas Hart 1889–1975 American painter
Be·o·wulf \ˈbā-ə-ˌwu̇lf\ legendary Scandinavian warrior and hero of the Old English poem *Beowulf*

Be·ring \ˈbir-iŋ, ˈber-\ Vitus 1681–1741 Danish navigator and explorer for Russia

Ber·lin \bər-ˈlin, ˌbər-\ Irving 1888–1989 American (Russian-born) composer and songwriter

Ber·li·oz \ˈber-lē-ˌōz\ (Louis-) Hector 1803–1869 French composer

Bern·hardt \ˈbərn-ˌhärt, ber-ˈnär\ Sarah 1844–1923 originally *Henriette-Rosine Ber·nard* \ber-ˈnär\ French actress

Ber·ni·ni \bər-ˈnē-nē\ Gian Lorenzo 1598–1680 Italian sculptor, architect, and painter

Bern·stein \ˈbərn-ˌstīn *also* -ˌstēn\ Leonard 1918–1990 American conductor and composer

Bes·se·mer \ˈbes-ə-mər\ Sir Henry 1813–1898 English engineer and inventor

Be·thune \bə-ˈthün, -ˈthyün\ Mary 1875–1955 née *McLeod* American educator

Beyle Marie-Henri — see STENDHAL

Bi·den \ˈbīd-ⁿn\ Joseph Robinette, Jr. 1942– vice president of the U.S. (2009–)

Bierce \ˈbirs\ Ambrose Gwinnett 1842–?1914 American author

Bi·ko \ˈbē-ˌkō\ (Bantu) Stephen 1946–1977 South African black nationalist

Bil·ly the Kid \ˈbil-ē-\ 1859?–1881 originally *William H. Bon·ney* \ˈbän-ē\ *, Jr.* or *Henry McCarty?* American outlaw

Bird \ˈbərd\ Larry 1956– American basketball player

Bis·marck \ˈbiz-ˌmärk\ Prince Otto Eduard Leopold von 1815–1898 1st chancellor of German empire (1871–90)

Bi·zet \bē-ˈzā\ Georges 1838–1875 originally *Alexandre-César-Léopold Bizet* French composer

Black Hawk \ˈblak-ˌhȯk\ 1767–1838 American Indian chief

Black·stone \ˈblak-ˌstōn, *chiefly British* -stən\ Sir William 1723–1780 English jurist

Black·well \ˈblak-ˌwel, -wəl\ Elizabeth 1821–1910 American (English-born) physician

Blair \ˈblar, ˈbler\ Tony 1953– *Anthony Charles Lynton Blair* British prime minister (1997–2007)

Blake \ˈblāk\ William 1757–1827 English poet and artist

Bloom·er \ˈblü-mər\ Amelia 1818–1894 née *Jenks* American social reformer

Boc·cac·cio \bō-ˈkäch-ē-ˌō, -ˈkäch-ō\ Giovanni 1313–1375 Italian author

Bohr \ˈbōr, ˈbȯr\ Niels 1885–1962 Danish physicist; Nobel Prize winner (1922)

Bo·leyn \bu̇-ˈlin, ˈbu̇l-ən\ Anne 1507?–1536 2nd wife of Henry VIII of England; mother of Elizabeth I

Bo·lí·var Si·món \sē-ˌmōn-bə-ˈlē-ˌvär, ˌsī-mən-ˈbäl-ə-vər\ 1783–1830 South American liberator

Bo·na·parte \ˈbō-nə-ˌpärt\ *or Italian* **Buo·na·par·te** \ˌbwȯn-ə-ˈpärt-ē\ Corsican family: Jérôme 1784–1860 king of Westphalia; Joseph 1768–1844 king of Naples and Spain; Louis 1778–1846 king of Holland; Lucien 1775–1840 prince of Canino; all brothers of Napoléon I

Bon·i·face \ˈbän-ə-fəs, -ˌfās\ name of 9 popes: especially **VIII** (*Benedetto Caetani*) *about* 1235 (or 1240)–1303 (pope 1294–1303)

Boniface Saint *about* 675–754 A.D. originally *Wynfrid* or *Wynfrith* English missionary in Germany

Boone \ˈbün\ Daniel 1734–1820 American pioneer

Booth \ˈbüth\ John Wilkes 1838–1865 American actor; assassin of Abraham Lincoln

Booth \ˈbüth, *chiefly British* ˈbüt͟h\ William 1829–1912 English founder of the Salvation Army

Bo·re·as \ˈbōr-ē-əs, ˈbȯr-\ god of the north wind in Greek mythology

Bor·gia \ˈbȯr-ˌjä, -jə, -zhə\ Cesare 1475 (or 1476)–1507 Italian cardinal and military leader; son of Rodrigo Borgia

Borgia Lucrezia 1480–1519 duchess of Ferrara; daughter of Rodrigo Borgia

Borgia Rodrigo — see Pope ALEXANDER VI

Bo·ro·din \ˌbȯr-ə-ˈdēn, ˌbär-\ Aleksandr Porfiryevich 1833–1887 Russian composer and chemist

Bosch \ˈbäsh, ˈbȯsh, *Dutch* ˈbäs, ˈbȯs\ Hieronymus *about* 1450–1516 Dutch painter

Bos·co \ˈbäs-kō, ˈbȯs-\ Saint Giovanni Melchior 1815–1888 Italian priest and founder of the Salesians

Bos·well \ˈbäz-ˌwel, -wəl\ James 1740–1795 Scottish biographer of Samuel Johnson

Bot·ti·cel·li \ˌbät-ə-ˈchel-ē\ Sandro 1445–1510 Italian painter

Bow·ie \ˈbü-ē, ˈbō-\ Jim 1796?–1836 *James Bowie* American popular hero of the Texas revolution

Boyle \ˈbȯil\ Robert 1627–1691 British physicist and chemist

Brad·bury \ˈbrad-ˌber-ē, -bə-rē, -brē\ Ray Douglas 1920–2012 American author

Brad·dock \ˈbrad-ək\ Edward 1695–1755 British general in America

Brad·ford \ˈbrad-fərd\ William 1590–1657 Pilgrim leader; 2nd governor of Plymouth colony

Brad·street \ˈbrad-ˌstrēt\ Anne *about* 1612–1672 American poet

Bra·dy \ˈbrād-ē\ Mathew B. 1823?–1896 American photographer

Brahe \ˌbrä; ˈbrä-hē, -hə\ Tycho 1546–1601 Danish astronomer

Brah·ma \ˈbräm-ə\ creator god of the Hindu sacred triad — compare SHIVA, VISHNU

Brahms \ˈbrämz\ Johannes 1833–1897 German composer

Braille \ˈbrāl, ˈbrī\ Louis 1809–1852 French blind teacher of the blind

Bran·deis \ˈbran-ˌdīs, -ˌdīz\ Louis Dembitz 1856–1941 American jurist

Brant \ˈbrant\ Joseph 1742–1807 *Thayendanegea* Mohawk Indian chief

Braun \ˈbrau̇n\ Wernher von 1912–1977 American (German-born) engineer

Brezh·nev \ˈbrezh-ˌnef\ Leonid Ilyich 1906–1982 Russian politician; 1st secretary of Communist party (1964–82); president of the U.S.S.R. (1960–64; 1977–82)

Bri·an Bo·ru \ˌbrī-ən-bə-ˈrü\ 941–1014 king of Ireland (1002–14)

Brig·id \ˈbrij-əd, ˈbrē-əd\ Saint *died about* 524–528 A.D. a patron saint of Ireland

Brit·ten \ˈbrit-ⁿn\ (Edward) Benjamin 1913–1976 English composer

Bron·të \ˈbränt-ē, ˈbrän-ˌtā\ family of English authors: Charlotte 1816–1855 and her sisters Emily 1818–1848 and Anne 1820–1849

Brooks \ˈbru̇ks\ Gwendolyn Elizabeth 1917–2000 American poet

Brown \ˈbrau̇n\ (James) Gordon 1951– British prime minister (2007–10)

Brown John 1800–1859 American abolitionist

Brow·ning \ˈbrau̇-niŋ\ Elizabeth Barrett 1806–1861 English poet

Browning Robert 1812–1889 English poet; husband of Elizabeth

Broz Josip — see TITO

Bruce the — see ROBERT I

Bruck·ner \ˈbru̇k-nər\ Anton 1824–1896 Austrian composer

Brue·ghel *or* **Breu·ghel** \ˈbrü-gəl, ˈbrȯi-\ Pieter *about* 1525–1569 *the Elder* Flemish painter

Brun·hild \ˈbrün-ˌhilt\ legendary Germanic queen won by Siegfried for Gunther

Bru·tus \ˈbrüt-əs\ Marcus Junius 85–42 B.C. Roman politician and one of Julius Caesar's assassins

Bry·an \ˈbrī-ən\ William Jennings 1860–1925 American lawyer and politician

Bry·ant \ˈbrī-ənt\ William Cullen 1794–1878 American poet

Bu·chan·an \byü-ˈkan-ən, bə-\ James 1791–1868 15th president of the U.S. (1857–61)

Buck \ˈbək\ Pearl S. 1892–1973 née *Sydenstricker* American author; Nobel Prize winner (1938)

Bud·dha \ˈbüd-ə, ˈbu̇d-\ *about* 563–*about* 483 B.C. originally *Siddhar·tha Gau·ta·ma* \si-ˈdär-tə-ˈgau̇t-ə-mə\ Indian founder of Buddhism

Buffalo Bill — see William Frederick CODY

Bunche \ˈbənch\ Ralph Johnson 1904–1971 American diplomat

Bun·yan \ˈbən-yən\ John 1628–1688 English preacher and author

Bunyan Paul — see PAUL BUNYAN

Bur·bank \ˈbər-ˌbaŋk\ Luther 1849–1926 American horticulturist

Bur·ger \ˈbər-gər\ Warren Earl 1907–1995 American jurist; chief justice U.S. Supreme Court (1969–86)

\ə\ **abut**	\au̇\ **out**	\i\ **tip**	\ȯ\ **saw**	\u̇\ **foot**
\ər\ **further**	\ch\ **chin**	\ī\ **life**	\ȯi\ **coin**	\y\ **yet**
\a\ **mat**	\e\ **pet**	\j\ **job**	\th\ **thin**	\yü\ **few**
\ā\ **take**	\ē\ **easy**	\ŋ\ **sing**	\t͟h\ **this**	\yu̇\ **cure**
\ä\ **cot, cart**	\g\ **go**	\ō\ **bone**	\ü\ **food**	\zh\ **vision**

Bur•goyne \'bər-ˌgȯin, ˌbər-'\ John 1722–1792 British general in America

Burke \'bərk\ Edmund 1729–1797 British statesman and author

Burns \'bərnz\ Robert 1759–1796 Scottish poet

Burn•side \'bərn-ˌsīd\ Ambrose Everett 1824–1881 American general

Burr \'bər\ Aaron 1756–1836 American politician; vice president of the U.S. (1801–05)

Bur•roughs \'bər-ˌōz, 'bə-ˌrōz\ Edgar Rice 1875–1950 American author

Bush \'bu̇sh\ George (Herbert Walker) 1924– 41st president of the U.S. (1989–93)

Bush George W. 1946– *George Walker Bush* 43rd president of the U.S. (2001–09); son of George Herbert Walker Bush

Byrd \'bərd\ Richard Evelyn 1888–1957 American admiral and polar explorer

By•ron \'bī-rən\ Lord 1788–1824 *George Gordon Byron,* 6th Baron *Byron* English poet

Cab•ot \'kab-ət\ John *about* 1450–*about* 1499 *Giovanni Caboto* Italian navigator and explorer for England

Ca•bri•ni \kə-'brē-nē\ Saint Frances Xavier 1850–1917 *Mother Cabrini* 1st American (Italian-born) saint (1946)

Cad•mus \'kad-məs\ founder of Thebes in Greek mythology

Caed•mon \'kad-mən\ *flourished* 658–680 A.D. English poet

Cae•sar \'sē-zər\ (Gaius) Julius 100?–44 B.C. Roman general, statesman, and writer

Cain \'kān\ son of Adam and Eve and brother of Abel in the Bible

Calamity Jane \-'jān\ 1852?–1903 *Martha Jane Burk* \'bərk\ née *Can•nary* \'kan-ə-rē\ American frontier figure

Cal•der \'kȯl-dər\ Alexander 1898–1976 American sculptor

Cal•houn \kal-'hün\ John Caldwell 1782–1850 American politician; vice president of the U.S. (1825–32)

Ca•lig•u•la \kə-'lig-yə-lə\ 12–41 A.D. *Gaius Caesar* Roman emperor (37–41)

Cal•li•o•pe \kə-'lī-ə-pē\ Muse of epic poetry in Greek mythology

Cal•vert \'kal-vərt\ George 1580?–1632 Baron *Baltimore* English colonist in America

Cal•vin \'kal-vən\ John 1509–1564 *Jean Calvin* or *Cauvin* French theologian and reformer

Ca•lyp•so \kə-'lip-sō\ sea nymph in Homer's *Odyssey* who keeps Odysseus for seven years on an island

Cam•er•on \'kam-ə-rən, 'kam-rən\ David (William Donald) 1966– British prime minister (2010–)

Ca•mus \kȧ-'mue\ Albert 1913–1960 French author; Nobel Prize winner (1957)

Ca•nute \kə-'nüt, -'nyüt\ *died* 1035 *Canute the Great* Danish king of England (1016–35); of Denmark (1018–35); of Norway (1028–35)

Ča•pek \'chäp-ˌek\ Karel 1890–1938 Czech author

Capet Hugh — see HUGH CAPET

Ca•pone \kə-'pōn\ Al 1899–1947 *Alphonse Capone* American gangster

Ca•ra•vag•gio \ˌkar-ə-'vä-jō\ 1571?–1610 originally *Michelangelo Merisi* Italian painter

Car•lyle \kär-'līl, 'kär-ˌ\ Thomas 1795–1881 Scottish essayist and historian

Car•ne•gie \'kär-nə-gē, kär-'neg-ē\ Andrew 1835–1919 American (Scottish-born) industrialist and philanthropist

Car•roll \'kar-əl\ Lewis 1832–1898 pseudonym of *Charles Lutwidge* \'lət-wij\ *Dodg•son* \'däj-sən, 'däd-\ English author and mathematician

Car•son \'kärs-n\ Kit 1809–1868 *Christopher Carson* American frontiersman and scout

Carson Rachel Louise 1907–1964 American biologist and writer

Car•ter \'kärt-ər\ Jimmy 1924– originally *James Earl Carter, Jr.* 39th president of the U.S. (1977–81); Nobel Prize winner (2002)

Car•tier \kär-'tyā, 'kärt-ē-ˌā\ Jacques 1491–1557 French navigator and explorer of Saint Lawrence River

Ca•ru•so \kə-'rü-sō, -zō\ En•ri•co \en-'rē-kō\ 1873–1921 Italian tenor

Car•ver \'kär-vər\ George Washington 1861?–1943 American agricultural chemist and agronomist

Ca•sals \kə-'sälz, -'zälz\ Pablo 1876–1973 Spanish-born cellist and conductor

Ca•sa•no•va \ˌkaz-ə-'nō-və, ˌkas-\ Giovanni Giacomo 1725–1798 Italian adventurer

Cas•san•dra \kə-'san-drə\ daughter of Priam in Greek mythology who is a prophetess but is fated never to be believed

Cas•satt \kə-'sat\ Mary 1845–1926 American painter

Cas•tor \'kas-tər\ mortal twin of Pollux in classical mythology

Cas•tro (Ruz) \'kas-trō(-'rüs), 'käs-\ Fi•del \fē-'del\ 1926– Cuban leader (1959–2008)

Castro (Ruz) Raúl Modesto 1931– Cuban leader (2008–); brother of Fidel Castro

Cath•er \'kath-ər\ Willa 1873–1947 American author

Cath•er•ine \'kath-rən, -ə-rən\ name of 1st, 5th, and 6th wives of Henry VIII of England: Catherine of Aragon 1485–1536; Catherine Howard 1520?–1542; Catherine Parr 1512–1548

Catherine I 1684–1727 wife of Peter the Great; empress of Russia (1725–27)

Catherine II 1729–1796 *Catherine the Great* empress of Russia (1762–96)

Cath•er•ine de Mé•di•cis \'kath-ə-rən-də-'mā-də-ˌsēs, -'med-ə-ˌchē\ 1519–1589 Italian *Ca•te•ri•na de' Me•di•ci* \ˌkä-te-'rē-nä-dā-'med-ē-ˌchē\ queen consort of Henry II of France (1547–59); regent of France (1560–74)

Cat•i•line \'kat-l-ˌīn\ *about* 108–62 B.C. Roman politician and conspirator

Ca•to \'kāt-ō\ Marcus Porcius 234–149 B.C. *Cato the Elder; Cato the Censor* Roman statesman

Cato Marcus Porcius 95–46 B.C. *Cato the Younger* Roman statesman; great-grandson of the preceding

Ca•tul•lus \kə-'təl-əs\ Gaius Valerius *about* 84–*about* 54 B.C. Roman poet

Cav•en•dish \'kav-ən-ˌdish\ Henry 1731–1810 English scientist

Cax•ton \'kak-stən\ William *about* 1422–1491 1st English printer

Ce•ci•lia \sə-'sēl-yə, -'sil-\ Saint *flourished* 3rd century A.D. Christian martyr; patron saint of music

Cel•li•ni \chə-'lē-nē\ Benvenuto 1500–1571 Italian goldsmith and sculptor

Cer•ber•us \'sər-bə-rəs, -brəs\ 3-headed dog in classical mythology who guards the entrance to Hades

Ce•res \'siər-ˌēz\ goddess of agriculture in Roman mythology — compare DEMETER

Cer•van•tes (Saa•ve•dra) \sər-'van-ˌtēz(-ˌsä-ə-'vä-drə)\ Miguel de 1547–1616 Spanish author

Cé•zanne \sā-'zan\ Paul 1839–1906 French painter

Cha•gall \shə-'gäl, -'gal\ Marc 1887–1985 Russian painter in France

Cham•ber•lain \'chām-bər-lən\ (Arthur) Neville 1869–1940 British prime minister (1937–40)

Chamberlain Wilt 1936–1999 *Wilton Norman Chamberlain* American basketball player

Cham•plain \sham-'plān, shäⁿ-'plaⁿ\ Samuel de 1567–1635 French navigator, explorer, and founder of Quebec

Chap•lin \'chap-lən\ Charlie 1889–1977 *Sir Charles Spencer Chaplin* British actor, director, and producer

Char•le•magne \'shär-lə-ˌmān\ *about* 742–814 A.D. *Charles the Great* or *Charles I* Frankish king (768–814); emperor of the West (800–814)

Charles \'chärlz\ name of 10 kings of France: especially **II** 823–877 A.D. *Charles the Bald* (reigned 840–77), Holy Roman emperor (875–77); **IV** 1294–1328 *Charles the Fair* (reigned 1322–28); **V** 1337–1380 *Charles the Wise* (reigned 1364–80); **VI** 1368–1422 *Charles the Mad* or *the Beloved* (reigned 1380–1422); **VII** 1403–1461 (reigned 1422–61); **IX** 1550–1574 (reigned 1560–74); **X** 1757–1836 (reigned 1824–30)

Charles name of 2 kings of Great Britain: **I** 1600–1649 (reigned 1625–49); **II** 1630–1685 (reigned 1660–85) son of Charles I

Charles 1948– prince of Wales; son of Elizabeth II

Charles I 1887–1922 *Charles Francis Joseph* emperor of Austria and (as *Charles IV*) king of Hungary (1916–18)

Charles V 1500–1558 Holy Roman emperor (1519–56); king of Spain as *Charles I* (1516–56)

Charles XII 1682–1718 king of Sweden (1697–1718)

Charles Edward — see STUART

Charles Mar•tel \mär-'tel\ *about* 688–741 A.D. grandfather of Charlemagne; Frankish ruler (719–41)

Char•on \'kar-ən, 'ker-\ boatman in Greek mythology who ferries the souls of the dead across the river Styx to Hades

Cha•teau•bri•and \sha-ˌtō-brē-'äⁿ\ (François-Auguste-) René 1768–1848 *Vicomte de Chateaubriand* French author

Chau•cer \'chȯ-sər\ Geoffrey *about* 1342–1400 English poet

Che•khov \'chek-ˌȯf, -ȯv\ Anton Pavlovich 1860–1904 Russian author

Che·ney \ˈchē-nē\ Richard Bruce 1941–   vice president of the U.S. (2001–09)
Cheops — see KHUFU
Ches·ter·field \ˈches-tər-ˌfēld\ 4th Earl of 1694–1773 *Philip Dormer Stanhope* English statesman and author
Ches·ter·ton \ˈches-tər-tən\ G. K. 1874–1936 *Gilbert Keith Chesterton* English author
Chiang Kai–shek \jē-ˈäng-ˈkī-ˈshek, ˈchang-\ 1887–1975 Chinese general and statesman; head of Chinese Nationalist government (1948–49; Taiwan, 1950–75)
Chi·ron \ˈkīr-ən, ˈkī-ˌrän\ wise centaur and tutor to many heroes in Greek mythology
Cho·pin \ˈshō-ˌpan, -ˌpa^{n}\ Frédéric François 1810–1849 Polish pianist and composer
Chou En–lai *or* **Zhou Enlai** \ˈjō-ˈen-ˈlī\ 1898–1976 Chinese Communist politician; premier (1949–76)
Chré·tien \krā-ˈtye^{n}\ (Joseph Jacques) Jean 1934–   prime minister of Canada (1993–2003)
Christ Jesus — see JESUS
Chris·tie \ˈkris-tē\ Dame Agatha 1890–1976 née *Miller* English author
Chry·sos·tom \ˈkris-əs-təm, kris-ˈäs-təm\ Saint John *about* 347–407 A.D. church father; patriarch of Constantinople
Chur·chill \ˈchər-ˌchil, ˈchərch-ˌhil\ Randolph Henry Spencer 1849–1895 *Lord Randolph Churchill* British statesman
Churchill Sir Winston Leonard Spencer 1874–1965 British prime minister (1940–45; 1951–55); Nobel Prize winner (1953); son of the preceding
Cic·ero \ˈsis-ə-ˌrō\ Marcus Tullius 106–43 B.C. Roman statesman, orator, and author
Cid, El \el-ˈsid\ *about* 1043–1099 *Rodrigo Díaz de Vi·var* \bē-ˈvär\ Spanish soldier and hero
Cir·ce \ˈsər-sē\ enchantress in Greek mythology who turns her victims into swine
Clark \ˈklärk\ George Rogers 1752–1818 American soldier and frontiersman
Clark William 1770–1838 American explorer (with Meriwether Lewis)
Clay \ˈklā\ Henry 1777–1852 American statesman and orator
Cle·men·ceau \ˌklem-ən-ˈsō, klā-mä^{n}-ˈsō\ Georges 1841–1929 French statesman; premier (1906–09; 1917–20)
Clemens Samuel Langhorne — see TWAIN
Clem·ent \ˈklem-ənt\ name of 14 popes
Cle·o·pa·tra \ˌklē-ə-ˈpa-trə, -ˈpā-, -ˈpä-\ 69–30 B.C. queen of Egypt (51–30)
Cleve·land \ˈklēv-lənd\ (Stephen) Grover 1837–1908 22nd and 24th president of the U.S. (1885–89; 1893–97)
Clin·ton \ˈklint-n\ Hillary Rodham 1947–   née *Rodham* U.S. secretary of state (2009–13); wife of William Clinton
Clinton William Jefferson 1946–   *Bill Clinton* 42nd president of the U.S. (1993–2001)
Clio \ˈklī-ō, ˈklē-\ Muse of history in Greek mythology
Clo·vis I \ˈklō-vəs\ *about* 466–511 A.D. Frankish king (481–511)
Cly·tem·nes·tra \ˌklīt-əm-ˈnes-trə\ wife of Agamemnon in Greek mythology
Cobb \ˈkäb\ Ty 1886–1961 *Tyrus Raymond Cobb* American baseball player
Co·chise \kō-ˈchēs\ 1812?–1874 Apache Indian chief
Coch·ran \ˈkäk-rən\ Jacqueline 1910?–1980 American aviator
Co·dy \ˈkōd-ē\ William Frederick 1846–1917 *Buffalo Bill* American scout and showman
Co·han \ˈkō-ˌhan\ George Michael 1878–1942 American actor, playwright, and songwriter
Cole·ridge \ˈkōl-rij, ˈkō-lə-rij\ Samuel Taylor 1772–1834 English poet and critic
Co·lette \kò-ˈlet\ 1873–1954 originally *Sidonie-Gabrielle Colette* French author
Co·lum·bus \kə-ˈləm-bəs\ Christopher 1451–1506 Italian navigator and discoverer of America for Spain (1492)
Con·fu·cius \kən-ˈfyü-shəs\ 551–479 B.C. Chinese philosopher
Con·rad \ˈkän-ˌrad\ Joseph 1857–1924 British (Ukrainian-born of Polish parents) author
Con·stan·tine I \ˈkän-stən-ˌtēn, -ˌtīn\ *after* 280?–337 A.D. *Constantine the Great* Roman emperor (306–37)
Cook \ˈku̇k\ Captain James 1728–1779 English navigator
Coo·lidge \ˈkü-lij\ (John) Calvin 1872–1933 30th president of the U.S. (1923–29)
Coo·per \ˈkü-pər, ˈku̇p-ər\ James Fen·i·more \ˈfen-ə-ˌmōr, -ˌmȯr\ 1789–1851 American author
Co·per·ni·cus \kō-ˈpər-ni-kəs\ Nicolaus 1473–1543 Polish astronomer
Cop·land \ˈkō-plənd\ Aaron 1900–1990 American composer
Cop·ley \ˈkäp-lē\ John Singleton 1738–1815 American painter
Corn·plan·ter \ˈkȯrn-ˌplant-ər\ *about* 1732–1836 *John O'Bail* Seneca Indian leader of partly European ancestry
Corn·wal·lis \kȯrn-ˈwäl-əs\ Charles 1738–1805 1st *Marquess Cornwallis* British general in America
Co·ro·na·do \ˌkȯr-ə-ˈnäd-ō, ˌkär-\ Francisco Vásquez de *about* 1510–1554 Spanish explorer and conquistador
Cor·tés *or* **Cor·tez** \kȯr-ˈtez, ˈkȯr-ˌ\ Hernán *or* Hernando 1485–1547 Spanish conqueror of Mexico
Cous·teau \kü-ˈstō\ Jacques (-Yves) 1910–1997 French marine explorer
Cow·per \ˈkü-pər, ˈku̇p-ər, ˈkau̇-pər\ William 1731–1800 English poet
Crane \ˈkrān\ Stephen 1871–1900 American author
Crazy Horse \ˈkrā-zē-ˌhȯrs\ 1842?–1877 *Ta-sunko-witko* Sioux Indian chief
Cres·si·da \ˈkres-əd-ə\ Trojan woman who in medieval legend is unfaithful to her lover Troilus
Crock·ett \ˈkräk-ət\ Davy 1786–1836 *David Crockett* American frontiersman and politician
Croe·sus \ˈkrē-səs\ *died* 546 B.C. king of Lydia (560–546)
Crom·well \ˈkräm-ˌwel, ˈkrəm-, -wəl\ Oliver 1599–1658 English general and statesman; lord protector of England (1653–58)
Cro·nus \ˈkrō-nəs\ Titan dethroned by his son Zeus in Greek mythology
Cum·mings \ˈkəm-ingz\ Edward Estlin 1894–1962 known as *e. e. cummings* American poet
Cu·pid \ˈkyü-pəd\ god of love in Roman mythology — compare EROS
Cu·rie \kyu̇-ˈrē, ˈkyu̇r-ē\ Marie 1867–1934 née *Sklodowska* French (Polish-born) chemist; Nobel Prize winner (1903, 1911)
Curie Pierre 1859–1906 French chemist; husband of Marie Curie; Nobel Prize winner (1903)
Cus·ter \ˈkəs-tər\ George Armstrong 1839–1876 American general
Cyb·e·le \ˈsib-ə-lē\ a nature goddess of ancient Asia Minor
Cy·ra·no de Ber·ge·rac \ˌsir-ə-ˌnō-də-ˈber-zhə-ˌrak\ Savinien 1619–1655 French satirist and playwright
Cyr·il \ˈsir-əl\ Saint *about* 827–869 A.D. apostle to the Slavs; brother of Methodius
Cy·rus II \ˈsī-rəs\ *about* 585–*about* 529 B.C. *Cyrus the Great* king of Persia (*about* 550–529)
Cyrus 424?–401 B.C. *the Younger* Persian prince and satrap
Dae·da·lus \ˈded-l-əs, ˈdēd-\ builder in Greek mythology of the Cretan labyrinth and inventor of wings by which he and his son Icarus escape imprisonment
Dahl \ˈdäl\ Roald 1916–1990 British author
Da·lai La·ma \ˌdäl-ī-ˈläm-ə\ 1935–   *Tenzin Gyatso* Tibetan religious and political leader
Da·lí \ˈdä-lē, dä-ˈlē\ Salvador 1904–1989 Spanish painter
Dal·ton \ˈdȯlt-n\ John 1766–1844 English chemist and physicist
Dam·o·cles \ˈdam-ə-ˌklēz\ courtier of ancient Syracuse held to have been seated at a banquet beneath a sword hung by one hair
Da·mon \ˈdā-mən\ legendary Sicilian who pledges his life for that of his condemned friend Pythias
Da·na \ˈdā-nə\ Richard Henry 1815–1882 American author
Dan·aë \ˈdan-ə-ˌē\ imprisoned princess in Greek mythology who is visited by Zeus as a shower of gold; mother of Perseus
Dan·iel \ˈdan-yəl\ prophet in the Bible who is held captive in Babylon and divinely delivered from a den of lions
Dan·te \ˈdän-tā, ˈdan-, -tē\ 1265–1321 *Dante Alighieri* Italian poet
Daph·ne \ˈdaf-nē\ nymph in Greek mythology who is transformed into a laurel tree to escape the pursuing Apollo
Dare \ˈdaər, ˈdeər\ Virginia 1587–? 1st child born in America of English parents
Da·ri·us I \də-ˈrī-əs\ 550–486 B.C. *Darius the Great* king of Persia (522–486)
Dar·row \ˈdar-ō\ Clarence Seward 1857–1938 American lawyer
Dar·win \ˈdär-wən\ Charles Robert 1809–1882 English naturalist

\ə\ **abut**	\au̇\ **out**	\i\ **tip**	\ȯ\ **saw**	\u̇\ **foot**
\ər\ **further**	\ch\ **chin**	\ī\ **life**	\ȯi\ **coin**	\y\ **yet**
\a\ **mat**	\e\ **pet**	\j\ **job**	\th\ **thin**	\yü\ **few**
\ā\ **take**	\ē\ **easy**	\ng\ **sing**	\t͟h\ **this**	\yu̇\ **cure**
\ä\ **cot, cart**	\g\ **go**	\ō\ **bone**	\ü\ **food**	\zh\ **vision**

Da•vid \ˈdā-vəd\ youth in the Bible who slays Goliath and succeeds Saul as king of Israel
David Saint *about* 520–600 patron saint of Wales
Da•vid \dä-ˈvēd\ Jacques-Louis 1748–1825 French painter
Da•vis \ˈdā-vəs\ Jefferson 1808–1889 president of the Confederate States of America (1861–65)
Davis Miles 1926–1991 American jazz musician
Da•vy \ˈdā-vē\ Sir Humphry 1778–1829 English chemist
Debs \ˈdebz\ Eugene Victor 1855–1926 American socialist and labor organizer
De•bus•sy \ˌdeb-yu̇-ˈsē, ˌdāb-; də-ˈbyü-sē\ (Achille-) Claude 1862–1918 French composer
De•ca•tur \di-ˈkāt-ər\ Stephen 1779–1820 American naval officer
De•foe \di-ˈfō\ Daniel 1660–1731 English author
De•gas \də-ˈgä\ (Hilaire-Germain-) Edgar 1834–1917 French painter
de Gaulle \di-ˈgōl, -ˈgȯl\ Charles (-André-Marie-Joseph) 1890–1970 French general; president of France's Fifth Republic (1958–69)
de Klerk \də-ˈklərk\ F. W. 1936– *Frederik Willem de Klerk* president of South Africa (1989–94); vice president (1994–96); Nobel Prize winner (1993)
De•la•croix \ˌdel-ə-ˈkrwä, -ˈkwä\ (Ferdinand-Victor-) Eugène 1798–1863 French painter
De•li•lah \di-ˈlī-lə\ mistress and betrayer of Samson in the Bible
De•me•ter \di-ˈmēt-ər\ goddess of agriculture in Greek mythology — compare CERES
de Mille \də-ˈmil\ Agnes George 1905–1993 American dancer and choreographer
de•Mille Cec•il \ˈses-əl\ Blount \ˈblənt\ 1881–1959 American film director and producer
De•mos•the•nes \di-ˈmäs-thə-ˌnēz\ 384–322 B.C. Athenian orator and statesman
Demp•sey \ˈdemp-sē\ Jack 1895–1983 originally *William Harrison Dempsey* American boxer
De•nis *or* **De•nys** \ˈden-əs, də-ˈnē\ Saint *died* 258? A.D. 1st bishop of Paris; patron saint of France
De Quin•cey \di-ˈkwin-sē, -ˈkwin-zē\ Thomas 1785–1859 English author
Des•cartes \dā-ˈkärt\ René 1596–1650 French mathematician and philosopher
de So•to \di-ˈsōt-ō\ Hernando *about* 1496–1542 Spanish explorer of Mississippi River (1540)
Dew•ey \ˈdü-ē, ˈdyü-\ George 1837–1917 American admiral
Dewey John 1859–1952 American philosopher and educator
Di•ana \dī-ˈan-ə\ ancient Italian goddess of the forest and of childbirth who was identified with Artemis in Roman mythology
Di•as *or* **Di•az** \ˈdē-ˌäsh\ Bartholomeu *about* 1450–1500 Portuguese navigator
Dick•ens \ˈdik-ənz\ Charles (John Huffam) 1812–1870 *Boz* \ˈbäz, ˈbōz\ English author
Dick•in•son \ˈdik-ən-sən\ Emily Elizabeth 1830–1886 American poet
Di•de•rot \dē-ˈdrō, ˈdēd-ə-ˌrō\ Denis 1713–1784 French philosopher and author
Di•do \ˈdīd-ō\ legendary queen of Carthage who falls in love with Aeneas and kills herself upon his departure
Di•Mag•gio \də-ˈmäzh-ē-ō, -ˈmaj-\ Joe 1914–1999 *Joseph Paul DiMaggio* American baseball player
Di•o•cle•tian \ˌdī-ə-ˈklē-shən\ 245–316 A.D. Roman emperor (284–305)
Di•og•e•nes \dī-ˈäj-ə-ˌnēz\ *died about* 320 B.C. Greek Cynic philosopher
Di•o•ny•sus \ˌdī-ə-ˈnī-səs, -ˈnē-\ god of wine and ecstasy in classical mythology
Dis \ˈdis\ god of the underworld in Roman mythology — compare PLUTO
Dis•ney \ˈdiz-nē\ Walt 1901–1966 *Walter Elias Disney* American film producer and cartoonist
Dis•rae•li \diz-ˈrā-lē\ Benjamin 1804–1881 Earl of *Bea•cons•field* \ˈbē-kənz-ˌfēld\ British politician and author; prime minister (1868; 1874–80)
Dix \ˈdiks\ Dorothea Lynde 1802–1887 American social reformer
Dodgson Charles Lutwidge — see CARROLL
Dom•i•nic \ˈdäm-ə-nik\ Saint *about* 1170–1221 Spanish-born founder of the Dominican order of friars
Do•mi•tian \də-ˈmish-ən\ 51–96 A.D. Roman emperor (81–96)
Don•i•zet•ti \ˌdän-əd-ˈzet-ē, ˌdōn-, -ə-ˈzet-\ Gaetano 1797–1848 Italian composer
Donne \ˈdən\ John 1572–1631 English poet and clergyman
Dos•to•yev•sky \ˌdäs-tə-ˈyef-skē, -ˈyev-\ Fyodor Mikhaylovich 1821–1881 Russian author
Doug•las \ˈdəg-ləs\ Stephen Arnold 1813–1861 American politician
Doug•lass \ˈdəg-ləs\ Frederick 1817–1895 American abolitionist
Doyle \ˈdȯil\ Sir Arthur Co•nan \ˈkō-nən, ˈkō-\ 1859–1930 British author and physician
Dra•co \ˈdrā-kō\ *flourished* 7th century B.C. Athenian lawgiver
Drake \ˈdrāk\ Sir Francis 1540 (or 1543)–1596 English navigator, explorer, and admiral
Drei•ser \ˈdrī-sər, -zər\ Theodore 1871–1945 American author
Drey•fus \ˈdrī-fəs, ˈdrā-\ Alfred 1859–1935 French army officer
Dry•den \ˈdrīd-n\ John 1631–1700 English author
DuBois \dü-ˈbȯis, dyü-\ William Edward Burghardt 1868–1963 American educator
Du•mas \dü-ˈmä, dyü-; ˈdü-ˌmä, ˈdyü-\ Alexandre 1802–1870 *Dumas père* \ˈpeər\ French author
Dumas Alexandre 1824–1895 *Dumas fils* \ˈfēs\ French author
Dun•bar \ˈdən-ˌbär\ Paul Laurence 1872–1906 American poet
Dun•can \ˈdəng-kən\ Isadora 1877–1927 American dancer
Dü•rer \ˈdu̇r-ər, ˈdyu̇r-, ˈdu̅e̅r-\ Albrecht 1471–1528 German painter and engraver
Du•se \ˈdü-zā\ Eleonora 1858–1924 Italian actress
Dvo•řák \də-ˈvȯr-ˌzhäk, ˈvȯr-ˌzhäk\ Antonín 1841–1904 Bohemian (Czech) composer
Ea•kins \ˈā-kənz\ Thomas 1844–1916 American artist
Ear•hart \ˈeər-ˌhärt, ˈiər-\ Amelia 1897–1937 American aviator
Earp \ˈərp\ Wyatt 1848–1929 American frontiersman and lawman
Ed•dy \ˈed-ē\ Mary Baker 1821–1910 American founder of the Christian Science religious faith
Ed•i•son \ˈed-ə-sən\ Thomas Alva 1847–1931 American inventor
Ed•ward \ˈed-wərd\ name of 8 post-Norman kings of England: **I** 1239–1307 *Edward Longshanks* (reigned 1272–1307); **II** 1284–1327 (reigned 1307–27); **III** 1312–1377 (reigned 1327–77); **IV** 1442–1483 (reigned 1461–70; 1471–83); **V** 1470–1483 (reigned 1483); **VI** 1537–1553 (reigned 1547–53) son of Henry VIII and Jane Seymour; **VII** 1841–1910 (reigned 1901–10) son of Queen Victoria; **VIII** 1894–1972 (reigned 1936; abdicated) *Duke of Windsor* son of George V
Edward 1330–1376 *the Black Prince* prince of Wales; son of Edward III
Edward 1003?–1066 *the Confessor* king of the English (1042–66)
Ed•wards \ˈed-wərdz\ Jonathan 1703–1758 American theologian
Ein•stein \ˈīn-ˌstīn\ Albert 1879–1955 American (German-born) physicist; Nobel Prize winner (1921)
Ei•sen•how•er \ˈīz-n-ˌhau̇-ər, -ˌhau̇r\ Dwight David 1890–1969 American general; 34th president of the U.S. (1953–61)
Elec•tra \i-ˈlek-trə\ sister of Orestes in Greek mythology who aids him in avenging their father's murder
El•gar \ˈel-ˌgär, -gər\ Sir Edward 1857–1934 English composer
Eli \ˈē-ˌlī\ early Hebrew judge and priest in the Bible
Eli•jah \i-ˈlī-jə\ Hebrew prophet of the 9th century B.C.
El•i•on \ˈel-ē-ən\ Gertrude Belle 1918–1999 American biochemist; Nobel Prize winner (1988)
El•iot \ˈel-ē-ət, ˈel-yət\ George 1819–1880 pseudonym of *Mary Ann Evans* English author
Eliot T. S. 1888–1965 *Thomas Stearns Eliot* British (American-born) poet and critic; Nobel prize winner (1948)
Elis•a•beth \i-ˈliz-ə-bəth\ mother of John the Baptist in the Bible
Eli•sha \i-ˈlī-shə\ Hebrew prophet in the Bible who is disciple and successor of Elijah
Eliz•a•beth I \i-ˈliz-ə-bəth\ 1533–1603 queen of England (1558–1603); daughter of Henry VIII and Anne Boleyn
Elizabeth II 1926– queen of the United Kingdom (1952–); daughter of George VI
El•ling•ton \ˈel-ing-tən\ Duke 1899–1974 originally *Edward Kennedy Ellington* American bandleader and composer
El•li•son \ˈel-ə-sən\ Ralph (Waldo) 1914–1994 American author
Em•er•son \ˈem-ər-sən\ Ralph Waldo 1803–1882 American essayist and poet
En•dym•i•on \em-ˈdim-ē-ən\ beautiful youth loved by the moon goddess Selene in Greek mythology

Eos \'ē-ˌäs\ goddess of the dawn in Greek mythology — compare AURORA
Ep·i·cu·rus \ˌep-i-'kyu̇r-əs\ 341–270 B.C. Greek philosopher
Eras·mus \i-'raz-məs\ Desiderius 1466?–1536 Dutch scholar
Er·a·to \'er-ə-ˌtō\ Muse of lyric and especially love poetry in Greek mythology
Erik the Red \'er-ik\ *flourished* 10th century originally *Erik Thor·vald·son* \'thȯr-väl-sən\ Norwegian explorer of Greenland coast (*about* 986); father of Leif Eriksson
Eriksson, Leif — see LEIF ERIKSSON
Eriny·es \i-'rin-ē-ˌēz\ *or* **Eu·men·i·des** \yü-'men-ə-ˌdēz\ the Furies in Greek mythology
Ernst \'eərnst, 'ərnst\ Max 1891–1976 German painter
Eros \'eər-ˌäs, 'iər-\ god of love in Greek mythology — compare CUPID
Esau \'ē-ˌsȯ\ son of Isaac and Rebekah and elder twin brother of Jacob in the Bible
Es·ther \'es-tər\ Hebrew woman in the Bible who as the queen of Persia delivers her people from destruction
Eu·clid \'yü-kləd\ *flourished about* 300 B.C. Greek mathematician
Eumenides — see ERINYES
Eu·rip·i·des \yu̇-'rip-ə-ˌdēz\ *about* 484–406 B.C. Greek playwright
Eu·ro·pa \yu̇-'rō-pə\ Phoenician princess in Greek mythology who is abducted by Zeus disguised as a white bull
Eu·ryd·i·ce \yu̇-'rid-ə-sē\ wife of Orpheus in Greek mythology
Eu·ter·pe \yü-'tər-pē\ Muse of music in Greek mythology
Eve \'ēv\ the first woman in biblical tradition
Eze·kiel \i-'zē-kyəl, -kē-əl\ Hebrew prophet of the 6th century B.C.
Ez·ra \'ez-rə\ Hebrew priest, scribe, and reformer of the 5th century B.C.
Fa·bi·us Max·i·mus Cunc·ta·tor \'fā-bē-əs-'mak-si-məs-ˌkəngk-tā-tər\ Quintus *died* 203 B.C. Roman general
Fahd \'fäd\ 1923–2005 king of Saudi Arabia (1982–2005)
Fahr·en·heit \'far-ən-ˌhīt, 'fär-\ Daniel Gabriel 1686–1736 German physicist
Far·a·day \'far-ə-ˌdā, -əd-ē\ Michael 1791–1867 English chemist and physicist
Far·mer \'fär-mər\ James Leonard 1920–1999 American civil rights leader
Far·ra·gut \'far-ə-gət\ David Glasgow 1801–1870 American admiral
Faulk·ner \'fȯk-nər\ William 1897–1962 American author; Nobel Prize winner (1949)
Faust *or* **Fau·stus** \'fau̇-stəs, 'fȯ-\ magician of German legend who sells his soul to the devil for knowledge and power
Fawkes \'fȯks\ Guy 1570–1606 English conspirator
Fe·li·pe \fā-'lē-pā\ 1968– king of Spain (2014–)
Fer·ber \'fər-bər\ Edna 1887–1968 American writer
Fer·di·nand I \'fərd-n-ˌand\ 1016 (or 1018)–1065 *Ferdinand the Great* king of Castile (1035–65); of León (1037–65)
Ferdinand V of Castile *or* **II** of Aragon 1452–1516 *Ferdinand the Catholic* king of Castile (1474–1504); of Aragon (1479–1516); of Naples (1504–16); founder of the Spanish monarchy; husband of Isabella I
Fer·mi \'feər-mē\ Enrico 1901–1954 American (Italian-born) physicist; Nobel Prize winner (1938)
Feyn·man \'fīn-mən\ Richard Phillips 1918–1988 American physicist; Nobel Prize winner (1965)
Fiel·ding \'fēl-diŋ\ Henry 1707–1754 English author
Fill·more \'fil-ˌmōr, -ˌmȯr\ Millard 1800–1874 13th president of the U.S. (1850–53)
Fitz·ger·ald \fits-'jer-əld\ Ella 1917–1996 American singer
Fitzgerald F. Scott 1896–1940 *Francis Scott Key Fitzgerald* American author
Fitz·Ger·ald \fits-'jer-əld\ Edward 1809–1883 English poet
Flau·bert \flō-'beər\ Gustave 1821–1880 French author
Flem·ing \'flem-iŋ\ Sir Alexander 1881–1955 British bacteriologist; Nobel Prize winner (1945)
Flo·ra \'flōr-ə, 'flȯr-\ goddess of flowers in Roman mythology
Flying Dutchman legendary Dutch mariner condemned to sail the seas until Judgment Day
Foch \'fȯsh, 'fäsh\ Ferdinand 1851–1929 French general; marshal of France (1918)
Ford \'fōrd, 'fȯrd\ Gerald Rudolph 1913–2006 38th president of the U.S. (1974–77)
Ford Henry 1863–1947 American automobile manufacturer
Fos·sey \'fȯs-ē, 'fäs-\ Dian 1932–1985 American zoologist
Fos·ter \'fȯs-tər, 'fäs-\ Stephen Collins 1826–1864 American songwriter
Fox \'fäks\ George 1624–1691 English founder of Society of Friends (Quakers)
Fran·cis \'fran-səs\ 1936– *Jorge Mario Bergoglio* pope (2013–)
Francis I 1494–1547 king of France (1515–47)
Francis II 1768–1835 last Holy Roman emperor (1792–1806); emperor of Austria (as *Francis I*) (1804–35)
Francis Ferdinand 1863–1914 archduke of Austria
Francis Joseph 1830–1916 emperor of Austria (1848–1916); king of Hungary (1867–1916)
Francis of As·si·si \ə-'sē-sē, -zē, -'sis-ē\ Saint 1181 (or 1182)–1226 Italian friar; founder of Franciscan order
Franck \'fräŋk\ César Auguste 1822–1890 French (Belgian-born) composer
Fran·co \'fräŋ-kō, 'fraŋ-\ Francisco 1892–1975 Spanish general, dictator, and head of Spanish state (1936–75)
Frank \'fraŋk\ Anne 1929–1945 Jewish (German-born) diarist during the Holocaust
Frank·lin \'fraŋ-klən\ Benjamin 1706–1790 American statesman, philosopher, and inventor
Fred·er·ick I \'fred-rik, -ə-rik\ *about* 1123–1190 *Frederick Bar·ba·ros·sa* \ˌbär-bə-'räs-ə, -'rȯs-\ Holy Roman emperor (1152–90)
Frederick II 1194–1250 Holy Roman emperor (1215–50); king of Sicily (1198–1250)
Frederick I 1657–1713 king of Prussia (1701–13)
Frederick II 1712–1786 *Frederick the Great* king of Prussia (1740–86)
Frederick IX 1899–1972 king of Denmark (1947–72)
Fré·mont \'frē-ˌmänt\ John Charles 1813–1890 American general and explorer
French \'french\ Daniel Chester 1850–1931 American sculptor
Freud \'frȯid\ Sigmund 1856–1939 Austrian neurologist; founder of psychoanalysis
Frig·ga \'frig-ə\ *or* **Frigg** \'frig\ wife of Odin and goddess of married love and the hearth in Norse mythology
Fron·te·nac (et Pal·lu·au) \'fränt-n-ˌak(-ˌā-pä-'lwʸō)\ Comte de 1622–1698 French colonial administrator in New France (Canada)
Frost \'frȯst\ Robert Lee 1874–1963 American poet
Ful·ler \'fu̇l-ər\ (Richard) Buckminster 1895–1983 American engineer and architect of the geodesic dome
Ful·ton \'fu̇lt-n\ Robert 1765–1815 American inventor
Ga·bri·el \'gā-brē-əl\ one of the four archangels named in Hebrew tradition — compare MICHAEL, RAPHAEL, URIEL
Ga·ga·rin \gə-'gär-ən\ Yu·ry \'yu̇r-ē\ Alekseyevich 1934–1968 Russian cosmonaut; 1st man in space (1961)
Gage \'gāj\ Thomas 1721–1787 British general in America
Gains·bor·ough \'gānz-ˌbər-ə, -bə-rə, -brə\ Thomas 1727–1788 English painter
Gal·a·had \'gal-ə-ˌhad\ knight of the Round Table in medieval legend who finds the Holy Grail
Gal·a·tea \ˌgal-ə-'tē-ə\ female figure carved by Pygmalion in Greek mythology and given life by Aphrodite
Ga·len \'gā-lən\ 129–*about* 216 A.D. Greek physician and writer
Ga·li·leo \ˌgal-ə-'lē-ō, -'lā-\ 1564–1642 *Galileo Ga·li·lei* \ˌgal-ə-'lā-ˌē\ Italian astronomer and physicist
Gall \'gȯl\ 1840?–1894 Sioux Indian leader
Ga·lois \gal-'wä\ Évariste 1811–1832 French mathematician
Gals·wor·thy \'gȯlz-ˌwər-t͟hē\ John 1867–1933 English author; Nobel Prize winner (1932)
Ga·ma \'gam-ə, 'gäm-\ Vasco da *about* 1460–1524 Portuguese navigator and explorer
Gan·dhi \'gän-dē, 'gan-\ Indira 1917–1984 Indian prime minister (1966–77; 1980–84); daughter of Jawaharlal Nehru
Gandhi Mohandas Karamchand 1869–1948 *Ma·hat·ma* \mə-'hät-mə, -'hat-\ *Gandhi* Indian nationalist leader
Gan·y·mede \'gan-i-ˌmēd\ cupbearer of the gods in Greek mythology
Gar·field \'gär-ˌfēld\ James Abram 1831–1881 20th president of the U.S. (1881)

\ə\ **abut**	\au̇\ **out**	\i\ **tip**	\ȯ\ **saw**	\u̇\ **foot**
\ər\ **further**	\ch\ **chin**	\ī\ **life**	\ȯi\ **coin**	\y\ **yet**
\a\ **mat**	\e\ **pet**	\j\ **job**	\th\ **thin**	\yü\ **few**
\ā\ **take**	\ē\ **easy**	\ŋ\ **sing**	\t͟h\ **this**	\yu̇\ **cure**
\ä\ **cot, cart**	\g\ **go**	\ō\ **bone**	\ü\ **food**	\zh\ **vision**

Gar·i·bal·di \ˌgar-ə-ˈbȯl-dē\ Giuseppe 1807–1882 Italian patriot
Gar·ri·son \ˈgar-ə-sən\ William Lloyd 1805–1879 American abolitionist
Gar·vey \ˈgär-vē\ Marcus Moziah 1887–1940 Jamaican black leader in America (1919–26)
Gates \ˈgāts\ Horatio *about* 1728–1806 American (British-born) Revolutionary general
Gates Bill 1955– *William Henry Gates III* American computer software manufacturer
Gau·guin \gō-ˈgaⁿ\ (Eugène-Henri-) Paul 1848–1903 French painter
Gauss \ˈgau̇s\ Carl Friedrich 1777–1855 German mathematician and astronomer
Gautama Buddha — see BUDDHA
Ga·wain \gə-ˈwān, ˈgä-ˌwān, ˈgau̇-ən\ nephew of King Arthur and knight of the Round Table in medieval legend
Gay \ˈgā\ John 1685–1732 English author
Geh·rig \ˈger-ig\ Lou 1903–1941 *Henry Louis Gehrig* American baseball player
Gei·sel \ˈgī-zəl\ Theodor Seuss 1904–1991 pseudonym *Dr. Seuss* \ˈsüs\ American author and illustrator
Gen·ghis Khan \ˌjeng-gə-ˈskän, ˌgeng-\ *about* 1162–1227 Mongol conqueror
George \ˈjȯrj\ Saint *about* 3rd century A.D. Christian martyr; patron saint of England
George name of 6 kings of Great Britain: **I** 1660–1727 (reigned 1714–27); **II** 1683–1760 (reigned 1727–60); **III** 1738–1820 (reigned 1760–1820); **IV** 1762–1830 (reigned 1820–30); **V** 1865–1936 (reigned 1910–36); **VI** 1895–1952 (reigned 1936–52) father of Elizabeth II
George I 1845–1913 king of Greece (1863–1913)
George II 1890–1947 king of Greece (1922–23; 1935–47)
George David Lloyd — see LLOYD GEORGE
Ge·ron·i·mo \jə-ˈrän-ə-ˌmō\ 1829–1909 Apache Indian leader
Gersh·win \ˈgərsh-wən\ George 1898–1937 American composer
Gib·bon \ˈgib-ən\ Edward 1737–1794 English historian
Gide \ˈzhēd\ André 1869–1951 French author; Nobel Prize winner (1947)
Gid·e·on \ˈgid-ē-ən\ Hebrew hero in the Bible
Gil·bert \ˈgil-bərt\ Sir William Schwenck 1836–1911 English librettist and poet; collaborated with Sir Arthur Sullivan
Gil·les·pie \gə-ˈles-pē\ Dizzy 1917–1993 *John Birks Gillespie* American jazz musician
Gins·burg \ˈginz-bərg\ Ruth Bader 1933– American jurist
Giot·to \ˈjȯt-tō, ˈjō-tō, jē-ˈät-ō\ 1266?–1337 *Giotto di Bondone* Florentine painter
Glad·stone \ˈglad-ˌstōn, *chiefly British* -stən\ William Ewart 1809–1898 British prime minister (1868–74; 1880–85; 1886; 1892–94)
Glenn \ˈglen\ John Herschel 1921– American astronaut; 1st American to orbit the earth (1962)
God·dard \ˈgäd-ərd\ Robert Hutchings 1882–1945 American physicist and inventor
Go·di·va \gə-ˈdī-və\ English earl's wife noted in legend for riding naked through Coventry to save its citizens from a tax levied by her husband
Goeb·bels \ˈgərb-əlz, ˈgœb-əls\ (Paul) Joseph 1897–1945 German Nazi propagandist
Goe·thals \ˈgō-thəlz\ George Washington 1858–1928 American engineer who directed the building of the Panama Canal
Goe·the \ˈgər-tə, ˈgœ̄-tə\ Johann Wolfgang von 1749–1832 German author
Gogh, van \van-ˈgō, -ˈgäk, -ˈkȯk\ Vincent Willem 1853–1890 Dutch painter
Go·gol \ˈgȯ-gəl, ˈgō-ˌgȯl\ Nikolay Vasilyevich 1809–1852 Russian author
Gol·ding \ˈgōl-ding\ William Gerald 1911–1993 English author; Nobel Prize winner (1983)
Gold·smith \ˈgōld-ˌsmith, ˈgōl-\ Oliver 1730–1774 British author
Go·li·ath \gə-ˈlī-əth\ Philistine giant in the Bible who is killed by David with a sling
Gom·pers \ˈgäm-pərz\ Samuel 1850–1924 American (British-born) labor leader
Goo·dall \ˈgu̇d-ˌȯl\ Jane 1934– British zoologist
Good·man \ˈgu̇d-mən\ Benny 1909–1986 *Benjamin David Goodman* American jazz clarinetist and bandleader
Good·year \ˈgu̇d-ˌyiər, ˈgu̇j-ˌiər\ Charles 1800–1860 American inventor
Gor·ba·chev \ˌgȯr-bə-ˈchȯf\ Mikhail Sergeyevich 1931– Soviet politician; 1st secretary of Communist party (1985–91); president of the U.S.S.R. (1990–91); Nobel Prize winner (1990)
Gore \ˈgōr, ˈgȯr\ Albert, Jr. 1948– vice president of the U.S. (1993–2001); Nobel Prize winner (2007)
Gor·gas \ˈgȯr-gəs\ William Crawford 1854–1920 American army surgeon
Gor·ky \ˈgȯr-kē\ Maksim 1868–1936 pseudonym of *Aleksey Maksimovich Pesh·kov* \ˈpesh-ˌkȯf, -ˌkȯv\ Russian author
Gou·nod \ˈgü-ˌnō\ Charles (-François) 1818–1893 French composer
Go·ya (y Lu·cien·tes) \ˈgȯi-ə(-ˌē-ˌlü-sē-ˌen-ˌtās)\ Francisco José de 1746–1828 Spanish painter
Grac·chus \ˈgrak-əs\ Gaius Sempronius 153?–121 B.C. and his brother Tiberius Sempronius 163?–133 B.C. *the Grac·chi* \ˈgrak-ˌī\ Roman statesmen
Gra·ham \ˈgrā-əm, ˈgra-əm, ˈgram\ Martha 1893–1991 American dancer and choreographer
Grant \ˈgrant\ Ulysses S. 1822–1885 originally *Hiram Ulysses Grant* American general; 18th president of the U.S. (1869–77)
Gray \ˈgrā\ Thomas 1716–1771 English poet
Gre·co, El \el-ˈgrek-ō, -ˈgrāk-, -ˈgrēk-\ 1541–1614 *Doménikos Theotokópoulos* Spanish (Cretan-born) painter
Gree·ley \ˈgrē-lē\ Horace 1811–1872 American journalist and politician
Greene \ˈgrēn\ (Henry) Graham 1904–1991 British author
Greene Nathanael 1742–1786 American Revolutionary general
Greg·o·ry \ˈgreg-rē, -ə-rē\ name of 16 popes: especially **I** Saint *about* 540–604 A.D. *Gregory the Great* (pope 590–604); **VII** Saint (*Hil·de·brand* \ˈhil-də-ˌbrand\) *about* 1020–1085 (pope 1073–85); **XIII** 1502–1585 (pope 1572–85)
Grey \ˈgrā\ Lady Jane 1537–1554 queen of England for nine days (1553)
Grey (Pearl) Zane 1872–1939 American author
Grieg \ˈgrēg, ˈgrig\ Edvard Hagerup 1843–1907 Norwegian composer
Grimm \ˈgrim\ Jacob 1785–1863 and his brother Wilhelm 1786–1859 German philologists and folklorists
Guin·e·vere \ˈgwin-ə-ˌviər, ˈgwen-\ wife of King Arthur and mistress of Lancelot in Arthurian legend
Gun·ther \ˈgu̇nt-ər\ Burgundian king and husband of Brunhild in Germanic legend
Gu·ten·berg \ˈgüt-n-ˌbərg\ Johannes *about* 1400–1468 German inventor of method of printing from movable type
Ha·dri·an \ˈhā-drē-ən\ 76–138 A.D. Roman emperor (117–138)
Ha·gar \ˈhā-ˌgär, -gər\ mistress of Abraham and mother of Ishmael in the Bible
Hag·gai \ˈhag-ē-ˌī, ˈhag-ˌī\ *or* **Ag·ge·us** \a-ˈgē-əs\ Hebrew prophet of the 6th century B.C.
Hai·le Se·las·sie \ˌhī-lē-sə-ˈlas-ē, -ˈläs-\ 1892–1975 emperor of Ethiopia (1930–36; 1941–74)
Hale \ˈhāl\ Edward Everett 1822–1909 American clergyman and author
Hale Nathan 1755–1776 American Revolutionary hero
Hal·ley \ˈhal-ē\ Edmond *or* Edmund 1656–1742 English astronomer and mathematician
Hal·sey \ˈhȯl-sē, -zē\ William Frederick 1882–1959 American admiral
Ham \ˈham\ son of Noah and ancestor of the Hamitic peoples in biblical tradition
Ha·man \ˈhā-mən\ Old Testament enemy of the Jews hanged for plotting their destruction
Ha·mil·car Bar·ca \hə-ˈmil-ˌkär-ˈbär-kə, ˈham-əl-\ 270?–229 (or 228) B.C. Carthaginian general; father of Hannibal
Ham·il·ton \ˈham-əl-tən, -əlt-n\ Alexander 1755–1804 American statesman
Hamilton Edith 1867–1963 American classicist
Ham·mar·skjöld \ˈham-ər-ˌshəld\ Dag 1905–1961 Swedish U.N. secretary-general (1953–61); Nobel Prize winner (1961, posthumously)
Ham·mu·ra·bi \ˌham-ə-ˈräb-ē\ *died about* 1750 B.C. king of Babylon (*about* 1792–50)
Ham·sun \ˈhäm-sən\ Knut 1859–1952 pseudonym of *Knut Pedersen* Norwegian author; Nobel Prize winner (1920)
Han·cock \ˈhan-ˌkäk\ John 1737–1793 American Revolutionary leader
Han·del \ˈhan-dl\ George Frideric 1685–1759 British (German-born) composer
Han·dy \ˈhan-dē\ W. C. 1873–1958 *William Christopher Handy* American blues musician and composer

Han·ni·bal \'han-ə-bəl\ 247–183? B.C. Carthaginian general
Har·de·ca·nute \ˌhärd-i-kə-'nüt, -'nyüt\ *about* 1019–1042 king of the English (1040–42); king of Denmark (1028–42)
Har·ding \'härd-iŋ\ Warren Gamaliel 1865–1923 29th president of the U.S. (1921–23)
Har·dy \'härd-ē\ Thomas 1840–1928 English author
Har·old I \'har-əld\ *died* 1040 *Harold Hare·foot* \'haər-ˌfu̇t, 'heər-\ king of the English (1035–40)
Harold II *about* 1022–1066 king of the English (1066)
Har·per \'här-pər\ Stephen (Joseph) 1959– prime minister of Canada (2006–)
Har·ris \'har-əs\ Joel Chandler 1848–1908 American author
Har·ri·son \'har-ə-sən\ Benjamin 1833–1901 23rd president of the U.S. (1889–93); grandson of W. H. Harrison
Harrison William Henry 1773–1841 American general; 9th president of the U.S. (1841)
Harte \'härt\ Bret 1836–1902 originally *Francis Brett Harte* American author
Har·vey \'här-vē\ William 1578–1657 English anatomist
Ha·vel \'hav-el\ Vá·clav \'vät-ˌsläf\ 1936–2011 Czech playwright and politician; president of Czech Republic (1993–2003)
Haw·king \'hȯ-kiŋ\ Stephen William 1942– British physicist
Haw·thorne \'hȯ-ˌthȯrn\ Nathaniel 1804–1864 American author
Haydn \'hīd-n\ Franz Joseph 1732–1809 Austrian composer
Hayes \'hāz\ Rutherford Birchard 1822–1893 19th president of the U.S. (1877–81)
Haz·litt \'haz-lət, 'hāz-\ William 1778–1830 English essayist
Hearst \'hərst\ William Randolph 1863–1951 American newspaper publisher
Hec·ate \'hek-ət-ē\ goddess associated especially with the underworld, night, and witchcraft in Greek mythology
Hec·tor \'hek-tər\ son of Priam and Hecuba; Trojan hero slain by Achilles in Greek mythology
Hec·u·ba \'hek-yə-bə\ wife of Priam and mother of Hector and Paris in Greek mythology
He·gel \'hā-gəl\ Georg Wilhelm Friedrich 1770–1831 German philosopher
Hei·deg·ger \'hī-ˌdeg-ər, 'hīd-i-gər\ Martin 1889–1976 German philosopher
Hei·ne \'hī-nə *also* -nē\ Heinrich 1797–1856 German author
Hei·sen·berg \'hī-zn-bərg\ Werner Karl 1901–1976 German physicist; Nobel Prize winner (1932)
Hel·en of Troy \ˌhel-ə-nəv-'trȯi\ wife of Menelaus whose abduction by Paris causes the Trojan War in Greek mythology
He·li·os \'hē-lē-ˌōs, -əs\ god of the sun in Greek mythology — compare SOL
Hell·man \'hel-mən\ Lillian 1905–1984 American playwright
Hem·ing·way \'hem-iŋ-ˌwā\ Ernest Miller 1899–1961 American author; Nobel Prize winner (1954)
Hen·ry \'hen-rē\ name of 8 kings of England: **I** 1068–1135 (reigned 1100–1135); **II** 1133–1189 (reigned 1154–89); **III** 1207–1272 (reigned 1216–72); **IV** 1366–1413 (reigned 1399–1413); **V** 1387–1422 (reigned 1413–22); **VI** 1421–1471 (reigned 1422–61; 1470–71); **VII** 1457–1509 (reigned 1485–1509); **VIII** 1491–1547 (reigned 1509–47)
Henry name of 4 kings of France: **I** *about* 1008–1060 (reigned 1031–60); **II** 1519–1559 (reigned 1547–59); **III** 1551–1589 (reigned 1574–89); **IV** 1553–1610 *Henry of Navarre* (reigned 1589–1610)
Henry O. 1862–1910 pseudonym of *William Sydney Porter* American author
Henry Patrick 1736–1799 American statesman and orator
Hen·son \'hen-sən\ Matthew Alexander 1866–1955 American arctic explorer
He·phaes·tus \hi-'fes-təs, -'fēs-\ god of fire and of metalworking in Greek mythology — compare VULCAN
He·ra \'hir-ə, 'hē-rə\ sister and wife of Zeus and goddess of women and marriage in Greek mythology — compare JUNO
Her·bert \'hər-bərt\ Victor 1859–1924 American (Irish-born) composer and conductor
Her·cu·les \'hər-kyə-ˌlēz\ *or* **Her·a·cles** \'her-ə-ˌklēz\ hero in classical mythology noted for his strength
Her·maph·ro·di·tus \hər-ˌmaf-rə-'dīt-əs\ son of Aphrodite and Hermes who in Greek mythology is combined with a nymph
Her·mes \'hər-ˌmēz, -mēz\ god of commerce, eloquence, invention, travel, and theft who serves as herald and messenger for the other gods in Greek mythology — compare MERCURY
He·ro \'hē-rō, 'hiər-ō\ priestess of Aphrodite loved by Leander in Greek mythology
Her·od \'her-əd\ 73–4 B.C. *Herod the Great* Roman king of Judea (37–4)
Herod An·ti·pas \'ant-ə-ˌpas, -pəs\ 21 B.C.–39 A.D. Roman tetrarch of Galilee (4 B.C.–39 A.D.); son of Herod the Great
He·rod·o·tus \hi-'räd-ə-təs\ *about* 484–*between* 430 *and* 420 B.C. Greek historian
Her·rick \'her-ik\ Robert 1591–1674 English poet
He·si·od \'hē-sē-əd, 'hes-ē-\ *flourished about* 800 B.C. Greek poet
Hes·se \'hes-ə\ Hermann 1877–1962 German author; Nobel Prize winner (1946)
Hes·tia \'hes-tē-ə; 'hes-chə, 'hesh-\ goddess of the hearth and domestic activity in Greek mythology — compare VESTA
Hey·er·dahl \'hā-ər-ˌdäl, 'hī-\ Thor 1914–2002 Norwegian explorer and author
Hi·a·wa·tha \ˌhī-ə-'wȯ-thə, ˌhē-ə-, -'wäth-ə\ legendary Iroquois Indian chief
Hick·ok \'hik-ˌäk\ Wild Bill 1837–1876 originally *James Butler Hickok* American frontiersman and U.S. marshal
Hildebrand — see GREGORY VII
Hil·la·ry \'hil-ə-rē\ Sir Edmund Percival 1919–2008 New Zealand mountaineer and explorer
Hil·ton \'hilt-n\ James 1900–1954 English novelist
Hin·den·burg \'hin-dən-ˌbərg, -ˌbu̇rg\ Paul von 1847–1934 German field marshal; president of Germany (1925–34)
Hip·poc·ra·tes \hip-'äk-rə-ˌtēz\ *about* 460–*about* 377 B.C. *father of medicine* Greek physician
Hi·ro·hi·to \ˌhir-ō-'hē-tō\ 1901–1989 emperor of Japan (1926–89)
Hit·ler \'hit-lər\ Adolf 1889–1945 German (Austrian-born) chancellor and dictator (1933–45)
Hobbes \'häbz\ Thomas 1588–1679 English philosopher
Ho Chi Minh \'hō-'chē-'min\ 1890–1969 originally *Nguyen Sinh Cung* Vietnamese nationalist; president of North Vietnam (1945–69)
Hodg·kin \'häj-kin\ Dorothy Mary 1910–1994 née *Crowfoot* British physicist; Nobel Prize winner (1964)
Ho·gan \'hō-gən\ Ben 1912–1997 *William Benjamin Hogan* American golfer
Ho·garth \'hō-ˌgärth\ William 1697–1764 English painter and engraver
Hol·bein \'hōl-ˌbīn, 'hȯl-\ Hans *the Elder* 1465?–1524 and his son Hans *the Younger* 1497?–1543 German painters
Hol·i·day \'häl-ə-ˌdā\ Billie 1915–1959 originally *Eleanora Fagan* American jazz singer
Hol·lande \ȯ-'län^d\ Francois (Gérard George Nicolas) 1954– president of France (2012–)
Holmes \'hōmz, 'hōlmz\ Oliver Wendell 1809–1894 American physician and author
Holmes Oliver Wendell, Jr. 1841–1935 American jurist; son of Oliver Wendell Holmes
Ho·mer \'hō-mər\ *flourished* 9th *or* 8th century B.C. Greek epic poet
Homer Winslow 1836–1910 American painter
Hooke \'hu̇k\ Robert 1635–1703 English scientist
Hook·er \'hu̇k-ər\ Thomas 1586?–1647 English Puritan clergyman and a founder of Connecticut
Hoo·ver \'hü-vər\ Herbert Clark 1874–1964 31st president of the U.S. (1929–33)
Hoover John Edgar 1895–1972 American criminologist; director of the Federal Bureau of Investigation (1924–72)
Hop·kins \'häp-kənz\ Gerard Manley 1844–1889 English poet
Hop·per \'häp-ər\ Grace 1906–1992 née *Murray* American admiral, mathematician, and computer scientist
Hor·ace \'hȯr-əs, 'här-\ 65–8 B.C. Roman poet
Ho·ra·tius \hə-'rā-shē-əs, -shəs\ hero in Roman legend noted for his defense of a bridge over the Tiber against the Etruscans
Ho·sea \hō-'zē-ə, -'zā-\ Hebrew prophet of the 8th century B.C.
Hou·di·ni \hü-'dē-nē\ Harry 1874–1926 originally *Erik Weisz* American magician
Hous·man \'hau̇-smən\ Alfred Edward 1859–1936 English classical scholar and poet
Hous·ton \'hyü-stən, 'yü-\ Sam 1793–1863 *Samuel Houston*

American politician; president of the Republic of Texas (1836–38; 1841–44)
How·e \ˈhau̇\ Elias 1819–1867 American inventor
Howe Julia 1819–1910 née *Ward* American suffragist and reformer
How·ells \ˈhau̇-əlz\ William Dean 1837–1920 American author
Hud·son \ˈhəd-sən\ Henry *about* 1565–1611 English navigator and explorer
Hugh Ca·pet \ˈkā-pət, ˈkap-ət, ka-ˈpā\ *about* 938–996 A.D. king of France (987–996)
Hughes \ˈhyüz *also* ˈyüz\ Charles Evans 1862–1948 chief justice of the U.S. Supreme Court (1930–41)
Hughes (James) Langston 1902–1967 American author
Hu·go \ˈhyü-gō, yü-\ Victor (-Marie) 1802–1885 French author
Hu Jin·tao \ˈhü-ˈjin-ˈtau̇\ 1942– Chinese Communist party leader (2002–12); president of China (2003–13)
Hume \ˈhyüm *also* ˈyüm\ David 1711–1776 Scottish philosopher
Hus *or* **Huss** \ˈhəs, ˈhu̇s\ Jan *about* 1370–1415 Czech religious reformer
Hus·sein \hü-ˈsān\ Saddam al-Tikriti 1937–2006 leader of Iraq (1979–2003)
Hussein I 1935–1999 king of Jordan (1952–99)
Hux·ley \ˈhək-slē\ Aldous Leonard 1894–1963 English author
Hy·ge·ia \hī-ˈjē-ə, -yə\ goddess of health in Greek mythology
Hy·men \ˈhī-mən\ god of marriage in Greek mythology
Hy·pe·ri·on \hī-ˈpir-ē-ən\ Titan and the father of Eos, Selene, and Helios in Greek mythology
Ib·sen \ˈib-sən, ˈip-\ Henrik 1828–1906 Norwegian playwright
Ic·a·rus \ˈik-ə-rəs\ son of Daedalus who falls into the sea when the wax of his artificial wings melts as he flies too near the sun
Ig·na·tius \ig-ˈnā-shē-əs, -shəs\ Saint 1491–1556 *Ignatius of Loy·o·la* \lȯi-ˈō-lə\ Spanish founder of the Society of Jesus (Jesuits)
In·no·cent \ˈin-ə-sənt\ name of 13 popes: especially **II** *died* 1143 (pope 1130–43); **III** 1160 (or 1161)–1216 (pope 1198–1216); **IV** *died* 1254 (pope 1243–54); **XI** 1611–1689 (pope 1676–89)
Iph·i·ge·nia \ˌif-ə-jə-ˈnī-ə\ daughter of Agamemnon nearly sacrificed by him to Artemis but saved by her in Greek mythology
Iris \ˈī-rəs\ goddess of the rainbow and a messenger of the gods in Greek mythology
Ir·ving \ˈər-viŋ\ Washington 1783–1859 American author
Isaac \ˈī-zik, -zək\ son of Abraham and father of Jacob in the Bible
Is·a·bel·la I \ˌiz-ə-ˈbel-ə\ 1451–1504 queen of Castile (1474–1504) and of Aragon (1479–1504); wife of Ferdinand V of Castile
Isa·iah \ī-ˈzā-ə\ Hebrew prophet of the 8th century B.C.
Ish·ma·el \ˈish-mē-əl, -mā-\ outcast son of Abraham and Hagar in the Bible
Isis \ˈī-səs\ ancient Egyptian nature goddess
Isol·de \i-ˈzōl-də\ legendary Irish princess married to King Mark of Cornwall and loved by Tristram
Ivan III \ē-ˈvän, ˈī-vən\ 1440–1505 *Ivan the Great* grand prince of Moscow (1462–1505)
Ivan IV 1530–1584 *Ivan the Terrible* ruler of Russia (1533–84) and 1st czar (1547–84)
Ives \ˈīvz\ Charles Edward 1874–1954 American composer
Jack·son \ˈjak-sən\ Andrew 1767–1845 American general; 7th president of the U.S. (1829–37)
Jackson Jesse Louis 1941– American clergyman and civil rights leader
Jackson Mahalia 1911–1972 American gospel singer
Jackson Thomas Jonathan 1824–1863 *Stonewall Jackson* American Confederate general
Ja·cob \ˈjā-kəb\ son of Isaac and Rebekah and younger twin brother of Esau in the Bible
James \ˈjāmz\ one of the 12 apostles and brother of the apostle John in the Bible
James *the Less* one of the 12 apostles in the Bible
James name of 2 kings of Great Britain: **I** 1566–1625 (reigned 1603–25); king of Scotland as *James VI* (reigned 1567–1625); **II** 1633–1701 (reigned 1685–88)
James Henry 1843–1916 British (American-born) author
James William 1842–1910 American psychologist and philosopher; brother of Henry James
James Edward — see STUART
Ja·nus \ˈjā-nəs\ god of gates, doors, and beginnings in Roman mythology and that is portrayed with two opposite faces
Ja·pheth \ˈjā-fəth\ son of Noah and ancestor of the Medes and Greeks in biblical tradition
Ja·son \ˈjās-ⁿn\ hero in Greek mythology noted for his successful quest of the Golden Fleece
Jay \ˈjā\ John 1745–1829 American jurist and statesman; 1st chief justice of the U.S. Supreme Court (1789–95)
Jef·fer·son \ˈjef-ər-sən\ Thomas 1743–1826 3rd president of the U.S. (1801–09)
Jen·ner \ˈjen-ər\ Edward 1749–1823 English physician
Jer·e·mi·ah \ˌjer-ə-ˈmī-ə\ Hebrew prophet of the 7th–6th century B.C.
Je·rome \jə-ˈrōm\ Saint *about* 347–419 (or 420) A.D. church father and biblical translator
Je·sus \ˈje-zəs, -zəz\ *or* **Jesus Christ** *about* 6 B.C.–*about* 30 A.D. source of the Christian religion and Savior in the Christian faith
Jez·e·bel \ˈjez-ə-ˌbel\ queen of Israel and wife of Ahab who is notable for her wickedness in the Bible
Ji·ang Ze·min \jē-ˈäŋ-zə-ˈmin\ 1926– Chinese Communist party leader (1989–2002) and president of China (1993–2003)
Joan of Arc \ˌjō-nə-ˈvärk\ Saint *about* 1412–1431 *the Maid of Orléans* French national heroine
Job \ˈjōb\ man in the Bible who endures afflictions with fortitude and faith
Jo·cas·ta \jō-ˈkas-tə\ queen of Thebes in Greek mythology who unknowingly marries her son Oedipus
Jo·el \ˈjō-əl\ Hebrew prophet in the Bible
John \ˈjän\ one of the 12 apostles and the traditional author of the 4th Gospel, three Epistles, and the Book of Revelation
John name of 21 popes: especially **XXIII** (*Angelo Giuseppe Roncalli*) 1881–1963 (pope 1958–63)
John 1167–1216 *John Lack·land* \ˈlak-ˌland\ king of England (1199–1216)
John of Gaunt \-ˈgȯnt, -ˈgänt\ 1340–1399 Duke of Lancaster; son of Edward III of England
John Paul name of 2 popes: especially **II** (Karol Wojtyla) 1920–2005 (pope 1978–2005)
John·son \ˈjän-sən\ Andrew 1808–1875 17th president of the U.S. (1865–69)
Johnson Jack 1878–1946 *John Arthur Johnson* American boxer
Johnson Lyndon Baines 1908–1973 36th president of the U.S. (1963–69)
Johnson Magic 1959– *Earvin Johnson, Jr.* American basketball player
Johnson Philip Cortelyou 1906–2005 American architect
Johnson Samuel 1709–1784 *Dr. Johnson* English lexicographer and author
John the Baptist Saint, 1st century A.D. prophet who in the Bible foretells Jesus' ministry and baptizes him
Jol·liet *or* **Jo·liet** \zhȯl-ˈyā\ Louis 1645–1700 French-Canadian explorer
Jo·nah \ˈjō-nə\ Hebrew prophet who in the Bible spends three days in the belly of a great fish
Jon·a·than \ˈjän-ə-thən\ son of Saul and friend of David in the Bible
Jones \ˈjōnz\ John Paul 1747–1792 originally *John Paul* American (Scottish-born) naval officer
Jon·son \ˈjän-sən\ Ben 1572–1637 *Benjamin Johnson* English author
Jop·lin \ˈjäp-lən\ Scott 1868–1917 American pianist and composer
Jor·dan \ˈjȯrd-ⁿn\ Michael Jeffrey 1963– American basketball player
Jo·seph \ˈjō-zəf *also* -səf\ son of Jacob who in the Bible rises to high office in Egypt after being sold into slavery by his brothers
Joseph Chief *about* 1840–1904 Nez Percé Indian chief
Joseph Saint, husband of Mary, the mother of Jesus, in the Bible
Jo·se·phine \ˈjō-zə-ˌfēn *also* -sə-\ 1763–1814 1st wife of Napoléon I; empress of France (1804–09)
Joseph of Ar·i·ma·thea \-ˌar-ə-mə-ˈthē-ə\ member of the Sanhedrin (supreme council) who in the Bible places the body of Jesus in his own tomb
Jo·se·phus \jō-ˈsē-fəs\ Flavius *about* 37–*about* 100 A.D. originally *Joseph Ben Matthias* Jewish historian
Josh·ua \ˈjäsh-wə, -ə-wə\ Hebrew leader in the Bible who succeeds Moses during the settlement of the Israelites in Canaan
Joyce \ˈjȯis\ James Augustine 1882–1941 Irish author
Juan Car·los \ˈhwän-ˈkär-ˌlōs, ˈwän-\ 1938– king of Spain (1975–2014)

Ju·dah \ˈjüd-ə\ son of Jacob and ancestor of one of the 12 tribes of Israel in the Bible

Ju·das \ˈjüd-əs\ *or* **Judas Is·car·i·ot** \-is-ˈkar-ē-ət\ one of the 12 apostles and betrayer of Jesus in the Bible

Ju·das Mac·ca·bae·us \ˈjud-ə-ˌsmak-ə-ˈbē-əs\ *died about* 161 B.C. Jewish patriot

Ju·lian \ˈjül-yən\ *about* 331–363 A.D. *Julian the Apostate* Roman emperor (361–63)

Jung \ˈyu̇ŋ\ Carl Gustav 1875–1961 Swiss psychologist

Ju·no \ˈjü-nō\ queen of heaven, wife of Jupiter, and goddess of light, birth, women, and marriage in Roman mythology — compare HERA

Ju·pi·ter \ˈjü-pət-ər\ chief god, husband of Juno, and god of light, of the sky and weather, and of the state in Roman mythology — compare ZEUS

Jus·tin·i·an I \ˌjə-ˈstin-ē-ən\ 483–565 A.D. *Justinian the Great* Byzantine emperor (527–565)

Ju·ve·nal \ˈjü-vən-ˡ\ 55 to 60–*about* 127 A.D. Roman satirist

Kaf·ka \ˈkäf-kə, ˈkaf-\ Franz 1883–1924 Czech-born author who wrote in German

Kalb \ˈkälp, ˈkalb\ Johann 1721–1780 Baron *de Kalb* \di-ˈkalb\ German general in American Revolutionary army

Ka·me·ha·me·ha I \kə-ˌmā-ə-ˈmā-hä\ 1758?–1819 *Kamehameha the Great* Hawaiian king (1795–1819)

Kant \ˈkant, ˈkänt\ Immanuel 1724–1804 German philosopher

Keats \ˈkēts\ John 1795–1821 English poet

Kel·ler \ˈkel-ər\ Helen Adams 1880–1968 American deaf and blind lecturer and author

Kel·vin \ˈkel-vən\ 1st Baron 1824–1907 *William Thomson* British mathematician and physicist

Kempis Thomas à — see THOMAS À KEMPIS

Ken·ne·dy \ˈken-əd-ē\ John Fitzgerald 1917–1963 35th president of the U.S. (1961–63); brother of R. F. Kennedy

Kennedy Robert Francis 1925–1968 American politician

Ke·o·kuk \ˈkē-ə-ˌkək\ 1780?–1848 American Indian chief

Kep·ler \ˈkep-lər\ Johannes 1571–1630 German astronomer

Ke·ren·sky \ˈker-ən-skē\ Aleksandr Fyodorovich 1881–1970 Russian revolutionary; head of provisional government (1917)

Ker·ry \ˈker-ē\ John (Forbes) 1943– American politician; U.S. Secretary of State (2013–)

Key \ˈkē\ Francis Scott 1779–1843 American lawyer and author of "The Star-Spangled Banner"

Keynes \ˈkānz\ John Maynard 1883–1946 Baron *Keynes of Tilton* English economist — **Keynes·ian** \ˈkān-zē-ən\ *adj or n*

Khayyám Omar — see OMAR KHAYYÁM

Khru·shchev \krush-ˈchóf, -ˈóf, -ˈchóv, -ˈóv, -ˈchef, -ˈef, ˈkrüsh-\ Ni·ki·ta \nə-ˈkēt-ə\ Sergeyevich 1894–1971 premier of U.S.S.R. (1958–64)

Khu·fu \ˈkü-ˌfü\ *or Greek* **Che·ops** \ˈkē-ˌäps\ *flourished* 25th century B.C. king of Egypt and pyramid builder

Kidd \ˈkid\ William *about* 1645–1701 *Captain Kidd* Scottish pirate

Kier·ke·gaard \ˈkir-kə-ˌgärd, -ˌgär, -ˌgór\ Søren Aabye 1813–1855 Danish philosopher and theologian

King \ˈkiŋ\ Billie Jean 1943– née *Moffitt* American tennis player

King Ernest Joseph 1878–1956 American admiral

King Martin Luther, Jr. 1929–1968 American clergyman and civil rights leader; Nobel Prize winner (1964)

Kip·ling \ˈkip-liŋ\ (Joseph) Rud·yard \ˈrəd-yərd, ˈrəj-ərd\ 1865–1936 English author; Nobel Prize winner (1907)

Kis·sin·ger \ˈkis-n-jər\ Henry Alfred 1923– American (German-born) government official; U.S. secretary of state (1973–77); Nobel Prize winner (1973)

Klee \ˈklā\ Paul 1879–1940 Swiss painter

Knox \ˈnäks\ John *about* 1514–1572 Scottish religious reformer

Koch \ˈkȯk, ˈkȯk, ˈkōk, ˈkōk, ˈkäk, ˈkäk\ Robert 1843–1910 German bacteriologist; Nobel Prize winner (1905)

Kohl \ˈkōl\ Helmut 1930– chancellor of Germany (1990–98)

Koś·ciusz·ko \ˌkäs-ē-ˈəs-ˌkō, kösh-ˈchúsh-kō\ Tadeusz 1746–1817 Polish patriot and general in American Revolutionary army

Krish·na \ˈkrish-nə\ deity or deified hero of later Hinduism worshiped as an incarnation of Vishnu

Ku·blai Khan \ˌkü-blə-ˈkän, -ˌblī-\ 1215–1294 founder of Mongol dynasty in China; grandson of Genghis Khan

La·fa·yette \ˌläf-ē-ˈet, ˌlaf-\ Marquis de 1757–1834 French general in American Revolutionary army

La Fon·taine \lə-ˌfän-ˈtān, -ˌfōⁿ-ˈten\ Jean de 1621–1695 French writer of fables

La·ius \ˈlā-əs, ˈlī-\ king of Thebes who in Greek mythology is slain by his son Oedipus

La·marck \lə-ˈmärk\ Chevalier de 1744–1829 *Jean-Baptiste de Monet* French naturalist

Lamb \ˈlam\ Charles 1775–1834 English author

Lan·ce·lot \ˈlan-sə-ˌlät\ knight of the Round Table and lover of Queen Guinevere in Arthurian legend

Lange \ˈlaŋ\ Dorothea 1895–1965 American photographer

Lang·land \ˈlaŋ-lənd\ William *about* 1330–*about* 1400 English poet

Lang·ley \ˈlaŋ-lē\ Samuel Pierpont 1834–1906 American astronomer and airplane pioneer

La·oc·o·ön \lā-ˈäk-ə-ˌwän\ Trojan priest in Greek mythology killed by sea serpents after warning against the wooden horse

Lao–tzu \ˈlau̇d-ˈzə\ *flourished* 6th century B.C. Chinese philosopher

La·place \lə-ˈpläs\ Pierre-Simon 1749–1827 Marquis *de Laplace* French astronomer and mathematician

La Roche·fou·cauld \lä-ˌrōsh-ˌfü-ˈkō, -ˌrōsh-\ François 1613–1680 Duc *de la Rochefoucauld* French author and moralist

La Salle \lə-ˈsal\ Sieur de 1643–1687 *René-Robert Cavelier* French explorer in North America

La·voi·sier \ləv-ˈwäz-ē-ˌā\ Antoine-Laurent 1743–1794 French chemist

Law·rence \ˈlȯr-əns, ˈlär-\ D.H. 1885–1930 *David Herbert Lawrence* English author

Lawrence Sir Thomas 1769–1830 English painter

Lawrence Thomas Edward 1888–1935 *Lawrence of Arabia* British archaeologist, soldier, and author

Laz·a·rus \ˈlaz-rəs, -ə-rəs\ brother of Mary and Martha who in the Bible is raised by Jesus from the dead

Lazarus beggar in the biblical parable of the rich man and the beggar

Lea·key \ˈlē-kē\ family of British anthropologists and paleontologists: Louis 1903–1972; his wife Mary 1913–1996 née *Nicol;* their son Richard 1944–

Le·an·der \lē-ˈan-dər\ youth in Greek mythology who swims the Hellespont nightly to visit his lover Hero

Le·da \ˈlēd-ə\ Spartan princess in Greek mythology who is visited by Zeus in the form of a swan

Lee \ˈlē\ Ann 1736–1784 English mystic and founder of Shaker society in the U.S.

Lee Henry 1756–1818 *Light-Horse Harry* American general

Lee Robert Edward 1807–1870 American Confederate general; son of the preceding

Leeu·wen·hoek *or* **Leu·wen·hoek** \ˈlā-vən-ˌhu̇k\ Antonie van 1632–1723 Dutch naturalist

Leib·niz \ˈlīb-nəts, ˈlīp-nits\ Gottfried Wilhelm 1646–1716 German philosopher and mathematician

Leif Er·iks·son \ˈlā-ˈver-ik-sən, ˈlē-ˈfer-\ *flourished* 1000 Norwegian explorer; son of Erik the Red

Le·nin \ˈlen-ən\ 1870–1924 originally *Vladimir Ilyich Ul·ya·nov* \ül-ˈyän-əf, -ˌóf, -ˌóv\ Russian Communist leader

Len·non \ˈlen-ən\ John Winston 1940–1980 British popular singer and songwriter

Leo \ˈlē-ō\ name of 13 popes: especially **I** Saint *died* 461 A.D. *Leo the Great* (pope 440–61); **III** Saint *died* 816 A.D. (pope 795–816); **XIII** 1810–1903 (pope 1878–1903)

Le·o·nar·do da Vin·ci \ˌlē-ə-ˈnär-dō-də-ˈvin-chē, ˌlā-\ 1452–1519 Italian painter, sculptor, architect, and engineer

Le·on·ca·val·lo \ˌlā-ˌōn-kə-ˈväl-ō\ Ruggero 1858–1919 Italian composer and librettist

Le·on·i·das \lē-ˈän-əd-əs\ *died* 480 B.C. Greek hero; king of Sparta (490?–480)

Lep·i·dus \ˈlep-əd-əs\ Marcus Aemilius *died* 13 (or 12) B.C. Roman triumvir (43–36)

Le·vi \ˈlē-ˌvī\ son of Jacob and ancestor of one of the 12 tribes of Israel in the Bible

Lew·is \ˈlü-əs\ C. S. 1898–1963 *Clive Staples Lewis* British author

Lewis John Llewellyn 1880–1969 American labor leader

\ə\ **abut**	\au̇\ **out**	\i\ **tip**	\ȯ\ **saw**	\u̇\ **foot**
\ər\ **further**	\ch\ **chin**	\ī\ **life**	\ȯi\ **coin**	\y\ **yet**
\a\ **mat**	\e\ **pet**	\j\ **job**	\th\ **thin**	\yü\ **few**
\ā\ **take**	\ē\ **easy**	\ŋ\ **sing**	\th\ **this**	\yu̇\ **cure**
\ä\ **cot, cart**	\g\ **go**	\ō\ **bone**	\ü\ **food**	\zh\ **vision**

Lewis Meriwether 1774–1809 American explorer (with William Clark)

Lewis (Harry) Sinclair 1885–1951 American author; Nobel Prize winner (1930)

Lin•coln \ˈliŋ-kən\ Abraham 1809–1865 16th president of the U.S. (1861–65)

Lind•bergh \ˈlind-ˌbərg, ˈlin-\ Charles Augustus 1902–1974 American aviator

Lin•nae•us \lə-ˈnē-əs, -ˈnā-\ Carolus 1707–1778 *Carl von Lin•né* \lə-ˈnā\ Swedish botanist

Lip•pi \ˈlip-ē\ Fra Fi•lip•po \fə-ˈlip-ō\ *about* 1406–1469 Florentine painter

Lis•ter \ˈlis-tər\ Joseph 1827–1912 English surgeon

Liszt \ˈlist\ Franz 1811–1886 Hungarian pianist and composer

Liv•ing•stone \ˈliv-iŋ-stən\ David 1813–1873 Scottish explorer and missionary in Africa

Livy \ˈliv-ē\ 59 B.C.–17 A.D. *Titus Livius* Roman historian

Lloyd George \ˈlȯid-ˈjȯrj\ David 1863–1945 Earl of *Dwy•for* \ˈdü-ē-ˌvȯr\ British prime minister (1916–22)

Locke \ˈläk\ John 1632–1704 English philosopher

Lo•hen•grin \ˈlō-ən-ˌgrin\ son of Parsifal and knight of the Holy Grail in German legend

Lon•don \ˈlən-dən\ Jack 1876–1916 *John Griffith London* American author

Long•fel•low \ˈlȯŋ-ˌfel-ō\ Henry Wads•worth \ˈwädz-wərth, -ˌwərth\ 1807–1882 American poet

Lo•re•lei \ˈlȯr-ə-ˌlī, ˈlȯr-\ siren in German legend whose singing lures boatmen to destruction on a reef in the Rhine River

Lot \ˈlät\ nephew of Abraham in the Bible whose wife turns into a pillar of salt after looking back on the doomed city of Sodom

Lou•is \ˈlü-ē, ˈlü-əs\ name of 18 kings of France: especially **IX** Saint 1214–1270 (reigned 1226–70); **XI** 1423–1483 (reigned 1461–83); **XII** 1462–1515 (reigned 1498–1515); **XIII** 1601–1643 (reigned 1610–43); **XIV** 1638–1715 (reigned 1643–1715); **XV** 1710–1774 (reigned 1715–74); **XVI** 1754–1793 (reigned 1774–92; guillotined); **XVII** 1785–1795 (nominally reigned 1793–95); **XVIII** 1755–1824 (reigned 1814–15; 1815–24)

Louis \ˈlü-əs\ Joe 1914–1981 originally *Joseph Louis Barrow* American boxer

Louis Napoléon — see NAPOLÉON III

Louis Phi•lippe \fi-ˈlēp\ 1773–1850 *the Citizen King* king of the French (1830–48)

Low \ˈlō\ Juliette 1860–1927 née *Gordon* American founder of the Girl Scouts

Low•ell \ˈlō-əl\ Amy 1874–1925 American poet and critic

Lowell James Russell 1819–1891 American author

Loyola — see IGNATIUS

Lu•cre•tius \lü-ˈkrē-shē-əs, -shəs\ *about* 96–*about* 55 B.C. *Titus Lucretius Carus* Roman poet and philosopher

Luke \ˈlük\ physician and companion of the apostle Paul and the traditional author of the 3rd Gospel and the Book of Acts

Lu•ther \ˈlü-thər\ Martin 1483–1546 German Reformation leader

Ly•on \ˈlī-ən\ Mary 1797–1849 American educator

Mac•Ar•thur \mə-ˈkär-thər\ Douglas 1880–1964 American general

Ma•cau•lay \mə-ˈkȯ-lē\ Thomas Babington 1800–1859 1st Baron *Macaulay* English historian, author, and statesman

Ma•chi•a•vel•li \ˌmak-ē-ə-ˈvel-ē\ Niccolò 1469–1527 Italian political philosopher

Mad•i•son \ˈmad-ə-sən\ James 1751–1836 4th president of the U.S. (1809–17)

Mae•ter•linck \ˈmāt-ər-ˌliŋk *also* ˈmet-, ˈmat-\ Count Maurice 1862–1949 Belgian author; Nobel Prize winner (1911)

Ma•gel•lan \mə-ˈjel-ən\ Ferdinand *about* 1480–1521 Portuguese navigator and explorer

Mah•ler \ˈmäl-ər\ Gustav 1860–1911 Austrian composer

Ma•jor \ˈmā-jər\ John 1943– prime minister of Great Britain (1990–97)

Mal•colm X \ˌmal-kə-ˈmeks\ 1925–1965 originally *Malcolm Little* American civil rights leader

Mal•o•ry \ˈmal-rē, -ə-rē\ Sir Thomas *flourished about* 1470 English author

Mal•thus \ˈmal-thəs\ Thomas Robert 1766–1834 English economist and demographer

Man•dela \man-ˈdel-ə\ Nelson Rolihlahla 1918–2013 South African black political leader; president of South Africa (1994–99); Nobel Prize winner (1993)

Ma•net \ma-ˈnā, mä-\ Édouard 1832–1883 French painter

Mann \ˈman\ Horace 1796–1859 American educator

Mann \ˈmän, ˈman\ Thomas 1875–1955 American (German-born) author; Nobel Prize winner (1929)

Mao Ze•dong *or* **Mao Tse–tung** \ˌmau̇d-zə-ˈdu̇ŋ, ˌmau̇-zə-, ˌmau̇t-sə-\ 1893–1976 Chinese Communist leader of the People's Republic of China (1949–76)

Ma•rat \mə-ˈrä\ Jean-Paul 1743–1793 French (Swiss-born) revolutionary

Mar•co•ni \mär-ˈkō-nē\ Guglielmo 1874–1937 Italian physicist and inventor; Nobel Prize winner (1909)

Marco Polo — see POLO

Mar•cus Au•re•lius \ˈmär-kəs-ȯ-ˈrēl-yəs\ 121–180 A.D. *Marcus Aurelius An•to•ni•nus* \ˌan-tə-ˈnī-nəs\ Roman emperor (161–80) and philosopher

Ma•ria The•re•sa \mə-ˌrē-ə-tə-ˈrā-sə, -ˈrā-zə\ 1717–1780 wife of Holy Roman Emperor Francis I; queen of Hungary and Bohemia (1740–80)

Ma•rie An•toi•nette \mə-ˈrē-ˌan-twə-ˈnet, -tə-ˈnet\ 1755–1793 wife of Louis XVI of France; daughter of the preceding

Mark \ˈmärk\ evangelist believed to be the author of the 2nd Gospel

Mark Antony — see ANTONY

Mar•lowe \ˈmär-ˌlō\ Christopher 1564–1593 English playwright

Mar•quette \mär-ˈket\ Jacques 1637–1675 *Père* \ˌpiər, ˌpear\ *Marquette* Jesuit missionary and French explorer in America

Mars \ˈmärz\ god of war in Roman mythology — compare ARES

Mar•shall \ˈmär-shəl\ George Catlett 1880–1959 American general and diplomat; Nobel Prize winner (1953)

Marshall John 1755–1835 American jurist; chief justice of the U.S. Supreme Court (1801–35)

Marshall Thurgood 1908–1993 American jurist

Martel Charles — see CHARLES MARTEL

Mar•tha \ˈmär-thə\ sister of Lazarus and Mary and friend of Jesus in the Bible

Mar•tial \ˈmär-shəl\ *about* 40–*about* 103 A.D. Roman poet and epigrammatist

Mar•tin \ˈmärt-n, mår-ˈtaⁿ\ Saint 316–397 A.D. *Martin of Tours* \-ˈtu̇r\ patron saint of France

Martin Paul 1938– prime minister of Canada (2003–06)

Marx \ˈmärks\ Karl Heinrich 1818–1883 German political philosopher and socialist

Mary \ˈmeər-ē, ˈmaər-ē, ˈmā-rē\ *Saint Mary; Virgin Mary* mother of Jesus

Mary sister of Lazarus and Martha in the Bible

Mary I 1516–1558 *Mary Tudor; Bloody Mary* queen of England (1553–58)

Mary II 1662–1694 joint British sovereign with William III (1689–94)

Mary Mag•da•lene \-ˈmag-də-ˌlēn, -ˌmag-də-ˈlē-nē\ woman in the Bible who is healed of evil spirits by Jesus and who later sees the risen Christ

Mary, Queen of Scots 1542–1587 *Mary Stuart* queen of Scotland (1542–67)

Ma•sca•gni \mä-ˈskän-yē, ma-\ Pietro 1863–1945 Italian composer

Mase•field \ˈmās-ˌfēld\ John 1878–1967 English author

Ma•son \ˈmās-n\ George 1725–1792 American Revolutionary statesman

Mas•sa•soit \ˌmas-ə-ˈsȯit\ *died* 1661 American Indian chief

Mas•se•net \ˌmas-n-ˈā, ma-ˈsnā\ Jules (-Émile-Frédéric) 1842–1912 French composer

Math•er \ˈmat͟h-ər, ˈmath-\ Cotton 1663–1728 American clergyman and author

Mather Increase 1639–1723 American clergyman and author; father of Cotton Mather

Ma•tisse \ma-ˈtēs, mə-\ Henri 1869–1954 French painter

Mat•thew \ˈmath-yü\ one of the 12 apostles and the traditional author of the 1st Gospel

Maugham \ˈmȯm\ (William) Somerset 1874–1965 English author

Mau•pas•sant \ˌmō-pə-ˈsäⁿ\ (Henri-René-Albert-) Guy de 1850–1893 French author

Max•i•mil•ian \ˌmak-sə-ˈmil-yən\ 1832–1867 emperor of Mexico (1864–67); brother of Francis Joseph I of Austria

Maximilian I 1459–1519 Holy Roman emperor (1493–1519)

Maximilian II 1527–1576 Holy Roman emperor (1564–76)

Max•well \ˈmak-ˌswel, -swəl\ James Clerk \ˈklärk\ 1831–1879 Scottish physicist

Mayo \ˈmā-ō\ William James 1861–1939 and his brother Charles Horace 1865–1939 American surgeons
Mays \ˈmāz\ Willie Howard 1931– American baseball player
Ma·za·rin \ˌmaz-ə-ˈraⁿ\ Jules 1602–1661 French cardinal and statesman
Maz·zi·ni \mät-ˈsē-nē, mäd-ˈzē-\ Giuseppe 1805–1872 Italian patriot and revolutionary
Mc·Car·thy \mə-ˈkärth-ē\ Joseph Raymond 1908–1957 American politician
Mc·Cart·ney \mə-ˈkärt-nē\ (James) Paul 1942– *Sir Paul McCartney* British singer and songwriter
Mc·Clel·lan \mə-ˈklel-ən\ George Brinton 1826–1885 American general
Mc·Clin·tock \mə-ˈklin-tək\ Barbara 1902–1992 American botanist; Nobel Prize winner (1983)
Mc·Cor·mick \mə-ˈkȯr-mik\ Cyrus Hall 1809–1884 American inventor of a mechanical reaper
Mc·Cul·lers \mə-ˈkəl-ərz\ Carson 1917–1967 née *Smith* American writer
Mc·Kin·ley \mə-ˈkin-lē\ William 1843–1901 25th president of the U.S. (1897–1901)
Mead \ˈmēd\ Margaret 1901–1978 American anthropologist
Meade \ˈmēd\ George Gordon 1815–1872 American general
Mea·ny \ˈmē-nē\ George 1894–1980 American labor leader
Me·dea \mə-ˈdē-ə\ enchantress in Greek mythology who helps Jason to win the Golden Fleece and kills her children when he deserts her
Medici Catherine de — see CATHERINE DE MÉDICIS
Medici Lorenzo de' 1449–1492 *Lorenzo the Magnificent* Florentine ruler, statesman, and patron of the arts
Me·du·sa \mi-ˈdü-sə, -ˈdyü-, -zə\ Gorgon in Greek mythology slain by Perseus
Med·ved·ev \mid-ˈvye-dif\ Dmitry Anatolyevich 1965– president of Russia (2008–12); prime minister (2012–)
Mel·pom·e·ne \mel-ˈpäm-ə-nē\ Muse of tragedy in Greek mythology
Mel·ville \ˈmel-ˌvil\ Herman 1819–1891 American author
Men·del \ˈmen-dl\ Gregor Johann 1822–1884 Austrian botanist
Men·de·le·yev \ˌmen-də-ˈlā-əf\ Dmitry Ivanovich 1834–1907 Russian chemist
Men·dels·sohn (–Bar·thol·dy) \ˈmen-dl-sən(-bär-ˈtȯl-dē, -ˈthȯl-)\ (Jakob Ludwig) Felix 1809–1847 German composer
Men·e·la·us \ˌmen-l-ˈā-əs\ king of Sparta, brother of Agamemnon, and husband of Helen of Troy in Greek mythology
Meph·is·toph·e·les \ˌmef-ə-ˈstäf-ə-ˌlēz\ chief devil in the Faust legend
Mer·ca·tor \ˌmər-ˈkāt-ər\ Gerhardus 1512–1594 originally *Gerhard Kremer* Flemish cartographer
Mer·cu·ry \ˈmər-kyə-rē, -kə-rē, -krē\ god of commerce, eloquence, travel, and theft who serves as herald and messenger of the other gods in Roman mythology — compare HERMES
Mer·e·dith \ˈmer-əd-əth\ George 1828–1909 English author
Mer·kel \ˈmer-kəl\ Angela (Dorothea) 1954– née *Kasner* chancellor of Germany (2005–)
Mer·lin \ˈmər-lən\ prophet and magician in Arthurian legend
Met·a·com \ˈmet-ə-ˌkäm\ *or* **King Philip** *about* 1638–1676 *Met·a·com·et* \ˌmet-ə-ˈkäm-ət\ American Indian chief; son of Massasoit
Me·tho·di·us \mə-ˈthōd-ē-əs\ Saint *about* 825–884 A.D. Apostle to the Slavs; brother of Cyril
Me·thu·se·lah \mə-ˈthüz-lə, -ˈthyüz-, -ə-lə\ ancestor of Noah who lived 969 years according to biblical tradition
Met·ter·nich \ˈmet-ər-nik, -nik\ Klemens (Wenzel Nepomuk Lothar) 1773–1859 Fürst (Prince) *von Metternich* Austrian statesman
Mey·er·beer \ˈmī-ər-ˌbiər, -ˌbeər\ Giacomo 1791–1864 originally *Jakob Liebmann Meyer Beer* German composer
Mfume \əm-ˈfü-mā\ Kweisi 1948– originally *Frizell Gray* American civil rights leader
Mi·cah \ˈmī-kə\ Hebrew prophet of the 8th century B.C.
Mi·chael \ˈmī-kəl\ one of the four archangels named in Hebrew tradition — compare GABRIEL, RAPHAEL, URIEL
Mi·chel·an·ge·lo \ˌmī-kə-ˈlan-jə-ˌlō, ˌmik-ə-ˈlan-, ˌmē-kə-ˈlän-\ 1475–1564 *Michelangelo di Lodovico Buonarroti Simoni* Italian sculptor, painter, architect, and poet
Mich·e·ner \ˈmich-nər, -ə-nər\ James Albert 1907?–1997 American author
Mi·das \ˈmīd-əs\ legendary king of Phrygia having the power to turn everything he touched into gold
Mill \ˈmil\ John Stuart 1806–1873 British philosopher and economist
Mil·lay \mil-ˈā\ Edna St. Vincent 1892–1950 American poet
Mil·ler \ˈmil-ər\ Arthur 1915–2005 American playwright
Mil·let \mē-ˈyā, mi-ˈlā\ Jean-François 1814–1875 French painter
Milne \ˈmiln, ˈmil\ A. A. 1882–1956 *Alan Alexander Milne* English author
Mil·ti·ades \mil-ˈtī-ə-ˌdēz\ *about* 544–489? B.C. *Miltiades the Younger* Athenian general
Mil·ton \ˈmilt-n\ John 1608–1674 English poet
Mi·ner·va \mə-ˈnər-və\ goddess of wisdom in Roman mythology — compare ATHENE
Mi·nos \ˈmī-nəs\ just king of Crete in Greek mythology who upon his death is made supreme judge of the underworld
Min·o·taur \ˈmin-ə-ˌtȯr, ˈmī-nə-\ monster in Greek mythology shaped half like a man and half like a bull
Min·u·it \ˈmin-yə-wət\ Peter *about* 1580–1638 Dutch colonial administrator in America
Mi·ró \mē-ˈrō\ Joan \zhu̇-ˈän\ 1893–1983 Spanish painter
Mitch·ell \ˈmich-əl\ Margaret 1900–1949 American author
Mitchell Maria 1818–1889 American astronomer
Mith·ras \ˈmith-rəs\ ancient Persian god of light who was the savior hero of an Iranian mystery cult for men flourishing in the late Roman Empire
Mit·ter·rand \ˌmē-ter-ˈäⁿ\ François (-Maurice) 1916–1996 president of France (1981–95)
Mne·mos·y·ne \ni-ˈmäs-n-ē\ goddess of memory and mother of the Muses by Zeus in Greek mythology
Mo·dred \ˈmō-drəd, ˈmäd-rəd\ knight of the Round Table and rebellious nephew of King Arthur in Arthurian legend
Mohammed — variant of MUHAMMAD
Mo·lière \mōl-ˈyeər, ˈmōl-ˌ\ 1622–1673 pseudonym of *Jean-Baptiste Poque·lin* \pō-ˈklaⁿ, -kə-ˈlaⁿ\ French actor and playwright
Mol·och \ˈmäl-ək, ˈmō-ˌläk\ *or* **Mol·ech** \ˈmäl-ək, ˈmō-ˌlek\ Semitic deity to whom children were sacrificed
Mo·lo·tov \ˈmäl-ə-ˌtȯf, ˈmȯl-, ˈmōl-, -ˌtȯv\ Vyacheslav Mikhaylovich 1890–1986 Soviet statesman
Mo·net \mō-ˈnā\ Claude 1840–1926 French painter
Mon·roe \mən-ˈrō\ James 1758–1831 5th president of the U.S. (1817–25)
Mon·taigne \män-ˈtān, mōⁿ-ˈtenʸ\ Michel (Eyquem) de 1533–1592 French essayist
Mont·calm (de Saint–Véran) \mänt-ˈkäm(-də-ˌsaⁿ-vā-ˈräⁿ), -ˈkälm-\ Marquis de 1712–1759 *Louis-Joseph de Montcalm-Grozon* French field marshal in Canada
Mon·tes·quieu \ˌmänt-əs-ˈkyü, -ˈkyər, -ˈkyœ\ Baron *de La Brède et de* 1689–1755 *Charles-Louis de Secondat* French political philosopher
Mon·tes·so·ri \ˌmänt-ə-ˈsōr-ē, -ˈsȯr-\ Maria 1870–1952 Italian physician and educator
Mon·te·ver·di \ˌmänt-ə-ˈveərd-ē, -ˈvərd-\ Claudio Giovanni Antonio 1567–1643 Italian composer
Mon·te·zu·ma II \ˌmänt-ə-ˈzü-mə\ 1466–1520 last Aztec emperor of Mexico (1502–20)
Moore \ˈmōr, ˈmȯr, ˈmu̇r\ Marianne 1887–1972 American poet
Moore Thomas 1779–1852 Irish poet
Mor·de·cai \ˈmȯrd-i-ˌkī\ cousin of Esther in the Bible who saves the Jews from the destruction planned by Haman
More \ˈmōr, ˈmȯr\ Sir Thomas 1478–1535 *Saint Thomas More* English statesman and author
Mor·gan \ˈmȯr-gən\ Sir Henry 1635–1688 English buccaneer
Morgan J. P. 1837–1913 *John Pierpont Morgan* American financier
Mor·pheus \ˈmȯr-fē-əs, -ˌfyüs, -ˌfüs\ god of dreams in Greek mythology
Mor·ris \ˈmȯr-əs, ˈmär-\ William 1834–1896 English poet, artist, and socialist
Mor·ri·son \ˈmȯr-ə-sən\ Toni 1931– originally *Chloe Anthony Wofford* American author; Nobel Prize winner (1993)

\ə\ **abut**	\au̇\ **out**	\i\ **tip**	\ȯ\ **saw**	\u̇\ **foot**
\ər\ **further**	\ch\ **chin**	\ī\ **life**	\ȯi\ **coin**	\y\ **yet**
\a\ **mat**	\e\ **pet**	\j\ **job**	\th\ **thin**	\yü\ **few**
\ā\ **take**	\ē\ **easy**	\ng\ **sing**	\th\ **this**	\yu̇\ **cure**
\ä\ **cot, cart**	\g\ **go**	\ō\ **bone**	\ü\ **food**	\zh\ **vision**

Morse \ˈmȯrs\ Samuel Finley Breese 1791–1872 American artist and inventor of the electrical telegraph
Mo·ses \ˈmō-zəz *also* -zəs\ Hebrew prophet and lawgiver who in the Bible is the liberator of the Israelites from Egypt
Moses Grandma 1860–1961 *Anna Mary Moses* née *Robertson* American painter
Mo·zart \ˈmōt-ˌsärt\ Wolfgang Amadeus 1756–1791 Austrian composer
Mu·bar·ak \mu̇-ˈbär-ək\ (Muhammad) Hosni 1929– president of Egypt (1981–2011)
Mu·ham·mad \mō-ˈham-əd, -ˈhäm- *also* mü-\ *about* 570–632 A.D. Arab prophet and founder of Islam
Mu·ham·mad \mu̇-ˈhäm-əd, -ˈham-\ Elijah 1897–1975 originally *Elijah Poole* American religious leader
Muir \ˈmyu̇r\ John 1838–1914 American (Scottish-born) naturalist
Mul·ro·ney \məl-ˈrü-nē\ (Martin) Brian 1939– prime minister of Canada (1984–93)
Mus·so·li·ni \ˌmü-sə-ˈlē-nē, ˌmu̇s-ə-\ Be·ni·to \bə-ˈnēt-ō\ 1883–1945 *Il Du·ce* \ēl-ˈdü-chā\ Italian Fascist premier (1922–43)
My·ron \ˈmī-rən\ *flourished about* 480–440 B.C. Greek sculptor
Na·bo·kov \nə-ˈbȯ-kəf, -ˌkȯf\ Vladimir Vladimirovich 1899–1977 American (Russian-born) author
Na·hum \ˈnā-əm, -həm\ Hebrew prophet of the 7th century B.C.
Na·o·mi \nā-ˈō-mē\ mother-in-law of the biblical heroine Ruth
Na·pier \ˈnā-pē-ər, -ˌpiər; nə-ˈpiər\ John 1550–1617 Scottish mathematician
Na·po·léon I \nə-ˈpōl-yən, -ˈpō-lē-ən\ *or* **Napoléon Bo·na·parte** \ˈbō-nə-ˌpärt\ 1769–1821 French general and emperor of the French (1804–15) — **Na·po·le·on·ic** \nə-ˌpō-lē-ˈän-ik\ *adj*
Napoléon III 1808–1873 *Louis-Napoléon* emperor of the French (1852–70); son of Louis Bonaparte and nephew of Napoléon I
Nar·cis·sus \När-ˈsis-əs\ beautiful youth in Greek mythology who pines away for love of his own reflection and is then transformed into the narcissus flower
Nash \ˈnash\ Ogden 1902–1971 American poet
Nas·ser \ˈnäs-ər, ˈnas-\ Ga·mal \gə-ˈmäl\ Ab·del \ˈab-dl\ 1918–1970 Egyptian politician; president of Egypt (1956–70)
Na·tion \ˈnā-shən\ Car·ry \ˈkar-ē\ Amelia 1846–1911 née *Moore* American temperance agitator
Nav·ra·ti·lo·va \ˌnav-rət-ə-ˈlō-və\ Martina 1956– American (Czech-born) tennis player
Neb·u·cha·drez·zar II \ˌneb-yə-kə-ˈdrez-ər, ˌneb-ə-kə-\ *or* **Neb·u·chad·nez·zar** \-kəd-ˈnez-\ *about* 630–*about* 561 B.C. Chaldean king of Babylon (605–562)
Ne·he·mi·ah \ˌnē-ə-ˈmī-ə, ˌnē-hə-\ Hebrew leader of the 5th century B.C.
Neh·ru \ˈneər-ˌü, ˈnā-ˌrü\ Ja·wa·har·lal \jə-ˈwä-hər-ˌläl\ 1889–1964 Indian nationalist; 1st prime minister of the Republic of India (1947–64)
Nel·son \ˈnel-sən\ Horatio 1758–1805 Viscount *Nelson* British admiral
Nem·e·sis \ˈnem-ə-səs\ goddess of reward and punishment in Greek mythology
Nep·tune \ˈnep-ˌtün, -ˌtyün\ god of the sea in Roman mythology — compare POSEIDON
Ne·ro \ˈnē-ˌrō, ˈniər-ˌō\ 37–68 A.D. Roman emperor (54–68)
Nes·tor \ˈnes-tər\ wise old counselor of the Greeks during the Trojan War in Greek mythology
Nev·el·son \ˈnev-əl-sən\ Louise *about* 1900–1988 originally *Leah Berliavsky* American (Russian-born) sculptor
New·man \ˈnü-mən, ˈnyü-\ John Henry 1801–1890 English cardinal and author
New·ton \ˈnüt-n, ˈnyüt-\ Sir Isaac 1642–1727 English mathematician and physicist
Nich·o·las \ˈnik-ləs, -ə-ləs\ Saint *flourished* 4th century A.D. Christian bishop
Nicholas I 1796–1855 czar of Russia (1825–55)
Nicholas II 1868–1918 czar of Russia (1894–1917)
Nick·laus \ˈnik-ləs\ Jack William 1940– American golfer
Nietz·sche \ˈnē-chə, -chē\ Friedrich Wilhelm 1844–1900 German philosopher
Night·in·gale \ˈnīt-n-ˌgāl, -iŋ-\ Florence 1820–1910 *Lady of the Lamp* English nurse and philanthropist
Ni·jin·sky \nə-ˈzhin-skē, -ˈjin-\ Vas·lav \ˈvät-släf\ Fomich 1890–1950 Russian dancer
Ni·ke \ˈnī-kē\ goddess of victory in Greek mythology
Nim·itz \ˈnim-əts\ Chester William 1885–1966 American admiral
Nim·rod \ˈnim-ˌräd\ ruler and mighty hunter in the Bible
Ni·o·be \ˈnī-ə-bē, nī-ˈō-bē\ bereaved mother in Greek mythology who while weeping for her slain children is turned into a stone from which her tears continue to flow
Nix·on \ˈnik-sən\ Richard Mil·hous \ˈmil-ˌhau̇s\ 1913–1994 37th president of the U.S. (1969–74)
No·ah \ˈnō-ə\ biblical builder of the ark in which he, his family, and living creatures of every kind survive the Flood
No·bel \nō-ˈbel\ Alfred Bernhard 1833–1896 Swedish manufacturer, inventor, and philanthropist
Nor·man \ˈnȯr-mən\ Jessye 1945– American soprano
Nos·tra·da·mus \ˌnäs-trə-ˈdā-məs, ˌnōs-trə-ˈdäm-əs\ 1503–1566 *Michel de Notredame* French physician, astrologer, and seer
Nu·re·yev \nu̇-ˈrā-yəf\ Rudolf Hametovich 1938–1993 Russian dancer
Oak·ley \ˈōk-lē\ Annie 1860–1926 originally *Phoebe Anne Oakley Moses* American sharpshooter
Oba·di·ah \ˌō-bə-ˈdī-ə\ Hebrew prophet of Old Testament times
Oba·ma \ō-ˈbäm-ə\ Barack Hussein, Jr. 1961– 44th president of the U.S. (2009–); Nobel Prize winner (2009)
Ober·on \ˈō-bə-ˌrän, -rən\ king of the fairies in medieval folklore and in Shakespeare's *A Midsummer Night's Dream*
O'·Ca·sey \ō-ˈkā-sē\ Sean 1880–1964 Irish playwright
Oce·anus \ō-ˈsē-ə-nəs\ god of the great outer sea that in Greek mythology encircles the earth
O'·Con·nor \ō-ˈkän-ər\ (Mary) Flannery 1925–1964 American author
O'Connor Sandra Day 1930– American jurist
Octavian — see AUGUSTUS
Odin \ˈōd-n\ *or* **Wo·den** \ˈwōd-n\ chief god, god of war, and patron of heroes in Norse mythology
Odys·seus \ō-ˈdish-ˌüs, -ˈdis-ˌyüs, -ˈdis-ē-əs\ *or* **Ulys·ses** \yü-ˈlis-ēz\ king of Ithaca in Greek mythology who after the Greek victory in the Trojan War wanders for 10 years before reaching home
Oe·di·pus \ˈed-ə-pəs, ˈēd-\ son of the king and queen of Thebes who in Greek mythology unknowingly kills his father and marries his mother as foretold by an oracle
Of·fen·bach \ˈȯf-ən-ˌbäk, -ˌbäk\ Jacques 1819–1880 French composer
Ogle·thorpe \ˈō-gəl-ˌthȯrp\ James Edward 1696–1785 English general and founder of Georgia
O'·Keeffe \ō-ˈkēf\ Georgia 1887–1986 American painter
Olaf I Trygg·va·son \ˈō-ləf . . . ˈtrig-və-sən\ *about* 964–*about* 1000 king of Norway (995–*about* 1000)
Olaf II Har·alds·son \ˈhar-əld-sən\ *about* 995–1030 *Saint Olaf* king of Norway (1016–28)
Olav V \ˈō-ləf\ 1903–1991 king of Norway (1957–91)
Oliv·i·er \ō-ˈliv-ē-ˌā\ Laurence Kerr 1907–1989 Baron *Olivier of Brighton* British actor and director
Omar Khay·yám \ˌō-ˌmär-ˌkī-ˈäm, -ˈyäm, -ˈam, -ˈyam\ 1048–?1131 Persian poet and astronomer
O'·Neill \ō-ˈnēl\ Eugene Gladstone 1888–1953 American playwright; Nobel Prize winner (1936)
Op·pen·hei·mer \ˈäp-ənˌhī-mər\ (Julius) Robert 1904–1967 American physicist
Ores·tes \ə-ˈres-tēz, ȯ-\ son of Agamemnon and Clytemnestra who in Greek mythology avenges his father's murder by slaying his mother and her lover
Or·pheus \ˈȯr-ˌfyüs, -fē-əs\ poet and musician in Greek mythology who almost rescues his wife Eurydice from Hades by charming Pluto and Persephone with his lyre
Or·well \ˈȯr-ˌwel, -wəl\ George 1903–1950 pseudonym of *Eric Arthur Blair* English author — **Or·well·ian** \ȯr-ˈwel-ē-ən\ *adj*
Osce·o·la \ˌäs-ē-ˈō-lə, ˌō-sē-\ *about* 1804–1838 Seminole Indian chief
Osi·ris \ō-ˈsī-rəs\ god of the underworld in ancient Egyptian mythology
Otis \ˈōt-əs\ James 1725–1783 American Revolutionary statesman
Ot·to I \ˈät-ō\ 912–973 A.D. *Otto the Great* German king (936–73) and Holy Roman emperor (962–73)
Ov·id \ˈäv-əd\ 43 B.C.–17 A.D. Roman poet
Ow·en \ˈō-ən\ Robert 1771–1858 Welsh social reformer
Ow·ens \ˈō-ənz\ Jesse 1913–1980 originally *James Cleveland Owens* American track-and-field athlete
Paine \ˈpān\ Thomas 1737–1809 American (English-born) political philosopher and author
Pa·le·stri·na \ˌpal-ə-ˈstrē-nə\ Giovanni Pierluigi da *about* 1525–1594 Italian composer

Pan \ˈpan\ god of pastures, flocks, and shepherds in Greek mythology who is usually represented as part goat

Pan·da·rus \ˈpan-də-rəs\ procurer of Cressida for Troilus during the Trojan War according to medieval legend

Pan·do·ra \pan-ˈdōr-ə, -ˈdȯr-\ woman in Greek mythology who opens a box and lets loose a swarm of evils upon mankind

Pank·hurst \ˈpangk-ˌhərst\ Emmeline 1858–1928 née *Goulden* English suffragist

Par·a·cel·sus \ˌpar-ə-ˈsel-səs\ 1493–1541 *Philippus Aureolus Theophrastus Bombastus von Hohenheim* Swiss-born alchemist and physician

Par·is \ˈpar-əs\ son of Priam whose abduction of Helen of Troy leads to the Trojan War in Greek mythology

Park \ˈpärk\ Mungo 1771–1806 Scottish explorer

Park·man \ˈpärk-mən\ Francis 1823–1893 American historian

Parks \ˈpärks\ Rosa 1913–2005 née *McCauley* American civil rights activist

Par·nell \pär-ˈnel\ Charles Stewart 1846–1891 Irish nationalist

Pas·cal \pas-ˈkal, pȧs-kȧl\ Blaise 1623–1662 French mathematician and philosopher

Pas·ter·nak \ˈpas-tər-ˌnak\ Boris Leonidovich 1890–1960 Russian author; Nobel Prize winner (1958)

Pas·teur \pas-ˈtər\ Louis 1822–1895 French chemist and microbiologist

Pat·rick \ˈpa-trik\ Saint *flourished* 5th century A.D. apostle and patron saint of Ireland

Pa·tro·clus \pə-ˈtrō-kləs, -ˈträk-ləs\ warrior in Greek mythology who is slain during the Trojan War by Hector and avenged by his friend Achilles

Pat·ton \ˈpat-ⁿn\ George Smith 1885–1945 American general

Paul \ˈpȯl\ Saint *died about* 67 A.D. Christian missionary and author of several New Testament epistles — **Paul·ine** \ˈpȯ-ˌlīn\ *adj*

Paul name of 6 popes: especially **III** 1468–1549 (pope 1534–49); **V** 1552–1621 (pope 1605–21); **VI** 1897–1978 (pope 1963–78)

Paul Bun·yan \ˈpȯl-ˈbən-yən\ giant lumberjack in American folklore

Pau·ling \ˈpȯ-ling\ Linus Carl 1901–1994 American chemist; Nobel Prize winner (1954, 1962)

Pav·lov \ˈpäv-ˌlȯf, ˈpav-, -ˌlȯv\ Ivan Petrovich 1849–1936 Russian physiologist; Nobel Prize winner (1904)

Pav·lo·va \ˈpav-lə-və, pav-ˈlō-və\ Anna 1881–1931 Russian ballerina

Peale \ˈpēl\ Charles Wilson 1741–1827 and his son Rembrandt 1778–1860 American painters

Pea·ry \ˈpiər-ē\ Robert Edwin 1856–1920 American arctic explorer

Peg·a·sus \ˈpeg-ə-səs\ winged horse in Greek mythology

Pei·sis·tra·tus *or* **Pi·sis·tra·tus** \pī-ˈsis-trət-əs, pə-\ *died* 527 B.C. tyrant of Athens

Pe·ña Nie·to \ˈpān-yä-ˈnyā-tō\ Enrique 1966– president of Mexico (2012–)

Pe·nel·o·pe \pə-ˈnel-ə-pē\ wife of Odysseus who in Greek mythology waits faithfully for him during his 20 years' absence

Penn \ˈpen\ William 1644–1718 English Quaker and founder of Pennsylvania

Pepys \ˈpēps\ Samuel 1633–1703 English diarist

Per·ce·val \ˈpər-sə-vəl\ knight in Arthurian legend who wins a sight of the Holy Grail

Per·i·cles \ˈper-ə-ˌklēz\ *about* 495–429 B.C. Athenian statesman

Per·ry \ˈper-ē\ Matthew Calbraith 1794–1858 American commodore

Perry Oliver Hazard 1785–1819 American naval officer; brother of the preceding

Per·seph·o·ne \pər-ˈsef-ə-nē\ daughter of Zeus and Demeter who in Greek mythology is abducted by Pluto and made his wife and queen

Per·seus \ˈpər-ˌsüs, -sē-əs\ son of Zeus and Danaë and slayer of Medusa in Greek mythology

Per·shing \ˈpər-shing, -zhing\ John Joseph 1860–1948 American general

Pé·tain \pā-ˈta^{n}\ (Henri-) Philippe 1856–1951 French general; marshal of France; premier of Vichy France (1940–44)

Pe·ter \ˈpēt-ər\ Saint *died about* 64 A.D. *Si·mon Peter* \ˈsī-mən-\ originally *Simon* one of the 12 apostles in the Bible

Peter I 1672–1725 *Peter the Great* czar of Russia (1682–1725)

Peter the Hermit *about* 1050–1115 French preacher of the First Crusade

Pe·trarch \ˈpē-ˌträrk, ˈpe-\ 1304–1374 Italian *Francesco Pe·trarca* \pā-ˈträr-kə\ Italian poet — **Pe·trarch·an** \pē-ˈträr-kən, pe-\ *adj*

Phae·dra \ˈfē-drə\ wife of Theseus in Greek mythology who falls in love with her stepson Hippolytus

Pha·ë·thon \ˈfā-ət-ⁿn; ˈfā-ə-tən, -ˌthän\ son of Helios in Greek mythology who drives his father's sun-chariot across the sky but loses control and is struck down with a thunderbolt by Zeus

Phid·i·as \ˈfid-ē-əs\ *about* 490–430 B.C. Greek sculptor

Phil·ip \ˈfil-əp\ Saint one of the 12 apostles in the Bible

Philip King — see METACOM

Philip name of 6 kings of France: especially **II** *or* **Philip Augustus** 1165–1223 (reigned 1179–1223); **IV** 1268–1314 (reigned 1285–1314) *Philip the Fair;* **VI** 1293–1350 (reigned 1328–50)

Philip name of 5 kings of Spain: especially **II** 1527–1598 (reigned 1556–98); **V** 1683–1746 (reigned 1700–24; 1724–46)

Philip II 382–336 B.C. king of Macedonia (359–336); father of Alexander the Great

Philip Prince 1921– Duke of *Edinburgh* consort of Elizabeth II of the United Kingdom

Phoebus — see APOLLO

Pi·cas·so \pi-ˈkäs-ō, -ˈkas-\ Pablo 1881–1973 Spanish painter and sculptor in France

Pick·ett \ˈpik-ət\ George Edward 1825–1875 American Confederate general

Pierce \ˈpiərs\ Franklin 1804–1869 14th president of the U.S. (1853–57)

Pi·late Pon·tius \ˈpän-chəs, ˈpən-chəs\ *died after* 36 A.D. Roman prefect of Judea (26–36)

Pin·dar \ˈpin-dər, -ˌdär\ *about* 522–*about* 438 B.C. Greek poet

Pi·ran·del·lo \ˌpir-ən-ˈdel-ō\ Luigi 1867–1936 Italian author; Nobel Prize winner (1934)

Pitt \ˈpit\ William 1708–1778 Earl of *Chatham; the Elder Pitt* British statesman

Pitt William 1759–1806 *the Younger Pitt* British prime minister (1783–1801; 1804–6); son of the preceding

Pi·us \ˈpī-əs\ name of 12 popes: especially **VII** 1742–1823 (pope 1800–23); **IX** 1792–1878 (pope 1846–78); **X** Saint 1835–1914 (pope 1903–14); **XI** 1857–1939 (pope 1922–39); **XII** 1876–1958 (pope 1939–58)

Pi·zar·ro \pə-ˈzär-ō\ Francisco *about* 1475–1541 Spanish conqueror of Peru

Planck \ˈplängk\ Max (Karl Ernst Ludwig) 1858–1947 German physicist; Nobel Prize winner (1918)

Pla·to \ˈplāt-ō\ *about* 428–348 (or 347) B.C. Greek philosopher

Plau·tus \ˈplȯt-əs\ *about* 254–184 B.C. Roman playwright

Pliny the Elder \ˈplin-ē\ 23–79 A.D. Roman scholar

Pliny the Younger 61 (or 62)–*about* 113 A.D. Roman author; nephew of the preceding

Plu·tarch \ˈplü-ˌtärk\ *about* 46–*after* 119 A.D. Greek biographer

Plu·to \ˈplüt-ō\ god of the underworld in Greek mythology — compare DIS

Po·ca·hon·tas \ˌpō-kə-ˈhänt-əs\ *about* 1595–1617 American Indian friend to the colonists at Jamestown; daughter of Powhatan

Poe \ˈpō\ Edgar Allan 1809–1849 American author

Polk \ˈpōk\ James Knox 1795–1849 11th president of the U.S. (1845–49)

Pol·lock \ˈpäl-ək\ Jackson 1912–1956 American painter

Pol·lux \ˈpäl-əks\ immortal twin of Castor in classical mythology

Po·lo \ˈpō-lō\ Mar·co \ˈmär-kō\ *about* 1254–1324 Venetian merchant and traveler

Pol·y·hym·nia \ˌpäl-i-ˈhim-nē-ə\ Muse of sacred song in Greek mythology

Poly·phe·mus \ˌpäl-ə-ˈfē-məs\ Cyclops in Greek mythology whom Odysseus blinds in order to escape from his cave

Pom·pa·dour \ˈpäm-pə-ˌdōr, -ˌdȯr, -ˌdu̇r\ Madame de 1721–1764 *Jeanne-Antoinette Poisson* mistress of Louis XV of France

Pom·pey the Great \ˈpäm-pē\ 106–48 B.C. Roman general and statesman

Ponce de Le·ón \ˌpäns-də-ˈlē-ən, ˌpän-sə-ˌdā-lē-ˈōn\ Juan 1460–1521 Spanish explorer of Florida (1513)

Pon·ti·ac \ˈpänt-ē-ˌak\ *about* 1720–1769 Ottawa Indian chief

\ə\ **abut**	\au̇\ **out**	\i\ **tip**	\ȯ\ **saw**	\u̇\ **foot**
\ər\ **further**	\ch\ **chin**	\ī\ **life**	\ȯi\ **coin**	\y\ **yet**
\a\ **mat**	\e\ **pet**	\j\ **job**	\th\ **thin**	\yü\ **few**
\ā\ **take**	\ē\ **easy**	\ng\ **sing**	\t͟h\ **this**	\yu̇\ **cure**
\ä\ **cot, cart**	\g\ **go**	\ō\ **bone**	\ü\ **food**	\zh\ **vision**

Pon·tius Pi·late — see PILATE
Pope \ˈpōp\ Alexander 1688–1744 English poet
Por·ter \ˈpōrt-ər, ˈpȯrt-\ Cole Albert 1891–1964 American composer and songwriter
Porter Katherine Anne 1890–1980 American author
Porter William Sydney — see O. HENRY
Po·sei·don \pə-ˈsīd-n\ god of the sea in Greek mythology — compare NEPTUNE
Pot·ter \ˈpät-ər\ (Helen) Beatrix 1866–1943 British author and illustrator
Pound \ˈpau̇nd\ Ezra Loomis 1885–1972 American poet
Pound·mak·er \ˈpau̇nd-ˌmā-kər\ 1826–1886 Cree Indian chief
Pow·ell \ˈpau̇-əl\ Adam Clayton, Jr. 1908–1972 American clergyman and politician
Powell Colin Luther 1937– American general; U.S. secretary of state (2001–05)
Powell John Wesley 1834–1902 American geologist and explorer
Pow·ha·tan \ˌpau̇-ə-ˈtan, pau̇-ˈhat-n\ 1550?–1618 American Indian chief; father of Pocahontas
Prax·it·e·les \prak-ˈsit-l-ˌēz\ *flourished* 370–330 B.C. Athenian sculptor
Pres·ley \ˈpres-lē, ˈprez-\ Elvis Aaron 1935–1977 American popular singer
Pri·am \ˈprī-əm, -ˌam\ king of Troy during the Trojan War and father of Hector and Paris in Greek mythology
Price \ˈprīs\ (Mary) Leontyne 1927– American soprano
Priest·ley \ˈprēst-lē\ Joseph 1733–1804 English clergyman and chemist
Pro·crus·tes \prə-ˈkrəs-tēz, pə-, prō-\ robber in Greek mythology who forces travelers to fit one of two unequally long beds by stretching their bodies or cutting off their legs
Pro·kof·iev \prə-ˈkȯf-yəf, -ˌyef, -ˌyev\ Sergey Sergeyevich 1891–1953 Russian composer
Pro·me·theus \prə-ˈme-thyüs, -thüs, -thē-əs\ Titan in Greek mythology whom Zeus tortures for giving fire to humans
Pro·tag·o·ras \prō-ˈtag-ə-rəs\ *about* 485–410 B.C. Greek philosopher and teacher
Pro·teus \ˈprō-ˌtyüs, -ˌtüs; ˈprōt-ē-əs\ sea god in Greek mythology capable of assuming different forms
Proust \ˈprüst\ Marcel 1871–1922 French novelist
Psy·che \ˈsī-kē\ princess in mythology loved by Cupid
Ptol·e·my \ˈtäl-ə-mē\ name of 15 kings of Egypt 323–30 B.C.
Ptolemy *flourished* 2nd century A.D. Greco-Egyptian astronomer, geographer, and mathematician in Alexandria
Puc·ci·ni \pü-ˈchē-nē\ Giacomo 1858–1924 Italian composer
Puck — see ROBIN GOODFELLOW
Pu·łas·ki \pə-ˈlas-kē, pyü-\ Kazimierz 1747–1779 Polish soldier in American Revolutionary army
Pu·lit·zer \ˈpu̇l-ət-sər, ˈpyü-lət-sər\ Joseph 1847–1911 American (Hungarian-born) journalist
Push·kin \ˈpu̇sh-kən\ Aleksandr Sergeyevich 1799–1837 Russian author
Pu·tin \ˈpüt-in\ Vladimir Vladimirovich 1952– president of Russia (2000–08); prime minister (2008–12); president (2012–)
Pyg·ma·lion \pig-ˈmāl-yən, -ˈmā-lē-ən\ sculptor in Greek mythology who creates Galatea
Pyr·a·mus \ˈpir-ə-məs\ legendary Babylonian youth who dies for the love of Thisbe
Py·thag·o·ras \pə-ˈthag-ə-rəs, pī-\ *about* 580–*about* 500 B.C. Greek philosopher and mathematician
Pyth·i·as \ˈpith-ē-əs\ condemned man in Greek legend whose life is spared when his friend Damon offers to take his place
Quin·til·ian \kwin-ˈtil-yən\ *about* 35–*about* 100 A.D. Roman rhetorician
Ra \ˈrä, ˈrȯ\ god of the sun and chief deity of ancient Egypt
Ra·be·lais \ˈrab-ə-ˌlā, ˌrab-ə-ˈlā\ François *about* 1483–1553 French author
Ra·bin \rä-ˈbēn\ Yitzhak 1922–1995 prime minister of Israel (1974–77; 1992–95); Nobel Prize winner (1994)
Ra·chel \ˈrā-chəl\ one of the wives of Jacob in the Bible
Rach·ma·ni·noff \räk-ˈmän-ə-ˌnȯf, rak-ˈman-, -ˌnȯv\ Sergey Vasilyevich 1873–1943 Russian composer and pianist
Ra·cine \ra-ˈsēn, rə-\ Jean (-Baptiste) 1639–1699 French playwright
Ra·leigh *or* **Ra·legh** \ˈrȯl-ē, ˈräl- *also* ˈral-\ Sir Walter 1554?–1618 English navigator, courtier, and writer
Ra·ma \ˈräm-ə\ deity or deified hero of later Hinduism worshiped as an incarnation of Vishnu
Ram·say \ˈram-zē\ Sir William 1852–1916 British chemist; Nobel Prize winner (1904)
Ram·ses \ˈram-ˌsēz\ *or* **Ram·e·ses** \ˈram-ə-ˌsēz\ name of 11 kings of Egypt: especially **II** (reigned 1279–1213 B.C.); **III** (reigned 1187–1156 B.C.)
Ran·dolph \ˈran-ˌdȯlf\ Asa Philip 1889–1979 American labor and civil rights leader
Ra·pha·el \ˈraf-ē-əl, ˈrā-fē-\ one of the four archangels named in Hebrew tradition — compare GABRIEL, MICHAEL, URIEL
Ra·pha·el \ˈraf-ē-əl, ˈrā-fē-, ˈräf-ē-\ 1483–1520 originally *Raffaello Sanzio* or *Santi* Italian painter
Ras·pu·tin \ra-ˈspyüt-n, -ˈspüt-, -ˈspu̇t-\ Grigory Yefimovich 1872–1916 Russian mystic
Ra·vel \rə-ˈvel, ra-\ (Joseph) Mau·rice \mȯ-ˈrēs\ 1875–1937 French composer
Rea·gan \ˈrā-gən, ˈrē-\ Ronald Wilson 1911–2004 40th president of the U.S. (1981–89)
Re·bek·ah \ri-ˈbek-ə\ wife of Isaac and mother of Jacob in the Bible
Red Cloud \ˈred-ˌklau̇d\ 1822–1909 Sioux Indian chief
Red Jack·et \ˈred-ˌjak-ət\ 1758?–1830 *Sagoyewatha* Seneca Indian chief
Reed \ˈrēd\ Walter 1851–1902 American army surgeon
Rehn·quist \ˈren-ˌkwist\ William Hubbs 1924–2005 American jurist; chief justice U.S. Supreme Court (1986–2005)
Re·marque \rə-ˈmärk\ Erich Maria 1898–1970 American (German-born) author
Rem·brandt \ˈrem-ˌbrant\ 1606–1669 *Rembrandt (Harmenszoon) van Rijn* Dutch painter
Rem·ing·ton \ˈrem-ing-tən\ Frederic 1861–1909 American painter and sculptor
Re·mus \ˈrē-məs\ legendary founder of Rome killed by his twin brother Romulus
Re·noir \ren-ˈwär, ˈren-ˌwär\ (Pierre-) Auguste 1841–1919 French painter
Re·vere \ri-ˈviər\ Paul 1735–1818 American patriot and silversmith
Reyn·olds \ˈren-ldz, -lz\ Sir Joshua 1723–1792 English painter
Rhodes \ˈrōdz\ Cecil John 1853–1902 British administrator and financier in South Africa
Rich·ard \ˈrich-ərd\ name of 3 kings of England: **I** 1157–1199 *Richard the Lion-Hearted* (reigned 1189–99); **II** 1367–1400 (reigned 1377–99); **III** 1452–1485 (reigned 1483–85)
Rich·ard·son \ˈrich-ərd-sən\ Samuel 1689–1761 English author
Ri·che·lieu \ˈrish-əl-ˌü, -ˌyü; rē-shə-ˈlyœ\ Duc de 1585–1642 originally *Armand-Jean du Plessis* French cardinal and statesman
Ride \ˈrīd\ Sally Kristen 1951–2012 American astronaut; first American woman in space
Rim·sky–Kor·sa·kov \ˌrim-skē-ˈkȯr-sə-ˌkȯf, -ˌkȯv, -ˌkȯr-sə-ˈ\ Nikolay Andreyevich 1844–1908 Russian composer
Ri·ve·ra \ri-ˈver-ə\ Diego 1886–1957 Mexican painter
Rob·ert I \ˈräb-ərt\ 1274–1329 *Robert the Bruce* \ˈbrüs\ king of Scotland (1306–29)
Rob·erts \ˈräb-ərts\ John Glover, Jr. 1955– American jurist; chief justice U.S. Supreme Court (2005–)
Robe·son \ˈrōb-sən\ Paul Bustill 1898–1976 American actor and singer
Robes·pierre \ˈrōbz-ˌpiər, -ˌpyeər; ˌrō-ˌbes-ˈpyeər\ Maximilien (-François-Marie-Isidore) de 1758–1794 French revolutionary
Rob·in Good·fel·low \ˌräb-ən-ˈgu̇d-ˌfel-ō\ *or* **Puck** \ˈpək\ mischievous sprite in English folklore
Rob·in Hood \ˌräb-ən-ˈhu̇d\ legendary English outlaw noted for his skill in archery and for his robbing the rich to help poor
Rob·in·son \ˈräb-ən-sən\ Edwin Arlington 1869–1935 American poet
Robinson Jackie 1919–1972 *Jack Roosevelt Robinson* American baseball player; 1st black player in the major leagues (1947–56)
Ro·cham·beau \ˌrō-ˌsham-ˈbō\ Comte de 1725–1807 originally *Jean-Baptiste-Donatien de Vimeur* French general in American Revolution
Rocke·fel·ler \ˈräk-i-ˌfel-ər, ˈräk-ˌfel-\ John Davison 1839–1937 and his son John Davison, Jr. 1874–1960 American oil magnates and philanthropists
Rod·gers \ˈräj-ərz\ Richard 1902–1979 American musical theater composer
Ro·din \ˈrō-ˌdaⁿ, -ˌdaⁿn\ (François-) Auguste (-René) 1840–1917 French sculptor
Roeb·ling \ˈrō-bling\ John Augustus 1806–1869 and his son

Washington 1837–1926 American civil engineers and designers of the Brooklyn Bridge

Rog•ers \ˈräj-ərz\ Will 1879–1935 *William Penn Adair Rogers* American actor and humorist

Ro•land \ˈrō-lənd\ stalwart defender of the Christians against the Saracens in the Charlemagne legends

Röl•vaag \ˈrōl-ˌväg\ Ole \ˈō-lə\ Ed•vart \ˈed-ˌvärt\ 1876–1931 American (Norwegian-born) educator and author

Ro•ma•nov \rō-ˈmän-əf, ˈrō-mə-ˌnäf\ Michael 1596–1645 1st czar (1613–45) of Russian Romanov dynasty (1613–1917)

Rom•mel \ˈräm-əl\ Erwin 1891–1944 German field marshal

Rom•u•lus \ˈräm-yə-ləs\ legendary founder of Rome who killed his twin brother Remus

Rönt•gen *or* **Roent•gen** \ˈrent-gən, ˈrənt-, -jən\ Wilhelm Conrad 1845–1923 German physicist; Nobel Prize winner (1901)

Roo•se•velt \ˈrō-zə-vəlt *(Roosevelts' usual pronunciation)*, -ˌvelt *also* ˈrü-\ (Anna) Eleanor 1884–1962 American humanitarian and writer; wife of Franklin Delano Roosevelt

Roosevelt Franklin Del•a•no \ˈdel-ə-ˌnō\ 1882–1945 32nd president of the U.S. (1933–45)

Roosevelt Theodore 1858–1919 26th president of the U.S. (1901–09); Nobel Prize winner (1906)

Root \ˈrüt, ˈru̇t\ Elihu 1845–1937 American lawyer and statesman; Nobel Prize winner (1912)

Ross \ˈrȯs\ Betsy 1752–1836 née *Griscom* reputed maker of 1st American flag

Ros•set•ti \rō-ˈzet-ē, -ˈset-\ Christina Georgina 1830–1894 English poet; sister of Dante Gabriel Rossetti

Rossetti Dante Gabriel 1828–1882 English painter and poet

Ros•si•ni \rō-ˈsē-nē, rə-\ Gioacchino Antonio 1792–1868 Italian composer

Ros•tand \rȯ-ˈstä^{n}, ˈräs-ˌtand\ Edmond 1868–1918 French playwright

Roth•schild \ˈrȯths-ˌchīld, ˈrȯth-, ˈrȯs-; *German* ˈrōt-ˌshilt\ Mayer Amschel 1744–1812 German financier

Rothschild Nathan Mayer 1777–1836 German financier in London; son of the preceding

Rous•seau \ru̇-ˈsō, ˈrü-ˌ\ Jean-Jacques 1712–1778 French (Swiss-born) philosopher and author

Row•ling \ˈrō-ling\ J. K. 1965– *Joanne Kathleen Rowling* British author

Ru•bens \ˈrü-bənz\ Peter Paul 1577–1640 Flemish painter

Ru•bin•stein \ˈrü-bən-ˌstīn\ An•ton \än-ˈtȯn\ Grigoryevich 1829–1894 Russian pianist and composer

Ru•dolph \ˈrü-ˌdȯlf\ Wilma Glodean 1940–1994 American athlete

Ru•pert \ˈrü-pərt\ Prince 1619–1682 English (German-born) royalist general and admiral

Rus•kin \ˈrəs-kən\ John 1819–1900 English art critic

Rus•sell \ˈrəs-əl\ Bertrand Arthur William 1872–1970 3rd Earl *Russell* English mathematician and philosopher; Nobel Prize winner (1950)

Russell Bill 1934– *William Felton Russell* American basketball player

Ruth \ˈrüth\ Moabite ancestor of King David in the Bible

Ruth Babe 1895–1948 *George Herman Ruth* American baseball player

Ruth•er•ford \ˈrə<u>th</u>-ər-fərd, ˈrə<u>th</u>-ə-, ˈrəth-\ Ernest 1871–1937 Baron *Rutherford* British physicist; Nobel Prize winner (1908)

Sa•bin \ˈsā-bin\ Albert Bruce 1906–1993 American (Polish-born) physician and microbiologist

Sac•a•ga•wea \ˌsak-ə-jə-ˈwē-ə\ 1786?–1812 Shoshone Indian guide to Lewis and Clark

Sā•dāt, \sə-ˈdat, -ˈdät\ (Muhammad) Anwar el- 1918–1981 president of Egypt (1970–81); Nobel Prize winner (1978)

Sa•gan \ˈsā-gən\ Carl Edward 1934–1996 American astronomer and science writer

Saint–Gau•dens \sānt-ˈgȯd-nz, sənt-\ Augustus 1848–1907 American (Irish-born) sculptor

Saint–Saëns \sa^{n}-ˈsä^{n}s\ (Charles-) Camille 1835–1921 French composer

Sal•a•din \ˈsal-əd-ən, ˌsal-ə-ˈdēn\ 1137 (or 1138)–1193 sultan of Egypt and Syria

Sal•in•ger \ˈsal-ən-jər\ J. D. 1919–2010 *Jerome David Salinger* American author

Salk \ˈsȯk, ˈsȯlk\ Jonas Edward 1914–1995 American physician and medical researcher

Sa•lo•me \sə-ˈlō-mē\ niece of Herod Antipas who in the Bible is given the head of John the Baptist as a reward for her dancing

Sa•mo•set \ˈsam-ə-ˌset, sə-ˈmäs-ət\ *died about* 1653 American Indian leader and friend of the Pilgrims

Sam•son \ˈsam-sən, ˈsamp-\ Hebrew hero in the Bible who wreaks havoc among the Philistines but is betrayed by Delilah

Sam•u•el \ˈsam-yəl, -yə-wəl\ Hebrew judge in the Bible who anoints Saul and then David king

Sand \ˈsand, ˈsä^{n}d, ˈsä^{n}nd, ˈsä^{n}\ George 1804–1876 pseudonym of *Amandin-Aurore-Lucie Dudevant* née *Dupin* French author

Sand•burg \ˈsand-ˌbərg, ˈsan-\ Carl 1878–1967 American author

Sang•er \ˈsang-ər\ Margaret 1883–1966 née *Higgins* American birth-control leader

San•ta Claus \ˈsant-ə-ˌklȯz, -ˌklȯs\ plump white-bearded and red-suited old man of modern folklore who delivers presents to good children at Christmastime

Sap•pho \ˈsaf-ō\ *flourished about* 610–*about* 580 B.C. Greek poet

Sa•rah \ˈser-ə, ˈsar-ə, ˈsā-rə\ wife of Abraham and mother of Isaac in the Bible

Sar•gent \ˈsär-jənt\ John Singer 1856–1925 American painter

Sar•ko•zy \ˌsär-kō-ˈzē\ Nicolas (Paul Stéphane) 1955– president of France (2007–12)

Sar•tre \ˈsärtr\ Jean-Paul 1905–1980 French philosopher and author

Sat•urn \ˈsat-ərn\ god of agriculture in Roman mythology

Saul \ˈsȯl\ 1st king of Israel in the Bible

Saul *or* **Saul of Tarsus** the apostle Paul

Sa•vo•na•ro•la \ˌsav-ə-nə-ˈrō-lə, sə-ˌvän-ə-ˈrō-\ Gi•ro•la•mo \ji-ˈrȯl-ə-ˌmō\ 1452–1498 Italian friar and reformer

Scar•lat•ti \skär-ˈlät-ē\ (Pietro) Alessandro 1660–1725 and his son (Giuseppe) Domenico 1685–1757 Italian composers

Sche•her•a•zade \shə-ˌher-ə-ˈzäd, -ˈzäd-ə, -ˈzäd-ē\ fictional sultana who narrates the tales in the *Arabian Nights' Entertainments*

Schil•ler \ˈshil-ər\ (Johann Christoph) Friedrich von 1759–1805 German poet and playwright

Schin•dler \ˈshind-lər\ Oskar 1908–1974 German humanitarian

Schoen•berg \ˈshərn-ˌbərg, ˈshœ̄n-ˌberk\ Arnold Franz Walter 1874–1951 American (Austrian-born) composer

Scho•pen•hau•er \ˈshō-pən-ˌhau̇-ər, -ˌhau̇r\ Arthur 1788–1860 German philosopher

Schu•bert \ˈshü-bərt, -ˌbert\ Franz Peter 1797–1828 Austrian composer

Schu•mann \ˈshü-ˌmän, -mən\ Robert Alexander 1810–1856 German composer

Schweit•zer \ˈshwīt-sər, ˈswīt-, ˈshvīt-\ Albert 1875–1965 French theologian, philosopher, physician, and music scholar; Nobel Prize winner (1952)

Scip•io Ae•mil•i•a•nus Af•ri•ca•nus Nu•man•ti•nus \ˈsip-ē-ˌō-i-ˌmil-ē-ˈā-nəs-ˌaf-rə-ˈkan-əs-ˌnü-mən-ˈtē-nəs, -ˌnyü-\ Publius Cornelius 185 (or 184)–129 B.C. *Scipio Africanus the Younger* Roman general; adopted grandson of Scipio Africanus the Elder

Scipio Africanus Publius Cornelius 236–184 (or 183) B.C. *Scipio Africanus the Elder* Roman general

Scott \ˈskät\ Dred \ˈdred\ 1795?–1858 American slave

Scott Robert Falcon 1868–1912 British polar explorer

Scott Sir Walter 1771–1832 Scottish author

Scott Winfield 1786–1866 American general

Seaborg \ˈsē-ˌbȯrg\ Glenn Theodore 1912–1999 American chemist; Nobel Prize winner (1951)

Se•at•tle *or* **Se•atlh** \sē-ˈat-l\ 1786?–1866 American Indian chief

See•ger \ˈsē-gər\ Peter 1919–2014 *Pete Seeger* American folksinger

Se•le•ne \sə-ˈlē-nē, -nə\ goddess of the moon in classical mythology

Se•leu•cus I Ni•ca•tor \sə-ˈlü-kəs-nī-ˈkāt-ər\ 358 (*or* 354)–281 B.C. Macedonian general and ruler (306–281) of an empire centering on Syria and Iran; founder of the Seleucid dynasty

Sen•e•ca \ˈsen-i-kə\ Lucius Annaeus 4 B.C.?–65 A.D. Roman philosopher, statesman, and playwright

Sen•nach•er•ib \sə-ˈnak-ə-rəb\ *died* 681 B.C. king of Assyria (704–681)

Se•quoyah *or* **Se•quoia** \si-ˈkwȯi-ə\ *about* 1760–1843 *George Guess* Cherokee Indian scholar

\ə\ **abut**	\au̇\ **out**	\i\ **tip**	\ȯ\ **saw**	\u̇\ **foot**
\ər\ **further**	\ch\ **chin**	\ī\ **life**	\ȯi\ **coin**	\y\ **yet**
\a\ **mat**	\e\ **pet**	\j\ **job**	\th\ **thin**	\yü\ **few**
\ā\ **take**	\ē\ **easy**	\ng\ **sing**	\<u>th</u>\ **this**	\yu̇\ **cure**
\ä\ **cot, cart**	\g\ **go**	\ō\ **bone**	\ü\ **food**	\zh\ **vision**

Ser·ra \ˈser-ə\ Junipero 1713–1784 Spanish missionary in Mexico and California

Se·ton \ˈsēt-n\ Saint Elizabeth Ann 1774–1821 *Mother Seton* née *Bayley* American religious leader

Seu·rat \sə-ˈrä\ Georges 1859–1891 French painter

Sew·ard \ˈsü-ərd, ˈsu̇-ərd, ˈsu̇rd\ William Henry 1801–1872 American statesman; U.S. secretary of state (1861–69)

Shack·le·ton \ˈshak-əl-tən\ Sir Ernest Henry 1874–1922 British polar explorer

Shake·speare \ˈshāk-ˌspiər\ William 1564–1616 English playwright and poet

Shaw \ˈshȯ\ George Bernard 1856–1950 British playwright; Nobel Prize winner (1925)

Shaw Robert Gould 1837–1863 American soldier

Shel·ley \ˈshel-ē\ Mary Woll·stone·craft \ˈwu̇l-stən-ˌkraft\ 1797–1851 née *Godwin* English novelist; wife of Percy Bysshe Shelley

Shelley Percy Bysshe \ˈbish\ 1792–1822 English poet

Shem \ˈshem\ eldest son of Noah and ancestor of the Semitic peoples in biblical tradition

Shep·ard \ˈshep-ərd\ Alan Bartlett, Jr. 1923–1998 American astronaut; 1st American in space (1961)

Sher·i·dan \ˈsher-əd-n\ Philip Henry 1831–1888 American general

Sheridan Richard Brins·ley \ˈbrinz-lē\ 1751–1816 British playwright

Sher·man \ˈshər-mən\ John 1823–1900 American statesman; brother of William Tecumseh Sherman

Sherman William Tecumseh 1820–1891 American general

Shi·va \ˈshiv-ə, ˈshē-və\ *or* **Si·va** \ˈshiv-ə, ˈsiv-; ˈshē-və, ˈsē-\ god of destruction and regeneration in the Hindu sacred triad — compare BRAHMA, VISHNU

Sho·sta·ko·vich \ˌshäs-tə-ˈkō-vich\ Dmitri Dmitrievich 1906–1975 Russian composer

Si·be·lius \sə-ˈbāl-yəs, -ˈbā-lē-əs\ Jean 1865–1957 Finnish composer

Sid·ney \ˈsid-nē\ Sir Philip 1554–1586 English poet

Sieg·fried \ˈsig-ˌfrēd, ˈsēg-\ *or* **Sig·urd** \ˈsig-u̇rd, -ərd\ hero in Germanic legend who slays a dragon guarding a gold hoard

Si·kor·sky \sə-ˈkȯr-skē\ Igor Ivan 1889–1972 American (Russian-born) aeronautical engineer

Si·mon \ˈsī-mən\ — see PETER

Simon *or* **Simon the Zealot** one of the 12 apostles in the Bible

Si·na·tra \sə-ˈnät-rə\ Frank 1915–1998 *Francis Albert Sinatra* American singer and actor

Sind·bad the Sailor \ˈsin-ˌbad-\ citizen of Baghdad whose adventures are narrated in the *Arabian Nights' Entertainments*

Sing·er \ˈsiŋ-ər\ Isaac Bashevis 1904–1991 American (Polish-born) author

Sis·y·phus \ˈsis-i-fəs\ king of Corinth in Greek mythology condemned to roll a heavy stone up a hill in Hades only to have it roll down again as it nears the top — **Sis·y·phe·an** \ˌsis-i-ˈfē-ən\ *adj*

Sit·ting Bull \ˌsit-iŋ-ˈbu̇l\ *about* 1831–1890 Sioux Indian chief

Smith \ˈsmith\ Adam 1723–1790 Scottish economist

Smith Bessie 1894?–1937 American blues singer

Smith John *about* 1580–1631 English colonist in America

Smith Joseph 1805–1844 American founder of the Mormon Church

Smol·lett \ˈsmäl-ət\ Tobias George 1721–1771 British author

Snead \ˈsnēd\ Sam 1912–2002 *Samuel Jackson Snead* American golfer

Soc·ra·tes \ˈsäk-rə-ˌtēz\ *about* 470–399 B.C. Greek philosopher

Sol \ˈsäl\ god of the sun in Roman mythology — compare HELIOS

Sol·o·mon \ˈsäl-ə-mən\ son of David and 10th century B.C. king of Israel noted for his wisdom

Sol·zhe·ni·tsyn \ˌsōl-zhə-ˈnēt-sən\ Aleksandr Isayevich 1918–2008 Russian author; Nobel Prize winner (1970)

Soph·o·cles \ˈsäf-ə-ˌklēz\ *about* 496–406 B.C. Greek playwright

Sou·sa \ˈsü-zə, ˈsü-sə\ John Philip 1854–1932 American bandmaster and composer

Spar·ta·cus \ˈspärt-ə-kəs\ *died* 71 B.C. Roman slave and gladiator; leader of a slave rebellion

Spen·ser \ˈspen-sər\ Edmund 1552 (*or* 1553)–1599 English poet

Spiel·berg \ˈspēl-bərg\ Steven 1947– American filmmaker

Spi·no·za \spin-ˈō-zə\ Benedict de 1632–1677 *Baruch Spinoza* Dutch philosopher of Portuguese-Jewish ancestry

Squan·to \ˈskwän-tō, ˈskwȯn-\ *died* 1622 American Indian friend of the Pilgrims

Sta·lin \ˈstäl-ən, ˈstal-, -ˌēn\ Joseph 1879–1953 originally *Iosif Vissarionovich Dzhu·gash·vi·li* \ˌjü-gəsh-ˈvē-lē\ Soviet Communist Party leader (1922–53), premier (1941–53), and dictator

Stan·dish \ˈstan-dish\ Myles *or* Miles 1584?–1656 English colonist in America

Stan·ley \ˈstan-lē\ Sir Henry Morton 1841–1904 British explorer

Stan·ton \ˈstant-n\ Elizabeth Cady 1815–1902 née *Cady* American suffragist

Steele \ˈstēl\ Sir Richard 1672–1729 English author

Stein \ˈstīn\ Gertrude 1874–1946 American author

Stein·beck \ˈstīn-ˌbek\ John Ernst 1902–1968 American author; Nobel Prize winner (1962)

Sten·dhal \sten-ˈdäl, stan-, *French* sta^{n}-ˈdȧl\ 1783–1842 pseudonym of *Marie-Henri Beyle* \ˈbel\ French author

Ste·phen \ˈstē-vən\ Saint *died about* 36 A.D. Christian martyr

Stephen *about* 1097–1154 *Stephen of Blois* king of England (1135–54)

Sterne \ˈstərn\ Laurence 1713–1768 English author

Steu·ben \ˈstü-bən, ˈstyü-, ˈshtȯi-\ Friedrich Wilhelm 1730–1794 Prussian-born general in American Revolutionary army

Ste·ven·son \ˈstē-vən-sən\ Adlai Ewing 1900–1965 American politician

Stevenson Robert Louis Balfour 1850–1894 Scottish author

Sto·ker \ˈstō-kər\ Bram 1847–1912 *Abraham Stoker* Irish author

Stowe \ˈstō\ Harriet Beecher 1811–1896 née *Beecher* American author

Stra·di·va·ri \ˌstrad-ə-ˈvär-ē, -ˈvar-, -ˈver-\ Antonio 1644?–1737 Italian violin maker

Strauss \ˈstrau̇s, ˈshtrau̇s\ Johann 1804–1849 and his sons Johann, Jr. 1825–1899 and Josef 1827–1870 Austrian composers

Strauss Ri·chard \ˈrik-ˌärt, ˈrik-\ 1864–1949 German composer

Stra·vin·sky \strə-ˈvin-skē\ Igor \ˈē-ˌgȯr\ Fyodorovich 1882–1971 American (Russian-born) composer

Stu·art \ˈstü-ərt, ˈstyü-, ˈstyu̇-, ˈstyu̇rt\ Charles Edward 1720–1788 *the Young Pretender; Bonnie Prince Charlie* claimant to the British throne; son of James Edward Stuart

Stuart Gilbert Charles 1755–1828 American painter

Stuart James Edward 1688–1766 *the Old Pretender* claimant to the British throne; son of James II

Stuart Jeb 1833–1864 *James Ewell Brown Stuart* American Confederate general

Stuy·ve·sant \ˈstī-və-sənt\ Peter *about* 1610–1672 Dutch colonial administrator in America

Sue·to·ni·us \swē-ˈtō-nē-əs, sü-ə-ˈtō-\ *about* 69–*after* 122 A.D. Roman biographer and historian

Sü·ley·man \ˈsü-lā-ˌmän, -li-\ 1494 (or 1495)–1566 *Süleyman the Magnificent* sultan of the Ottoman Empire (1520–66)

Sul·la \ˈsəl-ə\ 138–78 B.C. Roman general and statesman

Sul·li·van \ˈsəl-ə-vən\ Sir Arthur Seymour 1842–1900 English composer and collaborator with Sir William S. Gilbert

Sullivan Louis Henri 1856–1924 American architect

Sum·ner \ˈsəm-nər\ Charles 1811–1874 American statesman

Sun Yat–sen \ˈsu̇n-ˈyät-ˈsen\ 1866–1925 Chinese statesman

Swift \ˈswift\ Jonathan 1667–1745 English (Irish-born) author

Swin·burne \ˈswin-ˌbərn, -bərn\ Algernon Charles 1837–1909 English poet

Tac·i·tus \ˈtas-ət-əs\ Cornelius *about* 56–*about* 120 A.D. Roman historian

Taft \ˈtaft\ William Howard 1857–1930 27th president of the U.S. (1909–13); chief justice of the U.S. Supreme Court (1921–30)

Ta·gore \tə-ˈgȯr\ Ra·bin·dra·nath \rə-ˈbin-drə-ˌnät\ 1861–1941 Indian poet; Nobel Prize winner (1913)

Tall·chief \ˈtȯl-ˌchēf\ Maria 1925–2013 American dancer

Tal·ley·rand (–Pé·ri·gord) \ˈtal-ē-ˌrand(-ˌper-ə-ˈgȯr), -ˌran-, *French* tȧl-e-ˈrä^{n}-, tȧl-ˈrä^{n}-\ Charles-Maurice de 1754–1838 French statesman

Tam·er·lane — see TIMUR

Tan \ˈtan\ Amy 1952– American author

Tan·cred \ˈtaŋ-krəd\ 1078?–1112 Norman crusader

Ta·ney \ˈtȯ-nē\ Roger Brooke 1777–1864 American jurist; chief justice of the U.S. Supreme Court (1836–64)

Tan·ta·lus \ˈtant-l-əs\ king in Greek mythology condemned to stand up to his chin in a pool of water in Hades and beneath fruit-laden boughs only to have the water or fruit recede at each attempt to eat or drink

Tay·lor \ˈtā-lər\ Zachary 1784–1850 American general; 12th president of the U.S. (1849–50)

Tchai·kov·sky \chī-ˈkȯf-skē, chə-, -ˈkȯv-\ Pyotr Ilich 1840–1893 Russian composer

Te·cum·seh \tə-ˈkəm-sə, -ˈkəmp-, -sē\ 1768–1813 Shawnee Indian chief

Tek·a·kwitha \ˌtek-ə-ˈkwith-ə\ Ka·teri \ˈkät-ə-rē\ 1656–1680 *Lily of the Mohawks* beatified Mohawk Indian religious

Te·lem·a·chus \tə-ˈlem-ə-kəs\ son of Odysseus and Penelope who aids his father in the slaying of his mother's suitors

Ten·ny·son \ˈten-ə-sən\ Alfred 1809–1892 Baron *Tennyson* known as *Alfred, Lord Tennyson* English poet

Ter·ence \ˈter-əns\ *about* 195–159? B.C. Roman playwright

Te·re·sa \tə-ˈrē-sə, -ˈrā-\ Mother 1910–1997 beatified Albanian religious in India; Nobel Prize winner (1979)

Te·re·sa of Avi·la \tə-ˈrē-sə, -ˈrā-sə, -ˈrā-zə . . . ˈäv-ē-ˌlä\ Saint 1515–1582 Spanish Carmelite nun and mystic

Terp·sich·o·re \ˌtərp-ˈsik-ə-rē\ Muse of dancing and choral song in Greek mythology

Tes·la \ˈtes-lə\ Nikola 1856–1943 American (Croatian-born) electrical engineer and inventor

Thack·er·ay \ˈthak-rē, -ə-rē\ William Makepeace 1811–1863 English author

Tha·les \ˈthā-ˌlēz\ *flourished* 6th century B.C. Greek philosopher

Tha·lia \thə-ˈlī-ə\ Muse of comedy in Greek mythology

Thatch·er \ˈthach-ər\ Margaret Hilda 1925–2013 Baroness *Roberts of Kesteven née Roberts* British prime minister (1979–90)

The·mis·to·cles \thə-ˈmis-tə-ˌklēz\ *about* 524–*about* 460 B.C. Athenian general and statesman

The·oc·ri·tus \thē-ˈäk-rət-əs\ *about* 310–250 B.C. Greek poet

The·od·o·ric \thē-ˈäd-ə-rik\ 454–526 A.D. *Theodoric the Great* king of the Ostrogoths (471–526) and of Italy (493–526)

The·o·do·sius I \ˌthē-ə-ˈdō-shəs, -shē-əs\ 347–395 A.D. *Theodosius the Great* Roman general and emperor (379–395)

The·seus \ˈthē-ˌsüs, -sē-əs\ hero in Greek mythology who slays Procrustes and the Minotaur and conquers the Amazons

Thes·pis \ˈthes-pəs\ *flourished* 6th century B.C. Greek poet

The·tis \ˈthēt-əs\ sea goddess and mother of Achilles in Greek mythology

This·be \ˈthiz-bē\ legendary Babylonian maiden who dies for the love of Pyramus

Thom·as \ˈtäm-əs\ apostle in the Bible who demands proof of Jesus' resurrection

Thomas Clarence 1948– American jurist

Thomas Dyl·an \ˈdil-ən\ 1914–1953 Welsh poet

Thomas à Becket — see BECKET

Thomas à Kem·pis \ə-ˈkem-pəs, ä-ˈkem-\ 1379 (or 1380)–1471 Dutch ecclesiastic and author

Thomas Aquinas Saint — see AQUINAS

Thomp·son \ˈtäm-sən, ˈtämp-\ Benjamin 1753–1814 Count *Rum·ford* \ˈrəm-fərd, ˈrəmp-\ British (American-born) physicist and statesman

Thor \ˈthȯr\ god of thunder, weather, and crops in Norse mythology

Tho·reau \thə-ˈrō, thȯ-; ˈthȯr-ō\ Henry David 1817–1862 American author

Thorpe \ˈthȯrp\ Jim 1888–1953 *James Francis Thorpe* American athlete

Thu·cyd·i·des \thü-ˈsid-ə-ˌdēz, thyü-\ *died about* 401 B.C. Greek historian

Thur·ber \ˈthər-bər\ James Grover 1894–1961 American author

Ti·be·ri·us \tī-ˈbir-ē-əs\ 42 B.C.–37 A.D. Roman emperor (14–37)

Tim·o·thy \ˈtim-ə-thē\ a disciple of the apostle Paul

Tim·ur \ˈtim-ůr\ *or* **Tam·er·lane** \ˈtam-ər-ˌlān\ *or* **Tam·bur·laine** \ˈtam-bər-ˌlān\ 1336–1405 *Timur Lenk* Turkic conqueror

Tin·to·ret·to \ˌtin-tə-ˈret-ō\ *about* 1518–1594 *Jacopo Robusti* Italian painter

Ti·ta·nia \tə-ˈtān-yə, -ˈtän-, tī-ˈtān-\ queen of the fairies and wife of Oberon in Shakespeare's *A Midsummer Night's Dream*

Ti·tian \ˈtish-ən\ *about* 1488–1576 *Tiziano Vecellio* Italian painter

Ti·to \ˈtēt-ō\ 1892–1980 originally *Josip Broz* known as *Marshal Tito* Yugoslavian leader (1943–80)

Ti·tus \ˈtīt-əs\ disciple of the apostle Paul

Titus 39–81 A.D. Roman emperor (79–81)

Tocque·ville \ˈtōk-ˌvil, ˈtȯk-, ˈtäk-, -ˌvēl, -vəl\ Alexis (-Charles-Henri Clérel) de 1805–1859 French statesman and author

Tol·kien \ˈtōl-ˌkēn, ˈtōl-, ˈtäl-\ J. R. R. 1892–1973 *John Ronald Reuel Tolkien* British author

Tol·stoy \tōl-ˈstȯi, tōl-ˈ, täl-ˈ, ˈtōl-ˌ, ˈtōl-ˌ, ˈtäl-ˌ\ Leo 1828–1910 *Count Lev Nikolayevich Tolstoy* Russian author

Tor·que·ma·da \ˌtȯr-kə-ˈmäd-ə\ Tomás de 1420–1498 Spanish grand inquisitor

Tou·louse–Lau·trec (–Mon·fa) \tü-ˌlüz-lō-ˈtrek(-mō^{n}-ˈfa)\ Henri (-Marie-Raymond) de 1864–1901 French painter

Tous·saint–Lou·ver·ture \tü-ˌsa^{n}-ˌlü-ver-ˈtu̇r\ *about* 1743–1803 Haitian general and liberator

Toyn·bee \ˈtȯin-bē\ Arnold Joseph 1889–1975 British historian

Tra·jan \ˈtrā-jən\ 53–117 A.D. Roman emperor (98–117)

Tris·tram \ˈtris-trəm\ *or* **Tris·tan** \ˈtris-tən, -ˌtän, -ˌtan\ hero in medieval romance who drinks a love potion and falls in love with the Irish princess Isolde

Tri·ton \ˈtrīt-n\ sea god in Greek mythology who is half man and half fish

Troi·lus \ˈtrȯi-ləs, ˈtrō-ə-ləs\ son of Priam who in medieval legend loves Cressida but loses her to Diomedes

Trol·lope \ˈträl-əp\ Anthony 1815–1882 English author

Trots·ky \ˈträt-skē, ˈtrȯt-\ Leon 1879–1940 originally *Lev Davidovich Bronshtein* Russian Communist leader

Tru·deau \ˈtrü-dō, trü-ˈ\ Pierre Elliott 1919–2000 prime minister of Canada (1968–79; 1980–84)

Tru·man \ˈtrü-mən\ Harry S. 1884–1972 33rd president of the U.S. (1945–53)

Truth \ˈtrüth\ Sojourner *about* 1797–1883 American abolitionist

Tub·man \ˈtəb-mən\ Harriet *about* 1820–1913 American abolitionist

Tur·ge·nev \tu̇r-ˈgān-yəf\ Ivan Sergeyevich 1818–1883 Russian author

Tur·ner \ˈtər-nər\ J. M. W. 1775–1851 *Joseph Mallord William Turner* English painter

Turner Nat 1800–1831 American leader of a slave rebellion

Tut·ankh·a·men \ˌtü-ˌtang-ˈkäm-ən, -ˌtäng-\ originally *Tutankh·a·ten* \-ˌteng-ˈkät-ən\ *about* 1370–1352 B.C. king of Egypt (1361–52)

Tu·tu \ˈtü-ˌtü\ Desmond Mpilo 1931– South African clergyman and political activist; Nobel Prize winner (1984)

Twain \ˈtwān\ Mark 1835–1910 pseudonym of *Samuel Langhorne Clem·ens* \ˈklem-ənz\ American author

Tweed \ˈtwēd\ William Marcy 1823–1878 *Boss Tweed* American politician

Ty·ler \ˈtī-lər\ John 1790–1862 10th president of the U.S. (1841–45)

Ulysses — see ODYSSEUS

Up·dike \ˈəp-ˌdīk\ John Hoyer 1932–2009 American author

Ura·nia \yu̇-ˈrā-nē-ə, -nyə\ Muse of astronomy in Greek mythology

Ura·nus \ˈyu̇r-ə-nəs, yu̇-ˈrā-nəs\ the sky personified as a god and the father of the Titans in Greek mythology

Ur·ban \ˈər-bən\ name of 8 popes: especially **II** 1035–1099 (pope 1088–99)

Uri·el \ˈyu̇r-ē-əl\ one of the four archangels named in Hebrew tradition — compare GABRIEL, MICHAEL, RAPHAEL

Va·le·ri·an \və-ˈlir-ē-ən\ *died* 260 A.D. Roman emperor (253–260)

Van Bu·ren \van-ˈbyu̇r-ən, vən-\ Martin 1782–1862 8th president of the U.S. (1837–41)

Van·der·bilt \ˈvan-dər-ˌbilt\ Cornelius 1794–1877 American shipping and railroad magnate

Van Dyck *or* **Van·dyke** \van-ˈdīk, vən-\ Sir Anthony 1599–1641 Flemish painter

van Gogh Vincent — see GOGH, VAN

Ve·ga \ˈvā-gə\ Lo·pe \ˈlō-pā\ de 1562–1635 Spanish playwright

Ve·láz·quez \və-ˈlas-kəs\ Diego Rodríguez de Silva 1599–1660 Spanish painter

Ve·nus \ˈvē-nəs\ goddess of love and beauty in Roman mythology — compare APHRODITE

Ver·di \ˈveərd-ē\ Giuseppe 1813–1901 Italian composer

Vergil — see VIRGIL

Ver·meer \vər-ˈmer, -ˈmir\ Jan *or* Johannes 1632–1675 Dutch painter

Verne \ˈvərn, ˈvern\ Jules \ˈjülz, ˈzhu̇el\ 1828–1905 French author

Ve·ro·ne·se \ˌver-ə-ˈnā-sē, -ˈnā-zē\ Paolo 1528–1588 Italian painter

Ves·puc·ci \ve-ˈspü-chē\ Ame·ri·go \ˌäm-ə-ˈrē-gō\ 1454–1512

\ə\ **abut**	\au̇\ **out**	\i\ **tip**	\ȯ\ **saw**	\u̇\ **foot**
\ər\ **further**	\ch\ **chin**	\ī\ **life**	\ȯi\ **coin**	\y\ **yet**
\a\ **mat**	\e\ **pet**	\j\ **job**	\th\ **thin**	\yü\ **few**
\ā\ **take**	\ē\ **easy**	\ng\ **sing**	\th\ **this**	\yu̇\ **cure**
\ä\ **cot, cart**	\g\ **go**	\ō\ **bone**	\ü\ **food**	\zh\ **vision**

Amer·i·cus Ves·pu·cius \ə-ˈmer-ə-kəs-ˌves-ˈpyü-shəs, -shē-əs\ Italian navigator for Spain and namesake of America
Ves·ta \ˈves-tə\ goddess of the hearth in Roman mythology — compare HESTIA
Vic·tor Em·man·u·el I \ˈvik-tər-i-ˈman-yə-wəl, -ˈman-yəl\ 1759–1824 king of Sardinia (1802–21)
Victor Emmanuel II 1820–1878 king of Sardinia (1849–61); 1st king of Italy (1861–78)
Victor Emmanuel III 1869–1947 king of Italy (1900–46)
Vic·to·ria \vik-tōr-ē-ə, -ˈtȯr-\ 1819–1901 *Alexandrina Victoria* queen of the United Kingdom (1837–1901)
Vil·lon \vē-ˈōⁿ, -ˈyōⁿ\ François 1431–*after* 1463 French poet
Vin·cent de Paul \ˌvin-sənt-də-ˈpȯl\ Saint 1581–1660 French priest and founder of the Vincentians
Vinci, da Leonardo — see LEONARDO DA VINCI
Vir·gil *or* **Ver·gil** \ˈvər-jəl\ 70–19 B.C. Roman poet — **Vir·gil·ian** *also* **Ver·gil·ian** \ˌvər-ˈjil-ē-ən\ *adj*
Vish·nu \ˈvish-nü\ god of preservation in the Hindu sacred triad — compare BRAHMA, SHIVA
Vi·val·di \vi-ˈväl-dē, -ˈvȯl-\ Antonio 1678–1741 Italian composer
Vol·ta \ˈvōl-tə, ˈväl-, ˈvȯl-\ Alessandro 1745–1827 Italian physicist
Vol·taire \vōl-ˈtaər, vȯl-, väl-, -ˈteər\ 1694–1778 originally *François-Marie Arouet* French author
Vul·can \ˈvəl-kən\ god of fire and metalworking in Roman mythology — compare HEPHAESTUS
Wag·ner \ˈväg-nər\ (Wilhelm) Ri·chard \ˈrik-ˌärt, ˈrik-\ 1813–1883 German composer
Wal·cott \ˈwȯl-kət, -ˌkät\ Derek Alton 1930– West Indian author; Nobel Prize winner (1992)
Wa·le·sa \vä-ˈlen-sə\ Lech 1943– Polish labor leader and president of Poland (1990–95); Nobel Prize winner (1983)
Walk·er \ˈwȯk-ər\ Alice Malsenior 1944– American author
Wal·len·berg \ˈwäl-ən-ˌbərg\ Raoul 1912–?1947 Swedish diplomat and hero of the Holocaust
Wal·pole \ˈwȯl-ˌpōl, ˈwäl-\ Horace 1717–1797 4th Earl of *Or·ford* \ˈȯr-fərd\ English author
Wal·ton \ˈwȯlt-n\ Izaak \ˈī-zik, -zək\ 1593–1683 English author
War·ren \ˈwȯr-ən, ˈwär-\ Earl 1891–1974 American jurist; chief justice of the U.S. Supreme Court (1953–69)
War·ren \ˈwȯr-ən, ˈwär-\ Robert Penn 1905–1989 American author
Wash·ing·ton \ˈwȯsh-ing-tən, ˈwäsh-\ Book·er \ˈbu̇k-ər\ Tal·iaferro \ˈtäl-ə-vər\ 1856–1915 American educator
Washington George 1732–1799 American general; 1st president of the U.S. (1789–97)
Wat·son \ˈwät-sən\ James Dewey 1928– American geneticist; Nobel Prize winner (1962)
Watt \ˈwät\ James 1736–1819 Scottish inventor
Wayne \ˈwān\ Anthony 1745–1796 *Mad Anthony* American Revolutionary general
We·ber \ˈvā-bər\ Carl Maria von 1786–1826 German composer
Web·ster \ˈweb-stər\ Daniel 1782–1852 American statesman
Webster Noah 1758–1843 American lexicographer
Welles \ˈwelz\ (George) Orson 1915–1985 American film director and producer
Wel·ling·ton \ˈwel-ing-tən\ Duke of 1769–1852 *Arthur Wellesley; the Iron Duke* British general and statesman
Wel·ty \ˈwel-tē\ Eudora 1909–2001 American author
Wells \ˈwelz\ H. G. 1866–1946 *Herbert Gordon Wells* English author
Wes·ley \ˈwes-lē, ˈwez-\ John 1703–1791 English founder of Methodism
West \ˈwest\ Benjamin 1738–1820 American painter in England
Wes·ting·house \ˈwes-ting-ˌhau̇s\ George 1846–1914 American inventor and industrialist
Whar·ton \ˈhwȯrt-n, ˈwȯrt-\ Edith 1862–1937 née *Jones* American author
Wheat·ley \ˈwēt-lē, ˈhwēt-\ Phillis *about* 1753–1784 American (African-born) poet
Whis·tler \ˈhwis-lər, ˈwis-\ James (Abbott) McNeill 1834–1903 American artist
Whit·man \ˈhwit-mən, ˈwit-\ Walt 1819–1892 American poet
Whit·ney \ˈhwit-nē, ˈwit-\ Eli 1765–1825 American inventor
Whit·ti·er \ˈhwit-ē-ər, ˈwit-\ John Greenleaf 1807–1892 American poet
Wie·sel \vē-ˈzel, wē-\ Elie 1928– American (Romanian-born) author; Nobel Prize winner (1986)
Wilde \ˈwīld\ Oscar (Fingal O'Flahertie Wills) 1854–1900 Irish author
Wil·der \ˈwīl-dər\ Thornton Niven 1897–1975 American author
Wil·hel·mi·na \ˌwil-ˌhel-ˈmē-nə, ˌwil-ə-ˈmē-\ 1880–1962 queen of the Netherlands (1890–1948)
Wil·kins \ˈwil-kənz\ Roy 1901–1981 American civil rights leader
Wil·lard \ˈwil-ərd\ Emma 1787–1870 née *Hart* American educator
Wil·liam \ˈwil-yəm\ name of 4 kings of England: **I** *about* 1028–1087 *William the Conqueror* (reigned 1066–87); **II** *about* 1056–1100 *William Ru·fus* \ˈrü-fəs\ (reigned 1087–1100); **III** 1650–1702 (reigned 1689–1702); **IV** 1765–1837 (reigned 1830–37)
William I 1533–1584 *William the Silent* prince of Orange and founder of the Dutch Republic
William I 1797–1888 king of Prussia (1861–88) and emperor of Germany (1871–88)
William II 1859–1941 *Kaiser Wilhelm* emperor of Germany and king of Prussia (1888–1918; abdicated)
Wil·liam Tell \ˌwil-yəm-ˈtel\ legendary Swiss patriot sentenced to shoot an apple off his son's head
Wil·liams \ˈwil-yəmz\ Roger 1603?–1683 American (English-born) clergyman and founder of Rhode Island
Williams Ted 1918–2002 *Theodore Samuel Williams* American baseball player
Williams Tennessee 1911–1983 *Thomas Lanier Williams* American playwright
Williams Venus 1980– and her sister Serena 1981– American tennis players
Williams William Carlos 1883–1963 American poet and physician
Wil·son \ˈwil-sən\ August 1945–2005 American playwright
Wilson (Thomas) Wood·row \ˈwu̇d-rō\ 1856–1924 28th president of the U.S. (1913–21); Nobel Prize winner (1919)
Windsor Duke of — see EDWARD VIII
Win·throp \ˈwin-thrəp, ˈwint-\ John 1588–1649 English colonist in America; 1st governor of Massachusetts Bay Colony
Wo·den \ˈwōd-n\ — see ODIN
Wolfe \ˈwu̇lf\ James 1727–1759 British general
Wolfe Thomas Clayton 1900–1938 American author
Woll·stone·craft \ˈwu̇l-stən-ˌkraft\ Mary 1759–1797 English feminist and author; mother of Mary Wollstonecraft Shelley
Wol·sey \ˈwu̇l-zē\ Thomas *about* 1475–1530 English cardinal and statesman
Woods \ˈwu̇dz\ Tiger 1975– *Eldrick Woods* American golfer
Woolf \ˈwu̇lf\ Virginia 1882–1941 née *Stephen* English author
Words·worth \ˈwərdz-wərth, -ˌwərth\ William 1770–1850 English poet
Wo·vo·ka \wō-ˈvō-kə\ 1858?–1932 *Jack Wilson* Paiute Indian mystic
Wren \ˈren\ Sir Christopher 1632–1723 English architect
Wright \ˈrīt\ Frank Lloyd 1867–1959 American architect
Wright Or·ville \ˈȯr-vəl\ 1871–1948 and his brother Wilbur 1867–1912 American pioneers in aviation
Wright Richard 1908–1960 American author
Wyc·liffe \ˈwik-ˌlif, -ləf\ John *about* 1330–1384 English reformer and Bible translator
Wy·eth \ˈwī-əth\ Andrew Newell 1917–2009 American painter
Xa·vi·er \ˈzāv-yər, ˈzā-vē-ər, ig-ˈzā-\ Saint Francis 1506–1552 Spanish *Francisco Javier* Spanish Jesuit missionary
Xen·o·phon \ˈzen-ə-fən\ 431–*about* 350 B.C. Greek historian
Xer·xes I \ˈzərk-ˌsēz\ *about* 519–465 B.C. *Xerxes the Great* king of Persia (486–465); son of Darius I
Xi Jin·ping \ˈshē-ˈjin-ˈping\ 1953– Chinese Communist party leader (2012–); president of China (2013–)
Yeats \ˈyāts\ William Butler 1865–1939 Irish author
Yelt·sin \ˈyelt-sən, ˈyel-sin\ Boris Nikolayevich 1931–2007 president of Russia (1990–99)
Young \ˈyəng\ Brig·ham \ˈbrig-əm\ 1801–1877 American Mormon leader
Young Whitney Moore 1921–1971 American civil rights leader
Za·har·i·as \zə-ˈhar-ē-əs\ Babe Didrikson 1914–1956 *Mildred Ella Zaharias* née *Didrikson* American athlete
Zech·a·ri·ah \ˌzek-ə-ˈrī-ə\ Hebrew prophet of the 6th century B.C.
Zeng·er \ˈzeng-ər, ˈzeng-gər\ John Peter 1697–1746 American (German-born) journalist and printer
Ze·no of Ci·ti·um \ˈzē-nō-əv-ˈsish-ē-əm\ *about* 335–*about* 263 B.C. Greek philosopher and founder of Stoic school

Zeph•a•ni•ah \ˌzef-ə-ˈnī-ə\ Hebrew prophet of the 7th century B.C.

Zeph•y•rus \ˈzef-ə-rəs\ god of the west wind in Greek mythology

Zeus \ˈzüs\ chief god, ruler of the elements, and husband of Hera in Greek mythology — compare JUPITER

Zo•la \ˈzō-lə, ˈzō-ˌlä, zō-ˈlä\ Émile 1840–1902 French author

Zo•ro•as•ter \ˈzōr-ə-ˌwas-tər, ˈzȯr-\ *or* **Zar•a•thu•stra** \ˌzar-ə-ˈthüs-trə, -ˈthəs-\ *about* 628–*about* 551 B.C. founder of a Persian religion

Zwing•li \ˈzwing-lē, ˈswing-, -glē; ˈtsfing-lē\ Huldrych 1484–1531 Swiss Reformation leader

\ə\ **abut**	\au̇\ **out**	\i\ **tip**	\ȯ\ **saw**	\u̇\ **foot**
\ər\ **further**	\ch\ **chin**	\ī\ **life**	\ȯi\ **coin**	\y\ **yet**
\a\ **mat**	\e\ **pet**	\j\ **job**	\th\ **thin**	\yü\ **few**
\ā\ **take**	\ē\ **easy**	\ng\ **sing**	\th\ **this**	\yu̇\ **cure**
\ä\ **cot, cart**	\g\ **go**	\ō\ **bone**	\ü\ **food**	\zh\ **vision**

Geographical Names

This section constitutes a pronouncing dictionary of names of current, historical, mythological, and legendary places likely to be of interest to the student. It complements the general vocabulary by entering many adjectives and nouns derived from these names, such as **Florentine** at **Florence** and **Libyan** at **Libya.**

In the entries the letters [N], [E], [S], and [W], singly or in combination indicate direction and are not part of the name. They may represent either the direction (as *north*) or the adjective derived from it (as *northern*); thus, west-northwest of Santiago appears as [WNW] of Santiago and southern California appears as [S] California. The only other special abbreviations used in this section are U.S. for United States, and U.S.S.R. for Union of Soviet Socialist Republics.

Aa·chen \ˈäk-ən\ *or French* **Aix–la–Cha·pelle** \ˌäk-ˌslä-shə-ˈpel, ˌek-\ city [W] Germany [WSW] of Cologne

Aarhus — see ÅRHUS

Aba·dan \ˌäb-ə-ˈdän, ˌab-ə-ˈdan\ town [W] Iran on Abadan Island in delta of Shatt al Arab

Ab·er·deen \ˌab-ər-ˈdēn\ **1** *or* **Ab·er·deen·shire** \-ˌshir, -shər\ administrative area [NE] Scotland **2** city [NE] Scotland constituting an administrative area **(Aberdeen City)** — **Ab·er·do·ni·an** \-ˈdō-nē-ən\ *adj or n*

Ab·i·djan \ˌab-i-ˈjän\ city, seat of government of Ivory Coast

Ab·i·lene \ˈab-ə-ˌlēn\ city [NW] central Texas

Abruz·zi \ä-ˈbrüt-sē\ region central Italy on the Adriatic [E] of Latium; capital, L'Aquila

Abu Dha·bi \ˌäb-ü-ˈdäb-ē\ city, capital of United Arab Emirates

Abu·ja \ä-ˈbü-jä\ city, capital of Nigeria

Abyssinia — see ETHIOPIA

Aca·dia \ə-ˈkād-ē-ə\ *or French* **Aca·die** \á-ká-ˈdē\ NOVA SCOTIA — an early name

Acadia National Park section of coast of Maine including areas on Mount Desert Island & Isle au Haut

Aca·pul·co \ˌäk-ə-ˈpül-kō, ˌak-\ city [S] Mexico on the North Pacific

Ac·ar·na·nia \ˌak-ər-ˈnā-nē-ə, -ˈnā-nyə\ region [W] Greece on Ionian Sea

Accad — see AKKAD

Ac·cra \ə-ˈkrä\ city, capital of Ghana

Achaea \ə-ˈkē-ə\ *or* **Acha·ia** \ə-ˈkī-ə, -ˈkā-ə, -ˈkā-yə\ region [S] Greece in [N] Peloponnese

Ach·er·on \ˈak-ə-ˌrän, -rən\ a river of Hades in Greek mythology

Acon·ca·gua \ˌak-ən-ˈkäg-wə, ˌäk-, -əng-\ mountain 22,834 feet (6960 meters) [W] Argentina; highest in the Andes & Western Hemisphere

Açores — see AZORES

Ac·ti·um \ˈak-shē-əm, ˈak-tē-\ promontory & ancient town [W] Greece in [NW] Acarnania

Ada·na \ˈäd-ə-nə, -ˌnä; ə-ˈdän-ə\ city [S] Turkey

Ad·dis Aba·ba \ˌad-ə-ˈsab-ə-bə\ city, capital of Ethiopia

Ad·e·laide \ˈad-l-ˌād\ city, capital of South Australia

Aden \ˈäd-n, ˈād-, ˈad-\ **1** former British protectorate [S] Arabia [E] of Yemen **2** former British colony in [SW] Aden Protectorate **3** city & port [S] Yemen; formerly capital of People's Democratic Republic of Yemen

Aden, Gulf of arm of Indian Ocean between Yemen (Arabia) & Somalia (Africa)

Adi·ge \ˈäd-ə-ˌjā\ river 255 miles (410 kilometers) long [N] Italy flowing [SE] into the Adriatic

Ad·i·ron·dack \ˌad-ə-ˈrän-ˌdak\ mountains [NE] New York; highest Mount Marcy 5344 feet (1629 meters)

Ad·mi·ral·ty \ˈad-mrəl-tē, -mə-rəl-\ **1** island [SE] Alaska in [N] Alexander Archipelago **2** islands [W] Pacific [N] of New Guinea in Bismarck Archipelago; belong to Papua New Guinea

Adri·at·ic Sea \ˌā-drē-ˈat-ik, ˌad-rē-\ arm of Mediterranean between Italy & Balkan Peninsula

Ae·ge·an Sea \i-ˈjē-ən\ arm of Mediterranean between Asia Minor & Greece

Ae·gi·na \i-ˈjī-nə\ *or Greek* **Aí·yi·na** \ˈā-yē-ˌnä\ island & ancient state [SE] Greece in Saronic Gulf

Ae·o·lis \ˈē-ə-ləs\ *or* **Ae·o·lia** \ē-ˈō-lē-ə, -ˈōl-yə\ ancient country [NW] Asia Minor

Afars and the Issas, French Territory of the — see DJIBOUTI 1

Af·ghan·i·stan \af-ˈgan-ə-ˌstan\ country [W] Asia [E] of Iran; capital, Kabul

Af·ri·ca \ˈaf-ri-kə\ continent of Eastern Hemisphere [S] of the Mediterranean

Agana — see HAGÅTÑA

Agra \ˈäg-rə\ city [N] India in [W] Uttar Pradesh

Agri Dagi — see ARARAT

Aguas·ca·lien·tes \ˌäg-wə-ˌskäl-yen-ˌtās\ **1** state central Mexico **2** city, its capital, [NE] of Guadalajara

Agul·has, Cape \ə-ˈgəl-əs\ headland Republic of South Africa; most southerly point of Africa, at 34°50′ [S] latitude

Agulhas Current warm current of the Indian Ocean flowing [SW] along [SE] coast of Africa

Ahag·gar \ə-ˈhäg-ər, ˌä-hə-ˈgär\ *or* **Hog·gar** \ˈhäg-ər, hə-ˈgär\ mountains [S] Algeria in [W] central Sahara; highest peak 9842 feet (3000 meters)

Ah·mad·abad \ˈäm-əd-ə-ˌbäd\ city [W] India in Gujarat

Ah·waz \ä-ˈwäz\ city [SW] Iran

Aisne \ˈān\ river 165 miles (265 kilometers) long [N] France flowing from Argonne Forest into the Oise

Aix–la–Chapelle — see AACHEN

Aj·mer \ˌəj-ˈmiər, -ˈmeər\ city [NW] India in central Rajasthan [SW] of Delhi

Aki·ta \ä-ˈkēt-ə, ˈäk-i-ˌtä\ city Japan in [N] Honshu on Sea of Japan

Ak·kad *or* **Ac·cad** \ˈak-ˌad, ˈäk-ˌäd\ **1** [N] division of ancient Babylonia **2** *or* **Aga·de** \ə-ˈgäd-ə\ ancient city, its capital

Ak·ron \ˈak-rən\ city [NE] Ohio

Al·a·bama \ˌal-ə-ˈbam-ə\ state [SE] U.S.; capital, Montgomery — **Al·a·bam·i·an** \-ˈbam-ē-ən\ *or* **Al·a·bam·an** \-ˈbam-ən\ *adj or n*

Åland \ˈō-ˌländ\ *or* **Ah·ven·an·maa** \ˈäk-və-ˌnän-ˌmä, ˈä-və-\ archipelago [SW] Finland in Baltic Sea

Alas·ka \ə-ˈlas-kə\ **1** peninsula [SW] Alaska (state) [SW] of Cook Inlet **2** state of U.S. in [NW] North America; capital, Juneau **3** mountain range [S] Alaska (state) extending from Alaska Peninsula to Yukon boundary — **Alas·kan** \-kən\ *adj or n*

Alaska, Gulf of inlet of North Pacific off [S] Alaska between Alaska Peninsula on [W] & Alexander Archipelago on [E]

\ə\ **abut**	\aù\ **out**	\i\ **tip**	\ȯ\ **saw**	\u̇\ **foot**
\ər\ **further**	\ch\ **chin**	\ī\ **life**	\ȯi\ **coin**	\y\ **yet**
\a\ **mat**	\e\ **pet**	\j\ **job**	\th\ **thin**	\yü\ **few**
\ā\ **take**	\ē\ **easy**	\ng\ **sing**	\t͟h\ **this**	\yu̇\ **cure**
\ä\ **cot, cart**	\g\ **go**	\ō\ **bone**	\ü\ **food**	\zh\ **vision**

Al·ba Lon·ga \ˌal-bə-ˈlȯng-gə\ ancient city central Italy in Latium [SE] of Rome

Al·ba·nia \al-ˈbā-nē-ə, -nyə\ country [S] Europe in Balkan Peninsula on Adriatic; capital, Tirane

Al·ba·ny \ˈȯl-bə-nē\ city, capital of New York

Al·be·marle Sound \ˈal-bə-ˌmärl\ inlet of North Atlantic in [NE] North Carolina

Al·bert, Lake \ˈal-bərt\ lake [E] Africa between Uganda & Democratic Republic of the Congo in course of the Nile

Al·ber·ta \al-ˈbərt-ə\ province [W] Canada; capital, Edmonton — **Al·ber·tan** \-bərt-n\ *adj or n*

Albert Nile — see NILE

Al·bi·on \ˈal-bē-ən\ **1** the island of Great Britain **2** ENGLAND

Al·bu·quer·que \ˈal-bə-ˌkər-kē, -byə-\ city central New Mexico

Al·da·bra \ˈal-də-brə\ island (atoll) Seychelles, in [NW] Indian Ocean [N] of Madagascar

Al·der·ney \ˈȯl-dər-nē\ island in English Channel — see CHANNEL 2

Alep·po \ə-ˈlep-ō\ city [N] Syria

Aleu·tian \ə-ˈlü-shən\ islands [SW] Alaska extending in an arc 1700 miles (2735 kilometers) [W] from Alaska Peninsula

Al·ex·an·der \ˌal-ig-ˈzan-dər, ˌel-\ archipelago [SE] Alaska

Al·ex·an·dria \ˌal-ig-ˈzan-drē-ə, ˌel-\ **1** city [N] Virginia on the Potomac **2** city [N] Egypt on the Mediterranean — **Al·ex·an·dri·an** \-drē-ən\ *adj or n*

Al·ge·ria \al-ˈjir-ē-ə\ country [NW] Africa on the Mediterranean; capital, Algiers — **Al·ge·ri·an** \-ē-ən\ *adj or n*

Al·giers \al-ˈjiərz\ **1** Algeria especially as one of former Barbary States **2** city, capital of Algeria — **Al·ge·rine** \ˌal-jə-ˈrēn\ *adj or n*

Al·i·garh \ˌal-i-ˈgär\ city [N] India in [NW] Uttar Pradesh [N] of Agra

Al Jīzah — see GIZA

Al·lah·abad \ˈal-ə-hə-ˌbad, -ˌbäd\ city [N] India in [S] Uttar Pradesh [W] of Varanasi

Al·le·ghe·ny \ˌal-ə-ˈgā-nē\ mountains of Applachian system [E] U.S. in Pennsylvania, Maryland, Virginia, & West Virginia

Al·len·town \ˈal-ən-ˌtau̇n\ city [E] Pennsylvania

Al·maty \əl-ˈmät-ē\ *or* **Al·ma–Ata** \əl-ˈmä-ə-ˈtä\ city, former capital of Kazakhstan

Alps \ˈalps\ mountain system central Europe — see MONT BLANC

Al·sace \al-ˈsas, -sās, ˈal-ˌ\ *or German* **El·sass** \ˈel-ˌzäs\ *or ancient* **Al·sa·tia** \al-ˈsā-shē-ə, -shə\ region & former province [NE] France between Rhine River & Vosges Mountains — **Al·sa·tian** \al-ˈsā-shən\ *adj or n*

Al·sace–Lor·raine \-lə-ˈrān, -lȯ-ˈrān\ region [N] France [W] of the Rhine including Alsace & part of Lorraine

Al·tai *or* **Al·tay** \al-ˈtī\ mountain system central Asia between Outer Mongolia & [W] China & between Kazakhstan & Russia in Asia; highest peak about 15,000 feet (4570 meters)

Al·ta·mi·ra \ˌal-tə-ˈmir-ə\ caverns [N] Spain [WSW] of Santander

Al·to Adi·ge \ˌäl-tō-ˈäd-i-ˌjā\ *or* **South Ti·rol** \-tə-ˈrōl, -ˈtī-ˌrōl, -ˌtī-ˈ; -ˈtir-əl\ district [N] Italy in [S] Tirol in [N] Trentino-Alto Adige region

Al·to Pa·ra·ná \ˌal-tō-ˌpar-ə-ˈnä\ upper course of the Paraná

Ama·ga·sa·ki \ˌam-ə-gə-ˈsäk-ē\ city Japan in [W] central Honshu on Osaka Bay

Am·a·ril·lo \ˌam-ə-ˈril-ō, -ˈril-ə\ city [NW] Texas

Am·a·zon \ˈam-ə-ˌzän, -zən\ *or Portuguese and Spanish* **Ama·zo·nas** \ˌam-ə-ˈzō-nəs\ river about 3900 miles (6276 kilometers) long [N] South America flowing from Peruvian Andes into Atlantic in [N] Brazil

Am·a·zo·nia \ˌam-ə-ˈzō-nē-ə\ region [N] South America; basin of the Amazon

Amer·i·ca \ə-ˈmer-ə-kə\ **1** either continent (North America or South America) of Western Hemisphere **2** *or* **the Amer·i·cas** \-kəz\ lands of Western Hemisphere including North, Central & South America, & West Indies **3** UNITED STATES OF AMERICA

American Samoa *or* **Eastern Samoa** islands [SW] central Pacific; capital, Pago Pago (on Tutuila Island)

American Samoa National Park reservation at three locations in American Samoa

Am·man \ä-ˈmän, -ˈman\ city, capital of Jordan

Amoy — see XIAMEN

Am·rit·sar \ˌəm-ˈrit-sər\ city [N] India in [NW] Punjab

Am·ster·dam \ˈam-stər-ˌdam, ˈamp-\ city, official capital of the Netherlands

Amu Dar'·ya \ˌäm-ü-ˈdär-yə\ *or ancient* **Ox·us** \ˈäk-səs\ river over 1500 miles (2400 kilometers) long in central & [W] Asia flowing from the Pamirs into Aral Sea

Amur \ä-ˈmu̇r\ river about 1780 miles (2865 kilometers) long [E] Asia formed by junction of Shilka & Argun rivers flowing into the North Pacific at [N] end of Tatar Strait & forming part of boundary between China & Russia in Asia

An·a·heim \ˈan-ə-ˌhīm\ city [SW] California [E] of Long Beach

Aná·huac \ə-ˈnä-ˌwäk\ the central plateau of Mexico

An·a·to·lia \ˌan-ə-ˈtō-lē-ə, -ˈtōl-yə\ — see ASIA MINOR — **An·a·to·li·an** \-ən, -yən\ *adj or n*

An·chor·age \ˈang-kə-rij, -krij\ city [S] central Alaska; largest in state

An·co·hu·ma \ˌang-kə-ˈhü-mə, -ˈhyü-\ mountain peak 20,958 feet (6388 meters) [W] Bolivia; highest of Illampu

An·co·na \ang-ˈkō-nə, an-\ city central Italy, capital of Marche

An·da·lu·sia \ˌan-də-ˈlü-zhē-ə, -zhə\ *or Spanish* **An·da·lu·cía** \ˌan-də-ˈlü-ˈsē-ə\ region [S] Spain including Sierra Nevada & valley of the Guadalquivir — **An·da·lu·sian** \ˌan-də-ˈlü-zhən\ *adj or n*

An·da·man \ˈan-də-mən, -ˌman\ **1** islands India in Bay of Bengal [S] of Myanmar (Burma) & [N] of Nicobar Islands; in **Andaman and Nic·o·bar** \ˈnik-ə-ˌbär\ territory **2** sea, an arm of Bay of Bengal [S] of Myanmar (Burma) — **An·da·man·ese** \ˌan-də-mə-ˈnēz, -ˈnēs\ *adj or n*

An·des \ˈan-dēz, -ˌdēz\ mountain system [W] South America extending from Panama to Tierra del Fuego — see ACONCAGUA — **An·de·an** \ˈan-dē-ən, an-ˈ\ *adj* — **An·dine** \ˈan-ˌdēn, -ˌdīn\ *adj*

An·dhra Pra·desh \ˌän-drə-prə-ˈdāsh, -ˈdesh\ state [S] India [N] of Tamil Nadu bordering on Bay of Bengal; capital, Hyderabad

An·dor·ra \an-ˈdȯr-ə, -ˈdär-ə\ country [SW] Europe in [E] Pyrenees between France & Spain; capital, Andorra la Vella — **An·dor·ran** \-ən\ *adj or n*

An·dros **1** \ˈan-drəs\ island, largest of Bahamas **2** \ˈan-drəs, -ˌdräs\ island Greece in [N] Cyclades [SE] of Euboea

An·gel Falls \ˌān-jəl-\ waterfall 3212 feet (979 meters) [SE] Venezuela on Auyán-tepuí Mountain

An·gers \äⁿ-ˈzhā\ city [W] France [ENE] of Nantes

Ang·kor \ˈang-ˌkȯr\ ruins of ancient city [NW] Cambodia

An·gle·sey \ˈang-gəl-sē\ island [NW] Wales

An·glo–Egyp·tian Sudan \ˌang-glō-i-ˌjip-shən-\ former territory [NE] Africa under joint British & Egyptian rule; in 1956 formed republic of Sudan

An·go·la \ang-ˈgō-lə, an-\ *or formerly* **Portuguese West Africa** country [SW] Africa [S] of mouth of Congo River; until 1975 a dependency of Portugal; capital, Luanda — **An·go·lan** \-lən\ *adj or n*

An·gus \ˈang-gəs\ administrative area [E] Scotland

An·hui *or* **An·hwei** \ˈän-ˈhwā, -ˈwā\ province [E] China [W] of Jiangsu; capital, Hefei

An·i·ak·chak Crater \ˌan-ē-ˈak-ˌchak\ volcanic crater [SW] Alaska on Alaska Peninsula; crater 6 miles (10 kilometers) in diameter

An·jou \ˈan-ˌjü, äⁿ-ˈzhü\ region & former province [NW] France in valley of the Loire [SE] of Brittany; chief city, Angers

An·ka·ra \ˈang-kə-rə, ˈäng-\ *or formerly* **An·go·ra** \ang-ˈgōr-ə, an-, -ˈgȯr-\ city, capital of Turkey in [N] central Anatolia

An·na·ba \ə-ˈnäb-ə\ *or formerly* **Bône** \ˈbōn\ city [NE] Algeria

An·nam \a-ˈnam, ə-; ˈan-ˌam\ region & former kingdom [E] Indochina in central Vietnam; capital, Hue

An·nap·o·lis \ə-ˈnap-ləs, -ə-ləs\ city, capital of Maryland

An·shan \ˈän-ˈshän\ city [NE] China in [E] central Liaoning

An·ta·nan·a·ri·vo \ˌan-tə-ˌnan-ə-ˈrē-vō\ *or formerly* **Ta·nan·a·rive** \tə-ˈnan-ə-ˌrēv\ city, capital of Madagascar

Ant·arc·ti·ca \ant-ˈärk-ti-kə, ˈant-, -ˈärt-i-\ body of land around the South Pole; plateau covered by great ice cap

Antarctic Peninsula *or formerly* **Palm·er Peninsula** \ˌpäm-ər-, ˌpäl-mər-\ peninsula about 700 miles (1126 kilometers) long [W] Antarctica [S] of [S] end of South America

An·ti·gua \an-ˈtē-gə\ island British West Indies in the Leewards; with Barbuda constitutes independent country of **Antigua and Barbuda**; capital, Saint John's

Anti–Leb·a·non \ˈant-i-ˈleb-ə-nən, -nän\ mountains [SW] Asia on Lebanon–Syria border — see HERMON (Mount)

An·til·les \an-ˈtil-ēz\ the West Indies excluding Bahamas — see GREATER ANTILLES, LESSER ANTILLES — **An·til·le·an** \-ˈtil-ē-ən\ *adj*

An·ti·och \ˈant-ē-ˌäk\ city of ancient Syria on the Orontes; site in [W] central Turkey

An·trim \ˈan-trəm\ traditional county [E] Northern Ireland
Antung — see DANDONG
Ant·werp \ˈant-ˌwərp\ city [N] Belgium on the Scheldt
An·yang \ˈän-ˈyäŋ\ city [E] China in [N] Henan
An·zio \ˈan-zē-ō, ˈän-\ *or ancient* **An·ti·um** \ˈan-shē-əm\ Mediterranean seaport Italy in Latium [SSE] of Rome
Aomen — see MACAO
Ao·mo·ri \ˈau̇-mə-rē\ city [N] Japan in [NE] Honshu
Aoraki — see COOK (Mount)
Aos·ta \ä-ˈȯs-tə\ city [NW] Italy
Ap·en·nines \ˈap-ə-ˌnīnz\ mountain chain Italy extending length of the peninsula; highest peak Monte Corno ([NE] of Rome) 9560 feet (2897 meters) — **Ap·en·nine** \-ˌnīn\ *adj*
Apia \ə-ˈpē-ə\ town, capital of independent Samoa on Upolu Island
Apo, Mount \ˈäp-ō\ volcano Philippines in [SE] Mindanao 9692 feet (2954 meters); highest peak in the Philippines
Ap·pa·la·chia \ˌap-ə-ˈlā-chə, -ˈlach-ə, -ˈlā-shə\ region [E] U.S. including Appalachian Mountains from [S] central New York to central Alabama
Ap·pa·la·chian Mountains \ˌap-ə-ˈlā-chən, -ˈlach-ən, -ˈlā-shən\ mountain system [E] North America extending from [S] Quebec to central Alabama — see MITCHELL (Mount)
Apu·lia \ə-ˈpyül-yə, -ˈpyü-lē-ə\ — see PUGLIA — **Apu·lian** \ə-ˈpyül-yən, -ˈpyü-lē-ən\ *adj or n*
Aqa·ba, Gulf of \ˈäk-ə-bə, ˈak-\ arm of Red Sea [E] of Sinai Peninsula
Aquid·neck Island \ə-ˈkwid-ˌnek\ *or* **Rhode Island** \ˈrōd\ island [SE] Rhode Island in Narragansett Bay
Aq·ui·taine \ˈak-wə-ˌtān\ region of [SW] France
Aq·ui·ta·nia \ˌak-wə-ˈtā-nyə, -nē-ə\ a Roman division of [SW] Gaul
Ara·bia \ə-ˈrā-bē-ə\ peninsula of [SW] Asia including Saudi Arabia, Yemen, Oman, & Persian Gulf States
Ara·bi·an \ə-ˈrā-bē-ən\ **1** — see EASTERN DESERT **2** sea [NW] section of Indian Ocean between Arabia & India
Ara·ca·ju \ˌar-ə-kə-ˈzhü\ city [E] Brazil [NE] of Salvador
Arad \ä-ˈräd\ city [W] Romania
Ar·a·fu·ra \ˌar-ə-ˈfu̇r-ə\ sea between [N] Australia & [W] New Guinea
Ar·a·gon \ˈar-ə-ˌgän, -gən\ region [NE] Spain bordering on France — **Ar·a·go·nese** \ˌar-ə-gə-ˈnēz, -ˈnēs\ *adj or n*
Arak \är-ˈäk, ə-ˈrak\ city [SW] Iran [SW] of Tehran
Ar·al Sea \ˈar əl\ *or Russian* **Aral·sko·ye Mo·re** \ə-ˌral-skə-yə-ˈmȯr-ə, -yə\ inland sea [W] Asia between Kazakhstan & Uzbekistan; now smaller in area & split into sections
Ar·a·rat \ˈar-ə-ˌrat\ *or Turkish* **Ag·ri Da·gi** \ˌä-rē-dä-ˈē, ˌäg-rē-däg-ˈe\ mountain 16,946 feet (5165 meters) [E] Turkey near border of Iran
Ar·bil *or* **Ir·bīl** *or* **Er·bil** \ər-ˈbēl\ city [N] Iraq
Ar·ca·dia \är-ˈkād-ē-ə\ mountain region [S] Greece in central Peloponnese
Arch·es National Park \ˈär-chəz\ reservation [E] Utah
Arc·tic \ˈärk-tik, ˈärt-ik\ **1** ocean [N] of Arctic Circle **2** the Arctic Ocean and lands in it and adjacent to it **3** archipelago [N] Canada in Nunavut & Northwest Territories
Ar·da·bil *or* **Ar·de·bil** \ˌär-də-ˈbēl\ city [NW] Iran
Ar·dennes \är-ˈden\ wooded plateau [NE] France, [W] Luxembourg, & [SE] Belgium [E] of the Meuse
Are·ci·bo \ˌä-rā-ˈsē-bō\ city & port [N] Puerto Rico
Are·qui·pa \ˌar-ə-ˈkē-pə\ city [S] Peru
Ar·gen·ti·na \ˌär-jən-ˈtē-nə\ country [S] South America between the Andes & the South Atlantic [S] of the Pilcomayo; capital, Buenos Aires — **Argentine** \ˈär-jən-ˌtēn\ *adj or n* — **Argen·tin·ean** *or* **Argen·tin·i·an** \ˌär-jən-ˈtin-ē-ən\ *adj or n*
Ar·go·lis \ˌär-gə-lis\ district [S] Greece in [E] Peloponnese
Ar·gonne \är-ˈgän, ˈär-ˌ\ *or* **Argonne Forest** wooded plateau [NE] France [S] of the Ardennes between Meuse & Aisne rivers
Ar·gos \ˌär-ˌgäs, -gəs\ ancient Greek city & state [S] Greece in Argolis; site at present town of Argos
Ar·gyll and Bute \är-ˈgīl-\ administrative area [W] Scotland
År·hus *or* **Aar·hus** \ˈȯr-ˌhüs\ city & port Denmark in [E] Jutland
Ar·i·zo·na \ˌar-ə-ˈzō-nə\ state [SW] U.S.; capital, Phoenix — **Ar·i·zo·nan** \-nən\ *or* **Ar·i·zo·nian** \-nē-ən, -nyən\ *adj or n*
Ar·kan·sas \ˈär-kən-ˌsȯ; *1 is also* är-ˈkan-zəs\ **1** river 1450 miles (2334 kilometers) long [SW] central U.S. flowing [SE] into the Mississippi **2** state [S] central U.S.; capital, Little Rock — **Ar·kan·san** \är-ˈkan-zən\ *adj or n*
Ar·khan·gelsk \är-ˈkan-ˌgelsk\ *or* **Arch·an·gel** \ˈär-ˌkan-jəl\ city [N] Russia in Europe, on the Northern Dvina
Ar·ling·ton \ˈär-liŋ-tən\ city [N] Texas [E] of Fort Worth
Ar·magh \är-ˈmä, ˈär-ˌ\ traditional county [S] Northern Ireland
Ar·me·nia \är-ˈmē-nē-ə, -nyə\ **1** region [W] Asia in mountainous area [SE] of Black Sea & [SW] of Caspian Sea divided between Iran, Turkey, Armenia (country), & Azerbaijan **2** country [W] Asia, capital, Yerevan; a constituent republic of U.S.S.R. 1936–91 — see LESSER ARMENIA — **Ar·me·ni·an** \-nē-ən, -nyən\ *adj or n*
Arn·hem Land \ˈärn-ˌhem, ˈär-nəm\ region [N] Australia on [N] coast of Northern Territory
Ar·no \ˈär-nō\ river 150 miles (241 kilometers) long central Italy flowing through Florence into Ligurian Sea
Aru·ba \ə-ˈrü-bə\ internally self-governing Dutch island off [NW] Venezuela [NW] of Curaçao; chief town, Oranjestad
Arun·a·chal Pra·desh \ˌär-ə-ˌnäch-əl-prə-ˈdāsh, -desh\ *or formerly* **North East Frontier Agency** state [NE] India [N] of Assam; capital, Itanagar
Ar·vada \är-ˈvad-ə\ city [N] central Colorado
Asa·hi·ka·wa \ˌäs-ə-hē-ˈkä-wə\ *or* **Asa·hi·ga·wa** \-ˈgä-wə\ city Japan in central Hokkaido
As·cen·sion \ə-ˈsen-chən\ island South Atlantic; administratively part of St. Helena
Ash·ga·bat \ˈäsh-gə-ˌbät\ *or* **Ashkh·a·bad** \ˈash-kə-ˌbad, -ˌbäd\ city, capital of Turkmenistan
Asia \ˈā-zhə, -shə\ continent Eastern Hemisphere [N] of Equator — see EURASIA
Asia Mi·nor \-ˈmī-nər\ *or* **An·a·to·lia** \ˌan-ə-ˈtō-lē-ə, -ˈtōl-yə\ peninsula in modern Turkey between Black Sea on [N] & the Mediterranean on [S]
As·ma·ra \az-ˈmär-ə, -ˈmar-ə\ city, capital of Eritrea
As·sam \ə-ˈsam, a-; ˈas-ˌam\ state [NE] India on edge of the Himalaya [NW] of Myanmar; capital, Dispur — **As·sam·ese** \ˌas-ə-ˈmēz, -ˈmēs\ *adj or n*
As·syr·ia \ə-ˈsir-ē-ə\ ancient empire [W] Asia extending along the middle Tigris & over foothills to the [E]; early capital Calah, later capital Nineveh — **As·syr·i·an** \-ən\ *adj or n*
As·ta·na \ä-stä-ˈnä\ city, capital of Kazakhstan
As·tra·khan \ˈas-trə-ˌkan, -kən\ city Russia in Europe, on the Volga at head of its delta
As·tu·ri·as \ə-ˈstu̇r-ē-əs\ region [NW] Spain on Bay of Biscay
Asun·ción \ə-ˌsün-sē-ˈōn, ä-\ city, capital of Paraguay
As·wân \a-ˈswän, ä-\ city [S] Egypt on the Nile near site of **Aswân High Dam** which forms Lake Nasser
As·yût \ˌas-ē-ˈüt, ˌäs-\ city central Egypt on the Nile
Ata·ca·ma \ˌat-ə-ˈkäm-ə\ **1** desert [N] Chile between Copiapó & Peru border **2** — see PUNA DE ATACAMA
Atchaf·a·laya \ə-ˌchaf-ə-ˈlī-ə, ˌchaf-\ river 225 miles (362 kilometers) long [S] Louisiana flowing [S] into Gulf of Mexico; receives waters of Red & Mississippi rivers
Ath·a·bas·ca \ˌath-ə-ˈbas-kə\ river 765 miles (1231 kilometers) long [NE] Alberta flowing into **Lake Athabasca** on Alberta–Saskatchewan border
Ath·ens \ˈath-ənz\ city, capital of Greece — **Athe·nian** \ə-ˈthē-nē-ən, -nyən\ *adj or n*
At·lan·ta \ət-ˈlant-ə, at-\ city, capital of Georgia
At·lan·tic \ət-ˈlant-ik, at-\ ocean separating North America & South America from Europe & Africa; often divided into **North Atlantic Ocean** & **South Atlantic Ocean**
At·lan·tis \ət-ˈlant-əs, at-\ fabled island that was traditionally placed [W] of Strait of Gibraltar and that sank into the sea
At·las \ˈat-ləs\ mountains [NW] Africa extending from [SW] Morocco to [N] Tunisia
At·ti·ca \ˈat-i-kə\ region [E] Greece; chief city, Athens
Auck·land \ˈȯ-klənd\ city [N] New Zealand on [NW] North Island
Augs·burg \ˈȯgz-ˌbərg, ˈau̇gz-ˌbu̇rg\ city [S] Germany in [S] Bavaria [NW] of Munich
Au·gus·ta \ȯ-ˈgəst-ə, ə-\ city, capital of Maine
Au·la·vik National Park \ˈau̇-lə-ˌvik\ reservation Northwest Territories on [N] Banks Island
Au·ro·ra \ə-ˈrȯr-ə\ **1** city [N] central Colorado **2** city [NE] Illinois

\ə\ **abut**	\au̇\ **out**	\i\ **tip**	\ȯ\ **saw**	\u̇\ **foot**
\ər\ **further**	\ch\ **chin**	\ī\ **life**	\ȯi\ **coin**	\y\ **yet**
\a\ **mat**	\e\ **pet**	\j\ **job**	\th\ **thin**	\yü\ **few**
\ā\ **take**	\ē\ **easy**	\ŋ\ **sing**	\t͟h\ **this**	\yu̇\ **cure**
\ä\ **cot, cart**	\g\ **go**	\ō\ **bone**	\ü\ **food**	\zh\ **vision**

Auschwitz — see OSWIECIM
Aus·tin \'ös-tən, 'äs-\ city, capital of Texas
Austral — see TUBUAI
Aus·tral·asia \ˌös-trə-'lā-shə, ˌäs-, -'lā-shə\ Australia, Tasmania, New Zealand, & Melanesia — **Aus·tral·asian** \-zhən, -shən\ *adj or n*
Aus·tra·lia \ó-'strāl-yə, ä-, ə-\ **1** continent of Eastern Hemisphere [SE] of Asia **2** *or in full* **Commonwealth of Australia** independent country including continent of Australia & island of Tasmania; capital, Canberra — **Aus·tra·lian** \-yən\ *adj or n*
Australian Alps mountain range [SE] Australia in [E] Victoria & [SE] New South Wales; part of Great Dividing Range
Australian Capital Territory district [SE] Australia including two areas, one containing Canberra (capital of Australia) & the other on Jervis Bay; surrounded by New South Wales
Aus·tria \'ös-trē-ə, 'äs-\ country central Europe; capital, Vienna — **Aus·tri·an** \-ən\ *adj or n*
Aus·tria–Hun·ga·ry \-'həŋ-gə-rē\ dual monarchy 1867–1918 central Europe including what is now Austria, Hungary, the Czech Republic, Bukovina & Transylvania in Romania, Slovenia, Croatia, Galicia in Poland, & part of [NE] Italy — **Aus·tro–Hun·gar·i·an** \'ös-trō-ˌhəŋ-'gar-ē-ən, 'äs-, -'ger-\ *adj or n*
Aus·tro·ne·sia \ˌös-trə-'nē-zhə, ˌäs-, -'nē-shə\ **1** the islands of the South Pacific **2** area extending from Madagascar through Malay Peninsula & Malay Archipelago to Hawaii & Easter Island — **Aus·tro·ne·sian** \-zhən, -shən\ *adj or n*
Au·vergne \ō-'veərn, -'veərn-yə, -'vərn\ **1** region & former province [S] central France **2** mountains [S] central France in Massif Central; highest peak 6188 feet (1886 meters)
Au·yuit·tuq National Park \au̇-'yü-ə-ˌtək\ reservation [E] Nunavut in [E] Baffin Island
Ave·lla·ne·da \ˌav-ə-zhə-'nā-də\ city [E] Argentina on Río de la Plata [E] of Buenos Aires
Avon \'ā-vən, 'av-ən, *in the U.S. also* 'ā-ˌvän\ river 96 miles (154 kilometers) long central England flowing [WSW] past Stratford-upon-Avon into the Severn
Ayers Rock — see ULURU
Azer·bai·jan \ˌaz-ər-ˌbī-'jän, ˌäz-\ country [W] Asia & [SE] Europe, capital, Baku; a constituent republic of U.S.S.R. 1936–91
Azores \'ā-ˌzōrz, -ˌzȯrz, ə-'\ *or Portuguese* **Aço·res** \ə-'sōr-ēsh\ islands North Atlantic belonging to Portugal & lying 800 miles (1287 kilometers) [W] of Portuguese coast — **Azor·e·an** \ā-'zōr-ē-ən, ə-, -'zȯr-\ *adj or n*
Az·ov, Sea of \'az-ˌöf, 'äz-, -ˌäv\ gulf of Black Sea between Ukraine & Russia
Baalbek — see HELIOPOLIS
Ba·bel·thu·ap \ˌbäb-əl-'tü-ˌäp\ island [W] Pacific; chief island of Palau
Bab·y·lon \'bab-ə-lən, -ˌlän\ ancient city, capital of Babylonia; site about 55 miles (89 kilometers) [S] of Baghdad near the Euphrates — **Bab·y·lo·nian** \ˌbab-ə-'lō-nyən, -nē-ən\ *adj or n*
Bab·y·lo·nia \ˌbab-ə-'lō-nyə, -nē-ə\ ancient country [W] Asia in valley of lower Euphrates and Tigris rivers; capital, Babylon — **Bab·y·lo·nian** \-nyən, -nē-ən\ *adj or n*
Ba·co·lod \bäk-'ō-ˌlȯd\ city Philippines on Negros
Bac·tria \'bak-trē-ə\ ancient country [W] Asia between the Hindu Kush & upper Oxus in present [NE] Afghanistan — **Bac·tri·an** \-ən\ *adj or n*
Ba·den–Würt·tem·berg \ˌbäd-n-'wərt-əm-ˌbərg, -'wu̇rt-; -'vuert-əm-ˌberk\ state [SW] Germany [W] of Bavaria; capital, Stuttgart
Bad·lands National Park \'bad-ˌlandz-, -ˌlanz-\ reservation [SW] South Dakota [E] of Black Hills
Baf·fin \'baf-ən\ island [NE] Canada in Arctic Archipelago [N] of Hudson Strait
Baffin Bay inlet of the North Atlantic between [W] Greenland & [E] Baffin Island
Bagh·dad \'bag-ˌdad, ˌbäg-'däd\ city, capital of Iraq on the middle Tigris
Ba·guio \ˌbäg-ē-'ō\ city, former summer capital of the Philippines in [NW] central Luzon
Ba·ha·mas \bə-'häm-əz, *by outsiders also* -'hā-\ islands in North Atlantic [SE] of Florida; an independent country; capital, Nassau — **Ba·ha·mi·an** \-'hā-mē-ən, -'häm-ē-ən\ *or* **Ba·ha·man** \-'hā-mən, -'häm-ən\ *adj or n*
Bahia — see SALVADOR
Bah·rain \bä-'rān\ islands in Persian Gulf off coast of Arabia forming an independent country; capital, Manama
Bai·kal *or* **Bay·kal** \bī-'kȯl, -'käl\ lake Russia in Asia, in mountains [N] of Mongolia
Baile Atha Cliath — see DUBLIN
Ba·ja California \ˌbä-hä-\ **1** peninsula [NW] Mexico [W] of Gulf of California **2** state [NW] Mexico in [N] Baja California Peninsula; capital, Mexicali
Baja California Sur \'su̇r\ state [NW] Mexico in [S] Baja California Peninsula; capital, La Paz
Bakh·ta·ran \ˌbäk-tə-'rän\ city [W] Iran
Ba·ku \bä-'kü\ city, capital of Azerbaijan on Caspian Sea
Bakwanga — see MBUJI-MAYI
Bal·a·ton \'bal-ə-ˌtän, 'bȯl-ə-ˌtōn\ lake [W] Hungary
Balboa Heights \bal-ˌbō-ə-\ town Panama; former administrative center for Canal Zone
Bâle — see BASEL
Bal·e·ar·ic \ˌbal-ē-'ar-ik\ islands [E] Spain in the [W] Mediterranean — see MAJORCA, MINORCA, IBIZA
Ba·li \'bäl-ē\ island Indonesia off [E] end of Java — **Ba·li·nese** \ˌbäl-i-'nēz, ˌbal-, -'nēs\ *adj or n*
Bal·kans \'bȯl-kənz\ **1** *or* **Balkan Mountains** range [N] Bulgaria extending from Serbia border to Black Sea; highest 7793 feet (2375 meters) **2** *or* **Balkan Peninsula** peninsula [SE] Europe between Adriatic & Ionian seas on the [W] & Aegean & Black seas on the [E] **3** *or* **Balkan States** countries occupying the Balkan Peninsula: Slovenia, Croatia, Bosnia and Herzegovina, Macedonia, Serbia, Montenegro, Kosovo, Romania, Bulgaria, Albania, Greece, & Turkey (in Europe)
Bal·khash \bal-'kash, bäl-'käsh\ lake [E] Kazakhstan
Bal·tic Sea \'bȯl-tik\ arm of North Atlantic [N] Europe [E] of Scandinavian Peninsula
Bal·ti·more \'bȯl-tə-ˌmōr, -ˌmȯr; 'bȯl-tə-mər, 'bȯl-mər\ city [N] central Maryland
Ba·lu·chi·stan \bə-ˌlü-chə-'stan\ **1** arid region [S] Asia bordering on Arabian Sea in [SW] Pakistan & [SE] Iran **2** province [SW] Pakistan
Ba·ma·ko \ˌbäm-ə-'kō\ city, capital of Mali on the Niger
Bandar — see MACHILIPATNAM
Ban·dar Lam·pung \ˌbən-dər-'läm-pu̇ŋ\ city & port Indonesia in [S] Sumatra
Ban·dar Se·ri Be·ga·wan \ˌbən-dər-ˌser-ē-bə-'gä-wən\ town, capital of Brunei
Ban·dung \'bän-ˌdu̇ŋ\ city Indonesia in [W] Java [SE] of Jakarta
Banff National Park \'bamf\ reservation [SW] Alberta on [E] slope of Rocky Mountains
Ban·ga·lore \'baŋ-gə-ˌlōr, -ˌlȯr\ *or* **Ben·ga·lu·ru** \'beŋ-gə-ˌlü-rü\ city [S] India [W] of Madras, capital of Karnataka
Ban·gha·zi \bän-'gä-zē, bäŋ-, baŋ-, -'gaz-ē\ *or* **Ben·gha·zi** \ben-, beŋ-\ city [NE] Libya; formerly a capital of Libya
Bang·kok \'baŋ-ˌkäk, baŋ-'\ city, capital of Thailand
Ban·gla·desh \ˌbäŋ-glə-'desh, ˌbaŋ-, -'dāsh\ country [S] Asia [E] of India; formerly part of Pakistan; an independent republic since 1971; capital, Dhaka — see EAST PAKISTAN
Ban·gui \bäⁿ-'gē\ city, capital of Central African Republic
Ban·jul \'bän-ˌjül\ *or formerly* **Bath·urst** \'bath-ˌərst, -ərst\ city, capital of Gambia
Bao·ding *or* **Pao·ting** \'bau̇-'diŋ\ city [NE] China in Hebei [SW] of Beijing
Bao·tou *or* **Pao–t'ou** \'bau̇-'tō\ city [N] China in [SW] Inner Mongolia
Bar·ba·dos \bär-'bād-əs, -ōz, -äs, -ōs\ island British West Indies in Lesser Antilles; an independent country since 1966; capital, Bridgetown — **Bar·ba·di·an** \-'bād-ē-ən\ *adj or n*
Bar·ba·ry States \'bär-bə-rē, -brē\ the states of Morocco, Algeria, Tunisia, & Tripolitania while under Turkish rule
Bar·bu·da \bär-'büd-ə\ island British West Indies in the Leewards — see ANTIGUA
Bar·ce·lo·na \ˌbär-sə-'lō-nə\ city [NE] Spain on the Mediterranean; chief city of Catalonia
Ba·reil·ly *or* **Ba·re·li** \bə-'rā-lē\ city [N] India in [NW] central Uttar Pradesh
Ba·rents \'bar-əns, 'bär-\ sea comprising part of Arctic Ocean between Spitsbergen & Novaya Zemlya
Ba·ri \'bär-ē\ city [SE] Italy, capital of Puglia on the Adriatic
Bar·king \'bär-kiŋ\ borough of [E] Greater London, England
Bar·na·ul \ˌbär-nə-'ül\ city [S] Russia in Asia, on the Ob
Bar·net \'bär-nət\ borough of [N] Greater London, England
Baroda — see VADODARA
Bar·qui·si·me·to \ˌbär-kə-sə-'māt-ō\ city [NW] Venezuela
Bar·ran·qui·lla \ˌbar-ən-'kē-ə, -'kē-yə\ city [N] Colombia on the Magdalena
Barren Grounds treeless plains [N] Canada [W] of Hudson Bay

Bar·row, Point \ˈbar-ō\ most northerly point of Alaska & of U.S. at about 71°25′ [N] latitude
Ba·sel \ˈbäz-əl\ *or French* **Bâle** \ˈbäl\ city [NW] Switzerland
Ba·si·lan \bä-ˈsē-ˌlän\ **1** island [S] Philippines **2** city on the island
Bas·il·don \ˈbaz-əl-dən\ town [SE] England in Essex
Ba·si·li·ca·ta \bə-ˌzil-ə-ˈkät-ə, -ˌsil-\ region [S] Italy on Gulf of Taranto; capital, Potenza
Basque Country \ˈbask\ region [N] Spain on Bay of Biscay
Bas·ra \ˈbäs-rə, ˈbəs-, ˈbas-\ city [S] Iraq on Shatt al Arab
Bass \ˈbas\ strait separating Tasmania & continent of Australia
Bassein — see PATHEIN
Basse–Nor·man·die \ˌbȧs-ˌnȯr-mä^n-ˈdē\ region [N] France on English Channel
Basse·terre \bäs-ˈter\ town, capital of Saint Kitts & Nevis
Bas·tille \ba-ˈstēl\ medieval fortress, Paris; used as prison until destroyed by mobs on July 14, 1789
Basutoland — see LESOTHO
Ba·taan \bə-ˈtan, -ˈtän\ peninsula Philippines in [W] Luzon on [W] side of Manila Bay
Batavia — see JAKARTA
Bathurst — see BANJUL
Bat·on Rouge \ˌbat-n-ˈrüzh\ city, capital of Louisiana
Ba·var·ia \bə-ˈver-ē-ə, -ˈvar-\ *or German* **Bay·ern** \ˈbī-ərn\ state [SE] Germany bordering on the Czech Republic & Austria; capital, Munich — **Ba·var·i·an** \bə-ˈver-ē-ən, -ˈvar-\ *adj or n*
Ba·ya·mon \ˌbī-ə-ˈmōn\ city [NE] central Puerto Rico
Baykal — see BAIKAL
Beard·more \ˈbiərd-ˌmōr, -ˌmȯr\ glacier Antarctica, one of world's largest
Beau·fort \ˈbō-fərt\ sea comprising part of Arctic Ocean [NE] of Alaska & [NW] of Canada
Beau·mont \ˈbō-ˌmänt, bō-ˈ\ city [SE] Texas
Bech·u·a·na·land \ˌbech-ˈwän-ə-ˌland, -ə-ˈwän-\ **1** region [S] Africa [N] of Orange River **2** — see BOTSWANA
Bed·ford·shire \ˈbed-fərd-ˌshiər, -shər\ *or* **Bedford** county [SE] England
Bedloe's — see LIBERTY
Beer·she·ba \bir-ˈshē-bə, ber-\ town [S] Israel
Bei·jing \bā-ˈjiŋ\ *or* **Pe·king** \ˈpē-ˈkiŋ, ˈpā-\ city, capital of China
Bei·rut \bā-ˈrüt\ *or ancient* **Be·ry·tus** \bə-ˈrīt-əs\ city, capital of Lebanon
Be·la·rus \ˌbē-lə-ˈrüs, ˌbyel-ə\ country central Europe; capital, Minsk — see BELORUSSIA — **Be·la·ru·si·an** \-ˈrü-sē-ən, -ˈrəsh-ən\ *or* **Be·la·rus·sian** \-ˈrəsh-ən\ *adj or n*
Belau — see PALAU
Be·lém \bə-ˈlem\ *or* **Pa·rá** \pə-ˈrä\ city [N] Brazil on Pará River
Bel·fast \ˈbel-ˌfast, bel-ˈ\ city, capital of Northern Ireland
Belgian Congo — see CONGO 2
Bel·gium \ˈbel-jəm\ *or French* **Bel·gique** \bel-ˈzhēk\ *or Flemish* **Bel·gië** \ˈbel-gē-ə\ country [W] Europe; capital, Brussels — **Bel·gian** \ˈbel-jən\ *adj or n*
Bel·grade \ˈbel-ˌgrād, -ˌgräd, -ˌgrad, bel-ˈ\ *or* **Be·o·grad** \ˈbeü-ˌgräd\ city, capital of Serbia on the Danube
Be·lize \bə-ˈlēz\ *or Spanish* **Be·li·ce** \bä-ˈlē-sā\ **1** *or formerly* **British Hon·du·ras** \hän-ˈdu̇r-əs, -ˈdyu̇r-\ country Central America on the Caribbean; capital, Belmopan **2** city [E] Belize on the Caribbean
Belle·vue \ˈbel-ˌvyü\ city [W] Washington
Bel·mo·pan \ˌbel-mō-ˈpan\ city, capital of Belize
Be·lo Ho·ri·zon·te \ˈbā-lō-ˌhȯr-ə-ˈzänt-ē, ˈbel-ō-, -ˌhär-\ city [E] Brazil [N] of Rio de Janeiro
Be·lo·rus·sia \ˌbel-ō-ˈrəsh-ə, ˌbyel-\ *or* **Bye·lo·rus·sia** \bē-ˌel-ō-, ˌbyel-ō-\ former constituent republic of U.S.S.R.; became independent Belarus 1991
Beloye More — see WHITE SEA
Be·ne·lux \ˈben-l-ˌəks\ economic union comprising Belgium, Luxembourg, & the Netherlands; formed 1947
Ben·gal \ben-ˈgȯl, beŋ-\ region [S] Asia including delta of Ganges & Brahmaputra rivers; divided between West Bengal, India & Bangladesh — see EAST BENGAL, WEST BENGAL — **Ben·gal·ese** \ˌbeŋ-gə-ˈlēz, ˌben-, -ˈlēs\ *adj or n*
Bengal, Bay of arm of Indian Ocean between India & Myanmar (Burma)
Bengaluru — see BANGALORE
Benghazi — see BANGHAZI
Ben·guela Current \ben-ˈgwel-ə, ˈbeŋ-, -ˈgel-\ cold current of the Atlantic Ocean flowing [N] along [SW] coast of Africa
Be·nin \bə-ˈnin, -ˈnēn; ˈben-ən\ **1** *or formerly* **Da·ho·mey** \də-ˈhō-mē\ country [W] Africa on Gulf of Guinea; capital, Porto-Novo; seat of government, Cotonou **2** city [SW] Nigeria — **Ben·i·nese** \bə-ˌnin-ˈēz, -ˌnēn-; ˌben-i-ˈnēz, -ˈnēs\ *adj or n*
Benin, Bight of the [N] section of Gulf of Guinea
Ben Nev·is \ben-ˈnev-əs\ mountain 4406 feet (1343 meters) [W] Scotland in the Grampians; highest in Great Britain
Be·no·ni \bə-ˈnō-nē\ city [NE] Republic of South Africa
Ber·ga·mo \ˈbeər-gə-ˌmō, ˈbər-\ city [N] Italy in Lombardy [NE] of Milan
Ber·gen \ˈbər-gən, ˈbeər-\ city & port [SW] Norway
Be·ring \ˈbiər-iŋ, ˈbeər-\ **1** sea, an arm of the North Pacific between Alaska & [NE] Siberia **2** strait 53 miles (85 kilometers) wide between North America (Alaska) & Asia (Russia)
Berke·ley \ˈbər-klē\ city [W] California on San Francisco Bay [N] of Oakland
Berk·shire \ˈbərk-ˌshiər, -shər\ hills [W] Massachusetts; highest peak Mount Greylock 3491 feet (1064 meters)
Ber·lin \bər-ˈlin, ˌbər-\ city, capital of Germany; divided 1945–90 into East Berlin & West Berlin; comprises a state of present-day Germany — **Ber·lin·er** \-ˈlin-ər\ *n*
Berlin, East former city, capital of East Germany 1945–90
Berlin, West former city, West Germany; an enclave lying wholly within East Germany
Ber·mu·da \bər-ˈmyüd-ə, ˌbər-\ islands [W] North Atlantic [ESE] of Cape Hatteras; a British colony; capital, Hamilton — **Ber·mu·dan** \-ˈmyüd-n\ *or* **Ber·mu·di·an** \-ˈmyüd-ē-ən\ *adj or n*
Bern \ˈbərn, ˈbeərn\ city, capital of Switzerland — **Ber·nese** \bər-ˈnēz, ˌbər-, -ˈnēs\ *adj or n*
Berytus — see BEIRUT
Bes·kids \ˈbes-ˌkidz, be-ˈskēdz\ mountain ranges central Europe in the [W] Carpathians including **West Beskids** (in Poland, [NW] Slovakia, & [E] Czech Republic [W] of Tatra Mountains) & **East Beskids** (in [NE] Slovakia)
Bes·sa·ra·bia \ˌbes-ə-ˈrā-bē-ə\ region [SE] Europe between Dniester & Prut rivers now chiefly in Moldova — **Bes·sa·ra·bi·an** \-bē-ən\ *adj or n*
Beth·le·hem \ˈbeth-li-ˌhem, -lē-həm, -lē-əm\ town of ancient Palestine in Judea [SW] of Jerusalem; now in West Bank
Bex·ley \ˈbek-slē\ borough of [E] Greater London, England
Bezwada — see VIJAYAWADA
Bhav·na·gar \bau̇-ˈnəg-ər\ city [W] India in [S] Gujarat
Bho·pal \bō-ˈpäl\ city [N] central India [NW] of Nagpur, capital of Madhya Pradesh
Bhu·tan \bü-ˈtan, -ˈtän\ country [S] Asia in the Himalaya on [NE] border of India; capital, Thimphu — **Bhu·ta·nese** \ˌbüt-n-ˈēz, -ˈēs\ *adj or n*
Bi·af·ra, Bight of \bē-ˈaf-rə, bī-, -ˈäf-\ the [E] section of Gulf of Guinea in [W] Africa
Bia·ly·stok \bē-ˈäl-i-ˌstȯk\ city [NE] Poland
Bie·le·feld \ˈbē-lə-ˌfelt\ city [NW] central Germany [E] of Münster
Big Bend National Park reservation [SW] Texas on Rio Grande
Big Thicket wilderness area [E] Texas [NE] of Houston
Bi·har \bi-ˈhär\ state [E] India bordering on Nepal; capital, Patna
Bi·ki·ni \bə-ˈkē-nē\ island (atoll) [W] Pacific in Marshall Islands
Bil·bao \bil-ˈbä-ˌō, -ˈbau̇, -ˈbā-ō\ city [N] Spain
Bil·lings \ˈbil-iŋz\ city [S] central Montana; largest in state
Bio·ko \bē-ˈō-(ˌ)kō\ *or formerly* **Fer·nan·do Póo** \fər-ˌnan-(ˌ)dō-ˈpō\ island Equatorial Guinea in Bight of Biafra
Bir·ken·head \ˈbər-kən-ˌhed, ˌbər-kən-ˈ\ borough [NW] England
Bir·ming·ham \ˈbər-miŋ-ˌham, *British usually* -miŋ-əm\ **1** city [N] central Alabama **2** city [W] central England
Bisayas — see VISAYAN
Bis·cay, Bay of \ˈbis-ˌkā, -kē\ inlet of North Atlantic between [W] coast of France & [N] coast of Spain
Bis·cayne National Park \bis-ˈkān-, ˈbis-ˌ\ reservation [S] Florida
Bish·kek \bish-ˈkek\ *or 1926–91* **Frun·ze** \ˈfrün-zə\ city, capital of Kyrgyzstan
Bis·marck \ˈbiz-ˌmärk\ **1** city, capital of North Dakota **2** archipelago [W] Pacific [N] of [E] end of New Guinea
Bis·sau \bis-ˈau̇\ city, capital of Guinea-Bissau
Bi·thyn·ia \bə-ˈthin-ē-ə\ ancient country [NW] Asia Minor bor-

\ə\ abut	\au̇\ out	\i\ tip	\ȯ\ saw	\u̇\ foot
\ər\ further	\ch\ chin	\ī\ life	\ȯi\ coin	\y\ yet
\a\ mat	\e\ pet	\j\ job	\th\ thin	\yü\ few
\ā\ take	\ē\ easy	\ŋ\ sing	\t͟h\ this	\yu̇\ cure
\ä\ cot, cart	\g\ go	\ō\ bone	\ü\ food	\zh\ vision

dering on Sea of Marmara and Black Sea — **Bi·thyn·i·an** \-ē-ən\ *adj or n*

Black·burn \ˈblak-bərn, -ˌbərn\ borough NW England in Lancashire

Black Canyon of the Gun·ni·son National Park \ˈgən-ə-sən\ reservation SW central Colorado along the Gunnison River (150 miles or 241 kilometers flowing W & NW into the Colorado River)

Black Forest *or German* **Schwarz·wald** \ˈshfärts-ˌvält, ˈshwȯrt-ˌswȯld\ forested mountain region SW Germany along E bank of the upper Rhine

Black Hills mountains W South Dakota & NE Wyoming; highest Harney Peak 7242 feet (2207 meters)

Black·pool \ˈblak-ˌpül\ town NW England in Lancashire

Black Sea *or ancient* **Pon·tus Eux·i·nus** \ˌpän-təs-yük-ˈsī-nəs\ *or* **Pon·tus** \ˈpän-təs\ sea between Europe & Asia connected with Aegean Sea through the Bosporus, Sea of Marmara, & Dardanelles

Blae·nau Gwent \ˈblī-ˌnī-ˈgwent\ administrative area SE Wales

Blan·tyre \ˈblan-ˌtīr\ city S Malawi

Bloem·fon·tein \ˈblüm-fən-ˌtān, -ˌfän-\ city, judicial capital of the Republic of South Africa

Blue Nile river 850 miles (1368 kilometers) long Ethiopia & Sudan flowing NNW into the Nile at Khartoum

Blue Ridge E range of the Appalachians E U.S. extending from S Pennsylvania to N Georgia

Bo·bo–Diou·las·so \ˈbō-ˌbō-dyü-ˌlas-ō\ town W Burkina Faso

Bo·chum \ˈbō-kəm\ city W Germany in valley of the Ruhr

Bodh Ga·ya \ˈbȯd-ˈgī-ä\ village NE India in central Bihar

Boe·o·tia \bē-ˈō-shē-ə, -shə\ district E central Greece NW of Attica; chief ancient city, Thebes — **Boe·o·tian** \-shē-ən, -shən\ *adj or n*

Bo·go·tá \ˌbō-gə-ˈtȯ, -ˈtä\ city, capital of Colombia

Bo Hai *or* **Po Hai** \ˈbō-ˈhī\ *or* **Gulf of Chih·li** \ˈchē-lē, ˈjiər-ˈlē\ arm of Yellow Sea NE China N of Shandong Peninsula

Bo·he·mia \bō-ˈhē-mē-ə\ region W Czech Republic; once a kingdom & later a province; chief city, Prague

Boi·se \ˈbȯi-sē, -zē\ city, capital of Idaho

Boks·burg \ˈbäks-ˌbərg\ city NE Republic of South Africa

Bo·liv·ia \bə-ˈliv-ē-ə\ country W central South America; administrative capital, La Paz; constitutional capital, Sucre — **Bo·liv·ian** \-ē-ən\ *adj or n*

Bo·lo·gna \bə-ˈlōn-yə, -ˈlōn-ə\ city N Italy N of Florence, capital of Emilia-Romagna

Bol·ton \ˈbōlt-n\ town NW England in Greater Manchester

Bom·bay \bäm-ˈbā\ *or* **Mum·bai** \ˈməm-ˌbī\ city, capital of Maharashtra, India

Bône — see ANNABA

Bo·nin \ˈbō-nən\ *or* **Oga·sa·wa·ra** \ō-ˌgäs-ə-ˈwär-ə\ islands Japan in W Pacific SE of Honshu

Bonn \ˈbän, ˈbȯn\ city W Germany on the Rhine SSE of Cologne; formerly capital of West Germany

Bon·ne·ville Salt Flats \ˈbän-ə-ˌvil\ broad level area of desert NW Utah

Boo·thia \ˈbü-thē-ə\ peninsula N Nunavut, Canada W of Baffin Island; its N tip is most northerly point on North American mainland

Bor·deaux \bȯr-ˈdō\ city SW France on the Garonne

Bor·neo \ˈbȯr-nē-ˌō\ island Malay Archipelago SW of the Philippines

Bos·nia \ˈbäz-nē-ə\ region S Europe; with Herzegovina constitutes country of **Bosnia and Herzegovina**; formerly a constituent republic of Yugoslavia; capital, Sarajevo (in Bosnia) — **Bos·ni·an** \-nē-ən\ *adj or n*

Bos·po·rus \ˈbäs-pə-rəs, -prəs\ *or ancient* **Bosporus Thra·ci·us** \-ˈthrā-shē-əs, -shəs\ strait about 18 miles (29 kilometers) long between Turkey in Europe & Turkey in Asia connecting Sea of Marmara & Black Sea

Bos·ton \ˈbȯ-stən\ city, capital of Massachusetts — **Bos·to·nian** \bȯ-ˈstō-nē-ən, -nyən\ *adj or n*

Bot·a·ny Bay \ˈbät-n-ē, ˈbät-nē\ inlet of South Pacific SE Australia in New South Wales S of Sydney

Both·nia, Gulf of \ˈbäth-nē-ə\ arm of Baltic Sea between Sweden & Finland

Bo·tswa·na \bät-ˈswän-ə\ country S Africa N of Molopo River; formerly British protectorate of Bechuanaland; now an independent republic; capital, Gaborone

Boulder Dam — see HOOVER DAM

Bourgogne — see BURGUNDY

Bourne·mouth \ˈbȯrn-məth, ˈbȯrn-, ˈbu̇rn-\ town S England in Dorset on English Channel

Brad·ford \ˈbrad-fərd\ city N England

Brah·ma·pu·tra \ˌbräm-ə-ˈpü-trə, -ˈpyü-\ river 1800 miles (2900 kilometers) long S Asia flowing from the Himalaya in Tibet to delta of the Ganges

Bra·ila \brə-ˈē-lə\ city E Romania

Bramp·ton \ˈbramp-tən\ city SE Ontario

Bran·den·burg \ˈbran-dən-ˌbərg\ state E Germany bordering on Poland; capital, Potsdam

Bra·sí·lia \brə-ˈzil-yə\ city, capital of Brazil in Federal District

Bra·sov \bräsh-ˈȯv\ city central Romania

Bra·ti·sla·va \ˌbrat-ə-ˈsläv-ə, ˌbrät-\ city, capital of Slovakia

Bratsk \ˈbrätsk\ city S central Russia in Asia, NNE of Irkutsk

Braunschweig — see BRUNSWICK

Bra·zil \brə-ˈzil\ country E & central South America; capital, Brasília — **Bra·zil·ian** \brə-ˈzil-yən\ *adj or n*

Brazil Current warm current of the Atlantic Ocean flowing S along coast of Brazil

Braz·za·ville \ˈbraz-ə-ˌvil, ˈbräz-ə-ˌvēl\ city, capital of Republic of the Congo on W bank of Pool Malebo in lower Congo River

Bre·men \ˈbrem-ən, ˈbrā-mən\ **1** state NW Germany **2** city, its capital

Bren·ner \ˈbren-ər\ pass 4495 feet (1370 meters) in the Alps between Austria & Italy

Brent \ˈbrent\ borough of W Greater London, England

Bre·scia \ˈbresh-ə, ˈbrā-shə\ city N Italy in Lombardy

Breslau — see WROCLAW

Brest \ˈbrest\ **1** city SW Belarus **2** city NW France in Brittany

Bret·on, Cape \kāp-ˈbret-n, kə-ˈbret-, -ˈbrit-\ headland Canada; most easterly point of Cape Breton Island & of Nova Scotia

Bridg·end \ˌbrij-ˈend\ administrative area S Wales

Bridge·port \ˈbrij-ˌpōrt, -ˌpȯrt\ city SW Connecticut on Long Island Sound

Bridge·town \ˈbrij-ˌtau̇n\ city, capital of Barbados

Brigh·ton \ˈbrīt-n\ town S England in East Sussex on English Channel

Bris·bane \ˈbriz-bən, -ˌbān\ city E Australia, capital of Queensland

Bris·tol \ˈbris-tl\ **1** city SW England **2** channel between S Wales & SW England

Brit·ain \ˈbrit-n\ **1** the island of Great Britain **2** UNITED KINGDOM

British Columbia province W Canada on North Pacific coast; capital, Victoria

British Commonwealth — see COMMONWEALTH (the)

British Guiana — see GUYANA

British Honduras — see BELIZE 1

British Indian Ocean Territory British colony in Indian Ocean comprising Chagos Archipelago & formerly Aldabra, Farquhar, & Desroches islands (returned to Seychelles 1976)

British Isles island group W Europe comprising Great Britain, Ireland, & adjacent islands

British Solomon Islands former British protectorate comprising the Solomon Islands (except Bougainville, Buka, & adjacent small islands) & Santa Cruz Islands; capital, Honiara

British Somaliland former British protectorate E Africa bordering on Gulf of Aden; since 1960 part of Somalia

British Virgin Islands E islands of Virgin Islands group; a British dependency; capital, Road Town (on Tortola Island)

British West Indies islands of the West Indies belonging to the Commonwealth & including Jamaica, Trinidad and Tobago, & the Bahama, Cayman, Windward, Leeward, & British Virgin islands

Brit·ta·ny \ˈbrit-n-ē\ *or French* **Bre·tagne** \brə-ˈtänʸ\ region & former province NW France SW of Normandy

Brno \ˈbər-nō\ city SE Czech Republic, chief city of Moravia

Brom·ley \ˈbräm-lē\ borough of SE Greater London, England

Bronx \ˈbräŋs, ˈbräŋks\ *or* **The Bronx** borough of New York City on mainland NE of Manhattan Island

Brook·lyn \ˈbru̇k-lən\ borough of New York City at SW end of Long Island

Brooks Range \ˈbru̇ks\ mountains N Alaska

Bruce Peninsula National Park \ˈbrüs\ reservation SE Ontario

Bruges \ˈbrüzh, ˈbrüezh\ *or Flemish* **Brug·ge** \ˈbrüeg-ə\ city NW Belgium

Bru·nei \bru̇n-ˈī, ˈbrü-ˌnī\ sultanate NE Borneo; formerly a Brit-

ish protectorate; capital, Bandar Seri Begawan — **Bru·nei·an** \brü-'nī-ən\ *adj or n*
Bruns·wick \'brənz-wik\ *or German* **Braun·schweig** \'braün-ˌshwīg, -ˌshfīk\ city central Germany [W] of Berlin
Brus·sels \'brəs-əlz\ city, capital of Belgium
Bryansk \brē-'änsk\ city [W] Russia in Europe, [SW] of Moscow
Bryce Canyon National Park \'brīs\ reservation [S] Utah
Bu·ca·ra·man·ga \ˌbü-kə-rə-'mäng-gə\ city [N] Colombia [NNE] of Bogotá
Bu·cha·rest \'bü-kə-ˌrest, 'byü-\ city, capital of Romania
Bucheon — see PUCHON
Buck·ing·ham·shire \'bək-ing-əm-ˌshiər, -shər, *in the U.S. also* -ing-ˌham-\ *or* **Buckingham** county [SE] central England
Bu·da·pest \'büd-ə-ˌpest *also* 'byüd-, 'büd-, -ˌpesht\ city, capital of Hungary
Bue·nos Ai·res \ˌbwā-nə-'saər-ēz, ˌbō-nə-, -'seər-, -'sīr-\ city, capital of Argentina on Rio de la Plata
Buf·fa·lo \'bəf-ə-ˌlō\ city [W] New York on Lake Erie
Bu·jum·bu·ra \ˌbü-jəm-'bür-ə\ *or formerly* **Usum·bu·ra** \ˌü-səm-'bür-ə\ city, capital of Burundi
Bu·ka·vu \bü-'käv-ü\ city [E] Democratic Republic of the Congo
Bu·kha·ra \bü-'kär-ə, -'kar-, -'här-, -'har-\ *or* **Bu·xo·ro** \bü-'kor-ō\ city Uzbekistan [E] of the Amu Dar'ya
Bu·la·wayo \ˌbül-ə-'wā-ō, -'wī-\ city [SW] Zimbabwe
Bul·gar·ia \ˌbəl-'gar-ē-ə, bül-, -'ger-\ country [SE] Europe on Black Sea; capital, Sofia
Bur·bank \'bər-ˌbangk\ city [SW] California
Bur·gun·dy \'bər-gən-dē\ *or French* **Bour·gogne** \bür-'gōnʸ\ region [E] France; a former kingdom, duchy, & province — **Bur·gun·di·an** \bər-'gən-dē-ən, ˌbər-\ *adj or n*
Bur·ki·na Fa·so \bür-'kē-nə-'fäs-ō, bər-\ *or formerly* **Upper Vol·ta** \'vōl-tə, 'vōl-, 'väl-\ country [W] Africa [N] of Ivory Coast, Ghana, & Togo; capital, Ouagadougou
Bur·ling·ton \'bər-ling-tən\ city [NW] Vermont; largest in state
Burma — see MYANMAR
Bur·na·by \'bər-nə-bē\ city [SW] British Columbia
Bur·sa \bür-'sä, 'bər-sə\ city [NW] Turkey in Asia
Bu·run·di \bü-'rün-dē\ *or formerly* **Urun·di** \ü-'rün-dē\ country [E] central Africa; capital, Bujumbura — see RUANDA-URUNDI
Busan — see PUSAN
Bute \'byüt\ island [SW] Scotland in Firth of Clyde
Buxoro — see BUKHARA
Byd·goszcz \'bid-ˌgōshch, -ˌgōsh\ *or German* **Brom·berg** \'bräm-ˌbərg, 'brōm-ˌberk\ city [NW] central Poland
Byelorussia — see BELORUSSIA
Byzantium — see ISTANBUL
Cabo Verde — see CAPE VERDE
Caen \'käⁿ\ city [NW] France
Caer·phil·ly \kər-'fil-ē\ administrative area [SE] Wales
Cae·sa·rea \ˌsē-zə-'rē-ə; ˌses-ə-, ˌsez-ə-\ city of ancient Palestine in Samaria on the Mediterranean; Roman capital of Palestine
Ca·glia·ri \'käl-yə-rē\ city Italy, capital of Sardinia
Ca·guas \'käg-ˌwäs\ town [E] central Puerto Rico
Cai·ro \'kī-rō\ city, capital of Egypt — **Cai·rene** \kī-'rēn\ *adj or n*
Ca·la·bria \kə-'lā-brē-ə, -'läb-rē-\ **1** district of ancient Italy comprising area forming heel of peninsula of Italy; now [S] part of Puglia **2** *or ancient* **Brut·ti·um** \'brüt-ē-əm, 'brət-\ region [S] Italy occupying toe of peninsula of Italy; capital, Catanzaro — **Ca·la·bri·an** \kə-'lā-brē-ən, -'läb-rē-\ *adj or n*
Cal·cut·ta \kal-'kət-ə\ *or* **Kol·ka·ta** \kōl-'kä-tä\ city [E] India on Hugli River, capital of West Bengal — **Cal·cut·tan** \-'kət-n\ *adj or n*
Cal·e·do·nia \ˌkal-ə-'dō-nyə, -nē-ə\ — see SCOTLAND — **Cal·e·do·nian** \-nyən, -nē-ən\ *adj or n*
Cal·ga·ry \'kal-gə-rē\ city [SW] Alberta
Ca·li \'käl-ē\ city [W] Colombia
Cal·i·cut \'kal-i-kət\ *or* **Ko·zhi·kode** \'kō-zhə-ˌkōd\ city & port [SW] India
Cal·i·for·nia \ˌkal-ə-'fór-nyə\ state [SW] U.S.; capital, Sacramento — **Cal·i·for·nian** \-nyən\ *adj or n*
California, Gulf of arm of the North Pacific [NW] Mexico
California Current cold current of the North Pacific flowing [SE] along [W] coast of North America
Ca·llao \kə-'yä-ō, kə-'yaü\ city [W] Peru [W] of Lima
Cal·va·ry \'kalv-rē, -ə-rē\ *or Hebrew* **Gol·go·tha** \'gäl-gə-thə, gäl-'gäth-ə\ place outside ancient Jerusalem where Jesus was crucified
Ca·ma·güey \ˌkam-ə-'gwā\ city [E] central Cuba
Cam·bay, Gulf of — see KHAMBHAT (Gulf of)
Cam·ber·well \'kam-bər-ˌwel, -wəl\ city [SE] Australia in [S] Victoria [E] of Melbourne
Cam·bo·dia \kam-'bōd-ē-ə\ *or Khmer* **Kam·pu·chea** \ˌkam-pü-'chē-ə\ country [SE] Asia bordering on Gulf of Thailand; capital, Phnom Penh — **Cam·bo·di·an** \-ē-ən\ *adj or n*
Cam·bria \'kam-brē-ə\ — see WALES
Cam·bridge \'kām-brij\ **1** city [E] Massachusetts [W] of Boston **2** city [E] England in Cambridgeshire
Cam·bridge·shire \'kām-brij-ˌshiər, -shər\ *or* **Cambridge** county [E] England
Cam·den \'kam-dən\ **1** city [SW] New Jersey **2** borough of [N] Greater London, England
Cam·er·oon *or French* **Cam·er·oun** \ˌkam-ə-'rün\ country [W] equatorial Africa; capital, Yaoundé — **Cam·er·oo·nian** \-'rü-nē-ən, -'rü-nyən\ *adj or n*
Cam·er·oons \ˌkam-ə-'rünz\ region [W] Africa on [NE] Gulf of Guinea formerly administered by the British and French but now divided between Nigeria & Cameroon
Cam·pa·nia \kam-'pā-nyə, -nē-ə\ region [S] Italy bordering on Tyrrhenian Sea; capital, Naples — **Cam·pa·nian** \-nyən, -nē-ən\ *adj or n*
Cam·pe·che \kam-'pē-chē, käm-'pā-chā\ state [SE] Mexico in [W] Yucatán Peninsula; capital, Campeche
Cam·pi·nas \kam-'pē-nəs\ city [SE] Brazil [N] of São Paulo
Cam·po·bas·so \ˌkäm-pō-'bäs-ˌō\ city central Italy
Cam·po Gran·de \ˌkam-pü-'gran-də, -dē\ city [SW] Brazil
Cam·pos \'kam-pəs\ city [SE] Brazil [NE] of Rio de Janeiro
Cam Ranh Bay \'käm-'rän\ inlet of South China Sea [SE] Vietnam
Ca·naan \'kā-nən\ name used for region comprising part of or roughly equivalent to ancient Palestine — **Ca·naan·ite** \'kā-nə-ˌnīt\ *adj or n*
Can·a·da \'kan-ə-də\ country [N] North America; capital, Ottawa
Canadian Shield *or* **Lau·ren·tian Plateau** \lò-'ren-chən-\ plateau region [E] Canada & [NE] U.S. extending from Mackenzie Basin [E] to Davis Strait & [S] to [S] Quebec, [S] central Ontario, [NE] Minnesota, [N] Wisconsin, [NW] Michigan, & [NE] New York including the Adirondacks
Canal Zone *or* **Panama Canal Zone** strip of territory Panama; under U.S. control through 1999 for administration of the Panama Canal
Ca·nary \kə-'neər-ē\ islands in the North Atlantic off [NW] coast of Africa belonging to Spain; capital, Las Palmas
Ca·nav·er·al, Cape \kə-'nav-rəl, -ə-rəl\ *or 1963–73 officially* **Cape Ken·ne·dy** \-'ken-ə-dē\ headland [E] Florida in the North Atlantic on Canaveral Peninsula [E] of Indian River
Can·ber·ra \'kan-bə-rə, -brə, -ˌber-ə\ city, capital of Australia in Australian Capital Territory
Cannes \'kan, 'kän\ town & port [SE] France
Can·ta·bria \kän-'täb-rē-ə\ region [N] Spain on Bay of Biscay
Can·ter·bury \'kant-ər-ˌber-ē, 'kant-ə-, -bə-rē, -brē\ **1** city [SE] Australia in [E] New South Wales **2** city [SE] England in Kent
Can·ton \'kant-n\ city [NE] Ohio
Canton — see GUANGZHOU
Can·yon·lands National Park \'kan-yən-ˌlandz, -ˌlanz\ reservation [SE] Utah
Cape Bret·on Highlands National Park \kāp-ˌbret-n, kə-ˌbret-, -ˌbrit-\ reservation [NE] Nova Scotia near [N] end of Cape Breton Island
Cape Breton Island island [NE] Nova Scotia
Cape Coral city [SW] Florida
Cape of Good Hope **1** — see GOOD HOPE (Cape of) **2** *or* **Cape Province** *or before 1910* **Cape Colony** former province [S] Republic of South Africa; capital, Cape Town
Ca·per·na·um \kə-'pər-nē-əm\ city of ancient Palestine on [NW] shore of Sea of Galilee
Cape Town \'kāp-ˌtaün\ city Republic of South Africa, its legislative capital
Cape Verde \'vərd\ *or* **Ca·bo Ver·de** \ˌkä-bü-'verd-ə\ **1** islands in the North Atlantic off [W] Africa; a republic; capital, Praia; until 1975 belonged to Portugal **2** — see VERDE (Cape)

\ə\ **abut**	\aü\ **out**	\i\ **tip**	\ó\ **saw**	\ü\ **foot**
\ər\ **further**	\ch\ **chin**	\ī\ **life**	\ói\ **coin**	\y\ **yet**
\a\ **mat**	\e\ **pet**	\j\ **job**	\th\ **thin**	\yü\ **few**
\ā\ **take**	\ē\ **easy**	\ng\ **sing**	\th\ **this**	\yú\ **cure**
\ä\ **cot, cart**	\g\ **go**	\ō\ **bone**	\ü\ **food**	\zh\ **vision**

Cape York Peninsula \ˈyȯrk\ peninsula NE Australia in N Queensland
Capitol Reef National Park reservation S central Utah
Cap·pa·do·cia \ˌkap-ə-ˈdō-shə, -shē-ə\ ancient country & Roman province E Asia Minor; capital, Caesarea Mazaca
Ca·pri \ka-ˈprē, kə-; ˈkäp-rē, ˈkap-\ island Italy S of Bay of Naples
Ca·ra·cas \kə-ˈrak-əs, -ˈräk-\ city, capital of Venezuela
Car·diff \ˈkärd-əf\ **1** administrative area S Wales **2** city, capital of Wales
Ca·rib·be·an Sea \ˌkar-ə-ˈbē-ən, kə-ˈrib-ē-ən\ arm of the North Atlantic bounded on N & E by West Indies, on S by South America, & on W by Central America
Ca·rin·thia \kə-ˈrin-thē-ə, -ˈrint-\ region central Europe in E Alps in S Austria & Slovenia
Car·low \ˈkär-ˌlō\ county SE Ireland in Leinster
Carls·bad Caverns \ˈkärlz-ˌbad\ limestone caves SE New Mexico in **Carlsbad Caverns National Park**
Car·mar·then·shire \kär-ˈmär-t͟hən-ˌshiər, kər-, kə-, -shər\ *or* **Carmarthen** administrative area S Wales
Carmel, Mount \ˈkär-məl\ mountain ridge N Israel; highest point 1791 feet (546 meters)
Car·o·li·na \ˌkar-ə-ˈlī-nə\ English colony on E coast of North America founded 1663 & divided 1729 into North Carolina & South Carolina (the **Carolinas**) — **Car·o·lin·i·an** \-ˈlin-ē-ən\ *adj or n*
Ca·ro·li·na \ˌkär-ə-ˈlē-nə\ city NE central Puerto Rico
Car·o·line \ˈkar-ə-ˌlīn, -lən\ islands W Pacific E of S Philippines comprising Palau and the Federated States of Micronesia; formerly part of Trust Territory of the Pacific Islands
Car·pa·thi·an \kär-ˈpā-thē-ən\ mountains E central Europe along boundary between Slovakia & Poland & in N & central Romania; highest Gerlachovsky 8711 feet (2655 meters)
Carpathian Ruthenia — see RUTHENIA
Car·pen·tar·ia, Gulf of \ˌkär-pən-ˈter-ē-ə, -ˈtar-\ inlet of Arafura Sea N of Australia
Car·roll·ton \ˈkar-əl-tən\ city N Texas
Car·son City \ˈkärs-ⁿn\ city, capital of Nevada
Car·ta·ge·na \ˌkärt-ə-ˈgā-nə, -ˈhā-\ **1** city NW Colombia **2** city SE Spain
Car·thage \ˈkär-thij\ ancient city N Africa NE of modern Tunis; capital of an empire that included at greatest extent much of NW Africa, E Spain, & Sicily — **Car·tha·gin·ian** \ˌkär-thə-ˈjin-yən, -ˈjin-ē-ən\ *adj or n*
Ca·sa·blan·ca \ˌkas-ə-ˈblaŋ-kə, ˌkaz-\ *or Arabic* **Dar el Bei·da** \ˌdär-ˌel-bā-ˈdä\ city W Morocco on the North Atlantic
Cas·cade Range \kas-ˈkād, ˈkas-ˈkād\ mountains NW U.S. in Washington, Oregon, & N California — see RAINIER (Mount)
Cas·pi·an Sea \ˈkas-pē-ən\ salt lake between Europe & Asia about 90 feet (27 meters) below sea level
Cas·tile \kas-ˈtēl\ *or Spanish* **Cas·ti·lla** \kä-ˈstē-l^{y}ä, -ˈstē-yä\ region & ancient kingdom central & N Spain
Cas·tries \ka-ˈstrē, ˈkas-ˌtrēz\ city, capital of St. Lucia
Cat·a·lo·nia \ˌkat-ˡl-ˈō-nyə, -nē-ə\ *or Spanish* **Ca·ta·lu·ña** \ˌkät-ˡl-ˈü-nyə\ region NE Spain bordering on France & the Mediterranean; chief city, Barcelona — **Cat·a·lo·nian** \-ˈō-nyən, -nē-ən\ *adj or n*
Ca·ta·nia \kə-ˈtän-yə, -ˈtān-\ city Italy in E Sicily at foot of Mount Etna
Ca·tan·za·ro \ˌkät-ˌän-ˈzär-ˌō, -ˌänd-\ city S Italy
Ca·thay \ka-ˈthā, ka-\ CHINA — an old name
Cats·kill \ˈkat-ˌskil\ mountains in Appalachian system SE New York W of the Hudson
Cau·ca·sus \ˈkȯ-kə-səs\ **1** *or* **Cau·ca·sia** \kȯ-ˈkā-zhə, -shə\ region SE Europe between Black & Caspian seas **2** mountain system in Caucasus region — see ELBRUS (Mount)
Cav·an \ˈkav-ən\ county NE Ireland (republic) in Ulster
Cay·enne \kī-ˈen, kā-\ city, capital of French Guiana
Cay·man \kā-ˈman, ˈkā-, *attributively* ˈkā-mən\ islands British West Indies NW of Jamaica; a British colony; capital, George-town (on Grand Cayman Island)
Ce·bu \sā-ˈbü\ **1** island E central Philippines in Visayan Islands **2** city on E coast of Cebu Island
Ce·dar Rapids \ˈsēd-ər\ city E Iowa
Celebes — see SULAWESI
Celestial Empire the former Chinese Empire
Cel·le \ˈtsel-ə, ˈsel-ə\ city N central Germany NE of Hannover
Cel·tic \ˈkel-tik, ˈsel-\ sea inlet of the North Atlantic in British Isles SE of Ireland, SW of Wales, & W of Cornwall
Central African Republic country N central Africa; formerly the French territory of **Uban·gi–Sha·ri** \ü-ˈbaŋ-gē-ˈshär-ē, yü-, -ˈbaŋ-ē-\; capital, Bangui
Central America narrow portion of North America from S border of Mexico to South America — **Central American** *adj or n*
Centre \ˈsä^{n}tr^{ə}\ region central France
Ce·ram *or* **Se·ram** \ˈsā-ˌräm\ island E Indonesia in central Moluccas
Ce·re·dig·i·on \ˌker-ə-ˈdig-ē-ˌän\ administrative area SW Wales
Cé·vennes \sā-ˈven\ mountain range S France in SE Massif Central; highest peak Mount Mézenc 5755 feet (1754 meters)
Cey·lon \si-ˈlän, sā-\ **1** island in Indian Ocean off S India **2** — see SRI LANKA — **Cey·lon·ese** \ˌsā-lə-ˈnēz, ˌsē-lə-, ˌsel-ə-, -ˈnēs\ *adj or n*
Chad *or French* **Tchad** \ˈchad\ country N central Africa; capital, N'Djamana — **Chad·ian** \ˈchad-ē-ən\ *adj or n*
Chad, Lake shallow lake N central Africa at junction of boundaries of Chad, Niger, & Nigeria
Cha·gos \ˈchä-gəs\ archipelago central Indian Ocean; comprises British Indian Ocean Territory — see DIEGO GARCIA
Chal·cid·i·ce \kal-ˈsid-ə-sē\ peninsula NE Greece in E Macedonia
Chal·dea \kal-ˈdē-ə\ ancient region SW Asia on Euphrates River & Persian Gulf — **Chal·de·an** \-ˈdē-ən\ *adj or n* — **Chal·dee** \ˈkal-ˌdē\ *n*
Cham·pagne–Ar·denne \sham-ˈpān-är-ˈden\ region N France bordering on Belgium
Cham·plain, Lake \sham-ˈplān\ lake between New York & Vermont extending N into Quebec
Chan·di·garh \ˈchən-dē-gər\ city N India N of Delhi, constitutes a territory administered by the national government
Chan·dler \ˈchand-lər\ city SW central Arizona
Chang \ˈchäŋ\ *or traditionally* **Yang·tze** \ˈyaŋ-ˈsē; ˈyaŋt-sē, ˈyaŋkt-\ river 3965 miles (6380 kilometers) long central China flowing into East China Sea
Changan — see XI'AN
Ch'ang–chia–k'ou — see ZHANGJIAKOU
Ch'ang–chou — see ZHANGZHOU
Chang–chun \ˈchäŋ-ˈchu̇n\ city NE China, capital of Jilin
Chang·de *or* **Chang·te** \ˈchäŋ-ˈdə\ city SE central China in N Hunan
Chang·sha \ˈchäŋ-ˈshä\ city SE central China, capital of Hunan
Channel **1** — see SANTA BARBARA **2** **2** islands in English Channel including Jersey, Guernsey, & Alderney & belonging to United Kingdom
Channel Islands National Park reservation California off SW coast
Cha·pa·la \chə-ˈpäl-ə\ lake W central Mexico SE of Guadalajara
Charles \ˈchärlz\ river 47 miles (76 kilometers) long E Massachusetts
Charles, Cape cape E Virginia N of entrance to Chesapeake Bay
Charles·ton \ˈchärl-stən\ city, capital of West Virginia
Char·lotte \ˈshär-lət\ city S North Carolina
Charlotte Ama·lie \ə-ˈmäl-yə\ city, capital of Virgin Islands of the U.S.; on Saint Thomas Island
Char·lotte·town \ˈshär-lət-ˌtau̇n\ city, capital of Prince Edward Island, Canada
Chat·ta·noo·ga \ˌchat-ə-ˈnü-gə, ˌchat-ⁿn-ˈü-\ city SE Tennessee
Che·bok·sa·ry \ˌcheb-ˌäk-ˈsär-ē\ city central Russia in Europe on the Volga
Chech·nya \chech-ˈnyä, ˈchech-nyə\ area of SE Russia in Europe; capital, Grozny
Chekiang — see ZHEJIANG
Chelsea — see KENSINGTON AND CHELSEA
Che·lya·binsk \chel-ˈyä-bənsk\ city W Russia in Asia S of Sverdlovsk
Chemnitz \ˈkem-ˌnits, -nəts\ *or 1953–90* **Karl–Marx–Stadt** \ˌkärl-ˈmärk-ˌshtät, -ˌstät\ city E Germany SE of Leipzig
Chen–chiang — see ZHENJIANG
Cheng–chou — see ZHENGZHOU
Cheng·du *or* **Ch'eng–tu** \ˈchəŋ-ˈdü\ city SW central China, capital of Sichuan
Chennai — see MADRAS

Cher·no·byl \chər-ˈnō-bəl, cher-\ *or* **Chor·no·byl** \chȯr-ˈnō-bəl\ site [N] Ukraine of town abandoned after 1986 nuclear accident
Ches·a·peake Bay \ˈches-ˌpēk, -ə-ˌpēk\ inlet of the North Atlantic in Virginia & Maryland
Chesh·ire \ˈchesh-ər, ˈchesh-ˌiər\ *or* **Ches·ter** \ˈches-tər\ county [W] England bordering on Wales
Chev·i·ot \ˈchev-ē-ət, ˈchē-vē-ət\ hills along English–Scottish border
Chey·enne \shī-ˈan, -ˈen\ city, capital of Wyoming
Chhat·tis·garh \chə-ˈtēz-gər\ state central India; capital, Raipur
Chia–mu–ssu — see JIAMUSI
Chia·pas \chē-ˈäp-əs\ state [SE] Mexico; capital, Tuxtla Gutiérrez
Chi·ba \ˈchē-bə\ city [E] Japan in Honshu on Tokyo Bay
Chi·ca·go \shə-ˈkäg-ō, -ˈkȯg-\ city [NE] Illinois — **Chi·ca·go·an** \-ˈkäg-ə-wən, -ˈkȯg-\ *n*
Chi·chén It·zá \chə-ˌchen-ət-ˈsä\ ruined Mayan city [SE] Mexico in Yucatán [ESE] of Mérida
Ch'i–ch'i–ha–erh — see QIQIHAR
Chihli, Gulf of — see BO HAI
Chi·hua·hua \chə-ˈwä-wä, shə-, -wə\ **1** state [N] Mexico bordering on U.S. **2** city, its capital
Chile \ˈchil-ē\ country [SW] South America; capital, Santiago — **Chil·ean** \ˈchil-ē-ən, chə-ˈlā-ən\ *adj or n*
Chi–lung — see JILONG
Chim·bo·ra·zo \ˌchim-bə-ˈräz-ō, ˌshim-\ mountain 20,561 feet (6267 meters) [W] central Ecuador
Chimkent — see SHYMKENT
Chi·na, People's Republic of \ˈchī-nə\ country [E] Asia; capital, Beijing
China, Republic of — see TAIWAN
China Sea section of the [W] Pacific [E] & [SE] of China; divided at Taiwan Strait into **East China** & **South China** seas
Chinan — see JINAN
Chin–chou *or* **Chinchow** — see JINZHOU
Chi·os \ˈkī-ˌäs\ island Greece in the Aegean off [W] coast of Turkey
Chi·si·nau \ˌkē-shē-ˈnau̇\ *or 1940–91* **Ki·shi·nev** \ˈkish-i-ˌnef\ city, capital of Moldova
Chi·ta \chit-ˈä\ city [S] Russia in Asia, [E] of Lake Baikal
Chit·ta·gong \ˈchit-ə-ˌgäng, -ˌgȯng\ city [SE] Bangladesh on Bay of Bengal
Chkalov — see ORENBURG
Chong·jin *or* **Cheong·jin** \ˈchəŋ-ˌjin\ city & port [NE] North Korea on East Sea (Sea of Japan)
Chong·ju *or* **Cheong·ju** \ˈchəŋ-ˌjü\ city central South Korea
Chong·qing *or* **Ch'ung–ch'ing** \ˈchu̇ŋ-ˈchiŋ\ *or* **Chung·king** \ˈchu̇ŋ-ˈkiŋ\ city [SW] central China in [SE] Sichuan
Chon·ju *or* **Jeon·ju** \ˈjən-ˌjü\ city [W] South Korea
Chosen — see KOREA
Christ·church \ˈkrīs-ˌchərch, ˈkrīst-\ city New Zealand on [E] coast of South Island
Christ·mas \ˈkris-məs\ **1** island [E] Indian Ocean [SW] of Java; administered by Australia **2** — see KIRITIMATI
Ch'üan–chou *or* **Chuanchow** — see QUANZHOU
Chu–chou *or* **Chuchow** — see ZHUZHOU
Chu·la Vis·ta \ˌchü-lə-ˈvis-tə\ city [SW] California [S] of San Diego
Chuuk \ˈchu̇k\ *or* **Truk** \ˈtrək, ˈtru̇k\ islands central Carolines [W] Pacific; part of the Federated States of Micronesia
Ci·li·cia \sə-ˈlish-ə, -ˈlish-ē-ə\ ancient country [SE] Asia Minor on coast [S] of Taurus Mountains
Cin·cin·na·ti \ˌsin-sə-ˈnat-ē, -ˈnat-ə\ city [SW] Ohio on Ohio River
Cis·al·pine Gaul \sis-ˌal-ˌpīn-\ the part of Gaul lying [S] & [E] of the Alps
Citlaltepetl — see ORIZABA
Città del Vaticano — see VATICAN CITY
Ci·u·dad Gua·ya·na \ˌsē-ü-ˌt͟hät͟h-gwə-ˈyän-ə\ city [E] Venezuela
Ciudad Juá·rez *or* **Juárez** \ˈhwär-əs, ˈwär-\ city [N] Mexico in Chihuahua on Rio Grande opposite El Paso, Texas
Ciudad Trujillo — see SANTO DOMINGO
Clack·man·nan·shire \klak-ˈman-ən-ˌshir, -shər\ administrative area central Scotland
Clare \ˈklaər, ˈkleər\ county [W] Ireland in Munster
Clarks·ville \ˈklärks-ˌvil\ city [N] Tennessee
Clear·wa·ter \ˈklir-ˌwȯt-ər, -ˌwät-\ city [W] Florida on Gulf of Mexico
Cleve·land \ˈklēv-lənd\ city & port [NE] Ohio on Lake Erie
Clyde \ˈklīd\ river 106 miles (171 kilometers) long [SW] Scotland flowing into **Firth of Clyde** (estuary)
Clydes·dale \ˈklīdz-ˌdāl\ valley of upper Clyde River, Scotland
Cnossus — see KNOSSOS
Coa·hui·la \ˌkō-ə-ˈwē-lə, kwä-ˈwē-\ state [N] Mexico bordering on U.S.; capital, Saltillo
Coast Mountains mountain range [W] British Columbia; the [N] continuation of Cascade Range
Coast Ranges chain of mountain ranges [W] North America extending along Pacific coast through Vancouver Island into [S] Alaska to Kenai Peninsula & Kodiak Island
Co·chin China \ˌkō-chən-\ region [S] Vietnam
Cod, Cape \ˈkäd\ peninsula [SE] Massachusetts
Coim·ba·tore \ˌkȯim-bə-ˈtōr, -ˈtȯr\ city [S] India in [W] Tamil Nadu
Col·chis \ˈkäl-kəs\ ancient country bordering on Black Sea [S] of Caucasus Mountains; district now in [W] Republic of Georgia
Co·li·ma \kə-ˈlē-mə\ **1** state [SW] Mexico **2** city, its capital
Co·logne \kə-ˈlōn\ *or German* **Köln** \ˈkœln\ city [W] Germany on the Rhine
Co·lom·bia \kə-ˈləm-bē-ə\ country [NW] South America; capital, Bogotá — **Co·lom·bi·an** \-bē-ən\ *adj or n*
Co·lom·bo \kə-ˈləm-bō\ city, capital of Sri Lanka
Co·lón \kə-ˈlōn\ city Panama on the Caribbean
Colón Archipelago — see GALAPAGOS ISLANDS
Col·o·ra·do \ˌkäl-ə-ˈrad-ō, -ˈräd-\ **1** river 1450 miles (2334 kilometers) long [SW] U.S. & [NW] Mexico flowing from [N] Colorado into Gulf of California **2** desert [SE] California **3** plateau region [SW] U.S. [W] of Rocky Mountains **4** state [W] U.S.; capital, Denver — **Col·o·rad·an** \-ˈrad-n, -ˈräd-n\ *or* **Co·lo·ra·do·an** \-ˈrad-ə-wən, -ˈräd-\ *adj or n*
Colorado Springs city central Colorado [E] of Pikes Peak
Co·los·sae \kə-ˈlä-sē\ ancient city in [SW] Phrygia
Co·lum·bia \kə-ˈləm-bē-ə\ **1** river 1214 miles (1953 kilometers) long [SW] Canada & [NW] U.S. rising in [SE] British Columbia & flowing [C] & [W] into North Pacific **2** plateau in basin of Columbia River in [E] Washington, [E] Oregon, & [SW] Idaho **3** city, capital of South Carolina
Co·lum·bus \kə-ˈləm-bəs\ **1** city [W] Georgia **2** city, capital of Ohio
Commonwealth of Independent States association of the former constituent republics of the U.S.S.R. except for Lithuania, Latvia, & Estonia which didn't join & Georgia which withdrew 2009; formed 1991
Commonwealth, the *or* **Commonwealth of Nations** *or formerly* **British Commonwealth** association consisting of the United Kingdom and a number of its former dependencies
Co·mo, Lake \ˈkō-mō\ lake [N] Italy in Lombardy
Com·o·ros \ˈkäm-ə-ˌrōz\ islands off [SE] Africa [NW] of Madagascar; formerly a French possession; a republic (except for Mayotte Island remaining French) since 1975; capital, Moroni
Com·stock Lode \ˌkäm-ˌstäk\ gold & silver deposit at Virginia City, Nevada, discovered 1859
Con·a·kry \ˈkän-ə-krē\ city, capital of Guinea
Con·cord \ˈkäŋ-kərd\ **1** city, capital of New Hampshire **2** town [E] Massachusetts [NW] of Boston
Confederate States of America the 11 states of the U.S. during their secession from the Union 1860–65: Alabama, Arkansas, Florida, Georgia, Louisiana, Mississippi, North Carolina, South Carolina, Tennessee, Texas, & Virginia
Con·ga·ree National Park \ˈkäŋ-gə-ˌrē\ reservation central South Carolina
Con·go \ˈkäŋ-gō\ **1** *or* **Zaire** river more than 2700 miles (4344 kilometers) long [W] equatorial Africa flowing into the South Atlantic **2** *or* **Democratic Republic of the Congo** *or 1971–97* **Zaire** *or 1908–60* **Belgian Congo** country central Africa comprising most of basin [E] of lower Congo River; capital, Kinshasa **3** *or* **Republic of the Congo** *or formerly* **Middle Congo** country [W] central Africa [W] of lower Congo River; capital, Brazzaville — **Con·go·lese** \ˌkäŋ-gə-ˈlēz, -ˈlēs\ *adj or n*
Con·nacht \ˈkän-ˌȯt\ province [W] Ireland
Con·nect·i·cut \kə-ˈnet-i-kət\ **1** river 407 miles (655 kilome-

\ə\ abut	\au̇\ out	\i\ tip	\ȯ\ saw	\u̇\ foot
\ər\ further	\ch\ chin	\ī\ life	\ȯi\ coin	\y\ yet
\a\ mat	\e\ pet	\j\ job	\th\ thin	\yü\ few
\ā\ take	\ē\ easy	\ŋ\ sing	\t͟h\ this	\yu̇\ cure
\ä\ cot, cart	\g\ go	\ō\ bone	\ü\ food	\zh\ vision

ters) long [NE] U.S. flowing [S] from [N] New Hampshire into Long Island Sound **2** state [NE] U.S.; capital, Hartford

Con·stan·tine \ˈkän-stən-ˌtēn\ city [NE] Algeria

Constantinople — see ISTANBUL

Con·stan·tsa \kən-ˈstän-sə, -ˈstänt-\ city [SE] Romania

Con·wy \ˈkän-wē\ administrative area [N] Wales

Cook \ˈku̇k\ **1** inlet of the North Pacific [S] Alaska [W] of Kenai Peninsula **2** islands South Pacific [SW] of Society Islands belonging to New Zealand; capital, Avarua (on Rarotonga Island) **3** strait New Zealand between North Island & South Island

Cook, Mount *or Maori* **Ao·ra·ki** \au̇-ˈrä-kē\ mountain 12,316 feet (3754 meters) New Zealand in [W] central South Island in Southern Alps; highest in New Zealand

Co·pen·ha·gen \ˌkō-pən-ˈhā-gən, -ˈhäg-ən\ city, capital of Denmark

Coquilhatville — see MBANDAKA

Coral Sea arm of the [W] Pacific [NE] of Australia

Coral Springs city [SE] Florida [NW] of Fort Lauderdale

Cór·do·ba \ˈkȯr-də-bə, -ə-və\ **1** *or* **Cor·do·va** \ˈkȯrd-ə-və\ *or ancient* **Cor·du·ba** \ˈkȯrd-yə-bə, ˈkȯrd-u̇-bə\ city [S] Spain on the Guadalquivir **2** city [N] central Argentina

Cor·fu \kȯr-ˈfü; ˈkȯr-ˌfü, -ˌfyü\ island [NW] Greece in Ionian Islands

Cor·inth \ˈkȯr-ənth, ˈkär-, -ənttth\ **1** region of ancient Greece occupying most of Isthmus of Corinth & part of [NE] Peloponnese **2** ancient city, its capital; site [SW] of present city of Corinth — **Co·rin·thi·an** \kə-ˈrin-thē-ən, -ˈrint-\ *adj or n*

Corinth, Gulf of inlet of Ionian Sea central Greece [N] of the Peloponnese

Corinth, Isthmus of neck of land connecting the Peloponnese with rest of Greece

Cork \ˈkȯrk\ **1** county [S] Ireland in Munster **2** city [S] Ireland in County Cork

Corn·wall \ˈkȯrn-ˌwȯl, -wəl\ *or since 1974* **Cornwall and Isles of Scil·ly** \ˈsil-ē\ county [SW] England

Cor·o·man·del \ˌkȯr-ə-ˈman-dl, ˌkär-\ coast region [SE] India on Bay of Bengal

Co·ro·na \kə-ˈrō-nə\ city [SW] California [E] of Los Angeles

Cor·pus Chris·ti \ˌkȯr-pə-ˈskris-tē\ city & port [S] Texas

Cor·reg·i·dor \kə-ˈreg-ə-ˌdȯr\ island Philippines at entrance to Manila Bay

Cor·si·ca \ˈkȯr-si-kə\ *or French* **Corse** \kȯrs\ island France in the Mediterranean [N] of Sardinia — **Cor·si·can** \ˈkȯr-si-kən\ *adj or n*

Cos·ta Bra·va \ˌkäs-tə-ˈbräv-ə, ˌkȯs-, ˌkōs-\ coast region [NE] Spain on the Mediterranean extending [NE] from Barcelona

Costa del Sol \-del-ˈsȯl, -ˈsōl\ coast region [S] Spain on the Mediterranean extending [E] from Gibraltar

Cos·ta Me·sa \ˈkōs-tə-ˈmā-sə\ city [SW] California on Pacific coast

Cos·ta Ri·ca \ˌkäs-tə-ˈrē-kə, ˌkȯs-, ˌkōs-\ country Central America between Nicaragua & Panama; capital, San José — **Cos·ta Ri·can** \-ˈrē-kən\ *adj or n*

Côte d'A·zur \ˌkōt-də-ˈzu̇r\ region [SE] France on Mediterranean coast; part of the Riviera

Côte d'Ivoire — see IVORY COAST

Co·to·nou \ˌkōt-ə-ˈnü\ city, seat of government of Benin

Cots·wold \ˈkät-ˌswōld\ hills [SW] central England

Cov·en·try \ˈkäv-ən-trē, ˈkəv-\ city central England

Co·zu·mel \ˌkō-zə-ˈmel\ island [SE] Mexico off [NE] coast of Quintana Roo

Cracow — see KRAKOW

Cra·io·va \krə-ˈyō-və\ city [S] Romania

Cra·ter \ˈkrāt-ər\ lake [SW] Oregon in Cascade Range; main feature of **Crater Lake National Park** — see MAZAMA (Mount)

Crete \ˈkrēt\ island Greece in [E] Mediterranean; capital, Iráklion — **Cre·tan** \ˈkrēt-n\ *adj or n*

Cri·mea \krī-ˈmē-ə, krə-\ peninsula [E] Europe, extending into Black Sea — **Cri·me·an** \krī-ˈmē-ən, krə-\ *adj*

Cro·atia \krō-ˈā-shə, -shē-ə\ country [S] Europe; capital, Zagreb; formerly a constituent republic of Yugoslavia

Croy·don \ˈkrȯid-n\ borough of [S] Greater London, England

Cu·ba \ˈkyü-bə\ island in the West Indies; a republic; capital, Havana — **Cu·ban** \-bən\ *adj or n*

Cú·cu·ta \ˈkü-kət-ə\ city [N] Colombia

Cu·lia·cán \ˌkül-yə-ˈkän\ city [NW] Mexico, capital of Sinaloa

Cu·ma·ná \ˌkü-mə-ˈnä\ city [NE] Venezuela

Cum·ber·land \ˈkəm-bər-lənd\ former county [NW] England — see CUMBRIA

Cumberland Plateau mountain region [E] U.S.; part of [S] Appalachian Mountains [W] of Tennessee River extending from [S] West Virginia to [NE] Alabama

Cum·bria \ˈkəm-brē-ə\ county [NW] England including former counties of Cumberland & Westmorland — **Cum·bri·an** \-ən\ *adj or n*

Cumbrian Mountains range [NW] England chiefly in Cumbria

Cu·ra·çao \ˈku̇r-ə-ˌsō, ˈkyu̇r-, -ˌsau̇\ internally self-governing Dutch island in the [S] Caribbean; chief town, Willemstad

Cu·ri·ti·ba \ˌku̇r-ə-ˈtē-bə\ city [S] Brazil [SW] of São Paulo

Cush \ˈkəsh, ˈku̇sh\ ancient country [NE] Africa in upper valley of the Nile [S] of Egypt — **Cush·ite** \-ˌīt\ *n* — **Cush·it·ic** \ˌkəsh-ˈit-ik, ku̇sh-\ *adj*

Cut·tack \ˈkət-ək\ city [E] India in Orissa

Cuy·a·hoga Valley National Park \ˌkī-ə-ˈhō-gə\ reservation [NE] Ohio along the **Cuyahoga River** (100 miles or 161 kilometers flowing into Lake Erie)

Cyc·la·des \ˈsik-lə-ˌdēz\ islands Greece in [S] Aegean

Cymru — see WALES

Cy·prus \ˈsī-prəs\ island [E] Mediterranean [S] of Turkey; a republic; capital, Nicosia — **Cyp·ri·ot** \ˈsip-rē-ət, -rē-ˌät\ *or* **Cyp·ri·ote** \-ˌōt, -ət\ *adj or n*

Cy·re·na·ica \ˌsir-ə-ˈnā-ə-kə, ˌsī-rə-\ **1** ancient region [N] Africa on coast [W] of Egypt; capital, Cyrene **2** region [E] Libya; formerly a province — **Cy·re·na·i·can** \-kən\ *adj or n*

Czecho·slo·va·kia \ˌchek-ə-slō-ˈväk-ē-ə, -ˈvak-\ former country central Europe; capital, Prague; divided 1993 into Czech Republic & Slovakia — **Czecho·slo·vak** \-ˈslō-ˌväk, -ˌvak\ *adj or n* — **Czecho·slo·va·ki·an** \-slō-ˈväk-ē-ən, -ˈvak-\ *adj or n*

Czech Republic country central Europe; capital, Prague

Cze·sto·cho·wa \ˌchen-stə-ˈkō-və\ city [S] Poland

Dacca — see DHAKA

Da·cia \ˈdā-shə, -shē-ə\ ancient country & Roman province [SE] Europe roughly equivalent to Romania & Bessarabia

Da·dra and Na·gar Ha·ve·li \də-ˈdrä-ən-ˌnəg-ər-ə-ˌvel-ē\ territory India bordering on Gujarat & Maharashtra

Daegu — see TAEGU

Daejeon — see TAEJON

Da·ho·mey \də-ˈhō-mē\ — see BENIN — **Da·ho·man** \-mən\ *or* **Da·ho·me·an** *or* **Da·ho·mey·an** \-mē-ən\ *adj or n*

Da·kar \ˈdak-ˌär, də-ˈkär\ city, capital of Senegal

Da·ko·ta \də-ˈkōt-ə\ — see JAMES

Dakota Territory territory 1861–89 [NW] U.S. divided 1889 into states of North Dakota & South Dakota (the **Da·ko·tas**)

Da·lian *or* **Ta–lien** \ˈdäl-ˈyen\ *or* **Lü·da** *or* **Lü–ta** \ˈlīē-ˈdä\ *or* **Dai·ren** \ˈdī-ˈren\ city [NE] China in [S] Liaoning

Dal·las \ˈdal-əs, ˈda-lis\ city [NE] Texas

Dal·ma·tia \dal-ˈmā-shə, -shē-ə\ region [W] Balkan Peninsula on the Adriatic — **Dal·ma·tian** \-shən\ *adj or n*

Da·ly City \ˈdā-lē\ city [W] California [S] of San Francisco

Da·man and Diu \də-ˈmän-ən-ˈdē-ˌü, -ˈman-\ territory [W] India on Gulf of Khambhat

Da·mas·cus \də-ˈmas-kəs\ city, capital of Syria

Da·ma·vand \ˈdam-ə-ˌvand\ *or* **Dem·a·vend** \ˈdem-ə-ˌvend\ mountain 18,934 feet (5771 meters) [N] Iran [NE] of Tehran

Da Nang \dä-ˈnäng, ˈdä-\ *or formerly* **Tou·rane** \tü-ˈrän\ city [S] Vietnam in Annam [SE] of Hue

Dan·dong \ˈdän-ˈdu̇ng\ *or* **An·tung** \ˈän-ˈdu̇ng\ *or* **Tan–tung** \ˈdän-ˈdu̇ng\ city [NE] China in [SE] Liaoning

Dan·ube \ˈdan-yüb\ *or German* **Do·nau** \ˈdō-ˌnau̇\ river 1771 miles (2850 kilometers) long [S] Europe flowing from [S] Germany into Black Sea — **Da·nu·bi·an** \da-ˈnyü-bē-ən\ *adj*

Danzig — see GDANSK

Dar·da·nelles \ˌdärd-n-ˈelz\ *or* **Hel·les·pont** \ˈhel-ə-ˌspänt\ strait [NW] Turkey connecting Sea of Marmara & the Aegean

Dar el Beida — see CASABLANCA

Dar es Sa·laam \ˌdär-ˌes-sə-ˈläm\ city, historic capital of Tanzania

Darien, Isthmus of — see PANAMA (Isthmus of)

Dar·ling \ˈdär-ling\ river about 1700 miles (2735 kilometers) long [SE] Australia in Queensland & New South Wales flowing [SW] into the Murray

Dar·win \ˈdär-wən\ city Australia, capital of Northern Territory

Da·tong *or* **Ta·tung** \ˈdä-ˈtu̇ng\ city [NE] China in [N] Shanxi

Da·vao \ˈdäv-ˌau̇, dä-ˈvau̇\ city [S] Philippines in [E] Mindanao on **Davao Gulf** (inlet of the North Pacific)

Da·vis \ˈdā-vəs\ strait between [SW] Greenland & [E] Baffin Island connecting Baffin Bay & the North Atlantic

Day·ton \ˈdāt-n\ city [SW] Ohio

Dead Sea \ˈded\ salt lake between Israel & Jordan; 1312 feet (400 meters) below the level of the Mediterranean
Dear·born \ˈdiər-ˌbȯrn, -bərn\ city SE Michigan SW of Detroit
Death Valley \ˈdeth\ arid valley E California & S Nevada containing lowest point in U.S. (282 feet or 86 meters below sea level); most of area included in **Death Valley National Park**
De·bre·cen \ˈdeb-rət-ˌsen\ city E Hungary
Dec·can \ˈdek-ən, -ˌan\ plateau region S India
Del·a·ware \ˈdel-ə-ˌwaər, -ˌweər, -wər\ **1** river 296 miles (476 kilometers) long E U.S. flowing S from S New York into Delaware Bay **2** state E U.S.; capital, Dover — **Del·a·war·ean** *or* **Del·a·war·ian** \ˌdel-ə-ˈwar-ē-ən, -ˈwer-\ *adj or n*
Delaware Bay inlet of the North Atlantic between SW New Jersey & E Delaware
Del·hi \ˈdel-ē\ **1** territory N India W of Uttar Pradesh **2** city, its capital — see NEW DELHI
De·los \ˈdē-ˌläs\ island Greece in central Cyclades — **De·lian** \ˈdē-lē-ən, ˈdēl-yən\ *adj or n*
Del·phi \ˈdel-ˌfī\ ancient town central Greece in Phocis on S slope of Mount Parnassus
Denali, Denali National Park — see MCKINLEY (Mount)
Den·bigh·shire \ˈden-bē-ˌshiər, -shər\ administrative area N Wales
Den·mark \ˈden-ˌmärk\ country N Europe occupying most of Jutland & adjacent islands; capital, Copenhagen
Den·ver \ˈden-vər\ city, capital of Colorado
Der·by \ˈdär-bē, *chiefly in the U.S.* ˈdər-bē\ borough N central England in Derbyshire
Der·by·shire \ˈdär-bē-ˌshiər, -shər, *U.S. also* ˈdər-\ *or* **Derby** county N central England
Der·ry \ˈder-ē\ *or* **Lon·don·der·ry** \ˌlən-dən-ˈder-ē, ˈlən-dən-ˌ\ **1** traditional county NW Northern Ireland **2** seaport NW Northern Ireland
Des Moines \di-ˈmȯin\ city, capital of Iowa
De·troit \di-ˈtrȯit\ **1** river 31 miles (50 kilometers) long between Michigan & Ontario connecting Lake Saint Clair & Lake Erie **2** city SE Michigan
Dev·on \ˈdev-ən\ *or* **De·von·shire** \-ˌshiər, -shər\ county SW England
Dha·ka *or* **Dac·ca** \ˈdak-ə, ˈdäk-\ city, capital of Bangladesh
Dhau·la·gi·ri, Mount \ˌdau̇-lə-ˈgiər-ē\ mountain 26,810 feet (8172 meters) W central Nepal in the Himalaya
Di·a·mond Bar \ˈdī-mənd-ˌbär, ˈdī-ə-\ city S California E of Los Angeles
Di·e·go Gar·cia \dē-ˌā-gō-ˌgär-ˈsē-ə\ island in Indian Ocean; chief island of Chagos Archipelago
Di·jon \dē-ˈzhō^{n}\ city E France N of Lyon
Di·li \ˈdil-ē\ city & port, capital of East Timor
Di·nar·ic Alps \də-ˌnar-ik\ range of the E Alps in W Balkan Peninsula
Diospolis — see THEBES 1
District of Co·lum·bia \kə-ˈləm-bē-ə\ federal district E U.S. coextensive with city of Washington
Dix·ie \ˈdik-sē\ the states of the S U.S. and especially those which constituted the Confederate States of America
Djakarta — see JAKARTA
Dji·bou·ti *or* **Ji·bu·ti** \jə-ˈbüt-ē\ **1** *or formerly* **French Somaliland** *or later* **French Territory of the Afars and the Is·sas** \ä-ˈfär, -ˈfärz . . . ē-ˈsä, -ˈsäz\ republic E Africa on Gulf of Aden **2** city, its capital — **Dji·bou·ti·an** \jə-ˈbüt-ē-ən\ *adj or n*
Dnie·per \ˈnē-pər\ river 1420 miles (2285 kilometers) long flowing from Valdai Hills, Russia through Belarus & Ukraine into Black Sea
Dnies·ter \ˈnēs-tər\ river 877 miles (1411 kilometers) long W Ukraine & E Moldova flowing SE from the Carpathians into Black Sea
Dni·pro·pe·trovs'k *or* **Dne·pro·pe·trovsk** \də-ˌnyep-rə-pē-ˈtrȯfsk\ city E Ukraine
Do·dec·a·nese \dō-ˈdek-ə-ˌnēz, ˈdō-di-kə-, -ˌnēs\ islands Greece in the SE Aegean — see RHODES
Do·do·ma \dō-ˈdō-mä\ town, legislative capital of Tanzania
Do·ha \ˈdō-hä\ city & port, capital of Qatar on Persian Gulf
Do·lo·mites \ˈdō-lə-ˌmīts, ˈdäl-ə-\ *or Italian* **Do·lo·mi·ti** \ˌdȯ-lə-ˈmēt-ē\ range of the E Alps in NE Italy
Dom·i·ni·ca \ˌdäm-ə-ˈnē-kə\ island British West Indies in the Leewards; an independent republic; capital, Roseau
Do·min·i·can Republic \də-ˌmin-i-kən\ *or formerly* **San·to Do·min·go** \ˌsant-əd-ə-ˈming-gō\ country West Indies in E Hispaniola; capital, Santo Domingo — **Do·min·i·can** \də-ˈmin-i-kən\ *adj or n*
Don \ˈdän\ river 1224 miles (1969 kilometers) long S Russia in Europe flowing into Sea of Azov
Donau — see DANUBE
Don·e·gal \ˌdän-i-ˈgȯl, ˌdən-\ county NW Ireland (republic) in Ulster
Do·nets Basin \də-ˌnets\ *or* **Don·bass** *or* **Don·bas** \ˈdän-ˌbas\ region E Ukraine SW of **Donets River** (over 630 miles or 1014 kilometers flowing SE into Don River)
Do·netsk \də-ˈnetsk\ city E Ukraine in Donets Basin
Dor·set \ˈdȯr-sət\ *or* **Dor·set·shire** \-ˌshiər, -shər\ county S England on English Channel
Dort·mund \ˈdȯrt-ˌmu̇nt, -mənd\ city W Germany in the Ruhr
Dou·a·la \dü-ˈäl-ə\ city SW Cameroon
Doug·las \ˈdəg-ləs\ town British Isles, capital of Isle of Man
Dou·ro \ˈdōr-ü, ˈdȯr-\ *or Spanish* **Due·ro** \ˈdweər-ō\ *or ancient* **Du·ri·us** \ˈdu̇r-ē-əs, ˈdyu̇r-\ river 556 miles (895 kilometers) long N Spain & N Portugal flowing into the North Atlantic
Do·ver \ˈdō-vər\ **1** city, capital of Delaware **2** borough SE England in Kent on Strait of Dover
Dover, Strait of channel between SE England & N France; the most easterly section of English Channel
Down \ˈdau̇n\ traditional county SE Northern Ireland
Dow·ney \ˈdau̇-nē\ city SW California SE of Los Angeles
Dra·kens·berg \ˈdräk-ənz-ˌbərg\ mountain range E Republic of South Africa & Lesotho; highest peak Thabana Ntlenyana 11,425 feet (3482 meters)
Dres·den \ˈdrez-dən\ city E Germany in Saxony
Dry Tor·tu·gas \tȯr-ˈtü-gəz\ island group S Florida; site of **Dry Tortugas National Park**
Du·bayy *or* **Du·bai** \dü-ˈbī\ city United Arab Emirates on Persian Gulf
Dub·lin \ˈdəb-lən\ *or Gaelic* **Bai·le Atha Cli·ath** \blä-ˈklē-ə\ **1** county E Ireland in Leinster **2** city, capital of Ireland (republic) in County Dublin
Dud·ley \ˈdəd-lē\ borough W central England
Duis·burg \ˈdü-əs-ˌbərg; ˈdüz-ˌbərg, ˈdyüz-; *German* ˈdu̅e̅s-ˌbu̇rk\ city W Germany at junction of Rhine & Ruhr rivers
Du·luth \də-ˈlüth\ city & port NE Minnesota at W end of Lake Superior
Dum·fries and Gal·lo·way \ˌdəm-ˈfrēs-ənd-ˈgal-ə-ˌwā\ administrative area S Scotland
Dun·dee \ˌdən-ˈdē\ city E Scotland constituting an administrative area (**Dundee City**)
Dun·e·din \ˌdə-ˈnēd-ᵊn\ city New Zealand in SE South Island
Du·que de Ca·xi·as \ˌdü-kə-də-kə-ˈshē-əs\ city SE Brazil NW of Rio de Janeiro
Du·ran·go \du̇-ˈrang-gō, dyu̇-\ **1** state NW central Mexico **2** city, its capital
Dur·ban \ˈdər-bən\ city in the municipality of eThekwini E Republic of South Africa
Dur·ham \ˈdər-əm, ˈdə-rəm, ˈdu̇r-əm\ **1** city N central North Carolina **2** county N England on North Sea
Du·shan·be \dü-ˈsham-bē, dyü-, -ˈshäm-\ city, capital of Tajikistan
Düs·sel·dorf \ˈdüs-əl-ˌdȯrf, ˈdyüs-, ˈdu̅e̅s-\ city W Germany, capital of North Rhine-Westphalia
Dutch Borneo — see KALIMANTAN
Dutch Guiana — see SURINAME
Dzaudzhikau — see VLADIKAVKAZ
Dzer·zhinsk \dər-ˈzhinsk\ city central Russia in Europe
Ea·ling \ˈē-liŋ\ borough of W Greater London, England
East Africa region E Africa — usually considered to include Tanzania, Kenya, Uganda, Rwanda, Burundi, & Somalia
East An·glia \ˈaŋ-glē-ə\ region E England including Norfolk & Suffolk
East Ayrshire administrative area W Scotland
East Bengal the part of Bengal now in Bangladesh
East China Sea — see CHINA SEA
East Dunbartonshire administrative area W Scotland
Eas·ter \ˈē-stər\ island SE Pacific about 2000 miles (5200 kilometers) W of Chilean coast; belongs to Chile

\ə\ **abut**	\au̇\ **out**	\i\ **tip**	\ȯ\ **saw**	\u̇\ **foot**
\ər\ **further**	\ch\ **chin**	\ī\ **life**	\ȯi\ **coin**	\y\ **yet**
\a\ **mat**	\e\ **pet**	\j\ **job**	\th\ **thin**	\yü\ **few**
\ā\ **take**	\ē\ **easy**	\ŋ\ **sing**	\t͟h\ **this**	\yu̇\ **cure**
\ä\ **cot, cart**	\g\ **go**	\ō\ **bone**	\ü\ **food**	\zh\ **vision**

Eastern Cape province [SE] Republic of South Africa
Eastern Desert *or* **Arabian Desert** desert [E] Egypt
Eastern Ghats \ˈgȯts\ mountain chain [SE] India along coast
Eastern Samoa — see AMERICAN SAMOA
East Germany the former German Democratic Republic — see GERMANY
East Indies collective name for India, Indochina, and the Malay Archipelago — **East Indian** *adj or n*
East London city [S] Republic of South Africa
East Pakistan the former [E] division of Pakistan comprising [E] portion of Bengal; now the independent republic of Bangladesh
East Prussia region [N] Europe on the Baltic; formerly a part of Germany; divided 1945 between Poland & U.S.S.R. (Russia & Lithuania)
East Renfrewshire administrative area [W] Scotland
East River strait [SE] New York connecting upper New York Bay & Long Island Sound & separating Manhattan Island and Long Island
East Sea — see JAPAN (Sea of)
East Sus•sex \ˈsəs-iks, *U.S. also* -ˌeks\ county [SE] England
East Timor *or* **Ti•mor–Les•te** \ˈtē-mōr-ˈlesh-ˌtā\ country [SE] Asia; capital, Dili
Ebro \ˈā-brō\ river 565 miles (909 kilometers) long [NE] Spain flowing into the Mediterranean
Ec•ua•dor \ˈek-wə-ˌdȯr\ country [W] South America; capital, Quito — **Ec•ua•dor•an** \ˌek-wə-ˈdȯr-ən, -ˈdōr-\ *or* **Ec•ua•dor•ean** *or* **Ec•ua•dor•ian** \-ē-ən\ *adj or n*
Ed•in•burgh \ˈed-n-ˌbər-ə, -ˌbə-rə, -bə-rə, -brə\ city, capital of Scotland constituting an administrative area (**City of Edinburgh**)
Ed•mon•ton \ˈed-mən-tən\ city, capital of Alberta
Edo — see TOKYO
Edom \ˈēd-əm\ *or* **Id•u•maea** *or* **Id•u•mea** \ˌij-ə-ˈmē-ə\ ancient country [SW] Asia [S] of Dead Sea — **Edom•ite** \ˈēd-ə-ˌmīt\ *n*
Egypt \ˈē-jəpt\ country [NE] Africa & Sinai Peninsula of [SW] Asia bordering on Mediterranean & Red seas; capital, Cairo
Eilean Siar — see WESTERN ISLES
Eire — see IRELAND 2
Elam \ˈē-ləm\ ancient country [SW] Asia at head of Persian Gulf [E] of Babylonia; capital, Susa — **Elam•ite** \ˈē-lə-ˌmīt\ *n*
El•ba \ˈel-bə\ island Italy [E] of [N] Corsica off coast of Tuscany
Elbe \ˈel-bə, ˈelb\ *or Czech* **La•be** \ˈlä-be\ *or ancient* **Al•bis** \ˈal-bəs\ river 720 miles (1159 kilometers) long [N] Czech Republic & [N] Germany flowing [NW] into North Sea
El•bert, Mount \ˈel-bərt\ mountain 14,433 feet (4399 meters) [W] central Colorado; highest in Colorado & the Rocky Mountains
El•brus, Mount \el-ˈbrüz\ mountain 18,510 feet (5642 meters) [S] Russia in Europe in [NW] Caucasus Mountains
El•burz \el-ˈbu̇rz\ mountains [N] Iran
El Gîza — see GIZA
Elis \ˈē-ləs\ ancient country in [NW] Peloponnese, Greece
Elisabethville — see LUBUMBASHI
Eliz•a•beth \i-ˈliz-ə-bəth\ city [NE] New Jersey on Newark Bay
Elk Island National Park reservation [E] central Alberta
Ellás — see GREECE
Elles•mere \ˈelz-ˌmiər\ island [N] Canada in Nunavut
Ellice — see TUVALU
El•lis \ˈel-əs\ island between New Jersey & New York just [SW] of mouth of the Hudson; served as immigration station 1892–1954
El Mon•te \el-ˈmänt-ē\ city [SW] California [E] of Los Angeles
El Paso \el-ˈpas-ō\ city [W] Texas on Rio Grande
El Sal•va•dor \el-ˈsal-və-ˌdȯr, -ˌsal-və-ˈ\ country Central America bordering on the North Pacific; capital, San Salvador
Elsass — see ALSACE
Ely, Isle of \ˈē-lē\ district [E] England — see CAMBRIDGESHIRE
Emi•lia–Ro•ma•gna \ā-ˌmēl-yə-rō-ˈmän-yə\ region [N] Italy on the Adriatic [S] of the Po; capital, Bologna
En•field \ˈen-ˌfēld\ borough of [N] Greater London, England
En•gland \ˈiŋ-glənd *also* iŋ-lənd\ country [S] Great Britain; a division of United Kingdom; capital, London
English Channel arm of the North Atlantic between [S] England & [N] France
En•se•na•da \ˌen-sə-ˈnäd-ə\ city [NW] Mexico in Baja California
Ephra•im \ˈē-frē-əm\ **1** hilly region [N] Jordan [E] of River Jordan **2** — see ISRAEL — **Ephra•im•ite** \ˈē-frē-ə-ˌmīt\ *n*
Epi•rus \i-ˈpī-rəs\ region [NW] Greece on Ionian Sea
Equatorial Guinea *or formerly* **Spanish Guinea** country [W] Africa on Bight of Biafra including Mbini & Bioko; capital, Malabo
Erbil — see ARBIL
Ere•bus, Mount \ˈer-ə-bəs\ volcano 12,448 feet (3794 meters) Antarctica on Ross Island in [SW] Ross Sea
Er•furt \ˈeər-fərt, -ˌfu̇rt\ city central Germany [WSW] of Leipzig
Erie \ˈiər-ē\ **1** city [NW] Pennsylvania **2** canal New York between Hudson River at Albany & Lake Erie at Buffalo; built 1817–25; now superseded by New York State Barge Canal
Erie, Lake lake [E] central North America in U.S. & Canada; one of the Great Lakes
Er•in \ˈer-ən\ IRELAND — a poetic name
Er•i•trea \ˌer-ə-ˈtrē-ə, -ˈtrā-\ country [NE] Africa on Red Sea; capital, Asmara
Er Rif *or* **Er Riff** \er-ˈrif\ mountain region [N] Morocco on Mediterranean coast [E] of Strait of Gibraltar
Erz•ge•bir•ge \ˈerts-gə-ˌbir-gə\ mountains [E] central Germany & [NW] Czech Republic
Escaut — see SCHELDT
Es•con•di•do \ˌes-kən-ˈdēd-ō\ city [SW] California [N] of San Diego
Es•fa•han \ˌes-fä-ˈhän\ *or* **Is•fa•han** \ˌis-\ city [W] central Iran
Es•ki•se•hir \ˌes-ki-shə-ˈhiər\ city [W] central Turkey
España — see SPAIN
Española — see HISPANIOLA
Es•sen \ˈes-n\ city [W] Germany in the Ruhr
Es•sex \ˈes-iks\ county [SE] England on North Sea
Es•to•nia \e-ˈstō-nē-ə, -nyə\ country [E] Europe on Baltic Sea; capital, Tallinn; a constituent republic of U.S.S.R. 1940–91
eThe•kwi•ni \ˈe-te-ˌkwē-nē\ municipality Republic of South Africa including the city of Durban
Ethi•o•pia \ˌē-thē-ˈō-pē-ə\ **1** ancient country [NE] Africa [S] of Egypt **2** *or historically* **Ab•ys•sin•ia** \ˌab-ə-ˈsin-yə, -ˈsin-ē-ə\ country [E] Africa; a republic since 1975; capital, Addis Ababa
Et•na \ˈet-nə\ volcano 10,902 feet (3323 meters) Italy in [NE] Sicily
Etru•ria \i-ˈtru̇r-ē-ə\ ancient country central Italy coextensive with modern Tuscany & part of Umbria
Eu•boea \yu̇-ˈbē-ə\ island [E] Greece [NE] of Attica & Boeotia
Eu•phra•tes \yu̇-ˈfrāt-ēz\ river 1700 miles (2736 kilometers) long [SW] Asia flowing from [E] Turkey & uniting with the Tigris to form the Shatt al Arab
Eur•asia \yu̇-ˈrā-zhə, -shə\ landmass comprising Europe & Asia — **Eur•asian** \-zhən, -shən\ *adj or n*
Eu•rope \ˈyu̇r-əp\ continent of the Eastern Hemisphere between Asia & the North Atlantic
European Union *or formerly* **European Community** economic, scientific, & political organization consisting of Belgium, France, Italy, Luxembourg, Netherlands, Germany, Denmark, Greece, Ireland, United Kingdom, Spain, Portugal, Austria, Finland, Sweden, Cyprus, Czech Republic, Estonia, Hungary, Latvia, Lithuania, Malta, Poland, Slovakia, Slovenia, Bulgaria, Romania, & Croatia
Ev•ans•ville \ˈev-ənz-ˌvil\ city [SW] Indiana
Ev•er•est, Mount \ˈev-rəst, -ə-rəst\ mountain 29,035 feet (8850 meters) [S] Asia in the Himalaya on border between Nepal & Tibet; highest in the world
Ev•er•glades \ˈev-ər-ˌglādz\ swamp region [S] Florida now partly drained; [SW] part forms **Everglades National Park**
Ex•tre•ma•du•ra \ˌek-strə-mə-ˈdu̇r-ə\ region [W] Spain bordering on Portugal
Eyre, Lake \ˈaər, ˈeər\ intermittent lake central Australia in [N] South Australia
Faer•oe *or* **Far•oe** \ˈfaər-ō, ˈfeər-\ islands [NE] Atlantic [NW] of the Shetlands belonging to Denmark; capital, Tórshavn — **Faero•ese** \ˌfar-ə-ˈwēz, ˌfer-, -ˈwēs\ *adj or n*
Fair•banks \ˈfaər-ˌbaŋks, ˈfeər-\ city [E] central Alaska
Fai•sa•la•bad \ˌfī-ˌsäl-ə-ˈbäd, -ˌsal-ə-ˈbad\ *or formerly* **Ly•all•pur** \lē-ˌäl-ˈpu̇r\ city [NE] Pakistan [W] of Lahore
Fal•kirk \ˈfȯl-kərk\ administrative area central Scotland
Falk•land Islands \ˈfȯ-klənd-, ˈfȯl-\ *or Spanish* **Is•las Mal•vi•nas** \ˌēz-läz-mäl-ˈvē-näs\ islands [SW] Atlantic [E] of [S] end of Argentina; a British colony; capital, Stanley
Far East the countries of [E] Asia & the Malay Archipelago — usually considered as comprising the Asian countries bordering on the Pacific but sometimes as including also India, Sri Lanka, Bangladesh, Tibet, & Myanmar — **Far Eastern** *adj*
Far•go \ˈfär-gō\ city [E] North Dakota; largest in state
Fay•ette•ville \ˈfā-ət-ˌvil, ˈfed-vəl\ city [SE] central North Carolina
Fear, Cape \ˈfiər\ cape [SE] North Carolina at mouth of **Cape**

Fear River (202 miles or 325 kilometers flowing from central North Carolina into North Atlantic)
Federated Malay States former British protectorate (1895–1945) comprising states of Negri Sembilan, Pahang, Perak, & Selangor; now part of Malaysia
Fengtien — see SHENYANG
Fer•man•agh \fər-ˈman-ə\ traditional county [SW] Northern Ireland
Fernando Póo — see BIOKO
Fer•ra•ra \fə-ˈrär-ə\ city [N] Italy [NE] of Bologna
Fez \ˈfez\ *or* **Fès** \ˈfes\ city [N] central Morocco
Fife \ˈfīf\ *or* **Fife•shire** \-ˌshiər, -shər\ administrative area [E] Scotland
Fi•ji \ˈfē-jē\ islands [SW] Pacific; an independent country; capital, Suva — **Fi•ji•an** \-jē-ən\ *adj or n*
Fin•is•terre, Cape \ˌfin-ə-ˈsteər, -ˈster-ē\ cape [NW] Spain
Fin•land \ˈfin-lənd\ *or Finnish* **Suo•mi** \ˈswȯ-mē\ country [NE] Europe on Gulf of Bothnia and Gulf of Finland; capital, Helsinki — **Fin•land•er** \ˈfin-lənd-ər\ *n*
Finland, Gulf of arm of the Baltic between Finland & Estonia
Fiume — see RIJEKA
Flan•ders \ˈflan-dərz\ **1** region [W] Belgium & [N] France on North Sea **2** semiautonomous region [W] Belgium
Flat•tery, Cape \ˈflat-ə-rē\ cape [NW] Washington at entrance to Strait of Juan de Fuca
Flint \ˈflint\ city [SE] Michigan [NNW] of Detroit
Flint•shire \ˈflint-ˌshiər, -shər\ administrative area [NE] Wales
Flor•ence \ˈflȯr-əns, ˈflär-\ *or Italian* **Fi•ren•ze** \fē-ˈrent-sā\ *or ancient* **Flo•ren•tia** \flə-ˈren-chə, -chē-ə\ city central Italy, capital of Tuscany — **Flor•en•tine** \ˈflȯr-ən-ˌtēn, ˈflär-, -ˌtīn\ *adj or n*
Flo•res \ˈflōr-əs, ˈflȯr-\ island Indonesia in Lesser Sunda Islands
Flo•ri•a•nó•po•lis \ˌflōr-ē-ə-ˈnäp-ə-ləs, ˌflȯr-\ city [S] Brazil on an island [NE] of Porto Alegre
Flor•i•da \ˈflȯr-əd-ə, ˈflär-\ state [SE] U.S.; capital, Tallahassee — **Flo•rid•i•an** \flə-ˈrid-ē-ən\ *or* **Flor•i•dan** \ˈflȯr-əd-n, ˈflär-\ *adj or n*
Florida, Straits of channel between Florida Keys on [NW] & Cuba & Bahamas on [S] & [E] connecting Gulf of Mexico & North Atlantic
Florida Keys chain of islands off [S] tip of Florida
Fog•gia \ˈfȯ-jə, -jä\ city [SE] Italy in Puglia
Foochow — see FUZHOU
For•a•ker, Mount \ˈfȯr-i-kər, ˈfär-\ mountain 17,400 feet (5304 meters) [S] central Alaska in Alaska Range
Fo•ril•lon National Park \ˌfȯr-ē-ˈyōⁿ\ reservation Quebec in Gaspé Peninsula
For•mo•sa \fȯr-ˈmō-sə, fər-, -zə\ — see TAIWAN — **For•mo•san** \-sən, -zən\ *adj or n*
For•ta•le•za \ˌfȯrt-l-ˈā-zə\ city [NE] Brazil [NW] of Recife
Fort Col•lins \ˈkäl-ənz\ city [N] Colorado
Fort–de–France \ˌfȯrd-ə-ˈfräⁿs\ city French West Indies, capital of Martinique on [W] coast
Forth \ˈfōrth, ˈfȯrth\ river 116 miles (187 kilometers) long [S] central Scotland flowing [E] into North Sea through **Firth of Forth** (estuary)
Fort Knox \ˈnäks\ military reservation [N] central Kentucky [SSW] of Louisville; location of U.S. Gold Bullion Depository
Fort–Lamy — see N'DJAMENA
Fort Lau•der•dale \ˈlȯd-ər-ˌdāl\ city [SE] Florida on Atlantic
Fort Wayne \ˈwān\ city [NE] Indiana
Fort Worth \ˈwərth\ city [NE] Texas
Foxe Basin \ˈfäks\ inlet of North Atlantic [N] Canada [W] of Baffin Island
France \ˈfrans\ country [W] Europe between the English Channel & the Mediterranean; capital, Paris
Franche–Com•té \ˌfräⁿsh-kōⁿ-ˈtā\ region [E] France bordering on Switzerland
Frank•fort \ˈfrangk-fərt\ city, capital of Kentucky
Frank•furt \ˈfrangk-fərt, ˈfrängk-ˌfu̇rt\ *or in full* **Frankfurt am Main** \-äm-ˈmīn\ city [SW] central Germany on Main River
Frank•lin \ˈfrang-klən\ former district [N] Canada in Northwest Territories including Arctic Islands & Boothia & Melville peninsulas
Fra•ser \ˈfrā-zər, -zhər\ river 850 miles (1368 kilometers) long Canada in [S] central British Columbia flowing into North Pacific
Fred•er•ic•ton \ˈfred-rik-tən, -ə-rik-\ city, capital of New Brunswick
Free State *or formerly* **Or•ange Free State** \ˈȯr-inj, ˈär-, -ənj\ province [E] central Republic of South Africa
Free•town \ˈfrē-ˌtau̇n\ city, capital of Sierra Leone
Fre•mont \ˈfrē-ˌmänt\ city [W] California [SE] of Oakland
French Equatorial Africa former country [W] central Africa [N] of Congo River comprising a federation of Chad, Gabon, Middle Congo, & Ubangi-Shari territories
French Guiana country [N] South America on North Atlantic; a dependency of France; capital, Cayenne
French Guinea — see GUINEA
French Indochina — see INDOCHINA
French Morocco — see MOROCCO
French Polynesia islands in South Pacific belonging to France and including Society, Marquesas, Tuamotu, Gambier, & Tubuai groups; capital, Papeete
French Somaliland — see DJIBOUTI
French Sudan — see MALI
French Territory of the Afars and the Issas — see DJIBOUTI
French Togo — see TOGO
French West Indies islands of the West Indies belonging to France and including Guadeloupe, Martinique, Désirade, Les Saintes, Marie Galante, Saint Barthélemy, & part of Saint Martin
Fres•no \ˈfrez-nō\ city [S] central California
Fri•sian \ˈfrizh-ən, ˈfrē-zhən\ islands [N] Europe in North Sea including **West Frisian** islands off [N] Netherlands, **East Frisian** islands off [NW] Germany, & **North Frisian** islands off [N] Germany and [W] Denmark
Fri•u•li–Ve•ne•zia Giu•lia \frē-ˈü-lē-və-ˌnet-sē-ə-ˈjü-yə\ region [N] Italy; capital, Trieste
Frunze — see BISHKEK
Fu•ji, Mount \ˈfü-jē, ˈfyü-\ *or* **Fu•ji•ya•ma** \ˌfü-jē-ˈäm-ə, ˌfyü-, -ˈyäm-\ *or* **Fu•ji•san** \-jē-ˈsän\ mountain 12,388 feet (3776 meters) Japan in [S] central Honshu; highest in Japan
Fu•jian \ˈfü-ˈjän, -jē-ˈän\ *or* **Fu•kien** \ˈfü-ˈkyen, -kē-ˈen\ province [SE] China on Formosa Strait; capital, Fuzhou
Fu•ji•sa•wa \ˌfü-jē-ˈsä-wə\ city Japan in [SE] Honshu
Fu•ku•o•ka \ˌfü-kə-ˈwō-kə\ city Japan in [N] Kyushu
Fu•ku•ya•ma \ˌfü-kə-ˈyäm-ə\ city Japan in [SW] Honshu
Fu•na•bashi \ˌfü-nə-ˈbäsh-ē\ city Japan in [SE] Honshu on Tokyo Bay
Fu•na•fu•ti \ˌfü-nə-ˈfüt-ē, ˌfyü-, -ˈfyüt-\ city, capital of Tuvalu
Fun•dy, Bay of \ˈfən-dē\ inlet of North Atlantic [SE] Canada between New Brunswick & Nova Scotia
Fundy National Park reservation New Brunswick on Bay of Fundy
Fu•shun \ˈfü-ˈshu̇n\ city [NE] China in [NE] Liaoning
Fu•zhou \ˈfü-ˈjō\ *or* **Foo•chow** \ˈfü-ˈjō, -ˈchau̇\ *or formerly* **Min•how** \ˈmin-ˈhō\ city [SE] China, capital of Fujian
Ga•bon \ga-ˈbōⁿ\ country [W] equatorial Africa; capital, Libreville — **Gab•o•nese** \ˌgab-ə-ˈnēz, -ˈnēs\ *adj or n*
Ga•bo•rone \ˌgäb-ə-ˈrōn\ city, capital of Botswana
Gads•den Purchase \ˈgadz-dən\ tract of land [S] of Gila River in present Arizona & New Mexico purchased 1853 by the U.S. from Mexico
Gaeseong — see KAESONG
Ga•lá•pa•gos Islands \gə-ˈläp-ə-gəs, -ˈlap-\ *or* **Co•lón Archipelago** \kə-ˈlōn\ island group Ecuador in the Pacific about 600 miles (965 kilometers) [W] of mainland
Ga•lati \gə-ˈläts, -ˈlät-sē\ city [E] Romania on the Danube
Ga•la•tia \gə-ˈlā-shə, -shē-ə\ ancient country & Roman province central Asia Minor in region centering on modern Ankara, Turkey — **Ga•la•tian** \-shən\ *adj or n*
Ga•li•cia \gə-ˈlish-ə, -ˈlish-ē-ə\ **1** region [E] central Europe now divided between Poland & Ukraine **2** region [NW] Spain on North Atlantic — **Ga•li•cian** \-shən\ *adj or n*
Gal•i•lee \ˈgal-ə-ˌlē\ hilly region [N] Israel — **Gal•i•le•an** \ˌgal-ə-ˈlē-ən\ *adj or n*
Galilee, Sea of *or modern* **Lake Ti•be•ri•as** \tī-ˈbir-ē-əs\ *or biblical* **Lake of Gen•nes•a•ret** \gə-ˈnes-ə-ˌret, -rət\ *or* **Sea of Tiberias** lake [N] Israel on Syrian border traversed by Jordan River
Gal•lip•o•li \gə-ˈlip-ə-lē\ *or Turkish* **Ge•li•bo•lu Ya•ri•ma•da•si**

\ə\ abut	\au̇\ out	\i\ tip	\ȯ\ saw	\u̇\ foot
\ər\ further	\ch\ chin	\ī\ life	\ȯi\ coin	\y\ yet
\a\ mat	\e\ pet	\j\ job	\th\ thin	\yü\ few
\ā\ take	\ē\ easy	\ng\ sing	\t͟h\ this	\yu̇\ cure
\ä\ cot, cart	\g\ go	\ō\ bone	\ü\ food	\zh\ vision

\ˌgel-ə-bə-ˈlü-ˌyär-ə-ˌmäd-ə-ˈsē\ peninsula Turkey in Europe between the Dardanelles & Saros Gulf

Gal·way \ˈgȯl-ˌwā\ county [W] Ireland in Connacht

Gam·bia \ˈgam-bē-ə\ **1** river 700 miles (1126 kilometers) long [W] Africa **2** country [W] Africa; capital, Banjul — **Gam·bi·an** \-ən\ *adj or n*

Gand — see GHENT

Gan·ges \ˈgan-ˌjēz\ river 1550 miles (2494 kilometers) long [N] India flowing from the Himalaya [SE] & [E] to unite with the Brahmaputra & empty into Bay of Bengal through the vast **Ganges Delta** — see HUGLI — **Gan·get·ic** \gan-ˈjet-ik\ *adj*

Gan·su *or* **Kan·su** \ˈgän-ˈsü\ province [NW] China; capital, Lanzhou

Gao·xiong \ˈgau̇-ˈshyu̇ŋ\ *or* **Kao–hsiung** \ˈkau̇-ˈshyu̇ŋ, ˈgau̇-\ city [SW] Taiwan

Gar·da, Lake \ˈgärd-ə\ lake [N] Italy [NW] of Verona

Garden Grove city [SW] California [SW] of Los Angeles

Ga·ronne \gə-ˈrän, -ˈrōn\ river about 355 miles (571 kilometers) long [SE] France flowing into Gironde Estuary

Gary \ˈgaər-ē, ˈgeər-ē\ city [NW] Indiana on Lake Michigan

Gas·co·ny \ˈgas-kə-nē\ *or French* **Gas·cogne** \gȧ-ˈskōn^{y}\ region and former province [SW] France

Gas·pé \gas-ˈpā, ˈgas-ˌ\ peninsula [SE] Quebec [E] of mouth of the Saint Lawrence — **Gas·pe·sian** \ga-ˈspē-zhən\ *adj or n*

Gasteiz — see VITORIA

Gates·head \ˈgāts-ˌhed\ borough [N] England

Gates of the Arctic National Park reservation [N] central Alaska in Brooks Range

Gaul \ˈgȯl\ *or Latin* **Gal·lia** \ˈgal-ē-ə\ ancient country [W] Europe chiefly comprising region occupied by modern France & Belgium but at one time including also Po valley in [N] Italy — see CISALPINE GAUL, TRANSALPINE GAUL

Gau·teng \ˈgau̇-ˌteŋ\ province central [NE] Republic of South Africa

Ga·za Strip \ˈgäz-ə, ˈgaz-, ˈgāz-\ strip of land on [SE] Mediterranean Sea adjoining Sinai Peninsula; chief city, Gaza

Ga·zi·an·tep \ˌgäz-ē-ˌän-ˈtep, -än-\ city [S] Turkey

Gdansk \gə-ˈdänsk, -ˈdansk\ *or German* **Dan·zig** \ˈdan-sig, ˈdän-\ city [N] Poland on Gulf of Danzig

Gdyn·ia \gə-ˈdin-ē-ə\ city [N] Poland

Gebel Musa — see MUSA (Gebel)

Gee·long \jə-ˈlȯŋ\ city [SE] Australia in [S] Victoria

Gel·sen·kir·chen \ˌgel-zən-ˈkir-kən\ city [W] Germany in the Ruhr [W] of Dortmund

Ge·ne·ral San Mar·tín \ˌhā-nā-ˌräl-ˌsan-mär-ˈtēn\ city [E] Argentina [NW] of Buenos Aires

Ge·ne·va \jə-ˈnē-və\ city [SW] Switzerland on Lake Geneva — **Ge·ne·van** \-vən\ *adj or n*

Geneva, Lake *or* **Lake Le·man** \ˈlē-mən, ˈlem-ən, lə-ˈman\ *ancient* **Le·man·nus** \li-ˈman-əs\ *or* **Le·ma·nus** \li-ˈmān-əs\ lake on border between [SW] Switzerland & [E] France traversed by the Rhone

Gen·oa \ˈjen-ə-wə\ *or Italian* **Ge·no·va** \ˈje-nō-vä\ city [NW] Italy, capital of Liguria — **Gen·o·ese** \ˌjen-ə-ˈwēz, -ˈwēs\ *or* **Gen·o·vese** \-ə-ˈvēz, -ˈvēs\ *adj or n*

George·town \ˈjȯrj-ˌtau̇n\ **1** a [W] section of Washington, District of Columbia **2** city, capital of Guyana

George Town *or* **Pe·nang** \pə-ˈnaŋ\ city Malaysia, on an island in Peninsular Malaysia

Geor·gia \ˈjȯr-jə\ **1** state [SE] U.S.; capital, Atlanta **2** country [SW] Asia on Black Sea [S] of Caucasus Mountains; capital, Tbilisi; a constituent republic of U.S.S.R. 1936–91 — **Geor·gian** \ˈjȯr-jən\ *adj or n*

Georgia, Strait of channel Canada & U.S. between Vancouver Island & mainland [NW] of Puget Sound

Georgian Bay inlet of Lake Huron in [S] Ontario

Georgian Bay Islands National Park reservation Ontario in Georgian Bay

Ger·man·town \ˈjər-mən-ˌtau̇n\ a [NW] section of Philadelphia, Pennsylvania

Ger·ma·ny \ˈjərm-nē, -ə-nē\ country central Europe bordering on North & Baltic seas; capital, Berlin; divided into two republics 1940–90: the **Federal Republic of Germany** (capital, Bonn) & the **German Democratic Republic** (capital, East Berlin)

Ger·mis·ton \ˈjər-mə-stən\ city [NE] Republic of South Africa [E] of Johannesburg

Gha·na \ˈgän-ə, ˈgan-ə\ *or formerly* **Gold Coast** country [W] Africa on Gulf of Guinea; a republic; capital, Accra — **Gha·na·ian** \gä-ˈnā-ən, ga-, -yən; -ˈnī-ən\ *or* **Gha·ni·an** \ˈgän-ē-ən, ˈgän-yən, ˈgan-\ *adj or n*

Ghats \ˈgȯts\ two mountain chains [S] India — see EASTERN GHATS, WESTERN GHATS

Ghent \ˈgent\ *or Flemish* **Gent** \ˈkent\ *or French* **Gand** \ˈgä^{n}\ city [NW] central Belgium

Gi·bral·tar \jə-ˈbrȯl-tər\ British colony & fortress on [S] coast of Spain including Rock of Gibraltar

Gibraltar, Rock of headland on [S] coast of Spain in Gibraltar colony at [E] end of Strait of Gibraltar; highest point 1396 feet (426 meters) — see PILLARS OF HERCULES

Gibraltar, Strait of passage between Spain & Africa connecting North Atlantic & the Mediterranean

Gi·fu \ˈgē-ˌfü\ city Japan in central Honshu

Gi·jón \hē-ˈhōn\ city & port [NW] Spain on Bay of Biscay

Gi·la \ˈhē-lə\ river 630 miles (1014 kilometers) long [SW] New Mexico and [S] Arizona flowing [W] into the Colorado

Gil·bert \ˈgil-bərt\ **1** city [SW] central Arizona **2** islands Kiribati in [W] Pacific; until 1975 formed with Ellice Islands the British colony of **Gilbert and El·lice Islands** \ˈel-əs\ — see KIRIBATI, TUVALU

Gil·e·ad \ˈgil-ē-əd\ mountain region of ancient Palestine [E] of Jordan River; now in [NW] Jordan — **Gil·e·ad·ite** \-ē-ə-ˌdīt\ *n*

Gi·ronde \jə-ˈränd, zhə-; zhē-ˈrō^{n}d\ estuary [W] France formed by junction of Garonne & Dordogne rivers

Gi·za \ˈgē-zə\ *or* **El Gî·za** \el-\ *or* **Al Jī·zah** \al-jē-zə\ city [N] Egypt on the Nile [SW] of Cairo

Gla·cier Bay \ˌglā-shər-\ inlet [SE] Alaska at [S] end of Saint Elias Range in **Glacier Bay National Park**

Glacier National Park — see WATERTON-GLACIER INTERNATIONAL PEACE PARK

Glades \ˈglādz\ EVERGLADES

Glas·gow \ˈglas-kō, ˈglas-gō, ˈglaz-gō\ city [S] central Scotland on the Clyde constituting an administrative area (**Glasgow City**) — **Glas·we·gian** \glas-ˈwē-jən\ *adj or n*

Glen·dale \ˈglen-ˌdāl\ **1** city central Arizona [NW] of Phoenix **2** city [S] California [NE] of Los Angeles

Glouces·ter \ˈgläs-tər, ˈglȯs-\ city [SW] central England

Glouces·ter·shire \ˈgläs-tər-ˌshiər, ˈglȯs-, -shər\ *or* **Gloucester** county [SW] central England

Gnossus — see KNOSSOS

Goa \ˈgō-ə\ state India on [W] coast belonging before 1962 to Portugal; capital, Panaji

Go·bi \ˈgō-bē\ desert [E] central Asia in Mongolia & [N] China

Godthåb — see NUUK

Godwin Austen — see K2

Goi·â·nia \gȯi-ˈan-ē-ə\ city [SE] central Brazil [SW] of Brasília

Go·lan Heights \ˌgō-ˌlän, -lən\ hilly region between [NE] Israel & [SW] Syria

Gol·con·da \gäl-ˈkän-də\ ruined city central India [W] of Hyderabad

Gold Coast **1** coast region [W] Africa on [N] shore of Gulf of Guinea [E] of Ivory Coast **2** — see GHANA

Golden Gate strait [W] California connecting San Francisco Bay and North Pacific

Golden Horn inlet of the Bosporus, Turkey in Europe; harbor of Istanbul

Golgotha — see CALVARY

Gomel — see HOMYEL'

Go·mor·rah \gə-ˈmär-ə, -ˈmȯr-\ ancient city thought to be in the area now covered by the [SW] part of Dead Sea

Good Hope, Cape of \ˌgu̇d-ˈhōp\ cape [S] Republic of South Africa extending into South Atlantic

Go·rakh·pur \ˈgōr-ək-ˌpu̇r, ˈgȯr-\ city [NE] India in [E] Uttar Pradesh [N] of Varanasi

Gorki — see NIZHNIY NOVGOROD

Gor·lov·ka \gȯr-ˈlȯf-kə, -ˈlȯv-\ city [E] Ukraine in Donets Basin

Go·shen \ˈgō-shən\ district of ancient Egypt [E] of Nile Delta

Gö·te·borg \ˌyərt-ə-ˈbȯr-ē, *Swedish* ˌyœ-tə-ˈbȯry\ *or* **Goth·en·burg** \ˈgäth-ən-ˌbərg\ city & port [SW] Sweden

Got·land \ˈgät-ˌland, -lənd\ island Sweden in the Baltic; capital, Visby

Göt·ting·en \ˈgərt-iŋ-ən, ˈget-, ˈgœt-\ city central Germany [SSW] of Brunswick

Gram·pi·an \ˈgram-pē-ən\ hills [N] central Scotland — see BEN NEVIS

Gra·na·da \grə-ˈnäd-ə\ city [S] Spain in Andalusia

Grand Banks shoals in the [W] Atlantic [SE] of Newfoundland

Grand Canyon gorge of Colorado River [NW] Arizona; area largely in **Grand Canyon National Park**
Grand Canyon of the Snake — see HELLS CANYON
Grande, Rio — see RIO GRANDE
Grand Prairie city [NE] central Texas
Grand Rapids city [SW] Michigan
Grand Te·ton National Park \ˈtē-ˌtän\ reservation [NW] Wyoming [S] of Yellowstone National Park
Grass·lands National Park \ˈgras-ˌlandz\ reservation [SW] Saskatchewan
Gravenhage, 's — see HAGUE (The)
Graz \ˈgräts\ city [S] Austria
Great Australian Bight wide bay on [S] coast of Australia
Great Barrier Reef coral reef Australia off [NE] coast of Queensland
Great Basin region [W] U.S. between Sierra Nevada & Wasatch ranges including most of Nevada & parts of California, Idaho, Utah, Wyoming, & Oregon; has no drainage to ocean
Great Basin National Park reservation [E] Nevada
Great Bear lake Canada in Northwest Territories draining through Great Bear River into Mackenzie River
Great Brit·ain \ˈbrit-ᵊn\ **1** island [W] Europe [NW] of France comprising England, Scotland, & Wales **2** UNITED KINGDOM
Great Dividing Range mountain system [E] Australia & Tasmania extending [S] from Cape York Peninsula — see KOSCIUSKO (Mount)
Greater An·til·les \an-ˈtil-ēz\ group of islands of the West Indies including Cuba, Hispaniola, Jamaica, & Puerto Rico — see LESSER ANTILLES
Greater London the City of London & 32 surrounding boroughs
Greater Manchester metropolitan county [NW] England including city of Manchester
Greater Sunda — see SUNDA
Great Lakes **1** chain of five lakes (Superior, Michigan, Huron, Erie, & Ontario) central North America in U.S. & Canada **2** group of lakes [E] central Africa including Turkana, Albert, Victoria, Tanganyika, & Malawi
Great Plains elevated plains region [W] central U.S. & [W] Canada [E] of the Rockies; chiefly [W] of the 100th meridian extending from [W] Texas to [NE] British Columbia & [NW] Alberta
Great Rift Valley \ˈrift\ depression [SW] Asia & [E] Africa extending with several breaks from valley of the Jordan [S] to central Mozambique
Great Salt lake [N] Utah having saline waters & no outlet
Great Sand Dunes National Park reservation [S] Colorado
Great Slave lake [NW] Canada in [SE] Northwest Territories drained by Mackenzie River
Great Smoky mountains between [W] North Carolina & [E] Tennessee partly in **Great Smoky Mountains National Park**; highest Clingmans Dome 6643 feet (2025 meters)
Greece \ˈgrēs\ *or ancient* **Hel·las** \ˈhel-əs\ *or Greek* **El·lás** \e-ˈläs\ country [S] Europe at [S] end of Balkan Peninsula; capital, Athens
Green \ˈgrēn\ **1** mountains [E] North America in the Appalachians extending from [S] Quebec [S] through Vermont into [W] Massachusetts **2** river 730 miles (1175 kilometers) long [W] U.S. flowing from Wind River Range in [W] Wyoming [S] into the Colorado in [SE] Utah
Green Bay **1** inlet of [NW] Lake Michigan about 120 miles (193 kilometers) long in [NW] Michigan & [NE] Wisconsin **2** city [NE] Wisconsin
Green·land \ˈgrēn-lənd, -ˌland\ island in the North Atlantic off [NE] North America belonging to Denmark; capital, Nuuk
Greens·boro \ˈgrēnz-ˌbər-ə, -ˌbə-rə\ city [N] central North Carolina
Green·wich \ˈgrin-ij, ˈgren-, -ich\ [SE] borough of Greater London, England
Green·wich Village \ˌgren-ich-, ˌgrin-, -ij-\ section of New York City in Manhattan on lower [W] side
Gre·na·da \grə-ˈnād-ə\ island British West Indies in [S] Windwards; an independent country since 1974; capital, Saint George's
Gren·a·dines \ˌgren-ə-ˈdēnz\ islands West Indies in central Windwards; divided between Grenada & Saint Vincent and the Grenadines
Gre·no·ble \grə-ˈnō-bəl\ city [SE] France
Grisons — see GRAUBÜNDEN
Gro·ning·en \ˈgrō-ning-ən\ city [NE] Netherlands
Gros Morne National Park \grō-ˈmȯrn\ reservation Newfoundland along [W] coast
Groz·ny \ˈgrȯz-nē, ˈgräz-\ city [S] Russia in Europe [N] of Caucasus Mountains, capital of Chechnya
Gua·da·la·ja·ra \ˌgwäd-ə-lə-ˈhär-ə\ city [W] central Mexico, capital of Jalisco
Gua·dal·ca·nal \ˌgwäd-l-kə-ˈnal, ˌgwäd-ə-kə-\ island [W] Pacific in the [SE] Solomons
Gua·dal·qui·vir \ˌgwäd-l-ˈkwiv-ər, -ki-ˈviər\ river 408 miles (656 kilometers) long [S] Spain flowing into North Atlantic
Gua·da·lupe Mountains National Park \ˈgwäd-l-ˌüp\ reservation [W] Texas
Gua·de·loupe \ˈgwäd-l-ˌüp\ two islands, Basse-Terre (or Guadeloupe proper) & Grande-Terre, separated by a narrow channel in French West Indies in central Leewards; capital, Basse-Terre (on Basse-Terre Island)
Gua·di·a·na \ˌgwäd-ē-ˈän-ə, -ˈan-\ river 515 miles (829 kilometers) long [S] Spain & [SE] Portugal flowing into North Atlantic
Guaíra *or* **Guayra** — see SETE QUEDAS
Guam \ˈgwäm\ island [W] Pacific in [S] Mariana Islands belonging to U.S.; capital, Hagåtña — **Gua·ma·ni·an** \gwä-ˈmā-nē-ən\ *adj or n*
Gua·na·ba·coa \ˌgwän-ə-bə-ˈkō-ə\ city [W] Cuba
Gua·na·ba·ra Bay \ˌgwän-ə-ˈbar-ə, -ˈbär-\ inlet of South Atlantic [SE] Brazil on which city of Rio de Janeiro is situated
Gua·na·jua·to \ˌgwän-ə-ˈhwät-ō, -ˈwät-\ **1** state central Mexico **2** city, its capital
Guang·dong *or* **Kwang·tung** \ˈgwäng-ˈdu̇ng\ province [SE] China on South China Sea & Gulf of Tonkin; capital Guangzhou
Guang·xi Zhuang·zu \ˈgwäng-ˈshē-jə-ˈwäng-ˈzü\ *or* **Kwang·si–Chuang** \ˈgwäng-ˈshē-jə-ˈwäng\ region & former province [S] China; capital, Nanning
Guang·zhou *or* **Kuang–chou** \ˈgwäng-ˈjō\ *or* **Can·ton** \ˈkan-ˌtän, kan-ˈ\ city [SE] China, capital of Guangdong
Guan·ta·na·mo Bay \gwän-ˈtän-ə-ˌmō\ inlet of the Caribbean in [SE] Cuba; site of U.S. naval station
Gua·te·ma·la \ˌgwät-ə-ˈmä-lə\ **1** country Central America; a republic **2** *or* **Guatemala City** city, its capital — **Gua·te·ma·lan** \-lən\ *adj or n*
Gua·ya·quil \ˌgwī-ə-ˈkēl, -ˈkil\ city [W] Ecuador
Guay·na·bo \gwī-ˈnäb-ō\ city [NE] central Puerto Rico
Guern·sey \ˈgərn-zē\ island in English Channel — see CHANNEL 2
Guer·re·ro \gə-ˈreər-ō\ state [S] Mexico on North Pacific; capital, Chilpancingo
Gui·a·na \gē-ˈan-ə, -ˈän-ə; gī-ˈan-ə\ region [N] South America on the Atlantic bounded on [W] & [S] by Orinoco, Negro, & Amazon rivers; includes Guyana, French Guiana, Suriname, & adjacent parts of Brazil & Venezuela — **Gui·a·nan** \-ən\ *adj or n*
Gui·lin \ˈgwē-ˈlin\ *or* **Kwei·lin** *or* **Kuei–lin** \ˈgwā-ˈlin\ city [S] China in [NE] Guangxi Zhuangzu
Guin·ea \ˈgin-ē\ **1** region [W] Africa on the Atlantic extending along coast from Gambia to Angola **2** *or formerly* **French Guinea** country [W] Africa [N] of Sierra Leone & Liberia; a republic; capital, Conakry — **Guin·ean** \ˈgin-ē-ən\ *adj or n*
Guinea, Gulf of arm of the Atlantic [W] central Africa
Guin·ea–Bis·sau \ˌgin-ē-bis-ˈau̇\ *or formerly* **Portuguese Guinea** country [W] Africa on North Atlantic; capital, Bissau
Gui·yang \ˈgwē-ˈyäng\ *or* **Kuei–yang** \ˈgwā-ˈyäng\ city [S] China, capital of Guizhou
Gui·zhou \ˈgwē-ˈjō\ *or* **Kuei–chou** \ˈgwā-ˈjō\ *or* **Kwei·chow** \ˈgwā-ˈchau̇\ province [S] China [S] of Sichuan; capital, Guiyang
Gu·ja·rat *or* **Gu·je·rat** \ˌgü-jə-ˈrät, ˌgu̇j-ə-\ state [W] India [N] & [E] of Gulf of Khambhat; capital, Gandhinagar
Guj·ran·wa·la \ˌgu̇j-rən-ˈwäl-ə, ˌgu̇j-\ city [NE] Pakistan
Gulf States states of U.S. bordering on Gulf of Mexico: Florida, Alabama, Mississippi, Louisiana, and Texas
Gulf Stream warm ocean current of North Atlantic flowing from Gulf of Mexico [NE] along coast of U.S. to Nantucket Island and thence eastward
Gun·tur \gu̇n-ˈtu̇r\ city [E] India in central Andhra Pradesh
Gus·ta·vo A. Ma·de·ro \gu̇s-ˈtäv-ˌō-ˌä-mə-ˈder-ˌō\ city central Mexico [N] of Mexico City

\ə\ **a**bout	\au̇\ **ou**t	\i\ t**i**p	\ȯ\ s**aw**	\u̇\ f**oo**t
\ər\ f**ur**ther	\ch\ **ch**in	\ī\ l**i**fe	\ȯi\ c**oi**n	\y\ **y**et
\a\ m**a**t	\e\ p**e**t	\j\ **j**ob	\th\ **th**in	\yü\ f**ew**
\ā\ t**a**ke	\ē\ **ea**sy	\ng\ si**ng**	\t͟h\ **th**is	\yu̇\ c**u**re
\ä\ c**o**t, c**a**rt	\g\ **g**o	\ō\ b**o**ne	\ü\ f**oo**d	\zh\ vi**s**ion

Guy·ana \gī-ˈan-ə\ *or formerly* **British Guiana** country [N] South America on the Atlantic; a republic since 1970; capital, Georgetown
Gwa·li·or \ˈgwäl-ē-ˌȯr\ city [N] central India in [NW] Andhra Pradesh [SSE] of Agra
Gwangju — see KWANGJU
Gwyn·edd \ˈgwin-eth\ administrative area [NW] Wales
Habana, La — see HAVANA
Ha·chi·ō·ji \ˌhäch-ē-ˈō-jē\ city Japan in [SE] central Honshu
Hack·ney \ˈhak-nē\ borough of [N] Greater London, England
Ha·des \ˈhād-ēz, -ˌēz\ underground abode of the dead in Greek mythology
Ha·gåt·ña \hə-ˈgät-nyə\ *or formerly* **Aga·na** \ä-ˈgä-nyä\ town, capital of Guam
Hague, The \thə-ˈhāg\ *or Dutch* **'s Gra·ven·ha·ge** \ˌskräv-ən-ˈhäg-ə, ˌskräv-\ city [SW] Netherlands; seat of government of the Netherlands
Haidarabad — see HYDERABAD
Hai·fa \ˈhī-fə\ city & port [NW] Israel
Hai·kou \ˈhī-ˈkau̇, -ˈkō\ city [SE] China, capital of Hainan
Hai·nan \ˈhī-ˈnän\ island [SE] China in South China Sea; a province; capital, Haikou
Hai·phong \ˈhī-ˈfȯng\ city [N] Vietnam
Hai·ti \ˈhāt-ē\ **1** — see HISPANIOLA **2** country West Indies in [W] Hispaniola; capital, Port-au-Prince — **Hai·tian** \ˈhā-shən\ *adj or n*
Ha·ko·da·te \ˌhäk-ə-ˈdät-ē\ city & port Japan in [SW] Hokkaido
Ha·le·a·ka·la Crater \ˌhäl-ē-ˌäk-ə-ˈlä\ crater more than 2500 feet (762 meters) deep Hawaii in [E] Maui Island in **Haleakala National Park**
Hal·i·car·nas·sus \ˌhal-ə-kär-ˈnas-əs\ ancient city [SW] Asia Minor in [SW] Caria on Aegean Sea
Hal·i·fax \ˈhal-ə-ˌfaks\ city, capital of Nova Scotia
Hal·le \ˈhäl-ə\ city [E] central Germany [NW] of Leipzig
Hal·ma·hera \ˌhal-mə-ˈher-ə, ˌhäl-\ island [E] Indonesia; largest of the Moluccas
Ha·ma \ˈham-ˌä\ city [W] Syria
Ha·ma·dan \ˌham-ə-ˈdan, -ˈdän\ city [W] Iran
Ha·ma·ma·tsu \ˌhäm-ə-ˈmät-sü\ city Japan in [S] Honshu
Ham·burg \ˈham-ˌbərg, ˈhäm-ˌbu̇rg\ city [N] Germany on the Elbe; comprises a state of Germany — **Ham·burg·er** \-ˌbər-gər, -ˌbu̇r-\ *n*
Ham·hung *or* **Ham·heung** \ˈhäm-ˌhu̇ng\ city [E] central North Korea
Ham·il·ton \ˈham-əl-tən, -əlt-n\ **1** city [S] Ontario **2** town, capital of Bermuda
Ham·mer·smith and Ful·ham \ˈham-ər-ˌsmith-ənd-ˈfu̇l-əm\ borough of [SW] Greater London, England
Ham·mond \ˈham-ənd\ city [NW] Indiana
Hamp·shire \ˈhamp-ˌshiər, ˈham-, -shər\ county [S] England on English Channel
Hamp·ton \ˈhamp-tən, ˈham-\ city [SE] Virginia on Hampton Roads
Hampton Roads channel [SE] Virginia through which James & Elizabeth rivers flow into Chesapeake Bay
Hang·zhou \ˈhäng-ˈjō\ *or* **Hang–chou** \-ˈjō\ *or* **Hang·chow** \ˈhang-ˈchau̇, ˈhäng-ˌjō\ city [E] China, capital of Zhejiang
Han·kow \ˈhang-ˈkau̇, -ˈkō; ˈhäng-ˈkō\ former city [E] central China — see WUHAN
Han·no·ver *or* **Han·o·ver** \ˈhan-ˌō-vər, ˈhan-ə-vər; *German* hä-ˈnō-vər\ city [N] central Germany, capital of Lower Saxony
Ha·noi \ha-ˈnȯi, hə-, hä-\ city, capital of Vietnam
Han·yang \ˈhän-ˈyäng\ former city [E] central China — see WUHAN
Ha·ra·re \hə-ˈrä-ˌrā\ *or formerly* **Salis·bury** \ˈsȯlz-ˌber-ē, ˈsalz-, -bə-rē, -brē\ city, capital of Zimbabwe
Har·bin \ˈhär-bən, här-ˈbin\ *or* **Ha–erh–pin** \ˈhä-ˈer-ˈbin\ *or formerly* **Pin·kiang** \ˈbin-jē-ˈäng\ city [NE] China, capital of Heilongjiang
Har·in·gey \ˈhar-ing-gā\ borough of [N] Greater London, England
Har·lem \ˈhär-ləm\ section of New York City in [N] Manhattan
Har·ris·burg \ˈhar-əs-ˌbərg\ city, capital of Pennsylvania
Har·row \ˈhar-ō\ borough of [NW] Greater London, England
Hart·ford \ˈhärt-fərd\ city, capital of Connecticut on Connecticut River
Hart·le·pool \ˈhärt-lē-ˌpül\ borough [N] England
Ha·ry·a·na \ˌhə-rē-ˈän-ə\ state [N] India; capital, Chandigarh
Harz \ˈhärts\ mountains central Germany between Elbe & Leine rivers
Hat·ter·as, Cape \ˈhat-ə-rəs, ˈha-trəs\ cape, North Carolina on **Hatteras Island** (barrier island between Pamlico Sound and North Atlantic)
Haute–Nor·man·die \ˌōt-ˌnȯr-mäⁿ-ˈdē\ region [N] France on English Channel
Ha·vana \hə-ˈvan-ə\ *or Spanish* **La Ha·ba·na** \ˌlä-ä-ˈvän-ə, ˌlä-ˈvän-ə\ city, capital of Cuba — **Ha·van·an** \hə-ˈvan-ən\ *adj or n*
Hav·ant \ˈhav-ənt\ town [S] England
Ha·ver·ing \ˈhāv-ring, -ə-ring\ borough of [NE] Greater London, England
Ha·waii \hə-ˈwä-ē, -ˈwī-, -ˈwȯ-, -yē\ **1** *or formerly* **Sand·wich Islands** \ˌsan-ˌwich-, ˌsand-\ group of islands central Pacific belonging to U.S. **2** island, largest of the group **3** state of U.S. comprising Hawaiian Islands except Midway; capital, Honolulu
Hawaii Volcanoes National Park reservation Hawaii on Hawaii Island including Mauna Loa & Kilauea
Hay·ward \ˈhā-wərd\ city [W] California [SE] of Oakland
He·bei \ˈhəb-ˈā\ *or* **Hopeh** *or* **Hopei** \ˈhō-ˈbā\ province [NE] China; capital, Shijiazhuang
Heb·ri·des \ˈheb-rə-ˌdēz\ islands [W] Scotland in North Atlantic comprising **Outer Hebrides** (to [W]) and **Inner Hebrides** (to [E]) — see WESTERN ISLES — **Heb·ri·de·an** \ˌheb-rə-ˈdē-ən\ *adj or n*
He·fei *or* **Ho·fei** \ˈhəf-ˈā\ *or formerly* **Lu·chow** \ˈlü-ˈjō\ city [E] China, capital of Anhui [W] of Nanjing
Hei·long·jiang *or* **Hei·lung·kiang** \ˈhā-ˈlu̇ng-ˈjyäng\ province [NE] China in [N] Manchuria; capital, Harbin
He·jaz \hej-ˈaz, hij-\ region [W] Saudi Arabia on Red Sea
Hel·e·na \ˈhel-ə-nə\ city, capital of Montana
He·li·op·o·lis \ˌhē-lē-ˈäp-ə-ləs\ **1** either of two cities of ancient Egypt **2** city of ancient Syria; site at modern town of **Baal·bek** \ˈbā-əl-ˌbek, ˈbäl-ˌbek\ in [E] Lebanon [N] of Damascus
Hellas — see GREECE
Hellespont — see DARDANELLES
Hells Canyon \ˈhelz\ *or* **Grand Canyon of the Snake** canyon of Snake River on Idaho–Oregon boundary
Hel·sin·ki \ˈhel-ˌsing-kē, hel-ˈ\ *or Swedish* **Hel·sing·fors** \ˈhel-sing-ˌfȯrz\ city, capital of Finland
Helvetia — see SWITZERLAND — **Hel·ve·tian** \hel-ˈvē-shən\ *adj or n*
He·nan \ˈhən-ˈän\ *or* **Ho·nan** \ˈhō-ˈnän\ province [E] central China; capital, Zhengzhou
Hen·der·son \ˈhen-dər-sən\ city [S] Nevada
Heng·yang \ˈhəng-ˈyäng\ city [SE] central China in [SE] Hunan
Henry, Cape \ˈhen-rē\ headland [E] Virginia [S] of entrance to Chesapeake Bay
Her·mon, Mount \ˈhər-mən\ mountain 9232 feet (2814 meters) on Lebanon–Syria border; highest in Anti-Lebanon Mountains
Her·mo·si·llo \ˌer-mə-ˈsē-ō, -yō\ city [NW] Mexico, capital of Sonora
Hert·ford·shire \ˈhär-fərd-ˌshiər, *also* ˈhärt-, *in the U.S. also* ˈhərt-\ *or* **Hertford** county [SE] England
Her·ze·go·vi·na \ˌhert-sə-gō-ˈvē-nə, ˌhərt-\ *or* **Her·ce·go·vi·na** \ˈhert-sä-ˌgō-vē-nä\ region [S] Europe [S] of Bosnia; now part of Bosnia and Herzegovina
Hesse \ˈhes, ˈhes-ē\ *or German* **Hes·sen** \ˈhes-n\ state central Germany [E] of the Rhine & [N] of the Main; capital, Wiesbaden
Hi·a·le·ah \ˌhī-ə-ˈlē-ə\ city [SE] Florida [N] of Miami
Hibernia — see IRELAND
Hi·dal·go \hid-ˈal-gō\ state central Mexico; capital, Pachuca
Hi·ga·shi·ōsa·ka \hē-ˌgä-shē-ō-ˈsäk-ə\ city Japan in [S] Honshu
High·land \ˈhī-lənd\ administrative area [NW] Scotland
High·lands \ˈhī-ləndz, -lənz\ the mountainous [N] part of Scotland lying [N] & [W] of the Lowlands
High Plains the Great Plains especially from Nebraska southward
Hil·ling·don \ˈhil-ing-dən\ borough of [W] Greater London, England
Hi·ma·chal Pra·desh \hi-ˌmäch-əl-prə-ˈdesh, -ˈdāsh\ state [NW] India comprising two areas [NW] of Uttar Pradesh; capital, Simla
Hi·ma·la·ya, the \ˌhim-ə-ˈlā-ə; hə-ˈmäl-yə, -ˈmäl-ə-yə\ *or* **the Hi·ma·la·yas** \-əz, -yəz\ mountain system [S] Asia on border between India & Tibet & in Kashmir, Nepal, & Bhutan — see EVEREST (Mount) — **Hi·ma·la·yan** \ˌhim-ə-ˈlā-ən; hə-ˈmäl-yən, -ˈmäl-ə-yən\ *adj*
Hi·me·ji \hi-ˈmej-ē\ city Japan in [W] Honshu [WNW] of Kobe
Hin·du Kush \ˌhin-dü-ˈku̇sh, -ˈkəsh\ mountain range central

Asia [SW] of the Pamirs on border of Kashmir & in Afghanistan
Hin·du·stan \ˌhin-dü-ˈstan, -də-, -ˈstän\ **1** region [N] India [N] of the Deccan **2** historical name for India (country)
Hip·po \ˈhip-ō\ ancient city [N] Africa; chief town of Numidia
Hi·ra·ka·ta \ˌhir-ə-ˈkät-ə\ city Japan on Honshu
Hi·ro·shi·ma \ˌhir-ə-ˈshē-mə, hə-ˈrō-shə-mə\ city Japan in [SW] Honshu on Inland Sea
Hispalis — see SEVILLE
Hispania — see SPAIN
His·pan·io·la \ˌhis-pən-ˈyō-lə\ *or Spanish* **Es·pa·ño·la** \ˌes-ˌpän-ˈyō-lə\ *or formerly* **Hai·ti** \ˈhāt-ē\ *or* **San·to Do·min·go** \ˌsant-əd-ə-ˈmiŋ-gō\ island West Indies in Greater Antilles divided between Haiti on [W] & Dominican Republic on [E]
Ho·bart \ˈhō-ˌbärt\ city Australia, capital of Tasmania
Ho Chi Minh City \ˌhō-ˌchē-ˌmin-, -ˌshē-\ *or formerly* **Sai·gon** \sī-ˈgän, ˈsī-ˌ\ city [S] Vietnam
Hofei — see HEFEI
Hoggar — see AHAGGAR
Hoh·hot \ˈhō-ˈhōt\ *or* **Hu–ho–hao–t'e** \ˈhü-ˈhō-ˈhau̇-ˈtə\ city [N] China, capital of Inner Mongolia
Hok·kai·do \hä-ˈkīd-ō\ *or formerly* **Ye·zo** \ˈyez-ō\ island [N] Japan [N] of Honshu
Hol·land \ˈhäl-ənd\ **1** medieval county of Holy Roman Empire bordering on North Sea & comprising area now forming North Holland & South Holland provinces of the Netherlands **2** — see NETHERLANDS — **Hol·land·er** \-ən-dər\ *n*
Hol·ly·wood \ˈhäl-ē-ˌwu̇d\ **1** section of Los Angeles, California, [NW] of downtown district **2** city [SE] Florida
Hol·stein \ˈhōl-ˌstīn, -ˌstēn\ region [NW] Germany [S] of Jutland Peninsula adjoining Schleswig — see SCHLESWIG-HOLSTEIN
Holy Land the lands roughly equivalent to ancient Palestine including holy sites of the Jewish, Christian, & Islamic religions
Homs \ˈhȯmz, ˈhu̇ms\ city [W] Syria
Ho·myel' \hȯ-ˈmyel, k̲ō-\ *or* **Go·mel** \gō-ˈmel, -ˈmyel\ *or* **Ho·mel** \hȯ-\ city [SE] Belarus
Honan — see HENAN
Hon·du·ras \hän-ˈdu̇r-əs, -ˈdyu̇r-\ country Central America; capital, Tegucigalpa — **Hon·du·ran** \-ən\ *or* **Hon·du·ra·ne·an** *or* **Hon·du·ra·ni·an** \ˌhän-du̇-ˈrā-nē-ən, -dyu̇-\ *adj or n*
Hong Kong \ˈhäŋ-ˌkäŋ, -ˈkäŋ; ˈhȯŋ-ˌkȯŋ, -ˈkȯŋ\ *or Chinese* **Xiang·gang** *or* **Hsiang Kang** \ˈshyäŋ-ˈgäŋ\ special administrative region China including Hong Kong Island & Jiulong Peninsula; formerly a British colony with Victoria as capital
Ho·ni·a·ra \ˌhō-nē-ˈär-ə\ town, capital of Solomon Islands
Ho·no·lu·lu \ˌhän-l-ˈü-lü, ˌhōn-l-\ city, capital of Hawaii on Oahu Island
Hon·shu \ˈhän-shü\ *or* **Hon·do** \ˈhän-dō\ island Japan; largest of the four chief islands
Hood, Mount \ˈhu̇d\ mountain 11,235 feet (3424 meters) [NW] Oregon in Cascade Range
Hoo·ver Dam \ˌhü-vər\ *or* **Boul·der Dam** \ˌbōl-dər\ dam 726 feet (221 meters) high in Colorado River between Arizona & Nevada — see MEAD (Lake)
Hopeh *or* **Hopei** — see HEBEI
Ho·reb \ˈhōr-ˌeb, ˈhȯr-\ *or* **Si·nai** \ˈsī-ˌnī *also* -nē-ˌī\ mountain where according to the Bible the Law was given to Moses; generally thought to be on Sinai Peninsula
Hor·muz, Strait of \ˈhȯr-ˌməz, hȯr-ˈmüz\ strait [SW] Asia connecting Persian Gulf & Gulf of Oman
Horn, Cape \ˈhȯrn\ headland [S] Chile on Horn Island in Tierra del Fuego; the most southerly point of South America at 56° [S] latitude
Horn of Africa the easternmost projection of Africa -- variously used of Somalia, [SE] or all of Ethiopia, & sometimes Djibouti
Hos·pi·ta·let \ˌäs-ˌpit-l-ˈet, ˌhäs-\ city [NE] Spain
Hot Springs National Park reservation [SW] central Arkansas adjoining city of Hot Springs
Houns·low \ˈhau̇nz-ˌlō\ borough of [SW] Greater London, England
Hous·ton \ˈhyü-stən, ˈyü-\ city & port [SE] Texas
How·rah \ˈhau̇-rə\ city [E] India in West Bengal on Hugli River opposite Calcutta
Hsia–men — see XI'AMEN
Hsiang–t'an — see XIANGTAN
Huai·nan \hü-ī-ˈnän, ˈhwī-\ city [E] China in [N] central Anhui
Huang *or* **Hwang** \ˈhwäŋ\ *or* **Yellow** river 3396 miles (5464 kilometers) long [N] China flowing into Bo Hai
Huas·ca·rán \ˌwäs-kə-ˈrän\ mountain 22,205 feet (6768 meters) [W] Peru
Hu·bei \ˈhü-ˈbā\ *or* **Hu·peh** \ˈhü-ˈbē\ *or* **Hu·pei** \ˈhü-ˈbā, -ˈpā\ province [E] central China; capital, Wuhan
Hubli–Dharwad \ˌhu̇b-lē-ˌdär-ˈwäd\ city [SW] India in [W] Karnataka
Hud·ders·field \ˈhəd-ərz-ˌfēld\ town [N] England [NE] of Manchester
Hud·son \ˈhəd-sən\ **1** river 306 miles (492 kilometers) long [E] New York flowing [S] into New York Bay **2** bay of North Atlantic in [N] Canada **3** strait [NE] Canada connecting Hudson Bay & North Atlantic
Hue \ˈhwā, ˈwā, hü-ˈā, hyü-ˈā\ city central Vietnam in Annam
Hu·gli *or* **Hoo·ghly** \ˈhü-glē\ river 120 miles (193 kilometers) long [E] India flowing [S] into Bay of Bengal; most westerly channel of the Ganges in its delta
Hu–ho–hao–t'e — see HOHHOT
Hull \ˈhəl\ *or* **Kings·ton upon Hull** \ˈkiŋ-stən, ˈkiŋk-\ city [N] England
Hum·ber \ˈhəm-bər\ estuary [E] England formed by the Ouse & the Trent and flowing into North Sea
Hum·boldt \ˈhəm-ˌbōlt\ glacier [NW] Greenland
Humboldt Current — see PERU CURRENT
Hu·nan \ˈhü-ˈnän\ province [SE] central China; capital, Changsha
Hun·ga·ry \ˈhəŋ-grē, -gə-rē\ country central Europe; capital, Budapest
Hunt·ing·ton Beach city [SW] California [SE] of Los Angeles
Hunts·ville \ˈhəns-ˌvil, -vəl\ city [N] Alabama
Hu·ron, Lake \ˈhyu̇r-ən, ˈyu̇r-, -ˌän\ lake [E] central North America in U.S. & Canada; one of the Great Lakes
Hy·der·abad \ˈhīd-rə-ˌbad, -ə-rə-, -ˌbäd\ **1** *or* **Hai·dar·abad** *same*\ city [S] central India; capital of Andhra Pradesh **2** city [SE] Pakistan on the Indus
Hy·met·tus \hī-ˈmet-əs\ mountain ridge about 3370 feet (1027 meters) central Greece [E] & [SE] of Athens
Ia·si \ˈyäsh, ˈyäsh-ē\ city [NE] Romania
Iba·dan \i-ˈbäd-n, -ˈbad-\ city [SW] Nigeria
Ibe·ri·an \ī-ˈbir-ē-ən\ peninsula [SW] Europe occupied by Spain & Portugal
Ibi·za \ē-ˈvē-thə, -ˈbē-\ island Spain in Balearic Islands [SW] of Majorca
Ice·land \ˈī-slənd, -ˌsland\ island [SE] of Greenland between Arctic & North Atlantic oceans; capital, Reykjavik — **Ice·land·er** \-slən-dər, -ˌslan-dər\ *n*
Ichi·ka·wa \i-ˈchē-ˌkä-wə\ city Japan in [SE] Honshu [E] of Tokyo
Ida, Mount — see KAZ DAGI
Ida·ho \ˈīd-ə-ˌhō\ state [NW] U.S.; capital, Boise — **Ida·ho·an** \ˌīd-ə-ˈhō-ən\ *adj or n*
Idumaea *or* **Idumea** — see EDOM
If·ni \ˈif-nē\ former territory [SW] Morocco on North Atlantic; administered by Spain 1934–69; capital, Sidi Ifni
Igua·zú *or* **Igua·çu** \ˌē-gwä-ˈsü\ river 745 miles (1199 kilometers) long [S] Brazil flowing [W] into the Alto Paraná; contains **Iguazú Falls** (waterfall over 2 miles or 3.2 kilometers wide composed of numerous cataracts averaging 200 feet or 61 meters in height)
IJs·sel *or* **Ijs·sel** *or* **Ys·sel** \ˈī-səl\ river 70 miles (113 kilometers) long [E] Netherlands flowing out of Rhine [N] into IJsselmeer
IJs·sel·meer \ˌī-səl-ˈmeər\ *or* **Lake Ijs·sel** \ˈī-səl\ freshwater lake [N] Netherlands separated from North Sea by a dike; part of former Zuider Zee (inlet of North Sea)
Ika·ria \ˌē-kə-ˈrē-ə\ *or ancient* **Icar·ia** \ī-ˈker-ē-ə, -ˈkar-; ik-ˈer-, -ˈar-\ island Greece in central Aegean [W] of Samos
Île–de–France \ˌēl-də-ˈfräⁿs\ region [N] France containing Paris
Ilium *or* **Ilion** — see TROY
Illam·pu \ē-ˈäm-pü, -ˈyäm-\ *or* **So·ra·ta** \sə-ˈrät-ə\ mountain [W] Bolivia in the Andes [E] of Lake Titicaca — see ANCOHUMA
Il·li·nois \ˌil-ə-ˈnȯi *also* -ˈnȯiz\ state [N] central U.S.; capital, Springfield — **Il·li·nois·an** \-ˈnȯi-ən, -ˈnȯiz-\ *adj or n*
Il·lyr·ia \il-ˈir-ē-ə\ ancient country [S] Europe in Balkan Peninsula on the Adriatic — **Il·lyr·i·an** \-ē-ən\ *adj or n*

\ə\ **abut**	\au̇\ **out**	\i\ **tip**	\ȯ\ **saw**	\u̇\ **foot**
\ər\ **further**	\ch\ **chin**	\ī\ **life**	\ȯi\ **coin**	\y\ **yet**
\a\ **mat**	\e\ **pet**	\j\ **job**	\th\ **thin**	\yü\ **few**
\ā\ **take**	\ē\ **easy**	\ŋ\ **sing**	\t̲h̲\ **this**	\yu̇\ **cure**
\ä\ **cot, cart**	\g\ **go**	\ō\ **bone**	\ü\ **food**	\zh\ **vision**

Ilo·ilo \ˌē-lə-ˈwē-lō\ city central Philippines on [S] coast of Panay Island

Imperial Valley valley [SE] corner of California extending into Baja California, Mexico

In·chon *or* **In·cheon** \ˈin-ˌchən\ city South Korea on Yellow Sea

In·de·pen·dence \ˌin-də-ˈpen-dəns\ city [W] Missouri [E] of Kansas City

In·dia \ˈin-dē-ə\ **1** peninsula region (often called a subcontinent) [S] Asia [S] of the Himalaya between Bay of Bengal & Arabian Sea **2** country comprising major portion of the peninsula; capital, New Delhi **3** *or* **Indian Empire** before 1947 those parts of the Indian subcontinent under British rule or protection

In·di·an \ˈin-dē-ən\ **1** ocean [E] of Africa, [S] of Asia, [W] of Australia, & [N] of Antarctica **2** — see THAR

In·di·ana \ˌin-dē-ˈan-ə\ state [E] central U.S.; capital, Indianapolis — **In·di·an·an** \-ˈan-ən\ *or* **In·di·an·i·an** \-ˈan-ē-ən\ *adj or n*

In·di·a·nap·o·lis \ˌin-dē-ə-ˈnap-ləs, -ə-ləs\ city, capital of Indiana

Indian River lagoon 165 miles (266 kilometers) long [E] Florida between mainland & coastal islands

Indian Territory former territory [S] central U.S. in present state of Oklahoma

In·dies \ˈin-dēz\ **1** EAST INDIES **2** WEST INDIES

In·do·chi·na \ˈin-dō-ˈchī-nə\ **1** peninsula [SE] Asia including Myanmar, Malay Peninsula, Thailand, Cambodia, Laos, & Vietnam **2** *or* **French Indochina** former country [SE] Asia comprising area now forming Cambodia, Laos, & Vietnam — **Indo–Chi·nese** \-chī-ˈnēz, -ˈnēs\ *adj or n*

In·do·ne·sia \ˌin-də-ˈnē-zhə, -shə\ country [SE] Asia in Malay Archipelago comprising Sumatra, Java, [S] & [E] Borneo, Sulawesi, [W] New Guinea, [W] Timor, & many smaller islands; capital, Jakarta — see NETHERLANDS EAST INDIES — **In·do·ne·sian** \-zhən, -shən\ *adj or n*

In·dore \in-ˈdōr, -ˈdȯr\ city [W] central India in [W] Madhya Pradesh

In·dus \ˈin-dəs\ river 1800 miles (2897 kilometers) long [S] Asia flowing from Tibet [NW] & [SSW] through Pakistan into Arabian Sea

In·land \ˈin-ˌland, -lənd\ sea inlet of North Pacific in [SW] Japan between Honshu Island on [N] & Shikoku Island & Kyushu Island on [S]

Inner Hebrides — see HEBRIDES

Inner Mongolia region [N] China in [SE] Mongolia & [W] Manchuria; capital, Hohhot

Inns·bruck \ˈinz-ˌbru̇k, ˈins-\ city [W] Austria in Tirol

Inside Passage protected shipping route between Puget Sound, Washington, & Skagway, Alaska

In·ver·clyde \ˌin-vər-ˈklīd\ administrative area [W] Scotland

Io·ni·an \ī-ˈō-nē-ən\ **1** sea, an arm of the Mediterranean between [SE] Italy & [W] Greece **2** islands [W] Greece in Ionian Sea

Io·wa \ˈī-ə-wə\ state [N] central U.S.; capital, Des Moines — **Io·wan** \-wən\ *adj or n*

I–pin — see YIBIN

Ipoh \ˈē-pō\ city Malaysia [NNW] of Kuala Lumpur

Ips·wich \ˈip-swich\ town [SE] England

Iqa·lu·it \e-ˈkal-ü-ət\ town Canada on Baffin Island; capital of Nunavut

Iran \i-ˈran, -ˈrän; ī-ˈran\ *or formerly by outsiders* **Per·sia** \ˈpər-zhə\ country [SW] Asia [S] of Caspian Sea; capital, Tehran — **Ira·ni** \i-ˈran-ē, -ˈrän-\ *adj or n* — **Ira·nian** \i-ˈran-ē-ən, -ˈrän-, -ˈrān-\ *adj or n*

Iraq \i-ˈräk, -ˈrak\ country [SW] Asia in Mesopotamia; capital, Baghdad — **Iraqi** \-ˈräk-ē, -ˈrak-\ *adj or n*

Irbīl — see ARBIL

Ire·land \ˈīr-lənd\ **1** *or Latin* **Hi·ber·nia** \hī-ˈbər-nē-ə\ island [W] Europe in North Atlantic; one of the British Isles **2** *or* **Ei·re** \ˈer-ə\ country occupying major portion of the island; capital, Dublin

Irian — see NEW GUINEA

Irish \ˈīr-ish\ sea; an arm of North Atlantic between Great Britain & Ireland

Ir·kutsk \iər-ˈkütsk, ˌər-\ city [S] Russia in Asia, near Lake Baikal

Ir·ra·wad·dy \ˌir-ə-ˈwäd-ē\ river 1300 miles (2092 kilometers) long Myanmar (Burma) flowing [S] into Bay of Bengal

Ir·tysh \iər-ˈtish, ˌər-\ river over 2600 miles (4180 kilometers) long central Asia flowing [NW] & [N] from Altai Mountains in China, through Kazakhstan, & into the Ob' in Russia

Ir·vine \ˈər-ˌvīn\ city [SW] California

Isfahan — see ESFAHAN

Is·lam·abad \is-ˈläm-ə-ˌbäd, iz-ˈlam-ə-ˌbad\ city, capital of Pakistan

Isle of Anglesey administrative area [NW] Wales

Isle of Man — see MAN (Isle of)

Isle Roy·ale \ˈīl-ˈrȯi-əl, -ˈrȯil\ island Michigan in Lake Superior in **Isle Royale National Park**

Is·ling·ton \ˈiz-ling-tən\ borough of [N] Greater London, England

Is·ma·ilia \ˌiz-mā-ə-ˈlē-ə\ city [NE] Egypt on Suez Canal

Is·ra·el \ˈiz-rē-əl\ **1** kingdom in ancient Palestine comprising lands occupied by the Hebrew people **2** *or* **Northern Kingdom** *or* **Ephra·im** \ˈē-frē-əm\ the [N] part of the Hebrew kingdom after about 933 B.C. — see JUDAH **3** country [SW] Asia bordering on the Mediterranean; capital, Jerusalem; established 1948 — **Is·rae·li** \iz-ˈrā-lē\ *adj or n*

Is·tan·bul \ˌis-təm-ˈbül, -ˌtäm-, -ˌtam-, -ˌtän-\ *or formerly* **Con·stan·ti·no·ple** \ˌkän-ˌstant-n-ˈō-pəl\ *or ancient* **By·zan·tium** \bə-ˈzan-shəm, -shē-əm; -ˈzant-ē-əm\ city [NW] Turkey on Sea of Marmara & both sides of the Bosporus; former capital of Turkey

Is·tria \ˈis-trē-ə\ peninsula [S] central Europe extending into the [N] Adriatic; belongs to Croatia & Slovenia except for Trieste (to Italy) — **Is·tri·an** \-trē-ən\ *adj or n*

Italian Somaliland former country [E] Africa now part of Somalia

It·a·ly \ˈit-l-ē\ **1** peninsula about 760 miles (1223 kilometers) long [S] Europe extending into the Mediterranean between Adriatic & Tyrrhenian seas **2** country including the peninsula of Italy, Sicily, & Sardinia; capital, Rome

Itas·ca, Lake \ī-ˈtas-kə\ lake [NW] central Minnesota; source of the Mississippi

Ith·a·ca \ˈith-i-kə\ island [W] Greece in Ionian Islands

Iva·no·vo \i-ˈvän-ə-və\ city central Russia in Europe [WNW] of Nizhniy Novgorod

Ivory Coast *or French* **Côte d'Ivoire** \ˌkōt-dēv-ˈwär\ country [W] Africa on Gulf of Guinea; official capital, Yamoussoukro; seat of government, Abidjan

Iv·vav·ik National Park \ˈiv-ə-ˌvik\ reservation extreme [NW] Yukon

Iwo \ˈē-wō\ city [SW] Nigeria [NE] of Ibadan

Iwo Ji·ma \ˌē-wō-ˈjē-mə\ *or* **Iwo To** \-ˈtō\ island Japan in [W] Pacific in Volcano Islands about 759 miles (1221 kilometers) [S] of Tokyo

Izhevsk \ˈē-ˌzhefsk\ city [E] central Russia in Europe

Iz·mir \iz-ˈmiər\ *or formerly* **Smyr·na** \ˈsmər-nə\ city [W] Turkey

Ja·bal·pur \ˈjəb-əl-ˌpu̇r\ city central India in central Madhya Pradesh

Jack·son \ˈjak-sən\ city, capital of Mississippi

Jack·son·ville \ˈjak-sən-ˌvil\ city [NE] Florida

Jadotville — see LIKASI

Jaf·fa \ˈjaf-ə, ˈyaf-ə\ *or ancient* **Jop·pa** \ˈjäp-ə\ former city [W] Israel; now part of Tel Aviv

Jai·pur \ˈjī-ˌpu̇r\ city [NW] India, capital of Rajasthan

Ja·kar·ta *or* **Dja·kar·ta** \jə-ˈkär-tə\ *or formerly* **Ba·ta·via** \bə-ˈtā-vē-ə, -ˈtä-\ city, capital of Indonesia in [NW] Java

Ja·lan·dhar \ˈjəl-ən-dər\ city [N] India in Punjab [SE] of Amritsar

Jalapa — see XALAPA

Ja·lis·co \hə-ˈlis-kō\ state [W] central Mexico; capital, Guadalajara

Ja·mai·ca \jə-ˈmā-kə\ island West Indies in Greater Antilles; an independent country; capital, Kingston — **Ja·mai·can** \-kən\ *adj or n*

James \ˈjāmz\ **1** river in North Dakota & South Dakota — see DAKOTA **2** river 340 miles (547 kilometers) long Virginia flowing [E] into Chesapeake Bay

James Bay the [S] extension of Hudson Bay between [NE] Ontario & [W] Quebec

James·town \ˈjām-ˌstau̇n\ ruined village [E] Virginia on James River; first permanent English settlement in America (1607)

Jam·mu and Kashmir \ˈjəm-ˌü\ *or* **Kashmir** disputed territory [N] Indian subcontinent; claimed as a state (capital, Srinagar; winter capital, Jammu) & partly administered by India, but also claimed & partly controlled by Pakistan

Jam·na·gar \jäm-ˈnəg-ər\ city [W] India in [W] Gujarat

Jam·shed·pur \ˈjäm-ˌshed-ˌpu̇r\ city [E] India in Jharkhand

Ja·pan \jə-ˈpan, ji-, ja-\ **1** country [E] Asia comprising Honshu, Hokkaido, Kyushu, Shikoku, & other islands in the [W] Pacific; a constitutional monarchy; capital, Tokyo **2** warm current of the North Pacific flowing from [E] coast of the Philippines [N] along [E] coast of Japan & thence eastward

Japan, Sea of *also* **East Sea** arm of North Pacific between Japan & Asian mainland

Jas·per National Park \ˈjas-pər\ reservation [W] Alberta on [E] slope of Rocky Mountains

Ja·va \ˈjäv-ə, ˈjav-ə\ island Indonesia [SW] of Borneo; chief city, Jakarta — **Ja·van** \-ən\ *adj or n*

Jebel Musa — see MUSA (Jebel)

Jef·fer·son City \ˈjef-ər-sən\ city, capital of Missouri

Je·rez \hə-ˈrās\ *or in full* **Je·rez de la Fron·te·ra** \hə-ˈrez-də-lə-ˌfrən-ˈter-ə\ city [SW] Spain

Jer·i·cho \ˈjer-i-ˌkō\ city of ancient Palestine [N] of Dead Sea

Jer·sey \ˈjər-zē\ **1** island in English Channel — see CHANNEL 2 **2** NEW JERSEY — **Jer·sey·ite** \-zē-ˌīt\ *n*

Jersey City city [NE] New Jersey on Hudson River

Je·ru·sa·lem \jə-ˈrü-sə-ləm, -sləm; -ˈrüz-ə-ləm, -ˈrüz-ləm\ city [NW] of Dead Sea divided 1948–67 between Israel & Jordan; capital of Israel since 1950 & formerly of ancient kingdoms of Israel & Judah

Jhan·si \ˈjän-sē\ city [N] India in [S] Uttar Pradesh

Jhar·khand \ˈjär-kənd\ state [NE] India; capital, Ranchi

Jia·mu·si \jē-ˈä-ˈmü-ˈsē\ *or* **Chia–mu–ssu** \jē-ˈä-ˈmü-ˈsü\ *or* **Kia·mu·sze** \jē-ˈä-ˈmü-ˈsə\ city [NE] China in [E] Heilongjiang

Jiang·su *or* **Kiang·su** \jē-ˈäng-ˈsü\ province [E] China; capital, Nanjing

Jiang·xi *or* **Kiang·si** \jē-ˈäng-shē\ province [SE] China; capital, Nanchang

Jibuti — see DJIBOUTI

Jid·da \ˈjid-ə\ *or* **Jed·da** \ˈjed-ə\ city [W] Saudi Arabia in Hejaz on Red Sea; port for Mecca

Ji·lin \ˈjē-ˈlin\ *or* **Ki·rin** \ˈkē-ˈrin\ **1** province [NE] China; capital, Changchun **2** city in Jilin province

Ji·long *or* **Chi–lung** \ˈjē-ˈlu̇ŋ\ *or* **Kee·lung** \ˈkē-\ city & port [N] Taiwan

Ji·nan *or* **Chi·nan** *or* **Tsi·nan** \ˈjē-ˈnän\ city [E] China, capital of Shandong

Jin·zhou *or* **Chin–chou** *or* **Chin·chow** \ˈjin-ˈjō\ city [NE] China in [SW] Liaoning

Jiu·long \ˈjü-ˈlȯŋ\ *or* **Kow·loon** \ˈkau̇-ˈlün\ **1** peninsula [SE] China in Hong Kong opposite Hong Kong Island **2** city on Jiulong Peninsula

João Pes·soa \ˌzhau̇ⁿ-pə-ˈsō-ə, ˌzhau̇ⁿm-\ city [NE] Brazil [N] of Recife

Jodh·pur \ˈjäd-pər, -ˌpu̇r\ city [NW] India in central Rajasthan

Jo·han·nes·burg \jō-ˈhan-əs-ˌbərg, -ˈhän-\ city [NE] Republic of South Africa

Jo·hore Bah·ru \jə-ˈhōr-ˈbä-rü, -ˈhȯr-\ city Malaysia in [S] Peninsular Malaysia opposite Singapore Island

Jo·li·et \ˌjō-lē-ˈet\ city [NE] Illinois

Jor·dan \ˈjȯrd-n\ **1** river 200 miles (322 kilometers) long [SW] Asia rising in Syria & flowing [S] through Sea of Galilee into Dead Sea in Israel **2** *or formerly* **Trans·jor·dan** \trans-, tranz-, ˈtrans-, ˈtranz-\ country [SW] Asia in [NW] Arabia; capital, Amman — **Jor·da·ni·an** \jȯr-ˈdā-nē-ən\ *adj or n*

Josh·ua Tree National Park \ˈjäsh-ə-wə\ reservation [S] California

Juan de Fu·ca \ˌhwän-də-ˈfyü-kə, ˌwän-\ strait 100 miles (161 kilometers) long between Vancouver Island, British Columbia, & Olympic Peninsula, Washington

Juan Fer·nán·dez \ˌhwän-fər-ˈnan-dəs, ˌwän-\ group of three islands [SE] Pacific about 400 miles (645 kilometers) [W] of Chile; belongs to Chile

Juárez — see CIUDAD JUÁREZ

Ju·ba \ˈjü-bə, -ˌbä\ city, capital of South Sudan

Ju·dah \ˈjüd-ə\ kingdom [S] ancient Palestine; capital, Jerusalem — see ISRAEL

Ju·dea *or* **Ju·daea** \jü-ˈdē-ə, -ˈdā-\ region of ancient Palestine constituting the [S] division (Judah) of the country under Persian, Greek, & Roman rule — **Ju·de·an** \-ən\ *adj or n*

Jugoslavia — see YUGOSLAVIA

Juiz de Fo·ra \ˌzhwēzh-də-ˈfōr-ə, -ˈfȯr-\ city [E] Brazil [N] of Rio de Janeiro

Ju·neau \ˈjü-nō, jü-ˈ\ city, capital of Alaska

Jung·frau \ˈyu̇ŋ-ˌfrau̇\ mountain 13,642 feet (4158 meters) [SW] central Switzerland in Bernese Alps

Ju·ra \ˈju̇r-ə\ mountain range extending along boundary between France & Switzerland [N] of Lake Geneva

Jut·land \ˈjət-lənd\ **1** peninsula [N] Europe extending into North Sea & comprising mainland of Denmark & [N] portion of Schleswig-Holstein, Germany **2** the mainland of Denmark

Ka·bul \ˈkäb-əl, kä-ˈbül\ city, capital of Afghanistan

Kadiyevka — see STAKHANOV

Kae·song \ˈkā-ˌsȯŋ\ *or* **Gae·seong** \ˈgā-ˌsəŋ\ city North Korea [SE] of Pyongyang

Ka·go·shi·ma \ˌkäg-ə-ˈshē-mə, kä-ˈgō-shə-mə\ city Japan in [S] Kyushu

Kai·feng \ˈkī-ˈfəŋ\ city [E] central China in [NE] Henan

Ka Lae \kä-ˈlä-ā\ *or* **South Cape** *or* **South Point** most southerly point of Hawaii & of U.S.

Kal·a·ha·ri \ˌkal-ə-ˈhär-ē\ desert region [S] Africa [N] of Orange River in [S] Botswana & [NW] Republic of South Africa

Kalgan — see ZHANGJIAKOU

Ka·li·man·tan \ˌkal-ə-ˈman-ˌtan, ˌkäl-ə-ˈmän-ˌtän\ **1** BORNEO — its Indonesian name **2** the [S] & [E] portion of Borneo belonging to Indonesia; formerly (as **Dutch Borneo**) part of Netherlands East Indies

Kalinin — see TVER

Ka·li·nin·grad \kə-ˈlē-nən-ˌgrad, -nyən-\ *or German* **Kö·nigs·berg** \ˈkā-nigz-ˌbərg, ˈkərn-igz-, -ˌbeərg, *German* ˈkœ-niks-ˌberk\ city [W] Russia; formerly capital of East Prussia

Ka·lu·ga \kə-ˈlü-gə\ city Russia in Europe [WNW] of Oka

Kam·chat·ka \kam-ˈchat-kə\ peninsula 750 miles (1207 kilometers) long [NE] Russia in Asia between Sea of Okhotsk & Bering Sea

Kam·pa·la \käm-ˈpäl-ə\ city, capital of Uganda

Kampuchea — see CAMBODIA

Ka·nan·ga \kə-ˈnäŋ-gə\ *or formerly* **Lu·lua·bourg** \lü-ˈlü-ə-ˌbu̇rg, -ˌbu̇r\ city [S] central Democratic Republic of the Congo

Ka·na·za·wa \kə-ˈnäz-ə-wə, ˌkan-ə-ˈzä-wə\ city Japan in [W] Honshu [N] of Nagoya near Sea of Japan

Kan·chen·jun·ga \ˌkan-chən-ˈjəŋ-gə, -ˈju̇ŋ-\ mountain 28,209 feet (8598 meters) Nepal & Sikkim (India) in the Himalaya

Kan·da·har \ˈkan-də-ˌhär\ city [SE] Afghanistan

Ka·no \ˈkän-ō\ city [N] central Nigeria

Kan·pur \ˈkän-ˌpu̇r\ city [N] India in [S] Uttar Pradesh

Kan·sas \ˈkan-zəs\ state [W] central U.S.; capital, Topeka — **Kan·san** \-zən\ *adj or n*

Kansas City **1** city [NE] Kansas adjoining Kansas City, Missouri **2** city [W] Missouri

Kansu — see GANSU

Kao–hsiung — see GAOXIONG

Ka·ra·chi \kə-ˈräch-ē\ city [S] Pakistan on Arabian Sea

Karafuto — see SAKHALIN

Ka·ra·gan·da \ˌkär-ə-ˈgän-də\ *or* **Qa·ra·ghan·dy** \-dē\ city central Kazakhstan

Ka·raj \kə-ˈräj\ city [N] Iran [NW] of Tehran

Kar·a·ko·ram \ˌkar-ə-ˈkōr-əm, -ˈkȯr-\ mountain system [S] central Asia in [N] Kashmir & [NW] Tibet connecting the Himalaya & the Pamirs

Karakoram Pass mountain pass through Karakoram Range

Ka·ra Sea \ˈkär-ə\ arm of Arctic Ocean off [N] coast of Russia [E] of Novaya Zemlya

Ka·re·lia \kə-ˈrē-lē-ə, -ˈrēl-yə\ region [NE] Europe between Gulf of Finland & White Sea; now chiefly in Russia — **Ka·re·lian** \-ˈrē-lē-ən, -ˈrēl-yən\ *adj or n*

Karl–Marx–Stadt — see CHEMNITZ

Karls·ru·he \ˈkärlz-ˌrü-ə\ city [SW] Germany

Kar·na·ta·ka \kär-ˈnät-ə-kə\ *or formerly* **My·sore** \mī-ˈsōr, -ˈsȯr\ state [S] India; capital, Bangalore

Kar·roo \kə-ˈrü\ plateau region [W] Republic of South Africa [W] of Drakensberg Mountains; divided into **Little** (*or* **Southern**) **Karroo, Great** (*or* **Central**) **Karroo**, & **Northern Karroo**

Kashi \ˈkash-ē, ˈkäsh-\ *or* **Kash·gar** \ˈkash-ˌgär, ˈkäsh-\ city [W] China in [SW] Xinjiang Uygur

Ka·shi·wa \ˈkä-shē-ˌwä\ city Japan on Honshu

Kash·mir \ˈkash-ˌmiər, ˈkazh-, kash-ˈ, kazh-ˈ\ former princely state [N] Indian subcontinent; now part of Jammu and Kashmir — **Kash·miri** \kash-ˈmiər-ē, kazh-\ *adj or n*

Kas·sel \ˈkas-əl, ˈkäs-\ city central Germany [WNW] of Erfurt

Ka·thi·a·war \ˌkät-ē-ə-ˈwär\ peninsula [W] India in Gujarat [N] of Gulf of Khambhat

\ə\ **abut**	\au̇\ **out**	\i\ **tip**	\ȯ\ **saw**	\u̇\ **foot**
\ər\ **further**	\ch\ **chin**	\ī\ **life**	\ȯi\ **coin**	\y\ **yet**
\a\ **mat**	\e\ **pet**	\j\ **job**	\th\ **thin**	\yü\ **few**
\ā\ **take**	\ē\ **easy**	\ŋ\ **sing**	\t͟h\ **this**	\yu̇\ **cure**
\ä\ **cot, cart**	\g\ **go**	\ō\ **bone**	\ü\ **food**	\zh\ **vision**

Kath·man·du *or* **Kat·man·du** \ˌkat-ˌman-ˈdü, ˌkät-ˌmän-\ city, capital of Nepal
Kat·mai, Mount \ˈkat-ˌmī\ volcano 6715 feet (2047 meters) S Alaska in **Katmai National Park**
Ka·to·wi·ce \ˌkät-ə-ˈvēt-sə\ city S Poland WNW of Krakow
Kat·te·gat \ˈkat-i-ˌgat\ arm of North Sea between Sweden & E coast of Jutland Peninsula of Denmark
Kau·ai \ˈkau̇-ˌī\ island Hawaii NW of Oahu
Kau·nas \ˈkau̇-nəs, -ˌnäs\ *or Russian* **Kov·no** \ˈkȯv-nō\ city central Lithuania
Ka·wa·goe \kə-ˈwäg-ˌȯi\ city Japan on SE central Honshu
Ka·wa·gu·chi \ˌkä-wə-ˈgü-chē, kä-ˈwäg-u̇-chē\ city Japan in E Honshu N of Tokyo
Ka·wa·sa·ki \ˌkä-wə-ˈsäk-ē\ city Japan in E Honshu S of Tokyo
Kay·se·ri \ˌkī-zə-ˈrē\ city central Turkey
Ka·zakh·stan \kə-ˌzak-ˈstan; kə-ˌzäk-ˈstän, ˌkä-\ country NW central Asia; capital, Astana; a constituent republic of U.S.S.R. 1936–91
Ka·zan \kə-ˈzan, -ˈzän, -ˈzän-yə\ city E central Russia in Europe
Kazan Retto — see VOLCANO ISLANDS
Kaz Da·gi \ˌkäz-ˈdī\ *or* **Mount Ida** \ˈīd-ə\ mountain 5797 feet (1767 meters) NW Turkey in Asia SE of ancient Troy
Keelung — see JILONG
Kee·wa·tin \kē-ˈwāt-n\ former district N Canada in E Northwest Territories NW of Hudson Bay
Kej·im·ku·jik National Park \ˌkej-mə-ˈkü-jik, -ə-mə-\ reservation E Canada in SW Nova Scotia
Ke·me·ro·vo \ˈkem-ə-rə-və, -ˌrō-və, -rə-ˌvō\ city S Russia in Asia in Kuznetsk Basin
Ke·nai \ˈkē-ˌnī\ peninsula S Alaska E of Cook Inlet; site of **Kenai Fjords National Park**
Ke·ni·tra \kə-ˈnē-trə\ *or formerly* **Port Lyau·tey** \ˌpȯr-lē-ˌō-ˈtā, -ˈō-ˌ\ city N Morocco
Kennedy, Cape — see CANAVERAL (Cape)
Ken·sing·ton and Chel·sea \ˈken-zing-tən-ən-ˈchel-sē, ˈken-sing-\ borough of W Greater London, England
Kent \ˈkent\ county SE England — **Kent·ish** \ˈkent-ish\ *adj*
Ken·tucky \kən-ˈtək-ē\ state E central U.S.; capital, Frankfort — **Ken·tuck·i·an** \-ē-ən\ *adj or n*
Ken·ya \ˈken-yə, ˈkēn-\ **1** mountain 17,058 feet (5199 meters) central Kenya **2** country E Africa S of Ethiopia; capital, Nairobi — **Ken·yan** \-yən\ *adj or n*
Ker·a·la \ˈker-ə-lə\ state SW India bordering on Arabian Sea; capital, Trivandrum
Ker·gue·len \ˈkər-gə-lən, ˌkər-gə-ˈlen\ **1** archipelago S Indian Ocean belonging to France **2** chief island of the archipelago
Ker·man \kər-ˈmän, ker-\ city SE central Iran
Ker·ry \ˈker-ē\ county SW Ireland in Munster
Kes·te·ven, Parts of \ke-ˈstē-vən\ district E England
Kha·ba·rovsk \kə-ˈbär-əfsk\ city SE Russia in Asia on the Amur
Kham·bhat, Gulf of \ˈkəm-bət\ *or* **Gulf of Cam·bay** \kam-ˈbā\ inlet of Arabian Sea India N of Bombay
Khan·ka \ˈkang-kə\ lake E Asia between Russia & China
Khar·kiv \ˈkär-kəf, ˈkär-\ *or* **Khar·kov** \ˈkär-ˌkȯf, -kȯv, -kəf\ city NE Ukraine
Khar·toum \kär-ˈtüm\ city, capital of Sudan
Kher·son \keər-ˈsȯn\ city S Ukraine
Khy·ber \ˈkī-bər\ pass 33 miles (53 kilometers) long on border between Afghanistan & Pakistan WNW of Peshawar
Kiamusze — see JIAMUSI
Kiangsi — see JIANGXI
Kiangsu — see JIANGSU
Ki·bo \ˈkē-bō\ mountain peak 19,340 feet (5895 meters) NE Tanzania; highest peak of Kilimanjaro & highest point in Africa
Kiel \ˈkēl\ city N Germany, capital of Schleswig-Holstein
Kiel — see NORD-OSTSEE
Kiel·ce \kē-ˈelt-sā\ city S Poland S of Warsaw
Ki·ev \ˈkē-ˌef, -ˌev, -if\ *or Ukrainian* **Kyiv** \ˈkyē-ü\ city, capital of Ukraine
Ki·ga·li \ki-ˈgäl-ē\ city, capital of Rwanda
Ki·lau·ea \ˌkē-ˌlau̇-ˈā-ə\ volcanic crater Hawaii on Hawaii Island on E slope of Mauna Loa in Hawaii Volcanoes National Park
Kil·dare \kil-ˈdaər, -ˈdeər\ county E Ireland in Leinster
Kil·i·man·ja·ro \ˌkil-ə-mən-ˈjär-ō, -ˈjar-\ mountain NE Tanzania; highest in Africa — see KIBO
Kil·ken·ny \kil-ˈken-ē\ county SE Ireland in Leinster
Kil·lar·ney, Lakes of \kil-ˈär-nē\ three lakes SW Ireland in Kerry
Kim·ber·ley \ˈkim-bər-lē\ city central Republic of South Africa
Kings Canyon National Park \ˈkingz-\ reservation SE central California in Sierra Nevada N of Sequoia National Park
Kings·ton \ˈking-stən\ city, capital of Jamaica
Kingston upon Hull — see HULL
Kingston upon Thames \ˈtemz\ borough of SW Greater London, England
Kin·sha·sa \kin-ˈshäs-ə\ *or formerly* **Lé·o·pold·ville** \ˈlē-ə-ˌpōld-ˌvil, ˈlā-\ city, capital of Democratic Republic of the Congo
Kirghiz Soviet Socialist Republic *or* **Kirgiz Soviet Socialist Republic** \kir-ˈgēz\ former constituent republic of U.S.S.R.; became independent Kyrgyzstan 1991
Kir·i·bati \ˈkir-ə-ˌbas\ islands W Pacific including the Gilberts; an independent country; capital, Tarawa
Kirin — see JILIN
Ki·riti·mati \kə-ˈris-məs\ *or formerly* **Christ·mas** \ˈkris-məs\ island in Line Islands; largest atoll in the Pacific
Kir·kuk \kiər-ˈku̇k\ city NE Iraq
Ki·rov \ˈkē-ˌrȯf, -ˌrȯv, -rəf\ *or* **Vyat·ka** \vē-ˈat-kə, -ˈät-\ city central Russia in Europe N of Kazan
Ki·ro·vo·hrad \ˌkē-rə-və-ˈhrät\ *or* **Ki·ro·vo·grad** \ki-ˈrō-və-ˌgrad\ city S central Ukraine
Ki·san·ga·ni \ˌkē-sən-ˈgän-ē\ *or formerly* **Stan·ley·ville** \ˈstan-lē-ˌvil\ city NE Democratic Republic of the Congo
Kishinev — see CHISINAU
Ki·ta·kyu·shu \kē-ˌtä-kē-ˈü-shü\ city Japan in N Kyushu
Kitch·e·ner \ˈkich-nər, -ə-nər\ city Canada in SE Ontario
Klai·pe·da \ˈklī-pəd-ə\ *or* **Me·mel** \ˈmā-məl\ city & port W Lithuania
Klon·dike \ˈklän-ˌdīk\ region NW Canada in central Yukon in valley of **Klondike River** (90 miles or 145 kilometers flowing W into the Yukon River)
Klu·ane National Park \klü-ˈȯ-nē-, -ˈän-ē-\ reservation SW Yukon on Alaska border
Knos·sos *or* **Cnos·sus** \kə-ˈnäs-əs, ˈnäs-əs\ *or* **Gnos·sus** \gə-ˈnäs-əs, ˈnäs-əs\ ruined city, capital of ancient Crete near N coast
Knox·ville \ˈnäks-ˌvil, -vəl\ city E Tennessee
Ko·be \ˈkō-bē, -ˌbā\ city Japan in S Honshu
Ko·buk Valley National Park \kō-ˈbu̇k\ reservation NW Alaska N of Arctic Circle
Ko·chi \ˈkō-chē\ city Japan on S coast of Shikoku
Ko·di·ak \ˈkōd-ē-ˌak\ island S Alaska E of Alaska Peninsula
Kokand — see QŬQON
Ko·la \ˈkō-lə\ peninsula NW Russia in Europe between Barents & White seas
Ko·lar \kō-ˈlär\ city S India in SE Karnataka
Kol·ha·pur \ˈkō-lə-ˌpu̇r\ city W India in SW Maharashtra SSE of Bombay
Kolkata — see CALCUTTA
Köln — see COLOGNE
Ko·mo·do \kə-ˈmōd-ō\ island Indonesia in the Lesser Sundas W of Flores Island
Königsberg — see KALININGRAD
Kon·ya \kȯn-ˈyä\ city SW central Turkey
Koo·te·nay National Park \ˈküt-n-ˌā, -n-ē\ reservation SE British Columbia
Ko·rea \kə-ˈrē-ə, *especially South* kō-\ *or Japanese* **Cho·sen** \ˈchō-ˈsen\ former kingdom E Asia between Yellow Sea & East Sea (Sea of Japan); capital, Seoul; divided after World War II at 38th parallel into republics of **North Korea** (capital, Pyongyang) & **South Korea** (capital, Seoul)
Korea Bay arm of Yellow Sea between China & North Korea
Kos·ci·us·ko, Mount \ˌkäz-ē-ˈəs-kō\ mountain 7310 feet (2228 meters) SE Australia in SE New South Wales; highest in Great Dividing Range & in Australia
Ko·shi·ga·ya \kō-ˈshē-gä-yə; ˌkō-shig-ˈä-yə\ city Japan on Honshu
Ko·so·vo \ˈkō-sō-ˌvō, ˈkäs-ō-\ country S Europe in Balkan Peninsula; capital, Pristina
Kos·tro·ma \ˌkäs-trə-ˈmä\ city central Russia in Europe on the Volga
Ko·ta Bha·ru \ˌkōt-ə-ˈbär-ˌü, -ü\ city Malaysia in N Peninsular Malaysia
Kou·chi·bou·guac National Park \kü-ˌshē-bü-ˈgwäk\ reservation E New Brunswick along the coast
Kovno — see KAUNAS
Kowloon — see JIULONG

Kozhikode — see CALICUT
Krak·a·toa \ˌkrak-ə-ˈtō-ə\ *or* **Krak·a·tau** \-ˈtaů\ island & volcano Indonesia between Sumatra & Java
Kra·kow *or* **Cra·cow** \ˈkräk-ˌaů, ˈkrak-, ˈkräk-, -ō, *Polish* ˈkräk-ˌüf\ city S Poland
Kras·no·dar \ˈkras-nə-ˌdär\ city S Russia in Europe in N Caucasus
Kras·no·yarsk \ˌkras-nə-ˈyärsk\ city S central Russia in Asia on the upper Yenisey
Kre·feld \ˈkrā-ˌfelt\ city W Germany on the Rhine WSW of Essen
Kru·ger National Park \ˈkrü-gər\ game reserve NE Republic of South Africa on Mozambique border
Kru·gers·dorp \ˈkrü-gərz-ˌdȯrp\ city NE Republic of South Africa
Kry·vyy Rih \kri-ˌvē-ˈrik\ *or* **Kri·voy Rog** \ˌkri-ˌvȯi-ˈrōg, -ˈrȯk\ city SE central Ukraine
K2 \ˈkā-ˈtü\ *or* **God·win Aus·ten** \ˈgȯd-wən-ˈȯs-tən, ˈgäd-, -ˈäs-\ mountain 28,250 feet (8611 meters) N Kashmir in Karakoram Range; second highest in the world
Kua·la Lum·pur \ˌkwäl-ə-ˈlům-ˌpůr, -ˈləm-\ city, capital of Malaysia in Peninsular Malaysia
Kuang–chou — see GUANGZHOU
Kuei–chou — see GUIZHOU
Kuei–yang — see GUIYANG
Ku·ma·mo·to \ˌküm-ə-ˈmōt-ō\ city Japan in W Kyushu
Ku·ma·si \kü-ˈmäs-ē, -ˈmas-\ city S central Ghana
Kun·lun \ˈkün-ˈlün\ mountain system W China extending E from the Pamirs to SE Qinghai; highest peak 25,340 feet (7724 meters)
Kun·ming \ˈkůn-ˈmiŋ\ *or formerly* **Yun·nan** \yü-ˈnän\ *or* **Yun·nan·fu** \-ˈfü\ city S China, capital of Yunnan
Ku·ra·shi·ki \kü-ˈrä-shē-kē, ˌkůr-ə-ˈshē-kē\ city Japan in W Honshu WSW of Okayama
Kur·di·stan \ˌkůrd-ə-ˈstan, ˌkərd-\ region SW Asia chiefly in E Turkey, NW Iran, & N Iraq
Ku·re \ˈkůr-ē, ˈkyůr-ē, ˈkü-rā\ city Japan in SW Honshu on Inland Sea SE of Hiroshima
Kur·gan \kůr-ˈgan, -ˈgän\ city W Russia in Asia, SE of Yekaterinburg
Ku·ril *or* **Ku·rile** \ˈkyůr-ˌēl, kyů-ˈrēl\ islands Russia in North Pacific between S Kamchatka Peninsula & NE Hokkaido Island
Kur·nool \kər-ˈnül\ city S India in W Andhra Pradesh SSW of Hyderabad
Kursk \ˈkůrsk\ city SW Russia in Europe, N of Kharkiv, Ukraine
Ku·wait \kü-ˈwāt\ **1** country SW Asia in Arabia at head of Persian Gulf **2** city, its capital — **Ku·waiti** \-ˈwāt-ē\ *adj or n*
Kuybyshev — see SAMARA
Kuz·netsk Basin \kůz-ˈnetsk\ *or* **Kuz·bass** *or* **Kuz·bas** \ˈkůz-ˌbas\ basin of Tom River S Russia in Asia, extending from Tomsk to Novokuznetsk
Kwa·ja·lein \ˈkwäj-ə-lən, -ˌlān\ island (atoll) W Pacific in Ralik Chain of Marshall Islands
Kwang·ju *or* **Gwang·ju** \ˈgwäŋ-ˌjü\ city SW South Korea
Kwangsi–Chuang — see GUANGXI ZHUANGZU
Kwangtung — see GUANGDONG
Kwa·Zu·lu–Na·tal \kwä-ˈzü-lü-nä-ˈtäl\ province E Republic of South Africa between Drakensberg Mountains & Indian Ocean
Kweichow — see GUIZHOU
Kweilin *or* **Kuei–lin** — see GUILIN
Kyiv — see KIEV
Kyo·to \kē-ˈōt-ō\ city Japan in W central Honshu; formerly capital of Japan
Kyr·gyz·stan \ˌkir-gi-ˈstan, -ˈstän; ˈkir-gi-ˌ\ country W central Asia; capital, Bishkek; a constituent republic of U.S.S.R. 1936–91
Kyu·shu \kē-ˈü-shü\ island Japan S of W end of Honshu
Labe — see ELBE
Lab·ra·dor \ˈlab-rə-ˌdȯr\ **1** peninsula E Canada between Hudson Bay & North Atlantic divided between the provinces of Quebec & Newfoundland and Labrador **2** the part of the peninsula belonging to Newfoundland and Labrador — **Lab·ra·dor·ean** *or* **Lab·ra·dor·ian** \ˌlab-rə-ˈdȯr-ē-ən, -ˈdȯr-\ *adj or n*
Labrador Current cold current flowing S from Baffin Bay through Davis Strait past Labrador & Newfoundland
Lac·ca·dive \ˈlak-ə-ˌdēv, -ˌdīv\ islands India in Arabian Sea N of Maldive Islands
Lacedaemon — see SPARTA
La·co·nia \lə-ˈkō-nē-ə, -nyə\ ancient country S Greece in SE Peloponnese; capital, Sparta — **La·co·nian** \-nē-ən, -nyən\ *adj or n*
Lad·o·ga \ˈlad-ə-gə, ˈläd-\ lake W Russia in Europe, near Finland border
La·fay·ette \ˌlaf-ē-ˈet, ˌläf-\ city S Louisiana
La·gos \ˈlā-ˌgäs\ city & port, former capital of Nigeria
La Habana — see HAVANA
La·hon·tan, Lake \lə-ˈhänt-n\ prehistoric lake NW Nevada & NE California
La·hore \lə-ˈhōr, -ˈhȯr\ city Pakistan in E Punjab province
Lake Clark National Park \ˈklärk\ reservation S central Alaska WSW of Anchorage
Lake District region NW England containing many lakes & mountains
Lak·shad·weep \lək-ˈshäd-ˌwēp, ˌlək-shəd-ˈ\ territory India comprising the Laccadive Islands
La Mau·ri·cie National Park \lä-ˌmȯr-ē-ˈsē\ reservation S Quebec
Lam·beth \ˈlam-bəth, -ˌbeth\ borough of S Greater London, England
La·nai \lə-ˈnī\ island Hawaii W of Maui
Lan·ca·shire \ˈlaŋ-kə-ˌshiər, -shər\ *or* **Lan·cas·ter** \ˈlaŋ-kə-stər\ county NW England — **Lan·cas·tri·an** \laŋ-ˈkas-trē-ən, lan-\ *adj or n*
Lan·cas·ter \ˈlan-ˌkas-tər, ˈlaŋ-kəs-tər\ **1** city SW California NE of Los Angeles **2** city NW England
Land's End \ˈland-ˈzend, ˈlan-\ *or ancient* **Bo·le·ri·um** \bə-ˈlir-ē-əm\ cape SW England containing England's westernmost point
Lan·gue·doc \ˌlaŋ-gə-ˈdäk; ˌläⁿ-gə-ˈdȯk, ˌläⁿg-\ region & former province S France on the Mediterranean W of Provence
Lan·sing \ˈlan-siŋ\ city, capital of Michigan
La·nús \lə-ˈnüs\ city E Argentina S of Buenos Aires
Lan·zhou *or* **Lan–chou** \ˈlän-ˈjō\ city W central China, capital of Gansu
Laoighis \ˈlāsh, ˈlēsh\ *or* **Leix** \ˈlāsh, ˈlēsh\ *or formerly* **Queen's** \ˈkwēnz\ county central Ireland in Leinster
Laos \ˈlaůs, ˈlā-ˌäs, ˈlā-ˌōs\ country SE Asia in Indochina NE of Thailand; capital, Vientiane
La Paz \lə-ˈpaz, -ˈpäz, -ˈpäs\ city, administrative capital of Bolivia
Lap·land \ˈlap-ˌland, -lənd\ region N Europe above the Arctic Circle in N Norway, N Sweden, N Finland, & Kola Peninsula of Russia — **Lap·land·er** \-ˌlan-dər, -lən-\ *n*
La Pla·ta \lə-ˈplät-ə\ city E Argentina SE of Buenos Aires
L'Aqui·la \ˈläk-wi-lə, ˈlak-\ city central Italy NE of Rome
Las Pal·mas \lä-ˈspäl-məs\ city Spain in the Canary Islands on Grand Canary Island
La Spe·zia \lä-ˈspet-sē-ə\ city NW Italy in Liguria SE of Genoa
Las·sen Peak \ˈlas-n\ volcano 10,457 feet (3187 meters) N California at S end of Cascade Range in **Lassen Volcanic National Park**
Las Ve·gas \läs-ˈvā-gəs\ city SE corner of Nevada
Lat·a·kia \ˌlat-ə-ˈkē-ə\ city NW Syria
Latin America **1** Spanish America and Brazil **2** all of the Americas S of the U.S. — **Latin–American** *adj* — **Latin American** *n*
La·tium \ˈlā-shē-əm, -shəm\ *or Italian* **La·zio** \ˈlät-sē-ō\ region central Italy on Tyrrhenian Sea; capital, Rome
Lat·via \ˈlat-vē-ə\ country E Europe on Baltic Sea; capital, Riga; a constituent republic of U.S.S.R. 1940–91
Lau·ren·tian Mountains \lȯ-ˈren-chən-\ range E Canada in S Quebec N of the Saint Lawrence on S edge of Canadian Shield
Laurentian Plateau — see CANADIAN SHIELD
La·val \lə-ˈval\ city S Quebec NW of Montreal
League of Nations political organization established by the Allied powers at end of World War I; replaced by United Nations 1946
Leb·a·non \ˈleb-ə-nən, -ˌnän\ **1** *or ancient* **Lib·a·nus** \ˈlib-ə-nəs\ mountains Lebanon running parallel to coast; highest 10,131 feet (3088 meters) **2** country SW Asia on the Mediter-

\ə\ **abut**	\aů\ **out**	\i\ **tip**	\ȯ\ **saw**	\ů\ **foot**
\ər\ **further**	\ch\ **chin**	\ī\ **life**	\ȯi\ **coin**	\y\ **yet**
\a\ **mat**	\e\ **pet**	\j\ **job**	\th\ **thin**	\yü\ **few**
\ā\ **take**	\ē\ **easy**	\ŋ\ **sing**	\t͟h\ **this**	\yů\ **cure**
\ä\ **cot, cart**	\g\ **go**	\ō\ **bone**	\ü\ **food**	\zh\ **vision**

ranean; capital, Beirut — **Leb·a·nese** \ˌleb-ə-ˈnēz, -ˈnēs\ *adj or n*

Leeds \ˈlēdz\ city [N] England

Lee·ward \ˈlē-wərd\ **1** islands Hawaii extending [WNW] from main islands of the group **2** islands South Pacific in [W] Society Islands **3** islands West Indies in [N] Lesser Antilles

Le Ha·vre \lə-ˈhävr\ city [N] France on English Channel

Leices·ter \ˈles-tər\ city central England [ENE] of Birmingham

Leices·ter·shire \ˈles-tər-ˌshiər, -shər\ *or* **Leicester** county central England

Lein·ster \ˈlen-stər\ province [E] Ireland

Leip·zig \ˈlīp-sig, -sik\ city [E] central Germany in Saxony

Lei·trim \ˈlē-trəm\ county [NW] Ireland in Connacht

Leix — see LAOIGHIS

Leman, Lake *or* **Lemannus** *or* **Lemanus** — see GENEVA (Lake)

Lemberg — see L'VIV

Lem·nos \ˈlem-ˌnäs, -nəs\ *or Greek* **Lím·nos** \ˈlēm-ˌnȯs\ island Greece in the [N] Aegean

Le·na \ˈlē-nə, ˈlā-\ river about 2700 miles (4345 kilometers) long [E] central Russia in Asia, flowing [NE] & [N] into Arctic Ocean

Leningrad — see SAINT PETERSBURG 2

Le·ón \lā-ˈōn\ **1** city central Mexico in Guanajuato **2** region & ancient kingdom [NW] Spain

Léopoldville — see KINSHASA

Le Puglie — see PUGLIA

Les·bos \ˈlez-ˌbäs, -bəs\ *or* **Myt·i·le·ne** \ˌmit-l-ˈē-nē\ island Greece in the Aegean off [NW] coast of Turkey

Le·so·tho \lə-ˈsō-tō, ˈsü-ˌtü\ country [S] Africa surrounded by Republic of South Africa; formerly British territory of **Ba·su·to·land** \bə-ˈsüt-ə-ˌland\, now an independent monarchy; capital, Maseru

Lesser An·til·les \an-ˈtil-ēz\ islands in the West Indies including Virgin, Leeward, & Windward islands, Barbados, Trinidad, Tobago, & islands in the [S] Caribbean [N] of Venezuela — see GREATER ANTILLES

Lesser Armenia region [S] Turkey corresponding to ancient Cilicia

Lesser Sunda — see SUNDA

Le·vant \lə-ˈvant\ the countries bordering on the [E] Mediterranean — **Lev·an·tine** \ˈlev-ən-ˌtīn, -ˌtēn, lə-ˈvan-\ *adj or n*

Lew·i·sham \ˈlü-ə-shəm\ borough of [SE] Greater London, England

Lew·is with Har·ris \ˌlü-ə-swəth-ˈhar-əs, -swəth-\ island [NW] Scotland in Outer Hebrides

Lex·ing·ton \ˈlek-sing-tən\ city [N] central Kentucky

Ley·te \ˈlāt-ē\ island Philippines in Visayan Islands [S] of Samar

Lha·sa \ˈläs-ə, ˈlas-\ city [SW] China, capital of Tibet

Liao·ning \lē-ˈau̇-ˈning\ province [NE] China in [S] Manchuria; capital, Shenyang

Liao·yang \lē-ˈau̇-ˈyäng\ city [NE] China in central Liaoning [NE] of Anshan

Libanus — see LEBANON

Li·be·ria \lī-ˈbir-ē-ə\ country [W] Africa on North Atlantic; capital, Monrovia — **Li·be·ri·an** \-ē-ən\ *adj or n*

Lib·er·ty \ˈlib-ərt-ē\ *or formerly* **Bed·loe's** \ˈbed-ˌlōz\ island [SE] New York in Upper New York Bay; the Statue of Liberty is on it

Li·bre·ville \ˈlē-brə-ˌvil, -ˌvēl\ city, capital of Gabon

Lib·ya \ˈlib-ē-ə\ **1** the part of Africa [N] of the Sahara between Egypt & Gulf of Sidra — an ancient name **2** [N] Africa [W] of Egypt — an ancient name **3** country [N] Africa on the Mediterranean [W] of Egypt; capital, Tripoli — **Lib·y·an** \ˈlib-ē-ən\ *adj or n*

Libyan desert [N] Africa [W] of the Nile in Libya, Egypt, & Sudan

Li·do \ˈlēd-ō\ island Italy in Adriatic Sea

Liech·ten·stein \ˈlik-tən-ˌstīn, -ˌshtīn\ country [W] Europe between Austria & Switzerland; a principality; capital, Vaduz — **Liech·ten·stein·er** \-ˌstī-nər, -ˌshtī-\ *n*

Li·ège \lē-ˈezh, -ˈāzh\ *or Flemish* **Luik** \ˈlīk\ city [E] Belgium

Lif·fey \ˈlif-ē\ river 50 miles (80 kilometers) long [E] Ireland flowing into Dublin Bay

Li·gu·ria \lə-ˈgyu̇r-ē-ə\ region [NW] Italy; capital, Genoa — **Li·gu·ri·an** \-ē-ən\ *adj or n*

Ligurian Sea arm of the Mediterranean [N] of Corsica

Li·ka·si \li-ˈkäs-ē\ *or formerly* **Ja·dot·ville** \ˌzhad-ō-ˈvēl\ city [SE] Democratic Republic of the Congo

Lille \ˈlēl\ city [N] France

Li·lon·gwe \li-ˈlȯng-wā\ city, capital of Malawi

Li·ma \ˈlē-mə\ city, capital of Peru

Lim·burg \ˈlim-ˌbərg\ *or French* **Lim·bourg** \ˈlim-ˌbərg, la^{n}-ˈbu̇r\ region [W] Europe [E] of the Meuse in Belgium & Netherlands

Lim·er·ick \ˈlim-rik, -ə-rik\ county [SW] Ireland in Munster

Límnos — see LEMNOS

Li·mou·sin \ˌlē-mü-ˈza^{n}\ region [S] central France

Lim·po·po \lim-ˈpō-pō\ **1** river 1000 miles (1609 kilometers) long Africa flowing from [NE] Republic of South Africa into Indian Ocean in Mozambique **2** *or formerly* **Northern** province [NE] Republic of South Africa

Lin·coln \ˈling-kən\ **1** city, capital of Nebraska **2** city [E] England

Lin·coln·shire \ˈling-kən-ˌshiər, -shər\ *or* **Lincoln** county [E] England

Line \ˈlīn\ islands Kiribati [S] of Hawaii, formerly divided between U.S. & United Kingdom

Lip·a·ri \ˈlip-ə-rē\ islands Italy off [NE] Sicily

Li·petsk \ˈlē-ˌpetsk\ city [S] central Russia in Europe, [N] of Voronezh

Lis·bon \ˈliz-bən\ *or Portuguese* **Lis·boa** \lēzh-ˈvō-ə\ city, capital of Portugal

Lith·u·a·nia \ˌlith-ə-ˈwā-nē-ə, ˌlith-yə-, -nyə\ country [E] Europe; capital, Vilnius; a constituent republic of U.S.S.R. 1940–91

Lit·tle Rock \ˈlit-l-ˌräk\ city, capital of Arkansas

Liv·er·pool \ˈliv-ər-ˌpül\ city [NW] England on Mersey Estuary

Li·vo·nia \lə-ˈvō-nē-ə, -nyə\ **1** city [SE] Michigan [W] of Detroit **2** region [E] Europe on Baltic Sea in Latvia & Estonia

Lju·blja·na \lē-ˌü-blē-ˈän-ə\ city central Slovenia on Sava River

Lla·no Es·ta·ca·do \ˈlan-ō-ˌes-tə-ˈkäd-ō, ˈlän-\ *or* **Staked Plain** \ˈstākt-, ˈstāk-\ plateau region [SE] New Mexico & [NW] Texas

Lo·bam·ba \lō-ˈbäm-bə\ town, legislative capital of Swaziland

Lodz \ˈlüj, ˈlädz\ city central Poland [WSW] of Warsaw

Lo·fo·ten \ˈlō-ˌfōt-n\ islands [NW] Norway

Lo·gan, Mount \ˈlō-gən\ mountain 19,551 feet (5959 meters) [SW] Yukon in Saint Elias Range; highest in Canada & second highest in North America

Loire \lə-ˈwär\ river 634 miles (1020 kilometers) long central France flowing [NW] & [W] into Bay of Biscay

Lo·mas de Za·mo·ra \ˈlō-ˌmäz-də-zə-ˈmōr-ə, -ˈmȯr-\ city [E] Argentina [SW] of Buenos Aires

Lom·bar·dy \ˈläm-ˌbärd-ē, -bərd-\ *or Italian* **Lom·bar·dia** \ˌläm-bər-ˈdē-ə, ˌlōm-\ region [N] Italy [N] of Po River; capital, Milan

Lo·mé \lō-ˈmā\ city, capital of Togo

Lo·mond, Loch \ˈlō-mənd\ lake [S] central Scotland

Lon·don \ˈlən-dən\ **1** city [S] Ontario, Canada **2** city, capital of England & of United Kingdom on the Thames; comprises **City of London** & 12 inner boroughs of Greater London — **Lon·don·er** \-də-nər\ *n*

Londonderry — see DERRY

Long Beach city & port [SW] California [S] of Los Angeles

Long·ford \ˈlȯng-fərd\ county [E] central Ireland in Leinster

Long Island island 118 miles (190 kilometers) long [SE] New York [S] of Connecticut

Long Island Sound inlet of North Atlantic between Connecticut & Long Island, New York

Lon·gueuil \lȯng-ˈgāl\ city Canada in [S] Quebec [E] of Montreal

Lor·raine \lə-ˈrān, lȯ-\ region [NE] France around upper Moselle & Meuse rivers — see ALSACE-LORRAINE

Los An·ge·les \lȯ-ˈsan-jə-ləs *also* -ˈsang-gə-ləs\ city [SW] California

Lou·ise, Lake \lu̇-ˈēz\ lake [SW] Alberta in Banff National Park

Lou·i·si·ana \lu̇-ˌē-zē-ˈan-ə, ˌlü-ə-zē-, ˌlü-zē-\ state [S] U.S.; capital, Baton Rouge — **Lou·i·si·an·ian** \-ˈan-ē-ən, -ˈan-yən\ *or* **Lou·i·si·an·an** \-ˈan-ən\ *adj or n*

Louisiana Purchase area [W] central U.S. between Rocky Mountains & the Mississippi purchased 1803 from France

Lou·is·ville \ˈlü-i-ˌvil, -vəl\ city [N] Kentucky on the Ohio River

Lourenço Marques — see MAPUTO

Louth \ˈlau̇th\ county [E] Ireland in Leinster

Low Countries region [W] Europe comprising modern Belgium, Luxembourg, & the Netherlands

Low·ell \ˈlō-əl\ city [NE] Massachusetts

Lower California — see BAJA CALIFORNIA

Lower Canada former province, Canada in [S] & [E] parts of present-day Quebec

Lower 48 the continental states of the U.S. excluding Alaska

Lower Saxony *or German* **Nie·der·sach·sen** \ˌnēd-ər-ˈzäk-sən\ state [NW] Germany; capital, Hannover

Low·lands \ˈlō-ləndz, -lənz, -ˌlandz, -ˌlanz\ the central & [E] part of Scotland lying between the Highlands & the Southern Uplands

Lu·an·da \lu̇-ˈan-də\ city, capital of Angola

Lub·bock \ˈlə-bək\ city [NW] Texas

Lü·beck \ˈlü-ˌbek, ˈlue-\ city [N] Germany [NE] of Hamburg

Lu·blin \ˈlü-blən, -ˌblēn\ city [E] Poland [SE] of Warsaw

Lu·bum·ba·shi \ˌlü-büm-ˈbäsh-ē\ *or formerly* **Elis·a·beth·ville** \i-ˈliz-ə-bəth-ˌvil\ city [SE] Democratic Republic of the Congo

Lu·cerne, Lake of \lü-ˈsərn\ lake central Switzerland

Luchow — see HEFEI

Luck·now \ˈlək-ˌnau̇\ city [N] India, capital of Uttar Pradesh

Lüda — see DALIAN

Lu·dhi·a·na \ˌlu̇d-ē-ˈän-ə\ city [NW] India in Punjab [SE] of Amritsar

Luik — see LIÈGE

Luluabourg — see KANANGA

Lu·sa·ka \lü-ˈsäk-ə\ city, capital of Zambia

Lü·shun \ˈlü-ˈshün\ *or* **Port Ar·thur** \ˈär-thər\ city [NE] China in [S] Liaoning

Lusitania — see PORTUGAL

Lü–ta — see DALIAN

Lu·ton \ˈlüt-ᵊn\ town [SE] central England

Lux·em·bourg *or German* **Lux·em·burg** \ˈlək-səm-ˌbərg, ˈlu̇k-səm-ˌbu̇rg\ **1** country [W] Europe bordered by Belgium, France, & Germany; a grand duchy **2** city, its capital — **Lux·em·bourg·er** \-ˌbər-gər, -ˌbu̇r-\ *n* — **Lux·em·bourg·ian** \ˌlək-səm-ˈbər-gē-ən, ˌlu̇k-səm-ˈbu̇r-\ *adj*

Lu·zon \lü-ˈzän\ island [N] Philippines

L'viv \lə-ˈvē-ü, -ˈvēf\ *or* **L'vov** \lə-ˈvȯf, -ˈvȯv\ *or Polish* **Lwów** \lə-ˈvüf, -ˈvüv\ *or German* **Lem·berg** \ˈlem-ˌbərg, -ˌberg\ city [W] Ukraine

Lyallpur — see FAISALABAD

Ly·cia \ˈlish-ə, ˈlish-ē-ə\ ancient district & Roman province [SW] Asia Minor

Lyd·ia \ˈlid-ē-ə\ ancient country [W] Asia Minor on the Aegean; capital, Sardis — **Lyd·i·an** \-ē-ən\ *adj or n*

Lyon \ˈlyōⁿ\ *or* **Ly·ons** \lē-ˈōⁿ, ˈlī-ənz\ *or ancient* **Lug·du·num** \lu̇g-ˈdü-nəm, ˌləg-\ city [SE] central France

Maas — see MEUSE

Ma·cao *or Portuguese* **Ma·cau** \mə-ˈkau̇\ *or Chinese* **Ao·men** \ˈau̇-ˈmən\ **1** special administrative region on coast of [SE] China [W] of Hong Kong; formerly a Portuguese overseas territory **2** city & port Macao — **Mac·a·nese** \ˌmak-ə-ˈnēz, -ˈnēs\ *n*

Mac·e·do·nia \ˌmas-ə-ˈdō-nyə, -nē-ə\ **1** region [S] Europe in Balkan Peninsula in [NE] Greece, independent country of Macedonia, & [SW] Bulgaria including territory of ancient kingdom of Macedonia (**Mac·e·don** \ˈmas-əd-ən, -ə-ˌdän\) **2** country [S] central Balkan Peninsula; formerly a constituent republic of Yugoslavia; capital, Skopje — **Mac·e·do·nian** \ˌmas-ə-ˈdō-nyən, -nē-ən\ *adj or n*

Ma·ceió \ˌmas-ā-ˈō\ city [NE] Brazil

Mac·gil·li·cud·dy's Reeks \mə-ˌgil-ə-ˌkəd-ēz-ˈrēks\ mountains [SW] Ireland in Kerry; highest Carrantuohill 3414 feet (1041 meters)

Ma·chi·da \mə-ˈchē-də, ˈmä-chi-ˌdä\ city Japan on Honshu

Ma·chi·li·pat·nam \ˌməch-ə-lə-ˈpət-nəm\ *or* **Ban·dar** \ˈbən-dər\ city [SE] India in [E] Andhra Pradesh

Ma·chu Pic·chu \ˌmäch-ü-ˈpēk-chü\ site [SE] Peru of ancient Inca city [NW] of Cuzco

Mac·ken·zie \mə-ˈken-zē\ **1** river 1120 miles (1802 kilometers) long [NW] Canada flowing from Great Slave Lake [NW] into Beaufort Sea **2** former district [NW] Canada in [W] Northwest Territories in basin of Mackenzie River; area now split between Northwest Territories & Nunavut

Mack·i·nac, Straits of \ˈmak-ə-ˌnȯ\ channel [N] Michigan connecting Lake Huron & Lake Michigan

Ma·con \ˈmā-kən\ city central Georgia

Mad·a·gas·car \ˌmad-ə-ˈgas-kər\ *or formerly* **Mal·a·gasy Republic** \ˌmal-ə-ˌgas-ē\ island [W] Indian Ocean off [SE] Africa; capital, Antananarivo — **Mad·a·gas·can** \ˌmad-ə-ˈgas-kən\ *adj or n*

Ma·dei·ra \mə-ˈdir-ə, -ˈder-\ **1** river 2013 miles (3239 kilometers) long [W] Brazil flowing [NE] into the Amazon **2** islands in the North Atlantic [N] of the Canaries belonging to Portugal; capital, Funchal **3** island; chief of the Madeira group — **Ma·dei·ran** \-ən\ *adj or n*

Ma·dhya Pra·desh \ˌmäd-yə-prə-ˈdesh, -ˈdāsh\ state central India; capital, Bhopal

Mad·i·son \ˈmad-ə-sən\ city, capital of Wisconsin

Ma·dras \mə-ˈdras, -ˈdräs\ **1** — see TAMIL NADU **2** *or* **Chen·nai** \ˈchen-ˌī\ city [SE] India, capital of Tamil Nadu

Ma·drid \mə-ˈdrid\ city, capital of Spain

Ma·du·ra \mə-ˈdu̇r-ə\ island Indonesia [NE] of Java

Ma·du·rai \ˌmäd-ə-ˈrī\ *or* **Ma·du·ra** \ˈmaj-ə-rə\ city [S] India in [S] Tamil Nadu

Mag·da·len \ˈmag-də-lən\ *or French* **Ma·de·leine** \mäd-ˈlen, mä-də-\ islands Quebec in Gulf of Saint Lawrence

Mag·de·burg \ˈmäg-də-ˌbu̇rg, ˈmag-də-ˌbərg\ city central Germany [WSW] of Berlin; capital of Saxony-Anhalt

Ma·gel·lan, Strait of \mə-ˈjel-ən\ strait at [S] end of South America between mainland & Tierra del Fuego Archipelago

Mageröy — see NORTH CAPE

Mag·gio·re, Lake \mə-ˈjōr-ē, -ˈjȯr-\ lake [N] Italy & [S] Switzerland

Ma·ghreb *or* **Ma·ghrib** \ˈmäg-rəb\ [NW] Africa & at one time Spain — specifically the coastal areas of Morocco, Algeria, Tunisia, & sometimes Libya, but often used of those countries in their entirety

Mag·ni·to·gorsk \mag-ˈnēt-ə-ˌgȯrsk\ city [SW] Russia in Asia, on Ural River

Ma·hal·la el Ku·bra \mə-ˌhal-ə-el-ˈkü-brə\ city [N] Egypt in Nile Delta

Ma·ha·rash·tra \ˌmä-hə-ˈräsh-trə\ state [W] India on Arabian Sea; capital, Bombay

Ma·hi·lyow *or* **Mo·gi·lev** \mə-gil-ˈyȯf\ city [E] Belarus

Main \ˈmīn, ˈmān\ river 325 miles (523 kilometers) long [S] central Germany flowing [W] into the Rhine

Maine \ˈmān\ state [NE] U.S.; capital, Augusta

Mainz \ˈmīns\ city [W] Germany on the Rhine, capital of Rhineland-Palatinate

Ma·jor·ca \mə-ˈjȯr-kə, -ˈyȯr-\ *or Spanish* **Ma·llor·ca** \mə-ˈyȯr-kə\ island Spain; largest of the Balearic Islands — **Ma·jor·can** \-ˈjȯr-kən, -ˈyȯr-\ *adj or n*

Ma·ju·ro \mə-ˈju̇r-ō\ atoll [W] Pacific; contains capital of Marshall Islands

Ma·ka·lu \ˈmək-ə-ˌlü\ mountain 27,824 feet (8481 meters) [NE] Nepal in the Himalaya

Ma·kas·sar \mə-ˈkas-ər\ **1** strait Indonesia between Borneo & Sulawesi **2** *or formerly* **Ujung Pan·dang** \ˈü-ˌju̇ng-ˌpän-ˈdäng\ city Indonesia in [SW] Sulawesi

Ma·ke·yev·ka *or* **Ma·ki·yiv·ka** \mə-ˈkā-əf-kə, -yəf-\ city [E] Ukraine in Donets Basin

Ma·khach·ka·la \mə-ˌkäch-kə-ˈlä\ city [S] Russia in Europe, on the Caspian

Mal·a·bar Coast \ˈmal-ə-ˌbär\ region [SW] India on Arabian Sea in Karnataka & Kerala states

Ma·la·bo \mä-ˈläb-ō\ *or formerly* **San·ta Isa·bel** \ˌsan-tə-ˈiz-ə-bel\ city, capital of Equatorial Guinea

Ma·lac·ca, Strait of \mə-ˈlak-ə, -ˈläk-\ channel between [S] Malay Peninsula & island of Sumatra

Má·la·ga \ˈmal-ə-gə\ city [S] Spain in Andalusia

Ma·lang \mə-ˈläng\ city Indonesia in [E] Java

Ma·la·wi \mə-ˈlä-wē, -ˈlau̇-ē\ *or formerly* **Ny·asa·land** \nī-ˈas-ə-ˌland, nē-\ country [SE] Africa on Lake Malawi; a former British protectorate; capital, Lilongwe

Malawi, Lake *or* **Lake Nya·sa** \ˈnyä-sä, nī-ˈas-ə\ lake [SE] Africa in Malawi, Mozambique, & Tanzania

Ma·lay \mə-ˈlā, ˈmā-lā\ **1** archipelago [SE] Asia including Sumatra, Java, Borneo, Sulawesi, Moluccas, & Timor; usually considered to include the Philippines & sometimes New Guinea **2** peninsula [SE] Asia divided between Thailand & Malaysia

Ma·laya, Federation of \mə-ˈlā-ə, mā-\ former country [SE] Asia on Malay Peninsula; since 1963 part of Malaysia

Ma·lay·sia \mə-ˈlā-zhə, -shə, -zhē-ə, -shē-ə\ **1** a name formerly used for the Malay Archipelago **2** country [SE] Asia; a limited constitutional monarchy; capital, Kuala Lumpur — **Ma·lay·sian** \mə-ˈlā-zhən, -shən\ *adj or n*

Mal·dives \ˈmȯl-ˌdēvz, -ˌdīvz\ islands in Indian Ocean [S] of the Laccadives; formerly a sultanate under British protection; independent since 1965; capital, **Ma·le** \ˈmäl-ē\ — **Mal·div·i·an** \mȯl-ˈdiv-ē-ən\ *adj or n*

\ə\ abut	\au̇\ **out**	\i\ **tip**	\ȯ\ **saw**	\u̇\ **foot**
\ər\ **further**	\ch\ **chin**	\ī\ **life**	\ȯi\ **coin**	\y\ **yet**
\a\ **mat**	\e\ **pet**	\j\ **job**	\th\ **thin**	\yü\ **few**
\ā\ **take**	\ē\ **easy**	\ng\ **sing**	\th\ **this**	\yu̇\ **cure**
\ä\ **cot, cart**	\g\ **go**	\ō\ **bone**	\ü\ **food**	\zh\ **vision**

Ma·le·bo, Pool \mä-ˈlā-ˌbō\ expansion of Congo River between Democratic Republic of the Congo & Republic of the Congo

Ma·li \ˈmäl-ē, ˈmal-ē\ *or formerly* **French Sudan** country [W] Africa; capital, Bamako — **Ma·li·an** \-ē-ən\ *adj or n*

Malmö \ˈmal-ˌmər, ˈmal-ˌmœ̄\ city & port [SW] Sweden

Mal·ta \ˈmȯl-tə\ **1** islands in the Mediterranean [S] of Sicily; a former British colony; independent since 1964; capital, Valletta **2** island, chief of the group

Maluku — see MOLUCCAS

Malvinas, Islas — see FALKLAND ISLANDS

Mam·moth Cave \ˌmam-əth\ limestone caverns [SW] central Kentucky in **Mammoth Cave National Park**

Man, Isle of \ˈman\ island British Isles in Irish Sea; capital, Douglas; has own legislature & laws

Ma·na·do \mə-ˈnäd-ˌō\ city & port Indonesia on [NE] Sulawesi

Ma·na·gua \mə-ˈnäg-wə\ city, capital of Nicaragua

Ma·na·ma \mə-ˈnam-ə\ city, capital of Bahrain

Ma·naus \mə-ˈnau̇s\ city [W] Brazil on Rio Negro 12 miles (19 kilometers) above its junction with the Amazon

Man·ches·ter \ˈman-ˌches-tər, -chə-stər\ city [NW] England [ENE] of Liverpool — see GREATER MANCHESTER

Man·chu·kuo \ˈman-ˈchü-ˈkwō, man-ˈchü-ˌ\ former country (1931–45) [E] Asia in Manchuria & [E] Inner Mongolia; capital, Changchun

Man·chu·ria \man-ˈchu̇r-ē-ə\ region [NE] China [S] of the Amur — **Man·chu·ri·an** \man-ˈchu̇r-ē-ən\ *adj or n*

Man·da·lay \ˌman-də-ˈlā\ city central Myanmar (Burma)

Man·hat·tan \man-ˈhat-n, mən-\ **1** island [SE] New York in New York City **2** borough of New York City comprising chiefly Manhattan Island

Manihiki — see NORTHERN COOK

Ma·nila \mə-ˈnil-ə\ city, capital of Philippines

Ma·ni·pur \ˌman-ə-ˈpu̇r, ˌmən-\ state [NE] India between Assam & Myanmar; capital, Imphal

Man·i·to·ba \ˌman-ə-ˈtō-bə\ province central Canada; capital, Winnipeg — **Man·i·to·ban** \-ˈtō-bən\ *adj or n*

Man·i·tou·lin \ˌman-ə-ˈtü-lən\ island 80 miles (129 kilometers) long [S] Ontario in Lake Huron

Ma·ni·za·les \ˌman-ə-ˈzäl-əs, -ˈzal-\ city [W] central Colombia

Man·nar, Gulf of \mə-ˈnär\ inlet of Indian Ocean between Sri Lanka & [S] tip of India

Mann·heim \ˈman-ˌhīm, ˈmän-\ city [SW] Germany on the Rhine

Man·za·nil·lo \ˌman-zə-ˈnē-ō, -yō\ city [SW] Mexico in Colima

Ma·pu·to \mä-ˈpü-tō\ *or formerly* **Lou·ren·ço Mar·quez** \lə-ˌren-sō-ˌmär-ˈkes, -ˈmärks, -ˈmärk\ city, capital of Mozambique

Mar·a·cai·bo \ˌmar-ə-ˈkī-bō\ city [NW] Venezuela

Maracaibo, Lake the [S] extension of Gulf of Venezuela in [NW] Venezuela

Ma·ra·cay \ˌmär-ə-ˈkī\ city [N] Venezuela

Mar·a·thon \ˈmar-ə-ˌthän, -thən\ plain [E] Greece in Attica [NE] of Athens

Marche \ˈmärsh\ region central Italy on the Adriatic; capital, Ancona

Mar del Pla·ta \ˌmär-del-ˈplät-ə\ city & port [E] Argentina

Mar·i·ana \ˌmar-ē-ˈan-ə, ˌmer-\ islands [W] Pacific [N] of Caroline Islands including the Northern Mariana Islands & Guam

Ma·ri·a·nao \ˌmär-ē-ə-ˈnau̇\ city [W] Cuba [W] of Havana

Mariana Trench ocean trench [W] Pacific extending from [SE] of Guam to [NW] of Mariana Islands; deepest in world

Maritime Alps section of the [W] Alps [SE] France & [NW] Italy extending [N] from Mediterranean coast

Maritime Provinces *or* **the Maritimes** the Canadian provinces of New Brunswick, Nova Scotia, & Prince Edward Island & formerly thought by some to include Newfoundland and Labrador

Ma·ri·u·pol' \ˌmar-ē-ˈü-ˌpȯl\ *or 1949–89* **Zhda·nov** \zhe-ˈdä-nəf, ˈshtä-\ city [E] Ukraine on Sea of Azov

Mark·ham \ˈmär-kəm\ town [SE] Ontario

Markham, Mount mountain 14,275 feet (4351 meters) Antarctica [E] of Ross Ice Shelf

Mar·ma·ra, Sea of *or* **Sea of Mar·mo·ra** \ˈmär-mə-rə\ *or ancient* **Pro·pon·tis** \prə-ˈpänt-əs\ sea [NW] Turkey connected with Black Sea by the Bosporus & with Aegean Sea by the Dardanelles

Marne \ˈmärn\ river 325 miles (523 kilometers) long [NE] France flowing [W] into the Seine

Mar·que·sas \mär-ˈkā-zəz, -zəs, -səz, -səs\ islands South Pacific [N] of Tuamotu Archipelago in French Polynesia — **Mar·que·san** \-zən, -sən\ *adj or n*

Mar·ra·kech \mə-ˈräk-ish, ˌmar-ə-ˈkesh\ *or formerly* **Mo·roc·co** \mə-ˈräk-ō\ city central Morocco

Mar·seille \mär-ˈsā\ *or* **Mar·seilles** \mär-ˈsā, -ˈsālz\ *or ancient* **Mas·sil·ia** \mə-ˈsil-ē-ə\ city [SE] France

Mar·shall Islands \ˈmär-shəl\ islands [W] Pacific [E] of the Carolines; since 1986 an independent republic in association with the U.S.; capital, Majuro

Mar·tha's Vineyard \ˌmär-thəz\ island [SE] Massachusetts off [SW] coast of Cape Cod [WNW] of Nantucket

Mar·ti·nique \ˌmärt-n-ˈēk\ island West Indies in the Windwards; an overseas department of France; capital, Fort-de-France

Mary·land \ˈmer-ə-lənd\ state [E] U.S.; capital, Annapolis — **Mary·land·er** \-lən-dər, -ˌlan-\ *n*

Ma·san \ˈmäs-ˌän\ city South Korea [W] of Pusan

Mas·e·ru \ˈmaz-ə-ˌrü\ city, capital of Lesotho

Mash·had \mə-ˈshad\ city [NE] Iran

Ma·son–Dix·on Line \ˌmās-n-ˈdik-sən\ boundary between Maryland & Pennsylvania; was in part boundary between free & slave states

Masqat — see MUSCAT

Mas·sa·chu·setts \ˌmas-ə-ˈchü-səts, ˌmas-ˈchü-, -zəts\ state [NE] U.S.; capital, Boston

Mas·sif Cen·tral \ma-ˌsēf-ˌsen-ˈträl, -ˌsäⁿ-ˈträl\ plateau central France — see AUVERGNE, CÉVENNES

Mat·a·be·le·land \ˌmat-ə-ˈbē-lē-ˌland\ region [SW] Zimbabwe; chief town, Bulawayo

Ma·to Gros·so \ˌmat-ə-ˈgrō-sō\ plateau region [SW] Brazil; source of several rivers

Mat·su·do \mät-ˈsü-dō\ city Japan in [SE] Honshu [NE] of Tokyo

Ma·tsu·shi·ma \ˌmät-sü-ˈshē-mə, mät-ˈsü-shi-mə\ group of islets Japan off [N] Honshu [NE] of Sendai

Ma·tsu·ya·ma \ˌmät-sə-ˈyäm-ə\ city Japan in [W] Shikoku

Mat·ter·horn \ˈmat-ər-ˌhȯrn, ˈmät-\ mountain 14,691 feet (4478 meters) in Pennine Alps on border between Switzerland & Italy

Maui \ˈmau̇-ē\ island Hawaii [NW] of Hawaii Island

Mau·na Kea \ˌmau̇-nə-ˈkā-ə\ extinct volcano 13,796 feet (4205 meters) Hawaii in [N] central Hawaii Island

Mau·na Loa \ˌmau̇-nə-ˈlō-ə\ volcano 13,680 feet (4170 meters) Hawaii in [S] central Hawaii Island in Hawaii Volcanoes National Park

Mau·re·ta·nia *or* **Mau·ri·ta·nia** \ˌmȯr-ə-ˈtā-nē-ə, ˌmär-, -nyə\ ancient country [NW] Africa in modern Morocco & [W] Algeria — **Mau·re·ta·ni·an** *or* **Mau·ri·ta·nian** \-nē-ən, -nyən\ *adj or n*

Mauritania country [NW] Africa on North Atlantic [N] of Senegal River; capital, Nouakchott — **Mauritanian** *adj or n*

Mau·ri·tius \mȯ-ˈrish-əs, -ˈrish-ē-əs\ island in Indian Ocean [E] of Madagascar; an independent country; capital, Port Louis — **Mau·ri·tian** \-ˈrish-ən\ *adj or n*

Mawlamyine — see MOULMEIN

May, Cape \ˈmā\ cape [S] New Jersey at entrance to Delaware Bay

Mayo \ˈmā-ō\ county [NW] Ireland in Connacht

Ma·yon \mä-ˈyōn\ volcano 8077 feet (2462 meters) Philippines in [SE] Luzon

Ma·yotte \mä-ˈyät, -ˈyȯt\ island Comoros group; a French dependency

Ma·za·ma, Mount \mə-ˈzäm-ə\ prehistoric mountain [SW] Oregon the collapse of whose summit formed Crater Lake

Ma·za·tlán \ˌmäz-ə-ˈtlän, ˌmäs-\ city [W] Mexico in Sinaloa on the Pacific

Mba·bane \ˌem-bə-ˈbän-ā\ city, capital of Swaziland

Mban·da·ka \ˌem-ˌbän-ˈdäk-ə\ *or formerly* **Co·qui·lhat·ville** \ˌkō-kē-ˈat-ˌvil\ city [W] Democratic Republic of the Congo

Mbi·ni \əm-ˈbē-nē\ *or formerly* **Río Mu·ni** \ˌrē-ō-ˈmü-nē\ mainland portion of Equatorial Guinea on Gulf of Guinea

Mbu·ji–Ma·yi \əm-ˌbü-jē-ˈmī-ˌē\ *or formerly* **Ba·kwan·ga** \bə-ˈkwäng-gə\ city [S] Democratic Republic of the Congo

Mc·Al·len \mə-ˈkal-ən\ city [S] Texas

Mc·Kin·ley, Mount \mə-ˈkin-lē\ *or* **De·na·li** \də-ˈnäl-ē\ mountain 20,320 feet (6194 meters) [S] central Alaska in Alaska Range; highest in U.S. & in North America; in **Denali National Park**

Mead, Lake \ˈmēd\ reservoir [NW] Arizona & [SE] Nevada formed by Hoover Dam in Colorado River

Meath \ˈmēth, ˈmēth\ county [E] Ireland in Leinster

Mec·ca \ˈmek-ə\ city [W] Saudi Arabia, capital of Hejaz

Meck·len·burg–West Pomerania \ˈmek-lən-ˌbərg-\ state [NE] Germany on the Baltic; capital, Schwerin

Me·dan \mā-ˈdän\ city Indonesia in [NE] Sumatra
Me·de·llín \ˌmed-l-ˈēn, ˌmā-thā-ˈyēn\ city [NW] Colombia [NW] of Bogotá
Me·dia \ˈmēd-ē-ə\ ancient country & province of Persia
Me·di·na \mə-ˈdē-nə\ city [W] Saudi Arabia
Mediolanum — see MILAN
Med·i·ter·ra·nean \ˌmed-ə-tə-ˈrā-nē-ən, -nyən\ sea 2300 miles (3700 kilometers) long between Europe & Africa connecting with North Atlantic through Strait of Gibraltar
Mee·rut \ˈmā-rət, ˈmir-ət\ city [N] India in [NW] Uttar Pradesh
Me·gha·la·ya \ˌmā-gə-ˈlā-ə\ state [NE] India; capital, Shillong
Méjico — see MEXICO
Mek·nes \mek-ˈnes\ city [N] Morocco; former capital of the country
Me·kong \ˈmā-ˈkȯŋ, -ˈkäŋ\ river about 2600 miles (4184 kilometers) long [SE] Asia flowing from [E] Tibet [S] & [SE] into South China Sea in [S] Vietnam
Mel·a·ne·sia \ˌmel-ə-ˈnē-zhə, -shə\ islands of South Pacific [NE] of Australia & [S] of Micronesia including Bismarck Archipelago, the Solomons, Vanuatu, New Caledonia, & the Fijis
Mel·bourne \ˈmel-bərn\ city [SE] Australia, capital of Victoria
Mel·e·ke·ok \ˈmel-ə-ˌkā-ˌok\ town, capital of Palau
Me·los *or Greek* **Mí·los** \ˈmē-ˌläs\ island Greece in [SW] Cyclades — **Me·li·an** \ˈmē-lē-ən\ *adj or n*
Mel·ville \ˈmel-ˌvil\ **1** island [N] Canada in Parry Islands; split between Northwest Territories & Nunavut **2** peninsula in Nunavut
Me·mel \ˈmā-məl\ — see KLAIPEDA
Mem·phis \ˈmem-fəs, ˈmemp-\ **1** city [SW] Tennessee **2** ancient city [N] Egypt [S] of modern Cairo
Mem·phre·ma·gog, Lake \ˌmem-fri-ˈmā-ˌgäg\ lake 30 miles (48 kilometers) long on border between Quebec & Vermont
Men·do·ci·no, Cape \ˌmen-də-ˈsē-nō\ headland [NW] California
Menorca — see MINORCA
Mer·cia \ˈmər-shə, -shē-ə\ ancient Anglo-Saxon kingdom central England — **Mer·cian** \ˈmər-shən\ *adj or n*
Mé·ri·da \ˈmer-əd-ə\ city [SE] Mexico, capital of Yucatán
Mer·sey \ˈmər-zē\ river 70 miles (113 kilometers) long [NW] England flowing [NW] & [W] into Irish Sea through a large estuary
Mer·sey·side \ˈmər-zē-ˌsīd\ metropolitan county [NW] England; includes Liverpool
Mer·thyr Tyd·fil \ˈmər-thər-ˈtid-vil\ administrative area [S] Wales
Mer·ton \ˈmərt-n\ borough of [SW] Greater London, England
Me·sa \ˈmā-sə\ city [SW] central Arizona [E] of Phoenix
Me·sa·bi Range \mə-ˈsäb-ē\ region [NE] Minnesota that contains iron ore
Me·sa Verde National Park \ˌmā-sə-ˈvərd-ē, -ˈvərd\ reservation [SW] Colorado containing prehistoric cliff dwellings
Mes·o·po·ta·mia \ˌmes-ə-pə-ˈtā-mē-ə, -myə\ **1** region [SW] Asia between Euphrates & Tigris rivers **2** the entire Tigris-Euphrates valley — **Mes·o·po·ta·mian** \-mē-ən, -myən\ *adj or n*
Mes·quite \mə-ˈskēt\ city [NE] Texas [E] of Dallas
Mes·si·na \mə-ˈsē-nə\ city Italy in [NE] Sicily
Messina, Strait of channel between [NE] Sicily & [SW] tip of peninsula of Italy
Meuse \ˈmyüz, ˈmyərz, *French* mœz\ *or Dutch* **Maas** \ˈmäs\ river about 580 miles (933 kilometers) long [W] Europe flowing from [NE] France into North Sea in the Netherlands
Mex·i·cali \ˌmek-si-ˈkal-ē\ city [NW] Mexico, capital of Baja California
Mex·i·co \ˈmek-si-ˌkō\ *or Spanish* **Mé·ji·co** \ˈme-hē-kō\ **1** country [S] North America; capital Mexico City **2** *or* **Mexico City** city, its capital, in Federal District **3** state [S] central Mexico; capital, Toluca
Mexico, Gulf of inlet of North Atlantic [SE] North America
Mez·zo·gior·no \ˌmet-sō-ˈjȯr-nō, ˌmed-zō-\ the peninsula of Italy [S] of roughly the latitude of Rome
Mi·ami \mī-ˈam-ē, -ˈam-ə\ city [SE] Florida
Mich·i·gan \ˈmish-i-gən\ state [N] central U.S.; capital, Lansing — **Mich·i·gan·der** \ˌmish-i-ˈgan-dər\ *n* — **Mich·i·ga·ni·an** \ˌmish-ə-ˈgā-nē-ən, -ˈgan-ē-\ *n* — **Mich·i·gan·ite** \ˈmish-i-gə-ˌnīt\ *n*
Michigan, Lake lake [N] central U.S.; one of the Great Lakes
Mi·cho·a·cán \ˌmē-chə-wä-ˈkän\ state [SW] Mexico on North Pacific; capital, Morelia
Mi·cro·ne·sia \ˌmī-krə-ˈnē-zhə, -shə\ islands of the [W] Pacific [E] of the Philippines & [N] of Melanesia including Caroline, Kiribati, Mariana, & Marshall groups — **Mi·cro·ne·sian** \-zhən, -shən\ *adj or n*
Micronesia, Federated States of islands [W] Pacific in the Carolines comprising Kosrae, Pohnpei, Chuuk, & Yap; part of former Trust Territory of the Pacific Islands; republic in association with U.S.; capital, Palikir
Middle Congo — see CONGO 3
Middle East *or* **Mid·east** \ˌmid-ˈēst\ the countries of [SW] Asia & [N] Africa — usually considered as including the countries extending from Libya on the [W] to Afghanistan on the [E] — **Middle Eastern** *or* **Mid·east·ern** \ˈmid-ˈē-stərn\ *adj*
Mid·dles·brough \ˈmid-lz-brə\ town [N] England
Mi·di \mē-ˈdē\ the south of France
Mid·i·an \ˈmid-ē-ən\ ancient region [NW] Arabia [E] of Gulf of Aqaba — **Mid·i·an·ite** \-ē-ə-ˌnīt\ *n*
Mid·lands \ˈmid-ləndz, -lənz\ the central counties of England — see WEST MIDLANDS
Mid·lo·thi·an \mid-ˈlō-thē-ən\ administrative area [SE] Scotland; chief city, Edinburgh
Mid·way \ˈmid-ˌwā\ islands (atoll) central Pacific in Hawaiian group 1300 miles (2092 kilometers) [WNW] of Honolulu belonging to U.S.; not included in state of Hawaii
Mid·west *or* **Middle West** \ˈmid-ˈwest\ region [N] central U.S. including area around Great Lakes & in upper Mississippi valley from Ohio on the [E] to North Dakota, South Dakota, Nebraska, & Kansas on the [W] — **Mid·west·ern** \ˈmid-ˈwes-tərn\ *or* **Middle Western** *adj* — **Mid·west·ern·er** \ˈmid-ˈwes-tər-nər, -tə-nər\ *or* **Middle Westerner** *n*
Mi·lan \mə-ˈlan, -ˈlän\ *or Italian* **Mi·la·no** \mi-ˈlän-ō\ *or ancient* **Me·di·o·la·num** \ˌmed-ē-ō-ˈlā-nəm\ city [NW] Italy, capital of Lombardy — **Mil·a·nese** \ˌmil-ə-ˈnēz, -ˈnēs\ *adj or n*
Mílos — see MELOS
Mil·wau·kee \mil-ˈwȯ-kē\ city [SE] Wisconsin
Mi·nas Basin \ˌmī-nəs\ landlocked bay central Nova Scotia; [NE] extension of Bay of Fundy
Min·da·nao \ˌmin-də-ˈnä-ō, -ˈnau̇\ island [S] Philippines
Min·do·ro \min-ˈdōr-ō, -ˈdȯr-\ island central Philippines
Minhow — see FUZHOU
Min·ne·ap·o·lis \ˌmin-ē-ˈap-ləs, -ə-ləs\ city [SE] Minnesota
Min·ne·so·ta \ˌmin-ə-ˈsōt-ə\ state [N] central U.S.; capital, Saint Paul — **Min·ne·so·tan** \-ˈsōt-n\ *adj or n*
Mi·nor·ca \mə-ˈnȯr-kə\ *or Spanish* **Me·nor·ca** \mā-\ island Spain in Balearic Islands — **Mi·nor·can** \mə-ˈnȯr-kən\ *adj or n*
Minsk \ˈminsk\ city, capital of Belarus
Mi·que·lon \ˈmik-ə-ˌlän, *French* mēk-ˈlōⁿ, mēk-ə-\ island off [S] coast of Newfoundland belonging to France — see SAINT PIERRE
Mission Vie·jo \-vē-ˈā-hō\ city [SW] California
Mis·sis·sau·ga \ˌmis-ə-ˈsȯg-ə\ city Canada in [S] Ontario
Mis·sis·sip·pi \ˌmis-ə-ˈsip-ē, mis-ˈsip-ē\ **1** river 2340 miles (3765 kilometers) long central U.S. flowing into Gulf of Mexico — see ITASCA (Lake) **2** state [S] U.S.; capital, Jackson
Mis·sou·la \mə-ˈzü-lə\ city [W] Montana
Mis·sou·ri \mə-ˈzu̇r-ē, -ˈzu̇r-ə\ **1** river 2466 miles (3968 kilometers) long [W] U.S. flowing from [SW] Montana to the Mississippi in [E] Missouri **2** state central U.S.; capital, Jefferson City — **Mis·sou·ri·an** \-ˈzu̇r-ē-ən\ *adj or n*
Mitch·ell, Mount \ˈmich-əl\ mountain 6684 feet (2037 meters) [W] North Carolina in Black Mountains of the Appalachians; highest in U.S. [E] of the Mississippi
Mi·ya·za·ki \mē-ˌäz-ˈäk-ē, -ˌyäz-; mē-ˈäz-ə-kē, -ˈyäz-\ city Japan in [SE] Kyushu
Mi·zo·ram \mi-ˈzōr-əm\ state [NE] India; capital, Aizawl
Mo·ab \ˈmō-ˌab\ region Jordan [E] of Dead Sea; in biblical times a kingdom
Mo·bile \mō-ˈbēl, ˈmō-ˌbēl\ city [SW] Alabama on **Mobile Bay** (inlet of Gulf of Mexico)
Moçambique — see MOZAMBIQUE
Mo·de·na \ˈmȯd-n-ə, -n-ˌä\ city [N] Italy [SW] of Venice
Moe·sia \ˈmē-shə, -shē-ə\ ancient country & Roman province [S] of the Danube in modern Bulgaria & Serbia
Mog·a·di·shu \ˌmäg-ə-ˈdish-ü, -ˈdēsh-\ *or* **Mog·a·di·scio** \-ō\ city, capital of Somalia

\ə\ **abut**	\au̇\ **out**	\i\ **tip**	\ȯ\ **saw**	\u̇\ **foot**
\ər\ **further**	\ch\ **chin**	\ī\ **life**	\ȯi\ **coin**	\y\ **yet**
\a\ **mat**	\e\ **pet**	\j\ **job**	\th\ **thin**	\yü\ **few**
\ā\ **take**	\ē\ **easy**	\ŋ\ **sing**	\th\ **this**	\yu̇\ **cure**
\ä\ **cot, cart**	\g\ **go**	\ō\ **bone**	\ü\ **food**	\zh\ **vision**

Mogilev — see MAHILYOW
Mo·hen·jo–Da·ro \mō-ˌhen-jō-ˈdär-ō\ prehistoric city [S] Asia in valley of the Indus [NE] of modern Karachi, Pakistan
Mo·ja·ve *or* **Mo·ha·ve** \mə-ˈhäv-ē\ desert [S] California [SE] of [S] end of Sierra Nevada
Mo·ji \ˈmō-jē\ city Japan in [N] Kyushu
Mol·da·via \mäl-ˈdāv-ē-ə, -vyə\ **1** region [E] Europe in [NE] Romania & Moldova [W] of the Dniester **2** — see MOLDOVA — **Mol·da·vian** \-vē-ən, -vyən\ *adj or n*
Mol·do·va \mäl-ˈdō-və, mȯl-\ country [E] Moldavia region; capital Chisinau; formerly (as **Moldavia**) a constituent republic of the U.S.S.R.
Mo·li·se \ˈmȯ-li-ˌzā\ region central Italy on the Adriatic; capital, Campobasso
Mol·o·kai \ˌmäl-ə-ˈkī, ˌmō-lə-\ island Hawaii [ESE] of Oahu
Molotov — see PERM
Mo·luc·cas \mə-ˈlək-əz\ *or* **Spice Islands** \ˈspīs\ *or Indonesian* **Ma·lu·ku** \mə-ˈlü-kü\ islands Indonesia [E] of Sulawesi — **Mo·luc·ca** \mə-ˈlək-ə\ *adj* — **Mo·luc·can** \-ən\ *adj or n*
Mom·ba·sa \mäm-ˈbäs-ə\ city [S] Kenya on Mombasa Island
Mo·na·co \ˈmän-ə-ˌkō *also* mə-ˈnäk-ō\ country [W] Europe on Mediterranean coast of France; a principality; capital, Monaco — **Mo·na·can** \ˈmän-ə-kən, mə-ˈnäk-ən\ *adj or n* — **Mon·e·gasque** \ˌmän-i-ˈgask\ *adj or n*
Mon·a·ghan \ˈmän-ə-hən, -ˌhan\ county [NE] Ireland (republic) in Ulster
Mön·chen·glad·bach \ˌmœn-k̲ən-ˈglät-ˌbäk̲\ city [W] Germany
Mon·go·lia \män-ˈgōl-yə, mäng-, -ˈgō-lē-ə\ **1** region [E] Asia [E] of Altai Mountains; includes Gobi Desert **2** INNER MONGOLIA **3** *or* **Outer Mongolia** country [E] Asia comprising major portion of Mongolia; capital, Ulaanbaatar
Mon·mouth·shire \ˈmän-məth-ˌshiər, ˈmən-, -shər\ *or* **Monmouth** administrative area [SE] Wales bordering on England
Mon·ro·via \mən-ˈrō-vē-ə, ˌmən-\ city, capital of Liberia
Mon·tana \män-ˈtan-ə\ state [NW] U.S.; capital, Helena — **Mon·tan·an** \-ən\ *adj or n*
Mont Blanc \mō^n-ˈblä^n\ mountain 15,771 feet (4807 meters) [SE] France on Italian border; highest in the Alps
Mon·te·go Bay \män-ˈtē-gō\ city & port [NW] Jamaica on Montego Bay (inlet of the Caribbean)
Mon·te·ne·gro \ˌmänt-ə-ˈnē-grō, -ˈnā-\ country [S] Europe in Balkan Peninsula; capital, Podgorica — **Mon·te·ne·grin** \-grən\ *adj or n*
Mon·ter·rey \ˌmänt-ə-ˈrā\ city [NE] Mexico, capital of Nuevo León
Mon·te·vi·deo \ˌmänt-ə-və-ˈdā-ō, -ˈvid-ē-ˌō\ city, capital of Uruguay
Mont·gom·ery \mənt-ˈgəm-rē, mänt-, mən-, män-, -ˈgäm-, -ə-rē\ city, capital of Alabama
Mont·pe·lier \mänt-ˈpēl-yər, -ˈpil-\ city, capital of Vermont
Mon·tre·al \ˌmän-trē-ˈȯl, ˌmən-\ city [S] Quebec on Montreal Island in the Saint Lawrence
Mont–Saint–Mi·chel \mō^n-sa^n-mē-ˈshel\ islet [NW] France off coast of Brittany in Gulf of Saint-Malo
Mont·ser·rat \ˌmän-sə-ˈrat\ island British West Indies in the Leewards; capital, Plymouth
Mo·ra·via \mə-ˈrā-vē-ə\ region [E] Czech Republic; chief city, Brno
Mor·ay \ˈmər-ē, ˈmə-rē\ *or* **Mor·ay·shire** \-ˌshiər, -shər\ administrative area [NE] Scotland
Mo·re·los \mə-ˈrā-ləs\ state [S] central Mexico; capital, Cuernavaca
Mo·re·no Valley \mə-ˈrē-nō\ city [S] California
Mo·roc·co \mə-ˈräk-ō\ **1** country [NW] Africa; a kingdom; capital, Rabat; formerly divided into **French Morocco** (capital, Rabat), **Spanish Morocco** (capital, Tetuán) & **International Zone** of Tangier **2** — see MARRAKECH — **Mo·roc·can** \-ˈräk-ən\ *adj or n*
Mo·ro·ni \mȯ-ˈrō-nē\ city, capital of Comoros
Morris Jes·up, Cape \ˌmȯr-əs-ˈjes-əp, ˌmär-\ headland [N] Greenland in Arctic Ocean
Mos·cow \ˈmäs-ˌkau̇, -kō\ *or Russian* **Mos·kva** \mäsk-ˈvä\ city, capital of Russia, on Moskva River
Mo·selle \mō-ˈzel\ *or German* **Mo·sel** \ˈmō-zəl\ river about 340 miles (545 kilometers) long [E] France & [W] Germany flowing from Vosges Mountains into the Rhine at Koblenz
Mosquito Coast region Central America bordering on the Caribbean in [E] Honduras & [E] Nicaragua
Mo·sul \mō-ˈsül, ˈmō-səl\ city [N] Iraq on the Tigris
Moul·mein \mül-ˈmān, mōl-, -ˈmīn\ *or* **Maw·la·myine** \ˌmȯ-lə-ˈmyīn\ city [S] Myanmar (Burma) at mouth of the Salween
Mount Rainier National Park — see RAINIER (Mount)
Mount Rev·el·stoke National Park \ˈrev-əl-ˌstōk\ reservation [SE] British Columbia including Mount Revelstoke (over 7000 feet or 2130 meters)
Mo·zam·bique \ˌmō-zəm-ˈbēk\ *or Portuguese* **Mo·çam·bi·que** \ˌmü-səm-ˈbē-kə\ **1** channel [SE] Africa between Mozambique & Madagascar **2** *or formerly* **Portuguese East Africa** country [SE] Africa; formerly a dependency of Portugal; capital, Maputo
Mpu·ma·lan·ga \əm-ˌpü-mä-ˈläng-gä\ province [NE] Republic of South Africa
Mukden — see SHENYANG
Mul·tan \mu̇l-ˈtän\ city [NE] Pakistan [SW] of Lahore
Mumbai — see BOMBAY
Mu·nich \ˈmyü-nik\ *or German* **Mün·chen** \ˈmᵫn-k̲ən\ city [S] Germany, capital of Bavaria
Mun·ster \ˈmən-stər\ province [S] Ireland
Mün·ster \ˈmən-stər, ˈmün-, ˈmyün-, ˈmᵫn-\ city [W] Germany [NNE] of Dortmund
Mur·cia \ˈmər-shə, -shē-ə\ **1** region, province, & ancient kingdom [SE] Spain **2** city, its capital — **Mur·cian** \-shən\ *adj or n*
Mur·mansk \mu̇r-ˈmansk, -ˈmänsk\ city [NW] Russia in Europe on Barents Sea
Mur·ray \ˈmər-ē, ˈmə-rē\ river 1609 miles (2589 kilometers) long [SE] Australia flowing [W] from [E] Victoria into Indian Ocean in South Australia — see DARLING
Mur·rum·bidg·ee \ˌmər-əm-ˈbij-ē, ˌmə-rəm-\ river almost 1000 miles (1609 kilometers) long [SE] Australia in New South Wales flowing [W] into the Murray
Mu·sa, Ge·bel \ˌjeb-əl-ˈmü-sə\ mountain group [NE] Egypt in [S] Sinai Peninsula; highest Gebel Katherina 8652 feet (2637 meters) — see HOREB
Mu·sa, Je·bel \ˌjeb-əl-ˈmü-sə\ mountain 2775 feet (846 meters) [N] Morocco opposite Rock of Gibraltar — see PILLARS OF HERCULES
Mus·cat \ˈməs-ˌkät, -kət\ *or* **Mas·qat** \ˈməs-ˌkät\ city [E] Arabia; capital of Oman
Muscat and Oman — see OMAN
Mus·co·vy \mə-ˈskō-vē; ˈməs-kə-vē, -ˌkō-\ **1** the principality of Moscow (founded 1295) which in 15th century came to dominate Russia **2** RUSSIA — an old name
Myan·mar \ˈmyän-ˌmär\ *or unofficially* **Bur·ma** \ˈbər-mə\ country [SE] Asia; capital, Naypyidaw
My·ce·nae \mī-ˈsē-nē\ ancient city [S] Greece in [NE] Peloponnese [N] of Argos
My·ko·la·yiv \ˌmē-kə-ˈlä-yif\ *or* **Ni·ko·la·yev** \ˌnē-kə-ˈlä-yif\ city [S] Ukraine
Myk·o·nos \ˈmik-ə-ˌnōs\ island Greece in the Aegean in [NE] Cyclades
Myr·tle Beach \ˈmərt-l\ city [E] South Carolina on the Atlantic
My·sia \ˈmish-ə, ˈmish-ē-ə\ ancient country [NW] Asia Minor bordering on the Propontis
My·sore \mī-ˈsōr, -ˈsȯr\ **1** — see KARNATAKA **2** city in [S] Karnataka
Myt·i·le·ne \ˌmit-l-ˈē-nē\ **1** ancient city Greece on [E] coast of Lesbos Island; site at modern town of Mytilene **2** — see LESBOS
Nab·a·taea *or* **Nab·a·tea** \ˌnab-ə-ˈtē-ə\ ancient Arab kingdom [SE] of Palestine — **Nab·a·tae·an** *or* **Nab·a·te·an** \-ˈtē-ən\ *adj or n*
Na·be·rezh·nye Chel·ny \ˌnäb-ə-ˈrezh-nə-ˈchel-nē, -nyə-\ city [E] Russia in Europe
Na·ga·land \ˈnäg-ə-ˌland\ state [E] India [N] of Manipur in Naga Hills; capital, Kohima
Na·ga·no \nä-ˈgän-ō\ city Japan in [SE] Honshu [NW] of Tokyo
Na·ga·sa·ki \ˌnäg-ə-ˈsäk-ē, ˌnag-ə-ˈsak-ē\ city & port Japan in [W] Kyushu
Na·goya \nə-ˈgȯi-ə, ˈnäg-ə-ˌyä\ city Japan in [S] central Honshu
Nag·pur \ˈnäg-ˌpu̇r\ city [E] central India in [NE] Maharashtra
Na·ha \ˈnä-hä\ city Japan in Ryukyu Islands; capital of Okinawa
Na·huel Hua·pí \nä-ˌwel-wä-ˈpē\ lake [SW] Argentina in the Andes
Nai·ro·bi \nī-ˈrō-bē\ city, capital of Kenya
Najd — see NEJD
Na·mib·ia \nə-ˈmib-ē-ə\ *or formerly* **South–West Africa** country [SW] Africa, on South Atlantic; administered by South Africa 1919–90; capital, Windhoeck

Nan·chang \'nän-'chäŋ\ city [SE] China, capital of Jiangxi
Nan·cy \'nan-sē, nä^n-sē\ city [NE] France
Nanjing *or* **Nan·king** \'nan-'kiŋ, 'nän-\ city [E] China on the Chang (Yangtze), capital of Jiangsu
Nan·ning \'nän-'niŋ\ city [S] China, capital of Guangxi Zhuangzu
Nantes \'nans\ city [NW] France on the Loire
Nan·tuck·et \nan-'tək-ət\ island [SE] Massachusetts [S] of Cape Cod
Na·per·ville \'nā-pər-ˌvil\ city [NE] Illinois [W] of Chicago
Na·ples \'nā-pəlz\ *or Italian* **Na·po·li** \'näp-ə-lē\ *or ancient* **Ne·ap·o·lis** \nē-'ap-ə-ləs\ city [S] Italy on Bay of Naples — **Ne·a·pol·i·tan** \ˌnē-ə-'päl-ət-n\ *adj or n*
Na·ra \'när-ə\ city Japan in [W] central Honshu [E] of Osaka
Nar·ra·gan·sett Bay \ˌnar-ə-'gan-sət\ inlet of the North Atlantic [SE] Rhode Island
Nash·ville \'nash-ˌvil, -vəl\ city, capital of Tennessee
Nas·sau \'nas-ˌȯ\ city, capital of Bahamas on New Providence Island
Na·tal \nə-'tal, -'täl\ **1** city & port [NE] Brazil **2** former province [E] Republic of South Africa; now part of KwaZulu-Natal
Natch·ez Trace \'nach-əz\ pioneer road between Nashville & **Natchez** (city [SW] Mississippi on Mississippi River); constructed in early 19th century
Na·u·ru \nä-'ü-rü\ island (atoll) [W] Pacific; formerly a joint British, New Zealand, & Australian trust territory; an independent republic since 1968; capital, Yaren
Na·varre \nə-'vär\ *or Spanish* **Na·var·ra** \nə-'vär-ə\ region & former kingdom [N] Spain & [SW] France in [W] Pyrenees
Nax·ci·van \ˌnək-chi-'vän\ exclave of Azerbaijan separated from the rest of the country by Armenia
Nax·os \'nak-səs, -ˌsäs\ island Greece in the Aegean; largest of the Cyclades
Na·ya·rit \ˌnī-ə-'rēt\ state [W] Mexico on North Pacific; capital, Tepic
Nay·pyi·daw *or* **Nay Pyi Taw** \'nē-pyē-ˌdȯ\ site [S] central Myanmar (Burma) to which national capital was moved 2006
Naz·a·reth \'naz-rəth, -ə-rəth\ town of ancient Palestine in central Galilee; now a city of [N] Israel
N'Dja·me·na \ən-jä-mā-nä\ *or formerly* **Fort–La·my** \ˌfȯr-lə-'mē\ city, capital of Chad
Neagh, Lough \'nā\ lake Northern Ireland; largest in British Isles
Near East the countries of [NE] Africa & [SW] Asia; sometimes used interchangeably with Middle East which has become the more common term — **Near Eastern** *adj*
Neath and Port Talbot \'nēth-ənd-ˌpōrt-'tȯl-bət\ administrative area [S] Wales
Ne·bras·ka \nə-'bras-kə\ state central U.S.; capital, Lincoln — **Ne·bras·kan** \-kən\ *adj or n*
Neg·ev \'neg-ˌev\ *or* **Neg·eb** \-ˌeb\ desert region [S] Israel
Ne·gro \'nā-grō\ river 1400 miles (2253 kilometers) long in [E] Colombia & [N] Brazil flowing into the Amazon
Ne·gros \'nā-grōs\ island [S] central Philippines in Visayans
Neis·se \'nī-sə\ river 150 miles (256 kilometers) long [N] Europe flowing from [N] Czech Republic [N] into the Oder; forms part of boundary between Poland & Germany
Nejd \'nejd, 'nezhd\ *or* **Najd** \'najd, 'nazhd\ region central & [E] Saudi Arabia; capital, Riyadh
Nelson Mandela Bay municipality Republic of South Africa including the city of Port Elizabeth
Ne·pal \nə-'pȯl, -'päl, -'pal\ country Asia on [NE] border of India in the Himalaya; capital, Kathmandu — **Nep·a·lese** \ˌnep-ə-'lēz, -'lēs\ *adj or n* — **Ne·pali** \nə-'pȯl-ē, -'päl-, -'pal-\ *adj or n*
Neth·er·lands \'neth-ər-lənz, -ləndz\ **1** *or* **the Netherlands** *or Dutch* **Ne·der·land** \'nād-ər-ˌlänt\ *also* **Holland** country [NW] Europe on North Sea; a kingdom; capital, Amsterdam; seat of government, The Hague **2** LOW COUNTRIES — an historical usage — **Neth·er·land** \'neth-ər-lənd\ *adj* — **Neth·er·land·er** \-ˌlan-dər, -lən-\ *n* — **Neth·er·land·ish** \-dish\ *adj*
Netherlands An·til·les \an-'til-ēz\ former Dutch overseas territory of the West Indies; capital, Willemstad (on Curaçao)
Netherlands Indies former Dutch possessions in the East Indies including Indonesia
Ne·va \'nē-və, 'nā-\ river 40 miles (64 kilometers) long [W] Russia in Europe, flowing from Lake Ladoga into Gulf of Finland at Saint Petersburg
Ne·vada \nə-'vad-ə, -'väd-ə\ state [W] U.S.; capital, Carson City — **Ne·vad·an** \-'vad-n, -'väd-n\ *or* **Ne·vad·i·an** \-'vad-ē-ən, -'väd-\ *adj or n*
Ne·vis \'nē-vəs\ island British West Indies in the Leewards — see SAINT KITTS
Nevis, Ben — see BEN NEVIS
New Am·ster·dam \'am-stər-'dam, 'amp-\ town founded 1625 on Manhattan Island by the Dutch; renamed New York 1664 by the British
New·ark \'nü-ərk, 'nu̇-, 'nyü-, 'nyu̇-\ city & port [NE] New Jersey
New Bed·ford \'bed-fərd\ city & port [SE] Massachusetts
New Brit·ain \'brit-n\ island [W] Pacific, largest in Bismarck Archipelago
New Bruns·wick \'brənz-wik\ province [SE] Canada; capital, Fredericton
New Cal·e·do·nia \ˌkal-ə-'dō-nyə, -nē-ə\ island [SW] Pacific [SW] of Vanuatu; an overseas department of France; capital, Nouméa
New·cas·tle \'nü-ˌkas-əl, 'nyü-\ city [SE] Australia in [E] New South Wales
New·cas·tle up·on Tyne \nü-'kas-əl-ə-ˌpȯn-'tīn, nyü-, -ˌpän-, -pən-, 'nü-ˌ, 'nyü-ˌ\ city [N] England
New Del·hi \-'del-ē\ city, capital of India [S] of city of Delhi
New England section of [NE] U.S. comprising states of Maine, New Hampshire, Vermont, Massachusetts, Rhode Island, & Connecticut — **New En·gland·er** \-'iŋ-glən-dər *also* -'iŋ-lən-\ *n*
New·found·land \'nü-fən-dlənd, 'nyü-, -lənd, -ˌdland, -ˌland; ˌnü-fən-'dland, ˌnyü-, -'land\ island Canada in North Atlantic [E] of Gulf of Saint Lawrence — **New·found·land·er** \-ər\ *n*
Newfoundland and Labrador *or 1949–2001* **Newfoundland** province [E] Canada; capital, Saint John's
New France the possessions of France in North America before 1763
New Guin·ea \'gin-ē\ *or Indonesian* **Iri·an** \ˌir-ē-'än\ **1** island [W] Pacific [N] of [E] Australia divided between Indonesia & Papua New Guinea **2** the [NE] portion of the island of New Guinea together with Bismarck Archipelago, Bougainville, Buka, & adjacent small islands; now part of Papua New Guinea — **New Guin·ean** \'gin-ē-ən\ *adj or n*
New·ham \'nü-əm, 'nyü-\ borough of [E] Greater London, England
New Hamp·shire \'ham-shər, 'hamp-, -ˌshiər\ state [NE] U.S.; capital, Concord — **New Hamp·shire·man** \-mən\ *n* — **New Hamp·shir·ite** \-ˌīt\ *n*
New Ha·ven \'hā-vən\ city & port [S] Connecticut
New Hebrides — see VANUATU
New Jer·sey \'jər-zē\ state [E] U.S.; capital, Trenton — **New Jer·sey·an** \-ən\ *n* — **New Jer·sey·ite** \-ˌīt\ *n*
New Mex·i·co \'mek-si-ˌkō\ state [SW] U.S.; capital, Santa Fe — **New Mex·i·can** \-si-kən\ *adj or n*
New Neth·er·land \'neth-ər-lənd\ former Dutch colony (1613–64) North America along Hudson & lower Delaware rivers; capital, New Amsterdam
New Or·leans \'ȯr-lē-ənz; 'ȯrl-ənz, -yənz; ȯr-'lēnz\ city & port [SE] Louisiana between Lake Pontchartrain & Mississippi River
New·port \'nü-ˌpōrt, 'nyü-, -ˌpȯrt\ **1** administrative area [SE] Wales **2** city [SE] Wales in Newport administrative area
New·port News \ˌnü-ˌpōrt-'nüz, -ˌpȯrt-, -pərt-, ˌnyü...'nyüz\ city & port [SE] Virginia
New Prov·i·dence \'präv-əd-əns, -ə-ˌdens\ island [NW] central Bahamas; chief town, Nassau
New South Wales state [SE] Australia; capital, Sydney
New Spain former Spanish possessions in North America, Central America, West Indies, & the Philippines; capital, Mexico City
New Sweden former Swedish colony (1638–55) North America on [W] bank of Delaware River
New York \'yȯrk\ **1** state [NE] U.S.; capital, Albany **2** *or* **New York City** city [SE] New York; includes Bronx, Brooklyn, Manhattan, Queens, & Staten Island — **New York·er** \'yȯr-kər\ *n*
New Zea·land \'zē-lənd\ country [SW] Pacific [ESE] of Australia; capital, Wellington — **New Zea·land·er** \-lən-dər\ *n*
Ni·ag·a·ra Falls \nī-'ag-rə, -ə-rə\ falls New York & Ontario in **Niagara River** (flowing [N] from Lake Erie into Lake Ontario);

\ə\ abut	\au̇\ out	\i\ tip	\ȯ\ saw	\u̇\ foot
\ər\ further	\ch\ chin	\ī\ life	\ȯi\ coin	\y\ yet
\a\ mat	\e\ pet	\j\ job	\th\ thin	\yü\ few
\ā\ take	\ē\ easy	\ŋ\ sing	\th\ this	\yu̇\ cure
\ä\ cot, cart	\g\ go	\ō\ bone	\ü\ food	\zh\ vision

divided by Goat Island into Horseshoe, or Canadian, Falls (158 feet or 48 meters high) & American Falls (167 feet or 51 meters high)

Nia·mey \nē-ˈäm-ā, nyä-ˈmā\ city, capital of Niger

Ni·caea \nī-ˈsē-ə\ *or* **Nice** \ˈnīs\ ancient city [W] Bithynia; site at modern village of Iznik in [NW] Turkey — **Ni·cae·an** \nī-ˈsē-ən\ *adj or n* — **Ni·cene** \ˈnī-ˌsēn, nī-ˈsēn\ *adj*

Ni·ca·ra·gua \ˌnik-ə-ˈräg-wə\ **1** lake 102 miles (164 kilometers) long [S] Nicaragua **2** country Central America; capital, Managua — **Ni·ca·ra·guan** \-wən\ *adj or n*

Nice \ˈnēs\ *or ancient* **Ni·caea** \nī-ˈsē-ə\ city [SE] France on the Mediterranean

Nic·o·bar \ˈnik-ə-ˌbär\ islands India in Bay of Bengal [S] of the Andamans

Nic·o·sia \ˌnik-ə-ˈsē-ə\ city, capital of Cyprus

Niedersachsen — see LOWER SAXONY

Ni·ger \ˈnī-jər\ **1** river 2600 miles (4183 kilometers) long [W] Africa flowing into Gulf of Guinea **2** country [W] Africa [N] of Nigeria; capital, Niamey

Ni·ge·ria \nī-ˈjir-ē-ə\ country [W] Africa on Gulf of Guinea; capital, Abuja — **Ni·ge·ri·an** \-ē-ən\ *adj or n*

Nii·ga·ta \nē-ˈgät-ə, ˈnē-gə-ˌtä\ city Japan in [N] Honshu on Sea of Japan

Nii·hau \ˈnē-ˌhau̇\ island Hawaii [WSW] of Kauai

Nikolayev — see MYKOLAYIV

Nile \ˈnīl\ river about 4160 miles (6693 kilometers) long [E] Africa flowing from Lake Victoria in Uganda [N] into the Mediterranean in Egypt; in various sections called specifically **Vic·to·ria** \vik-ˈtōr-ē-ə, -ˈtȯr-\ *or* **Som·er·set** \ˈsəm-ər-sət, -ˌset\ **Nile** between Lake Victoria & Lake Albert; **Al·bert** \ˈal-bərt\ **Nile** between Lake Albert & Lake No; & **White Nile** from Lake No to Khartoum — see BLUE NILE

Nil·gi·ri \ˈnil-gə-rē\ hills [S] India in [W] Tamil Nadu

Nîmes \ˈnēm\ city [S] France [NW] of Marseille

Nin·e·veh \ˈnin-ə-və\ ancient city, capital of Assyria; ruins in [N] Iraq

Ning·xia Hui·zu \ˈning-shē-ˈä-ˈhwēd-ˈzü\ *or* **Ning·sia Hui** \ˈning-shē-ˈä-ˈhwē\ region [N] China; before 1954 part of former province of **Ningsia**

Nip·i·gon, Lake \ˈnip-ə-ˌgän\ lake Canada in [W] Ontario [N] of Lake Superior

Niš *or* **Nish** \ˈnish\ city [E] Serbia

Ni·shi·no·mi·ya \ˌnish-ə-ˈnō-mē-ˌä, -ˌyä\ city Japan in central Honshu [E] of Kobe

Ni·te·rói \ˌnēt-ə-ˈrȯi\ city [SE] Brazil on Guanabara Bay opposite Rio de Janeiro

Ni·ue \nē-ˈü-ā\ island [S] central Pacific; a self-governing territory of New Zealand

Nizh·niy Nov·go·rod *or* **Nizh·ni Novgorod** \ˌnizh-nē-ˈnäv-gə-ˌräd, -ˈnȯv-gə-rət\ *or formerly* **Gor·ki** \ˈgȯr-kē\ city central Russia in Europe, on the Volga [E] of Moscow

Nizh·ny Ta·gil *or* **Nizh·ni Tagil** \ˌnizh-nē-tə-ˈgil\ city [W] Russia in Asia, in the Urals

Nord–Ost·see \ˈnȯrt-ˌȯst-ˈzā\ *or* **Kiel** \ˈkēl\ ship canal 61 miles (98 kilometers) long [N] Germany connecting Baltic & North seas

Nord–Pas–de–Ca·lais \ˌnȯr-ˌpȧd-kȧ-ˈlā\ region northernmost France

Nor·folk \ˈnȯr-fək, *in the U.S. also* -ˌfȯk\ **1** city & port [SE] Virginia **2** county [E] England on North Sea

Nor·i·cum \ˈnȯr-i-kəm, ˈnär-\ ancient country & Roman province [S] central Europe [S] of the Danube in modern Austria & Germany

Nor·man·dy \ˈnȯr-mən-dē\ *or French* **Nor·man·die** \nȯr-mäⁿ-ˈdē\ region & former province [NW] France [NE] of Brittany; capital, Rouen

North **1** river, an estuary of the Hudson between [NE] New Jersey & [SE] New York **2** sea, an arm of North Atlantic [E] of Great Britain **3** island [N] New Zealand

North America continent of Western Hemisphere [NW] of South America & [N] of the Equator — **North American** *adj or n*

North·amp·ton \nȯrth-ˈam-tən, -ˈham-, -ˈamp-, -ˈhamp-\ city central England in Northamptonshire

North·amp·ton·shire \-ˌshiər, -shər\ *or* **Northampton** county central England

North Ayrshire administrative area [W] Scotland

North Cape **1** headland New Zealand at [N] end of North Island **2** headland [NE] Norway on **Ma·ger·öy** \ˌmäg-ə-ˈrəi\ Island

North Car·o·li·na \ˌkar-ə-ˈlī-nə\ state [E] U.S.; capital, Raleigh — **North Car·o·lin·ian** \-ˈlin-ē-ən, -ˈlin-yən\ *adj or n*

North Cas·cades National Park \kas-ˈkādz, ˈkas-ˌ\ area of glaciers and lakes [N] Washington in Cascades Range

North Da·ko·ta \də-ˈkōt-ə\ state [N] U.S.; capital, Bismarck — **North Da·ko·tan** \-ˈkōt-n\ *adj or n*

North East Frontier Agency — see ARUNACHAL PRADESH

North–East New Guinea the [NE] section of Papua New Guinea on New Guinea mainland

Northern — see LIMPOPO 2

Northern Cape province [W] Republic of South Africa

Northern Cook \ˈku̇k\ *or* **Ma·ni·hi·ki** \ˌmän-ə-ˈhē-kē\ islands [S] central Pacific [N] of Cook Islands

Northern Ireland region [N] Ireland; a division of United Kingdom; capital, Belfast

Northern Kingdom — see ISRAEL

Northern Mariana Islands islands [W] Pacific; commonwealth in association with U.S.; capital, Saipan

Northern Rhodesia — see ZAMBIA

Northern Territory territory [N] & central Australia; capital, Darwin

North Korea — see KOREA

North Lan·ark·shire \ˈlan-ərk-ˌshir, -shər\ administrative area [W] Scotland

North Las Vegas city [SE] Nevada

North Rhine–Westphalia *or German* **Nord·rhein–West·fa·len** \ˈnȯrt-ˌrīn-ˌvest-ˈfä-lən\ state [W] Germany; capital, Düsseldorf

North Slope region [N] Alaska between Brooks Range & Arctic Ocean

North·um·ber·land \nȯr-ˈthəm-bər-lənd\ county [N] England — **North·um·bri·an** \-ˈthəm-brē-ən\ *adj or n*

North·um·bria \nȯr-ˈthəm-brē-ə\ ancient country Great Britain between the Humber & Firth of Forth — **North·um·bri·an** \-brē-ən\ *adj or n*

North Vietnam — see VIETNAM

North West province [N] Republic of South Africa

North–West Frontier province Pakistan on Afghanistan border

Northwest Passage navigable sea route between North Atlantic & North Pacific along [N] coast of North America

Northwest Territories territory [N] Canada comprising the mainland [N] of 60° between Yukon & Nunavut, & the westernmost part of the Arctic Archipelago; capital, Yellowknife

North York \ˈyȯrk\ former city Canada in [SE] Ontario; now part of Toronto

North York·shire \ˈyȯrk-ˌshiər, -shər\ county [N] England

Nor·walk \ˈnȯr-ˌwȯk\ city [SW] California

Nor·way \ˈnȯr-ˌwā\ country [N] Europe in Scandinavia; a kingdom; capital, Oslo

Nor·we·gian \nȯr-ˈwē-jən\ sea between North Atlantic & Arctic oceans [W] of Norway

Nor·wich \ˈnȯr-wich; ˈnȯr-ich, ˈnär-\ city [E] England in Norfolk

Not·ting·ham \ˈnät-ing-əm, *in the U.S. also* -ˌham\ city [N] central England in Nottinghamshire

Not·ting·ham·shire \-ˌshiər, -shər\ *or* **Nottingham** county [N] central England

Nouak·chott \nu̇-ˈäk-ˌshät\ city, capital of Mauritania

Nou·méa \nü-ˈmā-ə\ city, capital of New Caledonia

No·va Igua·çu \ˌnȯ-və-ˌē-gwə-ˈsü\ city [SE] Brazil [NW] of Rio de Janeiro

No·va Sco·tia \ˌnō-və-ˈskō-shə\ province [SE] Canada; capital, Halifax — **No·va Sco·tian** \-ˈskō-shən\ *adj or n*

No·va·ya Zem·lya \ˌnō-və-yə-ˌzem-lē-ˈä\ two islands [N] of Russia in Europe, in Arctic Ocean between Barents & Kara seas

Nov·go·rod \ˈnäv-gə-ˌräd, ˈnȯv-gə-rət\ city [W] Russia in Europe [SSE] of Saint Petersburg

No·vi Sad \ˌnō-vē-ˈsäd\ city [N] Serbia on the Danube

No·vo·kuz·netsk \ˌnō-vō-ku̇z-ˈnetsk\ city [S] Russia in Asia at [S] end of Kuznetsk Basin

No·vo·si·birsk \ˌnō-vō-sə-ˈbiərsk\ city [S] Russia in Asia, on the Ob'

Nu·bia \ˈnü-bē-ə, ˈnyü-\ region [NE] Africa in valley of the Nile in [S] Egypt & [N] Sudan — **Nu·bi·an** \-bē-ən\ *adj or n*

Nubian desert [NE] Sudan [E] of the Nile

Nue·vo Le·ón \nu̇-ˌā-vō-lā-ˈōn\ state [N] Mexico; capital, Monterrey

Nu·ku·a·lo·fa \ˌnü-kə-wə-ˈlō-fə\ seaport, capital of Tonga

Nul·lar·bor Plain \ˈnəl-ə-ˌbȯr\ treeless area SW Australia in the states of Western Australia & South Australia

Nu·mid·ia \nu̇-ˈmid-ē-ə, nyu̇-\ ancient country N Africa E of Mauretania in modern Algeria; chief city, Hippo — **Nu·mid·i·an** \-ē-ən\ *adj or n*

Nu·na·vut \ˈnü-nə-ˌvüt\ territory N Canada comprising the mainland N of 60° between Northwest Territories & Hudson Bay & the easternmost & northernmost part of the Arctic Archipelago; capital, Iqaluit

Nu·rem·berg \ˈnu̇r-əm-ˌbərg, ˈnyu̇r-\ *or German* **Nürn·berg** \ˈnœrn-ˌberk\ city S central Germany in N Bavaria

Nu·ri·stan \ˌnu̇r-i-ˈstan\ mountainous area E Afghanistan

Nuuk \ˈnük\ *or Danish* **Godt·håb** \ˈgȯt-ˌhȯp\ town, capital of Greenland on SW coast

Nyasa, Lake — see MALAWI (Lake)

Nyasaland — see MALAWI

Oa·hu \ə-ˈwä-hü\ island Hawaii; site of Honolulu

Oak·land \ˈō-klənd\ city W California on San Francisco Bay E of San Francisco

Oa·xa·ca \wə-ˈhä-kə\ **1** state SE Mexico **2** city, its capital

Ob' \ˈäb, ˈȯb\ river over 2250 miles (3620 kilometers) long W central Russia in Asia flowing NW & N into **Gulf of Ob'** (inlet of Arctic Ocean)

Oce·a·nia \ˌō-shē-ˈan-ē-ə, -ˈä-nē-ə\ lands of the central & S Pacific: Micronesia, Melanesia, Polynesia including New Zealand, & by some thought to also include Australia & Malay Archipelago — **Oce·a·ni·an** \-ˈan-ē-ən, -ˈä-nē-\ *adj or n*

Ocean·side \ˈō-shən-ˌsīd\ city SW California NNW of San Diego

Oden·se \ˈōd-n-sə, ˈü-ən-zə\ city central Denmark on Fyn Island

Oder \ˈōd-ər\ *or* **Odra** \ˈō-drə\ river about 565 miles (909 kilometers) long central Europe flowing from E Czech Republic NW into Baltic Sea; forms part of boundary between Poland & Germany — see NEISSE

Odes·sa \ō-ˈdes-ə\ city S Ukraine on Black Sea

Odisha — see ORISSA

Of·fa·ly \ˈȯf-ə-lē, ˈäf-\ county central Ireland in Leinster

Ogasawara — see BONIN

Og·bo·mo·sho \ˌäg-bə-ˈmō-shō\ city W Nigeria

Ohio \ō-ˈhī-ō\ **1** river 981 miles (1578 kilometers) long E U.S. flowing from W Pennsylvania into the Mississippi **2** state E central U.S.; capital, Columbus — **Ohio·an** \ō-ˈhī-ə-wən\ *adj or n*

Oi·ta \ˈȯi-ˌtä, ō-ˈēt-ə\ city Japan in NE Kyushu

Oka·ya·ma \ˌō-kə-ˈyäm-ə\ city Japan in W Honshu on Inland Sea

Oka·za·ki \ˌō-kə-ˈzäk-ē\ city Japan in S central Honshu

Okee·cho·bee, Lake \ˌō-kē-ˈchō-bē\ lake S central Florida

Oke·fe·no·kee \ˌō-kē-fə-ˈnō-kē\ swamp SE Georgia & NE Florida

Okhotsk, Sea of \ō-ˈkätsk\ inlet of North Pacific E Russia in Asia, W of Kamchatka Peninsula & Kuril Islands

Oki·na·wa \ˌō-kə-ˈnä-wə, -ˈnau̇-ə\ **1** islands Japan in central Ryukyus; capital, Naha **2** island, chief of group — **Oki·na·wan** \-ˈnä-wən, -ˈnau̇-ən\ *adj or n*

Okla·ho·ma \ˌō-klə-ˈhō-mə\ state S U.S.; capital, Oklahoma City — **Okla·ho·man** \-mən\ *adj or n*

Oklahoma City city, capital of Oklahoma

Old Faithful geyser Yellowstone National Park NW Wyoming

Old·ham \ˈōl-dəm\ city NW England in Greater Manchester

Old Point Comfort cape SE Virginia N of entrance to Hampton Roads

Ol·du·vai Gorge \ˈōl-də-ˌvī\ canyon N Tanzania SE of Serengeti Plain; site of fossil beds

Olives, Mount of *or* **Ol·i·vet** \ˈäl-ə-ˌvet, ˌäl-ə-ˈ\ mountain ridge W Jordan on E side of Jerusalem

Olym·pia \ə-ˈlim-pē-ə, ō-\ **1** city, capital of Washington **2** plain S Greece in NW Peloponnese

Olym·pic \ə-ˈlim-pik, ō-\ mountains NW Washington on Olympic Peninsula, partly in **Olympic National Park**; highest Mt. Olympus 7965 feet (2428 meters)

Olym·pus \ə-ˈlim-pəs, ō-\ mountains NE Greece in Thessaly; home of the gods in Greek mythology

Oma·ha \ˈō-mə-ˌhȯ, -ˌhä\ **1** city E Nebraska **2** beach NW France; in World War II landing place of American army June 6, 1944

Oman \ō-ˈmän, -ˈman\ *or formerly* **Mus·cat and Oman** \ˈməs-ˌkat, -kət\ country SW Asia in SE Arabia; a sultanate; capital, Muscat — **Omani** \ō-ˈmän-ē\ *adj or n*

Oman, Gulf of arm of Arabian Sea between Oman & CE Iran

Om·dur·man \ˌäm-dər-ˈman, -ˈmän\ city central Sudan on left bank of the Nile opposite Khartoum

Omi·ya \ō-ˈmē-ə, ˈō-mē-ˌä\ city Japan in SE Honshu NW of Tokyo

Omsk \ˈȯmsk, ˈȯmpsk, ˈämsk, ˈämpsk\ city S Russia in Asia, at confluence of Irtysh & Om rivers

On·ta·ke \ōn-ˈtäk-ā\ mountain 10,049 feet (3063 meters) Japan in central Honshu

On·tar·io \än-ˈter-ē-ˌō\ **1** city SW California **2** province E Canada; capital, Toronto — **On·tar·i·an** \-ē-ən\ *adj or n*

Ontario, Lake lake E central North America in U.S. & Canada; one of the Great Lakes

Ophir \ˈō-fər\ a biblical land rich in gold; probably in Arabia

Oporto — see PORTO

Ora·dea \ȯ-ˈräd-ē-ə\ city NW Romania

Oral \ȯ-ˈräl\ *or* **Uralsk** \ü-ˈrälsk, yu̇-ˈralsk\ city W Kazakhstan on Ural River

Oran \ȯ-ˈrän\ city & port NW Algeria

Or·ange \ˈȯr-inj, ˈär-, -ənj\ **1** city SW California **2** river 1300 miles (2092 kilometers) long S Africa flowing W from Drakensberg Mountains into South Atlantic

Orange Free State — see FREE STATE

Ordzhonikidze — see VLADIKAVKAZ

Or·e·gon \ˈȯr-i-gən, ˈär-, -ˌgän\ state NW U.S.; capital, Salem — **Or·e·go·nian** \ˌȯr-i-ˈgō-nē-ən, ˌär-, -nyən\ *adj or n*

Oregon Trail pioneer route to the Pacific Northwest approximately 2000 miles (3225 kilometers) long from vicinity of Independence, Missouri, to Vancouver, Washington

Orel \ȯ-ˈrel, ȯr-ˈyȯl\ city SW Russia in Europe, S of Moscow

Oren·burg \ˈōr-ən-ˌbərg, ˈȯr-, -ˌbu̇rg\ *or formerly* **Chkalov** \chə-ˈkäl-əf\ city E Russia in Europe, on Ural River

Ori·no·co \ˌōr-ə-ˈnō-kō, ˌȯr-\ river 1336 miles (2150 kilometers) long Venezuela flowing into North Atlantic

Oris·sa \ȯ-ˈris-ə\ *or* **Odisha** \ȯ-ˈris-ə\ state E India; capital, Bhubaneswar

Ori·za·ba \ˌȯr-ə-ˈzäb-ə, ˌȯr-\ **1** *or* **Ci·tlal·te·petl** \sēt-ˌläl-ˈtā-ˌpet-l\ inactive volcano 18,700 feet (5700 meters) SE Mexico on Puebla–Veracruz border; highest point in Mexico & third highest in North America **2** city E Mexico in Veracruz state

Ork·ney Islands \ˈȯrk-nē\ islands N Scotland; an administrative area

Or·lan·do \ȯr-ˈlan-dō\ city E central Florida

Or·léans \ȯr-lā-ˈäⁿ\ city N central France

Oru·mi·yeh \-ˌu̇r-ü-ˈmē-yə\ city NW Iran

Osa·ka \ō-ˈsäk-ə\ city Japan in S Honshu

Os·lo \ˈäz-lō, ˈäs-\ city, capital of Norway

Os·sa, Mount \ˈäs-ə\ mountain 6490 feet (1967 meters) NE Greece in E Thessaly near Mount Pelion

Ostra·va \ˈȯ-strə-və\ city E Czech Republic in Moravia

Os·wie·cim \ˌȯsh-ˈfyen-chēm\ *or German* **Ausch·witz** \ˈau̇sh-ˌvits\ town S Poland W of Krakow; site of Nazi concentration camp during World War II

Otran·to, Strait of \ō-ˈtran-tō, ˈō-trən-ˌtō\ strait between SE Italy & Albania

Ot·ta·wa \ˈät-ə-ˌwä, -wə, -ˌwȯ\ city, capital of Canada in SE Ontario on Ottawa River

Oua·ga·dou·gou \ˌwäg-ə-ˈdü-ˌgü\ city, capital of Burkina Faso

Ouj·da \uzh-ˈdä\ city NE Morocco near Algerian border

Outer Hebrides — see HEBRIDES

Outer Mongolia — see MONGOLIA

Overland Park city NE Kansas S of Kansas City

Ovie·do \ˌō-vē-ˈā-t͟hō\ city NW Spain

Ox·ford \ˈäks-fərd\ city central England in Oxfordshire

Ox·ford·shire \ˈäks-fərd-ˌshiər, -shər\ *or* **Oxford** county central England

Oxus — see AMU DAR'YA

Ozark Plateau \ˈō-ˌzärk\ eroded tableland N Arkansas, S Missouri, & NE Oklahoma

Pa·cif·ic \pə-ˈsif-ik\ ocean extending from Arctic Circle to Antarctica & from W North America & W South America to E Asia & Australia; often divided into **North Pacific Ocean** & **South Pacific Ocean**

\ə\ abut	\au̇\ out	\i\ tip	\ȯ\ saw	\u̇\ foot
\ər\ further	\ch\ chin	\ī\ life	\ȯi\ coin	\y\ yet
\a\ mat	\e\ pet	\j\ job	\th\ thin	\yü\ few
\ā\ take	\ē\ easy	\ŋ\ sing	\t͟h\ this	\yu̇\ cure
\ä\ cot, cart	\g\ go	\ō\ bone	\ü\ food	\zh\ vision

Pacific Islands, Trust Territory of the former U.S. trust territory [W] Pacific comprising the Northern Mariana Islands (until 1978), the Federated States of Micronesia (until 1991), the Marshall Islands (until 1991), & Palau (until 1994)
Pacific Rim the countries bordering on or located in the Pacific Ocean — used especially of Asian countries on the Pacific
Pacific Rim National Park reservation [SW] British Columbia on Vancouver Island
Pa·dang \'pä-ˌdäng\ city & port Indonesia in [W] Sumatra
Pa·dre \'päd-rē, 'pad-\ island about 113 miles (182 kilometers) long [S] Texas in Gulf of Mexico
Padus — see PO
Pa·go Pa·go \ˌpäng-gō-'päng-gō, ˌpäng-ō-'päng-ō, ˌpäg-ō-'päg-ō\ town, capital of American Samoa on Tutuila Island
Pa·kan·ba·ru \ˌpäk-ən-'bär-ü\ city Indonesia in central Sumatra
Pak·i·stan \'pak-i-ˌstan, ˌpäk-i-'stän\ country [S] Asia in Indian subcontinent [NW] of India; until 1971 included also an [E] division [E] of India; capital, Islamabad — see EAST PAKISTAN — **Pak·i·stani** \-'stan-ē, -'stän-ē\ *adj or n*
Pal·at·i·nate \pə-'lat-n-ət\ *or German* **Pfalz** \'pfälts, 'fälts\ either of two districts [SW] Germany once ruled by counts of the Holy Roman Empire: **Rhenish Palatinate** *or German* **Rhein·pfalz** \'rīn-ˌpfälts, -ˌfälts\ (on the Rhine [E] of Saarland) & **Upper Palatinate** (on the Danube around Regensburg) — see RHINELAND-PALATINATE
Pa·lau \pə-'lau̇\ *or* **Be·lau** \bə-\ islands [W] Pacific; an independent republic in association with the U.S.; capital, Melekeok
Pa·la·wan \pə-'lä-wən, -ˌwän\ island [W] Philippines between South China & Sulu seas
Pa·lem·bang \ˌpäl-əm-'bäng\ city Indonesia in [SE] Sumatra
Pa·ler·mo \pə-'lər-mō, -'leər-\ city Italy, capital of Sicily
Pal·es·tine \'pal-ə-ˌstīn, -ˌstēn\ ancient region of varying and uncertain boundaries [SW] Asia bordering on [E] Mediterranean centered on what are now Israel, the West Bank, & the Gaza Strip and extending up to or [E] of Jordan River — **Pal·es·tin·ian** \ˌpal-ə-'stin-ē-ən, -'stin-yən\ *adj or n*
Pa·li·kir \ˌpäl-ē-'kir\ town, capital of Federated States of Micronesia
Pal·ma \'päl-mə\ *or* **Palma de Ma·llor·ca** \-ˌdā-mə-'yȯr-kə, -məl-\ city Spain on Majorca
Palm·dale \'päm-ˌdāl\ city [SW] California [NE] of Los Angeles
Palmer Peninsula — see ANTARCTIC PENINSULA
Pa·mirs \pə-'miərz\ elevated mountainous region central Asia in [E] Tajikistan & on borders of Xinjiang Uygur, Kashmir, & Afghanistan; many peaks over 20,000 feet (6096 meters)
Pam·li·co Sound \'pam-li-ˌkō\ inlet of the North Atlantic [E] North Carolina between mainland & offshore islands
Pam·plo·na \pam-'plō-nə\ city [N] Spain in Navarre
Pan·a·ma \'pan-ə-ˌmä, -ˌmȯ, ˌpan-ə-'\ **1** country [S] Central America **2** *or* **Panama City** city, its capital on North Pacific **3** canal 51 miles (82 kilometers) long Panama connecting North Atlantic & North Pacific oceans — **Pan·a·ma·ni·an** \ˌpan-ə-'mā-nē-ən\ *adj or n*
Panama, Isthmus of *or formerly* **Isthmus of Dar·i·en** \-ˌdar-ē-'en\ strip of land central Panama connecting North America & South America
Panama Canal Zone — see CANAL ZONE
Pa·nay \pə-'nī\ island Philippines in Visayan Islands; chief city, Iloilo
Pan·gaea \pan-'jē-ə\ hypothetical land area believed to have once connected the landmasses of the Southern Hemisphere with those of the Northern Hemisphere
Panjab — see PUNJAB
Pan·mun·jom *or* **Pan·mun·jeom** \ˌpän-ˌmün-'jəm\ village on border between North Korea & South Korea
Paoting — see BAODING
Pao–t'ou — see BAOTOU
Papal States *or* **States of the Church** temporal domain of the popes in central Italy 755–1870
Pa·pee·te \ˌpäp-ē-'āt-ē; pə-'pāt-ē, -'pēt-\ city Society Islands on Tahiti, capital of French Polynesia
Pap·ua, Territory of \'pap-yə-wə, 'päp-ə-wə\ former British territory comprising [SE] New Guinea & offshore islands; now part of Papua New Guinea
Papua New Guinea country [SW] Pacific combining former territories of Papua & New Guinea; formerly a United Nations trust territory administered by Australia; independent since 1975; capital, Port Moresby
Pará — see BELÉM
Par·a·guay \'par-ə-ˌgwī, -ˌgwā\ **1** river 1584 miles (2549 kilometers) long central South America flowing from Brazil [S] into the Paraná in Paraguay **2** country central South America; capital, Asunción — **Par·a·guay·an** \ˌpar-ə-'gwī-ən, -'gwā-ən\ *adj or n*
Par·a·mar·i·bo \ˌpar-ə-'mar-ə-ˌbō\ city, capital of Suriname
Pa·ra·ná \ˌpar-ə-'nä\ **1** river 2500 miles (4022 kilometers) long central South America flowing [S] from Brazil into Río de la Plata in Argentina **2** city [NE] Argentina on Paraná River
Par·is \'par-əs\ city, capital of France — **Pa·ri·sian** \pə-'rizh-ən, -'rēzh-\ *adj or n*
Par·ma \'pär-mə\ **1** city [NE] Ohio [S] of Cleveland **2** city [N] Italy in Emilia-Romagna [SE] of Milan
Par·nas·sus, Mount \pär-'nas-əs\ massif central Greece [N] of Gulf of Corinth; highest point 8061 feet (2457 meters)
Par·os \'par-ˌäs, 'per-\ island Greece in central Cyclades — **Par·i·an** \'par-ē-ən, 'per-\ *adj*
Par·ra·mat·ta \ˌpar-ə-'mat-ə\ city [SE] Australia in New South Wales [NW] of Sydney
Par·thia \'pär-thē-ə\ ancient country [SW] Asia in [NE] modern Iran — **Par·thi·an** \-thē-ən\ *adj or n*
Pas·a·de·na \ˌpas-ə-'dē-nə\ city [SW] California [E] of Glendale
Pat·a·go·nia \ˌpat-ə-'gō-nyə, -nē-ə\ barren region South America [S] of about 40° [S] latitude in [S] Argentina & [S] tip of Chile; sometimes considered to include Tierra del Fuego — **Pat·a·go·nian** \-nyən, -nē-ən\ *adj or n*
Pat·er·son \'pat-ər-sən\ city [NE] New Jersey [N] of Newark
Pa·thein \pə-'thān\ *or* **Bas·sein** \bə-'sān\ city [S] Myanmar
Pat·mos \'pat-məs\ island Greece in the Dodecanese [SSW] of Samos
Pat·na \'pət-nə\ city [NE] India on the Ganges, capital of Bihar
Pat·ras \pə-'tras, 'pa-trəs\ city [W] Greece in [N] Peloponnese on **Gulf of Patras** (inlet of Ionian Sea)
Pays de la Loire \ˌpād-lə-'lwär\ region [W] France containing the point where Loire River empties into the Atlantic
Pearl Harbor inlet of North Pacific in Hawaii on [S] coast of Oahu [W] of Honolulu
Peking — see BEIJING
Pe·li·on, Mount \'pē-lē-ən\ mountain 5089 feet (1551 meters) [NE] Greece in [E] Thessaly near Mount Ossa
Pel·o·pon·nese \'pel-ə-pə-ˌnēz, -ˌnēs\ *or* **Pel·o·pon·ne·sus** \ˌpel-ə-pə-'nē-səs\ *or* **Pel·o·pon·ne·sos** \-'ne-səs\ peninsula forming [S] part of mainland of Greece — **Pel·o·pon·ne·sian** \ˌpel-ə-pə-'nē-zhən, -shən\ *adj or n*
Pe·lo·tas \pə-'lōt-əs\ city [S] Brazil [SW] of Porto Alegre
Pem·broke Pines \'pem-ˌbrōk\ city [SE] Florida
Pem·broke·shire \'pem-bru̇k-ˌshiər, -shər\ administrative area [SW] Wales
Penang — see GEORGE TOWN
Pen·de·li·kón \ˌpen-ˌdel-ē-'kōn\ *or* **Pen·te·li·kon** \ˌpen-ˌtel-ē-'kän\ mountain 3638 feet (1109 meters) [E] Greece [NE] of Athens
Peninsular Malaysia territory [W] Malaysia comprising that part of Malaysia contained on Malay Peninsula
Pen·nine Chain \'pen-ˌīn\ mountains [N] England; highest Cross Fell 2930 feet (893 meters)
Penn·syl·va·nia \ˌpen-səl-'vā-nyə, -nē-ə\ state [E] U.S.; capital, Harrisburg
Pen·za \'pen-zə\ city [S] central Russia in Europe
People's Democratic Republic of Yemen — see YEMEN
People's Republic of China — see CHINA (People's Republic of)
Pe·o·ria \pē-'ȯr-ē-ə, -'ōr-\ city [N] central Illinois
Per·ga·mum \'pər-gə-məm\ *or* **Per·ga·mus** \-məs\ ancient Greek kingdom including most of Asia Minor; at its height 263–133 B.C.; capital, Pergamum (in what is now [W] Turkey)
Perm \'pərm, 'peərm\ *or formerly* **Mo·lo·tov** \'mäl-ə-ˌtȯf, 'mȯl-, 'mōl-, -ˌtȯv\ city [E] Russia in Europe
Pernambuco — see RECIFE
Per·pi·gnan \per-pē-'nyäⁿ\ city [S] France [SE] of Toulouse
Per·sep·o·lis \pər-'sep-ə-ləs\ city of ancient Persia; site in [SW] Iran [NE] of Shiraz
Persia — see IRAN
Per·sian Gulf \'pər-zhən\ arm of Arabian Sea between Iran & Arabia
Persian Gulf States Kuwait, Bahrain, Qatar, & United Arab Emirates
Perth \'pərth\ city, capital of Western Australia
Perth and Kin·ross \-kin-'rȯs\ administrative area [E] central Scotland

Pe·ru \pə-ˈrü\ country [W] South America; capital, Lima — **Pe·ru·vi·an** \pə-ˈrü-vē-ən\ *adj or n*
Peru Current *or* **Hum·boldt Current** \ˈhəm-ˌbōlt\ cold current of the South Pacific flowing [N] & [NW] along coast of [N] Chile, Peru, & Ecuador
Pe·ru·gia \pə-ˈrü-jə, -jē-ə\ city central Italy [SE] of Florence
Pe·sha·war \pə-ˈshä-wər, -ˈshau̇-ər\ city [N] Pakistan [ESE] of Khyber Pass
Pe·ta·re \pet-ˈär-ˌā\ city [N] Venezuela; a suburb of Caracas
Pe·tra \ˈpē-trə, ˈpe-trə\ ancient city [NW] Arabia; site in [SW] Jordan
Petrified Forest National Park reservation [E] Arizona
Petrograd — see SAINT PETERSBURG
Pe·tro·pav·lovsk \ˌpe-trə-ˈpav-ˌlȯfsk\ city [N] Kazakhstan
Pe·tro·za·vodsk \ˌpe-trə-zə-ˈvätsk\ city [NW] Russia in Europe
Pfalz — see PALATINATE
Phil·a·del·phia \ˌfil-ə-ˈdel-fyə, -fē-ə\ city [SE] Pennsylvania on Delaware River — **Phil·a·del·phian** \-fyən, -fē-ən\ *adj or n*
Phi·lae \ˈfī-lē\ former island [S] Egypt in the Nile above Aswân; now submerged in Lake Nasser
Phi·lip·pi \ˈfil-ə-ˌpī, fə-ˈlip-ˌī\ ancient town [NE] Greece
Phil·ip·pines \ˌfil-ə-ˈpēnz, ˈfil-ə-ˌ\ country, an archipelago approximately 500 miles (805 kilometers) off [SE] coast of Asia; capital, Manila — **Phil·ip·pine** \-ˈpēn, -ˌpēn\ *adj*
Phi·lis·tia \fə-ˈlis-tē-ə\ country [SW] ancient Palestine on the coast; the land of the Philistines
Phnom Penh \pə-ˈnȯm-ˈpen, ˈnȯm-, pə-ˈnäm-, ˈnäm-\ city, capital of Cambodia
Phoe·ni·cia \fi-ˈnish-ə, -ˈnēsh-, -ē-ə\ ancient country [SW] Asia on the Mediterranean in modern Syria & Lebanon
Phoe·nix \ˈfē-niks\ city, capital of Arizona
Phry·gia \ˈfrij-ə, ˈfrij-ē-ə\ ancient country [W] central Asia Minor
Pia·cen·za \pyä-ˈchen-sə, ˌpē-ə-ˈchen-\ city [N] Italy [SE] of Milan
Pic·ar·dy \ˈpik-ərd-ē\ *or French* **Pi·car·die** \pē-kär-dē\ region & former province [N] France [N] of Normandy
Pied·mont \ˈpēd-ˌmänt\ **1** plateau region [E] U.S. [E] of the Appalachians between [SE] New York & [NE] Alabama **2** *or Italian* **Pie·mon·te** \pyā-ˈmōn-tā\ region [NW] Italy; capital, Turin — **Pied·mon·tese** \ˌpēd-mən-ˈtēz, -män-, -ˈtēs\ *adj or n*
Pierre \ˈpiər\ city, capital of South Dakota
Pie·ter·mar·itz·burg \ˌpēt-ər-ˈmar-əts-ˌbərg\ city [E] Republic of South Africa in KwaZulu-Natal
Pigs, Bay of bay [W] Cuba on [S] coast
Pikes Peak \ˈpīks\ mountain 14,110 feet (4301 meters) [E] central Colorado in a range of the Rockies
Pillars of Her·cu·les \ˈhər-kyə-ˌlēz\ two promontories at [E] end of Strait of Gibraltar: Rock of Gibraltar (in Europe) & Jebel Musa (in Africa)
Pin·dus \ˈpin-dəs\ mountains [W] Greece [W] of Thessaly
Pinkiang — see HARBIN
Pi·rae·us \pī-ˈrē-əs\ *or Greek* **Pi·rai·évs** \ˌpē-rē-ˈefs\ city [E] Greece on Saronic Gulf; port for Athens
Pi·sa \ˈpē-zə, *Italian* ˈpē-sä\ city [W] central Italy [W] of Florence
Pit·cairn \ˈpit-ˌkaərn, -ˌkeərn\ island South Pacific [SE] of Tuamotu Archipelago; a British colony
Pitts·burgh \ˈpits-ˌbərg\ city [SW] Pennsylvania
Pla·no \ˈplān-ō\ city [NE] Texas [N] of Dallas
Pla·ta, Río de la \ˌrē-ō-ˌdel-ə-ˈplät-ə\ estuary of Paraná & Uruguay rivers between Uruguay & Argentina
Plov·div \ˈplȯv-ˌdif, -ˌdiv\ city [S] Bulgaria
Plym·outh \ˈplim-əth\ city & port [SW] England
Po \ˈpō\ *or ancient* **Pa·dus** \ˈpād-əs\ river 405 miles (652 kilometers) [N] Italy flowing into the Adriatic
Pod·go·ri·ca \ˈpȯd-ˌgȯr-ēt-sä\ city, capital of Montenegro
Po Hai — see BO HAI
Pohn·pei \ˈpōn-ˌpā\ island [W] Pacific in the [E] Carolines
Point Pe·lee National Park \ˌpȯint-ˈpē-lē\ reservation [SE] Ontario on Point Pelee (cape projecting into Lake Erie)
Poi·tou–Cha·rentes \pwä-ˈtü-shä-ˈrä^{n}t\ region [W] France on the Atlantic
Po·land \ˈpō-lənd\ country central Europe on Baltic Sea; capital, Warsaw
Pol·y·ne·sia \ˌpäl-ə-ˈnē-zhə, -shə\ islands of the central & [S] Pacific including Hawaii, the Line, Tuvalu, Phoenix, Tonga, Cook, & Samoa Islands, French Polynesia, & often New Zealand
Pom·er·a·nia \ˌpäm-ə-ˈrā-nē-ə, -ˈrā-nyə\ region [N] Europe on Baltic Sea; formerly in Germany, now mostly in Poland
Po·mo·na \pə-ˈmō-nə\ city [SW] California [E] of Los Angeles
Pom·peii \päm-ˈpā, -ˈpā-ˌē\ ancient city [S] Italy [SE] of Naples destroyed 79 A.D. by eruption of Vesuvius — **Pom·pe·ian** \-ˈpā-ən\ *adj or n*
Pon·ce \ˈpȯn-sā\ city & port [S] Puerto Rico
Pondicherry — see PUDUCHERRY
Pon·ta Del·ga·da \ˌpänt-ə-del-ˈgäd-ə, -ˈgad-\ city Portugal in the Azores on São Miguel Island
Pont·char·train, Lake \ˈpän-chər-ˌtrān, ˌpän-chər-ˈ\ lake [SE] Louisiana [E] of the Mississippi & [N] of New Orleans
Pon·ti·a·nak \ˌpän-tē-ˈä-ˌnäk\ city Indonesia on Borneo
Pon·tine Marshes \ˈpän-ˌtīn, -ˌtēn\ district central Italy in [SW] Latium; marshes now reclaimed
Pon·tus \ˈpänt-əs\ **1** ancient country & Roman province [NE] Asia Minor **2** *or* **Pontus Euxinus** — see BLACK SEA — **Pon·tic** \ˈpänt-ik\ *adj or n*
Poole \ˈpül\ town [S] England on English Channel
Pool Malebo — see MALEBO (Pool)
Poona — see PUNE
Po·po·ca·te·petl \ˌpō-pə-ˌkat-ə-ˈpet-l\ volcano 17,887 feet (5452 meters) [SE] central Mexico in Puebla
Port Arthur — see LÜSHUN
Port–au–Prince \ˌpōrt-ō-ˈprins, ˌpȯrt-, -ˈprans, -ˈpra^{n}s\ city, capital of Haiti
Port Eliz·a·beth \i-ˈliz-ə-bəth\ city in the municipality of Nelson Mandela Bay [S] Republic of South Africa in Eastern Cape
Port Jack·son \ˈjak-sən\ inlet of South Pacific [SE] Australia in New South Wales; harbor of Sydney
Port·land \ˈpōrt-lənd, ˈpȯrt-\ city [NW] Oregon
Port Lou·is \ˈlü-əs, ˈlü-ē, lu̇-ˈē\ city, capital of Mauritius
Port Lyautey — see KENITRA
Port Mores·by \ˈmōrz-bē, ˈmȯrz-\ city, capital of Papua New Guinea
Por·to \ˈpȯr-tü\ *or* **Opor·to** \ō-ˈpȯr-tü\ city [NW] Portugal
Por·to Ale·gre \ˌpōrt-ō-ə-ˈleg-rə, ˌpȯrt-\ city [S] Brazil
Port of Spain city [NW] Trinidad, capital of Trinidad and Tobago
Por·to–No·vo \ˌpōrt-ə-ˈnō-vō, ˌpȯrt-\ city, capital of Benin
Porto Rico — see PUERTO RICO
Port Phil·lip Bay \ˈfil-əp\ inlet of South Pacific [SE] Australia in Victoria; harbor of Melbourne
Port Said \sä-ˈēd, ˈsīd\ city [NE] Egypt on the Mediterranean at [N] end of Suez Canal
Ports·mouth \ˈpōrt-sməth, ˈpȯrt-\ **1** city [SE] Virginia **2** city [S] England on an island in English Channel
Port Su·dan \sü-ˈdan, -ˈdän\ city [NE] Sudan on Red Sea
Por·tu·gal \ˈpōr-chi-gəl, ˈpȯr-\ *or ancient* **Lu·si·ta·nia** \ˌlü-sə-ˈtā-nē-ə, -nyə\ country [SW] Europe; capital, Lisbon
Portuguese East Africa — see MOZAMBIQUE
Portuguese Guinea — see GUINEA-BISSAU
Portuguese India former Portuguese possession on [W] coast of India including Goa, Daman, & Diu; annexed to India 1962
Portuguese West Africa — see ANGOLA
Port–Vi·la \ˌpȯr-ˈvē-lä, -vē-ˈlä\ *or* **Vi·la** \ˈvē-lä, vē-ˈlä\ seaport, capital of Vanuatu
Po·ten·za \pə-ˈtent-sə; -ˈten-sə, -zə\ city [S] Italy
Po·to·mac \pə-ˈtō-mək, -mik\ river 287 miles (462 kilometers) long flowing from West Virginia into Chesapeake Bay & forming boundary between Maryland & Virginia
Po·wys \ˈpō-əs\ administrative area [E] central Wales
Poz·nan \ˈpōz-ˌnan-yə, ˈpȯz-, -ˌnän-yə, -ˌnan, -ˌnän\ city [W] central Poland
Prague \ˈpräg\ *or Czech* **Pra·ha** \ˈprä-hä\ city, capital of Czech Republic and formerly of Czechoslovakia
Praia \ˈprī-ə\ town, capital of Cape Verde
Prairie Provinces Alberta, Manitoba, & Saskatchewan
Pres·ton \ˈpres-tən\ city [NW] England
Pre·to·ria \pri-ˈtōr-ē-ə, -ˈtȯr-\ city, administrative capital of Republic of South Africa in the municipality of Tshwane
Prib·i·lof \ˈprib-ə-ˌlȯf\ islands Alaska in Bering Sea
Prince Al·bert National Park \ˈal-bərt\ reservation Canada in central Saskatchewan
Prince Ed·ward Island \ˌed-wərd\ island [SE] Canada in Gulf of Saint Lawrence; a province; capital, Charlottetown

\ə\ **abut**	\au̇\ **out**	\i\ **tip**	\ȯ\ **saw**	\u̇\ **foot**
\ər\ **further**	\ch\ **chin**	\ī\ **life**	\ȯi\ **coin**	\y\ **yet**
\a\ **mat**	\e\ **pet**	\j\ **job**	\th\ **thin**	\yü\ **few**
\ā\ **take**	\ē\ **easy**	\ng\ **sing**	\t͟h\ **this**	\yu̇\ **cure**
\ä\ **cot, cart**	\g\ **go**	\ō\ **bone**	\ü\ **food**	\zh\ **vision**

Prince Edward Island National Park reservation on [N] coast of Prince Edward Island
Prince Ru·pert's Land \'rü-pərts\ historical region [N] & [W] Canada comprising drainage basin of Hudson Bay
Prín·ci·pe \'prin-sə-pə\ island [W] Africa in Gulf of Guinea — see SÃO TOMÉ
Pris·ti·na \'prēsh-tē-ˌnä\ town, capital of Kosovo
Pro·ko·pyevsk \prə-'kȯp-yəfsk\ city [S] Russia in Asia
Propontis — see MARMARA (Sea of)
Pro·vence \prə-'vänˢ\ region & former province [SE] France on the Mediterranean
Prov·i·dence \'präv-əd-əns, -ə-ˌdens\ city, capital of Rhode Island
Pro·vo \'prō-vō\ city [N] central Utah
Prud·hoe Bay \'prüd-ō, 'prəd-\ inlet of Beaufort Sea [N] Alaska
Prus·sia \'prəsh-ə\ former kingdom &, later, state Germany; capital, Berlin — **Prus·sian** \-ən\ *adj or n*
Pu·chon \'pü-ˌchȯn\ *or* **Bu·cheon** \'bü-ˌchən\ city [NW] South Korea
Pu·du·cher·ry \'pü-dü-ˌcher-ē\ *or formerly* **Pon·di·cher·ry** \ˌpän-də-'cher-ē, -'sher-\ territory [SE] India; a settlement of French India before 1954
Pu·eb·la \pü-'eb-lə, 'pweb-, pyü-'eb-\ **1** state [SE] central Mexico **2** city, its capital
Puer·to Ri·co \ˌpȯrt-ə-'rē-kō, ˌpȯrt-, ˌpwert-\ *or formerly* **Por·to Ri·co** \ˌpōrt-, ˌpȯrt-\ island West Indies [E] of Hispaniola; a self-governing commonwealth associated with U.S.; capital, San Juan — **Puer·to Ri·can** \-'rē-kən\ *adj or n*
Pu·get Sound \ˌpyü-jət-\ arm of North Pacific [W] Washington
Pu·glia \'pül-yä\ *or* **Apu·lia** \ä-'pül-yä\ *or* **Le Pu·glie** \lə-pül-'yā\ region [SE] Italy bordering on the Adriatic Sea & Gulf of Taranto; capital, Bari
Pu·kas·kwa National Park \pü-'käs-kwə\ reservation Ontario bordering on Lake Superior
Pu·na de Ata·ca·ma \'pü-nə-ˌdā-ˌat-ə-'käm-ə, -ˌät-\ plateau region [NW] Argentina [NW] of San Miguel de Tucumán
Pu·ne *or* **Poo·na** \'pü-nə\ city [W] India in Maharashtra
Pun·jab *or* **Pan·jab** \ˌpən-'jäb, -'jab, 'pən-ˌ\ **1** region [NW] Indian subcontinent in Pakistan & [NW] India in valley of the Indus **2** *or* **Pun·jabi Su·ba** \ˌpən-ˌjäb-ē-'sü-bə, -ˌjab-\ state [NW] India in [E] Punjab region; capital, Chandigarh — see HARYANA **3** *or formerly* **West Punjab** province [NE] Pakistan
Pu·rus \pə-'rüs\ river about 2000 miles (3219 kilometers) long [NW] central South America in [SE] Peru & [NW] Brazil flowing into the Amazon
Pu·san \'pü-ˌsän\ *or* **Bu·san** \'bü-\ city South Korea on Korea Strait
Pyong·yang *or* **Pyeong·yang** \pē-'ȯng-ˌyäng, pē-'əng-, -ˌyang\ city, capital of North Korea
Pyr·e·nees \'pir-ə-ˌnēz\ mountains on French–Spanish border extending from Bay of Biscay to the Mediterranean; highest Pico de Aneto (Pic de Néthou) 11,168 feet (3404 meters)
Qaraghandy — see KARAGANDA
Qa·tar \'kät-ər, 'gät-, 'gət-\ country [E] Arabia on peninsula extending into Persian Gulf; an independent emirate; capital, Doha
Qing·dao \'ching-'dau̇\ *or* **Tsing·tao** \'ching-'dau̇, 'tsing-, 'sing-\ city [E] China in [E] Shandong
Qing·hai *or* **Tsing·hai** \'ching-'hī\ province [W] China [W] of Gansu; capital, Xining
Qi·qi·har \'chē-'chē-'här\ *or* **Ch'i–ch'i–ha–erh** \'chē-'chē-'hä-'ər\ city [NE] China in [W] Heilongjiang
Qom \'ku̇m\ city [NW] central Iran
Quan·zhou *or* **Ch'üan–chou** *or* **Chuan·chow** \chə-'wän-'jō\ city [SE] China in Fujian on Taiwan Strait
Que·bec \kwi-'bek, ki-\ *or French* **Qué·bec** \kā-bek\ **1** province [E] Canada **2** city, its capital, on the Saint Lawrence — **Que·bec·er** *or* **Que·beck·er** \kwi-'bek-ər, ki-\ *n*
Queens \'kwēnz\ borough of New York City on Long Island [E] of Brooklyn
Queen's — see LAOIGHIS
Queens·land \'kwēnz-ˌland, -lənd\ state [NE] Australia; capital, Brisbane — **Queens·land·er** \-ər\ *n*
Que·moy \kwi-'mȯi, ki-, 'kwē-ˌ\ island [E] China in Taiwan Strait
Que·ré·ta·ro \kə-'ret-ə-ˌrō\ **1** state central Mexico **2** city, its capital
Quet·ta \'kwet-ə\ city Pakistan in [N] Baluchistan
Que·zon City \'kā-ˌsȯn\ city Philippines in Luzon [NE] of Manila; former (1948–76) official capital of the Philippines
Quil·mes \'kēl-ˌmās, -ˌmes\ city [E] Argentina [SE] of Buenos Aires
Quin·ta·na Roo \kēn-ˌtän-ə-'rō\ state [SE] Mexico in [E] Yucatán; capital, Chetumal
Qui·to \'kē-tō\ city, capital of Ecuador
Qŭ·qon \kə-'kän\ *or* **Ko·kand** \kə-'känt\ city [E] Uzbekistan
Qut·ti·nir·paaq National Park \kə-'ti-nir-ˌpäk\ reservation [N] Nunavut on Ellesmere Island
Ra·bat \rə-'bät\ city, capital of Morocco
Ra·dom \'räd-ˌȯm\ city [E] central Poland
Rai·nier, Mount \rə-'niər, rā-\ mountain 14,410 feet (4392 meters) [W] central Washington in **Mount Rainier National Park**; highest in Cascade Mountains
Ra·ja·sthan \'räj-ə-ˌstän\ **1** state [NW] India bordering on Pakistan; capital, Jaipur **2** — see RAJPUTANA
Raj·kot \'räj-ˌkōt\ city [W] India in Gujarat
Raj·pu·ta·na \ˌräj-pə-'tän-ə\ *or* **Rajasthan** region [NW] India [S] of Punjab now largely included in Rajasthan state
Ra·leigh \'rȯ-lē, 'räl-ē\ city, capital of North Carolina
Ran·chi \'rän-chē\ city [E] India [NW] of Calcutta
Ran·cho Cu·ca·mon·ga \'ran-chō-ˌkü-kə-'məng-gə\ city [SW] California
Rand — see WITWATERSRAND
Range·ley Lakes \'rānj-lē\ chain of lakes [W] Maine & [N] New Hampshire
Rangoon — see YANGON
Rasht \'rasht\ city [NW] Iran
Rat \'rat\ islands [SW] Alaska in [W] Aleutians
Ra·wal·pin·di \ˌrä-wəl-'pin-dē, rau̇l-'pin-, rȯl-'pin-\ city [NE] Pakistan [NNW] of Lahore
Read·ing \'red-ing\ town [S] England
Re·ci·fe \rə-'sē-fə\ *or formerly* **Per·nam·bu·co** \ˌpər-nəm-'bü-kō, -'byü-, ˌper-nəm-'bü-\ city [NE] Brazil
Red \'red\ **1** river 1018 miles (1638 kilometers) long flowing [E] on Oklahoma–Texas boundary & into the Atchafalaya & the Mississippi in Louisiana **2** sea between Arabia & [NE] Africa
Red·bridge \'red-brij\ borough of [NE] Greater London, England
Red·wood National Park \'red-ˌwu̇d\ reservation [NW] California
Reg·gio \'rej-ō, 'rej-ē-ˌō\ **1** *or* **Reggio di Ca·la·bria** \-ˌdē-kə-'läb-rē-ə\ city [S] Italy on Strait of Messina **2** *or* **Reggio nel·l'Emi·lia** \-ˌnel-ə-'mēl-yə\ city [N] Italy [NW] of Bologna
Re·gi·na \ri-'jī-nə\ city, capital of Saskatchewan
Reims *or* **Rheims** \'rēmz, *French* 'raⁿs\ city [NE] France [ENE] of Paris
Ren·frew·shire \-ˌshiər, -shər\ administrative area [SW] Scotland
Rennes \'ren\ city [NW] France
Ré·union \rē-'yün-yən\ island [W] Indian Ocean [E] of Madagascar; an overseas department of France; capital, Saint-Denis
Revel — see TALLINN
Rey·kja·vik \'rāk-yə-ˌvik, -ˌvēk\ city, capital of Iceland
Rey·no·sa \rā-'nōs-ə\ city [NE] Mexico in Tamaulipas
Rheinpfalz — see PALATINATE
Rhine *or German* **Rhein** \'rīn\ *or French* **Rhin** \'raⁿ\ *or Dutch* **Rijn** \'rīn\ *or ancient* **Rhe·nus** \'rē-nəs\ river 820 miles (1320 kilometers) long [W] Europe flowing from [SE] Switzerland to North Sea in the Netherlands — **Rhen·ish** \'ren-ish, 'rē-nish\ *adj or n*
Rhine·land \'rīn-ˌland, -lənd\ *or German* **Rhein·land** \'rīn-ˌlänt\ the part of Germany [W] of the Rhine — **Rhine·land·er** \'rīn-ˌlan-dər, -lən-\ *n*
Rhineland–Palatinate *or German* **Rhein·land–Pfalz** \-'pfälts, -'fälts\ state [W] Germany chiefly [W] of the Rhine; capital, Mainz
Rhode Is·land \rō-'dī-lənd\ **1** *or officially* **Rhode Island and Providence Plantations** state [NE] U.S.; capital, Providence **2** — see AQUIDNECK ISLAND — **Rhode Is·land·er** \-lən-dər\ *n*
Rhodes \'rōdz\ **1** island Greece in the [SE] Aegean; chief island of the Dodecanese **2** city, its capital
Rhodesia — see ZIMBABWE
Rhon·dda \'rän-də, 'rän-thə, 'hrän-thə\ town [SE] Wales
Rhondda Cy·non Taff \'kən-ən-'taf\ administrative area [S] Wales
Rhone *or French* **Rhône** \'rōn\ *or ancient* **Rhod·a·nus** \'räd-n-əs\ river 505 miles (813 kilometers) long Switzerland & [SE] France
Rhône–Alpes \-'älp\ region [E] France bordering on Switzerland & Italy
Ri·bei·rão Prê·to \ˌrē-və-'rau̇ⁿ-'prā-tü\ city [SE] Brazil

Rich·mond \'rich-mənd\ **1** — see STATEN ISLAND **2** city, capital of Virginia **3** *or* **Richmond upon Thames** borough of [SW] Greater London, England
Rid·ing Mountain National Park \ˌrīd-iŋ\ reservation Canada in [SW] Manitoba
Rift Valley GREAT RIFT VALLEY
Ri·ga \'rē-gə\ city, capital of Latvia
Ri·je·ka *or* **Ri·e·ka** \rē-'ek-ə, -'yek-\ *or Italian* **Fiu·me** \'fyü-ˌmā, fē-'ü-\ city [W] Croatia
Rio \'rē-ō\ RIO DE JANEIRO
Rio de Ja·nei·ro \'rē-ō-ˌdā-zhə-'neər-ō, -ˌdē-, -də-, -jə-'neər-\ city [SE] Brazil on Guanabara Bay
Río de Oro \ˌrē-ōd-ē-'ōr-ō, -'ór-\ territory [NW] Africa comprising [S] zone of Western Sahara
Rio Grande \ˌrē-ō-'grand, -'grand-ē\ *or Mexican* **Río Bra·vo** \-'bräv-ō\ river 1885 miles (3034 kilometers) long [SW] U.S., forming part of U.S.–Mexico boundary, & flowing into Gulf of Mexico
Río Muni — see MBINI
Riv·er·side \'riv-ər-ˌsīd\ city [S] California
Riv·i·era \ˌriv-ē-'er-ə\ coast region [SE] France & [NW] Italy
Ri·yadh \rē-'yäd\ city, capital of Saudi Arabia
Ro·a·noke \'rō-ə-ˌnōk, 'rō-ˌnōk\ island North Carolina [S] of entrance to Albemarle Sound
Rob·son, Mount \'räb-sən\ mountain 12,972 feet (3954 meters) [W] Canada in [E] British Columbia; highest in the Canadian Rockies
Roch·es·ter \'räch-ə-stər, 'räch-ˌes-tər\ city [W] New York
Rock·ford \'räk-fərd\ city [N] Illinois [NW] of Chicago
Rocky Mountains \'räk-ē\ *or* **the Rock·ies** \'räk-ēz\ mountains [W] North America extending [SE] from [N] Alaska to central New Mexico — see ELBERT (Mount), ROBSON (Mount)
Rocky Mountain National Park reservation [N] Colorado
Ro·ma·nia \rú-'mā-nē-ə, rō-\ *or* **Ru·ma·nia** \rú-'mā-nē-ə\ country [SE] Europe on Black Sea; capital, Bucharest
Rome \'rōm\ **1** *or Italian* **Ro·ma** \'rō-mä\ city, capital of Italy **2** the Roman Empire
Ron·ces·va·lles \ˌrón-səs-'vī-əs\ commune [N] Spain in the Pyrenees
Roo·de·poort \'rōd-ə-ˌpórt\ city [NE] Republic of South Africa in Gauteng
Ro·sa·rio \rō-'zär-ē-ˌō, -'sär-\ city [E] central Argentina on the Paraná
Ros·com·mon \rä-'skäm-ən\ county central Ireland in Connacht
Ro·seau \rō-'zō\ seaport, capital of Dominica
Ross Sea \'rós\ arm of South Pacific extending into Antarctica [E] of Victoria Land
Ros·tock \'räs-ˌtäk, 'ró-ˌstók\ city [NE] Germany near Baltic coast
Ros·tov \rə-'stóf, -'stóv\ city [S] Russia in Europe on the Don
Rot·ter·dam \'rät-ər-ˌdam\ city & port [SW] Netherlands
Rou·baix \rü-'bā\ city [N] France [NE] of Lille
Rou·en \rü-'äⁿ, rü-'äⁿn\ city [N] France on the Seine
Ru·an·da–Urun·di \rú-ˌän-də-ú-'rün-dē\ former trust territory [E] central Africa bordering on Lake Tanganyika and administered by Belgium; divided 1962 into independent nations of Burundi (formerly Urundi) & Rwanda (formerly Ruanda)
Rudolf, Lake — see TURKANA (Lake)
Ruhr \'rúr\ industrial district [W] Germany [E] of the Rhine in valley of **Ruhr River** (146 miles or 235 kilometers long flowing [NW] & [W] into the Rhine)
Ru·me·lia \rü-'mēl-yə, -'mē-lē-ə\ a division of the old Ottoman Empire including Albania, Macedonia, & Thrace
Run·ny·mede \'rən-ē-ˌmēd\ meadow [S] England in Surrey on [S] bank of the Thames where Magna Carta was signed 1215
Rupert's Land PRINCE RUPERT'S LAND
Ru·se \'rü-sā\ city [NE] Bulgaria on the Danube
Rush·more, Mount \'rəsh-ˌmōr, -ˌmór\ mountain 5600 feet (1707 meters) [W] South Dakota in Black Hills [SW] of Rapid City
Rus·sia \'rəsh-ə\ **1** former empire largely coextensive with later U.S.S.R.; capital, Petrograd (Saint Petersburg) **2** UNION OF SOVIET SOCIALIST REPUBLICS **3** country [N] Asia (**Russia in Asia**) & [E] Europe (**Russia in Europe**) bordering on Arctic & North Pacific oceans & Baltic & Black seas; capital, Moscow; a constituent republic (**Russian Soviet Federated Socialist Republic** *or* **Soviet Russia**) of U.S.S.R. 1922–91
Ru·the·nia \rü-'thē-nyə, -nē-ə\ *or* **Car·pa·thi·an Ruthenia** \kär-'pā-thē-ən\ region [W] Ukraine [W] of the [N] Carpathians — **Ru·the·nian** \rü-'thē-nyən, -nē-ən\ *adj or n*
Ru·wen·zo·ri \ˌrü-ən-'zōr-ē, -'zór-\ mountain group [E] central Africa between Uganda & Democratic Republic of the Congo; highest Margherita Peak (highest peak of Mount Stanley) 16,763 feet (5109 meters)
Rwan·da *or chiefly formerly* **Ru·an·da** \rü-'än-də\ country [E] central Africa, until 1962 part of Ruanda–Urundi trust territory; capital, Kigali — **Rwan·dan** \rü-'än-dən\ *adj or n*
Rya·zan \ˌrē-ə-'zan-yə, -'zan\ city [W] Russia in Europe [SE] of Moscow
Ry·binsk \'rib-ənsk\ *or formerly* **Shcher·ba·kov** \ˌshcher-bə-'kóf, ˌsher-, -'kóv\ city central Russia in Europe [NNE] of Moscow
Ryu·kyu \rē-'ü-kyü, -'yü-, -kü\ islands Japan extending in an arc from Kyushu, Japan, to Taiwan, China — **Ryu·kyu·an** \-kyü-ən, -kü-ən\ *adj or n*
Saar \'sär, 'zär\ **1** river about 150 miles (241 kilometers) long Europe flowing from Vosges Mountains in [E] France into the Moselle in Germany **2** *or* **Saar·land** \'sär-ˌland, 'zär-\ district [W] Europe in valley of Saar River; a state of [W] Germany; capital, Saarbrücken
Sa·ba \'säb-ə\ internally self-governing Dutch island in West Indies; capital, The Bottom
Sachsen — see SAXONY
Sac·ra·men·to \ˌsak-rə-'ment-ō\ **1** river 382 miles (615 kilometers) long [N] California flowing [S] into Suisun Bay **2** city, capital of California
Sa·ga·mi Sea \sə-'gäm-ē\ inlet of North Pacific in central Honshu, Japan
Sa·ga·mi·ha·ra \sə-ˌgäm-ē-'här-ə\ city Japan on Honshu
Saguaro National Park reservation [SE] Arizona [E] of Tucson
Sag·ue·nay \'sag-ə-ˌnā, ˌsag-ə-'\ river 105 miles (169 kilometers) long Canada in [S] Quebec flowing from Lake Saint John [E] into the Saint Lawrence
Sa·hara \sə-'har-ə, -'her-, -'här-\ desert region [N] Africa [N] of Sudan region extending from North Atlantic coast to Red Sea or, as sometimes considered, to the Nile — **Sa·har·an** \-ən\ *adj*
Sa·hel \'sa-hil, sə-'hil\ the semidesert [S] edge of the Sahara that stretches from Mauritania to Chad
Saigon — see HO CHI MINH CITY
Saint Ber·nard \ˌsānt-bər-'närd, -bə-\ either of two mountain passes in the Alps: the **Great Saint Bernard** (8090 feet or 2468 meters between Italy & Switzerland [E] of Mont Blanc) & the **Little Saint Bernard** (7178 feet or 2188 meters between France & Italy [S] of Mont Blanc)
Saint Christopher — see SAINT KITTS
Saint Clair, Lake \'klaər, 'kleər\ lake [SE] Michigan & [SE] Ontario connected by **Saint Clair River** (about 40 miles or 64 kilometers long) with Lake Huron and draining by Detroit River into Lake Erie
Saint Croix \sānt-'krói, sənt-\ **1** river 129 miles (208 kilometers) long Canada & U.S. on border between New Brunswick & Maine **2** island West Indies; largest of Virgin Islands of the U.S.
Saint Eli·as, Mount \ˌsānt-l-'ī-əs\ mountain 18,008 feet (5489 meters) on Alaska–Yukon boundary in **Saint Elias Mountains** (range of the Coast Ranges)
Saint George's \'jór-jəz\ **1** channel British Isles between [SW] Wales & Ireland **2** town, capital of Grenada
Saint Gott·hard \sānt-'gät-ərd, -'gäth-, sənt-, ˌsaⁿ-gə-'tär\ **1** pass [S] central Switzerland in Saint Gotthard Range of the Alps **2** tunnel 3.5 miles (5.6 kilometers) long near the pass
Saint He·le·na \ˌsānt-l-'ē-nə, ˌsānt-hə-'lē-\ island South Atlantic; a British colony; capital, Jamestown
Saint Hel·ens \sānt-'hel-ənz, sənt-\ town [NW] England [ENE] of Liverpool
Saint Helens, Mount volcano about 8366 feet (2550 meters) [SW] Washington
Saint John \sānt-'jän, sənt-\ city Canada in [S] New Brunswick
Saint John's \sānt-'jänz, sənt-\ **1** city, capital of Antigua and Barbuda **2** *usually* **St. John's** city & port Canada, capital of Newfoundland and Labrador on [SE] Newfoundland
Saint Kitts \'kits\ *or* **Saint Chris·to·pher** \'kris-tə-fər\ island

British West Indies in the Leewards; with Nevis constitutes country of **Saint Kitts & Nevis**; capital, Basseterre (on Saint Kitts)

Saint Law•rence \sānt-ˈlȯr-əns, sənt-, -ˈlär-\ 1 river 760 miles (1223 kilometers) long [E] Canada in Ontario & Quebec bordering on U.S. in New York and flowing from Lake Ontario [NE] into the **Gulf of Saint Lawrence** (inlet of North Atlantic) 2 seaway Canada & U.S. in & along the Saint Lawrence between Lake Ontario & Montreal

Saint Lawrence Islands National Park reservation [SE] Ontario

Saint Lou•is \sānt-ˈlü-əs, sənt-\ city [E] Missouri on the Mississippi

Saint Lu•cia \sānt-ˈlü-shə, sənt-\ island British West Indies in the Windwards [S] of Martinique; an independent country; capital, Castries

Saint Mo•ritz \ˌsānt-mə-ˈrits, ˌsaⁿ-\ town [E] Switzerland

Saint Paul \ˈpȯl\ city, capital of Minnesota

Saint Pe•ters•burg \ˈpēt-ərz-ˌbərg\ 1 city [W] Florida 2 *or 1914–24* **Pet•ro•grad** \ˈpe-trə-ˌgrad\ *or 1924–91* **Le•nin•grad** \ˈlen-ən-ˌgrad\ city [W] Russia, on Gulf of Finland

Saint Pierre \sānt-ˈpiər, sənt-, -pē-ˈeər, *French* saⁿ-ˈpyer\ 1 island in North Atlantic off [S] Newfoundland; with nearby island of Miquelon constitutes French territory of **Saint Pierre and Miquelon** 2 town, capital of Saint Pierre and Miquelon

Saint Thom•as \ˈtäm-əs\ 1 island West Indies, one of Virgin Islands of the U.S.; chief town, Charlotte Amalie 2 — see SÃO TOMÉ

Saint–Tro•pez \ˌsaⁿ-trȯ-ˈpā\ town [SE] France on the Mediterranean

Saint Vin•cent \sānt-ˈvin-sənt, sənt-\ island British West Indies in the central Windwards; with [N] Grenadines constitutes independent country of **Saint Vincent and the Grenadines**; capital, Kingstown (on Saint Vincent)

Sai•pan \sī-ˈpan, -ˈpän, ˈsī-ˌ\ island [W] Pacific in [S] central Mariana Islands; contains capital of Northern Mariana Islands

Sa•kai \sä-ˈkī, ˈsä-\ city Japan in [S] Honshu on Osaka Bay

Sa•kha•lin \ˈsak-ə-ˌlēn, -lən; ˌsak-ə-ˈlēn\ *or formerly* **Sa•ghal•ien** \ˈsag-ə-ˌlēn, ˌsag-ə-ˈ\ *or Japanese* **Ka•ra•fu•to** \kə-ˈräf-ə-ˌtō\ island Russia in [W] Pacific [N] of Hokkaido, Japan; until 1945 divided between Japan & U.S.S.R.

Sa•la•do \sə-ˈläd-ō\ river 1120 miles (1802 kilometers) [N] Argentina flowing from the Andes [SE] into the Paraná

Sal•a•man•ca \ˌsal-ə-ˈmang-kə, ˌsäl-ə-ˈmäng-\ city [W] Spain [WNW] of Madrid

Sal•a•mis \ˈsal-ə-məs\ 1 ancient city Cyprus on [E] coast 2 island Greece in Saronic Gulf off Attica

Sa•lé \sal-ˈā\ city & port [NW] Morocco

Sa•lem \ˈsā-ləm\ 1 city, capital of Oregon 2 city [S] India in [N] Tamil Nadu [SW] of Madras

Sa•ler•no \sə-ˈlər-nō, -ˈleər-\ city [S] Italy on Gulf of Salerno

Sal•ford \ˈsȯl-fərd\ city [NW] England adjacent to Manchester

Sa•li•nas \sə-ˈlē-nəs\ city [W] California

Salisbury — see HARARE

Salonika — see THESSALONÍKI

Salop — see SHROPSHIRE

Sal•ta \ˈsäl-tə\ city [NW] Argentina

Salt Lake City city, capital of Utah

Sal•ton Sea \ˈsȯlt-n\ saline lake [SE] California

Sal•va•dor \ˈsal-və-ˌdȯr, ˌsal-və-ˈ\ *or formerly* **São Salvador** \saùⁿ-\ *or* **Ba•hia** \bä-ˈē-ə\ city [NE] Brazil on South Atlantic — **Sal•va•dor•an** \ˌsal-və-ˈdōr-ən, -ˈdȯr-\ *or* **Sal•va•do•re•an** *or* **Sal•va•do•ri•an** \-ē-ən\ *adj or n*

Sal•ween \ˈsal-ˌwēn\ river about 1500 miles (2415 kilometers) long [SE] Asia flowing from Tibet [S] into Bay of Bengal in Myanmar

Salz•burg \ˈsȯlz-ˌbərg, ˈsälz-, ˈsalz-, ˈsȯlts-, -ˌbu̇rg, *German* ˈzälts-ˌbu̇rk\ city [W] Austria [ESE] of Munich, Germany

Sa•mar \ˈsäm-ˌär\ island central Philippines in Visayan Islands

Sa•ma•ra \sə-ˈmär-ə\ *or 1935–91* **Kuy•by•shev** \ˈkwē-bə-ˌshef, ˈkü-ē-, -ˌshev\ city [E] Russia in Europe, on the Volga

Sa•mar•ia \sə-ˈmer-ē-ə, -ˈmar-\ 1 district of ancient Palestine [W] of the Jordan between Galilee & Judea 2 ancient city, its capital & capital of the Northern Kingdom (Israel)

Sam•a•rin•da \ˌsam-ə-ˈrin-də\ city Indonesia in [E] Borneo

Sam•ar•qand *or* **Sam•ar•kand** \ˈsam-ər-ˌkand\ city [E] Uzbekistan

Sam•ni•um \ˈsam-nē-əm\ ancient country [S] central peninsula of Italy [SE] of Latium — **Sam•nite** \ˈsam-ˌnīt\ *adj or n*

Sa•moa \sə-ˈmō-ə\ 1 islands [SW] central Pacific [N] of Tonga Islands; divided at longitude 171° [W] into American, or Eastern, Samoa & independent Samoa 2 *or formerly* **Western Samoa** islands [W] of American Samoa; an independent country; capital, Apia — **Sa•mo•an** \-ən\ *adj or n*

Sa•mos \ˈsā-ˌmäs\ island Greece in the Aegean off coast of Turkey [N] of the Dodecanese — **Sa•mi•an** \-mē-ən\ *adj or n*

Sam•o•thrace \ˈsam-ə-ˌthrās\ island Greece in the [NE] Aegean

San•aa *or* **San•'a** \ˈsan-ˌä, sän-ˈä\ city [SW] Arabia, capital of Yemen & formerly of Yemen Arab Republic

San An•dre•as Fault \ˌsan-an-ˈdrā-əs\ zone of faults California extending from [N] coast [SE] toward head of Gulf of California

San An•to•nio \ˌsan-ən-ˈtō-nē-ˌō\ city [S] Texas

San Ber•nar•di•no \ˌsan-ˌbər-nə-ˈdē-nō, -nər-ˈdē-\ city [SW] California [E] of Los Angeles

San Cris•tó•bal \ˌsan-kris-ˈtō-bəl\ city [W] Venezuela [SSW] of Lake Maracaibo

Sanc•ti Spi•ri•tus \ˌsäng-tē-ˈspir-ə-ˌtüs, ˌsängk-\ city [W] central Cuba

San Di•ego \ˌsan-dē-ˈā-gō\ city & port [SW] California

Sandwich Islands — see HAWAII

Sandy Hook peninsula [E] New Jersey extending [N]

San Fran•cis•co \ˌsan-frən-ˈsis-kō\ city [W] California on **San Francisco Bay** & North Pacific

San•i•bel \ˈsan-ə-bəl\ island [SW] Florida

San Isi•dro \ˌsan-ə-ˈsē-drō\ city [E] Argentina [NW] of Buenos Aires

San Joa•quin \ˌsan-wä-ˈkēn, -wȯ-\ river 350 miles (563 kilometers) long central California flowing [NW] into the Sacramento

San Jo•se \ˌsan-ə-ˈzā\ city [W] California [SE] of San Francisco

San Jo•sé \ˌsan-ə-ˈzā, -ō-ˈzā, -hō-ˈzā\ city, capital of Costa Rica

San Juan \san-ˈhwän, -ˈwän\ city, capital of Puerto Rico

San Lu•is Po•to•sí \ˌsän-lu̇-ˌē-ˌspōt-ə-ˈsē\ 1 state central Mexico 2 city, its capital

San Ma•ri•no \ˌsan-mə-ˈrē-nō\ 1 country [S] Europe on peninsula of Italy [ENE] of Florence near Adriatic Sea 2 town, its capital

San Mi•guel de Tu•cu•mán \ˌsan-mig-ˌel-də-ˌtü-kə-ˈmän\ *or* **Tu•cu•mán** \ˌtü-kə-ˈmän\ city [NW] Argentina

San Pe•dro Su•la \san-ˌpā-drō-ˈsü-lə\ city [NW] Honduras

San Sal•va•dor \san-ˈsal-və-ˌdȯr\ 1 *or formerly* **Wat•lings** \ˈwät-lingz\ island central Bahama Islands 2 city, capital of El Salvador

San•ta Ana \ˌsant-ə-ˈan-ə\ 1 city [SW] California [ESE] of Long Beach 2 city [NW] El Salvador [NW] of San Salvador

San•ta Bar•ba•ra \-ˈbär-brə, -bə-rə\ 1 city [S] California 2 *or* **Channel** islands California off [SW] coast

San•ta Clara \-ˈklar-ə, -ˈkler-ə\ 1 city [W] California [NW] of San Jose 2 city [W] central Cuba

San•ta Cla•ri•ta \-klə-ˈrēt-ə\ city [S] California

San•ta Cruz \-ˈkrüz\ city [E] Bolivia

San•ta Cruz de Te•ne•rife \-də-ˌten-ə-ˈrēf-ā, -ˈrēf, -ˈrif\ city Spain in [W] Canary Islands on Tenerife Island

San•ta Fe \ˌsant-ə-ˈfā\ 1 city, capital of New Mexico 2 city central Argentina

Santa Fe Trail pioneer route to the Southwest about 1200 miles (1930 kilometers) long used especially 1821–80 from vicinity of Kansas City, Missouri, to Santa Fe, New Mexico

Santa Isabel — see MALABO

San•ta Mar•ta \ˌsant-ə-ˈmärt-ə\ city [N] Colombia on the Caribbean

San•tan•der \ˌsän-ˌtän-ˈdeər, ˌsan-ˌtan-\ city [N] Spain [WNW] of Bilbao

San•ta Ro•sa \ˌsant-ə-ˈrō-zə\ city [W] California [N] of San Francisco

San•ti•a•go \ˌsant-ē-ˈäg-ō, ˌsänt-\ 1 city, capital of Chile 2 *or* **Santiago de los Ca•ba•lle•ros** \-də-ˌlōs-ˌkäb-ə-ˈyeər-ōs\ city [N] central Dominican Republic

Santiago de Cu•ba \-də-ˈkyü-bə\ city [SE] Cuba

San•to Do•min•go \ˌsant-əd-ə-ˈming-gō\ 1 — see HISPANIOLA 2 — see DOMINICAN REPUBLIC 3 *or formerly* **Ci•u•dad Tru•ji•llo** \ˌsē-ü-ˌthä-trü-ˈhē-ō, ˌsē-ü-ˌdad-\ city, capital of Dominican Republic

San•tos \ˈsant-əs\ city [SE] Brazil

São Lu•ís \ˌsaùⁿ-lü-ˈēs\ city [NE] Brazil on Maranhão Island

Saône \ˈsōn\ river [E] France flowing into the Rhone

São Pau•lo \saùⁿ-ˈpau̇-lü, saùⁿm-, -lō\ city [SE] Brazil

São Salvador — see SALVADOR

São To•mé *or* **São Tho•mé** \ˌsaùⁿt-ə-ˈmā, ˌsaùⁿnt-\ *or* **Saint**

Thom·as \sänt-ˈtäm-əs\ island [W] Africa in Gulf of Guinea; with Príncipe Island, forms country of **São Tomé and Príncipe**; capital, São Tomé; until 1975 a Portuguese colony
Sap·po·ro \ˈsäp-ə-ˌrō; sə-ˈpōr-ō, -ˈpȯr-\ city Japan on [W] Hokkaido
Saragossa — see ZARAGOZA
Sa·ra·je·vo \ˈsär-ə-ye-ˌvō\ city, capital of Bosnia and Herzegovina
Sa·ransk \sə-ˈränsk, -ˈransk\ city central Russia in Europe
Sa·ra·tov \sə-ˈrät-əf\ city [S] central Russia in Europe, on the Volga
Sar·din·ia \sär-ˈdin-ē-ə, -ˈdin-yə\ *or Italian* **Sar·de·gna** \sär-ˈdā-nyä\ island Italy in the Mediterranean [S] of Corsica; a region; capital, Cagliari — **Sar·din·ian** \-ˈdin-ē-ən, -ˈdin-yən\ *adj or n*
Sar·dis \ˈsärd-əs\ ancient city [W] Asia Minor, capital of Lydia
Sar·gas·so Sea \sär-ˌgas-ō\ area of comparatively still water in North Atlantic lying chiefly between 25° & 35° [N] latitude & 40° & 70° [W] longitude
Sa·ron·ic Gulf \sə-ˌrän-ik\ inlet of the Aegean [SE] Greece between Attica & Peloponnese
Sas·katch·e·wan \sə-ˈskach-ə-wən, sa-, -ˌwän\ province [W] Canada; capital, Regina
Sas·ka·toon \ˌsas-kə-ˈtün\ city Canada in central Saskatchewan
Sas·sa·ri \ˈsäs-ə-rē\ city Italy in [NW] Sardinia
Sau·di Arabia \ˌsau̇d-ē-ə-ˈrā-bē-ə, ˌsȯd-ē-, sä-ˌüd-ē-\ country [SW] Asia occupying largest part of Arabian Peninsula; a kingdom; capital, Riyadh — **Saudi** *adj or n* — **Saudi Arabian** *adj or n*
Sault Sainte Ma·rie Canals \ˌsü-ˌsānt-mə-ˈrē\ *or* **Soo Canals** \ˌsü-\ three ship canals, two in U.S. (Michigan) & one in Canada (Ontario), at rapids in Saint Marys River (70 miles or 115 kilometers long connecting Lake Superior & Lake Huron)
Sa·vaii \sə-ˈvī-ˌē\ island, largest in independent Samoa
Sa·van·nah \sə-ˈvan-ə\ city [E] Georgia
Sa·voy \sə-ˈvȯi\ *or French* **Sa·voie** \sȧ-ˈvwȧ\ region [SE] France [SW] of Switzerland bordering on Italy — **Sa·voy·ard** \sə-ˈvȯi-ˌärd, ˌsav-ˌȯi-ˈärd; ˌsav-ˌwä-ˈyär, -ˈyärd\ *adj or n*
Sax·o·ny \ˈsak-sə-nē, ˈsak-snē\ *or German* **Sach·sen** \ˈzäk-sən\ region [E] Germany [N] of the Erzgebirge — see LOWER SAXONY
Saxony An·halt \-ˈän-ˈhält\ state [NE] central Germany; capital, Magdeburg
Sca·fell Pike \ˌskȯ-ˈfel\ mountain 3210 feet (978 meters) [NW] England; highest in Cumbrian Mountains & in England
Scan·di·na·via \ˌskan-də-ˈnā-vē-ə, -vyə\ **1** peninsula [N] Europe occupied by Norway & Sweden **2** Denmark, Norway, Sweden, & thought by some to include also Iceland & Finland
Scar·bor·ough \ˈskär-ˌbər-ō\ former city Canada in [SE] Ontario; now part of Toronto
Scheldt \ˈskelt\ *or* **Schel·de** \ˈskel-də\ *or French* **Es·caut** \es-kō\ river 270 miles (434 kilometers) long [W] Europe flowing from [N] France through Belgium into North Sea in Netherlands
Schleswig–Hol·stein \ˈshles-wig-ˈhōl-ˌstīn, ˈsles-, -vik-ˈhōl-\ state [N] Germany consisting of Holstein & part of Schleswig; capital, Kiel
Schuyl·kill \ˈskü-kl, ˈskül-ˌkil\ river 131 miles (211 kilometers) long [SE] Pennsylvania flowing [SE] into the Delaware River at Philadelphia
Schwarzwald — see BLACK FOREST
Schwe·rin \shvā-ˈrēn\ city [N] Germany, capital of Mecklenburg-West Pomerania
Schweiz — see SWITZERLAND
Scil·ly \ˈsil-ē\ islands [SW] England off Land's End in county of Cornwall and Isles of Scilly
Sco·tia \ˈskō-shə\ SCOTLAND — the Medieval Latin name
Scot·land \ˈskät-lənd\ *or Latin* **Cal·e·do·nia** \ˌkal-ə-ˈdō-nyə, -nē-ə\ country [N] Great Britain; a division of United Kingdom; capital, Edinburgh
Scottish Borders administrative area [S] Scotland
Scotts·dale \ˈskäts-ˌdāl\ city [SW] central Arizona [E] of Phoenix
Scran·ton \ˈskrant-n\ city [NE] Pennsylvania
Scyth·ia \ˈsith-ē-ə, ˈsith-\ ancient country comprising parts of Europe & Asia in regions [N] & [NE] of Black Sea & [E] of Aral Sea — **Scyth·i·an** \-ē-ən\ *adj or n*
Se·at·tle \sē-ˈat-l\ city & port [W] Washington
Seine \ˈsān, ˈsen\ river 480 miles (772 kilometers) long [N] France flowing [NW] into English Channel
Sel·kirk \ˈsel-ˌkərk\ range of the Rocky Mountains [SE] British Columbia; highest peak, Mount Sir Sandford 11,555 feet (3522 meters)
Se·ma·rang \sə-ˈmär-ˌäng\ city Indonesia in central Java
Se·mey \ˈsem-ā\ *or* **Sem·i·pa·la·tinsk** \ˌsem-i-pə-ˈlä-ˌtinsk\ city [NE] Kazakhstan on the Irtysh
Sen·dai \sen-ˈdī, ˈsen-\ city Japan in [NE] Honshu
Sen·e·gal \ˌsen-i-ˈgȯl\ **1** river 1015 miles (1633 kilometers) long [W] Africa flowing [W] into North Atlantic **2** country [W] Africa; capital, Dakar — **Sen·e·ga·lese** \ˌsen-i-gə-ˈlēz, -ˈlēs\ *adj or n*
Sen·e·gam·bia \ˌsen-ə-ˈgam-bē-ə\ region [W] Africa around Senegal & Gambia rivers
Seongnam — see SONGNAM
Seoul \ˈsōl\ city, capital of South Korea
Se·quoia National Park \si-ˈkwȯi-ə\ reservation [SE] central California; includes Mount Whitney
Seram — see CERAM
Ser·bia \ˈsər-bē-ə\ country [S] Europe in Balkan Peninsula; capital, Belgrade
Serbia and Montenegro *or 1992–2003* **Yugoslavia** former country [S] Europe on Balkan Peninsula; capital, Belgrade
Ser·en·ge·ti Plain \ˌser-ən-ˈget-ē\ area [N] Tanzania including **Serengeti National Park**
Se·te Que·das \ˌsāt-ə-ˈkā-thəsh\ *or formerly* **Guai·ra** *or* **Guay·ra** \gwī-ˈrä\ former cataract in Alto Paraná on Brazil–Paraguay boundary; now submerged in dam-created lake
Se·vas·to·pol \sə-ˈvas-tə-ˌpōl, -ˌpȯl, -pəl; ˌsev-ə-ˈstō-pəl, -ˈstō-\ city & port [SW] Crimea, Ukraine
Sev·ern \ˈsev-ərn\ river 210 miles (338 kilometers) long Wales & England flowing from [E] central Wales into Bristol Channel
Se·ville \sə-ˈvil\ *or Spanish* **Se·vi·lla** \sā-ˈvē-ä, -yä\ *or ancient* **His·pa·lis** \ˈhis-pə-ləs\ city [SW] Spain
Sew·ard \ˈsü-ərd\ peninsula [W] Alaska projecting into Bering Sea
Sey·chelles \sā-ˈshel, -ˈshelz\ islands [W] Indian Ocean [NE] of Madagascar; formerly a British colony; became independent 1976; capital, Victoria (on Mahé Island)
's Gravenhage — see HAGUE (The)
Shaan·xi \ˈshän-ˈshē\ *or* **Shen·si** \ˈshen-ˈsē, ˈshən-ˈshē\ province [N] central China; capital, Xi'an
Sha·ba \ˈshäb-ə\ region [SE] Democratic Republic of the Congo; rich in mineral deposits
Shan·dong \ˈshän-ˈdȯŋ\ *or* **Shan·tung** \ˈshan-ˈtəŋ\ **1** peninsula [E] China extending into Yellow Sea **2** province [E] China including Shandong Peninsula; capital, Jinan
Shang·hai \shang-ˈhī\ city [E] China in [SE] Jiangsu
Shan·non \ˈshan-ən\ river 230 miles (370 kilometers) long [W] Ireland flowing [S] & [W] into North Atlantic
Shan·tou \ˈshän-ˈtō\ *or* **Swa·tow** \ˈswä-ˈtau̇\ city [SE] China in [E] Guangdong
Shan·xi \ˈshän-ˈshē\ *or* **Shan·si** \ˈshän-ˈsē, -ˈshē\ province [N] China bordering on Huang (Yellow) River; capital, Taiyuan
Shar·on, Plain of \shar-ən\ region Israel on coast between Mount Carmel & Jaffa
Shas·ta, Mount \ˈshas-tə\ mountain 14,162 feet (4316 meters) [N] California in Cascade Range
Shatt al Ar·ab \ˌshat-ˌal-ˈar-əb\ river 120 miles (193 kilometers) long [SE] Iraq formed by confluence of Euphrates & Tigris rivers & flowing [SE] into Persian Gulf
Shcherbakov — see RYBINSK
She·ba \ˈshē-bə\ ancient country [S] Arabia
She·chem \ˈshē-kəm, -ˌkem\ city of ancient Palestine in Samaria; site in present West Bank
Shef·field \ˈshef-ˌēld\ city [N] England
Shen·an·do·ah National Park \ˌshen-ən-ˈdō-ə, ˌshan-ə-ˈdō-ə\ reservation [N] Virginia in Blue Ridge Mountains
Shen·yang \ˈshən-ˈyäŋ\ *or* **Muk·den** \ˈmu̇k-dən, ˈmək-; ˈmu̇k-ˈden\ *or formerly* **Feng·tien** \ˈfəŋ-tē-ˈen\ city [NE] China, capital of Liaoning
Sher·wood Forest \ˌshər-ˌwu̇d\ ancient royal forest central England chiefly in Nottinghamshire
Shet·land Islands \ˈshet-lənd\ island group [N] Scotland [NE] of the Orkneys constituting an administrative area
Shi·jia·zhuang *or* **Shih–chia–chuang** \ˈshiər-jē-ˈäj-ˈwäŋ, ˈshē-jē-\ city [NE] China, capital of Hebei
Shi·ko·ku \shi-ˈkō-kü\ island [S] Japan [E] of Kyushu

\ə\ **abut**	\au̇\ **out**	\i\ **tip**	\ȯ\ **saw**	\u̇\ **foot**
\ər\ **further**	\ch\ **chin**	\ī\ **life**	\ȯi\ **coin**	\y\ **yet**
\a\ **mat**	\e\ **pet**	\j\ **job**	\th\ **thin**	\yü\ **few**
\ā\ **take**	\ē\ **easy**	\ng\ **sing**	\th\ **this**	\yu̇\ **cure**
\ä\ **cot, cart**	\g\ **go**	\ō\ **bone**	\ü\ **food**	\zh\ **vision**

Shim·la \ˈshim-lə\ *or* **Sim·la** \ˈsim-\ town [N] India, capital of Himachal Pradesh
Shi·raz \shi-ˈräz\ city [SW] Iran
Shi·zu·o·ka \ˌshiz-ə-ˈwō-kə, ˌshē-zə-ˈō-kə\ city Japan in central Honshu [SW] of Tokyo
Sho·la·pur \ˈshō-lə-ˌpu̇r\ city [W] India in [SE] Maharashtra [SE] of Bombay
Shreve·port \ˈshrēv-ˌpōrt, -ˌpȯrt\ city [NW] Louisiana on Red River
Shrop·shire \ˈshräp-shər, -ˌshir\ *or officially 1974–80* **Sal·op** \ˈsal-əp, -ˌäp\ county [W] England bordering on Wales
Shushan — see SUSA
Shym·kent \shim-ˈkent\ *or* **Chim·kent** \chim-\ city [S] Kazakhstan
Si·al·kot \sē-ˈäl-ˌkōt\ city [NE] Pakistan [NNE] of Lahore
Siam — see THAILAND
Siam, Gulf of — see THAILAND (Gulf of)
Sian — see XI'AN
Siangtan — see XIANGTAN
Si·be·ria \sī-ˈbir-ē-ə\ region [N] Asia in Russia between the Urals & North Pacific — **Si·be·ri·an** \-ē-ən\ *adj or n*
Si·chuan \ˈsē-ˈchwän\ *or* **Sze·chwan** \ˈsech-ˈwän, ˈsesh-\ province [SW] China; capital, Chengdu
Sic·i·ly \ˈsis-ə-lē, ˈsis-lē\ *or Italian* **Si·ci·lia** \sē-ˈchēl-yä\ island [S] Italy [SW] of toe of peninsula of Italy; a region; capital, Palermo — **Si·cil·ian** \sə-ˈsil-yən\ *adj or n*
Sid·ra, Gulf of \ˈsid-rə\ inlet of the Mediterranean on coast of Libya
Si·er·ra Le·one \sē-ˌer-ə-lē-ˈōn, ˌsir-ə-\ country [W] Africa on North Atlantic; capital, Freetown — **Sierra Le·on·ean** \-ˈō-nē-ən\ *adj or n*
Si·er·ra Ma·dre \sē-ˌer-ə-ˈmäd-rē\ mountain system Mexico including **Sierra Madre Oc·ci·den·tal** \-ˌäk-sə-ˌden-ˈtäl\ range [W] of the central plateau, **Sierra Madre Ori·en·tal** \-ˌōr-ē-ˌen-ˈtäl, -ˌȯr-\ range [E] of the plateau, & **Sierra del Sur** \sē-ˌer-ə-ˌdel-ˈsu̇r\ range to the [S]
Sierra Ne·vada \-nə-ˈvad-ə, -ˈväd-\ **1** mountain range [E] California & [W] Nevada — see WHITNEY (Mount) **2** mountain range [S] Spain; highest peak Mulhacén 11,410 feet (3478 meters), highest in Spain
Sik·kim \ˈsik-əm, -ˌim\ former country [SE] Asia on [S] slope of the Himalaya between Nepal & Bhutan; a state of Republic of India since 1975; capital, Gangtok
Si·le·sia \sī-ˈlē-zhə, sə-, -zhē-ə, -shə, -shē-ə\ region [E] central Europe in valley of the upper Oder bordering on Sudety Mountains; formerly chiefly in Germany now chiefly in [NE] Czech Republic & [SW] Poland — **Si·le·sian** \-zhən, -shən\ *adj or n*
Silk Road ancient trade route that extended from China to the Mediterranean Sea
Sim·birsk \sim-ˈbirsk\ *or 1924–91* **Ul·ya·novsk** \ül-ˈyän-əfsk\ city central Russia in Europe
Sim·coe, Lake \ˈsim-kō\ lake Canada in [SE] Ontario
Sim·fe·ro·pol \ˌsim-fə-ˈrō-pəl, ˌsimp-, -ˈrō-\ city [S] Ukraine in central Crimea Peninsula
Si·mi Valley \sē-ˈmē\ city [SW] California [W] of Los Angeles
Sim·plon \ˈsim-ˌplän\ **1** pass between Italy & Switzerland in Lepontine Alps **2** tunnel 12.5 miles (20 kilometers) long near the pass
Si·nai \ˈsī-ˌnī\ **1** — see HOREB **2** peninsula, extension of continent of Asia [NE] Egypt between Red Sea & the Mediterranean
Si·na·loa \ˌsē-nə-ˈlō-ə, ˌsin-ə-\ state [W] Mexico on Gulf of California; capital, Culiacán
Sind \ˈsind\ province [S] Pakistan in lower Indus River valley; chief city Karachi
Sin·ga·pore \ˈsing-ə-ˌpōr, -gə-, -ˌpȯr\ **1** island off [S] end of Malay Peninsula; an independent republic **2** city, its capital — **Sin·ga·por·ean** \ˌsing-ə-ˈpōr-ē-ən, -gə-, -ˈpȯr-\ *adj or n*
Sining — see XINING
Sinkiang–Uighur — see XINJIANG UYGUR
Sion — see ZION
Siracusa — see SYRACUSE
Sir·mi·lik National Park \ˈsər-mə-lik\ reservation [N] Nunavut, Canada on Baffin Island
Sjæl·land \ˈshel-ˌän\ *or* **Zea·land** \ˈzē-lənd\ island, largest of islands of Denmark; site of Copenhagen
Skag·ge·rak \ˈskag-ə-ˌrak\ arm of North Sea between [S] Norway & [N] Denmark
Skop·je \ˈskȯp-ˌyā\ city, capital of independent Macedonia
Skye \ˈskī\ island Scotland; one of the Inner Hebrides
Sky·ros \ˈskī-rəs, -ˌräs\ *or Greek* **Skí·ros** \ˈskē-ˌrȯs\ island Greece in Northern Sporades [E] of Euboea
Sla·vo·nia \slə-ˈvō-nē-ə, -nyə\ region [E] Croatia between Sava, Drava, & Danube rivers — **Sla·vo·nian** \-ne-ən, -nyən\ *adj or n*
Sli·go \ˈslī-gō\ county [N] Ireland (republic) in Connacht
Slo·va·kia \slō-ˈväk-ē-ə, -ˈvak-\ country central Europe; capital, Bratislava
Slo·ve·nia \slō-ˈvē-nē-ə, -nyə\ country [S] Europe [N] & [W] of Croatia; formerly a constituent republic of Yugoslavia; capital, Ljubljana — **Slo·ve·nian** \-nē-ən, -nyən\ *adj or n*
Smo·lensk \smō-ˈlensk\ city [W] Russia in Europe
Smyrna — see IZMIR
Snow·do·nia \snō-ˈdō-nē-ə, -nyə\ mountainous district [NW] Wales centering around **Snow·don** \ˈsnōd-n\ (massif 3560 feet or 1085 meters; highest point in Wales)
So·chi \ˈsō-chē\ city [S] Russia in Europe, on Black Sea
So·ci·e·ty \sə-ˈsī-ət-ē\ islands South Pacific in French Polynesia; capital, Papeete (on Tahiti)
So·co·tra \sə-ˈkō-trə\ island Yemen in Indian Ocean [E] of Gulf of Aden; capital, Tamridah
Sod·om \ˈsäd-əm\ ancient city thought to have been in the area now covered by the [SW] part of the Dead Sea
So·fia \ˈsō-fē-ə, ˈsȯ-, sō-ˈ\ city, capital of Bulgaria
So·ho \ˈsō-ˌhō\ district of central London, England
So·li·hull \ˌsō-li-ˈhəl\ town central England [SE] of Birmingham
Sol·o·mon \ˈsäl-ə-mən\ **1** islands [W] Pacific [E] of New Guinea divided between Papua New Guinea & independent **Solomon Islands** (capital, Honiara) **2** sea arm of Coral Sea [W] of the Solomons
So·ma·lia \sō-ˈmäl-ē-ə, sə-, -ˈmäl-yə\ country [E] Africa on Gulf of Aden & Indian Ocean; capital, Mogadishu — **So·ma·li·an** \-ˈmäl-ē-ən, -ˈmäl-yən\ *adj or n*
So·ma·li·land \sō-ˈmäl-ē-ˌland, sə-\ region [E] Africa comprising Somalia, Djibouti, & part of [E] Ethiopia
Som·er·set \ˈsəm-ər-ˌset, -sət\ *or* **Som·er·set·shire** \-ˌshiər, -shər\ county [SW] England
Somerset Nile — see NILE
Song·nam *or* **Seong·nam** \ˈsəng-ˈnäm\ city [NW] South Korea
So·no·ra \sə-ˈnōr-ə, -ˈnȯr-\ state [NW] Mexico bordering on U.S.; capital, Hermosillo
So·nor·an \sə-ˈnōr-ən, -ˈnȯr-\ *or* **Sonora** desert [SW] U.S. & [NW] Mexico in [S] Arizona, [SE] California, & [N] Sonora
Soo Canals — see SAULT SAINTE MARIE CANALS
Soochow — see SUZHOU
Sorata — see ILLAMPU
So·ro·ca·ba \ˌsōr-ə-ˈkab-ə, ˌsȯr-\ city [SE] Brazil [W] of São Paulo
Sos·no·wiec \säs-ˈnō-ˌvyets\ city [SW] Poland
South \ˈsau̇th\ island [S] New Zealand
South Africa, Republic of country [S] Africa; an independent republic; until 1961 (as **Union of South Africa**) a British dominion; administrative capital, Pretoria; legislative capital, Cape Town; judicial capital, Bloemfontein
South America continent of Western Hemisphere [SE] of North America & chiefly [S] of the Equator — **South American** *adj or n*
South·amp·ton \sau̇th-ˈam-tən, -ˈham-, -ˈamp-, -ˈhamp-\ city [S] England
South Australia state [S] Australia; capital, Adelaide — **South Australian** *adj or n*
South Ayrshire administrative area [W] Scotland
South Bend \ˈbend\ city [N] Indiana
South Cape *or* **South Point** — see KA LAE
South Car·o·li·na \ˌkar-ə-ˈlī-nə\ state [SE] U.S.; capital, Columbia — **South Car·o·lin·i·an** \-ˈlin-ē-ən, -ˈlin-yən\ *adj or n*
South China Sea — see CHINA SEA
South Da·ko·ta \də-ˈkōt-ə\ state [NW] central U.S.; capital, Pierre — **South Da·ko·tan** \-ˈkōt-n\ *adj or n*
South·end–on–Sea \ˌsau̇-ˌthend-än-ˈsē, -ȯn-\ resort [SE] England [E] of London
Southern Alps mountain range New Zealand in [W] South Island extending almost the length of the island
Southern Ocean the waters surrounding Antarctica including the [S] parts of the South Atlantic, South Pacific, & Indian oceans
Southern Rhodesia — see ZIMBABWE
Southern Yemen — see YEMEN
South Georgia island South Atlantic [E] of Tierra del Fuego; administered by Britain

South Korea — see KOREA

South Lanarkshire administrative area [W] Scotland

South Seas the areas of the Atlantic, Indian, & Pacific oceans in the Southern Hemisphere; especially, the South Pacific

South Shields \'shēldz, 'shēlz\ city [N] England

South Sudan country [E] Africa; capital, Juba

South Tirol — see ALTO ADIGE

South Vietnam — see VIETNAM

South·wark \'səth-ərk, 'sau̇th-wərk\ borough of [S] Greater London, England

South–West Africa — see NAMIBIA

South York·shire \'yȯrk-ˌshiər, -shər\ metropolitan county [N] England

Soviet Central Asia formerly used name for the portion of central & [SW] Asia belonging to U.S.S.R. & comprising the Kirghiz, Tadzhik, Turkmen, & Uzbek republics & thought by some to also include all or part of the Kazakh republic

Soviet Russia **1** — see RUSSIA **2** — see UNION OF SOVIET SOCIALIST REPUBLICS

Soviet Union — see UNION OF SOVIET SOCIALIST REPUBLICS

So·we·to \sō-'wāt-ō\ residential area [NE] Republic of South Africa adjoining [SW] Johannesburg

Spain \'spān\ *or Spanish* **Es·pa·ña** \ä-'spän-yä\ *or ancient* **His·pa·nia** \his-'pān-ē-ə, -'pān-yə, -'pan-\ country [SW] Europe in Iberian Peninsula; a kingdom; capital, Madrid

Spanish America **1** the Spanish-speaking countries of America **2** the parts of America settled & formerly governed by the Spanish

Spanish Guinea — see EQUATORIAL GUINEA

Spanish Main \'mān\ **1** the mainland of Spanish America especially along [N] coast of South America **2** the Caribbean Sea & adjacent waters especially when region was infested with pirates

Spanish Morocco — see MOROCCO

Spanish Sahara former Spanish territory [NW] Africa [SW] of Morocco comprising Río de Oro & Saguia el Hamra — see WESTERN SAHARA

Spar·ta \'spärt-ə\ *or* **Lac·e·dae·mon** \ˌlas-ə-'dē-mən\ ancient city [S] Greece in Peloponnese, capital of Laconia

Spey·er \'shpī-ər, 'spī-; 'shpīr, 'spīr\ *or English* **Spires** \'spīrz\ city [SW] Germany on the Rhine

Spice Islands — see MOLUCCAS

Spits·ber·gen \'spits-ˌbər-gən\ islands in Arctic Ocean [N] of Norway; chief island, West Spitsbergen — see SVALBARD

Split \'split\ city [S] Croatia

Spo·kane \spō-'kan\ city [E] Washington

Spor·a·des \'spȯr-ə-ˌdēz, 'spär-\ two island groups Greece in the Aegean: the **Northern Sporades** (chief island, Skyros, [E] of Euboea) & **Southern Sporades** (including Samos, Icaria, & the Dodecanese, off [SW] Turkey)

Sprat·ly \'sprat-lē\ islands central South China Sea; claimed by several countries

Spring·field \'spriŋ-ˌfēld\ **1** city, capital of Illinois **2** city [SW] Massachusetts on Connecticut River **3** city [SW] Missouri

Springs \'spriŋz\ city [NE] Republic of South Africa in Gauteng

Sri Lan·ka \srē-'läŋ-kə, 'srē-\ *or formerly* **Cey·lon** \si-'län, sā-\ country coextensive with island of Ceylon; an independent republic; capital, Colombo

Sri·na·gar \sri-'nəg-ər\ city, summer capital of Jammu and Kashmir, in [W] Kashmir

Staf·ford·shire \'staf-ərd-ˌshiər, -shər\ *or* **Stafford** county [W] central England

Staked Plain — see LLANO ESTACADO

Sta·kha·nov \stə-'kän-əf\ *or formerly* **Ka·di·yev·ka** \kə-'dē-yəf-kə\ city [E] Ukraine in Donets Basin

Stalingrad — see VOLGOGRAD

Stam·ford \'stam-fərd, 'stamp-\ city [SW] Connecticut

Stan·ley \'stan-lē\ town, capital of Falkland Islands

Stanley, Mount — see RUWENZORI

Stanleyville — see KISANGANI

Stat·en Island \'stat-n\ **1** island [SE] New York [SW] of mouth of the Hudson **2** *or formerly* **Rich·mond** \'rich-mənd\ borough of New York City including Staten Island

States of the Church — see PAPAL STATES

Stavropol — see TOL'YATTI

Stir·ling \'stər-liŋ\ administrative area central Scotland

Stock·holm \'stäk-ˌhōlm, -ˌhōm\ city, capital of Sweden

Stock·port \'stäk-ˌpōrt, -ˌpȯrt\ town [NW] England [S] of Manchester

Stock·ton \'stäk-tən\ city central California

Stoke on Trent \ˌstō-ˌkȯn-'trent, -ˌkän-\ city central England

Stone·henge \'stōn-ˌhenj, stōn-'henj\ assemblage of megaliths [S] England on Salisbury Plain

Stone Mountain mountain 1686 feet (514 meters) [NW] Georgia [E] of Atlanta

Straits Settlements former British crown colony [SE] Asia on Strait of Malacca comprising Singapore Island & George Town & Malacca settlements on Malay Peninsula

Stras·bourg \'sträs-ˌbu̇rg, 'sträz-, -ˌbərg\ city [NE] France

Strat·ford–upon–Avon \'strat-fərd\ town central England

Strom·bo·li \'sträm-bə-lē\ volcano 3038 feet (926 meters) Italy in Lipari Islands on Stromboli Island

Stutt·gart \'shtu̇t-ˌgärt, 'stu̇t-, 'stət-\ city [SW] Germany, capital of Baden-Württemberg

Styx \'stiks\ chief river of Hades in Greek mythology

Su·bic Bay \'sü-bik\ inlet of South China Sea in [W] Luzon, Philippines

Süchow **1** — see XUZHOU **2** — see YIBIN

Su·cre \'sü-krā\ city, constitutional capital of Bolivia

Su·dan \sü-'dan, -'dän\ **1** region [N] Africa [S] of the Sahara between the Atlantic & the upper Nile **2** country [NE] Africa [S] of Egypt; capital, Khartoum — see ANGLO-EGYPTIAN SUDAN — **Su·da·nese** \ˌsüd-n-'ēz, -'ēs\ *adj or n*

Su·de·ten \sü-'dāt-n\ *or* **Su·de·ten·land** \sü-'dāt-n-ˌland\ region [NE] Czech Republic in Sudety Mountains

Su·de·ty \'su̇d-et-ē, su̇-'det-\ mountains central Europe between Czech Republic & Poland

Su·ez \sü-'ez, 'sü-ˌez\ **1** city [NE] Egypt at [S] end of Suez Canal on **Gulf of Suez** (arm of Red Sea) **2** canal over 100 miles (161 kilometers) long [NE] Egypt across Isthmus of Suez

Suez, Isthmus of neck of land [NE] Egypt between Mediterranean & Red seas connecting Africa & Asia

Suf·folk \'səf-ək\ county [E] England on North Sea

Su·i·ta \sü-'ēt-ə\ city Japan in [S] Honshu [N] of Osaka

Su·la·we·si \ˌsü-lə-'wā-sē\ *or* **Ce·le·bes** \'sel-ə-ˌbēz, sə-'lē-bēz\ island Indonesia [E] of Borneo

Su·lu \'sü-lü\ archipelago [SW] Philippines [SW] of Mindanao — see BASILAN

Su·ma·tra \su̇-'mä-trə\ island [W] Indonesia [S] of Malay Peninsula — **Su·ma·tran** \-trən\ *adj or n*

Su·mer \'sü-mər\ the [S] division of ancient Babylonia — **Su·me·ri·an** \sü-'mer-ē-ən, -'mir-\ *adj or n*

Sun·belt \'sən-ˌbelt\ region [S] & [SW] U.S.

Sun·da \'sün-də\ **1** islands Malay Archipelago comprising the **Greater Sunda Islands** (Sumatra, Borneo, Java, Sulawesi, & adjacent islands) & the **Lesser Sunda Islands** (extending from Bali to Timor); with exception of [N] Borneo & East Timor belong to Indonesia **2** strait between Java & Sumatra

Sun·der·land \'sən-dər-lənd\ seaport [N] England on North Sea

Suomi — see FINLAND

Su·pe·ri·or, Lake \su̇-'pir-ē-ər\ lake [E] central North America in U.S. & Canada; largest of the Great Lakes

Su·ra·ba·ya \ˌsu̇r-ə-'bī-ə\ city Indonesia in [NE] Java

Su·ra·kar·ta \ˌsu̇r-ə-'kärt-ə\ city Indonesia in central Java

Su·rat \'su̇r-ət, sə-'rat\ city [W] India in [SE] Gujarat

Su·ri·na·me \ˌsu̇r-ə-'näm-ə\ *or formerly* **Dutch Guiana** country [N] South America on the Atlantic; capital, Paramaribo

Sur·rey \'sər-ē, 'sə-rē\ **1** county [SE] England [SW] of London **2** city Canada in [SW] British Columbia

Surts·ey \'sərt-ˌsā\ island Iceland off [S] coast

Su·sa \'sü-zə\ *or biblical* **Shu·shan** \'shü-shən, -ˌshan\ ancient city, capital of Elam; ruins in [SW] Iran

Sut·ton \'sət-n\ borough of [S] Greater London, England

Su·va \'sü-və\ city, capital of Fiji on Viti Levu Island

Su·wan·nee \sə-'wän-ē\ river 250 miles (400 kilometers) [SE] Georgia & [N] Florida flowing [SW] into Gulf of Mexico

Su·won \'sü-ˌwän\ city [NW] South Korea [S] of Seoul

Su·zhou \'sü-'jō\ *or* **Soo·chow** \'sü-'jō, -'chau̇\ *or formerly* **Wu·hsien** \'wü-shē-'en\ city [E] China in Jiangsu [W] of Shanghai

Sval·bard \'sfäl-ˌbär\ islands in Arctic Ocean including Spitsbergen under Norwegian administration

Sverdlovsk — see YEKATERINBURG

\ə\ **abut**	\au̇\ **out**	\i\ **tip**	\ȯ\ **saw**	\u̇\ **foot**
\ər\ **further**	\ch\ **chin**	\ī\ **life**	\ȯi\ **coin**	\y\ **yet**
\a\ **mat**	\e\ **pet**	\j\ **job**	\th\ **thin**	\yü\ **few**
\ā\ **take**	\ē\ **easy**	\ŋ\ **sing**	\t͟h\ **this**	\yu̇\ **cure**
\ä\ **cot, cart**	\g\ **go**	\ō\ **bone**	\ü\ **food**	\zh\ **vision**

Swa•bia \'swäb-ē-ə\ region & medieval county [SW] Germany

Swan•sea \'swän-zē\ **1** administrative area [S] Wales **2** city & port [S] Wales in Swansea administrative area

Swatow — see SHANTOU

Swa•zi•land \'swäz-ē-ˌland\ country [SE] Africa between Republic of South Africa & Mozambique; an independent kingdom; capital, Mbabane; legislative capital, Lobamba — **Swa•zi** \'swäz-ē\ *adj or n*

Swe•den \'swēd-ⁿn\ country [N] Europe on Scandinavian Peninsula bordering on Baltic Sea; a kingdom; capital, Stockholm

Swit•zer•land \'swit-sər-lənd\ *or Latin* **Hel•ve•tia** \hel-'vē-shə, -shē-ə\ *or French* **Suisse** \'swʸēs\ *or German* **Schweiz** \'shvīts\ *or Italian* **Sviz•ze•ra** \'zvēt-sä-rä\ country [W] Europe in the Alps; capital, Bern

Syd•ney \'sid-nē\ city [SE] Australia, capital of New South Wales

Syr•a•cuse \'sir-ə-ˌkyüs, -kyüz\ **1** city central New York **2** ancient city Italy in [SE] Sicily; site at modern city of **Si•ra•cu•sa** \ˌsē-rə-'kü-zə\

Syr Dar'•ya \sir-'där-yə\ river about 1370 miles (2204 kilometers) Tajikistan & [S] Kazakhstan flowing from Tian Shan [W] & [NW] into Aral Sea

Syr•ia \'sir-ē-ə\ **1** ancient region [SW] Asia bordering on the Mediterranean **2** former French mandate (1920–44) including present Syria & Lebanon **3** country [S] of Turkey; capital, Damascus — **Syr•i•an** \'sir-ē-ən\ *adj or n*

Syrian Desert desert region [N] Saudi Arabia, [SE] Syria, [W] Iraq, & [NE] Jordan

Szcze•cin \'shchet-ˌsēn\ city [NW] Poland on the Oder

Szechwan — see SICHUAN

Ta•bas•co \tə-'bas-kō\ state [SE] Mexico [SW] of Yucatán Peninsula; capital, Villahermosa

Ta•ble Bay \ˌtā-bəl\ harbor of Cape Town, Republic of South Africa

Ta•briz \tə-'brēz\ city [NW] Iran

Ta•co•ma \tə-'kō-mə\ city [W] Washington on Puget Sound

Tae•gu \'tā-gü, 'dā-\ *or* **Dae•gu** \'dā-\ city South Korea [NNW] of Pusan

Tae•jon \'tā-'jən, 'dā-\ *or* **Dae•jeon** \'dā-\ city South Korea [NW] of Taegu

Ta•gan•rog \'tag-ən-ˌräg\ city [SW] Russia in Europe, on a [NE] arm of Sea of Avov [W] of Rostov

Ta•gus \'tā-gəs\ *or Spanish* **Ta•jo** \'tä-hō\ *or Portuguese* **Te•jo** \'tā-zhü\ river 626 miles (1007 kilometers) long Spain & Portugal flowing [W] into North Atlantic

Ta•hi•ti \tə-'hēt-ē\ island South Pacific in French Polynesia in Society Islands; chief town, Papeete — **Ta•hi•tian** \-'hē-shən\ *adj or n*

T'ai–nan \'tī-'nän\ city [SW] Taiwan

Tai•pei \'tī-'pā, -'bā\ *or* **Tai•bei** \'tī-'bā\ city, capital of (Nationalist) Republic of China in [N] Taiwan

Tai•wan \'tī-'wän\ *or formerly* **For•mo•sa** \fȯr-'mō-sə, fər-, -zə\ **1** island off [SE] coast of mainland Asia; since 1949 seat of government of (Nationalist) Republic of China; capital, Taipei **2** strait between Taiwan & Fujian, China connecting East China & South China seas — **Tai•wan•ese** \ˌtī-wə-'nēz, -'nēs\ *adj or n*

Tai•yuan \'tī-yü-'än\ *or formerly* **Yang•ku** \'yäng-'kü\ city [N] China, capital of Shanxi

Tai•zhong \'tī-'jüng\ *or* **Tai•chung** \'tī-'chüng\ city [W] Taiwan

Tai•zhou *or* **T'ai–chou** \'tī-'jō\ city [E] China in central Jiangsu [NW] of Shanghai

Ta•jik•i•stan \tä-'jik-i-ˌstan, -'jēk-\ country [W] central Asia; capital, Dushanbe; a constituent republic (**Ta•dzhik•i•stan** *same*\ *or* **Ta•dzhik Soviet Socialist Republic** \tä-'jik, -'jēk\) of U.S.S.R. 1929–91

Ta•ka•ma•tsu \ˌtäk-ə-'mät-sü, tä-'käm-ət-ˌsü\ city Japan in [NE] Shikoku

Ta•kat•su•ki \tə-'kät-sü-kē\ city Japan in [S] Honshu

Ta•kli•ma•kan *or* **Ta•kla Ma•kan** \ˌtäk-lə-mə-'kän\ desert [W] China in Xinjiang Uygur

Ta–lien — see DALIAN

Tal•la•has•see \ˌtal-ə-'has-ē\ city, capital of Florida

Tal•la•hatch•ie \ˌtal-ə-'hach-ē\ river 230 miles (370 kilometers) long [N] Mississippi

Tal•linn \'tal-ən, 'täl-\ *or formerly* **Re•vel** \'rā-vəl\ city, capital of Estonia

Ta•mau•li•pas \ˌtäm-ˌaů-'lē-pəs, təm-\ state [NE] Mexico; capital, Ciudad Victoria

Tam•bov \täm-'bȯf, -'bȯv\ city [S] central Russia in Europe, [SE] of Moscow

Tam•il Na•du \ˌtam-əl-'näd-ü\ *or formerly* **Ma•dras** \mə-'dras, -'dräs\ state [S] India on Bay of Bengal; capital, Madras

Tam•pa \'tam-pə\ city [W] Florida on Tampa Bay

Tam•pe•re \'tam-pə-ˌrā, 'täm-\ city [SW] Finland

Tam•pi•co \tam-'pē-kō\ city [E] Mexico in [S] Tamaulipas

Tananarive — see ANTANANARIVO

Tan•gan•yi•ka \ˌtan-gən-'yē-kə, ˌtang-gən-, -gə-'nē-\ former country [E] Africa [S] of Kenya; became part of Tanzania 1964

Tanganyika, Lake lake [E] Africa between Tanzania & Democratic Republic of the Congo

Tang•shan \'täng-'shäng\ city [NE] China in [E] Hebei

Tan•ta \'tänt-ə\ city [N] Egypt in central delta of the Nile

Tan–tung — see DANDONG

Tan•za•nia \ˌtan-zə-'nē-ə, ˌtän-\ country [E] Africa on Indian Ocean; a republic formed 1964 by union of Tanganyika & Zanzibar; legislative capital Dodoma, historic capital, Dar es Salaam — **Tan•za•ni•an** \-'nē-ən\ *adj or n*

Taor•mi•na \taůr-'mē-nə\ city Italy in [NE] Sicily

Ta•ran•to \'tär-ən-ˌtō, tə-'rant-ō\ *or ancient* **Ta•ren•tum** \tə-'rent-əm\ city [SE] Italy on Gulf of Taranto

Ta•ra•wa \tə-'rä-wə\ island central Pacific containing capital of Kiribati

Ta•rim \'dä-'rēm, 'tä-\ river 1250 miles (2012 kilometers) long [W] China in Xinjiang Uygur flowing into a marshy depression

Tar•lac \'tär-ˌläk\ city Philippines in central Luzon

Tar•shish \'tär-shish\ ancient maritime country referred to in the Bible & often identified with Tartessus

Tar•sus \'tär-səs\ ancient city of [S] Asia Minor, capital of Cilicia; now a city of [S] Turkey

Tar•ta•ry \'tärt-ə-rē\ vast historical region in Asia & [E] Europe roughly extending from Sea of Japan (East Sea) to the Dnieper

Tar•tes•sus *or* **Tar•tes•sos** \tär-'tes-əs\ ancient kingdom on [SW] coast of Spain near mouth of the Guadalquivir — see TARSHISH

Tar•tu \'tär-ˌtü\ city [E] Estonia

Tash•kent \tash-'kent\ city, capital of Uzbekistan

Tas•man Sea \'taz-mən\ the part of the South Pacific between [SE] Australia & New Zealand

Tas•ma•nia \taz-'mā-nē-ə, -nyə\ *or earlier* **Van Die•men's Land** \van-'dē-mənz\ island [SE] Australia [S] of Victoria; a state; capital, Hobart — **Tas•ma•nian** \-nē-ən, -nyən\ *adj or n*

Ta•try \'tä-trē\ *or* **Ta•tra** \'tä-trə\ mountains [N] Slovakia & [S] Poland in central Carpathian Mountains

Tatung — see DATONG

Tau•rus \'tȯr-əs\ mountains [S] Turkey parallel to Mediterranean coast; highest more than 12,000 feet (3660 meters)

Tbi•li•si \tə-'bē-lə-sē, tə-bə-'lē-sē\ *or* **Tif•lis** \'tif-ləs, tə-'flēs\ city, capital of Republic of Georgia

Tchad — see CHAD

Te•gu•ci•gal•pa \tə-ˌgü-si-'gal-pə\ city, capital of Honduras

Teh•ran *or* **Te•he•ran** \ˌtā-ə-'ran, -'rän\ city, capital of Iran

Tel•a•nai•pura \ˌtel-ə-'nī-ˌpůr-ə\ city Indonesia in Sumatra

Tel Aviv \ˌtel-ə-'vēv\ city [W] Israel on the Mediterranean

Te•ne•ri•fe \ˌten-ə-'rē-'rē-fā, -'rēf, -'rif\ island Spain, largest of the Canary Islands

Ten•nes•see \ˌten-ə-'sē, 'ten-ə-ˌ\ state [E] central U.S.; capital, Nashville — **Ten•nes•se•an** *or* **Ten•nes•see•an** \ˌten-ə-'sē-ən\ *adj or n*

Te•re•si•na \ˌter-ə-'zē-nə\ city [NE] Brazil

Ter•ra No•va National Park \ˌter-ə-'nō-və\ reservation [E] Newfoundland

Té•tou•an \tā-'twäⁿ\ *or* **Te•tuán** \te-'twän, ˌtet-ə-'wän\ city [N] Morocco on the Mediterranean

Tex•as \'tek-səs, -siz\ state [S] U.S.; capital, Austin — **Tex•an** \-sən\ *adj or n*

Thai•land \'tī-ˌland, -lənd\ *or formerly* **Si•am** \sī-'am\ country [SE] Asia on Gulf of Thailand; capital, Bangkok — **Thai•land•er** \'tī-ˌlan-dər, -lən-dər\ *n*

Thailand, Gulf of *or formerly* **Gulf of Siam** arm of South China Sea between Indochina & Malay Peninsula

Thames \'temz\ river over 200 miles (322 kilometers) long [S] England flowing [E] from the Cotswolds into the North Sea

Thar \'tär\ *or* **Indian** desert [E] Pakistan & [NW] Republic of India [E] of Indus River

Thebes \'thēbz\ **1** *or ancient* **The•bae** \'thē-bē\ *or later* **Di•os•po•lis** \dī-'äs-pə-ləs\ ancient city [S] Egypt, capital of Upper Egypt on the Nile on site including modern towns of Karnak & Luxor **2** ancient city [E] Greece [NNW] of Athens on site of modern village of Thivai — **The•ban** \'thē-bən\ *adj or n*

Theodore Roosevelt National Park reservation W North Dakota

Thes·sa·lo·níki \ˌthes-ä-lō-ˈnē-kē\ *or formerly* **Sa·lon·i·ka** \sə-ˈlän-i-kə\ *or ancient* **Thes·sa·lo·ni·ca** \ˌthes-ə-lə-ˈnī-kə, -ˈlän-i-kə\ city N Greece in Macedonia — **Thes·sa·lo·nian** \-ˈlō-nē-ən, -ˈlō-nyən\ *adj or n*

Thes·sa·ly \ˈthes-ə-lē\ region central Greece between Pindus Mountains & the Aegean — **Thes·sa·lian** \thə-ˈsā-lē-ən, -ˈsāl-yən\ *adj or n*

The Vale of Gla·mor·gan \glə-ˈmȯr-gən\ administrative area S Wales

Thim·phu \ˈthim-pü\ city, capital of Bhutan

Thousand islands Canada & U.S. in the Saint Lawrence in Ontario & New York

Thousand Oaks city SW California W of Los Angeles

Thrace \ˈthrās\ *or ancient* **Thra·cia** \ˈthrā-shə, -shē-ə\ region SE Europe in Balkan Peninsula N of the Aegean now divided between Greece & Turkey; in ancient times extended N to the Danube — **Thra·cian** \ˈthrā-shən\ *adj or n*

Thu·rin·gia \thu̇-ˈrin-jē-ə\ region central Germany

Tian·jin \tē-ˈän-ˈjin\ *or* **Tien·tsin** \tē-ˈent-ˈsin, ˈtint-\ city NE China in Hebei

Tian Shan \tē-ˈän-ˈshän\ *or* **Tien Shan** \tē-ˈen-ˈshän\ mountain system central Asia extending NE from Pamirs into Xinjiang Uygur; highest Pobeda Peak (in Kyrgyzstan) 24,406 feet (7439 meters)

Ti·ber \ˈtī-bər\ *or Italian* **Te·ve·re** \ˈtā-vā-rā\ *or ancient* **Ti·ber·is** \ˈtī-bə-rəs\ river 252 miles (405 kilometers) long central Italy flowing through Rome into Tyrrhenian Sea

Tiberias, Lake — see GALILEE (Sea of)

Ti·bes·ti \tə-ˈbes-tē\ mountains N central Africa in central Sahara in NW Chad; highest 11,204 feet (3415 meters)

Ti·bet \tə-ˈbet\ *or* **Xi·zang** \ˈshēd-ˈzäŋ\ autonomous region SW China on high plateau N of the Himalaya; capital, Lhasa

Tier·ra del Fue·go \tē-ˈer-ə-ˌdel-fü-ˈā-gō, -fyü-\ **1** archipelago off S South America S of Strait of Magellan **2** chief island of the group; divided between Argentina & Chile

Tiflis — see TBILISI

Ti·gris \ˈtī-grəs\ river 1180 miles (1899 kilometers) long Turkey & Iraq flowing SSE & uniting with the Euphrates to form the Shatt al Arab

Ti·jua·na \ˌtē-ə-ˈwän-ə, tē-ˈwän-\ city NW Mexico on U.S. border in Baja California

Til·burg \ˈtil-ˌbərg\ city S Netherlands SE of Rotterdam

Tim·buk·tu \ˌtim-ˌbək-ˈtü, tim-ˈbək-ˌtü\ *or* **Tom·bouc·tou** \tō^{n}-bük-ˈtü\ town W Africa in Mali

Ti·mi·soa·ra \ˌtē-mish-ə-ˈwär-ə, -mish-ˈwär-\ city W Romania

Ti·mor \ˈtē-ˌmȯr, tē-ˈ\ island SE Asia SE of Sulawesi; W half formerly belonged to Netherlands and is now part of Indonesia, E half formerly belonged to Portugal and is now independent East Timor

Timor–Leste — see EAST TIMOR

Tip·pe·rary \ˌtip-ə-ˈrer-ē\ former county S Ireland in Munster; now divided into **Tipperary North** and **Tipperary South**

Ti·ra·ne *or* **Ti·ra·na** \ti-ˈrän-ə\ city, capital of Albania

Ti·rol *or* **Ty·rol** \tə-ˈrōl; ˈtī-ˌrōl, tī-ˈ; ˈtir-əl\ *or Italian* **Ti·ro·lo** \tē-ˈrȯ-lō\ region in E Alps in W Austria & NE Italy — **Ti·ro·le·an** \tə-ˈrō-lē-ən, tī-; ˌtir-ə-ˈ, ˌtī-rə-ˈ\ *or* **Tir·o·lese** \ˌtir-ə-ˈlēz, ˌtī-rə-, -ˈlēs\ *adj or n*

Ti·ruch·chi·rap·pal·li \ˌtir-ə-chə-ˈräp-ə-lē\ city S India in Tamil Nadu

Ti·ti·ca·ca, Lake \ˌtit-i-ˈkäk-ə\ lake on Bolivia–Peru boundary at altitude of 12,500 feet (3810 meters)

Tlax·ca·la \tlä-ˈskäl-ə\ state SE central Mexico; capital, Tlaxcala

To·ba·go \tə-ˈbā-gō\ island West Indies NE of Trinidad; part of independent Trinidad and Tobago — **To·ba·go·ni·an** \ˌtō-bə-ˈgō-nē-ən\ *n*

To·go \ˈtō-gō\ *or* **To·go·land** \-ˌland\ region W Africa on Gulf of Guinea between Benin & Ghana; until 1919 a German protectorate, then divided into two trust territories: British Togoland (in W, since 1957 part of Ghana) & French Togo (in E, since 1958 independent Togo; capital, Lomé) — **To·go·land·er** \-ˌlan-dər\ *n* — **To·go·lese** \ˌtō-gō-ˈlēz, -ˈlēs\ *adj or n*

To·ko·ro·za·wa \ˌtō-kə-ˈrō-zə-ˌwä\ city Japan on Honshu; a suburb of Tokyo

To·ku·shi·ma \ˌtō-kə-ˈshē-mə\ city Japan in E Shikoku

To·kyo \ˈtō-kē-ˌō\ *or formerly* **Edo** \ˈed-ō\ city, capital of Japan in SE Honshu on **Tokyo Bay** (inlet of North Pacific) — **To·kyo·ite** \ˈtō-kē-ˌō-ˌīt\ *n*

To·le·do \tə-ˈlēd-ō, -ˈlēd-ə\ **1** city NW Ohio **2** city central Spain SW of Madrid

To·lu·ca \tə-ˈlü-kə\ city central Mexico, capital of Mexico state

Tol'·yat·ti *or* **To·gliat·ti** \tȯl-ˈyät-ē\ *or formerly* **Stav·ro·pol** \stav-ˈrȯ-pəl, -ˈrō-\ city Russia in Europe, NW of Samara

Tombouctou — see TIMBUKTU

Tombstone city SE corner of Arizona

Tomsk \ˈtämsk, ˈtämpsk, ˈtȯmsk, ˈtȯmpsk\ city S central Russia in Asia

Ton·ga \ˈtäŋ-gə, ˈtäŋ-ə\ islands SW Pacific E of Fiji Islands; a kingdom; capital, Nukualofa — **Ton·gan** \-gən, -ən\ *adj or n*

Tong·hua *or* **T'ung–hua** \ˈtȯŋ-ˈhwä, -ˈwä\ city NE China in SW Jilin

Ton·kin, Gulf of \ˈtäŋ-kən\ arm of South China Sea E of N Vietnam

To·pe·ka \tə-ˈpē-kə\ city, capital of Kansas

Tor·bay \tȯr-ˈbā, ˈtȯr-\ town SW England on **Tor Bay** (inlet of English Channel)

Tor·faen \ˈtȯr-ˌvīn\ administrative area SE Wales

Torino — see TURIN

To·ron·to \tə-ˈränt-ō, -ˈränt-ə\ city, capital of Ontario

Tor·rance \ˈtȯr-əns, ˈtär-\ city SW California SSW of Los Angeles

Tor·re·ón \ˌtȯr-ē-ˈōn\ city N Mexico in SW Coahuila

Tor·res \ˈtȯr-əs\ strait between New Guinea & Cape York Peninsula, Australia

Tor·tu·ga \tȯr-ˈtü-gə\ island Haiti off N coast; a stronghold of pirates in 17th century

To·ruń \ˈtȯr-ˌün-yə, -ˌün\ city N Poland on the Vistula

Toscana — see TUSCANY

Tou·lon \tü-ˈlō^{n}\ city SE France ESE of Marseille

Tou·louse \tu̇-ˈlüz\ city S France on the Garonne

Tou·raine \tu̇-ˈrān, -ˈren\ region NW central France; chief city **Tours** \ˈtu̇r\

Tourane — see DA NANG

Tow·er Hamlets \ˈtau̇-ər-, ˈtau̇r-\ borough of E Greater London, England

To·ya·ma \tō-ˈyäm-ə\ city Japan in W central Honshu

To·yo·ha·shi \ˌtȯi-ə-ˈhäsh-ē\ city Japan in S Honshu

To·yo·na·ka \ˌtȯi-ə-ˈnä-kə\ city Japan on S Honshu

To·yo·ta \tȯi-ˈōt-ə\ city Japan on S Honshu

Tra·fal·gar, Cape \trə-ˈfal-gər, *Spanish* ˌträ-fäl-ˈgär\ headland SW Spain at W end of Strait of Gibraltar

Trans·al·pine Gaul \trans-ˌal-ˌpīn-, tranz-\ the part of Gaul included in modern France & Belgium

Transjordan — see JORDAN

Trans·vaal \trans-ˈväl, tranz-\ former province NE Republic of South Africa between Vaal & Limpopo rivers; capital, Pretoria

Tran·syl·va·nia \ˌtrans-əl-ˈvā-nyə, -nē-ə\ region W Romania — **Tran·syl·va·nian** \-nyən, -nē-ən\ *adj or n*

Transylvanian Alps a S extension of Carpathian Mountains in central Romania

Treb·i·zond \ˈtreb-ə-ˌzänd\ Greek empire 1204–1461, an offshoot of Byzantine Empire; at greatest extent included Crimea, Georgia, & N coast of Black Sea E of Sakarya River; capital, Trebizond (modern Trabon, in Turkey)

Tren·ti·no–Al·to Adi·ge \tren-ˈtē-ˌnō-ˌäl-ˌtō-ˈäd-i-ˌjā\ region N Italy; capital, **Tren·to** \ˈtren-ˌtō\

Tren·ton \ˈtrent-n\ city, capital of New Jersey

Trier \ˈtriər\ *or* **Treves** \ˈtrēvz\ city SW Germany on the Moselle

Tri·este \trē-ˈest, trē-ˈes-tē\ city NE Italy on the Adriatic

Trin·i·dad \ˈtrin-ə-ˌdad\ island West Indies off NE coast of Venezuela; with Tobago forms (since 1962) the country of **Trinidad and Tobago**; capital, Port of Spain — **Trin·i·da·di·an** \ˌtrin-ə-ˈdād-ē-ən, -ˈdad-\ *adj or n*

Trip·o·li \ˈtrip-ə-lē\ **1** city, capital of Libya **2** city NW Lebanon NNE of Beirut **3** Tripolitania when it was one of the Barbary States

Tri·pol·i·ta·nia \trip-ˌäl-ə-ˈtān-yə, ˌtrip-ə-lə-\ region NW Libya; chief city, Tripoli

\ə\ **abut**	\au̇\ **out**	\i\ **tip**	\ȯ\ **saw**	\u̇\ **foot**
\ər\ **further**	\ch\ **chin**	\ī\ **life**	\ȯi\ **coin**	\y\ **yet**
\a\ **mat**	\e\ **pet**	\j\ **job**	\th\ **thin**	\yü\ **few**
\ā\ **take**	\ē\ **easy**	\ŋ\ **sing**	\t͟h\ **this**	\yu̇\ **cure**
\ä\ **cot, cart**	\g\ **go**	\ō\ **bone**	\ü\ **food**	\zh\ **vision**

Tri·pu·ra \'trip-ə-rə\ state [E] India between Bangladesh & Assam; capital, Agartala
Tris·tan da Cu·nha \ˌtris-tən-də-'kü-nə\ island South Atlantic, chief of the Tristan da Cunha Islands (a dependency of the British colony of Saint Helena)
Tri·van·drum \triv-'an-drəm\ city [S] India [NW] of Cape Comorin, capital of Kerala
Tro·as \'trō-ˌas\ *or* **Tro·ad** \-ˌad\ territory surrounding ancient city of Troy in [NW] Mysia
Tro·bri·and \'trō-brē-ˌänd\ islands [SW] Pacific in Solomon Sea belonging to Papua New Guinea
Trond·heim \'trän-ˌhām\ city & port central Norway
Troy \'trȯi\ *or* **Il·i·um** \'il-ē-əm\ *or ancient* **Troja** \'trō-jə, -yə\ ancient city [NW] Asia Minor [SW] of the Dardanelles
Trucial States *or* **Trucial Oman** — see UNITED ARAB EMIRATES
Tru·ji·llo \trü-'hē-ō, -yō\ city [NW] Peru [NW] of Lima
Truk — see CHUUK
Tsaritsyn — see VOLGOGRAD
Tshwa·ne \'chwä-nā\ municipality Republic of South Africa including the city of Pretoria
Tsinan — see JINAN
Tsinghai — see QINGHAI
Tsingtao — see QINGDAO
Tu·a·mo·tu \ˌtü-ə-'mō-tü\ archipelago South Pacific in French Polynesia [E] of Society Islands
Tu·buai \tüb-'wä-ē\ *or* **Aus·tral** \'ȯs-trəl, 'äs-\ islands South Pacific in French Polynesia [S] of Tahiti
Tuc·son \tü-'sän, 'tü-ˌ\ city [SE] Arizona
Tucumán — see SAN MIGUEL DE TUCUMÁN
Tuk·tut No·gait National Park \'tu̇k-ˌtət-'näg-ˌgīd\ reservation [N] Northwest Territories on Nunavut border
Tu·la \'tü-lə\ city [W] Russia in Europe, [S] of Moscow
Tul·sa \'təl-sə\ city [NE] Oklahoma on Arkansas River
T'ung–hua — see TONGHUA
Tu·nis \'tü-nəs, 'tyü-\ **1** city, capital of Tunisia **2** Tunisia especially as one of the former Barbary States — **Tu·ni·sian** \tü-'nē-zhən, tyü-, -zhē-ən; -'nizh-ən, -ē-ən\ *adj or n*
Tu·ni·sia \tü-'nē-zhə, tyü-, -zhē-ə; -'nizh-ə, -ē-ə\ country [N] Africa on the Mediterranean [E] of Algeria; capital, Tunis — **Tu·nisian** \-zhən, -zhē-ən; -ən, -ē-ən\ *adj or n*
Tu·rin \'tu̇r-ən, 'tyu̇r-; tu̇-'rin, tyu̇-\ *or Italian* **To·ri·no** \tō-'rē-nō\ city [NW] Italy on the Po, capital of Piedmont
Tur·kana, Lake \tər-'kan-ə\ *or* **Lake Ru·dolf** \'rü-ˌdȯlf, -ˌdälf\ lake [N] Kenya in Great Rift Valley
Tur·key \'tər-kē\ country [W] Asia & [SE] Europe between Mediterranean & Black seas; capital, Ankara
Turk·men·i·stan \ˌtərk-'men-ə-ˌstan\ country central Asia bordering on Afghanistan, Iran, & Caspian Sea; capital, Ashgabat; a constituent republic (**Turk·men Soviet Socialist Republic** \ˌtərk-mən\ ) of U.S.S.R. 1925–91 — **Turk·me·ni·an** \ˌtərk-'mē-nē-ən\ *adj*
Turks and Cai·cos \ˌtərk-sən-'kā-kəs\ two groups of islands (Turks Islands & Caicos Islands) British West Indies at [SE] end of Bahamas; a British colony
Tur·ku \'tu̇r-kü\ city & port [SW] Finland
Tus·ca·ny \'təs-kə-nē\ *or Italian* **To·sca·na** \tō-'skän-ə\ region [NW] central Italy; capital, Florence
Tu·tu·ila \ˌtüt-ə-'wē-lə\ island South Pacific, chief of American Samoa group
Tu·va·lu \tü-'väl-ü, -'vär-\ *or formerly* **El·lice** \'el-əs\ islands [W] Pacific [N] of Fiji; an independent country; capital, Funafuti — see GILBERT
Tver' \'tver\ *or 1932–90* **Ka·li·nin** \kä-'lē-nin\ city Russia in Europe on the Volga
Twin Cities the cities of Minneapolis & Saint Paul, Minnesota
Tyne and Wear \'tī-nən-'dwiər, -'wiər\ metropolitan county [N] England; includes Newcastle upon Tyne
Tyre \'tīər\ ancient city, capital of Phoenicia; now a town of [S] Lebanon — **Tyr·i·an** \'tir-ē-ən\ *adj or n*
Tyrol — see TIROL
Ty·rone \tir-'ōn\ traditional county [W] central Northern Ireland
Tyr·rhe·ni·an Sea \tə-'rē-nē-ən\ part of the Mediterranean [SW] of Italy, [N] of Sicily, & [E] of Sardinia & Corsica
Tyu·men \tyü-'men\ city [W] Russia in Asia, [ENE] of Yekaterinburg
Tzu–kung — see ZIGONG
Tzu–po — see ZIBO
Ubangi–Shari — see CENTRAL AFRICAN REPUBLIC
Uca·ya·li \ˌü-kä-'yäl-ē\ river about 1000 miles (1609 kilometers) long central & [N] Peru
Udi·ne \'üd-i-ˌnā\ city [NE] Italy [NE] of Venice
Ufa \ü-'fä\ city [E] Russia in Europe, [NE] of Samara
Ugan·da \yü-'gan-də, -'gän-, -'gän-\ country [E] Africa [N] of Lake Victoria; capital, Kampala — **Ugan·dan** \-dən\ *adj or n*
Ujung Pandang — see MAKASSAR 2
Uk·ku·sik·sa·lik National Park \ˌü-kü-'sik-sə-lik\ reservation [E] mainland portion of Nunavut, Canada
Ukraine \yü-'krān, 'yü-ˌ\ country [E] Europe on [N] coast of Black Sea; capital, Kiev; a constituent republic of U.S.S.R. 1923–91
Ulaan·baa·tar *or* **Ulan Ba·tor** \ˌü-ˌlän-'bä-ˌtȯr\ *or formerly* **Ur·ga** \'u̇r-gə\ city, capital of Mongolia
Ulan–Ude \ˌü-ˌlän-u̇-'dā\ city [S] Russia in Asia, [E] of Lake Baikal
Ul·san \'ül-'sän\ city [SE] South Korea
Ul·ster \'əl-stər\ **1** region [N] Ireland (island) comprising Northern Ireland & [N] Ireland (republic); a province until 1921 **2** province [N] Ireland (republic) comprising counties Donegal, Cavan, & Monaghan **3** NORTHERN IRELAND
Ulu·ru \ü-'lü-rü\ *or* **Ayers Rock** \'erz\ outcrop central Australia in [SW] Northern Territory
Ulyanovsk — see SIMBIRSK
Um·bria \'əm-brē-ə\ region central Italy in the Apennines; capital, Perugia — **Um·bri·an** \-brē-ən\ *adj or n*
Un·ga·va \ˌən-'gav-ə\ **1** bay inlet of Hudson Strait [NE] Canada **2** peninsula region [NE] Canada in [N] Quebec
Union of South Africa — see SOUTH AFRICA (Republic of)
Union of Soviet Socialist Republics *or* **Soviet Union** *or* **Soviet Russia** country (1922–91) [E] Europe & [N] Asia; a union of 15 constituent republics; capital, Moscow
United Arab Emirates *or formerly* **Tru·cial States** \'trü-shəl\ *or* **Trucial Oman** country [E] Arabia on Persian Gulf; a federation of seven emirates; capital, Abu Dhabi
United Arab Republic former name (1961–71) of Egypt & previously (1958–61) of union of Egypt & Syria
United Kingdom *or in full* **United Kingdom of Great Britain and Northern Ireland** country [W] Europe in British Isles comprising England, Scotland, Wales, Northern Ireland, Channel Islands, & Isle of Man; capital, London
United Nations political organization established 1945 with headquarters (international territory) within New York City in [E] central Manhattan
United States of America *or* **United States** country North America bordering on North Atlantic, North Pacific, & Arctic oceans & including Hawaii; a federal republic; capital, Washington
Upper Canada former province, Canada in [S] part of present-day Ontario
Upper Volta — see BURKINA FASO
Ural \'yu̇r-əl\ **1** mountains [W] central Russia extending about 1640 miles (2640 kilometers) [S] from point near Kara Sea; usually considered to be dividing line between Europe & Asia; highest 6214 feet (1894 meters) **2** river over 1500 feet (2414 kilometers) long Russia flowing from [S] end of Ural Mountains into Caspian Sea
Uralsk \yu̇-'ralsk\ — see ORAL
Ura·wa \u̇-'rä-wə\ city Japan in central Honshu [N] of Tokyo
Uru·guay \'u̇r-ə-ˌgwī, 'yu̇r-; 'yu̇r-ə-ˌgwā\ **1** river about 1000 miles (1609 kilometers) long [SE] South America rising in Brazil & flowing into Río de la Plata **2** country [SE] South America; capital, Montevideo — **Uru·guay·an** \ˌu̇r-ə-'gwī-ən, ˌyu̇r-; ˌyu̇r-ə-'gwā-\ *adj or n*
Ürüm·qi \'ē-'rēm-'chē\ *or* **Urum·chi** \u̇-'ru̇m-chē, ˌu̇r-əm-'chē\ *or* **Wu–lu–mu–ch'i** \'wü-'lü-'mü-'chē\ city [NW] China, capital of Xinjiang Uygur
Urundi — see BURUNDI
Us·pa·lla·ta \ˌü-spə-'yät-ə, -'zhät-\ mountain pass 12,572 feet (3832 meters) [S] South America in the Andes between Argentina & Chile
Usumbura — see BUJUMBURA
Utah \'yü-ˌtȯ, -ˌtä\ state [W] U.S.; capital, Salt Lake City — **Utah·an** \'yü-ˌtȯ-ən, -ˌtȯn, -ˌtä-ən, -ˌtän\ *adj or n* — **Utahn** \-ˌtȯ-ən, -ˌtȯn, -ˌtä-ən, -ˌtän\ *n*
Utrecht \'yü-ˌtrekt\ city central Netherlands
Utsu·no·mi·ya \ˌüt-sə-'nō-mē-ˌä, -ˌyä\ city Japan in central Honshu [N] of Tokyo
Ut·ta·ra·khand \'ü-tä-rä-ˌkänd\ *or formerly* **Ut·ta·ran·chal** \'u̇t-ə-ˌrän-chəl\ state [N] India; capital Dehra Dun

Ut·tar Pra·desh \ˌu̇t-ər-prə-ˈdesh, -ˈdāsh\ state [N] India bordering on Tibet & Nepal; capital, Lucknow

Uz·bek·i·stan \u̇z-ˌbek-i-ˈstan, ˌəz-, -ˈstän\ country [W] central Asia between Aral Sea & Afghanistan; capital, Tashkent; a constituent republic (**Uz·bek Soviet Socialist Republic** \ˈu̇z-ˌbek, ˈəz-, u̇z-ˈ\) of U.S.S.R. 1924–91

Va·do·da·ra \və-ˈdō-də-ˌrä\ *or* **Ba·ro·da** \bə-ˈrō-də\ city [W] India in [SE] Gujarat

Va·duz \vä-ˈdüts\ town, capital of Liechtenstein

Va·len·cia \və-ˈlen-chə, -chē-ə, -ˈlen-sē-ə\ **1** region & ancient kingdom [E] Spain between Andalusia & Catalonia **2** city, its capital, on the Mediterranean **3** city [N] Venezuela [WSW] of Caracas

Val·la·do·lid \ˌval-əd-ə-ˈlid, -ˈlē\ city [NW] central Spain

Val·le d'Ao·sta \ˌväl-ā-dä-ˈös-tə\ region [NW] Italy bordering on France & Switzerland; capital, Aosta

Val·le·jo \və-ˈlā-ō\ city [W] California

Val·let·ta \və-ˈlet-ə\ city, capital of Malta

Val·pa·rai·so \ˌval-pə-ˈrī-zō, -ˈrā-\ *or Spanish* **Val·pa·ra·í·so** \ˌväl-pä-rä-ˈē-sō\ city, legislative capital of Chile

Van·cou·ver \van-ˈkü-vər\ **1** city [SW] Washington on Columbia River opposite Portland, Oregon **2** island [W] Canada in [SW] British Columbia **3** city [SW] British Columbia

Van Diemen's Land — see TASMANIA

Va·nu·a·tu \ˌvä-nü-ˈä-ˌtü\ *or formerly* **New Heb·ri·des** \-ˈheb-rə-ˌdēz\ islands [SW] Pacific [W] of Fiji; an independent republic; capital, Port-Vila

Va·ra·na·si \və-ˈrän-ə-sē\ city [N] India in [SE] Uttar Pradesh

Var·na \ˈvär-nə\ city & port [E] Bulgaria on Black Sea

Vat·i·can City \ˌvat-i-kən\ *or Italian* **Cit·tà del Va·ti·ca·no** \chēt-ˈtä-del-ˌvä-tē-ˈkä-nō\ independent papal state within city of Rome, Italy; created 1929

Vaughan \ˈvȯn, ˈvän\ city [SE] Ontario

Ve·ne·to \ˈven-ə-ˌtō, ˈvā-nə-\ region [NE] Italy; capital, Venice

Ven·e·zu·e·la \ˌven-əz-ə-ˈwā-lə, -əz-ˈwā-, -ˈwē-\ country [N] South America; capital, Caracas — **Ven·e·zu·e·lan** \-lən\ *adj or n*

Ven·ice \ˈven-əs\ *or Italian* **Ve·ne·zia** \və-ˈnet-sē-ə\ city [N] Italy on islands in Lagoon of Venice — **Ve·ne·tian** \və-ˈnē-shən\ *adj or n*

Ven·tu·ra \ven-ˈtu̇r-ə, -ˈtyu̇r-\ *or officially* **San Buen·a·ven·tu·ra** \ˌsan-ˌbwen-ə-ven-\ city & port [SW] California

Ve·ra·cruz \ˌver-ə-ˈkrüz, -ˈkrüs\ **1** state [E] Mexico; capital, Xalapa **2** city [E] Mexico in Veracruz state on Gulf of Mexico

Verde, Cape \ˈvərd\ *or* **Cape Vert** \ˈvərt\ promontory [W] Africa in Senegal; most westerly point of Africa

Ver·ee·ni·ging \fə-ˈrā-nə-ging, -nə-k̲ang\ city [NE] Republic of South Africa [S] of Johannesburg

Ver·mont \vər-ˈmänt\ state [NE] U.S.; capital, Montpelier — **Ver·mont·er** \-ər\ *n*

Ve·ro·na \və-ˈrō-nə\ city [N] Italy [W] of Venice

Ver·sailles \ˌvər-ˈsī, ver-\ city [N] France; suburb of Paris

Ve·su·vi·us \və-ˈsü-vē-əs\ volcano 4190 feet (1277 meters) [S] Italy near Bay of Naples

Vi·cen·te Ló·pez \və-ˌsent-ə-ˈlō-ˌpez\ city [E] Argentina

Vi·cen·za \vi-ˈchen-sə\ city [NE] Italy [W] of Venice

Vic·to·ria \vik-ˈtōr-ē-ə, -ˈtȯr-\ **1** city, capital of British Columbia on Vancouver Island **2** island [N] Canada in Arctic Archipelago [S] of Melville Sound; split between Northwest Territories & Nunavut **3** state [SE] Australia; capital, Melbourne **4** city & port Hong Kong — **Vic·to·ri·an** \-ē-ən\ *adj or n*

Victoria, Lake lake [E] Africa in Tanzania, Kenya, & Uganda

Victoria Falls waterfall 355 feet (108 meters) high [S] Africa in the Zambezi on border between Zambia & Zimbabwe

Victoria Nile — see NILE

Vi·en·na \vē-ˈen-ə\ *or German* **Wien** \ˈvēn\ city, capital of Austria on the Danube — **Vi·en·nese** \ˌvē-ə-ˈnēz, -ˈnēs\ *adj or n*

Vien·tiane \vyen-ˈtyän\ city, capital of Laos

Vie·ques \vē-ˈā-käs\ island Puerto Rico off [E] coast of main island

Viet·nam \vē-ˈet-ˈnäm, vyet-, ˌvē-ət-, vēt-, -ˈnam\ country [SE] Asia in Indochina; capital, Hanoi; established 1945–46 & divided 1954–75 at 17th parallel into republics of **North Vietnam** (capital, Hanoi) & **South Vietnam** (capital, Saigon)

Vi·go \ˈvē-ˌgō\ city & port [NW] Spain on **Vigo Bay** (inlet of North Atlantic)

Vi·ja·ya·wa·da \ˌvij-ə-yə-ˈwäd-ə\ *or formerly* **Bez·wa·da** \bez-ˈwäd-ə\ city [SE] India in [E] Andhra Pradesh

Vila — see PORT-VILA

Vil·ni·us \ˈvil-nē-əs\ *or Polish* **Wil·no** \ˈvil-nō\ *or Russian* **Vil·na** \ˈvil-nə\ *or* **Vil·no** \-nō\ city, capital of Lithuania

Vin·land \ˈvin-lənd\ a portion of [E] coast of North America visited & so called by Norse voyagers about 1000 A.D.; perhaps Newfoundland

Vin·ny·tsya *or* **Vin·ni·tsa** \ˈvin-ət-syə\ city [W] central Ukraine

Vin·son Massif \ˈvin-sən\ mountain 16,066 feet (4897 meters) [W] Antarctica in Ellsworth Mountains; highest in Antarctica

Vir·gin·ia \vər-ˈjin-yə, -ˈjin-ē-ə\ state [E] U.S.; capital, Richmond — **Vir·gin·ian** \-yən, -ē-ən\ *adj or n*

Virginia Beach city [SE] Virginia on North Atlantic

Vir·gin Islands \ˌvər-jən\ island group West Indies [E] of Puerto Rico — see BRITISH VIRGIN ISLANDS, VIRGIN ISLANDS OF THE UNITED STATES

Virgin Islands National Park reservation Saint John, Virgin Islands of the United States

Virgin Islands of the United States the [W] islands of the Virgin Islands group including Saint Croix, Saint John, & Saint Thomas; capital, Charlotte Amalie (on Saint Thomas)

Vi·sa·yan \və-ˈsī-ən\ *or* **Bi·sa·yas** \bə-ˈsī-əz\ islands central Philippines including Bohol, Cebu, Leyte, Masbate, Negros, Panay, & Samar

Vish·a·kha·pat·nam \vish-ˌäk-ə-ˈpət-nəm\ city & port [E] India in Andhra Pradesh

Vis·tu·la \ˈvis-chə-lə, ˈvish-; ˈvis-tə-lə\ *or Polish* **Wis·la** \ˈvē-slä\ river over 660 miles (1062 kilometers) long Poland flowing [N] from the Carpathians into Gulf of Danzig

Vi·ti Le·vu \ˌvēt-ē-ˈlev-ü\ island [SW] Pacific; largest of the Fiji group

Vi·to·ria \vi-ˈtōr-ē-ə, -ˈtȯr-\ *or* **Gas·teiz** \ˈgäsh-ˌtās\ city [N] Spain

Vi·tó·ria \vi-ˈtōr-ē-ə, -ˈtȯr-\ city [E] Brazil [NE] of Rio de Janeiro

Vit·syebsk \ˈvēts-yipsk\ *or* **Vi·tebsk** \ˈvē-ˌtipsk\ city [NE] Belarus

Vlad·i·kav·kaz \ˌvlad-ə-ˌkäf-ˈkäz, -ˈkaz\ *or 1932–43 & 1955–91* **Or·dzho·ni·kid·ze** \ˌȯr-ˌjän-ə-ˈkid-zə\ *or 1944–54* **Dzau·dzhi·kau** \dzau̇-ˈjē-ˌkau̇, zau̇-\ city [S] Russia in Europe, in the Caucasus

Vlad·i·vos·tok \ˌvlad-ə-və-ˈstäk, -ˈväs-ˌtäk\ city [SE] Russia in Asia at the tip of a peninsula

Voj·vo·dina \ˈvȯi-vȯ-ˌdē-nä\ province [N] Serbia

Volcano Islands *or* **Ka·zan Ret·to** \ˌkäz-ˌän-ˈret-ō\ island chain Japan in [W] Pacific [S] of Bonin Islands — see IWO JIMA

Vol·ga \ˈväl-gə, ˈvȯl-, ˈvōl-\ river 2293 miles (3689 kilometers) long [W] Russia flowing into Caspian Sea

Vol·go·grad \ˈväl-gə-ˌgrad, ˈvȯl-, ˈvōl-\ *or formerly* **Sta·lin·grad** \ˈstäl-ən-ˌgrad, ˈstal-\ *or earlier* **Tsa·ri·tsyn** \tsə-ˈrēt-sən, sə-\ city [S] Russia in Europe, on the Volga

Vol·ta \ˈväl-tə, ˈvōl-, ˈvȯl-\ river Ghana flowing into Bight of Benin and including **Lake Volta** (reservoir)

Vo·ro·nezh \və-ˈrō-nish\ city [SW] Russia in Europe, near Don River

Vo·ro·shi·lov·grad \ˌvȯr-ə-ˈshē-ləf-ˌgrad, ˌvär-, -ləv-\ city [E] Ukraine in Donets Basin

Vosges \ˈvōzh\ mountains [NE] France on [W] side of valley of the Rhine; highest 4672 feet (1424 meters)

Voy·a·geurs National Park \ˌvȯi-ə-ˈzhərz\ reservation [N] Minnesota on Canadian border

Vun·tut National Park \ˈvün-ˌtüt\ reservation [NW] Yukon on Alaska border

Vyatka — see KIROV

Wad·den·zee \ˌväd-n-ˈzā\ inlet of North Sea [N] Netherlands

Wai·ki·ki \ˌwī-ki-ˈkē\ resort section of Honolulu, Hawaii

Wa·ka·ya·ma \ˌwäk-ə-ˈyäm-ə\ city Japan in [SW] Honshu [SW] of Osaka

Wake \ˈwāk\ island North Pacific [N] of Marshall Islands; U.S. territory

Wa·la·chia *or* **Wal·la·chia** \wä-ˈlā-kē-ə\ region [S] Romania between Transylvanian Alps & the Danube

Wales \ˈwālz\ *or Welsh* **Cym·ru** \ˈkəm-rē\ *or Latin* **Cambria** principality [SW] Great Britain; a division of United Kingdom; capital, Cardiff

Wal·la·sey \ˈwäl-ə-sē\ town [NW] England on Irish Sea

Wal·lis and Fu·tu·na Islands \ˈwäl-əs-ənd-fü-ˈtü-nä\ French overseas territory [SW] Pacific [NE] of Fiji

\ə\ **abut**	\au̇\ **out**	\i\ **tip**	\ȯ\ **saw**	\u̇\ **foot**
\ər\ **further**	\ch\ **chin**	\ī\ **life**	\ȯi\ **coin**	\y\ **yet**
\a\ **mat**	\e\ **pet**	\j\ **job**	\th\ **thin**	\yü\ **few**
\ā\ **take**	\ē\ **easy**	\ng\ **sing**	\th̲\ **this**	\yu̇\ **cure**
\ä\ **cot, cart**	\g\ **go**	\ō\ **bone**	\ü\ **food**	\zh\ **vision**

Wal·lo·nia \wä-ˈlō-nē-ə\ semiautonomous region [S] Belgium
Wal·sall \ˈwȯl-ˌsȯl, -səl\ town [W] central England [NNW] of Birmingham
Wal·tham Forest \ˌwȯl-thəm-\ borough of [NE] Greater London, England
Wands·worth \ˈwändz-wərth, ˈwänz-\ borough of [SW] Greater London, England
Wan·ne–Eick·el \ˌvän-ə-ˈī-kəl\ city [W] Germany in the Ruhr
Wa·pusk National Park \ˈwä-ˌpu̇sk\ reservation [NE] Manitoba bordering Hudson Bay
War·ley \ˈwȯr-lē\ town [W] central England; a suburb of Birmingham
War·ren \ˈwȯr-ən, ˈwär-\ city [SE] Michigan [N] of Detroit
War·saw \ˈwȯr-ˌsȯ\ *or Polish* **War·sza·wa** \vär-ˈshäv-ə\ city, capital of Poland
War·wick·shire \ˈwär-ik-ˌshiər, -shər\ *or* **Warwick** county central England
Wa·satch \ˈwȯ-ˌsach\ range of the Rockies [SE] Idaho & [N] central Utah; highest Mount Timpanogos 12,008 feet or 3660 meters (in Utah)
Wash·ing·ton \ˈwȯsh-ing-tən, ˈwäsh-\ **1** state [NW] U.S.; capital, Olympia **2** city, capital of U.S.; coextensive with District of Columbia and collectively referred to as **Washington, D.C.** — **Wash·ing·to·nian** \ˌwȯsh-ing-ˈtō-nē-ən, ˌwäsh-, -nyən\ *adj or n*
Washington, Mount mountain 6288 feet (1916 meters) [N] New Hampshire; highest in White Mountains
Wa·ter·bury \ˈwȯt-ər-ˌber-ē, ˈwȯt-ə-, ˈwät-\ city [W] central Connecticut
Wa·ter·ford \ˈwȯt-ər-fərd, ˈwät-\ county [S] Ireland in Munster
Wa·ter·ton–Glacier International Peace Park \ˈwȯt-ər-tən-, ˈwät-\ international park, comprising **Waterton Lakes National Park** in [S] Alberta, and **Glacier National Park** in [NW] Montana
Watlings — see SAN SALVADOR
Wed·dell Sea \wə-ˈdel, ˈwed-l\ arm of the South Atlantic [E] of Antarctic Peninsula
Wei·mar Republic \ˈvī-ˌmär, ˈwī-\ the German republic 1919–33
Wel·land \ˈwel-ənd\ canal 27 miles (44 kilometers) long [SE] Ontario connecting Lake Erie & Lake Ontario
Wel·ling·ton \ˈwel-ing-tən\ city, capital of New Zealand in [SW] North Island
Wes·sex \ˈwes-iks\ ancient Anglian kingdom [S] England; capital, Winchester
West Australian Current warm ocean current flowing [N] off [W] coast of Australia
West Bank area Middle East [W] of Jordan River
West Bengal state [E] India; capital, Calcutta
West Brom·wich \ˈbrəm-ij, ˈbräm-, -ich\ town [W] central England [NW] of Birmingham
West Co·vi·na \kō-ˈvē-nə\ city [SW] California
West Dunbartonshire administrative area [W] Scotland
Western Australia state [W] Australia; capital, Perth
Western Cape province [SW] Republic of South Africa
Western Ghats \ˈgȯts\ chain of low mountains [SW] India
Western Isles *or* **Ei·lean Siar** \ˈel-ən-ˈshēər\ the Outer Hebrides constituting an administrative area of [W] Scotland
Western Sahara *or formerly* **Spanish Sahara** region [NW] Africa divided 1975 between Mauritania which gave up its claim in 1979 & Morocco which thereafter occupied the entire territory
Western Samoa — see SAMOA
West Germany the former Federal Republic of Germany — see GERMANY
West Indies islands lying between [SE] North America & [N] South America & comprising the Greater Antilles, Lesser Antilles, & Bahamas — **West Indian** *adj or n*
West Lothian administrative area [S] Scotland
West·meath \west-ˈmēth, wes-, -ˈmēth\ county [E] central Ireland in Leinster
West Midlands metropolitan county [W] central England
West·min·ster \ˈwest-ˌmin-stər\ **1** city [N] central Colorado [NW] of Denver **2** *or* **City of Westminster** borough of [W] central Greater London, England
West Pakistan the former [W] division of Pakistan now coextensive with Pakistan
West·pha·lia \west-ˈfāl-yə, -ˈfā-lē-ə, wes-\ region [NW] Germany [E] of the Rhine; now part of North Rhine-Westphalia — **Westpha·lian** \-ˈfāl-yən, -ˈfā-lē-ən\ *adj or n*
West Punjab — see PUNJAB 3
West Quod·dy Head \ˌkwäd-ē\ cape; most easterly point of Maine & of the Lower 48
West Sus·sex \ˈsəs-iks\ county [SE] England
West Valley City city [N] Utah [S] of Salt Lake City
West Virginia state [E] U.S.; capital, Charleston — **West Virginian** *adj or n*
West York·shire \ˈyȯrk-ˌshiər, -shər\ metropolitan county [NW] England
Wex·ford \ˈweks-fərd\ county [SE] Ireland in Leinster
White mountains [N] New Hampshire in the Appalachians — see WASHINGTON (Mount)
White·horse \ˈhwīt-ˌhȯrs, ˈwīt-\ city [NW] Canada, capital of Yukon
White Nile — see NILE
White Sea *or* **Be·lo·ye Mo·re** \ˌbel-ə-yə-ˈmȯr-yə\ inlet of Barents Sea [NW] Russia
Whit·ney, Mount \ˈhwit-nē, ˈwit-\ mountain 14,495 feet (4418 meters) [SE] central California in Sierra Nevada in Sequoia National Park; highest in U.S. outside of Alaska
Wich·i·ta \ˈwich-ə-ˌtȯ\ city [S] central Kansas on Arkansas River
Wichita Falls city [N] Texas
Wick·low \ˈwik-lō\ county [E] Ireland in Leinster
Wien — see VIENNA
Wies·ba·den \ˈvēs-ˌbäd-n, ˈvis-\ city [W] Germany on the Rhine [W] of Frankfurt, capital of Hesse
Wight, Isle of \ˈwīt\ island [S] England in English Channel
Wil·helms·ha·ven \ˌvil-ˌhelmz-ˈhäf-ən, ˈvil-əmz-ˌ\ city [NW] Germany [NW] of Bremen
Wil·lem·stad \ˈvil-əm-ˌstät\ city on Curaçao Island; formerly capital of Netherlands Antilles
Wil·liams·burg \ˈwil-yəmz-ˌbərg\ city [SE] Virginia; capital of Virginia 1699–1780; site of a restoration of the Colonial town
Wil·ming·ton \ˈwil-ming-tən\ city [N] Delaware; largest in state
Wilno — see VILNIUS
Wilt·shire \ˈwilt-ˌshiər, ˈwil-chər, ˈwilt-shər\ county [S] England
Wim·ble·don \ˈwim-bəl-dən\ section of Merton in Greater London, England
Wind Cave National Park reservation [SW] South Dakota in Black Hills
Win·der·mere \ˈwin-dər-ˌmiər, -də-\ lake [NW] England in Lake District
Wind·hoek \ˈvint-ˌhu̇k\ city, capital of Namibia
Wind·sor \ˈwin-zər\ city [S] Ontario on Detroit River
Wind·ward \ˈwin-dwərd\ islands West Indies in the [S] Lesser Antilles extending [S] from Martinique but not including Barbados, Tobago, or Trinidad
Win·ni·peg \ˈwin-ə-ˌpeg\ city, capital of Manitoba
Winnipeg, Lake lake [S] central Manitoba
Win·ni·pe·sau·kee, Lake \ˌwin-ə-pə-ˈsȯ-kē\ lake central New Hampshire
Win·ston–Sa·lem \ˌwin-stən-ˈsā-ləm\ city [N] central North Carolina
Wis·con·sin \wis-ˈkän-sən\ state [N] central U.S.; capital, Madison — **Wis·con·sin·ite** \-sə-ˌnīt\ *n*
Wisla — see VISTULA
Wit·wa·ters·rand \ˈwit-ˌwȯt-ərz-ˌrand, -ˌwät-, -ˌränd, -ˌränt\ *or* **Rand** \ˈrand, ˈränd, ˈränt\ ridge of gold-bearing rock [NE] Republic of South Africa
Wol·lon·gong \ˈwu̇l-ən-ˌgäng, -ˌgȯng\ city [SE] Australia in [E] New South Wales [S] of Sydney
Wol·ver·hamp·ton \ˈwu̇l-vər-ˌham-tən, -ˌhamp-\ town [W] central England [NW] of Birmingham
Won·san \ˈwən-ˌsän\ city North Korea on [E] coast
Wood Buffalo National Park reservation [N] Alberta & [SE] Northwest Territories
Worces·ter \ˈwu̇s-tər\ **1** city [E] central Massachusetts [W] of Boston **2** *or* **Worces·ter·shire** \-ˌshir, -shər\ county [W] central England
Wounded Knee locality [SW] South Dakota
Wran·gell, Mount \ˈrang-gəl\ volcano 14,163 feet (4317 meters) [S] Alaska in Wrangell Range; highest volcano in U.S.
Wrangell–Saint Eli·as National Park \-sānt-i-ˈlī-əs\ reservation [S] central Alaska [E] of Anchorage
Wrex·ham \ˈrek-səm\ administrative area [NE] Wales
Wro·claw \ˈvrȯt-ˌsläf, -ˌsläv\ *or German* **Bres·lau** \ˈbres-ˌlau̇\ city [SW] Poland in Silesia

Wu·chang \ˈwü-ˈchäŋ\ former city China — see WUHAN
Wu·han \ˈwü-ˈhän\ city [E] central China, capital of Hubei; formed from former cities of Hankow, Hanyang, & Wuchang
Wuhsien — see SUZHOU
Wu–lu–mu–ch'i — see ÜRÜMQI
Wup·per·tal \ˈvu̇p-ər-ˌtäl\ city [W] Germany in valley of the Ruhr [ENE] of Düsseldorf
Würt·tem·berg \ˈwərt-əm-ˌbərg, ˈwu̇rt-; ˈvᵫert-əm-ˌberk\ region [SW] Germany between Baden & Bavaria; chief city, Stuttgart; now part of Baden-Württemberg
Wy·o·ming \wī-ˈō-miŋ\ state [NW] U.S.; capital, Cheyenne — **Wy·o·ming·ite** \-miŋ-ˌīt\ *n*
Xa·la·pa *or* **Ja·la·pa** \hə-ˈlä-pə\ city [E] Mexico, capital of Veracruz
Xia·men *or* **Hsia–men** \shē-ˈä-ˈmən\ *or* **Amoy** \ä-ˈmȯi\ city [SE] China in [S] Fujian on two islands
Xi'·an *or* **Si·an** \ˈshē-ˈän\ *or formerly* **Chang·an** \ˈchäŋ-ˈän\ city [E] central China, capital of Shaanxi
Xianggang — see HONG KONG
Xiang·tan *or* **Hsiang–t'an** *or* **Siang·tan** \shē-ˈäŋ-ˈtän\ city [SE] China in Hunan
Xi·ning *or* **Si·ning** \ˈshē-ˈniŋ\ city [NW] China, capital of Qinghai
Xin·jiang Uy·gur *or* **Sin·kiang–Ui·ghur** \ˈshin-jē-ˈäŋ-ˈwē-gər\ region & former province [W] China; capital, Ürümqi
Xizang — see TIBET
Xu·zhou \ˈshü-ˈjō\ *or* **Hsü–chou** *or* **Sü·chow** \ˈshü-ˈjō, ˈsü-; ˈsü-ˈchau̇\ city [E] China in [NW] Jiangsu
Ya·kutsk \yə-ˈkütsk\ city [E] central Russia in Asia
Yal·ta \ˈyȯl-tə\ city & port on [S] coast of Crimea
Ya·lu \ˈyäl-ü\ *or* **Am·nok** \ˈam-ˌnäk\ river about 500 miles (804 kilometers) long [SE] Manchuria, China & North Korea flowing into Korea Bay
Ya·mous·sou·kro \ˌyä-mü-ˈsü-krō\ town central Ivory Coast, official capital of the country
Yangku — see TAIYUAN
Yan·gon \ˌyän-ˈgōn\ *or unofficially* **Ran·goon** \ran-ˈgün, raŋ-\ city, historic capital of Myanmar (Burma)
Yangtze — see CHANG
Yao \ˈyau̇\ city Japan in [S] Honshu [E] of Osaka
Yaoun·dé \yau̇n-ˈdā\ city, capital of Cameroon
Yap \ˈyap, ˈyäp\ island [W] Pacific in the [W] Carolines
Ya·ren \ˈyä-ˌren\ district of Nauru; site of government offices
Ya·ro·slavl \ˌyär-ə-ˈsläv-əl\ city central Russia in Europe, [NE] of Moscow
Ye·ka·te·rin·burg \yi-ˈkat-ə-rən-ˌbərg, yi-ˌkät-ə-rən-ˈbu̇rk\ *or 1924–91* **Sverd·lovsk** \sverd-ˈlȯfsk\ city [W] Russia in Asia, in central Ural Mountains
Yellow **1** — see HUANG **2** sea section of East China Sea between [N] China & Korea
Yel·low·knife \ˈyel-ə-ˌnīf\ town Canada, capital of Northwest Territories
Yel·low·stone National Park \ˈyel-ə-ˌstōn\ reservation [NW] Wyoming, [E] Idaho, & [S] Montana
Ye·men \ˈyem-ən\ country [S] Arabia bordering on Red Sea & Gulf of Aden; formed 1990 by merger of **Yemen Arab Republic** (capital, Sanaa) with **People's Democratic Republic of Yemen** *or* **Southern Yemen** (capital, Aden); capital, Sanaa — **Ye·me·ni** \ˈyem-ə-nē\ *adj or n* — **Ye·men·ite** \-ə-ˌnīt\ *n*
Yen·i·sey *or* **Yen·i·sei** \ˌyen-ə-ˈsā\ river over 2500 miles (4022 kilometers) long central Russia, flowing [N] into Arctic Ocean
Ye·re·van \ˌyer-ə-ˈvän\ city, capital of Armenia
Yezo — see HOKKAIDO
Yi·bin \ˈyē-ˈbēn\ *or* **I–pin** \ˈē-ˈbēn, -ˈpin\ *or formerly* **Sü·chow** \ˈshü-ˈjō, ˈsü-; ˈsü-ˈchau̇\ city central China in [S] Sichuan
Yog·ya·kar·ta \ˌyōg-yə-ˈkär-tə\ city Indonesia in [S] Java
Yo·ho National Park \ˈyō-hō\ reservation [W] Canada in [SE] British Columbia on Alberta boundary
Yo·ko·ha·ma \ˌyō-kə-ˈhäm-ə\ city Japan in [SE] Honshu on Tokyo Bay [S] of Tokyo
Yo·ko·su·ka \yō-ˈkȯ-sə-kə, -ˈkȯ-skə\ city Japan in [E] Honshu [W] of entrance to Tokyo Bay
Yon·kers \ˈyäŋ-kərz\ city [SE] New York [N] of New York City
York \ˈyȯrk\ city [N] England
York, Cape cape [NE] Australia in Queensland at [N] tip of Cape York Peninsula
Yo·sem·i·te Falls \yō-ˈsem-ət-ē\ waterfall [E] California in **Yosemite National Park** (reservation in the Sierra Nevada); includes two falls, the upper 1430 feet (436 meters) & the lower 320 feet (98 meters), connected by a series of cascades; total drop 2425 feet (739 meters)
Youngs·town \ˈyəŋ-ˌstau̇n\ city [NE] Ohio
Youth, Isle of island [W] Cuba in the Caribbean
Yssel — see IJSSEL
Yu·ca·tán \ˌyü-kə-ˈtan, -ˈtän\ **1** peninsula [SE] Mexico & [N] Central America including Belize & [N] Guatemala **2** state [SE] Mexico; capital, Mérida
Yu·go·sla·via *or earlier* **Ju·go·sla·via** \ˌyü-gō-ˈsläv-ē-ə\ **1** former country [S] Europe on the Adriatic consisting of Serbia, Montenegro, Slovenia, Croatia, Bosnia and Herzegovina, & Macedonia; capital, Belgrade **2** — see SERBIA AND MONTENEGRO — **Yu·go·slav** \ˌyü-gō-ˈsläv, -ˈslav\ *or* **Yu·go·sla·vi·an** \-ˈsläv-ē-ən\ *adj or n*
Yu·kon \ˈyü-ˌkän\ **1** river 1979 miles (3185 kilometers) long [NW] Canada & Alaska flowing into Bering Sea **2** territory [NW] Canada; capital, Whitehorse
Yun·nan \yü-ˈnän\ **1** province [SW] China bordering on Myanmar & Indochina; capital, Kunming **2** — see KUNMING
Yunnanfu — see KUNMING
Zab·rze \ˈzäb-zhā\ city [SW] Poland in Silesia
Za·ca·te·cas \ˌzak-ə-ˈtā-kəs, -ˈtek-əs\ **1** state [N] central Mexico **2** city; its capital
Zag·a·zig \ˈzag-ə-ˌzig\ city [N] Egypt [NNE] of Cairo
Za·greb \ˈzäg-ˌreb\ city, capital of Croatia
Za·he·dan \ˌzä-hi-ˈdän\ city [E] Iran
Zaire \zä-ˈiər\ **1** river in Africa — see CONGO 1 **2** country in Africa — see CONGO 2
Zam·be·zi *or* **Zam·be·si** \zam-ˈbē-zē\ river about 1700 miles (2735 kilometers) long [SE] Africa flowing from [NW] Zambia into Mozambique Channel
Zam·bia \ˈzam-bē-ə\ country [S] Africa [N] of the Zambezi; formerly the British protectorate of **Northern Rhodesia**; an independent republic since 1964; capital, Lusaka
Zam·bo·an·ga \ˌzam-bə-ˈwäŋ-gə\ city [S] Philippines in [SW] Mindanao
Zan·zi·bar \ˈzan-zə-ˌbär\ island Tanzania off [NE] Tanganyika coast; formerly a sultanate & British protectorate including also Pemba & other islands; became independent 1963; united 1964 with Tanganyika forming Tanzania
Za·po·rizh·zhya *or* **Za·po·ro·zh'ye** \ˌzäp-ə-ˈrȯ-zhə\ city [SE] Ukraine
Za·ra·go·za \ˌzar-ə-ˈgō-zə\ *or* **Sar·a·gos·sa** \ˌsar-ə-ˈgäs-ə\ city [NE] Spain in [W] Aragon
Zealand — see SJÆLLAND
Zhang·jia·kou \ˈjäŋ-jē-ˈä-ˈkō\ *or* **Ch'ang–chia–k'ou** \ˈchäŋ-jē-ˈä-ˈkō\ *or* **Kal·gan** \ˈkal-ˈgan\ city [NE] China in [NW] Hebei [NW] of Beijing
Zhang·zhou *or* **Chang–chou** \ˈjäŋ-ˈjō\ city [SE] China in [S] Fujian
Zhdanov — see MARIUPOL'
Zhe·jiang *or* **Che·kiang** \ˈjəj-ē-ˈäŋ\ province [E] China bordering on East China Sea; capital, Hangzhou
Zheng·zhou *or* **Cheng–chou** \ˈjəŋ-ˈjō\ city [NE] central China, capital of Henan
Zhen·jiang *or* **Chen–chiang** \ˈjən-jē-ˈäŋ\ city [E] China in [NW] central Jiangsu
Zhu·zhou *or* **Chu–chou** *or* **Chu·chow** \ˈjü-ˈjō\ city [SE] China in [E] Hunan
Zhy·to·myr *or* **Zhi·to·mir** \zhi-ˈtȯ-ˌmiər\ city [W] Ukraine
Zi·bo *or* **Tzu–po** \ˈdzə-ˈbō, ˈzə-\ city [E] China in central Shandong
Zi·gong *or* **Tzu–kung** *or* **Tze·kung** \ˈdzə-ˈgu̇ŋ, ˈzə-\ city [S] central China in [S] Sichuan
Zim·ba·bwe \zim-ˈbäb-wā, -wē\ *or before 1979* **Rho·de·sia** \rō-ˈdē-zhə, -zhē-ə\ *or* **Southern Rhodesia** country [S] Africa [S] of Zambezi River; capital, Harare — **Zim·ba·bwe·an** \-ən\ *adj or n*
Zi·on \ˈzī-ən\ *or* **Si·on** \ˈsī-ən\ the stronghold of Jerusalem conquered by David; site in ancient times of the Jewish Temple

\ə\ **abut**	\au̇\ **out**	\i\ **tip**	\ȯ\ **saw**	\u̇\ **foot**
\ər\ **further**	\ch\ **chin**	\ī\ **life**	\ȯi\ **coin**	\y\ **yet**
\a\ **mat**	\e\ **pet**	\j\ **job**	\th\ **thin**	\yü\ **few**
\ā\ **take**	\ē\ **easy**	\ŋ\ **sing**	\t͟h\ **this**	\yu̇\ **cure**
\ä\ **cot, cart**	\g\ **go**	\ō\ **bone**	\ü\ **food**	\zh\ **vision**

Zion National Park reservation [SW] Utah
Zla·to·ust \ˌzlät-ə-ˈüst\ city [W] Russia in Asia in the [S] Urals
Zom·ba \ˈzäm-bə\ city [S] Malawi [S] of Lake Malawi
Zui·der Zee \ˌzīd-ər-ˈzā, -ˈzē\ former inlet of North Sea [N] Netherlands; now (as IJsselmeer) partly reclaimed
Zu·lu·land \ˈzü-lü-ˌland\ territory [E] Republic of South Africa on Indian Ocean
Zu·rich \ˈzu̇r-ik\ city [N] Switzerland on **Lake of Zurich** (25 miles or 40 kilometers long)
Zwick·au \ˈtsfik-ˌau̇, ˈzwik-\ city [E] Germany [S] of Leipzig

Signs and Symbols

Astronomy

☉	the sun; Sunday
○ *or* ☽	the moon; Monday
●	new moon
☽, ◐, *or*)	first quarter
○	full moon
☾, ◑, *or* (	last quarter
☿	Mercury; Wednesday
♀	Venus; Friday
⊕ *or* ♁	Earth
♂	Mars; Tuesday
♃	Jupiter; Thursday
♄ *or* ♄	Saturn; Saturday
♅, ♅, *or* ♅	Uranus
♆, ♆, *or* ♆	Neptune
♇	Pluto
☄	comet
✱ *or* ✳	fixed star
☌	conjunction
□	quadrature
☍	opposition
	(for astrological symbols see ZODIAC table)

Biology

○	an individual, specifically, a female—used chiefly in inheritance charts
□	an individual, specifically, a male—used chiefly in inheritance charts
♀	female
♂ *or* ♁	male
×	crossed with; hybrid
+	wild type
P_1	parental generation usually consisting of two or more different pure strains
F_1	first filial generation, offspring of a mating between different P_1 strains
F_2	second filial generation, offspring of an $F_1 \times F_1$ mating

Business and Finance

a/c	account ⟨in a/c with⟩
@	at; each ⟨4 apples @ 5¢ = 20¢⟩
P	principal
i, r	rate of interest
n	number of periods (as of interest) and especially years
/ *or* ℔	per
c/o	care of
#	number if it precedes a numeral ⟨track #3⟩; pounds if it follows ⟨a 5 # sack of sugar⟩
℔	pound; pounds
%	percent
‰	per thousand
©	copyrighted
®	registered trademark
$	dollars
¢	cents
£	pounds

Chemistry

+	signifies "plus," "and," "together with"—used between the symbols of substances brought together for, or produced by, a reaction; placed to the right of a symbol above the line, it signifies a unit charge of positive electricity: Ca^{++} *or* Ca^{2+} denotes the ion of calcium, which carries two positive charges
−	signifies a unit charge of negative electricity when placed to the right of a symbol above the line: Cl^{-} denotes a chlorine ion carrying a negative charge; also used to indicate the removal of a part from a compound (as $-CO_2$)
–	signifies a single bond—used between the symbols of elements or groups which unite to form a compound (as H–O–H for H_2O)
·	—used to separate parts of a compound regarded as loosely joined (as $CuSO_4{\cdot}5H_2O$); the centered dot is also used to denote the presence of a single unpaired electron (as H·)
=	indicates a double bond; placed to the right of a symbol above the line, it signifies two unit charges of negative electricity (as $SO_4^{=}$, the negative ion of sulfuric acid, carrying two negative charges)
≡	signifies a triple bond or a triple negative charge
:	—used to indicate an unshared pair of electrons (as $:NH_3$); also sometimes used to indicate a double bond (as in $CH_2{:}CH_2$)
( )	marks groups within a compound [as in $C_6H_4(CH_3)_2$, the formula for xylene which contains two methyl groups (CH_3)]
⌬ *or* ⏣	denotes the benzene ring
=	gives or forms
→	gives, leads to, or is converted to
⇆	forms and is formed from, is in equilibrium with
↓	indicates precipitation of the substance
↑	indicates that the substance passes off as a gas
↔	indicates a reversible reaction or resonance structures
Δ	indicates that heat is required or produced
m, n, x	—used to indicate a variable or unknown number of atoms or groups especially in polymers [as in $(C_5H_8)_n$]
1, 2, etc.	—used to indicate various quantities (as mass number ⟨^{12}C⟩, atomic number ⟨$_6C$⟩, number of atoms or groups ⟨$(C_6H_5)_2$⟩, or quantity of electric charge ⟨Ca^{2+}⟩)
I, II, III, etc.	—used to indicate oxidation state ⟨Fe^{III}⟩
R	organic group

X halogen atom

Z atomic number (for element symbols see ELEMENT table)

Computers

? wildcard used especially to represent any single character in a keyword search (as in a search for "f?n" to find *fan, fin,* and *fun*)

* wildcard used especially to represent zero or more characters in a keyword search (as in a search for "key*" to find *key, keys, keyed, keying,* etc.)

@ at sign—used to introduce the domain name in an e-mail address

:-) *and* :-(etc. emoticons (e.g., smile, frown, etc.)

/ *or* \ —used to introduce or separate parts of a computer address

. dot—used to separate parts of a computer address or file name

⟨ ⟩ —used to enclose tags in a markup language (as ⟨title⟩Dictionary⟨/title⟩)

Mathematics

+ plus; positive ⟨$a + b = c$⟩—also used to indicate omitted figures or an approximation

− minus; negative

± plus or minus; positive or negative ⟨the square root of $4a^2$ is $\pm 2a$⟩ ⟨an age of 120,000 years ±12,000⟩

× multiplied by; times ⟨6 × 4 = 24⟩—also indicated by placing a dot between the factors ⟨6·4 = 24⟩ or by writing the factors one after the other, often enclosed in parentheses ⟨(4)(5)(3) = 60⟩ ⟨−4*abc*⟩

÷ *or* : divided by ⟨24 ÷ 6 = 4⟩—also indicated by writing the divisor under the dividend with a line between ⟨$\frac{24}{6} = 4$⟩ or by writing the divisor after the dividend with a slash between ⟨3/8⟩

E times 10 raised to an indicated exponent ⟨4.52E5 = 4.52×10^5⟩—used especially in electronic displays

= equals ⟨6 + 2 = 8⟩

≠ *or* ≠ is not equal to

> is greater than ⟨6 > 5⟩

< is less than ⟨3 < 4⟩

≧ *or* ≥ is greater than or equal to

≦ *or* ≤ is less than or equal to

≯ is not greater than

≮ is not less than

≈ is approximately equal to

≡ is identical to

∼ is similar to; the negation of; the negative of

≅ is congruent to

∝ varies directly as; is proportional to

: is to; the ratio of

∴ therefore

∞ infinity

∠ angle; the angle ⟨∠ ABC⟩

∟ right angle ⟨∟ *ABC*⟩

⊥ the perpendicular; is perpendicular to ⟨AB ⊥ CD⟩

∥ parallel; is parallel to ⟨AB ∥ CD⟩

⊙ *or* ○ circle

⌒ arc of a circle

△ triangle

□ square

▭ rectangle

$\sqrt{\ }$ *or* √ root—used without an index to indicate a square root (as in $\sqrt{4} = 2$) or with an index above the sign to indicate a higher degree (as in $\sqrt[3]{3}$, $\sqrt[5]{7}$); also denoted by a fractional index at the right of a number whose denominator expresses the degree of the root ⟨$3^{1/3} = \sqrt[3]{3}$⟩

( ) parentheses, [ ] brackets, { } braces —used to indicate associated quantities and the order of operations

— (when placed above quantities) vinculum

Δ the operation of finding the difference between two nearby values of a variable (as *y*) or of a function (as *f*) for two values of its independent variable (as *x*) differing by a small nonzero amount (as *h*) ⟨$\Delta y = y_2 - y_1$⟩ ⟨$\Delta f(x) = f(x + h) - f(x)$⟩

∫ integral; integral of ⟨$\int 2x dx = x^2 + C$⟩

$\int_b^a$ the integral taken from the value *b* to the value *a* of the variable

$\frac{df(x)}{dx}$ the derivative of the function *f*(*x*) with respect to *x*

s standard deviation of a sample taken from a population

σ standard deviation of a population

s^2 variance of a sample from a population

σ^2 variance

Σ sum; summation ⟨$\sum_{i=1}^{n} x_i = x_1 + x_2 + \ldots + x_n$⟩

$\bar{x}$ arithmetic mean of a sample of a variable *x*

μ (1) micrometer (2) arithmetic mean of a population

χ^2 chi-square

P probability

π pi; the number 3.14159265+; the ratio of the circumference of a circle to its diameter

Π product ⟨$\prod_{i=1}^{n} x_i = (x_1)(x_2) \ldots (x_n)$⟩

! factorial ⟨$n! = n(n-1)(n-2) \ldots 1$⟩

e or ϵ (1) the number 2.7182818+; the base of the natural system of logarithms (2) the eccentricity of a conic section

i the positive square root of minus one $\sqrt{-1}$

n an unspecified number (as an exponent) especially when integral

° degree ⟨60°⟩

′ minute; foot ⟨30′⟩—also used to distinguish between different values of the same variable or between different variables (as *a*′, *a*″, *a*‴)

″ second; inch ⟨30″⟩

^{0}, ^{1}, ^{2}, ^{3}, etc. —used as exponents placed above and at the right of an expression to indicate that it is raised to a power whose degree is indicated by the figure ⟨a^0 equals 1⟩ ⟨a^1 equals *a*⟩ ⟨a^2 is the square of *a*⟩

$^{-1}$, $^{-2}$, $^{-3}$, etc. —used as exponents placed above and at the right of an expression to indicate that the reciprocal of the expression is raised to the power whose degree is indicated by the figure ⟨a^{-1} equals $1/a$⟩ ⟨a^{-2} equals $1/a^2$⟩

θ angle or measure of an angle especially in radians

f function

f^{-1} the inverse of the function *f*

$|z|$ the absolute value of *z*

$[a_{ij}]$ matrix with element a_{ij} in the *i*th row and *j*th column

[*x*]	the greatest integer not greater than *x*
(*a*,*b*)	the open interval $a < x < b$
[*a*,*b*]	the closed interval $a \leq x \leq b$
$\aleph_0$	aleph-null
∍ *or* :	such that ⟨choose *a* and *b* ∍ *a* + *b* = 6⟩
∃	there exists ⟨∃ *a* ∍ *a* + 2 = 4⟩
∀	for every, for all ⟨∀ *a* ∍ *a* is a real number, $a^2 \geq 0$⟩
∪	union of two sets
∩	intersection of two sets
⊂	is included in, is a subset of
⊃	contains as a subset
∈ *or* ϵ	is an element of
∉	is not an element of
Λ *or* 0 *or* Ø *or* { }	empty set, null set

Miscellaneous

&	and
&c	et cetera, and so forth
" *or* "	ditto marks
/	slash (*or* diagonal) —used to mean "or" (as in *and/or*), "and/or" (as in *dead/wounded*), "per" (as in *feet/second*); used to indicate end of a line of verse; used to separate the figures of a date (4/4/73)
☞	index *or* fist
†	died—used especially in genealogies
+	cross (for variations see CROSS illustration)
☧	monogram from Greek XP signifying Christ
Ⓤ *or* Ⓚ	kosher certification
✡	Magen David
☥	ankh
℣	versicle
℟	response
✳	—used in Roman Catholic and Anglican service books to divide each verse of a psalm, indicating where the response begins
✠ *or* +	—used in some service books to indicate where the sign of the cross is to be made; also used by certain Roman Catholic and Anglican prelates as a sign of the cross preceding their signatures
LXX	Septuagint
f/ *or* *f*:	f-stop of a photographic lens
℞	take—used on prescriptions; prescription; treatment
☠	poison
☣	biohazard
☢ *or* ☢	radiation, radioactive materials
	fallout shelter
☮	peace
x *or* ×	by ⟨3 × 5 cards⟩
☯	yin and yang
♻	recycle, recyclable

Music

STAFFS AND CLEFS

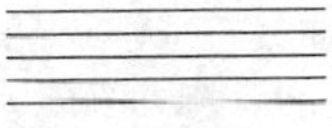
staff

treble clef, G clef—indicates that the second line from the bottom is the first G above middle C

bass clef, F clef—indicates that the second line from the top is the first F below middle C

NOTE LENGTHS AND RESTS

whole note, half note, quarter note, eighth note, sixteenth note

eighth notes, sixteenth notes (shown connected)

dots—a dotted note lasts half again as long as it would without the dot

triplets—three notes to be performed in the amount of time that two of those notes would ordinarily take

whole rest, half rest, quarter rest, eighth rest, sixteenth rest

TIME SIGNATURES AND MEASURES

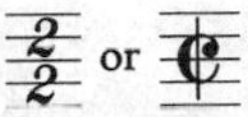

"two-two," cut time, alla breve—two beats per measure, each beat lasting a half note

"three-four"—three beats per measure, each beat lasting a quarter note

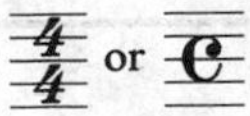

"four-four," common time—four beats per measure, each beat lasting a quarter note

"six-eight"—six beats per measure, each beat lasting an eighth note

bar lines—indicate the end of one measure and the beginning of the next

ACCIDENTALS

♯	sharp—raises a note one half step
♭	flat—lowers a note one half step
𝄪	double sharp—raises a note two half steps
𝄫	double flat—lowers a note two half steps
♮	natural—cancels the effect of a previous sharp, flat, etc.

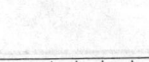

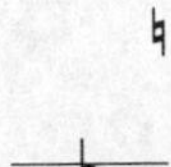
key signature—indicates the key of a piece or section by showing which notes will occur with sharps or flats throughout

DYNAMICS AND OTHER MARKS

pp p mp mf f ff — pianissimo (very soft), piano (soft), mezzo piano (medium soft), mezzo forte (medium loud), forte (loud), fortissimo (very loud)

crescendo (becoming louder), decrescendo (becoming softer)

accent marks—indicate that an individual note is to be played louder

staccato—indicates that a note should be performed very short, leaving a slight silence before the next note

hold—indicates that the note or notes below should be held longer than normal

tie—indicates that the first note should be held as long as the two notes combined

slur—indicates that each note should lead to the next smoothly

grace note—an extremely short note that doesn't affect the length of the following note

arpeggio—indicates that the notes of a chord should be played one after the other beginning at the bottom

tr trill—indicates that the marked note is performed several times in rapid alternation with the scale note immediately above it

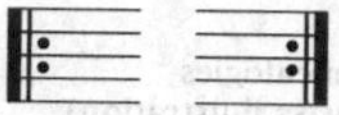
repeat signs—indicate that the music between the two signs should be repeated

Physics

α alpha particle
β beta particle, beta ray
γ gamma ray, photon
λ wavelength
μ micro-; micron; permeability
ν frequency; neutrino
σ conductivity; cross section; surface tension
φ luminous flux
Ω ohm
Å angstrom
c speed of light
e electron; electronic charge
n neutron
p proton
q charge; quark
X power of magnification

CIRCUIT ELEMENTS

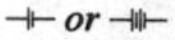 DC power, battery
 AC power, generator
 capacitor
 resistor
 inductor
 switch
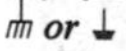 grounded connection

Reference Marks

* asterisk *or* star
† dagger
‡ double dagger
§ section *or* numbered clause
‖ parallels
¶ *or* ⁋ paragraph

Weather

◎ calm
○ clear
◐ cloudy (partly)
● cloudy (completely overcast)
 drifting or blowing snow
, drizzle
≡ fog 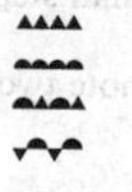
 front, cold
 warm 
 occluded
 stationary
 funnel clouds
∞ haze
 hurricane
 tropical storm
● rain
 sandstorm or dust storm
▽ shower(s)
 shower of rain
 snow
 thunderstorm

A Handbook of Style

Punctuation

Punctuation marks are used in English to separate groups of words for meaning and emphasis; to convey an idea of the variations of pitch, volume, pauses, and intonation of the spoken language; and to help avoid ambiguity. The uses of the standard punctuation marks are discussed and illustrated in the following pages.

’ Apostrophe

1. Indicates the possessive of nouns and indefinite pronouns. The possessive of singular nouns and some plural nouns is formed by adding *-’s*. The possessive of plural nouns ending in an *s* or *z* sound is usually formed by adding only an apostrophe; the possessive of irregular plurals is formed by adding *-’s*.

the boy’s mother	birds’ migrations
Douglas’s crimes	the Smiths’ house
anyone’s guess	people’s opinions
Arkansas’s capital	children’s laughter

2. Marks the omission of letters in contracted words and of digits in numerals.

didn’t	class of ’03
they’re	in the ’90s
she’d	

3. Often forms plurals of letters, figures, abbreviations, symbols, and words referred to as words.

dot your *i*’s and cross your *t*’s

three 8’s *or* three 8s

these Ph.D.’s *or* these Ph.D.s

has trouble pronouncing her *the*’s

[ ] Brackets

1. Enclose editorial comments or clarifications inserted into quoted material.

He wrote, “I ain’t [sic] going.”

2. Enclose insertions that supply missing letters or that alter the form of the original word.

Her letter continues, “If D[avid] won’t pay for your plane ticket, perhaps your uncle will.”

He dryly observed that they bought the stock because “they want[ed] to see themselves getting richer.”

3. Function as parentheses within parentheses.

Posner’s recent essays (like his earlier *Law and Literature* [1988]) bear this out.

: Colon

1. Introduces a word, phrase, or clause that acts as an appositive or identifies something that comes before it.

That year Dad’s old obsession was replaced with a new one: jazz.

The issue comes down to this: Will we offer a reduced curriculum, or will we simply cancel the program?

2. Introduces a list or series.

Three countries were represented: Britain, France, and Belgium.

3. Introduces a clause or phrase that explains, illustrates, clarifies, or restates what has gone before.

Dawn was breaking: the distant peaks were already glowing with the sun’s first rays.

4. Introduces lengthy quoted material set off from the rest of the text by indentation but not by quotation marks. It may also be used before a quotation enclosed by quotation marks in running text.

The *Rumpole* series has been well described as follows:

> Rumpled, disreputable, curmudgeonly barrister Horace Rumpole often wins cases despite the disdain of his more aristocratic colleagues. Fond of cheap wine (“Château Thames Embankment”) and
> . . .

The inscription reads: “To Mr. Richards, who inspires us to do our best.”

5. Separates elements in bibliographic and biblical references and in formulas used to express time and ratios.

Boston: Houghton Mifflin, 1997
Scientific American 240 (Jan.):122-33

John 4:10

8:30 a.m.

a ratio of 3:5

6. Separates titles and subtitles.

Southwest Stories: Tales from the Desert

7. Follows the salutation in formal correspondence.

Dear Judge Wright:

Ladies and Gentlemen:

Comma ,

1. Separates main clauses joined by a coordinating conjunction (such as *and, but, or, nor, so*), and occasionally very short clauses not joined by conjunctions.

She left a message, and he called her back that afternoon.

The trial lasted for nine months, but the jury took only four hours to reach its verdict.

She came, she saw, she conquered.

2. Sets off adverbial clauses and phrases that begin or interrupt a sentence. If the sentence can be easily read without a comma, the comma may be omitted.

When we heard the news, we whooped with joy.

The teacher, having taken attendance, told us to take out our homework.

In January the roof fell in.

As cars age they depreciate.

3. Sets off transitional words and phrases (such as *indeed, however*) and words that introduce examples (such as *namely, for example*).

Indeed, no one seemed to have heard of him.

The mystery, however, remains unsolved.

She plans to visit two countries, namely, Mexico and Belize.

4. Sets off contrasting expressions within a sentence.

This project will take six months, not six weeks.

5. Separates words, phrases, or clauses in a series. Many writers omit the comma before the last item in a series whenever this would not result in ambiguity.

Men, women[,] and children crowded aboard the train.

Her job required her to pack quickly, to travel often[,] and to have no personal life.

He came down the steps as reporters shouted questions, flashbulbs popped[,] and the crowd pushed closer.

6. Separates two or more adjectives that modify a noun. It is not used between two adjectives when the first adjective modifies the combination of the second adjective plus the noun it modifies.

in a calm, reflective manner

the harsh, damp, piercing wind

the lone bald eagle

a good used car

7. Sets off a nonrestrictive (nonessential) word, phrase, or clause that further identifies a preceding or following noun.

We visited Gettysburg, site of the famous battle.

A cherished landmark, the Hotel Sandburg was spared.

Its author, Maria Olevsky, was an expert diver.

8. Separates a direct quotation from a phrase identifying its source or speaker. The comma is omitted when the quotation ends with a question mark or exclamation point, and usually omitted when the quoted phrase itself is the subject or object of the larger sentence.

She answered, "I'm leaving."

"I suspect," Bob observed, "we'll be hearing more."

"How about another game?" Elaine piped up.

"The network is down" was the reply she feared.

9. Sets off words in direct address and mild interjections.

The facts, my friends, are very different.

You may go if you wish, Sam.

Ah, that's my idea of an excellent dinner.

10. Precedes a question added to a statement or command.

That's obvious, isn't it?

11. Indicates the omission of a word or phrase used earlier in the sentence. In short sentences, the comma may be omitted.

Eight councillors cast their votes for O'Reilly; six, for Mendez.

He critiqued my presentation and I his.

12. Is used to avoid ambiguity that might arise from adjacent words.

Under Mr. James, Madison High School flourished.

To Mary, Jane was someone special.

13. Groups numerals into units of three to separate thousands, millions, and so on. It is not used in street addresses, page numbers, and four-digit years.

2,000 case histories

a fee of $12,500

12537 Wilshire Blvd.

page 1415

numbering 3,450,000

in 3000 B.C.

14. Separates a surname from a following title or degree, and often from the abbreviations *Jr.* and *Sr.*

Sandra H. Cobb, Vice President

Lee Herman Melville, M.D.

Douglas Fairbanks, Jr. *or* Douglas Fairbanks Jr.

15. Sets off elements of an address (except for zip codes) and full dates. When only the month and year are given, the comma is usually omitted.

Write to Bureau of the Census, Washington, DC 20233.

On the way to Austin, Texas, our car broke down.

On July 4, 1776, the Continental Congress approved the Declaration of Independence.

In December 1903, the Wright brothers finally succeeded in keeping an airplane aloft for a few seconds.

16. Follows the salutation in informal correspondence and follows the word or words that conventionally come before the signature of a letter.

Dear Aunt Sarah,
Sincerely yours,

— Dash

1. Marks an abrupt change or break in the structure of a sentence.

The students seemed happy enough with the new plan, but the parents—there was the problem.

2. Is used in place of commas or parentheses to set off and emphasize explanatory or supplementary material. In general, no punctuation immediately precedes an opening dash or immediately follows a closing dash.

It will prevent corporations—large and small—from buying influence with campaign contributions.

3. Introduces defining phrases and lists.

The motion was then tabled—that is, removed indefinitely from consideration.

He speaks three languages—English, French, and Spanish.

4. Often precedes the attribution of a quotation, either immediately after the quotation or on the next line.

No one can make you feel inferior without your consent.—Eleanor Roosevelt

or

No one can make you feel inferior without your consent.

—Eleanor Roosevelt

. . . Ellipsis

1. Indicates the omission of one or more words within a quoted sentence. Omission of a word or phrase is indicated by three ellipsis points. If an entire sentence or more is omitted, the end punctuation of the preceding sentence (including a period) is followed by three ellipsis points. Punctuation used in the original that falls on either side of the ellipsis is often omitted; however, it may be retained, especially if this helps clarify the sentence structure. (The second and third examples below are shortened versions of the first.)

Is it so bad, then, to be misunderstood? Pythagoras was misunderstood, and Socrates, and Jesus, and Luther, and Copernicus, and Galileo, and Newton, and every pure and wise spirit that ever took flesh. To be great is to be misunderstood.—Emerson

Is it so bad, then, to be misunderstood? Pythagoras was misunderstood, and Socrates, and Jesus, . . . and every pure and wise spirit that ever took flesh.

Is it so bad, then, to be misunderstood? . . . To be great is to be misunderstood.

2. Indicates that one or more lines have been omitted from a poem. The row of ellipsis points usually matches the length of the line above.

When I heard the learned astronomer,
. . . .
How soon unaccountable I became tired and sick,
Til rising and gliding out I wandered off by myself,

3. Indicates faltering speech or an unfinished sentence in dialogue.

"I mean . . ." he stammered, "like . . . How?"

! Exclamation Point

Ends an emphatic phrase, sentence, or interjection.

Without a trace!

There is no alternative!

Encore!

- Hyphen

1. Is often used to link elements in compound words. Consult the dictionary in doubtful cases.

secretary-treasurer	spin-off
fleet-footed	light-year
middle-of-the-road	president-elect

2. Is used to separate a prefix, suffix, or combining form from an existing word if the base word is capitalized, and often when the base word is more than two syllables long, or when two identical letters would otherwise be adjacent to each other. Consult the dictionary in doubtful cases.

pre-Victorian	jewel-like
industry-wide	co-opted
recession-proof	anti-inflationary

3. Is used in most compound modifiers when placed before the noun.

the fresh-cut grass

a made-up excuse

her gray-green eyes

the well-worded sentence

4. Is used when different prefixes are employed with the same base word but separated by *and* or *or*.

pre- and postoperative care

anti- or pro-Revolutionary sympathies

early- and mid-20th-century painters

5. Is used in writing out compound numbers between 21 and 99.

forty-one years old

one hundred forty-one

his forty-first birthday

6. Is used in writing out fractions when they are employed as modifiers. Fractions that are not used as modifiers are often left open.

a one-half share

three fifths of the vote

7. Is used between numbers and dates with the meaning "(up) to and including."

pages 128-34

the years 1995-99

8. Is used as the equivalent of *to, and,* or *versus* to indicate linkage or opposition.

the New York-Paris flight

the Lincoln-Douglas debates

a final score of 7-2

9. Marks a division of a word at the end of a line of text.

In 1979 smallpox, formerly a great scourge, was declared eradicated by the World Health Organization.

Parentheses ( )

1. Enclose phrases and clauses that provide examples, explanations, or supplementary facts.

Nominations for principal officers (president, vice president, treasurer, and secretary) were approved.

Four computers (all outdated models) were replaced.

Although we like the restaurant (their pizza is the best), we haven't been there in several months.

2. Enclose numerals that confirm a spelled-out number.

Delivery will be made in thirty (30) days.

The fee is four thousand dollars ($4,000).

3. Enclose numbers or letters indicating individual items in a series within a sentence.

Sentences can be classified as (1) simple, (2) multiple or compound, and (3) complex.

4. Enclose abbreviations that follow their spelled-out forms, or spelled-out forms that follow their abbreviations.

the Food and Drug Administration (FDA)

the FDA (Food and Drug Administration)

5. Indicate alternative terms.

Please sign and return the enclosed form(s).

6. Often enclose cross-references and bibliographic references, as well as publishing data in bibliographic citations.

Specialized services are also available (see list below).

The diagram (Fig. 3) illustrates the action of the pump.

Subsequent studies (Braxton 1998; Roh and Weinglass 2002) have confirmed these findings.

3. See Stendhal, *Love* (New York: Penguin, 1975), 342.

7. Are used with other punctuation marks as follows: If an independent sentence is enclosed in parentheses, its first word is capitalized and a period is placed inside the parentheses. If the parenthetical expression occurs within a sentence, it is uncapitalized unless it is a quotation, and does not end with a period but may end with an exclamation point, a question mark, or quotation marks. No punctuation immediately precedes an opening parenthesis within a sentence; if punctuation is required, it follows the closing parenthesis.

The discussion was held in private. (The results are still confidential.)

This short section (musicians would call it the *bridge*) has the song's most distinctive harmonies.

She made the team (are you surprised?).

He was distraught ("This is the worst day of my life!") and refused to see anyone.

I'll get back to you tomorrow (Friday), when I have more details.

Period .

1. Ends a sentence or a sentence fragment that is neither a question nor an exclamation.

The bus left five minutes ago.

She asked if we liked to dance.

He said, "I haven't read that book yet."

Give it your best.

Unlikely. In fact, inconceivable.

2. Follows most abbreviations and some contractions.

Calif.	e.g.	Dr.
Sept.	p.m.	Jr.
etc.	dept.	Assn.

3. Is used with a person's initials.

F. Scott Fitzgerald

Robert E. Lee

4. Follows numerals and letters when used without parentheses in outlines and vertical lists.

I. Pollution
 A. Principal sources
  1. Industrial
  2. Residential
 B. Proposed solutions

? Question Mark

1. Ends a direct question but does not follow an indirect question.

What went wrong?

Was anyone seen in the area after 10 p.m.?

"When do they arrive?" she asked.

He asked when the store normally closed.

2. Ends a question that forms part of a sentence.

What was her motive? you may be asking.

I naturally wondered, Will it really work?

3. Indicates uncertainty about a fact.

Geoffrey Chaucer, English poet (1342?-1400)

" " Quotation Marks, Double

1. Enclose direct quotations but not indirect quotations.

"I'm leaving," she whispered. "This could last forever."

She whispered that she was leaving.

He asked, "What went wrong?"

The question is, What went wrong?

2. Enclose words or phrases borrowed from others, and words of obvious informality.

They required a "biodata summary"—that is, a résumé.

He called himself "emperor," but he was really just a dictator.

They were afraid the patient had "stroked out"—had had a stroke.

3. Enclose titles of articles in periodicals, poems, short stories, essays, chapters of books, and episodes of radio and television programs.

the article "In Search of Sleep" in *Newsweek*

"The Death of the Hired Man" by Robert Frost

Poe's "The Murders in the Rue Morgue"

Thoreau's famous essay "Civil Disobedience"

The Jungle Book's ninth chapter, "Rikki-tikki-tavi"

*M*A*S*H*'s finale, "Goodbye, Farewell and Amen"

4. Enclose lines of poetry run in with the text.

When Gilbert advised, "Stick close to your desks and never go to sea, / And you all may be rulers of the Queen's Navee!" this latest appointee was obviously paying attention.

5. Are used with other punctuation marks as follows: A period or comma is placed within the quotation marks. A colon or semicolon is placed outside them. A dash, question mark, or exclamation point is placed inside the quotation marks when it punctuates the quoted matter only, but outside when it punctuates the whole sentence.

He smiled and said, "I'm happy for you."

"Too easy," she shot back.

There was only one real "issue": noise.

She spoke of her "little cottage in the country"; she might better have called it a mansion.

"I can't see how—" he started to say.

Saturdays there were dances—"sock hops"—in the gym.

He asked, "When did she leave?"

What is the meaning of "the open door"?

She leaped into the air with a joyful "Whoopee!"

Save us from his "mercy"!

' ' Quotation Marks, Single

1. Enclose quoted material within quoted material.

The witness said, "I distinctly heard him say, 'Don't be late,' and then I heard the door close."

2. In British usage, may enclose quoted material, in which case a quotation within a quotation is set off by double quotation marks.

The witness said 'I distinctly heard him say, "Don't be late," and then I heard the door close.'

Semicolon ;

1. Separates related independent clauses joined without a coordinating conjunction.

Cream the butter and sugar; add the eggs and beat well.

The river overflowed its banks; roads vanished; freshly plowed fields turned into lakes.

2. Joins two clauses when the second includes a conjunctive adverb (such as *however, indeed, thus*) or a phrase that acts like one (such as *in that case, as a result, on the other hand*).

It won't be easy to sort out the facts; a decision must be made, however.

The case could take years; as a result, many plaintiffs will accept settlements.

3. Is often used before introductory expressions such as *for example, that is,* and *namely*.

We were fairly successful; that is, we raised more than a thousand dollars.

4. Separates phrases or items in a series when they contain commas.

The assets include $22 million in land, buildings, and equipment; $34 million in cash and investments; and $8 million in inventory.

The exhibition will travel to Washington, D.C.; Concord, N.H.; Portland, Ore.; and Oakland, Cal.

The votes against were: Precinct 1, 418; Precinct 2, 332; Precinct 3, 256.

5. Is placed outside quotation marks and parentheses.

They again demanded "complete autonomy"; the demand was again rejected.

She found him urbane and entertaining (if somewhat overbearing); he found her charmingly ingenuous.

Slash /

1. Separates alternatives and usually represents the words *or* or *and/or*.

alumni/ae his/her

2. Replaces the word *to* or *and* in some compound terms and ranges.

1998/99 *or* 1998–99

the May/June issue *or* the May–June issue

3. Separates lines of poetry that are run in with the text. A space usually precedes and follows the slash.

In Pope's words: "'Tis with our judgments as our watches, none / Go just alike, yet each believes his own."

4. Separates the elements in a numerical date, and numerators and denominators in fractions.

on 9/11/01 a 7/8-mile course

5. Represents the word *per* or *to* when used between units of measure or the terms of a ratio.

400,000 tons/year price/earnings ratio

29 mi/gal 20/20 vision

6. Punctuates some abbreviations.

w/o [*for* without]

c/o [*for* care of]

7. Punctuates Internet addresses.

http://www.Merriam-Webster.com/

Plurals

1. The plurals of most English words are formed by adding *-s* or *-es* to the singular; *-es* is added when the noun ends in *-s, -x, -z, -ch,* or *-sh.*

dog → dogs
race → races
voter → voters
book → books
grass → grasses
tax → taxes
blitz → blitzes
branch → branches
dish → dishes

2. The plurals of words that follow other patterns are given at the appropriate entries in the main section of this dictionary.

army → armies
woman → women
ox → oxen
foot → feet
phenomenon → phenomena
sheep → sheep
passerby → passersby
alumnus → alumni
elf → elves

Capitals and Italics

Words and phrases are capitalized or italicized to indicate that they have a special significance in particular contexts. The following rules and examples describe the most common uses of capitals and italics.

Beginnings

1. The first word of a sentence or sentence fragment is capitalized.

The play lasted nearly three hours.

How are you feeling?

So many people, so many opinions.

Bravo!

2. The first word of a direct quotation is capitalized. However, if the quotation is interrupted in mid-sentence, the second part does not begin with a capital.

Hart repeated, "We can only stay a few minutes."

"We can only stay a few minutes," repeated Hart, "but we'll come back tomorrow."

3. The first word of a sentence within a sentence that is not a direct quotation is usually capitalized. Examples include sayings and rules, unspoken or imaginary dialogue, and direct questions.

You know the saying "Fools rush in where angels fear to tread."

The first rule is, When in doubt, spell it out.

My first thought was, How can I avoid this assignment?

The question is, When can we go?

4. The first word of a line of poetry is traditionally capitalized. However, in modern poetry the line beginnings are often lowercased. The poem's original capitalization should always be retained.

The best lack all conviction, while the worst
Are full of passionate intensity.
—W. B. Yeats

If tributes cannot
be implicit
give me diatribes and the fragrance of iodine,
the corn oak acorn grown in Spain . . .
—Marianne Moore

5. In a letter, the first word of the salutation and the first of the words that conventionally come before the signature are capitalized.

Dear Catherine:

To whom it may concern:

Sincerely yours,

Proper Nouns and Adjectives

1. Names of persons and places, organizations and their members, conferences and councils, and historical periods and events are capitalized. When in doubt, consult a dictionary or encyclopedia.

Noah Webster	Yalta Conference
Christa McAuliffe	Council of Trent
New York City	Bronze Age
the Rotary Club	World War II
all Rotarians	Boston Tea Party

2. Derivatives of proper nouns are capitalized when used in their primary sense. If the derived term has taken on a specialized meaning, it is often lowercased. Consult the dictionary when in doubt.

Roman sculpture	chinaware
Edwardian era	french fries
Hodgkin's disease	quixotic

Legal Terms

3. Full names of high courts are capitalized. Short forms of such names are usually lowercased, as are names of city and county courts. However, both the full and short names of the U.S. Supreme Court are capitalized.

International Court of Justice

the state supreme court

Springfield municipal court

the county court

the Supreme Court of the United States

the Court

4. Full names of specific treaties, laws, and acts are capitalized.

Treaty of Versailles

First Amendment rights

Clean Air Act of 1990

5. Names of the plaintiff and defendant in legal case titles are italicized, as are short forms of case titles. The *v.* (for *versus*) may be roman or italic. When the party involved rather than the case itself is being discussed, the reference is not italicized.

Smith v. [*or* v.] *Jones*

a quick decision in the *Jones* case

She covered the Lemuel Jones trial for the newspaper.

People

6. Words designating languages, nationalities, peoples, races, religious groups, and tribes are capitalized. Designations based on skin color are usually lowercased.

Spanish	Iroquois
Spaniards	Asians
Muslims	blacks and Hispanics

7. Titles preceding the name of a person and epithets or nicknames used instead of a name are capitalized. However, titles following a name or used alone are usually lowercased.

President Lincoln

Honest Abe

King Henry VIII

Henry VIII, king of England

Marcia Ramirez, president of Logex Corp.

Logex Corp.'s president

8. Words of family relationship preceding or used in place of a person's name are capitalized; otherwise they are lowercased.

Uncle Fred	Mother's birthday
Cousin Julia	my mother's birthday

Religious Terms

9. Words designating the Supreme Being are capitalized. Plural references to deities are lowercased.

Allah	the Almighty
Brahma	in the eyes of God
Jehovah	the angry gods

10. Personal pronouns referring to the Supreme Being are often capitalized in religious writing.

God gave His Son

Scientific Terms

11. Names of planets and their satellites, stars, constellations, and other specific celestial objects are capitalized. However, the words *sun, earth,* and *moon* are usually lowercased unless they occur with other astronomical names.

Jupiter	Mars, Venus and Earth
the North Star	life on earth
Ursa Major	voyage to the moon

12. Genus terms in binomial scientific names in zoology and botany are capitalized and italicized. The species term that follows the genus term is lowercased and italicized, as are the names of races, varieties, or subspecies.

the California condor (*Gymnogyps californianus*)

a common buttercup (*Ranunculus acris*)

Otis asio naevius

13. Latin (New Latin) names of classes, families, and all groups above the genus level in zoology and botany are capitalized but not italicized. Their derivative nouns and adjectives are lowercased.

the class Gastropoda	the order Diptera
gastropod	dipteran flies
the family Mantidae	Thallophyta
mantid	thallophytic

14. Names of geological time divisions are capitalized. The generic terms that follow them are lowercased.

Mesozoic era

Paleocene epoch

Quaternary period

the Upper Cretaceous

Time Periods

15. Names of days of the week, months, and holidays and holy days are capitalized. Names of the seasons are lowercased.

Tuesday	Yom Kippur
January	Easter
Veterans Day	winter

Titles of Works

16. Words in titles of books, magazines, newspapers, plays, movies, long poems, and works of art such as paintings and sculpture are capitalized except for internal articles, coordinating conjunctions, prepositions, and the *to* of infinitives. Prepositions of four or more letters are often capitalized. The entire title is italicized. (Titles of articles in periodicals, short poems, short stories, essays, lectures, chapters of books, and episodes of radio and television programs are similarly capitalized but enclosed in quotation marks rather than italicized; see examples at "Quotation Marks, Double" on p. 1247.)

Of Mice and Men

Lawrence of Arabia

Publishers Weekly

Eliot's *The Waste Land*

USA Today

Monet's *Water-Lily Pool*

Miller's *The Crucible*

Rodin's *Thinker*

17. Titles of long musical compositions are usually capitalized and italicized; the titles of songs and short compositions are capitalized and enclosed in quotation marks, as are the popular names of longer works. The titles of compositions identified by their musical forms (such as *quartet, sonata, concerto*) are capitalized only, as are movements.

Mozart's *The Magic Flute*

the "Moonlight" Sonata

Ellington's *Black, Brown, and Beige*

his Violin Concerto in D

"My Funny Valentine"

Quartet in D, Op. 64, No. 5

Beethoven's "Für Elise"

the Adagietto movement

Trademarks

18. Registered trademarks, service marks, and brand names are capitalized.

Coke	Kleenex
Xerox	Walkman
Band-Aid	Levi's

Transportation

19. Names of ships, airplanes, and space vehicles are capitalized and italicized.

Titanic	*Challenger*
Spirit of St. Louis	*Apollo 13*

20. Names of train lines, types of aircraft, and space programs are capitalized but not italicized.

Metroliner	Concorde
Boeing 727	Pathfinder Program

Other Styling Conventions

1. Italics are often used for letters referred to as letters, words referred to as words, and numerals referred to as numerals.

The *g* in *align* is silent.

The word *slogan* evolved from Scottish Gaelic.

The first *2* and the last *0* are barely legible.

2. Foreign words and phrases are italicized.

"The cooking here is *wunderbar*!"